ISBN 978-0-8080-5364-4 (4-Volume Set)

2700 Lake Cook Road
Riverwoods, IL 60015
800 344 3734
CCHCPELink.com

Printed in the United States of America

SUSTAINABLE FORESTRY INITIATIVE
Certified Sourcing
www.sfiprogram.org
SFI-01681

This publication is designed to provide accurate and authoritative information in regard to the subject matter covered. It is sold with the understanding that the publisher is not engaged in rendering legal, accounting, or other professional service. If legal advice or other expert assistance is required, the services of a competent professional person should be sought.

Income
Tax Regulations

Including Proposed Regulations

As of January 13, 2023

Volume 1

§ 1.0-1–§ 1.436-1

Wolters Kluwer Editorial Staff Publication

FOREWORD

The federal income tax regulations are the official Treasury Department interpretation of the Internal Revenue Code and follow the number sequence of the Internal Revenue Code sections. Title 26 of the Code of Federal Regulations pertains to the Internal Revenue Code of 1986. Part 1 of Title 26 relates to federal income tax, Part 20 to estate taxes, Part 25 to gift taxes, Part 26 to the generation-skipping transfer tax, Part 31 to employment tax and withholding of income tax, and Part 301 to procedure and administration.

All regulations are written either by the Legislation and Regulations Division or the Employee Plans, Exempt Organizations Division of the Office of the Chief Counsel, IRS, and are approved by the Chief Counsel and the IRS Commissioner. The Treasury Department's Assistant Secretary for Tax Policy, or his deputy, has final approval over regulations.

Classes of Regulations

The three classifications of regulations are described below:

Proposed Regulations. Proposed regulations are issued to solicit public written comments, and public hearings are held if written requests are made.

Temporary Regulations. Temporary regulations are issued to provide guidance for the public and for IRS employees until final regulations are released. Public hearings are not held on temporary regulations.

Final Regulations. Final regulations are issued after public comments on proposed regulations are evaluated. Final regulations supersede any existing temporary regulations.

Finding Aids

A complete topical index to the final and temporary regulations begins on page 19,003; for proposed regulations, a complete topical index begins on page 73,001. A list indicating the subject of each part of the regulations for Title 26 of the Code, which is represented in the regulations reproduced in Volumes 1 through 4, appears at page 20,101. A list of irregularly numbered regulations giving the page on which the text of the regulation begins and the subject of the regulation is at page 20,201. A table of regulations that do not reflect changes made by recently enacted public laws appears at page 20,601.

January 2023

[The next page is 18,101.]

CONTENTS

TABLE OF CONTENTS

[The next page is 19,003.]

INDEX
FINAL AND TEMPORARY REGULATIONS UNDER
THE 1986 CODE

[References are to Reg. § numbers.]

[Index for Proposed Regulations Begins on Page 73,001.]

Index—Final and Temporary Regulations Under 1986 Code
[References are to Reg. § numbers.]

19,005

19,006

Index—Final and Temporary Regulations Under 1986 Code
[References are to Reg. § numbers.]

Index—Final and Temporary Regulations Under 1986 Code
[References are to Reg. § numbers.]

19,007

CHA

Index—Final and Temporary Regulations Under 1986 Code
[References are to Reg. § numbers.]

19,009

Index—Final and Temporary Regulations Under 1986 Code
[References are to Reg. § numbers.]

19,015

Index—Final and Temporary Regulations Under 1986 Code
[References are to Reg. § numbers.]

19,017

Index—Final and Temporary Regulations Under 1986 Code
[References are to Reg. § numbers.]

19,021

Index—Final and Temporary Regulations Under 1986 Code
[References are to Reg. § numbers.]

19,023

Index—Final and Temporary Regulations Under 1986 Code
[References are to Reg. § numbers.]

19,025

Index—Final and Temporary Regulations Under 1986 Code
[References are to Reg. § numbers.]

19,027

19,028

Index—Final and Temporary Regulations Under 1986 Code
[References are to Reg. § numbers.]

Index—Final and Temporary Regulations Under 1986 Code
[References are to Reg. § numbers.]

19,035

Index—Final and Temporary Regulations Under 1986 Code
[References are to Reg. § numbers.]

19,039

19,040

Index—Final and Temporary Regulations Under 1986 Code
[References are to Reg. § numbers.]

Index—Final and Temporary Regulations Under 1986 Code
[References are to Reg. § numbers.]

19,041

[The next page is 20,101.]

HOW TO LOCATE REGULATIONS

The INCOME TAX REGULATIONS volumes contain the final and temporary income, excise, estate and gift tax regulations, as well as the procedural and administrative regulations, under the Internal Revenue Code, i.e., Title 26 of the United States Code. They are arranged in strict Code sequence. To locate a particular regulation, always keep the Code section number in mind. This Code section number, in most instances, follows the decimal point in the regulation number.

> *Example 1:* § 1.641(a)-1 is an income tax regulation that explains or interprets Code section 641(a). It can be located in Volume 2.
>
> *Example 2:* § 31.3402(b)-1 is a withholding regulation that explains or interprets Code section 3402(b). It is among the regulations included in Volume 3.
>
> *Example 3:* § § 1.6655-1 and 301.6655-1 were both issued under Code section 6655. While § 301.6655-1 is merely a cross-reference to § 1.6655-1, it has been retained in the interest of completeness. Both of these regulation sections appear in Code order in Volume 3.

For a list of irregularly numbered regulations and their locations, see page 20,201.

Part Designation

The number preceding the decimal point in the regulation section number indicates the subject of the regulation. The following table indicates the subject of each part of the regulations for Title 26 of the United States Code that is represented in the regulations, which are reproduced in Volumes 1 through 3.

Part	Title
1	Final income tax regulations
4	Temporary regs. relating to foreign base company income
5	Temporary regs. under the Revenue Act of 1978
5c	Temporary regs. under the Economic Recovery Tax Act of 1981
5e	Temporary regs. on travel expenses of members of Congress
5f	Temporary regs. under the Tax Equity and Fiscal Responsibility Act of 1982
6a	Temporary regs. under the Omnibus Budget Reconciliation Act of 1981
7	Temporary regs. under the Tax Reform Act of 1976
8	Temporary regulation relating to charitable remainder trusts
11	Temporary regs. under the Employee Retirement Income Security Act of 1974
12	Temporary regs. under the Revenue Act of 1971
15A	Temporary regs. under the Installment Sales Revision Act of 1980
16	Temporary regs. under the Revenue Act of 1962
16A	Temporary regs. on the partial exclusion for certain conservation cost-sharing payments
18	Temporary regs. under the Subchapter S Revision Act of 1982
20	Estate taxes
25	Gift taxes
26	Tax on certain generation-skipping transfers
31	Withholding taxes
32	Temporary regulation pertaining to employment taxes
35	Temporary withholding regs. under TEFRA
35a	Temporary regs. concerning backup withholding
40	Excise tax procedural regulations
41	Excise tax on use of certain highway motor vehicles
42	Fuel stocks tax imposed by the Revenue Reconciliation Act of 1990
43	Excise tax on transportation by water
44	Excise tax on wagering
46	Excise tax regs. under the Tax Equity and Fiscal Responsibility Act of 1982
48, 145	Manufacturers and retailers excise tax
49, 148	Excise tax on communications and transportation by air
51	Branded prescription drug fee
52	Environmental tax regulations
53	Foundation and similar excise taxes
54	Pension excise taxes

Specially Located Regulations

Regulations from 31 C.F.R. Part 10, relating to practice before the IRS, are not included in the INCOME TAX REGULATIONS. For a list of regulations that have been proposed but not adopted, see the "List of Proposed Regulations" in Volume 4.

Subsequent Legislation

Not all regulations have been amended to reflect changes made in the related Code section by legislation. Check the Law Changes Not Yet in the Regulations Table (beginning on page 20,601) for regulations that do not reflect laws passed after the regulations were issued or amended.

[The next page is 20,201.]

IRREGULARLY NUMBERED REGULATIONS

There are a few exceptions to the standard method of numbering regulations. The following table indicates the page on which the text of the irregularly numbered regulation begins and the subject of the regulation. Unless otherwise indicated, regulations are part of Title 26 of the Code of Federal Regulations.

[The next page is 20,601.]

LAW CHANGES NOT YET IN THE REGULATIONS

There is a lapse of time between amendments to the Code and a corresponding change in the Regulations. This table shows those Regulations that do not yet reflect changes made in the Code. For a list of the designated or popular titles of Public Laws noted below, see the table beginning on page 20,301.

When a Regulation is adopted, it is reflected as a final Regulation. The reader, however, should always check this table to determine whether a particular Regulation has been amended for the latest change in the law.

Regulations Section	Public Law Making Changes Not Reflected
1.0-1	99-514
1.1-1	95-600, 97-34, 97-488, 99-514, 100-647, 103-66, 107-16, 108-27, 108-311, 112-240
1.1(i)-1T	100-647, 101-508, 105-34, 105-206, 107-16, 109-222, 110-28
1.2-1	99-514
1.2-2	93-597, 94-569, 97-448, 98-369, 99-514
1.3-1	94-12, 94-164, 94-455, 95-30, 95-600, 96-222, 97-34, 99-514
1.11-1	94-164, 94-455, 95-30, 95-600, 97-34, 98-369, 99-514, 100-203, 100-647, 115-97
1.15-1	95-30, 95-600, 97-34, 98-369, 99-514, 100-647, 107-16, 108-27
1.21-2	111-312
1.25-1T	99-514, 100-647, 101-239
1.25-2T	99-514, 100-647, 101-239, 104-188, 105-206, 107-16
1.25-3T	99-514, 100-647, 101-239, 103-66, 105-34
1.25-4T	99-514, 100-647, 101-239
1.25-5T	99-514, 100-647, 101-239
1.25-6T	99-514, 100-647, 101-239
1.25-7T	99-514, 100-647, 101-239
1.25-8T	99-514, 100-647, 101-239
1.25A-1	111-5, 111-312
1.25A-2	111-5, 111-312
1.25A-3	111-5, 111-312
1.25A-4	111-5
1.28-0	104-188, 106-170 (redesignated Code Sec. 28 as 45C)
1.28-1	100-647, 101-239, 102-227, 103-66, 104-188, 105-34, 106-170, 115-97 (redesignated Code Sec. 28 as 45C)
1.30-1	113-295 (repealed Code Sec. 30)
1.31-1	97-248, 97-354, 98-67, 98-369
1.31-2	(does not reflect current taxable wage base for FICA tax purposes)
1.32-2	96-222, 98-21, 98-369, 99-514, 100-647, 101-508, 103-66, 103-465, 104-7, 104-193, 105-34, 105-206, 107-16, 107-147, 109-135, 109-432, 110-245, 111-5, 111-226
1.37-1	98-21, 98-369, 99-514 (redesignated Code Sec. 37 as 22)
1.37-2	98-21, 98-369 (redesignated Code Sec. 37 as 22)
1.37-3	98-21, 98-369, 99-514 (redesignated Code Sec. 37 as 22)
1.41-3A	101-239, 103-66
1.41-5A, 1.41-7	101-239
1.41-6	112-240
1.42-1T	100-647, 101-239, 103-66
5c.44F-1	98-369 (redesignated Code Sec. 44F as 30), 99-514 (redesignated Code Sec. 30 as 41)
1.45G-1	114-113
1.46-1	100-647, 101-239, 101-508, 108-357, 109-58, 111-5, 111-148
1.46-2	96-222, 96-223, 97-34, 97-248, 97-354, 98-369, 101-508, 108-357, 109-58, 111-5, 111-148
1.46-3	97-34, 98-369, 99-514, 100-647, 101-508, 108-357, 109-58, 111-5, 111-148
1.46-4	97-34, 98-369, 99-514, 100-647, 101-508 (redesignated Code Sec. 46 as 50)
1.46-5	97-34, 98-369, 100-647, 101-508 (redesignated Code Sec. 46 as 47)
1.46-6	98-369, 99-514, 101-508 (redesignated Code Sec. 46 as 50)
1.47-1	97-34, 97-248, 98-369, 98-443, 99-121, 99-514, 100-647, 101-508, 104-188, 105-206 (redesignated Code Sec. 47 as 50)
1.47-2	91-676, 97-34, 97-248, 98-369, 98-443, 99-121, 99-514, 100-647, 101-508, 104-188 (redesignated Code Sec. 47 as 50)
1.47-3	97-34, 97-248, 98-369, 101-508, 104-188 (redesignated Code Sec. 47 as 50)
1.47-4	97-34, 97-248, 97-354, 98-369, 101-508 (redesignated Code Sec. 47 as 50)
1.47-5	97-34, 97-248, 98-369 (redesignated Code Sec. 47 as 50)
1.47-6	97-34, 97-248, 98-369 (redesignated Code Sec. 47 as 50)
1.48-1	101-508, 108-357, 109-58, 111-5, 111-148 (redesignated Code Sec. 48 as 46)
1.48-2	97-34, 97-248, 98-369, 99-514, 101-508, 108-357, 109-58 (redesignated Code Sec. 48 as 46)
1.48-3	94-12, 94-455, 95-600, 96-222, 96-223, 97-34, 97-248, 98-369, 101-508, 108-357, 109-58, 111-5, 111-148 (redesignated Code Sec. 48 as 46)
1.48-4	97-248, 98-369, 99-514, 101-508 (redesignated Code Sec. 48 as 50)
1.48-5	97-34, 97-354, 98-369, 101-508 (redesignated Code Sec. 48 as 46)
1.48-6	94-12, 97-34, 97-248, 98-369, 101-508 (redesignated Code Sec. 48 as 50)
1.48-9	97-34, 98-369, 101-508, 102-486, 108-357, 109-58, 109-432, 110-343, 111-5, 112-240
1.48-10	101-508 (redesignated Code Sec. 48 as 46)
1.48-12	101-508, 110-289, 115-97 (redesignated Code Sec. 48 as 47)
1.51-1	99-514, 100-203, 100-485, 100-647, 101-239, 101-508, 102-227, 103-66, 104-188, 105-34, 105-277, 106-170, 106-554, 107-147, 108-311, 109-432, 110-28, 110-246, 111-5, 111-147, 111-312, 112-240, 114-113
1.52-1	104-188
1.52-2	95-600, 98-369, 104-188
1.52-3	98-369, 101-508, 104-188
1.53-1	98-369 (repealed former Code Sec. 53; comparable provisions under Code Sec. 38), 108-357, 109-58, 109-59, 109-73, 109-135
1.53-2	98-369 (repealed former Code Sec. 53; comparable provisions under Code Sec. 39)

Regulations Section	Public Law Making Changes Not Reflected
1.408A-3	107-16, 109-222
1.412(b)-2	109-280
1.412(c)(1)-1, 1.412(c)(1)-2, 1.412(c)(1)-3	109-280
1.412(c)(2)-1	100-203, 107-16, 109-280
1.412(c)(3)-1	100-203, 103-465, 109-280
1.412(c)(3)-2	100-203, 109-280
11.412(c)-7	109-280
11.412(c)-11	100-203, 109-280
11.412(c)-12	100-203, 109-280
1.412(i)-1	109-280
1.421-1, 1.421-2	97-34, 101-508
1.423-1	98-369
1.423-1(b)	101-508
1.423-2(e)	99-514
1.423-2(i)(2), (j)	101-508
1.448-1, 1.448-1T	115-97
15A.453-1	100-203, 108-357
1.453-3	96-471
1.453-9	96-471, 98-369, 99-514
1.453A-1	106-170
1.455-6	94-455
1.456-7	94-455
1.460-5	111-240, 112-240
1.461-1	94-455
7.465-1	95-600, 96-222, 97-354, 98-369
7.465-2	95-600, 96-222, 97-354, 98-369
7.465-5	95-600, 96-222, 97-354, 98-369
1.467-7	108-27
1.468B-2, 1.468B-4, 1.468B-9	109-222
1.469-1	103-66, 104-188
1.469-2	103-66, 104-188
1.469-2T	104-188
1.469-3T	104-188
1.471-2	105-34
1.471-5	103-66
1.471-11	99-514, 100-203, 100-647
1.472-2(e)	98-369
1.472-2(f)	97-34
1.472-8	99-514
1.475(c)-1	105-206
1.482-1A	99-514
1.482-2A	99-514
1.501(a)-1	91-618, 92-418, 96-601, 96-605, 99-514, 100-203, 100-647
1.501(c)(2)-1	103-66
1.501(c)(3)-1	94-455, 98-369, 99-514, 100-203, 100-647, 101-73
1.501(c)(4)-1	99-514, 100-203, 100-647, 101-73, 104-168
1.501(c)(5)-1	94-455, 99-514, 100-203, 100-647, 101-73
1.501(c)(6)-1	89-800, 99-514, 100-203, 100-647, 101-73
1.501(c)(7)-1	94-568, 96-601, 99-514, 100-203, 100-647
1.501(c)(8)-1	94-568, 96-601, 99-514, 100-203, 100-647
1.501(c)(12)-1	96-605, 99-514, 100-203, 100-647
1.501(c)(14)-1	89-352, 99-514
1.501(c)(15)-1	99-514
1.501(c)(17)-1	99-514
1.501(c)(18)-1	99-514, 100-647, 107-16
1.501(c)(19)-1	97-248
1.501(c)(21)-1	102-486
1.501(c)(21)-2	102-486
1.501(e)-1	100-647
1.505(c)-1T	99-514, 103-66
1.507-6	98-369
1.511-1	95-30, 95-600, 96-222, 97-354, 98-369
1.511-4	100-647
1.512(b)-1	85-367, 88-380, 103-66, 104-188

Regulations Section	Public Law Making Changes Not Reflected
1.512(c)-1	85-367, 100-203
1.513-3	99-514
1.514(b)-1	99-514, 100-203, 100-647
1.514(c)-1	94-455, 95-345, 96-605, 98-369, 99-514, 100-203, 100-647, 103-66
1.514(e)-1	99-514, 100-203, 100-647
1.521-1	99-272
1.528-1—1.528-3	105-34
1.528-5	105-34
1.528-6	105-34
1.528-9	105-34
1.528-10	105-34
1.531-1	100-647, 103-66, 107-16, 108-27, 109-222, 111-312, 112-240
1.532-1	98-369, 99-514, 108-357 (repeal of Code Secs. 551-558), 109-135
1.535-1	98-369, 99-514, 109-135
1.535-2	98-369, 99-514, 109-135
1.535-3	94-12, 97-34, 101-508, 109-135
1.537-1	101-508
1.537-1(f)	104-188
1.541-1	88-272, 97-34, 99-514, 101-508, 103-66, 107-16, 108-27, 109-222, 111-312, 112-240
1.542-2	88-272, 89-809, 93-480, 95-600, 96-589, 97-248, 99-514
1.542-3	88-272, 89-809, 93-480, 95-600, 96-589, 97-248, 99-514
1.542-4	88-272, 93-480, 94-455
1.543-1	88-272, 88-484, 89-809, 94-455, 97-248, 98-369, 99-514, 100-647, 108-357, 113-295
1.543-2	88-272, 88-484, 94-455
1.544-1	88-272
1.544-4—1.544-7	88-272
1.545-1	89-809
1.545-2	94-455, 97-448, 99-514
1.545-3	101-508
1.551-1—1.551-2	108-357 (repealed Code Sec. 551)
1.561-1	108-357
1.561-2	87-403, 94-455
1.562-1	97-248, 99-514, 111-325
1.562-2	99-514, 111-325
1.563-1, 1.563-2	114-41
1.563-3	101-239, 114-41
1.564-1	94-455
1.581-3	87-722, 94-455
1.582-1	94-455, 98-369, 99-514, 100-647, 104-188
1.585-1(b)	104-188
1.585-4	99-514, 100-203, 100-647
1.591-1	97-34
1.594-1	98-369
1.612-4	99-514
1.612-5	99-514
1.613-1	108-357
1.613-2	89-809, 91-172, 94-12, 95-618, 108-357
1.613-4	95-618
1.613-5, 1.613-6	108-357
1.613A-5—1.613A-6	101-508
1.614-0	95-618
1.614-1	95-618
1.614-2	101-508
1.614-3	95-618
1.614-8	95-618
1.616-1	99-514
1.617-1—1.617-4	99-514
1.631-1(a)(4), (b)(1), (d)(4)	98-369
1.631-2	98-369
1.631-3	98-369, 99-514

Regulations Section	Public Law Making Changes Not Reflected
1.641(a)-0	95-600
1.641(a)-0(c)	98-369, 99-514, 100-647
1.641(a)-1	95-30, 104-188
1.641(a)-2	94-455, 99-514, 104-188, 110-28
1.641(b)-3	104-188, 110-28
1.641(c)-1	110-28
1.642(a)(3)-1—1.642(a)(3)-2	99-514
1.642(b)-1	107-134
1.642(c)-3	99-514
1.642(c)-5	98-369, 99-514, 100-647
1.642(c)-7	100-647
1.642(e)-1	97-34
1.642(f)-1	97-34
1.642(g)-1	94-455, 101-239
1.642(h)-1	91-172, 99-514
1.643(a)-1	97-248
1.643(a)-3	99-514, 105-34
1.643(a)-6	94-455, 99-514, 101-239, 104-188
1.643(a)-7	99-514
1.643(d)-1	94-455, 98-369, 99-514, 100-647, 104-188
1.643(d)-2	99-514, 105-34
1.652(b)-2	99-514
1.652(b)-3	99-514
1.652(c)-1	99-514, 105-34
1.652(c)-2	99-514, 105-34
1.652(c)-4	99-514, 105-34
1.661(a)-2(f)	98-369
1.661(c)-1	99-514
1.661(c)-2	99-514
1.662(b)-2	99-514
1.662(c)-1	99-514
1.662(c)-4	99-514
1.663(b)-1	105-34
1.663(b)-2	105-34
1.664-1	99-514, 105-34
1.664-1(f)	93-483, 94-455, 98-369, 100-647
8.1	95-600, 96-222, 96-605, 98-369, 100-647
1.664-2	105-34, 109-280
1.664-2(a)(5)	98-369
1.664-3	105-34, 109-280
1.664-3(a)(5)	98-369
1.665(a)-0A—1.665(a)-1A	94-455, 95-600, 105-34
1.665(b)-1A	94-455, 95-600, 105-34
1.665(b)-2A	94-455, 95-600
1.665(c)-1A	94-455, 95-600, 104-188, 105-34
1.665(d)-1A	94-455, 95-600, 104-188, 105-34
1.665(e)-1A	94-455, 95-600, 105-34
1.665(g)-2A	94-455, 95-600, 105-34
1.666(a)-1A	94-455, 95-600, 105-34
1.666(b)-1A	94-455, 95-600, 105-34
1.666(c)-1A	94-455, 95-600, 105-34
1.666(c)-2A	94-455, 95-600, 105-34
1.666(d)-1A	94-455, 95-600, 105-34
1.667(b)-1A	94-455, 95-600, 99-514, 105-34
1.671-2	99-514, 100-647
1.672(a)-1	99-514, 100-647, 101-508
1.672(c)-1	99-514, 100-647, 104-188
1.672(d)-1	99-514, 100-647
1.673(a)-1	99-514, 100-647
1.673(d)-1	99-514, 100-647
1.674(a)-1	99-514, 100-647, 105-34
1.674(b)-1	99-514, 100-647, 105-34
1.674(c)-1	99-514, 100-647
1.674(d)-1—1.674(d)-2	99-514, 100-647
1.675-1	99-514, 100-647
1.676(a)-1	99-514, 100-647

Regulations Section	Public Law Making Changes Not Reflected
1.676(b)-1	99-514, 100-647
1.677(a)-1	99-514, 100-647
1.677(b)-1	94-455, 99-514, 100-647
1.678(a)-1	99-514, 100-647
1.682(a)-1	115-97
1.682(b)-1	115-97
1.683-1—1.683-3	94-455
1.691(a)-1—1.691(a)-3	94-455, 95-600, 96-222, 96-471, 99-514, 100-203, 100-647
1.691(a)-5	94-455, 95-600, 96-222, 96-471, 99-514, 100-203, 100-647
1.691(c)-1	94-455, 95-600, 96-222, 96-471, 99-514, 100-203, 100-647, 104-188, 105-34, 107-16, 111-312
1.691(c)-2	94-455, 95-600, 96-222, 96-471, 99-514, 100-203, 100-647, 105-34
1.691(e)-1	94-455
1.692-1	98-259, 98-369, 99-514, 107-134
1.701-2	105-34
1.702-1	105-34, 108-27
1.702-1(a)(5)	99-514
1.702-3T(g)	99-514, 100-647
1.703-1	94-12, 94-455, 95-30, 96-589
1.704-4	105-34
1.706-1	94-455, 98-369, 105-34
1.706-1(c)	105-34
1.707-1	98-369
1.721-1	94-455, 105-34
1.722-1	94-455, 105-34
1.723-1	94-455
1.731-1	103-465, 105-34
1.731-1(a)(2)	105-34
1.732-2	106-170
1.734-1	98-369
1.735-1	98-369, 105-34
1.736-1	103-66
1.737-1	105-34
1.743-1	98-369
1.751-1	94-455, 95-600, 95-618, 97-448, 98-369, 103-66, 105-34, 106-170
1.761-2	96-222
1.801-2—1.801-8	98-369 (repealed and partially incorporated Code Sec. 801 as 816 and/or 817)
1.802-3	98-369 (repealed and substantially incorporated Code Sec. 802 as 801)
1.804-3	98-369 (repealed and partially incorporated Code Sec. 804 as 812)
1.804-4	98-369 (repealed and partially incorporated Code Sec. 804 as 805)
1.806-3	98-369 (repealed and partially incorporated Code Sec. 806 as 807)
1.809-2, 1.809-4—1.809-5	98-369 (repealed and partially incorporated Code Sec. 809 as 803 and/or 805)
1.810-2—1.810-3	98-369 (repealed and partially incorporated Code Sec. 810 as 807)
1.811-1—1.811-2	98-369 (repealed and partially incorporated Code Sec. 811 as 808)
1.812-1—1.812-8	98-369 (repealed and substantially incorporated Code Sec. 812 as 810)
1.815-1—1.815-6	98-369 (repealed and substantially incorporated Code Sec. 815 as 815)
1.817-1—1.817-4	98-369 (repealed and partially incorporated Code Sec. 817 as 818)
1.818-1—1.818-8	98-369 (repealed and partially incorporated Code Sec. 818 as 811)
1.819-1, 1.819-2	98-369 (repealed Code Sec. 819)
1.822-4	99-514 (redesignated Code Sec. 822 as 834)
1.822-8—1.822-12	99-514 (redesignated Code Sec. 822 as 834)

Regulations Section	Public Law Making Changes Not Reflected
1.826-1—1.826-7	99-514 (redesignated Code Sec. 826 as 835)
1.831-3	99-514
1.832-5	99-514
1.851-1	91-172, 94-12, 95-345, 99-514, 100-647
1.851-3—1.851-4	91-172, 94-12, 105-34
1.851-5—1.851-6	105-34
1.852-1	99-514
1.852-2	95-600, 99-514, 109-222, 115-97
1.852-3	105-34
1.852-4	98-369, 99-514, 105-34
1.852-5	99-514, 105-34
1.852-9	99-514
1.852-11	105-34
1.853-3	111-325
1.854-1	97-34, 98-369, 99-514
1.854-2	99-514
1.854-3	99-514
1.856-1	99-514
1.856-2	99-514, 105-34, 106-170, 115-141
1.856-3	99-514, 105-34, 115-141
1.856-4	99-514, 105-34, 115-141
1.856-4(b)(1), (2) and (5)	106-170
1.856-5	99-514
1.856-6	105-34, 106-170, 115-141
1.857-1	105-34
1.857-2	106-170
1.857-3	99-514
1.857-5	99-514, 105-34
1.857-6	98-369, 99-514, 105-34, 106-170
1.857-7	99-514, 105-34, 105-206
1.857-8	105-34
1.857-11	105-206
1.860E-1	104-188, 115-97
1.860G-2	104-188
1.861-1	94-455, 95-30, 95-600, 99-514, 100-647, 111-240
1.861-2	93-625, 95-600, 99-514, 101-508, 108-357, 111-226
1.861-3	87-834, 100-203, 100-647
1.861-4	105-34, 107-16
1.861-7	99-514
1.861-9T(g), 1.861-9T(h)	115-97
1.861-11T	108-357, 110-289, 111-226
1.861-15	95-600, 99-514
1.861-16	99-514
1.862-1	94-455, 95-30, 97-34, 99-514
1.863-4	105-34
1.864-2	105-34
1.864-3	99-514, 100-647
1.864-4	98-369, 100-647
1.864-5	111-240
1.864-6	98-369, 99-514, 100-647
1.864-7	98-369, 99-514, 100-647
1.864-8T	108-357
1.871-7	94-455, 98-369, 99-514, 100-647, 103-465, 109-222
1.871-8	94-455, 98-369, 99-514, 100-647, 103-66, 103-465
1.871-14	111-147
1.872-2	99-514, 100-647, 101-239
1.873-1	89-809, 92-580, 95-30, 98-369, 105-277
1.875-1	89-809
1.879-1	98-369, 99-514
1.881-1	98-369, 99-514, 103-66
1.881-2	98-369, 99-514, 103-66, 108-357
1.882-1	99-514, 100-647
1.882-2	100-647
1.883-1	94-164, 99-514, 100-647

Regulations Section	Public Law Making Changes Not Reflected
1.884-4(a)(2)	104-188
1.892-2T	100-647
1.893-1	100-647
1.894-1	99-514, 100-647
1.897-3	104-188
1.897-5T(c)(6)	100-647
1.901-1(a)	104-188, 105-34
1.901-1(f)	97-248, 98-369
1.902-3	94-455
1.902-4	94-455
1.907-0	110-343
1.907(a)-0	110-343
1.907(a)-1	103-66, 110-343
1.907(b)-1	103-66, 110-343
1.907(c)-1—1.907(c)-3	103-66, 110-343
1.907(d)-1	110-343
1.907(f)-1	110-343
1.911-1	99-514, 105-34, 109-222, 110-172
1.911-2	99-514, 105-34, 109-222, 110-172
1.911-3—1.911-6	99-514, 105-34, 109-222, 110-172
1.911-8	99-514, 105-34, 109-222, 111-172
1.912-1	86-707, 87-293, 100-647
1.921-1T, 1.921-2	106-519 (repealed Code Sec. 921)
1.927(a)-1T, 1.927(d)-2T	106-519 (repealed Code Sec. 927)
1.936-1	104-188
1.936-4—1.936-7	99-514, 100-647, 104-188
1.936-10	104-188
1.951-1	94-12, 94-455, 98-369, 99-514, 100-647, 103-66, 105-34
1.951-3	98-369, 103-66, 108-357
1.952-1(a)-(d)	99-509, 99-514, 100-647, 108-357
1.952-1(b)	105-34
1.952-2	108-357
1.953-1—1.953-2	98-369, 99-514, 100-647, 105-277, 106-170, 107-147, 109-222, 110-343
1.953-3—1.953-4	98-369, 99-514, 100-647, 105-277, 106-170, 107-147, 109-222, 110-343
1.953-5—1.953-6	98-369, 99-514, 100-647, 105-277, 106-170, 107-147, 109-222, 110-343
1.954-2	105-34, 105-277, 106-170, 107-147, 108-357, 109-222, 109-432, 110-343
1.954-3	103-66
1.954-4	98-369, 99-514, 106-170, 107-147, 109-222, 110-343
1.954-6	99-514, 103-66, 108-357
1.954-7, 1.954-8	99-514, 103-66
1.955-5	94-12
1.955-6	94-12
1.956-2	103-66, 105-34, 108-357
1.957-2	99-514
1.958-2	103-66
1.959-1—1.959-3	103-66
1.961-1	105-34
1.961-2	105-34
1.962-1	95-600, 100-647
1.970-1—1.970-3	94-455 (repeal of Code Sec. 972)
1.971-1	94-455 (repeal of Code Sec. 972)
1.988-1(a)(9)	105-34
1.988-3	103-66
1.988-5	103-66
1.989(b)-1	105-34
1.991-1	105-34, 105-206
1.992-1	98-369
1.992-1(f)	104-188
1.993-3(f)	103-66
1.995-1	94-455, 95-600, 98-369, 99-514, 100-647
1.995-1(a)	105-34, 105-206

Regulations Section	Public Law Making Changes Not Reflected
1.1402(a)-8(b)	94-455
1.1402(a)-11(a)	104-188
1.1402(a)-11(b)	95-615
1.1402(a)-12	99-514
1.1402(a)-15	94-455, 110-246
1.1402(b)-1	94-92, 94-455, 97-248, 98-21, 99-272, 99-509, 99-514, 101-508
1.1402(c)-3	98-369
1.1402(f)-1	95-216
1.1402(g)-1	94-455
1.1402(h)-1(a)	99-514, 101-239
1.1402(h)-1(c)	94-455, 100-647
1.1402(h)-1(d)	100-647
1.1403-1	98-369
1.1441-1, 1.1441-2, 1.1441-4	108-357
1.1445-2	109-222, 110-289
1.1445-4	110-289
1.1445-5	100-647, 103-66, 104-188, 109-222
1.1445-8	109-222
1.1502-1(g)	94-455
1.1502-3	94-12, 94-455, 95-600, 95-618, 96-222, 97-34, 97-448, 98-369, 100-647
1.1502-5	100-203
1.1502-24	97-34
1.1502-27	113-295
1.1502-47	98-369, 99-514
1.1502-81T	100-647
1.1503-1	88-272, 98-369, 99-514, 100-647, 101-239
1.1551-1	97-34, 99-514, 115-97
1.1561-0—1.1561-3	115-97
1.1563-2, 1.1563-3	108-357
20.0-1, 20.0-2	107-16, 111-312, 112-240
20.2001-1	107-16, 111-312, 112-240, 115-97
20.2011-1	94-455, 107-16, 107-134, 111-312, 112-240, 113-295
20.2011-2	94-455, 107-16, 107-134, 111-312, 112-240, 113-295
20.2012-1	107-16, 111-312, 112-240
20.2013-1	107-16, 111-312, 112-240
20.2013-2	94-455, 107-16, 111-312, 112-240
20.2013-3, 20.2013-4	107-16, 111-312, 112-240
20.2013-5, 20.2013-6	107-16, 111-312
20.2014-1	107-16, 111-312, 112-240
20.2014-2	107-16, 111-312
20.2014-3	107-16, 111-312, 112-240
20.2014-4	107-16, 111-312
20.2014-5	107-16, 111-312
20.2014-6—20.2014-7	107-16, 111-312, 112-240
20.2015-1	107-16, 111-312, 112-240
20.2016-1	107-16, 111-312, 112-240
20.2031-1(a), (b)	94-455, 95-600, 97-34, 97-448, 98-369, 99-514, 100-647, 101-508, 105-34, 105-206, 107-16, 111-312
20.2032A-3, 20.2032A-4, 20.2032A-8	97-34, 97-448, 98-369, 99-514, 100-647, 101-508, 105-34
20.2036-1	94-455, 95-600, 101-508
20.2038-1	94-455
20.2039-1(a)	93-406, 94-455
20.2039-2	97-34, 97-248, 97-448, 98-369, 99-514
20.2039-3	98-369, 99-514
20.2039-4, 20.2039-5	97-34, 97-248, 97-448, 98-369, 99-514
20.2040-1	94-455, 95-600, 96-222, 97-34
20.2053-10	107-16
20.2055-1, 20.2055-2	105-34
20.2055-3	107-16
20.2056(b)-1	105-34

Regulations Section	Public Law Making Changes Not Reflected
20.2056(b)-7	105-34
20.2056(b)-8	105-34
20.2056A-2	105-34
20.2056A-5, 20.2056A-6	107-16, 111-312
20.2056A-7	107-16
20.2101-1	107-16, 107-147, 111-312, 112-240
20.2102-1	104-188, 105-34, 107-16, 111-312, 112-240
20.2104-1(a)(3)	94-455
20.2105-1	100-647, 103-66, 105-34, 108-357
20.2105-1(i)	94-455 (extends the applicability of Code Sec. 861(a)(1)(A) and (c))
20.2105-1(j)	100-647, 103-66, 105-34
20.2105-1(m)	94-455 (repeal of Code Sec. 4912)
20.2106-1, 20.2106-2	107-16, 111-312, 112-240
20.2107-1	94-455, 104-191, 105-34, 107-16, 108-357, 111-312, 112-240
20.2204-1	94-455, 95-600
20.2204-2	94-455
20.2207A-1, 20.2207A-2	105-34
25.0-1	107-16, 111-312
25.2501-1	104-191, 105-34, 107-16, 108-357, 111-312, 114-113
25.2502-1	107-16, 111-312
25.2502-2	107-16, 111-312
25.2503-1	99-514, 107-16, 111-312
25.2503-2	105-34, 107-16, 111-312, 115-97
25.2503-3	95-600, 97-34
25.2504-1, 25.2504-2	107-16, 111-312
25.2511-1	107-16, 107-147, 111-312
25.2511-2, 25.2511-3	107-16, 107-147
25.2512-1	94-455
25.2513-3	97-34
25.2515-1—25.2515-4	94-455, 95-600
25.2516-1	98-369
25.2518-2	111-312
25.2522(c)-3	98-369
26.2642-1—26.2642-5	107-16, 110-312, 112-240
26.2654-1	105-206
26.2662-1	111-312
25.2701-1—25.2701-6	104-188
25.2702-1	104-188
31.3101-2	95-216
31.3111-2	95-216
31.3121(a)(1)-1	95-216, 101-508
31.3121(a)(2)-1	100-203
31.3121(a)(3)-1	98-21
31.3121(a)(5)-1	96-222, 96-499
31.3121(a)(6)-1	96-499
31.3121(a)(9)-1	98-21
31.3121(b)(3)-1	100-203
31.3121(b)(8)-2	98-21
31.3121(b)(19)-1	103-296
31.3121(b)(20)-1	104-188
31.3121(d)-1	95-600, 104-188
31.3121(i)-2, 31.3121(i)-3	100-203
31.3121(q)-1	100-203
31.3301-3	91-373, 92-329, 94-566, 100-203, 105-33
31.3302(a)-1	91-373, 92-329, 94-566
31.3302(c)-1	94-45, 94-455, 97-35
31.3302(d)-1	94-455
31.3306(a)-1	91-373, 94-566
31.3306(b)(1)-1	91-373, 94-566, 97-248
31.3306(b)(3)-1	98-21
31.3306(b)(5)-1	96-222
31.3306(b)(6)-1	96-499
31.3306(c)-2(c)	91-373, 94-566
31.3306(c)-3	91-373, 94-566

Regulations Section	Public Law Making Changes Not Reflected
31.3306(c)(1)-1	94-566
31.3306(c)(2)-1	94-566
31.3306(c)(7)-1, 31.3306(c)(8)-1	91-373
31.3306(c)(10)-2	91-373
31.3306(c)(18)-1	100-647
31.3306(i)-1	91-373
31.3306(j)-1	94-566
31.3306(k)-1	91-373
31.3401(a)-1T	98-369, 99-514, 100-647, 107-16
31.3401(a)(2)-1	101-239
31.3401(a)(12)-1	98-369, 98-397, 99-514, 100-203, 100-647, 107-16
31.3401(a)(14)-1	99-514, 100-647
31.3401(a)(15)-1	100-647
31.3401(c)-1(a)	94-455
31.3402(b)-1	94-455, 95-600, 97-34
31.3402(e)-1(d)	101-239
31.3402(f)(1)-1	99-514, 100-203
31.3402(f)(3)-1	100-203
31.3402(f)(4)-2	99-514, 100-203
31.3402(g)-1	103-66, 107-16
31.3402(i)-2	99-514
31.3402(o)-2	97-248
31.3402(p)-1	103-465, 107-16
31.3402(p)-1(b)(2)	100-203
31.3405(c)-1	107-16
35.3405-1T	98-369, 99-514, 100-647, 102-318
31.3406(a)-1	107-16
31.3406(c)-1	107-16
31.3406(d)-3	107-16
31.3406(d)-4	107-16
31.3406(d)-5	102-486
31.3406(e)-1	107-16
31.3406(g)-3	107-16
31.3406(h)-2	107-16
31.3501(a)-1T, Q-10 and A-10	103-66, 107-16
31.3507-1, 31.3507-2	111-226 (repealed Code Sec. 3507)
48.4041-3	101-508, 103-66, 104-188, 105-34, 109-59
48.4041-4	101-508, 103-66, 104-188, 105-34, 108-357, 109-59
48.4041-5, 48.4041-6	101-508, 103-66, 104-188, 105-34, 108-357, 109-59
48.4041-7	101-508, 103-66, 104-188, 105-34
48.4041-8	104-188, 105-34, 108-357, 109-59
48.4041-9	101-508, 102-240, 103-66, 109-59
48.4041-11	101-508, 103-66, 104-188, 105-2, 105-34, 108-357, 109-59
48.4041-13(c)	104-188
48.4041-19, 48.4041-20	101-508, 103-66, 105-34, 105-178, 108-357
48.4042-1	99-662, 100-647, 108-357
145.4051-1	98-369
145.4051-1(a)(4)	109-59
145.4051-1(c)(3)	105-34
145.4052-1(d)(8)(iii)	105-34
48.4061(a)-1—48.4061(a)-5	98-369 (Code Sec. 4061 stricken but regulations still in effect)
48.4061(b)-1, 48.4061(b)-2	98-369 (Code Sec. 4061 stricken but regulations still in effect)
48.4062(a)-1, 48.4062(b)-1	98-369 (Code Sec. 4062 stricken but regulations still in effect)
48.4063-1—48.4063-3	98-369 (Code Sec. 4063 stricken but regulations still in effect)
48.4064-1	101-508, 109-59
48.4071-1	108-357, 109-59
48.4071-2, 48.4071-3	108-357
48.4072-1	98-369, 108-357, 109-58
48.4073-1	98-369, 108-357
48.4073-2	108-357
48.4073-3	98-369, 108-357
48.4081-1(c)(3)(i)	108-357
48.4081-3	108-357, 109-59
48.4081-6	108-357
48.4082-1, 48.4082-4	108-357
48.4082-6	108-357, 109-59
48.4083-1	108-357
48.4101-1	108-357, 109-59, 109-280
48.4121-1(b), (d)(5)	97-119, 99-272
48.4161(a)-1	98-369, 109-59
48.4161(a)-3	98-369
48.4161(b)-1	98-369, 105-34, 108-357, 108-493
48.4161(b)-2	105-34, 108-357, 108-493
48.4216(b)-1(b)(5)	98-369
48.4216(b)-3(a)(4)	98-369
48.4216(b)-4(e)	98-369
48.4216(f)-1	98-369
48.4218-1	89-44, 95-227, 98-369 (repealed Code Secs. 4061 and 4141)
48.4218-5	89-44, 95-227
48.4221-7	95-618
48.4222(b)-1	105-34
48.4222(c)-1	101-508
48.4222(d)-1	105-34
49.4251-1—49.4251-2	89-44, 89-368, 90-285, 90-364, 91-172, 91-614, 96-499, 97-34, 97-248, 98-369, 101-508, 105-34, 105-206
49.4252-2, 49.4252-4—49.4252-5	89-44
49.4253-1, 49.4253-2	89-44
49.4253-3	89-44, 101-508
49.4253-4—49.4253-7, 49.4253-10	89-44
49.4253-11, 49.4253-12	89-44, 101-508
49.4254-1	89-44, 95-172
49.4254-2	89-44
49.4261-1	89-44, 91-258, 97-248, 101-508, 104-188, 105-2, 105-34
49.4261-3—49.4261-7	89-44, 91-258, 97-248, 101-508, 105-34
49.4261-8	89-44, 91-258, 97-248, 101-508, 104-188, 105-34
49.4261-9	89-44, 91-258, 97-248, 101-508, 105-34
49.4261-10	89-44, 91-258, 97-248, 101-508
49.4262(a)-1	89-44, 91-258, 97-248
49.4262(b)-1, 49.4262(c)-1	89-44, 97-248
49.4264(a)-1—49.4264(f)-1	91-258 (redesignated former Code Sec. 4264 as Code Sec. 4263)
49.4264(c)-1	91-258 (redesignated former Code Sec. 4264 as Code Sec. 4263), 105-34
49.4271-1	101-508
44.4401-1	93-499, 97-362
44.4411-1	93-499, 97-362
41.4481-1	108-357
52.4682-1	104-188, 105-34
52.4682-2	105-34
52.4682-4	105-34
44.4901-1(b)	93-499, 94-455, 97-362
44.4905-1, 44.4905-2	94-455
53.4940-1	98-369, 100-647, 109-280
53.4941(a)-1	109-280
53.4941(c)-1	109-280
53.4941(d)-3	100-647
53.4941(d)-4	96-608
53.4942(a)-1	97-34, 98-369, 109-280
53.4942(a)-2	97-34, 98-369, 99-514, 109-280
53.4942(a)-3	98-369
53.4942(b)-1	100-647

Regulations Section	Public Law Making Changes Not Reflected
53.4943-2	109-280
53.4943-4	98-369
53.4943-10	96-596, 109-280
53.4944-1, 53.4944-4	109-280
53.4945-1, 53.4945-2	109-280
53.4945-4	100-647
53.4945-5	98-369, 100-647, 109-280
53.4946-1	98-369, 99-514, 105-206
53.4947-1	105-34
53.4951-1	96-596
53.4952-1	96-596
53.4958-1	109-280
53.4958-2	111-148
53.4958-3, 53.4958-4	109-280
53.4963-1(a)-(c)	104-168, 109-280
54.4974-1	99-514
54.4975-1	104-188, 105-34, 109-280
54.4975-6	105-34, 109-280
54.4975-7	95-600, 99-514, 105-34, 107-16, 109-280
54.4975-11	99-514, 105-34, 107-16
54.4975-12	96-222, 105-34
54.4976-1T	99-514
54.4978-1T	99-514, 100-203, 100-647, 101-239, 105-34
54.4980B-7	111-5, 111-344, 112-40
20.6001-1, 25.6001-1	107-16, 111-312
20.6011-1, 25.6011-1	107-16
1.6011-2	98-369
301.6011-2	101-239, 105-34, 111-147
1.6012-1	99-514, 100-647, 105-34
1.6012-2	93-625
1.6012-3	96-589, 105-34
1.6013-1	99-514, 100-647
1.6013-2	100-647, 101-239, 105-206
1.6015-7	109-432
20.6018-1	94-455, 97-34, 98-369, 105-34, 107-16, 111-312
20.6018-2	107-16, 111-312
20.6018-3	94-455, 107-16, 111-312
20.6018-4	107-16, 111-312
25.6019-1—25.6019-2	105-34, 107-16, 111-312
25.6019-3—25.6019-4	107-16, 111-312
1.6031(b)-1T	105-34, 108-357
1.6031(c)-1T	105-34
1.6033-2	103-66, 104-168, 105-34, 107-276
1.6033-3	105-277
1.6034-1, 301.6034-1	109-280
1.6037-1	97-354, 98-369
1.6038A-6	104-188
1.6041-2	108-357
1.6041-3	108-173
1.6042-2	97-354, 98-67
1.6042-4	104-168
1.6044-2	98-67
1.6044-3	89-809
1.6044-5	104-168
1.6045-1	99-514, 100-647
1.6045-4	102-486
1.6045-4(o)	104-188
1.6046-1	100-647, 105-34
1.6047-1	97-248, 98-369, 107-16
1.6049-4	98-67, 109-58
1.6049-5	98-67, 99-514, 109-58, 109-222
1.6049-6(b)(1)(iii)	104-168
1.6049-7	109-58
1.6050A-1	104-188
1.6050I-1	100-690
1.6050I-1(f)(2)(i)	104-168
1.6050L-1	108-357, 109-280
1.6050P-1	104-134, 107-134
31.6051-1	103-465, 108-357
301.6058-1	95-600
301.6059-1	109-280
301.6061-1	105-206
20.6065-1(b)	94-455
25.6065-1(b)	94-455
1.6071-1	105-206
1.6072-3	95-628, 98-369
20.6075-1	107-16, 111-312
25.6075-1	107-16, 111-312, 112-240
1.6091-1	95-615, 97-34, 99-514, 100-203, 101-239
1.6091-3	95-615, 97-34, 99-514, 100-203, 101-239
1.6091-4	95-615, 97-34, 99-514, 100-203, 101-239
301.6096-1	96-223, 97-34, 97-414, 98-369, 103-66
301.6103(h)(2)-1	97-452, 98-21, 98-369, 98-378, 99-92, 99-335, 99-386, 99-514, 100-485, 100-647, 100-690, 101-239, 101-508, 104-168
301.6103(i)-1	97-452, 98-21, 98-369, 98-378, 99-92, 99-335, 99-386, 99-514, 100-485, 100-647, 100-690, 101-239, 101-508, 104-168, 107-134
301.6104(a)-1	106-230
301.6104(a)-6	106-230
301.6104(b)-1(b)	105-206, 106-230
301.6104(d)-0—301.6104(d)-3	106-230
301.6109-1	103-465, 105-206
301.6109-2	110-246
301.6110-1—301.6110-3	105-206
301.6110-7	105-206
301.6111-1T	105-34, 108-357
301.6111-2	108-357
20.6151-1(c)	92-5 (repealed Code Sec. 6312)
301.6159-1(b)	105-206
301.6159-1(c)	104-168, 108-357
300.3	109-222, 116-25
20.6161-1(a)	94-455
20.6161-2	94-455
20.6163-1	94-455
1.6164-2	97-248
1.6164-4	97-248
1.6164-8	97-248
20.6166-1	97-34, 105-34, 105-206, 107-16, 111-312, 112-240
20.6166A-1	97-34 (repealed Code Sec. 6166A)
20.6166A-2—20.6166A-3	94-455, 97-34 (repealed Code Sec. 6166A)
301.6201-1	94-12, 94-455, 98-369, 104-168
301.6211-1	94-455, 96-223, 100-418, 106-554
301.6212-1	99-514, 100-647, 105-206
301.6213-1	105-206
301.6213-1(e)	104-168
301.6224(c)-1	107-147
301.6224(c)-2	107-147
301.6229(f)-1	107-147
31.6302(c)-1	95-147, 98-369, 100-418, 100-647
40.6302(c)-1(e)	108-357, 111-237
301.6305-1(a)	104-193
301.6320-1	109-432, 114-94, 114-113, 116-25
301.6323(i)-1	99-514
20.6325-1	97-248
301.6330-1	109-432, 110-28, 114-113, 115-141, 116-25
301.6331-1	105-34, 105-206, 113-295
301.6331-2	105-26, 114-94
301.6334-1	115-97
301.6334-2	105-34
301.6334-3	105-34, 115-97
301.6335-1	105-206

Regulations Section	Public Law Making Changes Not Reflected
301.6336-1	116-25
301.6337-1	97-248
301.6340-1	105-206
301.6343-1	104-168, 105-206, 115-97
301.6343-2—301.6343-3	115-97
301.6361-1—301.6365-2	101-508 (repealed Code Secs. 6361-6365)
301.6401-1(a)(2)	98-369, 109-58, 115-97
301.6402-4	101-508, 106-554
301.6402-5	98-378, 101-508
301.6402-6	103-296
301.6404-1	94-455, 99-514, 100-647
301.6405-1	94-455, 99-514, 101-508, 106-554
1.6411-1—1.6411-3	94-455, 95-30, 97-34, 98-369, 99-514
48.6412-1, 48.6412-2	100-17, 101-508, 102-240, 105-178, 109-59
31.6413(c)-1	93-445, 94-455, 98-21, 98-67, 99-272
48.6416(b)(2)-1	109-59
48.6416(b)(2)-2	108-357, 109-280
48.6416(b)(2)-3	109-59
48.6416(c)-1	98-369 (repealed Code Sec. 6416(c))
48.6416(f)-1	105-34
48.6420-4	109-59
48.6421-1(c), 48.6421-2(c)	105-178
48.6421-3(b)(2)	105-178, 105-206
48.6421-4	108-357, 109-59
1.6425-2	99-499, 99-514, 115-97
48.6427-1	105-34, 109-59
48.6427-2	105-34, 108-357
48.6427-3	105-178, 105-206
48.6427-8	109-59
48.6427-9	109-59, 109-432
48.6427-11	109-59 (redesignation of Code Sec. 6427(l)(5) as Code Sec. 6427(l)(6))
301.6501(a)-1	98-369
301.6501(f)-1	88-272
301.6501(h)-1	95-600
301.6501(i)-1	94-455
301.6501(j)-1	95-628
301.6501(m)-1	95-30, 95-600, 95-628, 98-369, 99-514, 115-97
301.6501(n)-1	100-203
301.6503(a)-1	99-514
301.6503(b)-1	96-589, 101-508
301.6511(d)-2	95-600, 95-628, 99-514, 101-508
301.6511(d)-4	95-628, 97-34, 99-514
301.6511(f)-1	100-647
301.6512-1	96-223, 97-248, 100-418, 100-647
301.6532-1	96-589
301.6601-1	99-514, 105-34, 105-206
301.6601-1(e)	97-248, 105-34
301.6611-1	96-223, 97-248, 103-66, 105-34, 111-147
301.6621-1	99-514, 101-239, 101-508, 103-465, 105-206
301.6621-2T	101-239
301.6621-3	104-168, 105-34
301.6651-1	97-248, 99-514, 101-239, 104-168, 110-245
301.6652-1	97-248, 98-67, 98-397, 100-647
301.6652-1(d)	96-167, 97-248
301.6652-2	99-514, 100-203, 104-168, 104-188, 105-277, 106-230
301.6652-2(f)	105-34
301.6652-3	97-248, 104-188
301.6652-3(b)	105-34
301.6653-1	101-239
1.6654-1	97-34, 97-248, 98-369, 99-514, 100-203, 100-418, 100-647, 102-164, 103-66, 111-152
1.6654-2	97-34, 97-248, 99-514, 100-203, 100-418, 100-647, 102-164, 103-66, 103-465, 105-34, 105-277, 106-170, 111-152
1.6654-3	97-34, 97-248, 98-369, 99-514, 100-203, 100-418, 100-647, 102-164, 103-66
1.6655-1	99-514, 100-203, 100-418, 100-647, 102-318, 103-66
1.6655-2	99-514, 100-203, 100-418, 100-647, 102-318, 103-66, 103-465, 104-188, 106-170
1.6655-3	99-514, 100-203, 100-418, 100-647, 102-318, 103-66
1.6655-7	97-248, 103-66
301.6656-1	105-206
301.6657-1	100-647, 110-28, 111-198
301.6659-1	101-239 (repealed Code Sec. 6659)
1.6662-4(g)	105-34
1.6662-5	103-66, 109-280
301.6673-1	97-248, 99-514, 100-647, 101-239
31.6682-1	98-67
301.6685-1	104-168
301.6693-1	98-369, 100-647, 104-188, 104-191, 105-34
301.6708-1T	99-514
48.6715-1	108-357
301.6721-1	114-27
301.6721-1(f), (g)	109-280
301.6722-1	114-27
301.6724-1	102-486, 103-66, 109-280
301.6802-1	89-44
301.6863-2	100-647
301.6871(a)-1	96-589
301.6871(a)-2	96-589
301.6873-1	96-589
301.7122-1	109-222, 116-25
301.7207-1	97-248, 107-276
301.7272-1	109-59, 108-357
301.7422-1	104-168
301.7426-1	97-248, 105-206
301.7433-1	104-168, 105-206
301.7454-2	100-203, 104-168
301.7481-1	91-172, 100-647
301.7483-1	91-172
301.7502-1	89-713, 90-364, 95-147, 98-369, 104-168, 105-206
301.7513-1(c)	94-455
1.7519-1T	100-647
1.7519-1T(b)(1)	101-239
1.7519-2T	100-647, 101-239, 105-34
1.7519-2T(d)	101-239
301.7604-1	95-599, 96-223, 97-424, 98-369, 99-514, 100-647
301.7605-1(i)	98-369
301.7611-1, Q&A-16	105-206
301.7623-1	104-168, 116-25
301.7654-1	99-514
301.7701-6	107-16, 111-312, 112-240
301.7701-9	94-455
301.7701-13A	99-514, 100-647, 104-188, 108-357
301.7701-14	91-172
301.7701-17T	99-514
301.7701(b)-1, 301.7701(b)-5	108-357
301.7701(i)-1	108-357
1.7703-1	98-369, 108-311
1.7704-1	105-34, 105-206
301.7805-1(b)	104-168
301.7811-1	104-168
305.7871-1	98-369, 99-514, 100-203
301.9100-9T	101-508 (repeal Code Secs. 1101-1103)
301.9100-10T	101-508 (repeal Code Secs. 1101-1103)
301.9100-11T	101-508 (repeal Code Secs. 1101-1103)
301.9100-14T	98-369, 99-514, 100-647
301.9100-15T	98-369, 99-514, 100-647

[The next page is 21,001.]

INCOME TAX

Normal Tax and Surtax

EXPLANATION OF REGULATIONS

See p. 20,601 for regulations not amended to reflect law changes

[Reg. §1.0-1]

§1.0-1. Internal Revenue Code of 1954 and regulations.—(a) *Enactment of law.*—The Internal Revenue Code of 1954 which became law upon enactment of Public Law 591, 83d Congress, approved August 16, 1954, provides in part as follows:

Be it enacted by the Senate and House of Representatives of the United States of America in Congress assembled, That (a) *Citation.* (1) The provisions of this Act set forth under the heading "Internal Revenue Title" may be cited as the "Internal Revenue Code of 1954".

(2) The Internal Revenue Code enacted on February 10, 1939, as amended, may be cited as the "Internal Revenue Code of 1939".

(b) *Publication.*—This Act shall be published as volume 68A of the United States Statutes at Large, with a comprehensive table of contents and an appendix; but without an index or marginal references. The date of enactment, bill number, public law number, and chapter number, shall be printed as a headnote.

(c) *Cross reference.*—For saving provisions, effective date provisions, and other related provisions, see chapter 80 (sec. 7801 and following) of the Internal Revenue Code of 1954.

(d) *Enactment of Internal Revenue Title into law.*—The Internal Revenue Title referred to in subsection (a)(1) is as follows:

* * *

In general, the provisions of the Internal Revenue Code of 1954 are applicable with respect to taxable years beginning after December 31, 1953, and ending after August 16, 1954. Certain provisions of that Code are deemed to be included in the Internal Revenue Code of 1939. See section 7851.

(b) *Scope of regulations.*—The regulations in this part deal with (1) the income taxes imposed under subtitle A of the Internal Revenue Code of 1954, and (2) certain administrative provisions contained in subtitle F of such Code relating to such taxes. In general, the applicability of such regulations is commensurate with the applicability of the respective provisions of the Internal Revenue Code of 1954 except that with respect to the provisions of the Internal Revenue Code of 1954 which are deemed to be included in the Internal Revenue Code of 1939, the regulations relating to such provisions are applicable to certain fiscal years and short taxable years which are subject to the Internal Revenue Code of 1939. Those provisions of the regulations which are applicable to taxable years subject to the Internal Revenue Code of 1939 and the specific taxable years to which such provisions are so applicable are identified in each instance. The regulations in 26 CFR (1939) Part 39 (Regulations 118) are continued in effect until superseded by the regulations in this part. See Treasury Decision 6091, approved August 16, 1954 (19 F.R. 5167, C.B. 1954-2, 47). [Reg. §1.0-1.]

☐ [T.D. 6161, 2-3-56.]

DETERMINATION OF TAX LIABILITY

Tax on Individuals

[Reg. §1.1-1]

§1.1-1. Income tax on individuals.—(a) *General rule.*—(1) Section 1 of the Code imposes an income tax on the income of every individual who is a citizen or resident of the United States and, to the extent provided by section 871(b) or 877(b), on the income of a nonresident alien individual. For optional tax in the case of taxpayers with adjusted gross income of less than $10,000 (less than $5,000 for taxable years beginning before January 1, 1970) see section 3. The tax imposed is upon taxable income (determined by subtracting the allowable deductions from gross income). The tax is determined in accordance with the table contained in section 1. See subparagraph (2) of this paragraph for reference guides to the appropriate table for taxable years beginning on or after January 1, 1964, and before January 1, 1965, taxable years beginning after December 31, 1964, and before January 1, 1971, and taxable years beginning after December 31, 1970. In certain cases credits are allowed against the amount of the tax. See part IV (section 31 and following), subchapter A, chapter 1 of the Code. In general, the tax is payable upon the basis of returns rendered by persons liable therefor (subchapter A (sections 6001 and following), chapter 61 of the Code) or at the source of the income by withholding. For the computation of tax in the case of a joint return of a husband and wife, or a return of a surviving spouse, for taxable years beginning before January 1, 1971, see section 2. The computation of tax in such a case for taxable years beginning after December 31, 1970, is determined in accordance with the table contained in section 1(a) as amended by the Tax Reform Act of 1969. For other rates of tax on individuals, see section 5(a). For the imposition of an additional tax for the calendar years 1968, 1969, and 1970, see section 51(a).

(2)(i) For taxable years beginning on or after January 1, 1964, the tax imposed upon a single individual, a head of a household, a married individual filing a separate return, and estates and trusts is the tax imposed by section 1 determined in accordance with the appropriate table contained in the following subsection of section 1:

	Taxable years beginning in 1964	Taxable years beginning after 1964 but before 1971	Taxable years beginning after December 31, 1970. (References in this column are to the Code as amended by the Tax Reform Act of 1969)
Single individual	Sec. 1(a)(1)	Sec. 1(a)(2)	Sec. 1(c)
Head of a household	Sec. 1(b)(1)	Sec. 1(b)(2)	Sec. 1(b)
Married individual filing a separate return	Sec. 1(a)(1)	Sec. 1(a)(2)	Sec. 1(d)
Estates and trusts	Sec. 1(a)(1)	Sec. 1(a)(2)	Sec. 1(d)

(ii) For taxable years beginning after December 31, 1970, the tax imposed by section 1(d), as amended by the Tax Reform Act of 1969, shall apply to the income effectively connected with the conduct of a trade or business in the United States by a married alien individual who is a nonresident of the United States for all or part of the taxable year or by a foreign estate or trust. For such years the tax imposed by section 1(c), as amended by such Act, shall apply to the income effectively connected with the conduct of a trade or business in the United States by an unmarried alien individual (other than a surviving spouse) who is a nonresident of the United States for all or part of the taxable year. See paragraph (b)(2) of §1.871-8.

(3) The income tax imposed by section 1 upon any amount of taxable income is computed by adding to the income tax for the bracket in which that amount falls in the appropriate table in section 1 the income tax upon the excess of the amount over the bottom of the bracket at the rate indicated in such table.

(4) The provisions of section 1 of the Code, as amended by the Tax Reform Act of 1969, and of this paragraph may be illustrated by the following examples:

Example (1). A, an unmarried individual, had taxable income for the calendar year 1964 of $15,750. Accordingly, the tax upon such taxable income would be $4,507.50, computed as follows from the table in section 1(a)(1):

Tax on $14,000 (from table)	$3,790.00
Tax on $1,750 (at 41% as determined from the table)	717.50
Total tax on $15,750	$4,507.50

Example (2). Assume the same facts as in example (1), except the figures are for the calendar year 1965. The tax upon such taxable income would be $4,232.50, computed as follows from the table in section 1(a)(2):

Tax on $14,000 (from table) $3,550.00
Tax on $1,750 (at 39% as determined from the table) . . 682.50

Total tax on $15,750 . . . . $4,232.50

Example (3). Assume the same facts as in example (1), except the figures are for the calendar year 1971. The tax upon such taxable income would be $3,752.50, computed as follows from the table in section 1(c), as amended:

Tax on $14,000 (from table) $3,210.00
Tax on $1,750 (at 31% as determined from the table) . . 542.50

Total tax on $15,750 . . . . $3,752.50

(b) *Citizens or residents of the United States liable to tax.*—In general, all citizens of the United States, wherever resident, and all resident alien individuals are liable to the income taxes imposed by the Code whether the income is received from sources within or without the United States. Pursuant to section 876, a nonresident alien individual who is a bona fide resident of a section 931 possession (as defined in §1.931-1(c)(1) of this chapter) or Puerto Rico during the entire taxable year is, except as provided in section 931 or 933 with respect to income from sources within such possessions, subject to taxation in the same manner as a resident alien individual. As to tax on nonresident alien individuals, see sections 871 and 877.

(c) *Who is a citizen.*—Every person born or naturalized in the United States and subject to its jurisdiction is a citizen. For other rules governing the acquisition of citizenship, see chapters 1 and 2 of title III of the Immigration and Nationality Act (8 U.S.C. 1401-1459). For rules governing loss of citizenship, see sections 349 to 357, inclusive, of such Act (8 U.S.C. 1481-1489), *Schneider v. Rusk*, (1964) 377 U.S. 163, and Rev. Rul. 70-506, C.B. 1970-2, 1. For rules pertaining to persons who are nationals but not citizens at birth, e.g., a person born in American Samoa, see section 308 of such Act (8 U.S.C. 1408). For special rules applicable to certain expatriates who have lost citizenship with a principal purpose of avoiding certain taxes, see section 877. A foreigner who has filed his declaration of intention of becoming a citizen but who has not yet been admitted to citizenship by a final order of a naturalization court is an alien.

(d) *Effective/applicability date.*—The second sentence of paragraph (b) of this section applies to taxable years ending after April 9, 2008. [Reg. §1.1-1.]

□ [T.D. 6161, 2-3-56. *Amended by* T.D. 7117, 5-24-71; T.D. 7332, 12-20-74 *and* T.D. 9391, 4-4-2008.]

[Reg. §1.1(h)-1]

§1.1(h)-1. Capital gains look-through rule for sales or exchanges of interests in a partnership, S corporation, or trust.—(a) *In general.*—When an interest in a partnership held for more than one year is sold or exchanged, the transferor may recognize ordinary income (e.g., under section 751(a)), collectibles gain, section 1250 capital gain, and residual long-term capital gain or loss. When stock in an S corporation held for more than one year is sold or exchanged, the transferor may recognize ordinary income (e.g., under sections 304, 306, 341, 1254), collectibles gain, and residual long-term capital gain or loss. When an interest in a trust held for more than one year is sold or exchanged, a transferor who is not treated as the owner of the portion of the trust attributable to the interest sold or exchanged (sections 673 through 679) (a non-grantor transferor) may recognize collectibles gain and residual long-term capital gain or loss.

(b) *Look-through capital gain.*—(1) *In general.*—Look-through capital gain is the share of collectibles gain allocable to an interest in a partnership, S corporation, or trust, plus the share of section 1250 capital gain allocable to an interest in a partnership, determined under paragraphs (b)(2) and (3) of this section.

(2) *Collectibles gain.*—(i) *Definition.*—For purposes of this section, *collectibles gain* shall be treated as gain from the sale or exchange of a collectible (as defined in section 408(m) without regard to section 408(m)(3)) that is a capital asset held for more than 1 year.

(ii) *Share of collectibles gain allocable to an interest in a partnership, S corporation, or a trust.*—When an interest in a partnership, S corporation, or trust held for more than one year is sold or exchanged in a transaction in which all realized gain is recognized, the transferor shall recognize as collectibles gain the amount of net gain (but not net loss) that would be allocated to that partner (taking into account any remedial allocation under §1.704-3(d)), shareholder, or beneficiary (to the extent attributable to the portion of the partnership interest, S corporation stock, or trust interest transferred that was held for more than one year) if the partnership, S corporation, or trust transferred all of its collectibles for cash equal to the fair market value of the assets in a fully taxable transaction immediately before the transfer of

the interest in the partnership, S corporation, or trust. If less than all of the realized gain is recognized upon the sale or exchange of an interest in a partnership, S corporation, or trust, the same methodology shall apply to determine the collectibles gain recognized by the transferor, except that the partnership, S corporation, or trust shall be treated as transferring only a proportionate amount of each of its collectibles determined as a fraction that is the amount of gain recognized in the sale or exchange over the amount of gain realized in the sale or exchange. With respect to the transfer of an interest in a trust, this paragraph (b)(2) applies only to transfers by non-grantor transferors (as defined in paragraph (a) of this section). This paragraph (b)(2) does not apply to a transaction that is treated, for Federal income tax purposes, as a redemption of an interest in a partnership, S corporation, or trust.

(3) *Section 1250 capital gain.*—(i) *Definition.*—For purposes of this section, *section 1250 capital gain* means the capital gain (not otherwise treated as ordinary income) that would be treated as ordinary income if section 1250(b)(1) included all depreciation and the applicable percentage under section 1250(a) were 100 percent.

(ii) *Share of section 1250 capital gain allocable to interest in partnership.*—When an interest in a partnership held for more than one year is sold or exchanged in a transaction in which all realized gain is recognized, there shall be taken into account under section 1(h)(7)(A)(i) in determining the partner's unrecaptured section 1250 gain the amount of section 1250 capital gain that would be allocated (taking into account any remedial allocation under §1.704-3(d)) to that partner (to the extent attributable to the portion of the partnership interest transferred that was held for more than one year) if the partnership transferred all of its section 1250 property in a fully taxable transaction for cash equal to the fair market value of the assets immediately before the transfer of the interest in the partnership. If less than all of the realized gain is recognized upon the sale or exchange of an interest in a partnership, the same methodology shall apply to determine the section 1250 capital gain recognized by the transferor, except that the partnership shall be treated as transferring only a proportionate amount of each section 1250 property determined as a fraction that is the amount of gain recognized in the sale or exchange over the amount of gain realized in the sale or exchange. This paragraph (b)(3) does not apply to a transaction that is treated, for Federal income tax purposes, as a redemption of a partnership interest.

(iii) *Limitation with respect to net section 1231 gain.*—In determining a transferor partner's net section 1231 gain (as defined in section 1231(c)(3)) for purposes of section 1(h)(7)(B), the transferor partner's allocable share of section 1250 capital gain in partnership property shall not be treated as section 1231 gain, regardless of whether the partnership property is used in the trade or business (as defined in section 1231(b)).

(c) *Residual long-term capital gain or loss.*—The amount of residual long-term capital gain or loss recognized by a partner, shareholder of an S corporation, or beneficiary of a trust on account of the sale or exchange of an interest in a partnership, S corporation, or trust shall equal the amount of long-term capital gain or loss that the partner would recognize under section 741, that the shareholder would recognize upon the sale or exchange of stock of an S corporation, or that the beneficiary would recognize upon the sale or exchange of an interest in a trust (pre-look-through long-term capital gain or loss) minus the amount of look-through capital gain determined under paragraph (b) of this section.

(d) *Special rule for tiered entities.*—In determining whether a partnership, S corporation, or trust has gain from collectibles, such partnership, S corporation, or trust shall be treated as owning its proportionate share of the collectibles of any partnership, S corporation, or trust in which it owns an interest either directly or indirectly through a chain of such entities. In determining whether a partnership has section 1250 capital gain, such partnership shall be treated as owning its proportionate share of the section 1250 property of any partnership in which it owns an interest, either directly or indirectly through a chain of partnerships.

(e) *Notification requirements.*—Reporting rules similar to those that apply to the partners and the partnership under section 751(a) shall apply in the case of sales or exchanges of interests in a partnership, S corporation, or trust that cause holders of such interests to recognize collectibles gain and in the case of sales or exchanges of interests in a partnership that cause holders of such interests to recognize section 1250 capital gain. See §1.751-1(a)(3).

(f) *Examples.*—The following examples illustrate the requirements of this section:

Example 1. Collectibles gain. (i) *A* and *B* are equal partners in a personal service partnership (*PRS*). *B* transfers *B*'s interest in *PRS* to

T for $15,000 when *PRS*'s balance sheet (reflecting a cash receipts and disbursements method of accounting) is as follows:

	ASSETS	
	Adjusted Basis	Market Value
Cash	$3,000	$3,000
Loans Owed to Partnership	10,000	10,000
Collectibles	1,000	3,000
Other Capital Assets	6,000	2,000
Capital Assets	7,000	5,000
Unrealized Receivables	0	14,000
Total	$20,000	$32,000

	LIABILITIES AND CAPITAL	
Liabilities	$2,000	$2,000
Capital:		
A	9,000	15,000
B	9,000	15,000
Total	$20,000	$32,000

(ii) At the time of the transfer, *B* has held the interest in *PRS* for more than one year, and *B*'s basis for the partnership interest is $10,000 ($9,000 plus $1,000, *B*'s share of partnership liabilities). None of the property owned by *PRS* is section 704(c) property. The total amount realized by *B* is $16,000, consisting of the cash received, $15,000, plus $1,000, *B*'s share of the partnership liabilities assumed by *T*. See section 752. *B*'s undivided one-half interest in *PRS* includes a one-half interest in the partnership's unrealized receivables and a one-half interest in the partnership's collectibles.

(iii) If *PRS* were to sell all of its section 751 property in a fully taxable transaction for cash equal to the fair market value of the assets immediately prior to the transfer of *B*'s partnership interest to *T*, *B* would be allocated $7,000 of ordinary income from the sale of *PRS*'s unrealized receivables. Therefore, *B* will recognize $7,000 of ordinary income with respect to the unrealized receivables. The difference between the amount of capital gain or loss that the partner would realize in the absence of section 751 ($6,000) and the amount of ordinary income or loss determined under § 1.751-1(a)(2) ($7,000) is the partner's capital gain or loss on the sale of the partnership interest under section 741. In this case, the transferor has a $1,000 pre-look-through long-term capital loss.

(iv) If *PRS* were to sell all of its collectibles in a fully taxable transaction for cash equal to the fair market value of the assets immediately prior to the transfer of *B*'s partnership interest to *T*, *B* would be allocated $1,000 of gain from the sale of the collectibles. Therefore, *B* will recognize $1,000 of collectibles gain on account of the collectibles held by *PRS*.

(v) The difference between the transferor's pre-look-through long-term capital gain or loss (–$1,000) and the look-through capital gain determined under this section ($1,000) is the transferor's residual long-term capital gain or loss on the sale of the partnership interest. Under these facts, *B* will recognize a $2,000 residual long-term capital loss on account of the sale or exchange of the interest in *PRS*.

Example 2. Special allocations. Assume the same facts as in *Example 1*, except that under the partnership agreement, all gain from the sale of the collectibles is specially allocated to *B*, and *B* transfers *B*'s interest to *T* for $16,000. All items of income, gain, loss, or deduction of *PRS*, other than the gain from the collectibles, are divided equally between *A* and *B*. Under these facts, *B*'s amount realized is $17,000, consisting of the cash received, $16,000, plus $1,000, *B*'s share of the partnership liabilities assumed by *T*. See section 752. *B* will recognize $7,000 of ordinary income with respect to the unrealized receivables (determined under § 1.751-1(a)(2)). Accordingly, *B*'s pre-look-through long-term capital gain would be $0. If *PRS* were to sell all of its collectibles in a fully taxable transaction for cash equal to the fair market value of the assets immediately prior to the transfer of *B*'s partnership interest to *T*, *B* would be allocated $2,000 of gain from the sale of the collectibles. Therefore, *B* will recognize $2,000 of collectibles gain on account of the collectibles held by *PRS*. *B* will recognize a $2,000

residual long-term capital loss on account of the sale of *B*'s interest in *PRS*.

Example 3. Net collectibles loss ignored. Assume the same facts as in *Example 1*, except that the collectibles held by *PRS* have an adjusted basis of $3,000 and a fair market value of $1,000, and the other capital assets have an adjusted basis of $4,000 and a fair market value of $4,000. (The total adjusted basis and fair market value of the partnership's capital assets are the same as in *Example 1*.) If *PRS* were to sell all of its collectibles in a fully taxable transaction for cash equal to the fair market value of the assets immediately prior to the transfer of *B*'s partnership interest to *T*, *B* would be allocated $1,000 of loss from the sale of the collectibles. Because none of the gain from the sale of the interest in *PRS* is attributable to unrealized appreciation in the value of collectibles held by *PRS*, the net loss in collectibles held by *PRS* is not recognized at the time *B* transfers the interest in *PRS*. *B* will recognize $7,000 of ordinary income (determined under § 1.751-1(a)(2)) and a $1,000 long-term capital loss on account of the sale of *B*'s interest in *PRS*.

Example 4. Collectibles gain in an S corporation. (i) A corporation (*X*) has always been an S corporation and is owned by individuals *A*, *B*, and *C*. In 1996, *X* invested in antiques. Subsequent to their purchase, the antiques appreciated in value by $300. *A* owns one-third of the shares of *X* stock and has held that stock for more than one year. *A*'s adjusted basis in the *X* stock is $100. If *A* were to sell all of *A*'s *X* stock to *T* for $150, *A* would realize $50 of pre-look-through long-term capital gain.

(ii) If *X* were to sell its antiques in a fully taxable transaction for cash equal to the fair market value of the assets immediately before the transfer to *T*, *A* would be allocated $100 of gain on account of the sale. Therefore, *A* will recognize $100 of collectibles gain (look-through capital gain) on account of the collectibles held by *X*.

(iii) The difference between the transferor's pre-look-through long-term capital gain or loss ($50) and the look-through capital gain determined under this section ($100) is the transferor's residual long-term capital gain or loss on the sale of the S corporation stock. Under these facts, *A* will recognize $100 of collectibles gain and a $50 residual long-term capital loss on account of the sale of *A*'s interest in *X*.

Example 5. Sale or exchange of partnership interest where part of the interest has a short-term holding period. (i) *A*, *B*, and *C* form an equal partnership (*PRS*). In connection with the formation, *A* contributes $5,000 in cash and a capital asset with a fair market value of $5,000 and a basis of $2,000; *B* contributes $7,000 in cash and a collectible with a fair market value of $3,000 and a basis of $3,000; and *C* contributes $10,000 in cash. At the time of the contribution, *A* had held the contributed property for two years. Six months later, when *A*'s basis in *PRS* is $7,000, *A* transfers *A*'s interest in *PRS* to *T* for $14,000 at a time when *PRS*'s balance sheet (reflecting a cash receipts and disbursements method of accounting) is as follows:

	ASSETS	
	Adjusted Basis	Market Value
Cash	$22,000	$22,000
Unrealized Receivables	0	6,000
Capital Asset	2,000	5,000
Collectible	3,000	9,000
Capital Assets	5,000	14,000
Total	$27,000	$42,000

(ii) Although at the time of the transfer *A* has not held *A*'s interest in *PRS* for more than one year, 50 percent of the fair market value of *A*'s interest in *PRS* was received in exchange for a capital asset with a long-term holding period. Therefore, 50 percent of *A*'s interest in *PRS* has a long-term holding period. See § 1.1223-3(b)(1).

(iii) If *PRS* were to sell all of its section 751 property in a fully taxable transaction immediately before *A*'s transfer of the partnership interest, *A* would be allocated $2,000 of ordinary income. Accord-

ingly, *A* will recognize $2,000 ordinary income and $5,000 ($7,000 – $2,000) of capital gain on account of the transfer to *T* of *A*'s interest in *PRS*. Fifty percent ($2,500) of that gain is long-term capital gain and 50 percent ($2,500) is short-term capital gain. See § 1.1223-3(c)(1).

(iv) If the collectible were sold or exchanged in a fully taxable transaction immediately before *A*'s transfer of the partnership interest, *A* would be allocated $2,000 of gain attributable to the collectible. The gain attributable to the collectible that is allocable to the portion

Reg. § 1.1(h)-1(f)

of the transferred interest in *PRS* with a long-term holding period is $1,000 (50 percent of $2,000). Accordingly, *A* will recognize $1,000 of collectibles gain on account of the transfer of *A*'s interest in *PRS*.

(v) The difference between the amount of pre-look-through long-term capital gain or loss ($2,500) and the look-through capital gain ($1,000) is the amount of residual long-term capital gain or loss that *A* will recognize on account of the transfer of *A*'s interest in *PRS*. Under these facts, *A* will recognize a residual long-term capital gain of $1,500 and a short-term capital gain of $2,500.

(g) *Effective date.*—This section applies to transfers of interests in partnerships, S corporations, and trusts that occur on or after September 21, 2000. [Reg. § 1.1(h)-1.]

☐ [*T.D.* 8902, 9-20-2000.]

[Reg. §1.1(i)-1T]

§1.1(i)-1T. Questions and answers relating to the tax on unearned income of certain minor children (Temporary).

In general.

Q-1. To whom does section 1(i) apply?

A-1. Section 1(i) applies to any child who is under 14 years of age at the close of the taxable year, who has at least one living parent at the close of the taxable year, and who recognizes over $1,000 of unearned income during the taxable year.

Q-2. What is the effective date of section 1(i)?

A-2. Section 1(i) applies to taxable years of the child beginning after December 31, 1986.

Computation of tax.

Q-3. What is the amount of tax imposed by section 1 on a child to whom section 1(i) applies?

A-3. In the case of a child to whom section 1(i) applies, the amount of tax imposed by section 1 equals the greater of (A) the tax imposed by section 1 without regard to section 1(i) or (B) the sum of the tax that would be imposed by section 1 if the child's taxable income was reduced by the child's net unearned income, plus the child's share of the allocable parental tax.

Q-4. What is the allocable parental tax?

A-4. The allocable parental tax is the excess of (A) the tax that would be imposed by section 1 on the sum of the parent's taxable income plus the net unearned income of all children of such parent to whom section 1(i) applies, over (B) the tax imposed by section 1 on the parent's taxable income. Thus, the allocable parental tax is not computed with reference to unearned income of a child over 14 or a child under 14 with less than $1,000 of unearned income. *See* A-10 through A-13 for rules regarding the determination of the parent(s) whose taxable income is taken into account under section 1(i). *See* A-14 for rules regarding the determination of children of the parent whose net unearned income is taken into account under section 1(i).

Q-5. What is the child's share of the allocable parental tax?

A-5. The child's share of the allocable parental tax is an amount that bears the same ratio to the total allocable parental tax as the child's net unearned income bears to the total net unearned income of all children of such parent to whom section 1(i) applies. See A-14.

Example (1). During 1988, D, a 12 year old, receives $5,000 of unearned income and no earned income. D has no itemized deductions and is not eligible for a personal exemption. D's parents have two other children, E, a 15 year old, and F, a 10 year old. E has $10,000 of unearned income and F has $100 of unearned income. D's parents file a joint return for 1988 and report taxable income of $70,000. Neither D's nor his parent's taxable income is attributable to net capital gain. D's tax liability for 1988, determined without regard to section 1(i), is $675 on $4,500 of taxable income ($5,000 less $500 allowable standard deduction). In applying section 1(i), D's tax would be equal to the sum of (A) the tax that would be imposed on D's taxable income if it were reduced by any net unearned income, plus (B) D's share of the allocable parental tax. Only D's unearned income is taken into account in determining the allocable parental tax because E is over 14 and F has less than $1,000 of unearned income. *See* A-4. D's net unearned income is $4,000 ($4,500 taxable unearned income less $500). The tax imposed on D's taxable income as reduced by D's net unearned income is $75 ($500 × 15%). The allocable parental tax is $1,225, the excess of $16,957.50 (the tax on $74,000, the parent's taxable income plus D's net unearned income) over $15,732.50 (the tax on $70,000, the parent's taxable income). *See* A-4. Thus, D's tax under section 1(i)(1)(B) is $1,300 ($1,225 + $75). Since this amount is greater than the amount of D's tax liability as determined without regard to section 1(i), the amount of tax imposed on D for 1988 is $1,300. *See* A-3.

Example (2). H and W have 3 children, A, B, and C, who are all under 14 years of age. For the taxable year 1988, H and W file a joint return and report *taxable income of $129,750.* The tax imposed by section 1 on H and W is $35,355. A has $5,000 of net unearned income and B and C each have $2,500 of net unearned income during 1988. The allocable parental tax imposed on A, B, and C's combined net

unearned income of $10,000 is $3,300. This tax is the excess of $38,655, which is the tax imposed by section 1 on $139,750 ($129,750 + 10,000), over $35,355 (the tax imposed by section 1 on H and W's taxable income of $129,750). *See* A-4. Each child's share of the allocable parental tax is an amount that bears the same ratio to the total allocable parental tax as the child's net unearned income bears to the total net unearned income of A, B, and C. Thus, A's share of the allocable parental tax is $1,650

$$(\frac{5,000}{10,000} \times 3,300)$$

and B and C's share of the tax is $825

$$(\frac{2,500}{10,000} \times 3,300)$$ cash. *See* A-5.

Definition of net unearned income.

Q-6. What is net unearned income?

A-6. Net unearned income is the excess of the portion of adjusted gross income for the taxable year that is not "earned income" as defined in section 911(d)(2) (income that is not attributable to wages, salaries, or other amounts received as compensation for personal services), over the sum of the standard deduction amount provided for under section 63(c)(5)(A) ($500 for 1987 and 1988; adjusted for inflation thereafter), plus the greater of (A) $500 (adjusted for inflation after 1988) or (B) the amount of allowable itemized deductions that are directly connected with the production of unearned income. A child's net unearned income for any taxable year shall not exceed the child's taxable income for such year.

Example (3). A is a child who is under 14 years of age at the end of the taxable year 1987. Both of A's parents are alive at this time. During 1987, A receives $3,000 of interest from a bank savings account and earns $1,000 from a paper route and performing odd jobs. A has no itemized deductions for 1987. A's standard deduction is $1,000, which is an amount equal to A's earned income for 1987. Of this amount, $500 is applied against A's unearned income and the remaining $500 is applied against A's earned income. Thus, A's $500 of taxable earned income ($1,000 less the remaining $500 of the standard deduction) is taxed without regard to section 1(i); A has $2,500 of taxable unearned income ($3,000 gross unearned income less $500 of the standard deduction) of which $500 is taxed without regard to section 1(i). The remaining $2,000 of taxable unearned income is A's net unearned income and is taxed under section 1(i).

Example (4). B is a child who is subject to tax under section 1(i). B has $400 of earned income and $2,000 of unearned income. B has itemized deductions of $800 (net of the 2 percent of adjusted gross income (AGI) floor on miscellaneous itemized deductions under section 67) of which $200 are directly connected with the production of unearned income. The amount of itemized deductions that B may apply against unearned income is equal to the greater of $500 or the deductions directly connected with the production of unearned income. *See* A-6. Thus, $500 of B's itemized deductions are applied against the $2,000 of unearned income and the remaining $300 of deductions are applied against earned income. As a result, B has taxable earned income of $100 and taxable unearned income of $1,500. Of these amounts, all of the earned income and $500 of the unearned income are taxed without regard to section 1(i). The remaining $1,000 of unearned income is net unearned income and is taxed under section 1(i).

Unearned income subject to tax under section 1(i).

Q-7. Will a child be subject to tax under section 1(i) on net unearned income (as defined in section 1(i)(4) and A-6 of this section) that is attributable to property transferred to the child prior to 1987?

A-7. Yes. the tax imposed by section 1(i) on a child's net unearned income applies to any net unearned income of the child for taxable years beginning after December 31, 1986, regardless of when the underlying assets were transferred to the child.

Q-8. Will a child be subject to tax under section 1(i) on net unearned income that is attributable to gifts from persons other than the child's parents or attributable to assets resulting from the child's earned income?

A-8. Yes. The tax imposed by section 1(i) applies to all net unearned income of the child, regardless of the source of the assets that produced such income. Thus, the rules of section 1(i) apply to income attributable to gifts not only from the parents but also from any other source, such as the child's grandparents. Section 1(i) also applies to unearned income derived with respect to assets resulting from earned income of the child, such as interest earned on bank deposits.

Example (5). A is a child who is under 14 years of age at the end of the taxable year beginning on January 1, 1987. Both of A's parents are alive at the end of the taxable year. During 1987, A receives $2,000 in interest from his bank account and $1,500 from a paper route. Some of the interest earned by A from the bank account is attributable to

A's paper route earnings that were deposited in the account. The balance of the account is attributable to cash gifts from A's parents and grandparents and interest earned prior to 1987. Some cash gifts were received by A prior to 1987. A has no itemized deductions and is eligible to be claimed as a dependent on his parent's return. Therefore, for the taxable year 1987, A's standard deduction is $1,500, the amount of A's earned income. Of this standard deduction amount, $500 is allocated against unearned income and $1,000 is allocated against earned income. A's taxable unearned income is $1,500 of which $500 is taxed without regard to section 1(i). The remaining taxable unearned income of $1,000 is not unearned income and is taxed under section 1(i). The fact that some of A's unearned income is attributable to interest on principal created by earned income and gifts from persons other than A's parents or that some of the unearned income is attributable to property transferred to A prior to 1987, will not affect the tax treatment of this income under section 1(i). *See* A-8.

Q-9. For purposes of section 1(i), does income which is not earned income (as defined in section 911(d)(2)) include social security benefits or pension benefits that are paid to the child?

A-9. Yes. For purposes of section 1(i), earned income (as defined in section 911(d)(2)) does not include any social security or pension benefits paid to the child. Thus, such amounts are included in unearned income to the extent they are includible in the child's gross income.

Determination of the parent's taxable income.

Q-10. If a child's parents file a joint return, what is the taxable income that must be taken into account by the child in determining tax liability under section 1(i)?

A-10. In the case of parents who file a joint return, the parental taxable income to be taken into account in determining the tax liability of a child is the total taxable income shown on the joint return.

Q-11. If a child's parents are married and file separate tax returns, which parent's taxable income must be taken into account by the child in determining tax liability under section 1(i)?

A-11. For purposes of determining the tax liability of a child under section 1(i), where such child's parents are married and file separate tax returns, the parent whose taxable income is the greater of the two for the taxable year shall be taken into account.

Q-12. If the parents of a child are divorced, legally separated, or treated as not married under section 7703(b), which parent's taxable income is taken into account in computing the child's tax liability?

A-12. If the child's parents are divorced, legally separated, or treated as not married under section 7703(b), the taxable income of the custodial parent (within the meaning of section 152(e)) of the child is taken into account under section 1(i) in determining the child's tax liability.

Q-13. If a parent whose taxable income must be taken into account in determining a child's tax liability under section 1(i) files a joint return with a spouse who is not a parent of the child, what taxable income must the child take into account?

A-13. The amount of a parent's taxable income that a child must take into account for purposes of section 1(i) where the parent files a joint return with a spouse who is not a parent of the child is the total taxable income shown on such joint return.

Children of the parent.

Q-14. In determining a child's share of the allocable parental tax, is the net unearned income of legally adopted children, children related to such child by half-blood, or children from a prior marriage of the spouse of such child's parent taken into account in addition to the natural children of such child's parent?

A-14. Yes. In determining a child's share of the allocable parental tax, the net unearned income of all children subject to tax under section 1(i) and who use the same parent's taxable income as such child to determine their tax liability under section 1(i) must be taken into account. Such children are taken into account regardless of whether they are adopted by the parent, related to such child by half-blood, or are children from a prior marriage of the spouse of such child's parent.

Rules regarding income from a trust or similar instrument.

Q-15. Will the unearned income of a child who is subject to section 1(i) that is attributable to gifts given to the child under the Uniform Gift to Minors Act (UGMA) be subject to tax under section 1(i)?

A-15. Yes. A gift under the UGMA vests legal title to the property in the child although an adult custodian is given certain rights to deal with the property until the child attains majority. Any unearned income attributable to such a gift is the child's unearned income and is subject to tax under section 1(i), whether distributed to the child or not.

Q-16. Will a child who is a beneficiary of a trust be required to take into account the income of a trust in determining the child's tax liability under section 1(i)?

A-16. The income of a trust must be taken into account for purposes of determining the tax liability of a beneficiary who is subject to section 1(i) only to the extent it is included in the child's gross income for the taxable year under sections 652(a) or 662(a). Thus, income from a trust for the fiscal taxable year of a trust ending during 1987, that is included in the gross income of a child who is subject to section 1(i) and who has a calendar taxable year, will be subject to tax under section 1(i) for the child's 1987 taxable year.

Subsequent adjustments.

Q-17. What effect will a subsequent adjustment to a parent's taxable income have on the child's tax liability if such parent's taxable income was used to determine the child's tax liability under section 1(i) for the same taxable year?

A-17. If the parent's taxable income is adjusted and if, for the same taxable year as the adjustment, the child paid tax determined under section 1(i) with reference to that parent's taxable income, then the child's tax liability under section 1(i) must be recomputed using the parent's taxable income as adjusted.

Q-18. In the case where more than one child who is subject to section 1(i) uses the same parent's taxable income to determine their allocable parental tax, what effect will a subsequent adjustment to the net unearned income of one child have on the other child's share of the allocable parental tax?

A-18. If, for the same taxable year, more than one child uses the same parent's taxable income to determine their share of the allocable parental tax and a subsequent adjustment is made to one or more of such children's net unearned income, each child's share of the allocable parental tax must be recomputed using the combined net unearned income of all such children as adjusted.

Q-19. If a recomputation of a child's tax under section 1(i), as a result of an adjustment to the taxable income of the child's parents or another child's net unearned income, results in additional tax being imposed by section 1(i) on the child, is the child subject to interest and penalties on such additional tax?

A-19. Any additional tax resulting from an adjustment to the taxable income of the child's parents or the net unearned income of another child shall be treated as an underpayment of tax and interest shall be imposed on such underpayment as provided in section 6601. However, the child shall not be liable for any penalties on the underpayment resulting from additional tax's being imposed under section 1(i) due to such an adjustment.

Example (6). D and M are the parents of C, a child under the age of 14. D and M file a joint return for 1988 and report taxable income of $69,900. C has unearned income of $3,000 and no itemized deductions for 1988. C properly reports a total tax liability of $635 for 1988. This amount is the sum of the allocable parental tax of $560 on C's net unearned income of $2,000 (the excess of $3,000 over the sum of $500 standard deduction and the first $500 of taxable unearned income) plus $75 (the tax imposed on C's first $500 of taxable unearned income). *See* A-3. One year later, D and M's 1988 tax return is adjusted on audit by adding an additional $1,000 of taxable income. No adjustment is made to the amount reported as C's net unearned income for 1988. However, the adjustment to D and M's taxable income causes C's tax liability under section 1(i) for 1988 to be increased by $50 as a result of the phase-out of the 15 percent rate bracket. *See* A-20. In addition to this further tax liability, C will be liable for interest on the $50. However, C will not have to pay any penalty on the delinquent amount.

Miscellaneous rules.

Q-20. Does the phase-out of the parent's 15 percent rate bracket and personal exemptions under section 1(g), if applicable, have any effect on the calculation of the allocable parental tax imposed on a child's net unearned income under section 1(i)?

A-20. Yes. Any phase-out of the parent's 15 percent rate bracket or personal exemptions under section 1(g) is given full effect in determining the tax that would be imposed on the sum of the parent's taxable income and the total net unearned income of all children of the parent. Thus, any additional tax on a child's net unearned income resulting from the phase-out of the 15 percent rate bracket and the personal exemptions is reflected in the tax liability of the child.

Q-21. For purposes of calculating a parent's tax liability or the allocable parental tax imposed on a child, are other phase-outs, limitations, or floors on deductions or credits, such as the phase-out of the $25,000 passive loss allowance for rental real estate activities under section 469(i)(3) or the 2 percent of AGI floor on miscellaneous itemized deductions under section 67, affected by the addition of a child's net unearned income to the parent's taxable income?

A-21. No. A child's net unearned income is not taken into account in computing any deduction or credit for purposes of determining the parent's tax liability or the child's allocable parental tax. Thus, for example, although the amounts allowable to the parent as a charitable contribution deduction, medical expense deduction, section 212 deduction, or a miscellaneous itemized deduction are affected by the amount of the parent's adjusted gross income, the amount of these deductions that is allowed does not change as a result of the application of section 1(i) because the amount of the parent's adjusted gross income does not include the child's net unearned income. Similarly, the amount of itemized deductions that is allowed to a child does not change as a result of section 1(i) because section 1(i) only affects the amount of tax liability and not the child's adjusted gross income.

Q-22. If a child is unable to obtain information concerning the tax return of the child's parents directly from such parents, how may the child obtain information from the parent's tax return which is necessary to determine the child's tax liability under section 1(i)?

A-22. Under section 6103(e)(1)(A)(iv), a return of a parent shall, upon written request, be open to inspection or disclosure to a child of that individual (or the child's legal representative) to the extent necessary to comply with section 1(i). Thus, a child may request the Internal Revenue Service to disclose sufficient tax information about the parent to the child so that the child can properly file his or her return. [Temporary Reg. § 1.1(i)-1T.]

☐ [*T.D. 8158, 9-3-87.*]

[Reg. § 1.1-2]

§ 1.1-2. Limitation on tax.—(a) *Taxable years ending before January 1, 1971.*—For taxable years ending before January 1, 1971 the tax imposed by section 1 (whether by subsection (a) or subsection (b) thereof) shall not exceed 87 percent of the taxable income for the taxable year. For purposes of determining this limitation the tax under section 1(a) or (b) and the tax at the 87-percent rate shall each be computed before the allowance of any credits against the tax. Where the alternative tax on capital gains is imposed under section 1201(b), the 87-percent limitation shall apply only to the partial tax computed on the taxable income reduced by 50 percent of the excess of net long-term capital gains over net short-term capital losses. Where, for purposes of computations under the income averaging provisions, section 1201(b) is treated as imposing the alternative tax on capital gains computed under section 1304(e)(2), the 87-percent limitation shall apply only to the tax equal to the tax imposed by section 1, reduced by the amount of the tax imposed by section 1 which is attributable to capital gain net income for the computation year.

(b) *Taxable years beginning after December 31, 1970.*—If, for any taxable year beginning after December 31, 1970, an individual has earned taxable income which exceeds his taxable income as defined by section 1348, the tax imposed by section 1, as amended by the Tax Reform Act of 1969, shall not exceed the sum computed under the provisions of section 1348. For imposition of minimum tax for tax preferences see sections 56 through 58. [Reg. § 1.1-2.]

☐ [*T.D. 6161, 2-3-56. Amended by T.D. 6885, 6-1-66 and T.D. 7117, 5-24-71.*]

[Reg. § 1.1-3]

§ 1.1-3. Change in rates applicable to taxable year.—For computation of the tax for a taxable year during which a change in the tax rates occurs, see section [15]21 and the regulations thereunder. [Reg. § 1.1-3.]

☐ [*T.D. 6161, 2-3-56. Amended by T.D. 7117, 5-24-71.*]

[Reg. § 1.2-1]

§ 1.2-1. Tax in case of joint return of husband and wife or the return of a surviving spouse.—(a) *Taxable year ending before January 1, 1971.*—* * *

(b) *Taxable years beginning after December 31, 1970.*—(1) For taxable years beginning after December 31, 1970, in the case of a joint return of husband and wife, or the return of a surviving spouse as defined in section 2(a) of the Code as amended by the Tax Reform Act of 1969, the tax shall be determined in accordance with the table contained in section 1(a) of the Code as so amended. For rules relating to the filing of joint returns of husband and wife see section 6013 as amended and the regulations thereunder.

(2) The following computation illustrates the method of computing the tax of a husband and wife filing a joint return for calendar year 1971. If the combined gross income is $8,200, and the only deductions are the two exemptions of the taxpayers under section 151(b), as amended, and the standard deduction under section 141, as amended, the tax on the joint return for 1971, without regard to any credits against the tax, is $968.46, determined as follows:

1.	Gross income	. . . .	$8,200.00
2.	Less: Standard deduction, section 141	$1,066.00	
	Deduction for personal exemption, section 151	1,300.00	2,366.00
3.	Taxable income		$5,834.00
4.	Tax computed by the tax table provided under section 1(a) ($620 plus 19% of excess over $4,000)		968.46

(3) The limitation under section 1348 with respect to the maximum rate of tax on earned income shall apply to a married individual only if such individual and his spouse file a joint return for the taxable year.

(c) *Death of a spouse.*—If a joint return of a husband and wife is filed under the provisions of section 6013 and if the husband and wife have different taxable years solely because of the death of either spouse, the taxable year of the deceased spouse covered by the joint return shall, for the purpose of the computation of the tax in respect of such joint return, be deemed to have ended on the date of the closing of the surviving spouse's taxable year.

(d) *Computation of optional tax.*—For computation of optional tax in the case of a joint return or the return of a surviving spouse, see section 3 and the regulations thereunder.

(e) *Change in rates.*—For treatment of taxable years during which a change in the tax rates occurs see section 21 and the regulations thereunder. [Reg. § 1.2-1.]

☐ [*T.D. 6161, 2-3-56. Amended by T.D. 7117, 5-24-71.*]

[Reg. § 1.2-2]

§ 1.2-2. Definitions and special rules.—(a) *Surviving spouse.*—(1) If a taxpayer is eligible to file a joint return under the Internal Revenue Code of 1954 without regard to section 6013(a)(3) thereof for the taxable year in which his spouse dies, his return for each of the next two taxable years following the year of the death of the spouse shall be treated as a joint return for all purposes if all three of the following requirements are satisfied:

(i) He has not remarried before the close of the taxable year the return for which is sought to be treated as a joint return, and

(ii) He maintains as his home a household which constitutes for the taxable year the principal place of abode as a member of such household of a person who is (whether by blood or adoption) a son, stepson, daughter, or stepdaughter of the taxpayer, and

(iii) He is entitled for the taxable year to a deduction under section 151 (relating to deductions for dependents) with respect to such son, stepson, daughter, or stepdaughter.

(2) See paragraphs (c)(1) and (d) of this section for rules for the determination of when the taxpayer maintains as his home a household which constitutes for the taxable year the principal place of abode, as a member of such household, of another person.

(3) If the taxpayer does not qualify as a surviving spouse he may nevertheless qualify as a head of a household if he meets the requirements of § 1.2-2(b).

(4) The following example illustrates the provisions relating to a surviving spouse:

Example: Assume that the taxpayer meets the requirements of this paragraph for the years 1967 through 1971, and that the taxpayer, whose wife died during 1966 while married to him, remarried in 1968. In 1969, the taxpayer's second wife died while married to him, and he remained single thereafter. For 1967 the taxpayer will qualify as a surviving spouse, provided that neither the taxpayer nor the first wife was a nonresident alien at any time during 1966 and that she (immediately prior to her death) did not have a taxable year different from that of the taxpayer. For 1968 the taxpayer does not qualify as a surviving spouse because he remarried before the close of the taxable year. The taxpayer will qualify as a surviving spouse for 1970 and 1971, provided that neither the taxpayer nor the second wife was a nonresident alien at any time during 1969 and that she (immediately prior to her death) did not have a taxable year different from that of the taxpayer. On the other hand, if the taxpayer, in 1969, was divorced or legally separated from his second wife, the taxpayer will not qualify as a surviving spouse for 1970 or 1971, since he could not have filed a joint return for 1969 (the year in which his second wife died).

(b) *Head of household.*—(1) A taxpayer shall be considered the head of a household if, and only if, he is not married at the close of his taxable year, is not a surviving spouse, (as defined in paragraph (a) of this section), and (i) maintains as his home a household which constitutes for such taxable year the principal place of abode, as a member of such household, of at least one of the individuals described in subparagraph (3), or (ii) maintains (whether or not as his home) a household which constitutes for such taxable year the principal place of abode of one of the individuals described in subparagraph (4).

(2) Under no circumstances shall the same person be used to qualify more than one taxpayer as the head of a household for the same taxable year.

(3) Any of the following persons may qualify the taxpayer as a head of a household:

(i) A son, stepson, daughter, or stepdaughter of the taxpayer, or a descendant of a son or daughter of the taxpayer. For the purpose of determining whether any of the stated relationships exist, a legally adopted child of a person is considered a child of such person by blood. If any such person is not married at the close of the taxable year of the taxpayer, the taxpayer may qualify as the head of a household by reason of such person even though the taxpayer may not claim a deduction for such person under section 151, for example, because the taxpayer does not furnish more than half of the support of such person. However, if any such person is married at the close of the taxable year of the taxpayer, the taxpayer may qualify as the head of a household by reason of such person only if the taxpayer is entitled to a deduction for such person under section 151 and the regulations thereunder. In applying the preceding sentence there shall be disregarded any such person for whom a deduction is allowed under section 151 only by reason of section 152(c) (relating to persons covered by a multiple support agreement).

(ii) Any other person who is a dependent of the taxpayer, if the taxpayer is entitled to a deduction for the taxable year for such person under section 151 and paragraphs (3) through (8) of section 152(a) and the regulations thereunder. Under section 151 the taxpayer may be entitled to a deduction for any of the following persons:

(a) His brother, sister, stepbrother, or stepsister;

(b) His father or mother, or an ancestor of either;

(c) His stepfather or stepmother;

(d) A son or a daughter of his brother or sister;

(e) A brother or sister of his father or mother; or

(f) His son-in-law, daughter-in-law, father-in-law, mother-in-law, brother-in-law or sister-in-law;

if such person has a gross income of less than the amount determined pursuant to §1.151-2 applicable to the calendar year in which the taxable year of the taxpayer begins, if the taxpayer supplies more than one-half of the support of such person for such calendar year and if such person does not make a joint return with his spouse for the taxable year beginning in such calendar year. The taxpayer may not be considered to be a head of a household by reason of any person for whom a deduction is allowed under section 151 only by reason of sections 152(a)(9), 152(a)(10) or 152(c) (relating to persons not related to the taxpayer, persons receiving institutional care, and persons covered by multiple support agreements).

(4) The father or mother of the taxpayer may qualify the taxpayer as a head of a household, but only if the taxpayer is entitled to a deduction for the taxable year for such father or mother under section 151 (determined without regard to section 152(c)). For example, an unmarried taxpayer who maintains a home for his widowed mother may not qualify as the head of a household by reason of his maintenance of a home for his mother if his mother has gross income equal to or in excess of the amount determined pursuant to §1.151-2 applicable to the calendar year in which the taxable year of the taxpayer begins, or if he does not furnish more than one-half of the support of his mother for such calendar year. For this purpose, a person who legally adopted the taxpayer is considered the father or mother of the taxpayer.

(5) For the purpose of this paragraph, the status of the taxpayer shall be determined as of the close of the taxpayer's taxable year. A taxpayer shall be considered as not married if at the close of his taxable year he is legally separated from his spouse under a decree of divorce or separate maintenance, or if at any time during the taxable year the spouse to whom the taxpayer is married at the close of his taxable year was a nonresident alien.
A taxpayer shall be considered married at the close of his taxable year if his spouse (other than a spouse who is a nonresident alien) dies during such year.

(6) If the taxpayer is a nonresident alien during any part of the taxable year he may not qualify as a head of a household even though he may comply with the other provisions of this paragraph. See the regulations prescribed under section 871 for a definition of nonresident alien.

(c) *Household.*—(1) In order for a taxpayer to be considered as maintaining a household by reason of any individual described in paragraph (a)(1) or (b)(3) of this section, the household must actually constitute the home of the taxpayer for his taxable year. A physical change in the location of such home will not prevent a taxpayer from qualifying as a head of a household. Such home must also constitute the principal place of abode of at least one of the persons specified in such paragraph (a)(1) or (b)(3) of this section. It is not sufficient that the taxpayer maintain the household without being its occupant. The

taxpayer and such other person must occupy the household for the entire taxable year of the taxpayer. However, the fact that such other person is born or dies within the taxable year will not prevent the taxpayer from qualifying as a head of household if the household constitutes the principal place of abode of such other person for the remaining or preceding part of such taxable year. The taxpayer and such other person will be considered as occupying the household for such entire taxable year notwithstanding temporary absences from the household due to special circumstances. A nonpermanent failure to occupy the common abode by reason of illness, education, business, vacation, military service, or a custody agreement under which a child or stepchild is absent for less than six months in the taxable year of the taxpayer, shall be considered temporary absence due to special circumstances. Such absence will not prevent the taxpayer from being considered as maintaining a household if (i) it is reasonable to assume that the taxpayer or such other person will return to the household, and (ii) the taxpayer continues to maintain such household or a substantially equivalent household in anticipation of such return.

(2) In order for a taxpayer to be considered as maintaining a household by reason of any individual described in paragraph (b)(4) of this section, the household must actually constitute the principal place of abode of the taxpayer's dependent father or mother, or both of them. It is not, however, necessary for the purposes of such subparagraph for the taxpayer also to reside in such place of abode. A physical change in the location of such home will not prevent a taxpayer from qualifying as a head of a household. The father or mother of the taxpayer, however, must occupy the household for the entire taxable year of the taxpayer. They will be considered as occupying the household for such entire year notwithstanding temporary absences from the household due to special circumstances. For example, a nonpermanent failure to occupy the household by reason of illness or vacation shall be considered temporary absence due to special circumstances. Such absence will not prevent the taxpayer from qualifying as the head of a household if (i) it is reasonable to assume that such person will return to the household, and (ii) the taxpayer continues to maintain such household or a substantially equivalent household in anticipation of such return. However, the fact that the father or mother of the taxpayer dies within the year will not prevent the taxpayer from qualifying as a head of a household if the household constitutes the principal place of abode of the father or mother for the preceding part of such taxable year.

(d) *Cost of maintaining a household.*—A taxpayer shall be considered as maintaining a household only if he pays more than one-half the cost thereof for his taxable year. The cost of maintaining a household shall be the expenses incurred for the mutual benefit of the occupants thereof by reason of its operation as the principal place of abode of such occupants for such taxable year. The cost of maintaining a household shall not include expenses otherwise incurred. The expenses of maintaining a household include property taxes, mortgage interest, rent, utility charges, upkeep and repairs, property insurance, and food consumed on the premises. Such expenses do not include the cost of clothing, education, medical treatment, vacations, life insurance, and transportation. In addition, the cost of maintaining a household shall not include any amount which represents the value of services rendered in the household by the taxpayer or by a person qualifying the taxpayer as a head of a household or as a surviving spouse.

(e) *Certain married individuals living apart.*—For taxable years beginning after December 31, 1969, an individual who is considered as not married under section 143(b) shall be considered as not married for purposes of determining whether he or she qualifies as a single individual, a married individual, a head of household or a surviving spouse under sections 1 and 2 of the Code. [Reg. §1.2-2.]

☐ [T.D. 6161, 2-3-56. *Amended by* T.D. 6792, 1-14-65, *and* T.D. 7117, 5-24-71.]

[Reg. §1.3-1]

§1.3-1. Application of optional tax.—(a) *General rules.*—(1) For taxable years ending before January 1, 1970, an individual whose adjusted gross income is less than $5,000 (or a husband and wife filing a joint return whose combined adjusted gross income is less than $5,000) may elect to pay the tax imposed by section 3 in place of the tax imposed by section 1(a) or (b). For taxable years beginning after December 31, 1969 and before January 1, 1971 an individual whose adjusted gross income is less than $10,000 (or a husband and wife filing a joint return whose combined adjusted gross income is less than $10,000) may elect to pay the tax imposed by section 3 as amended by the Tax Reform Act of 1969 in place of the tax imposed by section 1(a) or (b). For taxable years beginning after December 31, 1970 an individual whose adjusted gross income is less than $10,000 (or a husband and wife filing a joint return whose combined adjusted gross income is less than $10,000) may elect to pay the tax imposed by section 3 as amended in place of the tax imposed by section 1 as amended. See §1.4-2 for the manner of making such election. A taxpayer may make such election regardless of the sources from which his income is derived and regardless of whether his income is computed by the cash method or the accrual method. See section 62 and the regulations thereunder for the determination of adjusted gross income. For the purpose of determining whether a taxpayer may elect to pay the tax under section 3, the amount of the adjusted gross income is controlling, without reference to the number of exemptions to which the taxpayer may be entitled. See section 4 and the regulations thereunder for additional rules applicable to section 3.

(2) The following examples illustrate the rule that section 3 applies only if the adjusted gross income is less than $10,000 ($5,000 for taxable years ending before January 1, 1970).

Example (1). A is employed at a salary of $9,200 for the calendar year 1970. In the course of such employment, he incurred travel expenses of $1,500 for which he was reimbursed during the year. Such items constitute his sole income for 1970. In such case the gross income is $10,700 but the amount of $1,500 is deducted from gross income in the determination of adjusted gross income and thus A's adjusted gross income for 1970 is $9,200. Hence, the adjusted gross income being less than $10,000, he may elect to pay his tax for 1970 under section 3. Similarly, in the case of an individual engaged in trade or business (excluding from the term "engaged in trade or business" the performance of personal services as an employee), there may be deducted from gross income in ascertaining adjusted gross income those expenses directly relating to the carrying on of such trade or business.

Example (2). If B has, as his only income for 1970, a salary of $11,600 and his spouse has no gross income, then B's adjusted gross income is $11,600 (not $11,600 reduced by exemptions of $1,250) and he is not, for such year, entitled to pay his tax under section 3. If, however, B has for 1970 a salary of $13,000 and incident to his employment he incurs expenses in the amount of $3,400 for travel, meals, and lodging while away from home, for which he is not reimbursed, the adjusted gross income is $13,000 minus $3,400 or $9,600. In such case his adjusted gross income being less than $10,000, B may elect to pay the tax under section 3. However, if B's wife has adjusted gross income of $400, the total adjusted gross income is $10,000. In such case, if B and his wife file a joint return, they may not elect to pay the optional tax since the combined adjusted gross income is not less than $10,000. B may nevertheless elect to pay the optional tax, but if he makes this election he must file a separate return and, since his wife has gross income, he may not claim an exemption for her in computing the optional tax.

(b) *Surviving spouse.*—The return of a surviving spouse is treated as a joint return for purposes of section 3. See section 2, and the regulations thereunder, with respect to the qualifications of a taxpayer as a surviving spouse. Accordingly, if the taxpayer qualifies as a surviving spouse and elects to pay the optional tax, he shall use the column in the tax table, appropriate to his number of exemptions, provided for cases in which a joint return is filed.

(c) *Use of tax table.*—(1) To determine the amount of the tax, the individual ascertains the amount of his adjusted gross income, refers to the appropriate table set forth in section 3 or the regulations thereunder, ascertains the income bracket into which such income falls, and, using the number of exemptions applicable to his case, finds the tax in the vertical column having at the top thereof a number corresponding to the number of exemptions to which the taxpayer is entitled.

(2) Section 3(b) (relating to taxable years beginning after December 31, 1964 and ending before January 1, 1970) contains 5 tables for use in computing the tax. Table I is to be used by a single person who is not a head of household. Table II is to be used by a head of household. Table III is to be used by married persons filing joint returns and by a surviving spouse. Table IV is to be used by married persons filing separate returns using the 10% standard deduction. Table V is to be used by married persons filing separate returns using the minimum standard deduction. For an explanation of the standard deduction see section 141 and the regulations thereunder.

(3) 30 tables are provided for use in computing the tax under the Tax Reform Act of 1969. Tables I through XV apply for taxable years beginning after December 31, 1969 and ending before January 1, 1971. Tables XVI through XXX apply for taxable years beginning after December 31, 1970. The standard deduction for Tables I through XV, applicable to taxable years beginning in 1970 is 10%. The standard deduction for Tables XVI through XXX, applicable to taxable years beginning in 1971 is 13%. For an explanation of the standard deduction and the low income allowance see section 141 as amended by the Tax Reform Act of 1969.

(4) In the case of married persons filing separate returns who qualify to use the optional tax imposed by section 3, such persons shall use the tax imposed by the table for the applicable year in accordance with the rules prescribed by sections 4(c) and 141 and the regulations thereunder governing the use and application of the standard deduction and the low income allowance.

(5) The tax shown in the tax tables set forth in section 3 or the regulations thereunder reflects full income splitting in the case of a joint return (including the return of a surviving spouse) and lesser income splitting in the case of a head of household. Therefore, it is possible for the tax shown in the tables relating to joint returns, or relating to a return of a head of a household, to be lower than that shown in the table for separate returns even though the amounts of adjusted gross income and the number of exemptions are the same. [Reg. §1.3-1.]

□ [T.D. 6161, 2-3-56. *Amended by T.D. 7117, 5-24-71.*]

Tax on Corporations

[Reg. §1.11-1]

§1.11-1. Tax on corporations.—(a) Every corporation, foreign or domestic, is liable to the tax imposed under section 11 except (1) corporations specifically excepted under such section from such tax: (2) corporations expressly exempt from all taxation under subtitle A of the Code (see section 501); and (3) corporations subject to tax under section 511(a). For taxable years beginning after December 31, 1966, foreign corporations engaged in trade or business in the United States shall be taxable under section 11 only on their taxable income which is effectively connected with the conduct of a trade or business in the United States (see section 882(a)(1)). For definition of the terms "corporations," "domestic," and "foreign," see section 7701(a)(3), (4), and (5), respectively. It is immaterial that a domestic corporation, and for taxable years beginning after December 31, 1966, a foreign corporation engaged in trade or business in the United States, which is subject to the tax imposed by section 11 may derive no income from sources within the United States. The tax imposed by section 11 is payable upon the basis of the returns rendered by the corporations liable thereto, except that in some cases a tax is to be paid at the source of the income. See subchapter A (sections 6001 and following), chapter 61 of the Code, and section 1442.

(b) The tax imposed by section 11 consists of a normal tax and a surtax. The normal tax and the surtax are both computed upon the taxable income of the corporation for the taxable year, that is, upon *the gross income of the corporation minus the deductions* allowed by chapter 1 of the Code. However, the deduction provided in section 242 for partially tax-exempt interest is not allowed in computing the taxable income subject to the surtax.

(c) The normal tax is at the rate of 22 percent and is applied to the taxable income for the taxable year. However, in the case of a taxable year ending after December 31, 1974, and before January 1, 1976, the normal tax is at the rate of 20 percent of so much of the taxable income as does not exceed $25,000 and at the rate of 22 percent of so much of the taxable income as does exceed $25,000 and is applied to the taxable income for the taxable year.

(d) The surtax is at the rate of 26 percent and is upon the taxable income (computed without regard to the deduction, if any, provided in section 242 for partially tax-exempt interest) in excess of $25,000. However, in the case of a taxable year ending after December 31, 1974, and before January 1, 1976, the surtax is upon the taxable income (computed as provided in the preceding sentence) in excess of $50,000. In certain circumstances the exemption from surtax may be disallowed in whole or in part. See sections 269, 1551, 1561, and 1564 and the regulations thereunder. For purposes of sections 244, 247, 804, 907, 922, and §§1.51-1 and 1.815-4, when the phrase "the sum of the normal tax rate and the surtax rate for the taxable year" is used in any such section, the normal tax rate for all taxable years beginning after December 31, 1963, and ending before January 1, 1976, shall be considered to be 22 percent.

(e) The computation of the tax on corporations imposed under section 11 may be illustrated by the following example:

Example. The X Corporation, a domestic corporation, has gross income of $86,000 for the calendar year 1964. The gross income includes interest of $5,000 on United States obligations for which a deduction under section 242 is allowable in determining taxable income subject to the normal tax. It has other deductions of $11,000. The tax of the X Corporation under section 11 for the calendar year is $28,400 ($15,400 normal tax and $13,000 surtax) computed as follows:

Computation of Normal Tax

Gross income		$86,000
Deductions:		
Partially tax-exempt interest	$5,000	
Other	11,000	16,000
Taxable income		70,000
Normal tax (22% of $70,000)		15,400

Computation of Surtax

Taxable income	$70,000
Add: Amount of partially tax-exempt interest deducted in computed taxable income	5,000
Taxable income subject to surtax	75,000
Less: Exemption from surtax	25,000
Excess of taxable income subject to surtax over exemption	50,000
Surtax (26% of $50,000)	$13,000

(f) For special rules applicable to foreign corporations engaged in trade or business within the United States, see section 882 and the regulations thereunder. For additional tax on personal holding companies, see part II of (section 541 and following), subchapter G, chapter 1 of the Code, and the regulations thereunder. For additional tax on corporations improperly accumulating surplus, see part I (section 531 and following), subchapter G, chapter 1 of the Code, and the regulations thereunder. For treatment of China Trade Act corporations, see sections 941 and 942 and the regulations thereunder. For treatment of Western Hemisphere trade corporations, see sections 921 and 922 and the regulations thereunder. For treatment of capital gains and losses, see subchapter P (sections 1201 and following), chapter 1 of the Code. For computation of the tax for a taxable year during which a change in the tax rates occurs, see section 21 and the regulations thereunder. [Reg. § 1.11-1.]

☐ [T.D. 6161, 2-3-56. *Amended by* T.D. 6237, 6-10-57; T.D. 6350, 1-6-59; T.D. 6407, 8-14-59; T.D. 6610, 8-30-62; T.D. 6681, 10-16-63, T.D. 7100, 3-19-71, T.D. 7181, 4-24-72, T.D. 7293, 11-27-73 *and* T.D. 7413, 3-25-76.]

Changes in Rates During a Taxable Year

[Reg. § 1.15-1]

§ 1.15-1. Changes in rate during a taxable year.—(a) Section 21 applies to all taxpayers, including individuals and corporations. It provides a general rule applicable in any case where (1) any rate of tax imposed by chapter 1 of the Code upon the taxpayer is increased or decreased, or any such tax is repealed, and (2) the taxable year includes the effective date of the change, except where that date is the first day of the taxable year. For example, the normal tax on corporations under section 11(b) was decreased from 30 percent to 22 percent in the case of a taxable year beginning after December 31, 1963. Accordingly, the tax for a taxable year of a corporation beginning on January 1, 1964, would be computed under section 11(b) at the new rate without regard to section 21. However, for any taxable year beginning before January 1, 1964, and ending on or after that date, the tax would be computed under section 21. For additional circumstances under which section 21 is not applicable, see paragraph (k) of this section.

(b) In any case in which section 21 is applicable, a tentative tax shall be computed by applying to the taxable income for the entire taxable year the rate for the period within the taxable year before the effective date of change, and another tentative tax shall be computed by applying to the taxable income for the entire taxable year the rate for the period within the taxable year on or after such effective date. The tax imposed on the taxpayer is the sum of—

(1) An amount which bears the same ratio to the tentative tax computed at the rate applicable to the period within the taxable year before the effective date of the change that the number of days in such period bears to the number of days in the taxable year, and

(2) An amount which bears the same ratio to the tentative tax computed at the rate applicable to the period within the taxable year on and after the effective date of the change that the number of days in such period bears to the number of days in the taxable year.

(c) If the rate of tax is changed for taxable years "beginning after" or "ending after" a certain date, the following day is considered the effective date of the change for purposes of section 21. If the rate is changed for taxable years "beginning on or after" a certain date, that date is considered the effective date of the change for purposes of section 21. This rule may be illustrated by the following examples:

Example (1). Assume that the law provides that a change in a certain rate of tax shall be effective only with respect to taxable years beginning after December 31, 1969. The effective date of change for purposes of section 21 is January 1, 1970, and section 21 must be applied to any taxable year which begins before and ends on or after January 1, 1970.

Example (2). Assume that the law provides that a change in a certain rate of tax shall be applicable only with respect to taxable years ending after December 31, 1970. For purposes of section 21, the effective date of change is January 1, 1971, and section 21 must be applied to any taxable year which begins before and ends on or after January 1, 1971.

Example (3). Assume that the law provides that a change in a certain rate of tax shall be effective only with respect to taxable years beginning on or after January 1, 1971. The effective date of change for purposes of section 21 is January 1, 1971, and section 21 must be applied to any taxable year which begins before and ends on or after January 1, 1971.

(d) If a tax is repealed, the repeal will be treated as a change of rate for purposes of section 21, and the rate for the period after the repeal (for purposes of computing the tentative tax with respect to that period) will be considered zero. For example, the Tax Reform Act of 1969 repealed section 1562, which imposed a 6 percent additional tax on controlled corporations electing multiple surtax exemptions, effective for taxable years beginning after December 31, 1974. For such controlled corporations having taxable years beginning in 1974 and ending in 1975, the rate for the period ending before January 1, 1975, would be 6 percent; the rate for the period beginning after December 31, 1974, would be zero. However, subject to the rules stated in this section, section 21 does not apply to the imposition of a new tax. For example, if a new tax is imposed for taxable years beginning on or after July 1, 1972, a computation under section 21 would not be required with respect to such new tax in the case of taxable years beginning before July 1, 1972, and ending on or after that date. If the effective date of the imposition of a new tax and the effective date of a change in rate of such tax fall in the same taxable year, section 21 is not applicable in computing the taxpayer's liability for such tax for such year unless the new tax is expressly imposed upon the taxpayer for a portion of his taxable year prior to the change in rate.

(e) If a husband and wife have different taxable years because of the death of either spouse, and if a joint return is filed with respect to the taxable years of each, then, for purposes of section 21, the joint return shall be treated as if the taxable years of both spouses ended on the date of the closing of the surviving spouse's taxable year. See section 6013(c), relating to treatment of joint return after death of either spouse. Accordingly, if a change in the rate of tax is effective during the taxable year of the surviving spouse, the tentative taxes with respect to the joint return shall be computed on the basis of the number of days during which each rate of tax was in effect for the taxable year of the surviving spouse.

(f) Section 21 applies whether or not the taxpayer has a taxable year of less than 12 months. Moreover, section 21 applies whether or not the taxable income for a taxable year of less than 12 months is required to be placed on an annual basis under section 443. If the taxable income is required to be computed under section 443(b) then the tentative taxes under section 21 are computed as provided in paragraph (1) or (2) of section 443(b) and are reduced as provided in those paragraphs. The tentative taxes so computed and reduced are then apportioned as provided in section 21(a)(2) to determine the tax for such taxable years as computed under section 21.

(g) If a taxpayer has made the election under section 441(f) (relating to computation of taxable income on the basis of an annual accounting period varying from 52 to 53 weeks), the rules provided in section 441(f)(2) shall be applicable for purposes of determining whether section 21 applies to the taxable year of the taxpayer. Where a taxpayer has made the election under section 441(f) and where section 21 applies to the taxable year of the taxpayer the computation under section 21(a)(2) shall be made upon the basis of the actual number of days in the taxable year and in each period thereof.

(h)(1) Section 21 is applicable only if the rate of tax imposed by chapter 1 changes. Sections in which rates of tax are specified or incorporated by reference include the following: 1, 2, 3, 11, 511, 531, 541, 821, 831, 871, 881, 1201 and 1348 (for taxable years beginning after December 31, 1970). Except as provided in subparagraph (3) of this paragraph, section 21 is not applicable with respect to changes in the law relating to deductions from gross income, exclusions from or inclusions in gross income, or other items taken into account in determining the amount or character of income subject to tax. Moreover, section 21 is not applicable with respect to changes in the law relating to credits against the tax or with respect to changes in the law relating to limitations on the amount of tax. Section 21 is applicable, however, to all those computations specified in the section providing the rate of tax which are implicit in determining the rate. For example, if one of the tax brackets in the tax tables under section 3 were to be changed, section 21 would be applicable to that change. Thus, if the bracket relating to "at least $4,200 but not less than $4,250" for heads of households should be changed to increase or decrease the last sum specified, with corresponding changes being made in subsequent brackets, section 21 would be applicable. The enactment of sections 1561 and 1562 is considered a change in section 11(d) which constitutes a change in rate for the period ending after December 31, 1963. The amendment of section 1561 and the repeal of section 1562 by the Tax Reform Act of 1969 is considered a change in section 11(d) which constitutes a change in rate for the period ending after December 31, 1974. The repeal of the 2 percent additional tax imposed under section 1503 on corporations filing consolidated returns constitutes a change in rate for the period ending after December 31, 1963. The addition to the Code of section 1348 (relating to 50 percent maximum rate on earned income) is a change in rate to which section 21(a) is applicable. The amendment of section 11(d) by the Tax Reduction Act of 1975 which increases to $50,000 the surtax exemption for a taxable year ending during 1975 constitutes a change in rate for such portion of the taxable year (if less than the entire taxable year) as follows December 31, 1974. Similarly, the return of the surtax exemption to $25,000 for a taxable year ending during 1976 constitutes a change in rate for such portion of the taxable year (if less than the entire taxable year) as follows December 31, 1975.

(2) Ordinarily, both the old and the new rates are applied to the same amount of taxable income. However, where the rate of tax is itself taken into account in determining taxable income (for example, the special deduction for Western Hemisphere trade corporations under section 922), the taxable income used in determining the tentative tax employing the rate before the effective date of change shall be determined by reference to that rate of tax, and the taxable income for the purpose of determining the tentative tax employing the rate for the period on and after the effective date of the change shall be determined by reference to the new tax rate.

(3) Section 21 is applicable with respect to changes in the law relating to the standard deduction for individuals provided in part IV of subchapter B and to the deduction for personal exemptions for individuals provided in part V of subchapter B.

(i) If the rate of tax changes more than once during the taxable year, section 21 is applicable to each change in rate. For example, if the rate of normal tax changed for taxable years beginning on or after March 1, 1954, and changed again for taxable years beginning on or after June 1, 1954, section 21 requires computation of 3 tentative taxes for any taxable year which began before March 1, 1954, and ended on or after June 1, 1954: One tentative tax at the rate in effect before the March 1 change; another tentative tax at the rate in effect from March 1 to May 31; and a third tentative tax at the rate in effect from June 1 to the end of the taxable year. The proportion of each such tentative tax taken into account in determining the tax imposed on the taxpayer is computed by reference to the portion of the taxable year before March 1, 1954, by reference to the portion of the taxable year from March 1, 1954, through May 31, 1954, and by reference to the portion of the taxable year from June 1, 1954, to the end of the taxable year, respectively.

(j)(1) If a change in the rate of one tax imposed by chapter 1 of the Code does not affect the amount of other taxes imposed by chapter 1 of the Code the other taxes may be determined without regard to section 21 and section 21 will be applied only to the tax for which a change in rate is made. However, if the change of rate of one tax does affect the amount of other taxes imposed under chapter 1 of the Code, then the computation of the taxes under chapter 1 of the Code, so affected shall be made by applying section 21. For example, if section 1201 applies to an individual taxpayer for a taxable year containing the effective date of a change in a rate of tax provided in section 1, then under section 21 the taxpayer must compute a tentative tax for each period for which a different rate of tax is effective under section 1. The tentative tax for each such period as computed under section 1201 will reflect the rate of tax provided by section 1 for such period.

(2) In certain cases chapter 1 of the Code provides that the particular tax to be imposed upon the taxpayer shall be one of several taxes, the basis of selection being the tax that is greater or lesser. See, for example, sections 821 and 1201. If in any such case the rate of any one of these taxes changes, then the tentative taxes computed as provided by section 21 for each period shall be computed employing the tax selected in accordance with the general rule of selection for such a case, at the rate of tax in effect for such period. Thus, if a change in the rate of the alternative tax under section 1201 is such that the alternative tax under section 1201 is applicable if the old rate is used and is not applicable if the new rate is used, one tentative tax will consist of the alternative tax under section 1201 and the other tentative tax will consist of the tax imposed by the other applicable sections of chapter 1 of the Code. The two tentative taxes so computed are then prorated in accordance with section 21(a)(2) and the sum of the proportionate amounts is the tax imposed for the taxable year under chapter 1 of the Code. See the examples in paragraph (n) of this section.

(k) Section 21 does not apply in the following situations:

(1) The provisions of section 21 do not apply to the imposition of the tax surcharge by section 51. The proration rules of section 51(a) apply in the case of a taxable year ending on or after the effective date of the surcharge and beginning before July 1, 1970.

(2) The provisions of section 21 do not apply to the imposition of the minimum tax for tax preferences by section 56. The proration rules of section 301(c) of the Tax Reform Act of 1969 (83 Stat. 586) apply in the case of a taxable year beginning in 1969 and ending in 1970.

(l) In computing the number of days each rate of tax is in effect during the taxable year for purposes of section 21(a)(2) the effective date of the change in rate shall be counted in the period for which the new rate is in effect.

(m) Any credits against tax, and any limitation in any credit against tax, shall be based upon the tax computed under section 21. For credits against tax, see Part IV (sections 31 and following), subchapter A, chapter 1 of the Code.

(n) The application of section 21 may be illustrated by the following examples: (See also the examples in § 1.1561-2A(a)(3).)

Example (1). A, a married taxpayer filing a joint return, reports his income on the basis of a fiscal year ending June 30. For his fiscal year ending June 30, 1970, A reports taxable income (exclusive of capital gains and losses) of $50,000 and net long-term capital gain (section 1201 gain (net capital gain for taxable years beginning after December 31, 1976)) of $75,000. The rate of tax on capital gains under section 1201(b) relating to the alternative tax has been increased from 25 percent to a maximum rate of 29$^{1}/_{2}$ percent with respect to gain in excess of $50,000 and the effective date of the change in rate is January 1, 1970. The income tax for the taxable year ended June 30, 1970, would be computed under section 21 as follows:

Tentative Tax

Taxable income exclusive of capital gains and losses	$50,000
Long-term capital gain	75,000
	$125,000
Deduct 50% of long-term capital gain	37,500
Taxable income	$87,500
Tax under section 1 (1969 and 1970 rates)	$37,690

Alternative tax under section 1201(b) (1969 rates)

Taxable income	
($50,000 + 50% of $75,000)	$87,500
Less 50% of long-term capital gain	37,500
Taxable income exclusive of capital gains	$50,000
Partial tax (tax on $50,000)	$17,060
Plus 25% of $75,000	18,750
Alternative tax under section 1201(b) at 1969 rates	$35,810

Alternative tax under section 1201(b) (1970 rates)
Step I

Taxable income		
($50,000 + 50% of $75,000)	$87,500	
Deduct 50% of net section 1201 gain	37,500	
	$50,000	
Tax on $50,000 (taxable income exclusive of capital gains)		$17,060

Step II

(a) Net section 1201 gain (net capital gain for taxable years beginning after December 31, 1976)	$75,000	
(b) Subsection (d) gain	$50,000	
25% of $50,000 (lesser of (a) or (b))		$12,500

Step III

(c) 29½% of $25,000 (excess of (a) over (b))	$7,375	
(d) Ordinary income	$50,000	
50% of net section 1201 gain	37,500	
	$87,500	
Tax on $87,500	$37,690	
Ordinary income	$50,000	
50% of subsection (d) gain	25,000	
	$75,000	
Tax on $75,000	30,470	
Difference	$7,220	
Lesser of (c) or (d)		$7,220
Alternative tax (total of 3 Steps) at rates effective on and after January 1, 1970		$36,780

Since the alternative tax is less than the tax imposed under section 1 for both the period in 1969 and the period in 1970, the alternative tax applies for both periods. Thus, since the effective date of the change in the rate of tax on capital gains is January 1, 1970, the old rate of alternative tax is effective for 184 days of the taxable year and the new rate of alternative tax is effective for 181 days of the taxable year. The alternative taxes are apportioned as follows:

1969—184/365 of $35,810	$18,052.16
1970—181/365 of $36,780	18,238.85
	$36,291.01
Tax surcharge (See §1.51-1(d)(1)(i))	2,729.28
Total tax for the taxable year	$39,020.29

Example (2). B, a single individual not a head of a household, has a taxable year ending March 31. For the taxable year ending March 31, 1971, B has adjusted gross income of $18,500. His computation of the tax is as follows:

1970 Tentative Tax

Adjusted gross income		$18,500
Less: Standard deduction	$1,000	
Personal exemption	625	1,625
Taxable income under 1970 deduction provisions		$16,875
Tax on $16,875 (1970 rates)		
Tax on first $16,000	$4,330	
42% of $875	367.50	
Tentative tax at rates and deduction provisions effective on or after January 1, 1970		$4,697.50

1971 Tentative Tax

Adjusted gross income		$18,500
Less: Standard deduction	1,500	
Personal exemption	650	2,150
Taxable income under 1971 deduction provisions		$16,350
Tax on $16,350 (1971 rates)		
Tax on first $16,000	$3,830	
34% of $350	119	
Tentative tax at rates and deduction provisions effective on or after January 1, 1971		$3,949

The 1970 and 1971 tentative taxes are apportioned as follows:

1970—275/365 of $4,697.50	$3,539.21
1971—90/365 of $3,949.00	973.73
	$4,512.94
Tax surcharge (See §1.51-1(d)(1)(i))	56.26
Total tax for the taxable year	$4,569.20

Example (3). H and W, husband and wife, have a foster child, C, who qualifies as a dependent under section 152(b)(2) for the period beginning after December 31, 1969. H and W file a joint return on the basis of a taxable year ending August 31. For the taxable year ending August 31, 1970, H and W have adjusted gross income of $12,500. Their computation of the tax imposed is as follows:

1969 Tentative Tax

Adjusted gross income		$12,500
Less: Standard deduction	$1,000	
Personal exemption (2)	1,200	2,200
Taxable income under 1969 deduction provision		$10,300
Taxable income reduced by one-half		$5,150

Tax on $5,150 (1969 rates)			
Tax on first $4,000		$690	
22% of $1,150		253	$943
Twice the tax on $5,150		$1,886	
Tentative tax at rates and deduction provisions effective on or after January 1, 1969			$1,886

1970 Tentative Tax

Adjusted gross income			$12,500
Less: Standard deduction		$1,000	
Personal exemption (3)		1,875	2,875
Taxable income under 1970 deduction provisions			$9,625
Tax on $9,625 (1970 rates)			
Tax on first $8,000		$1,380	
22% on $1,625		357.50	
Tentative tax at rates and deduction provision effective on or after January 1, 1970			$1,737.50
The 1969 and 1970 tentative taxes are apportioned as follows:			
1969—122/365 of $1,886			$630.39
1970—243/365 of $1,737.50			1,156.75
			$1,787.14
Tax surcharge (See § 1.51-1(d)(1)(i))			104.05
Total tax for the taxable year			$1,891.19

Example (4). B, a single individual with one exemption, reports his income on the basis of a fiscal year ending June 30. For fiscal year ending June 30, 1971, B reports adjusted gross income of $250,000, consisting of earned net income of $240,000 and investment income of $10,000. In addition, on April 24, 1971, stock was transferred to B pursuant to his exercise of a qualified stock option, and the fair market value of such stock at that time exceeded the option price by $175,000. This $175,000 constitutes an item of tax preference described in section 57(a)(6). B claims itemized deductions in the amount of $34,000. By reason of section 1348, the maximum rate of tax on earned taxable income for a taxable year beginning after 1970 but before 1972 is 60 percent. The income tax for the taxable year ending June 30, 1971, would be computed under section 21 as follows:

1970 Tentative Tax

Adjusted gross income			$250,000
Less: Itemized deductions		$34,000	
Personal exemption		625	34,625
Taxable income under 1970 deduction provisions			$215,375
Tax on $215,375 (1970 rates)			
Tax on first $100,000		$55,490	
70% of $115,375		80,762.50	
Tentative tax at rates and deduction provisions effective on or after January 1, 1970			$136,252.50
Minimum tax:			
Total tax preference items			$175,000.00
Less: Exemption		$30,000.00	
Income tax		136,252.50	166,252.50
Subject to 10% tax			$8,747.50
10% tax			$874.75
Total tentative tax ($136,252.50 + $874.75)			$137,127.25

1971 Tentative Tax

Adjusted gross income			$250,000
Less: Itemized deductions		$34,000	
Personal exemption		650	34,650
Taxable income under 1971 deduction provisions			$215,350
(a) Tax on highest amount of taxable income on which rate does not exceed 60% ($50,000) (1971 rates)			$20,190
(b) Earned taxable income:			
($215,350 × $240,000/$250,000)		$206,736	
Less: Tax preference offset:			
($175,000 – $30,000)		145,000	
		$61,736	
(c) 60% of the amount by which $61,736 exceeds $50,000			$7,041.60
(d) Tax on $215,350 (1971 rates)			
Tax on first $100,000		$53,090	
70% of $115,350		80,745	
Total		$133,835	
(e) Tax on $61,736 (1971 rates)			
Tax on first $60,000		$26,390	
64% of $1,736		1,111.04	
Total		$27,501.04	
(f) Excess of $133,835 over $27,501.04			$106,333.96
Tentative tax (total of Steps (a), (c), and (f)) at rates and deduction provisions effective on or after January 1, 1971			$133,565.56
Minimum tax:			
Total tax preference items			$175,000
Less: Exemption		$30,000	
Income tax		133,565.56	163,565.56
Subject to 10% tax			$11,434.44
10% tax			$1,143.44

Reg. § 1.15-1(n)

Total tentative tax ($133,565.56 + $1,143.44)		$134,709

The 1970 and 1971 tentative taxes are apportioned as follows:

1970—184/365 of $137,127.25		$69,127.16
1971—181/365 of $134,709		66,800.90
Total tax for the taxable year		$135,928.06

Example (5). The surtax exemption of corporation M (one of 4 subsidiary corporations of W corporation), which files its income tax returns on the basis of a fiscal year ending March 31, 1964, is less than $25,000, by reason of section 1561 of the Code applicable to taxable years ending after December 31, 1963, and beginning before January 1, 1975. The taxable income of corporation M is $100,000, and the amount of the surtax exemption determined under the new rule for the 1964 taxable year is $5,000 ($25,000 ÷ 5). M's income tax liability for the taxable year ending March 31, 1964, is computed as follows:

1963 Tentative Tax

Taxable income		$100,000
Normal tax on $100,000 (1963 rates)		
30% of $100,000	$30,000	
Surtax on $75,000 (1963 rates and $25,000 surtax exemption)		
22% of $75,000	16,500	
Total tentative tax at rates and surtax exemption effective before January 1, 1964		$46,500

1964 Tentative Tax

Taxable income		$100,000
Normal tax on $100,000 (1964 rates)		
22% of $100,000	$22,000	
Surtax on $95,000 (1964 rates and a $5,000 surtax exemption)		
28% of $95,000	26,600	
Total tentative tax at rates and surtax exemption effective after January 1, 1964		$48,600

The 1963 and 1964 tentative taxes are apportioned as follows:

1963—275/366 of $46,500		$34,938.52
1964—91/366 of $48,600		12,083.61
Total tax for the taxable year		$47,022.13

M has the same amount of taxable income in 1965. Its income tax liability for the fiscal year ending March 31, 1965, is computed as follows:

Taxable income		$100,000
Normal tax on $100,000 (1964 rates)		
22% of $100,000	$22,000	
Surtax on $95,000 (1964 rates and a $5,000 surtax exemption)		
28% of $95,000	26,600	
Total tentative tax at the 1964 rates		$48,600

1965 Tentative Tax

Taxable income		$100,000
Normal tax on $100,000 (1965 rates)		
22% of $100,000	$22,000	
Surtax on $95,000 (1965 rates and a $5,000 surtax exemption)		
26% of $95,000	24,700	
Total tentative tax at the 1965 rates		$46,700

The 1964 and 1965 tentative taxes are apportioned as follows:

1964—275/365 of $48,600		$36,616.44
1965—90/365 of $46,700		11,515.07
Total tax for the taxable year		$48,131.51

Example (6). Assume the same facts as in example (5), except that M elected the additional tax under section 1562 for its fiscal year ending March 31, 1964. M's tax liability is computed as follows:

1963 Tentative Tax

Taxable income		$100,000
Normal tax on $100,000 (1963 rates)		
30% of $100,000	$30,000	
Surtax on $75,000 (1963 rates and $25,000 surtax exemption)		
22% of $75,000	16,500	
Total tentative tax at rates and surtax exemption effective before January 1, 1964		$46,500

1964 Tentative Tax

Taxable income		$100,000
Normal tax on $100,000 (1964 rates)		
22% of $100,000	$22,000	
Surtax on $75,000 (1964 rates and $25,000 surtax exemption)		
28% of $75,000	21,000	
Additional tax on $25,000		
6% of $25,000	1,500	
Total tentative tax at rates and surtax exemption effective on and after January 1, 1964		$44,500

The 1963 and 1964 tentative taxes are apportioned as follows:

1963—275/366 of $46,500	$34,938.52
1964—91/366 of $44,500	11,064.21
Total tax for the taxable year	$46,002.73

Example (7). Corporation N files its income tax returns on the basis of a fiscal year ending June 30. For its taxable year ending in 1976, the taxable income of N is $100,000. N's income tax liability is determined for the period July 1, 1975, through December 31, 1975, by taking into account two rates of normal tax under section 11(b)(2)(A) and (B) and the increase to $50,000 in the surtax exemption under section 11(d). For the period January 1, 1976, through June 30, 1976, N's income tax liability is determined by taking into account the single normal tax rate under section 11(b)(1) and the $25,000 surtax exemption under section 11(d). N's tax liability for the taxable year ending June 30, 1976, is computed as follows:

1975 *Tentative Tax*

Taxable income		$100,000
Normal tax on $100,000 (1975 rates)		
20% of $25,000	$5,000	
22% of $75,000	16,500	
Surtax on $50,000 (1975 rates and $50,000 surtax exemption)		
26% of $50,000	$13,000	
Total tentative tax at rates and surtax exemption effective on and after January 1, 1975		$34,500

1976 *Tentative Tax*

Taxable income		$100,000
Normal tax on $100,000 (1976 rates)		
22% of $100,000	$22,000	
Surtax on $75,000 (1976 rates and $25,000 surtax exemption)		
26% of $75,000	19,500	
Total tentative tax at rates and surtax exemption effective on and after January 1, 1976		$41,500

The 1975 and 1976 tentative taxes are apportioned as follows:

1975—184/366 of $34,500	$17,344
1976—182/366 of $41,500	20,637
Total tax for the taxable year	$37,981

[Reg. § 1.15-1.]

☐ [*T.D.* 6161, 2-3-56. *Amended by T.D.* 6237, 6-10-57; *T.D.* 6350, 1-6-59; *T.D.* 6407, 8-14-59; *T.D.* 7164, 2-28-72; *T.D.* 7413, 3-25-76; *T.D.* 7528, 12-27-77; *and T.D.* 7728, 10-31-80. *Redesignated by T.D.* 9354, 8-13-2007.]

Credits Against Tax

[Reg. § 1.21-1]

§ 1.21-1. Expenses for household and dependent care services necessary for gainful employment.—(a) *In general.*—(1) Section 21 allows a credit to a taxpayer against the tax imposed by chapter 1 for employment-related expenses for household services and care (as defined in paragraph (d) of this section) of a qualifying individual (as defined in paragraph (b) of this section). The purpose of the expenses must be to enable the taxpayer to be gainfully employed (as defined in paragraph (c) of this section). For taxable years beginning after December 31, 2004, a qualifying individual must have the same principal place of abode (as defined in paragraph (g) of this section) as the taxpayer for more than one-half of the taxable year. For taxable years beginning before January 1, 2005, the taxpayer must maintain a household (as defined in paragraph (h) of this section) that includes one or more qualifying individuals.

(2) The amount of the credit is equal to the applicable percentage of the employment-related expenses that may be taken into account by the taxpayer during the taxable year (but subject to the limits prescribed in § 1.21-2). *Applicable percentage* means 35 percent reduced by 1 percentage point for each $2,000 (or fraction thereof) by which the taxpayer's adjusted gross income for the taxable year exceeds $15,000, but not less than 20 percent. For example, if a taxpayer's adjusted gross income is $31,850, the applicable percentage is 26 percent.

(3) Expenses may be taken as a credit under section 21, regardless of the taxpayer's method of accounting, only in the taxable year the services are performed or the taxable year the expenses are paid, whichever is later.

(4) The requirements of section 21 and §§ 1.21-1 through 1.21-4 are applied at the time the services are performed, regardless of when the expenses are paid.

(5) *Examples.*—The provisions of this paragraph (a) are illustrated by the following examples.

Example 1. In December 2007, B pays for the care of her child for January 2008. Under paragraph (a)(3) of this section, B may claim the credit in 2008, the later of the years in which the expenses are paid *and the services are performed.*

Example 2. The facts are the same as in *Example 1*, except that B's child turns 13 on February 1, 2008, and B pays for the care provided in January 2008 on February 3, 2008. Under paragraph (a)(4) of this section, the determination of whether the expenses are employment-related expenses is made when the services are performed. Assuming other requirements are met, the amount B pays will be an employment-related expense under section 21, because B's child is a qualifying individual when the services are performed, even though the child is not a qualifying individual when B pays the expenses.

(b) *Qualifying individual.*—(1) *In general.*—For taxable years beginning after December 31, 2004, a qualifying individual is—

(i) The taxpayer's dependent (who is a qualifying child within the meaning of section 152) who has not attained age 13;

(ii) The taxpayer's dependent (as defined in section 152, determined without regard to subsections (b)(1), (b)(2), and (d)(1)(B)) who is physically or mentally incapable of self-care and who has the same principal place of abode as the taxpayer for more than one-half of the taxable year; or

(iii) The taxpayer's spouse who is physically or mentally incapable of self-care and who has the same principal place of abode as the taxpayer for more than one-half of the taxable year.

(2) *Taxable years beginning before January 1, 2005.*—For taxable years beginning before January 1, 2005, a qualifying individual is—

(i) The taxpayer's dependent for whom the taxpayer is entitled to a deduction for a personal exemption under section 151(c) and who is under age 13;

(ii) The taxpayer's dependent who is physically or mentally incapable of self-care; or

(iii) The taxpayer's spouse who is physically or mentally incapable of self-care.

(3) *Qualification on a daily basis.*—The status of an individual as a qualifying individual is determined on a daily basis. An individual is not a qualifying individual on the day the status terminates.

(4) *Physical or mental incapacity.*—An individual is physically or mentally incapable of self-care if, as a result of a physical or mental defect, the individual is incapable of caring for the individual's hygiene or nutritional needs, or requires full-time attention of another person for the individual's own safety or the safety of others. The inability of an individual to engage in any substantial gainful activity or to perform the normal household functions of a homemaker or care for minor children by reason of a physical or mental

condition does not of itself establish that the individual is physically or mentally incapable of self-care.

(5) *Special test for divorced or separated parents or parents living apart.*—(i) *Scope.*—This paragraph (b)(5) applies to a child (as defined in section 152(f)(1) for taxable years beginning after December 31, 2004, and in section 151(c)(3) for taxable years beginning before January 1, 2005) who—

(A) Is under age 13 or is physically or mentally incapable of self-care;

(B) Receives over one-half of his or her support during the calendar year from one or both parents who are divorced or legally separated under a decree of divorce or separate maintenance, are separated under a written separation agreement, or live apart at all times during the last 6 months of the calendar year; and

(C) Is in the custody of one or both parents for more than one-half of the calendar year.

(ii) *Custodial parent allowed the credit.*—A child to whom this paragraph (b)(5) applies is the qualifying individual of only one parent in any taxable year and is the qualifying child of the custodial parent even if the noncustodial parent may claim the dependency exemption for that child for that taxable year. See section 21(e)(5). The custodial parent is the parent having custody for the greater portion of the calendar year. See section 152(e)(4)(A).

(6) *Example.*—The provisions of this paragraph (b) are illustrated by the following examples.

Example. C pays $420 for the care of her child, a qualifying individual, to be provided from January 2 through January 31, 2008 (21 days of care). On January 20, 2008, C's child turns 13 years old. Under paragraph (b)(3) of this section, C's child is a qualifying individual from January 2 through January 19, 2008 (13 days of care). C may take into account $260, the pro rata amount C pays for the care of her child for 13 days, under section 21. See § 1.21-2(a)(4).

(c) *Gainful employment.*—(1) *In general.*—Expenses are employment-related expenses only if they are for the purpose of enabling the taxpayer to be gainfully employed. The expenses must be for the care of a qualifying individual or household services performed during periods in which the taxpayer is gainfully employed or is in active search of gainful employment. Employment may consist of service within or outside the taxpayer's home and includes self-employment. An expense is not employment-related merely because it is paid or incurred while the taxpayer is gainfully employed. The purpose of the expense must be to enable the taxpayer to be gainfully employed. Whether the purpose of an expense is to enable the taxpayer to be gainfully employed depends on the facts and circumstances of the particular case. Work as a volunteer or for a nominal consideration is not gainful employment.

(2) *Determination of period of employment on a daily basis.*—(i) *In general.*—Expenses paid for a period during only part of which the taxpayer is gainfully employed or in active search of gainful employment must be allocated on a daily basis.

(ii) *Exception for short, temporary absences.*—A taxpayer who is gainfully employed is not required to allocate expenses during a short, temporary absence from work, such as for vacation or minor illness, provided that the care-giving arrangement requires the taxpayer to pay for care during the absence. An absence of 2 consecutive calendar weeks is a short, temporary absence. Whether an absence longer than 2 consecutive calendar weeks is a short, temporary absence is determined based on all the facts and circumstances.

(iii) *Part-time employment.*—A taxpayer who is employed part-time generally must allocate expenses for dependent care between days worked and days not worked. However, if a taxpayer employed part-time is required to pay for dependent care on a periodic basis (such as weekly or monthly) that includes both days worked and days not worked, the taxpayer is not required to allocate the expenses. A day on which the taxpayer works at least 1 hour is a day of work.

(3) *Examples.*—The provisions of this paragraph (c) are illustrated by the following examples:

Example 1. D works during the day and her husband, E, works at night and sleeps during the day. D and E pay for care for a qualifying individual during the hours when D is working and E is sleeping. Under paragraph (c)(1) of this section, the amount paid by D and E for care may be for the purpose of allowing D and E to be gainfully employed and may be an employment-related expense under section 21.

Example 2. F works at night and pays for care for a qualifying individual during the hours when F is working. Under paragraph (c)(1) of this section, the amount paid by F for care may be for the

purpose of allowing F to be gainfully employed and may be an employment-related expense under section 21.

Example 3. G, the custodial parent of two children who are qualifying individuals, hires a housekeeper for a monthly salary to care for the children while G is gainfully employed. G becomes ill and as a result is absent from work for 4 months. G continues to pay the housekeeper to care for the children while G is absent from work. During this 4-month period, G performs no employment services, but receives payments under her employer's wage continuation plan. Although G may be considered to be gainfully employed during her absence from work, the absence is not a short, temporary absence within the meaning of paragraph (c)(2)(ii) of this section, and her payments for household and dependent care services during the period of illness are not for the purpose of enabling her to be gainfully employed. G's expenses are not employment-related expenses, and she may not take the expenses into account under section 21.

Example 4. To be gainfully employed, H sends his child to a dependent care center that complies with all state and local requirements. The dependent care center requires payment for days when a child is absent from the center. H takes 8 days off from work as vacation days. Because the absence is less than 2 consecutive calendar weeks, under paragraph (c)(2)(ii) of this section, H's absence is a short, temporary absence. H is not required to allocate expenses between days worked and days not worked. The entire fee for the period that includes the 8 vacation days may be an employment-related expense under section 21.

Example 5. J works 3 days per week and her child attends a dependent care center (that complies with all state and local requirements) to enable her to be gainfully employed. The dependent care center allows payment for any 3 days per week for $150 or 5 days per week for $250. J enrolls her child for 5 days per week, and her child attends the care center for 5 days per week. Under paragraph (c)(2)(iii) of this section, J must allocate her expenses for dependent care between days worked and days not worked. Three-fifths of the $250, or $150 per week, may be an employment-related expense under section 21.

Example 6. The facts are the same as in *Example 5*, except that the dependent care center does not offer a 3-day option. The entire $250 weekly fee may be an employment-related expense under section 21.

(d) *Care of qualifying individual and household services.*—(1) *In general.*—To qualify for the dependent care credit, expenses must be for the care of a qualifying individual. Expenses are for the care of a qualifying individual if the primary function is to assure the individual's well-being and protection. Not all expenses relating to a qualifying individual are for the individual's care. Amounts paid for food, lodging, clothing, or education are not for the care of a qualifying individual. If, however, the care is provided in such a manner that the expenses cover other goods or services that are incidental to and inseparably a part of the care, the full amount is for care.

(2) *Allocation of expenses.*—If an expense is partly for household services or for the care of a qualifying individual and partly for other goods or services, a reasonable allocation must be made. Only so much of the expense that is allocable to the household services or care of a qualifying individual is an employment-related expense. An allocation must be made if a housekeeper or other domestic employee performs household duties and cares for the qualifying children of the taxpayer and also performs other services for the taxpayer. No allocation is required, however, if the expense for the other purpose is minimal or insignificant or if an expense is partly attributable to the care of a qualifying individual and partly to household services.

(3) *Household services.*—Expenses for household services may be employment-related expenses if the services are performed in connection with the care of a qualifying individual. The household services must be the performance in and about the taxpayer's home of ordinary and usual services necessary to the maintenance of the household and attributable to the care of the qualifying individual. Services of a housekeeper are household services within the meaning of this paragraph (d)(3) if the services are provided, at least in part, to the qualifying individual. Such services as are performed by chauffeurs, bartenders, or gardeners are not household services.

(4) *Manner of providing care.*—The manner of providing care need not be the least expensive alternative available to the taxpayer. The cost of a paid caregiver may be an expense for the care of a qualifying individual even if another caregiver is available at no cost.

(5) *School or similar program.*—Expenses for a child in nursery school, pre-school, or similar programs for children below the level of kindergarten are for the care of a qualifying individual and may be employment-related expenses. Expenses for a child in kindergarten or a higher grade are not for the care of a qualifying individual.

However, expenses for before-or after-school care of a child in kindergarten or a higher grade may be for the care of a qualifying individual.

(6) *Overnight camps.*—Expenses for overnight camps are not employment-related expenses.

(7) *Day camps.*—(i) The cost of a day camp or similar program may be for the care of a qualifying individual and an employment-related expense, without allocation under paragraph (d)(2) of this section, even if the day camp specializes in a particular activity. Summer school and tutoring programs are not for the care of a qualifying individual and the costs are not employment-related expenses.

(ii) A day camp that meets the definition of *dependent care center* in section 21(b)(2)(D) and paragraph (e)(2) of this section must comply with the requirements of section 21(b)(2)(C) and paragraph (e)(2) of this section.

(8) *Transportation.*—The cost of transportation by a dependent care provider of a qualifying individual to or from a place where care of that qualifying individual is provided may be for the care of the qualifying individual. The cost of transportation not provided by a dependent care provider is not for the care of the qualifying individual.

(9) *Employment taxes.*—Taxes under sections 3111 (relating to the Federal Insurance Contributions Act) and 3301 (relating to the Federal Unemployment Tax Act) and similar state payroll taxes are employment-related expenses if paid in respect of wages that are employment-related expenses.

(10) *Room and board.*—The additional cost of providing room and board for a caregiver over usual household expenditures may be an employment-related expense.

(11) *Indirect expenses.*—Expenses that relate to, but are not directly for, the care of a qualifying individual, such as application fees, agency fees, and deposits, may be for the care of a qualifying individual and may be employment-related expenses if the taxpayer is required to pay the expenses to obtain the related care. However, forfeited deposits and other payments are not for the care of a qualifying individual if care is not provided.

(12) *Examples.*—The provisions of this paragraph (d) are illustrated by the following examples:

Example 1. To be gainfully employed, K sends his 3-year old child to a pre-school. The pre-school provides lunch and snacks. Under paragraph (d)(1) of this section, K is not required to allocate expenses between care and the lunch and snacks, because the lunch and snacks are incidental to and inseparably a part of the care. Therefore, K may treat the full amount paid to the pre-school as for the care of his child.

Example 2. L, a member of the armed forces, is ordered to a combat zone. To be able to comply with the orders, L places her 10-year old child in boarding school. The school provides education, meals, and housing to L's child in addition to care. Under paragraph (d)(2) of this section, L must allocate the cost of the boarding school between expenses for care and expenses for education and other services not constituting care. Only the part of the cost of the boarding school that is for the care of L's child is an employment-related expense under section 21.

Example 3. To be gainfully employed, M employs a full-time housekeeper to care for M's two children, aged 9 and 13 years. The housekeeper regularly performs household services of cleaning and cooking and drives M to and from M's place of employment, a trip of 15 minutes each way. Under paragraph (d)(3) of this section, the chauffeur services are not household services. M is not required to allocate a portion of the expense of the housekeeper to the chauffeur services under paragraph (d)(2) of this section, however, because the chauffeur services are minimal and insignificant. Further, no allocation under paragraph (d)(2) of this section is required to determine the portion of the expenses attributable to the care of the 13-year old child (not a qualifying individual) because the household expenses are in part attributable to the care of the 9-year old child. Accordingly, the entire expense of employing the housekeeper is an employment-related expense. The amount that M may take into account as an employment-related expense under section 21, however, is limited to the amount allowable for one qualifying individual.

Example 4. To be gainfully employed, N sends her 9-year old child to a summer day camp that offers computer activities and recreational activities such as swimming and arts and crafts. Under paragraph (d)(7)(i) of this section, the full cost of the summer day camp may be for care.

Example 5. To be gainfully employed, O sends her 9-year old child to a math tutoring program for two hours per day during the

summer. Under paragraph (d)(7)(i) of this section, the cost of the tutoring program is not for care.

Example 6. To be gainfully employed, P hires a full-time housekeeper to care for her 8-year old child. In order to accommodate the housekeeper, P moves from a 2-bedroom apartment to a 3-bedroom apartment that otherwise is comparable to the 2-bedroom apartment. Under paragraph (d)(10) of this section, the additional cost to rent the 3-bedroom apartment over the cost of the 2-bedroom apartment and any additional utilities attributable to the housekeeper's residence in the household may be employment-related expenses under section 21.

Example 7. Q pays a fee to an agency to obtain the services of an au pair to care for Q's children, qualifying individuals, to enable Q to be gainfully employed. An au pair from the agency subsequently provides care for Q's children. Under paragraph (d)(11) of this section, the fee may be an employment-related expense.

Example 8. R places a deposit with a pre-school to reserve a place for her child. R sends the child to a different pre-school and forfeits the deposit. Under paragraph (d)(11) of this section, the forfeited deposit is not an employment-related expense.

(e) *Services outside the taxpayer's household.*—(1) *In general.*—The credit is allowable for expenses for services performed outside the taxpayer's household only if the care is for one or more qualifying individuals who are described in this section at—

(i) Paragraph (b)(1)(i) or (b)(2)(i); or

(ii) Paragraph (b)(1)(ii), (b)(2)(ii), (b)(1)(iii), or (b)(2)(iii) and regularly spend at least 8 hours each day in the taxpayer's household.

(2) *Dependent care centers.*—(i) *In general.*—The credit is allowable for services performed by a dependent care center only if—

(A) The center complies with all applicable laws and regulations, if any, of a state or local government, such as state or local licensing requirements and building and fire code regulations; and

(B) The requirements provided in this paragraph (e) are met.

(ii) *Definition.*—The term *dependent care center* means any facility that provides full-time or part-time care for more than six individuals (other than individuals who reside at the facility) on a regular basis during the taxpayer's taxable year, and receives a fee, payment, or grant for providing services for the individuals (regardless of whether the facility is operated for profit). For purposes of the preceding sentence, a facility is presumed to provide full-time or part-time care for six or fewer individuals on a regular basis during the taxpayer's taxable year if the facility has six or fewer individuals (including the taxpayer's qualifying individual) enrolled for full-time or part-time care on the day the qualifying individual is enrolled in the facility (or on the first day of the taxable year the qualifying individual attends the facility if the qualifying individual was enrolled in the facility in the preceding taxable year) unless the Internal Revenue Service demonstrates that the facility provides full-time or part-time care for more than six individuals on a regular basis during the taxpayer's taxable year.

(f) *Reimbursed expenses.*—Employment-related expenses for which the taxpayer is reimbursed (for example, under a dependent care assistance program) may not be taken into account for purposes of the credit.

(g) *Principal place of abode.*—For purposes of this section, the term *principal place of abode* has the same meaning as in section 152.

(h) *Maintenance of a household.*—(1) *In general.*—For taxable years beginning before January 1, 2005, the credit is available only to a taxpayer who maintains a household that includes one or more qualifying individuals. A taxpayer maintains a household for the taxable year (or lesser period) only if the taxpayer (and spouse, if applicable) occupies the household and furnishes over one-half of the cost for the taxable year (or lesser period) of maintaining the household. The household must be the principal place of abode for the taxable year of the taxpayer and the qualifying individual or individuals.

(2) *Cost of maintaining a household.*—(i) Except as provided in paragraph (h)(2)(ii) of this section, for purposes of this section, the term *cost of maintaining a household* has the same meaning as in § 1.2-2(d) without regard to the last sentence thereof.

(ii) The cost of maintaining a household does not include the value of services performed in the household by the taxpayer or by a qualifying individual described in paragraph (b) of this section or any expense paid or reimbursed by another person.

(3) *Monthly proration of annual costs.*—In determining the cost of maintaining a household for a period of less than a taxable year, the cost for the entire taxable year must be prorated on the basis of the

number of calendar months within that period. A period of less than a calendar month is treated as a full calendar month.

(4) *Two or more families.*—If two or more families occupy living quarters in common, each of the families is treated as maintaining a separate household. A taxpayer is maintaining a household if the taxpayer provides more than one-half of the cost of maintaining the separate household. For example, if two unrelated taxpayers with their respective children occupy living quarters in common and each taxpayer pays more than one-half of the household costs for each respective family, each taxpayer is treated as maintaining a household.

(i) Reserved.

(j) *Expenses qualifying as medical expenses.*—(1) *In general.*—A taxpayer may not take an amount into account as both an employment-related expense under section 21 and an expense for medical care under section 213.

(2) *Examples.*—The provisions of this paragraph (j) are illustrated by the following examples:

Example 1. S has $6,500 of employment-related expenses for the care of his child who is physically incapable of self-care. The expenses are for services performed in S's household that also qualify as expenses for medical care under section 213. Of the total expenses, S may take into account $3,000 under section 21. S may deduct the balance of the expenses, or $3,500, as expenses for medical care under section 213 to the extent the expenses exceed 7.5 percent of S's adjusted gross income.

Example 2. The facts are the same as in *Example 1*, however, S first takes into account the $6,500 of expenses under section 213. S deducts $500 as an expense for medical care, which is the amount by which the expenses exceed 7.5 percent of his adjusted gross income. S may not take into account the $6,000 balance as employment-related expenses under section 21, because he has taken the full amount of the expenses into account in computing the amount deductible under section 213.

(k) *Substantiation.*—A taxpayer claiming a credit for employment-related expenses must maintain adequate records or other sufficient evidence to substantiate the expenses in accordance with section 6001 and the regulations thereunder.

(l) *Effective/applicability date.*—This section and §§1.21-2 through 1.21-4 apply to taxable years ending after August 14, 2007. [Reg. §1.21-1.]

☐ [*T.D.* 9354, 8-13-2007.]

[Reg. §1.21-2]

§1.21-2. Limitations on amount creditable.—(a) *Annual dollar limitation.*—(1) The amount of employment-related expenses that may be taken into account under §1.21-1(a) for any taxable year cannot exceed—

(i) $2,400 ($3,000 for taxable years beginning after December 31, 2002, and before January 1, 2011) if there is one qualifying individual with respect to the taxpayer at any time during the taxable year; or

(ii) $4,800 ($6,000 for taxable years beginning after December 31, 2002, and before January 1, 2011) if there are two or more qualifying individuals with respect to the taxpayer at any time during the taxable year.

(2) The amount determined under paragraph (a)(1) of this section is reduced by the aggregate amount excludable from gross income under section 129 for the taxable year.

(3) A taxpayer may take into account the total amount of employment-related expenses that do not exceed the annual dollar limitation although the amount of employment-related expenses attributable to one qualifying individual is disproportionate to the total employment-related expenses. For example, a taxpayer with expenses in 2007 of $4,000 for one qualifying individual and $1,500 for a second qualifying individual may take into account the full $5,500.

(4) A taxpayer is not required to prorate the annual dollar limitation if a qualifying individual ceases to qualify (for example, by turning age 13) during the taxable year. However, the taxpayer may take into account only amounts that qualify as employment-related expenses before the disqualifying event. *See also* §1.21-1(b)(6).

(b) *Earned income limitation.*—(1) *In general.*—The amount of employment-related expenses that may be taken into account under section 21 for any taxable year cannot exceed—

(i) For a taxpayer who is not married at the close of the taxable year, the taxpayer's earned income for the taxable year; or

(ii) For a taxpayer who is married at the close of the taxable year, the lesser of the taxpayer's earned income or the earned income of the taxpayer's spouse for the taxable year.

(2) *Determination of spouse.*—For purposes of this paragraph (b), a taxpayer must take into account only the earned income of a spouse to whom the taxpayer is married at the close of the taxable year. The spouse's earned income for the entire taxable year is taken into account, however, even though the taxpayer and the spouse were married for only part of the taxable year. The taxpayer is not required to take into account the earned income of a spouse who died or was divorced or separated from the taxpayer during the taxable year. See §1.21-3(b) for rules providing that certain married taxpayers legally separated or living apart are treated as not married.

(3) *Definition of earned income.*—For purposes of this section, the term *earned income* has the same meaning as in section 32(c)(2) and the regulations thereunder.

(4) *Attribution of earned income to student or incapacitated spouse.*—(i) For purposes of this section, a spouse is deemed, for each month during which the spouse is a full-time student or is a qualifying individual described in §1.21-1(b)(1)(iii) or (b)(2)(iii), to be gainfully employed and to have earned income of not less than—

(A) $200 ($250 for taxable years beginning after December 31, 2002, and before January 1, 2011) if there is one qualifying individual with respect to the taxpayer at any time during the taxable year; or

(B) $400 ($500 for taxable years beginning after December 31, 2002, and before January 1, 2011) if there are two or more qualifying individuals with respect to the taxpayer at any time during the taxable year.

(ii) For purposes of this paragraph (b)(4), a full-time student is an individual who, during each of 5 calendar months of the taxpayer's taxable year, is enrolled as a student for the number of course hours considered to be a full-time course of study at an educational organization as defined in section 170(b)(1)(A)(ii). The enrollment for 5 calendar months need not be consecutive.

(iii) Earned income may be attributed under this paragraph (b)(4), in the case of any husband and wife, to only one spouse in any month.

(c) *Examples.*—The provisions of this section are illustrated by the following examples:

Example 1. In 2007, T, who is married to U, pays employment-related expenses of $5,000 for the care of one qualifying individual. T's earned income for the taxable year is $40,000 and her husband's earned income is $2,000. T did not exclude any dependent care assistance under section 129. Under paragraph (b)(1) of this section, T may take into account under section 21 only the amount of employment-related expenses that does not exceed the lesser of her earned income or the earned income of U, or $2,000.

Example 2. The facts are the same as in *Example 1* except that U is a full-time student at an educational organization within the meaning of section 170(b)(1)(A)(ii) for 9 months of the taxable year and has no earned income. Under paragraph (b)(4) of this section, U is deemed to have earned income of $2,250. T may take into account $2,250 of employment-related expenses under section 21.

Example 3. For all of 2007, V is a full-time student and W, V's husband, is an individual who is incapable of self-care (as defined in §1.21-1(b)(1)(iii)). V and W have no earned income and pay expenses of $5,000 for W's care. Under paragraph (b)(4) of this section, either V or W may be deemed to have $3,000 of earned income. However, earned income may be attributed to only one spouse under paragraph (b)(4)(iii) of this section. Under the limitation in paragraph (b)(1)(ii) of this section, the lesser of V's and W's earned income is zero. V and W may not take the expenses into account under section 21.

(d) *Cross-reference.*—For an additional limitation on the credit under section 21, see section 26. [Reg. §1.21-2.]

☐ [*T.D.* 9354, 8-13-2007.]

[Reg. §1.21-3]

§1.21-3. Special rules applicable to married taxpayers.—(a) *Joint return requirement.*—No credit is allowed under section 21 for taxpayers who are married (within the meaning of section 7703 and the regulations thereunder) at the close of the taxable year unless the taxpayer and spouse file a joint return for the taxable year. See section 6013 and the regulations thereunder relating to joint returns of income tax by husband and wife.

(b) *Taxpayers treated as not married.*—The requirements of paragraph (a) of this section do not apply to a taxpayer who is legally separated under a decree of divorce or separate maintenance or who is treated as not married under section 7703(b) and the regulations thereunder (relating to certain married taxpayers living apart). A taxpayer who is treated as not married under this paragraph (b) is not required to take into account the earned income of the taxpayer's spouse for purposes of applying the earned income limitation on the amount of employment-related expenses under §1.21-2(b).

(c) *Death of married taxpayer.*—If a married taxpayer dies during the taxable year and the survivor may make a joint return with respect to the deceased spouse under section 6013(a)(3), the credit is allowed for the year only if a joint return is made. If, however, the surviving spouse remarries before the end of the taxable year in which the deceased spouse dies, a credit may be allowed on the decedent spouse's separate return. [Reg. §1.21-3.]

☐ [T.D. 9354, 8-13-2007.]

[Reg. §1.21-4]

§1.21-4. Payments to certain related individuals.—(a) *In general.*—A credit is not allowed under section 21 for any amount paid by the taxpayer to an individual—

(1) For whom a deduction under section 151(c) (relating to deductions for personal exemptions for dependents) is allowable either to the taxpayer or the taxpayer's spouse for the taxable year;

(2) Who is a child of the taxpayer (within the meaning of section 152(f)(1) for taxable years beginning after December 31, 2004, and section 151(c)(3) for taxable years beginning before January 1, 2005) and is under age 19 at the close of the taxable year;

(3) Who is the spouse of the taxpayer at any time during the taxable year; or

(4) Who is the parent of the taxpayer's child who is a qualifying individual described in (1.21-1(b)(1)(i) or (b)(2)(i).

(b) *Payments to partnerships or other entities.*—In general, paragraph (a) of this section does not apply to services performed by partner-

ships or other entities. If, however, the partnership or other entity is established or maintained primarily to avoid the application of paragraph (a) of this section to permit the taxpayer to claim the credit, for purposes of section 21, the payments of employment-related expenses are treated as made directly to each partner or owner in proportion to that partner's or owner's ownership interest. Whether a partnership or other entity is established or maintained to avoid the application of paragraph (a) of this section is determined based on the facts and circumstances, including whether the partnership or other entity is established for the primary purpose of caring for the taxpayer's qualifying individual or providing household services to the taxpayer.

(c) *Examples.*—The provisions of this section are illustrated by the following examples:

Example 1. During 2007, X pays $5,000 to her mother for the care of X's 5-year old child who is a qualifying individual. The expenses otherwise qualify as employment-related expenses. X's mother is not her dependent. X may take into account under section 21 the amounts paid to her mother for the care of X's child.

Example 2. Y is divorced and has custody of his 5-year old child, who is a qualifying individual. Y pays $6,000 during 2007 to Z, who is his ex-wife and the child's mother, for the care of the child. The expenses otherwise qualify as employment-related expenses. Under paragraph (a)(4) of this section, Y may not take into account under section 21 the amounts paid to Z because Z is the child's mother.

Example 3. The facts are the same as in *Example 2*, except that Z is not the mother of Y's child. Y may take into account under section 21 the amounts paid to Z. [Reg. §1.21-4.]

☐ [T.D. 9354, 8-13-2007.]

→ *Code Sec. 22 was formerly Code Sec. 37. See Reg. §§1.37-1—1.37-3 for rules issued under former Code Sec. 37.*

→ *Code Sec. 24 was formerly Code Sec. 41. See Reg. §§1.41-0—1.41-8 for rules issued under former Code Sec. 41.*

[Reg. §1.24-1]

§1.24-1 Partial credit allowed for certain other dependents.—(a) *In general.*—For purposes of section 24(h)(4)(A), a taxpayer may be eligible to increase the credit determined under section 24(a) by $500 for a dependent of the taxpayer, as defined in section 152, other than a qualifying child described in section 24(c).

(b) *Applicability date.*—This section applies to taxable years beginning on or after October 13, 2020. [Reg. §1.24-1.]

☐ [T.D. 9913, 10-9-2020.]

[Reg. §1.25-1T]

§1.25-1T. Credit for interest paid on certain home mortgages (Temporary).—(a) *In general.*—Section 25 permits States and political subdivisions to elect to issue mortgage credit certificates in lieu of qualified mortgage bonds. An individual who holds a qualified mortgage credit certificate (as defined in §1.25-3T) is entitled to a credit against his Federal income taxes. The amount of the credit depends upon (1) the amount of mortgage interest paid or accrued during the year and (2) the applicable certificate credit rate. See §1.25-2T. The amount of the deduction under section 163 for interest paid or accrued during any taxable year is reduced by the amount of the credit allowable under section 25 for such year. See §1.163-6T. The holder of a qualified mortgage credit certificate may be entitled to additional withholding allowances. See section 3402(m) and the regulations thereunder.

(b) *Definitions.*—For purposes of §§1.25-2T through 1.25-8T and this section, the following definitions apply:

(1) *Mortgage.*—The term "mortgage" includes deeds of trust, conditional sales contracts, pledges, agreements to hold title in escrow, and any other form of owner financing.

(2) *State.*—(i) The term "State" includes a possession of the United States and the District of Columbia.

(ii) Mortgage credit certificates issued by or on behalf of any State or political subdivision ("governmental unit") by constituted authorities empowered to issue such certificates are the certificates of such governmental unit.

(3) *Qualified home improvement loan.*—The term "qualified home improvement loan" has the meaning given that term under section 103A(1)(6) and the regulations thereunder.

(4) *Qualified rehabilitation loan.*—The term "qualified rehabilitation loan" has the meaning given that term under section 103A(1)(7)(A) and the regulations thereunder.

(5) *Single-family and owner-occupied residences.*—The terms "single-family" and "owner-occupied" have the meaning given those terms under section 103A(1)(9) and the regulations thereunder.

(6) *Constitutional home rule city.*—The term "constitutional home rule city" means, with respect to any calendar year, any political subdivision of a State which, under a State constitution which was adopted in 1970 and effective on July 1, 1971, had home rule powers on the 1st day of the calendar year.

(7) *Targeted area residence.*—The term "targeted area residence" has the meaning given that term under section 103A(k) and the regulations thereunder.

(8) *Acquisition cost.*—The term "acquisition cost" has the meaning given that term under section 103A(1)(5) and the regulations thereunder.

(9) *Average area purchase price.*—The term "average area purchase price" has the meaning given that term under subparagraphs (2), (3), and (4) of section 103A(f) and the regulations thereunder. For purposes of this paragraph (b)(9), all determinations of average area purchase price shall be made with respect to residences as that term is defined in section 103A and the regulations thereunder.

(10) *Total proceeds.*—The "total proceeds" of an issue is the sum of the products determined by multiplying—

(i) The certified indebtedness amount of each mortgage credit certificate issued pursuant to such issue, by

(ii) The certificate credit rate specified in such certificate.

Each qualified mortgage credit certificate program shall be treated as a separate issue of mortgage credit certificates.

(11) *Residence.*—The term "residence" includes stock held by a tenant-stockholder in a cooperative housing corporation (as those terms are defined in section 216(b)(1) and (2)). It does not include property such as an appliance, a piece of furniture, a radio, *etc.*, which, under applicable local law, is not a fixture. The term also includes any manufactured home which has a minimum of 400 square feet of living space and a minimum width in excess of 102 inches and which is of a kind customarily used at a fixed location. The preceding sentence shall not apply for purposes of determining the average area purchase price for single-family residences, nor shall it apply for purposes of determining the State ceiling amount. The term "residence" does not, however, include recreational vehicles, campers, and other similar vehicles.

(12) *Related person.*—The term "related person" has the meaning given that term under section 103(b)(6)(C)(i) and §1.103-10(e)(1).

Credits Against Tax
See p. 20,601 for regulations not amended to reflect law changes
21,019

(13) *Date of issue.*—A mortgage credit certificate is considered issued on the date on which a closing agreement is signed with respect to the certified indebtedness amount.

(c) *Affidavits.*—For purposes of §§ 1.25-1T through 1.25-8T, an affidavit filed in connection with the requirements of §§ 1.25-1T through 1.25-8T shall be made under penalties of perjury. Applicants for mortgage credit certificates who are required by a lender or the issuer to sign affidavits must be informed that any fraudulent statement will result in (i) the revocation of the individual's mortgage credit certificate, and (ii) a $10,000 penalty under section 6709. Other persons required by a lender or an issuer to provide affidavits must receive similar notice. A person may not rely on an affidavit where that person knows or has reason to know that the information contained in the affidavit is false. [Temporary Reg. § 1.25-1T.]

☐ *[T.D. 8023, 5-3-85.]*

[Reg. § 1.25-2T]

§ 1.25-2T. Amount of credit (Temporary).—(a) *In general.*—Except as otherwise provided, the amount of the credit allowable for any taxable year to an individual who holds a qualified mortgage credit certificate is equal to the product of the certificate credit rate (as defined in paragraph (b)) and the amount of the interest paid or accrued by the taxpayer during the taxable year on the certified indebtedness amount (as defined in paragraph (c)).

(b) *Certificate credit rate.*—(1) *In general.*—For purposes of §§ 1.25-1T through 1.25-8T, the term "certificate credit rate" means the rate specified by the issuer on the mortgage credit certificate. The certificate credit rate shall not be less than 10 percent nor more than 50 percent.

(2) *Limitation in certain States.*—(i) In the case of a State which—

(A) Has a State ceiling for the calendar year in which an election is made that exceeds 20 percent of the average annual aggregate principal amount of mortgages executed during the immediately preceding 3 calendar years for single-family owner-occupied residences located within the jurisdiction of such State, or

(B) Issued qualified mortgage bonds in an aggregate amount less than $150 million for calendar year 1983,

the certificate credit rate for any mortgage credit certificate issued under such program shall not exceed 20 percent unless the issuing authority submits a plan to the Commissioner to ensure that the weighted average of the certificate credit rates in such mortgage credit certificate program does not exceed 20 percent and the Commissioner approves such plan. For purposes of determining the average annual aggregate principal amount of mortgages executed during the immediately preceding 3 calendar years for single-family owner-occupied residences located within the jurisdiction of such State, an issuer may rely upon the amount published by the Treasury Department for such calendar years. An issuer may rely on a different amount from that safe-harbor limitation where the issuer has made a more accurate and comprehensive determination of that amount. The weighted average of the certificate credit rates in a mortgage credit certificate program is determined by dividing the sum of the products obtained by multiplying the certificate credit rate of each certificate by the certified indebtedness amount with respect to that certificate by the sum of the certified indebtedness amounts of the certificates issued. See section 103A(g) and the regulations thereunder for the definition of the term "State ceiling".

(ii) The following example illustrates the application of this paragraph (b)(2):

Example. City Z issues four qualified mortgage credit certificates pursuant to its qualified mortgage credit certificate program. H receives a certificate with a certificate credit rate of 30 percent and a certified indebtedness amount of $50,000. I receives a certificate with a certificate credit rate of 25 percent and a certified indebtedness amount of $100,000. J and K each receive certificates with certificate credit rates of 10 percent; their certified indebtedness amounts are $50,000 and $100,000, respectively. The weighted average of the certificate credit rates is determined by dividing the sum of the products obtained by multiplying the certificate credit rate of each certificate by the certified indebtedness amount with respect to that certificate ((.3 × $50,000) + (.25 × $100,000) + (.1 × $50,000) + (.1 × $100,000)) by the sum of the certified indebtedness amounts of the certificates issued ($50,000 + $100,000 + $50,000 + $100,000)). Thus, the weighted average of the certificate credit rates is 18.33 percent ($55,000/$300,000).

(c) *Certified indebtedness amount.*—(1) *In general.*—The term "certified indebtedness amount" means the amount of indebtedness which is—

(i) Incurred by the taxpayer—

(A) To acquire his principal residence,

(B) As a qualified home improvement loan, or

(C) As a qualified rehabilitation loan, and

(ii) Specified in the mortgage credit certificate.

(2) *Example.*—The following example illustrates the application of this paragraph:

Example. On March 1, 1986, State X, pursuant to its qualified mortgage credit certificate program, provides a mortgage credit certificate to B. State X specifies that the maximum amount of the mortgage loan for which B may claim a credit is $65,000. On March 15, B purchases for $67,000 a single-family dwelling for use as his principal residence. B obtains from Bank M a mortgage loan for $60,000. State X, or Bank M acting on behalf of State X, indicates on B's mortgage credit certificate that the certified indebtedness amount of B's loan is $60,000. B may claim a credit under section 25(e) based on this amount.

(d) *Limitation on credit.*—(1) *Limitation where certificate credit rate exceeds 20 percent.*—(i) If the certificate credit rate of any mortgage credit certificate exceeds 20 percent, the amount of the credit allowed to the taxpayer by section 25(a)(1) for any year shall not exceed $2,000. Any amount denied under this paragraph (d)(1) may not be carried forward under section 25(e)(1) and paragraph (d)(2) of this section.

(ii) If two or more persons hold interests in any residence, the limitation of paragraph (d)(1)(i) shall be allocated among such persons in proportion to their respective interests in the residence.

(2) *Carryforward of unused credit.*—(i) If the credit allowable under section 25(a) and § 1.25-2T for any taxable year exceeds the applicable tax limit for that year, the excess (the "unused credit") will be a carryover to each of the 3 succeeding taxable years and, subject to the limitations of paragraph (d)(2)(ii), will be added to the credit allowable by section 25(a) and § 1.25-2T for that succeeding year.

(ii) The amount of the unused credit for any taxable year (the "unused credit year") which may be taken into account under this paragraph (d)(2) for any subsequent taxable year may not exceed the amount by which the applicable tax limit for that subsequent taxable year exceeds the sum of (i) the amount of the credit allowable under section 25(a) and § 1.25-1T for the current taxable year, and (ii) the sum of the unused credits which, by reason of this paragraph (d)(2), are carried to that subsequent taxable year and are attributable to taxable years before the unused credit year. Thus, if by reason of this paragraph (d)(2), unused credits from 2 prior taxable years are carried forward to a subsequent taxable year, the unused credit from the earlier of those 2 prior years must be taken into account before the unused credit from the later of those 2 years is taken into account.

(iii) For purposes of this paragraph (d)(2) the term "applicable tax limit" means the limitation imposed by section 26(a) for the taxable year reduced by the sum of the credits allowable for that year under section 21, relating to expenses for household and dependent care services necessary for gainful employment, section 22, relating to the credit for the elderly and the permanently disabled, section 23, relating to the residential energy credit, and section 24, relating to contributions to candidates for public office. The limitation imposed by section 26(a) for any taxable year is equal to the taxpayer's tax liability (as defined in section 26(b)) for that year.

(iv) The following examples illustrate the application of this paragraph (d)(2):

Example (1). (i) B, a calendar year taxpayer, holds a qualified mortgage credit certificate. For 1986 B's applicable tax limit (*i.e.,* tax liability) is $1,100. The amount of the credit under section 25(a) and § 1.25-2T for 1986 is $1,700. For 1986 B is not entitled to any of the credits described in sections 21 through 24. Under § 1.25-2T(d)(2), B's unused credit for 1986 is $600, and B is entitled to carry forward that amount to the 3 succeeding years.

(ii) For 1987 B's applicable tax limit is $1,500, the amount of the credit under section 25(a) and § 1.25-2T is $1,700, and the unused credit is $200. For 1988 B's applicable tax limit is $2,000, the amount of the credit under section 25(a) and § 1.25-2T is $1,300, and there is no unused credit. For 1987 and 1988 B is not entitled to any of the credits described in sections 21 through 24. No portion of the unused credit for 1986 may be used in 1987. For 1988 B is entitled to claim a credit of $2,000 under section 25(a) and § 1.25-2T, consisting of a $1,300 credit for 1988, the $600 unused credit for 1986, and $100 of the $200 unused credit for 1987. In addition, B may carry forward the remaining unused credit for 1987 ($100) to 1989 and 1990.

Example (2). The facts are the same as in Example (1) except that for 1988 B is entitled to a credit of $400 under section 23. B's applicable tax limit for 1988 is $1,600 ($2,000 less $400). For 1988 B is entitled to claim a credit of $1,600 under section 25(a) and § 1.25-2T, consisting of a $1,300 credit for 1988 and $300 of the unused credit for 1986. In addition, B may carry forward the remaining unused credits of $300 for 1986 to 1989 and of $200 for 1987 to 1989 and 1990. [Temporary Reg. § 1.25-2T.]

☐ *[T.D. 8023, 5-3-85.]*

Reg. § 1.25-2T(d)(2)(iv)

[Reg. §1.25-3]

§1.25-3. Qualified mortgage credit certificate.—(a) through (g)(1)(ii) [Reserved] For further guidance, see §1.25-3T(a) through (g)(1)(ii).

(g)(1)(iii) *Reissued certificate exception.*—See paragraph (p) of this section for rules regarding the exception in the case of refinancing existing mortgages.

(g)(2) through (o) [Reserved] For further guidance, see §1.25-3T(g)(2) through (o).

(p) *Reissued certificates for certain refinancings.*—(1) *In general.*—If the issuer of a qualified mortgage credit certificate reissues a certificate in place of an existing mortgage credit certificate to the holder of that existing certificate, the reissued certificate is treated as satisfying the requirements of this section. The period for which the reissued certificate is in effect begins with the date of the refinancing (that is, the date on which interest begins accruing on the refinancing loan).

(2) *Meaning of existing certificate.* For purposes of this paragraph (p), a mortgage credit certificate is an existing certificate only if it satisfies the requirements of this section. An existing certificate may be the original certificate, a certificate issued to a transferee under §1.25-3T(h)(2)(ii), or a certificate previously reissued under this paragraph (p).

(3) *Limitations on reissued certificate.* An issuer may reissue a mortgage credit certificate only if all of the following requirements are satisfied:

(i) The reissued certificate is issued to the holder of an existing certificate with respect to the same property to which the existing certificate relates.

(ii) The reissued certificate entirely replaces the existing certificate (that is, the holder cannot retain the existing certificate with respect to any portion of the outstanding balance of the certified mortgage indebtedness specified on the existing certificate).

(iii) The certified mortgage indebtedness specified on the reissued certificate does not exceed the remaining outstanding balance of the certified mortgage indebtedness specified on the existing certificate.

(iv) The reissued certificate does not increase the certificate credit rate specified in the existing certificate.

(v) The reissued certificate does not result in an increase in the tax credit that would otherwise have been allowable to the holder under the existing certificate for any taxable year. The holder of a reissued certificate determines the amount of tax credit that would otherwise have been allowable by multiplying the interest that was scheduled to have been paid on the refinanced loan by the certificate rate of the existing certificate. In the case of a series of refinancings, the tax credit that would otherwise have been allowable is determined from the amount of interest that was scheduled to have been paid on the original loan and the certificate rate of the original certificate.

(A) In the case of a refinanced loan that is a fixed interest rate loan, the interest that was scheduled to be paid on the refinanced loan is determined using the scheduled interest method described in paragraph (p)(3)(v)(C) of this section.

(B) In the case of a refinanced loan that is not a fixed interest rate loan, the interest that was scheduled to be paid on the refinanced loan is determined using either the scheduled interest method described in paragraph (p)(3)(v)(C) of this section or the hypothetical interest method described in paragraph (p)(3)(v)(C) of this section.

(C) The scheduled interest method determines the amount of interest for each taxable year that was scheduled to have been paid in the taxable year based on the terms of the refinanced loan including any changes in the interest rate that would have been required by the terms of the refinanced loan and any payments of principal that would have been required by the terms of the refinanced loan (other than repayments required as a result of any refinancing of the loan).

(D) The hypothetical interest method (which is available only for refinanced loans that are not fixed interest rate loans) determines the amount of interest treated as having been scheduled to be paid for a taxable year by constructing an amortization schedule for a hypothetical self-amortizing loan with level payments. The hypothetical loan must have a principal amount equal to the remaining outstanding balance of the certified mortgage indebtedness specified on the existing certificate, a maturity equal to that of the refinanced loan, and interest equal to the annual percentage rate (APR) of the refinancing loan that is required to be calculated for the Federal Truth in Lending Act.

(E) A holder must consistently apply the scheduled interest method or the hypothetical interest method for all taxable years beginning with the first taxable year the tax credit is claimed by the holder based upon the reissued certificate.

(4) *Examples.*—The following examples illustrate the application of paragraph (p)(3)(v) of this section:

Example 1. A holder of an existing certificate that meets the requirements of this section seeks to refinance the mortgage on the property to which the existing certificate relates. The final payment on the holder's existing mortgage is due on December 31, 2000; the final payment on the new mortgage would not be due until January 31, 2004. The holder requests that the issuer provide to the holder a reissued mortgage credit certificate in place of the existing certificate. The requested certificate would have the same certificate credit rate as the existing certificate. For each calendar year through the year 2000, the credit that would be allowable to the holder with respect to the new mortgage under the requested certificate would not exceed the credit allowable for that year under the existing certificate. The requested certificate, however, would allow the holder credits for the years 2001 through 2004, years for which, due to the earlier scheduled retirement of the existing mortgage, no credit would be allowable under the existing certificate. Under paragraph (p)(3)(v) of this section, the issuer may not reissue the certificate as requested because, under the existing certificate, no credit would be allowable for the years 2001 through 2004. The issuer may, however, provide a reissued certificate that limits the amount of the credit allowable in each year to the amount allowable under the existing certificate. Because the existing certificate would allow no credit after December 31, 2000, the reissued certificate could expire on December 31, 2000.

Example 2. (a) The facts are the same as *Example 1* except that the existing mortgage loan has a variable rate of interest and the refinancing loan will have a fixed rate of interest. To determine whether the limit under paragraph (p)(3)(v) of this section is met for any taxable year, the holder must calculate the amount of credit that otherwise would have been allowable absent the refinancing. This requires a determination of the amount of interest that would have been payable on the refinanced loan for the taxable year. The holder may determine this amount by—

(1) Applying the terms of the refinanced loan, including the variable interest rate or rates, for the taxable year as though the refinanced loan continued to exist; or

(2) Obtaining the amount of interest, and calculating the amount of credit that would have been available, from the schedule of equal payments that fully amortize a hypothetical loan with the principal amount equal to the remaining outstanding balance of the certified mortgage indebtedness specified on the existing certificate, the interest equal to the annual percentage rate (APR) of the refinancing loan, and the maturity equal to that of the refinanced loan.

(b) The holder must apply the same method for each taxable year the tax credit is claimed based upon the reissued mortgage credit certificate.

(5) *Coordination with Section 143(m)(3).* A refinancing loan underlying a reissued mortgage credit certificate that replaces a mortgage credit certificate issued on or before December 31, 1990, is not a federally subsidized indebtedness for the purposes of section 143(m)(3) of the Internal Revenue Code. [Reg. §1.25-3.]

☐ [T.D. 8692, 12-16-96.]

[Reg. §1.25-3T]

§1.25-3T. Qualified mortgage credit certificate (Temporary).—(a) *Definition of qualified mortgage credit certificate.*—For purposes of §§1.25-1T through 1.25-8T, the term "qualified mortgage credit certificate" means a certificate that meets all of the requirements of this section.

(b) *Qualified mortgage credit certificate program.*—A certificate meets the requirements of this paragraph if it is issued under a qualified mortgage credit certificate program (as defined in §1.25-4T).

(c) *Required form and information.*—A certificate meets the requirements of this paragraph if it is in the form specified in §1.25-6T and if all the information required by the form is specified on the form.

(d) *Residence requirement.*—(1) *In general.*—A certificate meets the requirements of this paragraph only if it is provided in connection with the acquisition, qualified rehabilitation, or qualified home improvement of a residence that is—

(i) A single-family residence (as defined in §1.25-1T(b)(5)) which, at the time the financing on the residence is executed or assumed, can reasonably be expected by the issuer to become (or, in the case of a qualified home improvement loan, to continue to be) the principal residence (as defined in section 1034 and the regulations thereunder) of the holder of the certificate within a reasonable time after the financing is executed or assumed, and

(ii) Located within the jurisdiction of the governmental unit issuing the certificate.

See section 103A(d) and the regulations thereunder for further definitions and requirements.

(2) *Certification procedure.*—The requirements of this paragraph will be met if the issuer or its agent obtains from the holder of the certificate and affidavit stating his intent to use (or, in the case of a qualified home improvement loan, that he is currently using and intends to continue to use) the residence as his principal residence within a reasonable time (*e.g.,* 60 days) after the mortgage credit certificate is issued and stating that the holder will notify the issuer of the mortgage credit certificate if the residence ceases to be his principal residence. The affidavit must also state facts that are sufficient for the issuer or his agent to determine whether the residence is located within the jurisdiction of the issuer that issued the mortgage credit certificate.

(e) *3-year requirement.*—(1) *In general.*—A certificate meets the requirements of this paragraph only if the holder of the certificate had no present ownership interest in a principal residence at any time during the 3-year period prior to the date on which the mortgage on the residence in connection with which the certificate is provided is executed. For purposes of the preceding sentence, the holder's interest in the residence with respect to which the certificate is being provided shall not be taken into account. See section 103A(e) and the regulations thereunder for further definitions and requirements.

(2) *Exceptions.*—Paragraph (e)(1) shall not apply with respect to—

(i) Any certificate provided with respect to a targeted area residence (as defined in §1.25-1T(b)(7)),

(ii) Any qualified home improvement loan (as defined in §1.25-1T(b)(3)), and

(iii) Any qualified rehabilitation loan (as defined in §1.25-1T(b)(4)).

(3) *Certification procedure.*—The requirements of paragraph (e)(1) will be met if the issuer or its agent obtains from the holder of the certificate an affidavit stating that he had no present ownership interest in a principal residence at any time during the 3-year period prior to the date on which the certificate is issued and the issuer or its agent obtains from the applicant copies of the applicant's Federal tax returns for the preceding 3 years and examines each statement to determine whether the applicant has claimed a deduction for taxes on property which was the applicant's principal residence pursuant to section 164(a)(1) or a deduction pursuant to section 163 for interest paid on a mortgage secured by property which was the applicant's principal residence. Where the mortgage is executed during the period between January 1 and February 15 and the applicant has not yet filed his Federal income tax return with the Internal Revenue Service, the issuer may, with respect to such year, rely on an affidavit of the applicant that the applicant is not entitled to claim deductions for taxes or interest on indebtedness with respect to property constituting his principal residence for the preceding calendar year. In the alternative, when applicable, the holder may provide an affidavit stating that one of the exceptions provided in paragraph (e)(2) applies.

(4) *Special rule.*—An issuer may submit a plan to the Commissioner for distributing certificates, in an amount not to exceed 10 percent of the proceeds of the issue, to individuals who do not meet the requirements of this paragraph. Such plan must describe a procedure for ensuring that no more than 10 percent of the proceeds of such issue will be used to provide certificates to such individuals. If the Commissioner approves the issuer's plan, certificates issued in accordance with the terms of that plan to holders who do not meet the 3-year requirement do not fail to satisfy the requirements of this paragraph.

(f) *Purchase price requirement.*—(1) *In general.*—A certificate meets the requirements of this paragraph only if the acquisition cost (as defined in §1.25-1T(b)(8)) of the residence, other than a targeted area residence, in connection with which the certificate is provided does not exceed 110 percent of the average area purchase price (as defined in §1.25-1T(b)(9)) applicable to that residence. In the case of a targeted area residence (as defined in §1.25-1T(b)(7)) the acquisition cost may not exceed 120 percent of the average area purchase price applicable to such residence. See section 103A(f) and the regulations thereunder for further definitions and requirements.

(2) *Certification procedure.*—The requirements of paragraph (f)(1) will be met if the issuer or its agent obtains affidavits executed by the seller and the buyer that state that these requirements have been met. Such affidavits must include an itemized list of—

(i) Any payments made by the buyer (or a related person) or for the benefit of the buyer,

(ii) If the residence is incomplete, an estimate of the reasonable cost of completing the residence, and

(iii) If the residence is purchased subject to a ground rent, the capitalized value of the ground rent.

The issuer or his agent must examine such affidavits and determine whether, on the basis of information contained therein, the purchase price requirement is met.

(g) *New mortgage requirement.*—(1) *In general.*—(i) A certificate meets the requirements of this paragraph only if the certificate is not issued in connection with the acquisition or replacement of an existing mortgage. Except in the case of a qualified home improvement loan, the certificate must be issued to an individual who did not have a mortgage (whether or not paid off) on the residence with respect to which the certificate is issued at any time prior to the execution of the mortgage.

(ii) *Exceptions.*—For purposes of this paragraph, a certificate used in connection with the replacement of—

(A) Construction period loans,

(B) Bridge loans or similar temporary initial financing, and

(C) In the case of a qualified rehabilitation loan, an existing mortgage,

shall not be treated as being used to acquire or replace an existing mortgage. Generally, temporary initial financing is any financing which has a term of 24 months or less. See section 103A(j)(1) and the regulations thereunder for examples illustrating the application of these requirements.

(2) *Certification procedure.*—The requirements of paragraph (g)(1) will be met if the issuer or its agent obtains from the holder of the certificate an affidavit stating that the mortgage being acquired in connection with the certificate will not be used to acquire or replace an existing mortgage (other than one that falls within the exceptions described in paragraph (g)(1)(ii)).

(h) *Transfer of mortgage credit certificates.*—(1) *In general.*—A certificate meets the requirements of this paragraph only if it is (i) not transferable or (ii) transferable only with the approval of the issuer.

(2) *Transfer procedure.*—A certificate that is transferred with the approval of the issuer is a qualified mortgage credit certificate in the hands of the transferee only if each of the following requirements is met:

(i) The transferee assumed liability for the remaining balance of the certified indebtedness amount in connection with the acquisition of the residence from the transferor,

(ii) The issuer issues a new certificate to the transferee, and

(iii) The new certificate meets each of the requirements of paragraphs (d), (e), (f), and (i) of this section based on the facts as they exist at the time of the transfer as if the mortgage credit certificate were being issued for the first time. For example, the purchase price requirement is to be determined by reference to the average area purchase price at the time of the assumption and not when the mortgage credit certificate was originally issued.

(3) *Statement on certificate.*—The requirements of paragraph (h)(1) will be met if the mortgage credit certificate states that the certificate may not be transferred or states that the certificate may not be transferred unless the issuer issues a new certificate in place of the original certificate.

(i) *Prohibited mortgages.*—(1) *In general.*—A certificate meets the requirements of this paragraph only if it is issued in connection with the acquisition of a residence none of the financing of which is provided from the proceeds of—

(i) A qualified mortgage bond (as defined under section 103A(c)(1) and the regulations thereunder), or

(ii) A qualified veterans' mortgage bond (as defined under section 103A(c)(3) and the regulations thereunder).

Thus, for example, if a mortgagor has a mortgage on his principal residence that was obtained from the proceeds of a qualified mortgage bond, a mortgage credit certificate issued to such mortgagor in connection with a qualified home improvement loan with respect to such residence is not a qualified mortgage credit certificate. If, however, the financing provided from the proceeds of the qualified mortgage bond had been paid off in full, the certificate would be a qualified mortgage credit certificate (assuming all the requirements of this paragraph are met).

(2) *Certification procedure.*—The requirements of paragraph (i)(1) will be met if the issuer or its agent obtains from the holder of the certificate an affidavit stating that no portion of the financing of the residence in connection with which the certificate is issued is provided from the proceeds of a qualified mortgage bond or a qualified veterans' mortgage bond.

(j) *Particular lenders.*—(1) *In general.*—Except as otherwise provided in paragraph (j)(2), a certificate meets the requirements of this paragraph only if the certificate is not limited to indebtedness incurred from particular lenders. A certificate is limited to indebtedness from particular lenders if the issuer, directly or indirectly, prohibits the holder of a certificate from obtaining financing from one or more lenders or requires the holder of a certificate to obtain financing from one or more lenders. For purposes of this paragraph, a lender is any person, including an issuer of mortgage credit certificates, that provides financing for the acquisition, qualified rehabilitation, or qualified home improvement of a residence.

(2) *Exception.*—A mortgage credit certificate that is limited to indebtedness incurred from particular lenders will not cease to meet the requirements of this paragraph if the Commissioner approves the basis for such limitation. The Commissioner may approve the basis for such limitation if the issuer establishes to the satisfaction of the Commissioner that it will result in a significant economic benefit to the holders of mortgage credit certificates (*e.g.,* substantially lower financing costs) compared to the result without such limitation.

(3) *Taxable bonds.*—The requirements of this paragraph do not prevent an issuer of mortgage credit certificates from issuing mortgage subsidy bonds (other than obligations described in section 103(a)) the proceeds of which are to be used to provide mortgages to holders of mortgage credit certificates provided that the holders of such certificates are not required to obtain financing from the proceeds of the bond issue. See §1.25-4T(h) with respect to permissible fees.

(4) *Lists of participating lenders.*—The requirements of this paragraph do not prohibit an issuer from maintaining a list of lenders that have stated that they will make loans to qualified holders of mortgage credit certificates, provided that (i) the issuer solicits such statements in a public notice similar to the notice described in §1.25-7T, (ii) lenders are provided a reasonable period of time in which to express their interest in being included in such a list, and (iii) holders of mortgage credit certificates are not required to obtain financing from the lenders on the list. If an issuer maintains such a list, it must update the list at least annually.

(5) *Certification procedure.*—The requirements of this paragraph will be met if (i) the issuer or its agent obtains from the holder of the certificate an affidavit stating that the certificate was not limited to indebtedness incurred from particular lenders or (ii) the issuer obtains a ruling from the Commissioner under paragraph (j)(2).

(6) *Examples.*—The following examples illustrate the application of this paragraph:

Example (1). Under its mortgage credit certificate program, County Z distributes all the certificates to be issued to a group of 60 participating lenders. Residents of County Z may obtain mortgage credit certificates only from the participating lenders and only in connection with the acquisition of mortgage financing from that lender or one of the other participating lenders. Certificates issued under this program do not meet the requirements of this paragraph since the certificates are limited to indebtedness incurred from particular lenders. The certificates, therefore, are not qualified mortgage credit certificates.

Example (2). In connection with its mortgage credit certificate program, County Y arranges with Bank P for a line of credit to be used to provide mortgage financing to holders of mortgage credit certificates. County Y, pursuant to paragraph (j)(4), maintains a list of lenders participating in the mortgage credit certificate program. County Y distributes the certificates directly to applicants. Holders of the certificates are not required to obtain mortgage financing through the line of credit or through a lender on the list of participating lenders. Certificates issued pursuant to County Y's program satisfy the requirements of this paragraph.

(k) *Developer certification.*—(1) *In general.*—A mortgage credit certificate that is allocated by the issuer to any particular development meets the requirements of this paragraph only if the developer provides a certification to the purchaser of the residence and the issuer stating that the purchase price of that residence is not higher than the price would be if the issuer had not allocated mortgage credit certificates to the development. The certification must be made by the developer if a natural person or, if not, by a duly authorized official of the developer.

(2) *Certification procedure.*—The requirements of this paragraph will be met if the issuer or its agent obtains from the holder of the certificate an affidavit stating that he has received from the developer the certification described in this paragraph.

(l) *Expiration.*—(1) *In general.*—A certificate meets the requirements of this paragraph if the certified indebtedness amount is incurred prior to the close of the second calendar year following the calendar year for which the issuer elected not to issue qualified mortgage bonds under §1.25-4T with respect to that issue of mortgage credit certificates. Thus, for example, if on October 1, 1984, an

issuing authority elects under §1.25-4T not to issue qualified mortgage bonds, a mortgage credit certificate provided under that program does not meet the requirements of this paragraph unless the indebtedness is incurred on or before December 31, 1986.

(2) *Issuer-imposed expiration dates.*—An issuer of mortgage credit certificates may provide that a certificate shall expire if the holder of the certificate does not incur certified indebtedness by a date that is prior to the expiration date provided in paragraph (l)(1). A certificate that expires prior to the date provided in paragraph (l)(1) may be reissued provided that the requirements of this paragraph are met.

(m) *Revocation.*—A certificate meets the requirements of this paragraph only if it has not been revoked. Thus, the credit provided by section 25 and §1.25-1T does not apply to interest paid or accrued following the revocation of a certificate. A certificate is treated as revoked when the residence to which the certificate relates ceases to be the holder's principal residence. An issuer may revoke a mortgage credit certificate if the certificate does not meet all the requirements of §1.25-3T(d), (e), (f), (g), (h), (i), (j), (k), and (n). The certificate is revoked by the issuer's notifying the holder of the certificate and the Internal Revenue Service that the certificate is revoked. The notice to the Internal Revenue Service shall be made as part of the report required by §1.25-8T(b)(2).

(n) *Interest paid to related person.*—(1) *In general.*—A certificate does not meet the requirements of this paragraph if interest on the certified indebtedness amount is paid to a person who is a related person to the holder of the certificate.

(2) *Certification procedure.*—The requirements of this paragraph will be met if the issuer or its agent obtains from the holder of the certificate an affidavit stating that a related person does not have, and is not expected to have, an interest as a creditor in the certified indebtedness amount.

(o) *Fraud.*—Notwithstanding any other provision of this section, a mortgage credit certificate does not meet the requirements of this section and, therefore, the certificate is not a qualified mortgage credit certificate for any calendar year, if the holder of the certificate provides a certification or any other information to the lender providing the mortgage or to the issuer of the certificate containing a material misstatement and such misstatement is due to fraud. In determining whether any misstatement is due to fraud, the rules generally applicable to underpayments of tax due to fraud (including rules relating to the statute of limitations) shall apply. See §1.6709-1T with respect to the penalty for filing negligent or fraudulent statements. [Temporary Reg. §1.25-3T.]

☐ [*T.D.* 8023, 5-3-85. *Amended by T.D.* 8502, 12-21-93 *and T.D.* 8692, 12-16-96.]

[Reg. §1.25-4T]

§1.25-4T. Qualified mortgage credit certificate program (Temporary).—(a) *In general.*—(1) *Definition of qualified mortgage credit certificate program.*—For purposes of §§1.25-1T through 1.25-8T, the term "qualified mortgage credit certificate program" means a program to issue qualified mortgage credit certificates which meets all of the requirements of paragraphs (b) through (i) of this section.

(2) *Requirements are a minimum.*—Except as otherwise provided in this section, the requirements of this section are minimum requirements. Issuers may establish more stringent criteria for participation in a qualified mortgage credit certificate program. Thus, for example, an issuer may target 30 percent of the proceeds of an issue of mortgage credit certificates to targeted areas. Further, issuers may establish additional eligibility criteria for participation in a qualified mortgage credit certificate program. Thus, for example, issuers may impose an income limitation designed to ensure that only those individuals who could not otherwise purchase a residence will benefit from the credit.

(3) Except as otherwise provided in this section and §1.25-3T, issuers may use mortgage credit certificates in connection with other Federal, State, and local programs provided that such use complies with the requirements of §1.25-3T(j). Thus, for example, a mortgage credit certificate may be issued in connection with the qualified rehabilitation of a residence part of the cost of which will be paid from the proceeds of a State grant.

(b) *Establishment of program.*—A program meets the requirements of this paragraph only if it is established by a State or political subdivision thereof for any calendar year for which it has the authority to issue qualified mortgage bonds.

(c) *Election not to issue qualified mortgage bonds.*—(1) *In general.*—A program meets the requirements of this paragraph only if the issuer elects, in the time and manner specified in this paragraph, not to issue an amount of qualified mortgage bonds that it may otherwise issue during the calendar year under section 103A and the regulations thereunder.

(2) *Manner of making election.*—On or before the earlier of the date of distribution of mortgage credit certificates under a program or December 31, 1987, the issuer must file an election not to issue an amount of qualified mortgage bonds. The election (and the certification (or affidavit) described in paragraph (d)) shall be filed with the Internal Revenue Service Center, Philadelphia, Pennsylvania 19255. The election should be titled "Mortgage Credit Certificate Election" and must include—

(i) The name, address, and TIN of the issuer,

(ii) The issuer's applicable limit, as defined in section 103A(g) and the regulations thereunder,

(iii) The aggregate amount of qualified mortgage bonds issued by the issuing authority during the calendar year,

(iv) The amount of the issuer's applicable limit that it has surrendered to other issuers during the calendar year,

(v) The date and amount of any previous elections under this paragraph for the calendar year, and

(vi) The amount of qualified mortgage bonds that the issuer elects not to issue.

(3) *Revocation of election.*—Any election made under this paragraph may be revoked, in whole or in part, at any time during the calendar year in which the election was made. The revocation, however, may not be made with respect to any part of the nonissued bond amount that has been used to issue mortgage credit certificates pursuant to the election. The revocation shall be filed with the Internal Revenue Service Center, Philadelphia, Pennsylvania 19255. The revocation should be titled "Revocation of Mortgage Credit Certificate Election" and must include—

(i) The name, address, and TIN of the issuer,

(ii) The nonissued bond amount as originally elected, and

(iii) The portion of the nonissued bond amount with respect to which the election is being revoked.

(4) *Special rule.*—If at the time that an issuer makes an election under this paragraph it does not know its applicable limit, the issuer may elect not to use all of its remaining authority to issue qualified mortgage bonds; this form of election will be treated as meeting the requirements of paragraph (c)(2) if, prior to the later of the end of the calendar year and December 31, 1985, the issuer amends its election so as to indicate the exact amount of qualified mortgage bond authority that it elected not to issue.

(5) *Limitation on nonissued bond amount.*—The amount of qualified mortgage bonds which an issuer elects not to issue may not exceed the issuer's applicable limit (as determined under section 103A(g) and the regulations thereunder). For example, a governmental unit that, pursuant to section 103A(g)(3), may issue $10 million of qualified mortgage bonds that elects to trade in $11 million in qualified mortgage bond authority has not met the requirements of this paragraph, and mortgage credit certificates issued pursuant to such election are not qualified mortgage credit certificates.

(d) *State certification requirement.*—(1) *In general.*—A program meets the requirements of this paragraph only if the State official designated by law (or, where there is no State official, the Governor) certifies, based on facts and circumstances as of the date on which the certification is requested, following a request for such certification, that the issue meets the requirements of section 103A(g) (relating to volume limitation) and the regulations thereunder. A copy of the State certification must be attached to the issuer's election not to issue qualified mortgage bonds, except that, in the case of elections made during calendar year 1984, the certification may be filed with the Service prior to July 8, 1985, provided that mortgage credit certificates may not be distributed until the certification is filed. In the case of any constitutional home rule city, the certification shall be made by the chief executive officer of the city.

(2) *Certification procedure.*—The official making the certification described in this paragraph (d) need not perform an independent investigation to determine whether the issuer has met the requirements of section 103A(g). In determining the aggregate amount of qualified mortgage bonds previously issued by that issuer during the calendar year the official may rely on copies of prior elections under paragraph (c) of this section made by the issuer for that year, together with an affidavit executed by an official of the issuer who is responsible for issuing bonds stating that the issuer has not, to date, issued any other issues of qualified mortgage bonds during the calendar year and stating the amount, if any, of the issuer's applicable limit that it has surrendered to other issuers during the calendar year; for any calendar year prior to 1985, the official may rely on an affidavit executed by a duly authorized official of the issuer who states the aggregate amount of qualified mortgage bonds issued by

the issuer during the year. In determining the aggregate amount of qualified mortgage bonds that the issuer has previously elected not to issue during that calendar year, the official may rely on copies of any elections not to issue qualified mortgage bonds filed by the issuer for that calendar year, together with an affidavit executed by an official of the issuer responsible for issuing mortgage credit certificates stating that the issuer has not, to date, made any other elections not to issue qualified mortgage bonds. If, based on such information, the certifying official determines that the issuer has not, as of the date on which the certification is provided, exceeded its applicable limit for the year, the official may certify that the issue meets the requirements of section 103A(g). The fact that the certification described in this paragraph (d) is provided does not ensure that the issuer has met the requirements of section 103A(g) and the regulations thereunder, nor does it preclude the application of the penalty for over-issuance of mortgage credit certificates if such over-issuance actually occurs. See § 1.25-5T.

(3) *Special rule.*—If within 30 days after the issuer files a proper request for the certification described in this paragraph (d) the issuer has not received from the State official designated by law (or, if there is no State official, the Governor) certification that the issue meets the requirements of section 103A(g) or, in the alternative, a statement that the issue does not meet such requirements, the issuer may submit, in lieu of the certification required by this paragraph (d), an affidavit executed by an officer of the issuer responsible for issuing mortgage credit certificates stating that—

(i) The issue meets the requirements of section 103A(g) and the regulations thereunder,

(ii) At least 30 days before the execution of the affidavit the issuer filed a proper request for the certification described in this paragraph (d), and

(iii) The State official designated by law (or, if there is no State official, the Governor) has not provided the certification described in this paragraph (d) or a statement that the issue does not meet such requirements.

For purposes of this paragraph, a request for certification is proper if the request includes the reports and affidavits described in paragraph (d)(2).

(e) *Information reporting requirement.*—(1) *Reports.*—With respect to mortgage credit certificates issued after September 30, 1985, a program meets the requirements of this paragraph only if the issuer submits a report containing the information concerning the holders of certificates issued during the preceding reporting period required by this paragraph. The report must be filed for each reporting period in which certificates (other than transferred certificates) are issued under the program. The issuer is not responsible for false information provided by a holder if the issuer did not know or have reason to know that the information was false. The report must be filed on the form prescribed by the Internal Revenue Service. If no form is prescribed, or if the form prescribed is not readily available, the issuer may use its own form provided that such form is in the format set forth in this paragraph and contains the information required by this paragraph. The report must be titled "Mortgage Credit Certificate Information Report" and must include the name, address, and TIN of the issuer, the reporting period for which the information is provided, and the following tables containing information concerning the holders of certificates issued during the reporting period for which the report is filed:

(i) A table titled "Number of Mortgage Credit Certificates by Income and Acquisition Cost" showing the number of mortgage credit certificates issued (other than those issued in connection with qualified home improvement and rehabilitation loans) according to the annualized gross income of the holders (categorized in the following intervals of income: $0-$9,999; $10,000-$19,999; $20,000-$29,999; $30,000-$39,999; $40,000-$49,999; $50,000-$74,999; and $75,000 or more) and according to the acquisition cost of the residences acquired in connection with the mortgage credit certificates (categorized in the following intervals of acquisition cost: $0-$19,999; $20,000-$39,999; $40,000-$59,999; $60,000-$79,999; $80,000-$99,999; $100,000-$119,999; $120,000-$149,999; $150,000-$199,999; and $200,000 or more). For each interval of income and acquisition cost the table must also be categorized according to—

(A) The aggregate amount of fees charged to holders to cover any administrative costs incurred by the issuer in issuing mortgage credit certificates, and

(B) The number of holders that—

(1) Did not have a present ownership interest in a principal residence at any time during the 3-year period ending on the date the mortgage credit certificate is executed (*i.e.*, satisfied the 3-year requirement) and purchased residences in targeted areas,

(2) Satisfied the 3-year requirement and purchased residences not located in targeted areas,

Reg. § 1.25-4T(e)(1)(i)(B)(2)

(3) Did have a present ownership interest in a principal residence at any time during the 3-year period ending on the date the mortgage credit certificate is executed (*i.e.*, did not satisfy the 3-year requirement) and purchased residences in targeted areas, and

(4) Did not satisfy the 3-year requirement and purchased residences not located in targeted areas.

(ii) A table titled "Volume of Mortgage Credit Certificates by Income and Acquisition Cost" containing data on—

(A) The total of the certified indebtedness amounts of the certificates issued (other than those issued in connection with qualified home improvement and rehabilitation loans);

(B) The sum of the products of the certified indebtedness amount and the certificate credit rate for each certificate (other than those issued in connection with qualified home improvement and rehabilitation loans) according to annualized gross income (categorized in the same intervals of income as the preceding table) and according to the acquisition cost of the residences acquired in connection with mortgage credit certificates (categorized in the same intervals of acquisition cost as the preceding table); and

(C) For each interval of income and acquisition cost, the information described in paragraph (e)(1)((ii)(A) and (B) categorized according to the holders that—

(1) Satisfied the 3-year requirement and purchased residences in targeted areas,

(2) Satisfied the 3-year requirement and purchased residences not located in targeted areas,

(3) Did not satisfy the 3-year requirement and purchased residences in targeted areas, and

(4) Did not satisfy the 3-year requirement and purchased residences not located in targeted areas.

(iii) A table titled "Mortgage Credit Certificates for Qualified Home Improvement and Rehabilitation Loans" showing the number of mortgage credit certificates issued in connection with qualified home improvement loans and qualified rehabilitation loans, the total of the certified indebtedness amount with respect to such certificates, and the sum of the products of the certified indebtedness amount and the certificate credit rate for each certificate; the information contained in the table must also be categorized according to whether the residences with respect to which the certificates were provided are located in targeted areas.

(2) *Format.*—If no form is prescribed by the Internal Revenue Service, or if the prescribed form is not readily available, the issuer must submit the report in the format specified in this paragraph (e)(2). The specified format of the report is the following:

MORTGAGE CREDIT CERTIFICATE INFORMATION REPORT

Name of issuer:
Address of issuer:
TIN of issuer:
Reporting period:

NUMBER OF MORTGAGE CREDIT CERTIFICATES
BY INCOME AND ACQUISITION COST

3-year Requirement: Annualized Gross Monthly Income of Borrowers		Satisfied		Not Satisfied		Totals	Fees
		Nontargeted Area	Targeted Area	Nontargeted Area	Targeted Area		
$ 0 —	9,999						
$ 10,000—	19,999						
$ 20,000—	29,999						
$ 30,000—	39,999						
$ 40,000—	49,999						
$ 50,000—	74,999						
$ 75,000 or more							
Total							
Acquisition Cost							
$ 0 —	19,999						
$ 20,000—	39,999						
$ 40,000—	59,999						
$ 60,000—	79,999						
$ 80,000—	99,999						
$ 100,000—	119,999						
$ 120,000—	149,999						
$ 150,000—	199,999						
$ 200,000 or more							
Total							

VOLUME OF MORTGAGE CREDIT CERTIFICATES BY INCOME AND ACQUISITION COST

		Holders Satisfying the 3-year Requirement			
		Nontargeted Area		Targeted Area	
Annualized Gross Monthly Income of Holders		Total of the Certified Indebtedness Amounts	Sum of Products of Certified Indebtedness Amounts and Credit Rates	Total of the Certified Indebtedness Amounts	Sum of Products of Certified Indebtedness Amounts and Credit Rates
$ 0 —	9,999				
$ 10,000—	19,999				
$ 20,000—	29,999				
$ 30,000—	39,999				
$ 40,000—	49,999				
$ 50,000—	74,999				
$ 75,000 or more					
Total					
Acquisition Cost					
$ 0 —	19,999				
$ 20,000—	39,999				
$ 40,000—	59,999				
$ 60,000—	79,999				
$ 80,000—	99,999				
$ 100,000—	119,999				
$ 120,000—	149,999				
$ 150,000—	199,999				
$ 200,000 or more					
Total					

Reg. § 1.25-4T(e)(1)(i)(B)(3)

VOLUME OF MORTGAGE CREDIT CERTIFICATES BY INCOME AND ACQUISITION COST

3-year Requirement Not Satisfied

	Nontargeted Area		Targeted Area		Totals	
Annualized Gross Monthly Income of Holders	Total of the Certified Indebtedness Amounts	Sum of Products of Certified Indebtedness Amounts and Credit Rates	Total of the Certified Indebtedness Amounts	Sum of Products of Certified Indebtedness Amounts and Credit Rates	Total Certified Indebtedness Amounts	Total Sum of Products of Certified Indebtedness Amounts and Credit Rates
$ 0 — 9,999						
$ 10,000— 19,999						
$ 20,000— 29,999						
$ 30,000— 39,999						
$ 40,000— 49,999						
$ 50,000— 74,999						
$ 75,000 or more						
Total						
Acquisition Cost						
$ 0 — 19,999						
$ 20,000— 39,999						
$ 40,000— 59,999						
$ 60,000— 79,999						
$ 80,000— 99,999						
$100,000— 119,999						
$120,000— 149,999						
$150,000— 199,999						
$200,000 or more						
Total						

MORTGAGE CREDIT CERTIFICATES FOR QUALIFIED HOME IMPROVEMENT AND REHABILITATION LOANS

	Nontargeted Area	Targeted Area	Totals
Home Improvement Loans			
Number of mortgage credit certificates			
Total of the certified indebtedness amounts			
Product of certified indebtedness amounts and credit rates			
Rehabilitation Loans			
Number of mortgage credit certificates			
Total of the certified indebtedness amounts			
Product of certified indebtedness amounts and credit rates			

(3) *Definitions and special rules.*—(i) For purposes of this paragraph the term "annualized gross income" means the borrower's gross monthly income multiplied by 12. Gross monthly income is the sum of monthly gross pay, any additional income from investments, pensions, Veterans Administration (VA) compensation, part-time employment, bonuses, dividends, interest, current overtime pay, net rental income, etc., and other income (such as alimony and child support, if the borrower chooses to disclose such income). Information with respect to gross monthly income may be obtained from available loan documents, *e.g.*, the sum of lines 23D and 23E on the Application for VA or FmHA Home Loan Guaranty or for HUD/FHA Insured Mortgage (VA Form 26-1802a, HUD 92900, Jan. 1982), or the total line from the Gross Monthly Income section of FHLMC Residential Loan Application form (FHLMC 65 Rev. 8/78).

(ii) For purposes of this paragraph, the term "reporting period" means each one year period beginning July 1 and ending June 30, except that issuers need not provide data with respect to the period prior to October 1, 1985.

(iii) For purposes of this paragraph, verification of information concerning a holder's gross monthly income by utilizing other available information concerning the holder's income (*e.g.*, Federal income tax returns) is not required. In determining whether the holder of a mortgage credit certificate acquiring a residence in a targeted area satisfies the 3-year requirement, the issuer may rely on a statement signed by the holder.

(4) *Time for filing.*—The report required by this paragraph shall be filed not later than the 15th day of the second calendar month after the close of the reporting period. The Commissioner may grant an extension of time for the filing of a report required by this paragraph if there is reasonable cause for the failure to file such report in a timely fashion. The report may be filed at any time before such date but must be complete based on facts and reasonable expectations as of the date the report is filed. The report need not be amended to reflect information learned subsequent to the date of filing, or to reflect changed circumstances with respect to any holder.

(5) *Place for filing.*—The report required by this paragraph is to be filed at the Internal Revenue Service Center, Philadelphia, Pennsylvania 19255

(f) *Policy statement.*—A program established pursuant to an election under paragraph (c) made after 1984 meets the requirements of this paragraph only if the applicable elected representative of the governmental unit—

(1) Which is the issuer, or

(2) On whose behalf the certificates were issued,

has published (after a public hearing following reasonable public notice) a policy statement described in §1.103A-2(1) by the last day of the year preceding the year in which the election under paragraph (c) is made, and a copy of such report has been submitted to the Commissioner on or before such last day. See §1.103A-2(1) for further definitions and requirements.

(g) *Targeted areas requirement.*—(1) *In general.*—A program meets the requirements of this paragraph only if—

(i) The portion of the total proceeds of the issue specified in paragraph (g)(2) is made available to provide mortgage credit certificates in connection with owner financing of targeted area residences for at least 1 year after the date on which mortgage credit certificates are first made available with respect to targeted area residences, and

Reg. §1.25-4T(g)(1)(i)

(ii) The issuer attempts with reasonable diligence to place such proceeds with qualified persons.

Mortgage credit certificates are considered first made available with respect to targeted area residences on the date on which the issuer first begins to accept applications for mortgage credit certificates provided under that issue.

(2) *Specified portion.*—(i) The specified portion of the total proceeds of an issue is the lesser of—

(A) 20 percent of the total proceeds, or

(B) 8 percent of the average annual aggregate principal amount of mortgages executed during the immediately preceding 3 calendar years for single-family, owner-occupied residences in targeted areas within the jurisdiction of the issuing authority.

For purposes of computing the required portion of the total proceeds specified in paragraph (g)(2)(i)(B) where such provision is applicable, an issuer may rely upon the safe-harbor formula provided in the regulations under section 103A(h).

(ii) See § 1.25-1T(b)(10)(ii) for the definition of "total proceeds".

(h) *Fees.*—(1) *In general.*—A program meets the requirements of this paragraph only if each applicant is required to pay, directly or indirectly, no fee other than those fees permitted under this paragraph.

(2) *Permissible fees.*—Applicants may be required to pay the following fees provided that they are reasonable:

(i) Points, origination fees, servicing fees, and other fees in amounts that are customarily charged with respect to mortgages not provided in connection with mortgage credit certificates.

(ii) Application fees, survey fees, credit report fees, insurance fees, or similar settlement or financing costs to the extent such amounts do not exceed the amounts charged in the area in cases where mortgages are not provided in connection with mortgage credit certificates. For example, amounts charged for FHA, VA, or similar private mortgage insurance on an individual's mortgage are permissible so long as such amounts do not exceed the amounts charged in the area with respect to a similar mortgage that is not provided in connection with a mortgage credit certificate, and

(iii) Other fees that, taking into account all the facts and circumstances, are reasonably necessary to cover any administrative costs incurred by the issuer or its agent in issuing mortgage credit certificates.

(i) *Qualified mortgage credit certificate.*—A program meets the requirement of this paragraph only if each mortgage credit certificate issued under the program meets each of the requirements of paragraphs (c) through (o) of § 1.25-3T.

(j) *Good faith compliance efforts.*—(1) *Eligibility requirements.*—(i) A program under which each of the mortgage credit certificates issued does not meet each of the requirements of paragraphs (c) through (o) of § 1.25-3T shall be treated as meeting the requirements of paragraph (i) of this section if each of the requirements of this paragraph (j)(1) is satisfied. A mortgage credit certificate program meets the requirements of this paragraph (j)(1) only if each of the following provisions is met:

(A) The issuer in good faith attempted to issue mortgage credit certificates only to individuals meeting each of the requirements of paragraphs (c) through (o) of § 1.25-3T. Good faith requires that agreements with lenders and agents and other relevant instruments contain restrictions that permit the approval of mortgage credit certificates only in accordance with the requirements of paragraphs (c) through (o) of § 1.25-3T. In addition, the issuer must establish reasonable procedures to ensure compliance with those requirements. Reasonable procedures include reasonable investigations by the issuer to determine whether individuals satisfy the requirements of paragraphs (c) through (o) of § 1.25-3T.

(B) 95 percent or more of the total proceeds of the issue were devoted to individuals with respect to whom, at the time that the certificate was issued, all the requirements of paragraphs (c) through (o) of § 1.25-3T were met. If a holder of a mortgage credit certificate fails to meet more than one of these requirements, the amount of the certificate (*i.e.,* the certificate credit rate multiplied by the certified indebtedness amount) issued to that individual will be taken into account only once in determining whether the 95-percent requirement is met. However, all of the defects in that individual's certificate must be corrected pursuant to paragraph (j)(1)(i)(C).

(C) Any failure to meet the requirements of paragraphs (c) *through (o) of § 1.25-3T is corrected within a reasonable* period after that failure is discovered. For example, if an individual fails to meet one or more of such requirements those failures can be corrected by revoking that individual's certificate.

(ii) *Examples.*—The following examples illustrate the application of this paragraph (j)(1):

Example (1). County X only distributes mortgage credit certificates to individuals who have contracted to purchase a principal residence. County X requires that applicants for mortgage credit certificates present the following information:

(i) An affidavit stating that the applicant intends to use the residence in connection with which the mortgage credit certificate is issued as his principal residence within a reasonable time after the certificate is issued by County X, that the applicant will notify the County if the residence ceases to be his principal residence, and facts that are sufficient for County X to determine whether the residence is located within the jurisdiction of County X,

(ii) An affidavit stating that the applicant had no present ownership interest in a principal residence at any time during the 3-year period prior to the date on which the certificate is issued,

(iii) Copies of the applicant's Federal tax returns for the preceding 3 years,

(iv) Affidavits from the seller of the residence with respect to which the certificate is issued and the applicant stating the purchase price of the residence, including an itemized list of (A) payments made by or for the benefit of the applicant, (B) if the residence is incomplete, an estimate of the reasonable cost of completing the residence, and (C) if the residence is subject to a ground rent, the capitalized value of the ground rent,

(v) An affidavit executed by the applicant stating that the mortgage being acquired in connection with the certificate will not be used to acquire or replace an existing mortgage,

(vi) An affidavit executed by the applicant stating that no portion of the financing for the residence in connection with which the certificate is issued is provided from the proceeds of a qualified mortgage bond or qualified veterans' mortgage bond and that no portion of the mortgage for the residence is provided by a person related to the applicant (as defined in § 1.25-3T(n)),

(vii) An affidavit executed by the applicant stating that the certificate was not limited to indebtedness incurred from particular lenders, and

(viii) In the case of a mortgage credit certificate allocated for use in connection with a particular development, an affidavit executed by the applicant stating that the applicant received from the developer a certification stating that the price of the residence with respect to which the certificate was issued is no higher than it would be without the use of a mortgage credit certificate.

County X examines the information submitted by the applicant to determine whether the requirements of paragraph (c), (d), (e), (f), (g), (i), (j), (k), and (n) of § 1.25-3T are met. County X determines that the certificate has not expired. The mortgage credit certificates issued by County X are in the form prescribed by § 1.25-6T and County X provides all the required information and statements. After determining that the applicant meets all these requirements County X issues a mortgage credit certificate to the applicant. This procedure for issuing mortgage credit certificates is sufficient evidence of the good faith of County X to meet the requirements of § 1.25-4T(j)(1)(i)(A).

Example (2). County W distributes preliminary mortgage credit certificates to individuals who have not entered into contracts to purchase a principal residence. County W issues preliminary certificates in the form prescribed by § 1.25-6T to those applicants that have submitted statements that they (i) intend to purchase a single-family residence located within the jurisdiction of County W which they will occupy as a principal residence, (ii) have had no present ownership interest in a principal residence within the preceding 3-year period, and (iii) will not use the certificate in connection with the acquisition or replacement of an existing mortgage. The certificates contain a maximum purchase price, the certificate credit rate, and a statement that the certificate will expire if the applicant does not enter into a closing agreement with respect to a loan within 6 months from the date of preliminary issuance. Holders of these certificates may apply for a mortgage loan from any lender. When the holder of the certificate applies for a loan the lender requires that he submit the following:

(i) An affidavit stating that the applicant intends to use the residence in connection with which the mortgage credit certificate is issued as his principal residence within a reasonable time after the certificate is issued by County W, that the applicant will notify the County if the residence ceases to be his principal residence, and facts that are sufficient for County W to determine whether the residence is located within the jurisdiction of County W,

(ii) An affidavit stating that the applicant had no present ownership interest in a principal residence at any time during the 3-year period prior to the date on which the certificate is issued,

(iii) Copies of the applicant's Federal tax returns for the preceding 3 years,

(iv) Affidavits from the seller of the residence with respect to which the certificate is issued and the applicant stating the purchase price of the residence, including an itemized list of (A) payments made by or for the benefit of the applicant, (B) if the residence is incomplete, an estimate of the reasonable cost of completing the residence, and (C) if the residence is subject to a ground rent, the capitalized value of the ground rent,

(v) An affidavit executed by the applicant stating that the mortgage being acquired in connection with the certificate will not be used to acquire or replace an existing mortgage,

(vi) An affidavit executed by the applicant stating that no portion of the financing for the residence in connection with which the certificate is issued is provided from the proceeds of a qualified mortgage bond or qualified veterans' mortgage bond and that no portion of the mortgage for the residence is provided by a person related to the applicant (as defined in §1.25-3T(n)),

(vii) An affidavit executed by the applicant stating that the certificate was not limited to indebtedness incurred from particular lenders, and

(viii) In the case of a mortgage credit certificate allocated for use in connection with a particular development, an affidavit executed by the applicant stating that the applicant received from the developer a certification stating that the price of the residence with respect to which the certificate was issued is no higher than it would be without the use of a mortgage credit certificate.
The lender then submits those affidavits, together with its statement as to the amount of the indebtedness incurred, to County W. After determining that the requirements of paragraphs (c), (d), (e), (f), (g), (i), (j), (k) and (n) of §1.25-3T are met and determining that the certificate has not expired, County W completes the mortgage credit certificate. This procedure for issuing mortgage credit certificates is sufficient evidence of the good faith of County W to meet the requirements of §1.25-4T(j)(1)(i)(A).

(2) *Program requirements.*—(i) A mortgage credit certificate program which fails to meet one or more of the requirements of paragraphs (b) through (h) of this section shall be treated as meeting such requirements if the requirements of this paragraph (j)(2) are satisfied. A mortgage credit certificate program meets the requirements of this paragraph (j)(2) only if each of the following provisions is met:

(A) The issuer in good faith attempted to meet all of the requirements of paragraphs (b) through (h) of this section. This good faith requirement will be met if all reasonable steps are taken by the issuer to ensure that the program complies with these requirements.

(B) Any failure to meet such requirements is due to inadvertent error, *e.g.*, mathematical error, after taking reasonable steps to comply with such requirements.

(ii) The following example illustrates the application of this paragraph (j)(2):
Example. City X issues an issue of mortgage credit certificates. However, despite taking all reasonable steps to determine accurately the size of the applicable limit, as provided in section 103A(g)(3) and the regulations thereunder, the limit is exceeded because the amount of the mortgages originated in the area during the past 3 years is incorrectly computed as a result of mathematical error. Such facts are sufficient evidence of the good faith of the issuer to meet the requirements of paragraph (j)(2). [Temporary Reg. §1.25-4T.]

☐ [*T.D. 8023, 5-3-85. Amended by T.D. 8048, 8-29-85.*]

[Reg. §1.25-5T]

§1.25-5T. Limitation on aggregate amount of mortgage credit certificates (Temporary).—(a) *In general.*—If the aggregate amount of qualified mortgage credit certificates (as defined in paragraph (b)) issued by an issuer under a qualified mortgage credit certificate program exceeds 20 percent of the nonissued bond amount (as defined in paragraph (c)), the provisions of paragraph (d) shall apply.

(b) *Aggregate amount of mortgage credit certificates.*—(1) *In general.*—The aggregate amount of qualified mortgage credit certificates issued under a qualified mortgage credit certificate program is the sum of the products determined by multiplying—

(i) The certified indebtedness amount of each qualified mortgage credit certificate issued under that program, by

(ii) The certificate credit rate with respect to such certificate.

(2) *Examples.*—The following examples illustrate the application of this paragraph (b):
Example (1). For 1986 City Q has a nonissued bond amount of $100 million. After making a proper election, Q issues 2,000 qualified mortgage credit certificates each with a certificate credit rate of 20 percent and a certified indebtedness amount of $50,000. The aggregate amount of qualified mortgage credit certificates is $20 million (2,000 × (.2 × $50,000)). Since this amount does not exceed 20 percent

of the nonissued bond amount (.2 × $100 million = $20 million), Q has complied with the limitation on the aggregate amount of mortgage credit certificates, provided that it does not issue any additional certificates.

Example (2). The facts are the same as in example (1) except that instead of issuing all its certificates at the 20 percent rate, Q issues (i) qualified mortgage credit certificates with a certificate credit rate of 10 percent and an aggregate principal amount of $25 million, (ii) qualified mortgage credit certificates with a certificate credit rate of 40 percent and an aggregate principal amount of $25 million, and (iii) qualified mortgage credit certificates with a certificate credit rate of 30 percent and an aggregate principal amount of $25 million. The aggregate amount of qualified mortgage credit certificates is $20 million (10 percent of $25 million) plus (40 percent of $25 million) plus (30 percent of $25 million)). Q has complied with the limitation on the aggregate amount of qualified mortgage credit certificates, provided that it does not issue any additional certificates pursuant to the same program.

(c) *Nonissued bond amount.*—The term "nonissued bond amount" means, with respect to any qualified mortgage credit certificate program, the amount of qualified mortgage bonds (as defined in section 103A(c)(1) and the regulations thereunder) which the issuer is otherwise authorized to issue and elects not to issue under section 25(c)(2) and §1.25-4T(b). The amount of qualified mortgage bonds which an issuing authority is authorized to issue is determined under section 103A(g) and the regulations thereunder; such determination shall take into account any prior elections by the issuer not to issue qualified mortgage bonds, the amount of any reduction in the State ceiling under paragraph (d) of this section, and the aggregate amount of qualified mortgage bonds issued by the issuer prior to its election not to issue qualified mortgage bonds.

(d) *Noncompliance with limitation on aggregate amount of mortgage credit certificates.*—(1) *In general.*—If the provisions of this paragraph apply, the State ceiling under section 103A(g)(4) and the regulations thereunder for the calendar year following the calendar year in which the Commissioner determines the correction amount for the State in which the issuer which exceeded the limitation on the aggregate amount of mortgage credit certificates is located shall be reduced by 1.25 times the correction amount with respect to such failure.

(2) *Correction amount.*—(i) The term "correction amount" means an amount equal to the excess credit amount divided by .20.

(ii) The term "excess credit amount" means the excess of—

(A) The credit amount for any mortgage credit certificate program, over

(B) The amount which would have been the credit amount for such program had such program met the requirements of section 25(d)(2) and paragraph (a) of this section.

(iii) The term "credit amount" means the sum of the products determined by multiplying—

(A) The certified indebtedness amount of each qualified mortgage credit certificate issued under the program, by

(B) The certificate credit rate with respect to such certificate.

(3) *Example.*—The following example illustrates the application of this paragraph:
Example. For 1987 City R has a nonissued bond amount of $100 million. City R issues all of its mortgage credit certificates with a certificate credit rate of 20 percent. City R issues certificates with an aggregate certified indebtedness amount of $120 million. The aggregate amount of mortgage credit certificates issued by City R is $24 million, which exceeds 20 percent of the nonissued bond amount. The State ceiling for the calendar year following the calendar year in which the Commissioner determines the correction amount is reduced by $25 million (the correction amount multiplied by 1.25). The correction amount is determined as follows: The credit amount is $24 million (.2 × $120 million); the amount which would have been the credit amount for the program had it met the requirements of section 25(d)(2) is $20 million (.2 × $100 million); the excess credit amount is $4 million ($24 million – $20 million); therefore, the correction amount is $20 million ($4 million/.2).

(4) *Cross references.*—See section 103A(g)(4) and the regulations thereunder with respect to the reduction of the applicable State ceiling. [Temporary Reg. §1.25-5T.]

☐ [*T.D. 8023, 5-3-85.*]

[Reg. §1.25-6T]

§1.25-6T. Form of qualified mortgage credit certificate (Temporary).—(a) *In general.*—Qualified mortgage credit certificates are to be issued on the form prescribed by the Internal Revenue Service. If no form is prescribed by the Internal Revenue Service, or if the form prescribed by the Internal Revenue Service is not readily available, the issuer may use its own form provided that such form contains the information required by this section. Each mortgage credit certificate must be issued in a form such that there are at least three copies of the form. One copy of the certificate shall be retained by the issuer; one copy shall be retained by the lender; and one copy shall be forwarded to the State official who issued the certification required by § 1.25-4T(d), unless that State official has stated in writing that he does not want to receive such copies.

(b) *Required information.*—Each qualified mortgage credit certificate must include the following information:

(1) The name, address, and TIN of the issuer,

(2) The date of the issuer's election not to issue qualified mortgage bonds pursuant to which the certificate is being issued,

(3) The number assigned to the certificate,

(4) The name, address, and TIN of the holder of the certificate,

(5) The certificate credit rate,

(6) The certified indebtedness amount,

(7) The acquisition cost of the residence being acquired in connection with the certificate,

(8) The average area purchase price applicable to the residence,

(9) Whether the certificate meets the requirements of § 1.25-3T(d), relating to residence requirement,

(10) Whether the certificate meets the requirements of § 1.25-3T(e), relating to 3-year requirement,

(11) Whether the certificate meets the requirements of § 1.25-3T(g), relating to new mortgage requirement,

(12) Whether the certificate meets the requirements of § 1.25-3T(i), relating to prohibited mortgages,

(13) Whether the certificate meets the requirements of § 1.25-3T(j), relating to particular lenders,

(14) Whether the certificate meets the requirements of § 1.25-3T(k), relating to allocations to particular developments,

(15) Whether the certificate meets the requirements of § 1.25-3T(n), relating to interest paid to related persons,

(16) Whether the residence in connection with which the certificate is issued is a targeted area residence,

(17) The date on which a closing agreement is signed with respect to the certified indebtedness amount,

(18) The expiration date of the certificate,

(19) A statement that the certificate is not transferable or a statement that the certificate may be transferred only if the issuer issues a new certificate, and

(20) A statement, signed under penalties of perjury by an authorized official of the issuer or its agent, that such person has made the determinations specified in paragraph (b)(9) through (16). [Temporary Reg. § 1.25-6T.]

☐ [T.D. 8023, 5-3-85.]

[Reg. § 1.25-7T]

§ 1.25-7T. Public notice (Temporary).—(a) *In general.*—At least 90 days prior to the issuance of any mortgage credit certificate under a qualified mortgage credit certificate program, the issuer shall provide reasonable public notice of—

(1) The eligibility requirements for such certificate,

(2) The methods by which such certificates are to be issued, and

(3) The other information required by this section.

(b) *Reasonable public notice.*—(1) *In general.*—Reasonable public notice means published notice which is reasonably designed to inform individuals who would be eligible to receive mortgage credit certificates of the proposed issuance. Reasonable public notice may be provided through newspapers of general circulation.

(2) *Contents of notice.*—The public notice required by paragraph (a) must include a brief description of the principal residence requirement, 3-year requirement, purchase price requirement, and new mortgage requirement. The notice must also provide a brief description of the methods by which the certificates are to be issued and the address and telephone number for obtaining further information. [Temporary Reg. § 1.25-7T.]

☐ [T.D. 8023, 5-3-85.]

[Reg. § 1.25-8T]

§ 1.25-8T. Reporting requirements (Temporary).—(a) *Lender.*—(1) *In general.*—Each person who makes a loan that is a certified indebtedness amount with respect to any mortgage credit certificate must file the report described in paragraph (a)(2) and must retain on *its books and records the information described in paragraph (a)(3).* The report described in paragraph (a)(2) is an annual report and must be filed on or before January 31 of the year following the calendar year to which the report relates. See section 6709(c) and the

regulations thereunder for the applicable penalties with respect to failure to file reports.

(2) *Information required.*—The report shall be submitted on Form 8329 and shall contain the information required therein. A separate Form 8329 shall be filed for each issue of mortgage credit certificates with respect to which the lender made mortgage loans during the preceding calendar year. Thus, for example, if during 1986 Bank M makes three mortgage loans which are certified indebtedness amounts with respect to State Z's January 15, 1986, issue of mortgage credit certificates, and two mortgage loans which are certified indebtedness amounts with respect to State Z's April 15, 1986, issue of mortgage credit certificates, and fifty mortgage loans which are certified indebtedness amounts with respect to County X's December 31, 1985, issue of mortgage credit certificates, Bank M must file three separate reports for calendar year 1986. The lender must submit the Form 8329 with the information required therein, including—

(i) The name, address, and TIN of the issuer of the mortgage credit certificates,

(ii) The date on which the election not to issue qualified mortgage bonds with respect to that mortgage credit certificate was made,

(iii) The name, address, and TIN of the lender, and

(iv) The sum of the products determined by multiplying—

(A) The certified indebtedness amount of each mortgage credit certificate issued under such program, by

(B) The certificate credit rate with respect to such certificate.

(3) *Recordkeeping requirements.*—Each person who makes a loan that is a certified indebtedness amount with respect to any mortgage credit certificate must retain the information specified in this paragraph (a)(3) on its books and records for 6 years following the year in which the loan was made. With respect to each loan the lender must retain the following information:

(i) The name, address, and TIN of each holder of a qualified mortgage credit certificate with respect to which a loan is made,

(ii) The name, address, and TIN of the issuer of such certificate, and

(iii) The date the loan for the certified indebtedness amount is closed, the certified indebtedness amount, and the certificate credit rate of such certificate.

(b) *Issuers.*—(1) *In general.*—Each issuer of mortgage credit certificates shall file the report described in paragraph (b)(2).

(2) *Quarterly reports.*—(i) Each issuer which elects to issue mortgage credit certificates shall file reports on Form 8330. These reports shall be filed on a quarterly basis, beginning with the quarter in which the election is made, and are due on the following dates: April 30 (for the quarter ending March 31), July 31 (for the quarter ending June 30), October 31 (for the quarter ending September 30), and January 31 (for the quarter ending December 31). For elections made prior to May 8, 1985, the first report need not be filed until July 31, 1985. An issuer shall file a separate report for each issue of mortgage credit certificates. In the quarter in which the last qualified mortgage credit certificate that may be issued under a program is issued, the issuer must state that fact on the report to be filed for that quarter; the issuer is not required to file any subsequent reports with respect to that program. See section 6709(c) for the penalties with respect to failure to file a report.

(ii) The report shall be submitted on Form 8330 and shall contain the information required therein, including—

(A) The name, address, and TIN of the issuer of the mortgage credit certificates,

(B) The date of the issuer's election not to issue qualified mortgage bonds with respect to the mortgage credit certificate program and the nonissued bond amount of the program,

(C) The sum of the products determined by multiplying—

(1) The certified indebtedness amount of each qualified mortgage credit certificate issued under that program during the calendar quarter, by

(2) The certificate credit rate with respect to such certificate, and

(D) A listing of the name, address, and TIN of each holder of a qualified mortgage credit certificate which has been revoked during the calendar quarter.

(c) *Extensions of time for filing reports.*—The Commissioner may grant an extension of time for the filing of a report required by this section if there is reasonable cause for the failure to file such report in a timely fashion.

(d) *Place for filing.*—The reports required by this section are to be filed at the Internal Revenue Service Center, Philadelphia, Pennsylvania 19255.

(e) *Cross reference.*—See section 6709 and the regulations thereunder with respect to the penalty for failure to file a report required by this section. [Temporary Reg. §1.25-8T.]

☐ [*T.D.* 8023, 5-3-85.]

[Reg. §1.25A-0]

§1.25A-0. Table of contents.—This section lists captions contained in §§1.25A-1, 1.25A-2, 1.25A-3, 1.25A-4, and 1.25A-5.

[Reg. §1.25A-0.]

☐ [*T.D.* 9034, 12-24-2002.]

[Reg. §1.25A-1]

§1.25A-1. Calculation of education tax credit and general eligibility requirements.—(a) *Amount of education tax credit.*—An individual taxpayer is allowed a nonrefundable education tax credit against income tax imposed by chapter 1 of the Internal Revenue Code for the taxable year. The amount of the education tax credit is the total of the Hope Scholarship Credit (as described in §1.25A-3) plus the Lifetime Learning Credit (as described in §1.25A-4). For limitations on the credits allowed by subpart A of part IV of subchapter A of chapter 1 of the Internal Revenue Code, see section 26.

(b) *Coordination of Hope Scholarship Credit and Lifetime Learning Credit.*—(1) *In general.*—In the same taxable year, a taxpayer may claim a Hope Scholarship Credit for each eligible student's qualified tuition and related expenses (as defined in §1.25A-2(d)) and a Lifetime Learning Credit for one or more other students' qualified tuition and related expenses. However, a taxpayer may not claim both a Hope Scholarship Credit and a Lifetime Learning Credit with respect to the same student in the same taxable year.

(2) *Hope Scholarship Credit.*—Subject to certain limitations, a Hope Scholarship Credit may be claimed for the qualified tuition and related expenses paid during a taxable year with respect to each eligible student (as defined in §1.25A-3(d)). Qualified tuition and related expenses paid during a taxable year with respect to one student may not be taken into account in computing the amount of the Hope Scholarship Credit with respect to any other student. In addition, qualified tuition and related expenses paid during a taxable year with respect to any student for whom a Hope Scholarship Credit is claimed may not be taken into account in computing the amount of the Lifetime Learning Credit.

(3) *Lifetime Learning Credit.*—Subject to certain limitations, a Lifetime Learning Credit may be claimed for the aggregate amount of qualified tuition and related expenses paid during a taxable year with respect to students for whom no Hope Scholarship Credit is claimed.

(4) *Examples.*—The following examples illustrate the rules of this paragraph (b):

Example 1. In 1999, Taxpayer A pays qualified tuition and related expenses for his dependent, B, to attend College Y during 1999. Assuming all other relevant requirements are met, Taxpayer A may claim either a Hope Scholarship Credit or a Lifetime Learning Credit with respect to dependent B, but not both. See §1.25A-3(a) and §1.25A-4(a).

Example 2. In 1999, Taxpayer C pays $2,000 in qualified tuition and related expenses for her dependent, D, to attend College Z during 1999. In 1999, Taxpayer C also pays $500 in qualified tuition and related expenses to attend a computer course during 1999 to improve Taxpayer C's job skills. Assuming all other relevant requirements are met, Taxpayer C may claim a Hope Scholarship Credit for the $2,000 of qualified tuition and related expenses attributable to dependent D (see §1.25A-3(a)) and a Lifetime Learning Credit (see §1.25A-4(a)) for the $500 of qualified tuition and related expenses incurred to improve her job skills.

Example 3. The facts are the same as in *Example 2*, except that Taxpayer C pays $3,000 in qualified tuition and related expenses for her dependent, D, to attend College Z during 1999. Although a Hope Scholarship Credit is available only with respect to the first $2,000 of qualified tuition and related expenses paid with respect to D (see §1.25A-3(a)), Taxpayer C may not add the $1,000 of excess expenses to her $500 of qualified tuition and related expenses in computing the amount of the Lifetime Learning Credit.

(c) *Limitation based on modified adjusted gross income.*—(1) *In general.*—The education tax credit that a taxpayer may otherwise claim is phased out ratably for taxpayers with modified adjusted gross income between $40,000 and $50,000 ($80,000 and $100,000 for married individuals who file a joint return). Thus, taxpayers with modified adjusted gross income above $50,000 (or $100,000 for joint filers) may not claim an education tax credit.

(2) *Modified adjusted gross income defined.*—The term *modified adjusted gross income* means the adjusted gross income (as defined in section 62) of the taxpayer for the taxable year increased by any amount excluded from gross income under section 911, 931, or 933 (relating to income earned abroad or from certain U.S. possessions or Puerto Rico).

(3) *Inflation adjustment.*—For taxable years beginning after 2001, the amounts in paragraph (c)(1) of this section will be increased for inflation occurring after 2000 in accordance with section 1(f)(3). If any amount adjusted under this paragraph (c)(3) is not a multiple of $1,000, the amount will be rounded to the next lowest multiple of $1,000.

(d) *Election.*—No education tax credit is allowed unless a taxpayer elects to claim the credit on the taxpayer's federal income tax return for the taxable year in which the credit is claimed. The election is made by attaching Form 8863, "Education Credits (Hope and Lifetime Learning Credits)," to the Federal income tax return.

(e) *Identification requirement.*—No education tax credit is allowed unless a taxpayer includes on the federal income tax return claiming the credit the name and the taxpayer identification number of the student for whom the credit is claimed. For rules relating to assessment for an omission of a correct taxpayer identification number, see section 6213(b) and (g)(2)(J).

(f) *Claiming the credit in the case of a dependent.*—(1) *In general.*—If a student is a claimed dependent of another taxpayer, only that taxpayer may claim the education tax credit for the student's qualified tuition and related expenses. However, if another taxpayer is eligible to, but does not, claim the student as a dependent, only the student may claim the education tax credit for the student's qualified tuition and related expenses.

(2) *Examples.*—The following examples illustrate the rules of this paragraph (f):

Example 1. In 1999, Taxpayer A pays qualified tuition and related expenses for his dependent, B, to attend University Y during 1999. Taxpayer A claims B as a dependent on his federal income tax return. Therefore, assuming all other relevant requirements are met, Taxpayer A is allowed an education tax credit on his federal income tax return, and B is not allowed an education tax credit on B's federal income tax return. The result would be the same if B paid the qualified tuition and related expenses. See §1.25A-5(a).

Example 2. In 1999, Taxpayer C has one dependent, D. In 1999, D pays qualified tuition and related expenses to attend University Z during 1999. Although Taxpayer C is eligible to claim D as a dependent on her federal income tax return, she does not do so. Therefore, assuming all other relevant requirements are met, D is allowed an education tax credit on D's federal income tax return, and Taxpayer C *is not allowed an education tax credit on her federal income tax return*, with respect to D's education expenses. The result would be the same if C paid the qualified tuition and related expenses on behalf of D. See §1.25A-5(b).

(g) *Married taxpayers.*—If a taxpayer is married (within the meaning of section 7703), no education tax credit is allowed to the taxpayer unless the taxpayer and the taxpayer's spouse file a joint Federal income tax return for the taxable year.

(h) *Nonresident alien taxpayers and dependents.*—If a taxpayer or the taxpayer's spouse is a nonresident alien for any portion of the taxable year, no education tax credit is allowed unless the nonresident alien is treated as a resident alien by reason of an election under section 6013(g) or (h). In addition, if a student is a nonresident alien, a taxpayer may not claim an education tax credit with respect to the qualified tuition and related expenses of the student unless the student is a claimed dependent (as defined in §1.25A-2(a)). [Reg. §1.25A-1.]

☐ [T.D. 9034, 12-24-2002.]

[Reg. §1.25A-2]

§1.25A-2. Definitions.—(a) *Claimed dependent.*—A *claimed dependent* means a dependent (as defined in section 152) for whom a deduction under section 151 is allowed on a taxpayer's federal income tax return for the taxable year. Among other requirements under section 152, a nonresident alien student must be a resident of a country contiguous to the United States in order to be treated as a dependent.

(b) *Eligible educational institution.*—(1) *In general.*—In general, an *eligible educational institution* means a college, university, vocational school, or other postsecondary educational institution that is—

(i) Described in section 481 of the Higher Education Act of 1965 (20 U.S.C. 1088) as in effect on August 5, 1997, (generally all accredited public, nonprofit, and proprietary postsecondary institutions); and

(ii) Participating in a federal financial aid program under title IV of the Higher Education Act of 1965 or is certified by the Department of Education as eligible to participate in such a program but chooses not to participate.

(2) *Rules on federal financial aid programs.*—For rules governing an educational institution's eligibility to participate in federal financial aid programs, see 20 U.S.C. 1070; 20 U.S.C. 1094; and 34 CFR 600 and 668.

(c) *Academic period.*—*Academic period* means a quarter, semester, trimester, or other period of study as reasonably determined by an eligible educational institution. In the case of an eligible educational institution that uses credit hours or clock hours, and does not have academic terms, each payment period (as defined in 34 CFR 668.4, revised as of July 1, 2002) may be treated as an academic period.

(d) *Qualified tuition and related expenses.*—(1) *In general.*—*Qualified tuition and related expenses* means tuition and fees required for the enrollment or attendance of a student for courses of instruction at an eligible educational institution.

(2) *Required fees.*—(i) *In general.*—Except as provided in paragraph (d)(3) of this section, the test for determining whether any fee is a qualified tuition and related expense is whether the fee is required to be paid to the eligible educational institution as a condition of the student's enrollment or attendance at the institution.

(ii) *Books, supplies, and equipment.*—Qualified tuition and related expenses include fees for books, supplies, and equipment used in a course of study only if the fees must be paid to the eligible educational institution for the enrollment or attendance of the student at the institution.

(iii) *Nonacademic fees.*—Except as provided in paragraph (d)(3) of this section, qualified tuition and related expenses include fees charged by an eligible educational institution that are not used directly for, or allocated to, an academic course of instruction only if the fee must be paid to the eligible educational institution for the enrollment or attendance of the student at the institution.

(3) *Personal expenses.*—Qualified tuition and related expenses do not include the costs of room and board, insurance, medical expenses (including student health fees), transportation, and similar personal, living, or family expenses, regardless of whether the fee must be paid to the eligible educational institution for the enrollment or attendance of the student at the institution.

(4) *Treatment of a comprehensive or bundled fee.*—If a student is required to pay a fee (such as a comprehensive fee or a bundled fee) to an eligible educational institution that combines charges for qualified tuition and related expenses with charges for personal expenses described in paragraph (d)(3) of this section, the portion of the fee that is allocable to personal expenses is not included in qualified tuition and related expenses. The determination of what portion of the fee relates to qualified tuition and related expenses and what

portion relates to personal expenses must be made by the institution using a reasonable method of allocation.

(5) *Hobby courses.*—Qualified tuition and related expenses do not include expenses that relate to any course of instruction or other education that involves sports, games, or hobbies, or any noncredit course, unless the course or other education is part of the student's degree program, or in the case of the Lifetime Learning Credit, the student takes the course to acquire or improve job skills.

(6) *Examples.*—The following examples illustrate the rules of this paragraph (d). In each example, assume that the institution is an eligible educational institution and that all other relevant requirements to claim an education tax credit are met. The examples are as follows:

Example 1. University V offers a degree program in dentistry. In addition to tuition, all students enrolled in the program are required to pay a fee to University V for the rental of dental equipment. Because the equipment rental fee must be paid to University V for enrollment and attendance, the tuition and the equipment rental fee are qualified tuition and related expenses.

Example 2. First-year students at College W are required to obtain books and other reading materials used in its mandatory first-year curriculum. The books and other reading materials are not required to be purchased from College W and may be borrowed from other students or purchased from off-campus bookstores, as well as from College W's bookstore. College W bills students for any books and materials purchased from College W's bookstore. The fee that College W charges for the first-year books and materials purchased at its bookstore is not a qualified tuition and related expense because the books and materials are not required to be purchased from College W for enrollment or attendance at the institution.

Example 3. All students who attend College X are required to pay a separate student activity fee in addition to their tuition. The student activity fee is used solely to fund on-campus organizations and activities run by students, such as the student newspaper and the student government (no portion of the fee covers personal expenses). Although labeled as a student activity fee, the fee is required for enrollment or attendance at College X. Therefore, the fee is a qualified tuition and related expense.

Example 4. The facts are the same as in *Example 3*, except that College X offers an optional athletic fee that students may pay to receive discounted tickets to sports events. The athletic fee is not required for enrollment or attendance at College X. Therefore, the fee is not a qualified tuition and related expense.

Example 5. College Y requires all students to live on campus. It charges a single comprehensive fee to cover tuition, required fees, and room and board. Based on College Y's reasonable allocation, sixty percent of the comprehensive fee is allocable to tuition and other required fees not allocable to personal expenses, and the remaining forty percent of the comprehensive fee is allocable to charges for room and board and other personal expenses. Therefore, only sixty percent of College Y's comprehensive fee is a qualified tuition and related expense.

Example 6. As a degree student at College Z, Student A is required to take a certain number of courses outside of her chosen major in Economics. To fulfill this requirement, Student A enrolls in a square dancing class offered by the Physical Education Department. Because Student A receives credit toward her degree program for the square dancing class, the tuition for the square dancing class is included in qualified tuition and related expenses.

[Reg. § 1.25A-2.]

☐ [*T.D.* 9034, 12-24-2002.]

[Reg. § 1.25A-3]

§ 1.25A-3. Hope Scholarship Credit.—(a) *Amount of the credit.*—(1) *In general.*—Subject to the phaseout of the education tax credit described in § 1.25A-1(c), the Hope Scholarship Credit amount is the total of—

(i) 100 percent of the first $1,000 of qualified tuition and related expenses paid during the taxable year for education furnished to an eligible student (as defined in paragraph (d) of this section) who is the taxpayer, the taxpayer's spouse, or any claimed *dependent during any academic period beginning in the taxable year* (or treated as beginning in the taxable year, see § 1.25A-5(e)(2)); plus

(ii) 50 percent of the next $1,000 of such expenses paid with respect to that student.

(2) *Maximum credit.*—For taxable years beginning before 2002, the maximum Hope Scholarship Credit allowed for each eligible student is $1,500. For taxable years beginning after 2001, the amounts used in paragraph (a)(1) of this section to determine the maximum credit will be increased for inflation occurring after 2000 in accordance with section 1(f)(3). If any amount adjusted under this para-

graph (a)(2) is not a multiple of $100, the amount will be rounded to the next lowest multiple of $100.

(b) *Per student credit.*—(1) *In general.*—A Hope Scholarship Credit may be claimed for the qualified tuition and related expenses of each eligible student (as defined in paragraph (d) of this section).

(2) *Example.*—The following example illustrates the rule of this paragraph (b). In the example, assume that all the requirements to claim an education tax credit are met. The example is as follows:

Example. In 1999, Taxpayer A has two dependents, B and C, both of whom are eligible students. Taxpayer A pays $1,600 in qualified tuition and related expenses for dependent B to attend a community college. Taxpayer A pays $5,000 in qualified tuition and related expenses for dependent C to attend University X. Taxpayer A may claim a Hope Scholarship Credit of $1,300 ($1,000 + (.50 × $600)) for dependent B, and the maximum $1,500 Hope Scholarship Credit for dependent C, for a total Hope Scholarship Credit of $2,800.

(c) *Credit allowed for only two taxable years.*—For each eligible student, the Hope Scholarship Credit may be claimed for no more than two taxable years.

(d) *Eligible student.*—(1) *Eligible student defined.*—For purposes of the Hope Scholarship Credit, the term *eligible student* means a student who satisfies all of the following requirements—

(i) *Degree requirement.*—For at least one academic period that begins during the taxable year, the student enrolls at an eligible educational institution in a program leading toward a postsecondary degree, certificate, or other recognized postsecondary educational credential;

(ii) *Work load requirement.*—For at least one academic period that begins during the taxable year, the student enrolls for at least one-half of the normal full-time work load for the course of study the student is pursuing. The standard for what is half of the normal full-time work load is determined by each eligible educational institution. However, the standard for half-time may not be lower than the applicable standard for half-time established by the Department of Education under the Higher Education Act of 1965 and set forth in 34 CFR 674.2(b) (revised as of July 1, 2002) for a half-time undergraduate student;

(iii) *Year of study requirement.*—As of the beginning of the taxable year, the student has not completed the first two years of postsecondary education at an eligible educational institution. Whether a student has completed the first two years of postsecondary education at an eligible educational institution as of the beginning of a taxable year is determined based on whether the institution in which the student is enrolled in a degree program (as described in paragraph (d)(1)(i) of this section) awards the student two years of academic credit at that institution for postsecondary course work completed by the student prior to the beginning of the taxable year. Any academic credit awarded by the eligible educational institution solely on the basis of the student's performance on proficiency examinations is disregarded in determining whether the student has completed two years of postsecondary education; and

(iv) *No felony drug conviction.*—The student has not been convicted of a federal or state felony offense for possession or distribution of a controlled substance as of the end of the taxable year for which the credit is claimed.

(2) *Examples.*—The following examples illustrate the rules of this paragraph (d). In each example, assume that the student has not been convicted of a felony drug offense, that the institution is an eligible educational institution unless otherwise stated, that the qualified tuition and related expenses are paid during the same taxable year that the academic period begins, and that a Hope Scholarship Credit has not previously been claimed for the student (see paragraph (c) of this section). The examples are as follows:

Example 1. Student A graduates from high school in June 1998 and is enrolled in an undergraduate degree program at College U for the 1998 Fall semester on a full-time basis. For the 1999 Spring semester, Student A again is enrolled at College U on a full-time basis. For the 1999 Fall semester, Student A is enrolled in less than half the normal full-time course work for her degree program. Because Student A is enrolled in an undergraduate degree program on at least a half-time basis for at least one academic period that begins during 1998 and at least one academic period that begins during 1999, Student A is an eligible student for taxable years 1998 and 1999 (including the 1999 Fall semester when Student A enrolls at College U on less than a half-time basis).

Example 2. Prior to 1998, Student B attended college for several years on a full-time basis. Student B transfers to College V for the 1998 Spring semester. College V awards Student B credit for some (but not all) of the courses he previously completed, and College V classifies Student B as a first-semester sophomore. During both the Spring and Fall semesters of 1998, Student B is enrolled in at least one-half the normal full-time work load for his degree program at College V. Because College V does not classify Student B as having completed the first two years of postsecondary education as of the beginning of 1998, Student B is an eligible student for taxable year 1998.

Example 3. The facts are the same as in *Example 2.* After taking classes on a half-time basis for the 1998 Spring and Fall semesters, Student B is enrolled at College V for the 1999 Spring semester on a full-time basis. College V classifies Student B as a second-semester sophomore for the 1999 Spring semester and as a first-semester junior for the 1999 Fall semester. Because College V does not classify Student B as having completed the first two years of postsecondary education as of the beginning of 1999, Student B is an eligible student for taxable year 1999. Therefore, the qualified expenses and required fees paid for the 1999 Spring semester and the 1999 Fall semester are taken into account in calculating any Hope Scholarship Credit.

Example 4. Prior to 1998, Student C was not enrolled at another eligible educational institution. At the time that Student C enrolls in a degree program at College W for the 1998 Fall semester, Student C takes examinations to demonstrate her proficiency in several subjects. On the basis of Student C's performance on these examinations, College W classifies Student C as a second-semester sophomore as of the beginning of the 1998 Fall semester. Student C is enrolled at College W during the 1998 Fall semester and during the 1999 Spring and Fall semesters on a full-time basis and is classified as a first-semester junior as of the beginning of the 1999 Spring semester. Because Student C was not enrolled in a college or other eligible educational institution prior to 1998 (but rather was awarded three semesters of academic credit solely because of proficiency examinations), Student C is not treated as having completed the first two years of postsecondary education at an eligible educational institution as of the beginning of 1998 or as of the beginning of 1999. Therefore, Student C is an eligible student for both taxable years 1998 and 1999.

Example 5. During the 1998 Fall semester, Student D is a high school student who takes classes on a half-time basis at College X. Student D is not enrolled as part of a degree program at College X because College X does not admit students to a degree program unless the student has a high school diploma or equivalent. Because Student D is not enrolled in a degree program at College X during 1998, Student D is not an eligible student for taxable year 1998.

Example 6. The facts are the same as in *Example 5.* In addition, during the 1999 Spring semester, Student D again attends College X but not as part of a degree program. Student D graduates from high school in June 1999. For the 1999 Fall semester, Student D enrolls in College X as part of a degree program, and College X awards Student D credit for her prior course work at College X. During the 1999 Fall semester, Student D is enrolled in more than one-half the normal full-time work load of courses for her degree program at College X. Because Student D is enrolled in a degree program at College X for the 1999 Fall term on at least a half-time basis, Student D is an eligible student for all of taxable year 1999. Therefore, the qualified tuition and required fees paid for classes taken at College X during both the 1999 Spring semester (during which Student D was not enrolled in a degree program) and the 1999 Fall semester are taken into account in computing any Hope Scholarship Credit.

Example 7. Student E completed two years of undergraduate study at College S. College S is not an eligible educational institution for purposes of the education tax credit. At the end of 1998, Student E enrolls in an undergraduate degree program at College Z, an eligible educational institution, for the 1999 Spring semester on a full-time basis. College Z awards Student E two years of academic credit for his previous course work at College S and classifies Student E as a first-semester junior for the 1999 Spring semester. Student E is treated as having completed the first two years of postsecondary education at an eligible educational institution as of the beginning of 1999. Therefore, Student E is not an eligible student for taxable year 1999.

Example 8. Student F received a degree in 1998 from College R. College R is not an eligible educational institution for purposes of the education tax credit. During 1999, Student F is enrolled in a graduate-degree program at College Y, an eligible educational institution, for the 1999 Fall semester on a full-time basis. By admitting Student F to its graduate program, College Y treats Student F as having completed the first two years of postsecondary education as of the beginning of 1999. Therefore, Student F is not an eligible student for taxable year 1999.

Example 9. Student G graduates from high school in June 2001. In January 2002, Student G is enrolled in a one-year postsecondary certificate program on a full-time basis to obtain a certificate as a travel agent. Student G completes the program in December 2002 and is awarded a certificate. In January 2003, Student G enrolls in a one-

year postsecondary certificate program on a full-time basis to obtain a certificate as a computer programer. Student G meets the degree requirement, the work load requirement, and the year of study requirement for the taxable years 2002 and 2003. Therefore, Student G is an eligible student for both taxable years 2002 and 2003.

(e) *Academic period for prepayments.*—(1) *In general.*—For purposes of determining whether a student meets the requirements in paragraph (d) of this section for a taxable year, if qualified tuition and related expenses are paid during one taxable year for an academic period that begins during January, February or March of the next taxable year (for taxpayers on a fiscal taxable year, use the first three months of the next taxable year), the academic period is treated as beginning during the taxable year in which the payment is made.

(2) *Example.*—The following example illustrates the rule of this paragraph (e). In the example, assume that all the requirements to claim a Hope Scholarship Credit are met. The example is as follows:

Example. Student G graduates from high school in June 1998. After graduation, Student G works full-time for several months to earn money for college. Student G is enrolled on a full-time basis in an undergraduate degree program at University W, an eligible educational institution, for the 1999 Spring semester, which begins in January 1999. Student G pays tuition to University W for the 1999 Spring semester in December 1998. Because the tuition paid by Student G in 1998 relates to an academic period that begins during the first three months of 1999, Student G's eligibility to claim a Hope Scholarship Credit in 1998 is determined as if the 1999 Spring semester began in 1998. Thus, assuming Student G has not been convicted of a felony drug offense as of December 31, 1998, Student G is an eligible student for 1998.

(f) *Effective date.*—The Hope Scholarship Credit is applicable for qualified tuition and related expenses paid after December 31, 1997, for education furnished in academic periods beginning after December 31, 1997. [Reg. § 1.25A-3.]

☐ [*T.D.* 9034, 12-24-2002 *(corrected* 4-1-2003).]

[Reg. § 1.25A-4]

§ 1.25A-4. Lifetime Learning Credit.—(a) *Amount of the credit.*—(1) *Taxable years beginning before January 1, 2003.*—Subject to the phaseout of the education tax credit described in § 1.25A-1(c), for taxable years beginning before 2003, the Lifetime Learning Credit amount is 20 percent of up to $5,000 of qualified tuition and related expenses paid during the taxable year for education furnished to the taxpayer, the taxpayer's spouse, and any claimed dependent during any academic period beginning in the taxable year (or treated as beginning in the taxable year, see § 1.25A-5(e)(2)).

(2) *Taxable years beginning after December 31, 2002.*—Subject to the phaseout of the education tax credit described in § 1.25A-1(c), for taxable years beginning after 2002, the Lifetime Learning Credit amount is 20 percent of up to $10,000 of qualified tuition and related expenses paid during the taxable year for education furnished to the taxpayer, the taxpayer's spouse, and any claimed dependent during any academic period beginning in the taxable year (or treated as beginning in the taxable year, see § 1.25A-5(e)(2)).

(3) *Coordination with the Hope Scholarship Credit.*—Expenses paid with respect to a student for whom the Hope Scholarship Credit is claimed are not eligible for the Lifetime Learning Credit.

(4) *Examples.*—The following examples illustrate the rules of this paragraph (a). In each example, assume that all the requirements to claim a Lifetime Learning Credit or a Hope Scholarship Credit, as applicable, are met. The examples are as follows:

Example 1. In 1999, Taxpayer A pays qualified tuition and related expenses of $3,000 for dependent B to attend an eligible educational institution, and Taxpayer A pays qualified tuition and related expenses of $4,000 for dependent C to attend an eligible educational institution. Taxpayer A does not claim a Hope Scholarship Credit with respect to either B or C. Although Taxpayer A paid $7,000 of qualified tuition and related expenses during the taxable year, Taxpayer A may claim the Lifetime Learning Credit with respect to only $5,000 of such expenses. Therefore, the maximum Lifetime Learning Credit Taxpayer A may claim for 1999 is $1,000 (.20 × $5,000).

Example 2. In 1999, Taxpayer D pays $6,000 of qualified tuition and related expenses for dependent E, and $2,000 of qualified tuition and related expenses for dependent F, to attend eligible educational institutions. Dependent F has already completed the first two years of postsecondary education. For 1999, Taxpayer D claims the maximum $1,500 Hope Scholarship Credit with respect to dependent E. In computing the amount of the Lifetime Learning Credit, Taxpayer D may not include any of the $6,000 of qualified tuition and related expenses paid on behalf of dependent E but may include the $2,000 of qualified tuition and related expenses of dependent F.

(b) *Credit allowed for unlimited number of taxable years.*—There is no limit to the number of taxable years that a taxpayer may claim a Lifetime Learning Credit with respect to any student.

(c) *Both degree and nondegree courses are eligible for the credit.*—(1) *In general.*—For purposes of the Lifetime Learning Credit, amounts paid for a course at an eligible educational institution are qualified tuition and related expenses if the course is either part of a postsecondary degree program or is not part of a postsecondary degree program but is taken by the student to acquire or improve job skills.

(2) *Examples.*—The following examples illustrate the rule of this paragraph (c). In each example, assume that all the requirements to claim a Lifetime Learning Credit are met. The examples are as follows:

Example 1. Taxpayer A, a professional photographer, enrolls in an advanced photography course at a local community college. Although the course is not part of a degree program, Taxpayer A enrolls in the course to improve her job skills. The course fee paid by Taxpayer A is a qualified tuition and related expense for purposes of the Lifetime Learning Credit.

Example 2. Taxpayer B, a stockbroker, plans to travel abroad on a "photo-safari" for his next vacation. In preparation for the trip, Taxpayer B enrolls in a noncredit photography class at a local community college. Because Taxpayer B is not taking the photography course as part of a degree program or to acquire or improve his job skills, amounts paid by Taxpayer B for the course are not qualified tuition and related expenses for purposes of the Lifetime Learning Credit.

(d) *Effective date.*—The Lifetime Learning Credit is applicable for qualified tuition and related expenses paid after June 30, 1998, for education furnished in academic periods beginning after June 30, 1998. [Reg. §1.25A-4.]

☐ [*T.D. 9034, 12-24-2002.*]

[Reg. §1.25A-5]

§1.25A-5. Special rules relating to characterization and timing of payments.—(a) *Educational expenses paid by claimed dependent.*—For any taxable year for which the student is a claimed dependent of another taxpayer, qualified tuition and related expenses paid by the student are treated as paid by the taxpayer to whom the deduction under section 151 is allowed.

(b) *Educational expenses paid by a third party.*—(1) *In general.*—Solely for purposes of section 25A, if a third party (someone other than the taxpayer, the taxpayer's spouse if the taxpayer is treated as married within the meaning of section 7703, or a claimed dependent) makes a payment directly to an eligible educational institution to pay for a student's qualified tuition and related expenses, the student is treated as receiving the payment from the third party and, in turn, paying the qualified tuition and related expenses to the institution.

(2) *Special rule for tuition reduction included in gross income of employee.*—Solely for purposes of section 25A, if an eligible educational institution provides a reduction in tuition to an employee of the institution (or to the spouse or dependent child of an employee, as described in section 132(h)(2)) and the amount of the tuition reduction is included in the employee's gross income, the employee is treated as receiving payment of an amount equal to the tuition reduction and, in turn, paying such amount to the institution.

(3) *Examples.*—The following examples illustrate the rules of this paragraph (b). In each example, assume that all the requirements to claim an education tax credit are met. The examples are as follows:

Example 1. Grandparent D makes a direct payment to an eligible educational institution for Student E's qualified tuition and related expenses. Student E is not a claimed dependent in 1999. For purposes of claiming an education tax credit, Student E is treated as receiving the money from her grandparent and, in turn, paying her qualified tuition and related expenses.

Example 2. Under a court-approved divorce decree, Parent A is required to pay Student C's college tuition. Parent A makes a direct payment to an eligible educational institution for Student C's 1999 tuition. Under paragraph (b)(1) of this section, Student C is treated as receiving the money from Parent A and, in turn, paying the qualified tuition and related expenses. Under the divorce decree, Parent B has custody of Student C for 1999. Parent B properly claims Student C as a dependent on Parent B's 1999 federal income tax return. Under paragraph (a) of this section, expenses paid by Student C are treated as paid by Parent B. Thus, Parent B may claim an education tax credit for the qualified tuition and related expenses paid directly to the institution by Parent A.

Example 3. University A, an eligible educational institution, offers reduced tuition charges to its employees and their dependent children. F is an employee of University A. F's dependent child, G,

enrolls in a graduate-level course at University A. Section 117(d) does not apply, because it is limited to tuition reductions provided for education below the graduate level. Therefore, the amount of the tuition reduction received by G is treated as additional compensation from University A to F and is included in F's gross income. For purposes of claiming a Lifetime Learning Credit, F is treated as receiving payment of an amount equal to the tuition reduction from University A and, in turn, paying such amount to University A on behalf of F's child, G.

(c) *Adjustment to qualified tuition and related expenses for certain excludable educational assistance.*—(1) *In general.*—In determining the amount of an education tax credit, qualified tuition and related expenses for any academic period must be reduced by the amount of any tax-free educational assistance allocable to such period. For this purpose, *tax-free educational assistance* means—

(i) A qualified scholarship that is excludable from income under section 117;

(ii) A veterans' or member of the armed forces' educational assistance allowance under chapter 30, 31, 32, 34 or 35 of title 38, United States Code, or under chapter 1606 of title 10, United States Code;

(iii) Employer-provided educational assistance that is excludable from income under section 127; or

(iv) Any other educational assistance that is excludable from gross income (other than as a gift, bequest, devise, or inheritance within the meaning of section 102(a)).

(2) *No adjustment for excludable educational assistance attributable to expenses paid in a prior year.*—A reduction is not required under paragraph (c)(1) of this section if the amount of excludable educational assistance received during the taxable year is treated as a refund of qualified tuition and related expenses paid in a prior taxable year. See paragraph (f)(5) of this section.

(3) *Scholarships and fellowship grants.*—For purposes of paragraph (c)(1)(i) of this section, a scholarship or fellowship grant is treated as a qualified scholarship excludable under section 117 except to the extent—

(i) The scholarship or fellowship grant (or any portion thereof) may be applied, by its terms, to expenses other than qualified tuition and related expenses within the meaning of section 117(b)(2) (such as room and board) and the student reports the grant (or the appropriate portion thereof) as income on the student's federal income tax return if the student is required to file a return; or

(ii) The scholarship or fellowship grant (or any portion thereof) must be applied, by its terms, to expenses other than qualified tuition and related expenses within the meaning of section 117(b)(2) (such as room and board) and the student reports the grant (or the appropriate portion thereof) as income on the student's federal income tax return if the student is required to file a return.

(4) *Examples.*—The following examples illustrate the rules of this paragraph (c). In each example, assume that all the requirements to claim an education tax credit are met. The examples are as follows:

Example 1. University X charges Student A, who lives on University X's campus, $3,000 for tuition and $5,000 for room and board. University X awards Student A a $2,000 scholarship. The terms of the scholarship permit it to be used to pay any of a student's costs of attendance at University X, including tuition, room and board, and other incidental expenses. University X applies the $2,000 scholarship against Student A's $8,000 total bill, and Student A pays the $6,000 balance of her bill from University X with a combination of savings and amounts she earns from a summer job. University X does not require A to pay any additional fees beyond the $3,000 in tuition in order to enroll in or attend classes. Student A does not report any portion of the scholarship as income on her federal income tax return. Since Student A does not report the scholarship as income, the scholarship is treated under paragraph (c)(3) of this section as a qualified scholarship that is excludable under section 117. Therefore, for purposes of calculating an education tax credit, Student A is treated as having paid only $1,000 ($3,000 tuition – $2,000 scholarship) in qualified tuition and related expenses to University X.

Example 2. The facts are the same as in *Example 1*, except that Student A reports the entire scholarship as income on the student's federal income tax return. Since the full amount of the scholarship may be applied to expenses other than qualified expenses (room and board) and Student A reports the scholarship as income, the exception in paragraph (c)(3) of this section applies and the scholarship is not treated as a qualified scholarship excludable under section 117. Therefore, for purposes of calculating an education tax credit, Student A is treated as having paid $3,000 of qualified tuition and related expenses to University X.

Example 3. The facts are the same as in *Example 1*, except that the terms of the scholarship require it to be used to pay tuition. Under paragraph (c)(3) of this section, the scholarship is treated as a qualified scholarship excludable under section 117. Therefore, for purposes of calculating an education tax credit, Student A is treated as having paid only $1,000 ($3,000 tuition – $2,000 scholarship) in qualified tuition and related expenses to University X.

Example 4. The facts are the same as in *Example 1*, except that the terms of the scholarship require it to be used to pay tuition or room and board charged by University X, and the scholarship amount is $6,000. Under the terms of the scholarship, Student A may allocate the scholarship between tuition and room and board in any manner. However, because room and board totals $5,000, that is the maximum amount that can be applied under the terms of the scholarship to expenses other than qualified expenses and at least $1,000 of the scholarship must be applied to tuition. Therefore, the maximum amount of the exception under paragraph (c)(3) of this section is $5,000 and at least $1,000 is treated as a qualified scholarship excludable under section 117 ($6,000 scholarship – $5,000 room and board). If Student A reports $5,000 of the scholarship as income on the student's federal income tax return, then Student A will be treated as having paid $2,000 ($3,000 tuition – $1,000 qualified scholarship excludable under section 117) in qualified tuition and related expenses to University X.

Example 5. The facts are the same as in *Example 1*, except that in addition to the scholarship that University X awards to Student A, University X also provides Student A with an education loan and pays Student A for working in a work/study job in the campus dining hall. The loan is not excludable educational assistance within the meaning of paragraph (c) of this section. In addition, wages paid to a student who is performing services for the payor are neither a qualified scholarship nor otherwise excludable from gross income. Therefore, Student A is not required to reduce her qualified tuition and related expenses by the amounts she receives from the student loan or as wages from her work/study job.

Example 6. In 1999, Student B pays University Y $1,000 in tuition for the 1999 Spring semester. University Y does not require Student B to pay any additional fees beyond the $1,000 in tuition in order to enroll in classes. Student B is an employee of Company Z. At the end of the academic period and during the same taxable year that Student B paid tuition to University Y, Student B provides Company Z with proof that he has satisfactorily completed his courses at University Y. Pursuant to an educational assistance program described in section 127(b), Company Z reimburses Student B for all of the tuition paid to University Y. Because the reimbursement from Company Z is employer-provided educational assistance that is excludable from Student B's gross income under section 127, the reimbursement reduces Student B's qualified tuition and related expenses. Therefore, for purposes of calculating an education tax credit, Student B is treated as having paid no qualified tuition and related expenses to University Y during 1999.

Example 7. The facts are the same as in *Example 6* except that the reimbursement from Company Z is not pursuant to an educational assistance program described in section 127(b), is not otherwise excludable from Student B's gross income, and is taxed as additional compensation to Student B. Because the reimbursement is not excludable educational assistance within the meaning of paragraph (c)(1) of this section, Student B is not required to reduce his qualified tuition and related expenses by the $1,000 reimbursement he received from his employer. Therefore, for purposes of calculating an education tax credit, Student B is treated as paying $1,000 in qualified tuition and related expenses to University Y during 1999.

(d) *No double benefit.*—Qualified tuition and related expenses do not include any expense for which a deduction is allowed under section 162, section 222, or any other provision of chapter 1 of the Internal Revenue Code.

(e) *Timing rules.*—(1) *In general.*—Except as provided in paragraph (e)(2) of this section, an education tax credit is allowed only for payments of qualified tuition and related expenses for an academic period beginning in the same taxable year as the year the payment is made. Except for certain individuals who do not use the cash receipts and disbursements method of accounting, qualified tuition and related expenses are treated as paid in the year in which the expenses are actually paid. See § 1.461-1(a)(1).

(2) *Prepayment rule.*—(i) *In general.*—If qualified tuition and related expenses are paid during one taxable year for an academic period that begins during the first three months of the taxpayer's next taxable year (i.e., in January, February, or March of the next taxable year for calendar year taxpayers), an education tax credit is allowed with respect to the qualified tuition and related expenses only in the taxable year in which the expenses are paid.

(ii) *Example.*—The following example illustrates the rule of this paragraph (e)(2). In the example, assume that all the requirements to claim an education tax credit are met. The example is as follows:

Example. In December 1998, Taxpayer A, a calendar year taxpayer, pays College Z $1,000 in qualified tuition and related expenses to attend classes during the 1999 Spring semester, which begins in January 1999. Taxpayer A may claim an education tax credit only in 1998 for payments made in 1998 for the 1999 Spring semester.

(3) *Expenses paid with loan proceeds.*—An education tax credit may be claimed for qualified tuition and related expenses paid with the proceeds of a loan only in the taxable year in which the expenses are paid, and may not be claimed in the taxable year in which the loan is repaid. Loan proceeds disbursed directly to an eligible educational institution will be treated as paid on the date the institution credits the proceeds to the student's account. For example, in the case of any loan issued or guaranteed as part of a federal student loan program under Title IV of the Higher Education Act of 1965, loan proceeds will be treated as paid on the date of disbursement (as defined in 34 CFR 668.164(a), revised as of July 1, 2002) by the eligible educational institution. If a taxpayer does not know the date the institution credits the student's account, the taxpayer must treat the qualified tuition and related expenses as paid on the last date for payment prescribed by the institution.

(4) *Expenses paid through third party installment payment plans.*—(i) *In general.*—A taxpayer, an eligible educational institution, and a third party installment payment company may enter into an agreement in which the company agrees to collect installment payments of qualified tuition and related expenses from the taxpayer and to remit the installment payments to the institution. If the third party installment payment company is the taxpayer's agent for purposes of paying qualified tuition and related expenses to the eligible educational institution, the taxpayer is treated as paying the qualified expenses on the date the company pays the institution. However, if the third party installment payment company is the eligible educational institution's agent for purposes of collecting payments of qualified tuition and related expenses from the taxpayer, the taxpayer is treated as paying the qualified expenses on the date the taxpayer pays the company.

(ii) *Example.*—The following example illustrates the rule of this paragraph (e)(4). The example is as follows:

Example. Student A, Company B, and College C enter into a written agreement in which Student A agrees to pay the tuition required to attend College C in 10 equal monthly installments to Company B. Under the written agreement, Student A is not relieved of her obligation to pay College C until Company B remits the payments to College C. Under the written agreement, Company B agrees to disburse the monthly installment payments to College C within 30 days of receipt. Because Company B acts as Student A's agent for purposes of paying qualified expenses to College C, Student A is treated as paying qualified expenses on the date Company B disburses payments to College C.

(f) *Refund of qualified tuition and related expenses.*—(1) *Payment and refund of qualified tuition and related expenses in the same taxable year.*—With respect to any student, the amount of qualified tuition and related expenses for a taxable year is calculated by adding all qualified tuition and related expenses paid for the taxable year, and subtracting any refund of such expenses received from the eligible educational institution during the same taxable year (including refunds of loan proceeds described in paragraph (f)(4) of this section).

(2) *Payment of qualified tuition and related expenses in one taxable year and refund in subsequent taxable year before return filed for prior taxable year.*—If, in a taxable year, a taxpayer or someone other than the taxpayer receives a refund (including refunds of loan proceeds described in paragraph (f)(4) of this section) of qualified tuition and related expenses paid on behalf of a student in a prior taxable year and the refund is received before the taxpayer files a federal income tax return for the prior taxable year, the amount of the qualified tuition and related expenses for the prior taxable year is reduced by the amount of the refund.

(3) *Payment of qualified tuition and related expenses in one taxable year and refund in subsequent taxable year.*—(i) *In general.*—If, in a taxable year (refund year), a taxpayer or someone other than the taxpayer receives a refund (including refunds of loan proceeds described in paragraph (f)(4) of this section) of qualified tuition and related expenses paid on behalf of a student for which the taxpayer claimed an education tax credit in a prior taxable year, the tax imposed by chapter 1 of the Internal Revenue Code for the refund year is increased by the recapture amount.

(ii) *Recapture amount.*—The recapture amount is the difference in tax liability for the prior taxable year (taking into account any redetermination of such tax liability by audit or amended return) that results when the tax liability for the prior year is calculated using the taxpayer's redetermined credit. The redetermined credit is computed by reducing the amount of the qualified tuition and related expenses taken into account in determining any credit claimed in the prior taxable year by the amount of the refund of the qualified tuition and related expenses (redetermined qualified expenses), and computing the allowable credit using the redetermined qualified expenses and the relevant facts and circumstances of the prior taxable year, such as modified adjusted gross income (redetermined credit).

(4) *Refund of loan proceeds treated as refund of qualified tuition and related expenses.*—If loan proceeds used to pay qualified tuition and related expenses (as described in paragraph (e)(3) of this section) during a taxable year are refunded by an eligible educational institution to a lender on behalf of the borrower, the refund is treated as a refund of qualified tuition and related expenses for purposes of paragraphs (f)(1), (2), and (3) of this section.

(5) *Excludable educational assistance received in a subsequent taxable year treated as a refund.*—If, in a taxable year, a taxpayer or someone other than the taxpayer receives any excludable educational assistance (described in paragraph (c)(1) of this section) for the qualified tuition and related expenses paid on behalf of a student during a prior taxable year (or attributable to enrollment at an eligible educational institution during a prior taxable year), the educational assistance is treated as a refund of qualified tuition and related expenses for purposes of paragraphs (f)(2) and (3) of this section. If the excludable educational assistance is received before the taxpayer files a Federal income tax return for the prior taxable year, the amount of the qualified tuition and related expenses for the prior taxable year is reduced by the amount of the excludable educational assistance as provided in paragraph (f)(2) of this section. If the excludable educational assistance is received after the taxpayer has filed a federal income tax return for the prior taxable year, any education tax credit claimed for the prior taxable year is subject to recapture as provided in paragraph (f)(3) of this section.

(6) *Examples.*—The following examples illustrate the rules of this paragraph (f). In each example, assume that all the requirements to claim an education tax credit are met. The examples are as follows:

Example 1. In January 1998, Student A, a full-time freshman at University X, pays $2,000 for qualified tuition and related expenses for a 16-hour work load for the 1998 Spring semester. Prior to beginning classes, Student A withdraws from 6 course hours. On February 15, 1998, Student A receives a $750 refund from University X. In September 1998, Student A pays University X $1,000 to enroll half-time for the 1998 Fall semester. Prior to beginning classes, Student A withdraws from a 2-hour course, and she receives a $250 refund in October 1998. Student A computes the amount of qualified tuition and related expenses she may claim for 1998 by:

(i) Adding all qualified expenses paid during the taxable year ($2,000 + 1,000 = $3,000);

(ii) Adding all refunds of qualified tuition and related expenses received during the taxable year ($750 + $250 = $1,000); and,

(iii) Subtracting paragraph (ii) of this *Example* 1 from paragraph (i) of this *Example* 1 ($3,000 − $1,000 = $2,000). Therefore, Student A's qualified tuition and related expenses for 1998 are $2,000.

Example 2. (i) In December 1998, Student B, a senior at College Y, pays $2,000 for qualified tuition and related expenses for a 16-hour work load for the 1999 Spring semester. Prior to beginning classes, Student B withdraws from a 4-hour course. On January 15, 1999, Student B files her 1998 income tax return and claims a $400 Lifetime Learning Credit for the $2,000 qualified expenses paid in 1998, which reduces her tax liability for 1998 by $400. On February 15, 1999, Student B receives a $500 refund from College Y.

(ii) Student B calculates the increase in tax for 1999 by—

(A) Calculating the redetermined qualified expenses for 1998 ($2,000 − $500 = $1,500);

(B) Calculating the redetermined credit for the redetermined qualified expenses ($1,500 × .20 = $300); and

(C) Calculating the difference in tax liability for 1998 resulting from the redetermined credit. Because Student B's tax liability for 1998 was reduced by the full amount of the $400 education tax credit claimed on her 1998 income tax return, the difference in tax liability can be determined by subtracting the redetermined credit from the credit claimed in 1998 ($400 − $300 = $100).

(iii) *Therefore, Student B must increase the tax on her 1999 Federal income tax return by $100.*

Example 3. In September 1998, Student C pays College Z $1,200 in qualified tuition and related expenses to attend evening classes during the 1998 Fall semester. Student C is an employee of Company R. On January 15, 1999, Student C files a federal income tax return for 1998 claiming a Lifetime Learning Credit of $240 (.20 × $1,200), which reduces Student C's tax liability for 1998 by $240. Pursuant to an educational assistance program described in section 127(b), Company R reimburses Student C in February 1999 for the $1,200 of qualified tuition and related expenses paid by Student C in 1998. The

$240 education tax credit claimed by Student C for 1998 is subject to recapture. Because Student C paid no net qualified tuition and related expenses for 1998, the redetermined credit for 1998 is zero. Student C must increase the amount of Student C's 1999 tax by the recapture amount, which is $240 (the difference in tax liability for 1998 resulting from the redetermined credit for 1998 ($0)). Because the $1,200 reimbursement relates to expenses for which the taxpayer claimed an education tax credit in a prior year, the reimbursement does not reduce the amount of any qualified tuition and related expenses that Student C paid in 1999.

[Reg. §1.25A-5.]

☐ [*T.D.* 9034, 12-24-2002 (*corrected* 4-1-2003).]

[Reg. §1.28-0]

§1.28-0. Credit for clinical testing expenses for certain drugs for rare diseases or conditions; table of contents.—In order to facilitate use of §1.28-1, this section lists the paragraphs, subparagraphs, and subdivisions contained in §1.28-1.

(a) General rule.

(b) Qualified clinical testing expenses.

  (1) In general.

  (2) Modification of section 41(b).

  (3) Exclusion for amounts funded by another person.

    (i) In general.

    (ii) Clinical testing in which taxpayer retains no rights.

    (iii) Clinical testing in which taxpayer retains substantial rights.

      (A) In general.

      (B) Drug by drug determination.

    (iv) Funding for qualified clinical testing expenses determinable only in subsequent taxable years.

  (4) Special rule governing the application of section 41(b) beyond its expiration date.

(c) Clinical testing.

  (1) In general.

  (2) Definition of "human clinical testing".

  (3) Definition of "carried out under" section 505(i).

(d) Definition and special rules.

  (1) Definition of "rare disease or condition".

    (i) In general.

    (ii) Cost of developing and making available the designated drug.

      (A) In general.

      (B) Exclusion of costs funded by another person.

      (C) Computation of cost.

      (D) Allocation of common costs. Costs for developing and making available the designated drug for both the disease or condition for which it is designated and one or more other diseases or conditions.

    (iii) Recovery from sales.

    (iv) Recordkeeping requirements.

  (2) Tax liability limitation.

    (i) Taxable years beginning after December 31, 1986.

    (ii) Taxable years beginning before January 1, 1987 and after December 31, 1983.

    (iii) Taxable years beginning before January 1, 1984.

  (3) Special limitations on foreign testing.

    (i) Clinical testing conducted outside the United States—In general.

    (ii) Insufficient testing population in the United States.

      (A) In general.

      (B) "Insufficient testing population".

      (C) "Unrelated to the taxpayer".

  (4) Special limitation for certain corporations.

    (i) Corporations to which section 936 applies.

    (ii) Corporations to which section 934(b) applies.

  (5) Aggregation of expenditures.

    (i) Controlled group of corporations: organizations under common control.

      (A) In general.

      (B) Definition of controlled group of corporations.

      (C) Definition of organization.

      (D) Determination of common control.

    (ii) Tax accounting periods used.

      (A) In general.

      (B) Special rule where the timing of clinical testing is manipulated.

    (iii) Membership during taxable year in more than one group.

    (iv) Intra-group transactions.

      (A) In general.

(B) In-house research expenses.
(C) Contract research expenses.
(D) Lease payments.
(E) Payments for supplies.
(6) Allocations.
  (i) Pass-through in the case of an S corporation.
  (ii) Pass-through in the case of an estate or trust.
  (iii) Pass-through in the case of a partnership.
    (A) In general.
    (B) Certain partnership non-business expenditures.
    (C) Apportionment.
  (iv) Year in which taken into account.
  (v) Credit allowed subject to limitation.
(7) Manner of making an election.
[Reg. § 1.28-0.]

□ [*T.D. 8232, 9-30-88.*]

[Reg. §1.28-1]

§1.28-1. Credit for clinical testing expenses for certain drugs for rare diseases or conditions.—(a) *General rule.*—Section 28 provides a credit against the tax imposed by chapter 1 of the Internal Revenue Code. The amount of the credit is equal to 50 percent of the qualified clinical testing expenses (as defined in paragraph (b) of this section) for the taxable year. The credit applies to qualified clinical testing expenses paid or incurred by the taxpayer after December 31, 1982, and before January 1, 1991. The credit may not exceed the taxpayer's tax liability for the taxable year (as determined under paragraph (d)(2) of this section).

(b) *Qualified clinical testing expenses.*—(1) *In general.*—Except as otherwise provided in paragraph (b)(3) of this section, the term "qualified clinical testing expenses" means the amounts which are paid or incurred during the taxable year which would constitute "qualified research expenses" within the meaning of section 41(b) (relating to the credit for increasing research activities) as modified by section 28(b)(1)(B) and paragraph (b)(2) of this section. For example, amounts paid or incurred for the acquisition of depreciable property used in the conduct of clinical testing (as defined in paragraph (c) of this section) are not qualified clinical testing expenses.

(2) *Modification of section 41(b).*—For purposes of paragraph (b)(1) of this section, section 41(b) is modified by substituting "clinical testing" for "qualified research" each place it appears in paragraph (2) of section 41(b) (relating to in-house research expenses) and paragraph (3) of section 41(b) (relating to contract research expenses). In addition, "100 percent" is substituted for "65 percent" in paragraph (3)(A) of section 41(b).

(3) *Exclusion for amounts funded by another person.*—(i) *In general.*—The term "qualified clinical testing expenses" shall not include any amount which would otherwise constitute qualified clinical testing expenses, to the extent such amount is funded by a grant, contract, or otherwise by another person (or any governmental entity). The determination of the extent to which an amount is funded shall be made in light of all the facts and circumstances. For a special rule regarding funding between commonly controlled businesses, see paragraph (d)(5)(iv) of § 1.28-1.

(ii) *Clinical testing in which taxpayer retains no rights.*—If a taxpayer conducting clinical testing with respect to the designated drug for another person retains no substantial rights in the clinical testing under the agreement providing for the clinical testing, the taxpayer's clinical testing expenses are treated as fully funded for purposes of section 28(b)(1)(C). Thus, for example, if the taxpayer incurs clinical testing expenses under an agreement that confers on another person the exclusive right to exploit the results of the clinical testing, those expenses do not constitute qualified clinical testing expenses because they are fully funded under this paragraph (b)(3)(ii). Incidental benefits to the taxpayer from the conduct of the clinical testing (for example, increased experience in the field of human clinical testing) do not constitute substantial rights in the clinical testing.

(iii) *Clinical testing in which taxpayer retains substantial rights.*—(A) *In general.*—If a taxpayer conducting clinical testing with respect to the designated drug for another person retains substantial rights in the clinical testing under the agreement providing for the clinical testing, the clinical testing expenses are funded to the extent of the payments (and fair market value of any property at the time of transfer) to which the taxpayer becomes entitled by conducting the clinical testing. *The taxpayers shall reduce the amount paid or incurred by the taxpayer for the clinical testing expenses that would, but for section 28(b)(1)(C), constitute qualified clinical testing expenses of the taxpayer by the amount of the funding determined under the preceding sentence. Rights retained in the clinical testing

are not treated as property for purposes of this paragraph (b)(3)(iii)(A). If the property that is transferred to the taxpayer is to be consumed in the clinical testing (for example, supplies), the taxpayer should exclude the value of that property from both the payments received and the expenses paid or incurred for the clinical testing.

(B) *Drug by drug determination.*—The provisions of this paragraph (b)(3) shall be applied separately to each designated drug tested by the taxpayer.

(iv) *Funding for qualified clinical testing expenses determinable only in subsequent taxable years.*—If, at the time the taxpayer files its return for a taxable year, it is impossible to determine to what extent some or all of the qualified clinical testing expenses may be funded, the taxpayer shall treat the clinical testing expenses as fully funded for purposes of that return. When the amount of funding for qualified clinical testing expenses is finally determined, the taxpayers should amend the return and any interim returns to reflect the amount of funding for qualified clinical testing expenses.

(4) *Special rule governing the application of section 41(b) beyond its expiration date.*—For purposes of section 28 and this section, section 41(b), as amended, and the regulations thereunder shall be deemed to remain in effect after December 31, 1988.

(c) *Clinical testing.*—(1) *In general.*—The term "clinical testing" means any human clinical testing which—

  (i) Is carried out under an exemption under section 505(i) of the Federal Food, Drug, and Cosmetic Act (21 U.S.C. 355(i)) and the regulations relating thereto (21 CFR Part 312) for the purpose of testing a drug for a rare disease or condition as defined in paragraph (d)(1) of this section,

  (ii) Occurs after the date the drug is designated as a drug for a rare disease or condition under section 526 of the Federal Food, Drug, and Cosmetic Act (21 U.S.C. 360bb),

  (iii) Occurs before the date on which an application for the designated drug is approved under section 505(b) of the Federal Food, Drug, and Cosmetic Act (21 U.S.C. 355(b)) or, if the drug is a biological product (other than a radioactive biological product intended for human use), before the date on which a license for such drug is issued under section 351 of the Public Health Services Act (42 U.S.C. 262), and

  (iv) Is conducted by or on behalf of the taxpayer to whom the designation under section 526 of the Federal Food, Drug, and Cosmetic Act applies.
Human clinical testing shall be taken into account under this paragraph (c)(1) only to the extent that the testing relates to the use of a drug for the rare disease or condition for which the drug was designated under section 526 of the Federal Food, Drug, and Cosmetic Act. For purposes of paragraph (c)(1)(i) of this section the testing under section 505(i) exemption procedures (21 CFR Part 312) of a biological product (other than a radioactive biological product intended for human use) pursuant to 21 CFR 601.21 is deemed to be carried out under an exemption under section 505(i) of the Federal Food, Drug, and Cosmetic Act.

(2) *Definition of "human clinical testing".*—Testing is considered to be human clinical testing only to the extent that it uses human subjects to determine the effect of the designated drug on humans and is necessary for the designated drug either to be approved under section 505(b) of the Federal Food, Drug, and Cosmetic Act and the regulations thereunder (21 CFR Part 314), or if the designated drug is a biological product (other than a radioactive biological product intended for human use), to be licensed under section 351 of the Public Health Services Act and the regulations thereunder (21 CFR Part 601). For purposes of this paragraph (c)(2), a human subject is an individual who is a participant in research, either as a recipient of the drug or as a control. A subject may be either a healthy individual or a patient.

(3) *Definition of "carried out under" section 505(i).*—Human clinical testing is not carried out under section 505(i) of the Federal Food, Drug, and Cosmetic Act and the regulations thereunder (21 CFR Part 312) unless the primary purpose of the human clinical testing is to ascertain the data necessary to qualify the designated drug for sale in the United States, and not to ascertain data unrelated or only incidentally related to that needed to qualify the designated drug. Whether or not this primary purpose test is met shall be determined in light of all of the facts and circumstances.

(d) *Definition and special rules*—.—(1) *Definition of "rare disease or condition".*—(i) *In general.*—The term "rare disease or condition" means any disease or condition which—

  (A) Afflicts 200,000 or fewer persons in the United States, or

  (B) Afflicts more than 200,000 persons in the United States but for which there is no reasonable expectation that the cost of developing and making available in the United States (as defined in section 7701(a)(9)) a drug for such disease or condition will be recovered from sales in the United States (as so defined) of such drug.

Determinations under paragraph (d)(1)(i)(B) of this section with respect to any drug shall be made on the basis of the facts and circumstances as of the date such drug is designated under section 526 of the Federal Food, Drug, and Cosmetic Act. Examples of diseases or conditions which in 1987 afflicted 200,000 or fewer persons in the United States are Duchenne dystrophy, one of the muscular dystrophies; Huntington's disease, and hereditary chorea; myoclonus; Tourette's syndrome; and amyotrophic lateral sclerosis (ALS or Lou Gehrig's disease).

(ii) *Cost of developing and making available the designated drug.*— (A) *In general.*—Except as otherwise provided in this paragraph (d)(1)(ii), the taxpayer's computation of the cost of developing and making available in the United States the designated drug shall include only the costs that the taxpayer (or any person whose right to make sales of the drug is directly or indirectly derived from the taxpayer, *e.g.,* a licensee or transferee) has incurred or reasonably expects to incur in developing and making available in the United States the designated drug for the disease or condition for which it is designated. For example, if, prior to designation under section 526, the taxpayer incurred costs of $125,000 to test the drug for the rare disease or condition for which it is subsequently designated and incurred $500,000 to test the same drug for other diseases, and if, on the date of designation, the taxpayer expects to incur costs of $1.2 million to test the drug for the rare disease or condition for which it is designated, the taxpayer shall include in its cost computation both the $125,000 incurred prior to designation and the $1.2 million expected to be incurred after designation to test the drug for the rare disease or condition for which it is designated. The taxpayer shall not include the $500,000 incurred to test the drug for other diseases.

(B) *Exclusion of costs funded by another person.*—In computing the cost of developing and making available in the United States the designated drug, the taxpayer shall not include any cost incurred or expected to be incurred by the taxpayer to the extent that the cost is funded or is reasonably expected to be funded (determined under the principles of paragraph (b)(3)) by a grant, contract, or otherwise by another person (or any governmental entity).

(C) *Computation of cost.*—The cost computation shall use only reasonable costs incurred after the first indication of an orphan application for the designated drug. Such costs shall include the costs of obtaining data needed, and of meetings to be held, in connection with a request for FDA assistance under section 525 of the Federal Food, Drug, and Cosmetic Act (21 U.S.C. 360aa) or a request for orphan designation under section 526 of that Act; costs of determining patentability of the drug; costs of screening animal and clinical studies; costs associated with preparation of a Notice of Claimed Investigational Exemption for a New Drug (IND) and a New Drug Application (NDA); costs of possible distribution of drug under a "treatment" protocol; costs of development of a dosage form; manufacturing costs; distribution costs; promotion costs; costs to maintain required records and reports; and costs of the taxpayer in acquiring the right to market a drug from the owner of that right prior to designation. The taxpayer shall also include general overhead, depreciation costs and premiums for insurance against liability losses to the extent that the taxpayer can demonstrate that these costs are properly allocable to the designated drug under the established standards of financial accounting and reporting of research and development costs.

(D) *Allocation of common costs. Costs for developing and making available the designated drug for both the disease or condition for which it is designated and one or more other diseases or conditions.*—In the case where the costs incurred or expected to be incurred in developing and making available the designated drug for the disease or condition for which it is designated are also incurred or expected to be incurred in developing and making available in the United States the same drug for one or more other diseases or conditions (whether or not they are also designated or expected to be designated), the costs shall be allocated between the cost of developing and making available the designated drug for the disease or condition for which the drug is designated and the cost of developing and making available the designated drug for the other diseases or conditions. The amount of the common costs to be allocated to the cost of developing and making available the designated drug for the disease or condition for which it is designated is determined by multiplying the common costs by a fraction the numerator of which is the sum of the expected amount of sales in the United States of the designated drug for the disease or condition for which the drug is designated and the denominator of which is the total expected amount of sales in the United States of the designated drug. For example, if prior to designation, the taxpayer incurs (among other costs) costs of $100,000 in

testing the designated drug for its toxic effect on animals (without reference to any disease or condition), and if the taxpayer expects to recover $500,000 from sales in the United States of the designated drug for disease X, the disease for which the drug is designated, and further expects to recover another $1.5 million from the sales in the United States of the designated drug for disease Y, the taxpayer must allocate a proportionate amount of the common costs of $100,000 to the cost of developing and making available the designated drug for both disease X and disease Y. Since the ratio of the expected amount of sales in the United States of the designated drug for disease X to the total of both the expected amount of sales in the United States of the designated drug for disease X and the expected amount of sales in the United States of the designated drug for disease Y is $500,000/$2,000,000, 25% of the common costs of $100,000 (*i.e.,* $25,000) is allocated to the cost of developing and making available the designated drug for disease X.

(iii) *Recovery from sales.*—In determining whether the taxpayer's cost described in paragraph (d)(1)(ii) of this section will be recovered from sales in the United States of the designated drug for the disease or condition for which the drug is designated, the taxpayer shall include anticipated sales by the taxpayer or any person whose right to make such sales is directly or indirectly derived from the taxpayer (such as a licensee or transferee). The anticipated sales shall be based upon the size of the anticipated patient population for which the designated drug would be useful, including the following factors: the degree of effectiveness and safety of the designated drug, if known; the projected fraction of the anticipated patient population expected to be given the designated drug and to continue to take it; other available agents and other types of therapy; the likelihood that superior agents will become available within a few years; and the number of years during which the designated drug would be exclusively available, *e.g.,* under a patent.

(iv) *Recordkeeping requirements.*—The taxpayer shall keep records sufficient to substantiate the cost and sales estimates made pursuant to this paragraph (d)(1). The records required by this paragraph (d)(1)(iv) shall be retained so long as the contents thereof may become material in the administration of section 28.

(2) *Tax liability limitation.*—(i) *Taxable years beginning after December 31, 1986.*—The credit allowed by section 28 shall not exceed the excess (if any) of—

(A) the taxpayer's regular tax liability for the taxable year (as defined in section 26(b)), reduced by the sum of the credits allowable under—

(1) Section 21 (relating to expenses for household and dependent care services necessary for gainful employment),

(2) Section 22 (relating to the elderly and permanently and totally disabled),

(3) Section 23 (relating to residential energy),

(4) Section 25 (relating to interest on certain home mortgages), and

(5) Section 27 (relating to taxes on foreign countries and possessions of the United States), over

(B) The tentative minimum tax for the taxable year (as determined under section 55(b)(1)).

(ii) *Taxable years beginning before January 1, 1987, and after December 31, 1983.*—The credit allowed by section 28 shall not exceed the taxpayer's tax liability for the taxable year (as defined in section 26(b) prior to its amendment by the Tax Reform Act of 1986 (Pub. Law 99-514)), reduced by the sum of the credits allowable under—

(A) Section 21 (relating to expenses for household and dependent care services necessary for gainful employment),

(B) Section 22 (relating to the elderly and permanently and totally disabled),

(C) Section 23 (relating to residential energy),

(D) Section 24 (relating to contributions to candidates for public office),

(E) Section 25 (relating to interest on certain home mortgages), and

(F) Section 27 (relating to the taxes on foreign countries and possessions of the United States).

(iii) *Taxable years beginning before January 1, 1984.*—The credit allowed by section 28 shall not exceed the amount of the tax imposed by chapter 1 of the Internal Revenue Code for the taxable year, reduced by the sum of the credits allowable under the following sections as designated prior to the enactment of the Tax Reform Act of 1984 (Pub. Law 98-369):

(A) Section 32 (relating to tax withheld at source on nonresident aliens and foreign corporations and on tax-free covenant bonds),

(B) Section 33 (relating to taxes of foreign countries and possessions of the United States),

(C) Section 37 (relating to the retirement income),

(D) Section 38 (relating to investment in certain depreciable property),

(E) Section 40 (relating to expenses of work incentive programs),

(F) Section 41 (relating to contributions to candidates for public office),

(G) Section 44 (relating to purchase of new principal residence),

(H) Section 44A (relating to expenses for household and dependent care services necessary for gainful employment),

(I) Section 44B (relating to employment of certain new employees),

(J) Section 44C (relating to residential energy),

(K) Section 44D (relating to producing fuel from a nonconventional source),

(L) Section 44E (relating to alcohol used as fuel),

(M) Section 44F (relating to increasing research activities), and

(N) Section 44G (relating to employee stock ownership).

The term "tax imposed by chapter 1," as used in this paragraph (d)(2)(iii) does not include any tax treated as not imposed by chapter 1 of the Internal Revenue Code under the last sentence of section 53(a).

(3) *Special limitations on foreign testing.*—(i) *Clinical testing conducted outside of the United States—In general.*—Except as otherwise provided in this paragraph (d)(3), expenses paid or incurred with respect to clinical testing conducted outside the United States (as defined in section 7701(a)(9)) are not eligible for credit under this section. Thus, for example, wages paid an employee clinical investigator for clinical testing conducted in medical facilities in the United States and Mexico generally must be apportioned between the clinical testing conducted within the United States and the clinical testing conducted outside the United States, and only the wages apportioned to the clinical testing conducted within the United States are qualified clinical testing expenses.

(ii) *Insufficient testing population in the United States.*—(A) *In general.*—If clinical testing is conducted outside of the United States because there is an insufficient testing population in the United States, and if the clinical testing is conducted by a United States person (as defined in section 7701(a)(30)) or is conducted by any other person unrelated to the taxpayer to whom the designation under section 526 of the Federal Food, Drug, and Cosmetic Act applies, then the expenses paid or incurred for clinical testing conducted outside of the United States are eligible for the credit provided by section 28.

(B) *"Insufficient testing population".*—The testing population in the United States is insufficient if there are not within the United States the number of available and appropriate human subjects needed to produce reliable data from the clinical investigation.

(C) *"Unrelated to the taxpayer".*—For the purpose of determining whether a person is unrelated to the taxpayer to whom the designation under section 526 of the Federal Food, Drug, and Cosmetic Act and the regulations thereunder applies, the rules of section 613A(d)(3) shall apply except that the number "5" in section 613A(d)(3)(A), (B), and (C) shall be deleted and the number "10" inserted in lieu thereof.

(4) *Special limitations for certain corporations.*—(i) *Corporations to which section 936 applies.*—Expenses paid or incurred for clinical testing conducted either inside or outside the United States by a corporation to which section 936 (relating to Puerto Rico and possessions tax credit) applies are not eligible for the credit under section 28.

(ii) *Corporations to which section 934(b) applies.*—For taxable years beginning before January 1, 1987, expenses paid or incurred for clinical testing conducted either inside or outside the United States by a corporation to which section 934(b) (relating to the limitation on reduction in income tax liability incurred to the Virgin Islands), as in effect prior to its amendment by the Tax Reform Act of 1986, applies are not eligible for the credit under section 28. For taxable years beginning after December 31, 1986, see section 1277(c)(1) of the Tax Reform Act of 1986 (100 Stat. 2600) which makes the rule set forth in the preceding sentence inapplicable with respect to corporations created or organized in the Virgin Islands only if (and so long as) an implementing agreement described in that section is in effect between the United States and the Virgin Islands.

(5) *Aggregation of expenditures.*—(i) *Controlled group of corporations; organizations under common control.*—(A) *In general.*—In deter-

mining the amount of the credit allowable with respect to an organization that at the end of its taxable year is a member of a controlled group of corporations or a member of a group of organizations under common control, all members of the group are treated as a single taxpayer and the credit (if any) allowable to the member is determined on the basis of its proportionate share of the qualified clinical testing expenses of the aggregated group.

(B) *Definition of controlled group of corporations.*—For purposes of this section, the term "controlled group of corporations" shall have the meaning given to the term by section 41(f)(5).

(C) *Definition of organization.*—For purposes of this section, an organization is a sole proprietorship, a partnership, a trust, an estate, or a corporation, that is carrying on a trade or business (within the meaning of section 162). For purposes of this section, any corporation that is a member of a commonly controlled group shall be deemed to be carrying on a trade or business if any other member of that group is carrying on any trade or business.

(D) *Determination of common control.*—Whether organizations are under common control shall be determined under the principles set forth in paragraphs (b)—(g) of 26 CFR § 1.52-1.

(ii) *Tax accounting periods used.*—(A) *In general.*—The credit allowable to a member of a controlled group of corporations or a group of organizations under common control is that member's share of the aggregate credit computed as of the end of such member's taxable year.

(B) *Special rule where the timing of clinical testing is manipulated.*—If the timing of clinical testing by members using different tax accounting periods is manipulated to generate a credit in excess of the amount that would be allowable if all members of the group used the same tax accounting period, the district director may require all members of the group to calculate the credit in the current taxable year and all future years by using the "conformed years" method. Each member computing a credit under the "conformed years" method shall compute the credit as if all members of the group had the same taxable year as the computing member.

(iii) *Membership during taxable year in more than one group.*—An organization may be a member of only one group for a taxable year. If, without application of this paragraph (d)(5)(iii), an organization would be a member of more than one group at the end of its taxable year, the organization shall be treated as a member of the group in which it was included for its preceding taxable year. If the organization was not included for its preceding taxable year in any group in which it could be included as of the end of its taxable year, the organization shall designate in its timely filed return the group in which it is being included. If the return for a taxable year is due before May 1, 1985, the organization may designate its group membership through an amended return for that year filed on or before April 30, 1985. If the organization does not so designate, then the district director with audit jurisdiction of the return will determine the group in which the business is to be included.

(iv) *Intra-group transactions.*—(A) *In general.*—Because all members of a group under common control are treated as a single taxpayer for purposes of determining the credit, transactions between members of the group are generally disregarded.

(B) *In-house research expenses.*—If one member of a group conducts clinical testing on behalf of another member, the member conducting the clinical testing shall include in its qualified clinical testing expenses any in-house research expenses for that work and shall not treat any amount received or accrued from the other member as funding the clinical testing. Conversely, the member for whom the clinical testing is conducted shall not treat any part of any amount paid or incurred as a contract research expense. For purposes of determining whether the in-house research for that work is clinical testing, the member performing the clinical testing shall be treated as carrying on any trade or business carried on by the member on whose behalf the clinical testing is performed.

(C) *Contract research expenses.*—If a member of a group pays or incurs contract research expenses to a person outside the group in carrying on the member's trade or business, that member shall include those expenses as qualified clinical testing expenses. However, if the expenses are not paid or incurred in carrying on any trade or business of that member, those expenses may be taken into account as contract research expenses by another member of the group provided that the other member—

(1) Reimburses the member paying or incurring the expenses, and

(2) Carries on a trade or business to which the clinical testing relates.

(D) *Lease payments.*—Amounts paid or incurred to another member of the group for the lease of personal property owned by a person outside the group shall be taken into account as in-house research expenses for purposes of section 28 only to the extent of the lesser of—

(1) The amount paid or incurred to the other member, or

(2) The amount of the lease expense paid to a person outside the group.

The amount paid or incurred to another member of the group for the lease of personal property owned by a member of the group is not taken into account for purposes of section 28.

(E) *Payment for supplies.*—Amounts paid or incurred to another member of the group for supplies shall be taken into account as in-house research expenses for purposes of section 28 only to the extent of the lesser of—

(1) The amount paid or incurred to the other member, or

(2) The amount of the other member's basis in the supplies.

(6) *Allocations.*—(i) *Pass-through in the case of an S corporation.*—In the case of an S corporation (as defined in section 1361), the amount of the credit for qualified clinical testing expenses computed for the corporation for any taxable year shall be allocated among the persons who are shareholders of the corporation during the taxable year according to the provisions of section 1366 and section 1377.

(ii) *Pass-through in the case of an estate or a trust.*—In the case of an estate or a trust, the amount of the credit for qualified clinical testing expenses computed for the estate or trust for any taxable year shall be apportioned between the estate or trust and the beneficiaries on the basis of the income of the estate or trust allocable to each.

(iii) *Pass-through in the case of a partnership.*—(A) *In general.*—In the case of a partnership, the credit for qualified clinical testing expenses computed for the partnership for any taxable year shall be apportioned among the persons who are partners during the taxable year in accordance with section 704 and the regulations thereunder.

(B) *Certain partnership non-business expenditures.*—A partner's share of an in-house research expense or contract research expense paid or incurred by a partnership other than in carrying on a trade or business of the partnership constitutes a qualified clinical testing expense of the partner if—

(1) The partner is entitled to make independent use of the result of the clinical testing, and

(2) The clinical testing expense paid or incurred in carrying on the clinical testing would have been paid or incurred by the partner in carrying on a trade or business of the partner if the partner had carried on the clinical testing that was in fact carried on by the partnership.

(C) *Apportionment.*—Qualified clinical testing expenses to which paragraph (d)(6)(iii)(B) of this section applies shall be apportioned among the persons who are partners during the taxable year in accordance with section 704 and the regulations thereunder. For purposes of section 28, these expenses shall be treated as paid or incurred directly by the partners rather than by the partnership. Thus, the partnership shall disregard these expenses in computing the credit to be apportioned under paragraph (d)(6)(iii)(A) of this section, and each partner shall aggregate the portion of these expenses allocated to the partner with other qualified clinical testing expenses of the partner in making the computations under section 28.

(iv) *Year in which taken into account.*—An amount apportioned to a person under paragraph (d)(6) of this section shall be taken into account by the person in the taxable year of such person in which or with which the taxable year of the corporation, estate, trust, or partnership (as the case may be) ends.

(v) *Credit allowed subject to limitation.*—Any person to whom any amount has been apportioned under paragraph (d)(6)(i), (ii), or (iii) of this section is allowed, subject to the limitation provided in section 28(d)(2), a credit for that amount.

(7) *Manner of making an election.*—To make an election to have section 28 apply for its taxable year, the taxpayer shall file Form 6765 (Credit for Increasing Research Activities (or for claiming the orphan drugs credit)) containing all the information required by that form. [Reg. § 1.28-1.]

☐ [T.D. 8232, 9-30-88.]

[Reg. § 1.30-1]

§ 1.30-1. Definition of qualified electric vehicle and recapture of credit for qualified electric vehicle.—(a) *Definition of qualified electric vehicle.*—A qualified electric vehicle is a motor vehicle that meets the requirements of section 30(c). Accordingly, a qualified electric vehicle

does not include any motor vehicle that has ever been used (for either personal or business use) as a non-electric vehicle.

(b) *Recapture of credit for qualified electric vehicle.*—(1) *In general.*—(i) *Addition to tax.*—If a recapture event occurs with respect to a taxpayer's qualified electric vehicle, the taxpayer must add the recapture amount to the amount of tax due in the taxable year in which the recapture event occurs. The recapture amount is not treated as income tax imposed on the taxpayer by chapter 1 of the Internal Revenue Code for purposes of computing the alternative minimum tax or determining the amount of any other allowable credits for the taxable year in which the recapture event occurs.

(ii) *Reduction of carryover.*—If a recapture event occurs with respect to a taxpayer's qualified electric vehicle, and if a portion of the section 30 credit for the cost of that vehicle was disallowed under section 30(b)(3)(B) and consequently added to the taxpayer's minimum tax credit pursuant to section 53(d)(1)(B)(iii), the taxpayer must reduce its minimum tax credit carryover by an amount equal to the portion of any minimum tax credit carryover attributable to the disallowed section 30 credit, multiplied by the recapture percentage for the taxable year of recapture. Similarly, the taxpayer must reduce any other credit carryover amounts (such as under section 469) by the portion of the carryover attributable to section 30, multiplied by the recapture percentage.

(2) *Recapture event.*—(i) *In general.*—A recapture event occurs if, within 3 full years from the date a qualified electric vehicle is placed in service, the vehicle ceases to be a qualified electric vehicle. A vehicle ceases to be a qualified electric vehicle if—

(A) The vehicle is modified so that it is no longer primarily powered by electricity;

(B) The vehicle is used in a manner described in section 50(b); or

(C) The taxpayer receiving the credit under section 30 sells or disposes of the vehicle and knows or has reason to know that the vehicle will be used in a manner described in paragraph (b)(2)(i)(A) or (B) of this section.

(ii) *Exception for disposition.*—Except as provided in paragraph (b)(2)(i)(C) of this section, a sale or other disposition (including a disposition by reason of an accident or other casualty) of a qualified electric vehicle is not a recapture event.

(3) *Recapture amount.*—The recapture amount is equal to the recapture percentage times the decrease in the credits allowed under section 30 for all prior taxable years that would have resulted solely from reducing to zero the cost taken into account under section 30 with respect to such vehicle, including any credits allowed attributable to section 30 (such as under sections 53 and 469).

(4) *Recapture date.*—The recapture date is the actual date of the recapture event unless a recapture event described in paragraph (b)(2)(i)(B) of this section occurs, in which case the recapture date is the first day of the recapture year.

(5) *Recapture percentage.*—For purposes of this section, the recapture percentage is—

(i) 100, if the recapture date is within the first full year after the date the vehicle is placed in service;

(ii) $66^{2}/_{3}$, if the recapture date is within the second full year after the date the vehicle is placed in service; or

(iii) $33^{1}/_{3}$, if the recapture date is within the third full year after the date the vehicle is placed in service.

(6) *Basis adjustment.*—As of the first day of the taxable year in which the recapture event occurs, the basis of the qualified electric vehicle is increased by the recapture amount and the carryover reductions taken into account under paragraphs (b)(1)(i) and (ii) of this section, respectively. For a vehicle that is of a character that is subject to an allowance for depreciation, this increase in basis is recoverable over the remaining recovery period for the vehicle beginning as of the first day of the taxable year of recapture.

(7) *Application of section 1245 for sales and other dispositions.*—For purposes of section 1245, the amount of the credit allowable under section 30(a) with respect to any qualified electric vehicle that is (or has been) of a character subject to an allowance for depreciation is treated as a deduction allowed for depreciation under section 167. Therefore, upon a sale or other disposition of a depreciable qualified electric vehicle, section 1245 will apply to any gain recognized to the extent the basis of the depreciable vehicle was reduced under section 30(d)(1) net of any basis increase described in paragraph (b)(6) of this section.

(8) *Examples.*—The following examples illustrate the provisions of this section:

Example 1. A, a calendar-year taxpayer, purchases and places in service for personal use on January 1, 1995, a qualified electric vehicle costing $25,000. On A's 1995 federal income tax return, A claims a credit of $2,500. On January 2, 1996, A sells the vehicle to an unrelated third party who subsequently converts the vehicle into a non-electric vehicle on October 15, 1996. There is no recapture upon the sale of the vehicle by A provided A did not know or have reason to know that the purchaser intended to convert the vehicle to non-electric use.

Example 2. B, a calendar-year taxpayer, purchases and places in service for personal use on October 11, 1994, a qualified electric vehicle costing $20,000. On B's 1994 federal income tax return, B claims a credit of $2,000, which reduces B's tax by $2,000. The basis of the vehicle is reduced to $18,000 ($20,000 – $2,000). On March 8, 1996, B sells the vehicle to a tax-exempt entity. Because B knowingly sold the vehicle to a tax-exempt entity described in section 50(b) in the second full year from the date the vehicle was placed in service, B must recapture $1,333 ($2,000 × 66²/₃ percent). This recapture amount increases B's tax by $1,333 on B's 1996 federal income tax return and is added to the basis of the vehicle as of January 1, 1996, the beginning of the taxable year in which the recapture event occurred.

Example 3. X, a calendar-year taxpayer, purchases and places in service for business use on January 1, 1994, a qualified electric vehicle costing $30,000. On X's 1994 federal income tax return, X claims a credit of $3,000, which reduces X's tax by $3,000. The basis of the vehicle is reduced to $27,000 ($30,000 – $3,000) prior to any adjustments for depreciation. On March 8, 1995, X converts the qualified electric vehicle into a gasoline-propelled vehicle. Because X modified the vehicle so that it is no longer primarily powered by electricity in the second full year from the date the vehicle was placed in service, X must recapture $2,000 ($3,000 × 66²/₃ percent). This recapture amount increases X's tax by $2,000 on X's 1995 federal income tax return. The recapture amount of $2,000 is added to the basis of the vehicle as of January 1, 1995, the beginning of the taxable year of recapture, and to the extent the property remains depreciable, the adjusted basis is recoverable over the remaining recovery period.

Example 4. The facts are the same as in *Example 3.* In 1996, X sells the vehicle for $31,000, recognizing a gain from this sale. Under paragraph (b)(7) of this section, section 1245 will apply to any gain recognized on the sale of a depreciable vehicle to the extent the basis of the vehicle was reduced by the section 30 credit net of any basis increase from recapture of the section 30 credit. Accordingly, the gain from the sale of the vehicle is subject to section 1245 to the extent of the depreciation allowance for the vehicle plus the credit allowed under section 30 ($3,000), less the previous recapture amount ($2,000). Any remaining amount of gain may be subject to other applicable provisions of the Internal Revenue Code.

(c) *Effective date.*—This section is effective on October 14, 1994. If the recapture date is before the effective date of this section, a taxpayer may use any reasonable method to recapture the benefit of any credit allowable under section 30(a) consistent with section 30 and its legislative history. For this purpose, the recapture date is defined in paragraph (b)(4) of this section. [Reg. § 1.30-1.]

☐ *[T.D. 8606, 8-2-95.]*

[Reg. § 1.31-1]

§ 1.31-1. Credit for tax withheld on wages.—(a) The tax deducted and withheld at the source upon wages under chapter 24 of the Internal Revenue Code of 1954 (or in the case of amounts withheld in 1954, under subchapter D, chapter 9 of the Internal Revenue Code of 1939) is allowable as a credit against the tax imposed by subtitle A of the Internal Revenue Code of 1954, upon the recipient of the income. If the tax has actually been withheld at the source, credit or refund shall be made to the recipient of the income even though such tax has not been paid over to the Government by the employer. For the purpose of the credit, the recipient of the income is the person subject to tax imposed under subtitle A upon the wages from which the tax was withheld. For instance, if a husband and wife domiciled in a State recognized as a community property State for Federal tax purposes make separate returns, each reporting for income tax purposes one-half of the wages received by the husband, each spouse is entitled to one-half of the credit allowable for the tax withheld at source with respect to such wages.

(b) The tax withheld during any calendar year shall be allowed as a credit against the tax imposed by subtitle A for the taxable year of the recipient of the income which begins in that calendar year. If such *recipient has more than one taxable year beginning in that calendar year,* the credit shall be allowed against the tax for the last taxable year so beginning. [Reg. § 1.31-1.]

☐ *[T.D. 6161, 2-3-56.]*

[Reg. § 1.31-2]

§ 1.31-2. Credit for "special refunds" of employee social security tax.—(a) *In general.*—(1) In the case of an employee receiving wages from more than one employer during the calendar year, amounts may be deducted and withheld as employee social security tax with respect to more than $3,600 of wages received during the calendar year 1954, and with respect to more than $4,200 of wages received during a calendar year after 1954. For example, employee social security tax may be deducted and withheld on $5,000 of wages received by an employee during a particular calendar year if the employee is paid wages in such year in the amount of $3,000 by one employer and in the amount of $2,000 by another employer. Section 6413(c) (as amended by section 202 of the Social Security Amendments of 1954 (68 Stat. 1089)), permits, under certain conditions, a so-called "special refund" of the amount of employee social security tax deducted and withheld with respect to wages paid to an employee in a calendar year after 1954 in excess of $4,200 ($3,600 for the calendar year 1954) by reason of the employee receiving wages from more than one employer during the calendar year. For provisions relating to the imposition of the employee tax and the limitation on wages, see with respect to the calendar year 1954, sections 1400 and 1426(a)(1) of the Internal Revenue Code of 1939 and, with respect to calendar years after 1954, sections 3101 and 3121(a)(1) of the Internal Revenue Code of 1954, as amended by sections 208(b) and 204(a), respectively, of the Social Security Amendments of 1954 (68 Stat. 1094, 1091).

(2) An employee who is entitled to a special refund of employee tax with respect to wages received during a calendar year and who is also required to file an income tax return for such calendar year (or for his last taxable year beginning in such calendar year) may obtain the benefits of such special refund only by claiming credit for such special refund in the same manner as if such special refund were an amount deducted and withheld as income tax at the source. For provisions for claiming special refunds for 1955 and subsequent years in the case of employees not required to file income tax returns, see section 6413(c) and the regulations thereunder. For provisions relating to such refunds for 1954, see 26 CFR (1939) § 408.802 (Regulations 128).

(3) The amount of the special refund allowed as a credit shall be considered as an amount deducted and withheld as income tax at the source under chapter 24 of the Internal Revenue Code of 1954, (or, in the case of a special refund for 1954, subchapter D, chapter 9 of the Internal Revenue Code of 1939). If the amount of such special refund when added to amounts deducted and withheld as income tax exceeds the taxes imposed by subtitle A of the Internal Revenue Code of 1954, the amount of the excess constitutes an overpayment of income tax under subtitle A, and interest on such overpayment is allowed to the extent provided under section 6611 upon an overpayment of income tax resulting from a credit for income tax withheld at source. See section 6401(b).

(b) *Federal and State employees and employees of certain foreign corporations.*—The provisions of this section shall apply to the amount of a special refund allowable to an employee of a Federal agency or a wholly owned instrumentality of the United States, to the amount of a special refund allowable to an employee of any State or political subdivision thereof (or any instrumentality of any one or more of the foregoing), and to the amount of a special refund allowable to employees of certain foreign corporations. See, with respect to such special refunds for 1954, section 1401(d)(4) of the Internal Revenue Code of 1939, and with respect to such special refunds for 1955 and subsequent years, section 6413(c)(2) of the Internal Revenue Code of 1954, as amended by section 202 of the Social Security Amendments of 1954. [Reg. § 1.31-2.]

☐ *[T.D. 6161, 2-3-56.]*

[Reg. § 1.32-2]

§ 1.32-2. Earned income credit for taxable years beginning after December 31, 1978.—(a) [Reserved].

(b) *Limitations.*—(1) [Reserved].

(2) *Married individuals.*—No credit is allowed by section 32 in the case of an eligible individual who is married (within the meaning of section 7703 and the regulations thereunder) unless the individual and spouse file a single return jointly (a joint return) for the taxable year (see section 6013 and the regulations thereunder relating to joint returns of income tax by husband and wife). The requirements of the preceding sentence do not apply to an eligible individual who is not considered as married under section 7703(b) and the regulations thereunder (relating to certain married individuals living apart).

(3) *Length of taxable year.*—No credit is allowed by section 32 in the case of a taxable year covering a period of less than 12 months.

However, the rule of the preceding sentence does not apply to a taxable year closed by reason of the death of the eligible individual.

(c) *Definitions.*—(1) [Reserved].

(2) *Earned income.*—For purposes of this section, earned income is computed without regard to any community property laws which may otherwise be applicable. Earned income is reduced by any net loss in earnings from self-employment. Earned income does not include amounts received as a pension, an annuity, unemployment compensation, or workmen's compensation, or an amount to which section 871(a) and the regulations thereunder apply (relating to income of nonresident alien individuals not connected with United States business).

(d) [Reserved].

(e) *Coordination of credit with advance payments.*—(1) *Recapture of excess advance payments.*—If any advance payment of earned income credit under section 3507 is made to an individual by an employer during any calendar year, then the total amount of these advance payments to the individual in that calendar year is treated as an additional amount of tax imposed (by Chapter 1 of the Code) upon the individual on the tax return for the individual's last taxable year beginning in that calendar year.

(2) *Reconciliation of payments advanced and credit allowed.*—Any additional amount of tax under paragraph (e)(1) of this section is not treated as a tax imposed by chapter 1 of the Internal Revenue Code for purposes of determining the amount of any credit (other than the earned income credit) allowable under part IV, subchapter A, chapter 1 of the Internal Revenue Code. [Reg. § 1.32-2.]

☐ [T.D. 7683, 3-12-80. *Redesignated by T.D.* 8448, 11-20-92. *Amended by T.D. 9045, 3-5-2003.*]

[Reg. § 1.32-3.]

§ 1.32-3. Eligibility requirements after denial of the earned income credit.—(a) *In general.*—A taxpayer who has been denied the earned income credit (EIC), in whole or in part, as a result of the deficiency procedures under subchapter B of chapter 63 (deficiency procedures) is ineligible to file a return claiming the EIC subsequent to the denial until the taxpayer demonstrates eligibility for the EIC in accordance with paragraph (c) of this section. If a taxpayer demonstrates eligibility for a taxable year in accordance with paragraph (c) of this section, the taxpayer need not comply with those requirements for any subsequent taxable year unless the Service again denies the EIC as a result of the deficiency procedures.

(b) *Denial of the EIC as a result of the deficiency procedures.*—For purposes of this section, denial of the EIC as a result of the deficiency procedures occurs when a tax on account of the EIC is assessed as a deficiency (other than as a mathematical or clerical error under section 6213(b)(1)).

(c) *Demonstration of eligibility.*—In the case of a taxpayer to whom paragraph (a) of this section applies, and except as otherwise provided by the Commissioner in the instructions for Form 8862, "Information To Claim Earned Income Credit After Disallowance," no claim for the EIC filed subsequent to the denial is allowed unless the taxpayer properly completes Form 8862, demonstrating eligibility for the EIC, and otherwise is eligible for the EIC. If any item of information on Form 8862 is incorrect or inconsistent with any item on the return, the taxpayer will be treated as not demonstrating eligibility for the EIC. The taxpayer must follow the instructions for Form 8862 to determine the income tax return to which Form 8862 must be attached. If the taxpayer attaches Form 8862 to an incorrect tax return, the taxpayer will not be relieved of the requirement that the taxpayer attach Form 8862 to the correct tax return and will, therefore, not be treated as meeting the taxpayer's obligation under paragraph (a) of this section.

(d) *Failure to demonstrate eligibility.*—If a taxpayer to whom paragraph (a) of this section applies fails to satisfy the requirements of paragraph (c) of this section with respect to a particular taxable year, the IRS can deny the EIC as a mathematical or clerical error under section 6213(g)(2)(K).

(e) *Special rule where one spouse denied EIC.*—The eligibility requirements set forth in this section apply to taxpayers filing a joint return where one spouse was denied the EIC for a taxable year prior to marriage and has not established eligibility as either an unmarried or married taxpayer for a subsequent taxable year.

(f) *Effective date.*—This section applies to returns claiming the EIC for taxable years beginning after December 31, 1997, where the EIC was denied for a taxable year beginning after December 31, 1996. [Reg. § 1.32-3.]

☐ [T.D. 8953, 6-22-2001.]

[Reg. § 1.34-1]

§ 1.34-1. Special rule for owners of certain business entities.—Amounts payable under sections 6420, 6421, and 6427 to a business entity that is treated as separate from its owner under § 1.1361-4(a)(8) (relating to certain qualified subchapter S subsidiaries) or § 301.7701-2(c)(2)(v) of this chapter (relating to certain wholly-owned entities) are, for purposes of section 34, treated as payable to the owner of that entity. [Reg. § 1.34-1.]

☐ [T.D. 9356, 8-15-2007.]

[Reg. § 1.36B-0]

§ 1.36B-0. Table of contents.—This section lists the captions contained in §§ 1.36B-1 through 1.36B-6.

(i) In general.
(ii) Withdrawal of consent.
(iii) Change in hardware or software requirements.
(iv) Examples.
(3) Required disclosures.
(i) In general.
(ii) Paper statement.
(iii) Scope and duration of consent.
(iv) Post-consent request for a paper statement.
(v) Withdrawal of consent.
(vi) Notice of termination.
(vii) Updating information.
(viii) Hardware and software requirements.
(4) Format.
(5) Notice.
(i) In general.
(ii) Undeliverable electronic address.
(iii) Corrected statement.
(6) Access period.
(7) Paper statements after withdrawal of consent.
§ 1.36B-6 *Minimum value.*
(a) In general.
(1) Employees.
(2) Related individuals
(i) In general.
(ii) Plans providing MV to employees.
(b) MV standard population.
(c) MV percentage.
(1) In general.
(2) Wellness program incentives.
(i) In general.
(ii) Example.
(3) Employer contributions to health savings accounts.
(4) Employer contributions to health reimbursement arrangements.
(5) Expected spending adjustments for health savings accounts and health reimbursement arrangements.
(d) Methods for determining MV.
(e) Scope of essential health benefits and adjustment for benefits not included in MV Calculator.
(f) Actuarial certification.
(1) In general.
(2) Membership in American Academy of Actuaries.
(3) Actuarial analysis.
(4) Use of MV Calculator.
(g) Effective/applicability date.
(1) In general.
(2) Exceptions. [Reg. § 1.36B-0.]

☐ [*T.D. 9590, 5-18-2012. Amended by T.D. 9663, 5-2-2014, T.D. 9745, 12-16-2015, T.D. 9804, 12-14-2016, T.D. 9822, 7-24-2017, T.D. 9867, 6-13-2019, T.D. 9912, 11-27-2020, T.D. 9912, 11-27-2020 and T.D. 9968, 10-11-2022.*]

[Reg. § 1.36B-1]

§ 1.36B-1. Premium tax credit definitions.—(a) *In general.*—Section 36B allows a refundable premium tax credit for taxable years ending after December 31, 2013. The definitions in this section apply to this section and § § 1.36B-2 through 1.36B-5.

(b) *Affordable Care Act.*—The term *Affordable Care Act* refers to the Patient Protection and Affordable Care Act, Public Law 111-148 (124 Stat. 119 (2010)), and the Health Care and Education Reconciliation Act of 2010, Public Law 111-152 (124 Stat. 1029 (2010)), as amended by the Medicare and Medicaid Extenders Act of 2010, Public Law 111-309 (124 Stat. 3285 (2010)), the Comprehensive 1099 Taxpayer Protection and Repayment of Exchange Subsidy Overpayments Act of 2011, Public Law 112-9 (125 Stat. 36 (2011)), the Department of Defense and Full-Year Continuing Appropriations Act, 2011, Public Law 112-10 (125 Stat. 38 (2011)), and the 3% Withholding Repeal and Job Creation Act, Public Law 112-56 (125 Stat. 711 (2011)).

(c) *Qualified health plan.*—The term *qualified health plan* has the same meaning as in section 1301(a) of the Affordable Care Act (42 U.S.C. 18021(a)) but does not include a catastrophic plan described in section 1302(e) of the Affordable Care Act (42 U.S.C. 18022(e)).

(d) *Family and family size.*—(1) *In general.*—A taxpayer's family means the individuals for whom a taxpayer properly claims a deduction for a personal exemption under section 151 for the taxable year. Family size means the number of individuals in the family. Family and family size may include individuals who are not subject to or are exempt from the penalty under section 5000A for failing to maintain minimum essential coverage.

(2) *Special rule for tax years to which section 151(d)(5) applies.*—For taxable years to which section 151(d)(5) applies, a taxpayer's family means the taxpayer, including both spouses in the case of a joint return, except for individuals who qualify as a dependent of another taxpayer under section 152, and any other individual for whom the taxpayer is allowed a personal exemption deduction and whom the taxpayer properly reports on the taxpayer's income tax return for the taxable year. For purposes of this paragraph (d)(2), an individual is reported on the taxpayer's income tax return if the individual's name and taxpayer identification number (TIN) are listed on the taxpayer's Form 1040 series return. *See* § 601.602 of this chapter.

(e) *Household income.*—(1) *In general.*—Household income means the sum of—

(i) A taxpayer's modified adjusted gross income (including the modified adjusted gross income of a child for whom an election under section 1(g)(7) is made for the taxable year);

(ii) The aggregate modified adjusted gross income of all other individuals who—

(A) Are included in the taxpayer's family under paragraph (d) of this section; and

(B) Are required to file a return of tax imposed by section 1 for the taxable year.

(2) *Modified adjusted gross income.*—Modified adjusted gross income means adjusted gross income (within the meaning of section 62) increased by—

(i) Amounts excluded from gross income under section 911;

(ii) Tax-exempt interest the taxpayer receives or accrues during the taxable year; and

(iii) Social security benefits (within the meaning of section 86(d)) not included in gross income under section 86.

(f) *Dependent.*—Dependent has the same meaning as in section 152.

(g) *Lawfully present.*—Lawfully present has the same meaning as in 45 CFR 155.20.

(h) *Federal poverty line.*—The Federal poverty line means the most recently published poverty guidelines (updated periodically in the **Federal Register** by the Secretary of Health and Human Services under the authority of 42 U.S.C. 9902(2)) as of the first day of the regular enrollment period for coverage by a qualified health plan offered through an Exchange for a calendar year. Thus, the Federal poverty line for computing the premium tax credit for a taxable year is the Federal poverty line in effect on the first day of the initial or annual open enrollment period preceding that taxable year. See 45 CFR 155.410. If a taxpayer's primary residence changes during a taxable year from one state to a state with different Federal poverty guidelines or married taxpayers reside in separate states with different Federal poverty guidelines (for example, Alaska or Hawaii and another state), the Federal poverty line that applies for purposes of section 36B and the associated regulations is the higher Federal poverty guideline (resulting in a lower percentage of the Federal poverty line for the taxpayers' household income and family size).

(i) [Reserved]

(j) *Advance credit payment.*—Advance credit payment means an advance payment of the premium tax credit as provided in section 1412 of the Affordable Care Act (42 U.S.C. 18082).

(k) *Exchange.*—Exchange has the same meaning as in 45 CFR 155.20.

(l) *Self-only coverage.*—Self-only coverage means health insurance that covers one individual and provides coverage for the essential health benefits as defined in section 1302(b)(1) of the Affordable Care Act (42 U.S.C. 18022).

(m) *Family coverage.*—Family coverage means health insurance that covers more than one individual and provides coverage for the essential health benefits as defined in section 1302(b)(1) of the Affordable Care Act (42 U.S.C. 18022).

(n) *Rating area.*—The term *rating area* has the same meaning as used in section 2701(a)(2) of the Public Health Service Act (42 U.S.C. 300gg(a)(2)) and 45 CFR 147.102(b).

(o) *Applicability dates.*—(1) Except for paragraphs (d)(2), (l), and (m) of this section, this section applies to taxable years ending after December 31, 2013.

(2) Paragraph (d)(2) of this section applies to taxable years ending on or after December 31, 2020.

(3) Paragraphs (l) and (m) of this section apply to taxable years beginning after December 31, 2018. Paragraphs (l) and (m) of

§1.36B-1 as contained in 26 CFR part 1 edition revised as of April 1, 2016, apply to taxable years ending after December 31, 2013, and beginning before January 1, 2019. [Reg. §1.36B-1.]

□ [T.D. 9590, 5-18-2012. *Amended by T.D. 9745, 12-16-2015, T.D. 9804, 12-14-2016 and T.D. 9912, 11-27-2020.]*

⫸→ *Caution: The amendments made to Reg. §1.36B-2, below, by T.D. 9867 generally apply for tax years beginning on or after January 1, 2020; see Reg. §1.36B-2(e)(3), below, for details.*

[Reg. §1.36B-2]

§1.36B-2. Eligibility for premium tax credit.—(a) *In general.*—An applicable taxpayer (within the meaning of paragraph (b) of this section) is allowed a premium assistance amount only for any month that one or more members of the applicable taxpayer's family (the applicable taxpayer or the applicable taxpayer's spouse or dependent)—

(1) Is enrolled in one or more qualified health plans through an Exchange; and

(2) Is not eligible for minimum essential coverage (within the meaning of paragraph (c) of this section) other than coverage described in section 5000A(f)(1)(C) (relating to coverage in the individual market).

(b) *Applicable taxpayer.*—(1) *In general.*—Except as otherwise provided in this paragraph (b), an applicable taxpayer is a taxpayer whose household income is at least 100 percent but not more than 400 percent of the Federal poverty line for the taxpayer's family size for the taxable year.

(2) *Married taxpayers must file joint return.*—(i) *In general.*—Except as provided in paragraph (b)(2)(ii) of this section, a taxpayer who is married (within the meaning of section 7703) at the close of the taxable year is an applicable taxpayer only if the taxpayer and the taxpayer's spouse file a joint return for the taxable year.

(ii) *Victims of domestic abuse and abandonment.*—Except as provided in paragraph (b)(2)(v) of this section, a married taxpayer satisfies the joint filing requirement of paragraph (b)(2)(i) of this section if the taxpayer files a tax return using a filing status of married filing separately and the taxpayer—

(A) Is living apart from the taxpayer's spouse at the time the taxpayer files the tax return;

(B) Is unable to file a joint return because the taxpayer is a victim of domestic abuse, as described in paragraph (b)(2)(iii) of this section, or spousal abandonment, as described in paragraph (b)(2)(iv) of this section; and

(C) Certifies on the return, in accordance with the relevant instructions, that the taxpayer meets the criteria of this paragraph (b)(2)(ii).

(iii) *Domestic abuse.*—For purposes of paragraph (b)(2)(ii) of this section, domestic abuse includes physical, psychological, sexual, or emotional abuse, including efforts to control, isolate, humiliate, and intimidate, or to undermine the victim's ability to reason independently. All the facts and circumstances are considered in determining whether an individual is abused, including the effects of alcohol or drug abuse by the victim's spouse. Depending on the facts and circumstances, abuse of the victim's child or another family member living in the household may constitute abuse of the victim.

(iv) *Abandonment.*—For purposes of paragraph (b)(2)(ii) of this section, a taxpayer is a victim of spousal abandonment for a taxable year if, taking into account all facts and circumstances, the taxpayer is unable to locate his or her spouse after reasonable diligence.

(v) *Three-year rule.*—Paragraph (b)(2)(ii) of this section does not apply if the taxpayer met the requirements of paragraph (b)(2)(ii) of this section for each of the three preceding taxable years.

(3) *Dependents.*—An individual is not an applicable taxpayer if another taxpayer may claim a deduction under section 151 for the individual for a taxable year beginning in the calendar year in which the individual's taxable year begins.

(4) *Individuals not lawfully present or incarcerated.*—An individual who is not lawfully present in the United States or is incarcerated (other than incarceration pending disposition of charges) is not eligible to enroll in a qualified health plan through an Exchange. However, the individual may be an applicable taxpayer if a family member is eligible to enroll in a qualified health plan. See sections 1312(f)(1)(B) and 1312(f)(3) of the Affordable Care Act (42 U.S.C. 18032(f)(1)(B) and (f)(3)) and §1.36B-3(b)(2).

(5) *Individuals lawfully present.*—If a taxpayer's household income is less than 100 percent of the Federal poverty line for the taxpayer's family size and the taxpayer or a member of the taxpayer's family is an alien lawfully present in the United States, the taxpayer is treated as an applicable taxpayer if—

(i) The lawfully present taxpayer or family member is not eligible for the Medicaid program; and

(ii) The taxpayer would be an applicable taxpayer if the taxpayer's household income for the taxable year was between 100 and 400 percent of the Federal poverty line for the taxpayer's family size.

(6) *Special rule for taxpayers with household income below 100 percent of the Federal poverty line for the taxable year.*—(i) *In general.*—A taxpayer (other than a taxpayer described in paragraph (b)(5) of this section) whose household income for a taxable year is less than 100 percent of the Federal poverty line for the taxpayer's family size is treated as an applicable taxpayer for the taxable year if—

(A) The taxpayer or a family member enrolls in a qualified health plan through an Exchange for one or more months during the taxable year;

(B) An Exchange estimates at the time of enrollment that the taxpayer's household income will be at least 100 percent but not more than 400 percent of the Federal poverty line for the taxable year;

(C) Advance credit payments are authorized and paid for one or more months during the taxable year; and

(D) The taxpayer would be an applicable taxpayer if the taxpayer's household income for the taxable year was at least 100 but not more than 400 percent of the Federal poverty line for the taxpayer's family size.

(ii) *Exceptions.*—This paragraph (b)(6) does not apply for an individual who, with intentional or reckless disregard for the facts, provides incorrect information to an Exchange for the year of coverage. A reckless disregard of the facts occurs if the taxpayer makes little or no effort to determine whether the information provided to the Exchange is accurate under circumstances that demonstrate a substantial deviation from the standard of conduct a reasonable person would observe. A disregard of the facts is intentional if the taxpayer knows the information provided to the Exchange is inaccurate.

(iii) Advance credit payments are authorized and paid for one or more months during the taxable year; and

(iv) The taxpayer would be an applicable taxpayer if the taxpayer's household income for the taxable year was between 100 and 400 percent of the Federal poverty line for the taxpayer's family size.

(7) *Computation of premium assistance amounts for taxpayers with household income below 100 percent of the Federal poverty line.*—If a taxpayer is treated as an applicable taxpayer under paragraph (b)(5) or (b)(6) of this section, the taxpayer's actual household income for the taxable year is used to compute the premium assistance amounts under §1.36B-3(d).

(c) *Minimum essential coverage.*—(1) *In general.*—Minimum essential coverage is defined in section 5000A(f) and regulations issued under that section. As described in section 5000A(f), government-sponsored programs, eligible employer-sponsored plans, grandfathered health plans, and certain other health benefits coverage are minimum essential coverage.

(2) *Government-sponsored minimum essential coverage.*—(i) *In general.*—An individual is eligible for government-sponsored minimum essential coverage if the individual meets the criteria for coverage under a government-sponsored program described in section 5000A(f)(1)(A) as of the first day of the first full month the individual may receive benefits under the program, subject to the limitation in paragraph (c)(2)(ii) of this section. The Commissioner may define eligibility for specific governmentsponsored programs further in additional published guidance, see §601.601(d)(2) of this chapter.

(ii) *Obligation to complete administrative requirements to obtain coverage.*—An individual who meets the criteria for eligibility for government-sponsored minimum essential coverage must complete the requirements necessary to receive benefits. An individual who fails by the last day of the third full calendar month following the event that establishes eligibility under paragraph (c)(2)(i) of this section to complete the requirements to obtain government-sponsored minimum essential coverage (other than a veteran's health care program) is treated as eligible for government-sponsored minimum essential coverage as of the first day of the fourth calendar month following the event that establishes eligibility.

(iii) *Special rule for coverage for veterans and other individuals under chapter 17 or 18 of Title 38, U.S.C.*—An individual is eligible for minimum essential coverage under a health care program under chapter 17 or 18 of Title 38, U.S.C. only if the individual is enrolled in

>>>→ *Caution: The amendments made to Reg. §1.36B-2, below, by T.D. 9867 generally apply for tax years beginning on or after January 1, 2020; see Reg. §1.36B-2(e)(3), below, for details.*

a health care program under chapter 17 or 18 of Title 38, U.S.C. identified as minimum essential coverage in regulations issued under section 5000A.

(iv) *Retroactive effect of eligibility determination.*—If an individual receiving advance credit payments is determined to be eligible for government-sponsored minimum essential coverage that is effective retroactively (such as Medicaid), the individual is treated as eligible for minimum essential coverage under that program no earlier than the first day of the first calendar month beginning after the approval.

(v) *Determination of Medicaid or Children's Health Insurance Program (CHIP) ineligibility.*—An individual is treated as not eligible for Medicaid, CHIP, or a similar program for a period of coverage under a qualified health plan if, when the individual enrolls in the qualified health plan, an Exchange determines or considers (within the meaning of 45 CFR 155.302(b)) the individual to be not eligible for Medicaid or CHIP. This paragraph (c)(2)(v) does not apply for an individual who, with intentional or reckless disregard for the facts, provides incorrect information to an Exchange for the year of coverage. A reckless disregard of the facts occurs if the taxpayer makes little or no effort to determine whether the information provided to the Exchange is accurate under circumstances that demonstrate a substantial deviation from the standard of conduct a reasonable person would observe. A disregard of the facts is intentional if the taxpayer knows that information provided to the Exchange is inaccurate.

(vi) *Examples.*—The following examples illustrate the provisions of this paragraph (c)(2):

Example 1. Delay in coverage effectiveness. On April 10, 2015, Taxpayer D applies for coverage under a government-sponsored health care program. D's application is approved on July 12, 2015, but her coverage is not effective until September 1, 2015. Under paragraph (c)(2)(i) of this section, D is eligible for government-sponsored minimum essential coverage on September 1, 2015.

Example 2. Time of eligibility. Taxpayer E turns 65 on June 3, 2015, and becomes eligible for Medicare. Under section 5000A(f)(1)(A)(i), Medicare is minimum essential coverage. However, E must enroll in Medicare to receive benefits. E enrolls in Medicare in September, which is the last month of E's initial enrollment period. Thus, E may receive Medicare benefits on December 1, 2015. Because E completed the requirements necessary to receive Medicare benefits by the last day of the third full calendar month after the event that establishes E's eligibility (E turning 65), under paragraph (c)(2)(i) and (c)(2)(ii) of this section E is eligible for government-sponsored minimum essential coverage on December 1, 2015, the first day of the first full month that E may receive benefits under the program.

Example 3. Time of eligibility, individual fails to complete necessary requirements. The facts are the same as in *Example 2*, except that E fails to enroll in the Medicare coverage during E's initial enrollment period. E is treated as eligible for government-sponsored minimum essential coverage under paragraph (c)(2)(ii) of this section as of October 1, 2015, the first day of the fourth month following the event that establishes E's eligibility (E turning 65).

Example 4. Retroactive effect of eligibility. In November 2014, Taxpayer F enrolls in a qualified health plan for 2015 and receives advance credit payments. F loses her part-time employment and on April 10, 2015 applies for coverage under the Medicaid program. F's application is approved on May 15, 2015, and her Medicaid coverage is effective as of April 1, 2015. Under paragraph (c)(2)(iv) of this section, F is eligible for government-sponsored minimum essential coverage on June 1, 2015, the first day of the first calendar month after approval.

Example 5. Determination of Medicaid ineligibility. In November 2014, Taxpayer G applies through the Exchange to enroll in health coverage for 2015. The Exchange determines that G is not eligible for Medicaid and estimates that G's household income will be 140 percent of the Federal poverty line for G's family size for purposes of determining advance credit payments. G enrolls in a qualified health plan and begins receiving advance credit payments. G experiences a reduction in household income during the year and his household income for 2015 is 130 percent of the Federal poverty line (within the Medicaid income threshold). However, under paragraph (c)(2)(v) of this section, G is treated as not eligible for Medicaid for 2015.

Example 6. Mid-year Medicaid eligibility redetermination. The facts are the same as in *Example 5*, except that G returns to the Exchange in July 2015 and the Exchange determines that G is eligible for Medicaid. Medicaid approves G for coverage and the Exchange discontinues G's advance credit payments effective August 1. Under paragraphs (c)(2)(iv) and (c)(2)(v) of this section, G is treated as not eligible for Medicaid for the months when G is covered by a qualified

health plan. G is eligible for government-sponsored minimum essential coverage for the months after G is approved for Medicaid and can receive benefits, August through December 2015.

(3) *Employer-sponsored minimum essential coverage.*—(i) *In general.*—(A) *Plans other than health reimbursement arrangements (HRAs) or other account-based group health plans described in paragraph (c)(3)(i)(B) of this section.*—For purposes of section 36B, an employee who may enroll in an eligible employer-sponsored plan (as defined in section 5000A(f)(2) and the regulations under that section) that is minimum essential coverage, and an individual who may enroll in the plan because of a relationship to the employee (a related individual), are eligible for minimum essential coverage under the plan for any month only if the plan is affordable and provides minimum value. Except for the Nonappropriated Fund Health Benefits Program of the Department of Defense, established under section 349 of the National Defense Authorization Act for Fiscal Year 1995 (Public Law 103–337; 10 U.S.C. 1587 note), government-sponsored minimum essential coverage is not an eligible employer-sponsored plan. The Nonappropriated Fund Health Benefits Program of the Department of Defense is considered eligible employer-sponsored coverage, but not government-sponsored coverage, for purposes of determining if an individual is eligible for minimum essential coverage under this section.

(B) *HRAs and other account-based group health plans integrated with individual health insurance coverage.*—An employee who is offered an HRA or other account-based group health plan that would be integrated with individual health insurance coverage (or Medicare Part A and B or Medicare Part C), within the meaning of §§54.9802-4 and 54.9815-2711(d)(4) of this chapter, if the employee enrolls in individual health insurance coverage (or Medicare Part A and B or Medicare Part C), and an individual who is offered the HRA or other account-based group health plan because of a relationship to the employee (a related HRA individual), are eligible for minimum essential coverage under an eligible employer-sponsored plan for any month for which the HRA or other account-based group health plan is offered if the HRA or other account-based group health plan is affordable for the month under paragraph (c)(5) of this section or if the employee does not opt out of and waive future reimbursements from the HRA or other account-based group health plan. An HRA or other account-based group health plan described in this paragraph (c)(3)(i)(B) that is affordable for a month under paragraph (c)(5) of this section is treated as providing minimum value for the month. For purposes of paragraphs (c)(3) and (5) of this section, the definitions under §54.9815-2711(d)(6) of this chapter apply.

(ii) *Plan year.*—For purposes of this paragraph (c)(3), a plan year is an eligible employer-sponsored plan's regular 12-month coverage period (or the remainder of a 12-month coverage period for a new employee or an individual who enrolls during a special enrollment period). The plan year for an HRA or other account-based group health plan described in paragraph (c)(3)(i)(B) of this section is the plan's 12-month coverage period (or the remainder of the 12-month coverage period for a newly eligible individual or an individual who enrolls during a special enrollment period).

(iii) *Eligibility for months during a plan year.*—(A) *Failure to enroll in plan.*—An employee or related individual may be eligible for minimum essential coverage under an eligible employer-sponsored plan for a month during a plan year if the employee or related individual could have enrolled in the plan for that month during an open or special enrollment period for the plan year. If an enrollment period relates to coverage for not only the upcoming plan year (or the current plan year in the case of an enrollment period other than an open enrollment period), but also coverage in one or more succeeding plan years, this paragraph (c)(3)(iii)(A) applies only to eligibility for the coverage in the upcoming plan year (or the current plan year in the case of an enrollment period other than an open enrollment period).

(B) *Waiting periods.*—An employee or related individual is not eligible for minimum essential coverage under an eligible employer-sponsored plan during a required waiting period before the coverage becomes effective.

(C) *Example.*—The following example illustrates the provisions of this paragraph (c)(3)(iii):

Example. (i) Taxpayer B is an employee of Employer X. X offers its employees a health insurance plan that has a plan year (within the meaning of paragraph (c)(3)(ii) of this section) from October 1 through September 30. Employees may enroll during an open season from August 1 to September 15. B does not enroll in X's plan for the plan year October 1, 2014, to September 30, 2015. In

Caution: *The amendments made to Reg. §1.36B-2, below, by T.D. 9867 generally apply for tax years beginning on or after January 1, 2020; see Reg. §1.36B-2(e)(3), below, for details.*

November 2014, B enrolls in a qualified health plan through an Exchange for calendar year 2015.

(ii) B could have enrolled in X's plan during the August 1 to September 15 enrollment period. Therefore, unless X's plan is not affordable for B or does not provide minimum value, B is eligible for minimum essential coverage under X's plan for the months that B is enrolled in the qualified health plan during X's plan year (January through September 2015).

(iv) Post-employment coverage.—A former employee (including a retiree), or an individual related (within the meaning of paragraph (c)(3)(i) of this section) to a former employee, who may enroll in eligible employer-sponsored coverage or in continuation coverage required under Federal law or a State law that provides comparable continuation coverage is eligible for minimum essential coverage under this coverage only for months that the former employee or related individual is enrolled in the coverage.

(v) Affordable coverage.—(A) *In general.*—(1) *Affordability for employee.*—Except as provided in paragraph (c)(3)(v)(A)(3) of this section, an eligible employer-sponsored plan is affordable for an employee if the portion of the annual premium the employee must pay, whether by salary reduction or otherwise (required contribution), for self-only coverage does not exceed the required contribution percentage (as defined in paragraph (c)(3)(v)(C) of this section) of the applicable taxpayer's household income for the taxable year. See paragraph (c)(5) of this section for rules for when an HRA or other account-based group health plan described in paragraph (c)(3)(i)(B) of this section is affordable for an employee for a month.

(2) Affordability for related individual.—Except as provided in paragraph (c)(3)(v)(A)(3) of this section, an eligible employer-sponsored plan is affordable for a related individual if the employee's required contribution for family coverage under the plan does not exceed the required contribution percentage, as defined in paragraph (c)(3)(v)(C) of this section, of the applicable taxpayer's household income for the taxable year. For purposes of this paragraph (c)(3)(v)(A)(2), an employee's required contribution for family coverage is the portion of the annual premium the employee must pay for coverage of the employee and all other individuals included in the employee's family, as defined in §1.36B-1(d), who are offered coverage under the eligible employer-sponsored plan.

(3) Employee safe harbor.—An eligible employer-sponsored plan is not affordable for an employee or a related individual for a plan year if, when the employee or a related individual enrolls in a qualified health plan for a period coinciding with the plan year (in whole or in part), an Exchange determines that the eligible employer-sponsored plan is not affordable for that plan year. This paragraph (c)(3)(v)(A)(3) does not apply to a determination made as part of the redetermination process described in 45 CFR 155.335 unless the individual receiving an Exchange redetermination notification affirmatively responds and provides current information about affordability. This paragraph (c)(3)(v)(A)(3) does not apply for an individual who, with intentional or reckless disregard for the facts, provides incorrect information to an Exchange concerning the portion of the annual premium for coverage for the employee or related individual under the plan. A reckless disregard of the facts occurs if the taxpayer makes little or no effort to determine whether the information provided to the Exchange is accurate under circumstances that demonstrate a substantial deviation from the standard of conduct a reasonable person would observe. A disregard of the facts is intentional if the taxpayer knows that the information provided to the Exchange is inaccurate. See paragraph (c)(5) of this section for an employee safe harbor that applies when an Exchange determines that an HRA or other account-based group health plan described in paragraph (c)(3)(i)(B) of this section is not affordable for an employee or a related HRA individual for the period of enrollment in a qualified health plan.

(4) Wellness program incentives.—Nondiscriminatory wellness program incentives offered by an eligible employer-sponsored plan that affect premiums are treated as earned in determining an employee's required contribution for purposes of affordability of an eligible employer-sponsored plan to the extent the incentives relate exclusively to tobacco use. Wellness program incentives that do not relate to tobacco use or that include a component unrelated to tobacco use are treated as not earned for this purpose. For purposes of this section, the term *wellness program incentive* has the same meaning as the term *reward* in §54.9802–1(f)(1)(i) of this chapter.

(5) Employer contributions to HRAs integrated with eligible employer-sponsored plans.—Amounts newly made available for the current plan year under an HRA that an employee may use to pay premiums, or may use to pay cost-sharing or benefits not covered by the primary plan in addition to premiums, reduce the employee's required contribution if the HRA would be integrated, within the meaning of §54.9815-2711(d)(2) of this chapter, with an eligible employer-sponsored plan for an employee enrolled in the plan. The eligible employer-sponsored plan and the HRA must be offered by the same employer. Employer contributions to an HRA described in this paragraph (c)(3)(v)(A)(5) reduce an employee's required contribution only to the extent the amount of the annual contribution is required under the terms of the plan or otherwise determinable within a reasonable time before the employee must decide whether to enroll in the eligible employer-sponsored plan.

(6) Employer contributions to cafeteria plans.—Amounts made available for the current plan year under a cafeteria plan, within the meaning of section 125, reduce an employee's or a related individual's required contribution if—

(i) The employee may not opt to receive the amount as a taxable benefit;

(ii) The employee may use the amount to pay for minimum essential coverage; and

(iii) The employee may use the amount exclusively to pay for medical care, within the meaning of section 213.

(7) Opt-out arrangements.—[Reserved]

(8) Multiple offers of coverage. An individual who has offers of coverage under eligible employer-sponsored plans from multiple employers, either as an employee or a related individual, has an offer of affordable coverage if at least one of the offers of coverage is affordable under paragraph (c)(3)(v)(A)(1) or (2) of this section.

(B) Affordability for part-year period.—Affordability under paragraph (c)(3)(v)(A) of this section is determined separately for each employment period that is less than a full calendar year or for the portions of an employer's plan year that fall in different taxable years of an applicable taxpayer (a part-year period). Coverage under an eligible employer-sponsored plan is affordable for a part-year period if the annualized required contribution for self-only coverage, in the case of an employee, or family coverage, in the case of a related individual, under the plan for the part-year period does not exceed the required contribution percentage of the applicable taxpayer's household income for the taxable year. The employee's annualized required contribution is the employee's required contribution for the part-year period times a fraction, the numerator of which is 12 and the denominator of which is the number of months in the part-year period during the applicable taxpayer's taxable year. Only full calendar months are included in the computation under this paragraph (c)(3)(v)(B).

(C) Required contribution percentage.—The required contribution percentage is 9.5 percent. For plan years beginning in a calendar year after 2014, the percentage will be adjusted by the ratio of premium growth to income growth for the preceding calendar year and may be further adjusted to reflect changes to the data used to compute the ratio of premium growth to income growth for the 2014 calendar year or the data sources used to compute the ratio of premium growth to income growth. Premium growth and income growth will be determined under published guidance, see §601.601(d)(2) of this chapter. In addition, the percentage may be adjusted for plan years beginning in a calendar year after 2018 to reflect rates of premium growth relative to growth in the consumer price index.

(D) Examples.—The following examples illustrate the provisions of this paragraph (c)(3)(v). Unless stated otherwise, in each example the taxpayer is single and has no dependents, the employer's plan is an eligible employer-sponsored plan and provides minimum value, the employee is not eligible for other minimum essential coverage, and the taxpayer, related individual, and employer-sponsored plan have a calendar taxable year:

(1) Example 1: Basic determination of affordability.—For all of 2023, taxpayer C works for an employer, X, that offers its employees and their spouses a health insurance plan under which, to enroll in self-only coverage, C must contribute an amount for 2023 that does not exceed the required contribution percentage of C's 2023 household income. Because C's required contribution for self-only coverage does not exceed the required contribution percentage of C's household income, under paragraph (c)(3)(v)(A)(1) of this section, X's plan is affordable for C, and C is eligible for minimum essential coverage for all months in 2023.

(2) Example 2: Basic determination of affordability for a related individual.—(i) The facts are the same as in paragraph (c)(3)(v)(D)(1) of this section (Example 1), except that C is married to J, they file a

>>→ *Caution: The amendments made to Reg. §1.36B-2, below, by T.D. 9867 generally apply for tax years beginning on or after January 1, 2020; see Reg. §1.36B-2(e)(3), below, for details.*

joint return, and to enroll C and J, X's plan requires C to contribute an amount for coverage for C and J for 2023 that exceeds the required contribution percentage of C's and J's household income. J does not work for an employer that offers employer-sponsored coverage.

(ii) J is a member of C's family as defined in §1.36B-1(d). Because C's required contribution for coverage of C and J exceeds the required contribution percentage of C's and J's household income, under paragraph (c)(3)(v)(A)(2) of this section, X's plan is unaffordable for J. Accordingly, J is not eligible for minimum essential coverage for 2023. However, under paragraph (c)(3)(v)(A)(1) of this section, X's plan is affordable for C, and C is eligible for minimum essential coverage for all months in 2023.

(3) *Example 3: Multiple offers of coverage.*—The facts are the same as in paragraph (c)(3)(v)(D)(2) of this section (Example 2), except that J works all year for an employer that offers employer-sponsored coverage to employees. J's required contribution for the cost of self-only coverage from J's employer does not exceed the required contribution percentage of C's and J's household income. Although the coverage offered by C's employer for C and J is unaffordable for J, the coverage offered by J's employer is affordable for J. Consequently, under paragraphs (c)(3)(v)(A)(1) and (8) of this section, J is eligible for minimum essential coverage for all months in 2023.

(4) *Example 4: Cost of covering individuals not part of taxpayer's family.*—(i) D and E are married, file a joint return, and have two children, F and G, under age 26. F is a dependent of D and E, but G is not. D works all year for an employer that offers employer-sponsored coverage to employees, their spouses, and their children under age 26. E, F, and G do not work for employers offering coverage. D's required contribution for self-only coverage under D's employer's coverage does not exceed the required contribution percentage of D's and E's household income. D's required contribution for coverage of D, E, F, and G exceeds the required contribution percentage of D's and E's household income, but D's required contribution for coverage of D, E, and F does not exceed the required contribution percentage of the household income.

(ii) E and F are members of D's family as defined in §1.36B-1(d). G is not a member of D's family under §1.36B-1(d), because G is not D's dependent. Under paragraph (c)(3)(v)(A)(1) of this section, D's employer's coverage is affordable for D because D's required contribution for self-only coverage does not exceed the required contribution percentage of D's and E's household income. D's employer's coverage also is affordable for E and F, because, under paragraph (c)(3)(v)(A)(2) of this section, D's required contribution for coverage of D, E, and F does not exceed the required contribution percentage of D's and E's household income. Although D's cost to cover D, E, F, and G exceeds the required contribution percentage of D's and E's household income, under paragraph (c)(3)(v)(A)(2) of this section, the cost to cover G is not considered in determining whether D's employer's coverage is affordable for E and F, regardless of whether G actually enrolls in the plan, because G is not in D's family. D, E, and F are eligible for minimum essential coverage for all months in 2023. Under paragraph (c)(4)(i) of this section, G is considered eligible for the coverage offered by D's employer only if G enrolls in the coverage.

(5) *Example 5: More than one family member with an employer offering coverage.*—(i) K and L are married, file a joint return, and have one dependent child, M. K works all year for an employer that offers coverage to employees, spouses, and children under age 26. L works all year for an employer that offers coverage to employees only. K's required contribution for self-only coverage under K's employer's coverage does not exceed the required contribution percentage of K's and L's household income. Likewise, L's required contribution for self-only coverage under L's employer's coverage does not exceed the required contribution percentage of K's and L's household income. However, K's required contribution for coverage of K, L, and M exceeds the required contribution percentage of K's and L's household income.

(ii) L and M are members of K's family as defined in §1.36B-1(d). Under paragraph (c)(3)(v)(A)(1) of this section, K's employer's coverage is affordable for K because K's required contribution for self-only coverage does not exceed the required contribution percentage of K's and L's household income. Similarly, L's employer's coverage is affordable for L, because L's required contribution for self-only coverage does not exceed the required contribution percentage of K's and L's household income. Thus, K and L are eligible for minimum essential coverage for all months in 2023. However, under paragraph (c)(3)(v)(A)(2) of this section, K's employer's coverage is unaffordable for M, because K's required contribution for coverage of K, L, and M exceeds the required contribution

percentage of K's and L's household income. Accordingly, M is not eligible for minimum essential coverage for 2023.

(6) *Example 6: Multiple offers of coverage for a related individual.*—(i) The facts are the same as in paragraph (c)(3)(v)(D)(5) of this section (Example 5), except that L works all year for an employer that offers coverage to employees, spouses, and children under age 26. L's required contribution for coverage of K, L, and M does not exceed the required contribution percentage of K's and L's household income.

(ii) Although M is not eligible for affordable employer coverage under K's employer's coverage, paragraph (c)(3)(v)(A)(8) of this section dictates that L's employer coverage must be evaluated to determine whether L's employer coverage is affordable for M. Under paragraph (c)(3)(v)(A)(2) of this section, L's employer's coverage is affordable for M, because L's required contribution for K, L, and M does not exceed the required contribution percentage of K's and L's household income. Accordingly, M is eligible for minimum essential coverage for all months in 2023.

(7) *Example 7: Determination of unaffordability at enrollment.*—(i) Taxpayer D is an employee of Employer X. In November 2013 the Exchange for D's rating area projects that D's 2014 household income will be $37,000. It also verifies that D's required contribution for self-only coverage under X's health insurance plan will be $3,700 (10 percent of household income). Consequently, the Exchange determines that X's plan is unaffordable. D enrolls in a qualified health plan and not in X's plan. In December 2014, X pays D a $2,500 bonus. Thus, D's actual 2014 household income is $39,500 and D's required contribution for coverage under X's plan is 9.4 percent of D's household income.

(ii) Based on D's actual 2014 household income, D's required contribution does not exceed 9.5 percent of household income and X's health plan is affordable for D. However, when D enrolled in a qualified health plan for 2014, the Exchange determined that X's plan was not affordable for D for 2014. Consequently, under paragraph (c)(3)(v)(A)(3) of this section, X's plan is not affordable for D and D is not eligible for minimum essential coverage under X's plan for 2014.

(8) *Example 8: Determination of unaffordability for plan year.*—The facts are the same as in paragraph (c)(3)(v)(D)(7) of this section (Example 7), except that X's employee health insurance plan year is September 1 to August 31. The Exchange for D's rating area determines in August 2014 that X's plan is unaffordable for D based on D's projected household income for 2014. D enrolls in a qualified health plan as of September 1, 2014. Under paragraph (c)(3)(v)(A)(3) of this section, X's plan is not affordable for D and D is not eligible for minimum essential coverage under X's plan for the coverage months September to December 2014 and January through August 2015.

(9) *Example 9: No affordability information affirmatively provided for annual redetermination.*—(i) The facts are the same as in paragraph (c)(3)(v)(D)(7) of this section (Example 7), except the Exchange redetermines D's eligibility for advance credit payments for 2015. D does not affirmatively provide the Exchange with current information regarding affordability and the Exchange determines that D's coverage is not affordable for 2015 and approves advance credit payments based on information from the previous enrollment period. In 2015, D's required contribution for coverage under X's plan is 9.4 percent of D's household income.

(ii) Because D does not respond to the Exchange notification and the Exchange makes an affordability determination based on information from an earlier year, the employee safe harbor in paragraph (c)(3)(v)(A)(3) of this section does not apply. D's required contribution for 2015 does not exceed 9.5 percent of D's household income. Thus, X's plan is affordable for D for 2015 and D is eligible for minimum essential coverage for all months in 2015.

(10) *Example 10: Determination of unaffordability for part of plan year (part-year period).*—(i) Taxpayer E is an employee of Employer X beginning in May 2015. X's employee health insurance plan year is September 1 to August 31. E's required contribution for self-only coverage for May through August is $150 per month ($1,800 for the full plan year). The Exchange for E's rating area projects E's household income for purposes of eligibility for advance credit payments as $18,000. E's actual household income for the 2015 taxable year is $20,000.

(ii) Under paragraph (c)(3)(v)(B) of this section, whether coverage under X's plan is affordable for E is determined for the remainder of X's plan year (May through August). E's required contribution for a full plan year ($1,800) exceeds 9.5 percent of E's household income (1,800/18,000 = 10 percent). Therefore, the Ex-

➤➤➤ Caution: *The amendments made to Reg. §1.36B-2, below, by T.D. 9867 generally apply for tax years beginning on or after January 1, 2020; see Reg. §1.36B-2(e)(3), below, for details.*

change determines that X's coverage is unaffordable for May through August. Although E's actual household income for 2015 is $20,000 (and E's required contribution of $1,800 does not exceed 9.5 percent of E's household income), under paragraph (c)(3)(v)(A)(3) of this section, X's plan is unaffordable for E for the part of the plan year May through August 2015. Consequently, E is not eligible for minimum essential coverage under X's plan for the period May through August 2015.

(11) *Example 11: Affordability determined for part of a taxable year (part-year period).*—(i) Taxpayer F is an employee of Employer X. X's employee health insurance plan year is September 1 to August 31. F's required contribution for self-only coverage for the period September 2014 through August 2015 is $150 per month or $1,800 for the plan year. F does not enroll in X's plan during X's open season but enrolls in a qualified health plan for September through December 2014. F does not request advance credit payments and does not ask the Exchange for his rating area to determine whether X's coverage is affordable for F. F's household income in 2014 is $18,000.

(ii) Because F is a calendar year taxpayer and Employer X's plan is not a calendar year plan, F must determine the affordability of X's coverage for the part-year period in 2014 (September-December) under paragraph (c)(3)(v)(B) of this section. F determines the affordability of X's plan for the September through December 2014 period by comparing the annual premiums ($1,800) to F's 2014 household income. F's required contribution of $1,800 is 10 percent of F's 2014 household income. Because F's required contribution exceeds 9.5 percent of F's 2014 household income, X's plan is not affordable for F for the part-year period September through December 2014 and F is not eligible for minimum essential coverage under X's plan for that period.

(iii) F enrolls in Exchange coverage for 2015 and does not ask the Exchange to approve advance credit payments or determine whether X's coverage is affordable. F's 2015 household income is $20,000.

(iv) F must determine if X's plan is affordable for the part-year period January 2015 through August 2015. F's annual required contribution ($1,800) is 9 percent of F's 2015 household income. Because F's required contribution does not exceed 9.5 percent of F's 2015 household income, X's plan is affordable for F for the part-year period January through August 2015 and F is eligible for minimum essential coverage for that period.

(12) *Example 12: Coverage unaffordable at year end.*—Taxpayer G is employed by Employer X. In November 2014, the Exchange for G's rating area determines that G is eligible for affordable employer-sponsored coverage for 2015. G nonetheless enrolls in a qualified health plan for 2015 but does not receive advance credit payments. G's 2015 household income is less than expected and G's required contribution for employer-sponsored coverage for 2015 exceeds 9.5 percent of G's actual 2015 household income. Under paragraph (c)(3)(v)(A)(1) of this section, G is not eligible for minimum essential coverage under X's plan for 2015.

(13) *Example 13: Wellness program incentives.*—(i) Employer X offers an eligible employer-sponsored plan with a nondiscriminatory wellness program that reduces premiums by $300 for employees who do not use tobacco products or who complete a smoking cessation course. Premiums are reduced by $200 if an employee completes cholesterol screening within the first six months of the plan year. Employee B does not use tobacco and the cost of his premiums is $3,700. Employee C uses tobacco and the cost of her premiums is $4,000.

(ii) Under paragraph (c)(3)(v)(A)(4) of this section, only the incentives related to tobacco use are counted toward the premium amount used to determine the affordability of X's plan. C is treated as having earned the $300 incentive for attending a smoking cessation course regardless of whether C actually attends the course. Thus, the required contribution for determining affordability for both Employee B and Employee C is $3,700. The $200 incentive for completing cholesterol screening is treated as not earned and does not reduce their required contribution.

(vi) *Minimum value.*—See §1.36B-6 for rules for determining whether an eligible employer-sponsored plan provides minimum value. An HRA or other account-based group health plan described in paragraph (c)(3)(i)(B) of this section that is affordable for a month under paragraph (c)(5) of this section is treated as providing minimum value for the month.

(vii) *Enrollment in eligible employer-sponsored plan.*—(A) *In general.*—Except as provided in paragraph (c)(3)(vii)(B) of this section, the requirements of affordability and minimum value do not apply

for months that an individual is enrolled in an eligible employer-sponsored plan.

(B) *Automatic enrollment.*—An employee or related individual is treated as not enrolled in an eligible employer-sponsored plan for a month in a plan year or other period for which the employee or related individual is automatically enrolled if the employee or related individual terminates the coverage before the later of the first day of the second full calendar month of that plan year or other period or the last day of any permissible opt-out period provided by the employer-sponsored plan or in regulations to be issued by the Department of Labor, for that plan year or other period.

(C) *Examples.*—The following examples illustrate the provisions of this paragraph (c)(3)(vii):

Example 1. Taxpayer H is employed by Employer X in 2014. H's required contribution for self-only employer coverage exceeds 9.5 percent of H's 2014 household income. H enrolls in X's calendar year plan for 2014. Under paragraph (c)(3)(vii)(A) of this section, H is eligible for minimum essential coverage for 2014 because H is enrolled in an eligible employer-sponsored plan for 2014.

Example 2. The facts are the same as in *Example 1*, except that H terminates plan coverage on June 30, 2014. Under paragraph (c)(3)(vii)(A) of this section, H is eligible for minimum essential coverage under X's plan for January through June 2014 but is not eligible for minimum essential coverage under X's plan for July through December 2014.

Example 3. The facts are the same as in *Example 1*, except that Employer X automatically enrolls H in the plan for calendar year 2015. H terminates the coverage on January 20, 2015. Under paragraph (c)(3)(vii)(B) of this section, H is not eligible for minimum essential coverage under X's plan for January 2015.

(4) *Special eligibility rules.*—(i) *Related individual.*—An individual who may enroll in minimum essential coverage because of a relationship to another person eligible for the coverage, but is not included in the family, as defined in §1.36B-1(d), of the other eligible person, is treated as eligible for such minimum essential coverage only for months that the related individual is enrolled in the coverage.

(ii) *Exchange unable to discontinue advance credit payments.*—(A) *In general.*—If an individual who is enrolled in a qualified health plan for which advance credit payments are made informs the Exchange that the individual is or will soon be eligible for other minimum essential coverage and that advance credit payments should be discontinued, but the Exchange does not discontinue advance credit payments for the first calendar month beginning after the month the individual informs the Exchange, the individual is treated as eligible for the other minimum essential coverage no earlier than the first day of the second calendar month beginning after the first month the individual may enroll in the other minimum essential coverage.

(B) *Medicaid or CHIP.*—If a determination is made that an individual who is enrolled in a qualified health plan for which advance credit payments are made is eligible for Medicaid or CHIP but the advance credit payments are not discontinued for the first calendar month beginning after the eligibility determination, the individual is treated as eligible for the Medicaid or CHIP no earlier than the first day of the second calendar month beginning after the eligibility determination.

(5) *Affordable HRA or other account-based group health plan.*—(i) *In general.*—Except as otherwise provided in this paragraph (c)(5), an HRA or other account-based group health plan described in paragraph (c)(3)(i)(B) of this section is affordable for a month if the employee's required HRA contribution (as defined in paragraph (c)(5)(ii) of this section) for the month does not exceed 1/12 of the product of the employee's household income for the taxable year and the required contribution percentage (as defined in paragraph (c)(3)(v)(C) of this section).

(ii) *Required HRA contribution.*—An employee's required HRA contribution is the excess of—

(A) The monthly premium for the lowest cost silver plan for self-only coverage of the employee offered in the Exchange for the rating area in which the employee resides, over

(B) The monthly self-only HRA or other account-based group health plan amount (or the monthly maximum amount available to the employee under the HRA or other account-based group health plan if the HRA or other account-based group health plan provides for reimbursements up to a single dollar amount regardless of whether an employee has self-only or other-than-self-only coverage).

»»→ *Caution: The amendments made to Reg. §1.36B-2, below, by T.D. 9867 generally apply for tax years beginning on or after January 1, 2020; see Reg. §1.36B-2(e)(3), below, for details.*

(iii) *Monthly amounts.*—(A) *Monthly lowest cost silver plan premium.*—For purposes of paragraph (c)(5)(ii)(A) of this section, the premium for the lowest cost silver plan is determined without regard to any wellness program incentive that affects premiums unless the wellness program incentive relates exclusively to tobacco use, in which case the incentive is treated as earned. If the premium differs for tobacco users and non-tobacco users, the premium for the lowest cost silver plan is the premium that applies to non-tobacco users. For the purpose of this paragraph (c)(5)(iii)(A), the term wellness program incentive has the same meaning as the term reward in 26 CFR 54.9802-1(f)(1)(i). A silver-level qualified health plan that is used for purposes of determining a taxpayer's lowest cost silver plan for self-only coverage under paragraph (c)(5)(ii)(A) of this section does not cease to be the taxpayer's lowest cost silver plan for self-only coverage solely because the plan terminates or closes to enrollment during the taxable year.

(B) *Monthly HRA amount.*—For purposes of paragraph (c)(5)(ii)(B) of this section, the monthly self-only HRA or other account-based group health plan amount is the self-only HRA or other account-based group health plan amount newly made available under the HRA for the plan year, divided by the number of months in the plan year the HRA or other account-based group health plan is available to the employee. The monthly maximum amount available to the employee under the HRA or other account-based group health plan is the maximum amount newly made available for the plan year to the employee under the plan, divided by the number of months in the plan year the HRA or other account-based group health plan is available to the employee.

(iv) *Employee safe harbor.*—An HRA or other account-based group health plan described in paragraph (c)(3)(i)(B) of this section is not affordable for a month for an employee or a related HRA individual if, when the employee or related HRA individual enrolls in a qualified health plan for a period coinciding with the period the HRA or other account-based group health plan is available to the employee or related HRA individual (in whole or in part), an Exchange determines that the HRA or other account-based group health plan is not affordable for the period of enrollment in the qualified health plan. This paragraph (c)(5)(iv) does not apply to a determination made as part of the redetermination process described in 45 CFR 155.335 unless the individual receiving an Exchange redetermination notification affirmatively responds and provides current information about affordability. This paragraph (c)(5)(iv) does not apply for an individual who, with intentional or reckless disregard for the facts, provides incorrect information to an Exchange concerning the relevant HRA or other account-based group health plan amount offered by the employee's employer. A reckless disregard of the facts occurs if the taxpayer makes little or no effort to determine whether the information provided to the Exchange is accurate under circumstances that demonstrate a substantial deviation from the standard of conduct a reasonable person would observe. A disregard of the facts is intentional if the taxpayer knows that the information provided to the Exchange is inaccurate.

(v) *Amounts used for affordability determination.*—Only amounts that are newly made available for the plan year of the HRA or other account-based group health plan described in paragraph (c)(3)(i)(B) of this section and determinable within a reasonable time before the beginning of the plan year of the HRA or other account-based health plan are considered in determining whether an HRA or other account-based group health plan described in paragraph (c)(3)(i)(B) of this section is affordable. Amounts made available for a prior plan year that carry over to the current plan year are not taken into account for purposes of this paragraph (c)(5). Similarly, amounts made available to account for amounts remaining in a different HRA or other account-based group health plan the employer previously provided to the employee and under which the employee is no longer covered are not taken into account for purposes of this paragraph (c)(5).

(vi) *Affordability for part-year period.*—Affordability under this paragraph (c)(5) is determined separately for each employment period that is less than a full calendar year or for the portions of the plan year of an employer's HRA or other account-based group health plan that fall in different taxable years of an applicable taxpayer. An HRA or other account-based group health plan described in paragraph (c)(3)(i)(B) of this section is affordable for a part-year period if the employee's annualized required HRA contribution for the part-year period does not exceed the required contribution percentage of the applicable taxpayer's household income for the taxable year. The employee's annualized required HRA contribution is the employee's required HRA contribution for the part-year period times a fraction,

the numerator of which is 12 and the denominator of which is the number of months in the part-year period during the applicable taxpayer's taxable year. Only full calendar months are included in the computation under this paragraph (c)(5)(vi).

(vii) *Related individual not allowed as a personal exemption deduction.*—A related HRA individual is treated as ineligible for minimum essential coverage under an HRA or other account-based group health plan described in paragraph (c)(3)(i)(B) of this section for months that the employee opted out of and waived future reimbursements from the HRA or other account-based group health plan and the employee is not allowed a personal exemption deduction under section 151 for the related HRA individual.

(viii) *Post-employment coverage.*—An individual who is offered an HRA or other account-based group health plan described in paragraph (c)(3)(i)(B) of this section, for months after an employee terminates employment with the employer offering the HRA or other account-based group health plan, is eligible for minimum essential coverage under the HRA or other account-based group health plan for months after termination of employment only if the employee does not forfeit or opt out of and waive future reimbursements from the HRA or other account-based group health plan for months after termination of employment.

(ix) *Examples.*—The following examples illustrate the provisions of this paragraph (c)(5). The required contribution percentage is defined in paragraph (c)(3)(v)(C) of this section and is updated annually. Because the required contribution percentage for 2020 has not yet been determined, the examples assume a required contribution percentage for 2020 of 9.78 percent.

(A) *Example 1: Determination of affordability*—(1) *Facts.* In 2020 Taxpayer A is single, has no dependents, and has household income of $28,000. A is an employee of Employer X for all of 2020. X offers its employees an HRA described in paragraph (c)(3)(i)(B) of this section that reimburses $2,400 of medical care expenses for single employees with no children (the self-only HRA amount) and $4,000 for employees with a spouse or children for the medical expenses of the employees and their family members. A enrolls in a qualified health plan through the Exchange in the rating area in which A resides and remains enrolled for all of 2020. The monthly premium for the lowest cost silver plan for self-only coverage of A that is offered in the Exchange for the rating area in which A resides is $500.

(2) *Conclusion.* A's required HRA contribution, as defined in paragraph (c)(5)(ii) of this section, is $300, the excess of $500 (the monthly premium for the lowest cost silver plan for self-only coverage of A) over $200 (1/12 of the self-only HRA amount provided by Employer X to its employees). In addition, 1/12 of the product of 9.78 percent and A's household income is $228 ($28,000 x .0978 = $2,738; $2,738/12 = $228). Because A's required HRA contribution of $300 exceeds $228 (1/12 of the product of 9.78 percent and A's household income), the HRA is unaffordable for A for each month of 2020 under paragraph (c)(5) of this section. If A opts out of and waives future reimbursements from the HRA, A is not eligible for minimum essential coverage under the HRA for each month of 2020 under paragraph (c)(3)(i)(B) of this section.

(B) *Example 2: Determination of affordability for a related HRA individual*—(1) *Facts.* In 2020 Taxpayer B is married and has one child who is a dependent of B for 2020. B has household income of $28,000. B is an employee of Employer X for all of 2020. X offers its employees an HRA described in paragraph (c)(3)(i)(B) of this section that reimburses $3,600 of medical care expenses for single employees with no children (the self-only HRA amount) and $5,000 for employees with a spouse or children for the medical expenses of the employees and their family members. B, B's spouse, and B's child enroll in a qualified health plan through the Exchange in the rating area in which B resides and they remain enrolled for all of 2020. No advance credit payments are made for their coverage. The monthly premium for the lowest cost silver plan for self-only coverage of B that is offered in the Exchange for the rating area in which B resides is $500.

(2) *Conclusion.* B's required HRA contribution, as defined in paragraph (c)(5)(ii) of this section, is $200, the excess of $500 (the monthly premium for the lowest cost silver plan for self-only coverage for B) over $300 (1/12 of the self-only HRA amount provided by Employer X to its employees). In addition, 1/12 of the product of 9.78 percent and B's household income for 2020 is $228 ($28,000 x .0978 = $2,738; $2,738/12 = $228). Because B's required HRA contribution of $200 does not exceed $228 (1/12 of the product of 9.78 percent and B's household income for 2020), the HRA is affordable for B under paragraph (c)(5) of this section, and B is eligible for minimum essential coverage under an eligible employer-sponsored plan for each month of 2020 under paragraph (c)(3)(i)(B) of this section. In addition, B's spouse and child are also eligible for minimum essential

coverage under an eligible employer-sponsored plan for each month of 2020 under paragraph (c)(3)(i)(B) of this section.

(C) *Example 3: Exchange determines that HRA is unaffordable*—(1) *Facts.* The facts are the same as in paragraph (c)(5)(ix)(B) of this section (*Example 2*), except that B, when enrolling in Exchange coverage for B's family, received a determination by the Exchange that the HRA was unaffordable, because B believed B's household income would be lower than it turned out to be. Consequently, advance credit payments were made for their 2020 coverage.

(2) *Conclusion.* Under paragraph (c)(5)(iv) of this section, the HRA is considered unaffordable for B, B's spouse, and B's child for each month of 2020 provided that B did not, with intentional or reckless disregard for the facts, provide incorrect information to the Exchange concerning the HRA.

(D) *Example 4: Affordability determined for part of a taxable year (part-year period)*—(1) *Facts.* Taxpayer C is an employee of Employer X. C's household income for 2020 is $28,000 X offers its employees an HRA described in paragraph (c)(3)(i)(B) of this section that reimburses medical care expenses of $3,600 for single employees without children (the self-only HRA amount) and $5,000 to employees with a spouse or children for the medical expenses of the employees and their family members. X's HRA plan year is September 1 to August 31 and C is first eligible to participate in the HRA for the period beginning September 1, 2020. C enrolls in a qualified health plan through the Exchange in the rating area in which C resides for all of 2020. The monthly premium for the lowest cost silver plan for self-only coverage of C that is offered in the Exchange for the rating area in which C resides for 2020 is $500.

(2) *Conclusion.* Under paragraph (c)(3)(vi) of this section, the affordability of the HRA is determined separately for the period September 1 through December 31, 2020, and for the period January 1 through August 31, 2021. C's required HRA contribution, as defined in paragraph (c)(5)(ii) of this section, for the period September 1 through December 31, 2020, is $200, the excess of $500 (the monthly premium for the lowest cost silver plan for self-only coverage for C) over $300 (1/12 of the self-only HRA amount provided by X to its employees). In addition, 1/12 of the product of 9.78 percent and C's household income is $228 ($28,000 x .0978 = $2,738; $2,738/12 = $228). Because C's required HRA contribution of $200 does not exceed $228, the HRA is affordable for C for each month in the period September 1 through December 31, 2020, under paragraph (c)(5) of this section. Affordability for the period January 1 through August 31, 2021, is determined using C's 2021 household income and required HRA contribution.

(E) *Example 5: Carryover amounts ignored in determining affordability*—(1) *Facts.* Taxpayer D is an employee of Employer X for all of 2020 and 2021. D is single. For each of 2020 and 2021, X offers its employees an HRA described in paragraph (c)(3)(i)(B) of this section that provides reimbursement for medical care expenses of $2,400 to single employees with no children (the self-only HRA amount) and $4,000 to employees with a spouse or children for the medical expenses of the employees and their family members. Under the terms of the HRA, amounts that an employee does not use in a calendar year may be carried over and used in the next calendar year. In 2020, D used only $1,500 of her $2,400 maximum reimbursement and the unused $900 is carried over and may be used by D in 2021.

(2) *Conclusion.* Under paragraph (c)(5)(v) of this section, only the $2,400 self-only HRA amount offered to D for 2021 is considered in determining whether D's HRA is affordable for D. The $900 carryover amount is not considered in determining the affordability of the HRA.

(d) *Applicability date.*—Paragraphs (b)(2) and (c)(3)(v)(C) of this section apply to taxable years beginning after December 31, 2013.

(e) *Applicability dates.*—(1) Except as provided in paragraphs (e)(2) through (5) of this section, this section applies to taxable years ending after December 31, 2013.

(2) Paragraph (b)(6)(ii), the last three sentences of paragraph (c)(2)(v), paragraph (c)(3)(i), paragraph (c)(3)(iii)(A), the last three sentences of paragraph (c)(3)(v)(A)(3), and paragraph (c)(4) of this section apply to taxable years beginning after December 31, 2016. Paragraphs (b)(6), (c)(3)(i), (c)(3)(iii)(A), and (c)(4) of §1.36B-2 as contained in 26 CFR part I edition revised as of April 1, 2016, apply to taxable years ending after December 31, 2013, and beginning before January 1, 2017.

(3) Paragraphs (c)(3)(i)(B) and (c)(5) of this section, and the last sentences of paragraphs (c)(3)(ii), (c)(3)(v)(A)(1) through (3), and (c)(3)(vi) of this section apply to taxable years beginning on or after January 1, 2020.

(4) Paragraph (c)(4)(i) of this section applies to taxable years ending on or after December 31, 2020.

(5) The first two sentences of paragraph (c)(3)(v)(A)(2), paragraph (c)(3)(v)(A)(8), the second sentence of paragraph (c)(3)(v)(B), paragraphs (c)(3)(v)(D)(1) through (6), and the first sentences of paragraphs (c)(3)(v)(D)(8) and (9) of this section apply to taxable years beginning after December 31, 2022. [Reg. §1.36B-2.]

☐ [T.D. 9590, 5-18-2012. *Amended by* T.D. 9611, 1-30-2013, T.D. 9683, 7-24-2014, T.D. 9745, 12-16-2015, T.D. 9804, 12-14-2016, T.D. 9822, 7-24-2017, T.D. 9867, 6-13-2019, T.D. 9912, 11-27-2020 *and* T.D. 9968, 10-11-2022 (*corrected* 12-1-2022).]

[Reg. §1.36B-3]

§1.36B-3. Computing the premium assistance credit amount.—(a) *In general.*—A taxpayer's premium assistance credit amount for a taxable year is the sum of the premium assistance amounts determined under paragraph (d) of this section for all coverage months for individuals in the taxpayer's family.

(b) *Definitions.*—For purposes of this section—
(1) The cost of a qualified health plan is the premium the plan charges; and
(2) The term *coverage family* means, in each month, the members of a taxpayer's family for whom the month is a coverage month.

(c) *Coverage month.*—(1) *In general.*—A month is a coverage month for an individual if—
(i) As of the first day of the month, the individual is enrolled in a qualified health plan through an Exchange;
(ii) The taxpayer pays the taxpayer's share of the premium for the individual's coverage under the plan for the month by the unextended due date for filing the taxpayer's income tax return for that taxable year, or the full premium for the month is paid by advance credit payments; and
(iii) The individual is not eligible for the full calendar month for minimum essential coverage (within the meaning of §1.36B-2(c)) other than coverage described in section 5000A(f)(1)(C) (relating to coverage in the individual market).

(2) *Certain individuals enrolled during a month.*—If an individual enrolls in a qualified health plan and the enrollment is effective on the date of the individual's birth, adoption, or placement for adoption or in foster care, or on the effective date of a court order, the individual is treated as enrolled as of the first day of that month for purposes of this paragraph (c).

(3) *Premiums paid for a taxpayer.*—Premiums another person pays for coverage of the taxpayer, taxpayer's spouse, or dependent are treated as paid by the taxpayer.

(4) *Appeals of coverage eligibility.*—A taxpayer who is eligible for advance credit payments pursuant to an eligibility appeal decision implemented under 45 CFR §155.545(c)(1)(ii) for coverage of a member of the taxpayer's coverage family who, based on the appeal decision, retroactively enrolls in a qualified health plan is considered to have met the requirement in paragraph (c)(1)(ii) of this section for a month if the taxpayer pays the taxpayer's share of the premiums for coverage under the plan for the month on or before the 120th day following the date of the appeals decision.

(5) *Examples.*—The following examples illustrate the provisions of this paragraph (c):
Example 1. (i) Taxpayer M is single with no dependents. In December 2013, M enrolls in a qualified health plan for 2014 and the Exchange approves advance credit payments. M pays M's share of the premiums. On May 15, 2014, M enlists in the U.S. Army and is eligible immediately for government-sponsored minimum essential coverage.
(ii) Under paragraph (c)(1) of this section, January through May 2014 are coverage months for M. June through December 2014 are not coverage months because M is eligible for minimum essential coverage for those months. Thus, under paragraph (a) of this section, M's premium assistance credit amount for 2014 is the sum of the premium assistance amounts for the months January through May.

Example 2. (i) Taxpayer N has one dependent, S. S is eligible for governmentsponsored minimum essential coverage. N is not eligible for minimum essential coverage. N enrolls in a qualified health plan for 2014 and the Exchange approves advance credit payments. On August 1, 2014, S loses eligibility for minimum essential coverage. N terminates enrollment in the qualified health plan that covers only N and enrolls in a qualified health plan that covers N and S for August through December 2014. N pays all premiums not covered by advance credit payments.
(ii) Under paragraph (c)(1) of this section, January through December of 2014 are coverage months for N and August through

December are coverage months for N and S. N's premium assistance credit amount for 2014 is the sum of the premium assistance amounts for these coverage months.

Example 3. (i) O and P are the divorced parents of T. Under the divorce agreement between O and P, T resides with P and P claims T as a dependent. However, O must pay premiums for health insurance for T. P enrolls T in a qualified health plan for 2014. O pays the portion of T's qualified health plan premiums not covered by advance credit payments.

(ii) Because P claims T as a dependent, P (and not O) may claim a premium tax credit for coverage for T. See § 1.36B-2(a). Under paragraph (c)(2) of this section, the premiums that O pays for coverage for T are treated as paid by P. Thus, the months when T is covered by a qualified health plan and not eligible for other minimum essential coverage are coverage months under paragraph (c)(1) of this section in computing P's premium tax credit under paragraph (a) of this section.

Example 4. Q, an American Indian, enrolls in a qualified health plan for 2014. Q's tribe pays the portion of Q's qualified health plan premiums not covered by advance credit payments. Under paragraph (c)(2) of this section, the premiums that Q's tribe pays for Q are treated as paid by Q. Thus, the months when Q is covered by a qualified health plan and not eligible for other minimum essential coverage are coverage months under paragraph (c)(1) of this section in computing Q's premium tax credit under paragraph (a) of this section.

(d) *Premium assistance amount.*—(1) *Premium assistance amount.*—The premium assistance amount for a coverage month is the lesser of—

(i) The premiums for the month, reduced by any amounts that were refunded in the same taxable year as the premium liability is incurred, for one or more qualified health plans in which a taxpayer or a member of the taxpayer's family enrolls (enrollment premiums); or

(ii) The excess of the adjusted monthly premium for the applicable benchmark plan (benchmark plan premium) over 1/12 of the product of a taxpayer's household income and the applicable percentage for the taxable year (the taxpayer's contribution amount).

(2) *Examples.*—The following examples illustrate the rules of paragraph (d)(1) of this section.

Example 1. Taxpayer Q is single and has no dependents. Q enrolls in a qualified health plan with a monthly premium of $400. Q's monthly benchmark plan premium is $500, and his monthly contribution amount is $80. Q's premium assistance amount for a coverage month is $400 (the lesser of $400, Q's monthly enrollment premium, and $420, the difference between Q's monthly benchmark plan premium and Q's contribution amount).

Example 2. (i) Taxpayer R is single and has no dependents. R enrolls in a qualified health plan with a monthly premium of $450. The difference between R's benchmark plan premium and contribution amount for the month is $420.

(ii) The issuer of R's qualified health plan is notified that R died on September 20. The issuer terminates coverage as of that date and refunds the remaining portion of the September enrollment premiums ($150) for R's coverage.

(iii) R's premium assistance amount for each coverage month from January through August is $420 (the lesser of $450 and $420). Under paragraph (d)(1) of this section, R's premium assistance amount for September is the lesser of the enrollment premiums for the month, reduced by any amounts that were refunded ($300 ($450 - $150)) or the difference between the benchmark plan premium and the contribution amount for the month ($420). R's premium assistance amount for September is $300, the lesser of $420 and $300.

Example 3. The facts are the same as in *Example 2* of this paragraph (d)(2), except that the qualified health plan issuer does not refund any enrollment premiums for September. Under paragraph (d)(1) of this section, R's premium assistance amount for September is $420, the lesser of $450 and $420.

(e) *Adjusted monthly premium.*—The adjusted monthly premium is the premium an issuer would charge for the applicable benchmark health plan to cover all members of the taxpayer's coverage family, adjusted *only for the age of each member of the coverage family* as allowed under section 2701 of the Public Health Service Act (42 U.S.C. 300gg). The adjusted monthly premium is determined without regard to any premium discount or rebate under the wellness discount demonstration project under section 2705(d) of the Public Health Service Act (42 U.S.C. 300gg-4(d)) and may not include any adjustments for tobacco use. The adjusted monthly premium for a coverage month is determined as of the first day of the month.

(f) *Applicable benchmark plan.*—(1) *In general.*—Except as otherwise provided in this paragraph (f), the applicable benchmark plan for

each coverage month is the second-lowest-cost silver plan (as described in section 1302(d)(1)(B) of the Affordable Care Act (42 U.S.C. 18022(d)(1)(B))) offered to the taxpayer's coverage family through the Exchange for the rating area where the taxpayer resides for—

(i) Self-only coverage for a taxpayer—

(A) Who computes tax under section 1(c) (unmarried individuals other than surviving spouses and heads of household) and is not allowed a deduction under section 151 for a dependent for the taxable year;

(B) Who purchases only self-only coverage for one individual; or

(C) Whose coverage family includes only one individual; and

(ii) Family coverage for all other taxpayers.

(2) *Family coverage.*—The applicable benchmark plan for family coverage is the second lowest-cost silver plan that would cover the members of the taxpayer's coverage family (such as a plan covering two adults if the members of a taxpayer's coverage family are two adults).

(3) *Silver-level plan not covering pediatric dental benefits.*—If one or more silver-level qualified health plans offered through an Exchange do not cover pediatric dental benefits, the premium for the applicable benchmark plan is determined based on the second lowest-cost option among—

(i) The silver-level qualified health plans that are offered by the Exchange to the members of the coverage family and that provide pediatric dental benefits; and

(ii) The silver-level qualified health plans that are offered by the Exchange to the members of the coverage family that do not provide pediatric dental benefits in conjunction with the second lowest-cost portion of the premium for a stand-alone dental plan (within the meaning of section 1311(d)(2)(B)(ii) of the Affordable Care Act (42 U.S.C. 18031(d)(2)(B)(ii)) offered by the Exchange to the members of the coverage family that is properly allocable to pediatric dental benefits determined under guidance issued by the Secretary of Health and Human Services.

(4) *Family members residing in different locations.*—If members of a taxpayer's coverage family reside in different locations, the taxpayer's benchmark plan premium is the sum of the premiums for the applicable benchmark plans for each group of coverage family members residing in different locations, based on the plans offered to the group through the Exchange where the group resides. If all members of a taxpayer's coverage family reside in a single location that is different from where the taxpayer resides, the taxpayer's benchmark plan premium is the premium for the applicable benchmark plan for the coverage family, based on the plans offered through the Exchange to the taxpayer's coverage family for the rating area where the coverage family resides.

(5) *Single or multiple policies needed to cover the family.*—(i) *Policy covering a taxpayer's family.*—If a silver-level plan or a stand-alone dental plan offers coverage to all members of a taxpayer's coverage family who reside in the same location under a single policy, the premium (or allocable portion thereof, in the case of a stand-alone dental plan) taken into account for the plan for purposes of determining the applicable benchmark plan under paragraphs (f)(1), (f)(2), and (f)(3) of this section is the premium for this single policy.

(ii) *Policy not covering a taxpayer's family.*—If a silver-level qualified health plan or a stand-alone dental plan would require multiple policies to cover all members of a taxpayer's coverage family who reside in the same location (for example, because of the relationships within the family), the premium (or allocable portion thereof, in the case of a standalone dental plan) taken into account for the plan for purposes of determining the applicable benchmark plan under paragraphs (f)(1), (f)(2), and (f)(3) of this section is the sum of the premiums (or allocable portion thereof, in the case of a stand-alone dental plan) for self-only policies under the plan for each member of the coverage family who resides in the same location.

(6) *Plan not available for enrollment.*—A silver-level qualified health plan or a stand-alone dental plan that is not open to enrollment by a taxpayer or family member at the time the taxpayer or family member enrolls in a qualified health plan is disregarded in determining the applicable benchmark plan.

(7) *Benchmark plan terminates or closes to enrollment during the year.*—A silver-level qualified health plan or a stand-alone dental plan that is used for purposes of determining the applicable benchmark plan under this paragraph (f) for a taxpayer does not cease to be the applicable benchmark plan for a taxable year solely because the plan or a lower cost plan terminates or closes to enrollment during the taxable year.

(8) *Only one silver-level plan offered to the coverage family.*—If there is only one silver-level qualified health plan or one stand-alone dental plan offered through an Exchange that would cover all members of a taxpayer's coverage family who reside in the same location (whether under one policy or multiple policies), that plan is used for purposes of determining the taxpayer's applicable benchmark plan.

(9) *Examples.*—The following examples illustrate the rules of this paragraph (f). Unless otherwise stated, in each example the plans are open to enrollment to a taxpayer or family member at the time of enrollment and are offered through the Exchange for the rating area where the taxpayer resides:

Example 1. Single taxpayer enrolls in Exchange coverage. Taxpayer A is single, has no dependents, and enrolls in a qualified health plan. The Exchange in the rating area in which A resides offers only silver-level qualified health plans that provide pediatric dental benefits. Under paragraphs (f)(1) and (f)(2) of this section, A's applicable benchmark plan is the second lowest cost silver plan providing self-only coverage for A.

Example 2. Single taxpayer enrolls with dependent child through an Exchange where all qualified health plans provide pediatric dental benefits. Taxpayer B is single and claims her 12-year old daughter, C, as a dependent. B purchases family coverage for herself and C. The Exchange in the rating area in which B and C reside offers qualified health plans that provide pediatric dental benefits but does not offer qualified health plans without pediatric dental benefits. Under paragraphs (f)(1) and (f)(2) of this section, B's applicable benchmark plan is the second lowest-cost silver plan providing family coverage to B and C.

Example 3. Single taxpayer enrolls with dependent child through an Exchange where one or more qualified health plans do not provide pediatric dental benefits. (i) Taxpayer D is single and claims his 10-year old son, E, as a dependent. The Exchange in the rating area in which D and E reside offers three silver-level qualified health plans, one of which provides pediatric dental benefits (S1) and two of which do not (S2 and S3), in which D and E may enroll. The Exchange also offers two stand-alone dental plans (DP1 and DP2) available to D and E. The monthly premiums allocable to essential health benefits for the silver-level plans are as follows:

S1 - $650
S2 - $620
S3 - $590

(ii) The monthly premiums, and the portion of the premium allocable to pediatric dental benefits, for the two dental plans are as follows:

DP1 - $50 ($20 allocable to pediatric dental benefits)
DP2 - $40 ($15 allocable to pediatric dental benefits)

(iii) Under paragraph (f)(3) of this section, D's applicable benchmark plan is the second lowest cost option among the following offered by the rating area in which D resides: silver-level qualified health plans providing pediatric dental benefits ($650 for S1) and the silver-level qualified health plans not providing pediatric dental benefits, in conjunction with the second lowest-cost portion of the premium for a stand-alone dental plan properly allocable to pediatric dental benefits ($590 for S3 in conjunction with $20 for DP1 = $610 and $620 for S2 in conjunction with $20 for DP1 = $640). Under paragraph (e) of this section, the adjusted monthly premium for D's applicable benchmark plan is $640.

Example 4. Single taxpayer enrolls with dependent adult through an Exchange where one or more qualified health plans do not provide pediatric dental benefits. (i) The facts are the same as in *Example 3*, except Taxpayer D's coverage family consists of D and D's 22-year old son, F, who is a dependent of D. The monthly premiums allocable to essential health benefits for the silver-level plans are as follows:

S1 - $630
S2 - $590
S3 - $580

(ii) Because no one in D's coverage family is eligible for pediatric dental benefits, $0 of the premium for a stand-alone dental plan is allocable to pediatric dental benefits in determining A's applicable benchmark plan. Consequently, under paragraphs (f)(1), (f)(2), and (f)(3) of this section, D's applicable benchmark plan is the second lowest-cost option among the following options offered by the rating area in which D resides: silver-level qualified health plans providing pediatric dental benefits ($630 for S1) and the silver-level qualified health plans not providing pediatric dental benefits, in conjunction with the second lowest-cost portion of the premium for a stand-alone dental plan properly allocable to pediatric dental benefits ($580 for S3 in conjunction with $0 for DP1 = $580 and $590 for S2 in conjunction with $0 for DP1 = $590). Under paragraph (e) of this section, the adjusted monthly premium for D's applicable benchmark plan is $590.

Example 5. Single taxpayer enrolls with dependent and nondependent. Taxpayer G is single and resides with his 25-year old daughter, H,

and with his 14-year old son, I. G may claim I, but not H, as a dependent. G, H, and I enroll in coverage through the Exchange in the rating area in which they all reside. The Exchange offers only silver-level plans providing pediatric dental benefits. Under paragraphs (f)(1) and (f)(2) of this section, G's applicable benchmark plan is the second lowest-cost silver plan covering G and I. However, H may qualify for a premium tax credit if H is otherwise eligible. See paragraph (h) of this section.

Example 6. Change in coverage family. Taxpayer J is single and has no dependents when she enrolls in a qualified health plan. The Exchange in the rating area in which she resides offers only silver-level plans that provide pediatric dental benefits. On August 1, J has a child, K, whom she claims as a dependent. J enrolls in a qualified health plan covering J and K effective August 1. Under paragraphs (f)(1) and (f)(2) of this section, J's applicable benchmark plan for January through July is the second lowest-cost silver plan providing self-only coverage for J, and J's applicable benchmark plan for the months August through December is the second lowest-cost silver plan covering J and K.

Example 7. Minimum essential coverage for some coverage months. Taxpayer L claims his 6-year old daughter, M, as a dependent. L and M are enrolled for the entire year in a qualified health plan that offers only silver-level plans that provide pediatric dental benefits. L, but not M, is eligible for government-sponsored minimum essential coverage for September to December. Thus, under paragraph (c)(1)(iii) of this section, January through December are coverage months for M, and January through August are coverage months for L. Because, under paragraphs (d) and (f)(1) of this section, the premium assistance amount for a coverage month is computed based on the applicable benchmark plan for that coverage month, L's applicable benchmark plan for January through August is the second lowest-cost option covering L and M. Under paragraph (f)(1)(i)(C) of this section, L's applicable benchmark plan for September through December is the second lowest-cost silver plan providing self-only coverage for M.

Example 8. Family member eligible for minimum essential coverage for the taxable year. The facts are the same as in *Example 7*, except that L is not eligible for government-sponsored minimum essential coverage for any months and M is eligible for government sponsored minimum essential coverage for the entire year. Under paragraph (f)(1)(i)(C) of this section, L's applicable benchmark plan is the second lowest-cost silver plan providing self-only coverage for L.

Example 9. Benchmark plan premium for a coverage family with family members who reside in different locations. (i) Taxpayer N's coverage family consists of N and her three dependents O, P, and Q. N, O, and P reside together but Q resides in a different location. The monthly applicable benchmark plan premium for N, O, and P is $1,000 and the monthly applicable benchmark plan premium for Q is $220.

(ii) Under paragraph (f)(4) of this section, because the members of N's coverage family reside in different locations, the monthly premium for N's applicable benchmark plan is the sum of $1,000, the monthly premiums for the applicable benchmark plan for N, O, and P, who reside together, and $220, the monthly applicable benchmark plan premium for Q, who resides in a different location than N, O, and P. Consequently, the premium for N's applicable benchmark plan is $1,220.

Example 10. Aggregation of silver-level policies for plans not covering a family under a single policy. (i) Taxpayers R and S are married and live with S's mother, T, whom they claim as a dependent. The Exchange for their rating area offers self-only and family coverage at the silver level through Issuers A, B, and C, which each offer only one silver-level plan. The silver-level plans offered by Issuers A and B do not cover R, S, and T under a single policy. The silver-level plan offered by Issuer A costs the following monthly amounts for self-only coverage of R, S, and T, respectively: $400, $450, and $600. The silver-level plan offered by Issuer B costs the following monthly amounts for self-only coverage of R, S, and T, respectively: $250, $300, and $450. The silver-level plan offered by Issuer C provides coverage for R, S, and T under one policy for a $1,200 monthly premium.

(ii) Under paragraph (f)(5) of this section, Issuer C's silver-level plan that covers R, S, and T under one policy ($1,200 monthly premium) and Issuer A's and Issuer B's silver-level plans that do not cover R, S and T under one policy are considered in determining R's and S's applicable benchmark plan. In addition, under paragraph (f)(5)(ii) of this section, in determining R's and S's applicable benchmark plan, the premium taken into account for Issuer A's plan is $1,450 (the aggregate premiums for self-only policies covering R ($400), S ($450), and T ($600) and the premium taken into account for Issuer B's plan is $1,000 (the aggregate premiums for self-only policies covering R ($250), S ($300), and T ($450). Consequently, R's and S's applicable benchmark plan is the Issuer C silver-level plan covering R's and S's coverage family and the premium for their applicable benchmark plan is $1,200.

Example 11. Benchmark plan premium for a taxpayer with family members who cannot enroll in one policy and who reside in different locations. (i) Taxpayer U's coverage family consists of U, U's mother, V, and U's two daughters, W and X. U and V reside together in Location 1 and W and X reside together in Location 2. The Exchange in the rating area in which U and V reside does not offer a silver-level plan that covers U and V under a single policy, whereas all the silver-level plans offered through the Exchange in the rating area in which W and X reside cover W and X under a single policy. Both Exchanges offer only silver-level plans that provide pediatric dental benefits. The silver plan offered by the Exchange for the rating area in which U and V reside that would cover U and V under self-only policies with the second-lowest aggregate premium costs $400 a month for self-only coverage for U and $600 a month for self-only coverage for V. The monthly premium for the second-lowest cost silver plan covering W and X that is offered by the Exchange for the rating area in which W and X reside is $500.

(ii) Under paragraph (f)(5)(ii) of this section, because multiple policies are required to cover U and V, the members of U's coverage family who reside together in Location 1, the premium taken into account in determining U's benchmark plan is $1,000, the sum of the premiums for the second-lowest aggregate cost of self-only policies covering U ($400) and V ($600) offered by the Exchange to U and V for the rating area in which U and V reside. Under paragraph (f)(5)(i) of this section, because all silver-level plans offered by the Exchange in which W and X reside cover W and X under a single policy, the premium for W and X's coverage that is taken into account in determining U's benchmark plan is $500, the second-lowest cost silver policy covering W and X that is offered by the Exchange for the rating area in which W and X reside. Under paragraph (f)(4) of this section, because the members of U's coverage family reside in different locations, U's monthly benchmark plan premium is $1,500, the sum of the premiums for the applicable benchmark plans for each group of family members residing in different locations ($1,000 for U and V, who reside in Location 1, plus $500 for W and X, who reside in Location 2).

Example 12. Qualified health plan closed to enrollment. Taxpayer Y has two dependents, Z and AA. Y, Z, and AA enroll in a qualified health plan through the Exchange for the rating area where the family resides. The Exchange, which offers only qualified health plans that include pediatric dental benefits, offers silver-level plans J, K, L, and M, which are, respectively, the first, second, third, and fourth lowest cost silver plans covering Y's family. When Y's family enrolls, Plan J is closed to enrollment. Under paragraph (f)(6) of this section, Plan J is disregarded in determining Y's applicable benchmark plan, and Plan L is used in determining Y's applicable benchmark plan.

Example 13. Benchmark plan closes to new enrollees during the year. (i) Taxpayers BB, CC, and DD each have coverage families consisting of two adults. In that rating area, Plan 2 is the second lowest cost silver plan and Plan 3 is the third lowest cost silver plan covering the two adults in each coverage family offered through the Exchange. The BB and CC families each enroll in a qualified health plan that is not the applicable benchmark plan (Plan 4) in November during the annual open enrollment period. Plan 2 closes to new enrollees the following June. Thus, on July 1, Plan 3 is the second lowest cost silver

plan available to new enrollees through the Exchange. The DD family enrolls in a qualified health plan in July.

(ii) Under paragraphs (f)(1), (f)(2), (f)(3), and (f)(7) of this section, the silver-level plan that BB and CC use to determine their applicable benchmark plan for all coverage months during the year is Plan 2. The applicable benchmark plan that DD uses to determine DD's applicable benchmark plan is Plan 3, because Plan 2 is not open to enrollment through the Exchange when the DD family enrolls.

Example 14. Benchmark plan terminates for all enrollees during the year. The facts are the same as in *Example 13*, except that Plan 2 terminates for all enrollees on June 30. Under paragraphs (f)(1), (f)(2), (f)(3), and (f)(7) of this section, Plan 2 is the silver-level plan that BB and CC use to determine their applicable benchmark plan for all coverage months during the year, and Plan 3 is the applicable benchmark plan that DD uses.

Example 15. Exchange offers only one silver-level plan. Taxpayer EE's coverage family consists of EE, his spouse FF, and their two dependent children GG and HH, who all reside together. The Exchange for the rating area in which they reside offers only one silver-level plan that EE's family may enroll in and the plan does not provide pediatric dental benefits. The Exchange also offers one stand-alone dental plan in which the family may enroll. Under paragraph (f)(8) of this section, the silver-level plan and the stand-alone dental plan offered by the Exchange are used for purposes of determining EE's applicable benchmark plan under paragraph (f)(3) of this section. Moreover, the lone silver-level plan and the lone stand-alone dental plan offered by the Exchange are used for purposes of determining EE's applicable benchmark plan regardless of whether these plans cover EE's family under a single policy or multiples policies.

(g) *Applicable percentage.*—(1) *In general.*—The applicable percentage multiplied by a taxpayer's household income determines the taxpayer's annual required share of premiums for the benchmark plan. The required share is divided by 12 and this monthly amount is subtracted from the adjusted monthly premium for the applicable benchmark plan when computing the premium assistance amount. The applicable percentage is computed by first determining the percentage that the taxpayer's household income bears to the Federal poverty line for the taxpayer's family size. The resulting Federal poverty line percentage is then compared to the income categories described in the table in paragraph (g)(2) of this section. An applicable percentage within an income category increases on a sliding scale in a linear manner and is rounded to the nearest one-hundredth of one percent. For taxable years beginning after December 31, 2014, the applicable percentages in the table will be adjusted by the ratio of premium growth to income growth for the preceding calendar year and may be further adjusted to reflect changes to the data used to compute the ratio of premium growth to income growth for the 2014 calendar year or the data sources used to compute the ratio of premium growth to income growth. Premium growth and income growth will be determined in accordance with published guidance, see § 601.601(d)(2) of this chapter. In addition, the applicable percentages in the table may be adjusted for taxable years beginning after December 31, 2018, to reflect rates of premium growth relative to growth in the consumer price index.

(2) *Applicable percentage table.*—

Household income percentage of Federal poverty line	Initial percentage	Final percentage
Less than 133%	2.0%	2.0%
At least 133% but less than 150%	3.0%	4.0%
At least 150% but less than 200%	4.0%	6.3%
At least 200% but less than 250%	6.3%	8.05%
At least 250% but less than 300%	8.05%	9.5%
At least 300% but not more than 400%	9.5%	9.5%

(3) *Examples.*—The following examples illustrate the rules of this paragraph (g):

Example 1. A's household income is 275 percent of the Federal Poverty line for A's family size for that taxable year. In the table in paragraph (g)(2) of this section, the initial percentage for a taxpayer with household income of 250 to 300 percent of the Federal poverty line is 8.05 and the final percentage is 9.5. A's Federal poverty line percentage of 275 percent is halfway between 250 percent and 300 percent. Thus, rounded to the nearest one-hundredth of one percent, A's applicable percentage is 8.78, which is halfway between the initial percentage of 8.05 and the final percentage of 9.5.

Example 2. (i) B's household income is 210 percent of the Federal poverty line for B's family size. In the table in paragraph (g)(2) of this section, the initial percentage for a taxpayer with household income of 200 to 250 percent of the Federal poverty line is 6.3 and the final percentage is 8.05. B's applicable percentage is 6.65, computed as follows.

(ii) Determine the excess of B's Federal poverty line percentage (210) over the initial household income percentage in B's range (200), which is 10. Determine the difference between the initial household

income percentage in the taxpayer's range (200) and the ending household income percentage in the taxpayer's range (250), which is 50. Divide the first amount by the second amount:

$$210 - 200 = 10$$
$$250 - 200 = 50$$
$$10/50 = .20$$

(iii) Compute the difference between the initial premium percentage (6.3) and the second premium percentage (8.05) in the taxpayer's range; $8.05 - 6.3 = 1.75$.

(iv) Multiply the amount in the first calculation (.20) by the amount in the second calculation (1.75) and add the product (.35) to the initial premium percentage in B's range (6.3), resulting in B's applicable percentage of 6.65:

$$.20 \times 1.75 = .35$$
$$6.3 + .35 = 6.65.$$

(h) *Plan covering more than one family.*—(1) *In general.*—If a qualified health plan covers more than one family under a single policy, each applicable taxpayer covered by the plan may claim a premium tax credit, if otherwise allowable. Each taxpayer computes the credit using that taxpayer's applicable percentage, household income, and the benchmark plan that applies to the taxpayer under paragraph (f) of this section. In determining whether the amount computed under paragraph (d)(1)(i) of this section (the premiums for the qualified health plan in which the taxpayer enrolls) is less than the amount computed under paragraph (d)(1)(i) of this section (the benchmark plan premium minus the product of household income and the applicable percentage), the premiums paid are allocated to each taxpayer in proportion to the premiums for each taxpayer's applicable benchmark plan.

(2) *Example.*—The following example illustrates the rules of this paragraph (h):

Example.·(i) Taxpayers A and B enroll in a single policy under a qualified health plan. B is A's 25-year old child who is not A's dependent. B has no dependents. The plan covers A, B, and A's two additional children who are A's dependents. The premium for the plan in which A and B enroll is $15,000. The premium for the second lowest cost silver family plan covering only A and A's dependents is $12,000 and the premium for the second lowest cost silver plan providing self-only coverage to B is $6,000. A and B are applicable taxpayers and otherwise eligible to claim the premium tax credit.

(ii) Under paragraph (h)(1) of this section, both A and B may claim premium tax credits. A computes her credit using her household income, a family size of three, and a benchmark plan premium of $12,000. B computes his credit using his household income, a family size of one, and a benchmark plan premium of $6,000.

(iii) In determining whether the amount in paragraph (d)(1)(i) of this section (the premiums for the qualified health plan A and B purchase) is less than the amount in paragraph (d)(1)(ii) of this section (the benchmark plan premium minus the product of household income and the applicable percentage), the $15,000 premiums paid are allocated to A and B in proportion to the premiums for their applicable benchmark plans. Thus, the portion of the premium allocated to A is $10,000 ($15,000 × $12,000/$18,000) and the portion allocated to B is $5,000 ($15,000 × $6,000/$18,000).

(i) [Reserved]

(j) *Additional benefits.*—(1) *In general.*—If a qualified health plan offers benefits in addition to the essential health benefits a qualified health plan must provide under section 1302 of the Affordable Care Act (42 U.S.C. 18022), or a State requires a qualified health plan to cover benefits in addition to these essential health benefits, the portion of the premium for the plan properly allocable to the additional benefits is excluded from the monthly premiums under paragraph (d)(1)(i) or (ii) of this section. Premiums are allocated to additional benefits before determining the applicable benchmark plan under paragraph (f) of this section.

(2) *Method of allocation.*—The portion of the premium properly allocable to additional benefits is determined under guidance issued by the Secretary of Health and Human Services. See section 36B(b)(3)(D).

(3) *Examples.*—The following examples illustrate the rules of this paragraph (j):

Example 1. (i) Taxpayer B enrolls in a qualified health plan that provides benefits in addition to essential health benefits (additional benefits). The monthly premiums for the plan in which B enrolls are $370, of which $35 is allocable to additional benefits. B's benchmark plan premium (determined after allocating premiums to additional benefits for all silver level plans) is $440, of which $40 is allocable to additional benefits. B's monthly contribution amount, which is the product of B's household income and the applicable percentage, is $60.

(ii) Under this paragraph (j), B's enrollment premiums and the benchmark plan premium are reduced by the portion of the premium that is allocable to the additional benefits provided under that plan. Therefore, B's monthly enrollment premiums are reduced to $335 ($370 - $35) and B's benchmark plan premium is reduced to $400 ($440 - $40). B's premium assistance amount for a coverage month is $335, the lesser of $335 (B's enrollment premiums, reduced by the portion of the premium allocable to additional benefits) and $340 (B's benchmark plan premium, reduced by the portion of the premium allocable to additional benefits ($400), minus B's $60 contribution amount).

Example 2. The facts are the same as in *Example 1* of this paragraph (j)(3), except that the plan in which B enrolls provides no benefits in addition to the essential health benefits required to be provided by the plan. Thus, under paragraph (j) of this section, B's benchmark plan premium ($440) is reduced by the portion of the premium allocable to additional benefits provided under that plan ($40). B's enrollment premiums ($370) are not reduced under this paragraph (j). B's premium assistance amount for a coverage month is $340, the lesser of $370 (B's enrollment premiums) and $340 (B's benchmark plan premium, reduced by the portion of the premium

allocable to additional benefits ($400), minus B's $60 contribution amount).

(k) *Pediatric dental coverage.*—(1) *In general.*—For purposes of determining the amount of the monthly premium a taxpayer pays for coverage under paragraph (d)(1)(i) of this section, if an individual enrolls in both a qualified health plan and a plan described in section 1311(d)(2)(B)(ii) of the Affordable Care Act (42 U.S.C. 13031(d)(2)(B)(ii)) (a stand-alone dental plan), the portion of the premium for the stand-alone dental plan that is properly allocable to pediatric dental benefits that are essential benefits required to be provided by a qualified health plan is treated as a premium payable for the individual's qualified health plan.

(2) *Method of allocation.*—The portion of the premium for a stand-alone dental plan properly allocable to pediatric dental benefits is determined under guidance issued by the Secretary of Health and Human Services.

(3) *Example.*—The following example illustrates the rules of this paragraph (k):

Example. (i) Taxpayer C and C's dependent, R, enroll in a qualified health plan. The premium for the plan in which C and R enroll is $7,200 ($600/month) (Amount 1). The plan does not provide dental coverage. C also enrolls in a stand-alone dental plan covering C and R. The portion of the premium for the dental plan allocable to pediatric dental benefits that are essential health benefits is $240 ($20 per month). The excess of the premium for C's applicable benchmark plan over C's contribution amount (the product of C's household income and the applicable percentage) is $7,260 ($605/month) (Amount 2).

(ii) Under this paragraph (k), the amount C pays for premiums (Amount 1) for purposes of computing the premium assistance amount is increased by the portion of the premium for the stand-alone dental plan allocable to pediatric dental benefits that are essential health benefits. Thus, the amount of the premiums for the plan in which C enrolls is treated as $620 for purposes of computing the amount of the premium tax credit. C's premium assistance amount for each coverage month is $605 (Amount 2), the lesser of Amount 1 (increased by the premiums allocable to pediatric dental benefits) and Amount 2.

(l) *Families including individuals not lawfully present.*—(1) *In general.*—If one or more individuals for whom a taxpayer is allowed a deduction under section 151 are not lawfully present (within the meaning of §1.36B-1(g)), the percentage a taxpayer's household income bears to the Federal poverty line for the taxpayer's family size for purposes of determining the applicable percentage under paragraph (g) of this section is determined by excluding individuals who are not lawfully present from family size and by determining household income in accordance with paragraph (l)(2) of this section.

(2) *Revised household income computation.*—(i) *Statutory method.*—For purposes of paragraph (l)(1) of this section, household income is equal to the product of the taxpayer's household income (determined without regard to this paragraph (l)(2)) and a fraction—

(A) The numerator of which is the Federal poverty line for the taxpayer's family size determined by excluding individuals who are not lawfully present; and

(B) The denominator of which is the Federal poverty line for the taxpayer's family size determined by including individuals who are not lawfully present.

(ii) *Comparable method.*—The Commissioner may describe a comparable method in additional published guidance, see §601.601(d)(2) of this chapter.

(m) *Applicability date.*—Paragraph (g)(1) of this section applies to taxable years beginning after December 31, 2013.

(n) *Effective/applicability date.*—(1) Except as provided in paragraphs (n)(2) and (3) of this section, this section applies to taxable years ending after December 31, 2013.

(2) Paragraphs (c)(4), (d)(1) and (d)(2) of this section apply to taxable years beginning after December 31, 2016. Paragraph (f) of this section applies to taxable years beginning after December 31, 2018. Paragraphs (d)(1) and (d)(2) of §1.36B-3, as contained in 26 CFR part I edition revised as of April 1, 2016, applies to taxable years ending after December 31, 2013, and beginning before January 1, 2017. Paragraph (f) of §1.36B-3, as contained in 26 CFR part I edition revised as of April 1, 2016, applies to taxable years ending after December 31, 2013, and beginning before January 1, 2019.

(3) Paragraph (d)(1)(i) of this section applies to taxable years beginning after December 31, 2022. [Reg. §1.36B-3.]

☐ [*T.D. 9590, 5-18-2012 (corrected 7-11-2012). Amended by T.D. 9683, 7-24-2014, T.D. 9745, 12-16-2015 (corrected 1-14-2016), T.D. 9804, 12-14-2016, T.D. 9822, 7-24-2017 and T.D. 9968, 10-11-2022.]*

[Reg. §1.36B-4]

§1.36B-4. Reconciling the premium tax credit with advance credit payments.—(a) *Reconciliation.*—(1) *Coordination of premium tax credit with advance credit payments.*—(i) *In general.*—A taxpayer must reconcile the amount of credit allowed under section 36B with advance credit payments on the taxpayer's income tax return for a taxable year. A taxpayer whose premium tax credit for the taxable year exceeds the taxpayer's advance credit payments may receive the excess as an income tax refund. A taxpayer whose advance credit payments for the taxable year exceed the taxpayer's premium tax credit owes the excess as an additional income tax liability.

(ii) *Allocation rules and responsibility for advance credit payments.*—(A) *In general.*—A taxpayer must reconcile all advance credit payments for coverage of any member of the taxpayer's family.

(B) *Individuals enrolled by a taxpayer and claimed as a personal exemption deduction by another taxpayer.*—(1) *In general.*—If a taxpayer (the enrolling taxpayer) enrolls an individual in a qualified health plan and another taxpayer (the claiming taxpayer) claims a personal exemption deduction for the individual (the shifting enrollee), then for purposes of computing each taxpayer's premium tax credit and reconciling any advance credit payments, the enrollment premiums and advance credit payments for the plan in which the shifting enrollee was enrolled are allocated under this paragraph (a)(1)(ii)(B) according to the allocation percentage described in paragraph (a)(1)(ii)(B)(2) of this section. If advance credit payments are allocated under paragraph (a)(1)(ii)(B)(4) of this section, the claiming taxpayer and enrolling taxpayer must use this same allocation percentage to calculate their §1.36B-3(d)(1)(ii) adjusted monthly premiums for the applicable benchmark plan (benchmark plan premiums). This paragraph (a)(1)(ii)(B) does not apply to amounts allocated under §1.36B-3(h) (qualified health plan covering more than one family) or if the shifting enrollee or enrollees are the only individuals enrolled in the qualified health plan. For purposes of this paragraph (a)(1)(ii)(B)(1), a taxpayer who is expected at enrollment in a qualified health plan to be the taxpayer filing an income tax return for the year of coverage with respect to an individual enrolling in the plan has enrolled that individual. For taxable years to which section 151(d)(5) applies, the claiming taxpayer is the taxpayer who properly includes the shifting enrollee in his or her family for the taxable year.

(2) *Allocation percentage.*—The enrolling taxpayer and claiming taxpayer may agree on any allocation percentage between zero and one hundred percent. If the enrolling taxpayer and claiming taxpayer do not agree on an allocation percentage, the percentage is equal to the number of shifting enrollees properly included in the enrolling taxpayer's family divided by the number of individuals enrolled by the enrolling taxpayer in the same qualified health plan as the shifting enrollee.

(3) *Allocating premiums.*—In computing the premium tax credit, the claiming taxpayer is allocated a portion of the enrollment premiums for the plan in which the shifting enrollee was enrolled equal to the enrollment premiums times the allocation percentage. The enrolling taxpayer is allocated the remainder of the enrollment premiums not allocated to one or more claiming taxpayers.

(4) *Allocating advance credit payments.*—In reconciling any advance credit payments, the claiming taxpayer is allocated a portion

of the advance credit payments for the plan in which the shifting enrollee was enrolled equal to the enrolling taxpayer's advance credit payments for the plan times the allocation percentage. The enrolling taxpayer is allocated the remainder of the advance credit payments not allocated to one or more claiming taxpayers. This paragraph (a)(1)(ii)(B)(4) only applies in situations in which advance credit payments are made for coverage of a shifting enrollee.

(5) *Premiums for the applicable benchmark plan.*—If paragraph (a)(1)(ii)(B)(4) of this section applies, the claiming taxpayer's benchmark plan premium is the sum of the benchmark plan premium for the claiming taxpayer's coverage family, excluding the shifting enrollee or enrollees, and the allocable portion. The allocable portion for purposes of this paragraph (a)(1)(ii)(B)(5) is the product of the benchmark plan premium for the enrolling taxpayer's coverage family if the shifting enrollee was a member of the enrolling taxpayer's coverage family and the allocation percentage. If the enrolling taxpayer's coverage family is enrolled in more than one qualified health plan, the allocable portion is determined as if the enrolling taxpayer's coverage family includes only the coverage family members who enrolled in the same plan as the shifting enrollee or enrollees. The enrolling taxpayer's benchmark plan premium is the benchmark plan premium for the enrolling taxpayer's coverage family had the shifting enrollee or enrollees remained a part of the enrolling taxpayer's coverage family, minus the allocable portion.

(C) *Responsibility for advance credit payments for an individual not reported on any taxpayer's return.*—If advance credit payments are made for coverage of an individual who is not included in any taxpayer's family, as defined in §1.36B-1(d), the taxpayer who attested to the Exchange to the intention to include such individual in the taxpayer's family as part of the advance credit payment eligibility determination for coverage of the individual must reconcile the advance credit payments.

(iii) *Advance credit payment for a month in which an issuer does not provide coverage.*—For purposes of reconciliation, a taxpayer does not have an advance credit payment for a month if the issuer of the qualified health plan in which the taxpayer or a family member is enrolled does not provide coverage for that month.

(2) *Credit computation.*—The premium assistance credit amount is computed on the taxpayer's return using the taxpayer's household income and family size for the taxable year. Thus, the taxpayer's contribution amount (household income for the taxable year times the applicable percentage) is determined using the taxpayer's household income and family size at the end of the taxable year. The applicable benchmark plan for each coverage month is determined under §1.36B-3(f).

(3) *Limitation on additional tax.*—(i) *In general.*—The additional tax imposed under paragraph (a)(1) of this section on a taxpayer whose household income is less than 400 percent of the Federal poverty line is limited to the amounts provided in the table in paragraph (a)(3)(ii) of this section (or successor tables). For taxable years beginning after December 31, 2014, the limitation amounts may be adjusted in published guidance, see §601.601(d)(2) of this chapter, to reflect changes in the consumer price index.

(ii) *Additional tax limitation table.*—

Household income percentage of Federal poverty line	Limitation amount for taxpayers whose tax is determined under section 1(c)	Limitation amount for all other taxpayers
Less than 200%	$ 300	$ 600
At least 200% but less than 300%	$ 750	$1,500
At least 300% but less than 400%	$1,250	$2,500

(iii) *Limitation on additional tax for taxpayers who claim a section 162(l) deduction for a qualified health plan.*—(A) *In general.*—A taxpayer who receives advance credit payments and deducts premiums for a qualified health plan under section 162(l) must use paragraph (a)(3)(iii)(B), and paragraph (a)(3)(iii)(C) or (D), of this section to determine the limitation on additional tax in this paragraph (a)(3) (limitation amount). Taxpayers must make this determination before calculating their section 162(l) deduction and premium tax credit. For additional rules for taxpayers who may claim a deduction under section 162(l) for a qualified health plan for which advance credit payments are made, see §1.162(l)-1.

(B) *Determining the limitation amount.*—A taxpayer described in paragraph (a)(3)(iii)(A) of this section must use the limitation amount for which the taxpayer qualifies under paragraph (a)(3)(iii)(C) or (D) of this section. The limitation amount determined under this paragraph (a)(3)(iii) replaces the limitation amount that would otherwise be determined under the additional tax limitation table in paragraph (a)(3)(ii) of this section. In applying paragraph (a)(3)(iii)(C) of this section, a taxpayer must first determine whether

he or she qualifies for the limitation amount applicable to taxpayers with household income of less than 200 percent of the Federal poverty line for the taxpayer's family size. If the taxpayer does not qualify to use the limitation amount applicable to taxpayers with household income of less than 200 percent of the Federal poverty line for the taxpayer's family size, the taxpayer must next determine whether he or she qualifies for the limitation applicable to taxpayers with household income of less than 300 percent of the Federal poverty line for the taxpayer's family size. If the taxpayer does not qualify to use the limitation amount applicable to taxpayers with household income of less than 300 percent of the Federal poverty line for the taxpayer's family size, the taxpayer must next determine whether he or she qualifies for the limitation applicable to taxpayers with household income of less than 400 percent of the Federal poverty line for the taxpayer's family size. If the taxpayer does not qualify to use the limitation amount applicable to taxpayers with household income of less than 200 percent, 300 percent, or 400 percent of the Federal poverty line for the taxpayer's family size, the limitation on additional tax under section 36B(f)(2)(B) does not apply to the taxpayer.

(C) *Requirements.*—A taxpayer meets the requirements of this paragraph (a)(3)(iii)(C) for a limitation amount if the taxpayer's household income as a percentage of the Federal poverty line is less than or equal to the maximum household income as a percentage of the Federal poverty line for which that limitation is available. Household income for this purpose is determined by using a section 162(l) deduction equal to the lesser of—

(1) The sum of the specified premiums for the plan not paid through advance credit payments, the limitation amount (determined without regard to paragraph (a)(1)(iii)(C)(2) of this section), and any deduction allowable under section 162(l) for premiums other than specified premiums, and

(2) The earned income from the trade or business with respect to which the health insurance plan is established.

(D) *Specified premiums not paid through advance credit payments.*—For purposes of paragraph (a)(3)(iii)(C) of this section, specified premiums not paid through advance credit payments means specified premiums, as defined in § 1.162(l)-1(a)(2), minus advance credit payments made with respect to the specified premiums.

(E) *Examples.*—For examples illustrating the rules of this paragraph (a)(3)(iii), see *Examples 13, 14,* and *15* of paragraph (a)(4) of this section.

(4) *Examples.*—The following examples illustrate the rules of this paragraph (a). In each example the taxpayer enrolls in a higher cost qualified health plan than the applicable benchmark plan:

Example 1. Household income increases. (i) Taxpayer A is single and has no dependents. The Exchange for A's rating area projects A's 2014 household income to be $27,925 (250 percent of the Federal poverty line for a family of one, applicable percentage 8.05). A enrolls in a qualified health plan. The annual premium for the applicable benchmark plan is $5,200. A's advance credit payments are $2,952, computed as follows: benchmark plan premium of $5,200 less contribution amount of $2,248 (projected household income of $27,925 × .0805) = $2,952.

(ii) A's household income for 2014 is $33,622, which is 301 percent of the Federal poverty line for a family of one (applicable percentage 9.5). Consequently, A's premium tax credit for 2014 is $2,006 (benchmark plan premium of $5,200 less contribution amount of $3,194 (household income of $33,622 × .095)). Because A's advance credit payments for 2014 are $2,952 and A's 2014 credit is $2,006, A has excess advance payments of $946. Under paragraph (a)(1) of this section, A's tax liability for 2014 is increased by $946. Because A's household income is between 300 percent and 400 percent of the Federal poverty line, if A's excess advance payments exceeded $1,250, under the limitation of paragraph (a)(3) of this section, A's additional tax liability would be limited to that amount.

Example 2. Household income increases, repayment limitation applies. The facts are the same as in *Example 1,* except that A's household income for 2014 is $43,560 (390 percent of the Federal poverty line for a family of one, applicable percentage 9.5). Consequently, A's premium tax credit for 2014 is $1,062 ($5,200 benchmark plan premium less contribution amount of $4,138 (household income of $43,560 × .095)). A's advance credit payments for 2014 are $2,952; therefore, A has excess advance payments of $1,890. Because A's household income is between 300 percent and 400 percent of the Federal poverty line, A's additional tax liability for the taxable year is $1,250 under the repayment limitation of paragraph (a)(3) of this section.

Example 3. Household income decreases. The facts are the same as in *Example 1,* except that A's actual household income for 2014 is $22,340 (200 percent of the Federal poverty line for a family of one, applicable percentage 6.3). Consequently, A's premium tax credit for 2014 is $3,793 ($5,200 benchmark plan premium less contribution amount of $1,407 (household income of $22,340 × .063)). Because A's advance credit payments for 2014 are $2,952, A is allowed an additional credit of $841 ($3,793 less $2,952).

Example 4. Family size decreases. (i) Taxpayers B and C are married and have two children, K and L (ages 17 and 20), whom they claim as dependents in 2013. The Exchange for their rating area projects their 2014 household income to be $63,388 (275 percent of the Federal poverty line for a family of four, applicable percentage 8.78). B and C enroll in a qualified health plan for 2014 that covers the four family members. The annual premium for the applicable benchmark plan is $14,100. B's and C's advance credit payments for 2014 are $8,535, computed as follows: benchmark plan premium of $14,100 less contribution amount of $5,565 (projected household income of $63,388 × .0878) = $8,535.

(ii) In 2014, B and C do not claim L as their dependent (and no taxpayer claims a personal exemption deduction for L). Consequently, B's and C's family size for 2014 is three, their household income of $63,388 is 332 percent of the Federal poverty line for a family of three (applicable percentage 9.5), and the annual premium for their applicable benchmark plan is $12,000. Their premium tax

credit for 2014 is $5,978 ($12,000 benchmark plan premium less $6,022 contribution amount (household income of $63,388 x .095)). Because B's and C's advance credit payments for 2014 are $8,535 and their 2014 credit is $5,978, B and C have excess advance payments of $2,557. B's and C's additional tax liability for 2014 under paragraph (a)(1) of this section, however, is limited to $2,500 under paragraph (a)(3) of this section.

Example 5. Repayment limitation does not apply. (i) Taxpayer D is single and has no dependents. The Exchange for D's rating area approves advance credit payments for D based on 2014 household income of $39,095 (350 percent of the Federal poverty line for a family of one, applicable percentage 9.5). D enrolls in a qualified health plan. The annual premium for the applicable benchmark plan is $5,200. D's advance credit payments are $1,486, computed as follows: benchmark plan premium of $5,200 less contribution amount of $3,714 (projected household income of $39,095 × .095) = $1,486.

(ii) D's actual household income for 2014 is $44,903, which is 402 percent of the Federal poverty line for a family of one. D is not an applicable taxpayer and may not claim a premium tax credit. Additionally, the repayment limitation of paragraph (a)(3) of this section does not apply. Consequently, D has excess advance payments of $1,486 (the total amount of the advance credit payments in 2014). Under paragraph (a)(1) of this section, D's tax liability for 2014 is increased by $1,486.

Example 6. Coverage for less than a full taxable year. (i) Taxpayer F is single and has no dependents. In November 2013, the Exchange for F's rating area projects F's 2014 household income to be $27,925 (250 percent of the Federal poverty line for a family of one, applicable percentage 8.05). F enrolls in a qualified health plan. The annual premium for the applicable benchmark plan is $5,200. F's monthly advance credit payment is $246, computed as follows: benchmark plan premium of $5,200 less contribution amount of $2,248 (projected household income of $27,925 × .0805) = $2,952; $2,952/12 = $246.

(ii) F begins a new job in August 2014 and is eligible for employer-sponsored minimum essential coverage for the period September through December 2014. F discontinues her Exchange coverage effective November 1, 2014. F's household income for 2014 is $28,707 (257 percent of the Federal poverty line for a family size of one, applicable percentage 8.25).

(iii) Under § 1.36B-3(a), F's premium assistance credit amount is the sum of the premium assistance amounts for the coverage months. Under § 1.36B-3(c)(1)(iii), a month in which an individual is eligible for minimum essential coverage other than coverage in the individual market is not a coverage month. Because F is eligible for employer-sponsored minimum essential coverage as of September 1, only the months January through August of 2014 are coverage months.

(iv) If F had 12 coverage months in 2014, F's premium tax credit would be $2,832 (benchmark plan premium of $5,200 less contribution amount of $2,368 (household income of $28,707 × .0825)). Because F has only eight coverage months in 2014, F's credit is $1,888 ($2,832/12 × 8). Because F does not discontinue her Exchange coverage until November 1, 2014, F's advance credit payments for 2014 are $2,460 ($246 × 10). Consequently, F has excess advance payments of $572 ($2,460 less $1,888) and F's tax liability for 2014 is increased by $572 under paragraph (a)(1) of this section.

Example 7. Changes in coverage months and applicable benchmark plan. (i) Taxpayer E claims one dependent, F. E is eligible for government-sponsored minimum essential coverage. E enrolls F in a qualified health plan for 2014. The Exchange for E's rating area projects E's 2014 household income to be $30,260 (200 percent of the Federal poverty line for a family of two, applicable percentage 6.3). The annual premium for E's applicable benchmark plan is $5,200. E's monthly advance credit payment is $275, computed as follows: benchmark plan premium of $5,200 less contribution amount of $1,906 (projected household income of $30,260 × .063) = $3,294; $3,294/12 = $275.

(ii) On August 1, 2014, E loses her eligibility for government-sponsored minimum essential coverage. E enrolls in the qualified health plan that covers F for August through December 2014. The annual premium for the applicable benchmark plan is $10,000. The Exchange computes E's monthly advance credit payments for the period September through December to be $675 as follows: benchmark plan premium of $10,000 less contribution amount of $1,906 (projected household income of $30,260 × .063) = $8,094; $8,094/12 = $675. E's household income for 2014 is $28,747 (190 percent of the Federal poverty line, applicable percentage 5.84).

(iii) Under § 1.36B-3(c)(1), January through July of 2014 are coverage months for F and August through December are coverage months for E and F. Under paragraph (a)(2) of this section, E must compute her premium tax credit using the premium for the applicable benchmark plan for each coverage month. E's premium assistance credit amount for 2014 is the sum of the premium assistance amounts for all coverage months. E reconciles her premium tax credit with advance credit payments as follows:

Advance credit payments (Jan. to July)	$1,925 ($275 × 7)
Advance credit payments (Aug. to Dec.)	3,375 ($675 × 5)
Total advance credit payments	5,300
Benchmark plan premium (Jan. to July)	3,033 (($5,200/12) × 7)
Benchmark plan premium (Aug. to Dec.)	4,167 (($10,000/12) × 5)
Total benchmark plan premium	7,200
Contribution amount (taxable year household income × applicable percentage)	1,679 ($28,747 × .0584)
Credit (total benchmark plan premium less contribution amount)	5,521

(iv) E's advance credit payments for 2014 are $5,300. E's premium tax credit is $5,521. Thus, E is allowed an additional credit of $221.

Example 8. Part-year coverage and changes in coverage months and applicable benchmark plan. (i) The facts are the same as in *Example 7*, except that F is eligible for government-sponsored minimum essential coverage for January and February 2014, and E enrolls F in a qualified health plan beginning in March 2014. Thus, March through July are coverage months for F and August through December are coverage months for E and F.

(ii) E reconciles her premium tax credit with advance credit payments as follows:

Advance credit payments (March to July)	$1,375 ($275 × 5)
Advance credit payments (Aug. to Dec.)	3,375 ($675 × 5)
Total advance credit payments	4,750
Benchmark plan premium (March to July)	2,167 (($5,200/12) × 5)
Benchmark plan premium (Aug. to Dec.)	4,167 (($10,000/12) × 5)
Total benchmark plan premium	6,334
Contribution amount for 10 coverage months (taxable year household income × applicable percentage × 10/12)	1,399 ($28,747 × .0584 × 10/12)
Credit (total benchmark plan premium less contribution amount)	4,935

(iii) E's advance credit payments for 2014 are $4,750. E's premium tax credit is $4,935. Thus, E is allowed an additional credit of $185.

Example 9. Advance credit payments for months an issuer does not provide coverage. (i) Taxpayer F enrolls in a qualified health plan for 2014 and the Exchange approves advance credit payments. F pays the portion of the premium not covered by advance credit payments for January through April of 2014 but fails to make payments in May, June, and July. As a result, the issuer of the qualified health plan initiates the 3-month grace period under section 1412(c)(2)(B)(iv)(II) of the Affordable Care Act and 45 CFR 156.270(d). During the grace period the issuer continues to receive advance credit payments on behalf of F. On July 1 the issuer rescinds F's coverage retroactive to the end of the first month of the grace period, May 31.

(ii) Under paragraph (a)(1)(iii) of this section, F does not take into account advance credit payments for June or July of 2014 when reconciling the premium tax credit with advance credit payments under paragraph (a)(1) of this section.

Example 10. Allocation percentage, agreement on allocation. (i) Taxpayers G and H are divorced and have two children, J and K. G enrolls herself and J and K in a qualified health plan for 2014. The premium for the plan in which G enrolls is $13,000. The Exchange in G's rating area approves advance credit payments for G based on a family size of three, an annual benchmark plan premium of $12,000, and projected 2014 household income of $58,590 (300 percent of the Federal poverty line for a family of three, applicable percentage 9.5). G's advance credit payments for 2014 are $6,434 ($12,000 benchmark plan premium less $5,566 contribution amount (household income of $58,590 x .095)). G's actual household income for 2014 is $58,900.

(ii) K lives with H for more than half of 2014 and H claims K as a dependent for 2014. G and H agree to an allocation percentage, as described in paragraph (a)(1)(ii)(B)(2) of this section, of 20 percent. Under the agreement, H is allocated 20 percent of the items to be allocated, and G is allocated the remainder of those items.

(iii) If H is eligible for a premium tax credit, H takes into account $2,600 of the premiums for the plan in which K was enrolled ($13,000 x .20) and $2,400 of G's benchmark plan premium ($12,000 x .20). In addition, H is responsible for reconciling $1,287 ($6,434 x .20) of the advance credit payments for K's coverage.

(iv) G's family size for 2014 includes only G and J and G's household income of $58,900 is 380 percent of the Federal poverty line for a family of two (applicable percentage 9.5). G's benchmark plan premium for 2014 is $9,600 (the benchmark premium for the plan covering G, J, and K ($12,000), minus the amount allocated to H ($2,400). Consequently, G's premium tax credit is $4,004 (G's benchmark plan premium of $9,600 minus G's contribution amount of $5,596 ($58,900 x .095)). G has an excess advance payment of $1,143 (the excess of the advance credit payments of $5,147 ($6,434 - $1,287 allocated to H) over the premium tax credit of $4,004).

Example 11. Allocation percentage, no agreement on allocation. (i) The facts are the same as in *Example 10* of paragraph (a)(4) of this section, except that G and H do not agree on an allocation percentage. Under paragraph (a)(1)(ii)(B)(2) of this section, the allocation percentage is 33 percent, computed as follows: the number of shifting enrollees, 1 (K), divided by the number of individuals enrolled by the enrolling taxpayer on the same qualified health plan as the shifting enrollee, 3 (G, J, and K). Thus, H is allocated 33 percent of the items to be allocated, and G is allocated the remainder of those items.

(ii) If H is eligible for a premium tax credit, H takes into account $4,290 of the premiums for the plan in which K was enrolled ($13,000 x .33). H, in computing H's benchmark plan premium, must include $3,960 of G's benchmark plan premium ($12,000 x .33). In addition, H is responsible for reconciling $2,123 ($6,434 x .33) of the advance credit payments for K's coverage.

(iii) G's benchmark plan premium for 2014 is $8,040 (the benchmark premium for the plan covering G, J, and K ($12,000), minus the amount allocated to H ($3,960). Consequently, G's premium tax credit is $2,444 (G's benchmark plan premium of $8,040 minus G's contribution amount of $5,596 ($58,900 x .095)). G has an excess advance credit payment of $1,867 (the excess of the advance credit payments of $4,311 ($6,434 - $2,123 allocated to H) over the premium tax credit of $2,444).

Example 12. Allocations for an emancipated child. Spouses L and M enroll in a qualified health plan with their child, N. L and M attest that they will claim N as a dependent and advance credit payments are made for the coverage of all three family members. However, N files his own return and claims a personal exemption deduction for himself for the taxable year. Under paragraph (a)(1)(ii)(B)(1) of this section, L and M are enrolling taxpayers, N is a claiming taxpayer, and all are subject to the allocation rules in paragraph (a)(1)(ii)(B) of this section.

Example 13. Taxpayer with advance credit payments allowed a section 162(l) deduction but not a limitation on additional tax. (i) In 2014, B, B's spouse, and their two dependents enroll in the applicable second lowest cost silver plan with an annual premium of $14,000. B's advance credit payments attributable to the premiums are $8,000. B is self-employed for all of 2014 and derives $75,000 of earnings from B's trade or business. B's household income without including a deduction under section 162(l) for specified premiums is $103,700. The Federal poverty line for a family the size of B's family is $23,550.

(ii) Because B received the benefit of advance credit payments and deducts premiums for a qualified health plan under section 162(l), B must determine whether B is allowed a limitation on additional tax under paragraph (a)(3)(iii) of this section. B begins by testing eligibility for the $600 limitation amount for taxpayers with household income at less than 200 percent of the Federal poverty line for the taxpayer's family size. B determines household income as a percentage of the Federal poverty line by taking a section 162(l) deduction equal to the lesser of $6,600 (the sum of the amount of premiums not paid through advance credit payments, $6,000 ($14,000 - $8,000), and the limitation amount, $600) and $75,000 (the earned income from the trade or business with respect to which the health insurance plan is established). The result is $97,100 ($103,700-$6,600) or 412 percent of the Federal poverty line for B's family size. Since 412 percent is not less than 200 percent, B may not use a $600 limitation amount.

(iii) B performs the same calculation for the $1,500 ($103,700 - $7,500 = $96,200 or 408 percent of the Federal poverty line) and $2,500 limitation amounts ($103,700 - $8,500 = $95,200 or 404 percent of the Federal poverty line), the amounts for taxpayers with household income of less than 300 percent or 400 percent, respectively, of the Federal poverty line for the taxpayer's family size, and determines that B may not use either of those limitation amounts. Because B does not meet the requirements of paragraph (a)(3)(iii) of this section for any of the limitation amounts in section 36B(f)(2)(B), B is not eligible for the limitation on additional tax for excess advance credit payments.

(iv) Although B may not claim a limitation on additional tax for excess advance credit payments, B may still be eligible for a premium tax credit. B would determine eligibility for the premium tax credit, the amount of the premium tax credit, and the section 162(l) deduction using the rules under section 36B and section 162(l), applying no limitation on additional tax.

Example 14. Taxpayer with advance credit payments allowed a section 162(l) deduction and a limitation on additional tax. (i) The facts are the same as in *Example 13* of paragraph (a)(4) of this section, except that B's household income without including a deduction under section 162(l) for specified premiums is $78,802.

(ii) Because B received the benefit of advance credit payments and deducts premiums for a qualified health plan under section 162(l), B must determine whether B is allowed a limitation on additional tax under paragraph (a)(3)(iii) of this section. B first determines that B does not meet the requirements of paragraph (a)(3)(iii)(C) of this section for using the $600 or $1,500 limitation amounts, the amounts for taxpayers with household income of less than 200 percent or 300 percent, respectively, of the Federal poverty line for the taxpayer's family size. That is because B's household income as a percentage of the Federal poverty line, determined by using a section 162(l) deduction for premiums for the qualified health plan equal to the lesser of the sum of the premiums for the plan not paid through advance credit payments and the limitation amount, and the earned income from the trade or business with respect to which the health insurance plan is established, is more than the maximum household income as a percentage of the Federal poverty line for which that limitation is available (using the $600 limitation, B's household income would be $72,202 ($78,802 – ($6,000 + $600)), which is 307 percent of the Federal poverty line for B's family size; and using the $1,500 limitation, B's household income would be $71,302 ($78,802 – ($6,000 + $1,500)), which is 303 percent of the Federal poverty line for B's family size).

(iii) However, B meets the requirements of paragraph (a)(3)(iii)(C) of this section using the $2,500 limitation amount for taxpayers with household income of less than 400 percent of the Federal poverty line for the taxpayer's family size. That is because B's household income as a percentage of the Federal poverty line by taking a section 162(l) deduction equal to the lesser of $8,500 (the sum of the amount of premiums not paid through advance credit payments, $6,000, and the limitation amount, $2,500) and $75,000 (the earned income from the trade or business with respect to which the health insurance plan is established), is $70,302 (299 percent of the Federal poverty line), which is below 400 percent of the Federal poverty line for B's family size, and is less than the maximum amount for which that limitation is available. Thus, B uses a limitation amount of $2,500 in computing B's additional tax on excess advance credit payments.

(iv) B may determine the amount of the premium tax credit and the section 162(l) deduction using the rules under section 36B and section 162(l), applying the $2,500 limitation amount determined above.

Example 15. Taxpayer with advance credit payments allowed a section 162(l) deduction and a limitation on additional tax limited to earned income from trade or business. (i) In 2017, C, C's spouse, and their two dependents enroll in the applicable second lowest cost silver plan with an annual premium of $14,000. C's advance credit payments attributable to the premiums are $8,000. C is self-employed for all of 2017 and derives $3,000 of earnings from C's trade or business. C's household income, without including a deduction under section 162(l) for specified premiums, is $39,100. The Federal poverty line for *a family the size of* C's family is $24,600.

(ii) Because C received the benefit of advance credit payments and deducts premiums for a qualified health plan under section 162(l), C must determine whether C is allowed a limitation on additional tax under paragraph (a)(3)(iii) of this section. C begins by testing eligibility for the $600 limitation amount for taxpayers with household income at less than 200 percent of the Federal poverty line for the taxpayer's family size. C determines household income as a percentage of the Federal poverty line by taking a section 162(l) deduction equal to the lesser of $6,600 (the sum of the amount of premiums not paid through advance credit payments, $6,000 ($14,000 - $8,000), and the limitation amount, $600), and C's earned income from the trade or business with respect to which the health insurance plan is established). The result is $36,100 ($39,100 - $3,000) or 147 percent of the Federal poverty line for C's family size. Because 147 percent is less than 200 percent, the limitation amount under paragraph (a)(3)(iii) of this section that C uses in computing C's additional tax on excess advance credit payments is $600.

(iii) C may determine the amount of the premium tax credit and the section 162(l) deduction using the rules under section 36B and section 162(l), applying the $600 limitation amount determined above.

(b) *Changes in filing status.*—(1) *In general.*—Except as provided in paragraph (b)(2) or (b)(3) of this section, a taxpayer whose marital status changes during the taxable year computes the premium tax credit by using the applicable benchmark plan or plans for the taxpayer's marital status as of the first day of each coverage month. The taxpayer's contribution amount (household income for the taxable year times the applicable percentage) is determined using the taxpayer's household income and family size at the end of the taxable year.

(2) *Taxpayers who marry during the taxable year.*—(i) *In general.*—Taxpayers who marry during and file a joint return for the taxable year may compute the additional tax imposed under paragraph (a)(1) of this section under paragraph (b)(2)(ii) of this section. Only taxpayers who are unmarried at the beginning of the taxable year and are married (within the meaning of section 7703) at the end of the taxable year, at least one of whom receives advance credit payments, may use this alternative computation.

(ii) *Alternative computation of additional tax liability.*—(A) *In general.*—The additional tax liability determined under this paragraph (b)(2)(ii) is equal to the excess of the taxpayers' advance credit payments for the taxable year over the amount of the alternative marriage-year credit. The alternative marriage-year credit is the sum of both taxpayers' alternative premium assistance amounts for the pre-marriage months and the premium assistance amounts for the marriage months. This paragraph (b)(2)(ii) may not be used to increase the additional premium tax credit computed under paragraph (a)(1)(i) of this section.

(B) *Alternative premium assistance amounts for pre-marriage months.*—Taxpayers compute the alternative premium assistance amounts for each taxpayer for each full or partial month the taxpayers are unmarried as described in paragraph (a)(2) of this section, except that each taxpayer treats the amount of household income as one-half of the actual household income for the taxable year and treats family size as the number of individuals in the taxpayer's family prior to the marriage. The taxpayers may include a dependent of the taxpayers for the taxable year in either taxpayer's family size for the pre-marriage months.

(C) *Premium assistance amounts for marriage months.*—Taxpayers compute the premium assistance amounts for each full month the taxpayers are married as described in paragraph (a)(2) of this section.

(3) *Taxpayers not married to each other at the end of the taxable year.*—Taxpayers who are married (within the meaning of section 7703) to each other during a taxable year but legally separate under a decree of divorce or of separate maintenance during the taxable year, and who are enrolled in the same qualified health plan at any time during the taxable year must allocate the benchmark plan premiums, the enrollment premiums, and the advance credit payments for the period the taxpayers are married during the taxable year. Taxpayers must also allocate these items if one of the taxpayers has a dependent enrolled in the same plan as the taxpayer's former spouse or enrolled in the same plan as a dependent of the taxpayer's former spouse. The taxpayers may allocate these items to each former spouse in any proportion but must allocate all items in the same proportion. If the taxpayers do not agree on an allocation that is reported to the IRS in accordance with the relevant forms and instructions, 50 percent of: the benchmark plan premiums; the enrollment premiums; and the advance credit payments for the married period, is allocated to each taxpayer. If for a period a plan covers only one of the taxpayers and no dependents, only one of the taxpayers and one or more dependents of that same taxpayer, or only one or more dependents of one of the taxpayers, then the benchmark plan premiums, the enrollment premiums, and the advance credit payments for that period are allocated entirely to that taxpayer.

(4) *Taxpayers filing returns as married filing separately or head of household.*—(i) *Allocation of advance credit payments.*—Except as provided in §1.36B-2(b)(2)(ii), the premium tax credit is allowed to married (within the meaning of section 7703) taxpayers only if they file joint returns. *See* §1.36B-2(b)(2)(i). Taxpayers who receive advance credit payments as married taxpayers and who do not file a joint return must allocate the advance credit payments for coverage under a qualified health plan equally to each taxpayer for any period the plan covers and in which advance credit payments are made for both taxpayers, only one of the taxpayers and one or more dependents of the other taxpayer, or one or more dependents of both taxpayers. If, for a period a plan covers, advance credit payments are made for only one of the taxpayers and no dependents, only one of the taxpayers and one or more dependents of that same taxpayer, or only one or more dependents of one of the taxpayers, the advance credit payments for that period are allocated entirely to that taxpayer. If one or both of the taxpayers is an applicable taxpayer eligible for a premium tax credit for the taxable year, the premium tax credit is computed by allocating the enrollment premiums under paragraph (b)(4)(ii) of this section. The repayment limitation described in paragraph (a)(3) of this section applies to each taxpayer based on the household income and family size reported on that taxpayer's return. This paragraph (b)(4) also applies to taxpayers who receive advance credit payments as married taxpayers and file a tax return using the head of household filing status.

(ii) *Allocation of premiums.*—If taxpayers who are married within the meaning of section 7703, without regard to section 7703(b), do not file a joint return, 50 percent of the enrollment premiums are allocated to each taxpayer. However, all of the enrollment premiums are allocated to only one of the taxpayers for a period in which a qualified health plan covers only that taxpayer and no dependents, only that taxpayer and one or more dependents of that taxpayer, or only one or more dependents of that taxpayer.

(5) *Examples.*—The following examples illustrate the provisions of this paragraph (b). In each example the taxpayer enrolls in a higher cost qualified health plan than the applicable benchmark plan:

Example 1. Taxpayers marry during the taxable year, general rule for computing additional tax. (i) P is a single taxpayer with no dependents. In 2013 the Exchange for the rating area where P resides determines that P's 2014 household income will be $40,000 (358 percent of the Federal poverty line, applicable percentage 9.5). P enrolls in a qualified health plan. The premium for the applicable benchmark plan is $5,200. P's monthly advance credit payment is $117, computed as follows: $5,200 benchmark plan premium minus contribution amount of $3,800 ($40,000 × .095) equals $1,400 (total advance credit payment); $1,400/12 = $117.

(ii) Q is a single taxpayer with two dependents. In 2013 the Exchange for the rating area where Q resides determines that Q's 2014 household income will be $35,000 (183 percent of the Federal poverty line, applicable percentage 5.52). Q enrolls in a qualified health plan. The premium for the applicable benchmark plan is $10,000. Q's monthly advance credit payment is $672, computed as follows: $10,000 benchmark plan premium minus contribution amount of $1,932 ($35,000 × .0552) equals $8,068 (total advance credit); $8,068/12 = $672.

(iii) P and Q marry on July 17, 2014 and enroll in a single policy for a qualified health plan covering four family members, effective August 1, 2014. The premium for the applicable benchmark plan is $14,000. Based on household income of $75,000 and a family size of four (325 percent of the Federal poverty line, applicable percentage 9.5), the Exchange approves advance credit payments of $573 per month, computed as follows: $14,000 benchmark plan premium minus contribution amount of $7,125 ($75,000 × .095) equals $6,875 (total advance credit); $6,875/12 = $573.

(iv) P and Q file a joint return for 2014 and report $75,000 in household income and a family size of four. P and Q compute their credit at reconciliation under paragraph (b)(1) of this section. They use the premiums for the applicable benchmark plans that apply for the months married and the months not married, and their contribution amount is based on their Federal poverty line percentage at the end of the taxable year. P and Q reconcile their premium tax credit with advance credit payments as follows:

Advance payments for P (Jan. to July)	$ 819
Advance payments for Q (Jan. to July)	4,704
Advance payments for P and Q (Aug. to Dec.)	2,865
Total advance payments	8,388
Benchmark plan premium for P (Jan. to July)	3,033
Benchmark plan premium for Q (Jan. to July)	5,833
Benchmark plan premium for P and Q (Aug. to Dec.)	5,833
Total benchmark plan premium	14,699
Contribution amount (taxable year household income × applicable percentage)	7,125
Credit (total benchmark plan premium less contribution amount)	7,574
Additional tax	814

(v) P's and Q's tax liability for 2014 is increased by $814 under paragraph (a)(1) of this section.

Example 2. Taxpayers marry during the taxable year, alternative computation of additional tax. (i) The facts are the same as in *Example 1*, except that P and Q compute their additional tax liability under paragraph (b)(2)(ii) of this section. P's and Q's additional tax is the excess of their advance credit payments for the taxable year ($8,388) over their alternative marriage-year credit, which is the sum of the alternative premium assistance amounts for the pre-marriage months and the premium assistance amounts for the marriage months.

(ii) P and Q compute the alternative marriage-year credit as follows:

Alternative premium assistance amounts for pre-marriage months	
Benchmark plan premium for P (Jan. to July)	$3,033 (($5,200/12) × 7)
Contribution amount (1/2 taxable year household income × applicable percentage) × 7/12)	$2,078 ($37,500 × .095 × 7/12)
Alternative premium assistance amount for P's pre-marriage months	$ 955 ($3,033 - $2,078)
Benchmark plan premium for Q (Jan. to July)	$5,833 (($10,000/12) × 7)
Contribution amount (1/2 taxable year household income × applicable percentage × 7/12)	$1,339 ($37,500 × .0612 × 7/12)
Alternative premium assistance amount for Q's pre-marriage months	$4,494 ($5,833 - $1,339)
Premium assistance amount for marriage months	
Benchmark plan premium for P and Q (Aug. to Dec.)	$5,833 (($14,000/12 × 5)
Contribution amount (taxable year household income × applicable percentage × 5/12)	$2,969 ($75,000 × .095 × 5/12)
Premium assistance amount for marriage months	$2,864 ($5,833 - $2,969)

Alternative marriage-year credit (sum of premium assistance amounts for pre-marriage months and marriage months): $955 + $4,494 + $2,864 = $8,313.

Reg. §1.36B-4(b)(5)

(iii) P and Q reconcile their premium tax credit with advance credit payments by determining the excess of their advance credit payments ($8,388) over their alternative marriage-year credit ($8,313). P and Q must increase their tax liability by $75 under paragraph (a)(1) of this section.

Example 3. Taxpayers marry during the taxable year, alternative computation of additional tax, alternative marriage-year tax credit exceeds advance credit payments. The facts are the same as in *Example 2*, except that the amount of P's and Q's advance credit payments is $8,301. Thus, their alternative marriage-year credit ($8,313) exceeds the amount of their advance credit payments ($8,301). Under paragraph (b)(2)(ii)(A) of this section, the amount of additional tax liability and additional tax credit that P and Q report on their tax return is $0.

Example 4. Taxpayers marry during the taxable year, alternative computation of additional tax. (i) Taxpayer R is single and has no dependents. In 2013, the Exchange for the rating area where R resides determines that R's 2014 household income will be $40,000 (358 percent of the Federal poverty line, applicable percentage 9.5). R enrolls in a qualified health plan. The premium for the applicable benchmark plan is $5,200. R's monthly advance credit payment is $117, computed as follows: $5,200 benchmark plan premium minus

Advance payments for R (Jan. to Sept.)
Advance payments for S (Jan. to Sept.)
Advance payments for R and S (Oct. to Dec.)

Total advance payments

(iv) R and S file a joint return for 2014 and report $62,000 in household income and a family size of two (410 percent of the FPL for a family of 2). Thus, under §1.36B-2(b)(2), R and S are not applicable taxpayers for 2014 and may not claim a premium tax credit for 2014. However, they compute their additional tax liability under paragraph (b)(2)(ii) of this section. R's and S's additional tax is the excess of their advance credit payments for the taxable year ($5,232) over their alternative marriage-year credit, which is the sum

Premium assistance amount for pre-marriage months

Benchmark plan premium for R (Jan. to Sept.)	$3,900 (($5,200/12) × 9)
Contribution amount ((1/2 taxable year household income × applicable percentage) × 9/12)	$2,053 ($31,000 × .0883 × 9/12)
Premium assistance amount for R's pre-marriage months	$1,847 ($3,900 - $2,053)
Benchmark plan premium for S (Jan. to Sept.)	$3,900 (($5,200/12) × 9)
Contribution amount ((1/2 taxable year household income × applicable percentage) × 9/12)	$2,053 ($31,000 × .0883 × 9/12)
Premium assistance amount for S's pre-marriage months	$1,847 ($3,900 - $2,053)

Premium assistance amount for marriage months $0

Alternative marriage-year credit (sum of premium assistance amounts for pre-marriage months and marriage months): $1,847 + 1,847 + 0 = $3,694.

(vi) R and S reconcile their premium tax credit with advance credit payments by determining the excess of their advance credit payments ($5,232) over their alternative marriage-year credit ($3,694). R and S must increase their tax liability by $1,538 under paragraph (a)(1) of this section.

Example 5. (i) *Taxpayers marry during the taxable year, no additional tax liability.* The facts are the same as in *Example 4*, except that S has no income and is enrolled in Medicaid for January through September 2014 and R's and S's household income for 2014 is $37,000 (245 percent of the Federal poverty line, applicable percentage 7.88). Their advance credit payments for 2014 are $2,707 ($1,053 for R for January to September and $1,654 for R and S for October to December). Their premium tax credit for 2014 is $3,484 (total benchmark premium of $6,400 less contribution amount of $2,916).

(ii) Because R's and S's premium tax credit of $3,484 exceeds their advance credit payments of $2,707, R and S are allowed an additional credit of $777. Although R and S marry in 2014, paragraph (b)(2) of this section (the alternative computation of additional tax for taxpayers who marry during the taxable year) does not apply because they do not owe additional tax for 2014.

Example 6. Taxpayers divorce during the taxable year, 50 percent allocation. (i) Taxpayers V and W are married and have two dependents. In 2013, the Exchange for the rating area where the family resides determines that their 2014 household income will be $76,000 (330 percent of the Federal poverty line for a family of 4, applicable percentage 9.5). V and W enroll in a qualified health plan for 2014. *The premium for the applicable benchmark plan is $14,100.* The Exchange approves advance credit payments of $573 per month, computed as follows: $14,100 benchmark plan premium minus V and W's contribution amount of $7,220 ($76,000 × .095) equals $6,880 (total advance credit); $6,880/12 = $573.

contribution amount of $3,800 ($40,000 × .095) = $1,400 (total advance credit); $1,400/12 = $117.

(ii) Taxpayer S is single with no dependents. In 2013, the Exchange for the rating area where S resides determines that S's 2014 household income will be $20,000 (179 percent of the Federal poverty line, applicable percentage 5.33). S enrolls in a qualified health plan. The premium for the applicable benchmark plan is $5,200. S's monthly advance credit payment is $345, computed as follows: $5,200 benchmark plan premium minus contribution amount of $1,066 ($20,000 × .0533) = $4,134 (total advance credit); $4,134/12 = $345.

(iii) R and S marry in September 2014 and enroll in a single policy for a qualified health plan covering them both, beginning October 1, 2014. The premium for the applicable benchmark plan is $10,000. Based on household income of $60,000 and a family size of two (397 percent of the Federal poverty line, applicable percentage 9.5), R's and S's monthly advance credit payment is $358, computed as follows: $10,000 benchmark plan premium minus contribution amount of $5,700 ($60,000 × .095) = $4,300; $4,300/12 = $358. R's and S's advance credit payments for 2014 are $5,232, computed as follows:

$1,053 ($117 × 9)
3,105 ($345 × 9)
1,074 ($358 × 3)
──────
5,232

of the alternative premium assistance amounts for the pre-marriage months and the premium assistance amounts for the marriage months. In this case, R and S have no premium assistance amounts for the married months because their household income is over 400 percent of the Federal poverty line for a family of 2.

(v) R and S compute their alternative marriage-year credit as follows:

(ii) V and W divorce on June 17, 2014, and obtain separate qualified health plans beginning July 1, 2014. V enrolls based on household income of $60,000 and a family size of three (314 percent of the Federal poverty line, applicable percentage 9.5). The premium for the applicable benchmark plan is $10,000. The Exchange approves advance credit payments of $358 per month, computed as follows: $10,000 benchmark plan premium minus V's contribution amount of $5,700 ($60,000 × .095) equals $4,300 (total advance credit); $4,300/12 = $358.

(iii) W enrolls based on household income of $16,420 and a family size of one (147 percent of the Federal poverty line, applicable percentage 3.82). The premium for the applicable benchmark plan is $5,200. The Exchange approves advance credit payments of $381 per month, computed as follows: $5,200 benchmark plan premium minus W's contribution amount of $627 ($16,420 × .0382) equals $4,573 (total advance credit); $4,573/12 = $381. V and W do not agree on an allocation of the premium for the applicable benchmark plan, the premiums for the plan in which they enroll, and the advance credit payments for the period they were married in the taxable year.

(iv) V and W each compute their credit at reconciliation under paragraph (b)(1) of this section, using the premiums for the applicable benchmark plans that apply to them for the months married and the months not married, and the contribution amount based on their Federal poverty line percentages at the end of the taxable year. Under paragraph (b)(3) of this section, because V and W do not agree on an allocation, V and W must equally allocate the benchmark plan premium ($7,050) and the advance credit payments ($3,438) for the six-month period January through June 2014 when they are married and enrolled in the same qualified health plan. Thus, V and W each are allocated $3,525 of the benchmark plan premium ($7,050/2) and $1,719 of the advance credit payments ($3,438/2) for January through June.

(v) V reports on his 2014 tax return $60,000 in household income and family size of three. W reports on her 2014 tax return $16,420 in household income and family size of one. V and W reconcile their premium tax credit with advance credit payments as follows:

	V	W
Allocated advance payments (Jan. to June)	$1,719	$1,719
Actual advance payments (July to Dec.)	2,148	2,286
Total advance payments	3,867	4,005
Allocated benchmark plan premium (Jan. to June)	3,525	3,525
Actual benchmark plan premium (July to Dec.)	5,000	2,600
Total benchmark plan premium	8,525	6,125
Contribution amount (taxable year household income × applicable percentage)	5,700	627
Credit (total benchmark plan premium less contribution amount)	2,825	5,498
Additional credit		1,493
Additional tax	1,042	

(vi) Under paragraph (a)(1) of this section, on their tax returns V's tax liability is increased by $1,042 and W is allowed $1,493 as additional credit.

Example 7. Taxpayers divorce during the taxable year, allocation in proportion to household income. (i) The facts are the same as in *Example 6*, except that V and W decide to allocate the benchmark plan premium ($7,050) and the advance credit payments ($3,438) for January through June 2014 in proportion to their household incomes (79 percent and 21 percent). Thus, V is allocated $5,570 of the benchmark plan premiums ($7,050 × .79) and $2,716 of the advance credit payments ($3,438 × .79), and W is allocated $1,481 of the benchmark plan premiums ($7,050 × .21) and $722 of the advance credit payments ($3,438 × .21). V and W reconcile their premium tax credit with advance credit payments as follows:

	V	W
Allocated advance payments (Jan. to June)	$2,716	$722
Actual advance payments (July to Dec.)	2,148	2,286
Total advance payments	4,864	3,008
Allocated benchmark plan premium (Jan. to June)	5,570	1,481
Actual benchmark plan premium (July to Dec.)	5,000	2,600
Total benchmark plan premium	10,570	4,081
Contribution amount (taxable year household income × applicable percentage)	5,700	627
Credit (total benchmark plan premium less contribution amount)	4,870	3,454
Additional credit	6	446

(ii) Under paragraph (a)(1) of this section, on their tax returns V is allowed an additional credit of $6 and W is allowed an additional credit of $446.

Example 8. Married taxpayers filing separate tax returns. (i) Taxpayers X and Y are married and have two dependents. In 2013, the Exchange for the rating area where the family resides determines that their 2014 household income will be $76,000 (330 percent of the Federal poverty line for a family of 4, applicable percentage 9.5). W and Y enroll in a qualified health plan for 2014. The premium for the applicable benchmark plan is $14,100. X's and Y's monthly advance credit payment is $573, computed as follows: $14,100 benchmark plan premium minus X's and Y's contribution amount of $7,220 ($76,000 × .095) equals $6,880 (total advance credit); $6,880/12 = $573.

(ii) X and Y file income tax returns for 2014 using a married filing separately filing status. X reports household income of $60,000 and a family size of three (314 percent of the Federal poverty line). Y reports household income of $16,420 and a family size of one (147 percent of the Federal poverty line).

(iii) Because X and Y are married but do not file a joint return for 2014, X and Y are not applicable taxpayers and are not allowed a premium tax credit for 2014. See §1.36B-2(b)(2). Under paragraph (b)(4) of this section, half of the advance credit payments ($6,880/2 = $3,440) is allocated to X and half is allocated to Y for purposes of determining their excess advance payments. The repayment limitation described in paragraph (a)(3) of this section applies to X and Y *based on the household income and family size reported on each return*. Consequently, X's tax liability for 2014 is increased by $2,500 and Y's tax liability for 2014 is increased by $600.

Example 9. (i) The facts are the same as in *Example 8* of paragraph (b)(5) of this section, except that X and Y live apart for over 6 months of the year and X properly files an income tax return as head of household. Under section 7703(b), X is treated as unmarried and therefore is not required to file a joint return. If X otherwise qualifies as an applicable taxpayer, X may claim the premium tax credit based on the household income and family size X reports on the return. Y is not an applicable taxpayer and is not eligible to claim the premium tax credit.

(ii) X must reconcile the amount of credit with advance credit payments under paragraph (a) of this section. The premium for the applicable benchmark plan covering X and his two dependents is $9,800. X's premium tax credit is computed as follows: $9,800 benchmark plan premium minus X's contribution amount of $5,700 ($60,000 × .095) equals $4,100.

(iii) Under paragraph (b)(4) of this section, half of the advance payments ($6,880/2 = $3,440) is allocated to X and half is allocated to Y. Thus, X is entitled to $660 additional premium tax credit ($4,100 - $3,440). Y has $3,440 excess advance payments, which is limited to $600 under paragraph (a)(3) of this section.

Example 10. (i) A is married to B at the close of 2014 and they have no dependents. A and B are enrolled in a qualified health plan for 2014 with an annual premium of $10,000 and advance credit payments of $6,500. A is not eligible for minimum essential coverage (other than coverage described in section 5000A(f)(1)(C)) for any month in 2014. A is a victim of domestic abuse as described in §1.36B-2(b)(2)(iii). At the time A files her tax return for 2014, A is unable to file a joint return with B for 2014 because of the domestic abuse. A certifies on her 2014 return, in accordance with relevant instructions, that she is living apart from B and is unable to file a joint return because of domestic abuse. Thus, under §1.36B-2(b)(2)(ii), A satisfies the joint return filing requirement in section 36B(c)(1)(C) for 2014.

(ii) A's family size for 2014 for purposes of computing the premium tax credit is one, and A is the only member of her coverage family. Thus, A's benchmark plan for all months of 2014 is the second lowest cost silver plan offered by the Exchange for A's rating area that covers A. A's household income includes only A's modified adjusted gross income. Under paragraph (b)(4)(ii) of this section, A takes into account $5,000 ($10,000 × .50) of the premiums for the plan in which she was enrolled in determining her premium tax credit. Further, A must reconcile $3,250 ($6,500 × .50) of the advance credit payments for her coverage under paragraph (b)(4)(i) of this section.

Reg. §1.36B-4(b)(5)

(c) *Applicability dates.*—Paragraphs (a)(1)(ii), (a)(3)(iii), (a)(4), *Examples 4, 10, 11, 12, 13, 14,* and *15,* (b)(3), (b)(4), and (b)(5), *Examples 9* and *10* apply to taxable years beginning after December 31, 2013. The last sentence of paragraph (a)(1)(ii)(B)(*1*), paragraph (a)(1)(ii)(B)(2), and paragraph (a)(1)(ii)(C) of this section apply to taxable years ending on or after December 31, 2020. [Reg. §1.36B-4.]

☐ [T.D. 9590, 5-18-2012 (*corrected* 7-11-2012). *Amended by* T.D. 9683, 7-24-2014, T.D. 9822, 7-24-2017 *and* T.D. 9912, 11-27-2020.]

[Reg. §1.36B-5]

§1.36B-5. Information reporting by Exchanges.—(a) *In general.*—An Exchange must report to the Internal Revenue Service (IRS) information required by section 36B(f)(3) and this section relating to individual market qualified health plans in which individuals enroll through the Exchange. No reporting is required under this section for enrollment in plans through the Small Business Health Options Exchange.

(b) *Individual filing a return.*—For purposes of this section, the terms *tax filer* and *responsible adult* describe the individual who is expected to be the taxpayer filing an income tax return for the year of coverage with respect to individuals enrolling in a qualified health plan. A tax filer is an individual on behalf of whom advance payments of the premium tax credit are made. A responsible adult is an individual on behalf of whom advance payments of the premium tax credit are not made. An individual may be a tax filer or responsible adult whether or not enrolled in coverage. If more than one family (within the meaning of §1.36B-1(d)) enrolls in the same qualified health plan, there is a tax filer or responsible adult for each family.

(c) *Information required to be reported.*—(1) *Information reported annually.*—An Exchange must report to the IRS the following information for each qualified health plan—

(i) The name, address, and taxpayer identification number (TIN), or date of birth if a TIN is not available, of the tax filer or responsible adult;

(ii) The name and TIN, or date of birth if a TIN is not available, of a tax filer's spouse;

(iii) The amount of the advance credit payments paid for coverage under the plan each month;

(iv) For plans for which advance credit payments are made, the premium (excluding the premium allocated to benefits in excess of essential health benefits, see §1.36B-3(j)) for the applicable benchmark plan for purposes of computing advance credit payments;

(v) Except as provided in paragraph (c)(3)(ii) of this section, for plans for which advance credit payments are not made, the premium (excluding the premium allocated to benefits in excess of essential health benefits, see §1.36B-3(j)) for the applicable benchmark plan that would apply to all individuals enrolled in the qualified health plan if advance credit payments were made for the coverage;

(vi) The name and TIN, or date of birth if a TIN is not available, and dates of coverage for each individual covered under the plan;

(vii) The coverage start and end dates of the qualified health plan;

(viii) The monthly premium for the plan in which the individuals enroll, however —

(A) The premium allocated to benefits in excess of essential health benefits is excluded, see §1.36B-3(j);

(B) The premium for a stand-alone dental plan allocated to pediatric dental benefits is added, see §1.36B-3(k), but if a family (within the meaning of §1.36B-1(d)) is enrolled in more than one qualified health plan, the pediatric dental premium is added to the premium for only one qualified health plan; and

(C) The amount is not reduced for advance credit payments;

(ix) The name of the qualified health plan issuer;

(x) The Exchange-assigned policy identification number;

(xi) The Exchange's unique identifier; and

(xii) Any other information specified by forms or instructions or in published guidance, see §601.601(d) of this chapter.

(2) *Information reported monthly.*—For each calendar month, an Exchange must report to the IRS for each qualified health plan, the information described in paragraph (c)(1) of this section and the following information—

(i) For plans for which advance credit payments are made—

(A) The names, TINs, or dates of birth if no TIN is available, of the individuals enrolled in the qualified health plan who are expected to be the tax filer's dependent; and

(B) Information on employment (to the extent this information is provided to the Exchange) consisting of—

(1) The name, address, and EIN of each employer of the tax filer, the tax filer's spouse, and each individual covered by the plan; and

(2) An indication of whether an employer offered affordable minimum essential coverage that provided minimum value, and, if so, the amount of the employee's required contribution for self-only coverage;

(ii) The unique identifying number the Exchange uses to report data that enables the IRS to associate the data with the proper account from month to month;

(iii) The issuer's employer identification number (EIN); and

(iv) Any other information specified by forms or instructions or in published guidance, see §601.601(d) of this chapter.

(3) *Special rules for information reported.*—(i) *Multiple families enrolled in a single qualified health plan.*—An Exchange must report the information specified in paragraphs (c)(1) and (c)(2) of this section for each family (within the meaning of §1.36B-1(d)) enrolled in a qualified health plan, including families submitting a single application or enrolled in a single qualified health plan. If advance credit payments are made for coverage under the plan, the enrollment premiums reported to each family under paragraph (c)(1)(viii) of this section are the premiums allocated to the family under §1.36B-3(h) (allocating enrollment premiums to each taxpayer in proportion to the premiums for each taxpayer's applicable benchmark plan).

(ii) *Alternative to reporting applicable benchmark plan.*—An Exchange satisfies the requirement in paragraph (c)(1)(v) of this section if, on or before January 1 of each year after 2014, the Exchange provides a reasonable method that a responsible adult may use to determine the premium (after adjusting for benefits in excess of essential health benefits) for the applicable benchmark plan that applies to the responsible adult's coverage family for the prior calendar year for purposes of determining the premium tax credit on the tax return.

(iii) *Partial month of coverage.*—(A) *In general.*—Except as provided in paragraph (c)(3)(iii)(B) of this section, if an individual is enrolled in a qualified health plan after the first day of a month, the amount reported for that month under paragraphs (c)(1)(iv), (c)(1)(v), and (c)(1)(viii) of this section is $0.

(B) *Certain mid-month enrollments.*—For information reporting that is due on or after January 1, 2019, if an individual's qualified health plan is terminated before the last day of a month, or if an individual is enrolled in coverage after the first day of a month and the coverage is effective on the date of the individual's birth, adoption, or placement for adoption or in foster care, or on the effective date of a court order, the amount reported under paragraphs (c)(1)(iv) and (c)(1)(v) of this section is the premium for the applicable benchmark plan for a full month of coverage (excluding the premium allocated to benefits in excess of essential health benefits), and the amount reported under paragraph (c)(1)(viii) of this section is the enrollment premium for the month, reduced by any amounts that were refunded.

(4) *Exemptions.*—For each calendar month, an Exchange must report to the IRS the name and TIN, or date of birth if a TIN is not available, of each individual for whom the Exchange has granted an exemption from coverage under section 5000A(e) and the related regulations, the months for which the exemption is in effect, and the exemption certificate number.

(d) *Time for reporting.*—(1) *Annual reporting.*—An Exchange must submit to the IRS the annual report required under paragraph (c)(1) of this section on or before January 31 of the year following the calendar year of coverage.

(2) *Monthly reporting.*—(i) *In general.*—Except as provided in paragraph (d)(2)(ii) of this section, an Exchange must submit to the IRS the monthly reports required under paragraphs (c)(2) and (c)(4) of this section on or before the 15th day following each month of coverage.

(ii) *Initial monthly reporting in 2014.*—Exchanges must submit to the IRS the initial monthly report required under paragraphs (c)(2) and (c)(4) of this section on a date that the Commissioner may establish in other guidance, see §601.601(d) of this section, but no earlier than June 15, 2014. The initial report must include cumulative information for enrollments for the period January 1, 2014, through the last day of the month preceding the month for submitting the initial monthly report.

(3) *Corrections to information reported.*—In general, an Exchange must correct erroneous or outdated monthly-reported information in the next monthly report. If the information must be corrected after the final monthly submission on January 15 following the coverage year, corrections should be submitted by the 15th day of the month

following the month in which the incorrect information is identified. However, no monthly report correction is permitted after April 15 following the year of coverage. Errors on the annual report must be corrected and reported to the IRS and to the individual recipient identified in paragraph (f) of this section as soon as possible.

(e) *Electronic reporting.*—An Exchange must submit the reports to the IRS required under this section in electronic format. The information reported monthly will be submitted to the IRS through the Department of Health and Human Services.

(f) *Annual statement to be furnished to individuals.*—(1) *In general.*—An Exchange must furnish to each tax filer or responsible adult (the recipient for purposes of paragraphs (f) and (g) of this section) a written statement showing—

(i) The name and address of the recipient and

(ii) The information described in paragraph (c)(1) of this section for the previous calendar year.

(2) *Form of statements.*—A statement required under this paragraph (f) may be made by furnishing to the recipient identified in the annual report either a copy of the report filed with the IRS or a substitute statement. A substitute statement must include the information required to be shown on the report filed with the IRS and must comply with requirements in published guidance (see §601.601(d)(2) of this chapter) relating to substitute statements. A reporting entity may use an IRS truncated taxpayer identification number as the identification number for an individual in lieu of the identification number appearing on the corresponding information report filed with the IRS.

(3) *Time and manner for furnishing statements.*—An Exchange must furnish the statements required under this paragraph (f) on or before January 31 of the year following the calendar year of coverage. If mailed, the statement must be sent to the recipient's last known permanent address or, if no permanent address is known, to the recipient's temporary address. For purposes of this paragraph (f)(3), an Exchange's first class mailing to the last known permanent address, or if no permanent address is known, the temporary address, discharges the Exchange's requirement to furnish the statement. An Exchange may furnish the statement electronically in accordance with paragraph (g) of this section.

(g) *Electronic furnishing of statements.*—(1) *In general.*—An Exchange required to furnish a statement under paragraph (f) of this section may furnish the statement to the recipient in an electronic format in lieu of a paper format. An Exchange that meets the requirements of paragraphs (g)(2) through (g)(7) of this section is treated as furnishing the statement in a timely manner.

(2) *Consent.*—(i) *In general.*—A recipient must have affirmatively consented to receive the statement in an electronic format. The consent may be made electronically in any manner that reasonably demonstrates that the recipient is able to access the statement in the electronic format in which it will be furnished. Alternatively, the consent may be made in a paper document that is confirmed electronically.

(ii) *Withdrawal of consent.*—The consent requirement of this paragraph (g)(2) is not satisfied if the recipient withdraws the consent and the withdrawal takes effect before the statement is furnished. An Exchange may provide that the withdrawal of consent takes effect either on the date the Exchange receives it or on another date no more than 60 days later. The Exchange may provide that a request by the recipient for a paper statement will be treated as a withdrawal of consent to receive the statement in an electronic format. If the Exchange furnishes a statement after the withdrawal of consent takes effect, the recipient has not consented to receive the statement in electronic format.

(iii) *Change in hardware or software requirements.*—If a change in the hardware or software required to access the statement creates a material risk that a recipient will not be able to access a statement, an Exchange must, prior to changing the hardware or software, notify the recipient. The notice must describe the revised hardware and software required to access the statement and inform the recipient that a new consent to receive the statement in the revised electronic format must be provided to the Exchange. After implementing the revised hardware and software, the Exchange must obtain a new consent or confirmation of consent from the recipient to receive the statement electronically.

(iv) *Examples.*—The following examples illustrate the rules of this paragraph (g)(2):

Example 1. Furnisher F sends Recipient R a letter stating that R may consent to receive the statement required under section 36B electronically on a web site instead of in a paper format. The letter contains instructions explaining how to consent to receive the statement electronically by accessing the web site, downloading and completing the consent document, and e-mailing the completed consent to F. The consent document posted on the web site uses the same electronic format that F will use for the electronically furnished statement. R reads the instructions and submits the consent in the manner provided in the instructions. R has consented to receive the statement required under section 36B electronically in the manner described in paragraph (g)(2)(i) of this section.

Example 2. Furnisher F sends Recipient R an e-mail stating that R may consent to receive the statement required under section 36B electronically instead of in a paper format. The e-mail contains an attachment instructing R how to consent to receive the statement required under section 36B electronically. The e-mail attachment uses the same electronic format that F will use for the electronically furnished statement. R opens the attachment, reads the instructions, and submits the consent in the manner provided in the instructions. R has consented to receive the statement required under section 36B electronically in the manner described in paragraph (g)(2)(i) of this section.

Example 3. Furnisher F posts a notice on its web site stating that Recipient R may receive the statement required under section 36B electronically instead of in a paper format. The web site contains instructions on how R may access a secure web page and consent to receive the statements electronically. R accesses the secure web page and follows the instructions for giving consent. R has consented to receive the statement required under section 36B electronically in the manner described in paragraph (g)(2)(i) of this section.

(3) *Required disclosures.*—(i) *In general.*—Prior to, or at the time of, a recipient's consent, an Exchange must provide to the recipient a clear and conspicuous disclosure statement containing each of the disclosures described in paragraphs (g)(3)(ii) through (g)(3)(viii) of this section.

(ii) *Paper statement.*—An Exchange must inform the recipient that the statement will be furnished on paper if the recipient does not consent to receive it electronically.

(iii) *Scope and duration of consent.*—An Exchange must inform the recipient of the scope and duration of the consent. For example, the Exchange must inform the recipient whether the consent applies to each statement required to be furnished after the consent is given until it is withdrawn or only to the first statement required to be furnished following the consent.

(iv) *Post-consent request for a paper statement.*—An Exchange must inform the recipient of any procedure for obtaining a paper copy of the recipient's statement after giving the consent described in paragraph (g)(2)(i) of this section and whether a request for a paper statement will be treated as a withdrawal of consent.

(v) *Withdrawal of consent.*—An Exchange must inform the recipient that—

(A) The recipient may withdraw consent by writing (electronically or on paper) to the person or department whose name, mailing address, telephone number, and e-mail address is provided in the disclosure statement;

(B) An Exchange will confirm the withdrawal and the date on which it takes effect in writing (either electronically or on paper); and

(C) A withdrawal of consent does not apply to a statement that was furnished electronically in the manner described in this paragraph (g) before the date on which the withdrawal of consent takes effect.

(vi) *Notice of termination.*—An Exchange must inform the recipient of the conditions under which the Exchange will cease furnishing statements electronically to the recipient.

(vii) *Updating information.*—An Exchange must inform the recipient of the procedures for updating the information needed to contact the recipient and notify the recipient of any change in the Exchange's contact information.

(viii) *Hardware and software requirements.*—An Exchange must provide the recipient with a description of the hardware and software required to access, print, and retain the statement, and the date when the statement will no longer be available on the web site. The Exchange must advise the recipient that the statement may be required to be printed and attached to a Federal, State, or local income tax return.

(4) *Format.*—The electronic version of the statement must contain all required information and comply with applicable published guidance (see §601.601(d) of this chapter) relating to substitute statements to recipients.

Reg. §1.36B-5(g)(4)

(5) *Notice.*—(i) *In general.*—If a statement is furnished on a web site, the Exchange must notify the recipient. The notice may be delivered by mail, electronic mail, or in person. The notice must provide instructions on how to access and print the statement and include the following statement in capital letters, "IMPORTANT TAX RETURN DOCUMENT AVAILABLE." If the notice is provided by electronic mail, this statement must be on the subject line of the electronic mail.

(ii) *Undeliverable electronic address.*—If an electronic notice described in paragraph (g)(5)(i) of this section is returned as undeliverable, and the Exchange cannot obtain the correct electronic address from the Exchange's records or from the recipient, the Exchange must furnish the notice by mail or in person within 30 days after the electronic notice is returned.

(iii) *Corrected statement.*—An Exchange must furnish a corrected statement to the recipient electronically if the original statement was furnished electronically. If the original statement was furnished through a web site posting, the Exchange must notify the recipient that it has posted the corrected statement on the web site in the manner described in paragraph (g)(5)(i) of this section within 30 days of the posting. The corrected statement or the notice must be furnished by mail or in person if—

(A) An electronic notice of the web site posting of an original statement or the corrected statement was returned as undeliverable; and

(B) The recipient has not provided a new e-mail address.

(6) *Access period.*—Statements furnished on a web site must be retained on the web site through October 15 of the year following the calendar year to which the statements relate (or the first business day after October 15, if October 15 falls on a Saturday, Sunday, or legal holiday). The furnisher must maintain access to corrected statements that are posted on the web site through October 15 of the year following the calendar year to which the statements relate (or the first business day after October 15, if October 15 falls on a Saturday, Sunday, or legal holiday) or the date 90 days after the corrected forms are posted, whichever is later.

(7) *Paper statements after withdrawal of consent.*—An Exchange must furnish a paper statement if a recipient withdraws consent to receive a statement electronically and the withdrawal takes effect before the statement is furnished. A paper statement furnished under this paragraph (g)(7) after the statement due date is timely if furnished within 30 days after the date the Exchange receives the withdrawal of consent.

(h) *Effective/applicability date.*—Except for the last sentence of paragraph (c)(3)(i) of this section and paragraph (c)(3)(iii) of this section, this section applies to taxable years ending after December 31, 2013. The last sentence of paragraph (c)(3)(i) of this section and paragraph (c)(3)(iii) of this section apply to taxable years beginning after December 31, 2018. Paragraph (c)(3) of § 1.36B-5 as contained in 26 CFR part I edition revised as of April 1, 2016, applies to information reporting for taxable years ending after December 31, 2013, and beginning before January 1, 2019. [Reg. § 1.36B-5.]

☐ [*T.D. 9590, 5-18-2012. Amended by T.D. 9663, 5-2-2014 and T.D. 9804, 12-14-2016.*]

[Reg. § 1.36B-6]

§1.36B-6. Minimum value.—(a) *In general.*—(1) *Employees.*—An eligible employer-sponsored plan provides minimum value (MV) for an employee of the employer offering the coverage only if—

(i) The plan's MV percentage, as defined in paragraph (c) of this section, is at least 60 percent based on the plan's share of the total allowed costs of benefits provided to the employee; and

(ii) The plan provides substantial coverage of inpatient hospital services and physician services.

(2) *Related individuals.*—(i) *In general.*—An eligible employer-sponsored plan provides MV for an individual who may enroll in the plan because of a relationship to an employee of the employer offering the coverage (a related individual) only if—

(A) The plan's MV percentage, as defined in paragraph (c) of this section, is at least 60 percent based on the plan's share of the total allowed costs of benefits provided to the related individual; and

(B) The plan provides substantial coverage of inpatient hospital services and physician services.

(ii) *Plans providing MV to employees.*—If an eligible employer-sponsored plan provides MV to an employee under paragraph (a)(1) of this section, the plan also provides MV for related individuals if—

(A) The scope of benefits is the same for the employee and related individuals; and

(B) Cost sharing (including deductibles, co-payments, coinsurance, and out-of-pocket maximums) under the plan is the same

for the employee and related individuals under the tier of coverage that would, if elected, include the employee and all related individuals (disregarding any differences in deductibles or out-of-pocket maximums that are attributable to a different tier of coverage, such as self plus one versus family coverage).

(b) *MV standard population.*—[Reserved]

(c) *MV percentage.*—(1) *In general.*—[Reserved]

(2) *Wellness program incentives.*—(i) *In general.*—Nondiscriminatory wellness program incentives offered by an eligible employer-sponsored plan that affect deductibles, copayments, or other cost-sharing are treated as earned in determining the plan's MV percentage if the incentives relate exclusively to tobacco use. Wellness program incentives that do not relate to tobacco use or that include a component unrelated to tobacco use are treated as not earned for this purpose. For purposes of this section, the term *wellness program incentive* has the same meaning as the term *reward* in § 54.9802–1(f)(1)(i) of this chapter.

(ii) *Example.*—The following example illustrates the rules of this paragraph (c)(2):

Example. (i) Employer X offers an eligible employer-sponsored plan that reduces the deductible by $300 for employees who do not use tobacco products or who complete a smoking cessation course. The deductible is reduced by $200 if an employee completes cholesterol screening within the first six months of the plan year. Employee B does not use tobacco and his deductible is $3,700. Employee C uses tobacco and her deductible is $4,000.

(ii) Under paragraph (c)(2)(i) of this section, only the incentives related to tobacco use are considered in determining the plan's MV percentage. C is treated as having earned the $300 incentive for attending a smoking cessation course regardless of whether C actually attends the course. Thus, the deductible for determining for the MV percentage for both Employees B and C is $3,700. The $200 incentive for completing cholesterol screening is disregarded.

(3) *Employer contributions to health savings accounts.*—Employer contributions for the current plan year to health savings accounts that are offered with an eligible employer-sponsored plan are taken into account for that plan year towards the plan's MV percentage.

(4) *Employer contributions to health reimbursement arrangements.*—Amounts newly made available for the current plan year under a health reimbursement arrangement that would be integrated within the meaning of Notice 2013-54 (2013-40 IRB 287), see § 601.601(d) of this chapter, with an eligible employer-sponsored plan for an employee enrolled in the plan are taken into account for that plan year towards the plan's MV percentage if the amounts may be used to reduce only cost-sharing for covered medical expenses. A health reimbursement arrangement counts toward a plan's MV percentage only if the health reimbursement arrangement and the eligible employer-sponsored plan are offered by the same employer. Employer contributions to a health reimbursement arrangement count for a plan year towards the plan's MV percentage only to the extent the amount of the annual contribution is required under the terms of the plan or otherwise determinable within a reasonable time before the employee must decide whether to enroll in the eligible employer-sponsored plan.

(5) *Expected spending adjustments for health savings accounts and health reimbursement arrangements.*—[Reserved]

(d) *Methods for determining MV.*—[Reserved]

(e) *Scope of essential health benefits and adjustment for benefits not included in MV Calculator.*—[Reserved]

(f) *Actuarial certification.*—[Reserved]

(1) *In general.*—[Reserved]

(2) *Membership in American Academy of Actuaries.*—[Reserved]

(3) *Actuarial analysis.*—[Reserved]

(4) *Use of MV Calculator.*—[Reserved]

(g) *Effective/applicability date—in general.*—(1) Except as provided in paragraph (g)(2) of this section, this section applies for taxable years ending after December 31, 2013.

(2) *Exceptions.*—(i) Paragraph (a)(1)(ii) of this section applies for plan years beginning after November 3, 2014; and

(ii) Paragraph (a)(2) of this section applies to taxable years beginning after December 31, 2022. [Reg. § 1.36B-6.]

☐ [*T.D. 9745, 12-16-2015. Amended by T.D. 9968, 10-11-2022.*]

➤ Caution: Reg. §1.37-1, below, was issued under former Code Sec. 37, which has been redesignated as Code Sec. 22.

[Reg. §1.37-1]

§1.37-1. General rules for the credit for the elderly.—(a) *In general.*—In the case of an individual, section 37 provides a credit against the tax imposed by chapter 1 of the Internal Revenue Code of 1954. This section and §§1.37-2 and 1.37-3 provide guidance in the computation of the credit for the elderly provided under section 37 for taxable years beginning after 1975. For rules relating to the computation of the retirement income credit provided under section 37 for taxable years beginning before 1976, see 26 CFR 1.37-1 through 1.37-5 (Rev. as of April 1, 1980). Note that section 403 of the Tax Reduction and Simplification Act of 1977 provides that a taxpayer may elect to compute the credit under section 37 for the taxpayer's first taxable year beginning in 1976 in accordance with the rules applicable to taxable years beginning before 1976.

(b) *Limitation on the amount of the credit.*—The credit allowed by section 37 for a taxable year shall not exceed the tax imposed by chapter 1 of the Code for the taxable year (reduced, in the case of a taxable year beginning before 1979, by the general tax credit allowed by section 42).

(c) *Married couples must file joint returns.*—If the taxpayer is married at the close of the taxable year, the credit provided by section 37 shall be allowed only if the taxpayer and the taxpayer's spouse file a joint return for the taxable year. The preceding sentence shall not apply in the case of a husband and wife who are not members of the same household at any time during the taxable year. For the determination of marital status, see section 143 and §1.143-1.

(d) *Nonresident aliens ineligible.*—No credit is allowed under section 37 to any individual for any taxable year during which that individual is at any time a nonresident alien unless the individual is treated, by reason of an election under section 6013(g) or (h), as a resident of the United States for that taxable year. [Reg. §1.37-1.]

☐ [T.D. 6161, 2-3-56. *Amended by T.D. 6633, 1-14-63; T.D. 6791, 1-5-65 and T.D. 7743, 12-19-80.*]

➤ Caution: Reg. §1.37-2, below, was issued under former Code Sec. 37, which has been redesignated as Code Sec. 22.

[Reg. §1.37-2]

§1.37-2. Credit for individuals age 65 or over.—(a) *In general.*—This section illustrates the computation of the credit for the elderly in the case of an individual who has attained the age of 65 before the close of the taxable year. This section shall not apply to an individual for any taxable year for which the individual makes the election described in section 37(e)(2) and paragraph (b) of §1.37-3.

(b) *Computation of credit.*—The credit for the elderly for an individual to whom this section applies equals 15 percent of the individual's "section 37 amount" for the taxable year. An individual's "section 37 amount" for a taxable year is the initial amount determined under section 37(b)(2), reduced as provided in section 37(b)(3) and (c)(1).

(c) *Examples.*—The computation of the credit for the elderly for individuals to whom this section applies may be illustrated by the following examples:

Example (1). A, a single individual who is 67 years old, has adjusted gross income of $8,000 for the calendar year 1977. A also receives social security payments of $1,450 during 1977. A does not itemize deductions. A's credit for the elderly is $120, computed as follows:

Initial amount under section 37(b)(2)		$2,500
Reductions required by Section 37(b)(3) and (c)(1):		
Social security payments	$1,450	
One-half the excess of adjusted gross income over $7,500	250	1,700

Section 37 amount	800
15% of $800	$120

A's tax from the tax tables, which reflect the allowance of the general tax credit, is $662. Accordingly, the limitation of section 37(c)(2) and paragraph (b) of §1.37-1 does not reduce A's credit for the elderly.

Example (2). H and W, who have both attained the age of 65, file a joint return for calendar year 1977. For that year H and W have adjusted gross income of $8,120; H also receives a railroad retirement pension of $1,550, and W receives social security payments of $1,200. H and W do not itemize deductions. The credit for the elderly allowed to H and W for 1977 is $139, computed as follows:

Initial amount under section 37(b)(2)		$3,750
Railroad retirement pension	$1,550	
Social security payments	1,200	2,750
Section 37 amount		1,000
15% of $1,000		150
Limitation based upon amount of tax (derived from tables reflecting allowance of general tax credit)		$139

Since the adjusted gross income of H and W is not greater than $10,000, no reduction of the initial amount is required under section 47(c)(1). [Reg. §1.37-2.]

☐ [T.D. 6161, 2-3-56. *Amended by T.D. 6791, 1-5-65 and T.D. 7743, 12-19-80.*]

➤ Caution: Reg. §1.37-3, below, was issued under former Code Sec. 37, which has been redesignated as Code Sec. 22.

[Reg. §1.37-3]

§1.37-3. Credit for individuals under age 65 who have public retirement system income.—(a) *In general.*—This section provides rules for the computation of the credit for the elderly under section 37(e) in the case of an individual who has not attained the age of 65 before the close of the taxable year and whose gross income for the taxable year includes retirement income within the meaning of paragraph (d)(1)(ii) of this section (*i.e.*, under a public retirement system). If such an individual is married within the meaning of section 143 at the close of the taxable year and the spouse of the individual has attained the age of 65 before the close of the taxable year, this section shall apply to the individual for the taxable year only if both spouses make the election described in paragraph (b) of this section. If both spouses make the election described in paragraph (b) of this section for the taxable year, the credit of each spouse shall be determined under the rules of this section. See paragraph (f)(2) of this section for a limitation on the effects of community property laws in making determinations and computations under section 37(e) and this section.

(b) *Election by certain married taxpayers.*—If a married individual under age 65 at the close of the taxable year has retirement income and the spouse of that individual has attained the age of 65 before the close of the taxable year, both spouses may elect to compute the credit provided by section 37 under the rules of section 37(e) and this section. The spouses shall signify the election on the return (or amended return) for the taxable year in the manner prescribed in the instructions accompanying the return. The election may be made at any time before the expiration of the period of limitation for filing claim for credit or refund for the taxable year. The election may be revoked without the consent of the Commissioner at any time before the expiration of that period by filing an amended return.

(c) *Computation of credit.*—The credit of an individual under section 37(e) and this section equals 15 percent of the individual's credit base for the taxable year. The credit base of an individual for a taxable year is the lesser of—

(1) The retirement income of the individual for the taxable year, or

(2) The amount determined under section 37(e)(5), as modified by section 37(e)(6) and (7).

(d) *Retirement income.*—(1) *General rule.*—(i) *For individuals 65 or over.*—Section 37(e)(4)(A) enumerates the kinds of income which may be treated as the retirement income of an individual who has attained the age of 65 before the close of the taxable year. They include income from pensions and annuities, interests, rents, dividends, certain bonds received under a qualified bond purchase plan, and certain individual retirement accounts or annuities.

(ii) *For individuals under 65.*—In the case of an individual who has not attained the age of 65 before the close of the taxable year, retirement income consists only of income from pensions and annuities (including disability annuity payments) under a public retirement system which arises from services performed by that individual or by a present or former spouse of that individual. The term "public retirement system" means a pension, annuity, or retirement, or similar fund or system established by the United States, a State, a possession of the United States, any political subdivision of any of the foregoing, or the District of Columbia.

(2) *Rents.*—For purposes of section 37(e)(4)(A)(iii), income from rents shall be the gross amount received, not reduced by depreciation or other expenses, except that beneficiaries of a trust or estate shall treat as retirement income only their proportionate shares of the taxable rents of the trust or estate. In the case of an amount received

⋙→ *Caution: Reg. §1.37-3, below, was issued under former Code Sec. 37, which has been redesignated as Code Sec. 22.*

for board and lodging, only the portion of the amount received for lodging is income from rents.

(3) *Disability annuity payments received by individual under age 65.*—Disability annuity payments received under a public retirement system by an individual under age 65 at the close of the taxable year shall not be treated as retirement income unless the payments are for periods after the date on which the individual reached minimum retirement age, that is, the age at which the individual would be eligible to receive a pension or annuity without regard to disability, and any of the following conditions is satisfied—

(i) The individual is precluded from seeking the benefits of section 105(d) (relating to certain disability payments) for that taxable year by reason of an irrevocable election;

(ii) The individual was not permanently and totally disabled at the time of retirement (and was not permanently and totally disabled either on January 1, 1976, or on January 1, 1977, if the individual retired before the later date on disability or under circumstances which entitled the individual to retire on disability); or

(iii) The payments are for periods after the individual reached mandatory retirement age.

For purposes of this paragraph, disability annuity payments include payments to an individual who retired on partial or temporary disability.

(4) *Compensation for personal services rendered during taxable year.*—Retirement income does not include any amount representing compensation for personal services rendered during the taxable year. For this purpose, amounts received as a pension shall not be treated as representing compensation for personal services rendered during the taxable year if the period of service during the taxable year is not substantial when compared with the total years of service. For example, an individual on the calendar year basis retires on November 30 after 5 years of service and receives a pension during the remainder of his taxable year. The pension is not treated as representing compensation for personal services rendered during such taxable year merely because it is paid by reason of the services of the individual for a period of 5 years which includes a portion of the taxable year.

(5) *Amounts not includible in gross income.*—Retirement income does not include any amount not includible in the gross income of the individual for the taxable year. For example, if a portion of an annuity is excluded from gross income under section 72, relating to annuities, that portion of the annuity is not retirement income; similarly, the portion of dividend income excluded from gross income under section 116, relating to the partial exclusion of dividends received by individuals is not retirement income.

(e) *Earned income.*—(1) *In general.*—The term "earned income" in section 37(e)(5)(B) generally has the same meaning as in section 911(b), except that earned income does not include any amount received as a pension or annuity. See section 911(b) and the regulations thereunder. Section 911(b) provides, in general, that earned income includes wages, salaries, professional fees, and other amounts received as compensation for personal services rendered.

(2) *Earned income from self-employment.*—For purposes of section 37(e)(5)(B), the earned income of a taxpayer from self-employment in a trade or business shall not exceed—

(i) The taxpayer's share of the net profits from the trade or business if capital is not a material income-producing factor in that trade or business; or

(ii) Thirty percent of the taxpayer's share of the net profits from the trade or business if capital is a material income-producing factor in that trade or business.

For other rules relating to the determination of earned income from self-employment in a trade or business, see section 911(b) and the regulations thereunder.

(3) *Disability annuity payments received by individuals under age 65.*—Disability annuity payments received under a public retirement system by an individual under age 65 at the close of the taxable year shall be treated as earned income for purposes of section 37(e)(5)(B) unless the payments are treated as retirement income under paragraph (d)(3) of this section.

(f) *Computation of credit under section 37(e) in the case of joint returns.*—(1) *In general.*—In the case of a joint return of husband and wife, the credit base of each spouse under section 37(e) is computed separately. The spouses then combine their credit bases and compute a single credit. The limitation in section 37(c)(2) and paragraph (b) of §1.37-1 on the amount of the credit is determined by reference to the joint tax liability of the spouses. Thus, regardless of whether a spouse would be liable for the tax imposed by chapter 1 of the Code if the joint return had not been filed, the credit base of that spouse is taken into account in computing the credit.

(2) *Community property laws.*—For taxable years beginning after 1977, married individuals filing joint returns shall disregard community property laws in making any determination or computation required under section 37(e) or this section. Each item of income is attributed in full to the spouse whose income it would have been in the absence of community property laws. Thus, if a 67-year old individual files a joint return with a 62-year old spouse for 1979 and the only income of the couple is from a public pension of the older spouse, that public pension is attributed in full to the older spouse for purposes of section 37(e) even though the applicable community property law may treat one-half of the pension as the income of the 62-year old spouse. Since the younger spouse consequently has no retirement income within the meaning of paragraph (d) of this section, the couple may not make the election described in paragraph (b) of this section.

(g) *Examples.*—The computation of the credit for the elderly under section 37(e) and this section is illustrated by the following examples:

Example (1). B, who is 62 years old and single, receives a fully taxable pension of $2,400 from a public retirement system during 1977. B performed the services giving rise to the pension. During that year, B also earns $2,650 from a part-time job. B receives no tax-exempt pension or annuity in 1977. Subject to the limitation of section 37(c)(2) and paragraph (b) of §1.37-1, B's credit for the elderly for 1977 under section 37(e) is $195, computed as follows:

Maximum retirement income level under section 37(e)(5)		$2,500
Earned income offset under section 37(e)(5)(B)(ii):		
Earned income in excess of $1,700	$950	
One-half of earned income in excess of $1,200, but not in excess of $1,700	250	
		1,200
Amount determined under section 37(e)(5)		1,300
Retirement income		2,400
Credit for the elderly (15 percent of $1,300)		$195

Example (2). During 1978 H, who is 67 years old, has earnings of $1,300 and retirement income (rents, interest, etc.) of $6,000. H also receives social security payments totalling $1,400. During 1978 W, who is 63 years old, earns $1,600 and receives a fully taxable pension of $1,400 from a public retirement system that constitutes retirement income. W performed the services giving rise to the pension. H and W file a joint return for 1978 and elect to compute the credit for the elderly under section 37(e). Under the applicable law these items of income are community income, and both spouses share equally in each item. Because H and W are filing a joint return, they disregard community property laws in computing their credit under section 37(e). The couple allocates $1,600 of the $3,750 referred to in section 37(e)(6) to W and $2,150 to H. Subject to the limitation of section 37(c)(2) and paragraph (b) of §1.37-1, their credit for the elderly is $315, computed as follows:

Credit base of H:		
Amount allocated to H under section 37(e)(6)		$2,150
Reductions required by section 37(e)(5):		
Social security payments	$1,400	
One-half of excess of earnings over $1,200	50	1,450
Amount determined under section 37(e)(5)		$700
Retirement income		6,000

>>>→ *Caution: Reg. §1.37-3, below, was issued under former Code Sec. 37, which has been redesignated as Code Sec. 22.*

Credit base of H	$700
Credit base of W:	
Amount allocated to W under section 37(e)(6)	$1,600
Reduction required by section 37(e)(5)(B):	
One-half of excess of earnings over $1,200 . . . . $200	
Amount determined under section 37(e)(5)	1,400
Retirement income	1,400
Credit base of W	$1,400
Computation of credit	
Credit base of H	$700
Credit base of W	1,400
Combined credit base	2,100
Credit for elderly (15 percent of $2,100)	$315

Example (3). (a) Assume the same facts as in example (2) of this paragraph, except that H and W live apart at all times during 1978 and file separate returns. Under these circumstances, H and W must give effect to the applicable community property law in determining their credits under section 37(e). Thus, each spouse must take into account one-half of each item of income.

(b) Subject to the limitation of section 37(c)(2) and paragraph (b) of §1.37-1, H's credit for the elderly is $157.50, computed as follows:

Maximum retirement income level under section 37(e)(7)		$1,875
Reductions required by section 37(e)(5):		
Social security payments	$700	
One-half of excess of earnings over $1,200 (taking into account one-half of combined earnings of $2,900)	125	825
Amount determined under section 37(e)(5)		$1,050
Retirement income		3,700
Credit of H (15 percent of $1,050)		$157.50

(c) Subject to the limitation of section 37(c)(2) and paragraph (b) of §1.37-1, W's credit for the elderly is computed as follows:

Maximum retirement income level under section 37(e)(7)		$1,875
Reductions required by section 37(e)(5):		
Social security payments	$ 700	
One-half of excess of earnings over $1,200	125	825
Amount determined under section 37(e)(5)		1,050
Retirement income (limited to W's share of public pension)		700
Credit of W (15 percent of $700)		$105

[Reg. §1.37-3.]

□ [*T.D. 6161, 2-3-56. Amended by T.D. 6722, 4-13-64; T.D. 6791, 1-5-65 and T.D. 7743, 12-19-80.*]

[Reg. §1.40-1]

§1.40-1. Questions and answers relating to the meaning of the term "qualified mixture" in section 40(b)(1).

Q-1. What is a "qualified mixture" within the meaning of section 40(b)(1)?

A-1. A "qualified mixture" is a mixture of alcohol and gasoline or of alcohol and a special fuel which (1) is sold by the taxpayer producing such mixture to any person for use as a fuel, or (2) is used as a fuel by the taxpayer producing such mixture.

Q-2. Must alcohol be present in a product in order for that product to be considered a mixture of alcohol and either gasoline or a special fuel?

A-2. No. A product is considered to be a mixture of alcohol and gasoline or of alcohol and a special fuel if the product is derived from alcohol and either gasoline or a special fuel even if the alcohol is chemically transformed in producing the product so that the alcohol is no longer present as a separate chemical in the final product, provided that there is no significant loss in the energy content of the alcohol. Thus, a product may be considered to be a "mixture of alcohol and gasoline or of alcohol and a special fuel" within the meaning of section 40(b)(1)(B) if such product is produced in a chemical reaction between alcohol and either gasoline or a special fuel. Similarly a product may be considered to be a "mixture of alcohol and gasoline or of alcohol and a special fuel" if such product is produced by blending a chemical compound derived from alcohol with either gasoline or a special fuel.

Thus, for example, a blend of gasoline and ethyl tertiary butyl ether (ETBE), a compound derived from ethanol (a qualified alcohol), in a chemical reaction in which there is no significant loss in the energy content of the ethanol, is considered for purposes of section 40(b)(1)(B) to be a mixture of gasoline and the ethanol used to produce the ETBE, even though the ethanol is chemically transformed in the production of ETBE and is not present in the final product. [Reg. §1.40-1.]

□ [*T.D. 8291, 3-6-90.*]

→ **Caution** *Code Sec. 41 was originally enacted as Code Sec. 44F and was redesignated first as Code Sec. 30 and later as Code Sec. 41.*

[Reg. §1.41-0]

§1.41-0. Table of contents.—This section lists the table of contents for §§1.41-1 through 1.41-9.

    (i) General rule.
    (ii) Limited exception.
  (4) Controlled groups.
 (d) Effective/applicability dates.
[Reg. § 1.41-0.]

☐ [*T.D. 8251, 5-16-89. Amended by T.D. 8930, 12-27-2000; T.D. 9104, 12-31-2003; T.D. 9205, 5-23-2005; T.D. 9296, 11-8-2006 T.D. 9401, 6-13-2008, T.D. 9528, 6-9-2011, T.D. 9717, 4-2-2015 and T.D. 9786, 10-3-2016.*]

[Reg. § 1.41-1]

§ 1.41-1. Credit for increasing research activities.—(a) *Amount of credit.*—The amount of a taxpayer's credit is determined under sec-

tion 41(a). For taxable years beginning after June 30, 1996, and at the election of the taxpayer, the portion of the credit determined under section 41(a)(1) may be calculated using the alternative incremental credit set forth in section 41(c)(4). For taxable years ending after December 31, 2006, and at the election of the taxpayer, the portion of the credit determined under section 41 (a)(1) may be calculated using either the alternative incremental credit set forth in section 41(c)(4), or the alternative simplified credit set forth in section 41(c)(5).

(b) *Introduction to regulations under section 41.*—(1) Sections 1.41-2 through 1.41-8 and 1.41-3A through 1.41-5A address only certain provisions of section 41. The following table identifies the provisions of section 41 that are addressed, and lists each provision with the section of the regulations in which it is covered.

Section of the regulation		Section of the Internal Revenue Code
§ 1.41-2	41(b)	
§ 1.41-3	41(c)	
§ 1.41-4	41(d)	
§ 1.41-5	41(e)	
§ 1.41-6	41(f)	
§ 1.41-7	41(f) 41(g)	
§ 1.41-8	41(c)	
§ 1.41-3A	41(c)	(taxable years beginning before January 1, 1990)
§ 1.41-4A	41(d)	(taxable years beginning before January 1, 1986)
§ 1.41-5A	41(e)	(taxable years beginning before January 1, 1987)

(2) Section 1.41-3A also addresses the special rule in section 221(d)(2) of the Economic Recovery Tax Act of 1981 relating to taxable years overlapping the effective dates of section 41. Section 41 was formerly designated as sections 30 and 44F. Sections 1.41-0 through 1.41-8 and 1.41-0A through 1.41-5A refer to these sections as section 41 for conformity purposes. Whether section 41, former section 30, or former section 44F applies to a particular expenditure depends upon when the expenditure was paid or incurred. [Reg. § 1.41-1.]

☐ [*T.D. 8251, 5-16-89. Amended by T.D. 8930, 12-27-2000 and T.D. 9401, 6-13-2008.*]

[Reg. § 1.41-2]

§ 1.41-2. Qualified research expenses.—(a) *Trade or business requirement.*—(1) *In general.*—An in-house research expense of the taxpayer or a contract research expense of the taxpayer is a qualified research expense only if the expense is paid or incurred by the taxpayer in carrying on a trade or business of the taxpayer. The phrase "in carrying on a trade or business" has the same meaning for purposes of section 41(b)(1) as it has for purposes of section 162; thus, expenses paid or incurred in connection with a trade or business within the meaning of section 174(a) (relating to the deduction for research and experimental expenses) are not necessarily paid or incurred in carrying on a trade or business for purposes of section 41. A research expense must relate to a particular trade or business being carried on by the taxpayer at the time the expense is paid or incurred in order to be a qualified research expense. For purposes of section 41, a contract research expense of the taxpayer is not a qualified research expense if the product or result of the research is intended to be transferred to another in return for license or royalty payments and the taxpayer does not use the product of the research in the taxpayer's trade or business.

(2) *New business.*—Expenses paid or incurred prior to commencing a new business (as distinguished from expanding an existing business) may be paid or incurred in connection with a trade or business but are not paid or incurred in carrying on a trade or business. Thus, research expenses paid or incurred by a taxpayer in developing a product the sale of which would constitute a new trade or business for the taxpayer are not paid or incurred in carrying on a *trade or business.*

(3) *Research performed for others.*—(i) *Taxpayer not entitled to results.*—If the taxpayer performs research on behalf of another person and retains no substantial rights in the research, that research shall not be taken into account by the taxpayer for purposes of section 41. See § 1.41-4A(d)(2).

(ii) *Taxpayer entitled to results.*—If the taxpayer in carrying on a trade or business performs research on behalf of other persons but retains substantial rights in the research, the taxpayer shall take

otherwise qualified expenses for that research into account for purposes of section 41 to the extent provided in § 1.41-4A(d)(3).

(4) *Partnerships.*—(i) *In general.*—An in-house research expense or a contract research expense paid or incurred by a partnership is a qualified research expense of the partnership if the expense is paid or incurred by the partnership in carrying on a trade or business of the partnership, determined at the partnership level without regard to the trade or business of any partner.

(ii) *Special rule for certain partnerships and joint ventures.*—(A) If a partnership or a joint venture (taxable as a partnership) is not carrying on the trade or business to which the research relates, then the general rule in paragraph (a)(4)(i) of this section would not allow any of such expenditures to qualify as qualified research expenses.

(B) Notwithstanding paragraph (a)(4)(ii)(A) of this section, if all the partners or venturers are entitled to make independent use of the results of the research, this paragraph (a)(4)(ii) may allow a portion of such expenditures to be treated as qualified research expenditures by certain partners or venturers.

(C) First, in order to determine the amount of credit that may be claimed by certain partners or venturers, the amount of qualified research expenditures of the partnership or joint venture is determined (assuming for this purpose that the partnership or joint venture is carrying on the trade or business to which the research relates).

(D) Second, this amount is reduced by the proportionate share of such expenses allocable to those partners or venturers who would not be able to claim such expenses as qualified research expenditures if they had paid or incurred such expenses directly. For this purpose such partners' or venturers' proportionate share of such expenses shall be determined on the basis of such partners' or venturers' share of partnership items of income or gain (excluding gain allocated under section 704(c)) which results in the largest proportionate share. Where a partner's or venturer's share of partnership items of income or gain (excluding gain allocated under section 704(c)) may vary during the period such partner or venturer is a partner or venturer in such partnership or joint venture, such share shall be the highest share such partner or venturer may receive.

(E) Third, the remaining amount of qualified research expenses is allocated among those partners or venturers who would have been entitled to claim a credit for such expenses if they had paid or incurred the research expenses in their own trade or business, in the relative proportions that such partners or venturers share deductions for expenses under section 174 for the taxable year that such expenses are paid or incurred.

(F) For purposes of section 41, research expenditures to which this paragraph (a)(4)(ii) applies shall be treated as paid or incurred directly by such partners or venturers. See § 1.41-7(a)(3)(ii) for special rules regarding these expenses.

(iii) The following examples illustrate the application of the principles contained in paragraph (a)(4)(ii) of this section.

Example (1). A joint venture (taxable as a partnership) is formed by corporations A, B, and C to develop and market a supercomputer. A and B are in the business of developing computers, and each has a 30 percent distributive share of each item of income, gain, loss, deduction, credit and basis of the joint venture. C, which is an investment banking firm, has a 40 percent distributive share of each item of income, gain, loss, deduction, credit and basis of the joint venture. The joint venture agreement provides that A's, B's and C's distributive shares will not vary during the life of the joint venture, liquidation proceeds are to be distributed in accordance with the partners' capital account balances, and any partner with a deficit in its capital account following the distribution of liquidation proceeds is required to restore the amount of such deficit to the joint venture. Assume in Year 1 that the joint venture incurs $100x of "qualified research expenses." Assume further that the joint venture cannot claim the research credit for such expenses because it is not carrying on the trade or business to which the research relates. In addition A, B, and C are all entitled to make independent use of the results of the research. First, the amount of qualified research expenses of the joint venture is $100x. Second, this amount is reduced by the proportionate share of such expenses allocable to C, the venturer which would not have been able to claim such expenses as qualified research expenditures if it had paid or incurred them directly, C's proportionate share of such expenses is $40x (40% of $100x). The reduced amount is $60x. Third, the remaining $60x of qualified research expenses is allocated between A and B in the relative proportions that A and B share deductions for expenses under section 174. A is entitled to treat $30x ((30% / (30% + 30%)) $60x) as a qualified research expense. B is also entitled to treat $30x ((30% / (30% + 30%)) $60x) as a qualified research expense.

Example (2). Assume the same facts as in example (1) except that the joint venture agreement provides that during the first 2 years of the joint venture, A and B are each allocated 10 percent of each item of income, gain, loss, deduction, credit and basis, and C is allocated 80 percent of each item of income, gain, loss, deduction, credit and basis. Thereafter the allocations are the same as in example (1). Assume for purposes of this example that such allocations have substantial economic effect for purposes of section 704(b). C's highest share of such items during the life of the joint venture is 80 percent. Therefore C's proportionate share of the joint venture's qualified research expenses is $80x (80% of $100x). The reduced amount of qualified research expenses is $20x ($100x − $80x). A is entitled to treat $10x ((10% / (10% + 10%)) $20x) as a qualified research expense in Year 1. B is also entitled to treat $10x ((10% / (10% + 10%)) $20x) as a qualified research expense in Year 1.

(b) *Supplies and personal property used in the conduct of qualified research.*—(1) *In general.*—Supplies and personal property (except to the extent provided in paragraph (b)(4) of this section) are used in the conduct of qualified research if they are used in the performance of qualified services (as defined in section 41(b)(2)(B), but without regard to the last sentence thereof) by an employee of the taxpayer (or by a person acting in a capacity similar to that of an employee of the taxpayer; see example (6) of §1.41-2(e)(5)). Expenditures for supplies or for the use of personal property that are indirect research expenditures or general and administrative expenses do not qualify as in-house research expenses.

(2) *Certain utility charges.*—(i) *In general.*—In general, amounts paid or incurred for utilities such as water, electricity, and natural gas used in the building in which qualified research is performed are treated as expenditures for general and administrative expenses.

(ii) *Extraordinary expenditures.*—To the extent the taxpayer can establish that the special character of the qualified research required additional extraordinary expenditures for utilities, the additional expenditures shall be treated as amounts paid or incurred for supplies used in the conduct of qualified research. For example, amounts paid for electricity used for general laboratory lighting are treated as general and administrative expenses, but amounts paid for electricity used in operating high energy equipment for qualified research (such as laser or nuclear research) may be treated as expenditures for supplies used in the conduct of qualified research to the extent the taxpayer can establish that the special character of the research required an extraordinary additional expenditure for electricity.

(3) *Right to use personal property.*—The determination of whether an amount is paid to or incurred for another person for the right to use personal property in the conduct of qualified research shall be made without regard to the characterization of the transaction as a lease under section 168(f)(8) (as that section read before it was repealed by the Tax Reform Act of 1986). See §5c.168(f)(8)-1(b).

(4) *Use of personal property in taxable years beginning after December 31, 1985.*—For taxable years beginning after December 31, 1985, amounts paid or incurred for the use of personal property are not qualified research expenses, except for any amount paid or incurred to another person for the right to use (time-sharing) computers in the conduct of qualified research. The computer must be owned and operated by someone other than the taxpayer, located off the taxpayer's premises, and the taxpayer must not be the primary user of the computer.

(c) *Qualified services.*—(1) *Engaging in qualified research.*—The term "engaging in qualified research" as used in section 41(b)(2)(B) means the actual conduct of qualified research (as in the case of a scientist conducting laboratory experiments).

(2) *Direct supervision.*—The term "direct supervision" as used in section 41(b)(2)(B) means the immediate supervision (first-line management) of qualified research (as in the case of a research scientist who directly supervises laboratory experiments, but who may not actually perform experiments). "Direct supervision" does not include supervision by a higher-level manager to whom first-line managers report, even if that manager is a qualified research scientist.

(3) *Direct support.*—The term "direct support" as used in section 41(b)(2)(B) means services in the direct support of either—

(i) Persons engaging in actual conduct of qualified research, or

(ii) Persons who are directly supervising persons engaging in the actual conduct of qualified research. For example, direct support of research includes the services of a secretary for typing reports describing laboratory results derived from qualified research, of a laboratory worker for cleaning equipment used in qualified research, of a clerk for compiling research data, and of a machinist for machining a part of an experimental model used in qualified research. Direct support of research activities does not include general administrative services, or other services only indirectly of benefit to research activities. For example, services of payroll personnel in preparing salary checks of laboratory scientists, of an accountant for accounting for research expenses, of a janitor for general cleaning of a research laboratory, or of officers engaged in supervising financial or personnel matters do not qualify as direct support of research. This is true whether general administrative personnel are part of the research department or in a separate department. Direct support does not include supervision. Supervisory services constitute "qualified services" only to the extent provided in paragraph (c)(2) of this section.

(d) *Wages paid for qualified services.*—(1) *In general.*—Wages paid to or incurred for an employee constitute in-house research expenses only to the extent the wages were paid or incurred for qualified services performed by the employee. If an employee has performed both qualified services and nonqualified services, only the amount of wages allocated to the performance of qualified services constitutes an in-house research expense. In the absence of another method of allocation that the taxpayer can demonstrate to be more appropriate, the amount of in-house research expense shall be determined by multiplying the total amount of wages paid to or incurred for the employee during the taxable year by the ratio of the total time actually spent by the employee in the performance of qualified services for the taxpayer to the total time spent by the employee in the performance of all services for the taxpayer during the taxable year.

(2) *"Substantially all".*—Notwithstanding paragraph (d)(1) of this section, if substantially all of the services performed by an employee for the taxpayer during the taxable year consist of services meeting the requirements of section 41(b)(2)(B)(i) or (ii), then the term "qualified services" means all of the services performed by the employee for the taxpayer during the taxable year. Services meeting the requirements of section 41(b)(2)(B)(i) or (ii) constitute substantially all of the services performed by the employee during a taxable year only if the wages allocated (on the basis used for purposes of paragraph (d)(1) of this section) to services meeting the requirements of section 41(b)(2)(B)(i) or (ii) constitute at least 80 percent of the wages paid to or incurred by the taxpayer for the employee during the taxable year.

(e) *Contract research expenses.*—(1) *In general.*—A contract research expense is 65 percent of any expense paid or incurred in carrying on a trade or business to any person other than an employee of the taxpayer for the performance on behalf of the taxpayer of—

(i) Qualified research as defined in §1.41-4 or 1.41-4A, whichever is applicable, or

(ii) Services which, if performed by employees of the taxpayer, would constitute qualified services within the meaning of section 41(b)(2)(B).

Where the contract calls for services other than services described in this paragraph (e)(1), only 65 percent of the portion of the amount paid or incurred that is attributable to the services described in this paragraph (e)(1) is a contract research expense.

(2) *Performance of qualified research.*—An expense is paid or incurred for the performance of qualified research only to the extent that it is paid or incurred pursuant to an agreement that—

(i) Is entered into prior to the performance of the qualified research,

(ii) Provides that research be performed on behalf of the taxpayer, and

(iii) Requires the taxpayer to bear the expense even if the research is not successful.

If an expense is paid or incurred pursuant to an agreement under which payment is contingent on the success of the research, then the expense is considered paid for the product or result rather than the performance of the research, and the payment is not a contract research expense. The previous sentence applies only to that portion of a payment which is contingent on the success of the research.

(3) *"On behalf of".*—Qualified research is performed on behalf of the taxpayer if the taxpayer has a right to the research results. Qualified research can be performed on behalf of the taxpayer notwithstanding the fact that the taxpayer does not have exclusive rights to the results.

(4) *Prepaid amounts.*—Notwithstanding paragraph (e)(1) of this section, if any contract research expense paid or incurred during any taxable year is attributable to qualified research to be conducted after the close of such taxable year, the expense so attributable shall be treated for purposes of section 41(b)(1)(B) as paid or incurred during the period during which the qualified research is conducted.

(5) *Examples.*—The following examples illustrate provisions contained in paragraphs (e)(1) through (4) of this section.

Example (1). A, a cash-method taxpayer using the calendar year as the taxable year, enters into a contract with B Corporation under which B is to perform qualified research on behalf of A. The contract requires A to pay B $300x, regardless of the success of the research. In 1982, B performs all of the research, and A makes full payment of $300x under the contract. Accordingly, during the taxable year 1982, $195x (65 percent of the payment of $300x) constitutes a contract research expense of A.

Example (2). The facts are the same as in example (1), except that B performs 50 percent of the research in 1983. Of the $195x of contract research expense paid in 1982, paragraph (e)(4) of this section provides that $97.5x (50 percent of $195x) is a contract research expense for 1982 and the remaining $97.5x is contract research expense for 1983.

Example (3). The facts are the same as in example (1), except that instead of calling for a flat payment of $300x, the contract requires A to reimburse B for all expenses plus pay B $100x. B incurs expenses attributable to the research as follows:

Labor	$90x
Supplies	20x
Depreciation on equipment	50x
Overhead	40x
Total	$200x

Under this agreement A pays B $300x during 1982. Accordingly, during taxable year 1982, $195x (65 percent of $300x) of the payment constitutes a contract research expense of A.

Example (4). The facts are the same as in example (3), except that A agrees to reimburse B for all expenses and agrees to pay B an additional amount of $100x, but the additional $100x is payable only if the research is successful. The research is successful and A pays B $300x during 1982. Paragraph (e)(2) of this section provides that the contingent portion of the payment is not an expense incurred for the performance of qualified research. Thus, for taxable year 1982, $130x (65 percent of the payment of $200x) constitutes a contract research expense of A.

Example (5). C conducts in-house qualified research in carrying on a trade or business. In addition, C pays D Corporation, a provider of computer services, $100x to develop software to be used in analyzing the results C derives from its research. Because the software services, if performed by an employee of C, would constitute qualified services, $65x of the $100x constitutes a contract research expense of C.

Example (6). C conducts in-house qualified research in carrying on C's trade or business. In addition, C contracts with E Corporation, a provider of temporary secretarial services, for the services of a secretary for a week. The secretary spends the entire week typing reports describing laboratory results derived from C's qualified research. C pays E $400 for the secretarial service, none of which constitutes wages within the meaning of section 41(b)(2)(D). These services, if performed by employees of C, would constitute qualified services within the meaning of section 41(b)(2)(B). Thus, pursuant to

paragraph (e)(1) of this section, $260 (65 percent of $400) constitutes a contract research expense of C.

Example (7). C conducts in-house qualified research in carrying on C's trade or business. In addition, C pays F, an outside accountant, $100x to keep C's books and records pertaining to the research project. The activity carried on by the accountant does not constitute qualified research as defined in section 41(d). The services performed by the accountant, if performed by an employee of C, would not constitute qualified services (as defined in section 41(b)(2)(B)). Thus, under paragraph (e)(1) of this section, no portion of the $100x constitutes a contract research expense. [Reg. §1.41-2.]

☐ [*T.D. 8251, 5-16-89. Amended by T.D. 8930, 12-27-2000.*]

[Reg. §1.41-3]

§1.41-3. Base amount for taxable years beginning on or after January 3, 2001.—(a) *New taxpayers.*—If, with respect to any credit year, the taxpayer has not been in existence for any previous taxable year, the average annual gross receipts of the taxpayer for the four taxable years preceding the credit year shall be zero. If, with respect to any credit year, the taxpayer has been in existence for at least one previous taxable year, but has not been in existence for four taxable years preceding the taxable year, then the average annual gross receipts of the taxpayer for the four taxable years preceding the credit year shall be the average annual gross receipts for the number of taxable years preceding the credit year for which the taxpayer has been in existence.

(b) *Special rules for short taxable years.*—(1) *Short credit year.*—If a credit year is a short taxable year, then the base amount determined under section 41(c)(1) (but not section 41(c)(2)) shall be modified by multiplying that amount by the number of months in the short taxable year and dividing the result by 12.

(2) *Short taxable year preceding credit year.*—If one or more of the four taxable years preceding the credit year is a short taxable year, then the gross receipts for such year are deemed to be equal to the gross receipts actually derived in that year multiplied by 12 and divided by the number of months in that year.

(3) *Short taxable year in determining fixed-base percentage.*—No adjustment shall be made on account of a short taxable year to the computation of a taxpayer's fixed-base percentage.

(c) *Definition of gross receipts.*—(1) *In general.*—For purposes of section 41, gross receipts means the total amount, as determined under the taxpayer's method of accounting, derived by the taxpayer from all its activities and from all sources (*e.g.*, revenues derived from the sale of inventory before reduction for cost of goods sold).

(2) *Amounts excluded.*—For purposes of this paragraph (c), gross receipts do not include amounts representing—

(i) Returns or allowances;

(ii) Receipts from the sale or exchange of capital assets, as defined in section 1221;

(iii) Repayments of loans or similar instruments (e.g., a repayment of the principal amount of a loan held by a commercial lender);

(iv) Receipts from a sale or exchange not in the ordinary course of business, such as the sale of an entire trade or business or the sale of property used in a trade or business as defined under section 1221(2);

(v) Amounts received with respect to sales tax or other similar state and local taxes if, under the applicable state or local law, the tax is legally imposed on the purchaser of the good or service, and the taxpayer merely collects and remits the tax to the taxing authority; and

(vi) Amounts received by a taxpayer in a taxable year that precedes the first taxable year in which the taxpayer derives more than $25,000 in gross receipts other than investment income. For purposes of this paragraph (c)(2)(vi), investment income is interest or distributions with respect to stock (other than the stock of a 20-percent owned corporation as defined in section 243(c)(2).

(3) *Foreign corporations.*—For purposes of section 41, in the case of a foreign corporation, gross receipts include only gross receipts that are effectively connected with the conduct of a trade or business within the United States, the Commonwealth of Puerto Rico, or other possessions of the United States. See section 864(c) and applicable regulations thereunder for the definition of effectively connected income.

(d) *Consistency requirement.*—(1) *In general.*—In computing the credit for increasing research activities for taxable years beginning after December 31, 1989, qualified research expenses and gross receipts taken into account in computing a taxpayer's fixed-base percentage and a taxpayer's base amount must be determined on a basis consistent with the definition of qualified research expenses and gross receipts for the credit year, without regard to the law in effect for the taxable years taken into account in computing the fixed-base percentage or the base amount. This consistency requirement applies even if the period for filing a claim for credit or refund has expired for any taxable year taken into account in computing the fixed-base percentage or the base amount.

(2) *Illustrations.*—The following examples illustrate the application of the consistency rule of paragraph (d)(1) of this section:

Example 1. (i) X, an accrual method taxpayer using the calendar year as its taxable year, incurs qualified research expenses in 2001. X wants to compute its research credit under section 41 for the tax year ending December 31, 2001. As part of the computation, X must determine its fixed-base percentage, which depends in part on X's qualified research expenses incurred during the fixed-base period, the taxable years beginning after December 31, 1983, and before January 1, 1989.

(ii) During the fixed-base period, X reported the following amounts as qualified research expenses on its Form 6765:

1984	$100x
1985	120x
1986	150x
1987	180x
1988	170x
Total	$720x

(iii) For the taxable years ending December 31, 1984, and December 31, 1985, X based the amounts reported as qualified research expenses on the definition of qualified research in effect for those taxable years. The definition of qualified research changed for taxable years beginning after December 31, 1985. If X used the definition of qualified research applicable to its taxable year ending December 31, 2001, the credit year, its qualified research expenses for the taxable years ending December 31, 1984, and December 31, 1985, would be reduced to $80x and $100x, respectively. Under the consistency rule in section 41(c)(5) and paragraph (d)(1) of this section, to compute the research credit for the tax year ending December 31, 2001, X must reduce its qualified research expenses for 1984 and 1985 to reflect the change in the definition of qualified research for taxable years beginning after December 31, 1985. Thus, X's total qualified research expenses for the fixed-base period (1984-1988) to be used in computing the fixed-base percentage is $80 + 100 + 150 + 180 + 170 = $680x.

Example 2. The facts are the same as in *Example 1*, except that, in computing its qualified research expenses for the taxable year ending December 31, 2001, X claimed that a certain type of expenditure incurred in 2001 was a qualified research expense. X's claim reflected a change in X's position, because X had not previously claimed that similar expenditures were qualified research expenses. The consistency rule requires X to adjust its qualified research expenses in computing the fixed-base percentage to include any similar expenditures not treated as qualified research expenses during the fixed-base period, regardless of whether the period for filing a claim for credit or refund has expired for any year taken into account in computing the fixed-base percentage.

(e) *Effective date.*—The rules in paragraphs (c) and (d) of this section are applicable for taxable years beginning on or after the date final regulations are published in the Federal Register. [Reg. § 1.41-3.]

☐ [T.D. 8930, 12-27-2000.]

[Reg. § 1.41-4]

§ 1.41-4. Qualified research for expenditures paid or incurred on or after January 3, 2001.—(a) *Qualified research.*—(1) *General rule.*—Research activities related to the development or improvement of a business component constitute qualified research only if the research activities meet all of the requirements of section 41(d)(1) and this section, and are not otherwise excluded under section 41(d)(3)(B) or (d)(4), or this section.

(2) *Requirements of section 41(d)(1).*—Research constitutes qualified research only if it is research—

(i) With respect to which expenditures may be treated as expenses under section 174, see § 1.174-2;

(ii) That is undertaken for the purpose of discovering information that is technological in nature, and the application of which is intended to be useful in the development of a new or improved business component of the taxpayer; and

(iii) Substantially all of the activities of which constitute elements of a process of experimentation that relates to a qualified purpose.

(3) *Undertaken for the purpose of discovering information.*—(i) *In general.*—For purposes of section 41(d) and this section, research must be undertaken for the purpose of discovering information that is technological in nature. Research is undertaken for the purpose of

discovering information if it is intended to eliminate uncertainty concerning the development or improvement of a business component. Uncertainty exists if the information available to the taxpayer does not establish the capability or method for developing or improving the business component, or the appropriate design of the business component.

(ii) *Application of the discovering information requirement.*—A determination that research is undertaken for the purpose of discovering information that is technological in nature does not require the taxpayer be seeking to obtain information that exceeds, expands or refines the common knowledge of skilled professionals in the particular field of science or engineering in which the taxpayer is performing the research. In addition, a determination that research is undertaken for the purpose of discovering information that is technological in nature does not require that the taxpayer succeed in developing a new or improved business component.

(iii) *Patent safe harbor.*—For purposes of section 41(d) and paragraph (a)(3)(i) of this section, the issuance of a patent by the Patent and Trademark Office under the provisions of 35 U.S.C. 151 (other than a patent for design issued under the provisions of 35 U.S.C. 171) is conclusive evidence that a taxpayer has discovered information that is technological in nature that is intended to eliminate uncertainty concerning the development or improvement of a business component. However, the issuance of such a patent is not a precondition for credit availability.

(4) *Technological in nature.*—For purposes of section 41(d) and this section, information is technological in nature if the process of experimentation used to discover such information fundamentally relies on principles of the physical or biological sciences, engineering, or computer science. A taxpayer may employ existing technologies and may rely on existing principles of the physical or biological sciences, engineering, or computer science to satisfy this requirement.

(5) *Process of experimentation.*—(i) *In general.*—For purposes of section 41(d) and this section, a process of experimentation is a process designed to evaluate one or more alternatives to achieve a result where the capability or the method of achieving that result, or the appropriate design of that result, is uncertain as of the beginning of the taxpayer's research activities. A process of experimentation must fundamentally rely on the principles of the physical or biological sciences, engineering, or computer science and involves the identification of uncertainty concerning the development or improvement of a business component, the identification of one or more alternatives intended to eliminate that uncertainty, and the identification and the conduct of a process of evaluating the alternatives (through, for example, modeling, simulation, or a systematic trial and error methodology). A process of experimentation must be an evaluative process and generally should be capable of evaluating more than one alternative. A taxpayer may undertake a process of experimentation if there is no uncertainty concerning the taxpayer's capability or method of achieving the desired result so long as the appropriate design of the desired result is uncertain as of the beginning of the taxpayer's research activities. Uncertainty concerning the development or improvement of the business component (e.g., its appropriate design) does not establish that all activities undertaken to achieve that new or improved business component constitute a process of experimentation.

(ii) *Qualified purpose.*—For purposes of section 41(d) and this section, a process of experimentation is undertaken for a qualified purpose if it relates to a new or improved function, performance, reliability or quality of the business component. Research will not be treated as conducted for a qualified purpose if it relates to style, taste, cosmetic, or seasonal design factors.

(6) *Substantially all requirement.*—In order for activities to constitute qualified research under section 41(d)(1), substantially all of the activities must constitute elements of a process of experimentation that relates to a qualified purpose. The substantially all requirement of section 41(d)(1)(C) and paragraph (a)(2)(iii) of this section is satisfied only if 80 percent or more of a taxpayer's research activities, measured on a cost or other consistently applied reasonable basis (and without regard to § 1.41-2(d)(2)), constitute elements of a process of experimentation for a purpose described in section 41(d)(3). Accordingly, if 80 percent (or more) of a taxpayer's research activities with respect to a business component constitute elements of a process of experimentation for a purpose described in section 41(d)(3), the substantially all requirement is satisfied even if the remaining 20 percent (or less) of a taxpayer's research activities with respect to the business component do not constitute elements of a process of experimentation for a purpose described in section 41(d)(3), so long as these remaining research activities satisfy the requirements of section 41(d)(1)(A) and are not otherwise excluded under section 41(d)(4).

The substantially all requirement is applied separately to each business component.

(7) *Use of computers and information technology.*—The employment of computers or information technology, or the reliance on principles of computer science or information technology to store, collect, manipulate, translate, disseminate, produce, distribute, or process data or information, and similar uses of computers and information technology does not itself establish that qualified research has been undertaken.

(8) *Illustrations.*—The following examples illustrate the application of paragraph (a)(5) of this section:

Example 1. (i) *Facts.* X is engaged in the business of developing and manufacturing widgets. X wants to change the color of its blue widget to green. X obtains from various suppliers several different shades of green paint. X paints several sample widgets, and surveys X's customers to determine which shade of green X's customers prefer.

(ii) *Conclusion.* X's activities to change the color of its blue widget to green are not qualified research under section 41(d)(1) and paragraph (a)(5) of this section because substantially all of X's activities are not undertaken for a qualified purpose. All of X's research activities are related to style, taste, cosmetic, or seasonal design factors.

Example 2. (i) *Facts.* The facts are the same as in *Example 1*, except that X chooses one of the green paints. X obtains samples of the green paint from a supplier and determines that X must modify its painting process to accommodate the green paint because the green paint has different characteristics from other paints X has used. X obtains detailed data on the green paint from X's paint supplier. X also consults with the manufacturer of X's paint spraying machines. The manufacturer informs X that X must acquire a new nozzle that operates with the green paint X wants to use. X tests the nozzles to ensure that they work as specified by the manufacturer of the paint spraying machines.

(ii) *Conclusion.* X's activities to modify its painting process are a separate business component under section 41(d)(2)(A). X's activities to modify its painting process to change the color of its blue widget to green are not qualified research under section 41(d)(1) and paragraph (a)(5) of this section. X did not conduct a process of evaluating alternatives in order to eliminate uncertainty regarding the modification of its painting process. Rather, the manufacturer of the paint machines eliminated X's uncertainty regarding the modification of its painting process. X's activities to test the nozzles to determine if the nozzles work as specified by the manufacturer of the paint spraying machines are in the nature of routine or ordinary testing or inspection for quality control.

Example 3. (i) *Facts.* X is engaged in the business of manufacturing food products and currently manufactures a large-shred version of a product. X seeks to modify its current production line to permit it to manufacture both a large-shred version and a fine-shred version of one of its food products. A smaller, thinner shredding blade capable of producing a fine-shred version of the food product, however, is not commercially available. Thus, X must develop a new shredding blade that can be fitted onto its current production line. X is uncertain concerning the design of the new shredding blade, because the material used in its existing blade breaks when machined into smaller, thinner blades. X engages in a systematic trial and error process of analyzing various blade designs and materials to determine whether the new shredding blade must be constructed of a different material from that of its existing shredding blade and, if so, what material will best meet X's functional requirements.

(ii) *Conclusion.* X's activities to modify its current production line by developing the new shredding blade meet the requirements of qualified research as set forth in paragraph (a)(2) of this section. Substantially all of X's activities constitute elements of a process of experimentation because X evaluated alternatives to achieve a result where the method of achieving that result, and the appropriate design of that result, were uncertain as of the beginning of the taxpayer's research activities. X identified uncertainties related to the development of a business component, and identified alternatives intended to eliminate these uncertainties. Furthermore, X's process of evaluating identified alternatives was technological in nature, and was undertaken to eliminate the uncertainties.

Example 4. (i) *Facts.* X is in the business of designing, developing and manufacturing automobiles. In response to government-mandated fuel economy requirements, X seeks to update its current model vehicle and undertakes to improve aerodynamics by lowering the hood of its current model vehicle. X determines, however, that lowering the hood changes the air flow under the hood, which changes the rate at which air enters the engine through the air intake system, and which reduces the functionality of the cooling system. X's engineers are uncertain how to design a lower hood to obtain the increased fuel economy, while maintaining the necessary air flow

under the hood. X designs, models, simulates, tests, refines, and retests several alternative designs for the hood and associated proposed modifications to both the air intake system and cooling system. This process enables X to eliminate the uncertainties related to the integrated design of the hood, air intake system, and cooling system, and such activities constitute eighty-five percent of X's total activities to update its current model vehicle. X then engages in additional activities that do not involve a process of evaluating alternatives in order to eliminate uncertainties. The additional activities constitute only fifteen percent of X's total activities to update its current model vehicle.

(ii) *Conclusion.* In general, if eighty percent or more of a taxpayer's research activities measured on a cost or other consistently applied reasonable basis constitute elements of a process of experimentation for a qualified purpose under section 41(d)(3)(A) and paragraph (a)(5)(ii) of this section, then the substantially all requirement of section 41(d)(1)(C) and paragraph (a)(2)(iii) of this section is satisfied. Substantially all of X's activities constitute elements of a process of experimentation because X evaluated alternatives to achieve a result where the method of achieving that result, and the appropriate design of that result, were uncertain as of the beginning of X's research activities. X identified uncertainties related to the improvement of a business component and identified alternatives intended to eliminate these uncertainties. Furthermore, X's process of evaluating the identified alternatives was technological in nature and was undertaken to eliminate the uncertainties. Because substantially all (in this example, eighty-five percent) of X's activities to update its current model vehicle constitute elements of a process of experimentation for a qualified purpose described in section 41(d)(3)(A), all of X's activities to update its current model vehicle meet the requirements of qualified research as set forth in paragraph (a)(2) of this section, provided that X's remaining activities (in this example, fifteen percent of X's total activities) satisfy the requirements of section 41(d)(1)(A) and are not otherwise excluded under section 41(d)(4).

Example 5. (i) *Facts.* X, a retail and distribution company, wants to upgrade its warehouse management software. X evaluates several of the alternative warehouse management software products available from vendors in the marketplace to determine which product will best serve X's technical requirements. X selects vendor V's software.

(ii) *Conclusion.* X's activities to select the software are not qualified research under section 41(d)(1) and paragraph (a)(5) of this section. X did not conduct a process of evaluating alternatives in order to eliminate uncertainty regarding the development of a business component. X's evaluation of products available from vendors is not a process of experimentation.

Example 6. (i) *Facts.* X wants to develop a new web application to allow customers to purchase its products online. X, after reviewing commercial software offered by various vendors, purchases a commercial software package of object-oriented functions from vendor Z that X can use in its web application (for example, a shopping cart). X evaluates the various object-oriented functions included in vendor Z's software package to determine which functions it can use. X then incorporates the selected software functions in its new web application software.

(ii) *Conclusion.* X's activities related to selecting the commercial software vendor with the object-oriented functions it wanted, and then selecting which functions to use, are not qualified research under section 41(d)(1) and paragraph (a)(5) of this section. In addition, incorporating the selected object-oriented functions into the new web application software being developed by X did not involve conducting a process of evaluating alternatives in order to eliminate uncertainty regarding the development of software. X's evaluation of products available from vendors and selection of software functions are not a process of experimentation.

Example 7. (i) *Facts.* In order to be more responsive to user online requests, X wants to develop software to balance the incoming processing requests across multiple web servers that run the same set of software applications. Without evaluating or testing any alternatives, X decides that a separate server will be used to distribute the workload across each of the web servers and that a round robin workload distribution algorithm is appropriate for its needs.

(ii) *Conclusion.* X's activities to develop the software are activities relating to the development of a separate business component under section 41(d)(2)(A). X's activities to develop the load distribution function are not qualified research under section 41(d)(1) and paragraph (a)(5) of this section. X did not conduct a process of evaluating different load distribution alternatives in order to eliminate uncertainty regarding the development of software. X's selection of a separate server and a round robin distribution algorithm is not a process of experimentation.

Example 8. (i) *Facts.* X must develop load balancing software across a server cluster supporting multiple web applications. X's web applications have high concurrency demands because of a dynamic, highly volatile environment. X is uncertain of the appropriate design of the load balancing algorithm, given that the existing evolutionary algorithms did not meet the demands of their highly volatile web environment. Therefore, X designs and systematically tests and evaluates several different algorithms that perform the load distribution functions.

(ii) *Conclusion.* X's activities to develop software are activities to develop a separate business component under section 41(d)(2)(A). X's activities involving the design, evaluation, and systematic testing of several new load balancing algorithms meet the requirements as set forth in paragraph (a)(5) of this section. X's activities constitute elements of a process of experimentation because X identified uncertainties related to the development of a business component, identified alternatives intended to eliminate those uncertainties, and evaluated one or more alternatives to achieve a result where the appropriate design was uncertain at the beginning of X's research activities.

Example 9. (i) *Facts.* X, a multinational manufacturer, wants to install an enterprise resource planning (ERP) system that runs off a single database so that X can track orders more easily, and coordinate manufacturing, inventory, and shipping among many different locations at the same time. In order to successfully install and implement ERP software, X evaluates its business needs and the technical requirements of the software, such as processing power, memory, storage, and network resources. X devotes the majority of its resources in implementing the ERP system to evaluating the available templates, reports, and other standard programs and choosing among these alternatives in configuring the system to match its business process and reengineering its business process to match the available alternatives in the ERP system. X also performs some data transfer from its old system, involving routine programming and one-to-one mapping of data to be exchanged between each system.

(ii) *Conclusion.* X's activities related to the ERP software including the data transfer are not qualified research under section 41(d)(1) and paragraph (a)(5) of this section. X did not conduct a process of evaluating alternatives in order to eliminate uncertainty regarding the development of software. X's activities in choosing between available templates, reports, and other standard programs and conducting data transfer are not elements of a process of experimentation.

Example 10. (i) *Facts.* Same facts as *Example 9* except that X determines that it must interface part of its legacy software with the new ERP software because the ERP software does not provide a particular function that X requires for its business. As a result, X must develop an interface between its legacy software and the ERP software, and X evaluates several data exchange software applications and chooses one of the available alternatives. X is uncertain as to how to keep the data synchronized between the legacy and ERP systems. Thus, X engages in systematic trial and error testing of several newly designed data caching algorithms to eliminate synchronization problems.

(ii) *Conclusion.* Substantially all of X's activities with respect to this ERP project do not satisfy the requirements for a process of experimentation. However, when the shrinking-back rule is applied, a subset of X's activities do satisfy the requirements for a process of experimentation. X's activities to develop the data caching software and keeping the data on the legacy and ERP systems synchronized meet the requirements of qualified research as set forth in paragraph (a)(2) of this section. Substantially all of X's activities to develop the specialized data caching and synchronization software constitute elements of a process of experimentation because X identified uncertainties related to the development of a business component, identified alternatives intended to eliminate those uncertainties, and evaluated alternatives to achieve a result where the appropriate design of that result was uncertain as of the beginning of the taxpayer's research activities.

(b) *Application of requirements for qualified research.*—(1) *In general.*—The requirements for qualified research in section 41(d)(1) and paragraph (a) of this section, must be applied separately to each business component, as defined in section 41(d)(2)(B). In cases involving development of both a product and a manufacturing or other commercial production process for the product, research activities relating to development of the process are not qualified research unless the requirements of section 41(d) and this section are met for the research activities relating to the process without taking into account the research activities relating to development of the product. Similarly, research activities relating to development of the product are not qualified research unless the requirements of section 41(d) and this section are met for the research activities relating to the product without taking into account the research activities relating to development of the manufacturing or other commercial production process.

(2) *Shrinking-back rule.*—The requirements of section 41(d) and paragraph (a) of this section are to be applied first at the level of the discrete business component, that is, the product, process, computer software, technique, formula, or invention to be held for sale, lease, or license, or used by the taxpayer in a trade or business of the taxpayer. If these requirements are not met at that level, then they apply at the most significant subset of elements of the product, process, computer software, technique, formula, or invention to be held for sale, lease, or license. This shrinking back of the product is to continue until either a subset of elements of the product that satisfies the requirements is reached, or the most basic element of the product is reached and such element fails to satisfy the test. This shrinking-back rule is applied only if a taxpayer does not satisfy the requirements of section 41(d)(1) and paragraph (a)(2) of this section with respect to the overall business component. The shrinking-back rule is not itself applied as a reason to exclude research activities from credit eligibility.

(3) *Illustration.*—The following example illustrates the application of this paragraph (b):

Example. X, a motorcycle engine builder, develops a new carburetor for use in a motorcycle engine. X also modifies an existing engine design for use with the new carburetor. Under the shrinking-back rule, the requirements of section 41(d)(1) and paragraph (a) of this section are applied first to the engine. If the modifications to the engine when viewed as a whole, including the development of the new carburetor, do not satisfy the requirements of section 41(d)(1) and paragraph (a) of this section, those requirements are applied to the next most significant subset of elements of the business component. Assuming that the next most significant subset of elements of the engine is the carburetor, the research activities in developing the new carburetor may constitute qualified research within the meaning of section 41(d)(1) and paragraph (a) of this section.

(c) *Excluded activities.*—(1) *In general.*—Qualified research does not include any activity described in section 41(d)(4) and paragraph (c) of this section.

(2) *Research after commercial production.*—(i) *In general.*—Activities conducted after the beginning of commercial production of a business component are not qualified research. Activities are conducted after the beginning of commercial production of a business component if such activities are conducted after the component is developed to the point where it is ready for commercial sale or use, or meets the basic functional and economic requirements of the taxpayer for the component's sale or use.

(ii) *Certain additional activities related to the business component.*—The following activities are deemed to occur after the beginning of commercial production of a business component—

(A) Preproduction planning for a finished business component;

(B) Tooling-up for production;

(C) Trial production runs;

(D) Trouble shooting involving detecting faults in production equipment or processes;

(E) Accumulating data relating to production processes; and

(F) Debugging flaws in a business component.

(iii) *Activities related to production process or technique.*—In cases involving development of both a product and a manufacturing or other commercial production process for the product, the exclusion described in section 41(d)(4)(A) and paragraphs (c)(2)(i) and (ii) of this section applies separately for the activities relating to the development of the product and the activities relating to the development of the process. For example, even after a product meets the taxpayer's basic functional and economic requirements, activities relating to the development of the manufacturing process still may constitute qualified research, provided that the development of the process itself separately satisfies the requirements of section 41(d) and this section, and the activities are conducted before the process meets the taxpayer's basic functional and economic requirements or is ready for commercial use.

(iv) *Clinical testing.*—Clinical testing of a pharmaceutical product prior to its commercial production in the United States is not treated as occurring after the beginning of commercial production even if the product is commercially available in other countries. Additional clinical testing of a pharmaceutical product after a product has been approved for a specific therapeutic use by the Food and Drug Administration and is ready for commercial production and sale is not treated as occurring after the beginning of commercial production if such clinical testing is undertaken to establish new functional uses, characteristics, indications, combinations, dosages, or delivery forms for the product. A functional use, characteristic, indication, combination, dosage, or delivery form shall be considered new only if such functional use, characteristic, indication, combination, dosage, or delivery form must be approved by the Food and Drug Administration.

(3) *Adaptation of existing business components.*—Activities relating to adapting an existing business component to a particular customer's requirement or need are not qualified research. This exclusion does not apply merely because a business component is intended for a specific customer.

(4) *Duplication of existing business component.*—Activities relating to reproducing an existing business component (in whole or in part) from a physical examination of the business component itself or from plans, blueprints, detailed specifications, or publicly available information about the business component are not qualified research. This exclusion does not apply merely because the taxpayer examines an existing business component in the course of developing its own business component.

(5) *Surveys, studies, research relating to management functions, etc.*—Qualified research does not include activities relating to—

(i) Efficiency surveys;

(ii) Management functions or techniques, including such items as preparation of financial data and analysis, development of employee training programs and management organization plans, and management-based changes in production processes (such as rearranging work stations on an assembly line);

(iii) Market research, testing, or development (including advertising or promotions);

(iv) Routine data collections; or

(v) Routine or ordinary testing or inspections for quality control.

(6) *Internal use software.*—(i) *General rule.*—Research with respect to software that is developed by (or for the benefit of) the taxpayer primarily for the taxpayer's internal use is eligible for the research credit only if—

(A) The research with respect to the software satisfies the requirements of section 41(d)(1);

(B) The research with respect to the software is not otherwise excluded under section 41(d)(4) (other than section 41(d)(4)(E)); and

(C) The software satisfies the high threshold of innovation test of paragraph (c)(6)(vii) of this section.

(ii) *Inapplicability of the high threshold of innovation test.*—This paragraph (c)(6) does not apply to the following:

(A) Software developed by (or for the benefit of) the taxpayer primarily for internal use by the taxpayer for use in an activity that constitutes qualified research (other than the development of the internal use software itself);

(B) Software developed by (or for the benefit of) the taxpayer primarily for internal use by the taxpayer for use in a production process to which the requirements of section 41(d)(1) are met; and

(C) A new or improved package of software and hardware developed together by the taxpayer as a single product (or to the costs to modify an acquired software and hardware package), of which the software is an integral part, that is used directly by the taxpayer in providing services in its trade or business. In these cases, eligibility for the research credit is to be determined by examining the combined hardware-software product as a single product.

(iii) *Software developed primarily for internal use.*—(A) *In general.*—Except as otherwise provided in paragraph (c)(6)(iv) of this section, software is developed by (or for the benefit of) the taxpayer primarily for the taxpayer's internal use if the software is developed for use in general and administrative functions that facilitate or support the conduct of the taxpayer's trade or business. Software that the taxpayer develops primarily for a related party's internal use will be considered internal use software. A related party is any corporation, trade or business, or other person that is treated as a single taxpayer with the taxpayer pursuant to section 41(f).

(B) *General and administrative functions.*—General and administrative functions are:

(1) *Financial management.*—Financial management functions are functions that involve the financial management of the taxpayer and the supporting recordkeeping. Financial management functions include, but are not limited to, functions such as accounts payable, accounts receivable, inventory management, budgeting, cash management, cost accounting, disbursements, economic analysis and forecasting, financial reporting, finance, fixed asset accounting, general ledger bookkeeping, internal audit, management accounting, risk management, strategic business planning, and tax.

(2) *Human resources management.*—Human resources management functions are functions that manage the taxpayer's workforce. Human resources management functions include, but are not limited to, functions such as recruiting, hiring, training, assigning personnel, and maintaining personnel records, payroll, and benefits.

(3) *Support services.*—Support services are other functions that support the day-to-day operations of the taxpayer. Support services include, but are not limited to, functions such as data processing, facility services (for example, grounds keeping, housekeeping, janitorial, and logistics), graphic services, marketing, legal services, government compliance services, printing and publication services, and security services (for example, video surveillance and physical asset protection from fire and theft).

(iv) *Software not developed primarily for internal use.*—Software is not developed primarily for the taxpayer's internal use if it is not developed for use in general and administrative functions that facilitate or support the conduct of the taxpayer's trade or business, such as —

(A) Software developed to be commercially sold, leased, licensed, or otherwise marketed to third parties; or

(B) Software developed to enable a taxpayer to interact with third parties or to allow third parties to initiate functions or review data on the taxpayer's system.

(v) *Time and manner of determination.*—For purposes of paragraphs (c)(6)(iii) and (iv) of this section, whether software is developed primarily for internal use or not developed primarily for internal use depends on the intent of the taxpayer and the facts and circumstances at the beginning of the software development. For example, software will not be considered internal use software solely because it is used internally for purposes of testing prior to commercial sale, lease, or license. If a taxpayer originally develops software primarily for internal use, but later makes improvements to the software with the intent to hold the improved software to be sold, leased, licensed, or otherwise marketed to third parties, or to interact with third parties or to allow third parties to initiate functions or review data on the taxpayer's system using the improved software, the improvements will be considered separate from the existing software and will not be considered developed primarily for internal use. Alternatively, if a taxpayer originally develops software to be sold, leased, licensed, or otherwise marketed to third parties, or to interact with third parties or to allow third parties to initiate functions or review data on the taxpayer's system, but later makes improvements to the software with the intent to use the software in general and administrative functions, the improvements will be considered separate from the existing software and will be considered developed primarily for internal use.

(vi) *Software developed for both internal use and to enable interaction with third parties (dual function software).*—(A) *Presumption of development primarily for internal use.*—Unless paragraph (c)(6)(vi)(B) or (C) of this section applies, software developed by (or for the benefit of) the taxpayer both for use in general and administrative functions that facilitate or support the conduct of the taxpayer's trade or business and to enable a taxpayer to interact with third parties or to allow third parties to initiate functions or review data on the taxpayer's system (dual function software) is presumed to be developed primarily for a taxpayer's internal use.

(B) *Identification of a subset of elements of software that only enables interaction with third parties.*—To the extent that a taxpayer can identify a subset of elements of dual function software that only enables a taxpayer to interact with third parties or allows third parties to initiate functions or review data (third party subset), the presumption under paragraph (c)(6)(vi)(A) of this section does not apply to such third party subset, and such third party subset is not developed primarily for internal use as described under paragraph (c)(6)(iv)(B) of this section.

(C) *Safe harbor for expenditures related to software developed for both internal use and to enable interaction with third parties.*—If, after the application of paragraph (c)(6)(vi)(B) of this section, there remains dual function software or a subset of elements of dual function software (dual function subset), a taxpayer may include 25 percent of the qualified research expenditures of such dual function software or dual function subset in computing the amount of the taxpayer's credit. This paragraph (c)(6)(vi)(C) applies only if the taxpayer's research activities related to the development or improvement of the dual function software or dual function subset constitute qualified research under section 41(d), without regard to section 41(d)(4)(E), and the dual function software or dual function subset's use by third parties or by the taxpayer to interact with third parties is reasonably anticipated to constitute at least 10 percent of the dual function software or the dual function subset's use. An objective, reasonable method within the taxpayer's industry must be used to estimate the

Reg. §1.41-4(c)(6)(vi)(C)

dual function software or dual function subset's use by third parties or by the taxpayer to interact with third parties. An objective, reasonable method may include, but is not limited to, processing time, amount of data transfer, and number of software user interface screens.

(D) *Time and manner of determination.*—A taxpayer must apply this paragraph (c)(6)(vi) based on the intent of the taxpayer and the facts and circumstances at the beginning of the software development.

(E) *Third party.*—For purposes of paragraphs (c)(6)(iv), (v), and (vi) of this section, the term *third party* means any corporation, trade or business, or other person that is not treated as a single taxpayer with the taxpayer pursuant to section 41(f). Additionally, for purposes of paragraph (c)(6)(iv)(B) of this section, third parties do not include any persons that use the software to support the general and administrative functions of the taxpayer.

(vii) *High threshold of innovation test.*—(A) *In general.*— Software satisfies this paragraph (c)(6)(vii) only if the taxpayer can establish that—

(1) The software is innovative;

(2) The software development involves significant economic risk; and

(3) The software is not commercially available for use by the taxpayer in that the software cannot be purchased, leased, or licensed and used for the intended purpose without modifications that would satisfy the requirements of paragraphs (c)(6)(vii)(A)(1) and (2) of this section.

(B) *Innovative.*—Software is innovative if the software would result in a reduction in cost or improvement in speed or other measurable improvement, that is substantial and economically significant, if the development is or would have been successful. This is a measurable objective standard, not a determination of the unique or novel nature of the software or the software development process.

(C) *Significant economic risk.*—The software development involves significant economic risk if the taxpayer commits substantial resources to the development and if there is substantial uncertainty, because of technical risk, that such resources would be recovered within a reasonable period. The term "substantial uncertainty" requires a higher level of uncertainty and technical risk than that required for business components that are not internal use software. This standard does not require technical uncertainty regarding whether the final result can ever be achieved, but rather whether the final result can be achieved within a timeframe that will allow the substantial resources committed to the development to be recovered within a reasonable period. Technical risk arises from uncertainty that is technological in nature, as defined in paragraph (a)(4) of this section, and substantial uncertainty must exist at the beginning of the taxpayer's activities.

(D) *Application of high threshold of innovation test.*—The high threshold of innovation test of paragraph (c)(6)(vii) of this section takes into account only the results anticipated to be attributable to the development of new or improved software at the beginning of the software development independent of the effect of any modifications to related hardware or other software. The implementation of existing technology by itself is not evidence of innovation, but the use of existing technology in new ways could be evidence of a high threshold of innovation if it resolves substantial uncertainty as defined in paragraph (c)(6)(vii)(C) of this section.

(viii) *Illustrations.*—The following examples illustrate provisions contained in this paragraph (c)(6). No inference should be drawn from these examples concerning the application of section 41(d)(1) and paragraph (a) of this section to these facts.

Example 1. Computer hardware and software developed as a single product—(i) *Facts.* X is a telecommunications company that developed high technology telephone switching hardware. In addition, X developed software that interfaces directly with the hardware to initiate and terminate a call, along with other functions. X designed and developed the hardware and software together.

(ii) *Conclusion.* The telecommunications software that interfaces directly with the hardware is part of a package of software and hardware developed together by the taxpayer that is used by the taxpayer in providing services in its trade or business. Accordingly, this paragraph (c)(6) does not apply to the software that interfaces directly with the hardware as described in paragraph (c)(6)(ii)(C) of this section, and eligibility for the research credit is determined by examining the combined software-hardware product as a single product.

Example 2. Internal use software; financial management—(i) *Facts.* X, a manufacturer, self-insures its liabilities for employee health benefits. X develops its own software to administer its self-insurance

reserves related to employee health benefits. At the beginning of the development, X does not intend to develop the software for commercial sale, lease, license, or to be otherwise marketed to third parties or to enable X to interact with third parties or to allow third parties to initiate functions or review data on X's system.

(ii) *Conclusion.* The software is developed for use in a general and administrative function because reserve valuation is a financial management function under paragraph (c)(6)(iii)(B)(1) of this section. Accordingly, the software is internal use software because it is developed for use in a general and administrative function.

Example 3. Internal use software; human resources management— (i) *Facts.* X, a manufacturer, develops a software module that interacts with X's existing payroll software to allow X's employees to print pay stubs and make certain changes related to payroll deductions over the internet. At the beginning of the development, X does not intend to develop the software module for commercial sale, lease, license, or to be otherwise marketed to third parties or to enable X to interact with third parties or to allow third parties to initiate functions or review data on X's system.

(ii) *Conclusion.* The employee access software module is developed for use in a general and administrative function because employee access software is a human resources management function under paragraph (c)(6)(iii)(B)(2) of this section. Accordingly, the software module is internal use software because it is developed for use in a general and administrative function.

Example 4. Internal use software; support services—(i) *Facts.* X, a restaurant, develops software for a website that provides information, such as items served, price, location, phone number, and hours of operation for purposes of advertising. At the beginning of the development, X does not intend to develop the website software for commercial sale, lease, license, or to be otherwise marketed to third parties or to enable X to interact with third parties or to allow third parties to initiate functions or review data on X's system. X intends to use the software for marketing by allowing third parties to review general information on X's website.

(ii) *Conclusion.* The software is developed for use in a general and administrative function because the software was developed to be used by X for marketing which is a support services function under paragraph (c)(6)(iii)(B)(3) of this section. Accordingly, the software is internal use software because it is developed for use in a general and administrative function.

Example 5. Internal use software—(i) *Facts.* X, a multinational manufacturer with different business and financial systems in each of its divisions, undertakes a software development project aimed at integrating the majority of the functional areas of its major software systems (Existing Software) into a single enterprise resource management system supporting centralized financial systems, human resources, inventory, and sales. X purchases software (New Software) upon which to base its enterprise-wide system. X has to develop software (Developed Software) that transfers data from X's legacy financial, human resources, inventory, and sales systems to the New Software. At the beginning of the development, X does not intend to develop the software for commercial sale, lease, license, or to be otherwise marketed to third parties or to enable X to interact with third parties or to allow third parties to initiate functions or review data on X's system.

(ii) *Conclusion.* The financial systems, human resource systems, inventory and sales systems are general and administrative functions under paragraph (c)(6)(iii)(B) of this section. Accordingly, the Developed Software is internal use software because it is developed for use in general and administrative functions.

Example 6. Internal use software; definition of third party—(i) *Facts.* X develops software to interact electronically with its vendors to improve X's inventory management. X develops the software to enable X to interact with vendors and to allow vendors to initiate functions or review data on the taxpayer's system. X defines the electronic messages that will be exchanged between X and the vendors. X's software allows a vendor to request X's current inventory of the vendor's product, and allows a vendor to send a message to X which informs X that the vendor has just made a new shipment of the vendor's product to replenish X's inventory. At the beginning of development, X does not intend to develop the software for commercial sale, lease, license, or to be otherwise marketed to third parties.

(ii) *Conclusion.* Under paragraph (c)(6)(vi)(E) of this section, X's vendors are not third parties for purposes of paragraph (c)(6)(iv) of this section. While X's software was developed to allow vendors to initiate functions or review data on the taxpayer's system, the software is not excluded from internal use software as set forth in paragraph (c)(6)(iv)(B) of this section because the software was developed to allow vendors to use the software to support X's inventory management, which is a general and administrative function of X.

Example 7. Not internal use software; third party interaction—(i) *Facts.* X, a manufacturer of various products, develops software for a website with the intent to allow third parties to access data on X's database, to order X's products and track the status of their orders online. At the beginning of the development, X does not intend to develop the website software for commercial sale, lease, license, or to be otherwise marketed to third parties.

(ii) *Conclusion.* The software is not developed primarily for internal use because it is not developed for use in a general and administrative function. X developed the software to allow third parties to initiate functions or review data on the taxpayer's system as provided under paragraph (c)(6)(iv)(B) of this section.

Example 8. Not internal use software; third party interaction—(i) *Facts.* X developed software that allows its users to upload and modify photographs at no charge. X earns revenue by selling advertisements that are displayed while users enjoy the software that X offers for free. X also developed software that has interfaces through which advertisers can bid for the best position in placing their ads, set prices for the ads, or develop advertisement campaign budgets. At the beginning of the development, X intended to develop the software to enable X to interact with third parties or to allow third parties to initiate functions on X's system.

(ii) *Conclusion.* The software for uploading and modifying photographs is not developed primarily for internal use because it is not developed for use in X's general and administrative functions under paragraph (c)(6)(iii)(A) of this section. The users and the advertisers are third parties for purposes of paragraph (c)(6)(iv) of this section. Furthermore, both the software for uploading and modifying photographs and the advertising software are not internal use software under paragraph (c)(6)(iv)(B) of this section because at the beginning of the development X developed the software with the intention of enabling X to interact with third parties or to allow third parties to initiate functions on X's system.

Example 9. Not internal use software; commercially sold, leased, licensed, or otherwise marketed—(i) *Facts.* X is a provider of cloud-based software. X develops enterprise application software (including customer relationship management, sales automation, and accounting software) to be accessed online and used by X's customers. At the beginning of development, X intended to develop the software for commercial sale, lease, license, or to be otherwise marketed to third parties.

(ii) *Conclusion.* The software is not developed primarily for internal use because it is not developed for use in a general and administrative function. X developed the software to be commercially sold, leased, licensed, or otherwise marketed to third parties under paragraph (c)(6)(iv)(A) of this section.

Example 10. Improvements to existing internal use software—(i) *Facts.* X has branches throughout the country and develops its own facilities services software to coordinate moves and to track maintenance requests for all locations. At the beginning of the development, X does not intend to develop the software for commercial sale, lease, license, or to be otherwise marketed to third parties or to enable X to interact with third parties or to allow third parties to initiate functions or review data on X's system. Several years after completing the development and using the software, X consults its business development department, which assesses the market for the software. X determines that the software could be sold at a profit if certain technical and functional enhancements are made. X develops the improvements to the software, and sells the improved software to third parties.

(ii) *Conclusion.* Support services, which include facility services, are general and administrative functions under paragraph (c)(6)(iii)(B) of this section. Accordingly, the original software is developed for use in general and administrative functions and is, therefore, developed primarily for internal use. However, the improvements to the software are not developed primarily for internal use because the improved software was not developed for use in a general and administrative function. X developed the improved software to be commercially sold, leased, licensed, or otherwise marketed to third parties under paragraphs (c)(6)(iv)(A) and (c)(6)(v) of this section.

Example 11. Dual function software; identification of a third party subset—(i) *Facts.* X develops software for use in general and administrative functions that facilitate or support the conduct of X's trade or business and to allow third parties to initiate functions. X is able to identify a third party subset. X incurs $50,000 of research expenditures for the software, 50% of which is allocable to the third party subset.

(ii) *Conclusion.* The software developed by X is dual function software. Because X is able to identify a third party subset, the third party subset is not presumed to be internal use software under paragraph (c)(6)(vi)(A) of this section. If X's research activities related to the third party subset constitute qualified research under section 41(d), and the allocable expenditures are qualified research expenditures under section 41(b), $25,000 of the software research expenditures allocable to the third party subset may be included in computing the amount of X's credit, pursuant to paragraph

(c)(6)(vi)(B) of this section. If, after the application of paragraph (c)(6)(vi)(B) of this section, there remains a dual function subset, X may determine whether paragraph (c)(6)(vi)(C) of this section applies.

Example 12. Dual function software; application of the safe harbor—(i) *Facts.* The facts are the same as in *Example 11,* except that X is unable to identify a third party subset. X uses an objective, reasonable method at the beginning of the software development to determine that the dual function software's use by third parties to initiate functions is reasonably anticipated to constitute 15% of the dual function software's use.

(ii) *Conclusion.* The software developed by X is dual function software. The software is presumed to be developed primarily for internal use under paragraph (c)(6)(vi)(A) of this section. Although X is unable to identify a third party subset, X reasonably anticipates that the dual function software's use by third parties will be at least 10% of the dual function software's use. If X's research activities related to the development or improvement of the dual function software constitute qualified research under section 41(d), without regard to section 41(d)(4)(E), and the allocable expenditures are qualified research expenditures under section 41(b), X may include $12,500 (25% of $50,000) of the software research expenditures of the dual function software in computing the amount of X's credit pursuant to paragraph (c)(6)(vi)(C) of this section.

Example 13. Dual function software; safe harbor inapplicable—(i) *Facts.* The facts are the same as in *Example 11,* except X is unable to identify a third party subset. X uses an objective, reasonable method at the beginning of the software development to determine that the dual function software's use by third parties to initiate functions is reasonably anticipated to constitute 5% of the dual function software's use.

(ii) *Conclusion.* The software developed by X is dual function software. The software is presumed to be developed primarily for X's internal use under paragraph (c)(6)(vi)(A) of this section. X is unable to identify a third party subset, and X reasonably anticipates that the dual function software's use by third parties will be less than 10% of the dual function software's use. X may only include the software research expenditures of the dual function software in computing the amount of X's credit if the software satisfies the high threshold of innovation test of paragraph (c)(6)(vii) of this section and X's research activities related to the development or improvement of the dual function software constitute qualified research under section 41(d), without regard to section 41(d)(4)(E), and the allocable expenditures are qualified research expenditures under section 41(b).

Example 14. Dual function software; identification of a third party subset and the safe harbor—(i) *Facts.* X develops software for use in general and administrative functions that facilitate or support the conduct of X's trade or business and to allow third parties to initiate functions and review data. X is able to identify a third party subset (Subset A). The remaining dual function subset of the software (Subset B) allows third parties to review data and provides X with data used in its general and administrative functions. X is unable to identify a third party subset of Subset B. X incurs $50,000 of research expenditures for the software, 50% of which is allocable to Subset A and 50% of which is allocable to Subset B. X determines, at the beginning of the software development, that the processing time of the third party use of Subset B is reasonably anticipated to account for 15% of the total processing time of Subset B.

(ii) *Conclusion.* The software developed by X is dual function software. Because X is able to identify a third party subset, such third party subset (Subset A) is not presumed to be internal use software under paragraph (c)(6)(vi)(A) of this section. If X's research activities related to the development or improvement of Subset A constitute qualified research under section 41(d), and the allocable expenditures are qualified research expenditures under section 41(b), the $25,000 of the software research expenditures allocable to Subset A may be included in computing the amount of X's credit pursuant to paragraph (c)(6)(vi)(B) of this section. Although X is unable to identify a third party subset of Subset B, 15% of Subset B's use is reasonably anticipated to be attributable to the use of Subset B by third parties. If X's research activities related to the development or improvement of Subset B constitute qualified research under section 41(d), without regard to section 41(d)(4)(E), and the allocable expenditures are qualified research expenditures under section 41(b), X may include $6,250 (25% x $25,000) of the software research expenditures of Subset B in computing the amount of X's credit, pursuant to paragraph (c)(6)(vi)(C) of this section.

Example 15. Internal use software; application of the high threshold of innovation test—(i) *Facts.* X maintained separate software applications for tracking a variety of human resource (HR) functions, including employee reviews, salary information, location within the hierarchy and physical location of employees, 401(k) plans, and insurance coverage information. X determined that improved HR efficiency could be achieved by redesigning its disparate software applications into one employee-centric system, and worked to develop that system. X also determined that commercially available database management systems did not meet all of the requirements of the proposed system. Rather than waiting several years for vendor offerings to mature and become viable for its purpose, X embarked upon the project utilizing older technology that was severely challenged with respect to data modeling capabilities. The improvements, if successful, would provide a reduction in cost and improvement in speed that is substantial and economically significant. For example, having one employee-centric system would remove the duplicative time and cost of manually entering basic employee information separately in each application because the information would only have to be entered once to be available across all applications. The limitations of the technology X was attempting to utilize required that X attempt to develop a new database architecture. X committed substantial resources to the project, but could not predict, because of technical risk, whether it could develop the database software in the timeframe necessary so that X could recover its resources in a reasonable period. Specifically, X was uncertain regarding the capability of developing, within a reasonable period, a new database architecture using the old technology that would resolve its technological issues regarding the data modeling capabilities and the integration of the disparate systems into one system. At the beginning of the development, X did not intend to develop the software for commercial sale, lease, license, or to be otherwise marketed to third parties or to enable X to interact with third parties or to allow third parties to initiate functions or review data on X's system.

(ii) *Conclusion.* The software is internal use software because it is developed for use in a general and administrative function. However, the software satisfies the high threshold of innovation test set forth in paragraph (c)(6)(vii) of this section. The software was intended to be innovative in that it would provide a reduction in cost or improvement in speed that is substantial and economically significant. In addition, X's development activities involved significant economic risk in that X committed substantial resources to the development and there was substantial uncertainty, because of technical risk, that the resources would be recovered within a reasonable period. Finally, at the time X undertook the development of the system, software meeting X's requirements was not commercially available for use by X.

Example 16. Internal use software; application of the high threshold of innovation test—(i) *Facts.* X undertook a software project to rewrite a legacy mainframe application using an object-oriented programming language, and to move the new application off the mainframe to a client/server environment. Both the object-oriented language and client/server technologies were new to X. This project was undertaken to develop a more maintainable application, which X expected would significantly reduce the cost of maintenance, and implement new features more quickly, which X expected would provide both significant improvements in speed and reduction in cost. Thus, the improvements, if successful, would provide a reduction in cost and improvement in speed that is substantial and economically significant. X also determined that commercially available systems did not meet the requirements of the proposed system. X was certain that it would be able to overcome any technological uncertainties and implement the improvements within a reasonable period. However, X was unsure of the appropriate methodology to achieve the improvements. At the beginning of the development, X does not intend to develop the software for commercial sale, lease, license, or to be otherwise marketed to third parties or to enable X to interact with third parties or to allow third parties to initiate functions or review data on X's system.

(ii) *Conclusion.* The software is internal use software because it is developed for use in a general and administrative function. X's activities do not satisfy the high threshold of innovation test of paragraph (c)(6)(vii) of this section. Although the software meets the requirements of paragraphs (c)(6)(vii)(A)(1) and (3) of this section, X's development activities did not involve significant economic risk under paragraph (c)(6)(vii)(A)(2) of this section. X did not have substantial uncertainty, because of technical risk, that the resources committed to the project would be recovered within a reasonable period.

Example 17. Internal use software; application of the high threshold of innovation test—(i) *Facts.* X wants to expand its internal computing power, and is aware that its PCs and workstations are idle at night, on the weekends, and for a significant part of any business day. Because the general and administrative computations that X needs to make could be done on workstations as well as PCs, X develops a *screen-saver*-like application that runs on employee computers. When employees' computers have been idle for an amount of time set by each employee, X's application goes back to a central server to get a new job to execute. This job will execute on the idle employee's computer until it has either finished, or the employee resumes working on his computer. The ability to use the idle employees' com-

puters would save X significant costs because X would not have to buy new hardware to expand the computing power. The improvements, if successful, would provide a reduction in cost that is substantial and economically significant. At the time X undertook the software development project, there was no commercial application available with such a capability. In addition, at the time X undertook the software development project, X was uncertain regarding the capability of developing a server application that could schedule and distribute the jobs across thousands of PCs and workstations, as well as handle all the error conditions that occur on a user's machine. X commits substantial resources to the project. X undertakes a process of experimentation to attempt to eliminate its uncertainty. At the beginning of the development, X does not intend to develop the software for commercial sale, lease, license, or to be otherwise marketed to third parties or to enable X to interact with third parties or to allow third parties to initiate functions or review data on X's system.

(ii) *Conclusion.* The software is internal use software because it is developed for use in a general and administrative function. However, the software satisfies the high threshold of innovation test as set forth in paragraph (c)(6)(vii) of this section. The software was intended to be innovative because it would provide a reduction in cost or improvement in speed that is substantial and economically significant. In addition, X's development activities involved significant economic risk in that X committed substantial resources to the development and there was substantial uncertainty that because of technical risk, such resources would be recovered within a reasonable period. Finally, at the time X undertook the development of the system, software meeting X's requirements was not commercially available for use by X.

Example 18. Internal use software; application of the high threshold of innovation test—(i) *Facts.* X, a multinational manufacturer, wants to install an enterprise resource planning (ERP) system that runs off a single database. However, to implement the ERP system, X determines that it must integrate part of its old system with the new because the ERP system does not have a particular function that X requires for its business. The two systems are general and administrative software systems. The systems have mutual incompatibilities. The integration, if successful, would provide a reduction in cost and improvement in speed that is substantial and economically significant. At the time X undertook this project, there was no commercial application available with such a capability. X is uncertain regarding the appropriate design of the interface software. However, X knows that given a reasonable period of time to experiment with various designs, X would be able to determine the appropriate design necessary to meet X's technical requirements and would recover the substantial resources that X commits to the development of the system within a reasonable period. At the beginning of the development, X does not intend to develop the software for commercial sale, lease, license, or to be otherwise marketed to third parties or to enable X to interact with third parties or to allow third parties to initiate functions or review data on X's system.

(ii) *Conclusion.* The software is internal use software because it is developed for use in a general and administrative function. X's activities do not satisfy the high threshold of innovation test of paragraph (c)(6)(vii) of this section. Although the software meets the requirements of paragraphs (c)(6)(vii)(A)(1) and (3) of this section, X's development activities did not involve significant economic risk under paragraph (c)(6)(vii)(A)(2) of this section. X did not have substantial uncertainty, because of technical risk, that the resources committed to the project would be recovered within a reasonable period.

(7) *Activities outside the United States, Puerto Rico, and other possessions.*—(i) *In general.*—Research conducted outside the United States, as defined in section 7701(a)(9), the Commonwealth of Puerto Rico and other possessions of the United States does not constitute qualified research.

(ii) *Apportionment of in-house research expenses.*—In-house research expenses paid or incurred for qualified services performed both in the United States, the Commonwealth of Puerto Rico and other possessions of the United States and outside the United States, the Commonwealth of Puerto Rico and other possessions of the United States must be apportioned between the services performed in the United States, the Commonwealth of Puerto Rico and other possessions of the United States and the services performed outside the United States, the Commonwealth of Puerto Rico and other possessions of the United States. Only those in-house research expenses apportioned to the services performed within the United States, the Commonwealth of Puerto Rico and other possessions of the United States are eligible to be treated as qualified research expenses, unless the in-house research expenses are wages and the 80 percent rule of § 1.41-2(d)(2) applies.

(iii) *Apportionment of contract research expenses.*—If contract research is performed partly in the United States, the Commonwealth of Puerto Rico and other possessions of the United States and partly outside the United States, the Commonwealth of Puerto Rico and other possessions of the United States, only 65 percent (or 75 percent in the case of amounts paid to qualified research consortia) of the portion of the contract amount that is attributable to the research activity performed in the United States, the Commonwealth of Puerto Rico and other possessions of the United States may qualify as a contract research expense (even if 80 percent or more of the contract amount is for research performed in the United States, the Commonwealth of Puerto Rico and other possessions of the United States).

(8) *Research in the social sciences, etc.*—Qualified research does not include research in the social sciences (including economics, business management, and behavioral sciences), arts, or humanities.

(9) *Research funded by any grant, contract, or otherwise.*—Qualified research does not include any research to the extent funded by any grant, contract, or otherwise by another person (or governmental entity). To determine the extent to which research is so funded, § 1.41-4A(d) applies.

(10) *Illustrations.*—The following examples illustrate provisions contained in paragraphs (c)(1) through (9) (excepting paragraphs (c)(6) of this section) of this section. No inference should be drawn from these examples concerning the application of section 41(d)(1) and paragraph (a) of this section to these facts. The examples are as follows:

Example 1. (i) *Facts.* X, a tire manufacturer, develops a new material to use in its tires. X conducts research to determine the changes that will be necessary for X to modify its existing manufacturing processes to manufacture the new tire. X determines that the new tire material retains heat for a longer period of time than the materials X currently uses for tires, and, as a result, the new tire material adheres to the manufacturing equipment during tread cooling. X evaluates several alternatives for processing the treads at cooler temperatures to address this problem, including a new type of belt for its manufacturing equipment to be used in tread cooling. Such a belt is not commercially available. Because X is uncertain of the belt design, X develops and conducts sophisticated engineering tests on several alternative designs for a new type of belt to be used in tread cooling until X successfully achieves a design that meets X's requirements. X then manufactures a set of belts for its production equipment, installs the belts, and tests the belts to make sure they were manufactured correctly.

(ii) *Conclusion.* X's research with respect to the design of the new belts to be used in its manufacturing of the new tire may be qualified research under section 41(d)(1) and paragraph (a) of this section. However, X's expenses to implement the new belts, including the costs to manufacture, install, and test the belts were incurred after the belts met the taxpayer's functional and economic requirements and are excluded as research after commercial production under section 41(d)(4)(A) and paragraph (c)(2) of this section.

Example 2. (i) *Facts.* For several years, X has manufactured and sold a particular kind of widget. X initiates a new research project to develop a new or improved widget.

(ii) *Conclusion.* X's activities to develop a new or improved widget are not excluded from the definition of qualified research under section 41(d)(4)(A) and paragraph (c)(2) of this section. X's activities relating to the development of a new or improved widget constitute a new research project to develop a new business component. X's research activities relating to the development of the new or improved widget, a new business component, are not considered to be activities conducted after the beginning of commercial production under section 41(d)(4)(A) and paragraph (c)(2) of this section.

Example 3. (i) *Facts.* X, a computer software development firm, owns all substantial rights in a general ledger accounting software core program that X markets and licenses to customers. X incurs expenditures in adapting the core software program to the requirements of C, one of X's customers.

(ii) *Conclusion.* Because X's activities represent activities to adapt an existing software program to a particular customer's requirement or need, X's activities are excluded from the definition of qualified research under section 41(d)(4)(B) and paragraph (c)(3) of this section.

Example 4. (i) *Facts.* The facts are the same as in *Example 3*, except that C pays X to adapt the core software program to C's requirements.

(ii) *Conclusion.* Because X's activities are excluded from the definition of qualified research under section 41(d)(4)(B) and paragraph (c)(3) of this section, C's payments to X are not for qualified research and are not considered to be contract research expenses under section 41(b)(3)(A).

Example 5. (i) *Facts.* The facts are the same as in *Example 3*, except that C's own employees adapt the core software program to C's requirements.

(ii) *Conclusion.* Because C's employees' activities to adapt the core software program to C's requirements are excluded from the definition of qualified research under section 41(d)(4)(B) and paragraph (c)(3) of this section, the wages C paid to its employees do not constitute in-house research expenses under section 41(b)(2)(A).

Example 6. (i) *Facts.* X manufacturers and sells rail cars. Because rail cars have numerous specifications related to performance, reliability and quality, rail car designs are subject to extensive, complex testing in the scientific or laboratory sense. B orders passenger rail cars from X. B's rail car requirements differ from those of X's other existing customers only in that B wants fewer seats in its passenger cars and a higher quality seating material and carpet that are commercially available. X manufactures rail cars meeting B's requirements.

(ii) *Conclusion.* X's activities to manufacture rail cars for B are excluded from the definition of qualified research. The rail car sold to B was not a new business component, but merely an adaptation of an existing business component that did not require a process of experimentation. Thus, X's activities to manufacture rail cars for B are excluded from the definition of qualified research under section 41(d)(4)(B) and paragraph (c)(3) of this section because X's activities represent activities to adapt an existing business component to a particular customer's requirement or need.

Example 7. (i) *Facts.* X, a manufacturer, undertakes to create a manufacturing process for a new valve design. X determines that it requires a specialized type of robotic equipment to use in the manufacturing process for its new valves. Such robotic equipment is not commercially available, and X, therefore, purchases the existing robotic equipment for the purpose of modifying it to meet its needs. X's engineers identify uncertainty that is technological in nature concerning how to modify the existing robotic equipment to meet its needs. X's engineers develop several alternative designs, and conduct experiments using modeling and simulation in modifying the robotic equipment and conduct extensive scientific and laboratory testing of design alternatives. As a result of this process, X's engineers develop a design for the robotic equipment that meets X's needs. X constructs and installs the modified robotic equipment on its manufacturing process.

(ii) *Conclusion.* X's research activities to determine how to modify X's robotic equipment for its manufacturing process are not excluded from the definition of qualified research under section 41(d)(4)(B) and paragraph (c)(3) of this section, provided that X's research activities satisfy the requirements of section 41(d)(1).

Example 8. (i) *Facts.* An existing gasoline additive is manufactured by Y using three ingredients, A, B, and C. X seeks to develop and manufacture its own gasoline additive that appears and functions in a manner similar to Y's additive. To develop its own additive, X first inspects the composition of Y's additive, and uses knowledge gained from the inspection to reproduce A and B in the laboratory. Any differences between ingredients A and B that are used in Y's additive and those reproduced by X are insignificant and are not material to the viability, effectiveness, or cost of A and B. X desires to use with A and B an ingredient that has a materially lower cost than ingredient C. Accordingly, X engages in a process of experimentation to develop, analyze and test potential alternative formulations of the additive.

(ii) *Conclusion.* X's activities in analyzing and reproducing ingredients A and B involve duplication of existing business components and are excluded from the definition of qualified research under section 41(d)(4)(C) and paragraph (c)(4) of this section. X's experimentation activities to develop potential alternative formulations of the additive do not involve duplication of an existing business component and are not excluded from the definition of qualified research under section 41(d)(4)(C) and paragraph (c)(4) of this section.

Example 9. (i) *Facts.* X, a manufacturing corporation, undertakes to restructure its manufacturing organization. X organizes a team to design an organizational structure that will improve X's business operations. The team includes X's employees as well as outside management consultants. The team studies current operations, interviews X's employees, and studies the structure of other manufacturing facilities to determine appropriate modifications to X's current business operations. The team develops a recommendation of proposed modifications which it presents to X's management. X's management approves the team's recommendation and begins to implement the proposed modifications.

(ii) *Conclusion.* X's activities in developing and implementing the new management structure are excluded from the definition of qualified research under section 41(d)(4)(D) and paragraph (c)(5) of this section. Qualified research does not include activities relating to management functions or techniques including management organization plans and management-based changes in production processes.

Example 10. (i) *Facts.* X, an insurance company, develops a new life insurance product. In the course of developing the product, X engages in research with respect to the effect of pricing and tax consequences on demand for the product, the expected volatility of interest rates, and the expected mortality rates (based on published data and prior insurance claims).

(ii) *Conclusion.* X's activities related to the new product represent research in the social sciences (including economics and business management) and are thus excluded from the definition of qualified research under section 41(d)(4)(G) and paragraph (c)(8) of this section.

(d) *Recordkeeping for the research credit.*—A taxpayer claiming a credit under section 41 must retain records in sufficiently usable form and detail to substantiate that the expenditures claimed are eligible for the credit. For the rules governing record retention, see § 1.6001-1. To facilitate compliance and administration, the IRS and taxpayers may agree to guidelines for the keeping of specific records for purposes of substantiating research credits.

(e) *Effective/applicability dates.*—Other than paragraph (c)(6) of this section, this section is applicable for taxable years ending on or after December 31, 2003. Paragraph (c)(6) of this section is applicable for taxable years beginning on or after October 4, 2016. For any taxable year that both ends on or after January 20, 2015 and begins before October 4, 2016, the IRS will not challenge return positions consistent with all of paragraph (c)(6) of this section or all of paragraph (c)(6) of this section as contained in the Internal Revenue Bulletin (IRB) 2015-5 (see *www.irs.gov/pub/irs-irbs/irb15-05.pdf*). For taxable years ending before January 20, 2015, taxpayers may choose to follow either all of § 1.41-4(c)(6) as contained in 26 CFR part 1 (revised as of April 1, 2003) and IRB 2001-5 (see www.irs.gov/pub/irs-irbs/irb01-05.pdf) or all of § 1.41-4(c)(6) as contained in IRB 2002-4 (see www.irs.gov/pub/irs-irbs/irb02-04.pdf). [Reg. § 1.41-4.]

☐ [*T.D. 8251*, 5-16-89. *Amended by T.D. 8930*, 12-27-2000, *T.D. 9104*, 12-31-2003 and *T.D. 9786*, 10-3-2016 (*corrected* 10-31-2016).]

[Reg. § 1.41-5]

§ 1.41-5. Basic research for taxable years beginning after December 31, 1986.—[Reserved]

☐ [*T.D. 8251*, 5-16-89. *Redesignated and amended by T.D. 8930*, 12-27-2000.]

[Reg. § 1.41-6]

§ 1.41-6. Aggregation of expenditures.—(a) *Controlled group of corporations; trades or businesses under common control.*—(1) *In general.*—To determine the amount of research credit (if any) allowable to a trade or business that at the end of its taxable year is a member of a controlled group, a taxpayer must—

(i) Compute the group credit in the manner described in paragraph (b) of this section; and

(ii) Allocate the group credit among the members of the group in the manner described in paragraph (c) of this section.

(2) *Consolidated groups.*—For special rules relating to consolidated groups, see paragraph (d) of this section.

(3) *Definitions.*—For purposes of this section—

(i) *Consolidated group* has the meaning set forth in § 1.1502-1(h).

(ii) *Controlled group* and *group* mean a controlled group of corporations, as defined in section 41(f)(5), or a group of trades or businesses under common control. For rules for determining whether trades or businesses are under common control, see § 1.52-1 (b) through (g).

(iii) *Credit year* means the taxable year for which the member is computing the credit.

(iv) *Group credit* means the research credit (if any) allowable to a controlled group.

(v) *Trade or business* means a sole proprietorship, a partnership, a trust, an estate, or a corporation that is carrying on a trade or business (within the meaning of section 162). Any corporation that is a member of a commonly controlled group shall be deemed to be carrying on a trade or business if any other member of that group is carrying on any trade or business.

(b) *Computation of the group credit.*—(1) *In general.*—All members of a controlled group are treated as a single taxpayer for purposes of computing the research credit. The group credit is computed by applying all of the section 41 computational rules on an aggregate basis. All members of a controlled group must use the same method of computation: the method described in section 41(a)(1), the alternative incremental credit (AIRC) method described in section 41(c)(4) (available for years beginning on or before December 31, 2008), or the alternative simplified credit (ASC) method described in section 41(c)(5), in computing the group credit for a credit year.

(2) *Start-up companies.*—(i) *In general.*—For purposes of computing the group credit, a controlled group is treated as a start-up company for purposes of section 41(c)(3)(B)(i) if—

(A) There was no taxable year beginning before January 1, 1984, in which a member of the group had gross receipts and either the same member or another member also had qualified research expenditures (QREs); or

(B) There were fewer than three taxable years beginning after December 31, 1983, and before January 1, 1989, in which a member of the group had gross receipts and either the same member or another member also had QREs.

(ii) *Example.*—The following example illustrates the principles of paragraph (b)(2)(i) of this section:

Example. A, B, and C, all of which are calendar year taxpayers, are members of a controlled group. During the 1983 taxable year, A had QREs, but no gross receipts; B had gross receipts, but no QREs; and C had no QREs or gross receipts. The 1984 taxable year was the first taxable year for which each of A, B, and C had both QREs and gross receipts. A, B, and C had both QREs and gross receipts in 1985, 1986, 1987, and 1988. Because the first taxable year for which each of A, B, and C had both QREs and gross receipts began after December 31, 1983, each of A, B, and C is a start-up company under section 41(c)(3)(B)(i) and each is a start-up company for purposes of computing the stand-alone entity credit. During the 1983 taxable year, at least one member of the group, A, had QREs and at least one member of the group, B, had gross receipts, thus, the group had both QREs and gross receipts in 1983. Therefore, the controlled group is not a start-up company because the first taxable year for which the group had both QREs and gross receipts did not begin after December 31, 1983, and there were not fewer than three taxable years beginning after December 31, 1983, and before January 1, 1989, in which a member of the group had gross receipts and QREs.

(iii) *First taxable year after December 31, 1993, for which the controlled group had QREs.*—In the case of a controlled group that is treated as a start-up company under section 41(c)(3)(B)(i) and paragraph (b)(2)(i) of this section, for purposes of determining the group's fixed-base percentage under section 41(c)(3)(B)(ii), the first taxable year after December 31, 1993, for which the group has QREs is the first taxable year in which at least one member of the group has QREs.

(iv) *Example.*—The following example illustrates the principles of paragraph (b)(2)(iii) of this section:

Example. D, E, and F, all of which are calendar year taxpayers, are members of a controlled group. The group is treated as a start-up company under section 41(c)(3)(B)(i) and paragraph (b)(2)(i) of this section. The first taxable year after December 31, 1993, for which D had QREs was 1994. The first taxable year after December 31, 1993, for which E had QREs was 1995. The first taxable year after December 31, 1993, for which F had QREs was 1996. Because the 1994 taxable year was the first taxable year after December 31, 1993, for which at least one member of the group, D, had QREs, for purposes of determining the group's fixed-based percentage under section 41(c)(3)(B)(ii), the 1994 taxable year was the first taxable year after December 31, 1993, for which the group had QREs.

(c) *Allocation of the group credit.*—The group credit is allocated to each member of the controlled group on a proportionate basis to its share of the aggregate of the qualified research expenses, basic research payments, and amounts paid or incurred to energy research consortiums taken into account for the taxable year by such controlled group for purposes of the credit. For purposes of paragraphs (c), (d), and (e) of this section, qualified research expenses, basic research payments, and amounts paid or incurred to energy research consortiums are collectively referred to as QREs.

(d) *Special rules for consolidated groups.*—(1) *In general.*—For purposes of applying paragraph (c) of this section, members of a consolidated group who are members of a controlled group are treated as a single member of the controlled group.

(2) *Start-up company status.*—A consolidated group's status as a start-up company and the first taxable year after December 31, 1993, for which a consolidated group has QREs are determined in accordance with the principles of paragraph (b)(2) of this section.

(3) *Special rule for allocation of group credit among consolidated group members.*—The portion of the group credit that is allocated to a consolidated group is allocated to each member of the consolidated group on a proportionate basis to its share of the aggregate of the QREs taken into account for the taxable year by such consolidated group for purposes of the credit.

(e) *Examples.*—The following examples illustrate the provisions of paragraphs (c) and (d) of this section.

Example 1. Controlled group. A, B, and C are a controlled group. A had $100x, B $300x, and C $500x of qualified research expenses for the year, totaling $900x for the group. A, in the course of its trade or business, also made a payment of $100x to an energy research consortium for energy research. The group's QREs total 1000x and the group calculated its total research credit to be $60x for the year. Based on each member's proportionate share of the controlled group's aggregate QREs, A is allocated $12x, B $18x, and C $30x of the credit.

Example 2. Consolidated group is a member of controlled group. The controlled group's members are D, E, F, G, and H. F, G, and H file a consolidated return and are treated as a single member (FGH) of the controlled group. D had $240x, E $360x, and FGH $600x of qualified research expenses for the year ($1,200x aggregate). The group calculated its research credit to be $100x for the year. Based on the proportion of each member's share of QREs to the controlled group's aggregate QREs for the taxable year D is allocated $20x, E $30x, and FGH $50x of the credit. The $50x of credit allocated to FGH is then allocated to the consolidated group members based on the proportion of each consolidated group member's share of QREs to the consolidated group's aggregate QREs. F had $120x, G $240x, and H $240x of QREs for the year. Therefore, F is allocated $10x, G is allocated $20x, and H is allocated $20x.

(f) *For taxable years beginning before January 1, 1990.*—For taxable years beginning before January 1, 1990, see § 1.41-6 as contained in 26 CFR part 1, revised April 1, 2005.

(g) *Tax accounting periods used.*—(1) *In general.*—The credit allowable to a member of a controlled group is that member's share of the group credit computed as of the end of that member's taxable year. In computing the group credit for a group whose members have different taxable years, a member generally should treat the taxable year of another member that ends with or within the credit year of the computing member as the credit year of that other member. For example, Q, R, and S are members of a controlled group of corporations. Both Q and R are calendar year taxpayers. S files a return using a fiscal year ending June 30. For purposes of computing the group credit at the end of Q's and R's taxable year on December 31, S's fiscal year ending June 30, which ends within Q's and R's taxable year, is treated as S's credit year.

(2) *Special rule when timing of research is manipulated.*—If the timing of research by members using different tax accounting periods is manipulated to generate a credit in excess of the amount that would be allowable if all members of the group used the same tax accounting period, then the appropriate Internal Revenue Service official in the operating division that has examination jurisdiction of the return may require each member of the group to calculate the credit in the current taxable year and all future years as if all members of the group had the same taxable year and base period as the computing member.

(h) *Membership during taxable year in more than one group.*—A trade or business may be a member of only one group for a taxable year. If, without application of this paragraph, a business would be a member of more than one group at the end of its taxable year, the business shall be treated as a member of the group in which it was included for its preceding taxable year. If the business was not included for its preceding taxable year in any group in which it could be included as of the end of its taxable year, the business shall designate in its timely filed (including extensions) return the group in which it is being included. If the return for a taxable year is due before July 1, 1983, the business may designate its group membership through an amended return for that year filed on or before June 30, 1983. If the business does not so designate, then the appropriate Internal Revenue Service official in the operating division that has examination jurisdiction of the return will determine the group in which the business is to be included.

(i) *Intra-group transactions.*—(1) *In general.*—Because all members of a group under common control are treated as a single taxpayer for purposes of determining the research credit, transfers between members of the group are generally disregarded.

(2) *In-house research expenses.*—If one member of a group performs qualified research on behalf of another member, the member performing the research shall include in its QREs any in-house research expenses for that work and shall not treat any amount received or accrued as funding the research. Conversely, the member for whom the research is performed shall not treat any part of any amount paid or incurred as a contract research expense. For purposes of determining whether the in-house research for that work is qualified research, the member performing the research shall be treated as carrying on any trade or business carried on by the member on whose behalf the research is performed.

(3) *Contract research expenses.*—If a member of a group pays or incurs contract research expenses to a person outside the group in carrying on the member's trade or business, that member shall include those expenses as QREs. However, if the expenses are not paid or incurred in carrying on any trade or business of that member, those expenses may be taken into account as contract research expenses by another member of the group provided that the other member—

(i) Reimburses the member paying or incurring the expenses; and

(ii) Carries on a trade or business to which the research relates.

(4) *Lease payments.*—The amount paid or incurred to another member of the group for the lease of personal property owned by a member of the group is not taken into account for purposes of section 41. Amounts paid or incurred to another member of the group for the lease of personal property owned by a person outside the group shall be taken into account as in-house research expenses for purposes of section 41 only to the extent of the lesser of—

(i) The amount paid or incurred to the other member; or

(ii) The amount of the lease expenses paid to the person outside the group.

(5) *Payment for supplies.*—Amounts paid or incurred to another member of the group for supplies shall be taken into account as in-house research expenses for purposes of section 41 only to the extent of the lesser of—

(i) The amount paid or incurred to the other member; or

(ii) The amount of the other member's basis in the supplies.

(j) *Effective/applicability dates.*—(1) *In general.*—Except for paragraph (d) of this section, these regulations are applicable for taxable years ending on or after May 24, 2005. Generally, a taxpayer may use any reasonable method of computing and allocating the credit (including use of the consolidated group rule contained in paragraph (d) of this section) for taxable years ending before May 24, 2005. However, paragraph (b) of this section, relating to the computation of the group credit, and paragraph (c) of this section, relating to the allocation of the group credit, (applied without regard to paragraph (d) of this section) will apply to taxable years ending on or after December 29, 1999, if the members of a controlled group, as a whole, claimed more than 100 percent of the amount that would be allowable under paragraph (b) of this section. In the case of a controlled group whose members have different taxable years and whose members use inconsistent methods of allocation, the members of the controlled group shall be deemed to have, as a whole, claimed more than 100 percent of the amount that would be allowable under paragraph (b) of this section.

(2) *Consolidated group rule.*—Paragraph (d) of this section is applicable for taxable years ending on or after November 9, 2006. For taxable years ending on or after May 24, 2005, and before November 9, 2006, see § 1.41-6T(d) as contained in 26 CFR part 1, revised April 1, 2006.

(3) *Taxable years ending on or before June 9, 2011.*—Paragraphs (b)(1), (c)(2), and (e) of this section are applicable for taxable years ending after June 9, 2011. For taxable years ending on or before June 9, 2011, see §§ 1.41-6T and 1.41-6 as contained in 26 CFR part 1, revised April 1, 2011.

(4) *Taxable years beginning after December 31, 2011.*—Paragraphs (c), (d)(1) and (3), (e), and (j)(4) and (5) of this section apply to taxable years beginning on or after April 2, 2018. For taxable years ending before April 2, 2018, see § 1.41-6T as contained in 26 CFR part 1, as revised April 1, 2017.

(5) *Taxable years beginning before January 1, 2012.*—See § 1.41-6 as contained in 26 CFR part 1, revised April 1, 2014. [Reg. § 1.41-6.]

□ [T.D. 9296, 11-8-2006 (corrected 12-6-2006). *Amended by* T.D. 9401, 6-13-2008, T.D. 9528, 6-9-2011, T.D. 9717, 4-2-2015 *and* T.D. 9832, 3-27-2018.]

[Reg. § 1.41-7]

§ 1.41-7. Special rules.—(a) *Allocations.*—(1) *Corporation making an election under subchapter S.*—(i) *Pass-through, for taxable years beginning after December 31, 1982, in the case of an S corporation.*—In the case of an S corporation (as defined in section 1361) the amount of research credit computed for the corporation shall be allocated to the shareholders according to the provisions of section 1366 and section 1377.

(ii) *Pass-through, for taxable years beginning before January 1, 1983, in the case of a subchapter S corporation.*—In the case of an electing small business corporation (as defined in section 1371 as that section read before the amendments made by the Subchapter S Revision Act of 1982), the amount of the research credit computed for the corporation for any taxable year shall be apportioned pro rata among the persons who are shareholders of the corporation on the last day of the corporation's taxable year.

(2) *Pass-through in the case of an estate or trust.*—In the case of an estate or trust, the amount of the research credit computed for the estate or trust for any taxable year shall be apportioned among the estate or trust and the beneficiaries on the basis of the income of the estate or trust allocable to each.

(3) *Pass-through in the case of a partnership*—(i) *In general.*—In the case of a partnership, the research credit computed for the partnership for any taxable year shall be apportioned among the persons who are partners during the taxable year in accordance with section 704 and the regulations thereunder. See, for example, § 1.704-1(b)(4)(ii). Because the research credit is an expenditure-based credit, the credit is to be allocated among the partners in the same proportion as section 174 expenditures are allocated for the year.

(ii) *Certain expenditures by joint ventures.*—Research expenses to which § 1.41-2(a)(4)(ii) applies shall be apportioned among the persons who are partners during the taxable year in accordance with the provisions of that section. For purposes of section 41, these expenses shall be treated as paid or incurred directly by the partners rather than by the partnership. Thus, the partnership shall disregard these expenses in computing the credit to be apportioned under paragraph (a)(3)(i) of this section, and in making the computations under section 41 each partner shall aggregate its distributive share of these expenses with other research expenses of the partner. The limitation on the amount of the credit set out in section 41(g) and in paragraph (c) of this section shall not apply because the credit is computed by the partner, not the partnership.

(4) *Year in which taken into account.*—An amount apportioned to a person under this paragraph shall be taken into account by the person in the taxable year of such person which or within which the taxable year of the corporation, estate, trust, or partnership (as the case may be) ends.

(5) *Credit allowed subject to limitation.*—The credit allowable to any person to whom any amount has been apportioned under paragraph (a)(1), (2) or (3)(i) of this section is subject to section 41(g) and sections 38 and 39 of the Code, if applicable

(b) *Adjustments for certain acquisitions and dispositions—Meaning of terms.*—For the meaning of "acquisition," "separate unit," and "major portion," see paragraph (b) of § 1.52-2. An "acquisition" includes an incorporation or a liquidation.

(c) *Special rule for pass-through of credit.*—The special rule contained in section 41(g) for the pass-through of the credit in the case of an individual who owns an interest in an unincorporated trade or business, is a partner in a partnership, is a beneficiary of an estate or trust, or is a shareholder in an S corporation shall be applied in accordance with the principles set forth in § 1.53-3.

(d) *Carryback and carryover of unused credits.*—The taxpayer to whom the credit is passed through under paragraph (c) of this section shall not be prevented from applying the unused portion in a carryback or carryover year merely because the entity that earned the credit changes its form of conducting business. [Reg. § 1.41-7.]

☐ [*T.D. 8251, 5-16-89. Redesignated by T.D. 8930, 12-27-2000.*]

[Reg. § 1.41-8]

§ 1.41-8. Alternative incremental credit applicable for taxable years beginning on or before December 31, 2008.—(a) *Determination of credit.*—At the election of the taxpayer, the credit determined under section 41(a)(1) equals the amount determined under section 41(c)(4).

(b) *Election.*—(1) *In general.*—A taxpayer may elect to apply the provisions of the alternative incremental research credit (AIRC) in section 41(c)(4) for any taxable year of the taxpayer beginning after June 30, 1996. If a taxpayer makes an election under section 41(c)(4), the election applies to the taxable year for which made and all subsequent taxable years unless revoked in the manner prescribed in paragraph (b)(3) of this section.

(2) *Time and manner of election.*—An election under section 41(c)(4) is made by completing the portion of Form 6765, "Credit for Increasing Research Activities," (or successor form) relating to the election of the AIRC, and attaching the completed form to the taxpayer's timely filed (including extensions) original return for the taxable year to which the election applies. An election under section 41(c)(4) may not be made on an amended return. An extension of time to make an election under section 41(c)(4) will not be granted under § 301.9100-3 of this chapter.

(3) *Revocation.*—An election under this section may not be revoked except with the consent of the Commissioner. A taxpayer is deemed to have requested, and to have been granted, the consent of the Commissioner to revoke an election under section 41(c)(4) if the taxpayer completes the portion of Form 6765, "Credit For Increasing Research Activities," (or successor form) relating to the amount determined under section 41(a)(1) (the regular credit) or the alternative simplified credit (ASC) and attaches the completed form to the taxpayer's timely filed (including extensions) original return for the year to which the revocation applies. An election under section 41(c)(4) may not be revoked on an amended return. An extension of time to revoke an election under section 41(c)(4) will not be granted under § 301.9100-3 of this chapter.

(4) *Special rules for controlled groups.*—(i) *In general.*—In the case of a controlled group of corporations, all the members of which are not included on a single consolidated return, an election (or revocation) must be made by the designated member by satisfying the requirements of paragraph (b)(2) or (b)(3) of this section (whichever applies), and such election (or revocation) by the designated member shall be binding on all the members of the group for the credit year to which the election (or revocation) relates. If the designated member fails to timely make (or revoke) an election, each member of the group must compute the group credit using the method used to compute the group credit for the immediately preceding credit year.

(ii) *Designated member.*—For purposes of this paragraph (b)(4), for any credit year, the term *designated member* means that member of the group that is allocated the greatest amount of the group credit under § 1.41-6(c) based on the amount of credit reported on the taxpayer's timely filed (including extensions) original Federal income tax return (even if that member subsequently is determined not to be the designated member). If the members of a group compute the group credit using different methods (the method described in section 41(a)(1), the AIRC method of section 41(c)(4) (available for years beginning on or before December 31, 2008), or the ASC method of section 41(c)(5)) and at least two members of the group qualify as the designated member, then the term *designated member* means that member that computes the group credit using the method that yields the greatest group credit. For example, A, B, C, and D are members of a controlled group but are not members of a consolidated group. For the 2008 taxable year (the credit year), the group credit using the method described in section 41(a)(1) is $10x. Under this method, A would be allocated $5x of the group credit, which would be the largest share of the group credit under this method. For the credit year, the group credit using the AIRC method is $15x. Under the AIRC method, B would be allocated $5x of the group credit, which is the largest share of the group credit computed using the AIRC method. For the credit year, the group credit using the ASC method is $10x. Under the ASC method, C would be allocated $5x of the group credit, which is the largest share of the group credit computed using the ASC method. Because the group credit is greatest using the AIRC method and B is allocated the greatest amount of credit under that method, B is the designated member. Therefore, if B makes a section 41(c)(4) election on its original timely filed return for the credit year, that election is binding on all members of the group for the credit year.

(5) *Effective/applicability dates.*—This section is applicable for taxable years ending after June 9, 2011. For taxable years ending on or before June 9, 2011, see § § 1.41-8 and 1.41-8T, as contained in 26 CFR part 1, revised April 1, 2011. [Reg. § 1.41-8.]

☐ [*T.D. 9296, 11-8-2006 (corrected 12-6-2006). Amended by T.D. 9401, 6-13-2008; and T.D. 9528, 6-9-2011.*]

[Reg. § 1.41-9]

§ 1.41-9. Alternative simplified credit.—(a) *Determination of credit.*—At the election of the taxpayer, the credit determined under section 41(a)(1) equals the amount determined under section 41(c)(5).

(b) *Election.*—(1) *In general.*—A taxpayer may elect to apply the provisions of the alternative simplified credit (ASC) in section 41(c)(5) for any taxable year of the taxpayer ending after December 31, 2006. If a taxpayer makes an election under section 41(c)(5), the election applies to the taxable year for which made and all subsequent taxable years unless revoked in the manner prescribed in paragraph (b)(3) of this section.

(2) *Time and manner of election.*—A taxpayer makes an election under section 41(c)(5) by completing the portion of Form 6765, "Credit for Increasing Research Activities," (or successor form) relating to the election of the ASC, and attaching the completed form to the taxpayer's timely filed (including extensions) original return for the taxable year to which the election applies. A taxpayer may make an election under section 41(c)(5) for a tax year on an amended return, but only if the taxpayer has not previously claimed a section

41(a)(1) credit on its original return or an amended return for that tax year, and only if that tax year is not closed by the period of limitations on assessment under section 6501(a). An extension of time to make an election under section 41(c)(5) will not be granted under §301.9100-3 of this chapter. A taxpayer that is a member of a controlled group in a tax year may not make an election under section 41(c)(5) for that tax year on an amended return if any member of the controlled group for that tax year previously claimed the research credit under section 41(a)(1) using a method other than the ASC on an original or amended return for that tax year. See paragraph (b)(4) of this section for additional rules concerning controlled groups. See also §1.41-6(b)(1) requiring that all members of the controlled group use the same method of computation.

(3) *Revocation.*—An election under this section may not be revoked except with the consent of the Commissioner. A taxpayer is deemed to have requested, and to have been granted, the consent of the Commissioner to revoke an election under section 41(c)(5) if the taxpayer completes the portion of Form 6765 (or successor form) relating to the credit determined under section 41(a)(1) (the regular credit) or the alternative incremental credit (AIRC) and attaches the completed form to the taxpayer's timely filed (including extensions) original return for the year to which the revocation applies. An election under section 41(c)(5) may not be revoked on an amended return. An extension of time to revoke an election under section 41(c)(5) will not be granted under §301.9100-3 of this chapter.

(4) *Special rules for controlled groups.*—(i) *In general.*—In the case of a controlled group of corporations, all the members of which are not included on a single consolidated return, an election (or revocation) must be made by the designated member by satisfying the requirements of paragraphs (b)(2) or (b)(3) of this section (whichever applies), and such election (or revocation) by the designated member shall be binding on all the members of the group for the credit year to which the election (or revocation) relates. If the designated member fails to timely make (or revoke) an election, each member of the group must compute the group credit using the method used to compute the group credit for the immediately preceding credit year.

(ii) *Designated member.*—For purposes of this paragraph (b)(4), for any credit year, the term *designated member* means that member of the group that is allocated the greatest amount of the group credit under §1.41-6(c) based on the amount of credit reported on the taxpayer's timely filed (including extensions) original Federal income tax return (even if that member subsequently is determined not to be the designated member). If the members of a group compute the group credit using different methods (the method described in section 41(a)(1), the AIRC method of section 41(c)(4), or the ASC method of section 41(c)(5)) and at least two members of the group qualify as the designated member, then the term *designated member* means that member that computes the group credit using the method that yields the greatest group credit. For example, A, B, C, and D are members of a controlled group but are not members of a consolidated group. For the 2011 taxable year (the credit year), the group credit using the method described in section 41(a)(1) is $10x. Under this method, A would be allocated $5x of the group credit, which would be the largest share of the group credit under this method. For the credit year, the group credit using the ASC method is $15x. Under the ASC method, C would be allocated $5x of the group credit, which is the largest share of the group credit computed using the ASC method. Because the group credit is greatest using the ASC method and C is allocated the greatest amount of credit under that method, C is the designated member. Therefore, if C makes a section 41(c)(5) election on its timely filed (including extensions) original return for the credit year, that election is binding on all members of the group for the credit year.

(c) *Special rules.*—(1) *Qualified research expenses (QREs) required in all years.*—Unless a taxpayer has QREs in each of the three taxable years preceding the taxable year for which the credit is being determined, the credit equals that percentage of the QREs for the taxable year provided by section 41(c)(5)(B)(ii).

(2) *Section 41(c)(6) applicability.*—QREs for the three taxable years preceding the credit year must be determined on a basis consistent with the definition of QREs for the credit year, without regard to the law in effect for the three taxable years preceding the credit year. This consistency requirement applies even if the period for filing a claim for credit or refund has expired for any of the three taxable years preceding the credit year.

(3) *Short taxable years.*—(i) *General rule.*—If one or more of the three taxable years preceding the credit year is a short taxable year, then the QREs for such year are deemed to be equal to the QREs actually paid or incurred in that year multiplied by 365 and divided by the number of days in that year. If a credit year is a short taxable year, then the average QREs for the three taxable years preceding the

credit year are modified by multiplying that amount by the number of days in the short taxable year and dividing the result by 365.

(ii) *Limited exception.*—Returns filed for taxable years ending after December 31, 2006, and before June 9, 2011, and for which the period of limitations has not expired, may be amended to apply the daily calculation for short taxable years provided in paragraph (3)(i) of this section in lieu of the monthly calculation for short taxable years provided in §1.41-9T(c)(4).

(4) *Controlled groups.*—For purposes of computing the group credit under §1.41-6, a controlled group must apply the rules of this paragraph (c) on an aggregate basis. For example, if the controlled group has QREs in each of the three taxable years preceding the taxable year for which the credit is being determined, the controlled group applies the credit computation provided by section 41(c)(5)(A) rather than section 41(c)(5)(B)(ii).

(d) *Effective/applicability dates.*—This section is applicable for taxable years ending after June 9, 2011. For taxable years ending on or before June 9, 2011, see §1.41-9T as contained in 26 CFR part 1, revised April 1, 2011. Paragraph (b)(2) of this section applies to elections with respect to taxable years ending on or after February 27, 2015. For taxable years ending before February 27, 2015, see §1.41-9T as contained in 26 CFR part 1, revised April 1, 2015. [Reg. §1.41-9.]

☐ [*T.D.* 9401, 6-13-2008. Amended by *T.D.* 9528, 6-9-2011, *T.D.* 9666, 6-2-2014 and *T.D.* 9712, 2-26-2015.]

[Reg. §1.41-0A]

§1.41-0A. Table of contents.—This section lists the paragraphs contained in §§1.41-0A, 1.41-3A, 1.41-4A and 1.41-5A.

(2) Research in the social sciences or humanities.

(f) Procedure for making an election to be treated as a qualified fund.

[Reg. §1.41-0A.]

☐ [*T.D. 8930, 12-27-2000.*]

[Reg. §1.41-3A]

§1.41-3A. Base period research expense.—(a) *Number of years in base period.*—The term "base period" generally means the 3 taxable years immediately preceding the year for which a credit is being determined ("determination year"). However, if the first taxable year of the taxpayer ending after June 30, 1981, ends in 1981 or 1982, then with respect to that taxable year the term "base period" means the immediately preceding taxable year. If the second taxable year of the taxpayer ending after June 30, 1981, ends in 1982 or 1983, then with respect to that taxable year the term "base period" means the 2 immediately preceding taxable years.

(b) *New taxpayers.*—If, with respect to any determination year, the taxpayer has not been in existence for the number of preceding taxable years that are included under paragraph (a) of this section in the base period for that year, then for purposes of paragraph (c)(1) of this section (relating to the determination of average qualified research expenses during the base period), the taxpayer shall be treated as—

(1) Having been in existence for that number of additional 12-month taxable years that is necessary to complete the base period specified in paragraph (a) of this section, and

(2) Having had qualified research expenses of zero in each of those additional years.

(c) *Definition of base period research expenses.*—For any determination year, the term "base period research expenses" means the greater of—

(1) The average qualified research expenses for taxable years during the base period, or

(2) Fifty percent of the qualified research expenses for the determination year.

(d) *Special rules for short taxable years.*—(1) *Short determination year.*—If the determination year for which a research credit is being taken is a short taxable year, the amount taken into account under paragraph (c)(1) of this section shall be modified by multiplying that amount by the number of months in the short taxable year and dividing the result by 12.

(2) *Short base period year.*—For purposes of paragraph (c)(1) of this section, if a year in the base period is a short taxable year, the qualified research expenses paid or incurred in the short taxable year are deemed to be equal to the qualified research expenses actually paid or incurred in that year multiplied by 12 and divided by the number of months in that year.

(3) *Years overlapping the effective dates of section 41 (section 44F).*—(i) *Determination years.*—If a determination year includes months before July 1981, the determination year is deemed to be a short taxable year including only the months after June 1981. Accordingly, paragraph (d)(1) of this section is applied for purposes of determining the base period expenses for such year. See section 221(d)(2) of the Economic Recovery Tax Act of 1981.

(ii) *Base period years.*—No adjustment is required in the case of a base period year merely because it overlaps June 30, 1981.

(4) *Number of months in a short taxable year.*—The number of months in a short taxable year is equal to the number of whole calendar months contained in the year plus fractions for any partially included months. The fraction for a partially included month is equal to the number of days in the month that are included in the short taxable year divided by the total number of days in that month. Thus, if a short taxable year begins on January 1, 1982, and ends on June 9, 1982, it consists of 5 and 9/30 months.

(e) *Examples.*—The following examples illustrate the application of this section.

Example (1). X Corp., an accrual-method taxpayer using the calendar year as its taxable year, is organized and begins carrying on a trade or business during 1979 and subsequently incurs qualified research expenses as follows:

1979	$ 10x
1980	150x
1/1/81—6/30/81	90x
7/1/81—12/31/81	110x
1982	250x
1983	450x

(i) *Determination year 1981.* For determination year 1981, the base period consists of the immediately preceding taxable year, calendar year 1980. Because the determination year includes months before July 1981, paragraph (d)(3)(i) requires that the determination year be treated as a short taxable year. Thus, for purposes of paragraph (c)(1), as modified by paragraph (d)(1), the average qualified research expenses for taxable years during the base period are $75x ($150x, the average qualified research expenses for the base period, multiplied by 6, the number of months in the determination year after June 30, 1981, and divided by 12). Because this amount is greater than the amount determined under paragraph (c)(2) (50 percent of the determination year's qualified research expense of $110x, or $55x), the amount of base period research expenses is $75x. The credit for determination year 1981 is equal to 25 percent of the excess of $110x (the qualified research expenditures incurred during the determination year including only expenditures accrued on or after July 1, 1981, through the end of the determination year) over $75x (the base period research expenses).

(ii) *Determination year 1982.* For determination year 1982, the base period consists of the 2 immediately preceding taxable years, 1980 and 1981. The amount determined under paragraph (c)(1) of this section (the average qualified research expenses for taxable years during the base period) is $175x (($150x + $90x + $110x) / 2). This amount is greater than the amount determined under paragraph (c)(2) (50 percent of $250x, or $125x). Accordingly, the amount of base period research expenses is $175x. The credit for determination year 1982 is equal to 25 percent of the excess of $250x (the qualified research expenses incurred during the determination year) over $175x (the base period research expenses).

(iii) *Determination year 1983.* For determination year 1983, the base period consists of the 3 immediately preceding taxable years 1980, 1981 and 1982. The amount determined under paragraph (c)(1) of this section (the average qualified research expenses for taxable years during the base period) is $200x (($150x + $200x + $250x) / 3). The amount determined under paragraph (c)(2) is $225x (50 percent of the $450x of qualified research expenses in 1983). Accordingly, the amount of base period research expenses is $225x. The credit for determination year 1983 is equal to 25 percent of the excess of $450x (the qualified research expenses incurred during the determination year) over $225x (the base period research expenses).

Example (2). Y, an accrual-basis corporation using the calendar year as its taxable year comes into existence and begins carrying on a trade or business on July 1, 1983. Y incurs qualified research expenses as follows:

7/1/83—12/31/83	$ 80x
1984	200x
1985	200x

(i) *Determination year 1983.* For determination year 1983, the base period consists of the 3 immediately preceding taxable years: 1980, 1981 and 1982. Although Y was not in existence during 1980, 1981 and 1982, Y is treated under paragraph (b) of this section as having been in existence during those years with qualified research expenses of zero. Thus, the amount determined under paragraph (c)(1) of this section (the average qualified research expenses for taxable years during the base period) is $0x (($0x + $0x + $0x) / 3). The amount determined under paragraph (c)(2) of this section is $40x (50 percent of $80x). Accordingly, the amount of base period research expenses is $40x. The credit for determination year 1983 is equal to 25 percent of the excess of $80x (the qualified research expenses incurred during the determination year) over $40x (the base period research expenses).

(ii) *Determination year 1984.* For determination year 1984, the base period consists of the 3 immediately preceding taxable years: 1981, 1982, and 1983. Under paragraph (b) of this section, Y is treated as having been in existence during years 1981 and 1982 with qualified research expenses of zero. Because July 1 through December 31, 1983 is a short taxable year, paragraph (d)(2) of this section requires that the qualified research expenses for that year be adjusted to $160x for purposes of determining the average qualified research expenses during the base period. The $160x results from the actual qualified research expenses for that year ($80x) multiplied by 12 and divided by 6 (the number of months in the short taxable year). Accordingly, the amount determined under paragraph (c)(1) of this section (the average qualified research expenses for taxable years during the base period) is $53-1/3x (($0x + $0x + $160x) / 3). The amount determined under paragraph (c)(2) of this section is $100x (50 percent of $200x). The amount of base period research expenses is $100x. The credit for determination year 1984 is equal to 25 percent of the excess of $200x (the qualified research expenses incurred during the determination year) over $100x (the base period research expenses).

(iii) *Determination year 1985.* For determination year 1985, the base period consists of the 3 immediately preceding taxable years: 1982, 1983, and 1984. Pursuant to paragraph (b) of this section, Y is treated as having been in existence during 1982 with qualified research expenses of zero. Because July 1 through December 31, 1982, is a short taxable year, paragraph (d)(2) of this section requires that the qualified research expense for that year be adjusted to $160x for purposes of determining the average qualified research expenses for taxable years during the base period. This $160x is the actual qualified research expense for that year ($80x) multiplied by 12 and divided by 6 (the number of months in the short taxable year). Accordingly, the amount determined under paragraph (c)(1) of this section (the average qualified research expenses for taxable years during the base period) is $120x (($0x + $160x + $200x) / 3). The amount determined under paragraph (c)(2) of this section is $100x (50 percent of $200x). The amount of base period research expenses is $120x. The credit for determination year 1985 is equal to 25 percent of the excess of $200x (the qualified research expenses incurred during the determination year) over $120x (the base period research expenses). [Reg. § 1.41-3A.]

☐ [*T.D. 8251, 5-16-89. Redesignated by T.D. 8930, 12-27-2000.*]

[Reg. § 1.41-4A]

§ 1.41-4A. Qualified research for taxable years beginning before January 1, 1986.—(a) *General rule.*—Except as otherwise provided in section 30(d) (as that section read before amendment by the Tax Reform Act of 1986) and in this section, the term "qualified research" means research, expenditures for which would be research and experimental expenditures within the meaning of section 174. Expenditures that are ineligible for the section 174 deduction elections are not expenditures for qualified research. For example, expenditures for the acquisition of land or depreciable property used in research, and mineral exploration costs described in section 174(d), are not expenditures for qualified research.

(b) *Activities outside the United States.*—(1) *In-house research.*—In-house research conducted outside the United States (as defined in section 7701(a)(9)) cannot constitute qualified research. Thus, wages paid to an employee scientist for services performed in a laboratory in the United States and in a test station in Antarctica must be apportioned between the services performed within the United States and the services performed outside the United States, and only the wages apportioned to the services conducted within the United States are qualified research expenses unless the 80 percent rule of § 1.41-2(d)(2) applies.

(2) *Contract research.*—If contract research is performed partly within the United States and partly without, only 65 percent of the portion of the contract amount that is attributable to the research performed within the United States can qualify as contract research expense (even if 80 percent or more of the contract amount was for research performed in the United States).

(c) *Social sciences or humanities.*—Qualified research does not include research in the social sciences or humanities. For purposes of section 30(d)(2) (as that section read before amendment by the Tax Reform Act of 1986) and of this section, the phrase "research in the social sciences or humanities" encompasses all areas of research other than research in a field of laboratory science (such as physics or biochemistry), engineering or technology. Examples of research in the social sciences or humanities include the development of a new life insurance contract, a new economic model or theory, a new accounting procedure or a new cookbook.

(d) *Research funded by any grant, contract, or otherwise.*—(1) *In general.*—Research does not constitute qualified research to the extent it is funded by any grant, contract, or otherwise by another person (including any governmental entity). All agreements (not only research contracts) entered into between the taxpayer performing the research and other persons shall be considered in determining the extent to which the research is funded. Amounts payable under any agreement that are contingent on the success of the research and thus considered to be paid for the product or result of the research (see § 1.41-2(e)(2)) are not treated as funding. For special rules regarding funding between commonly controlled businesses, see § 1.41-6(e).

(2) *Research in which taxpayer retains no rights.*—If a taxpayer performing research for another person retains no substantial rights in research under the agreement providing for the research, the research is treated as fully funded for purposes of section 41(d)(4)(H), and no expenses paid or incurred by the taxpayer in performing the research are qualified research expenses. For example, if the taxpayer performs research under an agreement that confers on another person the exclusive right to exploit the results of the research, the taxpayer is not performing qualified research because the research is treated as fully funded under this paragraph (d)(2). Incidental benefits to the taxpayer from performance of the research (for example, increased experience in a field of research) do not constitute substantial rights in the research. If a taxpayer performing research for another person retains no substantial rights in the research and if the

payments to the researcher are contingent upon the success of the research, neither the performer nor the person paying for the research is entitled to treat any portion of the expenditures as qualified research expenditures.

(3) *Research in which the taxpayer retains substantial rights.*—(i) *In general.*—If a taxpayer performing research for another person retains substantial rights in the research under the agreement providing for the research, the research is funded to the extent of the payments (and fair market value of any property) to which the taxpayer becomes entitled by performing the research. A taxpayer does not retain substantial rights in the research if the taxpayer must pay for the right to use the results of the research. Except as otherwise provided in paragraph (d)(3)(ii) of this section, the taxpayer shall reduce the amount paid or incurred by the taxpayer for the research that would, but for section 41(d)(4)(H), constitute qualified research expenses of the taxpayer by the amount of funding determined under the preceding sentence.

(ii) *Pro rata allocation.*—If the taxpayer can establish to the satisfaction of the district director—

(A) The total amount of research expenses,

(B) That the total amount of research expenses exceed the funding, and

(C) That the otherwise qualified research expenses (that is, the expenses which would be qualified research expenses if there were no funding) exceed 65 percent of the funding, then the taxpayer may allocate the funding pro rata to nonqualified and otherwise qualified research expenses, rather than allocating it 100 percent to otherwise qualified research expenses (as provided in paragraph (d)(3)(i) of this section). In no event, however, shall less than 65 percent of the funding be applied against the otherwise qualified research expenses.

(iii) *Project-by-project determination.*—The provisions of this paragraph (d)(3) shall be applied separately to each research project undertaken by the taxpayer.

(4) *Independent research and development under the Federal Acquisition Regulations System and similar provisions.*—The Federal Acquisition Regulations System and similar rules and regulations relating to contracts (fixed price, cost plus, etc.) with government entities provide for allocation of certain "independent research and development costs" and "bid and proposal costs" of a contractor to contracts entered into with that contractor. In general, any "independent research and development costs" and "bid and proposal costs" paid to a taxpayer by reason of such a contract shall not be treated as funding the underlying research activities except to the extent the "independent research and development costs" and "bid and proposal costs" are properly severable from the contract. See § 1.451-3(e); see also section 804(d)(2) of the Tax Reform Act of 1986.

(5) *Funding determinable only in subsequent taxable year.*—If at the time the taxpayer files its return for a taxable year, it is impossible to determine to what extent particular research performed by the taxpayer during that year may be funded, then the taxpayer shall treat the research as completely funded for purposes of completing that return. When the amount of funding is finally determined, the taxpayer should amend the return and any interim returns to reflect the proper amount of funding.

(6) *Examples.*—The following examples illustrate the application of the principles contained in this paragraph.

Example (1). A enters into a contract with B Corporation, a cash-method taxpayer using the calendar year as its taxable year, under which B is to perform research that would, but for section 41(d)(3)(H), be qualified research of B. The agreement calls for A to pay B $120x, regardless of the outcome of the research. In 1982, A makes full payment of $120x under the contract, B performs all the research, and B pays all the expenses connected with the research, as follows:

In-house research expenses	$ 100x
Outside research (amount B paid to third parties for research, 65 percent of which ($26x) is treated as a contract research expense of B)	40x
Overhead and other expenses	10x
Total	$150x

If B has no rights to the research, E is fully funded. Alternatively, assume that B retains the right to use the results of the research in carrying on B's business. Of B's otherwise qualified research expenses of $126x ($100x + $26x), $120x is treated as funded by A. Thus $6x ($126x − $120x) is treated as a qualified research expense of B. However, if B establishes the facts required under paragraph (d)(3) of this section, B can allocate the funding pro rata to nonqualified and otherwise qualified research expenses. Thus $100.8x ($120x ($126x/

Reg. § 1.41-4A(d)(6)

$150x)) would be allocated to otherwise qualified research expenses. B's qualified research expenses would be $25.2x ($126x – $100.8x). For purposes of the following examples (2), (3) and (4) assume that B retains substantial rights to use the results of the research in carrying on B's business.

Example (2). The facts are the same as in example (1) (assuming that B retains the right to use the results of the research in carrying on B's business) except that, although A makes full payment of $120x during 1982, B does not perform the research or pay the associated expenses until 1983. The computations are unchanged. However, B's qualified research expenses determined in example (1) are qualified research expenses during 1983.

Example (3). The facts are the same as in example (1) (assuming that B retains the right to use the results of the research in carrying on B's business) except that, although B performs the research and pays the associated expenses during 1982, A does not pay the $120x until 1983. The computations are unchanged and the amount determined in example (1) is a qualified research expense of B during 1982.

Example (4). The facts are the same as in example (1) (assuming that B retains the right to use the results of the research in carrying on B's business) except that, instead of agreeing to pay B $120x, A agrees to pay $100x regardless of the outcome and an additional $20x only if B's research produces a useful product. B's research produces a useful product and A pays B $120x during 1982. The $20x payment that is conditional on the success of the research is not treated as funding. Assuming that B establishes to the satisfaction of the district director the actual research expenses, B can allocate the funding to nonqualified and otherwise qualified research expenses. Thus $84x ($100x ($126x/$150x)) would be allocated to otherwise qualified research expenses. B's qualified research expenses would be $42x ($126x – $84x).

Example (5). C enters into a contract with D, a cash-method taxpayer using the calendar year as its taxable year, under which D is to perform research in which both C and D will have substantial rights. C agrees to reimburse D for 80 percent of D's expenses for the research. D performs part of the research in 1982 and the rest in 1983. At the time that D files its return for 1982, D is unable to determine the extent to which the research is funded under the provisions of this paragraph. Under these circumstances, D may not treat any of the expenses paid by D for this research during 1982 as qualified research expenses on its 1982 return. When the project is complete and D can determine the extent of funding, D should file an amended return for 1982 to take into account any qualified research expense for 1982. [Reg. § 1.41-4A.]

☐ *[T.D. 8251, 5-16-89. Redesignated and amended by T.D. 8930, 12-27-2000.]*

[Reg. § 1.41-5A]

§ 1.41-5A. Basic research for taxable years beginning before January 1, 1987.—(a) *In general.*—The amount expended for basic research within the meaning of section 30(e) (before amendment by the Tax Reform Act of 1986) equals the sum of money plus the taxpayer's basis in tangible property (other than land) transferred for use in the performance of basic research.

(b) *Trade or business requirement.*—Any amount treated as a contract research expense under section 30(e) (before amendment by the Tax Reform Act of 1986) shall be deemed to have been paid or incurred in carrying on a trade or business, if the corporation that paid or incurred the expense is actually engaged in carrying on some trade or business.

(c) *Prepaid amounts.*—(1) *In general.*—If any basic research expense paid or incurred during any taxable year is attributable to research to be conducted after the close of such taxable year, the expense so attributable shall be treated for purposes of section 30(b)(1)(B) (before amendment by the Tax Reform Act of 1986) as paid or incurred during the period in which the basic research is conducted.

(2) *Transfers of property.*—In the case of transfers of property to be used in the performance of basic research, the research in which that property is to be used shall be considered to be conducted ratably over a period beginning on the day the property is first so used and continuing for the number of years provided with respect to property of that class under section 168(c)(2) (before amendment by the Tax Reform Act of 1986). For example, if an item of property which is 3-year property under section 168(c) is transferred to a university for basic research on January 12, 1983, and is first so used by the university on March 1, 1983, then the research in which that property is used is considered to be conducted ratably from March 1, 1983, through February 28, 1986.

(d) *Written research agreement.*—(1) *In general.*—A written research agreement must be entered into prior to the performance of the basic research.

(2) *Agreement between a corporation and a qualified organization after June 30, 1983.*—(i) *In general.*—A written research agreement between a corporation and a qualified organization (including a qualified fund) entered into after June 30, 1983, shall provide that the organization shall inform the corporation within 60 days after the close of each taxable year of the corporation what amount of funds provided by the corporation pursuant to the agreement was expended on basic research during the taxable year of the corporation. In determining amounts expended on basic research, the qualified organization shall take into account the exclusions specified in section 30(e)(3) (before amendment by the Tax Reform Act of 1986) and in paragraph (e) of this section.

(ii) *Transfers of property.*—In the case of transfers of property to be used in basic research, the agreement shall provide that substantially all use of the property is to be for basic research, as defined in section 30(e)(3) (before amendment by the Tax Reform Act of 1986).

(3) *Agreement between a qualified fund and a qualified educational organization after June 30, 1983.*—A written research agreement between a qualified fund and a qualified educational organization (see section 30(e)(4)(B)(iii) (before amendment by the Tax Reform Act of 1986)) entered into after June 30, 1983, shall provide that the qualified educational organization shall furnish sufficient information to the qualified fund to enable the qualified fund to comply with the written research agreements it has entered into with grantor corporations, including the requirement set forth in paragraph (d)(2) of this section.

(e) *Exclusions.*—(1) *Research conducted outside the United States.*—If a taxpayer pays or incurs an amount for basic research to be performed partly within the United States and partly without, only 65 percent of the portion of the amount attributable to research performed within the United States can be treated as a contract research expense (even if 80 percent or more of the contract amount was for basic research performed in the United States).

(2) *Research in the social sciences or humanities.*—Basic research does not include research in the social sciences or humanities, within the meaning of § 1.41-4A(c).

(f) *Procedure for making an election to be treated as a qualified fund.*—In order to make an election to be treated as a qualified fund within the meaning of section 30(e)(4)(B)(iii) (before amendment by the Tax Reform Act of 1986) or as an organization described in section 41(e)(6)(D), the organization shall file with the Internal Revenue service center with which it files its annual return a statement that—

(1) Sets out the name, address, and taxpayer identification number of the electing organization (the "taxpayer") and of the organization that established and maintains the electing organization (the "controlling organization"),

(2) Identifies the election as an election under section 41(e)(6)(D) of the Code,

(3) Affirms that the controlling organization and the taxpayer are section 501(c)(3) organizations,

(4) Provides that the taxpayer elects to be treated as a private foundation for all Code purposes other than section 4940,

(5) Affirms that the taxpayer satisfies the requirement of section 41(e)(6)(D)(iii), and

(6) Specifies the date on which the election is to become effective.

If an election to be treated as a qualified fund is filed before February 1, 1982, the election may be made effective as of any date after June 30, 1981, and before January 1, 1986. If an election is filed on or after February 1, 1982, the election may be made effective as of any date on or after the date on which the election is filed. [Reg. § 1.41-5A.]

☐ *[T.D. 8251, 5-16-89. Redesignated and amended by T.D. 8930, 12-27-2000.]*

[Reg. § 1.42-0]

§ 1.42-0. Table of contents.—This section lists the paragraphs contained in §§ 1.42-1 through 1.42-19 and § 1.42-1T.

§ 1.42-1 Limitation on low-income housing credit allowed with respect to qualified low-income buildings receiving housing credit allocations from a State or local housing credit agency.

(a) through (g) [Reserved]

(h) Filing of forms.

(i) [Reserved]

(j) Effective dates.

§ 1.42-1T Limitation on low-income housing credit allowed with respect to qualified low income buildings receiving housing credit allocations from a State or local housing credit agency (temporary).

(a) In general.

(1) Determination of amount of low-income housing credit.

(2) Limitation on low-income housing credit allowed.

(b) The State housing credit ceiling.

(c) Apportionment of State housing credit ceiling among State and local housing credit agencies.

(1) In general.

(2) Primary apportionment.

(3) States with 1 or more constitutional home rule cities.

(i) In general.

(ii) Amount of apportionment to a constitutional home rule city.

(iii) Effect of apportionment to constitutional home rule cities on apportionment to other housing credit agencies.

(iv) Treatment of governmental authority within constitutional home rule city.

(4) Apportionment to local housing credit agencies.

(i) In general.

(ii) Change in apportionment during a calendar year.

(iii) Exchanges of apportionments.

(iv) Written records of apportionments.

(5) Set-aside apportionments for projects involving a qualified nonprofit organization.

(i) In general.

(ii) Projects involving a qualified nonprofit organization.

(6) Expiration of unused apportionments.

(d) Housing credit allocation made by State and local housing credit agencies.

(1) In general.

(2) Amount of a housing credit allocation.

(3) Counting housing credit allocations against an agency's aggregate housing credit dollar amount.

(4) Rules for when applications for housing credit allocations exceed an agency's aggregate housing credit dollar amount.

(5) Reduced or additional housing credit allocations.

(i) In general.

(ii) Examples.

(6) No carryover of unused aggregate housing credit dollar amount.

(7) Effect of housing credit allocations in excess of an agency's aggregate housing credit dollar amount.

(8) Time and manner for making housing credit allocations.

(i) Time.

(ii) Manner.

(iii) Certification.

(iv) Fee.

(v) No continuing agency responsibility.

(e) Housing credit allocation taken into account by owner of a qualified low-income building.

(1) Time and manner for taking housing credit allocation into account.

(2) First-year convention limitation on housing credit allocation taken into account.

(3) Use of excess housing credit allocation for increases in qualified basis.

(i) In general.

(ii) Example.

(4) Separate housing credit allocations for new buildings and increases in qualified basis.

(5) Acquisition of building for which a prior housing credit allocation has been made.

(6) Multiple housing credit allocations.

(f) Exception to housing credit allocation requirement.

(1) Tax-exempt bond financing.

(i) In general.

(ii) Determining use of bond proceeds.

(iii) Example.

(g) Termination of authority to make housing credit allocation.

(1) In general.

(2) Carryover of unused 1989 apportionment.

(3) Expiration of exception for tax-exempt bond financed projects.

(h) [Reserved]

(i) Transitional rules.

§1.42-2. Waiver of requirement that an existing building eligible for the low-income housing credit was last placed in service more than 10 years prior to acquisition by the taxpayer.

(a) Low-income housing credit for existing building

(b) Waiver of 10-year holding period requirement

(c) Waiver requirements

(1) Federally-assisted building

(2) Federal mortgage funds at risk

(3) Statement by the Department of Housing and Urban Development or the Farmers' Home Administration

(4) No prior credit allowed

(d) Application for waiver

(1) Time and manner

(2) Information required

(3) Other rules

(4) Effective date of waiver

(5) Attachment to return

(e) Effective date of regulations

§1.42-3 Treatment of buildings financed with proceeds from a loan under an Affordable Housing Program established pursuant to section 721 of the Financial Institutions Reform, Recovery, and Enforcement Act of 1989 (FIRREA).

(a) Treatment under sections 42(i) and 42(b).

(b) Effective date.

§1.42-4 Application of not-for-profit rules of section 183 to low-income housing credit activities.

(a) Inapplicability to section 42.

(b) Limitation.

(c) Effective date.

§1.42-5 Monitoring compliance with low-income housing credit requirements.

(a) Compliance monitoring requirement.

(1) In general.

(2) Requirements for a monitoring procedure.

(i) In general.

(ii) Order and form.

(iii) [Reserved]

(b) Recordkeeping and record retention provisions.

(1) Recordkeeping provision.

(2) Record retention provision.

(3) Inspection record retention provision.

(c) Certification and review provisions.

(1) Certification.

(2) Review.

(ii) [Reserved]

(iii) [Reserved]

(3) [Reserved]

(4) Exception for certain buildings.

(i) In general.

(ii) Agreement and review.

(iii) Example.

(5) Agency reports of compliance monitoring activities.

(d) Inspection provision.

(1) In general.

(2) Inspection standard.

(3) Exception from inspection provision.

(4) Delegation.

(e) Notification-of-noncompliance provisions.

(1) In general.

(2) Notice to owner.

(3) Notice to Internal Revenue Service.

(i) In general.

(ii) Agency retention of records.

(4) Correction period.

(f) Delegation of authority.

(1) Agencies permitted to delegate compliance monitoring functions.

(i) In general.

(ii) Limitations.

(2) Agencies permitted to delegate compliance monitoring functions to another Agency.

(g) Liability.

(h) Effective/applicability dates.

(1) In general.

(2) [Reserved]

§1.42-6 Buildings qualifying for carryover allocations.

(a) Carryover allocations.

(1) In general.

(2) 10 percent basis requirement.

(i) Allocation made before July 1.

(ii) Allocation made after June 30.

(b) Carryover-allocation basis.

(1) In general.

(2) Limitations.

(i) Taxpayer must have basis in land or depreciable property related to the project.

(ii) High cost areas.

(iii) Amounts not treated as paid or incurred.

(iv) Fees.

(3) Reasonably expected basis.

(2) Rental of next available unit in case of the average income test.

    (i) Basic rule.

    (ii) No requirement to comply with the next available unit rule in a specific order.

    (iii) Deep rent skewed projects.

    (iv) Limitation.

(d) Effect of current resident moving within building.

(e) Available unit rule applies separately to each building in a project.

(f) Result of noncompliance with available unit rule.

(g) Relationship to tax-exempt bond provisions.

(h) Examples.

(i) Applicability dates.

    (1) In general.

    (2) Applicability dates under the average income test.

§ 1.42-16 *Eligible basis reduced by federal grants.*

(a) In general.

(b) Grants do not include certain rental assistance payments.

(c) Qualifying rental assistance program.

(d) Effective date.

§ 1.42-17 *Qualified allocation plan*

(a) Requirements

    (1) In general [Reserved]

    (2) Selection criteria [Reserved]

    (3) Agency evaluation.

    (4) Timing of Agency evaluation.

      (i) In general.

      (ii) Time limit for placed-in-service evaluation.

    (5) Special rule for final determinations and certifications.

    (6) Bond-financed projects.

(b) Effective date.

§ 1.42-18 *Qualified Contracts.*

(a) Extended low-income housing commitment.

    (1) In general.

      (i) Extended use period.

      (ii) Termination of extended use period.

      (iii) Other non-acceptance.

      (iv) Eviction, gross rent increase concerning existing low-income tenants not permitted.

    (2) Exception.

(b) Definitions.

(c) Qualified contract purchase price formula.

    (1) In general.

      (i) Initial determination.

      (ii) Mandatory adjustment by the buyer and owner.

      (iii) Optional adjustment by the Agency and owner.

    (2) Low-income portion amount.

    (3) Outstanding indebtedness.

    (4) Adjusted investor equity.

      (i) Application of cost-of-living factor.

      (ii) Unadjusted investor equity.

      (iii) Qualified-contract cost-of-living adjustment.

      (iv) General rule.

      (v) Provision by the Commissioner of the qualified-contract cost-of-living adjustment.

      (vi) Methodology.

      (vii) Example.

    (5) Other capital contributions.

    (6) Cash distributions.

      (i) In general.

      (ii) Excess proceeds.

      (iii) Anti-abuse rule.

(d) Administrative discretion and responsibilities of the Agency.

    (1) In general.

    (2) Actual offer.

    (3) Debarment of certain appraisers.

(e) Effective / applicability date.

§ 1.42-19 *Average income test.*

(a) *Average income set-aside.*

(b) Definition of low-income unit and qualified group of units.

    (1) Definition of low-income unit.

    (2) Definition of qualified group of units.

    (3) Identification of qualified groups of units.

      (i) Average income set-aside test.

      (ii) Applicable fraction determinations.

      (iii) Identification of units.

(c) Procedures.

    (1) [Reserved]

(2) [Reserved]

(3) Designation of imputed income limitations.

    (i) Timing of designation.

    (ii) 10-percent increments.

    (iii) Continuity.

    (iv) [Reserved]

(4) [Reserved]

(d) Changing a unit's designated imputed income limitation.

    (1) Permitted changes.

      (i) Federally permitted changes.

      (ii) *Housing credit agency.*—(Agency)-permitted changes.

      (iii) Certain laws.

      (iv) Tenant movement.

      (v) Restoring compliance with average income requirements.

    (2) [Reserved]

(e) Examples.

(f) Applicability dates.

    (1) General rule.

    (2) Designations of occupied units.

    (3) Applicability of this section to taxable years beginning before January, 1 2023.

[Reg. § 1.42-0.]

☐ [T.D. 8302, 5-22-90. *Amended by T.D. 9755, 3-2-2016 and T.D. 9967, 10-7-2022.*]

[Reg. §1.42-1]

§ 1.42-1. Limitation on low-income housing credit allowed with respect to qualified low-income buildings receiving housing credit allocations from a State or local housing credit agency.—(a) through (g) [Reserved]. For further guidance, see § 1.42-1T(a) through (g).

(h) *Filing of forms.*—Unless otherwise provided in forms or instructions, a completed Form 8586, "Low-Income Housing Credit," (or any successor form) must be filed with the owner's Federal income tax return for each taxable year the owner of a qualified low-income building is claiming the low-income housing credit under section 42(a). Unless otherwise provided in forms or instructions, a completed Form 8609, "Low-Income Housing Credit Allocation and Certification," (or any successor form) must be filed by the building owner with the IRS. The requirements for completing and filing Forms 8586 and 8609 are addressed in the instructions to the forms.

(i) [Reserved].—For further guidance, see § 1.42-1T(i).

(j) *Effective dates.*—Section 1.42-1(n) applies to forms filed on or after November 7, 2005. The rules that apply for forms filed before November 7, 2005 are contained in § 1.42-1T(h) and § 1.42-1(h) (see 26 CFR part 1 revised as of April 1, 2003, and April 1, 2005). [Reg. § 1.42-1.]

☐ [T.D. 9112, 1-26-2004. *Amended by T.D. 9228, 11-4-2005.*]

[Reg. §1.42-1T]

§ 1.42-1T. Limitation on low-income housing credit allowed with respect to qualified low-income buildings receiving housing credit allocations from a State or local housing credit agency (temporary).—(a) *In general.*—(1) *Determination of amount of low-income housing credit.*—Section 42 provides that, for purposes of section 38, a low-income housing credit is determined for a building in an amount equal to the applicable percentage of the qualified basis of the qualified low-income building. In general, the credit may be claimed annually for a 10-year credit period, beginning with the taxable year in which the building is placed in service or, at the election of the taxpayer, the succeeding taxable year. If, after the first year of the credit period, the qualified basis of a building is increased in excess of the qualified basis upon which the credit was initially determined, the allowable credit with respect to such additional qualified basis is determined using a credit percentage equal to two-thirds of the applicable percentage for the initial qualified basis. The credit for additions to qualified basis is generally allowable for the remaining years in the 15-year compliance period which begins with the first taxable year of the credit period for the building. In general, the low-income housing credit is available with respect to buildings placed in service after December 31, 1986, in taxable years ending after that date. *See* section 42 for the definitions of "qualified low-income building", "applicable percentage", "qualified basis", "credit period", "compliance period", and for other rules relating to determination of the amount of the low-income housing credit.

(2) *Limitation on low-income housing credit allowed.*—Generally, the low-income housing credit determined under section 42 is allowed and may be claimed for any taxable year if, and to the extent that, the owner of a qualified low-income building receives a housing

credit allocation from a State or local housing credit agency. The aggregate amount of housing credit allocations that may be made in any calendar year by all housing credit agencies within a State is limited by a State housing credit ceiling, or volume cap, described in paragraph (b). The authority to make housing credit allocations within the State housing credit ceiling may be apportioned among the State and local housing credit agencies, under the rules prescribed in paragraph (c). Upon apportionment of the State housing credit volume cap, each State or local housing credit agency receives an aggregate housing credit dollar amount that may be used to make housing credit allocations among qualified low-income buildings located within an agency's geographic jurisdiction. The rules governing the making of housing credit allocations by any State or local housing credit agency are provided in paragraph (d). Housing credit allocations are required to be taken into account by owners of qualified low-income buildings under the rules prescribed in paragraph (e). Exceptions to the requirement that a qualified low-income building receive a housing credit allocation from a State or local housing credit agency are provided in paragraph (f). Rules regarding termination of the authority of State and local housing credit agencies to make housing credit allocations after December 31, 1989, are specified in paragraph (g). Rules concerning information reporting by State and local housing credit agencies and owners of qualified low-income buildings are provided in paragraph (h). Special statutory transitional rules are incorporated into this section of the regulations as described in paragraph (i) of this section.

(b) *The State housing credit ceiling.*—The aggregate amount of housing credit allocations that may be made in any calendar year by all State and local housing credit agencies within a State may not exceed the State's housing credit ceiling for such calendar year. The State housing credit ceiling for each State for any calendar year is equal to $1.25 multiplied by the State's population. A State's population for any calendar year is determined by reference to the most recent census estimate (whether final or provisional) of the resident population of the State released by the Bureau of the Census before the beginning of the calendar year for which the State's housing credit ceiling is set. Unless otherwise prescribed by applicable revenue procedure, determinations of population are based on the most recent estimates of population contained in the Bureau of the Census publication, "Current Population Reports, Series P-25: Population Estimates and Projections, Estimates of the Population of States". For purposes of this section, the District of Columbia and United States possessions are treated as States.

(c) *Apportionment of State housing credit ceiling among State and local housing credit agencies.*—(1) *In general.*—A State's housing credit ceiling for any calendar year is apportioned among the State and local housing credit agencies within such State under the rules prescribed in this paragraph. A "State housing credit agency" is any State agency specifically authorized by gubernatorial act or State statute to make housing credit allocations on behalf of the State and to carry out the provisions of section 42(h). A "local housing credit agency" is any agency of a political subdivision of the State that is specifically authorized by a State enabling act to make housing credit allocations on behalf of the State or political subdivision and to carry out the provisions of section 42(h). A "State enabling act" is any gubernatorial act, State statute, or State housing credit agency regulation (if authorized by gubernatorial act or State statute). A State enabling act enacted on or before October 22, 1986, the date of enactment of the Tax Reform Act of 1986, shall be given effect for purposes of this paragraph if such State enabling act expressly carries out the provisions of section 42(h).

(2) *Primary apportionment.*—Except as otherwise provided in paragraph (c)(3) and (4), a State's housing credit ceiling is apportioned in its entirety to the State housing credit agency. Such an apportionment is the "primary apportionment" of a State's housing credit ceiling. There shall be no primary apportionment of the State housing credit ceiling and no grants of housing credit allocations in such State until a State housing credit agency is authorized by gubernatorial act or State statute. If a State has more than one State housing credit agency, such agencies shall be treated as a single agency for purposes of the primary apportionment. In such a case, the State housing credit ceiling may be divided among the multiple State housing credit agencies pursuant to gubernatorial act or State statute.

(3) *States with 1 or more constitutional home rule cities.*—(i) *In general.*—Notwithstanding paragraph (c)(2), in any State with 1 or more constitutional home rule cities, a portion of the State housing credit ceiling is apportioned to each constitutional home rule city. In such a State, except as provided in paragraph (c)(4), the remainder of the State housing credit ceiling is apportioned to the State housing credit agency under paragraph (c)(2). *See* paragraph (c)(3)(iii). The term "constitutional home rule city" means, with respect to any

calendar year, any political subdivision of a State that, under a State constitution that was adopted in 1970 and effective on July 1, 1971, had home rule powers on the first day of the calendar year.

(ii) *Amount of apportionment to a constitutional home rule city.*—The amount of the State housing credit ceiling apportioned to a constitutional home rule city for any calendar year is an amount that bears the same ratio to the State housing credit ceiling for that year as the population of the constitutional home rule city bears to the population of the entire State. The population of any constitutional home rule city for any calendar year is determined by reference to the most recent census estimate (whether final or provisional) of the resident population of the constitutional home rule city released by the Bureau of the Census before the beginning of the calendar year for which the State housing credit ceiling is apportioned. However, determinations of the population of a constitutional home rule city may not be based on Bureau of the Census estimates that do not contain estimates for all of the constitutional home rule cities within the State. If no Bureau of the Census estimate is available for all such constitutional home rule cities, the most recent decennial census of population shall be relied on. Unless otherwise prescribed by applicable revenue procedure, determinations of population for constitutional home rule cities are based on estimates of population contained in the Bureau of the Census publication, "Current Population Reports, Series P-26: Local Population Estimates".

(iii) *Effect of apportionments to constitutional home rule cities on apportionments to other housing credit agencies.*—The aggregate amounts of the State housing credit ceiling apportioned to constitutional home rule cities under this paragraph (c)(3) reduce the State housing credit ceiling available for apportionment under paragraph (c)(2) or (4). Unless otherwise provided in a State constitutional amendment or by law changing the home rule provisions adopted in a manner provided by the State constitution, the power of the governor or State legislature to apportion the State housing credit ceiling among local housing credit agencies under paragraph (c)(4) shall not be construed as allowing any reduction of the portion of the State housing credit ceiling apportioned to a constitutional home rule city under this paragraph (c)(3). However, any constitutional home rule city may agree to a reduction in its apportionment of the State housing credit ceiling under this paragraph (c)(3), in which case the amount of the State housing credit ceiling not apportioned to the constitutional home rule city shall be available for apportionment under paragraph (c)(2) or (4).

(iv) *Treatment of governmental authority within constitutional home rule city.*—For purposes of determining which agency within a constitutional home rule city receives the apportionment of the State housing credit ceiling under this paragraph (c)(3), the rules of this paragraph (c) shall be applied by treating the constitutional home rule city as a "State", the chief executive officer of a constitutional home rule city as a "governor", and a city council as a "State legislature". A constitutional home rule city is also treated as a "State" for purposes of the set-aside requirement for housing credit allocations to projects involving a qualified nonprofit organization. *See* paragraph (c)(5) for rules governing set-aside requirements. In this connection, a constitutional home rule city may agree with the State housing credit agency to exchange an apportionment set aside for projects involving a qualified nonprofit organization for an apportionment that is not so restricted. In such a case, the authorizing gubernatorial act, State statute, or State housing credit agency regulation (if authorized by gubernatorial act or State statute) must ensure that the set-aside apportionment transferred to the State housing credit agency be used for the purposes described in paragraph (c)(5).

(4) *Apportionment to local housing credit agencies.*—(i) *In general.*—In lieu of the primary apportionment under paragraph (c)(2), all or a portion of the State housing credit ceiling may be apportioned among housing credit agencies of governmental subdivisions. Apportionments of the State housing credit ceiling to local housing credit agencies must be made pursuant to a State enabling act as defined in paragraph (c)(1). Apportionments of the State housing credit ceiling may be made to housing credit agencies of constitutional home rule cities under this paragraph (c)(4), in addition to apportionments made under paragraph (c)(3). Apportionments of the State housing credit ceiling under this paragraph (c)(4) need not be based on the population of political subdivisions and may, but are not required to, give balanced consideration to the low-income housing needs of the entire State.

(ii) *Change in apportionments during a calendar year.*—The apportionment of the State housing credit ceiling among State and local housing credit agencies under this paragraph (c)(4) may be changed after the beginning of a calendar year, pursuant to a State enabling act. No change in apportionments shall retroactively reduce the housing credit allocations made by any agency during such year. Any change in the apportionment of the State housing credit ceiling under this paragraph (c)(4) that occurs during a calendar year is effective only to the extent housing credit agencies have not previously made housing credit allocations during such year from their original apportionments of the State housing credit ceiling for such year. To the extent apportionments of the State housing credit ceiling to local housing credit agencies made pursuant to this paragraph (c)(4) for any calendar year are not used by such local agencies before a certain date (e.g., November 1) to make housing credit allocations in such year, the amount of unused apportionments may revert back to the State housing credit agency for reapportionment. Such reversion must be specifically authorized by the State enabling act.

(iii) *Exchanges of apportionments.*—Any State or local housing credit agency that receives an apportionment of the State housing credit ceiling for any calendar year under this paragraph (c)(4) may exchange part or all of such apportionment with another State or local housing credit agency to the extent no housing credit allocations have been made in such year from the exchanged portions. Such exchanges must be made with another housing credit agency in the same State and must be consistent with the State enabling act. If an apportionment set aside for projects involving a qualified nonprofit organization is transferred or exchanged, the transferee housing credit agency shall be required to use the set-aside apportionment for the purposes described in paragraph (c)(5).

(iv) *Written records of apportionments.*—All apportionments, exchanges of apportionments, and reapportionments of the State housing credit ceiling which are authorized by this paragraph (c)(4) must be evidenced in the written records maintained by each State and local housing credit agency.

(5) *Set-aside apportionments for projects involving a qualified nonprofit organization.*—(i) *In general.*—Ten percent of the State housing credit ceiling for a calendar year must be set aside exclusively for projects involving a qualified nonprofit organization (as defined in paragraph (c)(5)(ii)). Thus, at least 10 percent of apportionments of the State housing credit ceiling under paragraph (c)(2) and (3) must be used only to make housing credit allocations to buildings that are part of projects involving a qualified nonprofit organization. In the case of apportionments of the State housing credit ceiling under paragraph (c)(4), the State enabling act must ensure that the apportionment of at least 10 percent of the State housing credit ceiling be used exclusively to make housing credit allocations to buildings that are part of projects involving a qualified nonprofit organization. The State enabling act shall prescribe which housing credit agencies in the State receive apportionments that must be set aside for making housing credit allocations to buildings that are part of projects involving a qualified nonprofit organization. These set-aside apportionments may be distributed disproportionately among the State or local housing credit agencies receiving apportionments under paragraph (c)(4). The 10-percent set-aside requirement of this paragraph (c)(4) is a minimum requirement, and the State enabling act may set aside more than 10 percent of the State housing credit ceiling for apportionment to housing credit agencies for exclusive use in making housing credit allocations to buildings that are part of projects involving a qualified nonprofit organization.

(ii) *Projects involving a qualified nonprofit organization.*—The term "projects involving a qualified nonprofit organization" means projects with respect to which a qualified nonprofit organization is to materially participate (within the meaning of section 469(h)) in the development and continuing operation of the project throughout the 15-year compliance period. The term "qualified nonprofit organization" means any organization that is described in section 501(c)(3) or (4), is exempt from tax under section 501(a), and includes as one of its exempt purposes the fostering of low-income housing.

(6) *Expiration of unused apportionments.*—Apportionments of the State housing credit ceiling under this paragraph (c) for any calendar year may be used by housing credit agencies to make housing credit allocations only in such calendar year. Any part of an apportionment of the State housing credit ceiling for any calendar year that is not used for housing credit allocations in such year expires as of the end of such year and does not carry over to any other year. However, any part of an apportionment for 1989 that is not used to make a housing credit allocation in 1989 may be carried over to 1990 and used to make a housing credit allocation to a qualified low-income building described in section 42(n)(2)(B). See paragraph (g)(2).

(d) *Housing credit allocations made by State and local housing credit agencies.*—(1) *In general.*—This paragraph governs State and local housing credit agencies in making housing credit allocations to qualified low-income buildings. The amount of the apportionment of the State housing credit ceiling for any calendar year received by any State or local housing credit agency under paragraph (c) constitutes the agency's aggregate housing credit dollar amount for such year. The aggregate amount of housing credit allocations made in any

calendar year by a State or local housing credit agency may not exceed such agency's aggregate housing credit dollar amount for such year. A State or local housing credit agency may make housing credit allocations only to qualified low-income buildings located within the agency's geographic jurisdiction.

(2) *Amount of a housing credit allocation.*—In making a housing credit allocation, a State or local housing credit agency must specify a credit percentage, not to exceed the building's applicable percentage determined under section 42(b), and a qualified basis amount. The amount of the housing credit allocation for any building is the product of the specified credit percentage and the specified qualified basis amount. In specifying the credit percentage and qualified basis amount, the State or local housing credit agency shall not take account of the first-year conventions described in section 42(f)(2)(A) and (3)(B). A State or local housing credit agency may adopt rules or regulations governing conditions for specification of less than the maximum credit percentage and qualified basis amount allowable under section 42(b) and (c), respectively. For example, an agency may specify a credit percentage and a qualified basis amount of less than the maximum credit percentage and qualified basis amount allowable under section 42(b) and (c), respectively, when the financing and rental assistance from all sources for the project of which the building is a part is sufficient to provide the continuing operation of the building without the maximum credit amount allowable under section 42.

(3) *Counting housing credit allocations against an agency's aggregate housing credit dollar amount.*—The aggregate amount of housing credit allocations made in any calendar year by a State or local housing credit agency may not exceed such agency's aggregate housing credit dollar amount (i.e., the agency's apportionment of the State housing credit ceiling for such year). This limitation on the aggregate dollar amount of housing credit allocations shall be computed separately for set-aside apportionments received pursuant to paragraph (c)(5) of this section. Housing credit allocations count against an agency's aggregate housing credit dollar amount without regard to the amount or credit allowable to or claimed by an owner of a building in the taxable year in which the allocation is made or in any subsequent year. Thus, housing credit allocations (which are computed without regard to the first-year conventions as provided in paragraph (d)(2)) count in full against an agency's aggregate housing credit dollar amount, even though the first-year conventions described in section 42(f)(2)(A) and (3)(B) may reduce the amount of credit claimed by a taxpayer in the first year in which a credit is allowable. *See also* paragraph (e)(2). Housing credit allocations count against an agency's aggregate housing credit dollar amount only in the calendar year in which made and not in subsequent taxable years in the credit period or compliance period during which a taxpayer may claim a credit based on the original housing credit allocation. Since the aggregate amount of housing credit allocations made in any calendar year by a State or local housing credit agency may not exceed such agency's aggregate housing credit dollar amount, an agency shall at all times during a calendar year maintain a record of its cumulative allocations made during such year and its remaining unused aggregate housing credit dollar amount.

(4) *Rules for when applications for housing credit allocations exceed an agency's aggregate housing credit dollar amount.*—A State or local housing credit agency may adopt rules or regulations governing the awarding of housing credit allocations when an agency expects that applicants during a calendar year will seek aggregate allocations in excess of the agency's aggregate housing credit dollar amount. The State enabling act may provide uniform standards for the awarding of housing credit allocations when there is actual or anticipated excess demand from applicants in any calendar year.

(5) *Reduced or additional housing credit allocations.*—(i) *In general.*—A State or local housing credit agency may not reduce or rescind a housing credit allocation made to a qualified low-income building in the manner prescribed in paragraph (d)(8). Thus, a housing credit agency may not reduce or rescind a housing credit allocation made to a qualified low-income building which is acquired by a new owner who is entitled to a carryover of the allowable credit for such building under section 42(d)(7). A housing credit agency may make additional housing credit allocations to a building in any year in the building's compliance period, whether or not there are additions to qualified basis for which an increased credit is allowable under section 42(f)(3). Each additional housing credit allocation made to a building is treated as a separate allocation and is subject to the rules and requirements of this section. However, in the case of an additional housing credit allocation made with respect to additions to qualified basis for which an increased credit is allowable under section 42(f)(3), the amount of the allocation that counts against the agency's aggregate housing credit dollar amount shall be computed as if the specified credit percentage were unreduced in the manner

Reg. §1.42-1T(d)(5)(i)

prescribed in section 42(f)(3)(A) and the specified qualified basis amount were unreduced by the first-year convention prescribed in section 42(f)(3)(B).

    (ii) *Examples.*—The rules of paragraph (d)(5)(i) may be illustrated by the following examples:

    Example (1). For 1987, the County L Housing Credit Agency has an aggregate housing credit dollar amount of $2 million. D, an individual, places in service on July 1, 1987, a new qualified low-income building. As of the close of each month in 1987 in which the building is in service, the building consists of 100 residential rental units, of which 20 units are both rent-restricted and occupied by individuals whose income is 50 percent or less of area median gross income. The total floor space of the residential rental units is 120,000 square feet, and the total floor space of the low-income units is 20,000 square feet. The building is not Federally subsidized within the meaning of section 42(i)(2). As of the end of 1987, the building has eligible basis under section 42(d) of $1 million. Thus, the qualified basis of the building determined without regard to the first-year convention provided in section 42(f) is $166,666.67 (*i.e.*, $1 million eligible basis times 1/6, the floor space fraction which is required to be used instead of the larger unit fraction). However, the amount of the low-income housing credit determined for 1987 under section 42 reflects the first-year convention provided in section 42(f)(2). Since the building has the same floor space and unit fractions as of the close of each of the six months in 1987 during which it is in service, upon applying the first-year convention in section 42(f)(2), the qualified basis of the building in 1987 is $83,333.33 (*i.e.*, $1 million eligible basis times 1/12, the fraction determined under section 42(f)(2)(A)). Under paragraph (d)(2) of this section, the County L Housing Credit Agency may make a housing credit allocation by specifying a credit percentage, not to exceed 9 percent, and a qualified basis amount, which may be greater or less than the qualified basis of the building in 1987 as determined under section 42(c), without regard to the first-year convention provided in section 42(f)(2). If the County L Housing Credit Agency specifies a credit percentage of 8 percent and a qualified basis amount of $100,000, the amount of the housing credit allocation is $8,000. Under paragraph (d)(3) of this section, the County L Housing Credit Agency's aggregate housing credit dollar amount for 1987 is reduced by $8,000, notwithstanding that D is entitled to claim less than $8,000 of the credit in 1987 under the rules in paragraph (e) of this section. Under paragraph (e)(2), in 1987 D is entitled to claim only $4,000 of the credit, determined by applying the first-year convention of $6/12$ to the specified qualified basis amount contained in the housing credit allocation (*i.e.*, .08 × $100,000 × ($6/12$)).

    Example (2). The facts are the same as in *Example (1)* except that on July 1, 1988, the number of occupied low-income units increases to 50 units and the floor space of the occupied low-income units increases to 48,000 square feet. These occupancy fractions remain unchanged as of the close of each month remaining in 1988. Under section 42(c), the qualified basis of the building in 1988, without regard to the first-year convention in section 42(f)(3)(B), is $400,000 (*i.e.*, $1 million eligible basis times .4, the floor space fraction which is required to be used instead of the larger unit fraction). D's 1987 housing credit allocation from the County L Housing Credit Agency remains effective in 1988 and entitles D to a credit of $8,000 (*i.e.*, .08, the specified credit percentage, times $100,000, the specified qualified basis amount). With respect to the additional $300,000 of qualified basis which the 1987 housing credit allocation does not cover, D must apply to the County L Housing Credit Agency for an additional housing credit allocation. Assume that the County L Housing Credit Agency has a sufficient aggregate housing credit dollar amount for 1988 to make a housing credit allocation to D in 1988 by specifying a credit percentage of 9 percent and a qualified basis amount of $300,000. The amount of the housing credit allocation that counts against the County L Housing Credit Agency's aggregate housing credit dollar amount is $27,000 (*i.e.*, the amount counted (.09 times $300,000) is unreduced in the manner prescribed in section 42(f)(3)(A) and (B)). Since D's qualified basis in 1987 was $166,666.67, D is entitled to claim a credit in 1988 with respect to such basis of $14,000 (*i.e.*, .08 × $100,000, the 1987 credit allocation, + .09 × $66,666.67, the 1988 credit allocation). In addition, D is entitled to claim a credit in 1988 and subsequent years in the 15-year compliance period with respect to the additional $233,333.33 of qualified basis covered by the 1988 housing credit allocation. However, the allowable credit for 1988 with respect to this amount of additional qualified basis is subject to reductions prescribed in section 42(f)(3)(A) and (B). Thus, D is entitled in 1988 to a credit at a 6-percent rate applied to $116,666.67 of additional qualified basis, which is reduced to reflect the first-year convention. D's total allowable low-income housing credit in 1988 is $21,000 (*i.e.*, $14,000 with respect to original qualified basis + $7,000 with respect to 1988 additions to qualified basis). If the County L Housing Credit Agency had specified an 8-percent credit percentage in 1988 with respect to the qualified basis not covered by

the 1987 housing credit allocation to D, D's allowable credit with respect to the $233,333.33 of additions to qualified basis would not exceed, in 1988 and subsequent years, an amount determined by applying a specified credit percentage of 5.33 percent (*i.e.*, two-thirds of 8 percent). In 1988, D's specified qualified basis amount would be adjusted for the first-year convention.

    (6) *No carryover of unused aggregate housing credit dollar amount.*— Any portion of a State or local housing credit agency's aggregate housing credit dollar amount for any calendar year that is not used to make a housing credit allocation in such year may not be carried over to any other year, except as provided in paragraph (g). An agency may not permit owners of qualified low-income buildings to transfer housing credit allocations to other buildings. However, an agency may provide a procedure whereby owners may return to the agency, prior to the end of the calendar year in which housing credit allocations are made, unusable portions of such allocations. In such a case, an owner's housing credit allocation is deemed reduced by the amount of the allocation returned to the agency, and the agency may reallocate such amount to other qualified low-income buildings prior to the end of the year.

    (7) *Effect of housing credit allocations in excess of an agency's aggregate housing credit dollar amount.*—In the event that a State or local housing credit agency makes housing credit allocations in excess of its aggregate housing credit dollar amount for any calendar year, the allocations shall be deemed reduced (to the extent of such excess) for buildings in the reverse order in which such allocations were made during such year.

    (8) *Time and manner for making housing credit allocations.*— (i) *Time.*—Housing credit allocations are effective for the calendar year in which made in the manner prescribed in paragraph (d)(8)(ii). A State or local housing credit agency may not make a housing credit allocation to a qualified low-income building prior to the calendar year in which such building is placed in service. An agency may adopt its own procedures for receiving applications for housing credit allocations from owners of qualified low-income buildings. An agency may provide a procedure for making, in advance of a building's being placed in service, a binding commitment (*e.g.*, by contract, inducement resolution, or other means) to make a housing credit allocation in the calendar year in which a qualified low-income building is placed in service or in a subsequent calendar year. Any advance commitment shall not constitute a housing credit allocation for purposes of this section.

    (ii) *Manner.*—Housing credit allocations are deemed made when Part I of IRS Form 8609, Low-Income Housing Credit Allocation Certification, is completed and signed by an authorized official of the housing credit agency and mailed to the owner of the qualified low-income building. A copy of all completed (as to Part I) Form 8609 allocations along with a single completed Form 8610, Annual Low-Income Housing Credit Agencies Report, must also be mailed to the Internal Revenue Service not later than the 28th day of the second calendar month after the close of the calendar year in which the housing credit was allocated to the qualified low-income building. Housing credit allocations to a qualified low-income building must be made on Form 8609 and must include—

    (A) The address of the building;

    (B) The name, address, and taxpayer identification number of the housing credit agency making the housing credit allocation;

    (C) The name, address, and taxpayer identification number of the owner of the qualified low-income building;

    (D) The date of the allocation of housing credit;

    (E) The housing credit dollar amount allocated to the building on such date;

    (F) The specified maximum applicable credit percentage allocated to the building on such date;

    (G) The specified maximum qualified basis amount;

    (H) The percentage of the aggregate basis financed by tax-exempt bonds taken into account for purposes of the volume cap under section 146;

    (I) A certification under penalties of perjury by an authorized State or local housing credit agency official that the allocation is made in compliance with the requirements of section 42(h); and

    (J) Any additional information that may be required by Form 8609 or by an applicable revenue procedure.
See paragraph (h) for additional rules concerning filing of forms.

    (iii) *Certification.*—The certifying official for the State or local housing credit agency need not perform an independent investigation of the qualified low-income building in order to certify on Part I of Form 8609 that the housing credit allocation meets the requirements of section 42(h). For example, the certifying official may rely on information contained in an application for a low-income housing credit allocation submitted by the building owner which sets forth facts necessary to determine that the building is eligible for the low-income housing credit under section 42.

(iv) *Fee.*—A State or local housing credit agency may charge building owners applying for housing credit allocations a reasonable fee to cover the agency's administrative expenses for processing applications.

(v) *No continuing agency responsibility.*—The State or local housing credit agency need not monitor or investigate the continued compliance of a qualified low-income building with the requirements of section 42 throughout the applicable compliance period.

(e) *Housing credit allocation taken into account by owner of a qualified low-income building.*—(1) *Time and manner for taking housing credit allocation into account.*—An owner of a qualified low-income building may not claim a low-income housing credit determined under section 42 in any year in excess of an effective housing credit allocation received from a State or local housing credit agency. A housing credit allocation made to a qualified low-income building is effective with respect to any owner of the building beginning with the owner's taxable year in which the housing credit allocation is received. A housing credit allocation is deemed received in a taxable year, except as modified in the succeeding sentence, if that allocation is made (in the manner described in paragraph (d)(8)) not later than the earlier of (i) the 60th day after the close of the taxable year, or (ii) the close of the calendar year in which such taxable year ends. A housing credit allocation is deemed received in a taxable year ending in 1987, if such allocation is made (in the manner described in paragraph (d)(8)) on or before December 31, 1987. A housing credit allocation is not effective for any taxable year if received in a calendar year which ends prior to when the qualified low-income building is placed in service. A housing credit allocation made to a qualified low-income building remains effective for all taxable years in the compliance period.

(2) *First-year convention limitation on housing credit allocation taken into account.*—For purposes of the limitation that the allowable low-income housing credit may not exceed the effective housing credit allocation received from a State or local housing credit agency, as provided in paragraph (e)(1), the amount of the effective housing credit allocation shall be adjusted by applying the first-year convention provided in section 42(f)(2)(A) and (3)(B) and the percentage credit reduction provided in section 42(f)(3)(A). Under paragraph (d)(2) and (5), the State or local housing credit agency must specify the credit percentage and qualified basis amount, the product of which is the amount of the housing credit allocation, without taking account of the first-year convention described in section 42(f)(2)(A) and (3)(B) or the percentage credit reduction prescribed in section 42(f)(3)(A). However, for purposes of the limitation on the amount of the allowable low-income housing credit, as provided in paragraph (e)(1), in a taxable year in which the first-year convention applies to the amount of credit determined under section 42(a), the specified qualified basis amount shall be adjusted by the first-year convention fraction which is equal to the number of full months (during the first taxable year) in which the building was in service divided by 12. In addition, for purposes of the limitation on the amount of the allowable low-income housing credit, as provided in paragraph (e)(1), in a taxable year in which the reduction in credit percentage applies to additions to qualified basis, as prescribed in section 42(f)(3), the specified credit percentage shall be reduced by one-third. *See* examples in paragraph (d)(5)(ii) and (e)(3)(ii) of this section.

(3) *Use of excess housing credit allocation for increases in qualified basis.*—(i) *In general.*—If the housing credit allocation made to a qualified low-income building exceeds the amount of credit allowable with respect to such building in any taxable year (without regard to the first-year conventions under section 42(f)), such excess is not transferable to another qualified low-income building. However, if in a subsequent year there are increases in the qualified basis for which an increased credit is allowable under section 42(f)(3) at a reduced credit percentage, the original housing credit allocation (including the specified credit percentage and qualified basis amount) would be effective with respect to such increased credit.

(ii) *Example.*—The provisions of this paragraph (e)(3) may be illustrated by the following example:

Example. In 1987, a newly-constructed qualified low-income building receives a housing credit allocation of $90,000 based on a specified credit percentage of 9 percent and a specified qualified basis amount of $1,000,000. The building is placed in service in 1987, but the qualified basis in such year is only $800,000, resulting in an allowable credit in 1987 (determined without regard to the first-year conventions) of $72,000. In 1988, the qualified basis is increased to $1,100,000, resulting in an additional credit allowable under section 42(f)(3) (without regard to the first-year conventions) of $18,000 (*i.e.,* $300,000 × .06, or 2/3 of .09). The unused portion of the 1987 housing

credit allocation ($18,000) is effective in 1988 and in each subsequent year in the compliance period only with respect to the specified qualified basis for the 1987 housing credit allocation ($1,000,000). Thus, the owner is allowed to claim a credit in 1988 and in each subsequent year (without regard to the first-year conventions), based on the effective housing credit allocation from 1987, of $84,000 (*i.e.,* $72,000 + ($200,000 × .06). The owner of the qualified low-income building must obtain a new housing credit allocation in 1988 with respect to the additional $100,000 of qualified basis in order to claim a credit on such basis in 1988 and in each subsequent year. If the applicable first-year convention under section 42(f)(3)(B) entitled the owner in 1988 to only 1/2 of the otherwise applicable credit for the additions to qualified basis, under paragraph (e)(2) of this section the owner is allowed to claim a credit in 1988, based on the effective housing credit allocation from 1987, of $78,000 (*i.e.,* $72,000 + ($200,000 × .06 × .5)).

(4) *Separate housing credit allocations for new buildings and increases in qualified basis.*—Separate housing credit allocations must be received for each building with respect to which a housing credit may be claimed. Rehabilitation expenditures with respect to a qualified low-income building are treated as a separate new building under section 42(e) and must receive a separate housing credit allocation. Increases in qualified basis in a qualified low-income building are not generally treated as a new building for purposes of section 42. To the extent that a prior housing credit allocation received with respect to a qualified low-income building does not allow an increased credit with respect to an increase in the qualified basis of such building, an additional housing credit allocation must be received in order to claim a credit with respect to that portion of increase in qualified basis. *See* paragraph (e)(3) of this section. The amount of credit allowable with respect to an increase in qualified basis is subject to the credit percentage limitation of section 42(f)(3)(A) and the first-year convention of section 42(f)(3)(B). *See* paragraph (d)(5) of this section for a rule requiring that the State or local housing credit agency count a housing credit allocation made with respect to an increase in qualified basis as if the specified credit percentage were unreduced in the manner prescribed in section 42(f)(3) and the specified basis amount were unreduced by the first-year convention prescribed in section 42(f)(3)(B).

(5) *Acquisition of building for which a prior housing credit allocation has been made.*—If a carryover credit would be allowable to an acquirer of a qualified low-income building under section 42(d)(1), such acquirer need not obtain a new housing credit allocation with respect to such building. Under section 42(d)(7), the acquirer would be entitled to claim only such credits as would have been allowable to the prior owner of the building.

(6) *Multiple housing credit allocations.*—A qualified low-income building may receive multiple housing credit allocations from different housing credit agencies having overlapping jurisdictions. A qualified low-income building that receives a housing credit allocation set aside exclusively for projects involving a qualified nonprofit organization may also receive a housing credit allocation from a housing credit agency's aggregate housing credit dollar amount that is not so set aside.

(f) *Exception to housing credit allocation requirement.*—(1) *Tax-exempt bond financing.*—(i) *In general.*—No housing credit allocation is required in order to claim a credit under section 42 with respect to that portion of the eligible basis (as defined in section 42(d)) of a qualified low-income building that is financed with the proceeds of an obligation described in section 103(a) ("tax-exempt bond") which is taken into account for purposes of the volume cap under section 146. In addition, no housing credit allocation is required in order to claim a credit under section 42 with respect to the entire qualified basis (as defined in section 42(c)) of a qualified low-income building if 70 percent or more of the aggregate basis of the building and the land on which the building is located is financed with the proceeds of tax-exempt bonds which are taken into account for purposes of the volume cap under section 146. For purposes of this paragraph, "land on which the building is located" includes only land that is functionally related and subordinate to the qualified low-income building. *See* §1.103-8(b)(4)(iii) for the meaning of the term "functionally related and subordinate". For purposes of this paragraph, the basis of the land shall be determined using principles that are consistent with the rules contained in section 42(d).

(ii) *Determining use of bond proceeds.*—For purposes of determining the portion of proceeds of an issue of tax-exempt bonds used to finance (A) the eligible basis of a qualified low-income building, and (B) the aggregate basis of the building and the land on which the building is located, the proceeds of the issue must be allocated in the bond indenture or a related document (as defined in §1.103-13(b)(8)) in a manner consistent with the method used to allocate the net proceeds of the issue for purposes of determining whether 95 percent or more of the net proceeds of the issue are to be used for the exempt purpose of the issue. If the issuer is not consistent in making this allocation throughout the bond indenture and related documents, or if neither the bond indenture nor a related document provides an allocation, the proceeds of the issue will be allocated on a pro rata basis to all of the property financed by the issue, based on the relative cost of the property.

(iii) *Example.*—The provisions of this paragraph may be illustrated by the following example:

Example. In 1987, County K assigns $500,000 of its volume cap for private activity bonds under section 146 to a $500,000 issue of exempt facility bonds to provide a qualified residential rental project to be owned by A, an individual. The aggregate basis of the building and the land on which the building is located is $700,000. Under the terms of the bond indenture, the net proceeds of the issue are to be used to finance $490,000 of the eligible basis of the building. More than 70 percent of the aggregate basis of the qualified low-income building and the land on which the building is located is financed with the proceeds of tax-exempt bonds to which a portion of the volume cap under section 146 was allocated. Accordingly, A may claim a credit under section 42 without regard to whether any housing credit dollar amount was allocated to that building. If, instead, the aggregate basis of the building and land were $800,000, A would be able to claim the credit under section 42 without receiving a housing credit allocation for the building only to the extent that the credit is attributable to eligible basis of the building financed with tax-exempt bonds.

(g) *Termination of authority to make housing credit allocation.*—(1) *In general.*—No State or local housing credit agency shall receive an apportionment of a State housing credit ceiling for calendar years after 1989. Consequently, no housing credit allocations may be made after 1989, except as provided in paragraph (g)(2). Housing credit allocations made prior to January 1, 1990, remain effective after such date.

(2) *Carryover of unused 1989 apportionment.*—Any State or local housing credit agency that has an unused portion of its apportionment of the State housing credit ceiling for 1989 from which housing credit allocations have not been made in 1989 may carry over such unused portion into 1990. Such carryover portion of the 1989 apportionment shall be treated as the agency's apportionment for 1990. From this 1990 apportionment, the State or local housing credit agency may make housing credit allocations only to a qualified low-income building meeting the following requirements:

(i) The building must be constructed, reconstructed, or rehabilitated by the taxpayer seeking the allocation;

(ii) More than 10 percent of the reasonably anticipated cost of such construction, reconstruction, or rehabilitation must have been incurred as of January 1, 1989; and

(iii) The building must be placed in service before January 1, 1991.

(3) *Expiration of exception for tax-exempt bond financed projects.*—The exception to the requirement that a housing credit allocation be received with respect to any portion of the eligible basis of a qualified low-income building, as provided in paragraph (f), shall not apply to any building placed in service after 1989, unless such building is described in paragraph (g)(2)(i), (ii), and (iii).

(h) *Filing of forms.*—For further guidance, see § 1.42-1(h).

(i) *Transitional rules.*—The transitional rules contained in section 252(f)(1) of the Tax Reform Act of 1986 are incorporated into this section of the regulations for purposes of determining whether a qualified low-income building is entitled to receive a housing credit allocation or is excepted from the requirement that a housing credit allocation be received. Housing credit allocations made to qualified low-income buildings described in section 252(f)(1) shall not count against the State or local housing credit agency's aggregate housing credit dollar amount. The transitional rules contained in section 252(f)(2) of the Tax Reform Act of 1986 are incorporated into this section of the regulations for purposes of determining amounts available to certain State or local housing credit agencies for the making of housing credit allocations to certain qualified low-income housing projects. Amounts available to housing credit agencies under section 252(f)(2) shall be treated as special apportionments unavailable for housing credit allocations to qualified low-income buildings not described in section 252(f)(2). Housing credit allocations made from the special apportionments shall not count against the State or local credit agency's aggregate housing credit dollar amount. The set-aside requirements shall not apply to these special apportionments. The transitional rules contained in section 252(f)(3) of the Tax Reform Act of 1986 are incorporated in this section of the regulations for purposes of determining the amount of housing credit allocations received by certain qualified low-income buildings. Housing credit

allocations deemed received under section 252(f)(3) shall not count against the State or local housing credit agency's aggregate housing credit dollar amount. [Temporary Reg. § 1.42-1T.]

☐ [*T.D. 8144, 6-17-87. Amended by T.D. 9112, 1-26-2004.*]

[Reg. § 1.42-2]

§ 1.42-2. [Reserved].

☐ [*T.D. 8302, 5-22-90. Removed and reserved by T.D. 9849, 3-11-2019.*]

[Reg. § 1.42-3]

§ 1.42-3. Treatment of buildings financed with proceeds from a loan under an Affordable Housing Program established pursuant to section 721 of the Financial Institutions Reform, Recovery, and Enforcement Act of 1989 (FIRREA).—(a) *Treatment under sections 42(i) and 42(b).*—A below market loan funded in whole or in part with funds from an Affordable Housing Program established under section 721 of FIRREA is not, solely by reason of the Affordable Housing Program funds, a below market Federal loan as defined in section 42(i)(2)(D). Thus, any building with respect to which the proceeds of the loan are used during the tax year is not, solely by reason of the Affordable Housing Program funds, treated as a federally subsidized building for that tax year and subsequent tax years for purposes of determining the applicable percentage for the building under section 42(b).

(b) *Effective date.*—The rules set forth in paragraph (a) of this section are effective for loans made after August 8, 1989. [Reg. § 1.42-3.]

☐ [*T.D. 8368, 9-25-91.*]

[Reg. § 1.42-4]

§ 1.42-4. Application of not-for-profit rules of section 183 to low-income housing credit activities.—(a) *Inapplicability to section 42.*—In the case of a qualified low-income building with respect to which the low-income housing credit under section 42 is allowable, section 183 does not apply to disallow losses, deductions, or credits attributable to the ownership and operation of the building.

(b) *Limitation.*—Notwithstanding paragraph (a) of this section, losses, deductions, or credits attributable to the ownership and operation of a qualified low-income building with respect to which the low-income housing credit under section 42 is allowable may be limited or disallowed under other provisions of the Code or principles of tax law. *See, e.g.,* Sections 38(c), 163(d), 465, 469; *Knetsch v. United States,* 364 U.S. 361 (1960), 1961-1 C.B. 34 ("sham" or "economic substance" analysis); and *Frank Lyon Co. v. Commissioner,* 435 U.S. 561 (1978), 1978-1 C.B. 46 ("ownership" analysis).

(c) *Effective date.*—The rules set forth in paragraphs (a) and (b) of this section are effective with respect to buildings placed in service after December 31, 1986. [Reg. § 1.42-4.]

☐ [*T.D. 8420, 6-10-92.*]

[Reg. § 1.42-5]

§ 1.42-5. Monitoring compliance with low-income housing credit requirements.—(a) *Compliance monitoring requirement.*—(1) *In general.*—Under section 42(m)(1)(B)(iii), an allocation plan is not qualified unless it contains a procedure that the State or local housing credit agency ("Agency") (or an agent of, or other private contractor hired by, the Agency) will follow in monitoring for noncompliance with the provisions of section 42 and in notifying the Internal Revenue Service of any noncompliance of which the Agency becomes aware. These regulations only address compliance monitoring procedures required of Agencies. The regulations do not address forms and other records that may be required by the Service on examination or audit. For example, if a building is sold or otherwise transferred by the owner, the transferee should obtain from the transferor information related to the first year of the credit period so that the transferee can substantiate credits claimed.

(2) *Requirements for a monitoring procedure.*—(i) *In general.*—A procedure for monitoring for noncompliance under section 42(m)(1)(B)(iii) must include—

(A) The recordkeeping and record retention provisions of paragraph (b) of this section;

(B) The certification and review provisions of paragraph (c) of this section;

(C) The inspection provision of paragraph (d) of this section; and

(D) The notification-of-noncompliance provisions of paragraph (e) of this section.

(ii) *Order and form.*—A monitoring procedure will meet the requirements of section 42(m)(1)(B)(iii) if it contains the substance of these provisions. The particular order and form of the provisions in the allocation plan is not material. A monitoring procedure may contain additional provisions or requirements.

(b) *Recordkeeping and record retention provisions.*—(1) *Recordkeeping provision.*—Under the recordkeeping provision, the owner of a low-income housing project must be required to keep records for each qualified low-income building in the project that show for each year in the compliance period—

(i) The total number of residential rental units in the building (including the number of bedrooms and the size in square feet of each residential rental unit);

(ii) The percentage of residential rental units in the building that are low-income units;

(iii) The rent charged on each residential rental unit in the building (including any utility allowances);

(iv) The number of occupants in each low-income unit, but only if rent is determined by the number of occupants in each unit under section 42(g)(2) (as in effect before the amendments made by the Omnibus Budget Reconciliation Act of 1989);

(v) The low-income unit vacancies in the building and information that shows when, and to whom, the next available units were rented;

(vi) The annual income certification of each low-income tenant per unit. For an exception to this requirement, see section 42(g)(8)(B) (which provides a special rule for a 100 percent low-income building);

(vii) Documentation to support each low-income tenant's income certification (for example, a copy of the tenant's federal income tax return, Forms W-2, or verifications of income from third parties such as employers or state agencies paying unemployment compensation). For an exception to this requirement, see section 42(g)(8)(B) (which provides a special rule for a 100 percent low-income building). Tenant income is calculated in a manner consistent with the determination of annual income under section 8 of the United States Housing Act of 1937 ("Section 8"), not in accordance with the determination of gross income for federal income tax liability. In the case of a tenant receiving housing assistance payments under Section 8, the documentation requirement of this paragraph (b)(1)(vii) is satisfied if the public housing authority provides a statement to the building owner declaring that the tenant's income does not exceed the applicable income limit under section 42(g);

(viii) The eligible basis and qualified basis of the building at the end of the first year of the credit period; and

(ix) The character and use of the nonresidential portion of the building included in the building's eligible basis under section 42(d) (*e.g.,* tenant facilities that are available on a comparable basis to all tenants and for which no separate fee is charged for use of the facilities, or facilities reasonably required by the project).

(2) *Record retention provision.*—Under the record retention provision, the owner of a low-income housing project must be required to retain the records described in paragraph (b)(1) of this section for at least 6 years after the due date (with extensions) for filing the federal income tax return for that year. The records for the first year of the credit period, however, must be retained for at least 6 years beyond the due date (with extensions) for filing the federal income tax return for the last year of the compliance period of the building.

(3) *Inspection record retention provision.*—Under the inspection record retention provision, the owner of a low-income housing project must be required to retain the original local health, safety, or building code violation reports or notices that were issued by the State or local government unit (as described in paragraph (c)(1)(vi) of this section) for the Agency's inspection under paragraph (d) of this section. Retention of the original violation reports or notices is not required once the Agency reviews the violation reports or notices and completes its inspection, unless the violation remains uncorrected.

(c) *Certification and review provisions.*—(1) *Certification.*—Under the certification provision, the owner of a low-income housing project must be required to certify at least annually to the Agency that, for the preceding 12-month period—

(i) The project met the requirements of:

(A) The 20-50 test under section 42(g)(1)(A), the 40-60 test under section 42(g)(1)(B), or the 25-60 test under sections 42(g)(4) and 142(d)(6) for New York City, whichever minimum set-aside test was applicable to the project; and

(B) If applicable to the project, the 15-40 test under sections 42(g)(4) and 142(d)(4)(B) for "deep rent skewed" projects;

(ii) There was no change in the applicable fraction (as defined in section 42(c)(1)(B)) of any building in the project, or that there was a change, and a description of the change;

(iii) The owner has received an annual income certification from each low-income tenant, and documentation to support that

certification; or, in the case of a tenant receiving Section 8 housing assistance payments, the statement from a public housing authority described in paragraph (b)(1)(vii) of this section. For an exception to this requirement, see section 42(g)(8)(B) (which provides a special rule for a 100 percent low-income building);

(iv) Each low-income unit in the project was rent-restricted under section 42(g)(2);

(v) All units in the project were for use by the general public (as defined in §1.42-9), including the requirement that no finding of discrimination under the Fair Housing Act, 42 U.S.C. 3601-3619, occurred for the project. A finding of discrimination includes an adverse final decision by the Secretary of the Department of Housing and Urban Development (HUD), 24 CFR 180.680, an adverse final decision by a substantially equivalent state or local fair housing agency, 42 U.S.C. 3616a(a)(1), or an adverse judgment from a federal court;

(vi) The buildings and low-income units in the project were suitable for occupancy, taking into account local health, safety, and building codes (or other habitability standards), and the State or local government unit responsible for making local health, safety, or building code inspections did not issue a violation report for any building or low-income unit in the project. If a violation report or notice was issued by the governmental unit, the owner must attach a statement summarizing the violation report or notice or a copy of the violation report or notice to the annual certification submitted to the Agency under paragraph (c)(1) of this section. In addition, the owner must state whether the violation has been corrected;

(vii) There was no change in the eligible basis (as defined in section 42(d)) of any building in the project, or if there was a change, the nature of the change (*e.g.,* a common area has become commercial space, or a fee is now charged for a tenant facility formerly provided without charge);

(viii) All tenant facilities included in the eligible basis under section 42(d) of any building in the project, such as swimming pools, other recreational facilities, and parking areas, were provided on a comparable basis without charge to all tenants in the building;

(ix) If a low-income unit in the project became vacant during the year, that reasonable attempts were or are being made to rent that unit or the next available unit of comparable or smaller size to tenants having a qualifying income before any units in the project were or will be rented to tenants not having a qualifying income;

(x) If the income of tenants of a low-income unit in the building increased above the limit allowed in section 42(g)(2)(D)(ii), the next available unit of comparable or smaller size in the building was or will be rented to tenants having a qualifying income;

(xi) An extended low-income housing commitment as described in section 42(h)(6) was in effect (for buildings subject to section 7108(c)(1) of the Omnibus Budget Reconciliation Act of 1989, 103 Stat. 2106, 2308-2311), including the requirement under section 42(h)(6)(B)(iv) that an owner cannot refuse to lease a unit in the project to an applicant because the applicant holds a voucher or certificate of eligibility under section 8 of the United States Housing Act of 1937, 42 U.S.C. 1437f (for buildings subject to section 13142(b)(4) of the Omnibus Budget Reconciliation Act of 1993, 107 Stat. 312, 438-439); and

(xii) All low-income units in the project were used on a non-transient basis (except for transitional housing for the homeless provided under section 42(i)(3)(B)(iii) or single-room-occupancy units rented on a month-by-month basis under section 42(i)(3)(B)(iv)).

(2) *Review.*—The review provision must—

(i) Require that the Agency review the certifications submitted under paragraph (c)(1) of this section for compliance with the requirements of section 42;

(ii) Require that, with respect to each low-income housing project, the Agency conduct on-site inspections and review low-income certifications (including in that term the documentation supporting the low-income certifications and the rent records for tenants).

(iii) Require that the on-site inspections that the Agency must conduct satisfy both the requirements of §1.42-5(d) and the requirements in paragraph (c)(2)(iii)(A) through (D) of this section, and require that the low-income certification review that the Agency must perform satisfies the requirements in paragraphs (c)(2)(iii)(A) through (D) of this section. Paragraph (c)(2)(iii)(A) through (D) of this section provides rules determining how these on-site inspection requirements and how these low-income certification review requirements may be satisfied by an inspection or review, as the case may be, that includes only a sample of the low-income units.

(A) *Timing.*—The Agency must conduct on-site inspections of all buildings in the low-income housing project and must review low-income certifications of the low-income housing project—

(1) By the end of the second calendar year following the year the last building in the low-income housing project is placed in service; and

(2) At least once every 3 years thereafter.

(B) *Number of low-income units.*—The Agency must conduct on-site inspections and low-income certification review of not fewer than the minimum number of low-income units for the corresponding number of low-income units in the low-income housing project set forth in the table to paragraph (c)(2)(iii).

Table to Paragraph (c)(2)(iii)

Number of Low-Income Units in the Low-Income Housing Project	Number of Low-income Units Selected for Inspection or for Low-Income Certification Review (Minimum Unit Sample Size)
1	1
2	2
3	3
4	4
5-6	5
7	6
8-9	7
10-11	8
12-13	9
14-16	10
17-18	11
19-21	12
22-25	13
26-29	14
30-34	15
35-40	16
41-47	17
48-56	18
57-67	19
68-81	20
82-101	21
102-130	22
131-175	23
176-257	24
258-449	25
450-1,461	26
1,462-9,999	27

(C) *Selection of low-income units for inspection and low-income certifications for review.*—*(1)* *Random selection.*—The Agency must select in a random manner the low-income units to be inspected and the units whose low-income certifications are to be reviewed. Agencies generally may not select the same low-income units of a low-income housing project for on-site inspections and low-income certification review, because doing so would usually give prohibited advance notice. See paragraph (c)(2)(iii)(C)(2) of this section. An Agency may choose a different number of units for on-site inspections and for low-income certification review, provided the Agency chooses at least the minimum number of low-income units in each case. The Agency must select the units for inspections or low-income certification review separately and in a random manner.

(2) *Advance notification limited to reasonable notice.*—The Agency must select the low-income units to inspect and low-income certifications to review in a manner that does not give advance notice that a particular low-income unit (or low-income certifications for a particular low-income unit) will or will not be inspected (or reviewed) for a particular year. The Agency may notify the owner of the low-income units for on-site inspection only on the day of inspection. However, the Agency may give an owner reasonable notice that an inspection of the project and of not-yet-identified low-income units or review of low-income certifications will occur. The notice serves to enable the owner to assemble needed documentation for low-income certifications for review and to notify tenants of the possibility of physical inspection of their units.

(3) *Meaning of reasonable notice.*—For purposes of paragraph (c)(2)(iii)(C)(2) of this section, reasonable notice is generally no more than 15 days. The notice period begins on the date the Agency informs the owner that an on-site inspection of a project and low-income units or low-income certification review will occur. Notice of more than 15 days, however, may be reasonable in extraordinary circumstances that are beyond an Agency's control and that prevent an Agency from carrying out within 15 days an on-site inspection or low-income certification review. Extraordinary circumstances in-clude, but are not limited to, natural disasters and severe weather conditions. In the event of extraordinary circumstances that result in a reasonable-notice period longer than 15 days, an Agency must select the relevant units and conduct the same-day on-site inspection or low-income certification review as soon as practicable.

(4) *Alternative means of conducting on-site inspections – Use of the REAC protocol.*—An Agency may satisfy the requirements of paragraphs (c)(2)(ii) and (iii) of this section if the inspection is performed under the Department of Housing and Urban Development (HUD) Real Estate Assessment Center (REAC) protocol and the inspection satisfies the following requirements:

(i) Both vacant and occupied low-income units in a low-income housing project are included in the population of units from which units are selected for inspection;

(ii) The inspection complies with the procedural and substantive requirements of the REAC protocol, including the requirements of the most recent REAC Uniform Physical Condition Standards (UPCS) inspection software, or software accepted by HUD;

(iii) The inspection is performed by HUD or HUD-Certified REAC inspectors;

(iv) The inspection results are sent to HUD, the results are reviewed and scored within HUD's secure system without any involvement of the inspector who conducted the inspection, and HUD makes its inspection report available.

(5) *HUD Inspections that comply with the requirements of the REAC Protocol.*—If, consistent with the requirements of paragraph (c)(2)(iii)(4) of this section, an Agency conducts on-site inspections under the REAC protocol, then—

(i) Paragraph (c)(2)(iii)(A) of this section is applied as if it did not contain the word "all";

(ii) The number of low-income units required to be inspected under the REAC protocol satisfies the requirements of paragraph (c)(2)(iii)(B) of this section concerning the number of low-income units an Agency must inspect; and

(iii) The manner in which the low-income units are selected for inspection under the REAC protocol satisfies the requirements of paragraph (c)(2)(iii)(C) of this section.

(6) Income Certification Requirements for HUD Inspections that comply with the requirements of the REAC Protocol.—An agency that conducts on-site inspections under the REAC protocol is not excused from reviewing low-income certifications in accordance with paragraphs (c)(2)(ii) and (iii) of this section.

(7) Applicability of reasonable notice limitation when the same units are chosen for inspection and file review.—If the Agency chooses to select the same units for on-site inspections and low-income certification review, the Agency must complete both the inspections and review before the end of the day on which the units are selected. See paragraph (c)(2)(iii)(C)(*1*) and (*2*) of this section.

(D) Method of low-income certification review.—The Agency may review the low-income certifications wherever the owner maintains or stores the records (either on-site or off-site).

(3) Frequency and form of certification.—A monitoring procedure must require that the certifications and reviews of § 1.42-5(c)(1) and (c)(2)(i) be made at least annually covering each year of the 15-year compliance period under section 42(i)(1). The certifications must be made under penalties of perjury. A monitoring procedure may require certifications and reviews more frequently than every 12 months, provided that all months within each 12-month period are subject to certification.

(4) Exception for certain buildings.—(i) *In general.*—The review requirements under paragraph (c)(2)(ii) of this section may provide that owners are not required to submit, and the Agency is not required to review, the tenant income certifications, supporting documentation, and rent records for buildings financed by the Rural Housing Service (RHS), formerly known as Farmers Home Administration under the section 515 program, or buildings of which 50 percent or more of the aggregate basis (taking into account the building and the land) is financed with the proceeds of obligations the interest on which is exempt from tax under section 103 (tax-exempt bonds). In order for a monitoring procedure to except these buildings, the Agency must meet the requirements of paragraph (c)(4)(ii) of this section.

(ii) Agreement and review.—The Agency must enter into an agreement with the RHS or tax-exempt bond issuer. Under the agreement, the RHS or tax-exempt bond issuer must agree to provide information concerning the income and rent of the tenants in the building to the Agency. The Agency may assume the accuracy of the information provided by RHS or the tax-exempt bond issuer without verification. The Agency must review the information and determine that the income limitation and rent restriction of section 42(g)(1) and (2) are met. However, if the information provided by the RHS or tax-exempt bond issuer is not sufficient for the Agency to make this determination, the Agency must request the necessary additional income or rent information from the owner of the buildings. For example, because RHS determines tenant eligibility based on its definition of "adjusted annual income," rather than "annual income" as defined under Section 8, the Agency may have to calculate the tenant's income for section 42 purposes and may need to request additional income information from the owner.

(iii) Example.—The exception permitted under paragraph (c)(4)(i) and (ii) of this section is illustrated by the following example.

Example. An Agency selects for review buildings financed by the RHS. The Agency has entered into an agreement described in paragraph (c)(4)(ii) of this section with the RHS with respect to those buildings. In reviewing the RHS-financed buildings, the Agency obtains the tenant income and rent information from the RHS for 20 percent of the low-income units in each of those buildings. The Agency calculates the tenant income and rent to determine whether the tenants meet the income and rent limitation of section 42(g)(1) and (2). In order to make this determination, the Agency may need to request additional income or rent information from the owners of the RHS buildings if the information provided by the RHS is not sufficient.

(5) Agency reports of compliance monitoring activities.—The Agency must report its compliance monitoring activities annually on Form 8610, "Annual Low-Income Housing Credit Agencies Report."

(d) Inspection provision.—(1) *In general.*—Under the inspection provision, the Agency must have the right to perform an on-site inspection of any low-income housing project at least through the end of the compliance period of the buildings in the project. The inspection provision of this paragraph (d) is a separate requirement from any tenant file review under paragraph (c)(2)(ii) of this section.

(2) Inspection standard.—For the on-site inspections of buildings and low-income units required by paragraph (c)(2)(ii) of this section, the Agency must review any local health, safety, or building code violations reports or notices retained by the owner under paragraph (b)(3) of this section and must determine—

(i) Whether the buildings and units are suitable for occupancy, taking into account local health, safety, and building codes (or other habitability standards); or

(ii) Whether the buildings and units satisfy, as determined by the Agency, the uniform physical condition standards for public housing established by HUD (24 CFR 5.703). The HUD physical condition standards do not supersede or preempt local health, safety, and building codes. A low-income housing project under section 42 must continue to satisfy these codes and, if the Agency becomes aware of any violation of these codes, the Agency must report the violation to the Service. However, provided the Agency determines by inspection that the HUD standards are met, the Agency is not required under this paragraph (d)(2)(ii) to determine by inspection whether the project meets local health, safety, and building codes.

(3) Exception from inspection provision.—An Agency is not required to inspect a building under this paragraph (d) if the building is financed by the RHS under the section 515 program, the RHS inspects the building (under 7 CFR part 1930), and the RHS and Agency enter into a memorandum of understanding, or other similar arrangement, under which, the RHS agrees to notify the Agency of the inspection results.

(4) Delegation.—An Agency may delegate inspection under this paragraph (d) to an Authorized Delegate retained under paragraph (f) of this section. Such Authorized Delegate, which may include HUD or a HUD-approved inspector, must notify the Agency of the inspection results.

(e) Notification-of-noncompliance provisions.—(1) *In general.*—Under the notification-of-noncompliance provisions, the Agency must be required to give the notice described in paragraph (e)(2) of this section to the owner of a low-income housing project and the notice described in paragraph (e)(3) of this section to the Service.

(2) Notice to owner.—The Agency must be required to provide prompt written notice to the owner of a low-income housing project if the Agency does not receive the certification described in paragraph (c)(1) of this section, or does not receive or is not permitted to inspect the tenant income certifications, supporting documentation, and rent records described in paragraph (c)(2)(ii) of this section, or discovers by inspection, review, or in some other manner, that the project is not in compliance with the provisions of section 42.

(3) Notice to Internal Revenue Service.—(i) *In general.*—The Agency must be required to file Form 8823, "Low-Income Housing Credit Agencies Report of Noncompliance," with the Service no later than 45 days after the end of the correction period (as described in paragraph (e)(4) of this section, including extensions permitted under that paragraph) and no earlier than the end of the correction period, whether or not the noncompliance or failure to certify is corrected. The Agency must explain on Form 8823 the nature of the noncompliance or failure to certify and indicate whether the owner has corrected the noncompliance or failure to certify. Any change in either the applicable fraction or eligible basis under paragraph (c)(1)(ii) and (vii) of this section, respectively, that results in a decrease in the qualified basis of the project under section 42(c)(1)(A) is noncompliance that must be reported to the Service under this paragraph (e)(3). If an Agency reports on Form 8823 that a building is entirely out of compliance and will not be in compliance at any time in the future, the Agency need not file Form 8823 in subsequent years to report that building's noncompliance. If the noncompliance or failure to certify is corrected within 3 years after the end of the correction period, the Agency is required to file Form 8823 with the Service reporting the correction of the noncompliance or failure to certify.

(ii) Agency retention of records.—An Agency must retain records of noncompliance or failure to certify for 6 years beyond the Agency's filing of the respective Form 8823. In all other cases, the Agency must retain the certifications and records described in paragraph (c) of this section for 3 years from the end of the calendar year the Agency receives the certifications and records.

(4) Correction period.—The correction period shall be that period specified in the monitoring procedure during which an owner must supply any missing certifications and bring the project into compliance with the provisions of section 42. The correction period is not to exceed 90 days from the date of the notice to the owner described in paragraph (e)(2) of this section. An Agency may extend the correction period for up to 6 months, but only if the Agency determines there is good cause for granting the extension.

(f) *Delegation of authority.*—(1) *Agencies permitted to delegate compliance monitoring functions.*—(i) *In general.*—An Agency may retain an agent or other private contractor ("Authorized Delegate") to perform compliance monitoring. The Authorized Delegate must be unrelated to the owner of any building that the Authorized Delegate monitors. The Authorized Delegate may be delegated all of the functions of the Agency, except for the responsibility of notifying the Service under paragraphs (c)(5) and (e)(3) of this section. For example, the Authorized Delegate may be delegated the responsibility of reviewing tenant certifications and documentation under paragraph (c)(1) and (2) of this section, the right to inspect buildings and records as described in paragraph (d) of this section, and the responsibility of notifying building owners of lack of certification or noncompliance under paragraph (e)(2) of this section. The Authorized Delegate must notify the Agency of any noncompliance or failure to certify.

(ii) *Limitations.*—An Agency that delegates compliance monitoring to an Authorized Delegate under paragraph (f)(1)(i) of this section must use reasonable diligence to ensure that the Authorized Delegate properly performs the delegated monitoring functions. Delegation by an Agency of compliance monitoring functions to an Authorized Delegate does not relieve the Agency of its obligation to notify the Service of any noncompliance of which the Agency becomes aware.

(2) *Agencies permitted to delegate compliance monitoring functions to another Agency.*—An Agency may delegate all or some of its compliance monitoring responsibilities for a building to another Agency within the State. This delegation may include the responsibility of notifying the Service under paragraph (e)(3) of this section.

(g) *Liability.*—Compliance with the requirements of section 42 is the responsibility of the owner of the building for which the credit is allowable. The Agency's obligation to monitor for compliance with the requirements of section 42 does not make the Agency liable for an owner's noncompliance.

(h) *Effective/applicability dates.*—(1) *In general.*—Allocation plans must comply with these regulations by June 30, 1993. The requirement of section 42(m)(1)(B)(iii) that allocation plans contain a procedure for monitoring for noncompliance becomes effective on January 1, 1992, and applies to buildings for which a low-income housing credit is, or has been, allowable at any time. Thus, allocation plans must comply with section 42(m)(1)(B)(iii) prior to June 30, 1993, the effective date of these regulations. An allocation plan that complies with these regulations, with the notice of proposed rulemaking published in the Federal Register on December 27, 1991, or with a reasonable interpretation of section 42(m)(1)(B)(iii) will satisfy the requirements of section 42(m)(1)(B)(iii) for periods before June 30, 1993. Section 42(m)(1)(B)(iii) and these regulations do not require monitoring for whether a building or project is in compliance with the requirements of section 42 prior to January 1, 1992. However, if an Agency becomes aware of noncompliance that occurred prior to January 1, 1992, the Agency is required to notify the Service of that noncompliance. In addition, the requirements in paragraphs (b)(3) and (c)(1)(v), (vi), and (xi) of this section (involving recordkeeping and annual owner certifications) and paragraphs (c)(2)(ii)(B), (c)(2)(iii), and (d) of this section (involving tenant file reviews and physical inspections of existing projects, and the physical inspection standard) are applicable January 1, 2001. The requirement in paragraph (c)(2)(ii)(A) of this section (involving tenant file reviews and physical inspections of new projects) is applicable for buildings placed in service on or after January 1, 2001. The requirements in paragraph (c)(5) of this section (involving Agency reporting of compliance monitoring activities to the Service) and paragraph (e)(3)(i) of this section (involving Agency reporting of corrected noncompliance or failure to certify within 3 years after the end of the correction period) are applicable January 14, 2000.

(2) *Applicability dates.*—The requirements in paragraphs (c)(2)(ii) and (iii) and (c)(3) of this section apply beginning on February 26, 2019. A state housing credit agency is allowed a reasonable period of time to amend its qualified allocation plan, but must amend its qualified allocation plan no later than December 31, 2020. [Reg. §1.42-5.]

☐ [*T.D. 8430, 9-1-92. Amended by T.D. 8563, 9-30-94, T.D. 8859, 1-13-2000 (corrected 3-27-2000). T.D. 9753, 2-23-2016 and T.D. 9848, 2-22-2019.*]

[Reg. §1.42-6

§1.42-6. Buildings qualifying for carryover allocations.—(a) *Carryover allocations.*—(1) *In general.*—A carryover allocation is an allocation that meets the requirements of section 42(h)(1)(E) or (F). If the requirements of section 42(h)(1)(E) or (F) that are required to be satisfied by the close of a calendar year are not satisfied, the allocation is not valid and is treated as if it had not been made for that

calendar year. For example, if a carryover allocation fails to satisfy a requirement in §1.42-6(d) for making an allocation, such as failing to be signed or dated by an authorized official of an allocating agency by the close of a calendar year, the allocation is not valid and is treated as if it had not been made for that calendar year.

(2) *10 percent basis requirement.*—A carryover allocation may only be made with respect to a qualified building. A qualified building is any building which is part of a project if, by the date specified under paragraph (a)(2)(i) or (ii) of this section, a taxpayer's basis in the project is more than 10 percent of the taxpayer's reasonably expected basis in the project as of the close of the second calendar year following the calendar year the allocation is made. For purposes of meeting the 10 percent basis requirement, the determination of whether a building is part of a single-building project or multi-building project is based on whether the carryover allocation is made under section 42(h)(1)(E) (building-based allocation) or section 42(h)(1)(F) (project-based allocation). In the case of a multi-building project that receives an allocation under section 42(h)(1)(F), the 10 percent basis requirement is satisfied by reference to the entire project.

(i) *Allocation made before July 1.*—If a carryover allocation is made before July 1 of a calendar year, a taxpayer must meet the 10 percent basis requirement by the close of that calendar year. If a taxpayer does not meet the 10 percent basis requirement by the close of the calendar year, the carryover allocation is not valid and is treated as if it had not been made.

(ii) *Allocation made after June 30.*—If a carryover allocation is made after June 30 of a calendar year, a taxpayer must meet the 10 percent basis requirement by the close of the date that is 6 months after the date the allocation was made. If a taxpayer does not meet the 10 percent basis requirement by the close of the required date, the carryover allocation must be returned to the Agency. Unlike a carryover allocation made before July 1, if a taxpayer does not meet the 10 percent basis requirement by the close of the required date, the carryover allocation is treated as a valid allocation for the calendar year of allocation, but is included in the "returned credit component" for purposes of determining the State housing credit ceiling under section 42(h)(3)(C) for the calendar year following the calendar year of the allocation. See §1.42-14(d)(1).

(b) *Carryover-allocation basis.*—(1) *In general.*—Subject to the limitations of paragraph (b)(2) of this section, a taxpayer's basis in a project for purposes of section 42(h)(1)(E)(ii) or (F) (carryover-allocation basis) is the taxpayer's adjusted basis in land or depreciable property that is reasonably expected to be part of the project, whether or not these amounts are includible in eligible basis under section 42(d). Thus, for example, if the project is to include property that is not residential rental property, such as commercial space, the basis attributable to the commercial space, although not includible in eligible basis, is includible in carryover-allocation basis. The adjusted basis of land and depreciable property is determined under sections 1012 and 1016, and generally includes the direct and indirect costs of acquiring, constructing, and rehabilitating the property. Costs otherwise includible in carryover-allocation basis are not excluded by reason of having been incurred prior to the calendar year in which the carryover allocation is made.

(2) *Limitations.*—For purposes of determining carryover-allocation basis under paragraph (b)(1) of this section, the following limitations apply.

(i) *Taxpayer must have basis in land or depreciable property related to the project.*—A taxpayer has carryover-allocation basis to the extent that it has basis in land or depreciable property and the land or depreciable property is reasonably expected to be part of the project for which the carryover allocation is made. This basis includes all items that are properly capitalizable with respect to the land or depreciable property. For example, a nonrefundable downpayment for, or an amount paid to acquire an option to purchase, land or depreciable property may be included in carryover-allocation basis if properly capitalizable into the basis of land or depreciable property that is reasonably expected to be part of a project.

(ii) *High cost areas.*—Any increase in eligible basis that may result under section 42(d)(5)(C) from a building's location in a qualified census tract or difficult development area is not taken into account in determining carryover-allocation basis or reasonably expected basis.

(iii) *Amounts not treated as paid or incurred.*—An amount is not includible in carryover-allocation basis unless it is treated as paid or incurred under the method of accounting used by the taxpayer. For example, a cash method taxpayer cannot include construction costs in carryover-allocation basis unless the costs have been paid, and an accrual method taxpayer cannot include construction costs in carryover-allocation basis unless they have been properly accrued. See paragraph (b)(2)(iv) of this section for a special rule for fees.

(iv) *Fees.*—A fee is includible in carryover-allocation basis only to the extent the requirements of paragraph (b)(2)(iii) of this section are met and—

(A) The fee is reasonable;

(B) The taxpayer is legally obligated to pay the fee;

(C) The fee is capitalizable as part of the taxpayer's basis in land or depreciable property that is reasonably expected to be part of the project;

(D) The fee is not paid (or to be paid) by the taxpayer to itself; and

(E) If the fee is paid (or to be paid) by the taxpayer to a related person, and the taxpayer uses the cash method of accounting, the taxpayer could properly accrue the fee under the accrual method of accounting (considering, for example, the rules of section 461(h)). A person is a related person if the person bears a relationship to the taxpayer specified in sections 267(b) or 707(b)(1), or if the person and the taxpayer are engaged in trades or businesses under common control (within the meaning of subsections (a) and (b) of section 52).

(3) *Reasonably expected basis.*—Rules similar to the rules of paragraphs (a) and (b) of this section apply in determining the taxpayer's reasonably expected basis in a project (land and depreciable basis) as of the close of the second calendar year following the calendar year of the allocation.

(4) *Examples.*—The following examples illustrate the rules of paragraphs (a) and (b) of this section.

Example 1. (i) *Facts.* C, an accrual-method taxpayer, receives a carryover allocation from Agency, the state housing credit agency, in May of 2003. As of that date, C has not begun construction of the low-income housing building C plans to build. However, C has owned the land on which C plans to build the building since 1985. C's basis in the land is $100,000. C reasonably expects that by the end of 2005, C's basis in the project of which the building is to be a part will be $2,000,000. C also expects that because the project is located in a qualified census tract, C will be able to increase its basis in the project to $2,600,000. Before the close of 2003, C incurs $150,000 of costs for architects' fees and site preparation. C properly accrues these costs under its method of accounting and capitalizes the costs.

(ii) *Determination of carryover-allocation basis.* C's $100,000 basis in the land is includible in carryover-allocation basis even though C has owned the land since 1985. The $150,000 of costs C has incurred for architects' fees and site preparation are also includible in carryover-allocation basis. The expected increase in basis due to the project's location in a qualified census tract is not taken into account in determining C's carryover-allocation basis. Accordingly, C's carryover-allocation basis in the project of which the building is a part is $250,000.

(iii) *Determination of whether building is qualified.* C's reasonably expected basis in the project at the close of the second calendar year following the calendar year of allocation is $2,000,000. The expected increase in eligible basis due to the project's location in a qualified census tract is not taken into account in determining this amount. Because C's carryover-allocation basis is more than 10 percent of C's reasonably expected basis in the project of which the building is a part, the building for which C received the carryover allocation is a qualified building for purposes of section 42(h)(1)(E)(ii) and paragraph (a) of this section.

Example 2. (i) *Facts.* D, an accrual-method taxpayer, received a carryover allocation from Agency, the state housing credit agency of State X, on September 12, 2003. As of that date, D has not begun construction of the low-income housing building D plans to build and D does not have basis in the land on which D plans to build the building. From September 12, 2003, to the close of March 12, 2004, D incurs some costs related to the planned building, including architects' fees. As of the close of March 12, 2004, these costs do not exceed 10 percent of D's reasonably expected basis in the single-building project as of the close of 2005.

(ii) *Determination of whether building is qualified.* Because D's carryover-allocation basis as of the close of March 12, 2004, is not more than 10 percent of D's reasonably expected basis in the single-building project, the building is not a qualified building for purposes of section 42(h)(1)(E)(ii) and paragraph (a) of this section. Accordingly, the carryover allocation to D must be returned to the Agency. The allocation is valid for purposes of determining the amount of credit allocated by Agency from State X's 2003 State housing credit ceiling, but is included in the returned credit component of State X's 2004 housing credit ceiling.

(c) *Verification of basis by Agency.*—(1) *Verification requirement.*—An Agency that makes a carryover allocation to a taxpayer must verify that the taxpayer has met the 10 percent basis requirement of paragraph (a)(2) of this section.

(2) *Manner of verification.*—An Agency may verify that a taxpayer has incurred more than 10 percent of its reasonably expected basis in a project by obtaining a certification from the taxpayer, in writing and under penalty of perjury, that the taxpayer has incurred by the close of the calendar year of the allocation (for allocations made before July 1) or by the close of the date that is 6 months after the date the allocation is made (for allocations made after June 30) more than 10 percent of the reasonably expected basis in the project. The certification must be accompanied by supporting documentation that the Agency must review. Supporting documentation may include, for example, copies of checks or other records of payments. Alternatively, an Agency may verify that the taxpayer has incurred adequate basis by requiring that the taxpayer obtain from an attorney or certified public accountant a written certification to the Agency, that the attorney or accountant has examined all eligible costs incurred with respect to the project and that, based upon this examination, it is the attorney's or accountant's belief that the taxpayer has incurred more than 10 percent of its reasonably expected basis in the project by the close of the calendar year of the allocation (for allocations made before July 1) or by the close of the date that is 6 months after the date the allocation is made (for allocations made after June 30).

(3) *Time of verification.*—(i) *Allocations made before July 1.*—For a carryover allocation made before July 1, an Agency may require that the basis certification be submitted to or received by the Agency prior to the close of the calendar year of allocation or within a reasonable time following the close of the calendar year of allocation. The Agency will need to verify basis as provided in paragraph (c)(2) of this section to accurately complete the Form 8610, "Annual Low-Income Housing Credit Agencies Report," and the Schedule A (Form 8610), "Carryover Allocation of Low-Income Housing Credit," for the calendar year of the allocation. If the basis certification is not timely made, or supporting documentation is lacking, inadequate, or does not actually support the certification, the Agency should notify the taxpayer and try to get adequate documentation. If the Agency cannot verify before the Form 8610 is filed that the taxpayer has satisfied the 10 percent basis requirement for a carryover allocation made before July 1, the allocation is not valid and is treated as if it had not been made, and the carryover allocation should not be reported on the Schedule A (Form 8610).

(ii) *Allocations made after June 30.*—An Agency may require that the basis certification be submitted to or received by the Agency prior to the close of the date that is 6 months after the date the allocation was made or within a reasonable period of time following the close of the date that is 6 months after the date the allocation was made. The Agency will need to verify basis as provided in paragraph (c)(2) of this section. If the basis certification is not timely made, or supporting documentation is lacking, inadequate, or does not actually support the certification, the Agency should notify the taxpayer and try to get adequate documentation. If the Agency cannot verify that the taxpayer has satisfied the 10 percent basis requirement for a carryover allocation made after June 30, the allocation must be returned to the Agency. The carryover allocation is a valid allocation for the calendar year of the allocation, but is included in the returned credit component of the State housing credit ceiling for the calendar year following the calendar year of the allocation.

(d) *Requirements for making carryover allocations.*—(1) *In general.*—Generally, an allocation is made when an Agency issues the Form 8609, "Low-Income Housing Credit Allocation Certification," for a building. See § 1.42-1T(d)(8)(ii). An Agency does not issue the Form 8609 for a building until the building is placed in service. However, in cases where allocations of credit are made pursuant to section 42(h)(1)(E) (relating to carryover allocations for buildings) or section 42(h)(1)(F) (relating to carryover allocations for multiple-building projects), Form 8609 is not used as the allocating document because the buildings are not yet in service. When an allocation is made pursuant to section 42(h)(1)(E) or (F), the allocating document is the document meeting the requirements of paragraph (d)(2) of this section. In addition, when an allocation is made pursuant to section 42(h)(1)(F), the requirements of paragraph (d)(3) of this section must be met for the allocation to be valid. An allocation pursuant to section 42(h)(1)(E) or (F) reduces the state housing credit ceiling for the year in which the allocation is made, whether or not the Form 8609 is also issued in that year.

(2) *Requirements for allocation.*—An allocation pursuant to section 42(h)(1)(E) or (F) is made when an allocation document containing the following information is completed, signed, and dated by an authorized official of the Agency—

(i) The address of each building in the project, or if none exists, a specific description of the location of each building;

(ii) The name, address, and taxpayer identification number of the taxpayer receiving the allocation;

(iii) The name and address of the Agency;

(iv) The taxpayer identification number of the Agency;

(v) The date of the allocation;

(vi) The housing credit dollar amount allocated to the building or project, as applicable;

(vii) The taxpayer's reasonably expected basis in the project (land and depreciable basis) as of the close of the second calendar year following the calendar year in which the allocation is made;

(viii) For carryover allocations made before July 1, the taxpayer's basis in the project (land and depreciable basis) as of the close of the calendar year of the allocation and the percentage that basis bears to the reasonably expected basis in the project (land and depreciable basis) as of the close of the second calendar year following the calendar year of allocation;

(ix) The date that each building in the project is expected to be placed in service; and

(x) The Building Identification Number (B.I.N.) to be assigned to each building in the project. The B.I.N. must reflect the year an allocation is first made to the building, regardless of the year that the building is placed in service. This B.I.N. must be used for all allocations of credit for the building. For example, rehabilitation expenditures treated as a separate new building under section 42(e) should not have a separate B.I.N. if the building to which the rehabilitation expenditures are made has a B.I.N. In this case, the B.I.N. used for the rehabilitation expenditures shall be the B.I.N. previously assigned to the building, although the rehabilitation expenditures must have a separate Form 8609 for the allocation. Similarly, a newly constructed building that receives an allocation of credit in different calendar years must have a separate Form 8609 for each allocation. The B.I.N. assigned to the building for the first allocation must be used for the subsequent allocation.

(3) *Special rules for project-based allocations.*—(i) *In general.*—An allocation pursuant to section 42(h)(1)(F) (a project-based allocation) must meet the requirements of this section as well as the requirements of section 42(h)(1)(F), including the minimum basis requirement of section 42(h)(1)(E)(ii).

(ii) *Requirement of section 42(h)(1)(F)(i)(III).*—An allocation satisfies the requirement of section 42(h)(1)(F)(i)(III) if the Form 8609 that is issued for each building that is placed in service in the project states the portion of the project-based allocation that is applied to that building.

(4) *Recordkeeping requirements.*—(i) *Taxpayer.*—When an allocation is made pursuant to section 42(h)(1)(E) or (F), the taxpayer must retain a copy of the allocation document. The Form 8609 that reflects the allocation must be filed for the first taxable year that the credit is claimed and for each taxable year thereafter throughout the compliance period, whether or not a credit is claimed for the taxable year.

(ii) *Agency.*—The Agency must retain the original carryover allocation document made under paragraph (d)(2) of this section and file Schedule A (Form 8610) with the Agency's Form 8610 for the year the allocation is made. The Agency must also retain a copy of the Form 8609 that is issued to the taxpayer and file the original with the Agency's Form 8610 that reflects the year the form is issued.

(5) *Separate procedure for election of appropriate percentage month.*—If a taxpayer receives an allocation under section 42(h)(1)(E) or (F) and wishes to elect under section 42(b)(2)(A)(ii) to use the appropriate percentage for a month other than the month in which a building is placed in service, the requirements specified in §1.42-8 must be met for the election to be effective.

(e) *Special rules.*—The following rules apply for purposes of this section.

(1) *Treatment of partnerships and other flow-through entities.*—With respect to taxpayers that own projects through partnerships or other flow-through entities (e.g., S corporations, estates, or trusts), carryover-allocation basis is determined at the entity level using the rules provided by this section. In addition, the entity is responsible for providing to the Agency the certification and documentation required under the basis verification requirement in paragraph (c) of this section.

(2) *Transferees.*—If land or depreciable property that is expected to be part of a project is transferred after a carryover allocation has been made for a building that is reasonably expected to be part of the project, but by the close of the calendar year of the allocation (for allocations made before July 1) or by the close of the date that is 6 months after the date the allocation is made (for allocations made after June 30), the transferee's carryover-allocation basis is determined under the principles of this section and section 42(d)(7). See also Rev. Rul. 91-38, 1991-2 C.B. 3 (see §601.601(d)(2)(ii)(b) of this chapter). In addition, the transferee is treated as the taxpayer for

purposes of the basis verification requirement of this section, and therefore, is responsible for providing to the Agency the required certifications and documentation. [Reg. §1.42-6.]

☐ [*T.D. 8520, 3-2-94. Amended by T.D. 8859, 1-13-2000 and T.D. 9110, 12-31-2003.*]

[Reg. §1.42-7]

§1.42-7. Substantially bond-financed buildings.—[Reserved]

☐ [*T.D. 8520, 3-2-94.*]

[Reg. §1.42-8]

§1.42-8. Election of appropriate percentage month.—(a) *Election under section 42(b)(2)(A)(ii)(I) to use the appropriate percentage for the month of a binding agreement.*—(1) *In general.*—For purposes of section 42(b)(2)(A)(ii)(I), an agreement between a taxpayer and an Agency as to the housing credit dollar amount to be allocated to a building is considered binding if it—

(i) Is in writing;

(ii) Is binding under state law on the Agency, the taxpayer, and all successors in interest;

(iii) Specifies the type(s) of building(s) to which the housing credit dollar amount applies (i.e., a newly constructed or existing building, or substantial rehabilitation treated as a separate new building under section 42(e));

(iv) Specifies the housing credit dollar amount to be allocated to the building(s); and

(v) Is dated and signed by the taxpayer and the Agency during the month in which the requirements of paragraphs (a)(1)(i) through (iv) of this section are met.

(2) *Effect on state housing credit ceiling.*—Generally, a binding agreement described in paragraph (a)(1) of this section is an agreement by the Agency to allocate credit to the taxpayer at a future date. The binding agreement may include a reservation of credit or a binding commitment (under section 42(h)(1)(C)) to allocate credit in a future taxable year. A reservation or a binding commitment to allocate credit in a future year has no effect on the state housing credit ceiling until the year the Agency actually makes an allocation. However, if the binding agreement is also a carryover allocation under section 42(h)(1)(E) or (F), the state housing credit ceiling is reduced by the amount allocated by the Agency to the taxpayer in the year the carryover allocation is made. For a binding agreement to be a valid carryover allocation, the requirements of paragraph (a)(1) of this section and §1.42-6 must be met.

(3) *Time and manner of making election.*—An election under section 42(b)(2)(A)(ii)(I) may be made either as part of the binding agreement under paragraph (a)(1) of this section to allocate a specific housing credit dollar amount or in a separate document that references the binding agreement. In either case, the election must—

(i) Be in writing;

(ii) Reference section 42(b)(2)(A)(ii)(I);

(iii) Be signed by the taxpayer;

(iv) If it is in a separate document, reference the binding agreement that meets the requirements of paragraph (a)(1) of this section; and

(v) Be notarized by the 5th day following the end of the month in which the binding agreement was made.

(4) *Multiple agreements.*—(i) *Rescinded agreements.*—A taxpayer may not make an election under section 42(b)(2)(A)(ii)(I) for a building if an election has previously been made for the building for a different month. For example, assume a taxpayer entered into a binding agreement for allocation of a specific housing credit dollar amount to a building and made the election under section 42(b)(2)(A)(ii)(I) to apply the appropriate percentage for the month of the binding agreement. If the binding agreement subsequently is rescinded under state law, and the taxpayer enters into a new binding agreement for allocation of a specific housing credit dollar amount to the building, the taxpayer must apply to the building the appropriate percentage for the elected month of the rescinded binding agreement. However, if no prior election was made with respect to the rescinded binding agreement, the taxpayer may elect the appropriate percentage for the month of the new binding agreement.

(ii) *Increases in credit.*—The election under section 42(b)(2)(A)(ii)(I), once made, applies to any increase in the credit amount allocated for a building, whether the increase occurs in the same or in a subsequent year. However, in the case of a binding agreement (or carryover allocation that is treated as a binding agreement) to allocate a credit amount under section 42(e)(1) for substantial rehabilitation treated as a separate new building, a taxpayer may make the election under section 42(b)(2)(A)(ii)(I) notwithstanding that a prior election under section 42(b)(2)(A)(ii)(I) is in effect for a prior allocation of credit for a substantial rehabilitation that was previously placed in service under section 42(e).

(5) *Amount allocated.*—The housing credit dollar amount eventually allocated to a building may be more or less than the amount specified in the binding agreement. Depending on the Agency's determination pursuant to section 42(m)(2) as to the financial feasibility of the building (or project), the Agency may allocate a greater housing credit dollar amount to the building (provided that the Agency has additional housing credit dollar amounts available to allocate for the calendar year of the allocation) or the Agency may allocate a lesser housing credit dollar amount. Under section 42(h)(7)(D), in allocating a housing credit dollar amount, the Agency must specify the applicable percentage and maximum qualified basis of the building. The applicable percentage may be less, but not greater than, the appropriate percentage for the month the building is placed in service, or the month elected by the taxpayer under section 42(b)(2)(A)(ii)(I). Whether the appropriate percentage is the appropriate percentage for the 70-percent present value credit or the 30-percent present value credit is determined under section 42(i)(2) when the building is placed in service.

(6) *Procedures.*—(i) *Taxpayer.*—The taxpayer must give the original notarized election statement to the Agency before the close of the 5th calendar day following the end of the month in which the binding agreement is made. The taxpayer must retain a copy of the binding agreement and the election statement.

(ii) *Agency.*—The Agency must retain the original of the binding agreement and election statement and, to the extent required by Schedule A (Form 8610), "Carryover Allocation of Low-Income Housing Credit," account for the binding agreement and election statement on that schedule.

(7) *Examples.*—The following examples illustrate the provisions of this section. In each example, X is the taxpayer, Agency is the state housing credit agency, and the carryover allocations meet the requirements of §1.42-6 and are otherwise valid.

Example 1. (i) In August 2003, X and Agency enter into an agreement that Agency will allocate $100,000 of housing credit dollar amount for the low-income housing building X is constructing. The agreement is binding and meets all the requirements of paragraph (a)(1) of this section. The agreement is a reservation of credit, not an allocation, and therefore, has no effect on the state housing credit ceiling. On or before September 5, 2003, X signs and has notarized a written election statement that meets the requirements of paragraph (a)(3) of this section. The applicable percentage for the building is the appropriate percentage for the month of August 2003.

(ii) Agency makes a carryover allocation of $100,000 of housing credit dollar amount for the building on October 2, 2003. The carryover allocation reduces Agency's state housing credit ceiling for 2003. Due to unexpectedly high construction costs, when X places the building in service in July 2004, the product of the building's qualified basis and the applicable percentage for the building (the appropriate percentage for the month of August 2003) is $150,000, rather than $100,000. Notwithstanding that only $100,000 of credit was allocated for the building in 2003, Agency may allocate an additional $50,000 of housing credit dollar amount for the building from its state housing credit ceiling for 2004. The appropriate percentage for the month of August 2003 is the applicable percentage for the building for the entire $150,000 of credit allocated for the building, even though separate allocations were made in 2003 and 2004. Because allocations were made for the building in two separate calendar years, Agency must issue two Forms 8609, "Low-Income Housing Credit Allocation Certification," to X. One Form 8609 must reflect the $100,000 allocation made in 2003, and the other Form 8609 must reflect the $50,000 allocation made in 2004.

(iii) X gives the original notarized statement to Agency on or before September 5, 2003, and retains a copy of the binding agreement, election statement, and carryover allocation document.

(iv) Agency retains the original of the binding agreement, election statement, and 2003 carryover allocation document. Agency accounts for the binding agreement, election statement, and 2003 carryover allocation on the Schedule A (Form 8610) that it files for the 2003 calendar year. After the building is placed in service in 2004, and assuming other necessary requirements for issuing a Form 8609 are met (for example, taxpayer has certified all sources and uses of funds and development costs for the building under §1.42-17), Agency issues to X a copy of the Form 8609 reflecting the 2003 carryover allocation of $100,000. Agency files the original of this Form 8609 with the Form 8610, "Annual Low-Income Housing Credit Agencies Report," that it files for the 2004 calendar year. Agency also issues to X a copy of the Form 8609 reflecting the 2004 allocation of $50,000 and files the original of this Form 8609 with the Form 8610 that it files for the 2004 calendar year. Agency retains copies of the Forms 8609 that are issued to X.

Example 2. (i) In September 2003, X and Agency enter into an agreement that Agency will allocate $70,000 of housing credit dollar amount for rehabilitation expenditures that X is incurring and that X will treat as a new low-income housing building under section 42(e)(1). The agreement is binding and meets all the requirements of paragraph (a)(1) of this section. The agreement is a reservation of credit, not an allocation, and therefore, has no effect on Agency's state housing credit ceiling. On or before October 5, 2003, X signs and has notarized a written election statement that meets the requirements of paragraph (a)(3) of this section. The applicable percentage for the building is the appropriate percentage for the month of September 2003. Agency makes a carryover allocation of $70,000 of housing credit dollar amount for the building on November 15, 2003. The carryover allocation reduces by $70,000 Agency's state housing credit ceiling for 2003.

(ii) In October 2004, X and Agency enter into another binding agreement meeting the requirements of paragraph (a)(1) of this section. Under the agreement, Agency will allocate $50,000 of housing credit dollar amount for additional rehabilitation expenditures by X that qualify as a second separate new building under section 42(e)(1). On or before November 5, 2004, X signs and has notarized a written election statement meeting the requirements of paragraph (a)(3) of this section. On December 1, 2004, X receives a carryover allocation under section 42(h)(1)(E) for $50,000. The carryover allocation reduces by $50,000 Agency's state housing credit ceiling for 2004. The applicable percentage for the rehabilitation expenditures treated as the second separate new building is the appropriate percentage for the month of October 2004, not September 2003. The appropriate percentage for the month of September 2003 still applies to the allocation of $70,000 for the rehabilitation expenditures treated as first separate new building. Because allocations were made for the building in two separate calendar years, Agency must issue two Forms 8609 to X. One Form 8609 must reflect the $70,000 allocation made in 2003, and the other Form 8609 must reflect the $50,000 allocation made in 2004.

(iii) X gives the first original notarized statement to Agency on or before October 5, 2003, and retains a copy of the first binding agreement, election statement, and carryover allocation document issued in 2003. X gives the second original notarized statement to Agency on or before November 5, 2004, and retains a copy of the second binding agreement, election statement, and carryover allocation document issued in 2004.

(iv) Agency retains the original of the binding agreements, election statements, and carryover allocation documents. Agency accounts for the binding agreement, election statement, and 2003 carryover allocation on the Schedule A (Form 8610) that it files for the 2003 calendar year. Agency also accounts for the binding agreement, election statement, and 2004 carryover allocation on the Schedule A (Form 8610) that it files for the 2004 calendar year. After each separate new building is placed in service, and assuming other necessary requirements for issuing a Form 8609 are met (for example, taxpayer has certified all sources and uses of funds and development costs for the building under §1.42-17), the Agency will issue to X a copy of the Form 8609 reflecting the 2003 carryover allocation of $70,000 and a copy of the Form 8609 reflecting the 2004 carryover allocation of $50,000, respectively. Agency files the original of each Form 8609 with the Form 8610 that reflects the calendar year each Form 8609 is issued. Agency retains copies of the Forms 8609 that are issued to X.

(b) *Election under section 42(b)(2)(A)(ii)(II) to use the appropriate percentage for the month tax-exempt bonds are issued.*—(1) *Time and manner of making election.*—In the case of any building to which section 42(h)(4)(B) applies, an election under section 42(b)(2)(A)(ii)(II) to use the appropriate percentage for the month tax-exempt bonds are issued must—

(i) Be in writing;

(ii) Reference section 42(b)(2)(A)(ii)(II);

(iii) Specify the percentage of the aggregate basis of the building and the land on which the building is located that is financed with the proceeds of obligations described in section 42(h)(4)(A) (tax-exempt bonds);

(iv) State the month in which the tax-exempt bonds are issued;

(v) State that the month in which the tax-exempt bonds are issued is the month elected for the appropriate percentage to be used for the building;

(vi) Be signed by the taxpayer; and

(vii) Be notarized by the 5th day following the end of the month in which the bonds are issued.

(2) *Bonds issued in more than one month.*—If a building described in section 42(h)(4)(B) (substantially bond-financed building) is financed with tax-exempt bonds issued in more than one month, the taxpayer may elect the appropriate percentage for any month in

which the bonds are issued. Once the election is made, the appropriate percentage elected applies for the building even if all bonds are not issued in that month. The requirements of this paragraph (b), including the time limitation contained in paragraph (b)(1)(vii) of this section, must also be met.

(3) *Limitations on appropriate percentage.*—Under section 42(m)(2)(D), the credit allowable for a substantially bond-financed building is limited to the amount necessary to assure the project's feasibility. Accordingly, in making the determination under section 42(m)(2), an Agency may use an applicable percentage that is less, but not greater than, the appropriate percentage for the month the building is placed in service, or the month elected by the taxpayer under section 42(b)(2)(A)(ii)(II).

(4) *Procedures.*—(i) *Taxpayer.*—The taxpayer must provide the original notarized election statement to the Agency before the close of the 5th calendar day following the end of the month in which the bonds are issued. If an authority other than the Agency issues the tax-exempt bonds, the taxpayer must also give the Agency a signed statement from the issuing authority that certifies the information described in paragraphs (b)(1)(iii) and (iv) of this section. The taxpayer must also retain a copy of the election statement.

(ii) *Agency.*—The Agency must retain the original of the election statement and a copy of the Form 8609 that reflects the election statement. The Agency must file an additional copy of the Form 8609 with the Agency's Form 8610 that reflects the calendar year the Form 8609 is issued. [Reg. § 1.42-8.]

☐ [*T.D. 8520, 3-2-94. Amended by T.D. 9110, 12-31-2003.*]

[Reg. § 1.42-9]

§ 1.42-9. For use by the general public.—(a) *General rule.*—If a residential rental unit in a building is not for use by the general public, the unit is not eligible for a section 42 credit. A residential rental unit is for use by the general public if the unit is rented in a manner consistent with housing policy governing nondiscrimination, as evidenced by rules or regulations of the Department of Housing and Urban Development (HUD) (24 CFR subtitle A and Chapters I through XX). See HUD Handbook 4350.3 (or its successor). A copy of HUD Handbook 4350.3 may be requested by writing to: HUD, Directives Distribution Section, room B-100, 451 7th Street, SW, Washington, DC 20410.

(b) *Limitations.*—Notwithstanding paragraph (a) of this section, if a residential rental unit is provided only for a member of a social organization or provided by an employer for its employees, the unit is not for use by the general public and is not eligible for credit under section 42. In addition, any residential rental unit that is part of a hospital, nursing home, sanitarium, lifecare facility, trailer park, or intermediate care facility for the mentally and physically handicapped is not for use by the general public and is not eligible for credit under section 42.

(c) *Treatment of units not for use by the general public.*—The costs attributable to a residential rental unit that is not for use by the general public are not excludable from eligible basis by reason of the unit's ineligibility for the credit under this section. However, in calculating the applicable fraction, the unit is treated as a residential rental unit that is not a low-income unit. [Reg. § 1.42-9.]

☐ [*T.D. 8520, 3-2-94.*]

[Reg. § 1.42-10]

§ 1.42-10. Utility allowances.—(a) *Inclusion of utility allowances in gross rent.*—If the cost of any utility (other than telephone, cable television, or Internet) for a residential rental unit is paid directly by the tenant(s), and not by or through the owner of the building, the gross rent for that unit includes the applicable utility allowance determined under this section. For purposes of the preceding sentence, if the cost of a particular utility for a residential unit is paid pursuant to an actual-consumption submetering arrangement within the meaning of paragraph (e)(1) of this section, then that cost is treated as being paid directly by the tenant(s) and not by or through the owner of the building. This section only applies for purposes of determining gross rent under section 42(g)(2)(B)(ii) as to rent-restricted units.

(b) *Applicable utility allowances.*—(1) *Buildings assisted by the Rural Housing Service.*—If a building receives assistance from the Rural Housing Service (RHS-assisted building), the applicable utility allowance for all rent-restricted units in the building is the utility allowance determined under the method prescribed by the Rural Housing Service (RHS) for the building (whether or not the building or its tenants also receive other state or federal assistance).

(2) *Buildings with Rural Housing Service assisted tenants.*—If any tenant in a building receives RHS rental assistance payments (RHS tenant assistance), the applicable utility allowance for all rent-restricted units in the building (including any units occupied by tenants receiving rental assistance payments from the Department of Housing and Urban Development (HUD)) is the applicable RHS utility allowance.

(3) *Buildings regulated by the Department of Housing and Urban Development.*—If neither a building nor any tenant in the building receives RHS housing assistance, and the rents and utility allowances of the building are regulated by HUD (HUD-regulated buildings), the applicable utility allowance for all rent-restricted units in the building is the applicable HUD utility allowance.

(4) *Other buildings.*—If a building is neither an RHS-assisted nor a HUD-regulated building, and no tenant in the building receives RHS tenant assistance, the applicable utility allowance for rent-restricted units in the building is determined under the following methods.

(i) *Tenants receiving HUD rental assistance.*—The applicable utility allowance for any rent-restricted units occupied by tenants receiving HUD rental assistance payments (HUD tenant assistance) is the applicable Public Housing Authority (PHA) utility allowance established for the Section 8 Existing Housing Program.

(ii) *Other tenants.*—(A) *General rule.*—If none of the rules of paragraphs (b)(1), (2), (3), and (4)(i) of this section apply to determine the appropriate utility allowance for a rent-restricted unit, then the appropriate utility allowance for the unit is the applicable PHA utility allowance. However, if a local utility company estimate is obtained for any unit in the building in accordance with paragraph (b)(4)(ii)(B) of this section, that estimate becomes the appropriate utility allowance for all rent-restricted units of similar size and construction in the building. This local utility company estimate procedure is not available for and does not apply to units to which the rules of paragraph (b)(1), (2), (3), or (4)(i) of this section apply. However, if a local utility company estimate is obtained for any unit in the building under paragraph (b)(4)(ii)(B) of this section, a State or local housing credit agency (Agency) provides a building owner with an estimate for any unit in a building under paragraph (b)(4)(ii)(C) of this section, a cost estimate is calculated using the HUD Utility Schedule Model under paragraph (b)(4)(ii)(D) of this section, or a cost estimate is calculated by an energy consumption model under paragraph (b)(4)(ii)(E) of this section, then the estimate under paragraph (b)(4)(ii)(B), (C), (D), or (E) becomes the applicable utility allowance for all rent-restricted units of similar size and construction in the building. Paragraphs (b)(4)(ii)(B), (C), (D), and (E) of this section do not apply to units to which the rules of paragraphs (b)(1), (2), (3), or (4)(i) of this section apply.

(B) *Utility company estimate.*—Any interested party (including a low-income tenant, a building owner, or an Agency) may obtain a local utility company estimate for a unit. The estimate is obtained when the interested party receives, in writing, information from a local utility company providing the estimated cost of that utility for a unit of similar size and construction for the geographic area in which the building containing the unit is located. In the case of deregulated utility services, the interested party is required to obtain an estimate only from one utility company even if multiple companies can provide the same utility service to a unit. However, the utility company must offer utility services to the building in order for that utility company's rates to be used in calculating utility allowances. The estimate should include all component deregulated charges for providing the utility service. The local utility company estimate may be obtained by an interested party at any time during the building's extended use period (see section 42(h)(6)(D)) or, if the building does not have an extended use period, during the building's compliance period (see section 42(i)(1)). Unless the parties agree otherwise, costs incurred in obtaining the estimate are borne by the initiating party. The interested party that obtains the local utility company estimate (the initiating party) must retain the original of the utility company estimate and must furnish a copy of the local utility company estimate to the owner of the building (where the initiating party is not the owner), and the Agency that allocated credit to the building (where the initiating party is not the Agency). The owner of the building must make available copies of the utility company estimate to the tenants in the building.

(C) *Agency estimate.*—A building owner may obtain a utility estimate for each unit in the building from the Agency that has jurisdiction over the building provided the Agency agrees to provide the estimate. The estimate is obtained when the building owner receives, in writing, information from the Agency providing the estimated per-unit cost of the utilities for units of similar size and construction for the geographic area in which the building containing the units is located. The Agency estimate may be obtained by a building owner at any time during the building's extended use period (see section 42(h)(6)(D)). Costs incurred in obtaining the estimate are borne by the building owner. In establishing an accurate utility allowance estimate for a particular building, an Agency (or an agent or other private contractor of the Agency that is a qualified professional within the meaning of paragraph (b)(4)(ii)(E) of this section) must take into account, among other things, local utility rates, property type, climate and degree-day variables by region in the State, taxes and fees on utility charges, building materials, and mechanical systems. If the Agency uses an agent or other private contractor to calculate the utility estimates, the agent or contractor and the owner must not be related within the meaning of section 267(b) or 707(b). An Agency may also use actual utility company usage data and rates for the building. However, use of the Agency estimate is limited to the building's consumption data for the twelve-month period ending no earlier than 60 days prior to the beginning of the 90-day period under paragraph (c)(1) of this section and utility rates used for the Agency estimate must be no older than the rates in place 60 days prior to the beginning of the 90-day period under paragraph (c)(1) of this section. In the case of newly constructed or renovated buildings with less than 12 months of consumption data, the Agency (or an agent or other private contractor of the Agency that is a qualified professional within the meaning of paragraph (b)(4)(ii)(E) of this section) may use consumption data for the 12-month period of units of similar size and construction in the geographic area in which the building containing the units is located.

(D) *HUD Utility Schedule Model.*—A building owner may calculate a utility estimate using the "HUD Utility Schedule Model" that can be found on the Low-Income Housing Tax Credits page at *www.huduser.org/datasets/lihtc.html* (or successor URL). Utility rates used for the HUD Utility Schedule Model must be no older than the rates in place 60 days prior to the beginning of the 90-day period under paragraph (c)(1) of this section.

(E) *Energy consumption model.*—A building owner may calculate utility estimates using an energy and water and sewage consumption and analysis model (energy consumption model). The energy consumption model must, at a minimum, take into account specific factors including, but not limited to, unit size, building orientation, design and materials, mechanical systems, appliances, characteristics of the building location, and available historical data. The utility consumption estimates must be calculated by a properly licensed engineer or other qualified professional. The qualified professional and the building owner must not be related within the meaning of section 267(b) or 707(b). If a qualified professional is not a properly licensed engineer and if the building owner wants to utilize that qualified professional to calculate utility consumption estimates, then the owner must obtain approval from the Agency that has jurisdiction over the building. Further, regardless of the type of qualified professional, the Agency may approve or disapprove of the energy consumption model or require information before permitting its use. In addition, utility rates used for the energy consumption model must be no older than the rates in place 60 days prior to the beginning of the 90-day period under paragraph (c)(1) of this section.

(c) *Changes in applicable utility allowance.*—(1) *In general.*—If, at any time during the building's extended use period (as defined in section 42(h)(6)(D)), the applicable utility allowance for units changes, the new utility allowance must be used to compute gross rents of the units due 90 days after the change (the 90-day period). For example, if rent must be lowered because a local utility company estimate is obtained that shows a higher utility cost than the otherwise applicable PHA utility allowance, the lower rent must be in effect for rent due at the end of the 90-day period. A building owner using a utility company estimate under paragraph (b)(4)(ii)(B) of this section, the HUD Utility Schedule Model under paragraph (b)(4)(ii)(D) of this section, or an energy consumption model under paragraph (b)(4)(ii)(E) of this section must submit copies of the utility estimates to the Agency that has jurisdiction over the building and make the estimates available to all tenants in the building at the beginning of the 90-day period before the utility allowances can be used in determining the gross rent of rent-restricted units. An Agency may require *additional information from the owner during the 90-day period.* Any utility estimates obtained under the Agency estimate under paragraph (b)(4)(ii)(C) of this section must also be made available to all tenants in the building at the beginning of the 90-day period. The building owner must pay for all costs incurred in obtaining the estimates under paragraphs (b)(4)(ii)(B), (C), (D), and (E) of this section and providing the estimates to the Agency and the tenants. The building owner is not required to review the utility allowances, or implement new utility allowances, until the building has achieved 90 percent occupancy for a period of 90 consecutive days or the end of the first year of the credit period, whichever is earlier.

(2) *Annual review.*—A building owner must review at least once during each calendar year the basis on which utility allowances have been established and must update the applicable utility allowance in accordance with paragraph (c)(1) of this section. The review must take into account any changes to the building such as any energy conservation measures that affect energy consumption and changes in utility rates.

(d) *Record retention.*—The building owner must retain any utility consumption estimates and supporting data as part of the taxpayer's records for purposes of § 1.6001-1(a).

(e) *Actual-consumption submetering arrangements.*—(1) *Definition.*—For purposes of this section, an actual-consumption submetering arrangement for a utility in a residential unit possesses all of the following attributes:

(i) The utility consumed in the unit is described in paragraph (e)(1)(i)(A) or (e)(1)(i)(B) of this section;

(A) The utility is purchased from or through a local utility company by the building owner (or its agent or other party acting on behalf of the building owner).

(B) The utility is not purchased from or through a local utility company and is produced from a renewable source (within the meaning of paragraph (e)(1)(i)(C) of this section).

(C) For purposes of paragraph (e)(1)(i)(B) of this section, a utility is produced from a renewable source if—

(1) It is energy that is produced from energy property described in section 48;

(2) It is energy that is produced from a facility described in section 45(d)(1), (2), (3), (4), (6), (9), or (11); or

(3) It is a utility that is described in guidance published for this purpose in the Internal Revenue Bulletin (see § 601.601(d)(2)(ii) of this chapter).

(D) Determinations under paragraphs (e)(1)(i)(C)(1) and (2) of this section take into account only the manner in which the energy is produced and not who owns the energy property or the facility or whether the applicability of relevant portions of sections 45 and 48 has expired.

(ii) The tenants in the unit are billed for, and pay the building owner (or its agent or other party acting on behalf of the building owner) for, the unit's consumption of the utility;

(iii) The billed amount reflects the unit's actual consumption of the utility. In the case of sewerage charges, however, if the unit's sewerage charges are combined on the bill with water charges and the sewerage charges are determined based on the actual water consumption of the unit, then the bill is treated as reflecting the actual sewerage consumption of the unit; and

(iv) The rate at which the building owner bills for the utility satisfies the following requirements:

(A) To the extent that the utility consumed is described in paragraph (e)(1)(i)(A) of this section, the utility rate charged to the tenants of the unit does not exceed the rate incurred by the building owner for that utility; and

(B) To the extent that the utility consumed is described in paragraph (e)(1)(i)(B) of this section, the utility rate charged to the tenants of the unit does not exceed the highest rate that the tenants would have paid if they had obtained the utility from a local utility company. In determining whether a rate satisfies the preceding sentence, a building owner may rely on the rates published by local utility companies.

(2) *Administrative fees.*—If the owner charges a unit's tenants a fee for administering an actual-consumption submetering arrangement, the fee is not considered gross rent for purposes of section 42(g)(2). The preceding sentence, however, does not apply unless the fee is computed in the same manner for every unit receiving the same submetered utility service, nor does it apply to any amount by which the aggregate monthly fee or fees for all of the unit's utilities under one or more actual-consumption submetering arrangements exceed the greater of—

(i) Five dollars per month;

(ii) An amount (if any) designated by publication in the Internal Revenue Bulletin (see § 601.601(d)(2)(ii) of this chapter); or

(iii) The lesser of—

(A) The dollar amount (if any) specifically prescribed under a State or local law; or

(B) A maximum amount (if any) designated by publication in the Internal Revenue Bulletin (see § 601.601(d)(2)(ii) of this chapter). [Reg. § 1.42-10.]

☐ [*T.D. 8520, 3-2-94. Amended by T.D. 9420, 7-28-2008, T.D. 9755, 3-2-2016 and T.D. 9850, 2-27-2019.*]

Reg. § 1.42-10(e)(2)(iii)(B)

[Reg. §1.42-11]

§1.42-11. Provision of services.—(a) *General rule.*—The furnishing to tenants of services other than housing (whether or not the services are significant) does not prevent the units occupied by the tenants from qualifying as residential rental property eligible for credit under section 42. However, any charges to low-income tenants for services that are not optional generally must be included in gross rent for purposes of section 42(g).

(b) *Services that are optional.*—(1) *General rule.*—A service is optional if payment for the service is not required as a condition of occupancy. For example, for a qualified low-income building with a common dining facility, the cost of meals is not included in gross rent for purposes of section 42(g)(2)(A) if payment for the meals in the facility is not required as a condition of occupancy and a practical alternative exists for tenants to obtain meals other than from the dining facility.

(2) *Continual or frequent services.*—If continual or frequent nursing, medical, or psychiatric services are provided, it is presumed that the services are not optional and the building is ineligible for the credit, as is the case with a hospital, nursing home, sanitarium, lifecare facility, or intermediate care facility for the mentally and physically handicapped. See also §1.42-9(b).

(3) *Required services.*—(i) *General rule.*—The cost of services that are required as a condition of occupancy must be included in gross rent even if federal or state law requires that the services be offered to tenants by building owners.

(ii) *Exceptions.*—(A) *Supportive services.*—Section 42(g)(2)(B)(iii) provides an exception for certain fees paid for supportive services. For purposes of section 42(g)(2)(B)(iii), a supportive service is any service provided under a planned program of services designed to enable residents of a residential rental property to remain independent and avoid placement in a hospital, nursing home, or intermediate care facility for the mentally or physically handicapped. For a building described in section 42(i)(3)(B)(iii) (relating to transitional housing for the homeless) or section 42(i)(3)(B)(iv) (relating to single-room occupancy), a supportive service includes any service provided to assist tenants in locating and retaining permanent housing.

(B) *Specific project exception.*—Gross rent does not include the cost of mandatory meals in any federally-assisted project for the elderly and handicapped (in existence on or before January 9, 1989) that is authorized by 24 CFR part 278 to provide a mandatory meals program. [Reg. §1.42-11.]

☐ [*T.D.* 8520, 3-2-94. *Amended by T.D.* 8859, 1-13-2000.]

[Reg. §1.42-12]

§1.42-12. Effective dates and transitional rules.—(a) *Effective dates.*—(1) *In general.*—Except as provided in paragraphs (a)(2) and (a)(3) of this section, the rules set forth in §§1.42-6 and 1.42-8 through 1.42-12 are applicable on May 2, 1994. However, binding agreements, election statements, and carryover allocation documents entered into before May 2, 1994, that follow the guidance set forth in Notice 89-1, 1989-1 C.B. 620 (see §601.601(d)(2)(ii)(b) of this chapter) need not be changed to conform to the rules set forth in §§1.42-6 and 1.42-8 through 1.42-12.

(2) *Community Renewal Tax Relief Act of 2000.*—(i) *In general.*—Section 1.42-6 (a), (b)(4)(iii) *Example 1* and *Example 2*, (c), (d)(2)(viii), and (e)(2) are applicable for housing credit dollar amounts allocated after January 6, 2004. However, the rules in §1.42-6(a), (b)(4)(iii) *Example 1* and *Example 2*, (c), (d)(2)(viii), and (e)(2) may be applied by Agencies and taxpayers for housing credit dollar amounts allocated after December 31, 2000, and on or before January 6, 2004. Otherwise, subject to the applicable effective dates of the corresponding statutory provisions, the rules that apply for housing credit dollar amounts allocated on or before January 6, 2004, are contained in §1.42-6 in effect on and before January 6, 2004 (see 26 CFR part 1 revised as of April 1, 2003).

(3) *Electronic filing simplification changes.*—Sections 1.42-6(d)(4) and 1.42-8(a)(6)(i), (a)(6)(ii), (a)(7) *Example 1* and *Example 2*, (b)(4)(i), and (b)(4)(ii) are applicable for forms filed after January 6, 2004. The rules that apply for forms filed on or before January 6, 2004, are contained in §1.42-6 and §1.42-8 in effect on and before January 6, 2004 (see 26 CFR part 1 revised as of April 1, 2003).

(4) *Utility allowances.*—The first sentence in §1.42-10(a), §1.42-10(b)(1), (2), (3), and (4), the last two sentences in §1.42-10(b)(4)(ii)(A), the third, fourth, and fifth sentences in §1.42-10(b)(4)(ii)(B), §1.42-10(b)(4)(ii)(C), (D), and (E), and §1.42-10(c) and (d) are applicable to a building owner's taxable years

beginning on or after July 29, 2008. Taxpayers may rely on these provisions before the beginning of the building owner's taxable year beginning on or after July 29, 2008 provided that any utility allowances calculated under these provisions are effective no earlier than the first day of the building owner's taxable year beginning on or after July 29, 2008. The utility allowances provisions that apply to taxable years beginning before July 29, 2008 are contained in §1.42-10 (see 26 CFR part 1 revised as of April 1, 2008).

(5) *Additional effective dates affecting utility allowances.*—(i) The following provisions apply to a building owner's taxable years beginning on or after March 3, 2016—

    (A) The second sentence in §1.42-10(a);

    (B) Section 1.42-10(b)(3);

    (C) The first sentence in §1.42-10(b)(4)(ii)(A);

    (D) Section 1.42-10(b)(4)(ii)(E); and

    (E) Section 1.42-10(e), except as provided in paragraph (a)(5)(iii) of this section.

(ii) Except as provided in paragraph (a)(5)(iii) of this section, a building owner may apply the provisions described in paragraphs (a)(5)(i)(A) through (E) of this section to the building owner's taxable years beginning before March 3, 2016. Otherwise, the utility allowance provisions that apply to those taxable years are contained in §1.42-10, as contained in 26 CFR part 1, revised as of April 1, 2015.

(iii) The provisions in §1.42-10(e)(1)(i) introductory text, (e)(1)(i)(B) through (D), and (e)(1)(iv)(B) apply to a building owner's taxable years beginning on or after March 4, 2019. A building owner, however, may apply these provisions to earlier taxable years. Otherwise, the submetering provisions that apply to taxable years beginning after March 3, 2016, and before March 4, 2019, are contained in §1.42-10 and §1.42-10T as contained in 26 CFR part 1 revised as of April 1, 2016. In addition, a building owner may apply those submetering provisions to taxable years beginning before March 3, 2016.

(b) *Prior periods.*—Notice 89-1, 1989-1 C.B. 620 and Notice 89-6, 1989-1 C.B. 625 (see §601.601(d)(2)(ii)(b) of this chapter) may be applied for periods prior to May 2, 1994.

(c) *Carryover allocations.*—The rule set forth in §1.42-6(d)(4)(ii) relating to the requirement that state and local housing agencies file Schedule A (Form 8610), "Carryover Allocation of the Low-Income Housing Credit," is applicable for carryover allocations made after December 31, 1999. [Reg. §1.42-12.]

☐ [*T.D.* 8520, 3-2-94. *Amended by T.D.* 8859, 1-13-2000; *T.D.* 9110, 12-31-2003, *T.D.* 9420, 7-28-2008, *T.D.* 9755, 3-2-2016 *and T.D.* 9850, 2-27-2019.]

[Reg. §1.42-13]

§1.42-13. Rules necessary and appropriate; housing credit agencies' correction of administrative errors and omissions.—(a) *Publication of guidance.*—Under section 42(n), the Secretary has authority to prescribe regulations as may be necessary or appropriate to carry out the purposes of section 42. The Secretary may also provide guidance through various publications in the Internal Revenue Bulletin. (See §601.601(d)(2)(ii)(b) of this chapter.)

(b) *Correcting administrative errors and omissions.*—(1) *In general.*—An Agency may correct an administrative error or omission with respect to allocations and recordkeeping, as described in paragraph (b)(2) of this section, within a reasonable period after the Agency discovers the administrative error or omission. Whether a correction is made within a reasonable period depends on the facts and circumstances of each situation. Except as provided in paragraph (b)(3)(iii) of this section, an Agency need not obtain the prior approval of the Secretary to correct an administrative error or omission, if the correction is made in accordance with paragraph (b)(3)(i) of this section. The administrative errors and omissions to which this paragraph (b) applies are strictly limited to those described in paragraph (b)(2) of this section, and, thus, do not include, for example, any misinterpretation of the applicable rules and regulations under section 42. Accordingly, an Agency's allocation of a particular calendar year's low-income housing credit dollar amount made after the close of that calendar year, or the use of an incorrect population amount in calculating a State's housing credit ceiling for a calendar year are not administrative errors that can be corrected under this paragraph (b).

(2) *Administrative errors and omissions described.*—An administrative error or omission is a mistake that results in a document that inaccurately reflects the intent of the Agency at the time the document is originally completed or, if the mistake affects a taxpayer, a document that inaccurately reflects the intent of the Agency and the affected taxpayer at the time the document is originally completed. Administrative errors and omissions described in this paragraph (b)(2) include the following—

    (i) A mathematical error;

(ii) An entry on a document that is inconsistent with another entry on the same or another document regarding the same property, or taxpayer;

(iii) A failure in tracking the housing credit dollar amount an Agency has allocated (or that remains to be allocated) in the current calendar year (e.g., a failure to include in its State housing credit ceiling a previously allocated credit dollar amount that has been returned by a taxpayer);

(iv) An omission of information that is required on a document; and

(v) Any other type of error or omission identified by guidance published in the Internal Revenue Bulletin (see § 601.601(d)(2)(ii)(*b*) of this chapter) as an administrative error or omission covered by this paragraph (b).

(3) *Procedures for correcting administrative errors or omissions.*— (i) *In general.*—An Agency's correction of an administrative error or omission, as described in paragraph (b)(2) of this section, must amend the document so that the corrected document reflects the original intent of the Agency, or the Agency and the affected taxpayer, and complies with applicable rules and regulations under section 42.

(ii) *Specific procedures.*—If a document corrects a document containing an administrative error or omission that has not yet been filed with the Internal Revenue Service, the Agency, or the Agency and the affected taxpayer, should complete and file the corrected document as the original. When a document containing an administrative error or omission has already been filed with the Service, the Agency, or the Agency and the affected taxpayer, should refile a copy of the document containing the administrative error or omission, and prominently and clearly note the correction thereon or on an attached new document. The Agency should indicate at the top of the document(s) that the correction is being made under § 1.42-13 of the Income Tax Regulations.

(iii) *Secretary's prior approval required.*—Except as provided in paragraph (b)(3)(vi) of this section, an Agency must obtain the Secretary's prior approval to correct an administrative error or omission, as described in paragraph (b)(2) of this section, if the correction is not made before the close of the calendar year of the error or omission and the correction—

(A) Is a numerical change to the housing credit dollar amount allocated for the building or project;

(B) Affects the determination of any component of the State's housing credit ceiling under section 42(h)(3)(C); or

(C) Affects the State's unused housing credit carryover that is assigned to the Secretary under section 42(h)(3)(D).

(iv) *Requesting the Secretary's approval.*—To obtain the Secretary's approval under paragraph (b)(3)(iii) of this section, an Agency must submit a request for the Secretary's approval within a reasonable period after discovering the administrative error or omission, and must agree to any conditions that may be required by the Secretary under paragraph (b)(3)(v) of this section. When requesting the Secretary's approval, the Agency, or the Agency and the affected taxpayer, must file an application that complies with the requirements of this paragraph (b)(3)(iv). For further information on the application procedure see Rev. Proc. 93-1, 2003-1 I.R.B. 10 (or any subsequent applicable revenue procedure). (See § 601.601(d)(2)(ii)(*b*) of this chapter.) The application requesting the Secretary's approval must contain the following information—

(A) The name, address, and identification number of each affected taxpayer;

(B) The Building Identification Number (B.I.N.) and address of each building or project affected by the administrative error or omission;

(C) A statement explaining the administrative error or omission and the intent of the Agency, or of the Agency and the affected taxpayer, when the document was originally completed;

(D) Copies of any supporting documentation;

(E) A statement explaining the effect, if any, that a correction of the administrative error or omission would have on the housing credit dollar amount allocated for any building or project; and

(F) A statement explaining the effect, if any, that a correction of the administrative error or omission would have on the determination of the components of the State's housing credit ceiling under section 42(h)(3)(C) or on the State's unused housing credit carryover that is assigned to the Secretary under section 42(h)(3)(D).

(v) *Agreement to conditions.*—To obtain the Secretary's approval under paragraph (b)(3)(iii) of this section, an Agency, or the Agency and the affected taxpayer, must agree to the conditions the Secretary considers appropriate.

(vi) *Secretary's automatic approval.*—The Secretary grants automatic approval to correct an administrative error or omission described in paragraph (b)(2) of this section if—

(A) The correction is not made before the close of the calendar year of the error or omission and the correction is a numerical change to the housing credit dollar amount allocated for the building or multiple-building project;

(B) The administrative error or omission resulted in an allocation document (the Form 8609, "Low-Income Housing Credit Allocation Certification," or the allocation document under the requirements of section 42(h)(1)(E) or (F), and § 1.42-6(d)(2)) that either did not accurately reflect the number of buildings in a project (for example, an allocation document for a 10-building project only references 8 buildings instead of 10 buildings), or the correct information (other than the amount of credit allocated on the allocation document);

(C) The administrative error or omission does not affect the Agency's ranking of the building(s) or project and the total amount of credit the Agency allocated to the building(s) or project; and

(D) The Agency corrects the administrative error or omission by following the procedures described in paragraph (b)(3)(vii) of this section.

(vii) *How Agency corrects errors or omissions subject to automatic approval.*—An Agency corrects an administrative error or omission described in paragraph (b)(3)(vi) of this section by—

(A) Amending the allocation document described in paragraph (b)(3)(vi)(B) of this section to correct the administrative error or omission. The Agency will indicate on the amended allocation document that it is making the "correction under § 1.42-13(b)(3)(vii)." If correcting the allocation document requires including any additional B.I.N.(s) in the document, the document must include any B.I.N.(s) already existing for buildings in the project. If possible, the additional B.I.N.(s) should be sequentially numbered from the existing B.I.N.(s);

(B) Amending, if applicable, the Schedule A (Form 8610), "Carryover Allocation of the Low-Income Housing Credit," and attaching a copy of this schedule to Form 8610, "Annual Low-income Housing Credit Agencies Report," for the year the correction is made. The Agency will indicate on the schedule that it is making the "correction under § 1.42-13(b)(3)(vii)." For a carryover allocation made before January 1, 2000, the Agency must complete Schedule A (Form 8610), and indicate on the schedule that it is making the "correction under § 1.42-13(b)(3)(vii)";

(C) Amending, if applicable, the Form 8609 and attaching the original of this amended form to Form 8610 for the year the correction is made. The Agency will indicate on the Form 8609 that it is making the "correction under § 1.42-13(b)(3)(vii)"; and

(D) Mailing or otherwise delivering a copy of any amended allocation document and any amended Form 8609 to the affected taxpayer.

(viii) *Other approval procedures.*—The Secretary may grant automatic approval to correct other administrative errors or omissions as designated in one or more documents published either in the Federal Register or in the Internal Revenue Bulletin (see § 601.601(d)(2) of this chapter).

(c) *Examples.*—The following examples illustrate the scope of this section:

Example 1. Individual B applied to Agency X for a reservation of a low-income housing credit dollar amount for a building that is part of a low-income housing project. When applying for the low-income housing credit dollar amount, B informed Agency X that B intended to form Partnership Y to finance the project. After receiving the reservation letter and prior to receiving an allocation, B formed Partnership Y and sold partnership interests to a number of limited partners. B contributed the low-income housing project to Partnership Y in exchange for a partnership interest. B and Partnership Y informed Agency X of the ownership change. When actually allocating the housing credit dollar amount, Agency X sent Partnership Y a document listing B, rather than Partnership Y, as the building's owner. Partnership Y promptly notified Agency X of the error. After reviewing related documents, Agency X determined that it had incorrectly listed B as the building's owner on the allocation document. Since the parties originally intended that Partnership Y would receive the allocation as the owner of the building, Agency X may correct the error without obtaining the Secretary's approval, and insert Partnership Y as the building's owner on the allocation document.

Example 2. Agency Y allocated a lower low-income housing credit dollar amount for a low-income housing building than Agency Y originally intended. After the close of the calendar year of the allocation, B, the building's owner, discovered the error and promptly notified Agency Y. Agency Y reviewed relevant documents and agreed that an error had occurred. Agency Y and B must apply, as provided in paragraph (b)(3)(iv) of this section, for the Secretary's approval before Agency Y may correct the error.

(d) *Effective date.*—This section is effective February 24, 1994. However, an Agency may elect to apply these regulations to administrative errors or omissions that occurred before the publication of these regulations. Any reasonable method used by a State or local housing credit agency to correct an administrative error or omission prior to February 24, 1994 will be considered proper, provided that the method is consistent with the rules of section 42. Paragraphs (b)(3)(vi), (vii), and (viii) of this section are effective January 14, 2000. [Reg. § 1.42-13.]

☐ [*T.D. 8521, 2-23-94. Amended by T.D. 8859, 1-13-2000.*]

[Reg. § 1.42-14]

§ 1.42-14. Allocation rules for post-2000 State housing credit ceiling amount.—(a) *State housing credit ceiling.*—(1) *In general.*—The State housing credit ceiling for a State for any calendar year after 2000 is comprised of four components. The four components are—

(i) The unused State housing credit ceiling, if any, of the State for the preceding calendar year (the unused carryforward component);

(ii) The greater of—

(A) $1.75 ($1.50 for calendar year 2001) multiplied by the State population; or

(B) $2,000,000 (the population component);

(iii) The amount of State housing credit ceiling returned in the calendar year (the returned credit component); plus

(iv) The amount, if any, allocated to the State by the Secretary under section 42(h)(3)(D) from a national pool of unused credit (the national pool component).

(2) *Cost-of-living adjustment.*—(i) *General rule.*—For any calendar year after 2002, the $2,000,000 and $1.75 amounts in paragraph (a)(1)(ii) of this section are each increased by an amount equal to—

(A) The dollar amount; multiplied by

(B) The cost-of-living adjustment determined under section 1(f)(3) for the calendar year by substituting "calendar year 2001" for "calendar year 1992" in section 1(f)(3)(B).

(ii) *Rounding.*—Any increase resulting from the application of paragraph (a)(2)(i) of this section which, in the case of the $2,000,000 amount, is not a multiple of $5,000, is rounded to the next lowest multiple of $5,000, and which, in the case of the $1.75 amount, is not a multiple of 5 cents, is rounded to the next lowest multiple of 5 cents.

(b) *The unused carryforward component.*—The unused carryforward component of the State housing credit ceiling for any calendar year is the unused State housing credit ceiling, if any, of the State for the preceding calendar year. The unused State housing credit ceiling for any calendar year is the excess, if any, of—

(1) The sum of the population, returned credit, and national pool components for the calendar year; over

(2) The aggregate housing credit dollar amount allocated for the calendar year reduced by the housing credit dollar amounts allocated from the unused carryforward component for the calendar year.

(c) *The population component.*—The population component of the State housing credit ceiling of a State for any calendar year is determined pursuant to section 146(j). Thus, a State's population for any calendar year is determined by reference to the most recent census estimate, whether final or provisional, of the resident population of the State released by the Bureau of the Census before the beginning of the calendar year for which the State's housing credit ceiling is set. Unless otherwise prescribed by applicable revenue procedure, determinations of population are based on the most recent estimates of population contained in the Bureau of the Census publication, *Current Population Report, Series P-25; Population Estimates and Projections, Estimates of the Population of States.* For convenience, the Internal Revenue Service publishes the population estimates annually in the Internal Revenue Bulletin. (See § 601.601(d)(2)(ii)(*b*)).

(d) *The returned credit component.*—(1) *In general.*—The returned credit component of the State housing credit ceiling of a State for any calendar year equals the housing credit dollar amount returned during the calendar year that was validly allocated within the State in a prior calendar year to any project that does not become a qualified low-income housing project within the period required by section 42, or as required by the terms of the allocation. The returned credit component also includes credit allocated in a prior calendar year that is returned as a result of the cancellation of an allocation by mutual consent or by an Agency's determination that the amount allocated is not necessary for the financial feasibility of the project. For purposes of this section, credit is allocated within a State if it is

allocated from the State's housing credit ceiling by an Agency of the State or of a constitutional home rule city in the State.

(2) *Limitations and special rules.*—The following limitations and special rules apply for purposes of this paragraph (d).

(i) *General limitations.*—Notwithstanding any other provision of this paragraph (d), returned credit does not include any credit that was—

(A) Allocated prior to calendar year 1990;

(B) Allowable under section 42(h)(4) (relating to the portion of credit attributable to eligible basis financed by certain tax-exempt bonds under section 103); or

(C) Allocated during the same calendar year that it is received back by the Agency.

(ii) *Credit period limitation.*—Notwithstanding any other provision of this paragraph (d), an allocation of credit may not be returned any later than 180 days following the close of the first taxable year of the credit period for the building that received the allocation. After this date, credit that might otherwise be returned expires, and cannot be returned to or reallocated by any Agency.

(iii) *Three-month rule for returned credit.*—An Agency may, in its discretion, treat any portion of credit that is returned from a project after September 30 of a calendar year and that is not reallocated by the close of the calendar year as returned on January 1 of the succeeding calendar year. In this case, the returned credit becomes part of the returned credit component of the State housing credit ceiling for the succeeding calendar year. Any portion of credit that is returned from a project after September 30 of a calendar year that is reallocated by the close of the calendar year is treated as part of the returned credit component of the State housing credit ceiling for the calendar year that the credit was returned.

(iv) *Returns of credit.*—Subject to the limitations of paragraphs (d)(2)(i) and (ii) of this section, credit is returned to the Agency in the following instances in the manner described in paragraph (d)(3) of this section.

(A) *Building not qualified within required time period.*—If a building is not a qualified building within the time period required by section 42, it loses its credit allocation and the credit is returned. For example, a building is not qualified within the required time period if it is not placed in service within the period required by section 42 or if the project of which the building is a part fails to meet the minimum set-aside requirements of section 42(g)(1) by the close of the first year of the credit period. Also, a building that has received a post-June 30 carryover allocation is not qualified within the required time period if the taxpayer does not meet the 10 percent basis requirement by the date that is 6 months after the date the allocation was made (as described in § 1.42-6(a)(2)(ii)).

(B) *Noncompliance with terms of the allocation.*—If a building does not comply with the terms of its allocation, it loses the credit allocation and the credit is returned. The terms of an allocation are the written conditions agreed to by the Agency and the allocation recipient in the allocation document.

(C) *Mutual consent.*—If the Agency and the allocation recipient cancel an allocation of an amount of credit by mutual consent, that amount of credit is returned.

(D) *Amount not necessary for financial feasibility.*—If an Agency determines under section 42(m)(2) that an amount of credit allocated to a project is not necessary for the financial feasibility of the project and its viability as a qualified low-income housing project throughout the credit period, that amount of credit is returned.

(3) *Manner of returning credit.*—(i) *Taxpayer notification.*—After an Agency determines that a building or project no longer qualifies under paragraph (d)(2)(iv)(A), (B), or (D) of this section for all or part of the allocation it received, the Agency must provide written notification to the allocation recipient, or its successor in interest, that all or part of the allocation is no longer valid. The notification must also state the amount of the allocation that is no longer valid. The date of the notification is the date the credit is returned to the Agency. If an allocation is cancelled by mutual consent under paragraph (d)(2)(iv)(C) of this section, there must be a written agreement signed by the Agency, and the allocation recipient, or its successor in interest, indicating the amount of the allocation that is returned to the Agency. The effective date of the agreement is the date the credit is returned to the Agency.

(ii) *Internal Revenue Service notification.*—If a credit is returned within 180 days following the close of the first taxable year of a building's credit period as provided in paragraph (d)(2)(ii) of this section, and a Form 8609, *Low-Income Housing Credit Allocation Certifi-*

cation, has been issued for the building, the Agency must notify the Internal Revenue Service that the credit has been returned. If only part of the credit has been returned, this notification requirement is satisfied when the Agency attaches to an amended Form 8610, *Annual Low-Income Housing Credit Agencies Report*, the original of an amended Form 8609 reflecting the correct amount of credit attributed to the building together with an explanation for the filing of the amended Forms. The Agency must send a copy of the amended Form 8609 to the taxpayer that owns the building. If the building is not issued an amended Form 8609 because all of the credit allocated to the building is returned, notification to the Internal Revenue Service is satisfied by following the requirements prescribed in §1.42-5(e)(3) for filing a Form 8823, *Low-Income Housing Credit Agencies Report of Noncompliance.*

(e) *The national pool component.*—The national pool component of the State housing credit ceiling of a State for any calendar year is the portion of the National Pool allocated to the State by the Secretary for the calendar year. The national pool component for any calendar year is zero unless a State is a *qualified State.* (See paragraph (i) of this section for rules regarding the National Pool and the description of a qualified State.) A national pool component credit that is allocated during a calendar year and returned after the close of the calendar year may qualify as part of the returned credit component of the State housing credit ceiling for the calendar year that the credit is returned..

(f) *When the State housing credit ceiling is determined.*—For purposes of accounting for the State housing credit ceiling on Form 8610 and for purposes of determining the set-aside apportionment for projects involving qualified nonprofit organizations described in section 42(h)(5) and §1.42-1T(c)(5), the State housing credit ceiling for any calendar year is determined at the close of the calendar year.

(g) *Stacking order.*—Credit is treated as allocated from the various components of the State housing credit ceiling in the following order. The first credit allocated for any calendar year is treated as credit from the unused carryforward component of the State housing credit ceiling for the calendar year. After all of the credit in the unused carryforward component has been allocated, any credit allocated is treated as allocated from the sum of the population, returned credit, and national pool components of the State housing credit ceiling.

(h) *Nonprofit set-aside.*—(1) *Determination of set-aside.*—Under section 42(h)(5) and §1.42-1T(c)(5), at least 10 percent of a State housing credit ceiling in any calendar year must be set aside exclusively for projects involving qualified nonprofit organizations (the nonprofit set-aside). However, credit allocated from the nonprofit set-aside in a calendar year and returned in a subsequent calendar year does not retain its nonprofit set-aside character. The credit becomes part of the returned credit component of the State housing credit ceiling for the calendar year that the credit is returned and must be included in determining the nonprofit set-aside of the State housing credit ceiling for that calendar year. Similarly, credit amounts that are not allocated from the nonprofit set-aside in a calendar year and are returned in a subsequent calendar year become part of the returned credit component of the State housing credit ceiling for that year and are also included in determining the set-aside for that year.

(2) *Allocation rules.*—An Agency may allocate credit from any component of the State housing credit ceiling as part of the nonprofit set-aside and need not reserve 10 percent of each component for the nonprofit set-aside. Thus, an Agency may satisfy the nonprofit set-aside requirement of section 42(h)(5) and §1.42-1T(c)(5) in any calendar year by setting aside for allocation an amount equal to at least 10 percent of the total State housing credit ceiling for the calendar year.

(i) *National Pool.*—(1) *In general.*—The unused housing credit carryover of a State for any calendar year is assigned to the Secretary for inclusion in a national pool of unused housing credit carryovers (National Pool) that is reallocated among qualified States the succeeding calendar year. The assignment to the Secretary is made on Form 8610.

(2) *Unused housing credit carryover.*—The unused housing credit carryover of a State for any calendar year is the excess, if any, of—

(i) The unused carryforward component of the State housing credit ceiling for the calendar year; over

(ii) The total housing credit dollar amount allocated for the calendar year.

(3) *Qualified State.*—(i) *In general.*—The term *qualified State* means, with respect to any calendar year, any State that has allocated its entire State housing credit ceiling for the preceding calendar year and for which a request is made by the State, not later than May 1 of the calendar year, to receive an allocation of credit from the National Pool for that calendar year. Except as provided in paragraph (i)(3)(ii)

of this section, a State is not a qualified State in a calendar year if there remains any unallocated credit in its State housing credit ceiling at the close of the preceding calendar year that was apportioned to any Agency within the State for the calendar year.

(ii) *Exceptions.*—(A) *De minimis amount.*—If the amount remaining unallocated at the close of a calendar year is only a de minimis amount of credit, the State is a qualified State eligible to participate in the National Pool. For that purpose, a credit amount is de minimis if it does not exceed 1 percent of the aggregate State housing credit ceiling of the State for the calendar year.

(B) *Other circumstances.*—Pursuant to the authority under section 42(n), the Internal Revenue Service may determine that a State is a qualified State eligible to participate in the National Pool even though the State's unallocated credit is in excess of the 1 percent safe harbor set forth in paragraph (A) of this section. The Internal Revenue Service will make this determination based on all the facts and circumstances, weighing heavily the interests of the States who would otherwise qualify for the National Pool. The Internal Revenue Service will generally grant relief under this paragraph only where a State's unallocated credit is not substantial.

(iii) *Time and manner for making request.*—For further guidance as to the time and manner for making a request of housing credit dollar amounts from the National Pool by a qualified State, see Rev. Proc. 92-31, 1992-1 C.B. 775. (See 601.601(d)(2)(ii)(b)).

(4) *Formula for determining the National Pool.*—The amount allocated to a qualified State in any calendar year is an amount that bears the same ratio to the aggregate unused housing credit carryovers of all States for the preceding calendar year as that State's population for the calendar year bears to the population of all qualified States for the calendar year.

(j) *Coordination between Agencies.*—The Agency responsible for filing Form 8610 on behalf of all Agencies within a State and making any request on behalf of the State for credit from the National Pool (the Filing Agency) must coordinate with each Agency within the State to ensure that the various requirements of this section are complied with. For example, the Filing Agency of a State must ensure that all Agencies within the State that were apportioned a credit amount for the calendar year have allocated all of their respective credit amounts for the calendar year before the Filing Agency can make a request on behalf of the State for a distribution of credit from the National Pool.

(k) *Example.*—(1) The operation of the rules of this section is illustrated by the following examples. Unless otherwise stated in an example, Agency A is the sole Agency authorized to make allocations of housing credit dollar amounts in State M, all of Agency A's allocations are valid, and for calendar year 2003, Agency A has available for allocation a State housing credit ceiling consisting of the following housing credit dollar amounts:

A.	unused carryforward component	$50
B.	population component	$110
C.	returned credit component	$10
D.	national pool component	$0
Total		$170

(2) In addition, the $10 of returned credit component was returned before October 1, 2003.

Example 1—(i) *Additional facts.* By the close of 2003, Agency A had allocated $80 of the State M housing credit ceiling. Of the $80 allocated, $17 was allocated to projects involving qualified nonprofit organizations.

(ii) *Application of stacking rules.* The $80 of allocated credit is first treated as allocated from the unused carryforward component of the State housing credit ceiling. The $80 of allocated credit exceeds the $50 attributable to the unused carryforward component by $30. Because the unused carryforward component is fully utilized no credit will be forfeited by State M to the 2004 National Pool. The remaining $30 of allocated credit will next be treated as allocated from the $120 in credit determined by aggregating the population, returned credit, and national pool components ($110 + 10 + 0 = $120). The $90 of unallocated credit remaining in State M's 2003 State housing credit ceiling ($120 − 30 = $90) represents the unused carryforward component of State M's 2004 State housing credit ceiling. Under paragraph (i)(3) of this section, State M does not qualify for credit from the 2004 National Pool.

(iii) *Nonprofit set-aside.* Agency A allocated exactly the amount of credit to projects involving qualified nonprofit organizations as necessary to meet the nonprofit set-aside requirement ($17, 10% of the $170 ceiling).

Example 2—(i) *Additional facts.* By the close of 2003, Agency A had allocated $40 of the State M housing credit ceiling. Of the $40 allocated, $20 was allocated to projects involving qualified nonprofit organizations.

(ii) *Application of stacking rules.* The $40 of allocated credit is first treated as allocated from the unused carryforward component of the State housing credit ceiling. Because the $40 of allocated credit does not exceed the $50 attributable to the unused carryforward component, the remaining components of the State housing credit ceiling are unaffected. The $10 remaining in the unused carryforward component is assigned to the Secretary for inclusion in the 2004 National Pool. The $120 in credit determined by aggregating the population, returned credit, and national pool components becomes the unused carryforward component of State M's 2004 State housing credit ceiling. Under paragraph (i)(3) of this section, State M does not qualify for credit from the 2004 National Pool.

(iii) *Nonprofit set-aside.* Agency A allocated $3 more credit to projects involving qualified nonprofit organizations than necessary to meet the nonprofit set-aside requirement. This does not reduce the application of the 10% nonprofit set-aside requirement to the State M housing credit ceiling for calendar year 2004.

Example 3—(i) *Additional fact.* None of the applications for credit that Agency A received for 2003 are for projects involving qualified nonprofit organizations.

(ii) *Nonprofit set-aside.* Because at least 10% of the State housing credit ceiling must be set aside for projects involving a qualified nonprofit organization, Agency A can allocate only $153 of the $170 State housing credit ceiling for calendar year 2003 ($170 – 17 = $153). If Agency A allocates $153 of credit, the credit is treated as allocated $50 from the unused carryforward component and $103 from the sum of the population, returned credit, and national pool components. The $17 of unallocated credit that is set aside for projects involving qualified nonprofit organizations becomes the unused carryforward component of State M's 2004 State housing credit ceiling. Under paragraph (i)(3) of this section, State M does not qualify for credit from the 2004 National Pool.

Example 4—(i) *Additional facts.* The $10 of returned credit component was returned prior to October 1, 2003. However, a $40 credit that had been allocated in calendar year 2002 to a project involving a qualified nonprofit organization was returned to the Agency by a mutual consent agreement dated November 15, 2003. By the close of 2003, Agency A had allocated $170 of the State M's housing credit ceiling, including $17 of credit to projects involving qualified nonprofit organizations.

(ii) *Effect of three-month rule.* Under the three-month rule of paragraph (d)(2)(iii) of this section, Agency A may treat all or part of the $40 of previously allocated credit as returned on January 1, 2004. If Agency A treats all of the $40 amount as having been returned in calendar year 2004, the State M housing credit ceiling for 2003 is $170. This entire amount, including the $17 nonprofit set-aside, has been allocated in 2003. Under paragraph (i)(3) of this section, State M qualifies for the 2004 National Pool.

(iii) *If three-month rule not used.* If Agency A treats all of the $40 of previously allocated credit as returned in calendar year 2003, the State housing credit ceiling for the 2003 calendar year will be $210 of which $50 will be attributable to the returned credit component ($10 + $40 = $50). Because credit amounts allocated to a qualified nonprofit organization in a prior calendar year that are returned in a subsequent calendar year do not retain their nonprofit character, the nonprofit set-aside for calendar year 2003 is $21 (10% of the $210 State housing credit ceiling). The $170 that Agency A allocated during 2003 is first treated as allocated from the unused carryforward component of the State housing credit ceiling. The $170 of allocated credit exceeds the $50 attributable to the unused carryforward component by $120. Because the unused carryforward component is fully utilized no credit will be forfeited by State M to the 2004 National Pool. The remaining $120 of allocated credit will next be treated as allocated from the $160 in credit determined by aggregating the population, returned credit, and national pool components ($110 + 50 + 0 = $160). The $40 of unallocated credit (which includes $4 of unallocated credit from the $21 nonprofit set-aside) remaining in State M's 2003 housing credit ceiling ($160 – 120 = $40) represents the unused carryforward component of State M's 2004 housing credit ceiling. Under paragraph (i)(3) of this section, State M does not qualify for credit from the 2004 National Pool.

(l) *Effective dates.*—(1) *In general.*—Except as provided in paragraph (l)(2) of this section, the rules set forth in § 1.42-14 are applicable on January 1, 1994.

(2) *Community Renewal Tax Relief Act of 2000 changes.*—Paragraphs (a), (b), (c), (e), (i)(2) and (k) of this section are applicable *for housing credit dollar amounts allocated after January 6, 2004.* However, paragraphs (a), (b), (c), (e), (i)(2) and (k) of this section may be applied by Agencies and taxpayers for housing credit dollar amounts allocated after December 31, 2000, and on or before January 6, 2004. Otherwise, subject to the applicable effective dates of the

corresponding statutory provisions, the rules that apply for housing credit dollar amounts allocated on or before January 6, 2004, are contained in this section in effect on and before January 6, 2004 (see 26 CFR part 1 revised as of April 1, 2003). [Reg. § 1.42-14.]

☐ [*T.D. 8563, 9-30-94. Amended by T.D. 9110, 12-31-2003 (corrected 2-23-2004).*]

[Reg. § 1.42-15]

§ 1.42-15. Available unit rule.—(a) *Definitions.*—The following definitions apply to this section:

Applicable income limitation means the limitation applicable under section 42(g)(1) or, for deep rent skewed projects described in section 142(d)(4)(B), 40 percent of area median gross income.

Available unit rule means the rule in section 42(g)(2)(D)(ii).

Comparable unit means a residential unit in a low-income building that is comparably sized or smaller than an over-income unit or, for deep rent skewed projects described in section 142(d)(4)(B), any low-income unit. For purposes of determining whether a residential unit is comparably sized, a comparable unit must be measured by the same method used to determine qualified basis for the credit year in which the comparable unit became available.

Current resident means a person who is living in the low-income building.

Low-income unit is defined by section 42(i)(3)(A).

Nonqualified resident means a new occupant or occupants whose aggregate income exceeds the applicable income limitation.

Over-income unit means, in the case of a project with respect to which the taxpayer elects the requirements of section 42(g)(1)(A) or (B) (that is, the 20–50 or 40–60 tests), a low-income unit in which the aggregate income of the occupants of the unit increases above 140 percent of the applicable income limitation under section 42(g)(1)(A) and (B), or above 170 percent of the applicable income limitation for deep rent skewed projects described in section 142(d)(4)(B). In the case of a project with respect to which the taxpayer elects the requirements of section 42(g)(1)(C) (that is, the average income test), *over-income unit* means a residential unit described in § 1.42-19(b)(1)(i) through (iii) in which the aggregate income of the occupants of the unit increases above 140 percent (170 percent in case of deep rent skewed projects described in section 142(d)(4)(B)) of the greater of 60 percent of area median gross income or the imputed income limitation designated with respect to the unit under § 1.42-19(b).

Qualified resident means an occupant either whose aggregate income (combined with the income of all other occupants of the unit) does not exceed the applicable income limitation and who is otherwise a low-income resident under section 42, or who is a current resident.

(b) *General section 42(g)(2)(D)(i) rule.*—Except as provided in paragraph (c) of this section, notwithstanding an increase in the income of the occupants of a low-income unit above the applicable income limitation, if the income of the occupants initially met the applicable income limitation, and the unit continues to be rent-restricted—

(1) The unit continues to be treated as a low-income unit; and

(2) The unit continues to be included in the numerator and the denominator of the ratio used to determine whether a project satisfies the applicable minimum set-aside requirement of section 42(g)(1).

(c) *Exceptions.*—(1) *In general.*—A unit ceases to be treated as a low-income unit if it becomes an over-income unit and a nonqualified resident occupies any comparable unit that is available or that subsequently becomes available in the same low-income building. In other words, the owner of a low-income building must rent to qualified residents all comparable units that are available or that subsequently become available in the same building to continue treating the over-income unit as a low-income unit. Once the percentage of low-income units in a building (excluding the over-income units) equals the percentage of low-income units on which the credit is based, failure to maintain the over-income units as low-income units has no immediate significance. The failure to maintain the over-income units as low-income units, however, may affect the decision of whether or not to rent a particular available unit at market rate at a later time. A unit is not available for purposes of the available unit rule when the unit is no longer available for rent due to contractual arrangements that are binding under local law (for example, a unit is not available if it is subject to a preliminary reservation that is binding on the owner under local law prior to the date a lease is signed or the unit is occupied).

(2) *Rental of next available unit in case of the average income test.*—(i) *Basic rule.*—In the case of a project with respect to which the taxpayer elects the average income test, if a unit becomes an over-income unit within the meaning of paragraph (a) of this section, that unit ceases to be described in § 1.42-19(b)(1)(ii) if—

(A) Any residential rental unit (of a size comparable to, or smaller than, the over-income unit) is available, or subsequently becomes available, in the same low-income building; and

(B) That available unit is occupied by a new resident whose income exceeds the limitation described in paragraph (c)(2)(iv) of this section.

(ii) *No requirement to comply with the next available unit rule in a specific order.*—Where multiple units in a building are over-income units at the same time—

(A) The order in which available units are occupied makes no difference for purposes of complying with the rules in this section (next available unit rule); and

(B) In making imputed income limitation designations, the taxpayer must take into account the limitations described in paragraphs (c)(2)(iii) and (iv) of this section.

(iii) *Deep rent skewed projects.*—In the case of a project described in section 142(d)(4)(B) with respect to which the taxpayer elects the average income test, if a unit becomes an over-income unit within the meaning of paragraph (a) of this section, that unit ceases to be a unit described in §1.42-19(b)(1)(ii) if—

(A) Any residential unit described in §1.42-19(b)(1)(i) through (iii) is available, or subsequently becomes available, in the same low-income building; and

(B) That unit is occupied by a new resident whose income exceeds the lesser of 40 percent of area median gross income or the imputed income limitation designated with respect to that unit.

(iv) *Limitation.*—The limitation described in this paragraph (c)(2)(iv) is—

(A) In the case of a unit that was described in §1.42-19(b)(1)(i) through (iii) prior to becoming vacant, the imputed income limitation designated with respect to the available unit for the average income test under §1.42-19(b); and

(B) In the case of any other unit, the highest imputed income limitation that could be designated (consistent with section 42(g)(1)(C)(ii)(III)) for that available unit under §1.42-19(c) such that the average of all imputed income designations of residential units in the project does not exceed 60 percent of area median gross income (AMGI).

(v) *Example.*—The operation of paragraph (c)(2) of this section (that is, the next available unit rule for the average income test) is illustrated by the following example.

(A) *Facts.* (1) A single-building housing project received an allocation of housing credit dollar amount for 10 low-income units. The taxpayer who owns the project constructs the building with 10 identically sized units and elects the average income test. In the first year, the taxpayer intended to have 8 units that will qualify as low-income units (within the meaning of §1.42-19(b)(1)), and 2 units that are market-rate units. The taxpayer properly and timely designates the imputed income limitations for the 8 units as follows: 4 units at 80 percent of AMGI; and 4 units at 40 percent of AMGI.

Table 1 to Paragraph (c)(2)(v)(A)(1)

Unit Number	Imputed Income Limitation of the Unit
1	80 percent of AMGI
2	80 percent of AMGI
3	80 percent of AMGI
4	80 percent of AMGI
5	Market Rate
6	40 percent of AMGI
7	40 percent of AMGI
8	40 percent of AMGI
9	40 percent of AMGI
10	Market Rate

(2) In the first taxable year of the credit period (Year 1), the project is fully leased and occupied by income-qualified residents in Units ## 1-4 and 6-9. In Year 2, Unit # 1 and Unit # 6 become over-income. The tenant residing in Unit # 5 vacated that unit. Taxpayer then designated an imputed income limitation of 40 percent of AMGI for Unit #5. Later in Year 2, the tenant residing in Unit # 10 vacated that unit. Taxpayer designated an imputed income limitation of 80 percent of AMGI for Unit #10. After those designations, Unit # 10 was occupied by a new income-qualified tenant, and then later, Unit # 5 was occupied by a new income-qualified resident.

(B) *Analysis.* Taxpayer sought to maintain the status of the over-income units (Unit # 1 and Unit # 6) as units described in §1.42-19(b)(1)(ii). As the then-market rate units (Units ## 5 and 10) became available to rent, Taxpayer designated imputed income limitations for them at 40 percent and 80 percent of AMGI, respectively. Immediately after each designation, the average of the designations in the project does not exceed 60 percent AMGI. Pursuant to the rule in paragraph (c)(2)(ii) of this section, when there are multiple over-income units, Taxpayer is not required to rent the next-available units in a specific order, even though they may have different imputed income limitations. Thus, Taxpayer complied with the rules of the next available unit rule, and Unit #1 and Unit #6 maintain status as units described in §1.42-19(b)(1)(ii).

(d) *Effect of current resident moving within building.*—When a current resident moves to a different unit within the building, the newly occupied unit adopts the status of the vacated unit. Thus, if a current resident, whose income exceeds the applicable income limitation, moves from an over-income unit to a vacant unit in the same building, the newly occupied unit is treated as an over-income unit. The vacated unit assumes the status the newly occupied unit had immediately before it was occupied by the current resident.

(e) *Available unit rule applies separately to each building in a project.*—In a project containing more than one low-income building, the available unit rule applies separately to each building.

(f) *Result of noncompliance with available unit rule.*—If any comparable unit that is available or that subsequently becomes available is rented to a nonqualified resident, all over-income units for which the available unit was a comparable unit within the same building lose their status as low-income units; thus, comparably sized or larger over-income units would lose their status as low-income units.

(g) *Relationship to tax-exempt bond provisions.*—Financing arrangements that purport to be exempt-facility bonds under section 142 must meet the requirements of sections 103 and 141 through 150 for interest on the obligations to be excluded from gross income under section 103(a). This section is not intended as an interpretation under section 142.

(h) *Examples.*—The following examples illustrate this section:

Example 1. This example illustrates noncompliance with the available unit rule in a low-income building containing three over-income units. On January 1, 1998, a qualified low-income housing project, consisting of one building containing ten identically sized residential units, received a housing credit dollar amount allocation from a state housing credit agency for five low-income units. By the close of 1998, the first year of the credit period, the project satisfied the minimum set-aside requirement of section 42(g)(1)(B). Units 1, 2, 3, 4, and 5 were occupied by individuals whose incomes did not exceed the income limitation applicable under section 42(g)(1) and were otherwise low-income residents under section 42. Units 6, 7, 8, and 9 were occupied by market-rate tenants. Unit 10 was vacant. To avoid recapture of credit, the project owner must maintain five of the units as low-income units. On November 1, 1999, the certificates of annual income state that annual incomes of the individuals in Units 1, 2, and 3 increased above 140 percent of the income limitation applicable under section 42(g)(1), causing those units to become over-income units. On November 30, 1999, Units 8 and 9 became vacant. On December 1, 1999, the project owner rented Units 8 and 9 to qualified residents who were not current residents at rates meeting the rent restriction requirements of section 42(g)(2). On December 31, 1999, the project owner rented Unit 10 to a market-rate tenant. Because Unit 10, an available comparable unit, was leased to a market-rate tenant, Units 1, 2, and 3 ceased to be treated as low-income units. On that date, Units 4, 5, 8, and 9 were the only remaining low-income units. Because the project owner did not maintain five of the residential units as low-income units, the qualified basis in the building is reduced, and credit must be recaptured. If the project owner had rented Unit 10 to a qualified resident who was not a current resident, eight of the units would be low-income units. At that time, Units 1, 2, and 3, the over-income units, could be rented to market-rate tenants because the building would still contain five low-income units.

Example 2. This example illustrates the provisions of paragraph (d) of this section. A low-income project consists of one six-floor building. The residential units in the building are identically sized. The building contains two over-income units on the sixth floor and two vacant units on the first floor. The project owner, desiring to maintain the over-income units as low-income units, wants to rent the available units to qualified residents. J, a resident of one of the over-income units, wishes to occupy a unit on the first floor. J's income has recently increased above the applicable income limitation. The project owner permits J to move into one of the units on the first floor. Despite J's income exceeding the applicable income limitation, J is a qualified resident under the available unit rule because J is a current resident of the building. The unit newly occupied by J becomes an over-income unit under the available unit rule. The unit vacated by J assumes the status the newly occupied unit had immediately before J occupied the unit. The over-income units in the building continue to be treated as low-income units.

(i) *Applicability dates.*—(1) *In general.*—Except for paragraph (c)(2) of this section, this section applies to leases entered into or renewed on and after September 26, 1997.

(2) *Applicability dates under the average income test.*—The requirements of the second sentence of the definition of *over-income unit* in paragraph (a) of this section and paragraph (c)(2) of this section apply to taxable years beginning after December 31, 2022. A taxpayer may choose to apply this section to a taxable year beginning after October 12, 2022, and before January 1, 2023, provided that the taxpayer chooses to apply § 1.42-19 to the same taxable year. [Reg. § 1.42-15.]

☐ [T.D. 8732, 9-25-97. Amended by T.D. 9967, 10-7-2022.]

[Reg. § 1.42-16]

§ 1.42-16. Eligible basis reduced by federal grants.—(a) *In general.*—If, during any taxable year of the compliance period (described in section 42(i)(1)), a grant is made with respect to any building or the operation thereof and any portion of the grant is funded with federal funds (whether or not includible in gross income), the eligible basis of the building for the taxable year and all succeeding taxable years is reduced by the portion of the grant that is so funded.

(b) *Grants do not include certain rental assistance payments.*—A federal rental assistance payment made to a building owner on behalf or in respect of a tenant is not a grant made with respect to a building or its operation if the payment is made pursuant to—

(1) Section 8 of the United States Housing Act of 1937 (42 U.S.C. 1437f);

(2) A qualifying program of rental assistance administered under section 9 of the United States Housing Act of 1937 (42 U.S.C. 1437g); or

(3) A program or method of rental assistance as the Secretary may designate by publication in the Federal Register or in the Internal Revenue Bulletin (see § 601.601(d)(2) of this chapter).

(c) *Qualifying rental assistance program.*—For purposes of paragraph (b)(2) of this section, payments are made pursuant to a qualifying rental assistance program administered under section 9 of the United States Housing Act of 1937 to the extent that the payments—

(1) Are made to a building owner pursuant to a contract with a public housing authority with respect to units the owner has agreed to maintain as public housing units (PH-units) in the building;

(2) Are made with respect to units occupied by public housing tenants, provided that, for this purpose, units may be considered occupied during periods of short term vacancy (not to exceed 60 days); and

(3) Do not exceed the difference between the rents received from a building's PH-unit tenants and a pro rata portion of the building's actual operating costs that are reasonably allocable to the PH-units (based on square footage, number of bedrooms, or similar objective criteria), and provided that, for this purpose, operating costs do not include any development costs of a building (including developer's fees) or the principal or interest of any debt incurred with respect to any part of the building.

(d) *Effective date.*—This section is effective September 26, 1997. [Reg. § 1.42-16.]

☐ [T.D. 8731, 9-25-97.]

[Reg. § 1.42-17]

§ 1.42-17. Qualified allocation plan.—(a) *Requirements.*—(1) *In general.*—[Reserved]

(2) *Selection criteria.*—[Reserved]

(3) *Agency evaluation.*—Section 42(m)(2)(A) requires that the housing credit dollar amount allocated to a project is not to exceed the amount the Agency determines is necessary for the financial feasibility of the project and its viability as a qualified low-income housing project throughout the credit period. In making this determination, the Agency must consider—

(i) The sources and uses of funds and the total financing planned for the project. The taxpayer must certify to the Agency the full extent of all federal, state, and local subsidies that apply (or which the taxpayer expects to apply) to the project. The taxpayer must also certify to the Agency all other sources of funds and all development costs for the project. The taxpayer's certification should be sufficiently detailed to enable the Agency to ascertain the nature of the costs that will make up the total financing package, including subsidies and the anticipated syndication or placement proceeds to be raised. Development cost information, whether or not includible in eligible basis under section 42(d), that should be provided to the Agency includes, but is not limited to, site acquisition costs, construction contingency, general contractor's overhead and profit, architect's and engineer's fees, permit and survey fees, insurance premiums, real estate taxes during construction, title and recording fees, construction period interest, financing fees, organizational costs, rent-up and marketing costs, accounting and auditing costs, working capital and operating deficit reserves, syndication and legal fees, and developer fees;

(ii) Any proceeds or receipts expected to be generated by reason of tax benefits;

(iii) The percentage of the housing credit dollar amount used for project costs other than the costs of intermediaries. This requirement should not be applied so as to impede the development of projects in hard-to-develop areas under section 42(d)(5)(C); and

(iv) The reasonableness of the developmental and operational costs of the project.

(4) *Timing of Agency evaluation.*—(i) *In general.*—The financial determinations and certifications required under paragraph (a)(3) of this section must be made as of the following times—

(A) The time of the application for the housing credit dollar amount;

(B) The time of the allocation of the housing credit dollar amount; and

(C) The date the building is placed in service.

(ii) *Time limit for placed-in-service evaluation.*—For purposes of paragraph (a)(4)(i)(C) of this section, the evaluation for when a building is placed in service must be made not later than the date the Agency issues the Form 8609, "Low-Income Housing Credit Allocation Certification." The Agency must evaluate all sources and uses of funds under paragraph (a)(3)(i) of this section paid, incurred, or committed by the taxpayer for the project up until date the Agency issues the Form 8609.

(5) *Special rule for final determinations and certifications.*—For the Agency's evaluation under paragraph (a)(4)(i)(C) of this section, the taxpayer must submit a schedule of project costs. Such schedule is to be prepared on the method of accounting used by the taxpayer for federal income tax purposes, and must detail the project's total costs as well as those costs that may qualify for inclusion in eligible basis under section 42(d). For projects with more than 10 units, the schedule of project costs must be accompanied by a Certified Public Accountant's audit report on the schedule (an Agency may require an audited schedule of project costs for projects with fewer than 11 units). The CPA's audit must be conducted in accordance with generally accepted auditing standards. The auditor's report must be unqualified.

(6) *Bond-financed projects.*—A project qualifying under section 42(h)(4) is not entitled to any credit unless the governmental unit that issued the bonds (or on behalf of which the bonds were issued), or the Agency responsible for issuing the Form(s) 8609 to the project, makes determinations under rules similar to the rules in paragraphs (a)(3), (4), and (5) of this section.

(b) *Effective date.*—This section is effective on January 1, 2001. [Reg. § 1.42-17.]

☐ [T.D. 8859, 1-13-2000.]

[Reg. § 1.42-18]

§ 1.42-18. Qualified contracts.—(a) *Extended low-income housing commitment.*—(1) *In general.*—No credit under section 42(a) is allowed by reason of section 42 with respect to any building for the taxable year unless an extended low-income housing commitment (commitment) (as defined in section 42(h)(6)(B)) is in effect as of the end of such taxable year. A commitment must be in effect for the extended use period (as defined in paragraph (a)(1)(i) of this section).

(i) *Extended use period.*—The term *extended use period* means the period beginning on the first day in the compliance period (as defined in section 42(i)(1)) on which the building is part of a qualified low-income housing project (as defined in section 42(g)(1)) and ending on the later of—

(A) The date specified by the low-income housing credit agency (Agency) in the commitment; or

(B) The date that is 15 years after the close of the compliance period.

(ii) *Termination of extended use period.*—The extended use period for any building will terminate—

(A) On the date the building is acquired by foreclosure (or instrument in lieu of foreclosure) unless the Commissioner determines that such acquisition is part of an arrangement with the taxpayer ("the owner") a purpose of which is to terminate such period; or

(B) On the last day of the one-year period beginning on the date (after the 14th year of the compliance period) on which the owner submits a written request to the Agency to find a person to acquire the owner's interest in the low-income portion of the building if the Agency is unable to present during such period a qualified contract for the acquisition of the low-income portion of the building by any person who will continue to operate such portion as a qualified low-income building (as defined in section 42(c)(2)).

(iii) *Owner non-acceptance.*—If the Agency provides a qualified contract within the one-year period and the owner rejects or fails to act upon the contract, the building remains subject to the existing commitment.

(iv) *Eviction, gross rent increase concerning existing low-income tenants not permitted.*—Prior to the close of the three year period following the termination of a commitment, no owner shall be permitted to evict or terminate the tenancy (other than for good cause) of an existing tenant of any low-income unit, or increase the gross rent for such unit in a manner or amount not otherwise permitted by section 42.

(2) *Exception.*—Paragraph (a)(1)(ii)(B) of this section shall not apply to the extent more stringent requirements are provided in the commitment or under State law.

(b) *Definitions.*—For purposes of this section, the following terms are defined:

(1) As provided by section 42(h)(6)(G)(iii), *base calendar year* means the calendar year with or within which the first taxable year of the credit period ends.

(2) The *low-income portion* of a building is the portion of the building equal to the applicable fraction (as defined in section 42(c)(1)(B)) specified in the commitment for the building.

(3) The *fair market value of the non-low-income portion* of the building is determined at the time of the Agency's offer of sale of the building to the general public. The fair market value of the non-low-income portion also includes the fair market value of the land underlying the entire building (both the non-low-income portion and the lowincome portion). This valuation must take into account the existing and continuing requirements contained in the commitment for the building. The fair market value of the non-low-income portion also includes the fair market value of items of personal property not included in eligible basis under section 42(d) that convey under the contract with the building.

(4) *Qualifying building costs include.*—(i) Costs that are included in eligible basis of a low-income housing building under section 42(d) and that are included in the adjusted basis of depreciable property that is subject to section 168 and that is residential rental property for purposes of section 142(d) and § 1.103-8(b);

(ii) Costs that are included in eligible basis of a low-income housing building under section 42(d) and that are included in the adjusted basis of depreciable property that is subject to section 168 and that is used in a common area or is provided as a comparable amenity to all residential rental units in the building; and

(iii) Costs of the type described in paragraph (b)(4)(i) and (ii) of this section incurred after the first year of the low-income housing building's credit period under section 42(f).

(5) The *qualified contract amount* is the sum of the fair market value of the non-low-income portion of the building (within the meaning of section 42(h)(6)(F) and paragraph (b)(3) of this section) and the price for the low-income portion of the building (within the meaning of section 42(h)(6)(F) and paragraph (b)(2) of this section) as calculated in paragraph (c)(2) of this section. If this sum is not a multiple of $1,000, then when the Agency offers the building for sale

to the general public, the Agency may round up the offering price to the next highest multiple of $1,000.

(c) *Qualified contract purchase price formula.*—(1) *In general.*—For purposes of this section, *qualified contract* means a bona fide contract to acquire the building (within a reasonable period after the contract is entered into) for the qualified contract amount.

(i) *Initial determination.*—The qualified contract amount is determined at the time of the Agency's offer of sale of the building to the general public.

(ii) *Mandatory adjustment by the buyer and owner.*—The buyer and owner under a qualified contract must adjust the amount of the low-income portion of the qualified contract formula to reflect changes in the components of the qualified contract formula such as mortgage payments that reduce outstanding indebtedness between the time of the Agency's offer of sale to the general public and the building's actual sale closing date.

(iii) *Optional adjustment by the Agency and owner.*—The Agency and owner may agree to adjust the fair market value of the non low-income portion of the building after the Agency's offer of sale of the building to the general public and before the close of the one-year period described in paragraph (a)(1)(ii)(B) of this section. If no agreement between the Agency and owner is reached, the fair market value of the non-low-income portion of the building determined at the time of the Agency's offer of sale of the building to the general public remains unchanged.

(2) *Low-income portion amount.*—The low-income portion amount is an amount not less than the applicable fraction specified in the commitment, as defined in section 42(h)(6)(B)(i), multiplied by the total of—

(i) The outstanding indebtedness for the building (as defined in paragraph (c)(3) of this section); plus

(ii) The adjusted investor equity in the building for the calendar year (as defined in paragraph (c)(4) of this section); plus

(iii) Other capital contributions (as defined in paragraph (c)(5) of this section), not including any amounts described in paragraphs (c)(2)(i) and (ii) of this section; minus

(iv) Cash distributions from (or available for distribution from) the building (as defined in paragraph (c)(6) of this section).

(3) *Outstanding indebtedness.*—For purposes of paragraph (c)(2)(i) of this section, *outstanding indebtedness* means the remaining stated principal balance (which is initially determined at the time of the Agency's offer of sale of the building to the general public) of any indebtedness secured by, or with respect to, the building that does not exceed the amount of qualifying building costs described in paragraph (b)(4) of this section. Thus, any refinancing indebtedness or additional mortgages in excess of such qualifying building costs are not outstanding indebtedness for purposes of section 42(h)(6)(F) and this section. Examples of outstanding indebtedness include certain mortgages and developer fee notes (excluding developer service costs not included in eligible basis). Outstanding indebtedness does not include debt used to finance nondepreciable land costs, syndication costs, legal and accounting costs, and operating deficit payments. Outstanding indebtedness includes only obligations that are indebtedness under general principles of Federal income tax law and that are actually paid to the lender upon the sale of the building or are assumed by the buyer as part of the sale of the building.

(4) *Adjusted investor equity.*—(i) *Application of cost-of-living factor.*—For purposes of paragraph (c)(2)(ii) of this section, the *adjusted investor equity* for any calendar year equals the unadjusted investor equity, as described in paragraph (c)(4)(ii) of this section, multiplied by the qualified-contract cost-of-living adjustment for that year, as defined in paragraph (c)(4)(iii) of this section.

(ii) *Unadjusted investor equity.*—For purposes of this paragraph (c)(4), *unadjusted investor equity* means the aggregate amount of cash invested by owners for qualifying building costs described in paragraph (b)(4)(i) and (ii) of this section. Thus, equity paid for land, credit adjuster payments, Agency low-income housing credit application and allocation fees, operating deficit contributions, and legal, syndication, and accounting costs all are examples of cost payments that do not qualify as unadjusted investor equity. Unadjusted investor equity takes an amount into account only to the extent that, as of the beginning of the low-income building's credit period (as defined in section 42(f)(1)), there existed an obligation to invest the amount. Unadjusted investor equity does not include amounts included in the calculation of outstanding indebtedness as defined in paragraph (c)(3) of this section.

(iii) *Qualified-contract cost-of-living adjustment.*—For purposes of this paragraph (c)(4), the *qualified-contract cost-of-living adjustment for a calendar year* is the number that is computed under the general

Reg. § 1.42-18(c)(4)(iii)

rule in paragraph (c)(4)(iv) of this section or a number that may be provided by the Commissioner as described in paragraph (c)(4)(v) of this section.

(iv) *General rule.*—Except as provided in paragraph (c)(4)(v) of this section, the *qualified-contract cost-of-living adjustment* is the quotient of—

(A) The sum of the 12 monthly Consumer Price Index (CPI) values whose average is the CPI for the calendar year that precedes the calendar year in which the Agency offers the building for sale to the general public (The term "CPI for a calendar year" has the meaning given to it by section 1(f)(4) for purposes of computing annual inflation adjustments to the rate brackets.); divided by

(B) The sum of the 12 monthly CPI values whose average is the CPI for the base calendar year (within the meaning of section 1(f)(4)), unless that sum has been increased under paragraph (c)(4)(iii)(D) of this section.

(v) *Provision by the Commissioner of the qualified-contract cost-of-living adjustment.*—The Commissioner may publish in the Internal Revenue Bulletin (see § 601.601(d)(2) of this chapter) a process pursuant to which the Internal Revenue Service will compute the qualified-contract cost-of-living adjustment for a calendar year and make available the results of that computation.

(vi) *Methodology.*—The calculations in paragraph (c)(4)(iv) of this section are to be made in the following manner:

(A) The CPI data to be used for purposes of this paragraph (c)(4) are the not seasonally adjusted values of the CPI for all urban consumers. (The U.S. Department of Labor's Bureau of Labor Statistics (BLS) sometimes refers to these values as "CPI-U.") The BLS publishes the CPI data on-line (including a History Table that contains monthly CPI-U values for all years back to 1913). See *www.BLS.gov/data.*

(B) The quotient is to be carried out to 10 decimal places.

(C) The Agency may round adjusted investor equity to the nearest dollar.

(D) If the CPI for any calendar year (within the meaning of section 1(f)(4)) during the extended use period after the base calendar year exceeds by more than 5 percent the CPI for the preceding calendar year (within the meaning of section 1(f)(4)), then the sum described in paragraph (c)(4)(i)(B) is to be increased so that the excess is never taken into account under this paragraph (c)(4).

(vii) *Example.*—The following example illustrates the calculations described in this paragraph (c)(4):

Example. (i) *Facts.* Owner contributed $20,000,000 in equity to a building in 1997, which was the first year of the credit period for the building. In 2011, Owner requested Agency to find a buyer to purchase the building, and Agency offered the building for sale to the general public during 2011. The CPI for 1997 (within the meaning of section 1(f)(4)) is the average of the Consumer Price Index as of the close of the 12-month period ending on August 31, 1997. The sum of the CPI values for the twelve months from September 1996 through August 1997 is 1913.9. The CPI for 2010 (within the meaning of section 1(f)(4)) is the average of the Consumer Price Index as of the close of the 12-month period ending August 31, 2010. The sum of the CPI values for the twelve months from September 2009 through August 2010 is 2605.959. At no time during this period (after the base calendar year) did the CPI for any calendar year exceed the CPI for the preceding calendar year by more than 5 percent.

(ii) *Determination of adjusted investor equity.* The qualified-contract cost-of-living adjustment is 1.3615962171 (the quotient of 2605.959, divided by 1913.9). Owner's adjusted investor equity, therefore, is $27,231,924, which is $20,000,000, multiplied by 1.3615962171, rounded to the nearest dollar.

(5) *Other capital contributions.*—For purposes of paragraph (c)(2)(iii) of this section, other capital contributions to a low-income building are qualifying building costs described in paragraph (b)(4)(ii) of this section paid or incurred by the owner of the low-income building other than amounts included in the calculation of outstanding indebtedness or adjusted investor equity as defined in this section. For example, other capital contributions may include amounts incurred to replace a furnace after the first year of a low-income housing credit building's credit period under section 42(f), provided any loan used to finance the replacement of the furnace is not secured by the furnace or the building. Other capital contributions do not include expenditures for land costs, operating deficit payments, credit adjuster payments, and payments for legal, syndication, and accounting costs.

(6) *Cash distributions.*—(i) *In general.*—For purposes of paragraph (c)(2)(iv) of this section, the term *cash distributions from (or available for distribution from)* the building include—

(A) All distributions from the building to the owners or to persons whose relationship to the owner is described in section 267(b) or section 707(b)(1)), including distributions under section 301 (relating to distributions by a corporation), section 731 (relating to distributions by a partnership), or section 1368 (relating to distributions by an S corporation); and

(B) All cash and cash equivalents available for distribution at, or before, the time of sale, including, for example, reserve funds whether operating or replacement reserves, unless the reserve funds are legally required by mortgage restrictions, regulatory agreements, or third party contractual agreements to remain with the building following the sale.

(ii) *Excess proceeds.*—For purposes of paragraph (c)(6)(i) of this section, proceeds from the refinancing of indebtedness or additional mortgages that are in excess of qualifying building costs are not considered cash available for distribution.

(iii) *Anti-abuse rule.*—The Commissioner will interpret and apply the rules in this paragraph (c)(6) as necessary and appropriate to prevent manipulation of the qualified contract amount. For example, cash distributions include payments to owners or persons whose relation to owners is described in section 267(b) or section 707(b) for any operating expenses in excess of amounts reasonable under the circumstances.

(d) *Administrative discretion and responsibilities of the Agency.*—(1) *In general.*—An Agency may exercise administrative discretion in evaluating and acting upon an owner's request to find a buyer to acquire the building. An Agency may establish reasonable requirements for written requests and may determine whether failure to follow one or more applicable requirements automatically prevents a purported written request from beginning the one-year period described in section 42(h)(6)(I). If the one-year-period has already begun, the Agency may determine whether failure to follow one or more requirements suspends the running of that period. Examples of Agency administrative discretion include, but are not limited to, the following:

(i) Concluding that the owner's request lacks essential information and denying the request until such information is provided.

(ii) Refusing to consider an owner's representations without substantiating documentation verified with the Agency's records.

(iii) Determining how many, if any, subsequent requests to find a buyer may be submitted if the owner has previously submitted a request for a qualified contract and then rejected or failed to act upon a qualified contract presented by the Agency.

(iv) Assessing and charging the owner certain administrative fees for the performance of services in obtaining a qualified contract (for example, real estate appraiser costs).

(v) Requiring all appraisers involved in the qualified contract process to be State certified general appraisers that are acceptable to the Agency.

(vi) Specifying other conditions applicable to the qualified contract consistent with section 42 and this section.

(2) *Actual offer.*—Upon receipt of a written request from the owner to find a person to acquire the building, the Agency must offer the building for sale to the general public, based on reasonable efforts, at the determined qualified contract amount in order for the qualified contract to satisfy the requirements of this section unless the Agency has already identified a willing buyer who submitted a qualified contract to purchase the project.

(3) *Debarment of certain appraisers.*—Agencies shall not utilize any individual or organization as an appraiser if that individual or organization is currently on any list for active suspension or revocation for performing appraisals in any State or is listed on the Excluded Parties Lists System (EPLS) maintained by the General Services Administration for the United States Government found at *www.epls.gov.*

(e) *Effective date/applicability date.*—These regulations are applicable to owner requests to housing credit agencies on or after May 3, 2012 to obtain a qualified contract for the acquisition of a low-income housing credit building. [Reg. § 1.42-18.]

□ [T.D. 9587, 5-2-2012.]

[Reg. § 1.42-19]

§ 1.42-19. **Average income test.**—(a) *Average income set-aside.*—A project for residential rental property satisfies the average income test in section 42(g)(1)(C) for a taxable year if the project contains a qualified group of units (within the meaning of paragraph (b)(2) of this section) that constitutes 40 percent or more of the residential units in the project. (In the case of a project described in section 142(d)(6), "40 percent" in the preceding sentence is replaced with "25 percent.")

(b) *Definition of low-income unit and qualified group of units.*—(1) *Definition of low-income unit.*—For purposes of this section, a residential unit is a low-income unit if and only if—

(i) Such unit is rent-restricted (as defined in section 42(g)(2));

(ii) The individuals occupying such unit satisfy the imputed income limitation of that unit designated by the taxpayer in accordance with paragraphs (c)(3) and (d) of this section and with §1.42-19T(c) and §1.42-19T(c), or the unit meets the requirements under section 42(g)(2)(D);

(iii) No provision in section 42 (including section 42(i)(3)(B)-(E)) or in the regulations under section 42 denies low-income status to that unit; and

(iv) The unit is part of a qualified group of units under paragraph (b)(2) of this section.

(2) *Definition of qualified group of units.*—A group of residential units is a qualified group of units for a taxable year if and only if—

(i) Each unit in the group satisfies the requirements of paragraphs (b)(1)(i) through (iii) of this section; and

(ii) The average of the imputed income limitations of all of the units in the group does not exceed 60 percent of area median gross income (AMGI).

(3) *Identification of qualified groups of units.*—(i) *Average income set-aside test.*—For each taxable year in the extended use period, the taxpayer must identify a qualified group of units that constitute 40 percent or more of the residential units in the project. The requirements in paragraph (b)(3)(iii) of this section apply to these identifications.

(ii) *Applicable fraction determinations.*—For each taxable year in the extended use period, the taxpayer must identify a qualified group of units to be used in determining the applicable fractions for the buildings in the project.

(A) *Identification of the units in the qualified group of units used for determining applicable fractions.*—The residential units that are identified for purposes of this paragraph (b)(3)(ii) include the units that, under paragraph (b)(3)(i) of this section, are included in the qualified group of units identified for purposes of the set-aside qualification of the project. The taxpayer may identify additional units for inclusion in the group of units used in determining the applicable fractions for buildings in the project provided that the resulting group is a qualified group of units within the meaning of paragraph (b)(2) of this section.

(B) *Computing applicable fractions of buildings.*—For a taxable year, the applicable fraction of a building in a project is computed using the units that are in the particular building and that are also in the qualified group of units for the project identified for purposes of this paragraph (b)(3)(ii). The units included in the applicable fraction of a building do not have to be a qualified group of units on their own. See *Example 4* of paragraph (e) of this section.

(iii) *Identification of units.*—The recordkeeping and reporting requirements in §1.42-19T(c)(1) apply both to the identification of units that is required by paragraph (b)(3)(i) of this section and the identification of units that is described in paragraph (b)(3)(ii) of this section.

(c) *Procedures.*—(1) - (2) [Reserved]

(3) *Designation of imputed income limitations.*—(i) *Timing of designation.*—(A) Before a unit is first occupied as a low-income unit, or, except as provided in paragraph (c)(3)(i)(B) of this section, is first occupied under a changed income limit, the taxpayer must designate the unit's imputed income limitation or changed imputed income limitation.

(B) For an occupied unit that is subject to a change in imputed income limitation pursuant to paragraph (d) of this section, the taxpayer must designate the unit's changed imputed income limitation not later than the end of the taxable year in which the change occurs.

(ii) *10-percent increments.*—Under section 42(g)(1)(C)(ii)(III), a designation is valid only if it is one of the following: 20 percent, 30 percent, 40 percent, 50 percent, 60 percent, 70 percent, or 80 percent of AMGI.

(iii) *Continuity.*—Except as provided in paragraph (d) of this section, the imputed income limitation of a residential unit does not change.

(iv) [Reserved]

(4) [Reserved]

(d) *Changing a unit's designated imputed income limitation.*—(1) *Permitted changes.*—Notwithstanding paragraph (c)(3)(iii) of this section, the taxpayer may change the imputed income limitation of a unit in the following circumstances subject to the timing of designation requirement in paragraph (c)(3)(i)(B) of this section.

(i) *Federally permitted changes.*—Permission for the change is contained in IRS forms, instructions, or guidance published in the Internal Revenue Bulletin pursuant to §601.601(d)(2)(ii)(b) of this chapter.

(ii) *Housing credit agency (Agency)-permitted changes.*—The Agency with jurisdiction of the project has issued public written guidance that provides conditions for a permitted change and that applies to all average income test projects under the jurisdiction of the Agency.

(iii) *Certain laws.*—The change in designation is required or appropriate to enhance protections contained in the following, as amended—

(A) The Americans with Disabilities Act of 1990 (ADA), Pub. L. 101-336, 104 Stat. 328, 42 U.S.C. 12101, et seq.;

(B) The Fair Housing Amendments Act of 1988, Pub. L. 100-430, 102 Stat.1619, 42 U.S.C. 3601 et. seq.;

(C) The Violence Against Women Act of 1994, Pub. L. 103-322, 108 Stat. 1902, 34 U.S.C. 12291, et. seq.;

(D) The Rehabilitation Act of 1973, Pub. L. 93-112, 87 Stat. 394, 29 U.S.C. 701, et seq.; or

(E) Any other State, Federal, or local law or program that protects tenants and that is identified pursuant to paragraph (d)(1)(i) or (ii) of this section.

(iv) *Tenant movement.*—If a current income-qualified tenant moves to a different unit in the project—

(A) The unit to which the tenant moves has its imputed income designation, if any, changed to the limitation of the unit from which the tenant is moving; and

(B) The vacated unit takes on the prior limitation, if any, of the tenant's new unit.

(v) *Restoring compliance with average income requirements.*—If one or more units lose low-income status or if there is a change in the imputed income limitation of some unit and if either event would cause a previously qualifying group of units to cease to be described in paragraph (b)(2)(ii) of this section, then the taxpayer may designate an imputed income limitation for a market-rate unit or may reduce the existing imputed income limitations of one or more other units in the project in order to restore compliance with the average income requirement. The rule in this paragraph (d)(1)(v) may be applied to market-rate, vacant, or low-income units, but, in the case of occupied units, the current tenants must qualify under the new, lower imputed income limitation.

(2) [Reserved]

(e) *Examples.*—The operation of this section is illustrated by the following examples.

(1) *Example 1.*—(i) *Facts.* (A) A single-building housing project received an allocation of housing credit dollar amount. The taxpayer who owns the project elects the average income test, intending for the 10-unit building to have 100 percent low-income occupancy. The taxpayer properly and timely designates the imputed income limitations for the 10 units as follows: 5 units at 80 percent of AMGI; and 5 units at 40 percent of AMGI. Also, for the first credit year, the taxpayer follows proper procedure in identifying 4 units as the qualified group of units that are to be used for qualifying under the average income set-aside (Units ## 1, 2, 6, and 7). Additionally, for the first credit year, the taxpayer follows proper procedure in identifying all 10 units as the qualified group of units that are to be used for the applicable fraction determination. All of the units in the project are described in paragraphs (b)(1)(i) through (iii) of this section.

Table 1 to Paragraph (e)(1)(i)(A)

Unit Number	Imputed Income Limitation of the Unit
1	80 percent of AMGI
2	80 percent of AMGI
3	80 percent of AMGI

Unit Number	Imputed Income Limitation of the Unit
4	80 percent of AMGI
5	80 percent of AMGI
6	40 percent of AMGI
7	40 percent of AMGI
8	40 percent of AMGI
9	40 percent of AMGI
10	40 percent of AMGI

(B) In the first taxable year of the credit period (Year 1), the project is fully leased and occupied.

(ii) *Analysis.* The identified groups are qualified groups under paragraph (b)(2) of this section. All units in both of the groups are described in paragraphs (b)(1)(i) through (iii) of this section, and the averages of the imputed income limitations of both the 4-unit group (Units ## 1, 2, 6, and 7) and the 10-unit group do not exceed 60 percent of AMGI.

(A) *Average income set-aside.* The project qualifies under the average income set-aside because the identified group of 4 units (Units ## 1, 2, 6, and 7) is a qualified group of units that comprise at least 40% of the residential units in the project.

(B) *Qualified basis.* All 10 units in the identified qualified group of units are used in the applicable fraction determination when calculating qualified basis for purposes of determining the annual credit amount under section 42(a).

(2) *Example 2.*—(i) *Facts.* Assume the same facts as *Example 1* of paragraph (e)(1) of this section. In Year 2, Unit # 6 (which has a designated imputed income limitation of 40 percent of AMGI) becomes uninhabitable. Repair work on Unit # 6 is completed in Year 3. For Year 2, Taxpayer identifies the following as a qualified group of units that are to be used for both the set-aside requirement and the applicable fraction determination: Units ## 1–4 and 7–10. For Year 3, Taxpayer identifies all 10 units as the qualified group of units that are to be used for the set-aside requirement and the applicable fraction determination.

(ii) *Analysis.* For Year 2, the identified group is a qualified group under paragraph (b)(2) of this section. All 8 units in the group are described in paragraphs (b)(1)(i) through (iii) of this section, and the average of the imputed income limitations of the 8 units in the group of units does not exceed 60 percent of AMGI.

(A) *Average income set-aside.* For Year 2, the project qualifies for the average income set-aside because the project contains a qualified group of units that comprises at least 40% of the residential units in the project.

(B) *Qualified basis.* To determine qualified basis in Year 2, the 8 units in the identified qualified group of units are used in the applicable fraction determination when calculating qualified basis for purposes of determining the annual credit amount under section 42(a). Unit # 6 could not have been identified in the qualified group of units for use in the applicable fraction determination because its lack of habitability prevents it from being a low-income unit. Further, Taxpayer could not have identified all 9 of the habitable units to be used in the qualified group of units for the applicable fraction determination because the average of imputed income limitations of

those 9 exceeds 60 percent of AMGI. Taxpayer had a choice of which of Units ## 1–5 it was going to not identify for use in the applicable fraction determination. Omitting any one of them reduces the average limitation of the remaining group of 8 units to an amount that does not exceed 60 percent of AMGI. Given taxpayer's decision to leave out Unit #5, Units ## 1, 2, 3, 4, 7, 8, 9, and 10 are taken into account in the applicable fraction.

(C) *Recapture.* At the close of Year 2, Unit # 6's unsuitability for occupancy precludes it from being described in paragraph (b)(1)(iii) of this section. Unit # 6's resulting failure to be a low-income unit prevents it from being in a qualified group for purposes of computing the applicable fraction. The decline in the applicable fraction yields a decline in qualified basis, which results in credit recapture under section 42(j) for Year 2. Additionally, Unit # 5 is not a low-income unit because the taxpayer did not include it in the qualified group of units identified for determining the building's applicable fraction. The exclusion of Unit # 5 from the qualified group of units further reduces the applicable fraction for Year 2 and so reduces qualified basis for that year as well. Thus, this exclusion increases the credit recapture amount under section 42(j).

(D) *Restoration of habitability and of qualified basis.* As described in the facts in paragraph (e)(2)(i) of this section, in Year 3, after repair work is complete, the formerly uninhabitable Unit # 6 is again occupied by a qualified tenant at the same imputed income limitation, and the Taxpayer identifies all 10 units as the qualified group of units that are to be used for the set-aside requirement and the applicable fraction determination. The identified group is a qualified group under paragraph (b)(2) of this section. All 10 units in the group are described in paragraphs (b)(1)(i) through (iii) of this section, and the average of the imputed income limitations of the 10 units in the group of units does not exceed 60 percent of AMGI. For Year 3, all 10 units are included in the qualified group of units for purposes of the average income set-aside test and are a qualified group of units for the applicable fraction determination.

(3) *Example 3.*—(i) *Facts.* Assume the same facts as *Example 2* of paragraph (e)(2) of this section, except that the income for the tenant residing in Unit # 5 has declined so that tenant's income does not exceed 60 percent of AMGI. For Year 2, taxpayer timely redesignates Unit # 5 pursuant to the rule in paragraph (d)(1)(v) of this section so that the imputed income limitation is 60 percent of AMGI instead of 80 percent of AMGI. Taxpayer also makes revisions so that Unit # 5 is rent-restricted under the redesignated imputed income limitation. Taxpayer identifies 9 units (Units ## 1–5 and 7–10) as the qualified group of units that are to be used for the set-aside requirement and the applicable fraction determination.

Table 2 to Paragraph (e)(3)(i)

Unit Number	Imputed Income Limitation of the Unit
1	80 percent of AMGI
2	80 percent of AMGI
3	80 percent of AMGI
4	80 percent of AMGI
5	60 percent of AMGI
6	40 percent of AMGI
7	40 percent of AMGI
8	40 percent of AMGI
9	40 percent of AMGI
10	40 percent of AMGI

(ii) *Analysis.* For Year 2, the identified group is a qualified group under paragraph (b)(2) of this section. All 9 units in the group are described in paragraphs (b)(1)(i) through (iii) of this section, and the average of the imputed income limitations of the 9 units in the group of units does not exceed 60 percent of AMGI.

(A) *Average income set-aside.* For Year 2, project contains a qualified group of units that comprises at least 40% of the residential units in the project.

(B) *Qualified basis.* To determine qualified basis, all 9 units in the identified qualified group of units are used in the applicable fraction determination when calculating qualified basis for purposes of determining the annual credit amount under section 42(a). Unit # 6 could not have been identified in the qualified group of units for use in the applicable fraction determination because its lack of habitability prevents it from being a low-income unit. Thus, Units ## 1, 2, 3, 4, 5, 7, 8, 9, and 10 are taken into account in the applicable fraction determination.

Reg. § 1.42-19(e)(2)

(C) *Recapture*. At the close of Year 2, the amount of the qualified basis is less than the amount of the qualified basis at the close of Year 1, because Unit # 6's unsuitability for occupancy prohibits it from being a low-income unit. Unit # 6's failure to be a low-income unit results in a credit recapture amount under section 42(j) for Year 2 related to Unit #6. Because Units ## 1–5 and 7–10 are all included in the qualified group of units for use in the applicable fraction determination, Units ## 1-5 and 7-10 are included in qualified basis for Year 2 when determining the recapture amount.

(4) *Example 4.*—(i) *Facts*. (A) A multiple-building housing project consisting of two buildings received an allocation of housing credit dollar amount, and the taxpayer who owns the project elects the average income test. The taxpayer intends for the buildings (each containing 5 units) to have 100 percent low-income occupancy. The taxpayer properly and timely designates the imputed income limitations for the 10 units in Buildings 1 and 2 as follows: Building A contains 2 units at 80 percent of AMGI and 3 units at 40 percent of AMGI; and Building B contains 2 units at 40 percent of AMGI and 3 units at 80 percent of AMGI.

Table 3 to Paragraph (e)(4)(i)(A)

Building A, Unit Number	Imputed Income Limitation of the Unit
A1	80 percent of AMGI
A2	80 percent of AMGI
A3	40 percent of AMGI
A4	40 percent of AMGI
A5	40 percent of AMGI
Building B, Unit Number	
B1	40 percent of AMGI
B2	40 percent of AMGI
B3	80 percent of AMGI
B4	80 percent of AMGI
B5	80 percent of AMGI

(B) In the first taxable year of the credit period (Year 1), the project is fully leased and occupied. Also, for the first credit year, the taxpayer follows proper procedure in identifying all 10 units as a qualified group of units for the minimum set-aside and the applicable fraction determination.

(ii) *Analysis*. For Year 1, the identified group is a qualified group under paragraph (b)(2) of this section. All 10 units in the group are described in paragraphs (b)(1)(i) through (iii) of this section, and the average of the imputed income limitations of the 10 units in the group of units does not exceed 60 percent of AMGI.

(A) *Average income test*. The multiple-building project meets the average income test as the project contains a qualified group of units that comprises at least 40% of the residential units in the project. The fact that the average of the income limitations of the units in Building B exceeds 60 percent of AMGI does not impact this result.

(B) *Qualified basis*. To determine qualified basis, all 10 units in the identified qualified group of units across Building A and Building B are used in the applicable fraction determination when calculating qualified basis of each building for purposes of determining the annual credit amount under section 42(a). The fact that the average of the units in Building B exceeds 60 percent of AMGI does not impact the applicable fraction of Building B because the average of the identified group of units across both buildings does not exceed 60 percent of AMGI.

(5) *Example 5.*—(i) *Facts*. A single-building housing project received an allocation of housing credit dollar amount, and the taxpayer who owns the project elects the average income test. During Year 2 of the credit period, the tenant residing in a unit with a designated imputed income limitation of 40 percent of AMGI moves to a market-rate unit within the same project. The tenant's income continues to be at or below 40 percent of AMGI.

(ii) *Analysis*. Under the rule in paragraph (d)(1)(iv) of this section, when the current income-qualified tenant moves to a different unit in the project, the unit to which the tenant moves is eligible for the taxpayer to designate as a unit with a designated imputed income limitation of 40 percent of AMGI. If the taxpayer makes those designations, the unit vacated by the tenant takes on the prior limitation, if any, of the tenant's new unit. In this situation, the vacated unit formerly occupied by the tenant is now a market-rate unit.

(6) *Example 6.*—(i) *Facts*. A single-building housing project received an allocation of housing credit dollar amount, and the taxpayer who owns the project elects the average income test. During Year 2 of the credit period, the disability status under the ADA of a tenant changes, and therefore under the provisions of the ADA, the tenant now needs to reside in a different unit with different accommodations. The tenant currently resides in a unit with a designated imputed income limitation of 40 percent of AMGI. A unit that would meet the tenant's needs is available on the first-floor of the building, but it was previously a low-income unit with a designated imputed income limitation of 70 percent of AMGI and thus a higher maximum gross rent than the tenant's current unit. The tenant moves to the first-floor unit.

(ii) *Analysis*. The tenant's move was required under the ADA. Accordingly, the taxpayer is permitted to change the designation of the imputed income limitation of the first-floor unit so that the unit's designation is 40 percent of AMGI. Under paragraph (d)(1)(iv) of this section, the vacated unit takes on the prior limitation of 70 percent of AMGI of the tenant's new unit.

(f) *Applicability dates.*—(1) *In general.*—Except as provided in paragraph (f)(3) of this section, this section applies to taxable years beginning after December 31, 2022.

(2) *Designations of occupied units.*—(i) If a residential unit is occupied at the end of the most recent taxable year ending before the first taxable year to which this section applies and if the unit is to be taken into account as a low-income unit under this section as of the beginning of the first taxable year to which this section applies, then not later than the first day of such first taxable year, the taxpayer must designate an imputed income limitation for the unit. The first taxable year to which this section applies means the first taxable year beginning after December 31, 2022, if paragraph (f)(1) of this section applies, or the taxable year described in paragraph (f)(3) of this section if the taxpayer chooses to apply paragraph (f)(3) of this section.

(ii) The designation required by paragraph (f)(2)(i) of this section must comply with paragraph (c)(3)(ii) of this section and § 1.42-19T(c)(3)(iv), without taking into account § 1.42-19T(c)(4). Section 1.42-19T(c)(2) applies to these designations, except that the Agency may allow the notification to be made along with any other notifications for the first taxable year beginning after December 31, 2022.

(iii) The designated imputed income limitation for the unit may not be less than the income that the current occupant of the unit had when that occupancy began.

(3) *Applicability of this section to taxable years beginning before January 1, 2023.*—A taxpayer may choose to apply this section to a taxable year beginning after October 12, 2022, and before January 1, 2023, provided that the taxpayer chooses to apply § 1.42-15 to the same taxable year. [Reg. § 1.42-19.]

☐ [*T.D.* 9967, 10-7-2022 (corrected 11-10-2022 and 11-29-2022).]

[Reg. § 1.42-19T]

§ 1.42-19T. Average income test (temporary).
(a) -(b) [Reserved]

(c) *Procedures.*—(1) *Identification of low-income units for use in the average income set-aside test or the applicable fraction determination.*—(i) *In general.*—For a taxable year, a taxpayer must follow the procedures described in paragraph (c)(1)(ii) of this section to identify—

(A) A qualified group of units that satisfy the average income set-aside test; and

(B) A qualified group of units used to determine the applicable fraction.

(ii) *Recording and communicating.*—The procedures described in this paragraph (c)(1)(ii) are—

(A) Recording the identification in its books and records, where the identification must be retained for a period not shorter than the record retention requirement under § 1.42-5(b)(2); and

(B) Communicating the annual identifications to the applicable *housing credit agency* (Agency) as provided in paragraph (c)(2) of this section.

(2) *Notifications to the Agency with jurisdiction over a project.*— (i) *Agency flexibility.*—An Agency may establish the time and manner in which information is annually provided to it.

(ii) *Example.*—An Agency may allow a taxpayer to describe a current year's information by reporting differences from the previous year's information or by reporting that there are no such differences. Various Agencies may choose to apply this manner of reporting to the identity of a qualified group of units for use in the average income set-aside or applicable fraction determination, or the imputed income limits designated for the various units in a project.

(3) *Designation of imputed income limitations.*—(i) - (iii) [Reserved]

(iv) *Recording, retention, and annual communications related to designations.*—A taxpayer designates a unit's imputed income limitation by recording the limitation in its books and records, where it must be retained for a period not shorter than the record retention requirement under § 1.42-5(b)(2). The preceding sentence applies both to units whose first occupancy is as a low-income unit and to previously market-rate units that are converted to low-income status. The designation must also be communicated annually to the applicable Agency as provided in paragraph (c)(2) of this section.

(4) *Waiver for failure to comply with procedural requirements.*—On a case-by-case basis, the Agency has the discretion to waive in writing any failure to comply with the requirements of paragraph (c)(1) or (2) or (c)(3)(iv) of this section up to 180 days after discovery of the failure, whether by taxpayer or Agency. If an Agency exercises this discretion, then the relevant requirements are treated as having been satisfied. In such a case, the tax consequences under this section correspond to that deemed satisfaction.

(d) *Changing a unit's designated imputed income limitation.*— (1) [Reserved]

(2) *Process for changing a unit's designated imputed income limitation.* The taxpayer effects a change in a unit's imputed income limitation by recording the limitation in its books and records, where it must be retained for a period not shorter than the record retention requirement under § 1.42-5(b)(2). The new designation must also be communicated to the applicable Agency as provided in paragraph (c)(2) of this section and must become part of the annual report to the Agency of income designations. The prior designation must be retained in the books and records for the period specified in paragraph (c)(3)(iv) of this section. A designation under this paragraph (d)(2) is considered to be made in a manner consistent with paragraph (c)(3) of this section.

(e) [Reserved]

(f) *Applicability dates.*—(1) *In general.*—Except as provided in paragraph (f)(3) of this section, this section applies to taxable years beginning after December 31, 2022.

(2) *Designations of occupied units.*—(i) If a residential unit is occupied at the end of the most recent taxable year ending before the first taxable year to which this section applies and if the unit is to be taken into account as a low-income unit under this section as of the beginning of the first taxable year to which this section applies, then not later than the first day of such first taxable year, the taxpayer must designate an imputed income limitation for the unit. The first taxable year to which this section applies means the first taxable year beginning after December 31, 2022, if paragraph (f)(1) of this section applies, or the taxable year described in paragraph (f)(3) of this section if the taxpayer chooses to apply paragraph (f)(3) of this section.

(ii) The designation required by paragraph (f)(2)(i) of this section must comply with § 1.42-19(c)(3)(ii) and paragraph (c)(3)(iv) of this section, without taking into account paragraph (c)(4) of this section. Paragraph (c)(2) of this section applies to these designations, except that the Agency may allow the notification to be made along with any other notifications for the first taxable year beginning after December 31, 2022.

(iii) The designated imputed income limitation for the unit may not be less than the income that the current occupant of the unit had when that occupancy began.

(3) *Applicability of this section to taxable years beginning before January 1, 2023.*—A taxpayer may choose to apply this section to a taxable year beginning after October 12, 2022, and before January 1,

2023, provided that the taxpayer chooses to apply § 1.42-15 to the same taxable year.

(4) *Expiration date.*—The applicability of this section expires on October 7, 2025. [Reg. § 1.42-19T.]

☐ [T.D. 9967, 10-7-2022.]

[Reg. § 1.43-0]

§ 1.43-0. Table of contents.—This section lists the captions contained in § § 1.43-0 through 1.43-7.

(d) Costs paid or incurred prior to first injection.
    (1) In general.
    (2) First injection after filing of return for taxable year costs are allowable.
    (3) First injection more than 36 months after close of taxable year costs are paid or incurred.
    (4) Injections in volumes less than the volumes specified in the project plan.
    (5) Examples.
 (e) Other rules.
    (1) Anti-abuse rule.
    (2) Costs paid or incurred to acquire a project.
    (3) Examples.

§1.43-5. At-risk limitation. [Reserved]

§1.43-6. Election out of section 43.
 (a) Election to have the credit not apply.
    (1) In general.
    (2) Time for making the election.
    (3) Manner of making the election.
 (b) Election by partnerships and S corporations.

§1.43-7. Effective date of regulations.
[Reg. §1.43-0.]
   ☐ [T.D. 8448, 11-20-92.]

[Reg. §1.43-1]

§1.43-1. The enhanced oil recovery credit—general rules.—(a) *Claiming the credit.*—(1) *In general.*—The enhanced oil recovery credit (the "credit") is a component of the section 38 general business credit. A taxpayer that owns an operating mineral interest (as defined in §1.614-2(b)) in a property may claim the credit for qualified enhanced oil recovery costs (as described in §1.43-4) paid or incurred by the taxpayer in connection with a qualified enhanced oil recovery project (as described in §1.43-2) undertaken with respect to the property. A taxpayer that does not own an operating mineral interest in a property may not claim the credit. To the extent a credit included in the current year business credit under section 38(b) is unused under section 38, the credit is carried back or forward under the section 39 business credit carryback and carryforward rules.

(2) *Examples.*—The following examples illustrate the principles of this paragraph (a).

Example 1. Credit for operating mineral interest owner. In 1992, A, the owner of an operating mineral interest in a property, begins a qualified enhanced oil recovery project using cyclic steam. B, who owns no interest in the property, purchases and places in service a steam generator. B sells A steam, which A uses as a tertiary injectant described in section 193. Because A owns an operating mineral interest in the property with respect to which the project is undertaken, A may claim a credit for the cost of the steam. Although B owns the steam generator used to produce steam for the project, B may not claim a credit for B's costs because B does not own an operating mineral interest in the property.

Example 2. Credit for operating mineral interest owner. C and D are partners in CD, a partnership that owns an operating mineral interest in a property. In 1992, CD begins a qualified enhanced oil recovery project using cyclic steam. D purchases a steam generator and sells steam to CD. Because CD owns an operating mineral interest in the property with respect to which the project is undertaken, CD may claim a credit for the cost of the steam. Although D owns the steam generator used to produce steam for the project, D may not claim a credit for the costs of the steam generator because D paid these costs in a capacity other than that of an operating mineral interest owner.

(b) *Amount of the credit.*—A taxpayer's credit is an amount equal to 15 percent of the taxpayer's qualified enhanced oil recovery costs for the taxable year, reduced by the phase-out amount, if any, determined under paragraph (c) of this section.

(c) *Phase-out of the credit as crude oil prices increase.*—(1) *In general.*—The amount of the credit (determined without regard to this paragraph (c)) for any taxable year is reduced by an amount which bears the same ratio to the amount of the credit (determined without regard to this paragraph (c)) as—

    (i) The amount by which the reference price determined under section 29(d)(2)(C) for the calendar year immediately preceding the calendar year in which the taxable year begins exceeds $28 (as adjusted under paragraph (c)(2) of this section); bears to

    (ii) $6.

(2) *Inflation adjustment.*—(i) *In general.*—For any taxable year beginning in a calendar year after 1991, an amount equal to $28

multiplied by the inflation adjustment factor is substituted for the $28 amount under paragraph (c)(1)(i) of this section.

    (ii) *Inflation adjustment factor.*—For purposes of this paragraph (c), the inflation adjustment factor for any calendar year is a fraction, the numerator of which is the GNP implicit price deflator for the preceding calendar year and the denominator of which is the GNP implicit price deflator for 1990. The "GNP implicit price deflator" is the first revision of the implicit price deflator for the gross national product as computed and published by the Secretary of Commerce. As early as practicable, the inflation adjustment factor for each calendar year will be published by the Internal Revenue Service in the Internal Revenue Bulletin.

(3) *Examples.*—The following examples illustrate the principles of this paragraph (c).

Example 1. Reference price exceeds $28. In 1992, E, the owner of an operating mineral interest in a property, incurs $100 of qualified enhanced oil recovery costs. The reference price for 1991 determined under section 29(d)(2)(C) is $30 and the inflation adjustment factor for 1992 is 1. E's credit for 1992 determined without regard to the phase-out for crude oil price increases is $15 ($100 × 15%). In determining E's credit, the credit is reduced by $5 ($15 × ($30 − ($28 × 1))/6). Accordingly, E's credit for 1992 is $10 ($15 − $5).

Example 2. Inflation adjustment. In 1993, F, the owner of an operating mineral interest in a property, incurs $100 of qualified enhanced oil recovery costs. The 1992 reference price is $34, and the 1993 inflation adjustment factor is 1.10. F's credit for 1993 determined without regard to the phase-out for crude oil price increases is $15 ($100 × 15%). In determining F's credit, $30.80 (1.10 × $28) is substituted for $28, and the credit is reduced by $8 ($15 × ($34 − $30.80)/6). Accordingly, F's credit for 1993 is $7 ($15 − $8).

(d) *Reduction of associated deductions.*—(1) *In general.*—Any deduction allowable under chapter 1 for an expenditure taken into account in computing the amount of the credit determined under paragraph (b) of this section is reduced by the amount of the credit attributable to the expenditure.

(2) *Certain deductions by an integrated oil company.*—For purposes of determining the intangible drilling and development costs that an integrated oil company must capitalize under section 291(b), the amount allowable as a deduction under section 263(c) is the deduction allowable after paragraph (d)(1) of this section is applied. *See* §1.43-4(b)(2) (extent to which integrated oil company intangible drilling and development costs are qualified enhanced oil recovery costs).

(e) *Basis adjustment.*—For purposes of subtitle A, the increase in the basis of property which would (but for this paragraph (e)) result from an expenditure with respect to the property is reduced by the amount of the credit determined under paragraph (b) of this section attributable to the expenditure.

(f) *Passthrough entity basis adjustment.*—(1) *Partners' interests in a partnership.*—To the extent a partnership expenditure is not deductible under paragraph (d)(1) of this section or does not increase the basis of property under paragraph (e) of this section, the expenditure is treated as an expenditure described in section 705(a)(2)(B) (concerning decreases to basis of partnership interests). Thus, the adjusted bases of the partners' interests in the partnership are decreased (but not below zero).

(2) *Shareholders' stock in an S corporation.*—To the extent an S corporation expenditure is not deductible under paragraph (d)(1) of this section or does not increase the basis of property under paragraph (e) of this section, the expenditure is treated as an expenditure described in section 1367(a)(2)(D) (concerning decreases to basis of S corporation stock). Thus, the bases of the shareholders' S corporation stock are decreased (but not below zero).

(g) *Examples.*—The following examples illustrate the principles of paragraphs (d) through (f) of this section.

Example 1. Deductions reduced for credit amount. In 1992, G, the owner of an operating mineral interest in a property, incurs $100 of intangible drilling and development costs in connection with a qualified enhanced oil recovery project undertaken with respect to the property. G elects under section 263(c) to deduct these intangible drilling and development costs. The amount of the credit determined under paragraph (b) of this section attributable to the $100 of intangible drilling and development costs is $15 ($100 × 15%). Therefore, G's otherwise allowable deduction of $100 for the intangible drilling and development costs is reduced by $15. Accordingly, in 1992, G may deduct under section 263(c) only $85 ($100 − $15) for these costs.

Example 2. Integrated oil company deduction reduced. The facts are the same as in *Example 1*, except that G is an integrated oil company. As in *Example 1*, the amount of the credit determined under paragraph (b) of this section attributable to the $100 of intangible drilling and development costs is $15, and G's allowable deduction under section 263(c) is $85. Because G is an integrated oil company, G must capitalize $25.50 ($85 × 30%) under section 291(b). Therefore, in 1992, G may deduct under section 263(c) only $59.50 ($85 − $25.50) for these intangible drilling and development costs.

Example 3. Basis of property reduced. In 1992, H, the owner of an operating mineral interest in a property, pays $100 to purchase tangible property that is an integral part of a qualified enhanced oil recovery project undertaken with respect to the property. The amount of the credit determined under paragraph (b) of this section attributable to the $100 is $15 ($100 × 15%). Therefore, for purposes of subtitle A, H's basis in the tangible property is $85 ($100 − $15).

Example 4. Basis of interest in passthrough entity reduced. In 1992, I is a 50% partner in IJ, a partnership that owns an operating mineral interest in a property. IJ pays $200 to purchase tangible property that is an integral part of a qualified enhanced oil recovery project undertaken with respect to the property. The amount of the credit determined under paragraph (b) of this section attributable to the $200 is $30 ($200 × 15%). Therefore, for purposes of subtitle A, IJ's basis in the tangible property is $170 ($200 − $30). Under paragraph (f) of this section, the amount of the purchase price that does not increase the basis of the property ($30) is treated as an expenditure described in section 705(a)(2)(B). Therefore, I's basis in the partnership interest is reduced by $15 (I's allocable share of the section 705(a)(2)(B) expenditure ($30 × 50%)). [Reg. § 1.43-1.]

☐ [T.D. 8448, 11-20-92.]

[Reg. § 1.43-2]

§1.43-2. Qualified enhanced oil recovery project.—(a) *Qualified enhanced oil recovery project.*—A "qualified enhanced oil recovery project" is any project that meets all of the following requirements—

(1) The project involves the application (in accordance with sound engineering principles) of one or more qualified tertiary recovery methods (as described in paragraph (e) of this section) that is reasonably expected to result in more than an insignificant increase in the amount of crude oil that ultimately will be recovered;

(2) The project is located within the United States (within the meaning of section 638(1));

(3) The first injection of liquids, gases, or other matter for the project (as described in paragraph (c) of this section) occurs after December 31, 1990; and

(4) The project is certified under § 1.43-3.

(b) *More than insignificant increase.*—For purposes of paragraph (a)(1) of this section, all the facts and circumstances determine whether the application of a tertiary recovery method can reasonably be expected to result in more than an insignificant increase in the amount of crude oil that ultimately will be recovered. Certain information submitted as part of a project certification is relevant to this determination. *See* § 1.43-3(a)(3)(i)(D). In no event is the application of a recovery method that merely accelerates the recovery of crude oil considered an application of one or more qualified tertiary recovery methods that can reasonably be expected to result in more than an insignificant increase in the amount of crude oil that ultimately will be recovered.

(c) *First injection of liquids, gases, or other matter.*—(1) *In general.*— The "first injection of liquids, gases, or other matter" generally occurs on the date a tertiary injectant is first injected into the reservoir. The "first injection of liquids, gases, or other matter" does not include—

(i) The injection into the reservoir of any liquids, gases, or other matter for the purpose of pretreating or preflushing the reservoir to enhance the efficiency of the tertiary recovery method; or

(ii) Test or experimental injections.

(2) *Example.*—The following example illustrates the principles of this paragraph (c).

Example. Injections to pretreat the reservoir. In 1989, A, the owner of an operating mineral interest in a property, began injecting water into the reservoir for the purpose of elevating reservoir pressure to obtain miscibility pressure to prepare for the injection of miscible gas in connection with an enhanced oil recovery project. In 1992, A obtains miscibility pressure in the reservoir and begins injecting miscible gas into the reservoir. The injection of miscible gas, rather than the injection of water, is the first injection of liquids, gases, or other matter into the reservoir for purposes of determining whether the first injection of liquids, gases, or other matter occurs after December 31, 1990.

(d) *Significant expansion exception.*—(1) *In general.*—If a project for which the first injection of liquids, gases, or other matter (within the meaning of paragraph (c)(1) of this section) occurred before January 1, 1991, is significantly expanded after December 31, 1990, the expansion is treated as a separate project for which the first injection of liquids, gases, or other matter occurs after December 31, 1990.

(2) *Substantially unaffected reservoir volume.*—A project is considered significantly expanded if the injection of liquids, gases, or other matter after December 31, 1990, is reasonably expected to result in more than an insignificant increase in the amount of crude oil that ultimately will be recovered from reservoir volume that was substantially unaffected by the injection of liquids, gases, or other matter before January 1, 1991.

(3) *Terminated projects.*—Except as otherwise provided in this paragraph (d)(3), a project is considered significantly expanded if each qualified tertiary recovery method implemented in the project prior to January 1, 1991, terminated more than 36 months before implementing an enhanced oil recovery project that commences after December 31, 1990. Notwithstanding the provisions of the preceding sentence, if a project implemented prior to January 1, 1991, is terminated for less than 36 months before implementing an enhanced oil recovery project that commences after December 31, 1990, a taxpayer may request permission to treat the project that commences after December 31, 1990, as a significant expansion. Permission will not be granted if the Internal Revenue Service determines that a project was terminated to make an otherwise nonqualifying project eligible for the credit. For purposes of section 43, a qualified tertiary recovery method terminates at the point in time when the method no longer results in more than an insignificant increase in the amount of crude oil that ultimately will be recovered. All the facts and circumstances determine whether a tertiary recovery method has terminated. Among the factors considered is the project plan, the unit plan of development, or other similar plan. A tertiary recovery method is not necessarily terminated merely because the injection of the tertiary injectant has ceased. For purposes of this paragraph (d)(1), a project is implemented when costs that will be taken into account in determining the credit with respect to the project are paid or incurred.

(4) *Change in tertiary recovery method.*—If the application of a tertiary recovery method or methods with respect to an enhanced oil recovery project for which the first injection of liquids, gases, or other matter occurred before January 1, 1991, has not been terminated for more than 36 months, a taxpayer may request a private letter ruling from the Internal Revenue Service whether the application of a different tertiary recovery method or methods after December 31, 1990, that does not affect reservoir volume substantially unaffected by the previous tertiary recovery method or methods, is treated as a significant expansion. All the facts and circumstances determine whether a change in tertiary recovery method is treated as a significant expansion. Among the factors considered are whether the change in tertiary recovery method is in accordance with sound engineering principles and whether the change in method will result in more than an insignificant increase in the amount of crude oil that would be recovered using the previous method. A more intensive application of a tertiary recovery method after December 31, 1990, is not treated as a significant expansion.

(5) *Examples.*—The following examples illustrate the principles of this paragraph (d).

Example 1. Substantially unaffected reservoir volume. In January 1988, B, the owner of an operating mineral interest in a property, began injecting steam into the reservoir in connection with a cyclic steam enhanced oil recovery project. The project affected only a portion of the reservoir volume. In 1992, B begins cyclic steam injections with respect to reservoir volume that was substantially unaffected by the previous cyclic steam project. Because the injection of steam into the reservoir in 1992 affects reservoir volume that was substantially unaffected by the previous cyclic steam injection, the cyclic steam injection in 1992 is treated as a separate project for which the first injection of liquids, gases, or other matter occurs after December 31, 1990.

Example 2. Tertiary recovery method terminated more than 36 months. In 1982, C, the owner of an operating mineral interest cyclic steam injection as a method for the recovery of crude oil. The project was certified as a tertiary recovery project for purposes of the windfall profit tax. In May 1988, the application of the cyclic steam tertiary recovery method terminated. In July 1992, C begins drilling injection wells as part of a project to apply the steam drive tertiary recovery method with respect to the same project area affected by the cyclic steam method. C begins steam injections in September 1992. Because C commences an enhanced oil recovery project more than 36 months after the previous tertiary recovery method was terminated, the project is treated as a separate project for which the first injection of liquids, gases, or other matter occurs after December 31, 1990.

Example 3. Change in tertiary recovery method affecting substantially unaffected reservoir volume. In 1984, D, the owner of an operating mineral interest in a property implemented a tertiary recovery project using cyclic steam as a method for the recovery of crude oil. The project was certified as a tertiary recovery project for purposes of the windfall profit tax. D continued the cyclic steam injection until 1992, when the tertiary recovery method was changed from cyclic steam injection to steam drive. The steam drive affects reservoir volume that was substantially unaffected by the cyclic steam injection. Because the steam drive affects reservoir volume that was substantially unaffected by the cyclic steam injection, the steam drive is treated as a separate project for which the first injection of liquids, gases, or other matter occurs after December 31, 1990.

Example 4. Change in tertiary recovery method not affecting substantially unaffected reservoir volume. In 1988, E, the owner of an operating mineral interest in a property, undertook an immiscible nitrogen enhanced oil recovery project that resulted in more than an insignificant increase in the ultimate recovery of crude oil from the property. E continued the immiscible nitrogen project until 1992, when the project was converted from immiscible nitrogen displacement to miscible nitrogen displacement by increasing the injection of nitrogen to increase reservoir pressure. The miscible nitrogen displacement affects the same reservoir volume that was affected by the immiscible nitrogen displacement. Because the miscible nitrogen displacement does not affect reservoir volume that was substantially unaffected by the immiscible nitrogen displacement nor was the immiscible nitrogen displacement project terminated for more than 36 months before the miscible nitrogen displacement project was implemented, E must obtain a ruling whether the change from immiscible nitrogen displacement to miscible nitrogen displacement is treated as a separate project for which the first injection of liquids, gases, or other matter occurs after December 31, 1990. If E does not receive a ruling, the miscible nitrogen displacement project is not a qualified project.

Example 5. More intensive application of a tertiary recovery method. In 1989, F, the owner of an operating mineral interest in a property, undertook an immiscible carbon dioxide displacement enhanced oil recovery project. F began injecting carbon dioxide into the reservoir under immiscible conditions. The injection of carbon dioxide under immiscible conditions resulted in more than an insignificant increase in the ultimate recovery of crude oil from the property. F continues to inject the same amount of carbon dioxide into the reservoir until 1992, when new engineering studies indicate that an increase in the amount of carbon dioxide injected is reasonably expected to result in a more than insignificant increase in the amount of crude oil that would be recovered from the property as a result of the previous injection of carbon dioxide. The increase in the amount of carbon dioxide injected affects the same reservoir volume that was affected by the previous injection of carbon dioxide. Because the additional carbon dioxide injected in 1992 does not affect reservoir volume that was substantially unaffected by the previous injection of carbon dioxide and the previous immiscible carbon dioxide displacement method was not terminated for more than 36 months before additional carbon dioxide was injected, the increase in the amount of carbon dioxide injected into the reservoir is not a significant expansion. Therefore, it is not a separate project for which the first injection of liquids, gases, or other matter occurs after December 31, 1990.

(e) *Qualified tertiary recovery methods.*—(1) *In general.*—For purposes of paragraph (a)(1) of this section, a "qualified tertiary recovery method" is any one or any combination of the tertiary recovery methods described in paragraph (e)(2) of this section. To account for advances in enhanced oil recovery technology, the Internal Revenue Service may by revenue ruling prescribe that a method not described in paragraph (e)(2) of this section is a "qualified tertiary recovery method." In addition, a taxpayer may request a private letter ruling that a method not described in paragraph (e)(2) of this section or in a revenue ruling is a qualified tertiary recovery method. Generally, the methods identified in revenue rulings or private letter rulings will be limited to those methods that involve the displacement of oil from the reservoir rock by means of modifying the properties of the fluids in the reservoir or providing the energy and drive mechanism to force the oil to flow to a production well. The recovery methods described in paragraph (e)(3) of this section are not "qualified tertiary recovery methods."

(2) *Tertiary recovery methods that qualify.*—(i) *Thermal recovery methods.*—(A) *Steam drive injection.*—The continuous injection of steam into one set of wells (injection wells) or other injection source to effect oil displacement toward and production from a second set of wells (production wells);

(B) *Cyclic steam injection.*—The alternating injection of steam *and production of oil with condensed steam from the same well or* wells; and

(C) *In situ combustion.*—The combustion of oil or fuel in the reservoir sustained by injection of air, oxygen-enriched air, oxygen, or supplemental fuel supplied from the surface to displace unburned oil toward producing wells. This process may include the concurrent, alternating, or subsequent injection of water.

(ii) *Gas Flood recovery methods.*—(A) *Miscible fluid displacement.*—The injection of gas (*e.g.*, natural gas, enriched natural gas, a

liquified petroleum slug driven by natural gas; carbon dioxide, nitrogen, or flue gas) or alcohol into the reservoir at pressure levels such that the gas or alcohol and reservoir oil are miscible;

(B) *Carbon dioxide augmented waterflooding.*—The injection of carbonated water, or water and carbon dioxide, to increase waterflood efficiency;

(C) *Immiscible carbon dioxide displacement.*—The injection of carbon dioxide into an oil reservoir to effect oil displacement under conditions in which miscibility with reservoir oil is not obtained. This process may include the concurrent, alternating, or subsequent injection of water; and

(D) *Immiscible nonhydrocarbon gas displacement.*—The injection of nonhydrocarbon gas (*e.g.*, nitrogen) into an oil reservoir, under conditions in which miscibility with reservoir oil is not obtained, to obtain a chemical or physical reaction (other than pressure) between the oil and the injected gas or between the oil and other reservoir fluids. This process may include the concurrent, alternating, or subsequent injection of water.

(iii) *Chemical flood recovery methods.*—(A) *Microemulsion flooding.*—The injection of a surfactant system (*e.g.*, a surfactant, hydrocarbon, cosurfactant, electrolyte, and water) to enhance the displacement of oil toward producing wells; and

(B) *Caustic flooding.*—The injection of water that has been made chemically basic by the addition of alkali metal hydroxides, silicates, or other chemicals.

(iv) *Mobility control recovery method—Polymer augmented waterflooding.*—The injection of polymeric additives with water to improve the areal and vertical sweep efficiency of the reservoir by increasing the viscosity and decreasing the mobility of the water injected. Polymer augmented waterflooding does not include the injection of polymers for the purpose of modifying the injection profile of the wellbore or the relative permeability of various layers of the reservoir, rather than modifying the water-oil mobility ratio.

(3) *Recovery methods that do not qualify.*—The term "qualified tertiary recovery method" does not include—

(i) Waterflooding—The injection of water into an oil reservoir to displace oil from the reservoir rock and into the bore of the producing well;

(ii) Cyclic gas injection—The increase or maintenance of pressure by injection of hydrocarbon gas into the reservoir from which it was originally produced;

(iii) Horizontal drilling—The drilling of horizontal, rather than vertical, wells to penetrate hydrocarbon bearing formations;

(iv) Gravity drainage—The production of oil by gravity flow from drainholes that are drilled from a shaft or tunnel dug within or below the oil bearing zones; and

(v) Other methods—Any recovery method not specifically designated as a qualified tertiary recovery method in either paragraph (e)(2) of this section or in a revenue ruling or private letter ruling described in paragraph (e)(1) of this section.

(4) *Examples.*—The following examples illustrate the principles of this paragraph (e).

Example 1. Polymer augmented waterflooding. In 1992 G, the owner of an operating mineral interest in a property, begins a waterflood project with respect to the property. To reduce the relative permeability in certain areas of the reservoir and minimize water coning, G injects polymers to plug thief zones and improve the areal and vertical sweep efficiency of the reservoir. The injection of polymers into the reservoir does not modify the water-oil mobility ratio. Accordingly, the injection of polymers into the reservoir in connection with the waterflood project does not constitute polymer augmented waterflooding and the project is not a qualified enhanced oil recovery project.

Example 2. Polymer augmented waterflooding. In 1993 H, the owner of an operating mineral interest in a property, begins a caustic flooding project with respect to the property. Engineering studies indicate that the relative permeability of various layers of the reservoir may result in the loss of the injectant to thief zones, thereby reducing the areal and vertical sweep efficiency of the reservoir. As part of the caustic flooding project, H injects polymers to plug the thief zones and improve the areal and vertical sweep efficiency of the reservoir. Because the polymers are injected into the reservoir to improve the effectiveness of the caustic flooding project, the project is a qualified enhanced oil recovery project. [Reg. § 1.43-2.]

□ [*T.D. 8448, 11-20-92.*]

[Reg. § 1.43-3]

§1.43-3. Certification.—(a) *Petroleum engineer's certification of a project.*—(1) *In general.*—A petroleum engineer must certify, under penalties of perjury, that an enhanced oil recovery project meets the requirements of section 43(c)(2)(A). A petroleum engineer's certification must be submitted for each project. The petroleum engineer certifying a project must be duly registered or certified in any state.

(2) *Timing of certification.*—The operator of an enhanced oil recovery project or any other operating mineral interest owner designated by the operated ("designated owner") must submit a petroleum engineer's certification to the Internal Revenue Service Center, Austin, Texas, or such other place as may be designated by revenue procedure or other published guidance, not later than the last date prescribed by law (including extensions) for filing the operator's or designated owner's federal income tax return for the first taxable year for which the enhanced oil recovery credit (the "credit") is allowable. The operator may designate any other operating mineral interest owner (the "designated owner") to file the petroleum engineer's certification.

(3) *Content of certification.*—(i) *In general.*—A petroleum engineer's certification must contain the following information—

(A) The name and taxpayer identification number of the operator or the designated owner submitting the certification;

(B) A statement identifying the project, including its geographic location;

(C) A statement that the project involves a tertiary recovery method (as defined in section 43(c)(2)(A)(i)) and a description of the process used, including—

(1) A description of the implementation and operation of the project sufficient to establish that it is implemented and operated in accordance with sound engineering practices;

(2) If the project involves the application of a tertiary recovery method approved in a private letter ruling described in paragraph (e)(1) of section 1.43-2, a copy of the private letter ruling, and

(3) The date on which the first injection of liquids, gases, or other matter occurred or is expected to occur.

(D) A statement that the application of a qualified tertiary recovery method or methods is expected to result in more than an insignificant increase in the amount of crude oil that ultimately will be recovered, including—

(1) Data on crude oil reserve estimates covering the project area with and without the enhanced oil recovery process,

(2) Production history prior to implementation of the project and estimates of production after implementation of the project, and

(3) An adequate delineation of the reservoir, or portion of the reservoir, from which the ultimate recovery of crude oil is expected to be increased as a result of the implementation and operation of the project; and

(E) A statement that the petroleum engineer believes that the project is a qualified enhanced oil recovery project within the meaning of section 43(c)(2)(A).

(ii) *Additional information for significantly expanded projects.*—The petroleum engineer's certification for a project that is significantly expanded must in addition contain—

(A) If the expansion affects reservoir volume that was substantially unaffected by a previously implemented project, an adequate delineation of the reservoir volume affected by the previously implemented project;

(B) If the expansion involves the implementation of an enhanced oil recovery project more than 36 months after the termination of a qualified tertiary recovery method that was applied before January 1, 1991, the date on which the previous tertiary recovery method terminated and an explanation of the data or assumptions relied upon to determine the termination date;

(C) If the expansion involves the implementation of an enhanced oil recovery project less than 36 months after the termination of a qualified tertiary recovery method that was applied before January 1, 1991, a copy of a private letter ruling from the Internal Revenue Service that the project implemented after December 31, 1990 is treated as a significant expansion; or

(D) If the expansion involves the application after December 31, 1990, of a tertiary recovery method or methods that do not affect reservoir volume that was substantially unaffected by the application of a different tertiary recovery method or methods before January 1, 1991, a copy of a private letter ruling from the Internal Revenue Service that the change in tertiary recovery method is treated as a significant expansion.

(b) *Operator's continued certification of a project.*—(1) *In general.*—For each taxable year following the taxable year for which the petroleum engineer's certification is submitted, the operator or designated owner must certify, under penalties of perjury, that an enhanced oil recovery project continues to be implemented substantially in accor-

dance with the petroleum engineer's certification submitted for the project. An operator's certification must be submitted for each project.

(2) *Timing of certification.*—The operator or designated owner of an enhanced oil recovery project must submit an operator's certification to the Internal Revenue Service Center, Austin, Texas, or such other place as may be designated by revenue procedure or other published guidance, not later than the last date prescribed by law (including extensions) for filing the operator's or designated owner's federal income tax return for any taxable year after the taxable year for which the petroleum engineer's certification is filed.

(3) *Content of certification.*—An operator's certification must contain the following information—

(i) The name and taxpayer identification number of the operator or the designated owner submitting the certification;

(ii) A statement identifying the project, including its geographic location and the date on which the petroleum engineer's certification was filed;

(iii) A statement that the project continues to be implemented substantially in accordance with the petroleum engineer's certification (as described in paragraph (a) of this section) submitted for the project; and

(iv) A description of any significant change or anticipated change in the information submitted under paragraph (a)(3) of this section, including a change in the date on which the first injection of liquids, gases, or other matter occurred or is expected to occur.

(c) *Notice of project termination.*—(1) *In general.*—If the application of a tertiary recovery method is terminated, the operator or designated owner must submit a notice of project termination to the Internal Revenue Service.

(2) *Timing of notice.*—The operator or designated owner of an enhanced oil recovery project must submit the notice of project termination to the Internal Revenue Service Center, Austin, Texas, or such other place as may be designated by revenue procedure or other published guidance, not later than the last date prescribed by law (including extensions) for filing the operator's or designated owner's federal income tax return for the taxable year in which the project terminates.

(3) *Content of notice.*—A notice of project termination must contain the following information—

(i) The name and taxpayer identification number of the operator or the designated owner submitting the notice;

(ii) A statement identifying the project, including its geographic location and the date on which the petroleum engineer's certification was filed; and

(iii) The date on which the application of the tertiary recovery method was terminated.

(d) *Failure to submit certification.*—If a petroleum engineer's certification (as described in paragraph (a) of this section) or an operator's certification (as described in paragraph (b) of this section) is not submitted in the time or manner prescribed by this section, the credit will be allowed only after the appropriate certifications are submitted. [Reg. §1.43-3.]

☐ [*T.D. 8448*, 11-20-92.]

[Reg. §1.43-4]

§1.43-4. Qualified enhanced oil recovery costs.—(a) *Qualifying costs.*—(1) *In general.*—Except as provided in paragraph (e) of this section, amounts paid or incurred in any taxable year beginning after December 31, 1990, that are qualified tertiary injectant expenses (as described in paragraph (b)(1) of this section), intangible drilling and development costs (as described in paragraph (b)(2) of this section), and tangible property costs (as described in paragraph (b)(3) of this section) are "qualified enhanced oil recovery costs" if the amounts are paid or incurred with respect to an asset which is used for the primary purpose (as described in paragraph (c) of this section) of implementing an enhanced oil recovery project. Any amount paid or incurred in any taxable year beginning before January 1, 1991, in connection with an enhanced oil recovery project is not a qualified enhanced oil recovery cost.

(2) *Costs paid or incurred for an asset which is used to implement more than one qualified enhanced oil recovery project or for other activities.*—Any cost paid or incurred during the taxable year for an asset which is used to implement more than one qualified enhanced oil recovery project is allocated among the projects in determining the qualified enhanced oil recovery costs for each qualified project for the taxable year. Similarly, any cost paid or incurred during the taxable year for an asset which is used to implement a qualified enhanced oil recovery project and which is also used for other

activities (for example, an enhanced oil recovery project that is not a qualified enhanced oil recovery project) is allocated among the qualified enhanced oil recovery project and the other activities to determine the qualified enhanced oil recovery costs for the taxable year. *See* §1.613-5(a). Any cost paid or incurred for an asset which is used to implement a qualified enhanced oil recovery project and which is also used for other activities is not required to be allocated under this paragraph (a)(2) if the use of the property for nonqualifying activities is *de minimis* (*e.g*, not greater than 10%). Costs are allocated under this paragraph (a)(2) only if the asset with respect to which the costs are paid or incurred is used for the primary purpose of implementing an enhanced oil recovery project. *See* paragraph (c) of this section. Any reasonable allocation method may be used. A method that allocates costs based on the anticipated use in a project or activity is a reasonable method.

(b) *Costs defined.*—(1) *Qualified tertiary injectant expenses.*—For purposes of this section, "qualified tertiary injectant expenses" means any costs that are paid or incurred in connection with a qualified enhanced oil recovery project and that are deductible under section 193 for the taxable year. *See* section 193 and §1.193-1. Qualified tertiary injectant expenses are taken into account in determining the credit with respect to the taxable year in which the tertiary injectant expenses are deductible under section 193.

(2) *Intangible drilling and development costs.*—For purposes of this section, "intangible drilling and development costs" means any intangible drilling and development costs that are paid or incurred in connection with a qualified enhanced oil recovery project and for which the taxpayer may make an election under section 263(c) for the taxable year. Intangible drilling and development costs are taken into account in determining the credit with respect to the taxable year in which the taxpayer may deduct the intangible drilling and development costs under section 263(c). For purposes of this paragraph (b)(2), the amount of the intangible drilling and development costs for which an integrated oil company may make an election under section 263(c) is determined without regard to section 291(b).

(3) *Tangible property costs.*—(i) *In general.*—For purposes of this section, "tangible property costs" means an amount paid or incurred during a taxable year for tangible property that is an integral part of a qualified enhanced oil recovery project and that is depreciable or amortizable under chapter 1. An amount paid or incurred for tangible property is taken into account in determining the credit with respect to the taxable year in which the cost is paid or incurred.

(ii) *Integral part.*—For purposes of this paragraph (b), tangible property is an integral part of a qualified enhanced oil recovery project if the property is used directly in the project and is essential to the completeness of the project. All the facts and circumstances determine whether tangible property is used directly in a qualified enhanced oil recovery project and is essential to the completeness of the project. Generally, property used to acquire or produce the tertiary injectant or property used to transport the tertiary injectant to a project site is property that is an integral part of the project.

(4) *Examples.*—The following examples illustrate the principles of this paragraph (b). Assume for each of these examples that the qualified enhanced oil recovery costs are paid or incurred with respect to an asset which is used for the primary purpose of implementing an enhanced oil recovery project.

Example 1. Qualified costs—in general. (i) In 1992, X, a corporation, acquires an operating mineral interest in a property and undertakes a cyclic steam enhanced oil recovery project with respect to the property. X pays a fee to acquire a permit to drill and hires a contractor to drill six wells. As part of the project implementation, X constructs a building to serve as an office on the property and purchases equipment, including downhole equipment (*e.g.*, casing, tubing, packers, and sucker rods), pumping units, a steam generator, and equipment to remove gas and water from the oil after it is produced. X constructs roads to transport the equipment to the wellsites and incurs costs for clearing and draining the ground in preparation for the drilling of the wells. X purchases cars and trucks to provide transportation for monitoring the wellsites. In addition, X contracts with Y for the delivery of water to produce steam to be injected in connection with the cyclic steam project, and purchases storage tanks to store the water.

(ii) The leasehold acquisition costs are not qualified enhanced oil recovery costs. However, the costs of the permit to drill are intangible drilling and development costs that are qualified costs. The costs associated with hiring the contractor to drill, constructing roads, and clearing and draining the ground are intangible drilling and development costs that are qualified enhanced oil recovery costs. The downhole equipment, the pumping units, the steam generator, and the equipment to remove the gas and water from the oil after it is produced are used directly in the project and are essential to the completeness of the project. Therefore, this equipment is an integral part of the project and the costs of the equipment are qualified enhanced oil recovery costs. Although the building that X constructs as an office and the cars and trucks X purchases to provide transportation for monitoring the wellsites are used directly in the project, they are not essential to the completeness of the project. Therefore, the building and the cars and trucks are not an integral part of the project and their costs are not qualified enhanced oil recovery costs. The cost of the water X purchases from Y is a tertiary injectant expense that is a qualified enhanced oil recovery cost. The storage tanks X acquires to store the water are required to provide a proximate source of water for the production of steam. Therefore, the water storage tanks are an integral part of the project and the costs of the water storage tanks are qualified enhanced oil recovery costs.

Example 2. Diluent storage tanks. In 1992, A, the owner of an operating mineral interest, undertakes a qualified enhanced oil recovery project with respect to the property. A acquires diluent to be used in connection with the project. A stores the diluent in a storage tank that A acquires for that purpose. The storage tank provides a proximate source of diluent to be used in the tertiary recovery method. Therefore, the storage tank is used directly in the project and is essential to the completeness of the project. Accordingly, the storage tank is an integral part of the project and the cost of the storage tank is a qualified enhanced oil recovery cost.

Example 3. Oil storage tanks. In 1992, Z, a corporation and the owner of an operating mineral interest in a property, undertakes a qualified enhanced oil recovery project with respect to the property. Z acquires storage tanks that Z will use solely to store the crude oil that is produced from the enhanced oil recovery project. The storage tanks are not used directly in the project and are not essential to the completeness of the project. Therefore, the storage tanks are not an integral part of the enhanced oil recovery project and the costs of the storage tanks are not qualified enhanced oil recovery costs.

Example 4. Oil refinery. B, the owner of an operating mineral interest in a property, undertakes a qualified enhanced oil recovery project with respect to the property. Located on B's property is an oil refinery where B will refine the crude oil produced from the project. The refinery is not used directly in the project and is not essential to the completeness of the project. Therefore, the refinery is not an integral part of the enhanced oil recovery project.

Example 5. Gas processing plant. C, the owner of an operating mineral interest in a property, undertakes a qualified enhanced oil recovery project with respect to the property. A gas processing plant where C will process gas produced in the project is located on C's property. The gas processing plant is not used directly in the project and is not essential to the completeness of the project. Therefore, the gas processing plant is not an integral part of the enhanced oil recovery project.

Example 6. Gas processing equipment. The facts are the same as in *Example 5* except that C uses a portion of the gas processing plant to separate and recycle the tertiary injectant. The gas processing equipment used to separate and recycle the tertiary injectant is used directly in the project and is essential to the completeness of the project. Therefore, the gas processing equipment used to separate and recycle the tertiary injectant is an integral part of the enhanced oil recovery project and the costs of this equipment are qualified enhanced oil recovery costs.

Example 7. Steam generator costs allocated. In 1988, D, the owner of an operating mineral interest in a property, undertook a steam drive project with respect to the property. In 1992, D decides to undertake a steam drive project with respect to reservoir volume that was substantially unaffected by the 1988 project. The 1992 project is a significant expansion that is a qualified enhanced oil recovery project. D purchases a new steam generator with sufficient capacity to provide steam for both the 1988 project and the 1992 project. The steam generator is used directly in the 1992 project and is essential to the completeness of the 1992 project. Accordingly, the steam generator is an integral part of the 1992 project. Because the steam generator is also used to provide steam for the 1988 project, D must allocate the cost of the steam generator to the 1988 project and the 1992 project. Only the portion of the cost of the steam generator that is allocable to the 1992 project is a qualified enhanced oil recovery cost.

Example 8. Carbon dioxide pipeline. In 1992, E, the owner of an operating mineral interest in a property, undertakes an immiscible carbon dioxide displacement project with respect to the property. E constructs a pipeline to convey carbon dioxide to the project site. E contracts with F, a producer of carbon dioxide, to purchase carbon dioxide to be injected into injection wells in E's enhanced oil recovery project. The cost of the carbon dioxide is a tertiary injectant expense that is a qualified enhanced oil recovery cost. The pipeline is used by E to transport the tertiary injectant, that is, the carbon dioxide to the project site. Therefore, the pipeline is an integral part of the project. Accordingly, the cost of the pipeline is a qualified enhanced oil recovery cost.

Example 9. Water source wells. In 1992, G the owner of an operating mineral interest in a property, undertakes a polymer augmented waterflood project with respect to the property. G drills water wells to provide water for injection in connection with the project. The costs of drilling the water wells are intangible drilling and development costs that are paid or incurred in connection with the project. Therefore, the costs of drilling the water wells are qualified enhanced oil recovery costs.

Example 10. Leased equipment. In 1992, H, the owner of an operating mineral interest in a property undertakes a steam drive project with respect to the property. H contracts with I, a driller, to drill injection wells in connection with the project. H also leases a steam generator to provide steam for injection in connection with the project. The drilling costs are intangible drilling and development costs that are paid in connection with the project and are qualified enhanced oil recovery costs. The steam generator is used to produce the tertiary injectant. The steam generator is used directly in the project and is essential to the completeness of the project; therefore, it is an integral part of the project. The costs of leasing the steam generator are tangible property costs that are qualified enhanced oil recovery costs.

(c) *Primary purpose.*—(1) *In general.*—For purposes of this section, a cost is a qualified enhanced oil recovery cost only if the cost is paid or incurred with respect to an asset which is used for the primary purpose of implementing one or more enhanced oil recovery projects, at least one of which is a qualified enhanced oil recovery project. All the facts and circumstances determine whether an asset is used for the primary purpose of implementing an enhanced oil recovery project. For purposes of this paragraph (c), an enhanced oil recovery project is a project that satisfies the requirements of paragraphs (a)(1) and (2) of section 1.43-2.

(2) *Tertiary injectant costs.*—Tertiary injectant costs generally satisfy the primary purpose test of this paragraph (c).

(3) *Intangible drilling and development costs.*—Intangible drilling and development costs paid or incurred with respect to a well that is used in connection with the recovery of oil by primary or secondary methods are not qualified enhanced oil recovery costs. Except as provided in this paragraph (c)(3), a well used for primary or secondary recovery is not used for the primary purpose of implementing an enhanced oil recovery project. A well drilled for the primary purpose of implementing an enhanced oil recovery project is not considered to be used for primary or secondary recovery, notwithstanding that some primary or secondary production may result when the well is drilled, provided that such primary or secondary production is consistent with the unit plan of development or other similar plan. All the facts and circumstances determine whether primary or secondary recovery is consistent with the unit plan of development or other similar plan.

(4) *Tangible property costs.*—Tangible property costs must be paid or incurred with respect to property which is used for the primary purpose of implementing an enhanced oil recovery project. If tangible property is used partly in a qualified enhanced oil recovery project and partly in another activity, the property must be primarily used to implement the qualified enhanced oil recovery project.

(5) *Offshore drilling platforms.*—Amounts paid or incurred in connection with the acquisition, construction, transportation, erection, or installation of an offshore drilling platform (regardless of whether the amounts are intangible drilling and development costs) that is used in connection with the recovery of oil by primary or secondary methods are not qualified enhanced oil recovery costs. An offshore drilling platform used for primary or secondary recovery is not used for the primary purpose of implementing an enhanced oil recovery project.

(6) *Examples.*—The following examples illustrate the principles of this paragraph (c).

Example 1. Intangible drilling and development costs. In 1992, J incurs intangible drilling and development costs in drilling a well. J intends to use the well as an injection well in connection with an enhanced oil recovery project in 1994, but in the meantime will use the well in connection with a secondary recovery project. J may not take the intangible drilling and development costs into account in determining the credit because the primary purpose of a well used for secondary recovery is not to implement a qualified enhanced oil recovery project.

Example 2. Offshore drilling platform. K, the owner of an operating mineral interest in an offshore oil field located within the United States, constructs an offshore drilling platform that is designed to accommodate the primary, secondary, and tertiary development of the field. Subsequent to primary and secondary development of the field, K commences an enhanced oil recovery project that involves

the application of a qualified tertiary recovery method. As part of the enhanced oil recovery project, K drills injection wells from the offshore drilling platform K used in the primary and secondary development of the field and installs an additional separator on the platform. Because the offshore drilling platform was used in the primary and secondary development of the field and was not used for the primary purpose of implementing tertiary development of the field, costs incurred by K in connection with the acquisition, construction, transportation, erection, or installation of the offshore drilling platform are not qualified enhanced oil recovery costs. However, the costs K incurs for the additional separator are qualified enhanced oil recovery costs because the separator is used for the primary purpose of implementing tertiary development of the field. In addition, the intangible drilling and development costs K incurs in connection with drilling the injection wells are qualified enhanced oil recovery costs with respect to which K may claim the enhanced oil recovery credit.

(d) *Costs paid or incurred prior to first injection.*—(1) *In general.*—Qualified enhanced oil recovery costs may be paid or incurred prior to the date of the first injection of liquids, gases, or other matter (within the meaning of § 1.43-2(c)). If the first injection of liquids, gases, or other matter occurs on or before the date the taxpayer files the taxpayer's federal income tax return for the taxable year with respect to which the costs are allowable, the costs may be taken into account on that return. If the first injection of liquids, gases, or other matter is expected to occur after the date the taxpayer files that return, costs may be taken into account on that return if the Internal Revenue Service issues a private letter ruling to the taxpayer that so permits.

(2) *First injection after filing of return for taxable year costs are allowable.*—Except as provided in paragraph (d)(3) of this section, if the first injection of liquids, gases, or other matter occurs or is expected to occur after the date the taxpayer files the taxpayer's federal income tax return for the taxable year with respect to which the costs are allowable, the costs may be taken into account on an amended return (or in the case of a Coordinated Examination Program taxpayer, on a written statement treated as a qualified return) after the earlier of—

(i) The date the first injection of liquids, gases, or other matter occurs; or

(ii) The date the Internal Revenue Service issues a private letter ruling that provides that the taxpayer may take costs into account prior to the first injection of liquids, gases, or other matter.

(3) *First injection more than 36 months after close of taxable year costs are paid or incurred.*—If the first injection of liquids, gases, or other matter occurs more than 36 months after the close of the taxable year in which costs are paid or incurred, the taxpayer may take the costs into account in determining the credit only if the Internal Revenue Service issues a private letter ruling to the taxpayer that so provides.

(4) *Injections in volumes less than the volumes specified in the project plan.*—For purposes of this paragraph (d), injections in volumes significantly less than the volumes specified in the project plan, the unit plan of development, or another similar plan do not constitute the first injection of liquids, gases, or other matter.

(5) *Examples.*—The following examples illustrate the provisions of paragraph (d) of this section.

Example 1. First injection before return filed. In 1992, L, a calendar year taxpayer, undertakes a qualified enhanced oil recovery project on a property in which L owns an operating mineral interest. L incurs $1,000 of intangible drilling and development costs, which L may elect to deduct under section 263(c) for 1992. The first injection of liquids, gases, or other matter (within the meaning of § 1.43-2(c)) occurs in March 1993. L files a 1992 federal income tax return in April 1993. Because the first injection occurs before the filing of L's 1992 federal income tax return, L may take the $1,000 of intangible drilling and development costs into account in determining the credit for 1992 on that return.

Example 2. First injection after return filed. In 1993, M, a calendar year taxpayer, undertakes a qualified enhanced oil recovery project on a property in which M owns an operating mineral interest. M incurs $2,000 of intangible drilling and development costs, which M elects to deduct under section 263(c) for 1993. The first injection of liquids, gases, or other matter is expected to occur in 1995. M files a 1993 federal income tax return in April 1994. Because the first injection of liquids, gases, or other matter occurs after the date on which M's 1993 federal income tax return is filed in April 1994, M may take the $2,000 of intangible drilling and development costs into account on an amended return for 1993 after the earlier of the date the first injection of liquids, gases, or other matter occurs, or the date the Internal Revenue Service issues a private letter ruling that provides that M may take the $2,000 into account prior to first injection.

Example 3. First injection more than 36 months after taxable year. N, a calendar year taxpayer, owns an operating mineral interest in a property on which N undertakes an immiscible carbon dioxide displacement project. In 1994, N incurs $5,000 in connection with the construction of a pipeline to transport carbon dioxide to the project site. The first injection of liquids, gases, or other matter is expected to occur after the pipeline is completed in 1998. Because the first injection of liquids, gases, or other matter occurs more than 36 months after the close of the taxable year in which the $5,000 is incurred, N may take the $5,000 into account in determining the credit only if N receives a private letter ruling from the Internal Revenue Service that provides that N may take the $5,000 into account prior to first injection.

(e) *Other rules.*—(1) *Anti-abuse rule.*—Costs paid or incurred with respect to an asset that is acquired, used, or transferred in a manner designed to duplicate or otherwise unreasonably increase the amount of the credit are not qualified enhanced oil recovery costs, regardless of whether the costs would otherwise be creditable for a single taxpayer or more than one taxpayer.

(2) *Costs paid or incurred to acquire a project.*—A purchaser of an existing qualified enhanced oil recovery project may claim the credit for any section 43 costs in excess of the acquisition cost. However, costs paid or incurred to acquire an existing qualified enhanced oil recovery project (or an interest in an existing qualified enhanced oil recovery project) are not eligible for the credit.

(3) *Examples.*—The following examples illustrate the principles of paragraph (e) of this section.

Example 1. Duplicating or unreasonably increasing the credit. O owns an operating mineral interest in a property with respect to which a qualified enhanced oil recovery project is implemented. O acquires pumping units, rods, casing, and separators for use in connection with the project from an unrelated equipment dealer in an arm's length transaction. The equipment is used for the primary purpose of implementing the project. Some of the equipment acquired by O is used equipment. The costs paid by O for the used equipment are qualified enhanced oil recovery costs. O does not need to determine whether the equipment has been previously used in an enhanced oil recovery project.

Example 2. Duplicating or unreasonably increasing the credit. P and Q are co-owners of an oil property with respect to which a qualified enhanced oil recovery project is implemented. In 1992, P and Q jointly purchase a nitrogen plant to supply the tertiary injectant used in the project. P and Q claim the credit for their respective costs for the plant. In 1994, X, a corporation unrelated to P or Q, purchases the nitrogen plant and enters into an agreement to sell nitrogen to P and Q. Because this transaction duplicates or otherwise unreasonably increases the credit, the credit is not allowable for the amounts incurred by P and Q for the nitrogen purchased from X.

Example 3. Duplicating or unreasonably increasing the credit. The facts are the same as in *Example 2.* In addition, in 1995, P and Q reacquire the nitrogen plant from X. This constitutes the acquisition of property in a manner designed to duplicate or otherwise unreasonably increase the amount of the credit. Therefore, the credit is not allowable for amounts incurred by P and Q for the nitrogen plant purchased from X.

Example 4. Duplicating or unreasonably increasing the credit. R owns an operating mineral interest in a property with respect to which a qualified enhanced oil recovery project is implemented. R acquires a pump that is installed at the site of the project. After the pump has been placed in service for 6 months, R transfers the pump to a secondary recovery project and acquires a replacement pump for the tertiary project. The original pump is suited to the needs of the secondary recovery project and could have been installed there initially. The pumps have been acquired in a manner designed to duplicate or otherwise unreasonably increase the amount of the credit. Depending on the facts, the cost of one pump or the other may be a qualified enhanced oil recovery cost; however, R may not claim the credit with respect to the cost of both pumps.

Example 5. Acquiring a project. In 1993, S purchases all of T's interest in a qualified enhanced oil recovery project, including all of T's interest in tangible property that is an integral part of the project and all of T's operating mineral interest. In 1994, S incurs costs for additional tangible property that is an integral part of the project and which is used for the primary purpose of implementing the project. S also incurs costs for tertiary injectants that are injected in connection with the project. In determining the credit for 1994, S may take into account costs S incurred for tangible property and tertiary injectants. However, S may not take into account any amount that S paid for T's interest in the project in determining S's credit for any taxable year. [Reg. §1.43-4.]

☐ [*T.D.* 8448, 11-20-92.]

[Reg. §1.43-5]

§1.43-5. At-risk limitation.—[Reserved.]

☐ [*T.D.* 8448, 11-20-92.]

[Reg. §1.43-6]

§1.43-6. Election out of section 43.—(a) *Election to have the credit not apply.*—(1) *In general.*—A taxpayer may elect to have section 43 not apply for any taxable year. The taxpayer may revoke an election to have section 43 not apply for any taxable year. An election to have section 43 not apply (or a revocation of an election to have section 43 not apply) for any taxable year is effective only for the taxable year to which the election relates.

(2) *Time for making the election.*—A taxpayer may make an election under paragraph (a) of this section to have section 43 not apply (or revoke an election to have section 43 not apply) for any taxable year at any time before the expiration of the 3-year period beginning on the last date prescribed by law (determined without regard to extensions) for filing the return for the taxable year. The time for making the election (or revoking the election) is prescribed by section 43(e)(2) and may not be extended under §1.9100-1.

(3) *Manner of making the election.*—An election (or revocation) under paragraph (a)(1) of this section is made by attaching a statement to the taxpayer's federal income tax return or an amended return (or, in the case of a Coordinated Examination Program taxpayer, on a written statement treated as a qualified amended return) for the taxable year for which the election (or revocation) applies. The taxpayer must indicate whether the taxpayer is electing to not have section 43 apply or is revoking such an election and designate the project or projects to which the election (or revocation) applies. For any taxable year, the last election (or revocation) made by a taxpayer within the period prescribed in paragraph (a)(2) of this section determines whether section 43 applies for that taxable year.

(b) *Election by partnerships and S corporations.*—For partnerships and S corporations, an election to have section 43 not apply (or a revocation of an election to have section 43 not apply) for any taxable year is made, in accordance with the requirements of paragraph (a) of this section, by the partnership or S corporation with respect to the qualified enhanced oil recovery costs paid or incurred by the partnership or S corporation for the taxable year to which the election relates. [Reg. §1.43-6.]

☐ [*T.D.* 8448, 11-20-92.]

[Reg. §1.43-7]

§1.43-7. Effective date of regulations.—The provisions of §§1.43-1, 1.43-2 and 1.43-4 through 1.43-7 apply with respect to costs paid or incurred after December 31, 1991, in connection with a qualified enhanced oil recovery project. The provisions of §1.43-3 apply with respect to taxable years beginning after December 31, 1990. For costs paid or incurred after December 31, 1990, and before January 1, 1992, in connection with a qualified enhanced oil recovery project, taxpayers must take reasonable return positions taking into consideration the statute and its legislative history. [Reg. §1.43-7.]

☐ [*T.D.* 8448, 11-20-92.]

⟫⟫→ *Caution: Some of the provisions contained in former Code Sec. 44B, credit for employment of certain new employees, which was repealed by P.L. 98-369 (1984), are included in the expired targeted jobs credit under Code Sec. 51.*

[Reg. §1.44B-1]

§1.44B-1. Credit for employment of certain new employees.—(a) *In general.*—(1) *Targeted jobs credit.*—Under section 44B a taxpayer may elect to claim a credit for wages (as defined in section 51(c)) paid or incurred to members of a targeted group (as defined in section 51(d)). Generally, to qualify for the credit, the wages must be paid or incurred to members of a targeted group first hired after September 26, 1978. However, wages paid or incurred to a vocational rehabilitation referral (as defined in section 51(d)(2)) hired before September 27, 1978, may qualify for the credit if a credit under section 44B (as in effect prior to enactment of the Revenue Act of 1978) was claimed for

the individual by the taxpayer for a taxable year beginning before January 1, 1979. The amount of the credit shall be determined under section 51. Section 280C(b) (relating to the requirement that the deduction for wages be reduced by the amount of the credit) and the regulations thereunder will not apply to taxpayers who do not elect to claim the credit.

(2) *New job credit.*—Under section 44B (as in effect prior to enactment of the Revenue Act of 1978) a taxpayer may elect to claim as a credit the amount determined under sections 51, 52, and 53 (as in effect prior to enactment of the Revenue Act of 1978). Section 280C(b) (relating to the requirement that the deduction for wages be reduced

≫→ *Caution: Some of the provisions contained in former Code Sec. 44B, credit for employment of certain new employees, which was repealed by P.L. 98-369 (1984), are included in the expired targeted jobs credit under Code Sec. 51.*

by the amount of the credit) and the regulations thereunder will not apply to taxpayers who do not elect to claim the credit.

(b) *Time and manner of making election.*—The election to claim the targeted jobs credit and the new jobs credit is made by claiming the credit on an original return, or on an amended return, at any time before the expiration of the 3-year period beginning on the last date prescribed by law for filing the return for the taxable year (determined without regard to extensions). The election may be revoked within the above-described 3-year period by filing an amended return on which the credit is not claimed.

(c) *Elected by partnership, electing small business corporation, and members of a controlled group.*—In the case of a partnership, the election shall be made by the partnership. In the case of an electing small business corporation (as defined in section 1371(a)), the election shall be made by the corporation. In the case of a controlled group of corporations (within the meaning of section 52(a) and the regulations issued thereunder) not filing a consolidated return under section 1501, the election shall be made by each member of the group. In the case of an affiliated group filing a consolidated return under section 1501, the election shall be made by the group. [Reg. § 1.44B-1.]

☐ [*T.D.* 7921, 11-18-83.]

≫→ *Caution: Former Code Sec. 44F was redesignated as Code Sec. 30 and was redesignated again as Code Sec. 41.*

[Reg. § 5c.44F-1]

§ 5c.44F-1. Leases and T.D. 7921 research expenses.—For purposes of section 44F(b)(2)(A)(iii), the determination of whether any amount is paid or incurred to another person for the right to use personal property in the conduct of qualified research shall be made without regard to the characterization of the transaction as a lease under section 168(f)(8). See § 5c.168(f)(8)-1(b). [Temporary Reg. § 5c.44F-1.]

☐ [*T.D.* 7791, 10-20-81.]

[Reg. § 1.45D-0]

§ 1.45D-0. Table of contents.—This section lists the paragraphs contained in § 1.45D-1.

(1) In general.
(2) Population census tract location.
(E) Rental of real property for the GO Zone Targeted Population.
(10) Non-real estate qualified active low-income community business.
(i) Definition.
(ii) Payments of, or for, capital, equity or principal with respect to a non-real estate qualified active low-income community business.
(A) In general.
(B) Seventh year of the 7-year credit period.
(C) Amounts received from a qualifying entity.
(D) Definition of qualifying entity.
(e) Recapture.
(1) In general.
(2) Recapture event.
(3) Redemption.
(i) Equity investment in a C corporation.
(ii) Equity investment in an S corporation.
(iii) Capital interest in a partnership.
(4) Bankruptcy.
(5) Waiver of requirement or extension of time.
(i) In general.
(ii) Manner for requesting a waiver or extension.
(iii) Terms and conditions.
(6) Cure period.
(7) Example.
(f) Basis reduction.
(1) In general.
(2) Adjustment in basis of interest in partnership or S corporation.
(g) Other rules.
(1) Anti-abuse.
(2) Reporting requirements.
(i) Notification by CDE to taxpayer.
(A) Allowance of new markets tax credit.
(B) Recapture event.
(ii) CDE reporting requirements to Secretary.
(iii) Manner of claiming new markets tax credit.
(iv) Reporting recapture tax.
(3) Other Federal tax benefits.
(i) In general.
(ii) Low-income housing credit.
(4) Bankruptcy of CDE.
(h) Effective/applicability dates.
(1) In general.
(2) Exception for certain provisions.
(3) Targeted populations.
(4) Investments in non-real estate businesses.
[Reg. §1.45D-0.]

☐ [*T.D. 9560, 12-2-2011. Amended by T.D. 9600, 9-26-2012.*]

[Reg. §1.45D-1]

§1.45D-1. New markets tax credit.—(a) *Current year credit.*—The current year general business credit under section 38(b)(13) includes the new markets tax credit under section 45D(a).

(b) *Allowance of credit.*—(1) *In general.*—A taxpayer holding a qualified equity investment on a credit allowance date which occurs during the taxable year may claim the new markets tax credit determined under section 45D(a) and this section for such taxable year in an amount equal to the applicable percentage of the amount paid to a qualified community development entity (CDE) for such investment at its original issue. *Qualified equity investment* is defined in paragraph (c) of this section. *Credit allowance date* is defined in paragraph (b)(2) of this section. *Applicable percentage* is defined in paragraph (b)(3) of this section. A *CDE* is a qualified community development entity as defined in section 45D(c). The amount paid at original issue is determined under paragraph (b)(4) of this section.

(2) *Credit allowance date.*—The term *credit allowance date* means, with respect to any qualified equity investment—
(i) The date on which the investment is initially made; and
(ii) Each of the 6 anniversary dates of such date thereafter.

(3) *Applicable percentage.*—The *applicable percentage* is 5 percent for the first 3 credit allowance dates and 6 percent for the other 4 credit allowance dates.

(4) *Amount paid at original issue.*—The amount paid to the CDE for a qualified equity investment at its original issue consists of all amounts paid by the taxpayer to, or on behalf of, the CDE (including any underwriter's fees) to purchase the investment at its original issue.

(c) *Qualified equity investment.*—(1) *In general.*—The term *qualified equity investment* means any equity investment (as defined in paragraph (c)(2) of this section) in a CDE if—
(i) The investment is acquired by the taxpayer at its original issue (directly or through an underwriter) solely in exchange for cash;
(ii) Substantially all (as defined in paragraph (c)(5) of this section) of such cash is used by the CDE to make qualified low-income community investments (as defined in paragraph (d)(1) of this section); and
(iii) The investment is designated for purposes of section 45D and this section as a qualified equity investment or a non-real estate qualified equity investment (as defined in paragraph (c)(8) of this section) by the CDE on its books and records using any reasonable method.

(2) *Equity investment.*—The term *equity investment* means any stock (other than nonqualified preferred stock as defined in section 351(g)(2)) in an entity that is a corporation for Federal tax purposes and any capital interest in an entity that is a partnership for Federal tax purposes. See §§301.7701-1 through 301.7701-3 of this chapter for rules governing when a business entity, such as a business trust or limited liability company, is classified as a corporation or a partnership for Federal tax purposes.

(3) *Equity investments made prior to allocation.*—(i) *In general.*—Except as provided in paragraph (c)(3)(ii) of this section, an equity investment in an entity is not eligible to be designated as a qualified equity investment if it is made before the entity enters into an allocation agreement with the Secretary. An *allocation agreement* is an agreement between the Secretary and a CDE relating to a new markets tax credit allocation under section 45D(f)(2).

(ii) *Exceptions.*—Notwithstanding paragraph (c)(3)(i) of this section, an equity investment in an entity is eligible to be designated as a qualified equity investment or a non-real estate qualified equity investment under paragraph (c)(1)(iii) of this section if—

(A) *Allocation applications submitted by August 29, 2002.*
(1) The equity investment is made on or after April 20, 2001;
(2) The designation of the equity investment as a qualified equity investment is made for a credit allocation received pursuant to an allocation application submitted to the Secretary no later than August 29, 2002; and
(3) The equity investment otherwise satisfies the requirements of section 45D and this section; or

(B) *Other allocation applications.*
(1) The equity investment is made on or after the date the Secretary publishes a Notice of Allocation Availability (NOAA) in the **Federal Register;**
(2) The designation of the equity investment as a qualified equity investment is made for a credit allocation received pursuant to an allocation application submitted to the Secretary under that NOAA; and
(3) The equity investment otherwise satisfies the requirements of section 45D and this section.

(iii) *Failure to receive allocation.*—For purposes of paragraph (c)(3)(ii)(A) of this section, if the entity in which the equity investment is made does not receive an allocation pursuant to an allocation application submitted no later than August 29, 2002, the equity investment will not be eligible to be designated as a qualified equity investment. For purposes of paragraph (c)(3)(ii)(B) of this section, if the entity in which the equity investment is made does not receive an allocation under the NOAA described in paragraph (c)(3)(ii)(B)(1) of this section, the equity investment will not be eligible to be designated as a qualified equity investment.

(iv) *Initial investment date.*—If an equity investment is designated as a qualified equity investment in accordance with paragraph (c)(3)(ii) of this section, the investment is treated as initially made on the effective date of the allocation agreement between the CDE and the Secretary.

(4) *Limitations.*—(i) *In general.*—The term *qualified equity investment* does not include—
(A) Any equity investment issued by a CDE more than 5 years after the date the CDE enters into an allocation agreement (as defined in paragraph (c)(3)(i) of this section) with the Secretary; and

(B) Any equity investment by a CDE in another CDE, if the CDE making the investment has received an allocation under section 45D(f)(2).

(ii) *Allocation limitation.*—The maximum amount of equity investments issued by a CDE that may be designated under paragraph (c)(1)(iii) of this section by the CDE may not exceed the portion of the limitation amount allocated to the CDE by the Secretary under section 45D(f)(2).

(5) *Substantially all.*—(i) *In general.*—Except as provided in paragraph (c)(5)(v) of this section, the term *substantially all* means at least 85 percent. The substantially-all requirement must be satisfied for each annual period in the 7-year credit period using either the direct-tracing calculation under paragraph (c)(5)(ii) of this section, or the safe harbor calculation under paragraph (c)(5)(iii) of this section. For the first annual period, the substantially-all requirement is treated as satisfied if either the direct-tracing calculation under paragraph (c)(5)(ii) of this section, or the safe-harbor calculation under paragraph (c)(5)(iii) of this section, is performed on a single testing date and the result of the calculation is at least 85 percent. For each annual period other than the first annual period, the substantially-all requirement is treated as satisfied if either the direct-tracing calculation under paragraph (c)(5)(ii) of this section, or the safe harbor calculation under paragraph (c)(5)(iii) of this section, is performed every six months and the average of the two calculations for the annual period is at least 85 percent. For example, the CDE may choose the same two testing dates for all qualified equity investments regardless of the date each qualified equity investment was initially made under paragraph (b)(2)(i) of this section, provided the testing dates are six months apart. The use of the direct-tracing calculation under paragraph (c)(5)(ii) of this section (or the safe harbor calculation under paragraph (c)(5)(iii) of this section) for an annual period does not preclude the use of the safe harbor calculation under paragraph (c)(5)(iii) of this section (or the direct-tracing calculation under paragraph (c)(5)(ii) of this section) for another annual period, provided that a CDE that switches to a direct-tracing calculation must substantiate that the taxpayer's investment is directly traceable to qualified low-income community investments from the time of the CDE's initial investment in a qualified low-income community investment. For purposes of this paragraph (c)(5)(i), the *7-year credit period* means the period of 7 years beginning on the date the qualified equity investment is initially made. See paragraph (c)(6) of this section for circumstances in which a CDE may treat more than one equity investment as a single qualified equity investment.

(ii) *Direct-tracing calculation.*—The substantially-all requirement is satisfied if at least 85 percent of the taxpayer's investment is directly traceable to qualified low-income community investments as defined in paragraph (d)(1) of this section. The direct-tracing calculation is a fraction the numerator of which is the CDE's aggregate cost basis determined under section 1012 in all of the qualified low-income community investments that are directly traceable to the taxpayer's cash investment, and the denominator of which is the amount of the taxpayer's cash investment under paragraph (b)(4) of this section. For purposes of this paragraph (c)(5)(ii), cost basis includes the cost basis of any qualified low-income community investment that becomes worthless. See paragraph (d)(2) of this section for the treatment of amounts received by a CDE in payment of, or for, capital, equity or principal with respect to a qualified low-income community investment.

(iii) *Safe harbor calculation.*—The substantially-all requirement is satisfied if at least 85 percent of the aggregate gross assets of the CDE are invested in qualified low-income community investments as defined in paragraph (d)(1) of this section. The safe harbor calculation is a fraction the numberator of which is the CDE's aggregate cost basis determined under section 1012 in all of its qualified low-income community investments, and the denominator of which is the CDE's aggregate cost basis determined under section 1012 in all of its assets. For purposes of this paragraph (c)(5)(iii), cost basis includes the cost basis of any qualified low-income community investment that becomes worthless. See paragraph (d)(2) of this section for the treatment of amounts received by a CDE in payment of, or for, capital, equity or principal with respect to a qualified low-income community investment.

(iv) *Time limit for making investments.*—The taxpayer's cash investment received by a CDE is treated as invested in a qualified low-income community investment as defined in paragraph (d)(1) of this section only to the extent that the cash is so invested within the 12-month period beginning on the date the cash is paid by the *taxpayer (directly or through an underwriter) to the CDE.*

(v) *Reduced substantially-all percentage.*—For purposes of the substantially-all requirement (including the direct-tracing calculation under paragraph (c)(5)(ii) of this section and the safe harbor calcula-

tion under paragraph (c)(5)(iii) of this section), 85 percent is reduced to 75 percent for the seventh year of the 7-year credit period (as defined in paragraph (c)(5)(i) of this section).

(vi) *Examples.*—The following examples illustrate an application of this paragraph (c)(5):

Example 1. X is a partnership and a CDE that has received a $1 million new markets tax credit allocation from the Secretary. On September 1, 2004, X uses a line of credit from a bank to fund a $1 million loan to Y. The loan is a qualified low-income community investment under paragraph (d)(1) of this section. On September 5, 2004, A pays $1 million to acquire a capital interest in X. X uses the proceeds of A's equity investment to pay off the $1 million line of credit that was used to fund the loan to Y. X's aggregate gross assets consist of the $1 million loan to Y and $100,000 in other assets. A's equity investment in X does not satisfy the substantially-all requirement under paragraph (c)(5)(i) of this section using the direct-tracing calculation under paragraph (c)(5)(ii) of this section because the cash from A's equity investment is not used to make X's loan to Y. However, A's equity investment in X satisfies the substantially-all requirement using the safe harbor calculation under paragraph (c)(5)(iii) of this section because at least 85 percent of X's aggregate gross assets are invested in qualified low-income community investments.

Example 2. X is a partnership and a CDE that has received a new markets tax credit allocation from the Secretary. On August 1, 2004, A pays $100,000 for a capital interest in X. On August 5, 2004, X uses the proceeds of A's equity investment to make an equity investment in Y. X controls Y within the meaning of paragraph (d)(6)(ii)(B) of this section. For the annual period ending July 31, 2005, Y is a qualified active low-income community business (as defined in paragraph (d)(4) of this section). Thus, for that period, A's equity investment satisfies the substantially-all requirement under paragraph (c)(5)(i) of this section using the direct-tracing calculation under paragraph (c)(5)(ii) of this section. For the annual period ending July 31, 2006, Y no longer is a qualified active low-income community business. Thus, for that period, A's equity investment does not satisfy the substantially-all requirement using the direct-tracing calculation. However, during the entire annual period ending July 31, 2006, X's remaining assets are invested in qualified low-income community investments with an aggregate cost basis of $900,000. Consequently, for the annual period ending July 31, 2006, at least 85 percent of X's aggregate gross assets are invested in qualified low-income community investments. Thus, for the annual period ending July 31, 2006, A's equity investment satisfies the substantially-all requirement using the safe harbor calculation under paragraph (c)(5)(iii) of this section.

Example 3. X is a partnership and a CDE that has received a new markets tax credit allocation from the Secretary. On August 1, 2004, A and B each pay $100,000 for a capital interest in X. X does not treat A's and B's equity investments as one qualified equity investment under paragraph (c)(6) of this section. On September 1, 2004, X uses the proceeds of A's equity investment to make an equity investment in Y and X uses the proceeds of B's equity investment to make an equity investment in Z. X has no assets other than its investments in Y and Z. X controls Y and Z within the meaning of paragraph (d)(6)(ii)(B) of this section. For the annual period ending July 31, 2005, Y and Z are qualified active low-income community businesses (as defined in paragraph (d)(4) of this section). Thus, for the annual period ending July 31, 2005, A's and B's equity investments satisfy the substantially-all requirement under paragraph (c)(5)(i) of this section using either the direct-tracing calculation under paragraph (c)(5)(ii) of this section or the safe harbor calculation under paragraph (c)(5)(iii) of this section. For the annual period ending July 31, 2006, Y, but not Z, is a qualified active low-income community business. Thus, for the annual period ending July 31, 2006—

(1) X does not satisfy the substantially-all requirement using the safe harbor calculation under paragraph (c)(5)(iii) of this section;

(2) A's equity investment satisfies the substantially-all requirement using the direct-tracing calculation because A's equity investment is directly traceable to Y; and

(3) B's equity investment does not satisfy the substantially-all requirement because B's equity investment is traceable to Z.

Example 4. X is a partnership and a CDE that has received a new markets tax credit allocation from the Secretary. On November 1, 2004, A pays $100,000 for a capital interest in X. On December 1, 2004, B pays $100,000 for a capital interest in X. On December 31, 2004, X uses $85,000 from A's equity investment and $85,000 from B's equity investment to make a $170,000 equity investment in Y, a qualified active low-income community business (as defined in paragraph (d)(4) of this section). X has no assets other than its investment in Y. X determines whether A's and B's equity investments satisfy the substantially-all requirement under paragraph (c)(5)(i) of this section on December 31, 2004. The calculation for A's and B's equity investments is 85 percent using either the direct-tracing calculation under paragraph (c)(5)(ii) of this section or the safe harbor calculation under paragraph (c)(5)(iii) of this section. Therefore, for the annual periods ending October 31, 2005, and November 30, 2005, A's and B's equity investments, respectively, satisfy the substantially-all requirement under paragraph (c)(5)(i) of this section. For the subsequent annual period, X performs its calculations on December 31, 2005, and June 30, 2006. The average of the two calculations on December 31, 2005, and June 30, 2006, is 85 percent using either the direct-tracing calculation under paragraph (c)(5)(ii) of this section or the safe harbor calculation under paragraph (c)(5)(iii) of this section. Therefore, for the annual periods ending October 31, 2006, and November 30, 2006, A's and B's equity investments, respectively, satisfy the substantially-all requirement under paragraph (c)(5)(i) of this section.

(6) *Aggregation of equity investments.*—A CDE may treat any qualified equity investments issued on the same day as one qualified equity investment. If a CDE aggregates equity investments under this paragraph (c)(6), the rules in this section shall be construed in a manner consistent with that treatment.

(7) *Subsequent purchasers.*—A qualified equity investment includes any equity investment that would (but for paragraph (c)(1)(i) of this section) be a qualified equity investment in the hands of the taxpayer if the investment was a qualified equity investment in the hands of a prior holder.

(8) *Non-real estate qualified equity investment.*—If a qualified equity investment is designated as a non-real estate qualified equity investment under paragraph (c)(1)(iii) of this section, then the qualified equity investment may only satisfy the *substantially-all* requirement under paragraph (c)(5) of this section if the CDE makes qualified low-income community investments that are directly traceable (including investments made through one or more CDEs) to non-real estate qualified active low-income community businesses (as defined in paragraph (d)(10) of this section). The proceeds of a non-real estate qualified equity investment cannot be used for transactions involving a qualified active low-income community business that is not a non-real estate qualified active low-income community business.

(d) *Qualified low-income community investments.*—(1) *In general.*—The term *qualified low-income community investment* means any of the following:

(i) *Investment in a qualified active low-income community business or a non-real estate qualified active low-income community business.*—Any capital or equity investment in, or loan to, any qualified active low-income community business (as defined in paragraph (d)(4) of this section) or any non-real estate qualified active low-income community business (as defined in paragraph (d)(10) of this section).

(ii) *Purchase of certain loans from CDEs.*—(A) *In general.*—The purchase by a CDE (the ultimate CDE) from another CDE (whether or not that CDE has received an allocation from the Secretary under section 45D(f)(2)) of any loan made by such entity that is a qualified low-income community investment. A loan purchased by the ultimate CDE from another CDE is a qualified low-income community investment if it qualifies as a qualified low-income community investment either—

(1) At the time the loan was made; or

(2) At the time the ultimate CDE purchases the loan.

(B) *Certain loans made before CDE certification.*—For purposes of paragraph (d)(1)(ii)(A) of this section, a loan by an entity is treated as made by a CDE, notwithstanding that the entity was not a CDE at the time it made the loan, if the entity is a CDE at the time it sells the loan.

(C) *Intermediary CDEs.*—For purposes of paragraph (d)(1)(ii)(A) of this section, the purchase of a loan by the ultimate CDE from a CDE that did not make the loan (the second CDE) is treated as a purchase of the loan by the ultimate CDE from the CDE that made the loan (the originating CDE) if—

(1) The second CDE purchased the loan from the originating CDE (or from another CDE); and

(2) Each entity that sold the loan was a CDE at the time it sold the loan.

(D) *Examples.*—The following examples illustrate an application of this paragraph (d)(1)(ii):

Example 1. X is a partnership and a CDE that has received a new markets tax credit allocation from the Secretary. Y, a corporation, made a $500,000 loan to Z in 1999. In January of 2004, Y is certified as a CDE. On September 1, 2004, X purchases the loan from Y. At the time X purchases the loan, Z is a qualified active low-income community business under paragraph (d)(4)(i) of this section. Accordingly, the loan purchased by X from Y is a qualified low-

income community investment under paragraphs (d)(1)(ii)(A) and (B) of this section.

Example 2. The facts are the same as in *Example 1* except that on February 1, 2004, Y sells the loan to W and on September 1, 2004, W sells the loan to X. W is a CDE. Under paragraph (d)(1)(ii)(C) of this section, X's purchase of the loan from W is treated as the purchase of the loan from Y. Accordingly, the loan purchased by X from W is a qualified low-income community investment under paragraphs (d)(1)(ii)(A) and (C) of this section.

Example 3. The facts are the same as in *Example 2* except that W is not a CDE. Because W was not a CDE at the time it sold the loan to X, the purchase of the loan by X from W is not a qualified low-income community investment under paragraphs (d)(1)(ii)(A) and (C) of this section.

(iii) *Financial counseling and other services.*—Financial counseling and other services (as defined in paragraph (d)(7) of this section) provided to any qualified active low-income community business, or to any residents of a low-income community (as defined in section 45D(e)).

(iv) *Investments in other CDEs.*—(A) *In general.*—Any equity investment in, or loan to, any CDE (the second CDE) by a CDE (the primary CDE), but only to the extent that the second CDE uses the proceeds of the investment or loan—

(1) In a manner—

(i) That is described in paragraph (d)(1)(i) or (iii) of this section; and

(ii) That would constitute a qualified low-income community investment if it were made directly by the primary CDE;

(2) To make an equity investment in, or loan to, a third CDE that uses such proceeds in a manner described in paragraph (d)(1)(iv)(A)(1) of this section; or

(3) To make an equity investment in, or loan to, a third CDE that uses such proceeds to make an equity investment in, or loan to, a fourth CDE that uses such proceeds in a manner described in paragraph (d)(1)(iv)(A)(1) of this section.

(B) *Examples.*—The following examples illustrate an application of paragraph (d)(1)(iv)(A) of this section:

Example 1. X is a partnership and a CDE that has received a new markets tax credit allocation from the Secretary. On September 1, 2004, X uses $975,000 to make an equity investment in Y. Y is a corporation and a CDE. On October 1, 2004, Y uses $950,000 from X's equity investment to make a loan to Z. Z is a qualified active low-income community business under paragraph (d)(4)(i) of this section. Of X's equity investment in Y, $950,000 is a qualified low-income community investment under paragraph (d)(1)(iv)(A)(1) of this section.

Example 2. W is a partnership and a CDE that has received a new markets tax credit allocation from the Secretary. On September 1, 2004, W uses $975,000 to make an equity investment in X. On October 1, 2004, X uses $950,000 from W's equity investment to make an equity investment in Y. X and Y are corporations and CDEs. On October 5, 2004, Y uses $925,000 from X's equity investment to make a loan to Z. Z is a qualified active low-income community business under paragraph (d)(4)(i) of this section. Of W's equity investment in X, $925,000 is a qualified low-income community investment under paragraph (d)(1)(iv)(A)(2) of this section because X uses proceeds of W's equity investment to make an equity investment in Y, which uses $925,000 of the proceeds in a manner described in paragraph (d)(1)(iv)(A)(1) of this section.

Example 3. U is a partnership and a CDE that has received a new markets tax credit allocation from the Secretary. On September 1, 2004, U uses $975,000 to make an equity investment in V. On October 1, 2004, V uses $950,000 from U's equity investment to make an equity investment in W. On October 5, 2004, W uses $925,000 from V's equity investment to make an equity investment in X. On November 1, 2004, X uses $900,000 from W's equity investment to make an equity investment in Y. V, W, X, and Y are corporations and CDEs. On November 5, 2004, Y uses $875,000 from X's equity investment to make a loan to Z. Z is a qualified active low-income community business under paragraph (d)(4)(i) of this section. U's equity investment in V is not a qualified low-income community investment because X does not use proceeds of W's equity investment in a manner described in paragraph (d)(1)(iv)(A)(1) of this section.

(2) *Payments of, or for, capital, equity or principal.*—(i) *In general.*—Except as otherwise provided in this paragraph (d)(2), amounts received by a CDE in payment of, or for, capital, equity or principal with respect to a qualified low-income community investment must be reinvested by the CDE in a qualified low-income community investment no later than 12 months from the date of receipt to be treated as continuously invested in a qualified low-income community investment. If the amounts received by the CDE are equal to or greater than the cost basis of the original qualified low-income com-

Reg. § 1.45D-1(d)(2)(i)

munity investment (or applicable portion thereof), and the CDE reinvests, in accordance with this paragraph (d)(2)(i), an amount at least equal to such original cost basis, then an amount equal to such original cost basis will be treated as continuously invested in a qualified low-income community investment. In addition, if the amounts received by the CDE are equal to or greater than the cost basis of the original qualified low-income community investment (or applicable portion thereof), and the CDE reinvests, in accordance with this paragraph (d)(2)(i), an amount less than such original cost basis, then only the amount so reinvested will be treated as continuously invested in a qualified low-income community investment. If the amounts received by the CDE are less than the cost basis of the original qualified low-income community investment (or applicable portion thereof), and the CDE reinvests an amount in accordance with this paragraph (d)(2)(i), then the amount treated as continuously invested in a qualified low-income community investment will equal the excess (if any) of such original cost basis over the amounts received by the CDE that are not so reinvested. Amounts received by a CDE in payment of, or for, capital, equity or principal with respect to a qualified low-income community investment during the seventh year of the 7-year credit period (as defined in paragraph (c)(5)(i) of this section) do not have to be reinvested by the CDE in a qualified low-income community investment in order to be treated as continuously invested in a qualified low-income community investment.

(ii) *Subsequent reinvestments.*—In applying paragraph (d)(2)(i) of this section to subsequent reinvestments, the original cost basis is reduced by the amount (if any) by which the original cost basis exceeds the amount determined to be continuously invested in a qualified low-income community investment.

(iii) *Special rule for loans.*—Periodic amounts received during a calendar year as repayment of principal on a loan that is a qualified low-income community investment are treated as continuously invested in a qualified low-income community investment if the amounts are reinvested in another qualified low-income community investment by the end of the following calendar year.

(iv) *Example.*—The application of paragraphs (d)(2)(i) and (ii) of this section is illustrated by the following example:

Example. On April 1, 2003, A, B, and C each pay $100,000 to acquire a capital interest in X, a partnership. X is a CDE that has received a new markets tax credit allocation from the Secretary. X treats the 3 partnership interests as one qualified equity investment under paragraph (c)(6) of this section. In August 2003, X uses the $300,000 to make a qualified low-income community investment under paragraph (d)(1) of this section. In August 2005, the qualified low-income community investment is redeemed for $250,000. In February 2006, X reinvests $230,000 of the $250,000 in a second qualified low-income community investment and uses the remaining $20,000 for operating expenses. Under paragraph (d)(2)(i) of this section, $280,000 of the proceeds of the qualified equity investment is treated as continuously invested in a qualified low-income community investment. In December 2008, X sells the second qualified low-income community investment and receives $400,000. In March 2009, X reinvests $320,000 of the $400,000 in a third qualified low-income community investment. Under paragraphs (d)(2)(i) and (ii) of this section, $280,000 of the proceeds of the qualified equity investment is treated as continuously invested in a qualified low-income community investment ($40,000 is treated as invested in another qualified low-income community investment in March 2009).

(3) *Special rule for reserves.*—Reserves (not in excess of 5 percent of the taxpayer's cash investment under paragraph (b)(4) of this section) maintained by the CDE for loan losses or for additional investments in existing qualified low-income community investments are treated as invested in a qualified low-income community investment under paragraph (d)(1) of this section. Reserves include fees paid to third parties to protect against loss of all or a portion of the principal of, or interest on, a loan that is a qualified low-income community investment.

(4) *Qualified active low-income community business.*—(i) *In general.*—The term *qualified active low-income community business* means, with respect to any taxable year, a corporation (including a nonprofit corporation) or a partnership engaged in the active conduct of a qualified business (as defined in paragraph (d)(5) of this section), if the requirements of paragraphs (d)(4)(i)(A), (B), (C), (D), and (E) of this section are met (or in the case of an entity serving targeted populations, if the requirements of paragraphs (d)(4)(i)(D), (E), and (d)(9)(i) or (ii) of this section are met). Solely for purposes of this section, a nonprofit corporation will be deemed to be engaged in the active conduct of a trade or business if it is engaged in an activity that furthers its purpose as a nonprofit corporation.

(A) *Gross-income requirement.*—At least 50 percent of the total gross income of such entity is derived from the active conduct of

a qualified business (as defined in paragraph (d)(5) of this section) within any low-income community (as defined in section 45D(e)). An entity is deemed to satisfy this paragraph (d)(4)(i)(A) if the entity meets the requirements of either paragraph (d)(4)(i)(B) or (C) of this section, if "50 percent" is applied instead of 40 percent. In addition, an entity may satisfy this paragraph (d)(4)(i)(A) based on all the facts and circumstances. See paragraph (d)(4)(iv) of this section for certain circumstances in which an entity will be treated as engaged in the active conduct of a trade or business. See paragraph (d)(9) of this section for rules relating to targeted populations.

(B) *Use of tangible property.*—(1) *In general.*—At least 40 percent of the use of the tangible property of such entity (whether owned or leased) is within any low-income community. This percentage is determined based on a fraction the numerator of which is the average value of the tangible property owned or leased by the entity and used by the entity during the taxable year in a low-income community and the denominator of which is the average value of the tangible property owned or leased by the entity and used by the entity during the taxable year. Property owned by the entity is valued at its cost basis as determined under section 1012. Property leased by the entity is valued at a reasonable amount established by the entity. See paragraph (d)(9) of this section for rules relating to targeted populations.

(2) *Example.*—The application of paragraph (d)(4)(i)(B)(1) of this section is illustrated by the following example:

Example. X is a corporation engaged in the business of moving and hauling scrap metal. X operates its business from a building and an adjoining parking lot that X owns. The building and the parking lot are located in a low-income community (as defined in section 45D(e)). X's cost basis under section 1012 for the building and parking lot is $200,000. During the taxable year, X operates its business 10 hours a day, 6 days a week. X owns and uses 40 trucks in its business, which, on average, are used 6 hours a day outside a low-income community and 4 hours a day inside a low-income community (including time in the parking lot). The cost basis under section 1012 of each truck is $25,000. During non-business hours, the trucks are parked in the lot. Only X's 10-hour business days are used in calculating the use of tangible property percentage under paragraph (d)(4)(i)(B)(1) of this section. Thus, the numerator of the tangible property calculation is $600,000 (4/10 of $1,000,000 (the $25,000 cost basis of each truck times 40 trucks) plus $200,000 (the cost basis of the building and parking lot)) and the denominator is $1,200,000 (the total cost basis of the trucks, building, and parking lot), resulting in 50 percent of the use of X's tangible property being within a low-income community. Consequently, X satisfies the 40 percent use of tangible property test under paragraph (d)(4)(i)(B)(1) of this section.

(C) *Services performed.*—At least 40 percent of the services performed for such entity by its employees are performed in a low-income community. This percentage is determined based on a fraction the numerator of which is the total amount paid by the entity for employee services performed in a low-income community during the taxable year and the denominator of which is the total amount paid by the entity for employee services during the taxable year. If the entity has no employees, the entity is deemed to satisfy this paragraph (d)(4)(i)(C), and paragraph (d)(4)(i)(A) of this section, if the entity meets the requirement of paragraph (d)(4)(i)(B) of this section if "85 percent" is applied instead of 40 percent. See paragraph (d)(9) of this section for rules relating to targeted populations.

(D) *Collectibles.*—Less than 5 percent of the average of the aggregate unadjusted bases of the property of such entity is attributable to collectibles (as defined in section 408(m)(2)) other than collectibles that are held primarily for sale to customers in the ordinary course of business.

(E) *Nonqualified financial property.*—(1) *In general.*—Less than 5 percent of the average of the aggregate unadjusted bases of the property of such entity is attributable to *nonqualified financial property*. For purposes of the preceding sentence, the term *nonqualified financial property* means debt, stock, partnership interests, options, futures contracts, forward contracts, warrants, notional principal contracts, annuities, and other similar property except that such term does not include—

(i) Reasonable amounts of working capital held in cash, cash equivalents, or debt instruments with a term of 18 months or less (because the definition of *nonqualified financial property* includes debt instruments with a term in excess of 18 months, banks, credit unions, and other financial institutions are generally excluded from the definition of a *qualified active low-income community business*); or

(ii) Debt instruments described in section 1221(a)(4).

(2) *Construction of real property.*—For purposes of paragraph (d)(4)(i)(E)(1)(i) of this section, the proceeds of a capital or equity investment or loan by a CDE that will be expended for

construction of real property within 12 months after the date the investment or loan is made are treated as a reasonable amount of working capital.

(ii) *Proprietorships.*—Any business carried on by an individual as a proprietor is a qualified active low-income community business if the business would meet the requirements of paragraph (d)(4)(i) of this section if the business were incorporated.

(iii) *Portions of business.*—(A) *In general.*—A CDE may treat any trade or business (or portion thereof) as a qualified active low-income community business if the trade or business (or portion thereof) would meet the requirements of paragraph (d)(4)(i) of this section if the trade or business (or portion thereof) were separately incorporated and a complete and separate set of books and records is maintained for that trade or business (or portion thereof). However, the CDE's capital or equity investment or loan is not a qualified low-income community investment under paragraph (d)(1)(i) of this section to the extent the proceeds of the investment or loan are not used for the trade or business (or portion thereof) that is treated as a qualified active low-income community business under this paragraph (d)(4)(iii)(A).

(B) *Examples.*—The following examples illustrate an application of paragraph (d)(4)(iii) of this section:

Example 1. X is a partnership and a CDE that receives a new markets tax credit allocation from the Secretary. A pays $1 million for a capital interest in X. Z is a corporation that operates a supermarket that is not in a low-income community (as defined in section 45D(e)). X uses the proceeds of A's equity investment to make a loan to Z that Z will use to construct a new supermarket in a low-income community. Z will maintain a complete and separate set of books and records for the new supermarket. The proceeds of X's loan to Z will be used exclusively for the new supermarket. Assume that Z's new supermarket in the low-income community would meet the requirements to be a qualified active low-income community business under paragraph (d)(4)(i) of this section if it were separately incorporated. Pursuant to paragraph (d)(4)(iii)(A) of this section, X treats Z's new supermarket as the qualified active low-income community business. Accordingly, X's loan to Z is a qualified low-income community investment under paragraph (d)(1)(i) of this section.

Example 2. X is a partnership and a CDE that receives a new markets tax credit allocation from the Secretary. A pays $1 million for a capital interest in X. Z is a corporation that operates a liquor store in a low-income community (as defined in section 45D(e)). A liquor store is not a qualified business under paragraph (d)(5)(iii)(B) of this section. X uses the proceeds of A's equity investment to make a loan to Z that Z will use to construct a restaurant next to the liquor store. Z will maintain a complete and separate set of books and records for the new restaurant. The proceeds of X's loan to Z will be used exclusively for the new restaurant. Assume that Z's restaurant would meet the requirements to be a qualified active low-income community business under paragraph (d)(4)(i) of this section if it were separately incorporated. Pursuant to paragraph (d)(4)(iii) of this section, X treats Z's restaurant as the qualified active low-income community business. Accordingly, X's loan to Z is a qualified low-income community investment under paragraph (d)(1)(i) of this section.

Example 3. X is a partnership and a CDE that receives a new markets tax credit allocation from the Secretary. A pays $1 million for a capital interest in X. Z is a corporation that operates an insurance company in a low-income community (as defined in section 45D(e)). Five percent or more of the average of the aggregate unadjusted bases of Z's property is attributable to nonqualified financial property under paragraph (d)(4)(i)(E) of this section. Z's insurance operations include different operating units including a claims processing unit. X uses the proceeds of A's equity investment to make a loan to Z for use in Z's claims processing operations. Z will maintain a complete and separate set of books and records for the claims processing unit. The proceeds of X's loan to Z will be used exclusively for the claims processing unit. Assume that Z's claims processing unit would meet the requirements to be a qualified active low-income community business under paragraph (d)(4)(i) of this section if it were separately incorporated. Pursuant to paragraph (d)(4)(iii) of this section, X treats Z's claims processing unit as the qualified active low-income community business. Accordingly, X's loan to Z is a qualified low-income community investment under paragraph (d)(1)(i) of this section.

(iv) *Active conduct of a trade or business.*—(A) *Special rule.*—For purposes of paragraph (d)(4)(i) of this section, an entity will be treated as engaged in the active conduct of a trade or business if, at the time the CDE makes a capital or equity investment in, or loan to, the entity, the CDE reasonably expects that the entity will generate revenues (or, in the case of a nonprofit corporation, engage in an activity that furthers its purpose as a nonprofit corporation) within 3

years after the date the investment or loan is made. This paragraph (d)(4)(iv) applies only for purposes of determining whether an entity is engaged in the active conduct of a trade or business and does not apply for purposes of determining whether the gross-income requirement under paragraph (d)(4)(i)(A), (d)(9)(i)(B)(1)(i), or (d)(9)(ii)(C)(1)(i) of this section is satisfied.

(B) *Example.*—The application of paragraph (d)(4)(iv)(A) of this section is illustrated by the following example:

Example. X is a partnership and a CDE that receives a new markets tax credit allocation from the Secretary on July 1, 2004. X makes a ten-year loan to Y. Y is a newly formed entity that will own and operate a shopping center to be constructed in a low-income community. Y has no revenues but X reasonably expects that Y will generate revenues beginning in December 2005. Under paragraph (d)(4)(iv)(A) of this section, Y is treated as engaged in the active conduct of a trade or business for purposes of paragraph (d)(4)(i) of this section.

(5) *Qualified business.*—(i) *In general.*—Except as otherwise provided in this paragraph (d)(5), the term *qualified business* means any trade or business. There is no requirement that employees of a qualified business be residents of a low-income community.

(ii) *Rental of real property.*—The rental to others of real property located in any low-income community (as defined in section 45D(e)) is a qualified business if and only if the property is not residential rental property (as defined in section 168(e)(2)(A)) and there are substantial improvements located on the real property. However, a CDE's investment in or loan to a business engaged in the rental of real property is not a qualified low-income community investment under paragraph (d)(1)(i) of this section to the extent a lessee of the real property is described in paragraph (d)(5)(iii)(B) of this section.

(iii) *Exclusions.*—(A) *Trades or businesses involving intangibles.*—The term *qualified business* does not include any trade or business consisting predominantly of the development or holding of intangibles for sale or license.

(B) *Certain other trades or businesses.*—The term *qualified business* does not include any trade or business consisting of the operation of any private or commercial golf course, country club, massage parlor, hot tub facility, suntan facility, racetrack or other facility used for gambling, or any store the principal business of which is the sale of alcoholic beverages for consumption off premises.

(C) *Farming.*—The term *qualified business* does not include any trade or business the principal activity of which is farming (within the meaning of section 2032A(e)(5)(A) or (B)) if, as of the close of the taxable year of the taxpayer conducting such trade or business, the sum of the aggregate unadjusted bases (or, if greater, the fair market value) of the assets owned by the taxpayer that are used in such a trade or business, and the aggregate value of the assets leased by the taxpayer that are used in such a trade or business, exceeds $500,000. For purposes of this paragraph (d)(5)(iii)(C), two or more trades or businesses will be treated as a single trade or business under rules similar to the rules of section 52(a) and (b).

(6) *Qualifications.*—(i) *In general.*—Except as provided in paragraph (d)(6)(ii) of this section, an entity is treated as a qualified active low-income community business for the duration of the CDE's investment in the entity if the CDE reasonably expects, at the time the CDE makes the capital or equity investment in, or loan to, the entity, that the entity will satisfy the requirements to be a qualified active low-income community business under paragraph (d)(4)(i) of this section throughout the entire period of the investment or loan.

(ii) *Control.*—(A) *In general.*—If a CDE controls or obtains control of an entity at any time during the 7-year credit period (as defined in paragraph (c)(5)(i) of this section), the entity will be treated as a qualified active low-income community business only if the entity satisfies the requirements of paragraph (d)(4)(i) of this section throughout the entire period the CDE controls the entity.

(B) *Definition of control.*—Control means, with respect to an entity, direct or indirect ownership (based on value) or control (based on voting or management rights) of more than 50 percent of the entity. For purposes of the preceding sentence, the term *management rights* means the power to influence the management policies or investment decisions of the entity.

(C) *Disregard of control.*—For purposes of paragraph (d)(6)(ii)(A) of this section, the acquisition of control of an entity by a CDE is disregarded during the 12-month period following such acquisition of control (the 12-month period) if—

Reg. §1.45D-1(d)(6)(ii)(C)

(1) The CDE's capital or equity investment in, or loan to, the entity met the requirements of paragraph (d)(6)(i) of this section when initially made;

(2) The CDE's acquisition of control of the entity is due to financial difficulties of the entity that were unforeseen at the time the investment or loan described in paragraph (d)(6)(ii)(C)(1) of this section was made; and

(3) If the acquisition of control occurs before the seventh year of the 7-year credit period (as defined in paragraph (c)(5)(i) of this section), either—

(i) The entity satisfies the requirements of paragraph (d)(4) of this section by the end of the 12-month period; or

(ii) The CDE sells or causes to be redeemed the entire amount of the investment or loan described in paragraph (d)(6)(ii)(C)(1) of this section and, by the end of the 12-month period, reinvests the amount received in respect of the sale or redemption in a qualified low-income community investment under paragraph (d)(1) of this section. For this purpose, the amount treated as continuously invested in a qualified low-income community investment is determined under paragraphs (d)(2)(i) and (ii) of this section.

(7) *Financial counseling and other services.*—The term *financial counseling and other services* means advice provided by the CDE relating to the organization or operation of a trade or business.

(8) *Special rule for certain loans.*—(i) *In general.*—For purposes of paragraphs (d)(1)(i), (ii), and (iv) of this section, a loan is treated as made by a CDE to the extent the CDE purchases the loan from the originator (whether or not the originator is a CDE) within 30 days after the date the originator makes the loan if, at the time the loan is made, there is a legally enforceable written agreement between the originator and the CDE which—

(A) Requires the CDE to approve the making of the loan either directly or by imposing specific written loan underwriting criteria; and

(B) Requires the CDE to purchase the loan within 30 days after the date the loan is made.

(ii) *Example.*—The application of paragraph (d)(8)(i) of this section is illustrated by the following example:

Example. (i) X is a partnership and a CDE that has received a new markets tax credit allocation from the Secretary. On October 1, 2004, Y enters into a legally enforceable written agreement with W. Y and W are corporations but only Y is a CDE. The agreement between Y and W provides that Y will purchase loans (or portions thereof) from W within 30 days after the date the loan is made by W, and that Y will approve the making of the loans.

(ii) On November 1, 2004, W makes an $825,000 loan to Z pursuant to the agreement between Y and W. Z is a qualified active low-income community business under paragraph (d)(4) of this section. On November 15, 2004, Y purchases the loan from W for $840,000. On December 31, 2004, X purchases the loan from Y for $850,000.

(iii) Under paragraph (d)(8)(i) of this section, the loan to Z is treated as made by Y. Y's loan to Z is a qualified low-income community investment under paragraph (d)(1)(i) of this section. Accordingly, under paragraph (d)(1)(ii)(A) of this section, X's purchase of the loan from Y is a qualified low-income community investment in the amount of $850,000.

(9) *Targeted populations.*—For purposes of section 45D(e)(2), targeted populations that will be treated as a low-income community are individuals, or an identifiable group of individuals, including an Indian tribe, who are low-income persons as defined in paragraph (d)(9)(i) of this section or who are individuals who otherwise lack adequate access to loans or equity investments as defined in paragraph (d)(9)(ii) of this section.

(i) *Low-income persons.*—(A) *Definition.*—(1) *In general.*—For purposes of section 45D(e)(2) and this paragraph (d)(9), an individual shall be considered to be low-income if the individual's family income, adjusted for family size, is not more than—

(i) For metropolitan areas, 80 percent of the area median family income; and

(ii) For non-metropolitan areas, the greater of 80 percent of the area median family income, or 80 percent of the statewide non-metropolitan area median family income.

(2) *Area median family income.*—For purposes of paragraph (d)(9)(i)(A)(1) of this section, *area median family income* is determined in a manner consistent with the determinations of median family income under section 8 of the Housing Act of 1937, as amended. Taxpayers must use the annual estimates of median family income released by the Department of Housing and Urban Development (HUD) and may rely on those figures until 45 days after HUD releases a new list of income limits, or until HUD's effective date for the new list, whichever is later.

(3) *Individual's family income.*—For purposes of paragraph (d)(9)(i)(A)(1) of this section, an individual's family income is determined using any one of the following three methods for measuring family income:

(i) Household income as measured by the U.S. Census Bureau,

(ii) Adjusted gross income under section 62 as reported on Internal Revenue Service Form 1040. Adjusted gross income must include the adjusted gross income of any member of the individual's family (as defined in section 267(c)(4)) if the family member resides with the individual regardless of whether the family member files a separate return,

(iii) Household income determined under section 8 of the Housing Act of 1937, as amended.

(B) *Qualified active low-income community business requirements for low-income targeted populations.*—(1) *In general.*—An entity will not be treated as a qualified active low-income community business for low-income targeted populations unless—

(i) Except as provided in paragraph (d)(9)(i)(D)(2) of this section, at least 50 percent of the entity's total gross income for any taxable year is derived from sales, rentals, services, or other transactions with individuals who are low-income persons for purposes of section 45D(e)(2) and this paragraph (d)(9);

(ii) At least 40 percent of the entity's employees are individuals who are low-income persons for purposes of section 45D(e)(2) and this paragraph (d)(9); or

(iii) At least 50 percent of the entity is owned by individuals who are low-income persons for purposes of section 45D(e)(2) and this paragraph (d)(9).

(2) *Employee.*—The determination of whether an employee is a low-income person must be made at the time the employee is hired. If the employee is a low-income person at the time of hire, that employee is considered a low-income person for purposes of section 45D(e)(2) and this paragraph (d)(9) throughout the time of employment, without regard to any increase in the employee's income after the time of hire.

(3) *Owner.*—The determination of whether an owner is a low-income person must be made at the time the qualified low-income community investment is made, or at the time the ownership interest is acquired by the owner, whichever is later. If an owner is a low-income person at the time the qualified low-income community investment is made or at the time the ownership interest is acquired by the owner, whichever is later, that owner is considered a low-income person for purposes of section 45D(e)(2) and this paragraph (d)(9) throughout the time the ownership interest is held by that owner.

(4) *Derived from.*—For purposes of paragraph (d)(9)(i)(B)(1)(i) of this section, the term *derived from* includes gross income derived from:

(i) Payments made directly by low-income persons to the entity; and

(ii) Money and the fair market value of property or services provided to the entity primarily for the benefit of low-income persons, but only if the persons providing the money, property, or services do not receive a direct benefit from the entity (for this purpose, a contribution that benefits the general public is not a direct benefit).

(5) *Fair market value of sales, rentals, services, or other transactions.*—For purposes of paragraph (d)(9)(i)(B)(1)(i) of this section, an entity with gross income that is derived from sales, rentals, services, or other transactions with both non low-income persons and low-income persons may treat the gross income derived from the sales, rentals, services, or other transactions with low-income persons as including the full fair market value even if the low-income persons do not pay fair market value.

(C) *120-percent-income restriction.*—(1) *In general.*—(i) In no case will an entity be treated as a qualified active low-income community business under paragraph (d)(9)(i) of this section if the entity is located in a population census tract for which the median family income exceeds 120 percent of, in the case of a tract not located within a metropolitan area, the statewide median family income, or in the case of a tract located within a metropolitan area, the greater of statewide median family income or metropolitan area median family income (120-percent-income restriction).

(ii) The 120-percent-income restriction shall not apply to an entity located within a population census tract with a population of less than 2,000 if such tract is not located in a metropolitan area.

Reg. §1.45D-1(d)(6)(ii)(C)(1)

(iii) The 120-percent-income restriction shall not apply to an entity located within a population census tract with a population of less than 2,000 if such tract is located in a metropolitan area and more than 75 percent of the tract is zoned for commercial or industrial use. For this purpose, the 75 percent calculation should be made using the area of the population census tract. For purposes of this paragraph (d)(9)(i)(C)(*1*)(*iii*), property for which commercial or industrial use is a permissible zoning use will be treated as zoned for commercial or industrial use.

(2) Population census tract location.—(i) For purposes of the 120-percent-income restriction, an entity will be considered to be located in a population census tract for which the median family income exceeds 120 percent of the applicable median family income under paragraph (d)(9)(i)(C)(*1*)(*i*) of this section (non-qualifying population census tract) if at least 50 percent of the total gross income of the entity is derived from the active conduct of a qualified business (as defined in paragraph (d)(5) of this section) within one or more non-qualifying population census tracts (non-qualifying gross income amount); at least 40 percent of the use of the tangible property of the entity (whether owned or leased) is within one or more non-qualifying population census tracts (non-qualifying tangible property usage); and at least 40 percent of the services performed for the entity by its employees are performed in one or more non-qualifying population census tracts (non-qualifying services performance).

(ii) The entity is considered to have the non-qualifying gross income amount if the entity has non-qualifying tangible property usage or non-qualifying services performance of at least 50 percent instead of 40 percent.

(iii) If the entity has no employees, the entity is considered to have the nonqualifying gross income amount and non-qualifying services performance if at least 85 percent of the use of the tangible property of the entity (whether owned or leased) is within one or more non-qualifying population census tracts.

*(D) Rental of real property for low-income targeted populations.—(1) In general.—*An entity that rents to others real property for low-income targeted populations and that otherwise satisfies the requirements to be a qualified business under paragraph (d)(5) of this section will be treated as located in a low-income community for purposes of paragraph (d)(5)(ii) of this section if at least 50 percent of the entity's total gross income is derived from rentals to individuals who are low-income persons for purposes of section 45D(e)(2) and this paragraph (d)(9) or rentals to a qualified active low-income community business that meets the requirements for low-income targeted populations under paragraphs (d)(9)(i)(B)(*1*)(*i*) or (*ii*) and (d)(9)(i)(B)(*2*) of this section.

*(2) Special rule for entities whose sole business is the rental to others of real property.—*If an entity's sole business is the rental to others of real property under paragraph (d)(9)(i)(D)(*1*) of this section, then the gross income requirement in paragraph (d)(9)(i)(B)(*1*)(*i*) of this section will be considered satisfied if the entity is treated as being located in a low-income community under paragraph (d)(9)(i)(D)(*1*) of this section.

(ii) *Individuals who otherwise lack adequate access to loans or equity investments.—(A) In general.—*Paragraph (d)(9)(ii) of this section may be applied only with regard to qualified low-income community investments made under the increase in the new markets tax credit limitation pursuant to section 1400N(m)(2). Therefore, only CDEs with a significant mission of recovery and redevelopment of the Gulf Opportunity Zone (GO Zone) that receive an allocation from the increase described in section 1400N(m)(2) may make qualified low-income community investments from that allocation pursuant to the rules in paragraph (d)(9)(ii) of this section.

(B) *GO Zone Targeted Population.—*For purposes of the targeted populations rules under section 45D(e)(2), an individual otherwise lacks adequate access to loans or equity investments only if the individual was displaced from his or her principal residence as a result of Hurricane Katrina or the individual lost his or her principal source of employment as a result of Hurricane Katrina (GO Zone Targeted Population). In order to meet this definition, the individual's principal residence or principal source of employment, as applicable, must have been located in a population census tract within the GO Zone that contains one or more areas designated by the Federal Emergency Management Agency (FEMA) as flooded, having sustained extensive damage, or having sustained catastrophic damage as a result of Hurricane Katrina.

(C) *Qualified active low-income community business requirements for the GO Zone Targeted Population.—(1) In general.—*An entity will not be treated as a qualified active low-income community business for the GO Zone Targeted Population unless—

(i) At least 50 percent of the entity's total gross income for any taxable year is derived from sales, rentals, services, or other transactions with the GO Zone Targeted Population, low-income persons as defined in paragraph (d)(9)(i) of this section, or some combination thereof;

(ii) At least 40 percent of the entity's employees consist of the GO Zone Targeted Population, low-income persons as defined in paragraph (d)(9)(i) of this section, or some combination thereof; or

(iii) At least 50 percent of the entity is owned by the GO Zone Targeted Population, low-income persons as defined in paragraph (d)(9)(i) of this section, or some combination thereof.

*(2) Location.—(i) In general.—*In order to be a qualified active low-income community business under paragraph (d)(9)(ii)(C) of this section, the entity must be located in a population census tract within the GO Zone that contains one or more areas designated by FEMA as flooded, having sustained extensive damage, or having sustained catastrophic damage as a result of Hurricane Katrina (qualifying population census tract).

*(ii) Determination.—*For purposes of the preceding paragraph, an entity will be considered to be located in a qualifying population census tract if at least 50 percent of the total gross income of the entity is derived from the active conduct of a qualified business (as defined in paragraph (d)(5) of this section) within one or more qualifying population census tracts (gross income requirement); at least 40 percent of the use of the tangible property of the entity (whether owned or leased) is within one or more qualifying population census tracts (use of tangible property requirement); and at least 40 percent of the services performed for the entity by its employees are performed in one or more qualifying population census tracts (services performed requirement). The entity is deemed to satisfy the gross income requirement if the entity satisfies the use of tangible property requirement or the services performed requirement on the basis of at least 50 percent instead of 40 percent. If the entity has no employees, the entity is deemed to satisfy the services performed requirement and the gross income requirement if at least 85 percent of the use of the tangible property of the entity (whether owned or leased) is within one or more qualifying population census tracts.

(D) 200-percent-income restriction.—(1) In general.—(i) In no case will an entity be treated as a qualified active low-income community business under paragraph (d)(9)(ii) of this section if the entity is located in a population census tract for which the median family income exceeds 200 percent of, in the case of a tract not located within a metropolitan area, the statewide median family income, or, in the case of a tract located within a metropolitan area, the greater of statewide median family income or metropolitan area median family income (200-percent-income restriction).

(ii) The 200-percent-income restriction shall not apply to an entity located within a population census tract with a population of less than 2,000 if such tract is not located in a metropolitan area.

(iii) The 200-percent-income restriction shall not apply to an entity located within a population census tract with a population of less than 2,000 if such tract is located in a metropolitan area and more than 75 percent of the tract is zoned for commercial or industrial use. For this purpose, the 75 percent calculation should be made using the area of the population census tract. For purposes of this paragraph (d)(9)(ii)(D)(*1*)(*iii*), property for which commercial or industrial use is a permissible zoning use will be treated as zoned for commercial or industrial use.

(2) Population census tract location.—(i) For purposes of the 200-percent-income restriction, an entity will be considered to be located in a population census tract for which the median family income exceeds 200 percent of the applicable median family income under paragraph (d)(9)(ii)(D)(*1*)(*i*) of this section (non-qualifying population census tract) if— at least 50 percent of the total gross income of the entity is derived from the active conduct of a qualified business (as defined in paragraph (d)(5) of this section) within one or more non-qualifying population census tracts (non-qualifying gross income amount); at least 40 percent of the use of the tangible property of the entity (whether owned or leased) is within one or more non-qualifying population census tracts (non-qualifying tangible property usage); and at least 40 percent of the services performed for the entity by its employees are performed in one or more non-qualifying population census tracts (non-qualifying services performance).

(ii) The entity is considered to have the non-qualifying gross income amount if the entity has non-qualifying tangible property usage or non-qualifying services performance of at least 50 percent instead of 40 percent.

(iii) If the entity has no employees, the entity is considered to have the nonqualifying gross income amount and non-qualifying services performance if at least 85 percent of the use of the tangible property of the entity (whether owned or leased) is within one or more non-qualifying population census tracts.

Reg. §1.45D-1(d)(9)(ii)(D)(2)(iii)

(E) *Rental of real property for the GO Zone Targeted Population.*—The rental to others of real property for the GO Zone Targeted Population that otherwise satisfies the requirements to be a qualified business under paragraph (d)(5) of this section will be treated as located in a low-income community for purposes of paragraph (d)(5)(ii) of this section if at least 50 percent of the entity's total gross income is derived from rentals to the GO Zone Targeted Population, rentals to low-income persons as defined in paragraph (d)(9)(i) of this section, or rentals to a qualified active low-income community business that meets the requirements for the GO Zone Targeted Population under paragraph (d)(9)(ii)(C)(*1*)(*i*) or (*ii*) of this section.

(10) *Non-real estate qualified active low-income community business.*—(i) *Definition.*—The term *non-real estate qualified active low-income community business* means any qualified active low-income community business (as defined in paragraph (d)(4) of this section) whose predominant business activity does not include the development (including construction of new facilities and rehabilitation/enhancement of existing facilities), management, or leasing of real estate. For purposes of the preceding sentence, predominant business activity means a business activity that generates more than 50 percent of the business' gross income. The purpose of the capital or equity investment in, or loan to, the non-real estate qualified active low-income community business must not be connected to the development (including construction of new facilities and rehabilitation/enhancement of existing facilities), management, or leasing of real estate.

(ii) *Payments of, or for, capital, equity or principal with respect to a non-real estate qualified active low-income community business.*—(A) *In general.*—For purposes of paragraph (d)(2)(i) of this section, a portion of the amounts received by a CDE in payment of, or for, capital, equity, or principal with respect to a non-real estate qualified active low-income community business after year one of the 7-year credit period (as defined by paragraph (c)(5)(i) of this section) may be reinvested by the CDE in a qualifying entity (as defined in paragraph (d)(10)(ii)(D)). Any portion that the CDE chooses to reinvest in a qualifying entity must be reinvested by the CDE no later than 30 days from the date of receipt to be treated as continuously invested in a qualified low-income community investment for purposes of paragraph (d)(2)(i) of this section. If the amount reinvested in a qualifying entity exceeds the maximum aggregate portion of the non-real estate qualified equity investment, then the excess will not be treated as invested in a qualified low-income community investment. The maximum aggregate portion of the non-real estate qualified equity investment that may be reinvested into a qualifying entity, which will be treated as continuously invested in a qualified low-income community investment, may not exceed the following percentages of the non-real estate qualified equity investment in the following years:

(*1*) 15 percent in Year 2 of the 7-year credit period.

(*2*) 30 percent in Year 3 of the 7-year credit period.

(*3*) 50 percent in Year 4 of the 7-year credit period.

(*4*) 85 percent in Year 5 and Year 6 of the 7-year credit period.

(B) *Seventh year of the 7-year credit period.*—Amounts received by a CDE in payment of, or for, capital, equity, or principal with respect to a non-real estate qualified active low-income community business (as defined in paragraph (d)(10)(i) of this section) during the seventh year of the 7-year credit period do not have to be reinvested by the CDE in a qualified low-income community investment to be treated as continuously invested in a qualified low-income community investment.

(C) *Amounts received from qualifying entity.*—Except for the seventh year of the 7-year credit period under paragraph (d)(10)(ii)(B) of this section, amounts received from a qualifying entity must be reinvested by the CDE no later than 30 days from the date of receipt to be treated as continuously invested in a qualified low-income community investment.

(D) *Definition of qualifying entity.*—For purposes of paragraphs (d)(10)(ii) and (d)(10)(iii) of this section, a *qualifying entity* is—

(*1*) A certified community development financial institution (certified CDFI) that is a CDE under section 45D(c)(2)(B) (as defined by 12 CFR 1805.201), which is unrelated to the CDE making the investment in the certified CDFI within the meaning of section 267(b) or section 707(b)(1); or

(*2*) An entity designated by the Secretary by publication in the Internal Revenue Bulletin (see § 601.601(d)(2)(ii)(*b*) of this chapter).

(e) *Recapture.*—(1) *In general.*—If, at any time during the 7-year period beginning on the date of the original issue of a qualified equity investment in a CDE, there is a recapture event under para-

graph (e)(2) of this section with respect to such investment, then the tax imposed by Chapter 1 of the Internal Revenue Code for the taxable year in which the recapture event occurs is increased by the credit recapture amount under section 45D(g)(2). A recapture event under paragraph (e)(2) of this section requires recapture of credits allowed to the taxpayer who purchased the equity investment from the CDE at its original issue and to all subsequent holders of that investment.

(2) *Recapture event.*—There is a recapture event with respect to an equity investment in a CDE if—

(i) The entity ceases to be a CDE;

(ii) The proceeds of the investment cease to be used in a manner that satisfies the substantially-all requirement of paragraph (c)(1)(ii) of this section; or

(iii) The investment is redeemed or otherwise cashed out by the CDE.

(3) *Redemption.*—(i) *Equity investment in a C corporation.*—For purposes of paragraph (e)(2)(iii) of this section, an equity investment in a CDE that is treated as a C corporation for Federal tax purposes is redeemed when section 302(a) applies to amounts received by the equity holder. An equity investment is treated as cashed out when section 301(c)(2) or section 301(c)(3) applies to amounts received by the equity holder. An equity investment is not treated as cashed out when only section 301(c)(1) applies to amounts received by the equity holder.

(ii) *Equity investment in an S corporation.*—For purposes of paragraph (e)(2)(iii) of this section, an equity investment in a CDE that is an S corporation is redeemed when section 302(a) applies to amounts received by the equity holder. An equity investment in an S corporation is treated as cashed out when a distribution to a shareholder described in section 1368(a) exceeds the accumulated adjustments account determined under § 1.1368-2 and any accumulated earnings and profits of the S corporation.

(iii) *Capital interest in a partnership.*—In the case of an equity investment that is a capital interest in a CDE that is a partnership for Federal tax purposes, a pro rata cash distribution by the CDE to its partners based on each partner's capital interest in the CDE during the taxable year will not be treated as a redemption for purposes of paragraph (e)(2)(iii) of this section if the distribution does not exceed the CDE's *operating income* for the taxable year. In addition, a non-pro rata *de minimis* cash distribution by a CDE to a partner or partners during the taxable year will not be treated as a redemption. A non-pro rata de *minimis* cash distribution may not exceed the lesser of 5 percent of the CDE's *operating income* for that taxable year or 10 percent of the partner's capital interest in the CDE. For purposes of this paragraph (e)(3)(iii), with respect to any taxable year, *operating income* is the sum of:

(A) The CDE's taxable income as determined under section 703, except that—

(*1*) The items described in section 703(a)(1) shall be aggregated with the non-separately stated tax items of the partnership; and

(*2*) Any gain resulting from the sale of a capital asset under section 1221(a) or section 1231 property shall not be included in taxable income;

(B) Deductions under section 165, but only to the extent the losses were realized from qualified low-income community investments under paragraph (d)(1) of this section;

(C) Deductions under sections 167 and 168, including the additional first-year depreciation under section 168(k);

(D) Start-up expenditures amortized under section 195; and

(E) Organizational expenses amortized under section 709.

(4) *Bankruptcy.*—Bankruptcy of a CDE is not a recapture event.

(5) *Waiver of requirement or extension of time.*—(i) *In general.*—The Commissioner may waive a requirement or extend a deadline if such waiver or extension does not materially frustrate the purposes of section 45D and this section.

(ii) *Manner for requesting a waiver or extension.*—A CDE that believes it has good cause for a waiver or an extension may request relief from the Commissioner in a ruling request. The request should set forth all the relevant facts and include a detailed explanation describing the event or events relating to the request for a waiver or an extension. For further information on the application procedure for a ruling, see Rev. Proc. 2005-1 (2005-1 I.R.B. 1) or its successor revenue procedure (see § 601.601(d)(2) of this chapter).

(iii) *Terms and conditions.*—The granting of a waiver or an extension to a CDE under this section may require adjustments of the CDE's requirements under section 45D and this section as may be appropriate.

(6) *Cure period.*—If a qualified equity investment fails the substantially-all requirement under paragraph (c)(5)(i) of this section, the failure is not a recapture event under paragraph (e)(2)(ii) of this section if the CDE corrects the failure within 6 months after the date the CDE becomes aware (or reasonably should have become aware) of the failure. Only one correction is permitted for each qualified equity investment during the 7-year credit period under this paragraph (e)(6).

(7) *Example.*—The application of this paragraph (e) is illustrated by the following example:

Example. In 2003, A and B acquire separate qualified equity investments in X, a partnership. X is a CDE that has received a new markets tax credit allocation from the Secretary. X uses the proceeds of A's qualified equity investment to make a qualified low-income community investment in Y, and X uses the proceeds of B's qualified equity investment to make a qualified low-income community investment in Z. Y and Z are not CDEs. X controls both Y and Z within the meaning of paragraph (d)(6)(ii)(B) of this section. In 2003, Y and Z are qualified active low-income community businesses. In 2007, Y, but not Z, is a qualified active low-income community business and X does not satisfy the substantially-all requirement using the safe harbor calculation under paragraph (c)(5)(iii) of this section. A's equity investment satisfies the substantially-all requirement of paragraph (c)(1)(ii) of this section using the direct-tracing calculation of paragraph (c)(5)(ii) of this section because A's equity investment is traceable to Y. However, B's equity investment fails the substantially-all requirement using the direct-tracing calculation because B's equity investment is traceable to Z. Therefore, under paragraph (e)(2)(ii) of this section, there is a recapture event for B's equity investment (but not A's equity investment).

(f) *Basis reduction.*—(1) *In general.*—A taxpayer's basis in a qualified equity investment is reduced by the amount of any new markets tax credit determined under paragraph (b)(1) of this section with respect to the investment. A basis reduction occurs on each credit allowance date under paragraph (b)(2) of this section. This paragraph (f) does not apply for purposes of sections 1202, 1400B, and 1400F.

(2) *Adjustment in basis of interest in partnership or S corporation.*—The adjusted basis of either a partner's interest in a partnership, or stock in an S corporation, must be appropriately adjusted to take into account adjustments made under paragraph (f)(1) of this section in the basis of a qualified equity investment held by the partnership or S corporation (as the case may be).

(g) *Other rules.*—(1) *Anti-abuse.*—If a principal purpose of a transaction or a series of transactions is to achieve a result that is inconsistent with the purposes of section 45D and this section, the Commissioner may treat the transaction or series of transactions as causing a recapture event under paragraph (e)(2) of this section.

(2) *Reporting requirements.*—(i) *Notification by CDE to taxpayer.*—(A) *Allowance of new markets tax credit.*—A CDE must provide notice to any taxpayer who acquires a qualified equity investment in the CDE at its original issue that the equity investment is a qualified equity investment entitling the taxpayer to claim the new markets tax credit. The notice must be provided by the CDE to the taxpayer no later than 60 days after the date the taxpayer makes the investment in the CDE. The notice must contain the amount paid to the CDE for the qualified equity investment at its original issue and the taxpayer identification number of the CDE.

(B) *Recapture event.*—If, at any time during the 7-year period beginning on the date of the original issue of a qualified equity investment in a CDE, there is a recapture event under paragraph (e)(2) of this section with respect to such investment, the CDE must provide notice to each holder, including all prior holders, of the investment that a recapture event has occurred. The notice must be provided by the CDE no later than 60 days after the date the CDE becomes aware of the recapture event.

(ii) *CDE reporting requirements to Secretary.*—Each CDE must comply with such reporting requirements to the Secretary as the Secretary may prescribe.

(iii) *Manner of claiming new markets tax credit.*—A taxpayer may claim the new markets tax credit for each applicable taxable year by completing Form 8874, "New Markets Credit," and by filing Form 8874 with the taxpayer's Federal income tax return.

(iv) *Reporting recapture tax.*—If there is a recapture event with respect to a taxpayer's equity investment in a CDE, the taxpayer must include the credit recapture amount under section 45D(g)(2) on the line for recapture taxes on the taxpayer's Federal income tax return for the taxable year in which the recapture event under paragraph (e)(2) of this section occurs (or on the line for total tax, if

there is no such line for recapture taxes) and write *NMCR* (new markets credit recapture) next to the entry space.

(3) *Other Federal tax benefits.*—(i) *In general.*—Except as provided in paragraph (g)(3)(ii) of this section, the availability of Federal tax benefits does not limit the availability of the new markets tax credit. Federal tax benefits that do not limit the availability of the new markets tax credit include, for example:

(A) The rehabilitation credit under section 47;

(B) All deductions under sections 167 and 168, including the additional first-year depreciation under section 168(k), and the expense deduction for certain depreciable property under section 179; and

(C) All tax benefits relating to certain designated areas such as empowerment zones and enterprise communities under sections 1391 through 1397D, the District of Columbia Enterprise Zone under sections 1400 through 1400B, renewal communities under sections 1400E through 1400J, and the New York Liberty Zone under section 1400L.

(ii) *Low-income housing credit.*—If a CDE makes a capital or equity investment or a loan with respect to a qualified low-income building under section 42, the investment or loan is not a qualified low-income community investment under paragraph (d)(1) of this section to the extent the building's eligible basis under section 42(d) is financed by the proceeds of the investment or loan.

(4) *Bankruptcy of CDE.*—The bankruptcy of a CDE does not preclude a taxpayer from continuing to claim the new markets tax credit on the remaining credit allowance dates under paragraph (b)(2) of this section.

(h) *Effective/applicability dates.*.—(1) *In general.*—Except as provided in paragraphs (h)(2), (h)(3), and (h)(4) of this section, this section applies on or after December 22, 2004, and may be applied by taxpayers before December 22, 2004. The provisions that apply before December 22, 2004, are contained in §1.45D-1T (see 26 CFR part 1 revised as of April 1, 2003, and April 1, 2004).

(2) *Exception.*—Paragraph (d)(5)(ii) of this section as it relates to the restriction on lessees described in paragraph (d)(5)(iii)(B) of this section applies to qualified low-income community investments made on or after June 22, 2005.

(3) *Targeted populations.*—The rules in paragraph (d)(9) of this section and the last sentence in paragraph (d)(4)(iv)(A) of this section apply to taxable years ending on or after December 5, 2011. A taxpayer may apply the rules in paragraph (d)(9) of this section to taxable years ending before December 5, 2011 for designations made by the Secretary after October 22, 2004.

(4) *Investments in non-real estate businesses.*—Paragraphs (c)(8) and (d)(10) of this section apply to equity investments in CDEs made on or after September 28, 2012. [Reg. §1.45D-1.]

☐ [*T.D. 9171, 12-22-2004 (corrected 1-27-2005). Amended by T.D. 9560, 12-2-2011 and T.D. 9600, 9-26-2012.*]

[Reg. §1.45G-0]

§1.45G-0. Table of contents for the railroad track maintenance credit rules.—This section lists the table of contents for §1.45G-1.

§1.45G-1 Railroad track maintenance credit.

(a) In general.

(b) Definitions.

(1) Class II railroad and Class III railroad.

(2) Eligible railroad track.

(3) Eligible taxpayer.

(4) Qualifying railroad structure.

(5) Qualified railroad track maintenance expenditures.

(6) Rail facilities.

(7) Railroad-related property.

(8) Railroad-related services.

(9) Railroad track.

(10) Form 8900.

(11) Examples.

(c) Determination of amount of railroad track maintenance credit for the taxable year.

(1) General amount.

(2) Limitation on the credit.

(i) Eligible taxpayer is a Class II railroad or Class III railroad.

(ii) Eligible taxpayer is not a Class II railroad or Class III railroad.

(iii) No carryover of amount that exceeds limitation.

(3) Determination of amount of QRTME paid or incurred.

(i) In general.

(ii) Effect of reimbursements received from persons other than a Class II or Class III railroad.

    (4) Examples.

(d) Assignment of track miles.

    (1) In general.

    (2) Assignment eligibility.

    (3) Effective date of assignment.

    (4) Assignment information statement.

      (i) In general.

      (ii) Assignor.

      (iii) Assignee.

      (iv) Special rule for returns filed prior to November 9, 2007.

    (5) Special rules.

      (i) Effect of subsequent dispositions of eligible railroad track during the assignment year.

      (ii) Effect of multiple assignments of eligible railroad track miles during the same taxable year.

    (6) Examples.

(e) Adjustments to basis.

    (1) In general.

    (2) Basis adjustment made to railroad track.

    (3) Examples.

(f) Controlled groups.

    (1) In general.

    (2) Definitions.

      (i) Trade or business.

      (ii) Group and controlled group.

      (iii) Group credit.

      (iv) Consolidated group.

      (v) Credit year.

    (3) Computation of the group credit.

    (4) Allocation of the group credit.

    (5) Special rules for consolidated groups.

      (i) In general.

      (ii) Special rule for allocation of group credit among consolidated group members.

    (6) Tax accounting periods used.

      (i) In general.

      (ii) Special rule when timing of QRTME is manipulated.

    (7) Membership during taxable year in more than one group.

    (8) Intra-group transactions.

      (i) In general.

      (ii) Payment for QRTME.

(g) Effective/applicability date.

    (1) In general.

    (2) Taxable years ending before September 7, 2006.

    (3) Special rules for returns filed prior to November 9, 2007.

    (4) Taxable years beginning after December 31, 2011.

    (5) Taxable years beginning before January 1, 2012.

[Reg. §1.45G-0.]

   ☐ [*T.D. 9365*, 11-9-2007 *and T.D. 9717*, 4-2-2015.]

[Reg. §1.45G-1.]

§1.45G-1. Railroad track maintenance credit.—(a) *In general.*— For purposes of section 38, the railroad track maintenance credit (RTMC) for qualified railroad track maintenance expenditures (QRTME) paid or incurred by an eligible taxpayer during the taxable year is determined under this section. A taxpayer claiming the RTMC must do so by filing Form 8900, "Qualified Railroad Track Maintenance Credit," with its timely filed (including extensions) Federal income tax return for the taxable year the RTMC is claimed. Paragraph (b) of this section provides definitions of terms. Paragraph (c) of this section provides rules for computing the RTMC, including rules regarding limitations on the amount of the credit. Paragraph (d) of this section provides rules for assigning miles of railroad track. Paragraph (e) of this section contains rules for adjusting basis for the amount of the RTMC claimed by an eligible taxpayer. Paragraph (f) of this section contains rules for computing the amount of the RTMC in the case of a controlled group, and for the allocation of the group credit among members of the controlled group.

(b) *Definitions.*—For purposes of section 45G and this section, the following definitions apply:

    (1) *Class II railroad and Class III railroad* have the respective meanings given to these terms by the Surface Transportation Board (STB) without regard to the controlled group rules under section 45G(e)(2).

    (2) *Eligible railroad track* is railroad track (as defined in paragraph (b)(9) of this section) located within the United States that is owned or leased by a Class II railroad or Class III railroad at the close of its taxable year. For purposes of section 45G and this section, a Class II railroad or Class III railroad owns railroad track if the railroad track is subject to the allowance for depreciation under section 167 by the Class II railroad or Class III railroad.

    (3) *Eligible taxpayer* is—

      (i) A Class II railroad or Class III railroad during the taxable year;

      (ii) Any person that transports property using the rail facilities (as defined in paragraph (b)(6) of this section) of a Class II railroad or Class III railroad during the taxable year, but only is an eligible taxpayer with respect to the miles of eligible railroad track assigned to the person for that taxable year by that Class II railroad or Class III railroad under paragraph (d) of this section; or

      (iii) Any person that furnishes railroad-related property (as defined in paragraph (b)(7) of this section) or railroad-related services (as defined in paragraph (b)(8) of this section), to a Class II railroad or Class III railroad during the taxable year, but only is an eligible taxpayer with respect to the miles of eligible railroad track assigned to the person for that taxable year by that Class II railroad or Class III railroad under paragraph (d) of this section.

    (4) *Qualifying railroad structure* is property located within the United States that is described in the following STB property accounts in 49 CFR Part 1201, Subpart A:

      (i) Property Account 3, Grading.

      (ii) Property Account 4, Other right-of-way expenditures.

      (iii) Property Account 5, Tunnels and subways.

      (iv) Property Account 6, Bridges, trestles, and culverts.

      (v) Property Account 7, Elevated structures.

      (vi) Property Account 8, Ties.

      (vii) Property Account 9, Rails and other track material.

      (viii) Property Account 11, Ballast.

      (ix) Property Account 13, Fences, snowsheds, and signs.

      (x) Property Account 27, Signals and interlockers.

      (xi) Property Account 39, Public improvements; construction.

    (5) *Qualified railroad track maintenance expenditures (QRTME)* are expenditures for maintaining, repairing, and improving qualifying railroad structure (as defined in paragraph (b)(4) of this section) that is owned or leased as of January 1, 2005, by a Class II railroad or Class III railroad. These expenditures may or may not be chargeable to a capital account.

    (6) *Rail facilities* of a Class II railroad or Class III railroad are railroad yards, tracks, bridges, tunnels, wharves, docks, stations, and other related assets that are used in the transport of freight by a railroad and that are owned or leased by the Class II railroad or Class III railroad.

    (7) *Railroad-related property* is property that is provided directly to, and is unique to, a railroad and that, in the hands of a Class II railroad or Class III railroad, is described in—

      (i) The following STB property accounts in 49 CFR Part 1201, Subpart A:

        (A) Property Account 3, Grading;

        (B) Property Account 5, Tunnels and subways;

        (C) Property Account 22, Storage warehouses; and

      (ii) Asset classes 40.1 through 40.54 in the guidance issued by the Internal Revenue Service under section 168(i)(1) (for further guidance, for example, see Rev. Proc. 87-56 (1987-2 CB 674), and §601.601(d)(2)(ii)(*b*) of this chapter), except that any office building, any passenger train car, and any miscellaneous structure if such structure is not provided directly to, and is not unique to, a railroad are excluded from the definition of railroad-related property.

    (8) *Railroad-related services* are services that are provided directly to, and are unique to, a railroad and that relate to railroad shipping, loading and unloading of railroad freight, or repairs of rail facilities (as defined in paragraph (b)(6) of this section) or railroad-related property (as defined in paragraph (b)(7) of this section). Examples of railroad-related services are the transport of freight by rail; the loading and unloading of freight transported by rail; railroad bridge services; railroad track construction; providing railroad track material or equipment; locomotive leasing or rental; maintenance of railroad's right-of-way (including vegetation control); piggyback trailer ramping; rail deramping services; and freight train cars repair services. Examples of services that are not railroad-related services are general business services, such as, accounting and bookkeeping, marketing, legal services; janitorial services; office building rental; banking services (including financing of railroad-related property); and purchasing of, or services performed on, property not described in paragraph (b)(7) of this section.

    (9) Except as provided in paragraph (e)(2) of this section, *railroad track* is property described in STB property accounts 8 (ties), 9 (rails and other track material), and 11 (ballast) in 49 CFR part 1201, Subpart A. *Double track* is treated as multiple lines of railroad track, rather than as a single line of railroad track. Thus, one mile of single track is one mile, but one mile of double track is two miles.

(10) *Form 8900.*—If Form 8900 is revised or renumbered, any reference in this section to that form shall be treated as a reference to the revised or renumbered form.

(11) *Examples.*—The application of this paragraph (b) is illustrated by the following examples. In all examples, the taxpayers use a calendar taxable year, and are not members of a controlled group.

Example 1. A is a manufacturer that in 2006, transports its products by rail using the railroad tracks owned by B, a Class II railroad that owns 500 miles of railroad track within the United States on December 31, 2006. B properly assigns for purposes of section 45G 100 miles of eligible railroad track to A in 2006. A is an eligible taxpayer for 2006 with respect to the 100 miles of eligible railroad track.

Example 2. C is a bank that loans money to several Class III railroads. In 2006, C loans money to D, a Class III railroad, who in turn uses the loan proceeds to purchase track material. Because providing loans is not a service that is unique to a railroad, C is not providing railroad-related services and, thus, C is not an eligible taxpayer, even if D assigns miles of eligible railroad track to C for purposes of section 45G.

Example 3. E leases locomotives directly to Class I, Class II, and Class III railroads. In 2006, E leases locomotives to F, a Class II railroad that owns 200 miles of railroad track within the United States on December 31, 2006. F properly assigns for purposes of section 45G 200 miles of eligible railroad track to E. Because locomotives are property that is unique to a railroad, and E leases these locomotives directly to F in 2006, E is an eligible taxpayer for 2006 with respect to the 200 miles of eligible railroad track assigned to E by F.

Example 4. The facts are the same as in *Example 3*, except that E leases passenger trains, not locomotives, to F. Because passenger trains are not railroad-related property for purposes of section 45G, E is not an eligible taxpayer even if F assigns miles of eligible railroad track to E for purposes of section 45G.

(c) *Determination of amount of railroad track maintenance credit for the taxable year.*—(1) *General amount.*—Except as provided in paragraph (c)(2) of this section, for purposes of section 38, the RTMC determined under section 45G(a) for the taxable year is equal to 50 percent of the QRTME paid or incurred (as determined under paragraph (c)(3) of this section) by an eligible taxpayer during the taxable year.

(2) *Limitation on the credit.*—(i) *Eligible taxpayer is a Class II railroad or Class III railroad.*—If an eligible taxpayer is a Class II railroad or Class III railroad, the RTMC determined under paragraph (c)(1) of this section for the Class II railroad or Class III railroad for any taxable year must not exceed $3,500 multiplied by the sum of—

(A) The number of miles of eligible railroad track owned or leased by the Class II railroad or Class III railroad, reduced by the number of miles of eligible railroad track assigned under paragraph (d) of this section by the Class II railroad or Class III railroad to another eligible taxpayer for that taxable year; and

(B) The number of miles of eligible railroad track owned or leased by another Class II railroad or Class III railroad that are assigned under paragraph (d) of this section to the Class II railroad or Class III railroad for the taxable year.

(ii) *Eligible taxpayer is not a Class II railroad or Class III railroad.*—If an eligible taxpayer is not a Class II railroad or Class III railroad, the RTMC determined under paragraph (c)(1) of this section for the eligible taxpayer for any taxable year must not exceed $3,500 multiplied by the number of miles of eligible railroad track assigned under paragraph (d) of this section by a Class II railroad or Class III railroad to the eligible taxpayer for the taxable year.

(iii) *No carryover of amount that exceeds limitation.*—Amounts that exceed the limitation under paragraph (c)(2)(i) of this section or paragraph (c)(2)(ii) of this section, may never be carried over to another taxable year.

(3) *Determination of amount of QRTME paid or incurred.*—(i) *In general.*—The term *paid or incurred* means, in the case of a taxpayer using an accrual method of accounting, a liability incurred (within the meaning of §1.446-1(c)(1)(ii)). A liability may not be taken into account under section 45G and this section prior to the taxable year *during which the liability is incurred.* Any amount that an eligible taxpayer (assignee) pays a Class II railroad or Class III railroad (assignor) in exchange for an assignment of one or more miles of eligible railroad track under paragraph (d) of this section, is treated, for purposes of this section, as QRTME paid or incurred by the assignee, and not by the assignor, at the time and to the extent the assignor pays or incurs QRTME.

(ii) *Effect of reimbursements received from persons other than a Class II or Class III railroad.*—The amount of QRTME treated as paid or incurred during the taxable year by an eligible taxpayer under paragraphs (b)(3)(ii) and (iii) of this section shall be reduced by any amount to which the eligible taxpayer is entitled to be reimbursed, directly or indirectly, from persons other than a Class II or Class III railroad.

(4) *Examples.*—The application of this paragraph (c) is illustrated by the following examples. In all examples, the taxpayers use an accrual method of accounting and a calendar taxable year, and are not members of a controlled group.

Example 1. Computation of RTMC; section 45G credit limitation is not exceeded. (i) G is a Class II railroad that owns or has leased to it 1,000 miles of railroad track within the United States on December 31, 2006. H is a manufacturer that in 2006, transports its products by rail using the rail facilities of G. In 2006, for purposes of section 45G, G assigns 100 miles of eligible railroad track to H and does not make any other assignments of railroad track miles in 2006. H did not receive any other assignments of railroad track miles in 2006. During 2006, G incurred QRTME in the amount of $2.5 million and H incurred QRTME in the amount of $200,000.

(ii) For 2006, G determines the tentative amount of RTMC under paragraph (c)(1) of this section to be $1,250,000 (50% multiplied by $2,500,000 QRTME incurred by G during 2006). G further determines G's credit limitation under paragraph (c)(2)(i) of this section for 2006 to be $3,150,000 ($3,500 multiplied by 900 miles of eligible railroad track (1,000 miles owned by, or leased to, G on December 31, 2006, less 100 miles assigned by G to H in 2006)). Because G's tentative amount of RTMC does not exceed G's credit limitation amount for 2006, G may claim a RTMC for 2006 in the amount of $1,250,000.

(iii) For 2006, H determines the tentative amount of RTMC under paragraph (c)(1) of this section to be $100,000 (50% multiplied by $200,000 QRTME incurred by H during 2006). H further determines H's credit limitation under paragraph (c)(2)(ii) of this section for 2006 to be $350,000 ($3,500 multiplied by 100 miles of eligible railroad track assigned by G to H in 2006). Because H's tentative amount of RTMC does not exceed H's credit limitation amount for 2006, H may claim a RTMC in the amount of $100,000.

Example 2. Computation of RTMC; section 45G credit limitation is exceeded. (i) The facts are the same as in *Example 1*, except that G assigned for purposes of section 45G only 50 miles of railroad track to H in 2006 and, during 2006, H incurred QRTME in the amount of $400,000.

(ii) For 2006, G determines the tentative amount of RTMC under paragraph (c)(1) of this section to be $1,250,000 (50% multiplied by $2,500,000 QRTME incurred by G during 2006). G further determines G's credit limitation under paragraph (c)(2)(i) of this section for 2006 to be $3,325,000 ($3,500 multiplied by 950 miles of eligible railroad track (1,000 miles owned by, or leased to, G on December 31, 2006, less 50 miles assigned by G to H in 2006)). Because G's tentative amount of RTMC does not exceed G's credit limitation amount for 2006, G may claim a RTMC in the amount of $1,250,000

(iii) For 2006, H determines the tentative amount of RTMC under paragraph (c)(1) of this section to be $200,000 (50% multiplied by $400,000 QRTME incurred by H during 2006). H further determines H's credit limitation under paragraph (c)(2)(ii) of this section for 2006 to be $175,000 ($3,500 multiplied by 50 miles of eligible railroad track assigned by G to H in 2006). Because H's tentative amount of RTMC exceeds H's credit limitation amount for 2006, H may claim a RTMC in the amount of $175,000 (the credit limitation amount). Under paragraph (c)(2)(iii) of this section, there is no carryover of the $25,000 (the tentative amount of $200,000 less the credit limitation amount of $175,000) that exceeds the limitation.

Example 3. Railroad track miles assigned for payment. (i) J is a Class II railroad that owns or has leased to it 1,000 miles of railroad track within the United States on December 31, 2006. K is a corporation that sells ties, ballast, and other track material to Class I, Class II, and Class III railroads. During 2006, K sold these items to J and J incurred QRTME in the amount of $1 million. Also, on December 6, 2006, J assigned for purposes of section 45G 150 miles of eligible railroad track to K and K paid J $800,000 for that assignment. K did not pay or incur any other QRTME during 2006.

(ii) For 2006, in accordance with paragraph (c)(3)(ii) of this section, J is treated as having incurred QRTME in the amount of $200,000 ($1 million QRTME actually incurred by J less the $800,000 paid by K to J for the assignment of the railroad track miles in 2006). For 2006, J determines the tentative amount of RTMC under paragraph (c)(1) of this section to be $100,000 (50% multiplied by $200,000 QRTME treated as incurred by J during 2006). J further determines J's credit limitation amount under paragraph (c)(2)(i) of this section for 2006 to be $2,975,000 ($3,500 multiplied by 850 miles of eligible railroad track (1,000 miles owned by, or leased to, J on December 31, 2006, less 150 miles assigned by J to K in 2006)). Because J's tentative amount of RTMC does not exceed J's credit limitation amount for 2006, J may claim a RTMC in the amount of $100,000.

(iii) For 2006, K is an eligible taxpayer because, during 2006, K provided railroad-related property to J and received an assignment of eligible railroad track miles from J. Under paragraph (c)(3)(ii) of this section, K is treated as having incurred QRTME in the amount of $800,000 (the amount paid by K to J for the assignment of the railroad track miles in 2006). For 2006, K determines the tentative amount of RTMC under paragraph (c)(1) of this section to be $400,000 (50% multiplied by $800,000 QRTME treated as incurred by K during 2006). K further determines K's credit limitation amount under paragraph (c)(2)(ii) of this section for 2006 to be $525,000 ($3,500 multiplied by 150 miles of eligible railroad track assigned by J in 2006). Because K's tentative amount of RTMC does not exceed K's credit limitation amount for 2006, K may claim a RTMC in the amount of $400,000.

(iv) The results in this *Example 3* would be the same if K sold the ties, ballast, and other track material with a fair market value of $1 million to J for $200,000 in exchange for the assignment by J of 150 miles of eligible railroad track to K.

Example 4. Reimbursement of QRTME. (i) L is a Class III railroad that owns or has leased to it 500 miles of railroad track within the United States on December 31, 2006. M is a manufacturer that in 2006 transports its products by rail using the rail facilities of L. During 2006, L did not incur any QRTME. Also, in 2006, L assigned for purposes of section 45G 200 miles of eligible railroad track to M and agreed to reduce L's freight shipping rates to M by $250,000 in exchange for M upgrading these railroad track miles. Consequently, during 2006, M incurred QRTME of $500,000 to upgrade these 200 miles of railroad track and L reduced L's freight shipping rates for M by $250,000.

(ii) For 2006, M is an eligible taxpayer because, during 2006, M transported property using the rail facilities of L and received an assignment of eligible railroad track miles from L. The amount of QRTME paid or incurred by M during 2006 is $500,000 and is not reduced by the reimbursement of $250,000 by L to M because, under paragraph (c)(3)(ii) of this section, QRTME is not reduced by reimbursements from Class II or Class III railroads. For 2006, M determines the tentative amount of RTMC under paragraph (c)(1) of this section to be $250,000 (50% multiplied by $500,000 QRTME incurred by M during 2006). M further determines M's credit limitation amount under paragraph (c)(2)(ii) of this section for 2006 to be $700,000 ($3,500 multiplied by 200 miles of eligible railroad track assigned by L to M in 2006). Because M's tentative amount of RTMC does not exceed M's credit limitation amount for 2006, M may claim a RTMC in the amount of $250,000.

(d) *Assignment of track miles.*—(1) *In general.*—An assignment of any mile of eligible railroad track under this paragraph (d) is a designation by a Class II railroad or Class III railroad that is made solely for purposes of section 45G and this section of a specific number of miles of eligible railroad track as being assigned to another eligible taxpayer for a taxable year. A designation must be in writing and must include the name and taxpayer identification number of the assignee, and the information required under the rules of paragraph (d)(4)(iii)(B) of this section. A designation requires no transfer of legal title or other indicia of ownership of the eligible railroad track, and need not specify the location of any assigned mile of eligible railroad track. Further, an assigned mile of eligible railroad track need not correspond to any specific mile of eligible railroad track with respect to which the eligible taxpayer actually pays or incurs the QRTME.

(2) *Assignment eligibility.*—Only a Class II railroad or Class III railroad may assign a mile of eligible railroad track. If a Class II railroad or Class III railroad assigns a mile of eligible railroad track to an eligible taxpayer, the assignee is not permitted to reassign any mile of eligible railroad track to another eligible taxpayer. The maximum number of miles of eligible railroad track that may be assigned by a Class II railroad or Class III railroad for any taxable year is its total miles of eligible railroad track less the miles of eligible railroad track that the Class II railroad or Class III railroad retains for itself in determining its RTMC for the taxable year.

(3) *Effective date of assignment.*—If a Class II railroad or Class III railroad assigns a mile of eligible railroad track, the assignment is treated as being made by the Class II railroad or Class III railroad at the close of its taxable year in which the assignment was made. With respect to the assignee, the assignment of a mile of eligible railroad track is taken into account for the taxable year of the assignee that includes the date the assignment is treated as being made by the assignor Class II railroad or Class III railroad under this paragraph (d)(3).

(4) *Assignment information statement.*—(i) *In general.*—A taxpayer must file Form 8900, *"Qualified Railroad Track Maintenance Credit,"* with its timely filed (including extensions) Federal income tax return for the taxable year for which the taxpayer assigns any mile of eligible railroad track, even if the taxpayer is not itself claiming the RTMC for that taxable year.

(ii) *Assignor.*—Except as provided in paragraph (d)(4)(iv) of this section, a Class II railroad or Class III railroad (assignor) that assigns one or more miles of eligible railroad track during a taxable year to one or more eligible taxpayers must attach to the assignor's Form 8900 for that taxable year an information statement providing—

(A) The name and taxpayer identification number of each assignee;

(B) The total number of miles of the assignor's eligible railroad track;

(C) The number of miles of eligible railroad track assigned by the assignor to each assignee for the taxable year; and

(D) The total number of miles of eligible railroad track assigned by the assignor to all assignees for the taxable year.

(iii) *Assignee.*—Except as provided in paragraph (d)(4)(iv) of this section, an eligible taxpayer (assignee) that has received an assignment of miles of eligible railroad track during its taxable year from a Class II railroad or Class III railroad, and that claims the RTMC for that taxable year, must attach to the assignee's Form 8900 for that taxable year a statement—

(A) Providing the total number of miles of eligible railroad track assigned to the assignee for the assignee's taxable year; and

(B) Attesting that the assignee has in writing, and has retained as part of the assignee's records for purposes of § 1.6001-1(a), the following information from each assignor:

(1) The name and taxpayer identification number of each assignor.

(2) The date of each assignment made by each assignor (as determined under paragraph (d)(3) of this section) to the assignee;

(3) The number of miles of eligible railroad track assigned by each assignor to the assignee for the assignee's taxable year.

(iv) *Special rules for returns filed prior to November 9, 2007.*—If an eligible taxpayer's Federal income tax return for a taxable year beginning after December 31, 2004, and ending before November 9, 2007, was filed before December 13, 2007, and the eligible taxpayer is not filing an amended Federal income tax return for that taxable year pursuant to paragraph (g)(2) of this section before the eligible taxpayer's next filed original Federal income tax return, and the eligible taxpayer wants to apply paragraph (g)(2) of this section but did not include with that return the information specified in paragraph (d)(4)(ii) or (iii) of this section, as applicable, the eligible taxpayer must attach a statement containing the information specified in paragraph (d)(4)(ii) or (iii) of this section, as applicable, to either—

(A) The eligible taxpayer's next filed original Federal income tax return; or

(B) The eligible taxpayer's amended Federal income tax return that is filed pursuant to paragraph (g)(2) of this section, provided that amended Federal income tax return is filed by the eligible taxpayer before its next filed original Federal income tax return.

(5) *Special rules.*—(i) *Effect of subsequent dispositions of eligible railroad track during the assignment year.*—If a Class II railroad or Class III railroad assigns one or more miles of eligible railroad track that it owned or leased as of the actual date of the assignment, but does not own or lease any eligible railroad track at the close of the taxable year in which the assignment is made by the Class II railroad or Class III railroad, the assignment is not valid for that taxable year for purposes of section 45G and this section.

(ii) *Effect of multiple assignments of eligible railroad track miles during the same taxable year.*—If a Class II railroad or Class III railroad assigns more miles of eligible railroad track than it owned or leased as of the close of the taxable year in which the assignment is made by the Class II railroad or Class III railroad, the assignment is valid for purposes of section 45G and this section only with respect to the name of the assignee and the number of miles listed by the assignor Class II railroad or Class III railroad on the statement required under paragraph (d)(4)(ii) of this section and only to the extent of the maximum miles of eligible railroad track that may be assigned by the assignor Class II railroad or Class III railroad as determined under paragraph (d)(2) of this section. If the total number of miles on this statement exceeds the maximum miles of eligible railroad track that may be assigned by the assignor Class II railroad or Class III railroad (as determined under paragraph (d)(2) of this section), the total number of miles on the statement shall be reduced by the excess amount of miles. This reduction is allocated among each assignee listed on the statement in proportion to the total number of miles listed on the statement for that assignee.

(6) *Examples*.—The application of this paragraph (d) is illustrated by the following examples. In none of the examples are the taxpayers members of a controlled group:

Example 1. Assignor and assignee have the same taxable year. (i) N, a calendar year taxpayer, is a Class II railroad that owns 500 miles of railroad track within the United States on December 31, 2006. O, a calendar year taxpayer, is not a railroad, but is a taxpayer that provides railroad-related property to N during 2006. On November 7, 2006, N assigns for purposes of section 45G 300 miles of eligible railroad track to O. O receives no other assignment of eligible railroad track in 2006. O pays or incurs QRTME in the amount of $100,000 in November 2006, and $50,000 in February 2007. N and O each file Form 8900 with their timely filed Federal income tax returns for 2006 and attach the statement required by paragraph (d)(4)(ii) and (iii), respectively, of this section reporting the assignment of the 300 miles of eligible railroad track to O.

(ii) The assignment of the 300 miles of eligible railroad track made by N to O on November 7, 2006, is treated as made on December 31, 2006 (at the close of the N's taxable year). Consequently, the assignment is taken into account by O for O's taxable year ending on December 31, 2006. For 2006, O is an eligible taxpayer because, during 2006, O provides railroad-related property to N and receives an assignment of 300 eligible railroad track miles from N. For 2006, O determines the tentative amount of RTMC under paragraph (c)(1) of this section to be $50,000 (50% multiplied by $100,000 QRTME paid or incurred by O during 2006). O further determines the credit limitation amount under paragraph (c)(2)(ii) of this section for 2006 to be $1,050,000 ($3,500 multiplied by 300 miles of eligible railroad track assigned by N to O on December 31, 2006). Because O's tentative amount of RTMC does not exceed O's credit limitation amount for 2006, O may claim a RMTC for 2006 in the amount of $50,000.

Example 2. Assignor and assignee have different taxable years. (i) The facts are the same as in *Example 1*, except that O's taxable year ends on March 31.

(ii) The assignment of the 300 miles of eligible railroad track made by N to O on November 7, 2006, is treated as made on December 31, 2006. As a result, the assignment is taken into account by O for O's taxable year ending on March 31, 2007. Thus, for the taxable year ending on March 31, 2007, O determines the tentative amount of RMTC under paragraph (c)(1) of this section to be $75,000 (50% multiplied by $150,000 QRTME incurred by O during its taxable year ending March 31, 2007). Because O's tentative amount of RTMC does not exceed O's credit limitation amount for the taxable year ending March 31, 2007, O may claim a RMTC for the taxable year ending March 31, 2007, in the amount of $75,000.

Example 3. Assignment location differs from QRTME location. (i) P, a calendar-year taxpayer, is a Class III railroad that owns or has leased to it 200 miles of railroad track within the United States on December 31, 2006. P owns 50 miles of this railroad track and leases 150 miles of this railroad track from Q, a Class I railroad. On February 8, 2006, P assigns for purposes of section 45G 50 miles of eligible railroad track to R. R is not a railroad, but is a taxpayer that ships products using the 50 miles of eligible railroad track owned by P, and R paid $100,000 in 2006 to P to enable P to upgrade these 50 miles of eligible railroad track. In March 2006, P also assigns for purposes of section 45G 150 miles of eligible railroad track to S. S is not a railroad, but is a taxpayer that provides railroad-related property to P, and S paid $400,000 to P to enable P to upgrade P's 200 miles of eligible railroad track. For 2006, P pays or incurs QRTME in the amount of $500,000 to upgrade the 150 miles of eligible railroad track that it leases from Q and pays or incurs no QRTME on the 50 miles of eligible railroad track that it owns. For 2006, P receives no other assignment of eligible railroad track miles and did not retain any eligible railroad track miles for itself. Also, R and S do not pay or incur any other amounts that would qualify as QRTME during 2006. P, R, and S each file Form 8900 with their timely filed Federal income tax returns for 2006 and attach the statement required by paragraph (d)(4)(ii) or (iii) of this section, whichever applies, reporting the assignment of eligible railroad track by P to R or S in 2006.

(ii) For 2006, in accordance with paragraph (c)(3)(ii) of this section, P is treated as having incurred QRTME in the amount of $0 ($500,000 QRTME actually incurred by P less the $100,000 paid by R to P for the assignment of the 50 miles of eligible railroad track and the $400,000 paid by S to P for the assignment of the 150 miles of eligible railroad track). Further, P assigned all of its eligible railroad track miles to R and S for 2006. Accordingly, for 2006, P may not claim any RTMC.

(iii) For 2006, R is an eligible taxpayer because, during 2006, R ships property using the rail facilities of P and receives an assignment of 50 eligible railroad track miles from P. In accordance with paragraph (c)(3)(ii) of this section, R is treated as having incurred QRTME in the amount of $100,000 (the amount paid by R to P for the assignment of the eligible railroad track miles in 2006) even though

no work was performed on the 50 miles of eligible railroad track that was assigned by P to R. For 2006, R determines the tentative amount of RTMC under paragraph (c)(1) of this section to be $50,000 (50% multiplied by $100,000 QRTME treated as incurred by R during 2006). R further determines the credit limitation amount under paragraph (c)(2)(ii) of this section to be $175,000 ($3,500 multiplied by 50 miles of eligible railroad track assigned by P to R in 2006). Because R's tentative amount of RTMC does not exceed R's credit limitation amount for 2006, R may claim a RTMC for 2006 in the amount of $50,000.

(iv) For 2006, S is an eligible taxpayer because, during 2006, S provides railroad-related property to P and receives an assignment of 150 eligible railroad track miles from P. In accordance with paragraph (c)(3)(ii) of this section, S is treated as having incurred QRTME in the amount of $400,000 (amount paid by S to P for the assignment of the eligible railroad track miles in 2006). For 2006, S determines the tentative amount of RTMC under paragraph (c)(1) of this section to be $200,000 (50% multiplied by $400,000 QRTME treated as incurred by S during 2006). S further determines the credit limitation amount under paragraph (c)(2)(ii) of this section to be $525,000 ($3,500 multiplied by 150 miles of eligible railroad track assigned by P to S in 2006). Because S's tentative amount of RTMC does not exceed S's credit limitation amount for 2006, S may claim a RTMC for 2006 in the amount of $200,000.

Example 4. Multiple assignments of track miles. (i) T, a calendar-year taxpayer, is a Class III railroad that owns or has leased to it 200 miles of railroad track within the United States on December 31, 2006. T owns 75 miles of this railroad track and leases 125 miles of this railroad track from U, a Class I railroad. V and W are not railroads, but are both taxpayers that provide railroad-related services to T during 2006. On January 15, 2006, T assigns for purposes of section 45G 200 miles of eligible railroad track to V. V agrees to incur, in 2006, $1.4 million of QRTME to upgrade a portion of/segment of these 200 miles of eligible railroad track. Due to unexpected financial difficulties, V only incurs $250,000 of QRTME during 2006 and on May 15, 2006, T learns that V is unable to incur the remainder of the QRTME. On June 15, 2006, T assigns for purposes of section 45G the 200 miles of railroad track to W. In 2006, W incurs $1,100,000 of QRTME to upgrade a portion of/segment of the railroad track. For 2006, T receives no other assignment of eligible railroad track miles and did not retain any eligible railroad track miles for itself. V and W do not receive any other assignments of miles of eligible railroad track miles from a Class II railroad or Class III railroad during 2006. T and W each file Form 8900 with their timely filed Federal income tax returns for 2006, and attach the statement required by paragraph (d)(4)(ii) and (iii), respectively, of this section, reporting the assignment of 200 miles of eligible railroad track to W.

(ii) Because T did not retain any miles of eligible railroad track for itself for 2006, the maximum miles of eligible railroad track that may be assigned by T for 2006 is 200 miles pursuant to paragraph (d)(2) of this section. On the statement required by paragraph (d)(4)(ii) of this section, T assigned a total of 200 miles of eligible railroad track to W. Consequently, because T did not list V as an assignee on T's statement required by paragraph (d)(4)(ii) of this section, V did not receive an assignment of eligible railroad track miles from T during 2006 and V is not an eligible taxpayer for 2006. Thus, for 2006, V may not claim any RTMC even though V incurred QRTME in the amount of $250,000.

(iii) For 2006, W is an eligible taxpayer because, during 2006, W provides railroad-related services to T and receives an assignment of 200 eligible railroad track miles from T. W determines the tentative amount of RTMC under paragraph (c)(1) of this section to be $550,000 (50% multiplied by $1,100,000 QRTME incurred by W during 2006). W further determines the credit limitation amount under paragraph (c)(2)(ii) of this section to be $700,000 ($3,500 multiplied by the 200 miles of eligible railroad track assigned by T to W in 2006). Because W's tentative amount of RTMC does not exceed W's credit limitation amount for 2006, W may claim a RTMC for 2006 in the amount of $550,000.

Example 5. Multiple assignments of track miles. (i) Same facts as in *Example 4*, except T, to its Form 8900 for 2006, attaches the statement required by paragraph (d)(4)(ii) of this section assigning 200 miles of eligible railroad track to W and 200 miles of eligible railroad track to V.

(ii) Because T did not retain any miles of eligible railroad track for itself for 2006, the maximum miles of eligible railroad track that may be assigned by T for 2006 is 200 miles pursuant to paragraph (d)(2) of this section. However, on the statement required by paragraph (d)(4)(ii) of this section, T assigned a total of 400 miles of eligible railroad track (200 miles to W and 200 miles to V). Consequently, the 400 miles of eligible railroad track on this statement must be reduced to the 200 maximum miles of eligible railroad track available for assignment for 2006. Because the statement reports 200 miles of eligible railroad track assigned to each W and V, the reduction of 200 miles (400 total miles of eligible railroad track on the statement less 200 maximum miles of eligible railroad track available for assignment) is allocated pro-rata between W and V and, therefore, 100 miles each to W and V. Thus, pursuant to paragraph (d)(5)(ii) of this section, the number of miles of eligible railroad track assigned by T to W and V for 2006 is 100 miles each.

(iii) For 2006, V is an eligible taxpayer because, during 2006, V provides railroad-related services to T and receives an assignment of 100 eligible railroad track miles from T. V determines the tentative amount of RTMC under paragraph (c)(1) of this section to be $125,000 (50% multiplied by $250,000 QRTME incurred by V during 2006). V further determines the credit limitation amount under paragraph (c)(2)(ii) of this section to be $350,000 ($3,500 multiplied by the 100 miles of eligible railroad track assigned by T to V in 2006). Because V's tentative amount of RTMC does not exceed W's credit limitation amount for 2006, V may claim a RTMC for 2006 in the amount of $125,000.

(iv) For 2006, W is an eligible taxpayer because, during 2006, W provides railroad-related services to T and receives an assignment of 100 eligible railroad track miles from T. W determines the tentative amount of RTMC under paragraph (c)(1) of this section to be $550,000 (50% multiplied by $1,100,000 QRTME incurred by W during 2006). W further determines the credit limitation amount under paragraph (c)(2)(ii) of this section to be $350,000 ($3,500 multiplied by the 100 miles of eligible railroad track assigned by T to W in 2006). Because W's tentative amount of RTMC exceeds W's credit limitation amount for 2006, W may claim a RTMC for 2006 in the amount of $350,000 (the credit limitation). There is no carryover of the amount of $200,000 (the tentative amount of $550,000 less the credit limitation amount of $350,000).

(e) *Adjustments to basis.*—(1) *In general.*—All or some of the QRTME paid or incurred by an eligible taxpayer during the taxable year may be required to be capitalized under section 263(a) as a tangible asset or as an intangible asset. See, for example, §1.263(a)-4(d)(8), which requires capitalization of amounts paid or incurred by a taxpayer to produce or improve real property owned by another (except to the extent the taxpayer is selling services at fair market value to produce or improve the real property) if the real property can reasonably be expected to produce significant economic benefits for the taxpayer. The basis of the tangible asset or intangible asset includes the capitalized amount of the QRTME.

(2) *Basis adjustment made to railroad track.*—An eligible taxpayer must reduce the adjusted basis of any railroad track with respect to which the eligible taxpayer claims the RTMC. For purposes of section 45G(e)(3) and this paragraph (e)(2), the adjusted basis of any railroad track with respect to which the eligible taxpayer claims the RTMC is limited to the amount of QRTME, if any, that is required to be capitalized into the qualifying railroad structure or an intangible asset. The adjusted basis of the railroad track is reduced by the amount of the RTMC allowable (as determined under paragraph (c) of this section) by the eligible taxpayer for the taxable year, but not below zero. This reduction is taken into account at the time the QRTME is paid or incurred by an eligible taxpayer and before the depreciation deduction with respect to such railroad track is determined for the taxable year for which the RTMC is allowable. If all or some of the QRTME paid or incurred by an eligible taxpayer during the taxable year is capitalized under section 263(a) to more than one asset, whether tangible or intangible (for example, railroad track and bridges), the reduction to the basis of these assets under this paragraph (e)(2) is allocated among each of the assets subject to the reduction in proportion to the unadjusted basis of each asset at the time the QRTME is paid or incurred during that taxable year.

(3) *Examples.*—The application of this paragraph (e) is illustrated by the following examples. In each example, all taxpayers use a calendar taxable year, and no taxpayers are members of a controlled group.

Example 1. (i) X is a Class II railroad that owns 500 miles of railroad track within the United States on December 31, 2006. During 2006, X incurs $1 million of QRTME for maintaining this railroad track. X uses the track maintenance allowance method for track structure expenditures (for further guidance, see Rev. Proc. 2002-65 (2002-2 CB 700) and §601.601(d)(2)(ii)(*b*) of this chapter). Assume all of the $1 million QRTME is track structure expenditures and none of it was expended for new track structure.

(ii) For 2006, X determines the tentative amount of RTMC under paragraph (c)(1) of this section to be $500,000 (50% multiplied by $1 million QRTME incurred by X during 2006). X further determines the credit limitation amount under paragraph (c)(2)(i) of this section for 2006 to be $1,750,000 ($3,500 multiplied by 500 miles of eligible railroad track). Because X's tentative amount of RTMC does not exceed X's credit limitation amount for 2006, X may claim a RTMC for 2006 in the amount of $500,000.

(iii) Of the $1 million QRTME incurred by X during 2006, X determines under the track maintenance allowance method that

$750,000 is the track maintenance allowance under section 162 and $250,000 is the capitalized amount for the track structure. In accordance with paragraph (e)(2) of this section, X reduces the capitalized amount of $250,000 by the RTMC of $500,000 claimed by X for 2006, but not below zero. Thus, the capitalized amount of $250,000 is reduced to zero. X also deducts under section 162 a track maintenance allowance of $750,000 on its 2006 Federal income tax return.

Example 2. (i) Y is a Class II railroad that owns or has leased to it 500 miles of eligible railroad track within the United States on December 31, 2006. Z is not a railroad, but is a taxpayer that, in 2006, transports its products using the rail facilities of Y. In 2006, Y assigns for purposes of section 45G 300 miles of eligible railroad track to Z. Z does not receive any other assignments of eligible railroad track miles in 2006. During 2006, Z incurs QRTME in the amount of $1 million, and Y does not incur any QRTME. Y and Z each file Form 8900 with their timely filed Federal income tax returns for 2006 and attach the statement required by paragraph (d)(4)(ii) and (iii), respectively, of this section reporting the assignment of the 300 miles of eligible railroad track to Z.

(ii) For 2006, Z determines the tentative amount of RTMC under paragraph (c)(1) of this section to be $500,000 (50% multiplied by $1 million QRTME incurred by Z during 2006). Z further determines the credit limitation amount under paragraph (c)(2)(ii) of this section for 2006 to be $1,050,000 ($3,500 multiplied by 300 miles of eligible railroad track assigned by Y to Z in 2006). Because Z's tentative amount of RTMC does not exceed Z's credit limitation amount for 2006, Z may claim a RTMC for 2006 in the amount of $500,000.

(iii) For 2006, Z also must determine the portion of the $1 million QRTME that Z incurs that is required to be capitalized under section 263(a), and the portion that is a section 162 expense. Because Z is not a Class II railroad or Class III railroad, Z cannot use the track maintenance allowance method. Assume that all of the QRTME constitutes an intangible asset under §1.263(a)-4(d)(8) and, therefore, is required to be capitalized by Z under section 263(a) as an intangible asset. In accordance with paragraph (e)(2) of this section, Z reduces the capitalized amount of $1 million by the RTMC of $500,000 claimed by Z for 2006. Thus, the capitalized amount of $1 million for the intangible asset is reduced to $500,000. Further, pursuant to §1.167(a)-3(b)(1)(iv), Z may treat this intangible asset with an adjusted basis of $500,000 as having a useful life of 25 years for purposes of the depreciation allowance under section 167(a).

(f) *Controlled groups.*—(1) *In general.*—Pursuant to section 45G(e)(2), if an eligible taxpayer is a member of a controlled group of corporations, rules similar to the rules in §1.41-6T apply for determining the amount of the RTMC under section 45G(a) and this section. To determine the amount of RTMC (if any) allowable to a trade or business that at the end of its taxable year is a member of a controlled group, a taxpayer must—

(i) Compute the group credit in the manner described in paragraph (f)(3) of this section; and

(ii) Allocate the group credit among the members of the group in the manner described in paragraph (f)(4) of this section.

(2) *Definitions.*—For purposes of section 45G(e)(2) and paragraph (f) of this section—

(i) A *trade or business* is a sole proprietorship, a partnership, a trust, an estate, or a corporation that is carrying on a trade or business (within the meaning of section 162). Any corporation that is a member of a commonly controlled group shall be deemed to be carrying on a trade or business if any other member of that group is carrying on any trade or business;

(ii) *Group* and *controlled group* means a controlled group of corporations, as defined in section 41(f)(5), or a group of trades or businesses under common control. For rules for determining whether trades or businesses are under common control, see §1.52-1 (b) through (g);

(iii) *Group credit* means the RTMC (if any) allowable to a controlled group;

(iv) *Consolidated group* has the meaning set forth in §1.1502-1(h); and

(v) *Credit year* means the taxable year for which the member is computing the RTMC.

(3) *Computation of the group credit.*—All members of a controlled group are treated as a single taxpayer for purposes of computing the RTMC. The group credit is computed by applying all of the section 45G computational rules (including the rules set forth in this section) on an aggregate basis.

(4) *Allocation of the group credit.*—The group credit is allocated to each member of the controlled group on a proportionate basis to its share of the aggregate of the QRTMEs taken into account for the taxable year by such controlled group for purposes of the credit.

(5) *Special rules for consolidated groups.*—(i) *In general.*—For purposes of applying paragraph (f)(4) of this section, members of a consolidated group who are members of a controlled group are treated as a single member of the controlled group.

(ii) *Special rule for allocation of group credit among consolidated group members.*—The portion of the group credit that is allocated to a consolidated group is allocated to each member of the consolidated group on a proportionate basis to its share of the aggregate of the QRTMEs taken into account for the taxable year by such consolidated group for purposes of the credit.

(6) *Tax accounting periods used.*—(i) *In general.*—The credit allowable to a member of a controlled group is that member's share of the group credit computed as of the end of that member's taxable year. In computing the group credit for a group whose members have different taxable years, a member generally should treat the taxable year of another member that ends with or within the credit year of the computing member as the credit year of that other member. For example, Q, R, and S are members of a controlled group of corporations. Both Q and R are calendar year taxpayers. S files a return using a fiscal year ending June 30. For purposes of computing the group credit at the end of Q's and R's taxable year on December 31, S's fiscal year ending June 30, which ends within Q's and R's taxable year, is treated as S's credit year.

(ii) *Special rule when timing of QRTME is manipulated.*—If the timing of QRTME by members using different tax accounting periods is manipulated to generate a credit in excess of the amount that would be allowable if all members of the group used the same tax accounting period, then the appropriate Internal Revenue Service official in the operating division that has examination jurisdiction of the return may require each member of the group to calculate the credit in the current taxable year and all future years as if all members of the group had the same taxable year and base period as the computing member.

(7) *Membership during taxable year in more than one group.*—A trade or business may be a member of only one group for a taxable year. If, without application of this paragraph (f)(7), a business would be a member of more than one group at the end of its taxable year, the business shall be treated as a member of the group in which it was included for its preceding taxable year. If the business was not included for its preceding taxable year in any group in which it could be included as of the end of its taxable year, the business shall designate in its timely filed (including extensions) federal income tax return for the taxable year the group in which it is being included. If the business does not so designate, then the appropriate Internal Revenue Service official in the operating division that has examination jurisdiction of the return will determine the group in which the business is to be included. If the Federal income tax return for a taxable year beginning after December 31, 2004, and ending before November 9, 2007, was filed before December 13, 2007, and the business wants to apply paragraph (g)(2) of this section but did not designate its group membership in that return, the business must designate its group membership for that year either—

(i) In its next filed original Federal income tax return; or

(ii) In its amended Federal income tax return that is filed pursuant to paragraph (g)(2) of this section, provided that amended Federal income tax return is filed by the business before its next filed original Federal income tax return.

(8) *Intra-group transactions.*—(i) *In general.*—Because all members of a group under common control are treated as a single taxpayer for purposes of determining the RTMC, transfers between members of the group are generally disregarded.

(ii) *Payment for QRTME.*—Amounts paid or incurred by the owner (or lessor) of eligible railroad track to another member of the group for QRTME shall be taken into account as QRTME by the owner (or lessor) of the eligible railroad track for purposes of section 45G only to the extent of the lesser of—

(A) The amount paid or incurred to the other member; or

(B) The amount that would have been considered paid or incurred by the other member for the QRTME, if the QRTME was not reimbursed by the owner (or lessor) of the eligible railroad track.

(g) *Effective/applicability date.*—(1) *In general.*—Except as provided in paragraphs (g)(2) and (g)(3) of this section, this section applies to taxable years ending on or after September 7, 2006.

(2) *Taxable years ending before September 7, 2006.*—A taxpayer may apply this section to taxable years beginning after December 31, 2004, and ending before September 7, 2006, provided that the taxpayer applies all provisions in this section to the taxable year.

(3) *Special rules for returns filed prior to November 9, 2007.*—If a taxpayer's Federal income tax return for a taxable year beginning after December 31, 2004, and ending before November 9, 2007, was filed before December 13, 2007, and the taxpayer is not filing an amended Federal income tax return for that taxable year pursuant to paragraph (g)(2) of this section before the taxpayer's next filed original Federal income tax return, see paragraphs (d)(4)(iv) and (f)(7) of this section for the statements that must be attached to the taxpayer's next filed original Federal income tax return.

(4) *Taxable years beginning after December 31, 2011.*—Paragraphs (f)(4) and (5) and (g)(4) and (5) of this section apply to taxable years beginning on or after April 2, 2018. For taxable years ending before April 2, 2018, see §1.45G-1T as contained in 26 CFR part 1, as revised April 1, 2017.

(5) *Taxable years beginning before January 1, 2012.*—See §1.45-1 as contained in 26 CFR part 1, revised April 1, 2014. [Reg. §1.45G-1.]

☐ [*T.D. 9365, 11-9-2007, T.D. 9717, 4-2-2015 (corrected 4-24-2015). Amended by T.D. 9832, 3-27-2018.*]

(2) Carbon capture equipment components.
(3) Single process train.
(d) Industrial facility.
(1) Exclusion.
(2) Industrial source.
(3) Manufacturing process.
(4) Examples.
(i) Example 1.
(ii) Example 2.
(e) Electricity generating facility.
(f) Direct air capture facility.
(g) Qualified facility.
(1) Emissions and capture requirements.
(2) Examples.
(i) Example 1.
(ii) Example 2.
(iii) Example 3.
(iv) Example 4.
(v) Example 5.
(3) Annualization of first-year and last-year qualified carbon oxide emission and/or capture amounts.
(i) In general.
(ii) Calculation.
(iii) Consequences.
(4) Election for applicable facilities.
(i) Applicable facility.
(ii) Time and manner of making election.
(iii) Retroactive credit revocations.
(5) Retrofitted qualified facility or carbon capture equipment (80/20 Rule).
(h) Qualified enhanced oil or natural gas recovery project.
(1) Application of §§1.43-2 and 1.43-3.
(2) Required certification.
(3) Natural gas.
(4) Timely filing of petroleum engineer's certification.
(5) Carbon oxide injected in oil reservoir.
(6) Tertiary injectant.
(i) Section 45Q credit.
(j) *Form 8933.*
(k) Applicability date.
§1.45Q-3 Secure Geological Storage.
(a) In general.
(b) Requirements for secure geological storage.
(c) Documentation.
(d) Certification.
(e) Failure to submit complete documentation or certification.
(f) Applicability date.
§1.45Q-4 Utilization of Qualified Carbon Oxide.
(a) In general.
(b) Amount utilized.
(1) In general.
(2) Limitation.
(c) Lifecycle greenhouse gas emissions and lifecycle analysis (LCA).
(1) In general.
(2) LCA verification.
(3) Standards of adequate lifecycle analysis.
(4) Third-party independent review of LCA.
(5) Submission of the LCA.
(6) LCA review.
(d) Commercial market.
(e) Applicability date.
§1.45Q-5 Recapture of Credit.
(a) Recapture event.
(b) Ceases to be disposed of in secure geological storage or used as a tertiary injectant.
(c) Leaked amount of qualified carbon oxide.
(d) Qualified carbon oxide subject to recapture.
(e) Recapture amount.
(f) Recapture period.
(g) Application of recapture.
(1) In general.
(2) Calculation.
(3) Multiple units.
(4) Multiple taxpayers.
(i) In general.
(ii) Partnerships.
(A) General rule.
(B) Terminated partnerships.

(5) Reporting.
(6) Examples.
(i) Example 1.
(ii) Example 2.
(iii) Example 3.
(iv) Example 4.
(v) Example 5.
(vi) Example 6.
(h) Recapture in the event of deliberate removal from storage.
(1) In general.
(2) Recycled qualified carbon oxide.
(i) Limited exceptions.
(j) Applicability date.
[Reg. §1.45Q-0.]
☐ [*T.D. 9944*, 1-13-2021.]

[Reg. §1.45Q-1]

§1.45Q-1. Credit for Carbon Oxide Sequestration.—(a) *In general.*—For purposes of section 38 of the Internal Revenue Code (Code), the carbon oxide sequestration credit is determined under section 45Q of the Code and this section (section 45Q credit). Generally, the amount of the section 45Q credit and the party that is eligible to claim the credit depend on whether the taxpayer captures qualified carbon oxide using carbon capture equipment originally placed in service at a qualified facility before February 9, 2018, or on or after February 9, 2018, and whether the taxpayer disposes of the qualified carbon oxide in secure geological storage without using it as a tertiary injectant in a qualified enhanced oil or natural gas recovery project (disposal), uses it as a tertiary injectant in a qualified enhanced oil or natural gas recovery project and disposes of it in secure geological storage (injection), or utilizes it in a manner described in section 45Q(f)(5) and §1.45Q-4 (utilization). The section 45Q credit applies only with respect to qualified carbon oxide the capture and disposal, injection, or utilization of which is within the United States (within the meaning of section 638(1) of the Code) or a possession of the United States (within the meaning of section 638(2)).

(b) *Credit amount for carbon capture equipment originally placed in service before February 9, 2018.*—(1) *In general.*—For carbon capture equipment originally placed in service at a qualified facility before February 9, 2018, the amount of credit determined under section 45Q(a) and this section is the sum of—

(i) $20 per metric ton of qualified carbon oxide that is—

(A) Captured by the taxpayer at the qualified facility and disposed of by the taxpayer in secure geological storage, and

(B) Not used by the taxpayer as a tertiary injectant in a qualified enhanced oil or natural gas recovery project or utilized by the taxpayer in a manner described in section 45Q(f)(5) and §1.45Q-4, and

(ii) $10 per metric ton of qualified carbon oxide that is—

(A) Captured by the taxpayer at the qualified facility and used by the taxpayer as a tertiary injectant in a qualified enhanced oil or natural gas recovery project, and disposed of by the taxpayer in secure geological storage, or

(B) Captured by the taxpayer at the qualified facility and utilized by the taxpayer in a manner described in section 45Q(f)(5) and §1.45Q-4.

(2) *Inflation adjustment.*—In the case of any taxable year beginning in a calendar year after 2009, there is substituted for each dollar amount contained in paragraphs (b)(1)(i) and (ii) of this section an amount equal to the product of—

(i) Such dollar amount, multiplied by

(ii) The inflation adjustment factor for such calendar year determined under section 43(b)(3)(B) for such calendar year, determined by substituting "2008" for "1990."

(c) *Credit amount for carbon capture equipment originally placed in service on or after February 9, 2018.*—For carbon capture equipment originally placed in service at a qualified facility on or after February 9, 2018, the amount of credit determined under section 45Q(a)(3) and (4) and this section is the sum of—

(1) The applicable dollar amount (as determined under paragraph (d)(1) and (2) of this section) per metric ton of qualified carbon oxide that is captured during the 12-year period beginning on the date the equipment was originally placed in service, and is—

(i) Disposed of by the taxpayer in secure geological storage, and

(ii) Not used by the taxpayer as a tertiary injectant in a qualified enhanced oil or natural gas recovery project or utilized by the taxpayer in a manner described in section 45Q(f)(5) and §1.45Q-4; and

(2) The applicable dollar amount (as determined under paragraph (d)(3) and (4) of this section) per metric ton of qualified carbon oxide that is captured during the 12-year period beginning on the date the equipment was originally placed in service and is—

(i) Used by the taxpayer as a tertiary injectant in a qualified enhanced oil or natural gas recovery project and disposed of by the taxpayer in secure geological storage, or

(ii) Utilized by the taxpayer in a manner described in section 45Q(f)(5) and § 1.45Q-4.

(d) *Applicable dollar amount.*—In general, the applicable dollar amount depends on whether section 45Q(a)(3) and paragraph (c)(1) of this section applies or section 45Q(a)(4) and paragraph (c)(2) of this section applies, and the calendar year in which the taxable year begins.

(1) *Applicable dollar amount for any taxable year beginning in a calendar year after 2016 and before 2027 for qualified carbon oxide not used as a tertiary injectant or utilized.*—For purposes of section 45Q(a)(3) and paragraph (c)(1) of this section, the applicable dollar amount for each taxable year beginning in a calendar year after 2016 and before 2027 is:

Table 1 to paragraph (d)(1)

Year	Applicable Dollar Amount
2017	$22.66
2018	$25.70
2019	$28.74
2020	$31.77
2021	$34.81
2022	$37.85
2023	$40.89
2024	$43.92
2025	$46.96
2026	$50.00

(2) *Applicable dollar amount for any taxable year beginning in a calendar year after 2026 for qualified carbon oxide not used as a tertiary injectant or utilized.*—For purposes of section 45Q(a)(3) and paragraph (c)(1) of this section, the applicable dollar amount for any taxable year beginning in any calendar year after 2026 is an amount equal to the product of $50 and the inflation adjustment factor for the calendar year determined under section 43(b)(3)(B) for the calendar year, determined by substituting "2025" for "1990."

(3) *Applicable dollar amount for any taxable year beginning in a calendar year after 2016 and before 2027 for qualified carbon oxide used as a tertiary injectant or utilized.*—For purposes of section 45Q(a)(4) and paragraph (c)(2) of this section, the applicable dollar amount for each taxable year beginning in a calendar year after 2016 and before 2027 is:

Table 2 to paragraph (d)(3)

Year	Applicable Dollar Amount
2017	$12.83
2018	$15.29
2019	$17.76
2020	$20.22
2021	$22.68
2022	$25.15
2023	$27.61
2024	$30.07
2025	$32.54
2026	$35.00

(4) *Applicable dollar amount for any taxable year beginning in a calendar year after 2026 for qualified carbon oxide used as a tertiary injectant or utilized.*—For purposes of section 45Q(a)(4) and paragraph (c)(2) of this section, the applicable dollar amount for any taxable year beginning in any calendar year after 2026, is an amount equal to the product of $35 and the inflation adjustment factor for such calendar year determined under section 43(b)(3)(B) for such calendar year, determined by substituting "2025" for "1990."

(e) *Election to apply the $10 and $20 credit amounts in lieu of the applicable dollar amounts.*—For purposes of determining the carbon oxide sequestration credit under this section, a taxpayer may elect to have the dollar amounts applicable under section 45Q(a)(1) or (2) and paragraph (b) of this section apply in lieu of the dollar amounts applicable under section 45Q(a)(3) or (4)and paragraph (d) of this section for each metric ton of qualified carbon oxide which is captured by the taxpayer using carbon capture equipment which is originally placed in service at a qualified facility on or after February 9, 2018. The election must be made on a *Form 8933* (as defined in § 1.45Q-2(j)), and applies to all metric tons of qualified carbon oxide captured by the taxpayer using carbon capture equipment which is

originally placed in service at the qualified facility throughout the full 12-year credit period.

(f) *Application of section 45Q for certain carbon capture equipment placed in service before February 9, 2018.*—In the case of any carbon capture equipment placed in service before February 9, 2018, the credits under section 45Q(a)(1) and (2) and paragraph (b)(1)(i) and (ii) of this section apply with respect to qualified carbon oxide captured using such equipment before the end of the calendar year in which the Secretary of the Treasury or his delegate, in consultation with the Administrator of the Environmental Protection Agency (EPA), certifies that, during the period beginning after October 3, 2008, a total of 75,000,000 metric tons of qualified carbon oxide have been taken into account in accordance with section 45Q(a), as in effect on February 8, 2018, and section 45Q(a)(1) and (2). In general, a taxpayer may not claim credits under section 45Q(a)(1) and (2) in taxable years after the year in which the 75,000,000 metric ton limit is certified with respect to carbon capture equipment placed in service before February 9, 2018. However, see § 1.45Q-2(g)(4) regarding the election for applicable facilities to treat certain carbon capture equipment as having been placed in service on February 9, 2018 (section 45Q(f)(6) election).

(g) *Installation of additional carbon capture equipment.*—In general, the credit amounts for property placed in service before February 9, 2018, apply to a qualified facility at which carbon capture equipment was placed in service before February 9, 2018, subject to the limitations under paragraph (f) of this section. The same qualified facility may place additional carbon capture equipment in service on or after February 9, 2018. The additional carbon capture equipment is eligible to qualify for the section 45Q credit amounts for equipment placed in service on or after February 9, 2018.

(1) *Allocation of section 45Q credits for facilities installing additional carbon capture equipment.*—In the case of a qualified facility placed in service before February 9, 2018, for which additional carbon capture equipment is placed in service on or after February 9, 2018, the amount of qualified carbon oxide which is captured by the taxpayer is equal to—

(i) For purposes of section 45Q(a)(1)(A) and (2)(A), and paragraphs (b)(1)(i) and (ii) of this section, the lesser of the total amount of qualified carbon oxide captured at such facility for the taxable year, or the total amount of the carbon dioxide capture capacity of the carbon capture equipment in service at such facility on February 8, 2018, and

(ii) For purposes of section 45Q(a)(3)(A) and (4)(A), and paragraphs (c)(1) and (2) of this section, an amount (not less than zero) equal to the excess of the total amount of qualified carbon oxide captured at such facility for the taxable year, over the total amount of the carbon dioxide capture capacity of the carbon capture equipment in service at such facility on February 8, 2018.

(2) *Additional carbon capture equipment.*—A physical modification or equipment addition that results in an increase in the carbon dioxide capture capacity of existing carbon capture equipment constitutes the installation of additional carbon capture equipment. Increasing the amount of carbon dioxide captured without physically modifying existing carbon capture equipment or adding new equipment, for example, by merely operating the existing carbon capture equipment above the carbon dioxide capture capacity, does not constitute the installation of additional carbon capture equipment. For purposes of this section, the term *carbon dioxide capture capacity* means capture design capacity. Section 45Q credits attributable to qualified carbon oxide captured by additional carbon capture equipment that is placed in service on or after February 9, 2018, are not subject to the 75,000,000 metric ton limitation described in section 45Q(g) and paragraph (f) of this section.

(3) *New carbon capture equipment.*—A physical modification or equipment addition with a cost that satisfies the 80/20 Rule provided in § 1.45Q-2(g)(5) constitutes the installation of new carbon capture equipment rather than the installation of additional carbon capture equipment.

(4) *Examples.*—The following examples illustrate the rules of this paragraph (g):

(i) *Example 1.*—Taxpayer X owns qualified facility QF. In 2017, X placed in service three units of carbon capture equipment – CC1, CC2, and CC3 – to capture carbon dioxide emitted by QF. Each of CC1, CC2, and CC3 are capable of capturing 50,000 metric tons of carbon dioxide. In 2017, X entered into a binding written contract with Y to provide 80,000 metric tons of carbon dioxide annually for Y to dispose of in secure geological storage. X operates CC1 and CC2 to capture carbon dioxide pursuant to the binding written contract with Y, leaving CC3 idle. In 2020, X enters into a binding written contract with Z to provide 40,000 metric tons of carbon dioxide annually for Z to dispose of in secure geological storage. X operates CC3 to capture carbon dioxide pursuant to the binding written contract with Z. CC3 is not additional carbon capture equipment under paragraph (g)(2) of this section simply because it began operating CC3 in 2020. X merely increased the amount of carbon dioxide captured by existing carbon capture equipment. As a result, any section 45Q credits attributable to the carbon dioxide captured by CC3 and disposed of by Z are calculated under section 45Q(a)(1) and paragraph (b)(1)(i) of this section, and are subject to the 75,000,000 metric ton limitation described in section 45Q(g) and paragraph (f) of this section.

(ii) *Example 2.*—Assume the same facts as in Example 1, except that in 2019, X physically modified CC3 to enable CC3 to capture 100,000 metric tons of carbon dioxide. The physical modification to upgrade CC3 does not satisfy the 80/20 Rule in § 1.45Q-2(g)(5). In 2020 X enters into a binding written contract with Z to provide 80,000 metric tons of carbon dioxide annually for Z to dispose of in secure geological storage. X operates CC3 to capture carbon dioxide pursuant to the binding written contract with Z. Because the physical modification to upgrade CC3 does not satisfy the 80/20 Rule, the physical modification to upgrade CC3 is considered the installation of additional carbon capture equipment under paragraph (g)(2) of this section, rather than new carbon capture equipment under paragraph (g)(3) of this section. As a result, any section 45Q credits attributable to the first 50,000 metric tons of carbon dioxide captured by CC3 and disposed of by Z are calculated under section 45Q(a)(1) and paragraph (b)(1)(i) of this section, and are subject to the 75,000,000 metric ton limitation described in section 45Q(g) and paragraph (f) of this section. Any section 45Q credits attributable to additional carbon dioxide captured by CC3 and disposed of by Z in excess of those first 50,000 metric tons are calculated under section 45Q(a)(4) and paragraph (c)(2) of this section, and are not subject to the 75,000,000 metric ton limitation described in section 45Q(g) and paragraph (f) of this section.

(iii) *Example 3.*—Assume the same facts as in Example 2, except that the physical modification to CC3 satisfies the 80/20 Rule in § 1.45Q-2(g)(5). The physical modification to CC3 is considered the installation of new carbon capture equipment under paragraph (g)(3) of this section. As a result, any section 45Q credits attributable to carbon dioxide captured by CC3 and disposed of by Z are calculated under section 45Q(a)(4) and paragraph (c)(2) of this section, and are not subject to the 75,000,000 metric ton limitation described in section 45Q(g) and paragraph (f) of this section.

(h) *Eligibility for the section 45Q credit.*—The following rules determine who may claim the section 45Q credit.

(1) *Person to whom the section 45Q credit is attributable.*—In general, the person to whom the credit is attributable is the person who may claim the credit. Except as provided in paragraph (h)(3) of this section, the section 45Q credit is attributable to the following persons —

(i) *Equipment placed in service before February 9, 2018.*—In the case of qualified carbon oxide captured using carbon capture equipment that is originally placed in service at a qualified facility before February 9, 2018, the section 45Q credit is attributable to the person that captures and physically or contractually ensures the disposal, injection, or utilization of such qualified carbon oxide.

(ii) *Equipment placed in service on or after February 9, 2018.*—In the case of qualified carbon oxide captured using carbon capture equipment that is originally placed in service at a qualified facility on or after February 9, 2018, the section 45Q credit is attributable to the person that owns the carbon capture equipment and physically or contractually ensures the capture and disposal, injection, or utilization of such qualified carbon oxide. For each single process train of carbon capture equipment (as described in § 1.45Q-2(c)(3)), only one taxpayer will be considered the person to whom the credit is attributable under this paragraph (h)(1)(ii). That person will be the taxpayer who either physically ensures the capture and disposal, injection, or utilization of such qualified carbon oxide or contracts with others to capture and dispose, inject, or utilize such qualified carbon oxide.

(iii) *Reporting.*—The taxpayer described in this paragraph (h)(1) as eligible to claim the section 45Q credit must claim the credit on a *Form 8933*, "Carbon Dioxide Sequestration Credit," with the taxpayer's Federal income tax return or *Form 1065*, "U.S. Return of Partnership Income," for each taxable year for which the taxpayer is eligible. The taxpayer must provide the name and location of the qualified facilities at which the qualified carbon oxide was captured. If the taxpayer is claiming the section 45Q credit on an amended Federal income tax return, an amended *Form 1065*, or an administrative adjustment request under section 6227 (AAR), as applicable, the taxpayer must state AMENDED RETURN FOR SECTION 45Q

CREDIT at the top of the amended Federal income tax return, the amended *Form 1065*, or the AAR, as applicable. The amended Federal income tax return or the amended *Form 1065* must be filed, in any event, not later than the applicable period of limitations on filing an amended Federal income tax return or *Form 1065* is being filed. A BBA partnership may make a late election by filing an AAR on or before October 15, 2021, but in any event, not later than the period of limitations on filing an AAR under section 6227(c).

(2) *Contractually ensuring capture and disposal, injection, or utilization of qualified carbon oxide.*—In the case of qualified carbon oxide captured using carbon capture equipment which is originally placed in service at a qualified facility on or after February 9, 2018, a taxpayer is not required to physically carry out the capture and disposal, injection, or utilization of qualified carbon oxide to claim the section 45Q credit if the taxpayer contractually ensures in a binding written contract that the party that physically carries out the capture, disposal, injection, or utilization of the qualified carbon oxide does so in the manner required under section 45Q, this section and § § 1.45Q-2, 1.45Q-3, 1.45Q-4, and 1.45Q-5. A taxpayer may enter into a binding written contract with a general contractor that hires subcontractors to physically carry out the capture, disposal, injection, or utilization of the qualified carbon oxide, but the contract must bind the subcontractors to the requirements of this paragraph (h)(2). In the case of qualified carbon oxide captured using carbon capture equipment which is originally placed in service at a qualified facility before February 9, 2018, a taxpayer that contractually ensures the capture of the qualified carbon oxide is not eligible for the section 45Q credit. However, the taxpayer is not required to physically carry out the disposal, injection, or utilization of qualified carbon oxide to claim the section 45Q credit if the taxpayer contractually ensures in a binding written contract that the party that physically carries out the disposal, injection, or utilization of the qualified carbon oxide does so in the manner required under section 45Q, this section, and § § 1.45Q-2, 1.45Q-3, 1.45Q-4, and 1.45Q-5.

(i) *Binding written contract.*—A written contract is binding only if it is enforceable under State law against both the taxpayer and the party that physically carries out the capture, disposal, injection, or utilization of the qualified carbon oxide, or a predecessor or successor of either, and does not limit damages to a specified amount (for example, by use of a liquidated damages provision). For this purpose, a contractual provision that limits damages to an amount equal to at least five percent of the total contract price will not be treated as limiting damages to a specified amount. For additional guidance regarding the definition of a binding written contract, see § 1.168(k)-1(b)(4)(ii)(A)-(D).

(ii) *Multiple binding written contracts permitted.*—A taxpayer may enter into multiple binding written contracts with multiple parties for the capture, disposal, injection, or utilization of qualified carbon oxide. A party that physically carries out the capture, disposal, injection, or utilization of qualified carbon oxide may enter into multiple binding written contracts with multiple parties that own carbon capture equipment or capture or contractually ensure the capture of qualified carbon oxide.

(iii) *Contract provisions.*—Contracts ensuring the capture, disposal, injection, or utilization of qualified carbon oxide —

(A) Must include commercially reasonable terms and provide for enforcement of the party's obligation to perform the capture, disposal, injection, or utilization of the qualified carbon oxide;

(B) May, but are not required to, include long-term liability provisions, indemnity provisions, penalties for breach of contract, or liquidated damages provisions;

(C) May, but are not required to, include information including how many metric tons of qualified carbon oxide the parties agree to dispose of, inject, or utilize;

(D) May, but are not required to, include minimum quantities that the parties agree to dispose of, inject, or utilize;

(E) Must, in the case of qualified carbon oxide that is intended to be disposed of in secure geological storage and not used as a tertiary injectant in a qualified enhanced oil or natural gas recovery project, obligate the disposing party to comply with § § 1.45Q-3(b)(1) and (c), and, in the case of a recapture event, promptly inform the capturing party of all information that is pertinent to the recapture (e.g., location of leak, leaked amount of qualified carbon oxide, dollar value of section 45Q credit attributable to leaked qualified carbon oxide);

(F) Must, for qualified carbon oxide that is intended to be used as a tertiary injectant in a qualified enhanced oil or natural gas recovery, obligate the disposing party to comply with § 1.45Q-3(b)(2) and (c), and, in the case of a recapture event, promptly inform the capturing party of all information that is pertinent to recapture of the section 45Q credit as listed in § 1.45Q-5; and

(G) Must, for qualified carbon oxide that is intended to be utilized in a manner specified in §1.45Q-4, obligate the utilizing party to comply with §1.45Q-4.

(iv) *Pre-existing contracts.*—If a taxpayer entered into a contract for the capture, disposal, injection, or utilization of qualified carbon oxide prior to January 13, 2021, and that contract does not satisfy all of the requirements of this paragraph (h)(2), the taxpayer must amend its existing contract or execute a new contract that satisfies all of the requirements of this paragraph (h)(2) by July 12, 2021.

(v) *Reporting of contract information.*—The existence of each contract and the parties involved must be reported to the IRS annually. Each party to a contract must complete a signed *Form 8933* (as defined in §1.45-2(j)) and provide information required by the instructions to *Form 8933*. The party that contracts with the taxpayer claiming the credit must also provide that taxpayer with a signed *Form 8933* in accordance with the instructions to *Form 8933*. The taxpayer claiming the credit must attach and file all other signed *Forms 8933* received by each other party to the contract to its own signed *Form 8933*. Failure of the taxpayer claiming the credit to satisfy this reporting requirement in a taxable year will result in the inability of that taxpayer to claim the credit with respect to any qualified carbon oxide that is disposed of, injected, or utilized in that taxable year pursuant to that particular contract. In addition to any information stated as required on *Form 8933*, the report must include the following information—

(A) The name and taxpayer identification number of the taxpayer to whom the credit is attributable;

(B) The name and taxpayer identification number of each party with whom the taxpayer has entered into a contract to ensure the disposal, injection, or utilization of qualified carbon oxide;

(C) The date each contract to ensure the disposal, injection, or utilization of qualified carbon oxide was entered into;

(D) The number of metric tons of qualified carbon oxide each contracting party disposes of, injects, or utilizes on behalf of the contracting taxpayer each taxable year for reporting to the IRS; and

(E) For contracts for the disposal of qualified carbon oxide in secure geological storage or the use of qualified carbon oxide as a tertiary injectant in enhanced oil or natural gas recovery, the name of the operator, the field, unit, and reservoir, location by county and state, and identification number assigned to the facility by the EPA's electronic Greenhouse Gas Reporting Tool (e-GGRT ID number) for submission of the facility's 40 CFR Part 98 annual reports.

(vi) *Relationship with election to allow section 45Q credit.*—A taxpayer does not elect to allow all or a portion of the credit to any of the contracting parties merely by contracting with that party to ensure the disposal, injection, or utilization of qualified carbon oxide. Any election to allow all or a portion of the credit to be claimed by another party must be made separately pursuant to paragraph (h)(3) of this section.

(3) *Election to allow the section 45Q credit to another taxpayer.*—The taxpayer described in paragraph (h)(1) of this section as the person to whom the section 45Q credit is attributable (electing taxpayer) may elect to allow the person that enters into a contract with the electing taxpayer to dispose of the qualified carbon oxide (disposer), utilize the qualified carbon oxide (utilizer), or use the qualified carbon oxide as a tertiary injectant (injector) to claim the credit (credit claimant) (section 45Q(f)(3)(B) election). However, the electing taxpayer may not elect or otherwise allow the section 45Q credit to a contractor or subcontractor that physically captures carbon oxide on behalf of the taxpayer. For purposes of this paragraph (h)(3), the disposer or injector that is eligible to be a credit claimant is the party that obtains the permit to dispose of the qualified carbon oxide in secure geological storage. In the case of an injector that is itself a joint venture (not a federal tax partnership), only those taxpayers that hold a working interest in the joint venture may be credit claimants. A credit claimant may not allow the section 45Q credit to a subcontractor that performs the disposal, utilization, or injection for the credit claimant. The electing taxpayer may not claim any section 45Q credits that are allowable to a credit claimant. An electing taxpayer may elect to allow a credit claimant to claim the full amount or a partial amount of section 45Q credits arising during the taxable year. An electing taxpayer may elect to allow a single credit claimant or multiple credit claimants to claim section 45Q credits in the same taxable year. If an electing taxpayer elects to allow multiple credit claimants to claim section 45Q credits, the maximum amount of section 45Q credits allowable to each credit claimant is proportional to the amount of qualified carbon oxide disposed of, utilized, or used as a tertiary injectant by the credit claimant. A credit claimant may receive allowances of section 45Q credits from multiple electing taxpayers in the same taxable year. In the case of an electing taxpayer with multiple qualified facilities, the electing taxpayer must make a separate election for each qualified facility.

(i) *Example.*—Electing Taxpayer, E, captures 1,000,000 metric tons of qualified carbon oxide with carbon capture equipment that was placed in service in 2020. In 2021, E contracts with two companies, A and B, for the disposal of the qualified carbon oxide. E is eligible for a section 45Q credit at a rate of $22.68 per metric ton, for a total section 45Q credit of $22,680,000. E contractually ensures that A will dispose of 300,000 metric tons of qualified carbon oxide and that B will dispose of 700,000 metric tons of qualified carbon oxide. E may make a section 45Q(f)(3)(B) election to allow up to $6,804,000 of section 45Q credit to A and up to $15,876,000 of section 45Q credit to B, equal to the value of the number of metric tons each party has contracted to ensure disposal, multiplied by the credit value of the metric tons disposed of.

(ii) *Time and manner of making election.*—The electing taxpayer makes a section 45Q(f)(3)(B) election by filing a statement of election containing the information described in paragraph (h)(3)(iv) of this section with the taxpayer's Federal income tax return or *Form 1065* for each taxable year in which the credit arises. The section 45Q(f)(3)(B) election must be made in accordance with *Form 8933* no later than the time prescribed by law (including extensions) for filing the Federal income tax return or *Form 1065* for the year in which the credit arises. The election may not be filed with an amended Federal income tax return, an amended *Form 1065*, or an AAR, as applicable, after the prescribed date (including extensions) for filing the original Federal income tax return or *Form 1065* for the year, with the exception of amended Federal income tax returns, amended *Forms 1065*, or AARs, as applicable, for any taxable year ending after February 9, 2018, and beginning on or before January 13, 2021. The amended Federal income tax return or the amended *Form 1065* must be filed, in any event, not later than the applicable period of limitations on assessment for the taxable year for which the amended Federal income tax return or *Form 1065* is being filed. A BBA partnership may make a late election by filing an AAR on or before October 15, 2021, but in any event, not later than the period of limitations on filing an AAR under section 6227(c).

(iii) *Annual election.*—A section 45(Q)(f)(3)(B) election is only effective for the taxable year for which it is made. A new section 45Q(f)(3)(B) election must be made for each taxable year for which an electing taxpayer wishes to allow section 45Q credits to a credit claimant.

(iv) *Required information.*—For the section 45Q(f)(3)(B) election to be valid under paragraph (h)(3)(ii) of this section, the election statement of the electing taxpayer must be made on *Form 8933* and must indicate that an election is being made under section 45Q(f)(3)(B). The electing taxpayer must provide each credit claimant with a copy of the electing taxpayer's *Form 8933*. The electing taxpayer must, in addition to any information required on *Form 8933* set forth the following information—

(A) The electing taxpayer's name, address, taxpayer identification number, location, and e-GGRT ID number(s) (if available) of each qualified facility where qualified carbon oxide was captured;

(B) The full amount of credit attributable to the taxpayer prior to the election and the corresponding metric tons of qualified carbon oxide;

(C) The name, address, and taxpayer identification number of each credit claimant, and the name and location and e-GGRT ID number(s) (if available) of:

(i) Each secure geological storage site where the qualified carbon oxide is disposed of or injected, or

(ii) Each site where the qualified carbon oxide is utilized;

(D) The dollar amount of section 45Q credits the taxpayer is allowing each credit claimant to claim and the corresponding metric tons of qualified carbon oxide; and

(E) The dollar amount of section 45Q credits retained by the electing taxpayer and the corresponding metric tons of qualified carbon oxide.

(v) *Requirements for section 45Q credit claimant.*—For a section 45Q(f)(3)(B) election to be valid, the section 45Q credit claimant must include the following information on *Form 8933*—

(A) The name, address, taxpayer identification number of the credit claimant;

(B) The name, address, and taxpayer identification number of each taxpayer making an election under section 45Q(f)(3)(B) to allow the credit to the credit claimant;

(C) The name and location and e-GGRT ID number(s) (if available) of each qualified facility where qualified carbon oxide was captured;

(D) The name and location and e-GGRT ID number(s) (if available) of:

(i) Each secure geological storage site where the qualified carbon oxide is disposed of or injected, or

(ii) Each site where the qualified carbon oxide is utilized.

(E) The full dollar amount of section 45Q credits attributable to each electing taxpayer prior to the election and the corresponding metric tons of qualified carbon oxide;

(F) The dollar amount of section 45Q credits that each electing taxpayer is allowing the credit claimant to claim and the corresponding metric tons of qualified carbon oxide; and

(G) A copy of the electing taxpayer's *Form 8933*. The credit claimant must include this *Form 8933* with its timely filed Federal income tax return or *Form 1065* (including extensions). The election may not be filed with an amended Federal income tax return, an amended *Form 1065*, or an AAR, as applicable, after the prescribed date (including extensions) for filing the original Federal income tax return or *Form 1065* for the year, with the exception of amended Federal income tax returns, amended *Forms 1065*, or AARs, as applicable, for any taxable year ending after February 9, 2018, and beginning on or before January 13, 2021. The amended Federal income tax return or the amended *Form 1065* must be filed, in any event, not later than the applicable period of limitations on filing an amended Federal income tax return or *Form 1065*. In the case of a BBA partnership, the BBA partnership may make a late election by filing an AAR on or before October 15, 2021, but in any event, not later than the period of limitations on filing an AAR under section 6227(c).

(vi) *Failure to satisfy reporting requirements.*—With respect to any section 45Q(f)(3)(B) election, the failure of an electing taxpayer or a credit claimant to satisfy the requirements in paragraph (h)(3)(iv) or (v) in a taxable year will result in the inability to claim the credit with respect to any qualified carbon oxide that is disposed of, injected, or utilized in that taxable year pursuant to that particular election.

(i) *Applicability date.*—This section applies to taxable years beginning on or after January 13, 2021. Taxpayers may choose to apply this section for taxable years beginning on or after January 1, 2018, provided the taxpayer applies this section and §§ 1.45Q-2, 1.45Q-3, 1.45Q-4, and 1.45Q-5 in their entirety and in a consistent manner. [Reg. § 1.45Q-1.]

☐ [T.D. 9944, 1-13-2021.]

[Reg. § 1.45Q-2]

§ 1.45Q-2. Definitions for Purposes of §§ 1.45Q-1 through 1.45Q-5.—(a) *Qualified carbon oxide.*—The term *qualified carbon oxide* means—

(1) Any carbon dioxide which—

(i) Is captured from an industrial source by carbon capture equipment which is originally placed in service before February 9, 2018,

(ii) Would otherwise be released into the atmosphere as industrial emission of greenhouse gas or lead to such release, and

(iii) Is measured at the source of capture and verified at the point of disposal, injection, or utilization; or

(2) Any carbon dioxide or other carbon oxide which—

(i) Is captured from an industrial source by carbon capture equipment which is originally placed in service on or after February 9, 2018,

(ii) Would otherwise be released into the atmosphere as industrial emission of greenhouse gas or lead to such release, and

(iii) Is measured at the source of capture and verified at the point of disposal, injection, or utilization; or

(3) In the case of a direct air capture facility, any carbon dioxide that is captured directly from the ambient air and is measured at the source of capture and verified at the point of disposal, injection, or utilization.

(b) *Recycled carbon oxide.*—The term *qualified carbon oxide* includes the initial deposit of captured carbon oxide used as a tertiary injectant. Qualified carbon oxide does not include carbon oxide that is recaptured, recycled, and re-injected as part of the enhanced oil or natural gas recovery process.

(c) *Carbon capture equipment.*—In general, *carbon capture equipment* includes all components of property that are used to capture or process carbon oxide until the carbon oxide is transported for disposal, injection, or utilization. Except as described in paragraph (c)(2) of this section, carbon capture equipment generally does not include components of property used for transporting qualified carbon oxide for disposal, injection, or utilization. Carbon capture equipment that is originally placed in service at a qualified facility on or after February 9, 2018, may be owned by a taxpayer other than the taxpayer that owns the industrial facility at which the carbon capture equipment is placed in service.

(1) *Use of carbon capture equipment.*—Carbon capture equipment is equipment used for the purpose of—

(i) Separating, purifying, drying, and/or capturing carbon oxide that would otherwise be released into the atmosphere from an industrial facility;

(ii) Removing carbon oxide from the atmosphere via direct air capture; or

(iii) Compressing or otherwise increasing the pressure of carbon oxide.

(2) *Carbon capture equipment components.*—Carbon capture equipment generally includes components of property necessary to compress, treat, process, liquefy, pump or perform some other physical action to capture qualified carbon oxide. For purposes of this paragraph (c), carbon capture equipment includes a system of gathering and distribution lines that collect carbon oxide captured from a qualified facility or multiple qualified facilities that constitute a single project (as described in section 8.01 of Notice 2020-12, 2020-11 I.R.B. 495 (see § 601.601(d)(1) and (2)(ii) of this chapter)) for the purpose of transporting that carbon oxide away from the qualified facility or single project to a pipeline used to transport carbon oxide to or from one or more taxpayers and projects.

(3) *Single process train.*—All components that make up an independently functioning process train capable of capturing, processing, and preparing carbon oxide for transport will be treated as a single unit of carbon capture equipment.

(d) *Industrial facility.*—An *industrial facility* is a facility, including an electricity generating facility, that produces a carbon oxide stream from a fuel combustion source or fuel cell, a manufacturing process, or a fugitive carbon oxide emission source that, absent capture and disposal, injection, or utilization, would otherwise be released into the atmosphere as industrial emission of greenhouse gas or lead to such release.

(1) *Exclusion.*—An industrial facility does not include a facility that produces carbon dioxide from carbon dioxide production wells at natural carbon dioxide-bearing formations or a naturally occurring subsurface spring. For purposes of section 45Q, a carbon dioxide production well at natural carbon dioxide-bearing formations or a naturally occurring subsurface spring means a well that contains 90 percent or greater carbon dioxide by volume (90 percent test).

(2) *Exception for wells at natural carbon dioxide-bearing formations or a naturally occurring subsurface spring that contain a product other than carbon dioxide.*—A well meeting the 90 percent test will not be treated as a carbon dioxide production well at natural carbon dioxide-bearing formations or a naturally occurring subsurface spring if:

(i) The deposit contains a product, other than carbon oxide, that is commercially viable to extract and sell without taking into account the availability of a commercial market for the carbon oxide that is extracted or any section 45Q tax credit that might be available;

(ii) The taxpayer provides an attestation to paragraph (d)(2)(i) of this section from an independent registered engineer with experience in feasibility studies for extraction of gases from the subsurface;

(iii) A direct air capture facility (defined in section 45Q(e)(1)(A)) is not used to capture carbon oxide from the gas stream; and

(iv) Any carbon oxide extracted from the deposit is used as tertiary injectant in an enhanced oil or natural gas recovery project or as feedstock of a utilization project.

(2) *Industrial source.*—An *industrial source* is an emission of carbon oxide from an industrial facility.

(3) *Manufacturing process.*—A *manufacturing process* is a process involving the manufacture of one or more products, other than carbon oxide, that are intended to be sold at a profit, or are used for a commercial purpose (other than producing carbon oxide). All facts and circumstances with respect to the process and products are to be taken into account.

(4) *Examples.*—The following examples illustrate the rules of paragraph (d) of this section:

(i) *Example 1.*—A natural underground reservoir contains a gas that is comprised of 50 percent carbon dioxide and 50 percent methane by volume. The raw gas is not usable without the application of a separation process to create two gases that are primarily carbon dioxide and methane. Taxpayer B constructs processing equipment that separates the raw gas into carbon oxide and methane. The carbon dioxide is sold to a third party for use in a qualified enhanced oil recovery project. Some of the methane is used as fuel to power the processing equipment. The remainder of the methane is injected into the reservoir. The injection will increase the ultimate recovery of carbon dioxide. The injected methane can be produced later from the reservoir. At the end of the taxable year Taxpayer B has not secured a contract to sell methane and does not have any plans to use the methane for a commercial purpose other than producing carbon oxide. Because carbon dioxide is the only product manufactured that is intended to be sold at a profit or used for a commercial purpose, the separation process applied to the gases is not a manufacturing process within the meaning of paragraph (d)(3) of this section. The carbon dioxide captured by the process is not qualified carbon oxide.

(ii) *Example 2.*—(A) A natural underground reservoir contains a gas that is comprised of 95 percent carbon dioxide and 5 percent helium by volume. The raw gas is not usable without the application of a separation process to create two gases that are primarily carbon dioxide and helium. Taxpayer C determines that the extraction of helium is economically viable even if there were no commercial market for carbon dioxide or any section 45Q credit. An independent registered engineer attests to Taxpayer C's determination. Taxpayer C constructs processing equipment that separates the raw gas into carbon dioxide and helium. The helium is sold to various customers for use in commercial and industrial applications. The carbon dioxide is sold to a third party for use in a qualified enhanced oil recovery project. Any carbon dioxide which the third party cannot accept is returned to the reservoir or vented in accordance with applicable permits.

(B) Because the extraction of helium is economically viable even if there were no commercial market for carbon dioxide or any section 45Q credit, the reservoir will not be considered a natural carbon dioxide-bearing formation or a naturally occurring subsurface spring within the meaning of paragraph (d)(1) and the separation process applied to the gases is a manufacturing process within the meaning of paragraph (d)(3). Taxpayer C may claim the section 45Q credit with respect to the carbon dioxide sold to the third party and which the third party uses in a qualified enhanced oil recovery project during the taxable year. Taxpayer C may not claim the section 45Q credit with respect to the carbon dioxide that is returned to the reservoir or vented.

(e) *Electricity generating facility.*—An *electricity generating facility* is a facility described in section 45Q(d)(2)(A) or (B) of the Internal Revenue Code (Code) that is subject to depreciation under MACRS Asset Class 49.11 (Electric Utility Hydraulic Production Plant), 49.12 (Electric Utility Nuclear Production Plant), 49.13 (Electric Utility Steam Production Plant), or 49.15 (Electric Utility Combustion Turbine Production Plant).

(f) *Direct air capture facility.*—A *direct air capture facility* means any facility that uses carbon capture equipment to capture carbon oxide directly from the ambient air. It does not include any facility that captures carbon dioxide (1) that is deliberately released from naturally occurring subsurface springs or (2) using natural photosynthesis.

(g) *Qualified facility.*—A *qualified facility* means any industrial facility or direct air capture facility, the construction of which begins before January 1, 2026, and either at which construction of carbon capture equipment begins before that date, or the original planning and design for which includes installation of carbon capture equipment, and at which carbon capture equipment is placed in service that captures the requisite annual thresholds of carbon oxide described in paragraph (g)(1) of this section. See Notice 2020-12 (see § 601.601(d)(1) and (2)(ii) of this chapter), for guidance on the determination of when construction has begun on a qualified facility or on carbon capture equipment. For purposes of whether a facility satisfies the requisite annual carbon oxide capture thresholds described in paragraph (g)(1) of this section, a taxpayer may apply the rules of section 8.01 of Notice 2020-12 (see § 601.601(d)(1) and (2)(ii) of this chapter) to treat multiple facilities as a single facility.

(1) *Emissions and capture requirements.*—The carbon capture equipment placed in service at the qualified facility must capture—

(i) In the case of a facility, other than a direct air capture facility, which emits not more than 500,000 metric tons of carbon oxide into the atmosphere during the taxable year, at least 25,000 metric tons of qualified carbon oxide during the taxable year which is *utilized* in a manner consistent with section 45Q(f)(5) and § 1.45Q-4 (section 45Q(d)(2)(A) facility);

(ii) In the case of an electricity generating facility which is not a section 45Q(d)(2)(A) facility (section 45Q(d)(2)(B) facility), not less than 500,000 metric tons of qualified carbon oxide during the taxable year; and

(iii) In the case of a direct air capture facility or other facility that is not a section 45Q(d)(2)(A) facility or a section 45Q(d)(2)(B) facility, at least 100,000 metric tons of qualified carbon oxide during the taxable year.

(2) *Examples.*—The following examples illustrate the rules of paragraph (g) of this section:

(i) *Example 1.*—During the taxable year, an ethanol plant emits 200,000 metric tons of carbon dioxide. Carbon capture equipment located at the facility captures 35,000 metric tons of carbon dioxide, all of which are utilized in a manner consistent with section 45Q(f)(5) and § 1.45Q-4. The ethanol plant is a qualified facility under section 45Q(d)(2)(C) and § 1.45Q-2(g)(1)(i) during the taxable year because it met the requirement to capture at least 25,000 metric tons of qualified carbon oxide during the taxable year which were utilized in a manner consistent with section 45Q(f)(5) and § 1.45Q-4.

(ii) *Example 2.*—During the taxable year, an electricity generating facility emits 600,000 metric tons of carbon dioxide. Carbon capture equipment located at the facility captures a total of 450,000 metric tons of carbon dioxide. 50,000 metric tons of the captured carbon dioxide are utilized in a manner consistent with section 45Q(f)(5) and § 1.45Q-4, and 400,000 metric tons of the carbon dioxide are disposed of in secure geological storage. The electricity generating facility is not a qualified facility under section 45Q(d)(2)(B) during the taxable year because it did not capture at least 500,000 metric tons of qualified carbon oxide during the taxable year. Further, because the electricity generating facility emitted greater than 500,000 metric tons of carbon dioxide during the taxable year, but only captured 450,000 metric tons, it is not a qualified facility under section 45Q(d)(2)(A) and § 1.45Q-2(g)(1)(ii).

(iii) *Example 3.*—During the taxable year, a cement manufacturing plant emits 110,000 metric tons of carbon dioxide. Carbon capture equipment located at the plant captures 100,000 metric tons of carbon dioxide. 10,000 metric tons of the amount captured are utilized in a manner consistent with section 45Q(f)(5) and § 1.45Q-4, and 90,000 metric tons of carbon dioxide, are disposed of in secure geological storage. The cement manufacturing plant is a qualified facility during the taxable year because the carbon capture equipment located at the plant met the requirement under section 45Q(d)(2)(C) and § 1.45Q-2(g)(1)(i) to capture at least 100,000 metric tons of qualified carbon oxide during the taxable year.

(iv) *Example 4.*—Taxpayer X owns and operates three natural gas processing facilities (A, B, and C) that separate carbon dioxide from natural gas. A, B, and C are all located within several miles of each other. X installed carbon capture equipment by A, B, and C. Carbon dioxide captured by A, B, and C is collected via a single system of gathering and distribution lines for delivery to a transportation pipeline. X contracts with third-party Z for the use of carbon dioxide captured by A, B, and C as a tertiary injectant pursuant to a single contract. During the taxable year, equipment at A captures 30,000 metric tons of carbon dioxide, equipment at B captures 40,000 metric tons of carbon dioxide, and equipment at C captures 50,000 tons of carbon dioxide. All other factors listed in the single project rule in section 8.01 of Notice 2020-12 support the conclusion that A, B and C are a single facility. X may treat A, B, and C as a single facility under the rules of section 8.01 of Notice 2020-12 for purposes of determining whether the requirement under section 45Q(d)(2)(C) and § 1.45Q-2(g)(1)(i), to capture at least 100,000 metric tons of qualified carbon oxide during the taxable year is satisfied. If X treats A, B, and C as a single facility, the minimum capture requirement will be satisfied for the taxable year.

(3) *Annualization of first-year and last-year qualified carbon oxide emission and/or capture amounts.*—(i) *In general.*—For both the taxable year in which carbon capture equipment is placed in service at a qualified facility and the taxable year in which the 12-year period described in sections 45Q(a)(3)(A) and (4)(A) and § 1.45Q-1(c)(1) and (2) ends, annualization of the amount of qualified carbon oxide emitted and captured (or captured directly from the ambient air in the case of a direct air capture facility) is permitted to determine if the threshold requirements under paragraph (g)(1) of this section are satisfied. Such annualization may result in a facility being deemed to satisfy the threshold requirements under paragraph (g)(1) of this section for the year and may permit a taxpayer to claim section 45Q credits even though the amount of qualified carbon oxide emitted or captured in the first year or last year of the 12-year period is less than the threshold requirements under paragraph (g)(1) of this section.

(ii) *Calculation.*—Annualization is only available for the taxable year in which the carbon capture equipment is placed in service at the qualified facility and the taxable year in which the 12-year period described in sections 45Q(a)(3)(A) and (4)(A) and § 1.45Q-1(c)(1) and (2) ends. Annualized amounts must be calculated by—

(A) Determining the amount of qualified carbon oxide emitted and captured (or captured directly from the ambient air in the case of a direct air capture facility) during the taxable year in which the carbon capture equipment was placed in service at the qualified facility or the taxable year in which the 12-year period described in sections 45Q(a)(3)(A) and (4)(A) and §1.45Q-1(c)(1) and (2) ends,

(B) Dividing the amount of qualified carbon determined under paragraph (g)(3)(ii)(A) of this section by the number of days in the period either (I) beginning with the date on which the carbon capture equipment was placed in service at the qualified facility and ending with the last day of the taxable year containing that date, or (II) beginning with the first day of the taxable year in which the 12-year period described in sections 45Q(a)(3)(A) and (4)(A) and §1.45Q-1(c)(1) and (2) ends and ending with the last day of that 12-year period; and

(C) Multiplying by 365.

(iii) *Consequences.*—If the annualized amounts of qualified carbon oxide emitted and captured (or captured directly from the ambient air in the case of a direct air capture facility) as calculated under this formula meet the threshold requirements under paragraph (g)(1) of this section, the threshold requirements under paragraph (g)(1) of this section are deemed satisfied for the taxable year in which the carbon capture equipment was placed in service at the qualified facility or the taxable year in which the 12-year period described in sections 45Q(a)(3)(A) and (4)(A) and §1.45Q-1(c)(1) and (2) ends. The taxpayer may be eligible for a section 45Q credit for that taxable year but must calculate the credit based on actual amounts of qualified carbon oxide captured and disposed of, injected, or utilized during the taxable year.

(4) *Election for applicable facilities.*—In the case of an applicable facility, for any taxable year during which such facility captures not less than 500,000 metric tons of qualified carbon oxide, the taxpayer described in section 45Q(f)(3)(A)(ii) and §1.45Q-1(h)(1)(ii) (that is, the person that owns the carbon capture equipment and physically or contractually ensures the capture and disposal, injection or utilization of such qualified carbon oxide), may elect to have such facility, and any carbon capture equipment placed in service at such facility, deemed as having been placed in service on February 9, 2018 (section 45Q(f)(6) election). For purposes of whether a facility satisfies the 500,000 metric ton qualified carbon oxide capture threshold, a taxpayer may apply the rules of section 8.01 of Notice 2020-12 to treat multiple facilities as a single facility.

(i) *Applicable facility.*—An applicable facility means a qualified facility described in section 45Q(f)(6)(B) and §1.45Q-2(g) that was placed in service before February 9, 2018, for which no taxpayer claimed a section 45Q credit for qualified carbon oxide captured at the facility for any taxable year ending before February 9, 2018.

(ii) *Time and manner of making election.*—The taxpayer described §1.45Q-1(h)(1) makes a section 45Q(f)(6) election by filing a statement of election with the taxpayer's income tax return for each taxable year in which the credit arises. The section 45Q(f)(6) election must be made in accordance with *Form 8933* filed with the taxpayer's Federal income tax return for each taxable year in which the taxpayer makes the section 45Q(f)(6) election. The statement of election must, in addition to any information required on *Form 8933*, set forth the electing taxpayer's name, address, taxpayer identification number, location, and e-GGRT ID number(s) (if available) of the applicable facility.

(iii) *Retroactive credit revocations.*—A taxpayer may not file an amended Federal income tax return, an amended *Form 1065*, or an AAR, as applicable, for any taxable year ending before February 9, 2018, to revoke a prior claim of section 45Q credits.

(5) *Retrofitted qualified facility or carbon capture equipment (80/20 Rule).*—A qualified facility or carbon capture equipment may qualify as originally placed in service even if it contains some used components of property, provided the fair market value of the used components of property is not more than 20 percent of the qualified facility or carbon capture equipment's total value (that is, the cost of the new components of property plus the value of the used components of property) (80/20 Rule). In determining the value of the used components of property as compared to the new components, the general principles of Revenue Ruling 94-31 (see §601.601(d)(2)(i)(a) and (ii) of this chapter), will apply. The relevant unit of retrofitted carbon capture equipment for purposes of the 80/20 Rule is an independently functioning process train. For purposes of the 80/20 Rule, the cost of a new qualified facility or carbon capture equipment includes all properly capitalized costs of the new qualified facility or carbon capture equipment. Solely for purposes of the 80/20 Rule, properly capitalized costs of a new qualified facility or carbon capture equipment may, at the option of the taxpayer, include the cost of new equipment for a pipeline (the cost of equipment for a new pipeline, not equipment used to repair an existing pipeline) owned and used exclusively by that taxpayer to transport carbon oxides captured by

that taxpayer's qualified facility or carbon capture equipment that would otherwise be emitted into the atmosphere.

(h) *Qualified enhanced oil or natural gas recovery project.*—The term *qualified enhanced oil or natural gas recovery project* has the same meaning as a qualified enhanced oil recovery project under section 43(c)(2) of the Code and §1.43-2, by substituting crude oil or natural gas for crude oil in section 43(c)(2)(A)(i) and §§1.43-2 and 1.43-3.

(1) *Application of §§1.43-2 and 1.43-3.*—For purposes of applying §§1.43-2 and 1.43-3 with respect to a qualified enhanced oil or natural gas recovery project, the term enhanced oil or natural gas recovery is substituted for enhanced oil recovery, and the term oil or natural gas is substituted for oil.

(2) *Required certification.*—The qualified enhanced oil or natural gas recovery project must be certified under §1.43-3, even if no credit related to enhanced oil or natural gas recovery is claimed for the taxable year. For purposes of a natural gas project—

(i) The petroleum engineer's certification under §1.43-3(a)(3) and the operator's continued certification of a project under §1.43-3(b)(3) must include an additional statement that the certification is for purposes of the section 45Q carbon oxide sequestration tax credit;

(ii) The petroleum engineer's certification must be attached to a *Form 8933* and filed not later than the last date prescribed by law (including extensions) for filing the operator's or designated owner's Federal income tax return or *Form 1065* for the first taxable year in which qualified carbon oxide is injected into the reservoir; and

(iii) The operator's continued certification of a project must be attached to a *Form 8933* and filed not later than the last date prescribed by law (including extensions) for filing the operator's or designated owner's Federal income tax return or *Form 1065* for taxable years after the taxable year for which the petroleum engineer's certification is filed but not after the taxable year in which injection activity ceases and all injection wells are plugged and abandoned.

(3) *Natural gas.*—Natural gas has the same meaning as under section 613A(e)(2) of the Code.

(4) *Timely filing of petroleum engineer's certification.*—For purposes of this paragraph (h), if a section 45Q credit is claimed on an amended Federal income tax return, an amended *Form 1065*, or an AAR, as applicable, the petroleum engineer's certification for a natural gas project will be treated as filed timely if it is attached to a *Form 8933* that is submitted with such amended Federal income tax return, amended *Form 1065*, or AAR. With respect to a section 45Q credit that is claimed on a timely filed Federal income tax return or *Form 1065* for a taxable year ending after December 31, 2017, and beginning on or before January 13, 2021, for which the petroleum engineer's certification for a natural gas project was not submitted, the petroleum engineer's certification for a natural gas project will be treated as filed timely if it is attached to an amended *Form 8933* for such taxable year.

(5) *Carbon oxide injected in oil reservoir.*—Carbon oxide that is injected into an oil reservoir that is not a qualified enhanced oil recovery project under section 43(c)(2) due to circumstances such as the first injection of a tertiary injectant occurring before 1991, or because a petroleum engineer's certification was not timely filed, cannot be treated as qualified carbon oxide, disposed of in secure geological storage, or utilized in a manner described in section 45Q(f)(5). This rule will not apply to an oil reservoir if——

(i) The reservoir has permanently ceased oil production;

(ii) The operator has obtained an Underground Injection Control Class VI permit; and

(iii) The operator complies with 40 CFR Part 98 subpart RR.

(6) *Tertiary Injectant.*—For purposes of section 45Q, a tertiary injectant is qualified carbon oxide that is injected into and stored in a qualified enhanced oil or natural gas recovery project and contributes to the extraction of crude oil or natural gas. The term *tertiary injectant* has the same meaning as used in section 193(b)(1) of the Code.

(i) *Section 45Q credit.*—The term *section 45Q credit* means the carbon oxide sequestration credit determined under section 45Q of the Internal Revenue Code and §1.45Q-1.

(j) *Form 8933.*—The term *Form 8933* means Form 8933, Carbon Oxide Sequestration Credit, any successor form(s), pursuant to instructions to any of the foregoing (see §601.602 of this chapter), or other guidance. This definition of Form 8933 applies to this section and to §§1.45Q-1, 1.45Q-3, 1.45Q-4, and 1.45Q-5.

(k) *Applicability date.*—This section applies to taxable years beginning on or after January 13, 2021. Taxpayers may choose to apply this section for taxable years beginning on or after January 1, 2018, provided the taxpayer applies this section and §§ 1.45Q-1, 1.45Q-3, 1.45Q-4, and 1.45Q-5 in their entirety and in a consistent manner. [Reg. § 1.45Q-2.]

☐ [*T.D. 9944, 1-13-2021.*]

[Reg. § 1.45Q-3]

§ 1.45Q-3. Secure Geological Storage.—(a) *In general.*—To qualify for the section 45Q credit, a taxpayer must either physically or contractually dispose of captured qualified carbon oxide in secure geological storage in the manner provided in paragraph (b) of this section, or utilize qualified carbon oxide in a manner conforming with section 45Q(f)(5) of the Internal Revenue Code and § 1.45Q-4. Secure geological storage includes, but is not limited to, storage at deep saline formations, oil and gas reservoirs, and unminable coal seams.

(b) *Requirements for secure geological storage.*—For purposes of the section 45Q credit, qualified carbon oxide is considered disposed of by the taxpayer in secure geological storage such that the qualified carbon oxide does not escape into the atmosphere if the qualified carbon oxide is—

  (1) Injected into a well that

    (i) Complies with applicable Underground Injection Control or other regulations, located onshore or offshore under submerged lands within the territorial jurisdiction of States or federal waters, and

    (ii) Is not used as a tertiary injectant in a qualified enhanced oil or natural gas recovery project, in compliance with applicable requirements under 40 CFR Part 98 subpart RR; or

  (2) Injected into a well that

    (i) Complies with applicable Underground Injection Control or other regulations, is located onshore or offshore under submerged lands within the territorial jurisdiction of States or federal waters, and

    (ii) Is used as a tertiary injectant in a qualified enhanced oil or natural gas recovery project and stored in compliance with applicable requirements under 40 CFR Part 98 subpart RR, or the International Organization for Standardization (ISO) standards endorsed by the American National Standards Institute (ANSI) under CSA/ANSI ISO 27916:2019, Carbon dioxide capture, transportation and geological storage – Carbon dioxide storage using enhanced oil recovery (CO_2-EOR) (CSA/ANSI ISO 27916:2019).

(c) *Documentation.*—Documentation must be filed in accordance with *Form 8933*.

(d) *Certification.*—For qualified enhanced oil or natural gas recovery projects in which the taxpayer reported volumes of carbon oxide to the Environmental Protection Agency pursuant to 40 CFR Part 98 subpart RR, the taxpayer may self-certify the volume of qualified carbon oxide claimed for purposes of section 45Q. For qualified enhanced oil or natural gas recovery projects in which the taxpayer determined volumes pursuant to CSA/ANSI ISO 27916:2019, a taxpayer may prepare documentation as outlined in CSA/ANSI ISO 27916:2019 internally, but all such documentation must be provided to a qualified independent engineer or geologist, who then must certify that the documentation provided, including the mass balance calculations as well as information regarding monitoring and containment assurance, is accurate and complete. The qualified independent engineer or geologist certifying a project must be duly registered or certified in any State. The certification must contain an affidavit from the certifying engineer or geologist stating that he or she is independent from the taxpayer (and if a section 45Q(f)(3)(B) election has been made, the affidavit must state that he or she is independent from both the electing taxpayer and the credit claimant). Certifications must be made annually and under penalties of perjury. For any leaked amount of qualified carbon oxide (as defined in § 1.45Q-5(c)) that is determined pursuant to CSA/ANSI ISO 27916:2019, the certification must also include a statement that the quantity was determined in accordance with sound engineering principles. Taxpayers that capture qualified carbon oxide giving rise to the section 45Q credit must file *Form 8933* with a timely filed Federal income tax return or *Form 1065*, including extensions or for the purpose of this rule, amendments to Federal income tax returns, *Forms 1065*, or on AARs, as applicable. Taxpayers that dispose of, inject, or utilize qualified carbon oxide must also file *Form 8933* with a timely filed Federal income tax return or *Form 1065*, including extensions or for the purpose of this rule, amendments to Federal income tax returns, *Forms 1065*, or on AARs, as applicable. If the volume of carbon oxide certified and reported is a negative amount, see § 1.45Q-5 for rules regarding recapture.

(e) *Failure to submit complete documentation or certification.*—No section 45Q credit is allowed for any taxable year for which the taxpayer (including credit claimants) has failed to timely submit complete

documentation and certification that is required by this regulation or *Form 8933*. The credit will be allowed only for a taxable year for which complete documentation and certification has been timely submitted. Certifications for each taxable year must be submitted by the due date of the federal income tax return or *Form 1065* on which the section 45Q credit is claimed, including extensions. However, if a section 45Q credit is claimed on an amended Federal income tax return, an amended *Form 1065*, or an AAR, as applicable, certifications may also be submitted with such amended Federal income tax return, amended *Form 1065*, or AAR. Further, if a section 45Q credit was claimed on a timely filed Federal income tax return or *Form 1065* for a taxable year ending on or after January 1, 2018, and beginning on or before January 13, 2021, for which certifications were not submitted, such certifications may be submitted with a timely filed amended Federal income tax return, an amended *Form 1065*, or an AAR, as applicable, for such taxable year.

(f) *Applicability date.*—This section applies to taxable years beginning on or after January 13, 2021. Taxpayers may choose to apply this section for taxable years beginning on or after January 1, 2018, provided the taxpayer applies this section and §§ 1.45Q-1, 1.45Q-2, 1.45Q-4, and 1.45Q-5 in their entirety and in a consistent manner. [Reg. § 1.45Q-3.]

☐ [*T.D. 9944, 1-13-2021.*]

[Reg. § 1.45Q-4]

§ 1.45Q-4. Utilization of Qualified Carbon Oxide.—(a) *In general.*—For purposes of this section, *utilization of qualified carbon oxide* means—

  (1) The fixation of such qualified carbon oxide through photosynthesis or chemosynthesis, such as through the growing of algae or bacteria,

  (2) The chemical conversion of such qualified carbon oxide to a material or chemical compound in which such qualified carbon oxide is securely stored, or

  (3) The use of such qualified carbon oxide for any other purpose for which a commercial market exists (with the exception of use as a tertiary injectant in a qualified enhanced oil or natural gas recovery project), as described in paragraph (d) of this section.

(b) *Amount utilized.*—(1) *In general.*—For purposes of § 1.45Q-1(b)(ii) and (c)(2)(ii), the amount of qualified carbon oxide utilized by the taxpayer is equal to the metric tons of qualified carbon oxide which the taxpayer demonstrates, based upon an analysis of lifecycle greenhouse gas emissions (LCA), were—

    (i) Captured and permanently isolated from the atmosphere through use of a process described in paragraph (a) of this section, or

    (ii) Displaced from being emitted into the atmosphere through use of a process described in paragraph (a) of this section.

  (2) *Limitation.*—The amount determined under paragraph (b)(1) of this section cannot exceed the amount of qualified carbon oxide measured at the source of capture.

(c) *Lifecycle greenhouse gas emissions and lifecycle analysis (LCA).*—(1) *In general.*—For purposes of paragraph (b) of this section, the term lifecycle greenhouse gas emissions means the aggregate quantity of greenhouse gas emissions (including direct emissions and significant indirect emissions such as significant emissions from land use changes) related to the full product lifecycle, including all stages of product and feedstock production and distribution, from feedstock generation or extraction through the distribution and delivery and use of the finished product to the ultimate consumer, where the mass values for all greenhouse gases are adjusted to account for their relative global warming potential according to Table A-1 of 40 CFR Part 98 subpart A. Such emissions are expressed in carbon dioxide equivalent (CO_2-e).

  (2) *LCA verification.*—The taxpayer verifies the amount of qualified carbon oxide utilized through an LCA. The LCA must demonstrate that the proposed process results in a net reduction of carbon dioxide equivalents when compared to a comparison system. The results of the LCA must be documented in a written LCA report.

  (3) *Standards of adequate lifecycle analysis.*—The LCA report must be prepared in conformity with and contain documentation that conforms with International Organization for Standardization (ISO) 14040:2006, *Environmental management – Life cycle assessment – Principles and framework and ISO 14044:2006, Environmental management — Life cycle assessment — Requirements and guidelines*. The LCA may consist of direct and indirect data in conformity with ISO 14040:2006 and 14044:2006.

  (4) *Third-party independent review of LCA.*—The LCA report must be performed or verified by an independent third party. The LCA report must provide a statement documenting the qualifications of

the independent third party, including proof of appropriate U.S. or foreign professional license, an affidavit from the third party stating that it is independent from the taxpayer (if a section 45Q(f)(3)(B) election has been made, the affidavit must state that the third party is independent from both the electing taxpayer and the credit claimant), and the statement must be made under penalties of perjury. If an independent third-party review is conducted, then it must include an assessment of the model and supporting data.

(5) *Submission of the LCA.*—The taxpayer must submit the LCA report and third-party independent statement required by paragraph (c) of this section to the IRS and the Department of Energy. The taxpayer must also submit the model if the LCA is not verified by an independent third-party review.

(6) *LCA review.*—The LCA report will be subject to a technical review by the DOE. The IRS will determine whether to approve the LCA and will notify the taxpayer. The taxpayer must receive approval of its LCA prior to claiming the section 45Q credits for such taxable year on any federal income tax return. In addition to receiving approval of its LCA, the taxpayer must satisfy all other requirements of section 45Q and §§1.45Q-1, 1.45Q-2, and this section in order to be eligible to claim section 45Q credits.

(d) *Commercial market.*—A commercial market means a market in which a product, process, or service that utilizes carbon oxide is sold or transacted on commercial terms. A taxpayer must submit a statement attached to its *Form 8933* substantiating that a commercial market exists for its particular product, process, or service.

(e) *Applicability date.*—This section applies to taxable years beginning on or after January 13, 2021. Taxpayers may choose to apply this section for taxable years beginning on or after January 1, 2018, provided the taxpayer applies this section and §§1.45Q-1, 1.45Q-2, 1.45Q-3, and 1.45Q-5 in their entirety and in a consistent manner. [Reg. §1.45Q-4.]

☐ [*T.D. 9944*, 1-13-2021.]

[Reg. §1.45Q-5]

§1.45Q-5. Recapture of Credit.—(a) *Recapture event.*—A recapture event occurs when qualified carbon oxide for which a section 45Q credit has been previously claimed ceases to be disposed of in secure geological storage (as described in §1.45Q-3(b)), or used as a tertiary injectant during the recapture period. Recapture events are determined separately for each project involving the disposal or use of qualified carbon oxide as a tertiary injectant. A recapture event does not occur if some portion of qualified carbon oxide disposed of in the current year does not remain in secure storage at the end of the year. The amount of such carbon oxide that is securely stored in the current year is determined according to the applicable requirements of 40 CFR Part 98 subpart RR or CSA/ANSI ISO 27916:2019.

(b) *Ceases to be disposed of in secure geological storage or used as a tertiary injectant.*—Qualified carbon oxide for which a section 45Q credit has been previously claimed ceases to be disposed of in secure geological storage (as described in §1.45Q-3(b)), or used as a tertiary injectant, if the leaked amount of qualified carbon oxide in the taxable year exceeds the amount of qualified carbon oxide securely stored in that same taxable year.

(c) *Leaked amount of qualified carbon oxide.*—When a taxpayer that claimed a section 45Q credit with respect to qualified carbon oxide stored at a secure storage site, operator of the secure storage site, or regulatory agency with jurisdiction over the site determines that the qualified carbon oxide that was disposed of in secure geological storage has leaked to the atmosphere, the taxpayer or the party with whom the taxpayer contracted to ensure the secure geological storage of the qualified carbon oxide must quantify the metric tons of qualified carbon oxide that has leaked to the atmosphere pursuant to the requirements of 40 CFR Part 98 subpart RR or CSA/ANSI ISO 27916:2019. The quantity determined pursuant to CSA/ANSI ISO 27916:2019 must be certified by a qualified independent engineer or geologist, including a statement that the quantity was determined in accordance with sound engineering principles in the same manner as required in §1.45Q-3. The IRS will consider all available facts and circumstances, and may consult with the relevant regulatory agency with jurisdiction over such site, in verifying the amount of qualified carbon oxide that has leaked to the atmosphere. The verified amount is the leaked amount of qualified carbon oxide.

(d) *Qualified carbon oxide subject to recapture.*—The quantity of recaptured qualified carbon oxide (in metric tons) subject to recapture is the amount by which the leaked amount of qualified carbon oxide exceeds the amount of qualified carbon oxide securely stored in the taxable year. The leaked amount of qualified carbon oxide shall be subtracted from the amount of qualified carbon oxide that is securely

stored in the taxable year. If the leaked amount does not exceed the amount of qualified carbon oxide that is securely stored in the taxable year, then the taxpayer is entitled to a credit equal to the amount of qualified carbon oxide securely stored less the leaked amount in the taxable year, multiplied by the appropriate statutory credit rate.

(e) *Recapture amount.*—The recapture amount is equal to the product of the quantity of recaptured qualified carbon oxide (in metric tons) subject to recapture and the appropriate statutory credit rate.

(f) *Recapture period.*—The recapture period begins on the date of first injection of qualified carbon oxide for disposal in secure geological storage or use as a tertiary injectant for which a section 45Q credit was claimed. The recapture period ends on the earlier of three years after the last taxable year in which the taxpayer claimed a section 45Q credit or was eligible to claim a credit that it elected to carry forward or the date monitoring ends under the requirements of the standards described in §1.45Q-3(b)(1) or (2).

(g) *Application of recapture.*—(1) *In general.*—Any recapture amount must be taken into account in the taxable year in which it is identified and reported. If the leaked amount of qualified carbon oxide does not exceed the amount of qualified carbon oxide securely stored in the taxable year reported, there is no recapture amount and no further adjustments to prior taxable years are needed. If the leaked amount of qualified carbon oxide does exceed the amount of qualified carbon oxide securely stored in the taxable year reported, then the taxpayer must add the recapture amount to the amount of tax due in the taxable year in which the recapture event occurs.

(2) *Calculation.*—Recapture amounts are calculated on a last-in-first-out basis (LIFO), such that the leaked amount of qualified carbon oxide that exceeds the amount of qualified carbon oxide securely stored in the current taxable year will be deemed attributable first to the prior taxable year, then to taxable year before that, and then up to a maximum of the third preceding year.

(3) *Multiple units.*—In the event of a recapture event in which the leaked amount of qualified carbon oxide had been captured from multiple units of carbon capture equipment that were not under common ownership, the recapture amount must be allocated on a pro rata basis among the multiple units of carbon capture equipment. All taxpayers that claimed a section 45Q credit with respect to one or more of such units of carbon capture equipment are responsible for adding the recapture amount to their amount of tax due in the taxable year in which the recapture event occurs.

(4) *Multiple taxpayers.*—(i) *In general.*—In the event of a recapture event involving a leaked amount of qualified carbon oxide that is deemed attributable to qualified carbon oxide for which multiple taxpayers claimed section 45Q credits (for example, if ownership of the carbon capture equipment was transferred, or if a taxpayer made an election under section 45Q(f)(3)(B) to allow one or more credit claimants to claim a portion of the section 45Q credit), the recapture amount must be allocated on a pro rata basis among the taxpayers that claimed the section 45Q credits.

(ii) *Partnerships.*—(A) *General rule.*—For purposes of paragraph (g)(4)(i) of this section, if a partnership is one of the multiple taxpayers that claimed section 45Q credit amounts, the partnership and not its partners will be the taxpayer to which the pro rata recapture amount must be allocated. The partnership must allocate its pro rata recapture amount among its partners under §1.704-1(b)(4)(ii).

(B) *Terminated partnerships.*—If a partnership described in paragraph (g)(4)(ii)(A) of this section terminates under section 708(b)(1) prior to a recapture event, the partners of that terminated partnership at the time the section 45Q credit was claimed will be the taxpayers to which the pro rata recapture amount must be allocated.

(5) *Reporting.*—If a recapture event occurs during a project's recapture period, any taxpayer that claimed a section 45Q credit for that project must report the following information on a *Form 8933* filed with that taxpayer's Federal income tax return or *Form 1065* for the taxable year for which the recapture event occurred—
(A) The recapture amount (as defined in §1.45Q-5(e));
(B) The leaked amount of qualified carbon oxide (in metric tons) (as defined in §1.45Q-5(c));
(C) The statutory credit rate(s) at which the section 45Q credits were previously calculated; and
(D) A statement that describes how the taxpayer became aware of the recapture event, how the leaked amount was determined, and the identity and involvement of any regulatory agencies.

(6) *Examples.*—The following examples illustrate the principles of this paragraph (g):

(i) *Example 1.*—(A) A owns direct air capture Facility X. No other taxpayer has owned Facility X, and A has never allowed another taxpayer to claim any section 45Q credits with respect to qualified carbon oxide captured by Facility X. Facility X captured 100,000 metric tons of carbon dioxide in each of 2021, 2022, and 2023. All captured carbon dioxide was sold to B for use a tertiary injectant in a qualified enhanced oil recovery project. B provided contractual assurance that the carbon dioxide would be disposed of in secure geological storage. A claimed section 45Q credit amounts of $2,268,000 in 2021, $2,515,000 in 2022, and $2,761,000 in 2023 using the statutory rates in §1.45Q-1(d)(3). In 2024, A captured and sold another 100,000 metric tons of carbon dioxide to B, which B used as a tertiary injectant in a qualified enhanced oil recovery project. In late 2024, B determined that 10,000 metric tons of qualified carbon dioxide injected during 2021 had leaked from the containment area of the reservoir and were released into the atmosphere.

(B) Because the leakage determined in 2024 (10,000 metric tons) did not exceed the presumed amount stored in 2024 (100,000 metric tons), a recapture event did not occur in 2024. B's actual storage in 2024 is 90,000 metric tons of qualified carbon oxide. A's section 45Q credit for 2024 is $2,706,300 (net 90,000 metric tons of qualified carbon oxide captured, disposed of in secure geological storage, and used as a tertiary injectant multiplied by the statutory credit rate for 2024 of $30.07).

(ii) *Example 2.*—(A) Assume same facts as in Example 1. Additionally, in 2025, B determines that 190,000 metric tons of qualified carbon dioxide injected in 2021 and 2022 had leaked and were released into the atmosphere. No injection of carbon dioxide takes place in 2025.

(B) Because the leakage determined in 2025 (190,000 metric tons) exceeds the amount stored in 2025 (0 metric tons), a recapture event occurred in 2025. A's credit for 2025 is $0 because the net amount of carbon dioxide captured, disposed of in secure geological storage, and used as a tertiary injectant in 2025 was 0 metric tons. The 2025 recapture amount is calculated by multiplying the 190,000 metric tons of recaptured qualified carbon oxide by the appropriate statutory credit rate using the LIFO method. The first 90,000 metric tons of recaptured qualified carbon oxide is deemed attributable to 2024, and is recaptured at the 2024 statutory rate of $30.07 per metric ton. The remaining 100,000 metric tons of recaptured qualified carbon oxide are deemed attributable to 2023. The credits attributable to 2023 are recaptured at the 2023 statutory rate of $27.61 per metric ton. Thus, the total recapture amount is $5,467,300, and is added to A's tax due for 2025.

(iii) *Example 3.*—(A) Assume the same facts as in Example 2, except that A sells Facility X to C on January 1, 2024. C sells 100,000 metric tons of carbon dioxide captured by Facility X to B for use as a tertiary injectant in a qualified enhanced oil recovery project. C claims a section 45Q credit in 2024 of $2,706,300 (net 90,000 metric tons of qualified carbon oxide captured, disposed of in secure geological storage, and used as a tertiary injectant multiplied by the statutory credit rate for 2024 of $30.07).

(B) The total recapture amount in 2025 is the same $5,467,300 as in Example 2, but is allocated between A and C. The first 90,000 metric tons of recaptured qualified carbon oxide are deemed attributable to 2024. The credits that are attributable to 2024 are recaptured at the 2024 statutory rate of $30.07 per ton (for a recapture amount of $2,706,300). Because C claimed that amount of section 45Q credit in 2024, a recapture amount of $2,706,300 is added to C's tax due for 2025. The remaining 100,000 metric tons of recaptured qualified carbon oxide are deemed attributable to 2023. The credits that are attributable to 2023 are recaptured at the 2023 statutory rate of $27.61 per ton (for a recapture amount of $2,761,000). Because A claimed that amount of section 45Q credit in 2023, a recapture amount of $2,761,000 is added to A's tax due for 2025.

(iv) *Example 4.*—(A) Assume the same facts as in Example 2, except that in 2023, A made a section 45Q(f)(3)(B) election to allow B to claim one-half of the section 45Q credit for 2023. A and B each claimed $1,380,500 of section 45Q credit in 2023 (50,000 metric tons each multiplied by the 2023 statutory rate of $27.61).

(B) The total recapture amount in 2025 is the same $5,467,300 as in Example 2, but is allocated among A and B. The first 90,000 metric tons of recaptured qualified carbon oxide is deemed attributable to 2024. The section 45Q credit amounts attributable to 2024 are recaptured at the 2024 statutory rate of $30.07 per ton (for a recapture amount of $2,706,300). Because A claimed that amount of section 45Q credit in 2024, $2,706,300 is added to A's tax due for 2025. The remaining 100,000 metric tons of recaptured qualified carbon oxide is deemed attributable to 2023. The section 45Q credit amounts attributable to 2023 are recaptured at the 2023 statutory rate of $27.61 per ton (for a recapture amount of $2,761,000). Because A and B each claimed half of that amount ($1,380,500) of section 45Q credit in 2023, $1,380,500 is added to both A's and B's tax due for 2025. Thus, a

recapture amount of $4,086,800 is added to A's tax due for 2025, and a recapture amount of $1,380,500 is added to B's tax due for 2025.

(v) *Example 5.*—(A) Assume the same facts as in Example 2, except that the 100,000 metric tons of carbon dioxide sold to B in 2021, 2022, 2023, and 2024 for use as a tertiary injectant in a qualified enhanced oil recovery project were captured equally (50,000 metric tons per year) from qualified facilities owned by J and K. Neither J nor K made a section 45Q(f)(3)(B) election to allow B to claim the credit.

(B) Because the leakage determined in 2024 (10,000 metric tons) did not exceed the presumed amount stored in 2024 (100,000 metric tons) a recapture event did not occur in 2024. The total amount of section 45Q credit for 2024 is $2,706,300 (net 90,000 metric tons of qualified carbon oxide captured, disposed of in secure geological storage, and used as a tertiary injectant multiplied by the section 45Q credit rate for 2024 of $30.07). J and K may each claim half of this amount of section 45Q credit ($1,353,150) in 2024.

(C) The total recapture amount in 2025 is the same $5,467,300 as in Example 2, but is allocated between J and K. The section 45Q credit amounts relating to the first 90,000 metric tons of recaptured qualified carbon oxide are deemed attributable to 2024 and are recaptured at the 2024 statutory rate of $30.07 per ton (for a recapture amount of $2,706,300). Because J and K each claimed half of that amount ($1,353,150) of section 45Q credit in 2024, $1,353,150 is added to both J's and K's tax due for 2025. The section 45Q credit amounts relating to the remaining 100,000 metric tons of recaptured qualified carbon oxide are deemed attributable to 2023 and are recaptured at the 2023 statutory rate of $27.61 per ton (for a recapture amount of $2,761,000). Because J and K each claimed half of that amount ($1,380,500) of section 45Q credit in 2023, an additional $1,380,500 is added to both J's and Ks tax due for 2025. Thus, a total recapture amount of $2,733,650 is added to both J's and K's tax due for 2025.

(vi) *Example 6.*—(A) M owns Industrial Facility Z. No other taxpayer has ever owned Z, and M has never allowed another taxpayer to claim any section 45Q credits with respect to qualified carbon oxide captured from Z. M captured 1,000,000 metric tons of carbon dioxide annually in each of 2017, 2018, 2019, 2020, 2021, 2022, 2023, 2024, and 2025. All captured carbon dioxide was sold to N for use a tertiary injectant in a qualified enhanced oil recovery project. N provided contractual assurance that the carbon dioxide would be sequestered in secure geological storage. M claimed section 45Q credit amounts of $12,830,000 in 2017, $15,209,000 in 2018, $17,760,000 in 2019, $20,220,000 in 2020, $22,680,000 in 2021, $25,150,000 in 2022, $27,610,000 in 2023, $30,070,000 in 2024, and $32,540,000 in 2025 using the statutory rates in §1.45Q-1(d)(3). No injection of carbon oxides takes place in 2026. In 2026, N determined that 6,200,000 metric tons of qualified carbon dioxide previously injected had leaked from the containment area of the reservoir and were released into the atmosphere.

(B) Because the leakage determined in 2025 (6,200,000 metric tons) exceed the amount stored in 2026 (0 metric tons) a recapture event occurred in 2026. A's credit for 2026 is $0 because the net amount of carbon dioxide captured and used as a tertiary injectant in 2026 was 0 metric tons. The 2026 recapture amount is calculated by multiplying the 6,200,000 metric tons of recaptured qualified carbon oxide by the appropriate statutory credit rate using the LIFO method. The first 1,000,000 metric tons of recaptured qualified carbon oxide is deemed attributable to 2025, and is recaptured at the 2025 statutory rate of $32.54 per metric ton. The next 1,000,000 metric tons of recaptured qualified carbon oxide is deemed attributable to 2024, and is recaptured at the 2024 statutory rate of $30.07 per metric ton. The next 1,000,000 metric tons of recaptured qualified carbon oxide is deemed attributable to 2023, and is recaptured at the 2023 statutory rate of $27.16 per metric ton. The remaining 3,200,000 metric tons are not subject to recapture because of the three-year lookback limit in §1.45Q-1(g)(2). Thus, the total recapture amount is $89,770,000, and is added to A's tax due for 2026.

(h) *Recapture in the event of deliberate removal from storage.*—(1) *In general.*—If qualified carbon oxide for which a credit has been claimed is deliberately removed from a secure geological storage site, then a recapture event would occur in the year in which the qualified carbon oxide is removed from the storage site pursuant to §1.45Q-5(a).

(2) *Recycled qualified carbon oxide.*—If qualified carbon oxide for which a credit has been claimed is recaptured, recycled, and reinjected as part of the enhanced oil and natural gas recovery project, that qualified carbon oxide will be considered recycled carbon oxide under section 45Q(c)(2). If recycled carbon oxide is reinjected into the same qualified enhanced oil or natural gas recovery project it was originally injected into, it will not be considered deliberately removed from a secure geological storage site for purposes of paragraph (h)(1) of this section. If recycled carbon oxide is reinjected into

a different qualified enhanced oil or natural gas recovery project from the one it was initially injected into, or used for any other purpose, that qualified carbon oxide will be considered deliberately removed from a secure geological storage site for purposes of paragraph (h)(1) of this section.

(i) *Limited exceptions.*—A recapture event is not triggered in the event of a loss of containment of qualified carbon oxide resulting from actions not related to the selection, operation, or maintenance of the storage facility, such as volcanic activity or terrorist attack.

(j) *Applicability date.*—This section applies to taxable years beginning on or after January 13, 2021. Taxpayers may choose to apply this section for taxable years beginning on or after January 1, 2018, provided the taxpayer applies this section and §§1.45Q-1, 1.45Q-2, 1.45Q-3, and 1.45Q-4 in their entirety and in a consistent manner. [Reg. §1.45Q-5.]

☐ [*T.D.* 9944, 1-13-2021.]

[Reg. §1.45R-0]

§1.45R-0. Table of contents.—This section lists the table of contents for §§1.45R-1 through 1.45R-5.

☐ [*T.D.* 9672, 6-26-2014.]

[Reg. §1.45R-1]

§1.45R-1. Definitions.—(a) *Definitions.*—The definitions in this section apply to this section and §§1.45R-2, 1.45R-3, 1.45R-4, and 1.45R-5.

(1) *Average premium.*—The term *average premium* means an average premium for the small group market in the rating area in which the employee enrolls for coverage. The average premium for the small group market in a rating area is determined by the Secretary of Health and Human Services.

(2) *Composite billing.*—The term *composite billing* means a system of billing under which a health insurer charges a uniform premium for each of the employer's employees or charges a single aggregate premium for the group of covered employees that the employer then divides by the number of covered employees to determine the uniform premium.

(3) *Credit period.*—(i) *In general.*—The term *credit period* means, with respect to any eligible small employer (or any predecessor employer), the two-consecutive-taxable-year period beginning with the first taxable year beginning after 2013, for which the eligible small employer files an income tax return with an attached Form 8941, "Credit for Small Employer Health Insurance Premiums" (or files a Form 990-T, "Exempt Organization Business Income Tax Return," with an attached Form 8941 in the case of a tax-exempt eligible employer). For a transition rule for 2014, see §1.45R-3(i).

(ii) *Examples.*—The following examples illustrate the provisions of paragraph (a)(3)(i) of this section:

Example 1. (i) *Facts.* In 2014, an eligible small employer (Employer) that uses a calendar year as its taxable year begins to offer insurance through a SHOP Exchange. Employer has 4 employees and otherwise qualifies for the credit, but none of the employees enroll in the coverage offered by Employer through the SHOP Exchange. In mid-2015, the 4 employees enroll for coverage through the SHOP Exchange but Employer does not file Form 8941 or claim the credit. In 2016, Employer has 20 employees and all are enrolled in coverage offered through the SHOP Exchange. Employer files Form 8941 with Employer's 2016 tax return to claim the credit.

(ii) *Conclusion.* Employer's taxable year 2016 is the first year of the credit period. Accordingly, Employer's two-year credit period is 2016 and 2017.

Example 2. (i) *Facts.* Same facts as *Example 1*, but Employer files Form 8941 with Employer's 2015 tax return.

(ii) *Conclusion.* Employer's taxable year 2015 is the first year of the credit period. Accordingly, Employer's two-year credit period is 2015 and 2016 (and does not include 2017). Employer is entitled to a credit based on a partial year of SHOP Exchange coverage for Employer's taxable year 2015.

(4) *Eligible small employer.*—(i) The term *eligible small employer* means an employer that meets the requirements set forth in § 1.45R-2.

(ii) For the definition of tax-exempt eligible small employer, see paragraph (a)(19) of this section.

(iii) A farmers' cooperative described under section 521 that is subject to tax pursuant to section 1381, and otherwise meets the requirements of this paragraph (a)(4) and § 1.45R-2, is an eligible small employer.

(5) *Employee.*—(i) *In general.*—Except as otherwise specifically provided in this paragraph (a)(5), the term *employee* means an individual who is an employee of the eligible small employer under the common law standard. See § 31.3121(d)-1(c).

(ii) *Leased* employees. For purposes of this paragraph (a)(5), the term *employee* also includes a leased employee (as defined in section 414(n)).

(iii) *Certain individuals excluded.*—The term *employee* does not include independent contractors (including sole proprietors), partners in a partnership, shareholders owning more than two percent of an S corporation, and any owners of more than five percent of other businesses. The term *employee* also does not include family members of these owners and partners, including the employee-spouse of a shareholder owning more than two percent of the stock of an S corporation, the employee-spouse of an owner of more than five percent of a business, the employee-spouse of a partner owning more than a five percent interest in a partnership, and the employee-spouse of a sole proprietor, or any other member of the household of these owners and partners who qualifies as a dependent under section 152(d)(2)(H).

(iv) *Seasonal workers.*—The term *employee* does not include seasonal workers unless the seasonal worker provides services to the employer on more than 120 days during the taxable year.

(v) *Ministers.*—Whether a minister is an employee is determined under the common law standard for determining worker status. If, under the common law standard, a minister is not an employee, the minister is not an employee for purposes of this paragraph (a)(5) and is not taken into account in determining an employer's FTEs, and premiums paid for the minister's health insurance coverage are not taken into account in computing the credit. If, under the common law standard, a minister is an employee, the minister is an employee for purposes of this paragraph (a)(5), and is taken into account in determining an employer's FTEs, and premiums paid by the employer for the minister's health insurance coverage can be taken into account in computing the credit. Because the performance of services by a minister in the exercise of his or her ministry is not treated as employment for purposes of the Federal Insurance Contributions Act (FICA), compensation paid to the minister is not wages as defined under section 3121(a), and is not counted as wages for purposes of computing an employer's average annual wages.

(vi) *Former employees.*—Premiums paid on behalf of a former employee with no hours of service may be treated as paid on behalf of an employee for purposes of calculating the credit (see § 1.45R-3) provided that, if so treated, the former employee is also treated as an employee for purposes of the uniform percentage requirement (see § 1.45R-4). For the treatment of terminated employees for purposes of determining employer eligibility for the credit, see § 1.45R-2(c).

(6) *Employer-computed composite rate.*—The term *employer-computed composite rate* refers to a rate for a tier of coverage (such as employee-only, dependent or family) of a QHP that is the average rate determined by adding the premiums for that tier of coverage for all employees eligible to participate in the QHP (whether or not they actually receive coverage under the plan or under that tier of coverage) and dividing by the total number of such eligible employees. The employer-computed composite rate may be used in list billing to convert individual premiums for a tier of coverage into an employer-computed composite rate for that tier of coverage. See § 1.45R-4(b)(3).

(7) *Exchange.*—The term *Exchange* means an exchange as defined in 45 CFR 155.20.

(8) *Family member.*—The term *family member* is defined with respect to a taxpayer as a child (or descendant of a child); a sibling or step-sibling; a parent (or ancestor of a parent); a step-parent; a niece or nephew; an aunt or uncle; or a son-in-law, daughter-in-law, father-in-law, mother-in-law, brother-in-law or sister-in-law. A spouse of any of these family members is also considered a family member.

(9) *Full-time equivalent employee (FTE).*—The number of *full-time equivalent employees (FTEs)* is determined by dividing the total number of hours of service for which wages were paid by the employer to employees during the taxable year by 2,080. See § 1.45R-2(d) and (e) for permissible methods of calculating hours of service and the method for calculating the number of an employer's FTEs.

(10) *List billing.*—The term *list billing* refers to a system of billing under which a health insurer lists a separate premium for each employee based on the age of the employee or other factors.

(11) *Net premium payments.*—The term *net premium payments* means, in the case of an employer receiving a State tax credit or State subsidy for providing health insurance to its employees, the excess of the employer's actual premium payments over the State tax credit or State subsidy received by the employer. In the case of a State payment directly to an insurance company (or another entity licensed under State law to engage in the business of insurance), the employer's net premium payments are the employer's actual premium payments. If a State-administered program (such as Medicaid or another program that makes payments directly to a health care provider or insurance company on behalf of individuals and their families who meet certain eligibility guidelines) makes payments that are not contingent on the maintenance of an employer-provided group health plan, those payments are not taken into account in determining the employer's net premium payments.

(12) *Nonelective contribution.*—The term *nonelective contribution* means an employer contribution other than a contribution pursuant to a salary reduction arrangement under section 125.

(13) *Payroll taxes.*—For purposes of section 45R, the term *payroll taxes* means amounts required to be withheld as tax from the employees of a tax-exempt eligible small employer under section 3402, amounts required to be withheld from such employees under section 3101(b), and amounts of tax imposed on the tax-exempt eligible small employer under section 3111(b).

(14) *Qualified health plan or QHP.*—The term *qualified health plan* or the term *QHP* means a qualified health plan as defined in Affordable Care Act section 1301(a) (see 42 U.S.C. 18021(a)), but does not include a catastrophic plan described in Affordable Care Act section 1302(e) (see 42 U.S.C. 18022(e)).

(15) *Qualifying arrangement.*—The term *qualifying arrangement* means an arrangement that requires an eligible small employer to make a nonelective contribution on behalf of each employee who enrolls in a QHP offered to employees by the employer through a SHOP Exchange in an amount equal to a uniform percentage (not less than 50 percent) of the premium cost of the QHP.

(16) *Seasonal worker.*—The term *seasonal worker* means a worker who performs labor or services on a seasonal basis as defined by the Secretary of Labor, including (but not limited to) workers covered by 29 CFR 500.20(s)(1), and retail workers employed exclusively during holiday seasons. Employers may apply a reasonable, good faith interpretation of the term seasonal worker and a reasonable good faith interpretation of 29 CFR 500.20(s)(1) (including as applied by analogy to workers and employment positions not otherwise covered under 29 CFR 500.20(s)(1)).

(17) *SHOP dependent coverage.*—The term *SHOP dependent coverage* refers to coverage offered through SHOP separately to any individual who is or may become eligible for coverage under the terms of a group health plan offered through SHOP because of a relationship to a participant-employee, whether or not a dependent of the participant-employee under section 152 of the Internal Revenue Code. The term *SHOP dependent coverage* does not include coverage such as family coverage, which includes coverage of the participant-employee.

(18) *Small Business Health Options Program (SHOP).*—The term *Small Business Health Options Program (SHOP)* means an Exchange established pursuant to section 1311 of the Affordable Care Act and defined in 45 CFR 155.20.

(19) *State.*—The term *State* means a State as defined in section 7701(a)(10), including the District of Columbia.

(20) *Tax-exempt eligible small employer.*—The term *tax-exempt eligible small employer* means an eligible small employer that is exempt

from federal income tax under section 501(a) as an organization described in section 501(c).

(21) *Tier.*—The term *tier* refers to a category of coverage under a benefits package that varies only by the number of individuals covered. For example, employee-only coverage, dependent coverage, and family coverage would constitute three separate tiers of coverage.

(22) *Tobacco surcharge.*—The term *tobacco surcharge* means any allowable differential that is charged for insurance in the SHOP Exchange that is attributable to tobacco use as the term tobacco use is defined in 45 CFR 147.102(a)(1)(iv).

(23) *United States.*—The term *United States* means United States as defined in section 7701(a)(9).

(24) *Wages.*—The term *wages* for purposes of section 45R means wages as defined under section 3121(a) for purposes of the Federal Insurance Contributions Act (FICA), determined without regard to the social security wage base limitation under section 3121(a)(1).

(25) *Wellness program.*—The term *wellness program* for purposes of section 45R means a program of health promotion or disease prevention subject to the requirements of § 54.9802-1(f).

(b) *Effective/applicability date.*—This section is applicable for periods after 2013. For rules relating to certain plan years beginning in 2014, see § 1.45R-3(i). [Reg. § 1.45R-1.]

□ [T.D. 9672, 6-26-2014.]

[Reg. § 1.45R-2]

§ 1.45R-2. Eligibility for the credit.—(a) *Eligible small employer.*—To be eligible for the credit under section 45R, an employer must be an eligible small employer. In order to be an eligible small employer, with respect to any taxable year, an employer must have no more than 25 full-time equivalent employees (FTEs), must have in effect a qualifying arrangement, and the average annual wages of the employer's FTEs must not exceed an amount equal to twice the dollar amount in effect under § 1.45R-3(c)(2). For purposes of eligibility for the credit for taxable years beginning in or after 2014, a qualifying arrangement is an arrangement that requires an employer to make a nonelective contribution on behalf of each employee who enrolls in a qualified health plan (QHP) offered to employees through a small business health options program (SHOP) Exchange in an amount equal to a uniform percentage (not less than 50 percent) of the premium cost of the QHP. Notwithstanding the foregoing, an employer that is an agency or instrumentality of the federal government, or of a State, local or Indian tribal government, is not an eligible small employer if it is not an organization described in section 501(c) that is exempt from tax under section 501(a). An employer does not fail to be an eligible small employer merely because its employees are not performing services in a trade or business of the employer. An employer located outside the United States (including an employer located in a U.S. territory) must have income effectively connected with the conduct of a trade or business in the United States, and otherwise meet the requirements of this section, to be an eligible small employer. For eligibility standards for SHOP related to foreign employers, see 45 CFR 155.710. Paragraphs (b) through (f) of this section provide the rules for determining whether the requirements to be an eligible small employer are met, including rules related to identifying and counting the number of the employer's FTEs, counting the employees' hours of service, and determining the employer's average annual FTE wages for the taxable year. For rules on determining whether the uniform percentage requirement is met, see § 1.45R-4.

(b) *Application of section 414 employer aggregation rules.*—All employers treated as a single employer under section 414(b), (c), (m) or (o) are treated as a single employer for purposes of this section. Thus, all employees of a controlled group under section 414(b), (c) or (o), or an affiliated service group under section 414(m), are taken into account in determining whether any member of the controlled group or affiliated service group is an eligible small employer. Similarly, all wages paid to, and premiums paid for, employees by the members of the controlled group or affiliated service group are taken into account when determining the amount of the credit for a group treated as a single employer under these rules.

(c) *Employees taken into account.*—To be eligible for the credit, an employer must have employees as defined in § 1.45R-1(a)(5) during the taxable year. All such employees of the eligible small employer are taken into account for purposes of determining the employer's FTEs and average annual FTE wages. Employees include employees who terminate employment during the year for which the credit is being claimed, employees covered under a collective bargaining

agreement, and employees who do not enroll in a QHP offered by the employer through a SHOP Exchange.

(d) *Determining the hours of service performed by employees.*—(1) *In general.*—An employee's hours of service for a year include each hour for which an employee is paid, or entitled to payment, for the performance of duties for the employer during the employer's taxable year. It also includes each hour for which an employee is paid, or entitled to payment, by the employer on account of a period of time during which no duties are performed due to vacation, holiday, illness, incapacity (including disability), layoff, jury duty, military duty or leave of absence (except that no more than 160 hours of service are required to be counted for an employee on account of any single continuous period during which the employee performs no duties).

(2) *Permissible methods.*—In calculating the total number of hours of service that must be taken into account for an employee during the taxable year, eligible small employers need not use the same method for all employees, and may apply different methods for different classifications of employees if the classifications are reasonable and consistently applied. Eligible small employers may change the method for calculating employees' hours of service for each taxable year. An eligible small employer may use any of the following three methods.

(i) *Actual hours worked.*—An employer may use the actual hours of service provided by employees including hours worked and any other hours for which payment is made or due (as described in paragraph (d)(1) of this section).

(ii) *Days-worked equivalency.*—An employer may use a days-worked equivalency whereby the employee is credited with 8 hours of service for each day for which the employee would be required to be credited with at least one hour of service under paragraph (d)(1) of this section.

(iii) *Weeks-worked equivalency.*—An employer may use a weeks-worked equivalency whereby the employee is credited with 40 hours of service for each week for which the employee would be required to be credited with at least one hour of service under paragraph (d)(1) of this section.

(3) *Examples.*—The following examples illustrate the rules of paragraph (d) of this section:

Example 1. Counting hours of service by hours actually worked or for which payment is made or due. (i) *Facts.* An eligible small employer (Employer) has payroll records that indicate that Employee A worked 2,000 hours and that Employer paid Employee A for an additional 80 hours on account of vacation, holiday and illness. Employer uses the actual hours worked method described in paragraph (d)(2)(i) of this section.

(ii) *Conclusion.* Under this method of counting hours, Employee A must be credited with 2,080 hours of service (2,000 hours worked and 80 hours for which payment was made or due).

Example 2. Counting hours of service under days-worked equivalency. (i) *Facts.* Employee B worked from 8:00am to 12:00pm every day for 200 days. Employer uses the days-worked equivalency method described in paragraph (d)(2)(ii) of this section.

(ii) *Conclusion.* Under this method of counting hours, Employee B must be credited with 1,600 hours of service (8 hours for each day Employee B would otherwise be credited with at least 1 hour of service x 200 days).

Example 3. Counting hours of service under weeks-worked equivalency. (i) Facts. Employee C worked 49 weeks, took 2 weeks of vacation with pay, and took 1 week of leave without pay. Employer uses the weeks-worked equivalency method described in paragraph (d)(2)(iii) of this section.

(ii) *Conclusion.* Under this method of counting hours, Employee C must be credited with 2,040 hours of service (40 hours for each week during which Employee C would otherwise be credited with at least 1 hour of service x 51 weeks).

Example 4. Excluded employees. (i) *Facts.* Employee D worked 3 consecutive weeks at 32 hours per week during the holiday season. Employee D did not work during the remainder of the year. Employee E worked limited hours after school from time to time through the year for a total of 350 hours. Employee E does not work through the summer. Employer uses the actual hours worked method described in paragraph (d)(2)(i) of this section.

(ii) *Conclusion.* Employee D is a seasonal employee who worked for 120 days or less for Employer during the year. Employee D's hours are not counted when determining the hours of service of Employer's employees. Employee E works throughout most of the year and is not a seasonal employee. Employer counts Employee E's 350 hours of service during the year.

(e) *FTE Calculation.*—(1) *In general.*—The number of an employer's FTEs is determined by dividing the total hours of service, determined in accordance with paragraph (d) of this section, credited during the year to employees taken into account under paragraph (c) of this section (but not more than 2,080 hours for any employee) by 2,080. The result, if not a whole number, is then rounded to the next lowest whole number. If, however, after dividing the total hours of service by 2,080, the resulting number is less than one, the employer rounds up to one FTE.

(2) *Example.*—The following example illustrates the provisions of paragraph (e) of this section:

Example. Determining the number of FTEs. (i) *Facts.* A sole proprietor pays 5 employees wages for 2,080 hours each, pays 3 employees wages for 1,040 hours each, and pays 1 employee wages for 2,300 hours. One of the employees working 2,080 hours is the sole proprietor's nephew. The sole proprietor's FTEs would be calculated as follows: 8,320 hours of service for the 4 employees paid for 2,080 hours each (4 x 2,080); the sole proprietor's nephew is excluded from the FTE calculation; 3,120 hours of service for the 3 employees paid for 1,040 hours each (3 x 1,040); and 2,080 hours of service for the 1 employee paid for 2,300 hours (lesser of 2,300 and 2,080). The sum of the included hours of service equals 13,520 hours of service.

(ii) *Conclusion* The sole proprietor's FTEs equal 6 (13,520 divided by 2,080 = 6.5, rounded to the next lowest whole number).

(f) *Determining the employer's average annual FTE wages.*—(1) In general.—All wages paid to employees (including overtime pay) are taken into account in computing an eligible small employer's average annual FTE wages. The average annual wages paid by an employer for a taxable year is determined by dividing the total wages paid by the eligible small employer during the employer's taxable year to employees taken into account under paragraph (c) of this section by the number of the employer's FTEs for the year. The result is then rounded down to the nearest $1,000 (if not otherwise a multiple of $1,000). For purposes of determining the employer's average annual wages for the taxable year, only wages that are paid for hours of service determined under paragraph (d) of this section are taken into account.

(2) *Example.*—The following example illustrates the provision of paragraphs (e) and (f) of this section:

Example. (i) *Facts.* An employer has 26 FTEs with average annual wages of $23,000. Only 22 of the employer's employees enroll for coverage offered by the employer through a SHOP Exchange.

(ii) *Conclusion.* The hours of service and wages of all employees are taken into consideration in determining whether the employer is an eligible small employer for purposes of the credit. Because the employer does not have fewer than 25 FTEs for the taxable year, the employer is not an eligible small employer for purposes of this section, even if fewer than 25 employees (or FTEs) enroll for coverage through the SHOP Exchange.

(g) *Effective/applicability date.*—This section is applicable for periods after 2013. For transition rules relating to certain plan years beginning in 2014, see § 1.45R-3(i). [Reg. § 1.45R-2.]

☐ [*T.D. 9672, 6-26-2014.*]

[Reg. § 1.45R-3]

§ 1.45R-3. Calculating the credit.—(a) *In general.*—The tax credit available to an eligible small employer equals 50 percent of the eligible small employer's premium payments made on behalf of its employees under a qualifying arrangement, or in the case of a tax-exempt eligible small employer, 35 percent of the employer's premium payments made on behalf of its employees under a qualifying arrangement. The employer's tax credit is subject to the following adjustments and limitations:

(1) The average premium limitation for the small group market in the rating area in which the employee enrolls for coverage, described in paragraph (b) of this section;

(2) The credit phaseout described in paragraph (c) of this section;

(3) The net premium payment limitation in the case of State credits or subsidies described in paragraph (d) of this section;

(4) The payroll tax limitation for a tax-exempt eligible small employer described in paragraph (e) of this section;

(5) The two-consecutive-taxable year-credit period limitation, described in paragraph (f) of this section;

(6) The rules with respect to the premium payments taken into account, described in paragraph (g) of this section;

(7) The rules with respect to credits applicable to trusts, estates, regulated investment companies, real estate investment trusts and cooperatives described in paragraph (h) of this section; and

(8) The transition relief for 2014 described in paragraph (i) of this section.

(b) *Average premium limitation.*—(1) *In general.*—The amount of an eligible small employer's premium payments that is taken into account in calculating the credit is limited to the premium payments the employer would have made under the same arrangement if the average premium for the small group market in the rating area in which the employee enrolls for coverage were substituted for the actual premium.

(2) *Examples.*—The following examples illustrate the provisions of paragraph (b)(1) of this section:

Example 1. Comparing premium payments to average premium for small group market. (i) *Facts.* An eligible small employer (Employer) offers a health insurance plan with employee-only and SHOP dependent coverage through a small business options program (SHOP) Exchange. Employer has 9 full-time equivalent employees (FTEs) with average annual wages of $23,000 per FTE. All 9 employees are employees as defined under § 1.45R-1(a)(5). Six employees are enrolled in employee-only coverage and 5 of these 6 employees have also enrolled either one child or one spouse in SHOP dependent coverage. Employer pays 50% of the premiums for all employees enrolled in employee-only coverage and 50% of the premiums for all employees who enrolled family members in SHOP dependent coverage (and the employee is responsible for the remainder in each case). The premiums are $4,000 a year for employee-only coverage and $3,000 a year for each individual enrolled in SHOP dependent coverage. The average premium for the small group market in Employer's rating area is $5,000 for employee-only coverage and $4,000 for each individual enrolled in SHOP dependent coverage. Employer's premium payments for each FTE ($2,000 for employee-only coverage and $1,500 for SHOP dependent coverage) do not exceed 50 percent of the average premium for the small group market in Employer's rating area ($2,500 for employee-only coverage and $2,000 for each individual enrolled in SHOP dependent coverage).

(ii) *Conclusion.* The amount of premiums paid by Employer for purposes of computing the credit equals $19,500 ((6 x $2,000) plus (5 x $1,500)).

Example 2. Premium payments exceeding average premium for small group market. (i) *Facts.* Same facts as *Example* 1, except that the premiums are $6,000 for employee-only coverage and $5,000 for each dependent enrolled in coverage. Employer's premium payments for each employee ($3,000 for employee-only coverage and $2,500 for SHOP dependent coverage) exceed 50% of the average premium for the small group market in Employer's rating area ($2,500 for self-only coverage and $2,000 for family coverage).

(ii) *Conclusion.* The amount of premiums paid by Employer for purposes of computing the credit equals $25,000 ((6 x $2,500) plus (5 x $2,000)).

(c) *Credit phaseout.*—(1) *In general.*—The tax credit is subject to a reduction (but not reduced below zero) if the employer's FTEs exceed 10 or average annual FTE wages exceed $25,000. If the number of FTEs exceeds 10, the reduction is determined by multiplying the otherwise applicable credit amount by a fraction, the numerator of which is the number of FTEs in excess of 10 and the denominator of which is 15. If average annual FTE wages exceed $25,000, the reduction is determined by multiplying the otherwise applicable credit amount by a fraction, the numerator of which is the amount by which average annual FTE wages exceed $25,000 and the denominator of which is $25,000. In both cases, the result of the calculation is subtracted from the otherwise applicable credit to determine the credit to which the employer is entitled. For an employer with both more than 10 FTEs and average annual FTE wages exceeding $25,000, the total reduction is the sum of the two reductions.

(2) *$25,000 dollar amount adjusted for inflation.*—For taxable years beginning in a calendar year after 2013, each reference to "$25,000" in paragraph (c)(1) of this section is replaced with a dollar amount equal to $25,000 multiplied by the cost-of-living adjustment under section 1(f)(3) for the calendar year, determined by substituting "calendar year 2012" for "calendar year 1992" in section 1(f)(3)(B).

(3) *Examples.*—The following examples illustrate the provisions of paragraph (c) this section. For purposes of these examples, no employer is a tax-exempt organization and no other adjustments or limitations on the credit apply other than those adjustments and limitations explicitly set forth in the example.

Example 1. Calculating the maximum credit for an eligible small employer without an applicable credit phaseout. (i) *Facts.* An eligible small employer (Employer) has 9 FTEs with average annual wages of $23,000. Employer pays $72,000 in health insurance premiums for those employees (which does not exceed the total average premium for the small group market in the rating area), and otherwise meets the requirements for the credit.

(ii) *Conclusion.* Employer's credit equals $36,000 (50% x $72,000).

Example 2. Calculating the credit phaseout if the number of FTEs exceeds 10 or average annual wages exceed $25,000, as adjusted for infla-

tion. (i) *Facts.* An eligible small employer (Employer) has 12 FTEs and average annual FTE wages of $30,000 in a year when the amount in paragraph (c)(1) of this section, as adjusted for inflation, is $25,000. Employer pays $96,000 in health insurance premiums for its employees (which does not exceed the average premium for the small group market in the rating area) and otherwise meets the requirements for the credit.

(ii) *Conclusion.* The initial amount of the credit is determined before any reduction (50% x $96,000) = $48,000. The credit reduction for FTEs in excess of 10 is $6,400 ($48,000 x 2/15). The credit reduction for average annual FTE wages in excess of $25,000 is $9,600 ($48,000 x $5,000/$25,000), resulting in a total credit reduction of $16,000 ($6,400 + $9,600). Employer's total tax credit equals $32,000 ($48,000 - $16,000).

(d) *State credits and subsidies for health insurance.*—(1) *Payments to employer.*—If the employer is entitled to a State tax credit or a premium subsidy that is paid directly to the employer, the premium payment made by the employer is not reduced by the credit or subsidy for purposes of determining whether the employer has satisfied the requirement to pay an amount equal to a uniform percentage (not less than 50 percent) of the premium cost. Also, except as described in paragraph (d)(3) of this section, the maximum amount of the credit is not reduced by reason of a State tax credit or subsidy or by reason of payments by a State directly to an employer.

(2) *Payments to issuer.*—If a State makes payments directly to an insurance company (or another entity licensed under State law to engage in the business of insurance) to pay a portion of the premium for coverage of an employee enrolled for coverage through a SHOP Exchange, the State is treated as making these payments on behalf of the employer for purposes of determining whether the employer has satisfied the requirement to pay an amount equal to a uniform percentage (not less than 50 percent) of the premium cost of coverage. Also, except as described below in paragraph (d)(3) of this section, these premium payments by the State are treated as an employer contribution under this section for purposes of calculating the credit.

(3) *Credits may not exceed net premium payment.*—Regardless of the application of paragraphs (d)(1) and (2) of this section, in no event may the amount of the credit exceed the amount of the employer's net premium payments as defined in § 1.45R-1(a)(11).

(4) *Examples.*—The following examples illustrate the provisions of paragraphs (d)(1) through (3) of this section. For purposes of these examples, each employer is an eligible small employer that is not a tax-exempt organization and the eligible small employer's taxable year and plan year begin during or after 2014. No other adjustments or limitations on the credit apply other than those adjustments and limitations explicitly set forth in the example.

Example 1. State premium subsidy paid directly to employer. (i) *Facts.* The State in which an eligible small employer (Employer) operates provides a health insurance premium subsidy of up to 40% of the health insurance premiums for each eligible employee. The State pays the subsidy directly to Employer. Employer has one employee, Employee D. Employee D's health insurance premiums are $100 per month and are paid as follows: $80 by Employer and $20 by Employee D through salary reductions to a cafeteria plan. The State pays Employer $40 per month as a subsidy for Employer's payment of insurance premiums on behalf of Employee D. Employer is otherwise an eligible small employer that meets the requirements for the credit.

(ii) *Conclusion.* For purposes of calculating the credit, the amount of premiums paid by the employer is $80 per month (the premium payment by the Employer without regard to the subsidy from the State). The maximum credit is $40 ($80 x 50%).

Example 2. State premium subsidy paid directly to insurance company. (i) *Facts.* The State in which Employer operates provides a health insurance premium subsidy of up to 30% for each eligible employee. Employer has one employee, Employee E. Employee E is enrolled in employee-only coverage through a qualified health plan (QHP) offered by Employer through a SHOP Exchange. Employee E's health insurance premiums are $100 per month and are paid as follows: $50 by Employer; $30 by the State and $20 by the employee. The State pays the $30 per month directly to the insurance company and the insurance company bills Employer for the employer and employee's share, which equal $70 per month. Employer is otherwise an eligible small employer that meets the requirements for the credit.

(ii) *Conclusion.* For purposes of calculating the amount of the credit, the amount of premiums paid by Employer is $80 per month (the sum of Employer's payment and the State's payment). The maximum credit is $40 ($80 x 50%).

Example 3. Credit limited by employer's net premium payment. (i) *Facts.* The State in which Employer operates provides a health insurance premium subsidy of up to 50% for each eligible employee.

Employer has one employee, Employee F. Employee F is enrolled in employee-only coverage under the QHP offered to Employee F by Employer through a SHOP Exchange. Employee F's health insurance premiums are $100 per month and are paid as follows: $20 by Employer; $50 by the State and $30 by Employee F. The State pays the $50 per month directly to the insurance company and the insurance company bills Employer for the employer's and employee's shares, which total $50 per month. The amount of premiums paid by Employer (the sum of Employer's payment and the State's payment) is $70 per month, which is more than 50% of the $100 monthly premium payment. The amount of the premium for calculating the credit is also $70 per month.

(ii) *Conclusion.* The maximum credit without adjustments or limitations is $35 ($70 x 50%). Employer's net premium payment is $20 (the amount actually paid by Employer excluding the State subsidy). Because the credit may not exceed Employer's net premium payment, the credit is $20 (the lesser of $35 or $20).

(e) *Payroll tax limitation for tax-exempt eligible small employers.*—(1) *In general.*—For a tax-exempt eligible employer, the amount of the credit claimed cannot exceed the total amount of payroll taxes (as defined in § 1.45R-1(a)(13)) of the employer during the calendar year in which the taxable year begins.

(2) *Example.*—The following example illustrates the provisions of paragraph (e)(1) of this section. For purposes of this example, the eligible small employer's taxable year and plan year begin during or after 2014. No other adjustments or limitations on the credit apply other than those adjustments and limitations explicitly set forth in the example.

Example. Calculating the maximum credit for a tax-exempt eligible small employer. (i) *Facts.* Employer is a tax-exempt eligible small employer that has 10 FTEs with average annual wages of $21,000. Employer pays $80,000 in health insurance premiums for its employees (which does not exceed the average premium for the small group market in the rating area) and otherwise meets the requirements for the credit. The total amount of Employer's payroll taxes equals $30,000.

(ii) *Conclusion.* The initial amount of the credit is determined before any reduction: (35% x $80,000) = $28,000, and Employer's payroll taxes are $30,000. The total tax credit equals $28,000 (the lesser of $28,000 and $30,000).

(f) *Two-consecutive-taxable-year credit period limitation.*—The credit is available to an eligible small employer, including a tax-exempt eligible small employer, only during that employer's credit period. For a transition rule for 2014, see paragraph (i) of this section. To prevent the avoidance of the two-year limit on the credit period through the use of successor entities, a successor entity and a predecessor entity are treated as the same employer. For this purpose, the rules for identifying successor entities under § 31.3121(a)(1)-1(b) apply. Accordingly, for example, if an eligible small employer claims the credit for the 2014 and 2015 taxable years, that eligible small employer's credit period will have expired so that any successor employer to that eligible small employer will not be able to claim the credit for any subsequent taxable years.

(g) *Premium payments by the employer for a taxable year.*—(1) *In general.*—Only premiums paid by an eligible small employer or tax-exempt eligible small employer on behalf of each employee enrolled in a QHP or payments paid to the issuer in accordance with paragraph (d)(2) of this section are counted in calculating the credit. If an eligible small employer pays only a portion of the premiums for the coverage provided to employees (with employees paying the rest), only the portion paid by the employer is taken into account. Premiums paid on behalf of seasonal workers may be counted in determining the amount of the credit (even though seasonal worker wages and hours of service are not included in the FTE calculation and average annual FTE wage calculation unless the seasonal worker works for the employer on more than 120 days during the taxable year). Subject to the average premium limitation, premiums paid on behalf of an employee with respect to any individuals who are or may become eligible for coverage under the terms of the plan because of a relationship to the employee (including through family coverage or SHOP dependent coverage) may also be taken into account in determining the amount of the credit. (However, premiums paid for SHOP dependent coverage are not taken into account in determining whether the uniform percentage requirement is met, see § 1.45R-4(b)(5).)

(2) *Excluded amounts.*—(i) *Salary reduction amounts.*—Any premium paid pursuant to a salary reduction arrangement under a section 125 cafeteria plan is not treated as paid by the employer for purposes of section 45R and these regulations. For this purpose, premiums paid with employer-provided flex credits that employees may elect to receive as cash or other taxable benefits are treated as

paid pursuant to a salary reduction arrangement under a section 125 cafeteria plan.

(ii) *HSAs, HRAs, and FSAs.*—Employer contributions to, or amounts made available under, health savings accounts, reimbursement arrangements, and health flexible spending arrangements are not taken into account in determining the premium payments by the employer for a taxable year.

(h) *Rules applicable to trusts, estates, regulated investment companies, real estate investment trusts and cooperative organizations.*—Rules similar to the rules of section 52(d) and (e) and the regulations thereunder apply in calculating and apportioning the credit with respect to a trust, estate, a regulated investment company or real estate investment trusts or cooperative organization.

(i) *Transition rule for 2014.*—(1) *In general.*—This paragraph (i) applies if as of August 26, 2013, an eligible small employer offers coverage for a health plan year that begins on a date other than the first day of its taxable year. In such a case, if the eligible small employer has a health plan year beginning after January 1, 2014 but before January 1, 2015 (2014 health plan year) that begins after the start of its first taxable year beginning on or after January 1, 2014 (2014 taxable year), and the employer offers one or more QHPs to its employees through a SHOP Exchange as of the first day of its 2014 health plan year, then the eligible small employer is treated as offering coverage through a SHOP Exchange for its entire 2014 taxable year for purposes of section 45R if the health care coverage provided from the first day of the 2014 taxable year through the day immediately preceding the first day of the 2014 health plan year would have qualified for a credit under section 45R using the rules applicable to taxable years beginning before January 1, 2014. If the eligible small employer claims the section 45R credit in the 2014 taxable year, the 2014 taxable year begins the first year of the credit period.

(2) *Example.*—The following example illustrates the rule of this paragraph (i) of this section. For purposes of this example, it is assumed that the eligible small employer is not a tax-exempt organization and that no other adjustments or limitations on the credit apply other than those adjustments and limitations explicitly set forth in the example.

Example. (i) *Facts.* An eligible small employer (Employer) has a 2014 taxable year that begins January 1, 2014 and ends on December 31, 2014. As of August 26, 2013, Employer had a 2014 health plan year that begins July 1, 2014 and ends June 30, 2015. Employer offers a QHP through a SHOP Exchange the coverage under which begins July 1, 2014. Employer also provides other coverage from January 1, 2014 through June 30, 2014 that would have qualified for a credit under section 45R based on the rules applicable to taxable years beginning before 2014.

(ii) *Conclusion.* Employer may claim the credit at the 50% rate under section 45R for the entire 2014 taxable year using the rules under this paragraph (i) of this section. Accordingly, in calculating the credit, Employer may count premiums paid for the coverage from January 1, 2014 through June 30, 2014, as well as premiums paid for the coverage from July 1, 2014 through December 31, 2014. If Employer claims the credit for the 2014 taxable year, that taxable year is the first year of the credit period.

(j) *Effective/applicability date.*—This section is applicable for periods after 2013. For transition rules relating to certain plan years beginning in 2014, see paragraph (i) of this section. [Reg. § 1.45R-3.]

☐ [T.D. 9672, 6-26-2014.]

[Reg. § 1.45R-4]

§ 1.45R-4. Uniform percentage of premium paid.—(a) *In general.*—An eligible small employer must pay a uniform percentage (not less than 50 percent) of the premium for each employee enrolled in a qualified health plan (QHP) offered to employees by the employer through a small business health options program (SHOP) Exchange.

(b) *Employers offering one QHP.*—An employer that offers a single QHP through a SHOP Exchange must satisfy the requirements of this paragraph (b).

(1) *Employers offering one QHP, employee-only coverage, composite billing.*—For an eligible small employer offering employee-only coverage and using composite billing, the employer satisfies the requirements of this paragraph if it pays the same amount toward the premium for each employee receiving employee-only coverage under the QHP, and that amount is equal to at least 50 percent of the premium for employee-only coverage.

(2) *Employers offering one QHP, other tiers of coverage, composite billing.*—For an eligible small employer offering one QHP providing

at least one tier of coverage with a higher premium than employee-only coverage and using composite billing, the employer satisfies the requirements of this paragraph (b)(2) if it either—

(i) Pays an amount for each employee enrolled in that more expensive tier of coverage that is the same for all employees and that is no less than the amount that the employer would have contributed toward employee-only coverage for that employee, or

(ii) Meets the requirements of paragraph (b)(1) of this section for each tier of coverage that if offers.

(3) *Employers offering one QHP, employee-only coverage, list billing.*—For an eligible small employer offering one QHP providing only employee-only coverage and using list billing, the employer satisfies the requirements of this paragraph (b)(3) if either—

(i) The employer pays toward the premium an amount equal to a uniform percentage (not less than 50 percent) of the premium charged for each employee, or

(ii) The employer converts the individual premiums for employee-only coverage into an employer-computed composite rate for self-only coverage, and, if an employee contribution is required, each employee who receives coverage under the QHP pays a uniform amount toward the employee-only premium that is no more than 50 percent of the employer-computed composite rate for employee-only coverage.

(4) *Employers offering one QHP, other tiers of coverage, list billing.*—For an eligible small employer offering one QHP providing at least one tier of coverage with a higher premium than employee-only coverage and using list billing, the employer satisfies the requirements of this paragraph (b)(4) if it either—

(i) Pays toward the premium for each employee covered under each tier of coverage an amount equal to or exceeding the amount that the employer would have contributed with respect to that employee for employee-only coverage, calculated either based upon the actual premium that would have been charged by the insurer for that employee for employee-only coverage or based upon the employer-computed composite rate for employee-only coverage, or

(ii) Meets the requirements of paragraph (b)(3) of this section for each tier of coverage that it offers substituting the employer-computed composite rate for each tier of coverage for the employer-computed composite rate for employee-only coverage.

(5) *Employers offering SHOP dependent coverage.*—If SHOP dependent coverage is offered through the SHOP Exchange, the employer does not fail to satisfy the uniform percentage requirement by contributing a different amount toward that SHOP dependent coverage, even if that contribution is zero. For treatment of premiums paid on behalf of an employee's dependents, see § 1.45R-3(g)(1).

(c) *Employers offering more than one QHP.*—If an eligible small employer offers more than one QHP, the employer must satisfy the requirements of this paragraph (c). The employer may satisfy the requirements of this paragraph (c) in either of the following two ways:

(1) *QHP-by-QHP method.*—The employer makes payments toward the premium with respect to each QHP for which the employer is claiming the credit that satisfy the uniform percentage requirement under paragraph (b) of this section on a QHP-by-QHP basis (so that the amounts or percentages of premium paid by the employer for each QHP need not be identical, but the payments with respect to each QHP must satisfy paragraph (b) of this section); or

(2) *Reference QHP method.*—The employer designates a reference QHP and makes employer contributions in accordance with the following requirements—

(i) The employer determines a level of employer contributions for each employee such that, if all eligible employees enrolled in the reference QHP, the contributions would satisfy the uniform percentage requirement under paragraph (b) of this section, and

(ii) The employer allows each employee to apply an amount of employer contribution determined necessary to meet the uniform percentage requirement under paragraph (b) of this section either toward the reference QHP or toward the cost of coverage under any of the other available QHPs.

(d) *Tobacco surcharges and wellness program discounts or rebates.*—(i) *Tobacco surcharges.*—The tobacco surcharge and amounts paid by the employer to cover the surcharge are not included in premiums for purposes of calculating the uniform percentage requirement, nor are payments of the surcharge treated as premium payments for purposes of calculating the credit. The uniform percentage requirement is also applied without regard to employee payment of the tobacco surcharges in cases in which all or part of the employee tobacco surcharges are not paid by the employer.

(ii) *Wellness programs.*—If a plan of an employer provides a wellness program, for purposes of meeting the uniform percentage requirement any additional amount of the employer contribution attributable to an employee's participation in the wellness program over the employer contribution with respect to an employee that does not participate in the wellness program is not taken into account in calculating the uniform percentage requirement, whether the difference is due to a discount for participation or a surcharge for nonparticipation. The employer contribution for employees that do not participate in the wellness program must be at least 50 percent of the premium (including any premium surcharge for nonparticipation). However, for purposes of computing the credit, the employer contributions are taken into account, including those contributions attributable to an employee's participation in a wellness program.

(e) *Special rules regarding employer compliance with applicable State or local law.*—An employer will be treated as satisfying the uniform percentage requirement if the failure to otherwise satisfy the uniform percentage requirement is attributable solely to additional employer contributions made to certain employees to comply with an applicable State or local law.

(f) *Examples.*—The following examples illustrate the provisions of paragraphs (a) through (e) of this section:

Example 1. (i) *Facts.* An eligible small employer (Employer) offers a QHP on a SHOP Exchange, Plan A, which uses composite billing. The premiums for Plan A are $5,000 per year for employee-only coverage, and $10,000 for family coverage. Employees can elect employee-only or family coverage under Plan A. Employer pays $3,000 (60% of the premium) toward employee-only coverage under Plan A and $6,000 (60% of the premium) toward family coverage under Plan A.

(ii) *Conclusion.* Employer's contributions of 60% of the premium for each tier of coverage satisfy the uniform percentage requirement.

Example 2. (i) *Facts.* Same facts as *Example 1*, except that Employer pays $3,000 (60% of the premium) for each employee electing employee-only coverage under Plan A and pays $3,000 (30% of the premium) for each employee electing family coverage under Plan A.

(ii) *Conclusion.* Employer's contributions of 60% of the premium toward employee-only coverage and the same dollar amount toward the premium for family coverage satisfy the uniform percentage requirement, even though the percentage is not the same.

Example 3. (i) *Facts.* Employer offers two QHPs, Plan A and Plan B, both of which use composite billing. The premiums for Plan A are $5,000 per year for employee-only coverage and $10,000 for family coverage. The premiums for Plan B are $7,000 per year for employee-only coverage and $13,000 for family coverage. Employees can elect employee-only or family coverage under either Plan A or Plan B. Employer pays $3,000 (60% of the premium) for each employee electing employee-only coverage under Plan A, $3,000 (30% of the premium) for each employee electing family coverage under Plan A, $3,500 (50% of the premium) for each employee electing employee-only coverage under Plan B, and $3,500 (27% of the premium) for each employee electing family coverage under Plan B.

(ii) *Conclusion.* Employer's contributions of 60% (or $3,000) of the premiums for employee-only coverage and the same dollar amounts toward the premium for family coverage under Plan A, and of 50% (or $3,500) of the premium for employee-only of coverage and the same dollar amount toward the premium for family coverage under Plan B, satisfy the uniform percentage requirement on a QHP-by-QHP basis; therefore the employer's contributions to both plans satisfy the uniform percentage requirement.

Example 4. (i) *Facts.* Same facts as *Example 3*, except that Employer designates Plan A as the reference QHP. Employer pays $2,500 (50% of the premium) for each employee electing employee-only coverage under Plan A and pays $2,500 of the premium for each employee electing family coverage under Plan A or either employee-only or family coverage under Plan B.

(ii) *Conclusion.* Employer's contribution of 50% (or $2,500) toward the premium of each employee enrolled under Plan A or Plan B satisfies the uniform percentage requirement.

Example 5. (i) *Facts.* Employer receives a list billing premium quote with respect to Plan X, a QHP offered by Employer on a SHOP Exchange for health insurance coverage for each of Employer's four employees. For Employee L, age 20, the employee-only premium is $3,000 per year, and the family premium is $8,000. For Employees M, N and O, each age 40, the employee-only premium is $5,000 per year and the family premium is $10,000. The total employee-only premium for the four employees is $18,000 ($3,000 + (3 x 5,000)). Employer calculates an employer-computed composite employee-only rate of $4,500 ($18,000 / 4). Employer offers to make contributions such that each employee would need to pay $2,000 of the premium for employee-only coverage. Under this arrangement, Employer would contribute $1,000 toward employee-only coverage for L and $3,000 toward employee-only coverage for M, N, and O. In the event

an employee elects family coverage, Employer would make the same contribution ($1,000 for L or $3,000 for M, N, or O) toward the family premium.

(ii) *Conclusion.* Employer satisfies the uniform percentage requirement because it offers and makes contributions based on an employer-calculated composite employee-only rate such that, to receive employee-only coverage, each employee must pay a uniform amount which is not more than 50% of the composite rate, and it allows employees to use the same employer contributions toward family coverage.

Example 6. (i) *Facts.* Same facts as *Example 5*, except that Employer calculates an employer-computed composite family rate of $9,500 (($8,000 + 3 x 10,000) / 4) and requires each employee to pay $4,000 of the premium for family coverage.

(ii) *Conclusion.* Employer satisfies the uniform percentage requirement because it offers and makes contributions based on a calculated employee-only and family rate such that, to receive either employee-only or family coverage, each employee must pay a uniform amount which is not more than 50% of the composite rate for coverage of that tier.

Example 7. (i) *Facts.* Same facts as *Example 5*, except that Employer also receives a list billing premium quote from Plan Y with respect to a second QHP offered by Employer on a SHOP Exchange for each of Employer's 4 employees. Plan Y's quote for Employee L, age 20, is $4,000 per year for employee-only coverage or $12,000 per year for family coverage. For Employees M, N and O, each age 40, the premium is $7,000 per year for employee-only coverage or $15,000 per year for family coverage. The total employee-only premium under Plan Y is $25,000 ($4,000 + (3 x 7,000)). The employer-computed composite employee-only rate is $6,250 ($25,000 / 4). Employer designates Plan X as the reference plan. Employer offers to make contributions based on the employer-calculated composite premium for the reference QHP (Plan X) such that each employee has to contribute $2,000 to receive employee-only coverage through Plan X. Under this arrangement, Employer would contribute $1,000 toward employee-only coverage for L and $3,000 toward employee-only coverage for M, N, and O. In the event an employee elects family coverage through Plan X or either employee-only or family coverage through Plan Y, Employer would make the same contributions ($1,000 for L or $3,000 for M, N, or O) toward that coverage.

(ii) *Conclusion.* Employer satisfies the uniform percentage requirement because it offers and makes contributions based on the employer-calculated composite employee-only premium for the Plan X reference QHP such that, in order to receive employee-only coverage, each employee must pay a uniform amount which is not more than 50% of the employee-only composite premium of the reference QHP; it allows employees to use the same employer contributions toward family coverage in the reference QHP or coverage through another QHPs.

Example 8. (i) *Facts.* Employer offers employee-only and SHOP dependent coverage through a QHP to its three employees using list billing. All three employees enroll in the employee-only coverage, and one employee elects to enroll two dependents in SHOP dependent coverage. Employer contributes 100% of the employee-only premium costs, but only contributes 25% of the premium costs toward SHOP dependent coverage.

(ii) *Conclusion.* Employer's contribution of 100% toward the premium costs of employee-only coverage satisfies the uniform percentage requirement, even though Employer is only contributing 25% toward SHOP dependent coverage.

Example 9. (i) *Facts.* Employer has five employees. Employer is located in a State that requires employers to pay 50% of employees' premium costs, but also requires that an employee's contribution not exceed a certain percentage of the employee's monthly gross earnings from that employer. Employer offers to pay 50% of the premium costs for all its employees, and to comply with the State law, Employer contributes more than 50% of the premium costs for two of its employees.

(ii) *Conclusion.* Employer satisfies the uniform percentage requirement because its failure to otherwise satisfy the uniform percentage requirement is attributable solely to compliance with the applicable State or local law.

Example 10. (i) *Facts.* Employer has three employees who all enroll in employee-only coverage. Employer is located in a State that has a tobacco surcharge on the premiums of employees who use tobacco. One of Employer's employees smokes. Employer contributes 50% of the employee-only premium costs, but does not cover any of the tobacco surcharge for the employee who smokes.

(ii) *Conclusion.* Employer's contribution of 50% toward the premium costs of employee-only coverage satisfies the uniform percentage requirement. Tobacco surcharges are not factored into premiums when calculating the uniform percentage requirement.

Example 11. (i) *Facts.* Employer has five employees who all enroll in employee-only coverage. Employer offers a wellness program that reduces the employee share of the premium for employees who participate in the wellness program. Employer contributes 50% of the premium costs of employee-only coverage for employees who do not participate in the wellness program and 55% of the premium costs of employee-only coverage for employees who participate in the wellness program. Three of the five employees participate in the wellness program.

(ii) *Conclusion.* Employer's contribution of 50% toward the premium costs of employee-only coverage for the two employees who do not participate in the wellness program and 55% toward the premium costs of employee-only coverage for three employees who participate in the wellness program satisfies the uniform percentage requirement because the additional 5% contribution due to the employees' participation in the wellness program is not taken into account. However, the additional 5% contributions are taken into account for purposes of calculating the credit.

(g) *Effective/applicability date.*—This section is applicable for periods after 2013. For transition rules relating to certain plan years starting in 2014, see §1.45R-3(i). [Reg. §1.45R-4.]

☐ [*T.D. 9672, 6-26-2014.*]

[Reg. §1.45R-5]

§1.45R-5. Claiming the credit.—(a) *Claiming the credit.*—The credit is a general business credit. It is claimed on an eligible small employer's annual income tax return and offsets an employer's actual tax liability for the year. The credit is claimed by attaching Form 8941, "Credit for Small Employer Health Insurance Premiums," to the eligible small employer's income tax return or, in the case of a tax-exempt eligible small employer, by attaching Form 8941 to the employer's Form 990-T, "Exempt Organization Business Income Tax Return." To claim the credit, a tax-exempt eligible small employer must file a form 990-T with an attached Form 8941, even if a Form 990-T would not otherwise be required to be filed.

(b) *Estimated tax payments and alternative minimum tax (AMT) liability.*—An eligible small employer may reflect the credit in determining estimated tax payments for the year in which the credit applies in accordance with the estimated tax rules as set forth in sections 6654 and 6655 and the applicable regulations. An eligible small employer may also use the credit to offset the employer's alternative minimum tax (AMT) liability for the year, if any, subject to certain limitations based on the amount of the employer's regular tax liability, AMT liability and other allowable credits. See section 38(c)(1), as modified by section 38(c)(4)(B)(vi). However, an eligible small employer, including a tax-exempt eligible small employer, may not reduce its deposits and payments of employment tax (that is, income tax required to be withheld under section 3402, social security and Medicare tax under sections 3101 and 3111, and federal unemployment tax under section 3301) during the year in anticipation of the credit.

(c) *Reduction of section 162 deduction.*—No deduction under section 162 is allowed for the eligible small employer for that portion of the health insurance premiums that is equal to the amount of the credit under §1.45R-2.

(d) *Effective/applicability date.*—This section is applicable for periods after 2013. For rules relating to certain plan years beginning in 2014, see §1.45R-3(i). [Reg. §1.45R-5.]

☐ [*T.D. 9672, 6-26-2014.*]

[Reg. §1.46-1]

§1.46-1. Determination of amount.—(a) *Effective dates.*—(1) *In general.*—This section is effective for taxable years beginning after December 31, 1975. However, transitional rules under paragraph (g) of this section are effective for certain earlier taxable years.

(2) *Acts covered.*—This section reflects changes made by the following Acts of Congress:

Act and Section

Tax Reduction Act of 1975, section 301.
Tax Reform Act of 1976, section 802, 1701, 1703.
Revenue Act of 1978, section 311, 312, 315.
Energy Tax Act of 1978, section 301.
Economic Recovery Tax Act of 1981, section 212.
Technical Corrections Act of 1982, section 102(f).
Tax Reform Act of 1986, section 251.

(3) *Prior regulations.*—For taxable years beginning before January 1, 1976, see 26 CFR §1.46-1 (Rev. as of April 1, 1979). Those regulations do not reflect changes made by Pub. L. 89-384, Pub. L. 89-389, and Pub. L. 91-172.

(b) *General rule.*—The amount of investment credit (credit) allowed by section 38 for the taxable year is the portion of credit available

under section 46(a)(1) that does not exceed the limitation based on tax under section 46(a)(3).

(c) *Credit available.*—The credit available for the taxable year is the sum of—

(1) Unused credit carried over from prior taxable years under section 46(b) (carryovers),

(2) Amount of credit determined under section 46(a)(2) for the taxable year (credit earned), and

(3) Unused credit carried back from succeeding taxable years under section 46(b) (carrybacks).

(d) *Credit earned.*—The credit earned for the taxable year is the sum of the following percentages of qualified investment (as determined under section 46(c) and (d))—

(1) The regular percentage (as determined under section 46),

(2) For energy property, the energy percentage (as determined under section 46), and

(3) For the portion of the basis of a qualified rehabilitated building (as defined in §1.48-12(b)) that is attributable to qualified rehabilitation expenditures (as defined in §1.48-12(c)), the rehabilitation percentage (as determined under section 46(b)(4)).

(e) *Designation of credits.*—The credit available for the taxable year is designated as follows:

(1) The credit attributable to the regular percentage is the "regular credit".

(2) The credit attributable to the ESOP percentage is the "ESOP credit".

(3) The credit attributable to the energy percentage for energy property other than solar or wind is the "nonrefundable energy credit".

(4) The credit attributable to the energy percentage for solar or wind energy property is the "refundable energy credit".

(5) The credit attributable to the rehabilitation percentage for qualified rehabilitation expenditures is the rehabilitation investment credit.

(f) *Special rules for certain energy property.*—Energy property is defined in section 48(l). Under section 46(a)(2)(D), energy property that is section 38 property solely by reason of section 48(l)(1) qualifies only for the energy credit. Other energy property qualifies for both the regular credit (and, if applicable, the ESOP credit) and the energy credit. For limitation on the energy percentage for property financed by industrial development bonds, see section 48(l)(11).

(g) *Transitional rule for regular and ESOP credit.*—(1) *In general.*—Although section 46(a)(2) was amended by section 301(a)(1) of the Energy Tax Act of 1977 to eliminate the transitional rules under section 46(a)(2)(D), those rules still apply in certain instances. Section 46(a)(2)(D) was added by section 301(a) of the Tax Reduction Act of 1975 and amended by section 802(a) of the Tax Reform Act of 1976.

(2) *Regular credit.*—Under section 46(a)(2)(D), the regular credit is 10 percent and applies for the following property: (i) Property to which section 46(d) does not apply, the construction, reconstruction, or erection of which is completed by the taxpayer after January 21, 1975, but only to the extent of basis attributable to construction, reconstruction, or erection after that date.

(ii) Property to which section 46(d) does not apply, acquired by the taxpayer after January 21, 1975.

(iii) Qualified progress expenditures (as defined in section 46(d)) made after January 21, 1975.

(3) *ESOP credit.*—See section 48(m) for transitional rules limiting the period for which the ESOP percentage under section 46(a)(2)(E) applies. For prior statutes, see section 46(a)(2)(B) and (D), as added by section 301 of the Tax Reduction Act of 1975 and amended by section 802 of the Tax Reform Act of 1976.

(4) *Cross reference.*—(i) The principles of §1.48-2(b) and (c) apply in determining the portion of basis attributable to construction, reconstruction, or erection after January 21, 1975, and in determining the time when property is acquired.

(ii) Section 311 of the Revenue Act of 1978 made the 10 percent regular credit permanent.

(5) *Seven percent credit.*—To the extent that, under paragraph (g)(1) of this section, the 10 percent does not apply, the regular credit, in general, is 7 percent. For a special limitation on qualified investment for public utility property (other than energy property), see section 46(c)(3)(A).

(6) *Qualified progress expenditures.*—For progress expenditure property that is constructed, reconstructed, or erected by the taxpayer within the meaning of §1.48-2(b), the ten-percent credit applies in the year the property is placed in service to the portion of the

qualified investment that remains after reduction for qualified progress expenditures under section 46(c)(4), but only to the extent that the remaining qualified investment is attributable to construction, reconstruction, or erection after January 21, 1975. For progress expenditure property that is acquired by the taxpayer (within the meaning of §1.48-2(b)) after January 21, 1975, and placed in service after that date, the ten-percent credit applies in the year the property is placed in service to the entire portion of qualified investment that remains after reduction for qualified progress expenditures.

(h) *Tax liability limitation.*—(1) *In general.*—Section 46(a)(3) provides a tax liability limitation on the amount of credit allowed by section 38 (other than the refundable energy credit) for any taxable year. See section 46(a)(10)(C)(i). Tax liability is defined in paragraph (j) of this section.

The excess of available credit over the applicable tax liability limitation for the year is an unused credit which may be carried forward or carried back under section 46(b).

(2) *Regular and ESOP tax liability limitation.*—In general, the tax liability limitation for the regular and ESOP credits is the portion of tax liability that does not exceed $25,000 plus a percentage of the excess, as determined under section 46(a)(3)(B).

(3) *Nonrefundable energy credit tax liability limitation.*—(i) For nonrefundable energy credit carrybacks to a taxable year ending before October 1, 1978, the tax liability limitation is the portion of tax liability that does not exceed $25,000 plus a percentage of the excess, as determined under section 46(a)(3)(B).

(ii) For a taxable year ending after September 30, 1978, the tax liability limitation for available nonrefundable energy credit is 100 percent of the year's tax liability.

(4) *Alternative limitations.*—Alternative limitations apply for certain utilities, railroads, and airlines in determining the regular tax liability limitation and, for nonrefundable energy credit carrybacks to taxable years ending before October 1, 1978, the nonrefundable energy credit tax liability limitation. These alternative limitations do not apply in determining the energy tax liability limitation for a taxable year ending after October 1, 1978. The provisions listed below set forth the alternative limitations:

Code section, type, and years applicable

46(a)(6),[1] Utilities, Taxable years ending in 1975-1978.

46(a)(7),[2] Utilities, Taxable year ending in 1979.

46(a)(8), Railroads and Airlines, Taxable year ending in 1979 or 1980.

46(a)(8),[3] Railroads, Taxable years ending in 1977 or 1978.

46(a)(9),[3] Airlines, Taxable years ending in 1977 or 1978.

(i) [Reserved]

(j) *Tax liability.*—(1) *In general.*—"Tax liability" for purposes of the regular and ESOP credit and carrybacks of nonrefundable energy credit to a taxable year ending before October 1, 1978, means the liability for tax as defined in section 46(a)(4). For ordering of regular, ESOP, and nonrefundable energy credits, see paragraph (m) of this section. In addition to taxes excluded under section 46(a)(4), tax liability does not include tax resulting from recapture of credit under section 47 and the alternative minimum tax imposed by section 55. See sections 47(c) and 55(c)(1).

(2) *Certain nonrefundable energy credit.*—For a taxable year ending after September 30, 1978, "tax liability" for purposes of the nonrefundable energy credit is liability for tax, as defined in section 46(a)(4) and paragraph (j)(1) of this section, reduced by the regular and ESOP credit allowed for the taxable year. Thus, carrybacks of regular or ESOP credit to a taxable year may displace nonrefundable energy carryovers or credit earned taken into account in that year. However, carrybacks of regular, ESOP, or nonrefundable energy credit do not affect refundable energy credit which is treated as an overpayment of tax under section 6401(b). See paragraph (k) of this section.

(k) *Special rule for refundable energy credit.*—The amount of the refundable energy credit is determined under the rules of section 46 (other than section 46(a)(3)). However, to permit the refund, the refundable energy credit for purposes of the Internal Revenue Code (other than section 38, part IVB, and chapter 63 of the Code) is treated as allowed by section 39 and not by section 38. The refundable credit is not applied against tax liability for purposes of determining the tax liability limitation for other investment credits. Rather, it is treated as an overpayment of tax under section 6401(b).

(l) *FIFO rule.*—If the credit available for a taxable year is not allowed in full because of the tax liability limitation, special rules determine the order in which credits are applied. Under the first-in-first-out rule of section 46(a)(1) (FIFO), carryovers are applied against the tax liability limitation first. To the extent the tax liability limitation exceeds carryovers, credit earned, and carrybacks are then applied.

(m) *Special ordering rule.*—(1) *In general.*—Under section 46(a)(10)(A), the FIFO rule applies separately—

(i) First, with respect to regular and ESOP credits, and

(ii) Second, with respect to nonrefundable energy credit.

(2) *Regular and ESOP credit.*—Under §1.46-8(c)(9)(ii), regular and ESOP credits available are applied in the following order:

(i) Regular carryovers;

(ii) ESOP carryovers;

(iii) Regular credit earned;

(iv) ESOP credit earned;

(v) Regular carrybacks; and

(vi) ESOP carrybacks.

(3) *Example.*—For an example of the order of application of regular and ESOP credits, see §1.46-8(c)(9)(iii).

(n) *Examples.*—The following examples illustrate paragraphs (a) through (m) of this section.

Example (1). (a) Corporation M's regular credit available for its taxable year ending December 31, 1979 is as follows:

Regular carryovers	$5,000
Regular credit earned	10,000
Regular carrybacks	15,000
Credit available	$30,000

(b) M's "tax liability" for 1979 is $30,000. M's tax liability limitation for 1979 for the regular credit is $28,000, consisting of $25,000 plus 60 percent of the $5,000 of the "tax liability" in excess of $25,000.

(c) The regular carryovers and credit earned are allowed in full. However, only $13,000 of the regular carryback is allowed for 1979. The remaining $2,000 must be carried to the next year to which it may be carried under section 46(b).

Example (2). (a) For its taxable year ending December 31, 1980, corporation N has $30,000 regular credit earned and $9,000 nonrefundable energy credit earned. N has no carryovers to 1980 and no "tax liability" for pre-1980 years.

(b) N's "tax liability" for 1980 for the regular credit is $35,000. N's tax liability limitation for 1980 for the regular credit is $32,000, consisting of $25,000 plus 70 percent of the $10,000 of "tax liability" in excess of $25,000.

(c) The entire regular credit is allowed in 1980.

(d) N's "tax liability" for 1980 for the nonrefundable energy credit is $5,000, consisting of $35,000 less $30,000 regular credit allowed for 1980. N's *tax liability limitation* for 1980 for the nonrefundable energy credit is 100 percent of $5,000.

(e) $5,000 of the nonrefundable energy credit is allowed for 1980. The remaining $4,000 energy credit is an unused nonrefundable energy credit which must be carried to the next year to which it may be carried under section 46(b).

Example (3). (a) Assume the same facts as in example (2) except that in its taxable year ended December 31, 1981, N earns a regular credit of which it may carry back $2,000 to 1980.

(b) The $30,000 regular credit earned and $2,000 of the regular carryback is allowed for 1980. N's "tax liability" for 1980 for the nonrefundable energy credit is reduced to $3,000, consisting of $35,000 less $32,000 regular credit allowed for 1980. The nonrefundable energy credit allowed for 1980 is reduced to $3,000. The remaining $6,000 is an unused nonrefundable energy credit which must be carried to the next year to which it may be carried under section 46(b).

Example (4). (a) For its taxable year ending December 31, 1980, corporation P's regular credit earned is $20,000. P also has a $9,000 refundable energy credit for 1980. There are no carryovers or carrybacks to 1980.

(b) P's "tax liability" for 1980 for the regular credit is $25,000 which is also the tax liability limitation for the regular credit.

---

[1] Section 46(a)(6) was added by section 301(b)(2) of the Tax Reduction Act of 1975 and redesignated as section 46(a)(7) by section 302(a)(1) of the Tax Reform Act of 1976.

[2] Section 46(a)(7) was amended by section 312(b)(1) of the Revenue Act of 1978.

[3] These provisions were repealed by section 312(b)(2) of the Revenue Act of 1978.

(c) The entire $20,000 regular credit is allowed for 1980. The entire $9,000 refundable energy credit is treated as an overpayment of tax under section 6401(b), even though "tax liability" remains.

Example (5). Assume the same facts as in example (4), except that in the following year P earns a regular credit, $5,000 of which it may carry back to 1980. The $5,000 carryback is allowed in full in 1980.

Example (6). (i) Corporation X, a calendar year taxpayer, constructs a ship on which it begins construction on January 1, 1973, and which, when placed in service on December 31, 1980, has a basis of $450,000. Of that amount $100,000 is attributable to construction before January 22, 1975. X makes an election under section 46(d) (qualified progress expenditures) for taxable years after 1975.

(ii) For 1976, 1977, 1978, and 1979, qualified progress expenditures total $200,000. The ten-percent credit applies to those expenditures.

(iii) For 1980, qualified investment for the ship is $450,000. Under section 46(c)(4), X must reduce this amount by $200,000, the amount of qualified progress expenditures taken into account. The ten-percent credit applies to the portion of the remaining qualified investment attributable to construction after January 21, 1975 ($150,000). The seven-percent credit applies to the portion of qualified investment attributable to construction before January 22, 1975 ($100,000).

Example (7). (i) Corporation Y agrees to build a ship for Corporation X, which uses the calendar year. In 1973, Y begins construction of the ship which X acquires and places in service on December 31, 1980. X makes an election under section 46(d) for taxable years after 1974. The contract price is $400,000.

(ii) For 1975, 1976, 1977, 1978, and 1979, qualified progress expenditures total $250,000. The ten-percent credit applies to those expenditures.

(iii) For 1980, qualified investment for the ship is $400,000, which is the contract price. X must reduce qualified investment by $250,000, the amount of qualified progress expenditures. The ten-percent credit applies to the $150,000 of qualified investment that remains after reduction for qualified progress expenditures.

(o) *Married individuals.*—If a separate return is filed by a husband or wife, the tax liability limitation is computed by substituting a $12,500 amount for the $25,000 amount that applies under section 46(a)(3). However, this reduction of the $25,000 amount to $12,500 applies only if the taxpayer's spouse is entitled to a credit under section 38 for the taxable year of such spouse which ends with, or within, the taxpayer's taxable year. The taxpayer's spouse is entitled to a credit under section 38 either because of investment made in qualified property for such taxable year of the spouse (whether directly made by such spouse or whether apportioned to such spouse, for example, from an electing small business corporation, as defined in section 1371(b)), or because of an investment credit carryback or carryover to such taxable year. The determination of whether an individual is married shall be made under the principles of section 143 and the regulations thereunder.

(p) *Apportionment of $25,000 amount among component members of a controlled group.*—(1) *In general.*—In determining the tax liability limitation under section 46(a)(3) for corporations that are component members of a controlled group on a December 31, only one $25,000 amount is available to those component members for their taxable years that include that December 31. See subparagraph (2) of this paragraph for apportionment of such amount among such component members. See subparagraph (3) of this paragraph for definition of "component member".

(2) *Manner of apportionment.*—(i) In the case of corporations which are component members of a controlled group on a particular December 31, the $25,000 amount may be apportioned among such members for their taxable years that include such December 31 in any manner the component members may select, provided that each such member less than 100 percent of whose stock is owned, in the aggregate, by the other component members of the group on such December 31 consents to an apportionment plan. The consent of a component member to an apportionment plan with respect to a particular December 31 shall be made by means of a statement signed by a person duly authorized to act on behalf of the consenting member, stating that such member consents to the apportionment plan with respect to such December 31. The statement shall set forth *the name, address, employer identification number, and taxable year* of each component member of the group on such December 31, the amount apportioned to each such member under the plan, and the location of the Service Center where the statement is to be filed. The consent of more than one component member may be incorporated in a single statement. The statement shall be timely filed with the Service Center where the component member having the taxable year first ending on or after such December 31 files its return for such taxable year and shall be irrevocable after such filing. If two or more component members have the same such taxable year, a statement of consent may be filed by any one of such members. Such statement

shall be considered as timely filed if filed on or before the due date (including any extensions of time) of such member's income tax return which includes such December 31. Each component member of the group on such December 31 shall keep as a part of its records a copy of the statement containing all the required consents.

(ii) An apportionment plan adopted by a controlled group with respect to a particular December 31 shall be valid only for the taxable year of each member of the group which includes such December 31. Thus, a controlled group must file a separate consent to an apportionment plan with respect to each taxable year which includes a December 31 as to which an apportionment plan is desired.

(iii) If the apportionment plan is not timely filed, the $25,000 amount specified in section 46(a)(3) shall be reduced for each component member of the controlled group, for its taxable year which includes a December 31, to an amount equal to $25,000 divided by the number of component members of such group on such December 31.

(iv) If a component member of the controlled group makes its income tax return on the basis of a 52-53 week taxable year, the principles of section 441(f)(2)(A)(ii) and § 1.441-2 apply in determining the last day of such taxable year.

(3) *Definitions of controlled group of corporations and component member of controlled group.*—For the purpose of this paragraph, the terms "controlled group of corporations" and "component member" of a controlled group of corporations shall have the same meaning assigned to those terms in section 1563(a) and (b). For purposes of applying § 1.1563-1(b)(2)(ii)(c), an electing small business corporation shall be treated as an excluded member whether or not it is subject to the tax imposed by section 1378.

(4) *Members of a controlled group filing a consolidated return.*—If some component members of a controlled group join in filing a consolidated return pursuant to § 1.1502-3(a)(3), and other component members do not join, then, unless a consent is timely filed apportioning the $25,000 amount among the group filing the consolidated return and the other component members of the controlled group, each component member of the controlled group (including each component member which joins in filing the consolidated return) shall be treated as a separate corporation for purposes of equally apportioning the $25,000 amount under subparagraph (2)(iii) of this paragraph. In that case, the tax liability limitation for the group filing the consolidated return is computed by substituting for the $25,000 amount under section 46(a)(3) the total amount apportioned to each component member that joins in filing the consolidated return. If the affiliated group filing the consolidated return and the other component members of the controlled group adopt an apportionment plan, the affiliated group shall be treated as a single member for the purpose of applying subparagraph (2)(i) of this paragraph. Thus, for example, only one consent executed by the common parent to the apportionment plan is required for the group filing the consolidated return. If any component member of the controlled group which joins in the filing of the consolidated return is an organization to which section 593 applies or a cooperative organization described in section 1381(a), see paragraph (a)(3)(ii) of § 1.1502-3.

(5) *Examples.*—The provisions of this paragraph may be illustrated by the following examples:

Example (1). At all times during 1976 Smith, an individual, owns all the stock of corporations X, Y, and Z. Corporation X files an income tax return on a calendar year basis. Corporation Y files an income tax return on the basis of a fiscal year ending June 30. Corporation Z files an income tax return on the basis of a fiscal year ending September 30. On December 31, 1976, X, Y and Z are component members of the same controlled group. X, Y, and Z all consent to an apportionment plan in which the $25,000 amount is apportioned entirely to Y for its taxable year ending June 30, 1977 (Y's taxable year which includes December 31, 1976). Such consent is timely filed. For purposes of computing the credit under section 38, Y's tax liability limitation for its taxable year ending June 30, 1977, is so much of Y's tax liability as does not exceed $25,000, plus 50 percent of Y's tax liability in excess of $25,000. X's and Z's limitations for their taxable years ending December 31, 1976, and September 30, 1977, respectively, are equal to 50 percent of X's tax liability and 50 percent of Z's tax liability. On the other hand, if an apportionment plan is not timely filed, X's limitation would be so much of X's tax liability as does not exceed $8,333.33, plus 50 percent of X's liability in excess of $8,333.33, and Y's and Z's limitations would be computed similarly.

Example (2). At all times during 1976, Jones, an individual, owns all the outstanding stock of corporations P, Q, and R. Corporations Q and R both file returns for taxable years ending December 31, 1970. P files a consolidated return as a common parent for its fiscal year ending June 30, 1977, with its two wholly-owned subsidiaries N and

O. On December 31, 1976, N, O, P, Q, and R are component members of the same controlled group. No consent to an apportionment plan is filed. Therefore, each member is apportioned $5,000 of the $25,000 amount ($25,000 divided equally among the five members). The tax liability limitation for the group filing the consolidated return (P, N, and O) for the year ending June 30, 1977 (the consolidated taxable year within which December 31, 1976, falls) is computed by using $15,000 instead of the $25,000 amount. The $15,000 is arrived at by adding together the $5,000 amounts apportioned to P, N, and O.

(q) *Rehabilitation percentage.*—(1) *General rule.*—(i) *In general.*—Due to amendments made by the Tax Reform Act of 1986, different rules apply depending on when the property attributable to the qualified rehabilitated expenditures (as defined in §1.48-12(c)) is placed in service. Paragraph (q)(1)(ii) of this section contains the general rule relating to property placed in service after December 31, 1986. Paragraph (q)(1)(iii) of this section contains rules relating to property placed in service before January 1, 1987. Paragraph (q)(1)(iv) of this section contains rules relating to property placed in service after December 31, 1986, that qualifies for a transition rule.

(ii) *Property placed in service after December 31, 1986.*—Except as otherwise provided in paragraph (q)(1)(iv) of this section, in the case of section 38 property described in section 48(a)(1)(E) placed in service after December 31, 1986, the term "rehabilitation percentage" means—

(A) 10 percent in the case of qualified rehabilitation expenditures with respect to a qualified rehabilitated building other than a certified historic structure, and

(B) 20 percent in the case of qualified rehabilitation expenditures with respect to a certified historic structure.

(iii) *Property placed in service before January 1, 1987.*—For qualified rehabilitation expenditures (as defined in §1.48-12(c)) with respect to property placed in service before January 1, 1987, section 46(b)(4)(A) as in effect prior to the enactment of the Tax Reform Act of 1986 provided for a three-tier rehabilitation percentage. The applicable rehabilitation percentage for such expenditures depends on whether the qualified rehabilitated building is a "30-year building," a "40-year building," or a certified historic structure (as defined in section 48(g)(3) and §1.48-12(d)(1)). The rehabilitation percentage for such qualified rehabilitation expenditures incurred with respect to a qualified rehabilitated building is 15 percent to the extent that the building is a 30-year building (*i.e.*, at least 30 years, but less than 40 years, has elapsed between the date the physical work on the rehabilitation began and the date the building was first placed in service), 20 percent to the extent that the building is a 40-year building (*i.e.*, at least 40 years has so elapsed), and 25 percent for certified historic structures, regardless of age. See paragraph (q)(2)(ii) of this section for rules concerning buildings to which additions have been added.

(iv) *Property placed in service after December 31, 1986, that qualifies under the transition rules.*—In the case of section 38 property described in section 48(a)(1)(E) placed in service after December 31, 1986, and to which the amendments made by section 251 of the Tax Reform Act of 1986 do not apply because the transition rules in section 251(d) of that Act and §1.48-12(a)(2)(iv)(B) or (C) apply, the rehabilitation percentage for a "30-year building" (within the meaning of paragraph (q)(1)(iii) of this section) shall be 10 percent, the rehabilitation percentage for a "40-year building" (within the meaning of paragraph (q)(1)(iii) of this section) shall be 13 percent, and the rehabilitation percentage for a certified historic structure shall be 25 percent.

(2) *Special rules.*—(i) *Moved buildings.*—With respect to paragraph (q)(1)(ii) of this section, §1.48-12(b)(5) provides that a building (other than a certified historic structure) is not a qualified rehabilitated building unless it has been at the location where it is being rehabilitated since January 1, 1936. In addition, for purposes of paragraph (q)(1)(iii) and (iv) of this section, a building is not a "30-year building" unless it has been at the location where it is being rehabilitated for the thirty-year period immediately preceding the beginning of the rehabilitation process, and is not a "40-year building" unless it has been at the location where it is being rehabilitated for the forty-year period immediately preceding the beginning of the rehabilitation process.

(ii) *Building to which additions have been added.*—(A) *Property placed in service after December 31, 1986.*—For purposes of paragraph (q)(1)(ii) of this section, if part of a building meets the definition of a qualified rehabilitated building, and part of the building does not meet the definition of a qualified rehabilitated building because such part is an addition that was placed in service after December 31, 1935, the qualified rehabilitation expenditures made to the building must be allocated to the pre-1936 portion of the building and the post-1935 portion of the building using the principles in §1.48-12(c)(10)(ii). Qualified rehabilitation expenditures attributable to the post-1935 addition shall not qualify for the 10 percent rehabilitation percentage.

(B) *Property placed in service before January 1, 1987, and property qualifying for a transitional rule.*—For purposes of paragraph (q)(1)(iii) and (iv) of this section, if part of a building meets the definition of a "40-year building" and part of the building is an addition that was placed in service less than forty years before physical work on the rehabilitation began but more than thirty years before such date, then the qualified rehabilitation expenditures made to the building shall be allocated between the forty year old portion of the building and the thirty year old portion of the building, and a 20 percent rehabilitation percentage shall be applied to the forty year old portion of the building and a 15 percent rehabilitation percentage shall be applied to the thirty year old portion. This allocation shall be made using the principles in §1.48-12(c)(10)(ii). If an allocation cannot be made between the expenditures to the forty year old portion of the building and the thirty year old portion of the building, then the building will be considered to be a 30-year building. Furthermore, for purposes of this paragraph (q), a building (other than a certified historic structure) is not a qualified rehabilitated building to the extent of that portion of the building that is less than 30 years old. If rehabilitation expenditures are incurred with respect to an addition to a qualified rehabilitated building, but the addition is not considered to be part of the qualified rehabilitated building because the addition does not meet the age requirement in section 48(g)(1)(B) (as in effect prior to its amendment by the Tax Reform Act of 1986) and §1.48-12(b)(4)(i)(B), then no rehabilitation percentage will be applied to the expenditures attributable to the rehabilitation of the addition. Thus, for purposes of paragraph (q)(1)(iii) and (iv) of this section, it may be necessary to allocate rehabilitation expenditures incurred with respect to a building between the original portion of the building and the addition.

(iii) *Mixed-use buildings.*—If qualified rehabilitation expenditures are incurred for property that is excluded from section 38 property described in section 48(a)(1)(E) (because, for example, they are made with respect to a portion of the building used for lodging within the meaning of section 48(a)(3) and §1.48-1(h)), an allocation of the expenditures must be made between the expenditures that result in an addition to basis that is section 38 property and the expenditures that result in an addition to basis that is excluded from the definition of section 38 property since the rehabilitation percentage is applicable only to section 38 property. These allocations should be made using the principles contained in §1.48-12(c)(10)(ii).

(3) *Regular and energy percentages not to apply.*—The regular percentage and the energy percentage shall not apply to that portion of the basis of any building that is attributable to qualified rehabilitation expenditures (as defined in §1.48-12(c)).

(4) *Effective date.*—The rehabilitation percentage is applicable only to qualified rehabilitation expenditures (as defined in §1.48-12(c)). For rules relating to applicability of the regular percentage to qualified rehabilitation expenditures (as defined in §1.48-11(c)), see §1.48-11. [Reg. §1.46-1.]

☐ [*T.D. 6731, 5-7-64. Amended by T.D. 6931, 10-9-67; T.D. 6958, 6-20-68; T.D. 7181, 4-24-72; T.D. 7203, 8-24-72; T.D. 7564, 9-11-78; T.D. 7636, 8-9-79; T.D. 7751, 12-30-80; T.D. 8183, 3-1-88; T.D. 8233, 10-7-88 and T.D. 8996, 5-16-2002.*]

[Reg. §1.46-2]

§1.46-2. Carryback and carryover of unused credit.—(a) *Effective date.*—This section is effective for taxable years beginning after December 31, 1975. For taxable years beginning before January 1, 1976, see 26 CFR 1.46-2 (Rev. as of April 1, 1979).

(b) *In general.*—Under section 46(b)(1), unused credit may be carried back and carried over. Carrybacks and carryovers of unused credit are taken into account in determining the amount of credit available and the credit allowed for the taxable years to which they may be carried. In general, the application of the rules of this section to regular and ESOP credits are separate from their application to nonrefundable energy credits. For example, the limitations on carrybacks and carryovers of unused nonrefundable energy credit under section 46(b)(2) and (3), respectively, differ in amount from the limitations on the regular and ESOP credits because the tax liability limitations for those credits differ. See §1.46-1(h). For a further example, see the special ordering rule in §1.46-1(m). Section 46(b) does not apply to the refundable energy credit.

(c) *Unused credit.*—If carryovers and credit earned (as defined in §1.46-1(c)(1)) exceed the applicable tax liability limitation, the excess attributable to credit earned is an unused credit. The taxable year in which an unused credit arises is referred to as the "unused credit year".

(d) *Taxable years to which unused credit may be carried.*—An unused credit is a carryback to each of the 3 taxable years preceding the unused credit year and a carryover to each of the 7 taxable years succeeding the unused credit year. An unused credit must be carried first to the earliest of those 10 taxable years. An unused credit then must be carried to each of the other 9 taxable years (in order of time) to the extent that the unused credit was not absorbed during a prior taxable year because of the limitations under section 46(b)(2) and (3).

(e) *Special rule for pre-1971 years.*—(1) *In general.*—For unused credit years ending before January 1, 1971, unused credit is allowed a 10-year carryover rather than the 7-year carryover. The principles of paragraph (d) of this section apply to this 10-year carryover.

(2) *Cross reference.*—For limitations on the taxable years to which unused credit from pre-1971 credit years may be carried, see paragraph (g) of this section.

(f) *Limitations on carrybacks.*—Under the FIFO rule to section 46(a)(1), carryovers and credit earned are applied against the tax liability limitation before carrybacks. Thus, carrybacks to a taxable year may not exceed the amount by which the applicable tax liability limitation for that year exceeds the sum of carryovers to and credit earned for that year. Carrybacks from an unused credit year are applied against tax liability before carrybacks from a later unused credit year. To the extent an unused credit cannot be carried back to a

particular preceding taxable year, the unused credit must be carried to the next succeeding taxable year to which it may be carried.

(g) *Limitations on carryovers.*—(1) *General rule.*—Carryovers to a taxable year may not exceed the applicable tax liability limitation for that year. Carryovers from an unused credit year are applied before carryovers from a later unused credit year.

(2) *Exception.*—A 10-year carryover from a pre-1971 unused credit year may, under certain circumstances, be postponed to prevent a later-earned 7-year carryover from expiring. This exception does not extend the 10-year carryover period for pre-1971 unused credit. See section 46(b)(1)(D).

(h) *Examples.*—The following examples illustrate paragraphs (a) through (g) of this section.

Example (1). (a) Corporation M is organized on January 1, 1977 and files its income tax return on a calendar year basis. Assume the facts set forth in columns (1) and (2) of the following table. The determination of the regular credit allowed for each of the taxable years indicated is set forth in the remaining portions of the table.

	(1) Credit available	(2) Tax liability	(3) Per-cent	(4) Tax liability limitation* (remaining from col. (6) on preceding line)	(5) Credit allowed (lower of (1) or (4))	(6) Remaining tax liability limitation ((4)-(5))	(7) Unused credit ((1)-(5)) or (amount absorbed)
1977:							
A. Credit earned	$20,000	$45,000	50	$35,000	$20,000	$15,000	0
B. Carryback from 1978	*15,000	. .	.	[15,000]	15,000	. .	. .
1978:							
A. Credit earned	80,000	55,000	50	40,000	40,000	0	$20,000
Carryback to 1977	. .	. .	.	. .	. .	. .	(*15,000)
Carryover to 1979	. .	. .	.	. .	. .	. .	(*5,000)
1979:							
A. Carryover from 1978	* 5,000	50,000	60	40,000	6,000	35,000	. .
B. Credit earned	50,000	. .	.	[35,000]	35,000	0	15,000
Carryover to 1980	. .	. .	.	. .	. .	. .	(*15,000)
1980:							
A. Carryover from 1979	*15,000	55,000	70	46,000	15,000	31,000	. .
B. Credit earned	25,000	. .	.	[31,000]	25,000	6,000	0

* For line "A" each year: Lesser of (1) tax liability or (2) $25,000 + (percentage in col. (3) × [col. (2) − $25,000]). See, § 1.46-1(h). For other lines: Amount in col. (6) on preceding line.

Example (2). (a) Assume the same facts as in example (1) except for 1979 M earns a $35,000 nonrefundable energy credit. The following table shows the determinations for each year.

	(1) Credit available	(2) Tax liability (a) Regular	(2) (b) Energy ((2)(a)-(5)(R))	(3) Per-cent	(4) Tax liability limitation* (remaining from col. (6) on preceding line)	(5) Credit allowed (lower of (1) or (4))	(6) Remaining tax liability limitation ((4)-(5))	(7) Unused credit ((1)-(5)) or (amount absorbed)
1977:								
Regular:								
A. Credit earned	$20,000	$45,000	. . . . .	50	$35,000	$20,000R	$15,000	0
B. Carryback from 1978	*15,000	. . . . .	. . . . .	. . .	[15,000]	15,000R	0	. . .
1978:								
Regular:								
Carryback to 1977	. . . . .	. . . . .	. . . . .	. . .	. . . . .	. . . . .	. . . . .	(*15,000)
Carryover to 1979	. . . . .	. . . . .	. . . . .	. . .	. . . . .	. . . . .	. . . . .	(*5,000)
Energy:								
A. Carryback from 1979	*15,000	. . . . .	$15,000	100	15,000	15,000E	0	. . . . .
1979:								
Regular:								
A. Carryover from 1978	*5,000	50,000	. . . . .	60	40,000	5,000R	35,000	. . . . .
B. Credit earned	50,000	. . . . .	. . . . .	. . .	[35,000]	35,000R	0	15,000
Carryover to 1980	. . . . .	. . . . .	. . . . .	. . .	. . . . .	. . . . .	. . . . .	(*15,000)
Energy:								
A. Credit earned	35,000	. . . . .	10,000	100	10,000	10,000E	0	25,000
Carryback to 1978	. . . . .	. . . . .	. . . . .	. . .	. . . . .	. . . . .	. . . . .	(*15,000)
Carryover to 1980	. . . . .	. . . . .	. . . . .	. . .	. . . . .	. . . . .	. . . . .	(*10,000)
1980:								
Regular:								
A. Carryover from 1979	*15,000	55,000	. . . . .	70	46,000	15,000R	31,000	. . . . .
B. Credit earned	25,000	. . . . .	. . .		[31,000]	25,000R	6,000	0
Energy:								
A. Carryover from 1979	*10,000	. . . . .	15,000	100	15,000	10,000E	5,000	0

* See footnote to the chart in example (1).

Reg. §1.46-2(h)

(b) Although, in general, a nonrefundable energy credit may be carried back to taxable years ending before October 1, 1978, in this example the unused nonrefundable energy credit from 1979 may not be absorbed in 1977. The 1977 tax liability limitation for the nonrefundable energy credit is the same as it is for the regular credit, reduced by regular credit previously allowed for 1977. See §§ 1.46-1(h)(3) and 1.46-1(m).

Example (3). (a) Assume the same facts as in example (2) except M has regular credit of $37,000 for 1981 and M's tax liability for 1981 is $32,500. The determinations for 1980 and 1981 are set forth in the following table:

	(1)	(2) Tax liability		(3)	(4) Tax liability limitation* (remaining from col. (6) on preceding line)	(5)	(6) Remaining tax liability limitation ((4)-(5))	(7)
	Credit available	(a) Regular	(b) Energy ((2)(a)- (5)(R))	Per- cent		Credit allowed (lower of (1) or (4))		Unused credit ((1)-(5)) or (amount absorbed)
1979 (restated):								
Energy:								
To be carried over	...	...	...	...	...	...	...	$10,000
Carryover to 1980 ..	...	...	...	...	...	...	...	(*9,000)
Carryover to 1981 ..	...	...	...	...	...	...	...	(*1,000)
1980 (restated):								
Regular								
A. Carryover from 1979 .	$15,000	$55,000	...	70	$46,000	$15,000R	$31,000	...
C. Carryback from 1981 ..	*6,000	...	...	...	[6,000]	6,000R	0	...
Energy:								
A. Carryover from 1979 .	*9,000	...	$9,000	100	9,000	9,000E	...	...
1981:								
Regular:								
A. Credit earned	37,000	32,500	...	80	31,000	31,000R	0	6,000
Carryback to 1980								
....	...	...	...	...	...	...	...	(*6,000)
Energy:								
A. Carryover from 1979 .	*1,000	...	1,500	100	1,500	1,000E	500	0

* See footnote to chart under example (1).

(b) Allowance of the regular carryback in 1980 from 1981 requires that the computations for 1980 be restated. The energy tax liability limitation for 1980 is reduced from $15,000 (as determined in example (2)) to $9,000. Thus, $1,000 of the $10,000 energy credit allowed for 1980 is displaced by the regular carryback. That amount may not be carried back because there is no remaining energy tax liability limitation for the prior 3 years (see table in example (2)). It may be carried over to 1981 and allowed in full in that year.

(i) [Reserved]

(j) *Electing small business corporation.*—A shareholder of an electing small business corporation (as defined in section 1371(b)) may not take into account unused credit of the corporation attributable to unused credit years for which the corporation was not an electing small business corporation. However, a taxable year for which the corporation is an electing small business corporation is counted as a taxable year for determining the taxable years to which that unused credit may be carried.

(k) *Periods of less than 12 months.*—A fractional part of a year that is considered a taxable year under sections 441(b) and 7701(a)(23) is treated as a preceding or succeeding taxable year for determining under section 46(b) the taxable years to which an unused credit may be carried.

(l) *Corporate acquisitions.*—For carryover of unused credits in the case of certain corporate acquisitions, see section 381(c)(23). [Reg. § 1.46-2.]

☐ [T.D. 6731, 5-7-64. *Amended by* T.D. 6931, 10-9-67, T.D. 6958, 6-20-68, T.D. 7126, 6-9-71, T.D. 7203, 8-24-72, T.D. 7289, 11-5-73 *and* T.D. 7751, 12-30-80.]

[Reg. § 1.46-3]

§ 1.46-3. Qualified investment.—(a) *In general.*—(1) With respect to any taxable year, the qualified investment of the taxpayer is the aggregate (expressed in dollars) of (i) the applicable percentage of the basis of each new section 38 property placed in service by the taxpayer during such taxable year, plus (ii) the applicable percentage of the cost of each used section 38 property placed in service by the taxpayer during such taxable year. With respect to any section 38 property, qualified investment means the applicable percentage of the basis (or cost) of such property. Section 38 property placed in service by the taxpayer during the taxable year includes the tax-payer's share of the basis (or cost) of section 38 property placed in service by a partnership in the taxable year of such partnership ending with or within the taxpayer's taxable year. In the case of a shareholder of an electing small business corporation (as defined in section 1371(b)), or a beneficiary of an estate or trust, see §§ 1.48-5 and 1.48-6, respectively, for apportionment of the basis (or cost) of section 38 property placed in service by such corporation, estate, or trust. For the definitions of new section 38 property and used section 38 property, see §§ 1.48-2 and 1.48-3, respectively. See § 1.46-5 for special rules for progress expenditures property.

(2) The basis (or cost) of section 38 property placed in service during a taxable year shall not be taken into account in determining qualified investment for such year if such property is disposed of or otherwise ceases to be section 38 property during such year, except where § 1.47-3 applies. Thus, if individual A places in service during a taxable year section 38 property and later in the same year sells such property, the basis (or cost) of such property shall not be taken into account in determining A's qualified investment. On the other hand, if A places in service section 38 property during a taxable year and dies later in the same year, the basis (or cost) of such property would be taken into account in computing qualified investment. Similarly, if section 38 property is destroyed by fire in the same year in which it is placed in service and paragraph (h) of this section applies to reduce the basis (or cost) of replacement property, the basis (or cost) of the destroyed property would be taken into account in computing qualified investment. In order to determine whether sec-tion 38 property is disposed of or otherwise ceases to be section 38 property see § 1.47-2.

(3) Qualified investment is reduced in the case of property which is "public utility property" (see paragraph (h) of this section), and in the case of property of organizations to which section 593 applies, regulated investment companies or real estate investment trusts subject to taxation under subchapter M, chapter 1 of the Code, and cooperative organizations described in section 1381(a) (see § 1.46-4).

(b) *Applicable percentage.*—The applicable percentage to be applied to the basis (or cost) of property is $33^{1}/_3$ percent if the estimated useful life of the property is 3 years or more but less than 5 years; $66^{2}/_3$ percent if the estimated useful life is 5 years or more but less than 7 years; or 100 percent if the estimated useful life is 7 years or more. In the case of property which is not described in section 50, the preceding sentence shall be applied by substituting "4 years" for "3 years", "6 years" for "5 years", and "8 years" for "7 years". The provisions of this paragraph may be illustrated by the following example:

Example. Corporation Y acquires and places in service during 1972 the following new and used section 38 properties:

Property	Estimated useful life	Basis (or cost)
A (new)	4 years	$60,000
B (new)	10 years	90,000
C (new)	6 years	150,000
D (used)	3 years	30,000

Corporation Y's qualified investment for 1972 is $220,000 determined in the following manner:

Property	Basis (or cost)	Applicable percentage	Qualified investment
A	$60,000	33 $1/3$	$20,000
B	90,000	100	90,000
C	150,000	66 $2/3$	100,000
D	30,000	33 $1/3$	10,000
Total			$220,000

(c) *Basis or cost.*—(1) The basis of any new section 38 property shall be determined in accordance with the general rules for determining the basis of property. Thus, the basis of property would generally be its cost (see section 1012), unreduced by the adjustment to basis provided by section 48 (g) (1) with respect to property placed in service before January 1, 1964, and any other adjustment to basis, such as that for depreciation, and would include all items properly included by the taxpayer in the depreciable basis of the property, such as installation and freight costs. However, for purposes of determining qualified investment, the basis of new section 38 property constructed, reconstructed, or erected by the taxpayer shall not include any depreciation sustained with respect to any other property used in the construction, reconstruction, or erection of such new section 38 property. (See paragraph (b) (4) of §1.48-1.) If new section 38 property is acquired in exchange for cash and other property in a transaction described in section 1031 in which no gain or loss is recognized, the basis of the newly acquired property for purposes of determining qualified investment would be equal to the adjusted basis of the other property plus the cash paid. See §1.48-4 for the basis of property to a lessee where the lessor has elected to treat such lessee as a purchaser.

(2) The cost of any used section 38 property shall be determined in accordance with paragraph (b) of §1.48-3. However, the aggregate cost of used section 38 property which may be taken into account in any taxable year in computing qualified investment cannot exceed $50,000 (see paragraph (c) of §1.48-3).

(3) For reduction in the basis (or cost) of certain property which replaces other property which was destroyed or damaged by fire, storm, shipwreck, or other casualty, or which was stolen, see paragraph (h) of this section.

(d) *Placed in service.*—(1) For purposes of the credit allowed by section 38, property shall be considered placed in service in the earlier of the following taxable years:

(i) The taxable year in which, under the taxpayer's depreciation practice, the period for depreciation with respect to such property begins; or

(ii) The taxable year in which the property is placed in a condition or state of readiness and availability for a specifically assigned function, whether in a trade or business, in the production of income, in a tax-exempt activity, or in a personal activity. Thus, if property meets the conditions of subdivision (ii) of this subparagraph in a taxable year, it shall be considered placed in service in such year notwithstanding that the period for depreciation with respect to such property begins in a succeeding taxable year because, for example, under the taxpayer's depreciation practice such property is accounted for in a multiple asset account and depreciation is computed under an "averaging convention" (see §1.167(a)-10), or depreciation with respect to such property is computed under the completed contract method, the unit of production method, or the retirement method.

(2) In the case of property acquired by a taxpayer for use in his trade or business (or in the production of income), the following are examples of cases where property shall be considered in a condition or state of readiness and availability for a specifically assigned function:

(i) Parts are acquired and set aside during the taxable year for use as replacements for a particular machine (or machines) in order to avoid operational time loss.

(ii) Operational farm equipment is acquired during the taxable year and it is not practicable to use such equipment for its specifically assigned function in the taxpayer's business of farming until the following year.

(iii) Equipment is acquired for a specifically assigned function and is operational but is undergoing testing to eliminate any defects.

(iv) Reforestation expenditures (as defined in §1.194-3(c)) are incurred during the taxable year in connection with qualified timber property (as defined in §1.194-3(a)).

However, fruit-bearing trees and vines shall not be considered in a condition or state of readiness and availability for a specifically assigned function until they have reached an income-producing stage. Moreover, materials and parts acquired to be used in the construction of an item of equipment shall not be considered in a condition or state of readiness and availability for a specifically assigned function.

(3) Notwithstanding subparagraph (1) of this paragraph, property with respect to which an election is made under §1.48-4 to treat the lessee as having purchased such property shall be considered placed in service by the lessor in the taxable year in which possession is transferred to such lessee.

(4)(i) The credit allowed by section 38 with respect to any property shall be allowed only for the first taxable year in which such property is placed in service by the taxpayer. The determination of whether property is section 38 property in the hands of the taxpayer shall be made with respect to such first taxable year. Thus, if a taxpayer places property in service in a taxable year and such property does not qualify as section 38 property (or only a portion of such property qualifies as section 38 property) in such year, no credit (or a credit only as to the portion which qualifies in such year) shall be allowed to the taxpayer with respect to such property notwithstanding that such property (or a greater portion of such property) qualifies as section 38 property in a subsequent taxable year. For example, if a taxpayer places property in service in 1963 and uses the property entirely for personal purposes in such year, but in 1964 begins using the property in a trade or business, no credit is allowable to the taxpayer under section 38 with respect to such property. See §1.48-1 for the definition of section 38 property.

(ii) Notwithstanding subdivision (i) of this subparagraph, if, for the first taxable year in which property is placed in service by the taxpayer, the property qualifies as section 38 property but the basis of the property does not reflect its full cost for the reason that the total amount to be paid or incurred by the taxpayer for the property is indeterminate, a credit shall be allowed to the taxpayer for such first taxable year with respect to so much of the cost as is reflected in the basis of the property as of the close of such year, and an additional credit shall be allowed to the taxpayer for any subsequent taxable year with respect to the additional cost paid or incurred during such year and reflected in the basis of the property as of the close of such year. The estimated useful life used in computing each additional credit with respect to the property shall be the same as the estimated useful life used in computing the credit for the first taxable year in which the property was placed in service by the taxpayer. Assume, for example, that in 1964 X Corporation, a utility company which makes its return on the basis of a calendar year, enters into an agreement with Y Corporation, a builder, to construct certain utility facilities for a housing development built by Y. Assume further that part of the funds for the construction of the utility facilities is advanced by Y under a contract providing that X will repay the advances over a 10-year period in accordance with an agreed formula, after which no further amounts will be repayable by X even though the full amount advanced by Y has not been repaid. Assuming that the utility facilities are placed in service in 1964 and qualify as section 38 property, X is allowed a credit for 1964 with respect to its basis in the utility facilities at the close of 1964. For each succeeding taxable year X is allowed an additional credit with respect to the increase in the basis of the utility facilities resulting from the repayments to Y during such year.

(e) *Estimated useful life.*—(1) *In general.*—(i) With respect to assets placed in service by the taxpayer during any taxable year, for the purpose of computing qualified investment the estimated useful lives assigned to all assets which fall within a particular guideline class (within the meaning of Revenue Procedure 62-21) may be determined, at the taxpayer's option, under either subparagraph (2) or (3) of this paragraph. Thus, the taxpayer may assign estimated useful lives to all the assets falling in one guideline class in accordance with subparagraph (2) of this paragraph, and may assign estimated useful lives to all the assets falling within another guideline class in accordance with subparagraph (3) of this paragraph. See subparagraphs (4) and (5) of this paragraph for determination of estimated useful lives of assets not subject to subparagraph (2) or (3) of this paragraph.

(ii) Except as provided in subparagraph (7), this paragraph shall not apply to property described in section 50.

(2) *Class life system.*—The taxpayer may assign to each asset falling within a guideline class, which is placed in service during the taxable year, the class life of the taxpayer for the guideline class for such year as determined under section 4, Part II of Revenue Procedure 62-21. The preceding sentence may be applied to the assets falling within a guideline class irrespective of whether the taxpayer uses single asset accounts or multiple asset accounts in computing depreciation with respect to such assets and irrespective of whether the taxpayer chooses to have his depreciation allowance with respect to such assets examined under the rules provided in Revenue Procedure 62-21.

(3) *Individual useful life system.*—(i) The taxpayer may assign an individual estimated useful life to each asset falling within a guideline class which is placed in service during the taxable year. With respect to the assets falling within the guideline class which are placed in single asset accounts for purposes of computing depreciation, the estimated useful life used for each asset for that purpose shall be used in determining qualified investment. With respect to the assets falling within the guideline class which are placed in multiple asset accounts (including a guideline class account described in Revenue Procedure 62-21) for which a group, classified, or composite rate is used in computing depreciation (or in single asset accounts for which an average life rate is used), the determination of estimated useful life for each asset in the account shall be made individually on the best estimate obtainable on the basis of all the facts and circumstances. The individual estimated useful lives used for all the assets placed in a multiple asset account, when viewed together, must be consistent with the group, classified, or composite life used for the account for purposes of computing depreciation.

(ii) In determining the individual estimated useful lives of assets similar in kind contained in a multiple asset account (or in single asset accounts for which an average life rate is used), the taxpayer may (*a*) assign to each of such assets the average useful life of such assets used for purposes of computing depreciation, or (*b*) assign separate lives to such assets based on the estimated range of years taken into consideration in establishing the average useful life. Thus, for example, if a taxpayer places 9 similar trucks with an average estimated useful life of 7 years, based on an estimated range of 6 to 8 years (2 trucks with a useful life of 6 years, 5 trucks with a useful life of 7 years, and 2 trucks with a useful life of 8 years), in a multiple asset account for which a group rate is used in computing depreciation, he may either assign a useful life of 6 years to 2 of the trucks, 7 years to 5 of the trucks, and 8 years to 2 of the trucks, or he may assign the average useful life of the trucks (7 years) to each of the 9 trucks. Likewise, if a taxpayer places 100 telephone poles with an average useful life of 28 years, based on an estimated range of 3 to 40 years (2 with a useful life of less than 4 years, 3 with a useful life of 4 to 6 years, 4 with a useful life of 6 to 8 years, and 91 with a useful life of more than 8 years), in a multiple asset account for which a group rate is used in computing depreciation, he may either assign useful lives corresponding to the estimated range of years of the poles (i.e., a useful life of less than 4 years to 2 of the poles, etc.), or he may assign the average useful life of the poles (28 years) to each of the poles.

(iii) [Reserved]

(iv) For purposes of subdivision (ii) of this subparagraph, assets (other than "mass assets") shall not be considered as "similar in kind" in respect of other assets unless all such assets are substantially of the same value, nor shall used section 38 property be considered as "similar in kind" to new section 38 property.

(4) *Useful life of property subject to amortization.*—(i) *In general.*—In the case of property with respect to which amortization in lieu of depreciation is allowable, the term over which amortization deductions are taken shall be considered as the estimated useful life of such property.

(ii) *Qualified timber property.*—In the case of qualified timber property (within the meaning of section 194(c)(1)), the normal growing period of such property shall be considered its estimated useful life.

(5) *Useful life of property subject to certain methods of depreciation.*—If a taxpayer is using a method of depreciation, such as the unit of production or retirement method, which does not measure the useful life of the property in terms of years, he must estimate such useful life in years in order to compute his qualified investment.

(6) *Record requirements.*—The taxpayer shall maintain sufficient records to determine whether section 47 (relating to certain dispositions, etc., of section 38 property) applies with respect to any asset.

(7) *Section 50 property.*—(i) The provisions of this subparagraph and subparagraphs (4) and (6) of this paragraph shall apply to property which is described in section 50.

(ii) The estimated useful life of property for purposes of computing qualified investment shall be the useful life used or to be used by the taxpayer in computing the allowance for depreciation with respect to such property under section 167 for the taxable year in which the property is placed in service. Thus, if property is placed in service by a taxpayer in a taxable year but the period for depreciation with respect to such property does not begin until a succeeding taxable year (see paragraph (d)(1) of this section), the estimated useful life for purposes of computing qualified investment must be the estimated useful life that the taxpayer uses in computing the allowance for depreciation. See subdivision (iv) of this subparagraph for rules for determining the estimated useful life of property with respect to which the allowance for depreciation under section 167 is computed under the unit of production method, the income-forecast method, or any other method which does not measure the useful life of the property in terms of years.

(iii)(*a*) The estimated useful life of any section 38 property to which an election under section 167(m) applies shall be the asset depreciation period selected for such property under § 1.167(a)-11(b)(4), whether or not such property constitutes mass assets (as defined in § 1.47-1(e)(4)).

(*b*) The estimated useful life of any section 38 property to which an election under section 167(m) does not apply and which is placed in a multiple asset account for which a group, classified, or composite rate is used in computing depreciation (or in single asset accounts for which an average life rate is used) shall be determined individually for each asset on the best estimate obtainable on the basis of all the facts and circumstances. The individual estimated useful life for each asset placed in a multiple asset account (including a mass asset account) must be the same as the useful life of such asset used in determining the group, classified, or composite life for the account for purposes of computing depreciation. The individual estimated useful lives of assets similar in kind may be determined in accordance with subdivisions (ii) and (iv) of subparagraph (3) of this paragraph. In the case of mass assets, subdivision (iii) of subparagraph (3) of this paragraph shall apply.

(iv) [Reserved]

(f) *Partnerships.*—(1) *In general.*—In the case of a partnership, each partner shall take into account separately, for his taxable year with or within which the partnership taxable year ends, his share of the basis of partnership new section 38 property and his share of the cost of partnership used section 38 property placed in service by the partnership during such partnership taxable year. Each partner shall be treated as the taxpayer with respect to his share of the basis of partnership new section 38 property and his share of the cost of partnership used section 38 property. The estimated useful life to each partner of such property shall be deemed to be the estimated useful life of the property in the hands of the partnership. Partnership section 38 property shall not, by reason of each partner taking his share of the basis or cost into account, lose its character as either new section 38 property or used section 38 property, as the case may be. For computation of each partner's qualified investment for the energy credit for a qualified intercity bus, see § 1.48-9(q)(9)(iv).

(2) *Determination of partner's share.*—(i) Each partner's share of the basis (or cost) of any section 38 property shall be determined in accordance with the ratio in which the partners divide the general profits of the partnership (that is, the taxable income of the partnership as described in section 702(a)(9)) regardless of whether the partnership has a profit or a loss for its taxable year during which the section 38 property is placed in service. However, if the ratio in which the partners divide the general profits of the partnership changes during the taxable year of the partnership, the ratio effective for the date on which the property is placed in service shall apply.

(ii) Notwithstanding subdivision (i) of this subparagraph, if all related items of income, gain, loss, and deduction with respect to any item of partnership section 38 property are specially allocated in the same manner and if such special allocation is recognized under section 704(a) and (b) and paragraph (b) of § 1.704-1, then each partner's share of the basis of such item of new section 38 property or the cost of such item of used section 38 property shall be determined by reference to such special allocation effective for the date on which the property is placed in service.

(iii) Notwithstanding subdivisions (i) and (ii) of this subparagraph, if with respect to a partnership's taxable year the conditions set forth in (a) through (c) of this subdivision are satisfied with respect to a partner, then such partner shall not take into account the basis (or cost) of any section 38 property placed in service by the partnership during such taxable year. The conditions referred to in the preceding sentence are:

(a) Such partner's interest in the general profits of the partnership during the taxable year is 5 percent or less;

(b) Under the partnership agreement, such partner will retire from the partnership during the taxable year or within 7 years after the end of such year; and

(c) The partnership agreement provides that the basis (or cost) of section 38 property placed in service by the partnership during the taxable year shall not be taken into account by a partner described in (a) and (b) of this subdivision.

Any basis (or cost) of section 38 property which is not taken into account by a partner because of the provisions of this subdivision shall be taken into account by the other partners in accordance with subdivision (i) of this subparagraph.

(3) *Examples.*—This paragraph may be illustrated by the following examples:

Example (1). Partnership ABCD acquires and places in service on January 1, 1962, an item of new section 38 property, and acquires and places in service on September 1, 1962, another item of new section 38 property. The ABCD partnership and each of its partners reports income on the basis of the calendar year. Partners A, B, C, and D share partnership profits equally. Each partner's share of the basis of each new partnership section 38 property is 25 percent.

Example (2). Assume the same facts as in example (1) and the following additional facts: A dies on June 30, 1962, and B purchases

Property	Estimated useful life	Basis
Partnership MR		
Icemaker	8	$1,000
Soda Fountain	6	600
Sole Proprietorship		
Machine	4	300
Total		

A's interest as of such date. Each partner's share of the profits from January 1 to June 30 is 25 percent. From July 1 to December 31, B's share of the profits is 50 percent, and C and D's share of the profits is 25 percent each. For A's last taxable year (January 1 to June 30, 1962), A shall take into account 25 percent of the basis of the section 38 property placed in service on January 1, B shall take into account 25 percent of the basis of the section 38 property placed in service on January 1 and 50 percent of the basis of the section 38 property placed in service on September 1, C and D shall each take into account 25 percent of the basis of each new section 38 property placed in service by the partnership in 1962.

Example (3). Partnership MR is engaged in the business of renting soda fountain equipment and icemakers to restaurants. The partnership makes no elections under § 1.48-4 to treat its lessees as having purchased such property. Under the terms of the partnership agreements, the income, gain or loss on disposition, depreciation, and other deductions attributable to the icemakers are specially allocated 70 percent to partner M and 30 percent to partner R. In all other respects M and R share profits and losses equally. If the special allocation with respect to the icemakers is recognized under section 704(a) and (b) and paragraph (b) of § 1.704-1, the basis (or cost) of the icemakers which qualify as partnership section 38 property shall be taken into account 70 percent by M and 30 percent by R. The basis (or cost) of partnership section 38 property not subject to the special allocation shall be taken into account equally by M and R.

Example (4). Assume the same facts as in example (3) and the following additional facts: During November 1962, the partnership, which reports its income on the basis of a fiscal year ending May 31, acquires and places in service two items which qualify as new section 38 property, an icemaker and a soda fountain. The icemaker has an estimated useful life of 8 years to the partnership and a basis of $1,000. The soda fountain has an estimated useful life of 6 years to the partnership and a basis of $600. Partner M also owns and operates a business as a sole proprietorship and reports income on the calendar year basis. During 1963, M acquires and places in service in his sole proprietorship a machine which qualifies as new section 38 property. This machine has an estimated useful life of 4 years and a basis of $300. M owns no interest in any other partnerships, electing small business corporations, estates, or trusts. M's total qualified investment for 1963 is $1,000, computed as follows:

M's share of basis	Applicable percentage	Qualified investment
$700	100	$700
300	66 $2/3$	200
	33 $1/3$	100
		$1,000

(g) *Public utility property.*—(1) *In general.*—(i) *Scope of paragraph.*—This paragraph only applies to property described in section 50. For rules relating to public utility property not described in section 50, see 26 CFR Part 1 § 1.46-3(g) (as revised April 1, 1977). This paragraph does not reflect amendments to section 46(c) made after enactment of the Revenue Act of 1971.

(ii) *Amount of qualified investment.*—A taxpayer's qualified investment in section 38 property that is public utility property is 4/7 of the amount otherwise determined under this section.

(2) *Meaning and use of certain terms.*—For purposes of this paragraph—

(i) *Public utility property.*—"Public utility property" is property used by a taxpayer predominantly in a trade or business that is a public utility activity and property that is nonregulated communication property.

(ii) *Public utility activity.*—A "public utility activity" is any activity in which the goods or services described in section 46(c)(3)(B)(i), (ii), or (iii) are furnished or sold at regulated rates. If property is used by a taxpayer both in a public utility activity and in another activity, the characterization of such property is based on the predominant use of such property during the taxable year in which it is placed in service.

(iii) *Regulated rates.*—A taxpayer's rates are "regulated" if they are established or approved on a rate-of-return basis. Rates regulated on a rate-of-return basis are an authorization to collect revenues that cover the taxpayer's cost of providing goods or services, including a fair return on the taxpayer's investment in providing such goods or services, where the taxpayer's costs and investment are determined

by use of a uniform system of accounts prescribed by the regulatory body. A taxpayer's rates are not "regulated" if they are established or approved on the basis of maintaining competition within an industry, insuring adequate service to customers of an industry, or charging "reasonable" rates within an industry since the taxpayer is not authorized to collect revenues based on the taxpayer's cost of providing goods or services. Rates are considered to have been "established or approved" if a schedule of rates is filed with a regulatory body that has the power to approve such rates, even though the regulatory body takes no action on the filed schedule or generally leaves undisturbed rates filed by the taxpayer.

(iv) *Nonregulated communication property.*—"Nonregulated communication property" is property that is clearly the same type of property (and is used by the taxpayer predominantly for the same type of communication purposes) as communication property, but it is used by the taxpayer predominantly in a trade or business that is not a public utility activity. For purposes of this subdivision (iv), communication property is property ordinarily used for communication purposes by persons who provide regulated telephone or microwave communication services described in section 46(c)(3)(B)(iii). The determination of whether property is clearly of this same type and is used predominantly for these same communication purposes as communication property is made on the basis of the facts and circumstances of each particular case, including the current state of technology in the communications industry and the range and type of services permitted or required to be provided by the regulated telephone and microwave communication industry. As of 1978, wires or cables used predominantly to distribute to subscribers the signals of one or more television broadcast stations or cablecast stations (such as in a CATV system) are not used for the same type of communication purposes as communication property. Communication property includes microwave transmission equipment, private communication equipment (other than land mobile radio equipment for which the operator must obtain a license from the Federal Communications Commission), private switchboard (PBX) equipment, communications terminal equipment connected to telephone networks, data transmission equipment, and communications satellites. Communication property does not include (as of 1978) computer terminals or facsimile reproduction equipment that is connected to telephone lines to transmit data. It also does not include office furniture stands for communication property, tools, repair vehicles, and similar property, even if such property is exclusively used in providing regulated telephone or microwave communication services.

(3) *Leased property.*—Public utility property includes property which is leased to others by a taxpayer where the leasing of such property is part of the lessor's public utility activity. Thus, such leased property is public utility property even though the lessee uses such property in an activity which is not a public utility activity, and whether or not the lessor of such property makes a valid election under §1.48-4 to treat the lessee as having purchased such property for purposes of the credit allowed by section 38. Property leased by a lessor, where the leasing is not part of a public utility activity, to a lessee who uses such property predominantly in a public utility activity is public utility property for purposes of computing the lessor's or lessee's qualified investment with respect to such property.

(4) *Property used in both the production or transmission of gas and local distribution of gas.*—(i) With respect to properties of a taxpayer engaged in both the production or transmission of gas and the local distribution of gas, section 38 property shall be considered as used predominantly in the trade or business of the furnishing or sale of gas though a local distribution system if expenditures for such property are chargeable to any of the following accounts under either the uniform system of accounts prescribed for natural gas companies (class A and class B) by the Federal Power Commission, effective January 1, 1961, or the uniform system of accounts for class A and B gas utilities adopted in 1958 by the National Association of Railroad and Utility Commissioners (or would be chargeable to any of the following accounts if the taxpayer used either of such systems):

(*a*) Accounts 360 through 363, inclusive (Local Storage Plant), or

(*b*) Accounts 374 through 387, inclusive (Distribution Plant).

(ii) If expenditures for section 38 property are chargeable (or would be chargeable) to any of the following accounts under either of the systems named in subdivision (i) of this subparagraph, the determination of whether or not such property is used predominantly in the trade or business of the furnishing or sale of gas through a local distribution system shall be made under all the facts and circumstances relating to the actual use of such property in the year such property is placed in service:

(*a*) Accounts 304 through 320, inclusive (Manufactured Gas Production Plant), or

(*b*) Accounts 389 through 399, inclusive (General Plant). For example, if an office machine is used 55 percent of the time for billing customers of the taxpayer's local distribution system in the year in which it is placed in service, such office machine shall be considered as used predominantly in the trade or business of the furnishing or sale of gas through a local distribution system.

(5) *Certain submarine cable property.*—In the case of any interest in a submarine cable circuit which is property described in section 50 used to furnish telegraph service between the United States and a point outside the United States of a taxpayer engaged in furnishing international telegraph service (if the rates for such furnishing have been established or approved by a governmental unit, agency, instrumentality, commission, or similar body described in subparagraph (2) of this paragraph), the qualified investment shall not exceed the qualified investment attributable to so much of the interest of the taxpayer in the circuit as does not exceed 50 percent of all interests in the circuit.

(h) *Certain replacement property.*—(1)(i) If section 38 property is placed in service by the taxpayer to replace property (whether or not section 38 property) similar or related in service or use, which was destroyed or damaged before August 16, 1971, by fire, storm, shipwreck, or other casualty, or was stolen before such date, then for purposes of paragraph (a) of this section the basis (or cost) of the replacement section 38 property otherwise determined under paragraph (c) of this section shall be reduced by an amount equal to the lesser of—

(*a*) The amount of money, or the fair market value of other property, received as compensation, by insurance or otherwise, for the property which was destroyed, damaged, or stolen, or

(*b*) The adjusted basis of such destroyed, damaged, or stolen property (immediately before such destruction, damage, or theft).

(ii) For purposes of subdivision (i) of this subparagraph—

(*a*) Section 38 property placed in service after the due date (including extensions of time thereof) for filing the taxpayer's income tax return for the taxable year in which the other property was destroyed, damaged, or stolen shall not be considered as replacement section 38 property, and

(*b*) If the property which is destroyed, damaged, or stolen, is leased property, no other leased property shall be considered as replacement property with respect to the property destroyed, damaged, or stolen, in any case in which the lessor makes or made an election under section 48(d) (relating to election with respect to certain leased property) with respect to either the property destroyed, damaged, or stolen, the other leased property, or both.

(2) Subparagraph (1) of this paragraph shall not apply to replacement property if the reduction, under such subparagraph (1), in the basis (or cost) of such replacement property is less than the excess of—

(i) The qualified investment with respect to the destroyed, damaged, or stolen property, over

(ii) The recomputed qualified investment with respect to such property (determined under the principles of paragraph (a) of §1.47-1).

(3) This paragraph may be illustrated by the following examples:

Example (1). (i) A acquired and placed in service on January 1, 1962, machine No. 1, which qualified as section 38 property, with a basis of $30,000 and an estimated useful life of 6 years. The amount of qualified investment with respect to such machine was $20,000. On January 2, 1963, machine No. 1 is completely destroyed by fire. On January 1, 1963, the adjusted basis of such machine in A's hands is $24,500. On November 1, 1963, A receives $23,000 in insurance proceeds as compensation for the destroyed machine, and on December 15, 1963, A acquires and places in service machine No. 2, which qualifies as section 38 property, with a basis of $41,000 and an estimated useful life of 6 years to replace machine No. 1.

(ii) Under subparagraph (1) of this paragraph, the $41,000 basis of machine No. 2 is reduced, for purposes of paragraph (a) of this section, by $23,000 (that is, the $23,000 insurance proceeds since such amount is less than the $24,500 adjusted basis of machine No. 1 immediately before it was destroyed) to $18,000 since such reduction (that is, $23,000) is greater than the $20,000 reduction in qualified investment which would be made if paragraph (a) of §1.47-1 were to apply to machine No. 1 ($20,000 qualified investment less zero recomputed qualified investment).

Example (2). (i) The facts are the same as in example (1) except that on November 1, 1963, A receives only $19,000 in insurance proceeds as compensation for the destroyed machine.

(ii) The $41,000 basis of machine No. 2 is not reduced, for purposes of paragraph (a) of this section, under this paragraph since the $19,000 reduction which would have been made under this paragraph had it applied (that is, the $19,000 insurance proceeds since such amount is less than the $24,500 adjusted basis of machine No. 1 immediately before it was destroyed) is less than the $20,000 reduction in qualified investment which is made since paragraph (a) of §1.47-1 applies to machine No. 1 ($20,000 qualified investment less zero recomputed qualified investment). [Reg. §1.46-3.]

☐ [*T.D. 6731, 5-7-64. Amended by T.D. 6931, 10-9-67; T.D. 7203, 8-24-72; T.D. 7602, 3-20-79; T.D. 7927, 12-15-83; T.D. 7982, 10-5-84; T.D. 8183, 3-1-88 and T.D. 8474, 4-26-93.*]

[Reg. §1.46-4]

§1.46-4. Limitations with respect to certain persons.—(a) *Mutual savings institutions.*—In case of an organization to which section 593 applies (that is, a mutual savings bank, a cooperative bank, or a domestic building and loan association)—

(1) The qualified investment with respect to each section 38 property shall be 50 percent of the amount otherwise determined under §1.46-3, and

(2) The $25,000 amount specified in section 46(a)(2), relating to limitation based on amount of tax, shall be reduced by 50 percent of such amount.

For example, if a domestic building and loan association places in service on January 1, 1963, new section 38 property with a basis of $30,000 and an estimated useful life of 6 years, its qualified investment for 1963 with respect to such property computed under §1.46-3 is $20,000 (66⅔ percent of $30,000). However, under this paragraph such amount is reduced to $10,000 (50 percent of $20,000). If an organization to which section 593 applies is a member of an affiliated group (as defined in section 46(a)(5)), the $25,000 amount specified in section 46(a)(2) shall be reduced in accordance with the provisions of paragraph (f) of §1.46-1 before such amount is further reduced under this paragraph.

(b) *Regulated investment companies and real estate investment trusts.*— (1) In the case of a regulated investment company or a real estate investment trust subject to taxation under subchapter M, chapter 1 of the Code—

(i) The qualified investment with respect to each section 38 property otherwise determined under §1.46-3, and

(ii) The $25,000 amount specified in section 46(a)(2), relating to limitation based on amount of tax,

shall be reduced to such person's ratable share of each such amount. If a regulated investment company or a real estate investment trust is a member of an affiliated group (as defined in section 46(a)(5)), the $25,000 amount specified in section 46(a)(2) shall be reduced in accordance with the provisions of paragraph (f) of §1.46-1 before such amount is further reduced under this paragraph.

(2) A person's ratable share of the amount described in subparagraph (1)(i) and the amount described in subparagraph (1)(ii) of this paragraph shall be the ratio which—

(i) Taxable income for the taxable year, bears to

(ii) Taxable income for the taxable year plus the amount of the deduction for dividends paid taken into account under section 852(b)(2)(D) in computing investment company taxable income, or under section 857(b)(2)(B) (section 857(b)(2)(C), as then in effect, for taxable years ending before October 5, 1976) in computing real estate investment trust taxable income, as the case may be.

For purposes of the preceding sentence, taxable income means, in the case of a regulated investment company its investment company taxable income (within the meaning of section 852(b)(2)), and in the case of a real estate investment trust its real estate investment trust taxable income (within the meaning of section 857(b)(2)). In the case of a taxable year ending after October 4, 1976, real estate investment trust taxable income, for purposes of section 46(e) and this paragraph, is determined by excluding any net capital gain, and by computing the deduction for dividends paid without regard to capital gains dividends (as defined in section 857(b)(3)(C)). The amount of the deduction for dividends paid includes the amount of deficiency dividends (other than capital gains deficiency dividends) taken into account in computing investment company taxable income or real estate investment trust taxable income for the taxable year. See section 860(f) for the definition of deficiency dividends. For purposes of this paragraph only, in computing taxable income for a taxable year beginning before January 1, 1964, a regulated investment company or a real estate investment trust may compute depreciation deductions with respect to section 38 property placed in service before January 1, 1964, without regard to the reduction in basis of such property required under §1.48-7.

(3) This paragraph may be illustrated by the following example:

Example. (i) Corporation X, a regulated investment company subject to taxation under section 852 of the Code which makes its return on the basis of the calendar year, places in service on January 1, 1964, section 38 property with a basis of $30,000 and an estimated useful life of 6 years. Corporation X's investment company taxable income under section 852(b)(2) is $10,000 after taking into account a deduction for dividends paid of $90,000.

(ii) Under this paragraph, corporation X's qualified investment for the taxable year 1964 with respect to such property is $2,000, computed as follows: (*a*) $20,000 (qualified investment under §1.46-3), multiplied by (*b*) $10,000 (taxable income), divided by (*c*) $100,000 (taxable income plus the deduction for dividends paid). For 1964, the $25,000 amount specified in section 46(a)(2) is reduced to $2,500.

(c) *Cooperatives.*—(1) In the case of a cooperative organization described in section 1381(a)—

(i) The qualified investment with respect to each section 38 property otherwise determined under §1.46-3, and

(ii) The $25,000 amount specified in section 46(a)(2), relating to limitation based on amount of tax,

shall be reduced to such cooperative's ratable share of each such amount. If a cooperative organization described in section 1381(a) is a member of an affiliated group (as defined in section 46(a)(5)), the *$25,000 amount specified in section 46(a)(2)* shall be reduced in accordance with the provisions of paragraph (f) of §1.46-1 before such amount is further reduced under this paragraph.

(2) A cooperative's ratable share of the amount described in subparagraph (1)(i) and the amount described in subparagraph (1)(ii) of this paragraph shall be the ratio which—

(i) Taxable income for the taxable year, bears to

(ii) Taxable income for the taxable year plus the sum of (*a*) the amount of the deductions allowed under section 1382(b), (*b*) the amount of the deductions allowed under section 1382(c), and (*c*) amounts similar to the amounts described in (*a*) and (*b*) of this

subdivision the tax treatment of which is determined without regard to subchapter T, chapter 1 of the Code and the regulations thereunder.

Amounts similar to deductions allowed under section 1382(b) or (c) are, for example, in the case of a taxable year of a cooperative organization beginning before January 1, 1963, the amount of patronage dividends which are excluded or deducted and any nonpatronage distributions which are deducted under section 522(b)(1). In the case of a taxable year of a cooperative organization beginning after December 31, 1962, such amounts are the amount of patronage dividends and nonpatronage distributions which are excluded or deducted without regard to section 1382(b) or (c) because they are paid with respect to patronage occurring before 1963. For purposes of this paragraph only, in computing taxable income for a taxable year beginning before January 1, 1964, a cooperative may compute depreciation deductions with respect to section 38 property placed in service before January 1, 1964, without regard to the reduction in basis of such property required under §1.48-7.

(3) This paragraph may be illustrated by the following example:

Example. (i) Cooperative X, an organization described in section 1381(a) which makes its return on the basis of the calendar year, places in service on January 1, 1964, section 38 property with a basis of $30,000 and an estimated useful life of 6 years. Cooperative X's taxable income is $10,000 after taking into account deductions of $20,000 allowed under section 1382(b), deductions of $60,000 allowed under section 1382(c), and deductions of $10,000 allowed under section 522(b)(1)(B).

(ii) Under this paragraph, cooperative X's qualified investment for the taxable year 1964 with respect to such property is $2,000, computed as follows: (*a*) $20,000 (qualified investment under §1.46-3), multiplied by (*b*) $10,000 (taxable income), divided by (*c*) $100,000 (taxable income plus the sum of the deductions allowed under sections 1382(b), 1382(c), and 522(b)(1)(B)). For 1964, the $25,000 amount specified in section 46(a)(2) is reduced to $2,500.

(d) *Noncorporate lessors.*—(1) In the case of a lease entered into after September 22, 1971, a credit is allowed under section 38 to a noncorporate lessor of property with respect to the leased property only if—

(i) Such property has been manufactured or produced by the lessor in the ordinary course of his business, or

(ii) The term of the lease (taking into account any options to renew) is less than 50 percent of the estimated useful life of the property (determined under §1.46-3(e)), and for the period consisting of the first 12 months after the date on which the property is transferred to the lessee the sum of the deductions with respect to such property which are allowable to the lessor solely by reason of section 162 (other than rents and reimbursed amounts with respect to such property) exceeds 15 percent of the rental income produced by such property.

In the case of property of which a partnership is the lessor, the credit otherwise allowable under section 38 with respect to such property to any partner which is a corporation shall be allowed notwithstanding the first sentence of this subparagraph. For purposes of this subparagraph, an electing small business corporation (as defined in section 1371) shall be treated as a person which is not a corporation. This paragraph shall not apply to property used by the taxpayer in his trade or business (other than the leasing of property) for a period of at least 24 months preceding the day on which any lease of such property is entered into.

(2) For purposes of subparagraph (1)(ii) of this paragraph, if at the time the lessor files his income tax return for the taxable year in which the property is placed in service, the lessor is unable to show that the more-than-15-percent test has been satisfied, then no credit may be claimed by the lessor on such return with respect to such property unless (i) taking into account the lessor's obligations under the lease it is reasonable to believe that the more-than-15-percent test will be satisfied, and (ii) the lessor files a statement with his return from which it may be determined that he expects to satisfy the more-than-15-percent test. If the more-than-15-percent test is not satisfied with respect to the property, the taxpayer must file an amended return for the year in which the property is placed in service.

(3)(i) The more-than-15-percent test described in subparagraph (1)(ii) of this paragraph is based on the relationship of the expenses of the lessor relating to or attributable to the property to the gross income from rents of the taxpayer produced by the property. The test is applied with respect to such expenses and gross income as are properly attributable to the period consisting of the first 12 months after the date on which the property is transferred to the lessee. When more than one property is subject to a single lease and, pursuant to subparagraph (4) of this paragraph, the arrangement is considered to be a separate lease of each property, the test is applied separately to each such lease by making an apportionment of the payments received and expenses incurred with respect to each such property, considering all relevant factors. Such apportionment is made in accordance with any reasonable method selected and consistently applied by the taxpayer. For example, under subparagraph (4) of this paragraph, where a taxpayer leases an airplane which he owns to an airline along with a baggage truck, he is treated as having made two separate leases, one covering the airplane and one covering the baggage truck. Thus, the test will be applied by apportioning the related income and expenses between the two leases. Similarly, where a taxpayer leases a factory building erected by him containing section 38 property (machinery and equipment), the test will be applied to the taxpayer as though he had leased (to the lessee) the building and the section 38 property separately. Thus, the rental income and expenses are apportioned between the building and the section 38 property.

(ii) Only those deductions allowable solely by reason of section 162 are taken into account in applying the more-than-15-percent test. Hence, depreciation allowable by reason of section 167 (including amortization allowable in lieu of depreciation); interest allowable by reason of section 163; taxes allowable by reason of section 164; and depletion allowable by reason of section 611 are examples of deductions which are not taken into account in applying the test. Moreover, rents and reimbursed amounts paid or payable by the lessor are not taken into account notwithstanding that a deduction in respect of such rents or reimbursed amounts is allowable solely by reason of section 162. For purposes of this paragraph, a reimbursed amount is any expense for which the lessee or some other party is obligated to reimburse the lessor. Section 162 expenses paid or payable by any person other than the lessor are not taken into account unless the lessor is obligated to reimburse the person paying the expense. Further, if the lessee is obligated to pay to the lessor a charge for services which is separately stated or determinable, the expenses incurred by the lessor with respect to those services are not taken into account.

(iii) For purposes of the more-than-15-percent test, the gross income from rents of the lessor produced by the property is the total amount which is payable to the lessor by reason of the lease agreement other than reimbursements of section 162 expenses and charges for services which are separately stated or determinable. The fact that such amount depends, in whole or in part, on the sales or profits of the lessee or the performance of significant services by the lessor shall not affect the characterization of such amounts as gross income from rents for purposes of this paragraph. Gross income from rents also includes any taxes imposed on the lessor by local law but which are paid directly by the lessee on behalf of the lessor.

(4) For purposes of determining under this paragraph whether property is subject to a lease, the provisions of §1.57-3(d)(1) (relating to definition of a lease) shall apply. If a noncorporate lessor enters into two or more successive leases with respect to the same or substantially similar items of section 38 property, the terms of such leases shall be aggregated and such leases shall be considered one lease for the purpose of determining whether the term of such leases is less than 50 percent of the estimated useful life of the property subject to such leases. Thus, for example, if an individual owns an airplane with an estimated useful life of 7 years and enters into 3 successive 3-year leases of such airplane, such leases will be considered to be one lease for a term of 9 years for the purpose of determining whether the term of the lease is less than 3$^{1}/_{2}$ years (50 percent of the 7-year estimated useful life).

(5) The requirements of this paragraph shall not apply with respect to any property which is treated as section 38 property by reason of section 48(a)(1)(E). [Reg. §1.46-4.]

☐ [T.D. 6731, 5-7-64. Amended by T.D. 6958, 6-20-68; T.D. 7203, 8-24-72; T.D. 7767, 2-3-81; T.D. 7936, 1-17-84; and T.D. 8031, 6-27-85.]

[Reg. §1.46-5]

§1.46-5. Qualified progress expenditures.—(a) *Effective date.*—This section applies to taxable years ending after December 31, 1974. This section reflects amendments to the Internal Revenue Code made only by the Tax Reduction Act of 1975, the Tax Reform Act of 1976, and the Revenue Act of 1978.

(b) *General rule.*—Under section 46(d), a taxpayer may elect to take the investment credit for qualified progress expenditures (as defined in paragraph (g) of this section). In general, qualified progress expenditures are amounts paid (or incurred in the case of self-constructed property) for construction of progress expenditure property. The taxpayer must reasonably estimate that the property will take at least 2 years to construct and that the useful life of the property will be 7 years or more. Qualified progress expenditures *may not be taken into account if made before the later of* January 22, 1975, or the first taxable year to which an election under section 46(d) applies. In general, qualified progress expenditures are not allowed for the year property is placed in service, nor for the first year or any subsequent year recapture is required under section 47(a)(3). There is

a percentage limitation on qualified progress expenditures for taxable years beginning before January 1, 1980. For a special rule relating to transfers of progress expenditure property, see paragraph (r) of this section.

(c) *Reduction of qualified investment.*—Under section 46(c)(4), a taxpayer must reduce qualified investment for the year property is placed in service by qualified progress expenditures taken into account by that person or a predecessor. A "predecessor" of a taxpayer is a person whose election under section 46(d) carries over to the taxpayer under paragraph (o)(3) of this section.

(d) *Progress expenditure property.*—Progress expenditure property is property constructed by or for the taxpayer, with a normal construction period of 2 years or more. The taxpayer must reasonably believe that the property will be new section 38 property with a useful life of 7 years or more when placed in service. Whether property is progress expenditure property is determined on the basis of facts known at the close of the taxable year of the taxpayer in which construction begins (or, if later, at the close of the first taxable year to which an election under section 46(d) applies). For purposes of this paragraph (d), property is constructed by or for the taxpayer only if it is built or manufactured from materials and component parts. Accordingly, progress expenditure property does not include property such as orchards, vineyards, livestock, or motion picture films or videotapes.

(e) *Normal construction period.*—(1) *In general.*—(i) The normal construction period is the period the taxpayer reasonably expects will be required to construct the property. The period begins on the date physical work on construction of the property commences and ends on the date the property is available to be placed in service. The normal construction period does not include, however, construction before January 22, 1975, nor construction before the first day of the first taxable year for which an election under section 46(d) is in effect. Physical work on construction of property does not include preliminary activities such as planning, designing, preparing blueprints, exploring, or securing financing.

(ii) The determination of the time when physical work on construction commences is based on the facts and circumstances of each case. Physical work on construction of property may include the physical work done by a subcontractor on a component specifically designated as part of the property. Also, the commencement of physical work on construction may occur at a site different from the main site of construction of the property. For example, if a shipyard orders a turbine before it begins work on building a ship, the normal construction period of the ship is measured from the time the subcontractor commences physical work on construction of the turbine (if it is normal for such work to precede the work of the main contractor).

(iii) Generally, physical work on construction does not include physical activity that is not necessary to complete construction of the property, nor does it include physical work on construction of a building or other property that will not be new section 38 property when placed in service. Physical work on construction also does not include research and development activities in a laboratory or experimental setting.

(iv) The normal construction period of property ends on the date it is expected the property will be available to be placed in service. Property is considered available to be placed in service when construction is completed and the property is available for delivery to the site of its assigned function. It is not necessary that property be in a state of readiness for a specifically assigned function. Nor is it necessary that it actually be delivered to the site of its assigned function.

(2) *Estimates.*—Taxpayers should refer to normal industry practice in estimating the normal construction period of particular items. A different period may be used if special circumstances exist making it impractical to make the estimate on the basis of normal industry practice. The estimate must be based on information available at the close of the taxable year in which physical work on construction of the property begins, or, if later, at the close of the first taxable year for which an election under section 46(d) is in effect for the taxpayer. If the estimate is reasonable when made, the actual time it takes to complete the work is, in general, irrelevant in determining whether property is progress expenditure property. However, if there is a significant error in estimating the normal construction period, it may be evidence that the estimate was unreasonable when made. For taxable years ending after April 1, 1988, a taxpayer not relying on normal industry practice to estimate the normal construction period of particular property must attach to the tax return for the taxable year in which physical work on construction of the property begins (or, if later, the first taxable year for which an election under section 46(d) is in effect) a statement of the basis relied upon in estimating the normal construction period of the property.

(3) *Integrated unit.*—(i) In determining whether property has a normal construction period of 2 years or more, property that will be placed in service separately is to be considered separately. For example, if two ships are contracted for at the same time, each ship is considered separately under this paragraph. However, for property that will be placed in service as an integrated unit, the taxpayer must determine the normal construction period of the integrated unit. If the normal construction period of the integrated unit is 2 years or more, the normal construction period of each item of new section 38 property that is a part of the integrated unit is considered to be 2 years or more. Thus, the normal construction period of an integrated unit may be 2 years or more even if no part of the unit has a normal construction period of 2 years or more.

(ii) Property is part of an integrated unit only if the operation of that item is essential to the performance of the function to which the unit is assigned. Property essential to the performance of the function to which the unit is assigned includes property the use of which is significantly connected to that function and which effects the safe, proper, or efficient performance of the unit. Generally, property must be placed in service at the same time to be considered part of the same integrated unit. Properties are not an integrated unit, however, solely because they are to be placed in service at the same time.

(iii) The normal construction period for an integrated unit begins on the date the normal construction period of the first item of new section 38 property that is part of the unit begins. It is not necessary that physical work commence at the main construction site of the integrated unit.
The period ends on the date the last item of new section 38 property that is part of that unit is available to be placed in service. Property that is not new section 38 property, such as a building, is not considered part of an integrated unit for purposes of determining the normal construction period of that unit. For example, if a manufacturing plant has a normal construction period of two years or more but the equipment (*i.e.*, new section 38 property) to be installed in the plant has a normal construction period of less than two years, the plant and the equipment do not constitute an integrated unit with a construction period of two years or more and the equipment is not progress expenditure property.

(4) *Examples.*—The following examples illustrate this paragraph (e).

Example (1). On July 1, 1974, corporation X begins physical work on construction of a machine with an estimated useful life when placed in service of more than 7 years. For its taxable year ending June 30, 1975, X makes an election under section 46(d). For purposes of determining on June 30, 1975, whether the machine is "progress expenditure property", the normal construction period is treated as having begun on January 22, 1975. Thus, the machine will be considered to be progress expenditure property on June 30, 1975, only if the estimated time required to complete construction after June 30 is at least 18 months and 22 days (*i.e.*, 2 years less the period January 22, 1975, through June 30, 1975).

Example (2). (i) Corporation X constructs a pipeline in two sections and simultaneously begins physical work on construction of each section on January 1, 1976. One section extends from city M to city N. The other extends from city N to city O. Oil will be transferred to storage tanks at both city N and city O. Corporation X also begins construction on January 1, 1976, of a pumping station necessary to the operation of the pipeline from city M to city N. Construction of a pumping station necessary to the operation of the pipeline from city N to city O begins on June 30, 1977. For 1976, corporation X makes an election under section 46(d).

(ii) The section of pipeline from city M to city N and the associated pumping station will be available to be placed in service on January 1, 1977. Construction of the section of the pipeline from city N to city O will be completed on June 30, 1977. However, that section of the pipeline will not be available to be placed in service until completion of the associated pumping station on January 1, 1978.

(iii) The section of pipeline from city M to city N and the section from city N to city O must be considered separately in determining the normal construction period of the property. Each section will be placed in service separately. However, each section of the pipeline and the associated pumping station may be considered an integrated unit. The pumping stations are essential to the operation of each section of pipeline. Each section of pipeline and the associated pumping station are placed in service at the same time.

(iv) The section of pipeline from city M to city N and the associated pumping station are not progress expenditure property, because the normal construction period of that unit is only 1 year (January 1, 1976 to January 1, 1977).

(v) The section of pipeline from city N to city O and the associated pumping station are progress expenditure property, because the normal construction of that integrated unit is 2 years (January 1, 1976

to January 1, 1978). It is immaterial that neither the construction period of that section of pipeline (January 1, 1976 to June 30, 1977) nor the construction period of the associated pumping station (June 30, 1977 to January 1, 1978) is 2 years.

(vi) Assume the pumping station associated with the pipeline from city N to city O includes backup pumping equipment that will be used only if the primary pumping equipment fails. The backup equipment is part of the integrated unit because it serves to effect the safe or efficient performance of the unit.

(f) *New section 38 property with a 7-year useful life.*—(1) *In general.*—The taxpayer must determine if property will be new section 38 property with a useful life of 7 years or more when placed in service. The determination must be made at the close of the taxable year in which construction begins or, if later, at the close of the first taxable year to which an election under section 46(d) applies for the taxpayer.

(2) *Determination based on reasonably expected use.*—The determination of whether property will be "new section 38 property" (within the meaning of §§ 1.48-1 and 1.48-2) when placed in service must be based on the reasonably expected use of the property by the taxpayer. There is a presumption that property will be new section 38 property if it would be new section 38 property if placed in service by the taxpayer when the determination is made. For example, in determining if property is an integral part of manufacturing under section 48(a)(1)(B)(i), it will be presumed that property will be new section 38 property if the taxpayer is engaged in manufacturing when the determination is made. Also, significant steps taken to establish a trade or business will be evidence the taxpayer will be engaged in that trade or business when the property is placed in service.

(3) *Estimated useful life.*—The determination of whether property will have an estimated useful life of 7 years or more when placed in service must be made by applying the principles of § 1.46-3(e). If the estimated useful life is less than 7 years when the property is actually placed in service, the credit previously allowed under section 46(d) must be recomputed under section 47(a)(3)(B).

(g) *Definition of qualified progress expenditures.*—(1) *In general.*—A taxpayer's qualified progress expenditures are the sum of qualified progress expenditures for self-constructed property (determined under paragraph (h) of this section), plus qualified progress expenditures for non-self-constructed property (determined under paragraph (j) of this section). Only amounts includible under § 1.46-3(c) in the basis of new section 38 property may be considered as qualified progress expenditures.

(2) *Excluded amounts.*—Qualified progress expenditures do not include:

(i) In the case of non-self-constructed property, amounts incurred (whether or not paid)—

(A) Before the normal construction period begins, or

(B) Before the later of January 22, 1975, or the first day of the first taxable year for which an election under section 46(d) applies for the taxpayer;

(ii) In the case of self-constructed property, amounts chargeable to capital account—

(A) Before the normal construction period begins, or

(B) Before the later of January 22, 1975, or the first day of the first taxable year for which an election under section 46(d) applies for the taxpayer,

(See, however, section 46(d)(4)(A) and paragraph (h)(3)(i) of this section, relating to the time when amounts for component parts and materials are properly chargeable to capital account);

(iii) Expenditures with respect to particular property in the earlier of—

(A) The taxable year in which the property is placed in service, or

(B) The taxable year in which the taxpayer must recapture investment credit under section 47(a)(3) for the property or any subsequent year;

(iv) Expenditures for construction, reconstruction, or erection of property that is not section 38 property; or

(v) Amounts treated as an expense and deducted in the year paid or accrued.

(h) *Qualified progress expenditures for self-constructed property.*—(1) *In general.*—Qualified progress expenditures for self-constructed property (as defined in paragraph (k) of this section) are amounts properly chargeable to capital account in connection with that property. In general, amounts paid or incurred are chargeable to capital account if under the taxpayer's method of accounting they are properly includible in computing basis under § 1.46-3. Qualified progress expenditures for self-constructed property include both direct costs

Reg. § 1.46-5(h)(1)

(*e.g.*, labor, material, parts) and indirect costs (*e.g.*, overhead, insurance) associated with construction of property to the extent those costs are properly chargeable to capital account.

(2) *Property partially non-self-constructed.*—If an item of property is self-constructed because more than half of the construction expenditures are made directly by the taxpayer, then any expenditures (whether or not made directly by the taxpayer) for construction of that item of property are not subject to the limitations of section 46(d)(3)(B) and paragraph (j) of this section (relating to actual payment and progress in construction).

(3) *Time when amounts paid or incurred are properly chargeable to capital account.*—(i) In general, expenditures for component parts and materials to be used in construction of self-constructed property are not properly chargeable to capital account until consumed or physically attached in the construction process. Component parts and materials that have been neither consumed nor physically attached in the construction process, but which have been irrevocably allocated to construction of that property are properly chargeable to capital account. Component parts and materials designed specifically for the self-constructed property may be considered irrevocably allocated to construction of that property at the time of manufacture of the component parts and materials. Component parts and materials not designed specifically for the property may be considered irrevocably allocated to construction at the time of delivery to the construction site if they would be economically impractical to remove. For example, pumps delivered to sites of construction of a tundra pipeline may be treated as irrevocably allocated to that pipeline on the date of delivery, even if they would be usable, but for their location on the tundra, in connection with other property. Component parts and materials are not to be considered irrevocably allocated to use in self-constructed property until physical work on construction of that property has begun (as determined under paragraph (e)(1)(ii) of this section). Mere bookkeeping notations are not sufficient evidence that the necessary allocation has been made.

(ii) A taxpayer's procedure for determining the time when an expenditure is properly chargeable to capital account for self-constructed property is a method of accounting. Under section 446(e), the method of accounting, once adopted, may not be changed without consent of the Secretary.

(4) *Records requirement.*—The taxpayer shall maintain detailed records which permit specific identification of the amounts properly chargeable by the taxpayer during each taxable year to capital account for each item of self-constructed property.

(i) [Reserved].

(j) *Qualified progress expenditures for non-self-constructed property.*—(1) *In general.*—Qualified progress expenditures for non-self-constructed property (as defined in paragraph (l) of this section) are amounts actually paid by the taxpayer to another person for construction of the property, but only to the extent progress is made in construction. For example, such expenditures may include payments to the manufacturer of an item of progress expenditure property, payments to a contractor building progress expenditure property, or payments for engineering designs or blueprints that are drawn up during the normal construction period.

(2) *Property partially self-constructed.*—If an item of property is non-self-constructed, but a taxpayer uses its own employees to construct a portion of the property, expenditures for construction of that portion are made directly by the taxpayer (see § 1.46-5(h)(1)). Subject to the limitations of paragraph (g) of this section, those expenditures are qualified progress expenditures for non-self-constructed property if they satisfy the requirements of paragraph (j)(4), (5), and (6) of this section. Wages actually paid to the taxpayer's employees are presumed to correspond to progress in construction. Other amounts, including expenditures for materials, parts, and overhead, must be actually paid, not borrowed from the payee, and attributable to progress made in construction by the taxpayer.

(3) *Property constructed by more than one person.*—The percentage of completion limitation (as prescribed in paragraph (j)(6) of this section), including the presumption of ratable progress in construction, applies to an item of progress expenditure property as a whole. However, if several manufacturers or contractors do work in connection with the same property, the progress that each person makes toward completion of construction of the property must be determined separately. Section 46(d)(3)(B) is then applied separately to amounts paid to each manufacturer or contractor based on each person's progress in construction. For example, assume the taxpayer contracts with three persons to build an item of equipment. The taxpayer contracts with A to build the frame, B to build the motor, and C to assemble the frame and motor. Assume each contract represents $33^{1}/_{3}$ percent of the construction costs of the property. If,

within the taxable year in which construction begins, A and B each complete 50 percent of the construction of the frame and motor, respectively, amounts paid to A during that taxable year not in excess of $16^{2}/_{3}$ percent of the overall cost of the property, and amounts paid to B during that taxable year not in excess of $16^{2}/_{3}$ percent of the overall cost of the property, are qualified progress expenditures. Section 46(d)(3)(B) does not apply, however, to persons, such as lower-tier subcontractors, that do not have a direct contractual relationship with the taxpayer. If, in the above example, A engages a subcontractor to construct part of the frame, section 46(d)(3)(B) is applied only to amounts paid by the taxpayer to A, B, and C, but the portion of construction completed by A during a taxable year includes the portion completed by A's subcontractor.

(4) *Requirement of actual payment.*—Qualified progress expenditures for non-self-constructed property must be actually paid and not merely incurred. Amounts paid during the taxable year to another person for construction of non-self-constructed property may be in the form of money or property (*e.g.*, materials). However, property given as payment may be considered only to the extent it will be includible under § 1.46-3(c) in the basis of the non-self-constructed property when it is placed in service.

(5) *Certain borrowing disregarded.*—Qualified progress expenditures for non-self-constructed property do not include any amount paid to another person (the "payee") for construction if the amount is paid out of funds borrowed directly or indirectly from the payee. Amounts borrowed directly or indirectly from the payee by any person that is related to the taxpayer (within the meaning of section 267) or that is a member of the same controlled group of corporations (as defined in section 1563(a)) will be considered borrowed indirectly from the payee. Similarly, amounts borrowed under any financing arrangement that has the effect of making the payee a surety will be considered amounts borrowed indirectly by the taxpayer from the payee.

(6) *Percentage of completion limitation.*—(i) Under section 46(d)(3)(B)(ii), payments made in any taxable year may be considered qualified progress expenditures for non-self-constructed property only to the extent they are attributable to progress made in construction (percentage of completion limitation). Progress will generally be measured in terms of the manufacturer's incurred cost, as a fraction of the anticipated cost (as adjusted from year to year). Architectural or engineering estimates will be evidence of progress made in construction. Cost accounting records also will be evidence of progress. Progress will be presumed to occur not more rapidly than ratably over the normal construction period. However, the taxpayer may rebut the presumption by clear and convincing evidence of a greater percentage of completion.

(ii) If, after the first year of construction, there is a change in either the total cost to the taxpayer or the total cost of construction by another person, the taxpayer must recompute the percentage of completion limitation on the basis of revised cost. However, the recomputation will affect only amounts allowed as qualified progress expenditures in the taxable year in which the change occurs and in subsequent taxable years. The recomputation remains subject to the presumption of pro rata completion.

(iii) If, for any taxable year, the amount paid to another person for construction of an item of property under section 46(d)(3)(B)(i) exceeds the percentage of completion limitation in section 46(d)(3)(B)(ii), the excess is treated as an amount paid to the other person for construction for the succeeding taxable year. If for any taxable year the percentage of completion limitation for an item of property exceeds the amount paid to another during the taxable year for construction, the excess is added to the percentage of completion limitation for that property for the succeeding taxable year.

(iv) The taxpayer must maintain detailed records which permit specific identification of the amounts paid to each person for construction of each item of property and the percentage of construction completed by each person for each taxable year.

(7) *Example.*—The following example illustrates paragraph (j)(6) of this section.

Example. (i) Corporation X agrees to build an airplane for corporation Y, a calendar year taxpayer. The airplane is non-self-constructed progress expenditure property. Physical work on construction begins on January 1, 1980. The normal construction period for the airplane is five years and the airplane is delivered and placed in service on December 31, 1984.

(ii) The cost of construction to corporation X is $500,000. The contract price is $550,000. Corporation Y makes a $110,000 payment in each of the years 1980 and 1981, an $85,000 payment in 1982, a $135,000 payment in 1983, and a $110,000 payment in 1984.

(iii) For 1980, corporation Y makes an election under section 46(d). Progress is presumed to occur ratably over the 5-year construction period, which is 20 percent in each year. Twenty percent of the contract price is $110,000. The percentage of completion limitation for each year, thus, is $110,000.

(iv) For each of the years 1980 and 1981, the $110,000 payments may be treated as qualified progress expenditures. The payments equal the percentage of completion limitation.

(v) For 1982, the $85,000 payment may be treated as a qualified progress expenditure, because it is less than the percentage of completion limitation. The excess of the percentage of completion limitation ($110,000) over the 1982 payment ($85,000) is added to the percentage of completion limitation for 1983. One hundred and ten thousand dollars minus $85,000 equals $25,000. Twenty-five thousand dollars plus $110,000 equals $135,000, which is the percentage of completion limitation for 1983.

(vi) For 1983, the entire $135,000 payment may be treated as a qualifed progress expenditure. The payment equals the percentage of completion limitation for 1983.

(vii) For 1984, no qualified progress expenditures may be taken into account, because the airplane is placed in service in that year.

(viii) See example (2) of paragraph (r)(4) of this section for the result if Y sells its contract rights to the property on December 31, 1982.

(k) *Definition of self-constructed property.*—(1) *In general.*—Property is self-constructed property if it is reasonable to believe that more than half of the construction expenditures for the property will be made directly by the taxpayer. Construction expenditures made directly by the taxpayer include direct costs such as wages and materials and indirect costs such as overhead attributable to construction of the property. Expenditures for direct and indirect costs of construction will be treated as construction expenditures made directly by the taxpayer only to the extent that the expenditures directly benefit the construction of the property by employees of the taxpayer. Thus, wages paid to taxpayer's employees and expenditures for basic construction materials, such as sheet metal, lumber, glass, and nails, which are used by employees of the taxpayer to construct progress expenditure property, will be considered made directly by the taxpayer. Construction expenditures made by the taxpayer to a contractor or manufacturer, in general, will not be considered made directly by the taxpayer. Thus, the cost of component parts, such as boilers and turbines, which are purchased and merely installed or assembled by the taxpayer, will not be considered expenditures made directly by the taxpayer for construction. (*See* paragraph (h)(3) of this section to determine when such cost is properly chargeable to capital account.)

(2) *Time when determination made.*—The determination of whether property is self-constructed is to be made at the close of the taxable year in which physical work on construction of the property begins, or, if later, the close of the first taxable year to which an election under this section applies. Once it is reasonably estimated that more than half of construction expenditures will be made directly by the taxpayer, the fact the taxpayer actually makes half, or less than half, of the expenditures directly will not affect classification of the property as self-constructed property. Similarly, once a determination has been made, classification of property as self-constructed property is not affected by a change in circumstances in a later taxable year. However, a significant error unrelated to a change in circumstances may be evidence that the estimate was unreasonable when made.

(3) *Determination based on certain expenditures.*—For purposes of determining whether more than half of the expenditures for construction of an item of property will be made directly by the taxpayer, the taxpayer may take into account only expenditures properly includable by the taxpayer in the basis of the property under the provisions of § 1.46-3(c). Thus, property is self-constructed property only if more than half of the estimated basis of the property to be used for purposes of determining the credit allowed by section 38 is attributable to expenditures made directly by the taxpayer.

(l) *Definition of non-self-constructed property.*—Non-self-constructed property is property that is not self-constructed property. Thus, property is non-self-constructed property if it is reasonable to believe that only half, or less than half, of the expenditures for construction will be made directly by the taxpayer.

(m) *Alternative limitations for public utility, railroad, or airline property.*—The alternative limitations on qualified investment under section 46(a)(7) and (8) for public utility, railroad, or airline property (whichever applies) apply in determining the credit for qualified progress expenditures. The determination of whether progress expenditure property will be public utility, railroad, or airline property (whichever applies) when placed in service must be made at the close of the taxable year in which physical work on construction begins or, if later, at the close of the first taxable year for which an election

under section 46(d) is in effect. If, at that time, the taxpayer is in a trade or business as a public utility, railroad, or airline (as described in section 46(c)(3)(B) and 46(a)(8)(D) and (E), respectively), it is evidence the property will be public utility, railroad, or airline property when placed in service.

(n) *Leased property.*—A lessor of progress expenditure property may not elect under section 48(d) to treat a lessee (or a person who will be a lessee) as having made qualified progress expenditures.

(o) *Election.*—(1) *In general.*—The election under section 46(d)(6) to increase qualified investment by qualified progress expenditures may be made for any taxable year ending after December 31, 1974. Except as provided in paragraph (o)(2) of this section, the election is effective for the first taxable year for which it is made and for all taxable years thereafter unless it is revoked with the consent of the Commissioner. Except as provided in paragraphs (o)(2) and (3) of this section, the election applies to all qualified progress expenditures made by the taxpayer during the taxable year for construction of any progress expenditure property. Thus, the taxpayer may not make the election for one item of progress expenditure property and not for other items. If progress expenditure property is being constructed by or for a partnership, S corporation (as defined in section 1361(a)), trust, or estate, an election under section 46(d)(6) must be made separately by each partner or shareholder, or each beneficiary if the beneficiary, in determining his tax liability, would be allowed investment credit under section 38 for property subject to the election. The election may not be made by a partnership or S corporation, and may be made by a trust or estate only if the trust or estate, in determining its tax liability, would be allowed investment credit under section 38 for property subject to the election. The election of any partner, shareholder, beneficiary, trust, or estate will be effective for that person, even if a related partner, shareholder, beneficiary, trust, or estate does not make the election. An election made by a partner, shareholder, beneficiary, trust, or estate applies to all progress expenditure property of that person. For example, an election made by corporation X, which is a partner in the XYZ partnership, applies to progress expenditure property the corporation holds in its own capacity and also to its interest in progress expenditure property of the partnership.

(2) *Time and manner of making election.*—An election under section 46(d)(6) must be made on Form 3468 and filed with the original income tax return for the first taxable year ending after December 31, 1974 to which the election will apply. An election made before March 2, 1988, by filing a written statement (whether or not attached to the income tax return) will be considered valid. The election may not be made on an amended return filed after the time prescribed for filing the original return (including extensions) for that taxable year. However, an election under this section may be made or revoked by filing a statement with an amended return filed on or before May 31, 1988, if the due date for filing a return for the first taxable year to which the election applies is before May 31, 1988.

(3) *Carryover of election in certain transactions.*—In general, an election under section 48(d)(6) does not carry over to the transferee of progress expenditure property (or an interest therein). However, if under section 47(b) the property does not cease to be progress expenditure property because of the transfer, the election will carry over to the transferee. If so, the election will apply only to the property transferred. For rules relating to the determination of qualified progress expenditures of the transferee, see paragraph (r) of this section.

(p) *Partnerships, S corporations, trusts, or estates.*—(1) *In general.*—Each partner, shareholder, trust, estate, or beneficiary of a trust or estate that makes an election under section 46(d) shall take into account its share of qualified progress expenditures (determined under paragraph (p)(2) of this section) made by the partnership, S corporation, trust, or estate. In determining qualified investment for the year in which the property is placed in service, the basis of the property is apportioned as provided in § § 1.46-3(f), 1.48-6, or 1.48-5 (whichever applies). Each partner, shareholder, trust, estate, or beneficiary that made the election must reduce qualified investment under section 46(c)(4) for the year the property is placed in service by qualified progress expenditures taken into account by that person.

(2) *Determination of share of qualified progress expenditures.*—The share of qualified progress expenditures of each partner, shareholder, trust, estate, or beneficiary that makes an election under section 46(d) must be determined in accordance with the same ratio used under § § 1.46-3(f)(2), 1.48-5(a)(1), or 1.48-6(a)(1) (whichever applies) to determine its share of basis (or cost). The last sentence of § 1.46-3(f)(2)(i) must be applied by referring to the date on which qualified progress expenditures are paid or chargeable to capital amount (whichever is applicable).

(3) *Examples.*—The following examples illustrate this paragraph (p).

Example (1). (i) Corporation X contracts to build a ship for partnership AB that qualifies as progress expenditure property. The contract price is $100,000. Physical work on construction of the ship begins on January 1, 1980. The ship is placed in service on December 31, 1983.

(ii) The AB partnership reports income on the calendar year basis. Partners A and B share profits equally. For A's taxable year ending December 31, 1980, A makes an election under section 46(d). B does not make the election.

(iii) For each of the years 1980, 1981, 1982, and 1983, the AB partnership makes $25,000 payments to corporation X. The payments made in 1980, 1981, and 1982 are qualified progress expenditures. The 1983 payment is not a qualified progress expenditure, because the ship is placed in service in that year.

(iv) For each of the years 1980, 1981, and 1982, A may take into account qualified progress expenditures of $12,500 because A had a 50 percent partnership interest in each of those years.

(v) For 1983, qualified investment for the ship is $100,000. A and B's share are $50,000 each, because each had a 50 percent partnership interest in 1983. However, A must reduce its $50,000 share for 1983 by $37,500, the amount of qualified progress expenditures taken into account by A. B's share is not reduced, because B did not take into account qualified progress expenditures.

Example (2). (i) The facts are the same as in example (1) except that on June 30, 1983, the partnership agreement is amended to admit a new partner, C. The partners agree to share profits equally. There is no special allocation in effect under section 704 with respect to the ship.

(ii) For each of the years 1980, 1981, and 1982, A may take into account qualified progress expenditures of $12,500 because A has a 50 percent partnership interest in those years.

(iii) For 1983, A, B, and C's share of qualified investment is $33,333 each, because each had a 33 1/3 percent partnership interest in that year. A must reduce its share to zero, because it took $37,500 into account as qualified progress expenditures. In addition, the excess of the $37,500 over the $33,333 applied as a reduction is subject to recapture under section 47(a)(3)(B). B and C's shares are not reduced, because neither taxpayer took into account qualified progress expenditures.

(q) *Limitation on qualified progress expenditures for taxable years beginning before 1980.*—(1) *In general.*—(i) Under section 46(d)(7), qualified progress expenditures for any taxable year beginning before January 1, 1980, are limited. The taxpayer must apply the limitation under section 46(d)(7) on an item by item basis. In general, the taxpayer may take into account the applicable percentage (as determined under the table in section 46(d)(7)(A)) of qualified progress expenditures for each of those years. In addition, the taxpayer may take into account for each of those years 20 percent of qualified investment for each of the preceding taxable years determined without applying the limitations of section 46(d)(7).

(ii) The applicable percentage under section 46(d)(7)(A) may be applied only for one taxable year that ends within a calendar year in determining qualified investment for an item of progress expenditure property. For example, calendar year partners of a calendar year partnership may increase qualified investment for 1976 by 20 percent of qualified progress expenditures made in 1975 for an item of property. If the partnership incorporates in 1976 and the taxable year of the corporation begins on July 1, 1976, and ends on June 30, 1977, qualified investment of the corporation for its taxable year beginning on July 1, 1976, cannot be increased by 20 percent of the 1975 expenditure.

(2) *Example.*—The following example illustrates this paragraph (q).

Example. (i) Corporation X contracts with A on January 1, 1976, to build an electric generator that qualifies as non-self-constructed progress expenditure property. A will build the generator at a cost of $125,000. Corporation X agrees to pay A $150,000. Corporation X reports income on the calendar year basis. Corporation X makes an election under section 46(d) for 1976. Physical work on construction begins on January 1, 1976. Corporation X makes payments of $30,000 to A for construction of the generator in each of the years 1976, 1977, 1978, 1979, and 1980. A incurs a cost of $25,000 in each of those years for construction of the property. The property is placed in service in 1980.

(ii) For 1976, X may increase qualified investment by $12,000, 40 percent of the payment made in 1976.

(iii) For 1977, corporation X may increase qualified investment by $24,000. Eighteen thousand dollars of that amount is 60 percent of the 1977 payment. The remaining $6,000 is 20 percent of the $30,000 payment made in 1976.

(iv) For 1978, corporation X may increase qualified investment by $36,000. Twenty-four thousand dollars of that amount is 80 percent of the 1978 payment. The remaining $12,000 is 20 percent of the $30,000 payment made in 1976, plus 20 percent of the $30,000 payment made in 1977.

(v) For 1979, corporation X may increase qualified investment by $48,000. Thirty thousand dollars of that amount is 100 percent of the 1979 payment. The remaining $18,000 of that amount is 20 percent of the $30,000 payment made in each of the years 1976, 1977, and 1978.

(vi) Qualified investment for corporation X for 1980 is $30,000. The $30,000 is the basis (or cost) of the generator ($150,000), reduced by qualified progress expenditures allowed with respect to that property ($120,000).

(r) *Special rules for transferred property.*—(1) *In general.*—A transferee of progress expenditure property (or an interest therein) may take into account qualified progress expenditures for the property only if—

(i) The property is progress expenditure property in the hands of the transferee, and

(ii) The transferee makes an election under section 46(d) or the election made by the transferor (or its predecessor) carries over to the transferee under paragraph (o)(3) of this section.

(2) *Status as progress expenditure property.*—(i) If the transfer requires recapture under section 47(a)(3) and §1.47-1(g) (or would require recapture if the transferor had made an election under section 46(d)), then—

(A) For purposes of determining if the property is progress expenditure property in the hands of the transferee, the normal construction period for the property begins on the date of the transfer, or, if later, on the first day of the first taxable year for which the transferee makes an election under section 46(d), and

(B) For purposes of determining whether the property is self-constructed or non-self-constructed in the hands of the transferee, the amount paid or incurred for the transfer of the property will not be considered a construction expenditure made directly by the transferee.

(ii) If the transfer does not require recapture under section 47(a)(3) and §1.47-1(g), and the election carries over to the taxpayer under paragraph (o)(3) of this section, the property does not lose its status as progress expenditure property because of the transfer.

(3) *Amount of qualified progress expenditures for transferee.*—(i) If the transfer does not require recapture under section 47(a)(3) and §1.47-1(g), and the election carries over to the taxpayer under paragraph (o)(3) of this section, the transferee must determine its qualified progress expenditures—

(A) By using the same normal construction period used by the transferor,

(B) By treating the property as having the same status as self-constructed or non-self-constructed as the property had in the hands of the transferor, and

(C) In the case of non-self-constructed property, by taking into account any excess described in section 46(d)(4)(C)(i) (relating to the excess of payments over the percentage-of-completion limitation) or section 46(d)(4)(C)(ii) (relating to the excess of the percentage-of-completion limitation over the amount of payments) that the transferor would have taken into account with respect to that property.

(ii) If the transfer requires recapture under section 47(a)(3) and §1.47-1(g) (or would require recapture if the transferor had made an election under section 46(d)), the amount paid or incurred for the transfer will be considered a payment for construction of that property to the extent that—

(A) It is properly includible in the basis of the property under §1.46-3(c),

(B) The taxpayer can show the amount is attributable to construction costs paid or chargeable to capital account by the transferor or other person after physical work on construction of the property began, and

(C) It does not exceed the amount by which the transferor has increased qualified investment for qualified progress expenditures incurred with respect to the property (or would have increased qualified investment but for the "lesser of" limitation of section 46(d)(3)(B) or the absence of an election under section 46(d)), plus any amount that would have been treated as a qualified progress expenditure by the transferor had the property not been transferred. Once the status of the property as self-constructed or non-self-constructed property in the hands of the transferee has been determined, all rules under this section for determining the amount of qualified progress expenditures for that type of property apply. For example, if the property is non-self-constructed in the hands of the transferee, amounts merely incurred (but not paid) for the transfer are not taken into account as qualified progress expenditures. Actual payment is necessary (see paragraph (j)(3) of this section). In applying section

46(d)(3)(B)(ii), the amount paid or incurred for the transfer (to the extent that it qualifies as a payment for construction under the first sentence of this paragraph (r)(3)(ii)) is considered to be part of the overall cost to the transferee of construction by another person, and the portion of construction which is completed during the taxable year is determined by taking into account construction that was completed before the constructed property was acquired by the transferee. If the transferee makes an election under section 46(d) and this section for the taxable year in which the transfer occurs, then for purposes of applying the presumption in section 46(d)(4)(D) that construction is deemed to occur not more rapidly than ratably over the normal construction period, the transferee's normal construction period is considered to have begun on the date on which physical work on construction of the acquired property began.

(4) *Examples.*—The following examples illustrate this paragraph (r).

Example (1). Corporation X begins physical work on construction of progress expenditure property for corporation Y on January 1, 1976. Y accurately estimates a 3-year normal construction period and elects under section 48(d) on its return for its taxable year ending December 31, 1976. On January 1, 1978, Y sells the contract rights for construction of the property to corporation Z, which uses a fiscal year ending June 30. Qualified progress expenditures allowed to Y in 1976 and 1977 are subject to recapture under section 47(a)(3). Because Z's normal construction period for the property is less than 2 years (January 1, 1978 to January 1, 1979), the property is not progress expenditure property in Z's hands. Z may not elect progress expenditure treatment for the property.

Example (2). (i) Assume the same facts as in the example in paragraph (j)(7) of this section, except on December 31, 1982, Y sells its contract rights to the property for $340,000 to corporation Z, which also uses the calendar year. Z pays Y the full $340,000 on that date. The property is still to be placed in service on December 31, 1984, and will not be available for placing in service at an earlier date. Z makes payments to X of $135,000 on December 31, 1983, and $110,000 on December 31, 1984.

(ii) The investment credit allowed Y in 1980 and 1981 for qualified progress expenditures is subject to recapture under section 47(a)(3) and Y may not treat its $85,000 payment in 1982 as a qualified progress expenditure.

(iii) For purposes of determining if the airplane is qualified progress expenditure property with respect to Z, the normal construction period for the property for Z begins on December 31, 1982, the date of transfer. Since the remaining construction period is two years, the property is progress expenditure property if it otherwise qualifies in Z's hands.

(iv) Only $305,000 of the $340,000 payment to Y can qualify as a qualified progress expenditure, because only that amount is attributable to construction costs paid by Y and does not exceed the sum of the amount by which Y increased qualified investment in 1980 and 1981 for qualified progress expenditures ($220,000) and the amount that Y would have treated as a qualified progress expenditure in 1982 ($85,000).

(v) Assume that Z cannot establish that progress in construction has been completed more rapidly than ratably. If Z makes an election under section 46(d) for 1982, then for purposes of applying the percentage of completion limitation, Z's normal construction period is considered to begin on January 1, 1980. Progress is presumed to occur ratably over the 5-year construction period, which is 20 percent in each year.

(vi) For 1982, Z may treat the full $305,000 as a qualified progress expenditure because it is less than the percentage of completion limitation, $330,000 ($110,000 a year for 1980, 1981, and 1982).

(vii) For 1983, Z may treat the entire $135,000 payment as a qualified progress expenditure, since it does not exceed the percentage of completion limitation for that year, $135,000 ($110,000 plus the $25,000 excess from 1982).

(viii) For Z's taxable year ending December 31, 1984, no qualified progress expenditures may be taken into account because the property is placed in service during that year. [Reg. § 1.46-5.]

□ [*T.D.* 8183, 3-1-88.]

[Reg. § 1.46-6]

§ 1.46-6. Limitation in case of certain regulated companies.—(a) *In general.*—(1) *Scope of section.*—This section does not reflect amendments made to section 46 after enactment of the Revenue Act of 1971, other than the redesignation of section 46(e) as section 46(f) by the Tax Reduction Act of 1975.

(2) *Disallowance of credit.*—Under section 46(f), a credit otherwise allowable under section 38 ("credit") will be disallowed in certain cases with respect to "section 46(f) property" as defined in paragraph (b)(1) of this section. Paragraph (f) of this section describes circum-

stances under which a determination put into effect by a regulatory body will result in the disallowance of the credit. Such a determination will result in a disallowance only if section 46(f)(1) or (2) applies to such property and such determination affects the taxpayer's cost of service or rate base in a manner inconsistent with section 46(f)(1) or (2) (whichever is applicable).

(3) *General rules.*—The provisions of section 46(f)(1) and (2) are limitations on the treatment of the credit for ratemaking purposes and for purposes of the taxpayer's regulated books of account only. Under the provisions of section 46(f)(1), the credit may not be flowed through to income (*i.e.,* used to reduce taxpayer's cost of service) but in certain circumstances may be used to reduce rate base (provided that such reduction is restored not less rapidly than ratably). If an election is made under section 46(f)(2), the credit may be flowed through to income (but not more rapidly than ratably) and there may not be any reduction in rate base. If an election is made under section 46(f)(3), none of the limitations of section 46(f)(1) or (2) apply to certain section 46(f) property of the taxpayer. Thus, under the provisions of section 46(f)(3), no credit is disallowed if the credit is treated in any manner for ratemaking purposes, including any manner of treatment permitted under the limitations of section 46(f)(1) or (2).

(4) *Elections.*—For rules relating to the manner of making, on or before March 9, 1972, the three elections listed in section 46(f)(1), (2), and (3), see 26 CFR 12.3. For rules relating to the application of such elections, see paragraph (h) of this section.

(5) *Cross references.*—For rules with respect to the treatment of corporate reorganizations, asset acquisitions, and taxpayers subject to the jurisdiction of more than one regulatory body, etc., see paragraph (j) of this section.

(6) *Nonapplication of prior law.*—Under section 105(e) of the Revenue Act of 1971, section 203(e) of the Revenue Act of 1964, 78 Stat. 35, does not apply to section 46(f) property.

(b) *Definitions.*—For purposes of this section, the following definitions apply:

(1) *Section 46(f) property.*—"Section 46(f) property" is property described in section 50 that is—

(i) Public utility property within the meaning of section 46(c)(3)(B) (other than nonregulated communication property described in § 1.46-3(g)(2)(iv)) or

(ii) Property used predominantly in the trade or business of the furnishing or sale of steam through a local distribution system or of the transportation of gas or steam by pipeline, if the rates for the trade or business are regulated within the meaning of § 1.46-3(g)(2)(iii).

For purposes of determining whether property is used predominantly in the trade or business of transportation of gas by pipeline (or of transportation of gas by pipeline and of furnishing or sale of gas through a local distribution system), the rules prescribed in § 1.46-3(g)(4) apply except that accounts 365 through 371 inclusive (Transmission Plant) are added to the accounts listed in § 1.46-3(g)(4)(i).

(2) *Cost of service.*—(i)(A) For purposes of this section, "cost of service" is the amount required by a taxpayer to provide regulated goods or services. Cost of service includes operating expenses (including salaries, cost of materials, etc.), maintenance expenses, depreciation expenses, tax expenses, and interest expenses. For purposes of this section, any effect on a taxpayer's permitted return on investment that results from a reduction in the taxpayer's rate base does not constitute a reduction in cost of service, even though, as a technical ratemaking term, "cost of service" ordinarily includes a permitted return on investment. In addition, taking into account a deduction for the additional interest that the taxpayer would pay or accrue if the credit were unavailable in determining Federal income tax expense ("synchronization of interest") does not constitute a reduction in cost of service for purposes of section 46(f)(2). This adjustment to Federal income tax expense may be taken into account in determining cost of service for the regulated accounting period or periods that include the taxable year to which the adjustment relates or for any subsequent regulated accounting period.

(B) See paragraph (b)(3)(ii)(B) of this section for rules relating to the amount of additional interest that the taxpayer would pay or accrue if the credit were unavailable.

(ii) In determining whether, or to what extent, a credit has been used to reduce cost of service, reference shall be made to any accounting treatment that affects cost of service. Examples of such treatment include reducing by all or a portion of the credit the amount of Federal income tax expense taken into account for ratemaking purposes and reducing the depreciable bases of property by all or a portion of the credit for ratemaking purposes.

(3) *Rate base.*—(i) For purposes of this section, "rate base" is the monetary amount that is multiplied by a rate of return to determine the permitted return on investment.

(ii)(A) In determining whether, or to what extent, a credit has been used to reduce rate base, reference shall be made to any accounting treatment that affects rate base. In addition, in those cases in which the rate of return is based on the taxpayer's cost of capital, reference shall be made to any accounting treatment that reduces the permitted return on investment by treating the credit less favorably than the capital that would have been provided if the credit were unavailable. Thus, the credit may not be assigned a "cost of capital" rate that is less than the overall cost of capital rate, determined on the basis of a weighted average, for the capital that would have been provided if the credit were unavailable.

(B) For purposes of determining the cost of capital rate assigned to the credit and the amount of additional interest that the taxpayer would pay or accrue, the composition of the capital that would have been provided if the credit were unavailable may be determined—

(1) On the basis of all the relevant facts and circumstances; or

(2) By assuming for both such purposes that such capital would be provided solely by common shareholders, preferred shareholders, and long-term creditors in the same proportions and at the same rates of return as the capital actually provided to the taxpayer by such shareholders and creditors.

For purposes of this section, capital provided by long-term creditors does not include deferred taxes as described in section 167(l)(3)(G) or 168(e)(3)(B)(ii).

(C) If a taxpayer's overall rate of return is based on a deemed or hypothetical capital structure, paragraph (b)(3)(ii)(B) of this section shall be applied by treating the deemed or hypothetical capital as if it were the capital actually provided to the taxpayer and determining the composition of the capital that would have been provided if the credit were unavailable in a manner consistent with such treatment.

(iii) Whether, or to what extent, a credit has been used to reduce rate base for any period to which pre-June 23, 1986, rates apply will be determined under 26 CFR 1.46-6(b)(3) and (4) (revised as of April 1, 1985) if such a determination avoids disallowance of a credit that would be disallowed under paragraph (b)(3)(ii) or (4)(ii) of this section. For this purpose, a period to which pre-June 23, 1986, rates apply is any period for which the effect of the credit on rate base for ratemaking purposes is established under a determination put into effect (within the meaning of paragraph (f) of this section) before June 23, 1986.

(4) *Indirect reductions to cost of service or rate base.*—(i) Cost of service or rate base is also considered to have been reduced by reason of all or a portion of a credit if such reduction is made in an indirect manner.

(ii) One type of such indirect reduction is any ratemaking decision in which the credit is treated as operating income (subject to ratemaking regulation) or is treated less favorably than the capital that would have been provided if the credit were unavailable. For example, if the credit is accounted for as nonoperating income on a company's regulated books of account but a ratemaking decision has the effect of treating the credit as operating income in determining rate of return to common shareholders, then cost of service has been indirectly reduced by reason of the credit.

(iii) A second type of indirect reduction is any ratemaking decision intended to achieve an effect similar to a direct reduction to cost of service or rate base. In determining whether a ratemaking decision is intended to achieve this effect, consideration is given to all the relevant facts and circumstances of each case, including, but not limited to—

(A) The record of the proceeding,

(B) The regulatory body's orders or opinions (including any dissenting views), and

(C) The anticipated effect of the ratemaking decision on the company's revenues in comparison to a direct reduction to cost of service or rate base by reason of the investment tax credits available to the regulated company.

(iv) This subdivision (iv) describes a situation that is not an indirect reduction to cost of service or rate base by reason of all or a portion of a credit. The ratemaking treatment of credits may affect the financial condition of a company, including the company's ability to attract new capital, the cost of that capital, the company's future financial requirements, the market price of the company's securities, and the degree of risk attributable to investment in those securities. The financial condition may be reflected in certain customary financial indicators such as the comparative capital structure of the company, coverage ratios, price/earnings ratios, and price/book ratios.

Under the facts and circumstances test of paragraph (b)(4)(iii) of this section, the consideration of a company's financial condition by a regulatory body is not an indirect reduction to cost of service or rate base, even though such condition, as affected by the ratemaking treatment of the company's investment tax credits, is considered in the development of a reasonable rate of return on common shareholders' investment.

(c) *General rule.*—(1) *In general.*—Section 46(f)(1) applies to all of the taxpayer's section 46(f) property except property to which an election under section 46(f)(2) or (3) applies. Under section 46(f)(1), the credit for the taxpayer's section 46(f) property will be disallowed if—

(i) The taxpayer's cost of service for ratemaking purposes is reduced by reason of any portion of such credit, or

(ii) The taxpayer's rate base is reduced by reason of any portion of the credit and such reduction in rate base is not restored or is restored less rapidly than ratably within the meaning of paragraph (g) of this section.

(2) *Insufficient natural domestic supply.*—The provisions of paragraph (c)(1)(ii) of this section shall not apply to permit any reduction in taxpayer's rate base with respect to its "short supply property" if it made an election under the last sentence of section 46(f)(1) on or before March 9, 1972.

(3) *Short supply property.*—For purposes of this section, section 46(f) property is "short supply property" if—

(i) The property is described in paragraph (b)(1)(ii) of this section,

(ii) The regulatory body described in section 46(c)(3)(B) that has jurisdiction for ratemaking purposes with respect to such trade or business is an agency or instrumentality of the United States, and

(iii) This regulatory body makes a short supply determination and the determination is in effect on the date such property is placed in service.

(4) *Short supply determination.*—A short supply determination is made or revoked on the date of its publication in the FEDERAL REGISTER. It is a determination that the natural domestic supply of gas or steam is insufficient to meet the present and future requirements of the domestic economy.

(5) *Dates short supply determination in effect.*—(i) A short supply determination is considered to be in effect with respect to section 46(f) property placed in service at any time before the determination is revoked. However, a short supply determination made after June 18, 1979, is not considered to be in effect with respect to section 46(f) property placed in service before such determination was made.

(d) *Special rule for ratable flow-through.*—If an election was made under section 46(f)(2) on or before March 9, 1972, section 46(f)(2) applies to all of the taxpayer's section 46(f) property except property to which an election under section 46(f)(3) applies. Under section 46(f)(2), the credit for the taxpayer's section 46(f) property will be disallowed if—

(1) The taxpayer's cost of service, for ratemaking purposes or in its regulated books of account, is reduced by more than a ratable portion of such credit within the meaning of paragraph (g) of this section or

(2) The taxpayer's rate base is reduced by reason of any portion of such credit.

(e) *Flow-through property.*—If a taxpayer made an election under section 46(f)(3) on or before March 9, 1972, section 46(f)(1) and (2) do not apply to the taxpayer's section 46(f) property to which section 167(l)(2)(C) applies. In the case of an election under section 46(f)(3), a credit will not be disallowed, notwithstanding a determination by a regulatory body having jurisdiction over such taxpayer that reduces the taxpayer's cost of service or rate base by reason of such credit. In general, section 167(l)(2)(C) applies to property with respect to which a taxpayer may use a flow-through method of accounting (within the meaning of section 167(l)(3)(H)) to take into account the allowance for depreciation under section 167(a). Section 167(l)(2)(C) applies to property even though the taxpayer does not use a flow-through method of accounting with respect to the property. Section 167(l)(2)(C) does not apply to property if the taxpayer can not use a flow-through method of accounting with respect to the property. For example, section 167(l)(2)(C) does not apply to property with respect to which an election under section 167(l)(4)(A) applies. Thus, such property does not qualify for an election under section 46(f)(3).

(f) *Limitations.*—(1) *In general.*—This paragraph provides rules relating to limitations on the disallowance of credits under section 46(f)(4). Key terms are defined in paragraphs (f)(7), (8), and (9) of this section.

(2) *Disallowance postponed.*—There is no disallowance of a credit before the first final inconsistent determination is put into effect for the taxpayer's section 46(f) property.

(3) *Time of disallowance.*—A credit is disallowed—

(i) When the first final inconsistent determination is put into effect and

(ii) When any inconsistent determination (whether or not final) is put into effect after the first final inconsistent determination is put into effect.

(4) *Credits disallowed.*—A credit is disallowed for section 46(f) property placed in service (within the meaning of §1.46-3(d)) by the taxpayer—

(i) Before the date any inconsistent determination described in paragraph (f)(2) of this section is put into effect and

(ii) On or after such date and before the date a subsequent consistent determination (whether or not final) is put into effect.

(5) *Barred years.*—No amount of credit for a taxable year is disallowed under paragraph (f)(3) of this section if, for such year, assessment of a deficiency is barred by any law or rule of law.

(6) *Notification and other requirements.*—The taxpayer shall notify the district director of a disallowance of a credit under paragraph (f)(3) of this section within 30 days of the date that the applicable determination is put into effect. In the case of such a disallowance, the taxpayer shall recompute its tax liability for any affected taxable year, and such recomputation shall be made in the form of an amended return where necessary.

(7) *Determinations.*—For purposes of this paragraph, the term "determination" refers to a determination made with respect to section 46(f) property (other than property to which an election under section 46(f)(3) applies) by a regulatory body described in section 46(c)(3)(B) that determines the effect of the credit—

(i) For purposes of section 46(f)(1), on the taxpayer's cost of service or rate base for ratemaking purposes or

(ii) In the case of a taxpayer that made an election under section 46(f)(2), on the taxpayer's cost of service, for ratemaking purposes or in its regulated books of account, or on the taxpayer's rate base for ratemaking purposes.

A regulatory body does not have to take affirmative action to make a determination. Thus, a regulatory body's failure to take action on a rate schedule filed by a taxpayer is a determination if the rates can be put into effect without further action by the regulatory body.

(8) *Types of determinations.*—For purposes of this paragraph—

(i) The term "inconsistent" refers to a determination that is inconsistent with section 46(f)(1) or (2) (as the case may be). Thus, for example, a determination to reduce the taxpayer's cost of service by more than a ratable portion of the credit would be a determination that is inconsistent with section 46(f)(2). As a further example, such a determination would also be inconsistent if section 46(f)(1) applied because no reduction in cost of service is permitted under section 46(f)(1).

(ii) The term "consistent" refers to a determination that is *consistent with* section 46(f)(1) or (2) (as the case may be).

(iii) The term "final determination" means a determination with respect to which all rights to appeal or to request a review, a rehearing, or a redetermination have been exhausted or have lapsed.

(iv) The term "first final inconsistent determination" means the first final determination put into effect after December 10, 1971, that is inconsistent with section 46(f)(1) or (2) (as the case may be).

(9) *Put into effect.*—A determination is put into effect on the later of—

(i) The date it is issued (or, if a first final inconsistent determination, the date it becomes final) or

(ii) The date it becomes operative.

(10) *Examples.*—The provisions of this paragraph may be illustrated by the following examples:

Example (1). Corporation X, a calendar-year taxpayer engaged in a public utility activity is subject to the jurisdiction of regulatory body A. On September 15, 1971, X purchases section 46(f) property and places it in service on that date. For 1971, X takes the credit allowable by section 38 with respect to such property. X does not make any election permitted by section 46(f). On October 9, 1972, A makes a determination that X must account for the credit allowable under section 38 in a manner inconsistent with section 46(f)(1). The determination, which was the first determination by A after December 10, 1971, becomes final on January 1, 1973, and holds that X must retroactively adjust the manner in which it accounted for the credit allowable under section 38 starting with the taxable year that began on January 1, 1972. Since, under the provisions of paragraph (f)(8) of

this section, the determination by A is put into effect on January 1, 1973 (the date it becomes final), the credit is retroactively disallowed with respect to any of X's section 46(f) property placed in service before January 1, 1973, on any date which occurs during a taxable year with respect to which an assessment of a deficiency has not been barred by any law or rule of law. In addition, the credit is disallowed with respect to X's section 46(f) property placed in service on or after January 1, 1973, and before the date that a subsequent determination by A, which as to X is consistent with section 46(f)(1), is put into effect. Thus, X must amend its income tax return for 1971 to reflect the retroactive disallowance of the credit otherwise allowable under section 38 with respect to the section 46(f) property placed in service on September 15, 1971.

Example (2). The facts are the same as in example (1), except that the first inconsistent determination by A becomes final on April 5, 1972, and requires X to account for the credit for all taxable years beginning on or after January 1, 1973, in a manner inconsistent with section 46(f)(1). Under the provisions of paragraph (f)(8) of this section, the determination was put into effect on January 1, 1973 (the date it became operative). The result is the same as in example (1).

Example (3). The facts are the same as in example (1), except that on June 1, 1975, A issues a determination that X shall retroactively account for the credit allowable by section 38 in a manner consistent with the provisions of section 46(f)(1) for taxable years beginning on or after January 1, 1971. The determination becomes final on January 5, 1976, in the same form as originally issued. The result is the same as in example (1) with respect to property X places in service before June 1, 1975. The credit is allowed with respect to property X places in service on or after June 1, 1975 (the date that the consistent determination is put into effect).

(g) *Ratable methods.*—(1) *In general.*—Under this paragraph (g), rules are prescribed for purposes of determining whether or not, under section 46(f)(1), a reduction in the taxpayer's rate base with respect to the credit is restored less rapidly than ratably and whether or not under section 46(f)(2) the taxpayer's cost of service for ratemaking purposes is reduced by more than a ratable portion of such credit.

(2) *Regulated depreciation expense.*—What is "ratable" is determined by considering the period of time actually used in computing the taxpayer's regulated depreciation expense for the property for which a credit is allowed. "Regulated depreciation expense" is the depreciation expense for the property used by a regulatory body for purposes of establishing the taxpayer's cost of service for ratemaking purposes. Such period of time shall be expressed in units of years (or shorter periods), units of production, or machine hours and shall be determined in accordance with the individual useful life system or composite (or other group asset) account system actually used in computing the taxpayer's regulated depreciation expense. A method of restoring, or reducing, is ratable if the amount to be restored to rate base, or to reduce cost of service (as the case may be), is allocated ratably in proportion to the number of such units. Thus, for example, assume that the regulated depreciation expense is computed under the straight line method by applying a composite annual percentage rate to "original cost" (as defined for purposes of computing regulated depreciation expense). If, with respect to an item of section 46(f) property, the amount to be restored annually to rate base is computed by applying a composite annual percentage rate to the amount by which the rate base was reduced, then the restoration is ratable. Similarly, if cost of service is reduced annually by an amount computed by applying a composite annual percentage rate to the amount of the credit, cost of service is reduced by a ratable portion. If such composite annual percentage rate were revised for purposes of computing regulated depreciation expense beginning with a particular accounting period, the computation of ratable restoration or ratable portion (as the case may be) must also be revised beginning with such period. A composite annual percentage rate is determined solely by reference to the period of time actually used by the taxpayer in computing its regulated depreciation expense without reduction for salvage or other items such as over and under accruals. A composite annual percentage rate determined by taking into account salvage value or other items shall be considered to be ratable in the case of a determination (whether or not final) issued before March 22, 1979, and any rate order (whether or not final) that is entered into before June 20, 1979, in response to a rate case filed before April 23, 1979. For this purpose, the term "rate order" does not include an order by a regulatory body that perfunctorily adopts rates as filed if such rates are suspended or subject to rebate.

(h) *Elections.*—(1) *Applicability of elections.*—(i) Any election under section 46(f) applies to all of the taxpayer's property eligible for the election, whether or not the taxpayer is regulated by more than one regulatory body.

(ii) Section 46(f)(1) applies to all of the taxpayer's section 46(f) property in the absence of an election under either section 46(f)(2) or

(3). If an election is made under section 46(f)(2), section 46(f)(1) does not apply to any of the taxpayer's section 46(f) property.

(iii) An election made under the last sentence of section 46(f)(1) applies to that portion of the taxpayer's section 46(f) property to which section 46(f)(1) applies and which is short supply property within the meaning of paragraph (c)(2) of this section.

(iv) If a taxpayer makes an election under section 46(f)(2) and makes no election under section 46(f)(3), the election under section 46(f)(2) applies to all of the taxpayer's section 46(f) property.

(v) If a taxpayer makes an election under section 46(f)(3), such election applies to all of the taxpayer's section 46(f) property to which section 167(l)(2)(C) applies. Section 46(f)(1) or (2) (as the case may be) applies to that portion of the taxpayer's section 46(f) property that is not property to which section 167(l)(2)(C) applies. Thus, for example, if a taxpayer makes an election under section 46(f)(2) and also makes an election under section 46(f)(3), section 46(f)(3) applies to all of the taxpayer's section 46(f) property to which section 167(l)(2)(C) applies, and section 46(f)(2) applies to the remainder of the taxpayer's section 46(f) property.

(2) *Method of making elections.*—See 26 CFR 12.3 for rules relating to the method of making the elections described in section 46(f)(1), (2), or (3).

(i) [Reserved]

(j) *Reorganizations, asset acquisitions, multiple regulation, etc..*—(1) *Taxpayers not entirely subject to jurisdiction of one regulatory body.*—(i) If a taxpayer is required by a regulatory body having jurisdiction over less than all of its property to account for the credit under a determination that is inconsistent with section 46(f)(1) or (2) (as the case may be), such credit shall be disallowed only with respect to property subject to the jurisdiction of such regulatory body.

(ii) For purposes of this paragraph (j), a regulatory body is considered to have jurisdiction over property of a taxpayer if the property is included in the rate base for which the regulatory body determines an allowable rate of return for ratemaking purposes or if expenses with respect to the property are included in cost of service as determined by the regulatory body for ratemaking purposes. For example, if regulatory body A, having jurisdiction over 60 percent of an item of corporation X's section 46(f) property, makes a determination which is inconsistent with section 46(f), and if regulatory body B, having jurisdiction over the remaining 40 percent of such item of property, makes a consistent determination (or if the remaining 40 percent is not subject to the jurisdiction of any regulatory body), then 60 percent of the credit for such item will be disallowed. For a further example, if regulatory body A, having jurisdiction over 60 percent of X's section 46(f) property, has jurisdiction over 100 percent of a particular generator, 100 percent of the credit for such generator will be disallowed.

(iii) For rules which provide that the 3 elections under section 46(f) may not be made with respect to less than all of the taxpayer's property eligible for the election, see paragraph (h)(1)(i) of this section.

(2) [Reserved]

(k) *Treatment of accumulated deferred investment tax credits upon the deregulation of public utility property.*—(1) *Scope.*—(i) *In general.*—This paragraph (k) provides rules for the application of former sections 46(f)(1) and 46(f)(2) of the Internal Revenue Code to a taxpayer with respect to public utility property that ceases, whether by disposition, deregulation, or otherwise, to be public utility property with respect to the taxpayer and that is not described in paragraph (k)(1)(ii) of this section (deregulated public utility property).

(ii) *Exception.*—This paragraph (k) does not apply to property that ceases to be public utility property with respect to the taxpayer on account of an ordinary retirement within the meaning of §1.167(a)-11(d)(3)(ii).

(2) *Ratable amount.*—(i) *Restoration of rate base reduction.*—A reduction in the taxpayer's rate base on account of the credit with respect to public utility property that becomes deregulated public utility property is restored ratably during the period after the property becomes deregulated public utility property if the amount of the reduction remaining to be restored does not, at any time during the period, exceed the restoration percentage of the recoverable stranded cost of the property at such time. For this purpose—

(A) The stranded cost of the property is the cost of the property reduced by the amount of such cost that the taxpayer has recovered through regulated depreciation expense during the period before the property becomes deregulated public utility property;

(B) The recoverable stranded cost of the property at any time is the stranded cost of the property that the taxpayer will be permitted to recover through rates after such time; and

(C) The restoration percentage for the property is determined by dividing the reduction in rate base remaining to be restored

with respect to the property immediately before the property becomes deregulated public utility property by the stranded cost of the property.

(ii) *Cost of service reduction.*—Reductions in the taxpayer's cost of service on account of the credit with respect to public utility property that becomes deregulated public utility property are ratable during the period after the property becomes deregulated public utility property if the cumulative amount of the reduction during such period does not, at any time during the period, exceed the flowthrough percentage of the cumulative stranded cost recovery for the property at such time. For this purpose—

(A) The stranded cost of the property is the cost of the property reduced by the amount of such cost that the taxpayer has recovered through regulated depreciation expense during the period before the property becomes deregulated public utility property;

(B) The cumulative stranded cost recovery for the property at any time is the stranded cost of the property that the taxpayer has been permitted to recover through rates on or before such time; and

(C) The flowthrough percentage for the property is determined by dividing the amount of credit with respect to the property remaining to be used to reduce cost of service immediately before the property becomes deregulated public utility property by the stranded cost of the property.

(3) *Cross reference.*—See §1.168(i)-(3) for rules relating to the treatment of balances of excess deferred income taxes when public utility property becomes deregulated public utility property.

(4) *Effective/applicability dates.*—(i) *In general.*—Except as provided in paragraph (k)(4)(ii) of this section, this paragraph (k) applies to public utility property that becomes deregulated public utility property with respect to a taxpayer after December 21, 2005.

(ii) *Property that becomes public utility property of the transferee.*—This paragraph (k) does not apply to property that becomes deregulated public utility property with respect to a taxpayer an account of a transfer on or before March 20, 2008, if after the transfer the property is public utility property of the transferee.

(iii) *Application of regulation project (REG-104385-01).*—A reduction in the taxpayer's cost of service will be treated as ratable if it is consistent with the proposed rules in regulation project (REG-104385-01) (68 FR 10190) March 4, 2003, and occurs during the period beginning on March 5, 2003, and ending on the earlier of—

(A) The last date on which the utility's rates are determined under the rate order in effect on December 21, 2005; or

(B) December 21, 2007. [Reg. §1.46-6.]

☐ [*T.D. 7602, 3-20-79. Amended by T.D. 8089, 5-21-86 and T.D. 9387, 3-19-2008 (corrected 4-4-2008).*]

[Reg. §1.47-1]

§1.47-1. Recomputation of credit allowed by section 38.—(a) *General rule.*—(1) *In general.*—(i) If during the taxable year any section 38 property the basis (or cost) of which was taken into account, under paragraph (a) of §1.46-3, in computing the taxpayer's qualified investment is disposed of, or otherwise ceases to be section 38 property or becomes public utility property (as defined in paragraph (g) of §1.46-3) or is a qualifying commuter highway vehicle (as defined in paragraph (a) of §1.46-11) which undergoes a change in use (as defined in paragraph (m)(2) of this section) with respect to the taxpayer, before the close of the estimated useful life (as determined under subparagraph (2)(i) of this paragraph) which was taken into account in computing such qualified investment, then the credit earned for the credit year (as defined in subdivision (ii)(a) of this subparagraph) shall be recomputed under the principles of paragraph (a) of §1.46-1 and paragraph (a) of §1.46-3 substituting, in lieu of the estimated useful life of the property that was taken into account originally in computing qualified investment, the actual useful life of the property as determined under subparagraph (2)(ii) of this paragraph. There shall also be recomputed under the principles of §§1.46-1 and 1.46-2 the credit allowed for the credit year and for any other taxable year affected by reason of the reduction in credit earned for the credit year, giving effect to such reduction in the computation of carryovers or carrybacks of unused credit. If the recomputation described in the preceding sentence results in the aggregate in a decrease (taking into account any recomputations under this paragraph in respect of prior recapture years, as defined in subdivision (ii)(b) of this subparagraph) in the credits allowed for the credit year and for any other taxable year affected by the reduction in credit earned for the credit year, then the income tax for the recapture year shall be increased by the amount of such decrease in credits allowed. For treatment of such increase in tax, see paragraph (b) of this section. For rules relating to "disposition" and "cessation", see §1.47-2. For rules relating to certain exceptions to the application of this section, see §1.47-3. For special rules in the case of an electing small business corporation (as defined in section 1371(b)), an estate or trust, or a partnership, see respectively, §§1.47-4, 1.47-5, or 1.47-6. For rules applicable to energy property, see paragraph (h) of this section. For special rules relating to recomputation of credit allowed by section 38 if progress expenditure property (as defined in §1.46-5(d)) ceases to be progress expenditure property with respect to the taxpayer, see paragraph (g) of this section.

(ii) For purposes of this section and §§1.47-2 through 1.47-6—

(a) The term "credit year" means the taxable year in which section 38 property was taken into account in computing a taxpayer's qualified investment.

(b) The term "recapture year" means the taxable year in which section 38 property the basis (or cost) of which is taken into account in computing a taxpayer's qualified investment is disposed of, or otherwise ceases to be section 38 property or becomes public utility property with respect to the taxpayer, before the close of the estimated useful life which was taken into account in computing such qualified investment.

(c) The term "recapture determination" means a recomputation made under this paragraph.

(2) *Rules for applying subparagraph (1).*—For purposes of subparagraph (1) of this paragraph—

(i) In determining whether section 38 property is disposed of, or otherwise ceases to be section 38 property with respect to the taxpayer, before the close of the estimated useful life which was taken into account in computing the taxpayer's qualified investment, the term "estimated useful life" means the shortest life of the useful life category within which falls the estimated useful life which was assigned to such property under paragraph (e) of §1.46-3. Thus, section 38 property which is assigned, under paragraph (e) of §1.46-3, an estimated useful life of 6 years shall not be treated, for purposes of subparagraph (1) of this paragraph, as having been disposed of before the close of its estimated useful life if such property is sold 5 years (that is, the shortest life of the 5 years or more but less than 7 years useful life category) after the date on which it was placed in service. Likewise, section 38 property with an estimated useful life of 15 years which is placed in service on January 1, 1972, shall not be treated as having been disposed of before the close of its estimated useful life if such property is sold at any time after January 1, 1979 (that is, 7 years or more after the date on which it was placed in service).

(ii) In determining the recomputed qualified investment with respect to property which is disposed of or otherwise ceases to be section 38 property the term "actual useful life" means, except as otherwise provided in this section and §§1.47-2 through 1.47-6, the period beginning with the date on which the property was placed in service by the taxpayer and ending with the date of such disposition or cessation. See paragraph (c) of this section.

(iii) In determining the recomputed qualified investment with respect to property which ceases to be section 38 property with respect to the taxpayer after August 15, 1971, or which becomes public utility property after such date, such property shall be treated as if it were property described in section 50 at the time it was placed in service (whether or not it was property described in section 50 at such time). Thus, if property was placed in service on October 15, 1968, and was assigned an estimated useful life of 4 years, there would be no increase in tax under section 47 if the property were disposed of at any time after October 14, 1971, that is, 3 years or more after the property was placed in service.

(b) *Increase in income tax and reduction of investment credit carryover.*—(1) *Increase in tax.*—Except as provided in subparagraph (2) of this paragraph, any increase in income tax under this section shall be treated as income tax imposed on the taxpayer by chapter 1 of the Code for the recapture year notwithstanding that without regard to such increase the taxpayer has no income tax liability, has a net operating loss for such taxable year, or no income tax return was otherwise required for such taxable year.

(2) *Special rule.*—Any increase in income tax under this section shall not be treated as income tax imposed on the taxpayer by chapter 1 of the Code for purposes of determining the amount of the credits allowable to such taxpayer under—

(i) Section 33 (relating to taxes of foreign countries and possessions of United States),

(ii) Section 34 (relating to dividends received by individuals before January 1, 1965),

(iii) Section 35 (relating to partially tax-exempt interest received by individuals),

(iv) Section 37 (relating to retirement income), and

(v) Section 38 (relating to investment in certain depreciable property).

(3) *Reduction in credit allowed as a result of a net operating loss carryback.*—(i) If a net operating loss carryback from the recapture year or from any taxable year subsequent to the recapture year reduces the amount allowed as a credit under section 38 for any taxable year up to and including the recapture year, then there shall be a new recapture determination under paragraph (a) of this section for each recapture year affected, taking into account the reduced amount of credit allowed after application of the net operating loss carryback.

(ii) Subdivision (i) of this subparagraph may be illustrated by the following example:

Example (1). (a) X Corporation, which makes its returns on the basis of a calendar year, acquired and placed in service on January 1, 1962, an item of section 38 property with a basis of $10,000 and an estimated useful life of 8 years. The amount of qualified investment with respect to such asset was $10,000. For the taxable year 1962, X Corporation's credit earned of $700 (7 percent of $10,000) was allowed under section 38 as a credit against its liability for tax of $700. In 1963 and 1964 X Corporation had no liability for tax and placed in service no section 38 property. On January 3, 1963, such item of section 38 property was sold to Y Corporation. Since the actual useful life of such item was only one year, there was a recapture determination under paragraph (a) of this section. The income tax imposed by chapter 1 of the Code on X Corporation for the taxable year 1963 was increased by the $700 decrease in its credit earned for the taxable year 1962 (that is, $700 the original credit earned minus zero recomputed credit earned).

(b) For the taxable year 1965, X Corporation has a net operating loss which is carried back to the taxable year 1962 and reduces its liability for tax, as defined in paragraph (c) of §1.46-1, for such taxable year to $200. As a result of such net operating loss carryback, X Corporation's credit allowed under section 38 for the taxable year 1962 is limited to $200 and the excess of $500 ($700 credit earned minus $200 limitation based on amount of tax) is an investment credit carryover to the taxable year 1963.

(c) For 1965, there is a recapture determination under subdivision (i) of this subparagraph for the 1963 recapture year. The $700 increase in the income tax imposed on X Corporation for the taxable year 1963 is redetermined to be $200 (that is, the $200 credit allowed after taking into account the 1965 net operating loss minus zero credit which would have been allowed taking into account the 1963 recapture determination). In addition, X Corporation's $500 investment credit carryover to the taxable year 1963 is reduced by $500 ($700 minus $200) to zero and X Corporation is entitled to a $500 refund of the tax paid as a result of the 1963 determination.

Example (2). (a) X Corporation, which makes its returns on the basis of a calendar year, acquired and placed in service on January 1, 1962, an item of section 38 property with a basis of $10,000 and an estimated useful life of 8 years. The amount of qualified investment with respect to such asset was $10,000. For the taxable year 1962, X Corporation's credit earned of $700 (7 percent of $10,000) was allowed under section 38 as a credit against its liability for tax of $700. In 1963 and in 1964 X Corporation had no liability for tax and placed in service no section 38 property. On January 3, 1965, such item of section 38 property is sold to Y Corporation. For the taxable year 1965, X Corporation has a net operating loss which is carried back to the taxable year 1962 and reduces its liability for tax, as defined in paragraph (c) of §1.46-1, for such taxable year to $100.

(b) As a result of such net operating loss carryback, X Corporation's credit allowed under section 38 for the taxable year 1962 is limited to $100 and the excess of $600 ($700 credit earned minus $100 limitation based on amount of tax) is an investment credit carryover to the taxable year 1963.

(c) Since the actual useful life of the item of section 38 property sold to Y Corporation was only 3 years, there is a recapture determination under paragraph (a) of this section. X Corporation's $600 investment credit carryover to 1963 is reduced by $600 to zero. The income tax imposed by chapter 1 of the Code on X Corporation for the taxable year 1965 is increased by the $100 reduction in credit allowed by section 38 for 1962.

(4) *Statement of recomputation.*—The taxpayer shall attach to his income tax return for the recapture year a separate statement showing in detail the computation of the increase in income tax imposed on such taxpayer by chapter 1 of the Code and the reduction in any investment credit carryovers.

(c) *Date placed in service and date of disposition or cessation.*—(1) *General rule.*—For purposes of this section and §§1.47-2 through 1.47-6, in determining the actual useful life of section 38 property—

(i) Such property shall be treated as placed in service on the first day of the month in which such property is placed in service. The month in which property is placed in service shall be determined under the principles of paragraph (d) of §1.46-3.

(ii) If during the taxable year such property ceases to be section 38 property with respect to the taxpayer—

(a) As a result of the occurrence of an event on a specific date (for example, a sale, transfer, retirement or other disposition), such cessation shall be treated as having occurred on the actual date of such event.

(b) For any reason other than the occurrence of an event on a specific date (for example, because such property is used predominantly in connection with the furnishing of lodging during such taxable year), such cessation shall be treated as having occurred on the first day of such taxable year.

(2) *Special rule.*—Notwithstanding subparagraph (1) of this paragraph, if a taxpayer uses an averaging convention (see § 1.167(a)-10) in computing depreciation with respect to section 38 property, then, for purposes of this section and §§ 1.47-2 through 1.47-6, he may use the assumed dates of additions and retirements in determining the actual useful life of such property provided such assumed dates are used consistently for purposes of subpart B of part IV of subchapter A of chapter 1 of the Code with respect to all section 38 property for which such convention is used for purposes of depreciation. This subparagraph shall not apply in any case where from all the facts and circumstances it appears that the use of such assumed dates results in a substantial distortion of the investment credit allowed by section 38. Thus, for example, if the taxpayer computes depreciation under a convention under which the average of the beginning and ending balances of the asset account for the taxable year are taken into account, he may use July 1 as the assumed date of all additions and retirements to such account. Similarly, if the taxpayer computes depreciation under a convention under which the average of the beginning and ending balances of the asset account for each month is taken into account, he may use the date determined by reference to the weighted average of the monthly averages as the assumed date of all additions and retirements to such account.

(3) *Example.*—This paragraph may be illustrated by the following example:

Example. Assume that section 38 property is placed in service (within the meaning of paragraph (d) of § 1.46-3) on December 1, 1965 (thus the credit is treated as being earned in 1965) but under the taxpayer's depreciation practice the period for depreciation with respect to such property begins on January 1, 1966, and that the property is actually retired on December 2, 1970. Under the general rule of subparagraph (1) of this paragraph, the property is treated as placed in service on December 1, 1965, and as ceasing to be section 38 property with respect to the taxpayer on December 2, 1970, even though under the taxpayer's depreciation practice the period for depreciation with respect to such property begins on January 1, 1966, and terminates on January 1, 1971. However, under the special rule of subparagraph (2) of this paragraph the taxpayer may determine the actual useful life of the property by reference to the assumed dates of January 1, 1966, and January 1, 1971.

(d) *Examples.*—Paragraphs (a) through (c) of this section may be illustrated by the following examples:

Example (1). (i) X Corporation, which makes its returns on the basis of the calendar year, acquired and placed in service on January 1, 1962, three items of section 38 property each with a basis of $12,000 and an estimated useful life of 15 years. The amount of qualified investment with respect to each such asset was $12,000. For the taxable year 1962, X Corporation's credit earned of $2,520 was allowed under section 38 as a credit against its liability for tax of $4,000. On December 2, 1965, one of the items of section 38 property is sold to Y Corporation.

(ii) The actual useful life of the item of property which is sold on December 2, 1965, is three years and eleven months. The recomputed qualified investment with respect to such item of property is zero ($12,000 basis multiplied by zero applicable percentage) and X Corporation's recomputed credit earned for the taxable year 1962 is $1,680 (7 percent of $24,000). The income tax imposed by chapter 1 of the Code on X Corporation for the taxable year 1965 is increased by the $840 decrease in its credit earned for the taxable year 1962 (that is, $2,520 original credit earned minus $1,680 recomputed credit earned).

Example (2). (i) The facts are the same as in example (1) and in addition on December 1, 1966, a second item of section 38 property placed in service in the taxable year 1962 is sold to Y Corporation.

(ii) The actual useful life of the item of property which is sold on December 2, 1966, is four years and eleven months. The recomputed qualified investment with respect to such item of property is $4,000 ($12,000 basis multiplied by 33⅓ percent applicable percentage) and X Corporation's recomputed credit earned for the taxable year 1962 is $1,120 (7 percent of $16,000). The income tax imposed by chapter 1 of the Code on X Corporation for the taxable year 1966 is increased by $560 (that is, $1,400 ($2,520 original credit earned minus $1,120

recomputed credit earned) reduced by the $840 increase in tax for 1965).

Example (3). (i) The facts are the same as in example (1) except that for the taxable year 1962 X Corporation's liability for tax under section 46(a)(3) is only $1,520. Therefore, for such taxable year X Corporation's credit allowed under section 38 is limited to $1,520 and the excess of $1,000 ($2,520 credit earned minus $1,520 limitation based on amount of tax) is an unused credit. Of such $1,000 unused credit, $100 is allowed as a credit under section 38 for the taxable year 1963, $100 is allowed for 1964, and $800 is carried to the taxable year 1965.

(ii) The actual useful life of the item of property which is sold on December 2, 1965, is three years and eleven months. The recomputed qualified investment with respect to such item of property is zero ($12,000 basis multiplied by zero applicable percentage) and X Corporation's recomputed credit earned for the taxable year 1962 is $1,680 (7 percent of $24,000). If such $1,680 recomputed credit earned had been taken into account in place of the $2,520 original credit earned, X's credit allowed for 1962 would have been $1,520, and of the $160 unused credit from 1962 $100 would have been allowed as a credit under section 38 for 1963, and $60 would have been allowed for 1964. X Corporation's $800 investment credit carryover to the taxable year 1965 is reduced by $800 to zero. The income tax imposed by chapter 1 of the Code on X Corporation for the taxable year 1965 is increased by $40 (that is, the aggregate reduction in the credits allowed by section 38 for 1962, 1963, and 1964).

Example (4). (i) X Corporation, which makes its returns on the basis of the calendar year, acquired and placed in service on November 1, 1962, an item of section 38 property with a basis of $12,000 and an estimated useful life of 10 years. The amount of qualified investment with respect to such property was $12,000. For the taxable year 1962, X Corporation's credit earned of $840 was allowed under section 38 as a credit against its liability for tax of $840. For each of the taxable years 1963 and 1964 X Corporation's liability for tax was zero and its credit earned was $400; therefore, for each of such years its unused credit was $400. For the taxable year 1965 its liability for tax was $200 and its credit earned was zero; therefore, $200 of the $400 unused credit from 1963 was allowed as credit for 1965 and $600 ($200 from 1963 and $400 from 1964) is an investment credit carryover to 1966. On February 2, 1966, such item of section 38 property is sold to Y Corporation.

(ii) The actual useful life of such item of property is three years and three months. The recomputed qualified investment with respect to such property is zero ($12,000 basis multiplied by zero) and X Corporation's recomputed credit earned for the taxable year 1962 is zero. If such zero recomputed credit earned had been taken into account in place of the $840 original credit earned, the entire $400 unused credit from 1963 (including the $200 portion which was originally allowed as a credit for 1965) and the $400 unused credit from 1964 would have been allowed as investment credit carrybacks against X Corporation's liability for tax of $840 for 1962. (See § 1.46-2 for rules relating to the carryback of unused credits.)

(iii) Therefore, the $600 carryover from 1963 and 1964 to 1966 is eliminated and the income tax imposed by chapter 1 of the Code on X Corporation for the taxable year 1966 is increased by the $240 aggregate reduction in the credits allowed by section 38 for the taxable years 1962 and 1965 (that is, $1,040 credit allowed minus $800 which would have been allowed).

Example (5). (i) X Corporation, which makes its returns on the basis of the calendar year, acquired and placed in service on November 1, 1962, an item of section 38 property with a basis of $10,000 and an estimated useful life of 8 years. The amount of qualified investment with respect to such asset was $10,000. For the taxable year 1962, X Corporation's credit earned of $700 was allowed as a credit against its liability for tax. For each of the taxable years 1963, 1964, and 1965 X had no taxable income. On July 3, 1966, the item of section 38 property is sold to Y Corporation. For the taxable year 1966 X Corporation has a net operating loss of $3,000.

(ii) The actual useful life of the item of property is three years and eight months. The recomputed qualified investment with respect to such item of property is zero and X Corporation's recomputed credit earned for the taxable year 1962 is zero. Notwithstanding the $3,000 net operating loss for the taxable year 1966, the income tax imposed by chapter 1 of the Code on X Corporation for such year is $700 (that is, the decrease in its credit earned for the taxable year 1962).

(e) *Identification of property.*—(1) *General rule.*—(i) *Record requirements.*—In general, the taxpayer must maintain records from which he can establish, with respect to each item of section 38 property, the following facts:

(a) The date the property is disposed of or otherwise ceases to be section 38 property,

(b) The estimated useful life which was assigned to the property under paragraph (e) of § 1.46-3, *(c)* The month and the taxable year in which the property was placed in service, and

(d) The basis (or cost), actually or reasonably determined, of the property.

(ii) *Recapture determination.*—For purposes of determining whether section 38 property is disposed of, or otherwise ceases to be section 38 property with respect to the taxpayer, before the close of its estimated useful life, and for purposes of determining recomputed qualified investment, the taxpayer must establish from his records the facts required by subdivision (i) of this subparagraph.

(iii) *Examples.*—If the taxpayer fails to maintain records from which he can establish the facts required by subdivision (i) of this subparagraph, then this section shall be applied to the taxpayer in the manner indicated in the following examples:

Example (1). Corporation X, organized on January 1, 1964, files its income tax return on the basis of a calendar year. During the years 1964 and 1965, X places in service several items of machinery to which it assigns estimated useful lives of 8 years. X places the items of machinery in a composite account for purposes of computing depreciation. When X's 1966 return is being audited, X is unable to establish whether the items placed in service in 1964 and 1965 were still on hand at the end of 1966. Therefore, for purposes of paragraph (a) of this section, X is treated as having disposed of, in 1966, all of the items of machinery placed in service in 1964 and 1965.

Example (2). Corporation Y, organized on January 1, 1960, files its income tax return on the basis of a calendar year. During each of the years 1960 through 1965, Y places in service 4 items of machinery to each of which it assigns an estimated useful life of 8 years for depreciation purposes (and for purposes of computing qualified investment for relevant years). Y places the items of machinery in a composite account for purposes of computing depreciation (and for purposes of computing qualified investment for relevant years). When Y's 1965 return is being audited, Y can establish that it retired during 1965 only 6 items of this machinery. However, Y cannot establish the date on which these 6 items were placed in service, nor can Y establish that the items placed in service in 1963 or 1964 are still on hand as of the end of 1965. No previous recapture has taken place with respect to any of the items placed in service in 1963 or 1964. Assuming that paragraph (e)(2) and (3) of this section is not applicable, Y is treated, for purposes of paragraph (a) of this section, as having disposed of, in 1965, the 4 items placed in service in 1964, the most recent year before 1965 in which such property was placed in service, and 2 items from 1963, the next most recent year.

Example (3). The facts are the same as in example (2) except that when Y's 1966 return is being audited, Y can establish from its records that all 4 items placed in service in 1965 are still on hand and that only 3 items were retired in 1966. For purposes of paragraph (a) of this section, Y is treated as having disposed of, in 1966, the 2 remaining items of machinery placed in service in 1963, and one of the items placed in service in 1962.

(2) *Treatment of "mass assets".*—(i) If, in the case of mass assets (as defined in subparagraph (4) of this paragraph), it is impracticable for the taxpayer to maintain records from which he can establish with respect to each item of section 38 property the facts required by subparagraph (1) of this paragraph, and if he adopts other reasonable recordkeeping practices, consonant with good accounting and engineering practices, and consistent with his prior recordkeeping practices, then he may substitute data from an appropriate mortality dispersion table. An appropriate mortality dispersion table must be based on an acceptable sampling of the taxpayer's actual experience or other acceptable statistical or engineering techniques. In lieu of such mortality dispersion table, the taxpayer may use a standard mortality dispersion table prescribed by the Commissioner. If the taxpayer uses such standard mortality dispersion table for any taxable year, it must be used for all subsequent taxable years unless the taxpayer obtains the consent of the Commissioner to change. If mass assets are placed in a multiple asset account and if the depreciation rate for such account is based on the maximum expected life of the longest lived asset in such account, in applying a mortality dispersion table (including a standard mortality dispersion table) the average expected useful life of the mass assets in such account must be used.

(ii) Subdivision (i) of this subparagraph shall not apply with respect to assets placed in service in a taxable year ending on or after June 30, 1967, and beginning before January 1, 1971, or with respect to assets placed in service for a taxable year beginning after December 31, 1970, for which the taxpayer has not made the election provided by section 167(m), unless the estimated useful lives which were assigned to such assets for purposes of determining qualified investment—

(a) Were separate lives based on the estimated range of years taken into account in establishing the average useful life of assets similar in kind under paragraph (e)(3)(ii)(b) of §1.46-3, and

(b) Were determined by use of a mortality dispersion table (including a standard mortality dispersion table).

(iii) Any standard mortality dispersion table prescribed by the Commissioner shall be based on average useful life categories and with respect to each category shall contain 5 columns, the first 4 of which shall state the percentage of property assumed to have a useful life of—

Column (1): Less than 4 years,

Column (2): 4 years or more but less than 6 years,

Column (3): 6 years or more but less than 8 years, and

Column (4): 8 years or more.

The 5th column shall show the total qualified investment as a percentage and shall be used in connection with the determination to be made under §1.46-3(e)(3)(iii). In the case of a table which is to apply to property which is described in section 50 or to property which is treated as property described in section 50 under paragraph (a)(2)(iii), of this section shall be applied by substituting "3 years" for "4 years," "5 years" for "6 years," and "7 years" for "8 years."

(iv) Whenever the standard mortality dispersion table is used for a taxable year under subdivision (i) of this subparagraph (whether or not such table was used in determining qualified investment), the percentage of property shown in column (1) of the table shall (for purposes of section 47, this section, and §§1.47-2 through 1.47-6) be deemed to have been disposed of on the day before the expiration of the 4-year period beginning on the date on which it was considered as placed in service under §1.47-1(c); the percentage of property shown in column (2) of the table shall be deemed to have been disposed of on the day before the expiration of the 6-year period beginning on the date on which it was so considered as placed in service; and the percentage of property shown in column (3) shall be deemed to have been disposed of on the day before the expiration of the 8-year period beginning on the date on which it was so considered as placed in service. In applying this subdivision for purposes of recomputing qualified investment, the proper average useful life category shall be used whether or not such category was used in determining qualified investment. In the case of property which is described in section 50 or property which is treated as property described in section 50 under paragraph (a)(2)(iii) of this section (other than property the qualified investment with respect to which was determined by use of the standard or an appropriate mortality dispersion table), this subdivision shall be applied by substituting "3-year period" for "4-year period," "5-year period" for "6-year period," and "7-year period" for "8-year period."

(v) In lieu of using subdivision (iv) of this subparagraph for purposes of recomputing qualified investment, a taxpayer may, for the first recapture year (as defined in paragraph (a)(1)(ii)(b) of this section) to which such subdivision (iv) would otherwise apply with respect to any mass asset account, recompute qualified investment on the basis of the difference between *(a)* the proper total qualified investment based on the percentage shown in column (5) of the table, and *(b)* the total qualified investment actually claimed by the taxpayer for the year in which the property was placed in service.

Example. Assume that the taxpayer places in service during 1963 mass assets costing him $100,000, that he places these assets in a multiple asset account for which he properly claims a useful life of 6 years and a qualified investment of $66,667 ($\frac{2}{3} \times $100,000$), and that he is allowed an investment credit of $4,667.67. When the taxpayer's 1967 return is being audited he is unable to establish that any of the mass assets placed in service in 1963 were still on hand at the end of 1967. The taxpayer elects to use the standard mortality dispersion table prescribed by the Commissioner to determine the amount of recapture with respect to these mass assets. Assume that the table prescribed by the Commissioner shows with respect to mass assets with an average useful life of 6 years the following:

Percent of property assumed to have a useful life of—				
Less than 4 years	4 years or more, but less than 6 years	6 years or more, but less than 8 years	8 years or more	Total qualified investment (Percent)
(1)	(2)	(3)	(4)	(5)
15.87	34.13	34.13	15.87	50.00

Reg. §1.47-1(e)(2)(v)

(a) Under these circumstances 15.87 percent of the mass assets placed in service in 1963 are deemed to have been disposed of during 1967. With respect to these assets, the amount of qualified investment for 1963 was $10,580 ($15,870 × ²/₃) and the amount of credit earned was $740.60 (7% of $10,580), whereas the recomputed qualified investment is zero and the recomputed credit earned is zero. Thus, the tax imposed by chapter 1 of the Code for 1967 is increased by $740.60.

(b) No recapture determination is required for 1968 since no assets are deemed to have been disposed of in that year. During 1969, 34.13 percent of the mass assets placed in service in 1963 are deemed to have been disposed of. With respect to these assets, the amount of qualified investment for 1963 was $22,753.34 ($34,130 × ²/₃) and the amount of credit earned was $1,592.73 (7% of $22,753.34), whereas the recomputed qualified investment is $11,376.67 ($34,130 × ¹/₃ and the recomputed credit earned is $796.37 (7% of $11,376.67). Thus, the tax imposed by chapter 1 of the Code for 1969 is increased by $796.36 ($1,592.73 minus $796.37).

(c) If the taxpayer chooses to recompute qualified investment by using the method provided in subdivision (v) of this subparagraph, the increase in tax for 1967 (the first recapture year) would be $1,167.67, i.e., the original credit earned, $4,667.67, minus the recomputed credit earned, $3,500 (50%, the percentage shown in column (5), of $100,000 multiplied by 7%). As long as the same average useful life category reflects the taxpayer's experience for subsequent years, no recapture determination will be required for any future year, except as provided by subparagraph (3)(iv) of this paragraph.

(vi) Subdivision (i) of this subparagraph shall not apply with respect to section 38 property to which an election under section 167(m) applies unless the taxpayer assigns actual retirements of such section 38 property for all taxable years to the same vintage account for purposes of section 47 and for purposes of computing the allowance for depreciation under section 167. The assignment of actual retirements of section 38 property for a taxable year to particular vintage accounts may be made on the basis of an appropriate mortality dispersion table (based on an acceptable sampling of the taxpayer's actual experience or other statistical or engineering techniques) or on the basis of a standard mortality dispersion table prescribed by the Commissioner. If the taxpayer assigns actual retirements for any taxable year to particular vintage accounts on the basis of such standard mortality dispersion table, actual retirements for all subsequent taxable years must be assigned to particular vintage accounts on the basis of such table. Actual retirements of section 38 property for a taxable year shall be assigned to particular vintage accounts by—

(a) Determining the expected retirements for such taxable year from each vintage account containing such section 38 property, and

(b) Ratably allocating such actual retirements to each vintage account containing such section 38 property.

However, the unadjusted basis of retired assets assigned to any particular vintage account shall not exceed the unadjusted basis of the property contained in such account.

(3) *Special rules.*—(i) Taxpayers who properly determine estimated useful lives under § 1.46-3(e)(3)(ii)(b) or (iii) may treat such assets as having been disposed of or having ceased to be section 38 assets in the order of the estimated useful lives that were assigned to such assets. Thus, the asset that is first disposed of or first ceases to be section 38 property may be treated as the asset to which there was assigned the shortest estimated useful life; the next asset disposed of or ceasing to be section 38 property may be treated as the asset to which there was assigned the second shortest life, etc.

(ii) In the case of taxpayers who use the rule of subdivision (i) of this subparagraph with respect to mass assets for which the estimated useful life was determined under § 1.46-3(e)(3)(iii), if the dispersion shown by the mortality dispersion table effective for a taxable year subsequent to the credit year is the same as the dispersion shown by the mortality table that was effective for the credit year (for example, if the same average useful life on the standard mortality dispersion table reflects the taxpayer's experience for both such years), no recapture determination is required for such subsequent taxable year.

(iii) Notwithstanding subdivision (i) of this subparagraph, taxpayers who, for purposes of determining qualified investment, do not use a mortality dispersion table with respect to certain section 38 assets similar in kind but who consistently assign under paragraph (e)(3)(ii)(b) of § 1.46-3 to such assets separate lives based on the estimated range of years taken into consideration in establishing the average useful life of such assets, may select the order in which such assets shall be considered as having been disposed of, regardless of the taxable years in which such assets were placed in service. If a taxpayer uses the method provided in this subdivision to determine that any asset is considered as having been disposed of, then, in

addition to complying with the record requirements of subparagraph (1)(i) of this paragraph, such taxpayer must maintain records from which he can establish to the satisfaction of the district director that such asset has not previously been considered as having been disposed of. In addition, if, for any taxable year, a taxpayer uses the method provided in this subdivision for any asset, he must use for such year and for each subsequent taxable year (unless he obtains the district director's consent to change) with respect to all assets similar in kind to such asset—

(a) The method of determining estimated useful lives described in paragraph (e)(3)(ii)(b) of § 1.46-3, and

(b) The method he has selected under this subdivision for determining the order in which such assets are considered as having been disposed of.

A request by a taxpayer to obtain the district director's consent to change a system or method described in this subdivision with respect to assets similar in kind must be submitted to the district director on or before the last day of the taxable year with respect to which the change is sought.

(iv) Notwithstanding subdivisions (i), (ii), and (iii) of this subparagraph, there shall be taken into account separately any abnormal retirement of section 38 property of substantial value for which the estimated useful life was determined under § 1.46-3(e)(3)(ii)(b) or (iii). For definition of abnormal retirement, see paragraph (b) of § 1.167(a)-8.

(4) [Reserved]

(5) *Example.*—This paragraph may be illustrated by the following example:

Example. (i) Taxpayer A uses numerous small returnable containers in his business. It is impracticable for A to keep individual detailed records with respect to such containers which are mass assets. In 1965, A places in service 10 million containers purchased for $1 million, and reasonably determines that each of such containers has a basis of 10 cents. A places such containers in a multiple asset account to which is assigned a 5-year average useful life for purposes of computing depreciation. A has conducted an appropriate mortality study which shows that the containers have the following estimated useful lives:

Percent of assets	Useful life
10%	3 years
20	4
40	5
20	6
10	7

A assigns separate lives to such assets based on the estimated range of years taken into account in establishing the average useful life of such containers. The qualified investment with respect to such containers is $400,000 computed as follows:

Useful life	Basis	Applicable percentage	Qualified investment
4	$200,000	33¹/₃	$66,666
5	400,000	33¹/₃	133,334
6	200,000	66²/₃	133,334
7	100,000	66²/₃	66,666
			$400,000

A's credit earned for 1965 of $28,000 (7 percent times $400,000) is allowed as a credit under section 38 against A's liability for tax of $2 million. (For purposes of this example the computations of investment credit and recapture with respect to containers placed in service in years other than 1965 are omitted.) The mortality studies effective for 1966 and 1967 show that none of the containers placed in service in 1965 was retired.

(ii) A's mortality study effective with respect to 1968 shows that the containers are being retired as follows:

Percent of assets	Useful life
30%	3 years
20	4
30	5
10	6
10	7

Thus, the 1968 study shows that 30 percent of the 10 million containers placed in service in 1965 were retired in 1968. Under the rule of subparagraph (3)(i) of this paragraph, the 3 million containers are treated as consisting of the 1 million containers to which was assigned a 3-year useful life and the 2 million containers to which was assigned a 4-year useful life. Taking into account only the fact that 30 percent of the containers placed in service in 1965 had an actual life of less than 4 years, A's recomputed qualified investment for 1965 is $333,333 and his recomputed credit earned is $23,333. A's income tax for 1968 is increased by $4,667 ($28,000 original credit earned minus $23,333 recomputed credit earned).

(iii) The mortality study effective for 1969 shows the same results as the mortality study effective for 1968. Thus, it shows that 2 million containers were retired in 1969 (an actual life of 4 years). Under the rule of subparagraph (3)(i) of this paragraph such 2 million containers are treated as having been among 4,000,000 containers to which were assigned a 5-year useful life. Therefore, no recapture determination is required for 1969.

(iv) The mortality study effective for 1970 shows the same results as the mortality study effective for 1968. Thus, it shows that 3 million containers were retired in 1970 (an actual life of 5 years). Under the rule of subparagraph (3)(i) of this paragraph, the 3 million are treated as having been assigned useful lives as follows: 2 million as having been assigned a useful life of 5 years, and 1 million as having been assigned a useful life of 6 years. Taking into account only the fact that 10 percent of the containers placed in service in 1965 had an actual life of 5 years rather than the 6 years estimated useful life assigned to them, A's recomputed qualified investment is $300,000 and A's credit earned for 1965 is $21,000. Thus, taking into account the 1968 recapture determination, A's income tax for 1970 is increased by $2,333.

(f) *Public utility property.*—(1) *Recomputed qualified investment.*—In recomputing qualified investment with respect to section 38 property which becomes public utility property (as defined in paragraph (g) of § 1.46-3)—

(i) If such property becomes public utility property less than 3 years from the date on which it was placed in service, then such property shall be treated as public utility property for its entire useful life.

(ii) If such property becomes public utility property 3 years or more but less than 5 years from the date on which it was placed in service, then such property shall be treated as section 38 property which is not public utility property for the first 3 years of its estimated useful life and as public utility property for the remaining period of its estimated useful life.

(iii) If such property becomes public utility property 5 years or more but less than 7 years from the date on which it was placed in service, then such property shall be treated as section 38 property which is not public utility property for the first 5 years of its estimated useful life and as public utility property for the remaining period of its estimated useful life.

If property becomes public utility property before August 16, 1971, this subparagraph shall be applied by substituting "4 years" for "3 years," "6 years" for "5 years," and "8 years" for "7 years."

(2) *Examples.*—Subparagraph (1) of this paragraph may be illustrated by the following examples:

Example (1). (i) X Corporation, which makes its returns on the basis of the calendar year, acquired and placed in service on January 1, 1969, an item of section 38 property with a basis of $12,000 and an estimated useful life of 8 years. The amount of qualified investment with respect to such property was $12,000. For the taxable year 1969, X Corporation's credit earned was $840 (7 percent of $12,000) and for such taxable year X Corporation was allowed under section 38 a credit of $840 against its liability for tax. During the taxable year 1972 such property becomes public utility property (as defined in paragraph (g) of § 1.46-3) with respect to X Corporation.

(ii) Such item of section 38 property is treated as section 38 property which is not public utility property for the first 3 years of its 8-year estimated useful life and is treated as public utility property for the remaining 5 years. The recomputed qualified investment with respect to such item of section 38 property is $7,428, computed as follows:

$12,000 basis × 33¹/₃ percent applicable percentage	$4,000
$12,000 basis × 3/7 × 66²/₃ percent applicable percentage	3,428
Total recomputed qualified investment	$7,428

X Corporation's recomputed credit earned for the taxable year 1969 is $520 (7 percent of $7,428). The income tax imposed by chapter 1 of the Code on X Corporation for the taxable year 1972 is increased by the $320 decrease in its credit earned for the taxable year 1969 (that is, $840 original credit earned minus $520 recomputed credit earned).

Example (2). (i) The facts are the same as in example (1) and in addition the item of section 38 property which became public utility property in 1972 is sold to Y Corporation on January 2, 1975.

(ii) The actual useful life of such item of property is 6 years. For the first 3 years of its 8-year estimated useful life such item is treated as section 38 property which is not public utility property and for the remaining 3 years is treated as public utility property. The recomputed qualified investment with respect to such item of property is $5,714, computed as follows:

$12,000 basis × 33¹/₃ percent applicable percentage	$4,000
$12,000 basis × 3/7 × 33I/3 percent applicable percentage	1,714
Total recomputed qualified investment	$5,714

X Corporation's recomputed credit earned for the taxable year 1969 is $400 (7 percent of $5,714). The income tax imposed by chapter 1 of the Code on X Corporation for the taxable year 1975 is increased by $120 (that is, $440 ($840 original credit earned minus $400 recomputed credit earned) minus $320 increase in tax for 1969).

(g) *Special rules for progress expenditure property.*—Under section 47(a)(3), a recapture determination is required if property ceases to be progress expenditure property (as defined in § 1.46-5(d)). Property ceases to be progress expenditure property if it is sold or otherwise disposed of before it is placed in service. For example, cancellation of the contract for progress expenditure property or abandonment of the project by the taxpayer will be considered a "disposition" within the meaning of § 1.47-2. A cessation occurs if progress expenditure property ceases to be progress expenditure property that will be section 38 property with a useful life of 7 years or more when placed in service. In general, a sale and leaseback is treated as a cessation. However, see paragraph (g)(2) of § 1.47-3 for special rules for certain sale and leaseback transactions. Recapture determinations for progress expenditure property are to be made in a way similar to that provided under §§ 1.47-1 through 1.47-6. Reduction of qualified investment must begin with the most recent credit year (*i.e.*, the most recent taxable year the property is taken into account in computing qualified investment under § 1.46-3 or 1.46-5).

(h) *Special rules for energy property.*—(1) *In general.*—A recapture determination is required for the investment credit attributable to the energy percentage (energy credit) if property is (i) disposed of or (ii) otherwise ceases to be energy property (as defined in section 48(l)) with regard to the taxpayer before the close of the estimated useful life (as determined under paragraph (a)(2)(i) of this section) which was taken into account in computing qualified investment.

(2) *Dispositions.*—The term "disposition" is described in § 1.47-2(a)(1). A transfer of energy property that is a "disposition" requiring a recapture determination for the investment credit attributable to the regular percentage (regular credit) and the ESOP percentage (ESOP credit) will also be a "disposition" requiring a recapture determination for the energy credit.

(3)(i) *Cessation.*—The term "cessation" is described in § 1.47-2(a)(2). For energy property, a cessation occurs during a taxable year if, by reason of a change in use or otherwise, the property would not have qualified for an energy credit if placed in service during that year. A change in use will not require a recapture determination for the regular or ESOP credit unless, by reason of the change, the property would not have qualified for the regular or ESOP credit if placed in service during that year.

(ii) A qualified intercity bus described in § 1.48-9(q) must meet the predominant use test (of § 1.48-9(q)(7)) for the remainder of the taxable year from the date it is placed in service and for each taxable year thereafter. A cessation occurs in any taxable year in which the bus is no longer a qualifying bus under § 1.48-9(q)(6). A qualified intercity bus does not cease to be energy property for a taxable year subsequent to the one in which it was placed in service by reason of a decrease in operating capacity (see § 1.48-9(q)(9)) for that year compared to any prior taxable year.

(4) *Recordkeeping requirement.*—For recordkeeping requirements with respect to dispositions or cessations, the rules of paragraph (e)(1) of this section apply. For example, the taxpayer must maintain records for each recycling facility indicating the percentage of virgin materials used each year. See, § 1.48-9(g)(5)(ii).

(5) *Examples.*—The following examples illustrate this paragraph (h).

Example (1). (a) In 1980, corporation X, a calendar year taxpayer, acquires and places in service a computer that will perform solely energy conserving functions in connection with an existing industrial process. Assume the computer has a 10 year useful life and qualifies for both the regular and energy credits. In 1981, a change is made in the industrial process (within the meaning of § 1.48-9(l)(2)). However, for 1981 the computer continues to perform solely energy conserving functions. In 1982, the computer ceases to perform energy conserving functions and begins to perform a production related function.

(b) For 1981, a recapture determination is not required. For 1982, the entire energy credit must be recaptured, although none of the regular credit is recaptured. If in 1989 the computer first ceased to perform an energy conserving function, no part of the energy credit would be recaptured.

Reg. § 1.47-1(h)(5)

Example (2). Assume the same facts and conclusion as in example (1). Assume further that X sells the computer in 1985. A recapture determination is required for the regular credit.

Example (3). In 1981, corporation Y, a calendar year taxpayer, acquires and places in service recycling equipment. Assume the equipment has a 7-year useful life and qualifies for both the regular credit and energy credit. During the course of 1982, more than 10 percent of the material recycled is virgin material. The energy credit is recaptured in its entirety, although none of the regular credit is recaptured. See §1.48-9(g)(5)(B)(ii).

Example (4). In 1980, corporation Z, a calendar year taxpayer, acquires and places in service a boiler the primary fuel for which is an alternate substance. The boiler has a 7-year useful life. Assume the boiler is a structural component of a building within the meaning of §1.48-1(e)(2). Assume further that the boiler is not a part of a qualified rehabilitated building (as defined in section 48(g)(1)) or a single purpose agricultural or horticultural structure (as defined in section 48(p)). Z is allowed only an energy credit since the boiler is a structural component of a building. In 1984, Z modifies the boiler to use oil as the primary fuel. A recapture determination is required for the energy credit. See §1.48-9(c)(3).

(i) [Reserved].

(j) [Reserved].

(k) [Reserved].

(l) [Reserved].

(m) *Commuter highway vehicles.*—(1) *Recomputed qualified investment.*—(i) If a qualifying commuter highway vehicle (as defined in §1.46-11(a)) undergoes a change in use but does not cease to be section 38 property, qualified investment for that vehicle is recomputed as if the vehicle was section 38 property which is not a qualifying commuter highway vehicle for its entire useful life.

(ii) The following example illustrates this paragraph (m)(1).

Example. X Corporation, a calendar year taxpayer, acquired and placed in service on January 1, 1982, a qualifying commuter highway vehicle with a basis of $10,000 and which qualified as three year recovery property under section 168(c)(2)(A)(i). The amount of qualified investment for the vehicle under section 46(c)(1) and (6) is $10,000. For the taxable year 1982, X Corporation's credit earned was $1,000 (10 percent of $10,000) and X Corporation was allowed under section 38 a $1,000 credit against its 1982 tax liability. During the taxable year 1984, the vehicle undergoes a change in use but does not cease to be section 38 property. The vehicle is treated as section 38 property which is not a qualifying commuter highway vehicle for its entire useful life. The recomputed qualified investment for the vehicle is $6,000 (60 percent of $10,000) and X Corporation's recomputed credit earned is $600 (10 percent of $6,000). The income tax imposed by chapter 1 of the Code on X Corporation for 1984 is increased by the $400 decrease in its credit earned for 1982 ($1,000 – $600).

(2) *Change in use.*—(i) A qualifying commuter highway vehicle undergoes a change in use if the vehicle does not meet the commuter use requirement (as defined in §1.46-11(d)) for each computation period.

(ii) Each of the following is a computation period:

(A) The period beginning on the date the vehicle was placed in service and ending on the last day of the taxpayer's taxable year in which the vehicle was placed in service;

(B) Each of the taxpayer's taxable years beginning after the date the vehicle was placed in service and ending before the end of the first 36 months after the vehicle was placed in service; and

(C) The period at the end of the first 36 months after the vehicle was placed in service and beginning on the first day of the taxpayer's taxable year in which the end of those first 36 months falls.

(iii) The following example illustrates this paragraph (m)(2).

Example. (a) Z Corporation, a calendar year taxpayer, acquired and placed in service a qualifying commuter highway vehicle on January 15, 1979. Z Corporation used the vehicle as set forth in the following table:

Taxable year ending	Total miles	Commuter miles	Ratio
1979	10,000	9,000	.90
1980	10,000	8,000	.80
1981	10,000	8,000	.80
1982 (1-14)	1,000	100	.10

(b) The first computation period begins on the date the vehicle is placed in service, in this example 1-15-79, and ends 12-31-79. In that computation period, the ratio of commuter miles to total miles is .90 (9,000 miles ÷ 10,000 miles). Therefore, the vehicle meets the commuter use requirement for that period and has not undergone a change in use. Similar calculations for the computation periods 1-1-80 to 12-31-80 and 1-1-81 to 12-31-81 produce the same result.

(c) As of the computation period beginning 1-1-82 and ending 1-14-82, the ratio of commuter use to total mileage is .10 (100 miles ÷ 1,000 miles). Since that ratio is less than .80, the vehicle does not meet the commuter use requirement for the period and the vehicle has undergone a change in use. [Reg. §1.47-1.]

☐ [T.D. 6931, 10-9-67. *Amended by* T.D. 7203, 8-24-72; T.D. 7765, 1-19-81; T.D. 7982, 10-5-84; T.D. 8035, 7-18-85; T.D. 8183, 3-1-88 *and* T.D. 8474, 4-26-93.]

[Reg. §1.47-2]

§1.47-2. **"Disposition" and "cessation".**—(a) *General rule.*—(1) *"Disposition".*—For purposes of this section and §1.47-1 and §§1.47-3 through 1.47-6, the term "disposition" includes a sale in a sale-and-leaseback transaction, a transfer upon the foreclosure of a security interest and a gift, but such term does not include a mere transfer of title to a creditor upon creation of a security interest. See paragraph (g) of §1.47-3 for treatment of certain sale-and-leaseback transactions.

(2) *"Cessation".*—(i) A determination of whether section 38 property ceases to be section 38 property with respect to the taxpayer must be made for each taxable year subsequent to the credit year. Thus, in each such taxable year the taxpayer must determine, as if such property were placed in service in such taxable year, whether such property would qualify as section 38 property (within the meaning of §1.48-1) in the hands of the taxpayer for such taxable year.

(ii) Section 38 property does not cease to be section 38 property with respect to the taxpayer in any taxable year subsequent to the credit year merely because under the taxpayer's depreciation practice no deduction for depreciation with respect to such property is allowable to the taxpayer for the taxable year, provided that the property continues to be used in the taxpayer's trade or business (or in the production of income) and otherwise qualifies as section 38 property with respect to the taxpayer.

(iii) This subparagraph may be illustrated by the following examples:

Example (1). A, an individual who makes his returns on the basis of the calendar year, on January 1, 1962, acquired and placed in service in his trade or business an item of section 38 property with an estimated useful life of eight years. On January 1, 1965, A removes the item of section 38 property from use in his trade or business by converting such item to personal use. Therefore, no deduction for depreciation with respect to such item of property is allowable to A for the taxable year 1965. On January 1, 1965, such item of property ceases to be section 38 property with respect to A.

Example (2). On January 1, 1965, A placed in service an item of section 38 property with a basis of $10,000 and an estimated useful life of 4 years. A depreciates such item, which has a salvage value of $2,000 (after taking into account section 167(f)), on the declining balance method at a rate of 50 percent (that is, twice the straight line rate of 25 percent). With respect to such item, A is allowed deductions for depreciation of $5,000 for 1965, $2,500 for 1966, and $500 for 1967. A is not allowed a deduction for depreciation for 1968 although he continues to use such item in his trade or business. Such item does not cease to be section 38 property with respect to A in 1968.

(b) *Leased property.*—(1) *In general.*—For purposes of paragraph (a) of §1.47-1, generally the mere leasing of section 38 property by a lessor who took the basis of such property into account in computing his qualified investment for the credit year shall not be considered to be a disposition. However, in a case where a lease is treated as a sale for income tax purposes such transaction is considered to be a disposition. Leased section 38 property ceases to be section 38 property with respect to the lessor if, in any taxable year subsequent to the credit year, such property would not qualify as section 38 property (as defined in §1.48-1) in the hands of the lessor, the lessee, or any sublessee. Thus, if, in a taxable year subsequent to the credit year, a lessee uses the property predominantly outside the United States, such property shall be considered to have ceased to be section 38 property with respect to the lessor.

(2) *Where lessor elects to treat lessee as purchaser.*—For purposes of paragraph (a) of §1.47-1, if, under §1.48-4, the lessor of new section 38 property made a valid election to treat the lessee as having purchased such property for purposes of the credit allowed by section 38, the following rules apply in determining whether such property is disposed of, or otherwise ceases to be section 38 property with respect to the lessee:

(i) Generally, a mere disposition by the lessor of property subject to a lease shall not be considered to be a disposition by the lessee.

(ii) If the lessor makes a disposition of property subject to a lease to a person who may not, under §1.48-4, make a valid election to treat the lessee as having purchased such property for purposes of the credit allowed by section 38 (such as a person described in paragraph (a)(5) of §1.48-4), such property shall be considered to have ceased to be section 38 property with respect to the lessee on the date of such disposition.

(iii) If a lease is terminated and the property is transferred by the lessee to the lessor or to any other person, such transfer shall be considered to be a disposition by the lessee.

(iv) If the lessee actually purchases such property in the credit year or in a taxable year subsequent to the credit year, such purchase shall not be considered to be a disposition.

(v) The property ceases to be section 38 property with respect to the lessee if in any taxable year subsequent to the credit year such property would not qualify as section 38 property (as defined in §1.48-1) in the hands of the lessor, the lessee, or any sublessee. Thus, for example, if, in a taxable year subsequent to the credit year, a sublessee uses the property predominantly outside the United States, the property ceases to be section 38 property with respect to the lessee.

(c) *Reduction in basis of section 38 property.*—(1) *General rule.*—If, in the credit year or in any taxable year subsequent to the credit year, the basis (or cost) of section 38 property is reduced, for example, as a result of a refund of part of the cost of the property, then such section 38 property shall be treated as having ceased to be section 38 property with respect to the taxpayer to the extent of the amount of such reduction in basis (or cost) on the date the refund which results in such reduction in basis (or cost) is received or accrued, except that for purposes of §1.47-1(a) the actual useful life of the property treated as having ceased to be section 38 property shall be considered to be less than 3 years.

(2) *Example.*—Subparagraph (1) of this paragraph may be illustrated by the following example:

Example. (i) On January 1, 1962, A, a cash basis taxpayer, acquired from X Cooperative an item of section 38 property with a basis of $100 and an estimated useful life of 10 years which he placed in service on such date. The amount of qualified investment with respect to such asset was $100. For the taxable year 1962 A was allowed under section 38 a credit of $7 against his liability for tax. On June 1, 1963, A receives a $10 patronage dividend from X Cooperative with respect to such asset. Under paragraph (c)(2)(i) of §1.1385-1, the basis of the asset in A's hands is reduced by $10.

(ii) Under subparagraph (1) of this paragraph, on June 1, 1963, the item of section 38 property ceases to be section 38 property with respect to A to the extent of $10 of the original $100 basis.

(d) *Retirements.*—A retirement of section 38 property, including a normal retirement (as defined in paragraph (b) of §1.167(a)-8, relating to definition of normal and abnormal retirements), whether from a single asset account or a multiple asset account, and an abandonment, are dispositions for purposes of paragraph (a) of §1.47-1.

(e) *Conversion of section 38 property to personal use.*—(1) If, for any taxable year subsequent to the credit year—

(i) A deduction for depreciation is allowable to the taxpayer with respect to only a part of section 38 property because such property is partially devoted to personal use, and

(ii) The part of the property (expressed as a percentage of its total basis (or cost)) with respect to which a deduction for depreciation is allowable for such taxable year is less than the part of the property with respect to which a deduction for depreciation was allowable in the credit year, then such property shall be considered as having ceased to be section 38 property with respect to the taxpayer to such extent. Further, property ceases to be section 38 property with respect to the taxpayer to the extent that a deduction for depreciation thereon is disallowed under section 274 (relating to disallowance of certain entertainment, etc., expenses).

(2) *Examples.*—Subparagraph (1) of this paragraph may be illustrated by the following examples:

Example (1). (i) A, a calendar-year taxpayer, acquired and placed in service on January 1, 1962, an automobile with a basis of $2,400 and an estimated useful life of four years. In the taxable year 1962 the automobile was used by A 80 percent of the time in his trade or business and was used 20 percent of the time for personal purposes. Thus, for the taxable year 1962 only 80 percent of the basis of the automobile qualified as section 38 property since a deduction for depreciation was allowable to A only with respect to 80 percent of the basis of the automobile. In the taxable year 1963 the automobile is used by A only 60 percent of the time in his trade or business. Thus, for the taxable year 1963 a deduction for depreciation is allowable to A only with respect to 60 percent of the basis of the automobile.

(ii) Under subparagraph (1) of this paragraph, on January 1, 1963, the automobile ceases to be section 38 property with respect to A to the extent of 20 percent (80 percent minus 60 percent) of the $2,400 basis of the automobile.

Example (2). (i) The facts are the same as in example (1) and in addition for the taxable year 1964 a deduction for depreciation is allowable to A only with respect to 40 percent of the basis of the property.

(ii) Under subparagraph (1) of this paragraph, on January 1, 1964, the automobile ceases to be section 38 property with respect to A to the extent of 20 percent (60 percent minus 40 percent) of the $2,400 basis of the automobile. [Reg. §1.47-2.]

☐ [T.D. 6931, 10-9-67. *Amended by T.D. 7203, 8-24-72.*]

[Reg. §1.47-3]

§1.47-3. Exceptions to the application of §1.47-1.—(a) *In general.*—Notwithstanding the provisions of §1.47-2, relating to "disposition" and "cessation," paragraph (a) of §1.47-1 shall not apply if paragraph (b) of this section (relating to transfers by reason of death), paragraph (c) of this section (relating to property destroyed by casualty), paragraph (d) of this section (relating to reselection of used section 38 property), paragraph (e) of this section (relating to transactions to which section 381(a) applies), paragraph (f) of this section (relating to mere change in form of conducting a trade or business), paragraph (g) of this section (relating to sale-and-leaseback transactions), or paragraph (h) of this section (relating to certain property replaced after Apr. 18, 1969) applies with respect to such disposition or cessation.

(b) *Transfers by reason of death.*—(1) *General rule.*—Notwithstanding the provisions of §1.47-2, relating to "disposition" and "cessation", paragraph (a) of §1.47-1 shall not apply to a transfer of section 38 property by reason of the death of the taxpayer. Thus, for example, with respect to section 38 property held in joint tenancy, paragraph (a) of §1.47-1 shall not apply to the transfer of the deceased taxpayer's interest to the surviving joint tenant. If, under §1.48-4, the lessor of new section 38 property made a valid election to treat the lessee as having purchased such property for purposes of the credit allowed by section 38, paragraph (a) of §1.47-1 does not apply if, by reason of the death of the lessee, there is a termination of the lease and transfer of the leased property to the lessor, or there is an assignment of the lease and transfer of the leased property to another person. Moreover, paragraph (a) of §1.47-1 does not apply to the transfer of a partner's interest in a partnership, a beneficiary's interest in an estate or trust, or shares of stock of a shareholder of an electing small business corporation (as defined in section 1371(b)) by reason of the death of such partner, beneficiary, or shareholder. Paragraph (a) of §1.47-1 applies to a gift by a taxpayer prior to his death even if the value of such gift is included in his gross estate for estate tax purposes (such as, a gift in contemplation of death under section 2035). The effect of this subparagraph is that any section 38 property held by a taxpayer at the time of his death is deemed to have been held by him for its entire estimated useful life.

(2) *Examples.*—Subparagraph (1) of this paragraph may be illustrated by the following examples:

Example (1). (i) A, an individual, acquired and placed in service on January 1, 1962, an item of section 38 property with a basis of $10,000 and an estimated useful life of eight years. On April 28, 1963, A dies and, as a result of A's death, his interest in such item of section 38 property is transferred to a testamentary trust pursuant to A's will, and on February 1, 1967, the trust is terminated and the item of section 38 property is transferred to the beneficiaries of the trust.

(ii) Under subparagraph (1) of this paragraph, paragraph (a) of §1.47-1 does not apply to the transfer, as a result of A's death, of his interest in such item of section 38 property to the testamentary trust. Moreover, paragraph (a) of §1.47-1 does not apply to the February 1, 1967, transfer of such item of section 38 property by the trust to its beneficiaries.

Example (2). (i) X Corporation, an electing small business corporation (as defined in section 1371(b)) which makes its returns on the basis of a calendar year, acquired and placed in service during 1962 an item of section 38 property. On December 31, 1962, X Corporation had 10 shares of stock outstanding which were owned as follows: A owned eight shares and B owned two shares. On December 31, 1962, 80 percent of the basis of the item of section 38 property was apportioned to A and 20 percent to B. On June 1, 1964, A dies and, as a result of A's death, his eight shares of stock in X Corporation are transferred to his wife. On July 10, 1965, X Corporation sells the item of section 38 property to Y Corporation.

(ii) Under subparagraph (1) of this paragraph, paragraph (a) of §1.47-1 does not apply to the transfer, as a result of A's death, of his eight shares of stock in X Corporation to his wife. Moreover, with respect to the July 10, 1965, sale paragraph (a) of §1.47-1 applies only to the 20 percent of the basis of the item of section 38 property which was apportioned to B.

(c) *Property destroyed by casualty.*—(1) *Dispositions after April 18, 1969.*—Notwithstanding the provisions of §1.47-2, relating to "disposition" and "cessation", paragraph (a) of §1.47-1 shall not apply to property which, after April 18, 1969, and before August 16, 1971, is disposed of or otherwise ceases to be section 38 property with respect to the taxpayer on account of its destruction or damage by fire, storm, shipwreck, or other casualty, or by reason of its theft.

(2) *Dispositions before April 19, 1969.*—(i) In the case of property which, before April 19, 1969, is disposed of or otherwise ceases to be section 38 property with respect to the taxpayer on account of its destruction or damage by fire, storm, shipwreck or other casualty, or by reason of its theft, paragraph (a) of §1.47-1 shall apply except to the extent provided in subdivisions (ii) and (iii) of this subparagraph.

(ii) Paragraph (a) of §1.47-1 shall not apply if—

(a) Section 38 property is placed in service by the taxpayer to replace (within the meaning of paragraph (h) of §1.46-3) the destroyed, damaged, or stolen property, and

(b) The basis (or cost) of the section 38 property which is placed in service by the taxpayer to replace the destroyed, damaged, or stolen property is reduced under paragraph (h) of §1.46-3.

(iii) If property which would be section 38 property but for section 49 is placed in service by the taxpayer to replace the destroyed, damaged, or stolen property, then the provisions of paragraph (h) of this section (other than the requirement that the replacement take place within 6 months after the disposition) shall apply.

(3) *Examples.*—The provisions of subparagraph (2)(ii) of this paragraph may be illustrated by the following examples:

Example (1). (i) A acquired and placed in service on January 1, 1962, machine No. 1 which qualified as section 38 property with a basis of $30,000 and an estimated useful life of 6 years. The amount of qualified investment with respect to such machine was $20,000. For the taxable year 1962 A's credit earned of $1,400 was allowed under section 38 as a credit against its liability for tax. On January 1, 1963, machine No. 1 is completely destroyed by fire. On January 1, 1963, the adjusted basis of machine No. 1 in A's hands is $24,500. A receives $23,000 in insurance proceeds as compensation for the destroyed machine, and on February 15, 1964, A acquires and places in service machine No. 2, which qualifies as section 38 property, with a basis of $41,000 and an estimated useful life of six years to replace machine No. 1.

(ii) Under subparagraph (1) of this paragraph, paragraph (a) of §1.47-1 does not apply with respect to machine No. 1 since machine No. 2 is placed in service to replace machine No. 1 and the $41,000 basis of machine No. 2 is reduced, under paragraph (h) of §1.46-3, by $23,000. (See example (1) of paragraph (h)(3) of §1.46-3.)

Example (2). (i) The facts are the same as in example (1) except that A receives only $19,000 in insurance proceeds as compensation for the destroyed machine.

(ii) Although machine No. 2 is placed in service to replace machine No. 1, subparagraph (1) of this paragraph does not apply with respect to machine No. 1 since the basis of machine No. 2 is not reduced under paragraph (h) of §1.46-3. Paragraph (a) of §1.47-1 applies with respect to the January 1, 1963, destruction of machine No. 1. The actual useful life of machine No. 1 is one year. The recomputed qualified investment with respect to such machine is zero ($30,000 basis multiplied by zero applicable percentage) and A's recomputed credit earned for the taxable year 1962 is zero. The income tax imposed by chapter 1 of the Code on A for the taxable year 1963 is increased by $1,400.

(d) *Reselection of used section 38 property.*—(1) *Reselection.*—If—

(i) Used section 38 property (as defined in §1.48-3) the cost of which was taken into account in computing the taxpayer's qualified investment is disposed of, or otherwise ceases to be section 38 property with respect to the taxpayer, before the close of the estimated useful life which was taken into account in computing such qualified investment, and

(ii) For the taxable year in which the property described in subdivision (i) of this subparagraph was placed in service, the sum of (a) the cost of used section 38 property placed in service by the taxpayer, and (b) the cost of used section 38 property apportioned to such taxpayer exceeded $50,000,

then such taxpayer may treat the cost of any used section 38 property (regardless of its estimated useful life) which was not originally selected, under paragraph (c)(4) of §1.48-3, to be taken into account in computing qualified investment for such taxable year (or previously reselected under this subparagraph) as having been selected (in accordance with the principles of paragraph (c)(4)(ii) of §1.48-3) in place of the cost of the used section 38 property described in subdivision (i) of this subparagraph. Hereinafter such *reselected property* is referred to as "newly selected used section 38 property". For purposes of this subparagraph, the cost of used section 38 property apportioned to a taxpayer means the sum of the cost of used section 38 property apportioned to him by a trust, estate, or electing small

business corporation (as defined in section 1371(b)), and his share of the cost of partnership used section 38 property, with respect to the taxable year of such trust, estate, corporation or partnership ending with or within such taxpayer's taxable year. In the case of a taxpayer to whom paragraph (c)(2) of §1.48-3 applied for the taxable year in which the property described in subdivision (i) of this subparagraph was placed in service, a $25,000 amount shall be substituted for the $50,000 amount referred to in subdivision (ii)(b) of this subparagraph, and in the case of a member of an affiliated group (as defined in subparagraph (6) of §1.48-3(e)) the amount apportioned to such member under paragraph (e) of §1.48-3 shall be substituted for such $50,000 amount.

(2) *Application of paragraph (a) of §1.47-1.*—(i) If a taxpayer treats, under subparagraph (1) of this paragraph, the cost of any used section 38 property which was not originally selected as having been selected in place of the cost of used section 38 property described in subparagraph (1)(i) of this paragraph, then, notwithstanding the provisions of §1.47-2 (relating to "disposition" and "cessation"), paragraph (a) of §1.47-1 shall not apply to the property described in subparagraph (1)(i) of this paragraph to the extent of the cost of the newly selected used section 38 property.

(ii) If the cost of the used section 38 property described in subparagraph (1)(i) of this paragraph exceeds the cost of the newly selected used section 38 property, then the property described in subparagraph (1)(i) of this paragraph shall cease to be section 38 property with respect to the taxpayer to the extent of such excess.

(iii) If the newly selected used section 38 property is disposed of, or otherwise ceases to be section 38 property with respect to the taxpayer, before the close of the estimated useful life of the property described in subparagraph (1)(i) of this paragraph, then, unless he reselects other used section 38 property, paragraph (a) of §1.47-1 shall apply with respect to such newly selected used section 38 property. For purposes of recomputing qualified investment with respect to such newly selected used section 38 property the actual useful life shall be deemed to be the period beginning with the date on which the property described in subparagraph (1)(i) of this paragraph was placed in service by the taxpayer and ending with the date of the disposition or cessation with respect to such newly selected used section 38 property. See paragraph (c) of §1.47-1, relating to date placed in service and date of disposition or cessation.

(3) *Information requirement.*—(i) If in any taxable year this paragraph applies to a taxpayer, such taxpayer, shall attach to his income tax return for such taxable year a statement containing the information required by subdivision (ii) of this subparagraph.

(ii) The statement referred to in subdivision (i) of this subparagraph shall contain the following information:

(a) The taxpayer's name, address and taxpayer account number; and

(b) With respect to the originally selected used section 38 property and the newly selected used section 38 property, the month and year placed in service, cost, and estimated useful life.

(4) *Examples.*—This paragraph may be illustrated by the following examples:

Example (1). (i) X Corporation purchased and placed in service on January 1, 1962, machines No. 1 and No. 2, which qualified as used section 38 property, each with a cost of $50,000 and an estimated useful life of eight years. The aggregate cost of used section 38 property taken into account by X Corporation in computing its qualified investment for the taxable year 1962 could not exceed $50,000; therefore, under paragraph (c)(4) of §1.48-3, X selected the $50,000 cost of machine No. 1 to be taken into account in computing its qualified investment for the taxable year 1962. The qualified investment with respect to machine No. 1 was $50,000. For the taxable year 1962 X's credit earned of $3,500 was allowed under section 38 as a credit against its liability for tax. On January 2, 1965, X Corporation sells machine No. 1 to Y Corporation.

(ii) Under subparagraph (1) of this paragraph, X Corporation treats the $50,000 cost of machine No. 2 as having been selected to be taken into account in computing its qualified investment for the taxable year 1962 in place of the $50,000 cost of machine No. 1. Therefore, under subparagraph (2)(i) of this paragraph, paragraph (a) of §1.47-1 does not apply to the January 2, 1965, disposition of machine No. 1.

Example (2). (i) The facts are the same as in example (1) and in addition X Corporation, on December 2, 1966, sells machine No. 2 to Z Corporation.

(ii) Under subparagraph (2)(iii) of this paragraph, paragraph (a) of §1.47-1 applies with respect to the December 2, 1966, disposition of machine No. 2. The actual useful life of machine No. 2 is four years and eleven months (that is, the period beginning on January 1, 1962, and ending on December 2, 1966). The recomputed qualified investment with respect to machine No. 2 is $16,667 ($50,000 cost multiplied by 33¹/₃ percent applicable percentage) and X Corporation's recomputed credit earned for the taxable year 1962 is $1,167. The income tax imposed by chapter 1 of the Code on X Corporation for the taxable year 1966 is increased by the $2,333 decrease in its credit earned for the taxable year 1962 (that is, $3,500 original credit earned minus $1,167 recomputed credit earned).

Example (3). (i) The facts are the same as in example (1) except that machine No. 2 had a cost of $30,000.

(ii) Under subparagraph (1) of this paragraph, X Corporation treats the $30,000 cost of machine No. 2 as having been selected to be taken into account in computing its qualified investment for the taxable year 1962 in place of the $50,000 cost of machine No. 1. Therefore, under subparagraph (2)(i) of this paragraph, paragraph (a) of §1.47-1 does not apply to the January 2, 1965, disposition of machine No. 1 to the extent of $30,000 of the $50,000 cost of machine No. 1. However, under subparagraph (2)(ii) of this paragraph, paragraph (a) of §1.47-1 applies to the January 2, 1965, disposition of machine No. 1 to the extent of $20,000 (that is, $50,000 cost of machine No. 1 minus $30,000 cost of machine No. 2). The actual useful life of such $20,000 portion of machine No. 1 is three years (that is, the period beginning on January 1, 1962, and ending on January 2, 1965). The recomputed qualified investment with respect to the $20,000 portion of the cost of machine No. 1 is zero ($20,000 portion of the cost multiplied by zero applicable percentage) and X Corporation's recomputed credit earned for the taxable year 1962 is $2,100 (7 percent of $30,000). The income tax imposed by chapter 1 of the Code on X Corporation for the taxable year 1965 is increased by the $1,400 decrease in its credit earned for the taxable year 1962 (that is, $3,500 original credit earned minus $2,100 recomputed credit earned).

(e) *Transactions to which section 381(a) applies.*—(1) *General rule.*—Notwithstanding the provisions of §1.47-2, relating to "disposition" and "cessation", paragraph (a) of §1.47-1 shall not apply to a disposition of section 38 property in a transaction to which section 381(a) (relating to carryovers in certain corporate acquisitions) applies. If the section 38 property described in the preceding sentence is disposed of, or otherwise ceases to be section 38 property with respect to the acquiring corporation, before the close of the estimated useful life which was taken into account in computing the transferor corporation's qualified investment, then paragraph (a) of §1.47-1 shall apply to the acquiring corporation with respect to such section 38 property. For purposes of recomputing qualified investment with respect to such property its actual useful life shall be the period beginning with the date on which it was placed in service by the transferor corporation and ending with the date of the disposition by, or cessation with respect to, the acquiring corporation.

(2) *Examples.*—This paragraph may be illustrated by the following examples:

Example (1). (i) X Corporation, a wholly owned subsidiary of Y Corporation, acquired and placed in service on January 1, 1962, an item of section 38 property with a basis of $12,000 and an estimated useful life of eight years. Both X and Y make their returns on the basis of a calendar year. The qualified investment with respect to such item was $12,000. For the taxable year 1962 X Corporation's credit earned of $840 was allowed under section 38 as a credit against its liability for tax. On January 15, 1967, X Corporation is liquidated under section 332 and all of its properties, including the item of section 38 property, are transferred to Y Corporation. The bases of the properties in the hands of Y Corporation are determined under section 334(b)(1).

(ii) Under subparagraph (1) of this paragraph, paragraph (a) of §1.47-1 does not apply to the January 15, 1967, transfer to Y Corporation.

Example (2). (i) The facts are the same as in example (1) and in addition on February 2, 1968, Y Corporation sells the item of section 38 property to Z Corporation.

(ii) Under subparagraph (1) of this paragraph, paragraph (a) of §1.47-1 does not apply to the January 15, 1967, transfer to Y Corporation. However, paragraph (a) of §1.47 applies to the February 2, 1968, sale of the property by Y Corporation. The actual useful life of the property is six years and one month (that is, the period beginning on January 1, 1962, and ending on February 2, 1968).

(f) *Mere change in form of conducting a trade or business.*—(1) *General rule.*—(i) Notwithstanding the provisions of §1.47-2, relating to "disposition" and "cessation", paragraph (a) of §1.47-1 shall not apply to section 38 property which is disposed of, or otherwise ceases to be section 38 property with respect to the taxpayer, before the close of the estimated useful life which was taken into account in computing the taxpayer's qualified investment by reason of a mere change in the form of conducting the trade or business in which such section 38 property is used provided that conditions set forth in subdivision (ii) of this subparagraph are satisfied.

(ii) The conditions referred to in subdivision (i) of this subparagraph are as follows:

(*a*) The section 38 property described in subdivision (i) of this subparagraph is retained as section 38 property in the same trade or business,

(*b*) The transferor (or in a case where the transferor is a partnership, estate, trust, or electing small business corporation, the partner, beneficiary, or shareholder) of such section 38 property retains a substantial interest in such trade or business,

(*c*) Substantially all the assets (whether or not section 38 property) necessary to operate such trade of business are transferred to the transferee to whom such section 38 property is transferred, and

(*d*) The basis of such section 38 property in the hands of the transferee is determined in whole or in part by reference to the basis of such section 38 property in the hands of the transferor.

This subparagraph shall not apply to the transfer of section 38 property if paragraph (e) of this section, relating to transactions to which section 381 applies, applies with respect to such transfer.

(2) *Substantial interest.*—For purposes of this paragraph, a transferor (or in a case where the transferor is a partnership, estate, trust, or electing small business corporation, the partner, beneficiary, or shareholder) shall be considered as having retained a substantial interest in the trade or business only if, after the change in form, his interest in such trade or business—

(i) Is substantial in relation to the total interest of all persons, or

(ii) Is equal to or greater than his interest prior to the change in form.

Thus, where a taxpayer owns a 5-percent interest in a partnership, and, after the incorporation of that partnership, the taxpayer retains at least a 5-percent interest in the corporation, the taxpayer will be considered as having retained a substantial interest in the trade or business as of the date of the change in form.

(3) *Property held for the production of income.*—Subparagraph (1)(i) of this paragraph applies to section 38 property held for the production of income (within the meaning of section 167(a)(2)) as well as to section 38 property used in a trade or business.

(4) *Leased property.*—In a case where a lessor of new section 38 property made a valid election, under §1.48-4, to treat the lessee as having purchased such property for purposes of the credit allowed by section 38, in determining whether subparagraph (1)(i) of this paragraph applies to an assignment of the lease and transfer of possession of such property, the condition contained in subparagraph (1)(ii)(*d*) of this paragraph is not applicable.

(5) *Disposition or cessation.*—(i) If section 38 property described in subparagraph (1)(i) of this paragraph is disposed of by the transferee, or otherwise ceases to be section 38 property with respect to the transferee, before the close of the estimated useful life which was taken into account in computing the qualified investment of the transferor (or in a case where the transferor is a partnership, estate, trust, or electing small business corporation, the qualified investment of the partners, beneficiaries, or shareholders) then under paragraph (a) of §1.47-1 such property ceases to be section 38 property with respect to the transferor (or such partners, beneficiaries, or shareholders), and a recapture determination shall be made with respect to such property. For purposes of recomputing qualified investment with respect to such property, the actual useful life shall be the period beginning with the date on which it was placed in service by the transferor and ending with the date of the disposition by, or cessation with respect to, the transferee.

(ii) If in any taxable year the transferor (or in a case where the transferor is a partnership, estate, trust, or electing small business corporation, the partner, beneficiary, or shareholder) of the section 38 property described in subparagraph (1)(i) of this paragraph does not retain a substantial interest in the trade or business directly or indirectly (through ownership in other entities provided that such other entities' bases in such interest are determined in whole or in part by reference to the basis of such interest in the hands of the transferor) then, under paragraph (a) of §1.47-1, such property ceases to be section 38 property with respect to the transferor and he (or the partner, beneficiary, or shareholder) shall make a recapture determination. For purposes of recomputing qualified investment with respect to property described in this subdivision, its actual useful life shall be the period beginning with the date on which it was placed in service by the transferor and ending with the first date on which the transferor (or the partner, beneficiary, or shareholder) does not retain a substantial interest in the trade or business. Any taxpayer who seeks to establish his interest in a trade or business under the rule of this subdivision shall maintain adequate records to demonstrate his indirect interest in such trade or business after any such transfer or transfers.

(iii) In making a recapture determination under this subparagraph there shall be taken into account any prior recapture determinations with respect to the transferor in connection with the same property.

(iv) Notwithstanding subparagraph (1) of this paragraph and subdivision (ii) of this subparagraph in the case of a mere change in the form of a trade or business, if the interest of a taxpayer in the trade or business is reduced but such taxpayer has retained a substantial interest in such trade or business, paragraph (a)(2) of §1.47-4 (relating to electing small business corporations), paragraph (a)(2) of §1.47-5 (relating to estate or trusts) or paragraph (a)(2) of §1.47-6 (relating to partnerships) shall apply, as the case may be.

(6) *Examples.*—This paragraph may be illustrated by the following examples in each of which it is assumed that the transfer satisfies the conditions of subparagraph (1)(ii)(*a*), (*c*) and (*d*) of this paragraph.

Example (1). (i) On January 1, 1962, A, an individual, acquired and placed in service in his sole proprietorship an item of section 38 property with a basis of $12,000 and an estimated useful life of eight years. The qualified investment with respect to such item was $12,000. For the taxable year 1962 A's credit earned of $840 was allowed under section 38 as a credit against his liability for tax. On March 15, 1963, A transfers all of the assets used in his sole proprietorship to X Corporation, a newly formed corporation, in exchange for 45 percent of the stock of X Corporation.

(ii) Under subparagraph (1)(i) of this paragraph, paragraph (a) of §1.47-1 does not apply to the March 15, 1963, transfer to X Corporation.

Example 2. (i) The facts are the same as in example (1) and in addition on February 2, 1964, X Corporation sells the item of section 38 property to Y Corporation.

(ii) Under subparagraph (1)(i) of this paragraph, paragraph (a) of §1.47-1 does not apply to the March 15, 1963, transfer to X Corporation. However, under subparagraph (5)(i) of this paragraph, paragraph (a) of §1.47-1 applies to the February 2, 1964, sale of the item of section 38 property by X Corporation to Y Corporation. The actual useful life of the property is two years and one month (that is, the period beginning on January 1, 1962, and ending on February 2, 1964). The recomputed qualified investment with respect to such property is zero ($12,000 basis multiplied by zero applicable percentage) and A's recomputed credit earned for the taxable year 1962 is zero. The income tax imposed by chapter 1 of the Code on A for 1964 is increased by the $840 decrease in his credit earned for the taxable year 1962 (that is, $840 credit earned minus zero recomputed credit earned).

Example (3). (i) On January 1, 1962, partnership ABC, which makes its returns on the basis of a calendar year, acquired and placed in service an item of section 38 property with a basis of $20,000 and an estimated useful life of eight years. Partnership ABC has 10 partners who make their returns on the basis of a calendar year and share partnership profits equally. Each partner's share of the basis of such item of section 38 property is 10 percent, that is, $2,000. On March 15, 1963, partnership ABC transfers all of the assets used in its trade or business to the X Corporation, a newly formed corporation, in exchange for all of the stock of X Corporation and immediately thereafter transfers 10 percent of such stock to each of the 10 partners.

(ii) Under subparagraph (1)(i) of this paragraph, paragraph (a) of §1.47-1 does not apply to the March 15, 1963 transfer by the ABC Partnership to X Corporation.

Example (4). (i) The facts are the same as in example (3) except that partnership ABC transfers 10 percent of the stock in X Corporation to each of 8 partners, 20 percent to partner A, and cash to partner B.

(ii) Under subparagraph (1)(i) of this paragraph, with respect to all of the partners (including partner A) except partner B, paragraph (a) of §1.47-1 does not apply to the March 15, 1963, transfer by the ABC Partnership to X Corporation. Paragraph (a) of §1.47-1 applies with respect to partner B's $2,000 share of the item of section 38 property. See paragraph (a)(1) of §1.47-6.

Example (5). (i) X Corporation operates a manufacturing business and a separate personal service business. On January 1, 1962, X acquired and placed in service a truck, which qualified as section 38 property, in its manufacturing business. The truck had a basis of $10,000 and an estimated useful life of 8 years. On February 10, 1965, X transfers all the assets used in its manufacturing business to Partnership XY in exchange for 50 percent interest in such partnership.

(ii) Under subparagraph (1)(i) of this paragraph, paragraph (a) of §1.47-1 does not apply to the February 10, 1965, transfer to Partnership XY.

(g) *Sale-and-leaseback transactions.*—(1) *In general.*—Notwithstanding the provisions of §1.47-2, relating to "disposition" and "cessation", paragraph (a) of §1.47-1 shall not apply where section 38 property is disposed of and as part of the same transaction is leased back to the vendor even though gain or loss is recognized to the vendor-lessee and the property ceases to be subject to depreciation in his hands. If paragraph (a) of §1.47-1 applies with respect to such property subsequent to the transaction, the actual useful life shall

begin with the date on which such property was first placed in service by the vendor-lessee as owner.

(2) *Special rule for progress expenditure property.*—The sale and leaseback (or agreement or contract to leaseback) of progress expenditure property (including any contract rights to the property), in general, will be treated as a cessation described in section 47(a)(3)(A) with respect to the seller-lessee. However, a sale and leaseback (or agreement or contract to leaseback) will not be treated as a cessation to the extent qualified investment passed through to the lessee under section 48(d) in the year the property is placed in service equals or exceeds qualified progress expenditures for the property taken into account by the lessee. If a sale-leaseback transaction is treated as a cessation, qualified investment must be reduced and the credit recomputed, beginning with the most recent credit year (*i.e.*, the most recent year property is taken into account in computing qualified investment under §1.46-3 or 1.46-5). The amount of the reduction is the amount, if any, by which qualified progress expenditures taken into account by the lessee in all prior years exceeds qualified investment passed through to the lessee under section 48(d). This paragraph (g)(2) does not apply to any progress expenditure property that has been placed in service by a vendor-lessee (as described in paragraph (g)(1) of this section) prior to a sale-leaseback of that property in a transaction described in paragraph (g)(1) of this section.

»»→ *Caution: Reg. §1.47-3(h)(1) does not apply to tax years after 1978 (Rev. Rul. 88-96, 1988-2 CB 27).*

(h) *Certain property replaced after April 18, 1969.*—(1) *In general.*—(i) If section 38 property is disposed of and property which is, for purposes of section 1033 and regulations thereunder, similar or related in service or use to the property disposed of and which would be section 38 property but for the application of section 49 is placed in service to replace the property disposed of, the increase in income tax and adjustment of investment credit carryovers and carrybacks resulting from the recomputation under paragraph (a) of §1.47-1 shall be reduced (but not below zero) by the credit that would be allowed for the qualified investment of the replacement property (determined as if such property were section 38 property). The preceding sentence shall not apply unless the replacement takes place within 6 months after the disposition. If property otherwise qualifies as replacement property, it is immaterial that it is placed in service (for example, to undergo testing) before the replaced property is disposed of. The assignment by the taxpayer in his return of an estimated useful life to the replacement property in computing qualified investment will be considered a representation by the taxpayer that he expects to retain the replacement property for its entire estimated useful life. If such property is disposed of before the end of such life, then the circumstances surrounding the replacement will be examined to determine whether the taxpayer's representation was in good faith and, if appropriate, the qualified investment of the replacement property will be recomputed for the year of replacement using the actual useful life of such property.

(ii) The provisions of subdivision (i) of this subparagraph may be illustrated by the following example:

Example: On January 1, 1967, A, a calendar year taxpayer, acquired and placed in service a new machine with a basis of $100 and an estimated useful life of 8 years. A's qualified investment was $100 and his credit earned was $7, which was allowed as a credit against tax for 1967. On January 15, 1971, A disposed of the machine and replaced it with a similar new machine costing $75 and having an estimated useful life of 8 years. The new machine would be section 38 property but for section 49. Since the actual useful life of the original machine was at least 4 but less than 6 years, the recomputed qualified investment of the machine is $33.33 (33¹/₃ percent of $100) and under paragraph (a) of §1.47-1 the amount of recapture tax would be $4.67 ($7, the original credit earned, minus $2.33, the recomputed credit earned). However, under the provisions of this paragraph, the recapture tax is reduced (but not below zero) by the credit that would be allowed for the replacement property (determined as if such property were section 38 property). Under these facts the recapture tax is zero ($4.67, the recapture tax with respect to the original machine, minus $5.25, the credit that would be allowed on the new machine).

(2) *Leased property.*—Property disposed of may be replaced with property leased from another, provided (i) an election with respect to the newly leased property could be made under section 48(d) but for section 49, and (ii) the lessee obtains the lessor's written statement that he will not claim such property as replacement property under this paragraph. The statement of the lessor shall contain the information specified in subdivisions (i) through (vii) of §1.48-4(f)(1) and the statement (or a copy thereof) shall be retained in the records of the lessor and the lessee for a period of at least 3 years after the property is transferred to the lessee. [Reg. §1.47-3.]

☐ [*T.D. 6931,* 10-9-67. *Amended by T.D. 7126,* 6-9-71; *T.D. 7203,* 8-24-72 *and T.D. 8183,* 3-1-88.]

[Reg. §1.47-4]

§1.47-4. Electing small business corporations.—(a) *In general.*—(1) *Disposition or cessation in hands of corporation.*—If an electing small business corporation (as defined in section 1371(b)) or a former electing small business corporation disposes of any section 38 property (or if any section 38 property otherwise ceases to be section 38 property in the hands of the corporation) before the close of the estimated useful life which was taken into account in computing qualified investment with respect to such property, a recapture determination shall be made with respect to each shareholder who is treated, under §1.48-5, as a taxpayer with respect to such property. Each such recapture determination shall be made with respect to the pro rata share of the basis (or cost) of such property taken into account by such shareholder in computing his qualified investment. For purposes of each such recapture determination the actual useful life of such property shall be the period beginning with the date on which it was placed in service by the electing small business corporation and ending with the date of the disposition or cessation. In making a recapture determination under this subparagraph there shall be taken into account any prior recapture determinations made with respect to the shareholder in connection with the same property. For definition of "recapture determination" see paragraph (a)(1) of §1.47-1.

(2) *Disposition of shareholder's interest.*—(i) If—

(a) The basis (or cost) of section 38 property is apportioned, under §1.48-5, to a shareholder of an electing small business corporation who takes such basis (or cost) into account in computing his qualified investment, and

(b) After the end of shareholder's taxable year in which such apportionment was taken into account and before the close of the estimated useful life of the property, such shareholder's proportionate stock interest in such corporation is reduced (for example, by a sale or redemption, or by the issuance of additional shares) below the percentage specified in subdivision (ii) of this subparagraph,

then, on the date of such reduction such section 38 property ceases to be section 38 property with respect to such shareholder to the extent of the actual reduction in such shareholder's proportionate stock interest. (For example, if $100 of the basis of section 38 property was apportioned to a shareholder and if his proportionate stock interest is reduced from 60 percent to 30 percent (that is, 50 percent of his original interest), then such property shall be treated as having ceased to be section 38 property to the extent of $50.) Accordingly, a recapture determination shall be made with respect to such shareholder. For purposes of such recapture determination the actual useful life of such property shall be the period beginning with the date on which it was placed in service by the electing small business corporation and ending with the date on which it is treated as having ceased to be section 38 property with respect to the shareholder. In making a recapture determination under this subparagraph there shall be taken into account any prior recapture determination made with respect to the shareholder in connection with the same property.

(ii) The percentage referred to in subdivision (i)(b) of this subparagraph is $66\frac{2}{3}$ percent of the shareholder's proportionate stock interest in the corporation on the date of the apportionment under §1.48-5. However, once property has been treated under this subparagraph as having ceased to be section 38 property to any extent the percentage referred to shall be $33\frac{1}{3}$ percent of the shareholder's proportionate stock interest in the corporation on the date of the apportionment under §1.48-5.

(iii) In determining a shareholder's proportionate stock interest in a former electing small business corporation for purposes of this subparagraph, the shareholder shall be considered to own stock in such corporation which he owns directly or indirectly (through ownership in other entities provided such other entities' bases in such stock are determined in whole or in part by reference to the basis of such stock in the hands of the transferor). For example, if A, who owns all of the 100 shares of the outstanding stock of corporation X, a corporation which was formerly an electing small business corporation, transfers on November 1, 1966, 70 shares of X stock to corporation Y in exchange for 90 percent of the stock of Y in a transaction to which section 351 applies, then, for purposes of subdivision (i) of this subparagraph, A shall be considered to own 93 percent of the stock of X, 30 percent directly and 63 percent indirectly (i.e., 90 percent of 70). Any taxpayer who seeks to establish his interest in the stock of a former electing small business corporation

under the rule of this subdivision shall maintain adequate records to demonstrate his indirect interest in the corporation after any such transfer or transfers.

(b) *Election of a small business corporation under section 1372.*—(1) *General rule.*—If a corporation makes a valid election under section 1372 to be an electing small business corporation (as defined in section 1371(b)), then on the last day of the taxable year immediately preceding the first taxable year for which such election is effective, any section 38 property the basis (or cost) of which was taken into account in computing the corporation's qualified investment in taxable years prior to the first taxable year for which the election is effective (and which has not been disposed of or otherwise ceased to be section 38 property with respect to the corporation prior to such last day) shall be considered as having ceased to be section 38 property with respect to such corporation and §1.47-1 shall apply. However, if the corporation and each of the persons who are shareholders of the corporation on the first day of the first taxable year for which the election under section 1372 is to be effective, or on the date of such election, whichever is later, execute the agreement specified in subparagraph (2) of this paragraph, §1.47-1 shall not apply to any such section 38 property by reason of the election by the corporation under section 1372.

(2) *Agreement of shareholders and corporation.*—(i) The agreement referred to in subparagraph (1) of this paragraph shall be signed by the shareholders and the corporation, and shall recite that, in the event the section 38 property described in subparagraph (1) of this paragraph is later disposed of by, or ceases to be section 38 property with respect to, the corporation during a taxable year of the corporation for which the election under section 1372 is effective, each such signer agrees (a) to notify the district director of such disposition or cessation, and (b) to be jointly and severally liable to pay to the district director an amount equal to the increase in tax provided by section 47. The amount of such increase shall be determined as if such property had ceased to be section 38 property as of the last day of the taxable year immediately preceding the first taxable year for which the election under section 1372 is effective, except that the actual useful life (within the meaning of paragraph (a) of §1.47-1) of the property shall be considered to have ended on the date of the actual disposition by, or cessation in the hands of, the electing small business corporation.

(ii) The agreement shall set forth the name, address, and taxpayer account number of each party and the internal revenue district in which each such party files his or its income tax return for the taxable year which includes the last day of the corporation's taxable year immediately preceding the first taxable year for which the election under section 1372 is effective. The agreement may be signed on behalf of the corporation by any person who is duly authorized. The agreement shall be filed with the district director with whom the corporation files its income tax return for its taxable year immediately preceding the first taxable year for which the election under section 1372 is effective and shall be filed on or before the due date (including extensions of time) of such return. However, if the due date (including extensions of time) of such income tax return is on or before September 1, 1967, the agreement may be filed on or before December 31, 1967. For purposes of the two preceding sentences, the district director may, if good cause is shown, permit the agreement to be filed on a later date.

(c) *Examples.*—This section may be illustrated by the following examples in each of which it is assumed that X Corporation, an electing small business corporation which makes its returns on the basis of the calendar year, acquired and placed in service on June 1, 1962, three items of section 38 property. The basis and estimated useful life of each item of section 38 property are as follows:

Asset number	Basis	Estimated useful life
1	$30,000	4 years
2	30,000	6 years
3	30,000	8 years

On December 31, 1962, X Corporation had 20 shares of stock outstanding which were owned equally by A and B who make their returns on the basis of a calendar year. Under §1.48-5, the total bases of section 38 properties was apportioned to the shareholders of X Corporation as follows:

	Useful life category		
	4 to 6 years	6 to 8 years	8 years or more
Total bases	$30,000	$30,000	$30,000
Shareholder A (10/20)	$15,000	$15,000	$15,000
Shareholder B (10/20)	15,000	15,000	15,000

Reg. §1.47-4(c)

Assuming that during 1962 shareholders A and B did not place in service any section 38 property and that they did not own any interests in other electing small business corporations, partnerships, estates, or trusts, the qualified investment of each shareholder is $30,000, computed as follows:

Basis	Applicable percentage	Qualified investment
$15,000	33 $1/3$	$5,000
15,000	66 $2/3$	10,000
15,000	100	15,000
		$30,000

For the taxable year 1962, each shareholder's credit earned of $2,100 (7 percent of $30,000) was allowed under section 38 as a credit against his liability for tax.

Example (1). (i) On December 2, 1965, X Corporation sells asset No. 3 to Y Corporation.

(ii) The actual useful life of asset No. 3 is three years and six months. The recomputed qualified investment with respect to each shareholder's share of the basis of asset No. 3 is zero ($15,000 share of basis multiplied by zero applicable percentage) and for the taxable year 1962 each shareholder's recomputed credit earned is $1,050 (7 percent of $15,000). The income tax imposed by chapter 1 of the Code on each of the shareholders for the taxable year 1965 is increased by the $1,050 decrease in his credit earned for the taxable year 1962 (that is, $2,100 original credit earned minus $1,050 recomputed credit earned).

Example (2). (i) On December 3, 1964, shareholder A sells 5 of his 10 shares of stock in X Corporation to C, and on December 3, 1965, A sells his remaining 5 shares of stock to D. In addition, on January 2, 1966, X Corporation sells asset No. 3 to Y Corporation.

(ii) Under paragraph (a)(2) of this section, on December 3, 1964, 50 percent of the share of the basis of each of the three items of section 38 property ceases to be section 38 property with respect to shareholder A since immediately after the December 3, 1964, sale A's proportionate stock interest in X Corporation is reduced to 50 percent of the proportionate stock interest in X Corporation which he held on December 31, 1962. The actual useful life of the share of the basis of the section 38 properties which cease to be section 38 property with respect to A is two years and six months (that is, the period beginning with June 1, 1962, and ending with December 3, 1964). A's recomputed qualified investment with respect to such properties is $15,000, computed as follows:

Basis	Applicable percentage	Recomputed qualified investment
$7,500	33 $1/3$	$2,500
7,500	66 $2/3$	5,000
7,500	100	7,500
		$15,000

For the taxable year 1962 shareholder A's recomputed credit earned is $1,050 (7 percent of $15,000). The income tax imposed by chapter 1 of the Code on shareholder A for the taxable year 1964 is increased by the $1,050 decrease in his credit earned for the taxable year 1962 (that is, $2,100 original credit earned minus $1,050 recomputed credit earned).

(iii) Under paragraph (a)(2) of this section, on December 3, 1965, the remaining 50 percent of the share of the basis of each of the three items of section 38 property cease to be section 38 property with respect to shareholder A since immediately after the December 3, 1965, sale A's proportionate stock interest in X Corporation is reduced to zero. The actual useful life of the share of the bases of the section 38 properties which ceases to be section 38 property with respect to A is three years and six months (that is, the period beginning with June 1, 1962, and ending with December 3, 1965). A's recomputed qualified investment with respect to such properties is zero. For the taxable year 1962 shareholder A's recomputed credit earned is zero. The income tax imposed by chapter 1 of the Code on shareholder A for the taxable year 1965 is increased by $1,050 (that is, $2,100 ($2,100 original credit earned minus zero recomputed credit earned) reduced by the $1,050 increase in tax for 1964).

(iv) The actual useful life of asset No. 3 which was sold on January 2, 1966, is three years and seven months. The recomputed qualified investment with respect to B's share of the basis of asset No. 3 is zero ($15,000 share of basis multiplied by zero applicable percentage) and for the taxable year 1962, B's recomputed credit earned is $1,050 (7 percent of $15,000). The income tax imposed by chapter 1 of the Code

on shareholder B for the taxable year 1966 is increased by the $1,050 decrease in his credit earned for the taxable year 1962 ($2,100 original credit earned minus $1,050 recomputed credit earned). The sale of asset No. 3 on January 2, 1966, by X Corporation has no effect on A.

(d) *Termination or revocation of an election under section 1372.*—Section 38 property shall not be considered to be disposed of or to have ceased to be section 38 property solely by reason of a termination or revocation of a corporation's election under section 1372. [Reg. §1.47-4.]

☐ [*T.D.* 6931, 10-9-67.]

[Reg. §1.47-5]

§1.47-5. **Estates and trusts.**—(a) *In general.*—(1) *Disposition or cessation in hands of estate or trust.*—If an estate or trust disposes of any section 38 property (or if any section 38 property otherwise ceases to be section 38 property in the hands of the estate or trust) before the close of the estimated useful life which was taken into account in computing qualified investment with respect to such property, a recapture determination shall be made with respect to the estate or trust, and each beneficiary who is treated, under §1.48-6, as a taxpayer with respect to such property. Each such recapture determination shall be made with respect to the share of the basis (or cost) of such property taken into account by such estate or trust and such beneficiary in computing its or his qualified investment. For purposes of each such recapture determination the actual useful life of such property shall be the period beginning with the date on which it was placed in service by the estate or trust and ending with the date of the disposition or cessation. In making a recapture determination under this subparagraph with respect to a taxpayer there shall be taken into account any prior recapture determinations made with respect to such taxpayer in connection with the same property. For definition of "recapture determination" see paragraph (a)(1) of §1.47-1.

(2) *Disposition of interest.*—(i) If—

(*a*) The basis (or cost) of section 38 property is apportioned, under §1.48-6, to an estate or trust which, or to a beneficiary of an estate or trust who, takes such basis (or cost) into account in computing his qualified investment, and

(*b*) After the date on which such section 38 property was placed in service by the estate or trust and before the close of the estimated useful life of the property, such estate's, trust's, or such beneficiary's proportionate interest in the income of the estate or trust is reduced (for example, by a sale, or by the terms of the estate or trust instrument) below the percentage specified in subdivision (ii) of this subparagraph,

then, on the date of such reduction, such section 38 property ceases to be section 38 property with respect to such estate, trust, or beneficiary to the extent of the actual reduction in such estate's, trust's, or beneficiary's proportionate interest in the income of the estate or trust. (For example, if $100 of the basis of section 38 property was apportioned to a beneficiary and if his proportionate interest in the income of the estate or trust is reduced from 60 percent to 30 percent (that is, 50 percent of his original interest), then such property shall be treated as having ceased to be section 38 property to the extent of $50.) Accordingly, a recapture determination shall be made with respect to such estate, trust, or beneficiary. For purposes of such recapture determination the actual useful life of such property shall be the period beginning with the date on which it was placed in service by the estate or trust and ending with the date on which it is treated as having ceased to be section 38 property with respect to the estate, trust, or beneficiary. In making a recapture determination under this subparagraph there shall be taken into account any prior recapture determination made with respect to the estate, trust, or beneficiary in connection with the same property.

(ii) The percentage referred to in subdivision (i) (*b*) of this subparagraph is 66$2/3$ percent of the estate's, trust's, or beneficiary's proportionate interest in the income of the estate or trust for the taxable year of the apportionment under §1.48-6. However, once property has been treated under this subparagraph as having ceased to be section 38 property to any extent the percentage referred to shall be 33$1/3$ percent of the estate's, trust's, or beneficiary's proportionate interest in the income of the estate or trust for the taxable year of the apportionment under §1.48-6.

(iii) In determining a beneficiary's proportionate interest in the income of an estate or trust for purposes of this subparagraph, the beneficiary shall be considered to own any interest in such an estate or trust which he owns directly or indirectly (through ownership in other entities provided such other entities' bases in such interest are determined in whole or in part by reference to the basis of such interest in the hands of the beneficiary). For example, if A, whose proportionate interest in the income of trust X is 30 percent, transfers all of such interest to corporation Y in exchange for all of the stock of Y in a transaction to which section 351 applies, then, for purposes of subdivision (i) of this subparagraph, A shall be considered to own a 30-percent interest in trust X. Any taxpayer who seeks to establish his interest in an estate or trust under the rule of this subdivision shall maintain adequate records to demonstrate his indirect interest in the estate or trust after any such transfer or transfers.

(b) *Examples.*—Paragraph (a) of this section may be illustrated by the following examples in each of which it is assumed that XYZ

Total bases	
XYZ Trust	($10,000)
	($20,000)
Beneficiary A	($10,000)
	($20,000)

Assuming that during 1962 beneficiary A did not place in service any section 38 property and that he did not own any interests in other estates, trusts, electing small business corporations, or partnerships,

Basis
$15,000 . . . .
15,000 . . . .
15,000 . . . .

For the taxable year 1962, XYZ Trust and beneficiary A each had a credit earned of $2,100 (7 percent of $30,000). Each such credit earned was allowed under section 38 as a credit against the liability for tax.

Example (1). (i) On December 2, 1965, XYZ Trust sells asset No. 3 to X Corporation.

(ii) The actual useful life of asset No. 3 is three years and six months. The recomputed qualified investment with respect to XYZ Trust's and beneficiary A's share of the basis of asset No. 3 is zero ($15,000 share of basis multiplied by zero applicable percentage) and for the taxable year 1962, XYZ Trust's and beneficiary A's recomputed credit earned is $1,050 (7 percent of $15,000). The income tax imposed by chapter 1 of the Code on XYZ Trust and on beneficiary A for the taxable year 1965 is increased by the $1,050 decrease in his credit earned for the taxable year 1962 (that is, $2,100 original credit earned minus $1,050 recomputed credit earned).

Basis
$7,500 . . . .
7,500 . . . .
7,500 . . . .

For the taxable year 1962 beneficiary A's recomputed credit earned is $1,050 (7 percent of $15,000). The income tax imposed by chapter 1 of the Code on beneficiary A for the taxable year 1964 is increased by the $1,050 decrease in his credit earned for the taxable year 1962 (that is, $2,100 original credit earned minus $1,050 recomputed credit earned).

(iii) Under paragraph (a)(2) of this section, on December 3, 1965, the remaining 50 percent of the share of the basis of each of the three items of section 38 property ceases to be section 38 property with respect to beneficiary A since immediately after the December 3, 1965, sale A's proportionate interest in the income of XYZ Trust is reduced to zero. The actual useful life of the share of the basis of the section 38 properties which cease to be section 38 property with respect to A is three years and six months (that is, the period beginning with June 1, 1962, and ending with December 3, 1965). A's recomputed qualified investment with respect to such properties is zero. For the taxable year 1962 beneficiary A's recomputed credit earned is zero. The income tax imposed by chapter 1 of the Code on beneficiary A for the taxable year 1965 is increased by $1,050 (that is, $2,100 ($2,100 original credit earned minus zero recomputed credit earned) reduced by the $1,050 increase in tax for 1964).

(iv) The actual useful life of asset No. 3 which was sold on January 2, 1966, is three years and seven months. The recomputed qualified investment with respect to XYZ Trust's share of the basis of asset No.

Trust, which makes its returns on the basis of the calendar year, acquired and placed in service on June 1, 1962, three items of section 38 property. The basis and estimated useful life of each item of section 38 property are as follows:

Asset Number	Basis	Estimated useful life
1	$30,000	4 years
2	30,000	6 years
3	30,000	8 years

For the taxable year 1962 the income of XYZ Trust is $20,000, which is allocable equally to XYZ Trust and beneficiary A. Beneficiary A makes his returns on the basis of a calendar year. Under §1.48-6, the total bases of the section 38 properties was apportioned to XYZ Trust and beneficiary A as follows:

	Useful life category	
4 to 6 years	*6 to 8 years*	*8 years or more*
$30,000	$30,000	$30,000
15,000	15,000	15,000
15,000	15,000	15,000

the qualified investment of XYZ Trust and of beneficiary A is $30,000 each, computed as follows:

Applicable percentage	*Qualified investment*
33 1/3	$5,000
66 2/3	10,000
100	15,000
	$30,000

Example (2). (i) On December 3, 1964, beneficiary A sells 50 percent of his interest in the income of XYZ Trust to B, and on December 3, 1965, A sells his remaining 50 percent interest to C. In addition, on January 2, 1966, XYZ Trust sells asset No. 3 to Y Corporation.

(ii) Under paragraph (a)(2) of this section, on December 3, 1964, 50 percent of the basis of each of the three items of section 38 property ceases to be section 38 property with respect to beneficiary A since immediately after the December 3, 1964, sale A's proportionate interest in the income of XYZ Trust is reduced to 50 percent of his proportionate interest in the income of XYZ Trust for the taxable year 1962. The actual useful life of the share of the bases of the section 38 properties which cease to be section 38 property with respect to A is two years and six months (that is, the period beginning with June 1, 1962, and ending with December 3, 1964). Beneficiary A's recomputed qualified investment with respect to such properties is $15,000, computed as follows:

Applicable percentage	*Qualified investment*
33 1/3	$2,500
66 2/3	5,000
100	7,500
	$15,000

3 is zero ($15,000 share of basis multiplied by zero applicable percentage) and for the taxable year 1962, XYZ Trust's recomputed credit earned is $1,050 (7 percent of $15,000). The income tax imposed by chapter 1 of the Code on XYZ Trust for the taxable year 1966 is increased by the $1,050 decrease in its credit earned for the taxable year 1962 ($2,100 original credit earned minus $1,050 recomputed credit earned). The sale of asset No. 3 on January 2, 1966, has no effect on A. [Reg. §1.47-5.]

☐ [T.D. 6931, 10-9-67.]

[Reg. §1.47-6]

§1.47-6. Partnerships.—(a) *In general.*—(1) *Disposition or cessation in hands of partnership.*—If a partnership disposes of any partnership section 38 property (or if any partnership section 38 property otherwise ceases to be section 38 property in the hands of the partnership) before the close of the estimated useful life which was taken into account in computing qualified investment with respect to such property, a recapture determination shall be made with respect to each partner who is treated, under paragraph (f) of §1.46-3, as a taxpayer with respect to such property. Each such recapture determination shall be made with respect to the share of the basis (or cost) of such property taken into account by such partner in computing his qualified investment. For purposes of each such recapture determination the actual useful life of such property shall be the period beginning with the date on which it was placed in service by the partnership and ending with the date of the disposition or cessation. In making a recapture determination under this subparagraph there shall be taken into account any prior recapture determinations made with respect to the partner in connection with the same property. For definition of "recapture determination" see paragraph (a)(1) of § 1.47-1.

(2) *Disposition of partner's interest.*—(i) If—

(a) The basis (or cost) of partnership section 38 property is taken into account by a partner in computing his qualified investment, and

(b) After the date on which such partnership section 38 property was placed in service by the partnership and before the close of the estimated useful life of the property, such partner's proportionate interest in the general profits of the partnership (or in the particular item of property) is reduced (for example, by a sale, by a change in the partnership agreement, or by the admission of a new partner) below the percentage specified in subdivision (ii) of this subparagraph,

then, on the date of such reduction such partnership section 38 property ceases to be section 38 property with respect to such partner to the extent of the actual reduction in such partner's proportionate interest in the general profits of the partnership (or in the particular item of property). (For example, if $100 of the basis of section 38 property was taken into account by a partner and if his proportionate interest in the general profits of the partnership is reduced from 60 percent to 30 percent (that is, 50 percent of his original interest), then such property shall be treated as having ceased to be section 38 property to the extent of $50.) Accordingly, a recapture determination shall be made with respect to such partner. For purposes of such recapture determination the actual useful life of such property shall be the period beginning with the date on which it was placed in service by the partnership and ending with the date on which it is treated as having ceased to be section 38 property with respect to the partner. In making a recapture determination under this subpara-

Asset number	
1	
2	
3	

Partners A and B, who make their returns on the basis of a calendar year, share the profits and losses of ABC Partnership equally. Under

Asset No.	Estimated useful life
1	4 years
2	6 years
3	8 years

Assuming that during 1962 partners A and B did not place in service any section 38 property and that they did not own any interests in other partnerships, electing small business corporations, estates, or

Partnership asset No.	Share of basis
1	$15,000
2	15,000
3	15,000

For the taxable year 1962, each partner's credit earned of $2,100 (7 percent of $30,000) was allowed under section 38 as a credit against his liability for tax.

Example (1). (i) On December 2, 1965, ABC Partnership sells asset No. 3 to X Corporation.

(ii) The actual useful life of asset No. 3 is three years and six months. The recomputed qualified investment with respect to each partner's share of the basis of asset No. 3 is zero ($15,000 share of basis multiplied by zero applicable percentage) and for the taxable year 1962, each partner's recomputed credit earned is $1,050 (7 percent of $15,000). The income tax imposed by chapter 1 of the Code on each of the partners for the taxable year 1965 is increased by the $1,050 decrease in his credit earned for the taxable year 1962 (that is, $2,100 original credit earned minus $1,050 recomputed credit earned).

Reg. § 1.47-6(a)(2)(i)

graph there shall be taken into account any prior recapture determination made with respect to the partner in connection with the same property.

(ii) The percentage referred to in subdivision (i)(b) of this subparagraph is $66\frac{2}{3}$ percent of the partner's proportionate interest in the general profits of the partnership (or in the particular item of property) for the year in which such property was placed in service. However, once property has been treated under this subparagraph as having ceased to be section 38 property to any extent the percentage referred to shall be $33\frac{1}{3}$ percent of the partner's proportionate interest in the general profits of the partnership (or in the particular item of property) for the year in which such property was placed in service.

(iii) In determining a partner's proportionate interest in the general profits of a partnership for purposes of this subparagraph, the partner shall be considered to own any interest in such a partnership which he owns directly or indirectly (through ownership in other entities provided the other entities' bases in such interest are determined in whole or in part by reference to the basis of such interest in the hands of the partner). For example, if A, whose proportionate interest in the general profits of partnership X is 20 percent, transfers all of such interest to corporation Y in exchange for all of the stock of Y in a transaction to which section 351 applies, then, for purposes of subdivision (i) of this subparagraph, A shall be considered to own a 20-percent interest in partnership X. Any taxpayer who seeks to establish his interest in a partnership under the rule of this subdivision shall maintain adequate records to demonstrate his indirect interest in the partnership after any such transfer or transfers.

(b) *Examples.*—Paragraph (a) of this section may be illustrated by the following examples in each of which it is assumed that ABC Partnership, which makes its returns on the basis of the calendar year, acquired and placed in service on June 1, 1962, three items of section 38 property. The basis and estimated useful life of each item of section 38 property are as follows:

Basis	Estimated useful life
$30,000	4 years
30,000	6 years
30,000	8 years

paragraph (f)(2) of § 1.46-3, each partner's share of the basis of the partnership section 38 property is as follows:

		Partner's share of basis	
Basis		A 50%	B 50%
$30,000		$15,000	$15,000
30,000		15,000	15,000
30,000		15,000	15,000

trusts, the qualified investment of each partner is $30,000, computed as follows:

Applicable percentage	Qualified investment
$33\frac{1}{3}$	$5,000
$66\frac{2}{3}$	10,000
100	15,000
	$30,000

Example (2). (i) On December 3, 1964, partner A sells one-half of his 50 percent interest in ABC Partnership to C, and on December 3, 1965, A sells the remaining one-half of his interest to D. In addition, on January 2, 1966, ABC Partnership sells asset No. 3 to X Corporation.

(ii) Under paragraph (a)(2) of this section, on December 3, 1964, 50 percent of the basis of each of the three items of section 38 property ceases to be section 38 property with respect to partner A since immediately after the December 3, 1964, sale A's proportionate interest in the general profits of ABC Partnership is reduced to 50 percent of his proportionate interest in the general profits of ABC Partnership for 1962. The actual useful life of the share of the basis of each of the section 38 properties which cease to be section 38 property with respect to A is two years and six months (that is, the period beginning with June 1, 1962, and ending with December 3, 1964). Partner A's recomputed qualified investment with respect to such properties is $15,000, computed as follows:

Partnership asset No.	Share of basis	Applicable percentage	Qualified investment
1	$7,500	33 $^1/_3$	$2,500
2	7,500	66 $^2/_3$	5,000
3	7,500	100	7,500
			$15,000

For the taxable year 1962 partner A's recomputed credit earned is $1,050 (7 percent of $15,000). The income tax imposed by chapter 1 of the Code on partner A for the taxable year 1964 is increased by the $1,050 decrease in his credit earned for the taxable year 1962 (that is, $2,100 original credit earned minus $1,050 recomputed credit earned).

(iii) Under paragraph (a)(2) of this section, on December 3, 1965, the remaining 50 percent of the share of the basis of each of the three items of section 38 property ceases to be section 38 property with respect to partner A since immediately after the December 3, 1965, sale A's proportionate interest in the general profits of ABC Partnership is reduced to zero. The actual useful life of the share of the bases of the section 38 properties which cease to be section 38 property with respect to A is three years and six months (that is, the period beginning with June 1, 1962, and ending with December 3, 1965). A's recomputed qualified investment with respect to such properties is zero. For the taxable year 1962 partner A's recomputed credit earned is zero. The income tax imposed by chapter 1 of the Code on partner A for the taxable year 1965 is increased by $1,050 (that is, $2,520 ($2,520 original credit earned minus zero recomputed credit earned) reduced by the $1,050 increase in tax for 1964).

(iv) The actual useful life of asset No. 3 which was sold on January 2, 1966, is three years and seven months. The recomputed qualified investment with respect to partner B's share of the basis of asset No. 3 is zero ($15,000 share of basis multiplied by zero applicable percentage) and for the taxable year 1962, partner B's recomputed credit earned is $1,050 (7 percent of $15,000). The income tax imposed by chapter 1 of the Code on partner B for the taxable year 1966 is increased by the $1,050 decrease in his credit earned for the taxable year 1962 ($2,100 original credit earned minus $1,050 recomputed credit earned). The sale of asset No. 3 on January 2, 1966, has no effect on A. [Reg. § 1.47-6.]

☐ [T.D. 6931, 10-9-67.]

[Reg. § 1.47-7]

§ 1.47-7. Rehabilitation credit allocated over a 5-year period.— (a) *In general.*—For purposes of section 46, for any taxable year during the 5-year period beginning in the taxable year in which a qualified rehabilitated building, as defined in section 47(c)(1) and § 1.48-12(b), is placed in service, the rehabilitation credit for the taxable year is an amount equal to the ratable share for the taxable year, provided the requirements of section 47 are satisfied. Except as provided by section 13402(c)(2) of Public Law 115-97, 131 Stat. 2054 (2017), this section applies with respect to qualified rehabilitation expenditures, as defined in section 47(c)(2) and § 1.48-12(c), paid or incurred after December 31, 2017.

(b) *Ratable share.*—For purposes of paragraph (a) of this section, the term *ratable share* means, for any taxable year during the 5-year period described in such paragraph, the amount equal to 20 percent of the rehabilitation credit determined with respect to the qualified rehabilitated building, allocated ratably to each year during such period.

(c) *Rehabilitation credit determined.*—The term *rehabilitation credit determined* means the amount equal to 20 percent of the qualified rehabilitation expenditures, as defined in section 47(c)(2) and § 1.48-12(c), taken into account under section 47(b)(1) for the taxable year in which the qualified rehabilitated building is placed in service. However, if the taxpayer claims the additional first year depreciation for the qualified rehabilitation expenditures pursuant to § 1.168(k)-2(g)(9), the term *rehabilitation credit determined* means the amount equal to 20 percent of the remaining rehabilitated basis, as defined in § 1.168(k)-2(g)(9)(i)(B), of the qualified rehabilitated building for the taxable year in which such building is placed in service.

(d) *Coordination with section 50.*—For purposes of section 50 and § 1.50-1, the amount of the rehabilitation credit determined is the amount defined in paragraph (c) of this section.

(e) *Examples.*—The provisions of paragraphs (a) through (d) of this section are illustrated by the following examples. Assume that the additional first year depreciation deduction provided by section 168(k) is not allowed or allowable for the qualified rehabilitation expenditures.

(1) *Example 1: Rehabilitation Credit Determined and Ratable Share.*— Between February 1, 2021 and October 1, 2021, X, a calendar year C corporation, incurred qualified rehabilitation expenditures of $200,000 with respect to a qualified rehabilitated building. X placed the building in service on October 15, 2021. X's rehabilitation credit determined in 2021 under paragraph (c) of this section is $40,000 ($200,000 x 0.20). For purposes of section 46, for each taxable year during the 5-year period beginning in 2021, the ratable share allocated under paragraph (b) of this section for the year is $8,000 ($40,000 x 0.20).

(2) *Example 2: Coordination with section 50(c).*—The facts are the same as in paragraph (e)(1) of this section (Example 1). For purposes of determining the amount of X's basis adjustment in 2021 under section 50(c), the amount of the rehabilitation credit determined under paragraph (c) of this section is $40,000.

(3) *Example 3: Coordination with section 50(a).*—The facts are the same as in paragraph (e)(1) of this section (Example 1). In 2021 and 2022, X claimed the full amount of the ratable share allowed under section 46, or $8,000 per taxable year. X's total allowable ratable share for 2023 through 2025 is $24,000 ($8,000 allowable per taxable year). On November 1, 2023, X disposes of the qualified rehabilitated building. Under section 50(a)(1)(3)(iii), because the period of time between when the qualified rehabilitated building was placed in service is more than two, but less than 3 full years, the applicable recapture percentage is 60%. Based on these facts, X has an increase in tax of $9,600 under section 50(a) ($16,000 of credit claimed in 2021 and 2022 x 0.60) and has $3,200 of credits remaining in each of 2023 through 2025, after forgoing $4,800 in credits in each of the years 2023 through 2025 ($8,000 x 0.60).

(4) *Example 4: Coordination with section 50(d)(5) and § 1.50-1; C corporation lessee.*—X, a calendar year C corporation, leases nonresidential real property from Y. The property is a qualified rehabilitated building that is placed in service on October 15, 2021. Under paragraph (c) of this section, the amount of the rehabilitation credit determined is $100,000. Y elects under § 1.48-4 to treat X as having acquired the property. The shortest recovery period that could be available to the property under section 168 is 39 years. Because Y has elected to treat X as having acquired the property, Y does not reduce its basis in the property under section 50(c). Instead, pursuant to section 50(d)(5) and § 1.50-1, X, the lessee of the property, must include ratably in gross income over 39 years an amount equal to the rehabilitation credit determined with respect to such property.

(5) *Example 5: Coordination with section 50(d)(5) and § 1.50-1; partnership lessee.*—A and B, calendar year taxpayers, form a partnership, the AB partnership, that leases nonresidential real property from Y. The property is a qualified rehabilitated building that is placed in service on October 15, 2021. Under paragraph (c) of this section, the amount of the rehabilitation credit determined is $200,000. Y elects under § 1.48-4 to treat the AB partnership as having acquired the property. The shortest recovery period that could be available to the property under section 168 is 39 years. Because Y has elected to treat the AB partnership as having acquired the property, Y does not reduce its basis in the building under section 50(c). Instead, A and B, the ultimate credit claimants, as defined in § 1.50-1(b)(3)(ii), must include the amount of the rehabilitation credit determined under paragraph (c) of this section with respect to A and B ratably in gross income over 39 years, the shortest recovery period available with respect to such property.

(f) *Applicability date.*—This section applies to taxable years beginning on or after September 18, 2020. Taxpayers may choose to apply this section for taxable years beginning before September 18, 2020, provided the taxpayer applies this section in its entirety and in a consistent manner. [Reg. § 1.47-7.]

☐ [T.D. 9915, 9-16-2020.]

[Reg. § 1.48-1]

§ 1.48-1. Definition of section 38 property.—(a) *In general.*—Property which qualifies for the credit allowed by section 38 is known as "section 38 property". Except as otherwise provided in this section, the term "section 38 property" means property (1) with respect to which depreciation (or amortization in lieu of depreciation) is allowable to the taxpayer, (2) which has an estimated useful life of 3 years or more (determined as of the time such property is placed in service), and (3) which is (i) tangible personal property, (ii) other tangible property (not including a building and its structural components) but only if such other property is used as an integral part of manufacturing, production, or extraction, or as an integral part of furnishing transportation, communications, electrical energy, gas, water, or sewage disposal services by a person engaged in a trade or business of furnishing any such service, or is a research or storage facility used in connection with any of the foregoing activities, (iii) an elevator or escalator which satisfies the conditions of section 48(a)(1)(C), or (iv) in the case of a qualified rehabilitated building, that portion of the basis which is attributable to qualified rehabilitation expenditures. The determination of whether property qualifies as section 38 property in the hands of the taxpayer for purposes of the credit allowed by section 38 must be made with respect to the first taxable year in which such property is placed in service by the taxpayer. See paragraph (d) of §1.46-3. For the meaning of "estimated useful life", see paragraph (e) of §1.46-3. In the case of property which is not described in section 50, this paragraph shall be applied by substituting "4 years" for "3 years".

(b) *Depreciation allowable.*—(1) Property (with the exception of property described in section 48 (a)(1)(F) and paragraph (p) of this section) is not section 38 property unless a deduction for depreciation (or amortization in lieu of depreciation) with respect to such property is allowable to the taxpayer for the taxable year. A deduction for depreciation is allowable if the property is of a character subject to the allowance for depreciation under section 167 and the basis (or cost) of the property is recovered through a method of depreciation, including, for example, the unit of production method and the retirement method as well as methods of depreciation which measure the life of the property in terms of years. If property is placed in service (within the meaning of paragraph (d) of §1.46-3) in a trade or business (or in the production of income), but under the taxpayer's depreciation practice the period for depreciation with respect to such property begins in a taxable year subsequent to the taxable year in which such property is placed in service, then a deduction for depreciation shall be treated as allowable with respect to such property in the earlier taxable year (or years). Thus, for example, if a machine is placed in service in a trade or business in 1963, but the period for depreciation with respect to such machine begins in 1964, because the taxpayer uses an averaging convention (see §1.167(a)-10) in computing depreciation, then, for purposes of determining whether the machine qualifies as section 38 property, a deduction for depreciation shall be treated as allowable in 1963.

(2) If, for the taxable year in which property is placed in service, a deduction for depreciation is allowable to the taxpayer only with respect to a part of such property, then only the proportionate part of the property with respect to which such deduction is allowable qualifies as section 38 property for the purpose of determining the amount of credit allowable under section 38. Thus, for example, if property is used 80 percent of the time in a trade or business and is used 20 percent of the time for personal purposes, only 80 percent of the basis (or cost) of such property qualifies as section 38 property. Further, property does not qualify to the extent that a deduction for depreciation thereon is disallowed under section 274 (relating to disallowance of certain entertainment, etc., expenses).

(3) If the cost of property is not recovered through a method of depreciation but through a deduction of the full cost in one taxable year, for purposes of subparagraph (1) of this paragraph a deduction for depreciation with respect to such property is not allowable to the taxpayer. However, if an adjustment with respect to the income tax return for such taxable year requires the cost of such property to be recovered through a method of depreciation, a deduction for depreciation will be considered as allowable to the taxpayer.

(4) If depreciation sustained on property is not an allowable deduction for the taxable year but is added to the basis of property being constructed, reconstructed, or erected by the taxpayer, for purposes of subparagraph (1) of this paragraph a deduction for depreciation shall be treated as allowable for the taxable year with respect to the property on which depreciation is sustained. Thus, if $1,000 of depreciation sustained with respect to property no. 1, which is placed in service in 1964 by taxpayer A, is not allowable to A as a deduction for 1964 but is added to the basis of property being constructed by A (property no. 2), for purposes of subparagraph (1) of this paragraph a deduction for depreciation shall be treated as allowable to A for 1964 with respect to property no. 1. However, the $1,000 amount is not included in the basis of property no. 2 for purposes of determining A's qualified investment with respect to property no. 2. See paragraph (c)(1) of §1.46-3.

(c) *Definition of tangible personal property.*—If property is tangible personal property it may qualify as section 38 property irrespective of whether it is used as an integral part of an activity (or constitutes a research or storage facility used in connection with such activity) specified in paragraph (a) of this section. Local law shall not be

controlling for purposes of determining whether property is or is not "tangible" or "personal". Thus, the fact that under local law property is held to be personal property or tangible property shall not be controlling. Conversely, property may be personal property for purposes of the investment credit even though under local law the property is considered to be a fixture and therefore real property. For purposes of this section, the term "tangible personal property" means any tangible property except land and improvements thereto, such as buildings or other inherently permanent structures (including items which are structural components of such buildings or structures). Thus, buildings, swimming pools, paved parking areas, wharves and docks, bridges, and fences are not tangible personal property. Tangible personal property includes all property (other than structural components) which is contained in or attached to a building. Thus, such property as production machinery, printing presses, transportation and office equipment, refrigerators, grocery counters, testing equipment, display racks and shelves, and neon and other signs, which is contained in or attached to a building constitutes tangible personal property for purposes of the credit allowed by section 38. Further, all property which is in the nature of machinery (other than structural components of a building or other inherently permanent structure) shall be considered tangible personal property even though located outside a building. Thus, for example, a gasoline pump, hydraulic car lift, or automatic vending machine, although annexed to the ground, shall be considered tangible personal property.

(d) *Other tangible property.*—(1) *In general.*—In addition to tangible personal property, any other tangible property (but not including a building and its structural components) used as an integral part of manufacturing, production, or extraction, or as an integral part of furnishing transportation, communications, electrical energy, gas, water, or sewage disposal services by a person engaged in a trade or business of furnishing any such service, or which constitutes a research or storage facility used in connection with any of the foregoing activities, may qualify as section 38 property.

(2) *Manufacturing, production, and extraction.*—For purposes of the credit allowed by section 38, the terms "manufacturing", "production", and "extraction" include the construction, reconstruction, or making of property out of scrap, salvage, or junk material, as well as from new or raw material, by processing, manipulating, refining, or changing the form of an article, or by combining or assembling two or more articles, and include the cultivation of the soil, the raising of livestock, and the mining of minerals. Thus, section 38 property would include, for example, property used as an integral part of the extracting, processing, or refining of metallic and nonmetallic minerals, including oil, gas, rock, marble, or slate; the construction of roads, bridges, or housing; the processing of meat, fish or other foodstuffs; the cultivation of orchards, gardens, or nurseries; the operation of sawmills, the production of lumber, lumber products or other building materials; the fabrication or treatment of textiles, paper, leather goods, or glass; and the rebuilding, as distinguished from the mere repairing, of machinery.

(3) *Transportation and communications businesses.*—Examples of transportation businesses include railroads, airlines, bus companies, shipping or trucking companies, and oil pipeline companies. Examples of communications businesses include telephone or telegraph companies and radio or television broadcasting companies.

(4) *Integral part.*—In order to qualify for the credit, property (other than tangible personal property and research or storage facilities used in connection with any of the activities specified in subparagraph (1) of this paragraph) must be used as an integral part of one or more of the activities specified in subparagraph (1) of this paragraph. Property such as pavements, parking areas, inherently permanent advertising displays or inherently permanent outdoor lighting facilities, or swimming pools, although used in the operation of a business, ordinarily is not used as an integral part of any of such specified activities. Property is used as an integral part of one of the specified activities if it is used directly in the activity and is essential to the completeness of the activity. Thus, for example, in determining whether property is used as an integral part of manufacturing, all properties used by the taxpayer in acquiring or transporting raw materials or supplies to the point where the actual processing commences (such as docks, railroad tracks, and bridges), or in processing raw materials into the taxpayer's final product, would be considered as property used as an integral part of manufacturing. Specific examples of property which normally would be used as an integral part of one of the specified activities are blast furnaces, oil and gas pipelines, railroad tracks and signals, telephone poles, broadcasting towers, oil derricks, and fences used to confine livestock. Property shall be considered used as an integral part of one of the specified activities if so used either by the owner of the property or by the lessee of the property.

(5) *Research or storage facilities.*—(i) If property (other than a building and its structural components) constitutes a research or storage facility and if it is used in connection with an activity specified in subparagraph (1) of this paragraph, such property may qualify as section 38 property even though it is not used as an integral part of such activity. Examples of research facilities include wind tunnels and test stands. Examples of storage facilities include oil and gas storage tanks and grain storage bins. Although a research or storage facility must be used in connection with, for example, a manufacturing process, the taxpayer-owner of such facility need not be engaged in the manufacturing process.

(ii) In the case of property described in section 50, property will constitute a storage facility only if the facility is used principally for the bulk storage of fungible commodities. Bulk storage means the storage of a commodity in a large mass prior to its consumption or utilization. Thus, if a facility is used to store oranges that have been sorted and boxed, it is not used for bulk storage.

(e) *Definition of building and structural components.*—(1) Generally, buildings and structural components thereof do not qualify as section 38 property. See, however, section 48(a)(1)(E) and (g), and § 1.48-11 (relating to investment credit for qualified rehabilitated building). The term "building" generally means any structure or edifice enclosing a space within its walls, and usually covered by a roof, the purpose of which is, for example, to provide shelter or housing, or to provide working, office, parking, display, or sales space. The term includes, for example, structures such as apartment houses, factory and office buildings, warehouses, barns, garages, railway or bus stations, and stores. Such term includes any such structure constructed by, or for, a lessee even if such structure must be removed, or ownership of such structure reverts to the lessor, at the termination of the lease. Such term does not include (i) a structure which is essentially an item of machinery or equipment, or (ii) a structure which houses property used as an integral part of an activity specified in section 48(a)(1)(B)(i) if the use of the structure is so closely related to the use of such property that the structure clearly can be expected to be replaced when the property it initially houses is replaced. Factors which indicate that a structure is closely related to the use of the property it houses include the fact that the structure is specifically designed to provide for the stress and other demands of such property and the fact that the structure could not be economically used for other purposes. Thus, the term "building" does not include such structures as oil and gas storage tanks, grain storage bins, silos, fractionating towers, blast furnaces, basic oxygen furnaces, coke-ovens, brick kilns, and coal tipples.

(2) The term "structural components" includes such parts of a building as walls, partitions, floors, and ceilings, as well as any permanent coverings therefor such as paneling or tiling; windows and doors; all components (whether in, on, or adjacent to the building) of a central air conditioning or heating system, including motors, compressors, pipes and ducts; plumbing and plumbing fixtures, such as sinks and bathtubs; electric wiring and lighting fixtures; chimneys; stairs, escalators, and elevators, including all components thereof; sprinkler systems; fire escapes; and other components relating to the operation or maintenance of a building. However, the term "structural components" does not include machinery the sole justification for the installation of which is the fact that such machinery is required to meet temperature or humidity requirements which are essential for the operation of other machinery or the processing of materials or foodstuffs. Machinery may meet the "sole justification" test provided by the preceding sentence even though it incidentally provides for the comfort of the employees, or serves, to an insubstantial degree, areas where such temperature or humidity requirements are not essential. For example, an air conditioning and humidification system installed in a textile plant in order to maintain the temperature or humidity within a narrow optimum range which is critical in processing particular types of yarn or cloth is not included within the term "structural components". For special rules with respect to an elevator or escalator, the construction, reconstruction, or erection of which is completed by the taxpayer after June 30, 1963, or which is acquired after June 30, 1963, and the original use of which commences with the taxpayer and commences after such date, see section 48(a)(1)(C) and paragraph (m) of this section.

(f) *Intangible property.*—Intangible property, such as patents, copyrights, and subscription lists, does not qualify as section 38 property. The cost of intangible property, in the case of a patent or copyright, includes all costs of purchasing or producing the item patented or copyrighted. Thus, in the case of a motion picture or television film or tape, the cost of the intangible property includes manuscript and screenplay costs, the cost of wardrobe and set design, the salaries of cameramen, actors, directors, etc., and all other costs properly includible in the basis of such film or tape. In the case of a book, the cost of the intangible property includes all costs of producing the original copyrighted manuscript, including the cost of illustration, research,

and clerical and stenographic help. However, if tangible depreciable property is used in the production of such intangible property, see paragraph (b)(4) of this section.

(g) *Property used outside the United States.*—(1) *General rule.*—(i) Except as provided in subparagraph (2) of this paragraph, the term "section 38 property" does not include property which is used predominantly outside the United States (as defined in section 7701(a)(9)) during the taxable year. The determination of whether property is used predominantly outside the United States during the taxable year shall be made by comparing the period of time in such year during which the property is physically located outside the United States with the period of time in such year during which the property is physically located within the United States. If the property is physically located outside the United States during more than 50 percent of the taxable year, such property shall be considered used predominantly outside the United States during that year. If property is placed in service after the first day of the taxable year, the determination of whether such property is physically located outside the United States during more than 50 percent of the taxable year shall be made with respect to the period beginning on the date on which the property is placed in service and ending on the last day of such taxable year.

(ii) Since the determination of whether a credit is allowable to the taxpayer with respect to any property may be made only with respect to the taxable year in which the property is placed in service by the taxpayer, property used predominantly outside the United States during the taxable year in which it is placed in service cannot qualify as section 38 property with respect to such taxpayer, regardless of the fact that the property is permanently returned to the United States in a later year. Furthermore, if property is used predominantly in the United States in the year in which it is placed in service by the taxpayer, and a credit under section 38 is allowed with respect to such property, but such property is thereafter in any one year used predominantly outside the United States, such property ceases to be section 38 property with respect to the taxpayer and is subject to the application of section 47.

(iii) This subparagraph applies whether property is used predominantly outside the United States by the owner of the property, or by the lessee of the property. If property is leased and if the lessor makes a valid election under § 1.48-4 to treat the lessee as having purchased such property for purposes of the credit allowed by section 38, the determination of whether such property is physically located outside the United States during more than 50 percent of the taxable year shall be made with respect to the taxable year of the lessee; however, if the lessor does not make such an election, such determination shall be made with respect to the taxable year of the lessor.

(2) *Exceptions.*—The provisions of subparagraph (1) of this paragraph do not apply to—

(i) Any aircraft which is registered by the Administrator of the Federal Aviation Agency, and which (*a*) is operated, whether on a scheduled or nonscheduled basis, to and from the United States, or (*b*) is placed in service by the taxpayer during a taxable year ending after March 9, 1967, and is operated under contract with the United States: Provided, That use of the aircraft under the contract constitutes its principal use outside the United States during the taxable year. The term "to and from the United States" is not intended to exclude an aircraft which makes flights from one point in a foreign country to another such point, as long as such aircraft returns to the United States with some degree of frequency;

(ii) Rolling stock, of a domestic railroad corporation subject to part I of the Interstate Commerce Act, which is used within and without the United States. For purposes of this subparagraph, the term "rolling stock" means locomotives, freight and passenger train cars, floating equipment, and miscellaneous transportation equipment on wheels, the expenditures for which are chargeable (or, in the case of leased property, would be chargeable) to the equipment investment accounts in the uniform system of accounts for railroad companies prescribed by the Interstate Commerce Commission;

(iii) Any vessel documented under the laws of the United States which is operated in the foreign or domestic commerce of the United States. A vessel is documented under the laws of the United States if it is registered, enrolled, or licensed under the laws of the United States by the Commandant, United States Coast Guard. Vessels operated in the foreign or domestic commerce of the United States include those documented for use in foreign trade, coast-wise trade, or fisheries;

(iv) Any motor vehicle of a United States person (as defined in section 7701(a)(30)) which is operated to and from the United States with some degree of frequency;

(v) Any container of a United States person which is used in the transportation of property to and from the United States;

(vi) Any property (other than a vessel or an aircraft) of a U.S. person which is used for the purpose of exploring for, developing, removing, or transporting resources from the outer Continental Shelf (within the meaning of section 2 of the Outer Continental Shelf Lands Act, as amended and supplemented; 43 U.S.C., sec. 1331). Thus for example, offshore drilling equipment may be section 38 property;

(vii) Any property placed in service after December 31, 1965 which (a) is owned by a domestic corporation (other than a corporation entitled to the benefits of section 931 or 934(b)) or by a United States citizen (other than a citizen entitled to the benefits of section 931, 932, 933, or 934(c)), and (b) is used predominantly in a possession of the United States during the taxable year by such a corporation or such a citizen, or by a corporation created or organized in, or under the law of, a possession of the United States. Thus, property placed in service after December 31, 1965, which is owned by a domestic corporation not entitled to the benefits of section 931 or 934(b), which is leased to a corporation organized under the laws of a U.S. possession, and which is used by such lessee predominantly in a possession of the United States may qualify as section 38 property. However, property which is owned by a corporation not entitled to the benefits of section 931 or 934(b) but which is leased to a domestic corporation entitled to such benefits would not qualify as section 38 property. The determination of whether property is used predominantly in a possession of the United States during the taxable year shall be made under principles similar to those described in subparagraph (1) of this paragraph. For example, if a machine is placed in service in a possession of the United States on July 1, 1966 by a calendar year taxpayer and if it is physically located in such a possession during more than 50 percent of the period beginning on July 1, 1966 and ending on December 31, 1966, then such machine shall be considered used predominantly in a possession of the United States during the taxable year 1966;

(viii) Any communications satellite (as defined in section 103(3) of the Communications Satellite Act of 1962, 47 U.S.C., sec. 702(3)), or any interest therein, of a U.S. person;

(ix) Any cable which is property described in section 50, or any interest therein, of a domestic corporation engaged in furnishing telephone service to which section 46(c)(3)(B)(iii) applies (or of a wholly owned domestic subsidiary of such corporation), if such cable is part of a submarine cable system which constitutes part of a communications link exclusively between the United States and one or more foreign countries; and

(x) Any property described in section 50 (other than a vessel or an aircraft) of a United States person which is used in international or territorial waters for the purpose of exploring for, developing, removing, or transporting resources from ocean waters or deposits under such waters.

(h) *Property used for lodging.*—(1) *In general.*—(i) Except as provided in subparagraph (2) of this paragraph, the term "section 38 property" does not include property which is used predominantly to furnish lodging or is used predominantly in connection with the furnishing of lodging during the taxable year. Property used in the living quarters of a lodging facility, including beds and other furniture, refrigerators, ranges, and other equipment, shall be considered as used predominantly to furnish lodging. The term "lodging facility" includes an apartment house, hotel, motel, dormitory, or any other facility (or part of a facility) where sleeping accommodations are provided and let, except that such term does not include a facility used primarily as a means of transportation (such as an aircraft, vessel, or a railroad car) or used primarily to provide medical or convalescent services, even though sleeping accommodations are provided.

(ii) Property which is used predominantly in the operation of a lodging facility or in serving tenants shall be considered used in connection with the furnishing of lodging, whether furnished by the owner of the lodging facility or another person. Thus, for example, lobby furniture, office equipment, and laundry and swimming pool facilities used in the operation of an apartment house or in serving tenants would be considered used predominantly in connection with the furnishing of lodging. However, property which is used in furnishing, to the management of a lodging facility or its tenants, electrical energy, water, sewage disposal services, gas, telephone service, or other similar services shall not be treated as property used in connection with the furnishing of lodging. Thus, such items as gas and electric meters, telephone poles and lines, telephone station and switchboard equipment, and water and gas mains, furnished by a public utility would not be considered as property used in connection with the furnishing of lodging.

(iii) Notwithstanding any other provision of this paragraph (h), in the case of a qualified rehabilitated building (within the meaning of section 48(g)(1) and §1.48-12(b)), expenditures for property resulting in basis described in section 48(a)(1)(E) shall not be treated as section 38 property to the extent that such property is attributable to a portion of the building that is used for lodging or in connection with lodging. For example, if expenditures are incurred to rehabilitate a five story qualified rehabilitated building, three floors of which are used for apartments and two floors of which are used as commercial office space, the portion of the basis of the building attributable to qualified rehabilitated expenditures attributable to the commercial part of the building shall not be considered to be expenditures for property, or in connection with property, used predominantly for lodging. Allocation of expenditures between the two portions of the building are to be made using the principles contained in §1.48-12(c)(10)(ii).

(2) *Exceptions.*—(i) *Nonlodging commercial facility.*—A nonlodging commercial facility which is available to persons not using the lodging facility on the same basis as it is available to the tenants of the lodging facility shall not be treated as property which is used predominantly to furnish lodging or predominantly in connection with the furnishing of lodging. Examples of nonlodging commercial facilities include restaurants, drug stores, grocery stores, and vending machines located in a lodging facility.

(ii) *Property used by a hotel or motel.*—Property used by a hotel, motel, inn, or other similar establishment, in connection with the trade or business of furnishing lodging shall not be considered as property which is used predominantly to furnish lodging or predominantly in connection with the furnishing of lodging, provided that the predominant portion of the living accommodations in the hotel, motel, etc., is used by transients during the taxable year. For purposes of the preceding sentence, the term "predominant portion" means "more than one-half". Thus, if more than one-half of the living quarters of a hotel, motel, inn, or other similar establishment is used during the taxable year to accommodate tenants on a transient basis, none of the property used by such hotel, motel, etc., in the trade or business of furnishing lodging shall be considered as property which is used predominantly to furnish lodging or predominantly in connection with the furnishing of lodging. Accommodations shall be considered used on a transient basis if the rental period is normally less than 30 days.

(iii) *Coin-operated machines.*—In the case of property which is described in section 50, coin-operated vending machines and coin-operated washing machines and dryers shall not be considered as property which is used predominantly to furnish lodging or predominantly in connection with the furnishing of lodging.

(iv) *Certified historic structures.*—For purposes of this paragraph (h), regardless of the actual use of a certified historic structure, that portion of the basis of such certified historic structure which is attributable to qualified rehabilitation expenditures (as defined in §1.48-12(c)) shall not be considered as property which is either used predominantly to furnish lodging or predominantly in connection with the furnishing of lodging. Accordingly, such portion of the basis may qualify as section 38 property. (For the definition of "certified historic structure," see section 48(g)(3) and §1.48-12(d).)

(i) [Reserved]

(j) *Property used by certain tax-exempt organizations.*—The term "section 38 property" does not include property used by an organization (other than a cooperative described in section 521) which is exempt from the tax imposed by chapter 1 of the Code unless such property is used predominantly in an unrelated trade or business the income of which is subject to tax under section 511. If such property is debt-financed property as defined in section 514(b), the basis or cost of such property for purposes of computing qualified investment under section 46(c) shall include only that percentage of the basis or cost which is the same percentage as is used under section 514(a), for the year the property is placed in service, in computing the amount of gross income to be taken into account during such taxable year with respect to such property. The term "property used by an organization" means (1) property owned by the organization (whether or not leased to another person), and (2) property leased to the organization. Thus, for example, a data processing or copying machine which is leased to an organization exempt from tax would be considered as property used by such organization. Property (unless used predominantly in an unrelated trade or business) leased by another person to an organization exempt from tax or leased by such an organization to another person is not section 38 property to either the lessor or the lessee, and in either case the lessor may not elect under §1.48-4 to treat the lessee of such property as having purchased such property for purposes of the credit allowed by section 38. This paragraph shall not apply to property leased on a casual or short-term basis to an organization exempt from tax.

(k) *Property used by governmental units.*—The term "section 38 property" does not include property used by the United States, any State (including the District of Columbia) or political subdivision thereof, any international organization (as defined in section 7701(a)(18)) other than the International Telecommunications Satellite Consortium or any successor organization, or any agency or instrumentality of the United States, of any State or political subdivision thereof, or of any such international organization. The term "property used by the United States, etc." means (1) property owned by any such governmental unit (whether or not leased to another person), and (2) property leased to any such governmental unit. Thus, for example, a data processing or copying machine which is leased to any such governmental unit would be considered as property used by such governmental unit. Property leased by another person to any such governmental unit or leased by such governmental unit to another person is not section 38 property to either the lessor or the lessee, and in either case the lessor may not elect under §1.48-4 to treat the lessee of such property as having purchased such property for purposes of the credit allowed by section 38. This paragraph shall not apply to property leased on a casual or short-term basis to any such governmental unit.

(l) [Reserved]

(m) *Elevators and escalators.*—(1) *In general.*—Under section 48(a)(1)(C), an elevator or escalator qualifies as section 38 property if—

(i) The construction, reconstruction, or erection of the elevator or escalator is completed by the taxpayer after June 30, 1963, or

(ii) The elevator or escalator is acquired after June 30, 1963, and the original use of such elevator or escalator commences with the taxpayer and commences after such date.

In the case of construction, reconstruction, or erection of an elevator or escalator commenced before January 1, 1962, and completed after June 30, 1963, there shall be taken into account in determining the qualified investment under section 46(c) only that portion of the basis which is properly attributable to construction, reconstruction, or erection after December 31, 1961. Further, if the construction, reconstruction, or erection of such property is commenced after December 31, 1961, and is completed after June 30, 1963, the entire basis of the elevator or escalator shall be taken into account in determining qualified investment under section 46(c). Also, if an elevator or escalator is reconstructed by the taxpayer after June 30, 1963, the basis attributable to such reconstruction may be taken into account in determining the qualified investment under section 46(c), irrespective of the fact that the original construction or erection of such elevator or escalator may have occurred before January 1, 1962. Paragraph (b) of §1.48-2 shall be applied in determining the date of acquisition, original use, and basis attributable to construction, reconstruction, or erection.

(2) *Definition of elevators and escalators.*—For purposes of this section the term "elevator" means a cage or platform and its hoisting machinery for conveying persons or freight to or from different levels and functionally related equipment which is essential to its operation. The term includes, for example, guide rails and cables, motors and controllers, control panels and landing buttons, and elevator gates and doors, which are essential to the operation of the elevator. The term "elevator" does not, however, include a structure which is considered a building for purposes of the investment credit. The term "escalator" means a moving staircase and functionally related equipment which is essential to its operation. For purposes of determining qualified investment under section 46(c) and §1.46-3, the basis of an elevator or escalator does not include the cost of any structural alterations to the building, such as the cost of constructing a shaft or of making alterations to the floor, walls, or ceiling, even though such alterations may be necessary in order to install or modernize the elevator or escalator.

(3) *Examples.*—The provisions of this paragraph may be illustrated by the following examples:

Example (1). If an elevator with a total basis of $100,000 is completed after June 30, 1963, and the portion attributable to construction by the taxpayer after December 31, 1961, is determined by engineering estimates or by cost accounting records to be $30,000, only the $30,000 portion may be taken into account as an investment in new section 38 property in computing qualified investment.

Example (2). If construction of an elevator with a total basis of $90,000 is commenced by the taxpayer after December 31, 1961, and is completed after June 30, 1963, the entire basis of $90,000 may be taken into account as an investment in new section 38 property.

Example (3). The facts are the same as in example (2) except that construction of the elevator was completed before June 30, 1963. The elevator is not considered to be section 38 property.

Example (4). In 1964, a taxpayer reconditions an elevator, which had been constructed and placed in service in 1962 and which had an adjusted basis in 1964 of $75,000. The cost of reconditioning amounts to an additional $50,000. The basis of the elevator which may be taken into account in computing qualified investment in section 38 property is $50,000, irrespective of whether the taxpayer contracts to have it reconditioned or reconditions it himself, and irrespective of whether the materials used in the process are new in use.

(n) *Amortized property.*—Any property with respect to which an election under section 167(k), 169, 184, 187, or 188 applies shall not be treated as section 38 property. In the case of any property to which

section 169 applies, the preceding sentence shall apply only to so much of the adjusted basis of the property as (after the application of section 169(f)) constitutes the amortizable basis for purposes of section 169. This paragraph shall not apply to property with respect to which an election under section 167(k), 184, 187, or 188 applies unless such property is described in section 50.

(o) [Reserved]

(p) *Qualified timber property.*—(1) Qualified timber property (within the meaning of section 194(c)(1)) shall be treated as section 38 property to the extent of the portion of the basis of such property which is the amortizable basis (as defined in §1.194-3(b)) acquired during the taxable year and taken into account under section 194 (after applying the limitation of section 194(b)(1)). Such amortizable basis shall qualify as section 38 property whether or not an election is made under section 194. However, any portion of such amortizable basis which is attributable to property which otherwise qualifies as section 38 property shall not be treated as section 38 property under section 48(a)(1)(F) and this paragraph. For example, amortizable basis attributable to depreciation on equipment would not qualify as section 38 property under this paragraph if such equipment qualifies as section 38 property under sections 48(a)(1)(A) or (B). In determining the portion of amortizable basis which qualifies as section 38 property under this paragraph, the reduction in amortizable basis to account for depreciation sustained with respect to property used in the reforestation process (which otherwise qualifies as section 38 property) shall be applied before the $10,000 limitation on eligible costs under section 194(b)(1). For example, if in a taxable year a taxpayer incurs qualifying reforestation costs resulting in $12,000 of amortizable basis with respect to property for which an election is in effect, and $2,000 of these costs are attributable to depreciation of the taxpayer's equipment, such $12,000 would first be reduced by the $2,000 of depreciation, and the $10,000 limitation under section 194(b)(1) would be applied following such reduction.

(2) If a taxpayer makes an election to amortize reforestation expenditures under section 194, and allocates the $10,000 limitation among more than one property under §1.194-2(b)(2), then such allocation shall apply for purposes of determining the amortizable basis that qualifies as section 38 property under paragraph (p)(1) of this section. If no election is made under section 194, the taxpayer may select the manner in which the $10,000 limitation is to be allocated among the qualified timber properties. [Reg. §1.48-1.]

[*T.D.* 6731, 5-7-64. *Amended by T.D.* 6838, 7-19-65; *T.D.* 6958, 6-20-68; *T.D.* 6971, 9-11-68; *T.D.* 7203, 8-24-72; *T.D.* 7229, 12-20-72; *T.D.* 7927, 12-15-83; *T.D.* 8031, 6-27-85; *T.D.* 8233, 10-7-88 *and T.D.* 8474, 4-26-93 *(corrected 1-10-94).*]

[Reg. §1.48-2]

§1.48-2. New section 38 property.—(a) *In general.*—Section 48 (b) defines "new section 38 property" as section 38 property—

(1) The construction, reconstruction, or erection of which is completed by the taxpayer after December 31, 1961, or

(2) Which is acquired by the taxpayer after December 31, 1961, provided that the original use of such property commences with the taxpayer and commences after such date.

In the case of construction, reconstruction, or erection of such property commenced before January 1, 1962, and completed after December 31, 1961, there shall be taken into account as the basis of new section 38 property in determining qualified investment only that portion of the basis which is properly attributable to construction, reconstruction, or erection after December 31, 1961. See §1.148-1 for the definition of section 38 property.

(b) *Special rules for determining date of acquisition, original use, and basis attributable to construction, reconstruction, or erection.*—For purposes of paragraph (a) of this section, the principles set forth in paragraph (a)(1) and (2) of §1.167 (c)-1 shall be applied. Thus, for example, the following rules are applicable:

(1) Property is considered as constructed, reconstructed, or erected by the taxpayer if the work is done for him in accordance with his specifications.

(2) The portion of the basis of property attributable to construction, reconstruction, or erection after December 31, 1961, consists of all costs of construction, reconstruction, or erection allocable to the period after December 31, 1961, including the cost or other basis of materials entering into such work (but not including, in the case of reconstruction of property, the adjusted basis of the reconstructed property as of the time such reconstruction is commenced).

(3) It is not necessary that materials entering into construction, reconstruction, or erection be acquired after December 31, 1961, or that they be new in use.

(4) If construction or erection by the taxpayer began after December 31, 1961, the entire cost or other basis of such construction or erection may be taken into account as the basis of new section 38 property.

(5) Construction, reconstruction, or erection by the taxpayer begins when physical work is started on such construction, reconstruction, or erection.

(6) Property shall be deemed to be acquired when reduced to physical possession, or control.

(7) The term "original use" means the first use to which the property is put, whether or not such use corresponds to the use of such property by the taxpayer. For example, a reconditioned or rebuilt machine acquired by the taxpayer will not be treated as being put to original use by the taxpayer. The question of whether property is reconditioned or rebuilt property is a question of fact. Property will not be treated as reconditioned or rebuilt merely because it contains some used parts.

If the cost of reconstruction may properly either be capitalized and recovered through depreciation or charged against the depreciation reserve, such cost may be taken into account as the basis of new section 38 property even though it is charged against the depreciation reserve.

(c) *Examples.*—This section may be illustrated by the following examples:

Example (1). If a machine with a total cost of $100,000 is completed after December 31, 1961, and the portion attributable to construction by the taxpayer after December 31, 1961, is determined by engineering estimates or by cost accounting records to be $30,000, the $30,000 amount shall be taken into account by the taxpayer in computing qualified investment in new section 38 property.

Example (2). In 1965, a taxpayer reconditions a machine, which he constructed and placed in service in 1962 and which has an adjusted basis in 1965 of $10,000. The cost of reconditioning amounts to an additional $20,000. The basis of the machine which shall be taken into account in computing qualified investment in new section 38 property for 1965 is $20,000, whether he contracts to have it reconditioned or reconditions it himself, and irrespective of whether the materials used for reconditioning are new in use.

Example (3). In 1961, a taxpayer pays the entire purchase price of $10,000 for section 38 property to be delivered in 1962. In 1962 he takes possession of the property and commences the original use of the asset in that year. The $10,000 amount shall be taken into account in computing qualified investment in new section 38 property for 1962.

Example (4). A taxpayer, instead of reconditioning his old machine, buys a "factory reconditioned" or "rebuilt" machine in 1962 to replace it. The reconditioned or rebuilt machine is not new section 38 property since such taxpayer is not the first user of the machine. See, however, § 1.48-3 (relating to used section 38 property).

Example (5). In 1962, a taxpayer buys from X for $20,000 an item of section 38 property which has been previously used by X. The taxpayer in 1962 makes an expenditure on the property of $5,000 of the type that must be capitalized. Regardless of whether the $5,000 is added to the basis of such property or is capitalized in a separate account, such amount shall be taken into account by the taxpayer in computing qualified investment in new section 38 property for 1962. No part of the $20,000 purchase price may be taken into account for such purpose. See, however, § 1.48-3 (relating to used section 38 property).

(d) *Special rule for qualified rehabilitated buildings.*—Notwithstanding the rules in paragraphs (a) through (c) of this section, that portion of the basis of a qualified rehabilitated building attributable to qualified rehabilitation expenditures is treated as new section 38 property. See section 48(a)(1)(E) and (g), and § 1.48-11. [Reg. § 1.48-2.]

☐ [*T.D. 6731, 5-7-64. Amended by T.D. 8031, 6-27-85.*]

[Reg. § 1.48-3]

§ 1.48-3. Used section 38 property.—(a) *In general.*—(1) Section 48(c) provides that "used section 38 property" means section 38 property acquired by purchase after December 31, 1961, which is not "new section 38 property." See §§ 1.48-1 and 1.48-2, respectively, for definitions of section 38 property and new section 38 property. In determining whether property is acquired by purchase, the provisions of paragraph (c)(1) of § 1.179-3 shall apply, except that (i) "1961" shall be substituted for "1957", and (ii) the definition of "component member" of a controlled group of corporations in paragraph (d)(4) of this section shall be substituted for the definition of such term in paragraph (e) of § 1.179-3.

(2)(i) Property shall not qualify as used section 38 property if, after its acquisition by the taxpayer, it is used by (a) a person who used such property before such acquisition, or (b) a person who bears a relationship described in section 179 (d) (2) (A) or (B) to a person who used such property before such acquisition. Thus, for example, if property is used by a person and is later sold by him under a sale and leaseback arrangement, such property in the hands of the purchaser-lessor is not used section 38 property because the property, after its acquisition, is being used by the same person who used it before its acquisition. Similarly, where a lessee has been leasing

property and subsequently purchases it (whether or not the lease contains an option to purchase), such property is not used section 38 property with respect to the purchaser because the property is being used by the same person who used it before its acquisition. In addition, if property owned by a lessor is sold subject to the lease, or is sold upon the termination of the lease, the property will not qualify as used section 38 property with respect to the purchaser if, after the purchase, the property is used by a person who used the property as a lessee before the purchase.

(ii) For purposes of applying subdivision (i) of this subparagraph, property shall not be considered as used by a person before its acquisition if such property was used only on a casual basis by such person.

(iii) In determining whether a person bears a relationship described in section 179(d)(2)(A) or (B) to a person who used property before its acquisition by the taxpayer, the provisions of paragraph (c)(1)(i) and (ii) of § 1.179-3 shall apply, except that the definition of "component member" of a controlled group of corporations in paragraph (d)(4) of this section shall be substituted for the definition of such term in paragraph (e) of § 1.179-3.

(3) The provisions of this paragraph may be illustrated by the following examples:

Example (1). Corporation P acquires properties 1 and 2 in 1960 and uses them in its trade or business until 1962. In 1962, corporation P sells such properties to corporation Y, which leases back property 1 to corporation P and leases property 2 to corporation S, a wholly-owned subsidiary of corporation P. Property 1 is not used section 38 property in the hands of corporation Y because, after its acquisition by corporation Y, it is used by a person (corporation P) who used it prior to such acquisition. Property 2 is not used section 38 property because, after its acquisition by corporation Y, it is used by a person (corporation S) who is related, within the meaning of section 179(d)(2)(B), to a person (corporation P) who used it before such acquisition.

Example (2). In 1962, corporation L leases property from corporation M. In 1964, corporation L acquires the property that it previously had been leasing. The property acquired by corporation L is not used section 38 property because such property is used after such acquisition by the same person (corporation L) who used the property before its acquisition (corporation L).

Example (3). Corporation X buys property in 1962 and leases such property to corporation Y. Corporation X in 1965 sells the property to A subject to the lease. The property acquired by A is not used section 38 property if such property continues to be used by corporation Y, because corporation Y used the property before its acquisition by A.

Example (4). A owns a bulldozer which he rents out to a number of different users, including B. In 1962, B used the bulldozer from February 16 to March 12 and again on October 15 and 16. B purchases the bulldozer from A on December 1, 1962. The prior use of the property by B does not disqualify such property as used section 38 property to B, because he used such property only on a casual basis prior to its purchase.

(b) *Cost.*—(1) The cost of used section 38 property is equal to the basis of such property, but does not include so much of such basis as is determined by reference to the adjusted basis of other property (whether or not section 38 property) held at any time by the taxpayer acquiring such used section 38 property.

(2) If property (whether or not section 38 property) is disposed of by the taxpayer (other than by reason of its destruction or damage by fire, storm, shipwreck, or other casualty, or its theft) and used section 38 property similar or related in service or use is acquired as a replacement therefor in a transaction in which the basis of the replacement property is not determined by reference to the adjusted basis of the property replaced, then the cost of the used section 38 property so acquired shall be its basis reduced by the adjusted basis of the property replaced. The preceding sentence shall apply only if the taxpayer acquires (or enters into a contract to acquire) the replacement property within a period of 60 days before or after the date of the disposition.

(3) Notwithstanding subparagraphs (1) and (2) of this paragraph, the cost of used section 38 property shall not be reduced with respect to the adjusted basis of any property disposed of if, by reason of section 47, such disposition resulted in an increase of tax or a reduction of investment credit carrybacks or carryovers described in section 46(b).

(4) The provisions of this paragraph may be illustrated by the following examples:

Example (1). In 1972, A acquires machine 2 (an item of used section 38 property which has a sales price of $5,600) by trading in machine 1 (an item of section 38 property acquired in 1962), and by paying an additional $4,000 cash. The adjusted basis of machine 1 is $1,600. Under the provisions of sections 1012 and 1031(d), the basis of machine 2 is $5,600 ($1,600 adjusted basis of machine 1 plus cash expended of $4,000). The cost of machine 2 which may be taken into account in computing qualified investment for 1972 is $4,000 (basis of $5,600 less $1,600 adjusted basis of machine 1).

Example (2). The facts are the same as in example (1) except that machine 2 has a sales price of $6,000. The trade-in allowance on machine 1 is $2,000. The result is the same as in example (1), that is, the basis of machine 2 is $5,600 ($1,600 plus $4,000); therefore, the cost of machine 2 which may be taken into account in computing qualified investment for 1972 is $4,000 (basis of $5,600 less $1,600 adjusted basis of machine 1).

Example (3). On September 18, 1962, B sells truck 1, which he acquired in 1961 and which has an adjusted basis in his hands of $1,200. On October 15, 1962, he purchases for $2,000 truck 2 (an item of used section 38 property) as a replacement therefor. The cost of truck 2 which may be taken into account in computing qualified investment is $800 ($2,000 less $1,200).

Example (4). In 1962, C acquires property 1, an item of new section 38 property with a basis of $12,000 and a useful life of eight years or more. He is allowed a credit under section 38 of $840 (7 percent of $12,000) with respect to such property. In 1968, C acquires property 2 (an item of used section 38 property) by trading in property 1 and by paying an additional amount in cash. Section 47(a) applies to the disposition of property 1 and C's tax liability for 1968 is increased by $280. Since the application of section 47(a) results in an increase in tax, for purposes of computing qualified investment the cost of property 2 is not reduced by any part of the adjusted basis of the property traded in.

(c) *Dollar limitation.*—(1) *In general.*—Section 48(c)(2) provides that the aggregate cost of used section 38 property which may be taken into account for any taxable year in computing qualified investment under section 46(c)(1)(B) shall not exceed $50,000. If the total cost of used section 38 property exceeds $50,000, there must be selected, in the manner provided in subparagraph (4) of this paragraph, the particular items of used section 38 property the cost of which is to be taken into account in computing qualified investment. The cost of used section 38 property that may be taken into account by a person in applying the $50,000 limitation for any taxable year includes not only the cost of used section 38 property placed in service by such person during such taxable year, but also the cost of used section 38 property apportioned to such person. For purposes of this section, the cost of used section 38 property apportioned to any person means the cost of such property apportioned to him by a trust, estate, or electing small business corporation (as defined in section 1371(b)), and his share of the cost of partnership used section 38 property, with respect to the taxable year of such trust, estate, corporation or partnership ending with or within such person's taxable year. Thus, if an individual places in service during his taxable year used section 38 property with a cost of $25,000, if the cost of used section 38 property apportioned to him by an electing small business corporation for such year is $30,000, and if his share for such year of the cost of used section 38 property placed in service by a partnership is $20,000, he may select from the used section 38 property with a total cost of $75,000 the particular used section 38 property the cost of which he wishes to take into account. No part of the excess of $25,000 ($75,000 cost minus $50,000 annual limitation) may be taken into account in any other taxable year. For determining the amount of the cost to be apportioned by an electing small business corporation, see paragraph (a)(2) of §1.48-5; in the case of estates and trusts, see paragraph (a)(2) of §1.48-6. See paragraph (e) of this section for application of $50,000 limitation in the case of affiliated groups.

(2) *Married individuals filing separate returns.*—In the case of a husband or wife who files a separate return, the aggregate cost of used section 38 property which may be taken into account for the taxable year to which such return relates cannot exceed $25,000. The preceding sentence shall not apply, however, unless the taxpayer's spouse places in service (or is apportioned the cost of) used section 38 property for the taxable year of such spouse which ends with or within the taxpayer's taxable year. Thus, if a husband and wife who file separate returns on a calendar year basis both place in service used section 38 property during the taxable year, the maximum cost of used section 38 property which may be taken into account by each is $25,000. However, in such case, if only one spouse places in service (or is apportioned the cost of) used section 38 property during the taxable year, such spouse may take into account a maximum of $50,000 for such year. The determination of whether an individual is married shall be made under the principles of section 143 and the regulations thereunder.

(3) *Partnerships.*—In the case of a partnership, the aggregate cost of used section 38 property placed in service by the partnership (or apportioned to the partnership) which may be taken into account by the partners with respect to any taxable year of the partnership may not exceed $50,000. If such aggregate cost exceeds $50,000, the partnership must make a selection in the manner provided in subpara-

graph (4) of this paragraph. The $50,000 limitation applies to each partner, as well as to the partnership.

(4) *Selection of $50,000 cost.*—(i) If the sum of (a) the cost of used section 38 property placed in service during the taxable year by any person, (b) such person's share of the cost of partnership used section 38 property placed in service during the taxable year of a partnership ending with or within such person's taxable year, and (c) the cost of used section 38 property apportioned to such person for such taxable year by an electing small business corporation, estate, or trust, exceeds $50,000, such person must make a selection for such taxable year in the manner provided in subdivision (ii) of this subparagraph.

(ii) For purposes of computing qualified investment (or, in the case of a partnership, electing small business corporation, estate, or trust, for purposes of selecting used section 38 property the cost of which may be taken into account by the partners, shareholders, or estate or trust and its beneficiaries) any person to whom subdivision (i) of this subparagraph applies must select a total cost of $50,000 from (a) the cost of specific used section 38 property placed in service by such person, (b) such person's share of the cost of specific used section 38 property placed in service by a partnership, and (c) the cost of used section 38 property apportioned to such person by an electing small business corporation, estate, or trust. When a particular property is selected, the entire cost (or entire share of cost of a particular property in the case of partnership property) of such property must be taken into account unless, as a result of the selection of such particular property, the $50,000 limitation is exceeded. Likewise, in the case of an apportionment from an electing small business corporation, estate, or trust, when the cost in a particular useful life category is selected, the entire cost in such category must be taken into account unless, as a result of the selection of such cost, the $50,000 limitation is exceeded. Thus, if a person places in service during the taxable year three items of used section 38 property, each with a cost of $20,000, he must select the entire cost of two of the items and only $10,000 of the cost of the third item; he may not select a portion of the cost of each of the three items. The selection by any person shall be made by taking the cost of used section 38 property into account in computing qualified investment (or in selecting the used section 38 property the cost of which may be taken into account by the partners, etc.), and if such property was placed in service by such person, he must maintain records which permit specific identification of any item of used section 38 property selected.

(5) *Examples.*—The provisions of this paragraph may be illustrated by the following examples:

Example (1). H, who operates a sole proprietorship, purchases and places in service in 1963 used section 38 property with a cost of $60,000. His spouse, W, is a shareholder in an electing small business corporation which purchases and places in service during its fiscal year ending June 30, 1963, used section 38 property with a cost of $50,000. Both spouses file separate returns on a calendar year basis. W, as a 60 percent shareholder on the last day of the taxable year of the corporation, is apportioned $30,000 (60 percent of $50,000) of the cost of the used section 38 property placed in service by the corporation. The cost of used section 38 property that may be taken into account by H on his separate return is $25,000. The cost of used section 38 property that may be taken into account by W on her separate return is $25,000. On the other hand, if the corporation had made no investment in used section 38 property, H could take $50,000 of the $60,000 cost into account.

Example (2). Partners X, Y, and Z share the profits and losses of partnership XYZ in the ratio of 50 percent, 30 percent, and 20 percent, respectively. The partnership and each partner make returns on the basis of the calendar year. Each partner also operates a sole proprietorship. In 1963, the partnership and the partners purchase and place in service the following used section 38 property:

Property	Estimated useful life	Cost
Partnership XYZ		
Property No. 1	9 years	$10,000
Property No. 2	7 years	50,000
Property No. 3	7 years	50,000
Property No. 4	5 years	30,000
Partner X		
Property No. 5	6 years	$30,000
Partner Y		
Property No. 6	10 years	60,000
Partner Z		
Property No. 7	4 years	36,000

(i) *Selection by partnership.* In accordance with subparagraph (4)(ii) of this paragraph, the partnership selects property no. 1 and $40,000 of the cost of property no. 2 to be taken into account. Therefore, each partner's share of cost of the property selected by the partnership is as follows:

Property	Estimated useful life	Selected cost	X (50%)	Partner's share of cost Y (30%)	Z (20%)
No. 1	9 years	$10,000	$5,000	$3,000	$2,000
No. 2	7 years	40,000	20,000	12,000	8,000
Total		$50,000	$25,000	$15,000	$10,000

(ii) *Selection by partners.* In accordance with subparagraph (4)(ii) of this paragraph, the partners make the following selections: Partner X selects property No. 5 ($30,000), his share of the cost of property No. 1 ($5,000), and $15,000 of his share of the cost of property No. 2. Partner Y selects $50,000 of the cost of property No. 6, and no part of his share of the cost of partnership property. Partner Z, having an aggregate cost of used section 38 property of only $46,000 (partnership property of $10,000 and individually owned property of $36,000), takes into account the entire $46,000.

(iii) *Qualified investment of partner X.* X's total qualified investment in used section 38 property for 1963 is $35,000, computed as follows:

Property	Estimated useful life	Selected cost	Applicable percentage	Qualified investment
No. 1	9 years	$5,000	100	$5,000
No. 2	7 years	15,000	66 2/3	10,000
No. 5	6 years	30,000	66 2/3	20,000
Total		$50,000		$35,000

(iv) *Qualified investment of partner Y.* Y's total qualified investment in used section 38 property for 1963 is $50,000 (100 percent of $50,000) since he selected $50,000 of the cost of property No. 6 which has a useful life of 8 years or more.

(v) *Qualified investment of partner Z.* Z's total qualified investment in used section 38 property for 1963 is $19,333, computed as follows:

Property	Estimated useful life	Selected cost	Applicable percentage	Qualified investment
No. 1	9 years	$2,000	100	$2,000
No. 2	7 years	8,000	66 2/3	5,333
No. 7	4 years	36,000	33 1/3	12,000
Total		$46,000		$19,333

(d) *Dollar limitation for component members of a controlled group.*— (1) *In general.*—(i) Section 48(c)(2)(C) provides that the $50,000 limitation on the cost of used section 38 property which may be taken into account for any taxable year shall, in the case of component members of a controlled group (as defined in subparagraph (4) of this paragraph) on a particular December 31, be reduced for each such member by apportioning the $50,000 amount among such component members for their taxable years that include such December 31 in accordance with their respective amounts of used section 38 property which may be taken into account, that is, in accordance with the total cost of used section 38 property placed in service by each such member during its taxable year (without regard to the $50,000 limitation or the applicable percentages to be applied in computing qualified investment).

(ii) Except as otherwise provided in this paragraph, the $50,000 amount shall be apportioned among those corporations which are component members of the controlled group on a December 31. For the taxable year of each such member which includes such December 31, the cost of used section 38 property taken into account in computing qualified investment under section 46(c)(1)(B) shall not exceed the amount which bears the same ratio to $50,000 as the cost of used section 38 property placed in service by such member for such taxable year bears to the total cost of used section 38 property placed in service by all component members of the controlled group for their taxable years which include such December 31.

(iii) If a component member of the group makes its income tax return on the basis of a 52-53 week taxable year, the principles of section 441(f)(2)(A)(ii) and § 1.441-2 apply in determining the last day of such a taxable year.

(2) *Statement by the "filing member".*—For purposes of this paragraph, the term "filing member" with respect to a particular December 31 means the member (or members) of a controlled group which has, among those members of the group which are apportioned part of the $50,000 amount for their taxable years which include such December 31, the taxable year including such December 31 which ends on the earliest date. The filing member of the group shall attach to its income tax return a statement containing the name, address, and employer identification number of each component member of *the controlled group on such December 31 and a schedule* showing the computation of the apportionment of the $50,000 amount among the component members of the group. Each such other member shall retain as part of its records a copy of the statement containing the apportionment schedule. Except as otherwise provided in subpara-

graph (3)(ii) of this paragraph, each member which is apportioned part of the $50,000 amount shall take such apportioned amount into account in filing its return for its taxable year which includes such December 31.

(3) *Estimate of used section 38 property to be placed in service.*— (i) For purposes of subparagraphs (1) and (2) of this paragraph, if on the date (including extensions of time) for filing the income tax return of the filing member of the group with respect to a particular December 31, the total cost of used section 38 property actually placed in service by a component member of the group during such member's taxable year that includes such December 31 is not known, then such member shall estimate such cost. The estimate shall be made on the basis of the facts and circumstances known as of the time of the estimate. Any such estimate shall also be used in determining the total cost of used section 38 property placed in service by all component members for their taxable years including such December 31.

(ii) If an estimate is used by any component member of a controlled group pursuant to subdivision (i) of this subparagraph, each member may later file an original or amended return in which the apportionment of the $50,000 amount is based upon the cost of used section 38 property actually placed in service by all component members of the group during their taxable years which include such December 31. Such amended apportionment shall be made only if each component member of the group whose limitation would be changed files an original or amended return which reflects the amended apportionment based upon the cost of the used section 38 property actually placed in service by component members of the group. In such case, the new statement reflecting the amended apportionment shall be attached to the amended return of the filing member of the group, and a copy of such statement shall be retained by each such member pursuant to the requirements of subparagraph (2) of this paragraph.

(4) *Definitions of controlled group of corporations and component member of controlled group.*—For purposes of this section, the terms "controlled group of corporations" and "component member" of a controlled group of corporations shall have the same meaning assigned to those terms in section 1563(a) and (b), except that the phrase "more than 50 percent" shall be substituted for the phrase "at least 80 percent" each place it appears in section 1563(a)(1). For purposes of applying § 1.1563-1(b)(2)(ii)(c), an electing small business corporation shall be treated as an excluded member whether or not it is subject to the tax imposed by section 1378.

(5) *Members of controlled group filing a consolidated return.*—For the purpose of apportioning the $50,000 amount in the case of component members of a controlled group which join in filing a consolidated return, all such members shall be treated as though they were a single component member of the controlled group. Thus, in determining the limitation on the cost of used section 38 property which may be taken into account by the group filing the consolidated return, the apportionment provided in subparagraph (1)(ii) of this paragraph shall be made by using the aggregate cost of such property placed in service by all members of the group filing the consolidated return. If all component members of the controlled group join in filing a consolidated return, the group may select the items to be taken into account to the extent of an aggregate cost of $50,000; if some component members of the controlled group do not join in filing the consolidated return, then the members of the group which join in filing the consolidated return may select the items to be taken into account to the extent of the amount apportioned to such members under subparagraph (1)(ii) of this paragraph.

(6) *Examples.*—This paragraph may be illustrated by the following examples:

Example (1). (i) On December 31, 1970, corporations M, N, and O are component members of the same controlled group. The taxable years of M, N, and O end, respectively, on January 31, March 31, and April 30. During the respective taxable years of each corporation which include December 31, 1970, M places in service no used section 38 property, and N and O place in service used section 38 property with respective costs of $100,000 and $150,000. N is the "filing member" of the group since N, among the members (N and O) which are apportioned part of the $50,000 amount for their taxable years which include such December 31, has the taxable year ending on the earliest date.

(ii) The cost of used section 38 property taken into account by N for its taxable year ending March 31, 1971, may not exceed $20,000, that is, an amount which bears the same ratio to $50,000 as the cost of used section 38 property placed in service by N for its taxable year ($100,000) bears to the total cost of used section 38 property placed in service by all component members of the controlled group (M, N, and O) for their taxable years which include December 31, 1970 ($250,000). Similarly, the cost of used section 38 property taken into account by O for its taxable year ending April 30, 1971, may not exceed $30,000.

Example (2). (i) On December 31, 1971, corporations S and T are component members of the same controlled group. The taxable year of corporations S and T end, respectively, on January 31 and June 30. On April 15, 1972, S files an income tax return for its taxable year ending January 31, 1972, during which year it places in service used section 38 property costing $100,000. T estimates that it will place in service used section 38 property costing $150,000 during its taxable year ending June 30, 1972.

(ii) S, the "filing member" of the group, must file an apportionment schedule under which it may take into account as the cost of used section 38 property an amount not in excess of $20,000 ($100,000/$250,000 × $50,000). If T actually places in service during its taxable year used section 38 property costing more or less than $150,000, its income tax return for it taxable year ending June 30, 1972, may reflect the amended apportionment of the $50,000 limitation based upon the cost of used section 38 property actually placed in service by the group, provided that S attaches a new apportionment schedule to an amended return to reflect the amended apportionment. For example, if T places in service used section 38 property costing $200,000, the cost of used section 38 property taken into account by S and T for their respective taxable years could not exceed $16,667 ($100,000/$300,000 × $50,000) and $33,333 ($200,000/$300,000 × $50,000), respectively, under an amended apportionment. [Reg. §1.48-3.]

☐ [*T.D. 6731, 5-7-64. Amended by T.D. 7181, 4-24-72; T.D. 7820, 6-9-82 and T.D. 8996, 5-16-2002.*]

[Reg. §1.48-4]

§1.48-4. Election of lessor of new section 38 property to treat lessee as purchaser.—(a) *In general.*—(1) *Lessee treated as purchaser.*—Under section 48(d), a lessor of property may elect to treat the lessee of such property as having purchased such property (or, in the case of short-term lease property described in subparagraph (2) of this paragraph, a portion of such property) for purposes of the credit allowed by section 38 if the following conditions are satisfied:

(i) The property must be "section 38 property" in the hands of the lessor; that is, it must be property with respect to which depreciation (or amortization in lieu of depreciation) is allowable to the lessor, it must have a useful life of 3 years (4 years in the case of property which is not described in section 50) or more in his hands, and in every other respect it must meet the requirements of §1.48-1. Thus, for example, property leased by a municipality to a taxpayer for use in what is commonly known as an "industrial park" is not eligible for the election since, under paragraph (k) of §1.48-1, property used by a governmental unit is not section 38 property. In addition, property used by the lessee predominantly outside the United States is not eligible for the election since, under paragraph (g) of §1.48-1, such property is not section 38 property. For purposes of this subdivision, if the lessor is an estate or trust, depreciation (or amortization in lieu of depreciation) will be considered allowable to the estate or trust even if it is apportioned to the beneficiaries or other persons.

(ii) The property must be "new section 38 property" (within the meaning of §1.48-2) in the hands of the lessor, and the original use of such property must commence with the lessor. See paragraph (b) of this section for the application of the rules relating to "original use" in the case of leased property.

(iii) *The property would constitute "new section 38 property"* to the lessee if such lessee had actually purchased the property. Thus, the election is not available if the lessee is not the original user of the property. See paragraph (b) of this section for the application of the rules relating to "original use" in the case of leased property. See paragraph (d) of this section for the determination of the estimated useful life of leased property in the hands of the lessee.

(iv) A statement of election to treat the lessee as a purchaser has been filed in the manner and within the time provided in paragraph (f) or (g) of this section.

(v) The lessor is not a person referred to in section 46(d)(1), that is, a mutual savings bank, cooperative bank, or domestic building and loan association to which section 593 applies; a regulated investment company or real estate investment trust subject to taxation under subchapter M, chapter 1 of the Code; or a cooperative organization described in section 1381(a).

The election may be made on a property-by-property basis or a general election may be made with respect to each taxable year of a particular lessee. If the conditions of this subparagraph have been met, the lessee shall be treated as though he were the actual owner of all or a portion of the property for purposes of the credit allowed by section 38. Thus, the lessee shall be entitled to a credit allowed by section 38 with respect to such property for the taxable year in which he places such property in service, and the lessor shall not be entitled to a credit allowed by section 38 with respect to such property unless the property is short-term lease property (as defined in subparagraph (2) of this paragraph). Moreover, if the leased property is disposed of, or if it otherwise ceases to be section 38 property, the property will be subject to the provisions of section 47 (relating to early dispositions, etc.).

(2) *Short-term lease property.*—For purposes of this section, the term "short-term lease property" means property which—

(i) Is new section 38 property;

(ii) Has a class life (determined under section 167(m)) in excess of 14 years;

(iii) Is leased under a lease entered into after November 8, 1971, for a period which is less than 80 percent of the class life of such property; and

(iv) Is not leased subject to a net lease within the meaning of section 57(c)(1)(B) and the regulations thereunder.

The class life of property shall be determined under section 167(m) and the regulations prescribed in connection with that section, except that such class life shall be determined without regard to any variance from the class life permitted under such section. If a class life has not been prescribed for property under section 167(m) on the date such property is leased, the class life of the property shall be the estimated useful life used to compute the allowance for depreciation with respect to such property under section 167. For purposes of subdivision (iii) of this subparagraph, the period for which a lease is entered into shall be determined without regard to any option on the part of the lessee to extend or renew such lease, and without regard to any option on the part of the lessee to cancel the lease after a specified period if under the terms of such lease, such a cancellation would result in the imposition of a substantial penalty upon the lessee. Generally, a penalty equal to 25 percent of the total remaining rental payments due under the lease will be regarded as substantial.

(b) *Original use.*—For purposes of this section only, the lessor and the lessee may both be considered as the original users of an item of leased property. The determination of whether the lessor qualifies as the original user of leased property shall be made under paragraph (b)(7) of §1.48-2. The determination of whether the lessee qualifies as the original user of leased property shall be made, under paragraph (b)(7) of §1.48-2, as if the lessee actually purchased the property. Thus, the lessee would not be considered the original user of the property if it has been previously used by the lessor or another person, or if it is reconstructed, rebuilt, or reconditioned property. However, the lessee would be considered the original user if he is the first person to use the property for its intended function. Thus, the fact that the lessor may have, for example, tested, stored, or attempted to lease the property to other persons will not preclude the lessee from being considered the original user.

(c) *Qualified investment.*—(1) *In general.*—If a valid election is made under this section, the amount of qualified investment under section 46(c) with respect to the leased property shall be determined under this paragraph and paragraphs (d) and (e) of this section.

(2) *Nonshort-term lease property.*—In the case of property which is not short-term lease property, the lessee is treated as having acquired the entire property for an amount equal to—

(i) The fair market value of such property on the date possession is transferred to the lessee, or

(ii) If the property is leased by a component member of a controlled group to another component member of the same controlled group (within the meaning of paragraph (f)(4) of §1.46-1) on the date possession of the property is transferred to the lessee, the basis of the property in the hands of the lessor.

(3) *Short-term lease property.*—(i) In the case of short-term lease property, the lessee is treated as having acquired a portion of such property. The amount for which the lessee is treated as having acquired such portion is an amount equal to a fraction, the numerator of which is the term of the lease and the denominator of which is the class life of the property leased, of the amount for which the lessee would be treated as having acquired the property under subparagraph (2) of this paragraph if the property were not short-term lease property.

(ii) In the case of short-term lease property, the qualified investment of the lessor is an amount equal to his qualified investment in such property determined under section 46(c) multiplied by a fraction, the numerator of which is the class life of the property leased minus the term of the lease and the denominator of which is the class life of such property.

(4) *Example.*—The provisions of this paragraph may be illustrated by the following example:

Example. (a) On December 1, 1971, X corporation completed construction of an item of new section 38 property with a basis of $10,000. Under section 167(m), the property has a class life of 16 years. On December 1, 1971, X leases the property to individual A for 4 years and A immediately places the property in service. The lease is not a net lease within the meaning of section 57(c)(1)(B). On the date of the lease, the fair market value of the property is $12,000. The property would qualify as new section 38 property in A's hands if it had been purchased by A. Under this section, the property is short-terrm lease property. X makes the election under this section to treat A as having acquired a portion of the property.

(b) A is treated as having acquired from X a portion of the property for $3,000 (the fair market value of the property, $12,000, multiplied by a fraction, 4/16, the numerator of which is the term of the lease and the denominator of which is the class life of the leased property). Since under paragraph (d) of this section the useful life of such property in the hands of A is the same as the useful life of such property in the hands of X, and such useful life is at least 7 years, A's qualified investment with respect to the property is $3,000.

(c) The qualified investment of X is $7,500 (the qualified investment of X under section 46(c), $10,000, multiplied by a fraction, 12/16, the numerator of which is the class life of the leased property, 16 minus the term of the lease, 4, and the denominator of which is the class life of the property).

(d) *Estimated useful life of leased property.*—The estimated useful life to the lessee of property subject to the election shall be deemed to be the estimated useful life in the hands of the lessor for purposes of computing depreciation, regardless of the term of the lease. The lessor shall determine the estimated useful life of each leased property on an individual basis even though multiple asset accounts are used. However, in the case of assets similar in kind contained in a multiple asset account, the lessor shall assign to each of such assets the average useful life of such assets used in computing depreciation. Thus, for example, if during a taxable year a lessor leases 10 similar trucks with an average estimated useful life for depreciation purposes of 6 years, based on an estimated range of 5 to 7 years, he must assign a useful life of 6 years to each of the 10 trucks.

(e) *Lessor itself a lessee.*—(1) *In general.*—If the lessee of property is treated, under this section, as having purchased all or a portion of such property and if such lessee leases such property to a sublessee, the qualified investment with respect to such property in the hands of the sublessee shall be determined under paragraphs (c) and (d) of this section as if the original lessor had leased the property directly to the sublessee for the term of the sublessee's lease on the date possession of the property is transferred to the sublessee. For this purpose, property which is short-term lease property in the hands of the lessee shall be treated as short-term lease property in the hands of the sublessee regardless of whether such property is leased to the sublessee subject to a net lease (within the meaning of section 57(c)(1)(B)). In the case of property which is short-term lease property in the hands of the sublessee, the amount for which the lessee is treated as having acquired such property under paragraph (c) of this section shall be reduced by an amount equal to such amount multiplied by a fraction, the numerator of which is the term of the lease of the sublessee and the denominator of which is the term of the lease of the lessee.

(2) *Example.*—The provisions of this paragraph may be illustrated by the following example:

Example. (a) On December 1, 1971, corporation X completes construction of a machine at a cost of $10,000. The machine has a class life under section 167(m) of 20 years. On December 1, 1971, X

leases the machine to corporation Y for 12 years, and Y immediately subleases the machine to individual a for 8 years. X and Y are component members of the same controlled group. The lease between X and Y is not a net lease within the meaning of section 57(c)(1)(B). The fair market value of the property on December 1, 1971, is $16,000. Both X and Y make valid elections under this section.

(b) The property is short-term lease property and this paragraph applies.

(c) The qualified investment of A is $6,400. Such amount is determined by multiplying $16,000, the amount for which A would be treated under paragraph (c)(2) of this section as havng acquired the property if it were not short-term lease property, by 8/20.

(d) The qualified investment of Y is $2,000. Such amount is determined by multiplying $10,000, the amount for which Y would be treated under paragraph (c)(2) of this section as having acquired the property if it were not short-term lease property, by 12/20, and by reducing the amount so determined ($6,000) by 8/12 of such amount ($4,000) to $2,000.

(e) The qualified investment of X is $4,000. Such amount is determined by multiplying the amount of X's qualified investment determined under section 46(c) without regard to this section ($10,000) by 8/20.

(f) *Property-by-property election.*—(1) *Manner of making election.*—The election of a lessor with respect to a particular property (or properties) shall be made by filing a statement with the lessee, signed by the lessor and including the written consent of the lessee, containing the following information:

(i) The name, address, and taxpayer account number of the lessor and the lessee;

(ii) The district director's office with which the income tax returns of the lessor and the lessee are filed;

(iii) A description of each property with respect to which the election is being made;

(iv) The date on which possession of the property (or properties) is transferred to the lessee;

(v) The estimated useful life category of the property (or properties) in the hands of the lessor, that is, 3 years or more but less than 5 years, 5 years or more but less than 7 years, or 7 years or more;

(vi) The amount for which the lessee (or sublessee) is treated as having acquired the leased property under paragraph (c)(2) or (3) of this section; and

(vii) If the lessor is itself a lessee, the name, address, and taxpayer account number of the original lessor, and the district director's office with which the income tax return of such original lessor is filed.

(2) *Time for making election.*—The statement referred to in subparagraph (1) of this paragraph shall be filed with the lessee on or before the due date (including any extensions of time) of the lessee's return for the lessee's taxable year during which possession of the property is transferred to the lessee, except that if such taxable year ends after March 31, 1971, and before December 11, 1971, the statement shall be filed with the lessee on or before the due date (including any extensions of time) of the lessee's return for such taxable year, or on or before October 24, 1972, whichever is later.

(3) *Election is irrevocable.*—An election under this paragraph shall be irrevocable as of the time the statement referred to in subparagraph (1) of this paragraph is filed with the lessee.

(g) *General election.*—(1) *In general.*—In lieu of making elections on a property-by-property basis in the manner and time prescribed in paragraph (f) of this section, a lessor may, with respect to a particular taxable year of a particular lessee, make a general election to treat such lessee as having purchased all properties possession of which is transferred under lease by the lessor to the lessee during such taxable year of the lessee.

(2) *Manner and time for making general election.*—The general election of a lessor with respect to a taxable year of a lessee shall be made by filing a statement with the lessee, signed by the lessor and including the written consent of the lessee, on or before the due date (including any extensions of time) of the lessee's return for such taxable year, except that if such taxable year ends after March 31, 1971, and before December 11, 1971, the statement shall be filed with the lessee on or before the due date (including any extensions of time) of the lessee's return for such taxable year, or on or before October 24, 1972, whichever is later. Such statement of general election shall contain:

(i) The name, address, and taxpayer account number of the lessor and the lessee;

(ii) The taxable year of the lessee with respect to which such general election is made;

(iii) The district director's office with which the income tax returns of the lessor and the lessee are filed;

(iv) If the lessor is itself a lessee, the name, address, and taxpayer account number of the original lessor, and the district director's office with which the income tax return of such original lessor is filed.

(3) *Election is irrevocable.*—A general election under this paragraph shall be irrevocable as of the time the statement referred to in subparagraph (2) of this paragraph is filed with the lessee and shall be binding on the lessor and the lessee for the entire taxable year of the lessee with respect to which such general election is made.

(4) *Information requirement.*—If a lessor, with respect to a taxable year of the lessee, makes a general election under this paragraph, such lessor shall provide such lessee, on or before the date required for filing the statement under subparagraph (2) of this paragraph, with a statement (or statements) containing the information required by paragraph (f)(1)(iii), (iv), (v), and (vi) of this section with respect to all properties possession of which is transferred under lease by the lessor to the lessee during such taxable year.

(h) *Signature.*—The statement referred to in paragraph (f)(1) of (g)(2) of this section shall not be valid unless signed by both the lessor and the lessee. The signature of the lessee shall constitute the consent of the lessee to the election. The statement shall be signed by the taxpayer or a duly authorized agent of the taxpayer. For purposes of this section, a facsimile signature may be used in lieu of a signature manually executed and, if used, shall be as binding as a signature manually executed.

(i) [Reserved]

(j) *Record requirements.*—The lessor and the lessee shall keep as a part of their records the statement referred to in paragraph (f)(1), or the statements referred to in paragraphs (g)(2) and (g)(4), of this section. The lessor shall attach to his income tax return a summary statement of all property leased during his taxable year with respect to which an election is made. In the case of a taxable year ending after March 31, 1971, and before December 11, 1971, a summary statement may be filed on or before the due date (including any extensions of time) of the return or on or before October 24, 1972, whichever is later, with the Internal Revenue Service Center with which the return has been filed. Such summary statement shall contain the following information: (1) The name, address, and taxpayer account number of the lessor; and (2) in numerical account number order, each lessee's account number, name, and address, the estimated useful life category of the property (or, if applicable, the estimated useful life expressed in years), and the basis or fair market value of the property, whichever is applicable.

(k) *Adjustment of rental deductions.*—(1) *In general.*—The rules of this paragraph apply only to section 38 property placed in service before January 1, 1964, and with respect to any such property only for taxable years of a lessee beginning before January 1, 1964. If a lessor makes a valid election under this section with respect to property placed in service by the lessee before January 1, 1964, section 48(g) and §1.48-7 (relating to adjustments to basis of property) shall not apply to the lessor with respect to such property. Thus, the lessor is not required to reduce under section 48(g)(1) the basis of such property. However, if such an election is made, the deductions otherwise allowable under section 162 to the lessee for amounts paid or accrued to the lessor under the lease shall be adjusted in the manner provided in this paragraph. For special adjustments for taxable years beginning after December 31, 1963, see paragraph (m) of this section.

(2) *Decrease in rental deduction.*—(i) The deductions otherwise allowable under section 162 to the lessee for amounts paid or accrued to the lessor under the lease with respect to leased property placed in service before January 1, 1964, shall be decreased under subdivision (ii) or (iii) of this subparagraph, whichever is applicable, by an amount determined by reference to the credit earned on the leased property. The "credit earned" on the leased property is determined by multiplying the qualified investment (as defined in section 46(c)) with respect to such property by 7 percent. Thus, the credit earned (and the decrease in deductions) is determined without regard to the limitation based on tax which, under section 46(a)(2), may limit the amount of the credit the lessee may take into account in any one year.

(ii) If, in the case of property placed in service before January 1, 1964, the lessor, under paragraph (f)(1)(v) of this section, supplies the lessee with the useful life of such property expressed in years, then for each taxable year beginning before January 1, 1964, any part of which falls within a period beginning with the month in which the leased property is placed in service by the lessee and ending with the close of the estimated useful life of such property (as determined under paragraph (d) of this section), the lessee shall decrease the deduction otherwise allowable under section 162 for each such taxable year with respect to such property. The decrease for each such taxable year shall be equal to (a) the credit earned, divided by (b) the

estimated useful life of the property (expressed in months), multiplied by (c) the number of calendar months in which the leased property was held by the lessee during such taxable year. Thus, if leased property with a basis of $27,000 in the hands of a calendar-year lessee, and with an estimated useful life of 10 years, is placed in service by the lessee on July 15, 1963, the lessee must decrease his section 162 deduction with respect to the leased property for the taxable year 1963 by $94.50 ($1,890 credit earned, divided by 120, multiplied by 6).

(iii) If, in the case of property placed in service before January 1, 1964, the lessor, under paragraph (f)(1)(v) of this section, supplies the lessee with the useful life category of such property, then for each taxable year beginning before January 1, 1964, during a period equal to the shortest life of the useful life category used by the lessee in computing qualified investment under section 46(c) with respect to the leased property, the lessee shall decrease the deduction otherwise allowable under section 162 for such taxable year with respect to such property. The decrease for each such taxable year shall be equal to the credit earned divided by such shortest life, that is, 4, 6, or 8. Such decreases shall begin with the taxable year during which the lessee places the property in service. Thus, if leased property with a basis of $30,000 to the lessee, and an estimated useful life falling within the 4 years or more but less than 6 years useful life category, is placed in service by the lessee within the lessee's taxable year ending December 31, 1962, the lessee must decrease his section 162 deduction with respect to the leased property for each of the taxable years 1962 and 1963 by $175 ($700 credit earned divided by 4).

(iv) To the extent that a required decrease, under subdivision (ii) or (iii) of this subparagraph, is not taken into account for any taxable year beginning before January 1, 1964, because the deduction otherwise allowable under section 162 for such taxable year with respect to the leased property is less than the required decrease for such taxable year, then the balance of the required decrease not taken into account for such taxable year shall decrease the amount otherwise allowable as a deduction under section 162 with respect to such property for the next succeeding taxable year (or years) beginning before January 1, 1964, if any, for which a deduction is allowable with respect to such property. Thus, if the required decrease with respect to leased property is $200 for 1962 but the lessee's deduction otherwise allowable under section 162 for such taxable year with respect to such property is only $50, the balance of $150 must be applied in 1963 to decrease the deduction otherwise allowable to the lessee with respect to the leased property for such taxable year.

(v) See paragraph (b) of §1.48-7 for reduction of basis in the case of an actual purchase of leased property by a lessee (in a taxable year of such lessee beginning before January 1, 1964) who has been treated as a purchaser of such property under this section.

(3) *Increase in rental deductions on account of early dispositions, etc.*—(i) If, as a result of an early disposition, etc., in a taxable year beginning before January 1, 1964, with respect to leased property placed in service before such date, the lessee's tax is increased under section 47(a)(1) or (2), or an adjustment in a carryback or carryover is made under section 47(a)(3) by reduction of an unused credit, the rental deductions (if any) otherwise allowable under section 162 to such lessee for amounts paid or accrued to the lessor under the lease with respect to such property shall be increased in an amount equal to the total decreases previously made in the lessee's rental deductions under subparagraph (2) of this paragraph.

(ii) Except as provided in subdivision (iii) of this subparagraph, the increase in rental deductions described in subdivision (i) of this subparagraph shall be taken into account as an increase in rental deductions otherwise allowable under section 162 for the taxable year in which the early disposition, etc., occurred.

(iii) If, after the event which caused section 47(a)(1), (2), or (3) to apply, the lessee continues the use of the property in a trade or business or in the production of income, the increase in rental deduction described in subdivision (i) of this subparagraph shall be taken into account ratably over the remaining portion of the useful life of the property which was used in making the decreases in rental deductions with respect to the property under subparagraph (2) of this paragraph.

(iv) If subdivision (iii) of this subparagraph applies, and if, prior to the expiration of the useful life of the property used in making the decreases in rental deductions, the lease is terminated other than by actual purchase of the property by the lessee, any increase in rental deductions not previously taken into account shall be taken into account as an increase in rental deductions for the taxable year in which the lease is terminated. In the case of an actual purchase of the property by the lessee, see paragraph (e) of §1.48-7.

(l) *Examples.*—The provisions of this section may be illustrated by the following examples:

Example (1). X Corporation is engaged in the business of manufacturing and leasing new and reconstructed equipment which in its hands has an estimated useful life of 12 years. After December 31, 1961, X Corporation constructs machine no. 1 at a cost of $20,000 and reconstructs machine no. 2 at a cost of $5,000. On February 15, 1962, Y Corporation, a calendar-year taxpayer, leases both machines from X Corporation and places them in service. The fair market value of machine no. 1 on the date on which possession is transferred to Y is $25,200. Machine no. 1 would qualify as new section 38 property in Y's hands if it had been purchased by Y. If X elects to treat Y as the purchaser of machine no. 1, under paragraph (c)(2)(ii) of this section such machine will have a basis of $25,200 in Y's hands. Under paragraph (f)(1)(v) of this section, X supplies Y with an estimated useful life of 12 years (expressed in years rather than useful life category) with respect to machine no. 1 for purposes of determining Y's qualified investment. Y's credit earned with respect to the property is $1,764 (7 percent of $25,200). Under paragraph (k)(2)(ii) of this section, Y's deduction attributable to the leased property for 1962 will be decreased by $134.75 (credit earned of $1,764, divided by 144, multiplied by 11), and for 1963 such deduction will be decreased by $147 ($1,764, divided by 144, multiplied by 12). The election is not available with respect to machine no. 2 since a reconstructed machine would not constitute new section 38 property if Y had purchased it. In such case, while X cannot make the election to treat Y as a purchaser, X would be entitled to a credit under section 38 based on its expenditure of $5,000 as an investment in new section 38 property, since such amount represents cost of reconstruction after December 31, 1961.

Example (2). Assume the same facts as in example (1) except that under paragraph (f)(1)(v) of this section, X supplies Y with an estimated useful life category of 8 years or more (rather than an estimated useful life expressed in years) with respect to machine no. 1 for purposes of determining Y's qualified investment. Under paragraph (k)(2)(iii) of this section, Y's deduction attributable to the leased property will be decreased by $220.50 (credit earned of $1,764, divided by 8) for each of its taxable years of 1962 and 1963.

Example (3). Assume the same facts as in example (1) except that the lessee disposes of his interest in the lease on January 1, 1963, and that there is an increase in Y's tax for 1963 under section 47(a)(1) in the amount of $1,764. Under paragraph (k)(2) of this section, Y's deductions attributable to the leased property are decreased only in 1962, and the amount of such decrease is $134.75. In 1963 there shall be an increase of $134.75 in the deductions otherwise allowable under section 162 for such taxable year with respect to the leased property.

Example (4). Assume the same facts as in example (1) except that during the year 1963 the property was used by Y predominantly outside the United States within the meaning of paragraph (g) of § 1.48-1, and thereafter was used in Y's trade or business. Under paragraph (k)(3) of this section, the increase of $134.75 described in example (3) is taken into account ratably as an increase in rental deductions otherwise allowable under section 162 in the amount of $12.25 ($134.75 divided by 11 years) for 1963 and each of the 10 succeeding years.

(m) *Increase in rental deductions on account of section 203(a)(2)(B) of the Revenue Act of 1964.*—(1) *In general.*—(i) Under section 203(a)(2)(B) of the Revenue Act of 1964, if, for any taxable year of a lessee beginning before January 1, 1964, the rental deductions otherwise allowable under section 162 to such lessee for amounts paid or accrued to the lessor under the lease with respect to leased property placed in service before January 1, 1964, were decreased under paragraph (k)(2) of this section, such rental deductions shall be increased.

(ii) The increase in rental deductions described in subdivision (i) of this subparagraph shall be in an amount equal to the total decreases in the lessee's rental deductions previously made under paragraph (k)(2) of this section less any increases in rental deductions made under paragraph (k)(3) of this section.

(iii) Except as provided in subdivision (iv) of this subparagraph, the increase in rental deductions described in subdivision (i) of this subparagraph shall be taken into account ratably over the remaining portion of the useful life of the property commencing with the first day of the first taxable year beginning after December 31, 1963. For this purpose, the useful life of the property shall be the useful life used in making the decreases in rental deductions with respect to the property under paragraph (k)(2) of this section.

(iv) If the lease is terminated other than by the lessee's actual purchase of the property during a taxable year beginning after December 31, 1963, and before the end of the remaining useful life of the property used in making the decreases in rental deductions, the amount of the increase in rental deductions described in subdivision (i) of this subparagraph and not previously taken into account shall be allowed as a deduction for the taxable year in which such termination occurs.

(v) The rental deductions with respect to any section 38 property are not to be increased under this paragraph if the lessee dies in a taxable year beginning before January 1, 1964.

(vi) The increase in rental deductions described in subdivision (i) of this subparagraph shall ordinarily be taken into account by the lessee treated as the purchaser, that is, the lessee entitled to the credit. However, if the property under the lease is transferred by the lessee to a successor lessee in a transaction described in section 47(b) (other than a transfer by reason of death) under which the successor lessee assumes the lessee's obligations under the lease, such increase in rental deductions shall be taken into account by the successor lessee in the manner prescribed in this paragraph.

(2) *Examples.*—The operation of this paragraph may be illustrated by the following examples:

Example (1). (a) X Corporation acquired on January 1, 1962, an item of new section 38 property with a basis of $24,000 and with a useful life to the lessor of 10 years. Y Corporation, which makes its returns on the basis of a calendar year, leased such property from X Corporation and placed it in service on January 2, 1962. Under this section, X Corporation made a valid election to treat Y Corporation as having purchased such property for purposes of the credit allowed by section 38 and supplied the lessee with information that the property had a useful life of 10 years. The amount of the credit earned with respect to such property was $1,680 (7 percent of $24,000). For each of the taxable years 1962 and 1963, Y Corporation decreased, under paragraph (k)(2) of this section, its deductions otherwise allowable under section 162 with respect to such property by $168 ($1,680 multiplied by 12/120).

(b) For each of the taxable years 1964 through 1971, Y Corporation increases its deductions otherwise allowable under section 162 for amounts paid to X Corporation under the lease by $42 ($336 (that is, $168 multiplied by 2) divided by the remaining useful life of 8 years).

Example (2). (a) The facts are the same as in example (1) except that the lease is terminated on January 3, 1965.

(b) For the taxable year 1964, Y Corporation increases its deductions otherwise allowable under section 162 by $42.

(c) For the taxable year 1965, Y Corporation increases its deductions otherwise allowable under section 162 for the portion of the increase which had not been taken into account as of the time of the termination of the lease. Thus, the amount of such increase for the taxable year 1965 is $294 ($336 minus $42). [Reg. § 1.48-4.]

☐ [*T.D. 6731, 5-7-64. Amended by T.D. 6838, 7-19-65, T.D. 6953, 4-22-68, T.D. 7181, 4-24-72, and T.D. 7203, 8-24-72.*]

[Reg. § 1.48-5]

§ 1.48-5. **Electing small business corporations.**—(a) *In general..*—(1) In the case of an electing small business corporation (as defined in section 1371(b)), the basis of "new section 38 property" and the cost of "used section 38 property" placed in service during the taxable year shall be apportioned pro rata among the persons who are shareholders of such corporation on the last day of such corporation's taxable year. Section 38 property shall not (by reason of such apportionment) lose its character as new section 38 property or used section 38 property, as the case may be. The estimated useful life of such property in the hands of a shareholder shall be deemed to be the estimated useful life of such property in the hands of the electing small business corporation. The bases of all new section 38 properties which have a useful life falling within a particular useful life category shall be aggregated; likewise, the cost of all used section 38 properties which have a useful life falling within a particular useful life category shall be aggregated. The total bases of new section 38 properties within each useful life category and the total cost of used section 38 properties within each useful life category shall be apportioned separately. The useful life categories are: (i) 3 years or more but less than 5 years; (ii) 5 years or more but less than 7 years; and (iii) 7 years or more. There shall be apportioned to each person who is a shareholder of the electing small business corporation on the last day of the taxable year of such corporation, for his taxable year in which or with which the taxable year of such corporation ends, his pro rata share of the total bases of new section 38 properties within each useful life category, and his pro rata share of the total cost of used section 38 properties within each useful life category. In determining who are shareholders of an electing small business corporation on the last day of its taxable year, the rules of paragraph (d)(1) of § 1.1371-1 and of paragraph (a)(2) of § 1.1373-1 shall apply.

(2) The total cost of used section 38 property that may be apportioned by an electing small business corporation to its shareholders for any taxable year of such corporation shall not exceed $50,000. If the total cost of used section 38 property placed in service during the taxable year by the electing small business corporation exceeds $50,000, such corporation must select, under paragraph (c)(4) of § 1.48-3, the used section 38 property the cost of which is to be apportioned to its shareholders.

(3) A shareholder to whom the basis (or cost) of section 38 property is apportioned shall, for purposes of the credit allowed by

section 38, be treated as the taxpayer with respect to such property. Thus, the total cost of used section 38 property apportioned to him by the electing small business corporation must be taken into account as cost of used section 38 property in determining whether the $50,000 limitation on the cost of used section 38 property which may be taken into account by the shareholder in computing qualified investment for any taxable year is exceeded. If a shareholder takes into account in determining his qualified investment any portion of the basis (or cost) of section 38 property placed in service by an electing small business corporation and if such property subsequently is disposed of or otherwise ceases to be section 38 property in the hands of the corporation, such shareholder shall be subject to the provisions of section 47. See § 1.47-4.

(b) *Summary statement.*—An electing small business corporation shall attach to its return a statement showing the apportionment to each shareholder of the total bases of new, and the total cost of used, section 38 properties within each useful life category.

(c) *Example.*—This section may be illustrated by the following example:

Example. (1) X Corporation, an electing small business corporation which makes its return on the basis of the calendar year, acquires and places in service on June 1, 1962, three new assets which qualify as new section 38 property and three used assets which qualify as used section 38 property. The basis of each new, and the cost of each used, section 38 property and the estimated useful life of each property are as follows:

	Basis (or cost)	Estimated useful life
Asset No. 1 (new)	$30,000	4 years
Asset No. 2 (new)	30,000	4 years
Asset No. 3 (new)	30,000	8 years
Asset No. 4 (used)	12,000	6 years
Asset No. 5 (used)	12,000	6 years
Asset No. 6 (used)	12,000	8 years

On December 31, 1962, X Corporation has 10 shares of stock outstanding which are owned as follows: A owns 3 shares, B owns 2 shares, and C owns 5 shares.

(2) Under this section, the total bases of the new, and the total cost of the used, section 38 properties are apportioned to the shareholders of X Corporation as follows:

Useful life category	New— 4 to 6 years	New— 8 years or more	Used— 6 to 8 years	Used—8 years or more
Total bases or total cost	$60,000	$30,000	$24,000	$12,000
Shareholder A (3/10)	$18,000	$9,000	$7,200	$3,600
Shareholder B (2/10)	12,000	6,000	4,800	2,400
Shareholder C (5/10)	30,000	15,000	12,000	6,000

Assume that shareholders A, B, and C did not place in service during their taxable years in which falls December 31, 1962 (the last day of X Corporation's taxable year) any section 38 property and that such shareholders did not own any interests in other electing small business corporations, partnerships, estates, or trusts. Under section 46(c), the qualified investment of shareholder A is $23,400, of shareholder B is $15,600, and of shareholder C is $39,000, computed as follows:

Basis (or cost)	New or used	Applicable percentage	Qualified investment
		Shareholder A	
$18,000	(new)	× 33 1/3 percent	$6,000
9,000	(new)	× 100 percent	9,000
7,200	(used)	× 66 2/3 percent	4,800
3,600	(used)	× 100 percent	3,600
Total			$23,400

Basis (or cost)	New or used	Applicable percentage	Qualified investment
		Shareholder B	
$12,000	(new)	× 33 1/3 percent	$4,000
6,000	(new)	× 100 percent	6,000
4,800	(used)	× 66 2/3 percent	3,200
2,400	(used)	× 100 percent	2,400
Total			$15,600

		Shareholder C	
$30,000	(new)	× 33 1/3 percent	$10,000
15,000	(new)	× 100 percent	15,000
12,000	(used)	× 66 2/3 percent	8,000
6,000	(used)	× 100 percent	6,000
Total			$39,000

[Reg. § 1.48-5.]

☐ [*T.D. 6731, 5-7-64. Amended by T.D. 6931, 10-9-67, and T.D. 7203, 8-24-72.*]

[Reg. § 1.48-6]

§ 1.48-6. Estates and trusts.—(a) *In general.*—(1) In the case of an estate or trust, the basis of "new section 38 property" and the cost of "used section 38 property" placed in service during the taxable year shall be apportioned among the estate or trust and its beneficiaries on the basis of the income of such estate or trust allocable to each. Section 38 property shall not (by reason of such apportionment) lose its character as new section 38 property or used section 38 property, as the case may be. The estimated useful life of such property in the hands of a beneficiary shall be deemed to be the estimated useful life of such property in the hands of the estate or trust. The bases of all new section 38 properties which have a useful life falling within a particular useful life category shall be aggregated; likewise, the cost of all used section 38 properties which have a useful life falling within a particular useful life category shall be aggregated. The total bases of new section 38 properties within each useful life category and the total cost of used section 38 properties within each useful life category shall be apportioned separately. The useful life categories are: (i) 3 years or more but less than 5 years; (ii) 5 years or more but less than 7 years; and (iii) 7 years or more. There shall be apportioned to the estate or trust for its taxable year, and to each beneficiary of such estate or trust for his taxable year in which or with which the taxable year of such estate or trust ends, his share (as determined under paragraph (b) of this section) of the total bases of new section 38 properties within each useful life category, and his share of the total cost of used section 38 properties within each useful life category.

(2) The total cost of used section 38 property that may be apportioned among an estate or trust and its beneficiaries for any taxable year of such estate or trust shall not exceed $50,000. If the total cost of used section 38 property placed in service during the taxable year by the estate or trust exceeds $50,000, such estate or trust must select, under paragraph (c)(4) of § 1.48-3, the used section 38 property the cost of which is to be apportioned among such estate or trust and its beneficiaries.

(3) A beneficiary to whom the basis (or cost) of section 38 property is apportioned shall, for purposes of the credit allowed by section 38, be treated as the taxpayer with respect to such property. Thus, the total cost of used section 38 property apportioned to him by the estate or trust must be taken into account as cost of used section 38 property in determining whether the $50,000 limitation on the cost of used property which may be taken into account by the beneficiary in computing qualified investment for any taxable year is exceeded. If a beneficiary takes into account in determining his qualified investment any portion of the basis (or cost) of section 38 property placed in service by an estate or trust and if such property subsequently is disposed of or otherwise ceases to be section 38 property in the hands of the estate or trust, such beneficiary shall be subject to the provisions of section 47. See § 1.47-5.

(4) For purposes of this section, the term "beneficiary" includes heir, legatee, and devisee.

(5) If during the taxable year of an estate or trust a beneficiary's interest in the income of such estate or trust terminates, the basis (or cost) of section 38 property placed in service by such estate or trust after such termination shall not be apportioned to such beneficiary.

(b) *Share.*—A trust's, estate's, or beneficiary's share of the total bases of new section 38 properties, and the total cost of used section 38 properties, within a useful life category shall be—

(1) The total bases of new (or the total cost of used) section 38 properties which have a useful life falling within such useful life category placed in service in the taxable year of the estate or trust, multiplied by

(2) The amount of income allocable to such estate or trust or to such beneficiary for such taxable year, divided by

(3) The sum of the amounts of income allocable to such estate or trust and all its beneficiaries taken into account under subparagraph (2) of this paragraph.

(c) *Limitation based on amount of tax.*—In the case of an estate or trust, the $25,000 amount specified in section 46(a)(2), relating to limitation based on amount of tax, shall be reduced for the taxable year to—

(1) $25,000, multiplied by

(2) The qualified investment with respect to the total bases of new section 38 properties plus the qualified investment with respect to the total cost of used section 38 properties, apportioned to such estate or trust under paragraph (a) of this section, divided by

(3) The qualified investment with respect to the total bases of all new section 38 properties plus the qualified investment with respect to the total cost of all used section 38 properties, apportioned among such estate or trust and its beneficiaries.

For purposes of subparagraph (3) of this paragraph, cost of used section 38 property shall not be considered as apportioned to any beneficiary to the extent that such cost is not taken into account by such beneficiary in computing qualified investment in used section 38 property.

(d) *Summary statement.*—An estate or trust shall attach to its return a statement showing the apportionment to such estate or trust and to each beneficiary of the total bases of new, and the total cost of used, section 38 properties within each useful life category.

(e) *Example.*—This section may be illustrated by the following example:

Example. (1) XYZ Trust, which makes its return on the basis of the calendar year, acquires and places in service on June 1, 1962, three new assets which qualify as new section 38 property and three used assets which qualify as used section 38 property. The basis of the new, and the cost of the used, section 38 property and the estimated useful life of each property are as follows:

	Basis (or cost)	Estimated useful life
Asset No. 1 (new)	$30,000	4 years
Asset No. 2 (new)	30,000	4 years
Asset No. 3 (new)	30,000	8 years
Asset No. 4 (used)	12,000	6 years
Asset No. 5 (used)	12,000	6 years
Asset No. 6 (used)	12,000	8 years

For the taxable year 1962 the income of XYZ Trust is $20,000 which is allocable as follows: $10,000 to XYZ Trust, $6,000 to beneficiary A, and $4,000 to beneficiary B. Beneficiaries A and B make their returns on the basis of a calendar year.

(2) Under this section, the total bases of the new, and the total cost of the used, section 38 properties are apportioned to XYZ Trust and its beneficiaries as follows:

Useful life category	New— 4 to 6 years	New— 8 years or more	Used— 6 to 8 years	Used— 8 years or more
Total bases or total cost	$60,000	$30,000	$24,000	$12,000
XYZ Trust ($10,000 / 20,000)	$30,000	$15,000	$12,000	$6,000
Beneficiary A ($6,000 / 20,000)	18,000	9,000	7,200	3,600
Beneficiary B ($4,000 / 20,000)	12,000	6,000	4,800	2,400

Assume that beneficiary A placed in service during his taxable year 1962 new section 38 property with a basis of $10,000 and an estimated useful life of 8 years. Also, assume that beneficiary B did not place in service during his taxable year 1962 any section 38 property and that beneficiaries A and B did not own any interests in other trusts, estates, partnerships, or electing small business corporations. Under section 46(c), the qualified investment of XYZ Trust is $39,000, of beneficiary A is $33,400, and of beneficiary B is $15,600, computed as follows:

Basis (or cost)	New or used	XYZ Trust Applicable percentage	Qualified investment
$30,000	(new)	× 33¹/₃ percent	$10,000
15,000	(new)	× 100 percent	15,000
12,000	(used)	× 66²/₃ percent	8,000
6,000	(used)	× 100 percent	6,000
Total			$39,000

Beneficiary A

$18,000	(new)	× 33¹/₃ percent	$6,000
9,000	(new)	× 100 percent	9,000
7,200	(used)	× 66²/₃ percent	4,800
3,600	(used)	× 100 percent	3,600
			$23,400
$10,000	(new)	× 100 percent	$10,000
Total			$33,400

Beneficiary B

$12,000	(new)	× 33¹/₃ percent	$4,000
6,000	(new)	× 100 percent	6,000
4,800	(used)	× 66²/₃ percent	3,200
2,400	(used)	× 100 percent	2,400
Total			$15,600

(3) In the case of XYZ Trust, the $25,000 amount specified in section 46(a)(2) is reduced to $12,500, computed as follows: (i) $25,000, multiplied by (ii) $39,000 (qualified investment apportioned to the trust), divided by (iii) $78,000 (total qualified investment apportioned among such trust ($39,000), beneficiary A ($23,400), and beneficiary B ($15,600)). [Reg. §1.48-6.]

☐ [T.D. 6731, 5-7-64. *Amended by* T.D. 6931, 10-9-67; T.D. 6958, 6-20-68 *and* T.D. 7203, 8-24-72.]

[Reg. §1.48-9]

§1.48-9. Definition of energy property.—(a) *General rule.*—(1) *In general.*—Under section 48(l)(2), energy property means property that is described in at least one of 6 categories of energy property and that meets the other requirements of this section. If property is described in more than one of these categories, or is described more than once in a single category, only a single energy investment credit is allowed. In that case, the energy investment credit will be allowed under the category the taxpayer chooses by indicating the chosen category on Form 3468, Schedule B. The 6 categories of energy property are:

(i) alternative energy property,

(ii) solar or wind energy property,

(iii) specially defined energy property,

(iv) recycling equipment,

(v) shale oil equipment, and

(vi) equipment for producing natural gas from geopressured brine.

(2) *Depreciable property with 3-year useful life.*—Property is not energy property unless depreciation (or amortization in lieu of depreciation) is allowable and the property has an estimated useful life (determined at the time when the property is placed in service) of 3 years or more.

(3) *Effective date rules.*—To be energy property—

(i) If property is constructed, reconstructed or erected by the taxpayer, the construction, reconstruction, or erection must be completed after September 30, 1978, or

(ii) If the property is acquired, the original use of the property must (A) commence with the taxpayer and (B) commence after September 30, 1978, and before January 1, 1983.

For transitional rules, see section 48(m).

(4) *Cross references.*—(i) To determine if depreciation (or amortization in lieu of depreciation) is allowable for property, see § 1.48-1(b).

(ii) For the meaning of "estimated useful life", see § 1.46-3(e)(7).

(iii) The meaning of "acquired", "original use", "construction", "reconstruction", and "erection" is determined under the principles of § 1.48-2(b).

(iv) For the definition of energy investment credit (energy credit), see section 48(o)(2).

(v) For special rules relating to public utility property, see paragraph (n) of this section.

(b) *Relationship to section 38 property.*—(1) *In general.*—(i) Energy property is treated under section 48(l)(1) as meeting the general requirements for section 38 property set forth in section 48(a)(1). For example, structural components of a building may qualify for the energy credit. In addition, the exclusion from section 38 property under section 48(a)(3) (lodging limitation) does not apply to energy property. For purposes of the energy credit, energy property is treated as section 38 property solely by reason of section 48(l)(1). For example, if property ceases to be energy property, it ceases to be section 38 property for all purposes relating to the energy credit and, thus, is subject to recapture under section 47. See § 1.47-1(h).

(ii) See the effective date rules under paragraph (a)(3) of this section for limitations on the eligibility of property as energy property.

(iii) Section 48(l)(1) does not affect the character of property under sections of the Code outside the investment credit provisions. For example, structural components of a building that are treated as section 38 property under section 48(l)(1) remain section 1250 property and are not section 1245 property.

(2) *Other section 48 rules apply.*—(i) In general, section 48(a) otherwise applies in determining if energy property is section 38 property. Thus, energy property excluded from the definition of section 38 property under section 48(a) (except by reason of section 48(a)(1) or (a)(3)) is not eligible for the energy credit. For example, energy property used predominantly outside the United States (section 48(a)(2)) or used by tax exempt organizations (section 48(a)(4)), in general, is not treated as section 38 property for any purpose and thus, is not eligible for the energy credit.

(ii) Other rules of section 48, such as those for leased property under section 48(d), also apply to energy property.

(3) *Regular credit denied for certain energy property.*—In computing the amount of credit under section 46(a)(2), the regular percentage does not apply to any energy property which, but for section 48(l)(1), would not be section 38 property. See section 46(a)(2)(D). For example, energy property used for lodging (section 48(a)(3)) and, in general, structural components of a building (section 48(a)(1)(B)) are not eligible for the regular credit even though they may be eligible for the energy credit. However, a structural component of a qualified rehabilitated building (as defined in section 48(g)(1)) or a single purpose agricultural or horticultural structure (as defined in section 48(p)) may qualify for the regular credit without regard to section 48(l)(1).

(c) *Alternative energy property.*—(1) *In general.*—Alternative energy property means property described in paragraph (c)(3) through (10) of this section. In general alternative energy property includes certain property that uses an alternate substance as a fuel or feedstock or converts an alternate substance to a synthetic fuel and certain associated equipment.

(2) *Alternate substance.*—(i) An alternate substance is any substance or combination of substances other than an oil or gas substance. Alternate substances include coal, wood, and agricultural, industrial, and municipal wastes or byproducts. Alternate substances do not include synthetic fuels or other products that are produced from an alternate substance and that have undergone a chemical change as described in paragraph (c)(5)(ii) of this section. For example, methane produced from landfills is not an alternate substance; rather it is a synthetic fuel produced from an alternate substance. However, preparing an alternate substance for use as a fuel or feedstock or for conversion into a fuel does not create a new product if no chemical change occurs. For example, pelletizing, drying, compacting, and liquefying do not result in a new product if no chemical change occurs.

(ii) The term "oil or gas substance" means—

(A) oil or gas and

(B) any primary product of oil or gas.

(iii) For the definition of primary product of oil or gas, see § 1.993-3(g)(3)(i), (ii), and (vi). Thus, petrochemicals are not primary products of oil or gas.

(3) *Boiler.*—(i) A boiler that uses an alternate substance as its primary fuel is alternative energy property.

(ii) A boiler is a device for producing vapor from a liquid. Boilers, in general, have a burner in which fuel is burned. A boiler includes a fire box, boiler tubes, the containment shell, pumps, pressure and operating controls, and safety equipment, but not pollution control equipment (as defined in paragraph (c)(8) of this section).

(iii) A "primary fuel" is a fuel comprising more than 50 percent of the fuel requirement of an item of equipment, measured in terms of Btu's for the remainder of the taxable year from the date the equipment is placed in service and for each taxable year thereafter. Electricity and waste heat are not fuels. For example, electric boilers do not qualify as alternative energy property even if the electricity is derived from an alternate substance.

(4) *Burners.*—(i) A burner for a combustor other than a burner described in paragraph (c)(3)(ii) of this section is alternative energy property if the burner uses an alternate substance as its primary fuel (as defined in paragraph (c)(3)(iii) of this section).

(ii) A burner is the part of a combustor that produces a flame. A combustor is a process heater which includes ovens, kilns, and furnaces.

(iii) A burner includes equipment (such as conveyors, flame control devices, and safety monitoring devices) located at the site of the burner and necessary to bring the alternate substance to the burner.

(5) *Synthetic fuel production equipment.*—(i) Equipment (synthetic fuel equipment) that converts an alternate substance into a synthetic solid, liquid, or gaseous fuel (other than coke or coke gas) is alternative energy property. Synthetic fuel production equipment does not include equipment, such as an oxygen plant, that is not directly involved in the treatment of an alternate substance, but produces a substance that is, like the alternate substance, a basic feedstock or catalyst used in the conversion process. Equipment is not eligible if it is used beyond the point at which a substance usable as a fuel has been produced. Equipment is eligible only to the extent of the equipment's cost or basis allocable to the annual production of substances used as a fuel or used in the production of a fuel. For example, assume for the taxable year that 50 percent of the output of equipment is used to produce alcohol for production of whiskey and 50 percent is used to produce alcohol for use in a fuel mixture, such as gasohol. The alcohol production equipment qualifies as synthetic fuel equipment but only to the extent of one-half of its cost or basis. If, in a later taxable year, the equipment is used exclusively to produce whiskey, all of the equipment ceases to be synthetic fuel equipment.

(ii) A fuel is a material that produces usable heat upon combustion. To be "synthetic", the fuel either must differ significantly in chemical composition, as opposed to physical composition, from the alternate substance used to produce it or, in the case of solid fuel produced from biomass, the chemical change must consist of defiberization. Examples of synthetic fuels include alcohol derived from coal, peat, and vegetative matter, such as wood and corn, and methane from landfills.

(iii) Synthetic fuel equipment includes coal gasification equipment, coal liquefaction equipment, equipment for recovering methane from landfill, and equipment that converts biomass to a synthetic fuel.

(iv) Synthetic fuel equipment does not include equipment that merely mixes an alternate substance with another substance. For example, synthetic fuel equipment includes neither equipment that mixes coal and water to produce a slurry nor equipment that mixes alcohol and gasoline to produce gasohol. Equipment used to produce coke or coke gas, such as coke ovens, is also ineligible.

(6) *Modification equipment.*—(i) Alternative energy property includes equipment (modification equipment) designed to modify existing equipment. For the definition of "existing," see paragraph (l)(1)(i) of this section. To be eligible the modification must result in a substitution for the remainder of the taxable year from the date the equipment is placed in service and for each taxable year thereafter of the items in paragraph (c)(6)(ii)(A) or (B) of this section for all or a portion of the oil or gas substance used as a fuel or feedstock. As a result of the modification, the substituted alternate substance must comprise at least 25 percent of the fuel or feedstock (determined on the basis of Btu equivalency). If the modification also increases the capacity of the equipment, only the incremental cost (as defined in paragraph (k) of this section) of the equipment qualifies.

(ii) The substitutes for an oil or gas substance are—

(A) An alternate substance or

(B) A mixture of oil and an alternate substance.

(iii) Modification equipment does not include replacements for a boiler or burner. If the boiler or burner is replaced, the items must be described in paragraph (c)(3) or (4) of this section to qualify as alternative energy property. Modification may include, however, replacements of components of a boiler or burner, such as a heat exchanger.

(iv) The following examples illustrate this paragraph (c)(6).

Example (1). On January 1, 1980, corporation X is using oil to fuel its boiler. On June 1, 1980, X modifies the boiler to permit substitution of a coal and oil mixture for 40 percent of X's oil fuel needs. The mixture consists 75 percent of oil and 25 percent of coal. The equipment modifying the boiler does not qualify as modification equipment because the alternate substance comprises only 10 percent of the fuel.

Example (2). Assume the same facts as in example (1) except 75 percent of the mixture is coal. The equipment modifying the boiler qualifies.

Example (3). Assume the same facts as in example (2) except, instead of substituting an oil and coal mixture for 40 percent of X's oil fuel needs, X uses the modification to expand the boiler's fuel capacity by 40 percent using the mixture as additional fuel. The additional fuel mixture comprises only 28 percent of X's total fuel needs. Thus, even though 75 percent of the additional fuel mixture is an alternate substance, the boiler does not qualify as modification equipment because the alternate substance comprises only 21 percent of the total fuel.

(7) *Equipment using coal as feedstock.*—Equipment that uses coal (including lignite) to produce a feedstock for the manufacture of chemicals, such as petrochemicals, or other products is alternative energy property. Equipment is not eligible if it is not directly involved in the treatment of coal or a coal product, but produces a substance that is, like coal, a basic feedstock or catalyst used in the coal conversion process. Equipment is not eligible if it is used beyond the point at which the first product marketable as a feedstock has been produced. Equipment used to produce coke or coke gas, such as coke ovens, is ineligible.

(8) *Pollution control equipment.*—(i) Pollution control equipment is alternative energy property. Eligible equipment is limited to property or equipment to the extent it qualifies as a pollution control facility under section 103(b)(4)(F) and the regulations thereunder except that, if control of pollution is not the only significant purpose (within the meaning of those regulations), only the incremental cost (as defined in paragraph (k) of this section) of the equipment qualifies. However, if a Treasury decision changes the regulations under section 103(b)(4)(F) and, thus, the rules reflected in this subdivision (i), the rules as changed will apply as of the effective date of the Treasury decision.

(ii) To be eligible, the equipment must be required by a Federal, State, or local government regulation to be installed on, or used in connection with, eligible alternative energy property (as defined in paragraph (c)(8)(v) of this section).

(iii) Under section 48(l)(3)(D) equipment is not eligible if required by a Federal, State, or local government regulation in effect on October 1, 1978, to be installed on, or in connection with, property using coal (including lignite) as of October 1, 1978.

(iv) Under this subparagraph (8), pollution control equipment is required by regulation if it would be necessary to install the equipment to satisfy the requirements of any applicable law, including nuisance law. The pollution control equipment need not be specifically identified in the applicable law. If several different types of equipment may be used to comply with the applicable law, each type of equipment is considered necessary to satisfy the requirements of the law. An order permitting a taxpayer to delay compliance with any applicable law is disregarded.

(v) Under this subparagraph (8) "eligible alternative energy property" is energy property (as defined in section 48(l)(2)) described in paragraph (c)(3) through (7) of this section. If equipment otherwise qualifying as pollution control equipment is installed on, or used in connection with, both eligible alternative energy property and property other than eligible alternative energy property, only the incremental cost (as defined in paragraph (k) of this section) of the equipment qualifies.

(vi) *Examples.*—The following examples illustrate this subparagraph (8). Assume that the property or equipment in the examples are described in §1.103-8(g)(2)(ii) and that their only purpose is control of pollution.

Example (1). On October 1, 1978, corporation X acquires and places in service in State A a paper mill. The facility includes a boiler the primary fuel for which is wood chips. The facility includes equipment necessary to comply with pollution control standards in effect on October 1, 1978 in State A. This equipment qualifies as pollution control equipment.

Example (2). On October 1, 1978, corporation Y was burning coal at its facility in State B. The emissions from the facility exceeded State air pollution control requirements in effect on October 1, 1978.

On January 1, 1979, X installed cyclone separators to comply with the State pollution control requirements. The cyclone separators do not qualify as pollution control equipment.

Example (3). Assume the same facts as in example (2) except that Y installs a baghouse instead of cyclone separators to meet more stringent standards that take effect on December 31, 1978. The baghouse qualifies as pollution control equipment because the baghouse was not necessary to meet the standards in effect on October 1, 1978.

Example (4). On October 1, 1978, corporation Z is burning coal at its facility in State C. The emissions from that facility exceed State air pollution control standards in effect on October 1, 1978. C orders Z to install cyclone separators before January 1, 1979. However, C allows Z to operate its facility until January 1, 1979, under less stringent interim standards applicable only to Z. The separators do not qualify as pollution control equipment. The delayed compliance order is disregarded.

(9) *Handling and preparation equipment.*—(i) Alternative energy property includes equipment (handling and preparation equipment) used for unloading, transfer, storage, reclaiming from storage, or preparation of an alternate substance for use in eligible alternative energy property (as defined in paragraph (c)(9)(ii) of this section). Handling and preparation equipment must be located at the site the alternate substance is used as a fuel or feedstock. For example, equipment used to screen and prepare coal for use at a power plant qualifies if located at the plant. However, similar equipment located at the coal mine would not qualify.

(ii) Under this subparagraph (9), "eligible alternative energy property" is energy property (as defined in section 48(l)(2)) described in paragraph (c)(3) through (8) of this section. If equipment otherwise qualifying as handling and preparation equipment is installed on, or used in connection with, property other than eligible alternative energy property, only the incremental cost (as defined in paragraph (k) of this section) of the equipment qualifies.

(iii) The term "preparation" includes washing, crushing, drying, compacting, and weighing of an alternate substance. Handling and preparation equipment also includes equipment for shredding, chopping, pulverizing, or screening agricultural or forestry byproducts at the site of use.

(iv) Handling and preparation equipment does not include equipment, such as coal slurry pipelines and railroad cars, that transports a fuel or a feedstock to the site of its use.

(10) *Geothermal equipment.*—(i) Alternative energy property includes equipment (geothermal equipment) that produces, distributes, or uses energy derived from a geothermal deposit (as defined in §1.44C-2(h)).

(ii) In general, production equipment includes equipment necessary to bring geothermal energy from the subterranean deposit to the surface, including well-head and downhole equipment (such as screening or slotting liners, tubing, downhole pumps, and associated equipment). Reinjection wells required for production also may qualify. Production does not include exploration and development.

(iii) Distribution equipment includes equipment that transports geothermal steam or hot water from a geothermal deposit to the site of ultimate use. If geothermal energy is used to generate electricity, distribution equipment includes equipment that transports hot water from the geothermal deposit to a power plant. Distribution equipment also includes components of a heating system, such as pipes and ductwork that distribute within a building the energy derived from the geothermal deposit.

(iv) Geothermal equipment includes equipment that uses energy derived both from a geothermal deposit and from sources other than a geothermal deposit (dual use equipment). Such equipment, however, is geothermal equipment (A) only if its use of energy from sources other than a geothermal deposit does not exceed 25 percent of its total energy input in an annual measuring period and (B) only to the extent of its basis or cost allocable to its use of energy from a geothermal deposit during an annual measuring period. An "annual measuring period" for an item of dual use equipment is the 365 day period beginning with the day it is placed in service or a 365 day period beginning the day after the last day of the immediately preceding annual measuring period. The allocation of energy use required for purposes of paragraph (c)(10)(iv)(A) and (B) of this section may be made by comparing, on a Btu basis, energy input to dual use equipment from the geothermal deposit with energy input from other sources. However, the Commissioner may accept any other method that, in his opinion, accurately establishes the relative annual use by dual use equipment of energy derived from a geothermal deposit and energy derived from other sources.

(v) The existence of a backup system designed for use only in the event of a failure in the system providing energy derived from a geothermal deposit will not disqualify any other equipment. If geothermal energy is used to generate electricity, equipment using geothermal energy includes the electrical generating equipment, such as turbines and generators. However, geothermal equipment does not include any electrical transmission equipment, such as transmission lines and towers, or any equipment beyond the electrical transmission stage, such as transformers and distribution lines.

(vi) *Examples.*—The following examples illustrate this subparagraph (10):

Example (1). On October 1, 1979, corporation X, a calendar year taxpayer, places in service a system which heats its office building by circulating hot water heated by energy derived from a geothermal deposit through the building. Geothermal equipment includes the circulation system, including the pumps and pipes which circulate the hot water through the building.

Example (2). The facts are the same as in Example (1), except that corporation X also places in service a boiler to produce hot water for heating the building exclusively in the event of a failure of the geothermal equipment. Such a boiler is not geothermal equipment, but the existence of such a backup system does not serve to disqualify property eligible in Example (1).

Example (3). The facts are the same as in Example (1), except that the water heated by energy derived from a geothermal deposit is not hot enough to provide sufficient heat for the building. Therefore, the system includes an electric boiler in which the water is heated before being circulated in the heating system. Assume that, on a Btu basis, eighty percent of the total energy input to the circulating system during the 365 day period beginning on October 1, 1979, is energy derived from a geothermal deposit. The boiler is not geothermal equipment. For the 1979 taxable year, eighty percent of the circulating system is geothermal equipment because eighty percent of its basis or cost is allocable to use of energy from a geothermal deposit. If, in a subsequent taxable year, the basis or cost allocable to use of energy from a geothermal deposit falls below eighty percent, recapture may be required under section 47 and §1.47-1(h). Thus, if, on a Btu basis, only 70 percent of the total energy input to the circulating system for the 365 day period beginning October 1, 1980, is energy derived from a geothermal deposit, then there will be complete recapture of the credit during the 1980 taxable year. If, however, for that 365 day period, the portion of the total energy input that is derived from a geothermal deposit is less than 80 percent but greater than or equal to 75 percent, then only a proportional amount of credit will be recaptured during the 1980 taxable year. No additional credit is allowable in a subsequent taxable year, however, if the portion of the basis or cost allocable to use of energy from a geothermal deposit increases above what it was for a previous taxable year (see §1.46-3(d)(4)(i)).

Example (4). Corporation Y acquires a commercial vegetable dehydration system in 1981. The system operates by placing fresh vegetables on a conveyor belt and moving them through a dryer. The conveyor belt is powered by electricity. The dryer uses solely energy derived from a geothermal deposit. The dryer is geothermal equipment while the equipment powered by electricity does not qualify.

(d) *Solar energy property.*—(1) *In general.*—Energy property includes solar energy property. The term "solar energy property" includes equipment and materials (and parts related to the functioning of such equipment) that use solar energy directly to (i) generate electricity, (ii) heat or cool a building or structure, or (iii) provide hot water for use within a building or structure. Generally, those functions are accomplished through the use of equipment such as collectors (to absorb sunlight and create hot liquids or air), storage tanks (to store hot liquids), rockbeds (to store hot air), thermostats (to activate pumps or fans which circulate the hot liquids or air), and heat exchangers (to utilize hot liquids or air to create hot air or water). Property that uses, as an energy source, fuel or energy derived indirectly from solar energy, such as ocean thermal energy, fossil fuel, or wood, is not considered solar energy property.

(2) *Passive solar excluded.*—(i) Solar energy property excludes the materials and components of "passive solar systems," even if combined with "active solar systems."

(ii) An active solar system is based on the use of mechanically forced energy transfer, such as the use of fans or pumps to circulate solar generated energy.

(iii) A passive system is based on the use of conductive, convective, or radiant energy transfer. Passive solar property includes greenhouses, solariums, roof ponds, glazing, and mass or water trombe walls.

(3) *Electric generation equipment.*—Solar energy property includes equipment that uses solar energy to generate electricity, and includes storage devices, power conditioning equipment, transfer equipment, and parts related to the functioning of those items. In general, this process involves the transformation of sunlight into electricity through the use of such devices as solar cells or other collectors.

However, solar energy property used to generate electricity includes only equipment up to (but not including) the stage that transmits or uses electricity.

(4) *Pipes and ducts.*—Pipes and ducts that are used exclusively to carry energy derived from solar energy are solar energy property. Pipes and ducts that are used to carry both energy derived from solar energy and energy derived from other sources are solar energy property (i) only if their use of energy other than solar energy does not exceed 25 percent of their total energy input in an annual measuring period and (ii) only to the extent of their basis or cost allocable to their use of solar energy during an annual measuring period. (See paragraph (d)(6) of this section for the definition of "annual measuring period" and for rules relating to the method of allocation.)

(5) *Specially adapted equipment.*—Equipment that uses solar energy beyond the distribution stage is eligible only if specially adapted to use solar energy.

(6) *Auxiliary equipment.*—Solar energy property does not include equipment (auxiliary equipment), such as furnaces and hot water heaters, that use a source of power other than solar or wind energy to provide usable energy. Solar energy property does include equipment, such as ducts and hot water tanks, which is utilized by both auxiliary equipment and solar energy equipment (dual use equipment). Such equipment is solar energy property (i) only if its use of energy from sources other than solar energy does not exceed 25 percent of its total energy input in an annual measuring period and (ii) only to the extent of its basis or cost allocable to its use of solar or wind energy during an annual measuring period. An "annual measuring period" for an item of dual use equipment is the 365 day period beginning with the day it is placed in service or a 365 day period beginning the day after the last day of the immediately preceding annual measuring period. The allocation of energy use required for purposes of paragraph (d)(6)(i) and (ii) of this section may be made by comparing, on a Btu basis, energy input to dual use equipment from solar energy with energy input from other sources. However, the Commissioner may accept any other method that, in his opinion, accurately establishes the relative annual use by dual use equipment of solar energy and energy derived from other sources.

(7) *Solar process heat equipment.*—Solar energy property does not include equipment that uses solar energy to generate steam at high temperatures for use in industrial or commercial processes (solar process heat).

(8) *Example.*—The following example illustrates this paragraph (d).

Example. (a) In 1979, corporation X, a calendar year taxpayer, constructs an apartment building and purchases equipment to convert solar energy into heat for the building. Corporation X also installs an oil-fired water heater and other equipment to provide a backup source of heat when the solar energy equipment cannot meet the energy needs of the building. For purposes of this example, all equipment is placed in service on October 1, 1979. On a Btu basis, eighty percent of the total energy input to the dual use equipment during the 365 day period beginning October 1, 1979, is from solar energy.

(b) The items purchased, in addition to the water heater, include a roof solar collector, a heat exchanger, a hot water tank, a control component, pumps, pipes, fan-coil units, and valves. Assume the fan-coil units could be used with energy derived from an oil or gas substance without significant modification. All items are depreciable and have a useful life of three years or more. The use of the equipment to heat the building is the first use to which the equipment has been put.

(c) Water is pumped from the basement through pipes to the roof solar collector. Heated water returns through pipes to a heat exchanger which transfers heat to the water in the hot water tank.

(d) The hot water tank and the oil-fired water heater utilize the same distribution pipe. Pumps and valves at the points of connection between the hot water tank, the oil-fired water heater, and the distribution pipe regulate the auxiliary energy supply use. They also prevent the oil-fired water heater from heating water in the hot water tank.

(e) An integrated control component determines whether hot water from the hot water tank or from the oil-fired water heater is distributed to fan-coil units located throughout the building.

(f) The roof solar collector is solar energy property. The pump that moves the water to the roof collector and the pipes between the roof collector and the hot water tank qualify because they are solely related to transporting solar heated water. The hot water tank qualifies because it stores water heated solely by solar radiation. The heat exchanger also qualifies.

(g) The oil-fired water heater does not qualify as solar energy property because it is auxiliary equipment.

Reg. §1.48-9(d)(8)

(h) (i) Because the distribution pipe, the control component, and the pumps and valves serve the oil-fired water heater as well as the solar energy equipment, they qualify only to the extent of eighty percent of their cost or basis, the portion allocable to use of solar energy. If, in a subsequent taxable year, the basis or cost allocable to their use of solar energy falls below eighty percent, recapture may be required under section 47 and §1.47-1(h). Thus, if, on a Btu basis, only 70 percent of the total energy input to that equipment for the 365 day period beginning October 1, 1980, is from solar energy, then there will be complete recapture of the credit during the 1980 taxable year. If, however, for that 365 day period, the portion of that equipment's total energy input that is from solar energy is less than 80 percent but greater than or equal to 75 percent, then only a proportional amount of credit will be recaptured during the 1980 taxable year. No additional credit is allowable for that equipment in a subsequent taxable year, however, if the portion of its basis or cost allocable to use of solar energy increases above what it was for a previous taxable year (see §1.46-3(d)(4)(i)).

(ii) The fan-coil units do not qualify as solar energy property because they are not specially adapted to use energy derived from solar energy.

(e) *Wind energy property.*—(1) *In general.*—Energy property includes wind energy property. Wind energy property is equipment (and parts related to the functioning of that equipment) that performs a function described in paragraph (e)(2) of this section. In general, wind energy property consists of a windmill, wind-driven generator, storage devices, power conditioning equipment, transfer equipment, and parts related to the functioning of those items. Wind energy property does not include equipment that transmits or uses electricity derived from wind energy. In addition, limitations apply similar to those set forth in paragraph (d)(5), (6), and (8) of this section. For example, if equipment is used by both auxiliary equipment and wind energy equipment, such equipment is wind energy property only if its use of energy other than wind energy does not exceed 25 percent of its total energy input in an annual measuring period and only to the extent of its basis or cost allocable to its use of wind energy during an annual measuring period.

(2) *Eligible functions.*—Wind energy property is limited to equipment (and parts related to the functioning of that equipment) that—

(i) Uses wind energy to heat or cool, or provide hot water for use in, a building or structure, or

(ii) Uses wind energy to generate electricity (but not mechanical forms of energy).

(f) *Specially defined energy property.*—(1) *In general.*—Specially defined energy property means only those items described in paragraph (f)(4) through (14) of this section that meet the requirements of paragraph (f)(2) of this section. The items described in paragraph (f)(4) through (14) of this section also consist of related equipment, such as fans, pumps, ductwork, piping, and controls, the installation of which is necessary for the specified item to reduce the energy consumed or heat wasted by the process.

(2) *General requirements.*—To be eligible, each item described in paragraph (f)(4) through (14) of this section must be installed in connection with an existing industrial or commercial facility. In addition, the principal purpose of each of those items must be reduction of energy consumed or heat wasted in any existing industrial or commercial process. See section 48(l)(10) and paragraph (l) of this section. If an item performs more than one function, only the incremental cost (as defined in paragraph (k) of this section) of this equipment qualifies.

(3) *Industrial or commercial process.*—(i) A process is a means or method of producing a desired result by chemical, physical, or mechanical action. For example, equipment installed in connection with retail sales, general office use, and residential use are not used in a process within the meaning of this paragraph (f)(3).

(ii) An industrial process includes agricultural processes and thermal processes relating to production or manufacture, such as those involving boilers and furnaces.

(iii) A commercial process includes laundering and food preparation.

(iv) More than one process may be conducted in a single facility. The fact that several processes involved in the production of a product are integrated does not cause such integrated processes to be treated as one process. For example, in a food canning facility, producing prepared food from fresh vegetables is not one process but rather an integration of several processes including washing, cooking and canning.

(v) The following example illustrates this paragraph (f)(3).

Example. Corporation X, an advertising agency, acquires an automatic energy control system designed to reduce energy con-

sumed by heating and cooling its office building. Although the use of an office for X's business is a commercial activity, heating or cooling an office is not an industrial or commercial process. The automatic energy control system does not qualify because it does not reduce energy consumed in an industrial or commercial process.

(4) *Recuperators.*—Recuperators recover energy, usually in the form of waste heat from combustion exhaust gases, hot exiting product, or product cooling air, that is used to heat incoming combustion air, raw materials, or fuel. Recuperators are configurations of equipment consisting in part of fixed heat transfer surfaces between two gas flows, and include related baffles, dividers, entrance flanges, transition sections, and shells or cases enclosing the other components of the recuperator. In general, a fixed heat transfer surface absorbs heat from a gas or liquid flow or dissipates heat to the gas or liquid flow.

(5) *Heat wheels.*—Heat wheels recover energy, usually in the form of waste heat, from exhaust gases to preheat incoming gases. Heat wheels are items of equipment consisting in part of regenerators (which rotate between two gas flows) and related drive components, wiper seals, entrance flanges, and transition sections.

(6) *Regenerators.*—Regenerators are devices, such as clinker columns or chains, that recover energy by efficiently storing heat while exposed to high temperature gases and releasing heat while exposed to low temperature gases, fluids, or solids.

(7) *Heat exchangers.*—Heat exchangers recover energy, usually in the form of waste heat, from high temperature gases, liquids, or solids for transfer to low temperature gases, liquids, or solids. Heat exchangers consist in part of fixed heat transfer surfaces (described in paragraph (f)(4) of this section) separating two media. Heat exchange equipment does not include fluidized bed combustion equipment.

(8) *Waste heat boilers.*—Waste heat boilers use waste heat, usually in the form of combustion exhaust gases, as a substantial source of energy. A substantial source of energy is one that comprises more than 20 percent of the energy requirement on the basis of Btu's during the course of each taxable year (including the start-up year).

(9) *Heat pipes.*—Heat pipes recover energy, usually in the form of waste heat, from high temperature fluids to heat low temperature fluids. A heat pipe consists in part of sealed heat transfer chambers and a capillary structure. In general, the heat transfer chambers alternatively vaporize and condense a working fluid as it passes from one end of the chamber to the other.

(10) *Automatic energy control systems.*—Automatic energy control systems automatically reduce energy consumed in an industrial or commercial process for such purposes as environmental space conditioning (*i.e.,* lighting, heating, cooling or ventilating, etc.). Automatic energy control systems include, for example, automatic equipment settings controls, load shedding devices, and relay devices used as part of such system. Property such as computer hardware installed as a part of the energy control system also qualifies, but only to the extent of its incremental cost (as defined in paragraph (k) of this section).

(11) *Turbulators.*—Turbulators increase the rate of transfer of heat from combustion gases to heat exchange surfaces by increasing the turbulence in the gases. A turbulator is a baffle placed in a boiler firetube or in a heat exchange tube in industrial process equipment to deflect gases to the heat transfer surface.

(12) *Preheaters.*—Preheaters recover energy, usually in the form of waste heat, from either combustion exhaust gases or steam, to preheat incoming combustion air or boiler feedwater. A preheater consists in part of fixed heat transfer surfaces (described in paragraph (f)(4) of this section) separating two fluids.

(13) *Combustible gas recovery systems.*—Combustible gas recovery systems are items of equipment used to recover unburned fuel from combustion exhaust gases.

(14) *Economizers.*—Economizers are configurations of equipment used to reduce energy demand or recover energy from combustion exhaust gases and other high temperature sources to preheat boiler feedwater.

(15) *Other property added by the Secretary.*—[Reserved]

(g) *Recycling equipment.*—(1) *In general.*—Recycling equipment is equipment used exclusively to sort and prepare, or recycle, solid waste (other than animal waste) to recover usable raw materials ("recovery equipment") or to convert solid waste (including animal waste) into fuel or other useful forms of energy ("conversion equipment"). Recycling equipment may include certain other onsite related equipment.

(2) Recovery equipment.—Recovery equipment includes equipment that—

(i) Separates solid waste from a mixture of waste,

(ii) Applies a thermal, mechanical, or chemical treatment to solid waste to ensure the waste will properly respond to recycling, or

(iii) Recycles solid waste to recover usable raw materials, but not beyond occurrence of the first of the following:

(A) The point at which a material has been created that can be used in beginning the fabrication of an end-product in the same way as materials from a virgin substance. Examples are the fiber stage in textile recycling, the newsprint or paperboard stage in paper recycling, and the ingot stage for other metals (other than iron and steel). In the case of recycling iron or steel, recycling equipment does not include any equipment used to reduce solid waste to a molten state or any process thereafter.

(B) The point at which the material is a marketable product (*i.e.*, has a value other than for recycling) even if the material is not marketed by the taxpayer at that point.

(3) Conversion equipment.—Conversion equipment includes equipment that converts solid waste into a fuel or other usable energy, but not beyond the point at which a fuel, steam, electricity, hot water, or other useful form of energy has been created. Thus, combustors, boilers, and similar equipment may be eligible if used for a conversion process, but steam and heat distribution systems between the combustor or boiler and the point of use are not eligible.

(4) On-site related equipment.—Recycling equipment also includes onsite loading and transportation equipment, such as conveyors, integrally related to other recycling equipment. This equipment may include equipment to load solid waste into a sorting or preparation machine and also a conveyor belt system that transports solid waste from preparation equipment to other equipment in the recycling process.

(5) Solid waste.—(i) The term "solid waste" has the same meaning as in § 1.103-8(f)(2)(ii)(*b*), subject to the following exceptions and the other rules of this subparagraph (5):

(A) The date the equipment is placed in service is substituted in the first sentence of § 1.103-8(f)(2)(ii)(*b*) for the date of issue of the obligations, and

(B) Material that has a market value at the place it is located only by reason of its value for recycling is not considered to have a market value.

(ii) Solid waste may include a nominal amount of virgin materials, liquids, or gases, not to exceed 10 percent. If more than 10 percent of the material recycled during the course of any taxable year (including the "start up" year) consists of virgin material, liquids, or gases, the equipment ceases to be energy property and is subject to recapture under section 47. The determination of the portion of virgin material, liquids, or gases used is based on volume, weight, or Btu's, whichever is appropriate.

(6) Ineligible equipment.—Transportation equipment, such as trucks, that transfer solid waste between geographically separated sites (*e.g.*, the collection point and the recycling point) is not eligible. Steam and heat distribution systems are also ineligible.

(7) Increased recycling capacity.—If the equipment both replaces recycling capacity and increases that capacity at a particular site, only the incremental cost (as defined in paragraph (k) of this section) of increasing the capacity qualifies. Recycling capacity is determined by the ability to produce a product not previously produced by the taxpayer, or more of an existing product, in a way that does not lower overall production.

(8) Examples.—The following examples illustrate this paragraph (g).

Example (1). Corporation W recycles aluminum scrap metal. W owns a junk yard where it collects and crushes the metal into compact units. W's trucks bring the scrap metal from the junk yard to its main plant located 3 miles away. W's furnace equipment at the main plant reduces the scrap to the molten state and W's rolling equipment rolls the aluminum into sheets. The furnace qualifies, but for two separate reasons the rolling equipment does not qualify. First, the molten aluminum would be a marketable product if reduced to ingots prior to rolling. It is not necessary that W actually reduce the molten aluminum to ingots. Second, the molten aluminum could be used in the same way as virgin material.

Example (2). Corporation X manufactures newsprint using wood chips discarded during X's lumber operations. Assume X could sell the wood chips to other companies located a short distance from X's mill for use as a fuel. None of the equipment used to manufacture the newsprint qualifies.

Example (3). Assume the same facts as in example (2) except X uses old newspapers which have no value except for recycling in the area where X's mill is located. The equipment qualifies.

Example (4). Corporation Y recycles municipal waste. Assume the municipal waste is "solid waste" under paragraph (g)(5) of this section. During the first taxable year Y operates the equipment, Y uses 8,500 pounds of municipal waste and 1,500 pounds of virgin material and liquids. No energy credit is allowed for the equipment.

Example (5). Corporation Z owns a waste recovery facility. The corrugated paper portion of the waste stream is picked off a conveyor as it enters the facility. The corrugated paper is baled and sold as a secondary paper product. Z acquires shredding and air-classification equipment. Corrugated paper that is not removed from the conveyor belt enters the new equipment for production as a fuel. Z increases the input of corrugated paper so that the same amount of corrugated paper is removed from the conveyor to be baled. The excess paper that is not removed for baling enters the shredding and air-classification equipment. The new equipment qualifies.

(h) *Shale oil equipment.*—(1) *In general.*—Shale oil equipment used in mining or either surface or *in situ* processing qualifies as energy property. Shale oil equipment means equipment used exclusively to mine, or produce or extract oil from, shale rock.

(2) *Eligible processes.*—In general, processing equipment qualifies if used in or after the mining stage and up through the retorting process. Thus, eligible processes include crushing, loading into the retort, and retorting, but not hydrogenation, refining, or any process subsequent to retorting. However, with respect to *in situ* processing, eligible processes include creating the underground cavity.

(3) *Eligible equipment.*—Shale oil equipment includes—

(i) Heading jumbos, bulldozers, and scaling and bolting rigs used to create an underground cavity for *in situ* processing.

(ii) On-site water supply and treatment equipment and handling equipment for spent shale.

(iii) Crushing and screening plant equipment, such as hoppers, feeders, vibrating screens, and conveyors.

(iv) Briqueting plant equipment, such as hammer mills and vibratory pan feeders, and

(v) Retort equipment, including direct cooling and condensing equipment.

(i) [Reserved]

(j) *Natural gas from geopressured brine.*—Equipment used exclusively to extract natural gas from geopressured brine described in section 613A(b)(3)(C)(i) is energy property. Eligible equipment includes equipment used to separate the gas from saline water and remove other impurities from the gas. Equipment is eligible only up to the point the gas may be introduced into a pipeline.

(k) *Incremental cost.*—The term "incremental cost" means the excess of the total cost of equipment over the amount that would have been expended for the equipment if the equipment were not used for a qualifying purpose. For example, assume equipment costing $100 performs a pollution control function and another function. Assuming it would cost $60 solely to perform the nonqualifying function, the incremental cost would be $40.

(l) *Existing.*—(1) *In general.*—For purposes of section 48(l), the term "existing" means—

(i) When used in connection with a facility or equipment, 50 percent or more of the basis of that facility or equipment is attributable to construction, reconstruction, or erection before October 1, 1978, or

(ii) When used in connection with an industrial or commercial process, that process was carried on in the facility as of October 1, 1978.

(2) *Industrial or commercial process.*—(i) A process will be considered the same as the process carried on in the facility as of October 1, 1978, unless and until capitalizable expenditures are paid or incurred for modification of the process. The expenditures need not be capitalized in fact; it is sufficient if the taxpayer has an option or may elect to capitalize. In general, the date of change will be the date the expenditures are properly chargeable to capital account. If the taxpayer properly elects to expense a capitalizable expenditure, the date of change will be the date the expenditure could have been properly chargeable to capital account if the expenditure had been capitalized. Recapture will not occur by reason of a change in a process unless the process change also changes the use of the equipment. See example (1) of § 1.47-1(h)(5).

(m) *Quality and performance standards.*—(1) *In general.*—Energy property must meet quality and performance standards, if any, that have been prescribed by the Secretary (after consultation with the Secretary of Energy) and are in effect at the time of acquisition.

Reg. § 1.48-9(m)(1)

(2) *Time of acquisition.*—Under this paragraph (m) the time of acquisition is—

    (i) The date the taxpayer enters into a binding contract to acquire the property or

    (ii) For property constructed, reconstructed, or erected by the taxpayer, (A) the earlier of the date it begins construction, reconstruction, or erection of the property, or (B) the date the taxpayer and another person enter into a binding contract requiring each to construct, reconstruct, or erect property and place the property in service for an agreed upon use. See example under paragraph (m)(4) of this section.

    (3) *Binding contract.*—Under this paragraph (m), a binding contract to construct, reconstruct, or erect property, or to acquire property, is a contract that is binding at all times on the taxpayer under applicable State or local law. A binding contract to construct, reconstruct, or erect property or to acquire property, does not include a contract for preparation of architect's sketches, blueprints, or performance of any other activity not involving the beginning of physical work.

    (4) *Example.*—The following example illustrates this paragraph (m).

    Example. Corporation X owns a junk yard. Corporation Y manufactures recycling equipment and operates several recycling facilities. On January 1, 1979, X and Y enter into a written contract that is binding on both parties on that date and at all times thereafter. Under the contract's terms X will supply scrap metals to Y and Y agrees in return to build a recycling facility on land adjacent to the junk yard. Y will own and operate the facility using the scrap metal supplied by X, Y may treat the agreement as a binding contract under paragraph (m)(2) and (3) of this section. –

    (n) *Public utility property.*—(1) *Inclusions.*—Public utility property is included in both of the following categories of energy property:

    (i) Shale oil equipment and

    (ii) Equipment for producing natural gas from geopressured brine.

    (2) *Exclusions.*—Public utility property is excluded from each of the following categories of energy property:

    (i) Alternative energy property,

    (ii) Specially defined energy property,

    (iii) Solar or wind energy property, and

    (iv) Recycling equipment.

    (3) *Public utility property.*—The term "public utility property" has the meaning given in section 46(f)(5).

    (o) [Reserved].

    (p) [Reserved].

    (q) *Qualified intercity buses.*—(1) *In general.*—This paragraph (q) prescribes rules and definitions for purposes of section 48(l)(2)(A)(ix) and (16). Energy property includes qualified intercity buses of an eligible taxpayer, but only to the extent of the increase in the taxpayer's total operating seating capacity (operating capacity) under paragraphs (q)(9), (10), and (11) of this section. For application of recapture rules see § 1.47-1(h)(3)(ii).

    (2) *Eligible taxpayer.*—A taxpayer is an eligible taxpayer only if it is determined to be both—

    (i) A common carrier regulated by the Interstate Commerce Commission or an appropriate State agency and

    (ii) Engaged in the trade or business of furnishing intercity transportation by bus.

    (3) *Common carrier.*—The taxpayer is a common carrier only if the taxpayer holds itself out to the general public as providing passenger bus transportation for compensation over regular or irregular routes, or both.

    (4) *Appropriate State agency.*—A State agency is appropriate only if it has both—

    (i) Power to regulate intrastate transportation provided by a motor carrier, within the meaning of section 10521(b)(1) of the Revised Interstate Commerce Act (49 U.S.C. 10521(b)(1)), and

    (ii) Power to initiate an exemption proceeding under section 1025(b) of that Act (49 U.S.C. 10525(b)).

    (5) *Intercity transportation.*—Intercity transportation means intercity passenger transportation or intercity passenger charter service. Intercity transportation does not include transportation provided entirely within a municipality, contiguous municipalities, or within a zone that is adjacent to, and commercially a part of, the municipality or municipalities (within the meaning of section 10526(b)(1)) of the Revised Interstate Commerce Act (49 U.S.C. 10526(b)(1)). See 49 CFR Part 1048 regulations defining commercial zones under that statute).

    (6) *Definition of qualified intercity bus.*—A qualified intercity bus (qualifying bus) is an automobile bus—

    (i) The chassis and body of which are exempt (under section 4063(a)(6)) from the 10-percent excise tax generally imposed under section 4061(a) on trucks and buses.

    (ii) With a seating capacity of at least 36 passengers (in addition to the driver).

    (iii) With one or more baggage compartments, in an area separated from the passenger area, with an aggregate capacity of at least 200 cubic feet, and

    (iv) Which meets the predominant use test.

    (7) *Predominant use test.*—(i) A bus meets the predominant use test for a taxable year only if it meets the following conditions:

    (A) It is used on a full-time basis during the taxable year, and

    (B) At least 70 percent of the total miles driven are driven while furnishing intercity transportation.

    (ii) A bus driven from the end point of one trip to the beginning point of another trip ("deadheading"), both of which furnish intercity transportation of passengers, will be considered to have been driven while furnishing intercity transportation of passengers, even if no passengers are carried.

    (iii) A bus is considered used on a full-time basis in a taxable year if it was driven 10,000 miles in that year. If available, the best evidence of annual mileage is the difference between odometer readings at the beginning and end of each taxable year. If the bus was placed in service during the taxable year, or for a short taxable year described in section 441(b)(3), that 10,000 mile figure is prorated on a daily basis.

    (iv) If a qualifying bus fails to meet the predominant use test in a taxable year, a cessation occurs in that taxable year. See § 1.47-1(h)(3)(ii).

    (v) The following examples illustrate this paragraph (q)(7):

    Example (1). X, a bus company, used a bus for trips between city M and city N, a distance of 100 miles. These trips qualify as furnishing intercity transportation. During the taxable year, 300 round trips were run carrying passengers both ways and 75 trips were run carrying passengers from city M to city N immediately after each of which the bus was returned to city M for the next trip. The bus was also driven 20,000 miles to furnish passenger service which was local transportation. During the taxable year, the bus was driven a total of 100,000 miles. X makes the following calculations to determine if it met the predominant use test for the taxable year.

1. Total miles driven	100,000
2. Intercity miles driven:	
a. Passenger round trips (100 × 2 × 300)	60,000
b. Passenger one-way (75 × 100)	7,500
c. Non-passenger return trips (75 × 100)	7,500
3. Total intercity passenger miles (sum of lines 2a, b, and c)	75,000
4. 70% of line 1	70,000

Since line 1 is not less than 10,000 miles, the full-time use requirement is met. Since line 3 is greater than line 4, the 70 percent intercity mileage test is met. Thus, for the taxable year, the bus meets the predominant use test in paragraph (q)(7)(i) of this section.

    Example (2). The facts are the same as in example (1), except that the bus was placed in service on the last day of the taxable year. The bus was used to run one round trip, carrying passengers, between cities M and N. 10,000 miles × one day ÷ 365 days = 27.4 miles. Because, for the one day of the taxable year that the bus was in service, the bus was driven more than 27.4 miles, and all these miles were driven to furnish intercity transportation, it met the predominant use test for the taxable year.

    (8) *Leased buses.*—(i) A bus which is leased is energy property only if it meets the requirements of paragraph (q)(6)(i), (ii), and (iii) of this section, the lessee is an eligible taxpayer, and the bus meets the predominant use test in the hands of the lessee. If a leased bus is energy property, the energy credit is available only to the lessee unless paragraph (q)(8)(ii) of this section applies. The lessor must elect under section 48(d) for the lessee to claim the energy credit.

(ii) If a leased bus is energy property and, on or before October 9, 1984, either (A) the lessor and lessee enter into a lease and the lessee places the bus in service, or (B) the bus is not placed in service but the lessor and lessee enter into a binding contract under which the amount of the lease payments cannot be modified, then the energy credit is available to the lessor even if the lessor is not an eligible taxpayer.

(iii) Notwithstanding §1.47-2(b)(1) (relating to the effect of a disposition by the lessee on the credit claimed by the lessor), if, by reason of a lease or the termination of a lease, a bus is used in a taxable year subsequent to the credit year by a person other than the one whose increase in operating capacity determined the amount of qualified investment for the energy credit, a disposition of the bus under §1.47-1(h)(2) results. However, if the energy credit for a bus was earned in a taxable year and a lease of the bus which qualifies under section 168(f)(8) (safe-harbor lease) is entered into in a subsequent taxable year, the safe-harbor lease is not a disposition of the bus and the lessee under that lease is treated as the lessee for purposes of this paragraph (q)(8). For the requirement to file an amended return if the energy credit was allowed in a prior taxable year, see §5c.168(f)(8)-6(b)(2)(ii), (Temporary Income Tax Regulations under the Economic Recovery Tax Act of 1981). For the rule for determining whose operating capacity determines qualified investment for the energy credit, see paragraph (q)(9)(ii) of this section. For the rule for leases to related taxpayers, see paragraph (q)(10)(ii) of this section.

(9) *Operating capacity.*—(i) Qualified investment for a qualifying bus is taken into account for the energy credit only to the extent the bus increases the taxpayer's operating capacity. To increase operating capacity, a bus must be counted in operating capacity. The increase in a taxpayer's operating capacity is the excess of the taxpayer's operating capacity for the current taxable year over its operating capacity for the immediately preceding taxable year. Related taxpayers determine operating capacity on a group basis under paragraph (q)(10) of this section.

(ii) Operating capacity for a particular taxable year is determined by adding together the seating capacities of all intercity buses used by the taxpayer in that year and still owned by the taxpayer at the end of that year. An intercity bus is a bus which meets the chassis and body test and the predominant use test in paragraph (q)(6) of this section whether or not the bus is still in use at the end of the taxable year. In the case of a leased bus to which paragraph (q)(8) of this section applies, the lessee's operating capacity determines qualified investment for the energy credit.

(iii) The qualified investment for the energy credit for a qualifying bus is the bus's qualified investment for the regular credit multiplied by a fraction. The numerator of the fraction is the increase in the taxpayer's operating capacity for the taxable year. The denominator is the added operating capacity for the taxable year. Added operating capacity for the taxable year is determined for a taxpayer by adding together the seating capacities of the taxpayer's intercity buses included in operating capacity for the taxable year which were not included in operating capacity for the immediately preceding taxable year.

(iv) In the case of a partnership, each partner's qualified investment for the energy credit for a qualifying bus is the partner's qualified investment for the regular credit (determined under §1.46-3(f)) multiplied by the fraction referred to in paragraph (q)(9)(iii) of this section for the partnership, as determined for the partnership taxable year in which the bus is placed in service.

(v) The following example illustrates this paragraph (q)(9):

Example. Corporation Y is a calendar year bus company that is an eligible taxpayer under paragraph (q)(2) of this section. Based upon the facts as set forth in the following table, Y makes the following calculations to determine the energy credit earned in 1981:

1.	1980 operating capacity determined as of 12/31/80:	
	a. 5 intercity buses × 50 seats each	250
	b. Total 1980 operating capacity	250
2.	1981 operating capacity determined as of 12/31/81:	
	a. 2 1980 buses used on a full-time basis in 1981	100
	b. 1981 added capacity:	
	i. Qualifying buses:	
	Bus 1	45
	Bus 2	55
	Bus 3	50
	ii. Intercity bus not a qualifying bus	50
	iii. Total 1981 added capacity	200
	c. Total 1981 operating capacity	300
3.	1981 increase in operating capacity (line 2c – line 1b)	50
4.	Fraction for determining qualified investment attributable to increase in capacity (line 3 ÷ line 2(b)(iii))	$1/4$

Accordingly, the energy credit earned in 1981 for each of the qualifying buses is determined as follows:

Qualified investment for the regular credit	×	Line 4	×	Energy percentage	=	Energy credit earned
Bus 1: $15,000		$1/4$		10		$375
Bus 2: $20,000		$1/4$		10		500
Bus 3: $25,000		$1/4$		10		625
Total energy credit earned in 1981						$1,500

(10) *Related taxpayers.*—(i) Related taxpayers are treated as one taxpayer in determining the increase in operating capacity under paragraph (q)(9)(ii) of this section and in determining the qualified investment in qualified intercity buses for the energy credit under paragraph (q)(9)(iii) of this section. Related taxpayers are members of a group of trades or businesses that are under common control (as defined in §1.52-1(b)).

(ii) Related taxpayers make all computations relating to operating capacity on a group basis. Also, the determination of whether a bus meets the predominant use test is made on a group basis by aggregating bus usage by each member of the group. For example, if a bus is acquired by one member and used by that member for part of a taxable year and used by other members for the remainder, the combined usage is aggregated in determining whether the predominant use test is met. In addition, all related taxpayers are treated as one person in applying paragraph (q)(8) of this section (relating to leasing).

(iii) The energy credit earned for a qualifying bus is allocated to the member which acquired (or is a lessee treated under section 48(d) as having acquired) the bus whether or not that member had a separate increase in operating capacity for the taxable year.

(iv) Each member must make its own computation of the group's increase in operating capacity for the period comprising its taxable year. A member will make this computation as of the end of its taxable year ignoring different taxable years of other members. For the period comprising its taxable year, the member makes all calculations relating to group operating capacity, including the determination of full-time use by other members.

(v) Each member determines the composition of the group as of the end of that member's taxable year. For example, if X uses the calendar year and makes its computation as of December 31, 1981, and Y is a member of X's group at that time, Y's operating capacity determined as of the end of X's immediately preceding taxable year (December 31, 1980) is taken into account by X for 1980 even if Y was not a member of the group for any day prior to December 31, 1981.

(vi) The following example illustrates this paragraph (q)(10):

Example (a). Corporations X and Y are related taxpayers. In this example, each bus is a qualifying bus with a seating capacity of 50. Each bus owned at the close of either X's or Y's taxable year was used on a full-time basis for the relevant period corresponding to X's or Y's taxable year. Other facts are set forth in the following table:

	X	Y
Taxable year ends	Dec. 31	June 30.
Operating capacity for 1979.	5 buses	10 buses.
Buses added	3 buses Mar. 1, 1980	3 buses May 15, 1981.
Buses sold	2 buses Mar. 31, 1981	2 buses Sept. 30, 1980.
Cost of each added bus	$40,000	$60,000

(b) X makes the following calculations to determine the energy credit earned for calendar year 1980.

1.	1979 operating capacity determined as of 12/31/79:	
	a. Attributable to X (5 buses × 50 seats)	250
	b. Attributable to Y (10 buses × 50 seats)	500

c.   Total 1979 operating capacity   750

2.   1980 operating capacity determined as of 12/31/80:

    a.   X's 5 and Y's 8 1979 buses used on a full-time
basis in 1980 and still owned on 12/31/80   650

    b.   1980 added capacity (X's 3 buses × 50 seats) . . .   150

    c.   Total 1980 operating capacity   800

3.   1980 increase in operating capacity (line 2c – line 1c)   50

4.   Fraction in paragraph (q)(9)(iii) of this section (line 3 ÷
line 2b) 1/3

      Accordingly, X earned an energy credit of $4,000 in 1980
($40,000 × 1/3 × 10% × 3 buses).

      (c) Since in calendar year 1981 X placed no qualifying buses in
service, X earned no energy credit in 1981.

      (d) Since in the taxable year 7/1/79-6/30/80 Y placed no
qualifying buses in service, Y earned no energy credit in that taxable
year.

      (e) Y makes the following calculations to determine the energy
credit earned in the taxable year 7/1/80-6/30/81:

1.   Operating capacity for the taxable year ending
6/30/80 determined as of the close of that year:

    a.   Attributable to X (8 buses × 50 seats)   400

    b.   Attributable to Y (10 buses × 50 seats)   500

    c.   Total operating capacity for that year   900

2.   Operating capacity for the taxable year ending
6/30/81 determined as of the close of that year:

    a.   X's 6 and Y's 8 buses from prior taxable year
used on a full-time basis during current
taxable year and still owned on 6/30/81 . .   700

    b.   Capacity added during current taxable year
(Y's 3 buses × 50 seats)   150

    c.   Total operating capacity for that year   850

3.   Increase in operating capacity for taxable year
ending 6/30/81 (line 2c – line 1c) . . . .   (50)

      As determined for Y's taxable year ending 6/30/81 the group
experienced a decrease in operating capacity. Thus, no energy credit
is available for the buses Y placed in service in its taxable year ending
6/30/81.

      (11) *Section 381 (a) transactions.*—(i) in the case of a transaction
described in section 381(a), the operating capacity of each transferor
or distributor corporation, determined as of the date of distribution
or transfer (within the meaning of §1.381(b)-1(b)), shall reduce the
operating capacity of the acquiring corporation (determined without
this paragraph (q)(11)) for its first taxable year ending on or after that
date for purposes of determining the acquiring corporation's energy
credit for that year. This paragraph (q)(11) shall not apply to any case
to which paragraph (q)(10) of this section (dealing with related
taxpayers) applies.

      (ii) The following example illustrates this paragraph (q)(11):

      Example. X and Y are unrelated corporations which use the
calendar year. For 1981, each has an operating capacity of 250 seats (5
buses × 50 seats). X merges into Y on January 1, 1982. On May 1,
1982, Y retires and sells two buses and acquires four 50-seat qualifying buses at a cost of $40,000 each. All buses owned by Y on
December 31, 1982, are included in operating capacity. Y makes the
following calculations to determine the energy credit earned in taxable year 1982.

1.   Y's 1981 operating capacity determined as of
12/31/81   250

2.   1982 operating capacity determined as of 12/31/82
without this paragraph (q)(11):

    a.   X's 5 buses plus Y's 5 1981 buses less 2 retired
buses (8 buses × 50 seats)   400

    b.   1982 added capacity (4 buses × 50 seats)   200

    c.   Total   600

3.   Operating capacity of transferor (X) on 1/1/82   250

4.   Y's 1982 operating capacity (line 2c – line 3)   350

5.   1982 increase in operating capacity (line 4 – line 1)   100

6.   Fraction in paragraph (q)(9)(iii) of this section (line 5 ÷
line 2b) 1/2

7.   Energy credit earned in 1982 ($40,000 × 1/2 × 10% × 4
buses) $8,000

[Reg. §1.48-9.]

☐ [*T.D. 7765, 1-19-81. Amended by T.D. 7982, 10-5-84, T.D. 8014,
3-25-85 and T.D. 8147, 7-20-87.*]

[Reg. §1.48-10]

**§1.48-10. Single purpose agricultural or horticultural struc-
tures.**—(a) *In general.*—(1) *Scope.*—Under section 48(a)(1)(D), "section 38 property" includes single purpose agricultural and
horticultural structures, as defined in section 48(p) and paragraphs
(b) and (c) of this section. These structures are subject to a special rule
for recapture of the credit. See paragraph (g) of this section. For the
relation of this section to section 48(a)(1)(B) (other tangible property)
and to sections 1245 and 1250 (depreciation recapture), see paragraph
(h) of this section.

      (2) *Effective date.*—The provisions of section 48(a)(1)(D) and this
section apply to open taxable years ending after August 15, 1971.

      (b) *Definition of single purpose agricultural structure.*—(1) *In gen-
eral.*—Under section 48(p)(2), a single purpose agricultural structure
is any structure or enclosure that meets all of the following
requirements:

      (i) It is specifically designed and constructed exclusively for
permissible purposes (as defined in paragraph (b)(2) of this section).
See paragraph (d) of this section for the rule regarding "specifically
designed and constructed".

      (ii) It is specifically used exclusively for those permissible
purposes. See paragraph (e) of this section for the rules regarding
"specifically used".

      (iii) It houses equipment necessary to house, raise, and feed
livestock and their produce. See paragraph (b)(3) and (4) of this
section.

      (2) *Permissible purposes.*—The following are the only permissible
purposes for a single purpose agricultural structure:

      (i) Housing, raising, and feeding a particular type of livestock
and, at the taxpayer's option, its produce. The term "housing, raising,
and feeding" includes the full range of livestock breeding and raising
activities, including ancillary post-production activities (as defined in
paragraph (f) of this section). Thus, for example, use of a structure for
breeding livestock, or for producing eggs or livestock, is permitted.
The structure may also be used for storing feed or machinery, but
more than strictly incidental use for these purposes will disqualify
the structure. See paragraph (e)(1) of this section. For the special rule
concerning the permissible purposes for a milking parlor, see paragraph (b)(2)(iii) of this section.

      (ii) Housing required equipment (including any replace-
ments) as defined in paragraph (b)(4) of this section.

      (iii) If the structure is a dairy facility, it will qualify if it is used
for: (A) activities consisting of the production of milk or of the
production of milk and the housing, raising, or feeding dairy cattle,
and (B) housing equipment (including any replacements) necessary
for these activities. The term "housing, raising, or feeding" includes
the full range of dairy cattle breeding and raising activities including
ancillary post-production activities (as defined in paragraph (f) of
this section). The structure may also be used for storing feed or
machinery, but more than incidental use for these purposes will
disqualify the structure. See paragraph (e)(1) of this section.

      (3) *Livestock; particular type of livestock.*—(i) *Livestock.*—Livestock
qualifying as "section 38 property" under §1.48-1(l) constitutes livestock for purposes of this section. Thus, for example, horses are not
livestock for purposes of this section since they do not qualify as
"section 38 property" under §1.48-1(l). Under section 48(p)(6), poultry constitutes livestock for purposes of section 48(a)(1)(D). The term
"livestock" includes the offspring of livestock. "Livestock" is distinguished from the produce of livestock, such as milk and eggs held for
sale. For purposes of this section, eggs held for hatching and new-
born livestock are considered livestock. A structure used solely to
house produce of livestock or equipment necessary to house produce
of livestock will not qualify as a single purpose agricultural structure.
Thus, for example, a dairy facility used solely for storing milk will
not qualify.

      (ii) *Particular type of livestock.*—A structure qualifies as a single
purpose agricultural structure only if it is specifically designed,
constructed, and used exclusively for permissible purposes with
respect to one particular type of livestock. For purposes of this
section, each species is a different type except that all species of
poultry are considered to be of a single type. Thus, for example, a
structure specifically designed and constructed as a single purpose
hog-raising facility will not qualify if it is used to raise dairy cows,
but a structure specifically designed, constructed, and used to raise
poultry may house, raise, and feed both chickens and turkeys.

      (4) *Required equipment rule.*—(i) A single purpose agricultural
structure must also house equipment necessary to house, raise, and
feed the livestock ("required equipment"). Required equipment must
be an integral part of the structure, and includes, but is not limited to,
equipment necessary to contain the livestock, to provide them with
water or feed, and to control the temperature, lighting, and humidity
of the interior of the structure. For purposes of this section, equipment is an integral part of the structure if it is physically attached to
or a part of the structure. The useful life of the structure, however,
need not be contemporaneous with the life of the equipment it

houses. A structure without required equipment is not a single purpose agricultural structure.

(ii) A single purpose agricultural structure may, but is not required to, house equipment (for example, loading chutes) necessary to the conduct of ancillary post-production activities as defined in paragraph (e) of this section.

(5) *Livestock structure.*—In section 48(p)(2), the terms "single purpose livestock structure" and "single purpose agricultural structure" are interchangeable.

(c) *Definition of single purpose horticultural structure.*—(1) *In general.*—Under section 48(p)(3), a single purpose horticultural structure is any structure that meets both of the following requirements:

(i) It is a greenhouse or other structure specifically designed and constructed for permissible purposes (as defined in paragraph (c)(2) of this section). See paragraph (d) of this section for the rule regarding "specifically designed and constructed."

(ii) It is specifically used exclusively for those permissible purposes. See paragraph (e) of this section for the rules regarding "specifically used."

(2) *Permissible purposes.*—The following are the only permissible purposes for a single purpose horticultural structure:

(i) The commercial production of plants (including plant products such as flowers, vegetables, or fruit) in a greenhouse.

(ii) The commercial production of mushrooms.

(iii) A single purpose horticultural structure also may, but is not required to, house equipment necessary to carry out these permissible purposes listed in paragraph (c)(2)(i) and (ii) of this section.

(3) *Ancillary post-production activities.*—The terms "commercial production of plants" and "commercial production of mushrooms" include ancillary post-production activities (as defined in paragraph (f) of this section).

(d) *Specifically designed and constructed.*—A structure is specifically designed and constructed if it is not economic to design and construct the structure for the intended qualifying purpose and then use the structure for a different purpose. For example, if a hog raising structure is designed and constructed in accordance with a standard set of plans for such a structure provided by the Department of Agriculture, it would not be economic to use the structure for purposes other than hog raising.

(e) *Specifically used.*—There are two aspects of the specific use requirement—exclusive use and actual use.

(1) *Exclusive use.*—(i) A structure qualifies as a single purpose agricultural or horticultural structure only if it is used exclusively for the permitted purposes by reason of which it qualified for the credit. Thus—

(A) The structure may not be used for any nonpermissible purposes (for example, processing, marketing, or more than incidental use for storing feed or equipment) and

(B) It may not be put to any use other than the specific use by reason of which it qualifies for the credit.

(ii) For purposes of this section, the term "incidental use" means a use which is both related and subordinate to the qualifying purpose. Thus, for example, if feed is stored in an agricultural structure which will be used for raising hogs, the feed must be used only for the hogs in order to be related to the qualifying purpose. In determining whether use of the structure for feed storage is subordinate to the qualifying purpose, all of the facts and circumstances must be considered, including, with respect to feed storage, the following:

(A) Type of animal involved;

(B) Number of, and consumption rate for, each animal;

(C) Climate of area;

(D) Total volume of storage area; or

(E) Percentage of structure's total volume devoted to storage.

(iii) It will be presumed that the storage function is not subordinate to the qualifying purpose of the structure if more than one-third of the structure's total usable volume is devoted to storage. This presumption may be rebutted with clear and convincing evidence.

(iv) A structure may fail the exclusive use test if either of the requirements of paragraph (e)(1)(i) of this section is not met. Thus, for example, a horticultural structure that contains an area for processing plants or plant products will fail the exclusive use test because there is a nonpermissible use. An agricultural structure that is used to house more than one particular type of livestock fails the exclusive use test for the same reason. A change in the use of an agricultural structure from one species of livestock to another will cause the structure to fail the exclusive use test when the change

occurs. Thus, for example, a hog-raising facility which qualified for the credit when it was placed in service cannot later be modified and used for producing broiler chickens even if the structure would have qualified for the credit if it had been originally designed, constructed, and used exclusively for producing broiler chickens.

(2) *Actual use.*—(i) A single purpose agricultural or horticultural structure also must actually be used for the permissible purpose by reason of which it qualifies for the credit. "Actual use" means "placed in service" (as defined in §1.46-3(d)). Mere vacancy, on a temporary basis, will not disqualify the structure. Thus, for example, a structure that is designed and constructed as a hog-raising structure will not qualify if it is never placed in service for raising hogs. However, a turkey-raising facility will not be disqualified if the turkeys are all sent to a packing plant in November and the structure remains vacant until the next spring when newly hatched turkeys are placed in the structure to be raised.

(ii) For purposes of this section, "vacancy on a temporary basis" includes temporary vacancy caused by market fluctuations or other economic considerations and vacancy on a seasonal basis.

(f) *Work space; ancillary post-production activities.*—(1) *Permissible work space.*—Under section 48(p)(4), a single purpose agricultural or horticultural structure may contain work space only if it is used for—

(i) Stocking, caring for, or collecting livestock, plants, or mushrooms,

(ii) Maintenance of the structure, or

(iii) Maintenance or replacement of the equipment or stock enclosed by or contained in the structure.

Thus, for example, an eligible structure may not contain space devoted to processing or marketing or other nonpermissible purposes.

(2) *Ancillary post-production activities.*—The term "stocking, caring for, or collecting" the livestock, plants, or mushrooms includes ancillary post-production activities. These activities, therefore, constitute permissible purposes when carried on in conjunction with other permissible purposes, and a qualifying structure may contain work space devoted to such activities. Ancillary post-production activities include gathering, sorting, and loading livestock, plants, and mushrooms and packing unprocessed plants, mushrooms, and the live offspring and unprocessed produce of the livestock. Ancillary post-production activities do not include processing activities, such as slaughtering or packing meat, nor do they include marketing activities.

(g) *Special rule for recapture under section 47.*—Under section 48(p)(5), if a structure which qualifies for the credit under this section becomes ineligible because it ceases to be held for the specific use by reason of which it qualified (or it is used for other than that qualifying use) before the end of the applicable estimated useful life or period specified in section 47(a), then the investment credit previously allowed with respect to the structure may be partially or entirely recaptured under section 47. Unlike other property to which section 47 applies, single purpose structures may not be converted from one permissible use to another without recapture. See subparagraph (e)(2) of this section.

(h) *Relationship to other sections.*—(1) *Relation to section 48(a)(1)(B).*—All structures satisfying the requirements of section 48(a)(1)(B) and (a)(1)(D) will be considered to qualify under either provision.

(2) *Relationship to sections 1245 and 1250.*—For purposes of depreciation recapture, property to which section 48(a)(1)(D) applies is section 1245 property, except that property placed in service prior to January 1, 1981, may, at the option of the taxpayer, be treated as section 1250 property if depreciation deductions allowed were not under one of the methods authorized only for section 1245 property.

(i) [Reserved]

(j) *Examples.*—The provisions of this section may be illustrated by the following examples:

Example (1). A constructs a rectangular structure for use in an egg-producing facility. The structure has no windows. The walls and roof are made of corrugated steel and there is a door which is 4 feet wide and 8 feet tall at each end of the structure. At the end of each wall are louvered openings approximately 4 feet high and 8 feet long. These openings house thermostatically controlled fans. In the center of the walls are manually operated fresh-air openings. Corrugated steel "curtains" hang from the top of the openings so that the openings can be completely closed in cold weather, but the curtains can be propped open to admit fresh air. The building is well insulated. A has reinforced the roof with extra trusses and rafters and reinforced the building with extra wall studs. Two rows of cages are suspended from the rafters by thin steel girders and wires. The floor of the structure is a sloping concrete slab pierced with long troughs which run the length of the structure beneath the cages. The troughs are used for collection and disposal of chicken wastes. When this structure is placed in service it will qualify for an investment credit under this section.

Example (2). B constructs a greenhouse for the commercial production of plants. The greenhouse is a rectangular structure with translucent fiberglass walls and roof. The structure is equipped with an automatic temperature and humidity control system. Pipes were installed to carry water and liquid fertilizer to the plants and to release minute amounts of carbon dioxide into the air. When the structure was originally placed in service B used the entire structure for growing flowers commercially. In September 1978, B began to use the structure for growing tomatoes. Because of the success of the venture, in January 1979, B began to use the entire structure for growing tomatoes. In February 1980, B set up a small counter with a cash register at one end of the structure so that workers could sell tomatoes to customers at the greenhouse. Until February 1980, the structure would qualify for the credit under this section. The change in use from growing flowers to growing tomatoes will not affect the eligibility of the structure. Once the cash register is installed, however, the structure fails to meet both the exclusive use test of paragraph (e)(1) of this section and the work space rule of paragraph (f) of this section since a single purpose structure may not be used for marketing activities.

Example (3). C purchases a prefabricated structure and makes modifications so that the structure will meet C's requirements. C adds gates and constructs a partition which divides the structure into two parts. One part of the structure constitutes less than one-third of the total usable volume of the structure and is used to house feeder cattle while they are fed with hay. This part of the structure has a sloping concrete floor. The other part of the structure constitutes more than two-thirds of the total usable volume of the structure and is used to store the hay used to feed the cattle. This structure will not qualify for the credit since it fails the required equipment test. The structure does not contain equipment which is an integral part of the structure. This structure also fails the "specifically designed and constructed" test of paragraph (d) of this section since it would be economical to use the structure for purposes other than housing, raising, and feeding cattle (such as a general purpose barn, for example). Finally, the structure fails the incidental use test of paragraph (e) of this section because the storage function is presumptively not subordinate to the qualifying purpose since more than two-thirds of the structure's total usable volume is devoted to storage and none of the facts will serve to rebut the presumption. [Reg. § 1.48-10.]

☐ [*T.D. 7900, 7-18-83.*]

[Reg. § 1.48-11]

§1.48-11. Qualified rehabilitated building; expenditures incurred before January 1, 1982.—(a) *In general.*—Under section 48(a)(1)(E), that portion of the basis of a qualified rehabilitated building which is attributable to qualified rehabilitation expenditures qualifies as section 38 property. In general, property which is treated as section 38 property by reason of section 48(a)(1)(E) is treated as new section 38 property and therefore is not subject to the used property limitation. See §1.48-2(d). Section 48(g)(1) and paragraph (b) of this section define the term "qualified rehabilitated building". Section 48(g)(2) and paragraph (c) of this section define the term "qualified rehabilitation expenditure". Paragraph (d) of this section provides guidance for coordination of these provisions with other sections of the Code.

(b) *Definition of qualified rehabilitated building.*—(1) *In general.*—The term "qualified rehabilitated building" means any building and its structural components—

(i) Which has been rehabilitated (within the meaning of paragraph (b)(3) of this section),

(ii) Which was placed in service (within the meaning of §1.46-3(d)) by any person at any time before the beginning of the rehabilitation,

(iii) 75 percent or more of the existing external walls of which are retained in place as external walls (within the meaning of paragraph (b)(4) of this section) in the rehabilitation process, and

(iv) Which meets the twenty-year requirement in paragraph (b)(2) of this section.

In addition, a major portion of a building may be treated as a separate building for purposes of this paragraph if the requirements of paragraph (b)(5) of this section are met.

(2) *Twenty-year requirement.*—(i) *In general.*—A building is considered a qualified rehabilitated building only if a period of at least 20 years has elapsed between the date physical work on the rehabilitation of the building began, and the later of—

(A) The date the building was first placed in service (see §1.46-3(d)) by any person as a building, or

(B) The date the building was placed in service by any taxpayer in connection with a prior rehabilitation with respect to which a credit was allowed by reason of section 48(a)(1)(E).

(ii) *Vacant periods.*—The 20-year period includes periods during which a building was vacant or devoted to a personal use and is computed without regard to the number of owners or the identity of owners during the period.

(iii) *Physical work on a rehabilitation.*—For purposes of this section, "physical work on a rehabilitation" begins when actual construction begins. The term "physical work on a rehabilitation" does not include preliminary activities such as planning, designing, securing financing, exploring, researching, developing plans and specifications, or stabilizing a building to prevent deterioration (*e.g.*, placing boards over broken windows).

(iv) *Special rule.*—If a part of a building meets the twenty-years requirement in subdivision (i) of this subparagraph and a part (for example, an addition) does not, a rehabilitation of that part that meets the requirement may qualify for a credit only if that part constitutes a major portion (as defined in paragraph (b)(5) of this section) of the building.

(3) *Rehabilitation.*—(i) *In general.*—For purposes of this paragraph, rehabilitation includes renovation, restoration, or reconstruction. However, the term "rehabilitation" does not include enlargement (within the meaning of paragraph (c)(7)(ii) of this section), new construction, or the completion of new construction after a building has been placed in service. For purposes of this paragraph (b)(3), whether expenditures are attributable to the rehabilitation of an existing building, or to new construction, is determined upon all the facts and circumstances.

(ii) *Substantial rehabilitation.*—For a building to be considered rehabilitated, the rehabilitation must be substantial. Whether a rehabilitation is substantial is determined upon the basis of all the facts and circumstances. In general, to be substantial, the rehabilitation must do one of the following:

(A) materially extend the useful life of the building;

(B) significantly upgrade its usefulness (for either the same or a new use); or

(C) preserve it in a way that significantly improves its condition or enhances its historic value.

A substantial rehabilitation may vary in degree from gutting and extensive reconstruction of a building's major structural components to the cure of a substantial accumulation of major disrepairs. It may also include renovation, alteration, or remodelling for the conversion of a structurally sound building to a design and condition required for a new use. Cosmetic improvements alone, however, do not qualify as a substantial rehabilitation.

(iii) *Aggregation of rehabilitation.*—In the case where qualified rehabilitation expenditures are incurred with respect to a rehabilitation of a building by more than one person (*e.g.*, a lessor and a lessee, several lessees, or several condominium owners), the substantial rehabilitation requirement in this paragraph (b)(3) shall be applied by aggregating all the rehabilitation work done by such persons.

(iv) *Special rule for qualified rehabilitation expenditures treated as incurred by the taxpayer.*—In the case where qualified rehabilitation expenditures are treated as having been incurred by a taxpayer because of the application of paragraph (c)(3)(ii) of this section, the substantial rehabilitation test in paragraph (b)(3)(ii) of this section will be applied by aggregating the rehabilitation work done by the transferor and the transferee.

(v) *Examples.*—The provisions of this subparagraph (3) may be illustrated by the following examples:

Example (1). Taxpayer A is the owner of a 30-year-old building. The building is air conditioned by means of window air conditioning units. A replaces the window units with a central air conditioning system and no other rehabilitation is performed by A. The expenditures incurred by A did not materially extend the building's useful life, significantly upgrade its usefulness, or preserve it in a manner that significantly improves its condition or enhances its historic value. Although expenditures for replacement of window units with a central air conditioning system may constitute qualified expenditures as part of an overall rehabilitation, alone they do not qualify as a substantial rehabilitation and the building is not considered rehabilitated within the meaning of this subparagraph.

Example (2). Taxpayer B is the owner of a 10 story office building that is 35 years old. The building is in substantial disrepair and in order to modernize it as an office building B installs new plumbing, electrical wiring, and heating and air conditioning systems. In addition, the layout of each floor is changed by means of tearing down many existing interior walls and partitions and building new walls, partitions, and doors. Old plaster is removed from many walls and replaced by new wall covering. New windows and new flooring are installed throughout the building. The improvements made by B materially extend the useful life of the building and significantly upgrade its usefulness. The building is considered rehabilitated within the meaning of the facts and circumstances test in this subparagraph.

Example (3). Taxpayer C is the owner of a 100-year-old building that has substantial historic character, although the building is not a certified historic structure (as defined in section 191(d)(1) and the regulations thereunder). C uncovers and restores the original woodwork, wall coverings and molding throughout the building. The windows and doors are replaced with replicas of the original. The improvements made by C significantly preserve the building and significantly enhance its historic value. Thus, the building is considered rehabilitated within the meaning of this subparagraph.

(4) *Retention of 75 percent of external walls.*—(i) *In general.*—A building meets the requirements set forth in paragraph (b)(1)(iii) only if 75 percent or more of the existing external walls (as measured by the total area of the existing external walls) are retained in place as external walls in the rehabilitation process. For this purpose, the area of existing external walls includes the area of windows and doors.

(ii) *External wall.*—For purposes of this paragraph (b)(4), a wall includes both the supporting elements of the wall and the nonsupporting elements (*e.g.*, a curtain) of the wall. Except as otherwise provided in this paragraph (b)(4), the term "external wall" includes any wall that has one face exposed to the weather, earth, or an abutting wall erected on an adjacent property. An external wall also includes a shared wall (*i.e.*, a single wall shared with an adjacent building), generally referred to as a "party wall".

(iii) *Alternative rule.*—Notwithstanding the definition of external wall contained in paragraph (b)(4)(ii) of this section, in any case in which the building being rehabilitated would fail to meet the requirements of a qualified rehabilitation building if the definition of external wall in paragraph (b)(4)(ii) of this section were used, then the term "external wall" shall be defined as a wall, including its supporting elements, with one face exposed to the weather or earth, and a common wall shall not be treated as an external wall.

(iv) *Retained in place.*—An existing external wall is retained in place if the supporting elements of the wall are retained in place. An existing external wall is not retained in place if the supporting elements of the wall are replaced by new supporting elements. An external wall is retained in place, however, if the supporting elements are reinforced in the rehabilitation, provided that such supporting elements of the external wall are retained in place. An external wall is retained in place even though it is covered (e.g., with new siding). Moreover, the existing curtain may be replaced with a new curtain provided that the structural framework that provides for the support of the existing curtain is retained in place. An external wall is retained in place notwithstanding that the existing doors and windows in the wall are modified, eliminated, or replaced. A wall may be disassembled and reassembled so long as the same supporting elements are used when the wall is reassembled. Thus, for example, in the case of the brick wall, the wall is considered retained in place even though the original bricks are removed (for cleaning, *etc.*) and put back to form the wall.

(v) *Retention as an external wall.*—For purposes of meeting the 75 percent requirement of this subparagraph (4), an existing external wall must be retained in place as an external wall. If an addition is made that results in an existing external wall being converted into an internal wall, the wall is not retained in place as an external wall.

(vi) *Special rule.*—Solely for the purpose of meeting the 75 percent requirement of this subparagraph (4), the walls of an uncovered internal shaft designed solely to bring light or air into the center of a building which are completely surrounded by external walls of the building and which enclose space not designated for occupancy or other use by people (other than for maintenance or emergency) are not considered external walls. Thus, a wall of a light well in the center of an office building is not an external wall. However, walls surrounding an uncovered courtyard which is usable by the building's occupants, (*e.g.*, at lunch time) are external walls.

(vii) *Examples.*—The provisions of this subparagraph (4) may be illustrated by the following examples:

Example (1). Taxpayer A rehabilitated a building all of the walls of which consisted of wood siding attached to gypsum board sheets (which covered the studs). A covered the existing wood siding with aluminum siding in a part of a rehabilitation that otherwise qualified under this subparagraph. A satisfied the requirement that 75 percent of the existing external walls must be retained in place as external walls.

Example (2). Taxpayer B rehabilitated a building the external walls of which had a masonry curtain. The masonry on the wall face was replaced with a glass curtain. The steel beam and girders supporting the existing curtain were retained in place. B satisfied the requirement that 75 percent of the existing external walls must be retained in place as external walls.

Example (3). Taxpayer C rehabilitated a building which has two external walls measuring 75' × 20' and two other external walls measuring 100' × 20'. C tore down one of the larger walls, including its supporting elements, which accounted for more than 25% of the building's external walls and constructed a new wall. C has not satisfied the requirement that 75 percent of the existing external walls must be retained in place as external walls.

Example (4). The facts are the same as in example 3, except C does not tear down any walls, but makes an addition that results in one of the smaller walls becoming an internal wall. In addition, C enlarged 8 of the existing windows on the larger walls, increasing them from a size of 3' × 4' to 6' × 8'. Since the smaller wall accounts for less than 25 percent of the total wall area, C has satisfied the requirement that 75 percent of the existing external walls must be retained in place as external walls in the rehabilitation process. The enlargement of the existing windows on the larger wall does not change the result.

(5) *Major portion treated as separate building.*—(i) *In general.*— Where there is a separate rehabilitation of a major portion of a building, such major portion shall be treated as a separate building. Thus, such major portion may qualify as a qualified rehabilitated building if the requirements of this paragraph are met with respect to such major portion. Expenditures for property that services both a major portion of a building and another portion must be specifically allocated to each portion to the extent possible. If it is not possible to make such an allocation, the expenditures must be allocated to each portion on some reasonable basis. What constitutes a reasonable basis for an allocation depends on factors such as the type of improvement and how the improvement relates functionally to the building. For example, in the case of expenditures for an air conditioning system or a roof, a reasonable basis for allocating the expenditures would be the volume of the major portion served by the improvement relative to the volume of the other portion of the building served by the improvement.

(ii) *Major portion defined.*—Whether a part of a building constitutes a major portion of the building is determined upon the basis of all the facts and circumstances. A major portion must generally consist of clearly identifiable parts of a building (*e.g.*, a wing of a building or the first 5 stories of a 7 story building). The following factors shall be taken into account:

(A) Whether the portion comprises an entire leasehold interest or an entire ownership (*e.g.*, condominium) interest;

(B) Whether the portion (as measured by volume) is sufficiently large that it would be reasonable to treat it as a separate building; and

(C) Whether the portion is functionally different from other parts of the building.

(6) *Special rule for rehabilitation done in phases.*—If rehabilitation which is not continuous is determined under this subparagraph to be a single rehabilitation done in phases, the requirements of this paragraph (b) are to be applied with respect to the overall rehabilitation and not merely to a phase of the rehabilitation. In such case, a phase of a single overall rehabilitation will not be considered as "prior rehabilitation" for purposes of subparagraph (2)(i)(B) of this paragraph (b). Whether rehabilitation which is not continuous is a single rehabilitation that is done in phases is determined on the basis of all the facts and circumstances. Generally, however, to constitute a single rehabilitation that is done in phases, there must exist, prior to the time any rehabilitation work is commenced, a set of written plans describing generally all phases of the rehabilitation of the building and a reasonable expectation that all phases of the rehabilitation will be completed. Such written plans are not required to contain detailed working drawings or detailed specifications of the material to be used. In addition, the period between the time that physical work on the first phase of the overall rehabilitation begins and physical work on the last phase of the overall rehabilitation begins must be reasonable. In determining whether the rehabilitation is completed within a reasonable time, the fact that a building is occupied during the rehabilitation, the necessity of acquiring a lease (of additional portions of the building), and unforeseen delays shall be taken into account. Other factors that are relevant in determining whether rehabilitation is a single rehabilitation include the length of time between each phase of rehabilitation activities and the extent of rehabilitation activity in each phase.

(7) *Special rule for adjoining buildings that are combined.*—For purposes of this paragraph (b), if as part of a rehabilitation process two

or more adjoining buildings are combined and placed in service as a single building after the rehabilitation process, then all of the requirements of a qualified rehabilitated building in section 48(g)(1) and this section may be applied to the constituent adjoining buildings in the aggregate. Any party walls or abutting walls between the constituent buildings that would otherwise be treated as external walls (within the meaning of paragraph (b)(4)(ii) of this section) would not be treated as external walls of the building; the substantial rehabilitation test in paragraph (b)(3)(ii) of this section would be applied to the aggregate rehabilitation work with respect to all of the constituent buildings.

(c) *Definition of qualified rehabilitation expenditures.*—(1) *In general.*— Except as provided in subparagraph (2) of this paragraph, the term "qualified rehabilitation expenditure" means any amount—

(i) Properly chargeable to capital account (as described in subparagraph (2) of this paragraph),

(ii) Incurred after October 31, 1978, for depreciable or amortizable property (or additions or improvements to property) with a useful life of five years or more, and

(iii) Made in connection with the rehabilitation of a qualified rehabilitated building.

(2) *Chargeable to capital account.*—For purposes of paragraph (c)(1)(i) of this section, amounts paid or incurred are chargeable to capital account if under the taxpayer's method of accounting they are properly includible in computing basis under §1.46-3. Amounts treated as an expense and deducted in the year they are paid or incurred are not chargeable to capital account.

(3) *Incurred by the taxpayer.*—(i) *In general.*—Generally, to qualify for a credit under section 48(a)(1)(E), qualified rehabilitation expenditures must be incurred by the taxpayer after October 31, 1978. An expenditure is incurred for purposes of this paragraph on the date such expenditure would be considered incurred under the accrual method of accounting, regardless of the method of accounting used by the taxpayer with respect to other items of income and expense. If qualified rehabilitation expenditures are treated as having been incurred by a taxpayer under paragraph (c)(3)(ii) of this section, the taxpayer shall be treated as having incurred the expenditures on the date such expenditures were incurred by the transferor.

(ii) *Qualified rehabilitation expenditures treated as incurred by the taxpayer.*—(A) Where rehabilitation expenditures are incurred with respect to a building by a person (or persons) other than the taxpayer and the taxpayer acquires the building, or a portion of the building to which the expenditures are allocable, the taxpayer acquiring such property will be treated as having incurred the rehabilitation expenditures actually incurred by the transferor (or treated as incurred by the transferor under this paragraph (c)(3)(ii)) with respect to the acquired property, provided that—

(1) The building, or the portion of the building, acquired by the taxpayer was not used after the rehabilitation expenditures were incurred and prior to the date of acquisition by the taxpayer, and

(2) No credit with respect to such qualified rehabilitation expenditures is claimed by anyone other than the taxpayer acquiring the property.

For purposes of this paragraph (c)(3)(ii), use shall mean actual use, whether personal or business.

(B) The amount of qualified rehabilitation expenditures treated as incurred by the taxpayer under this paragraph is the lesser of—

(1) The qualified rehabilitation expenditures incurred before the date on which the taxpayer acquired the building (or portion thereof), to which the expenditures are attributable, or

(2) That portion of the taxpayer's cost or other basis for the property which is attributable to the qualified rehabilitation expenditures described in paragraph (c)(3)(B)(1) of this section incurred before such date.

For purposes of paragraph (c)(6)(ii) of this section, the amount of rehabilitation expenditures treated as incurred by the taxpayer under this paragraph (c)(3)(ii) shall not be considered to be part of the cost of acquiring a building or any interest in the building. The portion of the cost of acquiring a building (or an interest therein) which is not treated under this paragraph as qualified rehabilitation expenditures incurred by the taxpayer is not eligible for a rehabilitation investment credit. See paragraph (c)(6)(ii) of this section.

(C) See paragraph (b)(2)(iv) of this section for rules concerning the application of the substantial rehabilitation test to expenditures treated as incurred by the taxpayer.

(iii) *Examples.*—The provisions of this subparagraph may be illustrated by the following examples:

Example (1). In 1978, taxpayer A, a cash basis taxpayer, commenced the rehabilitation of a 30-year-old building. In June 1978, A

signed a contract with a plumbing contractor for replacement of the plumbing in the building. A agreed to pay the contractor as soon as the work was completed. The work was completed in September 1978, but A did not pay the amount due until November 1, 1978. The expenditures for the plumbing are not qualified rehabilitation expenditures because they were not incurred after October 31, 1978.

Example (2). B incurred qualified rehabilitation expenditures of $300,000 with respect to an existing building between January 1, 1980, and May 15, 1980, and then sold the building to C on June 1, 1980. If the property attributable to the expenditures was not placed in service by A during the period from January 1, 1980, to June 1, 1980, C will be treated as having incurred the expenditures.

(4) *Incurred for 5-year property.*—An expenditure is incurred for depreciable or amortizable property if the amount of the expenditure is added to the basis of property which is depreciable or amortizable under section 167. The determination of whether property has a useful life of five years or more is made by applying the principles of §1.46-3(e). In the case of expenditures for property made by a lessee, see sections 167 and 178 and the regulations thereunder for rules relating to whether improvements made to leased property are depreciable or amortizable.

(5) *Made in connection with the rehabilitation of a qualified rehabilitated building.*—Expenditures attributable to work done to facilities related to a building (*e.g.*, sidewalk, parking lot, landscaping) are not considered made in connection with a rehabilitation of a qualified rehabilitated building.

(6) *Certain expenditures excluded from qualified rehabilitation expenditures.*—The term "qualified rehabilitation expenditures" does not include the following expenditures:

(i) An expenditure for property which is "section 38 property" (determined without regard to section 48(a)(1)(E) and (1)).

(ii) The cost of acquiring a building or any interest in a building (including a leasehold interest) except as provided in paragraph (c)(3)(ii) of this section.

(iii) An expenditure attributable to enlargement of a building (as defined in paragraph (c)(7) of this section).

(iv) An expenditure attributable to rehabilitation of a certified historic structure (as defined in section 191(d)(1) and the regulations thereunder), unless the rehabilitation is a certified rehabilitation (as defined in paragraph (c)(8) of this section).

(7) *Expenditures for enlargement distinguished.*—(i) *In general.*— Expenditures attributable to an enlargement of an existing building do not qualify as qualified rehabilitated expenditures. A building is enlarged to the extent that the total volume of the building is increased. An increase in floor space resulting from interior remodelling is not considered an enlargement. Generally, the total volume of a building is equal to the product of the floor area of the base of the building and the height from the underside of the lowest floor (including the basement) to the average height of the finished roof (as it exists or existed). For this purpose, floor area is measured from the exterior faces of external walls (other than shared walls that are external walls) and from the centerline of shared walls that are external walls. In addition, a building is enlarged to the extent of any construction outside the exterior faces of the existing external wall of the building.

(ii) *Rehabilitation which includes enlargement.*—If expenditures for property only partially qualify as qualified rehabilitation expenditures because some of the expenditures are also attributable to the enlargement of the building, the expenditures must be apportioned between the original portion of the building and the enlargement. This allocation should be made using the principles contained in paragraph (b)(5)(i) of this section.

(8) *Certified rehabilitation.*—(i) *In general.*—For the purpose of this paragraph (c) of this section, the term "certified rehabilitation" means any rehabilitation of a certified historic building in a registered historic district which the Secretary of the Interior has certified to the Secretary as being consistent with the historic character of such building or the district in which such building is located.

(ii) *Revoked or invalidated certifications.*—If the Department of Interior revokes or otherwise invalidates a certification after it has been provided to a taxpayer, the decertified property will cease to be section 38 property described in section 48(a)(1)(E). Such cessation shall be effective as of the date the activity giving rise to the revocation or invalidation occurred. See section 47 for the rules applicable to property that ceases to be section 38 property.

(d) *Coordination with other provisions of the Code.*—(1) *Credit by lessees.*—(i) *Rehabilitation performed by lessor.*—A lessee may take the credit for rehabilitation performed by the lessor if the requirements of this section and section 48(d) are satisfied. For purposes of applying section 48(d), the fair market value of section 38 property described in section 48(a)(1)(E) shall be equal to that portion of the lessor's basis in a qualified rehabilitated building that is attributable to qualified rehabilitation expenditures.

(ii) *Rehabilitation performed by lessee.*—A lessee may take the credit for rehabilitation performed by the lessee, provided that the property (or improvements or additions to property) for which the rehabilitation expenditures are made is depreciable (or amortizable) by the lessee (see sections 167 and 178, and the regulations thereunder) and the requirements of this section are satisfied.

(2) *When credit may be claimed.*—The investment credit for qualified rehabilitation expenditures is allowed generally in the taxable year in which the property to which the rehabilitation expenditures is attributable is placed in service, provided the building is a qualified rehabilitated building for the taxable year. See §1.46-3(d). Under certain circumstances, however, the credit may be available prior to the date the property is placed in service. See section 46(d) and §1.46-5 (relating to qualified progress expenditures).

(3) *Recapture.*—If property described in section 48(a)(1)(E) is disposed of by the taxpayer, or otherwise ceases to be "section 38 property," recapture may result under section 47. Property will cease to be section 38 property, and therefore recapture may occur under section 47, in any case where the Department of Interior revokes or otherwise invalidates a certification of rehabilitation (see section 48(g)(2)(C)) after the property is placed in service because, for example, the taxpayer made modifications to the building inconsistent with Department of Interior standards.

(e) *Effective date.*—(1) *General rule.*—Except as provided in paragraph (e)(2) of this section, this §1.48-11 shall not apply to expenditures incurred after December 31, 1981.

(2) *Transitional rule.*—This §1.48-11 shall continue to apply to expenditures incurred after December 31, 1981, for the rehabilitation of a building if—

(i) The physical work on the rehabilitation began before January 1, 1982, and

(ii) The building does not meet the requirements of section 48(g)(1) of the Code as amended by the Economic Recovery Tax Act of 1981. [Reg. §1.48-11.]

☐ *[T.D. 8031, 6-27-85.]*

[Reg. §1.48-12]

§1.48-12. Qualified rehabilitated building; expenditures incurred after December 31, 1981.—(a) *General rule.*—(1) *In general.*—Under section 48(a)(1)(E), the portion of the basis of a qualified rehabilitated building that is attributable to qualified rehabilitation expenditures (within the meaning of section 48(g) and this section) is section 38 property. Property that is section 38 property by reason of section 48(a)(1)(E) is treated as new section 38 property and, therefore, is not subject to the used property limitation in section 48(c). Section 48(g)(1) and paragraph (b) of this section define the term "qualified rehabilitated building." Section 48(g)(2) and paragraph (c) of this section define the term "qualified rehabilitation expenditure." Section 48(g)(2)(B)(iv) and (3) and paragraph (d) of this section describe the rules applicable to "certified historic structures." Section 48(q) and paragraph (e) of this section provide rules concerning an adjustment to the basis of the rehabilitated building. Paragraph (f) of this section provides guidance for coordination of these provisions with other sections of the Code, including rules for determining when the rehabilitation credit may be claimed.

(2) *Effective dates and transition rules.*—(i) *In general.*—Except as otherwise provided in this paragraph (a)(2)(i), this section applies to expenditures incurred after December 31, 1981, in connection with the rehabilitation of a qualified rehabilitated building. (See paragraph (c)(3)(i) of this section for rules concerning the determination of when an expenditure is incurred.) If, however, physical work on the rehabilitation began before January 1, 1982, and the building does not meet the requirements of paragraph (b) of this section, the rules in §1.48-11 shall apply to the expenditures incurred after December 31, 1981, in connection with such rehabilitation. (See paragraph (b)(6)(i) of this section for rules determining when physical work on a rehabilitation begins.) The next to last sentence of paragraph (c)(8)(i) of this section applies to qualified rehabilitation expenditures that are qualified property under section 168(k)(2) or qualified New York Liberty Zone property under section 1400L(b) acquired by a taxpayer after September 10, 2001, and to qualified rehabilitation expenditures that are 50 percent bonus depreciation property under section 168(k)(4) acquired by a taxpayer after May 5, 2003. The last sentence of paragraph (c)(8)(i) of this section applies to qualified rehabilitation expenditures that are qualified property under section 168(k)(2) and

placed in service by a taxpayer during or after the taxpayer's taxable year that includes September 24, 2019. However, a taxpayer may choose to apply the last sentence in paragraph (c)(8)(i) of this section for qualified rehabilitation expenditures that are qualified property under section 168(k)(2) and acquired and placed in service after September 27, 2017, by the taxpayer during taxable years ending on or after September 28, 2017. A taxpayer may rely on the last sentence in paragraph (c)(8)(i) of this section in regulation project REG-104397-18 (2018-41 I.R.B. 558) (see §601.601(d)(2)(ii)(b) of this chapter) for qualified rehabilitation expenditures that are qualified property under section 168(k)(2) and acquired and placed in service after September 27, 2017, by the taxpayer during taxable years ending on or after September 28, 2017, and ending before the taxpayer's taxable year that includes September 24, 2019.

(ii) *Transition rules concerning ACRS lives.*—(A) For property placed in service before March 16, 1984, and any property subject to the exception set forth in section 111(g)(2) of Public Law 98-369 (Deficit Reduction Act of 1984), the references to "19 years" in paragraph (c)(4)(ii) and (7)(v) shall be replaced with "15 years" and the reference to "19-year real property" in paragraph (c)(4)(ii) shall be replaced with "15-year real property."

(B) Except as otherwise provided in paragraph (a)(2)(ii)(A) of this section, for property placed in service before May 9, 1985, and any property subject to the exception set forth in section 105(b)(2) and (5) of Public Law 99-121 (99 Stat. 501, 511), the references to "19 years" in paragraph (c)(4)(ii) and (7)(v) shall be replaced with "18 years" and the references to "19-year real property" in paragraph (c)(4)(ii) shall be replaced with "18-year real property."

(iii) *Transition rule concerning external wall definition.*—Notwithstanding the definition of external wall contained in paragraph (b)(3)(ii) of this section, in any case in which the written plans and specifications for a rehabilitation were substantially completed on or before June 28, 1985, and the building being rehabilitated would fail to meet the requirement of paragraph (b)(1)(iii) of this section if the definition of external wall in paragraph (b)(3)(ii) of this section were used, the term "external wall" shall be defined as a wall, including its supporting elements, with one face exposed to the weather or earth, and a common wall shall not be treated as an external wall. See paragraph (b)(2)(v) of this section for the definition of written plans and specifications.

(iv) *Transition rules concerning amendments made by the Tax Reform Act of 1986.*—(A) *In general.*—Except as otherwise provided in section 251(d) of the Tax Reform Act of 1986 and this paragraph (a)(2)(iv), the amendments made by section 251 of the Tax Reform Act of 1986 shall apply to property placed in service after December 31, 1986, in taxable years ending after that date, regardless of when the rehabilitation expenditures attributable to such property were incurred. If property attributable to qualified rehabilitation expenditures is incurred with respect to a rehabilitation to a building placed in service in segments or phases and some segments are placed in service before January 1, 1987, and the remaining segments are placed in service after December 31, 1986, the amendments under the Tax Reform Act would not apply to the property placed in service before January 1, 1987, but would apply to the segments placed in service after December 31, 1986, unless one of the transition rules in paragraph (a)(2)(iv)(B) or (C) of this section applies.

(B) *General transition rule.*—The amendments made by sections 251 and 201 of the Tax Reform Act of 1986 shall not apply to property that qualifies under section 251(d)(2), (3), or (4) of the Tax Reform Act of 1986. Property qualifies for the general transition rule in section 251(d)(2) of the Act if such property is placed in service before January 1, 1994, and if such property is placed in service as part of—

(1) A rehabilitation that was completed pursuant to a written contract that was binding on March 1, 1986, or (2) A rehabilitation incurred in connection with property (including any leasehold interest) acquired before March 2, 1986, or acquired on or after such date pursuant to a written contract that was binding on March 1, 1986, if—

(i) Parts 1 and 2 of the Historic Preservation Certificate Application were filed with the Department of Interior (or its designee) before March 2, 1986, or

(ii) The lesser of $1,000,000 or 5 percent of the cost of the rehabilitation is incurred before March 2, 1986, or is required to be incurred pursuant to a written contract which was binding on March 1, 1986.

(C) *Specific rehabilitations.*—See section 251(d)(3) and (4) of the Tax Reform Act of 1986 for additional rehabilitations that are exempted from the amendments made by sections 251 and 201 of the Tax Reform Act of 1986.

(b) *Definition of qualified rehabilitated building.*—(1) *In general.*—The term "qualified rehabilitated building" means any building and its structural components—

    (i) That has been substantially rehabilitated (within the meaning of paragraph (b)(2) of this section) for the taxable year,

    (ii) That was placed in service (within the meaning of § 1.46-3(d)) as a building by any person before the beginning of the rehabilitation, and

    (iii) That meets the applicable existing external wall retention test or the existing external wall and internal structural framework retention test in accordance with paragraph (b)(3) of this section.

The requirement in paragraph (b)(1)(iii) of this section does not apply to a certified historic structure. See paragraph (b)(4) and (5) of this section for additional requirements related to the definition of a qualified rehabilitated building.

    (2) *Substantially rehabilitated building.*—(i) *Substantial rehabilitation test.*—A building shall be treated as having been substantially rehabilitated for a taxable year only if the qualified rehabilitation expenditures (as defined in paragraph (c) of this section) incurred during any 24-month period selected by the taxpayer ending with or within the taxable year exceed the greater of—

        (A) the adjusted basis of the building (and its structural components), or

        (B) $5,000.

    (ii) *Date to determine adjusted basis of the building.*—(A) *In general.*—The adjusted basis of the building (and its structural components) shall be determined as of the beginning of the first day of the 24-month period selected by the taxpayer or the first day of the taxpayer's holding period of the building (within the meaning of section 1250(e)), whichever is later. For purposes of determining the holding period under section 1250(e), any reconstruction that is part of the rehabilitation shall be disregarded.

    (B) *Special rules.*—In the event that a building is not owned by the taxpayer, the adjusted basis of the building shall be determined as of the date that would have been used if the owner had been the taxpayer. The adjusted basis of a building that is being rehabilitated by a taxpayer other than the owner shall thus be determined as of the beginning of the first day of the 24-month period selected by the taxpayer or the first day of the owner's holding period, whichever is later. Therefore, if a building that is being rehabilitated by a lessee is sold subject to the lease prior to the date that the lessee has substantially rehabilitated the building, the lessee's adjusted basis is determined as of the beginning of the first day of the new lessor's holding period or the beginning of the first day of the 24-month period selected by the lessee (the taxpayer), whichever is later. If, therefore, the first day of the new lessor's holding period were later than the first day of the 24-month period selected by the lessee (the taxpayer), the lessee's adjusted basis for purposes of the substantial rehabilitation test would be the same as the adjusted basis of the new lessor as determined under paragraph (b)(2)(vii) of this section. If a building is sold after the date that a lessee has substantially rehabilitated the building with respect to the original lessor's adjusted basis, however, the lessee's basis may be determined as of the first day of the 24-month period selected by the lessee or the first day of the original lessor's holding period, whichever is later, and the transfer of the building will not affect the adjusted basis for purposes of the substantial rehabilitation test. The preceding sentence shall not apply, however, if the building is sold to the lessee or a related party within the meaning of section 267(b) or section 707(b)(1).

    (iii) *Adjusted basis of the building.*—(A) *In general.*—The term "adjusted basis of the building" means the aggregate adjusted basis (within the meaning of section 1011(a)) in the building (and its structural components) of all the parties who have an interest in the building.

    (B) *Special rules.*—In the case of a building that is leased to one or more tenants in whole or in part, the adjusted basis of the building is determined by adding the adjusted basis of the owner (lessor) in the building to the adjusted basis of the lessee (or lessees) in the leasehold and any leasehold improvements that are structural components of the building. Similarly, in the case of a building that is divided into condominium units, the adjusted basis of the building means the aggregate adjusted basis of all of the respective condominium owners (including the basis of any lessee in the leasehold and leasehold improvements) in the building (and its structural components). If the adjusted basis of a building would be determined in whole or in part by reference to the adjusted basis of a person or persons other than the taxpayer (*e.g.*, a rehabilitation by a lessee) and the taxpayer is unable to obtain the required information, the taxpayer must establish by clear and convincing evidence that the adjusted basis of such person or persons in the building on the date

specified in paragraph (b)(2)(ii) of this section is an amount that is less than the amount of qualified rehabilitation expenditures incurred by the taxpayer. If no such amount can be so established, the adjusted basis of the building will be deemed to be the fair market value of the building on the relevant date. For purposes of determining the adjusted basis of a building, the portion of the adjusted basis of a building that is allocable to an addition (within the meaning of paragraph (b)(4)(ii) of this section) to the building that does not meet the age requirement in paragraph (b)(4)(i) of this section shall be disregarded. (See paragraph (b)(2)(vii) of this section for the rule applicable to the determination of the adjusted basis of a building when qualified rehabilitation expenditures are treated as incurred by the taxpayer.)

    (iv) *Rehabilitation.*—Rehabilitation includes renovation, restoration, or reconstruction of a building, but does not include an enlargement (within the meaning of paragraph (c)(10) of this section) or new construction. The determination of whether expenditures are attributable to the rehabilitation of an existing building or to new construction shall be based upon all the facts and circumstances.

    (v) *Special rule for phased rehabilitation.*—In the case of any rehabilitation that may reasonably be expected to be completed in phases set forth in written architectural plans and specifications completed before the physical work on the rehabilitation begins, paragraphs (b)(2)(i), (ii), and (vii) of this section shall be applied by substituting "60-month period" for "24-month period." A rehabilitation may reasonably be expected to be completed in phases if it consists of two or more distinct stages of development. The determination of whether a rehabilitation consists of distinct stages and therefore may reasonably be expected to be completed in phases shall be made on the basis of all the relevant facts and circumstances in existence before physical work on the rehabilitation begins. For purposes of this paragraph and paragraph (a)(2)(iii) of this section, written plans that describe generally all phases of the rehabilitation process shall be treated as written architectural plans and specifications. Such written plans are not required to contain detailed working drawings or detailed specifications of the materials to be used. In addition, the taxpayer may include a description of work to be done by lessees in the written plans. For example, where the owner of a vacant four story building plans to rehabilitate two floors of the building and plans to require, as a condition of any lease, that tenants of the other two floors must rehabilitate those floors, the requirements of this paragraph (b)(2)(v) shall be met if the owner provides written plans for the rehabilitation work to be done by the owner and a description of the rehabilitation work that the tenants will be required to complete. The work required of the tenants may be described in the written plans in terms of minimum specifications (*e.g.*, as to lighting, wiring, materials, appearance) that must be met by such tenants. See paragraph (b)(6)(i) of this section for the definition of physical work on a rehabilitation.

    (vi) *Treatment of expenses incurred by persons who have an interest in the building.*—For purposes of the substantial rehabilitation test in paragraph (b)(2)(i) of this section, the taxpayer may take into account qualified rehabilitation expenditures incurred during the same rehabilitation process by any other person who has an interest in the building. Thus, for example, to determine whether a building has been substantially rehabilitated, a lessee may include the expenditures of the lessor and of other lessees; a condominium owner may include the expenditures incurred by other condominium owners; and an owner may include the expenditures of the lessees.

    (vii) *Special rules when qualified rehabilitation expenditures are treated as incurred by the taxpayer.*—In the case where qualified rehabilitation expenditures are treated as having been incurred by a taxpayer under paragraph (c)(3)(ii) of this section, the transferee shall be treated as having incurred the expenditures incurred by the transferor on the date that the transferor incurred the expenditures within the meaning of paragraph (c)(3)(i) of this section. For purposes of the substantial rehabilitation test in paragraph (b)(2)(i) of this section, the transferee's adjusted basis in the building shall be determined as of the beginning of the first day of a 24-month period, or the first day of the transferee's holding period, whichever is later, as provided in paragraph (b)(2)(ii) of this section. The transferee's basis as of the first day of the transferee's holding period for purposes of the substantial rehabilitation test in paragraph (b)(2)(i) of this section, however, shall be considered to be equal to the transferee's basis in the building on such date less—

    (A) The amount of any qualified rehabilitation expenditures incurred (or treated as having been incurred) by the transferor during the 24-month period that are treated as having been incurred by the transferee under paragraph (c)(3)(ii) of this section, and

    (B) The amount of qualified rehabilitation expenditures incurred before the transfer and during the 24-month period by any other person who has an interest in the building (*e.g.*, a lessee of the transferor).

The preceding sentence shall not apply, however, unless the transferee's basis in the building is determined with reference to (1) the transferee's cost of the building (including the rehabilitation expenditures), (2) the transferor's basis in the building (where such basis includes the amount of the expenditures), or (3) any other amount that includes the cost of the rehabilitation expenditures. In the event that the transferee's basis is determined with reference to an amount not described above (*e.g.*, transferee's basis in one building is determined with reference to the transferee's basis in another building under section 1031 (d)), the amount of the expenditures incurred by the transferor and treated as having been incurred by the transferee are not deducted from the transferee's basis for purposes of the substantial rehabilitation test. If a transferee's basis is determined under section 1014 or section 1022, any expenditures incurred by the decedent within the measuring period that are treated as having been incurred by the transferee under paragraph (c)(3)(ii) of this section shall decrease the transferee's basis for purposes of the substantial rehabilitation test.

(viii) *Statement of adjusted basis, measuring period, and qualified rehabilitation expenditures.*—In the case of any tax return filed after August 27, 1985, on which an investment tax credit for property, described in section 48 (a) (1) (E) is claimed, the taxpayer shall indicate by way of a marginal notation on, or a supplemental statement attached to, Form 3468—

(A) The beginning and ending dates for the measuring period selected by the taxpayer under section 48 (g) (1) (C) (i) and paragraph (b) (2) of this section,

(B) The adjusted basis of the building (within the meaning of paragraph (b) (2) (iii) or (vii) of this section) as of the beginning of such measuring period, and

(C) The amount of qualified rehabilitation expenditures incurred, and treated as incurred, respectively, during such measuring period.

Furthermore, for returns filed after August 27, 1985, if the adjusted basis of the building for purposes of the substantial rehabilitation test is determined in whole or in part by reference to the adjusted basis of a person, or persons, other than the taxpayer, (*e.g.*, a rehabilitation by a lessee), the taxpayer must attach to the Form 3468 filed with the tax return on which the credit is claimed a statement addressed to the District Director, signed by such third party, that states the first day of the third party's holding period and the amount of the adjusted basis of such third party in the building at the beginning of the measuring period or the first day of the holding period, whichever is later. If the taxpayer is unable to obtain the required information, that fact should be indicated and the taxpayer should state the manner in which the adjusted basis was determined and, if different, the fair market value of the building on the relevant date.

(ix) *Partnerships and S corporations.*—If a building is owned by a partnership (*i.e.*, the building is partnership property) or an S corporation, the substantial rehabilitation test shall be determined at the entity level. Thus, the entity shall compare the amount of qualified rehabilitation expenditures incurred during the measuring period against its basis in the building at the beginning of its holding period or the beginning of its measuring period, whichever is later. (See section 1223 (2) for rules concerning the determination of a partnership's holding period in the case of a contribution of property to the partnership meeting the requirements of section 721.) The adjusted basis of the building to a partnership shall be determined by taking into account any adjustments to the basis of the building made under section 743 and section 734. Any adjustments to the building's basis that are made under section 743 or section 734 after the beginning of the partnership's holding period, but before the end of the measuring period, shall be deemed for purposes of the substantial rehabilitation test to have been made on the first day of the partnership's holding period. However, in such case, the partnership's basis in the building shall be reduced by the amount of qualified rehabilitation expenditures incurred by the partnership. In the case of any tax return filed after January 9, 1989, on which a credit is claimed by a partner or a shareholder of an S corporation for rehabilitation expenditures incurred by a partnership or an S corporation, the partner or shareholder shall indicate on the Form 3468 on which the credit is claimed the name, address, and identification number of the partnership or S corporation that incurred the rehabilitation expenditures, and the partnership or S corporation shall, by way of a marginal notation on or a supplemental statement attached to the entity's return, provide the information required by paragraph (b)(2)(viii) of this section.

(x) *Examples.*—The following examples illustrate the application of the substantial rehabilitation test in this paragraph (b)(2):

Example (1). Assume that A, a calendar year taxpayer, purchases a building for $140,000 on January 1, 1982, incurs qualified

rehabilitation expenditures in the amount of $48,000 (at the rate of $4,000 per month) in 1982, $100,000 in 1983, and $20,000 (at the rate of $2,000 per month) in the first ten months of 1984, and places the rehabilitated building in service on October 31, 1984. Assume that A did not have written architectural plans and specifications describing a phased rehabilitation within the meaning of paragraph (b)(2)(v) of this section in existence prior to the beginning of physical work on the rehabilitation. For purposes of the substantial rehabilitation test in paragraph (b)(2) of this section, A may select any 24-consecutive-month measuring period that ends in 1984, the taxable year in which the rehabilitated building was placed in service. Assume that on A's 1984 return, A selects a measuring period beginning on February 1, 1982, and ending on January 31, 1984, and specifies that A's basis in the building (within the meaning of section 1011 (a)) was $144,000 on February 1, 1982 ($140,000 + $4,000). (The $4,000 of rehabilitation expenditures incurred during January 1982 are included in A's basis under section 1011 even though such property has not been placed in service.) The amount of qualified rehabilitation expenditures incurred during the measuring period was $146,000 ($44,000 from February 1 to December 31, 1982, plus $100,000 in 1983, plus $2,000 in January 1984). The building shall be treated as "substantially rehabilitated" within the meaning of this paragraph (b)(2) for A's 1984 taxable year because the $146,000 of expenditures incurred by A during the measuring period exceeded A's adjusted basis of $144,000 at the beginning of the period. If the other requirements of section 48 (g)(1) and this paragraph are met, the building is treated as a qualified rehabilitated building, and A can treat as qualified rehabilitation expenditures the amount of $168,000 (*i.e.*, $146,000 of expenditures incurred during the measuring period, $4,000 of expenditures incurred prior to the beginning of the measuring period as part of the rehabilitation process, and $18,000 of expenditures incurred after the measuring period during the taxable year within which the measuring period ends (See paragraph (c)(6) of this section.)). The result would generally be the same if the property attributable to the rehabilitation expenditures was placed in service as the expenditures were incurred, but A would have $148,000 of qualified rehabilitation expenditures for 1983 and $20,000 of qualified rehabilitation expenditures for 1984. (See paragraph (f)(2) of this section.)

Example (2). Assume the same facts as in example (1), except that additional rehabilitation expenditures are incurred after the portion of the basis of the building attributable to qualified rehabilitation expenditures was placed in service on October 31, 1984. Such expenditures are incurred through the end of 1984 and in 1985 when the portion of the basis attributable to the additional expenditures is placed in service. The fact that the building qualified as a substantially rehabilitated building for A's 1984 taxable year has no effect on whether the building is a qualified rehabilitated building for property placed in service in A's 1985 taxable year. In order to determine whether the building is a qualified rehabilitated building for A's 1985 taxable year, A must select a measuring period that ends in 1985 and compare the expenditures incurred within that period with the adjusted basis as of the beginning of the period. Solely for the purpose of determining whether the building was substantially rehabilitated for A's 1985 taxable year, expenditures incurred during 1983 and 1984, even though considered in determining whether the building was substantially rehabilitated in 1984, may also be used to determine whether the building was substantially rehabilitated for A's 1985 taxable year, provided the expenditures were incurred during any 24-month measuring period selected by A that ends in 1985.

Example (3). (i) Assume that B purchases a building for $100,000 on January 1, 1982, and leases the building to C who rehabilitates the building. Assume that C, a calendar year taxpayer, places the property with respect to which rehabilitation expenditures were made in service in 1982 and selects December 31, 1982, as the end of the measuring period for purposes of the substantial rehabilitation test. The beginning of the measuring period is January 2, 1982, the beginning of B's holding period under section 1250 (e), and the adjusted basis of the building is $100,000. Accordingly, if C incurred more than $100,000 of qualified rehabilitation expenditures during 1982, the building would be substantially rehabilitated within the meaning of paragraph (b)(2)(i) of this section.

(ii) Assume the facts of example (3)(i), except that after C begins physical work on the rehabilitation, but before C incurs $100,000 of expenditures, D acquires the building, subject to C's lease, from B for $200,000. D's holding period under section 1250 (e) begins on the day after D acquired the building, and C's adjusted basis for purposes of the substantial rehabilitation test is $200,000, less the amount of expenditures incurred by C before the transfer. (See paragraph (b)(2)(ii) and (vii) of this section.) Accordingly, if C incurred more than $200,000 (less the amount of expenditures incurred prior to the transfer) of qualified rehabilitation expenditures during 1982, the building would be substantially rehabilitated within the meaning of paragraph (b)(2) of this section. Under paragraph (b)(2)(ii)(B) of this section, however, C's adjusted basis for purposes of the substantial rehabilitation test would be $100,000 if C had substantially rehabilitated the building (*i.e.*, incurred more than $100,000 in rehabilitation expenditures) prior to B's sale to D.

Example (4). E owns a building with a basis of $10,000 and E incurs $5,000 of rehabilitation expenditures. Before completing the rehabilitation project, E sells the building to F for $30,000. Assume that F is treated under paragraph (c)(3)(ii) of this section as having incurred the $5,000 of rehabilitation expenditures actually incurred by E. Because F's basis in the building is determined under section 1011 with reference to F's $30,000 cost of the building (which includes the property attributable to E's rehabilitation expenditures), F's basis for purposes of the substantial rehabilitation test is $25,000 ($30,000 cost basis less $5,000 rehabilitation expenditures treated as if incurred by F). (See paragraph (b)(2)(vii) of this section.) F would thus be required to incur more than $20,000 of rehabilitation expenditures (in addition to the $5,000 incurred by E and treated as having been incurred by F) during a measuring period selected by F to satisfy the substantial rehabilitation test.

Example (5). G owns Building I with a basis of $10,000 and a fair market value of $20,000. H owns Building II with a basis of $5,000 and a fair market value of $20,000, with respect to which H has incurred $1,000 of rehabilitation expenditures. G and H exchange their buildings in a transaction that qualifies for nonrecognition treatment under section 1031. Assume that G is treated under paragraph (c)(3)(ii) of this section as having incurred $1,000 of rehabilitation expenditures. G's basis in Building II, computed under section 1031 (d), is $10,000. G's basis in Building II is not determined with reference to (A) the cost of Building II, (B) H's basis in Building II (including the cost of the rehabilitation expenditures) or (C) any other amount that includes the cost of the expenditures, but is instead determined with reference to G's basis in other property (Building I). Therefore, G's basis in Building II for purposes of the substantial rehabilitation test is not reduced by the $1,000 of rehabilitation expenditures treated as if incurred by G. (See paragraph (b)(2)(vii) of this section.) Accordingly, G's basis in Building II for purposes of the substantial rehabilitation test is $10,000, and G must incur additional rehabilitation expenditures in excess of $9,000 within a measuring period selected by G to satisfy the test.

(3) *Retention of existing external walls and internal structural framework.*—(i) *In general.*—(A) *Property placed in service after December 31, 1986.*—Except in the case of property that qualifies for the transition rules in paragraph (a)(2)(iv)(B) or (C) of this section, in the case of property that is placed in service after December 31, 1986, a building (other than a certified historic structure) meets the requirement in paragraph (b)(1)(iii) of this section only if in the rehabilitation process—

(1) 50 percent or more of the existing external walls of such building are retained in place as external walls;

(2) 75 percent or more of the existing external walls of such building are retained in place as internal or external walls, and

(3) 75 percent or more of the internal structural framework of such building (as defined in paragraph (b)(3)(iii) of this section) is retained in place.

(B) *Expenditures incurred before January 1, 1984, for property placed in service before January 1, 1987.*—With respect to rehabilitation expenditures incurred before January 1, 1984, for property that is either placed in service before January 1, 1987, or that qualifies for the transition rules in paragraph (a)(2)(iv)(B) or (C) of this section, a building meets the requirement in paragraph (b)(1)(iii) of this section only if 75 percent or more of the existing external walls of the building are retained in place as external walls in the rehabilitation process. If an addition to a building is not treated as part of a qualified rehabilitated building because it does not meet the 30-year requirement in paragraph (b)(4)(i)(B) of this section, then the external walls of such addition shall not be considered to be existing external walls of the building for purposes of section 48 (g)(1)(A)(iii) (as in effect prior to enactment of the Tax Reform Act of 1986), and this section.

(C) *Expenditures incurred after December 31, 1983, for property placed in service before January 1, 1987.*—With respect to expenditures incurred after December 31, 1983, for property that is either placed in service before January 1, 1987, or that qualifies for the transition rules in paragraph (a)(2)(iv)(B) or (C) of this section, the requirement of paragraph (b)(1)(iii) of this section is satisfied only if in the rehabilitation process either the existing external wall retention requirement in paragraph (b)(3)(i)(B) of this section is satisfied, or:

(1) 50 percent or more of the existing external walls of the building are retained in place as external walls,

(2) 75 percent or more of the existing external walls are retained in place as internal or external walls, and

(3) 75 percent or more of the existing internal structural framework of such building is retained in place.

(D) *Area of external walls and internal structural framework.*—The determinations required by paragraph (b)(3)(i)(A), (B), and (C) of this section shall be based upon the area of the external walls or internal structural framework that is retained in place compared to the total area of each prior to the rehabilitation. The area of the existing external walls and internal structural framework of a building shall be determined prior to any destruction, modification, or construction of external walls or internal structural framework that is undertaken by any party in anticipation of the rehabilitation.

(ii) *Definition of external wall.*—For purposes of this paragraph (b), a wall includes both the supporting elements of the wall and the nonsupporting elements (*e.g.*, a curtain, windows or doors) of the wall. Except as otherwise provided in this paragraph (b)(3), the term "external wall" includes any wall that has one face exposed to the weather, earth, or an abutting wall of an adjacent building. The term "external wall" also includes a shared wall (*i.e.*, a single wall shared with an adjacent building), generally referred to as a "party wall," provided that the shared wall has no windows or doors in any portion of the wall that does not have one face exposed to the weather, earth, or an abutting wall. In general, the term "external wall" includes only those external walls that form part of the outline or perimeter of the building or that surround an uncovered courtyard. Therefore, the walls of an uncovered internal shaft, designed solely to bring light or air into the center of a building, which are completely surrounded by external walls of the building and which enclose space not designated for occupancy or other use by people (other than for maintenance or emergency), are not considered external walls. Thus, for example, a wall of a light well in the center of a building is not an external wall. However, walls surrounding an outdoor space which is usable by people, such as a courtyard, are external walls.

(iii) *Definition of internal structural framework.*—For purposes of this section, the term "internal structural framework" includes all load-bearing internal walls and any other internal structural supports, including the columns, girders, beams, trusses, spandrels, and all other members that are essential to the stability of the building.

(iv) *Retained in place.*—An existing external wall is retained in place if the supporting elements of the wall are retained in place. An existing external wall is not retained in place if the supporting elements of the wall are replaced by new supporting elements. An external wall is retained in place, however, if the supporting elements are reinforced in the rehabilitation, provided that such supporting elements of the external wall are retained in place. An external wall also is retained in place if it is covered (*e.g.*, with new siding). Moreover, an external wall is retained in place if the existing curtain is replaced with a new curtain, provided that the structural framework that provides for the support of the existing curtain is retained in place. An external wall is retained in place notwithstanding that the existing doors and windows in the wall are modified, eliminated, or replaced. An external wall is retained in place if the wall is disassembled and reassembled, provided the same supporting elements are used when the wall is reassembled and the configuration of the external walls of the building after the rehabilitation is the same as it was before the rehabilitation process commenced. Thus, for example, a brick wall is considered retained in place even though the original bricks are removed (for cleaning, *etc.*) and replaced to form the wall. The principles of this paragraph (b)(3)(iv) shall also apply to determine whether internal structural framework of the building *is* retained in place.

(v) *Effect of additions.*—If an existing external wall is converted into an internal wall (*i.e.*, a wall that is not an external wall), the wall is not retained in place as an external wall for purposes of this section.

(vi) *Examples.*—The provisions of this paragraph (b)(3) may be illustrated by the following examples:

Example (1). Taxpayer A rehabilitated a building all of the walls of which consisted of wood siding attached to gypsum board sheets (which covered the supporting elements of the wall, *i.e.*, studs). A covered the existing wood siding with aluminum siding as part of a rehabilitation that otherwise qualified under this subparagraph. The addition of the aluminum siding does not affect the status of the existing external walls as external walls and they would be considered to have been retained in place.

Example (2). Taxpayer B rehabilitated a building, the external walls of which had a masonry curtain. The masonry on the wall face was replaced with a glass curtain. The steel beam and girders supporting the existing masonry curtain were retained in place. The walls of the building are considered to be retained in place as external walls, notwithstanding the replacement of the curtain.

Example (3). Taxpayer C rehabilitated a building that has two external walls measuring 75' × 20' and two other external walls measuring 100' × 20'. C demolished one of the larger walls, including its supporting elements and constructed a new wall. Because one of the larger walls represents more than 25 percent of the area of the building's external walls, C has not satisfied the requirement that 75 percent of the existing external walls must be retained in place as either internal or external walls. If however, C had not demolished the wall, but had converted it into an internal wall (*e.g.*, by building a new external wall), the building would satisfy the external wall requirements.

Example (4). The facts are the same as in example (3), except that C does not tear down any walls, but builds an addition that results in one of the smaller walls becoming an internal wall. In addition, C enlarged 8 of the existing windows on one of the larger walls, increasing them from a size of 3' × 4' to 6' × 8'. Since the smaller wall accounts for less than 25 percent of the total wall area, C has satisfied the requirement that 75 percent of the existing external walls must be retained in place as external walls in the rehabilitation process. The enlargement of the existing windows on the larger wall does not affect its status as an external wall.

Example (5). Taxpayer D rehabilitated a building that was in the center of a row of three buildings. The building being rehabilitated by D shares its side walls with the buildings on either side. The shared walls measure 100' × 20' and the rear and front walls measure 75' × 20'. As part of a rehabilitation, D tears down and replaces the front wall. Because the shared walls as well as the front and back walls are considered external walls and the front wall accounts for less than 25 percent of the total external wall area (including the shared walls), D has satisfied the requirement that 75 percent of the existing external walls must be retained in place as external walls in the rehabilitation process.

(4) *Age requirement.*—(i) *In general.*—(A) *Property placed in service after December 31, 1986.*—Except in the case of property that qualifies for the transition rules in paragraph (a)(2)(iv)(B) or (C) of this section, a building other than a certified historic structure shall not be considered a qualified rehabilitated building unless the building was first placed in service (within the meaning of §1.46-3(d)) before January 1, 1936.

(B) *Property placed in service before January 1, 1987, and property qualifying under a transition rule.*—In the case of property placed in service before January 1, 1987, and property that qualifies under the transition rules in paragraph (a)(2)(iv)(B) or (C) of this section, a building other than a certified historic structure is considered a qualified rehabilitated building only if a period of at least 30 years has elapsed between the date physical work on the rehabilitation of the building began and the date the building was first placed in service (within the meaning of §1.46-3(d)) as a building by any person.

(ii) *Additions.*—A building that was first placed in service before 1936 in the case described in paragraph (b)(4)(i)(A) of this section, or at least 30 years before physical work on the rehabilitation began in the case described in paragraph (b)(4)(i)(B) of this section, will not be disqualified because additions to such building have been added since 1936 in the case described in paragraph (b)(4)(i)(A) of this section, or are less than 30 years old in the case described in paragraph (b)(4)(i)(B). Such additions, however, shall not be treated as part of the qualified rehabilitated building. The term "addition" means any construction that resulted in any portion of an external wall becoming an internal wall, that resulted in an increase in the height of the building, or that increased the volume of the building.

(iii) *Vacant periods.*—The determinations required by paragraph (b)(4)(i) of this section include periods during which a building was vacant or devoted to a personal use and is computed without regard to the number of owners or the identity of owners during the period.

(5) *Location at which the rehabilitation occurs.*—A building, other than a certified historic structure, is not a qualified rehabilitated building unless it has been located where it is rehabilitated since before 1936 in the case described in paragraph (b)(4)(i)(A) of this section. Similarly, in the case described in paragraph (b)(4)(i)(B) of this section, a building, other than a certified historic structure, is not a qualified rehabilitated building unless it has been located where it is rehabilitated for the thirty-year period immediately preceding the date physical work on the rehabilitation began in the case of a "30-year building" or the forty-year period immediately preceding the date physical work on the rehabilitation began in the case of a "40-year building." (See §1.46-1 (q)(1)(iii) for the definitions of "30-year building" and "40-year building.")

(6) *Definition and special rule.*—(i) *Physical work on a rehabilitation.*—For purposes of this section, "physical work on a rehabilitation" begins when actual construction, or destruction in preparation for construction, begins. The term "physical work on a rehabilita-

tion," however, does not include preliminary activities such as planning, designing, securing financing, exploring, researching, developing plans and specifications, or stabilizing a building to prevent deterioration (*e.g.*, placing boards over broken windows).

(ii) *Special rule for adjoining buildings that are combined.*—For purposes of this paragraph (b), if as part of a rehabilitation process two or more adjoining buildings are combined and placed in service as a single building after the rehabilitation process, then, at the election of the taxpayer, all of the requirements for a qualified rehabilitated building in section 48(g)(1) and this section may be applied to the constituent adjoining buildings in the aggregate. For example, if such requirements are applied in the aggregate, any shared walls or abutting walls between the constituent buildings that would otherwise be treated as external walls (within the meaning of paragraph (b)(3) of this section) would not be treated as external walls of the building, and the substantial rehabilitation test in paragraph (b)(2) of this section would be applied to the aggregate expenditures with respect to all of the constituent buildings and to the aggregate adjusted basis of all of the constituent buildings. A taxpayer shall elect the special rule of this paragraph (b)(6)(ii) for adjoining buildings by indicating by way of a marginal notation on, or a supplemental statement attached to, the Form 3468 on which a credit is first claimed for qualified rehabilitation expenditures with respect to such buildings that such buildings are a single qualified rehabilitated building because of the application of the special rule in this paragraph (b)(6)(ii).

(c) *Definition of qualified rehabilitation expenditures.*—(1) *In general.*—Except as otherwise provided in paragraph (c)(7) of this section, the term "qualified rehabilitation expenditure" means any amount that is—

(i) Properly chargeable to capital account (as described in paragraph (c)(2) of this section),

(ii) Incurred by the taxpayer after December 31, 1981 (as described in paragraph (c)(3) of this section),

(iii) For property for which depreciation is allowable under section 168 and which is real property described in paragraph (c)(4) of this section, and

(iv) Made in connection with the rehabilitation of a qualified rehabilitated building (as described in paragraph (c)(5) of this section).

(2) *Chargeable to capital account.*—For purposes of paragraph (c)(1) of this section, amounts are chargeable to capital account if they are properly includible in computing basis of real property under §1.46-3(c). Amounts treated as an expense and deducted in the year they are paid or incurred or amounts that are otherwise not added to the basis of real property described in paragraph (c)(4) of this section do not qualify. For purposes of this paragraph (c), amounts incurred for architectural and engineering fees, site survey fees, legal expenses, insurance premiums, development fees, and other construction related costs, satisfy the requirement of this paragraph (c)(2) if they are added to the basis of real property that is described in paragraph (c)(4) of this section. Construction period interest and taxes that are amortized under section 189 (as in effect prior to its repeal by the Tax Reform Act of 1986) do not satisfy the requirement of this paragraph (c)(2). If, however, such interest and taxes are treated by the taxpayer as chargeable to capital account with respect to property described in paragraph (c)(4) of this section, they shall be treated in the same manner as other costs described in this paragraph (c)(2). Any construction period interest or taxes or other fees or costs incurred in connection with the acquisition of a building, any interest in a building, or land, are subject to paragraph (c)(7)(ii) of this section. See paragraph (c)(9) of this section for additional rules concerning interest.

(3) *Incurred by the taxpayer.*—(i) *In general.*—Qualified rehabilitation expenditures are incurred by the taxpayer for purposes of this section on the date such expenditures would be considered incurred under an accrual method of accounting, regardless of the method of accounting used by the taxpayer with respect to other items of income and expense. If qualified rehabilitation expenditures are treated as having been incurred by a taxpayer under paragraph (c)(3)(ii) of this section, the taxpayer shall be treated as having incurred the expenditures on the date such expenditures were incurred by the transferor.

(ii) *Qualified rehabilitation expenditures treated as incurred by the taxpayer.*—(A) Where rehabilitation expenditures are incurred with respect to a building by a person (or persons) other than the taxpayer and the taxpayer subsequently acquires the building, or a portion of the building to which some or all of the expenditures are allocable (*e.g.*, a condominium unit to which rehabilitation expenditures have been allocated), the taxpayer acquiring such property shall be treated as having incurred the rehabilitation expenditures actually incurred

Reg. §1.48-12(c)(3)(ii)(A)

by the transferor (or treated as incurred by the transferor under this paragraph (c)(3)(ii)) allocable to the acquired property, provided that—

(1) The building, or the portion of the building, acquired by the taxpayer was not used (or, if later, was not placed in service (as defined in paragraph (f)(2) of this section) after the rehabilitation expenditures were incurred and prior to the date of acquisition, and

(2) No credit with respect to such qualified rehabilitation expenditures is claimed by anyone other than the taxpayer acquiring the property.

For purposes of this paragraph (c)(3)(ii), use shall mean actual use, whether personal or business. In the case of a building that is divided into condominium units, expenditures attributable to the common elements shall be allocable to the individual condominium units in accordance with the principles of paragraph (c)(10)(ii) of this section. Furthermore, for purpose of this paragraph (c)(3)(ii), a condominium unit's share of the common elements shall not be considered to have been used (or placed in service) prior to the time that the particular condominium unit is used.

(B) The amount of rehabilitation expenditures described in paragraph (c)(3)(ii)(A) of this section treated as incurred by the taxpayer under this paragraph shall be the lesser of—

(1) The amount of rehabilitation expenditures incurred before the date on which the taxpayer acquired the building (or portion thereof) to which the rehabilitation expenditures are attributable, or

(2) The portion of the taxpayer's cost or other basis for the property that is properly allocable to the property resulting from the rehabilitation expenditures described in paragraph (c)(3)(ii)(B)(1) of this section.

(C) For purposes of this paragraph (c)(3)(ii), the amount of rehabilitation expenditures treated as incurred by the taxpayer under this paragraph (c) shall not be treated as costs for the acquisition of a building. The portion of the cost of acquiring a building (or an interest therein) that is not treated under this paragraph as qualified rehabilitation expenditures incurred by the taxpayer is not treated as section 38 property in the hands of the acquiring taxpayer. (See paragraph (c)(7)(ii) of this section.) (See paragraph (b)(2)(vii) for rules concerning the application of the substantial rehabilitation test when expenditures are treated as incurred by the taxpayer.)

(iii) *Examples.*—The provisions of this paragraph (c) may be illustrated by the following examples:

Example (1). In 1981, A, a taxpayer using the cash receipts and disbursements method of accounting, commenced the rehabilitation of a 30-year old building. In June 1981, A signed a contract with a plumbing contractor for replacement of the plumbing in the building. A agreed to pay the contractor as soon as the work was completed. The work was completed in December 1981, but A did not pay the amount due until January 15, 1982. The expenditures for the plumbing are not qualified rehabilitation expenditures (within the meaning of this paragraph (c)) because they were not incurred under an accrual method of accounting after December 31, 1981.

Example (2). B incurred qualified rehabilitation expenditures of $300,000 with respect to an existing building between January 1, 1982, and May 15, 1982, and then sold the building to C on June 1, 1982. The portion of the building to which the expenditures were allocable was not used by B or any other person during the period from January 1, 1982, to June 1, 1982, and neither B nor any other person claimed the credit. Consequently, C will be treated as having incurred the expenditures on the dates that B incurred the expenditures.

Example (3). D, a taxpayer using the cash receipts and disbursements method of accounting, begins the rehabilitation of a building on January 11, 1982. Prior to May 1, 1982, D makes rehabilitation expenditures of $16,000. On May 3, 1982, D sells the building, the land, and the property attributable to the rehabilitation expenditures to E for $35,000. The purchase price is properly allocable as follows:

land	$5,000
existing building	11,000
property attributable to rehabilitation expenditures	19,000
total purchase price	$35,000

The property attributable to the rehabilitation expenditures is placed in service by E on September 5, 1982. E may treat a portion of the $35,000 purchase price as rehabilitation expenditures paid or incurred by him. Since the rehabilitation expenditures paid by D ($16,000) are less than the portion of the purchase price properly allocable to property attributable to these expenditures ($19,000), E may treat only $16,000 as rehabilitation expenditures paid or incurred by him. The excess of the purchase price allocable to rehabilitation expenditures ($19,000) over the rehabilitation expenditures paid by D ($16,000), or $3,000, is treated as the cost of acquiring an interest in the building and is not a qualified rehabilitation expenditure treated as incurred by E.

Example (4). The facts are the same as in example (3), except that the purchase price properly allocable to the property attributable to rehabilitation expenditures is $15,000. Under these circumstances, E may treat only $15,000 of D's $16,000 expenditures as rehabilitation expenditures paid by D. The excess of the rehabilitation expenditures paid by D ($16,000) over the purchase price allocable to rehabilitation expenditures ($15,000), or $1,000, is treated as the cost of acquiring an interest in the building and is not a qualified rehabilitation expenditure treated as incurred by E.

(4) *Incurred for depreciable real property.*—(i) *Property placed in service after December 31, 1986.*—Except as otherwise provided in paragraph (c)(4)(ii) of this section (relating to certain property that qualifies under a transition rule), in the case of property placed in service after December 31, 1986, an expenditure is incurred for depreciable real property for purposes of paragraph (c)(1)(iii) of this section, only if it is added to the depreciable basis of depreciable property which is—

(A) Nonresidential real property,

(B) Residential rental property,

(C) Real property which has a class life of more than 12.5 years, or

(D) An addition or improvement to property described in paragraph (c)(4)(i)(A), (B), or (C) of this section.

For purposes of this paragraph (c)(4)(i), the terms "nonresidential real property", "residential rental property", and "class life" have the respective meanings given to such terms by section 168 and the regulations thereunder.

(ii) *Property placed in service before January 1, 1987, and property that qualifies under a transition rule.*—In the case of property placed in service before January 1, 1987, and property placed in service after December 31, 1986, that qualifies for the transition rules in paragraph (a)(2)(iv)(B) or (C) of this section, an expenditure attributable to such property shall be a qualified rehabilitation expenditure only if such expenditure is incurred for property that is real property (or additions or improvements to real property) with a recovery period (within the meaning of section 168 as in effect prior to its amendment by the Tax Reform Act of 1986) of 19 years (15 years for low-income housing) and if the other requirements of this paragraph (c) are met. For purposes of this section, an expenditure is incurred for recovery property having a recovery period of 19 years only if the amount of the expenditure is added to the basis of property which is 19-year real property or 15-year real property in the case of low-income housing. For purposes of this section, the term "low-income housing" has the meaning given such term by section 168 (c)(2)(F) (as in effect prior to the amendments made by the Tax Reform Act of 1986).

(5) *Made in connection with the rehabilitation of a qualified rehabilitated building.*—In order for an expenditure to be a qualified rehabilitation expenditure, such expenditure must be incurred in connection with a rehabilitation (as defined in paragraph (b)(2)(iv) of this section) of a qualified rehabilitated building. Expenditures attributable to work done to facilities related to a building (*e.g.*, sidewalk, parking lot, landscaping) are not considered made in connection with the rehabilitation of a qualified rehabilitated building.

(6) *When expenditures may be incurred.*—An expenditure is a qualified rehabilitation expenditure only if the building with respect to which the expenditures are incurred is substantially rehabilitated (within the meaning of paragraph (b)(2) of this section) for the taxable year in which the property attributable to the expenditures is placed in service (*i.e.*, the building is substantially rehabilitated during a measuring period ending with or within the taxable year in which a credit is claimed). (See paragraph (f)(2) of this section for rules relating to when property is placed in service.) Once the substantial rehabilitation test is met for a taxable year, the amount of qualified rehabilitation expenditures upon which a credit can be claimed for the taxable year is limited to expenditures incurred:

(i) Before the beginning of a measuring period during which the building was substantially rehabilitated that ends with or within the taxable year, provided that the expenditures were incurred in connection with the rehabilitation process that resulted in the substantial rehabilitation of the building;

(ii) Within a measuring period during which the building was substantially rehabilitated that ends with or within the taxable year, and

(iii) After the end of a measuring period during which the building was substantially rehabilitated but prior to the end of the taxable year with or within which the measuring period ends.

(7) *Certain expenditures excluded from qualified rehabilitation expenditures.*—The term "qualified rehabilitation expenditures" does not include the following expenditures:

(i) Except as otherwise provided in paragraph (c)(8) of this section, any expenditure with respect to which the taxpayer does not use the straight line method over a recovery period determined under section 168 (c) and (g).

(ii) The cost of acquiring a building, any interest in a building (including a leasehold interest), or land, except as provided in paragraph (c)(3)(ii) of this section.

(iii) Any expenditure attributable to an enlargement of a building (within the meaning of paragraph (c)(10) of this section).

(iv) Any expenditure attributable to the rehabilitation of a certified historic structure or a building located in a registered historic district, unless the rehabilitation is a certified rehabilitation. (See paragraph (d) of this section which contains definitions and special rules applicable to rehabilitations of certified historic structures and buildings located in registered historic districts.)

(v) Any expenditure of a lessee of a building or a portion of a building, if, on the date the rehabilitation is completed with respect to property placed in service by such lessee, the remaining term of the lease (determined without regard to any renewal period) is less than the recovery period determined under section 168(c) (or 19 years in the case of property placed in service before January 1, 1987, and property placed in service that qualifies under the transition rules in paragraph (a)(2)(iv)(B) or (C) of this section).

(vi) Any expenditure allocable to that portion of a building which is (or may reasonably be expected to be) tax-exempt use property (within the meaning of section 168 and the regulations thereunder), except that the exclusion in this paragraph (c)(7)(vi) shall not apply for purposes of determining whether the building is a substantially rehabilitated building under paragraph (b)(2) of this section.

(8) *Requirement to use straight line depreciation.*—(i) *Property placed in service after December 31, 1986.*—The requirement in section 48(g)(2)(B)(i) and paragraph (c)(7)(i) of this section to use straight line cost recovery does not apply to any expenditure to the extent that the alternative depreciation system of 168(g) applies to such expenditure by reason of section 168(g)(1)(B) or (C). In addition, the requirement in section 48(g)(2)(B)(i) and paragraph (c)(7)(i) of this section applies only to the depreciation of the portion of the basis of a qualified rehabilitated building that is attributable to qualified rehabilitation expenditures. However, see § 1.168(k)-1(f)(10) if the qualified rehabilitation expenditures are qualified property or 50-percent bonus depreciation property under section 168(k) and see § 1.1400L(b)-1(f)(9) if the qualified rehabilitation expenditures are qualified New York Liberty Zone property under section 1400L(b). Further, see § 1.168(k)-2(g)(9) if the qualified rehabilitation expenditures are qualified property under section 168(k), as amended by the Tax Cuts and Jobs Act, Public Law 115-97 (131 Stat. 2054 (December 22, 2017)).

(ii) *Property placed in service before January 1, 1987, and property placed in service after December 31, 1986, that qualifies for a transition rule.*—In the case of expenditures attributable to property placed in service before January 1, 1987, and property that qualifies for the transition rules in paragraph (a)(2)(iv)(B) or (C) of this section, the term "qualified rehabilitation expenditure" does not include an expenditure with respect to which an election was not made under section 168(b)(3) as in effect prior to its amendment by the Tax Reform Act of 1986, to use the straight line method of depreciation. In such case, the requirement that an election be made to use straight line cost recovery applies only to the cost recovery of the portion of the basis of a qualified rehabilitated building that is attributable to qualified rehabilitation expenditures. See section 168(f)(1), as in effect prior to its amendment by the Tax Reform Act of 1986, for rules relating to the use of different methods of cost recovery for different components of a building. In addition, such requirement shall not apply to any expenditure to the extent that section 168(f)(12) or (j), as in effect prior to the amendments made by the Tax Reform Act of 1986, applied to such expenditure.

(9) *Cost of acquisition.*—For purposes of paragraph (c)(7)(ii) of this section, cost of acquisition includes any interest incurred on indebtedness the proceeds of which are attributable to the acquisition of a building, an interest in a building, or land upon which a building exists. Interest incurred on a construction loan the proceeds of which are used for qualified rehabilitation expenditures, however, is not treated as a cost of acquisition.

(10) *Enlargement defined.*—(i) *In general.*—A building is enlarged to the extent that the total volume of the building is increased. An increase in floor space resulting from interior remodelling is not considered an enlargement. The total volume of a building is generally equal to the product of the floor area of the base of the building and the height from the underside of the lowest floor (including the basement) to the average height of the finished roof (as it exists or existed). For this purpose, floor area is measured from the exterior faces of external walls (other than shared walls that are external walls) and from the centerline of shared walls that are external walls.

(ii) *Rehabilitation that includes enlargement.*—If expenditures for property only partially qualify as qualified rehabilitation expenditures because some of the expenditures are attributable to the enlargement of the building, the expenditures must be apportioned between the original portion of the building and the enlargement. The expenditures must be specifically allocated between the original portion of the building and the enlargement to the extent possible. If it is not possible to make a specific allocation of the expenditures, the expenditures must be allocated to each portion on some reasonable basis. The determination of a reasonable basis for an allocation depends on factors such as the type of improvement and how the improvement relates functionally to the building. For example, in the case of expenditures for an air-conditioning system or a roof, a reasonable basis for allocating the expenditures among the two portions generally would be the volume of the building, excluding the enlargement, served by the air-conditioning system or the roof relative to the volume of the enlargement served by the improvement.

(d) *Rules applicable to rehabilitations of certified historic structures.*—(1) *Definition of certified historic structure.*—The term "certified historic structure" means any building (and its structural components) that is—

(i) Listed in the National Register of Historic Places ("National Register"); or

(ii) Located in a registered historic district and certified by the Secretary of the Interior to the Internal Revenue Service as being of historic significance to the district.

For purposes of this section, a building shall be considered to be a certified historic structure at the time it is placed in service if the taxpayer reasonably believes on that date the building will be determined to be a certified historic structure and has requested on or before that date a determination from the Department of Interior that such building is a certified historic structure within the meaning of this paragraph (d)(1)(i) or (ii) and the Department of Interior later determines that the building is a certified historic structure.

(2) *Definition of registered historic district.*—The term "registered historic district" means any district that is—

(i) Listed in the National Register, or

(ii)(A) Designated under a statute of the appropriate State or local government that has been certified by the Secretary of the Interior to the Internal Revenue Service as containing criteria that will substantially achieve the purpose of preserving and rehabilitating buildings of historic significance to the district, and (B) certified by the Secretary of the Interior as meeting substantially all of the requirements for the listing of districts in the National Register.

(3) *Definition of certified rehabilitation.*—The term "certified rehabilitation" means any rehabilitation of a certified historic structure that the Secretary of the Interior has certified to the Internal Revenue Service as being consistent with the historic character of the building and, where applicable, the district in which such building is located. The determination of the scope of a rehabilitation shall be made on the basis of all the facts and circumstances surrounding the rehabilitation and shall not be made solely on the basis of ownership. The Secretary of the Interior shall take all of the rehabilitation work performed as part of a single rehabilitation, including any post-certification work, into account in determining whether the rehabilitation complies with the Department of Interior standards for rehabilitation and whether the certification should be granted, revoked, or otherwise invalidated.

(4) *Revoked or invalidated certification.*—If the Department of Interior revokes or otherwise invalidates a certification after it has been issued to a taxpayer, the basis attributable to rehabilitation of the decertified property shall cease to be section 38 property described in section 48(a)(1)(E). Such cessation shall be effective as of the date the activity giving rise to the revocation or invalidation commenced. See section 47 for the rules applicable to property that ceases to be section 38 property.

(5) *Special rule for certain buildings located in registered historic districts.*—The exclusion in paragraph (c)(7)(iv) of this section does not apply to a building in a registered historic district if—

(i) Such building was not a certified historic structure during the rehabilitation process; and

(ii) The Secretary of the Interior certified to the Internal Revenue Service that such building was not of historic significance to the district.

In general, the certification referred to in paragraph (d)(5)(ii) of this section must be requested by the taxpayer prior to the time that physical work on the rehabilitation began. If, however, the certification referred to in paragraph (d)(5)(ii) of this section is requested by the taxpayer after physical work on the rehabilitation of the building has begun, the taxpayer must certify to the Internal Revenue Service that, prior to the date that physical work on the rehabilitation began, the taxpayer in good faith was not aware of the requirement of paragraph (d)(5)(ii) of this section. The certification referred to in the previous sentence must be attached to the Form 3468 filed with the tax return for the year in which the credit is claimed.

(6) *Special rule for certain rehabilitations begun before an area is designated as a registered historic district.*—In general, the exclusion from the definition of qualified rehabilitation expenditure in paragraph (c)(7)(iv) of this section applies to any rehabilitation expenditures that are incurred after a building becomes a certified historic structure within the meaning of section 48(g)(3)(A) and paragraph (d)(1) of this section or the area in which a building is located becomes a registered historic district within the meaning of section 48(g)(3)(B) and paragraph (d)(2) of this section. Rehabilitation expenditures incurred prior to such date, however, are not disqualified. In addition, rehabilitation expenditures made after the date the area in which a building is located becomes a registered historic district shall not be disqualified under paragraph (c)(7)(iv) of this section in any case in which physical work on the rehabilitation of a building begins prior to the date the taxpayer knows or has reason to know of an intention to nominate the area in which such building is located as a registered historic district. For purposes of this paragraph (d)(6), the taxpayer knows or has reason to know of such an intention if there is (A) a communication (written or oral) to the owner of any building within the district from the Department of the Interior, or any agency or instrumentality of the appropriate state or local government (or a designee of such agency or instrumentality) that the district in which the building is located is being considered for designation as a registered historic district, (B) a legal notice of such consideration published in a newspaper, or (C) a public meeting held to discuss such consideration. In order to take advantage of the special rule of this paragraph (d)(6), the taxpayer must attach to the Form 3468 filed for the taxable year in which the credit is claimed a statement that the taxpayer in good faith did not know, or have reason to know, of an intention to nominate the area in which the building is located as a registered historic district.

(7) *Notice of certification.*—(i) *In general.*—Except as otherwise provided in paragraph (d)(7)(ii) of this section, a taxpayer claiming the credit for rehabilitation of a certified historic structure (within the meaning of section 48(g)(3) and paragraph (d)(1) of this section) must attach to the Form 3468 filed with the tax return for the taxable year in which the credit is claimed a copy of the final certification of completed work by the Secretary of the Interior, and for returns filed after January 9, 1989, evidence that the building is a certified historic structure.

(ii) *Late certification.*—If the final certification of completed work has not been issued by the Secretary of the Interior at the time the tax return is filed for a year in which the credit is claimed, a copy of the first page of the Historic Preservation Certification Application—Part 2— Description of Rehabilitation (NPS Form 10-168a), with an indication that it has been received by the Department of the Interior or its designate, together with proof that the building is a certified historic structure (or that such status has been requested), must be attached to the Form 3468 filed with the return. A notice from the Department of the Interior or the State Historic Preservation Officer, stating that the nomination or application has been received, or a date-stamped nomination or application shall be sufficient indication that the nomination or application has been received. The building need not be either listed in the National Register or be determined to be of historic significance to a registered historic district at the time the return is filed for the year in which the credit is claimed. (See paragraph (d)(1) of this section.) The taxpayer must submit a copy of the final certification as an attachment to Form 3468 with the first income tax return filed after the receipt by the taxpayer of the certification. If the final certification is denied by the Department of Interior, the credit will be disallowed for any taxable year in which it was claimed. If the taxpayer fails to receive final certification of completed work prior to the date that is 30 months after the date that the taxpayer filed the tax return on which the credit was claimed, the taxpayer must submit a written statement to the District Director stating such fact prior to the last day of the 30th month, and the taxpayer shall be requested to consent to an agreement under section 6501(c)(4) extending the period of assessment for any tax relating to the time for which the credit was claimed. The procedure

permitted by the preceding sentence shall be used whenever the entire rehabilitation project is not fully completed by the date that is 30 months after the taxpayer filed the tax return upon which the credit was claimed (*e.g.* a phased rehabilitation) and the Secretary of the Interior has thus not yet certified the rehabilitation.

(iii) *Effective dates.*—Paragraph (d)(7)(i) of this section applies to returns for taxable years beginning before January 1, 2002. The requirement in the fourth sentence of paragraph (d)(7)(ii) of this section applies only if the first income tax return filed after receipt by the taxpayer of the certification is for a taxable year beginning before January 1, 2002. For rules applicable to returns for taxable years beginning after December 31, 2001, see paragraph (d)(7)(iv) of this section.

(iv) *Returns for taxable years beginning after December 31, 2001.*—(A) *In general.*—Except as otherwise provided in paragraph (d)(7)(ii) of this section and this paragraph (d)(7)(iv), a taxpayer claiming the credit for rehabilitation of a certified historic structure (within the meaning of section 47(c)(3) and paragraph (d)(1) of this section) for a taxable year beginning after December 31, 2001, must provide with the return for the taxable year in which the credit is claimed, the NPS project number assigned by, and the date of the final certification of completed work received from, the Secretary of the Interior. If a credit (including a credit for a taxable year beginning before January 1, 2002) is claimed under the late certification procedures of paragraph (d)(7)(ii) of this section and the first income tax return filed by the taxpayer after receipt of the certification is for a taxable year beginning after December 31, 2001, the taxpayer must provide the NPS project number assigned by, and the date of the final certification of completed work received from, the Secretary of the Interior with that return.

(B) *Reporting and recordkeeping requirements.*—The information required under paragraph (d)(7)(iv)(A) of this section must be provided on Form 3468 (or its successor) filed with the taxpayer's return. In addition, the taxpayer must retain a copy of the final certification of completed work for as long as its contents may become material in the administration of any internal revenue law.

(C) *Passthrough entities.*—In the case of a credit for qualified rehabilitation expenditures of a partnership, S corporation, estate, or trust, the requirements of this paragraph (d)(7)(iv) apply only to the entity. Each partner, shareholder or beneficiary claiming a credit for such qualified rehabilitation expenditures from a passthrough entity must, however, provide the employer identification number of the entity on Form 3468 (or its successor).

(e) *Adjustment to basis.*—(1) *General rule.*—Except as otherwise provided by this paragraph (e), if a credit is allowed with respect to property attributable to qualified rehabilitation expenditures incurred in connection with the rehabilitation of a qualified rehabilitated building, the increase in the basis of the rehabilitated property that would otherwise result from the qualified rehabilitation expenditures must be reduced by the amount of the credit allowed. See section 48(q) and the regulations thereunder for other rules concerning adjustments to basis in the case of section 38 property.

(2) *Special rule for certain property relating to certified historic structures.*—If a rehabilitation investment credit is allowed with respect to property that is placed in service before January 1, 1987, or property that qualifies for the transition rules in paragraph (a)(2)(iv)(B) or (C) of this section, and such property is attributable to qualified rehabilitation expenditures incurred in connection with the rehabilitation of a certified historic structure, the increase in the basis of the rehabilitated property that would otherwise result from the qualified rehabilitation expenditures must be reduced by one-half of the amount of the credit allowed.

(3) *Recapture of rehabilitation investment credit.*—If during any taxable year there is a recapture amount determined with respect to any credit that resulted in a basis adjustment under paragraph (e)(1) or (2) of this section, the basis of such building (immediately before the event resulting in such recapture) shall be increased by an amount equal to such recapture amount. For purposes of the preceding sentence, the term "recapture amount" means any increase in tax (or adjustment in carrybacks or carryovers) determined under section 47(a)(5).

(f) *Coordination with other provisions of the Code.*—(1) *Credit claimed by lessee for rehabilitation performed by lessor.*—A lessee may take the credit for rehabilitation performed by the lessor if the requirements of this section and section 48(d) are satisfied. For purposes of applying section 48(d), the fair market value of section 38 property described in section 48(a)(1)(E) shall be limited to that portion of the lessor's basis in the qualified rehabilitated building that is attributable to qualified rehabilitation expenditures. In the case of a portion of a building that is divided into more than one leasehold interest, the qualified rehabilitation expenditures attributable to the common elements shall be allocated to the individual leasehold interests in accordance with the principles of paragraph (c)(10)(ii) of this section. Furthermore, a leasehold interest's share of the common elements shall not be considered to have been placed in service prior to the time that the particular leasehold interest is placed in service.

(2) *When the credit may be claimed.*—(i) *In general.*—The investment credit for qualified rehabilitation expenditures is generally allowed in the taxable year in which the property attributable to the expenditure is placed in service, provided the building is a qualified rehabilitated building for the taxable year. See paragraph (b) of this section and section 46(c) and §1.46-3(d). Under certain circumstances, however, the credit may be available prior to the date the property is placed in service. See section 46(d) and §1.46-5 (relating to qualified progress expenditures). Solely for purposes of section 46(c), property attributable to qualified rehabilitation expenditures will not be treated as placed in service until the building with respect to which the expenditures are made meets the definition of a qualified rehabilitated building (as defined in section 48(g)(1) and paragraph (b) of this section) for the taxable year. Accordingly, in the first taxable year for which the building becomes a qualified rehabilitated building, the property described in section 48(a)(1)(E) attributable to expenditures described in paragraph (c) of this section shall be considered to be placed in service, if such property was considered placed in service under section 46(c) and the regulations thereunder without regard to this paragraph (f)(2)(i) in that taxable year or a prior taxable year. For purposes of the preceding sentence, the requirement in section 48(g)(1)(A)(iii) and paragraph (b)(3) of this section relating to the definition of a qualified rehabilitated building shall be deemed to be met if the taxpayer reasonably expects that no rehabilitation work undertaken during the remainder of the rehabilitation process will result in a failure to satisfy the requirements of paragraph (b)(3) of this section. If the requirements of paragraph (b)(3) are not satisfied, however, the credit shall be disallowed for the taxable year in which it was claimed. If a taxpayer fails to complete physical work on the rehabilitation prior to the date that is 30 months after the date that the taxpayer filed a tax return on which the credit is claimed, the taxpayer must submit a written statement to the District Director stating such fact prior to the last day of the 30th month, and shall be requested to consent to an agreement under section 6501(c)(4) extending the period of assessment for any tax relating to the item for which the credit was claimed.

(ii) *Section 38 property described in section 48(a)(1)(E).*—In the case of section 38 property described in section 48(a)(1)(E), the section 38 property is not the building. Instead, the section 38 property is the portion of the basis of the building that is attributable to qualified rehabilitation expenditures. Therefore, for example, for purposes of the determination of when such section 38 property is placed in service, a determination must be made regarding when property attributable to the a portion of the basis of the building attributable to qualified rehabilitation expenditures is placed in service. The issue of when the building is placed in service is thus not relevant. In fact, under this test, the building itself may never have been taken out of service during the rehabilitation process. If the building is rehabilitated over several years in stages (*e.g.*, by floors), section 38 property attributable to qualified rehabilitation expenditures to a qualified rehabilitated building placed in service in each taxable year shall, generally, be treated as a separate item of section 38 property.

(iii) *Example.*—The application of this paragraph (f)(2) may be illustrated by the following example:

Example. Assume that A, a calendar year taxpayer, purchases a four-story building on January 1, 1983, for $100,000, and incurs $10,000 of qualified rehabilitation expenditures in 1983 to rehabilitate floor one, $50,000 of qualified rehabilitation expenditures in 1984 to rehabilitate floor two, $70,000 of qualified rehabilitation expenditures in 1985 to rehabilitate floor three, and $60,000 of qualified rehabilitation expenditures in 1986 to rehabilitate floor four. Assume further that A places the property attributable to these expenditures in service on the last day of the year in which the respective expenditures were incurred and that the building is never taken out of service since as each floor is rehabilitated, the other three floors are *occupied by tenants. Under the rule in this paragraph (f)(2)*, the portion of the basis of the building that is attributable to qualified rehabilitation expenditures incurred with respect to floor one and two are deemed to be placed in service in 1985, because that is the first year that the substantial rehabilitation test described in paragraph (b) of this section is met ($120,000 of expenditures incurred by A during a measuring period ending on December 31, 1985 is greater than the $110,000 basis at the beginning of the period). Assume that as of December 31, 1985, at least 75 percent of the external walls of the building have been retained during the rehabilitation process and that A has a reasonable expectation that no work during the remain-

der of the rehabilitation process will result in less than 75 percent of the external walls being retained. A may claim a credit for A's 1985 taxable year on $130,000 of qualified rehabilitation expenditures ($10,000 in 1983, $50,000 in 1984, and $70,000 in 1985). (See paragraph (c)(6) of this section for rules applicable to when qualified expenditures may be incurred. In addition, see section 46(d) and §1.46-5 for rules relating to qualified progress expenditures.) The fact that the building was a qualified rehabilitated building for A's 1985 taxable year, however, has no effect on whether the building is a qualified rehabilitated building for A's 1986 taxable year. In order to determine whether A is entitled to claim a credit on A's 1986 return for the $60,000 of qualified rehabilitation expenditures incurred in 1986, A must select a measuring period ending in 1986 and must determine whether the building is a qualified rehabilitated building for that year. Solely for purposes of determining whether the building was substantially rehabilitated, expenditures incurred in 1984 and 1985, even though considered in determining whether the building was substantially rehabilitated for A's 1985 taxable year, may be used in addition to the expenditures incurred in 1986 to determine whether the building was substantially rehabilitated for A's 1986 taxable year, provided the expenditures were incurred during any measuring period selected by A that ends in 1986.

(3) *Coordination with section 47.*—If property described in section 48(a)(1)(E) is disposed of by the taxpayer, or otherwise ceases to be "section 38 property," section 47 may apply. Property will cease to be section 38 property, and therefore section 47 may apply, in any case in which the Department of Interior revokes or otherwise invalidates a certification of rehabilitation after the property is placed in service or a building (other than a certified historic structure) is moved from the place where it is rehabilitated after the property is placed in service. If, for example, the taxpayer made modifications to the building inconsistent with Department of Interior standards, the Secretary of the Interior might revoke the certification. In addition, if all or a portion of a substantially rehabilitated building becomes tax-exempt use property (see paragraph (c)(7)(vi) of this section) for the first time within five years after the credit is claimed, the credit will be recaptured under section 47 at that time as if the building or portion of the building which becomes tax-exempt use property had then been sold.

(g) *Effective/applicability date.*—This section applies on and after January 19, 2017. For rules before January 19, 2017, see §1.48-12 as contained in 26 CFR part 1 revised as of April 1, 2016. [Reg. §1.48-12.]

□ [*T.D.* 8233, 10-7-88. *Amended by T.D.* 8989, 4-23-2002; *T.D.* 9040, 1-30-2003, *T.D.* 9283, 8-28-2006, *T.D.* 9811, 1-18-2017 *and T.D.* 9874, 9-17-2019.]

[Reg. §1.50-1]

§1.50-1. Lessee's income inclusion following election of lessor of investment credit property to treat lessee as acquirer.—(a) *In general.*—Section 50(d)(5) provides that, for purposes of computing the investment credit, rules similar to the rules of former section 48(d) (relating to certain leased property) (as in effect on the day before the date of the enactment of the Revenue Reconciliation Act of 1990 (Public Law 101-508, 104 Stat. 1388 (November 5, 1990))) apply. This section provides rules similar to the rules of former section 48(d)(5) that the Secretary has determined shall apply for purposes of determining the inclusion in gross income required when a lessor elects to treat a lessee as having acquired investment credit property.

(b) *Coordination with basis adjustment rules.*—In the case of any property with respect to which an election is made under §1.48-4 by a lessor of investment credit property to treat the lessee as having acquired the property—

(1) *Basis adjustment.*—Section 50(c) does not apply with respect to such property.

(2) *Amount of credit included ratably in gross income.*—(i) *In general.*—A lessee of the property must include ratably in gross income, over the shortest recovery period which could be applicable under section 168 with respect to that property, an amount equal to the amount of the credit determined under section 46 with respect to that property. The ratable income inclusion under this paragraph begins on the date the investment credit property is placed in service and continues on each one year anniversary date thereafter until the end of the applicable recovery period. The lessee will include in gross income the amount of its credit determined under section 46 regardless of limitations on the amount of the credit allowed under section 38(c) based on the amount of the lessee's income tax.

(ii) *Special rule for the energy credit.*—In the case of any energy credit determined under section 48(a), paragraph (b)(2)(i) of this section applies only to the extent of 50 percent of the amount of the credit determined under section 46.

(3) *Special rule for partnerships and S corporations.*—(i) *In general.*—For purposes of paragraph (b)(2) of this section, if the lessee of the property is a partnership (other than an electing large partnership) or an S corporation, the gross income includible under such paragraph is not an item of partnership income to which the rules of subchapter K of Chapter 1, subtitle A of the Code apply or an item of S corporation income to which the rules of subchapter S of Chapter 1, subtitle A of the Code apply. Any partner or S corporation shareholder that is an ultimate credit claimant (as defined in paragraph (b)(3)(ii) of this section) is treated as a lessee that must include in gross income the amounts required under paragraph (b)(2) of this section in proportion to the credit determined under section 46 with respect to such partner or S corporation shareholder.

(ii) *Definition of ultimate credit claimant.*—For purposes of this section, the term *ultimate credit claimant* means any partner or S corporation shareholder that files (or that would file) Form 3468, "Investment Credit," with such partner's or S corporation shareholder's income tax return to claim an investment credit determined under section 46 with respect to such partner or S corporation shareholder.

(c) *Coordination with the recapture rules.*—(1) *In general.*—If section 50(a) requires an increase in the lessee's or the ultimate credit claimant's tax or a reduction in the carryback or carryover of an unused credit (or both) as a result of an early disposition (including a lease termination, etc.), of leased property for which an election had been made under § 1.48-4, the lessee or the ultimate credit claimant is required to include in gross income an amount equal to the excess, if any, of the amount of the credit that is not recaptured over the total increases in gross income previously made under paragraph (b)(2) of this section with respect to the property. Such amount is in addition to the amounts the lessee or the ultimate credit claimant previously included in gross income under paragraph (b)(2) of this section.

(2) *Income inclusion exceeds unrecaptured credit.*—If section 50(a) requires an increase in the lessee's or ultimate credit claimant's tax or a reduction in the carryback or carryover of an unused credit (or both) as a result of an early disposition (including a lease termination), etc., of leased property for which an election had been made under § 1.48-4, the lessee's or the ultimate credit claimant's gross income shall be reduced by an amount equal to the excess, if any, of the total increases in gross income previously included under paragraph (b)(2) of this section over the amount of the credit that is not recaptured.

(3) *Special rule for the energy credit.*—In the case of any energy credit determined under section 48(a), paragraphs (c)(1) and (2) of this section apply by substituting the phrase "50 percent of the amount of the credit that is not recaptured" for the phrase "the amount of the credit that is not recaptured."

(4) *Timing of income inclusion or reduction following recapture.*—Any adjustment required by paragraphs (c)(1) and (2) of this section is taken into account in the taxable year in which the property is disposed of or otherwise ceases to be investment credit property.

(d) *Election to accelerate income inclusion outside of the recapture period.*—(1) *In general.*—If after the recapture period described in section 50(a), but prior to the expiration of the recovery period described in paragraph (b)(2) of this section, there is a lease termination, the lessee otherwise disposes of the lease, or a partner or S corporation shareholder that is an ultimate credit claimant disposes of its entire interest, either direct or indirect, in a lessee partnership (other than an electing large partnership) or S corporation, the lessee, or, in the case of a partnership or S corporation, the ultimate credit claimant may irrevocably elect to take into account the remaining amount required to be included in gross income under this section in the taxable year of the disposition or termination.

(2) *Exceptions.*—The election provided under paragraph (d)(1) of this section is not available to—

(i) Lessees or ultimate credit claimants required by paragraph (c) of this section to account for the remaining amount required to be included in gross income after accounting for recapture in the taxable year in which the property was disposed of or otherwise ceased to be investment credit property under section 50(a); or

(ii) Former partners or S corporation shareholders that own no interest, either direct or indirect, in a lessee partnership or S corporation at the time of a lease termination or disposition.

(3) *Manner and time for making election.*—The election under paragraph (d)(1) of this section is made by including the remaining amount required to be included under this section in gross income in the taxable year of the lease termination or disposition or the disposition of the ultimate credit claimant's entire interest, either direct or indirect, in a partnership or S corporation. The election must be made

on or before the due date (including any extension of time) of the lessee's income tax return, or, in the case of a partnership or S corporation, the ultimate credit claimant's income tax return for the taxable year in which the lease termination or disposition or the disposition of the ultimate credit claimant's entire interest, either direct or indirect, in a partnership or S corporation occurs.

(e) *Examples.*—The provisions of this section may be illustrated by the following examples:

(1) *Example 1.* X, a calendar year C corporation, leases nonresidential real property from Y. The property is placed in service on October 1, 2016. Y elects under § 1.48-4 to treat X as having acquired the property. X's investment credit determined under section 46 for 2016 with respect to such property is $9,750. The shortest recovery period that could be available to the property under section 168 is 39 years. Because Y has elected to treat X as having acquired the property, Y does not reduce its basis in the property under section 50(c). Instead, X, the lessee of the property, must include ratably in gross income over 39 years an amount equal to the credit determined under section 46 with respect to such property. Under paragraph (b)(2) of this section, X's increase in gross income for each of the 39 years beginning with 2016 is $250 ($9,750/39 year recovery period).

(2) *Example 2.* The facts are the same as in *Example 1* in paragraph (e)(1) of this section, except that instead of nonresidential real property, X leases from Y solar energy equipment for which an energy credit under section 48 is determined under section 46. X's investment credit determined under section 46 for 2016 with respect to the property is $9,750. The shortest recovery period that could be available to the property under section 168 is 5 years. X, the lessee of the property, must include ratably in gross income over 5 years an amount equal to 50% of the credit determined under section 46 with respect to such property. Under paragraph (b)(2) of this section, X's increase in gross income for each of the 5 years beginning with 2016 is $975 ($4,875/5 year recovery period).

(3) *Example 3.* A and B, calendar year taxpayers, form a partnership, the AB partnership, that leases nonresidential real property from Y. The property is placed in service on October 1, 2016. Y elects under § 1.48-4 to treat the AB partnership as having acquired the property. A's investment credit determined under section 46 for 2016 is $3,900 and B's investment credit determined under section 46 for 2016 is $7,800 with respect to the property. The shortest recovery period that could be available to the property under section 168 is 39 years. Because Y has elected to treat the AB partnership as having acquired the property, Y does not reduce its basis in the building under section 50(c). Instead, A and B, the ultimate credit claimants, must include the amount of the credit determined with respect to A and B under section 46 ratably in gross income over 39 years, the shortest recovery period available with respect to such property. Therefore, A and B must include ratably in gross income over 39 years under paragraph (b)(2) of this section an amount equal to $3,900 and $7,800, respectively. Under paragraph (b)(2) of this section, A's increase in gross income for each of the 39 years beginning with 2016 is $100 ($3,900/39 year recovery period) and B's is $200 ($7,800/39 year recovery period). Because the gross income A and B are required to include under paragraph (b)(2) of this section is not an item of partnership income, the rules under subchapter K applicable to items of partnership income do not apply with respect to such income. In particular, A and B are not entitled to an increase in the outside basis of their partnership interests under section 705(a) and are not entitled to an increase in their capital accounts under section 704(b).

(4) *Example 4.* The facts are the same as in *Example 3* in paragraph (e)(3) of this section, except that on January 1, 2019, the lease between AB partnership and Y terminates (Y retains ownership of the property), which is a recapture event under section 50(a). A's and B's income tax for 2019 is increased under section 50(a) by $2,340 and $4,680, respectively (60% of $3,900 and $7,800, respectively, assuming that the aggregate decrease in the credits allowed under section 38 was the full amount of the investment credits determined as to A and B under section 46). Therefore, the amount of the unrecaptured credit as to A and B is $1,560 and $3,120, respectively (40% of $3,900 and $7,800, respectively). The amounts that A and B previously included in gross income under paragraph (b)(2) of this section are $300 ($100 for each of 2016, 2017, and 2018) and $600 ($200 for each of 2016, 2017, and 2018), respectively. A and B are required under paragraph (c)(1) of this section to include in gross income an amount equal to the excess of the credit that is not recaptured ($1,560 and $3,120, respectively) over the total increases in gross income previously made under paragraph (b)(2) of this section with respect to the property ($300 and $600, respectively). Therefore, A and B must include in gross income $1,260 and $2,520, respectively, in the taxable year of the lease termination (2019) in addition to the recapture amounts described above.

(5) *Example 5.* (i) The facts are the same as in *Example 4* in paragraph (e)(4) of this section, except that instead of nonresidential real

property, the AB partnership leases from Y solar energy equipment for which an energy credit under section 48 is determined under section 46. Because the shortest recovery period that could be available to the property under section 168 is 5 years, A and B are required under paragraph (b)(2)(ii) of this section to include ratably in gross income over 5 years an amount equal to 50% of the credit determined under section 46 with respect to such property (50% of $3,900/5, or $390, per year for A, and 50% of $7,800/5, or $780, per year for B).

(ii) The January 1, 2019 lease termination requires A's and B's income tax for 2019 to be increased under section 50(a) by $2,340 and $4,680, respectively (60% of $3,900 and $7,800, respectively). Therefore, the amount of the unrecaptured credit as to A and B is $1,560 and $3,120, respectively (40% of $3,900 and $7,800, respectively). Under paragraph (b)(2)(ii) of this section, the amounts A and B previously included in gross income are $1,170 ($390 for each of 2016, 2017, and 2018) and $2,340 ($780 for each of 2016, 2017, and 2018), respectively. A and B are entitled to a reduction in gross income under paragraph (c)(2) of this section equal to the excess of the total increases in gross income made under paragraph (b)(2)(ii) of this section ($1,170 and $2,340, respectively) over 50% of the amount of the credit that is not recaptured ($780 and $1,560, respectively). Therefore, A and B are entitled to a reduction in gross income in the amount of $390 and $780, respectively, in the taxable year of the lease termination (2019).

(6) *Example 6.* (i) The facts are the same as in *Example 3* in paragraph (e)(3) of this section, except that on December 1, 2021, A sells its entire interest to C, and on January 1, 2022, the lease between AB partnership and Y terminates. At the time of the lease termination, B is still a partner in the AB partnership. There is no recapture event under section 50(a) because both the lease termination and the disposition of A's interest in the partnership occurred outside of the recapture period.

(ii) At the time that A sold its interest in the AB partnership to C, A had previously included $500 ($100 for each of 2016-2020) in gross income under paragraph (b)(2) of this section. Under paragraph (b)(2) of this section, A must continue to include the remaining $3,400 (including $100 in 2021) in gross income ratably over the remaining portion of the applicable recovery period of 39 years. Alternatively, under paragraph (d)(1) of this section, A may irrevocably elect to include the remaining $3,400 in gross income in the taxable year that A sold its entire interest in the AB partnership to C (2021). Pursuant to paragraph (d)(2) of this section, A cannot make this election in the taxable year of the lease termination (2022).

(iii) At the time of the lease termination, B had previously included $1,200 ($200 for each of 2016-2021) in gross income under paragraph (b)(2) of this section. Under paragraph (b)(2) of this section, B must continue to include the remaining $6,600 required in gross income ratably over the remaining portion of the applicable recovery period of 39 years. Alternatively, under paragraph (d)(1) of this section, B may irrevocably elect to include the remaining $6,600 in gross income in the taxable year of the lease termination (2022).

(f) *Applicability date.*—This section applies to property placed in service on or after September 19, 2016. [Reg. § 1.50-1.]

☐ [T.D. 7203, 8-25-72. *Amended by T.D. 9776, 7-21-2016 and T.D. 9872, 7-17-2019.*]

[Reg. § 1.51-1]

§ 1.51-1. Amount of credit.—(a) *Determination of amount.*— (1) *General rule.*—Except as provided in paragraph (a)(2) of this section, the amount of the targeted jobs credit for purposes of section 38 (formerly designated section 44B) for the taxable year equals 50 percent of the qualified first-year wages (minus any qualified first-year wages paid to individuals while such individuals are qualified summer youth employees) plus 25 percent of the qualified second-year wages.

(2) *Special rule for employment of qualified summer youth employees.*—In the case of an employer who pays or incurs qualified wages after April 30, 1983, to a qualified summer youth employee beginning work for the employer after such date, the amount of the targeted jobs credit for the taxable year is equal to the amount determined under paragraph (a)(1) of this section plus an amount equal to 85 percent of the first $3,000 of qualified wages paid to each qualified summer youth employee during the taxable year. Such wages must be attributable to services rendered by the qualified summer youth employee during any 90-day period beginning on or after May 1 and ending on or before September 15.

(3) *Limitation.*—See section 38(c) for rules limiting the amount of the credit to a percentage of the amount of the taxpayer's net tax liability.

(b) *Definitions.*—(1) *Qualified wages.*—The term "qualified wages" means wages (as defined in paragraph (b)(4)) paid or incurred by the employer during the taxable year to individuals who are members of a targeted group (within the meaning of section 51(d)).

(2) *Qualified first-year wages.*—(i) *General rule.*—Except in the case of qualified summer youth employees, the term "qualified first-year wages" means the first $6,000 of wages (as defined in paragraph (b)(4) of this section) attributable to service rendered by a member of a targeted group during the 1-year period beginning with the day the individual first begins work for the employer. In the case of a vocational rehabilitation referral (as defined in section 51(d)(2)) who begins work for the employer before July 19, 1984, the one-year period begins with the day the individual begins work for the employer on or after the beginning of such individual's rehabilitation plan. However, with the exception of vocational rehabilitation referrals for whom the employer claimed a credit under section 44B (as in effect prior to enactment of the Revenue Act of 1978) for a taxable year beginning before January 1, 1979, members of a targeted group who are first hired after September 26, 1978, and before January 1, 1979, will be treated as if they first began work for the employer on January 1, 1979. The date on which the wages are paid is not determinative of whether the wages are first-year wages; rather, the wages must be attributed to the period during which the work was performed. See paragraph (f)(1) of this section for an additional limitation on the term "qualified first-year wages". (See examples (1), (2), (3), (4), (5), and (6) in paragraph (j) of this section for examples illustrating the application of the rules in this paragraph (b)(2)).

(ii) *Special rule for qualified summer youth employees.*—In the case of a qualified summer youth employee, qualified first-year wages for purposes of the 85 percent credit referred to in paragraph (a)(2) of this section include only wages attributable to services rendered by a qualified summer youth employee during any 90-day period beginning on or after May 1 and ending on or before September 15. If the individual is retained by the employer after the 90-day period and recertified as a member of another targeted group, the term "qualified first-year wages" for purposes of the 50 percent credit described by section 51(a)(1) has the meaning assigned that term in paragraph (b)(2)(i) of this section except that the $6,000 limitation for qualified first-year wages shall be reduced by wages up to, but not more than, $3,000 attributable to services rendered during the 90-day period.

(3) *Qualified second-year wages.*—The term "qualified second-year wages" means the first $6,000 of wages attributable to services rendered by a member of a targeted group, other than a qualified summer youth employee, during the 1-year period beginning on the day after the last day of the period for qualified first-year wages. The date on which the wages are paid is not determinative of whether the wages are second-year wages; rather, the wages must be attributed to the period during which the work was performed.

(4) *Wages.*—(i) *General rule.*—Except as otherwise provided in paragraph (b)(4)(ii) and (iii) of this section, the term "wages" shall only include amounts paid or incurred after December 31, 1978, for taxable years ending after December 31, 1978. For purposes of this section, the term "wages" has the meaning assigned such term by section 3306(b) (determined without regard to any dollar limitation contained in such subsection).

(ii) *Special rules.*—In the case of agricultural labor or railway labor, the term "wages" means unemployment insurance wages within the meaning of subparagraph (A) or (B) of section 51(h)(1). The term "wages" shall not include any amounts paid or incurred by an employer for any pay period to any individual for whom the employer receives federally funded payments for on-the-job training for such individual for such pay period. (See example (7) in paragraph (j) of this section.) The amount of wages which would otherwise be qualified wages under this section with respect to an individual for a taxable year shall be reduced by an amount equal to the amount of payments made to the employer (however utilized by such employer) with respect to such individual for such taxable year under a program established under section 414 of the Social Security Act. In addition, the term "wages" shall not include any amount paid or incurred by the employer in a taxable year beginning before January 1, 1982, to an individual with respect to whom the employer claims a credit under section 40 (relating to expenses of work incentive programs). For youths participating in a qualified cooperative education program:

(A) Section 3306(c)(10)(C) (relating to the definition of employment for certain students) does not apply in determining wages under this section; and

(B) The term "wages" shall include only those amounts paid or incurred by the employer that are attributable to services rendered by the individual while he or she meets the conditions specified in section 51(d)(8)(A). For purposes of the preceding sentence, an employee who met the requirement in section

51(d)(8)(A)(iv), dealing with economically disadvantaged status, when hired, shall be deemed to continuously meet the requirement in section 51(d)(8)(A)(iv) during the time the employee is in the cooperative education program. See also paragraph (e) of this section for rules relating to the exclusion of wages paid to certain individuals.

(iii) *Termination.*—The term "wages" shall not include any amount paid or incurred to an individual who begins work for the emloyer after December 31, 1985.

(5) *Special rule for eligible work incentive employees.*—In the case of an eligible work incentive employee (as defined in § 1.51-1(c)(4)), this paragraph (b) shall be applied for taxable years beginning after December 31, 1981, as if such employee had been a member of a targeted group for taxable years beginning before January 1, 1982. (See example (8) in paragraph (j) of this section.)

(c) *Members of targeted groups.*—(1) *In general.*—An individual is a member of a targeted group if the individual is certified as (i) a vocational rehabilitation referral, (ii) an economically disadvantaged youth, (iii) an economically disadvantaged Vietnam-era veteran, (iv) an SSI recipient, (v) a general assistance recipient, (vi) a youth participating in a cooperative education program, (vii) an economically disadvantaged ex-convict, (viii) an eligible work incentive employee, (ix) a qualified summer youth employee, or (x) an involuntarily terminated CETA employee. Except as provided below, see section 51(d) of this section for a definition of these groups. See paragraph (d) of this section for rules concerning the certification of individuals as members of one of these targeted groups.

(2) *Youths participating in a qualified cooperative education program.*—(i) *Student requirements.*—For an individual to qualify as a youth participating in a qualified cooperative education program, the individual must meet each of the following conditions (A) through (D)—

(A) The youth must have attained the age of 16 but not 20. (An individual reaching 19 will be treated as a youth participating in a qualified cooperative education program only for wages paid or incurred after November 26, 1979.)

(B) The youth must not have graduated from a high school or vocational school.

(C) The youth must be enrolled in and actively pursuing a qualified cooperative education program (as defined in paragraph (c)(2)(iii) of this section).

(D) With respect to wages paid or incurred after December 31, 1981, the youth must be a member of an economically disadvantaged family when initially hired.

(ii) *Economically disadvantaged family.*—See section 51(d)(11) for the rules relating to the determination of whether an individual is a member of an economically disadvantaged family.

(iii) *Qualified cooperative education program.*—The term "qualified cooperative education program" means a program of vocational education for individuals who (through written cooperative arrangements between a qualified school and one or more employers) receive instruction (including required academic instruction) by alternation of study in school with a job in any occupational field (but only if these two experiences are planned by the school and employer so that each contributes to the student's education and employability). See section 51(d)(8)(C) for the definition of a "qualified school." For purposes of this paragraph, the term "program of vocational education" means an organized educational program which is directly related to the preparation of individuals for employment, or for additional preparation for a career requiring other than a baccalaureate or advanced degree. An "organized educational program" means only instruction related to the occupation or occupations for which the students are in training or instruction necessary for students to benefit from such training. The student's employment contributes to his or her education and employability only if it is related to the occupation, or a cluster of closely related occupations, for which the student is in training in school. However, the student's employment need not be directly related to or in the same technical field as the training the student receives in school. For example, a student studying carpentry does not have to work as a carpenter for the program to constitute a "qualified cooperative education program." The program will qualify if, for example, the student works at a hardware store because the student's work would familiarize the student with the materials and tools used by carpenters. The program would not qualify, however, if the student works at a restaurant and generally performs tasks in such employment not related to carpentry.

(iv) *Actively pursuing.*—For purposes of this paragraph (c)(2), a youth will not be considered to be "actively pursuing" a school's qualified cooperative education program (within the meaning of

paragraph (c)(2)(iii) of this section) during summer vacation unless that school program continues during the summer vacation. Whether the school program continues during the summer vacation will be determined by examining the written agreement between the school and the employer. Thus, if a written agreement specifically covers the summer vacation period and provides for a significant degree of involvement by school personnel to provide supervision for the students in the program during that period, the school program will be considered to continue during the summer, regardless of whether classes are held during the vacation period.

(3) *General assistance recipients.*—In order for an individual to qualify as a general assistance recipient, the individual, or another member of the assistance unit (within the meaning of 45 CFR 205.40(a)(1)) that the individual is a member of, must receive assistance for a period of not less than 30 days ending within the preemployment period (as defined in section 51(d)(13)) from a qualified general assistance program. A qualified general assistance program is a program of a State or a political subdivision of a State that the Secretary (after consultation with the Secretary of Health and Human Services) has designated as providing general assistance (or similar assistance) which is based on need and consists of money payments or voucher or scrip. For purposes of the preceding sentences, a program qualifying as a general assistance program by reason of noncash assistance (*i.e.*, voucher or scrip) shall be so treated only with respect to amounts paid or incurred after July 1, 1982, to individuals beginning work for the employer after such date. For purposes of this subparagraph, the term "money" means cash or an instrument convertible into cash (*e.g.*, a check).

(4) *Eligible work incentive employees.*—An eligible work incentive employee means an individual who has been certified by the designated local agency (as defined in paragraph (d)(10) of this section) as—

(i) Being eligible for financial assistance under part A of title IV of the Social Security Act and as having continuously received such financial assistance during the 90-day period which immediately precedes the date on which such individual is hired by the employer, or

(ii) Having been placed in employment under a work incentive program established under section 432(b)(1) or 445 of the Social Security Act. The provisions of this paragraph (c)(4) are effective with respect to taxable years of the employer beginning after December 31, 1981. (See paragraph (b)(5) of this section for a special rule relating to eligible work incentive employees.)

(5) *Involuntarily terminated CETA employees.*—(i) *In general.*—An involuntarily terminated CETA employee is an individual who first began work for an employer after August 13, 1981, in taxable years of the employer ending after August 13, 1981, and is certified by the designated local agency (as defined in paragraph (d)(10) of this section) as having been involuntarily terminated after December 31, 1980, from employment financed in whole, or in part, under a program under part D of title II or title VI of the Comprehensive Employment and Training Act.

(ii) *Termination.*—Section 51(d)(10) and this paragraph (c)(5) shall not apply to any individual who begins work for the employer after December 31, 1982.

(d) *Certification.*—(1) *General rule.*—Except as otherwise provided in this paragraph, an individual shall not be treated as a member of a targeted group unless, on or before the day on which such individual begins work for the employer, the employer has received, or has requested in writing, a certification that the individual is a member of a targeted group from the designated local agency (as defined in paragraph (d)(10) of this section). In addition, the employer must receive a certification before the targeted jobs credit can be claimed. However, with respect to individuals who began work for the employer on or before May 11, 1982, the certification will be timely only if requested or received before the day the individual began work for the employer. In the case of a request in writing mailed via the United States Postal Service, the request shall be deemed to be made on the date of the postmark stamped on the cover in which such request was mailed to the designated local agency provided the request is mailed in accordance with the mailing requirements in § 301.7502-1(c) and delivered in accordance with the delivery requirements in § 301.7502-1(d). In the case of a deadline that but for this sentence would fall on a Saturday, Sunday, or a legal holiday, the deadline for making a timely request in writing for a certification or receiving a timely certification shall be the next succeeding day which is not a Saturday, Sunday, or legal holiday. (See section 7503 for the definition of "legal holiday.") See paragraph (d)(2) of this section for transitional rules applicable to certain employees who began work for the employer before September 26, 1981. See paragraph (d)(3) of this section for special rules applicable to cooperative education students and paragraph (d)(4) of this section for special rules applicable to eligible work incentive employees.

(2) *Timeliness of certification in the case of an individual to whom a written preliminary eligibility determination has been issued.*—If on or before the day on which an individual begins work for the employer, such individual has received from a designated local agency (or other agency or organization designated pursuant to a written agreement with such designated local agency) a written preliminary determination that such individual is a member of a targeted group, then such individual may be treated as a member of a targeted group if on or before the fifth day after the day such individual begins work for the employer such employer receives, or requests in writing, from the designated local agency a certification that such individual is a member of a targeted group. This paragraph (d)(2) only applies to individuals who begin work for the employer after July 18, 1984.

(3) *Transitional rules for certain employees who began work for the employer on or before September 26, 1981.*—In the case of an individual, other than a cooperative education student, who began work for the employer before June 29, 1981, the employer must either receive, or request in writing, a certification before July 23, 1981. In the case of an individual, other than a cooperative education student, who began work for the employer after June 28, 1981, and on or before September 26, 1981, the employer must either receive, or request in writing, a certification before September 26, 1981.

(4) *Cooperative education students.*—In the case of cooperative education students, the school administering the cooperative education program must issue the certification. Form 6199 is provided for this purpose. If the student begins work for the employer after September 26, 1981, see the general rule in § 1.51-1(d)(1) for the date when this certification must be received or requested. If the student begins work for the employer on or before September 26, 1981, the employer must receive the certification or request it in writing before September 26, 1981. In order for an employer to claim a credit on wages paid or incurred to a cooperative education student after December 31, 1981, the employer must receive or request in writing a determination that the student is a member of an economically disadvantaged family. A request for economic eligibility determination for a cooperative education student must be made in writing by the employer to the participating school. If the student begins work for the employer on or before September 26, 1981, the employer must receive or request in writing such determination before September 26, 1981. However, a request in writing on or after August 13, 1981, to a participating school for certification will be deemed to include a request for an economic eligibility determination. In addition, any certification issued by a school after August 13, 1981, will be deemed to be issued in response to a request for certification which includes a request for an economic eligibility determination. The rule in the preceding sentence does not eliminate the requirement that the employer receive a certification that includes an economic eligibility determination in order to claim a credit for wages paid or incurred after December 31, 1981. If a certification issued by a school after August 13, 1984, does not contain an economic eligibility determination and the employer wishes to claim a credit for wages paid or incurred after December 31, 1981, the employer must receive a completed certification before the date on which the credit is claimed.

(5) *Eligible work incentive employees.*—In the case of eligible work incentive employees, the employer must either receive, or request in writing, a certification within the time requirements of paragraph (d)(1), (2), or (3) of this section, whichever is applicable. Before October 12, 1981 (the date the Economic Recovery Tax Act of 1981 codified the State employment security agency as the designated local agency for certifying targeted groups), a certificate may be received or requested in writing from either the designated local agency (as defined in paragraph (d)(10) of this section) or the office or agency that properly issued certifications under former section 50B(h)(1) (relating to the work incentive credit).

(6) *Certifications that are not timely.*—Any certification that is not timely received or requested by the employer in accordance with the rules of this paragraph will be treated as invalid. Thus, the employer will not be allowed to claim a credit under section 51 with respect to any wages paid or incurred to an employee whose certification or request for certification is not timely. A timely request for certification does not eliminate the need for the employer to receive a certification before claiming the credit. In the case of a request for certification that was denied, resubmitted, and then approved, the timeliness of the request shall be determined by the timeliness of the first request.

(7) *Incorrect certification.*—(i) *In general.*—Except as otherwise provided in paragraph (d)(7)(ii) of this section, if an individual has been certified as a member of a targeted group, and such certification is based on false information provided by such individual, the certifi-

cation shall be revoked and wages paid by the employer after the date on which notice of revocation is received by the employer shall not be treated as qualified wages. For purposes of this paragraph, a certification will be revoked only if the individual would not have been certified had correct information been provided to the issuer of the certification. Thus, false information that is not material to an individual's eligibility as a member of a targeted group will not invalidate an otherwise valid certification.

(ii) *Employer's knowledge that the certification was incorrect.*—In the case of an employer who knew, or had reason to know, at the time of certification that the information provided to the designated local agency was false, none of the wages paid by such employer to an individual to whom an incorrect certification has been issued will be qualified wages.

(8) *Certifications issued to certain rehires.*—This paragraph (d)(8) applies in the case of an employee who first began work for the employer before August 13, 1981, and was dismissed and rehired by the employer. A certification received or requested by an employer with respect to such an employee will be considered timely only if there was a valid business reason, unrelated to the availability of the credit, for the dismissal and rehire and if the employer did not dismiss and then rehire the employee in order to meet the timing requirement with respect to certification. An individual who is dismissed and then rehired for the purpose described in the preceding sentence will be considered for purposes of section 51(d)(16) and this paragraph to have been continuously employed by the employer during the time between the dismissal and the rehire. Whether the employer was motivated by reason of the certification rules in section 51(d)(16) and this paragraph to dismiss and then rehire an employee is a question of fact to be determined from all the circumstances surrounding the dismissal and rehire. (See paragraph (e)(2) of this section for a separate rule disallowing the credit in the case of nonqualifying rehires.)

(9) *Individuals who continue to be employed by the same employer but as a member of another targeted group.*—This paragraph (d)(9) applies in the case of an employee who continues to be employed by the same employer but no longer qualifies as a member of the targeted group for which such employee was first certified (*e.g.*, the employee was originally certified as a qualified summer youth employee with respect to a ninety-day period between May 1 and September 15, but such ninety-day period has ended) In such case, the employer may request a certification that the employee is a member of another targeted group, and if any wages paid to such individual are qualified first-year wages or qualified second-year wages, the employer may be entitled to a targeted jobs credit with respect to such wages. The second certification will not be invalid merely because it was requested or received after the individual began work for the employer; only the first certification (for example, the certification with respect to an individual hired first as a qualified summer youth employee) must meet the requirement of section 51(d)(16) that a certification must be requested or received by an employer on or before the day on which the individual begins work for the employer. In the case of a former qualified summer youth employee or a youth participating in a qualified cooperative education program who is recertified as an economically disadvantaged youth, the term "hiring date" in section 51(d)(3)(B) does not mean the day the individual is hired by the employer but means the day the individual is certified as a member of the new targeted group. Accordingly, the age requirement of section 51(d)(3)(B) shall be applied as of the day the individual is certified as a member of the second targeted group. In addition, see section 51(d)(11) for rules concerning the viability of the original economic eligibility determination.

(10) *Certification where a trade or business has been transferred to a new employer.*—In the case of a transfer of a trade or business in which an individual who is a member of a targeted group is retained as an employee in the trade or business, the certification obtained for such employee by the transferor-employer will apply with respect to the transferee-employer.

(11) *Designated local agency.*—(i) *In general.*—For the period before October 12, 1981, the term "designated local agency" means the agency for any locality designated jointly by the Secretary and the Secretary of Labor to perform certifications of employees for employers in that locality. On or after October 12, 1981, the term "designated local agency" means a State employment security agency established in accordance with the Act of June 6, 1933, as amended (29 U.S.C. 49-49n).

(ii) *Jurisdiction.*—The designated local agency is the agency that has, pursuant to its charter, jurisdiction over the individual that is sought to be certified. Thus, any certification that is issued with respect to an individual who is not within the jurisdiction of the designated local agency that issued the certification will be invalid.

Notwithstanding any other provision of this section, a request in writing for certification to the appropriate designated local agency that is made before January 23, 1984, will be considered to be timely if it is made after an otherwise timely request in writing for certification was made to a designated local agency that does not have jurisdiction over the individual sought to be certified.

(e) *Certain ineligible individuals.*—(1) *Related individuals.*—For purposes of section 51(a), "qualified wages" does not include any amounts paid or incurred by a taxpayer to any of the following individuals:

(i) An individual who is related (within the meaning of any of paragraphs (1) through (8) of section 152(a)) to the taxpayer;

(ii) An individual who is a dependent (within the meaning of section 152(a)(9)) of the taxpayer;

(iii) An individual who is related (within the meaning of any of paragraphs (1) through (8) of section 152(a)) to a shareholder who owns (within the meaning of section 267(c)) more than 50 percent in value of the outstanding stock of the taxpayer, if the taxpayer is a corporation;

(iv) An individual who is a dependent (within the meaning of section 152(a)(9)) of a shareholder described in paragraph (e)(1)(iii) of this section;

(v) An individual who is a grantor, beneficiary or fiduciary of the taxpayer, if the taxpayer is an estate or trust;

(vi) An individual who is a dependent (within the meaning of section 152(a)(9)) of an individual described in paragraph (e)(1)(v) of this section; or

(vii) An individual who is related (within the meaning of any of paragraphs (1) through (8) of section 152(a)) to an individual described in paragraph (e)(1)(v) of this section.

(2) *Nonqualifying rehires.*—For purposes of section 51(a), "qualified wages" does not include wages paid to an employee who had been employed by the employer prior to the current hiring date of the employee if at any time during such prior employment the employee was not a member of a targeted group. The preceding sentence shall not apply to an employee who was previously timely certified as a member of a targeted group with respect to the same employer. An employee shall be treated as not having been a member of a targeted group if the certification requirements of section 51(d)(16) were not met. (See example (8) in paragraph (j) of this section.)

(3) *Effective date.*—The provisions of this paragraph (e) are effective with respect to employees first beginning work for an employer after August 13, 1981.

(f) *Limitations.*—(1) *Limitation on qualified first-year wages.*—With respect to taxable years beginning before January 1, 1982, the amount of the qualified first-year wages which may be taken into account for purposes of the targeted jobs credit for any taxable year shall not exceed 30 percent of the aggregate unemployment insurance wages paid by the employer during the calendar year ending in such taxable year. In the case of a group of trades or businesses under common control (as defined in §1.52-1(b)), the qualified first-year wages cannot exceed 30 percent of the aggregate unemployment insurance wages paid to all employees of that group of trades or businesses under common control during the calendar year ending in such taxable year. For this purpose, the term "unemployment insurance wages" has the same meaning given to the term "wages" as defined in §1.51-1(b)(4). In this case of agricultural or railway labor, see section 51(h)(1) for the applicable definition of unemployment insurance wages. (See examples (13) and (14) in paragraph (j) of this section.)

(2) *Remuneration must be for trade or business employment.*—Remuneration paid by an employer to an employee during any taxable year shall be taken into account only if more than one-half of the remuneration paid by the employer to an employee is for services in a trade or business of the employer. This determination shall be made by each employer without regard to section 52(a) or (b). Accordingly, employees of corporations that are members of a controlled group or employees of partnerships, proprietorships, and other trades or businesses (whether or not incorporated) which are under common control will be treated as being employed by each separate employer for this purpose. For this purpose, the term "year" means the taxable year of the employer. (See example (15) in paragraph (j) of this section.)

(g) *Election not to claim the targeted jobs credit.*—The election under section 51(j) (as amended by section 474(p) of the Tax Reform Act of 1984) not to claim the targeted jobs credit is available for taxable years beginning after December 31, 1983, and shall be made for the taxable year in which such credit is available by not claiming such credit on an original return or amended return at any time before the expiration of the 3-year period beginning on the last date prescribed by law for filing the return for the taxable year (determined without regard to extensions). The election may be revoked within the 3-year period by filing an amended return on which the credit is claimed.

(h) *Treatment of successor-employers.*—In the case of a successor-employer referred to in section 3306(b)(1), the determination of the amount of credit under this section with respect to wages paid by such successor-employer shall be made in the same manner as if such wages were paid by the predecessor-employer referred to in such section. Thus, the 1-year period referred to in §1.51-1(b)(2)(i) will be considered to begin with the day the employee first began work for the transferor-employer, and the amount of qualified first-year wages and qualified second-year wages paid or incurred with respect to the employee must be reduced by the amount of any such wages paid or incurred by the transferor-employer. (See examples (10) and (11) in paragraph (j) of this section.) Also, see paragraph (d)(10) of this section for rules concerning the viability of the employee's certification.

(i) *Treatment of employees performing services for other persons.*—No credit shall be determined under this section with respect to remuneration paid by an employer to an employee for services performed by such employee for another person unless the amount reasonably expected to be received by the employer for such services from such other person exceeds the remuneration paid by the employer to such employee for such services.

(j) *Examples.*—The application of this section may be illustrated by the following examples which, except as otherwise stated, assume that the limitations imposed by §§1.51-1(f)(2) and 1.53-3 are inapplicable:

Example (1). Corporation M is a calendar year, cash receipts and disbursements method taxpayer. A, an economically disadvantaged youth, first began work for Corporation M on October 1, 1978. Qualified first-year wages with respect to A are wages attributable to the period beginning on January 1, 1979 (since A was first hired after September 26, 1978, he is treated as having begun work on January 1, 1979) and ending on December 31, 1979. In the 1979 taxable year, Corporation M pays A $5,000 of qualified first-year wages attributable to services performed in 1979. Corporation M's allowable credit is equal to $2,500 (50 percent of $5,000).

Example (2). Assume the same facts as in example (1), except that in 1980 Corporation M pays to A $100 of wages attributable to services rendered in 1979. These wages will still be considered as qualified first-year wages, but the credit may not be claimed until the 1980 taxable year.

Example (3). Corporation O is a calendar year, cash receipts and disbursements method taxpayer. C, a vocational rehabilitation referral, first began work for Corporation O on July 1, 1978. Corporation O claimed a credit under section 44B (as in effect prior to enactment of the Revenue Act of 1978) for $3,000 of wages paid to C in the 1978 taxable year. Corporation O paid C $6,000 for services performed from January 1, 1979 to June 30, 1979. The period during which qualified first-year wages are determined begins on July 1, 1978, and ends on June 30, 1979. Amounts paid before January 1, 1979, however, are not taken into consideration in determining the amount of qualified first-year wages. Accordingly, only the wages attributable to services performed from January 1, 1979, through June 30, 1979, are considered as qualified first-year wages. Corporation O's allowable credit is equal to $3,000 (50 percent of $6,000).

Example (4). I first began work for Corporation Q, a cash receipts and disbursements method taxpayer, on January 1, 1981, and was not a member of a targeted group. On March 1, 1981, I was convicted of a felony and sentenced to prison. I quit work for Corporation Q, and served the prison sentence. On November 1, 1981, I again was hired by Corporation Q and began work on that date. On the November 1, 1981 hiring date, I was an economically disadvantaged ex-convict for whom Corporation Q received a certificate. Corporation Q paid I $500 of wages for services performed from November 1, 1981, to December 31, 1981, and $6,000 of wages for services performed during 1982. The $500 of wages paid for services performed from November 1, 1981, to December 31, 1981, would be qualified first-year wages because these qualified wages were paid for services performed during the 1-year period beginning on the date I first began work for Corporation Q (January 1, 1981). The $6,000 of wages paid for services performed during 1982 would be qualified second-year wages because these qualified wages were paid for services performed during the 1-year period beginning on the date after the first 1-year period. Accordingly, Corporation Q has an allowable credit of $250 attributable to qualified first-year wages and $1,500 attributable to qualified second-year wages.

Example (5). Assume the same facts as in example (4), except that all dates are 1 year later. Thus, I first began work for Corporation Q on January 1, 1982, was convicted on March 1, 1982, and was rehired on November 1, 1982. Under these facts, Q is not entitled to take a targeted jobs credit with respect to I's wages because I is a nonqualifying rehire.

Example (6). J, an economically disadvantaged youth, first began work for Corporation R, a calendar year cash receipts and disbursements method taxpayer, on December 1, 1979. On July 1, 1980, J was laid off by Corporation R and began work for Corporation S, which is unrelated to Corporation R, on July 2, 1980. On November 1, 1980, J again began work for Corporation R and continued working for Corporation R until January 1, 1982. At the time J first began work for Corporation S, J no longer met the qualifications of an economically disadvantaged youth. Corporation S may not claim a credit for wages paid to J because J was not a member of a targeted group at the time he began work for Corporation S. Corporation R, however, may claim a credit for wages paid to J because J was a member of a targeted group when he was hired by Corporation R. Corporation R's qualified first-year wages paid to J are the wages paid for services performed by J from December 1, 1979, to July 1, 1980, and from November 1, 1980, to November 30, 1980. Corporation R's qualified second-year wages paid to J are wages paid for services performed by J from December 1, 1980, to November 30, 1981. Corporation R may not claim a credit for wages paid for services performed by J after November 30, 1981.

Example (7). K, a member of a targeted group, first began work for Corporation T on January 1, 1979. For the pay periods from January 1, 1979, to March 31, 1979, Corporation T received federally funded payments for on-the-job training for K and paid wages of $2,000 to K. During the remainder of 1979 Corporation T paid wages of $7,000 to K. Corporation T may claim a credit on $6,000 of qualified first-year wages. Amounts paid to K by Corporation T during the pay periods for which Corporation T received federally funded payments for on-the-job training for K are not considered wages for purposes of the credit. However, Corporation T may consider $6,000 of the total $7,000 of wages paid after March 31, 1979, as qualified first-year wages.

Example (8). P first began work for Corporation X on January 1, 1981, as an individual who was certified to be an eligible employee for purposes of the WIN credit provided in section 40. Corporation X paid P $6,000 in wages during its taxable year beginning on January 1, 1981, and $6,000 of wages during its taxable year beginning on January 1, 1982. X can claim a targeted jobs credit for the wages paid in 1982 if the requirements of section 51 are met. For purposes of section 51(a), P's qualified first-year wages are the wages paid from January 1, 1981, to December 31, 1981, and P's qualified second-year wages are the wages paid from January 1, 1982, to December 31, 1982. Thus, Corporation X is only entitled to claim a targeted job credit based on P's qualified second-year wages.

Example (9). (i) L, 15 years of age, first began work for Corporation U on August 1, 1979. On September 3, 1979, L began her junior year in high school and enrolled in a qualified cooperative education program that was to run for her junior and senior years. On October 1, 1979, when L turned 16, she met all the requirements of § 1.51-1(c)(2)(i) and qualified as a youth participating in a qualified cooperative education program. Corporation U is entitled to claim a credit on wages paid or incurred for services performed by L after September 30, 1979, so long as L meets the requisite requirements. L's summer vacation began on June 1, 1980. Assume that the cooperative education program L was enrolled in did not continue during the summer vacation (*i.e.*, the written agreement between the employer and the school did not cover the summer vacation). Thus, during her summer vacation, L did not meet the requirement of actively pursuing a qualified cooperative education program. Accordingly, Corporation U may not claim a credit on wages paid for services performed by L during L's summer vacation. On September 2, 1980, L began her senior year, and again met all the requirements of § 1.51-1(c)(2)(i). She continued to meet these requirements until June 5, 1981, when she graduated from high school. Accordingly, Corporation U may claim a credit on wages paid for services performed after September 1, 1980, and before June 5, 1981.

(ii) Assume the same facts as in (i), above, except that all dates are 3 years later. Under these facts, U is not entitled to claim a targeted jobs credit with respect to any of L's wages because L has not been timely certified under section 51(d)(16) and § 1.51-1(d)(3).

Example (10). D began work for a drugstore owned by E as a sole proprietor on January 1, 1979, and was certified as a member of a targeted group with respect to E. On June 1, 1979, E sold the drugstore where D worked to F, who continued to operate the drugstore with D as an employee. D's qualification as a member of a targeted group is not required to be redetermined in order for F to qualify for the targeted jobs credit. F will take into account the certification of D's eligibility that was provided to E. F will have qualified first-year wages consisting of the first $6,000 of wages paid or incurred to D by E and F from January 1, 1979 to December 31, 1979 (reduced by any qualified wages paid or incurred by E to D from January 1, 1979, to May 31, 1979). F's qualified second-year wages will consist of the first

$6,000 of wages paid or incurred to D by F from January 1, 1980, to December 31, 1980.

Example (11). G began work in a machine shop owned by H as a sole proprietor on January 1, 1979, and was certified as a member of a targeted group with respect to H. On June 1, 1980, H transferred all the assets of the machine shop to newly formed Corporation P. Corporation P retained G as an employee in the machine shop. G's qualification as a member of a targeted group is not required to be redetermined in order for P to qualify for the targeted jobs credit. H has qualified first-year wages in the amount of the first $6,000 of wages paid or incurred to G by H from January 1, 1979, to December 31, 1979. Corporation P has qualified second-year wages in the amount of the first $6,000 of wages paid or incurred to G by H and Corporation P from January 1, 1980, to December 31, 1980 (reduced by any qualified second-year wages paid by H to G).

Example (12). W operates a retail store as a sole proprietor. On June 1, 1982, W hires S after receiving a written determination from a local community organization that S meets the requirements of an economically disadvantaged youth. W does not request a certification from the State employment security agency as to S's eligibility. W is not entitled to claim a credit with respect to wages paid to S because W did not receive, or request in writing, a certification from the State employment security agency as to S's eligibility on or before the day on which S began to work for W.

Example (13). Corporation V is a cash receipts and disbursements method taxpayer with a July 1 through June 30 taxable year. In the taxable year ending June 30, 1980, the aggregate unemployment insurance wages paid by V were $150,000. In calendar year 1979 the aggregate unemployment insurance wages paid by Corporation V were $110,000. Corporation V's qualified first-year wages are limited to 30 percent of the aggregate unemployment insurance wages paid by it in calendar year 1979 or $33,000 (30 percent of $110,000), even though the aggregate unemployment insurance wages paid by it in the taxable year ending June 30, 1980, were $150,000.

Example (14). Assume the same facts as in example (13), except that all dates are 3 years later. Since the limitation on qualified first-year wages does not apply to taxable years beginning after December 31, 1981, Corporation V's qualified first-year wages are $150,000.

Example (15). M operates a retail store as a sole proprietor. N and O, both members of a targeted group, first began work for M on January 1, 1979. M paid N total qualified first-year wages of $6,000 in 1979. Three thousand one hundred dollars of those wages were for services in M's retail store, and $2,900 of those wages were for services as M's maid. M paid O total qualified first-year wages of $6,000 in 1979. Three thousand dollars of those wages were for services in M's store and $3,000 of those wages were for services as M's chauffeur. M has an allowable credit of $3,000 in 1979 on all $6,000 of qualified first-year wages paid to N because more than one-half of the remuneration paid by M to N was for services in M's trade or business. M may not take into account the wages paid to O because not more than one-half of the remuneration paid by M to O was for services in M's trade or business. Accordingly, M may not claim a credit on wages paid to O. [Reg. § 1.51-1.]

☐ [T.D. 8062, 11-5-85.]

[Reg. § 1.52-1]

§ 1.52-1. Trades or businesses that are under common control.— (a) *Apportionment of new jobs credit among members of a group of trades or businesses that are under common control.—(1) Targeted jobs credit.—* (i) In the case of a group of trades or businesses that are under common control (within the meaning of paragraph (b) of this section) at any time during the calendar year, the amount of the targeted jobs credit (computed under section 51 as if all the organizations that are under common control are one trade or business) under section 4-1B must be apportioned among the members of the group on the basis of each member's proportionate share of the wages giving rise to such credit. If the group of trades or businesses that are under common control have different taxable years, the credit shall be computed as if all the organizations have the same taxable year as the organization for which a determination of the proportionate share of the credit is being made. For taxable years beginning before January 1, 1982, the amount of the qualified first-year wages cannot exceed 30 percent of the aggregate unemployment insurance wages paid by the group of trades or businesses under common control during the calendar year ending in the taxable year of the organization for which a determination of the proportionate share of the credit is being made. The limitations in section 53 and the regulations thereunder apply to each organization individually (although, in applying these limitations, an affiliated group of corporations electing to make a consolidated return shall be treated as one organization).

(ii) The application of the subparagraph may be illustrated by the following examples:

Example (1). (a) Corporation M and its three subsidiaries, Corporations N, O, and P, are a group of businesses that are under common control and each uses the cash receipts and disbursements method of accounting and has a calendar year taxable year. Corporations M, N, O, and P paid out the following amounts in unemployment insurance wages, qualified first-year wages and qualified second-year wages during 1980.

Corporation:	Unemployment insurance wages	Qualified 1st-year wages	Qualified 2d-year wages
M	$ 600,000	$184,000	$ 75,000
N	300,000	85,000	90,000
O	360,000	120,000	115,000
P	24,000	24,000	0
Total	1,284,000	413,000	280,000

(b) Since Corporations M, N, O, and P are under common control, the amount of qualified first-year wages paid by the group is limited to 30 percent of the aggregate unemployment insurance wages paid by the group in the calendar year ending in the group's taxable year. Since the qualified first-year wages of $413,000 exceeds 30% of the aggregate unemployment insurance wages, the group is limited to qualified first-year wages of $385,200 (30% of $1,284,000). The amount of the targeted jobs credit attributable to qualified first-

year wages is equal to $192,600 (50% of $385,200). The amount of the credit attributable to qualified second-year wages is equal to $70,000 (25% of $280,000).

(c) The credit is apportioned among Corporations M, N, O, and P on the basis of their proportionate share of the qualified first-year wages or qualified second-year wages giving rise to the credit. Each corporation's share of the credit attributable to qualified first-year wages would be computed as follows:

Corporation:

			Amount of credit
M	$192,600 ×	$\dfrac{\$184,000}{\$413,000}$	= $85,807.26
N	$192,600 ×	$\dfrac{\$85,000}{\$413,000}$	= $39,639.23
O	$192,600 ×	$\dfrac{\$120,000}{\$413,000}$	= $55,961.26
P	$192,600 ×	$\dfrac{\$ 24,000}{\$413,000}$	= $11,192.25

Each corporation's share of the credit attributable to qualified second-year wages is computed as follows:

Corporation:

			Amount of credit
M	$70,000 ×	$\dfrac{\$ 75,000}{\$280,000}$	= $18,750
N	$70,000 ×	$\dfrac{\$ 90,000}{\$280,000}$	= $22,500
O	$70,000 ×	$\dfrac{\$115,000}{\$280,000}$	= $28,750
P	$70,000 ×	$\dfrac{0}{\$280,000}$	= 0

Example (2). Assume the facts in example (1) with these additional facts. A, a member of a targeted group, worked for more than one of the members of the controlled group in the taxable year. A first began work for Corporation M on January 1, 1980, and later worked for Corporations N and O during 1980. For services rendered by A during 1980, the following wages were paid to A: Corporation M paid A $2,500 of qualified first-year wages: Corporation N paid A $1,500 of qualified first-year wages; Corporation O paid A $3,000 of

qualified first-year wages. Corporations M, N, and O paid A a total of $7,000 of wages during 1980. Only $6,000 of qualified first-year wages per year per employee may be taken into account for purposes of the credit. See § 1.51-1(d)(1). Since Corporations M, N, and O are treated as a single employer under section 52(a), the maximum $6,000 of qualified first-year wages paid A by the group must be apportioned among Corporations M, N, and O as follows:

Corporation:

			Qualified 1st-Year wages
M	$6,000 ×	$\dfrac{\$2,500}{\$7,000}$	= $2,142.86
N	$6,000 ×	$\dfrac{\$1,500}{\$7,000}$	= $1,285.71
O	$6,000 ×	$\dfrac{\$3,000}{\$7,000}$	= $2,571.48

Example (3). (a) Corporation Q and its two subsidiaries, Corporations R and S, are a group of businesses that are under common control and each uses the cash receipts and disbursements method of accounting. Corporation Q has a calendar year taxable year. Corporation R has a July 1 through June 30 taxable year. Corporation S has an

October 1 through September 30 taxable year. For purposes of determining Corporation R's proportionate share of the credit, the credit is computed as if Corporation Q and S have the same taxable year as Corporation R. Accordingly, Corporation R would compute its share of the credit for its 1979-1980 taxable year as set forth below.

Corporation:	Unemployment insurance wages, 1979	Qualified wages paid from July 1, 1979, to June 30, 1980	
		1st year wages	*2nd year wages*
Q	$500,000	$150,000	$80,000
R	300,000	110,000	50,000
S	100,000	25,000	10,000
Total	$900,000	$285,000	$140,000

(b) Since Corporations Q, R, and S are under common control, the amount of qualified first-year wages is limited to 30 percent of the aggregate unemployment insurance wages paid by the group during the calendar year ending in Corporation R's taxable year. Since the qualified first-year wages of $285,000 exceeds 30 percent of the aggregate unemployment insurance wages, the group is limited to qualified first-year wages of $270,000 (30% of $900,000). The amount of the targeted jobs credit attributable to qualified first-year wages paid by members of the group during the period of the taxpayer's taxable year is $135,000 (50% of $270,000). The amount of the credit attributable to qualified second-year wages paid or incurred by members of the group during the period of the taxpayer's taxable year is $35,000 (25% of $140,000).

(c) The credit is apportioned to Corporation R on the basis of its proportionate share of the qualified first-year wages and qualified second-year wages giving rise to the credit. Corporation R's share of the credit attributable to qualified first-year wages is $52,105.26

$$\$135,000 \times \frac{\$110,000}{\$285,000}$$

Corporation R's share of the credit attributable to qualified second-year wages is $12,500

$$\$35,000 \times \frac{\$50,000}{\$140,000}$$

Corporation:	1976	1977	Increase in FUTA wages in 1977 over 1976
T	$1,000,000	$1,015,000	+ $ 15,000
U	500,000	650,000	+150,000
V	600,000	580,000	−20,000
W	40,000	100,000	+60,000
Total	$2,140,000	$2,345,000	$205,000

(b) Since all employees of trades or businesses that are under common control are treated as employed by a single employer, the computations in section 51 are performed as if all the organizations which are under common control are one trade or business. Consequently, the amounts of the total unemployment insurance wages of the group in 1976 (i.e., $2,140,000) and 1977 (i.e., $2,345,000) are used to determine the increase in unemployment insurance wages in 1977 over the 1976 wage base. Since the amount equal to 102 percent of the 1976 unemployment insurance wages ($2,182,800) is greater than the amount equal to 50 percent of the 1977 unemployment insurance wages ($1,172,500), the increase in unemployment insurance wages in 1977 over the 1976 wage basis is $162,200 ($2,345,000 – $2,182,800). The limitations in section 51(c), (d), and (g) (as in effect prior to enactment of the Revenue Act of 1978) must also be computed as though all the organizations under common control are one trade or business. For purposes of this example, it is assumed that none of those limitations reduce the amount of increase in unemployment insurance wages. As a result, the amount of the new jobs credit allowed to the group of business is $81,100 (50% of $162,200).

(c) The credit is apportioned among Corporations T, U, and W on the basis of their proportionate contributions to the increase in unemployment insurance wages. No credit would be allowed to Corporation V because it did not contribute to the increase in the group's unemployment insurance wages. Corporation T's share of the credit would be $5,406.66 ($81,100 × ($15,000 ÷ $225,000 (i.e., $15,000 + $150,000 + $60,000))), Corporation U's share would be $54,066.67 ($81,100 × ($150,000 ÷ 225,000)), and Corporation W's share would be $21,626.67 ($81,100 × ($60,000 ÷ $225,000)).

(b) *Trades or businesses that are under common control.*—For purposes of this section, the term "trades or businesses that are under common control" means any group of trades or businesses that is either a "parent-subsidiary group under common control" as defined in paragraph (c) of this section, a "brother-sister group under common control" as defined in paragraph (d) of this section, or a "combined group under common control" as defined in paragraph (e) of this section. For purposes of this section and §§1.52-2 and 1.52-3, the term "organization" means a sole proprietorship, a partnership, a

Corporation R's share of the credit for its 1979-1980 taxable year is $64,605.26 ($52,105.26 + $12,500).

(2) *New jobs credit.*—In the case of a group of trades or businesses that are under common control at any time during the calendar year, the amount of the new jobs credit (computed under section 51 as if all the organizations that are under common control are one trade or business) under section 44B (as in effect prior to enactment of the Revenue Act of 1978) must be apportioned among the members of the group on the basis of each member's proportionate contribution to the increase in unemployment insurance wages for the entire group. The limitations in section 53 (as in effect prior to enactment of the Revenue Act of 1978) and the regulations thereunder apply to each organization individually (although, in applying these limitations, an affiliated group of corporations electing to make a consolidated return shall be treated as one organization). The application of this subparagraph may be illustrated by the following example:

Example. (a) Corporation T and its three subsidiaries, U, V, and W, are a group of businesses that are under common control and each has a calendar year taxable year. Corporations T, U, V, and W have paid out the following amounts in unemployment insurance wages during 1976 and 1977:

trust, an estate, or a corporation. An organization may be a member of only one group of trades or businesses under common control. If, without the application of this paragraph, an organization would be a member of more than one such group, that organization shall indicate in its timely filed return the group in which it is being included. If the organization does not so indicate, then the district director with audit jurisdiction of the organization's return will determine the group in which the organization is to be included.

(c) *Parent-subsidiary group under common control.*—(1) *In general.*— The term "parent-subsidiary group under common control" means one or more chains of organizations conducting trades or businesses that are connected through ownership of a controlling interest with a common parent organization if—

(i) A controlling interest in each of the organizations, except the common parent organization, is owned (directly and with the application of §1.414(c)-4(b)(1), relating to options) by one or more of the other organizations; and

(ii) The common parent organization owns (directly and with the application of §1.414(c)-4(b)(1), relating to options) a controlling interest in at least one of the other organizations, excluding, in computing the controlling interest, any direct ownership interest by the other organizations.

(2) *Controlling interest defined.*—For purposes of this paragraph, the term "controlling interest" means:

(i) In the case of a corporation, ownership of stock possessing more than 50 percent of the total combined voting power of all classes of stock entitled to vote or more than 50 percent of the total value of the shares of all classes of stock of the corporation;

(ii) In the case of a trust or estate, ownership of an actuarial interest (determined under paragraph (f) of this section) of more than 50 percent of the trust or estate;

(iii) In the case of a partnership, ownership or more than 50 percent of the profit interest or capital interest of the partnership; and

(iv) In the case of a sole proprietorship, ownership of the sole proprietorship.

Reg. §1.52-1(c)(2)(iv)

(d) *Brother-sister group under common control.*—(1) *In general.*—The term "brother-sister group under common control" means two or more organizations conducting trades or businesses if—

(i) The same five or fewer persons who are individuals, estates, or trusts own (directly and with the application of §1.414(c)-4), a controlling interest of each organization; and

(ii) Taking into account the ownership of each person only to the extent that person's ownership is identical with respect to each organization, such persons are in effective control of each organization.

The five or fewer persons whose ownership is considered for purposes of the controlling interest requirement for each organization must be the same persons whose ownership is considered for purposes of the effective control requirement.

(2) *Controlling interest defined.*—For purposes of this paragraph, the term "controlling interest" means:

(i) In the case of a corporation, ownership of stock possessing at least 80 percent of the total combined voting power of all classes of stock entitled to vote or at least 80 percent of the total value of the shares of all classes of stock of the corporation;

(ii) In case of a trust or estate, ownership of an actuarial interest (determined under paragraph (f) of this section) of at least 80 percent of the trust or estate;

(iii) In the case of a partnership, ownership of at least 80 percent of the profit interest or capital interest of the partnership; and

(iv) In the case of a sole proprietorship, ownership of the sole proprietorship.

(3) *Effective control defined.*—For purposes of this paragraph "effective control" means:

(i) In the case of a corporation, ownership of stock possessing more than 50 percent of the total combined voting power of all classes of stock entitled to vote or more than 50 percent of the total value of the shares of all classes of stock of the corporation;

(ii) In the case of a trust or estate, ownership of an actuarial interest (determined under paragraph (f) of this section) of more than 50 percent of the trust or estate;

(iii) In the case of a partnership, ownership of more than 50 percent of the profit interest or capital interest of the partnership; and

(iv) In the case of a sole proprietorship, ownership of the sole proprietorship.

(e) *Combined group under common control.*—The term "combined group under common control" means a group of three or more organizations, in which (1) each organization is a member of either a parent-subsidiary group under common control or brother-sister group under common control, and (2) at least one organization is the common parent organization of a parent-subsidiary group under common control and also a member of a brother-sister group under common control.

(f) *Actuarial interest.*—For purposes of this section, the actuarial interest of each beneficiary of a trust or estate shall be determined by assuming the maximum exercise of discretion by the fiduciary in favor of the beneficiary. The factors and method prescribed in §20.2031-7 or, for certain prior periods, §20.2031-7A of this chapter (Estate Tax Regulations) for use in ascertaining the value of an interest in property for estate tax purposes will be used to determine a beneficiary's actuarial interest.

(g) *Exclusion of certain interests and stock in determining control.*—In determining control under this paragraph, the term "interest" and the term "stock" do not include an interest that is treated as not outstanding under §1.414(c)-3. In addition, the term "stock" does not include treasury stock or nonvoting stock that is limited and preferred regarding dividends.

(h) *Transitional rule.*—(1) *In general.*—Paragraph (d) of this section, as amended by T.D. 8179, applies to all taxable years to which section 52(b) applies.

(2) *Election.*—In the case of taxable years ending before March 2, 1988:

(i) If, pursuant to paragraph (b) of this section, an organization indicated in a timely filed return that it chose to be a member of a brother-sister group under common control, and it is not a member of such group because of the amendments to paragraph (d) of this section made by T.D. 8179 such organization may make the choice described in paragraph (b) of this section by filing an amended return on or before September 2, 1988 if such organization would otherwise still be a member of more than one group of trades or businesses under common control, and

(ii) If an organization

(A) Is a member of a brother-sister group of trades or businesses under common control under §1.52-1(d)(1) as in effect

before amendment by T.D. 8179 ("old group"), for such taxable year and

(B) Is not such a member for such taxable year because of the amendments made by such Treasury decision,

such organization (whether or not a corporation) nevertheless will be treated as a member of such old group if all the organizations (whether or not corporations) that are members of the old group meet all the requirements of §1.1563-1(d)(3) with respect to such taxable year. [Reg. §1.52-1.]

☐ [*T.D. 7553, 7-20-78, Amended by T.D. 7921, 11-18-83, T.D. 7955, 5-10-84, T.D. 8179, 3-1-88 (corrected 3-14-88, 5-9-88 and 7-10-2019) and T.D. 8540, 6-9-94.*]

[Reg. §1.52-2]

§1.52-2. Adjustments for acquisitions and dispositions.—(a) *General rule.*—The provisions in this section only apply to the computation of the new jobs credit. If, after December 31, 1975, an employer acquires the major portion of a trade or business or the major portion of a separate unit of a trade or business, then, for purposes of computing the new jobs credit for any calendar year ending after the acquisition, both the amount of unemployment insurance wages and the amount of total wages considered to have been paid by the acquiring employer, for both the year in which the acquisition occurred and the preceding year, must be increased, respectively, by the amount of unemployment insurance wages and the amount of total wages paid by the predecessor employer that are attributable to the acquired portion of the trade or business or separate unit. If the predecessor employer informs the acquiring employer in writing of the amount of unemployment insurance wages and the amount of total wages attributable to the acquired portion of the trade or business that have been paid during the periods preceding the acquisition, then, for purposes of computing the credit for any calendar year ending after the acquisition the amount of unemployment insurance wages and the amount of total wages considered paid by the predecessor employer shall be decreased by those amounts. Regardless of whether the predecessor employer so informs the acquiring employer, the predecessor employer shall not be allowed a credit for the amount of any increase in the employment insurance wages or the total wages in the calendar year of the acquisition attributable to the acquired portion of the trade or business over the amount of such wages in the calendar year preceding the acquisition.

(b) *Meaning of terms.*—(1) *Acquisition.*—(i) For purposes of this section, the term "acquisition" includes a lease agreement if the effect of the lease is to transfer the major portion of the trade or business or of a separate unit of the trade or business for the period of the lease. For instance, if one company leases a factory (including equipment) to another company for a two-year period, the employees are retained by the second company, and the factory is used for the same general purposes as before, then for purposes of this section the lessee has acquired the lessor's trade or business for the period of the lease.

(ii) Neither the major portion of a trade or business nor the major portion of a separate unit of a trade or business is acquired merely by acquiring physical assets. The acquisition must transfer a viable trade or business.

(iii) Subdivision (ii) of this subparagraph may be illustrated by the following examples:

Example (1). R Company, a restaurant, sells its building and all its restaurant equipment to S Company and moves into a larger, more modern building across the street. R Company purchases new equipment, retains its name and continues to operate as a restaurant. S Company opens a new restaurant in the old R Company building. S Company has merely acquired the old R Company assets; it has not acquired any portion of R Company's business.

Example (2). The facts are the same as in *Example (1),* except that R Company also sells its name and goodwill to S Company and ceases to operate a restaurant business. S Company operates its restaurant using the old R Company name. In this situation, S Company has acquired R Company's business.

(2) *Separate unit.*—(i) A separate unit is a segment of a trade or business capable of operating as a self-sustaining enterprise with minor adjustments. The allocation of a portion of the goodwill of a trade or business to one of its segments is a strong indication that that segment is a separate unit.

(ii) The following examples are illustrations of the acquisition of a separate unit of a trade or business:

Example (1). The M Corporation, which has been engaged in the sale and repair of boats, leases the repair shop building and all the property used in its boat repair operations to the N Company for four years and gives the N Company a covenant not to compete in the boat repair business for the period of the lease. The N Company is considered to have acquired a separate unit of M Corporation's business for the period of the lease.

Example (2). (a) The P Company is engaged in the operation of a chain of department stores. There are eight divisions, each division is located in a different metropolitan area of the country, and each division operates under a different name. Although certain buying and merchandising functions are centralized, each division's day-to-day operations are independent of the others. The Q Corporation acquires all of the physical and intangible assets of one of the divisions, including the division's name. Other than making those minor adjustments necessary to give the division buying and merchandising departments, the Q Corporation allows the division to continue doing business in the same manner as it had been operating prior to the acquisition. The Q Corporation has acquired a separate unit of the P Company's business.

(b) The facts are the same as in (a) above, except that Q Corporation buys the division merely to obtain its store locations. Before the Q Corporation takes over, the division liquidates its inventory in a going-out-of-business sale. The Q Corporation has merely acquired assets in this transaction, not a separate unit of P Company's business.

Example (3). The R Company processes and distributes meat products. Both the processing division and the distributorship are self-sustaining, profitable operations. The acquisition of either the meat processing division or the distributorship would be an acquisition of a separate unit of the R Company's business.

Example (4). The S Corporation is engaged in the manufacture and sale of steel and steel products. S Corporation also owns a coal mine, which it operates for the sole purpose of supplying its coal requirements for its steel manufacturing operations. The acquisition of the coal mine would be an acquisition of a separate unit of the S Company's business.

Example (5). The T Company, which is engaged in the business of operating a chain of drug stores, sells its only downtown drug store to the V Company and agrees not to open another T Company store in the downtown area for five years. Included in the purchase price is an amount that is charged for the goodwill of the store location. The V Company has acquired a separate unit of the T Company's business.

Example (6). The W Company, which is engaged in the business of operating a chain of drug stores, sells one of its stores to the X Company, but continues to operate another drug store three blocks away. The X Company opens the store doing business under its own name. The X Company has not acquired a separate unit of the W Company's business.

Example (7). (a) The Y Corporation, which is engaged in the manufacture of mattresses, sells one of its three factories to the Z Company. At the time of the sale, the factory is capable of profitably manufacturing mattresses on its own. Z Company has acquired a separate unit of the Y Corporation.

(b) The facts are the same as in (a) above, except that a profitable manufacturing operation cannot be conducted in the factory standing on its own. Z Company has not acquired a separate unit of the Y Corporation.

Example (8). The O Construction Company is owned by A, B, and C, who are unrelated individuals. It owns equipment valued at 1.5 million dollars and construction contracts valued at 6 million dollars. A, wishing to start his own company, exchanges his interest in O Company for 2 million dollars of contracts and a sufficient amount of equipment to enable him to begin business immediately. A has acquired a separate unit of the O Company's business.

(3) *Major portion.*—All the facts and circumstances surrounding the transaction shall be taken into account in determining what constitutes a major portion of a trade or business (or separate unit). Factors to be considered include:

(i) The fair market value of the assets in the portion relative to the fair market value of the other assets of the trade or business (or separate unit);

(ii) The proportion of goodwill attributable to the portion of the trade or business (or separate unit);

(iii) The proportion of the number of employees of the trade or business (or separate unit) attributable to the portion in the periods immediately preceding the transaction; and

(iv) The proportion of the sales or gross receipts, net income, and budget of the trade or business (or separate unit) attributable to the portion. [Reg. §1.52-2.]

☐ [T.D. 7553, 7-20-78. Amended by T.D. 7921, 11-18-83.]

[Reg. §1.52-3]

§1.52-3. Limitations with respect to certain persons.—(a) *Mutual savings institutions.*—In the case of an organization to which section 593 applies (that is, a mutual savings bank, a cooperative bank or a domestic building and loan association), the amount of the targeted jobs credit (new jobs credit in the case of wages paid before 1979) allowable under section 44B shall be 50 percent of the amount otherwise determined under section 51, or, in the case of an organization under common control, under §1.52-1(a) and (b).

(b) *Regulated investment companies and real estate investment trusts.*—In the case of a regulated investment company or a real estate investment trust subject to taxation under subchapter M, chapter 1 of the Code, the amount of the targeted jobs credit (new jobs credit in the case of wages paid before 1979) allowable under section 44B shall be reduced to the company's or trust's ratable share of the credit. The ratable share shall be determined in accordance with rules similar to the rules provided in section 46(e)(2)(B) and the regulations thereunder. For purposes of computing the ratable share, the reduction of the deduction for wage or salary expenses under §1.280C-1 shall not be taken into account.

(c) *Cooperatives.*—(1) *Taxable years ending after October 31, 1978.*—For taxable years ending after October 31, 1978, in the case of a cooperative organization described in section 1381(a), rules similar to rules provided in section 46(h) and the regulations thereunder shall apply in determining the distribution of the amount of the targeted jobs credit (new jobs credit in the case of wages paid before 1979) allowable to the cooperative organization and its patrons under section 44B.

(2) *Taxable years ending before November 1, 1978.*—For taxable years ending before November 1, 1978, in the case of a cooperative organization described in section 1381(a), the amount of new jobs credit allowable under section 44B shall be reduced to the cooperative's ratable share of the credit. The ratable share shall be the ratio which the taxable income of the cooperative for the taxable year bears to its taxable income increased by the amount of the deductions allowed under section 1382(b) and (c). For purposes of computing the ratable share, the reduction of the deduction for wage or salary expenses under §1.280C-1 shall not be taken into account. [Reg. §1.52-3.]

☐ [T. D. 7553, 7-20-78. Amended by T. D. 7921, 11-18-83.]

⟫⟫→ *Caution: Reg. §1.53-1 was adopted under former Code Sec. 53 of the Internal Revenue Code of 1954. Current Code Sec. 38 contains provisions comparable to the former Code Sec. 53 limits on credits.*

[Reg. §1.53-1]

§1.53-1. Limitation based on amount of credit.—(a) *General rule.*—(1) *Targeted jobs credit.*—For taxable years beginning after December 31, 1978, the amount of the targeted jobs credit allowed by section 44B (as amended by the Revenue Act of 1978) shall not exceed 90 percent of the tax imposed by chapter 1, reduced by the credits enumerated in section 53(a).

(2) *New jobs credit.*—For taxable years beginning before January 1, 1979, the amount of the new jobs credit allowed by section 44B (as in effect prior to enactment of the Revenue Act of 1978) shall not exceed the tax imposed by chapter 1, reduced by the credits enumerated in section 53(a).

(b) *Special rule for 1978-79 fiscal year.*—In the case of a taxable year beginning before January 1, 1979, and ending after that date, the sum of the targeted jobs credit (determined without regard to the tax liability limitation in paragraph (a)(1) of this section) and the new jobs credit (determined without regard to the tax liability limitation in paragraph (a)(2) of this section) shall not exceed the tax imposed by chapter 1, reduced by the credits enumerated in section 53(a). [Reg. §1.53-1.]

☐ [T.D. 7921, 11-18-83.]

⟫⟫→ *Caution: Reg. §1.53-2 was adopted under former Code Sec. 53 of the Internal Revenue Code of 1954. Current Code Sec. 39 contains provisions comparable to the former Code Sec. 53 limits on carryovers of unused credits.*

[Reg. §1.53-2]

§1.53-2. Carryback and carryover of unused credit.—(a) *Allowance of unused credit as a carryback or carryover.*—(1) *In general.*—Section 53(b) (formerly designated as section 53(c) for taxable years beginning before 1979) provides for carrybacks and carryovers of unused targeted jobs credit (new jobs credit in the case of wages paid before 1979). An unused credit is the excess of the credit determined under section 51 for the taxable year over the limitations provided by Sec. 1.53-1 for such taxable year. Subject to the limitations contained in paragraph (b) of this section and paragraph (f) of section 1.53-3, an unused credit shall be added to the amount allowable as a credit under section 44B for the years to which an unused credit can be carried. The year with respect to which an unused credit arises shall be referred to in this section as the "unused credit year."

(2) *Taxable years to which unused credit may be carried.*—An unused targeted jobs credit (new jobs credit in the case of wages paid before

>>>→ Caution: *Reg. §1.53-2 was adopted under former Code Sec. 53 of the Internal Revenue Code of 1954. Current Code Sec. 39 contains provisions comparable to the former Code Sec. 53 limits on carryovers of unused credits.*

1979) shall be a new employee credit carryback to each of the 3 taxable years preceding the unused credit year and a new employee credit carryove to each of the 15 taxable years succeeding the unused credit year. An unused credit must be carried first to the earliest of the taxable years to which it may be carried, and then to each of the other taxable years (in order of time) to the extent that the unused credit may not be added (because of the limitation contained in paragraph (b) of this section) to the amount allowable as a credit under section 44B for a prior taxable year.

(b) *Limitations on allowance of unused credit.*—(1) *In general.*—The amount of the unused targeted jobs credit (new jobs credit in the case of wages paid before 1979) from any particular unused credit year which may be added under section 53(b)(1) (section 53(c)(1) in the case of a new jobs credit) to the amount allowable as a credit under section 44B for any of the preceding or succeeding taxable years to which such credit may be carried shall not exceed the amount by which the limitation in Sec 1.53-1 for such preceding or succeeding taxable year exceeds the sum of (i) the credit allowable under section 44B for such preceding or succeeding taxable year, and (ii) other unused credits carried to such preceding or succeeding taxable year which are attributable to unused credit years prior to the particular unused credit year. Thus, in determining the amount, if any, of an unused credit from a particular unused credit year which shall be added to the amount allowable as a credit for any preceding or succeeding taxable year, the credit earned for such preceding of succeeding taxable year, plus any unused credits originating in taxable years prior to the particular unused credit year, shall first be applied against the limitation based on amount of tax for such preceding or succeeding taxable year. To the extent the limitation based on amount of tax for the preceding or succeeding taxable year exceeds the sum of the credit earned for such year and other unused credits attributable to years prior to the particular unused credit year, the unused credit from the particular unused credit year shall be added to the amount allowable as a credit under section 44B for such preceding or succeeding year. If any portion of the unused credit is a carryback to a taxable year beginning before January 1, 1977, section 44B shall be deemed to have been in effect for such taxable year for purposes of allowing such carryback as a credit under section 44B. To the extent that an unused credit cannot be added for a particular preceding or succeeding taxable year because of the limitation contained in this paragraph, such unused credit shall be available as a carryback or carryover to the next succeeding taxable year to which it may be carried.

(2) *Special rules for an electing small business corporation.*—An unused targeted jobs credit (new jobs credit in the case of wages paid before 1979) under section 44B of a corporation which arises in an unused credit year for which the coporation is not an electing small business corporation (as defined in section 1371(b)) and which is a carryback or carryover to a taxable year for which the corporation is an electing small business corporation shall not be added to the amount allowable as a credit under section 44B to the shareholders of such corporation for any taxable year. However, a taxable year for which the corporation is an electing small business corporation shall be counted as a taxable year for purposes of determining the taxable years to which such unused credit may be carried.

(3) *Corporate acquisitions.*—For the carryover of unused credits under section 44B in the case of certain corporate acquisitions, see section 381(c)(26) and Sec. 1.381(c)(26)-1.

(4) *Examples.*—This paragraph may be illustrated by the following examples.

Example 1. In 1978, A, a calendar year taxpayer, had an unused new jobs credit of $2,000. In 1979, A has a targeted jobs credit of $2,000 and a tax liability imposed by chapter 1 of the Code of $4,000 after all credits listed in section 53(a) have been taken into account. The amount of A's targeted jobs credit allowable under section 44B for 1979 is 90 percent of A's tax liability. The amount of the new jobs credit that may be carried to 1979 is limited to $1,600 ($3,600 [90% of $4,000] – $2,000).

Example 2. In 1979, B, a calendar year taxpayer, has a tax liability imposed by chapter 1 of the Code of $10,000 after all credits listed in section 53(a) have been taken. B's targeted jobs credit for that taxable year is limited to 90 percent of his income tax liability of $9,000. B has a $15,000 targeted jobs credit in 1979 resulting in an unused targeted jobs credit of $5,000 for that year. In 1976 and 1977 B had tax liabilities imposed by chapter 1 of the Code of $3,000 and $4,000 respectively after all credits listed in section 53(a) had been taken. For purposes of carrying back an unused targeted jobs credit to a taxable year beginning before January 1, 1977, section 44B as amended by the Revenue Act of 1978 is deemed to have been in effect for such taxable year. Accordingly, the applicable tax liability limitation for 1976 would be governed by section 53(a) (as amended by the Revenue Act of 1978) which limits the amount of targeted jobs credit allowed to 90 percent of the tax imposed by chapter 1 of the Code after all credits listed in section 53(a) have been taken. B may carry back $2,700 (90% of 3,000) of the 1979 unused targeted jobs credit to 1976. B may carry back $4,000 of the unused targeted jobs credit to 1977 because section 53(a) as it applied to the 1977 taxable year limited the amount of the credit to 100 percent of the taxpayer's tax liability imposed by chapter 1 of the Code after all credits listed in section 53(a) had been taken.

[Reg. §1.53-2.]

□ [T.D. 7921, 11-18-83.]

>>>→ Caution: *Reg. §1.53-3 was adopted under former Code Sec. 53 of the Internal Revenue Code of 1954. Current Code Sec. 41 contains provisions comparable to the former Code Sec. 53 special rule for pass-through of credit.*

[Reg. §1.53-3]

§1.53-3. Separate rule for pass-through of jobs credit.—(a) *In general.*—Under section 53(b), in the case of a new jobs credit or targeted jobs credit earned under section 44B by a partnership, estate or trust, or subchapter S corporation, the amount of the credit that may be taken into account by a partner, beneficiary, or shareholder may not exceed a limitation under section 53(b) separately computed with respect to the partner's, beneficiary's, or shareholder's interest in the entity. A credit is subject to the limitation of section 53(b) with respect to a partner, beneficiary, or shareholder if it is earned by a partnership, estate or trust, or subchapter S corporation in a taxable year ending within, or ending before, a taxable year beginning before January 1, 1979 of the partner, beneficiary, or shareholder. See paragraph (f) of this section for rules on carryback or carryover of a credit subject to separate limitation. This section prescribes rules, under the authority of section 44B(b), relating to the computation of the separate limitation. For purposes of this section, references to section 53(a) and (b) are to that section as it existed before it was amended by the Revenue Act of 1978. This paragraph may be illustrated by the following examples:

Example 1. A, a calendar year taxpayer, is a partner in P, a calendar year partnership. A's pro rata portion of the credit earned by P in 1978 is $200. The $200 credit to be claimed on A's 1978 return is subject to the separate limitation in section 53(b) because the limitation applies to taxable years of the taxpayer beginning before January 1, 1979.

Example 2. B, a calendar year taxpayer, is a shareholder in Corporation M, a subchapter S corporation with a July to June fiscal year. B's prorata portion of the credit earned by Corporation M in its taxable year beginning in 1978 is $100. The $100 credit to be claimed on B's 1979 return is not subject to the separate limitation requirement of section 53(b) because the limitation only applies to taxable years of the taxpayer beginning before 1979, notwithstanding the credit was earned by Corporation M before 1979.

(b) *Application of credit earned.*—A credit earned under section 44B by a partnership, estate or trust, or subchapter S corporation shall be applied by a partner, beneficiary, or shareholder, to the extent allowed under section 53(b), before applying any other credit earned under section 44B. For example, if an individual has a new jobs credit from a proprietorship of $2,000 and from a partnership (after applying section 53(b)) of $1,800, but the credit must be limited under section 53(a) to $3,000, the entire $1,800 credit from the partnership would be applied before any part of the $2,000 amount is applied.

(c) *Amount of separate limitation.*—The amount of the separate limitation is equal to the partner's, beneficiary's, or shareholder's limitation under section 53(a) for the taxable year multiplied by a fraction. The numerator of the fraction is the portion of the taxpayer's taxable income for the year attributable to the taxpayer's interest in the entity. The denominator of the fraction is the taxpayer's total taxable income for the year reduced by the zero bracket amount, if any.

(d) *Portion of taxable income attributable to an interest in a partnership, estate or trust, or subchapter S corporation.*—(1) *General rule.*—The portion of a taxpayer's taxable income attributable to an interest in a partnership, estate or trust, or subchapter S corporation is the amount of income from that entity the taxpayer is required to include in gross income, reduced by—

(i) The amount of the deductions allowed to the taxpayer that are attributable to the taxpayer's interest in the entity; and

(ii) A proportionate share of the deductions allowed to the taxpayer not attributable to a specific activity (as defined in paragraph (e)).

If a deduction comprises both an item that is attributable to the taxpayer's interest in the entity and an item or items that are not attributable to the interest in the entity, and if the deduction is limited by a provision of the Code (such as section 170(b), relating to limitations on charitable contributions), the deduction must be prorated among the items taken into account in computing the deduc-

⟫⟫→ *Caution: Reg. §1.53-3 was adopted under former Code Sec. 53 of the Internal Revenue Code of 1954. Current Code Sec. 41 contains provisions comparable to the former Code Sec. 53 special rule for pass-through of credit.*

tion. For example, if an individual makes a charitable contribution of $5,000 and his distributive share of a partnership includes $2,000 in charitable contributions made by the partnership, and if the charitable contribution deduction is limited to $3,500 under section 170(b), then the portion of the deduction allowed to the taxpayer that is not attributable to a specific activity is $2,500 ($3,500 × ($5,000 ÷ $7,000)) and the portion of the deduction allowed to the taxpayer that is attributable to the interest in the partnership is $1,000 ($3,500 × ($2,000 ÷ $7,000)).

(2) *Deductions attributable to an interest in an entity.*—Examples of deductions that are attributable to the taxpayer's interest in an entity include (but are not limited to) a deduction under section 1202 attributable to a net capital gain passed through the entity, and a deduction attributable to a deductible item (such as a charitable contribution) that has been passed through the entity.

(3) *Computation of the proportionate share of deductions not attributable to a specific activity.*—The proportionate share of a deduction of the taxpayer not attributable to a specific activity is obtained by multiplying the amount of the deduction by a fraction. The numerator of the fraction is the income from the entity that the taxpayer is required to include in gross income, reduced by the amount of the deductions of the taxpayer that are attributable to the taxpayer's interest in the entity. The denominator is the taxpayer's gross income reduced by the amount of all the deductions attributable to specific activities.

(4) *Examples.*—The method of determining the amount of taxable income attributable to an interest in a partnership, estate or trust, or subchapter S corporation is illustrated by the following examples:

Example 1. (a) A, a single individual, is a shareholder in S Corporation, a subchapter S corporation. A is required to include the following amounts from S corporation is his gross income:

Salary	$3,000
Undistributed taxable income:	
Ordinary income	8,000
Net capital gain	2,000
Total	10,000
Total	13,000

A has income from other activities:

Ordinary income	6,000
Net capital gain	4,000
Total	10,000

(b) In order to determine the taxable income attributable to A's interest in S Corporation, it is necessary to reduce the amount of income from S Corporation that A is required to include in gross income by the amount of A's deductions attributable to the interest in S Corporation and by a proportionate share of A's deductions not attributable to a specific activity. These computations are made in paragraph (c) of this example. However, before the computation reducing A's income by a proportionate share of the deductions not attributable to a specific activity can be made, the ratio described in subparagraph (3) of this paragraph (d) must be determined. The numerator of the ratio (the amount of income from S Corporation that A is required to include in gross income, reduced by the amount of the deductions attributable to A's interest in S Corporation) is obtained in paragraph (c) of this example in the process of computing A's taxable income attributable to the interest in S Corporation. The determination of the denominator (A's gross income reduced by the amount of all deductions attributable to specific activities, however, require a separate computation, which follows:

Gross income:	
Income from S Corporation	$13,000
Income from other sources	10,000
Total	23,000
Less: Deductions attributable to specific activities:	
Section 1202 deduction (50 percent of $6,000)	3,000
A's gross income reduced by the amount of the deductions attributable to specific activities (denominator of the ratio for determining the proportionate share of deductions not attributable to a specific activity)	20,000

(c) Computation of the amount of A's taxable income attributable to the interest in S Corporation:

Income from S Corporation that A is required to include in gross income:	
Ordinary income	$11,000
Net capital gain	2,000
Total	13,000

Less: Deductions of the taxpayer attributable to the interest in S Corporation:	
Section 1202 deduction (50 pct. of $2,000)	1,000
(Numerator of the ratio for determining the proportionate share of deductions not attributable to a specific activity)	12,000
Less: Proportionate share of the deductions of the taxpayer not attributable to a specific activity:	
Personal exemption deduction ($750 × $12,000/$20,000)	450
Zero bracket amount ($2,200 × $12,000/$20,000)	1,320
Total	1,770
Portion of A's taxable income attributable to interest in S Corporation	10,230

Example 2. (a) C, a married individual with two children, is a partner in the CD Company. C's distributive share of the CD Company consists of the following:

Ordinary income (other than guaranteed payment)	$38,420
Guaranteed payment	20,000
Net long-term capital gain	6,000
Net short-term capital loss	2,000
Dividends qualifying for exclusion	100
Charitable contributions	500

C also has items of income from other sources and deductions, as follows:

Ordinary income	$21,680
Short-term capital gain	2,000
Dividends qualifying for exclusion	400
Deductions:	
Deductible medical expenses	16,000
Charitable contributions	4,000
Alimony	18,000
Interest and taxes on home	8,000
Loss relating to another specific activity	4,000

(b) In order to determine C's taxable income attributable to the interest in the partnership, it is necessary to reduce the amount of income from the partnership that C is required to include in gross income by the amount of C's deductions attributable to the interest in the partnership and by a proportionate share of C's deductions not attributable to a specific activity. These computations are made in paragraph (c) of this example. However, before the computation reducing C's income by a proportionate share of the deductions not attributable to a specific activity can be made, the ratio described in paragraph (d)(3) of this section must be determined. The numerator of the ratio is determined in paragraph (c) of this example in the process of computing C's taxable income attributable to the interest in the partnership. The denominator, however, requires a separate computation, reducing C's gross income by the amount of all deductions attributable to specific activities. This computation is as follows:

Gross income: Income from the partnership:		
Ordinary income		$58,420
Net long-term capital gain		6,000
Dividends	100	
Less: Proportionate share of dividend exclusion ($100 × $100/$500)	20	
		80
		64,500
Income from other sources:		
Ordinary income		21,680
Net short/term capital gain		2,000
Dividends	400	
Less: Proportionate share of dividend exclusion ($100 × $400/$500)	$80	
		320
		24,000
		88,500
Less: Deductions attributable to specific activities:		
Net short-term capital loss passed through the partnership		2,000
Loss related to another specific activity		4,000
Section 1202 deduction attributable to the interest in the partnership		2,000
Charitable contribution deduction passed through the partnership		500
		8,500

Reg. §1.53-3(d)(4)

»»→ *Caution: Reg. §1.53-3 was adopted under former Code Sec. 53 of the Internal Revenue Code of 1954. Current Code Sec. 41 contains provisions comparable to the former Code Sec. 53 special rule for pass-through of credit.*

C's gross income, reduced by the amount of the deductions attributable to specific activities (denominator of the ratio for determining the proportionate share of deductions not attributable to a specific activity) 80,000

(c) Computation of the amount of C's taxable income attributable to the interest in the partnership:

Distributive share of ordinary income (other than guaranteed payments)	$38,420
Guaranteed payment	20,000
Distributive share of dividends less share of exclusion	80
Distributive share of net long-term capital gain	6,000
	64,500

Section 1202 deduction (50 pct. of $4,000)	2,000
Charitable contribution passed through the partnership . . .	500
Net short-term capital loss passed through the partnership .	2,000
	4,500

(Numerator of the ratio for determining the proportionate share of deductions not attributable to a specific activity) . . . 60,000

Section 1202 deduction ($1,000 × $60,000/$80,000)	750
Deductible medical expenses ($16,000 × $60,000/$80,000) . .	12,000
Charitable contributions ($4,000 × $60,000/$80,000)	3,000
Alimony ($18,000 × $60,000/$80,000)	13,500
Interest and taxes on home ($8,000 × $60,000/$80,000)	6,000
Personal exemption deduction ($3,000 × $60,000/$80,000) . .	2,250
Total	37,500

Portion of C's taxable income attributable to the interest in the partnership 22,500

C has a deduction under section 1202 of $3,000. Of that deduction, $2,000 is attributable directly to C's interest in the partnership (50 percent of the net capital gain that would result from offsetting the $6,000 net long-term capital gain and the $2,000 net short-term capital loss that are attributable to C's interest in the partnership). Since the remaining $1,000 deduction under section 1202 cannot be attributed directly to either C's income from the partnership or any other specific activity, it must be treated as a deduction not attributable to a specific activity.

(e) *Deductions not attributable to a specific activity.*—(1) *Specific activity defined.*—A specific activity means a course of continuous conduct involving a particular line of endeavor, whether or not the activity is carried on for profit. Examples of a specific activity are:

(i) A trade or business carried on by the taxpayer;

(ii) A trade or business carried on by an entity in which the taxpayer has an interest;

(iii) An activity with respect to which the taxpayer is entitled to a deduction under section 212;

(iv) The operation of a farm as a hobby.

(2) *Types of deductions not attributable to a specific activity.*—Examples of deductions not attributable to a specific activity include charitable contributions made by the partner, beneficiary, or shareholder; medical expenses; alimony; interest on personal debts of the partner, beneficiary, or shareholder; and real estate taxes on the personal residence of the partner, beneficiary, or shareholder. For purposes of this section, in cases in which deductions are not itemized, the zero bracket amount is considered to be a deduction not attributable to a specific activity.

(f) *Carryback or carryover of credit subject to separate limitation.*—A credit subject to the separate limitation under section 53(b) that is carried back or carried over to a taxable year beginning before January 1, 1979, is also subject to the separate limitation in the carryback or carryover year. For purposes of the preceding sentence, a credit that is earned by a partnership, a trust, or estate, or a subchapter S corporation in a taxable year of such entity ending within, or after, the taxable year of a partner beneficiary or shareholder beginning after December 31, 1978, will not be subject to the separate limitation in section 53(b) with respect to such partner, beneficiary, or shareholder. The taxpayer to whom the credit has been passed through shall not be prevented from applying the unused portion in a carryback or carryover year merely because the entity that earned the credit changes its form of conducting business if the nature of its trade or business essentially remains the same. The computation of the separate limitation in such a case shall reflect the income attributable to the taxpayer's interest in the entity in its revised form. Thus, a shareholder carrying over a credit from a subchapter S corporation may include dividends declared by that corporation after the subchapter S election had been terminated as income attributable to that person's interest in the entity. Similarly, if a partnership incorporates in a carryover year, any income attributable to an interest in the corporation will be regarded, for purposes of computing the separate limitation under section 53(b), as income attributable to an interest in the entity. This paragraph may be illustrated by the following examples:

Example 1. A, a calendar year taxpayer, is a shareholder in Corporation M, a subchapter S corporation. In 1977, A's pro rata share of the new jobs credit earned by Corporation M was $10,000. A could only use $2,000 of the credit in 1977 because of the separate limitation under section 53(b). In 1978, A carries the unused credit over from 1977. The carryover credit is subject to the separate limitation under section 53(b).

Example 2. Assume the same facts as in example 1 except that the unused credit is carried over to 1979. The carryover credit is not subject to the separate limitation under section 53(b) because that limitation does not apply to taxable years of a taxpayer beginning after December 31, 1978.

Example 3. B, a calendar year taxpayer, is a shareholder in Corporation W, a subchapter S corporation. In 1979, B's pro rata share of the targeted jobs credit covered by Corporation W was $5,000 but B could only use $3,000 of the credit in 1979. B carries back the unused credit to 1978. The carryback credit is not subject to the separate limitation under section 53(b).

[Reg. §1.53-3.]

☐ [*T.D. 7560,* 12-28-78. *Redesignated and amended by T.D.* 7921, 11-18-83.]

Alternative Minimum Tax

[Reg. §1.55-1]

§1.55-1. Alternative minimum taxable income.—(a) *General rule for computing alternative minimum taxable income.*—Except as otherwise provided by statute, regulations, or other published guidance issued by the Commissioner, all Internal Revenue Code provisions that apply in determining the regular taxable income of a taxpayer also apply in determining the alternative minimum taxable income of the taxpayer.

(b) *Items based on adjusted gross income or modified adjusted gross income.*—In determining the alternative minimum taxable income of a taxpayer other than a corporation, all references to the taxpayer's adjusted gross income or modified adjusted gross income in determining the amount of items of income, exclusion, or deduction must be treated as references to the taxpayer's adjusted gross income or modified adjusted gross income as determined for regular tax purposes.

(c) *Effective date.*—These regulations are effective for taxable years beginning after December 31, 1993. [Reg. §1.55-1.]

☐ [*T.D.* 8569, 11-23-94.]

[Reg. §1.56-0]

§1.56-0. Table of contents to §1.56-1, adjustment for book income of corporations.

(a) Computation of the book income adjustment.

(C) Eligibility to make and manner of making election.

(D) Election or revocation of election made on an amended return.

(iv) Quarterly statement filed with the Securities and Exchange Commission (SEC).

(5) Computation of net book income using current earnings and profits.

(i) In general.

(ii) Current earnings and profits of a consolidated group.

(6) Additional rules for computation of net book income of a foreign corporate taxpayer.

(i) Adjusted net book income of a foreign taxpayer.

(ii) Effectively connected net book income of a foreign taxpayer.

(A) In general.

(B) Certain exempt amounts.

(iii) Computation of net book income of a foreign taxpayer using current earnings and profits.

(7) Examples.

(c) Applicable financial statement.

(1) In general.

(i) Statement required to be filed with the Securities and Exchange Commission (SEC).

(ii) Certified audited financial statement.

(iii) Financial statement provided to a government regulator.

(iv) Other financial statements.

(v) Required use of current earnings and profits.

(2) Election to treat net book income as equal to current earnings and profits for the taxable year.

(i) In general.

(ii) Time of making election.

(iii) Eligibility to make and manner of making election.

(iv) Election by common parent of consolidated group.

(v) Election or revocation of election made on an amended return.

(3) Priority among statements.

(i) In general.

(ii) Special priority rules for use of certified audited financial statements and other financial statements.

(iii) Priority among financial statements provided to a government regulator.

(iv) Statements of equal priority.

(A) In general.

(B) Exceptions to the general rule in paragraph (c)(3)(iv)(A).

(4) Use of financial statement for a substantial non-tax purpose.

(5) Special rules.

(i) Applicable financial statement of related corporations.

(A) Applicable financial statement of a consolidated group.

(B) Special rule for statements of equal priority.

(C) Special rule for related corporations.

(D) Anti-abuse rule.

(ii) Applicable financial statement of a foreign corporation with a United States trade or business.

(A) In general.

(B) Special rules for applicable financial statement of a trade or business of a foreign taxpayer.

(C) Special rule for statements of equal priority.

(D) Anti-abuse rule.

(iii) Supplement or amendment to an applicable financial statement.

(A) Excluding a restatement of net book income.

(B) Restatement of net book income.

(6) Examples.

(d) Adjustments to net book income.

(1) In general.

(2) Definitions.

(i) Historic practice.

(ii) Accounting literature.

(3) Adjustments for certain taxes.

(i) In general.

(ii) Exception for certain foreign taxes.

(iii) Certain valuation adjustments.

(iv) Examples.

(4) Adjustments to prevent omission or duplication.

(i) In general.

(ii) Special rule for depreciating an asset below its cost.

(iii) Consolidated group using current earnings and profits.

(iv) Restatement of a prior year's applicable financial statement.

(A) In general.

(B) Reconciliation of owner's equity in applicable financial statements.

(C) Use of different priority applicable financial statements in consecutive taxable years.

(D) First successor year defined.

(E) Exceptions.

(v) Adjustment for items previously taxed as subpart F income.

(vi) Adjustment for pooling of interests.

(vii) Adjustment for certain deferred foreign taxes.

(viii) Examples.

(5) Adjustments resulting from disclosure.

(i) Adjustment for footnote disclosure or other supplementary information.

(A) In general.

(B) Disclosures not specifically authorized in the accounting literature.

(ii) Equity adjustments.

(A) In general.

(B) Definition of equity adjustment.

(iii) Amount disclosed in an accountant's opinion.

(iv) Accounting method changes that result in cumulative adjustments to the current year's applicable financial statement.

(A) In general.

(B) Exception.

(v) Examples.

(6) Adjustments applicable to related corporations.

(i) Consolidated returns.

(A) In general.

(B) Corporations included in the consolidated Federal income tax return but excluded from the applicable financial statement.

(C) Corporations included in the applicable financial statement but excluded from the consolidated tax return.

(ii) Adjustment under the principles of section 482.

(iii) Adjustment for dividends received from section 936 corporations.

(A) In general.

(B) Treatment as foreign taxes.

(C) Treatment of taxes imposed on section 936 corporations.

(iv) Adjustment to net book income on sale of certain investments.

(v) Examples.

(7) Adjustments for foreign taxpayers with a United States trade or business.

(i) In general.

(ii) Example.

(8) Adjustment for corporations subject to subchapter F.

(e) Special rules.

(1) Cooperatives.

(2) Alaska Native Corporations.

(3) Insurance companies.

(4) Estimating the net book income adjustment for purposes of estimated tax liability.

(5) Effective/applicability date.

[Reg. § 1.56-0.]

☐ [T.D. 8138, 4-23-87. *Amended by T.D. 8197, 4-27-88. Redesignated and amended by T.D. 8307, 8-16-90. Amended by T.D. 9347, 8-6-2007.*]

[Reg. § 1.56(g)-0]

§ 1.56(g)-0. Table of Contents.—This section lists the paragraphs contained in § 1.56(g)-1.

§ 1.56(g)-1 Adjusted current earnings.
  (a) Adjustment for adjusted current earnings.
    (1) Positive adjustment.
    (2) Negative adjustment.
      (i) In general.
      (ii) Limitation on negative adjustments.
      (iii) Example.
    (3) Negative amounts.
    (4) Taxpayers subject to adjustment for adjusted current earnings.
    (5) General rule for applying Internal Revenue Code provisions in determining adjusted current earnings.
      (i) In general.
      (ii) Example.
    (6) Definitions.
      (i) Pre-adjustment alternative minimum taxable income.
      (ii) Adjusted current earnings.
      (iii) Earnings and profits.
    (7) Application to foreign corporations.
  (b) Depreciation allowed.
    (1) Property placed in service after 1989.
    (2) Property subject to new ACRS.
      (i) In general.
      (ii) Rules for computing the depreciation deduction.
      (iii) Example.
    (3) Property subject to original ACRS.
      (i) In general.
      (ii) Rules for computing the depreciation deduction.
      (iii) Example.
    (4) Special rule for certain section 168(f) property.
    (5) Certain property not subject to ACRS.
  (c) Inclusion in adjusted current earnings of items included in earnings and profits.
    (1) In general.
    (2) Certain amounts not taken into account in determining whether an item is permanently excluded.
    (3) Allowance of offsetting deductions.
    (4) Special rules.
      (i) Income from the discharge of indebtedness.
      (ii) Federal income tax refunds.
      (iii) Income earned on behalf of states and municipalities.
    (5) Treatment of life insurance contracts.
      (i) In general.
      (ii) Inclusion of inside buildup.
      (iii) Calculation of income on the contract.
      (iv) Treatment of distributions under the life insurance contract.
      (v) Treatment of death benefits.
      (vi) Other rules.
        (A) Term life insurance contracts without net surrender values.
        (B) Life insurance contracts involving divided ownership.
      (vii) Examples.
    (6) Partial list of income items excluded from gross income but included in earnings and profits.
    (7) Partial list of items excluded from both pre-adjustment alternative minimum taxable income and adjusted current earnings.
  (d) Disallowance of items not deductible in computing earnings and profits.
    (1) In general.
    (2) Deductions for certain dividends received.
      (i) Certain amounts deducted under sections 243 and 245.
      (ii) Special rules.
        (A) Dividends received from a foreign sales corporation.
        (B) Dividends received from a section 936 corporation.
      (iii) Special rule for certain dividends received by certain cooperatives.
    (3) Partial list of items not deductible in computing earnings and profits.
    (4) Partial list of items deductible for purposes of computing both pre-adjustment alternative minimum taxable income and adjusted current earnings.
  (e) Treatment of income items included, and deduction items not allowed, in computing pre-adjustment alternative minimum taxable income.
  (f) Certain other earnings and profits adjustments.
    (1) Intangible drilling costs.
    (2) Certain amortization provisions do not apply.
    (3) LIFO recapture adjustment.
      (i) In general.

      (ii) Beginning LIFO and FIFO inventory.
      (iii) Definitions.
        (A) LIFO recapture amount.
          (1) Definition.
          (2) Assets included.
        (B) FIFO method.
        (C) LIFO method.
        (D) Inventory amounts.
      (iv) Exchanges under sections 351 and 721.
      (v) Examples.
      (vi) Effective date.
    (4) Installment sales.
      (i) In general.
      (ii) Exception for prior dispositions.
      (iii) Special rules for obligations to which section 453A applies.
        (A) In general.
        (B) Limitation on application of installment method.
        (C) Treatment of the ineligible portion.
        (D) Treatment of the eligible portion.
        (E) Coordination with the pledge rule.
        (F) Example.
  (g) Disallowance of loss on exchange of debt pools. [RESERVED]
  (h) Policy acquisition expenses of life insurance companies.
    (1) In general.
    (2) Reasonably estimated life.
    (3) Reasonable allowance for amortization.
    (4) Safe harbor for public financial statements.
  (i) [RESERVED]
  (j) Depletion.
  (k) Treatment of certain ownership changes.
    (1) In general.
    (2) Definition of ownership change.
    (3) Determination of net unrealized built-in loss immediately before an ownership change.
    (4) Example.
  (l) [RESERVED]
  (m) Adjusted current earnings of foreign corporations.
    (1) In general.
    (2) Definitions.
      (i) Effectively connected pre-adjustment alternative minimum taxable income.
      (ii) Effectively connected adjusted current earnings.
    (3) Rules to determine effectively connected pre-adjustment alternative minimum taxable income and effectively connected adjusted current earnings.
    (4) Certain exempt amounts.
  (n) Adjustment for adjusted current earnings of consolidated groups.
    (1) Positive adjustments.
    (2) Negative adjustments.
      (i) In general.
      (ii) Limitation on negative adjustments.
    (3) Definitions.
      (i) Consolidated pre-adjustment alternative minimum taxable income.
      (ii) Consolidated adjusted current earnings.
    (4) Example.
  (o) [RESERVED]
  (p) Effective dates for corporate partners in partnerships.
    (1) In general.
    (2) Application of effective dates.
    (3) Example.
  (q) Treatment of distributions of property to shareholders.
    (1) In general.
    (2) Examples.
  (r) Elections to use simplified inventory methods to compute alternative minimum tax.
    (1) In general.
    (2) Effect of election.
      (i) Inventories.
      (ii) Modifications required.
        (A) In general.
        (B) Negative modifications allowed.
      (iii) LIFO recapture adjustment.
    (3) Time and manner of making election.
      (i) Prospective election.
      (ii) Retroactive election.
      (iii) Taxpayers under examination.

(A) In general.
   (1) Year of change under examination.
   (2) Other open years under examination.
(B) Statement required.
(C) Year of change.
(D) Treatment of additional tax liability.
  (iv) Election as method of accounting.
  (v) Untimely election to use simplified inventory method.
 (4) Example.
 (5) Election to use alternative minimum tax inventories to compute adjusted current earnings.
(s) Adjustment for alternative tax energy preference deduction.
 (1) In general.
 (2) Example.
[Reg. § 1.56(g)-0.]

☐ [*T.D. 8340, 3-14-91. Amended by T.D. 8454, 12-18-92.*]

[Reg. § 1.56(g)-1]

§ 1.56(g)-1. Adjusted current earnings.—(a) *Adjustment for adjusted current earnings.*—(1) *Positive adjustment.*—For taxable years beginning after December 31, 1989, the alternative minimum taxable income of any taxpayer described in paragraph (a)(4) of this section is increased by the adjustment for adjusted current earnings. The adjustment for adjusted current earnings is 75 percent of the excess, if any, of—

  (i) The adjusted current earnings (as defined in paragraph (a)(6)(ii) of this section) of the taxpayer for the taxable year over

  (ii) The pre-adjustment alternative minimum taxable income (as defined in paragraph (a)(6)(i) of this section) of the taxpayer for the taxable year.

(2) *Negative adjustment.*—(i) *In general.*—For taxable years beginning after December 31, 1989, the alternative minimum taxable income of any taxpayer is decreased, subject to the limitation of paragraph (a)(2)(ii) of this section, by 75 percent of the excess, if any, of pre-adjustment alternative minimum taxable income (as defined in paragraph (a)(6)(i) of this section), over adjusted current earnings (as defined in paragraph (a)(6)(ii) of this section).

  (ii) *Limitation on negative adjustments.*—The amount of the negative adjustment for any taxable year is limited to the excess, if any, of —

   (A) The aggregate increases in alternative minimum taxable income in prior years under paragraph (a)(1) of this section over

   (B) The aggregate decreases in alternative minimum taxable income in prior years under this paragraph (a)(2).
Any excess of pre-adjustment alternative minimum taxable income over adjusted current earnings that is not allowed as a negative adjustment for the taxable year because of the limitation in this paragraph (a)(2)(ii) is not applied to reduce any positive adjustment in any other taxable year.

  (iii) *Example.*—The following example illustrates the provisions of this paragraph (a)(2):

   (A) Corporation P is a calendar-year taxpayer and has pre-adjustment alternative minimum taxable income and adjusted current earnings in the following amounts for 1990 through 1993:

Year	Pre-adjustment alternative minimum taxable income	Adjusted current earnings
1990	$800,000	$700,000
1991	600,000	900,000
1992	500,000	400,000
1993	500,000	100,000

   (B) Under these facts, corporation P has the following positive and negative adjustments for adjusted current earnings:

Year	Negative adjustment	Positive adjustment
1990	-0-	-0-
1991	-0-	$225,000
1992	$75,000	-0-
1993	150,000	-0-

   (C) In 1990, P has a potential negative adjustment (before the cumulative limitation) of $75,000 (75 percent of the $100,000 excess of pre-adjustment alternative minimum taxable income over adjusted current earnings). Nonetheless, P is not permitted a negative adjustment because P had no prior increases in its alternative minimum taxable income due to an adjustment for adjusted current earnings.

   (D) In 1991, P has a positive adjustment of $225,000 (75 percent of the $300,000 excess of adjusted current earnings over pre-adjustment alternative minimum taxable income). P is not allowed to use the prior year's excess of pre-adjustment alternative minimum taxable income over adjusted current earnings to reduce its 1991 positive adjustment.

   (E) In 1992, P is permitted a negative adjustment of $75,000, the full amount of 75 percent of the $100,000 excess of pre-adjustment alternative minimum taxable income over adjusted current earnings for the taxable year. This is because P's prior cumulative increases in alternative minimum taxable income due to the positive adjustments for adjusted current earnings exceed the negative adjustment for the year.

   (F) In 1993, P has a potential negative adjustment (before the cumulative limitation) of $300,000 (75 percent of the $400,000 excess of pre-adjustment alternative minimum taxable income over adjusted current earnings). P's net cumulative increases in alternative minimum taxable income due to the adjustment for adjusted current earnings are $150,000 ($225,000 increase in 1991, less $75,000 decrease in 1992). Thus, P's negative adjustment in 1993 is limited to $150,000. P may not use the remaining portion ($150,000) of the negative adjustment for 1993 to reduce positive adjustments in other taxable years.

(3) *Negative amounts.*—In determining whether an excess exists under paragraph (a)(1) or (a)(2) of this section, a positive amount exceeds a negative amount by the sum of the absolute numbers, and a smaller negative amount exceeds a larger negative amount by the difference between the absolute numbers. Thus, for example, a positive amount of adjusted current earnings of $30 exceeds a negative amount (or loss) of pre-adjustment AMTI of $10 by the sum of the absolute numbers, or $40 (30 + 10). Accordingly, the adjustment for adjusted current earnings would be 75 percent of $40, or $30. In contrast, a negative amount of adjusted current earnings of $10 exceeds a negative amount (or loss) of pre-adjustment alternative minimum taxable income of $30 by the difference between the absolute numbers, or $20 (30 − 10). Accordingly, the adjustment for adjusted current earnings would be 75 percent of $20, or $15.

(4) *Taxpayers subject to adjustment for adjusted current earnings.*—The adjustment for adjusted current earnings applies to any corporation other than—

  (i) An S corporation as defined in section 1361,

  (ii) A regulated investment company as defined in section 851,

  (iii) A real estate investment trust as defined in section 856, or

  (iv) A real estate mortgage investment conduit as defined in section 860A.

(5) *General rule for applying Internal Revenue Code provisions in determining adjusted current earnings.*—(i) *In general.*—Except as otherwise provided by regulations or other guidance issued by the Internal Revenue Service, all Internal Revenue Code provisions that apply in determining the regular taxable income of a taxpayer also apply in determining adjusted current earnings. For example, the rules of part V of subchapter P (relating to original issue discount and similar matters) of the Code apply in determining the amount (and the timing) of any interest income included in adjusted current earnings under this section. In applying Code provisions, however, the adjustments of section 56(g) and this section are also taken into account. For example, in applying the capitalization provisions of section 263A, the amount of depreciation to be capitalized is based on the amount of depreciation allowed in computing adjusted current earnings.

  (ii) *Example.*—The following example illustrates the provisions of this paragraph (a)(5):

   (A) Corporation N is a calendar year manufacturer of golf clubs. N places new manufacturing equipment in service in 1990. The regular tax depreciation allowable for this equipment is $80,000; the pre-adjustment alternative minimum taxable income depreciation is $60,000; and the adjusted current earnings depreciation is $40,000. All of the golf clubs N produces in 1990 are unsold and are in ending inventory.

   (B) Pursuant to section 263A and § 1.263A-1(e)(3)(ii)(I), N must capitalize the depreciation allowed for the year for the new manufacturing equipment in the ending inventory of golf clubs. Thus, when N sells the golf clubs (or is deemed to have sold them under its normal method of accounting), the cost of goods sold attributable to the capitalized depreciation will be $80,000 in computing regular taxable income; $60,000 in computing pre-adjustment alternative minimum taxable income; and $40,000 in computing adjusted current earnings.

(6) *Definitions.*—The following terms have the following meanings for purposes of this section.

  (i) *Pre-adjustment alternative minimum taxable income.*—Pre-adjustment alternative minimum taxable income is the alternative minimum taxable income of the taxpayer for the taxable year, determined under section 55(b)(2), but without the adjustment for adjusted current earnings under section 56(g) and this section, without the alternative tax net operating loss deduction under section 56(a)(4), and without the alternative tax energy preference deduction under section 56(h).

(ii) *Adjusted current earnings.*—Adjusted current earnings is the pre-adjustment alternative minimum taxable income of the taxpayer for the taxable year, adjusted as provided in section 56(g) and this section. To the extent an amount is included (or deducted) in computing pre-adjustment alternative minimum taxable income for the taxable year (whether because an adjustment is made under section 56 or 58, because of a tax preference item under section 57, or because the item is reflected in taxable income), that amount is not again included (or deducted) in computing adjusted current earnings for the taxable year.

(iii) *Earnings and profits.*—Earnings and profits means current earnings and profits within the meaning of section 316(a)(2), that is, earnings and profits for the taxable year computed as of the close of the taxable year of the corporation without diminution by reason of any distributions made during the taxable year.

(7) *Application to foreign corporations.*—See paragraph (m) of this section for rules relating to the application of this section to foreign corporations.

(b) *Depreciation allowed.*—The depreciation deduction allowed in computing adjusted current earnings is determined under the rules of this paragraph (b). Generally, the rules for computing the adjusted current earnings depreciation deduction differ depending on the taxable year in which the property is placed in service and the method used in computing the depreciation deduction for taxable income purposes. See § 1.168(i)-1(k) for an election to use general asset accounts.

(1) *Property placed in service after 1989.*—The depreciation deduction for property placed in service in a taxable year beginning after December 31, 1989, is the amount determined by using the alternative depreciation system of section 168(g). This paragraph (b)(1) does not apply to property to which paragraph (b)(4) of this section applies (relating to certain property described in sections 168(f)(1) through (f)(4)).

(2) *Property subject to new ACRS.*—(i) *In general.*—This paragraph (b)(2) provides the rules for computing the depreciation deduction for property to which the amendments made by section 201 of the Tax Reform Act of 1986 (new ACRS) apply (generally property placed in service after December 31, 1986), and that is placed in service in a taxable year beginning before January 1, 1990. This paragraph (b)(2) does not apply to property described in paragraph (b)(4) of this section (relating to certain property described in sections 168(f)(1) through (f)(4)) or to property described in paragraph (b)(5)(i) of this section (relating to certain churning transactions described in section 168(f)(5)).

(ii) *Rules for computing the depreciation deduction.*—The depreciation deduction for property described in this paragraph (b)(2) is the amount determined by using—

(A) The adjusted basis of the property as determined in computing alternative minimum taxable income as of the close of the last taxable year beginning before January 1, 1990,

(B) The straight-line method, and

(C) The recovery period that consists of the remainder of the recovery period applicable to the property under the alternative depreciation system of section 168(g). Thus, the recovery period begins on the first day of the first taxable year beginning after December 31, 1989, and ends on the last day of the recovery period that would have applied had the recovery period for the property originally been determined under section 168(g). In determining the recovery period that would have applied, the property is deemed placed in service on the date it was considered placed in service under the depreciation convention that would have applied to the property under section 168(d).

(iii) *Example.*—The following example illustrates the provisions of this paragraph (b)(2).

Example. Corporation X, a calendar-year taxpayer, purchases and places in service on August 1, 1987, computer-based telephone central office switching equipment. This is the only item of depreciable property X places in service during 1987. Thus, the applicable convention under section 168(d) is the half-year convention. As of December 31, 1989, the adjusted basis of the property used in computing alternative minimum taxable income is $42,000. The recovery period that would have applied to the property under section 168(g)(2) is 9.5 years (from July 1, 1987 to December 31, 1996). Thus,

the recovery period for computing adjusted current earnings under section 56(g)(4)(A)(ii) and this paragraph (b)(2) begins on January 1, 1990, and ends on December 31, 1996. X's 1990 depreciation deduction for computing adjusted current earnings is $6,000, determined under the straight-line method by dividing $42,000 (adjusted basis) by 7 (recovery period).

(3) *Property subject to original ACRS.*—(i) *In general.*—This paragraph (b)(3) provides the rules for computing the depreciation deduction for property to which section 168 as in effect on the day before the date of enactment of the Tax Reform Act of 1986 (original ACRS) applies and that is placed in service in a taxable year beginning before January 1, 1990 (generally property that was placed in service after December 31, 1980 and before January 1, 1987). In determining whether original ACRS applies to property, the fact that the unadjusted basis of the property is reduced or eliminated under section 168(d)(4)(A)(i) of original ACRS is not taken into account. This paragraph (b)(3) does not apply to property described in paragraph (b)(4) or (b)(5)(i) of this section (relating to certain section 168(f) property).

(ii) *Rules for computing the depreciation deduction.*—The depreciation deduction for property described in this paragraph (b)(3) is the amount determined by using—

(A) The adjusted basis of the property as determined in computing taxable income as of the close of the last taxable year beginning before January 1, 1990,

(B) The straight-line method, and

(C) The recovery period that consists of the remainder of the recovery period applicable to the property under the alternative depreciation system of section 168(g). Thus, the recovery period begins on the first day of the first taxable year beginning after December 31, 1989, and ends on the last day of the recovery period that would have applied had the recovery period for the property originally been determined under section 168(g)(2). In determining the recovery period that would have applied, the property is deemed placed in service on the date it was considered placed in service under the depreciation convention that would have applied to the property under section 168(d) (without regard to section 168(d)(3)).

(iii) *Example.*—The following example illustrates the provisions of this paragraph (b)(3).

Example. Corporation Y, a calendar-year taxpayer, purchases and places in service on December 1, 1986, computer-based telephone central office switching equipment. The depreciation convention that would have applied to this property under section 168(d) (without regard to section 168(d)(3)) is the half-year convention. As of December 31, 1989, the adjusted basis of the property used in computing taxable income is $21,000. The recovery period for the property under section 168(g)(2) is 9.5 years (from July 1, 1986 to December 31, 1995). Thus, the recovery period for computing adjusted current earnings under section 56(g)(4)(A)(iii) and this paragraph (b)(3) begins on January 1, 1990, and ends on December 31, 1995. Y's 1990 depreciation deduction for computing adjusted current earnings is $3,500, determined under the straight-line method by dividing $21,000 (adjusted basis) by 6 (recovery period).

(4) *Special rule for certain section 168(f) property.*—The depreciation or amortization deduction for property described in section 168(f)(1) through (4) is determined in the same manner as used in computing taxable income, without regard to when the property is placed in service.

(5) *Certain property not subject to ACRS.*—The depreciation or amortization deduction for property not described in paragraphs (b)(1) through (4) of this section is determined in the same manner as used in computing taxable income. Thus, this paragraph (b)(5) applies to—

(i) Property placed in service after December 31, 1980, in a taxable year beginning before January 1, 1990, and that is excluded from the application of original ACRS or new ACRS by section 168(e)(4) of original ACRS or section 168(f)(5)(A)(i) of new ACRS, and

(ii) Property placed in service before January 1, 1981.

(c) *Inclusion in adjusted current earnings of items included in earnings and profits.*—(1) *In general.*—Except as otherwise provided in paragraph (c)(4) of this section, adjusted current earnings includes all income items that are permanently excluded from (i.e., not taken into account in determining) pre-adjustment alternative minimum taxable income but that are taken into account in determining earnings and profits. An income item is considered taken into account in determining pre-adjustment alternative minimum taxable income without regard to the timing of its inclusion. Thus, this paragraph (c)(1) does not apply to any income item that is, has been, or will be included in pre-adjustment alternative minimum taxable income. For example, a taxpayer eligible to use the completed contract method of accounting for long-term construction contracts does not take income (or expenses) into account in determining pre-adjustment alternative minimum taxable income for taxable years before the taxable year the contract is completed. The taxpayer is required under section 312(n)(6) to include income (and expenses) in earnings and profits throughout the term of the contract under the percentage of completion method. This paragraph (c)(1) does not require the income on the contract to be included in adjusted current earnings, however, because the income will be taken into account in the taxable year the contract is completed and therefore is considered to be taken into account in determining pre-adjustment alternative minimum taxable income.

(2) *Certain amounts not taken into account in determining whether an item is permanently excluded.*—The fact that proceeds from an income item may eventually be reflected in pre-adjustment alternative minimum taxable income of another taxpayer on the liquidation or disposal of a business, or similar circumstances, is not taken into account in determining whether the item is permanently excluded from pre-adjustment alternative minimum taxable income. Thus, for example, a corporation's adjusted current earnings include interest excluded from pre-adjustment alternative minimum taxable income under section 103 even though the interest might eventually be reflected in the pre-adjustment alternative minimum taxable income of a corporate shareholder as gain on the liquidation of the corporation.

(3) *Allowance of offsetting deductions.*—In determining adjusted current earnings under this paragraph (c), a deduction is allowed for all items that relate to income required to be included in adjusted current earnings under this paragraph (c) and that would be deductible in computing pre-adjustment alternative minimum taxable income if the income items to which the items of deduction relate were included in pre-adjustment alternative minimum taxable income for any taxable year. For example, deductions disallowed under section 265(a)(2) for the costs of carrying tax-exempt obligations, the interest on which is excluded from pre-adjustment alternative minimum taxable income under section 103 but is included in adjusted current earnings under this paragraph (c), are generally allowed as deductions in computing adjusted current earnings. Amounts deductible under this paragraph (c)(3) are taken into account using the taxpayer's method of accounting and are subject to any provisions or limitations of the Code that would have applied if the amounts had been deductible in determining pre-adjustment alternative minimum taxable income. For example, section 265(a)(2) may affect the timing of a deduction otherwise disallowed under section 265(a)(2).

(4) *Special rules.*—Adjusted current earnings does not include the following amounts.

(i) *Income from the discharge of indebtedness.*—Amounts that are excluded from gross income under section 108 of the Internal Revenue Code of 1986 or any corresponding provision of prior law (including the Bankruptcy Tax Act of 1980, case law, income tax regulations and administrative pronouncements).

(ii) *Federal income tax refunds.*—Refunds of federal income taxes.

(iii) *Income earned on behalf of states and municipalities.*—Amounts that are excluded from gross income under section 115.

(5) *Treatment of life insurance contracts.*—(i) *In general.*—This paragraph (c)(5) addresses the treatment of life insurance contracts in determining adjusted current earnings. These rules apply to life insurance contracts as defined in section 7702. Generally, death benefits under a life insurance contract are included in adjusted current earnings, and all other distributions (including surrenders) are taxed in accordance with the principles of section 72(e), taking into account the taxpayer's basis in the contract for purposes of adjusted current earnings. If the adjusted basis in the contract for purposes of adjusted current earnings exceeds the amount of death benefits received or the amount received when the contract is surrendered (increased by the amount of any outstanding policy loan), the resulting loss is allowed as a deduction under paragraph (c)(3) of this section in computing adjusted current earnings for the taxable year. In addition, undistributed income on the contract is included in adjusted current earnings as provided in paragraph (c)(5)(ii) of this section. Paragraph (c)(5)(vi)(A) of this section provides special rules for term insurance that has no net surrender value.

(ii) *Inclusion of inside buildup.*—Income on a life insurance contract with respect to a taxable year (or any shorter period either ending or beginning with the date of a distribution from the contract) is included in adjusted current earnings for the taxable year. Thus, income on the contract is calculated from the beginning of a taxable year to the date of any distribution, from immediately after any distribution to the date of the next distribution, and from the last distribution during the taxable year through the end of the taxable

year. Income on a life insurance contract is not included in adjusted current earnings for any taxable year in which the insured dies or the contract is completely surrendered for its entire net surrender value. Solely for purposes of computing adjusted current earnings, the taxpayer's adjusted basis in the contract (as determined under section 72(e)(6)) is increased to reflect any positive income on the contract included in adjusted current earnings under this paragraph (c)(5)(ii). The manner in which the income on the contract is determined for adjusted current earnings purposes is prescribed in paragraph (c)(5)(iii) of this section. If the income on the contract determined under paragraph (c)(5)(iii) of this section is a negative amount, income on the contract is not included in adjusted current earnings and no deduction from adjusted current earnings is allowed for the negative amount.

(iii) *Calculation of income on the contract.*—For purposes of determining adjusted current earnings, the income on a life insurance contract for any period, including a taxable year, is the excess, if any, of—

(A) The sum of the contract's net surrender value (as defined in section 7702(f)(2)(B)) at the end of the period, and any distributions under the contract during the period that, in accordance with the principles of section 72(e), are not taxed because they represent recoveries of the taxpayer's basis in the contract for adjusted current earnings, over

(B) The sum of the contract's net surrender value at the end of the preceding period, and any premiums paid under the contract during the period.

(iv) *Treatment of distributions under the life insurance contract.*—Any distribution under a life insurance contract (whether a partial withdrawal or an amount received on complete surrender of the contract) is included in adjusted current earnings in accordance with the principles of section 72(e), taking into account the taxpayer's basis in the contract for purposes of computing adjusted current earnings. The taxpayer's basis in the contract is equal to the basis at the end of the immediately preceding period, plus any premiums paid before the distribution. The taxpayer's basis in the contract for purposes of adjusted current earnings is reduced, in accordance with the principles of section 72(e), to the extent that the distribution is not included in adjusted current earnings because it represents a recovery of that basis.

(v) *Treatment of death benefits.*—The excess of the contractual death benefit of a life insurance contract over the taxpayer's adjusted basis in the contract for purposes of computing adjusted current earnings at the time of the insured's death is included in adjusted current earnings as provided by paragraph (c)(6)(i) of this section. The amount of the death benefit that is taken into account for adjusted current earnings includes the amount of any outstanding policy loan treated as forgiven or discharged by the insurance company upon the death of the insured.

(vi) *Other rules.*—(A) *Term life insurance contracts without net surrender values.*—Except as provided in this paragraph (c)(5)(vi), the requirements of paragraph (c)(5) of this section do not apply to term life insurance contracts that provide no net surrender value. Adjusted current earnings are reduced by any premiums paid under such a contract that are allocable to the taxable year. Any premiums paid that are not allocable to the taxable year must be included in the basis of the contract. The death benefit under such a term insurance contract is included in adjusted current earnings as provided by paragraph (c)(5)(v) of this section.

(B) *Life insurance contracts involving divided ownership.*—If the ownership of a life insurance contract is divided between different persons (for example, a split-dollar arrangement), the requirements of paragraph (c)(5) of this section apply to the separate ownership interests as though each interest were a separate contract.

(vii) *Examples.*—The following examples illustrate the provisions of this paragraph (c)(5).

Example 1. (i) On January 1, 1987, corporation X, a calendar-year taxpayer, purchased a flexible premium life insurance contract with a death benefit of $100,000 and planned annual gross premiums of $2,200 payable on January 1 of each year. The net surrender value of the contract at the end of 1987 and subsequent years, together with the cumulative premiums for the contract at the end of each year, are set forth in the following table:

Year	Cumulative Premiums Paid	Year-End Net Surrender Value
1987	$2,200	$2,420
1988	4,400	5,082
1989	6,600	8,010
1990	8,800	11,231
1991	11,000	14,774

(ii) Under paragraph (c)(5)(ii) of this section, X must include $1,021 in adjusted current earnings for 1990. The inclusion is computed by subtracting from the net surrender value of the contract at the end of the taxable year ($11,231) the sum of the net surrender value of the contract at the end of the preceding taxable year ($8,010) plus the premiums paid during the taxable year ($2,200). See paragraph (c)(5)(iii) of this section. For purposes of determining adjusted current earnings, X's adjusted basis in the contract would be increased at the end of 1990 from $8,800 to $9,821 to reflect the $1,021 inclusion. See paragraph (c)(5)(ii) of this section. The income under the contract attributable to taxable years prior to 1990 does not increase X's adjusted basis in the contract.

(iii) For 1991, the income on the contract included in adjusted current earnings is determined in the same manner as the preceding year, and there is a corresponding increase in X's adjusted basis in the contract. Thus, for 1991, the income on the contract is $1,343, which is determined by subtracting from the net surrender value of the contract at the end of the taxable year ($14,774) the sum of the net surrender value at the end of the preceding taxable year ($11,231) plus the premiums paid during the taxable year ($2,200). At the end of 1991, X's adjusted basis in the contract for adjusted current earnings is $13,364, which reflects the basis of the contract at the beginning of 1991, increased by the premium paid during the year ($2,200) and the income on the contract that has been included in adjusted current earnings for the taxable year ($1,343).

Example 2. The facts are the same as in example 1, except that, after the payment of the premium for 1991, the insured dies and X receives the $100,000 death benefit under the contract. Under paragraph (c)(5)(ii) of this section, no amount is included in adjusted current earnings for income on the contract for the taxable year in which the insured dies. Instead, under paragraph (c)(5)(v) of this section, X must include in adjusted current earnings for 1991 the excess of the death benefit ($100,000) over the adjusted basis in the contract for purposes of computing adjusted current earnings at the time of the insured's death ($12,021), which equals X's adjusted basis in the contract at the end of 1990 ($9,821), increased by X's premium payment for 1991 ($2,200).

Example 3. (i) The facts are the same as in example 1, except that in addition to making the $2,200 planned premium payment for 1992, X receives a $16,200 distribution under the contract on February 1, 1992, leaving a net surrender value of $915 immediately following the distribution. On March 1, 1992, X pays an additional premium of $5,000 under the contract. The net surrender value of the contract at the end of 1992 is $6,417.

(ii) Treatment of the distribution. Under paragraph (c)(5)(iv) of this section, the $16,200 distribution in 1992 is included in adjusted current earnings as an amount taxable in accordance with the principles of section 72(e) to the extent that the distribution ($16,200) exceeds X's adjusted basis for adjusted current earnings, as determined at the end of the immediately preceding period, and including premiums paid through the period ending on the date of the distribution ($15,564). Thus, X must include $636 in adjusted current earnings for 1992 as an amount taxable in accordance with the principles of section 72(e).

(iii) Determination of the income on the contract. Under paragraph (c)(5)(iii) of this section, for 1992, the income on the contract must be separately determined for the period beginning with the first day of the taxable year to the date of the distribution and for the period beginning immediately after the distribution to the end of the taxable year, using the contract's net surrender values at the beginning and end of each of these periods. The income on the contract for the period beginning on January 1, 1992 and ending on February 1, 1992 (the date of the distribution) is equal to the excess, if any, of (A) the sum of the net surrender value at the end of the period ($915) and the amount of the distribution that is allocable to X's basis in the contract for adjusted current earnings ($15,564), over (B) the sum of the net surrender value at the end of the preceding taxable year ($14,774) plus any premiums paid on the contract during the period ($2,200). Because the net result of this computation is a negative amount (($915 + $15,564) − ($14,774 + $2,200) = − $495), no income on the contract for the period ending with the date of the distribution is included in adjusted current earnings for 1992.

(iv) Under paragraph (c)(5)(ii), X must also determine the income on the contract for the period beginning immediately after the distribution through the end of the taxable year. The income on the contract for this period is $502, which is equal to the excess of the net surrender value at the end of the taxable year ($6,417) over the sum of the net surrender value at the end of the preceding period ($915), plus any premiums paid during the period ($5,000). At the end of 1992, X's adjusted basis in the contract for adjusted current earnings is $5,502, determined by adding the income on the contract ($502) and the premiums paid during the period ($5,000) to the basis at the end of the preceding period ($0).

(v) Thus, X must include a total of $1,138 ($636 + 502) in adjusted current earnings for 1992. This inclusion reflects both the undistributed income on the contract for the taxable year plus the amount of income from distributions under the contract that is taxed in accordance with the principles of section 72(e) using X's adjusted basis in the contract for adjusted current earnings.

(6) *Partial list of income items excluded from gross income but included in earnings and profits.*—The following is a partial list of items that are permanently excluded from pre-adjustment alternative minimum taxable income but that are included in earnings and profits, and are therefore included in adjusted current earnings under this paragraph (c).

(i) Proceeds of life insurance contracts that are excluded under section 101, to the extent provided in paragraph (c)(5)(v) or (c)(5)(vi) of this section.

(ii) Interest that is excluded under section 103.

(iii) Amounts received as compensation for injuries or sickness that are excluded under section 104.

(iv) Income taxes of a lessor of property that are paid by a lessee and are excluded under section 110.

(v) Income attributable to the recovery of an item deducted in computing earnings and profits in a prior year that is excluded under section 111.

(vi) Amounts received as proceeds from sports programs that are excluded under section 114.

(vii) Cost-sharing payments that are excluded under section 126, to the extent section 126(e) does not apply.

(viii) Interest on loans used to acquire employer securities that is excluded under section 133.

(ix) Financial assistance that is excluded under section 597.

(x) Amounts that are excluded from pre-adjustment alternative minimum taxable income as a result of an election under section 831(b) (allowing certain insurance companies to compute their pre-adjustment alternative minimum taxable income using only their investment income).

Items described in paragraph (c)(1) of this section must be included in earnings and profits (and therefore in adjusted current earnings) even if they are not identified in this paragraph (c)(6). The Commissioner may identify additional items described in paragraph (c)(1) in other published guidance.

(7) *Partial list of items excluded from both pre-adjustment alternative minimum taxable income and adjusted current earnings.*—The following is a partial list of items that are excluded from both pre-adjustment alternative minimum taxable income and adjusted current earnings, and for which no adjustment is allowed under this section.

(i) The value of improvements made by a lessee to a lessor's property that is excluded from the lessor's income under section 109.

(ii) Contributions to the capital of a corporation by a non-shareholder that are excluded from the corporation's income under section 118.

The Commissioner may identify additional items described in this paragraph (c)(7) in other published guidance.

(d) *Disallowance of items not deductible in computing earnings and profits*—.—(1) *In general.*—Except as otherwise provided in this paragraph (d), no deduction is allowed in computing adjusted current earnings for any items that are not taken into account in determining earnings and profits for any taxable year, even if the items are taken into account in determining pre-adjustment alternative minimum taxable income. These items therefore increase adjusted current earnings to the extent they are deducted in computing pre-adjustment alternative minimum taxable income. An item of deduction is considered taken into account without regard to the timing of its deductibility in computing earnings and profits. Thus, to the extent an item is, has been, or will be deducted for purposes of determining earnings and profits, it does not increase adjusted current earnings in the taxable year in which it is deducted for purposes of determining pre-adjustment alternative minimum taxable income. For example, a deduction allowed (in determining pre-adjustment alternative minimum taxable income) under section 196 for unused research credits allowable under section 41 is taken into account in computing earnings and profits because the costs that gave rise to the credit were deductible in computing earnings and profits when incurred. Therefore, the deduction does not increase adjusted current earnings. As a further example, payments by a United States parent corporation with respect to employees of certain foreign subsidiaries, which are deductible under section 176, are considered contributions to the capital of the foreign subsidiary for purposes of computing earnings and profits. Although the payments are not deductible in computing the earnings and profits of the United States parent corporation in the year incurred, the payments do increase the parent's basis in its stock in the foreign subsidiary. This basis increase will reduce any gain the parent may later realize for purposes of computing earnings and profits on the disposition of the stock of the foreign subsidiary. Therefore, the amount of the payment by the parent is considered taken into account in computing the earnings and profits of the parent and does not increase adjusted current earnings. Thus, only deduction items that are never taken into account in computing earnings and profits are disallowed in computing adjusted current earnings under this paragraph (d).

(2) *Deductions for certain dividends received.*—(i) *Certain amounts deducted under sections 243 and 245.*—Paragraph (d)(1) of this section does not apply to, and adjusted current earnings therefore are not increased by, amounts deducted under sections 243 and 245 that qualify as 100-percent deductible dividends under sections 243(a), 245(b) or 245(c), or to any dividend received from a 20-percent owned corporation (as defined in section 243(c)(2)), to the extent that the dividend giving rise to the deductions is attributable to earnings of the paying corporation that are subject to federal income tax. Earnings are considered subject to federal income tax if the earnings are included on the federal income tax return (that is filed or, if not, that should be filed) of an entity subject to United States taxation, even if there is no resulting United States tax liability (*e.g.*, because of net operating losses or tax credits, other than the credit provided for in section 936).

(ii) *Special rules.*—(A) [Reserved]

(B) *Dividends received from a section 936 corporation.*—In the case of a dividend received from a corporation eligible for the credit provided by section 936, only that part of the dividend that is attributable to income that is not eligible for the credit is attributable to earnings of the paying corporation that are subject to federal income tax. Dividends are deemed to be distributed first out of earnings and profits for the current taxable year of the section 936 corporation, to the extent thereof, and then out of the most recently accumulated earnings and profits, under the principles of section 316. With respect to a distribution of less than all of the earnings and profits for the current or any prior taxable year, the amount of the distribution attributable to income not eligible for the section 936 credit is determined on a pro rata basis. For example, assume that a section 936 corporation earns $100 of taxable income in its current taxable year, $10 of which is not eligible for the credit under section 936. If the section 936 corporation makes a distribution of $50 during that year, $5 of that distribution ($10 of income not eligible for the section 936 credit divided by $100 of income, times $50 distributed) is deemed to be attributable to earnings of the paying corporation that are subject to federal income tax.

(iii) *Special rule for certain dividends received by certain cooperatives.*—Paragraph (d)(1) of this section does not apply to, and adjusted current earnings do not include, any dividend received by any organization to which part I of subchapter T of the Code applies and that is engaged in the marketing of agricultural or horticultural products, if the dividend is paid by a FSC and is allowable as a deduction under section 245(c).

(3) *Partial list of items not deductible in computing earnings and profits.*—The following is a partial list of items that are not taken into account in computing earnings and profits and thus are not deductible in computing adjusted current earnings.

(i) Unrecovered losses attributable to certain damages that are deductible under section 186, to the extent those damages were previously deducted in computing earnings and profits.

(ii) The deduction for small life insurance companies allowed under section 806.

(iii) Dividends deductible under the following sections of the Code:

(A) Dividends received by corporations that are deductible under section 243, to the extent paragraph (d)(2)(i) of this section does not apply.

(B) Dividends received on certain preferred stock that are deductible under section 244.

(C) Dividends received from certain foreign corporations that are deductible under section 245, to the extent neither paragraph (d)(2)(i) nor (d)(2)(iii) of this section applies.

(D) Dividends paid on certain preferred stock of public utilities that are deductible under section 247.

(E) Dividends paid to an employee stock ownership plan that are deductible under section 404(k).

(F) Non-patronage dividends that are paid and deductible under section 1382(c)(1).

Items described in paragraph (d)(1) of this section are not taken into account in computing earnings and profits (and thus are not deductible in computing adjusted current earnings) even if they are not identified in this paragraph (d)(3). The Commissioner may identify additional items described in paragraph (d)(1) of this section in other published guidance.

(4) *Partial list of items deductible for purposes of computing both pre-adjustment alternative minimum taxable income and adjusted current earnings.*—The following is a partial list of items that are deductible for purposes of computing both pre-adjustment alternative minimum taxable income and adjusted current earnings, and for which no adjustment is allowed under this section.

(i) Payments by a United States corporation with respect to employees of certain foreign corporations that are deductible under section 176.

(ii) Dividends paid on deposits by thrift institutions that are deductible under section 591.

(iii) Life insurance policyholder dividends that are deductible under section 808.

(iv) Dividends paid by cooperatives that are deductible under sections 1382(b) or 1382(c)(2) and that are not paid with respect to stock.

The Commissioner may identify additional items described in this paragraph (d)(4) in other published guidance.

(e) *Treatment of income items included, and deduction items not allowed, in computing pre-adjustment alternative minimum taxable income.*—Adjusted current earnings includes any income item that is included in pre-adjustment alternative minimum taxable income, even if that income item is not included in earnings and profits for the taxable year. Except as specifically provided in paragraph (c)(3) or (c)(5) of this section, no deduction is allowed for an item in computing adjusted current earnings if the item is not deductible in computing pre-adjustment alternative minimum taxable income for the taxable year, even if the item is deductible in computing earnings and profits for the year. Thus, for example, capital losses in excess of capital gains for the taxable year are not deductible in computing adjusted current earnings for the taxable year.

(f) *Certain other earnings and profits adjustments.*—(1) *Intangible drilling costs.*—For purposes of computing adjusted current earnings, the amount allowable as a deduction for intangible drilling costs (as defined in section 263(c)) for amounts paid or incurred in taxable years beginning after December 31, 1989, is determined as provided in section 312(n)(2)(A). See section 56(h) for an additional adjustment to alternative minimum taxable income based on energy preferences for taxable years beginning after 1990.

(2) *Certain amortization provisions do not apply.*—For purposes of computing adjusted current earnings, sections 173 (relating to circulation expenditures) and 248 (relating to organizational expenditures) do not apply to amounts paid or incurred in taxable years beginning after December 31, 1989. If an election is made under section 59(e) to amortize circulation expenditures described in section 173 over a three-year period, the expenditures to which the election applies are deducted ratably over the three-year period for purposes of computing taxable income, pre-adjustment alternative minimum taxable income, and adjusted current earnings.

(3) *LIFO recapture adjustment.*—(i) *In general.*—Adjusted current earnings are generally increased or decreased by the increase or decrease in the taxpayer's LIFO recapture amount (as defined in paragraph (f)(3)(iii)(A) of this section) as of the close of each taxable year.

(ii) *Beginning LIFO and FIFO inventory.*—For purposes of computing the increase or decrease in the LIFO recapture amount, the beginning LIFO and FIFO inventory amounts for the first taxable year beginning after December 31, 1989, are—

(A) The ending LIFO inventory amount used in computing pre-adjustment alternative minimum taxable income for the last year beginning before January 1, 1990; and

(B) The ending FIFO inventory amount for the last year beginning before January 1, 1990, computed with the adjustments described in section 56 (other than the adjustment described in section 56(g)) and section 58, the items of tax preference described in section 57 and using the methods used in computing pre-adjustment alternative minimum taxable income.

(iii) Definitions

(A) *LIFO recapture amount.*—(1) *Definition.*—The taxpayer's LIFO recapture amount is the excess, if any, of—

(i) the inventory amount of its assets under the FIFO method, computed using the rules of this section; over

(ii) the inventory amount of its assets under the LIFO method, computed using the rules of this section.

(2) *Assets included.*—Only the assets for which the taxpayer uses the LIFO method to compute pre-adjustment alternative minimum taxable income are taken into account in determining the LIFO recapture amount.

(B) *FIFO Method.*—For purposes of this paragraph, the FIFO method is the first in, first out method described in section 471, determined by using—

(1) The retail method if that is the method the taxpayer uses in computing pre-adjustment alternative minimum taxable income; or

(2) The lower of cost or market method for all other taxpayers.

(C) *LIFO method.*—The LIFO method is the last in, first out method authorized by section 472.

(D) *Inventory amounts.*—Except as otherwise provided, inventory amounts are computed using the methods used in computing pre-adjustment alternative minimum taxable income. To the extent inventory is treated as produced or acquired during taxable years beginning after December 31, 1989, the inventory amount is determined with the adjustments described in sections 56 and 58 and the items of tax preference described in section 57. Thus, for example, the amount of depreciation to be capitalized under section 263A with respect to inventory produced in taxable years beginning after December 31, 1989, is based on the depreciation allowed under the rules of paragraph (b) of this section. See paragraph (a)(5) of this section.

(iv) *Exchanges under sections 351 and 721.*—For purposes of this section, any decrease in a transferor's LIFO recapture amount that

	1989
Ending inventory:	
A. FIFO	$500 [1]
B. LIFO	300 [2]
LIFO recapture amount:	
A − B	$200
Change in LIFO recapture amount and adjustment under paragraph (f)(3)	—

[1] Beginning FIFO inventory amount under paragraph (f)(3)(ii).
[2] Beginning LIFO inventory amount under paragraph (f)(3)(ii).

Example 2. (A) X Corporation, a calendar-year taxpayer, uses the LIFO method for purposes of computing pre-adjustment alternative minimum taxable income. X's LIFO recapture amount is $300 as of December 31, 1992, and is $200 as of December 31, 1993. Immediately prior to calculating its LIFO recapture amount as of December 31, 1993, X transfers inventory with an adjusted current earnings (ACE) basis of $500 to Y Corporation in an exchange to which section 351 applies. X determines that the $100 decrease in its LIFO recapture amount occurred as a result of its transfer of inventories to Y in the section 351 exchange. Thus, under paragraph (f)(3)(iv) of this section, X cannot decrease its adjusted current earnings by that amount. In computing its 1994 LIFO recapture adjustment, X will use $200 as its LIFO recapture amount as of December 31, 1993, even though it was not entitled to reduce adjusted current earnings by the $100 decrease in its LIFO recapture amount in 1993.

(B) For purposes of computing its ACE, Y takes a $500 carryover basis in the inventories received from X. If Y, a newly-formed calendar-year taxpayer, engages in no other inventory transactions in 1993 and adopts the LIFO inventory method on its 1993 tax return, it will have a LIFO recapture amount of $0 as of December 31, 1993 (because its FIFO inventory amount and its LIFO inventory amount are both $500). Assume that at December 31, 1994, Y has a LIFO recapture amount of $200 ($1,000 FIFO inventory amount—$800 LIFO inventory amount). Under paragraph (f)(3)(i) of this section, Y computes a LIFO recapture adjustment for 1994 of $200 ($200 − $0). If any portion of Y's $200 LIFO recapture adjustment occurs solely by reason of its carryover basis in the inventories it received from X, Y reduces its $200 LIFO recapture adjustment by that portion under paragraph (f)(3)(iv). In any event, however, Y will use its $200 LIFO recapture amount as of December 31, 1994, in computing its 1995 LIFO recapture adjustment.

(vi) *Effective date.*—Paragraph (f)(3) is effective for taxable years beginning after December 18, 1992. A taxpayer may choose to apply this paragraph, however, to all taxable years beginning after December 31, 1989.

(4) *Installment sales.*—(i) *In general.*—Adjusted current earnings are computed without regard to the installment method, except as provided in this paragraph (f)(4).

(ii) *Exception for prior dispositions.*—Paragraph (f)(4)(i) of this section does not apply to any disposition in a taxable year beginning before January 1, 1990, that is taken into account under the installment method for purposes of computing pre-adjustment alternative minimum taxable income. Thus, for any disposition in a taxable year beginning before January 1, 1990, the installment method applies in computing adjusted current earnings for taxable years beginning

occurs as a result of a transfer of inventories in an exchange to which section 351 or section 721 applies cannot be used to decrease the adjusted current earnings of the transferor. A decrease that is disallowed under the preceding sentence is instead carried over to reduce any LIFO recapture adjustment that the transferee (or its corporate partners, if section 721 applies) would otherwise make (in the absence of this paragraph (f)(3)(iv)) solely by reason of its carryover basis in inventories received in the section 351 or section 721 exchange. Nothing in this paragraph (f)(3)(iv), however, alters the computation of the LIFO recapture amount of the transferor or transferee as of the close of any taxable year.

(v) *Examples.*—The following examples illustrate the provisions of this paragraph (f)(3).

Example 1. M Corporation, a calendar-year taxpayer, uses the LIFO method of accounting for its inventory for purposes of computing pre-adjustment alternative minimum taxable income. M's ending LIFO inventory for all of its pools for purposes of computing pre-adjustment alternative minimum taxable income on December 31, 1989, is $300. M computes a $500 FIFO inventory amount on that date, after applying the provisions of section 263A along with the adjustments and preferences required in computing pre-adjustment alternative minimum taxable income. M's FIFO and LIFO ending inventory amounts at the close of its taxable years, its LIFO reserves, and its adjustment under this paragraph (f)(3), are as follows:

	1990	1991	1992
	$360	$560	$600
	180	320	440
	$180	$240	$160
	$(20)	$60	$(80)

after December 31, 1989, to the same extent it applies in determining pre-adjustment alternative minimum taxable income for the taxable year.

(iii) *Special rules for obligations to which section 453A applies.*—(A) *In general.*—The following special rules apply to any installment sale occurring in a taxable year beginning after December 31, 1989, that results in an installment obligation to which section 453A(a)(1) applies and with respect to which pre-adjustment alternative minimum taxable income is determined under the installment method. As explained in paragraph (f)(4)(iii)(B) of this section, for purposes of computing adjusted current earnings, a portion of the contract price is eligible for the installment method, and the remainder of the contract price is not eligible for the installment method. Payments under the obligation are allocated pro-rata between the two accounting methods.

(B) *Limitation on application of installment method.*—Only a portion of the contract price of an installment sale described in paragraph (f)(4)(iii)(A) of this section is eligible to be accounted for under the installment method for purposes of computing adjusted current earnings. The portion eligible for the installment method is equal to the total contract price of the sale multiplied by the applicable percentage (as determined under section 453A(c)(4)) for the taxable year of the sale. The remainder of the contract price is not eligible to be accounted for under the installment method for purposes of computing adjusted current earnings. The gross profit ratio is determined without regard to this bifurcated treatment of the sale.

(C) *Treatment of the ineligible portion.*—The gain on the sale that is taken into account in the taxable year of the sale for purposes of computing adjusted current earnings is equal to the gross profit ratio multiplied by the entire portion of the contract price that is ineligible for the installment method.

(D) *Treatment of the eligible portion.*—For purposes of calculating adjusted current earnings, the amount of gain recognized in a taxable year on the portion of the contract price that is eligible for the installment method is equal to—

(1) The amount of payments received during the taxable year, multiplied by

(2) The applicable percentage for the taxable year of the sale, multiplied by

(3) The gross profit ratio.

(E) *Coordination with the pledge rule.*—For purposes of determining the amount of payments received during the taxable year under paragraph (f)(4)(iii)(D), the rules of section 453A(d) (relating to the treatment of certain pledge proceeds as payments) apply. This

Reg. § 1.56(g)-1(f)(3)(iii)(B)

includes the rules under section 453A(d)(3) that relate to treating later payments as receipts of amounts on which tax has already been paid.

(F) *Example.*—The following example illustrates the provisions of this paragraph (f)(4)(iii):

(1) On January 1, 1990, corporation A, a calendar-year taxpayer, sells a building with an adjusted basis for purposes of computing adjusted current earnings of $10 million, for $5 million and an installment obligation bearing adequate stated interest with a principal amount of $20 million. The installment obligation calls for 4 annual payments of $5 million on January 1 of 1991, 1992, 1993 and 1994. A does not elect out of the installment method, and disposes of no other property under the installment method during 1990. No gain with respect to the sale is recaptured pursuant to section 1250.

(2) The gross profit percentage for purposes of computing adjusted current earnings on the sale is 60 percent, computed as follows: gross profit of $15 million ($25 million contract price less $10 million adjusted basis) divided by $25 million contract price. The applicable percentage on the sale is 75 percent, computed as follows: $15 million ($20 million of installment obligations arising during and outstanding at the end of 1990 less $5 million) divided by $20 million of installment obligations arising during and outstanding at the end of 1990. See section 453A(c)(4). The portion of the contract price eligible for accounting under the installment method for purposes of computing adjusted current earnings is $18.75 million, or $25 million total contract price times applicable percentage of 75 percent. The portion of the contract price ineligible for the installment method is $6.25 million, or $25 million less $18.75 million.

(3) In computing adjusted current earnings for 1990, A must include $3.75 million of the gain on the sale. This amount is equal to the portion of the contract price that is ineligible for the installment method times the gross profit ratio, or $6.25 million times 60 percent. A must also include $2.25 million of gain from the $5 million payment received in 1990. This amount is computed as follows: the eligible portion of the payment, $3.75 million ($5 million payment times the applicable percentage of 75 percent), times the gross profit ratio of 60 percent. Thus, the total amount of gain from the sale that A must include in adjusted current earnings for 1990 is $6 million ($3.75 million of gain from the portion of the contract price that is not eligible for the installment method, plus $2.25 million of gain from the 1990 payment).

(4) A does not pledge or otherwise accelerate payments on the note in any other taxable year. In computing adjusted current earnings for 1991, 1992, 1993 and 1994, A therefore includes $2.25 million of gain on the installment sale, computed as follows: $5 million payment times the applicable percentage of 75 percent, times the gross profit ratio of 60 percent.

(g) *Disallowance of loss on exchange of debt pools.*—[RESERVED]

(h) *Policy acquisition expenses of life insurance companies.*—(1) *In general.*—This paragraph (h) addresses the treatment of policy acquisition expenses of life insurance companies in determining adjusted current earnings. Policy acquisition expenses are those expenses that, under generally accepted accounting principles in effect at the time the expenses are incurred, are considered to vary with and to be primarily related to the acquisition of new and renewal insurance policies. Generally, these acquisition expenses must be capitalized and amortized for purposes of adjusted current earnings over the reasonably estimated life of the acquired policy, using a method that provides a reasonable allowance for amortization. This method of amortization is treated as if it applied to all taxable years in determining the amount of policy acquisition expenses deducted for adjusted current earnings. The rules in this paragraph (h) apply to any life insurance company, as defined in section 816(a).

(2) *Reasonably estimated life.*—The reasonably estimated life of an acquired policy is determined based on the facts with respect to each policy (such as the age, sex and health of the insured), and the company's experience (such as mortality, lapse rate and renewals) with similar policies. A company may treat as the reasonably estimated life of an acquired policy the period for amortizing expenses of the acquired policy that would be required by the Financial Accounting Standards Board (FASB) at the time the acquisition expenses are incurred. If the FASB has not established such a period, the period for amortizing acquisition expense of an acquired policy under guidelines issued by the American Institute of Certified Public Accountants in effect at the time the acquisition expenses are incurred may be treated as the reasonably estimated life of the acquired policy.

(3) *Reasonable allowance for amortization.*—For purposes of determining a reasonable allowance for amortization, a company may use a method that amortizes acquisition expenses in the same proportion that gross premiums and gross investment income for the taxable year bear to total anticipated receipts of gross premiums (including anticipated renewal premiums) and gross investment income to be realized over the reasonably estimated life of the policy.

(4) *Safe harbor for public financial statements.*—Any company that is required to file with the Securities and Exchange Commission (SEC) a financial statement with respect to the taxable year will be treated as having complied with paragraph (h)(1) of this section if it accounts for acquisition expenses for adjusted current earnings purposes in the same manner as it accounts for those expenses on its financial statements filed with the SEC.

(i) [RESERVED]

(j) *Depletion.*—For purposes of computing adjusted current earnings, the allowance for depletion with respect to any property placed in service in a taxable year beginning after December 31, 1989 is determined under the cost depletion method of section 611.

(k) *Treatment of certain ownership changes.*—(1) *In general.*—In the case of any corporation that has an ownership change as defined in paragraph (k)(2) of this section in a taxable year beginning after December 31, 1989, and that also has a net unrealized built-in loss (as defined in paragraph (k)(3) of this section) immediately before the ownership change, the adjusted basis of each asset of the corporation for purposes of computing adjusted current earnings following the ownership change shall be its proportionate share (determined on the basis of the respective fair market values of each asset) of the fair market value of the assets of the corporation immediately before the ownership change. The rules of §1.338-6(b), if otherwise applicable to the transaction, are applied in making this allocation of basis. If such rules apply, the limitations of §1.338-6(c)(1) and (2) also apply in allocating basis under this paragraph (k)(1).

(2) *Definition of ownership change.*—A corporation has an ownership change for purposes of section 56(g)(4)(G)(i) and this paragraph (k) if there is an ownership change under section 382(g) for purposes of computing the corporation's amount of taxable income that may be offset by pre-change losses or the regular tax liability that may be offset by pre-change credits. See §1.382-2T for rules to determine whether a corporation has an ownership change. Accordingly, in order for an ownership change to occur for purposes of this paragraph (k), a corporation must be a loss corporation as defined in §1.382-2(a)(1). In determining whether the corporation is a loss corporation, the determination of whether there is a net unrealized built-in loss is made by using the aggregate adjusted basis of the assets of the corporation used in computing taxable income. The aggregate adjusted basis of the corporation's assets for purposes of computing adjusted current earnings is not relevant in determining whether the corporation is a loss corporation. See part (iv) of the example in paragraph (k)(4) of this section.

(3) *Determination of net unrealized built-in loss immediately before an ownership change.*—In order to determine whether it has a net unrealized built-in loss for purposes of section 56(g)(4)(G)(ii) and paragraph (k)(1) of this section, a corporation that has an ownership change as defined in paragraph (k)(2) of this section must use the aggregate adjusted basis of its assets that it uses in computing its adjusted current earnings. The rules of section 382 (including sections 382(h)(3)(B)(i) and 382(h)(8)) otherwise apply in determining whether the corporation has a net unrealized built-in loss.

(4) *Example.*—The following example illustrates the provisions of this paragraph (k):

(i) Individual A has owned all the issued and outstanding stock of corporation L for the past 5 years. A sells all of his stock in L to unrelated individual B. On the date of the sale, L owns the following assets (all numbers are in millions):

Asset	Adjusted basis for computing taxable income	Adjusted basis for computing adjusted current earnings	Fair market value
x	$45	$50	$50
y	55	60	30
z	10	10	20
	$110	$120	$100

Reg. §1.56(g)-1(k)(4)(i)

For purposes of computing taxable income, L has a $500 million net operating loss carryforward to the taxable year in which the sale occurs. Therefore, L is a loss corporation. As a result of the transfer of shares of L from A to B, L has had an ownership change.

(ii) L has no net unrealized built-in loss for purposes of computing taxable income because the amount by which the aggregate adjusted basis of its assets for that purpose exceeds their fair market value is $10 million, which is less than 15 percent of their fair market value and is not greater than $10 million. See section 382(h)(3)(B)(i).

Asset		New adjusted basis
x	....	$50
y	....	30
z	....	20

L must use these new adjusted bases for all purposes in determining adjusted current earnings, including computing depreciation and any gain or loss on disposition.

(iv) If L did not have the net operating loss carryforward, and had no other loss or credit carryovers or other attributes described in §1.382-2(a)(1) for purposes of computing the amount of its taxable income that may be offset by pre-change losses or its regular tax liability that may be offset by pre-change credits, it would not have been a loss corporation on the date of the sale and therefore would not be treated as having had an ownership change for purposes of computing adjusted current earnings. This would be true even though L had a net unrealized built-in loss for purposes of computing adjusted current earnings. Therefore, this paragraph (k) would not have applied.

(l) [RESERVED]

(m) *Adjusted current earnings of a foreign corporation.*—(1) *In general.*—The alternative minimum taxable income of a foreign corporation is increased by 75 percent of the excess of—

(i) Its effectively connected adjusted current earnings for the taxable year; over

(ii) Its effectively connected pre-adjustment alternative minimum taxable income for the taxable year.

(2) *Definitions.*—(i) *Effectively connected pre-adjustment alternative minimum taxable income.*—Effectively connected preadjustment alternative minimum taxable income is the effectively connected taxable income of the foreign corporation for the taxable year, determined with the adjustments under sections 56 and 58 (except for the adjustment for adjusted current earnings, the alternative tax net operating loss and the alternative tax energy preference deduction) and increased by the tax preference items of section 57, but taking into account only items of income of the foreign corporation that are effectively connected (or treated as effectively connected) with the conduct of a trade or business in the United States, and any expense, loss or deduction that is properly allocated and apportioned to that income.

(ii) *Effectively connected adjusted current earnings.*—Effectively connected adjusted current earnings is the effectively connected pre-adjustment alternative minimum taxable income of the foreign corporation for the taxable year, adjusted under section 56(g) and this section, but taking into account only items of income of the foreign corporation that are effectively connected (or treated as effectively connected) with the conduct of a trade or business in the United States, and any expense, loss or deduction that is properly allocated and apportioned to that income.

(3) *Rules to determine effectively connected pre-adjustment alternative minimum taxable income and effectively connected adjusted current earnings.*—The principles of section 864(c) (and the regulations thereunder) and any other applicable provision of the Internal Revenue Code apply to determine whether items of income of the foreign corporation are effectively connected (or treated as effectively connected) with the conduct of a trade or business in the United States, and whether any expense, loss or deduction is properly allocated and apportioned to that income.

(4) *Certain exempt amounts.*—Effectively connected adjusted current earnings and effectively connected pre-adjustment alternative minimum taxable income do not include any item of income, or any expense, loss or deduction that is properly allocated and apportioned to income that is exempt from United States taxation under section 883 or an applicable income tax treaty. See section 894.

(n) *Adjustment for adjusted current earnings of consolidated groups.*—(1) *Positive adjustments.*—For taxable years beginning after December 31, 1989, the alternative minimum taxable income of a consolidated group (as defined in §1.1502-1T) is increased by 75 percent of the excess, if any, of—

(i) The consolidated adjusted current earnings for the taxable year, over

L, however, does have a net unrealized built-in loss for purposes of computing adjusted current earnings because the aggregate adjusted basis of its assets for that purpose exceeds their fair market value by $20 million, and that amount is greater than $10 million.

(iii) Under paragraph (k)(1) of this section, L must restate the adjusted basis of its assets for purposes of computing adjusted current earnings to their fair market values, as follows (all numbers are in millions):

(ii) The consolidated pre-adjustment alternative minimum taxable income for the taxable year.

(2) *Negative adjustments.*—(i) *In general.*—The alternative minimum taxable income of a consolidated group is decreased, subject to the limitation of paragraph (n)(2)(ii) of this section, by 75 percent of the excess, if any, of the consolidated pre-adjustment alternative minimum taxable income over consolidated adjusted current earnings.

(ii) *Limitation on negative adjustments.*—The amount of the negative adjustment for any taxable year shall be limited to the excess, if any, of—

(A) The aggregate increases in the alternative minimum taxable income of the group in prior years under this section, over

(B) The aggregate decreases in the alternative minimum taxable income of the group in prior years under this section.

(3) *Definitions.*—(i) *Consolidated pre-adjustment alternative minimum taxable income.*—Consolidated pre-adjustment alternative minimum taxable income is the consolidated taxable income (as defined in §1.1502-11) of a consolidated group for the taxable year, determined with the adjustments provided in sections 56 and 58 (except for the adjustment for adjusted current earnings and the alternative tax net operating loss determined under section 56(a)(4)) and increased by the preference items described in section 57.

(ii) *Consolidated adjusted current earnings.*—The consolidated adjusted current earnings of a consolidated group is the consolidated pre-adjustment alternative minimum taxable income of the consolidated group for the taxable year, adjusted as provided in section 56(g) and this section.

(4) *Example.*—The following example illustrates the provisions of this paragraph (n):

(i) P is the common parent of a consolidated group. In 1990, the group has consolidated pre-adjustment alternative minimum taxable income of $1,400,000 and consolidated adjusted current earnings of $1,600,000. Thus, the group has a consolidated adjustment for adjusted current earnings for 1990 of $150,000 (75 percent of the $200,000 excess of consolidated adjusted current earnings over consolidated pre-adjustment alternative minimum taxable income), and alternative minimum taxable income of $1,550,000 ($1,400,000 plus $150,000).

(ii) In 1991, the group has consolidated pre-adjustment alternative minimum taxable income of $1,500,000 and consolidated adjusted current earnings of $1,100,000. Thus, the group can reduce its alternative minimum taxable income by $150,000. The potential negative adjustment of $300,000 (75 percent of the $400,000 excess of consolidated pre-adjustment alternative minimum taxable income over consolidated adjusted current earnings) is limited to the $150,000 consolidated adjustment for adjusted current earnings taken into account in 1990.

(o) [RESERVED]

(p) *Effective dates for corporate partners in partnerships.*—(1) *In general.*—The provisions of this section apply to a corporate partner's distributive share of items of income and expense from a partnership for any taxable year of the partnership ending within or with any taxable year of the corporate partner beginning after December 31, 1989.

(2) *Application of effective dates.*—Solely for purposes of the effective date provisions of this section, a partnership event (such as placing property in service, paying or incurring a cost, or closing an installment sale) is deemed to occur on the last day of the partnership's taxable year.

(3) *Example.*—The following example illustrates the provisions of this paragraph (p):

(i) X is a calendar-year corporation that is a partner in P, an accrual-basis partnership with a taxable year ending March 31. During P's taxable year ending March 31, 1990, P earned ratably throughout the year interest income on tax-exempt obligations. In addition, P incurred intangible drilling costs in November 1989 and in February 1990.

(ii) X's adjusted current earnings for 1990 includes X's distributive share of the interest on the tax-exempt obligations earned by P for its taxable year ending March 31, 1990. This is true even though P earned a portion of the interest prior to January 1, 1990.

(iii) For purposes of computing X's adjusted current earnings for 1990, the adjustment provided in paragraph (f)(1) of this section applies to X's distributive share of P's November 1989 and February 1990 intangible drilling costs.

(q) *Treatment of distributions of property to shareholders.*—(1) *In general.*—If a distribution of an item of property by a corporation with respect to its stock gives rise to more than one adjustment to earnings and profits under section 312, all of the adjustments with respect to that item of property (including the adjustment described in section 312(c) with respect to liabilities to which the item is subject or which are assumed in connection with the distribution) are combined for purposes of determining the corporation's adjusted current earnings for the taxable year. If the amount included in pre-adjustment alternative minimum taxable income with respect to a distribution of an item of property exceeds the net increase in earnings and profits caused by the distribution, pre-adjustment alternative minimum taxable income is not reduced in computing adjusted current earnings. If the net increase in earnings and profits caused by a distribution of an item of property exceeds the amount included in pre-adjustment alternative minimum taxable income with respect to the distribution, that excess is added to pre-adjustment alternative minimum taxable income in computing adjusted current earnings.

(2) *Examples.*—The following examples illustrate the provisions of this paragraph (q).

(i) *Example 1.*—K corporation distributes property with a fair market value of $150 and an adjusted basis of $100. The adjusted basis is the same for purposes of computing taxable income, pre-adjustment alternative minimum taxable income, adjusted current earnings, and earnings and profits. Under section 312(a)(3), as modified by section 312(b)(2), K decreases its earnings and profits by the fair market value of the property, or $150. Under section 312(b)(1), K increases its earnings and profits by the excess of the fair market value of the property over its adjusted basis, or $50. As a result of the distribution, there is a net decrease in K's earnings and profits of $100. K recognizes $50 of gain under section 311(b) as a result of the distribution as if K sold the property for $150. K thus has no amount permanently excluded from pre-adjustment alternative minimum taxable income that is taken into account in determining current earnings and profits, and thus has no adjustment under paragraph (c)(1) of this section.

(ii) *Example 2.*—The facts are the same as in example 1, except that the distributee shareholder assumes a $190 liability in connection with the distribution. Under section 312(c)(1), K must adjust the adjustments to its earnings and profits under section 312(a) and (b) to account for the liability the shareholder assumes. K adjusts the $100 net decrease in its earnings and profits to reflect the $190 liability, resulting in an increase in its earnings and profits of $90. Because section 311(b)(2) makes the rules of section 336(b) apply, the fair market value of the property is not less than the amount of the liability, or $190. K therefore is treated as if it sold the property for $190, recognizing $90 of gain. K thus has no amount permanently excluded from pre-adjustment alternative minimum taxable income that is taken into account in determining current earnings and profits, and thus has no adjustment under paragraph (c)(1) of this section.

(r) *Elections to use simplified inventory methods to compute alternative minimum tax.*—(1) *In general.*—If a taxpayer makes an election under this paragraph (r) (and does not make the election in paragraph (r)(5) of this section), the rules of paragraph (r)(2) of this section apply in computing the taxpayer's pre-adjustment alternative minimum taxable income and adjusted current earnings.

(2) *Effect of election.*—(i) *Inventories.*—The taxpayer's inventory amounts as determined for purposes of computing taxable income are used for purposes of computing pre-adjustment alternative minimum taxable income and adjusted current earnings. Subject to the further modification described in paragraph (r)(2)(ii) of this section,

the taxpayer's cost of sales as determined for purposes of computing taxable income is also used for purposes of computing pre-adjustment alternative minimum taxable income and adjusted current earnings.

(ii) *Modifications required.*—(A) *In general.*—If a taxpayer makes an election under this paragraph (r), pre-adjustment alternative minimum taxable income and adjusted current earnings are computed with the modifications described in this paragraph. The items of adjustment under sections 56 and 58 and the items of tax preference under section 57 are computed without regard to the portion of those adjustments and preferences which, but for the election described in this paragraph, would have been capitalized in ending inventory. For example, pre-adjustment alternative minimum taxable income is increased by the excess of the depreciation allowable for the taxable year under section 168 for purposes of computing taxable income (determined without regard to section 263A) over the depreciation allowable for the taxable year under section 56(a)(1) and section 57 for purposes of computing pre-adjustment alternative minimum taxable income (determined without regard to section 263A). Similarly, adjusted current earnings is further increased by the excess of the depreciation allowable for the taxable year under section 56(a)(1) and section 57 for purposes of computing pre-adjustment alternative minimum taxable income (determined without regard to section 263A) over the depreciation allowable for the taxable year under section 56(g)(4)(A) for purposes of computing adjusted current earnings (determined without regard to section 263A). Thus, the modifications described in the preceding sentence do not duplicate amounts that are taken into account in computing pre-adjustment alternative minimum taxable income. See paragraph (a)(6)(ii) of this section.

(B) *Negative modifications allowed.*—An election under this paragraph (r) does not affect the taxpayer's ability to make negative adjustments. Thus, if an election is made under this paragraph (r) and the amount of any adjustment under section 56 or 58, determined after modification under paragraph (r)(2)(ii)(A) of this section, is a negative amount, then this amount reduces pre-adjustment alternative minimum taxable income or adjusted current earnings. However, no negative adjustment under this paragraph (r)(2)(ii)(B) is allowed for the items of tax preference under section 57.

(iii) *LIFO recapture adjustment.*—If a taxpayer makes an election under this paragraph (r) and uses the LIFO method for some assets, for purposes of computing the LIFO recapture adjustment under paragraph (f)(3) of this section for taxable years beginning after December 31, 1989—

(A) The LIFO inventory amount as determined for purposes of computing taxable income is used in lieu of the LIFO inventory amount as determined under paragraph (f)(3)(iii) of this section;

(B) The FIFO inventory amount is computed without regard to the adjustments under sections 56 (including the adjustments of section 56(g)(4)) and 58 and the items of tax preference of section 57; and

(C) The beginning LIFO and FIFO inventory amounts under paragraph (f)(3)(ii) of this section are the ending LIFO inventory amount as determined for purposes of computing taxable income and the ending FIFO inventory amount computed without regard to the adjustments under sections 56 (including the adjustments of section 56(g)(4)) and 58 and the items of tax preference of section 57 for the last taxable year beginning before January 1, 1990.

(3) *Time and manner of making election.*—(i) *Prospective election.*—(A) A prospective election under this paragraph (r) may be made by any taxpayer—

(1) That has computed pre-adjustment alternative minimum taxable income and adjusted current earnings for all prior taxable years in accordance with the method described in this paragraph (r); or

(2) That has not computed pre-adjustment alternative minimum taxable income and adjusted current earnings for all prior tax years in accordance with the method described in this paragraph (r), but for which the use of the method described in this paragraph (r) for all prior taxable years would not have changed the taxpayer's tax liability (as shown on returns filed as of the date the election is made) for any prior taxable year for which the period of limitations

under section 6501(a) has not expired (as of the date the election is made).

(B) A prospective election under this paragraph (r) may only be made by attaching a statement to the taxpayer's timely filed (including extensions) original Federal income tax return for any taxable year that is no later than its first taxable year to which this paragraph (r) applies and in which the taxpayer's tentative minimum tax (computed under the provisions of this paragraph (r)) exceeds its regular tax. However, in the case of a taxpayer described in paragraph (r)(3)(i)(A)(1) of this section that had tentative minimum tax in excess of its regular tax for any prior taxable year, the election may only be made by attaching a statement to its timely filed (including extensions) original Federal income tax return for the first taxable year ending after December 18, 1992. The statement must—

(1) Give the name, address and employer identification number of the taxpayer; and

(2) Identify the election as made under this paragraph (r).

(C) The determination of whether a taxpayer is described in paragraph (r)(3)(i)(A)(2) of this section is to be made as of the time the taxpayer makes a prospective election in accordance with the procedures in paragraph (r)(3)(i)(B) of this section.

(D) Any taxpayer described in paragraph (r)(3)(i)(A)(2) of this section that makes a prospective election will be deemed to have used the method described in this paragraph (r) in computing pre-adjustment alternative minimum taxable income and adjusted current earnings for all prior taxable years.

(ii) *Retroactive election.*—(A) A retroactive election under this paragraph (r) may be made by any taxpayer not described in paragraph (r)(3)(i)(A)(1) or (2) of this section. Except as provided in paragraph (r)(3)(iii) of this section, a retroactive election may only be made by attaching a statement to the taxpayer's amended Federal income tax return for the earliest taxable year for which the period of limitations under section 6501(a) has not expired and which begins after December 31, 1986. The amended return to which the election under this paragraph (r)(3)(ii) is attached must be filed no later than June 19, 1993.

(B) The amended return must contain the statement described in paragraph (r)(3)(i)(B) of this section. In addition, the statement must contain a representation that the taxpayer will modify its pre-adjustment alternative minimum taxable income and adjusted current earnings for all open taxable years in accordance with paragraph (r)(2) of this section. Upon this change in method of accounting, the taxpayer must include the entire adjustment required under section 481(a), if any, in pre-adjustment alternative minimum taxable income and adjusted current earnings on the amended return for the year of the election. The taxpayer must also reflect the method of accounting described in paragraph (r)(2) of this section on amended returns filed for all taxable years after the year of the election for which returns were originally filed before making the election (and for which the period of limitations under section 6501(a) has not expired).

(C) Provided a taxpayer meets the requirements of this paragraph (r), any change in method of accounting arising as a result of making a retroactive election will be treated as made with the advance consent of the Commissioner.

(D) Any retroactive election under this paragraph (r) that is made without filing amended returns required under this paragraph (r)(3)(ii) shall constitute a change in method of accounting made without the consent of the Commissioner.

(iii) *Taxpayers under examination.*—(A) *In general.*—A taxpayer that wishes to make a retroactive election under section (r)(3)(ii) of this section may use the procedures in paragraph (r)(3)(iii)(A)(1) or (2) in lieu of filing an amended return for any taxable year that is under examination by the Internal Revenue Service.

(1) *Year of change under examination.*—If the year of the change is under examination at the time the taxpayer timely makes the election, the taxpayer may (in lieu of filing an amended return for

the year of the change) furnish the written statement described in paragraph (r)(3)(iii)(B) of this section to the revenue agent responsible for examining the taxpayer's return no later than June 19, 1993. It is the taxpayer's responsibility to make a timely election either by furnishing the statement to the revenue agent or by filing amended returns by June 19, 1992.

(2) *Other open years under examination.*—If any other year for which the taxpayer must modify its pre-adjustment alternative minimum taxable income and adjusted current earnings (see paragraph (r)(3)(ii)(B) of this section) is examined, the taxpayer may (in lieu of filing an amended return) furnish the amount of the conforming adjustment to the revenue agent responsible for examining the taxpayer's return. It is the taxpayer's responsibility to timely modify its pre-adjustment alternative minimum taxable income and adjusted current earnings for each year other than the year of change, either by furnishing the amount of the adjustment to the revenue agent or by filing amended returns.

(B) *Statement required.*—The statement required under paragraph (r)(3)(iii)(A)(1) of this section must include all of the items required under paragraph (r)(3)(ii)(B) of this section, as well as—

(1) The caption "Election to use regular tax inventories for AMT purposes;"

(2) A description of the nature and amount of all items that would result in adjustments and that the taxpayer would have reported if the taxpayer had used the method described in this paragraph (r) for all prior taxable years for which the period of limitations under section 6501(a) has not expired and which begin after December 31, 1986; and

(3) The following declaration signed by the person authorized to sign the return for the taxpayer: "Under penalties of perjury, I declare that I have examined this written statement, and to the best of my knowledge and belief this written statement is true, correct, and complete."

(C) *Year of change.*—The year of change is the earliest taxable year for which the period of limitations under section 6501(a) has not expired at the time the statement is submitted to the appropriate revenue agent and that begins after December 31, 1986. Thus, the adjustments required to be included on the statement must include any adjustment under section 481(a) determined as if the method described in this paragraph (r) had been used in all taxable years prior to the year of change that begin after December 31, 1986.

(D) *Treatment of additional tax liability.*—Any additional tax liability that results from the adjustments identified in the written statement described in paragraph (r)(3)(iii)(B) of this section is treated as an additional amount of tax shown on an amended return.

(iv) *Election as method of accounting.*—The elections provided in paragraphs (r)(3)(i) and (ii) of this section constitute either adoptions of, or changes in, methods of accounting. These elections, once made, may be revoked only with the consent of the Commissioner in accordance with the rules of section 446(e) and § 1.446-1(e).

(v) *Untimely election to use simplified inventory method.*—If a taxpayer makes an election described in this paragraph (r) after the times set forth in paragraph (r)(3)(i) or (ii) of this section, the taxpayer must comply with the requirements of § 1.446-1(e)(3) in order to secure the consent of the Commissioner to change to the method of accounting prescribed in this paragraph (r). The taxpayer generally will be subject to terms and conditions designed to place the taxpayer in a position no more favorable than a taxpayer that timely complied with paragraph (r)(3)(i) or (ii) of this section, whichever is applicable.

(4) *Example.*—The following example illustrates the provisions of this paragraph (r).

Example. (i) Corporation L is a calendar year manufacturer of baseball bats and uses the LIFO method of accounting for inventories. During 1987, 1988, and 1989, L's cost of goods sold in computing taxable income was as follows:

	1987	1988	1989
Beginning LIFO inventory	$3,000	$4,000	$5,000
Purchases and other costs	9,000	9,000	9,000
Ending LIFO inventory	(4,000)	(5,000)	(6,000)
Cost of goods sold	$8,000	$8,000	$8,000

(ii) L has no preferences under section 57 during 1987, 1988 and 1989. L's sole adjustment in computing alternative minimum tax during 1987, 1988, and 1989 was the depreciation adjustment under

section 56(a)(1). Depreciation determined for both production and non-production assets under section 168 and under section 56(a)(1) during 1987, 1988, and 1989 was as follows:

	1987	1988	1989
Section 168 depreciation	$1,800	$1,800	$1,800
Section 56(a)(1) depreciation	(900)	(900)	(900)
Depreciation difference	$900	$900	$900
Portion of difference capitalized in the increase in inventory	(100)	(100)	$(100)
Adjustment required under section 56(a)(1)	$800	$800	$800

Reg. § 1.56(g)-1(r)(3)(i)(B)

(iii) In computing taxable income, a portion of each year's section 168 depreciation attributable to production assets is deducted currently and a portion is capitalized into the increase in ending inventory. For 1987, 1988, and 1989, L computed alternative minimum tax by deducting the cost of goods sold which was reflected in taxable income ($8,000) in accordance with paragraph (r)(2)(i) of this section. For 1987, 1988, and 1989, L also modified its adjustments under sections 56 and 58 and its preferences under section 57 to disregard the portion of any adjustment or preference that was capitalized in inventory. Thus, under section 56(a)(1), L increased alternative minimum taxable income during each year by $900.

(iv) L is eligible to make the election under paragraph (r)(1) of this section in accordance with paragraph (r)(3)(i) of this section (a prospective election).

(v) L must compute its LIFO recapture adjustment for each year by reference to—

(A) The FIFO inventory amount after applying the provisions of section 263A but before applying the adjustments of sections 56 and 58 and the items of preference in section 57; and

(B) The LIFO inventory amount used in computing taxable income.

(5) *Election to use alternative minimum tax inventories to compute adjusted current earnings.*—A taxpayer may elect under this paragraph (r)(5) to use the inventory amounts used to compute pre-adjustment alternative minimum taxable income in computing its adjusted current earnings. Rules similar to those of paragraphs (r)(2) and (r)(3) of this section apply for purposes of this election.

(s) *Adjustment for alternative tax energy preference deduction.*—(1) *In general.*—For purposes of computing adjusted current earnings, any taxpayer claiming a deduction under section 56(h) must properly decrease basis by the portion of the deduction allowed under section 56(h) which is attributable to adjustments under section 56(g)(4). In taxable years following the taxable year in which the section 56(h) deduction is claimed, basis recovery (including amortization, depletion, and gain on sale) must properly take into account this basis reduction.

(2) *Example.*—The following example illustrates the provisions of this paragraph (s):

Example. Corporation A, a calendar year taxpayer, incurs $100 of intangible drilling costs on January 1, 1994 and as a result of these intangible drilling costs A claims a deduction under section 56(h) of $40. Assume that $20 of A's deduction under section 56(h) is attributable to the adjustment under paragraph (f)(1) of this section. A must reduce by $20 the amount of intangible drilling costs to be amortized under paragraph (f)(1) of this section in 1995 through 1998 (the balance of the 60 month amortization period). [Reg. § 1.56(g)-1.]

☐ [T.D. 8340, 3-14-91. *Amended by T.D.* 8352, 6-26-91, T.D. 8454, 12-18-92, T.D. 8482, 8-6-93, T.D. 8566, 10-7-94, T.D. 8858, 1-5-2000, T.D. 8940, 2-12-2001 *and T.D.* 9849, 3-11-2019.]

⫸→ Caution: Reg. §12.8 was adopted under former Code Sec. 57 (repealed by P.L. 99-514).

[Reg. § 12.8]

§12.8. Elections with respect to net leases of real property.—(a) *In general.*—The elections described in this section are available for determining whether real property held by the taxpayer is subject to a net lease for purposes of section 57 (relating to items of tax preference for purposes of the minimum tax for tax preferences) or 163(d) (relating to limitation on interest on investment indebtedness). Under sections 57(c)(1)(A) and 163(d)(4)(A)(i), property will be considered to be subject to a net lease for a taxable year where the sum of the deductions of the lessor with respect to the property for the taxable year allowable solely by reason of section 162 (other than rents and reimbursed amounts with respect to the property) is less than 15 percent of the gross income from rents produced by the property (hereinafter referred to as the "expense test"). Under sections 57(c)(2) and 163(d)(7)(A), where a parcel of real property of the taxpayer is leased under two or more leases, the taxpayer may elect to apply the expense test set forth in sections 57(c)(1)(A) and 163(d)(4)(A)(i) by treating all leased portions of such property as subject to a single lease. Under sections 57(c)(3) and 163(d)(7)(B), at the election of the taxpayer, the expense test set forth in sections 57(c)(1)(A) and 163(d)(4)(A)(i) shall not apply with respect to real property of the taxpayer which has been in use for more than 5 years.

(b) *Election with respect to multiple leases of single parcel of real property.*—If a parcel of real property of the taxpayer is leased under two or more leases, the expense test referred to in paragraph (a) of this section shall, at the election of the taxpayer, be applied by treating all leased portions of such property as subject to a single lease. For purposes of this paragraph, the term "parcel of real property" includes adjacent properties each of which is subject to lease.

(c) *Election with respect to real property in use for more than five years.*—At the election of the taxpayer, the expense test referred to in paragraph (a) of this section shall not apply with respect to real property of the taxpayer which has been in use for more than five years. For this purpose, real property is in use only during the period that such property is both owned and used for commercial purposes by the taxpayer. If an improvement to the property was made during the time such property was owned by the taxpayer, and if, as a result of such improvement, the adjusted basis of such property was increased by 50 percent or more, use of such property for commercial purposes shall be deemed to have commenced for purposes of this paragraph as of the date such improvement was completed. An election under this paragraph shall apply to all real property of the taxpayer which has been in use for more than five years.

(d) *Procedure for making election.*—(1) *Time and scope of election.*—An election under paragraph (b) or (c) of this section shall be made for each taxable year to which such election is to apply. The election must be made before the later of (i) the time prescribed by law for filing the taxpayer's return for the taxable year for which the election is made (determined with regard to any extension of time) or (ii) August 31, 1973, but the election may not be made after the expiration of the time prescribed by law for the filing of a claim for credit or refund of tax with respect to the taxable year for which the election is to apply.

(2) *Manner of making election.*—Except as provided in the following sentence, an election by the taxpayer with respect to a taxable year shall be made by a statement containing the information described in paragraph (d)(3) of this section which is—

(i) Attached to the taxpayer's return or amended return for such taxable year,

(ii) Attached to a timely filed claim by the taxpayer for credit or refund of tax for such taxable year, or

(iii) Filed by the taxpayer with the director of the Internal Revenue Service Center where the return for such taxable year was filed.

In the case of a taxable year ending before July 1, 1973, no formal statement of election is necessary if the taxpayer's return took into account an election under paragraph (b) or (c) of this section; the taxpayer will be considered to have made an election in accordance with the manner in which leases with respect to parcels of real property described in paragraph (b) of this section, or leases of property which has been in use for more than 5 years as described in paragraph (c) of this section, are treated in the return.

(3) *Statement.*—The statement described in paragraph (d)(2) of this section shall contain the following information:

(i) The name, address, and taxpayer identification number of the taxpayer;

(ii) The taxable year to which the election is to apply if the statement is not attached to the return or a claim for credit or refund;

(iii) A description of any leases which are to be treated as a single lease; and

(iv) A description of any real property in use for more than five years to which the expense test is not to apply.

(4) *Revocation of election.*—An election made pursuant to this paragraph may be revoked within the time prescribed in paragraph (d)(1) of this section for making an election and may not be revoked thereafter. Any such revocation shall be made in the manner prescribed by paragraph (d)(2) of this section for the making of an election.

(e) *Election by members of partnership.*—Under section 703(b) (as amended by section 304(c) of the Revenue Act of 1971), any election under section 57(c) or 163(d)(7) with respect to property held by a partnership shall be made by each partner separately, rather than by the partnership. If an election made by a taxpayer under paragraph (b) of this section applies in whole or in part to property held by a partnership, the taxpayer shall, in applying the expense test referred to in paragraph (a) of this section, take into account his distributive share of the deductions of the partnership with respect to the property for the taxable year allowable solely by reason of section 162 (other than rents and reimbursed amounts with respect to the property) and also his distributive share of the partnership's rental income from such property for the taxable year. [Temporary Reg. §12.8.]

☐ [T.D. 7271, 4-11-73.]

[Reg. §1.57-0]

§1.57-0. Scope.—For purposes of the minimum tax for tax preferences (subtitle A, ch. I, pt. VI), the items of tax preference are:

(a) Excess investment interest,

(b) The excess of accelerated depreciation on section 1250 property over straight line depreciation,

(c) The excess of accelerated depreciation on section 1245 property subject to a net lease over straight line depreciation,

(d) The excess of the amortization deduction for certified pollution control facilities over the depreciation otherwise allowable,

(e) The excess of the amortization deduction for railroad rolling stock over the depreciation otherwise allowable,

(f) The excess of the fair market value of a share of stock received pursuant to a qualified or restricted stock option over the exercise price,

(g) The excess of the addition to the reserve for losses on bad debts of financial institutions over the amount which has been allowable based on actual experience,

(h) The excess of the percentage depletion deduction over the adjusted basis of the property, and

(i) The capital gains deduction allowable under section 1202 or an equivalent amount in the case of corporations.

Accelerated depreciation on section 1245 property subject to a net lease and excess investment interest are not items of tax preference in the case of a corporation, other than a personal holding company (as defined in section 542) and an electing small business corporation (as defined in section 1371(b)). In addition, excess investment interest is an item of tax preference only for taxable years beginning before January 1, 1972. Rules for the determination of the items of tax preference are contained in §§1.57-1 through 1.57-5. Generally, in the case of a nonresident alien or foreign corporation, the application of §§1.57-1 through 1.57-5 will be limited to cases in which the taxpayer has income effectively connected with the conduct of a trade or business within the United States. Special rules for the treatment of items of tax preference in the case of certain entities and the treatment of items of tax preference relating to income from sources outside the United States are provided in section 58 and in §§1.58-1 through 1.58-8. [Reg. §1.57-0.]

□ [*T.D. 7564, 9-11-78.*]

[Reg. §1.57-1]

§1.57-1. Items of tax preference defined.—(a) [Reserved]

(b) *Accelerated depreciation on section 1250 property.*—(1) *In general.*—Section 57(a)(2) provides that, with respect to each item of section 1250 property (as defined in section 1250(c)), there is to be included as an item of tax preference the amount by which the deduction allowable for the taxable year for depreciation or amortization exceeds the deduction which would have been allowable for the taxable year if the taxpayer had depreciated the property under the straight line method for each year of its useful life for which the taxpayer has held the property. The determination of the excess under section 57(a)(2) is made with respect to each separate item of section 1250 property. Accordingly, where the amount of depreciation which would have been allowable with respect to one item of section 1250 property if the taxpayer had originally used the straight line method exceeds the allowable depreciation or amortization with respect to such property, such excess may not be used to reduce the amount of the item of tax preference resulting from another item of section 1250 property.

(2) *Separate items of section 1250 property.*—The determination of what constitutes a separate item of section 1250 property is to be made on the facts and circumstances of each individual case. In general, each building (or component thereof, if the taxpayer uses the component method of computing depreciation) is a separate item of section 1250 property. However, for purposes of this section, assets placed in a group, classified, or composite account are to be treated as a single item by a taxpayer, provided that such account contains only property placed in service during a single taxable year. In addition, two or more items may be treated as one item of section 1250 property for purposes of this paragraph where, with respect to each such item: (i) the period for which depreciation is taken begins on the same date, (ii) the same estimated useful life has continually been used for purposes of taking depreciation or amortization, and (iii) the same method (and rate) of depreciation or amortization has continually been used. For example, assume a taxpayer constructed a 40-unit rental townhouse development and began taking declining

balance depreciation on all 40 units as of January 1, 1970, at a uniform rate and has consistently taken depreciation on all 40 units on this same basis. Although each townhouse is a separate item of section 1250 property, all 40 townhouses may be treated as one item of section 1250 property for purposes of the minimum tax since the conditions of subdivisions (i), (ii), and (iii) of this subparagraph are met. This would be true even if the 40 townhouses comprised two 20-unit developments located apart from each other. However, if the taxpayer constructed an additional development or new section on the existing development for which he began taking depreciation on July 1, 1970, at a uniform rate for all the additional units, the additional units and the original units may not be treated as one item of section 1250 property since the condition of subdivision (i) of this subparagraph is not met. Where a portion of an item of section 1250 property has been depreciated or amortized under a method (or rate) which is different from the method (or rate) under which the other portion or portions of such item have been depreciated or amortized, such portion is considered a separate item of section 1250 property for purposes of this paragraph.

(3) *Allowable depreciation or amortization.*—The phrase "deduction allowable for the taxable year for exhaustion, wear and tear, obsolescence, or amortization" and references in this paragraph to "allowable depreciation or amortization" include deductions allowable for the taxable year under sections 162, 167, 212, or 611 for the depreciation or amortization of section 1250 property. Such phrase does not include depreciation allowable in the year in which section 1250 property is disposed of. For the determination of "allowable depreciation or amortization" for taxable years in which the taxpayer has taken no deduction, see §1.1016-3(a)(2).

(4) *Straight line depreciation.*—(i) For purposes of computing the depreciation which would have been allowable for the taxable year if the taxpayer had depreciated the property under the straight line method for each taxable year of its useful life, the taxpayer must use the same useful life and salvage value as was used for the first taxable year in which the taxpayer depreciated or amortized the property (subject to redeterminations made pursuant to §1.167(a)-1(b) and (c)). If, however, for any taxable year, no useful life was used under the method of depreciation or amortization used or an artificial period was used, such as, for example, by application of section 167(k), or salvage value was not taken into account in determining the annual allowances, such as, for example, under the declining balance method, then, for purposes of computing the depreciation which would have been allowable under the straight line method for the taxable year—

(a) There is to be used the useful life and salvage value which would have been proper if depreciation had actually been determined under the straight line method (without reference to an artificial life) throughout the period the property was held, and

(b) Such useful life and such salvage value is to be determined by taking into account for each taxable year the same facts and circumstances as would have been taken into account if the taxpayer had used such method throughout the period the property was held.

If an election under §1.167(a)-11(f), §1.167(a)-12(e), or §1.167(a)-12(f) is applicable to the property, the salvage value of the property shall be determined in accordance with such election, and the asset depreciation period (or asset guideline period) applicable to the property pursuant to such election shall be considered to be the useful life of the property for the purposes of this section.

(ii) Where the taxpayer acquires property in a transaction to which section 381(a) applies or from another member of an affiliated group during a consolidated return year and an "accelerated" method of depreciation as described in section 167(b)(2), (3), or (4) or section 167(j)(1)(B) or (C) is permitted (see §1.381(c)(6)-1 and §1.1502-12(g)), the depreciation which would have been allowable under the straight line method is determined as if the property had been depreciated under the straight line method since depreciation was first taken on the property by the transferor of such property. In such cases, references in this paragraph to the period for which property is held or useful life of the property are treated as including the period beginning with the commencement of the original use of the property.

(iii) For purposes of section 57(a)(2), the straight line method includes the method of depreciation described in §1.167(b)-1 or any other method which provides for a uniform proration of the cost or other basis (less salvage value) of the property over the estimated useful life of the property to the taxpayer (in terms of years, hours of use, or other similar time units) or estimated number of units to be produced over the life of the property to the taxpayer. If a method other than the method described in §1.167(b)-1 is used, the estimated useful life or estimated units of production shall be determined in a manner consistent with subdivision (i) of this subparagraph.

(iv) In the case of property constructed by or improvements made by a lessee, the useful life is to be determined in accordance with §1.167(a)-4.

(5) *Application for partial period.*—If an item is section 1250 property for less than the entire taxable year, the allowable depreciation or amortization includes only the depreciation or amortization for that portion of the taxable year during which the item is section 1250 property and the amount of the depreciation which would have been allowable under the straight line method is determined only with regard to such portion of the taxable year.

Asset			
Building shell			
Partitions and walls			
Ceilings			
Electrical system			
Heating and air-conditioning system			

For purposes of computing the item of tax preference under this paragraph for the taxpayer, the partitions, walls, and ceilings may be grouped together and the electrical, heating, and air conditioning systems may be grouped together since the period for which depreciation is taken began with respect to the assets within these two

(6) *No section 1250 and basis adjustment.*—No adjustment is to be made as a result of the minimum tax either to the basis of section 1250 property or with respect to computations under section 1250.

(7) *Example.*—The principles of this paragraph may be illustrated by the following example:

Example. The taxpayer's only item of section 1250 property is an office building with respect to which operations were commenced on January 1, 1971. The taxpayer depreciates the component parts of the building on the declining balance method. The useful life and costs of the component parts for depreciation purposes are as follows:

Useful Life	Cost	Salvage Value
50	$400,000	$50,000
10	40,000	—0—
10	20,000	—0—
25	40,000	2,500
25	60,000	2,500

groups on the same date and the assets within each group have continually had the same useful life and have continually been depreciated under the same method (and rate).

(*a*) The taxpayer's 1971 item of tax preference under this paragraph would be determined as follows:

(1) Item of 1250 property	(2) Declining balance depreciation	(3) Straight line depreciation	(4) Excess of (2) over (3)
1. Shell	$12,000	$7,000	$5,000
2. Partitions, walls, ceilings	9,000	6,000	3,000
3. Electrical, heating and air-conditioning systems	6,000	3,800	2,200
1971 preference			$10,200

(*b*) Assuming the above facts are the same for 1974, the taxpayer's 1974 item of tax preference under this paragraph would be determined as follows:

(1) Item of 1250 property	(2) Declining balance depreciation	(3) Straight line depreciation	(4) Excess of (2) over (3)
1. Shell	$10,952	$7,000	$3,952
2. Partitions, walls, ceilings	5,529	8,000	None
3. Electrical, heating and air-conditioning systems	4,983	3,800	1,183
1974 preference			$5,135

(c) *Accelerated depreciation on section 1245 property subject to a net lease.*—(1) *In general.*—Section 57(a)(3) provides that, with respect to each item of section 1245 property (as defined in section 1245(a)(3)) which is the subject of a net lease for the taxable year, there is to be included as an item of tax preference the amount by which the deduction allowable for the taxable year for depreciation or amortization exceeds the deduction which would have been allowable for the taxable year if the taxpayer had depreciated the property under the straight line method for each year of its useful life for which the taxpayer has held the property. Except as provided in paragraph (b)(1)(ii) of this section the determination of the excess under section 57(a)(3) is made with respect to each separate item of section 1245 property. Accordingly, where the amount of depreciation which would have been allowable with respect to one item of section 1245 property if the taxpayer had originally used the straight line method exceeds the allowable depreciation or amortization with respect to such property, such excess may not be used to reduce the amount of the item of tax preference resulting from another item of section 1245 property.

(2) *Separate items of property.*—The determination of what constitutes a separate item of section 1245 property must be made on the facts and circumstances of each individual case. Such determination shall be made in a manner consistent with the principles expressed in paragraph (b)(2) of this section.

(3) *Allowable depreciation or amortization.*—The phrase "deduction allowable for the taxable year for exhaustion, wear and tear, obsolescence, or amortization" and references in this paragraph to "allowable depreciation or amortization" include deductions allowable for the taxable year under sections 162, 167 (including depreciation allowable under section 167 by reason of section 179), 169, 184, 185, 212, or 611 for the depreciation or amortization of section 1245 property. Such phrase does not include depreciation allowable in the year in which the section 1245 property is disposed of. Amortization of certified pollution control facilities under section 169, and amorti-

zation of railroad rolling stock under section 184 are not to be treated as amortization for purposes of section 57 (a)(3) to the extent such amounts are treated as an item of tax preference under section 57(a)(4) or (5) (see paragraphs (d) and (e) of this section). For the determination of "allowable depreciation or amortization" for taxable years in which the taxpayer has taken no deduction, see §1.1016-3(a)(2).

(4) *Straight line method of depreciation.*—The determination of the depreciation which would have been allowable under the straight line method shall be made in a manner consistent with paragraph(b)(4) of this section. Such amount shall include any amount allowable under section 167 by reason of section 179 (relating to additional first-year depreciation for small business).

(5) *Application for partial period.*—If an item is section 1245 property for less than the entire taxable year or subject to a net lease for less than the entire taxable year the allowable depreciation or amortization includes only the depreciation or amortization for that portion of the taxable year during which the item was both section 1245 property and subject to a net lease and the amount of the depreciation which would have been allowable under the straight line method is to be determined only with regard to such portion of the taxable year.

(6) *Net lease.*—Section 57(a)(3) applies only if the section 1245 property is the subject of a net lease for all or part of the taxable year. See §1.57-3 for the determination of when an item is considered the subject of a net lease.

(7) *No section 1245 and basis adjustment.*—No adjustment is to be made as a result of the minimum tax either to the basis of section 1245 property or with respect to computations under section 1245.

(8) *Nonapplicability to corporations.*—Section 57(a)(3) does not apply to a corporation other than an electing small business corporation

(as defined in section 1371(b)) and a personal holding company (as defined in section 542).

(d) *Amortization of certified pollution control facilities.*—(1) *In general.*—Section 57(a)(4) provides that, with respect to each certified pollution control facility for which an election is in effect under section 169, there is to be included as an item of tax preference the amount by which the deduction allowable for the taxable year under such section exceeds the depreciation deduction which would otherwise be allowable under section 167. The determination under section 57(a)(4) is made with respect to each separate certified pollution control facility. Accordingly, where the amount of the depreciation deduction which would otherwise be allowable under section 167 with respect to one facility exceeds the allowable amortization deduction under section 169 with respect to such facility, such excess may not be used to offset an item of tax preference resulting from another facility.

(2) *Separate facilities.*—The determination of what constitutes a separate facility must be made on the facts and circumstances of each individual case. Generally, each facility with respect to which a separate election is in effect under section 169 shall be treated as a separate facility for purposes of this paragraph. However, if the depreciation or amortization which would have been allowable without regard to section 169 with respect to any part of a facility is based on a different useful life, date placed in service, or method of depreciation or amortization from the other part or parts of such facility, such part is considered a separate facility for purposes of this paragraph. For example, if a building constitutes a certified pollution control facility and various component parts of the building have different useful lives, each group of component parts with the same useful life would be treated as a separate facility for purposes of this paragraph. Two or more facilities may be treated as one facility for purposes of this paragraph where, with respect to each such facility: (i) the initial amortization under section 169 commences on the same date, (ii) the facility is placed in service on the same date, (iii) the estimated useful life which would be the basis for depreciation or amortization other than section 169 has continually been the same, and (iv) the method of depreciation or amortization which could have been used without regard to section 169 could have continually been the same.

(3) *Amount allowable under section 169.*—For purposes of the determination of the amount of the deduction allowable under section 169, see section 169 and the regulations thereunder. Such amount, however, shall not include amortization allowable in the year in which the pollution control facility is disposed of.

(4) *Otherwise allowable deduction.*—(i) The determination of the amount of the depreciation deduction otherwise allowable under section 167 is made as if the taxpayer had depreciated the property under section 167 for each year of its useful life for which the property has been held. This amount may be determined under § 1.167(a)-11(c) if the property is eligible property (as defined in § 1.167(a)-11(b)(2)) and, during the taxable year in which the property was first placed in service, the taxpayer—

(a) Has made an election under § 1.167(a)-11(f) with respect to eligible property first placed in service in such taxable year, or

(b) Has placed no eligible property in service other than property described in § 1.167(a)-11(b)(5)(iii), (iv), or (v).

The amount determined pursuant to the preceding sentence shall be determined as if the taxpayer had depreciated the property in accordance with § 1.167(a)-11 for all years to which such section applies and during which the taxpayer held the property. This amount may be determined under § 1.167(a)-12(a)(5) if the property is qualified property (as defined in § 1.167(a)-12(a)(3)) and the taxpayer has made an election with respect to such property under § 1.167(a)-12(e). If the taxpayer has made an election under § 1.167(a)-12(f)(1) for a taxable year ending before January 1, 1971, this amount shall be determined for such year in accordance with such election. For purposes of this determination, any method selected by the taxpayer which would have been permissible under section 167 for such taxable year, including accelerated methods, may be used. Any additional amount which would have been allowable by reason of section 179 (relating to additional first-year depreciation for small business) may be included provided such amount is reflected in the determination made under this paragraph in subsequent years.

(ii) If a deduction for depreciation has not been taken by the taxpayer in any taxable year under section 167 with respect to the facility—

(a) There is to be used the useful life and salvage value which would have been proper under section 167,

(b) Such useful life and salvage value is determined by taking into account for each taxable year the same facts and circumstances as would have been taken into account if the taxpayer had used such method throughout the period the property has been held, and

(c) The date the property is placed in service is, for purposes of this section, deemed to be the first day of the first month for which the amortization deduction is taken with respect to the facility under section 169.

If, prior to the date amortization begins under section 169, a deduction for depreciation has been taken by the taxpayer in any taxable year under section 167 with respect to the facility, the useful life, salvage value, etc., used for that purpose is deemed to be the appropriate useful life, salvage value, etc., for purposes of this paragraph, with such adjustments as are appropriate in light of the facts and circumstances which would have been taken into account since the time the last such depreciation deduction was taken, unless it is established by clear and convincing evidence that some other useful life, salvage value, or date the property is placed in service is more appropriate.

(iii) For purposes of section (57)(a)(4) and this paragraph, if the deduction for amortization or depreciation which would have been allowable had no election been made under section 169 would have been—

(a) An amortization deduction based on the term of a leasehold or

(b) A depreciation deduction determined by reference to section 611,

such deduction is to be deemed to be a deduction allowable under section 167.

(iv) If a facility is subject to amortization under section 169 for less than the entire taxable year, the otherwise allowable depreciation deduction under section 167 shall be determined only with regard to that portion of the taxable year during which the election under section 169 is in effect.

(v) If less than the entire adjusted basis of a facility is subject to amortization under section 169, the otherwise allowable depreciation deduction under section 167 shall be determined only with regard to that portion of the adjusted basis subject to amortization under section 169.

(5) *No section 1245 and basis adjustment.*—No adjustment is to be made as a result of the minimum tax either to the basis of a certified pollution control facility or with respect to computations under section 1245.

(6) *Relationship to section 57(a)(3).*—See paragraph (c)(3) with respect to an adjustment in the amount treated as amortization under that provision where both paragraphs (3) and (4) of section 57(a) are applicable to the same item of property.

(7) *Example.*—The principles of this paragraph may be illustrated by the following example:

Example. A calendar year taxpayer has a certified pollution control facility on which an election is in effect under section 169 commencing with January 1, 1971. No part of the facility is section 1250 property. The original basis of the facility is $100,000 of which $75,000 constitutes amortizable basis. The useful life of the facility is 20 years. The taxpayer depreciates the $25,000 portion of the facility which is not amortizable basis under the double declining method and began taking depreciation on January 1, 1971.

(a) The taxpayer's 1971 item of tax preference under this paragraph would be determined as follows:

1. Amortization deduction	$15,000
2. Depreciation deduction on amortizable basis (double declining method)	7,500
1971 Preference (excess of 1 over 2)	$7,500

(b) If the taxpayer terminated his election under section 169 in 1972 effective as of July 1, 1972, the taxpayer's 1972 item of tax preference would be determined as follows:

1. Amortization deduction	$7,500
2. Depreciation deduction on amortizable basis:	

Full year ($75,000 (original basis) less $7,500 ("depreciation" to 1-1-72)
equals adjusted basis of $67,500; multiplied by .10 (double declining
rate)) $6,750

Portion of full year's depreciation attributable to amortization period (one-half)   3,375

1972 Preference (excess of 1 over 2) $4,125

(e) *Amortization of railroad rolling stock.*—(1) *In general.*—Section 57(a)(5) provides that, with respect to each unit of railroad rolling stock for which an election is in effect under section 184, there is to be included as an item of tax preference the amount by which the deduction allowable for the taxable year under such section exceeds the depreciation deduction which would otherwise be allowable under section 167. The determination under section 57(a)(5) is made with respect to each separate unit of rolling stock. Accordingly, where the amount of the depreciation deduction which would otherwise be allowable under section 167 with respect to one unit exceeds the allowable amortization deduction under section 184 with respect to such unit, such excess may not be used to offset an item of tax preference resulting from another unit.

(2) *Separate units of rolling stock.*—The determination of what constitutes a separate unit of rolling stock must be made on the facts and circumstances of each individual case. Such determination shall be made in a manner consistent with the manner in which the comparable determination is made with respect to separate certified pollution control facilities under paragraph (d)(2) of this section.

(3) *Amount allowable under section 184.*—For purposes of the determination of the amount of the deduction allowable under section 184, see section 184. Such amount, however, does not include amortization allowable in the year in which the rolling stock is disposed of.

(4) *Otherwise allowable deduction.*—The determination of the amount of the depreciation deduction otherwise allowable under section 167 is to be made in a manner consistent with the manner in which the comparable deduction with respect to certified pollution control facilities is determined under paragraph (d)(4) of this section.

(5) *No section 1245 or basis adjustment.*—No adjustment is to be made as a result of the minimum tax either to the basis of a unit of railroad rolling stock or with respect to computations under section 1245.

(6) *Relationship to section 57(a)(3).*—See paragraph (c)(3) of this section with respect to an adjustment in the amount treated as amortization under that provision where both paragraphs (3) and (5) of section 57(a) are applicable to the same item.

(f) *Stock options.*—(1) *In general.*—Section 57(a)(6) provides that with respect to each transfer of a share of stock pursuant to the exercise of a qualified stock option or a restricted stock option, there shall be included by the transferee as an item of tax preference the amount by which the fair market value of the share at the time of exercise exceeds the option price. The stock option item of tax preference is subject to tax under section 56(a) in the taxable year of the transferee in which the transfer is made.

(2) *Definitions.*—See generally § 1.421-7(e), (f), and (g) for the definitions of "option price," "exercise," and "transfer," respectively; however, in the case of a transfer of a share of stock pursuant to the exercise of a qualified stock option or a restricted stock option after the death of an employee by the estate of the decedent (or by a person who acquired the right to exercise such option by bequest or inheritance or by reason of the death of the decedent), the term "option price" shall, for purposes of this paragraph, include both the consideration paid by the estate (or such person) for such share of stock and so much of the basis of the option as is attributable to such share of stock. For the definition of a qualified stock option see section 422(b) and § 1.422-2. For the definition of a restricted stock option see section 424(b) and § 1.424-2. The definitions and special rules contained in section 425 and the regulations thereunder are applicable to this paragraph.

(3) *Fair market value.*—In accordance with the principles of section 83(a)(1), the fair market value of a share of stock received pursuant to the exercise of a qualified or restricted stock option is to be determined without regard to restrictions (other than nonlapse restrictions within the meaning of § 1.83-3(h)). Notwithstanding any valuation date given in section 83(a)(1), for purposes of this section, fair market value is determined as of the date the option is exercised.

(4) *Foreign source options.*—In the case of an option attributable to sources within any foreign country or possession, see section 58(g) and § 1.58-8.

(5) *Inapplicability in certain cases.*—(i) Section 57(a)(6) is inapplicable if during the same taxable year in which stock is transferred pursuant to the exercise of an option, the transferee makes a disposition (within the meaning of section 425(c)) of such stock. In the case of a nonresident alien, section 57(a)(6) is inapplicable to the extent the stock option is attributable (in accordance with the principles of sections 861 through 863 and the regulations thereunder) to sources without the United States.

(ii) Section 57(a)(6) is inapplicable if section 421(a) does not apply to the transfer because of employment requirements of section 422(a)(2) or section 424(a)(2).

(6) *Proportionate applicability.*—Where, by reason of section 422(b)(7) and (c)(3) (relating to percentage ownership limitations), only a portion of a transfer qualifies for application of section 421, the fair market value and option price shall be determined only with regard to that portion of the transfer which so qualifies.

(7) *No basis adjustment.*—No adjustment shall be made to the basis of the stock received pursuant to the exercise of a qualified or restricted stock option as a result of the minimum tax.

(g) *Reserves for losses on bad debts of financial institutions.*—(1) *In general.*—Section 57(a)(7) provides that, in the case of a financial institution to which section 585 or 593 (both relating to reserves for losses on loans) applies, there shall be included as an item of tax preference the amount by which the deduction allowable for the taxable year for a reasonable addition to a reserve for bad debts exceeds the amount that would have been allowable had the institution maintained its bad debt reserve for all taxable years on the basis of the institution's actual experience.

(2) *Taxpayers covered.*—Section 57(a)(7) applies only to an institution (or organization) to which section 585 or 593 applies. See sections 585(a) and 593(a) and the regulations thereunder for a description of those institutions.

(3) *Allowable deduction.*—For purposes of this paragraph, the amount of the deduction allowable for the taxable year for a reasonable addition to a reserve for bad debts is the amount of the deduction allowed under section 166(c) by reference to section 585 or 593.

(4) *Actual experience.*—(i) For purposes of this paragraph, the determination of the amount which would have been allowable had the institution maintained its reserve for bad debts on the basis of actual experience is the amount determined under section 585(b)(3)(A) and the regulations thereunder. For this purpose, the beginning balance for the first taxable year ending in 1970 is the amount which bears the same ratio to loans outstanding at the beginning of the taxable year as (a) the total bad debts sustained during the 5 preceding taxable years, adjusted for recoveries of bad debts during such period, bears to (b) the sum of the loans outstanding at the close of such 5 taxable years. The taxpayer may, however, select a more appropriate balance based on its actual experience during a shorter period subject to the approval of the district director upon examination of the return provided there are unusual circumstances which indicate that such period is more indicative of the taxpayer's actual loss experience. Any such selection and approval shall be made in a manner consistent with the selection and approval of a bad debt reserve method under § 1.166-1(b). In the case of an institution which has been in existence for less than 5 taxable years as of the beginning of the first taxable year ending in 1970, the above formula for determining the beginning balance is applied by substituting the number of taxable years for which the institution has been in existence as of the beginning of the taxable year for "5" each time it appears. If any taxable year utilized in the above formula for determining the beginning balance is a short taxable year the amount of the bad debts, adjusted for recoveries, for such taxable year is modified by dividing such amount by the number of days in the taxable year and multiplying the resulting amount by 365. The beginning balance for any subsequent taxable year is the amount of the beginning balance of the preceding taxable year, decreased by bad debt losses during such year, increased by recoveries of bad debts during such year and increased by the lower of the maximum amount determined under section 585(b)(3)(A) for such year or the amount of the deduction allowed for such year. The application of this subdivision (i) may be illustrated by the following example:

Example. The Y Bank, a calendar year taxpayer, uses the reserve method of accounting for bad debts. On December 31, 1969, Y determines the balance of its reserve for bad debts to the $70,000 under the percentage method. On the same date Y's 5-year moving average is $52,000. Y incurs net bad debt losses (bad debt losses less recoveries of bad debts) of $3,000 for each of the years 1970, 1971, and 1972, which it charges to its reserve for bad debts. Y's 6-year moving averages computed under section 585(b)(3)(A) at the close of 1970, 1971, and 1972 are $50,000, $49,000, and $51,000, respectively. Y's preference items are computed as follows based upon additional facts assumed:

		1970	1971	1972
1. Bad debt reserve—percentage method:				
	Balance beginning of year (closing balance prior				
(a)	year)	$70,000	$70,000	$68,000
(b)	Net bad debts charged to reserve	3,000	3,000	3,000
(c)	Subtotal	$67,000	$67,000	$65,000
(d)	Deduction allowed	3,000	1,000	4,000
(e)	Balance end of year	$70,000	$68,000	$69,000
2. Bad debt reserve—"actual experience":				
(a)	Beginning balance (for 1970, 5-year moving average; for other years, closing balance prior year)	$52,000	$50,000	$48,000
(b)	Net bad debts charged to reserve	$3,000	$3,000	$3,000
(c)	Subtotal	$49,000	$47,000	$45,000
(d)	Maximum amount under section 585(b)(3)(A) (6-year moving average minus (c))	$1,000	$2,000	$6,000
(e)	Deduction allowed (line 1(d))	3,000	1,000	4,000
(f)	Lower of (d) or (e)	1,000	1,000	4,000
(g)	Closing balance (line (c) + (f))	$50,000	$48,000	$49,000
3. Preference item under section 57(a)(7):				
(a)	Deduction allowed	$3,000	$1,000	$4,000
(b)	Maximum amount under section 585(b)(3)(A)	1,000	2,000	6,000
(c)	Preference item (excess of (a) over (b))	$2,000	0	0

(ii) In the case of a new institution whose first taxable year ends after 1969, its beginning balance for its reserve for bad debts, for purposes of this paragraph, is zero and its reasonable addition to the reserve for such taxable year is determined on the basis of the actual experience of similar institutions located in the area served by the taxpayer.

(h) *Depletion.*—(1) *In general.*—Section 57(a)(8) provides that with respect to each property (as defined in section 614), there is to be included as an item of tax preference the amount by which the deduction allowable for the taxable year under section 611 for depletion for the property exceeds the adjusted basis of the property at the end of the taxable year (determined without regard to the depletion deduction for that taxable year). The determination under section 57(a)(8) is made with respect to each separate property. Thus, for example, if one mineral property has an adjusted basis remaining at the end of the taxable year, such basis may not be used to reduce the amount of an item of tax preference resulting from another mineral property.

(2) *Allowable depletion.*—For the determination of the amount of the deduction for depletion allowable for the taxable year see section 611 and the regulations thereunder.

(3) *Adjusted basis.*—For the determination of the adjusted basis of the property at the end of the taxable year see section 1016 and the regulations thereunder.

(4) *No basis adjustment.*—No adjustment is to be made to the basis of property subject to depletion as a result of the minimum tax.

(i) *Capital gains.*—(1) *Taxpayers other than corporations.*—Section 57(a)(9)(A) provides that, in the case of a taxpayer other than a corporation, there is to be included as an item of tax preference one-half of the amount by which the taxpayer's net long-term capital gain for the taxable year exceeds the taxpayer's net short-term capital loss for the taxable year. For this purpose, for taxable years beginning after December 31, 1971, the taxpayer's net long-term capital gain does not include an amount equal to the deduction allowable under section 163 (relating to interest expense) by reason of subsection (d)(1)(C) of that section, and the excess described in the preceding sentence is reduced by an amount equal to the reduction of disallowed interest expense by reason of section 163(d)(2)(B). Furthermore, the net long-term capital gain of an estate or trust does not include capital gains described in section 642(c)(4). Included in the computation of the taxpayer's capital gains item of tax preference are amounts reportable by the taxpayer as distributive shares of gain or loss from partnerships, estates or trusts, electing small business corporations, common trust funds, etc. See section 58 and the regulations thereunder with respect to the above entities.

Example. For 1971, A, a calendar year individual taxpayer, recognized $50,000 from the sale of securities held for more than 6 months. In addition, A received a $15,000 dividend from X Fund, a regulated investment company, $12,000 of which was designated as a capital gain dividend by the company pursuant to section 852(b)(3)(C). The AB partnership recognized a gain of $20,000 from the sale of section 1231 property held by the partnership. The AB partnership agreement provides that A is entitled to 50 percent of the income and gains of the partnership. A had net short-term capital loss for the year of $10,000. A's 1971 capital gains item of tax preference is computed as follows:

Capital gain recognized from securities	$50,000
Capital gain dividend from regulated investment company	12,000
Distributive share of partnership capital gain	10,000
Total net long-term capital gain	$72,000
Less: net short-term capital loss	(10,000)
Excess of net long-term capital gain over net short-term capital loss	$62,000
One-half of above excess	$31,000

(2) *Corporations.*—(i) Section 57(a)(9)(B) provides that in the case of corporations there is to be included as an item of tax preference with respect to a corporation's net section 1201 gain an amount equal to the product obtained by multiplying the excess of the net long-term capital gain over the net short-term capital loss by a fraction. The numerator of this fraction is the sum of the normal tax rate and the surtax rate under section 11 minus the alternative tax rate under section 1201(a) for the taxable year, and the denominator of the fraction is the sum of the normal tax rate and the surtax rate under section 11 for the taxable year. Included in the above computation are amounts reportable by the taxpayer as distributive shares of gain or loss from partnerships, estates or trusts, common trust funds, etc. In certain cases the amount of the net section 1201 gain which results in

preferential treatment will be less than the amount determined by application of the statutory formula. Therefore, in lieu of the statutory formula, the capital gains item of tax preference for corporations may in all cases be determined by dividing—

(a) The amount of tax which would have been imposed under section 11 if section 1201 (a) did not apply minus—

(b) The amount of the taxes actually imposed by the sum of the normal tax rate plus the surtax rate under section 11. In case of foreign source capital gains and losses which are not taken into account pursuant to sections 58(g)(2)(B) and 1.58-8, the amount determined in the preceding sentence shall be multiplied by a fraction the numerator of which is the corporation's net section 1201 gain without regard to such gains and losses which are not taken into account and the denominator of which is the corporation's net section 1201 gain. The computation of the corporate capital gains item of tax preference may be illustrated by the following examples:

1. Tax under section 11:

Normal tax (0.22 × $60,000)		$13,200
Surtax (0.26 × $35,000)		9,100
		$22,300

2. Tax under section 1201(a)

Normal tax on ordinary income (0.22 × $10,000)	$2,200	
Tax on net section 1201 gain (0.30 × $50,000)	15,000	17,200

3. Excess $5,100
4. Normal tax rate plus surtax rate .... .48
5. Capital gains preference (line 3 divided by line 4) $10,625

Example (2). For 1971, A, a calendar year corporate taxpayer, has a loss from operations of $30,000 and net section 1201 gain of $150,000, none of which is subsection (d) gain (as defined in sec.

1. Tax under section 11:

Normal tax (0.22 × $120,000)		$26,400
Surtax (0.26 × $95,000)		24,700
		$51,100

2. Tax under section 1201(a)

Normal tax on ordinary income	None	
Tax on net section 1201 gain (0.30 × $150,000)	$45,000	45,000

3. Excess .... $ 6,100
4. Normal tax rate plus surtax rate .... .48
5. Capital gain preference (line 3 divided by line 4) $12,708

(ii) In the case of organizations subject to the tax imposed by section 511(a), mutual savings banks conducting a life insurance business (see sec. 594), life insurance companies (as defined in sec. 801), mutual insurance companies to which part II of subchapter L applies, insurance companies to which part III of subchapter L applies, regulated investment companies subject to tax under part I of subchapter M, real estate investment trusts subject to tax under part II of subchapter M, or any other corporation not subject to the taxes imposed by sections 11 and 1201(a), the capital gains item of tax preference may be computed in accordance with subdivision (i) of this subparagraph except that, in lieu of references to section 11, there is to be substituted the section which imposes the tax comparable to the tax imposed by section 11 and, in lieu of references to section 1201(a), there is to be substituted the section which imposes the alternative or special tax applicable to the capital gains of such corporation.

(iii) For purposes of this paragraph, where the net section 1201 gain is not in any event subject to the tax comparable to the

Example (1). For 1971, A, a calendar year corporate taxpayer, has ordinary income of $10,000 and net section 1201 gain of $50,000, none of which is subsection (d) gain (as defined in sec. 1201(d)) and none of which is attributable to foreign sources. A's 1971 capital gain item of tax preference may be computed as follows:

1201(d)) and none of which is attributable to foreign sources. A's 1971 capital gain item of tax preference may be computed as follows:

normal tax and the surtax under section 11, such as in the case of regulated investment companies subject to tax under subchapter M, such comparable tax shall be computed as if it were applicable to net section 1201 gain to the extent such gain is subject to the tax comparable to the alternative tax under section 1201(a). Thus, in the case of a regulated investment company subject to tax under subchapter M, the tax comparable to the normal tax and the surtax would be the tax computed under section 852(b)(1) determined as if the amount subject to tax under section 852(b)(3) were included in investment company taxable income. The principles of this subdivision (iii) may be illustrated by the following example:

Example. M, a calendar year regulated investment company, in 1971, has investment company taxable income (subject to tax under sec. 852(b)(1)) of $125,000 and net long-term capital gain of $800,000. M Company has no net short-term capital loss but has a deduction for dividends paid (determined with reference to capital gains only) of $700,000. M's 1971 capital gains item of tax reference is computed as follows:

1. Section 852(b)(1) tax computed as if it were applicable to all income including capital gains:

Amount subject to section 852(b)(1)		$125,000	
Net section 1201 gain	$800,000		
Less: Dividends paid deduction	700,000		
Net section 1201 gain subject to tax at the company level		100,000	
		$225,000	
Normal tax (0.22 × $225,000)			$ 49,500
Surtax (0.26 × 200,000)			52,000
			$101,500

2. Tax comparable to section 1201(a) tax section 852(b)(1) tax:

Normal tax (0.22 × 125,000)	$ 27,500		
Surtax (0.26 × 100,000)	26,000	$53,500	
Section 852(b)(3) tax (0.30 × 100,000)		30,000	$ 83,500

3. Excess $18,000
4. Normal tax rate plus surtax rate .... .48
5. Capital gains preference (line 3 divided by line 4) .... $ 37,500

(iv) For the computation of the capital gains item of tax preference in the case of an electing small business corporation (as defined in sec. 1371(b)), see section 1.58-4(c).

(3) *Nonresident aliens, foreign corporations.*—In the case of a nonresident alien individual or foreign corporation, there shall be included in computing the capital gains item of tax preference under section 57(a)(9) only those capital gains and losses included in the computation of income effectively connected with the conduct of a trade or business within the United States as provided in section 871(b) or 882. [Reg. § 1.57-1.]

☐ [T.D. 7564, 9-11-78.]

[Reg. § 1.57-5]

§ 1.57-5. Records to be kept.—(a) *In general.*—The taxpayer shall have available permanent records of all the facts necessary to determine with reasonable accuracy the amounts described in § 1.57-1. Such records shall include:

(1) In the case of amounts described in paragraph (a) of § 1.57-1: the amount and nature of indebtedness outstanding for the taxable year and the date or dates on which each such indebtedness was

incurred or renewed in any form; the amount expended for property held for investment during any taxable year during which such indebtedness was incurred or renewed; and the manner in which it was determined that property was or was not held for investment.

(2) In the case of amounts described in paragraphs (b), (c), (d), (e), and (h) of §1.57-1:

(i) The dates, and manner in which the property was acquired and placed in service,

(ii) The taxpayer's basis on the date the property was acquired and the manner in which the basis was determined,

(iii) An estimate of the useful life (in terms of months, hours of use, etc., whichever is appropriate) of the property on the date placed in service or an estimate of the number of units to be produced by the property on the date the property is placed in service, whichever is appropriate, and the manner in which such estimate was determined,

(iv) The amount and date of all adjustments by the taxpayer to the basis of the property and an explanation of the nature of such adjustments, and

(v) In the case of property which has an adjusted basis reflecting adjustments taken by another taxpayer with respect to the property or taken by the taxpayer with respect to other property, the information described in subdivisions (i) through (iv) above, with respect to such other property or other taxpayer.

(3) In the case of amounts described in paragraph (f) of §1.57-1, the fair market value of the shares of stock at the date of exercise of the option and the option price and the manner in which each was determined.

(4) In the case of amounts described in paragraph (g) of §1.57-1, the amount of debts written off and the amount of the loans outstanding for the taxable year and the 5 preceding taxable years or such shorter or longer period as is appropriate.

(b) *Net operating losses.*—The taxpayer shall have available permanent records for the first taxable year in which a portion of a net operating loss was attributable to items of tax preference (within the meaning of §1.56A-2(b)) and each succeeding taxable year in which there is a net operating loss or a net operating loss carryover a portion of which is so attributable. Such records shall include all the facts necessary to determine with reasonable accuracy the amount of deferred tax liability under section 56, including the amount of the net operating loss in each taxable year in which there are items of tax preference in excess of the minimum tax exemption (as determined under §1.58-1), the amount of the items of tax preference for each such taxable year, the amount by which each such net operating loss reduces taxable income in any taxable year, and the amount by which each such net operating loss is reduced in any taxable year. [Reg. §1.57-5.]

☐ *[T.D. 7564, 9-11-78. Amended by T.D. 8138, 4-23-87.]*

[Reg. §7.57(d)-1]

§7.57(d)-1. Election with respect to straight line recovery of intangibles.—(a) *Purpose.*—This section prescribes rules for making the election permitted under section 57(d)(2), as added by the Tax Reform Act of 1976. Under this election taxpayers may use cost depletion to compute straight line recovery of intangibles.

(b) *Election.*—The election under section 57(d) is subject to the following rules:

(1) The election is made within the time prescribed by law (including extensions thereof) for filing the return for the taxable year in which the intangible drilling costs are paid or incurred or, if later, by June 25, 1978.

(2) The election is made separately for each well. Thus, a taxpayer may make the election for only some of his or her wells.

(3) The election is made by using, for the well or wells to which the election applies, cost depletion to compute straight line recovery of intangibles for purposes of determining the amount of the preference under section 57(a)(11).

(4) The election may be made whether or not the taxpayer uses cost depletion in computing taxable income.

(5) The election is made by a partnership rather than by each partner.

(c) *Computation of cost depletion.*—For purposes of computing straight line recovery of intangibles through cost depletion, both depletable and depreciable intangible drilling and development costs for the taxable year are taken into account. They are treated as if capitalized, added to basis, and recovered under §1.611-2(a). Costs paid or incurred in other taxable years are not taken into account. [Temporary Reg. §7.57(d)-1.]

☐ *[T.D. 7541, 4-25-78. Amended by T.D. 8138, 4-23-87.]*

[Reg. §1.58-1]

§1.58-1. [Reserved].

☐ *[T.D. 7564, 9-11-78. Removed and reserved by T.D. 9849, 3-11-2019.]*

[Reg. §1.58-2]

§1.58-2. General rules for conduit entities; partnerships and partners.—(a) *General rules for conduit entities.*—Sections 1.58-3 through 1.58-6 provide rules under which items of tax preference of an estate, trust, electing small business corporation, common trust fund, regulated investment company, or real estate investment trust (referred to in this paragraph as the "conduit entity") are treated as items of tax preference of the beneficiaries, shareholders, participants, etc. (referred to in this paragraph as the "distributees"). Where an item of tax preference of a conduit entity is so apportioned to a distributee, the item of tax preference retains its character in the hands of the distributee and is adjusted to reflect: (1) the separate items of income and deduction of the distributee and (2) the tax status of the distributee as an individual, corporation, etc. For example, if a trust has $100,000 of capital gains for the taxable year, all of which are distributed to A, an individual, the item of tax preference apportioned to A under section 57(a)(9) (and §1.57-1(i)(1)) is $50,000. If, however, A had a net capital loss for the taxable year of $60,000 without regard to the distribution from the trust, the trust tax preference would be adjusted in the hands of A to reflect the separate items of income and deduction passed through to the distributee, or, in this case, to reflect the net section 1201 gain to A of $40,000. Thus, A's capital gains items of tax preference would be $20,000. By application of this rule, A, in effect, treats capital gains distributed to him from the trust the same as his other capital gains in computing his capital gains item of tax preference. If A had been a corporation, the trust tax preference would be adjusted both to reflect the capital loss and to reflect A's tax status by recomputing the capital gains item of tax preference (after adjustment for the capital loss) under section 57(a)(9)(B) and §1.57-1(i)(2). Similarly, if depreciation on section 1245 property subject to a net lease (as defined in section 57(a)(3) and §1.57-1(c)) is apportioned from a conduit entity to a corporation (other than a personal holding company or electing small business corporation), the amount so apportioned to the corporation is not treated as an item of tax preference to such corporation since such item is not an item of tax preference in the case of a corporation (other than a personal holding company or an electing small business corporation).

(b) *Partnerships and partners.*—(1) Section 701 provides that a partnership as such is not subject to the income tax imposed by chapter 1. Thus, a partnership as such is not subject to the minimum tax for tax preferences. Section 702 provides that, in determining his income tax, each partner is to take into account separately his distributive share of certain items of income, deductions, etc. of the partnership and other items of income, gain, loss, deduction, or credit of the partnership to the extent provided by regulations prescribed by the Secretary or his delegate. Accordingly, each partner, in computing his items of tax preference, must take into account separately those items of income and deduction of the partnership which enter into the computation of the items of tax preference in accordance with subparagraph (2) of this paragraph.

(2) Pursuant to section 702, each partner must, solely for purposes of the minimum tax for tax preferences (to the extent not otherwise required to be taken into account separately under section 702 and the regulations thereunder), take into account separately in the manner provided in subchapter K and the regulations thereunder those items of income and deduction of the partnership which enter into the computation of the items of tax preference specified in section 57 and the regulations thereunder. A partner must, for this purpose, take into account separately his distributive share of:

(i) Investment interest expense (as defined in section 57(b)(2)(D)) determined at the partnership level;

(ii) Investment income (as defined in section 57(b)(2)(B)) determined at the partnership level;

(iii) Investment expenses (as defined in section 57(b)(2)(C)) determined at the partnership level;

(iv) With respect to each section 1250 property (as defined in section 1250(c)), the amount of the deduction allowable for the taxable year for exhaustion, wear and tear, obsolescence, or amortization and the deduction which would have been allowable for the taxable year had the property been depreciated under the straight line method each taxable year of its useful life (determined without regard to section 167(k)) for which the partnership has held the property;

(v) With respect to each item of section 1245 property (as defined in section 1245(a)(3)) which is subject to a net lease, the amount of the deduction allowable for exhaustion, wear and tear, obsolescence, or amortization and the deduction which would have been allowable for the taxable year had the property been depreciated under the straight line method for each taxable year of its useful life for which the partnership has held the property;

(vi) With respect to each certified pollution control facility for which an election is in effect under section 169, the amount of the deduction allowable for the taxable year under such section and the deduction which would have been allowable under section 167 had no election been in effect under section 169;

(vii) With respect to each unit of railroad rolling stock for which an election is in effect under section 184, the amount of the deduction allowable for the taxable year under such section and the deduction which would have been allowable under section 167 had no election been in effect under section 184;

(viii) In the case of a partnership which is a financial institution to which section 585 or 593 applies, the amount of the deduction allowable for the taxable year for a reasonable addition to a reserve for bad debts and the amount of the deduction that would have been allowable for the taxable year had the institution maintained its bad debt reserve for all taxable years on the basis of actual experience; and

(ix) With respect to each mineral property, the deduction for depletion allowable under section 611 for the taxable year and the adjusted basis of the property at the end of the taxable year (determined without regard to the depreciation deduction for the taxable year).

If, pursuant to section 743 (relating to optional adjustment to basis), the basis of partnership property is adjusted with respect to a transferee partner due to an election being in effect under section 754 (relating to manner of electing optional adjustment), items representing amortization, depreciation, depletion, gain or loss, and the adjusted basis of property subject to depletion, described above, shall be adjusted to reflect the basis adjustment under section 743.

(3) The minimum tax is effective for taxable years ending after December 31, 1969. Thus, subparagraph (2) of this paragraph is inapplicable in the case of items of income or deduction paid or accrued in a partnership's taxable year ending on or before December 31, 1969. [Reg. § 1.58-2.]

☐ [T.D. 7564, 9-11-78.]

[Reg. § 1.58-3]

§ 1.58-3. Estates and trusts.—(a) *In general.*—(1) Section 58(c)(1) provides that the sum of the items of tax preference of an estate or trust shall be apportioned between the estate or trust and the beneficiary on the basis of the income of the estate or trust allocable to each. Income for this purpose is the income received or accrued by the trust or estate which is not subject to current taxation either in the hands of the trust or estate or the beneficiary by reason of an item of tax preference. The character of the amounts distributed is determined under section 652(b) or 662(b) and the regulations thereunder.

(2) Additional computations required by reason of excess distributions are to be made in accordance with the principles of sections 665-669 and the regulations thereunder.

(3) In the case of a charitable remainder annuity trust (as defined in section 664(d)(1) and § 1.664-2) or a charitable remainder unitrust (as defined in section 664(d)(2) and § 1.664-3), the determination of the income not subject to current taxation by reason of an item of tax preference is to be made as if such trust were generally subject to taxation. Where income of such a trust is not subject to current taxation in accordance with this section and is distributed to a beneficiary in a taxable year subsequent to the taxable year in which the trust received or accrued such income, the items of tax preference relating to such income are apportioned to the beneficiary in such subsequent year (without credit for minimum tax paid by the trust with respect to items of tax preference which are subject to the minimum tax by reason of section 664(c)).

(4) Items of tax preference apportioned to a beneficiary pursuant to this section are to be taken into account by the beneficiary in his taxable year within or with which ends the taxable year of the estate or trust during which it has such items of tax preference.

(5) Where a trust or estate has items of income or deduction which enter into the computation of the excess investment interest item of tax preference, but such items do not result in an item of tax preference at the trust or estate level, each beneficiary must take into account, in computing his excess investment interest, the portion of such items distributed to him. The determination of the portion of such items distributed to each beneficiary is made in accordance with the character rules of section 652(b) or section 662(b) and the regulations thereunder.

(6) Where, pursuant to subpart E of part 1 of subchapter J (sections 671-678), the grantor of a trust or another person is treated as the owner of any portion of the trust, there shall be included in computing the items of tax preference of such person those items of income, deductions, and credits against tax of the trust which are attributable to that portion of the trust to the extent such items are taken into account under section 671 and the regulations thereunder. Any remaining portion of the trust is subject to the provisions of this section.

(b) *Examples.*—The principles of this section may be illustrated by the following examples in each of which it is assumed that none of the distributions are accumulation distributions (see sections 665-669 and the regulations thereunder):

Example (1). Trust A, with one income beneficiary, has the following items of income and deduction without regard to the deduction for distributions:

Income:	
Business income	$200,000
Investment income	20,000
	$220,000
Deductions:	
Business deductions (nonpreference)	$100,000
Investment interest expense	80,000
	$180,000

Based on the above figures, the trust has $100,000 of taxable income without regard to items which enter into the computation of excess investment interest and the deduction for distributions. The trust also has $60,000 of excess investment interest, resulting in $40,000 of distributable net income. Thus, $60,000 of the $100,000 of noninvestment income is not subject to current taxation by reason of the excess investment interest.

(a) If $40,000 is distributed to the beneficiary, the beneficiary will normally be subject to tax on the full amount received and the "sheltered" portion of the income will remain at the trust level. Thus, none of the excess investment interest item of tax preference is apportioned to the beneficiary.

(b) If the beneficiary receives $65,000 from the trust, the beneficiary is still subject to tax on only $40,000 (the amount of the distributable net income) and, thus, is considered to have received $25,000 of business income "sheltered" by excess investment interest. Thus, $25,000 of the $60,000 of excess investment interest of the trust is apportioned to the beneficiary.

Example (2). Trust B has $150,000 of net section 1201 gain.

(a) If none of the gain is distributed to the beneficiaries, none of the capital gains item of tax preference is apportioned to the beneficiaries.

(b) If all or a part of the gain is distributed to the beneficiaries, a proportionate part of the capital gains item of tax preference is apportioned to the beneficiaries. If any of the beneficiaries are corporations the capital gains item of tax preference is adjusted in the hands of the corporations as provided in § 1.58-2(a).

Example (3). Trust C has taxable income of $200,000 computed without regard to depreciation on section 1250 property and the deduction for distributions. The depreciation on section 1250 property held by the trust is $160,000. The trust instrument provides for income to be retained by the trust in an amount equal to the depreciation on the property determined under the straight line method (which method has been used for this purpose for the entire period the trust has held the property) which, in this case, is equal to $100,000. The $60,000 excess of the accelerated depreciation of $160,000 over the straight line amount which would have resulted had the property been depreciated under that method for the entire period for which the trust has held the property is an item of tax preference pursuant to section 57(a)(2). Of the remaining $100,000 of net income of the trust (after the reserve for depreciation), 80 percent is distributed to the beneficiaries. Pursuant to sections 167(h) and 642(e), 80 percent of the remaining $60,0000 of depreciation deduction (or $48,000) is taken as a deduction directly by the beneficiaries and "shelters" the income received by the beneficiaries. Thus, the full $48,000 deduction taken by the beneficiaries is "excess accelerated depreciation" on section 1250 property and is an item of tax preference in the hands of the beneficiaries. None of the remaining $12,000 of "excess accelerated depreciation" is apportioned to the beneficiaries since this amount "shelters" income retained at the trust level.

Example (4). G creates a trust the ordinary income of which is payable to his adult son. Ten years from the date of the transfer, corpus is to revert to G. G retains no other right or power which would cause him to be treated as an owner under subpart E of part 1 of subchapter J (section 671 and following). Under the terms of the trust instrument and applicable local law capital gains must be applied to corpus. During the taxable year 1970 the trust has $200,000 income from dividends and interest and a net long-term capital gain of $100,000. Since the capital gain is held or accumulated for future distribution to G, he is treated under section 677(a)(2) as an owner of a portion of the trust to which the gain is attributable. Therefore, he must include the capital gain in the computation of his taxable income in 1970 and the capital gain item of tax preference is treated as being directly received by G. Accordingly, no adjustment is made to the trust's minimum tax exemption by reason of the capital gain.

Example (5). For its taxable year 1971 the trust referred to in example (4) has taxable income of $200,000 computed without regard to depreciation on section 1250 property and the deduction for distributions. The depreciation on section 1250 property held by the trust is $160,000. The trust instrument provides for income to be retained by the trust in an amount equal to the depreciation on the property determined for purposes of the Federal income tax. If the property had been depreciated under the straight line method for the entire period for which the trust held the property the resulting depreciation deduction would have been $100,000. The $60,000 excess is, therefore, an item of tax preference pursuant to section 57(a)(2) and §1.57-1(d). Since this amount of "income" is held or accumulated for future distributions to G, he is treated under section 677(a)(2) as an owner of a portion of the trust to which such income is attributable. Therefore, section 671 requires that in computing the tax liability of the grantor the income, deductions, and credits against tax of the trust which are attributable to such portion shall be taken into account. Thus, the grantor has received $160,000 of income and is entitled to a depreciation deduction in the same amount. The $60,000 item of tax preference resulting from the excess depreciation is treated as being directly received by G as he has directly received the income sheltered by that preference. Accordingly, no adjustment is made to the trust's minimum tax exemption by reason of such depreciation. [Reg. §1.58-3.]

☐ [T.D. 7564, 9-11-78.]

[Reg. §1.58-3T]

§1.58-3T. Treatment of non-alternative tax itemized deductions by trusts and estates and their beneficiaries in taxable years beginning after December 31, 1982.—For purposes of section 58(c), in taxable years beginning after December 31, 1982, itemized deductions of a trust or estate which are not alternative tax itemized deductions (as defined in section 55(e)(1)), shall be treated as items of tax preference and apportioned between trusts and their beneficiaries, and estates and their beneficiaries. [Temporary Reg. §1.58-3T.]

☐ [T.D. 8083, 4-22-86.]

[Reg. §1.58-4]

§1.58-4. Electing small business corporations.—(a) *In general.*—Section 58(d)(1) provides rules for the apportionment of the items of tax preference of an electing small business corporation among the shareholders of such corporation. Section 58(d)(2) provides rules for the imposition of the minimum tax on an electing small business corporation with respect to certain capital gains. For purposes of section 58(d) and this section, the items of tax preference are computed at the corporate level as if section 57 generally applied to the corporation. However, the items of tax preference so computed are treated as items of tax preference of the shareholders of such corporation and not as items of tax preference of such corporation (except as provided in paragraph (c) of this section). The items of tax preference specified in section 57(a)(1) and §1.57-1(a) (excess investment interest) and section 57(a)(3) and §1.57-1(c) (accelerated depreciation on section 1245 property subject to a net lease), while generally inapplicable to corporations, are included as items of tax preference in the case of an electing small business corporation.

(b) *Apportionment to shareholders.*—(1) The items of tax preference of an electing small business corporation, other than the capital gains item of tax preference described in paragraph (c) of this section, are apportioned pro rata among the shareholders of such corporation in a manner consistent with section 1374(c)(1). Thus, with respect to the items of tax preference of the electing small business corporation, there is to be treated as items of tax preference of each shareholder a pro rata share of such items computed as follows:

(i) Divide the total amount of such items of tax preference of the corporation by the number of days in the taxable year of the corporation, thus determining the daily amount of such items of tax preference.

(ii) Determine for each day the shareholder's portion of the daily amount of each such item of tax preference by applying to such amount the ratio which the stock owned by the shareholder on that day bears to the total stock outstanding on that day.

(iii) Total the shareholder's daily portions of each such item of tax preference of the corporation for its taxable year.

Amounts taken into account by shareholders in accordance with this paragraph are considered to consist of a pro rata share of each item of tax preference of the corporation. Thus, for example, if the corporation has $50,000 of excess investment interest and $150,000 of excess accelerated depreciation on section 1250 property and a shareholder, in accordance with this paragraph, takes into account $60,000 of the total $200,000 of tax preference items of the corporation, one-fourth ($50,000 ÷ $200,000) of the $60,000, or $15,000, taken into account by the shareholder is considered excess investment interest and three-fourths of the $60,000, or $45,000, is considered excess accelerated depreciation on section 1250 property.

(2) Items of tax preference apportioned to a shareholder pursuant to subparagraph (1) of this paragraph are taken into account by the shareholder for the shareholder's taxable year in which or with which the taxable year of the corporation ends, except that, in the case of the death of a shareholder during any taxable year of the corporation (during which the corporation is an electing small business corporation), the items of tax preference of the corporation for such taxable year are taken into account for the final taxable year of the shareholder.

(c) *Capital gains.*—(1) Capital gains of an electing small business corporation, other than those capital gains subject to tax under section 1378, do not result in an item of tax preference at the corporate level since, in applying the formula specified in sections 57(a)(9)(B) and 1.57-1(i)(2), the rate of tax on capital gains (and the resulting tax) at the corporate level is zero. Under section 1375(a) shareholders of an electing small business corporation take into account the capital gains of the corporation (including capital gains subject to tax under sec. 1378). Therefore, the computation of the capital gains item of tax preference at the shareholder level, with respect to such capital gains, is taken into account automatically by the operation of sections 57(a)(9) and 1.57-1(i). To avoid double inclusion of the capital gains item of tax preference by a shareholder with respect to capital gains subject to tax under section 1378, the capital gains item of tax preference which results at the corporate level by reason of section 58(d)(2) is not treated under section 58(d)(1) as an item of tax preference of the shareholders of the corporation.

(2) The capital gains item of tax preference of an electing small business corporation subject to the tax imposed by section 1378 is the excess of the amount of tax computed under section 1378(b)(2) over the sum of—

(i) The amount of tax that would be computed under section 1378(b)(2) if the following amount were excluded:

(a) That portion of the net section 1201 gain of the corporation described in section 1378(b)(1), or

(b) If section 1378(c)(3) applies, that portion of the net section 1201 gain attributable to the property described in section 1378(c)(3), and

(ii) The amount of tax imposed under section 1378 divided by the sum of the normal tax rate and the surtax rate under section 11 for the taxable year.

(3) The principles of this paragraph may be illustrated by the following example.

Example. Corporation X is a calendar year taxpayer and an electing small business corporation. For its taxable year 1971 the corporation has net section 1201 gain of $650,000 and taxable income of $800,000 (including the net section 1201 gain). Although X's election under section 1372(a) has been in effect for its three immediately preceding taxable years, X is subject to the tax imposed by section 1378 for 1971 since it has net section 1201 gain (in the amount of $200,000) attributable to property with a substituted basis. The tax computed under section 1378(b)(1) is $187,500 (30 percent of $650,000 – $25,000) and under section 1378(b)(2) is $377,500 (22 percent of $800,000 plus 26 percent of $775,000). By reason of the limitation imposed by section 1378(c) the tax actually imposed by section 1378 is $60,000 (30 percent of $200,000, the net section 1201 gain). The tax computed under section 1378(b)(2) with the modification required under subparagraph (2)(i) of this paragraph is $281,500 (22 percent of $600,000 plus 26 percent of $575,000). Thus, the 1971 capital gains item of tax preference of X is $75,000 computed as follows:

1. Tax computed under 1378(b)(2)	$377,500
2. Tax computed under 1378(b)(2) with modification	281,500
3. Excess	96,000
4. Tax actually imposed under 1378	60,000
5. Difference	36,000
6. Normal tax rate plus surtax rate	.48
7. Tax preference (line 5 ÷ line 6)	$75,000

In addition, each shareholder of X will take into account his distributive share of the $650,000 of net section 1201 gain of X less the taxes paid by X under sections 56 and 1378 on the gain. [Reg. §1.58-4.]

☐ [T.D. 7564, 9-11-78.]

[Reg. §1.58-5]

§1.58-5. Common trust funds.—Section 58(e) provides that each participant in a common trust fund (as defined in section 584 and the regulations thereunder) is to treat as items of tax preference his proportionate share of the items of tax preference of the fund computed as if the fund were an individual subject to the minimum tax. The participant's proportionate share of the items of tax preference of the fund is determined as if the participant had realized, or incurred, his pro rata share of items of income, gain, loss, or deduction of the fund directly from the source from which realized or incurred by the fund. The participant's pro rata share of such items is determined in a manner consistent with §1.584-2(c). Items of tax preference apportioned to a participant pursuant to this paragraph are taken into account by the participant for the participant's taxable year in which or with which the taxable year of the trust ends. [Reg. §1.58-5.]

☐ [T.D. 7564, 9-11-78.]

[Reg. §1.58-6]

§1.58-6. Regulated investment companies; real estate investment trusts.—(a) *In general.*—Section 58(f) provides rules with respect to the determination of the items of tax preference of regulated investment companies (as defined in section 851) and their shareholders and real estate investment trusts (as defined in section 856) and their shareholders, or holders of beneficial interest. In general, the items of tax preference of such companies and such trusts are determined at the company or trust level and the items of tax preference so determined (other than the capital gains item of tax preference (section 57(a)(9) and §1.57-1(i)) and, in the case of a real estate investment trust, accelerated depreciation on section 1250 property (section 57(a)(2) and §1.57-1(b))) are treated as items of tax preference of the shareholders or holders of beneficial interest, in the same proportion that the dividends (other than capital gains dividends) paid to each such shareholder, or holder of beneficial interest, bear to the taxable income of such company or such trust determined without regard to the deduction for dividends paid. In no case, however, is such proportion to be considered in excess of 100 percent. For example, if a regulated investment company has items of tax preference of $500,000 for the taxable year, none of which resulted from capital gains, and distributes dividends in an amount equal to 90 percent of its taxable income, each shareholder treats his share of 90 percent of the company's items of tax preference, or (a proportionate share of) $450,000, as items of tax preference of the shareholder. The remaining $50,000 constitutes items of tax preference of the company. Amounts treated under this paragraph as items of tax preference of the shareholders, or holders of beneficial interest, are deemed to be derived proportionately from each item of tax preference of the company or trust, other than the capital gains item of tax preference and, in the case of a real estate investment trust, accelerated depreciation on section 1250 property. Such amounts are taken into account by the shareholders, or holders of beneficial interest, in the same taxable year in which the dividends on which the apportionment is based are includible in income. The minimum tax exemption of the trust or company shall not be reduced because a portion of the trust's or company's items of tax preference are allocated to the shareholders or holders of beneficial interests.

(b) *Capital gains.*—Section 58(g)(1) provides that a regulated investment company or real estate investment trust does not treat as an item of tax preference the capital gains item of tax preference under section 57(a)(9) (and §1.57-1(i)) to the extent that such item is attributable to amounts taken into income by the shareholders of such company under section 852(b)(3) or by the shareholders or holders of beneficial interest of such trust under section 857(b)(3). Thus, such a company or trust computes its capital gains item of tax preference on the basis of its net section 1201 gain less the sum of (1) the capital gains dividend (as defined in section 852(b)(3)(C) or section 857(b)(3)(C)) for the taxable year of the company or trust plus (2), in the case of a regulated investment company, that portion of the

undistributed capital gains designated, pursuant to section 852(b)(3)(D) and the regulations thereunder, by the company to be includible in the shareholder's return as long-term capital gains for the shareholder's taxable year in which the last day of the company's taxable year falls. Amounts treated under section 852(b)(3) or 857(b)(3) as long-term capital gains of shareholders, or holders of beneficial interest, are automatically included, pursuant to section 57(a)(9) and §1.57-1(i), in the computation of the capital gains item of tax preference of the shareholders, or holders of beneficial interest.

(c) *Accelerated depreciation on section 1250 property.*—In the case of a real estate investment trust, all of the items of tax preference resulting from accelerated depreciation on section 1250 property held by the trust (section 57(a)(2) and §1.57-1(b)) are treated as items of tax preference of the trust, and, thus, none are treated as items of tax preference of the shareholder, or holder of beneficial interest. [Reg. §1.58-6.]

☐ [T.D. 7564, 9-11-78.]

[Reg. §1.58-7]

§1.58-7. Tax preferences attributable to foreign sources; preferences other than capital gains and stock options.—(a) *In general.*—Section 58(g)(1) provides that, except in the case of the stock options item of tax preference (section 57(a)(6) and §1.57-1 (f)) and the capital gains item of tax preference (section 57(a)(9) and §1.57-1 (i)), items of tax preference which are attributable to sources within any foreign country or possession of the United States shall, for purposes of section 56, be taken into account only to the extent that such items reduce the tax imposed by chapter 1 (other than the minimum tax under section 56) on income derived from sources within the United States. Items of tax preference from sources within any foreign country or possession of the United States reduce the chapter 1 tax on income from sources within the United States to the extent the deduction relating to such preferences, in combination with other foreign deductions, exceed the income from such sources and, in effect, offset income from sources within the United States. Items of tax preference, for this purpose, are determined after application of §1.57-4 (relating to limitation on amounts treated as items of tax preference). In the case of a taxpayer who deducted foreign taxes under section 164 for a taxable year, the provisions of this section shall be applied (without regard to section 275(a)(4)) as if he had elected the overall foreign tax credit limitation under section 904(a)(2) for such year.

(b) *Preferences attributable to foreign sources.*—(1) *Preferences other than excess investment interest.*—Except in the case of excess investment interest (see subparagraph (2) of this paragraph), an item of tax preference to which this section applies is attributable to sources within a foreign country or possession of the United States to the extent such item is attributable to a deduction properly allocable or apportionable to an item or class of gross income from sources within a foreign country or possession of the United States under the principles of section 862(b), or section 863, and the regulations thereunder. Where, in the case of income partly from sources within the United States and partly from sources within a foreign country or possession of the United States, taxable income is computed before apportionment to domestic and foreign sources, and is then apportioned by processes or formulas of general apportionment (pursuant to section 863(b) and the regulations thereunder), deductions attributable to such taxable income are considered to be proportionately from sources within the United States and within the foreign country or possession of the United States on the same basis as taxable income.

(2) *Excess investment interest.*—(i) *Per-country limitation.*—(a) In the case of a taxpayer on the per-country foreign tax credit limitation under section 904(a) for the taxable year, excess investment interest (as defined in section 57(b)(1)), and the resulting item of tax preference, is attributable to sources within a foreign country or a possession of the United States to the extent that investment interest expense attributable to income from sources within such foreign country or possession of the United States exceeds the net investment income from sources within such foreign country or such possession. For this purpose, net investment income from within a foreign country or possession of the United States is the excess (if any) of the

investment income from sources within such country or possession over the investment expenses attributable to income from sources within such country or such possession. For the definition of investment interest expense see section 57(b)(2)(D); for the definition of investment income see section 57(b)(2)(B); for the definition of investment expense see section 57(b)(2)(C).

(b) If the taxpayer's excess investment interest computed on a worldwide basis is less than the taxpayer's total separately determined excess investment interest (as defined in this subdivision (b)), the amount of the taxpayer's excess investment interest from each foreign country or possession is the amount which bears the same relationship to the taxpayer's excess investment interest from each such country or possession, determined without regard to this subdivision (b), as the taxpayer's worldwide excess investment interest bears to the taxpayer's total separately determined excess investment interest. For purposes of this subdivision (b), the taxpayer's total separately determined excess investment interest is the sum of the total excess investment interest determined without regard to this subdivision (b) plus the taxpayer's excess investment interest from sources within the United States determined in a manner consistent with (a) of this subdivision (i).

(ii) *Overall limitation.*—In the case of a taxpayer who has elected the overall foreign tax credit limitation under section 904(a)(2) for the taxable year, excess investment interest (as defined in section 57(b)(1)), and the resulting item of tax preference, is attributable to sources within any foreign country or possession of the United States to the extent that investment interest expense attributable to income from such sources exceeds the sum of (a) the net investment income from such sources plus (b) the excess, if any, of net investment income from sources within the United States over investment interest expense attributable to sources within the United States. For this purpose, net investment income from sources within any foreign country or possession of the United States is the excess (if any) of the investment income from all such sources over the investment expenses attributable to income from such sources. For the definition of investment interest expense see section 57(b)(2)(D); for the definition of investment income see section 57(b)(2)(B); for the definition of investment expense see section 57(b)(2)(C).

(iii) *Allocation of expenses.*—The determination of the investment interest expense and investment expenses attributable to a foreign country or possession of the United States is made in a manner consistent with subparagraph (1) of this paragraph.

(iv) *Attribution of certain interest deductions to foreign sources.*—Where net investment income from sources within any foreign country or possession has the effect of offsetting investment interest expense attributable to income from sources within the United States, the deductions for the investment interest expense so offset are, for purposes of §1.58-7(c) (relating to reduction in taxes on United States source income), treated as deductions attributable to income from sources within the foreign country or possession from which such net investment income is derived. Such an offset will occur where there is an excess of investment interest expense attributable to income from sources within the United States over net investment income from such sources and (a) in the case of a taxpayer on the per-country foreign tax credit limitation, an excess of net investment income from sources within a foreign country or possession of the United States over investment interest expense from within such foreign country or possession, or (b) in the case of a taxpayer who has elected the overall foreign tax credit limitation, there is an excess of net investment income from sources within foreign countries or possessions of the United States over investment interest expense attributable to income from within such sources.

(v) *Separate limitation on interest income.*—Where a taxpayer has income described in section 904(f)(2) (relating to interest income subject to the separate foreign tax credit limitation) or expenses attributable to such income, the determination of the excess investment interest resulting therefrom must be determined separately with respect to such income and the expenses properly allocable or apportionable thereto in the same manner as such determination is made in the case of a taxpayer on the per-country foreign tax credit limitation for the taxable year (see subdivision (i) of this subparagraph).

(vi) *Examples.*—The principles of this subparagraph may be illustrated by the following examples in each of which the taxpayer is an individual and a citizen of the United States:

Example (1). The taxpayer's only items of income and deduction relating to excess investment interest are as follows:

	United States	France	Germany	Total
Investment income from sources within	$150,000	$120,000	$180,000	$450,000
Investment expenses relating to income from sources within	(100,000)	(90,000)	(120,000)	(310,000)
Net investment income	$ 50,000	$ 30,000	$ 60,000	$140,000
Investment interest expense relating to income from sources within	($110,000)	($70,000)	($50,000)	($230,000)
(Excess) of investment interest expense over net investment income	($60,000)	($40,000)	* $ 10,000	($90,000)

* Excess of net investment income over investment interest expense.

(a) If the taxpayer has elected the overall foreign tax credit limitation, his excess investment interest from sources within any foreign countries or possessions of the United States determined under subdivision (ii) of this subparagraph is computed as follows:

Investment interest:			
French	($70,000)		
German	(50,000)		($120,000)
Net investment income:			
Investment income:			
French	$120,000		
German	180,000	$300,000	
Less:			
Investment expenses:			
French	($90,000)		
German	(120,000)	(210,000)	90,000
Excess of U.S. net income over investment interest expenses			0
Total foreign excess investment interest			($30,000)

(b) If the taxpayer is on the per-country foreign tax credit limitation, his excess investment interest from France and Germany determined under subdivision (i)(a) of this subparagraph is $40,000 and zero, respectively. Since the taxpayer's worldwide excess investment interest ($90,000) is less than his total separately determined

excess investment interest ($60,000 (U.S.) plus $40,000 (French) plus zero (German), or $100,000), the limitation in subdivision (i)(b) of this subparagraph applies and the excess investment interest attributable to France is limited as follows:

$$\frac{\text{Total worldwide excess (\$90,000)}}{\text{Total separately determined excess (\$100,000)}} \times \text{French excess (\$40,000)} = \$36,000$$

The taxpayer's total excess investment interest attributable to sources within any foreign country or possession of the United States is, thus, $36,000 ($36,000 (French) plus zero (German)). The taxpayer's excess investment interest attributable to sources within the United States is $54,000

$$\left(\frac{\$9,000}{\$100,000} \times \$60,000. \right).$$

Since, in making the latter determination, $6,000 of the $60,000 of U.S. investment interest expense in excess of U.S. net investment

	U.S.
Investment income from sources within:	$180,000
Investment expenses relating to income from sources within:	(120,000)
Net investment income:	$60,000
Investment interest expense relating to income from sources within:	($50,000)
(Excess) of investment interest expense over net investment income:	$10,000

(a) If the taxpayer has elected the overall limitation, his excess investment interest from sources within any foreign countries or

Foreign investment interest:		
French	($70,000)	
German	(110,000)	($180,000)
Foreign net investment income:		
French	$120,000	
German	150,000	$270,000
Less:		
Investment expenses:		
French	($90,000)	
German	(100,000)	(190,000)	80,000
Excess of U.S. net investment income over U.S. investment interest expense		$10,000
Excess investment interest attributable to foreign sources		($90,000)

(b) If the taxpayer has not elected the overall foreign tax credit limitation, his excess investment interest from France and Germany determined under subdivision (i) of this subparagraph (without regard to the limitation to worldwide excess investment interest) is $40,000 and $60,000, respectively, and his total separately determined excess investment interest is, thus, $100,000. Since the total separately determined excess would exceed the worldwide excess, the limitation to the worldwide excess in subdivision (i) applies and the excess investment interest is determined as follows:

France:
$$\frac{\$90,000}{\$100,000} \times \$40,000 = \$36,000$$

Germany:
$$\frac{\$90,000}{\$100,000} \times \$60,000 = \$54,000$$

Total excess investment interest attributable to sources within any foreign countries and possessions	$90,000

Example (3). Assume the same facts as in example (1) except that the taxpayer, in addition has investment income, investment expenses, and investment interest subject to the separate limitation under section 904(f).

(a) If the taxpayer has elected the overall foreign tax credit limitation, his excess investment interest from sources within any foreign countries or possessions of the United States determined under subdivision (ii) of this subparagraph is the same as in (a) of example (1) of this subdivision (vi). He then treats such amount as separately determined excess investment interest attributable to a *single foreign country* as determined under subdivision (i) of this subparagraph and proceeds as in (b) of example (1) of this subdivision (vi) treating items of income and deduction subject to section 904(f) and from each separate foreign country or possession separately in making the additional determinations under subdivisions (i) and (iv) of this subparagraph.

(b) If the taxpayer has not elected the overall foreign tax credit limitation, his excess investment interest from sources within any foreign country or possession of the United States would be determined in the same manner as in (b) of example (1) treating items of income and deduction which are subject to section 904(f) and from

income is, in effect, offset by German net investment income, for purposes of §1.58-7(c), $6,000 of interest deductions attributable to income from sources within the United States are, pursuant to subdivision (iv) of this subparagraph, treated as deductions attributable to income from sources within Germany.

Example (2). Assume the same facts as in example (1) except that the items of income and deduction in Germany and the United States are reversed. The worldwide excess investment interest, thus, remains $90,000 and the items of income and deduction relating to excess investment interest are as follows:

	France	Germany	Total
Investment income from sources within:	$120,000	$150,000	$450,000
Investment expenses relating to income from sources within:	(90,000)	(100,000)	(310,000)
Net investment income:	$30,000	$50,000	$140,000
Investment interest expense relating to income from sources within:	($70,000)	($110,000)	($230,000)
(Excess) of investment interest expense over net investment income:	($40,000)	($60,000)	($90,000)

possessions of the United States determined under subdivision (ii) of this subparagraph is determined as follows:

each separate foreign country or possession separately in making the determinations under subdivisions (i) and (iv) of this subparagraph.

(c) *Reduction in taxes on United States source income.*—(1) *Overall limitation.*—(i) *In general.*—If a taxpayer is on the overall foreign tax credit limitation under section 904(a)(2), the items of tax preference determined to be attributable to foreign sources under paragraph (b) of this section reduce the tax imposed by chapter 1 (other than the minimum tax imposed under section 56) on income from sources within the United States for the taxable year to the extent of the smallest of the following three amounts:

(a) Items of tax preference (other than stock options and capital gains) attributable to sources within a foreign country or possession of the United States,

(b) The excess (if any) of the total deductions properly allocable or apportionable to items or classes of gross income from sources within foreign countries and possessions of the United States over the gross income from such sources, or

(c) Taxable income from sources within the United States. See §1.58-7(b)(2)(iv) with respect to the attribution of certain interest deductions to foreign sources in cases involving the excess investment interest item of tax preference.

(ii) *Net operating loss.*—Where there is an overall net operating loss for the taxable year, to the extent that the lesser of the amounts determined under (a) or (b) of subdivision (i) of this subparagraph exceeds the taxpayer's taxable income from sources within the United States (and, therefore do not offset taxable income from sources within the United States for the taxable year) the amount of such excess is treated as "suspense preferences." Suspense preferences are converted to actual items of tax preference, arising in the loss year and subject to the provisions of section 56, as the net operating loss is used in other taxable years, in the form of a net operating loss deduction under section 172, to offset taxable income from sources within the United States. Suspense preferences which, in other taxable years, reduce taxable income from sources within any foreign country or possession of the United States lose their character as suspense preferences and, thus, are never converted into actual items of tax preference. The amount of the suspense preferences which are converted into actual items of tax preference is equal to that portion of the net operating loss attributable to the suspense preferences which offset taxable income from sources within the

United States in taxable years other than the loss year. The determination of the component parts of the net operating loss and the determination of the amount by which the portion of the net operating loss attributable to suspense preferences offsets taxable income from sources within the United States is made on a year-by-year basis in the same order as the net operating loss is used in accordance with section 172(b). Such determination is made by applying deductions attributable to U.S. source income first against such income and deductions attributable to foreign source income first against such foreign source income and in accordance with the following principles:

(a) Deductions attributable to items or classes of gross income from sources within the United States offset taxable income from sources within the United States before any remaining portion of the net operating loss;

(b) Deductions attributable to items or classes of gross income from sources within foreign countries or possessions of the United States offset taxable income from such sources before any remaining portion of the net operating loss;

(c) Deductions described in (b) of this subdivision (ii) which are not suspense preferences (referred to in this subparagraph as "other foreign deductions") offset taxable income from sources within foreign countries and possessions of the United States before suspense preferences; and

(d) Suspense preferences offset taxable income from sources within the United States before other foreign deductions.

For purposes of the above computations, taxable income is computed with the modifications specified in section 172(b)(2) or section 172(c), whichever is applicable. However, the amount of suspense preferences which are converted into actual items of tax preference in accordance with the above principles is reduced to the extent suspense preferences offset increases in taxable income from sources within the United States due to the modifications specified in section 172(b)(2) or section 172(c). For this purpose, suspense preferences are considered to offset an increase in taxable income due to the section 172(b)(2) modifications only after reducing taxable income computed before the section 172(b)(2) or section 172(c) modifications.

(iii) *Examples.*—The principles of this subparagraph may be illustrated by the following examples. In each example the taxpayer is an individual citizen of the United States and has elected the overall foreign tax credit limitation. Personal deductions and exemptions are disregarded for purposes of these examples.

Example (1). In 1974, the taxpayer has the following items of income and deduction:

United States taxable income:			
Gross income		$750,000	
Deductions		(250,000)	$500,000
Foreign source loss:			
Gross income		$200,000	
Deductions:			
Preference items (excess of percentage depletion over basis)	$550,000		
Other	50,000	(600,000)	(400,000)
Overall taxable income			$100,000

Pursuant to subdivision (i) of this subparagraph the smallest of (a) the items of tax preference attributable to the foreign sources ($550,000), (b) the foreign source loss ($400,000), or (c) the taxable income from sources within the United States ($500,000) reduces the tax imposed by chapter 1 (other than the minimum tax) on income from sources within the United States. Thus, $400,000 of the $550,000 of excess depletion is treated as an item of tax preference in 1974 subject to the minimum tax.

Example (2). Assume the same facts as in example (1) except that the gross income from sources within the United States is $350,000 resulting in U.S. taxable income of $100,000 and an overall net operating loss of $300,000. Pursuant to subdivision (i) of this subparagraph, $100,000 of the $550,000 excess depletion would be treated as an item of tax preference in 1974 subject to the minimum tax. In addition, pursuant to subdivision (ii) of this subparagraph, the excess of the items of tax preference from foreign sources ($550,000) or the foreign source loss ($400,000), whichever is less, over the U.S.

taxable income ($100,000), or, in this example, $300,000, is treated as suspense preferences.

(a) If, in 1971, the taxpayer's total items of income and deduction result in $350,000 of taxable income all of which is from sources within the United States, the entire $300,000 net operating loss, all of which is attributable to suspense preferences, is used to offset U.S. taxable income. Accordingly, the full $300,000 of suspense preferences are converted into actual items of tax preference arising in 1974 and are subject to tax under section 56.

(b) If the $350,000 in 1971 is modified taxable income resulting from the denial of a section 1202 capital gains deduction of $175,000 by reason of section 172(b)(2), the $300,000, otherwise treated as actual items of tax preference, is reduced by $125,000, i.e., the extent to which the suspense preferences offset U.S. taxable income attributable to the increase in taxable income resulting from the denial of the section 1202 deduction.

Example (3). In 1974, the taxpayer has the following items of income and deduction:

United States loss:			
Gross income		$ 75,000	
Deductions		(225,000)	
			($150,000)
Foreign loss:			
Gross income		$400,000	
Deductions:			
Preference items (excess of accelerated depreciation on section 1250 property over straight-line amount)	$200,000		
Other	550,000	($750,000)	
			(350,000)
Overall net operating loss			($500,000)

Since the nonpreference deductions reduce the foreign source income before the preference portion, the $350,000 foreign source loss consists of $200,000 of suspense preferences and $150,000 of other deductions. In 1971, 1972, and 1973 the taxpayer had taxable income from sources within the United States of $100,000, $200,000, and $300,000,

respectively and taxable income from sources within foreign countries of $80,000 each year. Of the $200,000 of suspense preferences, $150,000 are converted into actual items of tax preference, subject to the minimum tax in 1974, determined as follows:

		Taxable income		Foreign deductions	
[In thousands of dollars]					
Year—Explanation	U.S. source	Foreign source	U.S. deductions	Suspense preferences	Other
1971 End of year balance before section 58(g) computations	100	80	150	200	150
1. U.S. deductions against U.S. income	(100)	...	(100)	...	...
2. Other foreign deductions against foreign income	...	(80)	...	...	(80)
1972 End of year balance before section 58(g) computations	200	80	50	200	70
1. U.S. deductions against U.S. income	(50)		(50)		

[In thousands of dollars]

| Year—Explanation | Taxable income | | U.S. deductions | Foreign deductions | |
	U.S. source	Foreign source		Suspense preferences	Other
2. Other foreign deductions against income	. . .	(70)	. . .	. . .	(70)
3. Suspense preferences against foreign income	. . .	(10)	. . .	(10)	. . .
4. Suspense preferences against U.S. income	*(150)	. . .	. . .	* (150)	. . .
1973 End of year balance before section 58(g) computations	300	80	. . .	40	
1. U.S. deductions against U.S. income			Not applicable.		
2. Other foreign deductions against foreign income			Not applicable.		
3. Suspense preferences against foreign income	. . .	(40)	. . .	(40)	
4. Suspense preferences against U.S. income			Not applicable.		
Balances	300	40	. . .	. . .	. . .

* Suspense preferences converted to actual items of tax preference.

Example (4). In 1970, The taxpayer's total items of income and deduction, all of which are attributable to foreign sources, are as follows:

Foreign loss:			
Gross income			$400,000
Deductions			
Preferences (excess of accelerated depreciation on section 1250 property over straight-line)	$200,000		
Other deductions	$550,000	($750,000)	
Net operating loss			$350,000

Pursuant to subdivision (i) of this subparagraph, none of the preferences attributable to foreign sources reduce the tax imposed by chapter 1 (other than the minimum tax) on taxable income from sources within the United States. Pursuant to subdivision (ii) of this subparagraph, the $200,000 portion of the net operating loss resulting from the excess accelerated depreciation constitutes suspense preferences. No part of the net operating loss that is carried back to previous years is reduced in such previous years. In 1971 and 1972, the taxpayer's income (before the net operating loss deduction) consists of the following:

1971 taxable income:		
United States		$160,000
Foreign		70,000
Total		$230,000
1972 taxable income:		
United States		$25,000
Foreign		105,000
Total		$130,000

(a) In 1971, the conversion of suspense preferences into actual items of tax preference under section 58(g) (and this paragraph) and the imposition of the minimum tax on 1970 items of tax preference under section 56(b) (and §1.56A-2) are determined as follows:

Conversion of suspense preferences:

1970 NET OPERATING LOSS
(In thousands of dollars)

	U.S. Taxable Income $160	Foreign Taxable Income $70	U.S. Deductions . . .	Suspense Preferences $200	Other Foreign Deductions $150
1. U.S. deductions against U.S. income			Not applicable		
2. Other foreign deductions against foreign income		70			(70)
3. Suspense preference against foreign income . .			Not applicable		
4. Suspense preference against U.S. income	*(160)			(160)	
Balance to 1972		. . .	. . .	$40	$80

* Suspense preferences converted into actual items of tax preference.

Imposition of minimum tax on 1970 items of tax preference:

1970 NET OPERATING LOSS
(In thousands of dollars)

	1971 Taxable Income $230	Nonpreference portion $150	Preference portion . . .	Suspense portion $200
1. 1971 Conversion of *suspense preferences* pursuant to section 58(g)		30 [1]	$130	(160)
Adjusted NOL		$180	$130	$40
2. Nonpreference portion against taxable income	(180)	(180)		
3. Preference portion against taxable income	(50) [2]	. . .	(50)	. . .
Balance to 1972	. . .	. . .	$ 80	$40

[1] Represents the 1970 minimum tax exemption.
[2] Imposition of 1970 minimum tax (10% × $50,000 = $5,000).

(b) In 1972, the conversion of suspense preferences into actual items of tax preferences under section 58(g) (and this paragraph) and the imposition of the minimum tax on 1970 items of tax preference under section 56(b) (and §1.56A-2) are determined as follows:

Conversion of suspense preferences:

	U.S. Taxable Income $25	Foreign Taxable Income $105	U.S. Deductions ...	Suspense Preferences $40	Other Foreign Deductions $80
1. U.S. deduction against U.S. income			Not applicable		
2. Other foreign deductions against foreign income		(80)			(80)
3. Suspense preferences against foreign income		(25)		(25)	
4. Suspense preferences against U.S. income ...	(15)[1]	...	...	(15)	...
Balance	10				

1970 NET OPERATING LOSS (In thousands of dollars)

[1] Suspense preferences converted into actual items of tax preference.

Imposition of minimum tax on 1970 items of tax preference:

	1971 Taxable Income $130	Nonpreference portion ...	Preference portion $80	Suspense portion $40
1. 1972 Conversion of suspense preferences pursuant to section 58(g)	...	$25	15	(40)
Adjusted NOL		$25	$95	...
2. Nonpreference portion against taxable income	(25)	(25)	...	...
3. Preference portion against taxable income	(95)[1]	...	(95)	...
Balance	$10	...		...

1970 NET OPERATING LOSS (In thousands of dollars)

[1] Imposition of 1970 minimum tax (10% × $95,000 = $9,500).

(2) *Per-country limitation.*—(i) *In general.*—If a taxpayer is on the per-country foreign tax credit limitation for the taxable year, the amount by which the items of tax preference to which this section applies reduce the tax imposed by chapter 1 (other than the minimum tax under section 56) on income from sources within the United States is determined separately with respect to each foreign country or possession of the United States. Such determination is made in a manner consistent with subparagraph (1) of this paragraph as modified in subdivision (ii) of this subparagraph. In applying subparagraph (1)(i) of this paragraph to a taxpayer on the per-country limitation, if the total potential preference amounts (as defined in this subdivision (i)) exceed the taxpayer's taxable income from sources within the United States, then, for purposes of subparagraph (1)(i)(c) of this paragraph (relating to the U.S. taxable income limitation on the amount treated as a reduction of U.S. taxable income), the taxable income from sources within the United States which is reduced by potential preference amounts with respect to each foreign country or possession is an amount which bears the same relationship to such income as the potential preference amount with respect to such foreign country or possession bears to the total of the potential preference amounts with respect to all foreign countries and possessions. For purposes of this subparagraph, the potential preference amount with respect to a foreign country or possession is the lesser of the amount of foreign source preference (described in subparagraph (1)(i)(a) of this paragraph) attributable to such country or possession or the amount of foreign source loss (described in subparagraph (1)(i)(b) of this paragraph) attributable to such country or possession.

(ii) *Net operating loss.*—Where there is an overall net operating loss for the taxable year and the total of the potential preference amounts with respect to all foreign countries and possessions exceeds the taxpayer's taxable income from sources within the United States, the amount of such excess is treated as "suspense preferences". The suspense preferences are converted into actual items of tax preference, arising in the loss year and subject to the provisions of section 56, as the net operating loss is used in other taxable years, in the form of a net operating loss deduction under section 172, to offset taxable income from sources within the United States. Suspense preferences attributable to a foreign country or possession which, in other taxable years, reduce taxable income from sources within such country or possession or offset taxable income from sources within any other foreign country or possession lose their character as suspense preferences and, thus, are never converted into actual items of tax preference. The amount of the suspense preferences which are converted into actual items of tax preference is equal to that portion of the net operating loss attributable to the suspense preferences which offsets taxable income from sources within the United States in taxable years other than the loss year. The determination of the component parts of the net operating loss and the determination of

the amount by which the portion of the net operating loss attributable to the suspense preferences offsets taxable income from sources within the United States is made on a year-by-year basis in the same order as the net operating loss is used in accordance with section 172(b). Such determination is made by applying deductions attributable to United States source income first against such income and applying deductions attributable to income from sources within a foreign country or possession of the United States first against income from sources within such country or possession and in accordance with the following principles:

(a) Deductions attributable to items or classes of gross income from sources within the United States offset taxable income from sources within the United States before any remaining deductions;

(b) Deductions attributable to items or classes of gross income from sources within any foreign country or possession of the United States which are not suspense preferences (referred to in this paragraph as "other foreign deductions") offset taxable income from sources within such country or possession before any remaining deductions;

(c) Suspense preferences attributable to items or classes of gross income from sources within a foreign country or possession offset any remaining taxable income from sources within such foreign country or possession after application of (b) of this subdivision (ii) before any remaining deductions;

(d) Suspense preferences from each foreign country and possession (remaining after application of (c) of this subdivision (ii)) offset taxable income from sources within the United States (remaining after application of (a) of this subdivision (ii)) before other foreign deductions pro rata on the basis of the total of such suspense preferences;

(e) Other foreign deductions from each foreign country and possession (remaining after application of (b) of this subdivision (ii)) offset taxable income from sources within the United States (remaining after application of (a) and (d) of this subdivision (ii)) pro rata on the basis of the total of such other foreign deductions;

(f) Deductions attributable to income from sources within the United States (remaining after application of (a) of this subdivision (ii)) offset taxable income from sources within any foreign country or possession before any foreign deductions;

(g) Other foreign deductions from each foreign country and possession (remaining after application of (b) and (e) of this subdivision (ii)) offset taxable income from sources within any other foreign countries or possessions (remaining after application of (f) of this subdivision (ii)) pro rata on the basis of the total of such other foreign deductions; and

(h) Suspense preferences (remaining after the application of (c) and (d) of this subdivision (ii)) offset taxable income from sources within any foreign country or possession (remaining after the application of (f) and (g) of this subdivision (ii)) pro rata on the basis of the total of such suspense preferences.

For purposes of the above computations, taxable income is computed with the modifications specified in section 172(b)(2) or section 172(c), whichever is applicable. However, the amount of suspense preferences which are converted into actual items of tax preference in accordance with the above principles is reduced to the extent the suspense preferences offset increases in taxable income from sources within the United States due to the modifications specified in section 172(b)(2) or section 172(c). For this purpose, suspense preferences are considered to offset an increase in taxable income due to section 172(b)(2) or section 172(c) modifications only after reducing taxable income computed before such modifications.

(iii) *Examples.*—The principles of this subparagraph may be illustrated by the following examples in each of which the per-country foreign tax credit limitation is applicable. For purposes of these examples, personal deductions and exemptions are disregarded.

Example (1). The taxpayer has the following items of income and deduction for the taxable year 1971:

	United States	France	Germany	United Kingdom
Gross income	$180,000	$165,000	$50,000	$75,000
Deductions:				
Preferences	0	0	0	(45,000)
Other	(120,000)	(125,000)	(80,000)	(100,000)
Taxable income (or loss)	$60,000	$40,000	($30,000)	($70,000)

(a) Pursuant to subdivision (i) of this subparagraph, the potential preference amount in the case of the United Kingdom is the lesser of the preferences attributable to the United Kingdom ($45,000) or the excess of deductions over gross income from sources within the United Kingdom ($70,000) and the potential preference amounts in the case of France and Germany are zero in both cases since the preferences attributable to both countries are zero. Since the total potential preference amounts ($45,000) is less than the taxable income from sources within the United States ($60,000), no modification of U.S. taxable income is required. Thus, the amount by which the U.K. preferences reduce the tax on taxable income from sources within the United States, determined in a manner consistent with subparagraph (1)(i) of this paragraph, is the smallest of (1) the items of tax preference attributable to the United Kingdom ($45,000), (2) the excess of deductions over gross income attributable to the United Kingdom

($70,000), or (3) taxable income from sources within the United States ($60,000). The full $45,000 of U.K. preference items are, therefore, taken into account as items of tax preference in 1971 and subject to the minimum tax. Since there is no net operating loss, subdivision (ii) of this subparagraph does not apply.

(b) If the French taxable income is $15,000 instead of $40,000, a $25,000 net operating loss (on a worldwide basis) results. The determination of the foreign preference items pursuant to subdivision (i) of this subparagraph is the same as in (a) of this example. Subdivision (ii) of this subparagraph again does not apply since the total potential preference amounts ($45,000) is less than the U.S. taxable income ($60,000).

Example (2). For the taxable year 1972, the taxpayer has a net operating loss of $35,000 consisting of the following items of income and deduction:

	United States	France	Germany	United Kingdom	Belgium
Gross income	$250,000	$50,000	$60,000	$5,000	$45,000
Deductions:					
Preferences		(35,000)	(70,000)	(95,000)	
Other	(100,000)	(75,000)	(30,000)		(40,000)
Taxable income (or loss)	$150,000	($60,000)	($40,000)	($90,000)	$5,000

(a) Pursuant to subdivision (i) of this subparagraph the potential preference amount with respect to each country is the lesser of the amount shown as preferences with respect to such country or the amount of the loss from such country. Thus, the potential preference amounts in this case are:

France	$35,000
Germany	40,000
United Kingdom	90,000
Belgium	0
Total	$165,000

Since the total of the potential preference amounts exceeds the U.S. taxable income, in applying the principles of subparagraph (1)(i) of this paragraph, U.S. taxable income which is reduced by potential preference amounts with respect to each country is a pro rata amount based on the total potential preference amounts as follows:

France $\{ \dfrac{35,000}{165,000} \times \$150,000 \}$ $31,818

Germany $\{ \dfrac{40,000}{165,000} \times \$150,000 \}$ $36,364

United Kingdom $\{ \dfrac{90,000}{165,000} \times \$150,000 \}$ $81,818

Belgium $\{ \dfrac{0}{165,000} \times \$150,000 \}$ 0

$150,000

The amount by which the foreign preference items offset U.S. taxable income pursuant to subdivision (i) of this subparagraph is then determined as follows:

	(a) Preferences	(b) Loss	(c) U.S. taxable income	(d) Smallest of (a), (b), or (c)
France	$35,000	$60,000	$31,818	$31,818
Germany	70,000	40,000	36,364	36,364
United Kingdom	95,000	90,000	81,818	81,818
Belgium	-0-	-0-	-0-	-0-
				$150,000

Reg. § 1.58-7(c)(2)(iii)

Thus, $150,000 of the total foreign preference items will be taken into account pursuant to subdivision (i) of this subparagraph as items of tax preference in 1972 and subject to the provisions of section 56.

(b) Pursuant to subdivision (ii) of this subparagraph, the 1972 net operating loss of $35,000 will consist of suspense preferences of $15,000 and other foreign deductions of $20,000 attributable to each foreign country as shown below and determined as follows:

		Deductions					
		France		Germany		United Kingdom	Belgium
Explanation	United States	Preferences	Other	Preferences	Other	preferences	other
	$100,000	$35,000	$75,000	$70,000	$30,000	$95,000	$40,000
1. U.S. deductions against U.S. income ($250,000)	(100,000)						
2. Other foreign deductions against foreign income (per-country)[1]		(50,000)		...	(30,000)	...	(40,000)
3. Suspense preferences against remaining foreign income (per-country)		(30,000)	...	(5,000)	...		
4. Suspense preferences against remaining U.S. income:							
France $\frac{(35,000}{165,000} \times \$150,000)$		(31,818)					
Germany $\frac{(40,000}{165,000} \times \$150,000)$				(36,364)			
U.K. $\frac{(90,000}{165,000} \times \$150,000)$						(81,818)	
5. Other foreign deductions against remaining U.S. income (0)				Not applicable.			
6. U.S. deductions against other foreign income				Not applicable.			
7. Other foreign deductions against remaining foreign income ($5,000)	(5,000)		(5,000)				
8. Suspense preferences against remaining foreign income (0)				Not applicable.			
Balance (components of NOL)		3,182	20,000	3,636	....	8,182	

[1] Foreign income amounts before step 2 are; France—$50,000; Germany—$60,000; United Kingdom—$5,000; Belgium—$45,000.

Example (3). In 1973, the taxpayer has taxable income (computed without regard to the net operating loss deduction) from the following sources and in the following amounts:

United States	France	Germany	United Kingdom
$100,000	$60,000	$20,000	$30,000

In addition, the taxpayer has a net operating loss deduction of $235,000 resulting from a 1972 net operating loss consisting of the following amounts:

Deductions attributable to income from sources within the United States $25,000
Suspense preferences attributable to income from sources within France $75,000
Deductions other than suspense preferences attributable to income from sources within France $85,000
Deductions other than suspense preferences attributable to sources within the Netherlands $50,000

(a) Pursuant to subdivision (ii) of this subparagraph, the converted suspense preferences and the remaining portions of the 1972 net operating loss carried over to 1974 are computed as follows:

[In thousands of dollars]

	1973 income				1972 net operating loss			
	United States	France	Germany	United Kingdom	United States	French suspense preferences	French other deductions	Dutch other deductions
	100	60	20	30	25	75	85	50
U.S. deductions against U.S. income	(25)				(25)			
Other foreign deductions against foreign income (per-country)		(60)					(60)	
Suspense preferences against remaining foreign income (per-country)					Not applicable.			
Suspense preferences against remaining U.S. income	([1] 75)					(75)		
Other foreign deductions against remaining U.S. income					Not applicable.			
U.S. deductions against remaining foreign income					Not applicable.			
Other foreign deductions against remaining foreign income:								
French (25,000/75,000 × $50,000)		(16.7)					(16.7)	
Dutch (50,000/75,000 × $50,000)		(33.3)						(33.3)
Suspense preferences against remaining foreign income					Not applicable.			
Balance (1972 carryover to 1974)							8.3	16.7

[1] Suspense preferences converted to actual items of tax preferences.

(b) If, in 1972, there had been no items of tax preference without regard to the suspense preferences, the conversion of the suspense preferences in 1973 would result in a 1972 minimum tax liability under section 56(a) of $4,500 (10 percent × ($75,000 − $30,000)), all of which would have been deferred by reason of section 56(b). Further, by application of section 56(b) and §1.56A-2, $20,000 of the $45,000 preference portion of the 1972 net operating loss would be treated as having reduced taxable income in 1973 resulting in the imposition in 1973 of $2,000 of the deferred 1972 minimum tax liability.

(3) *Separate limitation under section 904(f).*—In the case of a taxpayer subject to the separate limitation on interest income under section 904(f), the provisions of this paragraph shall be applied in the same manner as in subparagraph (2) of this paragraph. If the taxpayer has elected the overall foreign tax credit limitation, subparagraph (2) of this paragraph shall be applied as if all income from sources within any foreign countries or possessions of the United States and deductions relating to income from such sources other than income or deductions subject to the separate limitation under section 904(f) were from a single foreign country.

Reg. §1.58-7(c)(3)

(4) *Carryover of excess taxes.*—For rules relating to carryover of excess taxes described in paragraph (1) of section 56(c) when suspense preferences are converted to actual items of tax preference, see §1.56A-5(f).

(5) *Character of amounts.*—Where the amounts from sources within a foreign country or possession of the United States (or all such countries or possessions in the case of a taxpayer who has elected the overall foreign tax credit limitation) which are treated as reducing chapter 1 tax on income from sources within the United States or as suspense preferences are less than the total items of tax preference described in subparagraph (1)(i)(a) of this paragraph attributable to such sources, the amounts so treated are considered derived proportionately from each such item of tax preference. [Reg. §1.58-7.]

☐ [*T.D. 7564, 9-11-78. Amended by T.D. 8138, 4-23-87.*]

[Reg. §1.58-8]

§1.58-8. Capital gains and stock options.—(a) *In general.*—Section 58(g)(2) provides that the items of tax preference specified in section 57 (a)(6), and §1.57-1(b) (stock options), and section 57(a)(9), and §1.57-1(i) (capital gains), which are attributable to sources within any foreign country or possession of the United States shall not be taken into account as items of tax preference if, under the tax laws of such country or possession, preferential treatment is not accorded:

(1) In the case of stock options, to the gain, profit, or other income realized from the transfer of shares of stock pursuant to the exercise of an option which is under United States tax law a qualified or restricted stock option (under section 422 or section 424); and

(2) In the case of capital gains, to gain from the sale or exchange of capital assets (or property treated as capital assets under United States tax law).

Where capital gains are not accorded preferential treatment within a foreign country, capital losses as well as capital gains from such country are not taken into account for purposes of the minimum tax.

(b) *Source of capital gains and stock options.*—Generally, in determining whether the capital gain or stock option item of tax preference is attributable to sources within any foreign country or possession of the United States, the principles of sections 861-863 and the regulations thereunder are applied. Thus, the stock option item of tax preference, representing compensation for personal services, is attributable, in accordance with §1.861-4, to sources within the country in which the personal services were performed. Where the capital gain item of tax preference represents gain from the purchase and sale of personal property, such gain is attributable, in accordance with §1.861-7, to sources within the country in which the property is sold. In accordance with paragraph (c) of §1.861-7, in any case in which the sales transaction is arranged in a particular manner for the primary purpose of tax avoidance, all factors of the transaction, such as negotiations, the execution of the agreement, the location of the property, and the place of payment, will be considered, and the sale will be treated as having been consummated at the place where the substance of the sale occurred.

(c) *Preferential treatment.*—For purposes of this section, gain, profit, or other income is accorded preferential treatment by a foreign country or possession of the United States if (1) recognition of the income, for foreign tax purposes, is deferred beyond the taxpayer's taxable year or comparable period for foreign tax purposes which coincide with the taxpayer's U.S. taxable year in cases where other items of profit, gain, or other income may not be deferred; (2) it is subject to tax at a lower effective rate (including no rate of tax) than other items of profit, gain, or other income, by means of a special rate of tax, artificial deductions, exemptions, exclusions, or similar reductions in the amount subject to tax; (3) it is subject to no significant amount of tax; or (4) the laws of the foreign country or possession by any other method provide tax treatment for such profit, gain, or other income more beneficial than the tax treatment otherwise accorded *income by such country or possession.* For the purpose of the preceding sentence, gain, profit, or other income is subject to no significant amount of tax if the amount of taxes imposed by the foreign country or possession of the United States is equal to less than 2.5 percent of the gross amount of such income.

(d) *Examples.*—The principles of this section may be illustrated by the following examples:

Example (1). The Bahamas imposes no income tax on individuals or corporations, whether resident or nonresident. Since capital gains are subject to no tax in the Bahamas, capital gains are considered to be accorded preferential treatment and will be taken into account for purposes of the minimum tax.

Example (2). In France, except in certain cases involving the sale of large blocks of stock, a nonresident individual is not subject to tax on isolated capital gains transactions. Since such capital gains are not subject to tax in France, they are considered to be accorded preferential treatment irrespective of the treatment accorded other capital gains in France and such gains will be taken into account for purposes of the minimum tax.

Example (3). In Germany, in the case of the sale within one taxable year of 1 percent or more of the shares of a corporation in which an individual taxpayer is regarded as holding a substantial interest, the gains on the sale of the large block of stock will be taxed as extraordinary income at one-half the ordinary income tax rate. Since these gains are taxed at a reduced rate of tax in comparison to other income, they are considered to be accorded preferential treatment and will be taken into account for purposes of the minimum tax.

Example (4). In Belgium, gains derived by an individual in the course of regular speculative transactions are taxed as ordinary income, but with an upper limit of 30 percent. Rates of tax on individuals in Belgium range from approximately 30 percent to approximately 60 percent. Since the gains on speculative transactions are taxed at a maximum rate which is more beneficial than the rates accorded to other income, such gains are considered to be accorded preferential treatment and will be taken into account for purposes of the minimum tax.

Example (5). In France, gains derived by a company on the sale of fixed assets held for less than 2 years are treated as short-term gains. The excess of short-term gains in any fiscal year is taxed at the full company tax rate of 50 percent. However, this tax may be paid in equal portions over the 5 years immediately following the realization of such short-term gains. Since recognition of the short-term gains for tax purposes is subject to deferral over a 5-year period, such gains are considered to be accorded preferential treatment and will be taken into account for purposes of the minimum tax.

Example (6). Also in France, in the case of the sale or exchange by a company of depreciable assets and nondepreciable assets owned for at least 2 years, the excess of long-term capital gains over long-term capital losses in a fiscal year is subject to an immediate tax at the reduced rate of 10 percent. Such excess, reduced by the 10-percent tax, is carried in a special reserve account on the taxpayer's books. If the excess is reinvested in other fixed assets within a stated period, no further tax is due. If the amounts in the special reserve are distributed, they will be treated as ordinary income for the fiscal year in which the distribution is made. Since such gains (other than those distributed in the same fiscal year they are realized) are subject to deferral or a reduced rate of tax, they are (except to the extent distributed in the year of realization) considered to be accorded preferential treatment and are taken into account for purposes of the minimum tax.

Example (7). In Sweden, in the case of gains derived by an individual on the sale of shares or bonds held for 5 years or less, 25 percent of the gains are taxed if the holding period is 4 to 5 years, 50 percent of the gain is taxed if the holding period is 3 to 4 years, and 75 percent of the gain is taxed if the holding period is 2 to 3 years. The gain is fully taxable at ordinary income rates if held for less than 2 years. Thus, gains on shares or bonds held for 2 years or more are considered accorded preferential treatment in Sweden since they are either subject to exemption or treatment comparable to the United States capital gains deduction and are taxed at a reduced rate. Thus, such gains are taken into account for purposes of the minimum tax.

Example (8). Pursuant to Article XIV of the United States-United Kingdom Income Tax Convention, a resident of the United States is exempt from United Kingdom tax on most capital gains. Since such capital gains are exempt from United Kingdom taxation, they are considered to be accorded preferential treatment and are taken into account for purposes of the minimum tax.

Example (9). An individual resident of the United States is desirous of selling his stock in a corporation listed on the New York Stock Exchange. He requests the stock certificates from his broker in the United States, travels to a foreign country, delivers the certificates to a broker in that country, and has the foreign broker execute the sale which takes place on the New York Stock Exchange. Since the sale was consummated in the United States, pursuant to paragraph (b) of this section and §1.861-7, the resulting capital gain item of tax preference is attributable to sources within the United States.

Example (10). Two individuals, both residing in the United States, negotiate and reach agreement in New York City for the sale of stock of a close corporation. Prior to the transfer of the stock, in order to avoid imposition of the minimum tax, both individuals travel to a foreign country which does not accord preferential treatment to capital gains, but imposes a 5 percent rate of income tax which would be fully creditable against United States tax under sections 901 and 904 if the capital gains were sourced in that country. The stock is actually transferred and consideration paid in the foreign country. Since the primary purpose of consummating the sale in the foreign country was the avoidance of tax, pursuant to paragraph (b) of this section, and §1.861-7(c), the resulting capital gain item of tax preference will be considered attributable to sources within the country in which the substance of sale took place or, in this case, the United States. [Reg. §1.58-8.]

☐ [*T.D. 7564, 9-11-78.*]

[Reg. §1.59-1]

§1.59-1. Optional 10-year writeoff of certain tax preferences.— (a) *In general.*—Section 59(e) allows any qualified expenditure to which an election under section 59(e) applies to be deducted ratably over the 10-year period (3-year period in the case of circulation expenditures described in section 173) beginning with the taxable year in which the expenditure was made (or, in the case of intangible drilling and development costs deductible under section 263(c), over the 60-month period beginning with the month in which the expenditure was paid or incurred).

(b) *Election.*—(1) *Time and manner of election.*—An election under section 59(e) shall only be made by attaching a statement to the taxpayer's income tax return (or amended return) for the taxable year in which the amortization of the qualified expenditures subject to the section 59(e) election begins. The statement must be filed no later than the date prescribed by law for filing the taxpayer's original income tax return (including any extensions of time) for the taxable year in which the amortization of the qualified expenditures subject to the section 59(e) election begins. Additionally, the statement must include the following information —

(i) The taxpayer's name, address, and taxpayer identification number; and

(ii) The type and amount of qualified expenditures identified in section 59(e)(2) that the taxpayer elects to deduct ratably over the applicable period described in section 59(e)(1).

(2) *Elected amount.*—A taxpayer may make an election under section 59(e) with respect to any portion of any qualified expenditure paid or incurred by the taxpayer in the taxable year to which the election applies. An election under section 59(e) must be for a specific dollar amount and the amount subject to an election under section 59(e) may not be made by reference to a formula. The amount elected under section 59(e) is properly chargeable to a capital account under section 1016(a)(20), relating to adjustments to basis of property.

(c) *Revocation.*—(1) *In general.*—An election under section 59(e) may be revoked only with the consent of the Commissioner. Such consent will only be granted in rare and unusual circumstances. The revocation, if granted, will be effective in the first taxable year in which the section 59(e) election was applicable. However, if the period of limitations for the first taxable year the section 59(e) election was applicable has expired, the revocation, if granted, will be effective in the earliest taxable year for which the period of limitations has not expired.

(2) *Time and manner for requesting consent.*—A taxpayer requesting the Commissioner's consent to revoke a section 59(e) election must submit the request prior to the end of the taxable year the applicable amortization period described in section 59(e)(1) ends. The application for consent to revoke the election must be submitted to the Internal Revenue Service in the form of a letter ruling request.

(3) *Information to be provided.*—A request to revoke a section 59(e) election must contain all of the information necessary to demonstrate the rare and unusual circumstances that would justify granting revocation.

(4) *Treatment of unamortized costs.*—The unamortized balance of the qualified expenditures subject to the revoked section 59(e) election as of the first day of the taxable year the revocation is effective is deductible in the year the revocation is effective (subject to the requirements of any other provision under the Code, regulations, or any other published guidance) and the taxpayer will be required to amend any federal income tax returns affected by the revocation.

(d) *Effective date.*—These regulations apply to a section 59(e) election made for a taxable year ending, or a request to revoke a section 59(e) election submitted, on or after December 22, 2004. [Reg. §1.59-1.]

☐ [*T.D. 9168, 12-21-2004.*]

Base Erosion and Anti-Abuse Tax

[Reg. §1.59A-0]

§1.59A-0. Table of contents.—This section contains a listing of the headings for §§1.59A-1, 1.59A-2, 1.59A-3, 1.59A-4, 1.59A-5, 1.59A-6, 1.59A-7, 1.59A-8, 1.59A-9 and 1.59A-10.

(5) Reductions in gross receipts.

(e) Base erosion percentage test.

  (1) In general.

  (2) Base erosion percentage test for banks and registered securities dealers.

    (i) In general.

    (ii) Aggregate groups.

    (iii) De minimis exception for banking and registered securities dealer activities.

  (3) Computation of base erosion percentage.

    (i) In general.

    (ii) Certain items not taken into account in denominator.

    (iii) Effect of treaties on base erosion percentage determination.

    (iv) Amounts paid or accrued between members of a consolidated group.

    (v) Deductions and base erosion tax benefits from partnerships.

    (vi) Mark-to-market positions.

    (vii) Reinsurance losses incurred and claims payments.

    (viii) Certain payments that qualify for the effectively connected income exception and another base erosion payment exception.

(f) Examples.

  (1) Example 1: Mark-to-market.

    (i) Facts.

    (ii) Analysis.

  (2) Example 2: Member leaving an aggregate group.

    (i) Facts.

    (ii) Analysis.

§ 1.59A-3 Base erosion payments and base erosion tax benefits.

(a) Scope.

(b) Base erosion payments.

  (1) In general.

  (2) Operating rules.

    (i) In general.

    (ii) Amounts paid or accrued in cash and other consideration.

    (iii) Transactions providing for net payments.

    (iv) Amounts paid or accrued with respect to mark-to-market position.

    (v) Coordination among categories of base erosion payments.

    (vi) Certain domestic passthrough entities.

      (A) In general.

      (B) Amount of base erosion payment.

      (C) Specified domestic passthrough.

      (D) Specified foreign related party.

    (vii) Transfers of property to related taxpayers.

    (viii) Reductions to determine gross income.

    (ix) Losses recognized on the sale or transfer of property.

  (3) Exceptions to base erosion payment.

    (i) Certain services cost method amounts.

      (A) In general.

      (B) Eligibility for the services cost method exception.

      (C) Adequate books and records.

      (D) Total services cost.

    (ii) Qualified derivative payments.

    (iii) Effectively connected income.

      (A) In general.

      (B) Application to certain treaty residents.

      (C) Application to partnerships.

    (iv) Exchange loss on a section 988 transaction.

    (v) Amounts paid or accrued with respect to TLAC securities and foreign TLAC securities.

      (A) In general.

      (B) Limitation on exclusion for TLAC securities.

      (C) Scaling ratio.

      (D) Average domestic TLAC securities amount.

      (E) Average TLAC long-term debt required amount.

      (F) Limitation on exclusion for foreign TLAC securities.

        (1) In general.

        (2) Foreign TLAC long-term debt required amount.

        (3) No specified minimum provided by local law.

        (4) Foreign TLAC security.

    (vi) Amounts paid or accrued in taxable years beginning before January 1, 2018.

    (vii) Business interest carried forward from taxable years beginning before January 1, 2018.

    (viii) Specified nonrecognition transactions.

      (A) In general.

      (B) Other property transferred to a foreign related party in a specified nonrecognition transaction.

      (C) Other property received from a foreign related party in certain specified nonrecognition transactions.

      (D) Definition of other property

      (E) Allocation of other property.

    (ix) Reinsurance losses incurred and claims payments.

      (A) In general.

      (B) Regulated foreign insurance company.

  (4) Rules for determining the amount of certain base erosion payments.

    (i) Interest expense allocable to a foreign corporation's effectively connected income.

      (A) Methods described in § 1.882-5.

      (B) U.S.-booked liabilities determination.

      (C) U.S.-booked liabilities in excess of U.S.-connected liabilities.

      (D) Election to use financial statements.

      (E) Coordination with certain tax treaties.

        (1) In general.

        (2) Hypothetical § 1.882-5 interest expense defined.

        (3) Consistency requirement.

      (F) Coordination with exception for foreign TLAC securities.

    (ii) Other deductions allowed with respect to effectively connected income.

    (iii) Depreciable property.

    (iv) Coordination with ECI exception.

    (v) Coordination with certain tax treaties.

      (A) Allocable expenses.

      (B) Internal dealings under certain income tax treaties.

    (vi) Business interest expense arising in taxable years beginning after December 31, 2017.

(c) Base erosion tax benefit.

  (1) In general.

  (2) Exception to base erosion tax benefit.

    (i) In general.

    (ii) Branch-level interest tax.

  (3) Effect of treaty on base erosion tax benefit.

  (4) Application of section 163(j) to base erosion payments.

    (i) Classification of payments or accruals of business interest expense based on the payee.

      (A) Classification of payments or accruals of business interest expense of a corporation.

      (B) Classification of payments or accruals of business interest expense by a partnership.

      (C) Classification of payments or accruals of business interest expense paid or accrued to a foreign related party that is subject to an exception.

        (1) ECI exception.

        (2) TLAC interest and interest subject to withholding tax.

    (ii) Ordering rules for business interest expense that is limited under section 163(j)(1) to determine which classifications of business interest expense are deducted and which classifications of business interest expense are carried forward.

      (A) In general.

      (B) Ordering rules for treating business interest expense deduction and disallowed business interest expense carryforwards as foreign related business interest expense, domestic related business interest expense, and unrelated business interest expense.

        (1) General ordering rule for allocating business interest expense deduction between classifications.

        (2) Ordering of business interest expense incurred by a corporation.

        (3) Ordering of business interest expense incurred by a partnership and allocated to a corporate partner.

  (5) Allowed deduction.

  (6) Election to waive allowed deductions.

    (i) In general.

    (ii) Time and manner for election to waive deduction.

      (A) In general.

      (B) Information required to make the election to waive allowed deductions.

    (iii) Effect of election to waive deduction.

      (A) In general.

        (1) Consistent treatment.

        (2) No allocation and apportionment of waived deductions.

        (3) Effect of waiver of deductions described in §§ 1.861-10 and 1.861-10T.

Reg. § 1.59A-0

(4) Effect of the election to waive deductions on the stock basis of a consolidated group member.

(B) Effect of the election to waive deductions disregarded for certain purposes.

(C) Not a method of accounting.

(D) Effect of the election in determining section 481(a) adjustments.

(iv) Rules applicable to partners and partnerships.

(A) In general.

(B) Rule for determining the adjusted basis of a partner's interest in a partnership.

(C) Rule for applying section 163(j).

(D) Limited application of election to waive deductions with respect to adjustments made pursuant to audit procedures under sections 6221 through 6241.

(v) Rule applicable to premium and other consideration paid or accrued by the taxpayer for any reinsurance payments that are taken into account under section 803(a)(1)(B) or 832(b)(4)(A).

(d) Examples.

(1) Example 1: Determining a base erosion payment.

(i) Facts.

(ii) Analysis.

(2) Example 2: Interest allocable under §1 882-5.

(i) Facts.

(ii) Analysis.

(3) Example 3: Interaction with section 163(j).

(i) Facts.

(ii) Analysis.

(A) Classification of business interest.

(B) Ordering rules for disallowed business interest expense carryforward.

(4) Example 4: Interaction with section 163(j); carryforward.

(i) Facts.

(ii) Analysis.

(A) Classification of business interest.

(B) Ordering rules for disallowed business interest expense carryforward.

(5) Example 5: Interaction with section 163(j); carryforward.

(i) Facts.

(ii) Analysis.

(6) Example 6: Interaction with section 163(j); partnership.

(i) Facts.

(ii) Partnership level analysis.

(iii) Partner level allocations analysis.

(iv) Partner level allocations for determining base erosion tax benefits.

(v) Computation of modified taxable income.

(7) Example 7: Transfers of property to related taxpayers.

(i) Facts.

(ii) Analysis.

(A) Year 1.

(B) Year 2.

(8) Example 8: Effect of election to waive deduction on method of accounting.

(i) Facts.

(ii) Analysis.

(9) Example 9: Change of accounting method when taxpayer has waived a deduction.

(i) Facts.

(ii) Analysis.

(A) Computation of the section 481(a) adjustment.

(B) Computation of basis adjustments.

§1.59A-4 Modified taxable income.

(a) Scope.

(b) Computation of modified taxable income.

(1) In general.

(2) Modifications to taxable income.

(i) Base erosion tax benefits.

(ii) Certain net operating loss deductions.

(3) Rule for holders of a residual interest in a REMIC.

(c) Examples.

(1) Example 1: Current year loss.

(i) Facts.

(ii) Analysis.

(2) Example 2: Net operating loss deduction

(i) Facts.

(ii) Analysis.

§1.59A-5 Base erosion minimum tax amount.

(a) Scope.

(b) Base erosion minimum tax amount.

(1) In general.

(2) Calculation of base erosion minimum tax amount.

(3) Credits that do not reduce regular tax liability.

(i) Taxable years beginning on or before December 31, 2025.

(ii) Taxable years beginning after December 31, 2025.

(c) Base erosion and anti-abuse tax rate.

(1) In general.

(i) Calendar year 2018.

(ii) Calendar years 2019 through 2025.

(iii) Calendar years after 2025.

(2) Increased rate for banks and registered securities dealers.

(i) In general.

(ii) De minimis exception to increased rate for banks and registered securities dealers.

(3) Application of section 15 to tax rates in section 59A.

(i) New tax.

(ii) Change in tax rate pursuant to section 59A(b)(1)(A).

(iii) Change in rate pursuant to section 59A(b)(2).

§1.59A-6 Qualified derivative payment.

(a) Scope.

(b) Qualified derivative payment.

(1) In general.

(2) Reporting requirements.

(i) In general.

(ii) Failure to satisfy the reporting requirement.

(iii) Reporting of aggregate amount of qualified derivative payments.

(iv) Transition period for qualified derivative payment reporting.

(3) Amount of any qualified derivative payment.

(i) In general.

(ii) Net qualified derivative payment that includes a payment that is a base erosion payment.

(c) Exceptions for payments otherwise treated as base erosion payments.

(d) Derivative defined.

(1) In general.

(2) Exceptions.

(i) Direct interest.

(ii) Insurance contracts.

(iii) Securities lending and sale-repurchase transactions.

(A) Multi-step transactions treated as financing.

(B) Special rule for payments associated with the cash collateral provided in a securities lending transaction or substantially similar transaction.

(C) Anti-abuse exception for certain transactions that are the economic equivalent of substantially unsecured cash borrowing.

(3) American depository receipts.

(e) Examples.

(1) Example 1: Notional principal contract as QDP.

(i) Facts.

(ii) Analysis.

(2) Example 2: Securities lending anti-abuse rule.

(i) Facts.

(ii) Analysis.

§1.59A-7 Application of base erosion and anti-abuse tax to partnerships.

(a) Scope.

(b) Application of section 59A to partnerships.

(c) Base erosion payment.

(1) Payments made by or to a partnership.

(2) Transfers of certain property.

(3) Transfers of a partnership interest.

(i) In general.

(ii) Transfers of a partnership interest by a partner.

(iii) Certain issuances of a partnership interest by a partnership.

(iv) Partnership interest transfers defined.

(4) Increased basis from a distribution.

(5) Operating rules applicable to base erosion payments.

(i) Single payment characterized as separate transactions.

(ii) Ordering rule with respect to transfers of a partnership interest.

(iii) Consideration for base erosion payment or property resulting in base erosion tax benefits.

(iv) Non-cash consideration.

(v) Allocations of income in lieu of deductions.

(d) Base erosion tax benefit for partners.

(1) In general.

(2) Exception for base erosion tax benefits of certain small partners.

☐ [T.D. 9885, 12-2-2019. Amended by T.D. 9910, 10-8-2020.]

[Reg. § 1.59A-1]

§ 1.59A-1. Base erosion and anti-abuse tax.—(a) *Purpose.*—This section and §§ 1.59A-2 through 1.59A-10 (collectively, the "section 59A regulations") provide rules under section 59A to determine the amount of the base erosion and anti-abuse tax. Paragraph (b) of this section provides definitions applicable to the section 59A regulations. Section 1.59A-2 provides rules regarding how to determine whether a taxpayer is an applicable taxpayer. Section 1.59A-3 provides rules regarding base erosion payments and base erosion tax benefits. Section 1.59A-4 provides rules for calculating modified taxable income. Section 1.59A-5 provides rules for calculating the base erosion minimum tax amount. Section 1.59A-6 provides rules relating to qualified derivative payments. Section 1.59A-7 provides rules regarding the application of section 59A to partnerships. Section 1.59A-8 is reserved for rules regarding the application of section 59A to certain expatriated entities. Section 1.59A-9 provides anti-abuse rules to prevent avoidance of section 59A. Finally, § 1.59A-10 provides the applicability date for the section 59A regulations.

(b) *Definitions.*—For purposes of this section and §§ 1.59A-2 through 1.59A-10, the following terms have the meanings provided in this paragraph (b).

(1) *Aggregate group.*—The term *aggregate group* means the group of corporations determined by—

(i) Identifying a controlled group of corporations as defined in section 1563(a), except that the phrase "more than 50 percent" is substituted for "at least 80 percent" each place it appears in section 1563(a)(1) and the determination is made without regard to sections 1563(a)(4) and (e)(3)(C), and

(ii) Once the controlled group of corporations is determined, excluding foreign corporations except with regard to income that is, or is treated as, effectively connected with the conduct of a trade or business in the United States under an applicable provision of the Internal Revenue Code or regulations published under 26 CFR chapter I. Notwithstanding the foregoing, if a foreign corporation is subject to tax on a net basis pursuant to an applicable income tax treaty of the United States, it is excluded from the controlled group of corporations except with regard to income taken into account in determining its net taxable income.

(2) *Applicable section 38 credits.*—The term *applicable section 38 credits* means the credits allowed under section 38 for the taxable year that are properly allocable to—

(i) The low-income housing credit determined under section 42(a),

(ii) The renewable electricity production credit determined under section 45(a), and

(iii) The investment credit determined under section 46, but only to the extent properly allocable to the energy credit determined under section 48.

(3) *Applicable taxpayer.*—The term *applicable taxpayer* means a taxpayer that meets the requirements set forth in § 1.59A-2(b).

(4) *Bank.*—The term *bank* has the meaning provided in section 581.

(5) *Base erosion and anti-abuse tax rate.*—The term *base erosion and anti-abuse tax rate* means the percentage that the taxpayer applies to its modified taxable income for the taxable year to calculate its base erosion minimum tax amount. See § 1.59A-5(c) for the base erosion and anti-abuse tax rate applicable for the relevant taxable year.

(6) *Business interest expense.*—The term *business interest expense*, with respect to a taxpayer and a taxable year, has the meaning provided in § 1.163(j)-1(b)(3).

(7) *Deduction.*—The term *deduction* means any deduction allowable under chapter 1 of subtitle A of the Internal Revenue Code.

(8) *Disallowed business interest expense carryforward.*—The term *disallowed business interest expense carryforward* has the meaning provided in § 1.163(j)-1(b)(11).

(9) *Domestic related business interest expense.*—The term *domestic related business interest expense* for any taxable year is the taxpayer's business interest expense paid or accrued to a related party that is not a foreign related party.

(10) *Foreign person.*—The term *foreign person* means any person who is not a United States person. For purposes of the preceding sentence, a United States person has the meaning provided in section 7701(a)(30), except that any individual who is a citizen of any possession of the United States (but not otherwise a citizen of the United States) and who is not a resident of the United States is not a United States person. See § 1.59A-7(b) for rules applicable to partnerships.

(11) *Foreign related business interest expense.*—The term *foreign related business interest expense* for any taxable year is the taxpayer's business interest expense paid or accrued to a foreign related party.

(12) *Foreign related party.*—The term *foreign related party* means a foreign person, as defined in paragraph (b)(10) of this section, that is a related party, as defined in paragraph (b)(17) of this section, with respect to the taxpayer. In addition, for purposes of § 1.59A-3(b)(4)(v)(B) (relating to internal dealings under certain income tax treaties), a foreign related party also includes the foreign corporation's home office or a foreign branch of the foreign corporation. See § 1.59A-7(b), (c), and (f) for rules applicable to partnerships.

(13) *Gross receipts.*—The term *gross receipts* has the meaning provided in § 1.448-1T(f)(2)(iv).

(14) *Member of an aggregate group.*—The term *member of an aggregate group* means a corporation that is included in an aggregate group, as defined in paragraph (b)(1) of this section.

(15) *Registered securities dealer.*—The term *registered securities dealer* means any dealer as defined in section 3(a)(5) of the Securities Exchange Act of 1934 that is registered, or required to be registered, under section 15 of the Securities Exchange Act of 1934.

(16) *Regular tax liability.*—The term *regular tax liability* has the meaning provided in section 26(b).

(17) *Related party.*—(i) *In general.*—A *related party*, with respect to an applicable taxpayer, is—

(A) Any 25-percent owner of the taxpayer;

(B) Any person who is related (within the meaning of section 267(b) or 707(b)(1)) to the taxpayer or any 25-percent owner of the taxpayer; or

(C) A controlled taxpayer within the meaning of § 1.482-1(i)(5) together with, or with respect to, the taxpayer.

(ii) *25-percent owner.*—With respect to any corporation, a *25-percent owner* means any person who owns at least 25 percent of—

(A) The total voting power of all classes of stock of the corporation entitled to vote; or

(B) The total value of all classes of stock of the corporation.

(iii) *Application of section 318.*—Section 318 applies for purposes of paragraphs (b)(17)(i) and (ii) of this section, except that—

(A) "10 percent" is substituted for "50 percent" in section 318(a)(2)(C); and

(B) Section 318(a)(3)(A) through (C) are not applied so as to consider a United States person as owning stock that is owned by a person who is not a United States person.

(18) *TLAC long-term debt required amount.*—The term *TLAC long-term debt required amount* means the specified minimum amount of debt that is required pursuant to 12 CFR 252.162(a).

(19) *TLAC securities amount.*—The term *TLAC securities amount* is the sum of the adjusted issue prices (as determined for purposes of § 1.1275-1(b)) of all TLAC securities issued and outstanding by the taxpayer, without regard to whether interest thereunder would be a base erosion payment absent § 1.59A-3(b)(3)(v).

(20) *TLAC security.*—The term *TLAC security* means an eligible internal debt security, as defined in 12 CFR 252.161.

(21) *Unrelated business interest expense.*—The term *unrelated business interest expense* for any taxable year is the taxpayer's business interest expense paid or accrued to a party that is not a related party. [Reg. § 1.59A-1.]

☐ [T.D. 9885, 12-2-2019. Amended by T.D. 9910, 10-8-2020.]

[Reg. § 1.59A-2]

§ 1.59A-2. Applicable taxpayer.—(a) *Scope.*—This section provides rules for determining whether a taxpayer is an applicable taxpayer. Paragraph (b) of this section defines an applicable taxpayer. Paragraph (c) of this section provides rules for determining whether a taxpayer is an applicable taxpayer by reference to the aggregate group of which the taxpayer is a member. Paragraph (d) of this section provides rules regarding the gross receipts test. Paragraph (e) of this section provides rules regarding the base erosion percentage test. Paragraph (f) of this section provides examples illustrating the rules of this section.

(b) *Applicable taxpayer.*—For purposes of section 59A, a taxpayer is an applicable taxpayer with respect to any taxable year if the taxpayer—

(1) Is a corporation, but not a regulated investment company, a real estate investment trust, or an S corporation;

(2) Satisfies the gross receipts test of paragraph (d) of this section; and

(3) Satisfies the base erosion percentage test of paragraph (e) of this section.

(c) *Aggregation rules.*—(1) *In general.*—Solely for purposes of this section and § 1.59A-4, a taxpayer that is a member of an aggregate group determines its gross receipts and its base erosion percentage on the basis of the aggregate group. For these purposes, transactions that occur between members of the taxpayer's aggregate group that were members of the aggregate group as of the time of the transaction are not taken into account. In the case of a foreign corporation that is a member of an aggregate group, only transactions that occur between members of the aggregate group and that relate to income effectively connected with, or treated as effectively connected with, the conduct of a trade or business in the United States are not taken into account for this purpose. In the case of a foreign corporation that is a member of an aggregate group and that is subject to tax on a net basis pursuant to an applicable income tax treaty of the United States, only transactions that occur between members of the aggregate group and that relate to income that is taken into account in determining its net taxable income are not taken into account for this purpose. For purposes of this paragraph (c)(1), each payment or accrual is treated as a separate transaction.

(2) *Aggregate group determined with respect to each taxpayer.*—(i) *In general.*—Solely for purposes of this section, an aggregate group is determined with respect to each taxpayer. As a result, the aggregate group of one taxpayer may be different than the aggregate group of another member of the taxpayer's aggregate group.

(ii) *Change in the composition of an aggregate group.*—A change in ownership of the taxpayer (for example, a sale of the taxpayer to a third party) does not cause the taxpayer to leave its own aggregate group. Instead, any members of the taxpayer's aggregate group before the change in ownership that are no longer members following the change in ownership are treated as having left the taxpayer's aggregate group, and any new members that become members of the taxpayer's aggregate group following the change in ownership are treated as having joined the taxpayer's aggregate group. A change in ownership of another member of the aggregate group of the taxpayer (for example, a sale of the member to a third party) may result in the member joining or leaving the aggregate group of the taxpayer. See paragraph (c)(4) of this section for the treatment of members joining or leaving the aggregate group of a taxpayer.

(3) *Taxable year of members of an aggregate group.*—Solely for purposes of this section, a taxpayer that is a member of an aggregate group measures the gross receipts and base erosion percentage of the aggregate group for a taxable year by reference to the taxpayer's gross receipts, base erosion tax benefits, and deductions for the taxable year and the gross receipts, base erosion tax benefits, and deductions of each member of the aggregate group for the taxable year of the member that ends with or within the taxpayer's taxable year.

(4) *Periods before and after a corporation is a member of an aggregate group.*—(i) *In general.*—Solely for purposes of this section, to determine the gross receipts and the base erosion percentage of the aggregate group of a taxpayer, the taxpayer takes into account only the portion of another corporation's taxable year during which the corporation is a member of the aggregate group of the taxpayer. The gross receipts, base erosion tax benefits, and deductions of a corporation that are properly included in the gross receipts and base erosion percentage of the aggregate group of a taxpayer are not reduced as a result of the member leaving the aggregate group of the taxpayer.

(ii) *Deemed taxable year-end.*—Solely for purposes of this paragraph (c), if a corporation leaves or joins the aggregate group of a taxpayer, the corporation is treated as ceasing to be a member of the aggregate group at the time of its taxable year-end, or becoming a member of the aggregate group immediately after the time of its taxable year-end, resulting from the transaction. For purposes of this paragraph (c), if a corporation joins or leaves an aggregate group in a transaction that does not result in the corporation having a taxable year-end, the corporation is treated as having a taxable year-end ("deemed taxable year-end") at the end of the day on which the transaction occurs.

(iii) *Items allocable to deemed taxable years before and after deemed taxable year-end.*—Solely for purposes of this paragraph (c), a corporation that has a deemed taxable year-end determines gross receipts, base erosion tax benefits, and deductions attributable to the deemed taxable year ending upon, or beginning immediately after, the deemed taxable year-end by either treating the corporation's books as closing ("deemed closing of the books") at the deemed taxable year-end or, in the case of items other than extraordinary items, allocating those items on a pro-rata basis without a closing of the books. Extraordinary items are allocated to the deemed taxable year ending upon, or beginning immediately after, the deemed taxable year-end based on the day that they are taken into account. For purposes of applying this paragraph (c)(4)(iii), extraordinary items that are attributable to a transaction that occurs during the portion of the corporation's day after the event resulting in the corporation joining or leaving the aggregate group are treated as taken into account at the beginning of the following day. Additionally, for purposes of applying this paragraph (c)(4)(iii), "extraordinary items" include the items enumerated in § 1.1502-76(b)(2)(ii)(C) as well as any other payment not made in the ordinary course of business that would be treated as a base erosion payment.

(5) *Short taxable year.*—(i) *Short period of the taxpayer.*—(A) *In general.*—Solely for purposes of this section, if a taxpayer has a taxable year of fewer than 12 months (a short period), the gross receipts, base erosion tax benefits, and deductions of the taxpayer are annualized by multiplying the total amount for the short period by 365 and dividing the result by the number of days in the short period.

(B) *Determining the gross receipts and base erosion percentage of the aggregate group of a taxpayer for a short period.*—When a taxpayer has a taxable year that is a short period and a member of the taxpayer's aggregate group does not have a taxable year that ends with or within the taxpayer's taxable year as a result of the taxpayer's short period, the taxpayer must use a reasonable approach to determine the gross receipts and base erosion percentage of its aggregate group for the short period. A reasonable approach should neither over-count nor under-count the gross receipts, base erosion tax benefits, and deductions of the aggregate group of the taxpayer. A reasonable approach does not include an approach that does not take into account the gross receipts, base erosion tax benefits, or deductions of the member. The taxpayer must consistently apply the reasonable approach. Examples of a reasonable approach may include an approach that takes into account 12 months of gross receipts, base erosion tax benefits, and deductions of the member by reference to—

(1) The 12-month period ending on the last day of the short period;

(2) The member's taxable year that ends nearest to the last day of the short period or that begins nearest to the first day of the short period; or

(3) An average of the two taxable years of the member ending before and after the short period.

(ii) *Short period of a member of the taxpayer's aggregate group.*—(A) *Multiple taxable years of a member of the taxpayer's aggregate group comprised of more than 12 months.*—If a member of a taxpayer's aggregate group has more than one taxable year ending with or within the taxpayer's taxable year, and the member's taxable years ending with or within the taxpayer's taxable year are comprised of more than 12 months in total, then the aggregate group member's gross receipts, base erosion tax benefits, and deductions are annualized for purposes of determining the gross receipts and base erosion percentage of the taxpayer's aggregate group. The aggregate group member's gross receipts, base erosion tax benefits, and deductions are annualized by multiplying the total amount for the member's taxable years by 365 and dividing the result by the total number of days in the multiple taxable years.

(B) *Short period or periods of a member of the taxpayer's aggregate group comprised of fewer than 12 months from change in taxable year.*—If, as a result of a member of a taxpayer's aggregate group changing its taxable year-end (other than as a result of the application of § 1.1502-76(a)), the member's taxable year or years ending with or within the taxpayer's taxable year are comprised of fewer than 12 months in total, then the aggregate group member's gross receipts, base erosion tax benefits, and deductions are annualized for purposes of determining the gross receipts and base erosion percentage of the taxpayer's aggregate group. The aggregate group member's gross receipts, base erosion tax benefits, and deductions are annualized by multiplying the total amount for the member's taxable year or years by 365 and dividing the result by the total number of days in the taxable year or years.

(iii) *Anti-abuse rule.*—If a taxpayer or a member of a taxpayer's aggregate group enters into a transaction (or series of transactions), plan, or arrangement with another corporation that is a member of the aggregate group or a foreign related party that has a principal purpose of changing the period taken into account under the gross receipts test or the base erosion percentage test to avoid applicable taxpayer status under paragraph (b) of this section, then the gross receipts test or base erosion percentage test, respectively, applies as if that transaction (or series of transactions), plan, or arrangement had not occurred.

(6) *Treatment of predecessors.*—(i) *In general.*—Solely for purposes of this section, in determining gross receipts under paragraph (d) of this section, any reference to a taxpayer includes a reference to any predecessor of the taxpayer. For this purpose, a predecessor is the distributor or transferor corporation in a transaction described in section 381(a) in which the taxpayer is the acquiring corporation. For purposes of determining the gross receipts of a predecessor that are taken into account by a taxpayer, the operating rules set forth in this paragraph (c) and in paragraph (d) of this section are applied to the same extent they were applied to the predecessor.

(ii) *No duplication.*—If the taxpayer or any member of its aggregate group is also a predecessor of the taxpayer or any member of its aggregate group, the gross receipts of each member are taken into account only once.

(7) *Partnerships.*—For the treatment of partnerships for purposes of determining gross receipts and base erosion tax benefits, see § 1.59A-7(e)(2) and (d), respectively.

(8) *Transition rule for aggregate group members with different taxable years.*—If the taxpayer has a different taxable year than another member of the taxpayer's aggregate group (other member), and the other member is eligible for the exception in § 1.59A-3(b)(3)(vi) (amounts paid or accrued in taxable years beginning before January 1, 2018) with respect to a taxable year ending with or within the taxpayer's taxable year ("excepted taxable year"), the excepted taxable year of the other member is not taken into account for purposes of paragraph (e) of this section. This rule applies solely for purposes of determining whether a taxpayer is an applicable taxpayer under this section.

(9) *Consolidated groups.*—For the treatment of consolidated groups for purposes of determining gross receipts and base erosion tax benefits, see § 1.1502-59A(b).

(d) *Gross receipts test.*—(1) *Amount of gross receipts.*—A taxpayer, or the aggregate group of which the taxpayer is a member, satisfies the gross receipts test of this section if it has average annual gross receipts of at least $500,000,000 for the three-taxable-year period ending with the preceding taxable year.

(2) *Taxpayer not in existence for entire three-year period.*—If a taxpayer was not in existence for the entire three-year period referred to in paragraph (d)(1) of this section, the taxpayer determines a gross receipts average for the period that it was in existence (which includes gross receipts in the current year).

(3) *Gross receipts of foreign corporations.*—With respect to any foreign corporation, only gross receipts that are taken into account in determining income that is, or is treated as, effectively connected with the conduct of a trade or business within the United States are taken into account for purposes of paragraph (d)(1) of this section. In the case of a foreign corporation that is a member of an aggregate group and that is subject to tax on a net basis pursuant to an applicable income tax treaty of the United States, the foreign corporation includes only gross receipts that are attributable to transactions taken into account in determining its net taxable income.

(4) *Gross receipts of an insurance company.*—Solely for purposes of this section, for any corporation that is subject to tax under subchapter L or any corporation that would be subject to tax under subchapter L if that corporation were a domestic corporation, gross receipts are reduced by return premiums (within the meaning of section 803(a)(1)(B) and section 832(b)(4)(A)), but are not reduced by any reinsurance premiums paid or accrued.

(5) *Reductions in gross receipts.*—For purposes of this section, gross receipts for any taxable year are reduced by returns and allowances made during that taxable year.

(6) *Gross receipts of consolidated groups.*—For purposes of this section, the gross receipts of a consolidated group are determined by aggregating the gross receipts of all of the members of the consolidated group. See § 1.1502-59A(b).

(e) *Base erosion percentage test.*—(1) *In general.*—A taxpayer, or the aggregate group of which the taxpayer is a member, satisfies the base erosion percentage test if its base erosion percentage is three percent or higher.

(2) *Base erosion percentage test for banks and registered securities dealers.*—(i) *In general.*—A taxpayer that is a member of an affiliated group (as defined in section 1504(a)(1)) that includes a bank (as defined in §1.59A-1(b)(4)) or a registered securities dealer (as defined in section §1.59A-1(b)(15)) satisfies the base erosion percentage test if its base erosion percentage is two percent or higher.

(ii) *Aggregate groups.*—An aggregate group of which a taxpayer is a member and that includes a bank or a registered securities dealer that is a member of an affiliated group (as defined in section 1504(a)(1)) is subject to the base erosion percentage threshold described in paragraph (e)(2)(i) of this section.

(iii) *De minimis exception for banking and registered securities dealer activities.*—An aggregate group that includes a bank or a registered securities dealer that is a member of an affiliated group (as defined in section 1504(a)(1)) is not treated as including a bank or registered securities dealer for purposes of paragraph (e)(2)(i) of this section for a taxable year, if, for that taxable year, the total gross receipts of the aggregate group attributable to the bank or the registered securities dealer (or attributable to all of the banks and registered securities dealers in the group, if more than one) represent less than two percent of the total gross receipts of the aggregate group, as determined under paragraph (d) of this section. When there is no aggregate group, a consolidated group that includes a bank or a registered securities dealer is not treated as including a bank or registered securities dealer for purposes of paragraph (e)(2)(i) of this section for a taxable year, if, for that taxable year, the total gross receipts of the consolidated group attributable to the bank or the registered securities dealer (or attributable to all of the banks or registered securities dealers in the group, if more than one) represent less than two percent of the total gross receipts of the consolidated group, as determined under paragraph (d) of this section.

(3) *Computation of base erosion percentage.*—(i) *In general.*—The taxpayer's base erosion percentage for any taxable year is determined by dividing—

(A) The aggregate amount of the taxpayer's (or in the case of a taxpayer that is a member of an aggregate group, the aggregate group's) base erosion tax benefits (as defined in §1.59A-3(c)(1)) for the taxable year, by

(B) The sum of—

(*1*) The aggregate amount of the deductions (including deductions for base erosion tax benefits described in §1.59A-3(c)(1)(i) and base erosion tax benefits described in §1.59A-3(c)(1)(ii)) allowable to the taxpayer (or in the case of a taxpayer that is a member of an aggregate group, any member of the aggregate group) under chapter 1 of Subtitle A for the taxable year;

(*2*) The base erosion tax benefits described in §1.59A-3(c)(1)(iii) with respect to any premiums or other consideration paid or accrued by the taxpayer (or in the case of a taxpayer that is a member of an aggregate group, any member of the aggregate group) to a foreign related party for any reinsurance payment taken

into account under sections 803(a)(1)(B) or 832(b)(4)(A) for the taxable year; and

(*3*) Any amount paid or accrued by the taxpayer (or in the case of a taxpayer that is a member of an aggregate group, any member of the aggregate group) resulting in a reduction of gross receipts described in §1.59A-3(c)(1)(iv) for the taxable year.

(ii) *Certain items not taken into account in denominator.*—Except as provided in paragraph (e)(3)(viii) of this section, the amount under paragraph (e)(3)(i)(B) of this section is determined by not taking into account—

(A) Any deduction allowed under section 172, 245A, or 250 for the taxable year;

(B) Any deduction for amounts paid or accrued for services to which the exception described in §1.59A-3(b)(3)(i) applies;

(C) Any deduction for qualified derivative payments that are not treated as base erosion payments by reason of §1.59A-3(b)(3)(ii);

(D) Any exchange loss within the meaning of §1.988-2 from a section 988 transaction as described in §1.988-1(a)(1) that is not treated as a base erosion payment by reason of §1.59A-3(b)(3)(iv);

(E) Any deduction for amounts paid or accrued to foreign related parties with respect to TLAC securities and foreign TLAC securities that are not treated as base erosion payments by reason of §1.59A-3(b)(3)(v);

(F) Any reinsurance losses incurred and claims payments described in §1.59A-3(b)(3)(ix); and

(G) Any deduction not allowed in determining taxable income for the taxable year.

(iii) *Effect of treaties on base erosion percentage determination.*—See §1.59A-3(c)(2) and (3).

(iv) *Amounts paid or accrued between members of a consolidated group.*—See §1.1502-59A(b).

(v) *Deductions and base erosion tax benefits from partnerships.*—See §1.59A-7(b), (d), and (e).

(vi) *Mark-to-market positions.*—For any position with respect to which the taxpayer (or in the case of a taxpayer that is a member of an aggregate group, a member of the aggregate group) applies a mark-to-market method of accounting for U.S. federal income tax purposes, the taxpayer must determine its gain or loss with respect to that position for any taxable year by combining all items of income, gain, loss, or deduction arising with respect to the position during the taxable year, regardless of how each item arises (including from a payment, accrual, or mark) for purposes of paragraph (e)(3) of this section. See paragraph (f)(1) of this section (*Example 1*) for an illustration of this rule. For purposes of section 59A, a taxpayer computes its losses resulting from positions subject to a mark-to-market regime under the Internal Revenue Code based on a single mark for the taxable year on the earlier of the last business day of the taxpayer's taxable year and the disposition (whether by sale, offset, exercise, termination, expiration, maturity, or other means) of the position, regardless of how frequently a taxpayer marks to market for other purposes. See §1.59A-3(b)(2)(iii) for the application of this rule for purposes of determining the amount of base erosion payments.

(vii) *Reinsurance losses incurred and claims payments.*—Except as provided in paragraph (e)(3)(ii)(F) of this section, amounts paid for losses incurred (as defined in section 832(b)(5)) and claims and benefits under section 805(a)(1) are taken into account for purposes of paragraph (e)(3)(i)(B)(*1*) of this section.

(viii) *Certain payments that qualify for the effectively connected income exception and another base erosion payment exception.*—Subject to paragraph (c) of this section (transactions that occur between members of the taxpayer's aggregate group), a payment that qualifies for the effectively connected income exception described in §1.59A-3(b)(3)(iii) and either the service cost method exception described in §1.59A-3(b)(3)(i), the qualified derivative payment exception described in §1.59A-3(b)(3)(ii), or the TLAC exception described in §1.59A-3(b)(3)(v) is not subject to paragraph (e)(3)(ii)(B), (C), or (E) of this section and those amounts are included in the denominator of the base erosion percentage if the foreign related party who received the payment is not a member of the aggregate group.

(f) *Examples.*—(1) *Example 1: Mark-to market.*—(i) *Facts.* (A) Foreign Parent (FP) is a foreign corporation that owns all of the stock of domestic corporation (DC). FP is a foreign related party of DC under §1.59A-1(b)(12). DC is a registered securities dealer that does not hold any securities for investment. On January 1 of year 1, DC enters into two interest rate swaps for a term of two years, one with unrelated Customer A as the counterparty (position A) and one with unrelated Customer B as the counterparty (position B). Each of the swaps provides for semiannual periodic payments to be made or received on June 30 and December 31. No party makes any payment to any other party upon initiation of either of the swaps (that is, they are entered into at-the-money). DC is required to mark-to-market positions A and B for U.S. federal income tax purposes. DC is a calendar year taxpayer.

(B) For position A in year 1, DC makes a payment of $150x on June 30, and receives a payment of $50x on December 31. There are no other payments in year 1. On December 31, position A has a value to DC of $110x (that is, position A is in-the-money by $110x).

(C) For position B in year 1, DC receives a payment of $120x on June 30, and makes a payment of $30x on December 31. There are no other payments in year 1. On December 31, position B has a value to DC of ($130x) (that is, position B is out-of-the-money by $130x).

(ii) *Analysis.* (A) With respect to position A, based on the total amount of payments made and received in year 1, DC has a net deduction of $100x. In addition, DC has a mark-to-market gain of $110x. As described in paragraph (e)(3)(vi) of this section, the mark-to-market gain of $110x is combined with the net deduction of $100x resulting from the payments. Therefore, with respect to position A, DC has a gain of $10x, and thus has no deduction in year 1 for purposes of section 59A.

(B) With respect to position B, based on the total amount of payments made and received in year 1, DC has net income of $90x. In addition, DC has a mark-to-market loss of $130x. As described in paragraph (e)(3)(vi) of this section, the mark-to-market loss of $130x is combined with the net income of $90x resulting from the payments. Therefore, with respect to position B, DC has a loss of $40x, and thus has a $40x deduction in year 1 for purposes of section 59A.

(2) *Example 2: Member leaving an aggregate group.*—(i) *Facts.* Parent Corporation wholly owns Corporation 1 and Corporation 2. Each corporation is a domestic corporation and a calendar-year taxpayer that does not file a consolidated return. The aggregate group of Corporation 1 includes Parent Corporation and Corporation 2. At noon on June 30, Year 1, Parent Corporation sells the stock of Corporation 2 to Corporation 3, an unrelated domestic corporation, in exchange for cash consideration. Before the acquisition, Corporation 3 was not a member of an aggregate group. Corporation 2 and Corporation 3 do not file a consolidated return.

(ii) *Analysis.* (A) For purposes of section 59A, to determine the gross receipts and base erosion percentage of the aggregate group of Corporation 1 for calendar Year 1, Corporation 2 is treated as having a taxable year-end at the end of the day on June 30, Year 1, as a result of the sale. Corporation 2 leaves the aggregate group of Corporation 1 and Parent Corporation at the end of the day on June 30, Year 1. The aggregate group of Corporation 1 takes into account only the gross receipts, base erosion tax benefits, and deductions of Corporation 2 allocable to the period from January 1 to the end of the day on June 30, Year 1, in accordance with paragraph (c)(4)(ii) and (iii) of this section. The same results apply to the aggregate group of Parent Corporation for calendar Year 1. See paragraph (d)(1) and (2) of this section for the periods taken into account in determining whether the taxpayer or its aggregate group satisfies the gross receipts test.

(B) For purposes of section 59A, to determine the gross receipts and base erosion percentage of the aggregate group of Corporation 2 for calendar Year 1, each of Parent Corporation, Corporation 1, and Corporation 3 are treated as having a taxable year-end at the end of the day on June 30, Year 1. Because Corporation 2 does not have a short taxable year, paragraph (c)(5)(i) of this section does not apply. The aggregate group of Corporation 2 takes into account the gross receipts, base erosion tax benefits, and deductions of Parent Corporation and Corporation 1 allocable to the period from January 1 to the end of the day on June 30, Year 1, and the gross receipts, base erosion tax benefits, and deductions of Corporation 3 allocable to the period from July 1 to December 31, Year 1 in accordance with paragraph (c)(4)(ii) and (iii) of this section. See paragraph (d)(1) and (2) of this section for the periods taken into account in determining whether the taxpayer or its aggregate group satisfies the gross receipts test. [Reg. §1.59A-2.]

☐ [*T.D. 9885, 12-2-2019. Amended by T.D. 9910, 10-8-2020.*]

[Reg. §1.59A-3]

§1.59A-3. Base erosion payments and base erosion tax benefits.—(a) *Scope.*—This section provides definitions and related rules regarding base erosion payments and base erosion tax benefits. Paragraph (b) of this section provides definitions and rules regarding base erosion payments. Paragraph (c) of this section provides rules for determining the amount of base erosion tax benefits. Paragraph (d) of this section provides examples illustrating the rules described in this section.

(b) *Base erosion payments.*—(1) *In general.*—Except as provided in paragraph (b)(3) of this section, a *base erosion payment* means—

(i) Any amount paid or accrued by the taxpayer to a foreign related party of the taxpayer and with respect to which a deduction is allowable under chapter 1 of subtitle A of the Internal Revenue Code;

(ii) Any amount paid or accrued by the taxpayer to a foreign related party of the taxpayer in connection with the acquisition of property by the taxpayer from the foreign related party if the character of the property is subject to the allowance for depreciation (or amortization in lieu of depreciation);

(iii) Any premium or other consideration paid or accrued by the taxpayer to a foreign related party of the taxpayer for any reinsurance payments that are taken into account under section 803(a)(1)(B) or 832(b)(4)(A); or

(iv) Any amount paid or accrued by the taxpayer that results in a reduction of the gross receipts of the taxpayer if the amount paid or accrued is with respect to—

(A) A surrogate foreign corporation, as defined in section 59A(d)(4)(C)(i), that is a related party of the taxpayer (but only if the corporation first became a surrogate foreign corporation after November 9, 2017); or

(B) A foreign person that is a member of the same expanded affiliated group, as defined in section 59A(d)(4)(C)(ii), as the surrogate foreign corporation.

(2) *Operating rules.*—(i) *In general.*—The determination of the amount paid or accrued, and the identity of the payor and recipient of any amount paid or accrued, is made under general U.S. federal income tax law.

(ii) *Amounts paid or accrued in cash and other consideration.*—For purposes of paragraph (b)(1) of this section, an amount paid or accrued includes an amount paid or accrued using any form of consideration, including cash, property, stock, a partnership interest, or the assumption of a liability, including any exchange transaction. A distribution of property that is not part of an exchange (such as a distribution under section 301, without regard to whether section 301(c)(1), (c)(2), or (c)(3) applies), is not received with respect to an amount paid or accrued and does not give rise to a base erosion payment. In contrast, a redemption of stock by a corporation within the meaning of section 317(b) (such as a redemption described in section 302(a) or (d) or section 306(a)(2)), or a transaction in which there is an exchange for stock (such as a section 304 or section 331 transaction), is an amount paid or accrued by the shareholder to the corporation (or by the acquiring corporation to the transferor in a section 304 transaction), without regard to the treatment of such transaction for U.S. federal income tax purposes. See paragraph (b)(3)(viii) of this section for an exception for specified nonrecognition transactions (as defined in paragraph (b)(3)(viii)(A) of this section).

(iii) *Transactions providing for net payments.*—Except as otherwise provided in paragraph (b)(2)(iv) of this section or as permitted by the Internal Revenue Code or the regulations, the amount of any base erosion payment is determined on a gross basis, regardless of any contractual or legal right to make or receive payments on a net basis. For this purpose, a right to make or receive payments on a net basis permits the parties to a transaction or series of transactions to settle obligations by offsetting any amounts to be paid by one party against amounts owed by that party to the other party. For example, any premium or other consideration paid or accrued by a taxpayer to a foreign related party for any reinsurance payments is not reduced by or netted against other amounts owed to the taxpayer from the foreign related party or by reserve adjustments or other returns.

(iv) *Amounts paid or accrued with respect to mark-to-market position.*—For any transaction with respect to which the taxpayer applies the mark-to-market method of accounting for U.S. federal income tax purposes, the rules set forth in §1.59A-2(e)(3)(vi) apply to determine the amount of the base erosion payment.

(v) *Coordination among categories of base erosion payments.*—A payment that does not satisfy the criteria of one category of base erosion payment may be a base erosion payment described in one of the other categories.

(vi) *Certain domestic passthrough entities.*—(A) *In general.*—If a taxpayer pays or accrues an amount that would be a base erosion payment except for the fact that the payment is made to a specified domestic passthrough, then the taxpayer will be treated as making a base erosion payment to each specified foreign related party for purposes of section 59A and §§1.59A-2 through 1.59A-10. This rule has no effect on the taxation of the specified domestic passthrough under subchapter J or subchapter M of the Code (as applicable).

(B) *Amount of base erosion payment.*—The amount of the base erosion payment is equal to the lesser of the amount paid or accrued by the taxpayer to or for the benefit of the specified domestic passthrough and the amount of the deduction allowed under section 561,

651, or 661 to the specified domestic passthrough with respect to amounts paid, credited, distributed, deemed distributed, or required to be distributed to a specified foreign related party.

(C) *Specified domestic passthrough.*—For purposes of this paragraph (b)(2)(vi), specified domestic passthrough means:

(1) A domestic trust that is not a grantor trust under subpart E of subchapter J of chapter 1 of the Code ("domestic trust") and which domestic trust is allowed a deduction under section 651 or section 661 with respect to amounts paid, credited, or required to be distributed to a specified foreign related party;

(2) A real estate investment trust (as defined in §1.856-1(a)) that pays, or is deemed to pay, a dividend to a specified foreign related party for which a deduction is allowed under section 561; or

(3) A regulated investment company (as defined in §1.851-1(a)) that pays, or is deemed to pay, a dividend to a specified foreign related party for which a deduction is allowed under section 561.

(D) *Specified foreign related party.*—For purposes of this paragraph (b)(2)(vi), specified foreign related party means, with respect to a specified domestic passthrough, any foreign related party of a taxpayer that is a direct or indirect beneficiary or shareholder of the specified domestic passthrough.

(vii) *Transfers of property to related taxpayers.*—If a taxpayer owns property of a character subject to the allowance for depreciation (or amortization in lieu of depreciation) with respect to which paragraph (c)(1)(ii) of this section applies, and the taxpayer sells, exchanges, or otherwise transfers the property to another taxpayer that is a member of an aggregate group that includes the taxpayer (taking into account §1.59A-7), any deduction for depreciation (or amortization in lieu of depreciation) by the transferee taxpayer remains subject to paragraph (c)(1)(ii) of this section to the same extent the amounts would have been so subject in the hands of the transferor. See paragraph (d)(7) of this section (*Example 7*) for an illustration of this rule.

(viii) *Reductions to determine gross income.*—For purposes of paragraphs (b)(1)(i) and (ii) of this section, any amount resulting in a reduction to determine gross income under section 61, including an amount properly treated as cost of goods sold under the Code, is not a base erosion payment.

(ix) *Losses recognized on the sale or transfer of property.*—If a taxpayer recognizes a loss on a sale or transfer of property to a foreign related party, the loss recognized with respect to the sale or transfer is not a deduction that would cause the payment to be treated as a base erosion payment under paragraph (b)(1)(i) of this section. However, if a taxpayer uses property to make a payment to a foreign related party and the payment otherwise meets the requirements of paragraph (b)(1) of this section, the amount of the payment that is treated as a base erosion payment equals the fair market value of the property at the time of the transfer.

(3) *Exceptions to base erosion payment.*—Paragraph (b)(1) of this section does not apply to the types of payments or accruals described in paragraphs (b)(3)(i) through (ix) of this section.

(i) *Certain services cost method amounts.*—(A) *In general.*—Amounts paid or accrued by a taxpayer to a foreign related party for services that meet the requirements in paragraph (b)(3)(i)(B) of this section, but only to the extent of the total services cost of those services. Thus, any amount paid or accrued to a foreign related party in excess of the total services cost of services eligible for the services cost method exception (the mark-up component) remains a base erosion payment. For this purpose, services are an activity as defined in §1.482-9(l)(2) performed by a foreign related party (the renderer) that provides a benefit as defined in §1.482-9(l)(3) to the taxpayer (the recipient).

(B) *Eligibility for the services cost method exception.*—To be eligible for the services cost method exception, all of the requirements of §1.482-9(b) must be satisfied, except that:

(1) The requirements of §1.482-9(b)(5) do not apply for purposes of determining eligibility for the service cost method exception in this section; and

(2) Adequate books and records must be maintained as described in paragraph (b)(3)(i)(C) of this section, instead of as described in §1.482-9(b)(6).

(C) *Adequate books and records.*—Permanent books of account and records must be maintained for as long as the costs with respect to the services are incurred by the renderer. The books and records must be adequate to permit verification by the Commissioner of the amount charged for the services and the total services costs incurred by the renderer, including a description of the services in question, identification of the renderer and the recipient of the services, calculation of the amount of profit mark-up (if any) paid for the services, and sufficient documentation to allow verification of the methods used to allocate and apportion the costs to the services in question in accordance with §1.482-9(k). For example, where a renderer incurs costs that are attributable to performing a service for the taxpayer that includes services eligible for the services cost method exception under this section (regardless of whether the taxpayer determined its payments for those services based on the services cost method) and another service that is not eligible for the services cost method exception, books and records must be maintained that show, among other things: the total amount of costs that are attributable to each of those services, the method chosen under §1.482-9(k) to apportion the costs between the service eligible for the services cost method under this section and the other service, and the application of that method in calculating the amount eligible for the services cost method exception. This paragraph (b)(3)(i)(C) does not affect the recordkeeping requirements imposed by any other provision, including §1.6001-1.

(D) *Total services cost.*—For purposes of this section, total services cost has the same meaning as total services costs in §1.482-9(j).

(ii) *Qualified derivative payments.*—Any qualified derivative payment as described in §1.59A-6.

(iii) *Effectively connected income.*—(A) *In general.*—Except as provided in paragraph (b)(3)(iii)(B) of this section, amounts paid or accrued to a foreign related party that are subject to U.S. federal income taxation as income that is, or is treated as, effectively connected with the conduct of a trade or business in the United States under an applicable provision of the Internal Revenue Code or regulations. Paragraph (b)(3)(iii) of this section applies only if the taxpayer receives a withholding certificate on which the foreign related party claims an exemption from withholding under section 1441 or 1442 because the amounts are effectively connected income.

(B) *Application to certain treaty residents.*—If a foreign related party determines its taxable income pursuant to the business profits provisions of an applicable income tax treaty, amounts paid or accrued to the foreign related party that are taken into account in determining its taxable income.

(C) *Application to partnerships.*—To the extent that paragraph (b)(3)(iii)(A) or (B) of this section would apply to a payment or accrual made directly by a taxpayer to a foreign related party, paragraph (b)(3)(iii)(A) or (B) of this section apply to an amount treated as paid or accrued by a taxpayer to a foreign related party under §1.59A-7(b) or (c) (generally applying aggregate principles to treat partnership transactions as partner level transactions for purposes of section 59A). The certification requirement in paragraph (b)(3)(iii)(A) of this section is met if the taxpayer receives a written statement from the foreign related party that is comparable to the certification provided in paragraph (b)(3)(iii)(A) of this section but based on the deemed transaction under §1.59A-7(b) or (c) and the extent to which paragraph (b)(3)(iii)(A) or (B) of this section would have applied to that deemed transaction. The taxpayer may rely on the written statement unless it has reason to know or actual knowledge that the statement is incorrect.

(iv) *Exchange loss on a section 988 transaction.*—Any exchange loss within the meaning of §1.988-2 from a section 988 transaction described in §1.988-1(a)(1) that is an allowable deduction and that results from a payment or accrual by the taxpayer to a foreign related party.

(v) *Amounts paid or accrued with respect to TLAC securities and foreign TLAC securities.*—(A) *In general.*—Except as provided in paragraph (b)(3)(v)(B) and (F) of this section, amounts paid or accrued to foreign related parties with respect to TLAC securities and foreign TLAC securities.

(B) *Limitation on exclusion for TLAC securities.*—The amount excluded under paragraph (b)(3)(v)(A) of this section is no greater than the product of the scaling ratio and amounts paid or accrued to foreign related parties with respect to TLAC securities for which a deduction is allowed.

(C) *Scaling ratio.*—For purposes of this paragraph (b)(3)(v), the scaling ratio for a taxable year of a taxpayer is a fraction the numerator of which is 115 percent of the average TLAC long-term debt required amount and the denominator of which is the average TLAC securities amount. The scaling ratio may in no event be greater than one.

(D) *Average TLAC securities amount.*—The average TLAC securities amount for a taxable year is the average of the TLAC securities amounts for the year, computed at regular time intervals in accordance with this paragraph. The TLAC securities amount used in calculating the average TLAC securities amount is computed on a monthly basis.

(E) *Average TLAC long-term debt required amount.*—The average TLAC longterm debt required amount for a taxable year is the average of the TLAC long-term debt required amounts, computed on a monthly basis.

(F) *Limitation on exclusion for foreign TLAC securities.*—(1) *In general.*—The amount excluded under paragraph (b)(3)(v)(A) of this section for foreign TLAC securities is limited to the extent that interest deducted by a U.S. trade or business or permanent establishment with respect to foreign TLAC securities exceeds the interest expense associated with the foreign TLAC long-term debt required amount, applying the scaling ratio principles set forth under paragraphs (b)(3)(v)(B) through (E) of this section.

(2) *Foreign TLAC long-term debt required amount.*—For purposes of paragraph (b)(3)(v) of this section, the term *foreign TLAC long-term debt required amount* means in the case of a trade or business or a permanent establishment in the United States, the lesser of—

(i) The specified minimum amount of debt, if any, required pursuant to a bank regulatory requirement imposed under the laws or regulations of a foreign country that are comparable to 12 CFR 252.160-167; or

(ii) The specified minimum amount of debt, if any, that would be required pursuant to 12 CFR 252.162(a) if the trade or business or permanent establishment were a U.S. person (as determined under Federal Reserve regulations).

(3) *No specified minimum provided by local law.*—For purposes of paragraph (b)(3)(v)(F)(2)(ii) of this section, if the bank regulatory requirements imposed under the laws or regulations of a foreign country do not specify a minimum amount, the limitation for purposes of paragraph (b)(3)(v)(F)(2) of this section is determined by reference solely to paragraph (b)(3)(v)(F)(2)(ii) of this section.

(4) *Foreign TLAC security.*—For purposes of paragraph (b)(3)(v) of this section, the term *foreign TLAC security* means an internal debt security issued under a bank regulatory requirement imposed under the laws or regulations of a foreign country that is comparable to 12 CFR 252.160-167. The laws or regulations of a foreign country are comparable to 12 CFR 252.160-167 if the requirement is imposed by a Financial Stability Board member state and those laws or regulations are substantially consistent with TLAC standards of the Financial Stability Board.

(vi) *Amounts paid or accrued in taxable years beginning before January 1, 2018.*—Any amount paid or accrued in taxable years beginning before January 1, 2018.

(vii) *Business interest carried forward from taxable years beginning before January 1, 2018.*—Any disallowed business interest described in section 163(j)(2) that is carried forward from a taxable year beginning before January 1, 2018.

(viii) *Specified nonrecognition transactions.*—(A) *In general.*—Subject to paragraph (b)(3)(viii)(B) and (C) of this section, any amount transferred to, or exchanged with, a foreign related party pursuant to a transaction to which sections 332, 351, 355, or 368 apply ("specified nonrecognition transaction"). See §1.59A-9(b)(4) for anti-abuse rules.

(B) *Other property transferred to a foreign related party in a specified nonrecognition transaction.*—If a taxpayer transfers other property (as defined in paragraph (b)(3)(viii)(D) of this section) to a foreign related party pursuant to a specified nonrecognition transaction, the other property is treated as an amount paid or accrued to which paragraph (b)(3) of this section does not apply, regardless of whether gain is recognized on the transaction.

(C) *Other property received from a foreign related party in certain specified nonrecognition transactions.*—If, in a transaction described in section 351, 355, or 368, the taxpayer transfers property and receives other property (as defined in paragraph (b)(3)(viii)(D) of this section) from a foreign related party, the property transferred by the taxpayer is treated as an amount paid or accrued to which paragraph (b)(3) of this section does not apply, regardless of whether gain is recognized on the transaction.

(D) *Definition of other property.*—Solely for purposes of this paragraph (b)(3)(viii), the term *other property* has the meaning of the phrase "other property or money" as used in section 351(b), with respect to a transaction to which section 351 applies, and as used in sections 356(a)(1)(B) and 361(b), with respect to a transaction to which sections 355 or 368 apply, as applicable, including liabilities

treated as money under section 357(b). However, the term *other property* does not include the sum of any money and the fair market value of any other property to which section 361(b)(3) applies. The term *other property* also includes liabilities that are assumed by the taxpayer in the specified nonrecognition transaction, but only to the extent of the amount of gain recognized under section 357(c).

(E) *Allocation of other property.*—Other property is treated as exchanged for property in a specified nonrecognition transaction in a manner consistent with U.S. federal income tax law. For purposes making the allocation under this paragraph (b)(3)(viii)(E), liabilities described in paragraph (b)(3)(viii)(D) of this section are treated as money received.

(ix) *Reinsurance losses incurred and claims payments.*—(A) *In general.*—Any amounts paid by a taxpayer subject to tax under subchapter L to a foreign related party that is a regulated insurance company under a reinsurance contract between the taxpayer and the regulated foreign insurance company for losses incurred (as defined in section 832(b)(5)) and claims and benefits under section 805(a)(1), to the extent that the amounts paid or accrued are properly allocable to amounts required to be paid by the regulated foreign insurance company (or indirectly through another regulated foreign insurance company), pursuant to an insurance, annuity, or reinsurance contract, to a person other than a related party. For purposes of this paragraph (b)(3)(ix), the determination of whether a contract is an insurance contract or an annuity contract is made without regard to sections 72(s), 101(f), 817(h), and 7702, provided that the contract is regulated as a life insurance or annuity contract in its jurisdiction of issuance and no policyholder, insured, annuitant or beneficiary with respect to the contract is a United States person.

(B) *Regulated foreign insurance company.*—The term regulated foreign insurance company means any foreign corporation which—

(1) Is subject to regulation as an insurance (or reinsurance) company by the country in which the corporation is created, organized, or maintains its registered office, and is licensed, authorized, or regulated by the applicable insurance regulatory body for that country to sell insurance, annuity, or reinsurance contracts to persons other than related parties in that country, and

(2) Would be subject to tax under subchapter L if it were a domestic corporation.

(4) *Rules for determining the amount of certain base erosion payments.*—The following rules apply in determining the amount that is a base erosion payment.

(i) *Interest expense allocable to a foreign corporation's effectively connected income.*—(A) *Methods described in §1.882-5.*—A foreign corporation that has interest expense allocable under section 882(c) to income that is, or is treated as, effectively connected with the conduct of a trade or business within the United States applying the method described in §1.882-5(b) through (d) or the method described in §1.882-5(e) has base erosion payments under paragraph (b)(1)(i) of this section for the taxable year equal to the sum of—

(1) The interest expense on a liability described in §1.882-5(a)(1)(ii)(A) or (B) (direct allocations) that is paid or accrued by the foreign corporation to a foreign related party;

(2) The interest expense on U.S.-booked liabilities, as described in §1.882-5(d)(2), determined by taking into account paragraph (b)(4)(i)(B) of this section, that is paid or accrued by the foreign corporation to a foreign related party; and

(3) The interest expense on U.S.-connected liabilities, as described in §1.882-5(d) or 1.882-5(e), in excess of interest expense on U.S.-booked liabilities as described in §1.882-5(d)(2), if any (hereafter, excess U.S.-connected liabilities), multiplied by a fraction, the numerator of which is the foreign corporation's average worldwide interest expense due to a foreign related party, and the denominator of which is the foreign corporation's average total worldwide interest expense. The numerator and denominator of this fraction are determined by translating interest expense into the functional currency of the foreign corporation using any reasonable method, consistently applied. Any interest expense that is interest expense on a U.S.-booked liability or is subject to a direct allocation is excluded from both the numerator and the denominator of the fraction.

(B) *U.S.-booked liabilities determination.*—For purposes of paragraph (b)(4)(i)(A) of this section, the determination of the interest expense on U.S.-booked liabilities, as described in §1.882-5(d)(2), is made without regard to whether the foreign corporation applies the method described in §1.882-5(b) through (d) or the method described in §1.882-5(e) for purposes of determining interest expense.

(C) *U.S.-booked liabilities in excess of U.S.-connected liabilities.*—For purposes of paragraph (b)(4)(i)(A)(2) of this section, if a foreign corporation has U.S.-booked liabilities, as described in §1.882-5(d)(2), in excess of U.S.-connected liabilities, as described in

§ 1.882-5(d) or § 1.882-5(e), the foreign corporation applies the scaling ratio pro-rata to all interest expense on U.S.-booked liabilities consistent with § 1.882-5(d)(4) for purposes of determining the amount of allocable interest expense on U.S.-booked liabilities that is a base erosion payment. This paragraph (b)(4)(i)(C) applies without regard to whether the foreign corporation applies the method described in § 1.882-5(b) through (d) or the method described in § 1.882-5(e) for purposes of determining its interest expense.

(D) *Election to use financial statements.*—A foreign corporation may elect to calculate the fraction described in paragraph (b)(4)(i)(A)(3) of this section on the basis of its applicable financial statement rather than U.S. tax principles. For purposes of this section, an applicable financial statement has the meaning provided in section 451(b)(3). The applicable financial statement must be the applicable financial statement of the foreign corporation, not a consolidated applicable financial statement. A foreign corporation makes this election in accordance with the requirements of Form 8991 (or successor).

(E) *Coordination with certain tax treaties.*—(1) *In general.*—If a foreign corporation elects to determine its taxable income pursuant to business profits provisions of an income tax treaty rather than provisions of the Internal Revenue Code, or the regulations published under 26 CFR chapter I, for determining effectively connected income, and the foreign corporation does not apply § 1.882-5 to allocate interest expense to a permanent establishment, then paragraph (b)(4)(i)(A) through (D) of this section applies to determine the amount of hypothetical § 1.882-5 interest expense that is a base erosion payment under paragraph (b)(1) of this section. Interest expense allowed to the permanent establishment in excess of the hypothetical § 1.882-5 interest expense, if any, is treated as an amount paid or accrued by the permanent establishment to the foreign corporation's home office or to another branch of the foreign corporation and is a base erosion payment to the extent that the payment or accrual is described under paragraph (b)(1) of this section.

(2) *Hypothetical § 1.882-5 interest expense defined.*—The hypothetical § 1.882-5 interest expense is equal to the amount of interest expense that would have been allocable under section 882(c) to income that is, or is treated as, effectively connected with the conduct of a trade or business within the United States if the foreign corporation determined interest expense in accordance with section § 1.882-5. However, the hypothetical § 1.882-5 interest expense shall not exceed the amount of interest expense allowed to the permanent establishment.

(3) *Consistency requirement.*—For purposes of determining the amount described in paragraph (b)(4)(i)(E)(2) of this section and applying paragraph (b)(4)(i)(A) through (D) of this section, the elections of § 1.882-5 must be applied consistently and are subject to the rules and limitations of § 1.882-5, including limitations on the time period in which an election may be made or revoked. If a foreign corporation otherwise meets the requirements for making or revoking an election under § 1.882-5, then solely for purposes of this section, the foreign corporation is treated as making or revoking the election in accordance with the requirements of Form 8991 (or successor) and its instructions.

(F) *Coordination with exception for foreign TLAC securities.*—For purposes of paragraph (b)(4)(i)(A) of this section, amounts paid or accrued to a foreign related party with respect to securities that are eligible for the foreign TLAC exception in paragraph (b)(3)(v) of this section are not treated as paid to a foreign related party.

(ii) *Other deductions allowed with respect to effectively connected income.*—A deduction allowed under § 1.882-4 for an amount paid or accrued by a foreign corporation to a foreign related party (including a deduction for an amount apportioned in part to effectively connected income and in part to income that is not effectively connected income) is a base erosion payment under paragraph (b)(1) of this section.

(iii) *Depreciable property.*—Any amount paid or accrued by a foreign corporation to a foreign related party of the taxpayer in connection with the acquisition of property by the foreign corporation from the foreign related party if the character of the property is subject to the allowance for depreciation (or amortization in lieu of depreciation) is a base erosion payment to the extent the property so acquired is used, or held for use, in the conduct of a trade or business within the United States.

(iv) *Coordination with ECI exception.*—For purposes of paragraph (b)(4) of this section, amounts paid or accrued to a foreign related party treated as effectively connected income (or, in the case of a foreign related party that determines taxable income pursuant to the business profits provisions of an applicable income tax treaty, such amounts that are taken into account in determining taxable income) are not treated as paid to a foreign related party.

(v) *Coordination with certain tax treaties.*—(A) *Allocable expenses.*—Except as provided in paragraph (b)(4)(i)(E) of this section with respect to interest, if a foreign corporation determines its taxable income on a net basis pursuant to an applicable income tax treaty rather than provisions of the Internal Revenue Code, or the regulations published under 26 CFR chapter I, for determining effectively connected income, then the foreign corporation must determine whether each allowable deduction is a base erosion payment under paragraph (b)(1) of this section.

(B) *Internal dealings under certain income tax treaties.*—Except as provided in paragraph (b)(4)(i)(E) of this section with respect to interest, if, pursuant to the terms of an applicable income tax treaty, a foreign corporation determines the profits attributable to a permanent establishment based on the assets used, risks assumed, and functions performed by the permanent establishment, then any deduction attributable to any amount paid or accrued (or treated as paid or accrued) by the permanent establishment to the foreign corporation's home office or to another branch of the foreign corporation (an "internal dealing") is a base erosion payment to the extent that the payment or accrual is described under paragraph (b)(1) of this section.

(vi) *Business interest expense arising in taxable years beginning after December 31, 2017.*—Any disallowed business interest expense described in section 163(j)(2) that resulted from a payment or accrual to a foreign related party that first arose in a taxable year beginning after December 31, 2017, is treated as a base erosion payment under paragraph (b)(1)(i) of this section in the year that the business interest expense initially arose. See paragraph (c)(4) of this section for rules that apply when business interest expense is limited under section 163(j)(1) in order to determine whether the disallowed business interest is attributed to business interest expense paid to a person that is not a related party, a foreign related party, or a domestic related party.

(c) *Base erosion tax benefit.*—(1) *In general.*—Except as provided in paragraph (c)(2) of this section, a base erosion tax benefit means:

(i) In the case of a base erosion payment described in paragraph (b)(1)(i) of this section, any deduction that is allowed under chapter 1 of subtitle A of the Internal Revenue Code for the taxable year with respect to that base erosion payment;

(ii) In the case of a base erosion payment described in paragraph (b)(1)(ii) of this section, any deduction allowed under chapter 1 of subtitle A of the Internal Revenue Code for the taxable year for depreciation (or amortization in lieu of depreciation) with respect to the property acquired with that payment;

(iii) In the case of a base erosion payment described in paragraph (b)(1)(iii) of this section, any reduction under section 803(a)(1)(B) in the gross amount of premiums and other consideration on insurance and annuity contracts for premiums and other consideration arising out of indemnity reinsurance, or any deduction under section 832(b)(4)(A) from the amount of gross premiums written on insurance contracts during the taxable year for premiums paid for reinsurance; or

(iv) In the case of a base erosion payment described in paragraph (b)(1)(iv) of this section, any reduction in gross receipts with respect to the payment in computing gross income of the taxpayer for the taxable year for purposes of chapter 1 of subtitle A of the Internal Revenue Code.

(2) *Exception to base erosion tax benefit.*—(i) *In general.*—Except as provided in paragraph (c)(3) of this section, any base erosion tax benefit attributable to any base erosion payment is not taken into account as a base erosion tax benefit if tax is imposed on that payment under section 871 or 881, and the tax has been deducted and withheld under section 1441 or 1442. If a payment is taken into account for purposes of the fraction described in paragraph (b)(4)(i)(A)(3) of this section, and tax is imposed on the payment under section 871 or 881, and the tax has been deducted and withheld under section 1441 or 1442, the payment is treated as not paid or accrued to a foreign related party.

(ii) *Branch-level interest tax.*—Except as provided in paragraph (c)(3) of this section, any base erosion tax benefit of a foreign corporation attributable to any base erosion payment determined under paragraph (b)(4)(i)(A)(3) of this section or attributable to interest expense in excess of the hypothetical section 1.882-5 interest expense determined under paragraph (b)(4)(i)(E)(1) of this section is not taken into account as a base erosion tax benefit to the extent of the amount of excess interest, as defined in § 1.884-4(a)(2), if any, on which tax is imposed on the foreign corporation under section 884(f) and § 1.884-4, if the tax is properly reported on the foreign corporation's income tax return and paid in accordance with § 1.884-4(a)(2)(iv).

(3) *Effect of treaty on base erosion tax benefit.*—If any treaty between the United States and any foreign country reduces the rate of

tax imposed by section 871 or 881, the amount of base erosion tax benefit that is not taken into account under paragraph (c)(2) of this section is equal to the amount of the base erosion tax benefit before the application of paragraph (c)(2) of this section multiplied by a fraction of—

(i) The rate of tax imposed under the treaty; over

(ii) The rate of tax imposed without regard to the treaty.

(4) *Application of section 163(j) to base erosion payments.*— (i) *Classification of payments or accruals of business interest expense based on the payee.*—The following rules apply for corporations and partnerships:

(A) *Classification of payments or accruals of business interest expense of a corporation.*—For purposes of this section, in the year that business interest expense of a corporation is paid or accrued the business interest expense is classified as foreign related business interest expense, domestic related business interest expense, or unrelated business interest expense.

(B) *Classification of payments or accruals of business interest expense by a partnership.*—For purposes of this section, in the year that business interest expense of a partnership is paid or accrued, the business interest expense that is allocated to a partner is classified separately with respect to each partner in the partnership as foreign related business interest expense, domestic related business interest expense, or unrelated business interest expense.

(C) *Classification of payments or accruals of business interest expense paid or accrued to a foreign related party that is subject to an exception.*—(1) *ECI exception.*—For purposes of paragraph (c)(4)(i)(A) and (B) of this section, business interest expense paid or accrued to a foreign related party to which the exception in paragraph (b)(3)(iii) of this section (effectively connected income) applies is classified as domestic related business interest expense.

(2) *TLAC interest and interest subject to withholding tax.*— For purposes of paragraph (c)(4)(i)(A) and (B) of this section, if the exception in paragraph (b)(3)(v) of this section (TLAC securities) or paragraph (c)(2) or (3) of this section (withholding tax) applies to business interest expense paid or accrued to a foreign related party, that business interest expense remains classified as foreign related business interest expense, and retains its classification as eligible for those exceptions, on a pro-rata basis with other foreign related business interest expense.

(ii) *Ordering rules for business interest expense that is limited under section 163(j)(1) to determine which classifications of business interest expense are deducted and which classifications of business interest expense are carried forward.*—(A) *In general.*—Section 163(j) and the regulations published under 26 CFR chapter I provide a limitation on the amount of business interest expense allowed as a deduction in a taxable year by a corporation or a partner in a partnership. In the case of a corporation with a disallowed business interest expense carryforward, the regulations under section 163(j) determine the ordering of the business interest expense deduction that is allowed on a year-by-year basis by reference first to business interest expense incurred in the current taxable year and then to disallowed business interest expense carryforwards from prior years. To determine the amount of base erosion tax benefit under paragraph (c)(1) of this section, this paragraph (c)(4)(ii) sets forth ordering rules that determine the amount of the deduction of business interest expense allowed under section 163(j) that is classified as paid or accrued to a foreign related party for purposes of paragraph (c)(1)(i) of this section. This paragraph (c)(4)(ii) also sets forth similar ordering rules that apply to disallowed business interest expense carryforwards for which a deduction is permitted under section 163(j) in a later year.

(B) *Ordering rules for treating business interest expense deduction and disallowed business interest expense carryforwards as foreign related business interest expense, domestic related business interest expense, and unrelated business interest expense.*—(1) *General ordering rule for allocating business interest expense deduction between classifications.*—For purposes of paragraph (c)(1) of this section, if a deduction for business interest expense is not subject to the limitation under section 163(j)(1) in a taxable year, the deduction is treated first as foreign related business interest expense and domestic related business interest expense (on a pro-rata basis), and second as unrelated business interest expense. The same principle applies to business interest expense of a partnership that is deductible at the partner level under § 1.163(j)-6(f).

(2) *Ordering of business interest expense incurred by a corporation.*—If a corporation's business interest expense deduction allowed for any taxable year is attributable to business interest expense paid or accrued in that taxable year and to disallowed business interest expense carryforwards from prior taxable years, the ordering

of business interest expense deduction provided in paragraph (c)(4)(ii)(B)(*1*) of this section among the classifications described therein applies separately for the carryforward amount from each taxable year, following the ordering set forth in § 1.163(j)-5(b)(2). Corresponding adjustments to the classification of disallowed business interest expense carryforwards are made consistent with this year-by-year approach. For purposes of section 59A and this section, an acquiring corporation in a transaction described in section 381(a) will succeed to and take into account the classification of any disallowed business interest expense carryforward. See § 1.381(c)(20)-1.

(3) *Ordering of business interest expense incurred by a partnership and allocated to a corporate partner.*—For a corporate partner in a partnership that is allocated a business interest expense deduction under § 1.163(j)-6(f), the ordering rule provided in paragraph (c)(4)(ii)(B)(*1*) of this section applies separately to the corporate partner's allocated business interest expense deduction from the partnership; that deduction is not comingled with the business interest expense deduction addressed in paragraph (c)(4)(ii)(B)(*1*) or (2) of this section or the corporate partner's items from any other partnership. Similarly, when a corporate partner in a partnership is allocated excess business interest expense from a partnership under the rules set forth in § 1.163(j)-6(f) and the excess interest expense becomes deductible to the corporate partner, that partner applies the ordering rule provided in paragraph (c)(4)(ii)(B)(*1*) of this section separately to that excess interest expense on a year-by-year basis. Corresponding adjustments to the classification of disallowed business interest expense carryforwards are made consistent with this year-by-year and partnership-by-partnership approach.

(5) *Allowed deduction.*—Solely for purposes of paragraph (c)(1) of this section, all deductions (and any premium or other consideration paid or accrued by the taxpayer for any reinsurance payments that are taken into account under section 803(a)(1)(B) or 832(b)(4)(A)) that could be properly claimed by a taxpayer for the taxable year (determined after giving effect to the taxpayer's permissible method of accounting and to any election, such as the election under section 173 to capitalize circulation expenditures or the election under section 168(g)(7) to use the alternative depreciation system of depreciation) are treated as allowed deductions under chapter 1 of subtitle A of the Internal Revenue Code.

(6) *Election to waive allowed deductions.*—(i) *In general.*—If a taxpayer elects to waive certain deductions, in whole or in part, pursuant to this paragraph (c)(6)(i), the amount of allowed deductions as described in paragraph (c)(5) of this section is reduced by the amounts that are properly waived. In order to make the election or increase the amount of the deduction waived, the taxpayer must determine that it could satisfy the requirements of § 1.59A-2(b) absent the election to waive certain deductions. For rules applicable to partners and partnerships, see paragraph (c)(6)(iv) of this section. For rules addressing waiver of premium or other consideration paid or accrued by a taxpayer for any reinsurance payments that are taken into account under section 803(a)(1)(B) or 832(b)(4)(A), see paragraph (c)(6)(v) of this section.

(ii) *Time and manner for election to waive deduction.*—(A) *In general.*—A taxpayer may make the election described in paragraph (c)(6)(i) of this section on its original filed Federal income tax return. In addition, a taxpayer may elect to waive deductions or increase the amount of deductions waived pursuant to the election described in paragraph (c)(6)(i) of this section on an amended Federal income tax return filed within the later of three years from the date the original return was filed, taking into account section 6501(b)(1), for the taxable year for which the election is made or the period described in section 6501(c)(4), or during the course of an examination of the taxpayer's income tax return for the relevant taxable year pursuant to procedures prescribed by the Commissioner. However, a taxpayer may not decrease the amount of deductions waived by the election, or otherwise revoke the election that is described in paragraph (c)(6)(i) of this section on any amended Federal income tax return or during the course of an examination. To make the election, a taxpayer must complete the appropriate part of Form 8991, *Tax on Base Erosion Payments of Taxpayers With Substantial Gross Receipts* (or successor), including the information described in paragraph (c)(6)(ii)(B) of this section and any other information required by the form or instructions. A taxpayer makes the election described in paragraph (c)(6)(i) of this section on an annual basis, and the taxpayer does not need the consent of the Commissioner if the taxpayer chooses not to make the election for a subsequent taxable year. The election described in paragraph (c)(6)(i) of this section may not be made in any other manner than as described in this paragraph (c)(6)(ii) (for example, by filing an application for a change in accounting method).

(B) *Information required to make the election to waive allowed deductions.*—To make this election, a taxpayer must maintain contemporaneous documentation and provide information related to each deduction waived as required by applicable forms and instructions issued by the Commissioner, including—

(1) A description of the item or property to which the deduction relates, including sufficient information to identify that item or property on the taxpayer's books and records;

(2) The date on which, or period in which, the waived deduction was paid or accrued;

(3) The provision of the Internal Revenue Code (and regulations, as applicable) that allows the deduction for the item or property to which the election relates;

(4) The amount of the deduction that is claimed for the taxable year with respect to the item or property;

(5) The amount of the deduction being waived for the taxable year with respect to the item or property;

(6) A description of where the deduction is reflected (or would have been reflected) on the Federal income tax return (such as a line number); and

(7) The name, Taxpayer Identification Number (or, if the foreign person does not have a Taxpayer Identification Number, the foreign equivalent), and country of organization of the foreign related party that is or will be the recipient of the payment that generates the deduction.

(iii) *Effect of election to waive deduction.*—(A) *In general.*— *(1) Consistent treatment.*—Except as otherwise provided in this paragraph (c)(6)(iii), any deduction waived under paragraph (c)(6)(i) of this section is treated as having been waived for all purposes of the Internal Revenue Code and regulations.

(2) No allocation and apportionment of waived deductions.— The waiver of deductions described in paragraph (c)(6)(i) of this section is treated as occurring before the allocation and apportionment of deductions under §§ 1.861-8 through 1.861-14T and 1.861-17 (such as for purposes of section 904).

(3) Effect of waiver of deductions described in §§ 1.861-10 and 1.861-10T.—To the extent that any waived deduction is interest expense that would have been directly allocated under the rules of § 1.861-10 or 1.861-10T and would have resulted in the reduction of value of any assets for purposes of allocating other interest expense under §§ 1.861-9 and 1.861-9T, the value of the assets is reduced to the same extent as if the taxpayer had not elected to waive the deduction.

(4) Effect of the election to waive deductions on the stock basis of a consolidated group member.—For purposes of § 1.1502-32, any deduction waived under paragraph (c)(6)(i) of this section is a non-capital, nondeductible expense under § 1.1502-32(b)(2)(iii).

(B) *Effect of the election to waive deductions disregarded for certain purposes.*—If a taxpayer makes the election to waive a deduction, in whole or in part, under paragraph (c)(6)(i) of this section, the election is disregarded for determining—

(1) The taxpayer's overall method of accounting, or the taxpayer's method of accounting for any item, under section 446;

(2) Whether a change in the taxpayer's overall plan of accounting or the taxpayer's treatment of a material item is a change in method of accounting under section 446(e) and § 1.446-1(e);

(3) The amount allowable under subtitle A of the Internal Revenue Code for depreciation or amortization for purposes of section 167(c) and section 1016(a)(2) or section 1016(a)(3) and any other adjustment to basis under section 1016(a);

(4) For purposes of applying the exclusive apportionment rule in § 1.861-17(b), the geographic source where the research and experimental activities which account for more than fifty percent of the amount of the deduction for research and experimentation was performed;

(5) The application of section 482;

(6) The amount of the taxpayer's earnings and profits; and

(7) Any other item as necessary to prevent a taxpayer from receiving the benefit of a waived deduction.

(C) *Not a method of accounting.*—The election described in paragraph (c)(6)(i) of this section is not a method of accounting under section 446.

(D) *Effect of the election in determining section 481(a) adjustments.*—A taxpayer making the election described in paragraph (c)(6)(i) of this section agrees that if the method of accounting for a waived deduction is changed, the amount of adjustment taken into account under section 481(a)(2) is determined without regard to the election described in paragraph (c)(6)(i) of this section. As a result, a waived deduction has no effect on the amount of a section 481(a) adjustment compared to what the adjustment would have been if the

deduction had not been waived. See paragraph (d)(9) of this section (*Example 9*).

(iv) *Rules applicable to partners and partnerships.*—(A) *In general.*—Except as provided in paragraph (c)(6)(iv)(D) of this section, deductions allocated to a corporate partner by a partnership may only be waived by the partner and not by the partnership, and then only to the extent the partner otherwise qualifies for the waiver under paragraph (c)(6) of this section. For purposes of complying with the documentation requirements in paragraph (c)(6)(ii)(B) of this section, the partner is not required to report the information in paragraphs (c)(6)(ii)(B)(2) and (3) of this section, and in lieu of reporting the information in paragraphs (c)(6)(ii)(B)(1) of this section, the partner is required to report the partnership from which the item is allocated.

(B) *Rule for determining the adjusted basis of a partner's interest in a partnership.*—If a partner elects to waive a deduction or increases the amount of deduction waived with respect to deductions allocated to it by a partnership, the partner treats the waived amount as a nondeductible expenditure under section 705(a)(2)(B).

(C) *Rule for applying section 163(j).*—If a partner waives a deduction pursuant to paragraph (c)(6)(iv)(A) of this section that was taken into account by the partnership in determining the partnership's adjusted taxable income for purposes of section 163(j), then the increase in the partner's income resulting from the waiver is treated by the partner (but not the partnership) as a partner basis item (as defined in § 1.163(j)-6(b)(2)) for purposes of section 163(j).

(D) *Limited application of election to waive deductions with respect to adjustments made pursuant to audit procedures under sections 6221 through 6241.*—Except as provided in this paragraph (c)(6)(iv)(D), a partner is not permitted to waive any adjustment by the Secretary to any partnership-related items that is made pursuant to subchapter C of chapter 63. A partner in a partnership subject to subchapter C of chapter 63 may only make an election to waive any increase in a deduction due to an adjustment made under subchapter C of chapter 63 that the partner takes into account under section 6225(c)(2)(A), 6226, or 6227 in a manner consistent with paragraph (c)(6) of this section. If the partner makes an election under paragraph (c)(6)(i) of this section, the partner will compute its additional reporting year tax (as described in § 301.6226-3 of this chapter) or amount due under § 301.6225-2(d)(2)(ii)(A) of this chapter taking into account the rules in paragraph (c)(6) of this section with respect to the increase in the deduction that is waived.

(v) *Rule applicable to premium and other consideration paid or accrued by the taxpayer for any reinsurance payments that are taken into account under section 803(a)(1)(B) or 832(b)(4)(A).*—For purposes of paragraph (c)(6)(i) of this section, a taxpayer may elect to waive (or increase the amount waived of) any premium or other consideration paid or accrued by the taxpayer for any reinsurance payments that are taken into account under section 803(a)(1)(B) or 832(b)(4)(A) that would be a base erosion tax benefit within the meaning of section 59A(c)(2)(A)(iii), in accordance with the rules and principles of this paragraph (c)(6).

(d) *Examples.*—The following examples illustrate the application of this section. For purposes of all the examples, assume that the taxpayer is an applicable taxpayer and all payments apply to a taxable year beginning after December 31, 2017.

(1) *Example 1: Determining a base erosion payment*—(i) *Facts.* FP is a foreign corporation that owns all of the stock of FC, a foreign corporation, and DC, a domestic corporation. FP has a trade or business in the United States with effectively connected income (USTB). DC owns FDE, a foreign disregarded entity. DC pays interest to FDE and FC. FDE pays interest to USTB. All interest paid by DC to FC and by FDE to USTB is deductible by DC in the current year for regular income tax purposes. FDE also acquires depreciable property from FP during the taxable year. FP's income from the sale of the depreciable property is not effectively connected with the conduct of FP's trade or business in the United States. DC and FP (based only on the activities of USTB) are applicable taxpayers under § 1.59A-2(b).

(ii) *Analysis.* The payment of interest by DC to FC is a base erosion payment under paragraph (b)(1)(i) of this section because the payment is made to a foreign related party and the interest payment is deductible. The payment of interest by DC to FDE is not a base erosion payment because the transaction is not a payment to a foreign person and the transaction is not a deductible payment. With respect to the payment of interest by FDE to USTB, if FP's USTB treats the payment of interest by FDE to USTB as income that is effectively connected with the conduct of a trade or business in the United States pursuant to section 864 or as profits attributable to a U.S. permanent establishment of a tax treaty resident, and if DC receives a withholding certificate from FP with respect to the payment, then the exception in paragraph (b)(3)(iii) of this section applies. Accordingly, the payment from DC, through FDE, to USTB is not a base erosion payment even though the payment is to the USTB of FP, a foreign related party. The acquisition of depreciable property by DC, through FDE, from FP is a base erosion payment under paragraph (b)(1)(ii) of this section because there is a payment to a foreign related party in connection with the acquisition by the taxpayer of property of a character subject to the allowance for depreciation and the exception in paragraph (b)(3)(iii) of this section does not apply because FP's income from the sale of the depreciable property is not effectively connected with the conduct of FP's trade or business in the United States. See § 1.59A-2 for the application of the aggregation rule with respect to DC and FP's USTB.

(2) *Example 2: Interest allocable under §1.882-5*—(i) *Facts.* FC, a foreign corporation, has income that is effectively connected with the conduct of a trade or business within the United States. FC determines its interest expense under the three-step process described in § 1.882-5(b) through (d) with a total interest expense of $125x. The total interest expense is comprised of interest expense of $100x on U.S.-booked liabilities ($60x paid to a foreign related party and $40x paid to unrelated persons) and $25x of interest on excess U.S.-connected liabilities. FC has average worldwide interest expense (not including interest expense on U.S.-booked liabilities) of $500x, of which $100x is interest expense paid to a foreign related party. FC is an applicable taxpayer with respect to its effectively connected income. Assume all of the interest expense is deductible in the current taxable year and that none of the interest is subject to the effectively connected income exception in paragraph (b)(3)(iii) of this section.

(ii) *Analysis.* Under paragraph (b)(4)(i) of this section, the total amount of interest expense determined under § 1.882-5 that is a base erosion payment is $65x ($60x + 5x). FC has $60x of interest on U.S.-booked liabilities that is paid to a foreign related party and that is treated as a base erosion payment under paragraph (b)(4)(i)(A)(2) of this section. Additionally, $5x of the $25x of interest expense on excess U.S.-connected liabilities is treated as a base erosion payment under paragraph (b)(4)(i)(A)(3) of this section ($25x * ($100x / $500x)).

(3) *Example 3: Interaction with section 163(j)*—(i) *Facts.* Foreign Parent (FP) is a foreign corporation that owns all of the stock of DC, a domestic corporation that is an applicable taxpayer. DC does not conduct a utility trade or business as described in section 163(j)(7)(A)(iv), an electing real property trade or business as described in section 163(j)(7)(B), or an electing farming business as described in section 163(j)(7)(C). In Year 1, DC has adjusted taxable income, as defined in section 163(j)(8), of $1000x and pays the following amounts of business interest expense: $420x that is paid to unrelated Bank, and $360x that is paid to FP. DC does not earn any business interest income or incur any floor plan financing interest expense in Year 1. None of the exceptions in paragraph (b)(3) of this section apply, and the interest is not subject to withholding.

(ii) *Analysis*—(A) *Classification of business interest.* In Year 1, DC is permitted to deduct only $300x of business interest expense under section 163(j)(1) ($1000x x 30%). Paragraph (c)(4)(ii)(B) of this section provides that for purposes of paragraph (c)(1) of this section the deduction is treated first as foreign related business interest expense and domestic related business interest expense (here, only FP); and second as unrelated business interest expense (Bank). As a result, the $300x of business interest expense that is permitted under section 163(j)(1) is treated entirely as the business interest paid to the related foreign party, FP. All of DC's $300x deductible interest is treated as an add-back to modified taxable income in the Year 1 taxable year for purposes of § 1.59A-4(b)(2)(i).

(B) *Ordering rules for disallowed business interest expense carryforward.* Under section 163(j)(2), the $480x of disallowed business interest ($420x + $360x - $300x) is carried forward to the subsequent year. Under paragraph (c)(4)(ii)(B)(1) and (2) of this section, the disallowed business interest carryforward is correspondingly treated first as unrelated business interest expense, and second pro-rata as foreign related business interest expense and domestic related business interest expense. As a result, $420x of the $480x disallowed business interest expense carryforward is treated first as business interest expense paid to Bank and the remaining $60x of the $480x disallowed business interest expense carryforward is treated as interest paid to FP and as an add-back to modified taxable income.

(4) *Example 4: Interaction with section 163(j); carryforward*—(i) *Facts.* The facts are the same as in paragraph (d)(3) of this section (the facts in *Example 3*), except that in addition, in Year 2, DC has adjusted taxable income of $250x, and pays the following amounts of business interest expense: $50x that is paid to unrelated Bank, and $45x that is paid to FP. DC does not earn any business interest income or incur any floor plan financing interest expense in Year 2. None of the exceptions in paragraph (b)(3) of this section apply.

(ii) *Analysis*—(A) *Classification of business interest.* In Year 2, for purposes of section 163(j)(1), DC is treated as having paid or accrued total business interest expense of $575x, consisting of $95x business

interest expense actually paid in Year 2 and $480x of business interest expense that is carried forward from Year 1. DC is permitted to deduct $75x of business interest expense in Year 2 under the limitation in section 163(j)(1) ($250x x 30%). Section 1.163(j)-5(b)(2) provides that, for purposes of section 163(j), the allowable business interest expense is first attributed to amounts paid or accrued in the current year, and then attributed to amounts carried over from earlier years on a first-in-first-out basis from the earliest year. Accordingly, the $75x of deductible business interest expense is deducted entirely from the $95x business interest expense incurred in Year 2 for section 163(j) purposes. Because DC's business interest expense deduction is limited under section 163(j)(1) and because DC's total business interest expense is attributable to more than one taxable year, paragraph (c)(4)(ii)(B)(2) of this section provides that the ordering rule in paragraph (c)(4)(ii)(B)(1) of this section is applied separately to each annual amount of section 163(j) disallowed business interest expense carryforward. With respect to the Year 2 layer, which is deducted first, paragraph (c)(4)(ii)(B) of this section provides that, for purposes of paragraph (c)(1) of this section, the Year 2 $75x deduction is treated first as foreign related business interest expense and domestic related business interest expense (here, only FP, $45x); and second as unrelated business interest expense (Bank, $30x). Consequentially, all of the $45x deduction of business interest expense that was paid to FP in Year 2 is treated as a base erosion tax benefit and an add-back to modified taxable income for the Year 2 taxable year for purposes of § 1.59A-4(b)(2)(i).

(B) *Ordering rules for disallowed business interest expense carryforward.* The disallowed business interest expense carryforward of $20x from Year 2 is correspondingly treated first as business interest expense paid to Bank under paragraph (c)(4)(i) of this section. The disallowed business interest expense carryforward of $480x from the Year 1 layer that is also not allowed as a deduction in Year 2 remains treated as $420x paid to Bank and $60 paid to FP.

(5) *Example 5: Interaction with section 163(j); carryforward*—(i) *Facts.* The facts are the same as in paragraph (d)(4) of this section (the facts in *Example 4*), except that in addition, in Year 3, DC has adjusted taxable income of $4000x and pays no business interest expense. DC does not earn any business interest income or incur any floor plan financing interest expense in Year 3.

(ii) *Analysis.* In Year 3, DC is treated as having paid or accrued total business interest expense of $500x, consisting of $480x of business interest expense that is carried forward from Year 1 and $20x of business interest expense that is carried forward from Year 2 for purposes of section 163(j)(1). DC is permitted to deduct $1200x of business interest expense in Year 3 under the limitation in section 163(j)(1) ($4000x x 30%). For purposes of section 163(j), DC is treated as first deducting the business interest expense from Year 1 then the business interest expense from Year 2. See § 1.163(j)-5(b)(2). Because none of DC's $500x business interest expense is limited under section 163(j), the stacking rule in paragraph (c)(4)(ii) of this section for allowed and disallowed business interest expense does not apply. For purposes of § 1.59A-4(b)(2)(i), DC's add-back to modified taxable income is $60x determined by the classifications in paragraph (c)(4)(i)(A) of this section ($60x treated as paid to FP from Year 1).

(6) *Example 6: Interaction with section 163(j); partnership*—(i) *Facts.* The facts are the same as in paragraph (d)(4) of this section (the facts in *Example 4*), except that in addition, in Year 2, DC forms a domestic partnership (PRS) with Y, a domestic corporation that is not related to DC within the meaning of § 1.59A-1(b)(17). PRS does not conduct a utility trade or business as described in section 163(j)(7)(A)(iv), an electing real property trade or business as described in section 163(j)(7)(B) or an electing farming business as described in section 163(j)(7)(C) subject to section 163(j). PRS is not a small business described in section 163(j)(3). DC and Y are equal partners in partnership PRS. In Year 2, PRS has ATI of $100x and $48x of business interest expense. $12x of PRS's business interest expense is paid to Bank, and $36x of PRS's business interest expense is paid to FP. PRS allocates the items comprising its $100x of ATI $50x to DC and $50x to Y. PRS allocates its $48x of business interest expense $24x to DC and $24x to Y. DC classifies its $24x of business interest expense as $6x unrelated business interest expense (Bank) and $18x as foreign related business interest expense (FP) under paragraph (c)(4)(i)(B) of this section. Y classifies its $24x of business interest expense as entirely unrelated business interest expense of Y (Bank and FP) under paragraph (c)(4)(i)(B) of this section. None of the exceptions in paragraph (b)(3) of this section apply.

(ii) *Partnership level analysis.* In Year 2, PRS's section 163(j) limit is 30 percent of its ATI, or $30x ($100x x 30 percent). Thus, PRS has $30x of deductible business interest expense and $18x of excess business interest expense ($48x - $30x). The $30x of deductible business interest expense is includible in PRS's non-separately stated income or loss, and is not subject to further limitation under section 163(j) at the partners' level.

(iii) *Partner level allocations analysis.* Pursuant to § 1.163(j)-6(f)(2), DC and Y are each allocated $15x of deductible business interest expense and $9x of excess business interest expense. At the end of Year 2, DC and Y each have $9x of excess business interest expense from PRS, which under §1.163(j)-6 is not treated as paid or accrued by the partner until such partner is allocated excess taxable income or excess business interest income from PRS in a succeeding year. Pursuant to §1.163(j)-6(e), DC and Y, in computing their limit under section 163(j), do not increase any of their section 163(j) items by any of PRS's section 163(j) items.

(iv) *Partner level allocations for determining base erosion tax benefits.* The $15x of deductible business interest expense allocated to DC is treated first as foreign related business interest expense (FP) under paragraph (c)(4)(ii)(B) of this section. DC's excess business interest expense from PRS of $9x is classified first as the unrelated business interest expense with respect to Bank ($6x) and then as the remaining portion of the business interest expense paid to FP ($3x, or $18x - $15x). Under paragraph (c)(4)(ii)(B)(3) of this section, these classifications of the PRS items apply irrespective of the classifications of DC's own interest expense as set forth in paragraph (d)(4) of this section (*Example 4*).

(v) *Computation of modified taxable income.* For Year 2, DC is treated as having incurred base erosion tax benefits of $60x, consisting of the $15x base erosion tax benefit with respect to its interest in PRS that is computed in paragraph (d)(6)(iii) of this section (*Example 6*) and $45x that is computed in paragraph (d)(4) of this section (*Example 4*).

(7) *Example 7: Transfers of property to related taxpayers*—(i) *Facts.* FP is a foreign corporation that owns all of the stock of DC1 and DC2, both domestic corporations. DC1 and DC2 are both members of the same aggregate group but are not members of the same consolidated tax group under section 1502. In Year 1, FP sells depreciable property to DC1. On the first day of the Year 2 tax year, DC1 sells the depreciable property to DC2.

(ii) *Analysis*—(A) *Year 1.* The acquisition of depreciable property by DC1 from FP is a base erosion payment under paragraph (b)(1)(ii) of this section because there is a payment to a foreign related party in connection with the acquisition by the taxpayer of property of a character subject to the allowance for depreciation.

(B) *Year 2.* The acquisition of the depreciable property in Year 2 by DC2 is not itself a base erosion payment because DC2 did not acquire the property from a foreign related party. However, under paragraph (b)(2)(viii) of this section any depreciation expense taken by DC2 on the property acquired from DC1 is a base erosion payment and a base erosion tax benefit under paragraph (c)(1)(ii) of this section because the acquisition of the depreciable property was a base erosion payment by DC1 and the property was sold to a member of the aggregate group; therefore, the depreciation expense continues as a base erosion tax benefit to DC2 as it would have been to DC1 if it continued to own the property.

(8) *Example 8: Effect of election to waive deduction on method of accounting*—(i) *Facts.* DC, a domestic corporation, purchased and placed in service a depreciable asset (Asset A) from a foreign related party on the first day of its taxable year 1 for $100x. DC elects to use the alternative depreciation system under section 168(g) to depreciate all properties placed in service during taxable year 1. Asset A is not eligible for the additional first year depreciation deduction. Beginning in taxable year 1, DC depreciates Asset A under the alternative depreciation system using the straight-line depreciation method, a 5-year recovery period, and the half-year convention. This depreciation method, recovery period, and convention are permissible for Asset A under section 168(g). On its timely filed original Federal income tax return for taxable year 1, DC does not elect to waive any deductions and DC claims a depreciation deduction of $10x for Asset A. On its timely filed original Federal income tax return for taxable year 2, DC does not elect to waive any deductions and DC claims a depreciation deduction of $20x for Asset A. During taxable year 3, DC files an amended return for taxable year 1 to elect to waive the depreciation deduction for Asset A and reports in accordance with paragraph (c)(6)(ii) of this section with its amended return for taxable year 1 that the amount of the waived depreciation deduction for Asset A is $10x and the amount of the claimed depreciation deduction is $0x.

(ii) *Analysis.* Pursuant to paragraph (c)(6)(iii)(B)(1) of this section, DC's election to waive the depreciation deduction for Asset A for taxable year 1 is disregarded for determining DC's method of accounting for Asset A. Accordingly, after DC's election to waive the depreciation deduction for Asset A for taxable year 1, DC's method of accounting for depreciation for Asset A continues to be the straight-line depreciation method, a 5-year recovery period, and the half-year convention. Pursuant to paragraph (c)(6)(iii)(C) of this section, the election made by DC in taxable year 3 on its amended return for taxable year 1 is not a method of accounting.

(9) *Example 9: Change of accounting method when taxpayer has waived a deduction*—(i) *Facts.* DC, a domestic corporation, purchased

and placed in service a depreciable asset (Asset B) from a foreign related party on the first day of its taxable year 1 for $100x. DC elects to use the alternative depreciation system under section 168(g) to depreciate all properties placed in service during taxable year 1. Asset B is not eligible for the additional first year depreciation deduction. Beginning in taxable year 1, DC depreciates Asset B under the alternative depreciation system using the straight-line depreciation method, a 10-year recovery period, and the half-year convention. Under this method of accounting, the depreciation deductions for Asset B are $5x for taxable year 1 and $10x for taxable year 2. However, for taxable years 1 and 2, DC elects to waive $3x and $6x, respectively, of the depreciation deductions for Asset B and reports the information required under paragraph (c)(6)(ii) of this section with its returns. In taxable year 3, DC realizes that the correct recovery period for Asset B is 5 years. If DC had used the correct recovery period for Asset B, the depreciation deductions for Asset B would have been $10x for taxable year 1 and $20x for taxable year 2. DC timely files a Form 3115 to change its method of accounting for Asset B from a 10-year recovery period to a 5-year recovery period, beginning with taxable year 3. DC was not under examination as of the date on which it timely filed this Form 3115.

(ii) *Analysis*—(A) *Computation of the section 481(a) adjustment.* In determining the net negative section 481(a) adjustment for this method change, DC compares the depreciation deductions under its present method of accounting to the depreciation deductions under its proposed method of accounting. Pursuant to paragraph (c)(6)(iii)(D) of this section, DC agreed that, by making the election to waive depreciation deductions for Asset B, DC will not take into account the fact that depreciation deductions for Asset B were waived under paragraph (c)(6)(i) of this section. Accordingly, DC's net negative section 481(a) adjustment for this method change is $15x, which is calculated by determining the difference between the depreciation deductions for Asset B for taxable years 1 and 2 under DC's present method of accounting ($15x) and the depreciation deductions that would have been allowable for Asset B for taxable years 1 and 2 under DC's proposed method of accounting ($30x).

(B) *Computation of basis adjustments.* Pursuant to paragraph (c)(6)(iii)(B)(3) of this section, DC's elections to waive the depreciation deductions for Asset B for taxable years 1 and 2 are disregarded for determining the amount allowable for depreciation for purposes of section 1016(a)(2). The amount allowable for depreciation of Asset B is determined based on the proper method of computing depreciation for Asset B. Accordingly, Asset B's adjusted basis at the end of taxable year 1 is $90x ($100x - $10x) and at the end of taxable year 2 is $70x ($90x - $20x). [Reg. §1.59A-3.]

☐ [*T.D. 9885, 12-2-2019. Amended by T.D. 9910, 10-8-2020.*]

[Reg. §1.59A-4]

§1.59A-4. Modified taxable income.—(a) *Scope.*—Paragraph (b)(1) of this section provides rules for computing modified taxable income. Paragraph (b)(2) of this section provides rules addressing how base erosion tax benefits and net operating losses affect modified taxable income. Paragraph (b)(3) of this section provides a rule for a holder of a residual interest in a REMIC. Paragraph (c) of this section provides examples illustrating the rules described in this section.

(b) *Computation of modified taxable income.*—(1) *In general.*—The term *modified taxable income* means a taxpayer's taxable income, as defined in section 63(a), determined with the additions described in paragraph (b)(2) of this section. Notwithstanding the foregoing, the taxpayer's taxable income may not be reduced to an amount less than zero as a result of a net operating loss deduction allowed under section 172. See paragraphs (c)(1) and (2) of this section (*Examples 1* and 2).

(2) *Modifications to taxable income.*—The amounts described in this paragraph (b)(2) are added back to a taxpayer's taxable income to determine its modified taxable income.

(i) *Base erosion tax benefits.*—The amount of any base erosion tax benefit as defined in §1.59A-3(c)(1).

(ii) *Certain net operating loss deductions.*—The base erosion percentage, as described in §1.59A-2(e)(3), of any net operating loss deduction allowed to the taxpayer under section 172 for the taxable year. For purposes of determining modified taxable income, the net operating loss deduction allowed does not exceed taxable income before taking into account the net operating loss deduction. See paragraph (c)(1) and (2) of this section (*Examples 1* and 2). The base erosion percentage for the taxable year that the net operating loss arose is used to determine the addition under this paragraph (b)(2)(ii). For a net operating loss that arose in a taxable year beginning before January 1, 2018, the base erosion percentage for the taxable year is zero.

(3) *Rule for holders of a residual interest in a REMIC.*—For purposes of paragraph (b)(1) of this section, the limitation in section 860E(a)(1) is not taken into account in determining the taxable income amount that is used to compute modified taxable income for the taxable year.

(c) *Examples.*—The following examples illustrate the rules of paragraph (b) of this section.

(1) *Example 1: Current year loss*—(i) *Facts.* A domestic corporation (DC) is an applicable taxpayer that has a calendar taxable year. In 2020, DC has gross income of $100x, a deduction of $80x that is not a base erosion tax benefit, and a deduction of $70x that is a base erosion tax benefit. In addition, DC has a net operating loss carryforward to 2020 of $400x that arose in 2016.

(ii) *Analysis.* DC's starting point for computing modified taxable income is $(50x), computed as gross income of $100x, less a deduction of $80x (non-base erosion tax benefit) and a deduction of $70x (base erosion tax benefit). Under paragraph (b)(2)(ii) of this section, DC's starting point for computing modified taxable income does not take into account the $400x net operating loss carryforward because the allowable deductions for 2020, not counting the NOL deduction, exceed the gross income for 2020. DC's modified taxable income for 2020 is $20x, computed as $(50x) + $70x base erosion tax benefit.

(2) *Example 2: Net operating loss deduction*—(i) *Facts.* The facts are the same as in paragraph (c)(1)(i) of this section (the facts in *Example 1*), except that DC's gross income in 2020 is $500x.

(ii) *Analysis.* DC's starting point for computing modified taxable income is $0x, computed as gross income of $500x, less: a deduction of $80x (non-base erosion tax benefit), a deduction of $70x (base erosion tax benefit), and a net operating loss deduction of $350x (which is the amount of taxable income before taking into account the net operating loss deduction, as provided in paragraph (b)(2)(ii) of this section ($500x - $150x)). DC's modified taxable income for 2020 is $70x, computed as $0x + $70x base erosion tax benefit. DC's modified taxable income is not increased as a result of the $350x net operating loss deduction in 2020 because the base erosion percentage of the net operating loss that arose in 2016 is zero under paragraph (b)(2)(ii) of this section. [Reg. §1.59A-4.]

☐ [*T.D.* 9885, 12-2-2019.]

[Reg. §1.59A-5]

§1.59A-5. Base erosion minimum tax amount.—(a) *Scope.*—Paragraph (b) of this section provides rules regarding the calculation of the base erosion minimum tax amount. Paragraph (c) of this section describes the base erosion and anti-abuse tax rate applicable to the taxable year.

(b) *Base erosion minimum tax amount.*—(1) *In general.*—For each taxable year, an applicable taxpayer must determine its base erosion minimum tax amount.

(2) *Calculation of base erosion minimum tax amount.*—With respect to any applicable taxpayer, the base erosion minimum tax amount for any taxable year is, the excess (if any) of—

(i) An amount equal to the base erosion and anti-abuse tax rate multiplied by the modified taxable income of the taxpayer for the taxable year, over

(ii) An amount equal to the regular tax liability as defined in §1.59A-1(b)(16) of the taxpayer for the taxable year, reduced (but not below zero) by the excess (if any) of—

(A) The credits allowed under chapter 1 of subtitle A of the Code against regular tax liability over

(B) The sum of the credits described in paragraph (b)(3) of this section.

(3) *Credits that do not reduce regular tax liability.*—The sum of the following credits are used in paragraph (b)(2)(ii)(B) of this section to limit the amount by which the credits allowed under chapter 1 of subtitle A of the Internal Revenue Code reduce regular tax liability—

(i) *Taxable years beginning on or before December 31, 2025.*—For any taxable year beginning on or before December 31, 2025—

(A) The credit allowed under section 38 for the taxable year that is properly allocable to the research credit determined under section 41(a);

(B) The portion of the applicable section 38 credits not in excess of 80 percent of the lesser of the amount of those applicable section 38 credits or the base erosion minimum tax amount (determined without regard to this paragraph (b)(3)(i)(B)); and

(C) Any credits allowed under sections 33, 37, and 53.

(ii) *Taxable years beginning after December 31, 2025.*—For any taxable year beginning after December 31, 2025, any credits allowed under sections 33, 37, and 53.

(c) *Base erosion and anti-abuse tax rate.*—(1) *In general.*—For purposes of calculating the base erosion minimum tax amount, the base erosion and anti-abuse tax rate is—

(i) *Calendar year 2018.*—For taxable years beginning in calendar year 2018, five percent.

(ii) *Calendar years 2019 through 2025.*—For taxable years beginning after December 31, 2018, through taxable years beginning before January 1, 2026, 10 percent.

(iii) *Calendar years after 2025.*—For taxable years beginning after December 31, 2025, 12.5 percent.

(2) *Increased rate for banks and registered securities dealers.*—(i) *In general.*—In the case of a taxpayer that is a member of an affiliated group (as defined in section 1504(a)(1)) that includes a bank or a registered securities dealer, the percentage otherwise in effect under paragraph (c)(1) of this section is increased by one percentage point.

(ii) *De minimis exception to increased rate for banks and registered securities dealers.*—Paragraph (c)(2)(i) of this section does not apply to a taxpayer that is a member of an affiliated group (as defined in section 1504(a)(1)) that includes a bank or registered securities dealer if, in that taxable year, the total gross receipts of the affiliated group attributable to the bank or the registered securities dealer (or attributable to all of the banks and registered securities dealers in the group, if more than one) represent less than two percent of the total gross receipts of the affiliated group, as determined under §1.59A-2(d).

(3) *Application of section 15 to tax rates in section 59A.*—(i) *New tax.*—Section 15 does not apply to any taxable year that includes January 1, 2018.

(ii) *Change in tax rate pursuant to section 59A(b)(1)(A).*—Section 15 does not apply to any taxable year that includes January 1, 2019.

(iii) *Change in rate pursuant to section 59A(b)(2).*—Section 15 applies to the change in tax rate pursuant to section 59A(b)(2)(A). [Reg. §1.59A-5.]

☐ [*T.D.* 9885, 12-2-2019.]

[Reg. §1.59A-6]

§1.59A-6. Qualified derivative payment.—(a) *Scope.*—This section provides additional guidance regarding qualified derivative payments. Paragraph (b) of this section defines the term qualified derivative payment. Paragraph (c) of this section provides guidance on certain payments that are not treated as qualified derivative payments. Paragraph (d) defines the term derivative for purposes of section 59A. Paragraph (e) of this section provides examples illustrating the rules of this section.

(b) *Qualified derivative payment.*—(1) *In general.*—A *qualified derivative payment* means any payment made by a taxpayer to a foreign related party pursuant to a derivative with respect to which the taxpayer—

(i) Recognizes gain or loss as if the derivative were sold for its fair market value on the last business day of the taxable year (and any additional times as required by the Internal Revenue Code or the taxpayer's method of accounting);

(ii) Treats any gain or loss so recognized as ordinary; and

(iii) Treats the character of all items of income, deduction, gain, or loss with respect to a payment pursuant to the derivative as ordinary.

(2) *Reporting requirements.*—(i) *In general.*—No payment is a qualified derivative payment under paragraph (b)(1) of this section for any taxable year unless the taxpayer (whether or not the taxpayer is a reporting corporation as defined in §1.6038A-1(c)) reports the information required in §1.6038A-2(b)(7)(ix) for the taxable year. To report its qualified derivative payments, a taxpayer must include the payment in the aggregate amount of qualified derivative payments on Form 8991 (or successor).

(ii) *Failure to satisfy the reporting requirement.*—If a taxpayer fails to satisfy the reporting requirement described in paragraph (b)(2)(i) of this section with respect to any payments, those payments are not eligible for the qualified derivative payment exception described in §1.59A-3(b)(3)(ii) and are base erosion payments unless an exception in §1.59A-3(b)(3) otherwise applies. A taxpayer's failure to report a payment as a qualified derivative payment does not impact the eligibility of any other payment which the taxpayer properly reported under paragraph (b)(2)(i) of this section from being a qualified derivative payment.

(iii) *Reporting of aggregate amount of qualified derivative payments.*—The aggregate amount of qualified derivative payments is the sum of the amount described in paragraph (b)(3) of this section for each derivative. To the extent that the taxpayer is treated as receiving a payment, as determined in §1.59-2(e)(3)(vi), for the taxable year with respect to a derivative, the payment is not included in the aggregate qualified derivative payments.

(iv) *Transition period for qualified derivative payment reporting.*— Before paragraph (b)(2)(i) of this section is applicable, a taxpayer will be treated as satisfying the reporting requirement described section 59A(h)(2)(B) to the extent that the taxpayer reports the aggregate amount of qualified derivative payments on Form 8991 (or successor). *See* §1.6038A-2(g) (applicability date for §1.6038A-2(b)(7)(ix)). Until paragraph (b)(2)(i) of this section is applicable, paragraph (b)(2)(ii) of this section will not apply to a taxpayer who reports the aggregate amount of qualified derivative payments in good faith.

(3) *Amount of any qualified derivative payment.*—(i) *In general.*— The amount of any qualified derivative payment excluded from the denominator of the base erosion percentage as provided in §1.59A-2(e)(3)(ii)(C) is determined as provided in §1.59A-2(e)(3)(vi).

(ii) *Net qualified derivative payment that includes a payment that is a base erosion payment.*—Any net amount determined in paragraph (b)(3)(i) of this section must be reduced by any gross items that are treated as a base erosion payment pursuant to paragraph (c) of this section.

(c) *Exceptions for payments otherwise treated as base erosion payments.*—A payment does not constitute a qualified derivative payment if—

(1) The payment would be treated as a base erosion payment if it were not made pursuant to a derivative, including any interest, royalty, or service payment; or

(2) In the case of a contract that has derivative and nonderivative components, the payment is properly allocable to the nonderivative component.

(d) *Derivative defined.*—(1) *In general.*—For purposes of this section, the term *derivative* means any contract (including any option, forward contract, futures contract, short position, swap, or similar contract) the value of which, or any payment or other transfer with respect to which, is (directly or indirectly) determined by reference to one or more of the following:

(i) Any share of stock in a corporation;

(ii) Any evidence of indebtedness;

(iii) Any commodity that is actively traded;

(iv) Any currency; or

(v) Any rate, price, amount, index, formula, or algorithm.

(2) *Exceptions.*—The following contracts are not treated as derivatives for purposes of section 59A.

(i) *Direct interest.*—A derivative contract does not include a direct interest in any item described in paragraph (d)(1)(i) through (v) of this section.

(ii) *Insurance contracts.*—A derivative contract does not include any insurance, annuity, or endowment contract issued by an insurance company to which subchapter L applies (or issued by any foreign corporation to which the subchapter would apply if the foreign corporation were a domestic corporation).

(iii) *Securities lending and sale-repurchase transactions.*— (A) *Multi-step transactions treated as financing.*—For purposes of paragraph (d)(1) of this section, a derivative does not include any securities lending transaction, sale-repurchase transaction, or substantially similar transaction that is treated as a secured loan for federal tax purposes. Securities lending transaction and sale-repurchase transaction have the meanings provided in §1.861-2(a)(7).

(B) *Special rule for payments associated with the cash collateral provided in a securities lending transaction or substantially similar transaction.*—For purposes of paragraph (d)(1) of this section, a derivative does not include the cash collateral component of a securities lending transaction (or the cash payments pursuant to a sale-repurchase transaction, or similar payments pursuant to a substantially similar transaction).

(C) *Anti-abuse exception for certain transactions that are the economic equivalent of substantially unsecured cash borrowing.*—For purposes of paragraph (d)(1) of this section, a derivative does not include any securities lending transaction or substantially similar transaction that is part of an arrangement that has been entered into with a principal purpose of avoiding the treatment of any payment with respect to that transaction as a base erosion payment and that provides the taxpayer with the economic equivalent of a substantially unsecured cash borrowing. The determination of whether the securities lending transaction or substantially similar transaction provides the taxpayer with the economic equivalent of a substantially

unsecured cash borrowing takes into account arrangements that effectively serve as collateral due to the taxpayer's compliance with any U.S. regulatory requirements governing such transaction.

(3) *American depository receipts.*—For purposes of section 59A, American depository receipts (or any similar instruments) with respect to shares of stock in a foreign corporation are treated as shares of stock in that foreign corporation.

(e) *Examples.*—The following examples illustrate the rules of this section.

(1) *Example 1: Notional principal contract as QDP*—(i) *Facts.* Domestic Corporation (DC) is a dealer in securities within the meaning of section 475. On February 1, 2019, DC enters into a contract (Interest Rate Swap) with Foreign Parent (FP), a foreign related party, for a term of five years. Under the Interest Rate Swap, DC is obligated to make a payment to FP each month, beginning March 1, 2019, in an amount equal to a variable rate determined by reference to the prime rate, as determined on the first business day of the immediately preceding month, multiplied by a notional principal amount of $50x. Under the Interest Rate Swap, FP is obligated to make a payment to DC each month, beginning March 1, 2019, in an amount equal to 5% multiplied by the same notional principal amount. The Interest Rate Swap satisfies the definition of a notional principal contract under §1.446-3(c). DC recognizes gain or loss on the Interest Rate Swap pursuant to section 475. DC reports the information required to be reported for the taxable year under §1.6038A-2(b)(7)(ix).

(ii) *Analysis.* The Interest Rate Swap is a derivative as described in paragraph (d) of this section because it is a contract that references the prime rate and a fixed rate for determining the amount of payments. The exceptions described in paragraph (c) of this section do not apply to the Interest Rate Swap. Because DC recognizes ordinary gain or loss on the Interest Rate Swap pursuant to section 475(d)(3), it satisfies the condition in paragraph (b)(1)(ii) of this section. Because DC satisfies the requirement relating to the information required to be reported under paragraph (b)(2) of this section, any payment to FP with respect to the Interest Rate Swap will be a qualified derivative payment. Therefore, under §1.59A-3(b)(3)(ii), the payments to FP are not base erosion payments.

(2) *Example 2: Securities lending anti-abuse rule*—(i) *Facts.* (A) Foreign Parent (FP) is a foreign corporation that owns all of the stock of domestic corporation (DC) and foreign corporation (FC). FP and FC are foreign related parties of DC under §1.59A-1(b)(12) but not members of DC's aggregate group. On January 1 of year 1, with a principal purpose of providing financing to DC without DC making a base erosion payment to FC, FC lends 100x U.S. Treasury bills with a remaining maturity of 11 months (Securities A) to DC (Securities Lending Transaction 1) for a period of six months. Pursuant to the terms of Securities Lending Transaction 1, DC is obligated to make substitute payments to FC corresponding to the interest payments on Securities A. DC does not post cash collateral with respect to Securities Lending Transaction 1, and no other arrangements of FC or DC effectively serve as collateral under any U.S. regulatory requirements governing the transaction. Immediately thereafter, DC sells Securities A for cash.

(B) On June 30 of year 1, FC lends 100x U.S. Treasury bills with a remaining maturity of 11 months (Securities B) to DC (Securities Lending Transaction 2) for a period of six months. Pursuant to the terms of Securities Lending Transaction 2, DC is obligated to make substitute payments to FC corresponding to the interest payments on Securities B. Immediately thereafter, DC sells Securities B for cash and uses the cash to purchase U.S. Treasury bills with a remaining maturity equal to the Securities A bills that DC then transfers to FC in repayment of Securities Lending Transaction 1.

(ii) *Analysis.* Securities Lending Transaction 1 and Securities Lending Transaction 2 are not treated as derivatives for purposes of paragraph (d)(1) of this section because the transactions are part of an arrangement that has been entered into with a principal purpose of avoiding the treatment of any payment with respect to Securities Lending Transaction 1 and Securities Lending Transaction 2 as a base erosion payment and provides DC with the economic equivalent of a substantially unsecured cash borrowing by DC. As a result, pursuant to paragraph (d)(2)(iii)(C) of this section, the substitute payments made by DC to FC with respect to Securities A and Securities B are not eligible for the exception in §1.59A-3(b)(3)(ii) (qualified derivative payment). [Reg. §1.59A-6.]

☐ [T.D. 9885, 12-2-2019.]

[Reg. §1.59A-7]

§1.59A-7. Application of base erosion and anti-abuse tax to partnerships.—(a) *Scope.*—This section provides rules regarding how partnerships and their partners are treated for purposes of making certain determinations under section 59A, including whether there is a base erosion payment or base erosion tax benefit. All references to partnerships in this section include domestic and foreign partnerships. This section applies to payments to a partnership and payments from a partnership as well as transfers of partnership interests (as defined in paragraph (c)(3)(iv) of this section). The aggregate principle described in this section does not override the treatment of partnership items under any Code section other than section 59A. The aggregate principles provided in this section apply without regard to any tax avoidance purpose relating to a particular partnership. See §1.701-2(e). Paragraph (b) of this section describes how the aggregate approach to partnerships applies for purposes of certain section 59A determinations. Paragraph (c) of this section provides rules for determining whether there is a base erosion payment with respect to a payment to or from a partnership. Paragraph (d) of this section provides rules for determining the base erosion tax benefits of a partner. Paragraph (e) of this section provides additional rules relating to the application of section 59A to partnerships. Paragraph (f) of this section provides a rule for determining whether a person is a foreign related party. Paragraph (g) of this section provides examples that illustrate the application of the rules of this section.

(b) *Application of section 59A to partnerships.*—The purpose of this section is to provide a set of operating rules for the application of section 59A to partnerships and partners in a manner consistent with the purposes of section 59A. Except for purposes of determining a partner's base erosion tax benefits under paragraph (d)(1) of this section and whether a taxpayer is a registered securities dealer under paragraph (e)(3) of this section, section 59A determinations are made at the partner level in the manner described in this section. The provisions of section 59A must be interpreted in a manner consistent with this approach. If a transaction is not specifically described in this section, whether the transaction gives rise to a base erosion payment or base erosion tax benefit is determined in accordance with the principles of this section and the purposes of section 59A.

(c) *Base erosion payment.*—For purposes of determining whether a taxpayer has made a base erosion payment as described in §1.59A-3(b), the taxpayer must treat a payment to or from a partnership as made to or from each partner and the assets and liabilities of the partnership as assets and liabilities of each partner. This paragraph (c) provides specific rules for determining whether a partner has made or received a payment, including as a result of a partnership interest transfer (as defined in paragraph (c)(3)(iv) of this section).

(1) *Payments made by or to a partnership.*—For purposes of determining whether a payment or accrual by a partnership is a base erosion payment described in §1.59A-3(b)(1)(i), any amount paid or accrued by the partnership (including any guaranteed payment described in section 707(c)) is treated as paid or accrued by each partner based on the partner's distributive share of the item of deduction with respect to that amount. For purposes of determining whether a payment or accrual to a partnership is a base erosion payment described in §1.59A-3(b)(1)(i) or (iii), any amount paid or accrued to the partnership (including any guaranteed payment described in section 707(c)) is treated as paid or accrued to each partner based on the partner's distributive share of the item of income with respect to that amount. See paragraph (e)(1) of this section to determine the partner's distributive share.

(2) *Transfers of certain property.*—When a partnership transfers property, each partner is treated as transferring its proportionate share of the property transferred for purposes of determining whether there is a base erosion payment described in §1.59A-3(b)(1)(ii) or (iv). When a partnership acquires property, each partner is treated as acquiring its proportionate share of the property acquired for purposes of determining whether there is a base erosion payment described in §1.59A-3(b)(1)(ii) or (iv). For purposes of this paragraph (c)(2), a transfer of property does not include a transfer of a partnership interest (as defined in paragraph (c)(3)(iv) of this section). See paragraph (c)(3) of this section for rules applicable to transfers of partnership interests. See paragraphs (g)(2)(v) and (vi) of this section (*Example 5* and *Example 6*) for examples illustrating the application of this paragraph (c)(2).

(3) *Transfers of a partnership interest.*—(i) *In general.*—A transfer of a partnership interest (as defined in paragraph (c)(3)(iv) of this section) is generally treated as a transfer by each partner in the partnership of its proportionate share of the partnership's assets to the extent of any change in its proportionate share of any partnership asset, as well as any assumption of associated liabilities by the partner. Paragraphs (c)(3)(ii) and (iii) of this section provide rules for applying the general rule to transfers of a partnership interest by a partner and issuances of a partnership interest by the partnership for contributed property, respectively. See paragraph (g)(2)(vii) of this section (*Example 7*) for an example illustrating the application of this paragraph (c)(3)(i).

(ii) *Transfers of a partnership interest by a partner.*—A transfer of a partnership interest (as defined in paragraph (c)(3)(iv) of this section) by a partner is treated as a transfer by the transferor to the recipient of the transferor's proportionate share of each of the partnership assets and an assumption by the recipient of the transferor's proportionate share of the partnership liabilities. If the partner's entire partnership interest is not transferred, only the proportionate share of each of the partnership assets and liabilities associated with the transferred partnership interest is treated as transferred and assumed. See paragraphs (g)(2)(iii), (iv), and (vi) of this section (*Example 3, Example 4,* and *Example 6*) for examples illustrating the application of this paragraph (c)(3)(ii).

(iii) *Certain issuances of a partnership interest by a partnership.*—If a partnership issues an interest in the partnership in exchange for a contribution of property to the partnership, the contributing partner is treated as exchanging a portion of the contributed property and assuming any liabilities associated with the transferred partnership interest for a portion of the partners' pre-contribution interests in the partnership's assets and the partners' assumption of any liabilities transferred to the partnership. For purposes of this paragraph (c)(3)(iii), a reference to the "partnership's assets" includes the assets contributed by the contributing partner and any other assets that are contributed to the partnership at the same time. Each partner whose proportionate share in a partnership asset (including the assets contributed to the partnership as part of the transaction) is reduced as a result of the transaction is treated as transferring the asset to the extent of the reduction, and each person who receives a proportionate share or an increased proportionate share in an asset as a result of the transaction is treated as receiving an asset to the extent of the increase, proportionately from the partners' reduced interests. For example, if a person contributes property to a partnership in which each of two existing partners has a 50 percent pro-rata interest in the partnership in exchange for a one-third pro-rata partnership interest, each of the pre-contribution partners is treated as transferring a one-third interest in their share of existing partnership assets to the contributing partner, and the contributing partner is treated as transferring a one-third interest in the contributed assets to each of the original partners. See paragraphs (g)(2)(i) and (ii) of this section (*Example 1* and *Example 2*) for additional examples illustrating the application of this paragraph (c)(3)(iii).

(iv) *Partnership interest transfers defined.*—For purposes of paragraphs (c)(3) and (4) of this section, a transfer of a partnership interest includes any issuance of a partnership interest by a partnership; any sale of a partnership interest; any increase or decrease in a partner's proportionate share of any partnership asset as a result of a contribution of property or services to a partnership, a distribution, or a redemption; or any other transfer of a proportionate share of any partnership asset (other than a transfer of a partnership asset that is not a partnership interest by the partnership to a person not acting in a partner capacity), whether by a partner or the partnership (including as a result of a deemed or actual sale or a capital shift).

(4) *Increased basis from a distribution.*—If a distribution of property from a partnership to a partner results in an increase in the tax basis of either the distributed property or other partnership property, such as under section 732(b) or 734(b), the increase in tax basis attributable to a foreign related party is treated as if it was newly purchased property acquired by the taxpayer (to the extent of its proportionate share) from the foreign related party that is placed in service when the distribution occurs. See §1.734-1(e). This increased basis treated as newly purchased property is treated as acquired with a base erosion payment, unless an exception in §1.59A-3(b) applies. For this purpose, in the case of a distribution to a foreign related party, the increased basis in the remaining partnership property that is treated as newly purchased property is entirely attributable to the foreign related party. In the case of a distribution to a taxpayer, the increased basis in the distributed property that is treated as newly purchased property is attributable to each foreign related party in proportion to the foreign related party's proportionate share of the asset immediately before the distribution. If the distribution is to a person other than a taxpayer or a foreign related party, there is no base erosion payment caused by the distribution under this paragraph (c)(4). See paragraphs (g)(2)(vii), (viii), and (ix) of this section (*Example 7, Example 8,* and *Example 9*) for examples illustrating the application of this paragraph (c)(4).

(5) *Operating rules applicable to base erosion payments.*—(i) *Single payment characterized as separate transactions.*—If a single transaction is partially characterized in one manner and partially characterized in another manner, each part of the transaction is separately analyzed. For example, if a contribution of property to a partnership is partially treated as a contribution and partially treated as a disguised sale, the contribution and sale are separately analyzed under paragraph (c) of this section.

(ii) *Ordering rule with respect to transfers of a partnership interest.*—If a partnership interest is transferred (within the meaning of paragraph (c)(3)(iv) of this section), paragraph (c)(3) of this section first applies to determine the assets deemed transferred by the transferor(s) to the transferee(s) and liabilities deemed assumed by the parties. Then, to the extent applicable (such as where a partnership makes a contribution in exchange for an interest in another partnership or when a partnership receives an interest in another partnership as a contribution to it), paragraph (c)(2) of this section applies for purposes of determining the proportionate share of the property received by the partners in a partnership. See paragraph (g)(2)(vi) of this section (*Example 6*) for an illustration of this rule.

(iii) *Consideration for base erosion payment or property resulting in base erosion tax benefits.*—When a partnership pays or receives property, services, or other consideration, each partner is deemed to pay or receive the property, services, or other consideration paid or received by the partnership for purposes of determining if there is a base erosion payment, except as otherwise provided in paragraph (c) of this section. See paragraphs (g)(2)(v) and (vi) of this section (*Example 5* and *Example 6*) for illustrations of this rule.

(iv) *Non-cash consideration.*—When both parties to a transaction use non-cash consideration, each party must separately apply paragraph (c) of this section to determine its base erosion payment with respect to each property. For example, if two partnerships, each with a domestic corporation and a foreign corporation as partners, all of whom are related, exchange depreciable property, each transfer of property would be separately analyzed to determine whether it is a base erosion payment.

(v) *Allocations of income in lieu of deductions.*—If a partnership adopts the curative method of making section 704(c) allocations under §1.704-3(c), an allocation of income to the partner to whom any built-in gain or built-in loss would be allocable under section 704(c) (the 704(c) partner), in an amount necessary to offset the effect of the ceiling rule (as defined in §1.704-3(b)(1)), in lieu of a deduction allocation to a partner other than the 704(c) partner (a non-704(c) partner), is treated as a deduction to the non-704(c) partner for purposes of section 59A in an amount equal to the income allocation. See paragraph (g)(2)(x) of this section (*Example 10*) for an example illustrating the application of this paragraph (c)(5)(v).

(d) *Base erosion tax benefit for partners.*—(1) *In general.*—A partner's distributive share of any deduction or reduction in gross receipts attributable to a base erosion payment (including as a result of sections 704(b) and (c), 707(a) and (c), 732(b) and (d), 734(b) and (d), 737, 743(b) and (d), and 751(b)) is the partner's base erosion tax benefit, subject to the exceptions in §1.59A-3(c)(2). See paragraph (e)(1) of this section to determine the partner's distributive share for purposes of section 59A. A partner's base erosion tax benefit may be more than the partner's base erosion payment. For example, if a partnership makes a payment to a foreign related party of its domestic partner to acquire a depreciable asset, and the partnership specially allocates more depreciation deductions to a partner than its proportionate share of the asset, the partner's base erosion tax benefit includes the specially allocated depreciation deduction even if the total allocated deduction exceeds the partner's share of the base erosion payment made to acquire the asset. Base erosion tax benefits are determined separately for each asset, payment, or accrual, as applicable, and are not netted with other items. A taxpayer determines its base erosion tax benefits for non-partnership items pursuant to §1.59A-3(c).

(2) *Exception for base erosion tax benefits of certain small partners.*—(i) *In general.*—For purposes of determining a partner's amount of base erosion tax benefits attributable to a base erosion payment made by a partnership, a partner does not take into account its distributive share of any base erosion tax benefits from the partnership for the taxable year if—

(A) The partner's interest in the partnership represents less than ten percent of the capital and profits of the partnership at all times during the taxable year;

(B) The partner is allocated less than ten percent of each partnership item of income, gain, loss, deduction, and credit for the taxable year; and

(C) The partner's interest in the partnership has a fair market value of less than $25 million on the last day of the partner's taxable year, determined using a reasonable method.

(ii) *Attribution.*—For purposes of paragraph (d)(2)(i) of this section, a partner's interest in a partnership or partnership item is determined by adding the interests of the partner and any related party of the partner (as determined under section 59A), taking into account any interest owned directly, indirectly, or through constructive ownership (applying the section 318 rules as modified by section 59A (except section 318(a)(3)(A) through (C) will also apply so as to

consider a United States person as owning stock that is owned by a person who is not a United States person), but excluding any interest to the extent already taken into account).

(e) *Other rules for applying section 59A to partnerships.*—(1) *Partner's distributive share.*—For purposes of section 59A, each partner's distributive share of an item of income or deduction of the partnership is determined under sections 704(b) and (c) and takes into account amounts determined under other provisions of the Code, including but not limited to sections 707(a) and (c), 732(b) and (d), 734(b) and (d), 737, 743(b) and (d), and 751(b). See §1.704-1(b)(1)(iii) regarding the application of section 482. These amounts are calculated separately for each payment or accrual on a property-by-property basis, including for purposes of section 704(c), and are not netted. For purposes of section 59A, a partner's distributive share of a reduction to determine gross income is equal to a proportionate amount of the partnership's reduction to determine gross income corresponding to the partner's share of the partnership gross receipts (as determined under paragraph (e)(2)(i) of this section) related to that reduction.

(2) *Gross receipts.*—(i) *In general.*—For purposes of section 59A, each partner in the partnership includes a share of partnership gross receipts in proportion to the partner's distributive share (as determined under sections 704(b) and (c)) of items of gross income that were taken into account by the partnership under section 703 or 704(c) (such as remedial or curative items under §1.704-3(c) or (d)).

(ii) *Foreign corporation.*—See §1.59A-2(d)(3) for gross receipts of foreign corporations.

(3) *Registered securities dealers.*—If a partnership, or a branch of the partnership, is a registered securities dealer, each partner is treated as a registered securities dealer unless the partner's interest in the registered securities dealer would satisfy the criteria for the exception in paragraph (d)(2) of this section. For purposes of applying the de minimis exception in §1.59A-2(e)(2)(iii), a partner takes into account its distributive share of the relevant partnership items.

(4) *Application of sections 163(j) and 59A(c)(3) to partners.*—See §1.59A-3(c)(4).

(5) *Tiered partnerships.*—In the case of one or more partnerships owning an interest in another partnership (or partnerships), the rules of this section apply successively to each partnership and its partners in the chain of ownership. Paragraphs (d)(2) and (f) of this section and the small partner exception in paragraph (e)(3) of this section apply only to a partner that is not itself a partnership.

(f) *Foreign related party.*—With respect to any person that owns an interest in a partnership, the related party determination in section 59A(g) applies at the partner level.

(g) *Examples.*—The following examples illustrate the application of this section.

(1) *Facts.*—The following facts are assumed for purposes of the examples.

(i) DC is a domestic corporation that is an applicable taxpayer for purposes section 59A.

(ii) FC is a foreign corporation that is a foreign related party with respect to DC.

(iii) UC is a domestic corporation that is not related to DC and FC.

(iv) Neither FC nor any partnership in the examples is (or is treated as) engaged in a U.S. trade or business or has a permanent establishment in the United States.

(v) All payments apply to a taxable year beginning after December 31, 2017.

(vi) Unless otherwise stated, all allocations are pro-rata and satisfy the requirements of section 704(b) and all the partners have equal interests in the partnership.

(vii) Unless otherwise stated, depreciable property acquired and placed in service by the partnership has a remaining recovery period of five years and is depreciated under the alternative depreciation system of section 168(g) using the straight line method. Solely for purposes of simplifying the calculations in these examples, assume the applicable convention rules in section 168(d) do not apply.

(viii) No exception under §1.59A-3(b) or (c) applies to any amount paid or accrued.

(2) *Examples.*—(i) *Example 1: Contributions to a partnership on partnership formation*—(A) *Facts.* DC and FC form partnership PRS, with each contributing depreciable property that has a fair market value and tax basis of $100x, Property A and Property B, respectively. Therefore, the property contributed by FC, Property B, will generate $20x of annual section 704(b) and tax depreciation deductions for five years. The depreciation deductions will be allocated $10x to each of DC and FC each year. Before the transactions, for purposes of section

59A, DC is treated as owning a 100 percent interest in Property A and a zero percent interest in Property B, and FC is treated as owning a 100 percent interest in Property B and a zero percent interest in Property A. After the formation of PRS, for purposes of section 59A, DC and FC are each treated as owning a 50 percent proportionate share of each of Property A and Property B.

(B) *Analysis.* The treatment of contributions of property in exchange for an interest in a partnership is described in paragraph (c)(3)(iii) of this section. Under paragraph (c)(3)(iii) of this section, DC is treated as exchanging a 50 percent interest in Property A for a 50 percent proportionate share of Property B. Under §1.59A-3(b)(1)(ii), the payment to acquire depreciable property, Property B, from FC is a base erosion payment. The base erosion tax benefit is the amount of depreciation allocated to DC with respect to Property B ($10x per year) and is not netted with any other partnership item pursuant to paragraph (d)(1) of this section.

(ii) *Example 2: Section 704(c) and remedial allocations*—(A) *Facts.* The facts are the same as in paragraph (g)(2)(i)(A) of this section (the facts in *Example 1*), except that Property B has a tax basis of $40x and PRS adopts the remedial method under §1.704-3(d).

(B) *Analysis.* The analysis and results are the same as in paragraph (g)(2)(i)(B) of this section (the analysis in *Example 1*), except that annual tax depreciation is $8x ($40x/5) and annual remedial tax deduction allocation to DC is $2x (with $2x of remedial income to FC) for five years. Both the tax depreciation and the remedial tax allocation to DC are base erosion tax benefits to DC under paragraph (d)(1) of this section.

(iii) *Example 3: Sale of a partnership interest without a section 754 election*—(A) *Facts.* UC and FC are equal partners in partnership PRS, the only asset of which is Property A, a depreciable property with a fair market value of $200x and a tax basis of $120x. PRS does not have any section 704(c) assets. DC purchases 50 percent of FC's interest in PRS for $50x. Prior to the sale, for section 59A purposes, FC is treated as owning a 50 percent proportionate share of Property A and DC is treated as owning no interest in Property A. Following the sale, for section 59A purposes, DC is treated as owning a 25 percent proportionate share of Property A, all of which is treated as acquired from FC. The partnership does not have an election under section 754 in effect. Property A will generate $24x of annual tax and section 704(b) depreciation deductions for five years. The depreciation deductions will be allocated $12x to UC and $6x to both FC and DC each year.

(B) *Analysis.* The sale of a partnership interest by a partner is analyzed under paragraph (c)(3)(ii) of this section. Under section (c)(3)(ii) of this section, FC is treated as selling to DC 25 percent of Property A. Under §1.59A-3(b)(1)(ii), the payment to acquire depreciable property is a base erosion payment. Under paragraph (d)(1) of this section, the base erosion tax benefit is the amount of depreciation allocated to DC with respect to the base erosion payment, which would be the depreciation deductions allocated to DC with respect to Property A. DC's annual $6x depreciation deduction is its base erosion tax benefit with respect to the base erosion payment.

(iv) *Example 4: Sale of a partnership interest with section 754 election*—(A) *Facts.* The facts are the same as in paragraph (g)(2)(iii)(A) of this section (the facts in *Example 3*), except that the partnership has an election under section 754 in effect. As a result of the sale, there is a $20x positive adjustment to the tax basis in Property A with respect to DC under section 743(b) (DC's $50x basis in the PRS interest less DC's $30x share of PRS's tax basis in Property A). The section 743(b) step-up in tax basis is recovered over a depreciable recovery period of five years. Therefore, DC will be allocated a total of $10x in annual depreciation deductions for five years, comprised of $6x with respect to DC's proportionate share of PRS's common tax basis in Property A ($30x over 5 years) and $4x with respect to the section 743(b) adjustment ($20x over 5 years).

(B) *Analysis.* The analysis is the same as in paragraph (g)(2)(iii)(B) of this section (the analysis in *Example 3*); however, because section 743(b) increases the basis in Property A for DC by $20x, DC is allocated additional depreciation deductions of $4x per year as a result of the section 743(b) adjustment and has an annual base erosion tax benefit of $10x ($6x plus $4x) for five years under paragraph (d)(1) of this section.

(v) *Example 5: Purchase of depreciable property from a partnership*—(A) *Facts.* The facts are the same as in paragraph (d)(2)(iii)(A) of this section (the facts in *Example 3*), except that instead of DC purchasing an interest in the partnership, DC purchases Property A from the partnership for $200x.

(B) *Analysis.* DC must analyze whether the purchase of the depreciable property from the partnership is a base erosion payment under paragraph (c)(2) of this section. Under paragraph (c)(2) of this section, DC is treated as acquiring FC's proportionate share of Property A from FC. Because DC paid the partnership for the partnership's interest in Property A, under paragraph (c)(5)(iii) of this section, DC is treated as paying FC for FC's proportionate share of

Property A. Under §1.59A-3(b)(1)(ii), the payment to FC to acquire depreciable property is a base erosion payment. DC's base erosion tax benefit is the amount of depreciation allocated to DC with respect to the base erosion payment, which in this case is the amount of depreciation deductions with respect to the property acquired with a base erosion payment, or the depreciation deductions from FC's (but not UC's) proportionate share of the asset. See §1.59A-7(d)(1).

(vi) *Example 6: Sale of a partnership interest to a second partnership*—(A) *Facts.* FC, UC1, and UC2 are equal partners in partnership PRS1. DC and UC3 are equal partners in partnership PRS2. UC1, UC2, and UC3 are not related to DC or FC. PRS1's sole asset is Property A, which is depreciable property with a fair market value and tax basis of $300x. FC sells its entire interest in PRS1 to PRS2 for $100. For section 59A purposes, FC's proportionate share of Property A prior to the sale is one-third. Following the sale, for section 59A purposes, PRS2's proportionate share of Property A is one-third and DC's proportionate share of Property A (through PRS2) is one-sixth (50 percent of one-third).

(B) *Analysis.* Under paragraph (c)(5)(ii) of this section (the ordering rule), FC's transfer of its interest in PRS1 is first analyzed under paragraph (c)(3) of this section to determine how the transfer of the partnership interest is treated. Then, paragraph (c)(2) of this section applies to analyze how the acquisition of property by PRS2 is treated. Under paragraph (c)(3)(ii) of this section, FC is deemed to transfer its proportionate share of PRS1's assets, which is one-third of Property A. Then, under paragraph (c)(2) of this section, DC is treated as acquiring its proportionate share of PRS2's proportionate share of Property A from FC, which is one-sixth (50 percent of one-third). Under paragraph (c)(5)(iii) of this section, DC is treated as paying for the property it is treated as acquiring from FC. Therefore, DC's deemed payment to FC to acquire depreciable property is a base erosion payment under §1.59A-3(b)(1)(ii). DC's base erosion tax benefit is equal to DC's distributive share of depreciation deductions that PRS2 allocates to DC attributable to Property A. See §1.59A-7(d)(1).

(vii) *Example 7: Distribution of cash by a partnership to a foreign related party*—(A) *Facts.* DC, FC, and UC are equal partners in a partnership, PRS, the assets of which consist of cash of $90x and a depreciable asset (Property A) with a fair market value of $180x and a tax basis of $60x. Each partner's interest in PRS has a fair market value of $90x ($270x/3) and a tax basis of $50x. Assume that all non-depreciable assets are capital assets, all depreciable assets are non-residential real property under section 168, and that no depreciation has been claimed prior to the transaction below. PRS has an election under section 754 in effect. PRS distributes the $90x of cash to FC in complete liquidation of its interest, resulting in gain to FC of $40x ($90x minus its tax basis in PRS of $50x) under section 731(a)(1) and an increase to the tax basis of Property A under section 734(b) of $40x. Prior to the distribution, for section 59A purposes, each partner had a one-third proportionate share of Property A. After the distribution, for section 59A purposes, the remaining partners each have a 50 percent proportionate share of Property A. Each partner's pro-rata allocation of depreciation deductions with respect to Property A is in proportion to each partner's proportionate share of Property A both before and after the distribution. Half of the depreciation deductions attributable to the $40x section 734(b) step-up will be allocated to DC. In addition, DC's proportionate share of Property A increased from one-third to one-half and therefore DC will be allocated depreciation deductions with respect to half of the original basis of $60x (or $30x) instead of one-third of $60x (or $20x).

(B) *Analysis.* Distributions of property that cause an increase in the tax basis of property that continues to be held by the partnership are analyzed under paragraph (c)(4) of this section. The $40x increase in the tax basis of Property A as a result of the distribution of cash to FC is treated as newly purchased property acquired from FC under paragraph (c)(4) of this section and therefore acquired with a base erosion payment under §1.59A-3(b)(1)(ii) to DC to the extent of DC's proportionate share. DC's base erosion tax benefit is the amount of DC's depreciation deductions attributable to that base erosion payment, which is DC's distributive share of the depreciation deductions with respect to the $40x increase in the tax basis of Property A. See §1.59A-7(d)(1). In addition, FC transferred a partnership interest to DC (as defined in paragraph (c)(3)(iv) of this section), which is analyzed under paragraph (c)(3)(i) of this section. Under paragraph (c)(3)(i) of this section, DC is deemed to acquire a one-sixth interest in Property A from FC (the increase in DC's proportionate share from one-third to one-half). DC's base erosion tax benefit from this additional one-sixth interest in Property A is the amount of DC's depreciation deductions attributable to this interest.

(viii) *Example 8: Distribution of property by a partnership to a taxpayer*—(A) *Facts.* The facts are the same as paragraph (g)(2)(vii)(A) of this section (the facts of *Example 7*), except that PRS's depreciable property consists of two assets, Property A having a fair market value of $90x and a tax basis of $60x and Property B having a fair market value of $90x and a tax basis of zero. Instead of distributing cash to FC, PRS distributes Property B to DC in liquidation of its interest, resulting in an increase in the basis of the distributed Property B to DC of $50x (from zero to $50x) under section 732(b) because DC's tax basis in the PRS interest was $50x. For section 59A purposes, prior to the distribution, each partner had a one-third proportionate share of Property B and after the distribution, the property is wholly owned by DC.

(B) *Analysis.* Distributions of property that cause an increase in the tax basis of property that is distributed to a taxpayer are analyzed under paragraph (c)(4) of this section. Under paragraph (c)(4) of this section, the $50x increase in tax basis is treated as newly purchased property that was acquired with a base erosion payment to the extent that the increase in tax basis is attributable to FC. Under paragraph (c)(4) of this section, the portion of the increase that is attributable to FC is the proportionate share of the Property B immediately before the distribution that was treated as owned by FC. Immediately before the distribution, FC had a one-third proportionate share of Property B. Accordingly, one-third of the $50x increase in the tax basis of Property B is treated as if it was newly purchased property acquired by DC from FC with a base erosion payment under §1.59A-3(b)(1)(ii). DC's base erosion tax benefit is the amount of DC's depreciation deductions with respect to the base erosion payment, which in this case is the depreciation deductions with respect to the one-third interest in the increased basis treated as newly purchased property deemed acquired from FC. See §1.59A-3(c)(1). In addition, PRS transferred Property B to DC, which is analyzed under paragraph (c)(2) of this section. Prior to the distribution, DC, FC, and UC each owned one-third of Property B. After the distribution, DC entirely owned Property B. Therefore, under paragraph (c)(2) of this section, DC is treated as acquiring one-third of Property B from FC. DC's depreciation deductions with respect to the one-third of Property B acquired from FC (without regard to the basis increase) is also a base erosion tax benefit.

(ix) *Example 9: Distribution of property by a partnership in liquidation of a foreign related party's interest*—(A) *Facts.* The facts are the same as paragraph (g)(2)(viii)(A) (the facts of *Example 8*), except that Property B is not distributed to DC and, instead, Property A is distributed to FC in liquidation of its interest, resulting in a tax basis in Property A of $50x in FC's hands under section 732(b) and a section 734(b) step-up in Property B of $10x (because Property A's tax basis was reduced from $60x to $50x), allocable to DC and UC. For section 59A purposes, prior to the distribution, each partner had a one-third proportionate share of Property B and after the distribution, DC and UC each have a one-half proportionate share of Property B.

(B) *Analysis.* Distributions of property that cause an increase in the tax basis of property that continues to be held by the partnership are analyzed under paragraph (c)(4) of this section. Under paragraph (c)(4) of this section, because the distribution of Property A to FC from PRS caused an increase in the tax basis of Property B, the entire $10x increase in tax basis is treated as newly purchased property that was acquired with a base erosion payment under §1.59A-3(b)(1)(ii). DC's base erosion tax benefit is the amount of DC's depreciation deductions attributable to the base erosion payment, which is DC's distributive share of the depreciation deductions with respect to the $10x increase in the tax basis of Property B. See §1.59A-7(d)(1). In addition, under paragraph (c)(3)(i) of this section, DC is deemed to acquire a one-sixth interest in Property B from FC (the increase in DC's proportionate share from one-third to one-half). While this increase is a base erosion payment under §1.59A-3(b)(1)(ii), there is no base erosion tax benefit from this additional one-sixth interest in Property B because the tax basis in Property B (without regard to the basis) is zero and therefore the increase in DC's proportionate share does not result in any additional depreciation deductions.

(x) *Example 10: Section 704(c) and curative allocations*—(A) *Facts.* The facts are the same as in paragraph (d)(2)(ii)(A) of this section (the facts in *Example 2*), except that DC's property is not depreciable, PRS uses the traditional method with curative allocations under §1.704-3(c), and the curative allocations are to be made from operating income. Also assume that the partnership has $20x of gross operating income in each year and a curative allocation of the operating income satisfies the "substantially the same effect" requirement of §1.704-3(c)(3)(iii)(A).

(B) *Analysis.* The analysis and results are the same as in paragraph (d)(2)(i)(B) of this section (the analysis in *Example 1*), except that actual depreciation is $8x ($40x/5) per year and the ceiling rule shortfall under §1.704-3(b)(1) of $2x per year is corrected with a curative allocation of income from DC to FC of $2x per year. Solely for U.S. federal income tax purposes, each year FC is allocated $12x of total operating income and DC is allocated $8x of operating income. Both the actual depreciation deduction to DC and the curative allocation of income from DC are base erosion tax benefits to DC under paragraphs (c)(5)(v) and (d)(1) of this section. [Reg. §1.59A-7.]

☐ [*T.D. 9885, 12-2-2019. Amended by T.D. 9910, 10-8-2020.*]

Reg. §1.59A-8

§1.59A-8. [Reserved].
[Reg. §1.59A-8.]
☐ [*T.D. 9885, 12-2-2019.*]

§1.59A-9. Anti-abuse and recharacterization rules.—(a) *Scope.*— This section provides rules for recharacterizing certain transactions according to their substance for purposes of applying section 59A and the section 59A regulations. Paragraph (b) of this section provides specific anti-abuse rules. Paragraph (c) of this section provides examples illustrating the rules of paragraph (b) of this section.

(b) *Anti-abuse rules.*—(1) *Transactions involving unrelated persons, conduits, or intermediaries.*—If a taxpayer pays or accrues an amount to one or more intermediaries (including an intermediary unrelated to the taxpayer) that would have been a base erosion payment if paid or accrued to a foreign related party, and one or more of the intermediaries makes (directly or indirectly) corresponding payments to or for the benefit of a foreign related party as part of a transaction (or series of transactions), plan, or arrangement that has as a principal purpose of avoiding a base erosion payment (or reducing the amount of a base erosion payment), the role of the intermediary or intermediaries is disregarded as a conduit, or the amount paid or accrued to the intermediary is treated as a base erosion payment, as appropriate.

(2) *Transactions to increase the amount of deductions taken into account in the denominator of the base erosion percentage computation.*—A transaction (or component of a transaction or series of transactions), plan, or arrangement that has a principal purpose of increasing the deductions taken into account for purposes of §1.59A-2(e)(3)(i)(B) (the denominator of the base erosion percentage computation) is disregarded for purposes of §1.59A-2(e)(3).

(3) *Transactions to avoid the application of rules applicable to banks and registered securities dealers.*—A transaction (or series of transactions), plan, or arrangement that occurs among related parties that has a principal purpose of avoiding the rules applicable to certain banks and registered securities dealers in §1.59A-2(e)(2) (base erosion percentage test for banks and registered securities dealers) or §1.59A-5(c)(2) (increased base erosion and anti-abuse tax rate for banks and registered securities dealers) is not taken into account for purposes of §1.59A-2(e)(2) or §1.59A-5(c)(2).

(4) *Nonrecognition transactions.*—If a transaction (or series of transactions), plan, or arrangement (the first transaction) increases the adjusted basis of property that the taxpayer acquires in a transaction (the second transaction) that qualifies for the specified nonrecognition transaction exception in §1.59A-3(b)(3)(viii)(A) (or would qualify, but for this paragraph (b)(4)), and a principal purpose of the first transaction was to increase the taxpayer's depreciation or amortization deductions without increasing the taxpayer's base erosion tax benefits, then §1.59A-3(b)(3)(viii)(A) does not apply to the property acquired in the second transaction to the extent of the increase in adjusted basis. For purposes of this paragraph (b)(4), if a transaction (or series of transactions), plan, or arrangement between related parties increases the adjusted basis of property within the six-month period before the taxpayer acquires the property, the transaction (or series of transactions), plan, or arrangement is deemed to have such a principal purpose.

(5) *Transactions involving derivatives on a partnership interest.*—If a taxpayer acquires a derivative on a partnership interest (or partnership assets) as part of a transaction (or series of transactions), plan, or arrangement that has as a principal purpose of avoiding a base erosion payment (or reducing the amount of a base erosion payment) and the partnership interest (or partnership assets) would have resulted in a base erosion payment had the taxpayer acquired that interest (or partnership asset) directly, then the taxpayer is treated as having a direct interest instead of a derivative interest for purposes of applying section 59A. This paragraph (b)(5), however, does not apply to a derivative, as defined in section 59A(h)(4)(A)(v), on a partnership asset to the extent the payment pursuant to the derivative qualifies for the exception for qualified derivative payments in §1.59A-3(b)(3)(ii) and §1.59A-6. A derivative interest in a partnership includes any contract (including any financial instrument) the value of which, or any payment or other transfer with respect to which, is (directly or indirectly) determined in whole or in part by reference to the partnership, including the amount of partnership distributions, the value of partnership assets, or the results of partnership operations.

(6) *Allocations to eliminate or reduce a base erosion payment.*—If a partnership receives (or accrues) an amount from a person not acting in a partner capacity (including a person who is not a partner) and

allocates the income or loss with respect to that amount to its partners with a principal purpose of avoiding a base erosion payment (or reducing the amount of a base erosion payment), then the taxpayer transacting (directly or indirectly) with the partnership will determine its base erosion payment as if the allocations had not been made and the items of income or loss had been allocated proportionately. The preceding sentence applies only when the allocations, in combination with any related allocations, do not change the economic arrangement of the partners to the partnership.

(c) *Examples.*—The following examples illustrate the application of this section.

(1) *Facts.*—The following facts are assumed for purposes of the examples.

(i) DC is a domestic corporation that is an applicable taxpayer for purposes section 59A.

(ii) FP is a foreign corporation that owns all the stock of DC.

(iii) None of the foreign corporations have income that is, or is treated as, effectively connected with the conduct of a trade or business in the United States under an applicable provision of the Internal Revenue Code or regulations thereunder.

(iv) All payments occur in a taxable year beginning after December 31, 2017.

(2) *Example 1: Substitution of payments that are not base erosion payments for payments that otherwise would be base erosion payments through a conduit or intermediary*—(i) *Facts.* FP owns Property 1 with a fair market value of $95x, which FP intends to transfer to DC. A payment from DC to FP for Property 1 would be a base erosion payment. Corp A is a domestic corporation that is not a related party with respect to DC. As part of a plan with a principal purpose of avoiding a base erosion payment, FP enters into an arrangement with Corp A to transfer Property 1 to Corp A in exchange for $95x. Pursuant to the same plan, Corp A transfers Property 1 to DC in exchange for $100x. Property 1 is subject to the allowance for depreciation (or amortization in lieu of depreciation) in the hands of DC.

(ii) *Analysis.* The arrangement between FP, DC, and Corp A is deemed to result in a $95x base erosion payment under paragraph (b)(1) of this section because DC's payment to Corp A would have been a base erosion payment if paid to a foreign related party, and Corp A makes a corresponding payment to FP as part of the series of transactions that has as a principal purpose of avoiding a base erosion payment.

(3) *Example 2: Alternative transaction to base erosion payment*—(i) *Facts.* The facts are the same as in paragraph (c)(2)(i) of this section (the facts in *Example 1*), except that DC does not purchase Property 1 from FP or Corp A. Instead, DC purchases Property 2 from Corp B, a domestic corporation that is not a related party with respect to DC and that originally produced or acquired Property 2 for Corp B's own account. Property 2 is substantially similar to Property 1, and DC uses Property 2 in substantially the same manner that DC would have used Property 1.

(ii) *Analysis.* Paragraph (b)(1) of this section does not apply to the transaction between DC and Corp B because Corp B does not make a corresponding payment to or for the benefit of FP as part of a transaction, plan, or arrangement.

(4) *Example 3: Alternative financing source*—(i) *Facts.* On Date 1, FP loaned $200x to DC in exchange for Note A. DC pays or accrues interest annually on Note A, and the payment or accrual is a base erosion payment within the meaning of § 1.59A-3(b)(1)(i). On Date 2, DC borrows $200x from Bank, a corporation that is not a related party with respect to DC, in exchange for Note B. The terms of Note B are substantially similar to the terms of Note A. DC uses the proceeds from Note B to repay Note A.

(ii) *Analysis.* Paragraph (b)(1) of this section does not apply to the transaction between DC and Bank because Bank does not make a corresponding payment to or for the benefit of FP as part of the series of transactions.

(5) *Example 4: Alternative financing source that is a conduit*—(i) *Facts.* The facts are the same as in paragraph (c)(4)(i) of this section (the facts in *Example 3*) except that in addition, as part of the same plan or arrangement as the Note B transaction and with a principal purpose of avoiding a base erosion payment, FP deposits $250x with Bank. The difference between the interest rate paid by Bank to FP on FP's deposit and the interest rate paid by DC to Bank is less than one percentage point. The interest rate charged by Bank to DC would have differed absent the deposit by FP.

(ii) *Analysis.* The transactions between FP, DC, and Bank are deemed to result in a base erosion payment under paragraph (b)(1) of this section because DC's payment to Bank would have been a base erosion payment if paid to a foreign related party, and Bank makes a corresponding payment to FP as part of the series of transactions that has as a principal purpose of avoiding a base erosion payment. See Rev. Rul. 87-89, 1987-2 C.B. 195, Situation 3.

(6) *Example 5: Intermediary acquisition*—(i) *Facts.* FP owns all of the stock of DC1 and DC2, each domestic corporations. FP is a manufacturer of lawn equipment. DC1 is in the trade or business of renting equipment to unrelated third parties. DC2 is a dealer in property that capitalizes its purchases into inventory and recovers the amount through cost of goods sold. Before Date 1, in the ordinary course of DC1's business, DC1 acquired depreciable property from FP that DC1 in turn rented to unrelated third parties. DC1's purchases from FP were base erosion payments within the meaning of § 1.59A-3(b)(1)(ii). On Date 1, with a principal purpose of avoiding a base erosion payment, FP and DC2 reorganized their operations so that DC2 acquires the lawn equipment from FP and immediately thereafter, DC2 resells the lawn equipment to DC1.

(ii) *Analysis.* The transactions between FP, DC1, and DC2 are deemed to result in a base erosion payment under paragraph (b)(1) of this section because DC1's payment to DC2 would have been a base erosion payment if paid directly to FP, and DC2 makes a corresponding payment to FP as part of a series of transactions, plan, or arrangement that has a principal purpose of avoiding a base erosion payment from DC1 to FP.

(7) *Example 6: Offsetting transactions to increase the amount of deductions taken into account in the denominator of the base erosion percentage computation*—(i) *Facts.* With a principal purpose of increasing the deductions taken into account by DC for purposes of § 1.59A-2(e)(3)(i)(B), DC enters into a long position with respect to Asset with Financial Institution 1 and simultaneously enters into a short position with respect to Asset with Financial Institution 2. Financial Institution 1 and Financial Institution 2 are not related to DC and are not related to each other.

(ii) *Analysis.* Paragraph (b)(2) of this section applies to the transactions between DC and Financial Institution 1 and DC and Financial Institution 2. These transactions are not taken into account for purposes of § 1.59A-2(e)(3)(i)(B) because the transactions have a principal purpose of increasing the deductions taken into account for purposes of § 1.59A-2(e)(3)(i)(B).

(8) *Example 7: Ordinary course transactions that increase the amount of deductions taken into account in the denominator of the base erosion percentage computation*—(i) *Facts.* DC, a financial institution, enters into a long position with respect to stock in Corporation with Person 1 and later on the same day enters into a short position with respect to stock in Corporation with Person 2. Person 1 and Person 2 are not related to DC and are not related to each other. DC entered into the positions in the ordinary course of its business and did not have a principal purpose of increasing the deductions taken into account by DC for purposes of § 1.59A-2(e)(3)(i)(B).

(ii) *Analysis.* Paragraph (b)(2) of this section does not apply because the transactions between DC and Person 1 and Person 2 were not entered into with a principal purpose of increasing the deductions taken into account by DC for purposes of § 1.59A-2(e)(3)(i)(B).

(9) *Example 8: Transactions to avoid the application of rules applicable to banks and registered securities dealers*—(i) *Facts.* DC owns all of the stock of DC1 and Bank (an entity defined in section 581). DC, DC1, and Bank are members of an affiliated group of corporations within the meaning of section 1504(a) that elect to file a consolidated U.S. federal income tax return. With a principal purpose of avoiding the rules of § 1.59A-2(e)(2) or § 1.59A-5(c)(2), DC and DC1 form a new partnership (PRS). DC contributes all of its stock of Bank, and DC1 contributes cash, to PRS. DC, DC1, and Bank do not materially change their business operations following the formation of PRS.

(ii) *Analysis.* Paragraph (b)(3) of this section applies to transactions with respect to Bank because the transactions with respect to PRS were entered into with a principal purpose of avoiding the rules of § 1.59A-2(e)(2) or § 1.59A-5(c)(2). The contribution of Bank to a PRS is not taken into account, and Bank will be deemed to be part of the affiliated group including DC and DC1 for purposes of § 1.59A-2(e)(2) and § 1.59A-5(c)(2).

(10) *Example 9: Transactions that do not avoid the application of rules applicable to banks and registered securities dealers*—(i) *Facts.* The facts are the same as the facts of paragraph (c)(9)(i) of this section (the facts of Example 8), except that DC sells 90 percent of the stock of Bank to an unrelated party in exchange for cash.

(ii) *Analysis.* Paragraph (b)(3) of this section does not apply to DC's sale of the stock of Bank because the sale was not made with a principal purpose of avoiding the rules of § 1.59A-2(e)(2) or § 1.59A-5(c)(2). Bank will not be treated as part of the affiliated group including DC and DC1 for purposes of § 1.59A-2(e)(2) and § 1.59A-5(c)(2).

(11) *Example 10: Acquisition of depreciable property in a nonrecognition transaction*—(i) *Facts.* U, which is not a related party with respect to FP or DC, owns Property 1 with an adjusted basis of $50x and a fair market value of $100x. On Date 1, FP purchases property, including Property 1, from U in exchange for cash, and then FP contributes

Property 1 to DC in an exchange described in section 351. Following the exchange, DC's basis in Property 1 is $100x.

(ii) *Analysis.* Paragraph (b)(4) of this section does not apply to DC's acquisition of Property 1 because the purchase of Property 1 from U (first transaction) did not have a principal purpose of increasing DC's adjusted basis of Property 1 without increasing DC's base erosion tax benefits. The transaction is economically equivalent to an alternative transaction under which FP contributed $100x to DC and then DC purchased Property 1 from U. Further, the second sentence of paragraph (b)(4) of this section (providing that certain transactions are deemed to have a principal purpose of increasing the adjusted basis of property acquired in a second transaction) does not apply because FP purchased Property 1 from an unrelated party.

(12) *Example 11: Transactions between related parties with a principal purpose of increasing the adjusted basis of property*—(i) *Facts.* The facts are the same as paragraph (c)(11)(i) of this section (the facts in *Example 10*), except that U is related to FP and DC.

(ii) *Analysis.* Paragraph (b)(4) of this section applies to DC's acquisition of Property 1 because the transaction that increased the adjusted basis of Property 1 (the purchase of Property 1 from U) was between related parties, and within six months DC acquired Property 1 from FP in a specified nonrecognition transaction. Accordingly, the purchase of property from U (first transaction) is deemed to have a principal purpose of increasing the adjusted basis of Property 1 that DC acquires in the second transaction – the contribution (a transaction that qualifies as a specified nonrecognition transaction in part and would wholly qualify but for the application of paragraph (b)(4) of this section). Accordingly, the exception in § 1.59A-3(b)(3)(viii)(A) for specified nonrecognition transactions does not apply to the contribution of Property 1 to DC to the extent of the increased adjusted basis from the first transaction ($50x), and DC's depreciation deductions with respect to Property 1 will be base erosion tax benefits to the extent of the $50x increase in adjusted basis in Property 1. [Reg. § 1.59A-9.]

☐ [*T.D.* 9885, 12-2-2019 (*corrected* 2-18-2020). *Amended by T.D.* 9910, 10-8-2020.]

[Reg. § 1.59A-10]

§ 1.59A-10. Applicability date.—(a) *General applicability date.*—Sections 1.59A-1 through 1.59A-9, other than the provisions described in the first sentence of paragraph (b) of this section, apply to taxable years ending on or after December 17, 2018. However, taxpayers may apply these regulations in their entirety for taxable years beginning after December 31, 2017, and ending before December 17, 2018. In lieu of applying the regulations referred to in the first sentence of this paragraph, taxpayers may apply the provisions matching § § 1.59A-1 through 1.59A-9 from the Internal Revenue Bulletin (IRB) 2019-02 (*https://www.irs.gov/irb/2019-02_IRB*) in their entirety for all taxable years beginning after December 31, 2017 and ending on or before December 6, 2019.

(b) *Exception.*—Sections 1.59A-2(c)(2)(ii) and (c)(4) through (6), 1.59A-3(b)(3)(iii)(C), 1.59A-3(c)(5) and (6), and 1.59A-9(b)(4) apply to taxable years beginning on or after October 9, 2020, and § § 1.59A-7(c)(5)(v) and 1.59A-9(b)(5) and (6) apply to taxable years ending on or after December 2, 2019. Taxpayers may apply those regulations in their entirety for taxable years beginning after December 31, 2017, and before their applicability date, provided that, once applied, taxpayers must continue to apply them in their entirety for all subsequent taxable years. Alternatively, taxpayers may apply only § 1.59A-3(c)(5) and (6) for taxable years beginning after December 31, 2017, and before their applicability date, provided that, once applied, taxpayers must continue to apply § 1.59A-3(c)(5) and (6) in their entirety for all subsequent taxable years. [Reg. § 1.59A-10.]

☐ [*T.D.* 9885, 12-2-2019. *Amended by T.D.* 9910, 10-8-2020.]

[The next page is 24,001.]

COMPUTATION OF TAXABLE INCOME

Definition of Gross Income, Adjusted Gross Income, Taxable Income, Etc.

See p. 20,601 for regulations not amended to reflect law changes

[Reg. §1.61-1]

§1.61-1. Gross income.—(a) *General definition.*—Gross income means all income from whatever source derived, unless excluded by law. Gross income includes income realized in any form, whether in money, property, or services. Income may be realized, therefore, in the form of services, meals, accommodations, stock, or other property, as well as in cash. Section 61 lists the more common items of gross income for purposes of illustration. For purposes of further illustration, §1.61-14 mentions several miscellaneous items of gross income not listed specifically in section 61. Gross income, however, is not limited to the items so enumerated.

(b) *Cross references.*—Cross references to other provisions of the Code are to be found throughout the regulations under section 61. The purpose of these cross references is to direct attention to the more common items which are included in or excluded from gross income entirely, or treated in some special manner. To the extent that another section of the Code or of the regulations thereunder, provides specific treatment for any item of income, such other provision shall apply notwithstanding section 61 and the regulations thereunder. The cross references do not cover all possible items.

(1) For examples of items specifically included in gross income, see part II (section 71 and following), subchapter B, chapter 1 of the Code.

(2) For examples of items specifically excluded from gross income, see part III (section 101 and following), subchapter B, chapter 1 of the Code.

(3) For general rules as to the taxable year for which an item is to be included in gross income, see section 451 and the regulations thereunder. [Reg. §1.61-1.]

☐ [T.D. 6272, 11-25-57.]

[Reg. §1.61-2]

§1.61-2. Compensation for services, including fees, commissions, and similar items.—(a) *In general.*—(1) Wages, salaries, commissions paid salesmen, compensation for services on the basis of a percentage of profits, commissions on insurance premiums, tips, bonuses (including Christmas bonuses), termination or severance pay, rewards, jury fees, marriage fees and other contributions received by a clergyman for services, pay of persons in the military or naval forces of the United States, retired pay of employees, pensions, and retirement allowances are income to the recipients unless excluded by law. Several special rules apply to members of the Armed Forces, National Oceanic and Atmospheric Administration, and Public Health Service of the United States; see paragraph (b) of this section.

(2) The Internal Revenue Code provides special rules including the following items in gross income:

(i) Distributions from employees' trusts, see sections 72, 402, and 403, and the regulations thereunder;

(ii) Compensation for child's services (in child's gross income), see section 73 and the regulations thereunder;

(iii) Prizes and awards, see section 74 and the regulations thereunder.

(3) Similarly, the Code provides special rules excluding the following items from gross income in whole or in part:

(i) Gifts, see section 102 and the regulations thereunder;

(ii) Compensation for injuries or sickness, see section 104 and the regulations thereunder;

(iii) Amounts received under accident and health plans, see section 105 and the regulations thereunder;

(iv) Scholarship and fellowship grants, see section 117 and the regulations thereunder;

(v) Miscellaneous items, see section 122.

(b) *Members of the Armed Forces, National Oceanic and Atmospheric Administration, and Public Health Service.*—(1) Subsistence and uniform allowances granted commissioned officers, chief warrant officers, warrant officers, and enlisted personnel of the Armed Forces, National Oceanic and Atmospheric Administration, and Public Health Service of the United States, and amounts received by them as commutation of quarters, are excluded from gross income. Similarly, the value of quarters or subsistence furnished to such persons is excluded from gross income.

(2) For purposes of this section, quarters or subsistence includes the following allowances for expenses incurred after December 31, 1993, by members of the Armed Forces, members of the commissioned corps of the National Oceanic and Atmospheric Administra-

tion, and members of the commissioned corps of the Public Health Service, to the extent that the allowances are not otherwise excluded from gross income under another provision of the Internal Revenue Code: a dislocation allowance, authorized by 37 U.S.C. 407; a temporary lodging allowance, authorized by 37 U.S.C. 405; a temporary lodging expense, authorized by 37 U.S.C. 404a; and a move-in housing allowance, authorized by 37 U.S.C. 405. No deduction is allowed under this chapter for any expenses reimbursed by such excluded allowances. For the exclusion from gross income of—

(i) Disability pensions, see section 104(a)(4) and the regulations thereunder;

(ii) Miscellaneous items, see section 122.

(3) The per diem or actual expense allowance, the monetary allowance in lieu of transportation, and the mileage allowance received by members of the Armed Forces, National Oceanic and Atmospheric Administration, and the Public Health Service, while in a travel status or on temporary duty away from their permanent stations, are included in their gross income except to the extent excluded under the accountable plan provisions of §1.62-2.

(c) *Payment to charitable, etc., organization on behalf of person rendering services.*—The value of services is not includible in gross income when such services are rendered directly and gratuitously to an organization described in section 170(c). Where, however, pursuant to an agreement or understanding, services are rendered to a person for the benefit of an organization described in section 170(c) and an amount for such services is paid to such organization by the person to whom the services are rendered, the amount so paid constitutes income to the person performing the services.

(d) *Compensation paid other than in cash.*—(1) *In general.*—Except as otherwise provided in paragraph (d)(6)(i) of this section (relating to certain property transferred after June 30, 1969), if services are paid for in property, the fair market value of the property taken in payment must be included in income as compensation. If services are paid for in exchange for other services, the fair market value of such other services taken in payment must be included in income as compensation. If the services are rendered at a stipulated price, such price will be presumed to be the fair market value of the compensation received in the absence of evidence to the contrary. For special rules relating to certain options received as compensation, see §§1.61-15, 1.83-7, and section 421 and the regulations thereunder. For special rules relating to premiums paid by an employer for an annuity contract which is not subject to section 403(a), see section 403(c) and the regulations thereunder and §1.83-8(a). For special rules relating to contributions made to an employees' trust which is not exempt under section 501, see section 402(b) and the regulations thereunder and §1.83-8(a).

(2) *Property transferred to employee or independent contractor.*—(i) Except as otherwise provided in section 421 and the regulations thereunder and §1.61-15 (relating to stock options), and paragraph (d)(6)(i) of this section, if property is transferred by an employer to an employee or if property is transferred to an independent contractor, as compensation for services, for an amount less than its fair market value, then regardless of whether the transfer is in the form of a sale or exchange, the difference between the amount paid for the property and the amount of its fair market value at the time of the transfer is compensation and shall be included in the gross income of the employee or independent contractor. In computing the gain or loss from the subsequent sale of such property, its basis shall be the amount paid for the property increased by the amount of such difference included in gross income.

(ii)(A) *Cost of life insurance on the life of the employee.*—Generally, life insurance premiums paid by an employer on the life of his employee where the proceeds of such insurance are payable to the beneficiary of such employee are part of the gross income of the employee. However, the amount includible in the employee's gross income is determined with regard to the provisions of section 403 and the regulations thereunder in the case of an individual contract issued after December 31, 1962, or a group contract, which provides incidental life insurance protection and which satisfies the requirements of section 401(g) and §1.401-9, relating to the nontransferability of annuity contracts. For example, if an employee or independent contractor is the owner (as defined in §1.61-22(c)(1)) of a life insurance contract and the payments with regard to such contract are not split-dollar loans under §1.7872-15(b)(1), the employee or independent contractor must include in income the amount of any such payments by the employer or service recipient with respect to such contract during any year to the extent that the employee's or independent contractor's rights to the life insurance contract are substantially vested (within the meaning of §1.83-3(b)). This result is the same regardless of whether the employee or independent contractor has at all times been the owner of the life insurance contract or the contract previously has been owned by the employer or service recipient as part of a split-dollar life insurance arrangement (as defined in §1.61-22(b)(1) or (2)) and was transferred by the employer or service recipient to the employee or independent contractor under §1.61-22(g). For the special rules relating to the includibility in an employee's gross income of an amount equal to the cost of certain group-term life insurance on the employee's life which is carried directly or indirectly by his employer, see section 79 and the regulations thereunder. For special rules relating to the exclusion of contributions by an employer to accident and health plans for the employees, see section 106 and the regulations thereunder.

(B) *Cost of group-term life insurance on the life of an individual other than an employee.*—The cost (determined under paragraph (d)(2) of §1.79-3) of group-term life insurance on the life of an individual other than an employee (such as the spouse or dependent of the employee) provided in connection with the performance of services by the employee is includible in the gross income of the employee.

(3) *Meals and living quarters.*—The value of living quarters or meals which an employee receives in addition to his salary constitutes gross income unless they are furnished for the convenience of the employer and meet the conditions specified in section 119 and the regulations thereunder. For the treatment of rental value of parsonages or rental allowance paid to ministers, see section 107 and the regulations thereunder; for the treatment of statutory subsistence allowances received by police, see section 120 and the regulations thereunder.

(4) *Stock and notes transferred to employee or independent contractor.*—Except as otherwise provided by section 421 and the regulations thereunder and §1.61-15 (relating to stock options), and paragraph (d)(6)(i) of this section, if a corporation transfers its own stock to an employee or independent contractor as compensation for services, the fair market value of the stock at the time of transfer shall be included in the gross income of the employee or independent contractor. Notes or other evidences of indebtedness received in payment for services constitute income in the amount of their fair market value at the time of the transfer. A taxpayer receiving as compensation a note regarded as good for its face value at maturity, but not bearing interest, shall treat as income as of the time of receipt its fair discounted value computed at the prevailing rate. As payments are received on such a note, there shall be included in income that portion of each payment which represents the proportionate part of the discount originally taken on the entire note.

(5) *Property transferred on or before June 30, 1969, subject to restrictions.*—Notwithstanding paragraph (d)(1), (2), or (4) of this section, if any property is transferred after September 24, 1959, by an employer to an employee or independent contractor as compensation for services, and such property is subject to a restriction which has a significant effect on its value at the time of transfer, the rules of §1.421-6(d)(2) shall apply in determining the time and the amount of compensation to be included in the gross income of the employee or independent contractor. This (5) is also applicable to transfers subject to a restriction which has a significant effect on its value at the time of transfer and to which §1.83-8(b) (relating to transitional rules with respect to transfers of restricted property) applies. For special rules relating to options to purchase stock or other property which are issued as compensation for services, see §1.61-15 and section 421 and the regulations thereunder.

(6) *Certain property transferred, premiums paid, and contributions made in connection with the performance of services after June 30, 1969.*—(i) *Exception.*—Paragraph (d)(1), (2), (4), and (5) of this section and §1.61-15 do not apply to the transfer of property (as defined in §1.83-3(e)) after June 30, 1969, unless §1.83-8 (relating to the applicability of section 83 and transitional rules) applies. If section 83 applies to a transfer of property, and the property is not subject to a restriction that has a significant effect on the fair market value of such property, then the rules contained in paragraph (d)(1), (2), and (4) of this section and §1.61-15 shall also apply to such transfer to the extent such rules are not inconsistent with section 83.

(ii) *Cross references.*—For rules relating to premiums paid by an employer for an annuity contract which is not subject to section 403(a), see section 403(c) and the regulations thereunder. For rules relating to contributions made to an employees' trust which is not exempt under section 501(a), see section 402(b) and the regulations thereunder. [Reg. §1.61-2.]

□ [*T.D. 6272*, 11-25-57. *Amended by T.D. 6416*, 9-24-59; *T.D. 6696*, 12-11-63; *T.D. 6856*, 10-19-65; *T.D. 6888*, 7-5-66; *T.D. 7554*, 7-21-78; *T.D. 7623*, 5-14-79; *T.D. 8256*, 7-5-89; *T.D. 8607*, 8-4-95 *and T.D. 9092*, 9-11-2003.]

[Reg. §1.61-3]

§1.61-3. Gross income derived from business.—(a) *In general.*—In a manufacturing, merchandising, or mining business, "gross income" means the total sales, less the cost of goods sold, plus any income from investments and from incidental or outside operations or sources. Gross income is determined without subtraction of depletion allowances based on a percentage of income to the extent that it exceeds cost depletion which may be required to be included in the amount of inventoriable costs as provided in §1.471-11 and without subtraction of selling expenses, losses or other items not ordinarily used in computing costs of goods sold or amounts which are of a type for which a deduction would be disallowed under section 162(c), (f), or (g) in the case of a business expense. The cost of goods sold should be determined in accordance with the method of accounting consistently used by the taxpayer. Thus, for example, an amount cannot be taken into account in the computation of cost of goods sold any earlier than the taxable year in which economic performance occurs with respect to the amount (see §1.446-1(c)(1)(ii)).

(b) *State contracts.*—The profit from a contract with a State or political subdivision thereof must be included in gross income. If warrants are issued by a city, town, or other political subdivision of a State, and are accepted by the contractor in payment for public work done, the fair market value of such warrants should be returned as income. If, upon conversion of the warrants into cash, the contractor does not receive and cannot recover the full value of the warrants so returned, he may deduct any loss sustained from his gross income for the year in which the warrants are so converted. If, however, he realizes more than the value of the warrants so returned, he must include the excess in his gross income for the year in which realized. [Reg. §1.61-3.]

□ [*T.D. 6272*, 11-25-57. *Amended by T.D. 7207*, 10-3-72; *T.D. 7285*, 9-14-73 *and T.D. 8408*, 4-9-92.]

[Reg. §1.61-4]

§1.61-4. Gross income of farmers.—(a) *Farmers using the cash method of accounting.*—A farmer using the cash receipts and disbursements method of accounting shall include in his gross income for the taxable year—

(1) The amount of cash and the value of merchandise or other property received during the taxable year from the sale of livestock and produce which he raised,

(2) The profits from the sale of any livestock or other items which were purchased,

(3) All amounts received from breeding fees, fees from rent of teams, machinery, or land, and other incidental farm income,

(4) All subsidy and conservation payments received which must be considered as income, and

(5) Gross income from all other sources.

The profit from the sale of livestock or other items which were purchased is to be ascertained by deducting the cost from the sales price in the year in which the sale occurs, except that in the case of the sale of purchased animals held for draft, breeding, or dairy purposes, the profits shall be the amount of any excess of the sales price over the amount representing the difference between the cost and the depreciation allowed or allowable (determined in accordance with the rules applicable under section 1016(a) and the regulations thereunder). However, see section 162 and the regulations thereunder with respect of the computation of taxable income on other than the crop method where the cost of seeds or young plants purchased for further development and cultivation prior to the sale is involved. Crop shares (whether or not considered rent under State law) shall be included in gross income as of the year in which the crop shares are reduced to money or the equivalent of money. See section 263A for rules regarding costs that are required to be capitalized.

(b) *Farmers using an accrual method of accounting.*—A farmer using an accrual method of accounting must use inventories to determine his gross income. His gross income on an accrual method is determined by adding the total of the items described in subparagraphs (1) through (5) of this paragraph and subtracting therefrom the total of the items described in subparagraphs (6) and (7) of this paragraph. These items are as follows:

(1) The sales price of all livestock and other products held for sale and sold during the year;

(2) The inventory value of livestock and products on hand and not sold at the end of the year;

(3) All miscellaneous items of income, such as breeding fees, fees from the rent of teams, machinery, or land, or other incidental farm income;

(4) Any subsidy or conservation payments which must be considered as income;

(5) Gross income from all other sources;

(6) The inventory value of the livestock and products on hand and not sold at the beginning of the year; and

(7) The cost of any livestock or products purchased during the year (except livestock held for draft, dairy, or breeding purposes, unless included in inventory).

All livestock raised or purchased for sale shall be added in the inventory at their proper valuation determined in accordance with the method authorized and adopted for the purpose. Livestock acquired for draft, breeding, or dairy purposes and not for sale may be included in the inventory (see subparagraphs (2), (6), and (7) of this paragraph) instead of being treated as capital assets subject to depreciation, provided such practice is followed consistently from year to year by the taxpayer. When any livestock included in an inventory are sold, their cost must not be taken as an additional deduction in computing taxable income, because such deduction is reflected in the inventory. See the regulations under section 471. See section 263A for rules regarding costs that are required to be capitalized. Crop shares (whether or not considered rent under State law) shall be included in gross income as of the year in which the crop shares are reduced to money or the equivalent of money.

(c) *Special rules for certain receipts.*—In the case of the sale of machinery, farm equipment, or any other property (except stock in trade of the taxpayer, or property of a kind which would properly be included in the inventory of the taxpayer if on hand at the close of the taxable year, or property held by the taxpayer primarily for sale to customers in the ordinary course of his trade or business), any excess of the proceeds of the sale over the adjusted basis of such property shall be included in the taxpayer's gross income for the taxable year in which such sale is made. See, however, section 453 and the regulations thereunder for special rules relating to certain installment sales. If farm produce is exchanged for merchandise, groceries, or the like, the market value of the article received in exchange is to be included in gross income. Proceeds of insurance, such as hail or fire insurance on growing crops, should be included in gross income to the extent of the amount received in cash or its equivalent for the crop injured or destroyed. See section 451(d) for special rule relating to election to include crop insurance proceeds in income for taxable year following taxable year of destruction. For taxable years beginning after July 12, 1972, where a farmer is engaged in producing crops and the process of gathering and disposing of such crops is not completed within the taxable year in which such crops are planted, the income therefrom may, with the consent of the Commissioner (see section 446 and the regulations thereunder), be computed upon the crop method. For taxable years beginning on or before July 12, 1972, where a farmer is engaged in producing crops which take more than a year from the time of planting to the time of gathering and disposing, the income therefrom may, with the consent of the Commissioner (see section 446 and the regulations thereunder), be computed upon the crop method. In any case in which the crop method is used, the entire cost of producing the crop must be taken as a deduction for the year in which the gross income from the crop is realized, and not earlier.

(d) *Definition of "farm".*—As used in this section, the term "farm" embraces the farm in the ordinarily accepted sense, and includes stock, dairy, poultry, fruit, and truck farms; also plantations, ranches, and all land used for farming operations. All individuals, partnerships, or corporations that cultivate, operate, or manage farms for gain or profit, either as owners or tenants, are designated as farmers. For more detailed rules with respect to the determination of whether or not an individual is engaged in farming, see § 1.175-3. For rules applicable to persons cultivating or operating a farm for recreation or pleasure, see sections 162 and 165, and the regulations thereunder.

(e) *Cross references.*—(1) For election to include Commodity Credit Corporation loans as income, see section 77 and regulations thereunder.

(2) For definition of gross income derived from farming for purposes of limiting deductibility of soil and water conservation expenditures, see section 175 and regulations thereunder.

(3) For definition of gross income from farming in connection with declarations of estimated income tax, see section 6073 and regulations thereunder. [Reg. § 1.61-4.]

☐ [*T.D. 6272, 11-25-57. Amended by T.D. 7198, 7-12-72 and T.D. 8729, 8-21-97.*]

[Reg. § 1.61-5]

§ 1.61-5. Allocations by cooperative associations; per-unit retain certificates—tax treatment as to cooperatives and patrons.—(a) *In general.*—Amounts allocated on the basis of the business done with or for a patron by a cooperative association, whether or not entitled to tax treatment under section 522, in cash, merchandise, capital stock, revolving fund certificates, retain certificates, certificates of indebtedness, letters of advice or in some other manner disclosing to the patron the dollar amount allocated, shall be included in the computation of the gross income of such patron for the taxable year in which received to the extent prescribed in paragraph (b) of this section, regardless of whether the allocation is deemed, for the purpose of section 522, to be made at the close of a preceding taxable year of the cooperative association. The determination of the extent of taxability of such amounts is in no way dependent upon the method of accounting employed by the patron or upon the method, cash, accrual, or otherwise, upon which the taxable income of such patron is computed.

(b) *Extent of taxability.*—(1) Amounts allocated to a patron on a patronage basis by a cooperative association with respect to products marketed for such patron, or with respect to supplies, equipment, or services, the cost of which was deductible by the patron under section 162 or section 212, shall be included in the computation of the gross income of such patron, as ordinary income, to the following extent:

(i) If the allocation is in cash, the amount of cash received.

(ii) If the allocation is in merchandise, the amount of the fair market value of such merchandise at the time of receipt by the patron.

(iii) If the allocation is in the form of revolving fund certificates, retain certificates, certificates of indebtedness, letters of advice, or similar documents, the amount of the fair market value of such document at the time of its receipt by the patron. For the purposes of this subdivision, any document containing an unconditional promise to pay a fixed sum of money on demand or at a fixed or determinable time shall be considered to have a fair market value at the time of its receipt by the patron, unless it is clearly established to the contrary. However, for the purposes of this subdivision, any document which is payable only in the discretion of the cooperative association, or which is otherwise subject to conditions beyond the control of the patron, shall be considered not to have any fair market value at the time of its receipt by the patron, unless it is clearly established to the contrary.

(iv) If the allocation is in the form of capital stock, the amount of the fair market value, if any, of such capital stock at the time of its receipt by the patron.

(2) If any allocation to which subparagraph (1) of this paragraph applies is received in the form of a document of the type described in subparagraph (1) (iii) or (iv) of this paragraph and is redeemed in full or in part or is otherwise disposed of, there shall be included in the computation of the gross income of the patron, as ordinary income, in the year of redemption or other disposition, the excess of the amount realized on the redemption or other disposition over the amount previously included in the computation of gross income under such subparagraph.

(3)(i) Amounts which are allocated on a patronage basis by a cooperative association with respect to supplies, equipment, or services, the cost of which was not deductible by the patron under section 162 or section 212, are not includible in the computation of the gross income of such patron. However, in the case of such amounts which are allocated with respect to capital assets (as defined in section 1221) or property used in the trade or business within the meaning of section 1231, such amounts shall, to the extent set forth in subparagraph (1) of the paragraph, to be taken into account by such patron in determining the cost of the property to which the allocation relates. Notwithstanding the preceding sentence, to the extent that such amounts are in excess of the unrecovered cost of such property, and to the extent that such amounts relate to such property which the patron no longer owns, they shall be included in the computation of the gross income of such patron.

(ii) If any patronage dividend is allocated to the patron in the form of a document of the type described in subparagraph (1)(iii) or (iv) of this paragraph, and if such allocation is with respect to capital assets (as defined in section 1221) or property used in the trade or business within the meaning of section 1231, any amount realized on the redemption or other disposition of such document which is in excess of the amount which was taken into account upon the receipt of the document by the patron shall be taken into account by such patron in the year of redemption or other disposition as an adjustment to basis or as an inclusion in the computation of gross income, as the case may be.

Reg. § 1.61-5(b)(3)(ii)

(iii) Any adjustment to basis in respect of an amount to which subdivision (i) or (ii) of this subparagraph applies shall be made as of the first day of the taxable year in which such amount is received.

(iv) The application of the provisions of this subparagraph may be illustrated by the following examples:

Example (1). On July 1, 1959, P, a patron of a cooperative association, purchases a tractor for use in his farming business from such association for $2,200. The tractor has an estimated useful life of

five years and an estimated salvage value of $200. P files his income tax returns on a calendar year basis and claims depreciation on the tractor for the year 1959 of $200 pursuant to his use of the straight-line method at the rate of $400 per year. On July 1, 1960, the cooperative association allocates to P with respect to his purchase of the tractor a dividend of $300 in cash. P will reduce his depreciation allowance with respect to the tractor for 1960 (and subsequent taxable years) to $333.33, determined as follows:

Cost of tractor, July 1, 1959		$2,200.00
Less: Depreciation for 1959 (6 mos.)	$200	
Adjustment as of January 1, 1960, for cash patronage dividend	300	
Salvage value	200	700.00
Basis for depreciation for the remaining 4½ years of estimated life		1,500.00
Basis for depreciation divided by the 4½ years of remaining life		333.33

Example (2). Assume the same facts as in example (1), except that on July 1, 1960, the cooperative association allocates a dividend to P with respect to his purchase of the tractor in the form of a revolving fund certificate having a face amount of $300. The certificate is redeemable in cash at the discretion of the directors of the association and is subject to diminution by any future losses of the association, and has no fair market value when received by P. Since the certificate had no fair market value when received by P, no amount with respect to such certificate was taken into account by him in the year 1960. In 1965, P receives $300 cash from the association in full redemption of the certificate. Prior to 1965, he had

recovered through depreciation $2,000 of the cost of the tractor, leaving an unrecovered cost of $200 (the salvage value). For the year 1965, the redemption proceeds of $300 are applied against the unrecovered cost of $200, reducing the basis to zero, and the balance of the redemption proceeds, $100, is includible in the computation of P's gross income.

Example (3). Assume the same facts as in example (2), except that the certificate is redeemed in full on July 1, 1962. The full $300 received on redemption of the certificate will be applied against the unrecovered cost of the tractor as of January 1, 1962, computed as follows:

Cost of tractor, July 1, 1959		$2,200
Less: Depreciation for 1959 (6 mos.)	$200	
Depreciation for 1960	400	
Depreciation for 1961	400	1,000
Unrecovered cost on January 1, 1962		$1,200
Adjustment as of January 1, 1962 for proceeds of the redemption of the revolving fund certificate		300
Unrecovered cost on January 1, 1962, after adjustment		$900
Less: Salvage value		200
Basis for depreciation on January 1, 1962		$700

If P uses the tractor in his business until June 30, 1964, he would be entitled to the following depreciation allowances with respect to the tractor:

For 1962	$280	
For 1963	280	
For 1964 (6 mos.)	$140	$700
Balance to be depreciated		0

Example (4). Assume the same facts as in example (3), except that P sells the tractor in 1961. The entire $300 received in 1962 in redemption of the revolving fund certificate is includible in the computation of P's gross income for the year 1962.

(c) *Special rule.*—If, for any taxable year ending before December 3, 1959, a taxpayer treated any patronage dividend received in the form of a document described in paragraph (b)(1)(iii) or (iv) of this section in accordance with the regulations then applicable (whether such dividend is subject to paragraph (b)(1) or (3) of this section), such taxpayer is not required to change the treatment of such patronage dividends for any such prior taxable year. On the other hand, the taxpayer may, if he so desires, amend his income tax returns to treat the receipt of such patronage dividend in accordance with the provisions of this section, but no provision in this paragraph shall be construed as extending the period of limitations within which a claim for credit or refund may be filed under section 6511.

(d) *Per-unit retain certificates; tax treatment of cooperative associations; distribution and reinvestment alternative.*—(1)(i) In the case of a taxable year to which this paragraph applies to a cooperative association, such association shall, in computing the amount paid or returned to a patron with respect to products marketed for such patron, take into account the stated dollar amount of any per-unit retain certificate (as defined in paragraph (g) of this section)—

(a) Which is issued during the payment period for such year (as defined in subparagraph (3) of this paragraph) with respect to such products,

(b) With respect to which the patron is a qualifying patron (as defined in subparagraph (2) of this paragraph), and

(c) Which clearly states the fact that the patron has agreed to treat the stated dollar amount thereof as representing a cash distribution to him which he has reinvested in the cooperative association.

(ii) No amount shall be taken into account by a cooperative association by reason of the issuance of a per-unit retain certificate to a patron who was not a qualifying patron with respect to such certificate. However, any amount paid in redemption of a per-unit retain certificate which was issued to a patron who was not a qualifying patron with respect to such certificate shall be taken into

account by the cooperative in the year of redemption, as an amount paid or returned to such patron with respect to products marketed for him. This subdivision shall apply only to per-unit retain certificates issued with respect to taxable years of the cooperative association to which this paragraph applied to the association (that is, taxable years with respect to which per-unit retain certificates were issued to one or more patrons who are qualifying patrons).

(2)(i) A patron shall be considered to be a "qualifying patron" with respect to a per-unit retain certificate if there is in effect an agreement between the cooperative association and such patron which clearly provides that such patron agrees to treat the stated dollar amounts of all per-unit retain certificates issued to him by the association as representing cash distributions which he has constructively received and which he has, of his own choice, reinvested in the cooperative association. Such an agreement may be included in a by-law of the cooperative which is adopted prior to the time the products to which the per-unit retain certificates relate are marketed. However, except where there is in effect a "written agreement" described in subdivision (ii) of this subparagraph, a patron shall not be considered to be a "qualifying patron" with respect to a per-unit retain certificate if it has been established by a determination of the Tax Court of the United States, or any other court of competent jurisdiction, which has become final, that the stated dollar amount of such certificate, or of a similar certificate issued under similar circumstances, to such patron or any other patron by the cooperative association, is not required to be included (as ordinary income) in the gross income of such patron, or such other patron, for the taxable year of the patron in which received.

(ii) The "written agreement" referred to in subdivision (i) of this subparagraph is an agreement in writing, signed by the patron, on file with the cooperative association, and revocable as provided in this subdivision. Unless such an agreement specifically provides to the contrary, it shall be effective for per-unit retain certificates issued with respect to the taxable year of the cooperative association in which the agreement is received by the association, and, unless revoked, for per-unit retain certificates issued with respect to all subsequent taxable years. A "written agreement" must be revocable by the patron at any time after the close of the taxable year in which it is made. To be effective, a revocation must be in writing, signed by the patron, and furnished to the cooperative association. A revocation shall be effective only for per-unit retain certificates issued with respect to taxable years of the cooperative association following the taxable year in which it is furnished to the association. Notwithstanding the preceding sentence, a revocation shall not be effective for per-unit retain certificates issued with respect to products marketed for the patron under a pooling arrangement in which such patron participated before such revocation. The following is an example of an agreement which would meet the requirements of this subparagraph: I agree that, for purposes of determining the amount I have received from this cooperative in payment for my goods, I shall treat the face amount of any per-unit retain certificates issued to me on and after . . . . as representing a cash distribution which I have constructively received and which I have reinvested in the cooperative.

(3) For purposes of this paragraph and paragraph (e) of this section, the payment period for any taxable year of the cooperative is the period beginning with the first day of such taxable year and ending with the 15th day of the 9th month following the close of such year.

(4) This paragraph shall apply to any taxable year of a cooperative association if, with respect to such taxable year, the association has issued per-unit retain certificates to one or more of its patrons who are qualifying patrons with respect to such certificates within the meaning of subparagraph (2) of this paragraph.

(e) *Tax treatment of cooperative association; taxable years for which paragraph (d) does not apply.*—(1) In the case of a taxable year to which paragraph (d) of this section does not apply to a cooperative association, such association shall, in computing the amount paid or returned to a patron with respect to products marketed for such patron, take into account the fair market value (at the time of issue) of any per-unit retain certificates which are issued by the association with respect to such products during the payment period for such taxable year.

(2) An amount paid in redemption of a per-unit retain certificate issued with respect to a taxable year of the cooperative association for which paragraph (d) of this section did not apply to the association, shall, to the extent such amount exceeds the fair market value of the certificate at the time of its issue, be taken into account by the association in the year of redemption, as an amount paid or returned to a patron with respect to products marketed for such patron.

(3) For purposes of this paragraph and paragraph (f)(2) of this section, any per-unit retain certificate containing an unconditional promise to pay a fixed sum of money on demand or at a fixed or determinable time shall be considered to have a fair market value at the time of its issue, unless it is clearly established to the contrary. On the other hand, any per-unit retain certificate (other than capital stock) which is redeemable only in the discretion of the cooperative association, or which is otherwise subject to conditions beyond the control of the patron, shall be considered not to have any fair market value at the time of its issue, unless it is clearly established to the contrary.

(f) *Tax treatment of patron.*—(1) The following rules apply for purposes of computing the amount includible in gross income with respect to a per-unit retain certificate which was issued to a patron by a cooperative association with respect to a taxable year of such association for which paragraph (d) of this section applies.

(i) If the patron is a qualifying patron with respect to such certificate (within the meaning of paragraph (d)(2) of this section), he shall, in accordance with his agreement, include (as ordinary income) the stated dollar amount of the certificate in gross income for his taxable year in which the certificate is received by him.

(ii) If the patron is not a qualifying patron with respect to such certificate, no amount is includible in gross income on the receipt of the certificate; however, any gain on the redemption, sale, or other disposition of such certificate shall, to the extent of the stated dollar amount thereof, be considered as gain from the sale or exchange of property which is not a capital asset.

(2) The amount of the fair market value of a per-unit retain certificate which is issued to a patron by a cooperative association with respect to a taxable year of the association for which paragraph (d) of this section does not apply shall be included, as ordinary income, in the gross income of the patron for the taxable year in which the certificate is received. Any gain on the redemption, sale, or other disposition of such a per-unit retain certificate shall, to the extent its stated dollar amount exceeds its fair market value at the time of issue, be treated as gain on the redemption, sale, or other disposition of property which is not a capital asset.

(g) *"Per-unit retain certificate" defined.*—For purposes of paragraphs (d), (e), and (f) of this section, the term "per-unit retain certificate" means any capital stock, revolving fund certificate, retain certificate, certificate of indebtedness, letter of advice, or other written notice—

(1) Which is issued to a patron with respect to products marketed for such patron;

(2) Which discloses to the patron the stated dollar amount allocated to him on the books of the cooperative association; and

(3) The stated dollar amount of which is fixed without reference to net earnings.

(h) *Effective date.*—This section shall not apply to any amount the tax treatment of which is prescribed in section 1385 and § 1.1385-1. Paragraphs (d), (e), and (f) of this section shall apply to per-unit retain certificates as defined in paragraph (g) of this section issued by a cooperative association during taxable years of the association beginning after April 30, 1966, with respect to products marketed for patrons during such years. [Reg. § 1.61-5.]

☐ [T.D. 6272, 11-25-57. *Amended by T.D. 6428*, 12-2-59; *T.D. 6643*, 4-1-63; *and T.D. 6855*, 10-14-65.]

[Reg. § 1.61-6]

§ 1.61-6. Gains derived from dealings in property.—(a) *In general.*—Gain realized on the sale or exchange of property is included in gross income, unless excluded by law. For this purpose property includes tangible items, such as a building, and intangible items, such as goodwill. Generally, the gain is the excess of the amount realized over the unrecovered cost or other basis for the property sold or exchanged. The specific rules for computing the amount of gain or loss are contained in section 1001 and the regulations thereunder. When a part of a larger property is sold, the cost or other basis of the entire property shall be equitably apportioned among the several parts, and the gain realized or loss sustained on the part of the entire property sold is the difference between the selling price and the cost or other basis allocated to such part. The sale of each part is treated as a separate transaction and gain or loss shall be computed separately on each part. Thus, gain or loss shall be determined at the time of sale of each part and not deferred until the entire property has been disposed of. This rule may be illustrated by the following examples:

Example (1). A, a dealer in real estate, acquires a 10-acre tract for $10,000, which he divides into 20 lots. The $10,000 cost must be equitably apportioned among the lots so that on the sale of each A can determine his taxable gain or deductible loss.

Example (2). B purchases for $25,000 property consisting of a used car lot and adjoining filling station. At the time, the fair market value of the filling station is $15,000 and the fair market value of the used car lot is $10,000. Five years later B sells the filling station for $20,000 at a time when $2,000 has been properly allowed as depreciation thereon. B's gain on this sale is $7,000, since $7,000 is the amount by which the selling price of the filling station exceeds the portion of the cost equitably allocable to the filling station at the time of purchase reduced by the depreciation properly allowed.

(b) *Nontaxable exchanges.*—Certain realized gains or losses on the sale or exchange of property are not "recognized", that is, are not included in or deducted from gross income at the time the transaction occurs. Gain or loss from such sales or exchanges is generally recognized at some later time. Examples of such sales or exchanges are the following:

(1) Certain formations, reorganizations, and liquidations of corporations, see sections 331, 333, 337, 351, 354, 355, and 361;

(2) Certain formations and distributions of partnerships, see sections 721 and 731;

(3) Exchange of certain property held for productive use or investment for property of like kind, see section 1031;

(4) A corporation's exchange of its stock for property, see section 1032;

(5) Certain involuntary conversions of property if replaced, see section 1033;

(6) Sale or exchange of residence if replaced, see section 1034;

(7) Certain exchanges of insurance policies and annuity contracts, see section 1035; and

(8) Certain exchanges of stock for stock in the same corporation, see section 1036.

(c) *Character of recognized gain.*—Under subchapter P, chapter 1 of the Code, relating to capital gains and losses, certain gains derived from dealings in property are treated specially, and under certain circumstances the maximum rate of tax on such gains is 25 percent, as provided in section 1201. Generally, the property subject to this treatment is a "capital asset" or treated as a "capital asset". For definition of such assets, see sections 1221 and 1231, and the regulations thereunder. For some of the rules either granting or denying this special treatment, see the following sections and the regulations thereunder:

(1) Transactions between partner and partnership, section 707;

(2) Sale or exchange of property used in the trade or business and involuntary conversions, section 1231;

(3) Payment of bonds and other evidences of indebtedness, section 1232;

(4) Gains and losses from short sales, section 1233;

(5) Options to buy or sell, section 1234;

(6) Sale or exchange of patents, section 1235;

(7) Securities sold by dealers in securities, section 1236;

(8) Real property subdivided for sale, section 1237;

(9) Amortization in excess of depreciation, section 1238;

(10) Gain from sale for certain property between spouses or between an individual and a controlled corporation, section 1239;

(11) Taxability to employee of termination payments, section 1240. [Reg. § 1.61-6.]

☐ [T.D. 6272, 11-25-57.]

[Reg. §1.61-7]

§1.61-7. Interest.—(a) *In general.*—As a general rule, interest received by or credited to the taxpayer constitutes gross income and is fully taxable. Interest income includes interest on savings or other bank deposits; interest on coupon bonds; interest on an open account, a promissory note, a mortgage, or a corporate bond or debenture; the interest portion of a condemnation award; usurious interest (unless by State law it is automatically converted to a payment on the principal); interest on legacies; interest on life insurance proceeds held under an agreement to pay interest thereon; and interest on refunds of Federal taxes. For rules determining the taxable year in which interest, including interest accrued or constructively received, is included in gross income, see section 451 and the regulations thereunder. For the inclusion of interest in income for the purpose of the retirement income credit, see section 37 and the regulations thereunder. For credit of tax withheld at source on interest on tax-free covenant bonds, see section 32 and the regulations thereunder. For rules relating to interest on certain deferred payments, see section 483 and the regulations thereunder.

(b) *Interest on Government obligations.*—(1) *Wholly tax-exempt interest.*—Interest upon the obligations of a State, Territory, or a possession of the United States, or any political subdivision of any of the foregoing, or of the District of Columbia, is wholly exempt from tax. Interest on certain United States obligations issued before March 1, 1941, is exempt from tax to the extent provided in the acts of Congress authorizing the various issues. See section 103 and the regulations thereunder.

(2) *Partially tax-exempt interest.*—Interest earned on certain United States obligations is partly tax exempt and partly taxable. For example, the interest on United States Treasury bonds issued before March 1, 1941, to the extent that the principal of such bonds exceeds $5,000, is exempt from normal tax but is subject to surtax. See sections 35 and 103, and the regulations thereunder.

(3) *Fully taxable interest.*—In general, interest on United States obligations issued on or after March 1, 1941, and obligations issued by any agency or instrumentality of the United States after that date, is fully taxable; but see section 103 and the regulations thereunder. A taxpayer using the cash receipts and disbursements method of accounting who owns United States savings bonds issued at a discount has an election as to when he will report the interest; see section 454 and the regulations thereunder.

(c) *Obligations bought at a discount; bonds bought when interest defaulted or accrued.*—When notes, bonds, or other certificates of indebtedness are issued by a corporation or the Government at a discount and are later redeemed by the debtor at the face amount, the original discount is interest, except as otherwise provided by law. See also paragraph (b) of this section for the rules relating to Government bonds. If a taxpayer purchases bonds when interest has been defaulted or when the interest has accrued but has not been paid, any interest which is in arrears but has accrued at the time of purchase is not income and is not taxable as interest if subsequently paid. Such payments are returns of capital which reduce the remaining cost basis. Interest which accrues after the date of purchase, however, is taxable interest income for the year in which received or accrued (depending on the method of accounting used by the taxpayer).

(d) *Bonds sold between interest dates; amounts received in excess of original issue discount; interest on life insurance.*—When bonds are sold between interest dates, part of the sales price represents interest accrued to the date of the sale and must be reported as interest income. Amounts received in excess of the original issue discount upon the retirement or sale of a bond or other evidence of indebtedness may under some circumstances constitute capital gain instead of ordinary income. See section 1232 and the regulations thereunder. Interest payments on amounts payable as employees' death benefits

(whether or not section 101(b) applies thereto) and on the proceeds of life insurance policies payable by reason of the insured's death constitute gross income under some circumstances. See section 101 and the regulations thereunder for details. Where accrued interest on unwithdrawn insurance policy dividends is credited annually and is subject to withdrawal annually by the taxpayer, such interest credits constitute gross income to such taxpayer as of the year of credit. However, if under the terms of the insurance policy the interest on unwithdrawn policy dividends is subject to withdrawal only on the anniversary date of the policy (or some other date specified therein), then such interest shall constitute gross income to the taxpayer for the taxable year in which such anniversary date (or other specified date) falls. [Reg. § 1.61-7.]

☐ [T.D. 6272, 11-25-57. *Amended by T.D. 6723, 4-20-64; and T.D. 6873, 1-24-66.*]

[Reg. §1.61-8]

§1.61-8. Rents and royalties.—(a) *In general.*—Gross income includes rentals received or accrued for the occupancy of real estate or the use of personal property. For the inclusion of rents in income for the purpose of the retirement income credit, see section 37 and the regulations thereunder. Gross income includes royalties. Royalties may be received from books, stories, plays, copyrights, trademarks, formulas, patents, and from the exploitation of natural resources, such as coal, gas, oil, copper, or timber. Payments received as a result of the transfer of patent rights may under some circumstances constitute capital gain instead of ordinary income. See section 1235 and the regulations thereunder. For special rules for certain income from natural resources, see subchapter I (611 and following), chapter 1 of the Code, and the regulations thereunder.

(b) *Advance rentals; cancellation payments.*—Except as provided in section 467 and the regulations thereunder, and except as otherwise provided by the Commissioner in published guidance (see §601.601(d)(2) of this chapter), gross income includes advance rentals, which must be included in income for the year of receipt regardless of the period covered or the method of accounting employed by the taxpayer. An amount received by a lessor from a lessee for cancelling a lease constitutes gross income for the year in which it is received, since it is essentially a substitute for rental payments. As to amounts received by a lessee for the cancellation of a lease, see section 1241 and the regulations thereunder.

(c) *Expenditures by lessee.*—As a general rule, if a lessee pays any of the expenses of his lessor such payments are additional rental income of the lessor. If a lessee places improvements on real estate which constitute, in whole or in part, a substitute for rent, such improvements constitute rental income to the lessor. Whether or not improvements made by a lessee result in rental income to the lessor in a particular case depends upon the intention of the parties, which may be indicated either by the terms of the lease or by the surrounding circumstances. For the exclusion from gross income of income (other than rent) derived by a lessor of real property on the termination of a lease, representing the value of such property attributable to buildings erected or other improvements made by a lessee, see section 109 and the regulations thereunder. For the exclusion from gross income of a lessor corporation of certain of its income taxes on rental income paid by a lessee corporation under a lease entered into before January 1, 1954, see section 110 and the regulations thereunder. [Reg. § 1.61-8.]

☐ [T.D. 6272, 11-25-57. *Amended by T.D. 8820, 5-17-99 and T.D. 9135, 7-7-2004.*]

[Reg. §1.61-9]

§1.61-9. Dividends.—(a) *In general.*—Except as otherwise specifically provided, dividends are included in gross income under sections 61 and 301. For the principal rules with respect to dividends includible in gross income, see section 316 and the regulations thereunder. As to distributions made or deemed to be made by regulated investment companies, see sections 851 through 855, and the regulations thereunder. As to distributions made by real estate investment trusts, see sections 856 through 858, and the regulations thereunder. See section 116 for the exclusion from gross income of $100 ($50 for dividends received in taxable years beginning before January 1, 1964) of dividends received by an individual, except those from certain corporations. Furthermore, dividends may give rise to a credit against tax under section 34, relating to dividends received by individuals (for dividends received on or before December 31, 1964), and under section 37, relating to retirement income.

(b) *Dividends in kind; stock dividends; stock redemptions.*—Gross income includes dividends in property other than cash, as well as cash dividends. For amounts to be included in gross income when distributions of property are made, see section 301 and the regulations thereunder. A distribution of stock, or rights to acquire stock, in the corporation making the distribution is not a dividend except under the circumstances described in section 305(b). However, the term "dividend" includes a distribution of stock, or rights to acquire stock, in a corporation other than the corporation making the distribution. For determining when distributions in complete liquidation shall be treated as dividends, see section 333 and the regulations thereunder. For rules determining when amounts received in exchanges under section 354 or exchanges and distributions under section 355 shall be treated as dividends, see section 356 and the regulations thereunder.

(c) *Dividends on stock sold.*—When stock is sold, and a dividend is both declared and paid after the sale, such dividend is not gross income to the seller. When stock is sold after the declaration of a dividend and after the date as of which the seller becomes entitled to the dividend, the dividend ordinarily is income to the seller. When stock is sold between the time of declaration and the time of payment of the dividend, and the sale takes place at such time that the purchaser becomes entitled to the dividend, the dividend ordinarily is income to him. The fact that the purchaser may have included the amount of the dividend in his purchase price in contemplation of receiving the dividend does not exempt him from tax. Nor can the purchaser deduct the added amount he advanced to the seller in anticipation of the dividend. That added amount is merely part of the purchase price of the stock. In some cases, however, the purchaser may be considered to be the recipient of the dividend even though he has not received the legal title to the stock itself and does not himself receive the dividend. For example, if the seller retains the legal title to the stock as trustee solely for the purpose of securing the payment of the purchase price, with the understanding that he is to apply the dividends received from time to time in reduction of the purchase price, the dividends are considered to be income to the purchaser. [Reg. § 1.61-9.]

☐ [*T.D. 6272, 11-25-57. Amended by T.D. 6598, 4-25-62; and T.D. 6777, 12-15-64.*]

[Reg. § 1.61-10]

§ 1.61-10. Alimony and separate maintenance payments; annuities; income from life insurance and endowment contracts.—(a) *In general.*—Alimony and separate maintenance payments, annuities, and income from life insurance and endowment contracts in general constitute gross income, unless excluded by law. Annuities paid by religious, charitable, and educational corporations are generally taxable to the same extent as other annuities. An annuity charged upon devised land is taxable to the donee-annuitant to the extent that it becomes payable out of the rents or other income of the land, whether or not it is a charge upon the income of the land.

(b) *Cross references.*—For the detailed rules relating to—

(1) Alimony and separate maintenance payments, see section 71 and the regulations thereunder;

(2) Annuities, certain proceeds of endowment and life insurance contracts, see section 72 and the regulations thereunder;

(3) Life insurance proceeds paid by reason of death of insured, employees' death benefits, see section 101 and the regulations thereunder;

(4) Annuities paid by employees' trusts, see section 402 and the regulations thereunder;

(5) Annuities purchased for employee by employer, see section 403 and the regulations thereunder. [Reg. § 1.61-10.]

☐ [*T.D. 6272, 11-25-57.*]

[Reg. § 1.61-11]

§ 1.61-11. Pensions.—(a) *In general.*—Pensions and retirement allowances paid either by the Government or by private persons constitute gross income unless excluded by law. Usually, where the taxpayer did not contribute to the cost of a pension and was not taxable on his employer's contributions, the full amount of the pension is to be included in his gross income. But see sections 72, 402, and 403, and the regulations thereunder. When amounts are received from other types of pensions, a portion of the payment may be excluded from gross income. Under some circumstances, amounts distributed from a pension plan in excess of the employee's contributions may constitute *long-term capital gain*, rather than ordinary income.

(b) *Cross references.*—For the inclusion of pensions in income for the purpose of the retirement income credit, see section 37 and the regulations thereunder. Detailed rules concerning the extent to which pensions and retirement allowances are to be included in or excluded from gross income are contained in other sections of the Code and the regulations thereunder. Amounts received as pensions or annuities under the Social Security Act (42 U.S.C. ch. 7) or the Railroad Retirement Act (45 U.S.C. ch. 9) are excluded from gross income. For

other partial and total exclusions from gross income, see the following:

(1) Annuities in general, section 72 and the regulations thereunder;

(2) Employees' annuities, sections 402 and 403 and the regulations thereunder;

(3) References to other acts of Congress exempting veterans' pensions and railroad retirement annuities and pensions, section 122. [Reg. § 1.61-11.]

☐ [*T.D. 6272, 11-25-57. Amended by T.D. 6598, 4-25-62; and T.D. 6777, 12-15-64.*]

[Reg. § 1.61-12]

§ 1.61-12. Income from discharge of indebtedness.—(a) *In general.*—The discharge of indebtedness, in whole or in part, may result in the realization of income. If, for example, an individual performs services for a creditor, who in consideration thereof cancels the debt, the debtor realizes income in the amount of the debt as compensation for his services. A taxpayer may realize income by the payment or purchase of his obligations at less than their face value. In general, if a shareholder in a corporation which is indebted to him gratuitously forgives the debt, the transaction amounts to a contribution to the capital of the corporation to the extent of the principal of the debt.

(b) *Proceedings under Bankruptcy Act.*—(1) Income is not realized by a taxpayer by virtue of the discharge, under section 14 of the Bankruptcy Act (11 U.S.C. 32), of his indebtedness as the result of an adjudication in bankruptcy, or by virtue of an agreement among his creditors not consummated under any provision of the Bankruptcy Act, if immediately thereafter the taxpayer's liabilities exceed the value of his assets. Furthermore, unless one of the principal purposes of seeking a confirmation under the Bankruptcy Act is the avoidance of income tax, income is not realized by a taxpayer in the case of a cancellation or reduction of his indebtedness under—

(i) A plan of a corporate reorganization confirmed under Chapter X of the Bankruptcy Act (11 U.S.C., ch. 10);

(ii) An "arrangement" or a "real property arrangement" confirmed under Chapter XI or XII, respectively, of the Bankruptcy Act (11 U.S.C., ch. 11, 12); or

(iii) A "wage earner's plan" confirmed under Chapter XIII of the Bankruptcy Act (11 U.S.C., ch. 13).

(2) For adjustment of basis of certain property in the case of cancellation or reduction of indebtedness resulting from a proceeding under the Bankruptcy Act, see the regulations under section 1016.

(c) *Issuance and repurchase of debt instruments.*—(1) *Issuance.*—An issuer does not realize gain or loss upon the issuance of a debt instrument. For rules relating to an issuer's interest deduction for a debt instrument issued with bond issuance premium, see § 1.163-13.

(2) *Repurchase.*—(i) *In general.*—An issuer does not realize gain or loss upon the repurchase of a debt instrument. However, if a debt instrument provides for payments denominated in, or determined by reference to, a nonfunctional currency, an issuer may realize a currency gain or loss upon the repurchase of the instrument. See section 988 and the regulations thereunder. For purposes of this paragraph (c)(2), the term *repurchase* includes the retirement of a debt instrument, the conversion of a debt instrument into stock of the issuer, and the exchange (including an exchange under section 1001) of a newly issued debt instrument for an existing debt instrument.

(ii) *Repurchase at a discount.*—An issuer realizes income from the discharge of indebtedness upon the repurchase of a debt instrument for an amount less than its adjusted issue price (within the meaning of § 1.1275-1(b)). The amount of discharge of indebtedness income is equal to the excess of the adjusted issue price over the repurchase price. See section 108 and the regulations thereunder for additional rules relating to income from discharge of indebtedness. For example, to determine the repurchase price of a debt instrument that is repurchased through the issuance of a new debt instrument, see section 108(e)(10).

(iii) *Repurchase at a premium.*—An issuer may be entitled to a repurchase premium deduction upon the repurchase of a debt instrument for an amount greater than its adjusted issue price (within the meaning of § 1.1275-1(b)). See § 1.163-7(c) for the treatment of repurchase premium.

(iv) *Effective date.*—This paragraph (c)(2) applies to debt instruments repurchased on or after March 2, 1998.

(d) *Cross references.*—For exclusion from gross income of—

(1) Income from discharge of indebtedness in certain cases, see sections 108 and 1017, and regulations thereunder;

(2) Forgiveness of Government payments to encourage exploration, development, and mining for defense purposes, see section 621 and regulations thereunder.

(e) *Cross reference.*—For rules relating to the treatment of liabilities on the sale or other disposition of encumbered property, see § 1.1001-2. [Reg. § 1.61-12.]

□ [*T.D.* 6272, 11-25-57. *Amended by T.D.* 6653, 5-22-63; *T.D.* 6984, 12-23-68; *T.D.* 7741, 12-11-80 *and T.D.* 8746, 12-30-97.]

[Reg. § 1.61-13]

§ 1.61-13. Distributive share of partnership gross income; income in respect of a decedent; income from an interest in an estate or trust.—(a) *In general.*—A partner's distributive share of patnership gross income (under section 702(c)) constitutes gross income to him. Income in respect of a decedent (under section 691) constitutes gross income to the recipient. Income from an interest in an estate or trust constitutes gross income under the detailed rules of part I (section 641 and following), subchapter J, chapter 1 of the Code. In many cases, these sections also determine who is to include in his gross income the income from an estate or trust.

(b) *Creation of sinking fund by corporation.*—If a corporation, for the sole purpose of securing the payment of its bonds or other indebtedness, places property in trust or sets aside certain amounts in a sinking fund under the control of a trustee who may be authorized to invest and reinvest such sums from time to time, the property or fund thus set aside by the corporation and held by the trustee is an asset of the corporation, and any gain arising therefrom is income of the corporation and shall be included as such in its gross income. [Reg. § 1.61-13.]

□ [*T.D.* 6272, 11-25-57.]

[Reg. § 1.61-14]

§ 1.61-14. Miscellaneous items of gross income.—(a) *In general.*—In addition to the items enumerated in section 61(a), there are many other kinds of gross income. For example, punitive damages such as treble damages under the antitrust laws and exemplary damages for fraud are gross income. Another person's payment of the taxpayer's income taxes constitutes gross income to the taxpayer unless excluded by law. Illegal gains constitute gross income. Treasure trove, to the extent of its value in United States currency, constitutes gross income for the taxable year in which it is reduced to undisputed possession.

(b) *Cross references.*—(1) Prizes and awards, see section 74 and regulations thereunder;

(2) Damages for personal injury or sickness, see section 104 and the regulations thereunder;

(3) Income taxes paid by lessee corporation, see section 110 and regulations thereunder;

(4) Scholarships and fellowship grants, see section 117 and regulations thereunder;

(5) Miscellaneous exemptions under other Acts of Congress, see section 122;

(6) Tax-free covenant bonds, see section 1451 and regulations thereunder.

(7) Notional principal contracts, see § 1.446-3. [Reg. § 1.61-14.]

□ [*T.D.* 6272, 11-25-57. *Amended by T.D.* 6856, 10-19-65 *and T.D.* 8491, 10-8-93.]

[Reg. § 1.61-15]

§ 1.61-15. Options received as payment of income.—(a) *In general.*—Except as otherwise provided in § 1.61-2(d)(6)(i) (relating to certain restricted property transferred after June 30, 1969), if any person receives an option in payment of an amount constituting compensation of such person (or any other person), such option is subject to the rules contained in § 1.421-6 for purposes of determining when income is realized in connection with such option and the amount of such income. In this regard, the rules of § 1.421-6 apply to an option received in payment of an amount constituting compensation regardless of the form of the transaction. Thus, the rules of § 1.421-6 apply to an option transferred for less than its fair market value in a transaction taking the form of a sale or exchange if the difference between the amount paid for the option and its fair market value at the time of transfer is the payment of an amount constituting compensation of the transferee or any other person. This section, for example, makes the rules of § 1.421-6 applicable to options granted in *whole or partial payment for services of an independent contractor.* If an amount money or property is paid for an option to which this paragraph applies, then the amount paid shall be part of the basis of such option.

(b) *Options to which paragraph (a) does not apply.*—(1) Paragraph (a) of this section does not apply to:

(i) An option which is subject to the rules contained in section 421; and

(ii) An option which is not granted as the payment of an amount constituting compensation, such as an option which is acquired solely as an investment (including an option which is part of an investment unit described in paragraph (b) of § 1.1232-3). For rules relating to the taxation of options described in this subdivision, see section 1234 and the regulations thereunder.

(2) If a person acquires an option which is not subject to the rules contained in section 421, and if such option has a readily ascertainable fair market value, such person may establish that such option was not acquired as payment of an amount constituting compensation by showing that the amount of money or its equivalent paid for the option equaled the readily ascertainable fair market value of the option. If a person acquires an option which is not subject to the rules contained in section 421, and if such option does not have a readily ascertainable fair market value, then to establish that such option was not acquired as payment of an amount constituting compensation, such person must show that, from an examination of all the surrounding circumstances, there was no reason for the option to have been granted as the payment of an amount constituting compensation. For example, such person must show that he had neither rendered nor was obligated to render substantial services in consideration for the granting of the option. In determining whether an option, such as an option acquired in connection with an obligation as part of an investment unit, has been granted as compensation for services, the ordinary services performed by an investor in his own self-interest in connection with his investing activities will not be treated as the consideration for the grant of the option. For example, if a small business investment company takes an active part in the management of its debtor small business company, the rendering of such management services will not be treated as the consideration for the granting of the option, provided such services are rendered for an independent consideration, or are merely protective of the small business investment company's investment in the borrower. See paragraph (c) of § 1.421-6 for the meaning of the term "readily ascertainable fair market value."

(c) *Statement required in connection with certain options.*—(1) Any person acquiring any option to purchase securities (other than an option described in subparagraph (2) of this paragraph) shall attach a statement to his income tax return for the taxable year in which the option was acquired. For the definition of the term "securities", see section 165(g)(2).

(2) The statement otherwise required by subparagraph (1) of this paragraph shall not be required with respect to the following options:

(i) Options subject to the rules contained in section 305(a) or section 421;

(ii) Options acquired as part of an investment unit consisting of an option and a debenture, note, or other similar obligation—

(a) If such unit is acquired as part of a public offering and the amount of money or its equivalent paid for such unit is not less than the public offering price, or

(b) If such unit is actively traded on an established market and the amount of money or its equivalent paid for such unit is not less than the price paid for such unit in contemporaneous purchases of such unit by persons independent of both the seller and the taxpayer;

(iii) Options acquired as part of a public offering, if the amount of money or its equivalent paid for such option is not less than the public offering price; and

(iv) Options which are actively traded on an established market and which are acquired for money or its equivalent at a price not less than the price paid for such options in contemporaneous purchases of such options by persons independent of both the seller and the taxpayer.

(3) The statement required by subparagraph (1) of this paragraph shall contain the following information:

(i) Name and address of the taxpayer;

(ii) Description of the securities subject to the option (including number of shares of stock);

(iii) Period during which the option is exercisable;

(iv) Whether the option had a readily ascertainable fair market value at date of grant; and

(v) Whether the option is subject to paragraph (a) of this section.

(4) If the statement required by subparagraph (1) of this paragraph indicates either that the option is not subject to paragraph (a) of this section, or that the option is subject to paragraph (a) of this section but that such option had a readily ascertainable fair market

value at date of grant, then such statement shall contain the following additional information:

    (i) Option price;

    (ii) Value at date of grant of securities subject to the option;

    (iii) Restrictions (if any) on exercise or transfer of option;

    (iv) Restrictions (if any) on transfer of securities subject to the option;

    (v) Value of the option (if readily ascertainable);

    (vi) How value of option was determined;

    (vii) Amount of money (or its equivalent) paid for the option;

    (viii) Person from whom the option was acquired;

    (ix) A concise description of the circumstances surrounding the acquisition of the option and any other factors relied upon by the taxpayer to establish that the option is not subject to paragraph (a) of this section, or, if the option is treated by the taxpayer as subject to paragraph (a) of this section, that the option had a readily ascertainable fair market value at date of grant.

(d) *Effective date.*—This section shall apply to options granted after July 11, 1963, other than options required to be granted pursuant to the terms of a written contract entered into on or before such date. [Reg. § 1.61-15.]

☐ [*T.D. 6696, 12-11-63. Amended by T.D. 6706, 3-2-64; T.D. 6984, 12-23-68 and T.D. 7554, 7-21-78.*]

[Reg. § 1.61-21]

§ 1.61-21. Taxation of fringe benefits.—(a) *Fringe benefits.*—(1) *In general.*—Section 61(a)(1) provides that, except as otherwise provided in subtitle A of the Internal Revenue Code of 1986, gross income includes compensation for services, including fees, commissions, fringe benefits, and similar items. For an outline of the regulations under this section relating to fringe benefits, see paragraph (a)(7) of this section. Examples of fringe benefits include: an employer-provided automobile, a flight on an employer-provided aircraft, an employer-provided free or discounted commercial airline flight, an employer-provided vacation, an employer-provided discount on property or services, an employer-provided membership in a country club or other social club, and an employer-provided ticket to an entertainment or sporting event.

(2) *Fringe benefits excluded from income.*—To the extent that a particular fringe benefit is specifically excluded from gross income pursuant to another section of subtitle A of the Internal Revenue Code of 1986, that section shall govern the treatment of that fringe benefit. Thus, if the requirements of the governing section are satisfied, the fringe benefits may be excludable from gross income. Examples of excludable fringe benefits include qualified tuition reductions provided to an employee (section 117(d)); meals or lodging furnished to an employee for the convenience of the employer (section 119); benefits provided under a dependent care assistance program (section 129); and no-additional-cost services, qualified employee discounts, working condition fringes, and de minimis fringes (section 132). Similarly, the value of the use by an employee of an employer-provided vehicle or a flight provided to an employee on an employer-provided aircraft may be excludable from income under section 105 (because, for example, the transportation is provided for medical reasons) if and to the extent that the requirements of that section are satisfied. Section 134 excludes from gross income "qualified military benefits." An example of a benefit that is not a qualified military benefit is the personal use of an employer-provided vehicle. The fact that another section of subtitle A of the Internal Revenue Code addresses the taxation of a particular fringe benefit will not preclude section 61 and the regulations thereunder from applying, to the extent that they are not inconsistent with such other section. For example, many fringe benefits specifically addressed in other sections of subtitle A of the Internal Revenue Code are excluded from gross income only to the extent that they do not exceed specific dollar or percentage limits, or only if certain other requirements are met. If the limits are exceeded or the requirements are not met, some or all of the fringe benefit may be includible in gross income pursuant to section 61. See paragraph (b)(3) of this section.

(3) *Compensation for services.*—A fringe benefit provided in connection with the performance of services shall be considered to have been provided as compensation for such services. Refraining from the performance of services (such as pursuant to a covenant not to compete) is deemed to be the performance of services for purposes of this section.

(4) *Person to whom fringe benefit is taxable.*—(i) *In general.*—A taxable fringe benefit is included in the income of the person performing the services in connection with which the fringe benefit is furnished. Thus, a fringe benefit may be taxable to a person even though that person did not actually receive the fringe benefit. If a fringe benefit is furnished to someone other than the service provider such benefit is considered in this section as furnished to the service provider, and use by the other person is considered use by the service provider. For example, the provision of an automobile by an employer to an employee's spouse in connection with the performance of services by the employee is taxable to the employee. The automobile is considered available to the employee and use by the employee's spouse is considered use by the employee.

    (ii) *All persons to whom benefits are taxable referred to as employees.*—The person to whom a fringe benefit is taxable need not be an employee of the provider of the fringe benefit, but may be, for example, a partner, director, or an independent contractor. For convenience, the term "employee" includes any person performing services in connection with which a fringe benefit is furnished, unless otherwise specifically provided in this section.

(5) *Provider of a fringe benefit referred to as an employer.*—The "provider" of a fringe benefit is that person for whom the services are performed, regardless of whether that person actually provides the fringe benefit to the recipient. The provider of a fringe benefit need not be the employer of the recipient of the fringe benefit, but may be, for example, a client or customer of the employer or of an independent contractor. For convenience, the term "employer" includes any provider of a fringe benefit in connection with payment for the performance of services, unless otherwise specifically provided in this section.

(6) *Effective date.*—Except as otherwise provided, this section is effective as of January 1, 1989 with respect to fringe benefits provided after December 31, 1988.

(7) *Outline of this section.*—The following is an outline of the regulations in this section relating to fringe benefits:

§ 1.61-21(a). *Fringe benefits.*
    (1) In general.
    (2) Fringe benefits excluded from income.
    (3) Compensation for services.
    (4) Person to whom fringe benefit is taxable.
    (5) Provider of a fringe benefit referred to as an employer.
    (6) Effective date.
    (7) Outline of this section.

§ 1.61-21(b). *Valuation of fringe benefits.*
    (1) In general.
    (2) Fair market value.
    (3) Exclusion from income based on cost.
    (4) Fair market value of the availability of an employer-provided vehicle.
    (5) Fair market value of chauffeur services.
    (6) Fair market value of a flight on an employer-provided piloted aircraft.
    (7) Fair market value of the use of an employer-provided aircraft for which the employer does not furnish a pilot.

§ 1.61-21(c). *Special valuation rules.*
    (1) In general.
    (2) Use of the special valuation rules.
    (3) Additional rules for using special valuation.
    (4) Application of section 414 to employers.
    (5) Valuation formulae contained in the special valuation rules.
    (6) Modification of the special valuation rules.
    (7) Special accounting rule.

§ 1.61-21(d). *Automobile lease valuation rule.*
    (1) In general.
    (2) Calculation of Annual Lease Value.
    (3) Services included in, or excluded from, the Annual Lease Value Table.
    (4) Availability of an automobile for less than an entire calendar year.
    (5) Fair market value.
    (6) Special rules for continuous availability of certain automobiles.
    (7) Consistency rules.

§ 1.61-21(e). *Vehicle cents-per-mile valuation rule.*
    (1) In general.
    (2) Definition of vehicle.
    (3) Services included in, or excluded from, the cents-per-mile rate.
    (4) Valuation of personal use only.
    (5) Consistency rules.

§ 1.61-21(f). *Commuting valuation rule.*
(1) In general.
(2) Special rules.
(3) Commuting value.
(4) Definition of vehicle.
(5) Control employee defined—Non-government employer.
(6) Control employee defined—Government employer.
(7) "Compensation" defined.

§ 1.61-21(g). *Non-commercial flight valuation rule.*
(1) In general.
(2) Eligible flights and eligible aircraft.
(3) Definition of a flight.
(4) Personal and non-personal flights.
(5) Aircraft valuation formula.
(6) Discretion to provide new formula.
(7) Aircraft multiples.
(8) Control employee defined—Non-government employer.
(9) Control employee defined—Government employer.
(10) "Compensation" defined.
(11) Treatment of former employees.
(12) Seating capacity rule.
(13) Erroneous use of the non-commercial flight valuation rule.
(14) Consistency rules.

§ 1.61-21(h). *Commercial flight valuation rule.*
(1) In general.
(2) Space-available flight.
(3) Commercial aircraft.
(4) Timing of inclusion.
(5) Consistency rules.

§ 1.61-21(i). [*Reserved*]

§ 1.61-21(j). *Valuation of meals provided at an employer-operated eating facility for employees.*
(1) In general.
(2) Valuation formula.

§ 1.61-21(k). *Commuting valuation rule for certain employees.*
(1) In general.
(2) Trip-by-trip basis.
(3) Commuting value.
(4) Definition of employer-provided transportation.
(5) Unsafe conditions.
(6) Qualified employee defined.
(7) Examples.
(8) Effective date.

(b) *Valuation of fringe benefits.*—(1) *In general.*—An employee must include in gross income the amount by which the fair market value of the fringe benefit exceeds the sum of—

(i) The amount, if any, paid for the benefit by or on behalf of the recipient, and

(ii) The amount, if any, specifically excluded from gross income by some other section of subtitle A of the Internal Revenue Code of 1986.

Therefore, for example, if the employee pays fair market value for what is received, no amount is includible in the gross income of the employee. In general, the determination of the fair market value of a fringe benefit must be made before subtracting out the amount, if any, paid for the benefit and the amount, if any, specifically excluded from gross income by another section of subtitle A. See paragraphs (d)(2)(ii) and (e)(1)(iii) of this section.

(2) *Fair market value.*—In general, fair market value is determined on the basis of all the facts and circumstances. Specifically, the fair market value of a fringe benefit is the amount that an individual would have to pay for the particular fringe benefit in an arm's-length transaction. Thus, for example, the effect of any special relationship that may exist between the employer and the employee must be disregarded. Similarly, an employee's subjective perception of the value of a fringe benefit is not relevant to the determination of the fringe benefit's fair market value nor is the cost incurred by the employer determinative of its fair market value. For special rules relating to the valuation of certain fringe benefits, see paragraph (c) of this section.

(3) *Exclusion from income based on cost.*—If a statutory exclusion phrased in terms of cost applies to the provision of a fringe benefit, *section 61 does not require the inclusion in the recipient's gross income of the difference between the fair market value and the excludable cost of that fringe benefit. For example, section 129 provides an exclusion from an employee's gross income for amounts contributed by an employer to a dependent care assistance program for employees. Even if the fair market value of the dependent care assistance exceeds the employer's cost, the excess is not subject to inclusion under section 61 and this section. However, if the statutory cost exclusion is a limited amount, the fair market value of the fringe benefit attributable to any excess cost is subject to inclusion. This would be the case, for example, where an employer pays or incurs a cost of more than $5,000 to provide dependent care assistance to an employee.

(4) *Fair market value of the availability of an employer-provided vehicle.*—(i) *In general.*—If the vehicle special valuation rules of paragraphs (d), (e), or (f) of this section do not apply with respect to an employer-provided vehicle, the value of the availability of that vehicle is determined under the general valuation principles set forth in this section. In general, that value equals the amount that an individual would have to pay in an arm's-length transaction to lease the same or comparable vehicle on the same or comparable conditions in the geographic area in which the vehicle is available for use. An example of a comparable condition is the amount of time that the vehicle is available to the employee for use, e.g., a one-year period. Unless the employee can substantiate that the same or comparable vehicle could have been leased on a cents-per-mile basis, the value of the availability of the vehicle cannot be computed by applying a cents-per-mile rate to the number of miles the vehicle is driven.

(ii) *Certain equipment excluded.*—The fair market value of a vehicle does not include the fair market value of any specialized equipment not susceptible to personal use or any telephone that is added to or carried in the vehicle, provided that the presence of that equipment or telephone is necessitated by, and attributable to, the business needs of the employer. However, the value of specialized equipment must be included, if the employee to whom the vehicle is available uses the specialized equipment in a trade or business of the employee other than the employee's trade or business of being an employee of the employer.

(5) *Fair market value of chauffeur services.*—(i) *Determination of value.*—(A) *In general.*—The fair market value of chauffeur services provided to the employee by the employer is the amount that an individual would have to pay in an arm's-length transaction to obtain the same or comparable chauffeur services in the geographic area for the period in which the services are provided. In determining the applicable fair market value, the amount of time, if any, the chauffeur remains on-call to perform chauffeur services must be included. For example, assume that A, an employee of corporation M, needs a chauffeur to be on-call to provide services to A during a twenty-four hour period. If during that twenty-four hour period, the chauffeur actually drives A for only six hours, the fair market value of the chauffeur services would have to be the value of having a chauffeur on-call for a twenty-four hour period. The cost of taxi fare or limousine service for the six hours the chauffeur actually drove A would not be an accurate measure of the fair market value of chauffeur services provided to A. Moreover, all other aspects of the chauffeur's services (including any special qualifications of the chauffeur (e.g., training in evasive driving skills) or the ability of the employee to choose the particular chauffeur) must be taken into consideration.

(B) *Alternative valuation with reference to compensation paid.*—Alternatively, the fair market value of the chauffeur services may be determined by reference to the compensation (as defined in paragraph (b)(5)(ii)) received by the chauffeur from the employer.

(C) *Separate valuation for chauffeur services.*—The value of chauffeur services is determined separately from the value of the availability of an employer-provided vehicle.

(ii) *Definition of compensation.*—(A) *In general.*—For purposes of this paragraph (b)(5)(ii), the term "compensation" means compensation as defined in section 414(q)(7) and the fair market value of nontaxable lodging (if any) provided by the employer to the chauffeur in the current year.

(B) *Adjustments to compensation.*—For purposes of this paragraph (b)(5)(ii), a chauffeur's compensation is reduced proportionately to reflect the amount of time during which the chauffeur performs substantial services for the employer other than as a chauffeur and is not on-call as a chauffeur. For example, assume a chauffeur is paid $25,000 a year for working a ten-hour day, five days a week and also receives $5,000 in nontaxable lodging. Further assume that during four hours of each day, the chauffeur is not on-call to perform services as a chauffeur because that individual is performing secretarial functions for the employer. Then, for purposes of determining the fair market value of this chauffeur's services, the employer may reduce the chauffeur's compensation by $4/10$ or $12,000 (.4 × ($25,000 + $5,000) = $12,000). Therefore, in this example, the fair market value of the chauffeur's services is $18,000 ($30,000 − $12,000).

However, for purposes of this paragraph (b)(5)(ii), a chauffeur's compensation is not to be reduced by any amounts paid to the chauffeur for time spent "on-call," even though the chauffeur actually performs other services for the employer during such time. For purposes of this paragraph (b)(5)(ii), a determination that a chauffeur is performing substantial services for the employer other than as a chauffeur is based upon the facts and circumstances of each situation. An employee will be deemed to be performing substantial services for the employer other than as a chauffeur if a certain portion of each working day is regularly spent performing other services for the employer.

(iii) *Calculation of chauffeur services for personal purposes of the employee.*—The fair market value of chauffeur services provided to the employee for personal purposes may be determined by multiplying the fair market value of chauffeur services, as determined pursuant to paragraph (b)(5)(i)(A) or (B) of this section, by a fraction, the numerator of which is equal to the sum of the hours spent by the chauffeur actually providing personal driving services to the employee and the hours spent by the chauffeur in "personal on-call time," and the denominator of which is equal to all hours the chauffeur spends in driving services of any kind paid for by the employer, including all hours that are "on-call."

(iv) *Definition of on-call time.*—For purposes of this paragraph, the term "on-call time" means the total amount of time that the chauffeur is not engaged in the actual performance of driving services, but during which time the chauffeur is available to perform such services. With respect to a round-trip, time spent by a chauffeur waiting for an employee to make a return trip is generally not treated as on-call time; rather such time is treated as part of the round-trip.

(v) *Definition of personal on-call time.*—For purposes of this paragraph, the term "personal on-call time" means the amount of time outside the employee's normal working hours for the employer when the chauffeur is available to the employee to perform driving services.

(vi) *Presumptions.*—(A) An employee's normal working hours will be presumed to consist of a ten hour period during which the employee usually conducts business activities for that employer.

(B) It will be presumed that if the chauffeur is on-call to provide driving services to an employee during the employee's normal working hours, then that on-call time will be performed for business purposes.

(C) Similarly, if the chauffeur is on-call to perform driving services to an employee after normal working hours, then that on-call time will be presumed to be "personal on-call time."

(D) The presumptions set out in paragraph (b)(5)(vi)(A), (B), and (C) of this section may be rebutted. For example, an employee may demonstrate by adequate substantiation that his or her normal working hours consist of more than ten hours. Furthermore, if the employee keeps adequate records and is able to substantiate that some portion of the driving services performed by the chauffeur after normal working hours is attributable to business purposes, then personal on-call time may be reduced by an amount equal to such personal on-call time multiplied by a fraction, the numerator of which is equal to the time spent by the chauffeur after normal working hours driving the employee for business purposes, and the denominator of which is equal to the total time spent by the chauffeur driving the employee after normal working hours for all purposes.

(vii) *Examples.*—The rules of this paragraph (b)(5) may be illustrated by the following examples:

Example (1). An employer makes available to employee A an automobile and a full-time chauffeur B (who performs no other services for A's employer) for an entire calendar year. Assume that the automobile lease valuation rule of paragraph (d) of this section is used and that the Annual Lease Value of the automobile is $9,250. Assume further that B's compensation for the year is $12,000 (as defined in section 414(q)(7)) and that B is furnished lodging with a value of $3,000 that is excludable from B's gross income. The maximum amount subject to inclusion in A's gross income for use of the automobile and chauffeur is therefore $24,250 ($12,000 + $3,000 + $9,250). If 70 percent of the miles placed on the automobile during the year are for A's employer's business, then $6,475 is excludable from A's gross income with respect to the automobile as a working condition fringe ($9,250 × .70). Thus, $2,775 is includible in A's gross income with respect to the automobile ($9,250 – $6,475). With respect to the chauffeur, if 20 percent of the chauffeur's time is spent actually driving A or being on-call to drive A for personal purposes, then $3,000 is includible in A's income (.20 × $15,000). Eighty percent of $15,000, or $12,000, is excluded from A's income as a working condition fringe.

Example (2). Assume the same facts as in example (1) except that in addition to providing chauffeur services, B is responsible for performing substantial non-chauffeur-related duties (such as clerical or secretarial functions) during which time B is not "on-call" as a chauffeur. If B spends only 75 percent of the time performing chauffeur services, then the maximum amount subject to inclusion in A's gross income for use of the automobile and chauffeur is $20,500 (($15,000 × .75) + $9,250). If B is actually driving A for personal purposes or is on-call to drive A for personal purposes for 20 percent of the time during which B is available to provide chauffeur services, then $2,250 is includible in A's gross income (.20 × $11,250). The income inclusion with respect to the automobile is the same as in example (1).

Example (3). Assume the same facts as in example (2) except that while B is performing non-chauffeur-related duties, B is on call as A's chauffeur. No part of B's compensation is excluded when determining the value of the benefit provided to A. Thus, as in example (1), $3,000 is includible in A's gross income with respect to the chauffeur.

(6) *Fair market value of a flight on an employer-provided piloted aircraft.*—(i) *In general.*—If the non-commercial flight special valuation rule of paragraph (g) of this section does not apply, the value of a flight on an employer-provided piloted aircraft is determined under the general valuation principles set forth in this paragraph.

(ii) *Value of flight.*—If an employee takes a flight on an employer-provided piloted aircraft and that employee's flight is primarily personal (see §1.162-2(b)(2)), the value of the flight is equal to the amount that an individual would have to pay in an arm's-length transaction to charter the same or a comparable piloted aircraft for that period for the same or a comparable flight. A flight taken under these circumstances may not be valued by reference to the cost of commercial airfare for the same or a comparable flight. The cost to charter the aircraft must be allocated among all employees on board the aircraft based on all the facts and circumstances unless one or more of the employees controlled the use of the aircraft. Where one or more employees control the use of the aircraft, the value of the flight shall be allocated solely among such controlling employees, unless a written agreement among all the employees on the flight otherwise allocates the value of such flight. Notwithstanding the allocation required by the preceding sentence, no additional amount shall be included in the income of any employee whose flight is properly valued under the special valuation rule of paragraph (g) of this section. For purposes of this paragraph (b)(6), "control" means the ability of the employee to determine the route, departure time and destination of the flight. The rules provided in paragraph (g)(3) of this section will be used for purposes of this section in defining a flight. Notwithstanding the allocation required by the preceding sentence, no additional amount shall be included in the income of an employee for that portion of any such flight which is excludible from income pursuant to section 132(d) or §1.132-5 as a working condition fringe.

(iii) *Examples.*—The rules of paragraph (b)(6) of this section may be illustrated by the following examples:

Example (1). An employer makes available to employees A and B a piloted aircraft in New York, New York. A wants to go to Los Angeles, California for personal purposes. B needs to go to Chicago, Illinois for business purposes, and then wants to go to Los Angeles, California for personal purposes. Therefore, the aircraft first flies to Chicago, and B deplanes and then boards the plane again. The aircraft then flies to Los Angeles, California where A and B deplane. The value of the flight to employee A will be no more than the amount that an individual would have to pay in an arm's length transaction to charter the same or a comparable piloted aircraft for the same or comparable flight from New York City to Los Angeles. No amount will be imputed to employee A for the stop at Chicago. As to employee B, the value of the personal flight will be no more than the value of the flight from Chicago to Los Angeles. Pursuant to the rules set forth in §1.132-5(k), the flight from New York to Chicago will not be included in employee B's income since that flight was taken solely for business purposes. The charter cost must be allocated between A and B, since both employees controlled portions of the flight. Assume that the employer allocates according to the relative value of each employee's flight. If the charter value of A's flight from New York City to Los Angeles is $1,000 and the value of B's flight from Chicago to Los Angeles is $600 and the value of the actual flight from New York to Chicago to Los Angeles is $1200, then the amount to be allocated to employee A is $750 ($1000/($1000 + $600) × $1200) and the amount to be allocated to employee B is $450 ($600/($1000 + $600) × $1200).

Example (2). Assume the same facts as in example (1), except that employee A also deplanes at Chicago, Illinois, but for personal purposes. The value of the flight to employee A then becomes the value of a flight from New York to Chicago to Los Angeles, i.e.,

$1200. Therefore, the amount to be allocated to employee A is $800 ($1200/($1200 + $600) × $1200) and the amount to be allocated to employee B is $400 ($600/($1200 + $600) × $1200).

(7) *Fair market value of the use of an employer-provided aircraft for which the employer does not furnish a pilot.*—(i) *In general.*—If the non-commercial flight special valuation rule of paragraph (g) of this section does not apply and if an employer provides an employee with the use of an aircraft without a pilot, the value of the use of the employer-provided aircraft is determined under the general valuation principles set forth in this paragraph (b)(7).

(ii) *Value of flight.*—In general, if an employee takes a flight on an employer-provided aircraft for which the employer does not furnish a pilot, the value of that flight is equal to the amount that an individual would have to pay in an arm's-length transaction to lease the same or comparable aircraft on the same or comparable terms for the same period in the geographic area in which the aircraft is used. For example, if an employer makes its aircraft available to an employee who will pilot the aircraft for a two-hour flight, the value of the use of the aircraft is the amount that an individual would have to pay in an arm's-length transaction to rent a comparable aircraft for that period in the geographic area in which the aircraft is used. As another example, assume that an employee uses an employer-provided aircraft to commute between home and work. The value of the use of the aircraft is the amount that an individual would have to pay in an arm's-length transaction to rent a comparable aircraft for commuting in the geographic area in which the aircraft is used. If the availability of the flight is of benefit to more than one employee, then such value shall be allocated among such employees on the basis of the relevant facts and circumstances.

(c) *Special valuation rules.*—(1) *In general.*—Paragraphs (d) through (k) of this section provide special valuation rules that may be used under certain circumstances for certain commonly provided fringe benefits. For general rules relating to the valuation of fringe benefits not eligible for valuation under the special valuation rules, or fringe benefits with respect to which the special valuation rules are not used, see paragraph (b) of this section.

(2) *Use of the special valuation rules.*—(i) *For benefits provided before January 1, 1993.*—The special valuation rules may be used for income tax, employment tax, and reporting purposes. The employer has the option to use any of the special valuation rules. However, an employee may only use a special valuation rule if the employer uses the rule. Moreover, an employee may only use the special rule that the employer uses to value the benefit provided; the employee may not use another special rule to value that benefit. The employee may always use general valuation rules based on facts and circumstances (see paragraph (b) of this section) even if the employer uses a special rule. If a special rule is used, it must be used for all purposes. If an employer properly uses a special rule and the employee uses the special rule, the employee must include in gross income the amount determined by the employer under the special rule reduced by the sum of—

(A) Any amount reimbursed by the employee to the employer, and

(B) Any amount excludable from income under another section of subtitle A of the Internal Revenue Code of 1986. If an employer properly uses a special rule and properly determines the amount of an employee's working condition fringe under section 132 and § 1.132-5 (under the general rule or under a special rule), and the employee uses the special valuation rule, the employee must include in gross income the amount determined by the employer less any amount reimbursed by the employee to the employer. The employer and employee may use the special rules to determine the amount of the reimbursement due the employer by the employee. Thus, if an employee reimburses an employer for the value of a benefit as determined under a special valuation rule, no amount is includible in the employee's gross income with respect to the benefit. The provisions of this paragraph are effective for benefits provided before January 1, 1993.

(ii) *For benefits provided after December 31, 1992.*—The special valuation rules may be used for income tax, employment tax, and reporting purposes. The employer has the option to use any of the special valuation rules. An employee may use a special valuation rule only if the employer uses that rule or the employer does not meet the condition of paragraph (c)(3)(ii)(A) of this section, but one of the other conditions of paragraph (c)(3)(ii) of this section is met. The employee may always use general valuation rules based on facts and circumstances (see paragraph (b) of this section) even if the employer uses a special rule. If a special rule is used, it must be used for all purposes. If an employer properly uses a special rule and the employee uses the special rule, the employee must include in gross

income the amount determined by the employer under the special rule reduced by the sum of—

(A) Any amount reimbursed by the employee to the employer; and

(B) Any amount excludable from income under another section of subtitle A of the Internal Revenue Code of 1986. If an employer properly uses a special rule and properly determines the amount of an employee's working condition fringe under section 132 and § 1.132-5 (under the general rule or under a special rule), and the employee uses the special valuation rule, the employee must include in gross income the amount determined by the employer less any amount reimbursed by the employee to the employer. The employer and employee may use the special rules to determine the amount of the reimbursement due the employer by the employee. Thus, if an employee reimburses an employer for the value of a benefit as determined under a special valuation rule, no amount is includible in the employee's gross income with respect to the benefit. The provisions of this paragraph are effective for benefits provided after December 31, 1992.

(iii) *Vehicle special valuation rules.*—(A) *Vehicle by vehicle basis.*—Except as provided in paragraphs (d)(7)(v) and (e)(5)(v) of this section, the vehicle special valuation rules of paragraphs (d), (e), and (f) of this section apply on a vehicle by vehicle basis. An employer need not use the same vehicle special valuation rule for all vehicles provided to all employees. For example, an employer may use the automobile lease valuation rule for automobiles provided to some employees, and the commuting and vehicle cents-per-mile valuation rules for automobiles provided to other employees. For purposes of valuing the use or availability of a vehicle, the consistency rules provided in paragraphs (d)(7) and (e)(5) of this section (relating to the automobile lease valuation rule and the vehicle cents-per-mile valuation rule, respectively) apply.

(B) *Shared vehicle usage.*—If an employer provides a vehicle to employees for use by more than one employee at the same time, such as with an employer-sponsored vehicle commuting pool, the employer may use any of the special valuation rules that may be applicable to value the use of the vehicle by the employees. The employer must use the same special valuation rule to value the use of the vehicle by each employee who shares such use. The employer must allocate the value of the use of the vehicle based on the relevant facts and circumstances among the employees who share use of the vehicle. For example, assume that an employer provides an automobile to four of its employees and that the employees use the automobile in an employer-sponsored vehicle commuting pool. Assume further that the employer uses the automobile lease valuation rule of paragraph (d) of this section and that the Annual Lease Value of the automobile is $5,000. The employer must treat $5,000 as the value of the availability of the automobile to the employees, and must apportion the $5,000 value among the employees who share the use of the automobile based on the relevant facts and circumstances. Each employee's share of the value of the availability of the automobile is then to be reduced by the amount, if any, of each employee's working condition fringe exclusion and the amount reimbursed by the employee to the employer.

(iv) *Commercial and noncommercial flight valuation rules.*—Except as otherwise provided, if either the commercial flight valuation rule or the non-commercial flight valuation rule is used, that rule must be used by an employer to value all eligible flights taken by all employees in a calendar year. See paragraph (g)(14) of this section for the applicable consistency rules.

(3) *Additional rules for using special valuation.*—(i) *Election to use special valuation rules for benefits provided before January 1, 1993.*—A particular special valuation rule is deemed to have been elected by the employer (and, if applicable, by the employee), if the employer (and, if applicable, the employee) determines the value of the fringe benefit provided by applying the special valuation rule and treats that value as the fair market value of the fringe benefit for income, employment tax, and reporting purposes. Neither the employer nor the employee must notify the Internal Revenue Service of the election. The provisions of this paragraph are effective for benefits provided before January 1, 1993.

(ii) *Conditions on the use of special valuation rules for benefits provided after December 31, 1992.*—Neither the employer nor the employee may use a special valuation rule to value a benefit provided after December 31, 1992, unless one of the following conditions is satisfied—

(A) The employer treats the value of the benefit as wages for reporting purposes within the time for filing the returns for the taxable year (including extensions) in which the benefit is provided;

(B) The employee includes the value of the benefit in income within the time for filing the returns for the taxable year (including extensions) in which the benefit is provided;

(C) The employee is not a control employee as defined in paragraphs (f)(5) and (f)(6) of this section; or

(D) The employer demonstrates a good faith effort to treat the benefit correctly for reporting purposes.

(4) *Application of section 414 to employers.*—For purposes of paragraphs (c) through (k) of this section, except as otherwise provided therein, the term "employer" includes all entities required to be treated as a single employer under section 414(b), (c), (m), or (o).

(5) *Valuation formulae contained in the special valuation rules.*—The valuation formulae contained in the special valuation rules are provided only for use in connection with those rules. Thus, when a special valuation rule is properly applied to a fringe benefit, the Commissioner will accept the value calculated pursuant to the rule as the fair market value of that fringe benefit. However, when a special valuation rule is not properly applied to a fringe benefit (see, for example, paragraph (g)(13) of this section), or when a special valuation rule is used to value a fringe benefit by a taxpayer not entitled to use the rule, the fair market value of that fringe benefit may not be determined by reference to any value calculated under any special valuation rule. Under the circumstances described in the preceding sentence, the fair market value of the fringe benefit must be determined pursuant to the general valuation rules of paragraph (b) of this section.

(6) *Modification of the special valuation rules.*—The Commissioner may, to the extent necessary for tax administration, add, delete, or modify any special valuation rule, including the valuation formulae contained herein, on a prospective basis by regulation, revenue ruling or revenue procedure.

(7) *Special accounting rule.*—If the employer is using the special accounting rule provided in Announcement 85-113 (1985-31 I.R.B. 31, August 5, 1985) (*see* §601.601(d)(2)(ii)(*b*) of this chapter) (relating to the reporting of and withholding on the value of noncash fringe benefits), benefits which are deemed provided in a subsequent calendar year pursuant to that rule are considered as provided in that subsequent calendar year for purposes of the special valuation rules. Thus, if a particular special valuation rule is in effect for a calendar year, it applies to benefits deemed provided during that calendar year under the special accounting rule.

(d) *Automobile lease valuation rule.*—(1) *In general.*—(i) *Annual Lease Value.*—Under the special valuation rule of this paragraph (d), if an employer provides an employee with an automobile that is available to the employee for an entire calendar year, the value of the benefit provided is the Annual Lease Value (determined under paragraph (d)(2) of this section) of that automobile. Except as otherwise provided, for an automobile that is available to an employee for less than an entire calendar year, the value of the benefit provided is either a pro-rated Annual Lease Value or the Daily Lease Value (both as defined in paragraph (d)(4) of this section), whichever is applicable. Absent any statutory exclusion relating to the employer-provided automobile (see, for example, section 132(a)(3) and §1.132-5(b)), the amount of the Annual Lease Value (or a pro-rated Annual Lease Value or the Daily Lease Value, as applicable) is included in the gross income of the employee.

(ii) *Definition of automobile.*—For purposes of this paragraph (d), the term "automobile" means any four-wheeled vehicle manufactured primarily for use on public streets, roads, and highways.

(2) *Calculation of Annual Lease Value.*—(i) *In general.*—The Annual Lease Value of a particular automobile is calculated as follows:

(A) Determine the fair market value of the automobile as of the first date on which the automobile is made available to any employee of the employer for personal use. For an automobile first made available to any employee for personal use prior to January 1, 1985, determine the fair market value as of January 1 of the first year the special valuation rule of this paragraph (d) is used with respect to the automobile. For rules relating to determination of the fair market value of an automobile for purposes of this paragraph (d), see paragraph (d)(5) of this section.

(B) Select the dollar range in column 1 of the Annual Lease Value Table, set forth in paragraph (d)(2)(iii) of this section, corresponding to the fair market value of the automobile. Except as otherwise provided in paragraphs (d)(2)(iv) and (v) of this section, the Annual Lease Value for each year of availability of the automobile is the corresponding amount in column 2 of the Table.

(ii) *Calculation of Annual Lease Value of automobile owned or leased by both an employer and an employee.*—(A) *Purchased automobiles.*—Notwithstanding anything in this section to the contrary, if an employee contributes an amount toward the purchase price of an automobile in return for a percentage ownership interest in the automobile, the Annual Lease Value or the Daily Lease Value, whichever is applicable, is determined by reducing the fair market value of the employer-provided automobile by the lesser of—

(1) The amount contributed, or

(2) An amount equal to the employee's percentage ownership interest multiplied by the unreduced fair market value of the automobile.

If the automobile is subsequently revalued, the revalued amount (determined without regard to this paragraph (d)(2)(ii)(A)) is reduced by an amount which is equal to the employee's percentage ownership interest in the vehicle. If the employee does not receive an ownership interest in the employer-provided automobile, then the Annual Lease Value or the Daily Lease Value, whichever is applicable, is determined without regard to any amount contributed. For purposes of this paragraph (d)(2)(ii)(A), an employee's ownership interest in an automobile will not be recognized unless it is reflected in the title of the automobile. An ownership interest reflected in the title of an automobile will not be recognized if under the facts and circumstances the title does not reflect the benefits and burdens of ownership.

(B) *Leased automobiles.*—Notwithstanding anything in this section to the contrary, if an employee contributes an amount toward the cost to lease an automobile in return for a percentage interest in the automobile lease, the Annual Lease Value or the Daily Lease Value, whichever is applicable, is determined by reducing the fair market value of the employer-provided automobile by the amount specified in the following sentence. The amount specified in this sentence is the unreduced fair market value of a vehicle multiplied by the lesser of—

(1) The employee's percentage interest in the lease, or

(2) A fraction, the numerator of which is the amount contributed and the denominator of which is the entire lease cost.

If the automobile is subsequently revalued, the revalued amount (determined without regard to this paragraph (d)(2)(ii)(B)) is reduced by an amount which is equal to the employee's percentage interest in the lease multiplied by the revalued amount. If the employee does not receive an interest in the automobile lease, then the Annual Lease Value or the Daily Lease Value, whichever is applicable, is determined without regard to any amount contributed. For purposes of this paragraph (d)(2)(ii)(B), an employee's interest in an automobile lease will not be recognized unless the employee is a named co-lessee on the lease. An interest in a lease will not be recognized if under the facts and circumstances the lease does not reflect the true obligations of the lessees.

(C) *Example.*—The rules of paragraph (d)(2)(ii)(A) and (B) of this section are illustrated by the following example:

Example. Assume that an employer pays $15,000 and an employee pays $5,000 toward the purchase of an automobile. Assume further that the employee receives a 25 percent interest in the automobile and is named as a co-owner on the title to the automobile. Under the rule of paragraph (d)(2)(ii)(A) of this section, the Annual Lease Value of the automobile is determined by reducing the fair market value of the automobile ($20,000) by the $5,000 employee contribution. Thus, the Annual Lease Value of the automobile under the table in paragraph (d)(2)(iii) of this section is $4,350. If the employee in this example does not receive an ownership interest in the automobile and is provided the use of the automobile for two years, the Annual Lease Value would be determined without regard to the $5,000 employee contribution. Thus, the Annual Lease Value would be $5,600. The $5,000 employee contribution would reduce the amount includible in the employee's income after taking into account the amount, if any, excluded from income under another provision of subtitle A of the Internal Revenue Code, such as the working condition fringe exclusion. Thus, if the employee places 50 percent of the mileage on the automobile for the employer's business each year, then the amount includible in the employee's income in the first year would be ($5,600 − 2,800 − 2,800), or $0, the amount includible in the employee's income in the second year would be ($5,600 − 2,800 − 2,200 ($5,000 − 2,800)) or $600 and the amount includible in the third year would be ($5,600 − 2,800) or $2,800 since the employee's contribution has been completely used in the first two years.

Reg. §1.61-21(d)(2)(ii)(C)

(iii) *Annual Lease Value Table.*

Automobile fair market value (1)	Annual Lease Value (2)
$0 to 999	$600
1,000 to 1,999	850
2,000 to 2,999	1,100
3,000 to 3,999	1,350
4,000 to 4,999	1,600
5,000 to 5,999	1,850
6,000 to 6,999	2,100
7,000 to 7,999	2,350
8,000 to 8,999	2,600
9,000 to 9,999	2,850
10,000 to 10,999	3,100
11,000 to 11,999	3,350
12,000 to 12,999	3,600
13,000 to 13,999	3,850
14,000 to 14,999	4,100
15,000 to 15,999	4,350
16,000 to 16,999	4,600
17,000 to 17,999	4,850
18,000 to 18,999	5,100
19,000 to 19,999	5,350
20,000 to 20,999	5,600
21,000 to 21,999	5,850
22,000 to 22,999	6,100
23,000 to 23,999	6,350
24,000 to 24,999	6,600
25,000 to 25,999	6,850
26,000 to 27,999	7,250
28,000 to 29,999	7,750
30,000 to 31,999	8,250
32,000 to 33,999	8,750
34,000 to 35,999	9,250
36,000 to 37,999	9,750
38,000 to 39,999	10,250
40,000 to 41,999	10,750
42,000 to 43,999	11,250
44,000 to 45,999	11,750
46,000 to 47,999	12,250
48,000 to 49,999	12,750
50,000 to 51,999	13,250
52,000 to 53,999	13,750
54,000 to 55,999	14,250
56,000 to 57,999	14,750
58,000 to 59,999	15,250

For vehicles having a fair market value in excess of $59,999, the Annual Lease Value is equal to: (.25 × the fair market value of the automobile) + $500.

(iv) *Recalculation of Annual Lease Value.*—The Annual Lease Values determined under the rules of this paragraph (d) are based on four-year lease terms. Therefore, except as otherwise provided in paragraph (d)(2)(v) of this section, the Annual Lease Value calculated by applying paragraph (d)(2)(i) or (ii) of this section shall remain in effect for the period that begins with the first date the special valuation rule of paragraph (d) of this section is applied by the employer to the automobile and ends on December 31 of the fourth full calendar year following that date. The Annual Lease Value for each subsequent four-year period is calculated by determining the fair market value of the automobile as of the first January 1 following the period described in the previous sentence and selecting the amount in column 2 of the Annual Lease Value Table corresponding to the appropriate dollar range in column 1 of the Table. If, however, the employer is using the special accounting rule provided in Announcement 85-113 (1985-31 I.R.B. 31, August 5, 1985) (relating to the reporting of and withholding on the value of noncash fringe benefits), the employer may calculate the Annual Lease Value for each subsequent four-year period as of the beginning of the special accounting period that begins immediately prior to the January 1 described in the previous sentence. For example, assume that pursuant to Announcement 85-113, an employer uses the special accounting rule. Assume further that beginning on November 1, 1988, the special accounting period is November 1 to October 31 and that the employer elects to use the special valuation rule of this paragraph (d) as of January 1, 1989. The employer may recalculate the Annual Lease Value as of November 1, 1992, rather than as of January 1, 1993.

(v) *Transfer of the automobile to another employee.*—Unless the primary purpose of the transfer is to reduce Federal taxes, if an employer transfers the use of an automobile from one employee to another employee, the employer may recalculate the Annual Lease Value based on the fair market value of the automobile as of January

1 of the calendar year of transfer. If, however, the employer is using the special accounting rule provided in Announcement 85-113 (1985-31 I.R.B. 31, August 5, 1985) (relating to the reporting of and withholding on the value of noncash fringe benefits), the employer may recalculate the Annual Lease Value based on the fair market value of the automobile as of the beginning of the special accounting period in which the transfer occurs. If the employer does not recalculate the Annual Lease Value, and the employee to whom the automobile is transferred uses the special valuation rule, the employee may not recalculate the Annual Lease Value.

(3) *Services included in, or excluded from, the Annual Lease Value Table.*—(i) *Maintenance and insurance included.*—The Annual Lease Values contained in the Annual Lease Value Table include the fair market value of maintenance of, and insurance for, the automobile. Neither an employer nor an employee may reduce the Annual Lease Value by the fair market value of any service included in the Annual Lease Value that is not provided by the employer, such as reducing the Annual Lease Value by the fair market value of a maintenance service contract or insurance. An employer or employee who wishes to take into account only the services actually provided with respect to an automobile may value the availability of the automobile under the general valuation rules of paragraph (b) of this section.

(ii) *Fuel excluded.*—(A) *In general.*—The Annual Lease Values do not include the fair market value of fuel provided by the employer, whether fuel is provided in kind or its cost is reimbursed by or charged to the employer. Thus, if an employer provides fuel, the fuel must be valued separately for inclusion in income.

(B) *Valuation of fuel provided in kind.*—The provision of fuel in kind may be valued at fair market value based on all the facts and circumstances or, in the alternative, it may be valued at 5.5 cents per mile for all miles driven by the employee. However, the provision of fuel in kind may not be valued at 5.5 cents per mile for miles driven outside the United States, Canada, or Mexico. For purposes of this section, the United States includes the United States, its possessions and its territories.

(C) *Valuation of fuel where cost reimbursed by or charged to an employer.*—The fair market value of fuel, the cost of which is reimbursed by or charged to an employer, is generally the amount of the actual reimbursement or the amount charged, provided the purchase of the fuel is at arm's-length.

(D) *Fleet-average cents-per-mile fuel cost.*—If an employer with a fleet of at least 20 automobiles that meets the requirements of paragraph (d)(5)(v)(D) of this section reimburses employees for the cost of fuel or allows employees to charge the employer for the cost of fuel, the fair market value of fuel provided to those automobiles may be determined by reference to the employer's fleet-average cents-per-mile fuel cost. The fleet-average cents-per-mile fuel cost is equal to the fleet-average per-gallon fuel cost divided by the fleet-average miles-per-gallon rate. The averages described in the preceding sentence must be determined by averaging the per-gallon fuel costs and miles-per-gallon rates of a representative sample of the automobiles in the fleet equal to the greater of ten percent of the automobiles in the fleet or 20 automobiles for a representative period, such as a two-month period. In lieu of determining the fleet-average cents-per-mile fuel cost, if an employer is using the fleet-average valuation rule of paragraph (d)(5)(v) of this section and if determining the amount of the actual reimbursement or the amount charged for the purchase of fuel would impose unreasonable administrative burdens on the employer, the provision of fuel may be valued under the rule provided in paragraph (d)(3)(ii)(B) of this section.

(iii) *Treatment of other services.*—The fair market value of any service not specifically identified in paragraph (d)(3)(i) of this section that is provided by the employer with respect to an automobile (other than the services of a chauffeur) must be added to the Annual Lease Value of the automobile in determining the fair market value of the benefit provided. See paragraph (b)(5) of this section for rules relating to the valuation of chauffeur services.

(4) *Availability of an automobile for less than an entire calendar year.*—(i) *Pro-rated Annual Lease Value used for continuous availability of at least 30 days.*—(A) *In general.*—Except as otherwise provided in paragraph (d)(4)(iv) of this section, for periods of continuous availability of at least 30 days, but less than an entire calendar year, the value of the availability of an automobile provided by an employer electing to use the automobile lease valuation rule of this paragraph (d) is the pro-rated Annual Lease Value. The pro-rated Annual Lease Value is calculated by multiplying the applicable Annual Lease Value by a fraction, the numerator of which is the number of days of availability and the denominator of which is 365.

(B) *Special rule for continuous availability of at least 30 days that straddles two reporting years.*—If an employee is provided with the continuous availability of an automobile for at least 30 days, but the continuous period straddles two calendar years (or two special accounting periods if the special accounting rule of Announcement 85-113 (1985-31 I.R.B. 31, August 5, 1985) (relating to the reporting of and withholding on noncash fringe benefits) is used), the pro-rated Annual Lease Value, rather than the Daily Lease Value, may be applied with respect to such period of continuous availability.

(ii) *Daily Lease Value used for continuous availability of less than 30 days.*—Except as otherwise provided in paragraph (d)(4)(iii) of this section, for periods of continuous availability of one or more but less than 30 days, the value of the availability of the employer-provided automobile is the Daily Lease Value. The Daily Lease Value is calculated by multiplying the applicable Annual Lease Value by a fraction, the numerator of which is four times the number of days of availability and the denominator of which is 365.

(iii) *Election to treat all periods as periods of at least 30 days.*—The value of the availability of an employer-provided automobile for a period of continuous availability of less than 30 days may be determined by applying the pro-rated Annual Lease Value by treating the automobile as if it had been available for 30 days, if doing so would result in a lower valuation than applying the Daily Lease Value to the shorter period of actual availability.

(iv) *Periods of unavailability.*—(A) *General rule.*—In general, a pro-rated Annual Lease Value (as provided in paragraph (d)(4)(i) of this section) is used to value the availability of an employer-provided automobile when the automobile is available to an employee for a continuous period of at least 30 days but less than the entire calendar year. Neither an employer nor an employee, however, may use a pro-rated Annual Lease Value when the reduction of Federal taxes is the primary reason the automobile is unavailable to an employee at certain times during the calendar year.

(B) *Unavailability for personal reasons of the employee.*—If an automobile is unavailable to an employee because of personal reasons of the employee, such as while the employee is on vacation, a pro-rated Annual Lease Value, if used, must not take into account such periods of unavailability. For example, assume that an automobile is available to an employee during the first five months of the year and during the last five months of the year. Assume further that the period of unavailability occurs because the employee is on vacation. The Annual Lease Value, if it is applied, must be applied with respect to the entire 12-month period. The Annual Lease Value may not be pro-rated to take into account the two-month period of unavailability.

(5) *Fair market value.*—(i) *In general.*—For purposes of determining the Annual Lease Value of an automobile under the Annual Lease Value Table, the fair market value of an automobile is the amount that an individual would have to pay in an arm's-length transaction to purchase the particular automobile in the jurisdiction in which the vehicle is purchased or leased. That amount includes all amounts attributable to the purchase of an automobile such as sales tax and title fees as well as the purchase price of the automobile. Any special relationship that may exist between the employee and the employer must be disregarded. Also, the employee's subjective perception of the value of the automobile is not relevant to the determination of the automobile's fair market value, and, except as provided in paragraph (d)(5)(ii) of this section, the cost incurred by the employer in connection with the purchase or lease of the automobile is not determinative of the fair market value of the automobile.

(ii) *Safe-harbor valuation rule.*—(A) *General rule.*—For purposes of calculating the Annual Lease Value of an automobile under this paragraph (d), the safe-harbor value of the automobile may be used as the fair market value of the automobile.

(B) *Automobiles owned by the employer.*—For an automobile owned by the employer, the safe-harbor value of the automobile is the employer's cost of purchasing the automobile (including sales tax, title, and other expenses attributable to such purchase), provided the purchase is made at arm's-length. Notwithstanding the preceding sentence, the safe-harbor value of this paragraph (d)(5)(ii)(B) is not available with respect to an automobile manufactured by the employer. Thus, for example, if one entity manufactures an automobile and sells it to an entity with which it is aggregated pursuant to paragraph (c)(4) of this section, this paragraph (d)(5)(ii)(B) does not apply to value the automobile by the aggregated employer. In this case, value must be determined under paragraph (d)(5)(i) of this section.

(C) *Automobiles leased by the employer.*—For an automobile leased but not manufactured by the employer, the safe-harbor value of the automobile is either the manufacturer's suggested retail price of the automobile less eight percent (including sales tax, title, and other expenses attributable to such purchase), or the value determined under paragraph (d)(5)(iii) of this section.

(iii) *Use of nationally recognized pricing sources.*—The fair market value of an automobile that is—

(A) Provided to an employee prior to January 1, 1985,

(B) Being revalued pursuant to paragraphs (d)(2)(iv) or (v) of this section, or

(C) A leased automobile being valued pursuant to paragraph (d)(5)(ii) of this section,

may be determined by reference to the retail value of such automobile as reported by a nationally recognized pricing source that regularly reports new or used automobile retail values, whichever is applicable. That retail value must be reasonable with respect to the automobile being valued. Pricing sources consist of publications and electronic data bases.

(iv) *Fair market value of special equipment.*—When determining the fair market value of an automobile, the employer may exclude the fair market value of any specialized equipment or telephone that is added to or carried in the automobile provided that the presence of that equipment or telephone is necessitated by, and attributable to, the business needs of the employer. The value of the specialized equipment must be included if the employee to whom the automobile is available uses the specialized equipment in a trade or business of the employee other than the employee's trade or business of being an employee of the employer.

(v) *Fleet-average valuation rule.*—(A) *In general.*—An employer with a fleet of 20 or more automobiles meeting the requirements of this paragraph (d)(5)(v) (including the business-use and fair market value conditions of paragraph (d)(5)(v)(D) of this section) may use a fleet-average value for purposes of calculating the Annual Lease Values of the automobiles in the fleet. The fleet-average value is the average of the fair market values of all automobiles in the fleet. The fair market value of each automobile in the fleet shall be determined, pursuant to the rules of paragraphs (d)(5)(i) through (iv) of this section, as of the date described in paragraph (d)(2)(i)(A) of this section.

Reg. §1.61-21(d)(5)(v)(A)

(B) *Period for use of rule.*—The fleet-average valuation rule of this paragraph (d)(5)(v) may be used by an employer as of January 1 of any calendar year following the calendar year in which the employer acquires a sufficient number of automobiles to total a fleet of 20 or more automobiles. The Annual Lease Value calculated for the automobiles in the fleet, based on the fleet-average value, shall remain in effect for the period that begins with the first January 1 the fleet-average valuation rule of this paragraph (d)(5)(v) is applied by the employer to the automobiles in the fleet and ends on December 31 of the subsequent calendar year. The Annual Lease Value for each subsequent two-year period is calculated by determining the fleet-average value of the automobiles in the fleet as of the first January 1 of such period. An employer may cease using the fleet-average valuation rule as of any January 1. If, however, the employer is using the special accounting rule provided in Announcement 85-113 (1985-31 I.R.B. 31, August 5, 1985) (relating to the reporting of and withholding on noncash fringe benefits), the employer may apply the rules of this paragraph (d)(5)(v)(B) on the basis of the special accounting period rather than the calendar year. (This is accomplished by substituting (*1*) the beginning of the special accounting period that begins immediately prior to the January 1 described in this paragraph (d)(5)(v)(B) for January 1 wherever it appears in this paragraph (d)(5)(v)(B) and (2) the end of such accounting period for December 31.) If the number of qualifying automobiles in the employer's fleet declines to fewer than 20 for more than 50 percent of the days in a year, then the fleet-average valuation rule does not apply as of January 1 of such year. In this case, the Annual Lease Value must be determined separately for each remaining automobile. The revaluation rules of paragraph (d)(2)(iv) and (v) of this section do not apply to automobiles valued under this paragraph (d)(5)(v).

(C) *Automobiles included in the fleet.*—An employer may include in a fleet any automobile that meets the requirements of this paragraph (d)(5)(v) and is available to any employee of the employer for personal use. An employer may include in the fleet only automobiles the availability of which is valued under the automobile lease valuation rule of this paragraph (d). An employer need not include in the fleet all automobiles valued under the automobile lease valuation rule. An employer may have more than one fleet for purposes of the fleet-average rule of this paragraph (d)(5)(v). For example, an employer may group automobiles in a fleet according to their physical type or use.

(D) *Limitations on use of fleet-average rule.*—The rule provided in this paragraph (d)(5)(v) may not be used for any automobile the fair market value of which (determined pursuant to paragraphs (d)(5)(i) through (iv) of this section as of the first date on which the automobile is made available to any employee of the employer for personal use) exceeds $50,000, as adjusted by section 280F(d)(7). The first such adjustment shall be for calendar year 2019. In addition, the rule provided in this paragraph (d)(5)(v) may only be used for automobiles that the employer reasonably expects will regularly be used in the employer's trade or business. For rules concerning when an automobile is regularly used in the employer's business, see paragraph (e)(1)(iv) of this section.

(E) *Additional automobiles added to the fleet.*—The fleet-average value in effect at the time an automobile is added to a fleet is treated as the fair market value of the additional automobile for purposes of determining the Annual Lease Value of the automobile until the fleet-average value changes pursuant to paragraph (d)(5)(v)(B) of this section.

(F) *Use of the fleet-average rule by employees.*—An employee may only use the fleet-average rule if it is used by the employer. If an employer uses the fleet-average rule, and the employee uses the special valuation rule of paragraph (d) of this section, the employee must use the fleet-average value determined by the employer.

(G) *Transition rule for 2018 and 2019.*—Notwithstanding paragraph (d)(5)(v)(B) of this section, an employer that did not qualify to use the fleet-average valuation rule prior to January 1, 2018, with respect to any automobile (including a truck or van) because the fair market value of the vehicle exceeded the inflation-adjusted maximum value requirement of paragraph (d)(5)(v)(D) of this section, as published by the Service in a notice or revenue procedure applicable to the year the vehicle was first made available to any employee of the employer, may adopt the fleet-average valuation rule for 2018 or 2019 with respect to the vehicle, provided the fair market value of the vehicle does not exceed $50,000 on January 1, 2018, or $50,400 on January 1, 2019, respectively.

(H) *Applicability date.*—Paragraphs (d)(5)(v)(D), and (G) of this section apply to taxable years beginning on or after February 5, 2020. Notwithstanding the first sentence of this paragraph (d)(5)(v)(H), any taxpayer may choose to apply paragraph (d)(5)(v)(G) of this section beginning on or after January 1, 2018.

(6) *Special rules for continuous availability of certain automobiles.*—(i) *Fleet automobiles.*—If an employer is using the fleet-average valuation rule of paragraph (d)(5)(v) of this section and the employer provides an employee with the continuous availability of an automobile from the same fleet during a period (though not necessarily the same fleet automobile for the entire period), the employee is treated as having the use of a single fleet automobile for the entire period, e.g., an entire calendar year. Thus, when applying the automobile lease valuation rule of this paragraph (d), the employer may treat the fleet-average value as the fair market value of the automobile deemed available to the employee for the period for purposes of calculating the Annual Lease Value (or pro-rated Annual Lease Value or Daily Lease Value, whichever is applicable) of the automobile. If an employer provides an employee with the continuous availability of more than one fleet automobile during a period, the employer may treat the fleet-average value as the fair market value of each automobile provided to the employee provided that the rules of paragraph (d)(5)(v)(D) of this section are satisfied.

(ii) *Demonstration automobiles.*—(A) *In general.*—If an automobile dealership provides an employee with the continuous availability of a demonstration automobile (as defined in §1.132-5(o)(3)) during a period (though not necessarily the same demonstration automobile for the entire period), the employee is treated as having the use of a single demonstration automobile for the entire period, e.g., an entire calendar year. If an employer provides an employee with the continuous availability of more than one demonstration automobile during a period, the employer may treat the value determined under paragraph (d)(6)(ii)(B) of this section as the fair market value of each automobile provided to the employee. For rules relating to the treatment as a working condition fringe of the qualified automobile demonstration use of a demonstration automobile by a full-time automobile salesman, see §1.132-5(o).

(B) *Determining the fair market value of a demonstration automobile.*—When applying the automobile lease valuation rule of this paragraph (d), the employer may treat the average of the fair market values of the demonstration automobiles which are available to an employee and held in the dealership's inventory during the calendar year as the fair market value of the demonstration automobile deemed available to the employee for the period for purposes of calculating the Annual Lease Value of the automobile. If under the facts and circumstances it is inappropriate to take into account, with respect to an employee, certain models of demonstration automobiles, the value of the benefit is determined without reference to the fair market values of such models. For example, assume that an employee has the continuous availability for an entire calendar year of one demonstration automobile, although not the same one for the entire year. Assume further that the fair market values of the automobiles in the dealership's inventory during the year range from $8,000 to $20,000. If there is not a substantial period (such as three months) during the year when the employee uses demonstration automobiles valued at less than $16,000, then those automobiles are not considered in determining the value of the benefit provided to the employee. In this case, the average of the fair market values of the demonstration automobiles in the dealership's inventory valued at $16,000 or more is treated as the fair market value of the automobile deemed available to the employee for the calendar year for purposes of calculating the Annual Lease Value of the automobile.

(7) *Consistency rules.*—(i) *Use of the automobile lease valuation rule by an employer.*—Except as provided in paragraph (d)(5)(v)(B) of this section, an employer may adopt the automobile lease valuation rule of this paragraph (d) for an automobile only if the rule is adopted to take effect by the later of—

(A) January 1, 1989, or

(B) The first day on which the automobile is made available to an employee of the employer for personal use (or, if the commuting valuation rule of paragraph (f) of this section is used when the automobile is first made available to an employee of the employer for personal use, the first day on which the commuting valuation rule is not used).

(ii) *An employer must use the automobile lease valuation rule for all subsequent years.*—Once the automobile lease valuation rule has been adopted for an automobile by an employer, the rule must be used by the employer for all subsequent years in which the employer makes the automobile available to any employee, except that the employer may, for any year during which (or for any employee for whom) use of the automobile qualifies for the commuting valuation rule of paragraph (f) of this section, use the commuting valuation rule with respect to the automobile.

(iii) *Use of the automobile lease valuation rule by an employee.*—An employee may adopt the automobile lease valuation rule for an automobile only if the rule is adopted—

(A) By the employer, and

(B) Beginning with the first day on which the automobile for which the employer (consistent with paragraph (d)(7)(i) of this section) adopted the rule is made available to that employee for personal use (or, if the commuting valuation rule of paragraph (f) of this section is used when the automobile is first made available to that employee for personal use, the first day on which the commuting valuation rule is not used).

(iv) *An employee must use the automobile lease valuation rule for all subsequent years.*—Once the automobile lease valuation rule has been adopted for an automobile by an employee, the rule must be used by the employee for all subsequent years in which the automobile for which the rule is used is available to the employee. However, the employee may, for any year during which use of the automobile qualifies for use of the commuting valuation rule of paragraph (f) of this section and for which the employer uses such rule, use the commuting valuation rule with respect to the automobile.

(v) *Replacement automobiles.*—Notwithstanding anything in this paragraph (d)(7) to the contrary, if the automobile lease valuation rule is used by an employer, or by an employer and an employee, with respect to a particular automobile, and a replacement automobile is provided to the employee for the primary purpose of reducing Federal taxes, then the employer, or the employer and the employee, using the rule must continue to use the rule with respect to the replacement automobile.

(e) *Vehicle cents-per-mile valuation rule.*—(1) *In general.*—(i) *General rule.*—Under the vehicle cents-per-mile valuation rule of this paragraph (e), if an employer provides an employee with the use of a vehicle that—

(A) The employer reasonably expects will be regularly used in the employer's trade or business throughout the calendar year (or such shorter period as the vehicle may be owned or leased by the employer), or

(B) Satisfies the requirements of paragraph (e)(1)(ii) of this section,

the value of the benefit provided in the calendar year is the standard mileage rate provided in the applicable Revenue Ruling or Revenue Procedure ("cents-per-mile rate") multiplied by the total number of miles the vehicle is driven by the employee for personal purposes. The cents-per-mile rate is to be applied prospectively from the first day of the taxable year following the date of publication of the applicable Revenue Ruling or Revenue Procedure. An employee who uses an employer-provided vehicle, in whole or in part, for a trade or business other than the employer's trade or business, may take a deduction for such business use based upon the vehicle cents-per-mile rule as long as such deduction is at the same standard mileage rate as that used in calculating the employee's income inclusion. The standard mileage rate must be applied to personal miles independent of business miles. Thus, for example, if the standard mileage rate were 24 cents per mile for the first 15,000 miles and 11 cents per mile for all miles over 15,000 and an employee drives 20,000 personal miles and 45,000 business miles in a year, the value of the personal use of the vehicle is $4,150 ((15,000 × $.24) + (5,000 × $.11)). For purposes of this section, the use of a vehicle for personal purposes is any use of the vehicle other than use in the employee's trade or business of being an employee of the employer.

(ii) *Mileage rule.*—A vehicle satisfies the requirements of this paragraph (e)(1)(ii) for a calendar year if—

(A) It is actually driven at least 10,000 miles in that year; and

(B) Use of the vehicle during the year is primarily by employees.

For example, if a vehicle is used by only one employee during the calendar year and that employee drives the vehicle at least 10,000 miles during the year, the vehicle satisfies the requirements of this paragraph (e)(1)(ii) even if all miles driven by the employee are personal. A vehicle is considered used during the year primarily by employees in accordance with the requirement of paragraph (e)(1)(ii)(B) of this section if employees use the vehicle on a consistent basis for commuting. If the employer does not own or lease the *vehicle during a portion of the year*, the 10,000 mile threshold is to be reduced proportionately to reflect the periods when the employer did not own or lease the vehicle. For purposes of this paragraph (e)(1)(ii), use of the vehicle by an individual (other than the employee) whose use would be taxed to the employee is not considered use by the employee.

(iii) *Limitation on use of the vehicle cents-per-mile valuation rule.*—(A) *In general.*—The value of the use of an automobile (as defined in paragraph (d)(1)(ii) of this section) may not be determined under the vehicle cents-per-mile valuation rule of this paragraph (e) for a calendar year if the fair market value of the automobile (deter-

mined pursuant to paragraphs (d)(5)(i) through (iv) of this section as of the first date on which the automobile is made available to any employee of the employer for personal use) exceeds $50,000, as adjusted by section 280F(d)(7). The first such adjustment shall be for calendar year 2019.

(B) *Application of limitation with respect to a vehicle owned by both an employer and an employee.*—If an employee contributes an amount towards the purchase price of a vehicle in return for a percentage ownership interest in the vehicle, for purposes of determining whether the limitation of this paragraph (e)(1)(iii) applies, the fair market value of the vehicle is reduced by the lesser of—

(1) The amount contributed, or

(2) An amount equal to the employee's percentage ownership interest multiplied by the unreduced fair market value of the vehicle.

If the employee does not receive an ownership interest in the employer-provided vehicle, then the fair market value of the vehicle is determined without regard to any amount contributed. For purposes of this paragraph (e)(1)(iii)(B), an employee's ownership interest in a vehicle will not be recognized unless it is reflected in the title of the vehicle. An ownership interest reflected in the title of a vehicle will not be recognized if under the facts and circumstances the title does not reflect the benefits and burdens of ownership.

(C) *Application of limitation with respect to a vehicle leased by both an employer and employee.*—If an employee contributes an amount toward the cost to lease a vehicle in return for a percentage interest in the vehicle lease, for purposes of determining whether the limitation of this paragraph (e)(1)(iii) applies, the fair market value of the vehicle is reduced by the amount specified in the following sentence. The amount specified in this sentence is the unreduced fair market value of a vehicle multiplied by the lesser of—

(1) The employee's percentage interest in the lease, or

(2) A fraction, the numerator of which is the amount contributed and the denominator of which is the entire lease cost.

If the employee does not receive an interest in the vehicle lease, then the fair market value is determined without regard to any amount contributed. For purposes of this paragraph (e)(1)(iii)(C), an employee's interest in a vehicle lease will not be recognized unless the employee is a named co-lessee on the lease. An interest in a lease will not be recognized if under the facts and circumstances, the lease does not reflect the true obligations of the lessees.

(iv) *Regular use in an employer's trade or business.*—Whether a vehicle is regularly used in an employer's trade or business is determined on the basis of all facts and circumstances. A vehicle is considered regularly used in an employer's trade or business for purposes of paragraph (e)(1)(i)(A) of this section if one of the following safe harbor conditions is satisfied:

(A) At least 50 percent of the vehicle's total annual mileage is for the employer's business; or

(B) The vehicle is generally used each workday to transport at least three employees of the employer to and from work in an employer-sponsored commuting vehicle pool. Infrequent business use of the vehicle, such as for occasional trips to the airport or between the employer's multiple business premises, does not constitute regular use of the vehicle in the employer's trade or business.

(v) *Application of rule to shared usage.*—If an employer regularly provides a vehicle to employees for use by more than one employee at the same time, such as with an employer-sponsored vehicle commuting pool, the employer may use the vehicle cents-per-mile valuation rule to value the use of the vehicle by each employee who shares such use. See § 1.61-21(c)(2)(ii)(B) for provisions relating to the allocation of the value of an automobile to more than one employee.

(2) *Definition of vehicle.*—For purposes of this paragraph (e), the term "vehicle" means any motorized wheeled vehicle manufactured primarily for use on public streets, roads, and highways. The term "vehicle" includes an automobile as defined in paragraph (d)(1)(ii) of this section.

(3) *Services included in, or excluded from, the cents-per-mile rate.*—(i) *Maintenance and insurance included.*—The cents-per-mile rate includes the fair market value of maintenance of, and insurance for, the vehicle. The cents-per-mile rate may not be reduced by the fair market value of any service included in the cents-per-mile rate but not provided by the employer. An employer or employee who wishes to take into account only the particular services provided with respect to a vehicle may value the availability of the vehicle under the general valuation rules of paragraph (b) of this section.

(ii) *Fuel provided by the employer.*—(A) *Miles driven in the United States, Canada, or Mexico.*—With respect to miles driven in the United States, Canada, or Mexico, the cents-per-mile rate includes the fair market value of fuel provided by the employer. If fuel is not provided by the employer, the cents-per-mile rate may be reduced by no more than 5.5 cents or the amount specified in any applicable Revenue Ruling or Revenue Procedure. For purposes of this section, the United States includes the United States, its possessions and its territories.

(B) *Miles driven outside the United States, Canada, or Mexico.*— With respect to miles driven outside the United States, Canada, or Mexico, the fair market value of fuel provided by the employer is not reflected in the cents-per-mile rate. Accordingly, the cents-per-mile rate may be reduced but by no more than 5.5 cents or the amount specified in any applicable Revenue Ruling or Revenue Procedure. If the employer provides the fuel in kind, it must be valued based on all the facts and circumstances. If the employer reimburses the employee for the cost of fuel or allows the employee to charge the employer for the cost of fuel, the fair market value of the fuel is generally the amount of the actual reimbursement or the amount charged, provided the purchase of fuel is at arm's length.

(iii) *Treatment of other services.*—The fair market value of any service not specifically identified in paragraph (e)(3)(i) of this section that is provided by the employer with respect to a vehicle is not reflected in the cents-per-mile rate. See paragraph (b)(5) of this section for rules relating to valuation of chauffeur services.

(4) *Valuation of personal use only.*—The vehicle cents-per-mile valuation rule of this paragraph (e) may only be used to value the miles driven for personal purposes. Thus, the employer must include an amount in an employee's income with respect to the use of a vehicle that is equal to the product of the number of personal miles driven by the employee and the appropriate cents-per-mile rate. The term "personal miles" means all miles for which the employee used the automobile except miles driven in the employee's trade or business of being an employee of the employer. Unless additional services are provided with respect to the vehicle (see paragraph (e)(3)(iii) of this section), the employer may not include in income a greater amount; for example, the employer may not include in income 100 percent (all business and personal miles) of the value of the use of the vehicle.

(5) *Consistency rules.*—(i) *Use of the vehicle cents-per-mile valuation rule by an employer.*—An employer must adopt the vehicle cents-per-mile valuation rule of this paragraph (e) for a vehicle to take effect by the first day on which the vehicle is used by an employee of the employer for personal use (or, if the commuting valuation rule of paragraph (f) of this section is used when the vehicle is first used by an employee of the employer for personal use, the first day on which the commuting valuation rule is not used).

(ii) *An employer must use the vehicle cents-per-mile valuation rule for all subsequent years.*—Once the vehicle cents-per-mile valuation rule has been adopted for a vehicle by an employer, the rule must be used by the employer for all subsequent years in which the vehicle qualifies for use of the rule, except that the employer may, for any year during which use of the vehicle qualifies for the commuting valuation rule of paragraph (f) of this section, use the commuting valuation rule with respect to the vehicle. If the vehicle fails to qualify for use of the vehicle cents-per-mile valuation rule during a subsequent year, the employer may adopt for such subsequent year and thereafter any other special valuation rule for which the vehicle then qualifies. If the employer elects to use the automobile lease valuation rule of paragraph (d) of this section for a period in which the automobile does not qualify for use of the vehicle cents-per-mile valuation rule, then the employer must comply with the requirements of paragraph (d)(7) of this section. For purposes of paragraph (d)(7) of this section, the first day on which the automobile with respect to which the vehicle cents-per-mile rule had been used fails to qualify for use of the vehicle cents-per-mile valuation rule may be deemed to be the first day on which the automobile is available to an employee of the employer for personal use.

(iii) *Use of the vehicle cents-per-mile valuation rule by an employee.*—An employee may adopt the vehicle cents-per-mile valuation rule for a vehicle only if the rule is adopted—

(A) By the employer, and

(B) Beginning with respect to the first day on which the vehicle for which the employer (consistent with paragraph (e)(5)(i) of this section) adopted the rule is available to that employee for personal use (or, if the commuting valuation rule of paragraph (f) of this section is used when the vehicle is first used by an employee for personal use, the first day on which the commuting valuation rule is not used).

(iv) *An employee must use the vehicle cents-per-mile valuation rule for all subsequent years.*—Once the vehicle cents-per-mile valuation rule has been adopted for a vehicle by an employee, the rule must be used by the employee for all subsequent years of personal use of the

vehicle by the employee for which the rule is used by the employer. However, see paragraph (f) of this section for rules relating to the use of the commuting valuation rule for a subsequent year.

(v) *Replacement vehicles.*—Notwithstanding anything in this paragraph (e)(5) to the contrary, if the vehicle cents-per-mile valuation rule is used by an employer, or by an employer and an employee, with respect to a particular vehicle, and a replacement vehicle is provided to the employee for the primary purpose of reducing Federal taxes, then the employer, or the employer and the employee, using the rule must continue to use the rule with respect to the replacement vehicle if the replacement vehicle qualifies for use of the rule.

(vi) *Transition rule for 2018 and 2019.*—For a vehicle first made available to any employee of an employer for personal use before calendar year 2018, an employer that did not qualify under this paragraph (e)(5) to adopt the vehicle cents-per-mile valuation rule on the first day on which the vehicle is used by the employee for personal use because the fair market value of the vehicle exceeded the inflation-adjusted limitation of paragraph (e)(1)(iii) of this section, as published by the Service in a notice or revenue procedure applicable to the year the vehicle was first used by the employee for personal use, may first adopt the vehicle cents-per-mile valuation rule for the 2018 or 2019 taxable year, provided the fair market value of the vehicle does not exceed $50,000 on January 1, 2018, or $50,400 on January 1, 2019, respectively. Similarly, for a vehicle first made available to any employee of the employer for personal use before calendar year 2018, if the commuting valuation rule of paragraph (f) of this section was used when the vehicle was first used by the employee for personal use, and the employer did not qualify to switch to the vehicle cents-per-mile valuation rule of this paragraph (e) on the first day on which the commuting valuation rule of paragraph (f) of this section was not used because the vehicle had a fair market value in excess of the inflation-adjusted limitation of paragraph (e)(1)(iii) of this section, as published by the Service in a notice or revenue procedure applicable to the year the commuting valuation rule was first not used, the employer may adopt the vehicle cents-per-mile valuation rule for the 2018 or 2019 taxable year, provided the fair market value of the vehicle does not exceed $50,000 on January 1, 2018, or $50,400 on January 1, 2019, respectively. However, in accordance with paragraph (e)(5)(ii) of this section, an employer that adopts the vehicle cents-per-mile valuation rule pursuant to this paragraph (e)(5)(vi) must continue to use the rule for all subsequent years in which the vehicle qualifies for use of the rule, except that the employer may, for any year during which use of the vehicle qualifies for the commuting valuation rule of paragraph (f) of this section, use the commuting valuation rule with regard to the vehicle.

(6) *Applicability date.*—Paragraphs (e)(1)(iii)(A) and (e)(5)(i) and (vi) of this section apply to taxable years beginning on or after February 5, 2020. Notwithstanding the first sentence of this paragraph (e)(6), any taxpayer may choose to apply paragraph (e)(5)(vi) of this section beginning on or after January 1, 2018.

(f) *Commuting valuation rule.*—(1) *In general.*—Under the commuting valuation rule of this paragraph (f), the value of the commuting use of an employer-provided vehicle may be determined pursuant to paragraph (f)(3) of this section if the following criteria are met by the employer and employees with respect to the vehicle:

(i) The vehicle is owned or leased by the employer and is provided to one or more employees for use in connection with the employer's trade or business and is used in the employer's trade or business;

(ii) For bona fide noncompensatory business reasons, the employer requires the employee to commute to and/or from work in the vehicle;

(iii) The employer has established a written policy under which neither the employee, nor any individual whose use would be taxable to the employee, may use the vehicle for personal purposes, other than for commuting or de minimis personal use (such as a stop for a personal errand on the way between a business delivery and the employee's home);

(iv) Except for de minimis personal use, the employee does not use the vehicle for any personal purpose other than commuting; and

(v) The employee required to use the vehicle for commuting is not a control employee of the employer (as defined in paragraphs (f)(5) and (6) of this section).

Personal use of a vehicle is all use of the vehicle by an employee that is not use in the employee's trade or business of being an employee of the employer. An employer-provided vehicle that is generally used each workday to transport at least three employees of the employer to and from work in an employer-sponsored commuting vehicle pool is deemed to meet the requirements of paragraphs (f)(1)(i) and (ii) of this section.

(2) *Special rules.*—Notwithstanding anything in paragraph (f)(1) of this section to the contrary, the following special rules apply—

(i) *Chauffeur-driven vehicles.*—If a vehicle is chauffeur-driven, the commuting valuation rule of this paragraph (f) may not be used to value the commuting use of any person (other than the chauffeur) who rides in the vehicle. (See paragraphs (d) and (e) of this section for other vehicle special valuation rules.) The special rule of this paragraph (f) may be used to value the commuting-only use of the vehicle by the chauffeur if the conditions of paragraph (f)(1) of this section are satisfied. For purposes of this paragraph (f)(2), an individual will not be considered a chauffeur if he or she performs non-driving services for the employer, is not available to perform driving services while performing such other services and whose only driving services consist of driving a vehicle used for commuting by other employees of the employer.

(ii) *Control employee exception.*—If the vehicle in which the employee is required to commute is not an automobile as defined in paragraph (d)(1)(ii) of this section, the restriction of paragraph (f)(1)(v) of this section (relating to control employees) does not apply.

(3) *Commuting value.*—(i) *$1.50 per one-way commute.*—If the requirements of this paragraph (f) are satisfied, the value of the commuting use of an employer-provided vehicle is $1.50 per one-way commute (e.g., from home to work or from work to home). The value provided in this paragraph (f)(3) includes the value of any goods or services directly related to the vehicle (e.g., fuel).

(ii) *Value per employee.*—If there is more than one employee who commutes in the vehicle, such as in the case of an employer-sponsored commuting vehicle pool, the amount includible in the income of each employee is $1.50 per one-way commute. Thus, the amount includible for each round-trip commute is $3.00 per employee. See paragraphs (d)(7)(vi) and (e)(5)(vi) of this section for use of the automobile lease valuation and vehicle cents-per-mile valuation special rules for valuing the use or availability of the vehicle in the case of an employer-sponsored vehicle or automobile commuting pool.

(4) *Definition of vehicle.*—For purposes of this paragraph (f), the term "vehicle" means any motorized wheeled vehicle manufactured primarily for use on public streets, roads, and highways. The term "vehicle" includes an automobile as defined in paragraph (d)(1)(ii) of this section.

(5) *Control employee defined—Non-government employer.*—For purposes of this paragraph (f), a control employee of a non-government employer is any employee—

(i) Who is a Board- or shareholder-appointed, confirmed, or elected officer of the employer whose compensation equals or exceeds $50,000,

(ii) Who is a director of the employer,

(iii) Whose compensation equals or exceeds $100,000, or

(iv) Who owns a one-percent or greater equity, capital, or profits interest in the employer.

For purposes of determining who is a one-percent owner under paragraph (f)(5)(iv) of this section, any individual who owns (or is considered as owning under section 318(a) or principles similar to section 318(a) for entities other than corporations) one percent or more of the fair market value of an entity (the "owned entity") is considered a one-percent owner of all entities which would be aggregated with the owned entity under the rules of section 414(b), (c), (m), or (o). For purposes of determining who is an officer or director with respect to an employer under this paragraph (f)(5), notwithstanding anything in this section to the contrary, if an entity would be aggregated with other entities under the rules of section 414(b), (c), (m), or (o), the officer definition (but not the compensation requirement) and the director definition apply to each such separate entity rather than to the aggregated employer. An employee who is an officer or a director of an entity (the "first entity") shall be treated as an officer or a director of all entities aggregated with the first entity under the rules of section 414(b), (c), (m), or (o). Instead of applying the control employee definition of this paragraph (f)(5), an employer may treat all, and only, employees who are "highly compensated" employees (as defined in §1.132-8(g)) as control employees for purposes of this paragraph (f).

(6) *Control employee defined—Government employer.*—For purposes of this paragraph (f), a control employee of a government employer is any—

(i) Elected official, or

(ii) Employee whose compensation equals or exceeds the compensation paid to a Federal Government employee holding a position at Executive Level V, determined under Chapter 11 of title 2, United States Code, as adjusted by section 5318 of Title 5 United States Code.

For purposes of this paragraph (f), the term "government" includes any Federal, state or local governmental unit, and any agency or instrumentality thereof. Instead of applying the control employee definition of paragraph (f)(6), an employer may treat all and only employees who are "highly compensated" employees (as defined in §1.132-8(f)) as control employees for purposes of this paragraph (f).

(7) *"Compensation" defined.*—For purposes of this paragraph (f), the term "compensation" has the same meaning as in section 414(q)(7). Compensation includes all amounts received from all entities treated as a single employer under section 414(b), (c), (m), or (o). Levels of compensation shall be adjusted at the same time and in the same manner as provided in section 415(d). The first such adjustment shall be for calendar year 1988.

(g) *Non-commercial flight valuation rule.*—(1) *In general.*—Under the non-commercial flight valuation rule of this paragraph (g), except as provided in paragraph (g)(12) of this section, if an employee is provided with a flight on an employer-provided aircraft, the value of the flight is calculated using the aircraft valuation formula of paragraph (g)(5) of this section. For purposes of this paragraph (g), the value of a flight on an employer-provided aircraft by an individual who is less than two years old is deemed to be zero. See paragraph (b)(1) of this section for rules relating to the amount includible in income when an employee reimburses the employee's employer for all or part of the fair market value of the benefit provided.

(2) *Eligible flights and eligible aircraft.*—The valuation rule of this paragraph (g) may be used to value flights on all employer-provided aircraft, including helicopters. The valuation rule of this paragraph (g) may be used to value international as well as domestic flights. The valuation rule of this paragraph (g) may not be used to value a flight on any commercial aircraft on which air transportation is sold to the public on a per-seat basis. For a special valuation rule relating to certain flights on commercial aircraft, see paragraph (h) of this section.

(3) *Definition of a flight.*—(i) *General rule.*—Except as otherwise provided in paragraph (g)(3)(iii) of this section (relating to intermediate stops), for purposes of this paragraph (g), a flight is the distance (in statute miles, i.e., 5,280 feet per statute mile) between the place at which the individual boards the aircraft and the place at which the individual deplanes.

(ii) *Valuation of each flight.*—Under the valuation rule of this paragraph (g), value is determined separately for each flight. Thus, a round-trip is comprised of at least two flights. For example, an employee who takes a personal trip on an employer-provided aircraft from New York City to Denver, then Denver to Los Angeles, and finally Los Angeles to New York City has taken three flights and must apply the aircraft valuation formula separately to each flight. The value of a flight must be determined on a passenger-by-passenger basis. For example, if an individual accompanies an employee and the flight taken by the individual would be taxed to the employee, the employee would be taxed on the special rule value of the flight by the employee and the flight by the individual.

(iii) *Intermediate stop.*—If a landing is necessitated by weather conditions, by an emergency, for purposes of refueling or obtaining other services relating to the aircraft, or for any other purpose unrelated to the personal purposes of the employee whose flight is being valued, that landing is an intermediate stop. Additional mileage attributable to an intermediate stop is not considered when determining the distance of an employee's flight.

(iv) *Examples.*—The rules of paragraph (g)(3)(iii) of this section may be illustrated by the following examples:

Example (1). Assume that an employee's trip originates in St. Louis, Missouri, with Seattle, Washington as its destination, but, because of weather conditions, the aircraft lands in Denver, Colorado, and the employee stays in Denver overnight. Assume further that the next day the aircraft flies to Seattle where the employee deplanes. The employee's flight is the distance between the airport in St. Louis and the airport in Seattle.

Example (2). Assume that a trip originates in New York, New York, with five passengers and that the aircraft makes a stop in Chicago, Illinois, so that one of the passengers can deplane for a purpose unrelated to the personal purposes of the other passengers whose flights are being valued. The aircraft then goes on to Los Angeles, California, where the other four passengers will deplane. The flight of the passenger who deplaned in Chicago is the distance between the airport in New York and the airport in Chicago. The stop in Chicago is disregarded as an intermediate stop, however, when measuring the flights taken by each of the other four passengers. Their flights would be the distance between the airport in New York and the airport in Los Angeles.

(4) *Personal and non-personal flights.*—(i) *In general.*—The valuation rule of this paragraph (g) applies to personal flights on employer-provided aircraft. A personal flight is one the value of which is not excludable under another section of subtitle A of the Internal Revenue Code of 1986, such as under section 132(d) (relating to a working condition fringe). However, solely for purposes of paragraphs (g)(4)(ii) and (g)(4)(iii) of this section, references to personal flights do not include flights a portion of which would not be excludable from income by reason of section 274(c).

(ii) *Trip primarily for employer's business.*—If an employee combines, in one trip, personal and business flights on an employer-provided aircraft and the employee's trip is primarily for the employer's business (see §1.162-2(b)(2)), the employee must include in income the excess of the value of all the flights that comprise the trip over the value of the flights that would have been taken had there been no personal flights but only business flights. For example, assume that an employee flies on an employer-provided aircraft from Chicago, Illinois, to Miami, Florida, for the employer's business and that from Miami the employee flies on the employer-provided aircraft to Orlando, Florida, for personal purposes and then flies back to Chicago. Assume further that the primary purpose of the trip is for the employer's business. The amount includible in income is the excess of the value of the three flights (Chicago to Miami, Miami to Orlando, and Orlando to Chicago), over the value of the flights that would have been taken had there been no personal flights but only business flights (Chicago to Miami and Miami to Chicago).

(iii) *Primarily personal trip.*—If an employee combines, in one trip, personal and business flights on an employer-provided aircraft and the employee's trip is primarily personal (see §1.162-2(b)(2)), the amount includible in the employee's income is the value of the personal flights that would have been taken had there been no business flights but only personal flights. For example, assume that an employee flies on an employer-provided aircraft from San Francisco, California, to Los Angeles, California, for the employer's business and that from Los Angeles the employee flies on an employer-provided aircraft to Palm Springs, California, primarily for personal reasons and then flies back to San Francisco. Assume further that the primary purpose of the trip is personal. The amount includible in the employee's income is the value of personal flights that would have been taken had there been no business flights but only personal flights (San Francisco to Palm Springs and Palm Springs to San Francisco).

(iv) *Application of section 274(c).*—The value of employer-provided travel outside the United States away from home may not be excluded from the employee's gross income as a working condition fringe, by either the employer or the employee, to the extent not deductible by reason of section 274(c). The valuation rule of this paragraph (g) applies to that portion of the value of any flight not excludable by reason of section 274(c). Such value is includible in income in addition to the amounts determined under paragraphs (g)(4)(ii) and (g)(4)(iii) of this section.

(v) *Flights by individuals who are not personal guests.*—If an individual who is not an employee of the employer providing the aircraft is on a flight, and the individual is not the personal guest of any employee of the employer, the flight by the individual is not taxable to any employee of the employer providing the aircraft. The rule in the preceding sentence applies where the individual is provided the flight by the employer for noncompensatory business reasons of the employer. For example, assume that G, an employee of company Y, accompanies A, an employee of company X, on company X's aircraft for the purpose of inspecting land under consideration for purchase by company X from company Y. The flight by G is not taxable to A. No inference may be drawn from this paragraph (g)(4)(v) concerning the taxation of a flight provided to an individual who is neither an employee of the employer nor a personal guest of any employee of the employer.

(5) *Aircraft valuation formula.*—Under the valuation rule of this paragraph (g), the value of a flight is determined under the base aircraft valuation formula (also known as the Standard Industry Fare Level formula or SIFL) by multiplying the SIFL cents-per-mile rates applicable for the period during which the flight was taken by the appropriate aircraft multiple (as provided in paragraph (g)(7) of this section) and then adding the applicable terminal charge. The SIFL cents-per-mile rates in the formula and the terminal charge are calculated by the Department of Transportation and are revised semi-annually. The base aircraft valuation formula in effect from January 1, 1989 through June 30, 1989, is as follows: a terminal charge of $26.48 plus ($.1449 per mile for the first 500 miles, $.1105 per mile for miles between 501 and 1500, and $.1062 per mile for miles over 1500). For example, if a flight taken on January 15, 1989, by a non-control employee on an employer-provided aircraft with a maximum certified takeoff weight of 26,000 lbs. is 2,000 miles long, the value of the flight determined under this paragraph (g)(5) is $100.36 ((.313 × (($.1449 × 500) + ($.1105 × 1,000) + ($.1062 × 500))) + $26.48). The aircraft valuation formula applies separately to each flight being valued under this paragraph (g). Therefore, the number of miles an employee has flown on employer-provided aircraft flights prior to the flight being valued does not affect the determination of the value of the flight.

(6) *Discretion to provide new formula.*—The Commissioner may prescribe a different base aircraft valuation formula by regulation, Revenue Ruling or Revenue Procedure in the event that the calculation of the Standard Industry Fare Level is discontinued.

(7) *Aircraft multiples.*—(i) *In general.*—The aircraft multiples are based on the maximum certified takeoff weight of the aircraft. When applying the aircraft valuation formula to a flight, the appropriate aircraft multiple is multiplied by the product of the applicable SIFL cents-per-mile rates multiplied by the number of miles in the flight and then the terminal charge is added to the product. For purposes of applying the aircraft valuation formula described in paragraph (g)(5) of this section, the aircraft multiples are as follows:

Maximum Certified Takeoff Weight of the Aircraft	Aircraft Multiple for a Control Employee	Aircraft Multiple for a Non-Control Employee
6,000 lbs. or less	62.5 percent	15.6 percent
6,001—10,000 lbs.	125 percent	23.4 percent
10,001—25,000 lbs.	300 percent	31.3 percent
25,001 lbs. or more	400 percent	31.3 percent

(ii) *Flights treated as provided to a control employee.*—Except as provided in paragraph (g)(12) of this section, any flight provided to an individual whose flight would be taxable to a control employee (as defined in paragraphs (g)(8) and (9) of this section) as the recipient shall be valued as if such flight had been provided to that control employee. For example, assume that the chief executive officer of an employer, his spouse, and his two children fly on an employer-provided aircraft for personal purposes. Assume further that the maximum certified takeoff weight of the aircraft is 12,000 lbs. The amount includible in the employee's income is 4 × ((300 percent × the applicable SIFL cents-per-mile rates provided in paragraph (g)(5) of this section multiplied by the number of miles in the flight) plus the applicable terminal charge).

(8) *Control employee defined—Non-government employer.*—(i) *Definition.*—For purposes of this paragraph (g), a control employee of a non-government employer is any employee—

(A) Who is a Board- or shareholder-appointed, confirmed, or elected officer of the employer, limited to the lesser of—

(1) One percent of all employees (increased to the next highest integer, if not an integer) or

(2) Ten employees;

(B) Who is among the top one percent most highly-paid employees of the employer (increased to the next highest integer, if not an integer) limited to a maximum of 50;

(C) Who owns a five-percent or greater equity, capital, or profits interest in the employer; or

(D) Who is a director of the employer.

(ii) *Special rules for control employee definition.*—(A) *In general.*—For purposes of this paragraph (g), any employee who is a family member (within the meaning of section 267(c)(4)) of a control employee is also a control employee. For purposes of paragraph (g)(8)(i)(B) of this section, the term "employee" does not include any individual unless such individual is a common-law employee, partner, or one-percent or greater shareholder of the employer. Pursuant to this paragraph (g)(8), an employee may be a control employee under more than one of the requirements listed in paragraphs (g)(8)(i)(A) through (D) of this section. For example, an employee may be both an officer under paragraph (g)(8)(i)(A) of this section and a highly-paid employee under paragraph (g)(8)(i)(B) of this section. In this case, for purposes of the officer limitation rule of paragraph (g)(8)(i)(A) of this section and the highly-paid employee limitation rule of paragraph (g)(8)(i)(B) of this section, the employee would be counted in applying both limitations. For purposes of determining the one-percent limitation under paragraphs (g)(8)(i)(A) and (B) of this section, an employer shall exclude from consideration employees described in § 1.132-8(b)(3). Instead of applying the control employee definition of this paragraph (g)(8), an employer may treat all (and only) employees who are "highly compensated" employees (as defined in § 1.132-8(f)) as control employees for purposes of this paragraph (g).

(B) *Special rules for officers, owners, and highly-paid control employees.*—In no event shall an employee whose compensation is less than $50,000 be a control employee under paragraph (g)(8)(i)(A) or (B) of this section. For purposes of determining who is a five-percent (or one-percent) owner under this paragraph (g)(8), any individual who owns (or is considered as owning under section 318(a) or principles similar to section 318(a) for entities other than corporations) five percent (or one-percent) or more of the fair market value of an entity (the "owned entity") is considered a five-percent (or one-percent) owner of all entities which would be aggregated with the owned entity under the rules of section 414(b), (c), (m), or (o). For purposes of determining who is an officer or director with respect to an employer under this paragraph (g)(8), notwithstanding anything in this section to the contrary, if the employer would be aggregated with other employers under the rules of section 414(b), (c), (m), or (o), the officer definition and the limitations and the director definition are applied to each such separate employer rather than to the aggregated employer. An employee who is an officer or director of one employer (the "first employer") shall not be counted as an officer or a director of any other employer aggregated with the first employer under the rules of section 414(b), (c), or (m). If applicable, the officer limitation rule of paragraph (g)(8)(i)(A) of this section is applied to employees in descending order of their compensation. Thus, if an employer has 11 board-appointed officers and the limit imposed under paragraph (g)(8)(i)(A) of this section is 10 officers, the employee with the least compensation of those officers would not be a control employee under paragraph (g)(8)(i)(A) of this section.

(9) *Control employee defined—Government employer.*—For purposes of this paragraph (g), a control employee of a government employer is any—

(i) Elected official, or

(ii) Employee whose compensation equals or exceeds the compensation paid to a Federal Government employee holding a position at Executive Level V, determined under Chapter 11 of title 2, United States Code, as adjusted by section 5318 of title 5 United States Code.

For purposes of paragraph (f), the term "government" includes any Federal, state or local governmental unit, and any agency or instrumentality thereof. Instead of applying the control employee definition of paragraph (f)(6), an employer may treat all and only employees who are "highly compensated" employees (as defined in § 1.132-8(f)) as control employees for purposes of this paragraph (f).

(10) *"Compensation" defined.*—For purposes of this paragraph (g), the term "compensation" has the same meaning as in section 414(q)(7). Compensation includes all amounts received from all entities treated as a single employer under section 414(b), (c), (m), or (o). Levels of compensation shall be adjusted at the same time and in the same manner as provided in section 415(d). The first such adjustment was for calendar year 1988.

(11) *Treatment of former employees.*—For purposes of this paragraph (g), an employee who was a control employee of the employer (as defined in this paragraph (g)) at any time after reaching age 55, or within three years of separation from the service of the employer, is a control employee with respect to flights taken after separation from the service of the employer. An individual who is treated as a control employee under this paragraph (g)(11) is not counted when determining the limitations of paragraph (g)(8)(i)(A) and (B) of this section. Thus, the total number of individuals treated as control employees under such paragraphs may exceed the limitations of such paragraphs to the extent that this paragraph (g)(11) applies.

(12) *Seating capacity rule.*—(i) *In general.*—(A) *General rule.*— Where 50 percent or more of the regular passenger seating capacity of an aircraft (as used by the employer) is occupied by individuals whose flights are primarily for the employer's business (and whose flights are excludable from income under section 132(d)), the value of a flight on that aircraft by any employee who is not flying primarily for the employer's business (or who is flying primarily for the employer's business but the value of whose flight is not excludable under section 132(d) by reason of section 274(c)) is deemed to be zero. See § 1.132-5 which limits the working condition fringe exclusion under section 132(d) to situations where the employee receives the flight in connection with the performance of services for the employer providing the aircraft.

(B) *Special rules.*—(1) *Definition of "employee".*—For purposes of this paragraph (g)(12), the term "employee" includes only employees of the employer, including a partner of a partnership, providing the aircraft and does not include independent contractors and directors of the employer. A flight taken by an individual other than an "employee" as defined in the preceding sentence is considered a flight taken by an employee for purposes of this paragraph (g)(12) only if that individual is treated as an employee pursuant to section 132(f)(1) or that individual's flight is treated as a flight taken by an employee pursuant to section 132(f)(2). If—

(i) A flight by an individual is not considered a flight taken by an employee (as defined in this paragraph (g)(12)(i)),

(ii) The value of that individual's flight is not excludable under section 132(d), and

(iii) The seating capacity rule of this paragraph (g)(12) otherwise applies,

then the value of the flight provided to such an individual is the value of a flight provided to a non-control employee pursuant to paragraph (g)(5) of this section (even if the individual who would be taxed on the value of the flight is a control employee).

(2) *Example.*—The special rules of paragraph (g)(12)(i)(B)(1) of this section are illustrated by the following example:

Example. Assume that 60 percent of the regular passenger seating capacity of an employer's aircraft is occupied by individuals whose flights are primarily for the employer's business and are excludable from income under section 132(d). If a control employee, his spouse, and his dependent child fly on the employer's aircraft for primarily personal reasons, the value of the three flights is deemed to be zero. If, however, the control employee's cousin were provided a flight on the employer's aircraft, the value of the flight taken by the cousin is determined by applying the aircraft valuation formula of paragraph (g)(5) of this section (including the terminal charge) and the non-control employee aircraft multiples of paragraph (g)(7) of this section.

(ii) *Application of 50-percent test to multiple flights.*—The seating capacity rule of this paragraph (g)(12) must be met both at the time the individual whose flight is being valued boards the aircraft and at the time the individual deplanes. For example, assume that employee A boards an employer-provided aircraft for personal purposes in New York, New York, and that at that time 80 percent of the regular passenger seating capacity of the aircraft is occupied by individuals whose flights are primarily for the employer's business (and whose flights are excludable from income under section 132(d)) ("the business passengers"). If the aircraft flies directly to Hartford, Connecticut where all of the passengers, including A, deplane, the requirements of the seating capacity rule of this paragraph (g)(12) have been satisfied. If instead, some of the passengers, including A, remain on the aircraft in Hartford and the aircraft continues on to Boston, Massachusetts, where they all deplane, the requirements of the seating capacity rule of this paragraph (g)(12) will not be satisfied with respect to A's flight from New York to Boston unless at least 50 percent of the seats comprising the aircraft's regular passenger seating capacity were occupied by the business passengers at the time A deplanes in Boston.

(iii) *Regular passenger seating capacity.*—(A) *General rule.*—Except as otherwise provided, the regular passenger seating capacity of an aircraft is the maximum number of seats that have at any time on or prior to the date of the flight been on the aircraft (while owned or leased by the employer). Except to the extent excluded pursuant to paragraph (g)(12)(v) of this section, regular seating capacity includes all seats which may be occupied by members of the flight crew. It is irrelevant that, on a particular flight, less than the maximum number of seats are available for use because, for example, some of the seats are removed.

(B) *Special rules.*—When determining the maximum number of seats that have at any time on or prior to the date of the flight been on the aircraft (while owned or leased by the employer), seats that could not at any time be legally used during takeoff and have not at any time been used during takeoff are not counted. As of the date an employer permanently reduces the seating capacity of an aircraft, the regular passenger seating capacity is the reduced number of seats on the aircraft. The previous sentence shall not apply if at any time within 24 months after such reduction any seats are added in the aircraft. Unless the conditions of this paragraph (g)(12)(iii)(B) are satisfied, jumpseats and removable seats used solely for purposes of flight crew training are counted for purposes of the seating capacity rule of this paragraph (g)(12).

(iv) *Examples.*—The rules of paragraph (g)(12)(iii) of this section are illustrated by the following examples:

Example (1). Employer A and employer B order the same aircraft, except that A orders it with 10 seats and B orders it with eight seats. A always uses its aircraft as a 10-seat aircraft; B always uses its aircraft as an eight-seat aircraft. The regular passenger seating capacity of A's aircraft is 10 and of B's aircraft is eight.

Example (2). Assume the same facts as in example (1), except that whenever A's chief executive officer and spouse use the aircraft eight seats are removed. Even if substantially all of the use of the aircraft is by the chief executive officer and spouse, the regular passenger seating capacity of the aircraft is 10.

Example (3). Assume the same facts as in example (1), except that whenever more than eight people want to fly in B's aircraft, two extra seats are added. Even if substantially all of the use of the aircraft occurs with eight seats, the regular passenger seating capacity of the aircraft is 10.

Example (4). Employer C purchases an aircraft with 12 seats. Three months later C remodels the interior of the aircraft and permanently removes four of the seats. Upon completion of the remodeling, the regular passenger seating capacity of the aircraft is eight. If, however, any seats are added within 24 months after the remodeling, the regular seating capacity of the aircraft is treated as 12 throughout the entire period.

(v) *Seats occupied by flight crew.*—When determining the regular passenger seating capacity of an aircraft, any seat occupied by a member of the flight crew (whether or not such individual is an employee of the employer providing the aircraft) shall not be counted, unless the purpose of the flight by such individual is not primarily to serve as a member of the flight crew. If the seat occupied by a member of the flight crew is not counted as a passenger seat pursuant to the previous sentence, such member of the flight crew is disregarded in applying the 50-percent test described in the first sentence of paragraph (g)(12)(i) of this section. For example, assume that prior to application of this paragraph (g)(12)(v) the regular passenger seating capacity of an aircraft is one. Assume further that an employee pilots the aircraft and that the employee's flight is not primarily for the employer's business. If the employee's spouse occupies the other seat for personal purposes, the seating capacity rule is not met and the value of both flights must be included in the employee's income. If, however, the employee's flight was primarily for the employer's business (unrelated to serving as a member of the flight crew), then the seating capacity rule is met and the value of the flight for the employee's spouse is deemed to be zero. If the employee's flight were primarily to serve as a member of the flight crew, then the seating capacity rule is not met and the value of a flight by any passenger for primarily personal reasons is not deemed to be zero.

(13) *Erroneous use of the non-commercial flight valuation rule.*—(i) *Certain errors in the case of a flight by a control employee.*—If—

(A) The non-commercial flight valuation rule of this paragraph (g) is applied by an employer or a control employee, as the case may be, on a return as originally filed or on an amended return on the grounds that either—

(1) The control employee is not in fact a control employee, or

(2) The aircraft is within a specific weight classification, and

(B) Either position is subsequently determined to be erroneous,

the valuation rule of this paragraph (g) is not available to value the flight taken by that control employee by the person or persons taking the erroneous position. With respect to the weight classifications, the previous sentence does not apply if the position taken is that the weight of the aircraft is greater than it is subsequently determined to be. If, with respect to a flight by a control employee, the seating capacity rule of paragraph (g)(12) of this section is used by an employer or the control employee, as the case may be, on a return as originally filed or on an amended return, the valuation rule of this paragraph (g) is not available to value the flight taken by that control employee by the person or persons taking the erroneous position.

(ii) *Value of flight excluded as a working condition fringe.*—If either an employer or an employee, on a return as originally filed or on an amended return, excludes from the employee's income or wages all or any part of the value of a flight on the grounds that the flight was excludable as a working condition fringe under section 132, and that position is subsequently determined to be erroneous, the valuation rule of this paragraph (g) is not available to value the flight taken by that employee by the person or persons taking the erroneous position. Instead, the general valuation rules of paragraph (b)(5) and (6) of this section apply.

(14) *Consistency rules.*—(i) *Use by employer.*—Except as otherwise provided in paragraph (g)(13) or paragraph (g)(14)(iii) of this section or in §1.132-5(m)(4), if the non-commercial flight valuation rule of

this paragraph (g) is used by an employer to value any flight provided in a calendar year, the rule must be used to value all flights provided to all employees in the calendar year.

(ii) *Use by employee.*—Except as otherwise provided in paragraph (g)(13) or (g)(14)(iii) of this section or in §1.132-5(m)(4), if the non-commercial flight valuation rule of this paragraph (g) is used by an employee to value a flight provided by an employer in a calendar year, the rule must be used to value all flights provided to the employee by that employer in the calendar year.

(iii) *Exception for entertainment flights provided to specified individuals after October 22, 2004.*—Notwithstanding the provisions of paragraph (g)(14)(i) of this section, an employer may use the general valuation rules of paragraph (b) of this section to value the entertainment use of an aircraft provided after October 22, 2004, to a specified individual. An employer who uses the general valuation rules of paragraph (b) of this section to value any entertainment use of an aircraft by a specified individual in a calendar year must use the general valuation rules of paragraph (b) of this section to value all entertainment use of aircraft provided to all specified individuals during that calendar year.

(A) *Specified individuals defined.*—For purposes of paragraph (g)(14)(iii) of this section, *specified individual* is defined in section 274(e)(2)(B) and §1.274-9(b).

(B) *Entertainment defined.*—For purposes of paragraph (g)(14)(iii) of this section, *entertainment* is defined in §1.274-2(b)(1).

(h) *Commercial flight valuation rule.*—(1) *In general.*—Under the commercial flight valuation rule of this paragraph (h), the value of a space-available flight (as defined in paragraph (h)(2) of this section) on a commercial aircraft is 25 percent of the actual carrier's highest unrestricted coach fare in effect for the particular flight taken. The rule of this paragraph (h) is available only to an individual described in §1.132-1(b)(1).

(2) *Space-available flight.*—The commercial flight valuation rule of this paragraph (h) is available to value a space-available flight. The term "space-available flight" means a flight on a commercial aircraft—

(i) Which is subject to the same types of restrictions customarily associated with flying on an employee "stand-by" or "space-available" basis, and

(ii) Which meets the definition of a no-additional-cost service under section 132(b), except that the flight is provided to an individual other than the employee or an individual treated as the employee under section 132(f). Thus, a flight is not a space-available flight if the employer guarantees the employee a seat on the flight or if the nondiscrimination requirements of section 132(h)(1) and §1.132-8 are not satisfied. A flight may be a space-available flight even if the airline that is the actual carrier is not the employer of the employee.

(3) *Commercial aircraft.*—If the actual carrier does not offer, in the ordinary course of its business, air transportation to customers on a per-seat basis, the commercial flight valuation rule of this paragraph (h) is not available. Thus, if, in the ordinary course of its line of business, the employer only offers air transportation to customers on a charter basis, the commercial flight valuation rule of this paragraph (h) may not be used to value a space-available flight on the employer's aircraft. If the commercial flight valuation rule is not available, the flight may be valued under the non-commercial flight valuation rule of paragraph (g) of this section.

(4) *Timing of inclusion.*—The date that the flight is taken is the relevant date for purposes of applying section 61(a)(1) and this section to a space-available flight on a commercial aircraft. The date of purchase or issuance of a pass or ticket is not relevant. Thus, this section applies to a flight taken on or after January 1, 1989, regardless of the date on which the pass or ticket for the flight was purchased or issued.

(5) *Consistency rules.*—(i) *Use by employer.*—If the commercial flight valuation rule of this paragraph (h) is used by an employer to value any flight provided in a calendar year, the rule must be used to value all flights eligible for use of the rule provided in the calendar year.

(ii) *Use by employee.*—If the commercial flight valuation rule of this paragraph (h) is used by an employee to value a flight provided by an employer in a calendar year, the rule must be used to value all flights provided by that employer eligible for use of the rule taken by such employee in the calendar year.

(i) [Reserved.]

(j) *Valuation of meals provided at an employer-operated eating facility for employees.*—(1) *In general.*—The valuation rule of this paragraph (j) may be used to value a meal provided at an employer-operated eating facility for employees (as defined in § 1.132-7). For rules relating to an exclusion for the value of meals provided at an employer-operated eating facility for employees, see section 132(e)(2) and § 1.132-7.

(2) *Valuation formula.*—(i) *In general.*—The value of all meals provided at an employer-operated eating facility for employees during a calendar year ("total meal value") is 150 percent of the direct operating costs of the eating facility determined separately with respect to such eating facility whether or not the direct operating costs test is applied separately to such eating facility under § 1.132-7(b)(2). For purposes of this paragraph (j), the definition of direct operating costs provided in § 1.132-7(b) and the adjustments specified in § 1.132-7(a)(2) apply. The taxable value of meals provided at an eating facility may be determined in two ways. The "individual meal subsidy" may be treated as the taxable value of a meal provided at the eating facility (see paragraph (j)(2)(ii) of this section) to a particular employee. Alternatively, the employer may allocate the "total meal subsidy" among employees (see paragraph (j)(2)(iii) of this section).

(ii) *"Individual meal subsidy" defined.*—The "individual meal subsidy" is determined by multiplying the amount paid by the employee for a particular meal by a fraction, the numerator of which is the total meal value and the denominator of which is the gross receipts of the eating facility for the calendar year and then subtracting the amount paid by the employee for the meal. The taxable value of meals provided to a particular employee during a calendar year, therefore, is the sum of the individual meal subsidies provided to the employee during the calendar year. This rule is available only if there is a charge for each meal selection and if each employee is charged the same price for any given meal selection.

(iii) *Allocation of "total meal subsidy".*—Instead of using the individual meal subsidy method provided in paragraph (j)(2)(ii) of this section, the employer may allocate the "total meal subsidy" (total meal value less the gross receipts of the facility) among employees in any manner reasonable under the circumstances. It will be presumed reasonable for an employer to allocate the total meal subsidy on a per-employee basis if the employer has information that would substantiate to the satisfaction of the Commissioner that each employee was provided approximately the same number of meals at the facility.

(k) *Commuting valuation rule for certain employees.*—(1) *In general.*—Under the rule of this paragraph (k), the value of the commuting use of employer-provided transportation may be determined under paragraph (k)(3) of this section if the following criteria are met by the employer and employee with respect to the transportation:

(i) The transportation is provided, solely because of unsafe conditions, to an employee who would ordinarily walk or use public transportation for commuting to or from work;

(ii) The employer has established a written policy (e.g., in the employer's personnel manual) under which the transportation is not provided for the employee's personal purposes other than for commuting due to unsafe conditions and the employer's practice in fact corresponds with the policy;

(iii) The transportation is not used for personal purposes other than commuting due to unsafe conditions; and

(iv) The employee receiving the employer-provided transportation is a qualified employee of the employer (as defined in paragraph (k)(6) of this section).

(2) *Trip-by-trip basis.*—The special valuation rule of this paragraph (k) applies on a trip-by-trip basis. If an employer and employee fail to meet the criteria of paragraph (k)(1) of this section with respect to any trip, the value of the transportation for that trip is not determined under paragraph (k)(3) of this section and the amount includible in the employee's income is determined by reference to the fair market value of the transportation.

(3) *Commuting value.*—(i) *$1.50 per one-way commute.*—If the requirements of this paragraph (k) are satisfied, the value of the commuting use of the employer-provided transportation is $1.50 per one-way commute (i.e., from home to work or from work to home).

(ii) *Value per employee.*—If transportation is provided to more than one qualified employee at the same time, the amount includible in the income of each employee is $1.50 per one-way commute.

(4) *Definition of employer-provided transportation.*—For purposes of this paragraph (k), "employer-provided transportation" means transportation by vehicle (as defined in paragraph (f)(4) of this section) that is purchased by the employer (or that is purchased by the employee and reimbursed by the employer) from a party that is not related to the employer for the purpose of transporting a quali-

fied employee to or from work. Reimbursements made by an employer to an employee to cover the cost of purchasing transportation (e.g., hiring cabs) must be made under a bona fide reimbursement arrangement.

(5) *Unsafe conditions.*—Unsafe conditions exist if a reasonable person would, under the facts and circumstances, consider it unsafe for the employee to walk to or from home, or to walk to or use public transportation at the time of day the employee must commute. One of the factors indicating whether it is unsafe is the history of crime in the geographic area surrounding the employee's workplace or residence at the time of day the employee must commute.

(6) *Qualified employee defined.*—(i) *In general.*—For purposes of this paragraph (k), a qualified employee is one who meets the following requirements with respect to the employer:

(A) The employee performs services during the current year, is paid on an hourly basis, is not claimed under section 213(a)(1) of the Fair Labor Standards Act of 1938 (as amended), 29 U.S.C. §§ 201-219 (FLSA), to be exempt from the minimum wage and maximum hour provisions of the FLSA, and is within a classification with respect to which the employer actually pays, or has specified in writing that it will pay, compensation for overtime equal to or exceeding one and one-half times the regular rate as provided by section 207 of the FLSA; and

(B) The employee does not receive compensation from the employer in excess of the amount permitted by section 414(q)(1)(C) of the Code.

(ii) *"Compensation" and "paid on an hourly basis" defined.*—For purposes of this paragraph (k), "compensation" has the same meaning as in section 414(q)(7). Compensation includes all amounts received from all entities treated as a single employer under section 414(b), (c), (m), or (o). Levels of compensation shall be adjusted at the same time and in the same manner as provided in section 415(d). If an employee's compensation is stated on an annual basis, the employee is treated as "paid on an hourly basis" for purposes of this paragraph (k) as long as the employee is not claimed to be exempt from the minimum wage and maximum hour provisions of the FLSA and is paid overtime wages either equal to or exceeding one and one-half the employee's regular hourly rate of pay.

(iii) *FLSA compliance required.*—An employee will not be considered a qualified employee for purposes of this paragraph (k), unless the employer is in compliance with the recordkeeping requirements concerning that employee's wages, hours, and other conditions and practices of employment as provided in section 211(c) of the FLSA and 29 CFR part 516.

(iv) *Issues arising under the FLSA.*—If questions arise concerning an employee's classification under the FLSA, the pronouncements and rulings of the Administrator of the Wage and Hour Division, Department of Labor are determinative.

(v) *Non-qualified employees.*—If an employee is not a qualified employee within the meaning of this paragraph (k)(6), no portion of the value of the commuting use of employer-provided transportation is excluded under this paragraph (k).

(7) *Examples.*—This paragraph (k) is illustrated by the following examples:

Example 1. A and B are word-processing clerks employed by Y, an accounting firm in a large metropolitan area, and both are qualified employees under paragraph (k)(6) of this section. The normal working hours for A and B are from 11:00 p.m. until 7:00 a.m. and public transportation, the only means of transportation available to A or B, would be considered unsafe by a reasonable person at the time they are required to commute from home to work. In response, Y hires a car service to pick up A and B at their homes each evening for purposes of transporting them to work. The amount includible in the income of both A and B is $1.50 for the one-way commute from home to work.

Example 2. Assume the same facts as in *Example 1*, except that Y also hires a car service to return A and B to their homes each morning at the conclusion of their shifts and public transportation would not be considered unsafe by a reasonable person at the time of day A and B commute to their homes. The value of the commute from work to home is includible in the income of both A and B by reference to fair market value since unsafe conditions do not exist for that trip.

Example 3. C is an associate for Z, a law firm in a metropolitan area. The normal working hours for C's law firm are from 9:00 a.m. until 6:00 p.m., but C's ordinary office hours are from 10:00 a.m. until 8:00 p.m. Public transportation, the only means of transportation available to C at the time C commutes from work to home during the evening, would be considered unsafe by a reasonable person. In response, Z hires a car service to take C home each evening. C does not receive annual compensation from Z in excess of the amount permitted by section 414(q)(1)(C) of the Code. However, C is treated as an employee exempt from the provisions of the FLSA and, accordingly, is not paid overtime wages. Therefore, C is not a qualified employee within the meaning of paragraph (k)(6) of this section. The value of the commute from work to home is includible in C's income by reference to fair market value.

(8) *Effective date.*—This paragraph (k) applies to employer-provided transportation provided to a qualified employee on or after July l, 1991. [Reg. §1.61-21.]

☐ [*T.D.* 8256, 7-5-89. *Amended by T.D.* 8389, 1-15-92, *T.D.* 8457, 12-29-92, *T.D.* 9597, 7-31-2012, *T.D.* 9849, 3-11-2019 *and T.D.* 9893, 2-4-2020.]

[Reg. §1.61-22.]

§1.61-22. Taxation of split-dollar life insurance arrangements.—(a) *Scope.*—(1) *In general.*—This section provides rules for the taxation of a splitdollar life insurance arrangement for purposes of the income tax, the gift tax, the Federal Insurance Contributions Act (FICA), the Federal Unemployment Tax Act (FUTA), the Railroad Retirement Tax Act (RRTA), and the Self-Employment Contributions Act of 1954 (SECA). For the Collection of Income Tax at Source on Wages, this section also provides rules for the taxation of a split-dollar life insurance arrangement, other than a payment under a split-dollar life insurance arrangement that is a split-dollar loan under §1.7872-15(b)(1). A split-dollar life insurance arrangement (as defined in paragraph (b) of this section) is subject to the rules of paragraphs (d) through (g) of this section, §1.7872-15, or general tax rules. For rules to determine which rules apply to a split-dollar life insurance arrangement, see paragraph (b)(3) of this section.

(2) *Overview.*—Paragraph (b) of this section defines a split-dollar life insurance arrangement and provides rules to determine whether an arrangement is subject to the rules of paragraphs (d) through (g) of this section, §1.7872-15, or general tax rules. Paragraph (c) of this section defines certain other terms. Paragraph (d) of this section sets forth rules for the taxation of economic benefits provided under a split-dollar life insurance arrangement. Paragraph (e) of this section sets forth rules for the taxation of amounts received under a life insurance contract that is part of a split-dollar life insurance arrangement. Paragraph (f) of this section provides rules for additional tax consequences of a split-dollar life insurance arrangement, including the treatment of death benefit proceeds. Paragraph (g) of this section provides rules for the transfer of a life insurance contract (or an undivided interest in the contract) that is part of a split-dollar life insurance arrangement. Paragraph (h) of this section provides examples illustrating the application of this section. Paragraph (j) of this section provides the effective date of this section.

(b) *Split-dollar life insurance arrangement.*—(1) *In general.*—A split-dollar life insurance arrangement is any arrangement between an owner and a non-owner of a life insurance contract that satisfies the following criteria—

(i) Either party to the arrangement pays, directly or indirectly, all or any portion of the premiums on the life insurance contract, including a payment by means of a loan to the other party that is secured by the life insurance contract;

(ii) At least one of the parties to the arrangement paying premiums under paragraph (b)(1)(i) of this section is entitled to recover (either conditionally or unconditionally) all or any portion of those premiums and such recovery is to be made from, or is secured by, the proceeds of the life insurance contract; and

(iii) The arrangement is not part of a group-term life insurance plan described in section 79 unless the group-term life insurance plan provides permanent benefits to employees (as defined in §1.79-0).

(2) *Special rule.*—(i) *In general.*—Any arrangement between an owner and a non-owner of a life insurance contract is treated as a split-dollar life insurance arrangement (regardless of whether the criteria of paragraph (b)(1) of this section are satisfied) if the arrangement is described in paragraph (b)(2)(ii) or (iii) of this section.

(ii) *Compensatory arrangements.*—An arrangement is described in this paragraph (b)(2)(ii) if the following criteria are satisfied—

(A) The arrangement is entered into in connection with the performance of services and is not part of a group-term life insurance plan described in section 79;

(B) The employer or service recipient pays, directly or indirectly, all or any portion of the premiums; and

(C) Either—

(1) The beneficiary of all or any portion of the death benefit is designated by the employee or service provider or is any person whom the employee or service provider would reasonably be expected to designate as the beneficiary; or

(2) The employee or service provider has any interest in the policy cash value of the life insurance contract.

(iii) *Shareholder arrangements.*—An arrangement is described in this paragraph (b)(2)(iii) if the following criteria are satisfied—

(A) The arrangement is entered into between a corporation and another person in that person's capacity as a shareholder in the corporation;

(B) The corporation pays, directly or indirectly, all or any portion of the premiums; and

(C) Either—

(1) The beneficiary of all or any portion of the death benefit is designated by the shareholder or is any person whom the shareholder would reasonably be expected to designate as the beneficiary; or

(2) The shareholder has any interest in the policy cash value of the life insurance contract.

(3) *Determination of whether this section or §1.7872-15 applies to a split-dollar life insurance arrangement.*—(i) *Split-dollar life insurance arrangements involving split-dollar loans under §1.7872-15.*—Except as provided in paragraph (b)(3)(ii) of this section, paragraphs (d) through (g) of this section do not apply to any split-dollar loan as defined in §1.7872-15(b)(1). Section 1.7872-15 applies to any such loan. See paragraph (b)(5) of this section for the treatment of a payment made by a non-owner under a split-dollar life insurance arrangement if the payment is not a split-dollar loan.

(ii) *Exceptions.*—Paragraphs (d) through (g) of this section apply (and §1.7872-15 does not apply) to any split-dollar life insurance arrangement if—

(A) The arrangement is entered into in connection with the performance of services, and the employer or service recipient is the owner of the life insurance contract (or is treated as the owner of the contract under paragraph (c)(1)(ii)(A)(1) of this section); or

(B) The arrangement is entered into between a donor and a donee (for example, a life insurance trust) and the donor is the owner of the life insurance contract (or is treated as the owner of the contract under paragraph (c)(1)(ii)(A)(2) of this section).

(4) *Consistency requirement.*—A split-dollar life insurance arrangement described in paragraph (b)(1) or (2) of this section must be treated in the same manner by the owner and the non-owner of the life insurance contract under either the rules of this section or §1.7872-15. In addition, the owner and non-owner must fully account for all amounts under the arrangement under paragraph (b)(5) of this section, paragraphs (d) through (g) of this section, or §1.7872-15.

(5) *Non-owner payments that are not split-dollar loans.*—If a non-owner of a life insurance contract makes premium payments (directly or indirectly) under a split-dollar life insurance arrangement, and the payments are neither split-dollar loans nor consideration for economic benefits described in paragraph (d) of this section, then neither the rules of paragraphs (d) through (g) of this section nor the rules in §1.7872-15 apply to such payments. Instead, general income tax, employment tax, self-employment tax, and gift tax principles apply to the premium payments. See, for example, §1.61-2(d)(2)(ii)(A).

(6) *Waiver, cancellation, or forgiveness.*—If a repayment obligation described in §1.7872-15(a)(2) is waived, cancelled, or forgiven at any time, then the parties must take the amount waived, cancelled, or forgiven into account in accordance with the relationships between the parties (for example, as compensation in the case of an employee-employer relationship).

(7) *Change in the owner.*—If payments made by a non-owner to an owner were treated as split-dollar loans under §1.7872-15 and the split-dollar life insurance arrangement is modified such that, after the modification, the non-owner is the owner (within the meaning of paragraph (c)(1) of this section) of the life insurance contract under the arrangement, paragraphs (d) through (g) of this section apply to the split-dollar life insurance arrangement from the date of the modification. The payments made (both before and after the modification) are not treated as split-dollar loans under §1.7872-15 on or after the date of the modification. The non-owner of the life insurance contract under the modified split-dollar life insurance arrangement must fully take into account all economic benefits provided under the arrangement under paragraph (d) of this section on or after the date of the modification. For the treatment of a transfer of the contract when the unmodified arrangement is governed by paragraphs (d) through (g) of this section, see paragraph (g) of this section.

(c) *Definitions.*—The following definitions apply for purposes of this section:

(1) *Owner.*—(i) *In general.*—With respect to a life insurance contract, the person named as the policy owner of such contract generally is the owner of such contract. If two or more persons are named as policy owners of a life insurance contract and each person has, at all times, all the incidents of ownership with respect to an undivided interest in the contract, each person is treated as the owner of a separate contract to the extent of such person's undivided interest. If two or more persons are named as policy owners of a life insurance contract but each person does not have, at all times, all the incidents of ownership with respect to an undivided interest in the contract, the person who is the first-named policy owner is treated as the owner of the entire contract.

(ii) *Special rule for certain arrangements.*—(A) *In general.*—Notwithstanding paragraph (c)(1)(i) of this section—

(1) An employer or service recipient is treated as the owner of a life insurance contract under a split-dollar life insurance arrangement that is entered into in connection with the performance of services if, at all times, the only economic benefit that will be provided under the arrangement is current life insurance protection as described in paragraph (d)(3) of this section; and

(2) A donor is treated as the owner of a life insurance contract under a split-dollar life insurance arrangement that is entered into between a donor and a donee (for example, a life insurance trust) if, at all times, the only economic benefit that will be provided under the arrangement is current life insurance protection as described in paragraph (d)(3) of this section.

(B) *Modifications.*—If an arrangement described in paragraph (c)(1)(ii)(A) of this section is modified such that the arrangement is no longer described in paragraph (c)(1)(ii)(A) of this section, the following rules apply:

(1). If, immediately after such modification, the employer, service recipient, or donor is the owner of the life insurance contract under the split-dollar life insurance arrangement (determined without regard to paragraph (c)(1)(ii)(A) of this section), the employer, service recipient, or donor continues to be treated as the owner of the life insurance contract.

(2). If, immediately after such modification, the employer, service recipient, or donor is not the owner of the life insurance contract under the split-dollar life insurance arrangement (determined without regard to paragraph (c)(1)(ii)(A) of this section), the employer, service recipient, or donor is treated as having made a transfer of the entire life insurance contract to the employee, service provider, or donee under the rules of paragraph (g) of this section as of the date of such modification.

(3) For purposes of this paragraph (c)(1)(ii)(B), entering into a successor split-dollar life insurance arrangement that has the effect of providing any economic benefit in addition to that described in paragraph (d)(3) of this section is treated as a modification of the prior split-dollar life insurance arrangement.

(iii) *Attribution rules for compensatory arrangements.*—For purposes of this section, if a split-dollar life insurance arrangement is entered into in connection with the performance of services, the employer or service recipient is treated as the owner of the life insurance contract if the owner (within the meaning of paragraph (c)(1)(i) of this section) of the life insurance contract under the split-dollar life insurance arrangement is—

(A) A trust described in section 402(b);

(B) A trust that is treated as owned (within the meaning of sections 671 through 677) by the employer or the service recipient;

(C) A welfare benefit fund within the meaning of section 419(e)(1); or

(D) A member of the employer or service recipient's controlled group (within the meaning of section 414(b)) or a trade or business that is under common control with the employer or service recipient (within the meaning of section 414(c)).

(iv) *Life insurance contracts owned by partnerships.*—[Reserved]

(2) *Non-owner.*—(i) *Definition.*—With respect to a life insurance contract, a non-owner is any person (other than the owner of such contract under paragraph (c)(1) of this section) that has any direct or indirect interest in such contract (but not including a life insurance company acting only in its capacity as the issuer of a life insurance contract).

(ii) *Example.*—The following example illustrates the provisions of this paragraph (c)(2):

Example. (i) On January 1, 2009, Employer R and Trust T, an irrevocable life insurance trust that is not treated under sections 671 through 677 as owned by a grantor or other person, enter into a split-dollar life insurance arrangement in connection with the performance of services under which R will pay all the premiums on the life insurance contract until the termination of the arrangement or the death of E, an employee of R. C, the beneficiary of T, is E's child. R is the owner of the contract under paragraph (c)(1)(i) of this section. E is the insured under the life insurance contract. Upon termination of the arrangement or E's death, R is entitled to receive the lesser of the aggregate premiums or the policy cash value of the contract and T will be entitled to receive any remaining amounts. Under the terms of the arrangement and applicable state law, the policy cash value is fully accessible by R and R's creditors but T has the right to borrow or withdraw at any time the portion of the policy cash value exceeding the amount payable to R.

(ii) Because E and T each have an indirect interest in the life insurance contract that is part of the split-dollar life insurance arrangement, each is a non-owner under paragraph (c)(2)(i) of this section. E and T each are provided economic benefits described in paragraph (d)(2) of this section pursuant to the split-dollar life insurance arrangement. Economic benefits are provided by owner R to E as a payment of compensation, and separately provided by E to T as a gift.

(3) *Transfer of entire contract or undivided interest therein.*—A transfer of the ownership of a life insurance contract (or an undivided interest in such contract) that is part of a split-dollar life insurance arrangement occurs on the date that a non-owner becomes the owner (within the meaning of paragraph (c)(1) of this section) of the entire contract or of an undivided interest in the contract.

(4) *Undivided interest.*—An undivided interest in a life insurance contract consists of an identical fractional or percentage interest or share in each right, benefit, and obligation with respect to the contract. In the case of any arrangement purporting to create undivided interests where, in substance, the rights, benefits or obligations are shared to any extent among the holders of such interests, the arrangement will be treated as a split-dollar life insurance arrangement.

(5) *Employment tax.*—The term employment tax means any tax imposed by, or collected under, the Federal Insurance Contributions Act (FICA), the Federal Unemployment Tax Act (FUTA), the Railroad Retirement Tax Act (RRTA), and the Collection of Income Tax at Source on Wages.

(6) *Self-employment tax.*—The term self-employment tax means the tax imposed by the Self-Employment Contributions Act of 1954 (SECA).

(d) *Economic benefits provided under a split-dollar life insurance arrangement.*—(1) *In general.*—In the case of a split-dollar life insurance arrangement subject to the rules of paragraphs (d) through (g) of this section, economic benefits are treated as being provided to the non-owner of the life insurance contract. The non-owner (and the owner for gift and employment tax purposes) must take into account the full value of all economic benefits described in paragraph (d)(2) of this section, reduced by the consideration paid directly or indirectly by the non-owner to the owner for those economic benefits. Depending on the relationship between the owner and the non-owner, the economic benefits may constitute a payment of compensation, a distribution under section 301, a contribution to capital, a gift, or a transfer having a different tax character. Further, depending on the relationship between or among a non-owner and one or more other persons (including a non-owner or non-owners), the economic benefits may be treated as provided from the owner to the non-owner and as separately provided from the non-owner to such other person or persons (for example, as a payment of compensation from an employer to an employee and as a gift from the employee to the employee's child).

(2) *Value of economic benefits.*—The value of the economic benefits provided to a non-owner for a taxable year under the arrangement equals—

(i) The cost of current life insurance protection provided to the non-owner as determined under paragraph (d)(3) of this section;

(ii) The amount of policy cash value to which the non-owner has current access within the meaning of paragraph (d)(4)(ii) of this section (to the extent that such amount was not actually taken into account for a prior taxable year); and

(iii) The value of any economic benefits not described in paragraph (d)(2)(i) or (ii) of this section provided to the non-owner (to the extent not actually taken into account for a prior taxable year).

(3) *Current life insurance protection.*—(i) *Amount of current life insurance protection.*—In the case of a split-dollar life insurance arrangement described in paragraph (d)(1) of this section, the amount of the current life insurance protection provided to the non-owner for a taxable year (or any portion thereof in the case of the first year or the last year of the arrangement) equals the excess of the death benefit of the life insurance contract (including paid-up additions thereto) over the total amount payable to the owner (including any outstanding policy loans that offset amounts otherwise payable to

Reg. § 1.61-22(d)(3)(i)

the owner) under the split-dollar life insurance arrangement, less the portion of the policy cash value actually taken into account under paragraph (d)(1) of this section or paid for by the non-owner under paragraph (d)(1) of this section for the current taxable year or any prior taxable year.

(ii) *Cost of current life insurance protection.*—The cost of current life insurance protection provided to the non-owner for any year (or any portion thereof in the case of the first year or the last year of the arrangement) equals the amount of the current life insurance protection provided to the non-owner (determined under paragraph (d)(3)(i) of this section) multiplied by the life insurance premium factor designated or permitted in guidance published in the Internal Revenue Bulletin (see § 601.601(d)(2)(ii) of this chapter).

(4) *Policy cash value.*—(i) *In general.*—For purposes of this paragraph (d), policy cash value is determined disregarding surrender charges or other similar charges or reductions. Policy cash value includes policy cash value attributable to paid-up additions.

(ii) *Current access.*—For purposes of this paragraph (d), a non-owner has current access to that portion of the policy cash value—

(A) To which, under the arrangement, the non-owner has a current or future right; and

(B) That currently is directly or indirectly accessible by the non-owner, inaccessible to the owner, or inaccessible to the owner's general creditors.

(5) *Valuation date.*—(i) *General rules.*—For purposes of this paragraph (d), the amount of the current life insurance protection and the policy cash value shall be determined on the same valuation date. The valuation date is the last day of the non-owner's taxable year, unless the owner and non-owner agree to instead use the policy anniversary date as the valuation date. Notwithstanding the previous sentence, if the split-dollar life insurance arrangement terminates during the taxable year of the non-owner, the value of such economic benefits is determined on the day that the arrangement terminates.

(ii) *Consistency requirement.*—The owner and non-owner of the split-dollar life insurance arrangement must use the same valuation date. In addition, the same valuation date must be used for all years prior to termination of the split-dollar life insurance arrangement unless the parties receive consent of the Commissioner to change the valuation date.

(iii) *Artifice or device.*—Notwithstanding paragraph (d)(5)(i) of this section, if any artifice or device is used to understate the amount of any economic benefit on the valuation date in paragraph (d)(5)(i) of this section, then, for purposes of this paragraph (d), the date on which the amount of the economic benefit is determined is the date on which the amount of the economic benefit is greatest during that taxable year.

(iv) *Special rule for certain taxes.*—For purposes of employment tax (as defined in paragraph (c)(5) of this section), self-employment tax (as defined in paragraph (c)(6) of this section), and sections 6654 and 6655 (relating to the failure to pay estimated income tax), the portions of the current life insurance protection and the policy cash value that are treated as provided by the owner to the non-owner shall be treated as so provided on the last day of the taxable year of the non-owner. Notwithstanding the previous sentence, if the split-dollar life insurance arrangement terminates during the taxable year of the non-owner, such portions of the current life insurance protection and the policy cash value shall be treated as so provided on the day that the arrangement terminates.

(6) *Examples.*—The following examples illustrate the rules of this paragraph (d). Except as otherwise provided, both examples assume the following facts: employer (R) is the owner (as defined in paragraph (c)(1)(i) of this section) and employee (E) is the non-owner (as defined in paragraph (c)(2)(i) of this section) of a life insurance contract that is part of a split-dollar life insurance arrangement that is subject to the provisions of paragraphs (d) through (g) of this section; the contract is a life insurance contract as defined in section 7702 and not a modified endowment contract as defined in section 7702A; R does not withdraw or obtain a loan of any portion of the policy cash value and does not surrender any portion of the life insurance contract; the compensation paid to E is reasonable; E is not provided any economic benefits described in paragraph (d)(2)(iii) of this section; E does not make any premium payments; E's taxable year is the calendar year; the value of the economic benefits is determined on the last day of E's taxable year; and E reports on E's Federal income tax return for each year that the split-dollar life insurance arrangement is in effect the amount of income required to be reported under paragraph (d) of this section. The examples are as follows:

Example 1. (i) *Facts.* On January 1 of year 1, R and E enter into the split-dollar life insurance arrangement. Under the arrangement, R

pays all of the premiums on the life insurance contract until the termination of the arrangement or E's death. The arrangement provides that upon termination of the arrangement or E's death, R is entitled to receive the lesser of the aggregate premiums paid or the policy cash value of the contract and E is entitled to receive any remaining amounts. Under the terms of the arrangement and applicable state law, the policy cash value is fully accessible by R and R's creditors but E has the right to borrow or withdraw at any time the portion of the policy cash value exceeding the amount payable to R. To fund the arrangement, R purchases a life insurance contract with constant death benefit protection equal to $1,500,000. R makes premium payments on the life insurance contract of $60,000 in each of years 1, 2, and 3. The policy cash value equals $55,000 as of December 31 of year 1, $140,000 as of December 31 of year 2, and $240,000 as of December 31 of year 3.

(ii) *Analysis.* Under the terms of the split-dollar life insurance arrangement, E has the right for year 1 and all subsequent years to borrow or withdraw the portion of the policy cash value exceeding the amount payable to R. Thus, under paragraph (d)(4)(ii) of this section, E has current access to such portion of the policy cash value for each year that the arrangement is in effect. In addition, because R pays all of the premiums on the life insurance contract, R provides to E all of the economic benefits that E receives under the arrangement. Therefore, under paragraph (d)(1) of this section, E includes in gross income the value of all economic benefits described in paragraphs (d)(2)(i) and (ii) of this section provided to E under the arrangement.

(iii) *Results for year 1.* For year 1, E is provided, under paragraph (d)(2)(ii) of this section, $0 of policy cash value (excess of $55,000 policy cash value determined as of December 31 of year 1 over $55,000 payable to R). For year 1, E is also provided, under paragraph (d)(2)(i) of this section, current life insurance protection of $1,445,000 ($1,500,000 minus $55,000 payable to R). Thus, E includes in gross income for year 1 the cost of $1,445,000 of current life insurance protection.

(iv) *Results for year 2.* For year 2, E is provided, under paragraph (d)(2)(ii) of this section, $20,000 of policy cash value ($140,000 policy cash value determined as of December 31 of year 2 minus $120,000 payable to R). For year 2, E is also provided, under paragraph (d)(2)(i) of this section, current life insurance protection of $1,360,000 ($1,500,000 minus the sum of $120,000 payable to R and the aggregate of $20,000 of policy cash value that E actually includes in income on E's year 1 and year 2 federal income tax returns). Thus, E includes in gross income for year 2 the sum of $20,000 of policy cash value and the cost of $1,360,000 of current life insurance protection.

(v) *Results for year 3.* For year 3, E is provided, under paragraph (d)(2)(ii) of this section, $40,000 of policy cash value ($240,000 policy cash value determined as of December 31 of year 3 minus the sum of $180,000 payable to R and $20,000 of aggregate policy cash value that E actually included in gross income on E's year 1 and year 2 federal income tax returns). For year 3, E is also provided, under paragraph (d)(2)(i) of this section, current life insurance protection of $1,260,000 ($1,500,000 minus the sum of $180,000 payable to R and $60,000 of aggregate policy cash value that E actually includes in gross income on E's year 1, year 2, and year 3 federal income tax returns). Thus, E includes in gross income for year 3 the sum of $40,000 of policy cash value and the cost of $1,260,000 of current life insurance protection.

Example 2. (i) *Facts.* The facts are the same as in *Example 1* except that E cannot directly or indirectly access any portion of the policy cash value, but the terms of the split-dollar life insurance arrangement or applicable state law provide that the policy cash value in excess of the amount payable to R is inaccessible to R's general creditors.

(ii) *Analysis.* Under the terms of the split-dollar life insurance arrangement or applicable state law, the portion of the policy cash value exceeding the amount payable to R is inaccessible to R's general creditors and E has a current or future right to that portion of the cash value. Thus, under paragraph (d)(4)(ii) of this section, E has current access to such portion of the policy cash value for each year that the arrangement is in effect. In addition, because R pays all of the premiums on the life insurance contract, R provides to E all of the economic benefits that E receives under the arrangement. Therefore, under paragraph (d)(1) of this section, E includes in gross income the value of all economic benefits described in paragraphs (d)(2)(i) and (ii) of this section provided to E under the arrangement.

(iii) *Results for years 1, 2 and 3.* The results for this example are the same as the results in *Example 1*.

(e) *Amounts received under the contract.*—(1) *In general.*—Except as otherwise provided in paragraph (f)(3) of this section, any amount received under a life insurance contract that is part of a split-dollar life insurance arrangement subject to the rules of paragraphs (d) through (g) of this section (including, but not limited to, a policy owner dividend, proceeds of a specified policy loan described in paragraph (e)(2) of this section, or the proceeds of a withdrawal from or partial surrender of the life insurance contract) is treated, to the extent provided directly or indirectly to a non-owner of the life insurance contract, as though such amount had been paid to the owner of the life insurance contract and then paid by the owner to the non-owner. The amount received is taxable to the owner in accordance with the rules of section 72. The non-owner (and the owner for gift tax and employment tax purposes) must take the amount described in paragraph (e)(3) of this section into account as a payment of compensation, a distribution under section 301, a contribution to capital, a gift, or other transfer depending on the relationship between the owner and the non-owner.

(2) *Specified policy loan.*—A policy loan is a specified policy loan to the extent—

(i) The proceeds of the loan are distributed directly from the insurance company to the non-owner;

(ii) A reasonable person would not expect that the loan will be repaid by the non-owner; or

(iii) The non-owner's obligation to repay the loan to the owner is satisfied or is capable of being satisfied upon repayment by either party to the insurance company.

(3) *Amount required to be taken into account.*—With respect to a non-owner (and the owner for gift tax and employment tax purposes), the amount described in this paragraph (e)(3) is equal to the excess of—

(i) The amount treated as received by the owner under paragraph (e)(1) of this section; over

(ii) The amount of all economic benefits described in paragraphs (d)(2)(ii) and (iii) of this section actually taken into account by the non-owner (and the owner for gift tax and employment tax purposes) plus any consideration described in paragraph (d)(1) of this section paid by the non-owner for such economic benefits described in paragraphs (d)(2)(ii) and (iii) of this section. The amount determined under the preceding sentence applies only to the extent that neither this paragraph (e)(3)(ii) nor paragraph (g)(1)(ii) of this section previously has applied to such economic benefits.

(f) *Other tax consequences.*—(1) *Introduction.*—In the case of a split-dollar life insurance arrangement subject to the rules of paragraphs (d) through (g) of this section, this paragraph (f) sets forth other tax consequences to the owner and non-owner of a life insurance contract that is part of the arrangement for the period prior to the transfer (as defined in paragraph (c)(3) of this section) of the contract (or an undivided interest therein) from the owner to the non-owner. See paragraph (g) of this section and § 1.83-6(a)(5) for tax consequences upon the transfer of the contract (or an undivided interest therein).

(2) *Investment in the contract.*—(i) *To the non-owner.*—A non-owner does not receive any investment in the contract under section 72(e)(6) with respect to a life insurance contract that is part of a split-dollar life insurance arrangement subject to the rules of paragraphs (d) through (g) of this section.

(ii) *To owner.*—Any premium paid by an owner under a split-dollar life insurance arrangement subject to the rules of paragraphs (d) through (g) of this section is included in the owner's investment in the contract under section 72(e)(6). No premium or amount described in paragraph (d) of this section is deductible by the owner (except as otherwise provided in § 1.83-6(a)(5)). Any amount paid by a non-owner, directly or indirectly, to the owner of the life insurance contract for current life insurance protection or for any other economic benefit under the life insurance contract is included in the owner's gross income and is included in the owner's investment in the life insurance contract for purposes of section 72(e)(6) (but only to the extent not otherwise so included by reason of having been paid by the owner as a premium or other consideration for the contract).

(3) *Treatment of death benefit proceeds.*—(i) *Death benefit proceeds to beneficiary (other than the owner).*—Any amount paid to a beneficiary (other than the owner) by reason of the death of the insured is excluded from gross income by such beneficiary under section 101(a) as an amount received under a life insurance contract to the extent such amount is allocable to current life insurance protection provided to the non-owner pursuant to the split-dollar life insurance arrangement, the cost of which was paid by the non-owner, or the value of which the non-owner actually took into account pursuant to paragraph (d)(1) of this section.

(ii) *Death benefit proceeds to owner as beneficiary.*—Any amount paid or payable to an owner in its capacity as a beneficiary by reason of the death of the insured is excluded from gross income of the owner under section 101(a) as an amount received under a life insurance contract to the extent such amount is not allocable to current life insurance protection provided to the non-owner pursuant to the split-dollar life insurance arrangement, the cost of which was paid by the non-owner, or the value of which the non-owner actually took into account pursuant to paragraph (d)(1) of this section.

(iii) *Transfers of death benefit proceeds.*—Death benefit proceeds paid to a party to a split-dollar life insurance arrangement (or the estate or beneficiary of that party) that are not excludable from that party's income under section 101(a) to the extent provided in paragraph (f)(3)(i) or (ii) of this section, are treated as transferred to that party in a separate transaction. The death benefit proceeds treated as so transferred will be taxed in a manner similar to other transfers. For example, if death benefit proceeds paid to an employee, the employee's estate, or the employee's beneficiary are not excludable from the employee's gross income under section 101(a) to the extent provided in paragraph (f)(3)(i) of this section, then such payment is treated as a payment of compensation by the employer to the employee.

(g) *Transfer of entire contract or undivided interest therein.*—(1) *In general.*—Upon a transfer within the meaning of paragraph (c)(3) of this section of a life insurance contract (or an undivided interest therein) to a non-owner (transferee), the transferee (and the owner (transferor) for gift tax and employment tax purposes) takes into account the excess of the fair market value of the life insurance contract (or the undivided interest therein) transferred to the transferee at that time over the sum of—

(i) The amount the transferee pays to the transferor to obtain the contract (or the undivided interest therein); and

(ii) The amount of all economic benefits described in paragraph (d)(2)(ii) and (iii) of this section actually taken into account by the transferee (and the transferor for gift tax and employment tax purposes), plus any consideration described in paragraph (d)(1) of this section paid by the transferee for such economic benefits described in paragraphs (d)(2)(ii) and (iii) of this section. The amount determined under the preceding sentence applies only to the extent that neither this paragraph (g)(1)(ii) nor paragraph (e)(3)(ii) of this section previously has applied to such economic benefits.

(2) *Determination of fair market value.*—For purposes of paragraph (g)(1) of this section, the fair market value of a life insurance contract is the policy cash value and the value of all other rights under such contract (including any supplemental agreements thereto and whether or not guaranteed), other than the value of current life insurance protection. Notwithstanding the preceding sentence, the fair market value of a life insurance contract for gift tax purposes is determined under § 25.2512-6(a) of this chapter.

(3) *Exception for certain transfers in connection with the performance of services.*—To the extent the ownership of a life insurance contract (or undivided interest in such contract) is transferred in connection with the performance of services, paragraph (g)(1) of this section does not apply until such contract (or undivided interest in such contract) is taxable under section 83. For purposes of paragraph (g)(1) of this section, fair market value is determined disregarding any lapse restrictions and at the time the transfer of such contract (or undivided interest in such contract) is taxable under section 83.

(4) *Treatment of non-owner after transfer.*—(i) *In general.*—After a transfer of an entire life insurance contract (except when such transfer is in connection with the performance of services and the transfer is not yet taxable under section 83), the person who previously had been the non-owner is treated as the owner of such contract for all purposes, including for purposes of paragraph (b) of this section and for purposes of § 1.61-2(d)(2)(ii)(A). After the transfer of an undivided interest in a life insurance contract (or, if later, at the time such transfer is taxable under section 83), the person who previously had been the non-owner is treated as the owner of a separate contract consisting of that interest for all purposes, including for purposes of paragraph (b) of this section and for purposes of § 1.61-2(d)(2)(ii)(A).

(ii) *Investment in the contract after transfer.*—(A) *In general.*—The amount treated as consideration paid to acquire the contract under section 72(g)(1), in order to determine the aggregate premiums paid by the transferee for purposes of section 72(e)(6)(A) after the transfer (or, if later, at the time such transfer is taxable under section 83), equals the greater of the fair market value of the contract or the sum of the amounts determined under paragraphs (g)(1)(i) and (ii) of this section.

(B) *Transfers between a donor and a donee.*—In the case of a transfer of a contract between a donor and a donee, the amount treated as consideration paid by the transferee to acquire the contract under section 72(g)(1), in order to determine the aggregate premiums paid by the transferee for purposes of section 72(e)(6)(A) after the transfer, equals the sum of the amounts determined under paragraphs (g)(1)(i) and (ii) of this section except that—

Reg. § 1.61-22(g)(4)(ii)(B)

(1) The amount determined under paragraph (g)(1)(i) of this section includes the aggregate of premiums or other consideration paid or deemed to have been paid by the transferor; and

(2) The amount of all economic benefits determined under paragraph (g)(1)(ii) of this section actually taken into account by the transferee does not include such benefits to the extent such benefits were excludable from the transferee's gross income at the time of receipt.

(C) *Transfers of an undivided interest in a contract.*—If a portion of a contract is transferred to the transferee, then the amount to be included as consideration paid to acquire the contract is determined by multiplying the amount determined under paragraph (g)(4)(ii)(A) of this section (as modified by paragraph (g)(4)(ii)(B) of this section, if the transfer is between a donor and a donee) by a fraction, the numerator of which is the fair market value of the portion transferred and the denominator of which is the fair market value of the entire contract.

(D) *Example.*—The following example illustrates the rules of this paragraph (g)(4)(ii):

Example. (i) In year 1, donor D and donee E enter into a split-dollar life insurance arrangement as defined in paragraph (b)(1) of this section. D is the owner of the life insurance contract under paragraph (c)(1) of this section. The life insurance contract is not a modified endowment contract as defined in section 7702A. In year 5, D gratuitously transfers the contract, within the meaning of paragraph (c)(3) of this section, to E. At the time of the transfer, the fair market value of the contract is $200,000 and D had paid $50,000 in premiums under the arrangement. In addition, by the time of the transfer, E had current access to $80,000 of policy cash value which was excludable from E's gross income under section 102.

(ii) E's investment in the contract is $50,000, consisting of the $50,000 of premiums paid by D. The $80,000 of policy cash value to which E had current access is not included in E's investment in the contract because such amount was excludable from E's gross income when E had current access to that policy cash value.

(iii) *No investment in the contract for current life insurance protection.*—Except as provided in paragraph (g)(4)(ii)(B) of this section, no amount allocable to current life insurance protection provided to the transferee (the cost of which was paid by the transferee or the value of which was provided to the transferee) is treated as consideration paid to acquire the contract under section 72(g)(1) to determine the aggregate premiums paid by the transferee for purposes of determining the transferee's investment in the contract under section 72(e) after the transfer.

(h) *Examples.*—The following examples illustrate the rules of this section. Except as otherwise provided, each of the examples assumes that the employer (R) is the owner (as defined in paragraph (c)(1) of this section) of a life insurance contract that is part of a split-dollar life insurance arrangement subject to the rules of paragraphs (d) through (g) of this section, that the employee (E) is not provided any economic benefits described in paragraph (d)(2)(iii) of this section, that the life insurance contract is not a modified endowment contract under section 7702A, that the compensation paid to E is reasonable, and that E makes no premium payments. The examples are as follows:

Example 1. (i) In year 1, R purchases a life insurance contract on the life of E. R is named as the policy owner of the contract. R and E enter into an arrangement under which R will pay all the premiums on the life insurance contract until the termination of the arrangement or E's death. Upon termination of the arrangement or E's death, R is entitled to receive the greater of the aggregate premiums or the policy cash value of the contract. The balance of the death benefit will be paid to a beneficiary designated by E.

(ii) Because R is designated as the policy owner of the contract, R is the owner of the contract under paragraph (c)(1)(i) of this section. In addition, R would be treated as the owner of the contract regardless of whether R were designated as the policy owner under paragraph (c)(1)(i) of this section because the split-dollar life insurance arrangement is described in paragraph (c)(1)(ii)(A)(1) of this section. E is a non-owner of the contract. Under the arrangement between R and E, a portion of the death benefit is payable to a beneficiary designated by E. The arrangement is a split-dollar life insurance arrangement under paragraph (b)(1) or (2) of this section. Because R pays all the premiums on the life insurance contract, R provides to E the entire amount of the current life insurance protection E receives under the arrangement. Therefore, for each year that the split-dollar life insurance arrangement is in effect, E must include in gross income under paragraph (d)(1) of this section the value of current life insurance protection described in paragraph (d)(2)(i) of this section provided to E in each year.

Example 2. (i) The facts are the same as in *Example 1* except that, upon termination of the arrangement or E's death, R is entitled to receive the lesser of the aggregate premiums or the policy cash value of the contract. Under the terms of the arrangement and applicable state law, the policy cash value is fully accessible by R and R's creditors but E has the right to borrow or withdraw at any time the portion of the policy cash value exceeding the amount payable to R.

(ii) Because R is designated as the policy owner, R is the owner of the contract under paragraph (c)(1)(i) of this section. E is a non-owner of the contract. For each year that the split-dollar life insurance arrangement is in effect, E has the right to borrow or withdraw at any time the portion of the policy cash value exceeding the amount payable to R. Thus, under paragraph (d)(4)(ii) of this section, E has current access to such portion of the policy cash value for each year that the arrangement is in effect. In addition, because R pays all the premiums on the life insurance contract, R provides to E all the economic benefits that E receives under the arrangement. Therefore, for each year that the split-dollar life insurance arrangement is in effect, E must include in gross income under paragraph (d)(1) of this section, the value of all economic benefits described in paragraph (d)(2)(i) and (ii) of this section provided to E in each year.

Example 3. (i) The facts are the same as in *Example 1* except that in year 5, R and E modify the split-dollar life insurance arrangement to provide that, upon termination of the arrangement or E's death, R is entitled to receive the greater of the aggregate premiums or one-half the policy cash value of the contract. Under the terms of the modified arrangement and applicable state law, the policy cash value is fully accessible by R and R's creditors but E has the right to borrow or withdraw at any time the portion of the policy cash value exceeding the amount payable to R.

(ii) For each year that the split-dollar life insurance arrangement is in effect, E must include in gross income under paragraph (d)(1) of this section the value of the economic benefits described in paragraph (d)(2)(i) of this section provided to E under the arrangement during that year. In year 5 (and subsequent years), E has the right to borrow or withdraw at any time the portion of the policy cash value exceeding the amount payable to R. Thus, under paragraph (d)(4)(ii) of this section, E has current access to such portion of the policy cash value. Thus, in year 5 (and each subsequent year), E must also include in gross income under paragraph (d)(1) of this section the value of the economic benefits described in paragraph (d)(2)(ii) of this section provided to E in each year.

(iii) The arrangement is not described in paragraph (c)(1)(ii)(A)(1) of this section after it is modified in year 5. Because R is the designated owner of the life insurance contract, R continues to be treated as the owner of the contract under paragraph (c)(1)(ii)(B)(1) of this section after the arrangement is modified. In addition, because the modification made by R and E in year 5 does not involve the transfer (within the meaning of paragraph (c)(3) of this section) of an undivided interest in the life insurance contract from R to E, the modification is not a transfer for purposes of paragraph (g) of this section.

Example 4. (i) The facts are the same as in *Example 2* except that in year 7, R and E modify the split-dollar life insurance arrangement to provide that, upon termination of the arrangement or E's death, R will be paid the lesser of 80 percent of the aggregate premiums or the policy cash value of the contract. Under the terms of the modified arrangement and applicable state law, the policy cash value is fully accessible by R and R's creditors but E has the right to borrow or withdraw at any time the portion of the policy cash value exceeding the lesser of 80 percent of the aggregate premiums paid by R or the policy cash value of the contract.

(ii) Commencing in year 7 (and in each subsequent year), E must include in gross income the economic benefits described in paragraph (d)(2)(ii) of this section as provided in this *Example 4(ii)* rather than as provided in *Example 2(ii)*. Thus, in year 7 (and in each subsequent year) E must include in gross income under paragraph (d) of this section, the excess of the policy cash value over the lesser of 80 percent of the aggregate premiums paid by R or the policy cash value of the contract (to the extent E did not actually include such amounts in gross income for a prior taxable year). In addition, in year 7 (and each subsequent year) E must also include in gross income the value of the economic benefits described in paragraph (d)(2)(i) of this section provided to E under the arrangement in each such year.

Example 5. (i) The facts are the same as in *Example 3* except that in year 7, E is designated as the policy owner. At that time, E's rights to the contract are substantially vested as defined in § 1.83-3(b).

(ii) In year 7, R is treated as having made a transfer (within the meaning of paragraph (c)(3) of this section) of the life insurance contract to E. E must include in gross income the amount determined under paragraph (g)(1) of this section.

(iii) After the transfer of the contract to E, E is the owner of the contract and any premium payments by R will be included in E's income under paragraph (b)(5) of this section and § 1.61-2(d)(2)(ii)(A) (unless R's payments are split-dollar loans as defined in § 1.7872-15(b)(1)).

Reg. §1.61-22(g)(4)(ii)(B)(1)

Example 6. (i) In year 1, E and R enter into a split-dollar life insurance arrangement as defined in paragraph (b)(2) of this section. Under the arrangement, R is required to make annual premium payments of $10,000 and E is required to make annual premium payments of $500. In year 5, a $500 policy owner dividend payable to E is declared by the insurance company. E directs the insurance company to use the $500 as E's premium payment for year 5.

(ii) For each year the arrangement is in effect, E must include in gross income the value of the economic benefits provided during the year, as required by paragraph (d)(2) of this section, over the $500 premium payments paid by E. In year 5, E must also include in gross income as compensation the excess, if any, of the $500 distributed to E from the proceeds of the policy owner dividend over the amount determined under paragraph (e)(3)(ii) of this section.

(iii) R must include in income the premiums paid by E during the years the split-dollar life insurance arrangement is in effect, including the $500 of the premium E paid in year 5 with proceeds of the policy owner dividend. R's investment in the contract is increased in an amount equal to the premiums paid by E, including the $500 of the premium paid by E in year 5 from the proceeds of the policy owner dividend. In year 5, R is treated as receiving a $500 distribution under the contract, which is taxed pursuant to section 72.

Example 7. (i) The facts are the same as in *Example 2* except that in year 10, E withdraws $100,000 from the cash value of the contract.

(ii) In year 10, R is treated as receiving a $100,000 distribution from the insurance company. This amount is treated as an amount received by R under the contract and taxed pursuant to section 72. This amount reduces R's investment in the contract under section 72(e). R is treated as paying the $100,000 to E as cash compensation, and E must include that amount in gross income less any amounts determined under paragraph (e)(3)(ii) of this section.

Example 8. (i) The facts are the same as in *Example 7* except E receives the proceeds of a $100,000 specified policy loan directly from the insurance company.

(ii) The transfer of the proceeds of the specified policy loan to E is treated as a loan by the insurance company to R. Under the rules of section 72(e), the $100,000 loan is not included in R's income and does not reduce R's investment in the contract. R is treated as paying the $100,000 of loan proceeds to E as cash compensation. E must include that amount in gross income less any amounts determined under paragraph (e)(3)(ii) of this section.

(i) [Reserved]

(j) *Effective date.*—(1) *General rule.*—(i) *In general.*—This section applies to any split-dollar life insurance arrangement (as defined in paragraph (b)(1) or (2) of this section) entered into after September 17, 2003.

(ii) *Determination of when an arrangement is entered into.*—For purposes of paragraph (j) of this section, a split-dollar life insurance arrangement is entered into on the latest of the following dates:

(A) The date on which the life insurance contract under the arrangement is issued;

(B) The effective date of the life insurance contract under the arrangement;

(C) The date on which the first premium on the life insurance contract under the arrangement is paid;

(D) The date on which the parties to the arrangement enter into an agreement with regard to the policy; or

(E) The date on which the arrangement satisfies the definition of a split-dollar life insurance arrangement (as defined in paragraph (b)(1) or (2) of this section).

(2) *Modified arrangements treated as new arrangements.*—(i) *In general.*—For purposes of paragraph (j)(1) of this section, if an arrangement entered into on or before September 17, 2003 is materially modified after September 17, 2003, the arrangement is treated as a new arrangement entered into on the date of the modification.

(ii) *Non-material modifications.*—The following is a non-exclusive list of changes that are not material modifications under paragraph (j)(2)(i) of this section (either alone or in conjunction with other changes listed in paragraphs (j)(2)(ii)(A) through (I) of this section)—

(A) A change solely in the mode of premium payment (for example, a change from monthly to quarterly premiums);

(B) A change solely in the beneficiary of the life insurance contract, unless the beneficiary is a party to the arrangement;

(C) A change solely in the interest rate payable under the life insurance contract on a policy loan;

(D) A change solely necessary to preserve the status of the life insurance contract under section 7702;

(E) A change solely to the ministerial provisions of the life insurance contract (for example, a change in the address to send payment);

(F) A change made solely under the terms of any agreement (other than the life insurance contract) that is a part of the split-dollar life insurance arrangement if the change is non-discretionary by the parties and is made pursuant to a binding commitment (whether set forth in the agreement or otherwise) in effect on or before September 17, 2003;

(G) A change solely in the owner of the life insurance contract as a result of a transaction to which section 381(a) applies and in which substantially all of the former owner's assets are transferred to the new owner of the policy;

(H) A change to the policy solely if such change is required by a court or a state insurance commissioner as a result of the insolvency of the insurance company that issued the policy; or

(I) A change solely in the insurance company that administers the policy as a result of an assumption reinsurance transaction between the issuing insurance company and the new insurance company to which the owner and the non-owner were not a party.

(iii) *Delegation to Commissioner.*—The Commissioner, in revenue rulings, notices, and other guidance published in the Internal Revenue Bulletin, may provide additional guidance with respect to other modifications that are not material for purposes of paragraph (j)(2)(i) of this section. See §601.601(d)(2)(ii) of this chapter. [Reg. §1.61-22.]

☐ [*T.D.* 9092, 9-11-2003 (*corrected* 11-7-2003).]

[Reg. §1.62-1]

§1.62-1. Adjusted gross income.—(a) [Reserved]
(b) [Reserved]

(c) *Deductions allowable in computing adjusted gross income.*—The deductions specified in section 62(a) for purposes of computing adjusted gross income are—

(1) Deductions set forth in §1.62-1T(c); and

(2) Deductions allowable under part VI, subchapter B, chapter 1 of the Internal Revenue Code, (section 161 and following) that consist of expenses paid or incurred by the taxpayer in connection with the performance of services as an employee under a reimbursement or other expense allowance arrangement (as defined in §1.62-2) with his or her employer. For the rules pertaining to expenses paid or incurred in taxable years beginning before January 1, 1989, *see* paragraphs (c)(2) and (f) (*see* §1.62-1T(c)(2) and (f) (as amended in 26 CFR part 1 §§1.61 to 1.169) revised April 1, 1992).

(d) through (h) [Reserved]

(i) *Effective date.*—Paragraph (c) of this section is effective for taxable years beginning on or after January 1, 1989. [Reg. §1.62-1.]

☐ [*T.D.* 8451, 12-4-92.]

[Reg. §1.62-1T]

§1.62-1T. Adjusted gross income (temporary).—(a) *Basis for determining the amount of certain deductions.*—The term "adjusted gross income" means the gross income computed under section 61 minus such of the deductions allowed by chapter 1 of the Code as are specified in section 62(a). Adjusted gross income is used as the basis for determining the following:

(1) The limitation on the amount of miscellaneous itemized deductions (under section 67).

(2) The limitation on the amount of the deduction for casualty losses (under section 165(h)(2)).

(3) The limitation on the amount of the deduction for charitable contributions (under section 170(b)(1)),

(4) The limitation on the amount of the deduction for medical and dental expenses (under section 213),

(5) The limitation on the amount of the deduction for qualified retirement contributions for active participants in certain pension plans (under section 219(g)), and

(6) The phase-out of the exemption from the disallowance of passive activity losses and credits (under section 469(i)(3)).

(b) *Double deduction not permitted.*—Section 62(a) merely specifies which of the deductions provided in chapter 1 of the Code shall be allowed in computing adjusted gross income. It does not create any new deductions. The fact that a particular item may be described in more than one of the paragraphs under section 62(a) does not permit the item to be deducted twice in computing adjusted gross income or taxable income.

(c) *Deductions allowable in computing adjusted gross income.*—The deductions specified in section 62(a) for purposes of computing adjusted gross income are:

(1) Deductions allowable under chapter 1 of the Code (other than by part VII (section 211 and following), subchapter B of such

chapter) that are attributable to a trade or business carried on by the taxpayer not consisting of services performed as an employee;

(2) [Reserved]

(3) For taxable years beginning after December 31, 1986, deductions allowable under section 162 that consist of expenses paid or incurred by a qualified performing artist (as defined in section 62 (b)) in connection with the performance by him or her of services in the performing arts as an employee;

(4) Deductions allowable under part VI as losses from the sale or exchange of property;

(5) Deductions allowable under part VI, section 212, or section 611 that are attributable to property held for the production of rents or royalties;

(6) Deductions for depreciation or depletion allowable under sections 167 or 611 to a life tenant of property or to an income beneficiary of property held in trust or to an heir, legatee, or devisee of an estate;

(7) Deductions allowed by section 404 for contributions on behalf of a self-employed individual;

(8) Deductions allowed by section 219 for contributions to an individual retirement account described in section 408(a), or for an individual retirement annuity described in section 408(b);

(9) Deductions allowed by section 402(e)(3) with respect to a lump-sum distribution;

(10) For taxable years beginning after December 31, 1972, deductions allowed by section 165 for losses incurred in any transaction entered into for profit though not connected with a trade or business, to the extent that such losses include amounts forfeited to a bank, mutual savings bank, savings and loan association, building and loan association, cooperative bank or homestead association as a penalty for premature withdrawal of funds from a time savings account, certificate of deposit, or similar class of deposit;

(11) For taxable years beginning after December 31, 1976, deductions for alimony and separate maintenance payments allowed by section 215;

(12) Deductions allowed by section 194 for the amortization of reforestation expenditures; and

(13) Deductions allowed by section 165 for the repayment (made in a taxable year beginning after December 28, 1980) to a trust described in paragraph (9) or (17) of section 501(c) of supplemental unemployment compensation benefits received from such trust if such repayment is required because of the receipt of trade readjustment allowances under section 231 or 232 of the Trade Act of 1974 (19 U.S.C. 2291 and 2292).

(d) *Expenses directly related to a trade or business.*—For the purpose of the deductions specified in section 62, the performance of personal services as an employee does not constitute the carrying on of a trade or business, except as otherwise expressly provided. The practice of a profession, not as an employee, is considered the conduct of a trade or business within the meaning of such section. To be deductible for the purposes of determining adjusted gross income, expenses must be those directly, and not those merely remotely, connected with the conduct of a trade or business. For example, taxes are deductible in arriving at adjusted gross income only if they constitute expenditures directly attributable to a trade or business or to property from which rents or royalties are derived. Thus, property taxes paid or incurred on real property used in a trade or business are deductible, but state taxes on net income are not deductible even though the taxpayer's income is derived from the conduct of a trade or business.

(e) *Reimbursed and unreimbursed employee expenses.*—(1) *In general.*—Expenses paid or incurred by an employee that are deductible from gross income under part VI in computing taxable income (determined without regard to section 67) and for which the employee is reimbursed by the employer, its agent, or third party (for whom the employee performs a benefit as an employee of the employer) under an express agreement for reimbursement or pursuant to an *express expense allowance arrangement* may be deducted from gross income in computing adjusted gross income. Except as provided in paragraph (e)(2) and (e)(4) of this section, for taxable years beginning after December 31, 1986, if the amount of a reimbursement made by an employer, its agent, or third party to an employee is less than the total amount of the business expenses paid or incurred by the employee, the determination of to which of the employee's business expenses the reimbursement applies and the amount of each expense that is covered by the reimbursement is made on the basis of all of the facts and circumstances of the particular case.

(2) *Facts and circumstances unclear on business expenses for meals and entertainment.*—If—

(i) The facts and circumstances do not make clear—

(A) That a reimbursement does not apply to business expenses for meals or entertainment, or

(B) The amount of business expenses for meals or entertainment that is covered by the reimbursement, and

(ii) the employee pays or incurs business expenses for meals or entertainment,

the amount of the reimbursement that applies to such expenses (or portion thereof with respect to which the facts and circumstances are unclear) shall be determined by multiplying the amount of the employee's business expenses for meals and entertainment (or portion thereof with respect to which the facts and circumstances are unclear) by a fraction, the numerator of which is the total amount of the reimbursement (or portion thereof with respect to which the facts and circumstances are unclear) and the denominator of which is the aggregate amount of all the business expenses of the employee (or portion thereof with respect to which the facts and circumstances are unclear).

(3) *Deductibility of unreimbursed expenses.*—The amount of expenses that is determined not to be reimbursed pursuant to paragraph (e)(1) or (2) of this section is deductible from adjusted gross income in determining the employee's taxable income subject to the limitations applicable to such expenses (*e.g.,* the 2-percent floor of section 67 and the 80-percent limitation on meal and entertainment expenses provided for in section 274(n)).

(4) *Unreimbursed expenses of State legislators.*—For taxable years beginning after December 31, 1986, any portion of the amount allowed as a deduction to State legislators pursuant to section 162(h)(1)(B) that is not reimbursed by the State or a third party shall be allocated between lodging and meals in the same ratio as the amounts allowable for lodging and meals under the Federal per diem applicable to the legislator's State capital at the end of the legislator's taxable year (see Appendix 1-A of the Federal Travel Regulations (FTR), which as of March 28, 1988, are contained in GSA Bulletin FPMR A-40, Supplement 20). For purposes of this paragraph (e)(4), the amount allowable for meals under the Federal per diem shall be the amount of the Federal per diem allowable for meals and incidental expenses reduced by $2 per legislative day (or other amount allocated to incidental expenses in 1-7.5(a)(2) of the FTR). The unreimbursed portion of each type of expense is deductible from adjusted gross income in determining the State legislator's taxable income subject to the limitations applicable to such expenses. For example, the unreimbursed portion allocable to meals shall be reduced by 20 percent pursuant to section 274(n) before being subjected to the 2-percent floor of section 67 for purposes of computing the taxable income of a State legislator. See § 1.67-1T(a)(2).

(5) *Expenses paid directly by an employer, its agent, or third party.*—In the case of an employer, its agent, or a third party who provides property or services to an employee or who pays an employee's expenses directly instead of reimbursing the employee, see section 132 and the regulations thereunder for the income tax treatment of such expenses.

(6) *Examples.*—The provisions of this paragraph (e) may be illustrated by the following examples:

Example (1). During 1987, A, an employee, while on business trips away form home pays $300 for travel fares, $200 for lodging and $100 for meals. In addition, A pays $50 for business meals in the area of his place of employment ("local meals"), $250 for continuing education courses, and $100 for business-related entertainment (other than meals). The total amount of the reimbursements received by A for his employee expenses from his employer is $750, and it is assumed that A's expenses meet the deductibility requirements of sections 162 and 274. A includes the amount of the reimbursement in his gross income. A's employer designates the reimbursement to cover in full A's expenses for travel fares, lodging, and meals while away from home, local meals, and entertainment, and no facts or circumstances indicate a contrary intention of the employer. Because the facts and circumstances make clear the amount of A's business expenses for meals and entertainment that is covered by the reimbursement, the reimbursement will be allocated to these expenses. In determining his adjusted gross income under section 62, A may deduct the full amount of the reimbursement for travel fares, lodging, and meals while away from home, local meals, and entertainment. In determining his taxable income under section 63, A may deduct his expenses for continuing education courses to the extent allowable by sections 67 and 162.

Example (2). Assume the facts are the same as in example (1) except that the facts and circumstances make clear that the reimbursement covers all types of deductible expenses but they do not make clear the amount of each type of expense that is covered by the reimbursement. The amount of the reimbursement that is allocated to A's business expenses for meals and entertainment is $187.50. This amount is determined by multiplying the total amount of A's business expenses for meals and entertainment ($250) by the ratio of A's total reimbursement to A's total business expenses ($750/$1,000).

The remaining amount of the reimbursement, $562.50 ($750 − $187.50), is allocated to A's business expenses other than meal and entertainment expenses. Therefore, in determining his adjusted gross income under section 62, A may deduct $750 for reimbursed business expenses (including meals and entertainment). In determining his taxable income under section 63, A may deduct (subject to the limitations and conditions of sections 67, 162, and 274) the un-reimbursed portion of his expenses for meals and entertainment ($62.50 ($250 − $187.50)), and other employee business expenses ($187.50 ($750 − $562.50)).

Example (3). Assume the facts are the same as in example (1) except that the amount of the reimbursement is $500. Assume further that the facts and circumstances make clear that the reimbursement covers $100 of expenses for meals and that the remaining $400 of the reimbursement covers all types of deductible expenses (including any expenses for meals in excess of the $100 already designated) other than expenses for entertainment. The amount of the reimbursement that is allocated to A's business expenses for meals and entertainment is $125. This amount is equal to the sum of the amount of the reimbursement that clearly applies to meals ($100) and the amount of the reimbursement with respect to which the facts are unclear that is allocated to meals ($25). The latter amount is determined by multiplying the total amount of A's business expenses for meals and entertainment with respect to which the facts are unclear ($50) by the ratio of A's total reimbursement with respect to which the facts are unclear to A's total business expenses with respect to which the facts are unclear ($400/$800). The remaining amount of the reimbursement, $375 ($500 − $125) is allocated to A's business expenses other than meals and entertainment. Therefore, in determining his adjusted gross income under section 62, A may deduct $500 for reimbursed business expenses (including meals). In determining his taxable income under section 63, A may deduct (subject to the limitations and conditions of sections 67, 162, and 274) the un-reimbursed portion of his expenses for meals ($25 ($150 − $125)), entertainment ($100), and other employee business expenses ($375 ($750 − $375)).

Example (4). During 1987 B, a research scientist, is employed by Corporation X. B gives a speech before members of Association Y, a professional organization of scientists, describing her most recent research findings. Pursuant to a reimbursement arrangement, Y reimburses B for the full amount of her travel fares to the site of the speech and for the full amount of her expenses for lodging and meals while there. B includes the amount of the reimbursement in her gross income. B may deduct the full amount of her travel expenses pursuant to section 62(a)(2)(A) in computing her adjusted gross income.

(f) [Reserved]

(g) *Moving expenses.*—For taxable years beginning after December 31, 1986, a taxpayer described in section 217(a) shall not take into account the deduction described in section 217 relating to moving expenses in computing adjusted gross income under section 62 even if the taxpayer is reimbursed for his or her moving expenses. Such a taxpayer shall include the amount of any reimbursement for moving expenses in income pursuant to section 82. The deduction described in section 217 shall be taken into account in computing the taxable income of the taxpayer under section 63. Pursuant to section 67(b)(6), the 2-percent floor described in section 67(a) does not apply to moving expenses.

(h) *Cross-reference.*—See 26 CFR 1.62-1 (Rev. as of April 1, 1986) with respect to pre-1987 deductions for travel, meal, lodging, transportation, and other trade or business expenses of an employee, reimbursed expenses of an employee, expenses of an outside sales-person, long-term capital gains, contributions described in section 405(c) to a bond purchase plan on behalf of a self-employed individual, moving expenses, amounts not received as benefits pursuant to section 1379(b)(3), and retirement bonds described in section 409 (allowed by section 219). [Temporary Reg. §1.62-1T.]

☐ [T.D. 8189, 3-25-88. Amended by T.D. 8276, 12-7-89; T.D. 8324, 12-14-90 and T.D. 8451, 12-4-92.]

[Reg. §1.62-2]

§1.62-2. Reimbursements and other expense allowance arrangements.—(a) *Table of contents.*—The contents of this section are as follows:

(b) *Scope.*—For purposes of determining "adjusted gross income," section 62(a)(2)(A) allows an employee a deduction for expenses allowed by Part VI (section 161 and following), subchapter B, chapter 1 of the Code, paid by the employee, in connection with the performance of services as an employee of the employer, under a reimbursement or other expense allowance arrangement with a payor (the employer, its agent, or a third party). Section 62(c) provides that an arrangement will not be treated as a reimbursement or other expense allowance arrangement for purposes of section 62(a)(2)(A) if (1) such arrangement does not require the employee to substantiate the expenses covered by the arrangement to the payor, or (2) such arrangement provides the employee the right to retain any amount in excess of the substantiated expenses covered under the arrangement. This section prescribes rules relating to the requirements of section 62(c).

(c) *Reimbursement or other expense allowance arrangement.*—(1) *Defined.*—For purposes of §§1.62-1, 1.62-1T and 1.62-2, the phrase "reimbursement or other expense allowance arrangement" means an arrangement that meets the requirements of paragraphs (d) (business connection), (e) (substantiation), and (f) (returning amounts in excess of expenses) of this section. A payor may have more than one arrangement with respect to a particular employee, depending on the facts and circumstances. See paragraph (d)(2) of this section (payor treated as having two arrangements under certain circumstances).

(2) *Accountable plans.*—(i) *In general.*—Except as provided in paragraph (c)(2)(ii) of this section, if an arrangement meets the requirements of paragraphs (d), (e), and (f) of this section, all amounts paid under the arrangement are treated as paid under an "accountable plan."

(ii) *Special rule for failure to return excess.*—If an arrangement meets the requirements of paragraphs (d), (e), and (f) of this section, but the employee fails to return, within a reasonable period of time, any amount in excess of the amount of the expenses substantiated in accordance with paragraph (e) of this section, only the amounts paid under the arrangement that are not in excess of the substantiated expenses are treated as paid under an accountable plan.

(3) *Nonaccountable plans.*—(i) *In general.*—If an arrangement does not satisfy one or more of the requirements of paragraphs (d), (e), or (f) of this section, all amounts paid under the arrangement are treated as paid under a "nonaccountable plan." If a payor provides a nonaccountable plan, an employee who receives payments under the plan cannot compel the payor to treat the payments as paid under an

accountable plan by voluntarily substantiating the expenses and returning any excess to the payor.

(ii) *Special rule for failure to return excess.*—If an arrangement meets the requirements of paragraphs (d), (e), and (f) of this section, but the employee fails to return, within a reasonable period of time, any amount in excess of the amount of the expenses substantiated in accordance with paragraph (e) of this section, the amounts paid under the arrangement that are in excess of the substantiated expenses are treated as paid under a nonaccountable plan.

(4) *Treatment of payments under accountable plans.*—Amounts treated as paid under an accountable plan are not reported as wages or other compensation on the employee's Form W-2, and are exempt from the withholding and payment of employment taxes (Federal Insurance Contributions Act (FICA), Federal Unemployment Tax Act (FUTA), Railroad Retirement Tax Act (RRTA), Railroad Unemployment Repayment Tax (RURT), and income tax). See paragraph (l) of this section for cross references.

(5) *Treatment of payments under nonaccountable plans.*—Amounts treated as paid under a nonaccountable plan are included in the employee's gross income, must be reported as wages or other compensation on the employee's Form W-2, and are subject to withholding and payment of employment taxes (FICA, FUTA, RRTA, RURT, and income tax). See paragraph (h) of this section. Expenses attributable to amounts included in the employee's gross income may be deducted, provided the employee can substantiate the full amount of his or her expenses (i.e., the amount of the expenses, if any, the reimbursement for which is treated as paid under an accountable plan as well as those for which the employee is claiming the deduction) in accordance with §1.274-5T and 1.274(d)-1 or §1.162-17, but only as a miscellaneous itemized deduction subject to the limitations applicable to such expenses (e.g., the 80-percent limitation on meal and entertainment expenses provided in section 274(n) and the 2-percent floor provided in section 67).

(d) *Business connection.*—(1) *In general.*—Except as provided in paragraphs (d)(2) and (d)(3) of this section, an arrangement meets the requirements of this paragraph (d) if it provides advances, allowances (including per diem allowances, allowances only for meals and incidental expenses, and mileage allowances), or reimbursements only for business expenses that are allowable as deductions by Part VI (section 161 and the following), subchapter B, chapter 1 of the Code, and that are paid or incurred by the employee in connection with the performance of services as an employee of the employer. The payment may be actually received from the employer, its agent, or a third party for whom the employee performs a service as an employee of the employer, and may include amounts charged directly or indirectly to the payor through credit card systems or otherwise. In addition, if both wages and the reimbursement or other expense allowance are combined in a single payment, the reimbursement or other expense allowance must be identified either by making a separate payment or by specifically identifying the amount of the reimbursement or other expense allowance.

(2) *Other bona fide expenses.*—If an arrangement provides advances, allowances, or reimbursements for business expenses described in paragraph (d)(1) of this section (i.e., deductible employee business expenses) and for other bona fide expenses related to the employer's business (e.g., travel that is not away from home) that are not deductible under Part VI (section 161 and the following), subchapter B, chapter 1 of the Code, the payor is treated as maintaining two arrangements. The portion of the arrangement that provides payments for the deductible employee business expenses is treated as one arrangement that satisfies this paragraph (d). The portion of the arrangement that provides payments for the nondeductible employee expenses is treated as a second arrangement that does not satisfy this paragraph (d) and all amounts paid under this second arrangement will be treated as paid under a nonaccountable plan. See paragraphs (c)(5) and (h) of this section.

(3) *Reimbursement requirement.*—(i) *In general.*—If a payor arranges to pay an amount to an employee regardless of whether the employee incurs (or is reasonably expected to incur) business expenses of a type described in paragraph (d)(1) or (d)(2) of this section, the arrangement does not satisfy this paragraph (d) and all amounts paid under the arrangement are treated as paid under a nonaccountable plan. See paragraphs (c)(5) and (h) of this section.

(ii) *Per diem allowances.*—An arrangement providing a per diem allowance for travel expenses of a type described in paragraph (d)(1) or (d)(2) of this section that is computed on a basis similar to that used in computing the employee's wages or other compensation (e.g., the number of hours worked, miles traveled, or pieces produced) meets the requirements of this paragraph (d) only if, on

December 12, 1989, the per diem allowance was identified by the payor either by making a separate payment or by specifically identifying the amount of the per diem allowance, or a per diem allowance computed on that basis was commonly used in the industry in which the employee is employed. See section 274(d) and §1.274(d)-1. A per diem allowance described in this paragraph (d)(3)(ii) may be adjusted in a manner that reasonably reflects actual increases in employee business expenses occurring after December 12, 1989.

(e) *Substantiation.*—(1) *In general.*—An arrangement meets the requirements of this paragraph (e) if it requires each business expense to be substantiated to the payor in accordance with paragraph (e)(2) or (e)(3) of this section, whichever is applicable, within a reasonable period of time. See §1.274-5T or §1.162-17.

(2) *Expenses governed by section 274(d).*—An arrangement that reimburses travel, entertainment, use of a passenger automobile or other listed property, or other business expenses governed by section 274(d) meets the requirements of this paragraph (e)(2) if information sufficient to satisfy the substantiation requirements of section 274(d) and the regulations thereunder is submitted to the payor. See §1.274-5. Under section 274(d), information sufficient to substantiate the requisite elements of each expenditure or use must be submitted to the payor. For example, with respect to travel away from home, §1.274-5(b)(2) requires that information sufficient to substantiate the amount, time, place, and business purpose of the expense must be submitted to the payor. Similarly, with respect to use of a passenger automobile or other listed property, §1.274-5(b)(6) requires that information sufficient to substantiate the amount, time, use, and business purpose of the expense must be submitted to the payor. See §1.274-5(g) and (j), which grant the Commissioner the authority to establish optional methods of substantiating certain expenses. Substantiation of the amount of a business expense in accordance with rules prescribed pursuant to the authority granted by §1.274-5(g) or (j) will be treated as substantiation of the amount of such expense for purposes of this section.

(3) *Expenses not governed by section 274(d).*—An arrangement that reimburses business expenses not governed by section 274(d) meets the requirements of this paragraph (e)(3) if information is submitted to the payor sufficient to enable the payor to identify the specific nature of each expense and to conclude that the expense is attributable to the payor's business activities. Therefore, each of the elements of an expenditure or use must be substantiated to the payor. It is not sufficient if an employee merely aggregates expenses into broad categories (such as "travel") or reports individual expenses through the use of vague, nondescriptive terms (such as "miscellaneous business expenses"). See §1.162-17(b).

(f) *Returning amounts in excess of expenses.*—(1) *In general.*—Except as provided in paragraph (f)(2) of this section, an arrangement meets the requirements of this paragraph (f) if it requires the employee to return to the payor within a reasonable period of time any amount paid under the arrangement in excess of the expenses substantiated in accordance with paragraph (e) of this section. The determination of whether an arrangement requires an employee to return amounts in excess of substantiated expenses will depend on the facts and circumstances. An arrangement whereby money is advanced to an employee to defray expenses will be treated as satisfying the requirements of this paragraph (f) only if the amount of money advanced is reasonably calculated not to exceed the amount of anticipated expenditures, the advance of money is made on a day within a reasonable period of the day that the anticipated expenditures are paid or incurred, and any amounts in excess of the expenses substantiated in accordance with paragraph (e) of this section are required to be returned to the payor within a reasonable period of time after the advance is received.

(2) *Per diem or mileage allowances.*—The Commissioner may, in his discretion, prescribe rules in pronouncements of general applicability under which a reimbursement or other expense allowance arrangement that provides per diem allowances providing for ordinary and necessary expenses of traveling away from home (exclusive of transportation costs to and from destination) or mileage allowances providing for ordinary and necessary expenses of local travel and transportation while traveling away from home will be treated as satisfying the requirements of this paragraph (f), even though the arrangement does not require the employee to return the portion of such allowance that relates to the days or miles of travel substantiated and that exceeds the amount of the employee's expenses deemed substantiated pursuant to rules prescribed under section 274(d), provided the allowance is paid at a rate for each day or mile of travel that is reasonably calculated not to exceed the amount of the employee's expenses or anticipated expenses and the employee is required to return to the payor within a reasonable period of time any portion of such allowance which relates to days or

miles of travel not substantiated in accordance with paragraph (e) of this section.

(g) *Reasonable period.*—(1) *In general.*—The determination of a reasonable period of time will depend on the facts and circumstances.

(2) *Safe harbors.*—(i) *Fixed date method.*—An advance made within 30 days of when an expense is paid or incurred, an expense substantiated to the payor within 60 days after it is paid or incurred, or an amount returned to the payor within 120 days after an expense is paid or incurred will be treated as having occurred within a reasonable period of time.

(ii) *Periodic statement method.*—If a payor provides employees with periodic statements (no less frequently than quarterly) stating the amount, if any, paid under the arrangement in excess of the expenses the employee has substantiated in accordance with paragraph (e) of this section, and requesting the employee to substantiate any additional business expenses that have not yet been substantiated (whether or not such expenses relate to the expenses with respect to which the original advance was paid) and/or to return any amounts remaining unsubstantiated within 120 days of the statement, an expense substantiated or an amount returned within that period will be treated as being substantiated or returned within a reasonable period of time.

(3) *Pattern of overreimbursements.*—If, under a reimbursement or other expense allowance arrangement, a payor has a plan or practice to provide amounts to employees in excess of expenses substantiated in accordance with paragraph (e) of this section and to avoid reporting and withholding on such amounts, the payor may not use either of the safe harbors provided in paragraph (g)(2) of this section for any years during which such plan or practice exists.

(h) *Withholding and payment of employment taxes.*—(1) *When excluded from wages.*—If an arrangement meets the requirements of paragraphs (d), (e), and (f) of this section, the amounts paid under the arrangement that are not in excess of the expenses substantiated in accordance with paragraph (e) of this section (i.e., the amounts treated as paid under an accountable plan) are not wages and are not subject to withholding and payment of employment taxes. If an arrangement provides advances, allowances, or reimbursements for meal and entertainment expenses and a portion of the payment is treated as paid under a nonaccountable plan under paragraph (d)(2) of this section due solely to section 274(n), then notwithstanding paragraph (h)(2)(ii) of this section, these nondeductible amounts are neither treated as gross income nor subject to withholding and payment of employment taxes.

(2) *When included in wages.*—(i) *Accountable plans.*—(A) *General rule.*—Except as provided in paragraph (h)(2)(i)(B) of this section, if the expenses covered under an arrangement that meets the requirements of paragraphs (d), (e), and (f) of this section are not substantiated to the payor in accordance with paragraph (e) of this section within a reasonable period of time or if any amounts in excess of the substantiated expenses are not returned to the payor in accordance with paragraph (f) of this section within a reasonable period of time, the amount which is treated as paid under a nonaccountable plan under paragraph (c)(3)(ii) of this section is subject to withholding and payment of employment taxes no later than the first payroll period following the end of the reasonable period. A payor may treat any amount not substantiated or returned within the periods specified in paragraph (g)(2) of this section as not substantiated or returned within a reasonable period of time.

(B) *Per diem or mileage allowances.*—(1) *In general.*—If a payor pays a per diem or mileage allowance under an arrangement that meets the requirements of paragraphs (d), (e), and (f) of this section, the portion, if any, of the allowance paid that relates to days or miles of travel substantiated in accordance with paragraph (e) of this section and that exceeds the amount of the employee's expenses deemed substantiated for such travel pursuant to rules prescribed under section 274(d) and §1.274(d)-1 or §1.274-5T(j) is treated as paid under a nonaccountable plan. See paragraph (c)(3)(ii) of this section. Because the employee is not required to return this excess portion, the reasonable period of time provisions of paragraph (g) of this section (relating to the return of excess amounts) do not apply to this excess portion.

(2) *Reimbursements.*—Except as provided in paragraph (h)(2)(i)(B)(4) of this section, in the case of a per diem or mileage allowance paid as a reimbursement at a rate for each day or mile of travel that exceeds the amount of the employee's expenses deemed substantiated for a day or mile of travel, the excess portion described in paragraph (h)(2)(i) of this section is subject to withholding and payment of employment taxes in the payroll period in which the payor reimburses the expenses for the days or miles of travel substantiated in accordance with paragraph (e) of this section.

(3) *Advances.*—Except as provided in paragraph (h)(2)(i)(B)(4) of this section, in the case of a per diem or mileage allowance paid as an advance at a rate for each day or mile of travel that exceeds the amount of the employee's expenses deemed substantiated for a day or mile of travel, the excess portion described in paragraph (h)(2)(i) of this section is subject to withholding and payment of employment taxes no later than the first payroll period following the payroll period in which the expenses with respect to which the advance was paid (i.e., the days or miles of travel) are substantiated in accordance with paragraph (e) of this section. The expenses with respect to which the advance was paid must be substantiated within a reasonable period of time. See paragraph (g) of this section.

(4) *Special rules.*—The Commissioner may, in his discretion, prescribe special rules in pronouncements of general applicability regarding the timing of withholding and payment of employment taxes on per diem and mileage allowances.

(ii) *Nonaccountable plans.*—If an arrangement does not satisfy one or more of the requirements of paragraphs (d), (e), or (f) of this section, all amounts paid under the arrangement are wages and are subject to withholding and payment of employment taxes when paid.

(i) *Application.*—The requirements of paragraphs (d)(business connection), (e)(substantiation), and (f)(returning amounts in excess of expenses) of this section will be applied on an employee-by-employee basis. Thus, for example, the failure by one employee to substantiate expenses under an arrangement in accordance with paragraph (e) of this section will not cause amounts paid to other employees to be treated as paid under a nonaccountable plan.

(j) *Examples.*—The rules contained in this section may be illustrated by the following examples.

Example (1). Reimbursement requirement. Employer S pays its engineers $200 a day. On those days that an engineer travels away from home on business for Employer S, Employer S designates $50 of the $200 as paid to reimburse the engineer's travel expenses. Because Employer S would pay an engineer $200 a day regardless of whether the engineer was traveling away from home, the arrangement does not satisfy the reimbursement requirement of paragraph (d)(3)(i) of this section. Thus, no part of the $50 Employer S designated as a reimbursement is treated as paid under an accountable plan. Rather, all payments under the arrangement are treated as paid under a nonaccountable plan. Employer S must report the entire $200 as wages or other compensation on the employees' Forms W-2 and must withhold and pay employment taxes on the entire $200 when paid.

Example (2). Reimbursement requirement, multiple arrangements. Airline T pays all its employees a salary. Airline T also pays an allowance under an arrangement that otherwise meets the requirements of paragraphs (d), (e), and (f) of this section to its pilots and flight attendants who travel away from their home base airports, whether or not they are "away from home." Because the allowance is paid only to those employees who incur (or are reasonably expected to incur) expenses of a type described in paragraph (d)(1) or (d)(2) of this section, the arrangement satisfies the reimbursement requirement of paragraph (d)(3)(i) of this section. Under paragraph (d)(2) of this section, Airline T is treated as maintaining two arrangements. The portion of the arrangement providing the allowances for away from home travel is treated as an accountable plan. The portion of the arrangement providing the allowances for non-away from home travel is treated as a nonaccountable plan. Airline T must report the non-away from home allowances as wages or other compensation on the employees' Forms W-2 and must withhold and pay employment taxes on these payments when paid.

Example (3). Reimbursement requirement. Corporation R pays all its salespersons a salary. Corporation R also pays a travel allowance under an arrangement that otherwise meets the requirements of paragraphs (d), (e), and (f) of this section. This allowance is paid to all salespersons, including salespersons that Corporation R knows, or has reason to know, do not travel away from their offices on Corporation R business and would not be reasonably expected to incur travel expenses. Because the allowance is not paid only to those employees who incur (or are reasonably expected to incur) expenses of a type described in paragraph (d)(1) or (d)(2) of this section, the arrangement does not satisfy the reimbursement requirement of paragraph (d)(3)(i) of this section. Thus, no part of the allowance Corporation R designated as a reimbursement is treated as paid under an accountable plan. Rather, all payments under the arrangement are treated as paid under a nonaccountable plan. Corporation R must report all payments under the arrangement as wages or other compensation on the employees' Forms W-2 and must withhold and pay employment taxes on the payments when paid.

Example (4). Separate arrangement, miscellaneous expenses. Under an arrangement that meets the requirements of paragraphs (d), (e), and (f) of this section, County U reimburses its employees for lodging and meal expenses incurred when they travel away from home on County U business. For its own convenience, County U also separately pays certain of its employees a $25 monthly allowance to cover the cost of small miscellaneous office expenses. County U does not require its employees to substantiate these miscellaneous expenses and does not require them to return the amounts by which the monthly allowance exceeds the miscellaneous expenses. The monthly allowance arrangement is a nonaccountable plan. County U must report the monthly allowances as wages or other compensation on the employees' Forms W-2 and must withhold and pay employment taxes on the monthly allowances when paid. The nonaccountable plan providing the monthly allowances is treated as separate from the accountable plan providing reimbursements for lodging and meal expenses incurred for travel away from home on County U business.

Example (5). Excessive advances. In anticipation of employee business expenses that Corporation V does not reasonably expect to exceed $400 in any quarter, Corporation V nonetheless advances $1,000 to Employee A for such expenses. Whenever Employee A substantiates an expense in accordance with paragraph (e) of this section, Corporation V provides an additional advance in an amount equal to the amount substantiated, thereby providing a continuing advance of $1,000. Because the amounts advanced under this arrangement are not reasonably calculated so as not to exceed the amount of anticipated expenditures and because the advance of money is not made on a day within a reasonable period of the day that the anticipated expenditures are paid or incurred, the arrangement is a nonaccountable plan. The arrangement fails to satisfy the requirements of paragraphs (d)(business connection) and (f) (reasonable calculation of advances) of this section. Thus, Corporation V must report the entire amount of each advance as wages or other compensation and must withhold and pay employment taxes on the entire amount of each advance when paid.

Example (6). Excess mileage advance. Under an arrangement that meets the requirements of paragraphs (d), (e), and (f) of this section, Employer W pays its employees a mileage allowance at a rate of 30 cents per mile (when the amount deemed substantiated for each mile of travel substantiated is 26 cents per mile) to cover automobile business expenses. The allowance is paid at a rate for each mile of travel that is reasonably calculated not to exceed the amount of the employee's expenses or anticipated expenses. Employer W does not require the return of the portion of the mileage allowance (4 cents) that exceeds the amount deemed substantiated for each mile of travel substantiated in accordance with paragraph (e) of this section. In June, Employer W advances Employee B $150 for 500 miles to be traveled by Employee B during the month. In July, Employee B substantiates 500 miles of business travel. The amount deemed substantiated by Employee B is $130. However, Employer W does not require Employee B to return the remaining $20 of the advance. No later than the first payroll period following the payroll period in which the business miles of travel are substantiated, Employer W must withhold and pay employment taxes on $20 (500 miles × 4 cents per mile).

Example (7). Excess per diem reimbursement. Under an arrangement that meets the requirements of paragraphs (d), (e), and (f) of this section, Employer X pays its employees a per diem allowance to cover lodging, meal, and incidental expenses incurred for travel away from home on Employer X business at a rate equal to 120 percent of the amount deemed substantiated for each day of travel to the localities to which the employees travel. Employer X does not require the employees to return the 20 percent by which the reimbursement for those expenses exceeds the amount deemed substantiated for each day of travel substantiated in accordance with paragraph (e) of this section. Employee C substantiates six days of business travel away from home: two days in a locality for which the amount deemed substantiated is $100 a day and four days in a locality for which the amount deemed substantiated is $125 a day. Employer X reimburses Employee C $840 for the six days of travel away from home (2 × (120% × $100) + 4 × (120% × $125)), and does not require Employee C to return the excess portion ($140 excess portion = (2 days × $20 ($120 – $100) + 4 days × $25 ($150 – $125)). For the payroll period in which Employer X reimburses the expenses, Employer X must withhold and pay employment taxes on $140.

Example (8). Return requirement. Employer Y provides expense allowances to certain of its employees to cover business expenses of a type described in paragraph (d)(1) of this section under an arrangement that requires the *employees to substantiate their expenses within a reasonable period of time and to return any excess amounts within a reasonable period of time.* Each time an employee returns an excess amount to Employer Y, however, Employer Y pays the employee a "bonus" equal to the amount returned by the employee. The

arrangement fails to satisfy the requirements of paragraph (f)(returning amounts in excess of expenses) of this section. Thus, Employer Y must report the entire amount of the expense allowance payments as wages or other compensation and must withhold and pay employment taxes on the payments when paid. Compare example (6)(where the employee is not required to return the portion of the mileage allowance that exceeds the amount deemed substantiated for each mile of travel substantiated).

Example (9). Timely substantiation. Employer Z provides a $500 advance to Employee D for a trip away from home on Employer Z business. Employee D incurs $500 in business expenses on the trip. Employer Z uses the periodic statement method safe harbor. At the end of the quarter during which the trip occurred, Employer Z sends a quarterly statement to Employee D stating that $500 was advanced to Employee D during the quarter and that no expenses were substantiated and no excess amounts returned. The statement advises Employee D that Employee D must substantiate any additional business expenses within 120 days of the date of the statement, and must return any unsubstantiated excess within the 120-day period. Employee D fails to substantiate any expenses or to return the excess within the 120-day period. Employer Z treats the $500 as wages and withholds and pays employment taxes on the $500. After the 120-day period has expired, Employee D substantiates the $500 in travel expenses in accordance with paragraph (e) of this section. Employer Z properly reported and withheld and paid employment taxes on the $500 and no adjustments may be made. Employee D must include the $500 in gross income and may deduct the $500 of expenses as a miscellaneous itemized deduction subject to the 2-percent floor provided in section 67.

(k) *Anti-abuse provision.*—If a payor's reimbursement or other expense allowance arrangement evidences a pattern of abuse of the rules of section 62(c) and this section, all payments made under the arrangement will be treated as made under a nonaccountable plan.

(l) *Cross references.*—For employment tax regulations relating to reimbursement and expense allowance arrangements, see §§31.3121(a)-3, 31.3231(e)-3, 31.3306(b)-2, and 31.3401(a)-4, which generally apply to payments made under reimbursement or other expense allowance arrangements received by an employee on or after July 1, 1990 with respect to expenses paid or incurred on or after July 1, 1990. For reporting requirements, see §1.6041-3(i), which generally applies to payments made under reimbursement or other expense allowance arrangements received by an employee on or after January 1, 1989 with respect to expenses paid or incurred on or after January 1, 1989.

(m) *Effective dates.*—This section generally applies to payments made under reimbursement or other expense allowance arrangements received by an employee in taxable years of the employee beginning on or after January 1, 1989, with respect to expenses paid or incurred in taxable years beginning on or after January 1, 1989. Paragraph (h) of this section generally applies to payments made under reimbursement or other expense allowance arrangements received by an employee on or after July 1, 1990 with respect to expenses paid or incurred on or after July 1, 1990. Paragraphs (d)(3)(ii) and (h)(2)(i)(B) of this section apply to payments made under reimbursement or other expense allowance arrangements received by an employee on or after January 1, 1991 with respect to expenses paid or incurred on or after January 1, 1991. Paragraph (e)(2) of this section applies to payments made under reimbursement or other expense allowance arrangements received by an employee with respect to expenses paid or incurred after December 31, 1997. [Reg. §1.62-2.]

☐ [T.D. 8324, 12-14-90. *Amended by* T.D. 8451, 12-4-92; T.D. 8666, 5-29-96; T.D. 8784, 9-30-98; T.D. 8864, 1-21-2000 *and* T.D. 9064, 6-30-2003.]

[Reg. §1.63-1]

§1.63-1. Change of treatment with respect to the zero bracket amount and itemized deductions.—(a) *In general.*—An individual who files a return on which the individual itemizes deductions in accordance with section 63(g) may later make a change of treatment by recomputing taxable income for the taxable year to which that return relates without itemizing deductions. Similarly, an individual who files a return on which the individual computes taxable income without itemizing deductions may later make a change of treatment by itemizing deductions in accordance with section 63(g) in recomputing taxable income for the taxable year to which that return relates.

(b) *No extension of time for claiming credit or refund.*—A change of treatment described in paragraph (a) of this section does not extend the period of time prescribed in section 6511 within which the taxpayer may make a claim for credit or refund of tax.

(c) *Special requirements if spouse filed separate return.*—(1) *Requirements.*—If the spouse of the taxpayer filed a separate return for a taxable year corresponding to the taxable year of the taxpayer, the taxpayer may not make a change of treatment described in paragraph (a) of this section for that year unless—

(i) The spouse makes a change of treatment on the separate return consistent with the change of treatment sought by the taxpayer; and

(ii) The taxpayer and the taxpayer's spouse file a consent in writing to the assessment of any deficiency of either spouse to the extent attributable to the change of treatment, even though the assessment of the deficiency would otherwise be prevented by the operation of any law or rule of law. The consent must be filed with the district director for the district in which the taxpayer applies for the change of treatment, and the period during which a deficiency may be assessed shall be established by agreement of the spouses and the district director.

(2) *Corresponding taxable year.*—A taxable year of one spouse corresponds to a taxable year of the other spouse if both taxable years end in the same calendar year. If the taxable year of one spouse ends with death, however, the corresponding taxable year of the surviving spouse is that in which the death occurs.

(d) *Inapplicable if tax liability has been compromised.*—The taxpayer may not make a change of treatment described in paragraph (a) of this section for any taxable year if—

(1) The tax liability of the taxpayer for the taxable year has been compromised under section 7122; or

(2) The tax liability of the taxpayer's spouse for a taxable year corresponding to the taxable year of the taxpayer has been compromised under section 7122. See paragraph (c)(2) of this section for the determination of a corresponding taxable year.

(e) *Effective date.*—This section applies to taxable years beginning after 1976. [Reg. §1.63-1.]

☐ [*T.D.* 7385, 1-3-79.]

[Reg. §1.63-2]

§1.63-2. Cross reference.—For rules with respect to charitable contribution deductions for nonitemizing taxpayers, see section 63(b)(1)(C) and (i) and section 170(i) of the Internal Revenue Code of 1954. [Reg. §1.63-2.]

☐ [*T.D.* 8002, 12-26-84.]

[Reg. §1.66-1]

§1.66-1. Treatment of community income.—(a) *In general.*—Married individuals domiciled in a community property state who do not elect to file a joint individual Federal income tax return under section 6013 generally must report half of the total community income earned by the spouses during the taxable year except at times when one of the following exceptions applies—

(1) The spouses live apart and meet the qualifications of §1.66-2.

(2) The Secretary denies a spouse the Federal income tax benefits resulting from community property law under §1.66-3, because that spouse acted as if solely entitled to the income and failed to notify his or her spouse of the nature and amount of the income prior to the due date for the filing of his or her spouse's return.

(3) A requesting spouse qualifies for traditional relief from the Federal income tax liability resulting from the operation of community property law under §1.66-4(a).

(4) A requesting spouse qualifies for equitable relief from the Federal income tax liability resulting from the operation of community property law under §1.66-4(b).

(b) *Applicability.*—(1) The rules of this section apply only to community income, as defined by state law. The rules of this section do not apply to income that is not community income. Thus, the rules of this section do not apply to income from property that was formerly community property, but in accordance with state law, has ceased to be community property, becoming, e.g., separate property or property held by joint tenancy or tenancy in common.

(2) When taxpayers report income under paragraph (a) of this section, *all* community income for the calendar year is treated in accordance with the rules provided by section 879(a). Unlike the other provisions under section 66, section 66(a) does not permit inclusion on an item-by-item basis.

(c) *Transferee liability.*—The provisions of section 66 do not negate liability that arises under the operation of other laws. Therefore, a spouse who is not subject to Federal income tax on community income may nevertheless remain liable for the unpaid tax (including additions to tax, penalties, and interest) to the extent provided by Federal or state transferee liability or property laws (other than community property laws). For the rules regarding the liability of

transferees, see sections 6901 through 6904 and the regulations thereunder. [Reg. §1.66-1.]

☐ [*T.D.* 9074, 7-9-2003.]

[Reg. §1.66-2]

§1.66-2. Treatment of community income where spouses live apart.—(a) Community income of spouses domiciled in a community property state will be treated in accordance with the rules provided by section 879(a) if all of the following requirements are satisfied—

(1) The spouses are married to each other at any time during the calendar year;

(2) The spouses live apart at all times during the calendar year;

(3) The spouses do not file a joint return with each other for a taxable year beginning or ending in the calendar year;

(4) One or both spouses have earned income that is community income for the calendar year; and

(5) No portion of such earned income is transferred (directly or indirectly) between such spouses before the close of the calendar year.

(b) *Living apart.*—For purposes of this section, living apart requires that spouses maintain separate residences. Spouses who maintain separate residences due to temporary absences are not considered to be living apart. Spouses who are not members of the same household under §1.6015-3(b) are considered to be living apart for purposes of this section.

(c) *Transferred income.*—For purposes of this section, transferred income does not include a de minimis amount of earned income that is transferred between the spouses. In addition, any amount of earned income transferred for the benefit of the spouses' child will not be treated as an indirect transfer to one spouse. Additionally, income transferred between spouses is presumed to be a transfer of earned income. This presumption is rebuttable.

(d) *Examples.*—The following examples illustrate the rules of this section:

Example 1. Living apart. H and W are married, domiciled in State A, a community property state, and have lived apart the entire year of 2002. W, who is in the Army, was stationed in Korea for the entire calendar year. During their separation, W intended to return home to H, and H intended to live with W upon W's return. H and W do not file a joint return for taxable year 2002. H and W may not report their income under this section because a temporary absence due to military service is not living apart as contemplated under this section.

Example 2. Transfer of earned income—de minimis exception. H and W are married, domiciled in State B, a community property state, and have lived apart the entire year of 2002. H and W are estranged and intend to live apart indefinitely. H and W do not file a joint return for taxable year 2002. H occasionally visits W and their two children, who live with W. When H visits, he often buys gifts for the children, takes the children out to dinner, and occasionally buys groceries or gives W money to buy the children new clothes for school. Both W and H have earned income in the year 2002 that is community income under the laws of State B. H and W may report their income on separate returns under this section.

Example 3. Transfer of earned income—source of transfer. H and W are married, domiciled in State C, a community property state, and have lived apart the entire year of 2002. H and W are estranged and intend to live apart indefinitely. H and W do not file a joint return for taxable year 2002. W provides H $1,000 a month from March 2002 through August 2002 while H is working part-time and seeking full-time employment. W is not legally obligated to make the $1,000 payments. W earns $75,000 in 2002 in wage income. W also receives $10,000 in capital gains income in December 2002. H wants to report his income in accordance with this section, alleging that the $6,000 that he received from W was not from W's earned income, but from the capital gains income W received in 2002. The facts and circumstances surrounding the periodic payments to H from W do not indicate that W made the payments out of her capital gains income. H and W may not report their income in accordance with this section, as the $6,000 W transferred to H is presumed to be from W's earned income, and H has not presented any facts to rebut the presumption. [Reg. §1.66-2.]

☐ [*T.D.* 9074, 7-9-2003.]

[Reg. §1.66-3]

§1.66-3. Denial of the Federal income tax benefits resulting from the operation of community property law where spouse not notified.—(a) *In general.*—The Secretary may deny the Federal income tax benefits of community property law to any spouse with respect to any item of community income if that spouse acted as if solely entitled to the income and failed to notify his or her spouse of the nature and amount of the income before the due date (including extensions) for the filing of the return of his or her spouse for the taxable year in which the item of income was derived. Whether a spouse has acted as if solely entitled to the item of income is a facts and circumstances determination. This determination focuses on whether the spouse used, or made available, the item of income for the benefit of the marital community.

(b) *Effect.*—The item of community income will be included, in its entirety, in the gross income of the spouse to whom the Secretary denied the Federal income tax benefits resulting from community property law. The tax liability arising from the inclusion of the item of community income must be assessed in accordance with section 6212 against this spouse.

(c) *Examples.*—The following examples illustrate the rules of this section:

Example 1. Acting as if solely entitled to income. (i) H and W are married and are domiciled in State A, a community property state. W's Form W-2 for taxable year 2000 showed wage income of $35,000. W also received a Form 1099-INT, "Interest Income," showing $1,000 W received in taxable year 2000. W's wage income was directly deposited into H and W's joint account, from which H and W paid bills and household expenses. W did not inform H of her interest income or the Form 1099-INT, but W gave H a copy of the W-2 when she received it in January 2001. W did not use her interest income for bills or household expenses. Instead W gave her interest income to her brother, who was unemployed. Neither the separate return filed by H nor the separate return filed by W included the interest income. In 2002, the IRS audits both H and W. The Internal Revenue Service (IRS) may raise section 66(b) as to W's interest income, denying W the Federal income tax benefit resulting from community property law as to this item of income.

(ii) H and W are married and are domiciled in State B, a community property state. For taxable year 2000, H receives $45,000 in wage income that H places in a separate account. H and W maintain separate residences. H's wage income is community income under the laws of State B. That same year, W loses her job, and H pays W's mortgage and household expenses for several months while W seeks employment. Neither H nor W files a return for 2000, the taxable year for which the IRS subsequently audits them. The IRS may not raise section 66(b) and deny H the Federal income tax benefits resulting from the operation of community property law as to H's wage income of $45,000, as H has not treated this income as if H were solely entitled to it.

Example 2. Notification of nature and amount of the income. H and W are married and domiciled in State C, a community property state. H and W do not file a joint return for taxable year 2001. H's and W's earned income for 2001 is community income under the laws of State C. H receives $50,000 in wage income in 2001. In January 2002, H receives a Form W-2 that erroneously states that H earned $45,000 in taxable year 2001. H provides W a copy of H's Form W-2 in February 2002. W files for an extension prior to April 15, 2002. H receives a corrected Form W-2 reflecting wages of $50,000 in May 2002. H provides a copy of the corrected Form W-2 to W in May 2002. W files a separate return in June 2002, but reports one half of $45,000 ($22,500) of wage income that H earned. H files a separate return reporting half of $50,000 ($25,000) in wage income. The IRS audits both H and W. Even if H had acted as if solely entitled to the wage income, the IRS may not raise section 66(b) as to this income because H notified W of the nature and amount of the income prior to the due date of W's return (including extensions).

[Reg. §1.66-3.]

□ [*T.D. 9074, 7-9-2003.*]

[Reg. §1.66-4]

§1.66-4. Request for relief from the Federal income tax liability resulting from the operation of community property law.—(a) *Traditional relief.*—(1) *In general.*—A requesting spouse will receive relief from the Federal income tax liability resulting from the operation of community property law for an item of community income if—

(i) The requesting spouse did not file a joint Federal income tax return for the taxable year for which he or she seeks relief;

(ii) The requesting spouse did not include in gross income for the taxable year an item of community income properly includible therein, which, under the rules contained in section 879(a), would be treated as the income of the nonrequesting spouse;

(iii) The requesting spouse establishes that he or she did not know of, and had no reason to know of, *the item of community income;* and

(iv) Taking into account all of the facts and circumstances, it is inequitable to include the item of community income in the requesting spouse's individual gross income.

(2) *Knowledge or reason to know.*—(i) A requesting spouse had knowledge or reason to know of an item of community income if he or she either actually knew of the item of community income, or if a reasonable person in similar circumstances would have known of the item of community income. All of the facts and circumstances are considered in determining whether a requesting spouse had reason to know of an item of community income. The relevant facts and circumstances include, but are not limited to, the nature of the item of community income, the amount of the item of community income relative to other income items, the couple's financial situation, the requesting spouse's educational background and business experience, and whether the item of community income was reflected on prior years' returns (e.g., investment income omitted that was regularly reported on prior years' returns).

(ii) If the requesting spouse is aware of the source of community income or the income-producing activity, but is unaware of the specific amount of the nonrequesting spouse's community income, the requesting spouse is considered to have knowledge or reason to know of the item of community income. The requesting spouse's lack of knowledge of the specific amount of community income does not provide a basis for relief under this section.

(3) *Inequitable.*—All of the facts and circumstances are considered in determining whether it is inequitable to hold a requesting spouse liable for a deficiency attributable to an item of community income. One relevant factor for this purpose is whether the requesting spouse benefitted, directly or indirectly, from the omitted item of community income. A benefit includes normal support, but does not include de minimis amounts. Evidence of direct or indirect benefit may consist of transfers of property or rights to property, including transfers received several years after the filing of the return. Thus, for example, if a requesting spouse receives from the nonrequesting spouse property (including life insurance proceeds) that is traceable to items of community income attributable to the nonrequesting spouse, the requesting spouse will have benefitted from those items of community income. Other factors may include, if the situation warrants, desertion, divorce or separation. Factors relevant to whether it would be inequitable to hold a requesting spouse liable, more specifically described under the applicable administrative procedure issued under section 66(c) (Revenue Procedure 2000-15 (2000-1 C.B. 447) (See §601.601(d)(2) of this chapter), or other applicable guidance published by the Secretary), are to be considered in making a determination under this paragraph.

(b) *Equitable relief.*—Equitable relief may be available when the four requirements of paragraph (a)(1) of this section are not satisfied, but it would be inequitable to hold the requesting spouse liable for the unpaid tax or deficiency. Factors relevant to whether it would be inequitable to hold a requesting spouse liable, more specifically described under the applicable administrative procedure issued under section 66(c) (Revenue Procedure 2000-15 (2000-1 C.B. 447), or other applicable guidance published by the Secretary), are to be considered in making a determination under this paragraph.

(c) *Applicability.*—Traditional relief under paragraph (a) of this section applies only to deficiencies arising out of items of omitted income. Equitable relief under paragraph (b) of this section applies to any deficiency or any unpaid tax (or any portion of either). Equitable relief is available only for the portion of liabilities that were unpaid as of July 22, 1998, and for liabilities that arise after July 22, 1998.

(d) *Effect of relief.*—When the requesting spouse qualifies for relief under paragraph (a) or (b) of this section, the IRS must assess any deficiency of the nonrequesting spouse arising from the granting of relief to the requesting spouse in accordance with section 6212.

(e) *Examples.*—The following examples illustrate the rules of this section:

Example 1. Item-by-item approach. H and W are married, living together, and domiciled in State A (a community property state). H and W file separate returns for taxable year 2002 on April 15, 2003. H earns $56,000 in wages, and W earns $46,000 in wages, in 2002. H reports half of his wage income as shown on his Form W-2, in the amount of $28,000, and half of W's wage income as shown on her Form W-2, in the amount of $23,000. W reports half of her wage income as shown on her W-2, in the amount of $23,000, and half of H's wage income as shown on his Form W-2, in the amount of $28,000. Neither H nor W reports W's income from her sole proprietorship of $34,000 or W's investment income of $5,000 for taxable year 2002. The Internal Revenue Service (IRS) proposes deficiencies with respect to H's and W's taxable year 2002 returns due to the omission of W's income from her sole proprietorship and investments. H timely requests relief under section 66(c). Because the IRS determines that H satisfies the four requirements of the traditional relief provision of section 66(c) with respect to W's omitted investment income, the IRS grants H's request for relief as to the omitted investment income. The IRS determines that H does not satisfy the four requirements of the traditional relief provision of section 66(c) as to W's sole proprietorship income. The IRS further determines that, under the equitable relief provision of section 66(c), it is not inequitable to hold H liable for the sole proprietorship income. Relief is applicable on an item-by-item basis. Thus, H is liable for the tax on half of his wage income in the amount of $28,000, half of W's wage income in the amount of $23,000, half of W's sole proprietorship income in the amount of $17,000, but none of W's investment income, for which H obtained relief under section 66(c). W is liable for the tax on half of H's wage income in the amount of $28,000, half of W's wage income in the amount of $23,000, half of W's sole proprietorship income in the amount of $17,000, and all of W's investment income in the amount of $5,000, because H obtained relief under section 66(c).

Example 2. Benefit. H and W are married, living together, and domiciled in State B (a community property state). Neither H nor W files a return for taxable year 2000. H earns $60,000 in 2000, which he deposits in a joint account. H and W pay the mortgage payment, household bills, and other family expenses out of the joint account. W earns $20,000 in 2000. W uses a portion of the $20,000 to make monthly loan payments on the family cars, but loses the remainder at the local racetrack. In 2002, the IRS audits H and W. H requests relief under section 66(c), stating that he did not know or have reason to know of W's additional income, as H travels extensively while W handles the family finances. Regardless of whether H had knowledge or reason to know of the source of W's income, H is not eligible for traditional relief under section 66(c) because H benefitted from W's income. H's benefit, the portion of W's income used to make monthly payments on the car loans, was more than a de minimis amount. While this benefit was not in excess of normal support, it is enough to preclude relief under the traditional relief provision of section 66(c). H may still qualify for equitable relief under section 66(c), depending on all of the facts and circumstances.

(f) *Fraudulent scheme.*—If the Secretary establishes that a spouse transferred assets to his or her spouse as part of a fraudulent scheme, relief is not available under this section. For purposes of this section, a fraudulent scheme includes a scheme to defraud the Secretary or another third party, such as a creditor, ex-spouse, or business partner.

(g) *Definitions.*—(1) *Requesting spouse.*—A requesting spouse is an individual who does not file a joint Federal income tax return with the nonrequesting spouse for the taxable year in question, and who requests relief from the Federal income tax liability resulting from the operation of community property law under this section for the portion of the liability arising from his or her share of community income for such taxable year.

(2) *Nonrequesting spouse.*—A nonrequesting spouse is the individual to whom the requesting spouse was married and whose income or deduction gave rise to the tax liability from which the requesting spouse seeks relief in whole or in part.

(h) *Effect of prior closing agreement or offer in compromise.*—A requesting spouse is not entitled to relief from the Federal income tax liability resulting from the operation of community property law under section 66 for any taxable year for which the requesting spouse has entered into a closing agreement (other than an agreement pursuant to section 6224(c) relating to partnership items) with the Secretary that disposes of the same liability that is the subject of the request for relief. In addition, a requesting spouse is not entitled to relief from the Federal income tax liability resulting from the operation of community property law under section 66 for any taxable year for which the requesting spouse has entered into an offer in compromise with the Secretary. For rules relating to the effect of closing agreements and offers in compromise, see sections 7121 and 7122, and the regulations thereunder.

(i) [Reserved]

(j) *Time and manner for requesting relief.*—(1) *Requesting relief.*—To request relief from the Federal income tax liability resulting from the operation of community property law under this section, a requesting spouse must file, within the time period prescribed in paragraph (j)(2) of this section, Form 8857, "Request for Innocent Spouse Relief" (or other specified form), or other written request, signed under penalties of perjury, stating why relief is appropriate. The requesting spouse must include the nonrequesting spouse's name and taxpayer identification number in the written request. The requesting spouse must also comply with the Secretary's reasonable requests for information that will assist the Secretary in identifying and locating the nonrequesting spouse.

(2) *Time period for filing a request for relief.*—(i) *Traditional relief.*—The earliest time for submitting a request for relief from the Federal income tax liability resulting from the operation of community prop-

erty law under paragraph (a) of this section, for an amount underreported on, or omitted from, the requesting spouse's separate return, is the date the requesting spouse receives notification of an audit or a letter or notice from the IRS stating that there may be an outstanding liability with regard to that year (as described in paragraph (j)(2)(iii) of this section). The latest time for requesting relief under paragraph (a) of this section is 6 months before the expiration of the period of limitations on assessment, including extensions, against the nonrequesting spouse for the taxable year that is the subject of the request for relief, unless the examination of the requesting spouse's return commences during that 6-month period. If the examination of the requesting spouse's return commences during that 6-month period, the latest time for requesting relief under paragraph (a) of this section is 30 days after the commencement of the examination.

(ii) *Equitable relief.*—The earliest time for submitting a request for relief from the Federal income tax liability resulting from the operation of community property law under paragraph (b) of this section is the date the requesting spouse receives notification of an audit or a letter or notice from the IRS stating that there may be an outstanding liability with regard to that year (as described in paragraph (j)(2)(iii) of this section). A request for equitable relief from the Federal income tax liability resulting from the operation of community property law under paragraph (b) of this section for a liability that is properly reported but unpaid is properly submitted with the requesting spouse's individual Federal income tax return, or after the requesting spouse's individual Federal income tax return is filed.

(iii) *Premature requests for relief.*—The Secretary will not consider a premature request for relief under this section. The notices or letters referenced in this paragraph (j)(2) do not include notices issued pursuant to section 6223 relating to TEFRA partnership proceedings. These notices or letters include notices of computational adjustment to a partner or partner's spouse (Notice of Income Tax Examination Changes) that reflect a computation of the liability attributable to partnership items of the partner or the partner's spouse.

(k) *Nonrequesting spouse's notice and opportunity to participate in administrative proceedings.*—(1) *In general.*—When the Secretary receives a request for relief from the Federal income tax liability resulting from the operation of community property law under this section, the Secretary must send a notice to the nonrequesting spouse's last known address that informs the nonrequesting spouse of the requesting spouse's request for relief. The notice must provide the nonrequesting spouse with an opportunity to submit any information for consideration in determining whether to grant the requesting spouse relief from the Federal income tax liability resulting from the operation of community property law. The Secretary will share with each spouse the information submitted by the other spouse, unless the Secretary determines that the sharing of this information will impair tax administration.

(2) *Information submitted.*—The Secretary will consider all of the information (as relevant to the particular relief provision) that the nonrequesting spouse submits in determining whether to grant relief from the Federal income tax liability resulting from the operation of community property law under this section. [Reg. §1.66-4.]

☐ [*T.D. 9074, 7-9-2003.*]

[Reg. §1.66-5]

§1.66-5. Effective date.—Sections 1.66-1 through 1.66-4 are applicable on July 10, 2003. In addition, §1.66-4 applies to any request for relief filed prior to July 10, 2003, for which the Internal Revenue Service has not issued a preliminary determination as of July 10, 2003. [Reg. §1.66-5.]

☐ [*T.D. 9074, 7-9-2003.*]

[Reg. §1.67-1T]

§1.67-1T. 2-percent floor on miscellaneous itemized deductions (temporary).—(a) *Type of expenses subject to the floor.*—(1) *In general.*—With respect to individuals, section 67 disallows deductions for miscellaneous itemized deductions (as defined in paragraph (b) of this section) in computing taxable income (i.e., so-called "below-the-line" deductions) to the extent that such otherwise allowable deductions do not exceed 2 percent of the individual's adjusted gross income (as defined in section 62 and the regulations thereunder). Examples of expenses that, if otherwise deductible, are subject to the 2-percent floor include but are not limited to—

(i) Unreimbursed employee expenses, such as expenses for transportation, travel fares and lodging while away from home, business meals and entertainment, continuing education courses, subscriptions to professional journals, union or professional dues, professional uniforms, job hunting, and the business use of the employee's home,

(ii) Expenses for the production or collection of income for which a deduction is otherwise allowable under section 212(1) and (2), such as investment advisory fees, subscriptions to investment advisory publications, certain attorneys' fees, and the cost of safe deposit boxes,

(iii) Expenses for the determination of any tax for which a deduction is otherwise allowable under section 212(3), such as tax counsel fees and appraisal fees, and

(iv) Expenses for an activity for which a deduction is otherwise allowable under section 183.

See section 62 with respect to deductions that are allowable in computing adjusted gross income (*i.e.,* so-called "above-the-line" deductions).

(2) *Other limitations.*—Except as otherwise provided in paragraph (d) of this section, to the extent that any limitation or restriction is placed on the amount of a miscellaneous itemized deduction, that limitation shall apply prior to the application of the 2-percent floor. For example, in the case of an expense for food or beverages, only 80 percent of which is allowable as a deduction because of the limitations provided in section 274(n), the otherwise deductible 80 percent of the expense is treated as a miscellaneous itemized deduction and is subject to the 2-percent limitation of section 67.

(b) *Definition of miscellaneous itemized deductions.*—For purposes of this section, the term "miscellaneous itemized deductions" means the deductions allowable from adjusted gross income in determining taxable income, as defined in section 63, other than—

(1) The standard deduction as defined in section 63(c),

(2) Any deduction allowable for impairment-related work expenses as defined in section 67(d),

(3) The deduction under section 72(b)(3) (relating to deductions if annuity payments cease before the investment is recovered),

(4) The deductions allowable under section 151 for personal exemptions,

(5) The deduction under section 163 (relating to interest),

(6) The deduction under section 164 (relating to taxes),

(7) The deduction under section 165(a) for losses described in subsection (c)(3) or (d) of section 165,

(8) The deduction under section 170 (relating to charitable contributions and gifts),

(9) The deduction under section 171 (relating to deductions for amortizable bond premiums),

(10) The deduction under section 213 (relating to medical and dental expenses),

(11) The deduction under section 216 (relating to deductions in connection with cooperative housing corporations),

(12) The deduction under section 217 (relating to moving expenses),

(13) The deduction under section 691(c) (relating to the deduction for estate taxes in the case of income in respect of the decedent),

(14) The deduction under 1341 (relating to the computation of tax if a taxpayer restores a substantial amount held under claim of right), and

(15) Any deduction allowable in connection with personal property used in a short sale.

(c) *Allocation of expenses.*—If a taxpayer incurs expenses that relate to both a trade or business activity (within the meaning of section 162) and a production of income or tax preparation activity (within the meaning of section 212), the taxpayer shall allocate such expenses between the activities on a reasonable basis.

(d) *Members of Congress.*—(1) *In general.*—With respect to the deduction for living expenses of Members of Congress referred to in section 162(a), the 2-percent floor described in section 67 and paragraph (a) of this section shall be applied to the deduction before the application of the $3,000 limitation on deductions for living expenses referred to in section 162(a). (For purposes of this paragraph (d), the term "Member(s) of Congress" includes any Delegate or Resident Commissioner.) The amount of miscellaneous itemized deductions of a Member of Congress that is disallowed pursuant to section 67 and paragraph (a) of this section shall be allocated between deductions for living expenses (within the meaning of section 162(a)) and other miscellaneous itemized deductions. The amount of deductions for living expenses of a Member of Congress that is disallowed pursuant to section 67 and paragraph (a) of this section is determined by multiplying the aggregate amount of such living expenses (determined without regard to the $3,000 limitation of section 162(a) but with regard to any other limitations) by a fraction, the numerator of which is the aggregate amount *disallowed pursuant to section 67 and paragraph (a) of this section with respect to miscellaneous itemized deductions of the Member of Congress* and the denominator of which is the amount of miscellaneous itemized deductions (including deductions for living expenses) of the Member of Congress (deter-

mined without regard to the $3,000 limitation of section 162(a) but with regard to any other limitations). The amount of deductions for miscellaneous itemized deductions (other than deductions for living expenses) of a Member of Congress that are disallowed pursuant to section 67 and paragraph (a) of this section is determined by multiplying the amount of miscellaneous itemized deductions (other than deductions for living expenses) of the Member of Congress (determined with regard to any limitations) by the fraction described in the preceding sentence.

(2) *Example.*—The provisions of this paragraph (d) may be illustrated by the following example:

Example. For 1987 A, a Member of Congress, has adjusted gross income of $100,000, and miscellaneous itemized deductions of $10,750 of which $3,750 is for meals, $3,000 is for other living expenses, and $4,000 is for other miscellaneous itemized deductions (none of which is subject to any percentage limitations other than the 2-percent floor of section 67). The amount of A's business meal expenses that are disallowed under section 274(n) is $750 ($3,750 × 20%). The amount of A's miscellaneous itemized deductions that are disallowed under section 67 is $2,000 ($100,000 × 2%). The portion of the amount disallowed under section 67 that is allocated to A's living expenses is $1,200. This portion is equal to the amount of A's deductions for living expenses allowable after the application of section 274(n) and before the application of section 67 ($6,000) multiplied by the ratio of A's total miscellaneous itemized deductions disallowed under section 67 to A's total miscellaneous itemized deductions, determined without regard to the $3,000 limitation of section 162(a) ($2,000/$10,000). Thus, after application of section 274(n) and section 67, A's deduction for living expenses is $4,800 ($6,750 − $750 − $1,200). However, pursuant to section 162(a), A may deduct only $3,000 of such expenses. The amount of A's other miscellaneous itemized deductions that are disallowed under section 67 is $800 ($4,000 × $2,000/$10,000). Thus, $3,200 ($4,000 − $800) of A's miscellaneous itemized deductions (other than deductions for living expenses) are allowable after application of section 67. A's total allowable miscellaneous itemized deductions are $6,200 ($3,000 + $3,200).

(e) *State legislators.*—See §1.62-1T(e)(4) with respect to rules regarding state legislator's expenses. [Temporary Reg. §1.67-1T.]

☐ [T.D. 8189, 3-25-88.]

[Reg. §1.67-2T]

§1.67-2T. Treatment of pass-through entities (temporary).—(a) *Application of section 67.*—This section provides rules for the application of section 67 to partners, shareholders, beneficiaries, participants, and others with respect to their interests in pass-through entities (as defined in paragraph (g) of this section). In general, an affected investor (as defined in paragraph (h) of this section) in a pass-through entity shall separately take into account as an item of income and as an item of expense an amount equal to his or her allocable share of the affected expenses (as defined in paragraph (i) of this section) of the pass-through entity for purposes of determining his or her taxable income. Except as provided in paragraph (e)(1)(ii)(B) of this section, the expenses so taken into account shall be treated as paid or incurred by the affected investor in the same manner as paid or incurred by the pass-through entity. For rules regarding the application of section 67 to affected investors in—

(1) Partnerships, S corporations, and grantor trusts, see paragraph (b) of this section,

(2) Real estate mortgage investment conduits, see paragraph (c) of this section,

(3) Common trust funds, see paragraph (d) of this section,

(4) Nonpublicly offered regulated investment companies, see paragraph (e) of this section, and

(5) Publicly offered regulated investment companies, see paragraph (p) of this section.

(b) *Partnerships, S corporations, and grantor trusts.*—(1) *In general.*—Pursuant to sections 702(a) and 1366(a) of the Code and the regulations thereunder, each partner of a partnership or shareholder of an S corporation shall take into account separately his or her distributive or pro rata share of any items of deduction of such partnership or corporation that are defined as miscellaneous itemized deductions pursuant to section 67(b). The 2-percent limitation described in section 67 does not apply to the partnership or corporation with respect to such deductions, but such deductions shall be included in the deductions of the partner or shareholder to which that limitation applies. Similarly, the limitation applies to the grantor or other person treated as the owner of a grantor trust with respect to items that are paid or incurred by a grantor trust and are treated as miscellaneous itemized deductions of the grantor or other person pursuant to subpart E, part 1, subchapter J, chapter 1 of the Code, but not to the trust itself. The 2-percent limitation applies to amounts otherwise deductible in taxable years of partners, shareholders, or grantors beginning after December 31, 1986, regardless of the taxable year of the partnership, corporation, or trust.

(2) *Example.*—The provisions of this paragraph (b) may be illustrated by the following example:

Example. P, a partnership, incurs $1,000 in expenses to which section 212 applies during its taxable year. A, an individual, is a partner in P. A's distributive share of the expenses to which section 212 applies is $20, determined without regard to the 2-percent limitation of section 67. Pursuant to section 702(a), A must take $20 of expenses to which section 212 applies into account in determining his income tax. Pursuant to section 67, in determining his taxable income A may deduct his miscellaneous itemized deductions (including his $20 distributive share of deductions from P) to the extent the total amount exceeds 2 percent of his adjusted gross income.

(c) *Real estate mortgage investment conduit.*—See §1.67-3T for rules regarding the application of section 67 to holders of interests in REMICs.

(d) *Common trust funds.*—(1) *In general.*—For purposes of determining the taxable income of an affected investor that is a participant in a common trust fund—

(i) The ordinary taxable income and ordinary net loss of the common trust fund shall be computed under section 584(d)(2) without taking into account any affected expenses, and

(ii) Each affected investor shall be treated as having paid or incurred an expense described in section 212 in an amount equal to the affected investor's proportionate share of the affected expenses.

The 2-percent limitation described in section 67 applies to amounts otherwise deductible in taxable years of participants beginning after December 31, 1986, regardless of the taxable year of the common trust fund.

(2) *Example.*—The provisions of this paragraph (d) may be illustrated by the following example:

Example. During 1987, the gross income and deductions of common trust fund C, a calendar year taxpayer, consist of the following items: (i) $50,000 of short-term capital gains; (ii) $150,000 of long-term capital gains; (iii) $1,000,000 of dividend income; (iv) $10,000 of deductions that are not affected expenses; and (v) $60,000 of deductions that are affected expenses. The proportionate share of Trust T in the income and losses of C is one percent. In computing its taxable income for 1987, T, a calendar year taxpayer, shall take into account the following items: (A) $500 of short-term capital gains (one percent of $50,000, C's short-term capital gains); (B) $1,500 of long-term capital gains (one percent of $150,000, C's long-term capital gains); (C) $9,900 of ordinary taxable income (one percent of $990,000, the excess of $100,000, C's gross income after excluding capital gains and losses, over $10,000, C's deductions that are not affected expenses); (D) $600 of expenses described in section 212 (one percent of $60,000, C's affected expenses).

(e) *Nonpublicly offered regulated investment companies.*—(1) *In general.*—For purposes of determining the taxable income of an affected investor that is a shareholder of a nonpublicly offered regulated investment company (as defined in paragraph (g)(3) of this section) during a calendar year—

(i) The current earnings and profits of the nonpublicly offered regulated investment company shall be computed without taking into account any affected RIC expenses that are allocated among affected investors, and

(ii) The affected investor shall be treated—

(A) As having received or accrued a dividend in an amount equal to the affected investor's allocable share of the affected RIC expenses of the nonpublicly offered regulated investment company for the calendar year, and

(B) As having paid or incurred an expense described in section 212 (or section 162 in the case of an affected investor that is a nonpublicly offered regulated investment company) in an amount equal to the affected investor's allocable share of the affected RIC expenses of the nonpublicly offered regulated investment company for the calendar year

in the affected investor's taxable year with which (or within which) the calendar year with respect to which the expenses are allocated ends. An affected investor's allocable share of the affected RIC expenses is the amount allocated to that affected investor pursuant to paragraph (k) of this section.

(2) *Shareholders that are not affected investors.*—A shareholder of a nonpublicly offered regulated investment company that is not an affected investor shall not take into account in computing its taxable income any amount of income or expense with respect to its allocable share of affected RIC expenses.

(3) *Example.*—The provisions of this paragraph (e) may be illustrated by the following example:

Example. During calendar year 1987, nonpublicly offered regulated investment company M distributes to individual shareholder A, a calendar year taxpayer, capital gain dividends of $1,000 and other dividends of $5,000. A's allocable share of the affected RIC expenses of M is $200. In computing A's taxable income for 1987, A shall take into account the following items: (i) $1,000 of long-term capital gains (the capital gain dividends received by A); (ii) $5,200 of dividend income (the sum of the other dividends received by A and A's allocable share of the affected RIC expenses of M); and (iii) $200 of expenses described in section 212 (A's allocable share of the affected RIC expenses of M). A is allowed a deduction for miscellaneous itemized deductions (including A's $200 allocable share of the affected RIC expenses of M, which is treated as an expense described in section 212) for 1987 only to the extent the aggregate of such deductions exceeds 2 percent of A's adjusted gross income for 1987.

(f) *Cross-reference.*—See §1.67-1T with respect to limitations on deductions for expenses described in section 212 (including amounts treated as such expenses under this section).

(g) *Pass-through entity.*—(1) *In general.*—Except as provided in paragraph (g)(2) of this section, for purposes of section 67(c) and this section, a pass-through entity is—

(i) A trust (or any portion thereof) to which subpart E, part 1, subchapter J, chapter 1 of the Code applies,

(ii) A partnership,

(iii) An S corporation,

(iv) A common trust fund described in section 584,

(v) A nonpublicly offered regulated investment company,

(vi) A real estate mortgage investment conduit, and

(vii) Any other person—

(A) Which is not subject to the income tax imposed by subtitle A, chapter 1, or which is allowed a deduction in computing such tax for distributions to owners or beneficiaries, and

(B) The character of the income of which may affect the character of the income recognized with respect to that person by its owners or beneficiaries.

Entities that do not meet the requirements of paragraph (g)(1)(vii)(A) and (B), such as qualified pension plans, individual retirement accounts, and insurance companies holding assets in separate asset accounts to fund variable contracts defined in section 817(d), are not described in this paragraph (g)(1).

(2) *Exception.*—For purposes of section 67(c) and this section, a pass-through entity does not include:

(i) An estate,

(ii) A trust (or any portion thereof) not described in paragraph (g)(1)(i) of this section,

(iii) A cooperative described in section 1381(a)(2), determined without regard to subparagraphs (A) and (C) thereof, or

(iv) A real estate investment trust.

(3) *Nonpublicly offered regulated investment company.*—(i) *In general.*—For purposes of this section, the term "nonpublicly offered regulated investment company" means a regulated investment company to which part I of subchapter M of the Code applies that is not a publicly offered regulated investment company.

(ii) *Publicly offered regulated investment company.*—For purposes of this section, the term "publicly offered regulated investment company" means a regulated investment company to which part I of subchapter M of the Code applies the shares of which are—

(A) Continuously offered pursuant to a public offering (within the meaning of section 4 of the Securities Act of 1933, as amended (15 U.S.C. 77a to 77aa)),

(B) Regularly traded on an established securities market, or

(C) Held by or for no fewer than 500 persons at all times during the taxable year.

(h) *Affected investor.*—(1) *In general.*—For purposes of this section, the term "affected investor" means a partner, shareholder, beneficiary, participant, or other interest holder in a pass-through entity at any time during the pass-through entity's taxable year that is—

(i) An individual (other than a nonresident alien whose income with respect to his or her interest in the pass-through entity is not effectively connected with the conduct of a trade or business within the United States);

(ii) A person, including a trust or estate, that computes its taxable income in the same manner as in the case of an individual; or

(iii) A pass-through entity if one or more of its partners, shareholders, beneficiaries, participants, or other interest holders is (A) a pass-through entity or (B) a person described in paragraph (h)(1)(i) or (ii) of this section.

(2) *Examples.*—The provisions of this paragraph (h) may be illustrated by the following examples:

Example (1). Corporation X holds shares of nonpublicly offered regulated investment company R in its capacity as a nominee or custodian for individual A, the beneficial owner of the shares. Because the owner of the shares for Federal income tax purposes is an individual, the shares are owned by an affected investor.

Example (2). Individual retirement account I owns shares of a nonpublicly offered regulated investment company. Because an individual retirement account is not a person described in paragraph (h)(1) of this section, the shares are not owned by an affected investor.

(i) *Affected expenses.*—(1) *In general.*—In general, for purposes of this section, the term "affected expenses" means expenses that, if paid or incurred by an individual, would be deductible, if at all, as miscellaneous itemized deductions as defined in section 67(b).

(2) *Special rule for nonpublicly offered regulated investment companies.*—In the case of a nonpublicly offered regulated investment company, the term "affected expenses" means only affected RIC expenses.

(j) *Affected RIC expenses.*—(1) *In general.*—In general, for purposes of this section, the term "affected RIC expenses" means the excess of—

(i) The aggregate amount of the expenses (other than expenses described in sections 62(a)(3) and 67(b) and § 1.67-1T(b)) paid or incurred in the calendar year that are allowable as a deduction in determining the investment company taxable income (without regard to section 852(b)(2)(D)) of the nonpublicly offered regulated investment company for a taxable year that begins or ends with or within the calendar year, over

(ii) The amount of expenses taken into account under paragraph (j)(1)(i) of this section that are allocable as part of a fee paid to an investment advisor or other person for a variety of services):

(A) Registration fees;

(B) Directors' or trustees' fees;

(C) Periodic meetings of directors, trustees, or shareholders;

(D) Transfer agent fees;

(E) Legal and accounting fees (other than fees for income tax return preparation or income tax advice); and

(F) Shareholder communications required by law (*e.g.*, the preparation and mailing of prospectuses and proxy statements). Expenses described in paragraph (j)(1)(ii)(A) through (F) of this section do not include, for example, expenses allocable to investment advice, marketing activities, shareholder communications and other services not specifically described in paragraph (j)(1)(ii)(A) through (F) of this section, and custodian fees.

(2) *Safe harbor.*—If a nonpublicly offered regulated investment company makes an election under this paragraph (j)(2), the affected RIC expenses for a calendar year shall be treated as equal to 40 percent of the amount determined under paragraph (j)(1)(i) of this section for that calendar year. The nonpublicly offered regulated investment company shall make the election by attaching to its income tax return for the taxable year that includes the last day of the first calendar year for which the nonpublicly offered regulated investment company makes the election a statement that it is making an election under paragraph (j)(2) of this section. An election made pursuant to this paragraph (j)(2) shall remain in effect for all subsequent calendar years unless revoked with the consent of the Commissioner.

(3) *Reduction for unused RIC expenses.*—The amount determined under paragraph (j)(1)(i) of this section shall be reduced by the nonpublicly offered regulated investment company's net operating loss, if any, for the taxable year ending with or within the calendar year. In computing the nonpublicly offered regulated investment company's net operating loss for purposes of this section, the deduction for dividends paid shall not be allowed and any net capital gain for the taxable year shall be excluded.

(4) *Exception.*—The affected RIC expenses of a nonpublicly offered regulated investment company will be treated as zero if the amount of its gross income for the calendar year (determined without regard to capital gain net income) is not greater than 1 percent of the sum of (i) such gross income and (ii) the amount of its interest income for the calendar year that is not includible in gross income pursuant to section 103.

(k) *Allocation of expenses among nonpublicly offered regulated investment company shareholders.*—(1) *General rule.*—A nonpublicly offered regulated investment company shall allocate to each of its affected investors that is a shareholder at any time during the calendar year,

the affected investor's allocable share of the affected RIC expenses of the nonpublicly offered regulated investment company for that calendar year. (See paragraph (m) of this section for rules regarding estimates with respect to the amount of an affected investor's share of affected RIC expenses upon which certain persons can rely for certain purposes.) A nonpublicly offered regulated investment company may use any reasonable method to make the allocation. A method of allocation shall not be reasonable if—

(i) The method can be expected to have the effect, if applied to all affected RIC expenses and all shareholders (whether or not affected investors), of allocating to the shareholders an amount of affected RIC expenses that is less than the affected RIC expenses of the nonpublicly offered regulated investment company for the calendar year,

(ii) The method can be expected to have the effect of allocating a disproportionately high share of the affected RIC expenses of the nonpublicly offered regulated investment company to (A) shareholders that are not affected investors or (B) affected investors, the amount of whose miscellaneous itemized deductions (including their allocable share of affected RIC expenses) exceeds the 2-percent floor described in section 67, or

(iii) A principal purpose of the method of allocation is to avoid allocating affected RIC expenses to persons described in paragraph (h)(1)(i) or (ii) of this section whose miscellaneous itemized deductions (inclusive of their allocable share of affected RIC expenses) may not exceed the 2-percent floor described in section 67.

(2) *Reasonable allocation method described.*—(i) *In general.*—The allocation method described in this paragraph (k)(2) shall be treated as a reasonable allocation method. Under the method described in this paragraph, an affected investor's allocable share of the affected RIC expenses of a nonpublicly offered regulated investment company is the amount that bears the same ratio to the amount of affected RIC expenses of the nonpublicly offered regulated investment company for the calendar year as—

(A) The amount of dividends paid to the affected investor during the calendar year, bears to

(B) The sum of—

(1) The aggregate amount of dividends paid by the nonpublicly offered regulated investment company during the calendar year to all shareholders, and

(2) Any amount on which tax is imposed under section 852(b)(1) for any taxable year of the nonpublicly offered regulated investment company ending within or with the calendar year.

(ii) *Exception.*—Paragraph (k)(2)(i) of this section does not apply if the amount of the deduction for dividends paid during the calendar year is zero.

(iii) *Dividends paid.*—For purposes of this paragraph (k)(2)—

(A) Dividends that are treated as paid during a calendar year pursuant to section 852(b)(7) are treated as paid during that calendar year and not during the succeeding calendar year.

(B) The term "dividends paid" does not include capital gain dividends (as defined in section 852(b)(3)(C)), exempt-interest dividends (as defined in section 852(b)(5)(A)), or any amount to which section 302(a) applies.

(C) The dividends paid during a calendar year is determined without regard to section 855(a).

(3) *Reasonable allocation made by District Director.*—If a nonpublicly offered regulated investment company does not make a reasonable allocation of affected RIC expenses to its affected investors as required by paragraph (k)(1) of this section, a reasonable allocation shall be made by the District Director of the internal revenue district in which the principal place of business or principal office or agency of the nonpublicly offered regulated investment company is located.

(4) *Examples.*—The provisions of this paragraph (k) may be illustrated by the following examples:

Example (1). Nonpublicly offered regulated investment company M, in calculating its investment company taxable income, claims a dividends paid deduction for a portion of redemption distributions (to which section 302(a) applies) to shareholders, as well as for nonredemption distributions. M allocates affected expenses among shareholders who have received nonredemption distributions by multiplying the amount of nonredemption distributions distributed to each shareholder by a fraction, the numerator of which is the affected RIC expenses of M and the denominator of which is M's investment company taxable income, determined on a calendar year basis and without regard to deductions described in section 852(b)(2)(D). No affected RIC expenses are allocated with respect to the redemption distributions. This allocation method can be expected to have the effect of allocating among the shareholders an amount of expenses that is less than the total amount of affected RIC expenses of M. Accordingly, the allocation method is not reasonable.

Example (2). Nonpublicly offered regulated investment company N has two classes of stock, a "capital" class and an "income" class. Owners of the capital class receive the benefit of all capital appreciation on the stocks owned by N, and bear the burden of certain capital expenditures of N; owners of the income class receive the benefit of all other income of N, and bear the burden of all expenses of N that are deductible under section 162. M allocates all affected RIC expenses among shareholders of the income class shares under a method that would be reasonable if the income class were the only class of N stock. Corporations and other shareholders that are not affected investors own a higher proportion of income class shares than of capital class shares. The affected RIC expenses of N are properly allocated among the shareholders who bear the burden of those expenses. Accordingly, the allocation method does not have the effect of allocating a disproportionately high share of the affected RIC expenses of N to shareholders that are not affected investors merely because a disproportionate share of income class shares are owned by shareholders that are not affected investors. The allocation method is reasonable.

Example (3). Nonpublicly offered regulated investment company O has two classes of stock, Class A and Class B. Shares of Class A, which may be purchased without payment of a sales or brokerage commission, are charged with the expenses of a Rule 12b-1 distribution plan of O. Shares of Class B, which may be purchased only upon payment of a sales or brokerage commission, are not charged with the expenses of the Rule 12b-1 distribution plan of O. O allocates all affected RIC expenses among shareholders of Class A and Class B shares under a method that would be reasonable if Class A or Class B shares, respectively, were the only class of O stock. The affected RIC expenses attributable to the Rule 12b-1 plan are allocated to the shareholders of Class A shares. Shareholders that are not affected investors own a higher proportion of Class A shares than of Class B shares. The affected RIC expenses of O are properly allocated among the shareholders who bear the burden of those expenses. Accordingly, the allocation method does not have the effect of allocating a disproportionately high share of the affected RIC expenses of O to shareholders that are not affected investors merely because a disproportionately high share of Class A shares are owned by persons that are not affected investors. The allocation method is reasonable.

Example (4). Assume the facts are the same as in example (3) except that a portion of the affected RIC expenses attributable to the Rule 12b-1 plan are allocated to the shareholders of Class B shares, and shareholders that are not affected investors own a higher proportion of Class B shares than of Class A shares. Thus, the affected RIC expenses are not allocated among the class of shareholders that bear the burden of the expenses. Accordingly, the allocation method has the effect of allocating a disproportionate share of the affected RIC expenses of O to the shareholders of Class B shares. Because shareholders that are not affected investors own a higher proportion of Class B shares than Class A shares, the method can be expected to allocate a disproportionately high share of the affected RIC expenses of O to shareholders that are not affected investors. Accordingly, the allocation method is not reasonable.

(l) *Affected RIC expenses not subject to backup withholding.*—The amount of dividend income that an affected investor in a nonpublicly offered regulated investment company is treated as having received or accrued under paragraph (e)(1)(ii) of this section is not subject to backup withholding under section 3406.

(m) *Reliance by nominees and pass-through investors on notices.*—(1) *General rule.*—Persons described in paragraph (m)(3) of this section may, for the purposes described in that paragraph (m)(3), treat an affected investor's allocable share of the affected RIC expenses of a nonpublicly offered regulated investment company as being equal to an amount determined by the nonpublicly offered regulated investment company on the basis of a reasonable estimate (*e.g.*, of allocable expenses as a percentage of dividend distributions or allocable expenses per share) that is (i) reported in writing by the nonpublicly offered regulated investment company to the person or (ii) reported in a newspaper or financial publication having a nationwide circulation (*e.g.*, the *Wall Street Journal* or *Standard and Poor's Weekly Dividend Record*).

(2) *Estimates must be reasonable.*—In general, for purposes of paragraph (m)(1) of this section, estimates of affected RIC expenses of a nonpublicly offered regulated investment company will be treated as reasonable only if the nonpublicly offered regulated investment company makes a reasonable effort to offset material understatements (or overstatements) of affected RIC expenses for a period by increasing (or decreasing) estimates of affected RIC expenses for a subsequent period. Understatements or overstatements of affected RIC expenses that are not material may be corrected by making offsetting adjustments in future periods, provided that understatements and overstatements are treated consistently.

(3) *Application.*—Paragraph (m)(1) of this section shall apply to the following persons for the following purposes:

(i) A nominee who, pursuant to section 6042(a)(1)(B) and paragraph (n)(2) of this section, is required to report dividends paid by a nonpublicly offered regulated investment company to the Internal Revenue Service and to the person to whom the payment is made, for purposes of reporting to the Internal Revenue Service and the person to whom the payment is made the amount of affected RIC expenses allocated to such person.

(ii) An affected investor to whom a nominee (to which paragraph (m)(3)(i) of this section applies) reports, for purposes of calculating the affected investor's taxable income and the amount of its affected expenses.

(iii) A shareholder that is a pass-through entity, for purposes of calculating its taxable income and the amount of its affected expenses.

(n) *Return of information and reporting to affected investors by a nonpublicly offered regulated investment company.*—(1) *In general.*—(i) *Return of information.*—A nonpublicly offered regulated investment company shall make an information return (*e.g.*, Form 1099-DIV, Dividends and Distributions, for 1987) with respect to each affected investor to which an allocation of affected RIC expenses is required to be made pursuant to paragraph (k) of this section and for which the nonpublicly offered regulated investment company is required to make an information return to the Internal Revenue Service pursuant to section 6042 (or would be required to make such information return but for the $10 threshold described in section 6042(a)(1)(A) and (B)). The nonpublicly offered regulated investment company shall make the information return for each calendar year and shall state separately on such return—

(A) The amount of affected RIC expenses required to be allocated to the affected investor for the calendar year pursuant to paragraph (k) of this section,

(B) The sum of—

(1) The aggregate amount of the dividends paid to the affected investor during the calendar year, and

(2) The amount of the affected RIC expenses required to be allocated to the affected investor for the calendar year pursuant to paragraph (k) of this section, and

(C) Such other information as may be specified by the form or its instructions.

(ii) *Statement to be furnished to affected investors.*—A nonpublicly offered regulated investment company shall provide to each affected investor for each calendar year (whether or not the nonpublicly offered regulated investment company is required to make an information return with respect to the affected investor pursuant to section 6042), a written statement showing the following information:

(A) The information described in paragraph (n)(1)(i) of this section with respect to the affected investor;

(B) The name and address of the nonpublicly offered regulated investment company;

(C) The name and address of the affected investor; and

(D) If the nonpublicly offered regulated investment company is required to report the amount of the affected investor's allocation of affected RIC expenses to the Internal Revenue Service pursuant to paragraph (n)(1)(i) of this section, a statement to that effect.

(iii) *Affected investor's shares held by a nominee.*—If an affected investor's shares in a nonpublicly offered regulated investment company are held in the name of a nominee, the nonpublicly offered regulated investment company may make the information return described in paragraph (n)(1)(i) of this section with respect to the nominee in lieu of the affected investor and may provide the written statement described in paragraph (n)(1)(ii) of this section to such nominee in lieu of the affected investor.

(2) *By a nominee.*—(i) *In general.*—Except as otherwise provided for in paragraph (n)(2)(iii) of this section, in any case in which a nonpublicly offered regulated investment company provides, pursuant to paragraph (n)(1)(iii) of this section, a written statement to the nominee of an affected investor for a calendar year, the nominee shall—

(A) If the nominee is required to make an information return pursuant to section 6042 (or would be required to make an information return but for the $10 threshold described in section 6042(a)(1)(A) and (B)), make an information return (*e.g.*, Form 1099-DIV, Dividends and Distributions, for 1987) for the calendar year with respect to each affected investor and state separately on such information return the information described in paragraph (n)(1)(i) of this section, and

(B) Furnish each affected investor with a written statement for the calendar year showing the information required by paragraph

Reg. §1.67-2T(n)(2)(i)(B)

(n)(2)(ii) of this section (whether or not the nominee is required to make an information return with respect to the affected investor pursuant to section 6042).

(ii) *Form of statement.*—The written statement required to be furnished for a calendar year pursuant to paragraph (n)(2)(i)(B) of this section shall show the following information:

(A) The affected investor's proportionate share of the items described in paragraph (n)(1)(i) of this section for the calendar year,

(B) The name and address of the nominee,

(C) The name and address of the affected investor, and

(D) If the nominee is required to report the affected investor's share of the allocable investment expenses to the Internal Revenue Service pursuant to paragraph (n)(2)(i)(A) of this section, a statement to that effect.

(iii) *Return not required.*—A nominee is not required to make an information return with respect to an affected investor pursuant to paragraph (n)(2)(i)(A) of this section if the nominee is excluded from the requirements of section 6042 pursuant to §1.6042-2(a)(1)(ii) or (iii).

(iv) *Statement not required.*—A nominee is not required to furnish a written statement to an affected investor pursuant to paragraph (n)(2)(i)(B) of this section if the nonpublicly offered regulated investment company furnishes the written statement to the affected investor pursuant to an agreement with the nominee described in §1.6042-2(a)(1)(iii).

(v) *Special rule.*—Paragraph (n)(1)(i) and (ii) of this section applies to a nonpublicly offered regulated investment company that agrees with the nominee to satisfy the requirements of section 6042 as described in §1.6042-2(a)(1)(iii) with respect to the affected investor.

(3) *Time and place for furnishing returns.*—The returns required by paragraph (n)(1)(i) and (2)(i)(A) of this section for any calendar year shall be filed at the time and place that a return required under section 6042 is required to be filed. See §1.6042-2(c).

(4) *Time for furnishing statements.*—The statements required by paragraph (n)(1)(ii) and (2)(i)(B) of this section to be furnished by a nonpublicly offered regulated investment company and a nominee, respectively, to an affected investor for a calendar year shall be furnished to such affected investor on or before January 31 of the following year.

(5) *Duplicative returns and statements not required.*—(i) *Information return.*—The requirements of paragraph (n)(1)(i) and (2)(i)(A) of this section for the making of an information return shall be met by the timely filing of an information return pursuant to section 6042 that contains the information required by paragraph (n)(1)(i).

(ii) *Written statement.*—The requirements of paragraph (n)(1)(ii) and (2)(i)(B) of this section for the furnishing of a written statement (including the statement required by paragraph (n)(1)(ii)(D) and (2)(ii)(D) of this section) shall be met by furnishing the affected investor a copy of the information return to which section 6042 applies (whether or not the nonpublicly offered regulated investment company or nominee is required to file an information return with respect to the affected investor pursuant to section 6042) that contains the information required by paragraph (n)(1)(ii) or (2)(ii), whichever is applicable, of this section. Nonpublicly offered regulated investment companies and nominees may use a substitute form that contains provisions substantially similar to those of the prescribed form if the nonpublicly offered regulated investment company or nominee complies with all revenue procedures relating to substitute forms in effect at the time. The statement shall be furnished either in person or in a statement mailed by first-class mail that includes adequate notice that the statement is enclosed. A statement shall be considered to be furnished to an affected investor within the meaning of this section if it is mailed to such affected investor at its last known address.

(o) *Return of information by a common trust fund.*—With respect to each affected investor to which paragraph (d) of this section applies, the common trust fund shall state on the return it is required to make pursuant to section 6032 for its taxable year, the following information:

(1) The amount of the affected investor's proportionate share of the affected expenses for the taxable year as described in paragraph (d)(1)(ii) of this section,

(2) The amount of the affected investor's proportionate share of ordinary taxable income or ordinary net loss for the taxable year determined pursuant to paragraph (d)(1)(i) of this section, and

(3) Such other information as may be specified by the form or its instructions.

(p) *Publicly offered regulated investment companies.*—[Reserved]

[Temporary Reg. §1.67-2T.]
☐ [*T.D.* 8189, 3-25-88.]

[Reg. §1.67-3]

§1.67-3. Allocation of expenses by real estate mortgage investment conduits.—(a) *Allocation of allocable investment expenses.*—[Reserved]

(b) *Treatment of allocable investment expenses.*—[Reserved]

(c) *Computation of proportionate share.*—[Reserved]

(d) *Example.*—[Reserved]

(e) *Allocable investment expenses not subject to backup withholding.*—[Reserved]

(f) *Notice to pass-through interest holders.*—(1) *Information required.*—A REMIC must provide to each pass-through interest holder to which an allocation of allocable investment expense is required to be made under §1.67-3T(a)(1) notice of the following—

(i) If, pursuant to paragraph (f)(2)(i) or (ii) of this section, notice is provided for a calendar quarter, the aggregate amount of expenses paid or accrued during the calendar quarter for which the REMIC is allowed a deduction under section 212;

(ii) If, pursuant to paragraph (f)(2)(ii) of this section, notice is provided to a regular interest holder for a calendar year, the aggregate amount of expenses paid or accrued during each calendar quarter that the regular interest holder held the regular interest in the calendar year and for which the REMIC is allowed a deduction under section 212; and

(iii) The proportionate share of these expenses allocated to that pass-through interest holder, as determined under §1.67-3T(c).

(2) *Statement to be furnished.*—(i) *To residual interest holder.*—For each calendar quarter, a REMIC must provide to each pass-through interest holder who holds a residual interest during the calendar quarter the notice required under paragraph (f)(1) of this section on Schedule Q (Form 1066), as required in §1.860F-4(e).

(ii) *To regular interest holder.*—For each calendar year, a single-class REMIC (as described in §1.67-3T(a)(2)(ii)(B)) must provide to each pass-through interest holder who held a regular interest during the calendar year the notice required under paragraph (f)(1) of this section. Quarterly reporting is not required. The information required to be included in the notice may be separately stated on the statement described in §1.6049-7(f) instead of on a separate statement provided in a separate mailing. See §1.6049-7(f)(4). The separate statement provided in a separate mailing must be furnished to each pass-through interest holder no later than the last day of the month following the close of the calendar year.

(3) *Returns to the Internal Revenue Service.*—(i) *With respect to residual interest holders.*—Any REMIC required under paragraphs (f)(1) and (2)(i) of this section to furnish information to any pass-through interest holder who holds a residual interest must also furnish such information to the Internal Revenue Service as required in §1.860F-4(e)(4).

(ii) *With respect to regular interest holders.*—A single-class REMIC (as described in §1.67-3T(a)(2)(ii)(B)) must make an information return on Form 1099 for each calendar year, with respect to each pass-through interest holder who holds a regular interest to which an allocation of allocable investment expenses is required to be made pursuant to §1.67-3T(a)(1) and (2)(ii). The preceding sentence applies with respect to a holder for a calendar year only if the REMIC is required to make an information return to the Internal Revenue Service with respect to that holder for that year pursuant to section 6049 and §1.6049-7(b)(2)(i) (or would be required to make an information return but for the $10 threshold described in section 6049(a)(1) and §1.6049-7(b)(2)(i)). The REMIC must state on the information return—

(A) The sum of—

(1) The aggregate amounts includible in gross income as interest (as defined in §1.6049-7(a)(1)(i) and (ii)), for the calendar year; and

(2) The sum of the amount of allocable investment expenses required to be allocated to the pass-through interest holder for each calendar quarter during the calendar year pursuant to §1.67-3T(a); and

(B) Any other information specified by the form or its instructions.

(4) *Interest held by nominees and other specified persons.*—(i) *Pass-through interest holder's interest held by a nominee.*—If a pass-through interest holder's interest in a REMIC is held in the name of a nominee, the REMIC may make the information return described in

paragraphs (f)(3)(i) and (ii) of this section with respect to the nominee in lieu of the pass-through interest holder and may provide the written statement described in paragraphs (f)(2)(i) and (ii) of this section to that nominee in lieu of the pass-through interest holder.

(ii) *Regular interests in a single-class REMIC held by certain persons.*—If a person specified in §1.6049-7(e)(4) holds a regular interest in a single-class REMIC (as described in §1.67-3T(a)(2)(ii)(B)), then the single-class REMIC must provide the information described in paragraphs (f)(1) and (f)(3)(ii)(A) and (B) of this section to that person with the information specified in §1.6049-7(e)(2) as required in §1.6049-7(e).

(5) *Nominee reporting.*—(i) *In general.*—In any case in which a REMIC provides information pursuant to paragraph (f)(4) of this section to a nominee of a pass-through interest holder for a calendar quarter or, as provided in paragraph (f)(2)(ii) of this section, for a calendar year—

(A) The nominee must furnish each pass-through interest holder with a written statement described in paragraph (f)(2)(i) or (ii) of this section, whichever is applicable, showing the information described in paragraph (f)(1) of this section; and

(B) The nominee must make an information return on Form 1099 for each calendar year, with respect to the pass-through interest holder and state on this information return the information described in paragraphs (f)(3)(ii)(A) and (B) of this section, if—

(1) The nominee is a nominee for a pass-through interest holder who holds a regular interest in a single-class REMIC (as described in §1.67-3T(a)(2)(ii)(B)); and

(2) The nominee is required to make an information return pursuant to section 6049 and §1.6049-7(b)(2)(i) and (b)(2)(ii)(B) (or would be required to make an information return but for the $10 threshold described in section 6049(a)(2) and §1.6049-7(b)(2)(i)) with respect to the pass-through interest holder.

(ii) *Time for furnishing statement.*—The statement required by paragraph (f)(5)(i)(A) of this section to be furnished by a nominee to a pass-through interest holder for a calendar quarter or calendar year must be furnished to this holder no later than 30 days after receiving the written statement described in paragraph (f)(2)(i) or (ii) of this section from the REMIC. If, however, pursuant to paragraph (f)(2)(ii) of this section, the information is separately stated on the statement described in §1.6049-7(f), then the information must be furnished to the pass-through interest holder in the time specified in §1.6049-7(f)(5).

(6) *Special rules.*—(i) *Time and place for furnishing returns.*—The returns required by paragraphs (f)(3)(ii) and (f)(5)(i)(B) of this section for any calendar year must be filed at the time and place that a return required under section 6049 and §1.6049-7(b)(2) is required to be filed. See §1.6049-4(g) and §1.6049-7(b)(2)(iv).

(ii) *Duplicative returns not required.*—The requirements of paragraphs (f)(3)(ii) and (f)(5)(i)(B) of this section for the making of an information return are satisfied by the timely filing of an information return pursuant to section 6049 and §1.6049-7(b)(2) that contains the information required by paragraph (f)(3)(ii) of this section. [Reg. §1.67-3.]

☐ [*T.D. 8431, 9-2-92.*]

[Reg. §1.67-3T]

§1.67-3T. Allocation of expenses by real estate mortgage investment conduits (temporary).—(a) *Allocation of allocable investment expenses.*—(1) *In general.*—A real estate mortgage investment conduit or REMIC (as defined in section 860D) shall allocate to each of its pass-through interest holders that holds an interest at any time during the calendar quarter the holder's proportionate share (as determined under paragraph (c) of this section) of the aggregate amount of allocable investment expenses of the REMIC for the calendar quarter.

(2) *Pass-through interest holder.*—(i) *In general.*—(A) *Meaning of term.*—Except as provided in paragraph (a)(2)(ii) of this section, the term "pass-through interest holder" means any holder of a REMIC residual interest (as defined in section 860G(a)(2)) that is—

(1) An individual (other than a nonresident alien whose income with respect to his or her interest in the REMIC is not effectively connected with the conduct of a trade or business within the United States),

(2) A person, including a trust or estate, that computes its taxable income in the same manner as in the case of an individual, or

(3) A pass-through entity (as defined in paragraph (a)(3) of this section) if one or more of its partners, shareholders, beneficiaries, participants, or other interest holders is (i) a pass-through entity or (ii) a person described in paragraph (a)(2)(i)(A)(1) or (2) of this section.

(B) *Examples.*—The provisions of this paragraph (a)(2)(i) may be illustrated by the following examples:

Example (1). Corporation X holds a residual interest in REMIC R in its capacity as a nominee or custodian for individual A, the beneficial owner of the interest Because the owner of the interest for Federal income tax purposes is an individual, the interest is owned by a pass-through interest holder.

Example (2). Individual retirement account I holds a residual interest in a REMIC. Because an individual retirement account is not a person described in paragraph (a)(2)(i)(A) of this section, the interest is not held by a pass-through interest holder.

(ii) *Single-class REMIC.*—(A) *In general.*—In the case of a single-class REMIC, the term "pass-through interest holder" means any holder of either—

(1) A REMIC regular interest (as defined in section 860G(a)(1)), or

(2) A REMIC residual interest,

that is described in paragraph (a)(2)(i)(A)(1), (2), or (3) of this section.

(B) *Single-class REMIC.*—For purposes of paragraph (a)(2)(ii)(A) of this section, a single-class REMIC is either—

(1) A REMIC that would be classified as an investment trust under §301.7701-4(c)(1) but for its qualification as a REMIC under section 860D and §1.860D-1T, or

(2) A REMIC that—

(i) Is substantially similar to an investment trust under §301.7701-4(c)(1), and

(ii) Is structured with the principal purposes of avoiding the requirement of paragraph (a)(1) and (2)(ii)(A) of this section to allocate allocable investment expenses to pass-through interest holders that hold regular interests in the REMIC.

For purposes of this paragraph (a)(2)(ii)(B), in determining whether a REMIC would be classified as an investment trust or is substantially similar to an investment trust, all interests in the REMIC shall be treated as ownership interests in the REMIC, without regard to whether or not they would be classified as debt for Federal income tax purposes in the absence of a REMIC election.

(C) *Examples.*—The provisions of paragraph (a)(2)(ii) of this section may be illustrated by the following examples:

Example (1). Corporation M transfers mortgages to a bank under a trust agreement as described in Example (2) of §301.7701-4(c)(2). There are two classes of certificates. Holders of class C certificates are entitled to receive 90 percent of the payments of principal and interest on the mortgages; holders of class D certificates are entitled to receive the remaining 10 percent. The two classes of certificates are identical except that, in the event of a default on the underlying mortgages, the payment rights of class D certificate holders are subordinated to the rights of class C certificate holders. M sells the class C certificates to investors and retains the class D certificates. The trust would be classified as an investment trust under §301.7701-4(c)(1) but for its qualification as a REMIC under section 860D. The class C certificates represent regular interests in the REMIC and the class D certificates represent residual interests in the REMIC. The REMIC is a single-class REMIC within the meaning of paragraph (a)(2)(ii)(B)(1) of this section and, accordingly, holders of both the class C and class D certificates who are described in paragraph (a)(2)(i)(A)(1), (2), or (3) of this section are treated as pass-through interest holders.

Example (2). Assume that the facts are the same as in Example (1) except that M structures the REMIC to include a second regular interest represented by class E certificates. The principal purpose of M in structuring the REMIC to include class E certificates is to avoid allocating allocable investment expenses to class C certificate holders. The class E certificate holders are entitled to receive the payments otherwise due the class D certificate holders until they have been paid a stated amount of principal plus interest. The fair market value of the class E certificate is ten percent of the fair market value of the class D certificate and, therefore, less than one percent of the fair market value of the REMIC. The REMIC would not be classified as an investment trust under §301.7701-4(c)(1) because the existence of the class E certificates is not incidental to the trust's purpose of facilitating direct investment in the assets of the trust. Nevertheless, because the fair market value of the class E certificates is de minimis, the REMIC is substantially similar to an investment trust under §301.7701-4(c)(1). In addition, avoidance of the requirement to allocate allocable investment expenses to regular interest holders is the principal purpose of M in structuring the REMIC to include class E certificates Therefore, the REMIC is a single-class REMIC within the meaning of paragraph (a)(2)(ii)(B)(2) of this section, and, accordingly, holders of both residual and regular interests who are described in paragraph (a)(2)(i)(A)(1), (2), or (3) of this section are treated as pass-through interest holders.

(3) *Pass-through entity.*—(i) *In general.*—Except as provided in paragraph (a)(3)(ii) of this section, for purposes of this section, a pass-through entity is—

(A) A trust (or any portion thereof) to which subpart E, part 1, subchapter J, chapter 1 of the Code applies,

(B) A partnership,

(C) An S corporation,

(D) A common trust fund described in section 584,

(E) A nonpublicly offered regulated investment company (as defined in paragraph (a)(5)(i) of this section),

(F) A REMIC, and

(G) Any other person—

(1) Which is not subject to income tax imposed by subtitle A, chapter 1, or which is allowed a deduction in computing such tax for distributions to owners or beneficiaries, and

(2) The character of the income of which may affect the character of the income recognized with respect to that person by its owners or beneficiaries.

Entities that do not meet the requirements of paragraph (a)(3)(i)(G)(1) and (2), such as qualified pension plans, individual retirement accounts, and insurance companies holding assets in separate asset accounts to fund variable contracts defined in section 817(d), are not described in this paragraph (a)(3)(i).

(ii) *Exception.*—For purposes of this section, a pass-through entity does not include—

(A) An estate,

(B) A trust (or any portion thereof) not described in paragraph (a)(3)(i)(A) of this section,

(C) A cooperative described in section 1381(a)(2), determined without regard to subparagraphs (A) and (C) thereof, or

(D) A real estate investment trust.

(4) *Allocable investment expenses.*—The term "allocable investment expenses" means the aggregate amount of the expenses paid or accrued in the calendar quarter for which a deduction is allowable under section 212 in determining the taxable income of the REMIC for the calendar quarter.

(5) *Nonpublicly offered regulated investment company.*—(i) *In general.*—For purposes of this section, the term "nonpublicly offered regulated investment company" means a regulated investment company to which part I of subchapter M of the Code applies that is not a publicly offered regulated investment company.

(ii) *Publicly offered regulated investment company.*—For purposes of this section, the term "publicly offered regulated investment company" means a regulated investment company to which part I of subchapter M of the Code applies, the shares of which are—

(A) Continuously offered pursuant to a public offering (within the meaning of section 4 of the Securities Act of 1933, as amended (15 U.S.C. 77a to 77aa)),

(B) Regularly traded on an established securities market, or

(C) Held by or for no fewer than 500 persons at all times during the taxable year.

(b) *Treatment of allocable investment expenses.*—(1) *By pass-through interest holders.*—(i) *Taxable year ending with calendar quarter.*—A pass-through interest holder whose taxable year is the calendar year or ends with a calendar quarter shall be treated as having—

(A) Received or accrued income, and

(B) Paid or incurred an expense described in section 212 (or section 162 in the case of a pass-through interest holder that is a regulated investment company), in an amount equal to the pass-through interest holder's proportionate share of the allocable investment expenses of the REMIC for those calendar quarters that fall within the holder's taxable year.

(ii) *Taxable year not ending with calendar quarter.*—A pass-through interest holder whose taxable year does not end with a calendar quarter shall be treated as having—

(A) Received or accrued income, and

(B) Paid or incurred an expense described in section 212 (or section 162 in the case of a pass-through interest holder that is a regulated investment company),

in an amount equal to the sum of—

(C) The pass-through interest holder's proportionate share of the allocable investment expenses of the REMIC for those calendar quarters that fall within the holder's taxable year, and

(D) For each calendar quarter that overlaps the *beginning or end of the taxable year,* the sum of the daily amounts of the allocable investment expenses allocated to the holder pursuant to paragraph (c)(1)(ii) of this section for the days in the quarter that fall within the holder's taxable year.

(2) *Proportionate share of allocable investment expenses.*—For purposes of paragraph (b) of this section, a pass-through interest holder's proportionate share of the allocable investment expenses is the amount allocated to the pass-through interest holder pursuant to paragraph (a)(1) of this section.

(3) *Cross-reference.*—See § 1.67-1T with respect to limitations on deductions for expenses described in section 212 (including amounts treated as such expenses under this section).

(4) *Interest income to holders of regular interests in certain REMICs.*—Any amount allocated under this section to the holder of a regular interest in a single-class REMIC (as described in paragraph (a)(2)(ii)(B) of this section) shall be treated as interest income.

(5) *No adjustment to basis.*—The basis of any holder's interest in a REMIC shall not be increased or decreased by the amount of the holder's proportionate share of allocable investment expenses.

(6) *Interest holders other than pass-through interest holders.*—An interest holder of a REMIC that is not a pass-through interest holder shall not take into account in computing its taxable income any amount of income or expense with respect to its proportionate share of allocable investment expenses.

(c) *Computation of proportionate share.*—(1) *In general.*—For purposes of paragraph (a)(1) of this section, a REMIC shall compute a pass-through interest holder's proportionate share of the REMIC's allocable investment expenses by—

(i) Determining the daily amount of the allocable investment expenses for the calendar quarter by dividing the total amount of such expenses by the number of days in that calendar quarter,

(ii) Allocating the daily amount of the allocable investment expenses to the pass-through interest holder in proportion to its respective holdings on that day, and

(iii) Totaling the interest holder's daily amount of allocable investment expenses for the calendar quarter.

(2) *Other holders taken into account.*—For purposes of paragraph (c)(1)(ii) of this section, a pass-through interest holder's proportionate share of the daily amount of the allocable investment expenses is determined by taking into account all holders of residual interests in the REMIC, whether or not pass-through interest holders.

(3) *Single-class REMIC.*—(i) *Daily allocation.*—In lieu of the allocation specified in paragraph (c)(1)(ii) of this section, a single-class REMIC (as described in paragraph (a)(2)(ii)(B) of this section) shall allocate the daily amount of the allocable investment expenses to each pass-through interest holder in proportion to the amount of income accruing to the holder with respect to its interest in the REMIC on that day.

(ii) *Other holders taken into account.*—For purposes of paragraph (c)(3)(i) of this section, the amount of the allocable investment expenses that is allocated on any day to each pass-through interest holder shall be determined by multiplying the daily amount of allocable investment expenses (determined pursuant to paragraph (c)(1)(i) of this section by a fraction, the numerator of which is equal to the amount of income that accrues (but not less than zero) to the pass-through interest holder on that day and the denominator of which is the total amount of income (as determined under paragraph (c)(3)(iii) of this section) that accrues to all regular and residual interest holders, whether or not pass-through interest holders, on that day.

(iii) *Total income accruing.*—The total amount of income that accrues to all regular and residual interest holders is the sum of—

(A) The amount includible under section 860B in the gross income (but not less than zero) of the regular interest holders, and

(B) The amount of REMIC taxable income (but not less than zero) taken into account under section 860C by the residual interest holders.

(4) *Dates of purchase and disposition.*—For purposes of this section, a pass-through interest holder holds an interest on the date of its purchase but not on the date of its disposition.

(d) *Example.*—The provisions of this section may be illustrated by the following example:

Example. (i) During the calendar quarter ending March 31, 1989, REMIC X, which is not a single-class REMIC, incurs $900 of allocable investment expenses. At the beginning of the calendar quarter, X has 4 residual interest holders, who hold equal proportionate shares, and 10 regular interest holders. The residual interest holders, all of whom have calendar-year taxable years, are as follows:

A, an individual,

C, a C corporation that is a nominee for individual I,

S, an S corporation, and

M, a C corporation that is not a nominee.

(ii) Except for A, all of the residual interest holders hold their interests in X for the entire calendar quarter. On January 31, 1989, A sells his interest to S. Thus, for the first month of the calendar quarter, each residual interest holder holds a 25 percent interest (100%/4 interest holders) in X. For the last two months, S's holding is increased to 50 percent and A's holding is decreased to zero. The daily amount of allocable investment expenses for the calendar quarter is $10 ($900/90 days).

(iii) The amount of allocable investment expenses apportioned to the residual interest holders is as follows:

(A) $75 ($10 × 25% × 30 days) is allocated to A for the 30 days that A holds an interest in X during the calendar quarter. A includes $75 in gross income in calendar year 1989. The amount of A's expenses described in section 212 is increased by $75 in calendar year 1989. A's deduction under section 212 (including the $75 amount of the allocation) is subject to the limitations contained in section 67.

(B) $225 ($10 × 25% × 90 days) is allocated to C. Because C is a nominee for I, C does not include $225 in gross income or increase its deductible expenses by $225. Instead, I includes $225 in gross income in calendar year 1989, her taxable year. The amount of I's expenses described in section 212 is increased by $225. I's deduction under section 212 (including the $225 amount of the allocation) is subject to the limitations contained in section 67.

(C) $375 (($10 × 25% × 30 days) + ($10 × 50% × 60 days)) is allocated to S. S includes in gross income $375 of allocable investment expenses in calendar year 1989. The amount of S's expenses described in section 212 for that taxable year is increased by $375. S allocates the $375 to its shareholders in accordance with the rules described in sections 1366 and 1377 in calendar year 1989. Thus, each shareholder of S includes its pro rata share of the $375 in gross income in its taxable year in which or with which calendar year 1989 ends. The amount of each shareholder's expenses described in section 212 is increased by the amount of the shareholder's allocation for the shareholder's taxable year in which or with which calender year 1989 ends. The shareholder's deduction under section 212 (including the allocation under this section) is subject to the limitations contained in section 67.

(D) No amount is allocated to M. However, M's interest is taken into account for purposes of determining the proportionate share of those residual interest holders to whom an allocation is required to be made.

(iv) No allocation is made to the 10 regular interest holders pursuant to paragraph (a) of this section. In addition, the interests held by these interest holders are not taken into account for purposes of determining the proportionate share of the residual interest holders to whom an allocation is required to be made.

(e) *Allocable investment expenses not subject to backup withholding.*— The amount of allocable investment expenses required to be allocated to a pass-through interest holder pursuant to paragraph (a)(1) of this section is not subject to backup withholding under section 3406.

(f) *Notice to pass-through interest holders.*—(1) *Information required.*— A REMIC must provide to each pass-through interest holder to which an allocation of allocable investment expense is required to be made under paragraph (a)(1) of this section notice of the following—

(i) If, pursuant to paragraph (f)(2)(i) or (ii) of this section, notice is provided for a calendar quarter, the aggregate amount of expenses paid or accrued during the calendar quarter for which the REMIC is allowed a deduction under section 212;

(ii) If, pursuant to paragraph (f)(2)(ii) of this section, notice is provided to a regular interest holder for a calendar year, the aggregate amount of expenses paid or accrued during each calendar quarter that the regular interest holder held the regular interest in the calendar year and for which the REMIC is allowed a deduction under section 212; and

(iii) The proportionate share of these expenses allocated to that pass-through interest holder, as determined under paragraph (c) of this section.

(2) *Statement to be furnished.*—(i) *To residual interest holder.*—For each calendar quarter, a REMIC shall provide to each pass-through interest holder who holds a residual interest during the calendar quarter the notice required under paragraph (f)(1) of this section on Schedule Q (Form 1066), as required in § 1.860F-4(e).

(ii) *To regular interest holder.*—(A) *In general.*—For each calendar year, a single-class REMIC (as described in paragraph (a)(2)(ii)(B) of this section) must provide to each pass-through interest holder who held a regular interest during the calendar year the notice required under paragraph (f)(1) of this section. Quarterly reporting is not required. The information required to be included in the notice may be separately stated on the statement described in § 1.6049-7(f) instead of on a separate statement provided in a separate mailing. See § 1.6049-7(f)(4). The separate statement provided in a separate

mailing must be furnished to each pass-through interest holder no later than the last day of the month following the close of the calendar year.

(B) *Special rule for 1987.*—The information required under paragraph (f)(2)(ii)(A) of this section for any calendar quarter of 1987 shall be mailed (or otherwise delivered) to each pass-through interest holder who holds a regular interest during that calendar quarter no later than March 28, 1988.

(3) *Returns to the Internal Revenue Service.*—(i) *With respect to residual interest holders.*—Any REMIC required under paragraphs (f)(1) and (2)(i) of this section to furnish information to any pass-through interest holder who holds a residual interest shall also furnish such information to the Internal Revenue Service as required in § 1.860F-4(e)(4).

(ii) *With respect to regular interest holders.*—A single-class REMIC (as described in paragraph (a)(2)(ii)(B) of this section) shall make an information return on Form 1099 for each calendar year beginning after December 31, 1987, with respect to each pass-through interest holder who holds a regular interest to which an allocation of allocable investment expenses is required to be made pursuant to paragraphs (a)(1) and (2)(ii) of this section. The preceding sentence applies with respect to a holder for a calendar year only if the REMIC is required to make an information return to the Internal Revenue Service with respect to that holder for that year pursuant to section 6049 and § 1.6049-7(b)(2)(i) (or would be required to make an information return but for the $10 threshold described in section 6049(a)(1) and § 1.6049-7(b)(2)(i)). The REMIC shall state on the information return—

(A) The sum of—

(1) The aggregate amounts includible in gross income as interest (as defined in § 1.6049-7(a)(1)(i) and (ii)), for the calendar year, and

(2) The sum of the amount of allocable investment expenses required to be allocated to the pass-through interest holder for each calendar quarter during the calendar year pursuant to paragraph (a) of this section, and

(B) Any other information specified by the form or its instructions.

(4) *Interest held by nominees and other specified persons.*—(i) *Pass-through interest holder's interest held by a nominee.*—If a pass-through interest holder's interest in a REMIC is held in the name of a nominee, the REMIC may make the information return described in paragraphs (f)(3)(i) and (ii) of this section with respect to the nominee in lieu of the pass-through interest holder and may provide the written statement described in paragraphs (f)(2)(i) and (ii) of this section to that nominee in lieu of the pass-through interest holder.

(ii) *Regular interests in a single-class REMIC held by certain persons.*—For calendar quarters and calendar years after December 31, 1991, if a person specified in § 1.6049-7(e)(4) holds a regular interest in a single-class REMIC (as described in paragraph (a)(2)(ii)(B) of this section), then the single-class REMIC must provide the information described in paragraphs (f)(1) and (f)(3)(ii)(A) and (B) of this section to that person with the information specified in § 1.6049-7(e)(2) as required in § 1.6049-7(e).

(5) *Nominee reporting.*—(i) *In general.*—In any case in which a REMIC provides information pursuant to paragraph (f)(4) of this section to a nominee of a pass-through interest holder for a calendar quarter or, as provided in paragraph (f)(2)(ii) of this section, for a calendar year—

(A) The nominee shall furnish each pass-through interest holder with a written statement described in paragraph (f)(2)(i) or (ii) of this section, whichever is applicable, showing the information described in paragraph (f)(1) of this section, and

(B) If—

(1) The nominee is a nominee for a pass-through interest holder who holds a regular interest in a single-class REMIC (as described in paragraph (a)(2)(ii)(B) of this section), and

(2) The nominee is required to make an information return pursuant to section 6049 and § 1.6049-7(b)(2)(i) and (b)(2)(ii)(B) (or would be required to make an information return but for the $10 threshold described in section 6049(a)(2) and § 1.6049-7(b)(2)(i)) with respect to the pass-through interest holder,
the nominee shall make an information return on Form 1099 for each calendar year beginning after December 31, 1987, with respect to the pass-through interest holder and state on this information return the information described in paragraph (f)(3)(ii)(A) and (B) of this section.

(ii) *Time for furnishing statement.*—The statement required by paragraph (f)(5)(i)(A) of this section to be furnished by a nominee to a pass-through interest holder for a calendar quarter or calendar year shall be furnished to this holder no later than 30 days after receiving the written statement described in paragraph (f)(2)(i) or (ii) of this section from the REMIC. If, however, pursuant to paragraph (f)(2)(ii) of this section, the information is separately stated on the statement described in §1.6049-7(f), then the information must be furnished to the pass-through interest holder in the time specified in §1.6049-7(f)(5).

(6) *Special rules.*—(i) *Time and place for furnishing returns.*—The returns required by paragraphs (f)(3)(ii) and (f)(5)(i)(B) of this section for any calendar year shall be filed at the time and place that a return required under section 6049 and §1.6049-7(b)(2) is required to be filed. See §1.6049-4(g) and §1.6049-7(b)(2)(iv).

(ii) *Duplicative returns not required.*—The requirements of paragraphs (f)(3)(ii) and (f)(5)(i)(B) of this section for the making of an information return shall be met by the timely filing of an information return pursuant to section 6049 and §1.6049-7(b)(2) that contains the information required by paragraph (f)(3)(ii) of this section. [Temporary Reg. §1.67-3T.]

☐ [T.D. 8186, 3-4-88. *Amended by T.D.* 8259, 9-6-89 *and T.D.* 8366, 9-27-91.]

[Reg. §1.67-4]

§1.67-4. Costs paid or incurred by estates or non-grantor trusts.—(a) *Deductions.*—(1) *Section 67(e) deductions.*—(i) *In general.*—An estate or trust (including the S portion of an electing small business trust) not described in §1.67-2T(g)(1)(i) (a non-grantor trust) must compute its adjusted gross income in the same manner as an individual, except that the following deductions (section 67(e) deductions) are allowed in arriving at adjusted gross income:

(A) Costs that are paid or incurred in connection with the administration of the estate or trust that would not have been incurred if the property were not held in such estate or trust; and

(B) Deductions allowable under section 642(b) (relating to the personal exemption) and sections 651 and 661 (relating to distributions).

(ii) *Not disallowed under section 67(g).*—Section 67(e) deductions are not itemized deductions under section 63(d) and are not miscellaneous itemized deductions under section 67(b). Therefore, section 67(e) deductions are not disallowed under section 67(g).

(2) *Deductions subject to 2-percent floor.*—A cost is not a section 67(e) deduction and thus is subject to both the 2-percent floor in section 67(a) and section 67(g) to the extent that it is included in the definition of miscellaneous itemized deductions under section 67(b), is incurred by an estate or non-grantor trust (including the S portion of an electing small business trust), and commonly or customarily would be incurred by a hypothetical individual holding the same property.

(b) *"Commonly" or "Customarily" Incurred.*—(1) *In general.*—In analyzing a cost to determine whether it commonly or customarily would be incurred by a hypothetical individual owning the same property, it is the type of product or service rendered to the estate or non-grantor trust in exchange for the cost, rather than the description of the cost of that product or service, that is determinative. In addition to the types of costs described as commonly or customarily incurred by individuals in paragraphs (b)(2), (3), (4), and (5) of this section, costs that are incurred commonly or customarily by individuals also include, for example, costs incurred in defense of a claim against the estate, the decedent, or the non-grantor trust that are unrelated to the existence, validity, or administration of the estate or trust.

(2) *Ownership costs.*—Ownership costs are costs that are chargeable to or incurred by an owner of property simply by reason of being the owner of the property. Thus, for purposes of section 67(e), ownership costs are commonly or customarily incurred by a hypothetical individual owner of such property. Such ownership costs include, but are not limited to, partnership costs deemed to be passed through to and reportable by a partner if these costs are defined as miscellaneous itemized deductions pursuant to section 67(b), condominium fees, insurance premiums, maintenance and lawn services, and automobile registration and insurance costs. Other expenses incurred merely by reason of the ownership of property may be fully deductible under other provisions of the Code, such as sections 62(a)(4), 162, or 164(a), which would not be miscellaneous itemized deductions subject to section 67(e).

(3) *Tax preparation fees.*—Costs relating to all estate and generationskipping transfer tax returns, fiduciary income tax returns, and the decedent's final individual income tax returns are not subject to the 2-percent floor. The costs of preparing all other tax returns (for example, gift tax returns) are costs commonly and customarily incurred by individuals and thus are subject to the 2-percent floor.

(4) *Investment advisory fees.*—Fees for investment advice (including any related services that would be provided to any individual

investor as part of an investment advisory fee) are incurred commonly or customarily by a hypothetical individual investor and therefore are subject to the 2-percent floor. However, certain incremental costs of investment advice beyond the amount that normally would be charged to an individual investor are not subject to the 2-percent floor. For this purpose, such an incremental cost is a special, additional charge that is added solely because the investment advice is rendered to a trust or estate rather than to an individual or attributable to an unusual investment objective or the need for a specialized balancing of the interests of various parties (beyond the usual balancing of the varying interests of current beneficiaries and remaindermen) such that a reasonable comparison with individual investors would be improper. The portion of the investment advisory fees not subject to the 2-percent floor by reason of the preceding sentence is limited to the amount of those fees, if any, that exceeds the fees normally charged to an individual investor.

(5) *Appraisal fees.*—Appraisal fees incurred by an estate or a non-grantor trust to determine the fair market value of assets as of the decedent's date of death (or the alternate valuation date), to determine value for purposes of making distributions, or as otherwise required to properly prepare the estate's or trust's tax returns, or a generation-skipping transfer tax return, are not incurred commonly or customarily by an individual and thus are not subject to the 2-percent floor. The cost of appraisals for other purposes (for example, insurance) is commonly or customarily incurred by individuals and is subject to the 2-percent floor.

(6) *Certain Fiduciary Expenses.*—Certain other fiduciary expenses are not commonly or customarily incurred by individuals, and thus are not subject to the 2-percent floor. Such expenses include without limitation the following: probate court fees and costs; fiduciary bond premiums; legal publication costs of notices to creditors or heirs; the cost of certified copies of the decedent's death certificate; and costs related to fiduciary accounts.

(c) *Bundled fees.*—(1) *In general.*—If an estate or a non-grantor trust pays a single fee, commission, or other expense (such as a fiduciary's commission, attorney's fee, or accountant's fee) for both costs that are subject to the 2-percent floor and costs (in more than a de minimis amount) that are not, then, except to the extent provided otherwise by guidance published in the Internal Revenue Bulletin, the single fee, commission, or other expense (bundled fee) must be allocated, for purposes of computing the adjusted gross income of the estate or non-grantor trust in compliance with section 67(e), between the costs that are subject to the 2-percent floor and those that are not.

(2) *Exception.*—If a bundled fee is not computed on an hourly basis, only the portion of that fee that is attributable to investment advice is subject to the 2-percent floor; the remaining portion is not subject to that floor.

(3) *Expenses Not Subject to Allocation.*—Out-of-pocket expenses billed to the estate or non-grantor trust are treated as separate from the bundled fee. In addition, payments made from the bundled fee to third parties that would have been subject to the 2-percent floor if they had been paid directly by the estate or non-grantor trust are subject to the 2-percent floor, as are any fees or expenses separately assessed by the fiduciary or other payee of the bundled fee (in addition to the usual or basic bundled fee) for services rendered to the estate or non-grantor trust that are commonly or customarily incurred by an individual.

(4) *Reasonable Method.*—Any reasonable method may be used to allocate a bundled fee between those costs that are subject to the 2-percent floor and those costs that are not, including without limitation the allocation of a portion of a fiduciary commission that is a bundled fee to investment advice. Facts that may be considered in determining whether an allocation is reasonable include, but are not limited to, the percentage of the value of the corpus subject to investment advice, whether a third party advisor would have charged a comparable fee for similar advisory services, and the amount of the fiduciary's attention to the trust or estate that is devoted to investment advice as compared to dealings with beneficiaries and distribution decisions and other fiduciary functions. The reasonable method standard does not apply to determine the portion of the bundled fee attributable to payments made to third parties for expenses subject to the 2-percent floor or to any other separately assessed expense commonly or customarily incurred by an individual, because those payments and expenses are readily identifiable without any discretion on the part of the fiduciary or return preparer.

(d) *Applicability date.*—This section applies to taxable years beginning after December 31, 2014. Paragraph (a) of this section applies to taxable years beginning after October 19, 2020. Taxpayers may choose to apply paragraph (a) of this section to taxable years beginning after December 31, 2017, and on or before October 19, 2020.[Reg. §1.67-4.]

☐ [T.D. 9664, 5-8-2014 (*amended* 7-16-2014). *Amended by T.D.* 9918, 10-16-2020.]

Items Specifically Included in Gross Income

[Reg. §1.71-1]

§1.71-1. Alimony and separate maintenance payments; income to wife or former wife.—(a) *In general.*—Section 71 provides rules for treatment in certain cases of payments in the nature of or in lieu of alimony or an allowance for support as between spouses who are divorced or separated. For convenience, the payee spouse will hereafter in this section be referred to as the "wife" and the spouse from whom she is divorced or separated as the "husband." See section 7701(a)(17). For rules relative to the deduction by the husband of periodic payments not attributable to transferred property, see section 215 and the regulations thereunder. For rules relative to the taxable status of income of an estate or trust in case of divorce, etc., see section 682 and the regulations thereunder.

(b) *Alimony or separate maintenance payments received from the husband.*—(1) *Decree of divorce or separate maintenance.*—(i) In the case of divorce or legal separation, paragraph (1) of section 71(a) requires the inclusion in the gross income of the wife of periodic payments (whether or not made at regular intervals) received by her after a decree of divorce or of separate maintenance. Such periodic payments must be made in discharge of a legal obligation imposed upon or incurred by the husband because of the marital or family relationship under a court order or decree divorcing or legally separating the husband and wife or a written instrument incident to such divorce status or legal separation status.

(ii) For treatment of payments attributable to property transferred (in trust or otherwise), see paragraph (c) of this section.

(2) *Written separation agreement.*—(i) Where the husband and wife are separated and living apart and do not file a joint income tax return for the taxable year, paragraph (2) of section 71(a) requires the inclusion in the gross income of the wife of periodic payments (whether or not made at regular intervals) received by her pursuant to a written separation agreement executed after August 16, 1954. The periodic payments must be made under the terms of the written separation agreement after its execution and because of the marital or family relationship. Such payments are includible in the wife's gross income whether or not the agreement is a legally enforceable instrument. Moreover, if the wife is divorced or legally separated subsequent to the written separation agreement, payments made under such agreement continue to fall within the provisions of section 71(a)(2).

(ii) For purposes of section 71(a)(2), any written separation agreement executed on or before August 16, 1954, which is altered or modified in writing by the parties in any material respect after that date will be treated as an agreement executed after August 16, 1954, with respect to payments made after the date of alteration or modification.

(iii) For treatment of payments attributable to property transferred (in trust or otherwise), see paragraph (c) of this section.

(3) *Decree for support.*—(i) Where the husband and wife are separated and living apart and do not file a joint income tax return for the taxable year, paragraph (3) of section 71(a) requires the inclusion in the gross income of the wife of periodic payments (whether or not made at regular intervals) received by her after August 16, 1954, from her husband under any type of court order or decree (including an interlocutory decree of divorce or a decree of alimony pendente lite) entered after March 1, 1954, requiring the husband to make the payments for her support or maintenance. It is not necessary for the wife to be legally separated or divorced from her husband under a court order or decree; nor is it necessary for the order or decree for support to be for the purpose of enforcing a written separation agreement.

(ii) For purposes of section 71(a)(3), any decree which is altered or modified by a court order entered after March 1, 1954, will be treated as a decree entered after such date.

(4) *Scope of section 71(a).*—Section 71(a) applies only to payments made because of the family or marital relationship in recognition of the general obligation to support which is made specific by the decree, instrument, or agreement. Thus, section 71(a) does not apply to that part of any periodic payment which is attributable to the repayment by the husband of, for example, a bona fide loan previously made to him by the wife, the satisfaction of which is specified in the decree, instrument, or agreement as a part of the general settlement between the husband and wife.

(5) *Year of inclusion.*—Periodic payments are includible in the wife's income under section 71(a) only for the taxable year in which received by her. As to such amounts, the wife is to be treated as if she makes her income tax returns on the cash receipts and disbursements method, regardless of whether she normally makes such returns on the accrual method. However, if the periodic payments described in section 71(a) are to be made by an estate or trust, such periodic payments are to be included in the wife's taxable year in which they are includible according to the rules as to income of estates and trusts provided in sections 652, 662, and 682, whether or not such payments are made out of the income of such estates or trusts.

(6) *Examples.*—The foregoing rules are illustrated by the following examples in which it is assumed that the husband and wife file separate income tax returns on the calendar year basis:

Example (1). W files suit for divorce from H in 1953. In consideration of W's promise to relinquish all marital rights and not to make public H's financial affairs, H agrees in writing to pay $200 a month to W during her lifetime if a final decree of divorce is granted without any provision for alimony. Accordingly, W does not request alimony and no provision for alimony is made under a final decree of divorce entered December 31, 1953. During 1954, H pays W $200 a month, pursuant to the promise. The $2,400 thus received by W is includible in her gross income under the provisions of section 71(a)(1). Under section 215, H is entitled to a deduction of $2,400 from his gross income.

Example (2). During 1945, H and W enter into an antenuptial agreement, under which, in consideration of W's relinquishment of all marital rights (including dower) in H's property, and, in order to provide for W's support and household expenses, H promises to pay W $200 a month during her lifetime. Ten years after their marriage, W sues H for divorce but does not ask for or obtain alimony because of the provision already made for her support in the antenuptial agreement. Likewise, the divorce decree is silent as to such agreement and H's obligation to support W. Section 71(a) does not apply to such a case. If, however, the decree were modified so as to refer to the antenuptial agreement, or if reference had been made to the antenuptial agreement in the court's decree or in a written instrument incident to the divorce status, section 71(a)(1) would require the inclusion in W's gross income of the payments received by her after the decree. Similarly, if a written separation agreement were executed after August 16, 1954, and incorporated the payment provisions of the antenuptial agreement, section 71(a)(2) would require the inclusion in W's income of payments received by W after W begins living apart from H, whether or not the divorce decree was subsequently entered and whether or not W was living apart from H when the separation agreement was executed, provided that such payments were made after such agreement was executed and pursuant to its terms. As to including such payments in W's income, if made by a trust created under the antenuptial agreement, regardless of whether referred to in the decree or a later instrument, or created pursuant to the written separation agreement, see section 682 and the regulations thereunder.

Example (3). H and W are separated and living apart during 1954. W sues H for support and on February 1, 1954, the court enters a decree requiring H to pay $200 a month to W for her support and maintenance. No part of the $200 a month support payments is includible in W's income under section 71(a)(3) or deductible by H under section 215. If, however, the decree had been entered after March 1, 1954, or had been altered or modified by a court order entered after March 1, 1954, the payments received by W after August 16, 1954, under the decree as altered or modified would be includible in her income under sections 71(a)(3) and deductible by H under section 215.

Example (4). W sues H for divorce in 1954. On January 15, 1954, the court awards W temporary alimony of $25 a week pending the final decree. On September 1, 1954, the court grants W a divorce and awards her $200 a month permanent alimony. No part of the $25 a week temporary alimony received prior to the decree is includible in W's income under section 71(a), but the $200 a month received during the remainder of 1954 by W is includible in her income for 1954. Under section 215, H is entitled to deduct such $200 payments from his income. If, however, the decree awarding W temporary alimony had been entered after March 1, 1954, or had been altered or modified by a court order entered after March 1, 1954, temporary alimony received by her after August 16, 1954, would be includible in her income under section 71(a)(3) and deductible by H under section 215.

(c) *Alimony and separate maintenance payments attributable to property.*—(1)(i) In the case of divorce or legal separation, paragraph (1) of section 71(a) requires the inclusion in the gross income of the wife of periodic payments (whether or not made at regular intervals) attributable to property transferred, in trust or otherwise, received by her after a decree of divorce or of separate maintenance. Such property must have been transferred in discharge of a legal obligation imposed upon or incurred by the husband because of the marital or family relationship under a decree of divorce or separate maintenance or under a written instrument incident to such divorce status or legal separation status.

(ii) Where the husband and wife are separated and living apart and do not file a joint income tax return for the taxable year, paragraph (2) of section 71(a) requires the inclusion in the gross income of the wife of periodic payments (whether or not made at regular intervals) received by her which are attributable to property transferred, in trust or otherwise, under a written separation agreement executed after August 16, 1954. The property must be transferred because of the marital or family relationship. The periodic payments attributable to the property must be received by the wife after the written separation agreement is executed.

(iii) The periodic payments received by the wife attributable to property transferred under subdivisions (i) and (ii) of this subparagraph and includible in her gross income are not to be included in the gross income of the husband.

(2) The full amount of periodic payments received under the circumstances described in section 71(a)(1), (2), and (3) is required to be included in the gross income of the wife regardless of the source of such payments. Thus, it matters not that such payments are attributable to property in trust, to life insurance, endowment, or annuity contracts, or to any other interest in property, or are paid directly or indirectly by the husband from his income or capital. For example, if in order to meet an alimony or separate maintenance obligation of $500 a month the husband purchases or assigns for the benefit of his wife a commercial annuity contract paying such amount, the full $500 a month received by the wife is includible in her income, and no part of such amount is includible in the husband's income or deductible by him. See section 72(k) and the regulations thereunder. Likewise, if property is transferred by the husband, subject to an annual charge of $5,000, payable to his wife in discharge of his alimony or separate maintenance obligation under the divorce or separation decree or written instrument incident to the divorce status or legal separation status or if such property is transferred pursuant to a written separation agreement and subject to a similar annual charge, the $5,000 received annually is, under section 71(a)(1) or (2), includible in the wife's income, regardless of whether such amount is paid out of income or principal of the property.

(3) The same rule applies to periodic payments attributable to property in trust. The full amount of periodic payments to which section 71(a)(1) and (2) applies is includible in the wife's income regardless of whether such payments are made out of trust income. Such periodic payments are to be included in the wife's income under section 71(a)(1) or (2) and are to be excluded from the husband's income even though the income of the trust would otherwise be includible in his income under subpart E, part I, subchapter J, chapter 1 of the Code, relating to trust income attributable to grantors and others as substantial owners. As to periodic payments received by a wife attributable to property in trust in cases to which section 71(a)(1) or (2) does not apply because the husband's obligation is not specified in the decree or an instrument incident to the divorce status or legal separation status or the property was not transferred under a written separation agreement, see section 682 and the regulations thereunder.

(4) Section 71(a)(1) or (2) does not apply to that part of any periodic payment attributable to that portion of any interest in property transferred in discharge of the husband's obligation under the decree or instrument incident to the divorce status or legal separation status, or transferred pursuant to the written separation agreement, which interest originally belonged to the wife. It will apply, however, if she received such interest from her husband in contemplation of or as an incident to the divorce or separation without adequate and full consideration in money or money's worth, other than the release of the husband or his property from marital obligations. An example of the first rule is a case where the husband and wife transfer securities, which were owned by them jointly, in trust to pay an annuity to the wife. In this case, the full amount of that part of the annuity received by the wife attributable to the husband's interest in the securities transferred in discharge of his obligation under the decree, or instrument incident to the divorce status or legal separation status, or transferred under the written separation agreement, is taxable to her under section 71(a)(1) or (2), while that portion of the annuity attributable to the wife's interest in the securities so transferred is taxable to her only to the extent it is out of trust income as provided in part I (sections 641 and following), subchapter J, chapter 1 of the Code. If, however, the husband's transfer to his wife is made before such property is transferred in discharge of his obligation under the decree or written instrument, or pursuant to the separation agreement in an *attempt to avoid the application of section 71(a)(1) or (2)* to part of *such payments received* by his wife, such transfers will be considered as a part of the same transfer by the husband of his property in discharge of his obligation or pursuant to such agreement. In such a case, section 71(a)(1) or (2) will be applied to the full amount received by the wife. As to periodic payments received under a joint purchase of a commercial annuity contract, see section 72 and the regulations thereunder.

(d) *Periodic and installment payments.*—(1) In general, installment payments discharging a part of an obligation the principal sum of which is, in terms of money or property, specified in the decree, instrument, or agreement are not considered "periodic payments" and therefore are not to be included under section 71(a) in the wife's income.

(2) An exception to the general rule stated in subparagraph (1) of this paragraph is provided, however, in cases where such principal sum, by the terms of the decree, instrument, or agreement, may be or is to be paid over a period ending more than 10 years from the date of such decree, instrument, or agreement. In such cases, the installment payment is considered a periodic payment for the purposes of section 71(a) but only to the extent that the installment payment, or sum of the installment payments, received during the wife's taxable year does not exceed 10 percent of the principal sum. This 10-percent limitation applies to installment payments made in advance but does not apply to delinquent installment payments for a prior taxable year of the wife made during her taxable year.

(3)(i) Where payments under a decree, instrument, or agreement are to be paid over a period ending 10 years or less from the date of such decree, instrument, or agreement, such payments are not installment payments discharging a part of an obligation the principal sum of which is, in terms of money or property, specified in the decree, instrument, or agreement (and are considered periodic payments for the purposes of section 71(a)) only if such payments meet the following two conditions:

(a) Such payments are subject to any one or more of the contingencies of death of either spouse, remarriage of the wife, or change in the economic status of either spouse, and

(b) Such payments are in the nature of alimony or an allowance for support.

(ii) Payments meeting the requirements of subdivision (i) are considered periodic payments for the purposes of section 71(a) regardless of whether—

(a) The contingencies described in subdivision (i)(a) are set forth in the terms of the decree, instrument, or agreement, or are imposed by local law, or

(b) The aggregate amount of the payments to be made in the absence of the occurrence of the contingencies described in subdivision (i)(a) of this subparagraph is explicitly stated in the decree, instrument, or agreement or may be calculated from the face of the decree, instrument, or agreement, or

(c) The total amount which will be paid may be calculated actuarially.

(4) Where payments under a decree, instrument, or agreement are to be paid over a period ending more than ten years from the date of such decree, instrument, or agreement, but where such payments meet the conditions set forth in subparagraph (3)(i) of this paragraph, such payments are considered to be periodic payments for the purpose of section 71 without regard to the rule set forth in subparagraph (2) of this paragraph. Accordingly, the rules set forth in subparagraph (2) of this paragraph are not applicable to such payments.

(5) The rules as to periodic and installment payments are illustrated by the following examples:

Example (1). Under the terms of a written instrument, H is required to make payments to W which are in the nature of alimony, in the amount of $100 a month for nine years. The instrument provides that if H or W dies the payments are to cease. The payments are periodic.

Example (2). The facts are the same as in example (1) except that the written instrument explicitly provides that H is to pay W the sum of $10,080 in monthly payments of $100 over a period of nine years. The payments are periodic.

Example (3). Under the terms of a written instrument, H is to pay W $100 a month over a period of nine years. The monthly payments are not subject to any of the contingencies of death of H or W, remarriage of W, or change in the economic status of H or W under the terms of the written instrument or by reason of local law. The payments are not periodic.

Example (4). A divorce decree in 1954 provides that H is to pay W $20,000 each year for the next five years, beginning with the date of the decree, and then $5,000 each year for the next ten years. Assuming the wife makes her returns on the calendar year basis, each payment received in the years 1954 to 1958, inclusive, is treated as a periodic payment under section 71(a)(1), but only to the extent of 10 percent of the principal sum of $150,000. Thus, for such taxable years, only $15,000 of the $20,000 received is includible under section 71(a)(1) in the wife's income and is deductible by the husband under section 215. For the years 1959 to 1968, inclusive, the full $5,000 received each year by the wife is includible in her income and is deductible from the husband's income.

(e) *Payments for support of minor children.*—Section 71(a) does not apply to that part of any periodic payment which, by the terms of the decree, instrument, or agreement under section 71(a), is specifically designated as a sum payable for the support of minor children of the husband. The statute prescribes the treatment in cases where an amount or portion is so fixed but the amount of any periodic payment is less than the amount of the periodic payment specified to be made. In such cases, to the extent of the amount which would be payable for the support of such children out of the originally specified periodic payment, such periodic payment is considered a payment for such support. For example, if the husband is by terms of the decree, instrument, or agreement required to pay $200 a month to his divorced wife, $100 of which is designated by the decree, instrument, or agreement to be for the support of their minor children, and the husband pays only $150 to his wife, $100 is nevertheless considered to be a payment by the husband for the support of his children. If, however, the periodic payments are received by the wife for the support and maintenance of herself and of minor children of the husband without such specific designation of the portion for the support of such children, then the whole of such amounts is includible in the income of the wife as provided in section 71(a). Except in cases of a designated amount or portion for the support of the husband's minor children, periodic payments described in section 71(a) received by the wife for herself and any other person or persons are includible in whole in the wife's income, whether or not the amount or portion for such other person or persons is designated. [Reg. §1.71-1.]

☐ [*T.D.* 6270, 11-16-57.]

[Reg. §1.71-1T]

§1.71-1T. Alimony and separate maintenance payments (temporary).—(a) *In general.*

Q-1. What is the income tax treatment of alimony or separate maintenance payments?

A-1. Alimony or separate maintenance payments are, under section 71, included in the gross income of the payee spouse and, under section 215, allowed as a deduction from the gross income of the payor spouse.

Q-2. What is an alimony or separate maintenance payment?

A-2. An alimony or separate maintenance payment is any payment received by or on behalf of a spouse (which for this purpose includes a former spouse) of the payor under a divorce or separation instrument that meets all of the following requirements:

(a) The payment is in cash (see A-5).

(b) The payment is not designated as a payment which is excludible from the gross income of the payee and nondeductible by the payor (see A-8).

(c) In the case of spouses legally separated under a decree of divorce or separate maintenance, the spouses are not members of the same household at the time the payment is made (see A-9).

(d) The payor has no liability to continue to make any payment after the death of the payee (or to make any payment as a substitute for such payment) and the divorce or separation instrument states that there is no such liability (see A-10).

(e) The payment is not treated as child support (see A-15).

(f) To the extent that one or more annual payments exceed $10,000 during any of the 6-post-separation years, the payor is obligated to make annual payments in each of the post-separation years (see A-19).

Q-3. In order to be treated as alimony or separate maintenance payments, must the payments be "periodic" as that term was defined prior to enactment of the Tax Reform Act of 1984 or be made in discharge of a legal obligation of the payor to support the payee arising out of a marital or family relationship?

A-3. No. The Tax Reform Act of 1984 replaces the old requirements with the requirements described in A-2 above. Thus, the requirements that alimony or separate maintenance payments be "periodic" and be made in discharge of a legal obligation to support arising out of a marital or family relationship have been eliminated.

Q-4. Are the instruments described in section 71(a) of prior law the same as divorce or separation instruments described in section 71, as amended by the Tax Reform Act of 1984?

A-4. Yes.

(b) *Specific requirements.*

Q-5. May alimony or separate maintenance payments be made in a form other than cash?

A-5. No. Only cash payments (including checks and money orders payable on demand) qualify as alimony or separate maintenance payments. Transfers of services or property (including a debt instrument of a third party or an annuity contract), execution of a debt instrument by the payor, or the use of property of the payor do not qualify as alimony or separate maintenance payments.

Q-6. May payments of cash to a third party on behalf of a spouse qualify as alimony or separate maintenance payments if the payments are pursuant to the terms of a divorce or separation instrument?

A-6. Yes. Assuming all other requirements are satisfied, a payment of cash by the payor spouse to a third party under the terms of the divorce or separation instrument will qualify as a payment of cash which is received "on behalf of a spouse". For example, cash payments of rent, mortgage, tax, or tuition liabilities of the payee spouse made under the terms of the divorce or separation instrument will qualify as alimony or separate maintenance payments. Any payments to maintain property owned by the payor spouse and used by the payee spouse (including mortgage payments, real estate taxes and insurance premiums) are not payments on behalf of a spouse even if those payments are made pursuant to the terms of the divorce or separation instrument. Premiums paid by the payor spouse for term or whole life insurance on the payor's life made under the terms of the divorce or separation instrument will qualify as payments on behalf of the payee spouse to the extent that the payee spouse is the owner of the policy.

Q-7. May payments of cash to a third party on behalf of a spouse qualify as alimony or separate maintenance payments if the payments are made to the third party at the written request of the payee spouse?

A-7. Yes. For example, instead of making an alimony or separate maintenance payment directly to the payee, the payor spouse may make a cash payment to a charitable organization if such payment is pursuant to the written request, consent or ratification of the payee spouse. Such request, consent or ratification must state that the parties intend the payment to be treated as an alimony or separate maintenance payment to the payee spouse subject to the rules of section 71, and must be received by the payor spouse prior to the date of filing of the payor's first return of tax for the taxable year in which the payment was made.

Q-8. How may spouses designate that payments otherwise qualifying as alimony or separate maintenance payments shall be excludible from the gross income of the payee and nondeductible by the payor?

A-8. The spouses may designate that payments otherwise qualifying as alimony or separate maintenance payments shall be nondeductible by the payor and excludible from gross income by the payee by so providing in a divorce or separation instrument (as defined in section 71(b)(2)). If the spouses have executed a written separation agreement (as described in section 71(b)(2)(B)), any writing signed by both spouses which designates otherwise qualifying alimony or separate maintenance payments as nondeductible and excludible and which refers to the written separation agreement will be treated as a written separation agreement (and thus a divorce or separation instrument) for purposes of the preceding sentence. If the spouses are subject to temporary support orders (as described in section 71(b)(2)(C)), the designation of otherwise qualifying alimony or separate payments as nondeductible and excludible must be made in the original or a subsequent temporary support order. A copy of the instrument containing the designation of payments as not alimony or separate maintenance payments must be attached to the payee's first filed return of tax (Form 1040) for each year in which the designation applies.

Q-9. What are the consequences if, at the time a payment is made, the payor and payee spouses are members of the same household?

A-9. Generally, a payment made at the time when the payor and payee spouses are members of the same household cannot qualify as an alimony or separate maintenance payment if the spouses are legally separated under a decree of divorce or of separate maintenance. For purposes of the preceding sentence, a dwelling unit formerly shared by both spouses shall not be considered two separate households even if the spouses physically separate themselves within the dwelling unit. The spouses will not be treated as members of the same household if one spouse is preparing to depart from the household of the other spouse, and does depart not more than one month after the date the payment is made. If the spouses are not legally separated under a decree of divorce or separate maintenance, a payment under a written separation agreement or a decree described in section 71(b)(2)(C) may qualify as an alimony or separate maintenance payment notwithstanding that the payor and payee are members of the same household at the time the payment is made.

Q-10. Assuming all other requirements relating to the qualification of certain payments as alimony or separate maintenance payments are met, what are the consequences if the payor spouse is required to continue to make the payments after the death of the payee spouse?

A-10. None of the payments before (or after) the death of the payee spouse qualify as alimony or separate maintenance payments.

Q-11. What are the consequences if the divorce or separation instrument fails to state that there is no liability for any period after the death of the payee spouse to continue to make any payments which would otherwise qualify as alimony or separate maintenance payments?

A-11. If the instrument fails to include such a statement, none of the payments, whether made before or after the death of the payee spouse, will qualify as alimony or separate maintenance payments.

Example (1). A is to pay B $10,000 in cash each year for a period of 10 years under a divorce or separation instrument which does not state that the payments will terminate upon the death of B. None of the payments will qualify as alimony or separate maintenance payments.

Example (2). A is to pay B $10,000 in cash each year for a period of 10 years under a divorce or separation instrument which states that the payments will terminate upon the death of B. In addition, under the instrument, A is to pay B or B's estate $20,000 in cash each year for a period of 10 years. Because the $20,000 annual payments will not terminate upon the death of B, these payments will not qualify as alimony or separate maintenance payments. However, the separate $10,000 annual payments will qualify as alimony or separate maintenance payments.

Q-12. Will a divorce or separation instrument be treated as stating that there is no liability to make payments after the death of the payee spouse if the liability to make such payments terminates pursuant to applicable local law or oral agreement?

A-12. No. Termination of the liability to make payments must be stated in the terms of the divorce or separation instrument.

Q-13. What are the consequences if the payor spouse is required to make one or more payments (in cash or property) after the death of the payee spouse as a substitute for the continuation of pre-death payments which would otherwise qualify as alimony or separate maintenance payments?

A-13. If the payor spouse is required to make any such substitute payments, none of the otherwise qualifying payments will qualify as alimony or separate maintenance payments. The divorce or separation instrument need not state, however, that there is no liability to make any such substitute payment.

Q-14. Under what circumstances will one or more payments (in cash or property) which are to occur after the death of the payee spouse be treated as a substitute for a continuation of payments which would otherwise qualify as alimony or separate maintenance payments?

A-14. To the extent that one or more payments are to begin to be made, increase in amount, or become accelerated in time as a result of the death of the payee spouse, such payments may be treated as a substitute for the continuation of payments terminating on the death of the payee spouse which would otherwise qualify as alimony or separate maintenance payments. The determination of whether or not such payments are a substitute for the continuation of payments which would otherwise qualify as alimony or separate maintenance payments, and of the amount of the otherwise qualifying alimony or separate maintenance payments for which any such payments are a substitute, will depend on all of the facts and circumstances.

Example (1). Under the terms of a divorce decree, A is obligated to make annual alimony payments to B of $30,000, terminating on the earlier of the expiration of 6 years or the death of B. B maintains custody of the minor children of A and B. The decree provides that at the death of B, if there are minor children of A and B remaining, A will be obligated to make annual payments of $10,000 to a trust, the income and corpus of which are to be used for the benefit of the children until the youngest child attains the age of majority. These facts indicate that A's liability to make annual $10,000 payments in trust for the benefit of his minor children upon the death of B is a substitute for $10,000 of the $30,000 annual payments to B. Accordingly, $10,000 of each of the $30,000 annual payments to B will not qualify as alimony or separate maintenance payments.

Example (2). Under the terms of a divorce decree, A is obligated to make annual alimony payments to B of $30,000, terminating on the earlier of the expiration of 15 years or the death of B. The divorce decree provides that if B dies before the expiration of the 15 year period, A will pay to B's estate the difference between the total amount that A would have paid had B survived, minus the amount actually paid. For example, if B dies at the end of the 10th year in which payments are made, A will pay to B's estate $150,000 ($450,000 – $300,000). These facts indicate that A's liability to make a lump sum payment to B's estate upon the death of B is a substitute for the full amount of each of the annual $30,000 payments to B. Accordingly,

none of the annual $30,000 payments to B will qualify as alimony or separate maintenance payments. The result would be the same if the lump sum payable at B's death were discounted by an appropriate interest factor to account for the prepayment.

(c) *Child support payments.*

Q-15. What are the consequences of a payment which the terms of the divorce or separation instrument fix as payable for the support of a child of the payor spouse?

A-15. A payment which under the terms of the divorce or separation instrument is fixed (or treated as fixed) as payable for the support of a child of the payor spouse does not qualify as an alimony or separate maintenance payment. Thus, such a payment is not deductible by the payor spouse or includible in the income of the payee spouse.

Q-16. When is a payment fixed (or treated as fixed) as payable for the support of a child of the payor spouse?

A-16. A payment is fixed as payable for the support of a child of the payor spouse if the divorce or separation instrument specifically designates some sum or portion (which sum or portion may fluctuate) as payable for the support of a child of the payor spouse. A payment will be treated as fixed as payable for the support of a child of the payor spouse if the payment is reduced (a) on the happening of a contingency relating to a child of the payor, or (b) at a time which can clearly be associated with such a contingency. A payment may be treated as fixed as payable for the support of a child of the payor spouse even if other separate payments specifically are designated as payable for the support of a child of the payor spouse.

Q-17. When does a contingency relate to a child of the payor?

A-17. For this purpose, a contingency relates to a child of the payor if it depends on any event relating to that child, regardless of whether such event is certain or likely to occur. Events that relate to a child of the payor include the following: the child's attaining a specified age or income level, dying, marrying, leaving school, leaving the spouse's household, or gaining employment.

Q-18. When will a payment be treated as to be reduced at a time which can clearly be associated with the happening of a contingency relating to a child of the payor?

A-18. There are two situations, described below, in which payments which would otherwise qualify as alimony or separate maintenance payments will be presumed to be reduced at a time clearly associated with the happening of a contingency relating to a child of the payor. In all other situations, reductions in payments will not be treated as clearly associated with the happening of a contingency relating to a child of the payor.

The first situation referred to above is where the payments are to be reduced not more than 6 months before or after the date the child is to attain the age of 18, 21, or local age of majority. The second situation is where the payments are to be reduced on two or more occasions which occur not more than one year before or after a different child of the payor spouse attains a certain age between the ages of 18 and 24, inclusive. The certain age referred to in the preceding sentence must be the same for each such child, but need not be a whole number of years.

The presumption in the two situations described above that payments are to be reduced at a time clearly associated with the happening of a contingency relating to a child of the payor may be rebutted (either by the Service or by taxpayers) by showing that the time at which the payments are to be reduced was determined independently of any contingencies relating to the children of the payor. The presumption in the first situation will be rebutted conclusively if the reduction is a complete cessation of alimony or separate maintenance payments during the sixth post-separation year (described in A-21) or upon the expiration of a 72-month period. The presumption may also be rebutted in other circumstances, for example, by showing that alimony payments are to be made for a period customarily provided in the local jurisdiction, such as a period equal to one-half the duration of the marriage.

Example: A and B are divorced on July 1, 1985, when their children, C (born July 15, 1970) and D (born September 23, 1972), are 14 and 12, respectively. Under the divorce decree, A is to make alimony payments to B of $2,000 per month. Such payments are to be reduced to $1,500 per month on January 1, 1991, and to $1,000 per month on January 1, 1995. On January 1, 1991, the date of the first reduction in payments, C will be 20 years 5 months and 17 days old. On January 1, 1995, the date of the second reduction in payments, D will be 22 years 3 months and 9 days old. Each of the reductions in payments is to occur not more than one year before or after a different child of A attains the age of 21 years and 4 months. (Actually, the reductions are to occur not more than one year before or after C and D attain *any* of the ages 21 years 3 months and 9 days through 21 years 5 months and 17 days.) Accordingly, the reductions will be presumed to clearly be associated with the happening of a contingency relating to C and D. Unless this presumption is rebutted, payments under the divorce decree equal to the sum of the reductions ($1,000 per month) will be treated as fixed for the support of the children of A and therefore will not quaify as alimony or separate maintenance payments.

(d) *Excess front-loading rules.*

Q-19. What are the excess front-loading rules?

A-19. The excess front-loading rules are two special rules which may apply to the extent that payments in any calendar year exceed $10,000. The first rule is a minimum term rule, which must be met in order for any annual payment, to the extent in excess of $10,000, to qualify as an alimony or separate maintenance payment (see A-2(f)). This rule requires that alimony or separate maintenance payments be called for, at a minimum, during the 6 "post-separation years". The second rule is a recapture rule which characterizes payments retrospectively by requiring a recalculation and inclusion in income by the payor and deduc tion by the payee of previously paid alimony or separate maintenance payments to the extent that the amount of such payments during any of the 6 "post-separation years" falls short of the amount of payments during a prior year by more than $10,000.

Q-20. Do the excess front-loading rules apply to payments to the extent that annual payments never exceed $10,000?

A-20. No. For example, A is to make a single $10,000 payment to B. Provided that the other requirements of section 71 are met, the payment will qualify as an alimony or separate maintenance payment. If A were to make a single $15,000 payment to B, $10,000 of the payment would qualify as an alimony or separate maintenance payment and $5,000 of the payment would be disqualified under the minimum term rule because payments were not to be made for the minimum period.

Q-21. Do the excess front-loading rules apply to payments received under a decree described in section 71(b)(2)(C)?

A-21. No. Payments under decrees described in section 71(b)(2)(C) are to be disregarded entirely for purposes of applying the excess front-loading rules.

Q-22. Both the minimum term rule and the recapture rule refer to 6 "post-separation years". What are the 6 "post-separation years"?

A-22. The 6 "post-separation years" are the 6 consecutive calendar years beginning with the first calendar year in which the payor pays to the payee an alimony or separate maintenance payment (except a payment made under a decree described in section 71(b)(2)(C)). Each year within this period is referred to as a "post-separation year". The 6-year period need not commence with the year in which the spouses separate or divorce, or with the year in which payments under the divorce or separation instrument are made, if no payments during such year qualify as alimony or separate maintenance payments. For example, a decree for the divorce of A and B is entered in October, 1985. The decree requires A to make monthly payments to B commencing November 1, 1985, but A and B are members of the same household until February 15, 1986 (and as a result, the payments prior to January 16, 1986, do not qualify as alimony payments). For purposes of applying the excess front-loading rules to payments from A to B, the 6 calendar years 1986 through 1991 are post-separation years. If a spouse has been making payments pursuant to a divorce or separation instrument described in section 71(b)(2)(A) or (B), a modification of the instrument or the substitution of a new instrument (for example, the substitution of a divorce decree for a written separation agreement) will not result in the creation of additional post-separation years. However, if a spouse has been making payments pursuant to a divorce or separation instrument described in section 71(b)(2)(C), the 6-year period does not begin until the first calendar year in which alimony or separate maintenance payments are made under a divorce or separation instrument described in section 71(b)(2)(A) or (B).

Q-23. How does the minimum term rule operate?

A-23. The minimum term rule operates in the following manner. To the extent payments are made in excess of $10,000, a payment will qualify as an alimony or separate maintenance payment only if alimony or separate maintenance payments are to be made in each of the 6 post-separation years. For example, pursuant to a divorce decree, A is to make alimony payments to B of $20,000 in each of the 5 calendar years 1985 through 1989. A is to make no payment in 1990. Under the minimum term rule, only $10,000 will qualify as an alimony payment *in each of the calendar years* 1985 through 1989. If the divorce decree also required A to make a $1 payment in 1990, the minimum term rule would be satisfied and $20,000 would be treated as an alimony payment in each of the calendar years 1985 through 1989. The recapture rule would, however, apply for 1990. For purposes of determining whether alimony or separate maintenance payments are to be made in any year, the possible termination of such payments upon the happening of a contingency (other than the passage of time) which has not yet occurred is ignored (unless such contingency may cause all or a portion of the payment to be treated as a child support payment).

Q-24. How does the recapture rule operate?

A-24. The recapture rule operates in the following manner. If the amount of alimony or separate maintenance payments paid in any post-separation year (referred to as the "computation year") falls short of the amount of alimony or separate maintenance payments paid in any prior post-separation year by more than $10,000, the payor must compute an "excess amount" for the computation year. The excess amount for any computation year is the sum of excess amounts determined with respect to each prior post-separation year. The excess amount determined with respect to a prior post-separation year is the excess of (1) the amount of alimony or separate maintenance payments paid by the payor spouse during such prior post-separation year, over (2) the amount of the alimony or separate maintenance payments paid by the payor spouse during the computation year plus $10,000. For purposes of this calculation, the amount of alimony or separate maintenance payments made by the payor spouse during any post-separation year preceding the computation year is reduced by any excess amount previously determined with respect to such year. The rules set forth above may be illustrated by the following example. A makes alimony payments to B of $25,000 in 1985 and $12,000 in 1986. The excess amount with respect to 1985 that is recaptured in 1986 is $3,000 ($25,000 – ($12,000 + $10,000)). For purposes of subsequent computation years, the amount deemed paid in 1985 is $22,000. If A makes alimony payments to B of $1,000 in 1987, the excess amount that is recaptured in 1987 will be $12,000. This is the sum of an $11,000 excess amount with respect to 1985 ($22,000 – ($1,000 + $10,000)) and a $1,000 excess amount with respect to 1986 ($12,000 – ($1,000 + $10,000)). If, prior to the end of 1990, payments decline further, additional recapture will occur. The payor spouse must include the excess amount in gross income for his/her taxable year beginning with or in the computation year. The payee spouse is allowed a deduction for the excess amount in computing adjusted gross income for his/her taxable year beginning with or in the computation year. However, the payee spouse must compute the excess amount by reference to the date when payments were made and not when payments were received.

Q-25. What are the exceptions to the recapture rule?

A-25. Apart from the $10,000 threshold for application of the recapture rule, there are three exceptions to the recapture rule. The first exception is for payments received under temporary support orders described in section 71(b)(2)(C) (see A-21). The second exception is for any payment made pursuant to a continuing liability over the period of the post-separation years to pay a fixed portion of the payor's income from a business or property or from compensation for employment or self-employment. The third exception is where the alimony or separate maintenance payments in any post-separation year cease by reason of the death of the payor or payee or the remarriage (as defined under applicable local law) of the payee before the close of the computation year. For example, pursuant to a divorce decree, A is to make cash payments to B of $30,000 in each of the calendar years 1985 through 1990. A makes cash payments of $30,000 in 1985 and $15,000 in 1986, in which year B remarries and A's alimony payments cease. The recapture rule does not apply for 1986 or any subsequent year. If alimony or separate maintenance payments made by A decline or cease during a post-separation year for any other reason (including a failure by the payor to make timely payments, a modification of the divorce or separation instrument, a reduction in the support needs of the payee, or a reduction in the ability of the payor to provide support) excess amounts with respect to prior post-separation years will be subject to recapture.

(e) *Effective dates.*

Q-26. When does section 71, as amended by the Tax Reform Act of 1984, become effective?

A-26. Generally, section 71, as amended, is effective with respect to divorce or separation instruments (as defined in section 71(b)(2)) executed after December 31, 1984. If a decree of divorce or separate maintenance executed after December 31, 1984, incorporates or adopts without change the terms of the alimony or separate maintenance payments under a divorce or separation instrument executed before January 1, 1985, such decree will be treated as executed before January 1, 1985. A change in the amount of alimony or separate maintenance payments or the time period over which such payments are to continue, or the addition or deletion of any contingencies or conditions relating to such payments is a change in the terms of the alimony or separate maintenance payments. For example, in November 1984, A and B executed a written separation agreement. In February 1985, a decree of divorce is entered in substitution for the written separation agreement. The decree of divorce does not change the terms of the alimony A pays to B. The decree of divorce will be treated as executed before January 1, 1985 and hence alimony payments under the decree will be subject to the rules of section 71 prior to amendment by the Tax Reform Act of 1984. If the amount or time period of the alimony or separate maintenance payments are not specified in the pre-1985 separation agreement or if the decree of divorce changes the amount or term of such payments, the decree of divorce will not be treated as executed before January 1, 1985, and alimony payments under the decree will be subject to the rules of section 71, as amended by the Tax Reform Act of 1984.

Section 71, as amended, also applies to any divorce or separation instrument executed (or treated as executed) before January 1, 1985 that has been modified on or after January 1, 1985, if such modification expressly provides that section 71, as amended by the Tax Reform Act of 1984, shall apply to the instrument as modified. In this case, section 71, as amended, is effective with respect to payments made after the date the instrument is modified [Temporary Reg. §1.71-1T.]

□ [*T.D. 7973, 8-30-84.*]

[Reg. §1.71-2]

§1.71-2. Effective date; taxable years ending after March 31, 1954, subject to the Internal Revenue Code of 1939.—Pursuant to section 7851(a)(1)(C), the regulations prescribed in §1.71-1, to the extent that they relate to payments under a written separation agreement executed after August 16, 1954, and to the extent that they relate to payments under a decree for support received after August 16, 1954, under a decree entered after March 1, 1954, shall also apply to taxable years beginning before January 1, 1954, and ending after August 16, 1954, although such years are subject to the Internal Revenue Code of 1939. [Reg. §1.71-2.]

□ [*T.D. 6270, 11-16-57.*]

[Reg. §1.72-1]

§1.72-1. Introduction.—(a) *General principle.*—Section 72 prescribes rules relating to the inclusion in gross income of amounts received under a life insurance, endowment, or annuity contract unless such amounts are specifically excluded from gross income under other provisions of chapter 1 of the Code. In general, these rules provide that amounts subject to the provisions of section 72 are includible in the gross income of the recipient except to the extent that they are considered to represent a reduction or return of premiums or other consideration paid.

(b) *Amounts to be considered as a return of premiums.*—For the purpose of determining the extent to which amounts received represent a reduction or return of premiums or other consideration paid, the provisions of section 72 distinguish between "amounts received as an annuity" and "amounts not received as an annuity". In general, "amounts received as an annuity" are amounts which are payable at regular intervals over a period of more than one full year from the date on which they are deemed to begin, provided the total of the amounts so payable or the period for which they are to be paid can be determined as of that date. See paragraph (b)(2) and (3) of §1.72-2. Any other amounts to which the provisions of section 72 apply are considered to be "amounts not received as an annuity." See §1.72-11.

(c) *"Amounts received as an annuity".*—(1) In the case of "amounts received as an annuity" (other than certain employees' annuities described in section 72(d) and in §1.72-13), a proportionate part of each amount so received is considered to represent a return of premiums or other consideration paid. The proportionate part of each annuity payment which is thus excludable from gross income is determined by the ratio which the investment in the contract as of the date on which the annuity is deemed to begin bears to the expected return under the contract as of that date. See §1.72-4.

(2) In the case of employees' annuities of the type described in section 72(d), no amount received as an annuity in a taxable year to which the Internal Revenue Code of 1954 applies is includible in the gross income of a recipient until the aggregate of all amounts received thereunder and excluded from gross income under the applicable income tax law exceeds the consideration contributed (or deemed contributed) by the employee under §1.72-8. Thereafter, all amounts so received are includible in the gross income of the recipient. See §1.72-13.

(d) *"Amounts not received as an annuity".*—In the case of "amounts not received as an annuity", if such amounts are received after an annuity has begun and during its continuance, amounts so received are generally includible in the gross income of the recipient. Amounts not received as an annuity which are received at any other time are generally includible in the gross income of the recipient only to the extent that such amounts, when added to all amounts previously received under the contract which were excludable from the gross income of the recipient under the income tax law applicable at the time of receipt, exceed the premiums or other consideration paid (see §1.72-11). However, if the aggregate of premiums or other consideration paid for the contract includes amounts for which a deduction was allowed under section 404 as contributions on behalf of an owner-employee, the amounts received under the circumstances of the preceding sentence shall be includible in gross income

until the amount so included equals the amount for which the deduction was so allowed. See paragraph (b) of §1.72-17.

(e) *Classification of recipients.*—For the purpose of the regulations under section 72, a recipient shall be considered an "annuitant" if he receives amounts under an annuity contract during the period that the annuity payments are to continue, whether for a term certain or during the continuing life or lives of the person or persons whose lives measure the duration of such annuity. However, a recipient shall be considered a "beneficiary" rather than an "annuitant" if the amounts he receives under a contract are received after the term of the annuity for a life or lives has expired and such amounts are paid by reason of the fact that the contract guarantees that payments of some minimum amount or for some minimum period shall be made. For special rules with respect to beneficiaries, see paragraphs (a)(1)(ii) and (c) of §1.72-11. [Reg. §1.72-1.]

□ [*T.D. 6211, 11-14-56. Amended by T.D. 6676, 9-16-63.*]

[Reg. §1.72-2]

§1.72-2. Applicability of section.—(a) *Contracts.*—(1) The contracts under which amounts paid will be subject to the provisions of section 72 include contracts which are considered to be life insurance, endowment, and annuity contracts in accordance with the customary practice of life insurance companies. For the purposes of section 72, however, it is immaterial whether such contracts are entered into with an insurance company. The term "endowment contract" also includes the "face-amount certificates" described in section 72(l).

(2) If two or more annuity obligations or elements to which section 72 applies are acquired for a single consideration, such as an obligation to pay an annuity to A for his life accompanied by an obligation to pay an annuity to B for his life, there being a single consideration paid for both obligations (whether paid by one or more persons in equal or different amounts, and whether paid in a single sum or otherwise), such annuity elements shall be considered to comprise a single contract for the purpose of the application of section 72 and the regulations thereunder. For rules relating to the allocation of investment in the contract in the case of annuity elements payable to two or more persons, see §1.72-6(b).

(3)(i) Sections 402 and 403 provide that certain distributions by employees' trusts and certain payments under employee plans are taxable under section 72. For taxable years beginning before January 1, 1964, section 72(e)(3), as in effect before such date, does not apply to such distributions or payments. For purposes of applying section 72 to such distributions and payments (other than those described in subdivision (iii) of this subparagraph), each separate program of the employer consisting of interrelated contributions and benefits shall be considered a single contract. Therefore, all distributions or payments (other than those described in subdivision (iii) of this subparagraph) which are attributable to a separate program of interrelated contributions and benefits are considered as received under a single contract. A separate program of interrelated contributions and benefits may be financed by the purchase from an insurance company of one or more group contracts or one or more individual contracts, or may be financed partly by the purchase of contracts from an insurance company and partly through an investment fund, or may be financed completely through an investment fund. A program may be considered separate for purposes of section 72 although it is only a part of a plan which qualifies under section 401. There may be several trusts under one separate program, or several separate programs may make use of a single trust. See, however, subdivision (iii) of this subparagraph for rules relating to what constitutes a "contract" for purposes of applying section 72 to distributions commencing before October 20, 1960.

(ii) The following types of benefits, and the contributions used to provide them, are examples of separate programs of interrelated contributions and benefits:

(a) Definitely determinable retirement benefits.

(b) Definitely determinable benefits payable prior to retirement in case of disability.

(c) Life insurance.

(d) Accident and health insurance.

However, retirement benefits and life insurance will be considered part of a single separate program of interrelated contributions and benefits to the extent they are provided under retirement income, endowment, or other contracts providing life insurance protection. See examples (6), (7), and (8) contained in subdivision (iv) of this subparagraph for illustrations of the principles of this subdivision. See, also, §1.72-15 for rules relating to the taxation of amounts received under an employee plan which provides both retirement benefits and accident and health benefits.

(iii) If any amount which is taxable under section 72 by reason of section 402 or 403 is actually distributed or made available to any person under an employees' trust or plan (other than the Civil Service Retirement Act (5 U.S.C. ch.14)) before October 20, 1960, section 72 shall, notwithstanding any other provisions in this subparagraph, be applied to all the distributions with respect to such person (or his beneficiaries) under such trust or plan (whether received before or after October 20, 1960) as though such distributions were provided under a single contract. For purposes of applying section 72 to distributions to which this subdivision applies, therefore, the term "contract" shall be considered to include the entire interest of an employee in each trust or plan described in sections 402 and 403 to the extent that distributions thereunder are subject to the provisions of section 72. Section 72 shall be applied to distributions received under the Civil Service Retirement Act in the manner prescribed in subdivision (i) of this subparagraph (see example (4) in subdivision (iv) of this subparagraph).

(iv) The application of this subparagraph may be illustrated by the following examples:

Example (1). On January 1, 1961, X Corporation established a noncontributory profit-sharing plan for its employees providing that the amount standing to the account of each participant will be paid to him at the time of his retirement and also established a contributory pension plan for its employees providing for the payment to each participant of a lifetime pension after retirement. The profit-sharing plan is designed to enable the employees to participate in the profits of X Corporation; the amount of the contributions to it are determined by reference to the profits of X Corporation; and the amount of any distribution is determined by reference to the amount of contributions made on behalf of any participant and the earnings thereon. On the other hand, the pension plan is designed to provide a lifetime pension for a retired employee; the amount of the pension is to be determined by a formula set forth in the plan; and the amount of contributions to the plan is the amount necessary to provide such pensions. In view of the fact that each of these plans constitutes a separate program of interrelated contributions and benefits, the distributions from each shall be treated as received under a separate contract. If these plans had been established before October 20, 1960, then, in the case of an employee who receives a distribution under the plans before October 20, 1960, the determination as to whether that distribution and all subsequent distributions to such employee are received under a single contract or under more than one contract shall be made by applying the rules in subdivision (iii) of this subparagraph. On the other hand, in the case of an employee who does not receive any distribution under these plans before October 20, 1960, the determination as to whether distributions to him are received under a single contract or under more than one contract shall be made in accordance with the rules illustrated by this example.

Example (2). On January 1, 1961, Z Corporation established a profit-sharing plan for its employees providing that any employee may make contributions, not in excess of 6 percent of his compensation, to a trust and that the employer would make matching contributions out of profits. Under the plan, a participant may receive a periodic distribution of the amount standing in his account during any period that he is absent from work due to a personal injury or sickness. On separation from service, the participant is entitled to receive a distribution of the balance standing in his account in accordance with one of several options. One option provides for the immediate distribution of one-half of the account and for the periodic distribution of the remaining one-half of the account. In addition, any participant may, after the completion of five years of participation, withdraw any part of his account, but in the case of such a withdrawal, the participant forfeits his rights to participate in the plan for a period of two years. Thus, a participant may receive distributions before separation from service; he may receive a distribution of a lump sum upon separation from service; he may also receive periodic distributions upon separation from service. However, since it is the total amount received under all the options that is interrelated with the contributions to the plan and not the amount received under any one option, this profit-sharing plan consists of only one separate program of interrelated contributions and benefits and all distributions under the plan (regardless of the option under which received) are treated as received under one contract. However, if, instead of providing that the amount standing in an employee's account would be paid to him during any period that he is absent from work due to a personal injury or sickness, the plan provided that a portion of the amount in the employee's account would be used to purchase incidental accident and health insurance, this plan would consist of two separate programs of interrelated contributions and benefits. The accident and health insurance, and the contributions used to purchase it, would be considered as one separate program of interrelated contributions and benefits and, therefore, a separate contract; whereas, the remaining contributions and benefits would be considered another separate program of interrelated contributions and benefits and, consequently, another separate contract.

Example (3). On January 1, 1961, N Corporation established a profit-sharing plan for its employees providing that the employees may make contributions, not in excess of 6 percent of their compensation, to a trust and that N Corporation would make matching contributions out of its profits. Under the plan, the employee may elect each year to have his and the employer's contributions for such year placed in either a savings arrangement or a retirement arrangement. Such an election is irrevocable. Under the savings arrangement, contributions to such arrangement for any one year and the earnings thereon will be distributed five years later. The retirement arrangement provides that all contributions thereto and the earnings thereon will be distributed when the employee is separated from the service of N Corporation. Since the distributions under the retirement arrangement are attributable solely to the contributions made to such arrangement and are not affected in any manner by contributions or distributions under the savings arrangement or any other plan, such distributions are treated as received under a separate program of interrelated contributions and benefits. Similarly, since distributions during any year under the savings arrangement are attributable only to contributions to such arrangement made during the fifth preceding year and not affected in any manner by any other contributions to or distributions from such arrangement or any other plan, the savings arrangement constitutes a series of separate programs of interrelated contributions and benefits. The contributions to the savings arrangement for any year and the distribution in a subsequent year based thereon constitute a separate contract for purposes of section 72.

Example (4). The Civil Service Retirement Act (5 U.S.C. ch. 14) which provides retirement benefits for participating employees, consists of a compulsory program and a voluntary program. Under the compulsory program, all participating employees are required to make certain contributions and, upon retirement, are provided retirement benefits computed on the basis of compensation and length of service. Under the voluntary program, such participating employees are permitted to make contributions in addition to those required under the compulsory program and, upon retirement, are provided additional retirement benefits computed on the basis of their voluntary contributions. Distributions received under the Act constitute distributions from two separate contracts for purposes of section 72. Distributions received under the compulsory program are considered as received under a separate program of interrelated contributions and benefits since they are computed solely under the compulsory program and are not affected by any contributions or distributions under the voluntary program or under any other plan. For similar reasons, distributions which are attributable to the voluntary contributions are considered as received under a separate program of interrelated contributions and benefits.

Example (5). On January 1, 1961, M Corporation established a contributory pension plan for its employees and created a trust to which it makes contributions to fund such plan. The plan provides that each participant will receive after age 65 a pension of $1\frac{1}{2}$ percent of his compensation for each year of service performed subsequent to the establishment of such plan. In order to fund part of the benefits under the plan, the trustee purchased a group annuity contract. The remaining part of the benefits are to be paid out of a separate investment fund. This pension plan constitutes a single program of interrelated contributions and benefits and, therefore, all distributions received by an employee under the plan are considered as received under a single contract for purposes of section 72.

Example (6). On January 1, 1961, Y Corporation established a noncontributory pension plan (including incidental death benefits) for its employees and created a trust to which it makes contributions to fund such plan. The plan provides that each participant will receive after age 65 a pension of $1\frac{1}{2}$ percent of his compensation for each year of service performed subsequent to the establishment of such plan. In addition, such plan provides for the payment of a death benefit if the employee dies before age 65. The trustee funded the death benefits through the purchase of a group term insurance policy and funded the retirement benefits through the purchase of a group annuity contract. Because of a subsequent change in funding from the deferred annuity method to the deposit administration method, the trustee purchased a second group annuity contract to provide the retirement benefits under the plan accruing after the effective date of the change in method of funding. Thus, retirement benefits distributed to an employee whose service with Y Corporation commenced before the effective date of the change in method of funding will be attributable to both group annuity contracts. This pension plan includes two separate programs of interrelated contributions and benefits. The death benefits, and the contributions required to provide them, are considered as one separate program of interrelated contributions and benefits; whereas, the retirement benefits, and the contributions required to provide them, are considered as another separate program of interrelated contributions and benefits. Therefore, any retirement benefits received by an employee, whether attributable to one or both of the group annuity contracts, shall be considered as received under a single contract for purposes of section 72. In determining the tax treatment of any such retirement benefits under section 72, no amount of the premiums used to purchase the group term insurance policy shall be taken into account, since such premiums, and the death benefits which they purchased, constitute a separate program of interrelated contributions and benefits.

Example (7). Assume the same facts as in example (6) except that, in lieu of funding the benefits in the manner described in that example, the trustee purchased individual retirement income contracts from an insurance company. Additional individual retirement income contracts are purchased in order to fund any increase in benefits resulting from increases in salary. Therefore, distributions to a particular employee may be attributable to a single retirement income contract or to more than one such contract. All distributions received by an employee under the pension plan, whether attributable to one or more retirement income contracts and whether made directly from the insurance company to the employee or made through the trustee, are considered as received under a single contract for purposes of section 72. For rules relating to the tax treatment of contributions and distributions under retirement income, endowment, or other life insurance contracts purchased by a trust described in section 401(a) and exempt under section 501(a), see paragraph (a)(2), (3), and (4) of §1.402(a)-1.

Example (8). Assume the same facts as in example (6) except that, in lieu of funding the benefits in the manner described in that example, the trustee funded the death benefits and part of the retirement benefits by purchasing individual retirement income contracts from an insurance company. The remaining part of the retirement benefits (such as any increase in benefits resulting from increases in salary) are to be paid out of a separate investment fund. This pension plan includes, with respect to each participant, two separate contracts for purposes of section 72. The retirement income contract purchased by the trust for each participant is a separate program of interrelated contributions and benefits and all distributions attributable to such contract (whether made directly from the insurance company to the employee or made through the trustee) are considered as received under a single contract. For rules relating to the tax treatment of contributions and distributions under retirement income, endowment, or other life insurance contracts purchased by a trust described in section 401(a) and exempt under section 501(a), see paragraph (a)(2), (3), and (4) of §1.402(a)-1. The remaining distributions under the plan are considered as received under another separate program of interrelated contributions and benefits.

(b) *Amounts.*—(1)(i) In general, the amounts to which section 72 applies are any amounts received under the contracts described in paragraph (a)(1). However, if such amounts are specifically excluded from gross income under other provisions of chapter 1 of the Internal Revenue Code, section 72 shall not apply for the purpose of including such amounts in gross income. For example, section 72 does not apply to amounts received under a life insurance contract if such amounts are paid by reason of the death of the insured and are excludable from gross income under section 101(a) of the Code. See also sections 101(d), relating to proceeds of life insurance paid at a date later than death, and 104(a)(4), relating to compensation for injuries or sickness.

(ii) Section 72 does not exclude from gross income any amounts received under an agreement to hold an amount and pay interest thereon. See §1.72-14(a). However, section 72 does apply to amounts received by a surviving annuitant under a joint and survivor annuity contract since such amounts are not considered to be paid by reason of the death of an insured. For a special deduction for the estate tax attributable to the inclusion of the value of the interest of a surviving annuitant under a joint and survivor annuity contract in the estate of the deceased primary annuitant, see section 691(d) and the regulations thereunder.

(2) Amounts subject to section 72 in accordance with subparagraph (1) are considered "amounts received as an annuity" only in the event that all of the following tests are met:

(i) They must be received on or after the "annuity starting date" as that term is defined in §1.72-4(b);

(ii) They must be payable in periodic installments at regular intervals (whether annually, semiannually, quarterly, monthly, weekly, or otherwise) over a period of more than one full year from the annuity starting date; and

(iii) Except as indicated in subparagraph (3), the total of the amounts payable must be determinable at the annuity starting date either directly from the terms of the contract or indirectly by the use of either mortality tables or compound interest computations, or both, in conjunction with such terms and in accordance with sound actuarial theory.

For the purpose of determining whether amounts subject to section 72(d) and §1.72-13 are "amounts received as an annuity," however, the provisions of subdivision (i) shall be disregarded. In addition, the term "amounts received as an annuity" does not include amounts received to which the provisions of §1.72-11(b) or (c) apply, relating to dividends and certain amounts received by a beneficiary in the nature of a refund. If an amount is to be paid periodically until a

fund plus interest at a fixed rate is exhausted, but further payments may be made thereafter because of earnings at a higher interest rate, the requirements of subdivision (iii) are met with respect to the payments determinable at the outset by means of computations involving the fixed interest rate, but any payments received after the expiration of the period determinable by such computations shall be taxable as dividends received after the annuity starting date in accordance with §1.72-11(b)(2).

(3)(i) Notwithstanding the requirement of subdivision (iii) of subparagraph (2), if amounts are to be received for a definite or determinable time (whether for a period certain or for a life or lives) under a contract which provides—

(a) That the amount of the periodic payments may vary in accordance with investment experience (as in certain profit-sharing plans), cost of living indices, or similar fluctuating criteria, or

(b) For specified payments the value of which may vary for income tax purposes, such as in the case of any annuity payable in foreign currency,

each such payment received shall be considered as an amount received as an annuity only to the extent that it does not exceed the amount computed by dividing the investment in the contract, as adjusted for any refund feature, by the number of periodic payments anticipated during the time that the periodic payments are to be made. If payments are to be made more frequently than annually, the amount so computed shall be multiplied by the number of periodic payments to be made during the taxable year for the purpose of determining the total amount which may be considered received as an annuity during such year. To this extent, the payments received shall be considered to represent a return of premiums or other consideration paid and shall be excludable from gross income in the taxable year in which received. See §1.72-4(d)(2), and (3). To the extent that the payments received under the contract during the taxable year exceed the total amount thus considered to be received as an annuity during such year, they shall be considered to be amounts not received as an annuity and shall be included in the gross income of the recipient. See section 72(e) and §1.72-11(b)(2).

(ii) For purposes of subdivision (i), the number of periodic payments anticipated during the time payments are to be made shall be determined by multiplying the number of payments to be made each year (a) by the number of years payments are to be made, or (b) if payments are to be made for a life or lives, by the multiple found by the use of the appropriate tables contained in §1.72-9, as adjusted in accordance with the table in §1.72-5(a)(2).

(iii) For an example of the computation to be made in accordance with this subparagraph and a special election which may be made in a taxable year subsequent to a taxable year in which the total payments received under a contract described in this subparagraph are less than the total of the amounts excludable from gross income in such year under subdivision (i), see §1.72-4(d)(3). [Reg. §1.72-2.]

☐ [*T.D.* 6211, 11-14-56. *Amended by T.D.* 6497, 10-19-60, *and by T.D.* 6885, 6-1-66.]

[Reg. §1.72-3]

§1.72-3. Excludable amounts not income.—In general, amounts received under contracts described in paragraph (a)(1) of §1.72-2 are not to be included in the income of the recipient to the extent that such amounts are excludable from gross income as the result of the application of section 72 and the regulations thereunder. [Reg. §1.72-3.]

☐ [*T.D.* 6211, 11-14-56.]

[Reg. §1.72-4]

§1.72-4. Exclusion ratio.—(a) *General rule.*—(1)(i) To determine the proportionate part of the total amount received each year as an annuity which is excludable from the gross income of a recipient in the taxable year of receipt (other than amounts received under (a) certain employee annuities described in section 72(d) and §1.72-13, or (b) certain annuities described in section 72(o) and §1.122-1), an exclusion ratio is to be determined for each contract. In general, this ratio is determined by dividing the investment in the contract as found under §1.72-6 by the expected return under such contract as found under §1.72-5. Where a single consideration is given for a particular contract which provides for two or more annuity elements, an exclusion ratio shall be determined for the contract as a whole by dividing the investment in such contract by the aggregate of the expected returns under all the annuity elements provided thereunder. However, where the provisions of paragraph (b)(3) of §1.72-2 apply to payments received under such a contract, see paragraph (b)(3) of §1.72-6. In the case of a contract to which §1.72-6(d) (relating to contracts in which amounts were invested both before July 1, 1986, and after June 30, 1986) applies, the exclusion ratio for purposes of this paragraph (a) is determined in accordance with §1.72-6(d) and, in particular, §1.72-6(d)(5)(i).

(ii) The exclusion ratio for the particular contract is then applied to the total amount received as an annuity during the taxable year by each recipient. See, however, paragraph (e)(3) of §1.72-5. Any excess of the total amount received as an annuity during the taxable year over the amount determined by the application of the exclusion ratio to such total amount shall be included in the gross income of the recipient for the taxable year of receipt.

(2) The principles of subparagraph (1) may be illustrated by the following example:

Example. Taxpayer A purchased an annuity contract providing for payments of $100 per month for a consideration of $12,650. Assuming that the expected return under this contract is $16,000 the exclusion ratio to be used by A is $12,650 ÷ [$]16,000; or 79.1 percent (79.06 rounded to the nearest tenth). If 12 such monthly payments are received by A during his taxable year, the total amount he may exclude from his gross income in such year is $949.20 ($1,200 × 79.1 percent). The balance of $250.80 ($1,200 less $949.20) is the amount to be included in gross income. If A instead received only five such payments during the year, he should exclude $395.50 ([$]500 × 79.1 percent) of the total amounts received.

For examples of the computation of the exclusion ratio in cases where two annuity elements are acquired for a single consideration, see paragraph (b)(1) of §1.72-6.

(3) The exclusion ratio shall be applied only to amounts received as an annuity within the meaning of that term under paragraph (b)(2) and (3) of §1.72-2. Where the periodic payments increase in amount after the annuity starting date in a manner not provided by the terms of the contract at such date, the portion of such payments representing the increase is not an amount received as an annuity. For the treatment of amounts not received as an annuity, see section 72(e) and §1.72-11. For special rules where paragraph (b)(3) of §1.72-2 applies to amounts received, see paragraph (d)(3) of this section.

(4) After an exclusion ratio has been determined for a particular contract, it shall be applied to any amounts received as an annuity thereunder unless or until one of the following occurs:

(i) The contract is assigned or transferred for a valuable consideration (see section 72(g) and paragraph (a) of §1.72-10);

(ii) The contract matures or is surrendered, redeemed, or discharged in accordance with the provisions of paragraph (c) or (d) of §1.72-11;

(iii) The contract is exchanged (or is considered to have been exchanged) in a manner described in paragraph (e) of §1.72-11.

(b) *Annuity starting date.*—(1) Except as provided in subparagraph (2) of this paragraph, the annuity starting date is the first day of the first period for which an amount is received as an annuity, except that if such date was before January 1, 1954, then the annuity starting date is January 1, 1954. The first day of the first period for which an amount is received as an annuity shall be whichever of the following is the later:

(i) The date upon which the obligations under the contract became fixed, or

(ii) The first day of the period (year, half-year, quarter, month, or otherwise, depending on whether payments are to be made annually, semiannually, quarterly, monthly, or otherwise) which ends on the date of the first annuity payment.

(2) Notwithstanding the provisions of paragraph (b)(1) of this section, the annuity starting date shall be determined in accordance with whichever of the following provisions is appropriate:

(i) In the case of a joint and survivor annuity contract described in section 72(i) and paragraph (b)(3) of §1.72-5, the annuity starting date is January 1, 1954, or the first day of the first period for which an amount is received as an annuity by the surviving annuitant, whichever is the later;

(ii) In the case of the transfer of an annuity contract for a valuable consideration, as described in section 72(g) and paragraph (a) of §1.72-10, the annuity starting date shall be January 1, 1954, or the first day of the first period for which the transferee received an amount as an annuity, whichever is the later;

(iii) If the provisions of paragraph (e) of §1.72-11 apply to an exchange of one contract for another, or to a transaction deemed to be such an exchange, the annuity starting date of the contract received (or deemed received) in exchange shall be January 1, 1954, or the first day of the first period for which an amount is received as an annuity under such contract, whichever is the later; and

(iv) In the case of an employee who has retired from work because of personal injuries or sickness, and who is receiving amounts under a plan that is a wage continuation plan under section 105(d) and §1.105-4, the annuity starting date shall be the date the employee reaches mandatory retirement age, as defined in §1.105-4(a)(3)(i)(B). (See, also §§1.72-15 and 1.105-6 for transitional and other special rules.)

(c) *Fiscal year taxpayers.*—Fiscal year taxpayers receiving amounts as annuities in a taxable year to which the Internal Revenue Code of

1954 applies shall determine the annuity starting date in accordance with section 72(c)(4) and this section. The annuity starting date for fiscal year taxpayers receiving amounts as an annuity in a taxable year to which the Internal Revenue Code of 1939 applies shall be January 1, 1954, except where the first day of the first period for which an amount is received by such a taxpayer as an annuity is subsequent thereto and before the end of a fiscal year to which the Internal Revenue Code of 1939 applied. In such case, the latter date shall be the annuity starting date. In all cases where a fiscal year taxpayer received an amount as an annuity in a taxable year to which the Internal Revenue Code of 1939 applied and subsequent to the annuity starting date determined in accordance with the provisions of this paragraph, such amount shall be disregarded for the purposes of section 72 and the regulations thereunder.

(d) *Exceptions to the general rule.*—(1) Where the provisions of section 72 would otherwise require an exclusion ratio to be determined, but the investment in the contract (determined under §1.72-6) is an amount of zero or less, no exclusion ratio shall be determined and all amounts received under such a contract shall be includible in the gross income of the recipient for the purposes of section 72.

(2) Where the investment in the contract is equal to or greater than the total expected return under such contract found under §1.72-5, the exclusion ratio shall be considered to be 100 percent and all amounts received as an annuity under such contract shall be excludable from the recipient's gross income. See, for example, paragraph (f)(1) of §1.72-5. In the case of a contract to which §1.72-6(d) (relating to contracts in which amounts were invested both before July 1, 1986, and after June 30, 1986) applies, this paragraph (d)(2) is applied in the manner prescribed in §1.72-6(d) and, in particular, §1.72-6(d)(5)(ii).

(3)(i) If a contract provides for payments to be made to a taxpayer in the manner described in paragraph (b)(3) of §1.72-2, the investment in the contract shall be considered to be equal to the expected return under such contract and the resulting exclusion ratio (100%) shall be applied to all amounts received as an annuity under such contract. For any taxable year, payments received under such a contract shall be considered to be amounts received as an annuity only to the extent that they do not exceed the portion of the investment in the contract which is properly allocable to that year and hence excludable from gross income as a return of premiums or other consideration paid for the contract. The portion of the investment in the contract which is properly allocable to any taxable year shall be determined by dividing the investment in the contract (adjusted for any refund feature in the manner described in paragraph (d) of §1.72-7) by the applicable multiple (whether for a term certain, life, or lives) which would otherwise be used in determining the expected return for such a contract under §1.72-5. The multiple shall be adjusted in accordance with the provisions of the table in paragraph (a)(2) of §1.72-5, if any adjustment is necessary, before making the above computation. If payments are to be made more frequently than annually and the number of payments to be made in the taxable year in which the annuity begins are less than the number of payments to be made each year thereafter, the amounts considered received as an annuity (as otherwise determined under this subdivision) shall not exceed, for such taxable year (including a short taxable year), an amount which bears the same ratio to the portion of the investment in the contract considered allocable to each taxable year as the number of payments to be made in the first year bears to the number of payments to be made in each succeeding year. Thus, if payments are to be made monthly, only seven payments will be made in the first taxable year, and the portion of the investment in the contract allocable to a full year of payments is $600, the amounts considered received as an annuity in the first taxable year cannot exceed $350 ($600 × 7/12). See subdivision (iii) of this subparagraph for an example illustrating the determination of the portion of the investment in the contract allocable to one taxable year of the taxpayer.

(ii) if subdivision (i) of this subparagraph applies to amounts received by a taxpayer and the total amount of payments he receives in a taxable year is less than the total amount excludable for such year under subdivision (i) of this subparagraph, the taxpayer may elect, in a succeeding taxable year in which he receives another payment, to redetermine the amounts to be received as an annuity during the current and succeeding taxable years. This shall be computed in accordance with the provisions of subdivision (i) of this subparagraph except that:

(a) The difference between the portion of the investment in the contract allocable to a taxable year, as found in accordance with subdivision (i) of this subparagraph, and the total payments actually received in the taxable year prior to the election shall be divided by the applicable life expectancy of the annuitant (or annuitants), found in accordance with the appropriate table in §1.72-9 (and adjusted in accordance with paragraph (a)(2) of §1.72-5), or by the remaining term of a term certain annuity, computed as of the first day of the

Reg. §1.72-4(d)(3)(ii)(a)

first period for which an amount is received as an annuity in the taxable year of the election; and

(b) The amount determined under (a) of this subdivision shall be added to the portion of the investment in the contract allocable to each taxable year (as otherwise found). To the extent that the total periodic payments received under the contract in the taxable year of the election or any succeeding taxable year does not equal this total sum, such payments shall be excludable from the gross income of the recipient. To the extent such payments exceed the sum so found, they shall be fully includible in the recipient's gross income. See subdivision (iii) of this subparagraph for an example illustrating the redetermination of amounts to be received as an annuity and subdivision (iv) of this subparagraph for the method of making the election provided by this subdivision.

(iii) The application of the principles of paragraph (d)(3)(i) and (ii) of this section may be illustrated by the following example:

Example. Taxpayer A, a 64 year old male, files his return on a calendar year basis and has a life expectancy of 15.6 years on June 30, 1954, the annuity starting date of a contract to which §1.72-2(b)(3) applies and which he purchased for $20,000. The contract provides for variable annual payments for his life. He receives a payment of $1,000 on June 30, 1955, but receives no other payment until June 30, 1957. He excludes the $1,000 payment from his gross income for the year 1955 since this amount is less than $1,324.50, the amount determined by dividing his investment in the contract ($20,000) by his life expectancy adjusted for annual payments, 15.1 (15.6-0.5), as of the original annuity starting date. Taxpayer A may elect, in his return for the taxable year 1957, to redetermine amounts to be received as an annuity under his contract as of June 30, 1956. For the purpose of determining the extent to which amounts received in 1957 or thereafter shall be considered amounts received as an annuity (to which a 100 percent exclusion ratio shall apply) he shall add $118.63 to the $1,324.50 originally determined to be receivable as an annuity under the contract, making a total of $1,443.13. This is determined by dividing the difference between what was excludable in 1955 and 1956, $2,649 (2 × $1,324.50) and what he actually received in those years ($1,000) by his life expectancy adjusted for annual payments, 13.9 (14.4 − 0.5), as of his age at his nearest birthday (66) on the first day of the first period for which he received an amount as an annuity in the taxable year of election (June 30, 1956). The result, $1,443.13, is excludable in that year and each year thereafter as an amount received as an annuity to which the 100% exclusion ratio applies. It will be noted that in this example the taxpayer received amounts less than the excludable amounts in two successive years and deferred making his election until the third year, and thus was able to accumulate the portion of the investment in the contract allocable to each taxable year to the extent he failed to receive such portion in both years. Assuming that he received $1,500 in the taxable year of his election, he would include $56.87 in his gross income and exclude $1,443.13 therefrom for that year.

(iv) If the taxpayer chooses to make the election described in subdivision (ii) of this subparagraph, he shall file with his return a statement that he elects to make a redetermination of the amounts excludable from gross income under his annuity contract in accordance with the provisions of paragraph (d)(3) of §1.72-4. This statement shall also contain the following information:

(a) The original annuity starting date and his age on that date,

(b) The date of the first day of the first period for which he received an amount in the current taxable year,

(c) The investment in the contract originally determined (as adjusted for any refund feature), and

(d) The aggregate of all amounts received under the contract between the date indicated in (a) of this subdivision and the day after the date indicated in (b) of this subdivision to the extent such amounts were excludable from gross income.

He shall include in gross income any amounts received during the taxable year for which the return is made in accordance with the redetermination made under this subparagraph.

(v) In the case of a contract to which §1.72-6(d) (relating to contracts in which amounts were invested both before July 1, 1986, and after June 30, 1986) applies, this paragraph (d)(3) is applied in the manner prescribed in §1.72-6(d) and, in particular, §1.72-6(d)(5)(iii). This application may be illustrated by the following example:

Example. B, a male calendar year taxpayer, purchases a contract which provides for variable annual payments for life and to which §1.72-2(b)(3) applies. The annuity starting date of the contract is June 30, 1990, when B is 64 years old. B receives a payment of $1,000 on June 30, 1991, but receives no other payment until June 30, 1993. B's total investment in the contract is $25,000. B's pre-July 1986 investment in the contract is $12,000. If B makes the election described in §1.72-6(d)(6), separate computations are required to determine the amounts received as an annuity and excludable from gross income with respect to the pre-July 1986 investment in the contract and the post-June 1986 investment in the contract. In the separate computations, B first determines the applicable portions of the total payment received which are allocable to the pre-July 1986 investment in the contract and the post-June 1986 investment in the contract. The portion of the payment received allocable to the pre-July 1986 investment in the contract is $480 ($12,000/$25,000 × $1,000). The portion of the payment received allocable to the post-June 1986 investment in the contract is $520 ($13,000/$25,000 × $1,000).

Second, B determines the pre-July 1986 investment in the contract and the post-June 1986 investment in the contract allocable to the taxable year by dividing the pre-July 1986 and post-June 1986 investments in the contract by the applicable life expectancy multiple. The life expectancy multiple applicable to pre-July 1986 investment in the contract is B's life expectancy as of the original annuity starting date adjusted for annual payments and is determined under Table I of §1.72-9 [15.1 (15.6 − 0.5)]. The life expectancy multiple applicable to post-June 1986 investment in the contract is determined under Table V of §1.72-9 (20.3 (20.8 − 0.5)). Thus, the pre-July 1986 investment in the contract allocable to each taxable year is $794.70 ($12,000 ÷ 15.1) and the post-June 1986 investment in the contract so allocable is $640.39 ($13,000 ÷ 20.3). Because the applicable portions of the total payment received in 1991 under the contract ($480 allocable to the pre-July 1986 investment in the contract and $520 allocable to the post-June 1986 investment in the contract) are treated as amounts received as an annuity and are excludable from gross income to the extent they do not exceed the portion of the corresponding investment in the contract allocable to 1991 ($794.70 pre-July 1986 investment in the contract and $640.39 post-June 1986 investment in the contract), the entire amount of each applicable portion of the total payment is excludable from gross income. B may elect, in the return filed for taxable year 1993, to redetermine amounts to be received as an annuity under the contract as of June 30, 1992. The extent to which the amounts received in 1993 or thereafter shall be considered amounts received as an annuity is determined as follows:

Pre-July 1986 investment in the contract allocable to taxable years 1991 and 1992 ($794.70 × 2)	$1,589.40
Less: Portion of total payments allocable to pre-July 1986 investment in the contract actually received as an annuity in taxable years 1991 and 1992	480.00
	1,109.40
Divided by: Life expectancy multiple applicable to pre-July 1986 investment in the contract for B, age 66 (14.4 − 0.5)	13.9
	79.81
Plus: Amount originally determined with respect to pre-July 1986 investment in the contract	794.70
Pre-July 1986 amount	874.51
Post-June 1986 investment in the contract allocable to taxable years 1991 and 1992 ($640.39 × 2)	$1,280.78
Less: Portion of total payments allocable to post-June 1986 investment in the contract actually received as an annuity in taxable years 1991 and 1992	520.00
	760.78
Divided by: Life expectancy multiple applicable to post-June 1986 investment in the contract for B, age 66 (19.2 − 0.5)	18.7
	40.68
Plus: Amount originally determined with respect to post-June 1986 investment in the contract	640.39
Post-June 1986 amount	681.07

Reg. §1.72-4(d)(3)(ii)(b)

(vi) The method of making an election to perform the separate computations illustrated in paragraph (d)(3)(v) of this section is described in §1.72-6(d)(6).

(e) *Exclusion ratio in the case of two or more annuity elements acquired for a single consideration.*—(1)(i) Where two or more annuity elements are provided under a contract described in paragraph (a)(2) of §1.72-2, an exclusion ratio shall be determined for the contract as a whole and applied to all amounts received as an annuity under any of the annuity elements. To obtain this ratio, the investment in the contract determined in accordance with §1.72-6 shall be divided by the aggregate of the expected returns found with respect to each of the annuity elements in accordance with §1.72-5. For this purpose, it is immaterial that payments under one or more of the annuity elements involved have not commenced at the time when an amount is first received as an annuity under one or more of the other annuity elements.

(ii) The exclusion ratio found under subdivision (i) of this subparagraph does not apply to:

(a) An annuity element payable to a surviving annuitant under a joint and survivor annuity contract to which section 72(i) and paragraphs (b)(3) and (e)(3) of §1.72-5 apply, or to

(b) A contract under which one or more of the constituent annuity elements provides for payments described in paragraph (b)(3) of §1.72-2.

For rules with respect to a contract providing for annuity elements described in (b) of this subdivision, see subparagraph (2) of this paragraph.

(2) If one or more of the annuity elements under a contract described in paragraph (a)(2) of §1.72-2 provides for payments to which paragraph (b)(3) of §1.72-2 applies:

(i) With respect to the annuity elements to which paragraph (b)(3) of §1.72-2 does not apply, an exclusion ratio shall be determined by dividing the portion of the investment in the entire contract which is properly allocable to all such elements (in the manner provided in paragraph (b)(3)(ii) of §1.72-6) by the aggregate of the

Monthly payment of $100 × 12 months equals annual payment of $1,200
Multiple shown in Table I, male, age 66 . . . .   14.4
Expected return ($1,200 × 14.4)   17,280

If, however, the taxpayer had purchased the contract after June 30, 1986, the expected return would be $23,040, determined by multiplying 19.2 (multiple shown in Table V, age 66) by $1,200.

(2)(i) If payments are to be made quarterly, semiannually, or annually, an adjustment of the applicable multiple shown in Table I or V (whichever is applicable) may be required. A further adjustment

expected returns thereunder and such ratio shall be applied in the manner described in subdivision (i) of subparagraph (1); and

(ii) With respect to the annuity elements to which paragraph (b)(3) of §1.72-2 does apply, the investment in the entire contract shall be reduced by the portion thereof found in subdivision (i) of this subparagraph and the resulting amount shall be used to determine the extent to which the aggregate of the payments received during the taxable year under all such elements is excludable from gross income. The amount so excludable shall be allocated to each recipient under such elements in the same ratio that the total of payments he receives each year bears to the total of the payments received by all such recipients during the year. The exclusion ratio with respect to the amounts so allocated shall be 100 percent. See paragraph (f)(2) of §1.72-5 and paragraph (b)(3) of §1.72-6.

(iii) In the case of a contract to which §1.72-6(d) (relating to contracts in which amounts were invested both before July 1, 1986, and after June 30, 1986) applies, this paragraph (e) is applied in the manner prescribed in §1.72-6(d) and, in particular, §1.72-6(d)(5)(iv). [Reg. §1.72-4.]

☐ [*T.D. 6211, 11-14-56. Amended by T.D. 7043, 6-1-70, T.D. 7352, 4-9-75, and T.D. 8115, 12-16-86.*]

[Reg. §1.72-5]

§1.72-5. **Expected return.**—(a) *Expected return for but one life.*—(1) If a contract to which section 72 applies provides that one annuitant is to receive a fixed monthly income for life, the expected return is determined by multiplying the total of the annuity payments to be received annually by the multiple shown in Table I or V (whichever is applicable) of §1.72-9 under the age (as of the annuity starting date) and, if applicable, sex of the measuring life (usually the annuitant's). Thus, where a male purchases a contract before July 1, 1986, providing for an immediate annuity of $100 per month for his life and, as of the annuity starting date (in this case the date of purchase), the annuitant's age at his nearest birthday is 66, the expected return is computed as follows:

may be required where the interval between the annuity starting date and the date of the first payment is less than the interval between future payments. Neither adjustment shall be made, however, if the payments are to be made more frequently than quarterly. The amount of the adjustment, if any, is to be found in accordance with the following table:

If the number of whole months from the annuity starting date to the first payment date is—	0-1	2	3	4	5	6	7	8	9	10	11	12
And payments under the contract are to be made:												
Annually	+0.5	+0.4	+0.3	+0.2	+0.1	0	0	−0.1	−0.2	−0.3	−0.4	−0.5
Semiannually	+.2	+.1	0	0	−.1	−.2						
Quarterly	+.1	0	−.1	...	...	...	...	...	...	...	...	...

Thus, for a male, age 66, the multiple found in Table I, adjusted for quarterly payments the first of which is to be made one full month after the annuity starting date, is 14.5 (14.4 + 0.1); for semiannual payments the first of which is to be made six full months from the annuity starting date, the adjusted multiple is 14.2 (14.4 − 0.2); for annual payments the first of which is to be made one full month from the annuity starting date, the adjusted multiple is 14.9 (14.4 + 0.5). If the annuitant in the example shown in subparagraph (1) of this paragraph were to receive an annual payment of $1,200 commencing 12 full months after his annuity starting date, the amount of the expected return would be $16,680 ($1,200 × 13.9 [14.4 − 0.5]). Similarly, for an annuitant, age 50, the multiple found in Table V, adjusted for quarterly payments the first of which is to be made one full month after the annuity starting date, is 33.2 (33.1 + 0.1); for semiannual payments the first of which is to be made six full months from the annuity starting date, the adjusted multiple is 32.9 (33.1 − 0.2); for annual payments the first of which is to be made one full month from the annuity starting date, the adjusted multiple is 33.6 (33.1 + 0.5).

(ii) Notwithstanding the table in subdivision (i) of this subparagraph, adjustments of multiples for early or other than monthly payments determined prior to February 19, 1956, under the table prescribed in paragraph 1(b)(4) of T.D. 6118 (19 FR 9897, C.B. 1955-1, 699), approved December 30, 1954, need not be redetermined.

(3) If the contract provides for fixed payments to be made to an annuitant until death or until the expiration of a specified limited period, whichever occurs earlier, the expected return of such temporary life annuity is determined by multiplying the total of the annuity payments to be received annually by the multiple shown in Table IV or VII (whichever is applicable) of §1.72-9 for the age (as of the annuity starting date) and, if applicable, sex of the annuitant and the nearest whole number of years in the specified period. For example, if a male annuitant, age 60 (at his nearest birthday), is to receive $60 per month for five years or until he dies, whichever is earlier, and there is no post-June 1986, investment in the contract, the expected return under such a contract is $3,456, computed as follows:

Monthly payments of $60 × 12 months equals annual payment of $720
Multiple shown in Table IV for male, age 60, for term of 5 years 4.8
Expected return for 5-year temporary life annuity of $720 per year ($720 × 4.8) $3,456

If the annuitant purchased the same contract after June 30, 1986, the expected return under the contract would be $3,528, computed as follows:

Monthly payments of $60 × 12 months equals annual payment of	$720.00
Multiple shown in Table VIII for annuitant, age 60, for term of 5 years	4.9
Expected return for 5-year temporary life annuity of $720 per year ($720 × 4.9)	$3,528.00

The adjustment provided by subparagraph (2) of this paragraph shall not be made with respect to the multiple found in Table IV or VIII (whichever is applicable).

(4) If the contract provides for payments to be made to an annuitant for the annuitant's lifetime, but the amount of the annual payments is to be decreased after the expiration of a specified limited period, the expected return is computed by considering the contract as a combination of a whole life annuity for the smaller amount plus a temporary life annuity for an amount equal to the difference between the larger and the smaller amount. For example, if a male annuitant, age 60, is to receive $150 per month for five years or until his earlier death, and is to receive $90 per month for the remainder of his lifetime after such five years, the expected return is computed as if the annuitant's contract consisted of a whole life annuity for $90 per month plus a five-year temporary life annuity of $60 per month. In such circumstances, the expected return if there is no post-June 1986 investment in the contract is computed as follows:

Monthly payments of $90 × 12 months equals annual payment of	$1,080
Multiple shown in Table I for male, age 60	18.2
Expected return for whole life annuity of $1,080 per year	$19,656
Expected return for 5-year temporary life annuity of $720 per year (as found in subparagraph (3) of this paragraph (a))	$3,456
Total expected return	$23,112

If the annuitant purchased the same contract after June 30, 1986, the expected return would be $29,664, computed as follows:

Monthly payments of $90 × 12 months equals annual payment of	$1,080
Multiple shown in Table V for annuitant, age 60	24.2
Expected return for whole life annuity of $1,080 per year	$26,136
Plus: Expected return for 5-year temporary life annuity of $720 per year (as found in subparagraph (3) of this paragraph (a))	$3,528
Total expected return	$29,664

If payments are to be made quarterly, semiannually, or annually, an appropriate adjustment of the multiple found in Table I or V (whichever is applicable) for the whole life annuity should be made in accordance with subparagraph (2) of this paragraph.

(5) If the contract described in subparagraph (4) of this paragraph provided that the amount of the annual payments to the annuitant were to be increased (instead of decreased) after the expiration of a specified limited period, the expected return would be computed as if the annuitant's contract consisted of a whole life annuity for the larger amount minus a temporary life annuity for an amount equal to the difference between the larger and smaller amount. Thus, if the annuitant described in subparagraph (4) of this paragraph were to receive $90 per month for five years or until his earlier death, and to receive $150 per month for the remainder of his lifetime after such five years, the expected return would be computed by subtracting the expected return under a five year temporary life annuity of $60 per month from the expected return under a whole life annuity of $150 per month. In such circumstances, the expected return if there is no post-June 1986 investment in the contract is computed as follows:

Monthly payments of $150 × 12 months equals annual payment of	$1,800
Multiple shown in Table I (male, age 60)	18.2
Expected return for annuity for whole life of $1,800 per year	$32,760
Less expected return for 5-year temporary life annuity of $720 per year (as found in subparagraph (3))	$3,456
Net expected return	$29,304

If the annuitant purchased the same contract after June 30, 1986, the expected return would be $40,032, computed as follows:

Monthly payments of $150 × 12 months equals annual payments of	$1,800
Multiple shown in Table V (age 60)	24.2
Expected return for annuity for whole life of $1,800 per year	$43,560
Less expected return for 5-year temporary life annuity of $720 per year (as found in subparagraph (3) of this paragraph (a))	$3,528
Net expected return	$40,032

If payments are to be made quarterly, semiannually, or annually, an appropriate adjustment of the multiple found in Table I or V (whichever is applicable) for the whole life annuity should be made in accordance with subparagraph (2) of this paragraph.

(b) *Expected return under joint and survivor and joint annuities.*— (1) In the case of a joint and survivor annuity contract involving two annuitants which provides the first annuitant with a fixed monthly income for life and, after the death of the first annuitant, provides an identical monthly income for life to a second annuitant, the expected return shall be determined by multiplying the total amount of the payments to be received annually by the multiple obtained from Table II or VI (whichever is applicable) of §1.72-9 under the ages (as of the annuity starting date) and, if applicable, sexes of the living annuitants. For example, a husband purchases a joint and survivor annuity contract providing for payments of $100 per month for life and, after his death, for the same amount to his wife for the remainder of her life. As of the annuity starting date his age at his nearest birthday is 70 and that of his wife at her nearest birthday is 67. If there is no post-June 1986 investment in the contract, the expected return is computed as follows:

Monthly payments of $100 × 12 months equals annual payment of	$1,200
Multiple shown in Table II (male, age 70, female, age 67)	19.7
Expected return ($1,200 × 19.7)	$23,640

If the annuitants purchased the same contract after June 30, 1986, the expected return would be $26,400, computed as follows:

Monthly payments of $100 × 12 months equals annual payment of	$1,200
Multiple shown in Table VI (ages 70, 67)	22.0
Expected return ($1,200 × 22.0)	$26,400

If payments are to be made quarterly, semiannually, or annually, an appropriate adjustment of the multiple found in Table II or VI (whichever is applicable) should be made in accordance with paragraph (a)(2) of this section.

Reg. §1.72-5(a)(4)

(2) If a contract of the type described in subparagraph (1) of this paragraph provides that a different (rather than an identical) monthly income is payable to the second annuitant, the expected return is computed in the following manner. The applicable multiple in Table II or VI (whichever is applicable) is first found as in the example in subparagraph (1) of this paragraph. The multiple applicable to the first annuitant is then found in Table I or V (whichever is applicable) as though the contract were for a single life annuity. The multiple from Table I or V is then subtracted from the multiple obtained from Table II or VI and the resulting multiple is applied to the total payments to be received annually under the contract by the second annuitant. The result is the expected return with respect to the second annuitant. The portion of the expected return with respect to payments to be made during the first annuitant's life is then computed by applying the multiple found in Table I or V to the total annual payments to be received by such annuitant under the contract. The expected returns with respect to each of the annuitants separately are then aggregated to obtain the expected return under the entire contract.

Example (1). A husband purchases a joint and survivor annuity providing for payments of $100 per month for his life and, after his death, payments to his wife of $50 per month for her life. As of the annuity starting date his age at his nearest birthday is 70 and that of his wife at her nearest birthday is 67. There is no post-June 1986 investment in the contract.

Multiple from Table II (male, age 70, female, age 67)	19.7
Multiple from Table I (male, age 70)	12.1
Difference (multiple applicable to second annuitant)	7.6
Portion of expected return, second annuitant ($600 × 7.6)	$4,560
Portion of expected return, first annuitant ($1,200 × 12.1)	$14,520
Expected return under the contract	$19,080

The expected return thus found, $19,080, is to be used in computing the amount to be excluded from gross income. Thus, if the investment in the contract in this example is $14,310, the exclusion ratio is $14,310 ÷ $19,080, or 75 percent. The amount excludable from each monthly payment made to the husband is 75 percent of $100, or $75, and the remaining $25 of each payment received by him shall be included in his gross income. After the husband's death, the amount excludable by the second annuitant (the surviving wife) would be 75 percent of each monthly payment of $50, or $37.50, and the remaining $12.50 of each payment shall be included in her gross income.

Example (2). If the same contract were purchased after June 30, 1986, the expected return would be $22,800, computed as follows:

Multiple from Table VI (ages 70, 67)	22.0
Multiple from Table V (age 70)	16.0
Difference (multiple applicable to second annuitant)	6.0
Portion of expected return, second annuitant ($600 × 6.0)	$3,600
Plus: Portion of expected return, first annuitant ($1,200 × 16.0)	$19,200
Expected return under the contract	$22,800

If the investment in the contract is $14,310, the exclusion ratio is $14,310 ÷ $22,800, or 62.8 percent. Thus, the husband would exclude $62.80 of each $100 payment received by him. After his death, his wife would exclude 62.8 percent, or $31.40, of each $50 monthly payment.

Example (3). If amounts were invested in the same contract both before July 1, 1986, and after June 30, 1986, and the election described in §1.72-6(d)(6) were made, two exclusion ratios would be determined pursuant to §1.72-6(d). Assume that the husband's total investment in the contract is $14,310 and that $7,310 is the pre-July 1986 investment in the contract. The pre-July 1986 exclusion ratio would be $7,310 ÷ $19,080, or 38.3 percent. The post-June 1986 exclusion ratio would be $7,000 ÷ $22,800, or 30.7 percent. The husband would exclude $69.00 ($38.30 + $30.70) of the $100 monthly payment received by him. The remaining $31.00 would be included in his gross income. After the husband's death, the amount excludable by his wife would be $34.50 (38.3 percent of $50 plus 30.7 percent of $50). The remaining $15.50 would be included in gross income.

The same method is used if the payments are to be increased after the death of the first annuitant. Thus, if the payments to be made until the husband's death were $50 per month and his widow were to receive $100 per month thereafter until her death, the 7.6 multiple in example (1) above would be applied to the $100 payments, yielding an expected return with respect to this portion of the annuity contract of $9,120 ($1,200 × 7.6). An expected return of $7,260 ($600 × 12.1) would be obtained with respect to the payments to be made to the husband, yielding a total expected return under the contract of $16,380 ($9,120 plus $7,260). If payments are to be made quarterly, semiannually, or annually, an appropriate adjustment of the multiples found in Tables I and II or Tables V and VI (whichever are applicable) should be made in accordance with paragraph (a)(2) of this section.

(3) In the case of a joint and survivor annuity contract in respect of which the first annuitant died in 1951, 1952, or 1953, and the basis of the surviving annuitant's interest in the contract was determinable under section 113(a)(5) of the Internal Revenue Code of 1939, such basis shall be considered the "aggregate of premiums or other consideration paid" by the surviving annuitant for the contract. (For rules governing this determination, see 26 CFR (1939) 39.22(b)(2)-2 and 39.113(a)(5)-1 (Regulations 118).) In determining such an annuitant's investment in the contract, such aggregate shall be reduced by any amounts received under the contract by the surviving annuitant before the annuity starting date, to the extent such amounts were excludable from his gross income at the time of receipt. The expected return of the surviving annuitant in such cases shall be determined in the manner prescribed in paragraph (a) of this section, as though the surviving annuitant alone were involved. For this purpose, the appropriate multiple for the survivor shall be obtained from Table I as of the annuity starting date determined in accordance with paragraph (b)(2)(i) of §1.72-4.

(4) If a contract involving two annuitants provides for fixed monthly payments to be made as a joint life annuity until the death of the first annuitant to die (in other words, only as long as both remain alive), the expected return under such contract shall be determined by multiplying the total of the annuity payments to be received annually under the contract by the multiple obtained from Table IIA or VIA (whichever is applicable) of §1.72-9 under the ages (as of the annuity starting date) and, if applicable, sexes of the annuitants. If, however, payments are to be made under the contract quarterly, semiannually, or annually, an appropriate adjustment of the multiple found in Table IIA or VIA shall be made in accordance with paragraph (a)(2) of this section.

(5) If a joint and survivor annuity contract involving two annuitants provides that a specified amount shall be paid during their joint lives and a different specified amount shall be paid to the survivor upon the death of whichever of the annuitants is the first to die, the following preliminary computation shall be made in all cases preparatory to determining the expected return under the contract:

(i) From Table II or VI (whichever is applicable), obtain the multiple under both of the annuitants' ages (as of the annuity starting date) and, if applicable, their appropriate sexes;

(ii) From Table IIA or VIA (whichever is applicable), obtain the multiple applicable to both annuitants' ages (as of the annuity starting date) and, if applicable, their appropriate sexes;

(iii) Apply the multiple found in subdivision (i) of this subparagraph to the total of the amounts to be received annually after the death of the first to die; and

(iv) Apply the multiple found in subdivision (ii) of this subparagraph to the difference between the total of amounts to be received annually before and the total of the amounts to be received annually after the death of the first to die.

If the original annual payment is in excess of the annual payment to be made after the death of the first to die, the expected return is the sum of the amounts determined under subdivisions (iii) and (iv) of this subparagraph. This may be illustrated by the following examples:

Example (1). A husband purchases a joint and survivor annuity providing for payments of $100 per month for as long as both he and his wife live, and, after the death of the first to die, payments to the survivor of $75 a month for life. As of the annuity starting date, his age at his nearest birthday is 70 and that of his wife at her nearest birthday is 67. If there is no post-June 1986 investment in the contract, the expected return under the contract is computed as follows:

Multiple from Table II (male age 70, female age 67)	19.7
Multiple from Table IIA (male age 70, female age 67)	9.3
Portion of expected return ($900 × 19.7—sum per year after first death)	$17,730
Plus: Portion of expected return ($300 × 9.3—amount of change in sum at first death)	$2,790
Expected return under the contract	$20,520

The total expected return in this example, $20,520, is to be used in computing the amount to be excluded from gross income. Thus, if the investment in the contract is $17,887, the exclusion ratio is $17,887 ÷ $20,520, or 87.2 percent. The amount excludable from each monthly payment made while both are alive is 87.2 percent of $100, or $87.20, and the remaining $12.80 of each payment shall be included in gross income. After the death of the first to die, the amount excludable by

the survivor shall be 87.2 percent of each monthly payment of $75, or $65.40, and the remaining $9.60 of each payment shall be included in gross income.

Example (2). Assume the same facts as in example (1), except that the contract is purchased after June 30, 1986.

The expected return under the contract is computed as follows:

Multiple from Table VI (ages 70, 67)	22.0
Multiple from Table VIA (ages 70, 67)	12.4
Portion of expected return ($900 × 22.0—sum per year after first death)	$19,800
Plus: Portion of expected return ($300 × 12.4—amount of change in sum at first death)	$3,720
Expected return under the contract	$23,520

Thus, if the investment in the contract is $17,887, the exclusion ratio is $17,887 ÷ $23,520, or 76.1 percent. The amount excludable from each monthly payment made while both are alive would be 76.1 percent of $100, or $76.10, and the remaining $23.90 of each payment would be included in gross income. After the death of the first to die, the amount excludable by the survivor would be 76.1 percent of each monthly payment of $75, or $57.08, and the remaining $17.92 of each payment would be included in gross income.

Example (3). Assume the same facts as in examples (1) and (2), except that the total investment in the contract is $17,887, and that the pre-July 1986 investment in the contract is $8,000. Assume also that one of the annuitants makes the election described in § 1.72-6(d)(6). Separate computations shall be performed pursuant to § 1.72-6(d) to determine the amount excludable from gross income. The pre-July 1986 exclusion ratio would be $8,000 ÷ $20,520, or 39 percent. The post-June 1986 exclusion ratio would be $9,887 ÷ $23,520, or 42 percent. The amount excludable from each monthly payment made while both are alive would be $81 ((.39 × 100) + (.42 × 100)), and the remaining $19 would be included in gross income. After the death of the first to die, the amount excludable by the survivor would be $60.75 ((.39 × 75) + (.42 × 75)), and the remaining $14.25 would be included in gross income.

If the original annual payment is less than the annual payment to be made after the death of the first to die, the expected return is the difference between the amounts determined under subdivisions (iii) and (iv) of this subparagraph. If, however, payments are to be made

quarterly, semiannually, or annually under the contract, the multiples obtained from both Tables II and IIA or Tables VI and VIA (whichever are applicable) shall first be adjusted in a manner prescribed in paragraph (a)(2) of this section.

(6) If a contract provides for the payment of life annuities to two persons during their respective lives and, after the death of one (without regard to which one dies first), provides that the survivor shall receive for life both his own annuity payments and the payments made formerly to the deceased person, the expected return shall be determined in accordance with paragraph (e)(4) of this section.

(7) If paragraph (b)(3) of § 1.72-2 applies to payments provided under a contract and this paragraph applies to such payments, the principles of this paragraph shall be used in making the computations described in paragraph (d)(3) of § 1.72-4. This may be illustrated by the following examples, examples (1) through (3) of which assume that there is no post-June 1986 investment in the contract:

Example (1). Taxpayer A, a male age 63, pays $24,000 for a contract which provides that the proceeds (both income and return of capital) from eight units of an investment fund shall be paid monthly to him for his life and that after his death the proceeds from six such units shall be paid monthly to B, a female age 55, for her life. The portion of the investment in the contract allocable to each taxable year of A is $955.20 and that allocable to each taxable year of B is $716.40. This is determined in the following manner:

Multiple from Table II (male, age 63, and female, age 55)	28.1
Number of units to be paid, in effect, as a joint and survivor annuity	× 6
Number of total annual unit payments anticipatable with respect to the joint and survivor annuity element	168.6
Multiple from Table I (male, age 63)	16.2
Number of units to be paid, in effect, as a single life annuity	× 2
Number of total annual unit payments anticipatable with respect to A alone	32.4
Total number of unit payments anticipatable	201
Portion of investment in the contract allocable to unit payments ($24,000 ÷ 201) on an annual basis	$119.40
Number of units payable to A while he continues to live	× 8
Portion of the investment in the contract allocable to each taxable year of A	$955.20
Portion of investment in the contract allocable to unit payments ($24,000 ÷ 201) on an annual basis	$119.40
Number of units payable to B for her life after A's death	× 6
Portion of the investment in the contract allocable to each taxable year of B	$716.40

For the purpose of the above computation it is immaterial whether or not A lives to or beyond the life expectancy shown for him in Table I.

Example (2). Assume that Taxpayer A in example (1) receives payments for five years which are at least as large as the portion of the investment in the contract allocable to such years, but in the sixth year he receives a total of only $626.40 rather than the $955.20 allocable to such year. A is 69 and B is 61 at the beginning of the first monthly period for which an amount is payable in the seventh taxable year. A makes the election in that year provided under paragraph (d)(3) of § 1.72-4. The difference between the portion of the investment in the contract allocable to the sixth year and the amount actually received in that year is $328.80 ($955.20 less $626.40). In this case, 139.2 unit payments are anticipatable (on an annual basis), since the appropriate multiple from Table II of § 1.72-9, 23.2, multiplied by the number of units payable, in effect, as a joint and survivor annuity yields this result (6 × 23.2). A's appropriate multiple from Table I of § 1.72-9 for the two units which will cease to be paid at his death is 12.6, and the total number of unit payments anticipatable (on an annual basis) is, therefore, 164.4 (2 × 12.6 plus 139.2). Dividing the

difference previously found ($328.80) by the total number of unit payments thus determined (164.4) indicates that A will have an additional allocation of the investment in the contract of $16 to the seventh and every succeeding full taxable year (8 units × $2), and B will have an additional allocation of the investment in the contract of $12 (6 units × $2) to each taxable year in which she received 12 monthly payments subsequent to the death of A. The total allocable to each taxable year of A is, therefore, $971.20, and that allocable to each taxable year of B will be $728.40.

Example (3). If, in example (2), A had died at the end of the fifth year, in the sixth year B would have received a payment of $469.80 (that portion of the $626.40 that A would have received which is in the same ratio that 6 units bear to 8 units) and would thus have received $246.60 less than the portion of the investment in the contract originally determined to be allocable to each of her taxable years. In these circumstances, B would be entitled to elect to redetermine the portion of the investment in the contract allocable to the taxable year of election and all subsequent years. The new amount allocable thereto would be found by dividing the $246.60 difference by her life expectancy as of the first day of the first period for which she received an amount as an annuity in the seventh year of the annuity contract, and adding the result to her originally determined allocation of $716.40.

Example (4). On July 1, 1986, Taxpayer C, age 60, pays $28,000 for a contract which provides that the proceeds (both income and return of capital) from 10 units of an investment fund shall be paid monthly to C for C's life and that after C's death the proceeds from 4 such units shall be paid monthly to D, age 57, for D's life. The portion of the investment in the contract allocable to each taxable year of C is $1,037.00 and that allocable to each taxable year of D is $414.80. This is determined as follows:

Multiple for Table VI (ages 60, 57)	31.2
Number of units to be paid, in effect, as a joint and survivor annuity	×4
Number of total annual unit payments anticipatable with respect to the joint and survivor annuity element	124.8
Multiple from Table V (age 60)	24.2
Number of units to be paid, in effect, as a single life annuity	×6
Number of total annual unit payments anticipatable with respect to C alone	145.2
Total number of unit payments anticipatable	270
Portion of investment in the contract allocable to unit payments ($28,000 ÷ 270) on an annual basis	103.70
Number of units payable to C while C continues to live	×10
Portion of the investment in the contract allocable to each taxable year of C	$1,037.00
Portion of investment in the contract allocable to unit payments ($28,000 ÷ 270) on an annual basis	$103.70
Number of units payable to D for D's life after C's death	×4
Portion of the investment in the contract allocable to each taxable year of D	$414.80

For purposes of the above computation it is immaterial whether or not C lives to or beyond the life expectancy shown in Table V.

Example (5). Assume the same facts as in example (4), except that C's total investment in the contract is $28,000, and C's pre-July 1986 investment in the contract is $16,000. If C makes the election described in §1.72-6(d)(6), separate computations are required to determine the amount excludable from gross income with respect to the pre-July 1986 investment in the contract and the post-June 1986 investment in the contract. The annuitant shall apply the appropriate pre-July 1986 and post-June 1986 life expectancy multiples to the applicable portions of the units to be paid as a joint and survivor annuity, and as a single life annuity.

Pre-July 1986 Computation (all references to unit payments are to the pre-July 1986 applicable portion of such payments):

Multiple from Table II (male, age 60, female, age 57)	27.6
Number of units to be paid, in effect, as a joint and survivor annuity	×4
Number of total annual unit payments anticipatable with respect to the joint and survivor annuity element	110.40
Multiple from Table I (male, age 60)	18.2
Number of units to be paid, in effect, as a single life annuity	×6
Number of total annual unit payments anticipatable with respect to C alone	109.20
Total number of unit payments anticipatable	219.6
Portion of pre-July 1986 investment in the contract allocable to unit payments ($16,000 ÷ 219.60) on an annual basis	$72.86
Number of units payable to C while C continues to live	×10
Portion of pre-July 1986 investment in the contract allocable to each taxable year of C	728.60
Portion of pre-July 1986 investment in the contract allocable to unit payments ($16,000 ÷ 219.60) on an annual basis	72.86
Number of units payable to D for D's life after C's death	×4
Portion of pre-July 1986 investment in the contract allocable to each taxable year of D	$291.44

Post-June 1986 Computation (all references to unit payments are to the post-June 1986 applicable portion of such payments):

Multiple from Table VI (ages 60, 57)	31.2
Number of units to be paid, in effect, as a joint and survivor annuity	×4
Number of total annual unit payments anticipatable with respect to the joint and survivor annuity element	$124.80
Multiple from Table V (age 60)	24.2
Number of units to be paid, in effect, as a single life annuity	×6
Number of total annual unit payments anticipatable with respect to C alone	145.20
Total number of unit payments anticipatable	270
Portion of post-June 1986 investment in the contract allocable to unit payments ($12,000 ÷ 270) on an annual basis	$44.44
Number of units payable to C while C continues to live	×10
Portion of post-June 1986 investment in the contract allocable to each taxable year of C	$444.40
Portion of post-June 1986 investment in the contract allocable to unit payments ($12,000 ÷ 270) on an annual basis	44.44
Number of units payable to D for D's life after C's death	×4
Portion of post-June 1986 investment in the contract allocable to each taxable year of D	$177.78

Total computation:

Total portion of the investment in the contract allocable to each taxable year of C ($728.60 + $444.40)	$1,173.00
Total portion of the investment in the contract allocable to each taxable year of D ($291.44 + $177.78)	$469.22

Example (6). Assume that taxpayer C in example (4) receives payments for four years which are at least as large as the portion of the investment in the contract allocable to such years, but in the fifth year receives a total of only $600 rather than the $1,037 allocable to such year. C is 65 and D is 62 at the beginning of the first monthly period for which an amount is payable in the sixth taxable year. C makes the election in that year provided under paragraph (d)(3) of §1.72-4. The difference between the portion of the investment in the contract allocable to the fifth year and the amount actually received in that year is $437 ($1,037 – $600). In this case, 106 unit payments are anticipatable with respect to the joint and survivor annuity element, since the appropriate multiple from Table VI of §1.72-9, 26.5, multiplied by the number of units payable, in effect, as a joint and survivor annuity yields this result (4 × 26.5). C's appropriate multiple from

Table V of §1.72-9 for the six units which will cease to be paid at C's death is 20.0, and the number of unit payments anticipatable with respect to C alone is 120 (6 × 20). The total number of unit payments anticipatable is, therefore, 226 (120 plus 106). Dividing the difference previously found ($437) by the total number of unit payments thus determined (226) indicates that C will have an additional allocation of the investment in the contract of $19.30 to the sixth and every succeeding full taxable year (10 units × $1.93), and D will have an additional allocation of the investment in the contract of $7.72 (4 units × $1.93) to each taxable year in which D receives 12 monthly payments subsequent to the death of C. The total allocable to each taxable year of C is, therefore, $1,056.30, and that allocable to each taxable year of D will be $422.52.

Example (7). If, in example (6), C had died at the end of the fourth year, in the fifth year D would have received a payment of $240 (that portion of the $600 that C would have received which is in the same ratio that 4 units bear to 10 units) and would thus have received $174.80 less than the portion of the investment in the contract allocable to each of D's taxable years. In these circumstances, D would be entitled to elect to redetermine the portion of the investment in the contract allocable to the taxable year of election and all subsequent years. The new amount allocable thereto would be found by dividing the $174.80 difference by D's life expectancy as of the first day of the first period for which D received an amount as an annuity in the sixth year of the annuity contract, and adding the result to D's originally determined allocation of $414.80.

(c) *Expected return for term certain.*—In the case of a contract providing for specific periodic payments which are to be paid for a term certain such as a fixed number of months or years, without regard to life expectancy, the expected return is determined by multiplying the fixed number of years or months for which payments are to be on or after the annuity starting date by the amount of the payment provided in the contract for each such period.

(d) *Expected return with respect to amount certain.*—In the case of contracts involving no life or lives as a measurement of their duration, but under which a determinable total amount is to be paid in installments of lesser amounts paid at periodic intervals, the expected return shall be the total amount guaranteed. If an amount is to be paid periodically until a fund plus interest at a fixed rate is exhausted, but further payments may be made thereafter because of earnings at a higher interest rate, this paragraph shall apply to the total amount anticipatable as a result of the amount of the fund plus the fixed interest thereon. Any amount which may be paid as the result of earnings at a greater interest rate shall be disregarded in determining the expected return. If such an amount is later received, it shall be considered an amount not received as an annuity after the annuity starting date. See paragraph (b)(2) of §1.72-11.

(e) *Expected return where two or more annuity elements providing for fixed payments are acquired for a single consideration.*—(1) In the case of a contract described in paragraph (a)(2) of §1.72-2, which provides for specified payments to be made under two or more annuity elements, the expected return shall be found for the contract as a whole by aggregating the expected returns found with respect to each annuity element. If individual life annuity elements are involved (including joint and survivor annuities where the primary annuitant died before January 1, 1954) the expected return for each of them shall be determined in the manner prescribed in paragraph (a) of this section. If joint and survivor annuity elements are involved, the expected return for such elements shall be determined under the appropriate subparagraph of paragraph (b) of this section. If terms certain or amounts certain are involved, the expected returns for such elements shall be determined under paragraph (c) or (d) of this section, respectively.

(2) The aggregate expected return found in accordance with the rules set forth in subparagraph (1) of this paragraph shall constitute the expected return for the contract as a whole. The investment in the contract shall be divided by the amount thus determined to obtain the exclusion ratio for the contract as a whole. This exclusion ratio shall be applied to all amounts received as a annuity under the contract by any recipient (in accordance with the provisions of §1.72-4), except in the case of amounts received by a surviving annuitant under a joint and survivor annuity element to which the provisions of section 72(i) and paragraph (b)(3) of this section would apply if it were a separate contract. See subparagraph (3) of this paragraph.

(3) In the case of a contract providing two or more annuity elements, one of which is a joint and survivor annuity element of the type described in section 72(i) and paragraph (b)(3) of this section, the general exclusion ratio for the contract as a whole, for the purpose of computations with respect to all the other annuity elements shall be determined in accordance with the principles of subparagraphs (1) and (2) of this paragraph. A special exclusion ratio

shall thereafter be determined for the surviving annuitant receiving payments under the annuity element described in section 72(i) and paragraph (b)(3) of this section by using the investment in the contract and the expected return determined in accordance with the provisions of paragraph (b)(3) of this section.

(4) In the case of a contract providing for payments to be made to two persons in the manner described in paragraph (b)(6) of this section, the expected return is to be computed as though there were two joint and survivor annuities under the same contract, in the following manner. First, the multiple appropriate to the ages (as of the annuity starting date) and, if applicable, sexes of the annuitants involved shall be found in Table II or VI (whichever is applicable) of §1.72-9 and adjusted, if necessary, in the manner described in paragraph (a)(2) of this section. Second, the multiple so found shall be applied to the sum of the payments to be made each year to both annuitants. The result is the expected return for the contract as a whole.

(5) For rules relating to expected return where two or more annuity elements are acquired for a single consideration and one or more of such elements does not specify a fixed payment for each period, see paragraph (f) of this section.

(f) *Expected return with respect to obligations providing for payments described in paragraph (b)(3) of §1.72-2.*—(1) If a contract to which section 72 applies provides only for payments to be made in a manner described in paragraph (b)(3) of §1.72-2, the expected return for such contract as a whole shall be an amount equal to the investment in the contract found in accordance with section 72(c)(1) and §1.72-6, as adjusted for any refund feature in accordance with §1.72-7.

(2) If a contract to which section 72 applies provides for annuity elements, one or more of which (but not all) provide for payments to be made in a manner described in paragraph (b)(3) of §1.72-2:

(i) With respect to the portion of the contract providing for annuity elements to which paragraph (b)(3) of §1.72-2 does not apply, the expected return shall be the aggregate of the expected returns found for each of such elements in accordance with the appropriate paragraph of this section; and

(ii) With respect to all annuity elements to which paragraph (b)(3) of §1.72-2 does apply, the expected return for all such elements shall be an amount equal to the portion of the investment in the contract allocable to such elements in accordance with the provisions of paragraph (e)(2)(ii) of §1.72-4 and paragraph (b)(3)(ii)(*b*) of §1.72-6.

(g) *Expected return with respect to contracts subject to §1.72-6(d).*—In the case of a contract to which §1.72-6(d) (relating to contracts in which amounts were invested both before July 1, 1986, and after June 30, 1986) applies, an expected return is computed using the multiples in Tables I through IV of §1.72-9 with respect to the pre-July 1986 investment in the contract and a second expected return is computed using the multiples in Tables V through VIII of §1.72-9 with respect to the post-June 1986 investment in the contract. [Reg. §1.72-5.]

☐ [T.D. 6211, 11-14-56. Amended by T.D. 8115, 12-16-86.]

[Reg. §1.72-6]

§1.72-6. **Investment in the contract.**—(a) *General rule.*—(1) For the purpose of computing the "investment in the contract", it is first necessary to determine the "aggregate amount of premiums or other consideration paid" for such contract. See section 72(c)(1). This determination is made as of the later of the annuity starting date of the contract or the date on which an amount is first received thereunder as an annuity. The amount so found is then reduced by the sum of the following amounts in order to find the investment in the contract:

(i) The total amount of any return of premiums or dividends received (including unrepaid loans or dividends applied against the principal or interest on such loans) on or before the date on which the foregoing determination is made, and

(ii) The total of any other amounts received with respect to the contract on or before such date which were excludable from the gross income for the recipient under the income tax law applicable at the time of receipt.

Amounts to which subdivision (ii) of this subparagraph applies shall include, for example, amounts considered to be return of premiums or other consideration paid under section 22(b)(2) of the Internal Revenue Code of 1939 and amounts considered to be an employer-provided death benefit under section 22(b)(1)(B) of such Code. For rules relating to the extent to which an employee or his beneficiary may include employer contributions in the aggregate amount of premiums or other consideration paid, see §1.72-8. If the aggregate amount of premiums or other consideration paid for the contract includes amounts for which deductions were allowed under section 404 as contributions on behalf of a self-employed individual, such amounts shall not be included in the investment in the contract.

(2) For the purpose of subparagraph (1) of this paragraph, amounts received subsequent to the receipt of an amount as an annuity or subsequent to the annuity starting date, whichever is the later, shall be disregarded. See, however, § 1.72-11.

(3) The application of this paragraph may be illustrated by the following examples:

Example (1). In 1950, B purchased an annuity contract for $10,000 which was to provide him with an annuity of $1,000 per year for life. He received $1,000 in each of the years 1950, 1951, 1952, and 1953, prior to the annuity starting date (January 1, 1954). Under the Internal Revenue Code of 1939, $300 of each of these payments (3% of $10,000) was includible in his gross income, and the remaining $700 was excludable therefrom during each of the taxable years mentioned. In computing B's investment in the contract as of January 1, 1954, the total amount excludable from his gross income during the years 1950 through 1953 ($2,800) must be subtracted from the consideration paid ($10,000). Accordingly, B's investment in the contract as of January 1, 1954, is $7,200 ($10,000 less $2,800).

Example (2). In 1945, C contracted for an annuity to be paid to him beginning December 31, 1960. In 1945 and in each successive year until 1960, he paid a premium of $5,000. Assuming he receives no payments of any kind under the contract until the date on which he receives the first annual payment as an annuity (December 31, 1960), his investment in the contract as of the annuity starting date (December 31, 1959) will be $75,000 ($5,000 paid each year for the 15 years from 1945 to 1959, inclusive).

Expectancy of A under Table I and § 1.72-5(a)(2), 11.6 (12.1 – 0.5), multiplied by $1,000	$11,600
Plus: Expectancy of B computed in a similar manner ($1,000 × 14.5 [15.0 – 0.5])	14,500
Total expected return	26,100

The exclusion ratio for both A and B is then $19,575, $26,100, or 75 percent. A and B shall each exclude from gross income three-fourths ($750) of each $1,000 annual payment received and shall include the remaining one-fourth ($250) of each $1,000 annual payment received in gross income.

Example (2). Assume the same facts as in example (1) except that of the total investment in the contract of $19,575, the pre-July 1986

Expectancy of A under Table I and § 1.72-5(a)(2), 11.6 (12.1 – 0.5), multiplied by $1,000	$11,600
Plus: Expectancy of B under Table I and § 1.72-5(a)(2), 14.5 (15.0 – 0.5), multiplied by $1,000	$14,500
Pre-July 1986 expected return	$26,100
Expectancy of A under Table V and § 1.72-5(a)(2), 15.5 (16.0 – 0.5), multiplied by $1,000	$15,500
Plus: Expectancy of B under Table V and § 1.72-5(a)(2), 15.5 (16.0 – 0.5), multiplied by $1,000	$15,500
Post-June 1986 expected return	$31,000
Pre-July 1986 exclusion ratio ($10,000 ÷ $26,100)	38.3
Post-June 1986 exclusion ratio ($9,575 ÷ 31,000)	30.9

A and B shall each exclude from gross income $692 (38.3 percent of $1,000 + 30.9 percent of $1,000) of each $1,000 payment and include the remaining $308 in gross income.

(2) In the case of a contract providing for specified annual annuity payments to be made to two persons during their joint lives and the payment of the aggregate of the two individual payments to the survivor for his life, the investment in the contract shall be allocated in accordance with the provisions of subparagraph (1) of this paragraph. For this purpose, the investment in the contract (without regard to the fact that differing amounts may have been contributed by the two annuitants) shall be divided by the expected return determined in accordance with paragraph (e)(4) of § 1.72-5. The resulting exclusion ratio shall then be applied to any amounts received as an annuity by either annuitant.

(3) In the case of a contract providing two or more annuity elements, one or more of which provides for payments to be made in a manner described in paragraph (b)(3) of § 1.72-2, the investment in the contract shall be allocated to the various annuity elements in the following manner.

(i) If all the annuity elements provide for payments to be made in the manner described in paragraph (b)(3) of § 1.72-2, the investment in the contract shall be allocated on the basis of the amounts received by each recipient by apportioning the amount determined to be excludable under that section to each recipient in the same ratio as the total of the amounts received by him in the taxable year bears to the total of the amounts received by all recipients during the same period; and

(ii) If one or more, but not all, of the annuity elements provide for payments to be made in a manner described in paragraph (b)(3) of § 1.72-2:

(a) With respect to all annuity elements to which that section does not apply, the investment in the contract for all such elements shall be the portion of the investment in the contract as a whole (found in accordance with the provisions of this section) which is properly allocable to all such elements; and

(b) With respect to all annuity elements to which paragraph (b)(3) of § 1.72-2 does apply, the investment in the contract for all

Example (3). Assume the same facts as in example (2), except that prior to the annuity starting date C has already received from the insurer dividends of $1,000 each in 1949, 1954, and 1959, such dividends not being includible in his gross income in any of those years. C's investment in the contract, as of the annuity starting date, will then be $72,000 ($75,000 – $3,000).

(b) *Allocation of the investment in the contract where two or more annuity elements are acquired for a single consideration.*—(1) In the case of a contract described in § 1.72-2(a)(2) which provides for two or more annuity elements, the investment in the contract determined under paragraph (a) shall be allocated to each of the annuity elements in the ratio that the expected return under each annuity element bears to the aggregate of the expected returns under all the annuity elements. The exclusion ratio for the contract as a whole shall be determined by dividing the investment in the contract (after adjustment for the present value of any or all refund features) by the aggregate of the expected returns under all the annuity elements. This may be illustrated by the following examples:

Example (1). If a contract provides for annuity payments of $1,000 per year for life (with no refund feature) to both A and B, a male and female, respectively, each 70 years of age as of the annuity starting date, such contract is acquired for consideration of $19,575 (without regard to whether paid by A, B, or both), and there is no post-June 1986 investment in the contract, the investment in the contract shall be allocated by determining the exclusion ratio for the contract as a whole in the following manner:

investment in the contract is $10,000. If the election described in § 1.72-6(d)(6) is made with respect to the contract, the investment in the contract shall be allocated by determining an exclusion ratio for the contract as a whole based on separately computed exclusion ratios with respect to the pre-July 1986 investment in the contract and the post-June 1986 investment in the contract in the following manner:

such elements shall be the investment in the contract as a whole (found in accordance with the provisions of this section) as reduced by the portion thereof determined under (a) of this subdivision.

For the purpose of determining, pursuant to (a) of this subdivision, the portion of the investment in the contract as a whole properly allocable to a particular annuity element, reference shall be made to the present value of such annuity element determined in accordance with paragraph (e)(1)(iii)(b) of § 1.101-2.

(iii) In the case of a contract to which paragraph (d) of this section applies, this paragraph (b) is applied in the manner prescribed in paragraph (d) and, in particular, paragraph (d)(5)(v) of this section.

(c) *Special rules.*—(1) For the special rule for determining the investment in the contract for a surviving annuitant in cases where the prior annuitant of a joint and survivor annuity contract died in 1951, 1952, or 1953, see paragraph (b)(3) of § 1.72-5.

(2) For special rules relating to the determination of the investment in the contract where employer contributions are involved, see § 1.72-8. See also paragraph (b) of § 1.72-16 for a special rule relating to the determination of the premiums or other consideration paid for a contract where an employee is taxable on the premiums paid for life insurance protection that is purchased by and considered to be a distribution from an exempt employees' trust.

(3) For the determination of an adjustment in investment in the contract in cases where a contract contains a refund feature, see § 1.72-7.

(4) In the case of "face-amount certificates" described in section 72(l), the amount of consideration paid for purposes of computing the investment in the contract shall include any amount added to the holder's basis by reason of section 1232(a)(3)(E) (relating to basis adjustment for amount of original issue discount ratably included in gross income as interest under section 1232(a)(3)).

(d) *Pre-July 1986 and post-June 1986 investment in the contract.*—(1) This paragraph (d) applies to an annuity contract if—

(i) The investment in the contract includes a pre-July 1986 investment in the contract and a post-June 1986 investment in the contract (both as defined in §1.72-6(d)(3));

(ii) The use of a multiple found in Tables I through VIII of §1.72-9 is required to determine the expected return under the contract; and

(iii) The election described in paragraph (d)(6) of this section is made with respect to the contract.

(2) In the case of an annuity contract to which this paragraph (d) applies—

(i) All computations required to determine the amount excludable from gross income shall be performed separately with respect to the pre-July 1986 investment in the contract and the post-June 1986 investment in the contract as if each such amount were the entire investment in the contract;

(ii) The multiples in Tables I through IV shall be used for computations involving the pre-July 1986 investment in the contract and the multiples in Tables V through VIII shall be used for computations involving the post-June 1986 investment in the contract; and

(iii) The amount excludable from gross income shall be the sum of the amounts determined under the separate computations required by paragraph (d)(2)(i) of this section.

(3) For purposes of the regulations under section 72, the pre-July 1986 investment in the contract and post-June 1986 investment in the contract are determined in accordance with the following rules:

(i)(A) Except as provided in §1.72-9, if the annuity starting date of the contract occurs before July 1, 1986, the pre-July 1986 investment in the contract is the total investment in the contract as of the annuity starting date;

(B) Except as provided in §1.72-9, if the annuity starting date of the contract occurs after June 30, 1986, and the contract does not provide for a disqualifying form of payment or settlement, the pre-July 1986 investment in the contract is the investment in the contract computed as of June 30, 1986, as if June 30, 1986, had been the later of the annuity starting date of the contract or the date on which an amount is first received thereunder as an annuity;

(C) If the annuity starting date of the contract occurs after June 30, 1986, and the contract provides, at the option of the annuitant or of any other person (including, in the case of an employee's annuity, an option exercisable only by, or with the consent of, the employer), for a disqualifying form of payment or settlement, the pre-July 1986 investment in the contract is zero (i.e., the total investment in the contract is post-June 1986 investment in the contract).

(ii) The post-June 1986 investment in the contract is the amount by which the total investment in the contract as of the annuity starting date exceeds the pre-July 1986 investment in the contract.

(iii) For purposes of paragraph (d)(3)(i) of this section, a disqualifying form of payment or settlement is any form of payment or settlement (whether or not selected) that permits the receipt of amounts under the contract in a form other than a life annuity. For example, each of the following options provides for a disqualifying form of payment or settlement:

(A) An option to receive a lump sum in full discharge of the obligation under the contract.

(B) An option to receive an amount under the contract after June 30, 1986, and before the annuity starting date.

(C) An option to receive an annuity for a period certain.

(D) An option to receive payments under a refund feature (within the meaning of paragraphs (b) and (c) of this section) that is substantially equivalent to an annuity for a period certain.

(E) An option to receive a temporary life annuity (within the meaning of §1.72-5(a)(3)) that is substantially equivalent to an annuity for a period certain.

An option to receive alternative forms of life annuity is not a disqualifying option for purposes of paragraph (d)(3)(i) of this section. Thus, if the sole options provided under a contract are a single life annuity and a joint and survivor life annuity, paragraph (d)(3)(i)(C) of this section does not apply to such contract.

(iv) For purposes of paragraph (d)(3)(iii) of this section, a refund feature is substantially equivalent to an annuity for a period certain if its value determined under Table VII of §1.72-9 exceeds 50 percent. Similarly, a temporary life annuity is substantially equivalent to an annuity for a period certain if the multiple determined under Table VIII of §1.72-9 exceeds 50 percent of the maximum duration of the annuity.

(4) In any separate computation under this paragraph (d), only the applicable portion of other amounts (such as the total expected return under the contract, or the total amount guaranteed under the contract as of the annuity starting date) shall be taken into account if the use of the entire amount in such computation is inconsistent with the use in the computation of only a portion of the investment in the contract. For example, such use is generally inconsistent if the computation requires a comparison of the investment in the contract and such other amount for the purpose of using the greater (or lesser) amount or the difference between the two. For purposes of the first sentence of this paragraph (d)(4), the applicable portion is the amount that bears the same ratio to the entire amount as the pre-July 1986, investment in the contract or the post-June 1986 investment in the contract, whichever is applicable, bears to the total investment in the contract as of the annuity starting date.

(5) *Application to particular computations.*—(i) In the case of a contract to which this paragraph (d) applies, the exclusion ratio for purposes of §1.72-4(a) is the sum of the exclusion ratios separately computed in accordance with this paragraph (d). The exclusion ratio with respect to the pre-July 1986 investment in the contract is determined by dividing the pre-July 1986 investment in the contract by the expected return as found under §1.72-5 by applying the appropriate multiples of Tables I through IV of §1.72-9. Similarly, the exclusion ratio with respect to the post-June 1986 investment in the contract is determined by dividing the post-June 1986 investment in the contract by the expected return as found under §1.72-5 by applying the appropriate multiples in Tables V through VIII of §1.72-9.

(ii) The applicability of §1.72-4(d)(2) to a contract to which this paragraph (d) applies shall be determined separately with respect to the post-June 1986 investment in the contract and the pre-July 1986 investment in the contract and in each such determination only the applicable portion of the total expected return under the contract shall be taken into account. If §1.72-4(d)(2) applies with respect to either such investment in the contract, the separately computed exclusion ratio shall be considered to be the applicable portion of 100 percent.

(iii) If §1.72-4(d)(3) applies to a contract to which this paragraph (d) applies—

(A) The applicable portions (as defined in paragraph (d)(4) of this section) of payments received under the contract for a taxable year shall be separately computed;

(B) The pre-July 1986 investment in the contract and the post-June 1986 investment in the contract shall be separately allocated to the taxable year; and

(C) The separate applicable portions of the payments received under the contract for the taxable year shall be considered to be amounts received as an annuity (for which the exclusion ratio is 100 percent) only to the extent they do not exceed the portions of the corresponding investments in the contract which are properly allocable to that year.

See the example in §1.72-4(d)(3)(v).

(iv) If §1.72-4(e) applies to a contract to which this paragraph (d) applies, the exclusion ratio shall be separately computed with respect to the pre-July 1986 investment in the contract and the post-June 1986 investment in the contract. For purposes of the separate computations under §1.72-4(e)(2)(ii), only the applicable portion of payments received shall be taken into account and the exclusion ratio (100%) shall be applied to the separately computed portion allocated to each participant.

(v) If paragraph (b)(3) of this section applies to a contract to which this paragraph (d) applies, separate allocations are required with respect to the pre-July 1986 investment in the contract and the post-June 1986 investment in the contract. For purposes of the separate computations required to determine the portion of the investment in the contract properly allocable to a particular annuity element, only the applicable portion of the present value of the annuity element determined in accordance with §1.101-2(e)(1)(iii)(b) is taken into account.

(vi) If §1.72-7 applies to a contract to which this paragraph (d) applies, separate computations are required to determine the adjustment to the pre-July 1986 investment in the contract and the post-June 1986 investment in the contract. For purposes of such separate computations, only the applicable portions of the amounts described in §1.72-7(b)(3)(ii), (c)(1)(ii)(B), (c)(2)(vii)(B), and (d)(1)(ii) are taken into account. Similarly, in the case of computations with respect to the guarantee of a specified amount under §1.72-7(d)(1), only the applicable portion of such amount is taken into account.

(6) This paragraph (d) applies to a contract only if the first taxpayer to receive an amount as an annuity under the contract elects to perform separate computations with respect to the pre-July 1986 investment in the contract and the post-June 1986 investment in the contract as if each such amount were the entire investment in contract. If two or more annuitants receive an amount as an annuity under the contract at the same time (such as under a joint-and-last-survivorship annuity contract), an election by one of the annuitants is treated as an election by each of the annuitants. The election is made by attaching a statement to the first return filed by the taxpayer for the first taxable year in which an amount is received as an annuity under the contract. The statement must indicate that the taxpayer is

electing to apply the provisions of paragraph (d) of §1.72-6, and must also contain the name, address, and taxpayer identification number of each annuitant under the contract, and the amount of the pre-July 1986 investment in the contract.

(7) If the investment in the contract includes a post-June 1986 investment in the contract and the election described in paragraph (d)(6) of this section is not made—

(i) The amount excludable from gross income shall be determined without regard to the separate computations described in this paragraph (d); and

(ii) Only the multiples found in Tables V through VIII shall be used in determining the amount excludable from gross income. [Reg. §1.72-6.]

☐ [*T.D. 6211, 11-14-56. Amended by T.D. 6676, 9-16-63, T.D. 7311, 3-29-74 and T.D. 8115, 12-16-86.*]

[Reg. §1.72-7]

§1.72-7. Adjustment in investment where a contract contains a refund feature.—(a) *Definition of a contract containing a refund feature.*—A contract to which section 72 applies, contains a refund feature if:

(1) The total amount receivable as an annuity under such contract depends, in whole or in part, on the continuing life of one or more persons,

(2) The contract provides for payments to be made to a beneficiary or the estate of an annuitant on or after the death of the annuitant if a specified amount or a stated number of payments has not been paid to the annuitant or annuitants prior to death, and

(3) Such payments are in the nature of a refund of the consideration paid. See paragraph (c)(1) of §1.72-11.

(b) *Adjustment of investment for the refund feature in the case of a single life annuity.*—Where a single life annuity contract to which section 72 applies contains a refund feature and the special rule of paragraph (d) of this section does not apply, the investment in the contract shall be adjusted in the following manner:

(1) Determine the number of years necessary for the guaranteed amount to be fully paid by dividing the maximum amount guaranteed as of the annuity starting date by the amount to be received annually under the contract to the extent such amount reduces the guaranteed amount. The number of years should be stated in terms of the nearest whole year, considering for this purpose a fraction of one-half or more as an additional whole year.

(2) Consult Table III or VII (whichever is applicable) of §1.72-9 for the appropriate percentage under the whole number of years found in subparagraph (1) of this paragraph and the age (as of the annuity starting date) and, if applicable, sex of the annuitant.

(3) Multiply the percentage found in subparagraph (2) of this paragraph by whichever of the following is the smaller: (i) the investment in the contract found in accordance with §1.72-6 or (ii) the total amount guaranteed as of the annuity starting date.

(4) Subtract the amount found in subparagraph (3) of this paragraph from the investment in the contract found in accordance with §1.72-6.

The resulting amount is the investment in the contract adjusted for the present value of the refund feature without discount for interest and is to be used in determining the exclusion ratio to be applied to the payments received as an annuity. The percentage found in Table III or VII shall not be adjusted in a manner described in paragraph (a)(2) of §1.72-5. These principles may be illustrated by the following examples:

Example (1). On January 1, 1954, a husband, age 65, purchased for $21,053, an immediate installment refund annuity payable $100 per month for life. The contract provided that in the event the husband did not live long enough to recover the full purchase price, payments were to be made to his wife until the total payments under the contract equaled the purchase price. The investment in the contract adjusted for the purpose of determining the exclusion ratio is computed in the following manner:

Cost of the annuity contract (investment in the contract, unadjusted)	$21,053
Amount to be received annually	$1,200
Number of years for which payment guaranteed ($21,053 divided by $1,200) . . .	17.5
Rounded to nearest whole number of years	18
Percentage located in Table III for age 65 (age of the annuitant as of the annuity starting date) and 18 (the number of whole years) (percent)	30
Subtract value of the refund feature to the nearest dollar (30% of $21,053)	$6,316
Investment in the contract adjusted for the present value of the refund feature without discount for interest	$14,737

Example (2). Assume the same facts as in example (1), except that the total investment in the contract was made after June 30, 1986. The investment in the contract adjusted for the purpose of determining the exclusion ratio is computed as follows:

Cost of the annuity contract (investment in the contract, unadjusted)	$21,053
Amount to be received annually	$1,200
Number of years for which payment guaranteed ($21,053÷$1,200)	17.5
Rounded to nearest whole number of years	18
Percentage in Table VII for age 65 and 18 years (percent)	15
Subtract value of the refund feature to the nearest dollar (15 percent of $21,053)	$3,158
Investment in the contract adjusted for the present value of the refund feature without discount for interest	$17,895

Example (3). Assume the same facts as in example (1), except that the pre-July 1986 investment in the contract is $10,000 and the post-June 1986 investment in the contract is $11,053. If the annuitant makes the election described in §1.72-6(d)(6), separate computations must be performed pursuant to §1.72-6(d) to determine the adjusted investment in the contract. The pre-July 1986 investment in the contract and the post-June 1986 investment in the contract adjusted for the purpose of determining the exclusion ratios are, respectively, $7,000 and $9,395, determined as follows:

Pre-July 1986 investment in the contract (unadjusted)	$10,000
Pre-July 1986 portion of the amount to be received annually ($10,000/$21,053×$1,200)	$570.00
Number of years for which payment guaranteed ($10,000÷$570)	17.50
Rounded to nearest whole number of years	18
Percentage in Table III for age 65 and 18 years (percent)	30
Subtract value of the refund feature to the nearest dollar (30 percent of $10,000)	$3,000
Pre-July 1986 investment in the contract adjusted for the present value of the refund feature without discount for interest	$7,000
Post-June 1986 investment in the contract (unadjusted)	$11,053
Post-June 1986 portion of the amount to be received annually ($11,053/$21,053×$1,200)	$630
Number of years for which payment guaranteed ($11,053÷$630)	17.54
Rounded to nearest whole number of years	18
Percentage in Table VII for age 65 and 18 years (percent)	15
Subtract value of the refund feature to the nearest dollar (15 percent of $11,053)	$1,658
Post-June 1986 investment in the contract adjusted for the present value of the refund feature without discount for interest	$9,395

If, in the above examples, the guaranteed amount had exceeded the investment in the contract (or applicable portion thereof), the percentage found in Table III or VII (whichever is applicable) should have been applied to the lesser of these amounts since any excess of the guaranteed amount over the investment in the contract (as found under §1.72-6) would not have constituted a refund of premiums or other consideration paid. In such a case, however, a different multiple might have been obtained from Table III or VII (whichever is applicable) since the number of years for which payments were guaranteed would have been greater.

(c) *Adjustment of investment for the refund feature in the case of a joint and survivor annuity.*—(1) Except as provided in paragraph (c)(2) of this section, if a joint and survivor annuity contract described in paragraph (b)(1), (2) or (6) of §1.72-5 contains a refund feature and the special rule of paragraph (d) of this section does not apply, the investment in the contract shall be adjusted in the following manner:

(i) Find the percentage determined under the following formula:

$$V = \frac{\sum_{t=0}^{N-1} \frac{d_{x+t}}{l_x}\left[(N-\tfrac{1}{2}-t) - P\left(\frac{T_{y+t+1} - T_{y+t+M+1}}{l_y}\right)\right]}{N}$$

In which:

V = The percentage, rounded to the nearest whole percent,

x = The age at the nearest birthday of the primary annuitant,

y = The age at the nearest birthday of the survivor annuitant,

N = The guaranteed amount divided by the annual annuity payable to the primary annuitant, rounded to the nearest integer,

P = The annual annuity continued to the survivor annuitant divided by the annual annuity payable to the primary annuitant,

$$M = \frac{N - \tfrac{1}{2} - t}{P}$$

l_x = The number of survivors at age x, $d = l_x - l_{x+1}$, and

$$T_x = \sum_{s=0}^{\infty} \tfrac{1}{2}(l_{x+s} + l_{x+s+1}).$$

(ii) Multiply the percentage found in paragraph (c)(1)(i) of this section by the lesser of (A) the investment in the contract found in accordance with §1.72-6, or (B) the total amount guaranteed as of the annuity starting date.

(iii) Subtract the amount found in paragraph (c)(1)(ii) of this section from the investment in the contract found in accordance with §1.72-6.

In the case of a contract providing for payments to be made to two persons in the manner described in paragraph (b)(6) of §1.72-5, this paragraph (c)(1) is applied as though the older person were the primary annuitant and the younger person were the survivor annuitant. For purposes of this paragraph (c)(1), the number of survivors at age_x (1_x) is determined under the following table:

x	lx	x	lx	x	lx
5	1000000.	42	982230.	79	665977.
6	999729.	43	981046.	80	637260.
7	999493.	44	979742.	81	607339.
8	999284.	45	978302.	82	575531.
9	999069.	46	976709.	83	541919.
10	998849.	47	974945.	84	506647.
11	998620.	48	972992.	85	469931.
12	998382.	49	970832.	86	432459.
13	998135.	50	968447.	87	394138.
14	997876.	51	966000.	88	355393.
15	997606.	52	963313.	89	316712.
16	997322.	53	960375.	90	278663.
17	997025.	54	957175.	91	242020.
18	996714.	55	953705.	92	207150.
19	996387.	56	949954.	93	174602.
20	996044.	57	945912.	94	144828.
21	995684.	58	941568.	95	118151.
22	995304.	59	936908.	96	94871.7
23	994905.	60	931903.	97	74863.6
24	994484.	61	926451.	98	58042.2
25	994041.	62	920540.	99	44176.1
26	993573.	63	914090.	100	32956.4
27	993080.	64	907011.	101	24044.8
28	992563.	65	899221.	102	17104.1
29	992024.	66	890428.	103	11815.5
30	991461.	67	880797.	104	7886.75
31	990876.	68	870298.	105	5054.94
32	990269.	69	858904.	106	3086.95
33	989638.	70	846565.	107	1778.82
34	988984.	71	832316.	108	955.465
35	988303.	72	816861.	109	470.955
36	987593.	73	800078.	110	208.668
37	986846.	74	781837.	111	80.7899
38	986055.	75	762012.	112	26.2340
39	985210.	76	740743.	113	6.69620
40	984298.	77	717689.	114	1.19385
41	983310.	78	692780.	115	.111460

(2) If the multiples in Tables I through IV of §1.72-9 are used to determine any portion of the expected return under a contract described in paragraph (c)(1) of this section, only the post-June 1986 investment in the contract (if any) shall be adjusted in the manner described in paragraph (c)(1) of this section, and the pre-July 1986 investment in the contract shall, in the case of a contract described in paragraph (b)(1) or (6) of §1.72-5, be adjusted in the following manner:

(i) Determine the number of years necessary for the guaranteed amount to be fully paid by dividing the maximum amount guaranteed as of the annuity starting date by the amount to be received annually under the contract. The number of years should be stated in terms of the nearest whole year, considering for this purpose a fraction of one-half or more as an additional whole year.

Number of years difference in age (2 male annuitants or 2 female annuitants)	Addition to older age in years
0 to 1, inclusive	9
2 to 3, inclusive	8
4 to 5, inclusive	7
6 to 8, inclusive	6
9 to 11, inclusive	5
12 to 15, inclusive	4
16 to 20, inclusive	3
21 to 27, inclusive	2
28 to 42, inclusive	1
Over 42	0

(v) Consult Table III for the appropriate percentage under the whole number of years found in subdivision (i) of this subparagraph and the age and sex of the elder annuitant as adjusted under subdivision (iv) of this subparagraph.

(vi) Subtract the percentage obtained in subdivision (v) of this subparagraph from the sum of the percentages found under subdivision (iii) of this subparagraph. If the result is less than one, subdivisions (vii) and (viii) of this subparagraph shall be disregarded and no adjustment made to the investment in the contract.

(vii) Multiply the percentage found in subdivision (vi) of this subparagraph by whichever of the following is the smaller: (A) the investment in the contract found in accordance with §1.72-6 or (B) the total amount guaranteed as of the annuity starting date.

Cost of the annuity contract (investment in the contract unadjusted)	$33,050
Guaranteed amount ($1,200 × 10)	$12,000
Percentage in Table III for male, age 70 (for female, age 75) for duration of the guarantee (10)	21
Percentage in Table III for female, age 40 (or male, age 35) for duration of the guarantee (10)	2
Sum of percentages obtained	23
Difference in years of age between two males, aged 70 and 35 (or 2 females, aged 75 and 40)	35
Addition, in years, to older age	1
Percentage in Table III for male one year older than A	22
Difference between percentages obtained (23 percent less 22 percent)	1
Value of the refund feature to the nearest dollar (1 percent of $12,000)	$120
Investment in the contract adjusted for present value of the refund feature	$32,930

Example (2). The facts are the same as in example (1), except that the total investment in the contract was made after June 30, 1986. A is 73 years of age, and B is A's 70 year old spouse. The percentage determined under the formula in paragraph (c)(1)(i) of this section is two percent. Thus, the amount determined under paragraph (c)(1)(ii) of this section is $240 (2 percent of $12,000), and the investment in the contract adjusted for the present value of the refund feature is $32,810 ($33,050 – $240).

(4) If an annuity described in paragraph (b) of §1.72-5 contains a refund feature and the manner of determining the adjustment to the investment in the contract (or to any part of such investment) is not *prescribed* or requires use of the formula in paragraph (c)(1)(i) of this section, the *Commissioner will determine* the amount of the adjustment upon request. The request must contain the date of birth of each annuitant, the guaranteed amount, the annual annuity payable to each annuitant, and the annuity starting date. Send the request to the Commissioner of Internal Revenue, Attention: OP:E:EP:GA, Washington, D.C. 20224.

(d) *Adjustment of investment in the contract where paragraph (b)(3) of §1.72-2 applies to payments.*—(1) If paragraph (b)(3) of §1.72-2 applies to payments to be made under a contract and this section also applies because of the provision for a refund feature, an adjustment shall be

(ii) Consult Table III of §1.72-9 for the appropriate percentages under the whole number of years found in subdivision (i) of this subparagraph and the age (as of the annuity starting date) and sex of each annuitant. If the annuitants are not of the same sex, substitute for the female annuitant a male annuitant 5 years younger, or for the male annuitant a female annuitant 5 years older, so that Table III will be entered in both cases with the ages of annuitants of the same sex.

(iii) Find the sum of the two percentages found in accordance with subdivision (ii) of this subparagraph.

(iv) To the age of the elder of the two annuitants (as determined under subdivision (ii) of this subparagraph), add the number of years (indicated in the table below) opposite the number of years by which such annuitants' ages differ:

(viii) Subtract the amount found in subdivision (vii) of this subparagraph from the investment in the contract found in accordance with §1.72-6.

(3) The principles of this paragraph (c) may be illustrated by the following examples:

Example (1). Prior to July 1, 1986, Taxpayer A, a 70-year old male, purchases a joint and last survivor annuity for $33,050. The contract provides for payments of $100 a month to be paid first to himself for life and then to B, his 40-year old daughter, if she survives him. The contract further provides that in the event both die before ten years' payments have been made, payments will be continued to C, a beneficiary, or to C's estate, until ten years' payments have been made. If there is no post-June 1986 investment in the contract, the investment in the contract adjusted for the purpose of determining the exclusion ratio is computed in the following manner:

made to the investment in the contract in accordance with this paragraph before making the computations required by paragraph (d)(3) of §1.72-4 and paragraph (b)(7) of §1.72-5. In the case of the guarantee of a specified amount, the adjustment shall be made by applying the appropriate multiple from Table III or VII (whichever is applicable), as otherwise determined under this section, to the investment in the contract or the guaranteed amount, whichever is the lesser. The guarantee period shall be found by dividing the amount guaranteed by an amount determined by placing the payments received during the first taxable year (to the extent such payments reduce the guaranteed amount) on an annual basis. Thus, if monthly payments are first received by a taxpayer on a calendar year basis in August, his total payments (to the extent that they reduce the guaranteed amount) for the taxable year would be divided by 5 and multiplied by 12. The guaranteed amount would then be divided by the result of this computation to obtain the guarantee period. If the contract merely guarantees that proceeds from a unit or units of a fund shall be paid for a fixed number of years or the life (or lives) of an annuitant (or annuitants), whichever is the longer, the fixed number of years is the guarantee period. The appropriate percentage in Table III or VII shall be applied to whichever of the following is the smaller: (i) the investment in the contract; or (ii) the product of the payments received in the first taxable year, placed on an annual basis, multiplied by the number of years for which payment of the proceeds of a unit or units is guaranteed.

(2) The principles of this paragraph may be illustrated by the following examples:

Example (1). Taxpayer A, a 50-year-old male, purchases for $25,000 a contract which provides for variable monthly payments to be paid to him for his life. The contract also provides that if he should die before receiving payments for fifteen years, payments shall continue according to the original formula to his estate or beneficiary until payments have been made for that period. Beginning with the month of September, A receives payments which total $450 for the first taxable year of receipt. This amount, placed on an annual basis, is $1,350 ($450 divided by 4, or $112.50; $112.50 multiplied by 12, or $1,350). If there is no post-June 1986 investment in the contract, the guaranteed amount is considered to be $20,250 ($1,350 × 15), and the multiple from Table III (found in the same manner as in paragraph (b) of this section), 9 percent, applied to $20,250 (since this amount is less than the investment in the contract), results in a refund adjustment of $1,822.50. The latter amount, subtracted from the investment in the contract of $25,000, results in an adjusted investment in the contract of $23,177.50. If A dies before receiving payments for 15 years and the remaining payments are made to B, his beneficiary, B shall exclude the entire amount of such payments from his gross income until the amounts so received by B, together with the amounts received by A and excludable from A's gross income, equal

or exceed $25,000. Any excess and any payments thereafter received by B shall be fully includible in gross income.

Example (2). Assume the same facts as in example (1), except that the total investment in the contract was made after June 20, 1986. The applicable multiple found in Table VII is 3 percent. When this is applied to the guaranteed amount of $20,250, it results in a refund adjustment of $607.50. The adjusted investment in the contract is $24,392.50 ($25,000 – $607.50).

(e) *Adjustment of the investment in the contract where more than one annuity element is provided for a single consideration.*—In the case of contracts to which paragraph (b) of § 1.72-6 applies for the purpose of allocating the investment in the contract to two or more annuity elements which are provided for a single consideration, if one or more of such elements involves a refund feature, the portion of the investment in the contract properly allocable to each such element shall be adjusted for the refund feature before aggregating all the investments in order to obtain the exclusion ratio which is to apply to the contract as a whole.

Example (1). If taxpayer A, an insured 70 years of age, upon maturity of an endowment policy which cost him a net amount of $86,000, elected a dual settlement consisting of (1) monthly payments for his life aggregating $4,146 per year with 10 years' payments certain, and (2) monthly payments for his 60 year old brother, B, aggregating $2,820 per year with 20 years' payments certain, the exclusion ratio to be used by both A and B if there is no post-June 1988 investment in the contract would be determined in the following manner:

A's expected return (A's payments per year of $4,146 multiplied by his life expectancy from Table 1 of 12.1)	$50,166.60
B's expected return (B's payments per year of $2,820 multiplied by his life expectancy from Table 1 of 18.2)	$51,324.00
Sum of expected returns to be used in determining exclusion ratio	$101,490.60
Percentage of total expected return attributable to A's expectancy of life ($50,166.60 ÷ $101,490.60)	49.4
Percentage of total expected return attributable to B's expectancy of life ($51,324/$101,490.60)	50.6
Portion of investment in the contract allocable to A's annuity (49.4 percent of $86,000)	$42,484.00
Portion of investment in the contract allocable to B's annuity (50.6 percent of $86,000)	$43,516.00
Value of the refund feature with respect to A's annuity (percentage from Table III for male, age 70, and duration 10, or 21 percent, multiplied by lesser of guaranteed amount and allocable portion of investment in the contract, $41,460)	$8,707.00
A's allocable portion of the investment in the contract adjusted for refund feature ($42,484 less $8,707.00)	$33,777.00
Value of the refund feature with respect to B's annuity (percentage from Table III for male, age 60, and duration 20, or 25 percent, multiplied by lesser of guaranteed amount and allocable portion of investment in the contract, $43,516)	$10,879.00
B's allocable portion of the investment in the contract adjusted for refund feature ($43,516 less $10,879.00)	$32,637.00
Sum of A's and B's allocable portions of the investment in the contract after adjustment for the refund feature	$66,414.00
Exclusion ratio for the contract as a whole (total adjusted investment in the contract, $66,414, divided by the total expected return from above, $101,490.60) (percent)	65.4

Example (2). Assume the same facts as in example (1) except that the total investment in the contract was made after June 30, 1986. The

exclusion ratio to be used by both A and B would be 56.9 percent, determined as follows:

A's expected return (A's payments per year of $41,146 multiplied by his life expectancy from Table V of 16.0)	$66,336.00
B's expected return (B's payments per year of $2,820 multiplied by his life expectancy from Table V of 24.2)	$68,244.00
Sum of expected returns to be used in determining exclusion ratio	$134,580.00
Percentage of total expected return attributable to A's expectancy of life ($66,336.00 ÷ $134,580.00)	49.3
Percentage of total expected return attributable to B's expectancy of life ($68,244.00 ÷ $134,580.00)	50.7
Portion of investment in the contract allocable to A's annuity (49.3 percent of $86,000)	$42,398.00
Portion of investment in the contract allocable to B's annuity (50.7 percent of $86,000)	$43,602.00
Value of the refund feature with respect to A's annuity (percentage from Table VII for age 70 and duration 10, or 11 percent, multiplied by lesser of the guaranteed amount and allocable portion of investment in the contract, $41,460)	$4,560.60
A's allocable portion of the investment in the contract adjusted for refund feature ($42,398 less $4,560.60)	$37,837.40
Value of the refund feature with respect to B's annuity (percentage from Table VII for age 60 and duration 20, or 11 percent, multiplied by lesser of guaranteed amount and allocable portion of investment in the contract, $43,602)	$4,796.22
B's allocable portion of the investment in the contract adjusted for refund feature ($43,602 less $4,796.22)	$38,805.78
Sum of A's and B's allocable portions of the investment in the contract after adjustment for the refund feature	$76,643.18
Exclusion ratio for the contract as a whole (total adjusted investment in the contract, $76,643.18, divided by the total expected return from above, $134,580.00) (percent)	56.9

(f) *Adjustment of investment in the contract with respect to contracts subject to § 1.72-6(d).*—In the case of a contract to which § 1.72-6(d) (relating to contracts in which amounts were invested both before July 1, 1986, and after June 30, 1986) applies, this section is applied in the manner prescribed in § 1.72-6(d) and, in particular, § 1.72-6(d)(5)(vi).

[Reg. § 1.72-7.]

☐ [T.D. 6211, 11-14-56. Amended by T.D. 8115, 12-16-86.]

[Reg. § 1.72-8]

§ 1.72-8. Effect of certain employer contributions with respect to premiums or other consideration paid or contributed by an employee.—(a) *Contributions in the nature of compensation.*—(1) *Amounts includible in gross income of employee under subtitle A of the Code or prior income tax laws.*—Section 72(f) provides that for the purposes of section 72(c), (d), and (e), amounts contributed by an employer for the benefit of an employee or his beneficiaries shall constitute consideration paid or contributed by the employee to the extent that such amounts were includible in the gross income of the employee under subtitle A of the Code or prior income tax laws. Amounts to which

this paragraph applies include, for example, contributions made by an employer to or under a trust or plan which fails to qualify under the provisions of section 401(a), provided that the employee's rights to such contributions are nonforfeitable at the time the contributions are made. See sections 402(b) and 403(c) and the regulations thereunder. This subparagraph also applies to premiums paid by an employer (other than premiums paid on behalf of an owner-employee) for life insurance protection for an employee if such premiums are includible in the gross income of the employee when paid. See § 1.72-16. However, such premiums shall only be considered as premiums and other consideration paid by the employee with respect to any benefits attributable to the contract providing the life insurance protection. See § 1.72-16.

(2) *Amounts not includible in gross income of employee at time contributed if paid directly to employee at that time.*—Except as provided in subparagraph (3) of this paragraph, section 72(f) provides that for the purposes of section 72(c), (d), and (e), amounts contributed by an employer for the benefit of an employee or his beneficiaries shall constitute consideration paid or contributed by the employee to the extent that such amounts would not have been includible in the gross

income of the employee at the time contributed had they been paid directly to the employee at that time. Amounts to which this subparagraph applies include, for example, contributions made by an employer after December 31, 1950, and before January 1, 1963, if made on account of foreign services rendered by an employee during a period in which the employee qualified as a bona fide resident of a foreign country under section 911(a) of the Internal Revenue Code of 1954, or under section 116(a) of the Internal Revenue Code of 1939. In such a case, it would be immaterial whether such contributions were made under a qualified plan or otherwise. See subparagraph (4) of this paragraph for rules governing the determination of the amount of employer foreign service contributions to which this subparagraph applies. On the other hand, if contributions are made by an employer to a qualified plan at a time when compensation paid directly to the employee concerned with respect to the same services rendered would have been includible in the gross income of the employee, such as in the case of an employee of a State government where contributions are made in 1955 with respect to services rendered by the employee prior to the year 1939, this subparagraph does not apply to such contributions.

(3) *Limitation.*—(i) *In general.*—Except as provided in subdivision (ii) of this subparagraph, the provisions of subparagraph (2) of this paragraph shall not apply to amounts which were contributed by the employer after December 31, 1962, and which would not have been includible in the gross income of the employee by reason of the application of section 911, if such amounts had been paid directly to the employee at the time of contribution. Employer contributions attributable to foreign services performed by the employee after December 31, 1962, do not constitute, for purposes of section 72(c), (d), and (e), consideration paid or contributed by the employee.

(ii) *Exception.*—The provisions of subdivision (i) of this subparagraph shall not apply to amounts which were contributed by the employer to provide pension or annuity credits (determined in accordance with the provisions of subparagraph (4) of this paragraph) to the extent such credits are—

(a) Attributable to foreign services performed before January 1, 1963, with respect to which the employee qualified for the benefits of section 911(a) (or corresponding provisions of prior revenue laws), and

(b) Provided pursuant to pension or annuity plan provisions in existence on March 12, 1962, and on that date applicable to such services. Amounts described in this subdivision constitute, for purposes of section 72(c), (d), and (e), consideration paid or contributed by the employee even though such amounts are contributed by the employer after December 31, 1962.

(4) *Determination of employer foreign service contributions which constitute consideration paid or contributed by the employee.*—For purposes of subparagraphs (2) and (3)(ii) of this paragraph, employer foreign service contributions which constitute, for purposes of section 72(c), (d), and (e), consideration paid or contributed by the employee shall be determined as follows:

(i) *Treatment of identifiable contributions.*—If, under the terms of the pension or annuity plan under which employer contributions were made, such contributions may be identified as—

(a) Attributable to foreign services performed before January 1, 1963, with respect to which the employee qualified for the benefits of section 911(a) (or corresponding provisions of prior revenue laws), and

(b) Made under pension or annuity plan provisions in existence on March 12, 1962, which were applicable to the services referred to in (a) of this subdivision on that date, the amount of employer contributions so identified shall be considered paid or contributed by the employee.

(ii) *Alternative rule for unidentifiable contributions.*—If employer contributions may not be identified in the manner described in subdivision (i) of this subparagraph, the amount of employer contributions attributable to foreign services performed before January 1, 1963, and considered paid or contributed by the employee shall be determined on the basis of an estimated allocation which is reasonable and consistent with the circumstances and the provisions of the pension or annuity plan under which such contributions are made. For example, if an employee's benefits under a pension or annuity plan, which is unchanged after March 12, 1962, are determined with respect to his basic compensation during his entire period of credited service, the amount of employer contributions considered paid or contributed by the employee shall be an amount which bears the same ratio to total employer contributions for such employee under the pension or annuity plan as his basic compensation attributable to foreign services performed before January 1, 1963, with respect to which he qualified for the benefits of section 911(a) (or corresponding provisions of prior revenue laws) bears to his total basic compensa-

tion. On the other hand, if an employee's benefits under a pension or annuity plan, which is unchanged after March 12, 1962, are determined with respect to his basic compensation during his final five years of credited service, the amount of employer contributions considered paid or contributed by the employee shall be an amount which bears the same ratio to total employer contributions for such employee as his number of years of credited service before January 1, 1963, with respect to which he qualified for the benefits of section 911(a) (or corresponding provisions of prior revenue laws) bears to his total number of years of credited service.

(5) *Amounts not includible in gross income of employee under subtitle A of the Code or prior income tax laws.*—Amounts contributed by an employer which were not includible in the gross income of the employee under subtitle A of the Code or prior income tax laws, but which would have been includible therein had they been paid directly to the employee, do not constitute consideration paid or contributed by the employee for the purposes of section 72. For example, contributions made by an employer under a qualified employees' trust or plan, which contributions would have been includible in the gross income of the employee had such contributions been paid to him directly as compensation, do not constitute consideration paid or contributed by the employee. Accordingly, the aggregate amount of premiums or other consideration paid or contributed by an employee, insofar as compensatory employer contributions are concerned, consists solely of the (i) sum of all amounts actually contributed by the employee, plus (ii) contributions in the nature of compensation which are deemed to be paid or contributed by the employee under this paragraph.

(b) *Contributions in the nature of death benefits.*—In the case of an employee's beneficiary, the aggregate amount of premiums or other consideration paid or deemed to be paid or contributed by the employee shall also include:

(1) Amounts (other than amounts paid as an annuity) to the extent such amounts are excludable from the beneficiary's gross income as a death benefit under section 101(b), and

(2) Any amount or amounts of death benefits which are treated as additional consideration contributed by the employee under section 101(b)(2)(D) and the regulations thereunder, or which were excludable from the beneficiary's gross income as a death benefit under section 22(b)(1)(B) of the Internal Revenue Code of 1939 and the regulations thereunder.

Accordingly, in the case of an employee's beneficiary, any such amount shall be added to any amount or amounts deemed paid or contributed by the employee under paragraph (a)(1) of this section and to any amounts actually contributed by the employee for the purpose of finding the aggregate amount of premiums or other consideration paid or contributed by the employee.

(c) *Amounts "made available" to an employee or his beneficiary.*—Any amount which, although not actually paid, is made available to and includible in the gross income of an employee or his beneficiary under the rules of sections 402 and 403 and the regulations thereunder, shall be considered an amount contributed by the employee and shall be aggregated with amounts, if any, to which paragraphs (a) and (b) of this section apply for the purpose of determining the aggregate amount of premiums or other consideration paid by the employee.

(d) *Amounts includible in gross income of employee when his rights under annuity contract change to nonforfeitable rights.*—Any amount which, by reason of section 403(d) and after the application of paragraph (b) of §1.403(b)-1, is required to be included in an employee's gross income for the year when his rights under an annuity contract change from forfeitable to nonforfeitable rights shall be considered an amount contributed by the employee and shall be aggregated with amounts, if any, to which paragraphs (a), (b), and (c) of this section apply for the purpose of determining the aggregate amount of premiums or other consideration paid or contributed by the employee for such annuity contract. In other words, if, under section 403(d), an employee of an organization exempt from tax under section 501(a) or 521(a) is required to include an amount in gross income by reason of his rights under an annuity contract changing from forfeitable to nonforfeitable rights, such amount, to the extent it is not excludable from gross income under paragraph (b) of §1.403(b)-1, shall be considered an amount contributed by such employee for the annuity contract. [Reg. §1.72-8.]

☐ [T.D. 6211, 11-14-56. Amended by T.D. 6665, 7-15-63 and T.D. 6783, 12-23-64.]

[Reg. §1.72-9]

§1.72-9. Tables.—The following tables are to be used in connection with computations under section 72 and the regulations thereunder. Tables I, II, IIA, III, and IV are to be used if the investment in the contract does not include a post-June 1986 investment in the contract (as defined in §1.72-6(d)(3)). Tables V, VI, VIA, VII, and VIII are to be used if the investment in the contract includes a post-June 1986 investment in the contract (as defined in §1.72-6(d)(3)).

In the case of a contract under which amounts are received as an annuity after June 30, 1986, a taxpayer receiving such amounts may elect to treat the entire investment in the contract as post-June 1986 investment in the contract and thus apply Tables V through VIII. A taxpayer may make the election for any taxable year in which such amounts are received by attaching to the taxpayer's return for such taxable year a statement that the taxpayer is electing under §1.72-9 to treat the entire investment in the contract as post-June 1986 investment in the contract. The statement must contain the taxpayer's name, address, and taxpayer identification number. The election is irrevocable and applies with respect to all amounts that the taxpayer receives as an annuity under the contract in the taxable year for which the election is made or in any subsequent taxable year. (Note that for purposes of the examples in §§1.72-4 through 1.72-11 the election described in this section is disregarded, (i.e., it is assumed that the taxpayer does not make an election under this section).)

See also §1.72-6(d)(3) for rules treating the entire investment in a contract as post-June 1986 investment in a contract if the annuity starting date of the contract is after June 30, 1986, and the contract provides for a disqualifying form of payment or settlement, such as an option to receive a lump sum in full discharge of the obligation under the contract. In addition, see §1.72-6(d) for special rules concerning the tables to be used and the separate computations required if the investment in the contract includes both a pre-July 1986 investment in the contract and a post-June 1986 investment in the contract and the election described in §1.72-6(d)(6) is made with respect to the contract.

TABLE I.—ORDINARY LIFE ANNUITIES—ONE LIFE—
EXPECTED RETURN MULTIPLES

Male	Female	Multiples	Male	Female	Multiples	Male	Female	Multiples
6	11	65.0	41	46	33.0	76	81	9.1
7	12	64.1	42	47	32.1	77	82	8.7
8	13	63.2	43	48	31.2	78	83	8.3
9	14	62.3	44	49	30.4	79	84	7.8
10	15	61.4	45	50	29.6	80	85	7.5
11	16	60.4	46	51	28.7	81	86	7.1
12	17	59.5	47	52	27.9	82	87	6.7
13	18	58.6	48	53	27.1	83	88	6.3
14	19	57.7	49	54	26.3	84	89	6.0
15	20	56.7	50	55	25.5	85	90	5.7
16	21	55.8	51	56	24.7	86	91	5.4
17	22	54.9	52	57	24.0	87	92	5.1
18	23	53.9	53	58	23.2	88	93	4.8
19	24	53.0	54	59	22.4	89	94	4.5
20	25	52.1	55	60	21.7	90	95	4.2
21	26	51.1	56	61	21.0	91	96	4.0
22	27	50.2	57	62	20.3	92	97	3.7
23	28	49.3	58	63	19.6	93	98	3.5
24	29	48.3	59	64	18.9	94	99	3.3
25	30	47.4	60	65	18.2	95	100	3.1
26	31	46.5	61	66	17.5	96	101	2.9
27	32	45.6	62	67	16.9	97	102	2.7
28	33	44.6	63	68	16.2	98	103	2.5
29	34	43.7	64	69	15.6	99	104	2.3
30	35	42.8	65	70	15.0	100	105	2.1
31	36	41.9	66	71	14.4	101	106	1.9
32	37	41.0	67	72	13.8	102	107	1.7
33	38	40.0	68	73	13.2	103	108	1.5
34	39	39.1	69	74	12.6	104	109	1.3
35	40	38.2	70	75	12.1	105	110	1.2
36	41	37.3	71	76	11.6	106	111	1.0
37	42	36.5	72	77	11.0	107	112	.8
38	43	35.6	73	78	10.5	108	113	.7
39	44	34.7	74	79	10.1	109	114	.6
40	45	33.8	75	80	9.6	110	115	.5
						111	116	0

TABLE II.—ORDINARY JOINT LIFE AND LAST SURVIVOR ANNUITIES—TWO LIVES—
EXPECTED RETURN MULTIPLES

Male	Female	6 / 11	7 / 12	8 / 13	9 / 14	10 / 15	11 / 16	12 / 17	13 / 18	14 / 19	15 / 20	16 / 21	17 / 22	18 / 23	19 / 24	20 / 25
6	11	73.5	73.0	72.6	72.2	71.8	71.4	71.0	70.7	70.4	70.0	69.7	69.5	69.2	68.9	68.7
7	12	73.0	72.6	72.1	71.7	71.3	70.9	70.5	70.1	69.8	69.4	69.1	68.8	68.5	68.3	68.0
8	13	72.6	72.1	71.6	71.2	70.8	70.4	70.0	69.6	69.2	68.9	68.5	68.2	67.9	67.6	67.3
9	14	72.2	71.7	71.2	70.7	70.3	69.9	69.4	69.0	68.7	68.3	67.9	67.6	67.3	67.0	66.7
10	15	71.8	71.3	70.8	70.3	69.8	69.4	68.9	68.5	68.1	67.7	67.4	67.0	66.7	66.4	66.1
11	16	71.4	70.9	70.4	69.9	69.4	68.9	68.5	68.0	67.6	67.2	66.8	66.5	66.1	65.8	65.4
12	17	71.0	70.5	70.0	69.4	68.9	68.5	68.0	67.5	67.1	66.7	66.3	65.9	65.5	65.2	64.8
13	18	70.7	70.1	69.6	69.0	68.5	68.0	67.5	67.1	66.6	66.2	65.8	65.4	65.0	64.6	64.2
14	19	70.4	69.8	69.2	68.7	68.1	67.6	67.1	66.6	66.1	65.7	65.3	64.8	64.4	64.0	63.7
15	20	70.0	69.4	68.9	68.3	67.7	67.2	66.7	66.2	65.7	65.2	64.8	64.3	63.9	63.5	63.1
16	21	69.7	69.1	68.5	67.9	67.4	66.8	66.3	65.8	65.3	64.8	64.3	63.8	63.4	63.0	62.6
17	22	69.5	68.8	68.2	67.6	67.0	66.5	65.9	65.4	64.8	64.3	63.8	63.4	62.9	62.5	62.0
18	23	69.2	68.5	67.9	67.3	66.7	66.1	65.5	65.0	64.4	63.9	63.4	62.9	62.4	62.0	61.5
19	24	68.9	68.3	67.6	67.0	66.4	65.8	65.2	64.6	64.0	63.5	63.0	62.5	62.0	61.5	61.0
20	25	68.7	68.0	67.3	66.7	66.1	65.4	64.8	64.2	63.7	63.1	62.6	62.0	61.5	61.0	60.6

Items Specifically Included in Gross Income
See p. 20,601 for regulations not amended to reflect law changes

TABLE II.—ORDINARY JOINT LIFE AND LAST SURVIVOR ANNUITIES—TWO LIVES—
EXPECTED RETURN MULTIPLES—Continued

Ages Male		21	22	23	24	25	26	27	28	29	30	31	32	33	34
Male	Female	26	27	28	29	30	31	32	33	34	35	36	37	38	39
6	11	68.4	68.2	68.0	67.8	67.6	67.5	67.3	67.1	67.0	66.8	66.7	66.6	66.5	66.4
7	12	67.8	67.5	67.3	67.1	66.9	66.7	66.5	66.4	66.2	66.1	65.9	65.8	65.7	65.6
8	13	67.1	66.8	66.6	66.4	66.2	66.0	65.8	65.6	65.4	65.3	65.1	65.0	64.9	64.7
9	14	66.4	66.2	65.9	65.7	65.4	65.2	65.0	64.8	64.7	64.5	64.3	64.2	64.1	63.9
10	15	65.8	65.5	65.2	65.0	64.7	64.5	64.3	64.1	63.9	63.7	63.6	63.4	63.3	63.1
11	16	65.1	64.8	64.6	64.3	64.1	63.8	63.6	63.4	63.2	63.0	62.8	62.6	62.5	62.3
12	17	64.5	64.2	63.9	63.6	63.4	63.1	62.9	62.7	62.4	62.2	62.0	61.9	61.7	61.5
13	18	63.9	63.6	63.3	63.0	62.7	62.4	62.2	61.9	61.7	61.5	61.3	61.1	60.9	60.8
14	19	63.3	63.0	62.7	62.3	62.0	61.8	61.5	61.2	61.0	60.8	60.6	60.4	60.2	60.0
15	20	62.7	62.4	62.0	61.7	61.4	61.1	60.8	60.6	60.3	60.1	59.8	59.6	59.4	59.2
16	21	62.2	61.8	61.4	61.1	60.8	60.5	60.2	59.9	59.6	59.4	59.1	58.9	58.7	58.5
17	22	61.6	61.2	60.9	60.5	60.2	59.8	59.5	59.2	58.9	58.7	58.4	58.2	57.9	57.7
18	23	61.1	60.7	60.3	59.9	59.6	59.2	58.9	58.6	58.3	58.0	57.7	57.5	57.2	57.0
19	24	60.6	60.2	59.7	59.4	59.0	58.6	58.3	57.9	57.6	57.3	57.0	56.8	56.5	56.3
20	25	60.1	59.6	59.2	58.8	58.4	58.0	57.7	57.3	57.0	56.7	56.4	56.1	55.8	55.6
21	26	59.6	59.1	58.7	58.3	57.9	57.5	57.1	56.7	56.4	56.0	55.7	55.4	55.1	54.9
22	27	59.1	58.7	58.2	57.7	57.3	56.9	56.5	56.1	55.8	55.4	55.1	54.8	54.5	54.2
23	28	58.7	58.2	57.7	57.2	56.8	56.4	55.9	55.5	55.2	54.8	54.4	54.1	53.8	53.5
24	29	58.3	57.7	57.2	56.8	56.3	55.8	55.4	55.0	54.6	54.2	53.8	53.5	53.2	52.8
25	30	57.9	57.3	56.8	56.3	55.8	55.3	54.9	54.4	54.0	53.6	53.2	52.9	52.5	52.2
26	31	57.5	56.9	56.4	55.8	55.3	54.8	54.4	53.9	53.5	53.1	52.7	52.3	51.9	51.6
27	32	57.1	56.5	55.9	55.4	54.9	54.4	53.9	53.4	53.0	52.5	52.1	51.7	51.3	50.9
28	33	56.7	56.1	55.5	55.0	54.4	53.9	53.4	52.9	52.4	52.0	51.5	51.1	50.7	50.3
29	34	56.4	55.8	55.2	54.6	54.0	53.5	53.0	52.4	52.0	51.5	51.0	50.6	50.2	49.8
30	35	56.0	55.4	54.8	54.2	53.6	53.1	52.5	52.0	51.5	51.0	50.5	50.1	49.6	49.2
31	36	55.7	55.1	54.4	53.8	53.2	52.7	52.1	51.6	51.0	50.5	50.0	49.5	49.1	48.7
32	37	55.4	54.8	54.1	53.5	52.9	52.3	51.7	51.1	50.6	50.1	49.5	49.1	48.6	48.1
33	38	55.1	54.5	53.8	53.2	52.5	51.9	51.3	50.7	50.2	49.6	49.1	48.6	48.1	47.6
34	39	54.9	54.2	53.5	52.8	52.2	51.6	50.9	50.3	49.8	49.2	48.7	48.1	47.6	47.1

Ages Male		35	36	37	38	39	40	41	42	43	44	45	46	47	48	49
Male	Female	40	41	42	43	44	45	46	47	48	49	50	51	52	53	54
6	11	66.3	66.2	66.1	66.0	65.9	65.9	65.8	65.7	65.7	65.6	65.6	65.5	65.5	65.5	65.4
7	12	65.4	65.3	65.3	65.2	65.1	65.0	64.9	64.9	64.8	64.8	64.7	64.7	64.6	64.6	64.5
8	13	64.6	64.5	64.4	64.3	64.2	64.1	64.1	64.0	64.0	63.9	63.8	63.8	63.7	63.7	63.7
9	14	63.8	63.7	63.6	63.5	63.4	63.3	63.2	63.2	63.1	63.0	63.0	62.9	62.9	62.8	62.8
10	15	63.0	62.9	62.8	62.7	62.6	62.5	62.4	62.3	62.2	62.2	62.1	62.0	62.0	61.9	61.9
11	16	62.2	62.1	61.9	61.8	61.7	61.6	61.5	61.4	61.4	61.3	61.2	61.2	61.1	61.0	61.0
12	17	61.4	61.3	61.1	61.0	60.9	60.8	60.7	60.6	60.5	60.4	60.4	60.3	60.2	60.2	60.1
13	18	60.6	60.5	60.3	60.2	60.1	60.0	59.9	59.8	59.7	59.6	59.5	59.4	59.4	59.3	59.2
14	19	59.8	59.7	59.5	59.4	59.3	59.1	59.0	58.9	58.8	58.7	58.6	58.6	58.5	58.4	58.4
15	20	59.0	58.9	58.7	58.6	58.4	58.3	58.2	58.1	58.0	57.9	57.8	57.7	57.6	57.6	57.5
16	21	58.3	58.1	57.9	57.8	57.6	57.5	57.4	57.2	57.1	57.0	56.9	56.8	56.8	56.7	56.6
17	22	57.5	57.3	57.2	57.0	56.8	56.7	56.6	56.4	56.3	56.2	56.1	56.0	55.9	55.8	55.7
18	23	56.8	56.6	56.4	56.2	56.0	55.9	55.7	55.6	55.5	55.4	55.2	55.1	55.1	55.0	54.9
19	24	56.0	55.8	55.6	55.4	55.3	55.1	54.9	54.8	54.7	54.5	54.4	54.3	54.2	54.1	54.0
20	25	55.3	55.1	54.9	54.7	54.5	54.3	54.1	54.0	53.8	53.7	53.6	53.5	53.4	53.3	53.2
21	26	54.6	54.4	54.1	53.9	53.7	53.5	53.4	53.2	53.0	52.9	52.8	52.6	52.5	52.4	52.3
22	27	53.9	53.6	53.4	53.2	53.0	52.8	52.6	52.4	52.2	52.1	51.9	51.8	51.7	51.6	51.5
23	28	53.2	52.9	52.7	52.5	52.2	52.0	51.8	51.6	51.5	51.3	51.1	51.0	50.9	50.7	50.6
24	29	52.5	52.3	52.0	51.7	51.5	51.3	51.1	50.9	50.7	50.5	50.3	50.2	50.0	49.9	49.8
25	30	51.9	51.6	51.3	51.0	50.8	50.5	50.3	50.1	49.9	49.7	49.6	49.4	49.2	49.1	49.0
26	31	51.2	50.9	50.6	50.3	50.1	49.8	49.6	49.4	49.2	49.0	48.8	48.6	48.4	48.3	48.1
27	32	50.6	50.3	50.0	49.7	49.4	49.1	48.9	48.6	48.4	48.2	48.0	47.8	47.6	47.5	47.3
28	33	50.0	49.6	49.3	49.0	48.7	48.4	48.2	47.9	47.7	47.5	47.2	47.1	46.9	46.7	46.5
29	34	49.4	49.0	48.7	48.3	48.0	47.7	47.5	47.2	47.0	46.7	46.5	46.3	46.1	45.9	45.7
30	35	48.8	48.4	48.1	47.7	47.4	47.1	46.8	46.5	46.2	46.0	45.8	45.5	45.3	45.2	45.0
31	36	48.2	47.8	47.5	47.1	46.8	46.4	46.1	45.8	45.6	45.3	45.0	44.8	44.6	44.4	44.2
32	37	47.7	47.3	46.9	46.5	46.1	45.8	45.5	45.2	44.9	44.6	44.3	44.1	43.9	43.7	43.4
33	38	47.2	46.7	46.3	45.9	45.5	45.2	44.8	44.5	44.2	43.9	43.7	43.4	43.2	42.9	42.7
34	39	46.7	46.2	45.8	45.4	45.0	44.6	44.2	43.9	43.6	43.3	43.0	42.7	42.5	42.2	42.0

TABLE II.—ORDINARY JOINT LIFE AND LAST SURVIVOR ANNUITIES—TWO LIVES—
EXPECTED RETURN MULTIPLES—Continued

Ages Male		50	51	52	53	54	55	56	57	58	59	60	61	62	63
Male	Female	55	56	57	58	59	60	61	62	63	64	65	66	67	68
6	11	65.4	65.4	65.3	65.3	65.3	65.3	65.3	65.2	65.2	65.2	65.2	65.2	65.2	65.2
7	12	64.5	64.5	64.4	64.4	64.4	64.4	64.3	64.3	64.3	64.3	64.3	64.3	64.3	64.2
8	13	63.6	63.6	63.5	63.5	63.5	63.5	63.4	63.4	63.4	63.4	63.4	63.4	63.3	63.3
9	14	62.7	62.7	62.7	62.6	62.6	62.6	62.5	62.5	62.5	62.5	62.5	62.5	62.4	62.4
10	15	61.8	61.8	61.8	61.7	61.7	61.7	61.6	61.6	61.6	61.6	61.6	61.5	61.5	61.5
11	16	61.0	60.9	60.9	60.8	60.8	60.8	60.7	60.7	60.7	60.7	60.6	60.6	60.6	60.6
12	17	60.1	60.0	60.0	59.9	59.9	59.9	59.8	59.8	59.8	59.8	59.7	59.7	59.7	59.7
13	18	59.2	59.1	59.1	59.0	59.0	58.9	58.9	58.9	58.9	58.8	58.8	58.8	58.8	58.8
14	19	58.3	58.2	58.2	58.2	58.1	58.1	58.0	58.0	58.0	57.9	57.9	57.9	57.9	57.9
15	20	57.4	57.4	57.3	57.3	57.2	57.2	57.1	57.1	57.1	57.0	57.0	57.0	57.0	56.9

Ages Male	Ages Female	50 / 55	51 / 56	52 / 57	53 / 58	54 / 59	55 / 60	56 / 61	57 / 62	58 / 63	59 / 64	60 / 65	61 / 66	62 / 67	63 / 68
16	21	56.5	56.5	56.4	56.4	56.3	56.3	56.2	56.2	56.2	56.1	56.1	56.1	56.1	56.0
17	22	55.7	55.6	55.5	55.5	55.4	55.4	55.3	55.3	55.3	55.2	55.2	55.1	55.1	55.1
18	23	54.8	54.7	54.7	54.6	54.6	54.5	54.5	54.4	54.4	54.3	54.3	54.3	54.2	54.2
19	24	53.9	53.9	53.8	53.7	53.7	53.6	53.6	53.5	53.5	53.4	53.4	53.4	53.3	53.3
20	25	53.1	53.0	52.9	52.8	52.8	52.7	52.7	52.6	52.6	52.5	52.5	52.4	52.4	52.4
21	26	52.2	52.1	52.0	52.0	51.9	51.8	51.8	51.7	51.7	51.6	51.6	51.5	51.5	51.5
22	27	51.4	51.3	51.2	51.1	51.0	51.0	50.9	50.8	50.8	50.7	50.7	50.6	50.6	50.6
23	28	50.5	50.4	50.3	50.2	50.2	50.1	50.0	50.0	49.9	49.8	49.8	49.7	49.7	49.7
24	29	49.7	49.6	49.5	49.4	49.3	49.2	49.1	49.1	49.0	49.0	49.0	48.9	48.8	48.8
25	30	48.8	48.7	48.6	48.5	48.4	48.3	48.3	48.2	48.1	48.1	48.1	48.0	48.0	47.9
26	31	48.0	47.9	47.8	47.7	47.6	47.5	47.4	47.3	47.3	47.2	47.1	47.1	47.0	47.0
27	32	47.2	47.1	46.9	46.8	46.7	46.6	46.5	46.5	46.4	46.3	46.2	46.2	46.1	46.1
28	33	46.4	46.3	46.1	46.0	45.9	45.8	45.7	45.6	45.5	45.4	45.4	45.3	45.2	45.2
29	34	45.6	45.4	45.3	45.2	45.1	44.9	44.8	44.7	44.7	44.6	44.6	44.4	44.4	44.3
30	35	44.8	44.6	44.5	44.4	44.2	44.1	44.0	43.9	43.8	43.7	43.7	43.6	43.6	43.5
31	36	44.0	43.9	43.7	43.6	43.4	43.3	43.2	43.1	43.0	42.9	42.8	42.7	42.6	42.6
32	37	43.3	43.1	42.9	42.8	42.6	42.5	42.4	42.2	42.1	42.0	41.9	41.9	41.8	41.7
33	38	42.5	42.3	42.1	42.0	41.8	41.7	41.5	41.4	41.3	41.2	41.1	41.0	40.9	40.8
34	39	41.8	41.6	41.4	41.2	41.0	40.9	40.7	40.6	40.5	40.4	40.3	40.2	40.1	40.0

Ages Male	Ages Female	64 / 69	65 / 70	66 / 71	67 / 72	68 / 73	69 / 74	70 / 75	71 / 76	72 / 77	73 / 78	74 / 79	75 / 80	76 / 81	77 / 82	78 / 83
6	11	65.1	65.1	65.1	65.1	65.1	65.1	65.1	65.1	65.1	65.1	65.1	65.1	65.1	65.1	65.1
7	12	64.2	64.2	64.2	64.2	64.2	64.2	64.2	64.2	64.2	64.2	64.2	64.2	64.2	64.1	64.1
8	13	63.3	63.3	63.3	63.3	63.3	63.3	63.3	63.3	63.3	63.3	63.2	63.2	63.2	63.2	63.2
9	14	62.4	62.4	62.4	62.4	62.4	62.4	62.3	62.3	62.3	62.3	62.3	62.3	62.3	62.3	62.3
10	15	61.5	61.5	61.5	61.5	61.4	61.4	61.4	61.4	61.4	61.4	61.4	61.4	61.4	61.4	61.4
11	16	60.6	60.6	60.6	60.5	60.5	60.5	60.5	60.5	60.5	60.5	60.5	60.5	60.5	60.5	60.5
12	17	59.7	59.6	59.6	59.6	59.6	59.6	59.6	59.6	59.6	59.6	59.6	59.6	59.5	59.5	59.5
13	18	58.8	58.7	58.7	58.7	58.7	58.7	58.7	58.7	58.7	58.7	58.6	58.6	58.6	58.6	58.6
14	19	57.8	57.8	57.8	57.8	57.8	57.8	57.8	57.7	57.7	57.7	57.7	57.7	57.7	57.7	57.7
15	20	56.9	56.9	56.9	56.9	56.9	56.8	56.8	56.8	56.8	56.8	56.8	56.8	56.8	56.8	56.8
16	21	56.0	56.0	56.0	56.0	55.9	55.9	55.9	55.9	55.9	55.9	55.9	55.9	55.9	55.9	55.8
17	22	55.1	55.1	55.1	55.0	55.0	55.0	55.0	55.0	55.0	55.0	55.0	54.9	54.9	54.9	54.9
18	23	54.2	54.2	54.1	54.1	54.1	54.1	54.1	54.1	54.0	54.0	54.0	54.0	54.0	54.0	54.0
19	24	53.3	53.2	53.2	53.2	53.2	53.2	53.2	53.1	53.1	53.1	53.1	53.1	53.1	53.1	53.1
20	25	52.4	52.3	52.3	52.3	52.3	52.2	52.2	52.2	52.2	52.2	52.2	52.2	52.2	52.1	52.1
21	26	51.4	51.4	51.4	51.4	51.3	51.3	51.3	51.3	51.3	51.3	51.3	51.2	51.2	51.2	51.2
22	27	50.5	50.5	50.5	50.5	50.4	50.4	50.4	50.4	50.4	50.3	50.3	50.3	50.3	50.3	50.3
23	28	49.6	49.6	49.6	49.5	49.5	49.5	49.5	49.5	49.4	49.4	49.4	49.4	49.4	49.4	49.4
24	29	48.7	48.7	48.7	48.6	48.6	48.6	48.6	48.5	48.5	48.5	48.5	48.5	48.5	48.4	48.4
25	30	47.8	47.8	47.8	47.7	47.7	47.7	47.6	47.6	47.6	47.6	47.6	47.5	47.5	47.5	47.5
26	31	46.9	46.9	46.8	46.8	46.8	46.8	46.7	46.7	46.7	46.7	46.6	46.6	46.6	46.6	46.6
27	32	46.0	46.0	45.9	45.9	45.9	45.8	45.8	45.8	45.8	45.7	45.7	45.7	45.7	45.7	45.7
28	33	45.1	45.1	45.1	45.0	45.0	44.9	44.9	44.9	44.9	44.8	44.8	44.8	44.8	44.8	44.8
29	34	44.3	44.2	44.2	44.1	44.1	44.0	44.0	44.0	44.0	43.9	43.9	43.9	43.9	43.9	43.8
30	35	43.4	43.3	43.3	43.2	43.2	43.1	43.1	43.1	43.1	43.0	43.0	43.0	43.0	42.9	42.9
31	36	42.5	42.4	42.4	42.3	42.3	42.3	42.2	42.2	42.2	42.1	42.1	42.1	42.1	42.0	42.0
32	37	41.6	41.6	41.5	41.5	41.4	41.4	41.3	41.3	41.3	41.2	41.2	41.2	41.2	41.1	41.1
33	38	40.8	40.7	40.7	40.6	40.5	40.5	40.4	40.4	40.4	40.3	40.3	40.3	40.3	40.2	40.2
34	39	39.9	39.9	39.8	39.7	39.7	39.6	39.6	39.5	39.5	39.4	39.4	39.4	39.4	39.3	39.3

TABLE II.—ORDINARY JOINT LIFE AND LAST SURVIVOR ANNUITIES—TWO LIVES—
EXPECTED RETURN MULTIPLES—Continued

Ages Male	Ages Female	79 / 84	80 / 85	81 / 86	82 / 87	83 / 88	84 / 89	85 / 90	86 / 91	87 / 92	88 / 93	89 / 94	90 / 95	91 / 96	92 / 97
6	11	65.1	65.1	65.1	65.1	65.1	65.1	65.1	65.1	65.1	65.0	65.0	65.0	65.0	65.0
7	12	64.1	64.1	64.1	64.1	64.1	64.1	64.1	64.1	64.1	64.1	64.1	64.1	64.1	64.1
8	13	63.2	63.2	63.2	63.2	63.2	63.2	63.2	63.2	63.2	63.2	63.2	63.2	63.2	63.2
9	14	62.3	62.3	62.3	62.3	62.3	62.3	62.3	62.3	62.3	62.3	62.3	62.3	62.3	62.3
10	15	61.4	61.4	61.4	61.4	61.4	61.4	61.4	61.4	61.4	61.4	61.4	61.4	61.4	61.4
11	16	60.5	60.5	60.5	60.5	60.5	60.5	60.4	60.4	60.4	60.4	60.4	60.4	60.4	60.4
12	17	59.5	59.5	59.5	59.5	59.5	59.5	59.5	59.5	59.5	59.5	59.5	59.5	59.5	59.5
13	18	58.6	58.6	58.6	58.6	58.6	58.6	58.6	58.6	58.6	58.6	58.6	58.6	58.6	58.6
14	19	57.7	57.7	57.7	57.7	57.7	57.7	57.7	57.7	57.7	57.7	57.7	57.7	57.7	57.7
15	20	56.8	56.8	56.8	56.8	56.8	56.8	56.7	56.7	56.7	56.7	56.7	56.7	56.7	56.7
16	21	55.8	55.8	55.8	55.8	55.8	55.8	55.8	55.8	55.8	55.8	55.8	55.8	55.8	55.8
17	22	54.9	54.9	54.9	54.9	54.9	54.9	54.9	54.9	54.9	54.9	54.9	54.9	54.9	54.9
18	23	54.0	54.0	54.0	54.0	54.0	54.0	54.0	54.0	54.0	54.0	54.0	54.0	54.0	53.9
19	24	53.1	53.1	53.1	53.0	53.0	53.0	53.0	53.0	53.0	53.0	53.0	53.0	53.0	53.0
20	25	52.1	52.1	52.1	52.1	52.1	52.1	52.1	52.1	52.1	52.1	52.1	52.1	52.1	52.1
21	26	51.2	51.2	51.2	51.2	51.2	51.2	51.2	51.2	51.2	51.2	51.2	51.2	51.2	51.2
22	27	50.3	50.3	50.3	50.3	50.3	50.2	50.2	50.2	50.2	50.2	50.2	50.2	50.2	50.2
23	28	49.4	49.3	49.3	49.3	49.3	49.3	49.3	49.3	49.3	49.3	49.3	49.3	49.3	49.3
24	29	48.4	48.4	48.4	48.4	48.4	48.4	48.4	48.4	48.4	48.4	48.4	48.4	48.4	48.4
25	30	47.5	47.5	47.5	47.5	47.5	47.5	47.5	47.5	47.4	47.4	47.4	47.4	47.4	47.4
26	31	46.6	46.6	46.6	46.6	46.5	46.5	46.5	46.5	46.5	46.5	46.5	46.5	46.5	46.5
27	32	45.7	45.6	45.6	45.6	45.6	45.6	45.6	45.6	45.6	45.6	45.6	45.6	45.6	45.6

Ages Male			79	80	81	82	83	84	85	86	87	88	89	90	91	92
Male	Female		84	85	86	87	88	89	90	91	92	93	94	95	96	97
28	33		44.7	44.7	44.7	44.7	44.7	44.7	44.7	44.7	44.7	44.7	44.7	44.7	44.7	44.7
29	34		43.8	43.8	43.8	43.8	43.8	43.8	43.8	43.8	43.8	43.7	43.7	43.7	43.7	43.7
30	35		42.9	42.9	42.9	42.9	42.9	42.9	42.8	42.8	42.8	42.8	42.8	42.8	42.8	42.8
31	36		42.0	42.0	42.0	42.0	42.0	41.9	41.9	41.9	41.9	41.9	41.9	41.9	41.9	41.9
32	37		41.1	41.1	41.1	41.1	41.0	41.0	41.0	41.0	41.0	41.0	41.0	41.0	41.0	41.0
33	38		40.2	40.2	40.2	40.2	40.1	40.1	40.1	40.1	40.1	40.1	40.1	40.1	40.1	40.1
34	39		39.3	39.3	39.3	39.3	39.2	39.2	39.2	39.2	39.2	39.2	39.2	39.2	39.2	39.2

Ages Male			93	94	95	96	97	98	99	100	101	102	103	104	105	106	107	108
Male	Female		98	99	100	101	102	103	104	105	106	107	108	109	110	111	112	113
6	11		65.0	65.0	65.0	65.0	65.0	65.0	65.0	65.0	65.0	65.0	65.0	65.0	65.0	65.0	65.0	65.0
7	12		64.1	64.1	64.1	64.1	64.1	64.1	64.1	64.1	64.1	64.1	64.1	64.1	64.1	64.1	64.1	64.1
8	13		63.2	63.2	63.2	63.2	63.2	63.2	63.2	63.2	63.2	63.2	63.2	63.2	63.2	63.2	63.2	63.2
9	14		62.3	62.3	62.3	62.3	62.3	62.3	62.3	62.3	62.3	62.3	62.3	62.3	62.3	62.3	62.3	62.3
10	15		61.4	61.4	61.4	61.4	61.4	61.4	61.4	61.4	61.4	61.4	61.4	61.4	61.4	61.4	61.4	61.4
11	16		60.4	60.4	60.4	60.4	60.4	60.4	60.4	60.4	60.4	60.4	60.4	60.4	60.4	60.4	60.4	60.4
12	17		59.5	59.5	59.5	59.5	59.5	59.5	59.5	59.5	59.5	59.5	59.5	59.5	59.5	59.5	59.5	59.5
13	18		58.6	58.6	58.6	58.6	58.6	58.6	58.6	58.6	58.6	58.6	58.6	58.6	58.6	58.6	58.6	58.6
14	19		57.7	57.7	57.7	57.7	57.7	57.7	57.7	57.7	57.7	57.7	57.7	57.7	57.7	57.7	57.7	57.7
15	20		56.7	56.7	56.7	56.7	56.7	56.7	56.7	56.7	56.7	56.7	56.7	56.7	56.7	56.7	56.7	56.7
16	21		55.8	55.8	55.8	55.8	55.8	55.8	55.8	55.8	55.8	55.8	55.8	55.8	55.8	55.8	55.8	55.8
17	22		54.9	54.9	54.9	54.9	54.9	54.9	54.9	54.9	54.9	54.9	54.9	54.9	54.9	54.9	54.9	54.9
18	23		53.9	53.9	53.9	53.9	53.9	53.9	53.9	53.9	53.9	53.9	53.9	53.9	53.9	53.9	53.9	53.9
19	24		53.0	53.0	53.0	53.0	53.0	53.0	53.0	53.0	53.0	53.0	53.0	53.0	53.0	53.0	53.0	53.0
20	25		52.1	52.1	52.1	52.1	52.1	52.1	52.1	52.1	52.1	52.1	52.1	52.1	52.1	52.1	52.1	52.1
21	26		51.2	51.2	51.2	51.2	51.2	51.2	51.1	51.1	51.1	51.1	51.1	51.1	51.1	51.1	51.1	51.1
22	27		50.2	50.2	50.2	50.2	50.2	50.2	50.2	50.2	50.2	50.2	50.2	50.2	50.2	50.2	50.2	50.2
23	28		49.3	49.3	49.3	49.3	49.3	49.3	49.3	49.3	49.3	49.3	49.3	49.3	49.3	49.3	49.3	48.3
24	29		48.4	48.4	48.4	48.4	48.4	48.4	48.4	48.4	48.4	48.4	48.4	48.4	48.4	48.4	48.3	48.3
25	30		47.4	47.4	47.4	47.4	47.4	47.4	47.4	47.4	47.4	47.4	47.4	47.4	47.4	47.4	47.4	47.4
26	31		46.5	46.5	46.5	46.5	46.5	46.5	46.5	46.5	46.5	46.5	46.5	46.5	46.5	46.5	46.5	46.5
27	32		45.6	45.6	45.6	45.6	45.6	45.6	45.6	45.6	45.6	45.6	45.6	45.6	45.6	45.6	45.6	45.6
28	33		44.7	44.6	44.6	44.6	44.6	44.6	44.6	44.6	44.6	44.6	44.6	44.6	44.6	44.6	44.6	44.6
29	34		43.7	43.7	43.7	43.7	43.7	43.7	43.7	43.7	43.7	43.7	43.7	43.7	43.7	43.7	43.7	43.7
30	35		42.8	42.8	42.8	42.8	42.8	42.8	42.8	42.8	42.8	42.8	42.8	42.8	42.8	42.8	42.8	42.8
31	36		41.9	41.9	41.9	41.9	41.9	41.9	41.9	41.9	41.9	41.9	41.9	41.9	41.9	41.9	41.9	41.9
32	37		41.0	41.0	41.0	41.0	41.0	41.0	41.0	41.0	41.0	41.0	41.0	41.0	41.0	41.0	41.0	41.0
33	38		40.1	40.1	40.1	40.1	40.1	40.1	40.1	40.1	40.1	40.1	40.1	40.1	40.1	40.1	40.1	40.0
34	39		39.2	39.2	39.2	39.2	39.2	39.2	39.2	39.2	39.2	39.2	39.2	39.1	39.1	39.1	39.1	39.1

TABLE II.—ORDINARY JOINT LIFE AND LAST SURVIVOR ANNUITIES—TWO LIVES—
EXPECTED RETURN MULTIPLES—Continued

Ages Male			35	36	37	38	39	40	41	42	43	44	45	46	47
Male	Female		40	41	42	43	44	45	46	47	48	49	50	51	52
35	40		46.2	45.7	45.3	44.8	44.4	44.0	43.6	43.3	43.0	42.6	42.3	42.0	41.8
36	41		45.7	45.2	44.8	44.3	43.9	43.5	43.1	42.7	42.3	42.0	41.7	41.4	41.1
37	42		45.3	44.8	44.3	43.8	43.4	42.9	42.5	42.1	41.8	41.4	41.1	40.7	40.4
38	43		44.8	44.3	43.8	43.3	42.9	42.4	42.0	41.6	41.2	40.8	40.5	40.1	39.8
39	44		44.4	43.9	43.4	42.9	42.4	41.9	41.5	41.0	40.6	40.2	39.9	39.5	39.2
40	45		44.0	43.5	42.9	42.4	41.9	41.4	41.0	40.5	40.1	39.7	39.3	38.9	38.6
41	46		43.6	43.1	42.5	42.0	41.5	41.0	40.5	40.0	39.6	39.2	38.8	38.4	38.0
42	47		43.3	42.7	42.1	41.6	41.0	40.5	40.0	39.6	39.1	38.7	38.2	37.8	37.5
43	48		43.0	42.3	41.8	41.2	40.6	40.1	39.6	39.1	38.6	38.2	37.7	37.3	36.9
44	49		42.6	42.0	41.4	40.8	40.2	39.7	39.2	38.7	38.2	37.7	37.2	36.8	36.4
45	50		42.3	41.7	41.1	40.5	39.9	39.3	38.8	38.2	37.7	37.2	36.8	36.3	35.9
46	51		42.0	41.4	40.7	40.1	39.5	38.9	38.4	38.0	37.3	36.8	36.3	35.9	35.4
47	52		41.8	41.1	40.4	39.8	39.2	38.6	38.0	37.5	36.9	36.4	35.9	35.4	35.0

Ages Male			48	49	50	51	52	53	54	55	56	57	58	59	60
Male	Female		53	54	55	56	57	58	59	60	61	62	63	64	65
35	40		41.5	41.3	41.0	40.8	40.6	40.4	40.3	40.1	40.0	39.8	39.7	39.6	39.5
36	41		40.8	40.6	40.3	40.1	39.9	39.7	39.5	39.3	39.2	39.0	38.9	38.8	38.6
37	42		40.2	39.9	39.6	39.4	39.2	39.0	38.8	38.6	38.4	38.3	38.1	38.0	37.9
38	43		39.5	39.2	39.0	38.7	38.5	38.3	38.1	37.9	37.7	37.5	37.3	37.2	37.1
39	44		38.9	38.6	38.3	38.0	37.8	37.6	37.3	37.1	36.9	36.8	36.6	36.4	36.3
40	45		38.3	38.0	37.7	37.4	37.1	36.9	36.6	36.4	36.2	36.0	35.9	35.7	35.5
41	46		37.7	37.3	37.0	36.7	36.5	36.2	36.0	35.7	35.5	35.3	35.1	35.0	34.8
42	47		37.1	36.8	36.4	36.1	35.8	35.6	35.3	35.1	34.8	34.6	34.4	34.2	34.1
43	48		36.5	36.2	35.8	35.5	35.2	34.9	34.7	34.4	34.2	33.9	33.7	33.5	33.3
44	49		36.0	35.6	35.3	34.9	34.6	34.3	34.0	33.8	33.5	33.3	33.0	32.8	32.6
45	50		35.5	35.1	34.7	34.4	34.0	33.7	33.4	33.1	32.9	32.6	32.4	32.2	31.9
46	51		35.0	34.6	34.2	33.8	33.5	33.1	32.8	32.5	32.2	32.0	31.7	31.5	31.3
47	52		34.5	34.1	33.7	33.3	32.9	32.6	32.2	31.9	31.6	31.4	31.1	30.9	30.6
48	53		34.0	33.6	33.2	32.8	32.4	32.0	31.7	31.4	31.1	30.8	30.5	30.2	30.0
49	54		33.6	33.1	32.7	32.3	31.9	31.5	31.2	30.8	30.5	30.2	29.9	29.6	29.4
50	55		33.2	32.7	32.3	31.8	31.4	31.0	30.6	30.3	29.9	29.6	29.3	29.0	28.8
51	56		32.8	32.3	31.8	31.4	30.9	30.5	30.1	29.8	29.4	29.1	28.8	28.5	28.2

Ages			48	49	50	51	52	53	54	55	56	57	58	59	60
	Male														
Male	Female		53	54	55	56	57	58	59	60	61	62	63	64	65
52	57		32.4	31.9	31.4	30.9	30.5	30.1	29.7	29.3	28.9	28.6	28.2	27.9	27.6
53	58		32.0	31.5	31.0	30.5	30.1	29.6	29.2	28.8	28.4	28.1	27.7	27.4	27.1
54	59		31.7	31.2	30.6	30.1	29.7	29.2	28.8	28.3	27.9	27.6	27.2	26.9	26.5
55	60		31.4	30.8	30.3	29.8	29.3	28.8	28.3	27.9	27.5	27.1	26.7	26.4	26.0
56	61		31.1	30.5	29.9	29.4	28.9	28.4	27.9	27.5	27.1	26.7	26.3	25.9	25.5
57	62		30.8	30.2	29.6	29.1	28.6	28.1	27.6	27.1	25.7	26.2	25.8	25.4	25.1
58	63		30.5	29.9	29.3	28.8	28.2	27.7	27.2	26.7	25.3	25.8	25.4	25.0	24.6
59	64		30.2	29.6	29.0	28.5	27.9	27.1	26.9	26.4	25.9	25.4	25.0	24.6	24.2
60	65		30.0	29.4	28.8	28.2	27.6	27.1	26.5	26.0	25.5	25.1	24.6	24.2	23.8

TABLE II.—ORDINARY JOINT LIFE AND LAST SURVIVOR ANNUITIES—TWO LIVES—
EXPECTED RETURN MULTIPLES—Continued

Male	Male / Female	61 / 66	62 / 67	63 / 68	64 / 69	65 / 70	66 / 71	67 / 72	68 / 73	69 / 74	70 / 75	71 / 76	72 / 77	73 / 78
35	40	39.4	39.3	39.2	39.1	39.0	38.9	38.9	38.8	38.8	38.7	38.7	38.6	38.6
36	41	38.5	38.4	38.3	38.2	38.2	38.1	38.0	38.0	37.9	37.9	37.8	37.8	37.7
37	42	37.7	37.6	37.5	37.4	37.3	37.3	37.2	37.1	37.1	37.0	36.9	36.9	36.9
38	43	36.9	36.8	36.7	36.6	36.5	36.4	36.4	36.3	36.2	36.2	36.1	36.0	36.0
39	44	36.2	36.0	35.9	35.8	35.7	35.6	35.5	35.5	35.4	35.3	35.3	35.2	35.2
40	45	35.4	35.3	35.1	35.0	34.9	34.8	34.7	34.6	34.6	34.5	34.4	34.4	34.3
41	46	34.6	34.5	34.4	34.2	34.1	34.0	33.9	33.8	33.8	33.7	33.6	33.5	33.5
42	47	33.9	33.7	33.6	33.5	33.4	33.2	33.1	33.0	33.0	32.9	32.8	32.7	32.7
43	48	33.2	33.0	32.9	32.7	32.6	32.5	32.4	32.3	32.3	32.2	32.1	32.0	31.9
44	49	32.5	32.3	32.1	32.0	31.8	31.7	31.6	31.5	31.4	31.3	31.2	31.1	31.1
45	50	31.8	31.6	31.4	31.3	31.1	31.0	30.8	30.7	30.6	30.5	30.4	30.4	30.3
46	51	31.1	30.9	30.7	30.5	30.4	30.2	30.1	30.0	29.9	29.8	29.7	29.6	29.5
47	52	30.4	30.2	30.0	29.8	29.7	29.5	29.4	29.3	29.1	29.0	28.9	28.8	28.7
48	53	29.8	29.5	29.3	29.2	29.0	28.8	28.7	28.5	28.4	28.3	28.2	28.1	28.0
49	54	29.1	28.9	28.7	28.5	28.3	28.1	28.0	27.8	27.7	27.6	27.5	27.4	27.3
50	55	28.5	28.3	28.1	27.8	27.6	27.5	27.3	27.1	27.0	26.9	26.7	26.6	26.5
51	56	27.9	27.7	27.4	27.2	27.0	26.8	26.6	26.5	26.3	26.2	26.0	25.9	25.8
52	57	27.3	27.1	26.8	26.6	26.4	26.2	26.0	25.8	25.7	25.5	25.4	25.2	25.1
53	58	26.8	26.5	26.2	26.0	25.8	25.6	25.4	25.2	25.0	24.8	24.7	24.6	24.4
54	59	26.2	25.9	25.7	25.4	25.2	25.0	24.7	24.6	24.4	24.2	24.0	23.9	23.8
55	60	25.7	25.4	25.1	24.9	24.6	24.4	24.1	23.9	23.8	23.6	23.4	23.3	23.1
56	61	25.2	24.9	24.6	24.3	24.1	23.8	23.6	23.4	23.2	23.0	22.8	22.6	22.5
57	62	24.7	24.4	24.1	23.8	23.5	23.3	23.0	22.8	22.6	22.4	22.2	22.0	21.9
58	63	24.3	23.9	23.6	23.3	23.0	22.7	22.5	22.2	22.0	21.8	21.6	21.4	21.3
59	64	23.8	23.5	23.1	22.8	22.5	22.2	21.9	21.7	21.5	21.2	21.0	20.9	20.7
60	65	23.4	23.0	22.7	22.3	22.0	21.7	21.4	21.2	20.9	20.7	20.5	20.3	20.1
61	66	23.0	22.6	22.2	21.9	21.6	21.3	21.0	20.7	20.4	20.2	20.0	19.8	19.6
62	67	22.6	22.2	21.8	21.5	21.1	20.8	20.5	20.2	19.9	19.7	19.5	19.2	19.0
63	68	22.2	21.8	21.4	21.1	20.7	20.4	20.1	19.8	19.5	19.2	19.0	18.7	18.5
64	69	21.9	21.5	21.1	20.7	20.3	20.0	19.6	19.3	19.0	18.7	18.5	18.2	18.0
65	70	21.6	21.1	20.7	20.3	19.9	19.6	19.2	18.9	18.6	18.3	18.0	17.8	17.5
66	71	21.3	20.8	20.4	20.0	19.6	19.2	18.8	18.5	18.2	17.9	17.6	17.3	17.1
67	72	21.0	20.5	20.1	19.6	19.2	18.8	18.5	18.1	17.8	17.5	17.2	16.9	16.7
68	73	20.7	20.2	19.8	19.3	18.9	18.5	18.1	17.8	17.4	17.1	16.8	16.5	16.2
69	74	20.4	19.9	19.5	19.0	18.6	18.2	17.8	17.4	17.1	16.7	16.4	16.1	15.8
70	75	20.2	19.7	19.2	18.7	18.3	17.9	17.5	17.1	16.7	16.4	16.1	15.8	15.5
71	76	20.0	19.5	19.0	18.5	18.0	17.6	17.2	16.8	16.4	16.1	15.7	15.4	15.1
72	77	19.8	19.2	18.7	18.2	17.8	17.3	16.9	16.5	16.1	15.8	15.4	15.1	14.8
73	78	19.6	19.0	18.5	18.0	17.5	17.1	16.7	16.2	15.8	15.5	15.1	14.8	14.4

TABLE II.—ORDINARY JOINT LIFE AND LAST SURVIVOR ANNUITIES—TWO LIVES—
EXPECTED RETURN MULTIPLES—Continued

Ages Male	Ages Female	74 / 79	75 / 80	76 / 81	77 / 82	78 / 83	79 / 84	80 / 85	81 / 86	82 / 87	83 / 88	84 / 89	85 / 90
35	40	38.6	38.5	38.5	38.5	38.4	38.4	38.4	38.4	38.4	38.4	38.3	38.3
36	41	37.7	37.6	37.6	37.6	37.6	37.5	37.5	37.5	37.5	37.5	37.5	37.4
37	42	36.8	36.8	36.7	36.7	36.7	36.7	36.6	36.6	36.6	36.6	36.6	36.6
38	43	36.0	35.9	35.9	35.9	35.8	35.8	35.8	35.8	35.7	35.7	35.7	35.7
39	44	35.1	35.1	35.0	35.0	35.0	34.9	34.9	34.9	34.9	34.8	34.8	34.8
40	45	34.3	34.2	34.2	34.1	34.1	34.1	34.1	34.0	34.0	34.0	34.0	34.0
41	46	33.4	33.4	33.3	33.3	33.3	33.2	33.2	33.2	33.2	33.1	33.1	33.1
42	47	32.6	32.6	32.5	32.5	32.4	32.4	32.4	32.3	32.3	32.3	32.3	32.3
43	48	31.8	31.8	31.7	31.7	31.6	31.6	31.5	34.5	31.5	31.5	31.4	31.4
44	49	31.0	30.9	30.9	30.8	30.8	30.8	30.7	30.7	30.7	30.6	30.6	30.6
45	50	30.2	30.1	30.1	30.0	30.0	29.9	29.9	29.9	29.8	29.8	29.8	29.8
46	51	29.4	29.4	29.3	29.2	29.2	29.2	29.1	29.1	29.0	29.0	29.0	28.9
47	52	28.7	28.6	28.5	28.5	28.4	28.4	28.3	28.3	28.2	28.2	28.2	28.1
48	53	27.9	27.8	27.8	27.7	27.6	27.6	27.5	27.5	27.5	27.4	27.4	27.4
49	54	27.2	27.1	27.0	26.9	26.9	26.8	26.8	26.7	26.7	26.6	26.6	26.6
50	55	26.4	26.3	26.3	26.2	26.1	26.1	26.0	26.0	25.9	25.9	25.8	25.8
51	56	25.7	25.6	25.5	25.5	25.4	25.3	25.3	25.2	25.2	25.1	25.1	25.0
52	57	25.0	24.9	24.8	24.7	24.7	24.6	24.5	24.5	24.4	24.4	24.3	24.3
53	58	24.3	24.2	24.1	24.0	23.9	23.9	23.8	23.7	23.7	23.6	23.6	23.5
54	59	23.6	23.5	23.4	23.3	23.2	23.2	23.1	23.0	23.0	22.9	22.9	22.8
55	60	23.0	22.9	22.8	22.7	22.6	22.5	22.4	22.3	22.3	22.2	22.2	22.1
56	61	22.3	22.2	22.1	22.0	21.9	21.8	21.7	21.6	21.6	21.5	21.5	21.4
57	62	21.7	21.6	21.5	21.3	21.2	21.1	21.1	21.0	20.9	20.8	20.8	20.7
58	63	21.1	21.0	20.8	20.7	20.6	20.5	20.4	20.3	20.2	20.2	20.1	20.0
59	64	20.5	20.4	20.2	20.1	20.0	19.9	19.8	19.7	19.6	19.5	19.4	19.4
60	65	19.9	19.8	19.6	19.5	19.4	19.3	19.1	19.0	19.0	18.9	18.8	18.7
61	66	19.4	19.2	19.1	18.9	18.8	18.7	18.5	18.4	18.3	18.3	18.2	18.1
62	67	18.8	18.7	18.5	18.3	18.2	18.1	18.0	17.8	17.7	17.7	17.6	17.5
63	68	18.3	18.1	18.0	17.8	17.6	17.5	17.4	17.3	17.2	17.1	17.0	16.9
64	69	17.8	17.6	17.4	17.3	17.1	17.0	16.8	16.7	16.6	16.5	16.4	16.3
65	70	17.3	17.1	16.9	16.7	16.6	16.4	16.3	16.2	16.0	15.9	15.8	15.8
66	71	16.9	16.6	16.4	16.3	16.1	15.9	15.8	15.6	15.5	15.4	15.3	15.2
67	72	16.4	16.2	16.0	15.8	15.6	15.4	15.3	15.1	15.0	14.9	14.8	14.7
68	73	16.0	15.7	15.5	15.3	15.1	15.0	14.8	14.6	14.5	14.4	14.3	14.2
69	74	15.8	15.3	15.1	14.9	14.7	14.5	14.3	14.2	14.0	13.9	13.8	13.7
70	75	15.2	14.9	14.7	14.5	14.3	14.1	13.9	13.7	13.6	13.4	13.3	13.2
71	76	14.8	14.5	14.3	14.1	13.8	13.6	13.5	13.3	13.1	13.0	12.8	12.7
72	77	14.5	14.2	13.9	13.7	13.5	13.2	13.0	12.9	12.7	12.5	12.4	12.3
73	78	14.1	13.8	13.6	13.3	13.1	12.9	12.7	12.5	12.3	12.1	12.0	11.8
74	79	13.8	13.5	13.2	13.0	12.7	12.5	12.3	12.1	11.9	11.7	11.6	11.4
75	80	13.5	13.2	12.9	12.6	12.4	12.2	11.9	11.7	11.5	11.4	11.2	11.0
76	81	13.2	12.9	12.6	12.3	12.1	11.8	11.6	11.4	11.2	11.0	10.8	10.7
77	82	13.0	12.6	12.3	12.1	11.8	11.5	11.3	11.1	10.8	10.7	10.5	10.3
78	83	12.7	12.4	12.1	11.8	11.5	11.2	11.0	10.7	10.5	10.3	10.1	10.0
79	84	12.5	12.2	11.8	11.5	11.2	11.0	10.7	10.5	10.2	10.0	9.8	9.6
80	85	12.3	11.9	11.6	11.3	11.0	10.7	10.4	10.2	10.0	9.7	9.5	9.3
81	86	12.1	11.7	11.4	11.1	10.7	10.5	10.2	9.9	9.7	9.5	9.3	9.1
82	87	11.9	11.5	11.2	10.8	10.5	10.2	10.0	9.7	9.4	9.2	9.0	8.8
83	88	11.7	11.4	11.0	10.7	10.3	10.0	9.7	9.5	9.2	9.0	8.7	8.5
84	89	11.6	11.2	10.8	10.5	10.1	9.8	9.5	9.3	9.0	8.7	8.5	8.3
85	90	11.4	11.0	10.7	10.3	10.0	9.6	9.3	9.1	8.8	8.5	8.3	8.1

TABLE II.—ORDINARY JOINT LIFE AND LAST SURVIVOR ANNUITIES—TWO LIVES—
EXPECTED RETURN MULTIPLES—Continued

Ages Male	Ages Female	86 / 91	87 / 92	88 / 93	89 / 94	90 / 95	91 / 96	92 / 97	93 / 98	94 / 99	95 / 100	96 / 101	97 / 102
35	40	38.3	38.3	38.3	38.3	38.3	38.3	38.3	38.3	38.3	38.3	38.3	38.3
36	41	37.4	37.4	37.4	37.4	37.4	37.4	37.4	37.4	37.4	37.4	37.4	37.4
37	42	36.5	36.5	36.5	36.5	36.5	36.5	36.5	36.5	36.5	36.5	36.5	36.5
38	43	35.7	35.7	35.6	35.6	35.6	35.6	35.6	35.6	35.6	35.6	35.6	35.6
39	44	34.8	34.8	34.8	34.8	34.8	34.8	34.7	34.7	34.7	34.7	34.7	34.7
40	45	33.9	33.9	33.9	33.9	33.9	33.9	33.9	33.9	33.9	33.9	33.9	33.9
41	46	33.1	33.1	33.1	33.0	33.0	33.0	33.0	33.0	33.0	33.0	33.0	33.0
42	47	32.2	32.2	32.2	32.2	32.2	32.2	32.2	32.2	32.2	32.1	32.1	32.1
43	48	31.4	31.4	31.4	31.3	31.3	31.3	31.3	31.3	31.3	31.3	31.3	31.3
44	49	30.6	30.5	30.5	30.5	30.5	30.5	30.5	30.5	30.5	30.5	30.5	30.4
45	50	29.7	29.7	29.7	29.7	29.7	29.7	29.7	29.6	29.6	29.6	29.6	29.6
46	51	28.9	28.9	28.9	28.9	28.9	28.8	28.8	28.8	28.8	28.8	28.8	28.8
47	52	28.1	28.1	28.1	28.1	28.0	28.0	28.0	28.0	28.0	28.0	28.0	28.0
48	53	27.3	27.3	27.3	27.3	27.2	27.2	27.2	27.2	27.2	27.2	27.2	27.2
49	54	26.5	26.5	26.5	26.5	26.5	26.4	26.4	26.4	26.4	26.4	26.4	26.4
50	55	25.8	25.7	25.7	25.7	25.7	25.7	25.6	25.6	25.6	25.6	25.6	25.6
51	56	25.0	25.0	24.9	24.9	24.9	24.9	24.9	24.9	24.8	24.8	24.8	24.8
52	57	24.3	24.2	24.2	24.2	24.1	24.1	24.1	24.1	24.1	24.1	24.1	24.0
53	58	23.5	23.5	23.4	23.4	23.4	23.4	23.4	23.3	23.3	23.3	23.3	23.3
54	59	22.8	22.7	22.7	22.7	22.7	22.6	22.6	22.6	22.6	22.6	22.6	22.5
55	60	22.1	22.0	22.0	22.0	21.9	21.9	21.9	21.9	21.8	21.8	21.8	21.8
56	61	21.4	21.3	21.3	21.3	21.2	21.2	21.2	21.1	21.1	21.1	21.1	21.1
57	62	20.7	20.6	20.6	20.6	20.5	20.5	20.5	20.4	20.4	20.4	20.4	20.4
58	63	20.0	19.9	19.9	19.9	19.8	19.8	19.8	19.8	19.7	19.7	19.7	19.7
59	64	19.3	19.3	19.2	19.2	19.2	19.1	19.1	19.1	19.0	19.0	19.0	19.0

Ages Male	Ages Female	98 / 103	99 / 104	100 / 105	101 / 106	102 / 107	103 / 108	104 / 109	105 / 110	106 / 111	107 / 112	108 / 113
35	40	38.3	38.3	38.3	38.3	38.3	38.3	38.2	38.2	38.2	38.2	38.2
36	41	37.4	37.4	37.4	37.4	37.4	37.4	37.4	37.4	37.4	37.4	37.3
37	42	36.5	36.5	36.5	36.5	36.5	36.5	36.5	36.5	36.5	36.5	36.5
38	43	35.6	35.6	35.6	35.6	35.6	35.6	35.6	35.6	35.6	35.6	35.6
39	44	34.7	34.7	34.7	34.7	34.7	34.7	34.7	34.7	34.7	34.7	34.7
40	45	33.9	33.8	33.8	33.8	33.8	33.8	33.8	33.8	33.8	33.8	33.8
41	46	33.0	33.0	33.0	33.0	33.0	33.0	33.0	33.0	33.0	33.0	33.0
42	47	32.1	32.1	32.1	32.1	32.1	32.1	32.1	32.1	32.1	32.1	32.1
43	48	31.3	31.3	31.3	31.3	31.3	31.3	31.3	31.3	31.3	31.3	31.3
44	49	30.4	30.4	30.4	30.4	30.4	30.4	30.4	30.4	30.4	30.4	30.4
45	50	29.6	29.6	29.6	29.6	29.6	29.6	29.6	29.6	29.6	29.6	29.6
46	51	28.8	28.8	28.8	28.8	28.8	28.8	28.8	28.8	28.8	28.8	28.7
47	52	28.0	28.0	28.0	28.0	28.0	28.0	28.0	27.9	27.9	27.9	27.9
48	53	27.2	27.2	27.2	27.2	27.2	27.1	27.1	27.1	27.1	27.1	27.1
49	54	26.4	26.4	26.4	26.4	26.4	26.3	26.3	26.3	26.3	26.3	26.3
50	55	25.6	25.6	25.6	25.6	25.6	25.6	25.6	25.6	25.5	25.5	25.5
51	56	24.8	24.8	24.8	24.8	24.8	24.8	24.8	24.8	24.8	24.8	24.7
52	57	24.0	24.0	24.0	24.0	24.0	24.0	24.0	24.0	24.0	24.0	24.0
53	58	23.3	23.3	23.3	23.3	23.3	23.3	23.2	23.2	23.2	23.2	23.2
54	59	22.5	22.5	22.5	22.5	22.5	22.5	22.5	22.5	22.5	22.5	22.5
55	60	21.8	21.8	21.8	21.8	21.8	21.8	21.8	21.8	21.8	21.7	21.7
56	61	21.1	21.1	21.1	21.1	21.1	21.1	21.0	21.0	21.0	21.0	21.0
57	62	20.4	20.4	20.4	20.4	20.3	20.3	20.3	20.3	20.3	20.3	20.3
58	63	19.7	19.7	19.7	19.6	19.6	19.6	19.6	19.6	19.6	19.6	19.6
59	64	19.0	19.0	19.0	19.0	19.0	18.9	18.9	18.9	18.9	18.9	18.9

Table II.—Ordinary Joint Life and Last Survivor Annuities—Two Lives—
Expected Return Multiples—Continued

Ages Male	Ages Female	86 / 91	87 / 92	88 / 93	89 / 94	90 / 95	91 / 96	92 / 97	93 / 98	94 / 99	95 / 100	96 / 101	97 / 102
60	65	18.7	18.6	18.6	18.5	18.5	18.5	18.4	18.4	18.4	18.4	18.3	18.3
61	66	18.1	18.0	17.9	17.9	17.9	17.8	17.8	17.8	17.7	17.7	17.7	17.7
62	67	17.4	17.4	17.3	17.3	17.2	17.2	17.1	17.1	17.1	17.1	17.0	17.0
63	68	16.8	16.8	16.7	16.7	16.6	16.6	16.5	16.5	16.5	16.4	16.4	16.4
64	69	16.2	16.2	16.1	16.1	16.0	16.0	15.9	15.9	15.9	15.8	15.8	15.8
65	70	15.7	15.6	15.5	15.5	15.4	15.4	15.3	15.3	15.3	15.2	15.2	15.2
66	71	15.1	15.0	15.0	14.9	14.8	14.8	14.7	14.7	14.7	14.6	14.6	14.6
67	72	14.6	14.5	14.4	14.4	14.3	14.2	14.2	14.1	14.1	14.1	14.1	14.0
68	73	14.1	14.0	13.9	13.8	13.8	13.7	13.6	13.6	13.6	13.5	13.5	13.5
69	74	13.6	13.5	13.4	13.3	13.2	13.2	13.1	13.1	13.0	13.0	13.0	12.9
70	75	13.1	13.0	12.9	12.8	12.7	12.7	12.6	12.5	12.5	12.5	12.4	12.4
71	76	12.6	12.5	12.4	12.3	12.2	12.2	12.1	12.1	12.0	12.0	11.9	11.9
72	77	12.1	12.0	11.9	11.8	11.8	11.7	11.6	11.6	11.5	11.5	11.4	11.4
73	78	11.7	11.6	11.5	11.4	11.3	11.3	11.2	11.1	11.0	11.0	11.0	10.9
74	79	11.3	11.2	11.1	11.0	10.9	10.8	10.7	10.7	10.6	10.6	10.5	10.5
75	80	10.9	10.8	10.7	10.5	10.5	10.4	10.3	10.2	10.2	10.1	10.1	10.0
76	81	10.5	10.4	10.3	10.2	10.1	10.0	9.9	9.8	9.7	9.7	9.7	9.6
77	82	10.2	10.0	9.9	9.8	9.7	9.5	9.5	9.4	9.3	9.3	9.2	9.2
78	83	9.8	9.7	9.5	9.4	9.3	9.2	9.1	9.0	9.0	8.9	8.9	8.8
79	84	9.5	9.3	9.2	9.1	8.9	8.8	8.8	8.7	8.6	8.5	8.5	8.4
80	85	9.2	9.0	8.9	8.7	8.6	8.5	8.4	8.3	8.3	8.2	8.1	8.1
81	86	8.9	8.7	8.6	8.4	8.3	8.2	8.1	8.0	7.9	7.9	7.8	7.7
82	87	8.6	8.4	8.3	8.1	8.0	7.9	7.8	7.7	7.6	7.5	7.5	7.4
83	88	8.3	8.2	8.0	7.9	7.7	7.6	7.5	7.4	7.3	7.2	7.2	7.1
84	89	8.1	7.9	7.8	7.6	7.5	7.3	7.2	7.1	7.0	7.0	6.9	6.8

Ages Male	Ages Female	98 / 103	99 / 104	100 / 105	101 / 106	102 / 107	103 / 108	104 / 109	105 / 110	106 / 111	107 / 112	108 / 113
60	65	18.3	18.3	18.3	18.3	18.3	18.3	18.3	18.2	18.2	18.2	18.2
61	66	17.7	17.7	17.6	17.6	17.6	17.6	17.6	17.6	17.6	17.6	17.5
62	67	17.0	17.0	17.0	17.0	17.0	17.0	16.9	16.9	16.9	16.9	16.9
63	68	16.4	16.4	16.4	16.3	16.3	16.3	16.3	16.3	16.3	16.3	16.2
64	69	15.8	15.8	15.7	15.7	15.7	15.7	15.7	15.7	15.7	15.7	15.6
65	70	15.2	15.2	15.1	15.1	15.1	15.1	15.1	15.1	15.1	15.0	15.0
66	71	14.6	14.6	14.5	14.5	14.5	14.5	14.5	14.5	14.5	14.4	14.4
67	72	14.0	14.0	14.0	14.0	13.9	13.9	13.9	13.9	13.9	13.9	13.8
68	73	13.5	13.4	13.4	13.4	13.4	13.4	13.3	13.3	13.3	13.3	13.2
69	74	12.9	12.9	12.9	12.8	12.8	12.8	12.8	12.8	12.8	12.7	12.7
70	75	12.4	12.4	12.3	12.3	12.3	12.3	12.3	12.2	12.2	12.2	12.1
71	76	11.9	11.9	11.8	11.8	11.8	11.8	11.7	11.7	11.7	11.7	11.6
72	77	11.4	11.4	11.3	11.3	11.3	11.3	11.2	11.2	11.2	11.2	11.1
73	78	10.9	10.9	10.9	10.8	10.8	10.8	10.7	10.7	10.7	10.7	10.6
74	79	10.5	10.4	10.4	10.4	10.3	10.3	10.3	10.3	10.2	10.2	10.1
75	80	10.0	10.0	9.9	9.9	9.9	9.8	9.8	9.8	9.8	9.7	
76	81	9.6	9.5	9.5	9.5	9.4	9.4	9.4	9.4	9.3	9.3	
77	82	9.2	9.1	9.1	9.1	9.0	9.0	9.0	8.9	8.9	8.9	
78	83	8.8	8.7	8.7	8.7	8.6	8.6	8.5	8.5	8.5	8.4	
79	84	8.4	8.4	8.3	8.3	8.2	8.2	8.2	8.1	8.1	8.0	
80	85	8.0	8.0	7.9	7.9	7.9	7.8	7.8	7.7	7.7	7.6	
81	86	7.7	7.6	7.6	7.6	7.5	7.5	7.4	7.4	7.3	7.3	
82	87	7.4	7.3	7.3	7.2	7.2	7.1	7.1	7.0	7.0	6.9	
83	88	7.1	7.0	6.9	6.9	6.8	6.8	6.7	6.7	6.7	6.6	
84	89	6.8	6.7	6.6	6.6	6.5	6.5	6.4	6.4	6.3		

TABLE II.—ORDINARY JOINT LIFE AND LAST SURVIVOR ANNUITIES—TWO LIVES—
EXPECTED RETURN MULTIPLES—Continued

Ages Male	Ages Female	86 / 91	87 / 92	88 / 93	89 / 94	90 / 95	91 / 96	92 / 97	93 / 98	94 / 99	95 / 100	96 / 101
85	90	7.9	7.7	7.5	7.4	7.2	7.1	7.0	6.9	6.8	6.7	6.6
86	91	7.7	7.5	7.3	7.1	7.0	6.8	6.7	6.6	6.5	6.4	6.4
87	92	7.5	7.3	7.1	6.9	6.8	6.6	6.5	6.4	6.3	6.2	6.1
88	93	7.3	7.1	6.9	6.7	6.6	6.4	6.3	6.2	6.1	6.0	5.9
89	94	7.1	6.9	6.7	6.5	6.4	6.2	6.1	6.0	5.9	5.8	5.7
90	95	7.0	6.8	6.6	6.4	6.2	6.1	5.9	5.8	5.7	5.6	5.5
91	96	6.8	6.6	6.4	6.2	6.1	5.9	5.8	5.7	5.5	5.4	5.3
92	97	6.7	6.5	6.3	6.1	5.9	5.8	5.6	5.5	5.4	5.3	5.2
93	98	6.6	6.4	6.2	6.0	5.8	5.7	5.5	5.4	5.2	5.1	5.0
94	99	6.5	6.3	6.1	5.9	5.7	5.5	5.4	5.2	5.1	5.0	4.9
95	100	6.4	6.2	6.0	5.8	5.6	5.4	5.3	5.1	5.0	4.9	4.7
96	101	6.4	6.1	5.9	5.7	5.5	5.3	5.2	5.0	4.9	4.7	4.6
97	102	6.3	6.1	5.8	5.6	5.4	5.2	5.1	4.9	4.8	4.6	4.5
98	103	6.2	6.0	5.8	5.5	5.3	5.1	5.0	4.8	4.7	4.5	4.4
99	104	6.2	5.9	5.7	5.5	5.2	5.1	4.9	4.7	4.6	4.4	4.3

Ages Male	Ages Female	97 / 102	98 / 103	99 / 104	100 / 105	101 / 106	102 / 107	103 / 108	104 / 109	105 / 110	106 / 111
85	90	6.6	6.5	6.4	6.4	6.3	6.2	6.2	6.1	6.1	6.0
86	91	6.3	6.2	6.2	6.1	6.0	6.0	5.9	5.9	5.8	5.7
87	92	6.1	6.0	5.9	5.8	5.8	5.7	5.6	5.6	5.5	5.4
88	93	5.8	5.8	5.7	5.6	5.5	5.5	5.4	5.3	5.3	5.1
89	94	5.6	5.5	5.5	5.4	5.3	5.2	5.2	5.1	5.0	
90	95	5.4	5.3	5.2	5.2	5.1	5.0	4.9	4.9	4.8	
91	96	5.2	5.1	5.1	5.0	4.9	4.8	4.7	4.6	4.5	
92	97	5.1	5.0	4.9	4.8	4.7	4.6	4.5	4.4		
93	98	4.9	4.8	4.7	4.6	4.5	4.4	4.3	4.2		
94	99	4.8	4.7	4.6	4.5	4.4	4.3	4.1			
95	100	4.6	4.5	4.4	4.3	4.2	4.1	4.0			
96	101	4.5	4.4	4.3	4.2	4.1	3.9				
97	102	4.4	4.3	4.1	4.0	3.9	3.7				
98	103	4.3	4.1	4.0	3.9	3.7					
99	104	4.1	4.0	3.9	3.7						

TABLE IIA.—ANNUITIES FOR JOINT LIFE ONLY—TWO LIVES—
EXPECTED RETURN MULTIPLES

Ages Male	Ages Female	6 / 11	7 / 12	8 / 13	9 / 14	10 / 15	11 / 16	12 / 17	13 / 18	14 / 19	15 / 20	16 / 21	17 / 22	18 / 23	19 / 24	20 / 25
6	11	56.6	56.1	55.7	55.1	54.6	54.1	53.5	52.9	52.3	51.7	51.1	50.5	49.8	49.1	48.4
7	12	56.1	55.7	55.2	54.7	54.2	53.7	53.1	52.6	52.0	51.4	50.8	50.2	49.5	48.9	48.2
8	13	55.7	55.2	54.8	54.3	53.8	53.3	52.8	52.2	51.6	51.1	50.5	49.9	49.2	48.6	47.9
9	14	55.1	54.7	54.3	53.8	53.3	52.9	52.3	51.8	51.3	50.7	50.1	49.5	48.9	48.3	47.7
10	15	54.6	54.2	53.8	53.3	52.9	52.4	51.9	51.4	50.9	50.3	49.8	49.2	48.6	48.0	47.4
11	16	54.1	53.7	53.3	52.9	52.4	52.0	51.5	51.0	50.5	50.0	49.4	48.8	48.3	47.7	47.1
12	17	53.5	53.1	52.8	52.3	51.9	51.5	51.0	50.6	50.1	49.6	49.0	48.5	47.9	47.3	46.7
13	18	52.9	52.6	52.2	51.8	51.4	51.0	50.6	50.1	49.6	49.1	48.6	48.1	47.5	47.0	46.4
14	19	52.3	52.0	51.6	51.3	50.9	50.5	50.1	49.6	49.2	48.7	48.2	47.7	47.2	46.6	46.1
15	20	51.7	51.4	51.1	50.7	50.3	50.0	49.6	49.1	48.7	48.2	47.8	47.3	46.8	46.2	45.7
16	21	51.1	50.8	50.5	50.1	49.8	49.4	49.0	48.6	48.2	47.8	47.3	46.8	46.3	45.8	45.3
17	22	50.5	50.2	49.9	49.5	49.2	48.8	48.5	48.1	47.7	47.3	46.8	46.4	45.9	45.4	44.9
18	23	49.8	49.5	49.2	48.9	48.6	48.3	47.9	47.5	47.2	46.8	46.3	45.9	45.4	45.0	44.5
19	24	49.1	48.9	48.6	48.3	48.0	47.7	47.3	47.0	46.6	46.2	45.8	45.4	45.0	44.5	44.0
20	25	48.4	48.2	47.9	47.7	47.4	47.1	46.7	46.4	46.1	45.7	45.3	44.9	44.5	44.0	43.6

TABLE IIA.—ANNUITIES FOR JOINT LIFE ONLY—TWO LIVES—
EXPECTED RETURN MULTIPLES—Continued

	Ages														
	Male	21	22	23	24	25	26	27	28	29	30	31	32	33	34
Male	Female	26	27	28	29	30	31	32	33	34	35	36	37	38	39
6	11	47.7	47.0	46.3	45.6	44.8	44.1	43.3	42.5	41.8	41.0	40.2	39.4	38.6	37.8
7	12	47.5	46.8	46.1	45.4	44.6	43.9	43.2	42.4	41.6	40.9	40.1	39.3	38.5	37.7
8	13	47.3	46.6	45.9	45.2	44.5	43.7	43.0	42.2	41.5	40.7	39.9	39.2	38.4	37.6
9	14	47.0	46.3	45.6	45.0	44.2	43.5	42.8	42.1	41.3	40.6	39.8	39.0	38.3	37.5
10	15	46.7	46.1	45.4	44.7	44.0	43.3	42.6	41.9	41.1	40.4	39.7	38.9	38.1	37.4
11	16	46.4	45.8	45.1	44.5	43.8	43.1	42.4	41.7	41.0	40.2	39.5	38.8	38.0	37.2
12	17	46.1	45.5	44.9	44.2	43.6	42.9	42.2	41.5	40.8	40.1	39.3	38.6	37.9	37.1
13	18	45.8	45.2	44.6	43.9	43.3	42.6	42.0	41.3	40.6	39.9	39.2	38.4	37.7	37.0
14	19	45.5	44.9	44.3	43.7	43.0	42.4	41.7	41.0	40.4	39.7	39.0	38.3	37.5	36.8
15	20	45.1	44.6	44.0	43.4	42.7	42.1	41.5	40.8	40.1	39.5	38.8	38.1	37.4	36.6
16	21	44.8	44.2	43.6	43.0	42.4	41.8	41.2	40.5	39.9	39.2	38.6	37.9	37.2	36.5
17	22	44.4	43.8	43.3	42.7	42.1	41.5	40.9	40.3	39.6	39.0	38.3	37.7	37.0	36.3
18	23	44.0	43.5	42.9	42.4	41.8	41.2	40.6	40.0	39.4	38.7	38.1	37.4	36.8	36.1
19	24	43.6	43.1	42.5	42.0	41.4	40.9	40.3	39.7	39.1	38.5	37.8	37.2	36.5	35.9
20	25	43.1	42.6	42.1	41.6	41.1	40.5	40.0	39.4	38.8	38.2	37.6	36.9	36.3	35.7
21	26	42.7	42.2	41.7	41.2	40.7	40.2	39.6	39.1	38.5	37.9	37.3	36.7	36.1	35.4
22	27	42.2	41.8	41.3	40.8	40.3	39.8	39.3	38.7	38.2	37.6	37.0	36.4	35.8	35.2
23	28	41.7	41.3	40.8	40.4	39.9	39.4	38.9	38.4	37.8	37.3	36.7	36.1	35.5	34.9
24	29	41.2	40.8	40.4	39.9	39.5	39.0	38.5	38.0	37.5	36.9	36.4	35.8	35.2	34.6
25	30	40.7	40.3	39.9	39.5	39.0	38.6	38.1	37.6	37.1	36.6	36.0	35.5	34.9	34.4
26	31	40.2	39.8	39.4	39.0	38.6	38.1	37.7	37.2	36.7	36.2	35.7	35.2	34.6	34.1
27	32	39.6	39.3	38.9	38.5	38.1	37.7	37.2	36.8	36.3	35.8	35.3	34.8	34.3	33.7
28	33	39.1	38.7	38.4	38.0	37.6	37.2	36.8	36.3	35.9	35.4	34.9	34.5	33.9	33.4
29	34	38.5	38.2	37.8	37.5	37.1	36.7	36.3	35.9	35.5	35.0	34.6	34.1	33.6	33.1
30	35	37.9	37.6	37.3	36.9	36.6	36.2	35.8	35.4	35.0	34.6	34.1	33.7	33.2	32.7
31	36	37.3	37.0	36.7	36.4	36.0	35.7	35.3	34.9	34.6	34.1	33.7	33.3	32.8	32.3
32	37	36.7	36.4	36.1	35.8	35.5	35.2	34.8	34.5	34.1	33.7	33.3	32.9	32.4	32.0
33	38	36.1	35.8	35.5	35.2	34.9	34.6	34.3	33.9	33.6	33.2	32.8	32.4	32.0	31.6
34	39	35.4	35.2	34.9	34.6	34.4	34.1	33.7	33.4	33.1	32.7	32.3	32.0	31.6	31.1

	Ages														
	Male	35	36	37	38	39	40	41	42	43	44	45	46	47	48	49
Male	Female	40	41	42	43	44	45	46	47	48	49	50	51	52	53	54
6	11	37.0	36.2	35.4	34.6	33.8	33.0	32.2	31.4	30.6	29.8	29.0	28.2	27.5	26.7	25.9
7	12	36.9	36.1	35.3	34.5	33.7	32.9	32.1	31.3	30.5	29.8	29.0	28.2	27.4	26.7	25.9
8	13	36.8	36.0	35.2	34.4	33.7	32.9	32.1	31.3	30.5	29.7	28.9	28.2	27.4	26.6	25.9
9	14	36.7	35.9	35.1	34.4	33.6	32.8	32.0	31.2	30.4	29.7	28.9	28.1	27.3	26.6	25.8
10	15	36.6	35.8	35.1	34.3	33.5	32.7	31.9	31.2	30.4	29.6	28.8	28.1	27.3	26.5	25.8
11	16	36.5	35.7	34.9	34.2	33.4	32.6	31.9	31.1	30.3	29.5	28.8	28.0	27.3	26.5	25.7
12	17	36.4	35.6	34.8	34.1	33.3	32.5	31.8	31.0	30.2	29.5	28.7	28.0	27.2	26.4	25.7
13	18	36.2	35.5	34.7	34.0	33.2	32.4	31.7	30.9	30.2	29.4	28.7	27.9	27.1	26.4	25.7
14	19	36.1	35.3	34.6	33.8	33.1	32.3	31.6	30.8	30.1	29.3	28.6	27.8	27.1	26.3	25.6
15	20	35.9	35.2	34.5	33.7	33.0	32.2	31.5	30.7	30.0	29.3	28.5	27.8	27.0	26.3	25.6
16	21	35.8	35.0	34.3	33.6	32.9	32.1	31.4	30.6	29.9	29.2	28.4	27.7	27.0	26.2	25.5
17	22	35.6	34.9	34.2	33.4	32.7	32.0	31.3	30.5	29.8	29.1	28.3	27.6	26.9	26.2	25.4
18	23	35.4	34.7	34.0	33.3	32.6	31.9	31.2	30.4	29.7	29.0	28.3	27.5	26.8	26.1	25.4
19	24	35.2	34.5	33.8	33.1	32.4	31.7	31.0	30.3	29.6	28.9	28.2	27.4	26.7	26.0	25.3
20	25	35.0	34.3	33.7	33.0	32.3	31.6	30.9	30.2	29.5	28.8	28.1	27.3	26.6	25.9	25.2
21	26	34.8	34.1	33.5	32.8	32.1	31.4	30.7	30.0	29.3	28.6	27.9	27.2	26.5	25.8	25.1
22	27	34.5	33.9	33.3	32.6	31.9	31.3	30.6	29.9	29.2	28.5	27.8	27.1	26.4	25.7	25.1
23	28	34.3	33.7	33.0	32.4	31.7	31.0	30.4	29.7	29.1	28.4	27.7	27.0	26.3	25.6	25.0
24	29	34.0	33.4	32.8	32.2	31.5	30.9	30.2	29.6	28.9	28.2	27.6	26.9	26.2	25.5	24.9
25	30	33.8	33.2	32.6	32.0	31.3	30.7	30.1	29.4	28.8	28.1	27.4	26.8	26.1	25.4	24.8
26	31	33.5	32.9	32.3	31.7	31.1	30.5	29.9	29.2	28.6	27.9	27.3	26.6	26.0	25.3	24.6
27	32	33.2	32.6	32.1	31.5	30.9	30.3	29.6	29.0	28.4	27.8	27.1	26.5	25.8	25.2	24.5
28	33	32.9	32.3	31.8	31.2	30.6	30.0	29.4	28.8	28.2	27.6	27.0	26.3	25.7	25.0	24.4
29	34	32.6	32.0	31.5	30.9	30.4	29.8	29.2	28.6	28.0	27.4	26.8	26.2	25.5	24.9	24.3
30	35	32.2	31.7	31.2	30.6	30.1	29.5	29.0	28.4	27.8	27.2	26.6	26.0	25.4	24.7	24.1
31	36	31.9	31.4	30.9	30.3	29.8	29.3	28.7	28.1	27.6	27.0	26.4	25.8	25.2	24.6	24.0
32	37	31.5	31.0	30.5	30.0	29.5	29.0	28.4	27.9	27.3	26.8	26.2	25.6	25.0	24.4	23.8
33	38	31.1	30.7	30.2	29.7	29.2	28.7	28.2	27.6	27.1	26.5	26.0	25.4	24.8	24.2	23.6
34	39	30.7	30.3	29.8	29.3	28.9	28.4	27.9	27.3	26.8	26.3	25.7	25.2	24.6	24.0	23.5

TABLE IIA.—ANNUITIES FOR JOINT LIFE ONLY—TWO LIVES—
EXPECTED RETURN MULTIPLES—Continued

	Ages														
	Male	50	51	52	53	54	55	56	57	58	59	60	61	62	63
Male	Female	55	56	57	58	59	60	61	62	63	64	65	66	67	68
6	*11*	25.2	24.4	23.7	22.9	22.2	21.5	20.8	20.1	19.4	18.7	18.0	17.4	16.7	16.1
7	12	25.1	24.4	23.6	22.9	22.2	21.5	20.8	20.1	19.4	18.7	18.0	17.4	16.7	16.1
8	13	25.1	24.4	23.6	22.9	22.2	21.4	20.7	20.0	19.4	18.7	18.0	17.4	16.7	16.1
9	14	25.1	24.3	23.6	22.9	22.1	21.4	20.7	20.0	19.3	18.7	18.0	17.3	16.7	16.1
10	15	25.0	24.3	23.6	22.8	22.1	21.4	20.7	20.0	19.3	18.6	18.0	17.3	16.7	16.1
11	16	25.0	24.3	23.5	22.8	22.1	21.4	20.7	20.0	19.3	18.6	18.0	17.3	16.7	16.1
12	17	25.0	24.2	23.5	22.8	22.1	21.4	20.7	20.0	19.3	18.6	18.0	17.3	16.7	16.0
13	18	24.9	24.2	23.5	22.7	22.0	21.3	20.6	19.9	19.3	18.6	17.9	17.3	16.7	16.0
14	19	24.9	24.1	23.4	22.7	22.0	21.3	20.6	19.9	19.2	18.6	17.9	17.3	16.6	16.0
15	20	24.8	24.1	23.4	22.7	22.0	21.3	20.6	19.9	19.2	18.5	17.9	17.3	16.6	16.0

Ages		50	51	52	53	54	55	56	57	58	59	60	61	62	63
Male	Male	55	56	57	58	59	60	61	62	63	64	65	66	67	68
Male	Female														
16	21	24.8	24.0	23.3	22.6	21.9	21.2	20.5	19.9	19.2	18.5	17.9	17.2	16.6	16.0
17	22	24.7	24.0	23.3	22.6	21.9	21.2	20.5	19.8	19.2	18.5	17.8	17.2	16.6	16.0
18	23	24.7	23.9	23.2	22.5	21.8	21.1	20.5	19.8	19.1	18.5	17.8	17.2	16.6	15.9
19	24	24.6	23.9	23.2	22.5	21.8	21.1	20.4	19.8	19.1	18.4	17.8	17.2	16.5	15.9
20	25	24.5	23.8	23.1	22.4	21.7	21.1	20.4	19.7	19.1	18.4	17.8	17.1	16.5	15.9
21	26	24.4	23.7	23.1	22.4	21.7	21.0	20.3	19.7	19.0	18.4	17.7	17.1	16.5	15.9
22	27	24.4	23.7	23.0	22.3	21.6	21.0	20.3	19.6	19.0	18.3	17.7	17.1	16.5	15.9
23	28	24.3	23.6	22.9	22.2	21.6	20.9	20.2	19.6	18.9	18.3	17.7	17.0	16.4	15.8
24	29	24.2	23.5	22.8	22.2	21.5	20.8	20.2	19.5	18.9	18.3	17.6	17.0	16.4	15.8
25	30	24.1	23.4	22.8	22.1	21.4	20.8	20.1	19.5	18.8	18.2	17.6	17.0	16.4	15.8
26	31	24.0	23.3	22.7	22.0	21.4	20.7	20.1	19.4	18.8	18.2	17.5	16.9	16.3	15.7
27	32	23.9	23.2	22.6	21.9	21.3	20.6	20.0	19.4	18.7	18.1	17.5	16.9	16.3	15.7
28	33	23.8	23.1	22.5	21.8	21.2	20.6	19.9	19.3	18.7	18.1	17.4	16.8	16.2	15.6
29	34	23.6	23.0	22.4	21.7	21.1	20.5	19.8	19.2	18.6	18.0	17.4	16.8	16.2	15.6
30	35	23.5	22.9	22.3	21.6	21.0	20.4	19.8	19.1	18.5	17.9	17.3	16.7	16.1	15.6
31	36	23.4	22.7	22.1	21.5	20.9	20.3	19.7	19.1	18.5	17.9	17.3	16.7	16.1	15.5
32	37	23.2	22.6	22.0	21.4	20.8	20.2	19.6	19.0	18.4	17.8	17.2	16.6	16.0	15.5
33	38	23.1	22.5	21.9	21.3	20.7	20.1	19.5	18.9	18.3	17.7	17.1	16.5	16.0	15.4
34	39	22.9	22.3	21.7	21.1	20.5	20.0	19.4	18.8	18.2	17.6	17.0	16.5	15.9	15.3

Ages		64	65	66	67	68	69	70	71	72	73	74	75	76	77	78
Male	Male	69	70	71	72	73	74	75	76	77	78	79	80	81	82	83
Male	Female															
6	11	15.5	14.9	14.3	13.7	13.1	12.6	12.0	11.5	11.0	10.5	10.0	9.6	9.1	8.7	8.2
7	12	15.5	14.9	14.3	13.7	13.1	12.6	12.0	11.5	11.0	10.5	10.0	9.6	9.1	8.7	8.2
8	13	15.5	14.9	14.3	13.7	13.1	12.6	12.0	11.5	11.0	10.5	10.0	9.6	9.1	8.7	8.2
9	14	15.5	14.9	14.3	13.7	13.1	12.6	12.0	11.5	11.0	10.5	10.0	9.5	9.1	8.7	8.2
10	15	15.4	14.8	14.3	13.7	13.1	12.6	12.0	11.5	11.0	10.5	10.0	9.5	9.1	8.7	8.2
11	16	15.4	14.8	14.2	13.7	13.1	12.6	12.0	11.5	11.0	10.5	10.0	9.5	9.1	8.7	8.2
12	17	15.4	14.8	14.2	13.7	13.1	12.5	12.0	11.5	11.0	10.5	10.0	9.5	9.1	8.6	8.2
13	18	15.4	14.8	14.2	13.6	13.1	12.5	12.0	11.5	11.0	10.5	10.0	9.5	9.1	8.6	8.2
14	19	15.4	14.8	14.2	13.6	13.1	12.5	12.0	11.5	11.0	10.5	10.0	9.5	9.1	8.6	8.2
15	20	15.4	14.8	14.2	13.6	13.1	12.5	12.0	11.5	11.0	10.5	10.0	9.5	9.1	8.6	8.2
16	21	15.4	14.8	14.2	13.6	13.1	12.5	12.0	11.5	11.0	10.5	10.0	9.5	9.1	8.6	8.2
17	22	15.4	14.8	14.2	13.6	13.0	12.5	12.0	11.5	10.9	10.5	10.0	9.5	9.1	8.6	8.2
18	23	15.3	14.7	14.2	13.6	13.0	12.5	12.0	11.4	10.9	10.4	10.0	9.5	9.1	8.6	8.2
19	24	15.3	14.7	14.1	13.6	13.0	12.5	12.0	11.4	10.9	10.4	10.0	9.5	9.1	8.6	8.2
20	25	15.3	14.7	14.1	13.6	13.0	12.5	11.9	11.4	10.9	10.4	10.0	9.5	9.0	8.6	8.2
21	26	15.3	14.7	14.1	13.5	13.0	12.5	11.9	11.4	10.9	10.4	9.9	9.5	9.0	8.6	8.2
22	27	15.3	14.7	14.1	13.5	13.0	12.4	11.9	11.4	10.9	10.4	9.9	9.5	9.0	8.6	8.2
23	28	15.2	14.6	14.1	13.5	13.0	12.4	11.9	11.4	10.9	10.4	9.9	9.5	9.0	8.6	8.2
24	29	15.2	14.6	14.0	13.5	12.9	12.4	11.9	11.4	10.9	10.4	9.9	9.5	9.0	8.6	8.2
25	30	15.2	14.6	14.0	13.5	12.9	12.4	11.9	11.4	10.9	10.4	9.9	9.5	9.0	8.6	8.2
26	31	15.1	14.6	14.0	13.4	12.9	12.4	11.9	11.3	10.8	10.4	9.9	9.4	9.0	8.6	8.2
27	32	15.1	14.5	14.0	13.4	12.9	12.4	11.8	11.3	10.8	10.4	9.9	9.4	9.0	8.6	8.2
28	33	15.1	14.5	13.9	13.4	12.9	12.3	11.8	11.3	10.8	10.3	9.9	9.4	9.0	8.6	8.1
29	34	15.0	14.5	13.9	13.4	12.8	12.3	11.8	11.3	10.8	10.3	9.9	9.4	9.0	8.5	8.1
30	35	15.0	14.4	13.9	13.3	12.8	12.3	11.8	11.3	10.8	10.3	9.8	9.4	9.0	8.5	8.1
31	36	14.9	14.4	13.8	13.3	12.8	12.2	11.7	11.2	10.8	10.3	9.8	9.4	8.9	8.5	8.1
32	37	14.9	14.3	13.8	13.3	12.7	12.2	11.7	11.2	10.7	10.3	9.8	9.4	8.9	8.5	8.1
33	38	14.8	14.3	13.8	13.2	12.7	12.2	11.7	11.2	10.7	10.2	9.8	9.3	8.9	8.5	8.1
34	39	14.8	14.2	13.7	13.2	12.7	12.2	11.7	11.2	10.7	10.2	9.8	9.3	8.9	8.5	8.1

TABLE IIA.—ANNUITIES FOR JOINT LIFE ONLY—TWO LIVES—
EXPECTED RETURN MULTIPLES—Continued

Ages		79	80	81	82	83	84	85	86	87	88	89	90	91	92	93
Male	Male	84	85	86	87	88	89	90	91	92	93	94	95	96	97	98
Male	Female															
6	11	7.8	7.4	7.1	6.7	6.3	6.0	5.7	5.4	5.1	4.8	4.5	4.2	4.0	3.7	3.5
7	12	7.8	7.4	7.1	6.7	6.3	6.0	5.7	5.4	5.1	4.8	4.5	4.2	4.0	3.7	3.5
8	13	7.8	7.4	7.0	6.7	6.3	6.0	5.7	5.4	5.1	4.8	4.5	4.2	4.0	3.7	3.5
9	14	7.8	7.4	7.0	6.7	6.3	6.0	5.7	5.4	5.1	4.8	4.5	4.2	4.0	3.7	3.5
10	15	7.8	7.4	7.0	6.7	6.3	6.0	5.7	5.4	5.1	4.8	4.5	4.2	4.0	3.7	3.5
11	16	7.8	7.4	7.0	6.7	6.3	6.0	5.7	5.4	5.1	4.8	4.5	4.2	4.0	3.7	3.5
12	17	7.8	7.4	7.0	6.7	6.3	6.0	5.7	5.4	5.1	4.8	4.5	4.2	4.0	3.7	3.5
13	18	7.8	7.4	7.0	6.7	6.3	6.0	5.7	5.3	5.1	4.8	4.5	4.2	4.0	3.7	3.5
14	19	7.8	7.4	7.0	6.7	6.3	6.0	5.7	5.3	5.0	4.8	4.5	4.2	4.0	3.7	3.5
15	20	7.8	7.4	7.0	6.7	6.3	6.0	5.7	5.3	5.0	4.8	4.5	4.2	4.0	3.7	3.5
16	21	7.8	7.4	7.0	6.7	6.3	6.0	5.7	5.3	5.0	4.8	4.5	4.2	4.0	3.7	3.5
17	22	7.8	7.4	7.0	6.7	6.3	6.0	5.7	5.3	5.0	4.8	4.5	4.2	4.0	3.7	3.5
18	23	7.8	7.4	7.0	6.7	6.3	6.0	5.7	5.3	5.0	4.8	4.5	4.2	4.0	3.7	3.5
19	24	7.8	7.4	7.0	6.7	6.3	6.0	5.7	5.3	5.0	4.8	4.5	4.2	4.0	3.7	3.5
20	25	7.8	7.4	7.0	6.7	6.3	6.0	5.6	5.3	5.0	4.8	4.5	4.2	4.0	3.7	3.5
21	26	7.8	7.4	7.0	6.7	6.3	6.0	5.6	5.3	5.0	4.8	4.5	4.2	4.0	3.7	3.5
22	27	7.8	7.4	7.0	6.7	6.3	6.0	5.6	5.3	5.0	4.8	4.5	4.2	4.0	3.7	3.5
23	28	7.8	7.4	7.0	6.6	6.3	6.0	5.6	5.3	5.0	4.8	4.5	4.2	4.0	3.7	3.5
24	29	7.8	7.4	7.0	6.6	6.3	6.0	5.6	5.3	5.0	4.7	4.5	4.2	4.0	3.7	3.5
25	30	7.8	7.4	7.0	6.6	6.3	6.0	5.6	5.3	5.0	4.7	4.5	4.2	4.0	3.7	3.5
26	31	7.8	7.4	7.0	6.6	6.3	6.0	5.6	5.3	5.0	4.7	4.5	4.2	4.0	3.7	3.5
27	32	7.7	7.4	7.0	6.6	6.3	5.9	5.6	5.3	5.0	4.7	4.5	4.2	4.0	3.7	3.5

Ages																
	Male	79	80	81	82	83	84	85	86	87	88	89	90	91	92	93
Male	Female	84	85	86	87	88	89	90	91	92	93	94	95	96	97	98
28	33	7.7	7.4	7.0	6.6	6.3	5.9	5.6	5.3	5.0	4.7	4.5	4.2	4.0	3.7	3.5
29	34	7.7	7.3	7.0	6.6	6.3	5.9	5.6	5.3	5.0	4.7	4.5	4.2	4.0	3.7	3.5
30	35	7.7	7.3	7.0	6.6	6.3	5.9	5.6	5.3	5.0	4.7	4.5	4.2	4.0	3.7	3.5
31	36	7.7	7.3	7.0	6.6	6.3	5.9	5.6	5.3	5.0	4.7	4.5	4.2	4.0	3.7	3.5
32	37	7.7	7.3	7.0	6.6	6.3	5.9	5.6	5.3	5.0	4.7	4.5	4.2	4.0	3.7	3.5
33	38	7.7	7.3	6.9	6.6	6.2	5.9	5.6	5.3	5.0	4.7	4.5	4.2	3.9	3.7	3.5
34	39	7.7	7.3	6.9	6.6	6.2	5.9	5.6	5.3	5.0	4.7	4.4	4.2	3.9	3.7	3.5

Ages																
	Male	94	95	96	97	98	99	100	101	102	103	104	105	106	107	108
Male	Female	99	100	101	102	103	104	105	106	107	108	109	110	111	112	113
6	11	3.3	3.1	2.9	2.7	2.5	2.3	2.1	1.9	1.7	1.5	1.3	1.2	1.0	0.8	0.7
7	12	3.3	3.1	2.9	2.7	2.5	2.3	2.1	1.9	1.7	1.5	1.3	1.2	1.0	0.8	0.7
8	13	3.3	3.1	2.9	2.7	2.5	2.3	2.1	1.9	1.7	1.5	1.3	1.2	1.0	0.8	0.7
9	14	3.3	3.1	2.9	2.7	2.5	2.3	2.1	1.9	1.7	1.5	1.3	1.2	1.0	0.8	0.7
10	15	3.3	3.1	2.9	2.7	2.5	2.3	2.1	1.9	1.7	1.5	1.3	1.2	1.0	0.8	0.7
11	16	3.3	3.1	2.9	2.7	2.5	2.3	2.1	1.9	1.7	1.5	1.3	1.2	1.0	0.8	0.7
12	17	3.3	3.1	2.9	2.7	2.5	2.3	2.1	1.9	1.7	1.5	1.3	1.2	1.0	0.8	0.7
13	18	3.3	3.1	2.9	2.7	2.5	2.3	2.1	1.9	1.7	1.5	1.3	1.2	1.0	0.8	0.7
14	19	3.3	3.1	2.9	2.7	2.5	2.3	2.1	1.9	1.7	1.5	1.3	1.2	1.0	0.8	0.7
15	20	3.3	3.1	2.9	2.7	2.5	2.3	2.1	1.9	1.7	1.5	1.3	1.2	1.0	0.8	0.7
16	21	3.3	3.1	2.9	2.7	2.5	2.3	2.1	1.9	1.7	1.5	1.3	1.2	1.0	0.8	0.7
17	22	3.3	3.1	2.9	2.7	2.5	2.3	2.1	1.9	1.7	1.5	1.3	1.2	1.0	0.8	0.7
18	23	3.3	3.1	2.9	2.7	2.5	2.3	2.1	1.9	1.7	1.5	1.3	1.2	1.0	0.8	0.7
19	24	3.3	3.1	2.9	2.7	2.5	2.3	2.1	1.9	1.7	1.5	1.3	1.2	1.0	0.8	0.7
20	25	3.3	3.1	2.9	2.7	2.5	2.3	2.1	1.9	1.7	1.5	1.3	1.2	1.0	0.8	0.7
21	26	3.3	3.1	2.9	2.7	2.5	2.3	2.1	1.9	1.7	1.5	1.3	1.2	1.0	0.8	0.7
22	27	3.3	3.1	2.9	2.7	2.5	2.3	2.1	1.9	1.7	1.5	1.3	1.2	1.0	0.8	0.7
23	28	3.3	3.1	2.9	2.7	2.5	2.3	2.1	1.9	1.7	1.5	1.3	1.2	1.0	0.8	0.7
24	29	3.3	3.1	2.9	2.7	2.5	2.3	2.1	1.9	1.7	1.5	1.3	1.2	1.0	0.8	0.7
25	30	3.3	3.1	2.9	2.7	2.5	2.3	2.1	1.9	1.7	1.5	1.3	1.2	1.0	0.8	0.7
26	31	3.3	3.1	2.9	2.7	2.5	2.3	2.1	1.9	1.7	1.5	1.3	1.2	1.0	0.8	0.7
27	32	3.3	3.1	2.9	2.7	2.5	2.3	2.1	1.9	1.7	1.5	1.3	1.2	1.0	0.8	0.7
28	33	3.3	3.1	2.9	2.7	2.5	2.3	2.1	1.9	1.7	1.5	1.3	1.2	1.0	0.8	0.7
29	34	3.3	3.1	2.9	2.7	2.5	2.3	2.1	1.9	1.7	1.5	1.3	1.2	1.0	0.8	0.7
30	35	3.3	3.1	2.9	2.7	2.5	2.3	2.1	1.9	1.7	1.5	1.3	1.2	1.0	0.8	0.7
31	36	3.3	3.1	2.9	2.7	2.5	2.3	2.1	1.9	1.7	1.5	1.3	1.2	1.0	0.8	0.7
32	37	3.3	3.1	2.9	2.7	2.5	2.3	2.1	1.9	1.7	1.5	1.3	1.2	1.0	0.8	0.7
33	38	3.3	3.1	2.9	2.7	2.5	2.3	2.1	1.9	1.7	1.5	1.3	1.2	1.0	0.8	0.7
34	39	3.3	3.1	2.9	2.7	2.5	2.3	2.1	1.9	1.7	1.5	1.3	1.2	1.0	0.8	0.7

TABLE IIA.—ANNUITIES FOR JOINT LIFE ONLY—TWO LIVES—
EXPECTED RETURN MULTIPLES—Continued

Ages														
	Male	35	36	37	38	39	40	41	42	43	44	45	46	47
Male	Female	40	41	42	43	44	45	46	47	48	49	50	51	52
35	40	30.3	29.9	29.4	29.0	28.5	28.0	27.5	27.0	26.5	26.0	25.5	24.9	24.4
36	41	29.9	29.5	29.0	28.6	28.2	27.7	27.2	26.7	26.2	25.7	25.2	24.7	24.2
37	42	29.4	29.0	28.6	28.2	27.8	27.3	26.9	26.4	25.9	25.5	25.0	24.4	23.9
38	43	29.0	28.6	28.2	27.8	27.4	27.0	26.5	26.1	25.6	25.2	24.7	24.2	23.7
39	44	28.5	28.2	27.8	27.4	27.0	26.6	26.2	25.8	25.3	24.8	24.4	23.9	23.4
40	45	28.0	27.7	27.3	27.0	26.6	26.2	25.8	25.4	25.0	24.5	24.1	23.6	23.1
41	46	27.5	27.2	26.9	26.5	26.2	25.8	25.4	25.0	24.6	24.2	23.8	23.3	22.9
42	47	27.0	26.7	26.4	26.1	25.8	25.4	25.0	24.6	24.2	23.8	23.4	23.0	22.6
43	48	26.5	26.2	25.9	25.6	25.3	25.0	24.6	24.2	23.9	23.5	23.1	22.7	22.2
44	49	26.0	25.7	25.5	25.2	24.8	24.5	24.2	23.8	23.5	23.1	22.7	22.3	21.9
45	50	25.5	25.2	25.0	24.7	24.4	24.1	23.8	23.4	23.1	22.7	22.4	22.0	21.6
46	51	24.9	24.7	24.4	24.2	23.9	23.6	23.3	23.0	22.7	22.3	22.0	21.6	21.2
47	52	24.4	24.2	23.9	23.7	23.4	23.1	22.9	22.6	22.2	21.9	21.6	21.2	20.9

Ages														
	Male	48	49	50	51	52	53	54	55	56	57	58	59	60
Male	Female	53	54	55	56	57	58	59	60	61	62	63	64	65
35	40	23.8	23.3	22.7	22.1	21.6	21.0	20.4	19.8	19.3	18.7	18.1	17.5	17.0
36	41	23.6	23.1	22.5	22.0	21.4	20.8	20.3	19.7	19.1	18.6	18.0	17.4	16.9
37	42	23.4	22.9	22.3	21.8	21.2	20.7	20.1	19.6	19.0	18.4	17.9	17.3	16.8
38	43	23.2	22.6	22.1	21.6	21.1	20.5	20.0	19.4	18.9	18.3	17.8	17.2	16.7
39	44	22.9	22.4	21.9	21.4	20.9	20.3	19.8	19.3	18.7	18.2	17.7	17.1	16.6
40	45	22.7	22.2	21.7	21.2	20.7	20.1	19.6	19.1	18.6	18.0	17.5	17.0	16.5
41	46	22.4	21.9	21.4	20.9	20.4	19.9	19.4	18.9	18.4	17.9	17.4	16.9	16.3
42	47	22.1	21.6	21.2	20.7	20.2	19.7	19.2	18.7	18.2	17.7	17.2	16.7	16.2
43	48	21.8	21.4	20.9	20.5	20.0	19.5	19.0	18.6	18.1	17.6	17.1	16.6	16.1
44	49	21.5	21.1	20.6	20.2	19.8	19.3	18.8	18.4	17.9	17.4	16.9	16.4	15.9
45	50	21.2	20.8	20.4	19.9	19.5	19.1	18.6	18.1	17.7	17.2	16.7	16.3	15.8
46	51	20.9	20.5	20.1	19.7	19.2	18.8	18.4	17.9	17.5	17.0	16.6	16.1	15.6
47	52	20.5	20.1	19.8	19.4	19.0	18.5	18.1	17.7	17.3	16.8	16.4	15.9	15.5
48	53	20.2	19.8	19.4	19.1	18.7	18.3	17.9	17.5	17.0	16.6	16.2	15.7	15.3
49	54	19.8	19.5	19.1	18.8	18.4	18.0	17.6	17.2	16.8	16.4	16.0	15.5	15.1
50	55	19.4	19.1	18.8	18.4	18.1	17.7	17.3	16.9	16.6	16.2	15.8	15.3	14.9
51	56	19.1	18.8	18.4	18.1	17.8	17.4	17.0	16.7	16.3	15.9	15.5	15.1	14.7

Ages		48	49	50	51	52	53	54	55	56	57	58	59	60
Male	Male	53	54	55	56	57	58	59	60	61	62	63	64	65
	Female													
52	57	18.7	18.4	18.1	17.8	17.4	17.1	16.8	16.4	16.0	15.7	15.3	14.9	14.5
53	58	18.3	18.0	17.7	17.4	17.1	16.8	16.4	16.1	15.8	15.4	15.1	14.7	14.3
54	59	17.9	17.6	17.3	17.0	16.8	16.4	16.1	15.8	15.5	15.1	14.8	14.4	14.1
55	60	17.5	17.2	16.9	16.7	16.4	16.1	15.8	15.5	15.2	14.9	14.5	14.2	13.9
56	61	17.0	16.8	16.6	16.3	16.0	15.8	15.5	15.2	14.9	14.6	14.3	13.9	13.6
57	62	16.6	16.4	16.3	15.9	15.7	15.4	15.1	14.9	14.6	14.3	14.0	13.7	13.4
58	63	16.2	16.0	15.8	15.5	15.3	15.1	14.8	14.5	14.3	14.0	13.7	13.4	13.1
59	64	15.7	15.5	15.3	15.1	14.9	14.7	14.4	14.2	13.9	13.7	13.4	13.1	12.8
60	65	15.3	15.1	14.9	14.7	14.5	14.3	14.1	13.9	13.6	13.4	13.1	12.8	12.6

TABLE IIA.—ANNUITIES FOR JOINT LIFE ONLY—TWO LIVES—
EXPECTED RETURN MULTIPLES—Continued

Ages		61	62	63	64	65	66	67	68	69	70	71	72	73
Male	Female	66	67	68	69	70	71	72	73	74	75	76	77	78
35	40	16.4	15.8	15.3	14.7	14.2	13.7	13.1	12.6	12.1	11.6	11.1	10.7	10.2
36	41	16.3	15.8	15.2	14.7	14.1	13.6	13.1	12.6	12.1	11.6	11.1	10.6	10.2
37	42	16.2	15.7	15.1	14.6	14.1	13.6	13.0	12.5	12.0	11.5	11.1	10.6	10.1
38	43	16.1	15.6	15.1	14.5	14.0	13.5	13.0	12.5	12.0	11.5	11.0	10.6	10.1
39	44	16.0	15.5	15.0	14.5	13.9	13.4	12.9	12.4	11.9	11.5	11.0	10.5	10.1
40	45	15.9	15.4	14.9	14.4	13.9	13.4	12.9	12.4	11.9	11.4	11.0	10.5	10.0
41	46	15.8	15.3	14.8	14.3	13.8	13.3	12.8	12.3	11.8	11.4	10.9	10.5	10.0
42	47	15.7	15.2	14.7	14.2	13.7	13.2	12.7	12.3	11.8	11.3	10.9	10.4	10.0
43	48	15.6	15.1	14.6	14.1	13.6	13.1	12.7	12.2	11.7	11.3	10.8	10.4	9.9
44	49	15.5	15.0	14.5	14.0	13.5	13.1	12.6	12.1	11.7	11.2	10.8	10.3	9.9
45	50	15.3	14.8	14.4	13.9	13.4	13.0	12.5	12.0	11.6	11.1	10.7	10.3	9.8
46	51	15.2	14.7	14.2	13.8	13.3	12.9	12.4	12.0	11.5	11.1	10.6	10.2	9.8
47	52	15.0	14.6	14.1	13.7	13.2	12.8	12.3	11.9	11.4	11.0	10.6	10.1	9.7
48	53	14.9	14.4	14.0	13.5	13.1	12.6	12.2	11.8	11.3	10.9	10.5	10.1	9.7
49	54	14.7	14.3	13.8	13.4	13.0	12.5	12.1	11.7	11.3	10.8	10.4	10.0	9.6
50	55	14.5	14.1	13.7	13.3	12.8	12.4	12.0	11.6	11.2	10.7	10.3	9.9	9.5
51	56	14.3	13.9	13.5	13.1	12.7	12.3	11.9	11.5	11.1	10.7	10.3	9.9	9.5
52	57	14.1	13.7	13.3	12.9	12.5	12.1	11.7	11.3	10.9	10.6	10.2	9.8	9.4
53	58	13.9	13.6	13.2	12.8	12.4	12.0	11.6	11.2	10.8	10.5	10.1	9.7	9.3
54	59	13.7	13.4	13.0	12.6	12.2	11.9	11.5	11.1	10.7	10.3	10.0	9.6	9.2
55	60	13.5	13.2	12.8	12.4	12.1	11.7	11.3	11.0	10.6	10.2	9.9	9.5	9.1
56	61	13.3	12.9	12.6	12.2	11.9	11.5	11.2	10.8	10.5	10.1	9.8	9.4	9.0
57	62	13.0	12.7	12.4	12.1	11.7	11.4	11.0	10.7	10.3	10.0	9.6	9.3	8.9
58	63	12.8	12.5	12.2	11.8	11.5	11.2	10.9	10.5	10.2	9.8	9.5	9.2	8.8
59	64	12.6	12.3	11.9	11.6	11.3	11.0	10.7	10.4	10.0	9.7	9.4	9.1	8.7
60	65	12.3	12.0	11.7	11.4	11.1	10.8	10.5	10.2	9.9	9.6	9.3	8.9	8.6
61	66	12.0	11.8	11.5	11.2	10.9	10.6	10.3	10.0	9.7	9.4	9.1	8.8	8.5
62	67	11.8	11.5	11.2	11.0	10.7	10.4	10.1	9.8	9.6	9.3	9.0	8.7	8.4
63	68	11.5	11.2	11.0	10.7	10.5	10.2	9.9	9.7	9.4	9.1	8.8	8.5	8.2
64	69	11.2	11.0	10.7	10.5	10.2	10.0	9.7	9.5	9.2	8.9	8.7	8.4	8.1
65	70	10.9	10.7	10.5	10.2	10.0	9.8	9.5	9.3	9.0	8.8	8.5	8.2	8.0
66	71	10.6	10.4	10.2	10.0	9.8	9.5	9.3	9.1	8.8	8.6	8.3	8.1	7.8
67	72	10.3	10.1	9.9	9.7	9.5	9.3	9.1	8.9	8.6	8.4	8.1	7.9	7.7
68	73	10.0	9.8	9.7	9.5	9.3	9.1	8.9	8.6	8.4	8.2	8.0	7.7	7.5
69	74	9.7	9.6	9.4	9.2	9.0	8.8	8.6	8.4	8.2	8.0	7.8	7.6	7.3
70	75	9.4	9.3	9.1	8.9	8.8	8.6	8.4	8.2	8.0	7.8	7.6	7.4	7.2
71	76	9.1	9.0	8.8	8.7	8.5	8.3	8.1	8.0	7.8	7.6	7.4	7.2	7.0
72	77	8.8	8.7	8.5	8.4	8.2	8.1	7.9	7.7	7.6	7.4	7.2	7.0	6.8
73	78	8.5	8.4	8.2	8.1	8.0	7.8	7.7	7.5	7.3	7.2	7.0	6.8	6.7

Items Specifically Included in Gross Income
See p. 20,601 for regulations not amended to reflect law changes

TABLE IIA.—ANNUITIES FOR JOINT LIFE ONLY—TWO LIVES—
EXPECTED RETURN MULTIPLES—Continued

Ages Male	Ages Female	74 / 79	75 / 80	76 / 81	77 / 82	78 / 83	79 / 84	80 / 85	81 / 86	82 / 87	83 / 88	84 / 89	85 / 90	86 / 91
35	40	9.7	9.3	8.9	8.5	8.1	7.7	7.3	6.9	6.6	6.2	5.9	5.6	5.3
36	41	9.7	9.3	8.9	8.4	8.0	7.7	7.3	6.9	6.6	6.2	5.9	5.6	5.3
37	42	9.7	9.3	8.8	8.4	8.0	7.6	7.3	6.9	6.5	6.2	5.9	5.6	5.3
38	43	9.7	9.2	8.8	8.4	8.0	7.6	7.2	6.9	6.5	6.2	5.9	5.6	5.3
39	44	9.6	9.2	8.8	8.4	8.0	7.6	7.2	6.9	6.5	6.2	5.9	5.6	5.3
40	45	9.6	9.2	8.8	8.4	8.0	7.6	7.2	6.9	6.5	6.2	5.9	5.5	5.2
41	46	9.6	9.2	8.7	8.3	7.9	7.6	7.2	6.8	6.5	6.2	5.8	5.5	5.2
42	47	9.5	9.1	8.7	8.3	7.9	7.5	7.2	6.8	6.5	6.2	5.8	5.5	5.2
43	48	9.5	9.1	8.7	8.3	7.9	7.5	7.2	6.8	6.5	6.1	5.8	5.5	5.2
44	49	9.5	9.0	8.6	8.2	7.9	7.5	7.1	6.8	6.4	6.1	5.8	5.5	5.2
45	50	9.4	9.0	8.6	8.2	7.8	7.5	7.1	6.8	6.4	6.1	5.8	5.5	5.2
46	51	9.4	9.0	8.6	8.2	7.8	7.4	7.1	6.7	6.4	6.1	5.8	5.5	5.2
47	52	9.3	8.9	8.5	8.1	7.8	7.4	7.1	6.7	6.4	6.1	5.8	5.5	5.2
48	53	9.3	8.9	8.5	8.1	7.7	7.4	7.0	6.7	6.4	6.0	5.7	5.4	5.1
49	54	9.2	8.8	8.4	8.1	7.7	7.3	7.0	6.7	6.3	6.0	5.7	5.4	5.1
50	55	9.1	8.8	8.4	8.0	7.7	7.3	7.0	6.6	6.3	6.0	5.7	5.4	5.1
51	56	9.1	8.7	8.3	8.0	7.6	7.3	6.9	6.6	6.3	6.0	5.7	5.4	5.1
52	57	9.0	8.6	8.3	7.9	7.6	7.2	6.9	6.6	6.2	5.9	5.6	5.3	5.1
53	58	8.9	8.6	8.2	7.9	7.5	7.2	6.9	6.5	6.2	5.9	5.6	5.3	5.0
54	59	8.9	8.5	8.2	7.8	7.5	7.1	6.8	6.5	6.2	5.9	5.6	5.3	5.0
55	60	8.8	8.4	8.1	7.7	7.4	7.1	6.8	6.4	6.1	5.8	5.6	5.3	5.0
56	61	8.7	8.4	8.0	7.7	7.3	7.0	6.7	6.4	6.1	5.8	5.5	5.3	5.0
57	62	8.6	8.3	7.9	7.6	7.3	7.0	6.7	6.4	6.1	5.8	5.5	5.2	5.0
58	63	8.5	8.2	7.9	7.5	7.2	6.9	6.6	6.3	6.0	5.7	5.5	5.2	4.9
59	64	8.4	8.1	7.8	7.5	7.1	6.8	6.5	6.3	6.0	5.7	5.4	5.2	4.9
60	65	8.3	8.0	7.7	7.4	7.1	6.8	6.5	6.2	5.9	5.6	5.4	5.1	4.9
61	66	8.2	7.9	7.6	7.3	7.0	6.7	6.4	6.1	5.9	5.6	5.3	5.1	4.8
62	67	8.1	7.8	7.5	7.2	6.9	6.6	6.4	6.1	5.8	5.5	5.3	5.0	4.8
63	68	8.0	7.7	7.4	7.1	6.8	6.6	6.3	6.0	5.7	5.5	5.2	5.0	4.7
64	69	7.8	7.6	7.3	7.0	6.7	6.5	6.2	5.9	5.7	5.4	5.2	4.9	4.7
65	70	7.7	7.4	7.2	6.9	6.6	6.4	6.1	5.9	5.6	5.4	5.1	4.9	4.7
66	71	7.6	7.3	7.1	6.8	6.5	6.3	6.0	5.8	5.5	5.3	5.1	4.8	4.6
67	72	7.4	7.2	6.9	6.7	6.4	6.2	6.0	5.7	5.5	5.2	5.0	4.8	4.6
68	73	7.3	7.0	6.8	6.6	6.3	6.1	5.9	5.6	5.4	5.2	4.9	4.7	4.5
69	74	7.1	6.9	6.7	6.4	6.2	6.0	5.8	5.5	5.3	5.1	4.9	4.7	4.5
70	75	7.0	6.8	6.5	6.3	6.1	5.9	5.7	5.4	5.2	5.0	4.8	4.6	4.4
71	76	6.8	6.6	6.4	6.2	6.0	5.8	5.6	5.3	5.1	4.9	4.7	4.5	4.3
72	77	6.6	6.4	6.3	6.1	5.9	5.7	5.5	5.3	5.0	4.9	4.7	4.5	4.3
73	78	6.5	6.3	6.1	5.9	5.7	5.5	5.3	5.1	5.0	4.8	4.6	4.4	4.2
74	79	6.3	6.1	6.0	5.8	5.6	5.4	5.2	5.0	4.9	4.7	4.5	4.3	4.1
75	80	6.1	6.0	5.8	5.6	5.5	5.3	5.1	4.9	4.8	4.6	4.4	4.2	4.1
76	81	6.0	5.8	5.6	5.5	5.3	5.2	5.0	4.8	4.7	4.5	4.3	4.1	4.0
77	82	5.8	5.6	5.5	5.3	5.2	5.0	4.9	4.7	4.5	4.4	4.2	4.1	3.9
78	83	5.6	5.5	5.3	5.2	5.0	4.9	4.7	4.6	4.4	4.3	4.1	4.0	3.8
79	84	5.4	5.3	5.2	5.0	4.9	4.7	4.6	4.5	4.3	4.2	4.0	3.9	3.7
80	85	5.2	5.1	5.0	4.9	4.7	4.6	4.5	4.4	4.2	4.1	3.9	3.8	3.6
81	86	5.0	4.9	4.8	4.7	4.6	4.5	4.3	4.2	4.1	3.9	3.8	3.7	3.6
82	87	4.9	4.8	4.7	4.5	4.4	4.3	4.2	4.1	4.0	3.8	3.7	3.6	3.5
83	88	4.7	4.6	4.5	4.4	4.3	4.2	4.1	3.9	3.8	3.7	3.6	3.5	3.4
84	89	4.5	4.4	4.3	4.2	4.1	4.0	3.9	3.8	3.7	3.6	3.5	3.4	3.3
85	90	4.3	4.2	4.1	4.1	4.0	3.9	3.8	3.7	3.6	3.5	3.4	3.3	3.2
86	91	4.1	4.1	4.0	3.9	3.8	3.7	3.6	3.6	3.5	3.4	3.3	3.2	3.1

TABLE IIA.—ANNUITIES FOR JOINT LIFE ONLY—TWO LIVES—
EXPECTED RETURN MULTIPLES—Continued

Ages												
	Male	87	88	89	90	91	92	93	94	95	96	97
Male	Female	92	93	94	95	96	97	98	99	100	101	102
35	40	5.0	4.7	4.4	4.2	3.9	3.7	3.5	3.3	3.1	2.9	2.7
36	41	5.0	4.7	4.4	4.2	3.9	3.7	3.5	3.3	3.1	2.9	2.7
37	42	5.0	4.7	4.4	4.2	3.9	3.7	3.5	3.3	3.1	2.9	2.7
38	43	5.0	4.7	4.4	4.2	3.9	3.7	3.5	3.3	3.1	2.9	2.6
39	44	5.0	4.7	4.4	4.2	3.9	3.7	3.5	3.3	3.0	2.8	2.6
40	45	5.0	4.7	4.4	4.2	3.9	3.7	3.5	3.3	3.0	2.8	2.6
41	46	5.0	4.7	4.4	4.2	3.9	3.7	3.5	3.2	3.0	2.8	2.6
42	47	4.9	4.7	4.4	4.2	3.9	3.7	3.5	3.2	3.0	2.8	2.6
43	48	4.9	4.7	4.4	4.1	3.9	3.7	3.5	3.2	3.0	2.8	2.6
44	49	4.9	4.7	4.4	4.1	3.9	3.7	3.4	3.2	3.0	2.8	2.6
45	50	4.9	4.6	4.4	4.1	3.9	3.7	3.4	3.2	3.0	2.8	2.6
46	51	4.9	4.6	4.4	4.1	3.9	3.7	3.4	3.2	3.0	2.8	2.6
47	52	4.9	4.6	4.4	4.1	3.9	3.7	3.4	3.2	3.0	2.8	2.6
48	53	4.9	4.6	4.4	4.1	3.9	3.6	3.4	3.2	3.0	2.8	2.6
49	54	4.9	4.6	4.3	4.1	3.9	3.6	3.4	3.2	3.0	2.8	2.6
50	55	4.8	4.6	4.3	4.1	3.9	3.6	3.4	3.2	3.0	2.8	2.6
51	56	4.8	4.6	4.3	4.1	3.8	3.6	3.4	3.2	3.0	2.8	2.6
52	57	4.8	4.5	4.3	4.1	3.8	3.6	3.4	3.2	3.0	2.8	2.6
53	58	4.8	4.5	4.3	4.0	3.8	3.6	3.4	3.2	3.0	2.8	2.6
54	59	4.8	4.5	4.3	4.0	3.8	3.6	3.4	3.2	3.0	2.8	2.6
55	60	4.7	4.5	4.3	4.0	3.8	3.6	3.4	3.2	3.0	2.8	2.6
56	61	4.7	4.5	4.2	4.0	3.8	3.6	3.3	3.1	2.9	2.8	2.6
57	62	4.7	4.5	4.2	4.0	3.8	3.5	3.3	3.1	2.9	2.7	2.6
58	63	4.7	4.4	4.2	4.0	3.7	3.5	3.3	3.1	2.9	2.7	2.5
59	64	4.6	4.4	4.2	3.9	3.7	3.5	3.3	3.1	2.9	2.7	2.5

Ages												
	Male	98	99	100	101	102	103	104	105	106	107	108
Male	Female	103	104	105	106	107	108	109	110	111	112	113
35	40	2.5	2.3	2.1	1.9	1.7	1.5	1.3	1.2	1.0	0.8	0.7
36	41	2.5	2.3	2.1	1.9	1.7	1.5	1.3	1.2	1.0	0.8	0.7
37	42	2.5	2.3	2.1	1.9	1.7	1.5	1.3	1.1	1.0	0.8	0.7
38	43	2.5	2.3	2.1	1.9	1.7	1.5	1.3	1.1	1.0	0.8	0.7
39	44	2.4	2.3	2.1	1.9	1.7	1.5	1.3	1.1	1.0	0.8	0.7
40	45	2.4	2.2	2.1	1.9	1.7	1.5	1.3	1.1	1.0	0.8	0.7
41	46	2.4	2.2	2.1	1.9	1.7	1.5	1.3	1.1	1.0	0.8	0.7
42	47	2.4	2.2	2.0	1.9	1.7	1.5	1.3	1.1	1.0	0.8	0.7
43	48	2.4	2.2	2.0	1.9	1.7	1.5	1.3	1.1	1.0	0.8	0.7
44	49	2.4	2.2	2.0	1.9	1.7	1.5	1.3	1.1	1.0	0.8	0.7
45	50	2.4	2.2	2.0	1.8	1.7	1.5	1.3	1.1	1.0	0.8	0.7
46	51	2.4	2.2	2.0	1.8	1.7	1.5	1.3	1.1	1.0	0.8	0.7
47	52	2.4	2.2	2.0	1.8	1.7	1.5	1.3	1.1	1.0	0.8	0.7
48	53	2.4	2.2	2.0	1.8	1.7	1.5	1.3	1.1	1.0	0.8	0.7
49	54	2.4	2.2	2.0	1.8	1.7	1.5	1.3	1.1	1.0	0.8	0.7
50	55	2.4	2.2	2.0	1.8	1.6	1.5	1.3	1.1	1.0	0.8	0.7
51	56	2.4	2.2	2.0	1.8	1.6	1.5	1.3	1.1	1.0	0.8	0.7
52	57	2.4	2.2	2.0	1.8	1.6	1.5	1.3	1.1	1.0	0.8	0.7
53	58	2.4	2.2	2.0	1.8	1.6	1.5	1.3	1.1	1.0	0.8	0.7
54	59	2.4	2.2	2.0	1.8	1.6	1.5	1.3	1.1	1.0	0.8	0.7
55	60	2.4	2.2	2.0	1.8	1.6	1.4	1.3	1.1	1.0	0.8	0.7
56	61	2.4	2.2	2.0	1.8	1.6	1.4	1.3	1.1	1.0	0.8	0.7
57	62	2.4	2.2	2.0	1.8	1.6	1.4	1.3	1.1	0.9	0.8	0.7
58	63	2.4	2.2	2.0	1.8	1.6	1.4	1.3	1.1	0.9	0.8	0.7
59	64	2.3	2.2	2.0	1.8	1.6	1.4	1.3	1.1	0.9	0.8	0.7

TABLE IIA.—ANNUITIES FOR JOINT LIFE ONLY—TWO LIVES—
EXPECTED RETURN MULTIPLES—Continued

Ages Male	Ages Female	87 / 92	88 / 93	89 / 94	90 / 95	91 / 96	92 / 97	93 / 98	94 / 99	95 / 100	96 / 101	97 / 102
60	65	4.6	4.4	4.1	3.9	3.7	3.5	3.3	3.1	2.9	2.7	2.5
61	66	4.6	4.3	4.1	3.9	3.7	3.5	3.3	3.1	2.9	2.7	2.5
62	67	4.5	4.3	4.1	3.9	3.7	3.5	3.3	3.1	2.9	2.7	2.5
63	68	4.5	4.3	4.1	3.8	3.6	3.4	3.2	3.0	2.9	2.7	2.5
64	69	4.5	4.2	4.0	3.8	3.6	3.4	3.2	3.0	2.8	2.7	2.5
65	70	4.4	4.2	4.0	3.8	3.6	3.4	3.2	3.0	2.8	2.6	2.5
66	71	4.4	4.2	4.0	3.8	3.6	3.4	3.2	3.0	2.8	2.6	2.4
67	72	4.3	4.1	3.9	3.7	3.5	3.3	3.1	3.0	2.8	2.6	2.4
68	73	4.3	4.1	3.9	3.7	3.5	3.3	3.1	2.9	2.8	2.6	2.4
69	74	4.2	4.0	3.8	3.6	3.5	3.3	3.1	2.9	2.7	2.6	2.4
70	75	4.2	4.0	3.8	3.6	3.4	3.2	3.1	2.9	2.7	2.5	2.4
71	76	4.1	3.9	3.8	3.6	3.4	3.2	3.0	2.9	2.7	2.5	2.3
72	77	4.1	3.9	3.7	3.5	3.3	3.2	3.0	2.8	2.7	2.5	2.3
73	78	4.0	3.8	3.7	3.5	3.3	3.1	3.0	2.8	2.6	2.5	2.3
74	79	3.9	3.8	3.6	3.4	3.3	3.1	2.9	2.8	2.6	2.4	2.3
75	80	3.9	3.7	3.5	3.4	3.2	3.0	2.9	2.7	2.6	2.4	2.2
76	81	3.8	3.6	3.5	3.3	3.2	3.0	2.8	2.7	2.5	2.4	2.2
77	82	3.7	3.6	3.4	3.3	3.1	3.0	2.8	2.6	2.5	2.3	2.2
78	83	3.7	3.5	3.4	3.2	3.1	2.9	2.7	2.6	2.4	2.3	2.1
79	84	3.6	3.4	3.3	3.1	3.0	2.8	2.7	2.5	2.4	2.2	2.1
80	85	3.5	3.4	3.2	3.1	2.9	2.8	2.6	2.5	2.3	2.2	2.0
81	86	3.4	3.3	3.1	3.0	2.9	2.7	2.6	2.4	2.3	2.1	2.0
82	87	3.3	3.2	3.1	2.9	2.8	2.7	2.5	2.4	2.2	2.1	2.0
83	88	3.2	3.1	3.0	2.9	2.7	2.6	2.5	2.3	2.2	2.0	1.9
84	89	3.1	3.0	2.9	2.8	2.7	2.5	2.4	2.3	2.1	2.0	1.9

Ages Male	Ages Female	98 / 103	99 / 104	100 / 105	101 / 106	102 / 107	103 / 108	104 / 109	105 / 110	106 / 111	107 / 112	108 / 113
60	65	2.3	2.1	2.0	1.8	1.6	1.4	1.3	1.1	0.9	0.8	0.7
61	66	2.3	2.1	2.0	1.8	1.6	1.4	1.2	1.1	0.9	0.8	0.7
62	67	2.3	2.1	1.9	1.8	1.6	1.4	1.2	1.1	0.9	0.8	0.7
63	68	2.3	2.1	1.9	1.7	1.6	1.4	1.2	1.1	0.9	0.8	0.7
64	69	2.3	2.1	1.9	1.7	1.6	1.4	1.2	1.1	0.9	0.8	0.7
65	70	2.3	2.1	1.9	1.7	1.6	1.4	1.2	1.1	0.9	0.8	0.7
66	71	2.3	2.1	1.9	1.7	1.5	1.4	1.2	1.1	0.9	0.8	0.7
67	72	2.2	2.1	1.9	1.7	1.5	1.4	1.2	1.0	0.9	0.7	0.7
68	73	2.2	2.0	1.9	1.7	1.5	1.4	1.2	1.0	0.9	0.7	0.7
69	74	2.2	2.0	1.8	1.7	1.5	1.3	1.2	1.0	0.9	0.7	0.6
70	75	2.2	2.0	1.8	1.7	1.5	1.3	1.2	1.0	0.9	0.7	0.6
71	76	2.2	2.0	1.8	1.6	1.5	1.3	1.2	1.0	0.9	0.7	0.6
72	77	2.1	2.0	1.8	1.6	1.5	1.3	1.1	1.0	0.8	0.7	0.6
73	78	2.1	1.9	1.8	1.6	1.4	1.3	1.1	1.0	0.8	0.7	0.6
74	79	2.1	1.9	1.7	1.6	1.4	1.3	1.1	1.0	0.8	0.7	0.6
75	80	2.1	1.9	1.7	1.6	1.4	1.3	1.1	1.0	0.8	0.7	
76	81	2.0	1.9	1.7	1.5	1.4	1.2	1.1	0.9	0.8	0.7	
77	82	2.0	1.8	1.7	1.5	1.4	1.2	1.1	0.9	0.8	0.7	
78	83	2.0	1.8	1.6	1.5	1.3	1.2	1.0	0.9	0.8	0.7	
79	84	1.9	1.8	1.6	1.5	1.3	1.2	1.0	0.9	0.8	0.7	
80	85	1.9	1.7	1.6	1.4	1.3	1.1	1.0	0.9	0.7	0.7	
81	86	1.8	1.7	1.5	1.4	1.3	1.1	1.0	0.8	0.7	0.6	
82	87	1.8	1.7	1.5	1.4	1.2	1.1	1.0	0.8	0.7	0.6	
83	88	1.8	1.6	1.5	1.3	1.2	1.1	0.9	0.8	0.7	0.6	
84	89	1.7	1.6	1.4	1.3	1.2	1.0	0.9	0.8	0.7		

TABLE IIA.—ANNUITIES FOR JOINT LIFE ONLY—TWO LIVES—
EXPECTED RETURN MULTIPLES—Continued

Ages		87	88	89	90	91	92	93	94	95	96
Male	Male										
Male	Female	92	93	94	95	96	97	98	99	100	101
85	90	3.1	2.9	2.8	2.7	2.6	2.5	2.3	2.2	2.1	1.9
86	91	3.0	2.8	2.7	2.6	2.5	2.4	2.3	2.1	2.0	1.9
87	92	2.9	2.8	2.6	2.5	2.4	2.3	2.2	2.1	1.9	1.8
88	93	2.8	2.7	2.6	2.4	2.3	2.2	2.1	2.0	1.9	1.7
89	94	2.6	2.6	2.5	2.4	2.2	2.1	2.0	1.9	1.8	1.7
90	95	2.5	2.4	2.4	2.3	2.2	2.0	1.9	1.8	1.7	1.6
91	96	2.4	2.3	2.2	2.2	2.1	2.0	1.9	1.7	1.6	1.5
92	97	2.3	2.2	2.1	2.0	2.0	1.9	1.8	1.7	1.6	1.5
93	98	2.2	2.1	2.0	1.9	1.9	1.8	1.7	1.6	1.5	1.4
94	90	2.1	2.0	1.9	1.8	1.7	1.7	1.6	1.5	1.4	1.3
95	100	1.9	1.9	1.8	1.7	1.6	1.6	1.5	1.4	1.3	1.2
96	101	1.8	1.7	1.7	1.6	1.5	1.5	1.4	1.3	1.2	1.1
97	102	1.7	1.6	1.6	1.5	1.4	1.4	1.3	1.2	1.1	1.1
98	103	1.6	1.5	1.4	1.4	1.3	1.3	1.2	1.1	1.0	1.0
99	104	1.4	1.4	1.3	1.3	1.2	1.1	1.2	1.0	1.0	0.9

Ages		97	98	99	100	101	102	103	104	105	106
Male	Male										
Male	Female	102	103	104	105	106	107	108	109	110	111
85	90	1.8	1.7	1.5	1.4	1.3	1.1	1.0	0.9	0.8	0.7
86	91	1.7	1.6	1.5	1.3	1.2	1.1	1.0	0.8	0.7	0.7
87	92	1.7	1.6	1.4	1.3	1.2	1.1	0.9	0.8	0.7	0.6
88	93	1.6	1.5	1.4	1.3	1.1	1.0	0.9	0.8	0.7	0.6
89	94	1.6	1.4	1.3	1.2	1.1	1.0	0.9	0.7	0.7	
90	95	1.5	1.4	1.3	1.2	1.0	0.9	0.8	0.7	0.6	
91	96	1.4	1.3	1.2	1.1	1.0	0.9	0.8	0.7	0.6	
92	97	1.4	1.3	1.1	1.0	0.9	0.8	0.7	0.7		
93	98	1.3	1.2	1.1	1.0	0.9	0.8	0.7	0.6		
94	99	1.2	1.1	1.0	0.9	0.8	0.7	0.7			
95	100	1.1	1.0	1.0	0.9	0.8	0.7	0.6			
96	101	1.1	1.0	0.9	0.8	0.7	0.7				
97	102	1.0	0.9	0.8	0.7	0.7	0.6				
98	103	0.9	0.8	0.7	0.7	0.6					
99	104	0.8	0.7	0.7	0.6						

TABLE III.—PERCENT VALUE OF REFUND FEATURE

Ages		Duration of guaranteed amount												
Male	Female	1 year	2 years	3 years	4 years	5 years	6 years	7 years	8 years	9 years	10 years	11 years	12 years	13 years
		Per-cent	Per-cent	Per-cent	Per-cent	Per-cent	Per-cent	Per-cent	Per-cent	Per-cent	Per-cent	Per-cent	Per-cent	Per-cent
6	11									1	1	1	1	1
7	12									1	1	1	1	1
8	13								1	1	1	1	1	1
9	14								1	1	1	1	1	1
10	15								1	1	1	1	1	1
11	16								1	1	1	1	1	1
12	17								1	1	1	1	1	1
13	18								1	1	1	1	1	1
14	19								1	1	1	1	1	1
15	20								1	1	1	1	1	1
16	21								1	1	1	1	1	1
17	22								1	1	1	1	1	1
18	23								1	1	1	1	1	1
19	24								1	1	1	1	1	1
20	25								1	1	1	1	1	1
21	26								1	1	1	1	1	1
22	27							1	1	1	1	1	1	1
23	28							1	1	1	1	1	1	1
24	29							1	1	1	1	1	1	1
25	30								1	1	1	1	1	1
26	31						1	1	1	1	1	1	1	1
27	32						1	1	1	1	1	1	1	1
28	33						1	1	1	1	1	1	1	1
29	34						1	1	1	1	1	1	1	2
30	35					1	1	1	1	1	1	1	2	2
31	36						1	1	1	1	1	1	2	2
32	37						1	1	1	1	1	1	2	2
33	38				1	1	1	1	1	1	1	2	2	2
34	39			1	1	1	1	1	1	1	2	2	2	2
35	40			1	1	1	1	1	1	1	2	2	2	2
36	41				1	1	1	1	1	1	2	2	2	3
37	42				1	1	1	1	1	2	2	2	3	3
38	43				1	1	1	1	1	2	2	2	3	3
39	44			1	1	1	1	2	2	2	2	3	3	3
40	45			1	1	1	1	2	2	2	3	3	3	4
41	46			1	1	1	1	2	2	2	3	3	3	4
42	47			1	1	1	2	2	2	3	3	4	4	4
43	48		1	1	1	1	2	2	2	3	3	4	4	4
44	49		1	1	1	1	2	2	3	3	3	4	4	5
45	50		1	1	1	2	2	3	3	4	4	5	5	5
46	51			1	1	1	2	2	3	3	4	4	5	5
47	52			1	1	1	2	2	3	4	4	5	5	6
48	53			1	1	2	2	2	3	4	5	5	6	6
49	54			1	1	2	2	3	3	4	5	6	6	7
50	55			1	1	2	2	3	3	4	5	6	7	7
51	56		1	1	2	3	3	4	4	5	6	6	7	8
52	57	1	1	2	2	3	3	4	5	5	6	7	8	8
53	58	1	1	2	2	3	4	4	5	6	7	7	8	9
54	59	1	1	2	2	3	4	4	5	6	7	8	9	10
55	60	1	1	2	2	3	3	4	5	6	7	8	9	10
56	61	1	1	2	3	4	4	5	6	7	8	9	10	11
57	62	1	1	2	3	4	5	6	7	8	9	10	11	12
58	63	1	2	2	3	4	5	6	7	8	9	10	12	13
59	64	1	2	3	4	5	6	7	8	9	10	11	12	14
60	65	1	2	3	4	5	6	7	8	10	11	12	13	15
61	66	1	2	3	4	5	6	8	9	10	12	13	14	16
62	67	1	2	3	4	6	7	8	10	11	12	14	15	17
63	68	1	2	3	5	6	7	8	10	12	13	15	16	18
64	69	1	3	4	5	7	8	9	11	13	14	16	17	19
65	70	1	3	4	6	7	9	10	12	13	15	17	19	20
66	71	1	3	4	6	8	9	11	13	14	16	18	20	22
67	72	2	3	5	6	8	10	12	14	15	17	19	21	23
68	73	2	3	5	7	9	11	13	14	16	18	21	23	25
69	74	2	4	6	7	9	11	13	16	18	20	22	24	26
70	75	2	4	6	8	10	12	14	17	19	21	23	26	28
71	76	2	4	6	9	11	13	15	18	20	22	25	27	29
72	77	2	5	7	9	12	14	16	19	21	24	26	29	31
73	78	2	5	7	10	12	15	18	20	23	25	28	30	33
74	79	3	5	8	11	13	16	19	22	24	27	30	32	35
75	80	3	6	8	11	14	17	20	23	26	29	31	34	37
76	81	3	6	9	12	15	18	21	24	27	30	33	36	39
77	82	3	7	10	13	16	20	23	26	29	32	35	38	41
78	83	4	7	11	14	17	21	24	28	31	34	37	40	43
79	84	4	8	11	15	19	22	26	29	33	36	39	42	45
80	85	4	8	12	16	20	24	27	31	34	38	41	44	47
81	86	4	9	13	17	21	25	29	33	36	40	43	46	49
82	87	5	9	14	18	23	27	31	35	38	42	45	48	51
83	88	5	10	15	19	24	28	33	37	40	44	47	50	53

Ages		Duration of guaranteed amount												
Male	Female	1 year	2 years	3 years	4 years	5 years	6 years	7 years	8 years	9 years	10 years	11 years	12 years	13 years
		Percent	Percent	Percent	Percent	Percent	Percent	Percent	Percent	Percent	Percent	Percent	Percent	Percent
84	89	5	11	16	21	26	30	34	38	42	46	49	52	55
85	90	6	11	17	22	27	32	36	41	44	48	51	55	57

TABLE III.—PERCENT VALUE OF REFUND FEATURE—Continued

Ages		Duration of guaranteed amount												
Male	Female	14 year	15 years	16 years	17 years	18 years	19 years	20 years	21 years	22 years	23 years	24 years	25 years	26 years
		Percent	Percent	Percent	Percent	Percent	Percent	Percent	Percent	Percent	Percent	Percent	Percent	Percent
6	11	1	1	1	1	1	1	1	1	1	1	2	2	2
7	12	1	1	1	1	1	1	1	1	1	1	2	2	2
8	13	1	1	1	1	1	1	1	1	1	1	2	2	2
9	14	1	1	1	1	1	1	1	1	1	1	2	2	2
10	15	1	1	1	1	1	1	1	1	1	2	2	2	2
11	16	1	1	1	1	1	1	1	1	1	2	2	2	2
12	17	1	1	1	1	1	1	1	1	1	2	2	2	2
13	18	1	1	1	1	1	1	1	1	2	2	2	2	2
14	19	1	1	1	1	1	1	1	1	2	2	2	2	2
15	20	1	1	1	1	1	1	1	1	2	2	2	2	2
16	21	1	1	1	1	1	1	1	2	2	2	2	2	2
17	22	1	1	1	1	1	1	1	2	2	2	2	2	2
18	23	1	1	1	1	1	1	2	2	2	2	2	2	2
19	24	1	1	1	1	1	2	2	2	2	2	2	2	2
20	25	1	1	1	1	1	2	2	2	2	2	2	2	3
21	26	1	1	1	1	2	2	2	2	2	2	2	3	3
22	27	1	1	1	1	2	2	2	2	2	2	3	3	3
23	28	1	1	1	2	2	2	2	2	2	2	3	3	3
24	29	1	1	1	2	2	2	2	2	2	3	3	3	3
25	30	1	1	2	2	2	2	2	2	3	3	3	3	3
26	31	1	2	2	2	2	2	2	3	3	3	3	3	4
27	32	2	2	2	2	2	2	3	3	3	3	3	4	4
28	33	2	2	2	2	2	3	3	3	3	3	4	4	4
29	34	2	2	2	2	2	3	3	3	3	4	4	4	5
30	35	2	2	2	2	3	3	3	3	4	4	4	5	5
31	36	2	2	2	3	3	3	3	4	4	4	5	5	5
32	37	2	2	2	3	3	3	3	4	4	5	5	5	6
33	38	2	2	3	3	3	4	4	4	5	5	5	6	6
34	39	3	3	3	3	4	4	4	5	5	5	6	6	7
35	40	3	3	3	4	4	4	4	5	5	6	6	7	7
36	41	3	3	4	4	4	4	5	5	5	6	6	7	8
37	42	3	3	4	4	4	4	5	5	6	6	7	7	8
38	43	3	4	4	4	4	5	5	6	6	7	7	8	9
39	44	4	4	4	4	5	5	6	6	7	7	8	9	9
40	45	4	4	5	5	6	6	7	7	8	8	9	9	10
41	46	4	5	5	6	6	7	7	8	8	9	9	10	11
42	47	5	5	5	6	6	7	8	8	9	9	10	11	12
43	48	5	5	6	6	7	8	8	9	9	10	11	12	12
44	49	5	6	6	7	7	8	9	9	10	11	12	12	13
45	50	6	6	7	7	8	9	9	10	11	12	12	13	14
46	51	6	7	7	8	9	9	10	11	12	12	13	14	15
47	52	7	7	8	9	9	10	11	12	12	13	14	15	16
48	53	7	8	8	9	10	11	12	12	13	14	15	16	17
49	54	8	8	9	10	11	11	12	13	14	15	16	17	18
50	55	8	9	10	11	11	12	13	14	15	16	17	18	20
51	56	9	10	10	11	12	13	14	15	16	17	18	20	21
52	57	9	10	11	12	13	14	15	16	17	18	20	21	22
53	58	10	11	12	13	14	15	16	17	19	20	21	22	24
54	59	11	12	13	14	15	16	17	18	20	21	22	24	25
55	60	11	13	14	15	16	17	18	20	21	22	24	25	26
56	61	12	13	15	16	17	18	20	21	22	24	25	27	28
57	62	13	14	16	17	18	20	21	22	24	25	27	28	30
58	63	14	15	17	18	19	21	22	24	25	27	28	30	31
59	64	15	16	18	19	21	22	24	25	27	28	30	31	33
60	65	16	18	19	20	22	24	25	27	28	30	32	33	35
61	66	17	19	20	22	23	25	27	28	30	32	33	35	37
62	67	18	20	22	23	25	27	28	30	32	33	35	37	38
63	68	20	21	23	25	26	28	30	32	33	35	37	39	40
64	69	21	23	24	26	28	30	32	33	35	37	39	41	42
65	70	22	24	26	28	30	32	33	35	37	39	41	42	44
66	71	24	26	28	29	31	33	35	37	39	41	43	44	46
67	72	25	27	29	31	33	35	37	39	41	43	45	46	48
68	73	27	29	31	33	35	37	39	41	43	45	47	48	50
69	74	28	30	33	35	37	39	41	43	45	47	48	50	52
70	75	30	32	34	37	39	41	43	45	47	49	50	52	54
71	76	32	34	36	39	41	43	45	47	49	51	52	54	56
72	77	34	36	38	41	43	45	47	49	51	53	54	56	58
73	78	35	38	40	43	45	47	49	51	53	55	56	58	59
74	79	37	40	42	45	47	49	51	53	55	57	58	60	61
75	80	39	42	44	47	49	51	53	55	57	58	60	62	63
76	81	41	44	46	49	51	53	55	57	59	60	62	63	65

Reg. §1.72-9

Ages		Duration of guaranteed amount												
Male	Female	14 year	15 years	16 years	17 years	18 years	19 years	20 years	21 years	22 years	23 years	24 years	25 years	26 years
		Per-cent	Per-cent	Per-cent	Per-cent	Per-cent	Per-cent	Per-cent	Per-cent	Per-cent	Per-cent	Per-cent	Per-cent	Per-cent
77	82	43	46	48	51	53	55	57	59	61	62	64	65	66
78	83	45	48	50	53	55	57	59	61	62	64	65	67	68
79	84	48	50	53	55	57	59	61	63	64	66	67	68	70
80	85	50	52	55	57	59	61	63	64	66	67	69	70	71
81	86	52	54	57	59	61	63	65	66	68	69	70	72	73
82	87	54	56	59	61	63	65	66	68	69	71	72	73	74
83	88	56	58	61	63	65	66	68	70	71	72	73	74	75
84	89	58	60	63	65	67	68	70	71	73	74	75	76	77
85	90	60	62	65	67	68	70	71	73	74	75	76	77	

TABLE III.—PERCENT VALUE OF REFUND FEATURE—Continued

Ages		Duration of guaranteed amount								
Male	Female	27 years	28 years	29 years	30 years	31 years	32 years	33 years	34 years	35 years
		Percent	Percent	Percent	Percent	Percent	Percent	Percent	Percent	Percent
6	11	2	2	2	2	2	2	2	2	2
7	12	2	2	2	2	2	2	2	2	3
8	13	2	2	2	2	2	2	2	2	3
9	14	2	2	2	2	2	2	2	3	3
10	15	2	2	2	2	2	2	3	3	3
11	16	2	2	2	2	2	2	3	3	3
12	17	2	2	2	2	2	3	3	3	3
13	18	2	2	2	2	2	3	3	3	3
14	19	2	2	2	2	3	3	3	3	3
15	20	2	2	2	3	3	3	3	3	3
16	21	2	2	3	3	3	3	3	3	4
17	22	2	2	3	3	3	3	3	4	4
18	23	2	3	3	3	3	3	4	4	4
19	24	3	3	3	3	3	4	4	4	4
20	25	3	3	3	3	4	4	4	4	5
21	26	3	3	3	4	4	4	4	5	5
22	27	3	3	4	4	4	4	5	5	5
23	28	3	3	4	4	4	5	5	5	5
24	29	3	4	4	4	5	5	5	5	6
25	30	4	4	4	5	5	5	6	6	6
26	31	4	4	5	5	5	6	6	6	7
27	32	4	5	5	5	6	6	6	7	7
28	33	5	5	5	6	6	6	7	7	8
29	34	5	5	6	6	6	7	7	8	8
30	35	5	6	6	6	7	7	8	8	9
31	36	6	6	6	7	7	8	8	9	9
32	37	6	7	7	7	8	8	9	10	10
33	38	7	7	7	8	8	9	10	10	11
34	39	7	8	8	9	9	10	10	11	12
35	40	8	8	9	9	10	10	11	12	12
36	41	8	9	9	10	10	11	12	13	13
37	42	9	9	10	11	11	12	13	13	14
38	43	9	10	11	11	12	13	13	14	15
39	44	10	11	11	12	13	14	14	15	16
40	45	11	11	12	13	14	15	15	16	17
41	46	11	12	13	14	15	16	16	17	18
42	47	12	13	14	15	16	17	18	18	19
43	48	13	14	15	16	17	18	19	20	21
44	49	14	15	16	17	18	19	20	21	22
45	50	15	16	17	18	19	20	21	22	23
46	51	16	17	18	19	20	21	22	24	25
47	52	17	18	19	20	21	23	24	25	26
48	53	18	19	20	22	23	24	25	26	28
49	54	19	21	22	23	24	25	27	28	29
50	55	21	22	23	24	26	27	28	29	31
51	56	22	23	25	26	27	28	30	31	32
52	57	23	25	26	27	29	30	31	33	34
53	58	25	26	28	29	30	32	33	34	36
54	59	26	28	29	31	32	33	35	36	38
55	60	28	29	31	32	34	35	36	38	39
56	61	29	31	32	34	35	37	38	40	41
57	62	31	33	34	36	37	39	40	41	43
58	63	33	34	36	37	39	40	42	43	45
59	64	35	36	38	39	41	42	44	45	47
60	65	36	38	40	41	43	44	46	47	48
61	66	38	40	41	43	44	46	47	49	50
62	67	40	42	43	45	46	48	49	51	52
63	68	42	44	45	47	48	50	51	52	54
64	69	44	46	47	49	50	52	53	54	55
65	70	46	47	49	50	52	53	55	56	57
66	71	48	49	51	52	54	55	56	58	59
67	72	50	51	53	54	56	57	58	59	61
68	73	52	53	55	56	57	59	60	61	62
69	74	53	55	56	58	59	60	62	63	64
70	75	55	57	58	60	61	62	63	64	65
71	76	57	59	60	61	63	64	65	66	67
72	77	59	60	62	63	64	65	66	67	68
73	78	61	62	64	65	66	67	68	69	70
74	79	63	64	65	66	67	68	69	70	71
75	80	64	66	67	68	69	70	71	72	72
76	81	66	67	68	69	70	71	72	73	
77	82	68	69	70	71	72	73	74		
78	83	69	70	71	72	73	74			
79	84	71	72	73	74	75				
80	85	72	73	74	75					
81	86	74	75	75						
82	87	75	76							
83	88	76								
84	89									

Reg. § 1.72-9

Ages		Duration of guaranteed amount								
Male	Female	27 years	28 years	29 years	30 years	31 years	32 years	33 years	34 years	35 years
		Percent	Percent	Percent	Percent	Percent	Percent	Percent	Percent	Percent
85	90									

Ages		Duration of guaranteed amount												
Male	Female	1 year	2 years	3 years	4 years	5 years	6 years	7 years	8 years	9 years	10 years	11 years	12 years	13 years	14 years
		Percent	Percent	Percent	Percent	Percent	Percent	Percent	Percent	Percent	Percent	Percent	Percent	Percent	Percent
86	91	6	12	18	24	29	34	38	43	47	50	54	57	59	62
87	92	7	13	19	25	31	36	40	45	49	52	56	59	61	64
88	93	7	14	21	27	32	38	42	47	51	55	58	61	63	66
89	94	8	15	22	28	34	40	45	49	53	57	60	63	65	68
90	95	8	16	23	30	36	42	47	51	55	59	62	65	67	70
91	96	9	17	25	32	38	44	49	53	57	61	64	67	69	71
92	97	9	18	26	34	40	46	51	55	59	63	66	69	71	73
93	98	10	20	28	36	42	48	53	58	62	65	68	70	73	75
94	99	11	21	30	37	44	50	55	60	64	67	70	72	74	76
95	100	12	22	31	39	46	52	58	62	66	69	72	74	76	78
96	101	12	24	33	42	49	55	60	64	68	71	73	76	78	79
97	102	13	25	35	44	51	57	62	66	70	73	75	77	79	
98	103	14	27	37	46	54	60	65	69	72	75	77	79		
99	104	15	29	40	49	56	62	67	71	74	77	79			
100	105	17	31	43	52	59	65	70	74	76	79				
101	106	18	33	46	55	63	68	73	76	79					
102	107	20	36	49	59	66	71	75	78						
103	108	22	40	53	62	69	74	78							
104	109	24	43	57	68	73	77								
105	110	27	48	61	70	76									
106	111	31	53	66	74										
107	112	35	58	71											
108	113	40	64												

Ages		Duration of guaranteed amount										
Male	Female	15 years	16 years	17 years	18 years	19 years	20 years	21 years	22 years	23 years	24 years	25 years
		Percent	Percent	Percent	Percent	Percent	Percent	Percent	Percent	Percent	Percent	Percent
86	91	64	66	68	70	72	73	74	75	76	77	
87	92	66	68	70	72	73	74	76	77	78		
88	93	68	70	72	73	75	76	77	78			
89	94	70	72	73	75	76	77	78				
90	95	72	73	75	76	77	79					
91	96	73	75	76	78	79						
92	97	75	76	78	79							
93	98	76	78	79								
94	99	78	79									
95	100	79										

TABLE IV.—TEMPORARY LIFE ANNUITIES[1]—ONE LIFE—EXPECTED RETURN MULTIPLES

| Ages | | Temporary period—maximum duration of annuity | | | | | | | | | |
Male	Female	1	2	3	4	5	6	7	8	9	10
0 to 8	0 to 13	1.0	2.0	3.0	4.0	5.0	6.0	7.0	8.0	8.9	9.9
9	14	1.0	2.0	3.0	4.0	5.0	6.0	7.0	8.0	8.9	9.9
10	15	1.0	2.0	3.0	4.0	5.0	6.0	7.0	8.0	8.9	9.9
11	16	1.0	2.0	3.0	4.0	5.0	6.0	7.0	8.0	8.9	9.9
12	17	1.0	2.0	3.0	4.0	5.0	6.0	7.0	8.0	8.9	9.9
13	18	1.0	2.0	3.0	4.0	5.0	6.0	7.0	8.0	8.9	9.9
14	19	1.0	2.0	3.0	4.0	5.0	6.0	7.0	8.0	8.9	9.9
15	20	1.0	2.0	3.0	4.0	5.0	6.0	7.0	8.0	8.9	9.9
16	21	1.0	2.0	3.0	4.0	5.0	6.0	7.0	8.0	8.9	9.9
17	22	1.0	2.0	3.0	4.0	5.0	6.0	7.0	8.0	8.9	9.9
18	23	1.0	2.0	3.0	4.0	5.0	6.0	7.0	8.0	8.9	9.9
19	24	1.0	2.0	3.0	4.0	5.0	6.0	7.0	8.0	8.9	9.9
20	25	1.0	2.0	3.0	4.0	5.0	6.0	7.0	8.0	8.9	9.9
21	26	1.0	2.0	3.0	4.0	5.0	6.0	7.0	8.0	8.9	9.9
22	27	1.0	2.0	3.0	4.0	5.0	6.0	7.0	8.0	8.9	9.9
23	28	1.0	2.0	3.0	4.0	5.0	6.0	7.0	8.0	8.9	9.9
24	29	1.0	2.0	3.0	4.0	5.0	6.0	7.0	7.9	8.9	9.9
25	30	1.0	2.0	3.0	4.0	5.0	6.0	7.0	7.9	8.9	9.9
26	31	1.0	2.0	3.0	4.0	5.0	6.0	7.0	7.9	8.9	9.9
27	32	1.0	2.0	3.0	4.0	5.0	6.0	7.0	7.9	8.9	9.9
28	33	1.0	2.0	3.0	4.0	5.0	6.0	7.0	7.9	8.9	9.9
29	34	1.0	2.0	3.0	4.0	5.0	6.0	6.9	7.9	8.9	9.9
30	35	1.0	2.0	3.0	4.0	5.0	6.0	6.9	7.9	8.9	9.9
31	36	1.0	2.0	3.0	4.0	5.0	6.0	6.9	7.9	8.9	9.9
32	37	1.0	2.0	3.0	4.0	5.0	6.0	6.9	7.9	8.9	9.9
33	38	1.0	2.0	3.0	4.0	5.0	6.0	6.9	7.9	8.9	9.9
34	39	1.0	2.0	3.0	4.0	5.0	5.9	6.9	7.9	8.9	9.8
35	40	1.0	2.0	3.0	4.0	5.0	5.9	6.9	7.9	8.9	9.8
36	41	1.0	2.0	3.0	4.0	5.0	5.9	6.9	7.9	8.9	9.8
37	42	1.0	2.0	3.0	4.0	5.0	5.9	6.9	7.9	8.8	9.8
38	43	1.0	2.0	3.0	4.0	5.0	5.9	6.9	7.9	8.8	9.8
39	44	1.0	2.0	3.0	4.0	4.9	5.9	6.9	7.9	8.8	9.8
40	45	1.0	2.0	3.0	4.0	4.9	5.9	6.9	7.8	8.8	9.7
41	46	1.0	2.0	3.0	4.0	4.9	5.9	6.9	7.8	8.8	9.7
42	47	1.0	2.0	3.0	4.0	4.9	5.9	6.9	7.8	8.8	9.7
43	48	1.0	2.0	3.0	4.0	4.9	5.9	6.9	7.8	8.8	9.7
44	49	1.0	2.0	3.0	4.0	4.9	5.9	6.8	7.8	8.7	9.7
45	50	1.0	2.0	3.0	3.9	4.9	5.9	6.8	7.8	8.7	9.6
46	51	1.0	2.0	3.0	3.9	4.9	5.9	6.8	7.8	8.7	9.6
47	52	1.0	2.0	3.0	3.9	4.9	5.9	6.8	7.7	8.7	9.6
48	53	1.0	2.0	3.0	3.9	4.9	5.9	6.8	7.7	8.6	9.5
49	54	1.0	2.0	3.0	3.9	4.9	5.8	6.8	7.7	8.6	9.5
50	55	1.0	2.0	3.0	3.9	4.9	5.8	6.8	7.7	8.6	9.5
51	56	1.0	2.0	3.0	3.9	4.9	5.8	6.7	7.7	8.6	9.4
52	57	1.0	2.0	3.0	3.9	4.9	5.8	6.7	7.6	8.5	9.4
53	58	1.0	2.0	2.9	3.9	4.9	5.8	6.7	7.6	8.5	9.3
54	59	1.0	2.0	2.9	3.9	4.8	5.8	6.7	7.6	8.4	9.3
55	60	1.0	2.0	2.9	3.9	4.8	5.8	6.7	7.5	8.4	9.2
56	61	1.0	2.0	2.9	3.9	4.8	5.7	6.6	7.5	8.4	9.2
57	62	1.0	2.0	2.9	3.9	4.8	5.7	6.6	7.5	8.3	9.1
58	63	1.0	2.0	2.9	3.9	4.8	5.7	6.6	7.4	8.3	9.1
59	64	1.0	2.0	2.9	3.9	4.8	5.7	6.5	7.4	8.2	9.0
60	65	1.0	2.0	2.9	3.8	4.8	5.6	6.5	7.3	8.1	8.9
61	66	1.0	2.0	2.9	3.8	4.7	5.6	6.5	7.3	8.1	8.8
62	67	1.0	2.0	2.9	3.8	4.7	5.6	6.4	7.2	8.0	8.8
63	68	1.0	2.0	2.9	3.8	4.7	5.6	6.4	7.2	7.9	8.7
64	69	1.0	1.9	2.9	3.8	4.7	5.5	6.3	7.1	7.9	8.6
65	70	1.0	1.9	2.9	3.8	4.6	5.5	6.3	7.1	7.8	8.5
66	71	1.0	1.9	2.9	3.8	4.6	5.4	6.2	7.0	7.7	8.4
67	72	1.0	1.9	2.9	3.7	4.6	5.4	6.2	6.9	7.6	8.3
68	73	1.0	1.9	2.8	3.7	4.6	5.4	6.1	6.8	7.5	8.2
69	74	1.0	1.9	2.8	3.7	4.5	5.3	6.1	6.8	7.4	8.0
70	75	1.0	1.9	2.8	3.7	4.5	5.3	6.0	6.7	7.3	7.9
71	76	1.0	1.9	2.8	3.7	4.5	5.2	5.9	6.6	7.2	7.8
72	77	1.0	1.9	2.8	3.6	4.4	5.2	5.8	6.5	7.1	7.6
73	78	1.0	1.9	2.8	3.6	4.4	5.1	5.8	6.4	7.0	7.5
74	79	1.0	1.9	2.8	3.6	4.3	5.0	5.7	6.3	6.8	7.3
75	80	1.0	1.9	2.7	3.5	4.3	5.0	5.6	6.2	6.7	7.1
76	81	1.0	1.9	2.7	3.5	4.2	4.9	5.5	6.1	6.5	7.0
77	82	1.0	1.9	2.7	3.5	4.2	4.8	5.4	5.9	6.4	6.8
78	83	1.0	1.9	2.7	3.4	4.1	4.7	5.3	5.8	6.2	6.6
79	84	1.0	1.8	2.7	3.4	4.1	4.7	5.2	5.7	6.1	6.4
80	85	1.0	1.8	2.6	3.4	4.0	4.6	5.1	5.5	5.9	6.2
81	86	1.0	1.8	2.6	3.3	3.9	4.5	5.0	5.4	5.7	6.0
82	87	1.0	1.8	2.6	3.3	3.9	4.4	4.8	5.2	5.6	5.8
83	88	.9	1.8	2.6	3.2	3.8	4.3	4.7	5.1	5.4	5.6
84	89	.9	1.8	2.5	3.2	3.7	4.2	4.6	4.9	5.2	5.4
85	90	.9	1.8	2.5	3.1	3.6	4.1	4.5	4.8	5.0	5.2
86	91	.9	1.8	2.5	3.1	3.6	4.0	4.3	4.6	4.8	5.0

[1] See footnote at end of table.

TABLE IV.—TEMPORARY LIFE ANNUITIES[1]—ONE LIFE—EXPECTED RETURN MULTIPLES—Continued

| Ages | | Temporary period—maximum duration of annuity | | | | | | | | | |
Male	Female	11	12	13	14	15	16	17	18	19	20
0 to 8	0 to 13	10.9	11.9	12.9	13.9	14.9	15.8	16.8	17.8	18.8	19.7
9	14	10.9	11.9	12.9	13.9	14.9	15.8	16.8	17.8	18.8	19.7
10	15	10.9	11.9	12.9	13.9	14.9	15.8	16.8	17.8	18.8	19.7
11	16	10.9	11.9	12.9	13.9	14.9	15.8	16.8	17.8	18.8	19.7
12	17	10.9	11.9	12.9	13.9	14.9	15.8	16.8	17.8	18.8	19.7
13	18	10.9	11.9	12.9	13.9	14.9	15.8	16.8	17.8	18.8	19.7
14	19	10.9	11.9	12.9	13.9	14.9	15.8	16.8	17.8	18.8	19.7

| Ages | | Temporary period—maximum duration of annuity ||||||||||
Male	Female	11	12	13	14	15	16	17	18	19	20
15	20	10.9	11.9	12.9	13.9	14.9	15.8	16.8	17.8	18.7	19.7
16	21	10.9	11.9	12.9	13.9	14.8	15.8	16.8	17.8	18.7	19.7
17	22	10.9	11.9	12.9	13.9	14.8	15.8	16.8	17.8	18.7	19.7
18	23	10.9	11.9	12.9	13.9	14.8	15.8	16.8	17.8	18.7	19.7
19	24	10.9	11.9	12.9	13.9	14.8	15.8	16.8	17.7	18.7	19.7
20	25	10.9	11.9	12.9	13.9	14.8	15.8	16.8	17.7	18.7	19.7
21	26	10.9	11.9	12.9	13.8	14.8	15.8	16.8	17.7	18.7	19.6
22	27	10.9	11.9	12.9	13.8	14.8	15.8	16.7	17.7	18.7	19.6
23	28	10.9	11.9	12.9	13.8	14.8	15.8	16.7	17.7	18.7	19.6
24	29	10.9	11.9	12.9	13.8	14.8	15.8	16.7	17.7	18.6	19.6
25	30	10.9	11.9	12.8	13.8	14.8	15.7	16.7	17.7	18.6	19.6
26	31	10.9	11.9	12.8	13.8	14.8	15.7	16.7	17.6	18.6	19.5
27	32	10.9	11.9	12.8	13.8	14.8	15.7	16.7	17.6	18.6	19.5
28	33	10.9	11.8	12.8	13.8	14.7	15.7	16.6	17.6	18.5	19.5
29	34	10.9	11.8	12.8	13.8	14.7	15.7	16.6	17.6	18.5	19.4
30	35	10.9	11.8	12.8	13.7	14.7	15.6	16.6	17.5	18.4	19.4
31	36	10.8	11.8	12.8	13.7	14.7	15.6	16.5	17.5	18.4	19.3
32	37	10.8	11.8	12.7	13.7	14.6	15.6	16.5	17.4	18.4	19.3
33	38	10.8	11.8	12.7	13.7	14.6	15.6	16.5	17.4	18.3	19.2
34	39	10.8	11.8	12.7	13.6	14.6	15.5	16.4	17.4	18.3	19.2
35	40	10.8	11.7	12.7	13.6	14.6	15.5	16.4	17.3	18.2	19.1
36	41	10.8	11.7	12.7	13.6	14.5	15.4	16.3	17.2	18.1	19.0
37	42	10.8	11.7	12.6	13.6	14.5	15.4	16.3	17.2	18.1	18.9
38	43	10.7	11.7	12.6	13.5	14.4	15.3	16.2	17.1	18.0	18.9
39	44	10.7	11.6	12.6	13.5	14.4	15.3	16.2	17.1	17.9	18.8
40	45	10.7	11.6	12.5	13.5	14.4	15.2	16.1	17.0	17.8	18.7
41	46	10.7	11.6	12.5	13.4	14.3	15.2	16.1	16.9	17.8	18.6
42	47	10.6	11.6	12.5	13.4	14.3	15.1	16.0	16.8	17.7	18.5
43	48	10.6	11.5	12.4	13.3	14.2	15.1	15.9	16.7	17.6	18.4
44	49	10.6	11.5	12.4	13.3	14.1	15.0	15.8	16.7	17.5	18.3
45	50	10.5	11.4	12.3	13.2	14.1	14.9	15.7	16.6	17.4	18.1
46	51	10.5	11.4	12.3	13.2	14.0	14.8	15.7	16.5	17.2	18.0
47	52	10.5	11.4	12.2	13.1	13.9	14.7	15.6	16.3	17.1	17.8
48	53	10.4	11.3	12.2	13.0	13.8	14.7	15.4	16.2	17.0	17.7
49	54	10.4	11.3	12.1	12.9	13.8	14.6	15.3	16.1	16.8	17.5
50	55	10.3	11.2	12.0	12.9	13.7	14.5	15.2	16.0	16.7	17.4
51	56	10.3	11.1	12.0	12.8	13.6	14.3	15.1	15.8	16.5	17.2
52	57	10.2	11.1	11.9	12.7	13.5	14.2	14.9	15.6	16.3	17.0
53	58	10.2	11.0	11.8	12.6	13.4	14.1	14.8	15.5	16.1	16.8
54	59	10.1	10.9	11.7	12.5	13.2	14.0	14.6	15.3	15.9	16.5
55	60	10.1	10.9	11.6	12.4	13.1	13.8	14.5	15.1	15.7	16.3
56	61	10.0	10.8	11.5	12.3	13.0	13.7	14.3	14.9	15.5	16.1
57	62	9.9	10.7	11.4	12.2	12.8	13.5	14.1	14.7	15.3	15.8
58	63	9.8	10.6	11.3	12.0	12.7	13.3	13.9	14.5	15.0	15.5
59	64	9.8	10.5	11.2	11.9	12.5	13.2	13.7	14.3	14.8	15.3
60	65	9.7	10.4	11.1	11.7	12.4	13.0	13.5	14.0	14.5	15.0
61	66	9.6	10.3	11.0	11.6	12.2	12.8	13.3	13.8	14.2	14.7
62	67	9.5	10.2	10.8	11.4	12.0	12.5	13.1	13.5	14.0	14.3
63	68	9.4	10.0	10.7	11.3	11.8	12.3	12.8	13.2	13.7	14.0
64	69	9.3	9.9	10.5	11.1	11.6	12.1	12.5	13.0	13.3	13.7
65	70	9.1	9.8	10.3	10.9	11.4	11.9	12.3	12.7	13.0	13.3
66	71	9.0	9.6	10.2	10.7	11.2	11.6	12.0	12.4	12.7	13.0
67	72	8.9	9.5	10.0	10.5	10.9	11.3	11.7	12.0	12.3	12.6
68	73	8.7	9.3	9.8	10.3	10.7	11.1	11.4	11.7	12.0	12.2
69	74	8.6	9.1	9.6	10.0	10.4	10.8	11.1	11.4	11.6	11.8
70	75	8.4	8.9	9.4	9.8	10.2	10.5	10.8	11.0	11.2	11.4
71	76	8.3	8.7	9.2	9.6	9.9	10.2	10.4	10.7	10.9	11.0
72	77	8.1	8.6	8.9	9.3	9.6	9.9	10.1	10.3	10.5	10.6
73	78	7.9	8.3	8.7	9.0	9.3	9.6	9.8	9.9	10.1	10.2
74	79	7.7	8.1	8.5	8.8	9.0	9.2	9.4	9.6	9.7	9.8
75	80	7.6	7.9	8.2	8.5	8.7	8.9	9.1	9.2	9.3	9.4
76	81	7.4	7.7	8.0	8.2	8.4	8.6	8.7	8.8	8.9	9.0
77	82	7.1	7.5	7.7	7.9	8.1	8.3	8.4	8.5	8.5	8.6
78	83	6.9	7.2	7.4	7.6	7.8	7.9	8.0	8.1	8.2	8.2
79	84	6.7	7.0	7.2	7.3	7.5	7.6	7.7	7.7	7.8	7.8
80	85	6.5	6.7	6.9	7.1	7.2	7.3	7.3	7.4	7.4	7.4
81	86	6.3	6.5	6.6	6.8	6.9	6.9	7.0	7.0	7.1	
82	87	6.0	6.2	6.4	6.5	6.5	6.6	6.7	6.7		
83	88	5.8	6.0	6.1	6.2	6.2	6.3	6.3			
84	89	5.6	5.7	5.8	5.9	5.9	6.0				
85	90	5.3	5.5	5.5	5.6	5.6					
86	91	5.1	5.2	5.3	5.3						

[1] See footnote at end of table.

TABLE IV.—TEMPORARY LIFE ANNUITIES[1]—ONE LIFE—EXPECTED RETURN MULTIPLES—Continued

| Ages | | Temporary period—maximum duration of annuity ||||||||||
Male	Female	21	22	23	24	25	26	27	28	29	30
0 to 8	0 to 13	20.7	21.7	22.7	23.6	24.6	25.6	26.5	27.5	28.4	29.4
9	14	20.7	21.7	22.7	23.6	24.6	25.5	26.5	27.5	28.4	29.4
10	15	20.7	21.7	22.7	23.6	24.6	25.5	26.5	27.5	28.4	29.4
11	16	20.7	21.7	22.6	23.6	24.6	25.5	26.5	27.4	28.4	29.3
12	17	20.7	21.7	22.6	23.6	24.6	25.5	26.5	27.4	28.4	29.3
13	18	20.7	21.7	22.6	23.6	24.6	25.5	26.5	27.4	28.4	29.3
14	19	20.7	21.7	22.6	23.6	24.5	25.5	26.4	27.4	28.3	29.3
15	20	20.7	21.6	22.6	23.6	24.5	25.5	26.4	27.4	28.3	29.2
16	21	20.7	21.6	22.6	23.6	24.5	25.5	26.4	27.3	28.3	29.2
17	22	20.7	21.6	22.6	23.5	24.5	25.4	26.4	27.3	28.2	29.2
18	23	20.7	21.6	22.6	23.5	24.5	25.4	26.3	27.3	28.2	29.1
19	24	20.6	21.6	22.5	23.5	24.4	25.4	26.3	27.2	28.1	29.1
20	25	20.6	21.6	22.5	23.5	24.4	25.3	26.3	27.2	28.1	29.0
21	26	20.6	21.5	22.5	23.4	24.4	25.3	26.2	27.1	28.0	28.9
22	27	20.6	21.5	22.5	23.4	24.3	25.3	26.2	27.1	28.0	28.9

Ages		Temporary period—maximum duration of annuity									
Male	Female	Years									
		21	22	23	24	25	26	27	28	29	30
23	28	20.6	21.5	22.4	23.4	24.3	25.2	26.1	27.0	27.9	28.8
24	29	20.5	21.5	22.4	23.3	24.2	25.2	26.1	27.0	27.8	28.7
25	30	20.5	21.4	22.4	23.3	24.2	25.1	26.0	26.9	27.8	28.6
26	31	20.5	21.4	22.3	23.2	24.1	25.0	25.9	26.8	27.7	28.5
27	32	20.4	21.3	22.3	23.2	24.1	25.0	25.8	26.7	27.6	28.4
28	33	20.4	21.3	22.2	23.1	24.0	24.9	25.8	26.6	27.5	28.3
29	34	20.3	21.2	22.1	23.0	23.9	24.8	25.7	26.5	27.4	28.2
30	35	20.3	21.2	22.1	23.0	23.8	24.7	25.6	26.4	27.2	28.1
31	36	20.2	21.1	22.0	22.9	23.8	24.6	25.5	26.3	27.1	27.9
32	37	20.2	21.1	21.9	22.8	23.7	24.5	25.4	26.2	27.0	27.8
33	38	20.1	21.0	21.9	22.7	23.6	24.4	25.2	26.0	26.8	27.6
34	39	20.0	20.9	21.8	22.6	23.5	24.3	25.1	25.9	26.7	27.4
35	40	20.0	20.8	21.7	22.5	23.3	24.2	25.0	25.7	26.5	27.2
36	41	19.9	20.7	21.6	22.4	23.2	24.0	24.8	25.6	26.3	27.0
37	42	19.8	20.6	21.5	22.3	23.1	23.9	24.6	25.4	26.1	26.8
38	43	19.7	20.5	21.4	22.2	23.0	23.7	24.5	25.2	25.9	26.6
39	44	19.6	20.4	21.2	22.0	22.8	23.6	24.3	25.0	25.7	26.4
40	45	19.5	20.3	21.1	21.9	22.6	23.4	24.1	24.8	25.5	26.1
41	46	19.4	20.2	21.0	21.7	22.5	23.2	23.9	24.6	25.2	25.9
42	47	19.3	20.1	20.8	21.6	22.3	23.0	23.7	24.3	25.0	25.6
43	48	19.2	19.9	20.7	21.4	22.1	22.8	23.4	24.1	24.7	25.3
44	49	19.0	19.8	20.5	21.2	21.9	22.6	23.2	23.8	24.4	25.0
45	50	18.9	19.6	20.3	21.0	21.7	22.3	22.9	23.5	24.1	24.6
46	51	18.7	19.4	20.1	20.8	21.5	22.1	22.7	23.2	23.8	24.3
47	52	18.6	19.3	19.9	20.6	21.2	21.8	22.4	22.9	23.4	23.9
48	53	18.4	19.1	19.7	20.4	21.0	21.5	22.1	22.6	23.1	23.5
49	54	18.2	18.9	19.5	20.1	20.7	21.2	21.7	22.2	22.7	23.1
50	55	18.0	18.7	19.3	19.8	20.4	20.9	21.4	21.9	22.3	22.7
51	56	17.8	18.4	19.0	19.6	20.1	20.6	21.0	21.5	21.9	22.3
52	57	17.6	18.2	18.7	19.3	19.8	20.2	20.7	21.1	21.5	21.8
53	58	17.4	17.9	18.5	19.0	19.4	19.9	20.3	20.7	21.0	21.3
54	59	17.1	17.7	18.2	18.7	19.1	19.5	19.9	20.2	20.6	20.8
55	60	16.9	17.4	17.9	18.3	18.7	19.1	19.5	19.8	20.1	20.3
56	61	16.6	17.1	17.5	18.0	18.4	18.7	19.0	19.3	19.6	19.8
57	62	16.3	16.8	17.2	17.6	18.0	18.3	18.6	18.9	19.1	19.3
58	63	16.0	16.5	16.9	17.2	17.6	17.9	18.1	18.4	18.6	18.8
59	64	15.7	16.1	16.5	16.8	17.1	17.4	17.7	17.9	18.1	18.2
60	65	15.4	15.8	16.1	16.4	16.7	17.0	17.2	17.4	17.5	17.7
61	66	15.1	15.4	15.7	16.0	16.3	16.5	16.7	16.9	17.0	17.1
62	67	14.7	15.0	15.3	15.6	15.8	16.0	16.2	16.3	16.4	16.5
63	68	14.4	14.6	14.9	15.1	15.3	15.5	15.7	15.8	15.9	16.0
64	69	14.0	14.3	14.5	14.7	14.9	15.0	15.2	15.3	15.3	15.4
65	70	13.6	13.8	14.1	14.2	14.4	14.5	14.6	14.7	14.8	14.9
66	71	13.2	13.4	13.6	13.8	13.9	14.0	14.1	14.2	14.2	14.3
67	72	12.8	13.0	13.2	13.3	13.4	13.5	13.6	13.7	13.7	13.7
68	73	12.4	12.6	12.7	12.8	12.9	13.0	13.1	13.1	13.2	13.2
69	74	12.0	12.1	12.3	12.4	12.4	12.5	12.6	12.6	12.6	12.6
70	75	11.6	11.7	11.8	11.9	12.0	12.0	12.0	12.1	12.1	12.1
71	76	11.2	11.3	11.3	11.4	11.5	11.5	11.5	11.6	11.6	
72	77	10.7	10.8	10.9	10.9	11.0	11.0	11.0	11.0		
73	78	10.3	10.4	10.4	10.5	10.5	10.5	10.5			
74	79	9.9	9.9	10.0	10.0	10.1	10.1				
75	80	9.5	9.5	9.6	9.6	9.6					
76	81	9.1	9.1	9.1	9.1						
77	82	8.6	8.7	8.7							
78	83	8.2	8.3								
79	84	7.8									

[1] The multiples in this table are not applicable to annuities for a term certain; for such cases see § 1.72-5(c).

TABLE V.—ORDINARY LIFE ANNUITIES; ONE LIFE—EXPECTED RETURN MULTIPLES

Age	Multiple	Age	Multiple
5	76.6	60	24.2
6	75.6	61	23.3
7	74.7	62	22.5
8	73.7	63	21.6
9	72.7	64	20.8
10	71.7	65	20.0
11	70.7	66	19.2
12	69.7	67	18.4
13	68.8	68	17.6
14	67.8	69	16.8
15	66.8	70	16.0
16	65.8	71	15.3
17	64.8	72	14.6
18	63.9	73	13.9
19	62.9	74	13.2
20	61.9	75	12.5
21	60.9	76	11.9
22	59.9	77	11.2
23	59.0	78	10.6
24	58.0	79	10.0
25	57.0	80	9.5
26	56.0	81	8.9
27	55.1	82	8.4
28	54.1	83	7.9
29	53.1	84	7.4
30	52.2	85	6.9
31	51.2	86	6.5
32	50.2	87	6.1
33	49.3	88	5.7
34	48.3	89	5.3
35	47.3	90	5.0
36	46.4	91	4.7
37	45.4	92	4.4
38	44.4	93	4.1
39	43.5	94	3.9
40	42.5	95	3.7
41	41.5	96	3.4
42	40.6	97	3.2
43	39.6	98	3.0
44	38.7	99	2.8
45	37.7	100	2.7
46	36.8	101	2.5
47	35.9	102	2.3
48	34.9	103	2.1
49	34.0	104	1.9
50	33.1	105	1.8
51	32.2	106	1.6
52	31.3	107	1.4
53	30.4	108	1.3
54	29.5	109	1.1
55	28.6	110	1.0
56	27.7	111	.9
57	26.8	112	.8
58	25.9	113	.7
59	25.0	114	.6
		115	.5

TABLE VI.—ORDINARY JOINT LIFE AND LAST SURVIVOR ANNUITIES; TWO LIVES—EXPECTED RETURN MULTIPLES

Ages	5	6	7	8	9	10	11	12	13	14
5	83.8	83.3	82.8	82.4	82.0	81.6	81.2	80.9	80.6	80.3
6	83.3	82.8	82.3	81.8	81.4	81.0	80.6	80.3	79.9	79.6
7	82.8	82.3	81.8	81.3	80.9	80.4	80.0	79.6	79.3	78.9
8	82.4	81.8	81.3	80.8	80.3	79.9	79.4	79.0	78.6	78.3
9	82.0	81.4	80.9	80.3	79.8	79.3	78.9	78.4	78.0	77.6
10	81.6	81.0	80.4	79.9	79.3	78.8	78.3	77.9	77.4	77.0
11	81.2	80.6	80.0	79.4	78.9	78.3	77.8	77.3	76.9	76.4
12	80.9	80.3	79.6	79.0	78.4	77.9	77.3	76.8	76.3	75.9
13	80.6	79.9	79.3	78.6	78.0	77.4	76.9	76.3	75.8	75.3
14	80.3	79.6	78.9	78.3	77.6	77.0	76.4	75.9	75.3	74.8
15	80.0	79.3	78.6	77.9	77.3	76.6	76.0	75.4	74.9	74.3
16	79.8	79.0	78.3	77.6	76.9	76.3	75.6	75.0	74.4	73.9
17	79.5	78.8	78.0	77.3	76.6	75.9	75.3	74.6	74.0	73.4
18	79.3	78.5	77.8	77.0	76.3	75.6	74.9	74.3	73.6	73.0
19	79.1	78.3	77.5	76.8	76.0	75.3	74.6	73.9	73.3	72.6
20	78.9	78.1	77.3	76.5	75.8	75.0	74.3	73.6	72.9	72.3
21	78.7	77.9	77.1	76.3	75.5	74.8	74.0	73.3	72.6	71.9
22	78.6	77.7	76.9	76.1	75.3	74.5	73.8	73.0	72.3	71.6
23	78.4	77.6	76.7	75.9	75.1	74.3	73.5	72.8	72.0	71.3
24	78.3	77.4	76.6	75.7	74.9	74.1	73.3	72.6	71.8	71.1
25	78.2	77.3	76.4	75.6	74.8	73.9	73.1	72.3	71.6	70.8
26	78.0	77.2	76.3	75.4	74.6	73.8	72.9	72.1	71.3	70.6
27	77.9	77.1	76.2	75.3	74.4	73.6	72.8	71.9	71.1	70.3
28	77.8	76.9	76.1	75.2	74.3	73.4	72.6	71.8	70.9	70.1
29	77.7	76.8	76.0	75.1	74.2	73.3	72.5	71.6	70.8	70.0
30	77.7	76.8	75.9	75.0	74.1	73.2	72.3	71.5	70.6	69.8
31	77.6	76.7	75.8	74.9	74.0	73.1	72.2	71.3	70.5	69.6
32	77.5	76.6	75.7	74.8	73.9	73.0	72.1	71.2	70.3	69.5
33	77.5	76.5	75.6	74.7	73.8	72.9	72.0	71.1	70.2	69.3
34	77.4	76.5	75.5	74.6	73.7	72.8	71.9	71.0	70.1	69.2
35	77.3	76.4	75.5	74.5	73.6	72.7	71.8	70.9	70.0	69.1
36	77.3	76.3	75.4	74.5	73.5	72.6	71.7	70.8	69.9	69.0
37	77.2	76.3	75.4	74.4	73.5	72.6	71.6	70.7	69.8	68.9
38	77.2	76.2	75.3	74.4	73.4	72.5	71.6	70.6	69.7	68.8
39	77.2	76.2	75.3	74.3	73.4	72.4	71.5	70.6	69.6	68.7
40	77.1	76.2	75.2	74.3	73.3	72.4	71.4	70.5	69.6	68.6
41	77.1	76.1	75.2	74.2	73.3	72.3	71.4	70.4	69.5	68.6
42	77.0	76.1	75.1	74.2	73.2	72.3	71.3	70.4	69.4	68.5
43	77.0	76.1	75.1	74.1	73.2	72.2	71.3	70.3	69.4	68.5
44	77.0	76.0	75.1	74.1	73.1	72.2	71.2	70.3	69.3	68.4
45	77.0	76.0	75.0	74.1	73.1	72.2	71.2	70.2	69.3	68.4
46	76.9	76.0	75.0	74.0	73.1	72.1	71.2	70.2	69.3	68.3
47	76.9	75.9	75.0	74.0	73.1	72.1	71.1	70.2	69.2	68.3
48	76.9	75.9	75.0	74.0	73.0	72.1	71.1	70.1	69.2	68.2
49	76.9	75.9	74.9	74.0	73.0	72.0	71.1	70.1	69.1	68.2
50	76.9	75.9	74.9	73.9	73.0	72.0	71.0	70.1	69.1	68.2
51	76.8	75.9	74.9	73.9	73.0	72.0	71.0	70.1	69.1	68.1
52	76.8	75.9	74.9	73.9	72.9	72.0	71.0	70.0	69.1	68.1
53	76.8	75.8	74.9	73.9	72.9	71.9	71.0	70.0	69.0	68.1
54	76.8	75.8	74.8	73.9	72.9	71.9	71.0	70.0	69.0	68.1
55	76.8	75.8	74.8	73.9	72.9	71.9	70.9	70.0	69.0	68.0
56	76.8	75.8	74.8	73.8	72.9	71.9	70.9	69.9	69.0	68.0
57	76.8	75.8	74.8	73.8	72.9	71.9	70.9	69.9	69.0	68.0
58	76.8	75.8	74.8	73.8	72.8	71.9	70.9	69.9	68.9	68.0
59	76.7	75.8	74.8	73.8	72.8	71.9	70.9	69.9	68.9	68.0
60	76.7	75.8	74.8	73.8	72.8	71.8	70.9	69.9	68.9	67.9
61	76.7	75.7	74.8	73.8	72.8	71.8	70.9	69.9	68.9	67.9
62	76.7	75.7	74.8	73.8	72.8	71.8	70.8	69.9	68.9	67.9
63	76.7	75.7	74.8	73.8	72.8	71.8	70.8	69.9	68.9	67.9
64	76.7	75.7	74.7	73.8	72.8	71.8	70.8	69.8	68.9	67.9
65	76.7	75.7	74.7	73.8	72.8	71.8	70.8	69.8	68.9	67.9
66	76.7	75.7	74.7	73.7	72.8	71.8	70.8	69.8	68.9	67.9
67	76.7	75.7	74.7	73.7	72.8	71.8	70.8	69.8	68.8	67.9
68	76.7	75.7	74.7	73.7	72.8	71.8	70.8	69.8	68.8	67.9
69	76.7	75.7	74.7	73.7	72.7	71.8	70.8	69.8	68.8	67.8
70	76.7	75.7	74.7	73.7	72.7	71.8	70.8	69.8	68.8	67.8
71	76.7	75.7	74.7	73.7	72.7	71.8	70.8	69.8	68.8	67.8
72	76.7	75.7	74.7	73.7	72.7	71.7	70.8	69.8	68.8	67.8
73	76.7	75.7	74.7	73.7	72.7	71.7	70.8	69.8	68.8	67.8
74	76.7	75.7	74.7	73.7	72.7	71.7	70.8	69.8	68.8	67.8
75	76.7	75.7	74.7	73.7	72.7	71.7	70.8	69.8	68.8	67.8
76	76.6	75.7	74.7	73.7	72.7	71.7	70.8	69.8	68.8	67.8
77	76.6	75.7	74.7	73.7	72.7	71.7	70.8	69.8	68.8	67.8
78	76.6	75.7	74.7	73.7	72.7	71.7	70.7	69.8	68.8	67.8
79	76.6	75.7	74.7	73.7	72.7	71.7	70.7	69.8	68.8	67.8
80	76.6	75.7	74.7	73.7	72.7	71.7	70.7	69.8	68.8	67.8
81	76.6	75.7	74.7	73.7	72.7	71.7	70.7	69.8	68.8	67.8
82	76.6	75.7	74.7	73.7	72.7	71.7	70.7	69.8	68.8	67.8
83	76.6	75.7	74.7	73.7	72.7	71.7	70.7	69.8	68.8	67.8
84	76.6	75.7	74.7	73.7	72.7	71.7	70.7	69.8	68.8	67.8
85	76.6	75.7	74.7	73.7	72.7	71.7	70.7	69.8	68.8	67.8
86	76.6	75.7	74.7	73.7	72.7	71.7	70.7	69.8	68.8	67.8
87	76.6	75.7	74.7	73.7	72.7	71.7	70.7	69.8	68.8	67.8
88	76.6	75.7	74.7	73.7	72.7	71.7	70.7	69.8	68.8	67.8
89	76.6	75.7	74.7	73.7	72.7	71.7	70.7	69.7	68.8	67.8
90	76.6	75.6	74.7	73.7	72.7	71.7	70.7	69.7	68.8	67.8
91	76.6	75.6	74.7	73.7	72.7	71.7	70.7	69.7	68.8	67.8
92	76.6	75.6	74.7	73.7	72.7	71.7	70.7	69.7	68.8	67.8
93	76.6	75.6	74.7	73.7	72.7	71.7	70.7	69.7	68.8	67.8
94	76.6	75.6	74.7	73.7	72.7	71.7	70.7	69.7	68.8	67.8
95	76.6	75.6	74.7	73.7	72.7	71.7	70.7	69.7	68.8	67.8
96	76.6	75.6	74.7	73.7	72.7	71.7	70.7	69.7	68.8	67.8
97	76.6	75.6	74.7	73.7	72.7	71.7	70.7	69.7	68.8	67.8
98	76.6	75.6	74.7	73.7	72.7	71.7	70.7	69.7	68.8	67.8
99	76.6	75.6	74.7	73.7	72.7	71.7	70.7	69.7	68.8	67.8

Reg. §1.72-9

Ages	5	6	7	8	9	10	11	12	13	14
100	76.6	75.6	74.7	73.7	72.7	71.7	70.7	69.7	68.8	67.8
101	76.6	75.6	74.7	73.7	72.7	71.7	70.7	69.7	68.8	67.8
102	76.6	75.6	74.7	73.7	72.7	71.7	70.7	69.7	68.8	67.8
103	76.6	75.6	74.7	73.7	72.7	71.7	70.7	69.7	68.8	67.8
104	76.6	75.6	74.7	73.7	72.7	71.7	70.7	69.7	68.8	67.8
105	76.6	75.6	74.7	73.7	72.7	71.7	70.7	69.7	68.8	67.8
106	76.6	75.6	74.7	73.7	72.7	71.7	70.7	69.7	68.8	67.8
107	76.6	75.6	74.7	73.7	72.7	71.7	70.7	69.7	68.8	67.8
108	76.6	75.6	74.7	73.7	72.7	71.7	70.7	69.7	68.8	67.8
109	76.6	75.6	74.7	73.7	72.7	71.7	70.7	69.7	68.8	67.8
110	76.6	75.6	74.7	73.7	72.7	71.7	70.7	69.7	68.8	67.8
111	76.6	75.6	74.7	73.7	72.7	71.7	70.7	69.7	68.8	67.8
112	76.6	75.6	74.7	73.7	72.7	71.7	70.7	69.7	68.8	67.8
113	76.6	75.6	74.7	73.7	72.7	71.7	70.7	69.7	68.8	67.8
114	76.6	75.6	74.7	73.7	72.7	71.7	70.7	69.7	68.8	67.8
115	76.6	75.6	74.7	73.7	72.7	71.7	70.7	69.7	68.8	67.8

TABLE VI.—ORDINARY JOINT LIFE AND LAST SURVIVOR ANNUITIES; TWO LIVES—EXPECTED RETURN MULTIPLES—Continued

Ages	15	16	17	18	19	20	21	22	23	24
15	73.8	73.3	72.9	72.4	72.0	71.6	71.3	70.9	70.6	70.3
16	73.3	72.8	72.3	71.9	71.4	71.0	70.7	70.3	70.0	69.6
17	72.9	72.3	71.8	71.3	70.9	70.5	70.0	69.7	69.3	69.0
18	72.4	71.9	71.3	70.8	70.4	69.0	69.5	69.9	68.7	68.3
19	72.0	71.4	70.9	70.4	69.8	69.4	68.9	68.5	68.1	67.7
20	71.6	71.0	70.5	69.9	69.4	68.8	68.4	67.9	67.5	67.1
21	71.3	70.7	70.0	69.5	68.9	68.4	67.9	67.4	66.9	66.5
22	70.9	70.3	69.7	69.0	68.5	67.9	67.5	66.9	66.4	65.9
23	70.6	70.0	69.3	68.7	68.1	67.5	66.9	66.4	65.9	65.4
24	70.3	69.6	69.0	68.3	67.7	67.1	66.5	65.9	65.4	64.9
25	70.1	69.3	68.6	68.0	67.3	66.7	66.1	65.5	64.9	64.4
26	69.8	69.1	68.3	67.6	67.0	66.3	65.7	65.1	64.5	63.9
27	69.6	68.8	68.1	67.3	66.7	66.0	65.3	64.7	64.1	63.5
28	69.3	68.6	67.8	67.1	66.4	65.7	65.0	64.3	63.7	63.1
29	69.1	68.4	67.6	66.8	66.1	65.4	64.7	64.0	63.3	62.7
30	69.0	68.2	67.4	66.6	65.8	65.1	64.4	63.7	63.0	62.3
31	68.8	68.0	67.2	66.4	65.6	64.8	64.1	63.4	62.7	62.0
32	68.6	67.8	67.0	66.2	65.4	64.6	63.8	63.1	62.4	61.7
33	68.5	67.6	66.8	66.0	65.2	64.4	63.6	62.8	62.1	61.4
34	68.3	67.5	66.6	65.8	65.0	64.2	63.4	62.6	61.9	61.1
35	68.2	67.4	66.5	65.6	64.8	64.0	63.2	62.4	61.6	60.9
36	68.1	67.2	66.4	65.5	64.7	63.8	63.0	62.2	61.4	60.6
37	68.0	67.1	66.2	65.4	64.5	63.7	62.8	62.0	61.2	60.4
38	67.9	67.0	66.1	65.2	64.4	63.5	62.7	61.8	61.0	60.2
39	67.8	66.9	66.0	65.1	64.2	63.4	62.5	61.7	60.8	60.0
40	67.7	66.8	65.9	65.0	64.1	63.3	62.4	61.5	60.7	59.9
41	67.7	66.7	65.8	64.9	64.0	63.1	62.3	61.4	60.5	59.7
42	67.6	66.7	65.7	64.8	63.9	63.0	62.2	61.3	60.4	59.6
43	67.5	66.6	65.7	64.8	63.8	62.9	62.1	61.2	60.3	59.4
44	67.5	66.5	65.6	64.7	63.8	62.9	62.0	61.1	60.2	59.3
45	67.4	66.5	65.5	64.6	63.7	62.8	61.9	61.0	60.1	59.2
46	67.4	66.4	65.4	64.6	63.6	62.7	61.8	60.9	60.0	59.1
47	67.3	66.4	65.4	64.5	63.6	62.6	61.7	60.8	59.9	59.0
48	67.3	66.3	65.4	64.4	63.5	62.6	61.6	60.7	59.8	58.9
49	67.2	66.3	65.3	64.4	63.5	62.5	61.6	60.7	59.7	58.8
50	67.2	66.2	65.3	64.3	63.4	62.5	61.5	60.6	59.7	58.8
51	67.2	66.2	65.3	64.3	63.4	62.4	61.5	60.5	59.6	58.7
52	67.1	66.2	65.2	64.3	63.3	62.4	61.4	60.5	59.6	58.6
53	67.1	66.2	65.2	64.2	63.3	62.3	61.4	60.4	59.5	58.6
54	67.1	66.1	65.2	64.2	63.2	62.3	61.3	60.4	59.5	58.5
55	67.1	66.1	65.1	64.2	63.2	62.3	61.3	60.4	59.4	58.5
56	67.0	66.1	65.1	64.1	63.2	62.2	61.3	60.3	59.4	58.4
57	67.0	66.1	65.1	64.1	63.2	62.2	61.2	60.3	59.3	58.4
58	67.0	66.0	65.1	64.1	63.1	62.2	61.2	60.3	59.3	58.4
59	67.0	66.0	65.0	64.1	63.1	62.1	61.2	60.2	59.3	58.3
60	67.0	66.0	65.0	64.1	63.1	62.1	61.2	60.2	59.2	58.3
61	67.0	66.0	65.0	64.0	63.1	62.1	61.1	60.2	59.2	58.3
62	66.9	66.0	65.0	64.0	63.1	62.1	61.1	60.2	59.2	58.2
63	66.9	66.0	65.0	64.0	63.0	62.1	61.1	60.1	59.2	58.2
64	66.9	65.9	65.0	64.0	63.0	62.0	61.1	60.1	59.2	58.2
65	66.9	65.9	65.0	64.0	63.0	62.0	61.1	60.1	59.1	58.2
66	66.9	65.9	64.9	64.0	63.0	62.0	61.1	60.1	59.1	58.2
67	66.9	65.9	64.9	64.0	63.0	62.0	61.0	60.1	59.1	58.1
68	66.9	65.9	64.9	64.0	63.0	62.0	61.0	60.1	59.1	58.1
69	66.9	65.9	64.9	63.9	63.0	62.0	61.0	60.0	59.1	58.1
70	66.9	65.9	64.9	63.9	63.0	62.0	61.0	60.0	59.1	58.1
71	66.9	65.9	64.9	63.9	62.9	62.0	61.0	60.0	59.1	58.1
72	66.9	65.9	64.9	63.9	62.9	62.0	61.0	60.0	59.0	58.1
73	66.8	65.9	64.9	63.9	62.9	62.0	61.0	60.0	59.0	58.1
74	66.8	65.9	64.9	63.9	62.9	62.0	61.0	60.0	59.0	58.1
75	66.8	65.9	64.9	63.9	62.9	61.9	61.0	60.0	59.0	58.1
76	66.8	65.9	64.9	63.9	62.9	61.9	61.0	60.0	59.0	58.0
77	66.8	65.9	64.9	63.9	62.9	61.9	61.0	60.0	59.0	58.0
78	66.8	65.8	64.9	63.9	62.9	61.9	61.0	60.0	59.0	58.0
79	66.8	65.8	64.9	63.9	62.9	61.9	61.0	60.0	59.0	58.0
80	66.8	65.9	64.9	63.9	62.9	61.9	60.9	60.0	59.0	58.0
81	66.8	65.8	64.9	63.9	62.9	61.9	60.9	60.0	59.0	58.0
82	66.8	65.8	64.9	63.9	62.9	61.9	60.9	60.0	59.0	58.0
83	66.8	65.8	64.9	63.9	62.9	61.9	60.9	60.0	59.0	58.0
84	66.8	65.8	64.8	63.9	62.9	61.9	60.9	60.0	59.0	58.0
85	66.8	65.8	64.8	63.9	62.9	61.9	60.9	60.0	59.0	58.0
86	66.8	65.8	64.8	63.9	62.9	61.9	60.9	60.0	59.0	58.0
87	66.8	65.8	64.8	63.9	62.9	61.9	60.9	60.0	59.0	58.0
88	66.8	65.8	64.8	63.9	62.9	61.9	60.9	60.0	59.0	58.0
89	66.8	65.8	64.8	63.9	62.9	61.9	60.9	60.0	59.0	58.0
90	66.8	65.8	64.8	63.9	62.9	61.9	60.9	60.0	59.0	58.0
91	66.8	65.8	64.8	63.9	62.9	61.9	60.9	60.0	59.0	58.0

Ages	15	16	17	18	19	20	21	22	23	24
92	66.8	65.8	64.8	63.9	62.9	61.9	60.9	59.9	59.0	58.0
93	66.8	65.8	64.8	63.9	62.9	61.9	60.9	59.9	59.0	58.0
94	66.8	65.8	64.8	63.9	62.9	61.9	60.9	59.9	59.0	58.0
95	66.8	65.8	64.8	63.9	62.9	61.9	60.9	59.9	59.0	58.0
96	66.8	65.8	64.8	63.9	62.9	61.9	60.9	59.9	59.0	58.0
97	66.8	65.8	64.8	63.9	62.9	61.9	60.9	59.9	59.0	58.0
98	66.8	65.8	64.8	63.9	62.9	61.9	60.9	59.9	59.0	58.0
99	66.8	65.8	64.8	63.9	62.9	61.9	60.9	59.9	59.0	58.0
100	66.8	65.8	64.8	63.9	62.9	61.9	60.9	59.9	59.0	58.0
101	66.8	65.8	64.8	63.9	62.9	61.9	60.9	59.9	59.0	58.0
102	66.8	65.8	64.8	63.9	62.9	61.9	60.9	59.9	59.0	58.0
103	66.8	65.8	64.8	63.9	62.9	61.9	60.9	59.9	59.0	58.0
104	66.8	65.8	64.8	63.9	62.9	61.9	60.9	59.9	59.0	58.0
105	66.8	65.8	64.8	63.9	62.9	61.9	60.9	59.9	59.0	58.0
106	66.8	65.8	64.8	63.9	62.9	61.9	60.9	59.9	59.0	58.0
107	66.8	65.8	64.8	63.9	62.9	61.9	60.9	59.9	59.0	58.0
108	66.8	65.8	64.8	63.9	62.9	61.9	60.9	59.9	59.0	58.0
109	66.8	65.8	64.8	63.9	62.9	61.9	60.9	59.9	59.0	58.0
110	66.8	65.8	64.8	63.9	62.9	61.9	60.9	59.9	59.0	58.0
111	66.8	65.8	64.8	63.9	62.9	61.9	60.9	59.9	59.0	58.0
112	66.8	65.8	64.8	63.9	62.9	61.9	60.9	59.9	59.0	58.0
113	66.8	65.8	64.8	63.9	62.9	61.9	60.9	59.9	59.0	58.0
114	66.8	65.8	64.8	63.9	62.9	61.9	60.9	59.9	59.0	58.0
115	66.8	65.8	64.8	63.9	62.9	61.9	60.9	59.9	59.0	58.0

TABLE VI.—ORDINARY JOINT LIFE AND LAST SURVIVOR ANNUITIES; TWO LIVES—EXPECTED RETURN MULTIPLES—Continued

Ages	25	26	27	28	29	30	31	32	33	34
25	63.9	63.4	62.9	62.5	62.1	61.7	61.3	61.0	60.7	60.4
26	63.4	62.9	62.4	61.9	61.5	61.1	60.7	60.4	60.0	59.7
27	62.9	62.4	61.9	61.4	60.9	60.5	60.1	59.7	59.4	59.0
28	62.5	61.9	61.4	60.9	60.4	60.0	59.5	59.1	58.7	58.4
29	62.1	61.5	60.9	60.4	59.9	59.4	59.0	58.5	58.1	57.7
30	61.7	61.1	60.5	60.0	59.4	58.9	58.4	58.0	57.5	57.1
31	61.3	60.7	60.1	59.5	59.0	58.4	57.9	57.4	57.0	56.5
32	61.0	60.4	59.7	59.1	58.5	58.0	57.4	56.9	56.4	56.0
33	60.7	60.0	59.4	58.7	58.1	57.5	57.0	56.4	55.9	55.5
34	60.4	59.7	59.0	58.4	57.7	57.1	56.5	56.0	55.5	54.9
35	60.1	59.4	58.7	58.0	57.4	56.7	56.1	55.6	55.0	54.5
36	59.9	59.1	58.4	57.7	57.0	56.4	55.8	55.1	54.6	54.0
37	59.6	58.9	58.1	57.4	56.7	56.0	55.4	54.8	54.2	53.6
38	59.4	58.6	57.9	57.1	56.4	55.7	55.1	54.4	53.8	53.2
39	59.2	58.4	57.7	56.9	56.2	55.4	54.7	54.1	53.4	52.8
40	59.0	58.2	57.4	56.7	55.9	55.2	54.5	53.8	53.1	52.4
41	58.9	58.0	57.2	56.4	55.7	54.9	54.2	53.5	52.8	52.1
42	58.7	57.9	57.1	56.2	55.5	54.7	53.9	53.2	52.5	51.8
43	58.6	57.7	56.9	56.1	55.3	54.5	53.7	52.9	52.2	51.5
44	58.4	57.6	56.7	55.9	55.1	54.3	53.5	52.7	52.0	51.2
45	58.3	57.4	56.6	55.7	54.9	54.1	53.3	52.5	51.7	51.0
46	58.2	57.3	56.5	55.6	54.8	53.9	53.1	52.3	51.5	50.7
47	58.1	57.2	56.3	55.5	54.6	53.8	52.9	52.1	51.3	50.5
48	58.0	57.1	56.2	55.3	54.5	53.6	52.8	51.9	51.1	50.3
49	57.9	57.0	56.1	55.2	54.4	53.5	52.6	51.8	51.0	50.1
50	57.8	56.9	56.0	55.1	54.2	53.4	52.5	51.7	50.8	50.0
51	57.8	56.9	55.9	55.0	54.1	53.3	52.4	51.5	50.7	49.8
52	57.7	56.8	55.9	55.0	54.1	53.2	52.3	51.4	50.5	49.7
53	57.6	56.7	55.8	54.9	54.0	53.1	52.2	51.3	50.4	49.6
54	57.6	56.7	55.7	54.8	53.9	53.0	52.1	51.2	50.3	49.4
55	57.5	56.6	55.7	54.7	53.8	52.9	52.0	51.1	40.2	49.3
56	57.5	56.5	55.6	54.7	53.8	52.8	51.9	51.0	50.1	49.2
57	57.4	56.5	55.6	54.6	53.7	52.8	51.9	50.9	50.0	49.1
58	57.4	56.5	55.5	54.6	53.6	52.7	51.8	50.9	50.0	49.1
59	57.4	56.4	55.5	54.5	53.6	52.7	51.7	50.8	49.9	49.0
60	57.3	56.4	55.4	54.5	53.6	52.6	51.7	50.8	49.8	48.9
61	57.3	56.4	55.4	54.5	53.5	52.6	51.6	50.7	49.8	48.9
62	57.3	56.3	55.4	54.4	53.5	52.5	51.6	50.7	49.7	48.8
63	57.3	56.3	55.3	54.4	53.4	52.5	51.6	50.6	49.7	48.7
64	57.2	56.3	55.3	54.4	53.4	52.5	51.5	50.6	49.6	48.7
65	57.2	56.3	55.3	54.3	53.4	52.4	51.5	50.5	49.6	48.7
66	57.2	56.2	55.3	54.3	53.4	52.4	51.5	50.5	49.6	48.6
67	57.2	56.2	55.3	54.3	53.3	52.4	51.4	50.5	49.5	48.6
68	57.2	56.2	55.2	54.3	53.3	52.4	51.4	50.4	49.5	48.6
69	57.1	56.2	55.2	54.3	53.3	52.3	51.4	50.4	49.5	48.5
70	57.1	56.2	55.2	54.2	53.3	52.3	51.4	50.4	49.4	48.5
71	57.1	56.2	55.2	54.2	53.3	52.3	51.3	50.4	49.4	48.5
72	57.1	56.1	55.2	54.2	53.2	52.3	51.3	50.4	49.4	48.4
73	57.1	56.1	55.2	54.2	53.2	52.3	51.3	50.3	49.4	48.4
74	57.1	56.1	55.2	54.2	53.2	52.3	51.3	50.3	49.4	48.4
75	57.1	56.1	55.1	54.2	53.2	52.2	51.3	50.3	49.3	48.4
76	57.1	56.1	55.1	54.2	53.2	52.2	51.3	50.3	49.3	48.4
77	57.1	56.1	55.1	54.2	53.2	52.2	51.3	50.3	49.3	48.4
78	57.1	56.1	55.1	54.1	53.2	52.2	51.2	50.3	49.3	48.4
79	57.1	56.1	55.1	54.1	53.2	52.2	51.2	50.3	49.3	48.4
80	57.1	56.1	55.1	54.1	53.2	52.2	51.2	50.3	49.3	48.3
81	57.0	56.1	55.1	54.1	53.2	52.2	51.2	50.3	49.3	48.3
82	57.0	56.1	55.1	54.1	53.2	52.2	51.2	50.3	49.3	48.3
83	57.0	56.1	55.1	54.1	53.2	52.2	51.2	50.3	49.3	48.3
84	57.0	56.1	55.1	54.1	53.2	52.2	51.2	50.3	49.3	48.3
85	57.0	56.1	55.1	54.1	53.2	52.2	51.2	50.2	49.3	48.3
86	57.0	56.1	55.1	54.1	53.1	52.2	51.2	50.2	49.3	48.3
87	57.0	56.1	55.1	54.1	53.1	52.2	51.2	50.2	49.3	48.3
88	57.0	56.1	55.1	54.1	53.1	52.2	51.2	50.2	49.3	48.3
89	57.0	56.1	55.1	54.1	53.1	52.2	51.2	50.2	49.3	48.3
90	57.0	56.1	55.1	54.1	53.1	52.2	51.2	50.2	49.3	48.3
91	57.0	56.1	55.1	54.1	53.1	52.2	51.2	50.2	49.3	48.3
92	57.0	56.1	55.1	54.1	53.1	52.2	51.2	50.2	49.3	48.3
93	57.0	56.1	55.1	54.1	53.1	52.2	51.2	50.2	49.3	48.3
94	57.0	56.0	55.1	54.1	53.1	52.2	51.2	50.2	49.3	48.3
95	57.0	56.0	55.1	54.1	53.1	52.2	51.2	50.2	49.3	48.3
96	57.0	56.0	55.1	54.1	53.1	52.2	51.2	50.2	49.3	48.3
97	57.0	56.0	55.1	54.1	53.1	52.2	51.2	50.2	49.3	48.3
98	57.0	56.0	55.1	54.1	53.1	52.2	51.2	50.2	49.3	48.3
99	57.0	56.0	55.1	54.1	53.1	52.2	51.2	50.2	49.3	48.3
100	57.0	56.0	55.1	54.1	53.1	52.2	51.2	50.2	49.3	48.3
101	57.0	56.0	55.1	54.1	53.1	52.2	51.2	50.2	49.3	48.3
102	57.0	56.0	55.1	54.1	53.1	52.2	51.2	50.2	49.3	48.3
103	57.0	56.0	55.1	54.1	53.1	52.2	51.2	50.2	49.3	48.3
104	57.0	56.0	55.1	54.1	53.1	52.2	51.2	50.2	49.3	48.3
105	57.0	56.0	55.1	54.1	53.1	52.2	51.2	50.2	49.3	48.3
106	57.0	56.0	55.1	54.1	53.1	52.2	51.2	50.2	49.3	48.3
107	57.0	56.0	55.1	54.1	53.1	52.2	51.2	50.2	49.3	48.3
108	57.0	56.0	55.1	54.1	53.1	52.2	51.2	50.2	49.3	48.3
109	57.0	56.0	55.1	54.1	53.1	52.2	51.2	50.2	49.3	48.3
110	57.0	56.0	55.1	54.1	53.1	52.2	51.2	50.2	49.3	48.3
111	57.0	56.0	55.1	54.1	53.1	52.2	51.2	50.2	49.3	48.3
112	57.0	56.0	55.1	54.1	53.1	52.2	51.2	50.2	49.3	48.3
113	57.0	56.0	55.1	54.1	53.1	52.2	51.2	50.2	49.3	48.3
114	57.0	56.0	55.1	54.1	53.1	52.2	51.2	50.2	49.3	48.3
115	57.0	56.0	55.1	54.1	53.1	52.2	51.2	50.2	49.3	48.3

TABLE VI.—ORDINARY JOINT LIFE AND LAST SURVIVOR ANNUITIES; TWO LIVES—EXPECTED RETURN MULTIPLES—Continued

Ages	35	36	37	38	39	40	41	42	43	44
35	54.0	53.5	53.0	52.6	52.2	51.8	51.4	51.1	50.8	50.5
36	53.5	53.0	52.5	52.0	51.6	51.2	50.8	50.4	50.1	49.8
37	53.0	52.5	52.0	51.5	51.0	50.6	50.2	49.8	49.5	49.1
38	52.6	52.0	51.5	51.0	50.5	50.0	49.6	49.2	48.8	48.5
39	52.2	51.6	51.0	50.5	50.0	49.5	49.1	48.6	48.2	47.8
40	51.8	51.2	50.6	50.0	49.5	49.0	48.5	48.1	47.6	47.2
41	51.4	50.8	50.2	49.6	49.1	48.5	48.0	47.5	47.1	46.7
42	51.1	50.4	49.8	49.2	48.6	48.1	47.5	47.0	46.6	46.1
43	50.8	50.1	49.5	48.8	48.2	47.6	47.1	46.6	46.0	45.6
44	50.5	49.8	49.1	48.5	47.8	47.2	46.7	46.1	45.6	45.1
45	50.2	49.5	48.8	48.1	47.5	46.9	46.3	45.7	45.1	44.6
46	50.0	49.2	48.5	47.8	47.2	46.5	45.9	45.3	44.7	44.1
47	49.7	49.0	48.3	47.5	46.8	46.2	45.5	44.9	44.3	43.7
48	49.5	48.8	48.0	47.3	46.6	45.9	45.2	44.5	43.9	43.3
49	49.3	48.5	47.8	47.0	46.3	45.6	44.9	44.2	43.6	42.9
50	49.2	48.4	47.6	46.8	46.0	45.3	44.6	43.9	43.2	42.6
51	49.0	48.2	47.4	46.6	45.8	45.1	44.3	43.6	42.9	42.2
52	48.8	48.0	47.2	46.4	45.6	44.8	44.1	43.3	42.6	41.9
53	48.7	47.9	47.0	46.2	45.4	44.6	43.9	43.1	42.4	41.7
54	48.6	47.7	46.9	46.0	45.2	44.4	43.6	42.9	42.1	41.4
55	48.5	47.6	46.7	45.9	45.1	44.2	43.4	42.7	41.9	41.2
56	48.3	47.5	46.6	45.8	44.9	44.1	43.3	42.5	41.7	40.9
57	48.3	47.4	46.5	45.6	44.8	43.9	43.1	42.3	41.5	40.7
58	48.2	47.3	46.4	45.5	44.7	43.8	43.0	42.1	41.3	40.5
59	48.1	47.2	46.3	45.4	44.5	43.7	42.8	42.0	41.2	40.4
60	48.0	47.1	46.2	45.3	44.4	43.6	42.7	41.9	41.0	40.2
61	47.9	47.0	46.1	45.2	44.3	43.5	42.6	41.7	40.9	40.0
62	47.9	47.0	46.0	45.1	44.2	43.4	42.5	41.6	40.8	39.9
63	47.8	46.9	46.0	45.1	44.2	43.3	42.4	41.5	40.6	39.8
64	47.8	46.8	45.9	45.0	44.1	43.2	42.3	41.4	40.5	39.7
65	47.7	46.8	45.9	44.9	44.0	43.1	42.2	41.3	40.4	39.6
66	47.7	46.7	45.8	44.9	44.0	43.1	42.2	41.3	40.4	39.5
67	47.6	46.7	45.8	44.8	43.9	43.0	42.1	41.2	40.3	39.4
68	47.6	46.7	45.7	44.8	43.9	42.9	42.0	41.1	40.2	39.3
69	47.6	46.6	45.7	44.8	43.8	42.9	42.0	41.1	40.2	39.3
70	47.5	46.6	45.7	44.7	43.8	42.9	41.9	41.0	40.1	39.2
71	47.5	46.6	45.6	44.7	43.8	42.8	41.9	41.0	40.1	39.1
72	47.5	46.6	45.6	44.7	43.7	42.8	41.9	40.9	40.0	39.1
73	47.5	46.5	45.6	44.6	43.7	42.8	41.8	40.9	40.0	39.0
74	47.5	46.5	45.6	44.6	43.7	42.7	41.8	40.9	39.9	39.0
75	47.4	46.5	45.5	44.6	43.6	42.7	41.8	40.8	39.9	39.0
76	47.4	46.5	45.5	44.6	43.6	42.7	41.7	40.8	39.9	38.9
77	47.4	46.5	45.5	44.6	43.6	42.7	41.7	40.8	39.8	38.9
78	47.4	46.4	45.5	44.5	43.6	42.6	41.7	40.7	39.8	38.9
79	47.4	46.4	45.5	44.5	43.6	42.6	41.7	40.7	39.8	38.9
80	47.4	46.4	45.5	44.5	43.6	42.6	41.7	40.7	39.8	38.8
81	47.4	46.4	45.4	44.5	43.5	42.6	41.6	40.7	39.8	38.8
82	47.4	46.4	45.4	44.5	43.5	42.6	41.6	40.7	39.7	38.8
83	47.4	46.4	45.4	44.5	43.5	42.6	41.6	40.7	39.7	38.8
84	47.4	46.4	45.4	44.5	43.5	42.6	41.6	40.7	39.7	38.8
85	47.4	46.4	45.4	44.5	43.5	42.6	41.6	40.7	39.7	38.8
86	47.3	46.4	45.4	44.5	43.5	42.5	41.6	40.6	39.7	38.8
87	47.3	46.4	45.4	44.5	43.5	42.5	41.6	40.6	39.7	38.7
88	47.3	46.4	45.4	44.5	43.5	42.5	41.6	40.6	39.7	38.7
89	47.3	46.4	45.4	44.4	43.5	42.5	41.6	40.6	39.7	38.7
90	47.3	46.4	45.4	44.4	43.5	42.5	41.6	40.6	39.7	38.7
91	47.3	46.4	45.4	44.4	43.5	42.5	41.6	40.6	39.7	38.7
92	47.3	46.4	45.4	44.4	43.5	42.5	41.6	40.6	39.7	38.7
93	47.3	46.4	45.4	44.4	43.5	42.5	41.6	40.6	39.7	38.7
94	47.3	46.4	45.4	44.4	43.5	42.5	41.6	40.6	39.7	38.7
95	47.3	46.4	45.4	44.4	43.5	42.5	41.6	40.6	39.7	38.7
96	47.3	46.4	45.4	44.4	43.5	42.5	41.6	40.6	39.7	38.7
97	47.3	46.4	45.4	44.4	43.5	42.5	41.6	40.6	39.6	38.7
98	47.3	46.4	45.4	44.4	43.5	42.5	41.6	40.6	39.6	38.7
99	47.3	46.4	45.4	44.4	43.5	42.5	41.5	40.6	39.6	38.7
100	47.3	46.4	45.4	44.4	43.5	42.5	41.5	40.6	39.6	38.7
101	47.3	46.4	45.4	44.4	43.5	42.5	41.5	40.6	39.6	38.7
102	47.3	46.4	45.4	44.4	43.5	42.5	41.5	40.6	39.6	38.7
103	47.3	46.4	45.4	44.4	43.5	42.5	41.5	40.6	39.6	38.7
104	47.3	46.4	45.4	44.4	43.5	42.5	41.5	40.6	39.6	38.7
105	47.3	46.4	45.4	44.4	43.5	42.5	41.5	40.6	39.6	38.7
106	47.3	46.4	45.4	44.4	43.5	42.5	41.5	40.6	39.6	38.7
107	47.3	46.4	45.4	44.4	43.5	42.5	41.5	40.6	39.6	38.7
108	47.3	46.4	45.4	44.4	43.5	42.5	41.5	40.6	39.6	38.7
109	47.3	46.4	45.4	44.4	43.5	42.5	41.5	40.6	39.6	38.7
110	47.3	46.4	45.4	44.4	43.5	42.5	41.5	40.6	39.6	38.7
111	47.3	46.4	45.4	44.4	43.5	42.5	41.5	40.6	39.6	38.7
112	47.3	46.4	45.4	44.4	43.5	42.5	41.5	40.6	39.6	38.7
113	47.3	46.4	45.4	44.4	43.5	42.5	41.5	40.6	39.6	38.7
114	47.3	46.4	45.4	44.4	43.5	42.5	41.5	40.6	39.6	38.7
115	47.3	46.4	45.4	44.4	43.5	42.5	41.5	40.6	39.6	38.7

TABLE VI.—ORDINARY JOINT LIFE AND LAST SURVIVOR ANNUITIES; TWO LIVES—EXPECTED RETURN MULTIPLES—Continued

Ages	45	46	47	48	49	50	51	52	53	54
45	44.1	43.6	43.2	42.7	42.3	42.0	41.6	41.3	41.0	40.7
46	43.6	43.1	42.6	42.2	41.8	41.4	41.0	40.6	40.3	40.0
47	43.2	42.6	42.1	41.7	41.2	40.8	40.4	40.0	39.7	39.3
48	42.7	42.2	41.7	41.2	40.7	40.2	39.8	39.4	39.0	38.7
49	42.3	41.8	41.2	40.7	40.2	39.7	39.3	38.8	38.4	38.1
50	42.0	41.4	40.8	40.2	39.7	39.2	38.7	38.3	37.9	37.5
51	41.6	41.0	40.4	39.8	39.3	38.7	38.2	37.8	37.3	36.9
52	41.3	40.6	40.0	39.4	38.8	38.3	37.8	37.3	36.8	36.4
53	41.0	40.3	39.7	39.0	38.4	37.9	37.3	36.8	36.3	35.8
54	40.7	40.0	39.3	38.7	38.1	37.5	36.9	36.4	35.8	35.3
55	40.4	39.7	39.0	38.4	37.7	37.1	36.5	35.9	35.4	34.9
56	40.2	39.5	38.7	38.1	37.4	36.8	36.1	35.6	35.0	34.4
57	40.0	39.2	38.5	37.8	37.1	36.4	35.8	35.2	34.6	34.0
58	39.7	39.0	38.2	37.5	36.8	36.1	35.5	34.8	34.2	33.6
59	39.6	38.8	38.0	37.3	36.6	35.9	35.2	34.5	33.9	33.3
60	39.4	38.6	37.8	37.1	36.3	35.6	34.9	34.2	33.6	32.9
61	39.2	38.4	37.6	36.9	36.1	35.4	34.6	33.9	33.3	32.6
62	39.1	38.3	37.5	36.7	35.9	35.1	34.4	33.7	33.0	32.3
63	38.9	38.1	37.3	36.5	35.7	34.9	34.2	33.5	32.7	32.0
64	38.8	38.0	37.2	36.3	35.5	34.8	34.0	33.2	32.5	31.8
65	38.7	37.9	37.0	36.2	35.4	34.6	33.8	33.0	32.3	31.6
66	38.6	37.8	36.9	36.1	35.2	34.4	33.6	32.9	32.1	31.4
67	38.5	37.7	36.8	36.0	35.1	34.3	33.5	32.7	31.9	31.2
68	38.4	37.6	36.7	35.8	35.0	34.2	33.4	32.5	31.8	31.0
69	38.4	37.5	36.6	35.7	34.9	34.1	33.2	32.4	31.6	30.8
70	38.3	37.4	36.5	35.7	34.8	34.0	33.1	32.3	31.5	30.7
71	38.2	37.3	36.5	35.6	34.7	33.9	33.0	32.2	31.4	30.5
72	38.2	37.3	36.4	35.5	34.6	33.8	32.9	32.1	31.2	30.4
73	38.1	37.2	36.3	35.4	34.6	33.7	32.8	32.0	31.1	30.3
74	38.1	37.2	36.3	35.4	34.5	33.6	32.8	31.9	31.1	30.2
75	38.1	37.1	36.2	35.3	34.5	33.6	32.7	31.8	31.0	30.1
76	38.0	37.1	36.2	35.3	34.4	33.5	32.6	31.8	30.9	30.1
77	38.0	37.1	36.2	35.3	34.4	33.5	32.6	31.7	30.8	30.0
78	38.0	37.0	36.1	35.2	34.3	33.4	32.5	31.7	30.8	29.9
79	37.9	37.0	36.1	35.2	34.3	33.4	32.5	31.6	30.7	29.9
80	37.9	37.0	36.1	35.2	34.2	33.4	32.5	31.6	30.7	29.8
81	37.9	37.0	36.0	35.1	34.2	33.3	32.4	31.5	30.7	29.8
82	37.9	36.9	36.0	35.1	34.2	33.3	32.4	31.5	30.6	29.7
83	37.9	36.9	36.0	35.1	34.2	33.3	32.4	31.5	30.6	29.7
84	37.8	36.9	36.9	35.0	34.2	33.2	32.3	31.4	30.6	29.7
85	37.8	36.9	36.0	35.1	34.1	33.2	32.3	31.4	30.5	29.6
86	38.8	36.9	36.0	35.0	34.1	33.2	32.3	31.4	30.5	29.6
87	37.8	36.9	35.9	35.0	34.1	33.2	32.3	31.4	30.5	29.6
88	37.8	36.9	35.9	35.0	34.1	33.2	32.3	31.4	30.5	29.6
89	37.8	36.9	35.9	35.0	34.1	33.2	32.3	31.4	30.5	29.6
90	37.8	36.9	35.9	35.0	34.1	33.2	32.3	31.3	30.5	29.6
91	37.8	36.8	35.9	35.0	34.1	33.2	32.2	31.3	30.4	29.5
92	37.8	36.8	35.9	35.0	34.1	33.2	32.2	31.3	30.4	29.5
93	37.8	36.8	35.9	35.0	34.1	33.1	32.2	31.3	30.4	29.5
94	37.8	36.8	35.9	35.0	34.1	33.1	32.2	31.3	30.4	29.5
95	37.8	36.8	35.9	35.0	34.0	33.1	32.2	31.3	30.4	29.5
96	37.8	36.8	35.9	35.0	34.0	33.1	32.2	31.3	30.4	29.5
97	37.8	36.8	35.9	35.0	34.0	33.1	32.2	31.3	30.4	29.5
98	37.8	36.8	35.9	35.0	34.0	33.1	32.2	31.3	30.4	29.5
99	37.8	36.8	35.9	35.0	34.0	33.1	32.2	31.3	30.4	29.5
101	37.8	36.8	35.9	35.0	34.0	33.1	32.2	31.3	30.4	29.5
102	37.8	36.8	35.9	35.0	34.0	33.1	32.2	31.3	30.4	29.5
103	37.7	36.8	35.9	34.9	34.0	33.1	32.2	31.3	30.4	29.5
104	37.7	36.8	35.9	34.9	34.0	33.1	32.2	31.3	30.4	29.5
105	37.7	36.8	35.9	34.9	34.0	33.1	32.2	31.3	30.4	29.5
106	37.7	36.8	35.9	34.9	34.0	33.1	32.2	31.3	30.4	29.5
107	37.7	36.8	35.9	34.9	34.0	33.1	32.2	31.3	30.4	29.5
108	37.7	36.8	35.9	34.9	34.0	33.1	32.2	31.3	30.4	29.5
109	37.7	36.8	35.9	34.9	34.0	33.1	32.2	31.3	30.4	29.5
110	37.7	36.8	35.9	34.9	34.0	33.1	32.2	31.3	30.4	29.5
111	37.7	36.8	35.9	34.9	34.0	33.1	32.2	31.3	30.4	29.5
112	37.7	36.8	35.9	34.9	34.0	33.1	32.2	31.3	30.4	29.5
113	37.7	36.8	35.9	34.9	34.0	33.1	32.2	31.3	30.4	29.5
114	37.7	36.8	35.9	34.9	34.0	33.1	32.2	31.3	30.4	29.5
115	37.7	36.8	35.9	34.9	34.0	33.1	32.2	31.3	30.4	29.5

TABLE VI.—ORDINARY JOINT LIFE AND LAST SURVIVOR ANNUITIES; TWO LIVES—EXPECTED RETURN MULTIPLES—Continued

Ages	55	56	57	58	59	60	61	62	63	64
55	34.4	33.9	33.5	33.1	32.7	32.3	32.0	31.7	31.4	31.1
56	33.9	33.4	33.0	32.5	32.1	31.7	31.4	31.0	30.7	30.4
57	33.5	33.0	32.5	32.0	31.6	31.2	30.8	30.4	30.1	29.8
58	33.1	32.5	32.0	31.5	31.1	30.6	30.2	29.9	29.5	29.2
59	32.7	32.1	31.6	31.1	30.6	30.1	29.7	29.3	28.9	28.6
60	32.3	31.7	31.2	30.6	30.1	29.7	29.2	28.8	28.4	28.0
61	32.0	31.4	30.8	30.2	29.7	29.2	28.7	28.3	27.8	27.4
62	31.7	31.0	30.4	29.9	29.3	28.8	28.3	27.6	27.3	26.9
63	31.4	30.7	30.1	29.5	28.9	28.4	27.6	27.3	26.9	26.4
64	31.1	30.4	29.8	29.2	28.6	28.0	27.4	26.9	26.4	25.9
65	30.9	30.2	29.5	28.9	28.2	27.6	27.1	26.5	26.0	25.5
66	30.6	29.9	29.2	28.6	27.9	27.3	26.7	26.1	25.6	25.1
67	30.4	29.7	29.0	28.3	27.6	27.0	26.4	25.8	25.2	24.7
68	30.2	29.5	28.8	28.1	27.4	26.7	26.1	25.5	24.9	24.3
69	30.1	29.3	28.6	27.8	27.1	26.5	25.8	25.2	24.6	24.0
70	29.9	29.1	28.4	27.6	26.9	26.2	25.6	24.9	24.3	23.7
71	29.7	29.0	28.2	27.5	26.7	26.0	25.3	24.7	24.0	23.4
72	29.6	28.8	28.1	27.3	26.5	25.8	25.1	24.4	23.8	23.1
73	29.5	28.7	27.9	27.1	26.4	25.6	24.9	24.2	23.5	22.9
74	29.4	28.6	27.8	27.0	26.2	25.5	24.7	24.0	23.3	22.7
75	29.3	28.5	27.7	26.9	26.1	25.3	24.6	23.8	23.1	22.4
76	29.2	28.4	27.6	26.8	26.0	25.2	24.4	23.7	23.0	22.3
77	29.1	28.3	27.5	26.7	25.9	25.1	24.3	23.6	22.8	22.1
78	29.1	28.2	27.4	26.6	25.8	25.0	24.2	23.4	22.7	21.9
79	29.0	28.2	27.3	26.5	25.7	24.9	24.1	23.3	22.6	21.8
80	29.0	28.1	27.3	26.4	25.6	24.8	24.0	23.2	22.4	21.7
81	28.9	28.1	27.2	26.4	25.5	24.7	23.9	23.1	22.3	21.6
82	28.9	28.0	27.2	26.3	25.5	24.6	23.8	23.0	22.3	21.5
83	28.8	28.0	27.1	26.3	25.4	24.6	23.8	23.0	22.2	21.4
84	28.8	27.9	27.1	26.2	25.4	24.5	23.7	22.9	22.1	21.3
85	28.8	27.9	27.0	26.2	25.3	24.5	23.7	22.8	22.0	21.3
86	28.7	27.9	27.0	26.1	25.3	24.5	23.6	22.8	22.0	21.2
87	28.7	27.8	27.0	26.1	25.3	24.4	23.6	22.8	21.9	21.1
88	28.7	27.8	27.0	26.1	25.2	24.4	23.5	22.7	21.9	21.1
89	28.7	27.8	26.9	26.1	25.2	24.4	23.5	22.7	21.9	21.1
90	28.7	27.8	26.9	26.1	25.2	24.3	23.5	22.7	21.8	21.0
91	28.7	27.8	26.9	26.0	25.2	24.3	23.5	22.6	21.8	21.0
92	28.6	27.8	26.9	26.0	25.2	24.3	23.5	22.6	21.8	21.0
93	28.6	27.8	26.9	26.0	25.1	24.3	23.4	22.6	21.8	20.9
94	28.6	27.7	26.9	26.0	25.1	24.3	23.4	22.6	21.7	20.9
95	28.6	27.7	26.9	26.0	25.1	24.3	23.4	22.6	21.7	20.9
96	28.6	27.7	26.9	26.0	25.1	24.2	23.4	22.6	21.7	20.9
97	28.6	27.7	26.8	26.0	25.1	24.2	23.4	22.5	21.7	20.9
98	28.6	27.7	26.8	26.0	25.1	24.2	23.4	22.5	21.7	20.9
99	28.6	27.7	26.8	26.0	25.1	24.2	23.4	22.5	21.7	20.9
100	28.6	27.7	26.8	26.0	25.1	24.2	23.4	22.5	21.7	20.8
101	28.6	27.7	26.8	25.9	25.1	24.2	23.4	22.5	21.7	20.8
102	28.6	27.7	26.8	25.9	25.1	24.2	23.3	22.5	21.7	20.8
103	28.6	27.7	26.8	25.9	25.1	24.2	23.3	22.5	21.7	20.8
104	28.6	27.7	26.8	25.9	25.1	24.2	23.3	22.5	21.6	20.8
105	28.6	27.7	26.8	25.9	25.1	24.2	23.3	22.5	21.6	20.8
106	28.6	27.7	26.8	25.9	25.1	24.2	23.3	22.5	21.6	20.8
107	28.6	27.7	26.8	25.9	25.1	24.2	23.3	22.5	21.6	20.8
108	28.6	27.7	26.8	25.9	25.1	24.2	23.3	22.5	21.6	20.8
109	28.6	27.7	26.8	25.9	25.1	24.2	23.3	22.5	21.6	20.8
110	28.6	27.7	26.8	25.9	25.1	24.2	23.3	22.5	21.6	20.8
111	28.6	27.7	26.8	25.9	25.0	24.2	23.3	22.5	21.6	20.8
112	28.6	27.7	26.8	25.9	25.0	24.2	23.3	22.5	21.6	20.8
113	28.6	27.7	26.8	25.9	25.0	24.2	23.3	22.5	21.6	20.8
114	28.6	27.7	26.8	25.9	25.0	24.2	23.3	22.5	21.6	20.8
115	28.6	27.7	26.8	25.9	25.0	24.2	23.3	22.5	21.6	20.8

Table VI.—Ordinary Joint Life and Last Survivor Annuities; Two Lives—Expected Return Multiples—Continued

Ages	65	66	67	68	69	70	71	72	73	74
65	25.0	24.6	24.2	23.8	23.4	23.1	22.8	22.5	22.2	22.0
66	24.6	24.1	23.7	23.3	22.9	22.5	22.2	21.9	21.6	21.4
67	24.2	23.7	23.2	22.8	22.4	22.0	21.7	21.3	21.0	20.8
68	23.8	23.3	22.8	22.3	21.9	21.5	21.2	20.8	20.5	20.2
69	23.4	22.9	22.4	21.9	21.5	21.1	20.7	20.3	20.0	19.6
70	23.1	22.5	22.0	21.5	21.1	20.6	20.2	19.8	19.4	19.1
71	22.8	22.2	21.7	21.2	20.7	20.2	19.8	19.4	19.0	18.6
72	22.5	21.9	21.3	20.8	20.3	19.8	19.4	18.9	18.5	18.2
73	22.2	21.6	21.0	20.5	20.0	19.4	19.0	18.5	18.1	17.7
74	22.0	21.4	20.8	20.2	19.6	19.1	18.6	18.2	17.7	17.3
75	21.8	21.1	20.5	19.9	19.3	18.8	18.3	17.8	17.3	16.9
76	21.6	20.9	20.3	19.7	19.1	18.5	18.0	17.5	17.0	16.5
77	21.4	20.7	20.1	19.4	18.8	18.3	17.7	17.2	16.7	16.2
78	21.2	20.5	19.9	19.2	18.6	18.0	17.5	16.9	16.4	15.9
79	21.1	20.4	19.7	19.0	18.4	17.8	17.2	16.7	16.1	15.6
80	21.0	20.2	19.5	18.9	18.2	17.6	17.0	16.4	15.9	15.4
81	20.8	20.1	19.4	18.7	18.1	17.4	16.8	16.2	15.7	15.1
82	20.7	20.0	19.3	18.6	17.9	17.3	16.6	16.0	15.5	14.9
83	20.6	19.9	19.2	18.5	17.8	17.1	16.5	15.9	15.3	14.7
84	20.5	19.8	19.1	18.4	17.7	17.0	16.3	15.7	15.1	14.5
85	20.5	19.7	19.0	18.3	17.6	16.9	16.2	15.6	15.0	14.4
86	20.4	19.6	18.9	18.2	17.5	16.8	16.1	15.5	14.8	14.2
87	20.4	19.6	18.8	18.1	17.4	16.7	16.0	15.4	14.7	14.1
88	20.3	19.5	18.8	18.0	17.3	16.6	15.9	15.3	14.6	14.0
89	20.3	19.5	18.7	18.0	17.2	16.5	15.8	15.2	14.5	13.9
90	20.2	19.4	18.7	17.9	17.2	16.5	15.8	15.1	14.5	13.8
91	20.2	19.4	18.6	17.9	17.1	16.4	15.7	15.0	14.4	13.7
92	20.2	19.4	18.6	17.8	17.1	16.4	15.7	15.0	14.3	13.7
93	20.1	19.3	18.6	17.8	17.1	16.3	15.6	14.9	14.3	13.6
94	20.1	19.3	18.5	17.8	17.0	16.3	15.6	14.9	14.2	13.6
95	20.1	19.3	18.5	17.8	17.0	16.3	15.6	14.9	14.2	13.5
96	20.1	19.3	18.5	17.7	17.0	16.2	15.5	14.8	14.2	13.5
97	20.1	19.3	18.5	17.7	17.0	16.2	15.5	14.8	14.1	13.5
98	20.1	19.3	18.5	17.7	16.9	16.2	15.5	14.8	14.1	13.4
99	20.0	19.2	18.5	17.7	16.9	16.2	15.5	14.7	14.1	13.4
100	20.0	19.2	18.4	17.7	16.9	16.2	15.4	14.7	14.0	13.4
101	20.0	19.2	18.4	17.7	16.9	16.1	15.4	14.7	14.0	13.3
102	20.0	19.2	18.4	17.6	16.9	16.1	15.4	14.7	14.0	13.3
103	20.0	19.2	18.4	17.6	16.9	16.1	15.4	14.7	14.0	13.3
104	20.0	19.2	18.4	17.6	16.8	16.1	15.4	14.6	13.9	13.3
105	20.0	19.2	18.4	17.6	16.8	16.1	15.3	14.6	13.9	13.3
106	20.0	19.2	18.4	17.6	16.8	16.1	15.3	14.6	13.9	13.2
107	20.0	19.2	18.4	17.6	16.8	16.1	15.3	14.6	13.9	13.2
108	20.0	19.2	18.4	17.6	16.8	16.1	15.3	14.6	13.9	13.2
109	20.0	19.2	18.4	17.6	16.8	16.1	15.3	14.6	13.9	13.2
110	20.0	19.2	18.4	17.6	16.8	16.0	15.3	14.6	13.9	13.2
111	20.0	19.2	18.4	17.6	16.8	16.0	15.3	14.6	13.9	13.2
112	20.0	19.2	18.4	17.6	16.8	16.0	15.3	14.6	13.9	13.2
113	20.0	19.2	18.4	17.6	16.8	16.0	15.3	14.6	13.9	13.2
114	20.0	19.2	18.4	17.6	16.8	16.0	15.3	14.6	13.9	13.2
115	20.0	19.2	18.4	17.6	16.8	16.0	15.3	14.6	13.9	13.2

TABLE VI.—ORDINARY JOINT LIFE AND LAST SURVIVOR ANNUITIES; TWO LIVES—EXPECTED RETURN MULTIPLES—Continued

Ages	75	76	77	78	79	80	81	82	83	84
75	16.5	16.1	15.8	15.4	15.1	14.9	14.6	14.4	14.2	14.0
76	16.1	15.7	15.4	15.0	14.7	14.4	14.1	13.9	13.7	13.5
77	15.8	15.4	15.0	14.6	14.3	14.0	13.7	13.4	13.2	13.0
78	15.4	15.0	14.6	14.2	13.9	13.5	13.2	13.0	12.7	12.5
79	15.1	14.7	14.3	13.9	13.5	13.2	12.8	12.5	12.3	12.0
80	14.9	14.4	14.0	13.5	13.2	12.8	12.5	12.2	11.9	11.6
81	14.6	14.1	13.7	13.2	12.8	12.5	12.1	11.8	11.5	11.2
82	14.4	13.9	13.4	13.0	12.5	12.2	11.8	11.5	11.1	10.9
83	14.2	13.7	13.2	12.7	12.3	11.9	11.5	11.1	10.8	10.5
84	14.0	13.5	13.0	12.5	12.0	11.6	11.2	10.9	10.5	10.2
85	13.8	13.3	12.8	12.3	11.8	11.4	11.0	10.6	10.2	9.9
86	13.7	13.1	12.6	12.1	11.6	11.2	10.8	10.4	10.0	9.7
87	13.5	13.0	12.4	11.9	11.4	11.0	10.6	10.1	9.8	9.4
88	13.4	12.8	12.3	11.8	11.3	10.8	10.4	10.0	9.6	9.2
89	13.3	12.7	12.2	11.6	11.1	10.7	10.2	9.8	9.4	9.0
90	13.2	12.6	12.1	11.5	11.0	10.5	10.1	9.6	9.2	8.8
91	13.1	12.5	12.0	11.4	10.9	10.4	9.9	9.5	9.1	8.7
92	13.1	12.5	11.9	11.3	10.8	10.3	9.8	9.4	8.9	8.5
93	13.0	12.4	11.8	11.3	10.7	10.2	9.7	9.3	8.8	8.4
94	12.9	12.3	11.7	11.2	10.6	10.1	9.6	9.2	8.7	8.3
95	12.9	12.3	11.7	11.1	10.6	10.1	9.6	9.1	8.6	8.2
96	12.9	12.2	11.6	11.1	10.5	10.0	9.5	9.0	8.5	8.1
97	12.8	12.2	11.6	11.0	10.5	9.9	9.4	8.9	8.5	8.0
98	12.8	12.2	11.5	11.0	10.4	9.9	9.4	8.9	8.4	8.0
99	12.7	12.1	11.5	10.9	10.4	9.8	9.3	8.8	8.3	7.9
100	12.7	12.1	11.5	10.9	10.3	9.8	9.2	8.7	8.3	7.8
101	12.7	12.1	11.4	10.8	10.3	9.7	9.2	8.7	8.2	7.8
102	12.7	12.0	11.4	10.8	10.2	9.7	9.2	8.7	8.2	7.7
103	12.6	12.0	11.4	10.8	10.2	9.7	9.1	8.6	8.1	7.7
104	12.6	12.0	11.4	10.8	10.2	9.6	9.1	8.6	8.1	7.6
105	12.6	12.0	11.3	10.7	10.2	9.6	9.1	8.5	8.0	7.6
106	12.6	11.9	11.3	10.7	10.1	9.6	9.0	8.5	8.0	7.5
107	12.6	11.9	11.3	10.7	10.1	9.6	9.0	8.5	8.0	7.5
108	12.6	11.9	11.3	10.7	10.1	9.5	9.0	8.5	8.0	7.5
109	12.6	11.9	11.3	10.7	10.1	9.5	9.0	8.4	7.9	7.5
110	12.6	11.9	11.3	10.7	10.1	9.5	9.0	8.4	7.9	7.4
111	12.5	11.9	11.3	10.7	10.1	9.5	8.9	8.4	7.9	7.4
112	12.5	11.9	11.3	10.6	10.1	9.5	8.9	8.4	7.9	7.4
113	12.5	11.9	11.2	10.6	10.0	9.5	8.9	8.4	7.9	7.4
114	12.5	11.9	11.2	10.6	10.0	9.5	8.9	8.4	7.9	7.4
115	12.5	11.9	11.2	10.6	10.0	9.5	8.9	8.4	7.9	7.4

Ages	85	86	87	88	89	90	91	92	93	94
85	9.6	9.3	9.1	8.9	8.7	8.5	8.3	8.2	8.0	7.9
86	9.3	9.1	8.8	8.6	8.3	8.2	8.0	7.8	7.7	7.6
87	9.1	8.8	8.5	8.3	8.1	7.9	7.7	7.5	7.4	7.2
88	8.9	8.6	8.3	8.0	7.8	7.6	7.4	7.2	7.1	6.9
89	8.7	8.3	8.1	7.8	7.5	7.3	7.1	6.9	6.8	6.6
90	8.5	8.2	7.9	7.6	7.3	7.1	6.9	6.7	6.5	6.4
91	8.3	8.0	7.7	7.4	7.1	6.9	6.7	6.5	6.3	6.2
92	8.2	7.8	7.5	7.2	6.9	6.7	6.5	6.3	6.1	5.9
93	8.0	7.7	7.4	7.1	6.8	6.5	6.3	6.1	5.9	5.8
94	7.9	7.6	7.2	6.9	6.6	6.4	6.2	5.9	5.8	5.6
95	7.8	7.5	7.1	6.8	6.5	6.3	6.0	5.8	5.6	5.4
96	7.7	7.3	7.0	6.7	6.4	6.1	5.9	5.7	5.5	5.3
97	7.6	7.3	6.9	6.6	6.3	6.0	5.8	5.5	5.3	5.1
98	7.6	7.2	6.8	6.5	6.2	5.9	5.6	5.4	5.2	5.0
99	7.5	7.1	6.7	6.4	6.1	5.8	5.5	5.3	5.1	4.9
100	7.4	7.0	6.6	6.3	6.0	5.7	5.4	5.2	5.0	4.8
101	7.3	6.9	6.6	6.2	5.9	5.6	5.3	5.1	4.9	4.7
102	7.3	6.9	6.5	6.2	5.8	5.5	5.3	5.0	4.8	4.6
103	7.2	6.8	6.4	6.1	5.8	5.5	5.2	4.9	4.7	4.5
104	7.2	6.8	6.4	6.0	5.7	5.4	5.1	4.8	4.6	4.4
105	7.1	6.7	6.3	6.0	5.6	5.3	5.0	4.8	4.5	4.3
106	7.1	6.7	6.3	5.9	5.6	5.3	5.0	4.7	4.5	4.2
107	7.1	6.6	6.2	5.9	5.5	5.2	4.9	4.6	4.4	4.2
108	7.0	6.6	6.2	5.8	5.5	5.2	4.9	4.6	4.3	4.1
109	7.0	6.6	6.2	5.8	5.5	5.1	4.8	4.5	4.3	4.1
110	7.0	6.6	6.2	5.8	5.4	5.1	4.8	4.5	4.3	4.0
111	7.0	6.5	6.1	5.7	5.4	5.1	4.8	4.5	4.2	4.0
112	7.0	6.5	6.1	5.7	5.4	5.0	4.7	4.4	4.2	3.9
113	6.9	6.5	6.1	5.7	5.4	5.0	4.7	4.4	4.2	3.9
114	6.9	6.5	6.1	5.7	5.3	5.0	4.7	4.4	4.1	3.9
115	6.9	6.5	6.1	5.7	5.3	5.0	4.7	4.4	4.1	3.9

TABLE VI.—ORDINARY JOINT LIFE AND LAST SURVIVOR ANNUITIES; TWO LIVES—EXPECTED RETURN MULTIPLES—Continued

Ages	95	96	97	98	99	100	101	102	103	104
95	5.3	5.1	5.0	4.8	4.7	4.6	4.5	4.4	4.3	4.2
96	5.1	5.0	4.8	4.7	4.5	4.4	4.3	4.2	4.1	4.0
97	5.0	4.8	4.7	4.5	4.4	4.3	4.1	4.0	3.9	3.8
98	4.8	4.7	4.5	4.4	4.2	4.1	4.0	3.9	3.8	3.7
99	4.7	4.5	4.4	4.2	4.1	4.0	3.8	3.7	3.6	3.5
100	4.6	4.4	4.3	4.1	4.0	3.8	3.7	3.6	3.5	3.3
101	4.5	4.3	4.1	4.0	3.8	3.7	3.6	3.4	3.3	3.2
102	4.4	4.2	4.0	3.9	3.7	3.6	3.4	3.3	3.2	3.1
103	4.3	4.1	3.9	3.8	3.6	3.5	3.3	3.2	3.0	2.9
104	4.2	4.0	3.8	3.7	3.5	3.3	3.2	3.1	2.9	2.8
105	4.1	3.9	3.7	3.6	3.4	3.2	3.1	2.9	2.8	2.7
106	4.0	3.8	3.6	3.5	3.3	3.1	3.0	2.8	2.7	2.5
107	4.0	3.8	3.6	3.4	3.2	3.1	2.9	2.7	2.6	2.4
108	3.9	3.7	3.5	3.3	3.1	3.0	2.8	2.7	2.5	2.3
109	3.8	3.6	3.4	3.3	3.1	2.9	2.7	2.6	2.4	2.3
110	3.8	3.6	3.4	3.2	3.0	2.8	2.7	2.5	2.3	2.2
111	3.8	3.5	3.3	3.2	3.0	2.8	2.6	2.4	2.3	2.1
112	3.7	3.5	3.3	3.1	2.9	2.8	2.6	2.4	2.2	2.1
113	3.7	3.5	3.3	3.1	2.9	2.7	2.5	2.4	2.2	2.0
114	3.7	3.5	3.3	3.1	2.9	2.7	2.5	2.3	2.1	2.0
115	3.7	3.4	3.2	3.0	2.8	2.7	2.5	2.3	2.1	1.9

Ages	105	106	107	108	109	110	111	112	113	114	115
105	2.5	2.4	2.3	2.2	2.1	2.0	2.0	1.9	1.8	1.8	1.8
106	2.4	2.3	2.2	2.1	2.0	1.9	1.8	1.7	1.7	1.6	1.6
107	2.3	2.2	2.1	1.9	1.8	1.7	1.7	1.6	1.5	1.5	1.4
108	2.2	2.1	1.9	1.8	1.7	1.6	1.5	1.5	1.4	1.3	1.3
109	2.1	2.0	1.8	1.7	1.6	1.5	1.4	1.3	1.3	1.2	1.1
110	2.0	1.9	1.7	1.6	1.5	1.4	1.3	1.2	1.1	1.1	1.0
111	2.0	1.8	1.7	1.5	1.4	1.3	1.2	1.1	1.0	.9	.9
112	1.9	1.7	1.6	1.5	1.3	1.2	1.1	1.0	.9	.8	.8
113	1.8	1.7	1.5	1.4	1.3	1.1	1.0	.9	.8	.7	.7
114	1.8	1.6	1.5	1.3	1.2	1.1	.9	.8	.7	.6	.6
115	1.8	1.6	1.4	1.3	1.1	1.0	.9	.8	.7	.6	.5

TABLE VIA.—ANNUITIES FOR JOINT LIFE ONLY; TWO LIVES—EXPECTED RETURN MULTIPLES

Ages	5	6	7	8	9	10	11	12	13	14
5	69.5	69.0	68.4	67.9	67.3	66.7	66.1	65.5	64.8	64.1
6	69.0	68.5	68.0	67.5	66.9	66.4	65.8	65.1	64.5	63.8
7	68.4	68.0	67.5	67.0	66.5	66.0	65.4	64.8	64.2	63.5
8	67.9	67.5	67.0	66.6	66.1	65.5	65.0	64.4	63.8	63.2
9	67.3	66.9	66.5	66.1	65.6	65.1	64.6	64.0	63.4	62.8
10	66.7	66.4	66.0	65.5	65.1	64.6	64.1	63.6	63.0	62.5
11	66.1	65.8	65.4	65.0	64.6	64.1	63.6	63.1	62.6	62.1
12	65.5	65.1	64.8	64.4	64.0	63.6	63.1	62.7	62.2	61.7
13	64.8	64.5	64.2	63.8	63.4	63.0	62.6	62.2	61.7	61.2
14	64.1	63.8	63.5	63.2	62.8	62.5	62.1	61.7	61.2	60.7
15	63.4	63.1	62.9	62.6	62.2	61.9	61.5	61.1	60.7	60.2
16	62.7	62.4	62.2	61.9	61.6	61.3	60.9	60.5	60.1	59.7
17	61.9	61.7	61.5	61.2	60.9	60.6	60.3	59.9	59.6	59.2
18	61.2	61.0	60.7	60.5	60.2	60.0	59.7	59.3	59.0	58.6
19	60.4	60.2	60.0	59.8	59.5	59.3	59.0	58.7	58.4	58.0
20	59.6	59.4	59.2	59.0	58.8	58.6	58.3	58.0	57.7	57.4
21	58.8	58.7	58.5	58.3	58.1	57.8	57.6	57.3	57.1	56.8
22	58.0	57.8	57.7	57.5	57.3	57.1	56.9	56.6	56.4	56.1
23	57.2	57.0	56.9	56.7	56.5	56.4	56.1	55.9	55.7	55.4
24	56.3	56.2	56.1	55.9	55.8	55.6	55.4	55.2	55.0	54.7
25	55.5	55.4	55.2	55.1	55.0	54.8	54.6	54.4	54.2	54.0
26	54.6	54.5	54.4	54.3	54.1	54.0	53.8	53.7	53.5	53.3
27	53.8	53.7	53.6	53.4	53.3	53.2	53.0	52.9	52.7	52.5
28	52.9	52.8	52.7	52.6	52.5	52.4	52.2	52.1	51.9	51.7
29	52.0	51.9	51.8	51.7	51.6	51.5	51.4	51.3	51.1	51.0
30	51.1	51.0	51.0	50.9	50.8	50.7	50.6	50.4	50.3	50.2
31	50.2	50.2	50.1	50.0	49.9	49.8	49.7	49.6	49.5	49.3
32	49.3	49.3	49.2	49.1	49.0	49.0	48.9	48.8	48.6	48.5
33	48.4	48.4	48.3	48.2	48.2	48.1	48.0	47.9	47.8	47.7
34	47.5	47.5	47.4	47.4	47.3	47.2	47.1	47.0	47.0	46.8
35	46.6	46.6	46.5	46.5	46.4	46.3	46.3	46.2	46.1	46.0
36	45.7	45.7	45.6	45.6	45.5	45.4	45.4	45.3	45.2	45.1
37	44.8	44.7	44.7	44.6	44.6	44.5	44.5	44.4	44.3	44.3
38	43.9	43.8	43.8	43.7	43.7	43.6	43.6	43.5	43.5	43.4
39	42.9	42.9	42.9	42.8	42.8	42.7	42.7	42.6	42.6	42.5
40	42.0	42.0	42.0	41.9	41.9	41.8	41.8	41.7	41.7	41.6
41	41.1	41.1	41.0	41.0	41.0	40.9	40.9	40.8	40.8	40.7
42	40.2	40.1	40.1	40.1	40.1	40.0	40.0	39.9	39.9	39.8
43	39.2	39.2	39.2	39.2	39.1	39.1	39.1	39.0	39.0	39.0
44	38.3	38.3	38.3	38.3	38.2	38.2	38.2	38.1	38.1	38.1
45	37.4	37.4	37.4	37.3	37.3	37.3	37.3	37.2	37.2	37.2
46	36.5	36.5	36.5	36.4	36.4	36.4	36.4	36.3	36.3	36.3
47	35.6	35.6	35.5	35.5	35.5	35.5	35.5	35.4	35.4	35.4
48	34.7	34.7	34.6	34.6	34.6	34.6	34.6	34.5	34.5	34.5
49	33.8	33.8	33.7	33.7	33.7	33.7	33.7	33.7	33.6	33.6
50	32.9	32.9	32.8	32.8	32.8	32.8	32.8	32.8	32.7	32.7
51	32.0	32.0	31.9	31.9	31.9	31.9	31.9	31.9	31.9	31.8
52	31.1	31.1	31.1	31.0	31.0	31.0	31.0	31.0	31.0	30.9
53	30.2	30.2	30.2	30.2	30.1	30.1	30.1	30.1	30.1	30.1
54	29.3	29.3	29.3	29.3	29.3	29.2	29.2	29.2	29.2	29.2
55	28.4	28.4	28.4	28.4	28.4	28.4	28.4	28.3	28.3	28.3
56	27.5	27.5	27.5	27.5	27.5	27.5	27.5	27.5	27.5	27.5
57	26.7	26.7	26.7	26.6	26.6	26.6	26.6	26.6	26.6	26.6
58	25.8	25.8	25.8	25.8	25.8	25.8	25.8	25.7	25.7	25.7
59	24.9	24.9	24.9	24.9	24.9	24.9	24.9	24.9	24.9	24.9
60	24.1	24.1	24.1	24.1	24.1	24.0	24.0	24.0	24.0	24.0
61	23.2	23.2	23.2	23.2	23.2	23.2	23.2	23.2	23.2	23.2
62	22.4	22.4	22.4	22.4	22.4	22.4	22.3	22.3	22.3	22.3
63	21.5	21.5	21.5	21.5	21.5	21.5	21.5	21.5	21.5	21.5
64	20.7	20.7	20.7	20.7	20.7	20.7	20.7	20.7	20.7	20.7
65	19.9	19.9	19.9	19.9	19.9	19.9	19.9	19.9	19.9	19.9
66	19.1	19.1	19.1	19.1	19.1	19.1	19.1	19.1	19.1	19.1
67	18.3	18.3	18.3	18.3	18.3	18.3	18.3	18.3	18.3	18.3
68	17.5	17.5	17.5	17.5	17.5	17.5	17.5	17.5	17.5	17.5
69	16.8	16.8	16.8	16.7	16.7	16.7	16.7	16.7	16.7	16.7
70	16.0	16.0	16.0	16.0	16.0	16.0	16.0	16.0	16.0	16.0
71	15.3	15.3	15.3	15.3	15.3	15.3	15.3	15.3	15.3	15.2
72	14.6	14.6	14.5	14.5	14.5	14.5	14.5	14.5	14.5	14.5
73	13.9	13.9	13.8	13.8	13.8	13.8	13.8	13.8	13.8	13.8
74	13.2	13.2	13.2	13.2	13.2	13.2	13.2	13.2	13.2	13.2
75	12.5	12.5	12.5	12.5	12.5	12.5	12.5	12.5	12.5	12.5
76	11.9	11.9	11.8	11.8	11.8	11.8	11.8	11.8	11.8	11.8
77	11.2	11.2	11.2	11.2	11.2	11.2	11.2	11.2	11.2	11.2
78	10.6	10.6	10.6	10.6	10.6	10.6	10.6	10.6	10.6	10.6
79	10.0	10.0	10.0	10.0	10.0	10.0	10.0	10.0	10.0	10.0
80	9.5	9.5	9.5	9.5	9.5	9.5	9.5	9.5	9.4	9.4
81	8.9	8.9	8.9	8.9	8.9	8.9	8.9	8.9	8.9	8.9
82	8.4	8.4	8.4	8.4	8.4	8.4	8.4	8.4	8.4	8.4
83	7.9	7.9	7.9	7.9	7.9	7.9	7.9	7.9	7.9	7.9
84	7.4	7.4	7.4	7.4	7.4	7.4	7.4	7.4	7.4	7.4
85	6.9	6.9	6.9	6.9	6.9	6.9	6.9	6.9	6.9	6.9
86	6.5	6.5	6.5	6.5	6.5	6.5	6.5	6.5	6.5	6.5
87	6.1	6.1	6.1	6.1	6.1	6.1	6.1	6.1	6.1	6.1
88	5.7	5.7	5.7	5.7	5.7	5.7	5.7	5.7	5.7	5.7
89	5.3	5.3	5.3	5.3	5.3	5.3	5.3	5.3	5.3	5.3
90	5.0	5.0	5.0	5.0	5.0	5.0	5.0	5.0	5.0	5.0
91	4.7	4.7	4.7	4.7	4.7	4.7	4.7	4.7	4.7	4.7
92	4.4	4.4	4.4	4.4	4.4	4.4	4.4	4.4	4.4	4.4
93	4.1	4.1	4.1	4.1	4.1	4.1	4.1	4.1	4.1	4.1
94	3.9	3.9	3.9	3.9	3.9	3.9	3.9	3.9	3.9	3.9
95	3.7	3.7	3.7	3.7	3.7	3.7	3.6	3.6	3.6	3.6
96	3.4	3.4	3.4	3.4	3.4	3.4	3.4	3.4	3.4	3.4
97	3.2	3.2	3.2	3.2	3.2	3.2	3.2	3.2	3.2	3.2
98	3.0	3.0	3.0	3.0	3.0	3.0	3.0	3.0	3.0	3.0
99	2.8	2.8	2.8	2.8	2.8	2.8	2.8	2.8	2.8	2.8
100	2.7	2.7	2.7	2.7	2.7	2.7	2.7	2.7	2.7	2.7

Ages	5	6	7	8	9	10	11	12	13	14
101	2.5	2.5	2.5	2.5	2.5	2.5	2.5	2.5	2.5	2.5
102	2.3	2.3	2.3	2.3	2.3	2.3	2.3	2.3	2.3	2.3
103	2.1	2.1	2.1	2.1	2.1	2.1	2.1	2.1	2.1	2.1
104	1.9	1.9	1.9	1.9	1.9	1.9	1.9	1.9	1.9	1.9
105	1.8	1.8	1.8	1.8	1.8	1.8	1.8	1.8	1.8	1.8
106	1.6	1.6	1.6	1.6	1.6	1.6	1.6	1.6	1.6	1.6
107	1.4	1.4	1.4	1.4	1.4	1.4	1.4	1.4	1.4	1.4
108	1.3	1.3	1.3	1.3	1.3	1.3	1.3	1.3	1.3	1.3
109	1.1	1.1	1.1	1.1	1.1	1.1	1.1	1.1	1.1	1.1
110	1.0	1.0	1.0	1.0	1.0	1.0	1.0	1.0	1.0	1.0
111	.9	.9	.9	.9	.9	.9	.9	.9	.9	.9
112	.8	.8	.8	.8	.8	.8	.8	.8	.8	.8
113	.7	.7	.7	.7	.7	.7	.7	.7	.7	.7
114	.6	.6	.6	.6	.6	.6	.6	.6	.6	.6
115	.5	.5	.5	.5	.5	.5	.5	.5	.5	.5

TABLE VIA.—ANNUITIES FOR JOINT LIFE ONLY; TWO LIVES—EXPECTED RETURN MULTIPLES—Continued

Ages	15	16	17	18	19	20	21	22	23	24
15	59.8	59.3	58.8	58.2	57.6	57.0	56.4	55.8	55.1	54.5
16	59.3	58.8	58.3	57.8	57.2	56.7	56.1	55.5	54.8	54.2
17	58.8	58.3	57.8	57.3	56.8	56.3	55.7	55.1	54.5	53.9
18	58.2	57.8	57.3	56.9	56.4	55.9	55.3	54.7	54.2	53.5
19	57.6	57.2	56.8	56.4	55.9	55.4	54.9	54.4	53.8	53.2
20	57.0	56.7	56.3	55.9	55.4	54.9	54.5	53.9	53.4	52.8
21	56.4	56.1	55.7	55.3	54.9	54.5	54.0	53.5	53.0	52.4
22	55.8	55.5	55.1	54.7	54.4	53.9	53.5	53.0	52.5	52.0
23	55.1	54.8	54.5	54.2	53.8	53.4	53.0	52.6	52.1	51.6
24	54.5	54.2	53.9	53.5	53.2	52.8	52.4	52.0	51.6	51.1
25	53.8	53.5	53.2	52.9	52.6	52.2	51.9	51.5	51.1	50.6
26	53.0	52.8	52.5	52.3	52.0	51.6	51.3	50.9	50.5	50.1
27	52.3	52.1	51.8	51.6	51.3	51.0	50.7	50.3	50.0	49.6
28	51.5	51.3	51.1	50.9	50.6	50.3	50.0	49.7	49.4	49.0
29	50.8	50.6	50.4	50.2	49.9	49.7	49.4	49.1	48.8	48.4
30	50.0	49.8	49.6	49.4	49.2	49.0	48.7	48.4	48.1	47.8
31	49.2	49.0	48.9	48.7	48.5	48.3	48.0	47.8	47.5	47.2
32	48.4	48.2	48.1	47.9	47.7	47.5	47.3	47.1	46.8	46.5
33	47.6	47.4	47.3	47.1	47.0	46.8	46.6	46.3	46.1	45.9
34	46.7	46.6	46.5	46.3	46.2	46.0	45.8	45.6	45.4	45.2
35	45.9	45.8	45.7	45.5	45.4	45.2	45.1	44.9	44.7	44.4
36	45.0	44.9	44.8	44.7	44.6	44.4	44.3	44.1	43.9	43.7
37	44.2	44.1	44.0	43.9	43.8	43.6	43.5	43.3	43.2	43.0
38	43.3	43.2	43.1	43.0	42.9	42.8	42.7	42.5	42.4	42.2
39	42.4	42.4	42.3	42.2	42.1	42.0	41.9	41.7	41.6	41.4
40	41.6	41.5	41.4	41.3	41.2	41.1	41.0	40.9	40.8	40.6
41	40.7	40.6	40.5	40.5	40.4	40.3	40.2	40.1	40.0	39.8
42	39.8	39.7	39.7	39.6	39.5	39.4	39.4	39.3	39.1	39.0
43	38.9	38.9	38.8	38.7	38.7	38.6	38.5	38.4	38.3	38.2
44	38.0	38.0	37.9	37.9	37.8	37.7	37.7	37.6	37.5	37.4
45	37.1	37.1	37.0	37.0	36.9	36.9	36.8	36.7	36.6	36.5
46	36.2	36.2	36.2	36.1	36.1	36.0	35.9	35.9	35.8	35.7
47	35.3	35.3	35.3	35.2	35.2	35.1	35.1	35.0	34.9	34.9
48	34.5	34.4	34.4	34.4	34.3	34.3	34.2	34.2	34.1	34.0
49	33.6	33.5	33.5	33.5	33.4	33.4	33.4	33.3	33.2	33.2
50	32.7	32.7	32.6	32.6	32.6	32.5	32.5	32.4	32.4	32.3
51	31.8	31.8	31.8	31.7	31.7	31.7	31.6	31.6	31.5	31.5
52	30.9	30.9	30.9	30.9	30.8	30.8	30.8	30.7	30.7	30.6
53	30.0	30.0	30.0	30.0	30.0	29.9	29.9	29.9	29.8	29.8
54	29.2	29.2	29.1	29.1	29.1	29.1	29.0	29.0	29.0	28.9
55	28.3	28.3	28.3	28.3	28.2	28.2	28.2	28.2	28.1	28.1
56	27.4	27.4	27.4	27.4	27.4	27.3	27.3	27.3	27.3	27.2
57	26.6	26.6	26.5	26.5	26.5	26.5	26.5	26.5	26.4	26.4
58	25.7	25.7	25.7	25.7	25.7	25.6	25.6	25.6	25.6	25.6
59	24.9	24.8	24.8	24.8	24.8	24.8	24.8	24.8	24.7	24.7
60	24.0	24.0	24.0	24.0	24.0	23.9	23.9	23.9	23.9	23.9
61	23.2	23.2	23.1	23.1	23.1	23.1	23.1	23.1	23.1	23.0
62	22.3	22.3	22.3	22.3	22.3	22.3	22.3	22.2	22.2	22.2
63	21.5	21.5	21.5	21.5	21.5	21.4	21.4	21.4	21.4	21.4
64	20.7	20.7	20.7	20.6	20.6	20.6	20.6	20.6	20.6	20.6
65	19.9	19.8	19.8	19.8	19.8	19.8	19.8	19.8	19.8	19.8
66	19.1	19.0	19.0	19.0	19.0	19.0	19.0	19.0	19.0	19.0
67	18.3	18.3	18.3	18.3	18.2	18.2	18.2	18.2	18.2	18.2
68	17.5	17.5	17.5	17.5	17.5	17.5	17.5	17.5	17.4	17.4
69	16.7	16.7	16.7	16.7	16.7	16.7	16.7	16.7	16.7	16.7
70	16.0	16.0	16.0	16.0	16.0	16.0	15.9	15.9	15.9	15.9
71	15.2	15.2	15.2	15.2	15.2	15.2	15.2	15.2	15.2	15.2
72	14.5	14.5	14.5	14.5	14.5	14.5	14.5	14.5	14.5	14.5
73	13.8	13.8	13.8	13.8	13.8	13.8	13.8	13.8	13.8	13.8
74	13.2	13.1	13.1	13.1	13.1	13.1	13.1	13.1	13.1	13.1
75	12.5	12.5	12.5	12.5	12.5	12.5	12.5	12.5	12.5	12.5
76	11.8	11.8	11.8	11.8	11.8	11.8	11.8	11.8	11.8	11.8
77	11.2	11.2	11.2	11.2	11.2	11.2	11.2	11.2	11.2	11.2
78	10.6	10.6	10.6	10.6	10.6	10.6	10.6	10.6	10.6	10.6
79	10.0	10.0	10.0	10.0	10.0	10.0	10.0	10.0	10.0	10.0
80	9.4	9.4	9.4	9.4	9.4	9.4	9.4	9.4	9.4	9.4
81	8.9	8.9	8.9	8.9	8.9	8.9	8.9	8.9	8.9	8.9
82	8.4	8.4	8.4	8.4	8.4	8.4	8.4	8.4	8.4	8.4
83	7.9	7.9	7.9	7.9	7.9	7.9	7.9	7.9	7.8	7.8
84	7.4	7.4	7.4	7.4	7.4	7.4	7.4	7.4	7.4	7.4
85	6.9	6.9	6.9	6.9	6.9	6.9	6.9	6.9	6.9	6.9
86	6.5	6.5	6.5	6.5	6.5	6.5	6.5	6.5	6.5	6.5
87	6.1	6.1	6.1	6.1	6.1	6.1	6.1	6.1	6.1	6.1
88	5.7	5.7	5.7	5.7	5.7	5.7	5.7	5.7	5.7	5.7
89	5.3	5.3	5.3	5.3	5.3	5.3	5.3	5.3	5.3	5.3
90	5.0	5.0	5.0	5.0	5.0	5.0	5.0	5.0	5.0	5.0
91	4.7	4.7	4.7	4.7	4.7	4.7	4.7	4.7	4.7	4.7
92	4.4	4.4	4.4	4.4	4.4	4.4	4.4	4.4	4.4	4.4

Ages	15	16	17	18	19	20	21	22	23	24
93	4.1	4.1	4.1	4.1	4.1	4.1	4.1	4.1	4.1	4.1
94	3.9	3.9	3.9	3.9	3.9	3.9	3.9	3.9	3.9	3.9
95	3.6	3.6	3.6	3.6	3.6	3.6	3.6	3.6	3.6	3.6
96	3.4	3.4	3.4	3.4	3.4	3.4	3.4	3.4	3.4	3.4
97	3.2	3.2	3.2	3.2	3.2	3.2	3.2	3.2	3.2	3.2
98	3.0	3.0	3.0	3.0	3.0	3.0	3.0	3.0	3.0	3.0
99	2.8	2.8	2.8	2.8	2.8	2.8	2.8	2.8	2.8	2.8
100	2.7	2.7	2.7	2.7	2.7	2.7	2.7	2.7	2.7	2.7
101	2.5	2.5	2.5	2.5	2.5	2.5	2.5	2.5	2.5	2.5
102	2.3	2.3	2.3	2.3	2.3	2.3	2.3	2.3	2.3	2.3
103	2.1	2.1	2.1	2.1	2.1	2.1	2.1	2.1	2.1	2.1
104	1.9	1.9	1.9	1.9	1.9	1.9	1.9	1.9	1.9	1.9
105	1.8	1.8	1.8	1.8	1.8	1.8	1.8	1.8	1.8	1.8
106	1.6	1.6	1.6	1.6	1.6	1.6	1.6	1.6	1.6	1.6
107	1.4	1.4	1.4	1.4	1.4	1.4	1.4	1.4	1.4	1.4
108	1.3	1.3	1.3	1.3	1.3	1.3	1.3	1.3	1.3	1.3
109	1.1	1.1	1.1	1.1	1.1	1.1	1.1	1.1	1.1	1.1
110	1.0	1.0	1.0	1.0	1.0	1.0	1.0	1.0	1.0	1.0
111	.9	.9	.9	.9	.9	.9	.9	.9	.9	.9
112	.8	.8	.8	.8	.8	.8	.8	.8	.8	.8
113	.7	.7	.7	.7	.7	.7	.7	.7	.7	.7
114	.6	.6	.6	.6	.6	.6	.6	.6	.6	.6
115	.5	.5	.5	.5	.5	.5	.5	.5	.5	.5

TABLE VIA.—ANNUITIES FOR JOINT LIFE ONLY; TWO LIVES—EXPECTED RETURN MULTIPLES—Continued

Ages	25	26	27	28	29	30	31	32	33	34
25	50.2	49.7	49.2	48.6	48.1	47.5	46.9	46.2	45.6	44.9
26	49.7	49.2	48.7	48.2	47.7	47.1	46.5	45.9	45.3	44.6
27	49.2	48.7	48.3	47.8	47.3	46.7	46.2	45.6	45.0	44.3
28	48.6	48.2	47.8	47.3	46.8	46.3	45.8	45.2	44.6	44.0
29	48.1	47.7	47.3	46.8	46.4	45.9	45.4	44.8	44.3	43.7
30	47.5	47.1	46.7	46.3	45.9	45.4	44.9	44.4	43.9	43.3
31	46.9	46.5	46.2	45.8	45.4	44.9	44.5	44.0	43.5	42.9
32	46.2	45.9	45.6	45.2	44.8	44.4	44.0	43.5	43.0	42.5
33	45.6	45.3	45.0	44.6	44.3	43.9	43.5	43.0	42.6	42.1
34	44.9	44.6	44.3	44.0	43.7	43.3	42.9	42.5	42.1	41.6
35	44.2	44.0	43.7	43.4	43.1	42.7	42.4	42.0	41.6	41.1
36	43.5	43.3	43.0	42.7	42.4	42.1	41.8	41.4	41.0	40.6
37	42.8	42.5	42.3	42.1	41.8	41.5	41.2	40.8	40.5	40.1
38	42.0	41.8	41.6	41.4	41.1	40.8	40.6	40.2	39.9	39.5
39	41.3	41.1	40.9	40.7	40.4	40.2	39.9	39.6	39.3	39.0
40	40.5	40.3	40.1	39.9	39.7	39.5	39.2	39.0	38.7	38.4
41	39.7	39.5	39.4	39.2	39.0	38.8	38.5	38.3	38.0	37.7
42	38.9	38.8	38.6	38.4	38.3	38.1	37.8	37.6	37.4	37.1
43	38.1	38.0	37.8	37.7	37.5	37.3	37.1	36.9	36.7	36.4
44	37.3	37.2	37.0	36.9	36.7	36.6	36.4	36.2	36.0	35.8
45	36.5	36.3	36.2	36.1	36.0	35.8	35.6	35.5	35.3	35.1
46	35.6	35.5	35.4	35.3	35.2	35.0	34.9	34.7	34.5	34.4
47	34.8	34.7	34.6	34.5	34.4	34.3	34.1	34.0	33.8	33.6
48	34.0	33.9	33.8	33.7	33.6	33.5	33.4	33.2	33.1	32.9
49	33.1	33.0	33.0	32.9	32.8	32.7	32.6	32.4	32.3	32.2
50	32.3	32.2	32.1	32.1	32.0	31.9	31.8	31.7	31.5	31.4
51	31.4	31.4	31.3	31.2	31.2	31.1	31.0	30.9	30.8	30.6
52	30.6	30.5	30.5	30.4	30.3	30.3	30.2	30.1	30.0	29.9
53	29.7	29.7	29.6	29.6	29.5	29.5	29.4	29.3	29.2	29.1
54	28.9	28.9	28.8	28.8	28.7	28.6	28.6	28.5	28.4	28.3
55	28.1	28.0	28.0	27.9	27.9	27.8	27.8	27.7	27.6	27.5
56	27.2	27.2	27.1	27.1	27.0	27.0	26.9	26.9	26.8	26.7
57	26.4	26.3	26.3	26.3	26.2	26.2	26.1	26.1	26.0	25.9
58	25.5	25.5	25.5	25.4	25.4	25.4	25.3	25.3	25.2	25.1
59	24.7	24.7	24.6	24.6	24.6	24.5	24.5	24.5	24.4	24.3
60	23.9	23.8	23.8	23.8	23.8	23.7	23.7	23.6	23.6	23.5
61	23.0	23.0	23.0	23.0	22.9	22.9	22.9	22.8	22.8	22.7
62	22.2	22.2	22.2	22.1	22.1	22.1	22.1	22.0	22.0	21.9
63	21.4	21.4	21.3	21.3	21.3	21.3	21.3	21.2	21.2	21.2
64	20.6	20.6	20.5	20.5	20.5	20.5	20.5	20.4	20.4	20.4
65	19.8	19.8	19.7	19.7	19.7	19.7	19.7	19.6	19.6	19.6
66	19.0	19.0	19.0	18.9	18.9	18.9	18.9	18.9	18.8	18.8
67	18.2	18.2	18.2	18.2	18.2	18.1	18.1	18.1	18.1	18.1
68	17.4	17.4	17.4	17.4	17.4	17.4	17.4	17.3	17.3	17.3
69	16.7	16.7	16.7	16.6	16.6	16.6	16.6	16.6	16.6	16.6
70	15.9	15.9	15.9	15.9	15.9	15.9	15.9	15.9	15.8	15.8
71	15.2	15.2	15.2	15.2	15.2	15.2	15.2	15.1	15.1	15.1
72	14.5	14.5	14.5	14.5	14.5	14.5	14.5	14.4	14.4	14.4
73	13.8	13.8	13.8	13.8	13.8	13.8	13.8	13.8	13.7	13.7
74	13.1	13.1	13.1	13.1	13.1	13.1	13.1	13.1	13.1	13.1
75	12.5	12.5	12.5	12.4	12.4	12.4	12.4	12.4	12.4	12.4
76	11.8	11.8	11.8	11.8	11.8	11.8	11.8	11.8	11.8	11.8
77	11.2	11.2	11.2	11.2	11.2	11.2	11.2	11.2	11.2	11.1
78	10.6	10.6	10.6	10.6	10.6	10.6	10.6	10.6	10.6	10.5
79	10.0	10.0	10.0	10.0	10.0	10.0	10.0	10.0	10.0	10.0
80	9.4	9.4	9.4	9.4	9.4	9.4	9.4	9.4	9.4	9.4
81	8.9	8.9	8.9	8.9	8.9	8.9	8.9	8.9	8.9	8.9
82	8.4	8.4	8.3	8.3	8.3	8.3	8.3	8.3	8.3	8.3
83	7.8	7.8	7.8	7.8	7.8	7.8	7.8	7.8	7.8	7.8
84	7.4	7.4	7.4	7.4	7.4	7.4	7.4	7.4	7.4	7.4
85	6.9	6.9	6.9	6.9	6.9	6.9	6.9	6.9	6.9	6.9
86	6.5	6.5	6.5	6.5	6.5	6.5	6.5	6.5	6.5	6.5
87	6.1	6.1	6.1	6.1	6.1	6.1	6.1	6.1	6.1	6.1
88	5.7	5.7	5.7	5.7	5.7	5.7	5.7	5.7	5.7	5.7
89	5.3	5.3	5.3	5.3	5.3	5.3	5.3	5.3	5.3	5.3
90	5.0	5.0	5.0	5.0	5.0	5.0	5.0	5.0	5.0	5.0
91	4.7	4.7	4.7	4.7	4.7	4.7	4.7	4.7	4.7	4.7
92	4.4	4.4	4.4	4.4	4.4	4.4	4.4	4.4	4.4	4.4
93	4.1	4.1	4.1	4.1	4.1	4.1	4.1	4.1	4.1	4.1
94	3.9	3.9	3.9	3.9	3.9	3.9	3.9	3.9	3.9	3.9
95	3.6	3.6	3.6	3.6	3.6	3.6	3.6	3.6	3.6	3.6
96	3.4	3.4	3.4	3.4	3.4	3.4	3.4	3.4	3.4	3.4
97	3.2	3.2	3.2	3.2	3.2	3.2	3.2	3.2	3.2	3.2
98	3.0	3.0	3.0	3.0	3.0	3.0	3.0	3.0	3.0	3.0
99	2.8	2.8	2.8	2.8	2.8	2.8	2.8	2.8	2.8	2.8
100	2.7	2.7	2.7	2.7	2.7	2.7	2.7	2.7	2.7	2.7
101	2.5	2.5	2.5	2.5	2.5	2.5	2.5	2.5	2.5	2.5
102	2.3	2.3	2.3	2.3	2.3	2.3	2.3	2.3	2.3	2.3
103	2.1	2.1	2.1	2.1	2.1	2.1	2.1	2.1	2.1	2.1
104	1.9	1.9	1.9	1.9	1.9	1.9	1.9	1.9	1.9	1.9
105	1.8	1.8	1.8	1.8	1.8	1.8	1.8	1.8	1.8	1.8
106	1.6	1.6	1.6	1.6	1.6	1.6	1.6	1.6	1.6	1.6
107	1.4	1.4	1.4	1.4	1.4	1.4	1.4	1.4	1.4	1.4
108	1.3	1.3	1.3	1.3	1.3	1.3	1.3	1.3	1.3	1.3
109	1.1	1.1	1.1	1.1	1.1	1.1	1.1	1.1	1.1	1.1
110	1.0	1.0	1.0	1.0	1.0	1.0	1.0	1.0	1.0	1.0
111	.9	.9	.9	.9	.9	.9	.9	.9	.9	.9
112	.8	.8	.8	.8	.8	.8	.8	.8	.8	.8
113	.7	.7	.7	.7	.7	.7	.7	.7	.7	.7
114	.6	.6	.6	.6	.6	.6	.6	.6	.6	.6
115	.5	.5	.5	.5	.5	.5	.5	.5	.5	.5

TABLE VIA.—ANNUITIES FOR JOINT LIFE ONLY; TWO LIVES—EXPECTED RETURN MULTIPLES—Continued

Ages	35	36	37	38	39	40	41	42	43	44
35	40.7	40.2	39.7	39.2	38.6	38.0	37.4	36.8	36.2	35.5
36	40.2	39.7	39.3	38.7	38.2	37.7	37.1	36.5	35.9	35.2
37	39.7	39.3	38.8	38.3	37.8	37.3	36.7	36.2	35.6	34.9
38	39.2	38.7	38.3	37.9	37.4	36.9	36.3	35.8	35.2	34.6
39	38.6	38.2	37.8	37.4	36.9	36.4	35.9	35.4	34.9	34.3
40	38.0	37.7	37.3	36.9	36.4	36.0	35.5	35.0	34.5	34.0
41	37.4	37.1	36.7	36.3	35.9	35.5	35.1	34.6	34.1	33.6
42	36.8	36.5	36.2	35.8	35.4	35.0	34.6	34.1	33.7	33.2
43	36.2	35.9	35.6	35.2	34.9	34.5	34.1	33.7	33.2	32.8
44	35.5	35.2	34.9	34.6	34.3	34.0	33.6	33.2	32.8	32.3
45	34.8	34.6	34.3	34.0	33.7	33.4	33.0	32.7	32.3	31.8
46	34.1	33.9	33.7	33.4	33.1	32.8	32.5	32.1	31.8	31.4
47	33.4	33.2	33.0	32.8	32.5	32.2	31.9	31.6	31.2	30.8
48	32.7	32.5	32.3	32.1	31.8	31.6	31.3	31.0	30.7	30.3
49	32.0	31.8	31.6	31.4	31.2	30.9	30.7	30.4	30.1	29.8
50	31.3	31.1	30.9	30.7	30.5	30.3	30.0	29.8	29.5	29.2
51	30.5	30.4	30.2	30.0	29.8	29.6	29.4	29.2	28.9	28.6
52	29.7	29.6	29.5	29.3	29.1	28.9	28.7	28.5	28.3	28.0
53	29.0	28.9	28.7	28.6	28.4	28.2	28.1	27.9	27.6	27.4
54	28.2	28.1	28.0	27.8	27.7	27.5	27.4	27.2	27.0	26.8
55	27.4	27.3	27.2	27.1	27.0	26.8	26.7	26.5	26.3	26.1
56	26.7	26.6	26.5	26.3	26.2	26.1	26.0	25.8	25.6	25.4
57	25.9	25.8	25.7	25.6	25.5	25.4	25.2	25.1	24.9	24.8
58	25.1	25.0	24.9	24.8	24.7	24.6	24.5	24.4	24.2	24.1
59	24.3	24.2	24.1	24.1	24.0	23.9	23.8	23.6	23.5	23.4
60	23.5	23.4	23.4	23.3	23.2	23.1	23.0	22.9	22.8	22.7
61	22.7	22.6	22.6	22.5	22.4	22.4	22.3	22.2	22.1	22.0
62	21.9	21.9	21.8	21.7	21.7	21.6	21.5	21.4	21.3	21.2
63	21.1	21.1	21.0	21.0	20.9	20.8	20.8	20.7	20.6	20.5
64	20.3	20.3	20.2	20.2	20.1	20.1	20.0	20.0	19.9	19.8
65	19.6	19.5	19.5	19.4	19.4	19.3	19.3	19.2	19.1	19.1
66	18.8	18.8	18.7	18.7	18.6	18.6	13.5	18.5	18.4	18.4
67	18.0	18.0	18.0	17.9	17.9	17.9	17.8	17.8	17.7	17.6
68	17.3	17.3	17.2	17.2	17.2	17.1	17.1	17.0	17.0	16.9
69	16.5	16.5	16.5	16.5	16.4	16.4	16.4	16.3	16.3	16.2
70	15.8	15.8	15.8	15.7	15.7	15.7	15.6	15.6	15.6	15.5
71	15.1	15.1	15.1	15.0	15.0	15.0	15.0	14.9	14.9	14.9
72	14.4	14.4	14.4	14.3	14.3	14.3	14.3	14.2	14.2	14.2
73	13.7	13.7	13.7	13.7	13.7	13.6	13.6	13.6	13.6	13.5
74	13.1	13.0	13.0	13.0	13.0	13.0	13.0	12.9	12.9	12.9
75	12.4	12.4	12.4	12.4	12.3	12.3	12.3	12.3	12.3	12.2
76	11.8	11.8	11.7	11.7	11.7	11.7	11.7	11.7	11.6	11.6
77	11.1	11.1	11.1	11.1	11.1	11.1	11.1	11.1	11.0	11.0
78	10.5	10.5	10.5	10.5	10.5	10.5	10.5	10.5	10.5	10.4
79	10.0	10.0	9.9	9.9	9.9	9.9	9.9	9.9	9.9	9.9
80	9.4	9.4	9.4	9.4	9.4	9.4	9.4	9.3	9.3	9.3
81	8.9	8.8	8.8	8.8	8.8	8.8	8.8	8.8	8.8	8.8
82	8.3	8.3	8.3	8.3	8.3	8.3	8.3	8.3	8.3	8.3
83	7.8	7.8	7.8	7.8	7.8	7.8	7.8	7.8	7.8	7.8
84	7.3	7.3	7.3	7.3	7.3	7.3	7.3	7.3	7.3	7.3
85	6.9	6.9	6.9	6.9	6.9	6.9	6.9	6.9	6.9	6.9
86	6.5	6.5	6.5	6.5	6.4	6.4	6.4	6.4	6.4	6.4
87	6.1	6.0	6.0	6.0	6.0	6.0	6.0	6.0	6.0	6.0
88	5.7	5.7	5.7	5.7	5.7	5.7	5.7	5.6	5.6	5.6
89	5.3	5.3	5.3	5.3	5.3	5.3	5.3	5.3	5.3	5.3
90	5.0	5.0	5.0	5.0	5.0	5.0	5.0	5.0	5.0	5.0
91	4.7	4.7	4.7	4.7	4.7	4.7	4.7	4.7	4.6	4.6
92	4.4	4.4	4.4	4.4	4.4	4.4	4.4	4.4	4.4	4.4
93	4.1	4.1	4.1	4.1	4.1	4.1	4.1	4.1	4.1	4.1
94	3.9	3.9	3.9	3.9	3.9	3.9	3.9	3.9	3.9	3.9
95	3.6	3.6	3.6	3.6	3.6	3.6	3.6	3.6	3.6	3.6
96	3.4	3.4	3.4	3.4	3.4	3.4	3.4	3.4	3.4	3.4
97	3.2	3.2	3.2	3.2	3.2	3.2	3.2	3.2	3.2	3.2
98	3.0	3.0	3.0	3.0	3.0	3.0	3.0	3.0	3.0	3.0
99	2.8	2.8	2.8	2.8	2.8	2.8	2.8	2.8	2.8	2.8
100	2.7	2.7	2.7	2.7	2.7	2.7	2.7	2.7	2.6	2.6
101	2.5	2.5	2.5	2.5	2.5	2.5	2.5	2.5	2.5	2.5
102	2.3	2.3	2.3	2.3	2.3	2.3	2.3	2.3	2.3	2.3
103	2.1	2.1	2.1	2.1	2.1	2.1	2.1	2.1	2.1	2.1
104	1.9	1.9	1.9	1.9	1.9	1.9	1.9	1.9	1.9	1.9
105	1.8	1.8	1.8	1.8	1.8	1.8	1.8	1.8	1.8	1.8
106	1.6	1.6	1.6	1.6	1.6	1.6	1.6	1.6	1.6	1.6
107	1.4	1.4	1.4	1.4	1.4	1.4	1.4	1.4	1.4	1.4
108	1.3	1.3	1.3	1.3	1.3	1.3	1.3	1.3	1.3	1.3
109	1.1	1.1	1.1	1.1	1.1	1.1	1.1	1.1	1.1	1.1
110	1.0	1.0	1.0	1.0	1.0	1.0	1.0	1.0	1.0	1.0
111	.9	.9	.9	.9	.9	.9	.9	.9	.9	.9
112	.8	.8	.8	.8	.8	.8	.8	.8	.8	.8
113	.7	.7	.7	.7	.7	.7	.7	.7	.7	.7
114	.6	.6	.6	.6	.6	.6	.6	.6	.6	.6
115	.5	.5	.5	.5	.5	.5	.5	.5	.5	.5

TABLE VIA.—ANNUITIES FOR JOINT LIFE ONLY; TWO LIVES—EXPECTED RETURN MULTIPLES—Continued

Ages	45	46	47	48	49	50	51	52	53	54
45	31.4	30.9	30.5	30.0	29.4	28.9	28.3	27.7	27.1	26.5
46	30.9	30.5	30.0	29.6	29.1	28.5	28.0	27.4	26.9	26.3
47	30.5	30.0	29.6	29.2	28.7	28.2	27.7	27.1	26.6	26.0
48	30.0	29.6	29.2	28.7	28.3	27.8	27.3	26.8	26.3	25.7
49	29.4	29.1	28.7	28.3	27.9	27.4	26.9	26.5	25.9	25.4
50	28.9	28.5	28.2	27.4	27.4	27.0	26.5	26.1	25.6	25.1
51	28.3	28.0	27.7	27.3	26.9	26.5	26.1	25.7	25.2	24.7
52	27.7	27.4	27.1	26.8	26.5	26.1	25.7	25.3	24.8	24.4
53	27.1	26.9	26.6	26.3	25.9	25.6	25.2	24.8	24.4	24.0
54	26.5	26.3	26.0	25.7	25.4	25.1	24.7	24.4	24.0	23.6
55	25.9	25.7	25.4	25.1	24.9	24.6	24.2	23.9	23.5	23.2
56	25.2	25.0	24.8	24.6	24.3	24.0	23.7	23.4	23.1	22.7
57	24.6	24.4	24.2	24.0	23.7	23.5	23.2	22.9	22.6	22.2
58	23.9	23.7	23.5	23.3	23.1	22.9	22.6	22.4	22.1	21.7
59	23.2	23.1	22.9	22.7	22.5	22.3	22.1	21.8	21.5	21.2
60	22.5	22.4	22.2	22.1	21.9	21.7	21.5	21.2	21.0	20.7
61	21.8	21.7	21.6	21.4	21.2	21.1	20.9	20.6	20.4	20.2
62	21.1	21.0	20.9	20.7	20.6	20.4	20.2	20.0	19.8	19.6
63	20.4	20.3	20.2	20.1	19.9	19.8	19.6	19.4	19.2	19.0
64	19.7	19.6	19.5	19.4	19.3	19.1	19.0	18.8	18.6	18.5
65	19.0	18.9	18.8	18.7	18.6	18.5	18.3	18.2	18.0	17.9
66	18.3	18.2	18.1	18.0	17.9	17.8	17.7	17.6	17.4	17.3
67	17.6	17.5	17.4	17.3	17.3	17.2	17.1	16.9	16.8	16.7
68	16.9	16.8	16.7	16.7	16.6	16.5	16.4	16.3	16.2	16.1
69	16.2	16.1	16.1	16.0	15.9	15.8	15.8	15.7	15.6	15.4
70	15.5	15.4	15.4	15.3	15.3	15.2	15.1	15.0	14.9	14.8
71	14.8	14.8	14.7	14.7	14.6	14.5	14.5	14.4	14.3	14.2
72	14.1	14.1	14.1	14.0	14.0	13.9	13.8	13.8	13.7	13.6
73	13.5	13.5	13.4	13.4	13.3	13.3	13.2	13.2	13.1	13.0
74	12.8	12.8	12.8	12.7	12.7	12.7	12.6	12.6	12.5	12.4
75	12.2	12.2	12.2	12.1	12.1	12.1	12.0	12.0	11.9	11.9
76	11.6	11.6	11.6	11.5	11.5	11.5	11.4	11.4	11.3	11.3
77	11.0	11.0	11.0	10.9	10.9	10.9	10.8	10.8	10.8	10.7
78	10.4	10.4	10.4	10.4	10.3	10.3	10.3	10.2	10.2	10.2
79	9.9	9.8	9.8	9.8	9.8	9.8	9.7	9.7	9.7	9.6
80	9.3	9.3	9.3	9.3	9.2	9.2	9.2	9.2	9.1	9.1
81	8.8	8.8	8.7	8.7	8.7	8.7	8.7	8.7	8.6	8.6
82	8.3	8.2	8.2	8.2	8.2	8.2	8.2	8.2	8.1	8.1
83	7.8	7.8	7.7	7.7	7.7	7.7	7.7	7.7	7.7	7.6
84	7.3	7.3	7.3	7.3	7.3	7.2	7.2	7.2	7.2	7.2
85	6.8	6.8	6.8	6.8	6.8	6.8	6.8	6.8	6.8	6.7
86	6.4	6.4	6.4	6.4	6.4	6.4	6.4	6.4	6.3	6.3
87	6.0	6.0	6.0	6.0	6.0	6.0	6.0	6.0	6.0	5.9
88	5.6	5.6	5.6	5.6	5.6	5.6	5.6	5.6	5.6	5.6
89	5.3	5.3	5.3	5.3	5.3	5.3	5.2	5.2	5.2	5.2
90	5.0	4.9	4.9	4.9	4.9	4.9	4.9	4.9	4.9	4.9
91	4.6	4.6	4.6	4.6	4.6	4.6	4.6	4.6	4.6	4.6
92	4.4	4.4	4.4	4.3	4.3	4.3	4.3	4.3	4.3	4.3
93	4.1	4.1	4.1	4.1	4.1	4.1	4.1	4.1	4.1	4.1
94	3.9	3.9	3.8	3.8	3.8	3.8	3.8	3.8	3.8	3.8
95	3.6	3.6	3.6	3.6	3.6	3.6	3.6	3.6	3.6	3.6
96	3.4	3.4	3.4	3.4	3.4	3.4	3.4	3.4	3.4	3.4
97	3.2	3.2	3.2	3.2	3.2	3.2	3.2	3.2	3.2	3.2
98	3.0	3.0	3.0	3.0	3.0	3.0	3.0	3.0	3.0	3.0
99	2.8	2.8	2.8	2.8	2.8	2.8	2.8	2.8	2.8	2.8
100	2.6	2.6	2.6	2.6	2.6	2.6	2.6	2.6	2.6	2.6
101	2.5	2.5	2.5	2.5	2.5	2.5	2.5	2.5	2.5	2.5
102	2.3	2.3	2.3	2.3	2.3	2.3	2.3	2.3	2.3	2.3
103	2.1	2.1	2.1	2.1	2.1	2.1	2.1	2.1	2.1	2.1
104	1.9	1.9	1.9	1.9	1.9	1.9	1.9	1.9	1.9	1.9
105	1.8	1.8	1.8	1.8	1.8	1.8	1.8	1.8	1.8	1.8
106	1.6	1.6	1.6	1.6	1.6	1.6	1.6	1.6	1.6	1.6
107	1.4	1.4	1.4	1.4	1.4	1.4	1.4	1.4	1.4	1.4
108	1.3	1.3	1.3	1.3	1.3	1.3	1.3	1.3	1.3	1.3
109	1.1	1.1	1.1	1.1	1.1	1.1	1.1	1.1	1.1	1.1
110	1.0	1.0	1.0	1.0	1.0	1.0	1.0	1.0	1.0	1.0
111	.9	.9	.9	.9	.9	.9	.9	.9	.9	.9
112	.8	.8	.8	.8	.8	.8	.8	.8	.8	.8
113	.7	.7	.7	.7	.7	.7	.7	.7	.7	.7
114	.6	.6	.6	.6	.6	.6	.6	.6	.6	.6
115	.5	.5	.5	.5	.5	.5	.5	.5	.5	.5

TABLE VIA.—ANNUITIES FOR JOINT LIFE ONLY; TWO LIVES—EXPECTED RETURN MULTIPLES—Continued

Ages	55	56	57	58	59	60	61	62	63	64
55	22.7	22.3	21.9	21.4	20.9	20.4	19.9			
56	22.3	21.9	21.5	21.1	20.6	20.1	19.6			
57	21.9	21.5	21.1	20.7	20.3	19.8	19.3	.4		
58	21.4	21.1	20.7	20.3	19.9	19.5	19.0		18.8	18.3
59	20.9	20.6	20.3	19.9	19.5	19.1	18.7	18.	18.3	18.0
60	20.4	20.1	19.8	19.5	19.1	18.7	18.3	17.9	18.0	17.8
61	29.9	19.6	19.3	19.0	18.7	18.3	17.9	17.5	17.7	17.5
62	19.4	19.1	18.8	18.5	18.2	17.9	17.5	17.1	7.4	17.3
63	18.8	18.6	18.3	18.0	17.7	17.4	17.1	16.8		17.0
64	18.3	18.0	17.8	17.5	17.3	17.0	16.7	16.3		16.7
65	17.7	17.5	17.3	17.0	16.8	16.5	16.2	15.9		16.3
66	17.1	16.9	16.7	16.5	16.3	16.0	15.8	15.5	1.	16.0
67	16.5	16.3	16.2	16.0	15.8	15.5	15.3	15.0	14.7	15.6
68	15.9	15.8	15.6	15.4	15.2	15.0	14.8	14.6	14.3	5.3
69	15.3	15.2	15.0	14.9	14.7	14.5	14.3	14.1	13.9	
70	14.7	14.6	14.5	14.3	14.2	14.0	13.8	13.6	13.4	
71	14.1	14.0	13.9	13.8	13.6	13.5	13.3	13.1	12.9	
72	13.5	13.4	13.3	13.2	13.1	12.9	12.8	12.6	12.4	
73	13.0	12.9	12.8	12.7	12.5	12.4	12.3	12.1	12.0	1.
74	12.4	12.3	12.2	12.1	12.0	11.9	11.8	11.6	11.5	11.
75	11.8	11.7	11.7	11.6	11.5	11.4	11.3	11.1	11.0	10.9
76	11.2	11.2	11.1	11.0	10.9	10.9	10.3	10.6	10.5	10.4
77	10.7	10.6	10.6	10.5	10.4	10.3	10.3	10.2	10.0	9.9
78	10.1	10.1	10.0	10.0	9.9	9.8	9.8	9.7	9.6	9.5
79	9.6	9.6	9.5	9.5	9.4	9.3	9.3	9.2	9.1	9.0
80	9.1	9.0	9.0	9.0	8.9	8.9	8.8	8.7	8.7	8.6
81	8.6	8.5	8.5	8.5	8.4	8.4	8.3	8.3	8.2	8.1
82	8.1	8.1	8.0	8.0	8.0	7.9	7.9	7.8	7.8	7.7
83	7.6	7.6	7.6	7.5	7.5	7.5	7.4	7.4	7.3	7.3
84	7.2	7.1	7.1	7.1	7.1	7.0	7.0	7.0	6.9	6.9
85	6.7	6.7	6.7	6.7	6.6	6.6	6.6	6.5	6.5	6.5
86	6.3	6.3	6.3	6.3	6.2	6.2	6.2	6.2	6.1	6.1
87	5.9	5.9	5.9	5.9	5.9	5.8	5.8	5.8	5.8	5.7
88	5.6	5.5	5.5	5.5	5.5	5.5	5.5	5.4	5.4	5.4
89	5.2	5.2	5.2	5.2	5.2	5.1	5.1	5.1	5.1	5.1
90	4.9	4.9	4.9	4.9	4.9	4.8	4.8	4.8	4.8	4.8
91	4.6	4.6	4.6	4.6	4.6	4.5	4.5	4.5	4.5	4.5
92	4.3	4.3	4.3	4.3	4.3	4.3	4.3	4.2	4.2	4.2
93	4.1	4.1	4.0	4.0	4.0	4.0	4.0	4.0	4.0	4.0
94	3.8	3.8	3.8	3.8	3.8	3.8	3.8	3.8	3.8	3.7
95	3.6	3.6	3.6	3.6	3.6	3.6	3.6	3.6	3.5	3.5
96	3.4	3.4	3.4	3.4	3.4	3.4	3.4	3.3	3.3	3.3
97	3.2	3.2	3.2	3.2	3.2	3.2	3.2	3.2	3.1	3.1
98	3.0	3.0	3.0	3.0	3.0	3.0	3.0	3.0	3.0	3.0
99	2.8	2.8	2.8	2.8	2.8	2.8	2.8	2.8	2.8	2.8
100	2.6	2.6	2.6	2.6	2.6	2.6	2.6	2.6	2.6	2.6
101	2.5	2.4	2.4	2.4	2.4	2.4	2.4	2.4	2.4	2.4
102	2.3	2.3	2.3	2.3	2.3	2.3	2.3	2.3	2.3	2.2
103	2.1	2.1	2.1	2.1	2.1	2.1	2.1	2.1	2.1	2.1
104	1.9	1.9	1.9	1.9	1.9	1.9	1.9	1.9	1.9	1.9
105	1.8	1.8	1.8	1.8	1.8	1.8	1.7	1.7	1.7	1.7
106	1.6	1.6	1.6	1.6	1.6	1.6	1.6	1.6	1.6	1.6
107	1.4	1.4	1.4	1.4	1.4	1.4	1.4	1.4	1.4	1.4
108	1.3	1.3	1.3	1.3	1.3	1.3	1.3	1.3	1.3	1.3
109	1.1	1.1	1.1	1.1	1.1	1.1	1.1	1.1	1.1	1.1
110	1.0	1.0	1.0	1.0	1.0	1.0	1.0	1.0	1.0	1.0
111	.9	.9	.9	.9	.9	.9	.9	.9	.9	.9
112	.8	.8	.8	.8	.8	.8	.8	.8	.8	.8
113	.7	.7	.7	.7	.7	.7	.7	.7	.7	.7
114	.6	.6	.6	.6	.6	.6	.6	.6	.6	.6
115	.5	.5	.5	.5	.5	.5	.5	.5	.5	.5

TABLE VIA.—ANNUITIES FOR JOINT LIFE ONLY; TWO LIVES—EXPECTED RETURN MULTIPLES—Continued

Ages	65	66	67	68	69	70	71	72	73	74
65	14.9	14.5	14.1	13.7	13.3	12.9	12.5	12.0	11.6	11.2
66	14.5	14.2	13.8	13.4	13.1	12.6	12.2	11.8	11.4	11.0
67	14.1	13.8	13.5	13.1	12.8	12.4	12.0	11.6	11.2	10.8
68	13.7	13.4	13.1	12.8	12.5	12.1	11.7	11.4	11.0	10.6
69	13.3	13.1	12.8	12.5	12.1	11.8	11.4	11.1	10.7	10.4
70	12.9	12.6	12.4	12.1	11.8	11.5	11.2	10.8	10.5	10.1
71	12.5	12.2	12.0	11.7	11.4	11.2	10.9	10.5	10.2	9.9
72	12.0	11.8	11.6	11.4	11.1	10.8	10.5	10.2	9.9	9.6
73	11.6	11.4	11.2	11.0	10.7	10.5	10.2	9.9	9.7	9.4
74	11.2	11.0	10.8	10.6	10.4	10.1	9.9	9.6	9.4	9.1
75	10.7	10.5	10.4	10.2	10.0	9.8	9.5	9.3	9.1	8.8
76	10.3	10.1	9.9	9.8	9.6	9.4	9.2	9.0	8.8	8.5
77	9.8	9.7	9.5	9.4	9.2	9.0	8.8	8.6	8.4	8.2
78	9.4	9.2	9.1	9.0	8.8	8.7	8.5	8.3	8.1	7.9
79	8.9	8.8	8.7	8.6	8.4	8.3	8.1	8.0	7.8	7.6
80	8.5	8.4	8.3	8.2	8.0	7.9	7.8	7.6	7.5	7.3
81	8.0	8.0	7.9	7.9	7.7	7.5	7.4	7.3	7.1	7.0
82	7.6	7.5	7.5	7.4	7.3	7.2	7.1	6.9	6.8	6.7
83	7.2	7.1	7.1	7.0	6.9	6.8	6.7	6.6	6.5	6.4
84	6.8	6.7	6.7	6.6	6.5	6.4	6.4	6.3	6.2	6.0
85	6.4	6.4	6.3	6.2	6.2	6.1	6.0	5.9	5.8	5.7
86	6.0	6.0	5.9	5.9	5.8	5.8	5.7	5.6	5.5	5.4
87	5.7	5.6	5.6	5.6	5.5	5.4	5.4	5.3	5.2	5.2
88	5.3	5.3	5.3	5.2	5.2	5.1	5.1	5.0	5.0	4.9
89	5.0	5.0	5.0	4.9	4.9	4.8	4.8	4.7	4.7	4.6
90	4.7	4.7	4.7	4.6	4.6	4.6	4.5	4.5	4.4	4.4
91	4.5	4.4	4.4	4.4	4.3	4.3	4.3	4.2	4.2	4.1
92	4.2	4.2	4.1	4.1	4.1	4.1	4.0	4.0	3.9	3.9
93	3.9	3.9	3.9	3.9	3.9	3.8	3.8	3.8	3.7	3.7
94	3.7	3.7	3.7	3.7	3.6	3.6	3.6	3.6	3.5	3.5
95	3.5	3.5	3.5	3.5	3.4	3.4	3.4	3.4	3.3	3.3
96	3.3	3.3	3.3	3.3	3.3	3.2	3.2	3.2	3.2	3.1
97	3.1	3.1	3.1	3.1	3.1	3.1	3.0	3.0	3.0	3.0
98	2.9	2.9	2.9	2.9	2.9	2.9	2.9	2.9	2.8	2.8
99	2.8	2.8	2.8	2.7	2.7	2.7	2.7	2.7	2.7	2.6
100	2.6	2.6	2.6	2.6	2.6	2.5	2.5	2.5	2.5	2.5
101	2.4	2.4	2.4	2.4	2.4	2.4	2.4	2.4	2.3	2.3
102	2.2	2.2	2.2	2.2	2.2	2.2	2.2	2.2	2.2	2.2
103	2.1	2.1	2.1	2.1	2.1	2.0	2.0	2.0	2.0	2.0
104	1.9	1.9	1.9	1.9	1.9	1.9	1.9	1.9	1.9	1.9
105	1.7	1.7	1.7	1.7	1.7	1.7	1.7	1.7	1.7	1.7
106	1.6	1.6	1.6	1.6	1.6	1.6	1.6	1.6	1.5	1.5
107	1.4	1.4	1.4	1.4	1.4	1.4	1.4	1.4	1.4	1.4
108	1.3	1.3	1.3	1.3	1.3	1.3	1.3	1.3	1.3	1.3
109	1.1	1.1	1.1	1.1	1.1	1.1	1.1	1.1	1.1	1.1
110	1.0	1.0	1.0	1.0	1.0	1.0	1.0	1.0	1.0	1.0
111	.9	.9	.9	.9	.9	.9	.9	.9	.9	.9
112	.8	.8	.8	.8	.8	.8	.8	.8	.8	.8
113	.7	.7	.7	.7	.7	.6	.6	.6	.6	.6
114	.6	.6	.6	.6	.6	.6	.5	.5	.5	.5
115	.5	.5	.5	.5	.5	.5	.5	.5	.5	.5

TABLE VIA.—ANNUITIES FOR JOINT LIFE ONLY; TWO LIVES—EXPECTED RETURN MULTIPLES—Continued

Ages	75	76	77	78	79	80	81	82	83	84
75	8.6	8.3	8.0	7.7	7.4	7.1	6.6	6.5	6.2	5.9
76	8.3	8.0	7.8	7.5	7.2	6.9	6.7	6.4	6.1	5.8
77	8.0	7.8	7.6	7.3	7.0	6.8	6.5	6.2	5.9	5.7
78	7.7	7.5	7.3	7.0	6.8	6.6	6.3	6.0	5.8	5.5
79	7.4	7.2	7.0	6.8	6.6	6.3	6.1	5.9	5.6	5.4
80	7.1	6.9	6.8	6.6	6.3	6.1	5.9	5.7	5.5	5.2
81	6.8	6.7	6.5	6.3	6.1	5.9	5.7	5.5	5.3	5.1
82	6.5	6.4	6.2	6.0	5.9	5.7	5.5	5.3	5.1	4.9
83	6.2	6.1	5.9	5.8	5.6	5.5	5.3	5.1	4.9	4.7
84	5.9	5.8	5.7	5.5	5.4	5.2	5.1	4.9	4.7	4.6
85	5.6	5.5	5.4	5.3	5.2	5.0	4.9	4.7	4.6	4.4
86	5.4	5.3	5.1	5.0	4.9	4.8	4.7	4.5	4.4	4.2
87	5.1	5.0	4.9	4.8	4.7	4.6	4.4	4.3	4.2	4.1
88	4.8	4.7	4.6	4.5	4.4	4.3	4.2	4.1	4.0	3.9
89	4.5	4.5	4.4	4.3	4.2	4.1	4.0	3.9	3.8	3.7
90	4.3	4.2	4.2	4.1	4.0	3.9	3.8	3.8	3.7	3.5
91	4.1	4.0	4.0	3.9	3.8	3.7	3.7	3.6	3.5	3.4
92	3.9	3.8	3.7	3.7	3.6	3.6	3.5	3.4	3.3	3.2
93	3.7	3.6	3.6	3.5	3.4	3.4	3.3	3.2	3.2	3.1
94	3.5	3.4	3.4	3.3	3.3	3.2	3.2	3.1	3.0	3.0
95	3.3	3.2	3.2	3.2	3.1	3.1	3.0	3.0	2.9	2.8
96	3.1	3.1	3.0	3.0	3.0	2.9	2.9	2.8	2.8	2.7
97	2.9	2.9	2.9	2.9	2.8	2.8	2.7	2.7	2.6	2.6
98	2.8	2.8	2.7	2.7	2.7	2.6	2.5	2.6	2.5	2.5
99	2.6	2.6	2.6	2.6	2.5	2.5	2.5	2.4	2.4	2.3
100	2.5	2.5	2.4	2.4	2.4	2.4	2.3	2.3	2.3	2.2
101	2.3	2.3	2.3	2.3	2.2	2.2	2.2	2.2	2.1	2.1
102	2.2	2.1	2.1	2.1	2.1	2.1	2.0	2.0	2.0	2.0
103	2.0	2.0	2.0	2.0	1.9	1.9	1.9	1.9	1.9	1.8
104	1.8	1.8	1.8	1.8	1.8	1.8	1.8	1.7	1.7	1.7
105	1.7	1.7	1.7	1.7	1.6	1.6	1.6	1.6	1.6	1.6
106	1.5	1.5	1.5	1.5	1.5	1.5	1.5	1.5	1.5	1.4
107	1.4	1.4	1.4	1.4	1.4	1.4	1.3	1.3	1.3	1.3
108	1.3	1.2	1.2	1.2	1.2	1.2	1.2	1.2	1.2	1.2
109	1.1	1.1	1.1	1.1	1.1	1.1	1.1	1.1	1.1	1.1
110	1.0	1.0	1.0	1.0	1.0	1.0	1.0	1.0	1.0	1.0
111	.9	.9	.9	.9	.9	.9	.9	.9	.8	.8
112	.8	.8	.8	.7	.7	.7	.7	.7	.7	.7
113	.6	.6	.6	.6	.6	.6	.6	.6	.6	.6
114	.5	.5	.5	.5	.5	.5	.5	.5	.5	.5
115	.5	.5	.5	.5	.5	.5	.5	.5	.5	.5

Ages	85	86	87	88	89	90	91	92	93	94
85	4.2	4.1	3.9	3.8	3.6	3.4	3.3	3.2	3.0	2.9
86	4.1	3.9	3.8	3.6	3.5	3.3	3.2	3.1	2.9	2.8
87	3.9	3.8	3.6	3.5	3.4	3.2	3.1	3.0	2.8	2.7
88	3.8	3.6	3.5	3.4	3.2	3.1	3.0	2.9	2.8	2.6
89	3.6	3.5	3.4	3.2	3.1	3.0	2.9	2.8	2.7	2.6
90	3.4	3.3	3.2	3.1	3.0	2.9	2.8	2.7	2.6	2.5
91	3.3	3.2	3.1	3.0	2.9	2.8	2.7	2.6	2.5	2.4
92	3.2	3.1	3.0	2.9	2.8	2.7	2.6	2.5	2.4	2.3
93	3.0	2.9	2.8	2.8	2.7	2.6	2.5	2.4	2.3	2.3
94	2.9	2.8	2.7	2.6	2.6	2.5	2.4	2.3	2.3	2.2
95	2.8	2.7	2.6	2.5	2.5	2.4	2.3	2.2	2.2	2.1
96	2.6	2.6	2.5	2.4	2.4	2.3	2.2	2.2	2.1	2.0
97	2.5	2.5	2.4	2.3	2.3	2.2	2.2	2.1	2.0	2.0
98	2.4	2.4	2.3	2.2	2.2	2.1	2.1	2.0	2.0	1.9
99	2.3	2.2	2.2	2.1	2.1	2.0	2.0	1.9	1.9	1.8
100	2.2	2.1	2.1	2.0	2.0	1.9	1.9	1.9	1.8	1.8
101	2.1	2.0	2.0	1.9	1.9	1.9	1.8	1.8	1.7	1.7
102	1.9	1.9	1.9	1.8	1.8	1.8	1.7	1.7	1.6	1.6
103	1.8	1.8	1.8	1.7	1.7	1.7	1.6	1.6	1.5	1.5
104	1.7	1.7	1.6	1.6	1.6	1.5	1.5	1.5	1.5	1.4
105	1.6	1.5	1.5	1.5	1.5	1.4	1.4	1.4	1.4	1.3
106	1.4	1.4	1.4	1.4	1.4	1.3	1.3	1.3	1.3	1.2
107	1.3	1.3	1.3	1.3	1.2	1.2	1.2	1.2	1.2	1.2
108	1.2	1.2	1.2	1.1	1.1	1.1	1.1	1.1	1.1	1.1
109	1.1	1.1	1.0	1.0	1.0	1.0	1.0	1.0	1.0	1.0
110	.9	.9	.9	.9	.9	.9	.9	.9	.9	.9
111	.8	.8	.8	.8	.8	.8	.8	.8	.8	.8
112	.7	.7	.7	.7	.7	.7	.7	.7	.7	.7
113	.6	.6	.6	.6	.6	.6	.6	.6	.6	.6
114	.5	.5	.5	.5	.5	.5	.5	.5	.5	.5
115	.5	.5	.5	.5	.5	.5	.5	.5	.5	.5

TABLE VIA.—ANNUITIES FOR JOINT LIFE ONLY; TWO LIVES—EXPECTED RETURN MULTIPLES—Continued

Ages	95	96	97	98	99	100	101	102	103	104
95	2.0	2.0	1.9	1.8	1.8	1.7	1.6	1.6	1.5	1.4
96	2.0	1.9	1.9	1.8	1.7	1.7	1.6	1.5	1.5	1.4
97	1.9	1.9	1.8	1.7	1.7	1.6	1.6	1.5	1.4	1.3
98	1.8	1.8	1.7	1.7	1.6	1.6	1.5	1.5	1.4	1.3
99	1.8	1.7	1.7	1.6	1.6	1.5	1.5	1.4	1.4	1.3
100	1.7	1.7	1.6	1.6	1.5	1.5	1.4	1.4	1.3	1.3
101	1.6	1.6	1.6	1.5	1.5	1.4	1.4	1.3	1.3	1.2
102	1.6	1.5	1.5	1.5	1.4	1.4	1.3	1.3	1.2	1.2
103	1.5	1.5	1.4	1.4	1.4	1.3	1.3	1.2	1.2	1.1
104	1.4	1.4	1.3	1.3	1.3	1.3	1.2	1.2	1.1	1.1
105	1.3	1.3	1.3	1.2	1.2	1.2	1.2	1.1	1.1	1.0
106	1.2	1.2	1.2	1.2	1.1	1.1	1.1	1.1	1.0	1.0
107	1.1	1.1	1.1	1.1	1.1	1.0	1.0	1.0	1.0	.9
108	1.0	1.0	1.0	1.0	1.0	1.0	1.0	.9	.9	.9
109	1.0	.9	.9	.9	.9	.9	.9	.9	.8	.8
110	.9	.9	.8	.8	.8	.8	.8	.8	.8	.8
111	.8	.8	.8	.8	.7	.7	.7	.7	.7	.7
112	.7	.7	.7	.7	.7	.7	.7	.7	.6	.6
113	.6	.6	.6	.6	.6	.6	.6	.6	.6	.6
114	.5	.5	.5	.5	.5	.5	.5	.5	.5	.5
115	.5	.5	.5	.5	.5	.5	.5	.5	.5	.5

Ages	105	106	107	108	109	110	111	112	113	114	115
105	1.0	1.0	.9	.9	.8	.7	.7	.6	.6	.5	.5
106	1.0	.9	.9	.8	.8	.7	.7	.6	.6	.5	.5
107	.9	.9	.8	.8	.7	.7	.7	.6	.6	.5	.5
108	.9	.8	.8	.8	.7	.7	.7	.6	.5	.5	.5
109	.8	.8	.7	.7	.7	.7	.6	.6	.5	.5	.5
110	.7	.7	.7	.7	.7	.6	.6	.6	.5	.5	.5
111	.7	.7	.7	.6	.6	.6	.6	.5	.5	.5	.5
112	.6	.6	.6	.6	.6	.6	.5	.5	.5	.5	.5
113	.6	.6	.6	.5	.5	.5	.5	.5	.5	.5	.5
114	.5	.5	.5	.5	.5	.5	.5	.5	.5	.5	.5
115	.5	.5	.5	.5	.5	.5	.5	.5	.5	.5	.5

TABLE VII.—PERCENT VALUE OF REFUND FEATURE; DURATION OF GUARANTEED AMOUNT

Age	Years—									
	1	2	3	4	5	6	7	8	9	10
5	0	0	0	0	0	0	0	0	0	0
6	0	0	0	0	0	0	0	0	0	0
7	0	0	0	0	0	0	0	0	0	0
8	0	0	0	0	0	0	0	0	0	0
9	0	0	0	0	0	0	0	0	0	0
10	0	0	0	0	0	0	0	0	0	0
11	0	0	0	0	0	0	0	0	0	0
12	0	0	0	0	0	0	0	0	0	0
13	0	0	0	0	0	0	0	0	0	0
14	0	0	0	0	0	0	0	0	0	0
15	0	0	0	0	0	0	0	0	0	0
16	0	0	0	0	0	0	0	0	0	0
17	0	0	0	0	0	0	0	0	0	0
18	0	0	0	0	0	0	0	0	0	0
19	0	0	0	0	0	0	0	0	0	0
20	0	0	0	0	0	0	0	0	0	0
21	0	0	0	0	0	0	0	0	0	0
22	0	0	0	0	0	0	0	0	0	0
23	0	0	0	0	0	0	0	0	0	0
24	0	0	0	0	0	0	0	0	0	0
25	0	0	0	0	0	0	0	0	0	0
26	0	0	0	0	0	0	0	0	0	0
27	0	0	0	0	0	0	0	0	0	0
28	0	0	0	0	0	0	0	0	0	0
29	0	0	0	0	0	0	0	0	0	0
30	0	0	0	0	0	0	0	0	0	0
31	0	0	0	0	0	0	0	0	0	0
32	0	0	0	0	0	0	0	0	0	0
33	0	0	0	0	0	0	0	0	0	0
34	0	0	0	0	0	0	0	0	0	0
35	0	0	0	0	0	0	0	0	0	0
36	0	0	0	0	0	0	0	0	0	0
37	0	0	0	0	0	0	0	0	0	1
38	0	0	0	0	0	0	0	0	0	1
39	0	0	0	0	0	0	0	0	1	1
40	0	0	0	0	0	0	0	1	1	1
41	0	0	0	0	0	0	0	1	1	1
42	0	0	0	0	0	0	1	1	1	1
43	0	0	0	0	0	0	1	1	1	1
44	0	0	0	0	0	1	1	1	1	1
45	0	0	0	0	0	1	1	1	1	1
46	0	0	0	0	1	1	1	1	1	1
47	0	0	0	0	1	1	1	1	1	1
48	0	0	0	1	1	1	1	1	1	2
49	0	0	0	1	1	1	1	1	1	2
50	0	0	0	1	1	1	1	1	1	2
51	0	0	0	1	1	1	1	1	2	2
52	0	0	0	1	1	1	1	1	2	2
53	0	0	1	1	1	1	1	2	2	2
54	0	0	1	1	1	1	1	2	2	2
55	0	0	1	1	1	1	2	2	2	3
56	0	0	1	1	1	1	2	2	2	3
57	0	1	1	1	1	2	2	2	3	3
58	0	1	1	1	1	2	2	2	3	3
59	0	1	1	1	1	2	2	3	3	4
60	0	1	1	1	2	2	2	3	3	4
61	0	1	1	1	2	2	3	3	4	4
62	0	1	1	2	2	2	3	4	4	5
63	0	1	1	2	2	3	3	4	5	6
64	0	1	1	2	2	3	4	4	5	6
65	0	1	2	2	3	3	4	5	6	6
66	1	1	2	2	3	4	5	5	6	7
67	1	1	2	3	3	4	5	6	7	8
68	1	1	2	3	4	5	6	7	8	9
69	1	1	2	3	4	5	6	7	8	10
70	1	2	3	4	5	6	7	8	9	11
71	1	2	3	4	5	6	8	9	10	12
72	1	2	3	4	6	7	8	10	11	13
73	1	2	4	5	6	8	9	11	13	14
74	1	3	4	5	7	9	10	12	14	16
75	1	3	4	6	8	9	11	13	15	17
76	2	3	5	7	9	10	12	15	17	19
77	2	4	5	7	9	12	14	16	18	21
78	2	4	6	8	10	13	15	18	20	23
79	2	4	7	9	11	14	17	19	22	25
80	2	5	7	10	13	15	18	21	24	27
81	3	5	8	11	14	17	20	23	26	29
82	3	6	9	12	15	19	22	25	28	32
83	3	7	10	13	17	20	24	27	31	34
84	4	7	11	15	19	22	26	30	33	37
85	4	8	12	16	20	24	28	32	36	40
86	4	9	13	18	22	27	31	35	39	42
87	5	10	15	20	24	29	33	37	41	45
88	5	11	16	21	26	31	36	40	44	48
89	6	12	18	23	28	33	38	43	47	50
90	7	13	19	25	31	36	41	45	49	53
91	7	14	21	27	33	38	43	48	52	55
92	8	15	22	29	35	40	45	50	54	58
93	9	17	24	31	37	43	48	52	56	60
94	9	18	26	33	39	45	50	54	58	62
95	10	19	27	35	41	47	52	57	60	64
96	11	20	29	36	43	49	54	59	62	66
97	11	21	30	38	45	51	56	61	64	68
98	12	23	32	40	47	53	58	63	66	69

Reg. §1.72-9

Age	Years—									
	1	2	3	4	5	6	7	8	9	10
99	13	24	34	42	49	55	60	65	68	71
100	14	26	36	44	52	58	63	67	70	73
101	14	27	38	47	54	60	65	69	72	75
102	15	29	40	49	56	62	67	71	74	77
103	17	31	42	52	59	65	69	73	76	78
104	18	33	45	55	62	67	72	75	78	80
105	19	36	48	58	65	70	74	77	80	82
106	21	38	51	61	68	73	77	79	82	84
107	23	42	55	64	71	75	79	81	84	85
108	25	45	58	67	73	78	81	83	85	87
109	28	49	62	71	76	80	83	85	87	88
110	31	52	66	74	79	82	85	87	88	89
111	34	57	70	77	82	85	87	88	90	91
112	37	61	73	80	84	87	88	90	91	92
113	41	66	77	83	86	88	90	91	92	93
114	45	70	80	85	88	90	92	93	93	94
115	50	75	83	88	90	92	93	94	94	95

TABLE VII.—PERCENT VALUE OF REFUND FEATURE; DURATION OF GUARANTEED AMOUNT—Continued

Age	11	12	13	14	15	16	17	18	19	20
5	0	0	0	0	0	0	0	0	0	0
6	0	0	0	0	0	0	0	0	0	0
7	0	0	0	0	0	0	0	0	0	0
8	0	0	0	0	0	0	0	0	0	0
9	0	0	0	0	0	0	0	0	0	0
10	0	0	0	0	0	0	0	0	0	0
11	0	0	0	0	0	0	0	0	0	0
12	0	0	0	0	0	0	0	0	0	0
13	0	0	0	0	0	0	0	0	0	0
14	0	0	0	0	0	0	0	0	0	0
15	0	0	0	0	0	0	0	0	0	0
16	0	0	0	0	0	0	0	0	0	0
17	0	0	0	0	0	0	0	0	0	0
18	0	0	0	0	0	0	0	0	0	0
19	0	0	0	0	0	0	0	0	0	0
20	0	0	0	0	0	0	0	0	0	1
21	0	0	0	0	0	0	0	0	0	1
22	0	0	0	0	0	0	0	0	1	1
23	0	0	0	0	0	0	0	1	1	1
24	0	0	0	0	0	0	0	1	1	1
25	0	0	0	0	0	0	1	1	1	1
26	0	0	0	0	0	0	1	1	1	1
27	0	0	0	0	0	1	1	1	1	1
28	0	0	0	0	1	1	1	1	1	1
29	0	0	0	0	1	1	1	1	1	1
30	0	0	0	1	1	1	1	1	1	1
31	0	0	0	1	1	1	1	1	1	1
32	0	0	1	1	1	1	1	1	1	1
33	0	0	1	1	1	1	1	1	1	1
34	0	1	1	1	1	1	1	1	1	1
35	0	1	1	1	1	1	1	1	1	1
36	1	1	1	1	1	1	1	1	1	1
37	1	1	1	1	1	1	1	1	1	1
38	1	1	1	1	1	1	1	1	1	2
39	1	1	1	1	1	1	1	1	2	2
40	1	1	1	1	1	1	1	2	2	2
41	1	1	1	1	1	1	2	2	2	2
42	1	1	1	1	1	2	2	2	2	2
43	1	1	1	1	2	2	2	2	2	3
44	1	1	1	2	2	2	2	2	3	3
45	1	1	2	2	2	2	2	3	3	3
46	1	2	2	2	2	2	3	3	3	3
47	1	2	2	2	2	2	3	3	3	4
48	2	2	2	2	2	3	3	3	4	4
49	2	2	2	2	3	3	3	4	4	4
50	2	2	2	3	3	3	3	4	4	5
51	2	2	3	3	3	3	4	4	4	5
52	2	2	3	3	3	4	4	5	5	5
53	2	3	3	3	4	4	5	5	5	6
54	3	3	3	4	4	4	5	5	6	7
55	3	3	4	4	4	5	5	6	7	7
56	3	3	4	4	5	5	6	7	7	8
57	3	4	4	5	5	6	6	7	8	9
58	4	4	5	5	6	6	7	8	9	9
59	4	5	5	6	6	7	8	9	9	10
60	4	5	6	6	7	8	9	10	10	11
61	5	6	6	7	8	9	10	10	11	13
62	5	6	7	8	9	10	11	12	13	14
63	6	7	8	9	10	11	12	13	14	15
64	7	8	8	9	10	12	13	14	15	17
65	7	8	9	10	12	13	14	15	17	18
66	8	9	10	12	13	14	15	17	18	20
67	9	10	11	13	14	15	17	18	20	22
68	10	11	13	14	15	17	19	20	22	24
69	11	12	14	15	17	19	20	22	24	26
70	12	14	15	17	19	20	22	24	26	28
71	13	15	17	18	20	22	24	26	28	30
72	15	17	18	20	22	24	26	28	30	32
73	16	18	20	22	24	26	28	31	33	35
74	18	20	22	24	26	28	31	33	35	37
75	19	22	24	26	28	31	33	35	38	40
76	21	24	26	28	31	33	36	38	40	43
77	23	26	28	31	33	36	38	41	43	45
78	25	28	31	33	36	38	41	43	46	48
79	28	30	33	36	38	41	44	46	48	51
80	30	33	36	38	41	44	46	49	51	53
81	32	35	38	41	44	47	49	51	54	56
82	35	38	41	44	47	49	52	54	56	58
83	38	41	44	47	49	52	54	57	59	61
84	40	44	47	49	52	55	57	59	61	63
85	43	46	49	52	55	57	59	62	63	65
86	46	49	52	55	57	60	62	64	66	67
87	48	52	55	57	60	62	64	66	68	69
88	51	54	57	60	62	64	66	68	70	71
89	54	57	60	62	65	67	68	70	72	73
90	56	59	62	64	67	69	70	72	74	75
91	59	62	64	67	69	71	72	74	75	76
92	61	64	66	69	71	72	74	75	77	78
93	63	66	68	70	72	74	75	77	78	79
94	65	68	70	72	74	75	77	78	79	80
95	67	69	72	74	75	77	78	79	81	82
96	69	71	73	75	77	78	80	81	82	83
97	70	73	75	77	78	80	81	82	83	84
98	72	74	76	78	79	81	82	83	84	85

| Age | Years— | | | | | | | | | |
	11	12	13	14	15	16	17	18	19	20
99	74	76	78	79	81	82	83	84	85	86
100	75	78	79	81	82	83	84	85	86	86
101	77	79	81	82	83	84	85	86	87	87
102	79	81	82	83	84	85	86	87	88	88
103	80	82	83	85	86	87	87	88	89	89
104	82	84	85	86	87	88	88	89	90	90
105	84	85	86	87	88	89	89	90	90	91
106	85	86	87	88	89	90	90	91	91	92
107	87	88	89	89	90	91	91	92	92	93
108	88	89	90	90	91	92	92	93	93	93
109	89	90	91	92	92	93	93	93	94	94
110	90	91	92	92	93	93	94	94	94	95
111	92	92	93	93	94	94	95	95	95	95
112	93	93	94	94	95	95	95	96	96	96
113	94	94	95	95	95	96	96	96	96	97
114	95	95	95	96	96	96	97	97	97	97
115	95	96	96	96	97	97	97	97	97	98

TABLE VII.—PERCENT VALUE OF REFUND FEATURE; DURATION OF GUARANTEED AMOUNT—Continued

Age	21	22	23	24	25	26	27	28	29	30
5	0	0	0	0	0	0	0	0	0	0
6	0	0	0	0	0	0	0	0	0	0
7	0	0	0	0	0	0	0	0	0	0
8	0	0	0	0	0	0	0	0	0	1
9	0	0	0	0	0	0	0	0	1	1
10	0	0	0	0	0	0	0	1	1	1
11	0	0	0	0	0	0	1	1	1	1
12	0	0	0	0	0	0	1	1	1	1
13	0	0	0	0	0	1	1	1	1	1
14	0	0	0	0	1	1	1	1	1	1
15	0	0	0	1	1	1	1	1	1	1
16	0	0	1	1	1	1	1	1	1	1
17	0	0	1	1	1	1	1	1	1	1
18	0	1	1	1	1	1	1	1	1	1
19	1	1	1	1	1	1	1	1	1	1
20	1	1	1	1	1	1	1	1	1	1
21	1	1	1	1	1	1	1	1	1	1
22	1	1	1	1	1	1	1	1	1	1
23	1	1	1	1	1	1	1	1	1	1
24	1	1	1	1	1	1	1	1	1	1
25	1	1	1	1	1	1	1	1	1	1
26	1	1	1	1	1	1	1	1	1	1
27	1	1	1	1	1	1	1	1	1	2
28	1	1	1	1	1	1	1	1	2	2
29	1	1	1	1	1	1	1	2	2	2
30	1	1	1	1	1	1	2	2	2	2
31	1	1	1	1	1	2	2	2	2	2
32	1	1	1	1	2	2	2	2	2	2
33	1	1	1	2	2	2	2	2	2	2
34	1	1	2	2	2	2	2	2	2	3
35	1	2	2	2	2	2	2	2	3	3
36	2	2	2	2	2	2	2	3	3	3
37	2	2	2	2	2	2	3	3	3	3
38	2	2	2	2	2	3	3	3	3	4
39	2	2	2	2	3	3	3	3	4	4
40	2	2	3	3	3	3	3	4	4	4
41	2	3	3	3	3	3	4	4	4	5
42	3	3	3	3	3	4	4	4	5	5
43	3	3	3	4	4	4	4	5	5	6
44	3	3	4	4	4	4	5	5	6	6
45	3	4	4	4	5	5	5	6	6	7
46	4	4	4	5	5	5	6	6	7	7
47	4	4	5	5	5	6	6	7	7	8
48	4	5	5	5	6	6	7	7	8	9
49	5	5	5	6	6	7	8	8	9	10
50	5	5	6	6	7	8	8	9	10	10
51	5	6	6	7	8	8	9	10	11	11
52	6	7	7	8	8	9	10	11	11	12
53	7	7	8	8	9	10	11	12	13	14
54	7	8	8	9	10	11	12	13	14	15
55	8	9	9	10	11	12	13	14	15	16
56	9	9	10	11	12	13	14	15	16	18
57	9	10	11	12	13	14	15	17	18	19
58	10	11	12	13	14	16	17	18	19	21
59	11	12	13	15	16	17	18	20	21	22
60	12	14	15	16	17	19	20	21	23	24
61	14	15	16	17	19	20	22	23	25	26
62	15	16	18	19	20	22	23	25	27	28
63	16	18	19	21	22	24	25	27	29	30
64	18	19	21	23	24	26	28	29	31	33
65	20	21	23	25	26	28	30	31	33	35
66	21	23	25	27	28	30	32	34	35	37
67	23	25	27	29	31	32	34	36	38	40
68	25	27	29	31	33	35	37	38	40	42
69	28	29	31	33	35	37	39	41	43	44
70	30	32	34	36	38	40	42	43	45	47
71	32	34	36	38	40	42	44	46	47	49
72	35	37	39	41	43	45	46	48	50	51
73	37	39	41	43	45	47	49	51	52	54
74	40	42	44	46	48	50	51	53	54	56
75	42	44	46	48	50	52	54	55	57	58
76	45	47	49	51	53	54	56	58	59	60
77	47	50	51	53	55	57	58	60	61	62
78	50	52	54	56	57	59	61	62	63	64
79	53	55	56	58	60	61	63	64	65	66
80	55	57	59	60	62	63	65	66	67	68
81	58	59	61	63	64	66	67	68	69	70
82	60	62	63	65	66	68	69	70	71	72
83	62	64	66	67	68	70	71	72	73	74
84	65	66	68	69	70	71	72	73	74	75
85	67	68	70	71	72	73	74	75	76	77
86	69	70	72	73	74	75	76	77	77	78
87	71	72	73	75	76	76	77	78	79	80
88	73	74	75	76	77	78	79	80	80	81
89	74	76	77	78	79	79	80	81	81	82
90	76	77	78	79	80	81	81	82	83	83
91	78	79	79	80	81	82	83	83	84	84
92	79	80	81	82	82	83	84	84	85	85
93	80	81	82	83	83	84	85	85	86	86
94	81	82	83	84	84	85	85	86	86	87
95	82	83	84	85	85	86	86	87	87	88
96	83	84	85	86	86	87	87	88	88	88
97	84	85	86	86	87	87	88	88	89	89
98	85	86	87	87	88	88	89	89	89	90

Reg. § 1.72-9

Age	21	22	23	24	25	26	27	28	29	30
99	86	87	87	88	88	89	89	90	90	90
100	87	88	88	89	89	90	90	90	91	91
101	88	89	89	90	90	90	91	91	91	92
102	89	89	90	90	91	91	91	92	92	92
103	90	90	91	91	91	92	92	92	93	93
104	91	91	91	92	92	92	93	93	93	93
105	91	92	92	92	93	93	93	94	94	94
106	92	93	93	93	93	94	94	94	94	95
107	93	93	94	94	94	94	95	95	95	95
108	94	94	94	94	95	95	95	95	95	96
109	94	95	95	95	95	95	96	96	96	96
110	95	95	95	96	96	96	96	96	96	96
111	96	96	96	96	96	96	97	97	97	97
112	96	96	96	97	97	97	97	97	97	97
113	97	97	97	97	97	97	97	98	98	98
114	97	97	97	98	98	98	98	98	98	98
115	98	98	98	98	98	98	98	98	98	98

TABLE VII.—PERCENT VALUE OF REFUND FEATURE; DURATION OF GUARANTEED AMOUNT—Continued

Age	Years—									
	31	32	33	34	35	36	37	38	39	40
5	0	1	1	1	1	1	1	1	1	1
6	0	1	1	1	1	1	1	1	1	1
7	1	1	1	1	1	1	1	1	1	1
8	1	1	1	1	1	1	1	1	1	1
9	1	1	1	1	1	1	1	1	1	1
10	1	1	1	1	1	1	1	1	1	1
11	1	1	1	1	1	1	1	1	1	1
12	1	1	1	1	1	1	1	1	1	1
13	1	1	1	1	1	1	1	1	1	1
14	1	1	1	1	1	1	1	1	1	1
15	1	1	1	1	1	1	1	1	1	1
16	1	1	1	1	1	1	1	1	1	1
17	1	1	1	1	1	1	1	1	1	1
18	1	1	1	1	1	1	1	1	1	1
19	1	1	1	1	1	1	1	1	1	2
20	1	1	1	1	1	1	1	2	2	2
21	1	1	1	1	1	1	2	2	2	2
22	1	1	1	1	1	2	2	2	2	2
23	1	1	1	2	2	2	2	2	2	2
24	1	1	2	2	2	2	2	2	2	2
25	1	2	2	2	2	2	2	2	2	3
26	2	2	2	2	2	2	2	2	3	3
27	2	2	2	2	2	2	2	3	3	3
28	2	2	2	2	2	2	3	3	3	3
29	2	2	2	2	2	3	3	3	3	4
30	2	2	2	3	3	3	3	3	4	4
31	2	2	3	3	3	3	3	4	4	4
32	2	3	3	3	3	3	4	4	4	5
33	3	3	3	3	3	4	4	4	5	5
34	3	3	3	3	4	4	4	5	5	5
35	3	3	3	4	4	4	5	5	5	6
36	3	4	4	4	4	5	5	5	6	6
37	4	4	4	4	5	5	6	6	6	7
38	4	4	5	5	5	6	6	7	7	8
39	4	5	5	5	6	6	7	7	8	8
40	5	5	5	6	6	7	7	8	8	9
41	5	5	6	6	7	7	8	9	9	10
42	6	6	6	7	7	8	9	9	10	11
43	6	7	7	8	8	9	9	10	11	12
44	7	7	8	8	9	10	10	11	12	13
45	7	8	8	9	10	10	11	12	13	14
46	8	9	9	10	11	11	12	13	14	15
47	9	9	10	11	12	12	13	14	15	16
48	9	10	11	12	13	14	15	16	17	18
49	10	11	12	13	14	15	16	17	18	19
50	11	12	13	14	15	16	17	18	20	21
51	12	13	14	15	16	17	19	20	21	22
52	13	14	15	17	18	19	20	21	23	24
53	15	16	17	18	19	20	22	23	24	26
54	16	17	18	19	21	22	23	25	26	28
55	17	18	20	21	22	24	25	27	28	30
56	19	20	21	23	24	26	27	29	30	32
57	20	22	23	25	26	28	29	31	32	34
58	22	24	25	27	28	30	31	33	34	36
59	24	25	27	28	30	32	33	35	36	38
60	26	27	29	31	32	34	35	37	38	40
61	28	29	31	33	34	36	37	39	40	42
62	30	32	33	35	36	38	40	41	42	44
63	32	34	35	37	39	40	42	43	45	46
64	34	36	38	39	41	42	44	45	47	48
65	37	38	40	42	43	45	46	47	49	50
66	39	41	42	44	45	47	48	50	51	52
67	41	43	45	46	48	49	50	52	53	54
68	44	45	47	48	50	51	52	54	55	56
69	46	48	49	51	52	53	54	56	57	58
70	48	50	51	53	54	55	57	58	59	60
71	51	52	54	55	56	57	59	60	61	62
72	53	54	56	57	58	59	60	62	62	63
73	55	57	58	59	60	61	62	63	64	65
74	57	59	60	61	62	63	64	65	66	67
75	59	61	62	63	64	65	66	67	68	69
76	62	63	64	65	66	67	68	69	69	70
77	64	65	66	67	68	69	70	70	71	72
78	66	67	68	69	70	70	71	72	73	73
79	67	68	69	70	71	72	73	73	74	75
80	69	70	71	72	73	74	74	75	76	76
81	71	72	73	74	74	75	76	76	77	78
82	73	74	74	75	76	77	77	78	78	79
83	74	75	76	77	77	78	79	79	80	80
84	76	77	77	78	79	79	80	80	81	81
85	78	78	79	79	80	81	81	82	82	83
86	79	80	80	81	81	82	82	83	83	84
87	80	81	81	82	83	83	83	84	84	85
88	82	82	83	83	84	84	85	85	85	86
89	83	83	84	84	85	85	85	86	86	87
90	84	84	85	85	86	86	86	87	87	87
91	85	85	86	86	87	87	87	88	88	88
92	86	86	87	87	87	88	88	88	89	89
93	87	87	87	88	88	88	89	89	89	90
94	87	88	88	88	89	89	89	90	90	90
95	88	88	89	89	89	90	90	90	91	91
96	89	89	89	90	90	90	91	91	91	91
97	89	90	90	90	91	91	91	91	92	92
98	90	90	91	91	91	91	92	92	92	92

Reg. §1.72-9

Age	Years—									
	31	32	33	34	35	36	37	38	39	40
99	91	91	91	92	92	92	92	92	93	93
100	91	92	92	92	92	92	93	93	93	93
101	92	92	92	93	93	93	93	93	94	94
102	92	93	93	93	93	94	94	94	94	94
103	93	93	93	94	94	94	94	94	94	95
104	94	94	94	94	94	95	95	95	95	95
105	94	94	95	95	95	95	95	95	95	95
106	95	95	95	95	95	95	96	96	96	96
107	95	95	96	96	96	96	96	96	97	97
108	96	96	96	96	96	97	97	97	97	97
109	96	96	96	97	97	97	97	97	97	97
110	97	97	97	97	97	97	98	98	98	98
111	97	97	97	98	98	98	98	98	98	98
112	97	97	98	98	98	98	98	98	98	98
113	98	98	98	98	98	98	98	98	98	99
114	98	98	98	98	98	98	98	98	99	99
115	98	98	98	99	99	99	99	99	99	99

TABLE VIII.—TEMPORARY LIFE ANNUITIES; [1] ONE LIFE—EXPECTED RETURN MULTIPLES
(See footnote at end of tables)
Temporary Period—Maximum Duration of Annuity

Age	Years—									
	1	2	3	4	5	6	7	8	9	10
5	1.0	2.0	3.0	4.0	5.0	6.0	7.0	8.0	9.0	10.0
6	1.0	2.0	3.0	4.0	5.0	6.0	7.0	8.0	9.0	10.0
7	1.0	2.0	3.0	4.0	5.0	6.0	7.0	8.0	9.0	10.0
8	1.0	2.0	3.0	4.0	5.0	6.0	7.0	8.0	9.0	10.0
9	1.0	2.0	3.0	4.0	5.0	6.0	7.0	8.0	9.0	10.0
10	1.0	2.0	3.0	4.0	5.0	6.0	7.0	8.0	9.0	10.0
11	1.0	2.0	3.0	4.0	5.0	6.0	7.0	8.0	9.0	10.0
12	1.0	2.0	3.0	4.0	5.0	6.0	7.0	8.0	9.0	10.0
13	1.0	2.0	3.0	4.0	5.0	6.0	7.0	8.0	9.0	10.0
14	1.0	2.0	3.0	4.0	5.0	6.0	7.0	8.0	9.0	10.0
15	1.0	2.0	3.0	4.0	5.0	6.0	7.0	8.0	9.0	10.0
16	1.0	2.0	3.0	4.0	5.0	6.0	7.0	8.0	9.0	10.0
17	1.0	2.0	3.0	4.0	5.0	6.0	7.0	8.0	9.0	10.0
18	1.0	2.0	3.0	4.0	5.0	6.0	7.0	8.0	9.0	10.0
19	1.0	2.0	3.0	4.0	5.0	6.0	7.0	8.0	9.0	10.0
20	1.0	2.0	3.0	4.0	5.0	6.0	7.0	8.0	9.0	10.0
21	1.0	2.0	3.0	4.0	5.0	6.0	7.0	8.0	9.0	10.0
22	1.0	2.0	3.0	4.0	5.0	6.0	7.0	8.0	9.0	10.0
23	1.0	2.0	3.0	4.0	5.0	6.0	7.0	8.0	9.0	10.0
24	1.0	2.0	3.0	4.0	5.0	6.0	7.0	8.0	9.0	10.0
25	1.0	2.0	3.0	4.0	5.0	6.0	7.0	8.0	9.0	10.0
26	1.0	2.0	3.0	4.0	5.0	6.0	7.0	8.0	9.0	10.0
27	1.0	2.0	3.0	4.0	5.0	6.0	7.0	8.0	9.0	10.0
28	1.0	2.0	3.0	4.0	5.0	6.0	7.0	8.0	9.0	10.0
29	1.0	2.0	3.0	4.0	5.0	6.0	7.0	8.0	9.0	10.0
30	1.0	2.0	3.0	4.0	5.0	6.0	7.0	8.0	9.0	10.0
31	1.0	2.0	3.0	4.0	5.0	6.0	7.0	8.0	9.0	10.0
32	1.0	2.0	3.0	4.0	5.0	6.0	7.0	8.0	9.0	10.0
33	1.0	2.0	3.0	4.0	5.0	6.0	7.0	8.0	9.0	10.0
34	1.0	2.0	3.0	4.0	5.0	6.0	7.0	8.0	9.0	10.0
35	1.0	2.0	3.0	4.0	5.0	6.0	7.0	8.0	9.0	10.0
36	1.0	2.0	3.0	4.0	5.0	6.0	7.0	8.0	9.0	10.0
37	1.0	2.0	3.0	4.0	5.0	6.0	7.0	8.0	9.0	9.9
38	1.0	2.0	3.0	4.0	5.0	6.0	7.0	8.0	9.0	9.9
39	1.0	2.0	3.0	4.0	5.0	6.0	7.0	8.0	9.0	9.9
40	1.0	2.0	3.0	4.0	5.0	6.0	7.0	8.0	8.9	9.9
41	1.0	2.0	3.0	4.0	5.0	6.0	7.0	8.0	8.9	9.9
42	1.0	2.0	3.0	4.0	5.0	6.0	7.0	8.0	8.9	9.9
43	1.0	2.0	3.0	4.0	5.0	6.0	7.0	7.9	8.9	9.9
44	1.0	2.0	3.0	4.0	5.0	6.0	7.0	7.9	8.9	9.9
45	1.0	2.0	3.0	4.0	5.0	6.0	7.0	7.9	8.9	9.9
46	1.0	2.0	3.0	4.0	5.0	6.0	6.9	7.9	8.9	9.9
47	1.0	2.0	3.0	4.0	5.0	6.0	6.9	7.9	8.9	9.9
48	1.0	2.0	3.0	4.0	5.0	6.0	6.9	7.9	8.9	9.9
49	1.0	2.0	3.0	4.0	5.0	6.0	6.9	7.9	8.9	9.8
50	1.0	2.0	3.0	4.0	5.0	5.9	6.9	7.9	8.9	9.8
51	1.0	2.0	3.0	4.0	5.0	5.9	6.9	7.9	8.9	9.8
52	1.0	2.0	3.0	4.0	5.0	5.9	6.9	7.9	8.8	9.8
53	1.0	2.0	3.0	4.0	5.0	5.9	6.9	7.9	8.8	9.8
54	1.0	2.0	3.0	4.0	4.9	5.9	6.9	7.9	8.8	9.8
55	1.0	2.0	3.0	4.0	4.9	5.9	6.9	7.8	8.8	9.7
56	1.0	2.0	3.0	4.0	4.9	5.9	6.9	7.8	8.8	9.7
57	1.0	2.0	3.0	4.0	4.9	5.9	6.9	7.8	8.8	9.7
58	1.0	2.0	3.0	4.0	4.9	5.9	6.9	7.8	8.7	9.7
59	1.0	2.0	3.0	4.0	4.9	5.9	6.8	7.8	8.7	9.6
60	1.0	2.0	3.0	3.9	4.9	5.9	6.8	7.8	8.7	9.6
61	1.0	2.0	3.0	3.9	4.9	5.9	6.8	7.7	8.7	9.6
62	1.0	2.0	3.0	3.9	4.9	5.8	6.8	7.7	8.6	9.5
63	1.0	2.0	3.0	3.9	4.9	5.8	6.8	7.7	8.6	9.5
64	1.0	2.0	3.0	3.9	4.9	5.8	6.7	7.6	8.5	9.4
65	1.0	2.0	3.0	3.9	4.9	5.8	6.7	7.6	8.5	9.3
66	1.0	2.0	2.9	3.9	4.8	5.8	6.7	7.6	8.4	9.3
67	1.0	2.0	2.9	3.9	4.8	5.7	6.6	7.5	8.4	9.2
68	1.0	2.0	2.9	3.9	4.8	5.7	6.6	7.5	8.3	9.1
69	1.0	2.0	2.9	3.9	4.8	5.7	6.6	7.4	8.2	9.0
70	1.0	2.0	2.9	3.9	4.8	5.6	6.5	7.3	8.1	8.9
71	1.0	2.0	2.9	3.8	4.7	5.6	6.5	7.3	8.1	8.8
72	1.0	2.0	2.9	3.8	4.7	5.6	6.4	7.2	8.0	8.7
73	1.0	2.0	2.9	3.8	4.7	5.5	6.3	7.1	7.9	8.6
74	1.0	1.9	2.9	3.8	4.6	5.5	6.3	7.0	7.7	8.4
75	1.0	1.9	2.9	3.8	4.6	5.4	6.2	6.9	7.6	8.3
76	1.0	1.9	2.8	3.7	4.6	5.4	6.1	6.8	7.5	8.1
77	1.0	1.9	2.8	3.7	4.5	5.3	6.0	6.7	7.3	7.9
78	1.0	1.9	2.8	3.6	4.5	5.2	5.9	6.6	7.2	7.7
79	1.0	1.9	2.8	3.6	4.4	5.1	5.8	6.4	7.0	7.5
80	1.0	1.9	2.8	3.6	4.4	5.1	5.7	6.3	6.8	7.3
81	1.0	1.9	2.8	3.6	4.3	5.0	5.6	6.1	6.6	7.0
82	1.0	1.9	2.7	3.5	4.2	4.9	5.4	6.0	6.4	6.8
83	1.0	1.9	2.7	3.5	4.1	4.8	5.3	5.8	6.2	6.5
84	1.0	1.8	2.7	3.4	4.1	4.6	5.2	5.6	6.0	6.3
85	1.0	1.8	2.6	3.3	4.0	4.5	5.0	5.4	5.7	6.0
86	1.0	1.8	2.6	3.3	3.9	4.4	4.8	5.2	5.5	5.7
87	.9	1.8	2.5	3.2	3.8	4.3	4.7	5.0	5.3	5.5
88	.9	1.8	2.5	3.1	3.7	4.1	4.5	4.8	5.0	5.2
89	.9	1.8	2.5	3.1	3.6	4.0	4.3	4.6	4.8	4.9
90	.9	1.7	2.4	3.0	3.4	3.8	4.1	4.4	4.5	4.7
91	.9	1.7	2.4	2.9	3.3	3.7	4.0	4.2	4.3	4.4
92	.9	1.7	2.3	2.8	3.2	3.5	3.8	4.0	4.1	4.2
93	.9	1.7	2.3	2.7	3.1	3.4	3.6	3.8	3.9	4.0
94	.9	1.6	2.2	2.7	3.0	3.3	3.5	3.6	3.7	3.8
95	.9	1.6	2.2	2.6	2.9	3.1	3.3	3.4	3.5	3.6
96	.9	1.6	2.1	2.5	2.8	3.0	3.2	3.3	3.3	3.4

Age	Years—									
	1	2	3	4	5	6	7	8	9	10
97	.9	1.6	2.1	2.4	2.7	2.9	3.0	3.1	3.2	3.2
98	.9	1.5	2.0	2.4	2.6	2.8	2.9	3.0	3.0	3.0
99	.9	1.5	2.0	2.3	2.5	2.6	2.7	2.8	2.8	2.8
100	.9	1.5	1.9	2.2	2.4	2.5	2.6	2.6	2.6	2.7
101	.8	1.4	1.8	2.1	2.3	2.4	2.4	2.5	2.5	2.5
102	.8	1.4	1.8	2.0	2.1	2.2	2.3	2.3	2.3	2.3
103	.8	1.4	1.7	1.9	2.0	2.1	2.1	2.1	2.1	2.1
104	.8	1.3	1.6	1.8	1.9	1.9	1.9	1.9	1.9	1.9
105	.8	1.3	1.5	1.7	1.7	1.8	1.8	1.8	1.8	1.8
106	.8	1.2	1.4	1.5	1.6	1.6	1.6	1.6	1.6	1.6
107	.7	1.1	1.3	1.4	1.4	1.4	1.4	1.4	1.4	1.4
108	.7	1.1	1.2	1.3	1.3	1.3	1.3	1.3	1.3	1.3
109	.7	1.0	1.1	1.1	1.1	1.1	1.1	1.1	1.1	1.1
110	.7	.9	1.0	1.0	1.0	1.0	1.0	1.0	1.0	1.0
111	.6	.8	.9	.9	.9	.9	.9	.9	.9	.9
112	.6	.7	.8	.8	.8	.8	.8	.8	.8	.8
113	.6	.6	.7	.7	.7	.7	.7	.7	.7	.7
114	.5	.6	.6	.6	.6	.6	.6	.6	.6	.6
115	.5	.5	.5	.5	.5	.5	.5	.5	.5	.5

TABLE VIII.—TEMPORARY LIFE ANNUITIES; [1] ONE LIFE—EXPECTED RETURN MULTIPLES—Continued
(See footnote at end of tables)
Temporary Period—Maximum Duration of Annuity

Age	11	12	13	14	15	16	17	18	19	20
5	11.0	12.0	13.0	14.0	15.0	16.0	17.0	18.0	19.0	19.9
6	11.0	12.0	13.0	14.0	15.0	16.0	17.0	18.0	19.0	19.9
7	11.0	12.0	13.0	14.0	15.0	16.0	17.0	18.0	19.0	19.9
8	11.0	12.0	13.0	14.0	15.0	16.0	17.0	18.0	18.9	19.9
9	11.0	12.0	13.0	14.0	15.0	16.0	17.0	18.0	18.9	19.9
10	11.0	12.0	13.0	14.0	15.0	16.0	17.0	18.0	18.9	19.9
11	11.0	12.0	13.0	14.0	15.0	16.0	17.0	17.9	18.9	19.9
12	11.0	12.0	13.0	14.0	15.0	16.0	17.0	17.9	18.9	19.9
13	11.0	12.0	13.0	14.0	15.0	16.0	17.0	17.9	18.9	19.9
14	11.0	12.0	13.0	14.0	15.0	16.0	16.9	17.9	18.9	19.9
15	11.0	12.0	13.0	14.0	15.0	16.0	16.9	17.9	18.9	19.9
16	11.0	12.0	13.0	14.0	15.0	16.0	16.9	17.9	18.9	19.9
17	11.0	12.0	13.0	14.0	15.0	15.9	16.9	17.9	18.9	19.9
18	11.0	12.0	13.0	14.0	15.0	15.9	16.9	17.9	18.9	19.9
19	11.0	12.0	13.0	14.0	15.0	15.9	16.9	17.9	18.9	19.9
20	11.0	12.0	13.0	14.0	14.9	15.9	16.9	17.9	18.9	19.9
21	11.0	12.0	13.0	14.0	14.9	15.9	16.9	17.9	18.9	19.9
22	11.0	12.0	13.0	14.0	14.9	15.9	16.9	17.9	18.9	19.9
23	11.0	12.0	13.0	13.9	14.9	15.9	16.9	17.9	18.9	19.9
24	11.0	12.0	13.0	13.9	14.9	15.9	16.9	17.9	18.9	19.9
25	11.0	12.0	13.0	13.9	14.9	15.9	16.9	17.9	18.9	19.9
26	11.0	12.0	12.9	13.9	14.9	15.9	16.9	17.9	18.9	19.9
27	11.0	12.0	12.9	13.9	14.9	15.9	16.9	17.9	18.9	19.9
28	11.0	12.0	12.9	13.9	14.9	15.9	16.9	17.9	18.9	19.8
29	11.0	12.0	12.9	13.9	14.9	15.9	16.9	17.9	18.9	19.8
30	11.0	11.9	12.9	13.9	14.9	15.9	16.9	17.9	18.8	19.8
31	11.0	11.9	12.9	13.9	14.9	15.9	16.9	17.9	18.8	19.8
32	11.0	11.9	12.9	13.9	14.9	15.9	16.9	17.9	18.8	19.8
33	11.0	11.9	12.9	13.9	14.9	15.9	16.9	17.8	18.8	19.8
34	10.9	11.9	12.9	13.9	14.9	15.9	16.8	17.8	18.8	19.8
35	10.9	11.9	12.9	13.9	14.9	15.9	16.8	17.8	18.8	19.7
36	10.9	11.9	12.9	13.9	14.9	15.8	16.8	17.8	18.8	19.7
37	10.9	11.9	12.9	13.9	14.9	15.8	16.8	17.8	18.7	19.7
38	10.9	11.9	12.9	13.9	14.8	15.8	16.8	17.8	18.7	19.7
39	10.9	11.9	12.9	13.9	14.8	15.8	16.8	17.7	18.7	19.6
40	10.9	11.9	12.9	13.8	14.8	15.8	16.7	17.7	18.7	19.6
41	10.9	11.9	12.9	13.8	14.8	15.8	16.7	17.7	18.6	19.6
42	10.9	11.9	12.8	13.8	14.8	15.7	16.7	17.6	18.6	19.5
43	10.9	11.9	12.8	13.8	14.8	15.7	16.7	17.6	18.6	19.5
44	10.9	11.8	12.8	13.8	14.7	15.7	16.6	17.6	18.5	19.4
45	10.9	11.8	12.8	13.8	14.7	15.7	16.6	17.5	18.5	19.4
46	10.9	11.8	12.8	13.7	14.7	15.6	16.6	17.5	18.4	19.3
47	10.8	11.8	12.8	13.7	14.7	15.6	16.5	17.5	18.4	19.3
48	10.8	11.8	12.7	13.7	14.6	15.6	16.5	17.4	18.3	19.2
49	10.8	11.8	12.7	13.7	14.6	15.5	16.4	17.4	18.3	19.2
50	10.8	11.7	12.7	13.6	14.6	15.5	16.4	17.3	18.2	19.1
51	10.8	11.7	12.7	13.6	14.5	15.4	16.3	17.2	18.1	19.0
52	10.8	11.7	12.6	13.6	14.5	15.4	16.3	17.2	18.0	18.9
53	10.7	11.7	12.6	13.5	14.4	15.3	16.2	17.1	18.0	18.8
54	10.7	11.6	12.6	13.5	14.4	15.3	16.2	17.0	17.9	18.7
55	10.7	11.6	12.5	13.4	14.3	15.2	16.1	16.9	17.8	18.6
56	10.7	11.6	12.5	13.4	14.3	15.1	16.0	16.8	17.6	18.4
57	10.6	11.5	12.4	13.3	14.2	15.1	15.9	16.7	17.5	18.3
58	10.6	11.5	12.4	13.3	14.1	15.0	15.8	16.6	17.4	18.1
59	10.6	11.4	12.3	13.2	14.0	14.9	15.7	16.4	17.2	17.9
60	10.5	11.4	12.3	13.1	13.9	14.7	15.5	16.3	17.0	17.7
61	10.5	11.3	12.2	13.0	13.8	14.6	15.4	16.1	16.8	17.5
62	10.4	11.3	12.1	12.9	13.7	14.5	15.2	15.9	16.6	17.2
63	10.3	11.2	12.0	12.8	13.6	14.3	15.0	15.7	16.3	17.0
64	10.3	11.1	11.9	12.7	13.4	14.1	14.8	15.5	16.1	16.7
65	10.2	11.0	11.8	12.5	13.2	13.9	14.6	15.2	15.8	16.3
66	10.1	10.9	11.6	12.4	13.1	13.7	14.4	14.9	15.5	16.0
67	10.0	10.8	11.5	12.2	12.9	13.5	14.1	14.7	15.2	15.6
68	9.9	10.6	11.4	12.0	12.7	13.3	13.3	14.3	14.8	15.3
69	9.8	10.5	11.2	11.8	12.4	13.0	13.5	14.0	14.4	14.8
70	9.6	10.3	11.0	11.6	12.2	12.7	13.2	13.7	14.0	14.4
71	9.5	10.2	10.8	11.4	11.9	12.4	12.9	13.3	13.6	13.9
72	9.4	10.0	10.6	11.2	11.7	12.1	12.5	12.9	13.2	13.5
73	9.2	9.8	10.4	10.9	11.4	11.8	12.1	12.5	12.7	13.0
74	9.0	9.6	10.1	10.6	11.0	11.4	11.7	12.0	12.3	12.5
75	8.8	9.4	9.9	10.3	10.7	11.0	11.3	11.6	11.8	12.0
76	8.6	9.1	9.6	10.0	10.3	10.6	10.9	11.1	11.3	11.4
77	8.4	8.9	9.3	9.7	10.0	10.2	10.5	10.6	10.8	10.9
78	8.2	8.6	9.0	9.3	9.6	9.8	10.0	10.2	10.3	10.4
79	7.9	8.3	8.7	9.0	9.2	9.4	9.5	9.7	9.8	9.8
80	7.7	8.0	8.3	8.6	8.8	9.0	9.1	9.2	9.3	9.3
81	7.4	7.7	8.0	8.2	8.4	8.5	8.6	8.7	8.8	8.8
82	7.1	7.4	7.6	7.8	8.0	8.1	8.2	8.2	8.3	8.3
83	6.8	7.1	7.3	7.4	7.5	7.6	7.7	7.8	7.8	7.8
84	6.5	6.7	6.9	7.0	7.1	7.2	7.3	7.3	7.3	7.4
85	6.2	6.4	6.6	6.7	6.7	6.8	6.8	6.9	6.9	6.9
86	5.9	6.1	6.2	6.3	6.4	6.4	6.4	6.5	6.5	6.5
87	5.6	5.8	5.9	5.9	6.0	6.0	6.0	6.1	6.1	6.1
88	5.3	5.4	5.5	5.6	5.6	5.6	5.7	5.7	5.7	5.7
89	5.1	5.1	5.2	5.3	5.3	5.3	5.3	5.3	5.3	5.3
90	4.8	4.9	4.9	4.9	5.0	5.0	5.0	5.0	5.0	5.0
91	4.5	4.6	4.6	4.6	4.7	4.7	4.7	4.7	4.7	4.7
92	4.3	4.3	4.3	4.4	4.4	4.4	4.4	4.4	4.4	4.4
93	4.0	4.1	4.1	4.1	4.1	4.1	4.1	4.1	4.1	4.1
94	3.8	3.8	3.9	3.9	3.9	3.9	3.9	3.9	3.9	3.9
95	3.6	3.6	3.6	3.6	3.7	3.7	3.7	3.7	3.7	3.7
96	3.4	3.4	3.4	3.4	3.4	3.4	3.4	3.4	3.4	3.4

Age	Years—									
	11	12	13	14	15	16	17	18	19	20
97	3.2	3.2	3.2	3.2	3.2	3.2	3.2	3.2	3.2	3.2
98	3.0	3.0	3.0	3.0	3.0	3.0	3.0	3.0	3.0	3.0
99	2.8	2.8	2.8	2.8	2.8	2.8	2.8	2.8	2.8	2.8
100	2.7	2.7	2.7	2.7	2.7	2.7	2.7	2.7	2.7	2.7
101	2.5	2.5	2.5	2.5	2.5	2.5	2.5	2.5	2.5	2.5
102	2.3	2.3	2.3	2.3	2.3	2.3	2.3	2.3	2.3	2.3
103	2.1	2.1	2.1	2.1	2.1	2.1	2.1	2.1	2.1	2.1
104	1.9	1.9	1.9	1.9	1.9	1.9	1.9	1.9	1.9	1.9
105	1.8	1.8	1.8	1.8	1.8	1.8	1.8	1.8	1.8	1.8
106	1.6	1.6	1.6	1.6	1.6	1.6	1.6	1.6	1.6	1.6
107	1.4	1.4	1.4	1.4	1.4	1.4	1.4	1.4	1.4	1.4
108	1.3	1.3	1.3	1.3	1.3	1.3	1.3	1.3	1.3	1.3
109	1.1	1.1	1.1	1.1	1.1	1.1	1.1	1.1	1.1	1.1
110	1.0	1.0	1.0	1.0	1.0	1.0	1.0	1.0	1.0	1.0
111	.9	.9	.9	.9	.9	.9	.9	.9	.9	.9
112	.8	.8	.8	.8	.8	.8	.8	.8	.8	.8
113	.7	.7	.7	.7	.7	.7	.7	.7	.7	.7
114	.6	.6	.6	.6	.6	.6	.6	.6	.6	.6
115	.5	.5	.5	.5	.5	.5	.5	.5	.5	.5

TABLE VIII.—TEMPORARY LIFE ANNUITIES; [1] ONE LIFE—EXPECTED RETURN MULTIPLES—Continued
(See footnote at end of tables)
Temporary Period—Maximum Duration of Annuity

Age	Years—									
	21	22	23	24	25	26	27	28	29	30
5	20.9	21.9	22.9	23.9	24.9	25.9	26.9	27.9	28.9	29.9
6	20.9	21.9	22.9	23.9	24.9	25.9	26.9	27.9	28.9	29.9
7	20.9	21.9	22.9	23.9	24.9	25.9	26.9	27.9	28.9	29.9
8	20.9	21.9	22.9	23.9	24.9	25.9	26.9	27.9	28.9	29.9
9	20.9	21.9	22.9	23.9	24.9	25.9	26.9	27.9	28.9	29.8
10	20.9	21.9	22.9	23.9	24.9	25.9	26.9	27.9	28.8	29.8
11	20.9	21.9	22.9	23.9	24.9	25.9	26.9	27.9	28.8	29.8
12	20.9	21.9	22.9	23.9	24.9	25.9	26.9	27.8	28.8	29.8
13	20.9	21.9	22.9	23.9	24.9	25.9	26.9	27.8	28.8	29.8
14	20.9	21.9	22.9	23.9	24.9	25.9	26.8	27.8	28.8	29.8
15	20.9	21.9	22.9	23.9	24.9	25.9	26.8	27.8	28.8	29.8
16	20.9	21.9	22.9	23.9	24.9	25.8	26.8	27.8	28.8	29.8
17	20.9	21.9	22.9	23.9	24.9	25.8	26.8	27.8	28.8	29.8
18	20.9	21.9	22.9	23.9	24.8	25.8	26.8	27.8	28.8	29.7
19	20.9	21.9	22.9	23.9	24.8	25.8	26.8	27.8	28.8	29.7
20	20.9	21.9	22.9	23.8	24.8	25.8	26.8	27.8	28.7	29.7
21	20.9	21.9	22.9	23.8	24.8	25.8	26.8	27.8	28.7	29.7
22	20.9	21.9	22.8	23.8	24.8	25.8	26.8	27.7	28.7	29.7
23	20.9	21.9	22.8	23.8	24.8	25.8	26.7	27.7	28.7	29.7
24	20.9	21.8	22.8	23.8	24.8	25.8	26.7	27.7	28.7	29.6
25	20.9	21.8	22.8	23.8	24.8	25.7	26.7	27.7	28.6	29.6
26	20.8	21.8	22.8	23.8	24.8	25.7	26.7	27.7	28.6	29.6
27	20.8	21.8	22.8	23.8	24.7	25.7	26.7	27.6	28.6	29.5
28	20.8	21.8	22.8	23.7	24.7	25.7	26.6	27.6	28.6	29.5
29	20.8	21.8	22.8	23.7	24.7	25.7	26.6	27.6	28.5	29.5
30	20.8	21.8	22.7	23.7	24.7	25.6	26.6	27.5	28.5	29.4
31	20.8	21.8	22.7	23.7	24.6	25.6	26.6	27.5	28.4	29.4
32	20.8	21.7	22.7	23.7	24.6	25.6	26.5	27.5	28.4	29.3
33	20.8	21.7	22.7	23.6	24.6	25.5	26.5	27.4	28.4	29.3
34	20.7	21.7	22.7	23.6	24.6	25.5	26.4	27.4	28.3	29.2
35	20.7	21.7	22.6	23.6	24.5	25.5	26.4	27.3	28.2	29.2
36	20.7	21.6	22.6	23.5	24.5	25.4	26.3	27.3	28.2	29.1
37	20.7	21.6	22.6	23.5	24.4	25.4	26.3	27.2	28.1	29.0
38	20.6	21.6	22.5	23.4	24.4	25.3	26.2	27.1	28.0	28.9
39	20.6	21.5	22.5	23.4	24.3	25.2	26.1	27.0	27.9	28.8
40	20.6	21.5	22.4	23.3	24.3	25.2	26.1	27.0	27.8	28.7
41	20.5	21.4	22.4	23.3	24.2	25.1	26.0	26.9	27.7	28.6
42	20.5	21.4	22.3	23.2	24.1	25.0	25.9	26.8	27.6	28.5
43	20.4	21.3	22.2	23.2	24.0	24.9	25.8	26.6	27.5	28.3
44	20.4	21.3	22.2	23.1	24.0	24.8	25.7	26.5	27.3	28.2
45	20.3	21.2	22.1	23.0	23.9	24.7	25.6	26.4	27.2	28.0
46	20.2	21.1	22.0	22.9	23.8	24.6	25.4	26.2	27.0	27.8
47	20.2	21.1	21.9	22.8	23.6	24.5	25.3	26.1	26.8	27.6
48	20.1	21.0	21.8	22.7	23.5	24.3	25.1	25.9	26.6	27.4
49	20.0	20.9	21.7	22.6	23.4	24.2	25.0	25.7	26.4	27.1
50	19.9	20.8	21.6	22.4	23.2	24.0	24.8	25.5	26.2	26.9
51	19.8	20.7	21.5	22.3	23.1	23.8	24.6	25.3	25.9	26.6
52	19.7	20.6	21.4	22.1	22.9	23.6	24.3	25.0	25.7	26.3
53	19.6	20.4	21.2	22.0	22.7	23.4	24.1	24.7	25.3	25.9
54	19.5	20.3	21.0	21.8	22.5	23.2	23.8	24.4	25.0	25.6
55	19.3	20.1	20.8	21.6	22.2	22.9	23.5	24.1	24.6	25.2
56	19.2	19.9	20.6	21.3	22.0	22.6	23.2	23.7	24.3	24.7
57	19.0	19.7	20.4	21.1	21.7	22.3	22.8	23.4	23.8	24.3
58	18.8	19.5	20.2	20.8	21.4	21.9	22.5	22.9	23.4	23.8
59	18.6	19.3	19.9	20.5	21.1	21.6	22.0	22.5	22.9	23.2
60	18.4	19.0	19.6	20.2	20.7	21.2	21.6	22.0	22.4	22.7
61	18.1	18.7	19.3	19.8	20.3	20.7	21.1	21.5	21.8	22.1
62	17.8	18.4	18.9	19.4	19.9	20.3	20.6	21.0	21.2	21.5
63	17.5	18.1	18.5	19.0	19.4	19.8	20.1	20.4	20.6	20.8
64	17.2	17.7	18.1	18.6	18.9	19.3	19.5	19.8	20.0	20.2
65	16.8	17.3	17.7	18.1	18.4	18.7	18.9	19.2	19.3	19.5
66	16.5	16.9	17.3	17.6	17.9	18.1	18.3	18.5	18.7	18.8
67	16.1	16.4	16.8	17.1	17.3	17.5	17.7	17.9	18.0	18.1
68	15.6	16.0	16.3	16.5	16.7	16.9	17.1	17.2	17.3	17.4
69	15.2	15.5	15.7	16.0	16.1	16.3	16.4	16.5	16.6	16.7
70	14.7	15.0	15.2	15.4	15.5	15.7	15.8	15.8	15.9	15.9
71	14.2	14.4	14.6	14.8	14.9	15.0	15.1	15.2	15.2	15.2
72	13.7	13.9	14.1	14.2	14.3	14.4	14.4	14.5	14.5	14.5
73	13.2	13.3	13.5	13.6	13.7	13.7	13.8	13.8	13.8	13.9
74	12.6	12.8	12.9	13.0	13.0	13.1	13.1	13.1	13.2	13.2
75	12.1	12.2	12.3	12.4	12.4	12.5	12.5	12.5	12.5	12.5
76	11.5	11.6	11.7	11.8	11.8	11.8	11.8	11.9	11.9	11.9
77	11.0	11.1	11.1	11.2	11.2	11.2	11.2	11.2	11.2	11.2
78	10.4	10.5	10.5	10.6	10.6	10.6	10.6	10.6	10.6	10.6
79	9.9	9.9	10.0	10.0	10.0	10.0	10.0	10.0	10.0	10.0
80	9.4	9.4	9.4	9.4	9.5	9.5	9.5	9.5	9.5	9.5
81	8.8	8.9	8.9	8.9	8.9	8.9	8.9	8.9	8.9	8.9
82	8.3	8.4	8.4	8.4	8.4	8.4	8.4	8.4	8.4	8.4
83	7.8	7.9	7.9	7.9	7.9	7.9	7.9	7.9	7.9	7.9
84	7.4	7.4	7.4	7.4	7.4	7.4	7.4	7.4	7.4	7.4
85	6.9	6.9	6.9	6.9	6.9	6.9	6.9	6.9	6.9	6.9
86	6.5	6.5	6.5	6.5	6.5	6.5	6.5	6.5	6.5	6.5
87	6.1	6.1	6.1	6.1	6.1	6.1	6.1	6.1	6.1	6.1
88	5.7	5.7	5.7	5.7	5.7	5.7	5.7	5.7	5.7	5.7
89	5.3	5.3	5.3	5.3	5.3	5.3	5.3	5.3	5.3	5.3
90	5.0	5.0	5.0	5.0	5.0	5.0	5.0	5.0	5.0	5.0
91	4.7	4.7	4.7	4.7	4.7	4.7	4.7	4.7	4.7	4.7
92	4.4	4.4	4.4	4.4	4.4	4.4	4.4	4.4	4.4	4.4
93	4.1	4.1	4.1	4.1	4.1	4.1	4.1	4.1	4.1	4.1
94	3.9	3.9	3.9	3.9	3.9	3.9	3.9	3.9	3.9	3.9
95	3.7	3.7	3.7	3.7	3.7	3.7	3.7	3.7	3.7	3.7
96	3.4	3.4	3.4	3.4	3.4	3.4	3.4	3.4	3.4	3.4

Age	Years—									
	21	22	23	24	25	26	27	28	29	30
97	3.2	3.2	3.2	3.2	3.2	3.2	3.2	3.2	3.2	3.2
98	3.0	3.0	3.0	3.0	3.0	3.0	3.0	3.0	3.0	3.0
99	2.8	2.8	2.8	2.8	2.8	2.8	2.8	2.8	2.8	2.8
100	2.7	2.7	2.7	2.7	2.7	2.7	2.7	2.7	2.7	2.7
101	2.5	2.5	2.5	2.5	2.5	2.5	2.5	2.5	2.5	2.5
102	2.3	2.3	2.3	2.3	2.3	2.3	2.3	2.3	2.3	2.3
103	2.1	2.1	2.1	2.1	2.1	2.1	2.1	2.1	2.1	2.1
104	1.9	1.9	1.9	1.9	1.9	1.9	1.9	1.9	1.9	1.9
105	1.8	1.8	1.8	1.8	1.8	1.8	1.8	1.8	1.8	1.8
106	1.6	1.6	1.6	1.6	1.6	1.6	1.6	1.6	1.6	1.6
107	1.4	1.4	1.4	1.4	1.4	1.4	1.4	1.4	1.4	1.4
108	1.3	1.3	1.3	1.3	1.3	1.3	1.3	1.3	1.3	1.3
109	1.1	1.1	1.1	1.1	1.1	1.1	1.1	1.1	1.1	1.1
110	1.0	1.0	1.0	1.0	1.0	1.0	1.0	1.0	1.0	1.0
111	.9	.9	.9	.9	.9	.9	.9	.9	.9	.9
112	.8	.8	.8	.8	.8	.8	.8	.8	.8	.8
113	.7	.7	.7	.7	.7	.7	.7	.7	.7	.7
114	.6	.6	.6	.6	.6	.6	.6	.6	.6	.6
115	.5	.5	.5	.5	.5	.5	.5	.5	.5	.5

TABLE VIII.—TEMPORARY LIFE ANNUITIES; [1] ONE LIFE—EXPECTED RETURN MULTIPLES—Continued
(See footnote at end of tables)
Temporary Period—Maximum Duration of Annuity

Age	\\ \\ Years—									
	31	32	33	34	35	36	37	38	39	40
5	30.8	31.8	32.8	33.8	34.8	35.8	36.8	37.7	38.7	39.7
6	30.8	31.8	32.8	33.8	34.8	35.8	36.8	37.7	38.7	39.7
7	30.8	31.8	32.8	33.8	34.8	35.8	36.7	37.7	38.7	39.7
8	30.8	31.8	32.8	33.8	34.8	35.7	36.7	37.7	38.7	39.7
9	30.8	31.8	32.8	33.8	34.8	35.7	36.7	37.7	38.7	39.6
10	30.8	31.8	32.8	33.8	34.7	35.7	36.7	37.7	38.6	39.6
11	30.8	31.8	32.8	33.8	34.7	35.7	36.7	37.7	38.6	39.6
12	30.8	31.8	32.8	33.7	34.7	35.7	36.7	37.6	38.6	39.6
13	30.8	31.8	32.7	33.7	34.7	35.7	36.6	37.6	38.6	39.5
14	30.8	31.8	32.7	33.7	34.7	35.7	36.6	37.6	38.6	39.5
15	30.8	31.7	32.7	33.7	34.7	35.6	36.6	37.6	38.5	39.5
16	30.8	31.7	32.7	33.7	34.6	35.6	36.6	37.5	38.5	39.4
17	30.7	31.7	32.7	33.7	34.6	35.6	36.5	37.5	38.5	39.4
18	30.7	31.7	32.7	33.6	34.6	35.6	36.5	37.5	38.4	39.4
19	30.7	31.7	32.6	33.6	34.6	35.5	36.5	37.4	38.4	39.3
20	30.7	31.7	32.6	33.6	34.5	35.5	36.4	37.4	38.3	39.3
21	30.7	31.6	32.6	33.6	34.5	35.5	36.4	37.4	38.3	39.2
22	30.6	31.6	32.6	33.5	34.5	35.4	36.4	37.3	38.2	39.2
23	30.6	31.6	32.5	33.5	34.4	35.4	36.3	37.3	38.2	39.1
24	30.6	31.5	32.5	33.5	34.4	35.3	36.3	37.2	38.1	39.0
25	30.6	31.5	32.5	33.4	34.3	35.3	36.2	37.1	38.1	39.0
26	30.5	31.5	32.4	33.4	34.3	35.2	36.2	37.1	38.0	38.9
27	30.5	31.4	32.4	33.3	34.2	35.2	36.1	37.0	37.9	38.8
28	30.5	31.4	32.3	33.3	34.2	35.1	36.0	36.9	37.8	38.7
29	30.4	31.4	32.3	33.2	34.1	35.0	35.9	36.8	37.7	38.6
30	30.4	31.3	32.2	33.1	34.1	35.0	35.8	36.7	37.6	38.5
31	30.3	31.2	32.2	33.1	34.0	34.9	35.8	36.6	37.5	38.3
32	30.3	31.2	32.1	33.0	33.9	34.8	35.6	36.5	37.4	38.2
33	30.2	31.1	32.0	32.9	33.8	34.7	35.5	36.4	37.2	38.0
34	30.1	31.0	31.9	32.8	33.7	34.6	35.4	36.2	37.1	37.9
35	30.1	31.0	31.8	32.7	33.6	34.4	35.3	36.1	36.9	37.7
36	30.0	30.9	31.7	32.6	33.5	34.3	35.1	35.9	36.7	37.4
37	29.9	30.8	31.6	32.5	33.3	34.1	34.9	35.7	36.5	37.2
38	29.8	30.7	31.5	32.3	33.2	34.0	34.7	35.5	36.2	37.0
39	29.7	30.5	31.4	32.2	33.0	33.8	34.5	35.3	36.0	36.7
40	29.6	30.4	31.2	32.0	32.8	33.6	34.3	35.0	35.7	36.4
41	29.4	30.2	31.0	31.8	32.6	33.3	34.1	34.7	35.4	36.0
42	29.3	30.1	30.9	31.6	32.4	33.1	33.8	34.4	35.1	35.7
43	29.1	29.9	30.7	31.4	32.1	32.8	33.5	34.1	34.7	35.3
44	28.9	29.7	30.5	31.2	31.9	32.5	33.2	33.8	34.3	34.9
45	28.8	29.5	30.2	30.9	31.6	32.2	32.8	33.4	33.9	34.4
46	28.5	29.3	30.0	30.6	31.3	31.9	32.4	33.0	33.5	33.9
47	28.3	29.0	29.7	30.3	30.9	31.5	32.0	32.5	33.0	33.4
48	28.1	28.7	29.4	30.0	30.6	31.1	31.6	32.1	32.5	32.9
49	27.8	28.4	29.0	29.6	30.2	30.7	31.1	31.5	31.9	32.3
50	27.5	28.1	28.7	29.2	29.7	30.2	30.6	31.0	31.4	31.7
51	27.2	27.8	28.3	28.8	29.3	29.7	30.1	30.4	30.7	31.0
52	26.8	27.4	27.9	28.4	28.8	29.2	29.5	29.8	30.1	30.3
53	26.5	27.0	27.4	27.9	28.3	28.6	28.9	29.2	29.4	29.6
54	26.1	26.5	27.0	27.4	27.7	28.0	28.3	28.5	28.7	28.9
55	25.6	26.1	26.5	26.8	27.1	27.4	27.6	27.8	28.0	28.1
56	25.2	25.6	25.9	26.2	26.5	26.7	26.9	27.1	27.2	27.3
57	24.7	25.0	25.3	25.6	25.8	26.0	26.2	26.3	26.5	26.5
58	24.1	24.4	24.7	25.0	25.2	25.3	25.5	25.6	25.7	25.7
59	23.6	23.8	24.1	24.3	24.4	24.6	24.7	24.8	24.9	24.9
60	23.0	23.2	23.4	23.6	23.7	23.8	23.9	24.0	24.0	24.1
61	22.3	22.5	22.7	22.9	23.0	23.1	23.1	23.2	23.2	23.3
62	21.7	21.9	22.0	22.1	22.2	22.3	22.3	22.4	22.4	22.4
63	21.0	21.1	21.3	21.4	21.4	21.5	21.5	21.6	21.6	21.6
64	20.3	20.4	20.5	20.6	20.6	20.7	20.7	20.7	20.8	20.8
65	19.6	19.7	19.8	19.8	19.9	19.9	19.9	19.9	19.9	20.0
66	18.9	19.0	19.0	19.1	19.1	19.1	19.1	19.1	19.1	19.1
67	18.2	18.2	18.3	18.3	18.3	18.3	18.3	18.3	18.4	18.4
68	17.4	17.5	17.5	17.5	17.5	17.6	17.5	17.6	17.6	17.6
69	16.7	16.7	16.8	16.8	16.8	16.8	16.8	16.8	16.8	16.8
70	16.0	16.0	16.0	16.0	16.0	16.0	16.0	16.0	16.0	16.0
71	15.3	15.3	15.3	15.3	15.3	15.3	15.3	15.3	15.3	15.3
72	14.6	14.6	14.6	14.6	14.6	14.6	14.6	14.6	14.6	14.6
73	13.9	13.9	13.9	13.9	13.9	13.9	13.9	13.9	13.9	13.9
74	13.2	13.2	13.2	13.2	13.2	13.2	13.2	13.2	13.2	13.2
75	12.5	12.5	12.5	12.5	12.5	12.5	12.5	12.5	12.5	12.5
76	11.9	11.9	11.9	11.9	11.9	11.9	11.9	11.9	11.9	11.9
77	11.2	11.2	11.2	11.2	11.2	11.2	11.2	11.2	11.2	11.2
78	10.6	10.6	10.6	10.6	10.6	10.6	10.6	10.6	10.6	10.6
79	10.0	10.0	10.0	10.0	10.0	10.0	10.0	10.0	10.0	10.0
80	9.5	9.5	9.5	9.5	9.5	9.5	9.5	9.5	9.5	9.5
81	8.9	8.9	8.9	8.9	8.9	8.9	3.9	8.9	8.9	8.9
82	8.4	8.4	8.4	8.4	8.4	8.4	8.4	8.4	8.4	8.4
83	7.9	7.9	7.9	7.9	7.9	7.9	7.9	7.9	7.9	7.9
84	7.4	7.4	7.4	7.4	7.4	7.4	7.4	7.4	7.4	7.4
85	6.9	6.9	6.9	6.9	6.9	6.9	6.9	6.9	6.9	6.9
86	6.5	6.5	6.5	6.5	6.5	6.5	6.5	6.5	6.5	6.5
87	6.1	6.1	6.1	6.1	6.1	6.1	6.1	6.1	6.1	6.1
88	5.7	5.7	5.7	5.7	5.7	5.7	5.7	5.7	5.7	5.7
89	5.3	5.3	5.3	5.3	5.3	5.3	5.3	5.3	5.3	5.3
90	5.0	5.0	5.0	5.0	5.0	5.0	5.0	5.0	5.0	5.0
91	4.7	4.7	4.7	4.7	4.7	4.7	4.7	4.7	4.7	4.7
92	4.4	4.4	4.4	4.4	4.4	4.4	4.4	4.4	4.4	4.4
93	4.1	4.1	4.1	4.1	4.1	4.1	4.1	4.1	4.1	4.1
94	3.9	3.9	3.9	3.9	3.9	3.9	3.9	3.9	3.9	3.9
95	3.7	3.7	3.7	3.7	3.7	3.7	3.7	3.7	3.7	3.7
96	3.4	3.4	3.4	3.4	3.4	3.4	3.4	3.4	3.4	3.4

Age	Years— 31	32	33	34	35	36	37	38	39	40
97	3.2	3.2	3.2	3.2	3.2	3.2	3.2	3.2	3.2	3.2
98	3.0	3.0	3.0	3.0	3.0	3.0	3.0	3.0	3.0	3.0
99	2.8	2.8	2.8	2.8	2.8	2.8	2.8	2.8	2.8	2.8
100	2.7	2.7	2.7	2.7	2.7	2.7	2.7	2.7	2.7	2.7
101	2.5	2.5	2.5	2.5	2.5	2.5	2.5	2.5	2.5	2.5
102	2.3	2.3	2.3	2.3	2.3	2.3	2.3	2.3	2.3	2.3
103	2.1	2.1	2.1	2.1	2.1	2.1	2.1	2.1	2.1	2.1
104	1.9	1.9	1.9	1.9	1.9	1.9	1.9	1.9	1.9	1.9
105	1.8	1.8	1.8	1.8	1.8	1.8	1.8	1.8	1.8	1.8
106	1.6	1.6	1.6	1.6	1.6	1.6	1.6	1.6	1.6	1.6
107	1.4	1.4	1.4	1.4	1.4	1.4	1.4	1.4	1.4	1.4
108	1.3	1.3	1.3	1.3	1.3	1.3	1.3	1.3	1.3	1.3
109	1.1	1.1	1.1	1.1	1.1	1.1	1.1	1.1	1.1	1.1
110	1.0	1.0	1.0	1.0	1.0	1.0	1.0	1.0	1.0	1.0
111	.9	.9	.9	.9	.9	.9	.9	.9	.9	.9
112	.8	.8	.8	.8	.8	.8	.8	.8	.8	.8
113	.7	.7	.7	.7	.7	.7	.7	.7	.7	.7
114	.6	.6	.6	.6	.6	.6	.6	.6	.6	.6
115	.5	.5	.5	.5	.5	.5	.5	.5	.5	.5

1 The multiples in this table are not applicable to annuities for a term certain; for such cases see paragraph (c) of §1.72-5.

If (a) the terms of the contract involve a life or lives, and are such that the above tables cannot be correctly applied, and (b) the amounts received under the contract are at least partly "amounts received as an annuity" under a contract to which section 72 applies, the taxpayer may submit with his return an actuarial computation based upon the applicable annuity table (described below) with ages set back one year, showing the appropriate factors applied in his case, subject to the approval of the Commissioner upon examination of such return. The applicable annuity table is the 1937 Standard Annuity Table (if the investment in the contract does not include a post-June 1986 investment in the contract) or the gender-neutral version of the 1983 Basic Table (if the investment in the contract includes a post-June 1986 investment in the contract). In the case of a contract to which §1.72-6(d) (relating to contracts in which amounts were invested both before July 1, 1986, and after June 30, 1986) applies, the actuarial computation shall be based on both tables in accordance with the principles of §1.72-6(d). Computations involving factors to compensate for the effects of contingencies other than mortality, such as marriage or remarriage, re-employment, recovery from disability, or the like, will not be approved. [Reg. §1.72-9.]

☐ [T.D. 6211, 11-14-56. Amended by T.D. 6233, 5-14-57 and T.D. 8115, 12-16-86.]

[Reg. §1.72-10]

§1.72-10. Effect of transfer of contracts on investment in the contract.—(a) If a contract to which section 72 applies, or any interest therein, is transferred for a valuable consideration, by assignment or otherwise, only the actual value of the consideration given for such transfer and the amount of premiums or other consideration subsequently paid by the transferee shall be included in the transferee's aggregate of premiums or other consideration paid. In accordance with the provisions of section 72(g)(3) and paragraph (b) of §1.72-4, an annuity starting date shall be determined for the transferee without regard to the annuity starting date, if any, of the transferor. In determining the transferee's investment in the contract, the aggregate amount of premiums or other consideration paid shall be reduced by all amounts received by the transferee before the receipt of an amount as an annuity or before the annuity starting date, whichever is the later, to the extent that such amounts were excludable from his gross income under the applicable income tax law at the time of receipt. For the treatment of amounts received by the transferee subsequent to both the annuity starting date and the date of receipt of a payment as an annuity, but not received as annuity payments, see §1.72-11. For a limitation on adjustments to the basis of annuity contracts sold, see section 1021

(b) In the case of a transfer of such a contract without valuable consideration, the annuity starting date and the expected return under the contract shall be determined as though no such transfer had taken place. See paragraph (b) of §1.72-4. The transferee shall include the aggregate of premiums or other consideration paid or deemed to have been paid by his transferor in the aggregate of premiums or other consideration as though paid by him. In determining the transferee's investment in the contract, the transferee's aggregate amount of premiums or other consideration paid (as so found) shall be reduced by all amounts either received or deemed to have been received by himself or his transferor before the annuity starting date, or before the date on which an amount is first received as an annuity, whichever is the later, to the extent that such amounts were excludable from the gross income of the actual recipient under the applicable income tax law at the time of receipt. For treatment of amounts received subsequent to both the above dates by such transferee, but not received as annuity payments, see §1.72-11. [Reg. §1.72-10.]

☐ [T.D. 6211, 11-14-56.]

[Reg. §1.72-11]

§1.72-11. Amounts not received as annuity payments.—(a) Introductory.—(1) This section applies to amounts received under a contract to which section 72 applies if either:

(i) Paragraph (b) of §1.72-2 is inapplicable to such amounts.

(ii) Paragraph (b) of §1.72-2 is applicable but the annuity payments received differ either in amount, duration, or both, from those originally provided under the contract, or

(iii) Paragraph (b) of §1.72-2 is applicable, but such annuity payments are received by a beneficiary after the death of an annuitant (or annuitants) in full discharge of the obligation under the contract and solely because of a guarantee.

The payments referred to in subdivision (i) of this subparagraph include all amounts other than "amounts received as an annuity" as that term is defined in paragraph (b)(2) and (3) of §1.72-2. If such amounts are received as dividends or payments in the nature of dividends, or as a return of premiums, see paragraph (b) of this section. If such amounts are paid in full discharge of the obligation under the contract and are in the nature of a refund of the consideration, see paragraph (c) of this section. If such amounts are paid upon the surrender, redemption, or maturity of the contract, see paragraph (d) of this section. The payments referred to in subdivision (ii) of this subparagraph include all annuity payments which are paid as the result of a modification or an exchange of the annuity obligations originally provided under a contract for different annuity obligations (whether or not such modification or exchange is accompanied by the payment of an amount to which subdivision (i) of this subparagraph applies). If the duration of the new annuity obligations differs from the duration of the old annuity obligations, paragraph (e) of this section applies to the new annuity obligations and paragraph (d) of this section applies to any lump sum payment received. If, however, the duration of the new annuity obligations is the same as the duration of the old obligations, paragraph (f) of this section applies to the new obligations and to any lump sum received in connection therewith. The annuity payments referred to in subdivision (iii) of this subparagraph are annuity payments which are made to a beneficiary after the death of annuitant (or annuitants) in full discharge of the obligations under a contract because of a provision in the contract requiring the payment of a guaranteed amount or minimum number of payments for a fixed period; see paragraph (c) of this section.

(2) The principles of this section apply, to the extent appropriate thereto, to amounts paid which are taxable under section 72 (except, for taxable years beginning before January 1, 1964, section 72(e)(3)) in accordance with sections 402 and 403 and the regulations thereunder. However, if contributions used to purchase the contract include amounts for which a deduction was allowed under section 404 as contributions on behalf of an owner-employee, the rules of this section are modified by the rules of paragraph (b) of §1.72-17. Further, in applying the provisions of this section, the aggregate premiums or other consideration paid shall not include contributions on behalf of self-employed individuals to the extent that deductions were allowed under section 404 for such contributions. Nor shall the aggregate of premiums or other consideration paid include amounts used to purchase life, accident, health, or other insurance protection for an owner-employee. See paragraph (b)(4) of §1.72-16 and paragraph (c) of §1.72-17. The principles of this section also apply to payments made in the manner described in paragraph (b)(3)(i) of §1.72-2.

(b) Amounts received in the nature of dividends or similar distributions.—(1) if dividends (or payments in the nature of dividends or a return of premiums or other consideration) are received under a contract to which section 72 applies and such payments are received before the annuity starting date or before the date on which an amount is first received as an annuity, whichever is the later; such payments are includible in the gross income of the recipient only to the extent that they, taken together with all previous payments received under the contract which were excludable from the gross income of the recipient under the applicable income tax law, exceed the aggregate of premiums or other consideration paid or deemed to have been paid by the recipient. Such payments shall also be subtracted from the consideration paid (or deemed paid) both for the purpose of determining an exclusion ratio to be applied to subsequent amounts paid as an annuity and for the purpose of determining the applicability of section 72(d) and §1.72-13, relating to employee contributions recoverable in three years.

(2) If dividends or payments in the nature of dividends are paid under a contract to which section 72 applies and such payments are received on or after the annuity starting date or the date on which an amount is first received as an annuity, whichever is later, such payments shall be fully includible in the gross income of the recipient. The receipt of such payments shall not affect the aggregate of premiums or other consideration paid nor the amounts contributed or deemed to have been contributed by an employee as otherwise calculated for purposes of section 72. Since the investment in the contract and the expected return are not affected by a payment which is fully includible in the gross income of the recipient under this rule, the exclusion ratio will not be affected by such payment and will continue to be applied to amounts received as annuity payments in the future as though such payment had not been made. This subparagraph shall apply to amounts received under a contract described in paragraph (b)(3)(i) of §1.72-2 to the extent that the amounts received exceed the portion of the investment in the contract allocable to each taxable year in accordance with paragraph (d)(3) of §1.72-4. Hence, such excess is fully includible in the gross income of the recipient.

(c) *Amounts received in the nature of a refund of the consideration under a contract and in full discharge of the obligation thereof.*—(1) Any amount received under a contract to which section 72 applies, if it is at least in part a refund of the consideration paid, including amounts paya-

ble to a beneficiary after the death of an annuitant by reason of a provision in the contract for a life annuity with minimum period of payments certain or with a minimum amount which must be paid in any event, shall be considered an amount received in the nature of a refund of the consideration paid for such contract. If such an amount is in full discharge of an obligation to pay a fixed amount (whether in a lump sum or otherwise) or to pay amounts for a fixed number of years (including amounts described in paragraph (b)(3)(i) of §1.72-2), it shall be included in the gross income of the recipient only to the extent that it, when added to amounts previously received under the contract which were excludable from gross income under the law applicable at the time of receipt, exceeds the aggregate of premiums or other consideration paid. See section 73(e)(2)(A). This paragraph shall not apply if the total of the amounts to be paid in discharge of the obligation can in any event exceed the total of the annuity payments which would otherwise fully discharge the obligation. For rules to be applied in such a case, see paragraph (e) of this section.

(2) The principles of subparagraph (1) of this paragraph may be illustrated by the following examples:

Example (1). A, a male employee, retired on December 31, 1954, at the age of 60. A life annuity of $75 per month was payable to him beginning January 31, 1955. The annuity contract guaranteed that if A did not live for at least ten years after his retirement his beneficiary, B, would receive the monthly payments for any balance of such ten year period which remained at the date of A's death. Under section 72, A was deemed to have paid $3,600 toward the cost of the annuity. A lived for five years after his retirement receiving a total of $4,500 in annuity payments. After A's death, B began receiving the monthly payments of $75 beginning with the January 31, 1960 payment. B will exclude such payments from his gross income throughout 1960, 1961, and 1962, and will exclude only $18 of the first payment in 1963 from his gross income for that year. Thereafter, B will include the entire amount of all such payments in his gross income for the taxable year of receipt. This result is determined as follows:

A's investment in the contract (unadjusted)		$3,600
Multiple from Table III of §1.72-9 for male, age 60, where duration of guaranteed amount is 10 years (percent)	11	
Subtract value of the refund feature to the nearest dollar (11 percent of $3,600)		396
Investment in the contract adjusted for the present value of the refund feature without discount for interest		3,204
Aggregate of premiums or other consideration paid		3,600
A's exclusion ratio ($3,204 ÷ $16,380 [$900 × 18.2]) (percent)	19.6	
Subtract amount excludable during five years A received payments (19.6 percent of $4,500 [$900 × 5])		882
Remainder of aggregate of premiums or other consideration paid excludable from gross income of B under section 72(e)		2,718

As a result of the above computation, the number of payments to B which will exhaust the remainder of consideration paid which is excludable from gross income of the recipient is 36⁶/₂₅ ($2,718 ÷ $75) and B will exclude the payments from his gross income for three years, then exclude only $18 of the first payment for the fourth year from his gross income, and thereafter include the entire amount of all payments he receives in his gross income.

Example (2). The facts are the same as in example (1), except that B, the beneficiary, elects to receive $50 per month for his life in lieu of the payments guaranteed under the original contractual obligation. Since such amounts will be received as an annuity and may, because of the length of time B may live, exceed the amount guaranteed, they are not amounts to which this paragraph applies. See paragraph (e) of this section.

Example (3). The facts are the same as in example (1), except that B, the beneficiary, elects to receive the remaining guaranteed amount in installments which are larger or smaller than the $75 per month provided until, under the terms of the contract, the guaranteed amount is exhausted. The rule of subparagraph (1) of this paragraph and the computation illustrated in example (1) apply to such installments since the total of such installments will not exceed the original amount guaranteed to be paid at A's death in any event.

Example (4). C pays $12,000 for a contract providing that he is to be paid an annuity of $1,000 per year for 15 years. His exclusion ratio is therefore 80 percent ($12,000 ÷ $15,000). He directs that the annuity is to be paid to D, his beneficiary, if he should die before the full 15 year period has expired. C dies after 5 years and D is paid $1,000 in 1960. D will include $200 ($1,000 − $800 [80 percent of $1,000]) in his

gross income for the taxable year in which he receives the $1,000 since section 72(e) and this section do not apply to the annuity payments made in accordance with the provisions and during the term of the contract. D will continue with the same exclusion ratio used by C (80 percent).

Example (5). In 1954, E paid $50,000 into a fund and was promised an annual income for life the amount of which would depend in part upon the earnings realized from the investment of the fund in accordance with an agreed formula. The contract also specified that if E should die before ten years had elapsed, his beneficiary, F, would be paid the amounts determined annually under the formula until ten payments had been received by E and F together. E died in 1960, having received five payments totaling $30,000. Assuming that $22,000 of this amount was properly excludable from E's gross income prior to his death, F will exclude from his gross income the payments he receives until the taxable year in which his total receipts from the fund exceed $28,000 ($50,000 − $22,000). F will include any excess over the $28,000 in his gross income for that taxable year. Thereafter, F will include in his gross income the entire amount of any payments made to him from the fund.

Example (6). Assume the facts are the same as in example (1), except that the total investment in the contract is made after June 30, 1986, that A is to receive payments under the life annuity contract beginning on January 31, 1987, and that B will begin to receive the monthly payments on January 31, 1992. B will exclude the $75 monthly payments from gross income throughout 1992, 1993, and 1994. B will exclude only the first two monthly payments and $21 of the third monthly payment in 1995. This is determined as follows:

A's investment in the contract (unadjusted)	$3,600
Multiple from Table VII, age 60, 10 years (percent)	4
Subtract value of the refund feature (4 percent of $3,600)	$144
Investment in the contract adjusted for the present value of the refund feature without discount for interest	$3,456
Aggregate of premiums or other consideration paid	$3,600.00
A's exclusion ratio ($3,456 ÷ $21,780 [$900 × 24.2]) (percent)	15.9
Subtract amount excludable during five years A received payments (15.9 percent of $4,500 [$900 × 5])	$715.50
Remainder of aggregate of premiums or other consideration paid excludable from gross income of B under section 72(e)	$2,884.50

As a result of the above computation, the number of payments to B which will exhaust the remainder of consideration paid which is excludable from gross income of the recipient is $38^{23}/_{50}$ ($2,884.50 ÷ 75) and B will exclude the payments from gross income for three years, then exclude only the first two monthly payments and $34.50 of the third. Thereafter B shall include the entire amount of all payments received in gross income.

(3) For the purpose of applying the rule contained in subparagraph (1) of this paragraph, it is immaterial whether the recipient of the amount received in full discharge of the obligation is the same person as the recipient of amounts previously received under the contract which were excludable from gross income, except in the case of a contract transferred for a valuable consideration, with respect to which see paragraph (a) of § 1.72-10. For the limit on the tax, for taxable years beginning before January 1, 1964, attributable to the receipt of a lump sum to which this paragraph applies, see paragraph (g) of this section.

(d) *Amounts received upon the surrender, redemption, or maturity of a contract.*—(1) Any amount received upon the surrender, redemption, or maturity of a contract to which section 72 applies, which is not received as an annuity under the rules of paragraph (b) of § 1.72-2, shall be included in the gross income of the recipient to the extent that it, when added to amounts previously received under the contract and which were excludable from the gross income of the recipient under the law applicable at the time of receipt, exceeds the aggregate of premiums or other consideration paid. See section 72(e)(2)(B). If amounts are to be received as an annuity, whether in lieu of or in addition to amounts described in the preceding sentence, such amounts shall be included in the gross income of the recipient in accordance with the provisions of paragraph (e) or (f) of this section, whichever is applicable. The rule stated in the first sentence of this paragraph shall not apply to payments received as an annuity or otherwise after the date of the first receipt of an amount as an annuity subsequent to the maturity, redemption, or surrender of the original contract. If amounts are so received and are other than amounts received as an annuity, they are includible in the gross income of the recipient. See section 72(e)(1)(A) and paragraph (b)(2).

(2) For the purpose of applying the rule contained in subparagraph (1) of this paragraph, it is immaterial whether the recipient of the amount received upon the surrender, redemption, or maturity of the contract is the same as the recipient of amounts previously received under the contract which were excludable from gross income, except in the case of a contract transferred for a valuable consideration, with respect to which see paragraph (a) of § 1.72-10. For the limit on the amount of tax, for taxable years beginning before January 1, 1964, attributable to the receipt of certain lump sums to which this paragraph applies, see paragraph (g) of this section.

(e) *Periodic payments received for a different term.*—If, after the date on which an amount is first received as an annuity under a contract to which section 72 applies, the terms of the contract are modified or the annuity obligations are exchanged so that periodic payments are to be received for a different term than originally provided under the contract (whether or not accompanied by the receipt of a lump sum to which paragraph (d) of this section applies), the rules of this paragraph shall apply to such payments. Hence, the provisions of section 72(e) and paragraphs (b), (c), (d), and (f) of this section are inapplicable for the purpose of determining the includibility of such payments in gross income and the general principles of section 72 with respect to the use of an exclusion ratio shall be applied to such payments as if they were provided under a new contract received in exchange for the contract providing the original annuity payments. If such payments are received as the result of the surrender, redemption, or discharge of a contract to which section 72 applies, they shall

be considered to be received as an annuity under a contract exchanged for the contract whose redemption, surrender, or discharge was involved. For the purpose of determining the extent to which the payments so received are to be included in the gross income of the recipient, an exclusion ratio shall be determined for such contract as of the later of January 1, 1954, or the first day of the first period for which an amount is received as an annuity thereunder, whichever is the later. See paragraph (b) of § 1.72-4. In determining the investment in the contract for this purpose, any lump sum amount received at the time of the exchange shall not be considered an amount to which paragraph (a)(2) of § 1.72-6 applies. However, such lump sum shall be subtracted from the aggregate of premiums or other consideration paid to the extent it is excludable as an amount not received as an annuity under this section as if it were an amount received before the annuity starting date of the contract obtained in exchange.

(f) *Periodic payments received for the same term after a lump sum withdrawal.*—(1) If, after the date of the first receipt of a payment as an annuity, the annuitant receives a lump sum and is thereafter to receive annuity payments in a reduced amount under the contract for the same term, life, or lives as originally specified in the contract, a portion of the contract shall be considered to have been surrendered or redeemed in consideration of the payment of such lump sum and the exclusion ratio originally determined for the contract shall continue to apply to the amounts received as an annuity without regard to the fact that such amounts are less than the original amounts which were to be paid periodically. The lump sum shall be includible in the gross income of the recipient in accordance with the provisions of subparagraph (2) of this paragraph. However, except in the case of amounts to which sections 402 and 403 apply, the tax, for taxable years beginning before January 1, 1964, attributable to the inclusion of all or part of the lump sum in gross income shall not exceed the amount determined under section 72(e)(3) and paragraph (g) of this section. For taxable years beginning after December 31, 1963, such amounts may be taken into account in computations under sections 1301 through 1305 (relating to income averaging).

(2) There shall be excluded from gross income that portion of the lump sum which bears the same ratio to the aggregate premiums or other consideration paid for the contract, as reduced by all amounts previously received under the contract and excludable from the gross income of the recipient under the applicable income tax law, as:

(i) In the case of payments to be made in the manner described in paragraph (b)(2) of § 1.72-2, the amount of the reduction in the annuity payments to be made thereafter bears to the annuity payments originally provided under the contract, or

(ii) In the case of a contract providing for payments to be made in the manner described in paragraph (b)(3)(i) of § 1.72-2, the amount of the reduction in the number of units per period to be paid thereafter bears to the number of units per period payable under the contract immediately before the lump sum withdrawal.

(3) This paragraph may be illustrated by the following examples:

Example (1). Taxpayer A pays $20,000 for an annuity contract providing for payments to him of $100 per month for his life. At the annuity starting date he has a life expectancy of 20 years. His expected return is therefore $24,000 and the exclusion ratio is five-sixths. He continues to receive the original annuity payments for 5 years, receiving a total of $6,000, and properly excludes a total of $5,000 from his gross income in his income tax returns for those years. At the beginning of the next year, A agrees with the insurer to take a reduced annuity of $75 per month and a lump sum payment of $4,000 in cash. Of the lump sum he receives, he will include $250 and exclude $3,750 from his gross income for his taxable year of receipt, determined as follows:

Aggregate of premiums or other consideration paid	$20,000
Less amounts received as an annuity to the extent they were excludable from A's income	5,000
Remainder of the consideration	$15,000
Ratio of the reduction in the amount of the annuity payments to the original annuity payments	25/$100 or ¼
Lump sum received	$4,000
Less one-fourth of the remainder of the consideration (¼ of $15,000)	3,750
Portion of the lump sum includible in gross income	$250

For taxable years beginning before January 1, 1964, the limit on tax of section 72(e)(3), as in effect before such date, applies to the portion of the lump sum includible in gross income. For taxable years beginning after December 31, 1963, such portion may be taken into account in computations under sections 1301 through 1305 (relating to income averaging). If, in this example, the annuity were a pension payable to A as a retired *employee,* but the facts were otherwise the same (assuming that, for instance, the $20,000 aggregate of premiums or other consideration paid were A's contributions as determined under section 72(f) and § 1.72-8) the result would be the same except

that the tax attributable to the inclusion of the $250 in A's gross income, for taxable years beginning before January 1, 1964, would not be limited by section 72(e)(3), as in effect before such date. If such a lump sum is received in a taxable year beginning after December 31, 1963, the portion of such sum includible in gross income may be taken into account in computations under sections 1301 through 1305 (relating to income averaging).

Example (2). Taxpayer B pays $30,000 for a contract providing for monthly payments to be made to him for 15 years with respect to the principal and earnings of 10 units of an investment fund. B receives

$12,000 during the first 5 years of participation and of this amount he has properly excluded a total of $10,000 from his gross income in his income returns for the taxable years, since $2,000 of $2,400 he received in each such year represented his investment divided by the term of the annuity ($30,000 ÷ 15). At the beginning of the 6th year, B agrees to take $11,000 in a lump sum and thereafter to accept the payments arising with respect to five units for the remaining 10 years

of payments in full discharge of the original obligations of the contract. B shall include $1,000 in his gross income for the 6th year as the result of the lump sum he receives and allocates $1,000 of his original investment in the contract to each of the remaining 10 years with respect to the payments which will continue, determined as follows:

Aggregate of premiums or other consideration paid	$30,000
Total amount received and excludable from gross income	10,000
Remainder of the consideration	$20,000
Ratio of units discontinued to the total units originally provided	5/10, or 1/2
Lump sum received at the time of reduction in the number of units to be paid	$11,000
Less one-half of the remainder of the consideration (1/2 of $20,000)	10,000
Portion of the lump sum received and includible in gross income	$1,000
Remainder of the consideration less the portion of such remainder attributable to the excludable portion of the lump sum ($20,000 − $10,000)	$10,000
Remainder of the consideration properly allocable to each taxable year for the remaining 10 years ($10,000 ÷ 10)	1,000

For the taxable years beginning before January 1, 1964, the limit on tax of section 72(e)(3), as in effect before such date, applies to the portion of the lump sum received and includible in gross income. For taxable years beginning after December 31, 1963, such portion may be taken into account in computations under sections 1301 through 1305 (relating to income averaging).

(g) *Limit on tax attributable to the receipt of a lump sum.*—(1) For taxable years beginning before January 1, 1964, if the entire amount of the proceeds received upon the redemption, maturity, surrender, or discharge of a contract to which section 72 applies is received in a lump sum and paragraph (c), (d), or (f) of this section is applicable in determining the portion of such amount which is includible in gross income, the tax attributable to such portion shall not exceed the tax which would have been attributable thereto had such portion been received ratably in the taxable year in which received and the 2 preceding taxable years. The amount of tax attributable to the includible portion of the lump sum received shall be the lesser of:

(i) The difference between the amount of tax for the taxable year of receipt computed by including such portion in gross income and the amount of tax for such taxable year computed by excluding such portion from gross income; or

(ii) The difference between the total amount of tax for the taxable year of receipt and the 2 preceding taxable years computed by including one-third of such portion in gross income for each of the 3 taxable years, and the total amount of the tax for the taxable year of receipt and the 2 preceding taxable years computed by entirely excluding such portion from the gross income of all 3 taxable years.

For the definition of "taxable year", see section 441(b). This subparagraph shall not apply, for taxable years beginning before January 1, 1964, to payments excepted from the application of section 72(e)(3), as in effect before such date, under the provisions of section 402 or 403. See paragraph (a) of § 1.72-2 and paragraph (d) of § 1.72-14.

(2) For taxable years beginning after December 31, 1963, any amount includible in gross income to which this section relates may be taken into account in computations under sections 1301 through 1305 (relating to income averaging).

(h) *Amounts deemed to be paid or received by a transferee.*—Amounts deemed to have been paid or received by a transferee for the purposes of § 1.72-10 shall also be deemed to have been so paid or received by such transferee for the purposes of this section. Thus, if a donee is deemed to have paid the premiums or other consideration actually paid by his transferor for the purposes of section 72(g) and paragraph (b) of § 1.72-10, such consideration shall be deemed premiums or other consideration paid by the donee for the purposes of this section. [Reg. § 1.72-11.]

☐ [*T.D. 6211, 11-14-56. Amended by T.D. 6676, 9-16-63, T.D. 6885, 6-1-66 and T.D. 8115, 12-16-86.*]

[Reg. § 1.72-12]

§ 1.72-12. Effect of taking an annuity in lieu of a lump sum upon the maturity of a contract.—If a contract to which section 72 applies provides for the payment of a lump sum in full discharge of the obligation thereunder and the obligee entitled thereto, prior to receiving any portion of such lump sum and within 60 days after the date on which such lump sum first becomes payable, exercises an option or irrevocably agrees with the obligor to take, in lieu thereof, payments which will constitute "amounts received as an annuity", as that term is defined in paragraph (b) of § 1.72-2, no part of such lump sum shall be deemed to have been received by the obligee at the time he was first entitled thereto merely because he would have been

entitled to such amount had he not exercised the option or made such an agreement with the obligor. [Reg. § 1.72-12.]

☐ [*T.D. 6211, 11-14-56.*]

[Reg. § 1.72-13]

§ 1.72-13. Special rule for employee contributions recoverable in three years.—(a) *Amounts received as an annuity.*—(1) Section 72(d) provides a special rule for the treatment of amounts received as an annuity by an employee (or by the beneficiary or beneficiaries of an employee) under a contract to which section 72 applies. This special rule is applicable only in the event that:

(i) At least part of the consideration paid for the contract is contributed by the employer, and

(ii) The aggregate amount receivable as an annuity under such contract by the employee (or by his beneficiary or beneficiaries if the employee died before any amount was received as an annuity under the contract) within the 3-year period beginning on the date (whether or not before January 1, 1954) on which an amount is first received as an annuity equals or exceeds the total consideration contributed (or deemed contributed under section 72 (f) and § 1.72-8) by the employee as of such date as reduced by all amounts previously received and excludable from the gross income of the recipient under the applicable income tax law.

In such an event, section 72(d) provides that all amounts received as an annuity under the contract during a taxable year to which the Code applies shall be excluded from gross income until the total of the amounts excluded under that section plus all amounts excluded under prior income tax laws equals or exceeds the consideration contributed (or deemed contributed) by the employee. The excess, if any, and all amounts received by any recipient thereafter (whether or not received as an annuity), shall be fully included in gross income. See paragraph (b) of this section.

(2) If the aggregate amount receivable as an annuity under the contract within three years from the date on which an amount is first received as an annuity thereunder will not equal or exceed the consideration contributed (or deemed contributed) by the employee in accordance with the provisions of § 1.72-8, computed as of such date, the special rule of section 72(d) shall not apply to amounts received as an annuity under the contract and the general rules of section 72 shall apply thereto.

(3) The aggregate of the amounts receivable as an annuity within the prescribed 3-year period shall be the total of all annuity payments anticipatable by an employee (or a beneficiary or beneficiaries of an employee, if the employee died before any amount was received as an annuity) under the contract as a whole as defined in paragraph (a) of § 1.72-2. See paragraph (a)(3) of § 1.72-2 for rules for determining what constitutes "the contract" in the case of distributions from an employees' trust or plan.

(4) If subparagraphs (1) and (3) of this paragraph apply to amounts received as an annuity under a contract, the rule prescribed in subparagraph (1) of this paragraph shall apply to all amounts so received thereunder regardless of the fact that they may be payable (i) to more than one beneficiary, (ii) for the same or different intervals, (iii) in different sums, or (iv) for a different period certain, life, or lives.

(5) For purposes of section 72(d), contributions which are made with respect to a self-employed individual and which are allowed as a deduction under section 404(a) are not considered contributions by the employee, but such contributions are considered contributions by the employer. A contribution which is deemed paid in a prior taxable year under the provisions of section 404(a)(6) shall be considered made with respect to a self-employed individual if the individual on

whose behalf the contribution is made was self-employed for the taxable year in which the contribution is deemed paid, whether or not such individual is self-employed at the time the contribution is actually paid. Contributions with respect to a self-employed individual who is an owner-employee used to purchase life, accident, health, or other insurance protection for such owner-employee shall not be treated as consideration for the contract contributed by the employee in computing the employee contributions for purposes of section 72(d).

(b) *Amounts not received as an annuity.*—If the rule of paragraph (a) applies to a contract and, after the date on which an annuity payment is first received, amounts are received other than as an annuity under such contract in a taxable year to which the Code applies, they shall be included in the gross income of the recipient in accordance with the provisions of § 1.72-11. Thus, if such amounts are received as a dividend or a similar distribution after the date on which an amount is first received as an annuity under the contract, they shall be included in the gross income of the recipient (in accordance with section 72(e)(1)(A) and paragraph (b)(2) of § 1.72-11). All other amounts not received as an annuity shall be included in the gross income of the recipient in accordance with the provisions of section 72(e)(1)(B) and paragraph (c), (d), or (f), whichever is applicable, of § 1.72-11. See section 72(e)(2).

(c) *Amounts received after the exhaustion of employee contributions.*—(1) Amounts received under a contract to which the rule of paragraph (a) of this section applies (whether or not such amounts are received as an annuity) shall be included in the gross income of the recipient if such amounts are received after the date on which the aggregate of all amounts excluded from gross income by the recipients under section 72(d) and prior income tax laws equalled or exceeded the consideration contributed (or deemed contributed) by the employee.

(2) If the rule of paragraph (a) of this section applies to amounts received by an employee (or his beneficiary or beneficiaries) under a joint and survivor annuity contract, payments made to a prior annuitant may entirely exhaust the amounts excludable from gross income. In such case, amounts paid to the surviving annuitant (or annuitants) shall be included in gross income by such recipients.

(d) *Application of section 72(d) to a contract, trust, or plan providing for payments in a manner described in paragraph (b)(3)(i) of § 1.72-2.*—For the purpose of applying section 72(d) and this section, any amount received in the nature of a periodic payment under a contract, trust, or plan which provides for the payment of amounts in a manner described in paragraph (b)(3)(i) of § 1.72-2 shall be considered an amount received as an annuity notwithstanding the provisions of any other section of the regulations under section 72. The special exclusion rule of section 72(d) and paragraph (a) of this section shall apply to all amounts so received if the first amount received, when multiplied by the number of periodic payments to be made within the three years beginning on the date of its receipt, results in an amount in excess of the aggregate premiums or other consideration contributed (or deemed contributed) by the employee as of that date. If more than one series of periodic payments is to be paid under the same contract, trust, or plan, all payments anticipatable, whether because fixed in amount or determinable in the manner described in the preceding sentence, shall be aggregated for the purpose of determining the applicability of section 72(d) to the contract, trust, or plan as a whole.

(e) *Inapplicability of section 72(d) and this section.*—Section 72(d) and this section do not apply to:

(1) Amounts received as proceeds of a life insurance contract to which section 101(a) applies, nor to

(2) Amounts paid to a surviving annuitant under a joint and survivor annuity contract to which paragraph (b)(3) of § 1.72-5 applies, nor to

(3) Amounts paid to an annuitant under chapter 73 of title 10 of the United States Code with respect to which section 72(o) and § 1.122-1 apply.

See also paragraph (d) of § 1.72-14. [Reg. § 1.72-13.]

☐ [*T.D.* 6211, 11-14-56. *Amended by T.D.* 6497, 10-19-60, *T.D.* 6676, 9-16-63 *and T.D.* 7043, 6-1-70.]

[Reg. § 1.72-14]

§ 1.72-14. Exceptions from application of principles of section 72.—(a) *Payments of interest.*—If any amount is received under an agreement to pay interest on a sum or sums held by the obligor, such amount shall not be excludable from the gross income of the recipient under the provisions of section 72 to the extent that it is an actual interest payment. See section 72(j). An amount shall be considered to be held under an agreement to pay interest thereon if the amount payable after the term of the annuity (whether for a term certain or

for a life or lives) is substantially equal to or larger than the aggregate amount of premiums or other consideration paid therefor. For this purpose, however, the aggregate amount of premiums or other consideration paid shall include all contributions made by an employer and not merely those to which section 72(f) applies.

(b) *Alimony payments.*—To the extent that payments made to a wife are includible in her gross income by reason of either or both sections 71 and 682, they shall not be excluded from the wife's gross income under the principles of section 72 although made under a contract to which that section applies. However, section 72 shall apply in the case of amounts received under such a contract if a husband and wife are entitled to make and do make a single return jointly.

(c) *Certain "face-amount certificates.".*—The principles of section 72 do not apply to "face-amount certificates" described in section 72(l) which were issued before January 1, 1955.

(d) *Employer plans.*—The provisions of §§ 1.72-1 to 1.72-13, inclusive, shall be disregarded to the extent that they are inconsistent with the treatment of amounts received provided in section 402 (relating to the taxability of a beneficiary of an employee's trust), section 403 (relating to the taxation of employee annuities), or the regulations under either of such sections. [Reg. § 1.72-14.]

☐ [*T.D.* 6211, 11-14-56.]

[Reg. § 1.72-15]

§ 1.72-15. Applicability of section 72 to accident or health plans.—(a) *Applicability of section.*—This section provides the rules for determining the taxation of amounts received from an employer-established plan which provides for distributions that are taxable under section 72 (or for distributions that are taxable under section 402(a)(2) or (e), or section 403(a)(2), in the case of lump sum distributions) and which also provides for distributions that may be excludable from gross income under section 104 or 105 as accident or health benefits. For example, this section will apply to a pension plan described in section 401 and exempt under section 501 which provides for the payment of pensions at retirement and the payment of an earlier pension in the event of permanent disability. This section will also apply to a profit-sharing plan described in section 401 and exempt under section 501 which provides for periodic distribution of the amount standing to the account of a participant during any period that the participant is absent from work due to a personal injury or sickness and for the distribution of any balance standing to the account of the participant upon his separation from service. For purposes of this section, the term "contributions of the employee" includes contributions by the employer which were includible in the employee's gross income. Paragraphs (d), (h), and (i) of this section apply for taxable years beginning on or after January 1, 2015.

(b) *General rule.*—Section 72 does not apply to any amount received as an accident or health benefit, and the tax treatment of any such amount shall be determined under sections 104 and 105. See paragraphs (c) and (d) of this section, paragraph (d) of § 1.104-1, and §§ 1.105-1 through 1.105-5. Section 72 (or, in the case of certain total distributions, section 402(a)(2) or section 403(a)(2)) does apply to any amount which is received under a plan to which this section applies and which is not an accident or health benefit. See paragraph (e) of this section.

(c) *Accident or health benefits attributable to employee contributions.*—(1) If a plan to which this section applies provides that any portion of the accident or health benefits is attributable to the contributions of the employee to such plan, then such portion of such benefits is excludable from gross income under section 104(a)(3) and paragraph (d) of § 1.104-1. Neither section 72 nor section 105 applies to any accident or health benefits (whether paid before or after retirement) attributable to contributions of the employee. Since such portion is excludable under section 104(a)(3), such portion is not subject to the dollar limitation of section 105(d) and if such portion is payable after the retirement of the employee, it is excludable without regard to the provisions of § 1.105-4 and section 72.

(2) In determining the taxation of any amounts received as accident or health benefits from a plan to which this section applies, the first step is to determine the portion, if any, of the contributions of the employee which is used to provide the accident or health benefits and the portion of the accident or health benefits attributable to such portion of the employee's contributions. If such a plan expressly provides that the accident or health benefits are provided in whole or in part by employee contributions and the portion of employee contributions to be used for such purpose, the contributions so used will be treated as used to provide accident or health benefits. However, if the plan does not expressly provide that the accident or health benefits are to be provided with employee contributions and the portion of employee contributions to be used for such purpose, it will be presumed that none of the employee contri-

butions is used to provide such benefits. Thus, in the case of a contributory pension plan, it will be presumed that the disability pension is provided by employer contributions, unless the plan expressly provides otherwise, or in the case of a contributory profit-sharing plan providing that a portion of the amount standing to the account of each participant will be used to purchase accident or health insurance, it will be presumed that such insurance is purchased with employer contributions, unless the plan expressly provides otherwise. Similarly, unless the plan expressly provides otherwise, it will be presumed that if a contributory profit-sharing plan provides for periodic distributions from the account of a participant during any absence from work because of a personal injury or sickness, all such distributions which do not exceed the contributions of the employer plus earnings thereon are provided by employer contributions.

(3) Any employee contributions that are treated under subparagraph (2) of this paragraph as used to provide accident or health benefits shall not be included for any purpose under section 72 as employee contributions or as aggregate premiums or other consideration paid. Thus, in the case of a pension plan, or in the case of a profit-sharing plan providing that a portion of the amount standing to the account of each participant will be used to purchase accident or health insurance, any employee whose contributions are so used must make the adjustment provided by this subparagraph irrespective of whether such employee receives any accident or health benefits under such plan. However, in the case of a profit-sharing plan providing for periodic distributions from the account of a participant during any absence from work because of a personal injury or sickness, and adjustment under this subparagraph is required only when an employee receives distributions in excess of the employer contributions and earnings thereon or receives distributions consisting in whole or in part of his own contributions.

(4) If any of the employee contributions are treated under subparagraph (2) of this paragraph as used to provide any of the accident or health benefits, the portion of the benefits attributable to employee contributions shall be determined in accordance with § 1.105-1. Any accident or health benefits that are excludable under section 104(a)(3) shall not be included in the expected return for purposes of section 72.

(d) *Accident or health benefits attributable to employer contributions.*— Any amounts received as accident or health benefits and not attributable to contributions of the employee are includible in gross income except to the extent that the amounts are excludable from gross income under section 105(b) or (c) and the regulations under those sections. See § 1.402(a)-1(e) for rules relating to the use of a qualified plan under section 401(a) to pay premiums for accident or health insurance.

(e) *Other benefits under the plan.*—The taxability of amounts that are received under a plan to which this section applies and that are not accident or health benefits is determined under section 72 (or, in the case of certain total distributions, under section 402(a)(2) or section 403(a)(2)) without regard to any exclusion or inclusion of accident or health benefits under sections 104 and 105. For example, the investment in the contract or aggregate premiums paid is determined without regard to the exclusion of any amount under section 104 or 105, and the annuity starting date is determined without regard to the receipt of any accident or health benefits. However, if any employee contributions are used to provide any accident or health benefits, the investment in the contract or aggregate premiums paid must be adjusted as provided in paragraph (c)(3) of this section.

(f) [Reserved]

(g) *Payments to or on behalf of a self-employed individual.*—A self-employed individual is not considered an employee for purposes of section 105, relating to amounts received by employees under accident and health plans, nor for purposes of excluding under section 104(a)(3) amounts received by him under an accident and health plan as referred to in section 105(e). See section 105(g) and paragraph (a) of § 1.105-1. Therefore, the other paragraphs of this section are not applicable to amounts received by or on behalf of a self-employed individual. Except where accident or health benefits are provided through an insurance contract or an arrangement having the effect of insurance, all amounts received by or on behalf of a self-employed individual from a plan described in section 401(a) and exempt under section 501(a) or a plan described in section 403(a) shall be taxed as otherwise provided in section 72, 402, or 403. If the accident or health benefits are paid under an insurance contract or under an arrangement having the effect of insurance, section 104(a)(3) shall apply. Section 72 shall not apply to any amounts received under such circumstances.

(h) *Medical benefits for retired employees, etc.*—See § 1.402(a)-1(e)(2) for rules relating to the payment of medical benefits described in section 401(h) under a qualified pension or annuity plan.

(i) *Special rules.*—(1) *In general.*—For purposes of section 72(b) and (d) and this section, the taxpayer must maintain such records as are necessary to substantiate the amount treated as an investment in the taxpayer's annuity contract.

(2) *Delegation to Commissioner.*—The Commissioner may prescribe a form and instructions with respect to the taxpayer's past and current treatment of amounts received under section 72 or 105, and the taxpayer's computation, or recomputation, of the taxpayer's investment in his or her annuity contract. This form may be required to be filed with the taxpayer's returns for years in which the amounts are excluded under section 72 or 105. [Reg. § 1.72-15.]

☐ [T.D. 6485, 7-29-60. *Amended by* T.D. 6676, 9-16-63, T.D. 6722, 4-13-64, T.D. 6770, 11-16-64, T.D. 7352, 4-9-75, T.D. 9665, 5-9-2014 *and* T.D. 9849, 3-11-2019.]

[Reg. § 1.72-16]

§ 1.72-16. **Life insurance contracts purchased under qualified employee plans.**—(a) *Applicability of section.*—This section provides rules for the tax treatment of premiums paid under qualified pension, annuity, or profit-sharing plans for the purchase of life insurance contracts and rules for the tax treatment of the proceeds of such a life insurance contract and of annuity contracts purchased under such plans. For purposes of this section, the term "life insurance contract" means a retirement income, an endowment, or other contract providing life insurance protection. The rules of this section apply to plans covering only common-law employees as well as to plans covering self-employed individuals.

(b) *Treatment of cost of life insurance protection.*—(1) The rules of this paragraph are applicable to any life insurance contract—

(i) Purchased as a part of a plan described in section 403(a), or

(ii) Purchased by a trust described in section 401(a) which is exempt from tax under section 501(a) if the proceeds of such contract are payable directly or indirectly to a participant in such trust or to a beneficiary of such participant.

The proceeds of a contract described in subdivision (ii) of this subparagraph will be considered payable indirectly to a participant or beneficiary of such participant where they are payable to the trustee but under the terms of the plan the trustee is required to pay over all of such proceeds to the beneficiary.

(2) If under a plan or trust described in subparagraph (1) of this paragraph, amounts which were allowed as a deduction under section 404, or earnings of the trust, are applied toward the purchase of a life insurance contract described in subparagraph (1) of this paragraph, the cost of the life insurance protection under such contract shall be included in the gross income of the participant for the taxable year or years in which such contributions or earnings are so applied.

(3) If the amount payable upon death at any time during the year exceeds the cash value of the insurance policy at the end of the year, the entire amount of such excess is considered current life insurance protection. The cost of such insurance will be considered to be a reasonable net premium cost, as determined by the Commissioner, for such amount of insurance for the appropriate period.

(4) The amount includible in the gross income of the employee under this paragraph shall be considered as premiums or other consideration paid or contributed by the employee only with respect to any benefits attributable to the contract (within the meaning of paragraph (a)(3) of § 1.72-2) providing the life insurance protection. However, if under the rules of this paragraph an owner-employee is required to include any amounts in his gross income, such amounts shall not in any case be treated as part of his investment in the contract.

(5) The determination of the cost of life insurance protection may be illustrated by the following example:

Example. An annual premium policy purchased by a qualified trust for a common-law employee provides an annuity of $100 per month upon retirement at age 65, with a minimum death benefit of $10,000. The insurance payable if death occurred in the first year would be $10,000. The cash value at the end of the first year is 0. The net insurance is therefore $10,000 minus 0, or $10,000. Assuming that the Commissioner has determined that a reasonable net premium cost for the employee's age is $5.85 per $1,000, the premium for $10,000 of life insurance is therefore $58.50, and this is the amount to be reported as income by the employee for his taxable year in which the premium is paid. The balance of the premium is the amount contributed for the annuity, which is not taxable to the employee under a plan meeting the requirements of section 401(a), except as provided under section 402(a). Assuming that the cash value at the end of the second year is $500, the net insurance would then be $9,500 for the second year. With a net 1-year term rate of $6.30 for the employee's age in the second year, the amount to be reported as income to the employee would be $59.85.

(6) This paragraph shall not apply if the trust has a right under any circumstances to retain any part of the proceeds of the life insurance contract. But see paragraph (c)(4) of this section relating to the taxability of the distribution of such proceeds to a beneficiary.

(c) *Treatment of proceeds of life insurance and annuity contracts.*—(1) If under a qualified pension, annuity, or profit-sharing plan, there is purchased either—

(i) A life insurance contract described in paragraph (b)(1) of this section, and the employee either paid the cost of the insurance or was taxable on the cost of the insurance under paragraph (b) of this section, or

(ii) An annuity contract,

the amounts payable under any such contract by reason of the death of the employee are taxable under the rules of subparagraph (2) of this paragraph, except in the case of a joint and survivor annuity.

(2)(i) In the case of an annuity contract, the death benefit is the accumulation of the premiums (plus earnings thereon) which is intended to fund pension or other deferred benefits under a pension, annuity, or profit-sharing plan. Such death benefits are not in the nature of life insurance and are not excludable from gross income under section 101(a).

(ii) In the case of a life insurance contract under which there is a reserve accumulation which is intended to fund pension or other deferred benefits under a pension, annuity, or profit-sharing plan, such reserve accumulation constitutes the source of the cash value of the contract and approximates the amount of such cash value. The portion of the proceeds paid upon the death of the insured employee which is equal to the cash value immediately before death is not excludable from gross income under section 101(a). The remaining portion, if any, of the proceeds paid to the beneficiary by reason of the death of the insured employee—that is, the amount in excess of the cash value—constitutes current insurance protection and is excludable under section 101(a).

(iii) The death benefit under an annuity contract, or the portion of the death proceeds under a life insurance contract which is equal to the cash value of the contract immediately before death, constitutes a distribution under the plan consisting in whole or in part of deferred compensation and is taxable to the beneficiary in accordance with section 72(m)(3) and the provisions of this paragraph, except to the extent that the limited exclusion from income provided in section 101(b) is applicable.

(iv) In the case of a life insurance contract under which the benefits are paid at a date or dates later than the death of the employee, section 101(d) is applicable only to the portion of the benefits which is attributable to the amount excludable under section 101(a). The portion of such benefits which is attributable to the cash value of the contract immediately before death is taxable under section 72, and in such case, any amount excludable under section 101(b) is treated as additional consideration paid by the employee in accordance with section 101(b)(2)(D).

(3) The application of the rules under subparagraph (2) of this paragraph with respect to the taxability of proceeds of a life insurance contract paid by reason of the death of an insured common-law employee who has paid no contributions under the plan is illustrated by the following examples:

Example (1).

Total face amount of the contract payable in a lump sum at time of death	$25,000
Cash value of the contract immediately before death	11,000
Excess over cash value, excludable under section 101(a)	$14,000
Cash value subject to limited exclusion under section 101(b)	$11,000
Excludable under section 101(b) (assuming that there is no other death benefit paid by or on behalf of any employer with respect to the employee)	5,000
Balance taxable in accordance with section 402(a)(2) or 403(a)(2) (assuming a total distribution in one taxable year of the distributee)	$6,000
Portion of premiums taxed to employee under the provisions of paragraph (b) of this section and considered as contributions of the employee	940
Balance taxable as long-term capital gain	$5,060

Example (2). The facts are the same as in example (1), except that the contract provides that the beneficiary may elect within 60 days after the death of the employee either to take the $25,000 or to receive 10 annual installments of $3,000 each, and the beneficiary elects to receive the 10 installments. In addition, the employee's rights to the cash value immediately before his death were forfeitable at least to the extent of $5,000. Section 101(d) is applicable to the amount excludable under section 101(a), that is, $14,000. The portion of each annual installment of $3,000 which is attributable to this $14,000 is determined by allocating each installment in accordance with the ratio which this $14,000 bears to the total amount which was payable at death ($25,000). Accordingly, the portion of each annual installment which is subject to section 101(d) is $1,680 (14/25 of $3,000), of which $1,400 (1/10 of $14,000) is excludable under section 101(a), and the remaining $280 is includable in the gross income of the beneficiary. However, if the beneficiary is a surviving spouse as defined in section 101(d)(3), the exclusion provided by section 101(d)(1)(B) is applicable to such $280. The remaining portion of each annual $3,000 installment, $1,320, is attributable to the cash value of the contract and is treated under section 72, as follows:

Amount actually contributed by the employee	$0
Amount considered contributed by employee by reason of section 101(b)	5,000
Portion of premiums taxed to employee under the provisions of paragraph (b) of this section and considered as contributions of the employee	940
Investment in the contract	$5,940
Expected return, 10 × $1,320	$13,200
Exclusion ratio, $5,940 ÷ $13,200	0.45
Annual exclusion, 0.45 × $1,320	$594

Accordingly, $594 of the $1,320 portion of each annual installment is excludable each year under section 72, and the remaining $726 is includible. Thus, if the beneficiary is not a surviving spouse, a total of $1,006 ($280 plus $726) of each annual $3,000 installment is includible in income each year. If the beneficiary is a surviving spouse, and can exclude all of the $280 under section 101(d)(1)(B), the amount includible in gross income each year is $726 of each annual $3,000 installment.

(4) If an employee neither paid the total cost of the life insurance protection provided under a life insurance contract, nor was taxable under paragraph (b) of this section with respect thereto, no part of the proceeds of such a contract which are paid to the beneficiaries of the employee as a death benefit is excludable under section 101(a). The entire distribution is taxable to the beneficiaries under section 402(a) or 403(a) except to the extent that a limited exclusion may be allowable under section 101(b). [Reg. § 1.72-16.]

☐ [*T.D.* 6676, 9-16-63.]

[Reg. § 1.72-17]

§ 1.72-17. Special rules applicable to owner-employees.—(a) *In general.*—Under section 401(c) and section 403(a), certain self-employed individuals may participate in qualified pension, annuity, and profit-sharing plans, and the amounts received by such individuals from such plans are taxable under section 72. Section 72(m) and this section contain special rules for the taxation of amounts received from qualified pension, profit-sharing, or annuity plans covering an owner-employee. For purposes of section 72 and the regulations thereunder, the term "employee" shall include the self-employed individual who is treated as an employee by section 401(c)(1) (see paragraph (b) of § 1.401-10), and the term "owner-employee" has the meaning assigned to it in section 401(c)(3) (see paragraph (d) of § 1.401-10). See also paragraph (a)(2) of § 1.401-10 for the rule for determining when a plan covers an owner-employee. For purposes of this section, a self-employed individual may not treat as consideration for the contract contributed by the employee any contributions under the plan for which deductions were allowed under section 404 and which, consequently, are considered employer contributions.

(b) *Certain amounts received before annuity starting date.*—(1) The rules of this paragraph are applicable to amounts received from a qualified pension, profit-sharing, or annuity plan by an employee (or his beneficiary) who is or was an owner-employee with respect to such plan when such amounts—

(i) Are received before the annuity starting date; and

(ii) Are not received as an annuity.

For the definition of annuity starting date, see paragraph (b) of § 1.72-4 and subparagraph (4) of this paragraph. As to what constitutes amounts not received as an annuity, see paragraphs (c) and (d) of § 1.72-11.

(2) Amounts to which this paragraph applies shall be included in the recipient's gross income for the taxable year in which received. However, the sum of the amounts so included under this subparagraph in all taxable years shall not exceed the aggregate deductions allowed under section 404 for premiums or other consideration paid under the plan on behalf of the employee while he was an owner-employee, including any such deductions taken in the taxable year of receipt.

(3) Any amounts to which this paragraph applies and which are not includible in gross income under the rules of subparagraph (2) of this paragraph shall be subject to the provisions of section 72(e) and § 1.72-11. However, for taxable years beginning before January 1, 1964, section 72(e)(3), as in effect before such date, shall not apply to such amounts. For taxable years beginning after December 31, 1963, such amounts (other than amounts subject to a penalty under section 72(m)(5) and paragraph (e) of this section) may be taken into account in computations under sections 1301 through 1305 (relating to income averaging).

(4) Under section 401(d)(4), a qualified pension, profit-sharing, or annuity plan may not provide for distributions to an owner-employee before he reaches age $59\frac{1}{2}$ years, except in the case of his earlier disability. Therefore, in the case of a distribution from a qualified plan to an individual for whom contributions have been made to the plan as an owner-employee, the annuity starting date cannot be prior to the time such individual attains the age $59\frac{1}{2}$ years unless he is entitled to benefits before reaching such age because of his disability. For taxable years beginning after December 31, 1966, see section 72(m)(7) and paragraph (f) of this section for the meaning of disabled. For taxable years beginning before January 1, 1967, see section 213(g)(3) for the meaning of disabled.

(5) The rules of this paragraph are not applicable to amounts credited to an individual in his capacity as a policyholder of an annuity, endowment, or life insurance contract which are in the nature of a dividend or refund of premium, and which are applied in accordance with paragraph (a)(4) of § 1.404(a)-8 towards the purchase of benefits under the policy.

(6) The rules of this paragraph may be illustrated by the following example:

Example. B, a self-employed individual, received $8,000 as a distribution under a qualified pension plan before the annuity starting date. At the time of such distribution, $10,000 had been contributed (the whole amount being allowed as a deduction) under the plan on behalf of such individual while he was a common-law employee and $5,000 had been contributed under the plan on his behalf while he was an owner-employee, of which $2,500 was allowed as a deduction. In addition, B had contributed $1,000 on his own behalf as an employee under the plan. Of the $8,000, $2,500 (the amount allowed as a deduction with respect to contributions on behalf of the individual while he was an owner-employee) is includible in gross income under subparagraph (2) of this paragraph. With respect to the remaining $5,500, B has a basis of $3,500, consisting of the $2,500 contributed on his behalf while he was an owner-employee which was not allowed as a deduction and the $1,000 which B contributed as an employee. The difference between the $5,500 and B's basis of $3,500, or $2,000, is includible in gross income under section 72(e).

(c) *Amounts paid for life, accident, health, or other insurance.*— Amounts used to purchase life, accident, health, or other insurance protection for an owner-employee shall not be taken into account in computing the following:

(1) The aggregate amount of premiums or other consideration paid for the contract for purposes of determining the investment in the contract under section 72(c)(1)(A) and § 1.72-6;

(2) The consideration for the contract contributed by the employee for purposes of section 72(d)(1) and § 1.72-13, which provide the method of taxing employees' annuities where the employees's contributions will be recoverable within 3 years; and

(3) The aggregate premiums or other consideration paid for purposes of section 72(e)(1)(B) and § 1.72-11, which provide the rules for taxing amounts not received as annuities prior to the annuity starting date.

The cost of such insurance protection will be considered to be a reasonable net premium cost, as determined by the Commissioner, for the appropriate period.

(d) *Amounts constructively received.*—(1) If during any taxable year an owner-employee assigns or pledges (or agrees to assign or pledge) any portion of his interest in a trust described in section 401(a) which is exempt from tax under section 501(a), or any portion of the value of a contract purchased as part of a plan described in section 403(a), such portion shall be treated as having been received by such owner-employee as a distribution from the trust or as an amount received under the contract during such taxable year.

(2) If during any taxable year an owner-employee receives, either directly or indirectly, any amount from any insurance company as a loan under a contract purchased by a trust described in section 401(a) which is exempt from tax under section 501(a) or purchased as part of a plan described in section 403(a), and issued by such insurance company, such amount shall be treated as an amount received under the contract during such taxable year. An owner-employee will be considered to have received an amount under a contract if a premium, which is otherwise in default, is paid by the insurance company in the form of a loan against the cash surrender value of the contract. Further, an owner-employee will be considered to have received an amount to which this subparagraph applies if an amount is received from the issuer of a face-amount certificate as a loan under such a certificate purchased as part of a qualified trust or plan.

(e) *Penalties applicable to certain amounts received by owner-employees.*—(1)(i) The rules of this paragraph are applicable to amounts, to the extent includible in gross income, received from a trust described in section 401(a) or under a plan described in section 403(a) by or on behalf of an individual who is or has been an owner-employee with respect to such plan or trust—

(a) Which are received before the owner-employee reaches the age $59\frac{1}{2}$ years and which are attributable to contributions paid on behalf of such owner-employee (whether or not paid by him) while he was an owner-employee (see subdivision (ii) of this subparagraph),

(b) Which are in excess of the benefits provided for such owner-employee under the plan formula (see subdivision (iii) of this subparagraph), or

(c) Which are received by reason of a distribution of the owner-employee's entire interest under the provisions of section 401(e)(2)(E), relating to excess contributions on behalf of an owner-employee which are willfully made.

(ii) The amounts referred to in subdivision (i)(a) of this subparagraph do not include—

(a) Amounts received by reason of the owner-employee becoming disabled, or

(b) Amounts received by the owner-employee in his capacity as a policyholder of an annuity, endowment, or life insurance contract which are in the nature of a dividend or similar distribution. Amounts attributable to contributions paid on behalf of an owner-employee and which are paid to a person other than the owner-employee before the owner-employee dies or reaches the age $59\frac{1}{2}$ shall be considered received by the owner-employee for purposes of this paragraph. For taxable years beginning after December 31, 1966, see section 72(m)(7) and paragraph (f) of this section for the meaning of disabled. For taxable years beginning before January 1, 1967, see section 213(g)(3) for the meaning of disabled. For taxable years beginning after December 31, 1968, if an amount is not included in the amounts referred to in subdivision (i)(a) of this subparagraph solely by reason of the owner-employee becoming disabled and if a penalty would otherwise be applicable with respect to all or a portion of such amount, then for the taxable year in which such amount is received, there must be submitted with the owner-employee's income tax return a doctor's statement as to the impairment, and a statement by the owner-employee with respect to the effect of such impairment upon his substantial gainful activity and the date such impairment occurred. For taxable years which are subsequent to the first taxable year beginning after December 31, 1968, with respect to which the statements referred to in the preceding sentence are submitted, the owner-employee may, in lieu of such statements, submit a statement declaring the continued existence (without substantial diminution) of the impairment and its continued effect upon his substantial gainful activity.

(iii) This paragraph applies to amounts described in subdivision (i) (b) of this subparagraph (relating to excess benefits) even though a portion of such amounts may be attributable to contributions made on behalf of an individual while he was not an owner-employee and even though the amounts are received by his successor. However, these amounts do not include the portion of a distribution to which section 402(a)(2) or 403(a)(2) (relating to certain total distributions in one taxable year) applies.

(iv)(a) For purposes of subdivision (i) (a) of this subparagraph, the portion of any distribution or payment attributable to contributions on behalf of an employee-participant while he was an owner-employee includes the contributions made on his behalf while he was an owner-employee and the increments in value attributable to such contributions.

(b) The increments in value of an individual's account may be allocated to contributions on his behalf while he was an owner-employee either by maintaining a separate account, or an accounting, which reflects the actual increment attributable to such contributions, or by the method described in (c) of this subdivision.

(c) Where an individual is covered under the same plan both as an owner-employee and as a nonowner-employee, the portion of the increment in value of his interest attributable to contributions made on his behalf while he was an owner-employee may be determined by multiplying the total increment in value in his account by a fraction. The numerator of the fraction is the total contributions made on behalf of the individual as an owner-employee, weighted for the number of years that each contribution was in the plan. The denominator is the total contributions made on behalf of the individual, whether or not an owner-employee, weighted for the number of years each contribution was in the plan. The contributions are weighted for the number of years in the plan by multiplying each contribution by the number of years it was in the plan. For purposes of this computation, any forfeiture allocated to the account of the individual is treated as a contribution to the account made at the time so allocated.

(d) The method described in (c) of this subdivision may be illustrated by the following example:

Example. B was a member of the XYZ Partnership and a participant in the partnership's profit-sharing plan which was created in 1963. Until the end of 1967, B's interest in the partnership was less than 10 percent. On January 1, 1968, B obtained an interest in excess of 10 percent in the partnership and continued to participate in the profit-sharing plan until 1972. During 1972, prior to the time he attained the age of $59\frac{1}{2}$ years and during a time when he was not disabled, B withdrew his entire interest in the profit-sharing plan. At that time his interest was $15,000, $9,600 contributions and $5,400 increment attributable to the contributions. The portion of the increment attributable to contributions while B was an owner-employee is $667.80, determined as follows:

	A	B	C
		No. of years contribution was in trust	Contribution weighted for years in trust $(A \times B)$
	Contribution		
1972	$1,000	0	0
1971	800	1	$800
1970	1,200	2	2,400
1969	600	3	1,800
1968	200	4	800
1967	400	5	2,000
1966	2,000	6	12,000
1965	1,000	7	7,000
1964	1,500	8	12,000
1963	900	9	8,100
	$9,600		$46,900

Total weighted contributions as owner-employee
(1968-1972) — $5,800
Total weighted contributions — $46,900

$$\$5,400 \times \frac{\$5,800}{\$46,900} = \$667.80$$

(2)(i) If the aggregate of the amounts to which this paragraph applies received by any person in his taxable year equals or exceeds $2,500, the tax with respect to such amount shall be the greater of—

(a) The increase in tax attributable to the inclusion of the amounts so received in his gross income for the taxable year in which received, or

(b) 110 percent of the aggregate increase in taxes, for such taxable year and the four immediately preceding taxable years, which would have resulted if such amounts had been included in such person's gross income ratably over such taxable years. However, if deductions were allowed under section 404 for contributions to the plan on behalf of the individual as an owner-employee for less than four prior taxable years (whether or not consecutive), the number of immediately preceding taxable years taken into account shall be the number of prior taxable years in which such deductions were allowed.

(ii) If the aggregate of the amounts to which this paragraph applies received by any person in his taxable year is less than $2,500, the tax with respect to such amounts shall be 110 percent of the increase in tax which results from including such amounts in the person's gross income for the taxable year in which received.

(3)(i) For purposes of making the ratable inclusion computations of subparagraph (2) (i) of this paragraph, the taxable income of the recipient for each taxable year involved (notwithstanding section 63, relating to definition of taxable income) shall be treated as being not less than the amount required to be treated as includible in the taxable year pursuant to the ratable inclusion.

(ii) For purposes of subparagraph (2) (i) (a) and (ii) of this paragraph, the recipient's taxable income (notwithstanding section 63, relating to definition of taxable income) shall be treated as being not less than the aggregate of the amounts to which this paragraph applies reduced by the deductions allowed the recipient for such taxable year under section 151 (relating to deductions for personal exemptions).

(iii) In any case in which the application of subdivision (i) or (ii) of this subparagraph results in an increase in taxable income for any taxable year, the resulting increase in taxes imposed by section 1 or 3 for such taxable year shall be reduced by the credits against tax provided by section 31 (tax withheld on wages) and section 39 (certain uses of gasoline and lubricating oil), but shall not be reduced by any other credits against tax.

(4) The application of the rules of subparagraphs (2) (i) and (3) of this paragraph may be illustrated by the following example:

Example. B, a sole proprietor and a calendar-year basis taxpayer, established a qualified pension trust to which he made annual contributions for 10 years of 10 percent of his earned income. B withdrew his entire interest in the trust during 1973 when he was 55 years old and not disabled and for which, without regard to the distribution, he had a net operating loss and for which he is allowed under section 151 a deduction for one personal exemption. The portion of the distribution includible in B's gross income is $25,750. In addition, B had a net operating loss for 1972. The other three taxable years involved in the computation under subparagraph (2)(i) of this paragraph were years of substantial income. For purposes of determining B's increase in tax attributable to the receipt of the $25,750 (before the application of the provisions of subparagraph (2)(i)(b) of this paragraph), B's taxable income for the year he received the $25,750 is treated, under subparagraph (3)(ii) of this paragraph, as being $25,000 ($25,750 minus $750, the amount of the deduction allowed for each personal exemption under section 151 for 1973). For purposes of determining whether 110 percent of the aggregate increase in taxes which would have resulted if 20 percent of the amount of the withdrawal had been included in B's gross income for the year of receipt and for each of the 4 preceding taxable years is greater (and thus is the amount of his increase in tax attributable to the receipt of the $25,750), B's taxable income for the taxable year of receipt, and for the immediately preceding taxable year, is treated, under subparagraph (3)(i) of this paragraph, as being $5,150 ($25,750 divided by 5).

(f) *Meaning of disabled.*—(1) For taxable years beginning after December 31, 1966, section 72(m)(7) provides that an individual shall be considered to be disabled if he is unable to engage in any substantial gainful activity by reason of any medically determinable physical or mental impairment which can be expected to result in death or to be of long-continued and indefinite duration. In determining whether an individual's impairment makes him unable to engage in any substantial gainful activity, primary consideration shall be given to the nature and severity of his impairment. Consideration shall also be given to other factors such as the individual's education, training, and work experience. The substantial gainful activity to which section 72(m)(7) refers is the activity, or a comparable activity, in which the individual customarily engaged prior to the arising of the disability (or prior to retirement if the individual was retired at the time the disability arose).

(2) Whether or not the impairment in a particular case constitutes a disability is to be determined with reference to all the facts in

Reg. §1.72-17(e)(1)(iii)(b)

the case. The following are examples of impairments which would ordinarily be considered as preventing substantial gainful activity:

(i) Loss of use of two limbs;

(ii) Certain progressive diseases which have resulted in the physical loss or atrophy of a limb, such as diabetes, multiple sclerosis, or Buerger's disease;

(iii) Diseases of the heart, lungs, or blood vessels which have resulted in major loss of heart or lung reserve as evidenced by X-ray, electro-cardiogram, or other objective findings, so that despite medical treatment breathlessness, pain, or fatigue is produced on slight exertion, such as walking several blocks, using public transportation, or doing small chores;

(iv) Cancer which is inoperable and progressive;

(v) Damage to the brain or brain abnormality which has resulted in severe loss of judgment, intellect, orientation, or memory;

(vi) Mental diseases (e.g. psychosis or severe psychoneurosis) requiring continued institutionalization or constant supervision of the individual;

(vii) Loss or diminution of vision to the extent that the affected individual has a central visual acuity of no better than 20/200 in the better eye after best correction, or has a limitation in the fields of vision such that the widest diameter of the visual fields subtends an angle no greater than 20 degrees;

(viii) Permanent and total loss of speech;

(ix) Total deafness uncorrectible by a hearing aid.

The existence of one or more of the impairments described in this subparagraph (or of an impairment of greater severity) will not, however, in and of itself always permit a finding that an individual is disabled as defined in section 72(m)(7). Any impairment, whether of lesser or greater severity, must be evaluated in terms of whether it does in fact prevent the individual from engaging in his customary or any comparable substantial gainful activity.

(3) In order to meet the requirements of section 72(m)(7), an impairment must be expected either to continue for a long and indefinite period or to result in death. Ordinarily, a terminal illness because of disease or injury would result in disability. Indefinite is used in the sense that it cannot reasonably be anticipated that the impairment will, in the foreseeable future, be so diminished as no longer to prevent substantial gainful activity. For example, an individual who suffers a bone fracture which prevents him from working for an extended period of time will not be considered disabled, if his recovery can be expected in the foreseeable future; if the fracture persistently fails to knit, the individual would ordinarily be considered disabled.

(4) An impairment which is remediable does not constitute a disability within the meaning of section 72(m)(7). An individual will not be deemed disabled if, with reasonable effort and safety to himself, the impairment can be diminished to the extent that the individual will not be prevented by the impairment from engaging in his customary or any comparable substantial gainful activity.

(g) *Years to which this section applies.*—This section applies to taxable years ending before September 3, 1974. For taxable years ending after September 2, 1974, see §1.72-17A. [Reg. §1.72-17.]

□ [*T.D. 6676, 9-16-63. Amended by T.D. 6885, 6-1-66, T.D. 6985, 12-26-68, T.D. 7114, 5-17-71 and T.D. 7636, 8-9-79.*]

[Reg. §1.72-17A]

§1.72-17A. Special rules applicable to employee annuities and distributions under deferred compensation plans to self-employed individuals and owner-employees.—(a) *In general.*—Section 72(m) and this section contain special rules for the taxation of amounts received from qualified pension, profit-sharing, or annuity plans covering an owner-employee. This section applies to such amounts for taxable years of the recipient ending after September 2, 1974, unless another date is specified. For purposes of this section, the term "employee" shall include the self-employed individual who is treated as an employee by section 401(c)(1), and the term "owner-employee" has the meaning assigned to it in section 401(c)(3). Paragraph (b) of this section provides rules dealing with the computation of consideration paid by self-employed individuals and paragraph (c) of this section provides rules dealing with such computation when insurance is purchased for owner-employees. Paragraph (d) of this section provides rules for constructive receipt and, for purposes of these rules, treats as an owner-employee an individual for whose benefit an individual retirement account or annuity described in section 408(a) or (b) is maintained after December 31, 1974. Paragraph (e) of this section provides rules for penalties provided by section 72(m)(5) with respect to certain distributions received by owner-employees or their successors. Paragraph (f) of this section provides rules for determining whether a person is disabled within the meaning of section 72(m)(7). See §1.72-16, relating to life insurance contracts purchased under qualified employee plans, for rules under section 72(m)(3).

(b) *Computation of consideration paid by self-employed individuals.*—Under section 72(m)(2), consideration paid or contributed for the contract by any self-employed individual shall for purposes of section 72 be deemed not to include any contributions paid or contributed under a plan described in paragraph (a), or any other plan of deferred compensation described in section 404(a) (whether or not qualified), if the contributions are—

(1) Paid under such plan with respect to a time during which the employee was an employee only by reason of sections 401(c)(1) and 404(a)(8), and

(2) Deductible under section 404 by the employer, including an employer within the meaning of sections 401(c)(4) and 404(a)(8), of such self-employed individual at the time of such payment, or subsequent to such time of payment.

For purposes of this paragraph the term "consideration paid or contributed for the contract" has the same meaning as under subparagraphs (1), (2), and (3) of paragraph (c) of this section.

(c) *Amounts paid for life, accident, health, or other insurance.*—Under section 72(m)(2), amounts used to purchase life, accident, health, or other insurance protection for an owner-employee shall not be taken into account in computing the following:

(1) The aggregate amount of premiums or other consideration paid for the contract for purposes of determining the investment in the contract under section 72(c)(1)(A) and §1.72-6;

(2) The consideration for the contract contributed by the employee for purposes of section 72(d)(1) and §1.72-13, which provide the method of taxing employee's annuities where the employee's contributions will be recoverable within 3 years; and

(3) The aggregate premiums or other consideration paid for purposes of section 72(e)(1)(B) and §1.72-11, which provide the rules for taxing amounts not received as annuities prior to the annuity starting date.

The cost of such insurance protection will be considered to be a reasonable net premium cost, as determined by the Commissioner, for the appropriate period.

(d) *Amounts constructively received.*—(1) The references in this paragraph (d) to section 72(m)(4) are to that section as in effect on August 13, 1982. Section 236(b)(1) of the Tax Equity and Fiscal Responsibility Act of 1982 (96 Stat. 324) repealed section 72(m)(4), generally effective for assignments, pledges and loans made after August 13, 1982, and added section 72(p). See section 72(p) and §1.72(p)-1 for rules governing the income tax treatment of certain assignments, pledges and loans from qualified employer plans made after August 13, 1982.

(2) Under section 72(m)(4)(A), if during any taxable year an owner-employee assigns or pledges (or agrees to assign or pledge) any portion of his interest in a trust described in section 401(a) which is exempt from tax under section 501(a), or any portion of the value of a contract purchased as part of a plan described in section 403(a), such portion shall be treated as having been received by such owner-employee as a distribution from the trust or as an amount received under the contract during such taxable year.

(3)(i) Under paragraphs (4)(A) and (6) of section 72(m), if after December 31, 1974, during any taxable year an individual for whose benefit an individual retirement account or annuity described in section 408(a) or (b) is maintained assigns or pledges (or agrees to assign or pledge) any portion of his interest in such account or annuity, such portion shall be treated as having been received by such individual as a distribution from such account or trust during such taxable year. See subsections (d) and (f) of section 408 and the regulations thereunder for the tax treatment of an amount treated as a distribution under this subparagraph.

(ii) Notwithstanding subdivision (i) of this subparagraph, if an individual retirement account or annuity, or portion thereof, is subject to the additional tax imposed by section 408(f), that amount shall be deemed not to be a distribution under section 72(m)(4)(A) and subdivision (i) of this subparagraph.

(4) Under section 72(m)(4)(B), if during any taxable year an owner-employee receives, either directly or indirectly, any amount from any insurance company as a loan under a contract purchased by a trust described in section 401(a) which is exempt from tax under section 501(a) or purchased as part of a plan described in section 403(a), and issued by such insurance company, such amount shall be treated as an amount received under the contract during such taxable year. An owner-employee will be considered to have received an amount under a contract if a premium, which is otherwise in default, is paid by the insurance company in the form of a loan against the cash surrender value of the contract. Further, an owner-employee will be considered to have received an amount to which this subparagraph applies if an amount is received from the issuer of a face-amount certificate as a loan under such certificate purchased as part of a qualified trust or plan.

(e) *Penalties applicable to certain amounts received with respect to owner-employees under section 72(m)(5).*—(1)(i) For taxable years of the recipient beginning after December 31, 1975, if any person receives an amount to which subparagraph (2) of this paragraph applies, his tax under chapter 1 for the taxable year in which such amount is received shall be increased by an amount equal to 10 percent of the portion of the amount so received which is includible in his gross income for such taxable year.

(ii) For taxable years of the recipient beginning before January 1, 1976, see subparagraph (3) of this paragraph.

(2)(i) This subparagraph is applicable to amounts, to the extent includible in gross income, received from a qualified trust described in section 401(a) or under a plan described in section 403(a) by or on behalf of an individual who is or has been an owner-employee with respect to such trust or plan—

(A) Which are received before the owner-employee reaches the age of $59\frac{1}{2}$ years, and which are attributable to contributions paid on behalf of such owner-employee by his employer (that is employer contributions within the meaning of section 401(c)(5)(A) and the increments in value attributable to such employer contributions) and the increments in value attributable to contributions made by him as an owner-employee while he was an owner-employee (that is, the increments attributable to owner-employee contributions within the meaning of section 401(c)(5)(B), but not such contributions; see subdivision (ii) of this subparagraph).

(B) Which are in excess of the benefits provided for such owner-employee under the plan formula (see subdivision (iii) of this subparagraph), or

(C) Which are subject to the transitional rules with respect to willful excess contributions made on behalf of an owner-employee in his employer's taxable years which begin before January 1, 1976 (see subdivision (v) of this subparagraph).

(ii) The amounts referred to in subdivision (i)(A) of this subparagraph do not include—

(A) Amounts received by reason of the owner-employee becoming disabled (see paragraph (f) of this section).

(B) Amounts received by the owner-employee in his capacity as a policyholder of an annuity, endowment, or life insurance contract which are in the nature of a dividend or similar distribution, or

(C) Amounts attributable to contributions (and increments in value thereon) made for years for which the recipient was not an owner-employee.

If an amount is not included in the amounts referred to in subdivision (i)(A) of this subparagraph solely by reason of the owner-employee's becoming disabled and if a penalty would otherwise be applicable with respect to all or a portion of such amount, then for the owner-employee's taxable year in which such amount is received, there must be submitted with his income tax return a doctor's statement as to the impairment, and a statement by the owner-employee with respect to the effect of such impairment upon his substantial gainful activity and the date such impairment occurred. For taxable years which are subsequent to the first taxable year with respect to which the statements referred to in the preceding sentence are submitted, the owner-employee may, in lieu of such statements, submit a statement declaring the continued existence (without substantial diminution) of the impairment and its continued effect upon his substantial gainful activity.

(iii) This subparagraph applies to amounts described in subdivision (i)(B) of this subparagraph (relating to benefits in excess of the plan formula) even though a portion of such amounts may be attributable to contributions made on behalf of an individual while he was not an owner-employee and even if he is deceased and the amounts are received by his successor.

(iv)(A) The rules described in subdivisions (i)(A) and (iii) of this subparagraph, relating to the treatment under section 72(m)(5)(A)(i) of certain premature distributions, may be illustrated by the following example:

Example. (1) A was a member of the X partnership, consisting of partners A through I, and a participant in the partnership's qualified profit-sharing plan which was established on January 1, 1972. A's taxable years, the X partnership's taxable years, the plan years, and other relevant years are all calendar years at all relevant times. For the three calendar years 1972 through 1974, A was an owner-employee in the X partnership. On January 1, 1975, new partners J and K became partners in the X partnership, and as of that date, each of partners A through K held a 1/11 interest in the capital and profits of the X partnership. On that date, A became a partner who was not an owner-employee. A continued in this status for the 2 calendar years 1975 and 1976. On January 1, 1977, when A was 50 years old and not disabled, he liquidated his interest in the X partnership and became an employee of an unrelated employer. On that date, A received a distribution representing his entire interest in the X partnership's plan of $54,000 cash in violation of the plan provision required by section 401(d)(4)(B). As of that date, the distribution was attributable to the following sources and times, computed by the plan in a manner consistent with the subparagraph:

Calendar years	X contributions on behalf of A deductible under sec. 404 A	A's contributions made as an employee B	Increments in value attributable to column A yearly contributions C	Increments in value attributable to column B yearly contributions D
1977	0	0	0	0
1976	$7,500	$2,500	$900	$300
1975	7,500	2,500	4,000	1,300
1974	7,500	2,500	1,800	700
1973	2,500	2,500	1,200	1,200
1972	2,500	2,500	1,300	1,300
Totals	$27,500	$12,500	$9,200	$4,800

(2) The amount of the $54,000 distribution to which subdivision (i)(A) of this subparagraph applies is $20,000, computed as follows:

X contributions on behalf of A made in years A was an owner-employee:

1974	$7,500
1973	2,500
1972	2,500
Total	$12,500

Increments in value attributable to such contributions:

1974	1,800
1973	1,200
1972	1,300
Total	$4,300

Increments in value attributable to contributions made by A as an employee for years in which he was an owner-employee:

1974	700
1973	1,200
1972	1,300
Total	$3,200
Grand Total	$20,000

In this example, the $20,000 amount computed above would be includible in A's gross income for 1977 and would be subject to the 10 percent tax described in subparagraph (1)(i) of this paragraph.

(3) Subdivision (i)(A) of this subparagraph does not apply to the contributions made by X on behalf of A for 1976 and 1975 ($7,500 each year, totaling $15,000) nor to the increments in value attributable to those contributions ($900 for 1976 and $4,000 for 1975, totaling $4,900) because A was not an owner-employee with respect to these two years 1976 and 1975, on account of which these employer contributions were made. For the same reason, subdivision (i)(A) of this subparagraph does not apply to the increments in value attributable to A's contributions for 1976 and 1975 ($300 and $1,300, respectively, totaling $1,600).

See section 4972(c) for the amount of employee contributions which is permitted to be contributed by an owner-employee (as an employee) without subjecting an owner-employee to the tax on excess contributions.

(4) Subdivision (i)(A) of this subparagraph does not apply to the contributions made by A, as an employee during the years when he was an owner-employee ($2,500 during each of the years 1972, 1973, and 1974, totaling $7,500), because the distribution was received in a taxable year of A ending after September 2, 1974; see subparagraph (3) of this paragraph. Furthermore, because the distribution of the amount of A's contributions ($12,500) constitutes consideration for the contract paid by A for purposes of section 72, the $7,500 amount described in the preceding sentence is not includible in his gross income, and that amount is not subject to the rules of this subparagraph; see subdivision (i) of this subparagraph, and paragraphs (b) and (c) of this section.

(B) The increments in value of an individual's account may be allocated to contributions on his behalf, by his employer or by such individual as an owner-employee, while he was an owner-employee either by maintaining a separate account, or an accounting, which reflects the actual increment attributable to such contributions, or by the method described in (C) of this subdivision.

1982	. . . .		
1981	. . . .		
1980	. . . .		
1979	. . . .		
1978	. . . .		
1977	. . . .		
1976	. . . .		
1975	. . . .		
1974	. . . .		
1973	. . . .		
Total	. . . .		

Total weighted contributions as owner-employee (1978-1982) = $5,800.

$$5,400 \times \frac{\$5,800}{\$46,900} = \$667.80$$

(E)(1) The rules set forth in subdivision (iv)(E)(2) of this subparagraph shall be used to determine the amounts to which subdivision (i)(A) of this subparagraph applies in the case of a distribution of less than the entire balance of the employee's account from a plan in which he has been covered at different times as owner-employee or as an employee other than an owner-employee.

(2) Distributions or payments from a plan for any employee taxable year shall be deemed to be attributable to contributions to the plan, and increments thereon, in the following order—

(i) Excess contributions, within the meaning of section 4972(b), designated as such by the trustee;

(ii) Employee contributions;

(iii) Employer contributions, other than those described in (i), and the increments in value attributable to the employee's own contributions and his employer's contributions on the basis of the taxable years of his employer in succeeding order of time whether or not the employee was an owner-employee for any such year.

For purposes of (iii) of this subdivision, the time of contributions made on the basis of any employer taxable year shall take into account the rule specified in section 404(a)(6), relating to time when contributions deemed made.

(v) The amounts referred to in subdivision (i)(C) of this subparagraph are amounts which are received by reason of a distribution of the owner-employee's entire interest under the provisions of section 401(e)(2)(E), as in effect on September 1, 1974, relating to

(C) Where an individual is covered under the same plan both as an owner-employee and as a non-owner-employee, the portion of the increment in value of his interest attributable to contributions made on his behalf while he was an owner-employee may be determined by multiplying the total increment in value in his account by a fraction. The numerator of the fraction is the total contributions made on behalf of the individual as an owner-employee, weighted for the number of years that each contribution was in the plan. The denominator is the total contributions made on behalf of the individual, whether or not as an owner-employee, weighted for the number of years each contribution was in the plan. The contributions are weighted for the number of years in the plan by multiplying each contribution by the number of years it was in the plan. For purposes of this computation, any forfeiture allocated to the account of the individual is treated as a contribution to the account made at the time so allocated. For purposes of this computation, where the individual has received a prior distribution from such account, an appropriate adjustment must be made to reflect such prior distribution.

(D) The method described in (C) of this subdivision may be illustrated by the following example:

Example. B was a member of the XYZ Partnership and a participant in the partnership's profit-sharing plan which was created in 1973. Until the end of 1977, B's interest in the partnership was less than 10 percent. On January 1, 1978, B obtained an interest in excess of 10 percent in the partnership and continued to participate in the profit-sharing plan until 1982. During 1982, prior to the time he attained the age of 59 1/2 years and during a time when he was not disabled, B, who had not received any prior plan distributions, withdrew his entire interest in the profit-sharing plan. At the time his interest was $15,000, $9,600 contributions and $5,400 increment attributable to the contributions. The portion of the increment attributable to contributions while B was an owner-employee is $667.80, determined as follows:

Contribution A	Number of years contribution was in trust B	Contribution weighted for years in trust (A × B) C
$1,000	0	0
800	1	800
1,200	2	2,400
600	3	1,800
200	4	800
400	5	2,000
2,000	6	12,000
1,000	7	7,000
1,500	8	12,000
900	9	8,100
9,600	. . . .	46,900

Total weighted contributions = $46,900.

excess contributions on behalf of an owner-employee which are willfully made. Notwithstanding the preceding sentence, an owner-employee's entire interest in all plans with respect to which he is an owner-employee (within the meaning of subsections (d)(8)(C) and (e)(2)(E)(ii) of section 401, as in effect on September 1, 1974) does not include any distribution or payment attributable to his employer's contributions or his own contributions made with respect to his employer's taxable years beginning after December 31, 1975. However, his entire interest in all plans does include all of the distribution or payment attributable to his employer's contributions and his own contributions made with respect to all of his employer's taxable years beginning before January 1, 1976, if any portion thereof is attributable in whole or in part to such a willful excess contribution and such entire interest is received because of a willful excess contribution pursuant to section 401(e)(2)(E)(ii). A distribution or payment is described in the preceding sentence even though it is received in an owner-employee's taxable year beginning after December 31, 1975. For purposes of computing the increments in value attributable to employer taxable years which begin before January 1, 1976, and such increments attributable to such years beginning after December 31, 1975, the rules specified in subdivision (iv)(B), (C), (D), and (E) of this subparagraph shall be applied to the extent applicable.

(3)(i) For taxable years of the recipient beginning before January 1, 1976, the tax with respect to amounts to which subparagraph (2) of this paragraph applies shall be computed under subparagraphs (B),

Reg. §1.72-17A(e)(3)(i)

(C), (D), and (E) of section 72(m)(5) as such subparagraphs were in effect prior to the amendments made by subsections (g)(1) and (2)(A) of section 2001 of the Employee Retirement Income Security Act of 1974 (88 Stat. 957) except as provided in subdivisions (ii) and (iii) of this subparagraph (see paragraph (e) of §1.72-17). For purposes of the preceding sentence, amounts to which subparagraph (2) of this paragraph applies in the case of an amount described in section 72(m)(5)(A)(i) shall be determined under subdivisions (ii) and (ii) of §1.72-17(e)(1), except as provided in subdivision (ii) of this sub-paragraph. For purposes of the first sentence of this subdivision, amounts to which subparagraph (2) of this paragraph applies in the case of an amount described in section 72(m)(5)(A)(ii) shall be determined under subdivisions (i)(b) and (iii) of §1.72-17(e)(1), except as provided in subdivision (iii) of this subparagraph.

(ii) For purposes of applying section 72(m)(5)(A)(i), after the amendment made by section 2001(h)(3) of such Act, and subdivisions (i)(a) and (ii) of §1.72-17(e)(1), to a distribution or payment received in recipient taxable years ending after September 2, 1974, and beginning before January 1, 1976, with respect to contributions made on behalf of an owner-employee which were made by him as an owner-employee (that is, employee contributions within the meaning of section 401(c)(5)(B)) the portion of any distribution or payment attributable to such contributions shall not include such contributions but shall include the increments in value attributable to such contributions.

(iii) For purposes of applying section 72(m)(5)(D) and subdivisions (i)(b) and (iii) of §1.72-17(e)(1) to recipient taxable years beginning after December 31, 1973, and beginning before January 1, 1976, in the case of distributions or payments made after December 31, 1973, the amounts to which section 402(a)(2) or 403(a)(2) applies after the amendments made by section 2005(b)(1) and (2) of such Act (88 Stat. 990 and 991) (which are amounts to which subdivision (i)(b) of §1.72-17(e)(1) does not apply) shall be deemed to be the amount which is treated as a gain from the sale or exchange of a capital asset held for more than 6 months under either of such sections.

(f) *Meaning of disabled.*—(1) Section 72(m)(7) provides that an individual shall be considered to be disabled if he is unable to engage in any substantial gainful activity by reason of any medically determinable physical or mental impairment which can be expected to result in death or to be of long-continued and indefinite duration. In determining whether an individual's impairment makes him unable to engage in any substantial gainful activity, primary consideration shall be given to the nature and severity of his impairment. Consideration shall also be given to other factors such as the individual's education, training, and work experience. The substantial gainful activity to which section 72(m)(7) refers is the activity, or a comparable activity, in which the individual customarily engaged prior to the arising of the disability or prior to retirement if the individual was retired at the time the disability arose.

(2) Whether or not the impairment in a particular case constitutes a disability is to be determined with reference to all the facts in the case. The following are examples of impairments which would ordinarily be considered as preventing substantial gainful activity:

(i) Loss of use of two limbs;

(ii) Certain progressive diseases which have resulted in the physical loss or atrophy of a limb, such as diabetes, multiple sclerosis, or Buerger's disease;

(iii) Diseases of the heart, lungs, or blood vessels which have resulted in major loss of heart or lung reserve as evidenced by X-ray, electrocardiogram, or other objective findings, so that despite medical treatment breathlessness, pain, or fatigue is produced on slight exertion, such as walking several blocks, using public transportation, or doing small chores;

(iv) Cancer which is inoperable and progressive;

(v) Damage to the brain or brain abnormality which has resulted in severe loss of judgment, intellect, orientation, or memory;

(vi) Mental diseases (e.g., psychosis or severe psychoneurosis) requiring continued institutionalization or constant supervision of the individual;

(vii) Loss or diminution of vision to the extent that the affected individual has a central visual acuity of no better than 20/200 in the better eye after best correction, or has a limitation in the fields of vision such that the widest diameter of the visual fields subtends an angle no greater than 20 degrees;

(viii) Permanent and total loss of speech;

(ix) Total deafness uncorrectible by a hearing aid.

The existence of one or more of the impairments described in this subparagraph (or of an impairment of greater severity) will not, however, in and of itself always permit a finding that an individual is disabled as defined in section 72(m)(7). Any impairment, whether of lesser or greater severity, must be evaluated in terms of whether it does in fact prevent the individual from engaging in his customary or any comparable substantial gainful activity.

(3) In order to meet the requirements of section 72(m)(7), an impairment must be expected either to continue for a long and indefinite period or to result in death. Ordinarily, a terminal illness because of disease or injury would result in disability. The term "indefinite" is used in the sense that it cannot reasonably be anticipated that the impairment will, in the foreseeable future, be so diminished as no longer to prevent substantial gainful activity. For example, an individual who suffers a bone fracture which prevents him from working for an extended period of time will not be considered disabled, if his recovery can be expected in the foreseeable future; if the fracture persistently fails to knit, the individual would ordinarily be considered disabled.

(4) An impairment which is remediable does not constitute a disability within the meaning of section 72(m)(7). An individual will not be deemed disabled if, with reasonable effort and safety to himself, the impairment can be diminished to the extent that the individual will not be prevented by the impairment from engaging in his customary or any comparable substantial gainful activity. [Reg. §1.72-17A.]

☐ [T.D. 7636, 8-9-79. *Amended by T.D. 8894, 7-28-2000 and T.D. 9849,* 3-11-2019.]

[Reg. §1.72-18]

§1.72-18. Treatment of certain total distributions with respect to self-employed individuals.—(a) *In general.*—The Self-Employed Individuals Tax Retirement Act of 1962 permits self-employed individuals to be treated as employees for purposes of participation in pension, profit-sharing, and annuity plans described in sections 401(a) and 403(a). In general, amounts received by a distributee or payee which are attributable to contributions made on behalf of a participant while he was self-employed are taxed in the same manner as amounts which are attributable to contributions made on behalf of a common-law employee. However, such amounts which are paid in one taxable year representing the total distributions payable to a distributee or payee with respect to an employee, are not eligible for the capital gains treatment of section 402(a)(2) or 403(a)(2). This section sets forth the treatment of such distributions, except where such a distribution is subject to the penalties of section 72(m)(5) and paragraph (3) of §1.72-17.

(b) *Distributions to which this section applies.*—(1)(i) Except as provided in subparagraphs (2) and (3) of this paragraph, this section applies to amounts distributed to a distributee in one taxable year of the distributee in the case of an employees' trust described in section 401 (a) which is exempt under section 501 (a), or to amounts paid to a payee in one taxable year of the payee in the case of an annuity plan described in section 403 (a), which constitute the total distributions payable, or the total amounts payable, to the distributee or payee with respect to an employee.

(ii) For the total distributions or amounts payable to a distributee or payee to be considered paid within one taxable year of the distributee or payee for purposes of this section, all amounts to the credit of the employee-participant through the end of such taxable year which are payable to the distributee or payee must be distributed or paid within such taxable year. Thus, the provisions of this section are not applicable to a distribution or payment to a distributee or payee if the trust or plan retains any amounts after the close of such taxable year which are payable to the same distributee or payee even though the amounts retained may be attributable to contributions on behalf of the employee-participant while he was a common-law employee in the business with respect to which the plan was established.

(iii) For purposes of this section, the total amounts payable to a distributee or the amounts to the credit of the employee do not include United States Retirement Plan Bonds held by a trust to the credit of the employee. Thus, a distribution to a distributee by a qualified trust may constitute a distribution to which this section applies even though the trust retains retirement plan bonds registered in the name of the employee on whose behalf the distribution is made which are to be distributed to the same distributee. Moreover, the proceeds of a retirement bond received as part of a distribution which constitutes the total distributions payable to the distributee are not entitled to the special tax treatment of this section.

(iv) If the amounts payable to a distributee from a qualified trust with respect to an employee-participant includes an annuity contract, such contract must be distributed along with all other amounts payable to the distributee in order to have a distribution to which this section applies. However, the proceeds of an annuity contract received in a total distribution will not be entitled to the tax treatment of this section unless the contract is surrendered in the taxable year of the distributee in which the total distribution was received.

(v) In the case of a qualified annuity plan, the term "total amounts" means all annuities payable to a payee. If more than one annuity contract is received under the plan by a distributee, this section shall not apply to an amount received on surrender of any such contracts unless all contracts under the plan payable to the payee are surrendered within one taxable year of the payee.

(vi)(a) The provisions of this section are applicable where the total amounts payable to a distributee or payee are paid within one taxable year of the distributee or payee whether or not a portion of the employee-participant's interest which is payable to another distributee or payee is paid within the same taxable year. However, a distributee or payee who, in prior taxable years received amounts (except amounts described in (b) of this subdivision) after the employee-participant ceases to be eligible for additional contributions to be made on his behalf, does not receive a distribution or payment to which this section applies, even though the total amount remaining to be paid to such distributee or payee with respect to such employee is paid within one taxable year. On the other hand, a distribution to a distributee or payee prior to the time that the employee-participant ceases to be eligible for additional contributions on his behalf does not preclude the application of this section to a later distribution to the same distributee or payee.

(b) The receipt of an amount which constitutes—

(1) A payment in the nature of a dividend or similar distribution to an individual in his capacity as a policyholder of an annuity, endowment, or life insurance contract, or

(2) A return of excess contributions which were not willfully made,

does not prevent the application of this section to a total distribution even though the amount is received after the employee-participant ceases to be eligible for additional contributions and in a taxable year other than the taxable year in which the total amount is received.

(vii) For purposes of this section, the total amounts payable to a distributee or payee, or the amounts to the credit of the employee, do not include any amounts which have been placed in a separate account for the funding of medical benefits described in section 401(h) as defined in paragraph (a) of § 1.401-14. Thus, a distribution by a qualified trust or annuity plan may constitute a distribution to which this section applies even though amount attributable to the funding of section 401(h) medical benefits as defined in paragraph (a) of § 1.401-14 are not so distributed.

(2) This section shall apply—

(i) Only if the distribution or payment is made—

(a) On account of the employee's death at any time,

(b) After the employee has attained the age 59 1/2 years, or

(c) After the employee has become disabled; and

(ii) Only to so much of the distribution or payment as is attributable to contributions made on behalf of an employee while he was a self-employed individual in the business with respect to which the plan was established. Any distribution or payment, or any portion thereof, which is not so attributable shall be subject to the rules of taxation which apply to any distribution or payment that is attributable to contributions on behalf of common-law employees. For taxable years beginning after December 31, 1966, see section 72(m)(7) and paragraph (f) of § 1.72-17 for the meaning of disabled. For taxable years beginning before January 1, 1967, see section 213(g)(3) for the meaning of disabled. For taxable years beginning after December 31, 1968, if this section is applicable by reason of the distribution or payment being made after the employee has become disabled, then for the taxable year in which the amounts to which this section applies are distributed or paid, there shall be submitted with the recipient's income tax return a doctor's statement as to the nature and effect of the employee's impairment.

(3) This section shall not apply to—

(i) Distributions or payments to which the penalty provisions of section 72(m)(5) and paragraph (e) of § 1.72-17 apply,

(ii) Distributions or payments from a trust or plan made to or on behalf of an individual prior to the time such individual ceases to be eligible for additional contributions (except the contribution attributable to the last year of service) to be made to the trust or plan on his behalf as a self-employed individual, and

(iii) Distributions or payments made to the employee from a plan or trust unless contributions which were allowed as a deduction under section 404 have been made on behalf of such employee as a self-employed individual under such trust or plan for 5 or more taxable years (whether or not consecutive) prior to the taxable year in which such distributions or payments are made. Distributions or payments to which this section does not apply by reason of this subdivision are taxed as otherwise provided in section 72. However, for taxable years beginning before January 1, 1964, section 72(e)(3), as in effect before such date, is not applicable. For taxable years beginning after December 31, 1963, such distributions or payments may be taken into account in computations under sections 1301 through 1305 (relating to income averaging).

(4) The portion of any distribution or payment attributable to contributions on behalf of an employee-participant while he was self-employed includes the contributions made on his behalf while he was self-employed and the increments in value attributable to such contributions. Where the amounts to the credit of an employee-participant include amounts attributable to contributions on his behalf while he was a self-employed individual and amounts attributable to contributions on his behalf while he was a common-law employee, the increment in value attributable to the employee-participant's interest shall be allocated to the contributions on his behalf while he was self-employed either by maintaining a separate account, or an accounting, which reflects the actual increment attributable to such contributions, or by the method described in paragraph (e)(1)(iv)(c) of § 1.72-17. However, if the latter method is used, the numerator of the fraction is the total contributions made on behalf of the individual as a self-employed individual, weighted for the number of years that each contribution was in the plan.

(c) *Amounts includible in gross income.*—(1) Where a total distribution or payment to which this section applies is made to one distributee or payee and includes the total amount remaining to the credit of the employee-participant on whose behalf the distribution or payment was made, the distributee or payee shall include in gross income an amount equal to the portion of the distribution or payment which exceeds the employee-participant's investment in the contract. For purposes of this paragraph, the investment in the contract shall be reduced by any amounts previously received from the plan or trust by or on behalf of the employee-participant which were excludable from gross income as a return of the investment in the contract.

(2) In the case of a distribution to which this section applies and which is made to more than one distributee or payee, each element of the amounts to the credit of an employee-participant shall be allocated among the several distributees or payees on the basis of the ratio of the value of the distributee's or payee's distribution or payment to the total amount to the credit of the employee-participant. The elements to be so allocated include the investment in the contract, the increments in value, and the portion of the amounts to the credit of the employee-participant which is attributable to the contributions on behalf of the employee-participant while he was a self-employed individual.

(d) *Computation of tax.*—(1) The tax attributable to the amounts to which this section applies for the taxable year in which such amounts are received is the greater of—

(i) 5 times the increase in tax which would result from the inclusion in gross income of the recipient of 20 percent of so much of the amount so received as is includible in gross income, or

(ii) 5 times the increase which would result if the taxable income of the recipient for such taxable year equaled 20 percent of the excess of the aggregate of the amounts so received and includible in gross income over the amount of the deductions allowed the recipient for such taxable year under section 151 (relating to deduction for personal exemptions).

In any case in which the application of subdivision (ii) of this subparagraph results in an increase in taxable income for any taxable year, the resulting increase in taxes imposed by section 1 or 3 for such taxable year shall be reduced by the credit against tax provided by section 31 (tax withheld on wages), but shall not be reduced by any other credits against tax.

(2) The application of the rules of this paragraph may be illustrated by the following example:

Example. B, a sole proprietor and a calendar-year basis taxpayer, established a qualified pension trust to which he made annual contributions for 10 years of 10 percent of his earned income. B withdrew his entire interest in the trust during 1973, for which year, without regard to the distribution, he had a net operating loss and is allowed under section 151 a deduction for one personal exemption. At the time of the withdrawal, B was 64 years old. The amount of the distribution that is includible in his gross income is $25,750. Because of B's net operating loss the tax attributable to the distribution is determined under the rule of subparagraph (1)(ii) of this paragraph. For purposes of determining the tax attributable to the $25,750, B's taxable income for 1973 is treated, under subparagraph (1)(ii) of this paragraph, as being 20 percent of $25,000 ($25,750 minus $750, the amount of the deduction allowed for each personal exemption under section 151 for 1973). Thus, under subparagraph (1) of this paragraph, the tax attributable to the $25,750 would be 5 times the increase which would result if the taxable income of B for the taxable year he received such amount equaled $5,000. B has had no amounts withheld from wages and thus is not entitled to reduce the increase in taxes by the credit against tax provided in section 31 and may not reduce the increase in taxes by any other credits against tax. [Reg. § 1.72-18.]

☐ [T.D. 6676, 9-16-63. *Amended by* T.D. 6722, 4-13-64, T.D. 6885, 6-1-66, *T.D.* 6985, 12-26-68, *T.D.* 7114, 5-17-71 *and* T.D. 9849, 3-11-2019.]

[Reg. § 1.72(e)-1T]

§ 1.72(e)-1T. Treatment of distributions where substantially all contributions are employee contributions (Temporary).

Q-1: How did the Tax Reform Act (TRA) of 1984 change the law with regard to the treatment of non-annuity distributions (i.e., amounts distributed prior to the annuity starting date and not received as annuities) from a qualified plan that is treated as a single contract under section 72 and under which substantially all of the contributions are employee contributions?

A-1: (a) Prior to the amendment of section 72(e) by the TRA of 1984, non-annuity distributions from such a qualified plan generally were allocable, first, to nondeductible employee contributions and thus were not includible in gross income. After distributions equaled the balance of nondeductible employee contributions, further non-annuity distributions generally were includible in gross income.

(b) Pursuant to section 72(e)(7), as added by the TRA of 1984, non-annuity distributions from such a qualified plan that are allocable to investment in the plan after August 13, 1982 (as determined in accordance with section 72(e)(5)(B)), generally will be treated, first, as allocable to income and, second, as allocable to nondeductible employee contributions. Distributions allocable to income are includible in gross income. Distributions allocable to nondeductible employee contributions are not includible in gross income.

Q-2: To which qualified plans and contracts does section 72(e)(7) apply?

A-2: Section 72 (e)(7) applies to any plan or contract under which substantially all of the contributions are employee contributions if—

(a) Such plan is described in section 401(a) and the related trust or trusts are exempt from tax under section 501(a); or

(b) Such contract is—

(1) Purchased by a trust described in (a) above,

(2) Purchased as part of a plan described in section 403(a), or

(3) Described in section 403(b).

Q-3: What is the definition of a qualified plan or contract under which substantially all of the contributions are employee contributions?

A-3: (a) A qualified plan or contract under which substantially all of the contributions are employee contributions is a plan or contract with respect to which 85 percent or more of the total contributions during the "representative period" are employee contributions. The "representative period" means the five-plan-year period preceding the plan year during which a distribution occurs. However, if less than 85 percent of the total contributions for all plan years during which the plan or contract is in existence prior to the plan year of distribution are employee contributions, then the plan or contract is not one with respect to which substantially all of the contributions are employee contributions.

(b) For purposes of the 85 percent test, contributions made to a predecessor plan or contract are aggregated with contributions made to the plan or contract to which the 85 percent test is being applied (the successor plan or contract). For purposes of the preceding sentence, a predecessor plan or contract is a plan or contract the terms of which are substantially the same as the successor plan or contract.

Q-4: What is the definition of employee contributions for purposes of section 72(e)(7)?

A-4: For purposes of section 72(e)(7), employee contributions are those amounts contributed by the employee and those amounts considered contributed by the employee under section 72(f). For example, amounts contributed to a section 401(k) qualified cash or deferred arrangement, pursuant to an employee's election to defer such amounts, are employer contributions to the extent that such amounts are not currently includible in gross income. In addition, deductible employee contributions under section 72(o) are disregarded in their entirety (i.e., treated as neither employee contributions nor employer contributions) in determining whether substantially all the contributions are employee contributions.

Q-5: How is the 85 percent test of section 72(e)(7) applied to a qualified plan or contract?

A-5: (a) Except as provided in paragraphs (b), (c), and (d), the 85 percent test is applied separately with respect to each contract under section 72.

(b) If a single qualified plan described in section 401(a) or section 403(a) comprises more than one contract under section 72, regardless of whether such plan includes multiple trusts or combinations of profit-sharing and pension features, these contracts are aggregated for purposes of applying the 85 percent test. Thus, if substantially all of the contributions under a qualified plan comprising two contracts under section 72 are employee contributions, section 72(e)(5)(D) shall not apply to non-annuity distributions under either of the contracts.

(c) With respect to the plans maintained by the Federal Government or by instrumentalities of the Federal Government, the 85 percent test shall be applied by aggregating all such plans. This aggregation rule applies only to those plans that are actively administered by the Federal Government or an instrumentality thereof. Thus, if a plan of the Federal Government is administered by a commercial financial institution, it would not be aggregated with other plans of the Federal Government and its instrumentalities for purposes of applying the 85 percent test.

(d) In the case of a contract described in section 403(b), the 85 percent test is applied separately to each such contract.

Q-6: Is a loan from a qualified plan or contract described in section 72(e)(7) treated as a distribution under section 72(e)(4)(A)?

A-6: Yes. Pursuant to section 72(e)(4)(A), if an employee receives, either directly or indirectly, any amount as a loan from a qualified plan or contract described in section 72(e)(7), such amount shall be treated as a distribution from the plan or contract of an amount not received as an annuity. Similarly, if an employee assigns or pledges, or agrees to assign or pledge, any portion of the value of any qualified plan or contract, such portion shall be treated as a distribution from the plan or contract of an amount not received as an annuity.

Q-7: Does the five percent penalty for premature distributions from annuity contracts, as described in section 72(q), apply to distributions from a qualified plan or contract described in section 72(e)(7)?

A-7: No.

Q-8: When is section 72(e)(7) effective?

A-8: Section 72(e)(7) is effective for amounts received or loans made on or after October 17, 1984. For purposes of this effective date provision, loan amounts outstanding on October 16, 1984, which are renegotiated, extended, renewed, or revised after that date generally are treated as loans made on the date of the renegotiation, etc. [Temporary Reg. § 1.72(e)-1T.]

☐ [T.D. 8073, 1-29-86.]

[Reg. § 1.72(p)-1]

§ 1.72(p)-1. Loans treated as distributions.—The questions and answers in this section provide guidance under section 72(p) pertaining to loans from qualified employer plans (including government plans and tax-sheltered annuities and employer plans that were formerly qualified). The examples included in the questions and answers in this section are based on the assumption that a bona fide loan is made to a participant from a qualified defined contribution plan pursuant to an enforceable agreement (in accordance with paragraph (b) of Q&A-3 of this section), with adequate security and with an interest rate and repayment terms that are commercially reasonable. (The particular interest rate used, which is solely for illustration, is 8.75 percent compounded annually.) In addition, unless the contrary is specified, it is assumed in the examples that the amount of the loan does not exceed 50 percent of the participant's nonforfeitable account balance, the participant has no other outstanding loan (and had no prior loan) from the plan or any other plan maintained by the participant's employer or any other person required to be aggregated with the employer under section 414(b), (c) or (m), and the loan is not excluded from section 72(p) as a loan made in the ordinary course of an investment program as described in Q&A-18 of this section. The regulations and examples in this section do not provide guidance on whether a loan from a plan would result in a prohibited transaction under section 4975 of the Internal Revenue Code or on whether a loan from a plan covered by Title I of the Employee Retirement Income Security Act of 1974 (88 Stat. 829) (ERISA) would be consistent with the fiduciary standards of ERISA or would result in a prohibited transaction under section 406 of ERISA. The questions and answers are as follows:

Q-1: In general, what does section 72(p) provide with respect to loans from a qualified employer plan?

A-1: (a) *Loans.* Under section 72(p), an amount received by a participant or beneficiary as a loan from a qualified employer plan is treated as having been received as a distribution from the plan (a deemed distribution), unless the loan satisfies the requirements of Q&A-3 of this section. For purposes of section 72(p) and this section, a loan made from a contract that has been purchased under a qualified employer plan (including a contract that has been distributed to the participant or beneficiary) is considered a loan made under a qualified employer plan.

(b) *Pledges and assignments.* Under section 72(p), if a participant or beneficiary assigns or pledges (or agrees to assign or pledge) any portion of his or her interest in a qualified employer plan as security for a loan, the portion of the individual's interest assigned or pledged (or subject to an agreement to assign or pledge) is treated as a loan from the plan to the individual, with the result that such portion is subject to the deemed distribution rule described in paragraph (a) of this Q&A-1. For purposes of section 72(p) and this section, any assignment or pledge of (or agreement to assign or to pledge) any portion of a participant's or beneficiary's interest in a contract that has been purchased under a qualified employer plan (including a contract that has been distributed to the participant or beneficiary) is considered an assignment or pledge of (or agreement to assign or pledge) an interest in a qualified employer plan. However, if all or a portion of a participant's or beneficiary's interest in a qualified employer plan is pledged or assigned as security for a loan from the plan to the participant or the beneficiary, only the amount of the loan received by the participant or the beneficiary, not the amount pledged or assigned, is treated as a loan.

Q-2: What is a qualified employer plan for purposes of section 72(p)?

A-2: For purposes of section 72(p) and this section, a qualified employer plan means—

(a) A plan described in section 401(a) which includes a trust exempt from tax under section 501(a);

(b) An annuity plan described in section 403(a);

(c) A plan under which amounts are contributed by an individual's employer for an annuity contract described in section 403(b);

(d) Any plan, whether or not qualified, established and maintained for its employees by the United States, by a State or political subdivision thereof, or by an agency or instrumentality of the United States, a State or a political subdivision of a State; or

(e) Any plan which was (or was determined to be) described in paragraph (a), (b), (c), or (d) of this Q&A-2.

Q-3: What requirements must be satisfied in order for a loan to a participant or beneficiary from a qualified employer plan not to be a deemed distribution?

A-3: (a) *In general.* A loan to a participant or beneficiary from a qualified employer plan will not be a deemed distribution to the participant or beneficiary if the loan satisfies the repayment term requirement of section 72(p)(2)(B), the level amortization requirement of section 72(p)(2)(C), and the enforceable agreement requirement of paragraph (b) of this Q&A-3, but only to the extent the loan satisfies the amount limitations of section 72(p)(2)(A).

(b) *Enforceable agreement requirement.* A loan does not satisfy the requirements of this paragraph unless the loan is evidenced by a legally enforceable agreement (which may include more than one document) and the terms of the agreement demonstrate compliance with the requirements of section 72(p)(2) and this section. Thus, the agreement must specify the amount and date of the loan and the repayment schedule. The agreement does not have to be signed if the agreement is enforceable under applicable law without being signed. The agreement must be set forth either—

(1) In a written paper document; or

(2) In a document that is delivered through an electronic medium under an electronic system that satisfies the requirements of §1.401(a)-21 of this chapter.

Q-4: If a loan from a qualified employer plan to a participant or beneficiary fails to satisfy the requirements of Q&A-3 of this section, when does a deemed distribution occur?

A-4: (a) *Deemed distribution.* For purposes of section 72, a deemed distribution occurs at the first time that the requirements of Q&A-3 of this section are not satisfied, in form or in operation. This may occur at the time the loan is made or at a later date. If the terms of the loan do not require repayments that satisfy the repayment term requirement of section 72(p)(2)(B) or the level amortization requirement of section 72(p)(2)(C), or the loan is not evidenced by an enforceable agreement satisfying the requirements of paragraph (b) of Q&A-3 of this section, the entire amount of the loan is a deemed distribution under section 72(p) at the time the loan is made. If the loan satisfies the requirements of Q&A-3 of this section except that the amount loaned exceeds the limitations of section 72(p)(2)(A), the amount of the loan in excess of the applicable limitation is a deemed distribution under section 72(p) at the time the loan is made. If the loan initially satisfies the requirements of section 72(p)(2)(A), (B) and (C) and the enforceable agreement requirement of paragraph (b) of Q&A-3 of this section, but payments are not made in accordance with the terms applicable to the loan, a deemed distribution occurs as a result of the failure to make such payments. See Q&A-10 of this

section regarding when such a deemed distribution occurs and the amount thereof and Q&A-11 of this section regarding the tax treatment of a deemed distribution.

(b) *Examples.* The following examples illustrate the rules in paragraph (a) of this Q&A-4 and are based upon the assumptions described in the introductory text of this section:

Example 1. (i) A participant has a nonforfeitable account balance of $200,000 and receives $70,000 as a loan repayable in level quarterly installments over five years.

(ii) Under section 72(p), the participant has a deemed distribution of $20,000 (the excess of $70,000 over $50,000) at the time of the loan, because the loan exceeds the $50,000 limit in section 72(p)(2)(A)(i). The remaining $50,000 is not a deemed distribution.

Example 2. (i) A participant with a nonforfeitable account balance of $30,000 borrows $20,000 as a loan repayable in level monthly installments over five years.

(ii) Because the amount of the loan is $5,000 more than 50% of the participant's nonforfeitable account balance, the participant has a deemed distribution of $5,000 at the time of the loan. The remaining $15,000 is not a deemed distribution. (Note also that, if the loan is secured solely by the participant's account balance, the loan may be a prohibited transaction under section 4975 because the loan may not satisfy 29 CFR 2550.408b-1(f)(2).)

Example 3. (i) The nonforfeitable account balance of a participant is $100,000 and a $50,000 loan is made to the participant repayable in level quarterly installments over seven years. The loan is not eligible for the section 72(p)(2)(B)(ii) exception for loans used to acquire certain dwelling units.

(ii) Because the repayment period exceeds the maximum five-year period in section 72(p)(2)(B)(i), the participant has a deemed distribution of $50,000 at the time the loan is made.

Example 4. (i) On August 1, 2002, a participant has a nonforfeitable account balance of $45,000 and borrows $20,000 from a plan to be repaid over five years in level monthly installments due at the end of each month. After making monthly payments through July 2003, the participant fails to make any of the payments due thereafter.

(ii) As a result of the failure to satisfy the requirement that the loan be repaid in level monthly installments, the participant has a deemed distribution. See paragraph (c) of Q&A10 of this section regarding when such a deemed distribution occurs and the amount thereof.

Q-5: What is a principal residence for purposes of the exception in section 72(p)(2)(B)(ii) from the requirement that a loan be repaid in five years?

A-5: Section 72(p)(2)(B)(ii) provides that the requirement in section 72(p)(2)(B)(i) that a plan loan be repaid within five years does not apply to a loan used to acquire a dwelling unit which will within a reasonable time be used as the principal residence of the participant (a principal residence plan loan). For this purpose, a principal residence has the same meaning as a principal residence under section 121.

Q-6: In order to satisfy the requirements for a principal residence plan loan, is a loan required to be secured by the dwelling unit that will within a reasonable time be used as the principal residence of the participant?

A-6: A loan is not required to be secured by the dwelling unit that will within a reasonable time be used as the participant's principal residence in order to satisfy the requirements for a principal residence plan loan.

Q-7: What tracing rules apply in determining whether a loan qualifies as a principal residence plan loan?

A-7: The tracing rules established under section 163(h)(3)(B) apply in determining whether a loan is treated as for the acquisition of a principal residence in order to qualify as a principal residence plan loan.

Q-8: Can a refinancing qualify as a principal residence plan loan?

A-8: (a) *Refinancings.* In general, no, a refinancing cannot qualify as a principal residence plan loan. However, a loan from a qualified employer plan used to repay a loan from a third party will qualify as a principal residence plan loan if the plan loan qualifies as a principal residence plan loan without regard to the loan from the third party.

(b) *Example.* The following example illustrates the rules in paragraph (a) of this Q&A-8 and is based upon the assumptions described in the introductory text of this section:

Example. (i) On July 1, 2003, a participant requests a $50,000 plan loan to be repaid in level monthly installments over 15 years. On August 1, 2003, the participant acquires a principal residence and pays a portion of the purchase price with a $50,000 bank loan. On September 1, 2003, the plan loans $50,000 to the participant, which the participant uses to pay the bank loan.

(ii) Because the plan loan satisfies the requirements to qualify as a principal residence plan loan (taking into account the tracing rules of section 163(h)(3)(B)), the plan loan qualifies for the exception in section 72(p)(2)(B)(ii).

Q-9: Does the level amortization requirement of section 72(p)(2)(C) apply when a participant is on a leave of absence without pay?

A-9: (a) *Leave of absence*. The level amortization requirement of section 72(p)(2)(C) does not apply for a period, not longer than one year (or such longer period as may apply under section 414(u) and paragraph (b) of this Q&A-9), that a participant is on a bona fide leave of absence, either without pay from the employer or at a rate of pay (after applicable employment tax withholdings) that is less than the amount of the installment payments required under the terms of the loan. However, the loan (including interest that accrues during the leave of absence) must be repaid by the latest permissible term of the loan and the amount of the installments due after the leave ends must not be less than the amount required under the terms of the original loan.

(b) *Military service*. In accordance with section 414(u)(4), if a plan suspends the obligation to repay a loan made to an employee from the plan for any part of a period during which the employee is performing service in the uniformed services (as defined in 38 U.S.C. chapter 43), whether or not qualified military service, such suspension shall not be taken into account for purposes of section 72(p) or this section. Thus, if a plan suspends loan repayments for any part of a period during which the employee is performing military service described in the preceding sentence, such suspension shall not cause the loan to be deemed distributed even if the suspension exceeds one year and even if the term of the loan is extended. However, the loan will not satisfy the repayment term requirement of section 72(p)(2)(B) and the level amortization requirement of section 72(p)(2)(C) unless loan repayments resume upon the completion of such period of military service and the loan is repaid thereafter by amortization in substantially level installments over a period that ends not later than the latest permissible term of the loan.

(c) *Latest permissible term of a loan*. For purposes of this Q&A-9, the latest permissible term of a loan is the latest date permitted under section 72(p)(2)(B) (i.e., five years from the date of the loan, assuming that the replacement loan does not qualify for the exception at section 72(p)(2)(B)(ii) for principal residence plan loans) plus any additional period of suspension permitted under paragraph (b) of this Q&A-9.

(d) *Examples*. The following examples illustrate the rules of this Q&A-9 and are based upon the assumptions described in the introductory text of this section:

Example 1. (i) On July 1, 2003, a participant with a nonforfeitable account balance of $80,000 borrows $40,000 to be repaid in level monthly installments of $825 each over 5 years. The loan is not a principal residence plan loan. The participant makes 9 monthly payments and commences an unpaid leave of absence that lasts for 12 months. The participant was not performing military service during this period. Thereafter, the participant resumes active employment and resumes making repayments on the loan until the loan is repaid. The amount of each monthly installment is increased to $1,130 in order to repay the loan by June 30, 2008.

(ii) Because the loan satisfies the requirements of section 72(p)(2), the participant does not have a deemed distribution. Alternatively, section 72(p)(2) would be satisfied if the participant continued the monthly installments of $825 after resuming active employment and on June 30, 2008 repaid the full balance remaining due.

Example 2. (i) The facts are the same as in *Example 1*, except the participant was on leave of absence performing service in the uniformed services (as defined in chapter 43 of title 38, United States Code) for two years and the rate of interest charged during this period of military service is reduced to 6 percent compounded annually under 50 App. Section 526 (relating to the Soldiers' and Sailors' Civil Relief Act Amendments of 1942). After the military service ends

on April 2, 2006, the participant resumes active employment on April 19, 2006, continues the monthly installments of $825 thereafter, and on June 30, 2010 repays the full balance remaining due ($6,487).

(ii) Because the loan satisfies the requirements of section 72(p)(2) and paragraph (b) of this Q&A-9, the participant does not have a deemed distribution. Alternatively, section 72(p)(2) would also be satisfied if the amount of each monthly installment after April 19, 2006, is increased to $930 in order to repay the loan by June 30, 2010 (without any balance remaining due then).

Q-10: If a participant fails to make the installment payments required under the terms of a loan that satisfied the requirements of Q&A-3 of this section when made, when does a deemed distribution occur and what is the amount of the deemed distribution?

A-10: (a) *Timing of deemed distribution*. Failure to make any installment payment when due in accordance with the terms of the loan violates section 72(p)(2)(C) and, accordingly, results in a deemed distribution at the time of such failure. However, the plan administrator may allow a cure period and section 72(p)(2)(C) will not be considered to have been violated if the installment payment is made not later than the end of the cure period, which period cannot continue beyond the last day of the calendar quarter following the calendar quarter in which the required installment payment was due.

(b) *Amount of deemed distribution*. If a loan satisfies Q&A-3 of this section when made, but there is a failure to pay the installment payments required under the terms of the loan (taking into account any cure period allowed under paragraph (a) of this Q&A-10), then the amount of the deemed distribution equals the entire outstanding balance of the loan (including accrued interest) at the time of such failure.

(c) *Example*. The following example illustrates the rules in paragraphs (a) and (b) of this Q&A-10 and is based upon the assumptions described in the introductory text of this section:

Example. (i) On August 1, 2002, a participant has a nonforfeitable account balance of $45,000 and borrows $20,000 from a plan to be repaid over 5 years in level monthly installments due at the end of each month. After making all monthly payments due through July 31, 2003, the participant fails to make the payment due on August 31, 2003 or any other monthly payments due thereafter. The plan administrator allows a threemonth cure period.

(ii) As a result of the failure to satisfy the requirement that the loan be repaid in level installments pursuant to section 72(p)(2)(C), the participant has a deemed distribution on November 30, 2003, which is the last day of the three-month cure period for the August 31, 2003 installment. The amount of the deemed distribution is $17,157, which is the outstanding balance on the loan at November 30, 2003. Alternatively, if the plan administrator had allowed a cure period through the end of the next calendar quarter, there would be a deemed distribution on December 31, 2003 equal to $17,282, which is the outstanding balance of the loan at December 31, 2003.

Q-11: Does section 72 apply to a deemed distribution as if it were an actual distribution?

A-11: (a) *Tax basis*. If the employee's account includes after-tax contributions or other investment in the contract under section 72(e), section 72 applies to a deemed distribution as if it were an actual distribution, with the result that all or a portion of the deemed distribution may not be taxable.

(b) *Section 72(t) and (m)*. Section 72(t) (which imposes a 10 percent tax on certain early distributions) and section 72(m)(5) (which imposes a separate 10 percent tax on certain amounts received by a 5-percent owner) apply to a deemed distribution under section 72(p) in the same manner as if the deemed distribution were an actual distribution.

»»→ Caution: *Reg. §1.72(p)-1, Q&A-12, below, prior to amendment by T.D. 9169, contains a cross reference to Reg. §1.401(k)-1 before amendment by T.D. 9169, applicable generally for plan years beginning before January 1, 2006.*

Q-12: Is a deemed distribution under section 72(p) treated as an actual distribution for purposes of the qualification requirements of section 401, the distribution provisions of section 402, the distribution restrictions of section 401(k)(2)(B) or 403(b)(11), or the vesting requirements of §1.411(a)-7(d)(5) (which affects the application of a graded vesting schedule in cases involving a prior distribution)?

A-12: No; thus, for example, if a participant in a money purchase plan who is an active employee has a deemed distribution under

section 72(p), the plan will not be considered to have made an in-service distribution to the participant in violation of the qualification requirements applicable to money purchase plans. Similarly, the deemed distribution is not eligible to be rolled over to an eligible retirement plan and is not considered an impermissible distribution of an amount attributable to elective contributions in a section 401(k) plan. See also §1.402(c)-2, Q&A-4(d) and §1.401(k)-1(d)(6)(ii).

»»→ Caution: *Reg. §1.72(p)-1, Q&A-12, below, as amended by T.D. 9169, updates a cross reference to Reg. §1.401(k)-1 that was amended by T.D. 9169, applicable generally for plan years beginning on or after January 1, 2006.*

Q-12: Is a deemed distribution under section 72(p) treated as an actual distribution for purposes of the qualification requirements of section 401, the distribution provisions of section 402, the distribution restrictions of section 401(k)(2)(B) or 403(b)(11), or the vesting requirements of §1.411(a)-7(d)(5) (which affects the application of a graded vesting schedule in cases involving a prior distribution)?

A-12: No; thus, for example, if a participant in a money purchase plan who is an active employee has a deemed distribution under

section 72(p), the plan will not be considered to have made an in-service distribution to the participant in violation of the qualification requirements applicable to money purchase plans. Similarly, the deemed distribution is not eligible to be rolled over to an eligible retirement plan and is not considered an impermissible distribution of an amount attributable to elective contributions in a section 401(k) plan. See also §1.402(c)-2, Q&A-4(d) and §1.401(k)-1(d)(5)(iii).

Q-13: How does a reduction (offset) of an account balance in order to repay a plan loan differ from a deemed distribution?

A-13: (a) *Difference between deemed distribution and plan loan offset amount.*—(1) Loans to a participant from a qualified employer plan can give rise to two types of taxable distributions—

(i) A deemed distribution pursuant to section 72(p); and

(ii) A distribution of an offset amount.

(2) As described in Q&A-4 of this section, a deemed distribution occurs when the requirements of Q&A-3 of this section are not satisfied, either when the loan is made or at a later time. A deemed distribution is treated as a distribution to the participant or beneficiary only for certain tax purposes and is not a distribution of the accrued benefit. A distribution of a plan loan offset amount (as defined in §1.402(c)-2, Q&A-9(b)) occurs when, under the terms governing a plan loan, the accrued benefit of the participant or beneficiary is reduced (offset) in order to repay the loan (including the enforcement of the plan's security interest in the accrued benefit). A distribution of a plan loan offset amount could occur in a variety of circumstances, such as where the terms governing the plan loan require that, in the event of the participant's request for a distribution, a loan be repaid immediately or treated as in default.

(b) *Plan loan offset.* In the event of a plan loan offset, the amount of the account balance that is offset against the loan is an actual distribution for purposes of the Internal Revenue Code, not a deemed distribution under section 72(p). Accordingly, a plan may be prohibited from making such an offset under the provisions of section 401(a), 401(k)(2)(B) or 403(b)(11) prohibiting or limiting distributions to an active employee. See §1.402(c)-2, Q&A-9(c), *Example 6.* See also Q&A-19 of this section for rules regarding the treatment of a loan after a deemed distribution.

Q-14: How is the amount includible in income as a result of a deemed distribution under section 72(p) required to be reported?

A-14: The amount includible in income as a result of a deemed distribution under section 72(p) is required to be reported on Form 1099-R (or any other form prescribed by the Commissioner).

Q-15: What withholding rules apply to plan loans?

A-15: To the extent that a loan, when made, is a deemed distribution or an account balance is reduced (offset) to repay a loan, the amount includible in income is subject to withholding. If a deemed distribution of a loan or a loan repayment by benefit offset results in income at a date after the date the loan is made, withholding is required only if a transfer of cash or property (excluding employer securities) is made to the participant or beneficiary from the plan at the same time. See §§35.3405-1, f-4, and 31.3405(c)-1, Q&A-9 and Q&A11, of this chapter for further guidance on withholding rules.

Q-16: If a loan fails to satisfy the requirements of Q&A-3 of this section and is a prohibited transaction under section 4975, is the deemed distribution of the loan under section 72(p) a correction of the prohibited transaction?

A-16: No, a deemed distribution is not a correction of a prohibited transaction under section 4975. See §§141.4975-13 and 53.4941(e)-1(c)(1) of this chapter for guidance concerning correction of a prohibited transaction.

Q-17: What are the income tax consequences if an amount is transferred from a qualified employer plan to a participant or beneficiary as a loan, but there is an express or tacit understanding that the loan will not be repaid?

A-17: If there is an express or tacit understanding that the loan will not be repaid or, for any reason, the transaction does not create a debtor-creditor relationship or is otherwise not a bona fide loan, then the amount transferred is treated as an actual distribution from the plan for purposes of the Internal Revenue Code, and is not treated as a loan or as a deemed distribution under section 72(p).

Q-18: If a qualified employer plan maintains a program to invest in residential mortgages, are loans made pursuant to the investment program subject to section 72(p)?

A-18: (a) Residential mortgage loans made by a plan in the ordinary course of an investment program are not subject to section 72(p) if the property acquired with the loans is the primary security for such loans and the amount loaned does not exceed the fair market value of the property. An investment program exists only if the plan has established, in advance of a specific investment under the pro-*gram*, that a certain percentage or amount of plan assets will be invested in residential mortgages *available* to persons purchasing the property who satisfy commercially customary financial criteria. A loan will not be considered as made under an investment program if—

(1) Any of the loans made under the program matures upon a participant's termination from employment;

(2) Any of the loans made under the program is an earmarked asset of a participant's or beneficiary's individual account in the plan; or

(3) The loans made under the program are made available only to participants or beneficiaries in the plan.

(b) Paragraph (a)(3) of this Q&A-18 shall not apply to a plan which, on December 20, 1995, and at all times thereafter, has had in effect a loan program under which, but for paragraph (a)(3) of this Q&A-18, the loans comply with the conditions of paragraph (a) of this Q&A-18 to constitute residential mortgage loans in the ordinary course of an investment program.

(c) No loan that benefits an officer, director, or owner of the employer maintaining the plan, or their beneficiaries, will be treated as made under an investment program.

(d) This section does not provide guidance on whether a residential mortgage loan made under a plan's investment program would result in a prohibited transaction under section 4975, or on whether such a loan made by a plan covered by Title I of ERISA would be consistent with the fiduciary standards of ERISA or would result in a prohibited transaction under section 406 of ERISA. See 29 CFR 2550.408b-1.

Q-19: If there is a deemed distribution under section 72(p), is the interest that accrues thereafter on the amount of the deemed distribution an indirect loan for income tax purposes and what effect does the deemed distribution have on subsequent loans?

A-19: (a) *General rule.* Except as provided in paragraph (b) of this Q&A-19, a deemed distribution of a loan is treated as a distribution for purposes of section 72. Therefore, a loan that is deemed to be distributed under section 72(p) ceases to be an outstanding loan for purposes of section 72, and the interest that accrues thereafter under the plan on the amount deemed distributed is disregarded for purposes of applying section 72 to the participant or the beneficiary. Even though interest continues to accrue on the outstanding loan (and is taken into account for purposes of determining the tax treatment of any subsequent loan in accordance with paragraph (b) of this Q&A-19), this additional interest is not treated as an additional loan (and thus, does not result in an additional deemed distribution) for purposes of section 72(p). However, a loan that is deemed distributed under section 72(p) is not considered distributed for all purposes of the Internal Revenue Code. See Q&A-11 through Q&A-16 of this section.

(b) *Effect on subsequent loans*—(1) *Application of section 72(p)(2)(A).* A loan that is deemed distributed under section 72(p) (including interest accruing thereafter) and that has not been repaid (such as by a plan loan offset) is considered outstanding for purposes of applying section 72(p)(2)(A) to determine the maximum amount of any subsequent loan to the participant or beneficiary.

(2) *Additional security for subsequent loans.* If a loan is deemed distributed to a participant or beneficiary under section 72(p) and has not been repaid (such as by a plan loan offset), then no payment made thereafter to the participant or beneficiary is treated as a loan for purposes of section 72(p)(2) unless the loan otherwise satisfies section 72(p)(2) and this section and either of the following conditions is satisfied:

(i) There is an arrangement among the plan, the participant or beneficiary, and the employer, enforceable under applicable law, under which repayments will be made by payroll withholding. For this purpose, an arrangement will not fail to be enforceable merely because a party has the right to revoke the arrangement prospectively.

(ii) The plan receives adequate security from the participant or beneficiary that is in addition to the participant's or beneficiary's accrued benefit under the plan.

(3) *Condition no longer satisfied.* If, following a deemed distribution that has not been repaid, a payment is made to a participant or beneficiary that satisfies the conditions in paragraph (b)(2) of this Q&A-19 for treatment as a plan loan and, subsequently, before repayment of the second loan, the conditions in paragraph (b)(2) of this Q&A-19 are no longer satisfied with respect to the second loan (for example, if the loan recipient revokes consent to payroll withholding), the amount then outstanding on the second loan is treated as a deemed distribution under section 72(p).

Q-20: May a participant refinance an outstanding loan or have more than one loan outstanding from a plan?

A-20: (a) *Refinancings and multiple loans*—(1) *General rule.* A participant who has an outstanding loan that satisfies section 72(p)(2) and this section may refinance that loan or borrow additional amounts if, under the facts and circumstances, the loans collectively satisfy the amount limitations of section 72(p)(2)(A) and the prior loan and the additional loan each satisfy the requirements of section 72(p)(2)(B) and (C) and this section. For this purpose, a refinancing includes any situation in which one loan replaces another loan.

(2) *Loans that repay a prior loan and have a later repayment date.* For purposes of section 72(p)(2) and this section (including the amount limitations of section 72(p)(2)(A)), if a loan that satisfies section 72(p)(2) is replaced by a loan (a replacement loan) and the term of the replacement loan ends after the latest permissible term of the loan it replaces (the replaced loan), then the replacement loan and the replaced loan are both treated as outstanding on the date of the

Reg. §1.72(p)-1

transaction. For purposes of the preceding sentence, the latest permissible term of the replaced loan is the latest date permitted under section 72(p)(2)(C) (i.e., five years from the original date of the replaced loan, assuming that the replaced loan does not qualify for the exception at section 72(p)(2)(B)(ii) for principal residence plan loans and that no additional period of suspension applied to the replaced loan under Q&A-9(b) of this section). Thus, for example, if the term of the replacement loan ends after the latest permissible term of the replaced loan and the sum of the amount of the replacement loan plus the outstanding balance of all other loans on the date of the transaction, including the replaced loan, fails to satisfy the amount limitations of section 72(p)(2)(A), then the replacement loan results in a deemed distribution. This paragraph (a)(2) does not apply to a replacement loan if the terms of the replacement loan would satisfy section 72(p)(2) and this section determined as if the replacement loan consisted of two separate loans, the replaced loan (amortized in substantially level payments over a period ending not later than the last day of the latest permissible term of the replaced loan) and, to the extent the amount of the replacement loan exceeds the amount of the replaced loan, a new loan that is also amortized in substantially level payments over a period ending not later than the last day of the latest permissible term of the replacement loan.

(b) *Examples.* The following examples illustrate the rules of this Q&A-20 and are based on the assumptions described in the introductory text of this section:

Example 1. (i) A participant with a vested account balance that exceeds $100,000 borrows $40,000 from a plan on January 1, 2005, to be repaid in 20 quarterly installments of $2,491 each. Thus, the term of the loan ends on December 31, 2009. On January 1, 2006, when the outstanding balance on the loan is $33,322, the loan is refinanced and is replaced by a new $40,000 loan from the plan to be repaid in 20 quarterly installments. Under the terms of the refinanced loan, the loan is to be repaid in level quarterly installments (of $2,491 each) over the next 20 quarters. Thus, the term of the new loan ends on December 31, 2010.

(ii) Under section 72(p)(2)(A), the amount of the new loan, when added to the outstanding balance of all other loans from the plan, must not exceed $50,000 reduced by the excess of the highest outstanding balance of loans from the plan during the 1-year period ending on December 31, 2005 over the outstanding balance of loans from the plan on January 1, 2006, with such outstanding balance to be determined immediately prior to the new $40,000 loan. Because the term of the new loan ends later than the term of the loan it replaces, under paragraph (a)(2) of this Q&A-20, both the new loan and the loan it replaces must be taken into account for purposes of applying section 72(p)(2), including the amount limitations in section 72(p)(2)(A). The amount of the new loan is $40,000, the outstanding balance on January 1, 2006 of the loan it replaces is $33,322, and the highest outstanding balance of loans from the plan during 2005 was $40,000. Accordingly, under section 72(p)(2)(A), the sum of the new loan and the outstanding balance on January 1, 2006 of the loan it replaces must not exceed $50,000 reduced by $6,678 (the excess of the $40,000 maximum outstanding loan balance during 2005 over the $33,322 outstanding balance on January 1, 2006, determined immediately prior to the new loan) and, thus, must not exceed $43,322. The sum of the new loan ($40,000) and the outstanding balance on January 1, 2006 of the loan it replaces ($33,322) is $73,322. Since $73,322 exceeds the $43,322 limit under section 72(p)(2)(A) by $30,000, there is a deemed distribution of $30,000 on January 1, 2006.

(iii) However, no deemed distribution would occur if, under the terms of the refinanced loan, the amount of the first 16 installments on the refinanced loan were equal to $2,907, which is the sum of the $2,491 originally scheduled quarterly installment payment amount under the first loan, plus $416 (which is the amount required to repay, in level quarterly installments over 5 years beginning on January 1, 2006, the excess of the refinanced loan over the January 1, 2006 balance of the first loan ($40,000 minus $33,322 equals $6,678)), and the amount of the 4 remaining installments was equal to $416. The refinancing would not be subject to paragraph (a)(2) of this Q&A-20 because the terms of the new loan would satisfy section 72(p)(2) and this section (including the substantially level amortization requirements of section 72(p)(2)(B) and (C)) determined as if the new loan consisted of 2 loans, one of which is in the amount of the first loan ($33,322) and is amortized in substantially level payments over a period ending December 31, 2009 (the last day of the term of the first loan) and the other of which is in the additional amount ($6,678) borrowed under the new loan. Similarly, the transaction also would not result in a deemed distribution (and would not be subject to paragraph (a)(2) of this Q&A-20) if the terms of the refinanced loan provided for repayments to be made in level quarterly installments (of $2,990 each) over the next 16 quarters.

Example 2. (i) The facts are the same as in *Example 1*(i), except that the applicable interest rate used by the plan when the loan is refinanced is significantly lower due to a reduction in market rates of interest and, under the terms of the refinanced loan, the amount of

the first 16 installments on the refinanced loan is equal to $2,848 and the amount of the next 4 installments on the refinanced loan is equal to $406. The $2,848 amount is the sum of $2,442 to repay the first loan by December 31, 2009 (the term of the first loan), plus $406 (which is the amount to repay, in level quarterly installments over 5 years beginning on January 1, 2006 the $6,678 excess of the refinanced loan over the January 1, 2006 balance of the first loan).

(ii) The transaction does not result in a deemed distribution (and is not subject to paragraph (a)(2) of this Q&A-20) because the terms of the new loan would satisfy section 72(p)(2) and this section (including the substantially level amortization requirements of section 72(p)(2)(B) and (C)) determined as if the new loan consisted of 2 loans, one of which is in the amount of the first loan ($33,322) and is amortized in substantially level payments over a period ending December 31, 2009 (the last day of the term of the first loan) and the other of which is in the additional amount ($6,678) borrowed under the new loan. The transaction would also not result in a deemed distribution (and not be subject to paragraph (a)(2) of this Q&A-20) if the terms of the new loan provided for repayments to be made in level quarterly installments (of $2,931 each) over the next 16 quarters.

Q-21: Is a participant's tax basis under the plan increased if the participant repays the loan after a deemed distribution?

A-21: (a) *Repayments after deemed distribution.* Yes, if the participant or beneficiary repays the loan after a deemed distribution of the loan under section 72(p), then, for purposes of section 72(e), the participant's or beneficiary's investment in the contract (tax basis) under the plan increases by the amount of the cash repayments that the participant or beneficiary makes on the loan after the deemed distribution. However, loan repayments are not treated as aftertax contributions for other purposes, including sections 401(m) and 415(c)(2)(B).

(b) *Example.* The following example illustrates the rules in paragraph (a) of this Q&A-21 and is based on the assumptions described in the introductory text of this section:

Example. (i) A participant receives a $20,000 loan on January 1, 2003, to be repaid in 20 quarterly installments of $1,245 each. On December 31, 2003, the outstanding loan balance ($19,179) is deemed distributed as a result of a failure to make quarterly installment payments that were due on September 30, 2003 and December 31, 2003. On June 30, 2004, the participant repays $5,147 (which is the sum of the three installment payments that were due on September 30, 2003, December 31, 2003, and March 31, 2004, with interest thereon to June 30, 2004, plus the installment payment due on June 30, 2004). Thereafter, the participant resumes making the installment payments of $1,245 from September 30, 2004 through December 31, 2007. The loan repayments made after December 31, 2003 through December 31, 2007 total $22,577.

(ii) Because the participant repaid $22,577 after the deemed distribution that occurred on December 31, 2003, the participant has investment in the contract (tax basis) equal to $22,577 (14 payments of $1,245 each plus a single payment of $5,147) as of December 31, 2007.

Q-22: When is the effective date of section 72(p) and the regulations in this section?

A-22: (a) *Statutory effective date.* Section 72(p) generally applies to assignments, pledges, and loans made after August 13, 1982.

(b) *Regulatory effective date.* This section applies to assignments, pledges, and loans made on or after January 1, 2002.

(c) *Loans made before the regulatory effective date*—(1) *General rule.* A plan is permitted to apply Q&A-19 and Q&A-21 of this section to a loan made before the regulatory effective date in paragraph (b) of this Q&A-22 (and after the statutory effective date in paragraph (a) of this Q&A-22) if there has not been any deemed distribution of the loan before the transition date or if the conditions of paragraph (c)(2) of this Q&A-22 are satisfied with respect to the loan.

(2) *Consistency transition rule for certain loans deemed distributed before the regulatory effective date.*—(i) The rules in this paragraph (c)(2) of this Q&A-22 apply to a loan made before the regulatory effective date in paragraph (b) of this Q&A-22 (and after the statutory effective date in paragraph (a) of this Q&A-22) if there has been any deemed distribution of the loan before the transition date.

(ii) The plan is permitted to apply Q&A-19 and Q&A-21 of this section to the loan beginning on any January 1, but only if the plan reported, in Box 1 of Form 1099-R, for a taxable year no later than the latest taxable year that would be permitted under this section (if this section had been in effect for all loans made after the statutory effective date in paragraph (a) of this Q&A-22), a gross distribution of an amount at least equal to the initial default amount. For purposes of this section, the initial default amount is the amount that would be reported as a gross distribution under Q&A-4 and Q&A-10 of this section and the transition date is the January 1 on which a plan begins applying Q&A-19 and Q&A-21 of this section to a loan.

(iii) If a plan applies Q&A-19 and Q&A-21 of this section to such a loan, then the plan, in its reporting and withholding on or after the transition date, must not attribute investment in the contract (tax basis) to the participant or beneficiary based upon the initial default amount.

(iv) This paragraph (c)(2)(iv) of this Q&A-22 applies if—

(A) The plan attributed investment in the contract (tax basis) to the participant or beneficiary based on the deemed distribution of the loan;

(B) The plan subsequently made an actual distribution to the participant or beneficiary before the transition date; and

(C) Immediately before the transition date, the initial default amount (or, if less, the amount of the investment in the contract so attributed) exceeds the participant's or beneficiary's investment in the contract (tax basis). If this paragraph (c)(2)(iv) of this Q&A-22 applies, the plan must treat the excess (the loan transition amount) as a loan amount that remains outstanding and must include the excess in the participant's or beneficiary's income at the time of the first actual distribution made on or after the transition date.

(3) *Examples.* The rules in paragraph (c)(2) of this Q&A-22 are illustrated by the following examples, which are based on the assumptions described in the introductory text of this section (and, except as specifically provided in the examples, also assume that no distributions are made to the participant and that the participant has no investment in the contract with respect to the plan). *Example 1, Example 2,* and *Example 4* of this paragraph (c)(3) of this Q&A-22 illustrate the application of the rules in paragraph (c)(2) of this Q&A-22 to a plan that, before the transition date, did not treat interest accruing after the initial deemed distribution as resulting in additional deemed distributions under section 72(p). *Example 3* of this paragraph (c)(3) of this Q&A-22 illustrates the application of the rules in paragraph (c)(2) of this Q&A-22 to a plan that, before the transition date, treated interest accruing after the initial deemed distribution as resulting in additional deemed distributions under section 72(p). The examples are as follows:

Example 1. (i) In 1998, when a participant's account balance under a plan is $50,000, the participant receives a loan from the plan. The participant makes the required repayments until 1999 when there is a deemed distribution of $20,000 as a result of a failure to repay the loan. For 1999, as a result of the deemed distribution, the plan reports, in Box 1 of Form 1099-R, a gross distribution of $20,000 (which is the initial default amount in accordance with paragraph (c)(2)(ii) of this Q&A-22) and, in Box 2 of Form 1099-R, a taxable amount of $20,000. The plan then records an increase in the participant's tax basis for the same amount ($20,000). Thereafter, the plan disregards, for purposes of section 72, the interest that accrues on the loan after the 1999 deemed distribution. Thus, as of December 31, 2001, the total taxable amount reported by the plan as a result of the deemed distribution is $20,000 and the plan's records show that the participant's tax basis is the same amount ($20,000). As of January 1, 2002, the plan decides to apply Q&A-19 of this section to the loan. Accordingly, it reduces the participant's tax basis by the initial default amount of $20,000, so that the participant's remaining tax basis in the plan is zero. Thereafter, the amount of the outstanding loan is not treated as part of the account balance for purposes of section 72. The participant attains age 59½ in the year 2003 and receives a distribution of the full account balance under the plan consisting of $60,000 in cash and the loan receivable. At that time, the plan's records reflect an offset of the loan amount against the loan receivable in the participant's account and a distribution of $60,000 in cash.

(ii) For the year 2003, the plan must report a gross distribution of $60,000 in Box 1 of Form 1099-R and a taxable amount of $60,000 in Box 2 of Form 1099-R.

Example 2. (i) The facts are the same as in *Example 1,* except that in 1999, immediately prior to the deemed distribution, the participant's account balance under the plan totals $50,000 and the participant's tax basis is $10,000. For 1999, the plan reports, in Box 1 of Form 1099-R, a gross distribution of $20,000 (which is the initial default amount in accordance with paragraph (c)(2)(ii) of this Q&A-22) and reports, in Box 2 of Form 1099-R, a taxable amount of $16,000 (the $20,000 deemed distribution minus $4,000 of tax basis ($10,000 times ($20,000/$50,000)) allocated to the deemed distribution). The plan then records an increase in tax basis equal to the $20,000 deemed distribution, so that the participant's remaining tax basis as of December 31, 1999, totals $26,000 ($10,000 minus $4,000 plus $20,000). Thereafter, the plan disregards, for purposes of section 72, the interest that accrues on the loan after the 1999 deemed distribution. Thus, as of December 31, 2001, the total taxable amount reported by the plan as a result of the deemed distribution is $16,000 and the plan's records show that the participant's tax basis is $26,000. As of January 1, 2002, the plan decides to apply Q&A19 of this section to the loan. Accordingly, it reduces the participant's tax basis by the initial default amount of $20,000, so that the participant's remaining tax basis in the plan is $6,000. Thereafter, the amount of the outstanding loan is not treated as part of the account balance for purposes of section

72. The participant attains age 59½ in the year 2003 and receives a distribution of the full account balance under the plan consisting of $60,000 in cash and the loan receivable. At that time, the plan's records reflect an offset of the loan amount against the loan receivable in the participant's account and a distribution of $60,000 in cash.

(ii) For the year 2003, the plan must report a gross distribution of $60,000 in Box 1 of Form 1099-R and a taxable amount of $54,000 in Box 2 of Form 1099-R.

Example 3. (i) In 1993, when a participant's account balance in a plan is $100,000, the participant receives a loan of $50,000 from the plan. The participant makes the required loan repayments until 1995 when there is a deemed distribution of $28,919 as a result of a failure to repay the loan. For 1995, as a result of the deemed distribution, the plan reports, in Box 1 of Form 1099-R, a gross distribution of $28,919 (which is the initial default amount in accordance with paragraph (c)(2)(ii) of this Q&A-22) and, in Box 2 of Form 1099-R, a taxable amount of $28,919. For 1995, the plan also records an increase in the participant's tax basis for the same amount ($28,919). Each year thereafter through 2001, the plan reports a gross distribution equal to the interest accruing that year on the loan balance, reports a taxable amount equal to the interest accruing that year on the loan balance reduced by the participant's tax basis allocated to the gross distribution, and records a net increase in the participant's tax basis equal to that taxable amount. As of December 31, 2001, the taxable amount reported by the plan as a result of the loan totals $44,329 and the plan's records for purposes of section 72 show that the participant's tax basis totals the same amount ($44,329). As of January 1, 2002, the plan decides to apply Q&A-19 of this section. Accordingly, it reduces the participant's tax basis by the initial default amount of $28,919, so that the participant's remaining tax basis in the plan is $15,410 ($44,329 minus $28,919). Thereafter, the amount of the outstanding loan is not treated as part of the account balance for purposes of section 72. The participant attains age 59½ in the year 2003 and receives a distribution of the full account balance under the plan consisting of $180,000 in cash and the loan receivable equal to the $28,919 outstanding loan amount in 1995 plus interest accrued thereafter to the payment date in 2003. At that time, the plan's records reflect an offset of the loan amount against the loan receivable in the participant's account and a distribution of $180,000 in cash.

(ii) For the year 2003, the plan must report a gross distribution of $180,000 in Box 1 of Form 1099-R and a taxable amount of $164,590 in Box 2 of Form 1099-R ($180,000 minus the remaining tax basis of $15,410).

Example 4. (i) The facts are the same as in *Example 1,* except that in 2000, after the deemed distribution, the participant receives a $10,000 hardship distribution. At the time of the hardship distribution, the participant's account balance under the plan totals $50,000. For 2000, the plan reports, in Box 1 of Form 1099-R, a gross distribution of $10,000 and, in Box 2 of Form 1099-R, a taxable amount of $6,000 (the $10,000 actual distribution minus $4,000 of tax basis ($10,000 times ($20,000/$50,000)) allocated to this actual distribution). The plan then records a decrease in tax basis equal to $4,000, so that the participant's remaining tax basis as of December 31, 2000, totals $16,000 ($20,000 minus $4,000). After 1999, the plan disregards, for purposes of section 72, the interest that accrues on the loan after the 1999 deemed distribution. Thus, as of December 31, 2001, the total taxable amount reported by the plan as a result of the deemed distribution plus the 2000 actual distribution is $26,000 and the plan's records show that the participant's tax basis is $16,000. As of January 1, 2002, the plan decides to apply Q&A-19 of this section to the loan. Accordingly, it reduces the participant's tax basis by the initial default amount of $20,000, so that the participant's remaining tax basis in the plan is reduced from $16,000 to zero. However, because the $20,000 initial default amount exceeds $16,000, the plan records a loan transition amount of $4,000 ($20,000 minus $16,000). Thereafter, the amount of the outstanding loan, other than the $4,000 loan transition amount, is not treated as part of the account balance for purposes of section 72. The participant attains age 59½ in the year 2003 and receives a distribution of the full account balance under the plan consisting of $60,000 in cash and the loan receivable. At that time, the plan's records reflect an offset of the loan amount against the loan receivable in the participant's account and a distribution of $60,000 in cash.

(ii) In accordance with paragraph (c)(2)(iv) of this Q&A22, the plan must report in Box 1 of Form 1099-R a gross distribution of $64,000 and in Box 2 of Form 1099-R a taxable amount for the participant for the year 2003 equal to $64,000 (the sum of the $60,000 paid in the year 2003 plus $4,000 as the loan transition amount).

(d) *Effective date for Q&A-19(b)(2) and Q&A-20.* Q&A-19(b)(2) and Q&A-20 of this section apply to assignments, pledges, and loans made on or after January 1, 2004. [Reg. § 1.72(p)-1.]

☐ [T.D. 8894, 7-28-2000. *Amended by* T.D. 9021, 12-2-2002 *(corrected* 2-27-2003); T.D. 9169, 12-28-2004 *and* T.D. 9294, 10-19-2006.]

[Reg. §1.73-1]

§1.73-1. Services of child.—(a) Compensation for personal services of a child shall, regardless of the provisions of State law relating to who is entitled to the earnings of the child, and regardless of whether the income is in fact received by the child, be deemed to be the gross income of the child and not the gross income of the parent of the child. Such compensation, therefore, shall be included in the gross income of the child and shall be reflected in the return rendered by or for such child. The income of a minor child is not required to be included in the gross income of the parent for income tax purposes. For requirements for making the return by such child, or for such child by his guardian, or other person charged with the care of his person or property, see section 6012.

(b) In the determination of taxable income or adjusted gross income, as the case may be, all expenditures made by the parent or the child attributable to amounts which are includible in the gross income of the child and not of the parent solely by reason of section 73 are deemed to have been paid or incurred by the child. In such determination, the child is entitled to take deductions not only for expenditures made on his behalf by his parent which would be commonly considered as business expenses, but also for other expenditures such as charitable contributions made by the parent in the name of the child and out of the child's earnings.

(c) For purposes of section 73, the term "parent" includes any individual who is entitled to the services of the child by reason of having parental rights and duties in respect of the child. See section 6201(c) and the regulations in Part 301 of this chapter (Regulations on Procedure and Administration) for assessment of tax against the parent in certain cases. [Reg. §1.73-1.]

☐ [T.D. 6211, 11-14-56.]

[Reg. §1.74-1]

§1.74-1. Prizes and awards.—(a) *Inclusion in gross income.*—(1) Section 74(a) requires the inclusion in gross income of all amounts received as prizes and awards, unless such prizes or awards qualify as an exclusion from gross income under subsection (b), or unless such prize or award is a scholarship or fellowship grant excluded from gross income by section 117. Prizes and awards which are includible in gross income include (but are not limited to) amounts received from radio and television giveaway shows, door prizes, and awards in contests of all types, as well as any prizes and awards from an employer to an employee in recognition of some achievement in connection with his employment.

(2) If the prize or award is not made in money but is made in goods or services, the fair market value of the goods or services is the amount to be included in income.

(b) *Exclusion from gross income.*—Section 74(b) provides an exclusion from gross income of any amount received as a prize or award, if (1) such prize or award was made primarily in recognition of past achievements of the recipient in religious, charitable, scientific, educational, artistic, literary, or civic fields; (2) the recipient was selected without any action on his part to enter the contest or proceedings; and (3) the recipient is not required to render substantial future services as a condition to receiving the prize or award. Thus, such awards as the Nobel prize and the Pulitzer prize would qualify for the exclusion. Section 74(b) does not exclude prizes or awards from an employer to an employee in recognition of some achievement in connection with his employment.

(c) *Scholarships and fellowship grants.*—See section 117 and the regulations thereunder for provisions relating to scholarships and fellowship grants. [Reg. §1.74-1.]

☐ [T.D. 6137, 7-6-55.]

[Reg. §1.75-1]

§1.75-1. Treatment of bond premiums in case of dealers in tax-exempt securities.—(a) *In general.*—(1) Section 75 requires certain adjustments to be made by dealers in securities with respect to premiums paid on municipal bonds which are held for sale to customers in the ordinary course of the trade or business. The adjustments depend upon the method of accounting used by the taxpayer in computing the gross income from the trade or business. See paragraphs (b) and (c) of this section.

(2) The term "municipal bond" under section 75 means any obligation issued by a government or political subdivision thereof if the interest on the obligation is excludable from gross income under section 103. However, such term does not include an obligation—

(i) If the earliest maturity or call date of the obligation is more than 5 years from the date of acquisition by the taxpayer or the obligation is sold or otherwise disposed of by the taxpayer within 30 days after the date of acquisition by him, and

(ii) If, in case of an obligation acquired after December 31, 1957, the amount realized upon its sale (or, in the case of any other disposition, its fair market value at the time of disposition) is higher than its adjusted basis.

For purposes of this subparagraph, the amount realized on the sale of the obligation, or the fair market value of the obligation, shall not include any amount attributable to interest, and the adjusted basis shall be computed without regard to any adjustment for amortization of bond premium required under section 75 and section 1016(a)(6). For purposes of determining whether the obligation is sold or otherwise disposed of by the taxpayer within 30 days after the date of its acquisition by him, it is immaterial whether or not such 30-day period is entirely within one taxable year.

(3) The term "cost of securities sold" means the amount ascertained by subtracting the inventory value of the closing inventory of a taxable year from the sum of the inventory value of the opening inventory for such year and the cost of securities and other property purchased during such year which would properly be included in the inventory of the taxpayer if on hand at the close of the taxable year.

(b) *Inventories not valued at cost.*—(1) In the case of a dealer in securities who computes gross income from his trade or business by the use of inventories and values such inventories on any basis other than cost, the adjustment required by section 75 is, except as provided in subparagraph (2) of this paragraph, the reduction of "cost of securities sold" by the amount equal to the amortizable bond premium which would be disallowed as a deduction under section 171(a)(2) with respect to the municipal bond if the dealer were an ordinary investor holding such bond. Such amortizable bond premium is computed under section 171(b) by reference to the cost or other original basis of the bond on the date of acquisition (determined without regard to section 1013, relating to inventory value on a subsequent date).

(2) With respect to an obligation acquired after December 31, 1957, which has as its earliest maturity or call date a date more than five years from the date on which it was acquired by the taxpayer, the following rules shall apply:

(i) If the taxpayer holds the obligation at the end of the taxable year, he is not required by section 75 to reduce the "cost of securities sold" for such year with respect to the obligation.

(ii) If the taxpayer sells or otherwise disposes of the obligation during the taxable year, he shall reduce the "cost of securities sold" for the taxable year of the sale or disposition unless he sold the obligation for more than its adjusted basis or otherwise disposed of it when its fair market value was more than its adjusted basis. For purposes of determining whether or not the taxpayer sold the obligation for more than its adjusted basis, or otherwise disposed of it when its fair market value was more than its adjusted basis, the amount realized on the sale of the obligation, or the fair market value of the obligation, shall not include any amount attributable to interest, and the adjusted basis shall be computed without regard to any adjustment for amortization of bond premium required under sections 75 and 1016(a)(6). The amount of the reduction referred to in the first sentence of this subdivision is the total amount by which the adjusted basis of the obligation would be required to be reduced under section 1016(a)(5) were the obligation subject to the amortizable bond premium provisions of section 171; that is, the amount of the amortizable bond premium attributable to the period during which the obligation was held which would be disallowed as a deduction under section 171(a)(2) if the taxpayer were an ordinary investor.

(3) This paragraph may be illustrated by the following examples:

Example (1). X, a dealer in securities who values his inventories on a basis other than cost, makes his income tax returns on the calendar year basis. On July 1, 1954, he bought, for $1,060 each, three municipal bonds (A, B, and C) having a face obligation of $1,000, and maturing on July 1, 1959. Bond A is sold on December 31, 1954, bond B is sold on December 31, 1955, and bond C is sold on June 30, 1956. For each bond the amortizable bond premium to maturity is $60, the period from date of acquisition to maturity is 60 months, and the amortizable bond premium per month is $1. The adjustment for each of the years 1954, 1955, and 1956 is as follows:

| Bond | Date acquired | Date Sold | Adjustment to "cost of securities sold" for— | | |
			1954	1955	1956
A	July 1, 1954	Dec. 31, 1954	$6	—	—
B	July 1, 1954	Dec. 31, 1955	6	$12	—
C	July 1, 1954	June 30, 1956	6	12	$6
		Total	$18	$24	$6

Example (2). Y is a dealer in securities who values his inventories on a basis other than cost. He makes his income tax returns on the calendar year basis. On January 1, 1958, Y bought five bonds (D, E, F, G, and H) issued by various municipalities. Each bond has a face obligation of $1,000 and was purchased for $1,060. The interest on each is excludable from gross income under section 103. Bonds D, E, and F mature on December 31, 1962, and bonds G and H mature on December 31, 1967. The amortizable bond premium per month is $1 with respect to bonds D, E, and F, and is $.50 with respect to bonds G and H. The following table indicates the reduction in "cost of securities sold" which Y should make for the years shown, assuming that he sells the bonds on the dates and for the prices set forth:

Bond	Date sold	Sale price	Adjustment to "cost of securities sold" for — 1958	1959	1960
D	Feb. 1, 1959	$1,090	$12	$1	..
E	Jan. 30, 1958	1,100	None	..	..
F	Jan. 30, 1958	1,000	1	..	..
G	Dec. 31, 1960	1,065	None	None	None
H	Dec. 31, 1960	1,050	None	None	$18
			$13	$1	$18

An adjustment to "cost of securities sold" must be made with respect to bond D (even though it was ultimately sold at a gain) because the bond neither had an earliest maturity or call date of more than 5 years from the date on which Y acquired it, nor was it disposed of within 30 days after such date. An adjustment must be made for the years 1958 and 1959 since section 75(a)(1) requires that an adjustment be made with respect to such a bond at the close of each taxable year in which it is held. On the other hand, since bonds E, F, G, and H either were disposed of within 30 days after the date of such acquisition or had an earliest maturity or call date more than 5 years from the date of acquisition, and were acquired after December 31, 1957, it is necessary to determine whether Y disposed of them at a loss so as to require an adjustment under section 75. No adjustment is necessary with respect to bonds E and G because they were sold at a gain. An adjustment to "cost of securities sold" is required with respect to bonds F and H because they were sold at a loss. As in the case of bond D, an adjustment with respect to bond F is made in 1958 in accordance with section 75(a)(1); however, the adjustment with respect to bond H is made entirely in 1960, the taxable year in which Y sold that bond, in accordance with the last sentence of section 75(a). If Y had acquired bonds before January 1, 1958, it would be unnecessary to determine whether they were disposed of at a loss since that factor is significant only with respect to bonds acquired on or after that date.

(c) *Inventories not used or inventories valued at cost.*—(1) In the case of a dealer in securities who computes gross income from his trade or business without the use of inventories or by use of inventories valued at cost, the adjustment required by section 75 is a reduction of the adjusted basis of each municipal bond sold or otherwise disposed of during the taxable year. The amount of such reduction is the total amount by which the adjusted basis of the bond would be required to be reduced under section 1016(a)(5) were the bond subject to the amortizable bond premium provisions of section 171; that is, the amount of the amortizable bond premium attributable to the period during which the bond was held which would be disallowed as a deduction under section 171(a)(2) if the taxpayer were an ordinary investor.

(2) Subparagraph (1) of this paragraph may be illustrated by the following example:

Example. Z, a dealer in securities who values his inventories on the basis of cost, makes his income tax returns on the calendar year basis. On January 1, 1954, he buys, for $1,060 each, three municipal bonds (I, J, and K) having a face obligation of $1,000, and maturing on January 1, 1959. Bond I is sold on December 31, 1954, bond J is sold on June 30, 1955, and bond K is sold on December 31, 1956. For each bond, the amortizable bond premium to maturity is $60, the period from the date of acquisition to maturity is 60 months, and the amortizable bond premium per month is $1.

Bond	Date acquired	Date sold	Adjustment for— 1954	1955	1956
I	Jan. 1, 1954	Dec. 31, 1954	$12	...	...
J	Jan. 1, 1954	June 30, 1955	None	$18	...
K	Jan. 1, 1954	Dec. 31, 1956	None	None	$36

(d) *Bonds acquired before July 1, 1950.*—Under section 203(c) of the Revenue Act of 1950, adjustment is required for a municipal bond acquired before July 1, 1950, only with respect to taxable years beginning on or after that date. Accordingly, if the municipal bond was acquired before July 1, 1950, then for purposes of section 75 the amortizable bond premium under section 171 must be computed after adjusting the bond premium to the extent proper to reflect unamortized bond premium for so much of the holding period (as determined under section 1223) as precedes the taxable year of the dealer beginning on or after July 1, 1950. Thus, in example (1) of paragraph (b) and in the example in paragraph (c) of this section, the first taxable year beginning on or after July 1, 1950, is, for each dealer, the taxable year beginning January 1, 1951. If each dealer had purchased for $1,060 on April 1, 1950, a municipal bond having a face obligation of $1,000 and maturing April 1, 1955, and had sold such bond on February 28, 1955, the adjustment under section 75 would be computed as follows:

	Dealer X	Dealer Z
Bond premium	$60	$60
Adjustment for holding period prior to January 1, 1951	9	9
Amortizable bond premium to maturity, as adjusted	$51	$51
Amortizable bond premium per month	$1	$1
Total adjustments under sec. 22(o), 1939 Code, for years 1951-1953	36	None
Adjustment under sec. 75 for 1954	12	None
Adjustment under sec. 75 for 1955	2	50

[Reg. §1.75-1.]

☐ [*T.D. 6137, 7-6-55. Amended by T.D. 6647, 4-10-63.*]

[Reg. §1.77-1]

§1.77-1. Election to consider Commodity Credit Corporation loans as income.—A taxpayer who receives a loan from the Commodity Credit Corporation may, at his election, include the amount of such loan in his gross income for the taxable year in which the loan is received. If a taxpayer makes such an election (or has made such an election under section 123 of the Internal Revenue Code of 1939 or under section 223(d) of the Revenue Act of 1939 (53 Stat. 897)), then for subsequent taxable years he shall include in his gross income all amounts received during those years as loans from the Commodity Credit Corporation, unless he secures the permission of the Commissioner to change to a different method of accounting. Application for permission to change such method of accounting and the basis upon which the return is made shall be filed with the Commissioner of Internal Revenue, Washington 25, D.C., within 90 days after the beginning of the taxable year to be covered by the return. [Reg. §1.77-1.]

☐ [*T.D. 6137, 7-6-55.*]

[Reg. §1.77-2]

§1.77-2. Effect of election to consider commodity credit loans as income.—(a) If a taxpayer elects or has elected under section 77, section 123 of the Internal Revenue Code of 1939, or section 223(d) of the Revenue Act of 1939 (53 Stat. 897), as amended, to include in his gross income the amount of a loan from the Commodity Credit Corporation for the taxable year in which it is received, then—

(1) No part of the amount realized by the Commodity Credit Corporation upon the sale or other disposition of the commodity pledged for such loan shall be recognized as income to the taxpayer, unless the taxpayer receives an amount in addition to that advanced to him as the loan, in which event such additional amount shall be

included in the gross income of the taxpayer for the taxable year in which it is received, and

(2) No deductible loss to the taxpayer shall be recognized on account of any deficiency realized by the Commodity Credit Corporation on such loan if the taxpayer was relieved from liability for such deficiency.

(b) The application of paragraph (a) of this section may be illustrated by the following example:

Example. A, a taxpayer who elected for his taxable year 1952 to include in gross income amounts received as loans from the Commodity Credit Corporation, received as loans $500 in 1952, $700 in 1953, and $900 in 1954. In 1956 all the pledged commodity was sold by the Commodity Credit Corporation for an amount $100 and $200 less than the loans with respect to the commodity pledged in 1952 and 1953, respectively, and for an amount $150 greater than the loan with respect to the commodity pledged in 1954. A, in making his return for 1956, shall include in gross income the sum of $150 if it is received during that year, but will not be allowed a deduction for the deficiencies of $100 and $200 unless he is required to satisfy such deficiencies and does satisfy them during that year. [Reg. § 1.77-2.]

☐ [*T.D. 6137, 7-6-55.*]

[Reg. § 1.78-1]

§ 1.78-1. Gross up for deemed paid foreign tax credit.—(a) *Taxes deemed paid by certain domestic corporations treated as a dividend.*—If a domestic corporation chooses to have the benefits of the foreign tax credit under section 901 for any taxable year, an amount that is equal to the U.S. dollar amount of foreign income taxes deemed to be paid by the corporation for the year under section 960 (in the case of section 960(d), determined without regard to the phrase "80 percent of" in section 960(d)(1)) is, to the extent provided by this section, treated as a dividend (a *section 78 dividend*) received by the domestic corporation from the foreign corporation. A section 78 dividend is treated as a dividend for all purposes of the Code, except that it is not treated as a dividend for purposes of section 245 or 245A, and does not increase the earnings and profits of the domestic corporation or decrease the earnings and profits of the foreign corporation. Any reduction under section 907(a) of the foreign income taxes deemed paid with respect to combined foreign oil and gas income does not affect the amount treated as a section 78 dividend. See § 1.907(a)-1(e)(3). Similarly, any reduction under section 901(e) of the foreign income taxes deemed paid with respect to foreign mineral income does not affect the amount treated as a section 78 dividend. See § 1.901-3(a)(2)(i), (b)(2)(i)(b), and (d) *Example 8.* Any reduction under section 6038(c)(1)(B) in the foreign taxes paid or accrued by a foreign corporation is taken into account in determining foreign taxes deemed paid and the amount treated as a section 78 dividend. See, for example, § 1.6038-2(k)(5) *Example 1.* To the extent provided in the Code, section 78 does not apply to any tax not allowed as a credit. See, for example, sections 901(j)(3), 901(k)(7), 901(l)(4), 901(m)(6), and 908(b). For rules on determining the source of a section 78 dividend in computing the limitation on the foreign tax credit under section 904, see §§ 1.861-3(a)(3), 1.862-1(a)(1)(ii), and 1.904-5(m)(6). For rules on assigning a section 78 dividend to a separate category, see § 1.904-4.

(b) *Date on which section 78 dividend is received.*—A section 78 dividend is considered received by a domestic corporation on the date on which—

(1) The corporation includes in gross income under section 951(a)(1)(A) the amounts by reason of which there are deemed paid under section 960(a) the foreign income taxes that give rise to that section 78 dividend, notwithstanding that the foreign income taxes may be carried back or carried over to another taxable year and deemed to be paid or accrued in such other taxable year under section 904(c); or

(2) The corporation includes in gross income under section 951A(a) the amounts by reason of which there are deemed paid under section 960(d) the foreign income taxes that give rise to that section 78 dividend.

(c) *Applicability date.*—This section applies to taxable years of foreign corporations that begin after December 31, 2017, and to taxable years of United States shareholders in which or with which such taxable years of foreign corporations end. The second sentence of paragraph (a) of this section also applies to section 78 dividends that are received after December 31, 2017, by reason of taxes deemed paid under section 960(a) with respect to a taxable year of a foreign corporation beginning before January 1, 2018. [Reg. § 1.78-1.]

☐ [*T.D. 6805, 3-8-65. Amended by T.D. 7120, 6-3-71, T.D. 7481, 4-15-77, T.D. 7490, 6-10-77, T.D. 7649, 10-17-79, T.D. 7961, 6-20-84, T.D. 9849, 3-11-2019 and T.D. 9866, 6-14-2019.*]

[Reg. § 1.79-0]

§ 1.79-0. Group-term life insurance—definitions of certain terms.—The following definitions apply for purposes of section 79, this section, and §§ 1.79-1, 1.79-2, and 1.79-3.

Carried directly or indirectly. A policy of life insurance is "carried directly or indirectly" by an employer if—

(a) The employer pays any part of the cost of the life insurance directly or through another person; or

(b) The employer or two or more employers arrange for payment of the cost of the life insurance by their employees and charge at least one employee less than the cost of his or her insurance, as determined under Table I of § 1.79-3(d)(2), and at least one other employee more than the cost of his or her insurance, determined in the same way.

Employee. An "employee" is—

(a) A person who performs services if his or her relationship to the person for whom services are performed is the legal relationship of employer and employee described in § 31.3401(c)-1; or

(b) A full-time life insurance salesperson described in section 7701(a)(20); or

(c) A person who formerly performed services as an employee. A person who formerly performed services as an employee and currently performs services for the same employer as an independent contractor is considered an employee only with respect to insurance provided because of the person's former services as an employee.

Group of employees. A "group of employees" is all employees of an employer, or less than all employees if membership in the group is determined solely on the basis of age, marital status, or factors related to employment. Examples of factors related to employment are membership in a union some or all of whose members are employed by the employer, duties performed, compensation received, and length of service. Ordinarily the purchase of something other than group-term life insurance is not a factor related to employment. For example, if an employer provides credit life insurance to all employees who purchase automobiles, these employees are not a "group of employees" because membership is not determined solely on the basis of age, marital status, or factors related to employment. On the other hand, participation in an employer's pension, profit-sharing, or accident and health plan is considered a factor related to employment even if employees are required to contribute to the cost of the plan. Ownership of stock in the employer corporation is not a factor related to employment. However, participation in an employer's stock bonus plan may be a factor related to employment and a "group of employees" may include employees who own stock in the employer corporation.

Permanent benefit. A "permanent benefit" is an economic value extending beyond one policy year (for example, a paid-up or cash surrender value) that is provided under a life insurance policy. However, the following features are not permanent benefits:

(a) A right to convert (or continue) life insurance after group life insurance coverage terminates;

(b) Any other feature that provides no economic benefit (other than current insurance protection) to the employee; or

(c) A feature under which term life insurance is provided at a level premium for a period of five years or less.

Policy. The term "policy" includes two or more obligations of an insurer (or its affiliates) that are sold in conjunction. Obligations that are offered or available to members of a group of employees are sold in conjunction if they are offered or available because of the employment relationship. The actuarial sufficiency of the premium charged for each obligation is not taken into account in determining whether the obligations are sold in conjunction. In addition, obligations may be sold in conjunction even if the obligations are contained in separate documents, each document is filed with and approved by the applicable state insurance commission, or each obligation is independent of any other obligation. Thus, a group of individual contracts under which life insurance is provided to a group of employees may be a policy. Similarly, two benefits provided to a group of employees, one term life insurance and the other a permanent benefit, may be a policy, even if one of the benefits is provided only to employees who decline the other benefit. However, an employer may elect to treat two or more obligations each of which provides no permanent benefits as separate policies if the premiums are properly allocated among such policies. An employer also may elect to treat an obligation which provides permanent benefits as a separate policy if—

(1) The insurer sells the obligation directly to the employee who pays the full cost thereof;

(2) The participation of the employer with respect to sales of the obligation to employees is limited to selection of the insurer and the type of coverage and to sales assistance activities such as providing employee lists to the insurer, permitting the insurer to use the employer's premises for solicitation, and collecting premiums through payroll deduction;

(3) The insurer sells the obligation on the same terms and in substantial amounts to individuals who do not purchase (and whose employers do not purchase) any other obligation from the insurer; and

(4) No employer-provided benefit is conditioned on purchase of the obligation. [Reg. § 1.79-0.]

☐ [*T.D. 7623, 5-14-79. Amended by T.D. 7917, 10-6-83.*]

[Reg. §1.79-1]

§1.79-1. Group-term life insurance—general rules.—(a) *What is group-term life insurance?*.—Life insurance is not group-term life insurance for purposes of section 79 unless it meets the following conditions:

(1) It provides a general death benefit that is excludable from gross income under section 101(a).

(2) It is provided to a group of employees.

(3) It is provided under a policy carried directly or indirectly by the employer.

(4) The amount of insurance provided to each employee is computed under a formula that precludes individual selection. This formula must be based on factors such as age, years of service, compensation, or position. This condition may be satisfied even if the amount of insurance provided is determined under a limited number of alternative schedules that are based on the amount each employee elects to contribute. However, the amount of insurance provided under each schedule must be computed under a formula that precludes individual selection.

(b) *May group-term life insurance be combined with other benefits?*.—No part of the life insurance provided under a policy that provides a permanent benefit is group-term life insurance unless—

(1) The policy or the employer designates in writing the part of the death benefit provided to each employee that is group-term life insurance; and

(2) The part of the death benefit that is provided to an employee and designated as the group-term life insurance benefit for any policy year is not less than the difference between the total death benefit provided under the policy and the employee's deemed death benefit (DDB) at the end of the policy year determined under paragraph (d)(3) of this section.

(c) *May a group include fewer than 10 employees?*.—(1) As a general rule, life insurance provided to a group of employees cannot qualify as group-term life insurance for purposes of section 79 unless, at some time during the calendar year, it is provided to at least 10 full-time employees who are members of the group of employees. For purposes of this rule, all life insurance provided under policies carried directly or indirectly by the employer is taken into account in determining the number of employees to whom life insurance is provided.

(2) The general rule of paragraph (c)(1) of this section does not apply if the following conditions are met:

(i) The insurance is provided to all full-time employees of the employer or, if evidence of insurability affects eligibility, to all full-time employees who provide evidence of insurability satisfactory to the insurer.

(ii) The amount of insurance provided is computed either as a uniform percentage of compensation or on the basis of coverage brackets established by the insurer. However, the amount computed under either method may be reduced in the case of employees who do not provide evidence of insurability satisfactory to the insurer. In general, no bracket may exceed $2\frac{1}{2}$ times the next lower bracket and the lowest bracket must be at least 10 percent of the highest bracket. However, the insurer may establish a separate schedule of coverage brackets for employees who are over age 65, but no bracket in the over-65 schedule may exceed $2\frac{1}{2}$ times the next lower bracket and the lowest bracket in the over-65 schedule must be at least 10 percent of the highest bracket in the basic schedule.

(iii) Evidence of insurability affecting an employee's eligibility for insurance or the amount of insurance provided to that employee *is limited* to a medical questionnaire completed by the employee that does not require a *physical examination*.

(3) The general rule of paragraph (c)(1) of this section does not apply if the following conditions are met:

(i) The insurance is provided under a common plan to the employees of two or more unrelated employers.

(ii) The insurance is restricted to, but mandatory for, all employees of the employer who belong to or are represented by an organization (such as a union) that carries on substantial activities in addition to obtaining insurance.

(iii) Evidence of insurability does not affect an employee's eligibility for insurance or the amount of insurance provided to that employee.

(4) For purposes of paragraphs (c)(2) and (3) of this section, employees are not taken into account if they are denied insurance for the following reasons:

(i) They are not eligible for insurance under the terms of the policy because they have not been employed for a waiting period, specified in the policy, which does not exceed six months.

(ii) They are part-time employees. Employees whose customary employment is for not more than 20 hours in any week, or 5 months in any calendar year, are presumed to be part-time employees.

(iii) They have reached the age of 65.

(5) For purposes of paragraph (c)(1) and (2) of this section, insurance is considered to be provided to an employee who elects not to receive insurance unless, in order to receive the insurance, the employee is required to contribute to the cost of benefits other than term life insurance. Thus, if an employee could receive term life insurance by contributing to its cost, the employee is taken into account in determining whether the insurance is provided to 10 or more employees even if such employee elects not to receive the insurance. However, an employee who must contribute to the cost of permanent benefits to obtain term life insurance is not taken into account in determining whether the term life insurance is provided to 10 or more employees unless the term life insurance is actually provided to such employee.

(d) *How much must an employee receiving permanent benefits include in income?*.—(1) *In general.*—If an insurance policy that meets the requirements of this section provides permanent benefits to an employee, the cost of the permanent benefits reduced by the amount paid for permanent benefits by the employee is included in the employee's income. The cost of the permanent benefits is determined under the formula in paragraph (d)(2) of this section.

(2) *Formula for determining cost of the permanent benefits.*—In each policy year the cost of the permanent benefits for any particular employee must be no less than—

$$X \ (DDB_2 - DDB_1)$$

where—

DDB_2 is the employee's deemed death benefit at the end of the policy year;

DDB_1 is the employee's deemed death benefit at the end of the preceding policy year; and

X is the net single premium for insurance (the premium for one dollar of paid-up, whole-life insurance) at the employee's attained age at the beginning of the policy year.

(3) *Formula for determining deemed death benefit.*—The deemed death benefit (DDB) at the end of any policy year for any particular employee is equal to—

$$R/Y$$

where—

R is the net level premium reserve at the end of that policy year for all benefits provided to the employee by the policy or, if greater, the fair market value of the policy at the end of that policy year; and

Y is the net single premium for insurance (the premium for one dollar of paid-up, whole life insurance) at the employee's age at the end of that policy year.

(4) *Mortality tables and interest rates used.*—For purposes of paragraphs (d)(2) and (d)(3) of this section, the net level premium reserve (R) and the net single premium (X or Y) shall be based on the 1958 CSO mortality Table and 4 percent interest.

(5) *Dividends.*—If an insurance policy that meets the requirements of this section provides permanent benefits, part or all of the dividends under the policy may be includible in the employee's income. If the employee pays nothing for the permanent benefits, all dividends under the policy that are actually or constructively received by the employee are includible in the employee's income. In all other cases, the amount of dividends included in the employee's income is equal to—

$$(D + C) - (PI + DI + AP)$$

where—

D is the total amount of dividends actually or constructively received under the policy by the employee in the current and all preceding taxable years of the employee;

C is the total cost of the permanent benefits for the current and all preceding taxable years of the employee determined under the formulas in paragraphs (d)(2) and (6) of this section;

PI is the total amount of premium included in the employee's income under paragraph (d)(1) of this section for the current and all preceding taxable years of the employee;

DI is the total amount of dividends included in the employee's income under this paragraph (d)(5) in all preceding taxable years of the employee; and

AP is the total amount paid for permanent benefits by the employee in the current and all preceding taxable years of the employee.

(6) *Different policy and taxable years.*—(i) If a policy year begins in one employee taxable year and ends in another employee taxable year, the cost of the permanent benefits, determined under the formula in paragraph (d)(2) of this section, is allocated between the employee taxable years.

(ii) The cost of permanent benefits for a policy year is allocated first to the employee taxable year in which the policy year begins. The cost of permanent benefits allocated to that policy year is equal to—

$$F \times C$$

where—

F is the fraction of the premium for that policy year that is paid on or before the last day of the employee taxable year; and

C is the cost of permanent benefits for the policy year determined under the formula in paragraph (d)(2) of this section.

(iii) Any part of the cost of permanent benefits that is not allocated to the employee taxable year in which the policy year begins is allocated to the subsequent employee taxable year.

(iv) The cost of permanent benefits for an employee taxable year is the sum of the costs of permanent benefits allocated to that year under paragraphs (d)(6)(ii) and (iii) of this section.

(7) *Example.* The provisions of this paragraph may be illustrated by the following example:

Example. An employer provides insurance to employee A under a policy that meets the requirements of this section. Under the policy, A, who is 47 years old, received $70,000 of group-term life insurance and elects to receive a permanent benefit under the policy. A pays $2 for each $1,000 of group-term life insurance through payroll deductions and the employer pays the remainder of the premium for the group-term life insurance. The employer also pays one half of the premium specified in the policy for the permanent benefit. A pays the other half of the permanent benefit through payroll deductions. The policy specifies that the annual premium paid for the permanent benefit is $300. However, the amount of premium allocated to the permanent benefit by the formula in paragraph (d)(2) of this section is $350. A is a calendar year taxpayer; the policy year begins January 1. In year 2000, $200 is includible in A's income because of insurance provided by the employer. This amount is computed as follows:

(1)	Cost of permanent benefits	$350
(2)	Amounts considered paid by A for permanent benefits ($1/2 \times $300)	150
(3)	Line (1) minus line (2)	200
(4)	Cost of $70,000 of group-term life insurance under Table I of §1.79-3	126
(5)	Cost of $50,000 of group-term life insurance under Table I of §1.79-3	90
(6)	Cost of group-term insurance in excess of $50,000 (line (4) minus line (5))	36
(7)	Amount considered paid by A for group-term life insurance (70 × $2)	140
(8)	Line (6) minus line (7) (but not less than 0)	0
(9)	Amount includible in income (line (3) plus line (8))	200

(e) *What is the effect of state law limits?.*—Section 79 does not apply to life insurance in excess of the limits under applicable state law on the amount of life insurance that can be provided to an employee under a single contract of group-term life insurance.

(f) *Cross references.*—(1) See section 79(b) and §1.79-2 for rules relating to group-term life insurance provided to certain retired individuals.

(2) See section 61(a) and the regulations thereunder for rules relating to life insurance not meeting the requirements of section 79, this section, or §1.79-2, such as insurance provided on the life of a non-employee (for example, an employee's spouse), insurance not provided as compensation for personal services performed as an employee, insurance not provided under a policy carried directly or indirectly by the employer, or permanent benefits.

(3) See section 106 and §1.106-1 for rules relating to certain insurance that does not provide general death benefits, such as travel insurance or accident and health insurance (including amounts payable under a double indemnity clause or rider).

(g) [Reserved]

(h) *Effective date.*—Section 1.79-0 applies to insurance provided in employee taxable year beginning on or after January 1, 1977 (except as provided in 26 CFR 1.79-1(g) (revised as of April 1, 1983) with respect to insurance provided in employee taxable years beginning in 1977). Sections 1.79-1 through 1.79-3 apply to insurance provided in employee taxable years beginning after December 31, 1982. See 26 CFR 1.79-1 through 1.79-3 (revised as of April 1, 1983) for rules applicable to insurance provided in employee taxable years beginning before January 1, 1983. [Reg. §1.79-1.]

☐ [T.D. 6888, 7-5-66. *Amended by* T.D. 6999, 1-17-69, T.D. 7132, 7-13-71, T.D. 7236, 12-27-72, T.D. 7623, 5-14-79, T.D. 7917, 10-6-83; T.D. 7924, 12-1-83; T.D. 8821, 5-28-99 *and* T.D. 9223, 8-26-2005.]

[Reg. §1.79-2]

§1.79-2. Exceptions to the rule of inclusion.—(a) *In general.*—(1) Section 79(b) provides exceptions for the cost of group-term life insurance provided under certain policies otherwise described in section 79(a). The policy or policies of group-term life insurance which are described in section 79(a) but which qualify for one of the exceptions set forth in section 79(b) are described in paragraphs (b) through (d) of this section. Paragraph (b) of this section discusses the exception provided in section 79(b)(1); paragraph (c) of this section discusses the exception provided in section 79(b)(2); and paragraph (d) of this section discusses the exception provided in section 79(b)(3).

(2)(i) If a policy of group-term life insurance qualifies for an exception provided by section 79(b), then the amount equal to the cost of such insurance is excluded from the application of the provisions of section 79(a).

(ii) If a policy, or portion of a policy of group-term life insurance qualifies for an exception provided by section 79(d), the amount (if any) paid by the employee toward the purchase of such insurance is not to be taken into account as an amount referred to in section 79(a)(2). In the case of a policy or policies of group-term life insurance which qualify for an exception provided by section 79(b)(1) or (3), the amount paid by the employee which is not to be taken into account as an amount referred to in section 79(a)(2) is the amount paid by the employee for the particular policy or policies of group-term life insurance which qualify for an exception provided under such section. If the exception provided in section 79(b)(2) is applicable only to a portion of the group-term life insurance on the employee's life, the amount considered to be paid by the employee toward the purchase of such portion is the amount equal to the excess of the cost of such portion of the insurance over the amount otherwise includible in the employee's gross income with respect to the group-term life insurance on his life carried directly or indirectly by such employer.

(iii) The rules of this subparagraph may be illustrated by the following example:

Example. A is an employee of X Corporation and is also an employee of Y Corporation, a subsidiary of X Corporation. A is provided, under a separate plan arranged by each of his employers, group-term life insurance on his life. During his taxable year, under the group-term life insurance plan of X Corporation, A is provided $60,000 of group-term life insurance on his life, and A pays $360.00 toward the purchase of such insurance. Under the group-term life insurance plan of Y Corporation, A is provided $65,000 of group-term life insurance on his life, but does not pay any part of the cost of such insurance. At the beginning of his taxable year, A terminates his employment with the X Corporation after he has reached the retirement age with respect to such employer, and the policy carried by the X Corporation qualifies for the exception provided by section 79(b)(1). For that taxable year, the cost of the group-term life insurance on A's life which is provided under the plan of X Corporation is not taken into account in determining the amount includible in A's gross income under section 79(a), and A may not take into account as an amount described in section 79(a)(2) the $360.00 he pays toward the purchase of such insurance.

(b) *Retired and disabled employees.*—(1) *In general.*—Section 79(b)(1) provides an exception for the cost of group-term life insurance on the life of an individual which is provided under a policy or policies otherwise described in section 79(a) if the individual has terminated his employment (as defined in subparagraph (2) of this paragraph) with such employer and either has reached the retirement age with respect to such employer (as defined in subparagraph (3) of this paragraph, or has become disabled (as defined in subparagraph (4)(i) of this paragraph). If an individual who has terminated his employment attains retirement age or has become disabled during his taxable year, or if an employee who has attained retirement age or has become disabled terminates his employment during the taxable year, the exception provided by section 79(b)(1) applies only to the portion of the cost of group-term life insurance which is provided subsequent to the happening of the last event which qualifies the policy of insurance on the employee's life for the exception provided in such section.

(2) *Termination of employment.*—For purposes of section 79(b)(1), an individual has terminated his employment with an employer providing such individual group-term life insurance when such individual no longer renders services to that employer as an employee of such employer.

(3) *Retirement age.*—For purposes of section 79(b)(1) and this section, the meaning of the term "retirement age" is determined in accordance with the following rules—

(i)(a) If the employee is covered under a written pension or annuity plan of the employer providing such individual group-term life insurance on his life (whether or not such plan is qualified under section 401(a) or 403(a)), then his retirement age shall be considered to be the earlier of

(1) The earliest age indicated by such plan at which an active employee has the right (or an inactive individual would have the right had he continued in employment) to retire without disability and without the consent of his employer and receive immediate retirement benefits computed at either the full rate or a rate proportionate to completed service as set forth in the normal retirement formula of the plan, i.e., without actuarial or similar reduction because of retirement before some later specified age, or

(2) The age at which it has been the practice of the employer to terminate, due to age, the services of the class of employees to which the individual has belonged.

(b) For purposes of (a) of this subdivision, if an employee is covered under more than one pension or annuity plan of the employer, his retirement age shall be determined with regard to that plan which covers that class of employees of the employer to which the employee last belonged. If the class of employees to which the employee last belonged is covered under more than one pension or annuity plan, then the employee's retirement age shall be determined with regard to that plan which covers the greatest number of the employer's employees.

(ii) In the absence of a written employee's pension or annuity plan described in subdivision (i) of this subparagraph, retirement age is the age, if any, at which it has been the practice of the employer to terminate, due to age, the services of the class of employees to which the particular employee last belonged, provided such age is reasonable in view of all the pertinent facts and circumstances.

(iii) If neither subdivision (i) or (ii) of this subparagraph applies, the retirement age is considered to be age 65.

(4) *Disabled.*—(i) For taxable years beginning after December 31, 1966, an individual is considered disabled for purposes of section 79(b)(1) and subparagraph (1) of this paragraph if he is disabled within the meaning of section 72(m)(7) and paragraph (f) of § 1.72-17. For taxable years beginning before January 1, 1967, an individual is considered disabled for purposes of section 79(b)(1) and subparagraph (1) of this paragraph if he is disabled within the meaning of section 213(g)(3), relating to the meaning of disabled, but the determination of the individual's status shall be made without regard to the provisions of section 213(g)(4), relating to the determination of status.

(ii)(a) In any taxable year in which an individual seeks to apply the exception set forth in section 79(b)(1) by reason of his being disabled within the meaning of subdivision (i) of this subparagraph, and in which the aggregate amount of insurance on the individual's life subject to the rule of inclusion set forth in section 79(a) but determined without regard to the amount of any insurance subject to any exception set forth in section 79(b), is greater than $50,000 of such insurance, the substantiation required by (b) or (c) of this subdivision must be submitted with the individual's tax return.

(b) For the first taxable year for which the individual seeks to apply the exception set forth in section 79(b)(1) by reason of his being disabled within the meaning of subdivision (i) of this subparagraph, there must be submitted with his income tax return a doctor's statement as to his impairment. There must also be submitted with the return a statement by the individual with respect to the effect of the impairment upon his substantial gainful activity, and the date such impairment occurred. For subsequent taxable years, the taxpayer may, in lieu of such statements, submit a statement declaring the continued existence (without substantial diminution) of the impairment and its continued effect upon his substantial gainful activity.

(c) In lieu of the substantiation required to be submitted by (b) of this subdivision for the taxable year, the individual may submit a signed statement issued to him by the insurer to the effect that the individual is disabled within the meaning of subdivision (i) of this paragraph. Such statement must set forth the basis for the insurer's determination that the individual was so disabled, and, for the first taxable year in which the individual is so disabled, the date such disability occurred.

(c) *Employer or charity a beneficiary.*—(1) *General rule.*—Section 79(b)(2) provides an exception with respect to the amounts referred to in section 79(a) for the cost of any portion of the group-term life insurance on the life of an employee provided during part or all of the taxable year of the employee under which the employer is directly or indirectly the beneficiary, or under which a person described in section 170(c) (relating to definition of charitable contributions) is the sole beneficiary, for the entire period during such taxable year for which the employee receives such insurance.

(2) *Employer is a beneficiary.*—For purposes of section 79(b)(2) and subparagraph (1) of this paragraph, the determination of whether the employer is directly or indirectly the beneficiary under a policy or policies of group-term life insurance depends upon the facts and circumstances of the particular case. Such determination is not made solely with regard to whether the employer possesses all the incidents of ownership in the policy. Thus, for example, if the employer is the nominal beneficiary under a policy of group-term life insurance on the life of his employee but there is an arrangement whereby the employer is required to pay over all (or a portion) of the proceeds of such policy to the employee's estate or his beneficiary, the employer is not considered a beneficiary under such policy (or such portion of the policy).

(3) *Charity a beneficiary.*—(i) For purposes of section 79(b)(2) and subparagraph (1) of this paragraph, a person described in section 170(c) is a beneficiary under a policy providing group-term life insurance if such person is designated the beneficiary under the policy by any assignment or designation of beneficiary under the policy which, under the law of the jurisdiction which is applicable to the policy, has the effect of making such person the beneficiary under such policy (whether or not such designation is revocable during the taxable year). Such a designation may be made by the employee with respect to any portion of the group-term life insurance on his life. However, no deduction is allowed under section 170, relating to charitable, etc., contributions and gifts, with respect to any such assignment or designation.

(ii) A person described in section 170(c) must be designated the sole beneficiary under the policy or portion of the policy. Such requirement is satisfied if the person described in section 170(c) is the beneficiary under such policy or portion of the policy, and there is no contingent or similar beneficiary under such policy or such portion other than a person described in section 170(c). A general "preference beneficiary clause" in a policy governing payment where there is no designated beneficiary in existence at the death of the employee will not of itself be considered to create a contingent or similar beneficiary. A person described in section 170(c) may be designated the beneficiary under a portion of the policy if such person is designated the sole beneficiary under a beneficiary designation which is expressed, for example, as a fraction of the amount of insurance on the insured's life.

(iii) If a person described in section 170(c) is designated, before May 1, 1964, the beneficiary under the policy (or portion thereof) and such person remains the beneficiary for the period beginning May 1, 1964, and ending with the close of the first taxable year of the employee ending after April 30, 1964, such person shall be treated as the beneficiary under the policy (or the portion thereof) for the period beginning January 1, 1964, and ending April 30, 1964.

(d) *Insurance contracts purchased under qualified employee plans.*—(1) Section 79(b)(3) provides an exception with respect to the cost of any group-term life insurance which is provided under a life insurance contract purchased as a part of a plan described in section 403(a), or purchased by a trust described in section 401(a) which is exempt from tax under section 501(a) if the proceeds of such contract are payable directly or indirectly to a participant in such trust or to a beneficiary of such participant. The provisions of sections 72(m)(3) and § 1.72-13 apply to the cost of such group-term life insurance, and, therefore, no part of such cost is excluded from the gross income of the employee by reason of the provisions of section 79.

Reg. § 1.79-2(d)(1)

(2) Whether the life insurance protection on an employee's life is provided under a qualified employee plan referred to in subparagraph (1) of this paragraph depends upon the provisions of such plan. In determining whether a pension, profit-sharing, stock bonus, or annuity plan satisfies the requirements for qualification set forth in sections 401(a) or 403(a), only group-term life insurance which is provided under such plan is taken into account. [Reg. § 1.79-2.]

☐ [*T.D. 6888, 7-5-66. Amended by T.D. 6919, 5-17-67, T.D. 6985, 12-26-68 and T.D. 7623, 5-14-79.*]

[Reg. § 1.79-3]

§ 1.79-3. Determination of amount equal to cost of group-term life insurance.—(a) *In general.*—This section prescribes the rules for determining the amount equal to the cost of group-term life insurance on an employee's life which is to be included in his gross income pursuant to the rule of inclusion set forth in section 79(a). Such amount is determined by—

(1) Computing the cost of the portion of the group-term life insurance on the employee's life to be taken into account (determined in accordance with the rules set forth in paragraph (b) of this section) for each "period of coverage" (as defined in paragraph (c) of this section) and aggregating the costs so determined, then

(2) Reducing the amount determined under subparagraph (1) of this paragraph by the amount determined in accordance with the rules set forth in paragraph (e) of this section, relating to the amount paid by the employee toward the purchase of group-term life insurance.

(b) *Determination of the portion of the group-term life insurance on the employee's life to be taken into account.*—(1) For each "period of coverage" (as defined in paragraph (c) of this section), the portion of the group-term life insurance to be taken into account in computing the amount includible in an employee's gross income for purposes of paragraph (a)(1) of this section is the sum of the proceeds payable upon the death of the employee under each policy, or portion of a policy, of group-term life insurance on such employee's life to which the rule of inclusion set forth in section 79(a) applies, less $50,000 of such insurance. Thus, the amount of any proceeds payable under a policy, or portion of a policy, which qualifies for one of the exceptions to the rule of inclusion provided by section 79(b) is not taken into account. For the regulations relating to such exceptions to the rule of inclusion, see § 1.79-2.

(2) For purposes of making the computation required by subparagraph (1) of this paragraph in any case in which the amount payable under the policy, or portion thereof, varies during the period of coverage, the amount payable under such policy during such period is considered to be the average of the amount payable under such policy at the beginning and the end of such period.

(3)(i) For purposes of making the computation required by subparagraph (1) of this paragraph in any case in which the amount payable under the policy is not payable as a specific amount upon the death of the employee in full discharge of the liability of the insurer, and such form of payment is not one of alternative methods of payment, the amount payable under such policy is the present value of the agreement by the insurer under the policy to make the payments to the beneficiary or beneficiaries entitled to such amounts upon the employee's death. For each period of coverage, such present value is to be determined as if the first and last day of such period is the date of death of the employee.

(ii) The present value of the agreement by the insurer under the policy to make payments shall be determined by the use of the mortality tables and interest rate employed by the insurer with respect to such a policy in calculating the amount held by the insurer (as defined in section 101(d)(2)), unless the Commissioner otherwise determines that a particular mortality table and interest rate, representative of the mortality table and interest rate used by commercial insurance companies with respect to such policies, shall be used to determine the present value of the policy for purposes of this subdivision.

(iii) For purposes of making the computation required by subdivision (i) of this subparagraph in any case in which it is necessary to determine the age of an employee's beneficiary and such beneficiary remains the same (under the policy, or the portion of the policy, with respect to which the determination of the present value of the agreement of the insurer to pay benefits is being made) for the entire period during the employee's taxable year for which such policy is in effect, the age of such beneficiary is such beneficiary's age at his nearest birthday on June 30th of the calendar year.

(iv) If the policy of group-term life insurance on the employee's life is such that the present value of the agreement by the insurer under the policy to pay benefits cannot be determined by the rules prescribed in this subparagraph, the taxpayer may submit with his return a computation of such present value, consistent with the actuarial and other assumptions set forth in this subparagraph, showing the appropriate factors applied in his case. Such computation shall be subject to the approval of the Commissioner upon examination of such return.

(c) *Period of coverage.*—For purposes of this section, the phrase "period of coverage" means any one calendar month period, or part thereof, during the employee's taxable year during which the employee is provided group-term life insurance on his life to which the rule of inclusion set forth in section 79(a) applies. The phrase "part thereof" as used in the preceding sentence means any continuous period which is less than the one calendar month period referred to in the preceding sentence for which premiums are charged by the insurer.

(d) *The cost of the portion of the group-term life insurance on an employee's life.*—(1) This paragraph sets forth the rules for determining the cost, for each period of coverage, of the portion of the group-term life insurance on the employee's life to be taken into account in computing the amount includible in the employee's gross income for purposes of paragraph (a)(1) of this section. The portion of the group-term life insurance on the employee's life to be taken into account is determined in accordance with the provisions of paragraph (b) of this section. Table I, which is set forth in subparagraph (2) of this paragraph, determines the cost for each $1,000 of such portion of the group-term life insurance on the employee's life for each one-month period. The cost of the portion of the group-term life insurance on the employee's life for each period of coverage of one month is obtained by multiplying the number of thousand dollars of such insurance computed to the nearest tenth which is provided during such period by the appropriate amount set forth in Table 1. In any case in which group-term life insurance is provided for a period of coverage of less than one month, the amount set forth in Table I is prorated over such period of coverage.

(2) For the cost of group-term life insurance provided after June 30, 1999, the following table sets forth the cost of $1,000 of group-term life insurance provided for one month, computed on the basis of 5-year age brackets. See 26 CFR 1.79-3(d)(2) in effect prior to July 1, 1999, and contained in the 26 CFR part 1 edition revised as of April 1, 1999, for a table setting forth the cost of group-term life insurance provided before July 1, 1999. For purposes of Table I, the age of the employee is the employee's attained age on the last day of the employee's taxable year.

TABLE I.—UNIFORM PREMIUMS FOR $1,000 OF GROUP-TERM LIFE INSURANCE PROTECTION

5-year age bracket	Cost per $1,000 of protection for one month
Under 25	$0.05
25 to 29	.06
30 to 34	.08
35 to 39	.09
40 to 44	.10
45 to 49	.15
50 to 54	.23
55 to 59	.43
60 to 64	.66
65 to 69	1.27
70 and above	2.06

(3) The net premium cost of group-term life insurance as provided in Table I of subparagraph (2) of this paragraph applies only to the cost of group-term life insurance subject to the rule of inclusion set forth in section 79(a). Therefore, such net premium cost is not applicable to the determination of the cost of group-term life insurance provided under a policy which is not subject to such rule of inclusion.

(e) *Effective date.*—(1) *General effective date for table.*—Except as provided in paragraph (e)(2) of this section, the table in paragraph (d)(2) of this section is applicable July 1, 1999. Until January 1, 2000, an employer may calculate imputed income for all its employees under age 30 using the 5-year age bracket for ages 25 to 29.

(2) *Effective date for table for purposes of § 1.79-0.*—For a policy of life insurance issued under a plan in existence on June 30, 1999, which would not be treated as carried directly or indirectly by an employer under § 1.79-0 (taking into account the Table I in effect on that date), until January 1, 2003, an employer may use either the table in paragraph (d)(2) of this section or the table in effect prior to July 1, 1999 (as described in paragraph (d)(2) of this section) for determining if the policy is carried directly or indirectly by the employer.

(f) *Amount paid by the employee toward the purchase of group-term life insurance.*—(1) Except as otherwise provided in subparagraph (2) of this paragraph, if an employee pays any amount toward the purchase of group-term life insurance provided for a taxable year which is subject to the rule of inclusion set forth in section 79(a), the sum of all such amounts is the amount referred to in section 79(a)(2) and paragraph (a)(2) of this section. The rule of the preceding sentence applies even though the payments made by the employee are made with respect to a period of coverage during which no portion of the group-term life insurance on his life is taken into account under paragraph (b)(1) of this section.

(2) In determining the amount paid by the employee for purposes of section 79(a)(2) and paragraph (a)(2) of this section, there is not taken into account any amounts paid by the employee for group-term life insurance provided (or to be provided) for a different taxable year (other than amounts applicable to regular pay periods extending into the next taxable year). Thus, for example, if part of an employee's payment during a taxable year represents a prepayment for insurance to be provided after his retirement, such part does not reduce the amount includible in his gross income for the current taxable year. Furthermore, in determining such amount, there is not taken into account any amount paid by an employee toward the purchase of group-term life insurance which qualifies for one of the exceptions described in section 79(b). The amount paid by an employee toward the purchase of group-term life insurance which qualifies for one of the exceptions described in section 79(b) is determined under the rules of paragraph (a)(2) of § 1.79-2.

(3) If payments are made by the employer and his employees to provide group-term life insurance which is subject to the rule of inclusion set forth in section 79(a) as well as to provide other benefits for the employees, and if the amount paid by the employee toward the purchase of such insurance cannot be determined by the provisions of the policy or plan under which such benefits are provided, then the determination of the portion of the cost of group-term life insurance (computed in accordance with the provisions of this section) which is attributable to the contributions of the employee shall be made in accordance with the provisions of this subparagraph. The amount paid by the employee toward the purchase of all the group-term life insurance on his life for his taxable year (or for the portion of his taxable year if such portion is the basis of the computation) under such group policy shall be an amount determined first by ascertaining the total amount paid by all employees who are covered for multiple benefits which is allocable toward the purchase of group-term life insurance on their lives for the year, and then by ascertaining the pro rata portion of such total amount attributable to the individual employee. The total amount paid by all employees who are covered for multiple benefits which is allocable toward the purchase of group-term life insurance on their lives with respect to such year shall be an amount which bears the same ratio to the total amount paid by all employees for multiple benefits with respect to such year as the aggregate premiums paid to the insurer for group-term life insurance on such employees' lives with respect to such year bears to the aggregate premiums paid to the insurer for such multiple benefits with respect to such year. The pro rata portion of such total amount attributable to the individual employee for the cost of group-term life insurance on his life shall be an amount which bears the same ratio to the total amount paid by all employees which is allocable towards the purchase of group-term insurance on their lives with respect to such year as the amount of group-term life insurance on the life of the employee at a specified time during the year, as determined by the employer, bears to the total amount of *group-term life* insurance on the lives of all employees insured for such multiple benefits at such time.

(g) *Effect of provision of other benefits.*—(1) *In general.*—This paragraph discusses the effect of the provision of certain benefits other than group-term life insurance on the life of the employee if the provision of such benefits is contingent upon the underwriting of group-term life insurance on the employee's life to which the rule of inclusion set forth in section 79(a) applies.

(2) *Dependent coverage.*—An amount equal to the cost of group-term life insurance on the life of the spouse or other family member of the employee which is provided under a policy of group-term life insurance carried directly or indirectly by his employer is not subject to the provisions of section 79 since it is not on the life of the employee. See paragraph (d)(2)(ii)(b) of § 1.61-2 for rules regarding the tax treatment of such insurance.

(3) *Disability provisions.*—Payments made for disability benefits provided under a group-term life insurance contract are considered to constitute payments made for accident and health insurance. Thus, employer contributions to provide such benefits are excluded from gross income by reason of the provisions of section 106.

(4) *Cost of other benefits.*—If a benefit described in this paragraph is provided under a policy under which both the employer and his employees contribute, then, except as otherwise provided in this subparagraph, the employer and the employees will be treated as contributing toward the payment of such benefit at the same rate as they contribute toward the cost of group-term life insurance on the employees' lives. A separate allocation of employer and employee contributions for such benefits is permissible only if—

(i) Such separate allocation is set forth in the group policy and is applicable to all the employees covered under such policy;

(ii) Such separate allocation is followed in transactions between the insurer and the group-policyholder; and

(iii) The allocation set forth in the policy satisfies the requirements of the law of the jurisdiction which is applicable to the contract regarding any minimum or maximum contribution rate by the employer or the employees. [Reg. § 1.79-3.]

☐ [T.D. 6888, 7-5-66. Amended by T.D. 7623, 5-14-79; T.D. 7924, 12-1-83; T.D. 8273, 11-17-89; T.D. 8424, 7-29-92 and T.D. 8821, 5-28-99.]

[Reg. § 1.79-4T]

§ 1.79-4T. Questions and answers relating to the nondiscrimination requirements for group-term life insurance (Temporary).

Q-1: When does section 79, as amended by the Tax Reform Act of 1984, become effective?

A-1: (a) Generally, section 79, as amended, applies to taxable years (of the employee receiving insurance coverage) beginning after December 31, 1983. There are, however, several exceptions to this effective date where there is coverage under a group-term life insurance plan of the employer that was in existence on January 1, 1984, or a comparable successor to such a plan maintained by the employer or a successor employer.

(b) First, the new rules of section 79(b) and (e), that require the inclusion in income of a retired employee of amounts attributable to the cost of group-term life insurance in excess of $50,000 and that include former employees within the definition of the term "employee" will not apply to any employee who retired from employment on or before January 1, 1984.

(c) Second, in the case of an individual who retires after January 1, 1984, and before January 1, 1987, the new rules of section 79(b) and (e) do not apply if (1) the individual attained age 55 on or before January 1, 1984, and (2) the plan was maintained by the same employer who employed the individual during 1983, or by a successor employer.

(d) Third, in the case of an individual who retires after December 31, 1986, the new rules of section 79(b) and (e) do not apply if (1) the individual attained age 55 on or before January 1, 1984, (2) the plan was maintained by the same employer who employed the individual during 1983, or by a successor employer, and (3) the plan is not, after December 31, 1986, a discriminatory group-term life insurance plan (not taking into account any group-term life insurance coverage provided to employees who retired before January 1, 1987).

(e) For purposes of determining whether a plan is, after December 31, 1986, a discriminatory group-term life insurance plan, there shall be ignored any insurance coverage provided pursuant to a state law requirement that an insurer continue to provide insurance coverage for a period of time not in excess of two months following the termination of a policy.

Q-2: What is meant by a "group-term life insurance plan of the employer that was in existence on January 1, 1984"?

A-2: A group-term life insurance plan of the employer was in existence on January 1, 1984, only if the group policy or policies providing group-term life insurance benefits under the plan were executed on or before January 1, 1984, and were not terminated prior to such date. The applicability of section 79, as amended, to an employee will not be affected by the transfer of the employee between employers treated as a single employer under section 79(d)(7) if the employee continues, after the transfer, to be provided with group-term life insurance benefits under a plan that is comparable (determined under the principles set forth in Q&A 3) to the plan provided by the former employer.

Q-3: When is a plan of group-term life insurance a "comparable successor" to another such plan?

A-3: A plan of group-term life insurance will be a comparable successor to another plan of group-term life insurance (the first plan) only if the plan does not differ from the first plan in any significant aspect with respect to individuals who are potentially eligible for benefits provided under the grandfather provisions in Q&A 1. These individuals consist of those persons who are covered under a plan of group-term life insurance of the employer that was in existence on January 1, 1984, or a comparable successor to such a plan maintained by the employer or a successor employer, and who either retired on or before January 1, 1984, or who both attained age 55 on or before January 1, 1984, and were employed by the employer maintaining the plan (or a predecessor of that employer) during the year 1983. Accordingly, if significant additional or reduced benefits are provided only to individuals who are not described in the preceding sentence, the plan will be considered a comparable successor plan. A plan will not fail to be a comparable successor plan merely because the employer purchases a policy or policies identical to the employer's first plan from a different insurance company. If the new plan provides significant additional or reduced benefits (either as to the type or amount available) to employees, or provides benefits to a category of employees that was formerly excluded from participating in the plan, the plan is generally not a comparable successor to the first plan. However, a plan will not be considered as providing significant additional or reduced benefits merely because a participant's coverage is based on a percentage of compensation and the participant's compensation for the taxable year has been increased or decreased. Furthermore, a plan will not be considered a non-comparable successor plan merely because it is amended, either to decrease benefits provided to key employees or to increase benefits provided to non-key employees, solely in order to comply with the nondiscrimination requirements of section 79(d). Finally, a plan will not be considered a non-comparable successor plan merely because a policy that is part of a discriminatory plan is terminated in order to end discriminatory coverage.

Q-4: For purposes of determining the effective date of section 79, as amended by the Tax Reform Act of 1984, what is a "successor employer"?

A-4: A successor employer is an employer who employs a group of individuals formerly employed by another employer as a result of a business merger, acquisition or division.

Q-5: Under what circumstances will separate policies of group-term life insurance of an employer be considered to be a single plan in determining whether the employer's plan of group-term life insurance is discriminatory?

A-5: All policies providing group-term life insurance to a common key employee or key employees (as defined in this Q&A) carried directly or indirectly by an employer (or by a group of employers described in section 79(d)(7)) will be considered as a single plan for purposes of determining whether an employer's group-term life insurance plan is discriminatory. For example, if a key employee receives $50,000 of group-term life insurance coverage under one policy and the same key employee receives an additional $250,000 of coverage under a separate group-term life insurance policy, the two policies will be treated as a single plan in determining whether the group-term life insurance provided by the employer is discriminatory. If it is discriminatory, the key employees covered by either policy will not receive the benefit of section 79(a)(1) or section 79(c) for either policy. The result is the same even if each policy, considered alone, would be nondiscriminatory. A policy that provides group-term life insurance to a key employee and a policy under which the same key employee is eligible to receive group-term life insurance upon separation from service will be considered to provide group-term life insurance to a common key employee. In addition, an employer may treat two or more policies that do not provide group-term life insurance to a common key employee as constituting a single plan for purposes of satisfying the nondiscrimination provisions of section 79(d). For example, if the employer provides group-term life insurance coverage for non-key employees under one policy and provides group-term life insurance coverage for key employees under a second policy, the two policies may be considered together in determining whether the requirements of section 79(d) are satisfied with regard to the second policy. For purposes of this section, the term "key employee" has the meaning given to such term by paragraph (1) of section 416(i), except that subparagraph (A)(iv) of such paragraph shall be applied by not taking into account employees described in section 79(d)(3)(B) who are not participants in the plan. For purposes of this section, all references to "plan year" or "plan years" in section 416(g)(4)(C) and section 416(i) shall be deleted and replaced with "taxable year of the employer" or "taxable years of the employer," respectively.

Q-6: In the case of a discriminatory group-term life insurance plan, what amounts should be included in the gross income of a key employee?

A-6: (a) In the case of a discriminatory group-term life insurance plan, each key employee must include in gross income for the taxable year the cost of his or her insurance benefit for that year provided by the employer under the plan.

(b) The cost of group-term life insurance coverage provided by an employer for a key employee during the employee's taxable year is determined by apportioning the net premium (group premium less policy dividends, premium refunds or experience rating credits) allocable to the group-term life insurance coverage during the key employee's taxable year, less the actual cost allocated to other key employees pursuant to the method described in the subparagraph (d) of this answer, if applicable, among the covered employees. In the event that the employer has other forms and types of coverage with the same insurer, the employer must make a reasonable allocation of the total premiums paid to the insurer. For example, where an employer has both health insurance coverage and a plan of group-term life insurance with the same insurer, and there is no volume discount, the net premium for the plan of group-term life insurance must include the excess, if any, of the payments the employer makes for the health insurance coverage over the payments the employer would make for such coverage if the plan of group-term life insurance for which this calculation is being made did not exist.

(c) In general, the portion of the net premium for group-term life insurance that should be apportioned to a key employee, other than a key employee to whom the method in subparagraph (d) of this answer is applicable, is determined by (1) calculating a "tabular" premium for the entire group (with the exception of all key employees to whom the method in subparagraph (d) of this answer is applicable), in the manner described below, (2) determining the ratio of the total actual net premium (less the actual cost allocated to key employees pursuant to the method in the subparagraph (d) of this answer) to the total tabular premium and (3) multiplying the tabular premium for the key employee at his or her attained age by such ratio. Thus, if the total actual net premium is 125 percent of the total tabular premium for all covered employees and the tabular premium at the key employee's attained age is $2.00 per thousand per month, the cost for such employee would be $2.50 per thousand per month ($2.00 times 125 percent). For these purposes the table used to calculate tabular premiums will be determined as follows:

(i) If the group policy contains a reasonable table (based on recognized mortality assumptions) of premium rates on an attained age basis (which table may use age brackets not exceeding five years) with reference to which the group premium is determined, such table will be used;

(ii) If such table is not available, the 1960 Basic Group Table published by the Society of Actuaries will be used.

(d) In cases where the mortality charge for group-term life insurance coverage provided to a key employee is calculated separately by the insurer (for example, where the charge for the coverage provided to a key employee is based on a medical examination) and the amount of such mortality charge plus a proportionate share of the loading charge for the coverage provided to the group is higher than the amount that would be allocable to such employee under the allocation method in subparagraph (c) the cost of group-term life insurance coverage for that employee shall be that higher amount.

Q-7: Must all active and former employees be considered in applying the coverage tests in section 79(d)(3) to determine whether or not a plan of group-term life insurance is discriminatory with respect to coverage?

A-7: No. Generally, a plan of group-term life insurance which covers both active and former employees will not satisfy the nondiscrimination requirements of section 79(d) unless the coverage tests in section 79(d)(3) are satisfied with respect to both the active and the former employees of the employer, except to the extent they are excluded from tests for discrimination by application of the grandfather provisions set forth in Q&A 1. However, for purposes of determining whether a plan is discriminatory with respect to coverage, the coverage tests must be applied separately to active and former employees. In addition, if the plan limits participation by former employees to employees who retired from employment with the employer, then only retired employees must be considered in applying the coverage tests to former employees. Also, in applying the coverage tests in section 79(d)(3), the employer may make reasonable mortality assumptions regarding former employees who are not covered under the plan but must be considered in applying the coverage tests. Furthermore, only those former employees who terminated employment on or after the earliest date of termination from employment for any former employee covered by the plan must be considered. Finally, for purposes of determining whether a plan of group-term life insurance of the employer (or a successor employer) that was in existence on January 1, 1984 (or a comparable successor to such a plan) is discriminatory, after December 31, 1986, with respect to group-term life insurance coverage for former employees, coverage provided to employees who retired on or before December 31, 1986, shall not be taken into account.

Q-8: Will a group-term life insurance plan be considered discriminatory if active employees receive greater benefits as a percentage of compensation than former employees, or vice versa?

A-8: No. For purposes of determining whether a plan is discriminatory with respect to the type and amount of benefits available, insurance coverage for former employees must be tested separately from insurance coverage for active employees. For example, a group-term life insurance plan that provides group-term life insurance benefits equal to 200 percent of compensation for all active employees and 100 percent of final compensation (based on the average annual compensation for the final five years) for all former employees would satisfy the nondiscrimination requirements of section 79(d). However, a group-term life insurance plan that provides group-term life insurance benefits equal to 200 percent of compensation for all active employees and 100 percent of final compensation (based on the average annual compensation for the final five years) only for key employees who are no longer employed by the employer (or a successor employer) would not satisfy the nondiscrimination requirement of section 79(d)(2)(A).

Q-9: Under what circumstances will the amount of benefits available under a plan of group-term life insurance be considered not to discriminate in favor of participants who are key employees?

A-9: A plan of group-term life insurance will be considered not to discriminate in favor of participants who are key employees, as to the amount of benefits available, if the plan provides a fixed amount of insurance which is the same for all covered employees. In other circumstances, the determination of whether a plan is nondiscriminatory will be based on all of the facts and circumstances. Such plans will be considered not to discriminate in favor of participants who are key employees, as to the amount of benefits available, if the plan contains no group of employees described in the following sentence that, if tested separately, would fail to satisfy the requirements of section 79(d)(2)(A). The group subject to separate testing under the preceding sentence consists of a key employee and all other participants (including other key employees) who receive, under the plan, an amount of insurance (as a multiple of compensation (either total compensation or the basic or regular rate of compensation)) that is equal to or greater than the amount of insurance received by such key employee. As described in Q&As 7&8, active and former employees are tested separately under section 79(d)(2)(A).

Example: Assume that a plan of group-term life insurance has 500 participants, 10 of whom are key employees. Under the plan, 400 of the non-key employees receive an amount of insurance equal to 100 percent of compensation, while all of the key employees and 90 of the non-key employees receive an amount of insurance equal to 200 percent of compensation. The plan will be considered not to discriminate in favor of the participants who are key employees because, tested separately, the group of participants receiving an amount of insurance equal to or greater then 200 percent of compensation would satisfy the requirements of section 79(d)(2)(A) (by reason of section 79(d)(3)(A)(ii)). If one of the key employees received an amount of insurance equal to 300 percent of compensation, the plan would be considered to discriminate in favor of participants who are key employees, because, tested separately, the group consisting of the single key employee receiving an amount of insurance equal to or greater than 300 percent of compensation would fail to satisfy the requirements of section 79(d)(2)(A).

In determining the groups of employees that are tested separately for this purpose, allowance shall be made for reasonable differences in amount of insurance (as a multiple of compensation) due to rounding, the use of compensation brackets or other similar factors. Thus, if a plan bases group-term life insurance coverage on "compensation brackets," it is not intended that any participants will be treated as receiving an amount of insurance (as a multiple of compensation) that is greater (or less) than that of any other participant merely because the first participant's compensation is at the lower (or higher) end of a compensation bracket while the second participant's compensation is at the higher (or lower) end of a compensation bracket. However, any compensation brackets utilized by a plan will be examined to determine if the brackets, or compensation groupings, result in discrimination in favor of key employees. In addition, a plan does not meet the requirements for nondiscrimination as to the type and amount of benefits available under the plan unless all types of benefits (including permanent benefits) and all terms and conditions with respect to such benefits which are available to any participant who is a key employee are also available on a nondiscriminatory basis to non-key employee participants.

Q-10: How is additional coverage purchased by employees under a plan of group-term life insurance treated for purposes of determining whether a plan of group-term life insurance is discriminatory?

A-10: (a) The extent to which employees purchase additional coverage under a plan of group-term life insurance is not taken into account for purposes of determining whether a plan of group-term life insurance is discriminatory. For example, a plan providing insurance to all employees of 1 times annual compensation, which gives all employees the option to purchase additional insurance of 1 times annual compensation at their own expense, would not be considered discriminatory as to the type and amount of benefits available, even if the group (or groups) of participants who purchase additional insurance, if tested separately, would not satisfy the requirements of section 79(d)(2)(A). Solely for this purpose, the choice of an amount of group-term life insurance as a benefit under a cafeteria plan will be treated as the purchase of group-term life insurance by an employee. If additional insurance coverage is available to any key employee that is not available, or a nondiscriminatory basis, to non-key employees, the plan will be considered discriminatory, even if the full cost of such additional insurance coverage is paid by the employee(s) electing such benefits.

(b) If the employer bears a part of the expense of any additional coverage that is purchased by an employee under a plan of group-term life insurance, the additional insurance shall be treated, in part, as an amount of insurance provided by the employer under the plan and, in part, as an amount of insurance purchased by the employee. Except to the extent provided in subparagraph (a) above, the portion of insurance treated as an amount of insurance purchased by the employee is not taken into account for purposes of determining whether the plan is discriminatory. Whether such insurance (together with any other insurance provided by the employer under the plan) will cause the plan to be considered to discriminate in favor of participants who are key employees is determined under the rules of Q&A 9.

Q-11: What effect do the provisions of section 79(d)(1) have if a plan of group-term life insurance is discriminatory for only part of a year?

A-11: If a plan of group-term life insurance is discriminatory at any time during the key employee's taxable year, then it is a discriminatory group-term life insurance plan for that taxable year and the provisions of section 79(d)(1) will be applicable with respect to all group-term life insurance costs allocable to that employee for that year.

Q-12: Are the section 79(d) provisions independent from the requirements contained in Treas. Reg. §1.79-1?

A-12: Yes. Treas. Reg. §1.79-1(c)(1) provides that life insurance provided to a group of employees cannot qualify as group-term life insurance if it is provided to less than ten full-time employees unless certain requirements are satisfied. The satisfaction of these requirements does not guarantee that the plan will be nondiscriminatory, and vice versa. Treas. Reg. §1.79-1(a)(4) provides that life insurance is not group-term life insurance unless the amount of insurance provided to each employee is computed under a formula that precludes individual selection. The mere fact that a life insurance policy is nondiscriminatory is not determinative as to whether the policy precludes individual selection, and vice versa. [Temporary Reg. §1.79-4T.]

☐ [T.D. 8073, 1-29-86.]

[Reg. §1.82-1]

§1.82-1. Payments for or reimbursements of expenses of moving from one residence to another residence attributable to employment or self-employment.—(a) *Reimbursements in gross income.*—(1) *In general.*—Any amount received or accrued, directly or indirectly, by an individual as a payment for or reimbursement of expenses of moving from one residence to another residence attributable to employment or self-employment is includible in gross income under section 82 as compensation for services in the taxable year received or accrued. For rules relating to the year a deduction may be allowed for expenses of moving from one residence to another residence, see section 217 and the regulations thereunder.

(2) *Amounts received or accrued as reimbursement or payment.*—For purposes of this section, amounts are considered as being received or accrued by an individual as reimbursement or payment whether received in the form of money, property, or services. A cash basis taxpayer will include amounts in gross income under section 82 when they are received or treated as received by him. Thus, for example, if an employer moves an employee's household goods and personal effects from the employee's old residence to his new residence using the employer's facilities, the employee is considered as having received a payment in the amount of the fair market value of the services furnished at the time the services are furnished by the employer. If the employer pays a mover for moving the employee's

household goods and personal effects, the employee is considered as having received the payment at the time the employer pays the mover, rather than at the time the mover moves the employee's household goods and effects. Where an employee receives a loan or advance from an employer to enable him to pay his moving expenses, the employee will not be deemed to have received a reimbursement of moving expenses until such time as he accounts to his employer if he is not required to repay such loan or advance and if he makes such accounting within a reasonable time. Such loan or advance will be deemed to be a reimbursement of moving expenses at the time of such accounting to the extent used by the employee for such moving expenses.

(3) *Direct or indirect payments or reimbursements.*—For purposes of this section amounts are considered as being received or accrued whether received directly (paid or provided to an individual by an employer, a client, a customer, or similar person) or indirectly (paid to a third party on behalf of an individual by an employer, a client, a customer, or similar person). Thus, if an employer pays a mover for the expenses of moving an employee's household goods and personal effects from one residence to another residence, the employee has indirectly received a payment which is includible in his gross income under section 82.

(4) *Expenses of moving from one residence to another residence.*—An expense of moving from one residence to another residence is any expenditure, cost, loss, or similar item paid or incurred in connection with a move from one residence to another residence. Moving expenses include (but are not limited to) any expenditure, cost, loss, or similar item directly or indirectly resulting from the acquisition, sale, or exchange of property, the transportation of goods or property, or travel (by the taxpayer or any other person) in connection with a change in residence. Such expenses include items described in section 217(b) (relating to the definition of moving expenses), irrespective of the dollar limitations contained in section 217(b)(3) and the conditions contained in section 217(c), as well as items not described in section 217(b), such as a loss sustained on the sale or exchange of personal property, storage charges, taxes, or expenses of refitting rugs or draperies.

(5) *Attributable to employment or self-employment.*—Any amount received or accrued from an employer, a client, a customer, or similar person in connection with the performance of services for such employer, client, customer, or similar person, is attributable to employment or self-employment. Thus, for example, if an employer reimburses an employee for a loss incurred on the sale of the employee's house, reimbursement is attributable to the performance of services if made because of the employer-employee relationship. Similarly, if an employer in order to prevent an employee's sustaining a loss on a sale of a house acquires the property from the employee at a price in excess of fair market value, the employee is considered to have received a payment attributable to employment to the extent that such payment exceeds the fair market value of the property.

(b) *Effective date.*—(1) *In general.*—Except as provided in subparagraph (2) of this paragraph, paragraph (a) of this section is applicable only to amounts received or accrued in taxable years beginning after December 31, 1969.

(2) *Election with respect to payments or reimbursements for expenses paid or incurred before January 1, 1971.*—Paragraph (a) of this section does not apply with respect to moving expenses paid or incurred before January 1, 1971, in connection with the commencement of work by an employee at a new principal place of work where such employee had been notified by his employer on or before December 19, 1969, of such move and the employee makes an election under paragraph (h) of §1.217-2. [Reg. §1.82-1.]

☐ [*T.D. 7195, 7-10-72. Amended by T.D. 7578, 12-19-78.*]

[Reg. §1.83-1]

§1.83-1. Property transferred in connection with the performance of services.—(a) *Inclusion in gross income.*—(1) *General rule.*— Section 83 provides rules for the taxation of property transferred to an employee or independent contractor (or beneficiary thereof) in connection with the performance of services by such employee or independent contractor. In general, such property is not taxable under section 83(a) until it has been transferred (as defined in §1.83-3(a)) to such person and become substantially vested (as defined in §1.83-3(b)) in such person. In that case, the excess of—

(i) The fair market value of such property (determined without regard to any lapse restriction, as defined in §1.83-3(*i*)) at the time that the property becomes substantially vested, over

(ii) The amount (if any) paid for such property,

shall be included as compensation in the gross income of such employee or independent contractor for the taxable year in which the

property becomes substantially vested. Until such property becomes substantially vested, the transferor shall be regarded as the owner of such property, and any income from such property received by the employee or independent contractor (or beneficiary thereof) or the right to the use of such property by the employee or independent contractor constitutes additional compensation and shall be included in the gross income of such employee or independent contractor for the taxable year in which such income is received or such use is made available. This paragraph applies to a transfer of property in connection with the performance of services even though the transferor is not the person for whom such services are performed.

(2) *Life insurance.*—The cost of life insurance protection under a life insurance contract, retirement income contract, endowment contract, or other contract providing life insurance protection is taxable generally under section 61 and the regulations thereunder during the period such contract remains substantially nonvested (as defined in §1.83-3(b)). For the taxation of life insurance protection under a split-dollar life insurance arrangement (as defined in §1.61-22(b)(1) or (2)), see §1.61-22.

(3) *Cross references.*—For rules concerning the treatment of employers and other transferors of property in connection with the performance of services, see section 83(h) and §1.83-6. For rules concerning the taxation of beneficiaries of an employees' trust that is not exempt under section 501(a), see section 402(b) and the regulations thereunder.

(b) *Subsequent sale, forfeiture, or other disposition of nonvested property.*—(1) If substantially nonvested property (that has been transferred in connection with the performance of services) is subsequently sold or otherwise disposed of to a third party in an arm's length transaction while still substantially nonvested, the person who performed such services shall realize compensation in an amount equal to the excess of—

(i) The amount realized on such sale or other disposition, over

(ii) The amount (if any) paid for such property.

Such amount of compensation is includible in his gross income in accordance with his method of accounting. Two preceding sentences also apply when the person disposing of the property has received it in a non-arm's length transaction described in paragraph (c) of this section. In addition, section 83(a) and paragraph (a) of this section shall thereafter cease to apply with respect to such property.

(2) If substantially nonvested property that has been transferred in connection with the performance of services to the person performing such services is forfeited while still substantially nonvested and held by such person, the difference between the amount paid (if any) and the amount received upon forfeiture (if any) shall be treated as an ordinary gain or loss. This paragraph (b)(2) does not apply to property to which §1.83-2(a) applies.

(3) This paragraph (b) shall not apply to, and no gain shall be recognized on, any sale, forfeiture, or other disposition described in this paragraph to the extent that any property received in exchange therefor is substantially nonvested. Instead, section 83 and this section shall apply with respect to such property received (as if it were substituted for the property disposed of).

(c) *Dispositions of nonvested property not at arm's length.*—If substantially nonvested property (that has been transferred in connection with the performance of services) is disposed of in a transaction which is not at arm's length and the property remains substantially nonvested, the person who performed such services realizes compensation equal in amount to the sum of any money and the fair market value of any substantially vested property received in such disposition. Such amount of compensation is includible in his gross income in accordance with his method of accounting. However, such amount of compensation shall not exceed the fair market value of the property disposed of at the time of disposition (determined without regard to any lapse restriction), reduced by the amount paid for such property. In addition, section 83 and these regulations shall continue to apply with respect to such property, except that any amount previously includible in gross income under this paragraph (c) shall thereafter be treated as an amount paid for such property. For example, if in 1971 an employee pays $50 for a share of stock which has a fair market value of $100 and is substantially nonvested at that time and later in 1971 (at a time when the property still has a fair market value of $100 and is still substantially nonvested) the employee disposes of, in a transaction not at arm's length, the share of stock to his wife for $10, the employee realizes compensation of $10 in 1971. If in 1972, when the share of stock has a fair market value of $120, it becomes substantially vested, the employee realizes additional compensation in 1972 in the amount of $60 (the $120 fair market value of the stock less both the $50 price paid for the stock and the $10 taxed as compensation in 1971). For purposes of this paragraph, if substantially nonvested property has been transferred to a person other than the person who performed the services, and the transferee dies holding the property while the property is still substantially nonvested and while the person who performed the services is alive, the transfer which results by reason of the death of such transferee is a transfer not at arm's length.

(d) *Certain transfers upon death.*—If substantially nonvested property has been transferred in connection with the performance of services and the person who performed such services dies while the property is still substantially nonvested, any income realized on or after such death with respect to such property under this section is income in respect of a decedent to which the rules of section 691 apply. In such a case the income in respect of such property shall be taxable under section 691 (except to the extent not includible under section 101(b)) to the estate or beneficiary of the person who performed the services, in accordance with section 83 and the regulations thereunder. However, if an item of income is realized upon such death before July 21, 1978, because the property became substantially vested upon death, the person responsible for filing decedent's income tax return for decedent's last taxable year may elect to treat such item as includible in gross income for decedent's last taxable year by including such item in gross income on the return or amended return filed for decedent's last taxable year.

(e) *Forfeiture after substantial vesting.*—If a person is taxable under section 83(a) when the property transferred becomes substantially vested and thereafter the person's beneficial interest in such property is nevertheless forfeited pursuant to a lapse restriction, any loss incurred by such person (but not by a beneficiary of such person) upon such forfeiture shall be an ordinary loss to the extent the basis in such property has been increased as a result of the recognition of income by such person under section 83(a) with respect to such property.

(f) *Examples.*—The provisions of this section may be illustrated by the following examples:

Example (1). On November 1, 1978, X corporation sells to E, an employee, 100 shares of X corporation stock at $10 per share. At the time of such sale the fair market value of the X corporation stock is $100 per share. Under the terms of the sale each share of stock is subject to a substantial risk of forfeiture which will not lapse until November 1, 1988. Evidence of this restriction is stamped on the face of E's stock certificates, which are therefore nontransferable (within the meaning of §1.83-3(d)). Since in 1978 E's stock is substantially nonvested, E does not include any of such amount in his gross income as compensation in 1978. On November 1, 1988, the fair market value of the X corporation stock is $250 per share. Since the X corporation stock becomes substantially vested in 1988, E must include $24,000 (100 shares of X corporation stock × $250 fair market value per share less $10 price paid by E for each share) as compensation for 1988. Dividends paid by X to E on E's stock after it was transferred to E on November 1, 1973, are taxable to E as additional compensation during the period E's stock is substantially nonvested and are deductible as such by X.

Example (2). Assume the facts are the same as in example (1), except that on November 1, 1985, each share of stock of X corporation in E's hands could as a matter of law be transferred to a bona fide purchaser who would not be required to forfeit the stock if the risk of forfeiture materialized. In the event, however, that the risk materializes, E would be liable in damages to X. On November 1, 1985, the fair market value of the X corporation stock is $230 per share. Since E's stock is transferable within the meaning of §1.83-3(d) in 1985, the stock is substantially vested and E must include $22,000 (100 shares of X corporation stock × $230 fair market value per share less $10 price paid by E for each share) as compensation for 1985.

Example (3). Assume the facts are the same as in example (1) except that, in 1984 E sells his 100 shares of X corporation stock in an arm's length sale to I, an investment company, for $120 per share. At the time of this sale each share of X corporation's stock has a fair market value of $200. Under paragraph (b) of this section, E must include $11,000 (100 shares of X corporation stock × $120 amount realized per share less $10 price paid by E per share) as compensation for 1984 notwithstanding that the stock remains nontransferable and is still subject to a substantial risk of forfeiture at the time of such sale. Under §1.83-4(b)(2), I's basis in the X corporation stock is $120 per share. [Reg. §1.83-1.]

☐ [T.D. 7554, 7-21-78. *Amended by* T.D. 9092, 9-11-2003.]

[Reg. §1.83-2]

§1.83-2. Election to include in gross income in year of transfer.—(a) *In general.*—If property is transferred (within the meaning of §1.83-3(a)) in connection with the performance of services, the person performing such services may elect to include in gross income under section 83(b) the excess (if any) of the fair market value of the property at the time of transfer (determined without regard to any lapse restriction, as defined in §1.83-3(i)) over the amount (if any) paid for such property, as compensation for services. The fact that

the transferee has paid full value for the property transferred, realizing no bargain element in the transaction, does not preclude the use of the election as provided for in this section. If this election is made, the substantial vesting rules of section 83(a) and the regulations thereunder do not apply with respect to such property, and except as otherwise provided in section 83(d)(2) and the regulations thereunder (relating to the cancellation of a nonlapse restriction), any subsequent appreciation in the value of the property is not taxable as compensation to the person who performed the services. Thus, property with respect to which this election is made shall be includible in gross income as of the time of transfer, even though such property is substantially nonvested (as defined in §1.83-3(b)) at the time of transfer, and no compensation will be includible in gross income when such property becomes substantially vested (as defined in §1.83-3(b)). In computing the gain or loss from the subsequent sale or exchange of such property, its basis shall be the amount paid for the property increased by the amount included in gross income under section 83(b). If property for which a section 83(b) election is in effect is forfeited while substantially nonvested, such forfeiture shall be treated as a sale or exchange upon which there is realized a loss equal to the excess (if any) of—

(1) The amount paid (if any) for such property, over,

(2) The amount realized (if any) upon such forfeiture.

If such property is a capital asset in the hands of the taxpayer, such loss shall be a capital loss. A sale or other disposition of the property that is in substance a forfeiture, or is made in contemplation of a forfeiture, shall be treated as a forfeiture under the two immediately preceding sentences.

(b) *Time for making election.*—Except as provided in the following sentence, the election referred to in paragraph (a) of this section shall be filed not later than 30 days after the date the property was transferred (or, if later, January 29, 1970) and may be filed prior to the date of transfer. Any statement filed before February 15, 1970, which was amended not later than February 16, 1970, in order to make it conform to the requirements of paragraph (e) of this section, shall be deemed a proper election under section 83(b).

(c) *Manner of making election.*—The election referred to in paragraph (a) of this section is made by filing one copy of a written statement with the internal revenue office with which the person who performed the services files his return.

(d) *Additional copies.*—The person who performed the services shall also submit a copy of the statement referred to in paragraph (c) of this section to the person for whom the services are performed. In addition, if the person who performs the services and the transferee of such property are not the same person, the person who performs the services shall submit a copy of such statement to the transferee of the property.

(e) *Content of statement.*—The statement shall be signed by the person making the election and shall indicate that it is being made under section 83(b) of the Code, and shall contain the following information:

(1) The name, address and taxpayer identification number of the taxpayer;

(2) A description of each property with respect to which the election is being made;

(3) The date or dates on which the property is transferred and the taxable year (for example. "calendar year 1970" or "fiscal year ending May 31, 1970") for which such election was made;

(4) The nature of the restriction or restrictions to which the property is subject;

(5) The fair market value at the time of transfer (determined without regard to any lapse restriction, as defined in §1.83-3(i)) of each property with respect to which the election is being made;

(6) The amount (if any) paid for such property; and

(7) With respect to elections made after July 21, 1978, a statement to the effect that copies have been furnished to other persons as provided in paragraph (d) of this section.

(f) *Revocability of election.*—An election under section 83(b) may not be revoked except with the consent of the Commissioner. Consent will be granted only in the case where the transferee is under a mistake of fact as to the underlying transaction and must be requested within 60 days of the date on which the mistake of fact first became known to the person who made the election. In any event, a mistake as to the value, or decline in the value, of the property with respect to which an election under section 83(b) has been made or a failure to perform an act contemplated at the time of transfer of such property does not constitute a mistake of fact.

(g) *Effective/applicability date.*—Paragraph (c) of this section applies to property transferred on or after January 1, 2016. [Reg. §1.83-2.]

☐ [T.D. 7554, 7-21-78. *Amended by* T.D. 9779, 7-25-2016.]

[Reg. §1.83-3]

§1.83-3. Meaning and use of certain terms.—(a) *Transfer.*—(1) *In general.*—For purposes of section 83 and the regulations thereunder, a transfer of property occurs when a person acquires a beneficial ownership interest in such property (disregarding any lapse restriction, as defined in §1.83-3(i)). For special rules applying to the transfer of a life insurance contract (or an undivided interest therein) that is part of a split-dollar life insurance arrangement (as defined in §1.61-22(b)(1) or (2)), see §1.61-22(g).

(2) *Option.*—The grant of an option to purchase certain property does not constitute a transfer of such property. However, see §1.83-7 for the extent to which the grant of the option itself is subject to section 83. In addition, if the amount paid for the transfer of property is an indebtedness secured by the transferred property, on which there is no personal liability to pay all or a substantial part of such indebtedness, such transaction may be in substance the same as the grant of an option. The determination of the substance of the transaction shall be based upon all the facts and circumstances. The factors to be taken into account include the type of property involved, the extent to which the risk that the property will decline in value has been transferred, and the likelihood that the purchase price will, in fact, be paid. See also §1.83-4(c) for the treatment of forgiveness of indebtedness that has constituted an amount paid.

(3) *Requirement that property be returned.*—Similarly, no transfer may have occurred where property is transferred under conditions that require its return upon the happening of an event that is certain to occur, such as the termination of employment. In such a case, whether there is, in fact, a transfer depends upon all the facts and circumstances. Factors which indicate that no transfer has occurred are described in paragraph (a)(4), (5) and (6) of this section.

(4) *Similarity to option.*—An indication that no transfer has occurred is the extent to which the conditions relating to a transfer are similar to an option.

(5) *Relationship to fair market value.*—An indication that no transfer has occurred is the extent to which the consideration to be paid the transferee upon surrendering the property does not approach the fair market value of the property at the time of surrender. For purposes of paragraph (a)(5) and (6) of this section, fair market value includes fair market value determined under the rules of §1.83-5(a)(1), relating to the valuation of property subject to nonlapse restrictions. Therefore, the existence of a nonlapse restriction referred to in §1.83-5(a)(1) is not a factor indicating no transfer has occurred.

(6) *Risk of loss.*—An indication that no transfer has occurred is the extent to which the transferee does not incur the risk of a beneficial owner that the value of the property at the time of transfer will decline substantially. Therefore, for purposes of this (6), risk of decline in property value is not limited to the risk that any amount paid for the property may be lost.

(7) *Examples.*—The provisions of this paragraph may be illustrated by the following examples:

Example (1). On January 3, 1971, X corporation sells for $500 to S, a salesman of X, 10 shares of stock in X corporation with a fair market value of $1,000. The stock is nontransferable and subject to return to the corporation (for $500) if S's sales do not reach a certain level by December 31, 1971. Disregarding the restriction concerning S's sales (since the restriction is a lapse restriction), S's interest in the stock is that of a beneficial owner and therefore a transfer occurs on January 3, 1971.

Example (2). On November 17, 1972, W sells to E 100 shares of stock in W corporation with a fair market value of $10,000 in exchange for a $10,000 note without personal liability. The note requires E to make yearly payments of $2,000 commencing in 1973. E collects the dividends, votes the stock and pays the interest on the note. However, he makes no payments towards the face amount of the note. Because E has no personal liability on the note, and since E is making no payments towards the face amount of the note, the likelihood of E paying the full purchase price is in substantial doubt. As a result, E has not incurred the risks of a beneficial owner that the value of the stock will decline. Therefore, no transfer of the stock has occurred on November 17, 1972, but an option to purchase the stock has been granted to E.

Example (3). On January 3, 1971, X corporation purports to transfer to E, an employee, 100 shares of stock in X corporation. The X stock is subject to the sole restriction that E must sell such stock to X on termination of employment for any reason for an amount which is equal to the excess (if any) of the book value of the X stock at termination of employment over book value on January 3, 1971. The stock is not transferable by E and the restrictions on transfer are stamped on the certificate. Under these facts and circumstances, there is no transfer of the X stock within the meaning of section 83.

Example (4). Assume the same facts as in example (3) except that E paid $3,000 for the stock and that the restriction required E upon termination of employment to sell the stock to M for the total amount of dividends that have been declared on the stock since September 2, 1971, or $3,000 whichever is higher. Again, under the facts and circumstances, no transfer of the X stock has occurred.

Example (5). On July 4, 1971, X corporation purports to transfer to G an employee, 100 shares of X stock. The stock is subject to the sole restriction that upon termination of employment G must sell the stock to X for the greater of its fair market value at such time or $100, the amount G paid for the stock. On July 4, 1971 the X stock has a fair market value of $100. Therefore, G does not incur the risk of a beneficial owner that the value of the stock at the time of transfer ($100) will decline substantially. Under these facts and circumstances, no transfer has occurred.

(b) *Substantially vested and substantially nonvested property.*—For purposes of section 83 and the regulations thereunder, property is substantially nonvested when it is subject to a substantial risk of forfeiture, within the meaning of paragraph (c) of this section, and is nontransferable, within the meaning of paragraph (d) of this section. Property is substantially vested for such purposes when it is either transferable or not subject to a substantial risk of forfeiture.

(c) *Substantial risk of forfeiture.*—(1) *In general.*—For purposes of section 83 and these regulations, whether a risk of forfeiture is substantial or not depends upon the facts and circumstances. Except as set forth in paragraphs (j) and (k) of this section, a substantial risk of forfeiture exists only if rights in property that are transferred are conditioned, directly or indirectly, upon the future performance (or refraining from performance) of substantial services by any person, or upon the occurrence of a condition related to a purpose of the transfer if the possibility of forfeiture is substantial. Property is not transferred subject to a substantial risk of forfeiture if at the time of transfer the facts and circumstances demonstrate that the forfeiture condition is unlikely to be enforced. Further, property is not transferred subject to a substantial risk of forfeiture to the extent that the employer is required to pay the fair market value of a portion of such property to the employee upon the return of such property. The risk that the value of property will decline during a certain period of time does not constitute a substantial risk of forfeiture. A nonlapse restriction, standing by itself, will not result in a substantial risk of forfeiture. A restriction on the transfer of property, whether contractual or by operation of applicable law, will result in a substantial risk of forfeiture only if and to the extent that the restriction is described in paragraph (j) or (k) of this section. For this purpose, transfer restrictions that will not result in a substantial risk of forfeiture include, but are not limited to, restrictions that if violated, whether by transfer or attempted transfer of the property, would result in the forfeiture of some or all of the property, or liability by the employee for any damages, penalties, fees, or other amount.

(2) *Illustrations of substantial risks of forfeiture.*—The regularity of the performance of services and the time spent in performing such services tend to indicate whether services required by a condition are substantial. The fact that the person performing services has the right to decline to perform such services without forfeiture may tend to establish that services are insubstantial. Where stock is transferred to an underwriter prior to a public offering and the full enjoyment of such stock is expressly or impliedly conditioned upon the successful completion of the underwriting, the stock is subject to a substantial risk of forfeiture. Where an employee receives property from an employer subject to a requirement that it be returned if the total earnings of the employer do not increase, such property is subject to a substantial risk of forfeiture. On the other hand, requirements that the property be returned to the employer if the employee is discharged for cause or for committing a crime will not be considered to result in a substantial risk of forfeiture. An enforceable requirement that the property be returned to the employer if the employee accepts a job with a competing firm will not ordinarily be considered to result in a substantial risk of forfeiture unless the particular facts and circumstances indicate to the contrary. Factors which may be taken into account in determining whether a covenant not to compete constitutes a substantial risk of forfeiture are the age of the employee, the availability of alternative employment opportunities, the likelihood of the employee's obtaining such other employment, the degree of skill possessed by the employee, the employee's health, and the practice (if any) of the employer to enforce such covenants. Similarly, rights in property transferred to a retiring employee subject to the sole requirement that it be returned unless he renders consulting services upon the request of his former employer will not be considered subject to a substantial risk of forfeiture unless he is in fact expected to perform substantial services.

(3) *Enforcement of forfeiture condition.*—In determining whether the possibility of forfeiture is substantial in the case of rights in property transferred to an employee of a corporation who owns a significant amount of the total combined voting power or value of all classes of stock of the employer corporation or of its parent corporation, there will be taken into account (i) the employee's relationship to other stockholders and the extent of their control, potential control and possible loss of control of the corporation, (ii) the position of the employee in the corporation and the extent to which he is subordinate to other employees, (iii) the employee's relationship to the officers and directors of the corporation, (iv) the person or persons who must approve the employee's discharge, and (v) past actions of the employer in enforcing the provisions of the restrictions. For example, if an employee would be considered as having received rights in property subject to a substantial risk of forfeiture, but for the fact that the employee owns 20 percent of the single class of stock in the transferor corporation, and if the remaining 80 percent of the class of stock is owned by an unrelated individual (or members of such an individual's family) so that the possibility of the corporation enforcing a restriction on such rights is substantial, then such rights are subject to a substantial risk of forfeiture. On the other hand, if 4 percent of the voting power of all the stock of a corporation is owned by the president of such corporation and the remaining stock is so diversely held by the public that the president, in effect, controls the corporation, then the possibility of the corporation enforcing a restriction on rights in property transferred to the president is not substantial, and such rights are not subject to a substantial risk of forfeiture.

(4) *Examples.*—The rules contained in paragraph (c)(1) of this section may be illustrated by the following examples. In each example it is assumed that, if the conditions on transfer are not satisfied, the forfeiture provision will be enforced.

Example (1). On November 1, 1971, corporation X transfers in connection with the performance of services to E, an employee, 100 shares of corporation X stock for $90 per share. Under the terms of the transfer, E will be subject to a binding commitment to resell the stock to corporation X at $90 per share if he leaves the employment of corporation X for any reason prior to the expiration of a 2-year period from the date of such transfer. Since E must perform substantial services for corporation X and will not be paid more than $90 for the stock, regardless of its value, if he fails to perform such services

during such 2-year period, E's rights in the stock are subject to a substantial risk of forfeiture during such period.

Example (2). On November 10, 1971, corporation X transfers in connection with the performance of services to a trust for the benefit of employees, $100x. Under the terms of the trust any child of an employee who is an enrolled full-time student at an accredited educational institution as a candidate for a degree will receive an annual grant of cash for each academic year the student completes as a student in good standing, up to a maximum of four years. E, an employee, has a child who is enrolled as a full-time student at an accredited college as a candidate for a degree. Therefore, E has a beneficial interest in the assets of the trust equalling the value of four cash grants. Since E's child must complete one year of college in order to receive a cash grant, E's interest in the trust asssets are subject to a substantial risk of forfeiture to the extent E's child has not become entitled to any grants.

Example (3). On November 25, 1971, corporation X gives to E, an employee, in connection with his performance of services to corporation X, a bonus of 100 shares of corporation X stock. Under the terms of the bonus arrangement E is obligated to return the corporation X stock to corporation X if he terminates his employment for any reason. However, for each year occurring after November 25, 1971, during which E remains employed with corporation X, E ceases to be obligated to return 10 shares of the corporation X stock. Since in each year occurring after November 25, 1971, for which E remains employed he is not required to return 10 shares of corporation X's stock, E's rights in 10 shares each year for 10 years cease to be subject to a substantial risk of forfeiture for each year he remains so employed.

Example (4). (a) Assume the same facts as in example (3) except that for each year occurring after November 25, 1971, for which E remains employed with corporation X, X agrees to pay, in redemption of the bonus shares given to E if he terminates employment for any reason, 10 percent of the fair market value of each share of stock on the date of such termination of employment. Since corporation X will pay E 10 percent of the value of his bonus stock for each of the 10 years after November 25, 1971, in which he remains employed by X, and the risk of a decline in value is not a substantial risk of forfeiture, E's interest in 10 percent of such bonus stock becomes substantially vested in each of those years.

(b) The following chart illustrates the fair market value of the bonus stock and the fair market value of the portion of bonus stock that becomes substantially vested on November 25, for the following years:

| | Fair market value of: | |
| | (I) All stock | (II) Portion of stock that becomes vested |
Year		
1972	$200	$20
1973	300	30
1974	150	15
1975	150	15
1976	100	10

If E terminates his employment on July 1, 1977, when the fair market value of the bonus stock is $100, E must return the bonus stock to X, and X must pay, in redemption of the bonus stock, $50 (50 percent of the value of the bonus stock on the date of termination of employment). E has recognized income under section 83(a) and §1.83-1(a) with respect to 50 percent of the bonus stock, and E's basis in that portion of the stock equals the amount of income recognized, $90. Under §1.83-1(e), the $40 loss E incurred upon forfeiture ($90 basis less $50 redemption payment) is an ordinary loss.

Example (5). On January 7, 1971, corporation X, a computer service company, transfers to E, 100 shares of coporation X stock for $50. E is a highly compensated salesman who sold X's products in a three-state area since 1960. At the time of transfer each share of X stock has a fair market value of $100. The stock is transferred to E in connection with his termination of employment with X. Each share of X stock is subject to the sole condition that E can keep such share only if he does not engage in competition with X for a 5-year period in the three-state area where E had previously sold X's products. E, who is 45 years old, has no intention of retiring from the work force. In order to earn a salary comparable to his current compensation, while preventing the risk of forfeiture from arising, E will have to expend a substantial amount of time and effort in another industry or market to establish the necessary business contacts. Thus, under these facts and circumstances E's rights in the stock are subject to a substantial risk of forfeiture.

Example 6. On April 3, 2013, Y corporation grants to Q, an officer of Y, a nonstatutory option to purchase Y common stock. Although the option is immediately exercisable, it has no readily ascertainable fair market value when it is granted. Under the option, Q has the right to purchase 100 shares of Y common stock for $10 per share, which is the fair market value of a Y share on the date of grant of the

option. On August 1, 2013, Y sells its common stock in an initial public offering. Pursuant to an underwriting agreement entered into in connection with the initial public offering, Q agrees not to sell, otherwise dispose of, or hedge any Y common stock from August 1 through February 1 of 2014 ("the lock-up period"). Q exercises the option and Y shares are transferred to Q on November 15, 2013, during the lock-up period. The underwriting agreement does not impose a substantial risk of forfeiture on the Y shares acquired by Q because the provisions of the agreement do not condition Q's rights in the shares upon anyone's future performance (or refraining from performance) of substantial services or on the occurrence of a condition related to the purpose of the transfer of shares to Q. Accordingly, neither section 83(c)(3) nor the imposition of the lock-up period by the underwriting agreement precludes taxation under section 83 when the shares resulting from exercise of the option are transferred to Q.

Example 7. Assume the same facts as in *Example 6*, except that on August 1, 2013, Y also adopts an insider trading compliance program, under which, as applied to 2013, insiders (such as Q) may trade Y shares only during a limited number of days following each quarterly earnings release ("a trading window"). Under the program, if Q trades Y shares outside a trading window without Y's permission, Y has the right to terminate Q's employment. However, the exercise of the nonstatutory options outside a trading window for Y shares is not prohibited under the insider trading compliance program. Q fully exercises the option, and Y shares are transferred to Q, on November 15, 2013. The exercise of the option occurs outside a trading window, and, on the date of exercise, Q is in possession of material nonpublic information concerning Y that would subject him to liability under Rule 10b-5 under the Securities Exchange Act of 1934 if Q sold the Y shares while in possession of such information.

Neither the insider trading compliance program nor the potential liability under Rule 10b-5 impose a substantial risk of forfeiture on the Y shares acquired by Q because the provisions of the program and Rule 10b-5 do not condition Q's rights in the shares upon anyone's future performance (or refraining from performance) of substantial services or on the occurrence of a condition related to the purpose of the transfer of shares to Q. Accordingly, none of section 83(c)(3), the imposition of the trading windows by the insider trading compliance program, and the potential liability under Rule 10b-5 preclude taxation under section 83 when the shares resulting from exercise of the option are transferred to Q.

(d) *Transferability of property.*—For purposes of section 83 and the regulations thereunder, the rights of a person in property are transferable if such person can transfer any interest in the property to any person other than the transferor of the property, but only if the rights in such property of such transferee are not subject to a substantial risk of forfeiture. Accordingly, property is transferable if the person performing the services or receiving the property can sell, assign, or pledge (as collateral for a loan, or as security for the performance of an obligation, or for any other purpose) his interest in the property to any person other than the transferor of such property and if the transferee is not required to give up the property or its value in the event the substantial risk of forfeiture materializes. On the other hand, property is not considered to be transferable merely because the person performing the services or receiving the property may designate a beneficiary to receive the property in the event of his death.

(e) *Property.*—For purposes of section 83 and the regulations thereunder, the term "property" includes real and personal property other than either money or an unfunded and unsecured promise to pay money or property in the future. The term also includes a beneficial interest in assets (including money) which are transferred or set aside from the claims of creditors of the transferor, for example, in a trust or escrow account. See, however, § 1.83-8(a) with respect to employee trusts and annuity plans subject to section 402(b) and section 403(c). In the case of a transfer of a life insurance contract, retirement income contract, endowment contract, or other contract providing life insurance protection, or any undivided interest therein, the policy cash value and all other rights under such contract (including any supplemental agreements thereto and whether or not guaranteed), other than current life insurance protection, are treated as property for purposes of this section. However, in the case of the transfer of a life insurance contract, retirement income contract, endowment contract, or other contract providing life insurance protection, which was part of a split-dollar arrangement (as defined in § 1.61-22(b)) entered into (as defined in § 1.61-22(j)) on or before September 17, 2003, and which is not materially modified (as defined in § 1.61-22(j)(2)) after September 17, 2003, only the cash surrender value of the contract is considered to be property. Where rights in a contract providing life insurance protection are substantially nonvested, see § 1.83-1(a)(2) for rules relating to the taxation of the cost of life insurance protection.

(f) *Property transferred in connection with the performance of services.*—Property transferred to an employee or an independent contractor (or beneficiary thereof) in recognition of the performance of, or the refraining from performance of, services is considered transferred in connection with the performance of services within the meaning of section 83. The existence of other persons entitled to buy stock on the same terms and conditions as an employee, whether pursuant to a public or private offering may, however, indicate that in such circumstances a transfer to the employee is not in recognition of the performance of, or the refraining from performance of, services. The transfer of property is subject to section 83 whether such transfer is in respect of past, present, or future services.

(g) *Amount paid.*—For purposes of section 83 and the regulations thereunder, the term "amount paid" refers to the value of any money or property paid for the transfer of property to which section 83 applies, and does not refer to any amount paid for the right to use such property or to receive the income therefrom. Such value does not include any stated or unstated interest payments. For rules regarding the calculation of the amount of unstated interest payments, see § 1.483-1(c). When section 83 applies to the transfer of property pursuant to the exercise of an option, the term "amount paid" refers to any amount paid for the grant of the option plus any amount paid as the exercise price of the option. For rules regarding the forgiveness of indebtedness treated as an amount paid, see § 1.83-4(c).

(h) *Nonlapse restriction.*—For purposes of section 83 and the regulations thereunder, a restriction which by its terms will never lapse (also referred to as a "nonlapse restriction") is a permanent limitation on the transferability of property—

(i) Which will require the transferee of the property to sell, or offer to sell, such property at a price determined under a formula, and

(ii) Which will continue to apply to and be enforced against the transferee or any subsequent holder (other than the transferor).

A limitation subjecting the property to a permanent right of first refusal in a particular person at a price determined under a formula is a permanent nonlapse restriction. Limitations imposed by registration requirements of State or Federal security laws or similar laws imposed with respect to sales or other dispositions of stock or securities are not nonlapse restrictions. An obligation to resell or to offer to sell property transferred in connection with the performance of services to a specific person or persons at its fair market value at the time of such sale is not a nonlapse restriction. See § 1.83-5(c) for examples of nonlapse restrictions.

(i) *Lapse restriction.*—For purposes of section 83 and the regulations thereunder, the term "lapse restriction" means a restriction other than a nonlapse restriction as defined in paragraph (h) of this section, and includes (but is not limited to) a restriction that carries a substantial risk of forfeiture.

(j) *Sales which may give rise to suit under section 16(b) of the Securities Exchange Act of 1934.*—(1) *In general.*—For purposes of section 83 and the regulations thereunder if the sale of property at a profit within six months after the purchase of the property could subject a person to suit under section 16(b) of the Securities Exchange Act of 1934, the person's rights in the property are treated as subject to a substantial risk of forfeiture and as not transferable until the earlier of (i) the expiration of such six-month period, or (ii) the first day on which the sale of such property at a profit will not subject the person to suit under section 16(b) of the Securities Exchange Act of 1934. However, whether an option is "transferable by the optionee" for purposes of § 1.83-7(b)(2)(i) is determined without regard to section 83(c)(3) and this paragraph (j).

(2) *Examples.*—The provisions of this paragraph may be illustrated by the following examples:

Example (1). On January 1, 1983, X corporation sells to P, a beneficial owner of 12% of X corporation stock, in connection with P's performance of services, 100 shares of X corporation stock at $10 per share. At the time of the sale the fair market value of the X corporation stock is $100 per share. P, as a beneficial owner of more than 10% of X corporation stock, is liable to suit under section 16(b) of the Securities Exchange Act of 1934 for recovery of any profit from any sale and purchase or purchase and sale of X corporation stock within a six-month period, but no other restrictions apply to the stock. Because the section 16(b) restriction is applicable to P, P's rights in the 100 shares of stock purchased on January 1, 1983, are treated as subject to a substantial risk of forfeiture and as not transferable through June 29, 1983. P chooses not to make an election under section 83(b) and therefore does not include any amount with respect to the stock purchase in gross income as compensation on the date of purchase. On June 30, 1983, the fair market value of X corporation stock is $250 per share. P must include $24,000 (100 shares of X corporation stock × $240 ($250 fair market value per share less $10 price paid by P for each share)) in gross income as compensation on June 30, 1983. If, in this example, restrictions other than section 16(B) applied to the stock, such other restrictions (but not section 16(b)) would be taken into account in determining whether the stock is subject to a substantial risk of forfeiture and is nontransferable for periods after June 29, 1983.

Example (2). Assume the same facts as in example (1) except that P is not an insider on or after May 1, 1983, and the section 16(b) restriction does not apply beginning on that date. On May 1, 1983, P must include in gross income as compensation the difference between the fair market value of the stock on that date and the amount paid for the stock.

Example (3). Assume the same facts as in example (1) except that on June 1, 1983, X corporation sells to P an additional 100 shares of X corporation stock at $20 per share. At the time of the sale the fair market value of the X corporation stock is $150 per share. On June 30, 1983, P must include $24,000 in gross income as compensation with respect to the January 1, 1983 purchase. On November 30, 1983, the fair market value of X corporation stock is $200 per share. Accordingly, on that date P must include $18,000 (100 shares of X corporation stock × $180 ($200 fair market value per share less $20 price paid for P each share)) in gross income as compensation with respect to the June 1, 1983 purchase.

Example 4. (i) On June 3, 2013, Y corporation grants to Q, an officer of Y, a nonstatutory option to purchase Y common stock. Y stock is traded on an established securities market. Although the option is immediately exercisable, it has no readily ascertainable fair market value when it is granted. Under the option, Q has the right to purchase 100 shares of Y common stock for $10 per share, which is the fair market value of a Y share on the date of grant of the option.

The grant of the option is not one that satisfies the requirements for a transaction that is exempt from section 16(b) of the Securities Exchange Act of 1934. On December 15, 2013, Y stock is trading at more than $10 per share. On that date, Q fully exercises the option, paying the exercise price in cash, and receives 100 Y shares. Q's rights in the shares received as a result of the exercise are not conditioned upon the future performance of substantial services. Because no exemption from section 16(b) was available for the June 3, 2013 grant of the option, the section 16(b) liability period expires on December 1, 2013. Accordingly, the section 16(b) liability period expires *before* the date that Q exercises the option and the Y common stock is transferred to Q. Thus, the shares acquired by Q pursuant to the exercise of the option are not subject to a substantial risk of forfeiture under section 83(c)(3) as a result of section 16(b). As a result, section 83(c)(3) does not preclude taxation under section 83 when the shares acquired pursuant to the December 15, 2013 exercise of the option are transferred to Q.

(ii) Assume the same facts as in paragraph (i) of this *Example 4* except that Q exercises the nonstatutory option on October 30, 2013 when Y stock is trading at more than $10 per share. The shares acquired are subject to a substantial risk of forfeiture under section 83(c)(3) as a result of section 16(b) through December 1, 2013.

(iii) Assume the same facts as in paragraph (i) of this *Example 4* except that on November 5, 2013, Q also purchases 100 shares of Y common stock on the public market. The purchase of the shares is not a transaction exempt from section 16(b) of the Securities Exchange Act of 1934. Because no exemption from section 16(b) was available for the November 5, 2013 purchase of shares, the section 16(b) liability period with respect to such shares will last for a period of six months after the November 5, 2013 purchase of shares. Notwithstanding the nonexempt purchase of Y common stock on November 5, 2013, the shares acquired by Q pursuant to the December 15, 2013 exercise of the option are not subject to a substantial risk of forfeiture under section 83(c)(3) as a result of section 16(b). As a result, section 83(c)(3) does not preclude taxation under section 83 when the shares acquired pursuant to the December 15, 2013 exercise of the option are transferred to Q.

(k) For purposes of section 83 and the regulations thereunder, property is subject to substantial risk of forfeiture and is not transferable so long as the property is subject to a restriction on transfer to comply with the "Pooling-of-Interests Accounting" rules set forth in Accounting Series Release Numbered 130 ((10/5/72) 37 FR 20937; 17 CFR 211.130) and Accounting Series Release Numbered 135 ((1/18/73) 38 FR 1734; 17 CFR 211.135).

(l) *Effective/applicability date.*—This section applies to property transferred on or after January 1, 2013. For rules relating to property transferred before that date, see § 1.83-3 as contained in 26 CFR part 1 (as of April 1, 2012). [Reg. § 1.83-3.]

☐ [*T.D.* 7554, 7-21-78. *Amended by T.D.* 8042, 8-5-85; *T.D.* 9092, 9-11-2003; *T.D.* 9223, 8-26-2005 *and T.D.* 9659, 2-25-2014.]

[Reg. § 1.83-4]

§ 1.83-4. Special rules.—(a) *Holding period.*—Under section 83(f), the holding period of transferred property to which section 83(a) applies shall begin just after such property is substantially vested. However, if the person who has performed the services in connection with which property is transferred has made an election under section 83(b), the holding period of such property shall begin just after the date such property is transferred. If property to which section 83 and the regulations thereunder apply is transferred at arm's length, the holding period of such property in the hands of the transferee shall be determined in accordance with the rules provided in section 1223.

(b) *Basis.*—(1) Except as provided in paragraph (b) (2) of this section, if property to which section 83 and the regulations thereunder apply is acquired by any person (including a person who acquires such property in a subsequent transfer which is not at arm's length), while such property is still substantially nonvested, such person's basis for the property shall reflect any amount paid for such property and any amount includible in the gross income of the person who performed the services (including any amount so includible as a result of a *disposition* by the person who acquired such property). Such basis shall also reflect any adjustments to basis provided under sections 1015, 1016, and 1022.

(2) If property to which § 1.83-1 applies is transferred at arm's length, the basis of the property in the hands of the transferee shall be determined under section 1012 and the regulations thereunder.

(c) *Forgiveness of indebtedness treated as an amount paid.*—If an indebtedness that has been treated as an amount paid under § 1.83-1 (a) (1) (ii) is subsequently cancelled, forgiven or satisfied for an amount less than the amount of such indebtedness, the amount that is not, in fact, paid shall be includible in the gross income of the service

provider in the taxable year in which such cancellation, forgiveness or satisfaction occurs.

(d) *Effective/applicability date.*—The provisions in this section are applicable for taxable years beginning on or after July 21, 1978. The provisions of paragraph (b)(1) of this section relating to section 1022 are effective on and after January 19, 2017. [Reg. § 1.83-4.]

☐ [*T.D.* 7554, 7-21-78. *Amended by T.D.* 9811, 1-18-2017.]

[Reg. § 1.83-5]

§ 1.83-5. Restrictions that will never lapse.—(a) *Valuation.*—For purposes of section 83 and the regulations thereunder, in the case of property subject to a nonlapse restriction (as defined in § 1.83-3(h)), the price determined under the formula price will be considered to be the fair market value of the property unless established to the contrary by the Commissioner, and the burden of proof shall be on the Commissioner with respect to such value. If stock in a corporation is subject to a nonlapse restriction which requires the transferee to sell such stock only at a formula price based on book value, a reasonable multiple of earnings or a reasonable combination thereof, the price so determined will ordinarily be regarded as determinative of the fair market value of such property for purposes of section 83. However, in certain circumstances the formula price will not be considered to be the fair market value of property subject to such a formula price restriction, even though the formula price restriction is a substantial factor in determining such value. For example, where the formula price is the current book value of stock, the book value of the stock at some time in the future may be a more accurate measure of the value of the stock than the current book value of the stock for purposes of determining the fair market value of the stock at the time the stock becomes substantially vested.

(b) *Cancellation.*—(1) *In general.*—Under section 83(d) (2), if a nonlapse restriction imposed on property that is subject to section 83 is cancelled, then, unless the taxpayer establishes—

(i) That such cancellation was not compensatory, and

(ii) That the person who would be allowed a deduction, if any, if the cancellation were treated as compensatory, will treat the transaction as not compensatory, as provided in paragraph (c) (2) of this section, the excess of the fair market value of such property (computed without regard to such restriction) at the time of cancellation, over the sum of—

(iii) The fair market value of such property (computed by taking the restriction into account) immediately before the cancellation, and

(iv) The amount, if any, paid for the cancellation,

shall be treated as compensation for the taxable year in which such cancellation occurs. Whether there has been a noncompensatory cancellation of a nonlapse restriction under section 83 (d) (2) depends upon the particular facts and circumstances. Ordinarily the fact that the employee or independent contractor is required to perform additional services or that the salary or payment of such a person is adjusted to take the cancellation into account indicates that such cancellation has a compensatory purpose. On the other hand, the fact that the original purpose of a restriction no longer exists may indicate that the purpose of such cancellation is noncompensatory. Thus, for example, if a so-called "buy-sell" restriction was imposed on a corporation's stock to limit ownership of such stock and is being cancelled in connection with a public offering of the stock, such cancellation will generally be regarded as noncompensatory. However, the mere fact that the employer is willing to forego a deduction under section 83(h) is insufficient evidence to establish a noncompensatory cancellation of a nonlapse restriction. The refusal by a corporation or shareholder to repurchase stock of the corporation which is subject to a permanent right of first refusal will generally be treated as a cancellation of a nonlapse restriction. The preceding sentence shall not apply where there is no nonlapse restriction, for example, where the price to be paid for the stock subject to the right of first refusal is the fair market value of the stock. Section 83 (d) (2) and this (1) do not apply where immediately after the cancellation of a nonlapse restriction the property is still substantially nonvested and no section 83 (b) election has been made with respect to such property. In such a case the rules of section 83 (a) and § 1.83-1 shall apply to such property.

(2) *Evidence of noncompensatory cancellation.*—In addition to the information necessary to establish the factors described in paragraph (b) (1) of this section, the taxpayer shall request the employer to furnish the taxpayer with a written statement indicating that the employer will not treat the cancellation of the nonlapse restriction as a compensatory event, and that no deduction will be taken with respect to such cancellation. The taxpayer shall file such written statement with his income tax return for the taxable year in which or with which such cancellation occurs.

(c) *Examples.*—The provisions of this section may be illustrated by the following examples:

Example (1). On November 1, 1971, X corporation whose shares are closely held and not regularly traded, transfers to E, an employee, 100 shares of X corporation stock subject to the condition that, if he desires to dispose of such stock during the period of his employment, he must resell the stock to his employer at its then existing book value. In addition, E or E's estate is obligated to offer to sell the stock at his retirement or death to his employer at its then existing book value. Under these facts and circumstances, the restriction to which the shares of X corporation stock are subject is a nonlapse restriction. Consequently, the fair market value of the X stock is includible in E's gross income as compensation for taxable year 1971. However, in determining the fair market value of the X stock, the book value formula price will ordinarily be regarded as being determinative of such value.

Example (2). Assume the facts are the same as in example (1), except that the X stock is subject to the condition that if E desires to dispose of the stock during the period of his employment he must resell the stock to his employer at a multiple of earnings per share that is in this case a reasonable approximation of value at the time of transfer to E. In addition, E or E's estate is obligated to offer to sell the stock at his retirement or death to his employer at the same multiple of earnings. Under these facts and circumstances, the restriction to which the X corporation stock is subject is a nonlapse restriction. Consequently, the fair market value of the X stock is includible in E's gross income for taxable year 1971. However, in determining the fair market value of the X stock, the multiple-of-earnings formula price will ordinarily be regarded as determinative of such value.

Example (3). On January 4, 1971, X corporation transfers to E, an employee, 100 shares of stock in X corporation. Each such share of stock is subject to an agreement between X and E whereby E agrees that such shares are to be held solely for investment purposes and not for resale (a so-called investment letter restriction). E's rights in such stock are substantially vested upon transfer, causing the fair market value of each share of X corporation stock to be includible in E's gross income as compensation for taxable year 1971. Since such an investment letter restriction does not constitute a nonlapse restriction, in determining the fair market value of each share, the investment letter restriction is disregarded.

Example (4). On September 1, 1971, X corporation transfers to B, an independent contractor, 500 shares of common stock in X corporation in exchange for B's agreement to provide services in the construction of an office building on property owned by X corporation. X corporation has 100 shares of preferred stock outstanding and an additional 500 shares of common stock outstanding. The preferred stock has a liquidation value of $1,000x, which is equal to the value of all assets owned by X. Therefore, the book value of the common stock in X corporation is $0. Under the terms of the transfer, if B wishes to dispose of the stock, B must offer to sell the stock to X for 150 percent of the then existing book value of B's common stock. The stock is also subject to a substantial risk of forfeiture until B performs the agreed-upon services. B makes a timely election under section 83(b) to include the value of the stock in gross income in 1971. Under these facts and circumstances, the restriction to which the shares of X corporation common stock are subject is a nonlapse restriction. In determining the fair market value of the X common stock at the time of transfer, the book value formula price would ordinarily be regarded as determinative of such value. However, the fair market value of X common stock at the time of transfer, subject to the book value restriction, is greater than $0 since B was willing to agree to provide valuable personal services in exchange for the stock. In determining the fair market value of the stock, the expected book value after construction of the office building would be given great weight. The likelihood of completion of construction would be a factor in determining the expected book value after completion of construction. [Reg. § 1.83-5.]

☐ [*T.D.* 7554, 7-21-78.]

[Reg. § 1.83-6]

§ 1.83-6. Deduction by employer.—(a) *Allowance of deduction.*—(1) *General rule.*—In the case of a transfer of property in connection with the performance of services, or a compensatory cancellation of a nonlapse restriction described in section 83(d) and § 1.83-5, a deduction is allowable under section 162 or 212 to the person for whom the services were performed. The amount of the deduction is equal to the amount included as compensation in the gross income of the service provider under section 83(a), (b), or (d)(2), but only to the extent the amount meets the *requirements of section 162 or 212 and the regulations thereunder.* The deduction is allowed only for the taxable year of that person in which or with which ends the taxable year of the service provider in which the amount is included as compensation. For purposes of this paragraph, any amount excluded from gross income under section 79 or section 101(b) or subchapter N is considered to have been included in gross income.

(2) *Special rule.*—For purposes of paragraph (a)(1) of this section, the service provider is deemed to have included the amount as compensation in gross income if the person for whom the services were performed satisfies in a timely manner all requirements of section 6041 or section 6041A, and the regulations thereunder, with respect to that amount of compensation. For purposes of the preceding sentence, whether a person for whom services were performed satisfies all requirements of section 6041 or section 6041A, and the regulations thereunder, is determined without regard to § 1.6041-3(c) (exception for payments to corporations). In the case of a disqualifying disposition of stock described in section 421(b), an employer that otherwise satisfies all requirements of section 6041 and the regulations thereunder will be considered to have done so timely for purposes of this paragraph (a)(2) if Form W-2 or Form W-2c, as appropriate, is furnished to the employee or former employee, and is filed with the federal government, on or before the date on which the employer files the tax return claiming the deduction relating to the disqualifying disposition.

(3) *Exceptions.*—Where property is substantially vested upon transfer, the deduction shall be allowed to such person in accordance with his method of accounting (in conformity with sections 446 and 461). In the case of a transfer to an employee benefit plan described in § 1.162-10(a) or a transfer to an employees' trust or annuity plan described in section 404(a)(5) and the regulations thereunder, section 83(h) and this section do not apply.

(4) *Capital expenditure, etc.*—No deduction is allowed under section 83(h) to the extent that the transfer of property constitutes a capital expenditure, an item of deferred expense, or an amount properly includible in the value of inventory items. In the case of a capital expenditure, for example, the basis of the property to which such capital expenditure relates shall be increased at the same time and to the same extent as any amount includible in the employee's gross income in respect of such transfer. Thus, for example, no deduction is allowed to a corporation in respect of a transfer of its stock to a promoter upon its organization, notwithstanding that such promoter must include the value of such stock in his gross income in accordance with the rules under section 83.

(5) *Transfer of life insurance contract (or an undivided interest therein).*—(i) *General rule.*—In the case of a transfer of a life insurance contract (or an undivided interest therein) described in § 1.61-22(c)(3) in connection with the performance of services, a deduction is allowable under paragraph (a)(1) of this section to the person for whom the services were performed. The amount of the deduction, if allowable, is equal to the sum of the amount included as compensation in the gross income of the service provider under § 1.61-22(g)(1) and the amount determined under § 1.61-22(g)(1)(ii).

(ii) *Effective date.*—(A) *General rule.*—Paragraph (a)(5)(i) of this section applies to any split-dollar life insurance arrangement (as defined in § 1.61-22(b)(1) or (2)) entered into after September 17, 2003. For purposes of this paragraph (a)(5), an arrangement is entered into as determined under § 1.61-22(j)(1)(ii).

(B) *Modified arrangements treated as new arrangements.*—If an arrangement entered into on or before September 17, 2003 is materially modified (within the meaning of § 1.61-22(j)(2)) after September 17, 2003, the arrangement is treated as a new arrangement entered into on the date of the modification.

(6) *Effective date.*—Paragraphs (a)(1) and (2) of this section apply to deductions for taxable years beginning on or after January 1, 1995. However, taxpayers may also apply paragraphs (a)(1) and (2) of this section when claiming deductions for taxable years beginning before that date if the claims are not barred by the statute of limitations. Paragraphs (a)(3) and (4) of this section are effective as set forth in § 1.83-8(b).

(b) *Recognition of gain or loss.*—Except as provided in section 1032, at the time of a transfer of property in connection with the performance of services the transferor recognizes gain to the extent that the transferor receives an amount that exceeds the transferor's basis in the property. In addition, at the time a deduction is allowed under section 83(h) and paragraph (a) of this section, gain or loss is recognized to the extent of the difference between (i) the sum of the amount paid plus the amount allowed as a deduction under section 83(h), and (ii) the sum of the taxpayer's basis in the property plus any amount recognized pursuant to the previous sentence.

(c) *Forfeitures.*—If, under section 83(h) and paragraph (a) of this section, a deduction, an increase in basis, or a reduction of gross income was allowable (disregarding the reasonableness of the amount of compensation) in respect of a transfer of property and such property is subsequently forfeited, the amount of such deduction, increase in basis or reduction of gross income shall be includible in the gross income of the person to whom it was allowable for the taxable year of forfeiture. The basis of such property in the hands of the person to whom it is forfeited shall include any such amount includible in the gross income of such person, as well as any amount such person pays upon forfeiture.

(d) *Special rules for transfers by shareholders.*—(1) *Transfers.*—If a shareholder of a corporation transfers property to an employee of such corporation or to an independent contractor (or to a beneficiary thereof), in consideration of services performed for the corporation, the transaction shall be considered to be a contribution of such property to the capital of such corporation by the shareholder, and immediately thereafter a transfer of such property by the corporation to the employee or independent contractor under paragraphs (a) and (b) of this section. For purposes of this (1), such a transfer will be considered to be in consideration for services performed for the corporation if either the property transferred is substantially nonvested at the time of transfer or an amount is includible in the gross income of the employee or independent contractor at the time of transfer under §1.83-1(a)(1) or §1.83-2(a). In the case of such a transfer, any money or other property paid to the shareholder for such stock shall be considered to be paid to the corporation and transferred immediately thereafter by the corporation to the shareholder as a distribution to which section 302 applies. For special rules that may apply to a corporation's transfer of its own stock to any person in consideration of services performed for another corporation or partnership, see §1.1032-3. The preceding sentence applies to transfers of stock and amounts paid for such stock occurring on or after May 16, 2000.

(2) *Forfeiture.*—If, following a transaction described in paragraph (d)(1) of this section, the transferred property is forfeited to the shareholder, paragraph (c) of this section shall apply both with respect to the shareholder and with respect to the corporation. In addition, the corporation shall, in the taxable year of forfeiture be allowed a loss (or realize a gain) to offset any gain (or loss) realized under paragraph (b) of this section. For example, if a shareholder transfers property to an employee of the corporation as compensation, and as a result the shareholder's basis of $200x in such property is allocated to his stock in such corporation and such corporation recognizes a short-term capital gain of $800x, and is allowed a deduction of $1,000x on such transfer, upon a subsequent forfeiture of the property to the shareholder, the shareholder shall take $200x into gross income, and the corporation shall take $1,000x into gross income and be allowed a short-term capital loss of $800x.

(e) *Options.*—[Reserved.]

(f) *Reporting requirements.*—[Reserved.]
[Reg. §1.83-6.]

☐ [T.D. 7554, 7-21-78. *Amended by* T.D. 8599, 7-18-95; T.D. 8883, 5-11-2000 *and* T.D. 9092, 9-11-2003.]

[Reg. §1.83-7]

§1.83-7. Taxation of nonqualified stock options.—(a) *In general.*—If there is granted to an employee or independent contractor (or beneficiary thereof) in connection with the performance of services, an option to which section 421 (relating generally to certain qualified and other options) does not apply, section 83(a) shall apply to such grant if the option has a readily ascertainable fair market value (determined in accordance with paragraph (b) of this section) at the time the option is granted. The person who performed such services realizes compensation upon such grant at the time and in the amount determined under section 83(a). If section 83(a) does not apply to the grant of such an option because the option does not have a readily ascertainable fair market value at the time of grant, sections 83(a) and 83(b) shall apply at the time the option is exercised or otherwise disposed of, even though the fair market value of such option may have become readily ascertainable before such time. If the option is exercised, sections 83(a) and 83(b) apply to the transfer of property pursuant to such exercise, and the employee or independent contractor realizes compensation upon such transfer at the time and in the amount determined under section 83(a) or 83(b). If the option is sold or otherwise disposed of in an arm's length transaction, sections 83(a) and 83(b) apply to the transfer of money or other property received in the *same manner* as sections 83(a) and 83(b) would have applied to the transfer of property pursuant to an exercise of the option. The preceding sentence does not apply to a sale or other disposition of the option to a person related to the service provider that occurs on or after July 2, 2003. For this purpose, a person is related to the service provider if—

(1) The person and the service provider bear a relationship to each other that is specified in section 267(b) or 707(b)(1), subject to the modifications that the language "20 percent" is used instead of "50 percent" each place it appears in sections 267(b) and 707(b)(1), and section 267(c)(4) is applied as if the family of an individual includes the spouse of any member of the family; or

(2) The person and the service provider are engaged in trades or businesses under common control (within the meaning of section 52(a) and (b)); provided that a person is not related to the service provider if the person is the service recipient with respect to the option or the grantor of the option.

(b) *Readily ascertainable defined.*—(1) *Actively traded on an established market.*—Options have a value at the time they are granted, but that value is ordinarily not readily ascertainable unless the option is actively traded on an established market. If an option is actively traded on an established market, the fair market value of such option is readily ascertainable for purposes of this section by applying the rules of valuation set forth in §20.2031-2.

(2) *Not actively traded on an established market.*—When an option is not actively traded on an established market, it does not have a readily ascertainable fair market value unless its fair market value can otherwise be measured with reasonable accuracy. For purposes of this section, if an option is not actively traded on an established market, the option does not have a readily ascertainable fair market value when granted unless the taxpayer can show that all of the following conditions exist:

(i) The option is transferable by the optionee;

(ii) The option is exercisable immediately in full by the optionee;

(iii) The option or the property subject to the option is not subject to any restriction or condition (other than a lien or other condition to secure the payment of the purchase price) which has a significant effect upon the fair market value of the option; and

(iv) The fair market value of the option privilege is readily ascertainable in accordance with paragraph (b)(3) of this section.

(3) *Option privilege.*—The option privilege in the case of an option to buy is the opportunity to benefit during the option's exercise period from any increase in the value of property subject to the option during such period, without risking any capital. Similarly, the option privilege in the case of an option to sell is the opportunity to benefit during the exercise period from a decrease in the value of property subject to the option. For example, if at some time during the exercise period of an option to buy, the fair market value of the property subject to the option is greater than the option's exercise price, a profit may be realized by exercising the option and immediately selling the property so acquired for its higher fair market value. Irrespective of whether any such gain may be realized immediately at the time an option is granted, the fair market value of an option to buy includes the value of the right to benefit from any future increase in the value of the property subject to the option (relative to the option exercise price), without risking any capital. Therefore, the fair market value of an option is not merely the difference that may exist at a particular time between the option's exercise price and the value of the property subject to the option, but also includes the value of the option privilege for the remainder of the exercise period. Accordingly, for purposes of this section, in determining whether the fair market value of an option is readily ascertainable, it is necessary to consider whether the value of the entire option privilege can be measured with reasonable accuracy. In determining whether the value of the option privilege is readily ascertainable, and in determining the amount of such value when such value is readily ascertainable, it is necessary to consider—

(i) Whether the value of the property subject to the option can be ascertained;

(ii) The probability of any ascertainable value of such property increasing or decreasing; and

(iii) The length of the period during which the option can be exercised.

(c) *Reporting requirements.*—[Reserved]

(d) *Effective dates.*—This section applies on and after July 2, 2003. For transactions prior to that date, see §1.83-7 as published in 26 CFR Part 1 (revised as of April 1, 2003). [Reg. §1.83-7.]

☐ [T.D. 7554, 7-21-78. *Amended by* T.D. 9067, 7-1-2003 *and* T.D. 9148, 8-9-2004.]

[Reg. §1.83-8]

§1.83-8. Applicability of section and transitional rules.—(a) *Scope of section 83.*—Section 83 is not applicable to—

(1) A transaction concerning an option to which section 421 applies;

(2) A transfer to or from a trust described in section 401(a) for the benefit of employees or their beneficiaries, or a transfer under an annuity plan that meets the requirements of section 404(a)(2) for the benefit of employees or their beneficiaries;

(3) The transfer of an option without a readily ascertainable fair market value (as defined in §1.83-7(b)(1)); or

(4) The transfer of property pursuant to the exercise of an option with a readily ascertainable fair market value at the date of grant. Section 83 applies to a transfer to or from a trust or under an annuity plan for the benefit of employees, independent contractors, or their

beneficiaries (except as provided in paragraph (a)(2) of this section), but to the extent a transfer is subject to section 402(b) or 403(c), section 83 applies to such a transfer only as provided for in section 402(b) or 403(c).

(b) *Transitional rules.*—(1) *In general.*—Except as otherwise provided in this paragraph, section 83 and the regulations thereunder shall apply to property transferred after June 30, 1969.

(2) *Binding written contracts.*—Section 83 and the regulations thereunder shall not apply to property transferred pursuant to a binding written contract entered into before April 22, 1969. For purposes of this paragraph, a binding written contract means only a written contract under which the employee or independent contractor has an enforceable right to compel the transfer of property or to obtain damages upon the breach of such contract. A contract which provides that a person's right to such property is contingent upon the happening of an event (including the passage of time) may satisfy the requirements of this paragraph. However, if the event itself, or the determination of whether the event has occurred, rests with the board of directors or any other individual or group acting on behalf of the employer (other than an arbitrator), the contract will not be treated as giving the person an enforceable right for purposes of this paragraph. The fact that the board of directors has the power (either expressly or impliedly) to terminate employment of an officer pursuant to a contract that contemplates the completion of services over a fixed or ascertainable period does not negate the existence of a binding written contract. Nor will the binding nature of the contract be negated by a provision in such contract which allows the employee or independent contractor to terminate the contract for any year and receive cash instead of property if such election would cause a substantial penalty, such as a forfeiture of part or all of the property received in connection with the performance of services in an earlier year.

(3) *Options granted before April 22, 1969.*—Section 83 shall not apply to property received upon the exercise of an option granted before April 22, 1969.

(4) *Certain written plans.*—Section 83 shall not apply to property transferred (whether or not by the exercise of an option) before May 1, 1970, pursuant to a written plan adopted and approved before July 1, 1969. A plan is to be considered as having been adopted and approved before July 1, 1969, only if prior to such date the transferor of the property undertook an ascertainable course of conduct which under applicable State law does not require further approval by the board of directors or the stockholders of any corporation. For example, if a corporation transfers property to an employee in connection with the performance of services pursuant to a plan adopted and approved before July 1, 1969, by the board of directors of such corporation, it is not necessary that the stockholders have adopted or approved such plan if State law does not require such approval. However, such approval is necessary if required by the articles of incorporation or the by-laws or if, by its terms, such plan will not become effective without such approval.

(5) *Certain options granted pursuant to a binding written contract.*—Section 83 shall not apply to property transferred before January 1, 1973, upon the exercise of an option granted pursuant to a binding written contract (as defined in paragraph (b)(2) of this section) entered into before April 22, 1969, between a corporation and the transferor of such property requiring the transferor to grant options to employees of such corporation (or a subsidiary of such corporation) to purchase a determinable number of shares of stock of such corporation, but only if the transferee was an employee of such corporation (or a subsidiary of such corporation) on or before April 22, 1969.

(6) *Certain tax free exchanges.*—Section 83 shall not apply to property transferred in exchange for (or pursuant to the exercise of a conversion privilege contained in) property transferred before July 1, 1969, or in exchange for property to which section 83 does not apply (by reason of paragraphs (1), (2), (3), or (4) of section 83(i)), if section 354, 355, 356, or 1036 (or so much of section 1031 as relates to section 1036) applies, or if gain or loss is not otherwise required to be recognized upon the exercise of such conversion privilege, and if the property received in such exchange is subject to restrictions and conditions substantially similar to those to which the property given in such exchange was subject. [Reg. § 1.83-8.]

☐ [*T.D. 7554, 7-21-78.*]

[Reg. § 1.84-1]

§ 1.84-1. Transfer of appreciated property to political organizations.—(a) *Transfer defined.*—A transfer after May 7, 1974, of property

to a political organization (as defined in section 527(e)(1), and including a newsletter fund to the extent provided under section 527(g)) is treated as a sale of the property to the political organization if the fair market value of the property exceeds its adjusted basis. The transferor is treated as having realized an amount equal to the fair market value of the property on the date of the transfer. For purposes of this section, a transfer is any assignment, conveyance, or delivery of property other than a bona fide sale for an adequate and full consideration in money or money's worth, whether the transfer is in trust or otherwise, whether the transfer is direct or indirect and whether the property is real or personal, tangible or intangible. Thus, for example, a sale at less than fair market value (other than an ordinary trade discount), or a receipt of property by a political organization under an agency agreement entitling the organization to sell the property and retain all or a portion of the proceeds of the sale, is a transfer within the meaning of this section. The term "transfer" also includes an illegal contribution of property.

(b) *Amount realized.*—A transferor to whom this section applies realizes an amount equal to the fair market value of the property on the date of the transfer. For purposes of this section, the definition of fair market value set forth in § 1.170A-1(c)(2) and (3) is incorporated by reference.

(c) *Amount recognized.*—A transferor to whom this section applies is treated as having sold the property to the political organization on the date of the transfer. Therefore, the rules of chapter 1 of subtitle A (relating to income tax) apply to the gain realized under this section as if this gain were an amount realized upon the sale of the property. These rules include those of section 55 and section 56 (relating to minimum tax for tax preference), section 306 (relating to disposition of certain stock), section 1201 (relating to the alternative tax on certain capital gains), section 1245 (relating to gain from dispositions of certain depreciable property), and section 1250 (relating to gain from dispositions of certain depreciable realty).

(d) *Holding period.*—The holding period of property transferred to a political organization to which this section applies begins on the day after the date of acquisition of the property by the political organization. [Reg. § 1.84-1.]

☐ [*T.D. 7671, 2-5-80.*]

[Reg. § 1.85-1]

§ 1.85-1. Unemployment compensation.—(a) *Introduction.*—Section 85 prescribes rules relating to the inclusion in gross income of unemployment compensation (as defined in paragraph (b)(1) of this section) paid in taxable years beginning after December 31, 1978 pursuant to governmental programs. In general, these rules provide that unemployment compensation paid pursuant to governmental programs is includible in the gross income of a taxpayer if the taxpayer's modified adjusted gross income (as defined in paragraph (b)(2) of this section) exceeds a statutory base amount (as defined in paragraph (b)(3) of this section). If there is such an excess, however, the amount included in gross income is limited under paragraph (c)(1) of this section to the lesser of one-half of such excess or the amount of the unemployment compensation. If such taxpayer's modified adjusted gross income does not exceed the applicable statutory base amount, none of the unemployment compensation is included in the taxpayer's gross income.

(b) *Definitions.*—(1) *Unemployment compensation.*—(i) *General rule.*—Except as provided in paragraph (b)(1)(iii) of this section, the term "unemployment compensation" means any amount received under a law of the United States, or of a State, which is in the nature of unemployment compensation. Thus, section 85 applies only to unemployment compensation paid pursuant to governmental programs and does not apply to amounts paid pursuant to private nongovernmental unemployment compensation plans (which are includible in income without regard to section 85). Generally, unemployment compensation programs are those designed to protect taxpayers against the loss of income caused by involuntary layoff. Ordinarily, unemployment compensation is paid in cash and on a periodic basis. The amount of the payments is usually computed in accordance with a formula based on the taxpayer's length of prior employment and wages. Such payments, however, may be made in a lump sum or other than in cash or on some other basis.

(ii) *Disability and worker's compensation payments.*—Amounts in the nature of unemployment compensation also include cash disability payments made pursuant to a governmental program as a substitute for cash unemployment payments to an unemployed taxpayer who is ineligible for such payments solely because of the disability. Usually these disability payments are paid in the same weekly amount and for the same period as the unemployed compensation benefits to which the unemployed taxpayer otherwise would have been entitled. Amounts received under workmen's compensation acts as compensation for personal injuries or sickness are not amounts in the nature of unemployment compensation. See section 104(a)(1) relating to the exclusion from gross income of such amounts.

(iii) *Employee contributions to a governmental plan.*—If a governmental unemployment compensation program is funded in part by an employee's contribution which is not deductible by the employee, an amount paid to such employee under the program is not to be considered unemployment compensation until an amount equal to the total nondeductible contributions paid by the employee to such program has been paid to such employee.

(iv) *Examples of governmental unemployment compensation programs.*—Governmental unemployment compensation programs include (but are not limited to) programs established under:

(A) A State law approved by the Secretary of Labor pursuant to section 3304 of the Internal Revenue Code of 1954.

(B) Chapter 85 of Title 5, United States Code, relating to unemployment compensation for Federal employees generally and for ex-servicemen.

(C) Trade Act of 1974, sections 231 and 232 (19 U.S.C. 2291 and 2292).

(D) Disaster Relief Act of 1974, section 407 (42 U.S.C. 5177).

(E) The Airline Deregulation Act of 1978 (49 U.S.C. 1552 (b)).

(F) The Railroad Unemployment Insurance Act, section 2 (45 U.S.C. 352).

(2) *Modified adjusted gross income.*—The term "modified adjusted gross income" means the sum of the following amounts:

(i) Adjusted gross income (as defined in section 62);

(ii) All disability payments of the type that are eligible for exclusion from gross income under section 105(d); and

(iii) All amounts of unemployment compensation as (defined in paragraph (b)(1) of this section).

(3) *Base amount.*—The term "base amount" means—

(i) $25,000 in the case of a joint return under section 6013.

(ii) Zero in the case of a taxpayer who—

(A) Is married (within the meaning of section 143) at the close of the taxable year,

(B) Does not file a joint return for such taxable year, and

(C) Does not live apart (as defined in paragraph (b)(4) of this section) from his or her spouse at all times during the taxable year.

(iii) $20,000 in the case of all other taxpayers.

(4) *Living apart.*—A taxpayer does not "live apart" from his or her spouse at all times during a taxable year if for any period during the taxable year the taxpayer is a member of the same household as such taxpayer's spouse. A taxpayer is a member of a household for any period, including temporary absences due to special circumstances, during which the household is the taxpayer's place of abode. A temporary absence due to special circumstances includes a nonpermanent absence caused by illness, education, business, vacation, or military service.

(c) *Limitations.*—(1) *General rule.*—If for a taxable year, a taxpayer's modified adjusted gross income does not exceed the applicable statutory base amount, no amount of unemployment compensation is included in gross income for the taxable year. If there is such an excess, the taxpayer includes in gross income for the taxable year the lesser of the following:

(i) One-half of the excess of the taxpayer's modified adjusted gross income over such taxpayer's base amount, or

(ii) The amount of unemployment compensation.

(2) *Exception for fraudulently received unemployment compensation.*—If a taxpayer fraudulently receives unemployment compensation under any governmental unemployment compensation program, then the entire amount of such fraudulently received unemployment compensation must be included in the taxpayer's gross income for the taxable year in which the benefits were received. Thus, the limitation in section 85 and in paragraph (c)(1) of this section, does not apply to such amounts.

(3) *Examples.*—The application of this paragraph may be illustrated by the following examples:

Example (1). H and W are married taxpayers who for calendar year 1979 file a joint income tax return. During 1979 H receives $4,500

of disability income that is eligible for an exclusion under section 105(d). W works for part of 1979 and receives $20,000 as compensation and also receives $5,000 of unemployment compensation in 1979. Assume that H and W's adjusted gross income is $20,000. The modified adjusted gross income of H & W is $29,500 ($4,500 + $20,000 + $5,000). Since their modified adjusted gross income ($29,500) is greater than their base amount ($25,000), some of the unemployment compensation received by W must be included in their gross income on their 1979 joint income tax return. Under paragraph (c)(1) of this section, of the $5,000 which is unemployment compensation, the lesser of $2,250 (($29,500 − 25,000) ÷ 2) or $5,000 must be included in their gross income. Thus, $2,250 of the $5,000 received by F in 1979 is included in the gross income of H and W on their joint income tax return for 1979.

Example (2). Assume the same facts in example (1) except H receives $5,000 of disability income that is eligible for an exclusion under section 105(d) and W receives $28,000 as compensation, and $4,000 which is unemployment compensation. Assume that H and W's adjusted gross income is $23,000. The modified adjusted gross income of H and W is $37,000 ($4,000 + $28,000 + $5,000). Since their modified adjusted gross income ($37,000) is greater than their base amount ($25,000), all of the unemployment compensation received by W must be included in their gross income on their 1979 joint income tax return. Under paragraph (c)(1) of this section, of the $4,000 which is unemployment compensation, the lesser of $6,000 (($37,000 − $25,000) ÷ 2) or $4,000 must be included in their gross income. Thus, all of the $4,000 unemployment compensation received by W is included in the gross income of H and W on their joint income tax return for 1979.

(d) *Cross reference.*—See section 6050B, relating to the requirement that every person who makes payments of unemployment compensation aggregating $10 or more to any individual during any calendar year file an information return with the Internal Revenue Service. [Reg. §1.85-1.]

☐ [T.D. 7705, 7-8-80.]

[Reg. §1.88-1]

§1.88-1. Nuclear decommissioning costs.—(a) *In general.*—Section 88 provides that the amount of nuclear decommissioning costs directly or indirectly charged to the customers of a taxpayer that is engaged in the furnishing or sale of electric energy generated by a nuclear power plant must be included in the gross income of such taxpayer in the same manner as amounts charged for electric energy. For this purpose, decommissioning costs directly or indirectly charged to the customers of a taxpayer include all decommissioning costs that consumers are liable to pay by reason of electric energy furnished by the taxpayer during the taxable year, whether payable to the taxpayer, a trust, State government, or other entity, and even though the taxpayer may not control the investment or current expenditure of the amount and the amount may not be paid to the taxpayer at the time decommissioning costs are incurred. However, decommissioning costs payable to a taxpayer holding a qualified leasehold interest (as described in paragraph (b)(2)(ii) of §1.468A-1) are included in the gross income of such taxpayer, and not in the gross income of the lessor.

(b) *Examples.*—The following examples illustrate the application of the principles of paragraph (a) of this section:

Example (1). X corporation, an accrual method taxpayer engaged in the sale of electric energy generated by a nuclear power plant owned by X, is authorized by the public utility commission of State A to collect nuclear decommissioning costs from ratepayers residing in State A. With respect to the sale of electric energy, X includes in income amounts that have been billed to customers as well as estimated unbilled amounts that relate to energy provided by X after the previous billing but before the end of the taxable year ("accrued unbilled amounts"). The decommissioning costs are included in the monthly bills provided by X to its ratepayers and the entire amount billed is remitted directly to X. Under paragraph (a) of this section, the decommissioning costs must be included in the gross income of X in the same manner as amounts charged for electric energy (i.e., by including in income decommissioning costs that relate to amounts billed as well as decommissioning costs that relate to accrued unbilled amounts). The same rule would apply if the decommissioning costs charged to ratepayers were separately billed and the amounts billed were remitted to State A to be held in trust for the purpose of decommissioning the nuclear power plant owned by X. In that case, X must include in gross income decommissioning costs that relate to amounts billed as well as decommissioning costs that relate to accrued unbilled amounts.

Example (2). Assume the same facts as in Example (1), except that X and M, a municipality located in State A, have entered into a life-of-unit contract pursuant to which (i) M is entitled to 20 percent of the electric energy generated by the nuclear power plant owned by X, and (ii) M is obligated to pay 20 percent of the plant operating costs, including decommissioning costs, incurred by X. Under paragraph (a) of this section, the decommissioning costs that relate to electric energy consumed or distributed by M during any taxable year must be included in the gross income of X for such taxable year. The result contained in this example would be the same if M was a State or an agency or instrumentality of a State or a political subdivision thereof.

(c) *Cross reference.*—For special rules relating to the deduction for amounts paid to a nuclear decommissioning fund, see § 1.468A-1 through § 1.468A-8.

(d) *Effective date.*—(1) Section 88 and this section apply to nuclear decommissioning costs directly or indirectly charged to the customers of a taxpayer on or after July 18, 1984, and with respect to taxable years ending on or after such date.

(2) If the amount of nuclear decommissioning costs directly or indirectly charged to the customers of a taxpayer before July 18, 1984, was includible in gross income in a different manner than amounts charged for electric energy, such amounts must be included in gross income for the taxable year in which includible in gross income under the method of accounting of the taxpayer that was in effect when such amount was charged to customers. [Reg. § 1.88-1.]

☐ [*T.D.* 8184, 2-29-88.]

[The next page is 25,001.]

Items Specifically Excluded from Gross Income

See p. 20,601 for regulations not amended to reflect law changes

[Reg. §1.101-1]

§1.101-1. Exclusion from gross income of proceeds of life insurance contracts payable by reason of death.—*(a)(1) In general.*—Section 101(a)(1) states the general rule that the proceeds of life insurance policies, if paid by reason of the death of the insured, are excluded from the gross income of the recipient. Death benefit payments having the characteristics of life insurance proceeds payable by reason of death under contracts, such as workmen's compensation insurance contracts, endowment contracts, or accident and health insurance contracts, issued on or before December 31, 1984, are covered by this provision. The exclusion from gross income allowed by section 101(a) applies whether payment is made to the estate of the insured or to any beneficiary (individual, corporation, or partnership) and whether it is made directly or in trust. The extent to which this exclusion applies in cases where life insurance policies have been transferred for a valuable consideration is stated in section 101(a)(2) and in paragraph (b) of this section. In cases where the proceeds of a life insurance policy, payable by reason of the death of the insured, are paid other than in a single sum at the time of such death, the amounts to be excluded from gross income may be affected by the provisions of section 101(c) (relating to amounts held under agreements to pay interest) or section 101(d) (relating to amounts payable at a date later than death). See §§1.101-3 and 1.101-4. However, neither section 101(c) nor section 101(d) applies to a single sum payment which does not exceed the amount payable at the time of death even though such amount is actually paid at a date later than death. If the life insurance contract is an employer-owned life insurance contract within the definition of section 101(j)(3), the amount to be excluded from gross income may be affected by the provisions of section 101(j).

(2) Cross references.—For rules governing the taxability of insurance proceeds constituting benefits payable on the death of an employee—

(i) Under pension, profit-sharing, or stock bonus plans described in section 401(a) and exempt from tax under section 501(a), or under annuity plans described in section 403(a), see section 72(m)(3) and paragraph (c) of §1.72-16;

(ii) Under annuity contracts to which §1.403(b)-3 applies, see §1.403(b)-7; or

(iii) Under eligible State deferred compensation plans described in section 457(b), see paragraph (c) of §1.457-1.

For the definition of a life insurance company, see section 801.

(b) *Transfers of life insurance policies.*—*(1) Transfer of an interest in a life insurance contract for valuable consideration.*—*(i) In general.*—In the case of a transfer of an interest in a life insurance contract for valuable consideration, including a reportable policy sale for valuable consideration, the amount of the proceeds attributable to the interest that is excludable from gross income under section 101(a)(1) is limited under section 101(a)(2) to the sum of the actual value of the consideration for the transfer paid by the transferee and the premiums and other amounts subsequently paid by the transferee with respect to the interest. For exceptions to this general rule for certain transfers for valuable consideration that are not reportable policy sales, see paragraph (b)(1)(ii) of this section. The application of section 101(d), (f) or (j), which is not addressed in paragraph (b) of this section, may further limit the amount of the proceeds excludable from gross income.

(ii) Exceptions.—(A) *Exception for carryover basis transfers.*—The limitation described in paragraph (b)(1)(i) of this section does not apply to the transfer of an interest in a life insurance contract for valuable consideration if each of the following requirements are satisfied. First, the transfer is not a reportable policy sale. Second, the basis of the interest, for the purpose of determining gain or loss with respect to the transferee, is determinable in whole or in part by reference to the basis of the interest in the hands of the transferor (see section 101(a)(2)(A)). Third, paragraph (b)(1)(ii)(B) of this section does not apply. In the case of a transfer described in this paragraph (b)(1)(ii)(A), *the amount of the proceeds* attributable to the interest that is excludable from gross income under section 101(a)(1) is limited to the sum of the amount that would have been excludable by the transferor if the transfer had not occurred and the premiums and other amounts subsequently paid by the transferee with respect to the interest. The preceding sentence applies without regard to whether the interest previously has been transferred and the nature of any prior transfer of the interest.

(B) *Exception for transfers to certain persons.*—(1) *In general.*—The limitation described in paragraph (b)(1)(i) of this section does not apply to the transfer of an interest in a life insurance contract for valuable consideration if both of the following requirements are satisfied. First, the transfer is not a reportable policy sale and the interest was not previously transferred for valuable consideration in a reportable policy sale. Second, the interest is transferred to the insured, a partner of the insured, a partnership in which the insured is a partner, or a corporation in which the insured is a shareholder or officer (see section 101(a)(2)(B)).

(2) Transfers to certain persons subsequent to a reportable policy sale.—Except as provided in paragraph (b)(1)(ii)(B)(3) of this section, if a transfer of an interest in a life insurance contract would be described in paragraph (b)(1)(ii)(B)(1) of this section, but for the fact that the interest previously was transferred for valuable consideration in a reportable policy sale (whether in the immediately preceding transfer or an earlier transfer), then the amount of the proceeds attributable to the interest that is excludable from gross income under section 101(a)(1) is limited to the sum of—

(i) The higher of the amount that would have been excludable by the transferor if the transfer had not occurred or the actual value of the consideration for the transfer paid by the transferee; and

(ii) The premiums and other amounts subsequently paid by the transferee with respect to the interest.

(3) Transfers to the insured subsequent to a reportable policy sale.—*(i)* Except as provided in paragraph (b)(1)(ii)(B)(3)(ii) of this section, to the extent that an interest (or portion of an interest) in a life insurance contract that was transferred for valuable consideration in a reportable policy sale subsequently is transferred to the insured for valuable consideration, the limitations described in paragraph (b)(1)(i) of this section and paragraph (b)(1)(ii)(B)(2) of this section do not apply. To the extent that fair market value is not paid by the insured for the transferred interest, the transfer of the portion of the interest with a value in excess of the consideration paid will be treated as a gift under the bargain sale rule in paragraph (b)(2)(iii) of this section.

(ii) This paragraph (b)(1)(ii)(B)(3)(ii) applies with respect to an interest described in paragraph (b)(1)(ii)(B)(3)(i) of this section (or portion of such an interest) that subsequently is transferred by the insured to any other person. If all subsequent transfers of the interest (or portion of the interest) are gratuitous transfers that are not reportable policy sales, the amount of the proceeds excluded from gross income is determined under paragraph (b)(2)(i) of this section, taking into account the application of paragraph (b)(1)(ii)(B)(3)(i) of this section to the insured's acquisition of the interest. If any subsequent transfer of the interest (or portion of the interest) is for valuable consideration or is a reportable policy sale, the amount of the policy proceeds excludable from gross income is determined in accordance with paragraph (b) of this section; if the amount that would have been excludable from gross income by the insured following the transaction described in paragraph (b)(1)(ii)(B)(3)(i) of this section if no subsequent transfer had occurred is relevant, that amount is determined under paragraph (b)(1)(ii)(B)(2) of this section. Paragraph (g)(8) (*Example 8*) of this section and paragraph (g)(9) (*Example 9*) of this section illustrate the application of this paragraph (b)(1)(ii)(B)(3)(ii).

(2) Other transfers.—*(i) Gratuitous transfer of an interest in a life insurance contract.*—To the extent that a transfer of an interest in a life insurance contract is gratuitous, including a reportable policy sale that is not for valuable consideration, the amount of the proceeds attributable to the interest that is excludable from gross income under section 101(a)(1) is limited to the sum of the amount of the proceeds attributable to the gratuitously transferred interest that would have been excludable by the transferor if the transfer had not occurred and the premiums and other amounts subsequently paid by the transferee with respect to the interest. However, if an interest in a life insurance contract is transferred gratuitously to the insured, and that interest has not previously been transferred for value in a reportable policy sale, the entire amount of the proceeds attributable to the interest transferred to the insured is excludable from gross income.

(ii) Partial transfers.—When only part of an interest in a life insurance contract is transferred, the transferor's exclusion is ratably apportioned between or among the several parts. If multiple parts of an interest are transferred, the transfer of each part is treated as a separate transaction, with each transaction subject to the rule under paragraph (b) of this section that is applicable to the type of transfer involved.

(iii) Bargain sales.—When the transfer of an interest in a life insurance contract is in part a transfer for valuable consideration and

in part a gratuitous transfer, the transfer of each part is treated as a separate transaction for purposes of determining the amount of the proceeds attributable to the interest that is excludable from gross income under section 101(a)(1). Each separate transaction is subject to the rule under paragraph (b) of this section that is applicable to the type of transfer involved.

(3) *Determination of amounts paid by the transferee.*—For purposes of paragraphs (b)(1) and (2) of this section, in determining the amounts, if any, of consideration paid by the transferee for the transfer of an interest in a life insurance contract and premiums and other amounts subsequently paid by the transferee with respect to that interest, the amounts paid by the transferee are reduced, but not below zero, by amounts received by the transferee under the life insurance contract that are not received as an annuity, to the extent excludable from gross income under section 72(e).

(c) *Reportable policy sale.*—(1) *In general.*—Except as provided in paragraph (c)(2) of this section, a reportable policy sale for purposes of this section and section 6050Y is any direct or indirect acquisition of an interest in a life insurance contract if the acquirer has, at the time of the acquisition, no substantial family, business, or financial relationship with the insured apart from the acquirer's interest in the life insurance contract.

(2) *Exceptions.*—None of the following transactions is a reportable policy sale:

(i) A transfer of an interest in a life insurance contract between entities with the same beneficial owners, if the ownership interest of each beneficial owner in the transferor entity does not vary by more than a 20 percent ownership interest from that beneficial owner's ownership interest in the transferee entity. In a series of transfers, the prior sentence is applied by comparing the beneficial owners' ownership interest in the first transferor entity and the last transferee entity. For purposes of this paragraph (c)(2)(i), each beneficial owner of a trust is deemed to have an ownership interest determined by the broadest possible exercise of a trustee's discretion in that beneficial owner's favor. Paragraph (g)(13) (*Example 13*) of this section provides an illustration of the application of this paragraph (c)(2)(i).

(ii) A transfer between corporations that are members of an affiliated group (as defined in section 1504(a)) that files a consolidated U.S. income tax return for the taxable year in which the transfer occurs.

(iii) The indirect acquisition of an interest in a life insurance contract by a person if—

(A) A partnership, trust, or other entity in which an ownership interest is being acquired directly or indirectly holds the interest in the life insurance contract and acquired that interest before January 1, 2019, or acquired that interest in a reportable policy sale reported in compliance with section 6050Y(a) and § 1.6050Y-2; or

(B) Immediately before the acquisition, no more than 50 percent of the gross value of the assets (as determined under paragraph (f)(4) of this section) of the partnership, trust, or other entity that directly or indirectly holds the interest in the life insurance contract, and in which an ownership interest is being directly acquired, consists of life insurance contracts, provided that, after the acquisition, with respect to that partnership, trust, or other entity, the person indirectly acquiring the interest in the life insurance contract and his or her family members own, in the aggregate—

(1) With respect to an S corporation, stock possessing 5 percent or less of the total combined voting power of all classes of stock entitled to vote and 5 percent or less of the total value of shares of all classes of stock of the S corporation;

(2) With respect to a trust or decedent's estate, 5 percent or less of the corpus and 5 percent or less of the annual income (taking into account, for the purpose of determining any person's ownership interest, the maximum amount of income and corpus that could be distributed to or held for the benefit of that person); or

(3) With respect to a partnership or other entity that is not a corporation or a trust, 5 percent or less of the capital interest and 5 percent or less of the profits interest.

(iv) The acquisition of a life insurance contract by an insurance company that issues a life insurance contract in an exchange pursuant to section 1035.

(v) The acquisition of a life insurance contract by a policyholder in an exchange pursuant to section 1035, if the policyholder has a substantial family, business, or financial relationship with the insured, apart from its interest in the life insurance contract, at the time of the exchange.

(d) *Substantial relationship.*—(1) *Substantial family relationship.*—For purposes of this section, a substantial family relationship means the relationship between an individual and any family member of that individual as defined in paragraph (f)(3) of this section. In addition, a

substantial family relationship exists between an individual and his or her former spouse with regard to the transfer of an interest in a life insurance contract to (or in trust for the benefit of) that former spouse incident to divorce.

(2) *Substantial business relationship.*—For purposes of this section, a substantial business relationship between the insured and the acquirer exists in each of the following situations:

(i) The insured is a key person (as defined in section 264) of, or materially participates (within the meaning of section 469) in, an active trade or business as an owner, employee, or contractor, and at least 80 percent of that trade or business is owned (directly or indirectly, through one or more partnerships, trusts, or other entities) by the acquirer or the beneficial owners of the acquirer.

(ii) The acquirer acquires an active trade or business and acquires the interest in the life insurance contract either as part of that acquisition or from a person owning significant property leased to the acquired trade or business or life insurance policies held to facilitate the succession of the ownership of the business if—

(A) The insured—

(1) Is an employee within the meaning of section 101(j)(5)(A) of the acquired trade or business immediately preceding the acquisition (for purposes of this paragraph (d)(2)(ii)(A)(1), however, the reference in section 101(j)(5)(A) to highly compensated employee within the meaning of section 414(q) does not include a former employee); or

(2) Was a director, highly compensated employee, or highly compensated individual within the meaning of section 101(j)(2)(A)(ii) of the acquired trade or business, and the acquirer, immediately after the acquisition, has ongoing financial obligations to the insured with respect to the insured's employment by the trade or business (for example, the life insurance contract is maintained by the acquirer to fund current or future retirement, pension, or survivorship obligations based on the insured's relationship with the entity or to fund a buy-out of the insured's interest in the acquired trade or business); and

(B) The acquirer either carries on the acquired trade or business or uses a significant portion of the acquired business assets in an active trade or business that does not include investing in interests in life insurance contracts.

(3) *Substantial financial relationship.*—For purposes of this section, a substantial financial relationship between the insured and the acquirer exists in each of the following situations:

(i) The acquirer (directly or indirectly, through one or more partnerships, trusts, or other entities of which it is a beneficial owner) has, or the beneficial owners of the acquirer have, a common investment (other than the interest in the life insurance contract) with the insured and a buy-out of the insured's interest in the common investment by the co-investor(s) after the insured's death is reasonably foreseeable.

(ii) The acquirer maintains the life insurance contract on the life of the insured to provide funds to purchase assets of or to satisfy liabilities of the insured or the insured's estate, heirs, legatees, or other successors in interest, or to satisfy other liabilities arising upon or by reason of the death of the insured.

(iii) The acquirer is an organization described in sections 170(c), 2055(a), and 2522(a) that previously received from the insured either financial support in a substantial amount or significant volunteer support or that meets other requirements prescribed in guidance published in the Internal Revenue Bulletin (see § 601.601(d)(2) of this chapter) for establishing that a substantial financial relationship exists between the insured and the organization.

(4) *Special rules.*—Paragraphs (d)(4)(i), (ii), and (iii) of this section apply for purposes of determining whether a substantial relationship (whether family, business, or financial) exists under paragraph (d)(1), (2), or (3) of this section, respectively.

(i) *Indirect acquisitions.*—The acquirer of an interest in a life insurance contract in an indirect acquisition is deemed to have a substantial business or financial relationship with the insured if the direct holder of the interest in the life insurance contract has a substantial business or financial relationship with the insured immediately before and after the date the acquirer acquires its interest.

(ii) *Acquisitions by certain persons.*—The sole fact that an acquirer is a partner of the insured, a partnership in which the insured is a partner, or a corporation in which the insured is a shareholder or officer, is not sufficient to establish a substantial business or financial relationship with the insured. In addition, an acquirer need not be a partner of the insured, a partnership in which the insured is a partner, or a corporation in which the insured is a shareholder or officer to have a substantial business or financial relationship with the insured.

(iii) *Acquisitions by those with differing types of substantial relationships.*—A substantial family, business, or financial relationship exists between the insured and a partnership, trust, or other entity if each beneficial owner of that partnership, trust, or other entity has a substantial family, business, or financial relationship with the insured. For example, a substantial family, business, or financial relationship exists between the insured and a trust if each trust beneficiary is a family member of the insured or an organization described in paragraph (d)(3)(iii) of this section.

(e) *Interest in a life insurance contract.*—(1) *Definition.*—For purposes of this section and section 6050Y, the term *interest in a life insurance contract* means the interest held by any person that has taken title to or possession of the life insurance contract (also referred to as a life insurance policy), in whole or part, for state law purposes, including any person that has taken title or possession as nominee for another person, and the interest held by any person that has an enforceable right to receive all or a part of the proceeds of a life insurance contract or to any other economic benefits of the policy as described in §20.2042-1(c)(2) of this chapter, such as the enforceable right to designate a contract beneficiary. Any person named as the owner in the life insurance contract generally is the owner (or an owner) of the contract and holds an interest in the contract.

(2) *Transfer of an interest in a life insurance contract.*—For purposes of this section and section 6050Y, the term *transfer of an interest in a life insurance contract* means the transfer of any interest in the life insurance contract, including any transfer of title to, possession of, or legal or beneficial ownership of the life insurance contract itself. The creation of an enforceable right to receive all or a part of the proceeds of a life insurance contract constitutes the transfer of an interest in the life insurance contract. The following events are not a transfer of an interest in a life insurance contract: the revocable designation of a beneficiary of the policy proceeds (until the designation becomes irrevocable other than by reason of the death of the insured); the pledging or assignment of a policy as collateral security; and the issuance of a life insurance contract to a policyholder, other than the issuance of a policy in an exchange pursuant to section 1035.

(3) *Acquisition of an interest in a life insurance contract.*—For purposes of this section and section 6050Y, the acquisition of an interest in a life insurance contract may be direct or indirect.

(i) *Direct acquisition of an interest in a life insurance contract.*—For purposes of this section and section 6050Y, the transfer of an interest in a life insurance contract results in the direct acquisition of the interest by the transferee (acquirer).

(ii) *Indirect acquisition of an interest in a life insurance contract.*—For purposes of this section and section 6050Y, an indirect acquisition of an interest in a life insurance contract occurs when a person (acquirer) becomes a beneficial owner of a partnership, trust, or other entity that holds (whether directly or indirectly) the interest (whether legal or beneficial) in the life insurance contract. For purposes of this paragraph (e)(3)(ii), the term *other entity* does not include a C corporation, unless more than 50 percent of the gross value of the assets of the C corporation consists of life insurance contracts (as determined under paragraph (f)(4) of this section) immediately before the indirect acquisition.

(f) *Definitions.*—The following definitions apply for purposes of this section:

(1) *Beneficial owner.*—A beneficial owner of a partnership, trust, or other entity is an individual or C corporation with an ownership interest in that entity. The interest may be held directly or indirectly, through one or more other partnerships, trusts, or other entities. For instance, an individual that directly owns an interest in a partnership (P1), which directly owns an interest in another partnership (P2), is an indirect beneficial owner of P2 and any assets or other entities owned by P2 directly or indirectly. For purposes of this paragraph (f)(1), the beneficial owners of a trust include those who may receive current distributions of trust income or corpus and those who could receive distributions if the trust were to terminate currently.

(2) *C corporation.*—The term *C corporation* has the meaning given to it in section 1361(a)(2).

(3) *Family member.*—With respect to any individual, the term *family member* refers to any person described in paragraphs (f)(3)(i) through (vi) of this section. For purposes of this paragraph (f)(3), full effect is given to a legal adoption, and a step-child is deemed to be a descendant. The family members of an individual include:

(i) The individual;

(ii) The individual's spouse or a person with whom the individual is in a registered domestic partnership, civil union, or other similar relationship established under state law;

(iii) Any parent, grandparent, or great-grandparent of the individual or of the person described in paragraph (f)(3)(ii) of this section and any spouse of such parent, grandparent, or great-grandparent, or person with whom the parent, grandparent, or great-grandparent is in a registered domestic partnership, civil union, or other similar relationship established under state law;

(iv) Any lineal descendant of the individual or of any person described in paragraph (f)(3)(ii) or (iii) of this section;

(v) Any spouse of a lineal descendant described in paragraph (f)(3)(iv) of this section and any person with whom such a lineal descendant is in a registered domestic partnership, civil union, or other similar relationship established under state law; and

(vi) Any lineal descendant of a person described in paragraph (f)(3)(v) of this section.

(4) *Gross value of assets.*—(i) *Determination of gross value of assets.*—Except as provided in paragraph (f)(4)(ii) or (iii) of this section, for purposes of paragraphs (c)(2)(iii)(B) and (e)(3)(ii) of this section, the term *gross value of assets* means, with respect to any entity, the fair market value of the entity's assets, including assets beneficially owned by the entity under paragraph (f)(1) of this section as a beneficial owner of a partnership, trust, or other entity.

(ii) *Determination of gross value of assets of publicly traded entity.*—For purposes of determining the gross value of assets of an entity that is publicly traded, if the entity's annual Form 10-K filed with the United States Securities and Exchange Commission (or equivalent annual filing if the entity is publicly traded in a non-U.S. jurisdiction) for the period immediately preceding a person's acquisition of an ownership interest in the entity does not contain information demonstrating that more than 50 percent of the gross value of the entity's assets consists of life insurance contracts, that person may assume that no more than 50 percent of the gross value of the entity's assets consists of life insurance contracts, unless that person has actual knowledge or reason to know that more than 50 percent of the gross value of the entity's assets consists of life insurance contracts.

(iii) *Safe harbor definition of gross value of assets.*—An entity may choose to determine the gross value of all the entity's assets for purposes of this section using the following alternative definition of *gross value of assets*:

(A) In the case of assets that are life insurance policies or annuity or endowment contracts that have cash values, the cash surrender value as defined in section 7702(f)(2)(A); and

(B) In the case of assets not described in paragraph (f)(4)(iii)(A) of this section, the adjusted bases (within the meaning of section 1016) of such assets.

(5) *Transfer for valuable consideration.*—A transfer for valuable consideration means any transfer of an interest in a life insurance contract for cash or other consideration reducible to a money value.

(g) *Examples.*—The application of this section is illustrated by the following examples. Each example assumes that the transferee did not receive any amounts under the life insurance contract other than the amounts described in the examples. With the exception of paragraph (g)(7) (*Example 7*) of this section, the bargain sale rules set forth in paragraph (b)(2)(iii) of this section do not apply in the examples because the consideration paid for the policy transferred is fair market value:

(1) *Example 1.* A is the initial policyholder of a $100,000 insurance policy on A's life. A sells the policy to B, A's child, for $6,000, its fair market value. B is not a partner in a partnership in which A is a partner. B receives the proceeds of $100,000 upon the death of A. Because the transfer to B was for valuable consideration, and none of the exceptions in paragraph (b)(1)(ii) of this section applies, the amount of the proceeds B may exclude from B's gross income under this section is limited under paragraph (b)(1)(i) of this section to $6,000 plus any premiums and other amounts paid by B with respect to the policy subsequent to the transfer.

(2) *Example 2.* The facts are the same as in *Example 1* in paragraph (g)(1) of this section except that, before A's death, B gratuitously transfers the policy back to A. A's estate receives the proceeds of $100,000 on A's death. Because the transfer from B to A is a gratuitous transfer to the insured, and the preceding transfer from A to B was not a reportable policy sale, the amount of the proceeds A's estate may exclude from gross income under this section is not limited by paragraph (b)(2)(i) of this section.

(3) *Example 3.* The facts are the same as in *Example 1* in paragraph (g)(1) of this section except that, before A's death, B sells the policy back to A for its fair market value. A's estate receives the proceeds of $100,000 on A's death. The transfer from A to B is not a reportable policy sale because the acquirer B has a substantial family relationship with the insured, A. The transfer from B to A also is not a reportable policy sale because the acquirer A has a substantial family relationship with the insured, A. Accordingly, paragraph

(b)(1)(ii)(B)(*1*) of this section applies to the transfer to A, and the amount of the proceeds A's estate may exclude from gross income is not limited by paragraph (b) of this section.

(4) *Example 4.* A is the initial policyholder of a $100,000 insurance policy on A's life. A transfers the policy for $6,000, its fair market value, to an individual, C, who does not have a substantial family, business, or financial relationship with A. The transfer from A to C is a reportable policy sale. C receives the proceeds of $100,000 on A's death. The amount of the proceeds C may exclude from C's gross income under this section is limited under paragraph (b)(1)(i) of this section to $6,000 plus any premiums and other amounts paid by C with respect to the policy subsequent to the transfer.

(5) *Example 5.* The facts are the same as in *Example 4* in paragraph (g)(4) of this section, except that before A's death, C transfers the policy to D, a partner of A who co-owns real property with A, for $8,000, the policy's fair market value. D receives the proceeds of $100,000 on A's death. The transfer from C to D is not a reportable policy sale because the acquirer D has a substantial financial relationship with the insured, A. However, because that transfer follows a reportable policy sale (the transfer from A to C), the amount of the proceeds that D may exclude from gross income under this section is limited by paragraph (b)(1)(ii)(B)(2) of this section to the sum of—

(i) The higher of the amount C could have excluded had the transfer to D not occurred ($6,000 plus any premiums and other amounts paid by C with respect to the policy subsequent to the transfer to C, as described in *Example 4* in paragraph (g)(4) of this section) or the actual value of the consideration for that transfer paid by D ($8,000); and

(ii) Any premiums and other amounts paid by D with respect to the policy subsequent to the transfer to D.

(6) *Example 6.* The facts are the same as in *Example 4* in paragraph (g)(4) of this section, except that before A's death, C transfers the policy back to A for $8,000, its fair market value. A's estate receives the proceeds of $100,000 on A's death. The transfer from C to A is not a reportable policy sale because the acquirer A has a substantial family relationship with the insured, A. Although the transfer follows a reportable policy sale (the initial transfer from A to C), A's estate may exclude all of the policy proceeds from gross income because paragraph (b)(1)(ii)(B)(3)(*i*) of this section applies and, therefore, the amount of the proceeds that A may exclude from gross income is not limited by paragraph (b)(1)(i) of this section or (b)(1)(ii)(B)(2) of this section.

(7) *Example 7.* The facts are the same as in *Example 6* in paragraph (g)(6) of this section, except that C transfers the policy back to A for $4,000, rather than its fair market value of $8,000. A's estate receives the proceeds of $100,000 on A's death. Because A did not pay fair market value for the policy, the transfer is bifurcated and treated as a bargain sale under paragraph (b)(2)(iii) of this section. A therefore is treated as having purchased 50% of the policy interest for valuable consideration equal to fair market value and as having received 50% of the policy interest in a gratuitous transfer. The transfer from C to A is not a reportable policy sale because the acquirer, A, has a substantial family relationship with the insured, A, but the transfer from C to A follows a reportable policy sale (the transfer from A to C).

(i) *Treatment of policy interest purchased by A.* A's estate may exclude from income all of the policy proceeds related to the 50% policy interest transferred for valuable consideration ($50,000) because, under paragraph (b)(1)(ii)(B)(3)(*i*) of this section, the amount of the proceeds that may be excluded from gross income is not limited by paragraph (b)(1)(i) of this section or (b)(1)(ii)(B)(2) of this section.

(ii) *Treatment of policy interest gratuitously transferred to A.* The amount of the policy proceeds related to the 50% policy interest transferred gratuitously that A's estate may exclude from income is limited under paragraph (b)(2)(i) of this section to the sum of the amount C could have excluded with respect to 50% of the policy had the transfer back to A not occurred (that is, 50% of the $6,000 that C paid A for the policy, plus 50% of any premiums and other amounts paid by C with respect to the policy subsequent to the transfer to C), plus 50% of any premiums and other amounts paid by A with respect to the policy subsequent to the transfer to A.

(8) *Example 8.* The facts are the same as in *Example 6* in paragraph (g)(6) of this section, except that, before A's death, A gratuitously transfers 50% of the policy interest to B, A's child, and sells 50% of the policy interest for its fair market value to an individual, E, who does not have a substantial family, business, or financial relationship with A. B and E each receive $50,000 of the proceeds on A's death. Paragraph (b)(1)(ii)(B)(3)(*ii*) of this section applies to determine the amount of the proceeds that B and E may exclude from gross income because the policy interests transferred to B and E were first transferred for valuable consideration in a reportable policy sale (the transfer by A to C) and then transferred to the insured, A, for fair market value.

(i) *Treatment of policy interest transferred to B.* With respect to the portion of the policy interest transferred to B, because the transfer to B was the only transfer subsequent to the transfer to A and the transfer to B was gratuitous and not a reportable policy sale, under paragraph (b)(1)(ii)(B)(3)(*ii*) of this section, the amount of the policy proceeds excludable from gross income by B is determined under paragraph (b)(2)(i) of this section, taking into account the application of paragraph (b)(1)(ii)(B)(3)(*i*) of this section to A's acquisition of the interest. Under paragraph (b)(2)(i) of this section, the amount of the proceeds B may exclude is limited to the sum of the amount A could have excluded had the transfer to B not occurred, and any premiums and other amounts paid by B with respect to the policy subsequent to the transfer to B. As described in *Example 6* in paragraph (g)(6) of this section, under paragraph (b)(1)(ii)(B)(3)(*i*) of this section, the amount of the proceeds that A may exclude from gross income is not limited by paragraph (b)(1)(i) of this section or (b)(1)(ii)(B)(2) of this section. Accordingly, the amount of the proceeds that B may exclude from gross income is not limited by paragraph (b) of this section.

(ii) *Treatment of policy interest transferred to E.* With respect to the portion of the policy interest transferred to E, because the transfer to E was not gratuitous and was a reportable policy sale, under paragraph (b)(1)(ii)(B)(3)(*ii*) of this section, the amount of the policy proceeds excludable from gross income by E is determined in accordance with paragraph (b) of this section. Accordingly, because the transfer to E was for valuable consideration, the amount excludable from gross income by E is limited by paragraph (b)(1)(i) of this section unless an exception in paragraph (b)(1)(ii) of this section applies. Because the transfer from A to E is a reportable policy sale, none of the exceptions in paragraph (b)(1)(ii) of this section apply. Therefore, the amount of the proceeds E may exclude from gross income under this section is limited by paragraph (b)(1)(i) of this section to the sum of the consideration paid by E and the premiums and other amounts paid by E with respect to the policy subsequent to the transfer to E.

(9) *Example 9.* The facts are the same as in *Example 8* in paragraph (g)(8) of this section, except that, before A's death, B transfers B's policy interest to Partnership F, whose partners are A and other family members of A, in exchange for a partnership interest in Partnership F. Partnership F receives $50,000 of the proceeds on A's death. With respect to the policy interest transferred to Partnership F, paragraph (b)(1)(ii)(B)(3)(*ii*) of this section applies to determine the amount of the proceeds that Partnership F may exclude from gross income for the reasons described in *Example 8* in paragraph (g)(8) of this section.

(i) *Treatment of policy interest transferred to Partnership F.* The transfer to Partnership F was not a reportable policy sale. However, because the transfer to Partnership F was not gratuitous, the amount of the policy proceeds excludable from gross income by Partnership F is determined in accordance with paragraph (b) of this section as if the amount that would have been excludable from gross income by A following the transfer to A, if no subsequent transfer had occurred, was determined under paragraph (b)(1)(ii)(B)(2) of this section. Because B's transfer to Partnership F was a transfer for valuable consideration to a partnership in which the insured is a partner that was preceded by a reportable policy sale (the transfer to C), the amount of the proceeds Partnership F may exclude from gross income under this section is limited under paragraph (b)(1)(ii)(B)(2) of this section to the higher of the amount that would have been excludable by B if the transfer to Partnership F had not occurred or the actual value of the consideration for the policy paid by Partnership F, plus any premiums and other amounts paid by Partnership F with respect to the policy subsequent to the transfer to Partnership F.

(ii) *Amount that B could have excluded.* Because the transfer from A to B was a gratuitous transfer, the amount of the proceeds B could have excluded from gross income under this section if the transfer to Partnership F had not occurred is limited under paragraph (b)(2)(i) of this section to the sum of the amount A could have excluded had the transfer to B not occurred, and any premiums and other amounts paid by B with respect to the policy subsequent to the transfer to B.

(iii) *Amount that A could have excluded.* As described in paragraph (g)(9)(i) of this section, the amount of the proceeds A could have excluded under this section if the transfer to B had not occurred must be determined under paragraph (b)(1)(ii)(B)(2) of this section in accordance with paragraph (b)(1)(ii)(B)(3)(*ii*) of this section. Under paragraph (b)(1)(ii)(B)(2) of this section, the amount that would have been excludable by A is limited to the higher of the amount that would have been excludable by C if the transfer to A had not occurred ($6,000 plus premiums and other amounts subsequently paid by C) or the actual value of the consideration for the policy paid by A ($8,000), plus any premiums and other amounts paid by A with respect to the policy subsequent to the transfer to A.

(10) *Example 10.* A is the initial policyholder of a $100,000 insurance policy on A's life. A contributes the policy to Corporation X in exchange for stock. Corporation X's basis in the policy is determinable in whole or in part by reference to A's basis in the policy.

Corporation X conducts an active trade or business that it wholly owns, and A materially participates in that active trade or business as an employee of Corporation X. Corporation X receives the proceeds of $100,000 on A's death. A's contribution of the policy to Corporation X is not a reportable policy sale because Corporation X has a substantial business relationship with A under paragraph (d)(2)(i) of this section. Although Corporation X's basis in the policy is determinable in whole or in part by reference to A's basis in the policy, paragraph (b)(1)(ii)(A) of this section does not apply because the insured, A, is a shareholder of Corporation X and the other requirements under paragraph (b)(1)(ii)(B) of this section are satisfied. Accordingly, paragraph (b)(1)(ii)(B) of this section applies, and paragraph (b)(1)(ii)(A) of this section is inapplicable. Under paragraph (b)(1)(ii)(B)(1) of this section, Corporation X's exclusion is not limited by paragraph (b) of this section.

(11) *Example 11.* The facts are the same as in *Example 10* in paragraph (g)(10) of this section, except that Corporation X transfers its active trade or business and the policy on A's life to Corporation Y in a tax-free reorganization at a time when A is still employed by Corporation X, but is no longer a shareholder of Corporation X. Corporation Y's basis in the policy is determinable in whole or in part by reference to Corporation X's basis in the policy, and Corporation Y carries on the trade or business acquired from Corporation X. Corporation Y receives the proceeds of $100,000 on A's death. The transfer from Corporation X to Corporation Y is not a reportable policy sale because Corporation Y has a substantial business relationship with A under paragraph (d)(2)(ii) of this section. The amount of the proceeds that Corporation Y may exclude from gross income is limited under paragraph (b)(1)(ii)(A) of this section to the sum of the amount that would have been excludable by Corporation X had the transfer to Corporation Y not occurred, plus any premiums and other amounts paid by Corporation Y with respect to the policy subsequent to the transfer. Accordingly, because Corporation X's exclusion is not limited by paragraph (b) of this section, as described in *Example 10* in paragraph (g)(10) of this section, Corporation Y's exclusion is not limited by paragraph (b) of this section.

(12) *Example 12.* A is the initial policyholder of a $100,000 insurance policy on A's life. A contributes the policy to a C corporation, Corporation W, in exchange for stock. After the acquisition, A owns less than 20% of the outstanding stock of Corporation W and owns stock possessing less than 20 % of the total combined voting power of all stock of Corporation W and is therefore not a key person with respect to Corporation W under section 264(e)(3). Corporation W's basis in the policy is determinable in whole or in part by reference to A's basis in the policy. However, no substantial family, business, or financial relationship exists between A and Corporation W, so A's contribution of the policy to Corporation W is a reportable policy sale. Corporation W receives the proceeds of $100,000 on A's death. Under paragraph (b)(1)(i) of this section, the amount of the proceeds Corporation W may exclude from gross income is limited to the actual value of the stock exchanged for the policy, plus any premiums and other amounts paid by Corporation W with respect to the policy subsequent to the transfer. The exceptions in paragraph (b)(1)(ii) of this section do not apply because the transfer to Corporation W is a reportable policy sale.

(13) *Example 13.* Partnership X and Partnership Y are owned by individuals A, B, and C. A holds 40% of the capital and profits interest of Partnership X and 20% of the capital and profits interest of Partnership Y. B holds 35% of the capital and profits interest of Partnership X and 40% of the capital and profits interest of Partnership Y. C holds 25% of the capital and profits interest of Partnership X and 40% of the capital and profits interest of Partnership Y. Partnership X is the initial policyholder of a $100,000 insurance policy on the life of A. Partnership Y purchases the policy from Partnership X. Under paragraph (c)(2)(i) of this section, this transfer is not a reportable policy sale because the ownership interest of each beneficial owner in Partnership X does not vary from that owner's interest in Partnership Y by more than a 20% ownership interest. A's ownership varies by a 20% interest, B's ownership varies by a 5% interest, and C's ownership varies by a 15% interest.

(14) *Example 14.* Partnership X conducts an active trade or business and is the initial policyholder of a $100,000 insurance policy on the life of its full-time employee, A. A materially participates in Partnership X's active trade or business in A's capacity as an employee. Individual B acquires a *10% profits interest* in Partnership X in exchange for a cash payment of $1,000,000. Under paragraphs (d)(1) through (3) of this section, B does not have a substantial family, business, or financial relationship with A. Under paragraph (d)(4)(i) of this section, however, B is deemed to have a substantial business relationship with A because, under paragraph (d)(2)(i) of this section, Partnership X (the direct policyholder) has a substantial business relationship with A. Accordingly, although the acquisition of the 10% partnership interest by B is an indirect acquisition of a 10% interest in the insurance policy covering A's life, the acquisition is not a reportable policy sale.

(15) *Example 15.* The facts are the same as in *Example 14* in paragraph (g)(14) of this section, except that A is no longer an employee of Partnership X, and Partnership X has no substantial family, business, or financial relationship with A, when B acquires the profits interest in Partnership X. Also, B acquires only a 5% profits interest in exchange for a cash payment of $500,000. Partnership X does not own an interest in any other life insurance policies, and the gross value of its assets is $10 million. Although neither Partnership X nor B has a substantial family, business, or financial relationship with A at the time of B's indirect acquisition of an interest in the policy covering A's life, because B's profits interest in Partnership X does not exceed 5%, and because no more than 50% of Partnership X's asset value consists of life insurance contracts, the exception in paragraph (c)(2)(iii)(B) of this section applies, and B's indirect acquisition of an interest in the policy covering A's life is not a reportable policy sale.

(16) *Example 16.* A is the initial policyholder of a $100,000 insurance policy on A's life. A sells the policy for its fair market value. As a result of the sale, Bank X holds legal title to the life insurance contract as the nominee of Partnership B, and Partnership B has the enforceable right to designate the contract beneficiary. Under paragraphs (d)(1) through (4) of this section, neither Bank X nor Partnership B has a substantial family, business, or financial relationship with the insured, A, at the time of the sale. Accordingly, the transfer of legal title to the policy to Bank X is a reportable policy sale under paragraph (c)(1) of this section, unless an exception set forth in paragraph (c)(2) of this section applies. The same is true of the transfer of the economic benefits of the policy to Partnership B. At a later date, Partnership B sells its economic interest in the policy to Partnership C for fair market value. Bank X continues to hold legal title to the life insurance contract, but now holds it as Partnership C's nominee. Partnership C has no substantial family, business, or financial relationship with the insured, A, under paragraphs (d)(1) through (4) of this section at the time of the transfer. Accordingly, Partnership C's acquisition of the economic interest in the policy from Partnership B is a reportable policy sale under paragraph (c)(1) of this section, unless an exception set forth in paragraph (c)(2) of this section applies. [Reg. § 1.101-1.]

□ [*T.D.* 6280, 12-16-57. *Amended by T.D.* 6783, 12-23-64 *T.D.* 7836, 9-23-82, *T.D.* 9340, 7-23-2007 *and T.D.* 9879, 10-25-2019 (corrected 12-12-2019).]

[Reg. § 1.101-2]

§ 1.101-2. Employees' death benefits.—(a) *In general.*—(1) Section 101(b) states the general rule that amounts up to $5,000 which are paid to the beneficiaries or the estate of an employee, or former employee, by or on behalf of an employer and by reason of the death of the employee shall be excluded from the gross income of the recipient. This exclusion from gross income applies whether payment is made to the estate of the employee or to any beneficiary (individual, corporation, or partnership), whether it is made directly or in trust, and whether or not it is made pursuant to a contractual obligation of the employer. The exclusion applies whether payment is made in a single sum or otherwise, subject to the provisions of section 101(c), relating to amounts held under an agreement to pay interest thereon (see § 1.101-3). The exclusion from gross income also applies to any amount not actually paid which is otherwise taxable to a beneficiary of an employee because it was made available as a distribution from an employee's trust.

(2) The exclusion does not apply to amounts constituting income payable to the employee during his life as compensation for his services, such as bonuses or payments for unused leave or uncollected salary, nor to certain other amounts with respect to which the deceased employee possessed, immediately before his death, a nonforfeitable right to receive the amounts while living (see section 101(b)(2)(B) and paragraph (d) of this section). Further, the exclusion does not apply to amounts received as an annuity under a joint and survivor annuity obligation where the employee was the primary annuitant and the annuity starting date occurred before the death of the employee (see section 101(b)(2)(C) and paragraph (e)(1)(ii) of this section). In the case of amounts received by a beneficiary as an annuity (but not as a survivor under a joint and survivor annuity with respect to which the employee was the primary annuitant), the exclusion is applied indirectly by means of the provisions of section 72 and the regulations thereunder (see section 101(b)(2)(D) and paragraph (e)(1)(iii) and (iv) of this section). Thus, for example, the exclusion applies to amounts which are received by a survivor of an employee retired on disability under the provisions of the Civil service retirement law (5 U.S.C. 8301 or any former corresponding provisions of law) or the Retired Serviceman's Family Protection Plan or Survivor Benefit Plan (10 U.S.C. 1431 et seq.), provided such employee dies before attaining mandatory retirement age (as defined in § 1.105-4(a)(3)(i)(B)).

(3) The total amount excludable with respect to any employee may not exceed $5,000, regardless of the number of employers or the

number of beneficiaries. For allocation of the exclusion among beneficiaries, see paragraph (c) of this section. For rules governing the taxability of benefits payable on the death of an employee under pension, profit-sharing, or stock bonus plans described in section 401(a) and exempt under section 501(a), under annuity plans described in section 403(a), or under annuity contracts to which paragraph (a) or (b) of §1.403(b)-1 applies, see sections 72(m)(3), 402(a), and 403 and the regulations thereunder.

(b) *Payments under certain employee benefit plans.*—(1) *In general.*—Where a payment is made by reason of the death of an employee by an employer-provided welfare fund or a trust, including a stock bonus, pension, or profit-sharing trust described in section 401(a), or by an insurance company (if such payment does not constitute "life insurance" within the purview of section 101(a)), the payment shall be considered to have been made by or on behalf of the employer to the extent that it exceeds amounts contributed by, or deemed contributed by, the deceased employee.

(2) *Cross references.*—For provisions governing the taxability of distributions payable on the death of an employee participant—

(i) Under a trust described in section 401(a) and exempt from tax under section 501(a), see paragraph (c) of §1.72-16 and paragraph (a)(5) of §1.402(a)-1;

(ii) Under an annuity plan described in section 403(a), see paragraph (c) of §1.72-16 and paragraph (c) of §1.403(a)-1;

(iii) Under annuity contracts to which paragraph (a) or (b) of §1.403(b)-1 applies, see paragraph (c)(2) and (3) of §1.403(b)-1;

(iv) Under eligible State deferred compensation plans described in section 457(b), see paragraph (c) of §1.457-1.

(c) *Allocation of the exclusion.*—(1) Where the aggregate payments by or on behalf of an employer or employers as death benefits to the beneficiaries or the estate of the deceased employee exceed $5,000, the $5,000 exclusion shall be apportioned among them in the same proportion as the amount received by or the present value of the amount payable to each bears to the total death benefits paid or payable by or on behalf of the employer or employers.

(2) The application of the rule in subparagraph (1) of this paragraph may be illustrated by the following example:

Example. The M Corporation, the employer of A, a deceased employee who died November 30, 1954, makes payments in 1955 to the beneficiaries of A as follows: $5,000 to W, A's widow, $2,000 to B, the son of A, and $3,000 to C, the daughter of A. No other amounts are paid by any other employer of A to his estate or beneficiaries. By application of the apportionment rule stated above, W, the widow, will exclude $2,500 ($5,000/$10,000, or one-half, of $5,000); B, the son, will exclude $1,000 ($2,000/$10,000, or one-fifth, of $5,000); and C, the daughter, will exclude $1,500 ($3,000/$10,000 or three-tenths, of $5,000).

(d) *Nonforfeitable rights.*—(1) Except as provided in subparagraphs (3) and (4) of this paragraph, the exclusion provided by section 101(b) does not apply to amounts with respect to which the deceased employee possessed, immediately before his death, a nonforfeitable right to receive the amounts while living. Section 101(b)(2)(B). For the purpose of section 101(b) and this paragraph, an employee shall be considered to have had a nonforfeitable right with respect to—

(i) Any amount to which he would have been entitled—

(*a*) If he had made an appropriate election or demand, or

(*b*) Upon termination of his employment (see examples (5) and (6) of subparagraph (2) of this paragraph); or

(ii) The present value (immediately before his death) of—

(*a*) Amounts payable as an annuity (as defined in paragraph (b) of §1.72-2, whether immediate or deferred) by or on behalf of the employer (see example (1) of subparagraph (2) of this paragraph), or

(*b*) Amounts which would have been so payable if the employee had terminated his employment and continued to live; or

(iii) Any amount to the extent it is paid in lieu of amounts described in either subdivision (i) or (ii) of this subparagraph. See examples (2), (3), and (4) of subparagraph (2) of this paragraph. For purposes of subdivision (iii) of this subparagraph, any amount paid in discharge of an obligation which arose solely because of the existence of a particular fact or circumstance subsequent to the employee's death shall not be considered an amount paid in lieu of amounts described in subdivision (i) or (ii) of this subparagraph. Subdivision (iii) of this subparagraph shall apply, however, to the extent indicated therein, to amounts payable without regard to any such contingency (to the extent that such amounts are equal to or less than those described in subdivisions (i) and (ii) of this subparagraph which are not paid). See paragraph (e)(1)(iii)(*b*) of this section for rules with respect to finding the present value of an annuity immediately before the employee's death.

(2) The application of paragraph (d)(1) of this section may be illustrated by the following examples, in which it is assumed that the plans are not "qualified plans" and that no employer is an organization referred to in section 170(b)(1)(A)(ii) or (vi) or a religious organization (other than a trust) which is exempt from tax under section 501(a):

Example (1). A, who was a participant under the X Company pension plan, retired on December 31, 1953. He had made no contributions to the plan. Upon his retirement, he became entitled to monthly payments of $100 payable for life, or 120 months certain. A died on October 31, 1954, having received 10 monthly payments of $100 each. After his death, the monthly payments became payable to his estate for the remaining 110 months certain. No exclusion from gross income is allowed to A's estate (or any beneficiary who receives the right to such payments from the estate), since the employee's right to the monthly payments was nonforfeitable at the date of his death. It will be noted that in this example it is unnecessary to consider the present value of the annuity to A just before his death since the payments to be made include only those certain to be made in any event under the plan whether or not A continued to live.

Example (2). C, a participant under the Y Company pension plan, died on December 15, 1954, while actively in the employment of the company, survived by a widow and minor children. Because of his years of service, he would have been entitled to an annuity for life, his own contributions to the plan and interest thereon being guaranteed, if he had retired or terminated his employment at a time immediately before his death. The plan further provides that—(a) if, but only if, an employee is survived by a widow and minor children, his widow is to receive an annuity for her life without regard to whether or not the employee had begun his annuity; (b) any payments made with respect to his widow's annuity are to reduce the guaranteed amount to an equal extent; and (c) if the employee is not so survived, the guaranteed amount is payable to his beneficiary or estate, but no amount is payable to anyone with respect to what would have been the widow's annuity. In view of these provisions, that portion of the present value of the annuity payable to C's widow which exceeds the guaranteed amount shall be considered paid neither as an amount, nor in lieu of an amount, which C had a nonforfeitable right to receive while living. The reason for this result is that the payment of such excess is contingent upon C's begin survived by a widow and minor children, a circumstance existing subsequent to his death. Conversely, to the extent that the present value of the annuity payable to C's widow does not exceed the guaranteed amount, annuity payments attributable to such present value shall be considered paid in lieu of an amount which C had a nonforfeitable right to receive while living.

Example (3). D, a participant under the Y Company pension plan, died on January 1, 1955, while actively in the employment of the company. The Y Company plan provides that where an employee dies in service, the present value of the accumulated credits which he could have obtained at that time if he had instead separated from the service shall be paid in a single sum to his surviving spouse or to his estate if no widow survives him. The present value of D's accumulated credits, at the time of his death, was $10,000. However, the plan also provides that a surviving spouse may elect to take, in lieu of a single sum, an annuity the present value of which exceeds such sum by $2,500. D's widow elects to receive an annuity (the present value of which is $12,500). Therefore, $2,500 is an amount to which the exclusion of section 101(b) and this section shall apply.

Example (4). A, an employee of the X Company, continues to work after reaching the normal retirement age of 60 years, although he could have retired at that age and obtained an annuity of $3,000 per year for his life. A is not entitled to any part of the annuity while he is employed and receiving compensation. A dies at the age of 67 while still in active employment. Since he had passed normal retirement age, his additional years of service did not entitle him to a larger annuity at age 67 than that which he could have obtained at age 60. However, the plan of the X Company provides that in the event of an employee's death prior to separation from the service, his widow is to be paid an annuity for her life in the same amount per year as that which the employee could have obtained if he had instead retired but if no widow survives him, the present value of the annuity which the employee could have obtained at a time just before his death is to be paid to a named beneficiary or the estate of the employee. Assuming that the present value of the annuity to A's widow, whose age is 61, is $36,000 and the present value of the annuity which would have been payable to A at age 67 if he had then retired is $23,500, the present value of the widow's annuity, to the extent of $23,500, is an amount which is payable in lieu of amounts which the employee had a nonforfeitable right to receive while living because it does not exceed the value of his nonforfeitable rights and is not otherwise paid. On the other hand, the $12,500 excess of the value of the widow's annuity ($36,000) over the value of the employee's annuity ($23,500) is an amount to which section 101(b) applies since the employee had no right to any part of it. If no other death benefits are payable, a $5,000 exclusion is available (see section 101(b)(2)(D) and paragraph (e) of this section).

Example (5). The trustee of the X Corporation noncontributory profit-sharing plan is required under the provisions of the plan to pay to the beneficiary of B, an employee of the X Corporation who died on July 1, 1955, the benefit due on account of the death of B. The provisions of the profit-sharing plan give each participating employee in case of termination of employment a 10-percent vested interest in the amount accumulated in his account for each year of participation in the plan. In case of death, the entire credit in the participant's account is to be paid to his beneficiary. At the time of B's death, he had been a participant for three years and the accumulation in his account was $8,000. After his death this amount is paid to his beneficiary. At the time of B's death, the amount distributable to him on account of termination of employment would have been $2,400 (30 percent of $8,000). The difference of $5,600 ($8,000 minus $2,400), payable to the beneficiary of B, is an amount payable solely by reason of B's death. Accordingly, $5,000 of the $5,600 may be excluded from the gross income of the beneficiary receiving such payment (assuming no other death benefits are involved). However, if it is assumed that the facts are the same as above, except that at the time of his death B has been a participant for 6 years, the amount distributable to him on account of termination of employment would have been $4,800 (60 percent of $8,000). The difference of $3,200 ($8,000 minus $4,800), payable to B's beneficiary, is an amount payable solely by reason of B's death. Accordingly, only $3,200 may be excluded from the gross income of the beneficiary receiving such payment (assuming no other death benefits are involved).

Example (6). The X Corporation instituted a trust, forming part of a pension plan, for its employees, the cost thereof being borne entirely by the corporation. The plan provides, in part, that after 10 or more years of service and attaining the age of 55, an employee can elect to retire and receive benefits before the normal retirement date contingent upon the employer's approval. If he retires without the employer's consent, or voluntarily leaves the company, no benefits are or will be payable. The plan further provides that if the employee is involuntarily separated or dies before retirement, he or his beneficiary, respectively, will receive a percentage of the reserve provided for the employee in the trust fund on the following basis: 10 to 15 years of service, 25 percent; 15 to 20 years of service, 50 percent; 20 to 25 years of service, 75 percent; 25 or more years of service, 100 percent. A, an employee of the X Corporation for 17 years, died at the age of 56 while in the employ of the corporation. At the time of his death, $15,000 was the reserve provided for him in the trust. His beneficiary receives $7,500, an amount equal to 50 percent of the reserve provided for A's retirement; accordingly, $5,000 of the $7,500 may be excluded from the gross income of the beneficiary receiving such payment (assuming no other death benefits are involved) since A, prior to his death, had only a forfeitable right to receive $7,500.

(3)(i) Notwithstanding the rule stated in subparagraph (1) of this paragraph and illustrated in subparagraph (2) of this paragraph, the exclusion from gross income provided by section 101(b) applies to the receipt of certain amounts, paid under "qualified" plans, with respect to which the deceased employee possessed, immediately before his death, a nonforfeitable right to receive the amounts while living (see section 101(b)(2)(B)(i) and (ii)). The payments to which this exclusion applies are—

(a) "Total distributions payable" by a stock bonus, pension, or profit-sharing trust described in section 401(a) which is exempt from tax under section 501(a), and

(b) "Total amounts" paid under an annuity contract under a plan described in section 403(a),

provided such distributions or amounts are paid in full within one taxable year of the distributee (see example (3) of subdivision (ii) of this subparagraph). For the purposes of applying section 101(b), "total distributions payable" means the balance to the credit of an employee which becomes payable to a distributee on account of the employee's death, either before or after separation from the service (see section 402(a)(3)(C), the regulations thereunder, and examples (2) and (4) of subdivision (ii) of this subparagraph); and "total amounts" means the balance to the credit of an employee which becomes payable to the payee by reason of the employee's death, either before or after separation from the service (see section 403(a)(2)(B), the regulations thereunder, and example (1) of subdivision (ii) of this subparagraph). See subparagraph (4) of this paragraph relating to the exclusion of amounts which are received under annuity contracts purchased by certain exempt organizations and with respect to which the deceased employee possessed, immediately before his death, a nonforfeitable right to receive the amounts while living.

(ii) The application of the provisions of subdivision (i) of this subparagraph may be illustrated by the following examples:

Example (1). The widow of an employee elects, under a noncontributory "qualified" plan, to receive in a lump sum the present value of the annuity which C, the deceased employee, could have obtained at a time just before his death if he had retired at that time. Such present value is $6,000. Of this amount, $5,000 is excludable from the widow's gross income despite the fact that C had a nonforfeitable right to the amount in lieu of which the payment is made, since such payment is an amount to which subdivision (i) of this subparagraph applies (assuming no other death benefits are involved).

Example (2). The trustee of the X Corporation noncontributory, "qualified", profit-sharing plan is required under the provisions of the plan to pay to the beneficiary of B, an employee of the X Corporation who died on July 1, 1955, the benefit due on account of the death of B. The provisions of the profit-sharing plan give each participating employee, in case of termination of employment, a 10 percent vested interest in the amount accumulated in his account for each year of participation in the plan, but, in case of death, the entire credit to the participant's account is to be paid to his beneficiary. At the time of B's death, he had been a participant for five years. The accumulation in his account was $8,000, and the amount which would have been distributable to him in the event of termination of employment was $4,000 (50 percent of $8,000). After his death, $8,000 is paid to his beneficiary in a lump sum. (It may be noted that these are the same facts as in example (5) of subparagraph (2) of this paragraph except that the employee has been a participant for five years instead of three and the plan is a "qualified" plan.) It is immaterial that the employee had a nonforfeitable right to $4,000, because the payment of the $8,000 to the beneficiary is the payment of the "total distributions payable" within one taxable year of the distributee to which subdivision (i) of this subparagraph applies. Assuming no other death benefits are involved, the beneficiary may exclude $5,000 of the $8,000 payment from gross income.

Example (3). The facts are the same as in example (2) except that the beneficiary is entitled to receive only the $4,000 to which the employee had a nonforfeitable right and elects, 30 days after B's death, to receive it over a period of ten years. Since the "total distributions payable" are not paid within one taxable year of the distributee, no exclusion from gross income is allowable with respect to the $4,000.

Example (4). The X Corporation instituted a trust, forming part of a "qualified" profit-sharing plan for its employees, the cost thereof being borne entirely by the corporation. The plan provides, in part, that if, after 10 or more years of service, an employee leaves the employ of the corporation, either voluntarily or involuntarily, before retirement, a percentage of the reserve provided for the employee in the trust fund will be paid to the employee as follows: 10 to 15 years of service, 25 percent; 15 to 20 years of service, 50 percent; 20 to 25 years of service, 75 percent; 25 or more years of service, 100 percent. The plan further provides that if an employee dies before reaching retirement age, his beneficiary will receive a percentage of the reserve provided for the employee in the trust fund, on the same basis as shown in the preceding sentence. A, an employee of the X Corporation for 17 years, died before attaining retirement age while in the employ of the corporation. At the time of his death, $15,000 was the reserve provided for him in the trust fund. His beneficiary receives $7,500 in a lump sum, an amount equal to 50 percent of the reserve provided for A's retirement. The beneficiary may exclude from gross income (assuming no other death benefits are involved) $5,000 of the $7,500, since the latter amount constitutes "total distributions payable" paid within one taxable year of the distributee, to which subdivision (i) of this subparagraph applies.

(4)(i) Notwithstanding the rule stated in subparagraph (1) of this paragraph and illustrated in subparagraph (2) of this paragraph, the exclusion from gross income under section 101(b) also applies (but only to the extent provided in the next sentence) to amounts with respect to which the deceased employee possessed, immediately before his death, a nonforfeitable right to receive the amounts while living—

(a) If such amounts are paid under an annuity contract purchased by an employer which is an organization referred to in section 170(b)(1)(A)(ii) or (vi) or which is a religious organization (other than a trust) and which is exempt from tax under section 501(a);

(b) If such amounts are paid as part of a "total payment" with respect to the deceased employee; and

(c) If such "total payment" is paid in full within one taxable year of the payee beginning after December 31, 1957.

However, the amount that is excludable under section 101(b) by reason of this subparagraph shall not exceed an amount which bears the same ratio to the amount which would be includible in the payee's gross income if it were not for the second sentence of section 101(b)(2)(B) and this subparagraph, as the amount contributed by the employer for the annuity contract that was excludable from the deceased employee's gross income under paragraph (b) of §1.403(b)-1 bears to the total amount contributed by the employer for the annuity contract. See section 101(b)(2)(B)(iii). For purposes of this subparagraph, a "total payment" means a payment of the balance to the credit of an employee with respect to all "section 403(b) annuities" purchased by the employer which becomes payable to the payee by reason of the employee's death, either before or after separation from the service. An annuity contract will be regarded as a "section 403(b) annuity" if any amount contributed (or considered as contributed under paragraph (b)(2) of §1.403(b)-1) by the employer for such contract was excludable from the employee's gross income under paragraph (b) of §1.403(b)-1. Under this definition, therefore, an annuity contract may be regarded as a "section 403(b) annuity" even though some of the employer's contributions for the contract were not excludable from the employee's gross income under paragraph (b) of §1.403(b)-1 because, for example, the employer was not an exempt organization when such contributions were paid. For purposes of computing the ratio described in this subdivision in such a case, the total amount contributed by the employer for the contract includes the amounts contributed by the employer when it was not an exempt organization.

(ii) This subparagraph does not relate to any amounts with respect to which the deceased employee did not possess, immediately before his death, a nonforfeitable right to receive the amounts while living. Such amounts are excludable under the provisions of section 101(b) without regard to section 101(b)(2)(B) and this subparagraph. Thus, if a "total payment" received by a beneficiary of a deceased employee under an annuity contract purchased by an organization described in subdivision (i)(a) of this subparagraph consists both of amounts with respect to which the deceased employee possessed, immediately before his death, a nonforfeitable right to receive the amounts while living and of amounts with respect to which the deceased employee did not possess such a nonforfeitable right, only those amounts with respect to which the deceased employee possessed such a nonforfeitable right are amounts to which this subparagraph applies. Therefore, for purposes of computing the ratio described in subdivision (i) of this subparagraph in such a case, there shall be taken into account only the employer contributions attributable to those amounts with respect to which the deceased employee possessed, immediately before his death, a nonforfeitable right to receive the amounts while living. See example (e) of subdivision (v) of this subparagraph. In no event, however, may the total amount excludable under section 101(b) with respect to any employee exceed $5,000 (see paragraph (a)(3) of this section).

(iii)(a) In any case when the deceased employee's interest in the employer's contributions for an annuity contract was forfeitable at the time the contributions were made but, at a subsequent date prior to his death, such interest changed to a nonforfeitable interest, then, for purposes of computing the ratio described in subdivision (i) of this subparagraph, the cash surrender value of the contract on the date of the change (except to the extent attributable to employee contributions) shall be considered as the amount contributed by the employer for the contract. In such a case, if only part of the deceased employee's interest in the annuity changed from a forfeitable to a nonforfeitable interest, then only the corresponding part of the case surrender value of the contract on the date of the change shall be considered as the amount contributed by the employer for the contract. Similarly, if part of the deceased employee's interest in the annuity contract changed from a forfeitable to a nonforfeitable interest on a particular date and another part of his interest so changed on a subsequent date, it is necessary, in order to compute the amount contributed by the employer for the contract, to first determine (under the rules in the preceding sentence) the amount that is considered as the amount contributed by the employer with respect to each change, and then to add these amounts together. For purposes of computing the ratio described in subdivision (i) of this subparagraph in all of the above cases, the amount contributed by the employer that was excludable from the employee's gross income under paragraph (b) of §1.403(b)-1 is that amount which, under paragraph (b)(2) of such section, was considered as employer contributions and which, under such paragraph (b) of §1.403-1, was excludable from the deceased employee's gross income for the taxable year in which the change occurred.

(b) This subdivision (iii) may be illustrated by the following examples:

Example (1). X Organization contributed $4,000 toward the purchase of an annuity contract for A, an employee who died in 1970. At the time they were made, A's interest in such contributions was forfeitable. A made no contributions toward the purchase of the annuity contract. On January 1, 1960, A's entire interest in the annuity contract changed to a *nonforfeitable interest. At the time of such change, the cash surrender value of the contract was $5,000.* For purposes of the ratio described in subdivision (i) of this subparagraph, the total amount contributed by X Organization for the annuity contract is $5,000. If any part of such $5,000 was excludable under

paragraph (b) of §1.403(b)-1 from A's gross income for his taxable year in which the change occurred, the amount so excludable shall be considered as the amount contributed for the contract by the employer that was excludable from the employee's gross income under paragraph (b) of §1.403(b)-1.

Example (2). Assume the same facts as in example (1) except that only one-half of A's interest in the annuity contract changed to a nonforfeitable interest on January 1, 1960, and that no other part of his interest so changed during his lifetime. For purposes of the ratio described in subdivision (i) of this subparagraph, the total amount contributed by X Organization for the annuity contract is $2,500 (¹/₂ of the cash surrender value of the annuity contract on the date of the change). To the extent such $2,500 was, under paragraph (b) of §1.403(b)-1, excludable from A's gross income for the taxable year of the change, it is considered as the amount contributed by the employer that was excludable under paragraph (b) of §1.403(b)-1.

Example (3). Assume the same facts as in example (1) except that one-half of A's interest in the annuity contract changed to a nonforfeitable interest on January 1, 1960, and the other half of his interest changed to a nonforfeitable interest on January 1, 1965. On January 1, 1965, the cash surrender value of the annuity contract was $6,000. For purposes of the ratio described in subdivision (i) of this subparagraph, the total amount contributed by X organization for the annuity contract is $5,500 (*i.e.*, ¹/₂ × $5,000 plus ¹/₂ × $6,000). The amount contributed by the employer that was excludable from A's gross income under paragraph (b) of §1.403(b)-1 is an amount equal to the sum of the amount that was, under such paragraph, excludable from A's gross income for the taxable year during which the first change occurred and the amount that was, under such paragraph, excludable from A's gross income for the taxable year in which the second change occurred.

(iv) For purposes of this subparagraph, an annuity contract will be considered to have been purchased by an employer which is an organization referred to in section 170(b)(1)(A)(ii) or (vi) or which is a religious organization (other than a trust) and which is exempt from tax under section 501(a), if any of the contributions paid toward the purchase price of such contract by the employer were paid at a time when the employer was such an organization. Thus an annuity contract may be regarded as purchased by such an organization even though part of the organization's contributions for such annuity contract were paid at a time when the organization was not such an exempt organization.

(v) The application of this subparagraph may be illustrated by the following examples:

Example (1). The widow of A, a deceased employee, elects, under an annuity contract purchased for A by X Organization, to receive in a lump sum the present value of such annuity contract as of the date of A's death. Such present value is $6,000 and is received by the widow in a taxable year beginning after December 31, 1957. X Organization contributed $3,000 toward the purchase of the annuity contract and A contributed $2,000 toward such purchase. A's interest in X Organization's contributions was nonforfeitable at the time such contributions were made. Thus, just before his death, A's entire interest in the annuity contract was a nonforfeitable interest and, if he had retired at that time, he could have received the present value of $6,000. The whole amount of the $3,000 contributed by X Organization for the annuity contract was excludable from A's gross income under paragraph (b) of §1.403(b)-1. This annuity contract was the only annuity contract purchased by X Organization for A and was not purchased as part of a qualified plan. However, all the contributions paid by X Organization were paid at a time when X Organization was an organization referred to in section 170(b)(1)(A)(ii) and exempt from tax under section 501(a). The amount that A's widow may exclude from gross income (assuming no other death benefits) is computed in the following manner:

(a)	Amount includible in gross income without regard to second sentence of section 101(b)(2)(B) ($6,000 minus $2,000 contributed for contract by A)	$4,000
(b)	Total employer contributions for the contract . . .	$3,000
(c)	Amount of employer contributions for the contract that was excludable under paragraph (b) of §1.403(b)-1	$3,000
(d)	Percent of total employer contributions for the contract that were excludable under paragraph (b) of §1.403(b)-1 ((c) ÷ (b))	100%
(e)	Amount to which section 101(b) exclusion applies ((d) × (a))	$4,000

Example (2). The facts are the same as in example (1) except that only $2,000 of X Organization's contributions for the annuity contract was excludable from A's gross income under paragraph (b) of §1.403(b)-1 and that the remaining $1,000 was includible in A's gross income for the taxable years during which such amounts were contributed by X Organization. The amount that A's widow may exclude from gross income (assuming no other death benefits) is computed in the following manner:

(a)	Amount includible in gross income without regard to second sentence of section 101(b)(2)(B) ($6,000 minus $2,000 contributed for contract by A and $1,000 of X organization's contributions includible in A's gross income)	$3,000
(b)	Total employer contributions for the contract . . .	$3,000
(c)	Amount of employer contributions for the contract that was excludable under paragraph (b) of §1.403(b)-1	$2,000
(d)	Percent of total employer contributions for the contract that were excludable under paragraph (b) of §1.403(b)-1 ((c) ÷ (b))	67%
(e)	Amount to which section 101(b) exclusion applies ((d) × (a))	$2,000

Example (3). The widow of B, a deceased employee, elects, under an annuity contract purchased for B by Y Organization, to receive in a lump sum the present value of such annuity contract as of the date of B's death. Such present value is $6,000 and is received by the widow in a taxable year beginning after December 31, 1957. Y Organization contributed $4,000 toward the purchase of the contract; whereas B made no contributions toward the purchase of the contract. This annuity contract was the only annuity contract purchased by Y Organization for B and was not purchased as part of a "qualified" plan. However, all the contributions paid by Y Organization were paid at a time when it was an organization referred to in section 170(b)(1)(A)(ii) and exempt from tax under section 501(a). B's interest in Y Organization's contributions was, at the time they were paid, forfeitable. However, prior to his death, one-half of B's interest in the annuity contract changed from a forfeitable to a nonforfeitable interest. Therefore, just before his death, B could have obtained $3,000 under the annuity contract if he had retired at that time. On the date of the change, the cash surrender value of the annuity contract was $5,000. As a result of the change, $1,500 was, under paragraph (b) of §1.403(b)-1, excludable from B's gross income, and $600 was includible in his gross income for the taxable year in which the change occurred. Part of the value of the annuity contract on the date of the change was attributable to contributions made by Y Organization prior to January 1, 1958, and, consequently, was neither excludable from B's gross income under paragraph (b) of §1.403(b)-1 nor includible in B's gross income (see paragraph (b) of §1.403(d)-1). The amount that B's widow may exclude from gross income (assuming no other death benefits) is computed in the following manner:

(a)	Amount of "total payment" with respect to which A had a forfeitable right at time of death. (¹/₂ × $6,000)	$3,000
(b)	Amount includible in gross income without regard to second sentence of section 101(b)(2)(B) (¹/₂ × $6,000 less $600 includible in B's gross income for year when his rights changed to nonforfeitable rights)	$2,400
(c)	Total employer contributions for the contract (¹/₂ of cash surrender value of contract on date B's rights changed to nonforfeitable rights)	$2,500
(d)	Amount of employer contributions for the contract that was excludable under paragraph (b) of §1.403(b)-1	$1,500
(e)	Percent of total employer contributions for the contract that were excludable under paragraph (b) of §1.403(b)-1 ((d) ÷ (c))	60%
(f)	Amount to which section 101(b) exclusion applies by reason of the second sentence of section 101(b)(2)(B) ((e) × (b))	$1,440
(g)	Total amount to which section 101(b) exclusion applies ((a) + (f))	$4,440

(e) *Annuity payments.*—(1) Where death benefits are paid in the form of annuity payments, the following rules shall govern for purposes of the exclusion provided in section 101(b):

(i) The exclusion from gross income provided by section 101(b) does not apply to amounts, paid as an annuity, with respect to which the employee possessed, immediately before his death, a nonforfeitable right to receive the amounts while living, or to amounts paid as an annuity in lieu thereof. See paragraph (d) of this section.

(ii) Under section 101(b)(2)(C), no exclusion is allowable for amounts received by a surviving annuitant under a joint and survivor's annuity contract if the annuity starting date (as defined in section 72(c)(4) and paragraph (b) of §1.72-4) occurs before the death of the employee. If the annuity starting date occurs after the death of the employee, the joint and survivor's annuity contract shall be

treated as an annuity to which section 101(b)(2)(D) applies. See subdivision (iii) of this subparagraph.

(iii)(a) Subject to the other limitations stated in section 101(b) and in this section (see section 101(b)(2)(D)), the amount to which the exclusion of section 101(b) shall apply, with respect to "amounts received as an annuity" (as defined in paragraph (b) of §1.72-2), shall be the amount by which the present value of the annuity to be paid to the beneficiary, computed as of the date of the employee's death, exceeds the value (if any) of whichever of the following is the larger:

(1) Amounts contributed by the employee (determined in accordance with the provisions of section 72 and the regulations thereunder), or

(2) Amounts with respect to which the employee possessed, immediately before his death, a nonforfeitable right to receive the amounts while living, or amounts paid in lieu thereof (see paragraph (d) of this section).

(b) The present value of an annuity (immediately before the death of the employee), to the employee, or (immediately after the death of the employee), to his estate or beneficiary, shall be determined as follows:

(1) In the case of an annuity paid by an insurance company or by an organization (other than an insurance company) regularly engaged in issuing annuity contracts with an insurance company as the coinsurer or reinsurer of the obligations under the contract, by use of the discount interest rates and mortality tables used by the insurance company involved to determine the installment benefits; and

(2) In the case of an annuity issued after November 23, 1984, to which paragraph (e)(1)(ii)(b)(1) of this section is not applicable, by use of the appropriate tables in §20.2031-7 of this chapter (Estate Tax Regulations).

(iv) Any amount subject to section 101(b)(2)(D) which is excludable under section 101(b) (see subdivision (iii) of this subparagraph) shall, for purposes of section 72, be treated as additional consideration paid by the employee. See paragraph (d) of §1.72-8.

(v) Where more than one beneficiary, or more than one death benefit, is involved, the exclusion provided by section 101(b) shall be apportioned to the various beneficiaries and benefits in accordance with the proportion that the present value of each benefit bears to the total present value of all the benefits.

(2) The application of the principles of this paragraph may be illustrated by the following examples:

Example (1). (i) A died on January 1, 1969. Under the plan of the X Corporation, W, who is the widow of employee A, and who is 55 years old at the time of A's death, is entitled to an immediate annuity of $2,000 per year during her life and C, the minor child of A, is entitled to receive $1,000 per year for 15 years. A made no contributions under the plan and died while still employed by the X Corporation. At the time of A's death, the amount in his account is $18,000. Under the terms of the plan, this amount would have been distributable to him on account of voluntary termination of employment, but would not have been payable after his death except in the form of the annuities just described. This amount, accordingly, constitutes a nonforfeitable interest in lieu of which the annuities are paid. The exclusion does not apply, except to the extent that the present value of the annuities exceeds $18,000, whether or not the plan is "qualified", since the total of the amount in A's account will not be paid within one taxable year of the distributees. See subparagraph (1)(i) of this paragraph.

(ii) The computation of the exclusion applicable to the interests of W and C (assuming that the payments will not be made by an insurance company or some other organization regularly engaged in issuing annuity contracts) is, by application of the tables in §20.2031-7 of this chapter (Estate Tax Regulations) [Reg. §20.2031-7 of this chapter is reproduced at ¶2391.05 and Reg. §20.2031-10 is reproduced at ¶2391.10.—CCH.], as follows: The present value of W's interest is $26,243.60, determined by multiplying the annual payment of $2,000 by 13.1218 (the factor for a person aged 55); the present value of C's interest is $11,517.40, determined by multiplying the yearly payment of $1,000 by 11.5174 (the factor in Table II for payments for a term certain of 15 years). The present value of both annuities is $37,761 and (assuming no other death benefits are involved), the total amount excludable is $5,000, because the total present value of the annuities exceeds the employee's nonforfeitable interest by more than $5,000 ($37,761 minus $18,000 equal $19,761). The exclusion allocable to W's interest is $26,243.60/$37,761 times $5,000 or $3,474.96; the exclusion allocable to C's interest is $11,517.40/$37,761 times $5,000, or $1,525.04. That portion of the death benefit exclusion as so determined for each beneficiary is to be treated as consideration paid by the employee for purposes of section 72.

Example (2). The facts are the same as in example (1), except that the nonforfeitable interest of A, at the time of his death, amounted to $33,761. Since the present value of both annuities ($37,761) exceeds the value of such nonforfeitable interest by only $4,000, the latter amount is the total amount excludable from the gross income of the beneficiaries. This $4,000 exclusion is to be divided in the same proportions as those indicated in example (1). Thus, the exclusion allocable to W's interest is $26,243.60/$37,761 times $4,000, or $2,779.97; and the exclusion allocable to the interest of C is $11,517.40/$37,761 times $4,000, or $1,220.03. That portion of the death benefit exclusion as so determined for each beneficiary is to be treated as consideration paid by the employee for purposes of section 72.

(f) *Distributions on behalf of a self-employed individual.*—(1) Under sections 401(c)(1) and 403(a)(3), certain self-employed individuals may be covered by a pension or profit-sharing plan described in section 401(a) and exempt under section 501(a) or under an annuity plan described in section 403(a). However, a payment pursuant to the provisions of any such plan by reason of the death of an individual who participated in such a plan as a self-employed individual immediately before his retirement or death to the beneficiary or estate of such individual does not qualify for the exclusion provided by section 101(b).

(2) The application of this paragraph may be illustrated by the following examples:

Example (1). From 1950 to 1965, A was an employee of B, a sole proprietor. In 1963, B established a qualified pension plan covering A and all other persons who had been employed by B for more than 3 years. In 1965, A acquired from B a 40-percent interest in the capital and profits of the business. A continued to participate in the pension plan as a self-employed individual. In 1970, A died and his widow, in compliance with one of the provisions of the pension plan, elected to receive all of the benefits accrued to A prior to his death in a lump-sum distribution. As A participated in the plan as a self-employed individual immediately prior to his death, A's widow may not exclude any portion of such distribution from her gross income under section 101(b).

Example (2). A, an attorney, is employed by the X Company in their legal department. He is covered by the pension plan that X has established for its employees. Under the terms of A's contract of employment with X, A is permitted to carry on the private practice of law in his off-duty hours. A establishes his own pension plan with respect to his earnings from his private practice. On A's death, his widow elected to receive a lump-sum distribution with respect to any benefits accrued to A under both X's pension plan and A's own pension plan. To the extent that such payment otherwise complies with the requirements of section 101(b), up to $5,000 of the amount paid by X may be excluded from her gross income. No part of the distribution from A's own pension plan may be excluded from her gross income under section 101(b) because A participated in the plan as a self-employed individual immediately before his death. [Reg. §1.101-2.]

☐ [*T.D.* 6280, 12-16-57. *Amended by T.D.* 6722, 4-13-64, *T.D.* 6783, 12-23-64, *T.D.* 7043, 6-1-70, *T.D.* 7352, 4-9-75, *T.D.* 7428, 8-13-76, *T.D.* 7836, 9-23-82, *T.D.* 7955, 5-10-84 *and T.D.* 8540, 6-9-94.]

[Reg. §1.101-3]

§1.101-3. Interest payments.—(a) *Applicability of section 101(c).*—Section 101(c) provides that if any amount excluded from gross income by section 101(a) (relating to life insurance proceeds) or section 101(b) (relating to employees' death benefits) is held under an agreement to pay interest thereon, the interest payments shall be included in gross income. This provision applies to payments made (either by an insurer or by or on behalf of an employer) of interest earned on any amount so excluded from gross income which is held without substantial diminution of the principal amount during the period when such interest payments are being made or credited to the beneficiaries or estate of the insured or the employee. For example, if a monthly payment is $100, of which $99 represents interest and $1 represents diminution of the principal amount, the principal amount shall be considered held under an agreement to pay interest thereon and the interest payment shall be included in the gross income of the recipient. Section 101(c) applies whether the election to have an amount held under an agreement to pay interest thereon is made by the insured or employee or by his beneficiaries or estate, and whether or not an interest rate is explicitly stated in the agreement. Section 101(d), relating to the payment of life insurance proceeds at a date later than death, shall not apply to any amount to which section 101(c) applies. See section 101(d)(4). However, both section 101(c) and section 101(d) may apply to payments received under a single life insurance contract. For provisions relating to the application of this rule to payments received under a permanent life insurance policy with a family income rider attached, see paragraph (h) of §1.101-4.

(b) *Determinations of "present value".*—For the purpose of determining whether section 101(c) or section 101(d) applies, the present value

(at the time of the insured's death) of any amount which is to be paid at a date later than death shall be determined by the use of the interest rate and mortality tables used by the insurer in determining the size of the payments to be made. [Reg. §1.101-3.]

☐ [*T.D.* 6280, 12-16-57. *Amended by T.D.* 6577, 10-27-61.]

[Reg. §1.101-4]

§1.101-4. Payment of life insurance proceeds at a date later than death.—(a) *In general.*—(1)(i) Section 101(d) states the provisions governing the exclusion from gross income of amounts (other than those to which section 101(c) applies) received under a life insurance contract and paid by reason of the death of the insured which are paid to a beneficiary on a date or dates later than the death of the insured. However, if the amounts payable as proceeds of life insurance to which section 101(a)(1) applies cannot in any event exceed the amount payable at the time of the insured's death, such amounts are fully excludable from the gross income of the recipient (or recipients) without regard to the actual time of payment and no further determination need be made under this section. Section 101(d)(1)(A) provides an exclusion from gross income of any amount determined by a proration, under applicable regulations, of "an amount held by an insurer with respect to any beneficiary". The quoted phrase is defined in section 101(d)(2). For the regulations governing the method of computation of this proration, see paragraphs (c) through (f) of this section. The prorated amounts are to be excluded from the gross income of the beneficiary regardless of the taxable year in which they are actually received (see example (2) of subparagraph (2) of this paragraph).

(ii) Section 101(d)(1)(B) provides an additional exclusion where life insurance proceeds are paid to the surviving spouse of an insured. For purposes of this exclusion, the term "surviving spouse" means the spouse of the insured as of the date of death, including a spouse legally separated, but not under a decree of absolute divorce (section 101(d)(3)). To the extent that the total payments, under one or more agreements, made in excess of the amounts determined by proration under section 101(d)(1)(A) do not exceed $1,000 in the taxable year of receipt, they shall be excluded from the gross income of the surviving spouse (whether or not payment of any part of such amounts is guaranteed by the insurer). Amounts excludable under section 101(d)(1)(B) are not "prorated" amounts.

(2) The principles of this paragraph may be illustrated by the following examples:

Example (1). A surviving spouse elects to receive all of the life insurance proceeds with respect to one insured, amounting to $150,000, in ten annual installments of $16,500 each, based on a certain guaranteed interest rate. The prorated amount is $15,000 ($150,000 ÷ 10). As the second payment, the insurer pays $17,850, which exceeds the guaranteed payment by $1,350 as the result of earnings of the insurer in excess of those required to pay the guaranteed installments. The surviving spouse shall include $1,850 in gross income and exclude $16,000—determined in the following manner:

Fixed payment (including guaranteed interest)	$16,500
Excess interest	1,350
Total payment	17,850
Prorated amount	15,000
Excess over prorated amount	2,850
Annual excess over prorated amount excludable under section 101(d)(1)(B)	$1,000
Amount includible in gross income	1,850

Example (2). Assume the same facts as in example (1), except that the third and fourth annual installments, totalling $33,000 (2 × $16,500), are received in a single subsequent taxable year of the surviving spouse. The prorated amount of $15,000 of each annual installment, totalling $30,000, shall be excluded even though the spouse receives more than one annual installment in the single subsequent taxable year. However, the surviving spouse is entitled to only one exclusion of $1,000 under section 101(d)(1)(B) for each taxable year of receipt. The surviving spouse shall include $2,000 in her gross income for the taxable year with respect to the above installment payments ($33,000 less the sum of $30,000 plus $1,000).

Example (3). Assume the same facts as in example (1), except that the surviving spouse dies before receiving all ten annual installments and the remaining installments are paid to her estate or beneficiary. In such a case, $15,000 of each installment would continue to be excludable from the gross income of the recipient, but any amounts received in excess thereof would be fully includible.

(b) *Amount held by an insurer.*—(1) For the purpose of the proration referred to in section 101(d)(1), an "amount held by an insurer with respect to any beneficiary" means an amount equal to the present value to such beneficiary (as of the date of death of the insured) of an agreement by the insurer under a life insurance policy (whether as an option or otherwise) to pay such beneficiary an amount or amounts at a date or dates later than the death of the insured (section 101(d)(2)). The present value of such agreement is to be computed as if the agreement under the life insurance policy had been entered into on the date of death of the insured, except that such value shall be determined by the use of the mortality table and interest rate used by the insurer in calculating payments to be made to the beneficiary under such agreement. Where an insurance policy provides an option for the payment of a specific amount upon the death of the insured in full discharge of the contract, such lump sum is the amount held by the insurer with respect to all beneficiaries (or their beneficiaries) under the contract. See, however, paragraph (e) of this section.

(2) In the case of two or more beneficiaries, the "amount held by the insurer" with respect to each beneficiary depends on the relationship of the different benefits payable to such beneficiaries. Where the amounts payable to two or more beneficiaries are independent of each other, the "amount held by the insurer with respect to each beneficiary" shall be determined and prorated over the periods involved independently. Thus, if a certain amount per month is to be paid to A for his life, and, concurrently, another amount per month is to be paid to B for his life, the "amount held by the insurer" shall be determined and prorated for both A and B independently, but the aggregate shall not exceed the total present value of such payments to both. On the other hand, if the obligation to pay B was contingent on his surviving A, the "amount held by the insurer" shall be considered an amount held with respect to both beneficiaries simultaneously. Furthermore, it is immaterial whether B is a named beneficiary or merely the ultimate recipient of payments for a term of years. For the special rules governing the computation of the proration of the "amount held by an insurer" in determining amounts excludable under the provisions of section 101(d), see paragraphs (c) to (f), inclusive, of this section.

(3) Notwithstanding any other provision of this section, if the policy was transferred for a valuable consideration, the total "amount held by an insurer" cannot exceed the sum of the consideration paid plus any premiums or other consideration paid subsequent to the transfer if the provisions of section 101(a)(2) and paragraph (b) of §1.101-1 limit the excludability of the proceeds to such total.

(c) *Treatment of payments for life to a sole beneficiary.*—If the contract provides for the payment of a specified lump sum, but, pursuant to an agreement between the beneficiary and the insurer, payments are to be made during the life of the beneficiary in lieu of such lump sum, the lump sum shall be divided by the life expectancy of the beneficiary determined in accordance with the mortality table used by the insurer in determining the benefits to be paid. Moreover, if payments are to be made to the estate or beneficiary of the primary beneficiary in the event that the primary beneficiary dies before receiving a certain number of payments or a specified total amount, such lump sum shall be reduced by the present value (at the time of the insured's death) of amounts which may be paid by reason of the guarantee, in accordance with the provisions of paragraph (e) of this section, before making this calculation. To the extent that payments received in each taxable year do not exceed the amount found from the above calculation, they are "prorated amounts" of the "amount held by an insurer" and are excludable from the gross income of the beneficiary without regard to whether he lives beyond the life expectancy used in making the calculation. If the contract in question does not provide for the payment of a specific lump sum upon the death of the insured as one of the alternative methods of payment, the present value (at the time of the death of the insured) of the payments to be made the beneficiary, determined in accordance with the interest rate and mortality table used by the insurer in determining the benefits to be paid, shall be used in the above calculation in lieu of a lump sum.

(d) *Treatment of payments to two or more beneficiaries.*—(1) *Unrelated payments.*—If payments are to be made to two or more beneficiaries, but the payments to be made to each are to be made without regard to whether or not payments are made or continue to be made to the other beneficiaries, the present value (at the time of the insured's death) of such payments to each beneficiary shall be determined independently for each such beneficiary. The present value so determined shall then be divided by the term for which the payments are to be made. If the payments are to be made for the life of the beneficiary, the divisor shall be the life expectancy of the beneficiary. To the extent that payments received by a beneficiary do not exceed the amount found from the above calculation, they are "prorated amounts" of the "amount held by an insurer" with respect to such beneficiary and are excludable from the gross income of the beneficiary without regard to whether he lives beyond any life expectancy used in making the calculation. For the purpose of the calculation described above, both the "present value" of the payments to be

made periodically and the "life expectancy" of a beneficiary shall be determined in accordance with the interest rate and mortality table used by the insurer in determining the benefits to be paid. If payments are to be made to the estate or beneficiary of a primary beneficiary in the event that such beneficiary dies before receiving a certain number of payments or a specified total amount, the "present value" of payments to such beneficiary shall not include the present value (at the time of the insured's death) of amounts which may be paid by reason of such a guarantee. See paragraph (e) of this section.

(2) *Related payments.*—If payments to be made to two or more beneficiaries are in the nature of a joint and survivor annuity (as described in paragraph (b) of §1.72-5), the present value (at the time of the insured's death) of the payments to be made to all such beneficiaries shall be divided by the life expectancy of such beneficiaries as a group. To the extent that the payments received by a beneficiary do not exceed the amount found from the above calculation, they are "prorated amounts" of the "amount held by an insurer" with respect to such beneficiary and are excludable from the gross income of the beneficiary without regard to whether all the beneficiaries involved live beyond the life expectancy used in making the calculation. For the purpose of the calculation described above, both the "present value" of the payments to be made periodically and the "life expectancy" of all the beneficiaries as a group shall be determined in accordance with the interest rate and mortality table used by the insurer in determining the benefits to be paid. If the contract provides that certain payments are to be made in the event that all the beneficiaries of the group die before a specified number of payments or a specified total amount is received by them, the present value of payments to be made to the group shall not include the present value (at the time of the insured's death) of amounts which may be paid by reason of such a guarantee. See paragraph (e) of this section.

(3) *Payments to secondary beneficiaries.*—Payments made by reason of the death of a beneficiary (or beneficiaries) under a contract providing that such payments shall be made in the event that the beneficiary (or beneficiaries) die before receiving a specified number of payments or a specified total amount shall be excluded from the gross income of the recipient to the extent that such payments are made solely by reason of such guarantee.

(e) *Treatment of present value of guaranteed payments.*—In the case of payments which are to be made for a life or lives under a contract providing that further amounts shall be paid upon the death of the primary beneficiary (or beneficiaries) in the event that such beneficiary (or beneficiaries) die before receiving a specified number of payments or a specified total amount, the present value (at the time of the insured's death) of all payments to be made under the contract shall not include, for purposes of prorating the amount held by the insurer, the present value of the payments which may be made to the estate or beneficiary of the primary beneficiary. In such a case, any lump sum amount used to measure the value of the amount held by an insurer with respect to the primary beneficiary must be reduced by the value at the time of the insured's death of any amounts which may be paid by reason of the guarantee provided for a secondary beneficiary or the estate of the primary beneficiary before prorating such lump sum over the life or lives of the primary beneficiaries. Such present value (of the guaranteed payment) shall be determined by the use of the interest rate and mortality tables used by the insurer in determining the benefits to be paid.

(f) *Treatment of payments not paid periodically.*—Payments made to beneficiaries other than periodically shall be included in the gross income of the recipients, but only to the extent that they exceed amounts payable at the time of the death of the insured to each such beneficiary or, where no such amounts are specified, the present value of such payments at that time.

(g) *Examples.*—The principles of this section may be illustrated by the following examples:

Example (1). A life insurance policy provides for the payment of $20,000 in a lump sum to the beneficiary at the death of the insured. Upon the death of the insured, the beneficiary elects an option to leave the proceeds with the company for five years and then receive payment of $24,000, having no claim of right to any part of such sum before the entire five years have passed. Upon the payment of the larger sum, $24,000, the beneficiary shall include $4,000 in gross income and exclude $20,000 therefrom. If it is assumed that the same insurer has determined the benefits to be paid, the same result would obtain if no lump sum amount were provided for at the death of the insured and the beneficiary were to be paid $24,000 five years later. In neither of these cases would the surviving spouse be able to exclude any additional amount from gross income since both cases involve an amount held by an insurer under an agreement to pay interest thereon to which section 101(c) applies, rather than an amount to be paid periodically after the death of the insured to which section 101(d) applies.

Example (2). A life insurance policy provides that $1,200 per year shall be paid the sole beneficiary (other than a surviving spouse) until a fund of $20,000 and interest which accrues on the remaining balance is exhausted. A guaranteed rate of interest is specified, but excess interest may be credited according to the earnings of the insurer. Assuming that the fund will be exhausted in 20 years if only the guaranteed interest is actually credited, the beneficiary shall exclude $1,000 of each installment received ($20,000 divided by 20) and any installments received, whether by the beneficiary or his estate or beneficiary, in excess of 20 shall be fully included in the gross income of the recipient. If, instead, the excess interest were to be paid each year, any portion of each installment representing an excess over $1,000 would be fully includible in the recipient's gross income. Thus, if an installment of $1,350 were received, $350 of it would be included in gross income.

Example (3). Assume that the sole life insurance policy of a decedent provides only for the payment of $5,000 per year for the life of his surviving spouse, beginning with the insured's death. If the present value of the proceeds, determined by reference to the interest rate and the mortality table used by the insurance company, is $60,000, and such beneficiary's life expectancy is 20 years, $3,000 of each $5,000 payment ($60,000 divided by 20) is excludable as the prorated portion of the "amount held by an insurer". For each taxable year in which a payment is made, an additional $1,000 is excludable from the gross income of the surviving spouse. Hence, if she receives only one $5,000 payment in her taxable year, only $1,000 is includible in her gross income in that year with respect to such payment ($5,000 less the total amount excludable, $4,000). Assuming that the policy also provides for payments of $2,000 per year for 10 years to the daughter of the insured, the present value of the payments to the daughter is to be computed separately for the purpose of determining the excludable portion of each payment to her. Assuming that such present value is $15,000, $1,500 of each payment of $2,000 received by the daughter is excludable from her gross income ($15,000 divided by 10). The remaining $500 shall be included in the gross income of the daughter.

Example (4). Beneficiaries A and B, neither of whom is the surviving spouse of the insured, are each to receive annual payments of $1,800 for each of their respective lives upon the death of the insured. The contract does not provide for payments to be made in any other manner. Assuming that the present value of the payments to be made to A, whose life expectancy according to the insurer's mortality table is 30 years, is $36,000, A shall exclude $1,200 of each payment received ($36,000 divided by 30). Assuming that the present value of the payments to be made to B, whose life expectancy according to the insurer's mortality table is 20 years, is $27,000, B shall exclude $1,350 of each payment received ($27,000 divided by 20).

Example (5). A life insurance policy provides for the payment of $76,500 in a lump sum to the beneficiary, A, at the death of the insured. Upon the insured's death, however, A selects an option for the payment of $2,000 per year for her life and for the same amount to be paid after her death to B, her daughter, for her life. Assuming that since A is 51 years of age and her daughter is 28 years of age, the insurer determined the amount of the payments by reference to a mortality table under which the life expectancy for the lives of both A and B, joint and survivor, is 51 years, $1,500 of each $2,000 payment to either A or B ($76,500 divided by 51, or $1,500) shall be excluded from the gross income of the recipient. However, if A is the surviving spouse of the insured and no other contracts of insurance whose proceeds are to be paid to her at a date later than death are involved, A shall exclude the entire payment of $2,000 in any taxable year in which she receives but one such payment because of the additional exclusion under section 101(d)(1)(B).

Example (6). Beneficiaries A and B, neither of whom is the surviving spouse of the insured, are each to receive annual payments of $1,800 for each of their respective lives upon the death of the insured, but after the death of either, the survivor is to receive the payments formerly made to the deceased beneficiary until the survivor dies. Assuming that the life expectancy, joint and survivor, of A and B in accordance with the mortality table used by the insurer is 32 years and assuming that the total present value of the benefits to both (determined in accordance with the interest rate used by the insurer), is $80,000. A and B shall each exclude $1,250 of each installment of $1,800 ($80,000 divided by the life expectancy, 32, multiplied by the fraction of the annual payment payable to each, one-half) until the death of either. Thereafter, the survivor shall exclude $2,500 of each installment of $3,600 ($80,000 divided by 32).

Example (7). A life insurance policy provides for the payment of $75,000 in a lump sum to the beneficiary, A, at the death of the insured. A, upon the insured's death, however, selects an option for the payment of $4,000 per year for life, with a guarantee that any part of the $75,000 lump sum not paid to A before his death shall be paid to B (or his estate), A's beneficiary. Assuming that, under the criteria used by the insurer in determining the benefits to be paid, the present value of the guaranteed amount to B is $13,500 and that A's life expectancy is 25 years, the lump sum shall be reduced by the present value of the guarantee to B ($75,000 less $13,500 or $61,500) and divided by A's life expectancy ($61,500 divided by 25, or $2,460). Hence, $2,460 of each $4,000 payment is excludable from A's gross income. If A is the surviving spouse of the insured and no other contracts of insurance whose proceeds are to be paid to her at a date later than death are involved, A shall exclude $3,460 of each $4,000 payment from gross income in any taxable year in which but one such payment is received. Under these facts, if any amount is paid to B by reason of the fact that A dies before receiving a total of $75,000, the residue of the lump sum paid to B shall be excluded from B's gross income since it is wholly in lieu of the present value of such guarantee plus the present value of the payments to be made to the first beneficiary, and is therefore entirely an "amount held by an insurer" paid at a date later than death (see paragraph (d)(3) of this section).

Example (8). Assume that an insurance policy does not provide for the payment of a lump sum, but provides for the payment of $1,200 per year for a beneficiary's life upon the death of the insured, and also provides that if ten payments are not made to the beneficiary before death a secondary beneficiary (whether named by the insured or by the first beneficiary) shall receive the remainder of the ten payments in similar installments. If, according to the criteria used by the insurance company in determining the benefits, the present value of the payments to the first beneficiary is $12,000 and the life expectancy of such beneficiary is 15 years, $800 of each payment received by the first beneficiary is excludable from gross income. Assuming that the same figures obtain even though the payments are to be made at the rate of $100 per month, the yearly exclusion remains the same unless more or less than twelve months' installments are received by the beneficiary in a particular taxable year. In such a case two-thirds of the total received in the particular taxable year with respect to such beneficiary shall be excluded from gross income. Under either of the above alternatives, any amount received by the second beneficiary by reason of the guarantee of ten payments is fully excludable from the beneficiary's gross income since it is wholly in lieu of the present value of such guarantee plus the present value of the payments to be made to the first beneficiary and is therefore entirely an "amount held by an insurer" paid at a date later than death (see paragraph (d)(3) of this section).

(h) *Applicability of both section 101(c) and 101(d) to payments under a single life insurance contract.*—(1) *In general.*—Section 101(d) shall not apply to interest payments on any amount held by an insurer under an agreement to pay interest thereon (see sections 101(c) and 101(d)(4) and §1.101-3). On the other hand, both section 101(c) and section 101(d) may be applicable to payments received under a single life insurance contract, if such payments consist both of interest on an amount held by an insurer under an agreement to pay interest thereon and of amounts held by the insurer and paid on a date or dates later than the death of the insured. One instance when both section 101(c) and section 101(d) may be applicable to payments received under a single life insurance contract is in the case of a permanent life insurance policy with a family income rider attached. A typical family income rider is one which provides additional term insurance coverage for a specified number of years from the register date of the basic policy. Under the policy with such a rider, ith B) nsured dies at any time during the term period, the beneficiary is entitled to receive (i) monthly payments of a specified amount commencing as of the date of death and continuing for the balance of the term period, and (ii) a lump sum payment of the proceeds under the basic policy to be paid at the end of the term period. If the insured dies after the expiration of the term period, the beneficiary receives only the proceeds under the basic policy. If the insured dies before the expiration of the term period, part of each monthly payment received by the beneficiary during the term period consists of interest on the proceeds of the basic policy (such proceeds being retained by the insurer until the end of the term period). The remaining part consists of an installment (principal plus interest) of the proceeds of the term insurance purchased under the family income rider. The amount of term insurance which is provided under the family income rider is, therefore, that amount which, at the date of the insured's death, will provide proceeds sufficient to fund such remaining part of each monthly payment. Since the proceeds under the basic policy are held by the insurer until the end of the term period, that portion of each monthly payment which consists of interest on such proceeds is interest on an amount held by an insurer under an agreement to pay interest thereon and is includible in gross income under section 101(c). On the other hand, since the remaining portion of each monthly payment consists of an installment payment (principal plus interest) of the proceeds of the term insurance, it is a payment of an amount held by the insurer and paid on a date later than the death of the insured to which section 101(d) and this section applies (including the $1,000 exclusion allowed the surviving spouse under section 101(d)(1)(B)). The proceeds of the basic policy, when received in a lump sum at the end of the term period, are excludable from gross income under section 101(a).

(2) *Example of tax treatment of amounts received under a family income rider.*—The following example illustrates the application of the principles contained in subparagraph (1) of this paragraph to payments received under a permanent life insurance policy with a family income rider attached:

Example. The sole life insurance policy of the insured provides for the payment of $100,000 to the beneficiary (the insured's spouse) on his death. In addition, there is attached to the policy a family income rider which provides that, if the insured dies before the 20th anniversary of the basic policy, the beneficiary shall receive (i)

monthly payments of $1,000 commencing on the date of the insured's death and ending with the payment prior to the 20th anniversary of the basic policy, and (ii) a single payment of $100,000 payable on the 20th anniversary of the basic policy. On the date of the insured's death, the beneficiary (surviving spouse of the insured) is entitled to 36 monthly payments of $1,000 and to the single payment of $100,000 on the 20th anniversary of the basic policy. The value of the proceeds of the term insurance at the date of the insured's death is $28,409.00 (the present value of the portion of the monthly payments to which section 101(d) applies computed on the basis that the interest rate used by the insurer in determining the benefits to be paid under the contract is $2^1/4$ percent). The amount of each monthly payment of $1,000 which is includible in the beneficiary's gross income is determined in the following manner:

(a)	Total amount of monthly payment	$1,000.00
(b)	Amount includible in gross income under section 101(c) as interest on the $100,000 proceeds under the basic policy held by the insurer until 20th anniversary of the basic policy (computed on the basis that the interest rate used by the insurer in determining the benefits to be paid under the contract is $2^1/4$ percent)	185.00
(c)	Amount to which section 101(d) applies ((a) minus (b))	815.00
(d)	Amount excludable from gross income under section 101(d) ($28,409 ÷ 36)	789.14
(e)	Amount includible in gross income under section 101(d) without taking into account the $1,000 exclusion allowed the beneficiary as the surviving spouse ((c) minus (d))	25.86

The beneficiary, as the surviving spouse of the insured, is entitled to exclude the amounts otherwise includible in gross income under section 101(d) (item (e)) to the extent such amounts do not exceed $1,000 in the taxable year of receipt. This exclusion is not applicable, however, with respect to the amount of each payment which is includible in gross income under section 101(c) (item (b)). In this example, therefore, the beneficiary must include $185 of each monthly payment in gross income (amount includible under section 101(c)), but may exclude the $25.86 which is otherwise includible under section 101(d). The payment of $100,000 which is payable to the beneficiary on the 20th anniversary of the basic policy will be entirely excludable from gross income under section 101(a).

(3) *Limitation on amount considered to be an "amount held by an insurer".*—See paragraph (b)(3) of this section for a limitation on the amount which shall be considered an "amount held by an insurer" in the case of proceeds of life insurance which are paid subsequent to the transfer of the policy for a valuable consideration.

(4) *Effective date.*—The provisions of this paragraph are applicable only with respect to amounts received during the taxable years beginning after October 28, 1961, irrespective of the date of the death of the insured. [Reg. § 1.101-4.]

□ [*T.D. 6280, 12-16-57. Amended by T.D. 6577, 10-27-61.*]

[Reg. § 1.101-5]

§1.101-5. [Reserved].

□ [*T.D. 6280, 12-16-57. Removed and reserved by T.D. 9849, 3-11-2019.*]

[Reg. § 1.101-6]

§1.101-6. Effective date.—(a) Except as otherwise provided in paragraph (h)(4) of § 1.101-4, the provisions of section 101 of the Internal Revenue Code of 1954 and §§ 1.101-1, 1.101-2, 1.101-3 and 1.101-4 are applicable only with respect to amounts received by reason of the death of an insured or an employee occurring after August 16, 1954. In the case of such amounts, these sections are applicable even though the receipt of such amounts occurred in a taxable year beginning before January 1, 1954, to which the Internal Revenue Code of 1939 applies.

(b) Notwithstanding paragraph (a) of this section, for purposes of determining whether a transfer of an interest in a life insurance contract is a reportable policy sale or a payment of death benefits is a payment of reportable death benefits subject to the reporting requirements of section 6050Y and §§ 1.6050Y-1 through 1.6050Y-4, § 1.101-1(b) through (g) apply to reportable policy sales made after December 31, 2018, and to reportable death benefits paid after December 31, 2018. For any other purpose, including for purposes of determining the amount of the proceeds of life insurance contracts payable by reason of death excluded from gross income under section 101, § 1.101-1(b) through (g) apply to amounts paid by reason of the death of the insured under a life insurance contract, or interest therein, transferred after October 31, 2019. However, under section 7805(b)(7), a taxpayer may apply the rules set forth in § 1.101-1(b) through (g) of the final regulations, in their entirety, with respect to all amounts paid by reason of the death of the insured under a life insurance contract, or interest therein, transferred after December 31, 2017, and on or before October 31, 2019. [Reg. § 1.101-6.]

□ [*T.D. 6280, 12-16-57. Amended by T.D. 6577, 10-27-61, T.D. 9849, 3-11-2019 and T.D. 9879, 10-25-2019.*]

[Reg. § 1.101-7]

§1.101-7. Mortality table used to determine exclusion for deferred payments of life insurance proceeds.—(a) *Mortality Table.*—Notwithstanding any provision of § 1.101-4 that otherwise would permit the use of a mortality table not described in this section, the mortality table set forth in § 1.72-7(c)(1) must be used to determine—

(1) The amount held by an insurer with respect to a beneficiary for purposes of section 101(d)(2) and § 1.101-4; and

(2) The period or periods with respect to which payments are to be made for purposes of section 101(d)(1) and § 1.101-4.

(b) *Examples.*—The principles of this section may be illustrated by the following examples:

Example (1). A life insurance policy provides only for the payment of $5,000 per year for the life of the beneficiary, A, beginning with the insured's death. If A is 59 years of age at the time of the insured's death, the period with respect to which the payments are to be made is 25 years. This period is determined by using the mortality table set forth in § 1.72-7(c)(1), and is shown in Table V of § 1.72-9 (which contains life expectancy tables determined using this mortality table). If the present value of the proceeds, determined by reference to the interest rate used by the insurance company and the mortality table set forth in § 1.72-7(c)(1), is $75,000, $3,000 of each $5,000 payment ($75,000 divided by 25) is excluded from the gross income of A.

Example (2). A life insurance policy provides for the payment of $82,500 in a lump sum to the beneficiary, A, at the death of the insured. Upon the insured's death, however, A selects an option for the payment of $2,000 per year for life and for the same amount to be paid after A's death to B for B's life. If A is 51 years of age and B is 28 years of age at the death of the insured, the period with respect to which the payments are to be made is 55 years. This period is determined by using the mortality table set forth in § 1.72-7(c)(1), and is shown in Table VI of § 1.72-9 (which contains life expectancy tables determined using this mortality table). Accordingly, $1,500 of each $2,000 payment ($82,500 divided by 55) is excluded from the gross income of the recipient.

(c) *Effective date.*—This section applies to amounts received with respect to deaths occurring after October 22, 1986, in taxable years ending after October 22, 1986. [Reg. § 1.101-7.]

□ [*T.D. 8161, 9-18-87. Amended by T.D. 8272, 11-17-89.*]

[Reg. § 1.102-1]

§1.102-1. Gifts and inheritances.—(a) *General rule.*—Property received as a gift, or received under a will or under statutes of descent and distribution, is not includible in gross income, although the income from such property is includible in gross income. An amount of principal paid under a marriage settlement is a gift. However, see section 71 and the regulations thereunder for rules relating to alimony or allowances paid upon divorce or separation. Section 102 does not apply to prizes and awards (see section 74 and § 1.74-1) nor to scholarships and fellowship grants (see section 117 and the regulations thereunder).

(b) *Income from gifts and inheritances.*—The income from any property received as a gift, or under a will or statute of descent and distribution shall not be excluded from gross income under paragraph (a) of this section.

(c) *Gifts and inheritances of income.*—If the gift, bequest, devise, or inheritance is of income from property, it shall not be excluded from gross income under paragraph (a) of this section. Section 102 provides a special rule for the treatment of certain gifts, bequests, devises, or inheritances which by their terms are to be paid, credited, or distributed at intervals. Except as provided in section 663(a)(1) and paragraph (d) of this section, to the extent any such gift, bequest, devise, or inheritance is paid, credited, or to be distributed out of income from property, it shall be considered a gift, bequest, devise, or inheritance of income from property. Section 102 provides the same treatment for amounts of income from property which is paid, credited, or to be distributed under a gift or bequest whether the gift or bequest is in terms of a right to payments at intervals (regardless of income) or is in terms of a right to income. To the extent the amounts in either case are paid, credited, or to be distributed at intervals out of income, they are not to be excluded under section 102 from the taxpayer's gross income.

(d) *Effect of subchapter J.*—Any amount required to be included in the gross income of a beneficiary under sections 652, 662, or 668 shall be treated for purposes of this section as a gift, bequest, devise, or inheritance of income from property. On the other hand, any amount excluded from the gross income of a beneficiary under section 663(a)(1) shall be treated for purposes of this section as property acquired by gift, bequest, devise, or inheritance.

(e) *Income taxed to grantor or assignor.*—Section 102 is not intended to tax a donee upon the same income which is taxed to the grantor of a trust or assignor of income under section 61 or sections 671 through 677, inclusive. [Reg. § 1.102-1.]

☐ [*T.D. 6220, 12-28-56.*]

»»→ *Caution: Code Sec. 103 has been amended to remove special exempt bond issue rules and provide similar rules in Code Secs. 141-150.*

[Reg. § 1.103-1]

§1.103-1. Interest upon obligations of a State, Territory, etc.—
(a) Interest upon obligations of a State, territory, a possession of the United States, the District of Columbia, or any political subdivision thereof (hereinafter collectively or individually referred to as "State or local governmental unit") is not includable in gross income except as provided under section 103(c) and (d) and the regulations thereunder.

(b) Obligations issued by or on behalf of any State or local governmental unit by constituted authorities empowered to issue such obligations are the obligations of such a unit. However, section 103(a)(1) and this section do not apply to industrial development bonds except as otherwise provided in section 103(c). See section 103(c) and § § 1.103-7 through 1.103-12 for the rules concerning interest paid on industrial development bonds. See section 103(d) for rules concerning interest paid on arbitrage bonds. Certificates issued by a political subdivision for public improvements (such as sewers, sidewalks, streets, etc.) which are evidence of special assessments against specific property, which assessments become a lien against such property and which the political subdivision is required to enforce, are, for purposes of this section, obligations of the political subdivision even though the obligations are to be satisfied out of special funds and not out of general funds or taxes. The term "political subdivision", for purposes of this section denotes any division of any State or local governmental unit which is a municipal corporation or which has been delegated the right to exercise part of the sovereign power of the unit. As thus defined, a political subdivision of any State or local governmental unit may or may not, for purposes of this section, include special assessment districts so created, such as road, water, sewer, gas, light, reclamation, drainage, irrigation, levee, school, harbor, port improvement, and similar districts and divisions of any such unit. [Reg. § 1.103-1.]

☐ [*T.D. 6220, 12-28-56. Amended by T.D. 7199, 7-31-72.*]

[Reg. § 5f.103-1]

§ 5f.103-1. Obligations issued after December 31, 1982, required to be in registered form (Temporary).—(a) *Registration; general rule.*—Interest on a registration-required obligation (as defined in paragraph (b) of this section) shall not be exempt from tax notwithstanding section 103(a) or any other provision of law, exclusive of any treaty obligation of the United States, unless the obligation is issued in registered form (as defined in paragraph (c) of this section).

(b) *Registration-required obligation.*—For purposes of this section, the term "registration-required obligation" means any obligation except any one of the following:

(1) An obligation not of a type offered to the public. The determination as to whether an obligation is not of a type offered to the public shall be based on whether similar obligations are in fact publicly offered or traded.

(2) An obligation that has a maturity at the date of issue of not more than 1 year.

(3) An obligation issued before January 1, 1983. An obligation first issued before January 1, 1983, shall not be considered to have been issued on or after that date merely as a result of the existence of a right on the part of the holder of such obligation to convert the obligation from registered form into bearer form, or as a result of the exercise of such a right.

(4) An obligation described in § 5f.163-1(c) (relating to certain *obligations issued to foreign persons*).

(c) *Registered form.*—(1) *General rule.*—An obligation issued after January 20, 1987, pursuant to a binding contract entered into after January 20, 1987, is in registered form if—

(i) The obligation is registered as to both principal and any stated interest with the issuer (or its agent) and transfer of the obligation may be effected only by surrender of the old instrument and either the reissuance by the issuer of the old instrument to the new holder or the issuance by the issuer of a new instrument to the new holder,

(ii) The right to the principal of, and stated interest on, the obligation may be transferred only through a book entry system maintained by the issuer (or its agent) (as described in paragraph (c)(2) of this section), or

(iii) The obligation is registered as to both principal and any stated interest with the issuer (or its agent) and may be transferred through both of the methods described in subdivisions (i) and (ii).

(2) *Special rule for registration of a book entry obligation.*—An obligation shall be considered transferable through a book entry system if the ownership of an interest in the obligation is required to be reflected in a book entry, whether or not physical securities are issued. A book entry is a record of ownership that identifies the owner of an interest in the obligation.

(d) *Effective date.*—The provisions of this section shall apply to obligations issued after December 31, 1982, unless issued on an exercise of a warrant for the conversion of a convertible obligation if such warrant or obligation was offered or sold outside the United States without registration under the Securities Act of 1933 and was issued before August 10, 1982.

(e) *Special rules.*—The following special rules apply to obligations issued after January 20, 1987, pursuant to a binding contract entered into after January 20, 1987.

(1) An obligation that is not in registered form under paragraph (c) of this section is considered to be in bearer form.

(2) An obligation is not considered to be in registered form as of a particular time if it can be transferred at that time or at any time until its maturity by any means not described in paragraph (c) of this section.

(3) An obligation that as of a particular time is not considered to be in registered form by virtue of subparagraph (2) of this paragraph (e) and that, during a period beginning with a later time and ending with the maturity of the obligation, can be transferred only by a means described in paragraph (c) of this section, is considered to be in registered form at all times during such period.

(f) *Examples.*—The application of this section may be illustrated by the following examples:

Example (1). Municipality X publicly offers its general debt obligations to United States persons. The obligations have a maturity at issue exceeding 1 year. The obligations are registration-required obligations under § 5f.103-1(b). When individual A buys an obligation, X issues an obligation in A's name evidencing A's ownership of the principal and interest under the obligation. A can transfer the obligation only by surrendering the obligation to X and by X issuing a new instrument to the new holder. The obligation is issued in registered form.

Example (2). Municipality Y issues a single obligation on January 4, 1983 to Bank M provided that (i) Bank M will not at any time transfer any interest in the obligation to any person unless the transfer is recorded on Municipality Y's records (except by means of a transfer permitted in (ii) of this example) and (ii) interests in the obligation that are sold by Bank M (and any persons who acquire interests from M) will be reflected in book entries. C, an individual, buys an interest in Y's obligation from Bank M. Bank M receives the interest or principal payments with respect to C's interest in the obligation as agent for C. Bank M records interests in the Municipality Y obligation as agent of Municipality Y. Any transfer of C's interest must be reflected in a book entry in accordance with Bank M's agreement

>>>→ *Caution: Code Sec. 103 has been amended to remove special exempt bond issue rules and provide similar rules in Code Secs. 141-150.*

with Municipality Y. Since C's interest can only be transferred through a book entry system maintained by the issuer (or its agent), the obligation is considered issued in registered form. Interest received by C is excludable from gross income under section 103(a).

Example (3). Municipality Z wishes to sell its debt obligations having a maturity in excess of 1 year. The obligations are sold to Bank N, O, and P, all of which are located in Municipality Z. By their terms the obligations are freely transferable, although each of the banks has stated that it acquired the obligations for purposes of investment and not for resale. Obligations similar to the obligations sold by Municipality Z are traded in the market for municipal securities. The obligations issued by Municipality Z are of a type offered to the public and are therefore registration-required under § 5f.103-1(b).

Example (4). Corporation A issues an obligation that is registered with the corporation as to both principal and any stated interest. Transfer may be effected by the surrender of the old instrument and either the reissuance by the issuer of the old instrument to the new holder or the issuance by the issuer of a new instrument to the new holder. The obligation can be converted into a form in which the right to the principal of, or stated interest on, the obligation may be effected by physical transfer of the obligation. Under § 5f.103-1(c) and (e), the obligation is not considered to be in registered form and is considered to be in bearer form.

Example (5). Corporation B issues its obligations in a public offering in bearer definitive form. Beginning at X months after the issuance of the obligations, a purchaser (either the original purchaser or a purchaser in the secondary market) may deliver the definitive bond in bearer form to the issuer in exchange for a registration receipt evidencing a book entry record of the ownership of the obligation. The issuer maintains the book entry system. The purchaser identified in the book entry as the owner of record has the right to receive a definitive bearer obligation at any time. Under § 5f.103-1(c) and (e), the obligation is not considered to be issued in registered form and is considered to be issued in bearer form. All purchasers of the obligation are considered to hold an obligation in bearer form.

Example (6). Corporation C issues obligations in bearer form. A foreign person purchases a definitive bearer obligation and then sells it to a United States person. At the time of the sale, the United States person delivers the bearer obligation to Corporation C and receives an obligation that is identical except that the obligation is registered as to both principal and any stated interest with the issuer or its agent and may be transferred at all times until its maturity only through a means described in § 5f.103-1(c). Under § 5f.103-1(e), the obligation is considered to be in registered form from the time it is delivered to Corporation C until its maturity.

(g) *Cross-references.*—See section 103A(j)(1), for the registration requirement of certain mortgage subsidy bonds issued after December 31, 1981, and § 6a.103A-1(a)(5) for the definition of registered form for such obligations issued after December 31, 1981, and on or before December 31, 1982. See also section 103(h) (requiring registration of certain energy bonds issued on or after October 18, 1979). [Temporary Reg. § 5f.103-1.]

☐ [*T.D. 7852,* 11-9-82. *Amended by T.D. 8111,* 12-16-86.]

[Reg. § 1.103-2]

§ 1.103-2. [Reserved].

☐ [*T.D. 6220,* 12-28-56. *Amended by T.D. 8129,* 3-10-87. *Removed and reserved by T.D. 9849,* 3-11-2019.]

[Reg. § 1.103-3]

§ 1.103-3. [Reserved].

☐ [*T.D. 6220,* 12-28-56. *Removed and reserved by T.D. 9849,* 3-11-2019.]

[Reg. § 1.103-4]

§ 1.103-4. [Reserved].

☐ [*T.D. 6220,* 12-28-56. *Removed and reserved by T.D. 9849,* 3-11-2019.]

[Reg. § 1.103-5]

§ 1.103-5. [Reserved].

☐ [*T.D. 6220,* 12-28-56. *Removed and reserved by T.D. 9849,* 3-11-2019.]

[Reg. § 1.103-6]

§ 1.103-6. [Reserved].

☐ [*T.D. 6220,* 12-28-56. *Removed and reserved by T.D. 9849,* 3-11-2019.]

[Reg. § 1.103-7]

§ 1.103-7. Industrial development bonds.—(a) *In general.*—Under section 103(c)(1) and this section, an industrial development bond issued after April 30, 1968, shall be treated as an obligation not described in section 103(a)(1) and § 1.103-1. Accordingly, interest paid on such a bond is includable in gross income unless the bond was issued by a State or local governmental unit to finance certain exempt facilities (see section 103(c)(4) and § 1.103-8), to finance an industrial park (see section 103(c)(5) and § 1.103-9), or as part of an exempt small issue (see section 103(c)(6) and § 1.103-10). For applicable rules when an industrial development bond is held by a substantial user (or a person related to a substantial user) of such an exempt facility, or an industrial park, or a facility financed with the proceeds of such an exempt small issue, see section 103(c)(7) and § 1.103-11. See also § 1.103-12 for the transitional provisions concerning the interest paid on certain industrial development bonds issued before January 1, 1969, and certain other industrial development bonds. Even if section 103(c) does not prevent a bond from being treated as an obligation described in section 103(a)(1) and § 1.103-1, such bond shall nevertheless be treated as an obligation which is not described in section 103(a)(1) and § 1.103-1 if under section 103(d) it is an arbitrage bond. For purposes of section 103(c), the term "issue" includes a single obligation such as a single note issued in connection with a bank loan as well as a series of notes or bonds.

(b) *Industrial development bonds.*—(1) *Definition.*—For purposes of this section, the term "industrial development bond" means any obligation—

(i) Which is issued as part of an issue all or a major portion of the proceeds of which are to be used directly or indirectly in any trade or business carried on by any person who is not an exempt person (as defined in subparagraph (2) of this paragraph), and

(ii) The payment of the principal or interest on which, under the terms of such obligation or any underlying arrangement (as described in subparagraph (4) of this paragraph), is in whole or in major part (*i.e.*, major portion)—

(a) Secured by any interest in property used or to be used in a trade or business,

(b) Secured by any interest in payments in respect of property used or to be used in a trade or business, or

(c) To be derived from payments in respect of property, or borrowed money, used or to be used in a trade or business.

See subparagraphs (3) and (4) of this paragraph for the trade or business test and the security interest test respectively, See § 1.103-8(a)(6) to determine the amount of proceeds of an issue for which the amount payable during each annual period over the term of the issue is less than the amount of interest accruing thereon in such period, *e.g.*, in the case of an issue sold by the issuer for less than its face amount.

(2) *Exempt person.*—The term "exempt person" means a governmental unit as defined in this subparagraph, or an organization which is described in section 501(c)(3) and this subparagraph and is exempt from taxation under section 501(a). For purposes of this subparagraph, the term "governmental unit" means a State or local governmental unit (as defined in § 1.103-1). For purposes of this subparagraph, the term "governmental unit" also includes the United States of America (or an agency or instrumentality of the United States of America), but only in the case of obligations (i) issued on or before August 3, 1972, or (ii) issued after August 3, 1972, with respect to which a bond resolution or any other official action was taken and in reliance on such action either (a) construction of such facility to be financed with such obligations commenced or (b) a binding contract was entered into, or an irrevocable bid was submitted, prior to August 3, 1972, or (iii) issued after August 3, 1972, with respect to a program approved by Congress prior to such date but only if (a) a portion of such program has been financed by obligations issued prior to such date, to which section 103(a) applied pursuant to a ruling issued by the Commissioner or his delegate prior to such date and (b) construction of one or more facilities comprising a part of such program commenced prior to such date. For purposes of this subparagraph, a tax-exempt organization is an exempt person only with respect to a trade or business it carries on which is not an unrelated trade or business. Whether a particular trade or business carried on by a tax-exempt organization is an unrelated trade or business is determined by applying the rules of section 513(a) (relating to general rule for unrelated trade or business) and the regulations thereunder to the tax-exempt organization without regard to whether the organization is an organization subject to the tax imposed by section 511 (relating to imposition of tax on unrelated business income of charitable, etc., organizations).

➤➤➤ *Caution: Code Sec. 103 has been amended to remove special exempt bond issue rules and provide similar rules in Code Secs. 141-150.*

(3) *Trade or business test.*—(i) The trade or business test relates to the use of the proceeds of a bond issue. The test is met if all or a major portion of the proceeds of a bond issue is used in a trade or business carried on by a nonexempt person. For example, if all or a major portion of the proceeds of a bond issue is to be loaned to one or more private business users, or is to be used to acquire, construct, or reconstruct facilities to be leased or sold to such private business users, and such proceeds or facilities are to be used in trades or businesses carried on by them, such proceeds are to be used in a trade or business carried on by persons who are not exempt persons, and the debt obligations comprising the bond issue satisfy the trade or business test. If, however, less than a major portion of the proceeds of an issue is to be loaned to nonexempt persons or is to be used to acquire or construct facilities which will be used in a trade or business carried on by a nonexempt person, the debt obligations will not be industrial development bonds. Also, when publicly-owned facilities which are intended for general public use, such as toll roads or bridges, are constructed with the proceeds of a bond issue and used by nonexempt persons in their trades or businesses on the same basis as other members of the public, such use does not constitute a use in the trade or business of a nonexempt person for purposes of the trade or business test.

(ii) In determining whether a debt obligation meets the trade or business test, the indirect, as well as the direct, use of the proceeds is to be taken into account. For example, the debt obligations comprising a bond issue do not fail to satisfy the trade or business test merely because the State or local governmental unit uses the proceeds to engage in a series of financing transactions for property to be used by private business users in trades or businesses carried on by them. Similarly, if such proceeds are to be used to construct facilities to be leased or sold to any nonexempt person for use in a trade or business it carries on, such proceeds are to be used in a trade or business carried on by a nonexempt person and the debt obligations comprising such issue satisfy the trade or business test. If such proceeds are to be used to construct facilities to be leased or sold to an exempt person who will, in turn, lease or sell the facilities to a nonexempt person for use in a trade or business, such proceeds are to be used in a trade or business carried on by a nonexempt person and the debt obligations comprising such issue satisfy the trade or business test. In addition, proceeds will be treated as being used in the trade or business of a nonexempt person in situations involving other arrangements, whether in a single transaction or in a series of transactions, whereby a nonexempt person uses property acquired with the proceeds of a bond issue in its trade or business.

(iii) The use of more than 25 percent of the proceeds of an issue of obligations in the trades or businesses of nonexempt persons will constitute the use of a major portion of such proceeds in such manner. In the case of the direct or indirect use of the proceeds of an issue of obligations or the direct or indirect use of a facility constructed, reconstructed, or acquired with such proceeds, the use by all nonexempt persons in their trades or businesses must be aggregated to determine whether the trade or business test is satisfied. If more than 25 percent of the proceeds of a bond issue is used in the trades or businesses of nonexempt persons, the trade or business test is satisfied. For special rules with respect to the acquisition of the output of facilities, see subparagraph (5) of this paragraph.

(4) *Security interest test.*—The security interest test relates to the nature of the security for, and the source of, the payment of either the principal or interest on a bond issue. The nature of the security for, and the source of, the payment may be determined from the terms of the bond indenture or on the basis of an underlying arrangement. An underlying arrangement to provide security for, or the source of, the payment of the principal or interest on an obligation may result from separate agreements between the parties or may be determined on the basis of all the facts and circumstances surrounding the issuance of the bonds. The property which is the security for, or the source of, the payment of either the principal or interest on a debt obligation need not be property acquired with bond proceeds. The security interest test is satisfied if, for example, a debt obligation is secured by unimproved land or investment securities used, directly or indirectly, in any trade or business carried on by any private business user. A pledge of the full faith and credit of a State or local governmental unit will not prevent a debt obligation from otherwise satisfying the security interest test. For example, if the payment of either the principal or interest on a bond issue is secured by both a pledge of the full faith and credit of a State or local governmental unit and any interest in property used or to be used in a trade or business, the bond issue satisfies the security interest test. For rules with respect to the acquisition of the output of facilities, see subparagraph (5) of this paragraph.

(5) *Trade or business test and security interest test with respect to certain output contracts.*—(i) The use by one or more nonexempt persons of a major portion of the subparagraph (5) output of facilities such as electric energy, gas, or water facilities constructed, reconstructed, or acquired with the proceeds of an issue satisfies the trade or business test and the security interest test if such use has the effect of transferring to nonexempt persons the benefits of ownership of such facilities, and the burdens of paying the debt service on governmental obligations used directly or indirectly to finance such facilities, so as to constitute the indirect use by them of a major portion of such proceeds. Such benefits and burdens are transferred and a major portion of the proceeds of an issue is used indirectly by the users of the subparagraph (5) output of such a facility which is owned and operated by an exempt person where—

(a)(1) One nonexempt person agrees pursuant to a contract to take, or to take or pay for, a major portion (more than 25 percent) of the subparagraph (5) output (within the meaning of subdivision (ii) of this subparagraph) of such a facility (whether or not conditional upon the production of such output) or (2) two or more nonexempt persons, each of which pays annually a guaranteed minimum payment exceeding 3 percent of the average annual debt service with respect to the obligations in question, agree, pursuant to contracts, to take, or to take or pay for, a major portion (more than 25 percent) of the subparagraph (5) output of such a facility (whether or not conditioned upon the production of such output), and

(b) Payment made or to be made with respect to such contract or contracts by such nonexempt person or persons exceeds a major part (more than 25 percent) of the total debt service with respect to such issue of obligations.

(ii) For purposes of this subparagraph—

(a) Where a contract described in subdivision (i) of this subparagraph may be extended by the issuer of obligations described therein, the term of the contract shall be considered to include the period for which such contract may be so extended.

(b) The subparagraph (5) output of a facility shall be determined by multiplying the number of units produced or to be produced by the facility in one year by the number of years in the contract term of the issue of obligations issued to provide such facility. The number of units produced or to be produced by a facility in one year shall be determined by reference to its nameplate capacity (or where there is no nameplate capacity, its maximum capacity) without any reduction for reserves or other unutilized capacity. The contract term of an issue begins on the date the output of a facility is first taken, pursuant to a take or a take or pay contract, by a nonexempt person and ends on the latest maturity date of any obligation of the issue (determined without regard to any optional redemption dates). If, however, on or before the date of issue of a prior issue of governmental obligations issued to provide a facility, the issuer makes a commitment in the bond indenture or related document to refinance such prior issue with one or more subsequent issues of governmental obligations, then the contract term of the issue shall be determined with regard to the latest redemption date of any obligation of the last such refinancing issue with respect to such facility (determined without regard to any optional redemption dates). Where it appears that the term of an issue (or the terms of 2 or more issues) is extended for purposes of extending the contract term of an issue and thereby increasing the subparagraph (5) output of the facility provided by such issue, the subparagraph (5) output of such facility shall be determined by the Commissioner without regard to the provisions of this subdivision (b).

(c) The total debt service with respect to an issue of obligations shall be the total dollar amount (excluding any penalties) payable with respect to such issue over its entire term. The entire term of an issue begins on its date of issue and ends on the latest maturity date of any obligation of the issue (determined without regard to any optional redemption dates). If, however, on or before the date of issue of a prior issue of governmental obligations the issuer makes a commitment of the bond indenture or related document to refinance such prior issue with one or more subsequent issues of governmental obligations, the entire term of the issue shall be determined with regard to the latest redemption date of any obligation of the last such refinancing issue (determined without regard to any optional redemption dates).

(d) Two or more nonexempt persons who are related persons (within the meaning of section 103(c)(6)(C)) shall be treated as one nonexempt person.

(c) *Examples.*—The application of the rules contained in section 103(c)(2) and (3) and paragraph (b) of this section are illustrated by the following examples:

Example (1). State A and corporation X enter into an arrangement under which A is to provide a factory which X will lease for 20 years. The arrangement provides (1) that A will issue $10 million of bonds, (2) that the proceeds of the bond issue will be used to purchase land and to construct and equip a factory in accordance with X's specifica-

>>>→ *Caution: Code Sec. 103 has been amended to remove special exempt bond issue rules and provide similar rules in Code Secs. 141-150.*

tions, (3) that X will rent the facility (land, factory, and equipment) for 20 years at an annual rental equal to the amount necessary to amortize the principal and pay the interest on the outstanding bonds, and (4) that such payments by X and the facility itself will be the security for the bonds. The bonds are industrial development bonds since they are part of an issue of obligations (1) all of the proceeds of which are to be used (by purchasing land and constructing and equipping the factory) in a trade or business by a nonexempt person, and (2) the payment of the principal and interest on which is secured by the facility and payments to be made with respect thereto.

Example (2). The facts are the same as in example (1) except that (1) X will purchase the facility, and (2) annual payments equal to the amount necessary to amortize the principal and pay the interest on the outstanding bonds will be made by X. The bonds are industrial development bonds for the reasons set forth in example (1).

Example (3). State B and corporation X enter into an arrangement under which B is to loan $10 million to X. The arrangement provides (1) that B will issue $10 million of bonds, (2) that the proceeds of the bond issue will be loaned to X to provide additional working capital and to finance the acquisition of certain new machinery, (3) that X will repay the loan in annual installments equal to the amount necessary to amortize the principal and pay the interest on the outstanding bonds, and (4) that the payments on the loan and the machinery will be the security for only the payment of the principal on the bonds. The bonds are industrial development bonds since they are part of an issue of obligations (1) all of the proceeds of which are to be used in a trade or business by a nonexempt person, and (2) the payment of the principal on which is secured by payments to be made in respect of property to be used in a trade or business. The result would be the same if only the payment of the interest on the bonds were secured by payments on the loan and machinery.

Example (4). The facts are the same as in example (1), (2), or (3) except that the annual payments required to be made by corporation X exceed the amount necessary to amortize the principal and pay the interest on the outstanding bonds. The bonds are industrial development bonds for the reasons set forth in such examples. The fact that corporation X is required to pay an amount in excess of the amount necessary to pay the principal and interest on the bonds does not affect their status as industrial development bonds. Similarly, if the annual payments required to be made by corporation X were sufficient to pay only a major portion of either the principal or the interest on the outstanding bonds, the bonds would be industrial development bonds for the reasons set forth in such examples.

Example (5). The facts are the same as in example (1), (2), (3), or (4) except that the issuer is a political subdivision which has taxing power and the bonds are general obligation bonds. Since both the trade or business and the security interest tests are met, the bonds are industrial development bonds notwithstanding the fact that they constitute an unconditional obligation of the issuer payable from its general revenues.

Example (6). (a) State C issues its general obligation bonds to purchase land and construct a hotel for use by the general public (*i.e.*, tourists, visitors, travelers on business, etc.). The bond indenture provides (1) that C will own and operate the project for the period required to redeem the bonds, and (2) that the project itself and the revenues derived therefrom are the security for the bonds. The bonds are not industrial development bonds since (1) the proceeds are to be used by an exempt person in a trade or business carried on by such person, and (2) a major portion of such proceeds is not to be used, directly or indirectly, in a trade or business carried on by a nonexempt person. Use of the hotel by hotel guests who are travelling in connection with trades or businesses of nonexempt persons is not an indirect use of the hotel by such nonexempt persons for purposes of section 103(c).

(b) The facts are the same as in paragraph (a) of this example except that corporation Y enters into a long-term agreement with C that Y will rent more than one-fourth of the rooms on an annual basis for a period approximately equal to one half of the term of the bonds. The bonds are industrial development bonds because (1) a major portion of the proceeds used to construct the hotel is to be used in the trade or business of corporation Y (a nonexempt person), and (2) a major portion of the principal and interest on such issue will be derived from payments in respect of the property used in the trade or business of Y.

Example (7). (a) State D and corporation Y enter into an agreement under which Y will lease for 20 years three floors of a 12-story office building to be constructed by D on land which it will acquire. D will occupy the grade floor and the remaining eight floors of the building. The portion of the costs of acquiring the land and constructing the building which are allocated to the space to be leased by Y is not in excess of 25 percent of the total costs of acquiring the land and constructing the building. Such costs, whether attributable to the acquisition of land or the construction of the building, were allocated to leased space in the same proportion that the reasonable rental value of such leased space bears to the reasonable rental value of the entire building. From the facts and circumstances presented, it is determined that such allocation was reasonable. The arrangement between D and Y provides that D will issue $10 million of bonds, that the proceeds of the bond issue will be used to purchase land and construct an office building, that Y will lease the designated floor space for 20 years at its reasonable rental value, and that such rental payments and the building itself shall be security for the bonds. The bonds are not industrial development bonds since a major portion of the proceeds is not to be used, directly or indirectly, in the trade or business of a nonexempt person.

(b) The facts are the same as in paragraph (a) of this example except that corporation Y will lease 4 floors, and the costs allocated to these floors are in excess of 25 percent of D's investment in the land and building. The bonds are industrial development bonds because (1) a major portion of the building is to be used in the trade or business of a nonexempt person, and (2) a major portion of the principal and interest on such issue is secured by the rental payments on the building.

Example (8). The facts are the same as in paragraph (b) of example (7) except that, instead of leasing any space to corporation Y, State D will lease the 4 floors to numerous unrelated private business users to be used in their trades or businesses. No lease will have a term exceeding 2 years. A major portion of the principal and interest will be paid from the revenues that D will derive from such leases. The fact that the activities of D, an exempt person, may amount to a trade or business of leasing property is not material, and the bonds are industrial development bonds for the reasons set forth in paragraph (b) of example (7). The result would be the same in the case of long-term leases.

Example (9). State E issues its obligations to finance the construction of dormitories for educational institution Z which is an organization described in section 501(c)(3) and exempt from tax under section 501(a). The dormitories are to be owned and operated by Z and their operation does not constitute an unrelated trade or business. The bonds are not industrial development bonds since the proceeds are to be used by an exempt person in a trade or business carried on by such person which is not an unrelated trade or business, as determined by applying section 513(a) to Z.

Example (10). State F issues its obligations to finance the construction of a toll road and the cost of erecting related facilities such as gasoline service stations and restaurants. Such related facilities represent less than 25 percent of the total cost of the project and are to be leased or sold to nonexempt persons. The toll road is to be owned and operated by F. The revenues from the toll road and from the rental of related facilities are the security for the bonds. The bonds are not industrial development bonds since a major portion of the proceeds is not to be used, directly or indirectly, in the trades or businesses of nonexempt persons. The fact that vehicles owned by nonexempt persons engaged in their trades or businesses may use the road in common with, or as a part of, the general public is not material.

Example (11). City G issues its obligations to finance the construction of a municipal auditorium which it will own and operate. The use of the auditorium will be open to anyone who wishes to use it for a short period of time on a rate-scale basis. The rights of such a user are only those of a transient occupant rather than the full legal possessory interests of a lessee. It is anticipated that the auditorium will be used by schools, church groups, and fraternities, and numerous commercial organizations. The revenues from the rentals of the auditorium and the auditorium building itself will be the security for the bonds. The bonds are not industrial development bonds because such use is not a use in the trade or business of a nonexempt person.

Example (12). The facts are the same as in example (11) except that one nonexempt person will have a 20-year rental agreement providing for exclusive use of the entire auditorium for more than three months of each year at a rental comparable to that charged short-term users. The bonds are industrial development bonds since such use is a use in the trade or business of a nonexempt person and, therefore, a major portion of the proceeds of the issue will be used in the trade or business of a nonexempt person and a major portion of the principal or interest on such issue will be secured by a facility used in such trade or business and by payments with respect to such facility.

Example (13). In order to construct an electric generating facility of a size sufficient to take advantage of the economies of scale: (1) City H will issue $50 million of its 25-year bonds and Z (a privately owned electric utility) will use $100 million of its funds for construction of a facility they will jointly own as tenants in common. (2) Each of the participants will share in the ownership, output, and operating expenses of the facility in proportion to its contribution to the cost of the facility, that is, one-third by H and two-thirds by Z. (3) H's bonds

➤➤➤ *Caution: Code Sec. 103 has been amended to remove special exempt bond issue rules and provide similar rules in Code Secs. 141-150.*

will be secured by H's ownership in the facility and by revenues to be derived from the sale of H's share of the annual output of the facility. (4) Because H will need only 50 percent of its share of the annual output of the facility, it agrees to sell to Z 25 percent of its share of such annual output for a period of 20 years pursuant to a contract under which Z agrees to take or pay for such power in all events. The facility will begin operation, and Z will begin to receive power, 4 years after the City H obligations are issued. The contract term of the issue will, therefore, be 21 years. (5) H also agrees to sell the remaining 25 percent of its share of the annual output to numerous other private utilities under a prevailing rate schedule including demand charges. (6) No contracts will be executed obligating any person other than Z to purchase any specified amount of the power for any specified period of time and no one such person (other than Z) will pay a demand charge or other minimum payment under conditions which, under paragraph (b)(5) of this section, result in a transfer of the benefits of ownership and the burdens of paying the debt service on obligations used directly or indirectly to provide such facilities. The bonds are not industrial development bonds because H's one-third interest in the facility (financed with bond proceeds) shall be treated as a separate property interest and, although 25 percent of H's interest in the annual output of the facility will be used directly or indirectly in the trade or business of Z, a nonexempt person, under the rule of paragraph (b)(5) of this section, such portion constitutes less than a major portion of the subparagraph (5) output of the facility. If more than 25 percent of the subparagraph (5) output of the facility were to be sold to Z pursuant to the take or pay contract, the bonds would be industrial development bonds since they would be secured by H's ownership in the facility and revenues therefrom, and under the rules of paragraph (b)(5) of this section a major portion of the proceeds of the bond issue would be used in the trade or business of Z, a nonexempt person.

Example (14). J, a political subdivision of a State, will issue several series of bonds from time to time and will use the proceeds to rehabilitate urban areas. More than 25 percent of the proceeds of each issue will be used for the rehabilitation and construction of buildings which will be leased or sold to nonexempt persons for use in their trades or businesses. There is no limitation either on the number of issues or the aggregate amount of bonds which may be outstanding. No group of bondholders has any legal claim prior to any other bondholders or creditors with respect to specific revenues of J, and there is no arrangement whereby revenues from a particular project are paid into a trust or constructive trust, or sinking fund, or are otherwise segregated or restricted for the benefit of any group of bondholders. There is, however, an unconditional obligation by J to pay the principal and interest on each issue of bonds. Further, it is apparent that J requires the revenues from the lease or sale of buildings to nonexempt persons in order to pay in full the principal and interest on the bonds in question. The bonds are industrial development bonds because a major portion of the proceeds will be used in the trades or businesses of nonexempt persons and, pursuant to an underlying arrangement, payment of the principal and interest is, in major part, to be derived from payments in respect of property or borrowed money used in the trades or businesses of nonexempt persons.

Example (15). Power Authority K, a political subdivision created by the legislature in state X to own and operate certain power generating facilities, sells all of the power from its existing facilities to four private utility systems under contracts executed in 1970, whereby such four systems are required to take or pay for specified portions of the total power output until the year 2000. Currently, existing facilities supply all of the present needs of the four utility systems but their future power requirements are expected to increase substantially. K issues 20-year general obligation bonds to construct a large nuclear generating facility. A fifth private utility system contracts with K to take or pay for 30 percent of the subparagraph (5) output of the new facility. The balance of the power output of the new facility will be available for sale as required, but initially it is not anticipated there will be any need for such power. The revenues from the contract with the fifth private utility system will be sufficient to pay less than 25 percent of the principal or interest on the bonds. The balance, which will exceed 25 percent of the principal or interest on such bonds, will be paid from revenue from the contracts with the four systems from sale of power produced by the old facilities. The bonds will be industrial development bonds because a major portion of the proceeds will be used in the trade or business of a nonexempt person, and payment of the principal and interest, pursuant to an underlying arrangement, will be derived in major part from payments in respect of property used in the trades or businesses of nonexempt persons.

(d) *Certain refunding issues.*—(1) *General rule.*—In the case of an issue of obligations issued to refund the outstanding face amount of an issue of obligations, the proceeds of the refunding issue will be considered to be used for the purpose for which the proceeds of the issue to be refunded were used. The rules of this subparagraph shall apply regardless of the date of issuance of the issue to be refunded and shall apply to refunding issues to be issued to refund prior refunding issues.

(2) *Obligations issued prior to effective date.*—In the case of an issue of obligations issued to refund the outstanding face amount of an issue of obligations issued on or before April 30, 1968 (or before January 1, 1969, if the transitional rules of § 1.103-12 are applicable) which would have been industrial development bonds within the meaning of section 103(c)(2) had they been issued after such date, the refunding issue shall not be considered to be an issue of industrial development bonds if it does not make funds available for any purpose other than the debt service on the obligations. For rules as to arbitrage bonds, see section 103(d).

(3) *Examples.*—The provisions of this paragraph may be illustrated by the following examples:

Example (1). In 1969, State A issued $20 million of 20-year revenue bonds the proceeds of which were used to construct a sports facility which qualifies as an exempt facility described in section 103(c)(4)(B) and paragraph (c) of § 1.103-8. The sports facility will be owned and operated by X, a nonexempt person, for the use of the general public. In 1975, A issues $15 million of revenue bonds in order to refund the outstanding face amount of the 1969 issue. Since the proceeds of the 1969 issue were used for an exempt facility, the proceeds of the 1975 refunding issue will be considered to be used for the same purposes and section 103(c)(1) shall not apply to the 1975 refunding issue. The result would have been the same if the original issue had been issued in 1965. For rules as to a refunding obligation held by substantial users of facilities constructed with the proceeds of the issue refunded, see section 103(c)(7) and § 1.103-11.

Example (2). In 1967, prior to the effective date of section 103(c), City B issued $10 million of revenue bonds the proceeds of which were used to construct a manufacturing facility for corporation Y, a nonexempt person. Lease payments by Y were security for the bonds. In 1975, B issues $7 million of revenue bonds in order to retire the outstanding face amount of the 1967 issue. The interest rate of the 1975 issue is one and one-half percentage points lower than the interest rate on the 1967 issue. Both issues sold at par. All of the terms of the 1975 issue are the same as the terms of the 1967 issue with the exception of the interest rate. The 1975 refunding issue will not be considered to be an issue of industrial development bonds since the refunding issue will not make funds available for any purpose other than the debt service on the outstanding obligations.

Example (3). The facts are the same as in example (2) except that the interest rate on the refunding issue is the same as the interest rate on the issue to be refunded. Assume further that City B issued the 1975 refunding issue in order to extend the term of the obligations issued in 1967 as the result of its inability to pay such obligations due to insufficient revenues. The results will be the same as in example (2) for the reasons stated therein. [Reg. § 1.103-7.]

☐ [*T.D. 7199, 7-31-72. Amended by T.D. 7869, 1-12-83.*]

[Reg. § 1.103-8]

§ 1.103-8. Interest on bonds to finance certain exempt facilities.—(a) *In general.*—(1) *General rule.*—(i) Under section 103(b)(4), interest paid on an issue of obligations issued by a State or local governmental unit (as defined in § 1.103-1) is not includable in gross income if substantially all of the proceeds of such issue is to be used to provide one or more of the exempt facilities listed in subparagraphs (A) through (G) of section 103(b)(4) and in this section. However, interest on an obligation of such issue is includable in gross income if the obligation is held by a substantial user or a related person (as described in section 103(b)(8) and § 1.103-11). If substantially all of the proceeds of a bond issue is to be used to provide such exempt facilities, the debt obligations are treated as obligations described in section 103(a)(1) and § 1.103-1 even though such obligations are industrial development bonds as defined in section 103(b)(2) and § 1.103-7. Substantially all of the proceeds of an issue of governmental obligations are used to provide an exempt facility if 90 percent or more of such proceeds are so used. For purposes of this "substantially all" test, two rules apply. First, proceeds are reduced by amounts properly allocable on a pro rata basis between providing the exempt facility and other uses of the proceeds. Second, amounts used to provide an exempt facility include amounts paid or incurred which are chargeable to the facility's capital account or would be so chargeable either with a proper election by a taxpayer (for example, under section 266) or but for a proper election by a taxpayer to deduct such amounts. In the event the amount payable with respect to an issue during each annual period over its term is less than the amount of interest accruing thereon in such period, *e.g.*, in the case of

»»→ Caution: *Code Sec. 103 has been amended to remove special exempt bond issue rules and provide similar rules in Code Secs. 141-150.*

an issue sold by the issuer for less than its face amount, see paragraph (a)(6) of this section to determine the amount of proceeds of the issue.

(ii) The provisions of subdivision (i) of this subparagraph shall also apply to an issue of obligations substantially all of the proceeds of which is to be used to provide exempt facilities described in this section and for either or both of the following purposes: (*a*) to acquire or develop land as the site for an industrial park described in section 103(b)(5) and §1.103-9, (*b*) to provide facilities to be used by an exempt person.

(iii) Section 103(b)(4) only becomes applicable where the bond issue meets both the trade or business and the security interest tests so that obligations are industrial development bonds within the meaning of section 103(b)(2). For rules as to exempt facilities including property functionally related and subordinate to such facilities, see subparagraph (3) of this paragraph. For rules with respect to the ultimate use of proceeds of obligations, see paragraph (4) of this subparagraph. For rules which limit the application of the provisions of this section see subparagraph (5) of this paragraph. For the interrelationship of the rules provided in this section and the exemption for certain small issues provided in section 103(b)(6), see §1.103-10.

(2) *Public use requirement.*—To qualify under section 103(b)(4) and this section as an exempt facility, a facility must serve or be available on a regular basis for general public use, or be a part of a facility so used, as contrasted with similar types of facilities which are constructed for the exclusive use of a limited number of nonexempt persons in their trades or businesses. For example, a private dock or wharf owned by or leased to, and serving only a single manufacturing plant would not qualify as a facility for general public use, but a hangar or repair facility at a municipal airport, or a dock or a wharf, would qualify even if it is owned by, or leased or permanently assigned to, a nonexempt person provided that such nonexempt person directly serves the general public, such as a common passenger carrier or freight carrier. Similarly, an airport owned or operated by a nonexempt person for general public use is a facility for public use, as is a dock or wharf which is part of a public port. However, a landing strip which, by reason of a formal or informal agreement or by reason of geographic location, will not be available for general public use does not satisfy the public use requirement. Sewage or solid waste disposal facilities and air or water pollution control facilities, described in sections 103(b)(4)(E) and (F) and paragraphs (f) and (g) of this section, will be treated in all events as serving a general public use although they may be part of a nonpublic facility such as a manufacturing facility used in the trade or business of a nonexempt user.

(3) *Functionally related and subordinate.*—An exempt facility includes any land, building, or other property functionally related and subordinate to such facility. Property is not functionally related and subordinate to a facility if it is not of a character and size commensurate with the character and size of such facility. Since substantially all of the proceeds of a bond issue must be used for the exempt facility (or for any combination of exempt facilities, industrial parks, and facilities to be used by exempt persons), including property functionally related and subordinate thereto, an insubstantial amount of the proceeds of a bond issue may be used for facilities which are neither exempt facilities (or a combination of exempt facilities, industrial parks and facilities to be used by exempt persons) nor functionally related and subordinate to exempt facilities. Thus, for example, where substantially all of the proceeds of an urban redevelopment bond issue are to be used by a State urban redevelopment agency for residential real property for family units within the meaning of section 103(b)(4)(A) and paragraph (b) of this section, an insubstantial amount may be used for an industrial or commercial project or for any other purpose that is not functionally related and subordinate to the residential real property for family units.

(4) *Ultimate use of proceeds.*—The question whether substantially all of the proceeds of an issue of obligations are to be used to provide one or more of the exempt facilities listed in subparagraphs (A) through (G) of section 103(b)(4) and in this section is to be resolved by reference to the ultimate use of such proceeds. For example, such proceeds will be treated as used to provide residential rental property whether the State or local governmental unit (i) constructs such property and leases or sells it to any person who is not an exempt person for use in such person's trade or business or leasing such property; (ii) lends the proceeds to any such person for such purpose; or (iii) lends the proceeds to banks or other financial institutions in order to increase the supply of funds for mortgage lending under conditions requiring such banks or other financial institutions to use such proceeds only for further lending for residential rental property.

(5) *Limitation.*—(i) A facility qualifies under this section only to the extent that there is a valid reimbursement allocation under

§1.150-2 with respect to expenditures that are incurred before the issue date of the bonds to provide the facility and that are to be paid with the proceeds of the issue. In addition, if the original use of the facility begins before the issue date of the bonds, the facility does not qualify under this section if any person that was a substantial user of the facility at any time during the 5-year period before the issue date or any related person to that user receives (directly or indirectly) 5 percent or more of the proceeds of the issue for the user's interest in the facility and is a substantial user of the facility at any time during the 5-year period after the issue date, unless—

(A) An official intent for the facility is adopted under §1.150-2 within 60 days after the date on which acquisition, construction, or reconstruction of that facility commenced; and

(B) For an acquisition, no person that is a substantial user or related person after the acquisition date was also a substantial user more than 60 days before the date on which the official intent was adopted.

(ii) A facility, the original use of which commences (or the acquisition of which occurs) on or after the issue date of bonds to provide that facility, qualifies under this section only to the extent that an official intent for the facility is adopted under §1.150-2 by the issuer of the bonds within 60 days after the commencement of the construction, reconstruction, or acquisition of that facility. Temporary construction or other financing of a facility prior to the issuance of the bonds to provide that facility will not cause that facility to be one that does not qualify under this paragraph (a)(5)(ii).

(iii) For purposes of paragraph (a)(5)(i) of this section, *substantial user* has the meaning used in section 147(a)(1), *related person* has the meaning used in section 144(a)(3), and a user that is a governmental unit within the meaning of §1.103-1 is disregarded.

(iv) Except to the extent provided in §§1.142-4(d), 1.148-11A(i), and 1.150-2(j), this paragraph (a)(5) applies to bonds issued after June 30, 1993, and sold before July 8, 1997. See §1.142-4(d) for rules relating to bonds sold on or after July 8, 1997.

(6) *Deep discount obligations.*—(i) Except as otherwise provided in paragraph (a)(7) of this section, the proceeds of any issue of obligations sold by the issuer after June 4, 1982, shall include any imputed proceeds of the issue. The imputed proceeds of an issue equal the sum of the amounts of imputed proceeds for each annual period (hereinafter, bond year) over the term of the issue.

(ii) The amount of imputed proceeds for a bond year equals—

(*a*) The sum of the amounts of interest that will accrue with respect to each obligation that is part of the issue in such year, reduced (but not below zero) by

(*b*) The sum of the amounts of principal and interest that become payable with respect to the issue in that bond year.

(iii) Interest will be deemed to accrue with respect to an obligation on an amount that, as of the commencement of that year, is equal to the sum of—

(*a*) The purchase price (as defined in §1.103-13(d)(2)) allocable to the obligation and

(*b*) The aggregate of the amounts of interest accruing in each prior bond year with respect to the obligation, reduced by all amounts that became payable with respect to the obligation in prior bond years. Any amount that becomes payable during the 30 day period following any bond year will be deemed to have become payable in such bond year. Thus, to the extent interest on an obligation accruing during a bond year does not become payable within 30 days from the end of such year, it is treated as reinvested under the same terms as the obligation. For purposes of this subparagraph (6), the rate at which such interest accrues is equal to the yield of the obligation. Yield is computed in the same manner as set forth in §1.103-13(c)(1)(ii) for computing yield on governmental obligations (assuming annual compounding of interest). Such computations shall be made without regard to optional call dates.

(7) *Deep discount obligations; special rules.*—(i) There are no imputed proceeds with respect to an obligation if—

(*a*) The obligation does not have a stated interest rate (determinable at the date of issue) that increases over the term of the obligation, and

(*b*) The purchase price of the obligation is at least 95 percent of its face amount.
At the option of the issuer, any obligation described in the preceeding sentence may be disregarded in computing the imputed proceeds of the issue. Payments with respect to such obligations are also disregarded in determining the amount payable with respect to the issue in that bond year. If each obligation which is part of an issue is described in this subdivision (i), there are no imputed proceeds with respect to the issue.

(ii) If the actual rate at which interest is to accrue over the term of an obligation is indeterminable at the date of issue then, in

⧐⧐⧐ Caution: *Code Sec. 103 has been amended to remove special exempt bond issue rules and provide similar rules in Code Secs. 141-150.*

computing the yield of the obligation for purposes of this paragraph, such rate shall be determined as if the conditions as of the date of issue will not change over the term of the obligation. Thus, for example, if interest on an obligation is to be paid semiannually at a rate equal to 80 percent of the yield on six month Treasury bills at the most recent public sale immediately prior to the corresponding interest payment date and the yield on six month Treasury bills sold immediately preceding the issue date is 10 percent, then the six month Treasury bill rate is deemed to be a constant 10 percent for purposes of determining the amount of imputed proceeds of the issue. Therefore, all interest payments on the obligation would be deemed to be made at a rate of 8 percent.

(8) *Examples.*—The principles of this paragraph may be illustrated by the following examples:

Example (1). State A issues its bonds and plans to use substantially all of the proceeds from such bond issue to purchase land and build a facility which will be used for one of the purposes described in section 103(b)(4) and this section. The arrangement provides that (1) A will issue bonds with a face amount of $21 million and with all accrued interest payable annually, the proceeds of which (after deducting bond election costs, costs of publishing notices, attorneys' fees, printing costs, trustees' fees for fiscal agents, and similar expenses) will be $20 million; (2) $18 million of the proceeds of the bond issue will be used to purchase land and to construct such facility; (3) $2 million of the proceeds will be used for an unrelated

Date	Purchase price plus accumulated interest
Aug. 1, 1983	$18,627,639.69
Aug. 1, 1984	20,490,403.68
Aug. 1, 1985	22,539,444.03
Aug. 1, 1986	24,793,388.43
Aug. 1, 1987	27,272,727.27
Total imputed proceeds	

Therefore, proceeds of the issue equal $27,272,727.27 less issuance costs. Substantially all of the bond proceeds are not used to provide an exempt facility, and section 103(b)(1) applies to the issue.

Example (3). The facts are the same as example (2) except that the issue has a face amount and purchase price of $18,500,000. The issue also provides for one payment in addition to the redemption payment, in the amount of $10,267,668 payable on or after August 1, 1986, one year before maturity. Section 103(b)(1) applies to the issue.

Example (4). On July 1, 1982, City E sells an issue of industrial development bonds to provide for a convention facility, as described

facility which will be used by X, a nonexempt person, in a separate trade or business and for a purpose not described in section 103(b)(4) or (5); (4) X will rent both facilities for 20 years at an annual rental equal to the amount necessary to amortize the principal and pay the interest annually on the outstanding bonds; and (5) such payments by X and the facilities will be the security for the bonds. On these facts, substantially all of the proceeds will be used in connection with an exempt facility described in section 103(b)(4) and this section. Accordingly, section 103(b)(1) does not apply to the bonds unless such bonds are thereafter held by a person who is a substantial user of the facilities or a related person within the meaning of section 103(b)(13) and § 1.103-11.

Example (2). On July 1, 1982, State B sells an issue of its obligations to an underwriter in anticipation of a public offering. The initial offering price is $18,627,639.69 of which $17,000,000 is to be used to construct a pollution control facility described in section 103(b)(4)(F). X Corporation, a nonexempt person, is to use the facility and, in exchange, is obligated to pay an amount equal to the face amount of the issue when it becomes due. The obligations are issued on August 1, 1982. The face amount of the issue is $30,000,000. The issue is a term issue with all obligations maturing on August 1, 1987. The issue bears no stated rate of interest; there are no interest coupons on the obligations. The bonds are industrial development bonds with a yield (based upon annual compounding) of ten percent. Based on these facts, the amount of imputed proceeds with respect to the issue is determined as follows:

Interest	Imputed proceeds
$1,862,763.97	$1,862,763.97
2,049,040.37	2,049,040.37
2,253,944.40	2,253,944.40
2,479,338.84	2,479,338.84
2,727,272.73	0
	$8,645,087.58

in section 103(b)(4)(C). Assume that the bonds are issued on that date as well. The issue has a face amount of $15,240,000 and a purchase price of $11,929,382.53. The estimated cost of the facility is $11,000,000. The bonds are "zero coupon" bonds, *i.e.,* there are no interest coupons. Each series is initially offered for less than 95 percent of its face amount. The issue matures serially over a five year period, with each series being allocated a part of the purchase price of the issue. The following chart indicates the purchase price and yield for each series and debt service for the issue:

[Amount allocable to each series]

Date	1983 series at 8 percent	1984 series at 8.5 percent	1985 series at 8.75 percent	1986 series at 9.25 percent	1987 series at 9.75 percent	Interest accruing on issue*	Amount due	Imputed proceeds
July 1, 1983	• 2,939,814.82	2,697,020.54	2,468,629.60	2,228,732.51	1,595,185.06	. . .	. . .	0
	235,185.18	229,246.75	216,005.09	206,157.76	155,530.54	1,042,125.32	3,175,000	. . .
July 1, 1984	. . .	2,926,267.29	2,684,634.69	2,434,890.27	1,750,715.60	. . .	. . .	0
	. . .	248,732.71	234,905.54	225,227.35	170,694.77	879,560.37	3,175,000	. . .
July 1, 1985	. . .	. . .	2,919,540.23	2,660,117.62	1,921,410.37	. . .	. . .	0
	. . .	. . .	255,459.77	246,060.88	187,337.51	688,858.16	3,175,000	. . .
July 1, 1986				2,906,178.50	2,108,747.88	. . .	. . .	0
	. . .	. . .	. . .	266,821.50	205,602.92	474,424.42	3,175,000	. . .
July 1, 1987				. . .	2,314,350.80	. . .	. . .	0
	. . .	. . .	. . .	. . .	225,649.20	*225,649.20	2,540,000	. . .
Total	. . .	. . .	. . .	. . .	. . .		15,240,000	. . .

* This column (Interest accruing on the issue) contains the sums of the interest that accrues on each series in each bond year. The amount of interest accruing on the issue is computed by adding the amount of interest accruing on each series outstanding for that bond year (the bottom number in the line for each bond year). The amount of interest annually accruing on each series also is added to the purchase price of the series to determine the amount of interest accruing in subsequent year, inasmuch as there are no payments with respect to the outstanding series prior to maturity. Thus, the "principal" amount, of the top of the two numbers given in such line for each bond year, is the purchase price allocable to that series plus the amount of interest that accrued on that series in prior years.

There are no imputed proceeds because the amount payable on the issue in each bond year exceeds the total amount of interest accruing on the issue during such bond year. Section 103(b)(1) does not apply to the bonds unless such bonds are held by a person who is a substantial user of the facility or a related person within the meaning of section 103(b)(13) and § 1.103-11.

Example (5). On July 1, 1982, City C issues industrial development bonds in the face amount of $30 million to construct a sports facility described in section 103(b)(4)(B) to be leased to D, a nonexempt person, with payments on the bonds secured by the lease. C receives $30 million in exchange for the bonds which will be used to provide the facility. The bonds mature on July 1, 2002. Each bond provides for an annual interest payment equal to ten percent of the face amount of the bond, with the last payment thereon (on July 1, 2002) including a return of the principal amount of the bond. The proceeds of the issue are $30 million. Section 103(b)(1) does not apply

to the bonds unless such bonds are held by a person who is a substantial user of the facility or a related person within the meaning of section 103(b)(13) and § 1.103-11.

Example (6). The facts are the same as example (5) except that each bond provides for an annual interest payment equal to nine percent of its face amount and is sold with the option to tender the bond to D for purchase at par 5 years after the sale date of July 1, 1982 (*i.e.,* the bonds are sold with a "put" option). Such bonds also provide a put option annually thereafter. There are no imputed proceeds (without regard to § 1.103-8(a)(7)), and the result is the same as example (5).

Example (7). On July 1, 1982, City F sells an issue of industrial development bonds in the face amount of $20 million to acquire a parking facility as described in section 103(b)(4)(D). The estimated cost of the facility is $17,800,000. The issue is issued on the same date and will mature serially over the following ten years. Each bond that

≫→ Caution: Code Sec. 103 has been amended to remove special exempt bond issue rules and provide similar rules in Code Secs. 141-150.

is part of the issue bears annual interest coupons, each of which is in an amount equal to ten percent of the face amount of the bond. Each maturity has a face amount of $2,000,000. The issue is initially offered to the public for $19,700,000, allocable to each maturity as follows:

Maturity	Purchase price
July 1, 1983	$1,990,000
July 1, 1984	$1,980,000
July 1, 1985	$1,980,000
July 1, 1986	$1,970,000
July 1, 1987	$1,970,000
July 1, 1988	$1,970,000
July 1, 1989	$1,960,000
July 1, 1990	$1,960,000
July 1, 1991	$1,960,000
July 1, 1992	$1,960,000

Based on the foregoing issue proceeds equal $19,700,000 less issuance costs. There are no imputed proceeds with respect to this issue inasmuch as each bond pays interest at a constant rate in each bond year and the purchase price of each bond is at least 95 percent of its face amount. Substantially all of the proceeds are to be used to provide the exempt facility. Accordingly, section 103(b)(1) does not apply to the bonds unless such bonds are thereafter held by a person who is a substantial user of the facility or a related person within the meaning of section 103(b)(13) and § 1.103-11.

(b) *Residential rental property.*—(1) *General rule for obligations issued after April 24, 1979.*—Section 103(b)(1) shall not apply to any obligation which is issued after April 24, 1979, and is part of an issue substantially all of the proceeds of which are to be used to provide a residential rental project in which 20 percent or more of the units are to be occupied by individuals or families of low or moderate income (as defined in paragraph (b)(8)(v) of this section. In the case of a targeted area project, the minimum percentage of units which are to be occupied by individuals of low or moderate income is 15 percent. See generally § 1.103-7 for rules relating to refunding issues.

(2) *Registration requirement.*—Any obligation (including any refunding obligation) issued after December 31, 1981, to provide a residential rental project must be issued as part of an issue, each obligation of which is in registered form (as defined in paragraph (b)(8)(ii) of this section).

(3) *Transitional rule.*—For purposes of this section, obligations issued after April 24, 1979, may be treated as issued before April 25, 1979, if the transitional requirements of section 1104 of the Mortgage Subsidy Bond Tax Act of 1980 (94 Stat. 2670) are satisfied.

(4) *Residential rental project.*—(i) *In general.*—A residential rental project is a building or structure, together with any functionally related and subordinate facilities, containing one or more similarly constructed units—

(a) Which are used on other than a transient basis, and

(b) Which satisfy the requirements of paragraph (b)(5)(i) of this section and are available to members of the general public in accordance with the requirement of paragraph (a)(2) of this section.

Substantially all of each project must contain such units and functionally related and subordinate facilities. Hotels, motels, dormitories, fraternity and sorority houses, rooming houses, hospitals, nursing homes, sanitariums, rest homes, and trailer parks and courts for use on a transient basis are not residential rental projects.

(ii) *Multiple buildings.*—(a) Proximate buildings or structures (hereinafter "buildings") which have similarly constructed units are treated as part of the same project if they are owned for Federal tax purposes by the same person and if the buildings are financed pursuant to a common plan.

(b) Buildings are proximate if they are located on a single tract of land. The term "tract" means any parcel or parcels of land which are contiguous except for the interposition of a road, street, stream or similar property. Otherwise, parcels are contiguous if their boundaries meet at one or more points.

(c) A common plan of financing exists if, for example, all such buildings are provided by the same issue or several issues subject to a common indenture.

(iii) *Functionally related and subordinate facilities.*—Under paragraph (a)(3) of this section, facilities that are functionally related and subordinate to residential rental projects include facilities for use by the tenants, for example, swimming pools, other recreational facilities, parking areas, and other facilities which are reasonably required for the project, for example, heating and cooling equipment, trash disposal equipment or units for resident managers or maintenance personnel.

(iv) *Owner-occupied residences.*—For purposes of section 103(b)(4)(A) and this paragraph (b), the term "residential rental project" does not include any building or structure which contains fewer than five units, one unit of which is occupied by an owner of the units.

(5) *Requirements must be continuously satisfied.*—(i) *Rental requirement.*—Once available for occupancy, each unit (as defined in paragraph (b)(8)(i) of this section) in a residential rental project must be rented or available for rental on a continuous basis during the longer of—

(a) the remaining term of the obligation, or

(b) the qualified project period (as defined in paragraph (b)(7) of this section).

(ii) *Low or moderate income occupancy requirement.*—Individuals or families of low or moderate income must occupy that percentage of completed units in such project applicable to the project under paragraph (b)(1) of this section continuously during the qualified project period. For this purpose, a unit occupied by an individual or family who at the commencement of the occupancy is of low or moderate income is treated as occupied by such an individual or family during their tenancy in such unit, even though they subsequently cease to be of low or moderate income. Moreover, such unit is treated as occupied by an individual or family of low or moderate income until reoccupied, other than for a temporary period, at which time the character of the unit shall be redetermined. In no event shall such temporary period exceed 31 days.

(6) *Effect of post-issuance noncompliance.*—(i) *In general.*—Unless corrected within a reasonable period, noncompliance with the requirements of this paragraph (b) shall cause the project to be treated as other than a project described in section 103(b)(4)(A) and this paragraph (b) as of the date of issue. After an issue to provide such project ceases to qualify, subsequent conformity with the requirements will not alter the taxable status of such issue.

(ii) *Correction of noncompliance.*—If the issuer corrects any noncompliance arising from events occurring after the issuance of the obligation within a reasonable period, such noncompliance (*e.g.*, an unauthorized sublease) shall not cause the project to be a project not described in this paragraph (b). A reasonable period is at least 60 days after such error is first discovered or would have been discovered by the exercise of reasonable diligence.

(iii) *Involuntary loss.*—(a) The requirements of paragraph (b) shall cease to apply to a project in the event of involuntary noncompliance caused by fire, seizure, requisition, foreclosure, transfer of title by deed in lieu of foreclosure, change in a Federal law or an action of a Federal agency after the date of issue which prevents an issuer from enforcing the requirements of this paragraph, or condemnation or similar event but only if, within a reasonable period, either the obligation used to provide such project is retired or amounts received as a consequence of such event are used to provide a project which meets the requirements of section 103(b)(4)(A) and this paragraph (b).

(b) The provisions of paragraph (b)(6)(iii)(a) of this section shall cease to apply to a project subject to foreclosure, transfer of title by deed in lieu of foreclosure or similar event if, at anytime during that part of the qualified project period subsequent to such event, the obligor on the acquired purpose obligation (as defined in § 1.103-13(b)(4)(iv)(a)) or a related person (as defined in § 1.103-10(e)) obtains an ownership interest in such project for tax purposes.

(7) *Qualified project period.*—The term "qualified project period" means—

(i) For obligations issued after April 24, 1979, and prior to September 4, 1982, a period of 20 years commencing on the later of the date that the project becomes available for occupancy or the date of issue of the obligations. The requirement of paragraph (b)(5)(ii) of this section shall be deemed met if the owner of the project contracts with a Federal or state agency to maintain at least 20 percent (or 15 percent in the case of targeted areas) of the units for low or moderate income individuals or families (as defined in paragraph (b)(8)(v) of this section) for 20 years in consideration for rent subsidies for such individuals or families for such period.

(ii) For obligations issued after September 3, 1982, a period beginning on the later of the first day on which at least 10 percent of the units in the project are first occupied or the date of issue of an obligation described in section 103(b)(4)(A) and this paragraph and ending on the later of the date—

(a) Which is 10 years after the date on which at least 50 percent of the units in the project are first occupied,

(b) Which is a qualified number of days after the date on which any of the units in the project is first occupied, or

⟫→ *Caution: Code Sec. 103 has been amended to remove special exempt bond issue rules and provide similar rules in Code Secs. 141-150.*

(c) On which any assistance provided with respect to the project under section 8 of the United States Housing Act of 1937 terminates. For purposes of this paragraph (b)(7)(ii), the term "qualified number of days" means 50 percent of the total number of days comprising the term of the obligation with the longest maturity in the issue used to provide the project. In the case of a refunding of such an issue, the longest maturity is equal to the sum of the period the prior issue was outstanding and the longest term of any refunding obligations.

(8) *Other definitions.*—For purposes of this paragraph—

(i) *Unit.*—The term "unit" means any accommodation containing separate and complete facilities for living, sleeping, eating, cooking, and sanitation. Such accommodations may be served by centrally located equipment, such as air conditioning or heating. Thus, for example, an apartment containing a living area, a sleeping area, bathing and sanitation facilities, and cooking facilities equipped with a cooking range, refrigerator, and sink, all of which are separate and distinct from other apartments, would constitute a unit.

(ii) *In registered form.*—The term "in registered form" has the same meaning as in section 6049. With respect to obligations issued after December 31, 1982, such term shall have the same meaning as prescribed in section 103(j) (including the regulations thereunder).

(iii) *Targeted area project.*—The term "targeted area project" means a project located in a qualified census tract (as defined in §6a.103A-2(b)(4)) or in an area of chronic economic distress (as defined in §6a.103A-2(b)(5)).

(iv) *Building or structure.*—The term "building or structure" generally means a discrete edifice or other man-made construction consisting of an independent foundation, outer walls, and roof. A single unit which is not an entire building but is merely a part of a building is not a building or structure within the meaning of this section. As such, while single townhouses are not buildings if their foundation, outer walls, and roof are not independent, detached houses and rowhouses are buildings.

(v) *Low or moderate income.*—Individuals and families of low or moderate income shall be determined in a manner consistent with determinations of lower income families under section 8 of the United States Housing Act of 1937, as amended, except that the percentage of median gross income which qualifies as low or moderate income shall be 80 percent. Therefore, occupants of a unit are considered individuals or families of low or moderate income only if their adjusted income (computed in the manner prescribed with §1.167(k)-3(b)(3)) does not exceed 80 percent of the median gross income for the area. Notwithstanding the foregoing, the occupants of a unit shall not be considered to be of low or moderate income if all the occupants are students (as defined in section 151(e)(4)), no one of whom is entitled to file a joint return under section 6013. The method of determining low or moderate income in effect on the date of issue will be determinative for such issue, even if such method is subsequently changed. In the event programs under §8(f) of the Housing Act of 1937, as amended, are terminated prior to the date of issue, the applicable method shall be that in effect immediately prior to the date of such termination.

(9) *Examples.*—The following examples illustrate the application of this paragraph (b).

Example (1). In August 1982, City X issues $10 million of registered bonds with a term of 20 years to be used to finance the construction of an apartment building to be available to members of the general public. X loans the proceeds of the bonds to Corporation M, the tax owner of the project. The loan is secured by a promissory note from M and a mortgage on the project. The mortgage requires annual payments sufficient to amortize the principal and interest on the bonds. Corporation M maintains 20 percent of the units in the project for low or moderate income individuals and meets all of the requirements of this section until 2002, at which time M converts the project to offices. The bonds are industrial development bonds, but because the proceeds are used for construction of residential rental property, which is an exempt facility under section 103(b)(4)(A) and paragraph (b) of this section, section 103(b)(1) does not apply.

Example (2). The facts are the same as in example (1), except that the building is constructed adjacent to a factory, and the factory employees are to be given preference in selecting tenants. The bonds are industrial development bonds and the facility is not an exempt facility under section 103(b)(4)(A) and paragraph (b) of this section because *it is not a facility constructed for use by the general public.*

Example (3). The facts are the same as in example (1), except that the proceeds of the obligation are provided to N, a cooperative housing corporation, to finance the construction of a cooperative housing project. N sells stock in such cooperative to shareholders, some of whom occupy the units in the cooperative and some of whom rent the units to other persons. Such project is not a residential rental project within the meaning of section 103(b)(4)(A) and §1.103-8(b) because less than all of the units in the building are used for rental. Further, the bonds are mortgage subsidy bonds under section 103A because more than a significant portion of the proceeds are used to provide financing for residences, some of which are owner-occupied and some of which are used in the trade or business of rental.

Example (4). On February 1, 1984, County Z issues registered obligations with a term of 3 years and loans the proceeds to Corporation V to construct a garden apartment project for tenants who are 65 years or older. The mortgage on the project secures the loan. At the end of 3 years, V obtains permanent financing for the project from a commercial lender. The project is not a targeted area project. V has not contracted with any Federal or state agency to provide rental assistance under section 8 of the United States Housing Act of 1937. As a condition for providing financing for construction, Z requires that the deed to the project contain a covenant that requires the project be used for elderly tenants and restricts occupancy of 20 percent of the units in the project to individuals or families of low or moderate income. Further, the deed provides that "Such covenant shall run with and bind the land, from the date that ten percent of the units in the project are first occupied until ten years after the date that at least half the units are first occupied. The right to enforce these restrictions is vested in County Z." In 1990, however, less than 20 percent of the units are occupied by families or individuals of low or moderate incomes, and three months after learning of this condition County Z had not commenced enforcement of the covenant. Although on the date of issue the proceeds of the obligation were used to provide a residential rental project, the obligation will not be treated as providing a residential rental project within the meaning of section 103(b)(4)(A) as of February 1, 1984, because the project did not meet the requirements of this paragraph for at least 10 years after at least 50 percent of the units are first occupied.

Example (5). On January 15, 1983, State X issues registered obligations with a term of 15 years, the proceeds of which are loaned to Corporation P to construct an apartment building. The project will be a "targeted area project", within the meaning of §1.103-8(b)(8)(iii). Corporation P intends to rent all the units to individuals for their residences, maintaining 15 percent of the units in the project for individuals having low or moderate incomes, for 15 years. In 1988, however, Corporation P converts 80 percent of the units to condominiums. Corporation P repays the loan to State X which, in turn, redeems the obligations. The obligations are not used to provide a residential rental project within the meaning of section 103(b)(4)(A), and all the interest paid or to be paid on such obligations will be includible in gross income.

Example (6). On January 15, 1984, State Z issues registered obligations with a term of 15 years the proceeds of which will be used to acquire and renovate a residential apartment building. Z sells the project to Corporation U and receives a 30-year mortgage. On June 1, 1985, the first occupants of the project commence their tenancies. At least 50 percent of the units in the project are occupied on July 1, 1985. On January 15, 1988, Z issues 35-year refunding bonds the proceeds of which are used to retire the obligations issued in 1984. The prior issue will be discharged by March 15, 1988. In order to meet the requirement of §1.103-8(b)(5)(ii), at least 20 percent of such units must be occupied by individuals of low or moderate income until January 1, 2005.

Example (7). The facts are the same as in example (6) except that in 1987, the apartment building is substantially destroyed by fire. The building was insured at its fair market value. U does not intend to reconstruct the building but uses a portion of the insurance proceeds to repay the unpaid balance of the mortgage. Z uses this amount to redeem the outstanding bonds at the first available call date. Since the project was substantially destroyed by fire and the outstanding bonds are retired at the first available call date, the requirements of section 103(b)(4)(A) and this paragraph (b) are satisfied with respect to the obligations.

Example (8). The facts are the same as in example (6) except that in 1987 U defaults on the mortgage, and Z obtains title to the project with out instituting foreclosure proceedings. Z sells the project to S and uses the proceeds to retire the outstanding bonds. Since S did not obtain the project with obligations described in section 103(b)(4), S is not required to meet the requirements of section 103(b)(4)(A) and this paragraph. Further, the 1984 obligations are obligations described in section 103(b)(4)(A).

Example (9). In September 1983, State W issues $10 million of registered bonds with a term of 3 years, the proceeds of which are to be loaned to Corporation V to finance the construction of an apartment building in a rural community. At the end of 3 years, V obtains permanent financing from Federal Agency T. Agency T will not

»»→ Caution: Code Sec. 103 has been amended to remove special exempt bond issue rules and provide similar rules in Code Secs. 141-150.

allow the deed to contain any restrictive covenant relating to the use of the project. Under Federal law, however, T requires that V maintain all of the units in the project for rental to low-income farmworkers for the term of the mortgage, which is 20 years. Further, the mortgage between T and V provides that if T determines that low-income housing is no longer required in the community in which the project is constructed then the repayment of the mortgage may be accelerated. T determines as of the date of issue that low-income housing will be needed in the community for at least 20 years. In 1987, the project fails to meet the requirements of section 1.103-8(b)(5)(ii), relating to occupancy by individuals or families of low or moderate income. Further, T does not require V to correct the failure. Based on the foregoing, the bonds issued by W will be treated as described in section 103(b)(4)(A).

Example (10). The facts are the same as in example (9) except that in 1987, the Federal law is amended to provide that Agency T may not enforce its low-income occupancy requirement. The result is the same.

Example (11). The facts are the same as in example (9) except that in 1987 Agency T determines that due to a change in circumstances in the community in which the project is located low-income rental housing is no longer required. As such, T requires V to repay the mortgage. Since the obligations have been repaid, W has no legal right to enforce the requirements of paragraph (b) with respect to the project. Subsequent nonconformity of the project with the requirements of §1.103-8(b) under these circumstances will not cause the obligations issued by W to be industrial development bonds within the meaning of section 103(b)(1).

(10) *Obligations issued before April 25, 1979.*—(i) *General rules.*—Section 103(b)(1) shall not apply to obligations issued before April 25, 1979, which are part of an issue substantially all of the proceeds of which are to be used to provide residential real property for family units. In order to qualify under this paragraph (b) as an exempt facility, the facility must satisfy the public use requirement of paragraph (a)(2) of this section by being available for use by members of the general public.

(ii) *Family units defined.*—For purposes of this paragraph (b) the term "family unit" means a building or any portion thereof which contains complete living facilities which are to be used on other than a transient basis by one or more persons, and facilities functionally related and subordinate thereto. Thus, an apartment which is to be used on other than a transient basis as a residence by a single person or by a family and which contains complete facilities for living, sleeping, eating, cooking, and sanitation, constitutes a family unit. Such a unit may be served by centrally located machinery and equipment as in a typical apartment building. To qualify as a family unit, the living facilities must be a separate, self-contained building or constitute one unit in a building substantially all of which consists of similar units, together with functionally related and subordinate facilities and areas. Hotels, motels, dormitories, fraternity and sorority houses, rooming houses, hospitals, sanitariums, rest homes, and trailer parks and courts for use on a transient basis do not constitute residential real property for family units.

(iii) *Functionally related and subordinate facilities.*—Under paragraph (a)(3) of this section, facilities which are functionally related and subordinate to residential real property actually used for family units include, for example, facilities for use by the occupants such as a swimming pool, a parking area, and recreational facilities.

(c) *Sports facilities.*—(1) *General rule.*—Section 103(b)(4)(B) provides that section 103(b)(1) shall not apply to obligations issued by a State or local governmental unit which are part of an issue substantially all of the proceeds of which are to be used to provide sports facilities. In order to qualify as an exempt facility under section 103(b)(4)(B) and this paragraph, the facility must satisfy the public use requirement of paragraph (a)(2) of this section by being available for use by members of the general public either as participants or as spectators.

(2) *Sports facility defined.*—(i) For purposes of section 103(b)(4)(B) and this paragraph, the term "sport facilities" includes both outdoor and indoor facilities. The facility may be designed either as a spectator or as a participation facility. For example, the term includes both indoor and outdoor stadiums for baseball, football, ice hockey, or other sports events, as well as facilities for the participation of the general public in sports activities, such as golf courses, ski slopes, swimming pools, tennis courts, and gymnasiums. The term does not include, however, facilities such as a golf course, swimming pool, or tennis court, which are constructed for use by members of a private club or as integral or subordinate parts of a hotel or motel, or the use of which will be restricted to a special class or group or to guests of a particular hotel or motel, since they are not

facilities for the use of the general public as required by paragraph (a)(2) of this section.

(ii) Under paragraph (a)(3) of this section, facilities which are functionally related and subordinate to a sports facility, such as a parking lot, clubhouse, ski slope warming house, bath house, or ski tow, are considered to be part of a sports facility. A ski lodge which consists primarily of overnight accommodations is not functionally related and subordinate to a sports facility.

(d) *Convention or trade show facilities.*—(1) *General rule.*—Section 103(b)(4)(C) provides that section 103(b)(1) shall not apply to obligations issued by a State or local governmental unit which are a part of an issue substantially all of the proceeds of which are to be used to provide convention or trade show facilities. In order to qualify under section 103(b)(4)(C) and this paragraph as an exempt facility, the facility must satisfy the public use requirement of paragraph (a)(2) of this section by being available for an appropriate charge or rental, on a rate scale basis, for use by members of the general public. The public use requirement is not satisfied if the use of a convention or trade show facility is limited by long-term leases to a single user or group of users.

(2) *Convention or trade show facilities defined.*—For purposes of section 103(b)(4)(C) and this paragraph, the term "convention or trade show facilities" means special-purpose buildings or structures, such as meeting halls and display areas, which are generally used to house a convention or trade show, including, under paragraph (a)(3) of this section, facilities functionally related and subordinate to such facilities such as parking lots or railroad sidings. A hotel or motel which is available to the general public, whether or not it is intended primarily to house persons attending or participating in a convention or trade show, is neither a convention or trade show facility nor functionally related and subordinate thereto.

(e) *Certain transportation facilities.*—(1) *General rule.*—Section 103(b)(4)(D) provides that section 103(b)(1) shall not apply to obligations issued by a State or local governmental unit which are part of an issue substantially all of the proceeds of which are to be used to provide (i) airports, docks, wharves, mass commuting facilities, or public parking facilities, or (ii) storage or training facilities directly related to any such facility. In order to qualify under section 103(b)(4)(D) and this paragraph as an exempt facility, the facility must satisfy the public use requirement of paragraph (a)(2) of this section by being available for use by members of the general public or for use by common carriers or charter carriers which serve members of the general public. A dock or wharf which is part of a public port (or a public port to be constructed in accordance with a plan which has been finally adopted on the date the obligations in question are issued) satisfies the public use test. A parking lot will be available for use by the general public unless more than an insubstantial portion thereof will be used exclusively by or for the benefit of a nonexempt person by reason of a formal or informal agreement or by reason of the remote geographic location of the facility.

(2) *Definitions.*—For purposes of section 103(b)(4)(D) and this paragraph—

(i) With respect to bonds sold at or before 5:00 p.m. EST on December 29, 1978, an airport includes service accommodations for the public such as terminals, retail stores in such terminals, runways, hangars, loading facilities, repair shops, parking areas, and facilities which, under paragraph (a)(3) of this section, are functionally related and subordinate to the airport, such as facilities for the preparation of in-flight meals, restaurants, and accommodations for temporary or overnight use by passengers, and other facilities functionally related to the needs or convenience of passengers, shipping companies, and airlines. The term "airport" does not include a landing strip which, by reason of a formal or informal agreement, or by reason of geographic location, will not be available for general public use.

(ii) With respect to bonds sold after 5:00 p.m. EST on December 29, 1978—

(a) An airport includes facilities which are directly related and essential to—

(1) Servicing aircraft or enabling aircraft to take off and land, or

(2) Transferring passengers or cargo to or from aircraft. A facility does not satisfy either of the foregoing requirements if the facility need not be located at, or in close proximity to, the take-off and landing area in order to perform its function. Examples of facilities which satisfy those requirements are terminals, runways, hangars, loading facilities, repair shops, and land-based navigation aids such as radar installations.

(b) Under paragraph (a)(3) of this section, an airport includes facilities other than those described in paragraph (e)(2)(ii)(a) only if they are functionally related and subordinate to an airport (as

>>> *Caution: Code Sec. 103 has been amended to remove special exempt bond issue rules and provide similar rules in Code Secs. 141-150.*

defined in paragraph (e)(2)(ii)(*a*). A facility (or part thereof) is not functionally related and subordinate to an airport if the facility (or part thereof)—

(1) Is not of a character and size commensurate with the character and size of the airport at or adjacent to which the facility is located, or

(2) Is not located at or adjacent to that airport.

A facility may satisfy the character and size requirement although it provides minimal benefits to other airports. For example, a facility for the preparation of in-flight meals which has capacity sufficient to prepare all in-flight meals for aircraft departing the airport where the facility is located qualifies although some meals may be consumed in transit between other airports. Other examples of facilities functionally related and subordinate to an airport are restaurants and retail stores located in terminals, ground transportation parking areas, and accommodations for temporary or overnight use by passengers. Unimproved land (including agricultural land) that is adjacent to an airport and that is impaired by a significant level of airport noise is functionally related and subordinate to the airport if after its acquisition that land will not be converted to a use that is incompatible with the level of airport noise. Adjacent land with existing improvements also may be functionally related and subordinate to an airport by reason of impairment by a significant level of airport noise but only if the use of such land before its acquisition is incompatible with the airport noise level, its use after acquisition is to be compatible, and the post-acquisition use will be essentially different from the pre-acquisition use. Notwithstanding the foregoing, an interest in such improved land acquired solely to mitigate damages attributable to airport noise is treated as functionally related and subordinate to the airport. Thus, for example, amounts allocated to imposing a servitude on improved land adjacent to an airport restricting its future use to uses compatible with airport noise are treated as amounts allocated to property functionally related and subordinate to an airport. For the purpose of determining whether land is impaired by a significant level of airport noise, any generally accepted noise estimating methodology may be used. For example, a Noise Exposure Forecast (NEF), a method for composite noise rating recommended by the Federal Aviation Administration to measure the impact of airport noise, may be used for this purpose. Compatibility may be determined by reference to regulations or general guidelines published by the Federal Aviation Administration under section 102 of the Aviation Safety and Noise Abatement Act of 1979 (49 U.S.C. 2102), or sections 11(3)(C) and 18(a)(4) of the Airport and Airway Development Act of 1970, as amended (49 U.S.C. 1711(3)(C) and 1718 (a)(4)), concerning uses of land impaired by a significant level of airport noise, or, where available, by reference to the airport compatibility plan specifically addressing what constitutes a compatible use of that land.

(*c*) As an illustration of the rules of this paragraph (e)(2)(ii), an office building (or office space within a building) or a computer facility, either of which serves a system-wide or regional function of an airline, is not considered part of an airport since that facility is not described in either paragraph (e)(2)(ii)(*a*) or (*b*). However, a maintenance or overhaul facility which services aircraft is considered part of an airport under paragraph (e)(2)(ii)(*a*) since that facility is directly related and essential to servicing aircraft and must be located where aircraft take off and land in order to perform its function.

(*d*) A hotel located at or adjacent to an airport satisfies the requirements of paragraph (e)(2)(ii)(*b*), that is, it is of a character and size commensurate with the character and size of the airport at or adjacent to which it is located, if the number of guest rooms in the hotel is reasonable for the size of the airport, taking into account the current and projected passenger usage of the terminal facility. If the hotel contains meeting rooms, the number and size of these rooms must be in reasonable proportion to the number of guest rooms in the hotel. Limited recreational facilities will not prevent the hotel from being of a character and size commensurate with the character and size of the airport.

(iii) A dock or wharf includes property which, under paragraph (a)(3) of this section, is functionally related and subordinate to a dock or wharf such as the structure alongside which a vessel docks, the equipment needed to receive and to discharge cargo and passengers from the vessel, such as cranes and conveyors, related storage, handling, office, and passenger areas, and similar facilities.

(iv) A mass commuting facility includes real property together with improvements and personal property used therein, such as machinery, equipment, and furniture, serving the general public commuting on a day-to-day basis by bus, subway, rail, ferry, or other conveyance which moves over prescribed routes. Such property also includes terminals and facilities which, under paragraph (a)(3) of this section, are functionally related and subordinate to the mass commuting facility, such as parking garages, car barns, and repair shops. Use of mass commuting facilities by noncommuters in common with

commuters is immaterial. Thus, a terminal leased to a common carrier bus line which serves both commuters and long distance travellers would qualify as an exempt facility.

(3) *Related storage and training facility.*—Section 103(b)(4)(D) includes only those storage and training facilities which are both (i) directly related to a facility to which subparagraph (1)(i) or (ii) of this paragraph applies and (ii) physically located on or adjacent to such a facility. For example, a storage facility would include a grain elevator, silo, warehouse, or oil and gas storage tank used in connection with a dock or wharf and located on or adjacent to such dock or wharf. Similarly, a training facility would include a building located at or adjacent to an airport for the training of flight personnel or a paved area immediately adjoining a bus garage used to train bus drivers.

(4) *Examples.*—The principles of this paragraph may be illustrated by the following examples:

Example (1). B Airport Authority, a political subdivision of State A, owns and operates B Airport. B Airport Authority adds several runways. In view of the expanded area impaired by significant levels of airport noise, the Authority proposes to issue bonds the proceeds of which are to be used to acquire a hospital located adjacent to the airport. The noise level on the acquired property is 40 NEF. By reference to a noise exposure map setting forth noncompatible land uses and by reference to guidelines published by the Federal Aviation Administration, it is established that continued use of the land for a hospital is not compatible with the noise level. Prior to issuing the bonds, B contracts to lease the property to Corporation C to be used for warehouse space. Within 18 months of the bonds' issuance C will remodel the hospital (previously owned by D, who is unrelated to C) with its own funds and rent the facility as a warehouse. Use as a warehouse is determined to be compatible with the level of airport noise impairing the land. The improved land and prospective revenues from the facility's rental are security for the proposed issuance. Based on the foregoing, the acquired land satisfies the public use test. Furthermore, it is functionally related and subordinate to the airport because the improvements are to be used in an essentially different manner than prior to the land's acquisition. The bonds are industrial development bonds. However, section 103(b)(1) does not apply unless the provisions of section 103(b)(8) and § 1.103-11 apply.

Example (2). The facts are the same as in Example (1) except that a substantial portion of the proceeds of the bond issue is allocated to the acquisition of a limited interest in an additional tract of land (also impaired by airport noise measured at 40 NEF) on which an office building stands. The limited interest holds B harmless for damages caused by airport noise and restricts uses of the tract after the building is retired to those compatible with noise levels caused by the airport. Based on the foregoing, such interest satisfies the public use test. Furthermore, the interest is functionally related and subordinate to the airport because it is solely to mitigate damage attributable to airport noise, in part by restricting future land uses. The bonds are industrial development bonds. However, section 103(b)(1) does not apply unless the provisions of section 103(b)(8) or § 1.103-11 apply.

Example (3). On June 1, 1980, M Airport Authority, a political subdivision of State O, issues obligations, the proceeds of which are loaned to X Corporation, a nonexempt person. X uses the proceeds to construct a hotel adjacent to the main terminal building at M Airport. X will be unconditionally liable for repayment of the proposed obligations. The hotel will be used to provide temporary and overnight accommodations for airline passengers using M Airport. The number of rooms in the hotel is reasonable for an airport of M's size, taking into account the current and projected passenger usage of the terminal facility. In addition to guest rooms, the hotel will contain a restaurant, small retail stores (such as a gift shop and newsstand), and limited recreation facilities (such as a swimming pool). The hotel will also contain several multipurpose rooms suitable for use as meeting rooms. The number and size of these rooms will be in reasonable proportion to the number and size of the guest rooms in the hotel. Use of the guest rooms, restaurant and stores, recreational facilities, and meeting rooms by air passengers arriving at or departing from M Airport will be incidental to the use of the hotel by air passengers for temporary and overnight accommodations. The hotel is of a character and size commensurate with the character and size of M Airport. Consequently, applying the provisions of § 1.103-8(e)(2) the hotel is functionally related and subordinate to M Airport. The obligations are industrial development bonds. Section 103(b)(1) does not apply to the obligations, however, unless the provisions of section 103(b)(10) and § 1.103-11 apply.

Example (4). On June 1, 1980, N Airport Authority, a political subdivision of State P, issues obligations, the proceeds of which are loaned to Y Corporation, a nonexempt person. Y uses the proceeds to construct a hotel adjacent to the main terminal building at N Airport.

➤➤➤ *Caution: Code Sec. 103 has been amended to remove special exempt bond issue rules and provide similar rules in Code Secs. 141-150.*

Y Corporation will be unconditionally liable for repayment of the proposed obligations. The hotel will contain extensive recreational facilities, including a large roof-top swimming pool, tennis courts, and a health club. In addition, facilities for conferences consisting of a ballroom-sized meeting room capable of being partitioned by movable panels and several smaller meeting rooms will be constructed. The number of rooms in the hotel will substantially exceed the number which is reasonable based on the current and projected passenger usage of the terminal facility. Because of the presence of extensive recreational and conference facilities, as well as the presence of an excessive number of rooms at the hotel, the hotel fails to be of a character and size commensurate with the character and size of N Airport. The result would be the same if the hotel did not have extensive recreational facilities. Consequently, the hotel is not functionally related and subordinate to N Airport under §1.103-8(e)(2). The obligations are industrial development bonds and interest thereon is not excluded from gross income by reason of subsection (a)(1) or (b)(4) of section 103.

(f) *Certain public utility facilities.*—(1) *General rule.*—(i) Section 103 (b)(4)(E) provides that section 103(c)(1) shall not apply to obligations issued by a State or local governmental unit which are part of an issue substantially all of the proceeds of which are to be used to provide sewage disposal facilities, solid waste disposal facilities, or facilities for the local furnishing of electric energy or gas. In order to qualify under section 103(b)(4)(E) as an exempt facility, the facility must satisfy the public use requirement of paragraph (a)(2) of this section. A public utility facility described in this subparagraph (with the exception of sewage and solid waste disposal facilities which will be treated in all events as serving the general public) will satisfy the public use requirement only if such facility, or the output thereof, is available for use by members of the general public.

(ii) A facility for the local furnishing of electric energy or gas is, for purposes of applying the public use test in paragraph (a)(2) of this section, available for use by members of the general public if (*a*) the owner or operator of the facility is obligated, by a legislative enactment, local ordinance, regulation, or the equivalent thereof, to furnish electric energy or gas to all persons who desire such services and who are within the service area of the owner or operator of such facility, and (*b*) it is reasonably expected that such facility will serve or be available to a large segment of the general public in such service area. For rules with respect to facilities for furnishing of water, see paragraph (h) of this section.

(2) *Definitions.*—For purposes of section 103(b)(4)(E) and this paragraph—

(i) The term "sewage disposal facilities" means any property used for the collection, storage, treatment, utilization, processing, or final disposal of sewage.

(ii) The term "facilities for the local furnishing of electric energy or gas" means property which—

(*a*) Is either property of a character subject to the allowance for depreciation provided in section 167 or land,

(*b*) Is used to produce, collect, generate, transmit, store, distribute, or convey electric energy or gas,

(*c*) Is used in the trade or business of furnishing electric energy or gas, and

(*d*) Is a part of a system providing service to the general populace of one or more communities or municipalities, but in no event more than 2 contiguous counties (or a political equivalent) whether or not such counties are located in one state.

For purposes of this subdivision, a city which is not within, or does not consist of, one or more counties (or a political equivalent) shall be treated as a county (or a political equivalent). A facility for the generation of electric energy otherwise qualifying under this subdivision will not be disqualified because it is connected to a system for interconnection with other public utility systems for the emergency transfer of electric energy. The facilities need not be located in the area served by them. Also, the term "facilities for local furnishing of electric energy or gas" does not include coal, oil, gas, nuclear cores, or other materials performing a similar function.

(g) *Air or water pollution control facilities.*—(1) *General rule.*—Section 103(b)(4)(F) provides that section 103(b)(1) shall not apply to obligations issued by a State or local governmental unit which are part of an issue substantially all of the proceeds of which are to be used to provide air or water pollution control facilities. Such facilities are in all events treated as serving the general public and, thus, satisfy the public use requirement of paragraph (a)(2) of this section.

(2) *Definitions.*—(i) For purposes of section 103(b)(4)(F) and this paragraph, property is a pollution control facility to the extent that the test of either subdivision (iii) or (iv) of this subparagraph is satisfied, but only if—

(*a*) It is property which is described in subdivision (ii) of this subparagraph and is either of a character subject to the allowance for depreciation provided in section 167 or land, and

(*b*) Either (1) a Federal, State, or local agency exercising jurisdiction has certified that the facility, as designed, is in furtherance of the purpose of abating or controlling atmospheric pollutants or contaminants, or water pollution, as the case may be, or (2) the facility is designed to meet or exceed applicable Federal, State, and local requirements for the control of atmospheric pollutants or contaminants, or water pollution, as the case may be, in effect at the time the obligations, the proceeds of which are to be used to provide such facilities, are issued.

(ii) Property is described in this subdivision if it is property to be used, in whole or in part, to abate or control water or atmospheric pollution or contamination by removing, altering, disposing, or storing pollutants, contaminants, wastes, or heat. In the case of property to be used to control water pollution, such property includes the necessary intercepting sewers, pumping, power, and other equipment, and their appurtenances. For rules relating to facilities which remove pollutants from fuel or certain other items, see subdivision (vi) of this subparagraph.

(iii) In the case of an expenditure for property which is designed for no significant purpose other than the control of pollution, the total expenditure for such property satisfies the test of this subdivision. Thus, where property which is to serve no function other than the control of pollution is to be added to an existing manufacturing or production facility, the total expenditure for such property satisfies the test of this subdivision. Also, if an expenditure for property would not be made but for the purpose of controlling pollution, and if the expenditure has no significant purpose other than the purpose of pollution control, the total expenditure for such property satisfies the test of this subdivision even though such property serves one or more functions in addition to its function as a pollution control facility.

(iv) In the case of property to be placed in service for the purpose of controlling pollution and for a significant purpose other than controlling pollution, only the incremental cost of such facility satisfies the test of this subdivision. The "incremental cost" of property is the excess of its total cost over that portion of its cost expended for a purpose other than the control of pollution.

(v) An expenditure has a significant purpose other than the control of pollution if it results in an increase in production or capacity, or in a material extension of the useful life of a manufacturing or production facility of a part thereof.

(vi) [Reserved]

(h) *Water facilities.*—(1) *General rule.*—Section 103(b)(4)(G) provides that section 103(b)(1) shall not apply to obligations issued by a State or local governmental unit which are part of an issue substantially all of the proceeds of which are to be used to provide facilities for the furnishing of water which are available, on reasonable demand, to members of the general public. A water facility will satisfy the public use test of paragraph (a)(2) of this section if it will provide water, on reasonable demand, to any member of the general public within the service area of the water system of which such facility is a part.

(2) *Definition.*—For purposes of section 103(b)(4)(G) and this paragraph, the "water facilities" include artesian wells, reservoirs, dams, related equipment and pipelines, and other facilities used to furnish water for domestic, industrial, irrigation, or other purposes.

(3) *Effective date.*—The provisions of this paragraph apply in the case of facilities provided by obligations issued after January 1, 1969. In the case of facilities provided by obligations issued on or before such date to which section 103(b) is applicable, the provisions of paragraph (f) of this section shall apply. For such purposes, wherever the term "local furnishing of electric energy or gas" appears in paragraph (f) of this section, such term shall be deemed to read "local furnishing of electric energy, gas, or water."

(i) *Examples.*—The application of section 103(b)(4) and this section are illustrated by the following examples:

Example (1). City B plans to issue $10 million of bonds to be used to construct a sports stadium. The revenues from the facility and the facility itself will be the security for the bonds. A professional football team rents the facility on a long-term lease for part of the year and a professional baseball team rents the sports facility for the remainder of the year. Tickets are sold by the teams to the general public. The bonds are industrial development bonds, but since the proceeds are used for a spectator facility for general public use, which is an exempt facility under section 103(b)(4)(B) and paragraph (c) of this section, section 103(b)(1) does not apply unless the provisions of section 103(b)(8) and §1.103-11 apply.

⋙→ *Caution: Code Sec. 103 has been amended to remove special exempt bond issue rules and provide similar rules in Code Secs. 141-150.*

Example (2). City C plans to issue $10 million of bonds to be used to construct a convention hall which it will own. City C plans to lease the convention hall for 25 years to corporation Y, a nonexempt person, which will operate and maintain it. The terms of the lease obligate Y to make the convention hall generally available for civic, business, and recreational shows, meetings, performances, and similar activities serving or benefiting the community. Lease payments from Y and the facility will be security for the bonds. The bonds are industrial development bonds, but since the proceeds are to be used for a facility for general public use, which is an exempt facility under section 103(b)(4)(C) and paragraph (d) of this section, section 103(b)(1) does not apply unless the provisions of section 103(b)(8) and § 1.103-11 apply.

Example (3). City D issues $100 million of its bonds and uses the proceeds to finance construction of an airport for the use of the general public. D will own and operate the airport. A major portion of the rentable space in the terminal building is leased on a long-term basis to common carrier and non-scheduled airlines. The bonds will be secured by the airport landing and runway charges and by payments with respect to such long-term leases from such commercial airlines. Such commercial airline payments are expected to constitute more than 50 percent of the total revenues from the airport. The bonds are industrial development bonds, but since the proceeds are to be used for an airport for use by the general public and by carriers serving the general public, which is an exempt facility under section 103(b)(4)(D) and paragraph (e) of this section, section 103(b)(1) does not apply unless the provisions of section 103(b)(8) and § 1.103-11 apply. The result would be the same if D hired an airport management firm to operate the airport.

Example (4). City E issues $6 million of its bonds and uses the proceeds to finance construction of a landing strip for airplanes to be located adjacent to the factories of corporations Y and Z. The landing strip will be used in the trades or businesses of Y and Z and by any member of the general public wishing to use it. However, due to its location, general public use will be negligible. The lease payments by Y and Z for the use of the facility are the security for the bonds. The bonds are industrial development bonds and the facility is not an exempt facility under section 103(b)(4)(D) and paragraph (c) of this section because it is not a facility constructed for general public use.

Example (5). State F and corporation Z enter into an arrangement which provides that F will issue $10 million of its bonds and use the proceeds to construct a facility for Z the only purpose of which is to control air and water pollution at Z's plant. The principal and interest on the bonds will be secured by the charges which F will impose on Z. The bonds are industrial development bonds, but since the proceeds are to be used for air and water pollution facilities designed to abate pollution by private persons, such facilities are for the benefit of the general public and are exempt facilities under section 103(b)(4)(F) and paragraph (g) of this section. Accordingly, section 103(b)(1) does not apply unless the provisions of section 103(b)(8) and § 1.103-11 apply.

Example (6). City G issues $20 million of its bonds and will use $6 million to finance residential rental property which qualifies as an exempt facility under section 103(b)(4)(A) and paragraph (b) of this section, $9 million to finance construction of a stadium which qualifies as an exempt facility under section 103(b)(4)(B) and paragraph (c) of this section, and $5 million for convention facilities which qualify as exempt facilities under section 103(b)(4)(C) and paragraph (d) of this section. The facilities will be used in the trades or businesses of nonexempt persons and rental payments with respect to such facilities and the facilities themselves will be the security for the bonds. The bonds are industrial development bonds, but since all the proceeds are to be used for facilities which are exempt facilities under section 103(b)(4), section 103(b)(1) does not apply unless the provisions of section 103(b)(10) and § 1.103-11 apply. The result would be the same, if; instead of using $9 million to finance construction of a stadium, the $9 million were used to finance construction of a capitol building. [Reg. § 1.103-8].

☐ [T.D. 7199, 7-31-72. *Amended by T.D. 7362, 6-17-75; T.D. 7511, 9-30-77; T.D. 7737, 11-14-80; T.D. 7840, 10-12-82; T.D. 7848, 11-10-82; T.D. 7869, 1-12-83; T.D. 8476, 6-14-93; T.D. 8538, 5-5-94; T.D. 8718, 5-8-97 and T.D. 9546, 8-18-2011.]*

[Reg. § 1.103-9]

§ 1.103-9. Interest on bonds to finance industrial parks.— (a) *General rule.—*(1) Under section 103(c)(5), interest paid on an issue of obligations issued by a State or local governmental unit (as defined in § 1.103-1) is not includable in gross income if substantially all of the proceeds of such issue is to be used to finance the acquisition or development of land as the site for an industrial park (referred to in this section as "industrial park bonds"). However, interest on an obligation of such an issue is includable in gross income if the obligation is held by a substantial user or a related

person (as described in section 103(c)(7) and § 1.103-11). If substantially all of the proceeds of a bond issue is to be so used to finance an industrial park, the debt obligations are treated as obligations described in section 103(a)(1) and § 1.103-1 even though such obligations are industrial development bonds within the meaning of section 103(c)(2) and § 1.103-7. Whether substantially all of the proceeds of an issue of governmental obligations are used to finance an industrial park is determined consistently with the rules for exempt facilities in § 1.103-8 (a)(1)(i).

(2) The provisions of subparagraph (1) of this paragraph shall also apply to an issue of obligations substantially all of the proceeds of which is to be used to acquire or develop land as the site for an industrial park described in section 103(c)(5) and this section and for either or both of the following purposes: (i) to finance exempt facilities described in section 103(c)(4) and § 1.103-8, (ii) to finance facilities to be used by an exempt person.

(3) Section 103(c)(5) only becomes applicable where the bond issue meets both the trade or business and the security interest tests so that the obligations are industrial development bonds within the meaning of section 103(c)(2). For the interrelationship of the rules provided in this section and the exemption for certain small issues provided in section 103(c)(6), see § 1.103-10.

(b) *Definition of an industrial park.—*For purposes of section 103(c)(5) and this section, the term "industrial park" means a tract of land, other than a tract of land intended for use by a single enterprise, suitable primarily for use as building sites by a group of enterprises engaged in industrial, distribution, or wholesale businesses if either—

(1) The control and administration of the tract is vested in an exempt person (within the meaning of paragraph (b)(2) of § 1.103-7), or

(2) The uses of the tract are normally (i) regulated by protective minimum restrictions, ordinarily including the size of individual sites, parking and loading regulations, and building setback lines, and (ii) designed to be compatible, under a comprehensive plan, with the community in which the industrial park is located and with the uses of the surrounding land.

(c) *Development of land defined.—*For purposes of section 103(c)(5) and this section, the term "development of land" includes the provision of certain improvements to an industrial park site if such improvements are incidental to the use of the land as an industrial park. Such incidental improvements include the building or installation of incidental water, sewer, sewage and waste disposal, drainage, or similar facilities (whether surface, subsurface, or both). Such incidental improvements include the provision of incidental transportation facilities, such as hard-surface roads (including curbs and gutters) and railroad spurs and sidings; power distribution facilities, such as gas and electric lines; and communication facilities. The provision of structures or buildings of any kind is not included within the meaning of the term "development of land," except for those structures or buildings which are necessary in connection with the incidental improvements encompassed by the term, such as, for example, a water pumphouse and storage tank needed in connection with the incidental provision of water facilities in an industrial park.

(d) *Examples.—*The applications of the rules contained in section 103(c)(5) and this section are illustrated by the following examples:

Example (1). City A and corporation X, Y, and Z (unrelated companies) enter into an arrangement under which A is to acquire a tract of land suitable for use as an industrial park. The arrangement provides that: (1) A will issue $10 million of bonds to be used for the acquisition and development of a suitable tract of land; (2) the tract will be controlled and administered by A, pursuant to a comprehensive zoning plan, for the use of a group of enterprises; (3) A will install necessary water, sewer, and drainage facilities on the tract; (4) A will sell substantial portions of the developed tract to X for use as a factory site and to Y for use as a warehouse site; (5) A will lease a sizeable portion of the tract to Z for 20 years as a distribution center site; and (6) the developed tract and the proceeds from the sale or lease of parts of the tract will be the security for the bonds. The bonds are industrial development bonds. Since, however, the proceeds of the issue are to be used for the acquisition and development of a tract of land as the site for an industrial park under section 103(c)(5), section 103(c)(1) does not apply unless the provisions of section 103(c)(7) and § 1.103-11 apply.

Example (2). The facts are the same as in example (1) except that $1 million of the proceeds of the $10 million issue are to be used for the construction of a factory by corporation W or X. The bonds are industrial development bonds. Under these circumstances, substantially all of the proceeds are treated as used or to be used for the acquisition and development of a tract of land as the site for an industrial park described in section 103(c)(5). Accordingly, section

>>>→ *Caution: Code Sec. 103 has been amended to remove special exempt bond issue rules and provide similar rules in Code Secs. 141-150.*

103(c)(1) does not apply unless the provisions of section 103(c)(7) and §1.103-11 apply. [Reg. §1.103-9.]

☐ [*T.D. 7199, 7-31-72. Amended by T.D. 7511, 9-30-77.*]

[Reg. §1.103-10]

§1.103-10. Exemption for certain small issues of industrial development bonds.—(a) *In general.*—Section 103(b)(6) applies to certain industrial development bond issues (referred to in this section as "exempt small issues") and bonds issued to refund certain issues (referred to in this section as "exempt small refunding issues"). If an issue is an exempt small issue or an exempt small refunding issue, then under the requirements of section 103(b)(6) and this section the interest paid on the debt obligations is not includable in gross income, and the obligations are treated as obligations described in section 103(a)(1) and §1.103-1, even though such obligations are industrial development bonds as defined in section 103(b)(2) and §1.103-7. However, interest on an obligation of such an issue is includable in gross income if the obligation is held by a substantial user of the financial facilities or a related person (as described in section 103(b)(7) and §1.103-11). Section 103(b)(6) only becomes applicable where the bond issue meets both the trade or business and the security interest tests so that the obligations are industrial development bonds within the meaning of section 103(b)(2). For bonds issued before January 1, 1979, in taxable years ending before such date, and for capital expenditures made before January 1, 1979, with respect to such bonds, paragraphs (b), (c), and (d) of this section shall be applied by substituting $5 million for $10 million.

(b) *Small issue exemption.*—(1) *$1 million or less.*—Section 103(b)(6)(A) provides that section 103(b)(1) shall not apply to any debt obligation issued by a State or local governmental unit as part of an issue where—

(i) The aggregate authorized face amount of such issue (determined by aggregating the outstanding face amount of any prior exempt small issues described in paragraph (d) of this section and the face amount of the issue of obligations in question) is $1 million or less; and

(ii) Substantially all of the proceeds of such issue is to be used for the acquisition, construction, reconstruction, or improvement of land or property of a character subject to the allowance for depreciation under section 167. Proceeds which are loaned to a borrower for use as working capital or to finance inventory are not used in the manner described in the preceding sentence. Whether substantially all of the proceeds of an issue of governmental obligations are used in such manner is determined consistently with the rules for exempt facilities in §1.103-8(a)(1)(i). Any obligation which is an industrial development bond within the meaning of section 103(b)(2) and which satisfies the $1 million small issue exemption requirements is an exempt small issue. See paragraph (c)(1) of this section for the treatment of refunding issues of $1 million or less.

(2) *$10 million or less.*—(i) Under section 103(b)(6)(D), the issuing State or local governmental unit may elect to have an aggregate authorized face amount of $10 million or less, in lieu of the $1 million exemption otherwise provided for in section 103(b)(6)(A), with respect to issues of obligations that are industrial development bonds (within the meaning of section 103(b)(2)) issued after October 24, 1968. If the election is made in a timely manner, the bonds will be treated as obligations of a State or local governmental unit described in section 103(a)(1) and §1.103-1 if the sum of—

(a) The aggregate face amount of the issue including the aggregate outstanding face amount of any prior $1 million or $10 million exempt small issues taken into account under section 103(b)(6)(B) and paragraph (d) of this section, and

(b) The aggregate amount of "section 103(b)(6)(D) capital expenditures" (within the meaning of paragraph (b)(2)(ii) of this section),

is $10 million or less. In the case of an issue of obligations that qualified for exemption uner section 103(b)(6)(A) and this paragraph, if a section 103(b)(6)(D) capital expenditure made after the date of issue has the effect of making taxable the interest on the issue, under section 103(b)(6)(G) the loss of tax exemption for the interest shall begin only with the date on which the expenditure that caused the issue to cease to qualify under the $10 million limit was paid or incurred. See paragraph (b)(2)(vi) of this section for the time and manner in which the issuer may elect the $10 million exemption. See section 103(b)(6)(H) and paragraph (c)(2) of this section for the treatment of certain refinancing issues of $10 million or less.

(ii) The term "section 103(b)(6)(D) capital expenditure" is defined in this subdivision. Special rules for applying such definition in the case of certain expenditures paid or incurred by a State or local governmental unit are prescribed in subdivision (iii) of this subparagraph. Except as excluded by subdivision (iv) or (v) of this subparagraph, an expenditure (regardless of how paid, whether in cash, notes, or stock in a taxable or nontaxable transaction) is a section 103(b)(6)(D) capital expenditure if—

(a) The capital expenditure was financed other than out of the proceeds of issues to the extent such issues are taken into account under paragraph (b)(2)(i)(a) of this section.

(b) The capital expenditures were paid or incurred during the 6-year period which begins 3 years before the date of issuance of the issue in question and ends 3 years after such date,

(c) The principal user of the facility in connection with which the property resulting from the capital expenditures is used and the principal user of the facility financed by the proceeds of the issue in question is the same person or are two or more related persons (as defined in section 103(b)(6)(C) and paragraph (e) of this section),

(d) Both facilities referred to in (c) of this subdivision were (during the period described in (b) of this subdivision or a part thereof) located in the same incorporated municipality or in the same county (outside of the incorporated municipalities in such county), and

(e) The capital expenditures were properly chargeable to the capital account of any person or State or local governmental unit (whether or not such person is the principal user of the facility or a related person) determined, for this purpose, without regard to any rule of the Code which permits expenditures properly chargeable to capital account to be treated as current expenses. With respect to obligations issued on or after August 8, 1972, determinations under the preceding sentence shall be made by including any expenditure which may, under any rule or election under the Code, be treated as a capital expenditure (whether or not such expenditure is so treated). With respect to obligations issued on or after August 8, 1972, for purposes of this subparagraph, capital expenditures made with respect to a contiguous or integrated facility which is located on both sides of a border between two or more political jurisdictions are made with respect to a facility located in all such jurisdictions and, therefore, shall be treated as if they were made in each such political jurisdiction.

(iii) Amounts properly chargeable to capital account under subdivision (ii)(e) of this subparagraph include capital expenditures made by a State or local governmental unit with respect to an exempt facility or an industrial park, within the 6-year period described in subdivision (ii)(b) of this subparagraph, out of the proceeds of bond issues to which section 103(b)(1) did not apply by reason of section 103(b)(4) or (5) (relating to certain exempt activities and industrial parks). Thus, for example, the cost to the lessor of a leased plant site financed out of the proceeds of an issue for an exempt air pollution control facility under section 103(b)(4)(F) and paragraph (g) of §1.103-8 would constitute a section 103(b)(6)(D) capital expenditure. However, in the case of an industrial park, only the land costs allocated on an area basis to the plant site and the actual cost of any improvements made on the plant site, or to be used principally in connection with the actual plant site occupied by a principal user or a related person, shall be taken into account as capital expenditures. Where the actual amount of capital expenditures made with respect to a facility by a person (including a State or local governmental unit) other than the user of such facility (or a related person) cannot be ascertained, the fair market value of the property with respect to which the capital expenditures were made, at the time of such capital expenditures, shall be deemed to be the amount of such capital expenditures. In the case of a transaction which is not in form a purchase but which is treated as a purchase for Federal income tax purposes, the purchase price for Federal income tax purposes shall constitute a capital expenditure.

(iv) A section 103(b)(6)(D) capital expenditure shall not include any "excluded expenditure" described in subdivision (a) through (e) of this subdivision (iv):

(a) A capital expenditure is an excluded expenditure if either it is made by a public utility company which is not the principal user of the facility financed by the proceeds of the issue in question (or a related person) with respect to property of such company, or it is made by a State or local governmental unit with respect to property of such unit, and if in either case it meets all of the following three conditions: Such property of such company or unit (as the case may be) must be used to provide gas, water, sewage disposal services, electric energy, or telephone service. Such property must be installed in, or connected to, the facility but must not consist of property which is such an integral part of the facility that the cost of such property is ordinarily included as part of the acquisition, construction, or reconstruction cost of such facility. Such property must be of a type normally paid for by the user (or a related person) in the form of periodic fees based upon time or use.

(b) A capital expenditure is an excluded expenditure if it is made by a person other than the user, a related person, or a State or

»»→ *Caution: Code Sec. 103 has been amended to remove special exempt bond issue rules and provide similar rules in Code Secs. 141-150.*

local governmental unit and if it is made with respect to tangible personal property (within the meaning of paragraph (c) of §1.48-1), or intangible personal property, leased to the user (or a related person) of a facility. However, the preceding sentence shall apply only if such personal property is leased by the manufacturer of such tangible or intangible personal property, or by a person in the trade or business of leasing property the same as, or similar to, such personal property, and only if, pursuant to general business practice, property of such type is ordinarily the subject of a lease.

(c) A capital expenditure is an excluded expenditure if it is made to replace property damaged or destroyed by fire, storm, or other casualty, to the extent that these expenditures do not exceed in dollar amount the fair market value (determined immediately before the casualty) of the property replaced.

(d) A capital expenditure is an excluded expenditure if it is required by a change made after the date of issue in a Federal or State law, or a local ordinance which has general application, or if it is required by a change made after such date in rules and regulations of general application issued under such law or ordinance.

(e) A capital expenditure is an excluded expenditure if it is required by or arises out of circumstances which could not reasonably be foreseen on the date of issue or which arise out of a mistake of law or fact. However, the aggregate dollar amount taken into account under this subdivision (e) with respect to any issue may not exceed $1,000,000. With respect to expenditures incurred prior to December 11, 1971, the dollar amount specified in the preceding sentence shall be $250,000.

(v)(a) If the assets of a corporation are acquired by another corporation in a transaction to which section 381(a) (relating to carryovers in certain corporate acquisitions) applies, the exchange of consideration by the acquiring corporation for such assets is not a section 103(b)(6)(D) capital expenditure by such acquiring corporation.

(b) However, if an exchange referred to in (a) of this subdivision occurs during the 6-year period beginning 3 years before the date of issuance of an issue of obligations and ending 3 years after such date, the transferor and transferee shall be treated as having been related persons for the portion of such 6-year period preceding the date of the exchange for purposes of determining whether section 103(b)(6)(D) capital expenditures have been made. For purposes of this subdivision (b), the date of an exchange to which section 381 applies shall be the date of distribution or transfer within the meaning of paragraph (b) of §1.381(b)-1.

(c) If section 351 (a) applies to a transfer of property to a corporation solely in exchange for its stock or securities, the issuance of such stock or securities in such exchange is not a section 103(b)(6)(D) capital expenditure by such corporation.

(d) However, if such a transfer referred to in (c) of this subdivision occurs during the 6-year period beginning 3 years before the date of issuance of an issue of obligations and ending 3 years after such date, and if, with respect to the property transferred, expenditures made within such period would have been section 103(b)(6)(D) capital expenditures if the transferor and transferee had been related persons for such period, then such capital expenditures shall be considered to be section 103(b)(6)(D) capital expenditures made by the transferee. In addition, if a transferor and transferee are related persons immediately following such transfer, such transferor and transferee shall also be treated as having been related persons for the portion of such 6-year period preceding the date of such transfer.

(e) For purposes of this subdivision (v), the term "issue of obligations" means an issue being tested for purposes of qualifying or continuing to qualify under an election pursuant to section 103(b)(6)(D) as to which an amount which would be a section 103(b)(6)(D) capital expenditure solely by reason of (b) or (d) of the subdivision must be taken into account.

(f) If with respect to an issue of obligations an expenditure would not have been a section 103(b)(6)(D) capital expenditure but for the application of (b) or (d) of this subdivision, and if such section 103(b)(6)(D) capital expenditure has the effect of making taxable the interest on an issue of obligations which qualified for exemption under section 103(b)(6)(A) and this paragraph, the loss of tax exemption for such interest shall begin not earlier than the date of such exchange or transfer referred to in this subdivision (v).

(vi) The issuer may make the election provided by section 103(b)(6)(D) and this paragraph (b)(2) (assuming that the bonds otherwise qualify under section 103(b)(6)) by noting the election affirmatively at or before the time of issuance of the issue in question on its books or records with respect to the issue. The term "books or records" includes the bond resolution or other similar legislation for the issue in question as well as the bond transcript or other compilation of bond and bond-related documents. If the issuer fails to make an election at the time and in the manner prescribed in this para-

graph (b)(2), the issue will not be treated as described in section 103(b)(6)(D), and interest thereon will be includible in gross income.

(c) *Refunding or refinancing issue exemption.*—(1) *$1 million or less refunding issue.*—Section 103(b)(6)(A) also provides that section 103(b)(1) shall not apply to any debt obligation issued by a State or local governmental unit as part of an issue the aggregate authorized face amount of which is $1 million or less, if substantially all of the proceeds of such issue are to be used—

(i) To redeem part or all of a prior issue substantially all of the proceeds of which were used to acquire, construct, reconstruct, or improve land or property of a character subject to the allowance for depreciation, or

(ii) To redeem part or all of a prior exempt small refunding issue.

(2) *$10 million or less refinancing issue.*—Section 103(b)(6)(H) provides that section 103(b)(1) shall not apply to any debt obligation issued by a governmental unit as part of an issue which is $10 million or less if the condition of section 103(b)(6)(H) is met and if substantially all of the proceeds are to be used—

(i) To redeem part or all of one or more prior exempt small issues, or

(ii) To redeem part or all of one or more prior exempt small refunding issues.

The condition of section 103(b)(6)(H) is that an election by the issuer of the $10 million exemption in lieu of the $1 million limit for a refunding issue may be made only if each prior issue being redeemed is an issue which qualified either for the $1 million exemption or, by reason of an election under section 103(b)(6)(D), for the $10 million exemption. In addition, in applying the capital expenditures test under section 103(b)(6)(D)(ii) and paragraph (b)(2)(i)(b) of this section to refinancing issues, section 103(b)(6)(D) capital expenditures are taken into account only for purposes of determining whether prior issues which were made under the section 103(b)(6)(D) election qualified under section 103(b)(6)(A) and would have continued to qualify under that section but for the redemption.

(d) *Certain prior issues taken into account.*—(1) *In general.*—Section 103(b)(6)(B) provides, in effect, that if (i) a prior issue specified in subparagraph (2) of this paragraph is an exempt small issue (including for this purpose an exempt small refunding issue) under section 103(b)(6)(A) and this section, and (ii) such prior issue is outstanding at the time of issuance of a subsequent issue, then in determining the aggregate face amount of such subsequent issue (for purposes of determining whether such issue is a $1 million or $10 million exempt small issue under section 103(b)(6)(A) and this section) there shall be taken into account the outstanding face amount of such prior exempt small issue. For purposes of this paragraph, the outstanding face amount of a prior exempt small issue does not include the face amount of any obligation which is to be redeemed from the proceeds of such subsequent issue.

(2) *Prior issues specified.*—The face amount of an outstanding prior exempt small issue is taken into account under subparagraph (1) of this paragraph if—

(i) The proceeds of both the prior exempt small issue and of the subsequent issue (whether or not the State or local governmental unit issuing such obligation is the same unit for each such issue) are or will be used primarily with respect to facilities located or to be located in the same incorporated municipality or located or to be located in the same county outside of an incorporated municipality in such county (and for purposes of this subdivision, on or after August 8, 1972, a contiguous or integrated facility which is located on both sides of a border between two or more political jurisdictions shall be treated as if it is entirely within each such political jurisdiction), and

(ii) The principal user of the financed facilities referred to in subdivision (i) of this subparagraph is or will be the same person or two or more related persons (as defined in section 103(b)(6)(C) and paragraph (e) of this section).

(3) *Rules of application.*—The rules of this paragraph shall apply—

(i) Only in the case of outstanding prior exempt small issues which are industrial development bonds to which section 103(b)(1) would have applied but for the provisions of section 103(b)(6). Thus, for example, the provisions of this paragraph do not apply in respect of a prior issue of obligations issued on or before April 30, 1968. In addition, the provisions of this paragraph do not apply in respect of a prior issue for an exempt facility under section 103(b)(4) and §1.103-8, or for an industrial park under section 103(b)(5) and §1.103-9, whether or not the issue might also have qualified as an exempt small issue under section 103(b)(6)(A) and this section.

»»→ Caution: Code Sec. 103 has been amended to remove special exempt bond issue rules and provide similar rules in Code Secs. 141-150.

(ii) To all prior exempt small issues which meet the requirements of this paragraph. Thus, for example, in determining the aggregate face amount of an issue under section 103(b)(6)(A), the outstanding face amount of prior $1 million or $10 million exempt small issues which meet the requirements of this paragraph shall be taken into account in determining the aggregate face amount of a subsequent issue being tested for the $1 million small issue exemption. Similarly, in determining the aggregate face amount of an issue under section 103(b)(6)(A) and (D), the outstanding face amount of prior $1 million or $10 million exempt small issues which meet the requirements of this paragraph shall be taken into account in determining the aggregate face amount of a subsequent issue being tested for the $10 million small issue exemption.

(e) *Related persons.*—For purposes of section 103(b) and §§1.103-7 through 1.103-11, the term "related person" means a person who is related to another person if, on the date of issue of an issue of obligations—

(1) The relationship between such persons would result in a disallowance of losses under section 267 (relating to disallowance of losses, etc., between related taxpayers) and section 707(b) (relating to losses disallowed, etc., between partners and controlled partnerships) and the regulations thereunder, or

(2) Such persons are members of the same controlled group of corporations, as defined in section 1563(a), relating to definition of controlled group of corporations (except that "more than 50 percent" shall be substituted for "at least 80 percent" each place it appears in section 1563(a)) and the regulations thereunder.

(f) *Disqualification of certain small issues.*—(1) Section 103(b)(6) shall not apply to any obligation issued after April 24, 1979, which is part of an issue, a significant portion of the proceeds of which are to be used directly or indirectly to provide residential real property for family units. For purposes of the preceding sentence, the term "residential real property for family units" means residential rental projects (within the meaning of §1.103-8(b)) and owner-occupied residences (within the meaning of section 103A).

(2) For purposes of paragraph (f)(1), a significant portion of the proceeds of an issue are used to provide residential real property for family units if 5 percent or more of the proceeds are so used.

(g) *Examples.*—The application of the rules contained in section 103(b)(6) and this section are illustrated by the following examples:

Example (1). County A and corporation X enter into an arrangement under which the county will provide a factory which X will lease for 25 years. The arrangement provides (1) that A will issue $1 million of bonds on March 1, 1970, (2) that the proceeds of the bond issue will be used to acquire land in County A (but not in an incorporated municipality) and to construct and equip a factory on such land in accordance with X's specifications, (3) that X will rent the facility for 25 years at an annual rental equal to the amount necessary to amortize the principal and pay the interest on the outstanding bonds, and (4) that such payments by X and the facility itself shall be the security for the bonds. Although the bonds issued are industrial development bonds, the bonds are an exempt small issue under section 103(b)(6)(A) and this section since the aggregate authorized face amount of the bond issue is $1 million or less and all of the proceeds of the bond issue are to be used to acquire and improve land and acquire and construct depreciable property. The result would be the same if the arrangement provided that X would purchase the facility from A.

Example (2). The facts are the same as in example (1) except that, instead of acquiring land and constructing a new factory, the arrangement provides that A will acquire a vacant existing factory building and rebuild and equip the building in accordance with X's specifications. The bonds are an exempt small issue for the same reasons as in example (1).

Example (3). The facts are the same as in example (1) or (2) except that the financed facilities are additions to facilities which were financed by an issue of bonds to which section 103(c)(1) does not apply because such bonds were issued prior to May 1, 1968, or were subject to the transitional provisions of §1.103-12. The bonds are an exempt small issue since neither of the prior bond issues are taken into account under section 103(b)(6)(B) and this section in determining the status of industrial development bonds which are issued after April 30, 1968, and which are not subject to the transitional provisions of §1.103-12.

Example (4). The facts are the same as in example (1) except that, subsequently, corporation X proposes to County A that A built a $400,000 warehouse located in Town M (an unincorporated town located in County A) for X under terms similar to the factory arrangement described in example (1). On the proposed issue date of the subsequent bond issue, $600,000 of the first exempt small issue will be outstanding. If A issues $400,000 of bonds for such purposes,

the bonds will be an exempt small issue under section 103(b)(6) and this section since, under the rules of section 103(b)(6)(B) and paragraph (d) of this section, if the aggregate authorized face amount of the new issue and the outstanding prior exempt small issue will be $1 million or less, the new issue will be an exempt small issue. If, however, the aggregate authorized face amount of the prior issue outstanding on the date of the subsequent issue were in excess of $600,000, the subsequent issue would not qualify as an exempt small issue because (1) the combined aggregate face amount of the outstanding prior issue and the new issue would be in excess of $1 million, (2) the facilities financed by both issues are to be located in unincorporated areas in the same county, (3) the same taxpayer will be the principal user of both facilities, and (4) but for the rules of section 103(b)(6)(B) and paragraph (d) of this section the prior issue would be an exempt small issue.

Example (5). The facts are the same as in example (1) except that subsequently corporation X proposes to City P and City R (incorporated municipalities located in County A) that P and R each issue bonds and each build $1 million facilities to be located in Cities P and R for the use of X under terms similar to the arrangement in example (1). Each of the $1 million issues will be an exempt small issue because each proposed facility is located within a different incorporated municipality and the proceeds of the prior outstanding exempt small issue were used to construct facilities outside of an incorporated area.

Example (6). The facts are the same as in example (1) except that $95,000 of the $1 million will be used by the corporation as working capital. The bonds are an exempt small issue for the same reason as in example (1) since substantially all of the proceeds will be used for the acquisition of land and the construction of depreciable property.

Example (7). The facts are the same as in example (1) except that on November 1, 1969, County A issued $10 million of industrial development bonds, all of the proceeds of which were issued for the acquisition of land as the site for an industrial park within the meaning of section 103(c)(5) and §1.103-9. The proceeds of the $1 million of bonds issued in 1970 will be used to construct a factory for corporation X to be located in the industrial park. The bonds issued in 1970 are industrial development bonds within the meaning of section 103(b)(2) and §1.103-7. Since, however, the prior 1969 issue is not an issue to which section 103(b)(6)(A) applied (see paragraph (d)(3)(i) of this section), the bonds issued in 1970 are an exempt small issue for the reasons stated in example (1).

Example (8). County B enters into three separate arrangements with three unrelated corporations whereby the county will provide separate storage facilities for each corporation. The arrangement provides (1) that the county will issue bonds and loan to each corporation $250,000 of the proceeds which will be used to acquire land in the county and to construct the facilities, (2) that the rental payments by the corporations will be equal to the amount necessary to amortize the principal and pay the interest on any outstanding bonds issued by the county, and (3) that the payments by the corporations and the facilities themselves shall be the security for the industrial development bonds. For convenience, the county issues one series of bonds in the face amount of $750,000 rather than three separate series of bonds of $250,000 each. The issue is an exempt small issue under section 103(c)(6)(A) and paragraph (b)(1) of this section since the aggregate authorized face amount of the bond issue is $1 million or less, and all of the proceeds of the bond issue are to be used to acquire and improve land and acquire and construct depreciable property.

Example (9). City C and corporation Y enter into an arrangement under which C will provide a factory which Y will lease for 25 years. The arrangement provides (1) that C will issue $4 million of bonds on March 1, 1969, after making the election under section 103(b)(6)(D) and paragraph (b)(2) of this section, (2) that the proceeds of the bond issue will be used to acquire land in the city and to construct and equip a factory on such land in accordance with Y's specifications, (3) that Y will rent the facilities for 25 years at an annual rental equal to the amount necessary to amortize the principal and pay the interest on the outstanding bonds, (4) that such payments by Y and the facility itself shall be the security for the bonds, and (5) that, if corporation Y pays or incurs capital expenditures in excess of $1 million within 3 years from the date of issue which disqualify the bonds as an exempt small issue under section 103(b)(6)(D), it will either furnish funds to C to redeem such bonds at par or at a premium, or increase the rental payments to C in an amount sufficient to pay a premium interest rate. Although the bonds issued are industrial development bonds, they are an exempt small issue under section 103(b)(6)(A) by reason of the election under section 103(b)(6)(D) and paragraph (b)(2) of this section, since the aggregate authorized face amount of the bond issue is $5 million or less and all of the proceeds of the bond issue are to be used to acquire and improve land and acquire and construct depreciable property. The

Reg. §1.103-10(g)

>>> → *Caution: Code Sec. 103 has been amended to remove special exempt bond issue rules and provide similar rules in Code Secs. 141-150.*

provisions for redemption of the bonds or an increase in rental if the bonds are disqualified as an exempt small issue under section 103(b)(6)(A) will not disqualify an otherwise valid election under section 103(b)(6)(D) and paragraph (b)(2) of this section.

Example (10). The facts are the same as in example (9) except that corporation Y subsequently proposed to the city that it build a $1 million warehouse next to the plant for the use of Y under terms similar to the factory arrangement. Assume further that the factory building was completed by March 1, 1970, and that on January 15, 1972, the proposed issue date of the subsequent bond issue, $2 million of the first exempt small issue will be outstanding. In determining the aggregate authorized face amount of the new issue, the original face amount of a prior outstanding issue must be reduced by that portion which is to be redeemed before it is added to the face amount of the new issue. Therefore, if the city issues $3 million of bonds to redeem the remaining $2 million of bonds and to construct the warehouse, the bonds will be an exempt small issue under section 103(b)(6)(A) if an election is made under section 103(b)(6)(D) and paragraph (b)(2) of this section since (1) the face amount of the new issue ($3 million), plus (2) the face amount of the prior outstanding exempt small issue minus the amount of such issue to be refunded ($2 million minus $2 million), plus (3) capital expenditures during the preceding three years financed other than out of the proceeds of outstanding issues to which section 103(b)(6)(A) and paragraph (b) of this section applied ($2 million), do not exceed $5 million. If, however, the amount of the January 15, 1972, issue were $3¹/₂ million, the issue would not qualify as an exempt small issue under section 103(b)(6)(A) and paragraph (b)(2) of this section.

Example (11). The facts are the same as in example (9), except that on June 15, 1971, Y purchases from an unrelated motor carrier business a warehouse terminal in the same city at a cost of $250,000 and tractor-trailers and other automotive equipment based at the terminal at a cost of $1 million. This subsequent expenditure by Y has the effect of making the interest on the city C bonds includible in the gross income of the holders of such bonds as of June 15, 1971, because the face amount of the March 1, 1969, issue ($4 million) plus the subsequent capital expenditures within three years of the date of issue ($1,250,000) exceed $5 million. (See section 103(b)(6)(D) and paragraph (b)(2)(i) of this section.)

Example (12). The facts are the same as in example (9), except that in March, 1970, Y will move $3 million of additional used machinery and equipment into the factory from its factory in another city. The expenditures for such machinery and equipment were incurred by Y more than 3 years prior to the date of issue of the bonds. The transfer of such used equipment into city C does not constitute a section 103(c)(6)(D) capital expenditure within the meaning of paragraph (b)(2)(ii) of this section since the expenditures with respect to such property were incurred more than three years prior to the date of issue of the bonds. Had the capital expenditures with respect to such property been incurred during the 6-year period beginning 3 years before the date of issue of the bonds and in the 3 years after such date, they would constitute section 103(b)(6)(D) capital expenditures.

Example (13). The facts are the same as in example (9), except that in March, 1970, corporation Y enters into an arrangement with respect to machinery and equipment to be used in the facility. The arrangement is labeled by the parties as a lease but is treated as a sale for Federal income tax purposes. The amount treated as the purchase price of the machinery and equipment is a section 103(b)(6)(D) capital expenditure.

Example (14). On February 1, 1970, city D issues $5 million of its bonds to finance construction of an addition to the manufacturing plant of corporation Z. The bonds will be secured by the facility and lease payments to be made by Z which will be sufficient to pay the principal and interest on such bonds. Assume that the bonds qualify as an exempt small issue under section 103(b)(6)(A) pursuant to an election under section 103(b)(6)(D) and paragraph (b)(2) of this section. On February 1, 1971, D plans to issue $1 million of its bonds to construct a pollution control facility to be leased to Z for use at its manufacturing plant. The rental payments from the lease will be sufficient to pay the principal and interest on the bonds. The bonds will be secured by such facility and the lease payments. Capital expenditures for the pollution control facility will be paid or incurred beginning before February 1, 1973. Although the pollution control facility is an exempt facility under section 103(b)(4)(F) and paragraph (g) of §1.103-8, amounts used for the pollution control facility shall be considered to be a section 103(b)(6)(D) capital expenditure and the interest on the February 1, 1970, issue will become taxable as of the date such capital expenditure began to be paid or incurred. See section 103(b)(6)(G) and paragraph (b)(2)(i) of this section.

Example (15). On February 1, 1970, city E issues $500,000 of its bonds to acquire and develop an industrial park within the meaning of section 103(b)(5) and paragraph (b) of §1.103-9. The park consists of 100 acres and is divided into one 50 acre plant site and 4 smaller sites. The aggregate acquisition cost of the undeveloped land is $150,000 or an average per acre cost of $1,500. Roads, sidewalks, sewers, utilities, sewage, and waste disposal facilities serving the entire industrial park cost $300,000. On September 1, 1970, E leases to corporation Y for 30 years the 50 acre plant site (with an allocated cost of $75,000) and a railroad spur track from the railroad right of way to Y's plant site for Y's exclusive use. The spur track was constructed using $50,000 of the proceeds of the industrial park bond issue. E also proposes to issue on September 1, 1970, $4,875,000 of its bonds to construct and equip a building on the leased plant site to be leased to Y at an additional rental sufficient to pay the principal and interest on this issue of bonds. The September 1, 1970, issue will be an exempt small issue under section 103(c)(6)(A) pursuant to an election under section 103(b)(6)(D) and paragraph (b)(2) of this section since the sum of the amount of the second issue ($4,875,000) and the capital expenditures allocated to the plant site ($75,000 for 50 acres of land plus $50,000 for the railroad spur tract, totalling $125,000) does not exceed $5 million. The sum of $300,000 which was spent in development of the industrial park provided facilities which will serve or benefit the users generally and hence under paragraph (b)(2)(iii) of this section is not considered to have provided facilities as to which Y will be the principal user.

Example (16). On June 1, 1970, corporation Z simultaneously enters into separate arrangements with city F and city G under which each city will issue a $5 million exempt small issue of bonds the proceeds of which will be used by Z to construct separate facilities in each city. By June 1, 1971, the facilities have been completed in the respective cities. On January 1, 1972, cities F and G, through a valid legal proceeding, merge into a new city FG. Since in this case F and G were separate cities on June 1, 1970 (the date of the bond issues), the factories are not considered to be located in the same incorporated municipality. Accordingly, each $5 million issue by city F and G will continue to qualify as an exempt small issue.

Example (17). On June 1, 1973, city H issues an exempt small issue of $4.75 million to finance a facility of corporation S to be located in city H. On October 1, 1974, S and corporation T, previously unrelated to S, consummated a statutory merger which qualifies as a reorganization described in section 368(a)(1)(A) and thus as a transaction described in section 381(a). In the transaction, T transferred to S assets with a fair market value of $1.5 million in exchange for stock of S, $300,000 of securities of S, and $100,000 cash. On March 23, 1971, T made $400,000 of capital expenditures for an addition to its factory located in city H. For purposes of testing the H issue of June 1, 1973, such expenditures would have been section 103(b)(6)(D) capital expenditures if T and S had been related persons. Under the provisions of paragraph (b)(2)(v)(a) of this section, the exchange of $1.5 million of stock, securities, and cash by S does not constitute a section 103(b)(6)(D) capital expenditure. Since, however, S and T are treated as related persons starting three years prior to the date of issue of the obligations, the $400,000 of expenditures by T constitute section 103(b)(6)(D) capital expenditures. Thus, the interest on the June 1, 1973, issue of obligations would become taxable (since the $5 million limit would be exceeded) on the date of the merger.

Example (18). In 1965 City I issues $10 million of industrial development bonds to construct and equip a factory for corporation Z. In 1975 the remaining principal amount of the bonds outstanding is $4.1 million. If I issues $4.5 million of bonds to redeem the balance of the prior issue, and for other purposes, such issue cannot qualify as an exempt small issue under section 103(b)(6)(D) and paragraph (b)(2) of this section even though at the time of issue the interest on the 1965 bonds was tax-exempt since the prior issue must be one which qualified under section 103(b)(6)(A) and this section. Further, the 1975 issue will be an issue of industrial development bonds notwithstanding the provisions of paragraph (d)(2) of §1.103-7 which provides that certain bonds issued to refund an issue of obligations issued on or before April 30, 1968 (or January 1, 1969, in certain cases) will not be so treated. Paragraph (d)(2) of §1.103-7 is not applicable because the 1975 issue makes funds available for a purpose other than the debt service obligation on the 1965 bonds.

Example (19). In 1969 City J issues $4 million of industrial development bonds which qualify as an exempt small issue under section 103(b)(6)(A) pursuant to an election under section 103(b)(6)(D) and paragraph (b)(2) of this section. In 1971, by reason of a $2 million addition to the factory built with the proceeds of the issue, the 1969 exempt small issue loses its tax-exempt status. In 1972, the city issues a $5 million issue to redeem the prior 1969 issue. The redemption issue will not qualify as an exempt small issue since the prior 1969 issue did not continue to qualify under section 103(b)(6)(A) and this section. [Reg. §1.103-10.]

☐ [*T.D. 7199, 7-31-72. Amended by T.D. 7511, 9-30-77, T.D. 7840, 10-12-82 and T.D. 8086, 5-1-86.*]

⇨ Caution: Code Sec. 103 has been amended to remove special exempt bond issue rules and provide similar rules in Code Secs. 141-150.

[Reg. §1.103-11]

§1.103-11. Bonds held by substantial users.—(a) *In general.*—Section 103(c)(4), (5), or (6) (relating respectively to interest on bonds to finance certain exempt facilities, interest on bonds to finance industrial parks, and the exemption for certain small issues of industrial development bonds) does not apply, as provided in section 103(c)(7), with respect to any obligation for any period during which such obligation is held either by a person who is a substantial user of the facilities with respect to which the proceeds of such obligation were used or by a related person (within the meaning of section 103(c)(6)(C) and paragraph (e) of §1.103-10). Therefore, in such a case, interest paid on such an obligation is includable in the gross income of a substantial user (or related person) for any period during which such obligation is held by such user (or related person).

(b) *Substantial user.*—In general, a substantial user of a facility includes any nonexempt person who regularly uses a part of such facility in his trade or business. However, unless a facility, or a part thereof, is constructed, reconstructed, or acquired specifically for a nonexempt person or persons, such a nonexempt person shall be considered to be a substantial user of a facility only if (1) the gross revenue derived by such user with respect to such facility is more than 5 percent of the total revenue derived by all users of such facility or (2) the amount of area of the facility occupied by such user is more than 5 percent of the entire usable area of the facility. Under certain facts and circumstances, where a nonexempt person has a contractual or preemptive right to the exclusive use of property or a portion of property, such person may be a substantial user of such property. A substantial user may also be a lessee or sublessee of all or any portion of the facility. A licensee or similar person may also be a substantial user where his use is regular and is not merely a casual, infrequent, or sporadic use of the facility. Absent special circumstances, individuals who are physically present on or in the facility as employees of a substantial user shall not be deemed to be substantial users.

(c) *Examples.*—The application of section 103(c)(7) and this section are illustrated by the following examples:

Example (1). Pursuant to an arrangement with corporation X, county A issues $4 million of its bonds (an exempt small issue under section 103(c)(6)(A) pursuant to an election under section 103(c)(6)(D) and paragraph (b)(2) of §1.103-10) and will use the proceeds to finance construction of a manufacturing facility which is to be leased to X for an annual rental of $500,000. X subleases space to a restaurant operator at an annual rental of $25,000 for the operation of a canteen and lunch counter for the convenience of X's employees. The canteen is required to be open at least five days each week (except holidays) from 8:30 A.M. to 5:00 P.M., and the lunch counter must be in operation during the noon hour. The canteen regularly sells cigarettes, candy, and soft drinks, and uses advertising displays and dispensers with product names. The space physically occupied and the amount of revenue derived by the restaurant operator are more than 5 percent of the respective amounts with respect to the entire facility. Both X and the restaurant operator are substantial users. However, absent special circumstances none of X's employees, the employees of the restaurant operator, or the customers or salesmen who regularly visit the premises to do business either with X or the restaurant operator are substantial users. Similarly, the manufacturers, distributors, and dealers of products sold in the canteen ordinarily are not substantial users.

Example (2). The facts are the same as in example (1) except that X rents food and beverage vending machines from a local dealer. The machines are regularly serviced by the local dealer under a contract with X. Title to and ownership of the machines are retained by the dealer. The local dealer is not deemed to be a substantial user if the revenue derived by such dealer from, and the space occupied by, such machines do not exceed 5 percent of the respective amounts with respect to the entire facility.

Example (3). City B proposes to issue $2 million of bonds which qualify as an exempt small issue under section 103(c)(6)(A) pursuant to an election under section 103(c)(6)(D) and paragraph (b)(2) of §1.103-10 in order to construct a medical building for certain physicians and dentists. The facility will contain thirty offices to be leased on equal terms and for the same rental rates to each physician or dentist for use in his trade or business. Each physician or dentist will be a substantial user of the facility since the facility is being constructed specifically for such physicians and dentists. The result would be the same in the case of an office building for general commercial use.

Example (4). City C proposes to expand the airport it owns and operates with the proceeds of its bonds which qualify as bonds issued for an exempt facility under section 103(c)(4)(D) and paragraph (e) of §1.103-8 and which are secured by a pledge of airport revenues. The airport is serviced by several commercial airlines which have long-term agreements with C for the use of runways, terminal space, and hangar and storage facilities. Each of the airlines either occupies more than 5 percent of the usable space of, or derives more than 5 percent of the revenue derived with respect to, the airport. C also leases counter and vehicle servicing and parking areas to car rental companies, space for restaurants, kiosks for the sale of newspapers and magazines, and space for the operations of a charter plane company. The latter operates its own planes, offers flying lessons and services, and stores private planes for local businesses and individuals. An airport limousine company has an exclusive franchise for passenger pick-up at the terminal. Other taxi, transfer, freight, and express companies regularly deliver passengers and freight to the terminal but do not have space regularly assigned to them, nor do they have operating agreements with C. Various business concerns have advertising product displays in the terminal building. In addition to regular telephone service, coin-operated telephones, provided by the telephone company, are located throughout the terminal, at locations specified by C. None of the above exceed the 5 percent limitations of paragraph (b) of this section and the bond proceeds will not be specifically used for any of them. Only the commercial airlines, which violate the 5 percent limitations, are substantial users of the airport.

Example (5). City D issues $25 million of its revenue bonds and will use $10 million of the proceeds to finance construction of a sports facility which qualifies as an exempt facility under section 103(c)(4)(B) and paragraph (c) of §1.103-8, $8 million to acquire and develop land as the site for an industrial park within the meaning of section 103(c)(5) and §1.103-9, and $7 million to finance the construction of an office building to be used exclusively by the city, an exempt person. The revenues from the sports facility and the industrial park and all the facilities themselves will be the security for the bonds. The sports facility and the industrial park sites will be used in the trades or businesses of nonexempt persons. The bonds are industrial development bonds, but under the provisions of paragraph (a)(1) of §1.103-8 and paragraph (a) of §1.103-9, the interest on the $25 million issue will not be includable in gross income. However, the interest on bonds held shall be includable in the gross income of a substantial user of either the sports facility or the industrial park if such substantial user holds any of the obligations of the $25 million issue. The 5 percent limitations of paragraph (b) of this section are applied separately with respect to each facility.

Example (6). Authority E issues $4 million of bonds which qualify as an exempt small issue under section 103(c)(6)(A) pursuant to an election under section 103(c)(6)(D) and paragraph (b)(2) of §1.103-10 in order to construct a bank building on the grounds of an airport. In addition, E issues $40 million to expand the airport. The bank will not derive revenue in excess of 5 percent of the revenue derived with respect to the airport nor will it occupy more than 5 percent of the usable area of such airport. The bank will be a substantial user of the bank building constructed with the proceeds of the $4 million issue since the facility was constructed specifically for the bank. However, the bank will not be a substantial user with respect to the airport because it does not exceed the 5 percent limitations of paragraph (b) of this section. Had E issued one issue of $44 million in order to expand the airport and construct a bank building, the bank would be a substantial user of the entire facility since the $44 million issue was being used to construct a facility a portion of which was specifically for the bank. [Reg. §1.103-11.]

☐ [T.D. 7199, 7-31-72.]

[Reg. §1.103-16]

§1.103-16. Obligations of certain volunteer fire departments.—(a) *General rule.*—An obligation of a volunteer fire department issued after December 31, 1980, shall be treated as an obligation of a political subdivision of a State for purposes of section 103(a)(1) of—

(1) The volunteer fire department is a qualified volunteer fire department within the meaning of paragraph (b) of this section, and

(2) Substantially all of the proceeds of the issue of which the obligation is a part are to be used for the acquisition, construction, reconstruction, or improvement of a fire house or fire truck used or to be used by the qualified volunteer fire department.

An obligation of a volunteer fire department shall not be treated as an obligation of a political subdivision of a State for purposes of section 103(a)(1) unless both conditions set forth in this paragraph (a) are satisfied. Thus, for example, if an obligation is issued by an ambulance and rescue squad that is a qualified volunteer fire department as required by paragraph (a)(1) of this section, but substantially all of the proceeds of the issue of which the obligation is a part are to be used for the furnishing of emergency medical services, rather than for the purposes specified in paragraph (a)(2) of this section, the obligation shall not be treated as an obligation of a political subdivision of a State for purposes of section 103(a)(1).

»»→ *Caution: Code Sec. 103 has been amended to remove special exempt bond issue rules and provide similar rules in Code Secs. 141-150.*

(b) *Definition of qualified volunteer fire department.*—For purposes of this section, the term "qualified volunteer fire department" means an organization—

(1) That is organized and operated to provide firefighting services or emergency medical services in an area within the jurisdiction of a political subdivision, and

(2) That is required to furnish firefighting services by written agreement with the political subdivision, and

(3) That serves persons in an area within the jurisdiction of the political subdivision that is not provided with any other firefighting services. The requirement of paragraph (b)(2) of this section that a qualified volunteer fire department be required to furnish firefighting services by written agreement with the political subdivision may be satisfied by an ordinance or statute of the political subdivision that establishes, regulates, or funds the volunteer fire department. A volunteer fire department does not fail to satisfy the requirement of paragraph (b)(3) of this section by furnishing or receiving firefighting services on an emergency basis, or by cooperative agreement with other fire departments, to or from areas outside of the area that the volunteer fire department is organized and operated to serve. The fact that tax revenues of a political subdivision served by a volunteer fire department contribute toward the support of the volunteer fire department in the form of salary, purchase of equipment, or other defrayment of expenses will not prevent the volunteer fire department from being a "qualified volunteer fire department" within the meaning of this paragraph (b). Moreover, an obligation of a volunteer fire department receiving such support may qualify as an obligation of a political subdivision within the meaning of section 103(a)(1) independently of section 103(i) and this section if the requirements of section 103(a)(1) are satisfied. See §1.103-1(b) for rules relating to qualification under section 103(a)(1).

(c) *"Substantially all" test.*—Substantially all of the proceeds of an issue are used for the purposes specified in paragraph (a)(2) of this section if 90 percent or more of the proceeds are so used. Thus, for example, if more than 10 percent of the proceeds of an obligation issued by a qualified volunteer fire department are used for the purchase of an ambulance or for rescue equipment not to be used in providing fire fighting services, interest on the obligation is not exempt from tax under section 103(i) and this section. In computing this percentage—

(1) Costs are allocated between providing a firehouse or firetruck and other uses of the proceeds on a pro rata basis; and

(2) The rules set forth in §1.103-8(a)(1)(i), relating to amounts allocable to exempt and nonexempt uses and amounts chargeable to capital account, apply.

(d) *Refunding issues.*—An obligation which is part of an issue issued by a qualified volunteer fire department after December 31, 1980, part or all of the proceeds of which issue are used directly or indirectly to pay principal, interest, call premium, or reasonable incidental costs of refunding a prior issue qualifies as an obligation of a political subdivision under section 103(i) and this section only if—

(1) The prior issue was issued by a qualified volunteer fire department;

(2) Substantially all of the proceeds of the prior issue were used for the purposes described in paragraph (a)(2) of this section;

(3) The prior issue was issued after December 31, 1980; and

(4) The refunding issue is issued not more than 180 days before the date on which the last obligation of the prior issue is discharged (within the meaning of §1.103-13(b)(11)).

(e) *Examples.*—The provisions of this section may be illustrated by the following examples:

Example (1). The County M Volunteer Fire and Rescue Association provides firefighting, ambulance, and emergency medical services in County M. The board of county commissioners of County M contracts with the County M Volunteer Fire and Rescue Association for these services, and County M is not served by any other firefighting association. On August 1, 1981, the Association issues an obligation for funds to purchase a new fire truck, a new ambulance, and rescue equipment not to be used for fighting fires. Funds to be used for the purchase of the ambulance and rescue equipment constitute more than 10 percent of the proceeds of the obligation. Thus, substantially all of the proceeds of the obligations are not used for one of the purposes described in paragraph (a)(2) of this section. Although the County M Volunteer Fire and Rescue Association is a qualified volunteer fire department under paragraph (b) of this section because it provides firefighting and emergency medical services in an area within County M which is not provided with any other firefighting services and is required to provide these services by written agreement with County M, the August 1, 1981, obligation of County M Volunteer Fire and Rescue Association will not be treated as an obligation of a political subdivision of a State under section 103(i) and paragraph (a) of this section because substantially all of the proceeds of the obligation are not to be used for a purpose described in section 103(i)(1)(B) and paragraph (a)(2) of this section. Accordingly, interest on the August 1, 1981, obligation of County M Volunteer Fire and Rescue Association is not exempt from gross income under section 103(a)(1).

Example (2). County N Volunteer Fire Department provides firefighting services in County N by contract with the county, which is not served by any other firefighting association. On June 15, 1982, County N Volunteer Fire Department issues its obligation for funds to construct an addition to its firehouse to house a rescue squad, the rescue squad's vehicle, and rescue equipment not to be used in firefighting. Although the County N Volunteer Fire Department is a qualified volunteer fire department under paragraph (b) of this section, interest on its June 15, 1982, obligation will not be exempt from tax under section 103(i) and this section because the proceeds of this obligation will not be used for the purposes described in paragraph (a) of this section.

Example (3). The County O Volunteer Fire and Rescue Association provides firefighting, ambulance, and emergency medical services in County O. The board of county commissioners of County O contracts with the County O Volunteer Fire and Rescue Association for these services, and County O is not served by any other firefighting association. On September 1, 1983, the Association issues its obligations for funds to construct a new building to house its firefighting, ambulance, and rescue functions. Although the ambulance and rescue equipment will occupy space in the projected facility, the cost allocable on a pro rata basis to providing housing for the ambulance and rescue equipment represents less than 10 percent of the proceeds of the obligations. Thus, substantially all of the proceeds of the obligations are used for one of the purposes described in paragraph (a)(2) of this section. The County O Volunteer Fire and Rescue Association is a qualified volunteer fire department under paragraph (b) of this section because it provides firefighting and emergency medical services in an area within County O which is not provided with any other firefighting services and is required to provide these services by written agreement with County O. The obligations of County O Volunteer Fire and Rescue Association will be treated as obligations of a political subdivision of a State under section 103(i) and paragraph (a) of this section because the obligations are those of a qualified volunteer fire department and because substantially all of the proceeds of the obligations are to be used for a purpose described in section 103(i)(1)(B) and paragraph (a)(2) of this section. Accordingly, interest on the September 1, 1983, issue of obligations of County O Volunteer Fire and Rescue Association is exempt from gross income under section 103(a)(1). [Reg. §1.103-16.]

☐ [*T.D.* 7901, 7-19-83.]

»»→ *Caution: Code Sec. 103A has been repealed. Similar exempt bond issue rules have been provided in Code Secs. 141-150.*

[Reg. §6a.103A-1]

§6a.103A-1. Interest on mortgage subsidy bonds (Temporary).—(a) *In general.*—(1) *Mortgage subsidy bond.*—A mortgage subsidy bond shall be treated as an obligation not described in section 103(a)(1) or (a)(2). Thus, the interest on a mortgage subsidy bond is includible in gross income and subject to Federal income taxation.

(2) *Exceptions.*—Any qualified mortgage bond and any qualified veterans' mortgage bond shall not be treated as a mortgage subsidy bond. See §6a.103A-2 with respect to requirements of qualified mortgage bonds and §6a.103A-3 with respect to requirements of qualified veterans' mortgage bonds.

(3) *Additional requirement.*—In addition to the requirements of §6a.103A-2, §6a.103A-3, and this section, qualified mortgage bonds and qualified veterans' mortgage bonds shall be subject to the requirements of section 103(c) and the regulations thereunder.

(4) *Advance refunding.*—On or after December 5, 1980, no tax-exempt obligation may be issued for the advance refunding of a mortgage subsidy bond (determined without regard to section 103A(b)(2) or §6a.103A-1(a)(2)). An obligation issued for the re-funding of a mortgage subsidy bond will be considered to be an advance refunding obligation if it is issued more than 180 days before the prior issue is discharged.

(5) *Registration.*—Any obligation that is part of a qualified mortgage bond issue or qualified veterans' mortgage bond issue and which is issued after December 31, 1981, must be in registered form. The term "in registered form" has the same meaning as in §1.6049-2(d). Thus, in general, an obligation is issued in registered form if it is registered as to both principal and interest and if its

»»→ *Caution: Code Sec. 103A has been repealed. Similar exempt bond issue rules have been provided in Code Secs. 141-150.*

transfer must be effected by the surrender of the old instrument to the issuer and by either the reissuance of the old instrument to a new holder or the issuance of a new instrument to a new holder.

(b) *Definitions.*—For purposes of §6a.103A-2, §6a.103A-3, and this section the following definitions apply:

(1) *Mortgage subsidy bond.*—(i) The term "mortgage subsidy bond" means any obligation which is issued as part of an issue a significant portion of the proceeds of which is to be used directly or indirectly to provide mortgages on owner-occupied residences.

(ii) For purposes of subdivision (i), a significant portion of the proceeds of an issue is used to provide mortgages if 5 percent or more of the proceeds are so used.

(2) *Mortgage.*—The term "mortgage" includes deeds of trust, conditional sales contracts, pledges, agreements to hold title in escrow, and any other form of owner financing.

(3) *Bond.*—The term "bond" means any obligation. The term "obligation" means any evidence of indebtedness.

(4) *State.*—(i) The term "State" includes a possession of the United States and the District of Columbia.

(ii) For purposes of subdivision (i), obligations issued by or on behalf of any State or local governmental unit by constituted authorities empowered to issue such obligations are the obligations of such governmental unit. See §1.103-1(b).

(5) *Proceeds.*—The term "proceeds" includes original proceeds and investment proceeds. The terms "original proceeds" and "investment proceeds" shall have the same meaning as in §1.103-13(b)(2). Unless otherwise provided in §6a.103A-2 or this section, however, amounts earned from the investment of proceeds which are derived from qualified mortgage bonds in nonmortgage investments may not be commingled for the purposes of accounting for expenditures with other non-bond amounts, and such proceeds are investment proceeds even though not treated as investment proceeds for purposes of section 103(c). Repayments of principal on mortgages shall be treated as proceeds of an issue. Amounts (such as State appropriations or surplus funds) which are provided by the issuer or a private lender in conjunction with a qualified mortgage bond or a qualified veterans' mortgage bond shall not be treated as proceeds of a mortgage subsidy bond under this section. However, fees which are paid by a participating financial institution pursuant to an agreement with the issuer whereby such institution receives the right to originate or service mortgages and which are retained by an issuer are treated as original proceeds of the issue. Amounts provided by the issuer or a private lender may be treated as proceeds of an issue for purposes of section 103(c).

(6) *Single-family and owner-occupied residences.*—Except for purposes of §6a.103A-2(g) and (h)(2)(ii), the terms "single-family" and "owner-occupied," when used with respect to residences, include two-, three-, and four-family residences—

(i) One unit of which is occupied by the owner of the units, and

(ii) Which were first occupied as a residence at least 5 years before the mortgage is executed. [Temporary Reg. §6a.103A-1.]

☐ [*T.D. 7780, 6-29-81. Amended by T.D. 7794, 11-5-81.*]

[Reg. §1.103A-2]

§1.103A-2. Qualified mortgage bond.—

(a)-(j) [Reserved]

(k) *Information reporting requirement.*—(1) *In general.*—An issue meets the requirements of this paragraph only if the issuer in good faith attempted to meet the information reporting requirements of this paragraph. Except as otherwise provided in paragraph (k)(5)(iv), the requirements of this paragraph apply to qualified veterans' mortgage bonds issued after July 18, 1984, and to qualified mortgage bonds issued after December 31, 1984. With respect to bonds issued after December 31, 1986, see the regulations under section 149(e).

(2) *Information required.*—(i) The issuer must, based on information and reasonable expectations determined as of the date of issue, submit on Form 8038 the information required therein; the issuer need not, however, include the information required by Form 8038 that is relevant only to obligations described in section 103(l)(1) and the regulations thereunder. The information that must be submitted includes—

(A) The name, address, and employer identification number of the issuer,

(B) The date of issue,

(C) The face amount of each obligation which is part of the issue,

(D) The total purchase price of the issue,

(E) The amount allocated to a reasonably required reserve or replacement fund,

(F) The amount of lendable proceeds,

(G) The stated interest rate of each maturity,

(H) The term of each maturity,

(I) In the case of an issue of qualified mortgage bonds, whether the issuer has elected under section §6a.103A-2(i)(4)(v) to pay arbitrage to the United States,

(J) In the case of an issue of qualified mortgage bonds, the issuer's market limitation as of the date of issue (as defined in §6a.103A-2(g)), the amount of qualified mortgage bonds that the issuer has elected not to issue under section 25(c)(2) and the regulations thereunder, and the aggregate amount of qualified mortgage bonds issued to date by the issuer during the calendar year, and

(K) In the case of an issue of qualified veterans' mortgage bonds, the issuer's State veterans limit (as defined in section 103A(o)(3)(B) and the regulations thereunder) and the aggregate amount of qualified veterans' mortgage bonds issued to date by the issuer during the calendar year and prior to the date of issue of the issue for which the Form 8038 is being submitted.

(ii) With respect to issues issued after December 31, 1984, the issuer must submit a report containing information on the borrowers of the original proceeds of such issues. The report must be filed for each reporting period in which the original proceeds of any of such issues are used to provide mortgages. The issuer is not responsible for false information provided by a borrower if the issuer did not know or have reason to know that the information was false. The report must be filed on the form prescribed by the Internal Revenue Service. If no form is prescribed, or if the form prescribed is not readily available, the issuer may use its own form provided that such form is in the format set forth in paragraph (k)(3) and contains the information required by this paragraph (k)(2)(ii). The report must be titled "Qualified Mortgage Bond Information Report" or "Qualified Veterans' Mortgage Bond Information Report", and must include the name, address, and TIN of the issuer, the reporting period for which the information is provided, and the following tables containing information concerning the borrowers of the original proceeds of the issues subject to the requirements of this paragraph (k)(2)(ii) with respect to mortgages provided during the reporting period for which the report is filed:

(A) A table titled "Number of Mortgage Loans by Income and Acquisition Cost" showing the number of mortgage loans (other than those issued in connection with qualified home improvement and rehabilitation loans) made during the reporting period according to the annualized gross income of the borrowers (categorized in the following intervals of income: $0 - $9,999; $10,000 - $19,999; $20,000 - $29,999; $30,000 - $39,999; $40,000 - $49,999; $50,000 -$74,999; and $75,000 or more) and according to the acquisition cost of each residence being financed (categorized in the following intervals of acquisition cost: $0 - $19,999; $20,000 - $39,999; $40,000 - $59,999; $60,000 - $79,999; $80,000 - $99,999; $100,000 - $119,999; $120,000 - $149,999; $150,000 - $199,999; and $200,000 or more). For each interval of income and acquisition cost the table must also be categorized according to the number of borrowers that—

(1) Did not have a present ownership interest in a principal residence at any time during the 3-year period ending on the date the mortgage is executed (*i.e.,* satisfied the 3-year requirement) and purchased residences in targeted areas,

(2) Satisfied the 3-year requirement and purchased residences not located in targeted areas,

(3) Did have a present ownership interest in a principal residence at any time during the 3-year period ending on the date the mortgage is executed (*i.e.,* did not satisfy the 3-year requirement) and purchased residences in targeted areas, and

(4) Did not satisfy the 3-year requirement and purchased residences not located in targeted areas.

With respect to issues of qualified veterans' mortgage bonds, for each interval of income and acquisition cost the table need only be categorized according to the number of borrowers that satisfied the 3-year requirement and the number of borrowers that failed to satisfy the 3-year requirement.

(B) A table titled "Volume of Mortgage Loans by Income and Acquisition Cost" showing the total principal amount of the mortgage loans (other than qualified home improvement and rehabilitation loans) provided during the reporting period according to annualized gross income (categorized in the same intervals of income as the preceding table) and according to the acquisition cost of the residences acquired (categorized in the same acquisition cost intervals as the preceding table). For each interval of income and acquisi-

»»→ Caution: *Code Sec. 103A has been repealed. Similar exempt bond issue rules have been provided in Code Secs. 141-150.*

tion cost the table must also be categorized according to the total principal amount of the mortgage loans of borrowers that—

(1) Satisfied the 3-year requirement and purchased residences in targeted areas,

(2) Satisfied the 3-year requirement and purchased residences not located in targeted areas,

(3) Did not satisfy the 3-year requirement and purchased residences in targeted areas, and

(4) Did not satisfy the 3-year requirement and purchased residences not located in targeted areas.

With respect to issues of qualified veterans' mortgage bonds, for each interval of income and acquisition cost the table need only be categorized according to the total principal amount of the mortgage loans of borrowers that satisfied the 3-year requirement and the total principal amount of the mortgage loans of borrowers that did not satisfy the 3-year requirement.

(C) For issues other than qualified veterans' mortgage bonds, a table titled "Mortgage Subsidy Bonds for Qualified Home Improvement and Rehabilitation Loans" showing the number of borrowers obtaining qualified home improvement loans and qualified rehabilitation loans and the total of the principal amounts of such loans; the information contained in the table must also be categorized according to whether the residences with respect to which the loans were provided are located in targeted areas.

(3) *Format.*—(i) With respect to the report required by paragraph (k)(2)(ii), if no form is prescribed by the Internal Revenue Service, or if the prescribed form is not readily available, the issuer must submit the report in the format specified in this paragraph (k)(3).

(ii) With respect to issues of qualified mortgage bonds, the format of the report specified in paragraph (k)(3) is the following:

QUALIFIED MORTGAGE BOND INFORMATION REPORT
Name of issuer:
Address of issuer:
TIN of issuer:
Reporting period:
NUMBER OF MORTGAGE LOANS BY INCOME AND ACQUISITION COST

3-year Requirement: Annualized Gross Monthly Income of Borrowers		Satisfied		Not Satisfied		Totals
		Nontargeted Area	Targeted Area	Nontargeted Area	Targeted Area	
$ 0 —	9,999					
$ 10,000—	19,999					
$ 20,000—	29,999					
$ 30,000—	39,999					
$ 40,000—	49,999					
$ 50,000—	74,999					
$ 75,000 or more						
Total						
Acquisition Cost						
$ 0 —	19,999					
$ 20,000—	39,999					
$ 40,000—	59,999					
$ 60,000—	79,999					
$ 80,000—	99,999					
$100,000—	119,999					
$120,000—	149,999					
$150,000—	199,999					
$200,000 or more						
Total						

VOLUME OF MORTGAGE LOANS BY INCOME AND ACQUISITION COST

3-year Requirement: Annualized Gross Monthly Income of Borrowers		Satisfied		Not Satisfied		Totals
		Nontargeted Area	Targeted Area	Nontargeted Area	Targeted Area	
$ 0 —	9,999					
$ 10,000—	19,999					
$ 20,000—	29,999					
$ 30,000—	39,999					
$ 40,000—	49,999					
$ 50,000—	74,999					
$ 75,000 or more						
Total						
Acquisition Cost						
$ 0 —	19,999					
$ 20,000—	39,999					
$ 40,000—	59,999					
$ 60,000—	79,999					
$ 80,000—	99,999					
$100,000—	119,999					
$120,000—	149,999					
$150,000—	199,999					
$200,000 or more						
Total						

MORTGAGE SUBSIDY BONDS FOR QUALIFIED HOME IMPROVEMENT AND REHABILITATION LOANS

	Nontargeted Area	Targeted Area	Totals
Number of qualified home improvement loans			
Volume of qualified home improvement loans			
Number of qualified rehabilitation loans			
Volume of qualified rehabilitation loans			

(iii) The format of the report specified in paragraph (k)(3) for qualified veterans' mortgage bonds is the following:

QUALIFIED VETERANS' MORTGAGE BOND INFORMATION REPORT
Name of issuer:
Address of issuer:
TIN of issuer:
Reporting period:
NUMBER OF MORTGAGE LOANS BY INCOME AND ACQUISITION COST

Reg. §1.103A-2(k)(2)(ii)(B)(1)

>»»→ *Caution: Code Sec. 103A has been repealed. Similar exempt bond issue rules have been provided in Code Secs. 141-150.*

3-year Requirement: Annualized Gross Monthly Income of Borrowers		Satisfied	Not Satisfied	Totals
$ 0 —	9,999			
$ 10,000—	19,999			
$ 20,000—	29,999			
$ 30,000—	39,999			
$ 40,000—	49,999			
$ 50,000—	74,999			
$ 75,000 or more				
Total				
Acquisition Cost				
$ 0 —	19,999			
$ 20,000—	39,999			
$ 40,000—	59,999			
$ 60,000—	79,999			
$ 80,000—	99,999			
$100,000—	119,999			
$120,000—	149,999			
$150,000—	199,999			
$200,000 or more				
Total				

VOLUME OF MORTGAGE LOANS BY INCOME AND ACQUISITION COST

3-year Requirement: Annualized Gross Monthly Income of Borrowers		Satisfied	Not Satisfied	Totals
$ 0 —	9,999			
$ 10,000—	19,999			
$ 20,000—	29,999			
$ 30,000—	39,999			
$ 40,000—	49,999			
$ 50,000—	74,999			
$ 75,000 or more				
Total				
Acquisition Cost				
$ 0 —	19,999			
$ 20,000—	39,999			
$ 40,000—	59,999			
$ 60,000—	79,999			
$ 80,000—	99,999			
$100,000—	119,999			
$120,000—	149,999			
$150,000—	199,999			
$200,000 or more				
Total				

(4) *Definitions and special rules.*—(i) For purposes of this paragraph the term "annualized gross income" means the borrower's gross monthly income multiplied by 12. Gross monthly income is the sum of monthly gross pay, any additional income from investments, pensions, Veterans Administration (VA) compensation, part-time employment, bonuses, dividends, interest, current overtime pay, net rental income, etc., and other income (such as alimony and child support, if the borrower has chosen to disclose such income). Information with respect to gross monthly income may be obtained from available loan documents, *e.g.*, the sum of lines 23D and 23E on the Application for VA or FmHA Home Loan Guaranty or for HUD/FHA Insured Mortgage (VA Form 26-1802a, HUD 92900, Jan. 1982), or the total line from the Gross Monthly Income section of FHLMC Residential Loan Application form (FHLMC 65 Rev. 8/78). With respect to obligations issued prior to October 1, 1985, issuers may submit data based on annualized gross income or, instead, based on the adjusted income (as defined in § 1.167(k)-3(b)(3)) of the mortgagor's family for the previous calendar year. If data is submitted based on adjusted income, the issuer must note this fact in the report.

(ii) For purposes of this paragraph, the term "reporting period" means the following periods:

(A) The period beginning January 1, 1985, and ending on September 30, 1985,

(B) The period beginning on October 1, 1985, and ending June 30, 1986, and

(C) After June 30, 1986, each 1-year period beginning July 1 and ending June 30.

(iii) See the regulations under section 103(l) for the definitions of the terms "date of issue", "maturity", and "term of issue".

(iv) For purposes of this paragraph, verification of information concerning a borrower's gross monthly income with other available information concerning the borrower's income (*e.g.*, Federal income tax returns) is not required. In determining whether a borrower acquiring a residence in a targeted area satisfies the 3-year requirement, the issuer may rely on a statement signed by the borrower.

(5) *Time for filing.*—(i) The report required by paragraph (k)(2)(i) shall be filed not later than the 15th day of the second calendar month after the close of the calendar quarter in which the obligation is issued. The statement may be filed at any time before such date but must be complete based on facts and reasonable expectations as of the date of issue. The statement need not be amended to report information learned subsequent to the date of issue or to reflect changed circumstances with respect to the issuer.

(ii) The report required by paragraph (k)(2)(ii) (relating to use of proceeds) shall be filed not later than the 15th day of the second calendar month after the close of the reporting period, except that the report for the reporting period ending September 30, 1985, is due not later than February 15, 1986. The report may be filed at any time before such date but must be complete based on facts and reasonable expectations as of the date the report is filed. The report need not be amended to reflect information learned subsequent to the date the report is filed or to reflect changed circumstances with respect to any borrower.

(iii) The Commissioner may grant an extension of time for the filing of a report required by paragraph (k)(2)(i) or (ii) if there is reasonable cause for the failure to file such report in a timely fashion.

(iv) An issue of qualified veterans' mortgage bonds issued after July 18, 1984, and prior to January 1, 1985, will be treated as satisfying the information reporting requirement of this paragraph if a Form 8038 with respect to the issue is properly filed not later than February 15, 1985; the report described in paragraph (k)(2)(ii) need not be filed with respect to such issues.

(6) *Place for filing.*—The reports required by paragraph (k)(2)(i) and (ii) are to be filed at the Internal Revenue Service Center, Philadelphia, Pennsylvania 19255.

(l) *Policy statement.*—(1) *In general.*—(i) For obligations issued after December 31, 1984, an issue meets the requirements of this paragraph only if the applicable elected representative of the governmental unit which is the issuer (or on behalf of which the issuing authority is empowered to issue qualified mortgage bonds) has published (after a public hearing following reasonable public notice) the report described in paragraph (l)(3) by the last day of the year preceding the year in which such issue is issued and a copy of such report has been submitted to the Commissioner on or before such last day. The Commissioner may grant an extension of time for publishing and filing the report if there is reasonable cause for the failure to

>>>→ *Caution: Code Sec. 103A has been repealed. Similar exempt bond issue rules have been provided in Code Secs. 141-150.*

publish or file such report in a timely fashion. The requirements of this paragraph will be treated as met if the issuer in good faith attempted to meet the policy statement requirements of this paragraph.

(ii) With respect to reports required by paragraph (l)(1)(i) to be published and submitted to the Commissioner not later than December 31, 1984, the Commissioner has determined that there is reasonable cause for the failure to publish or file such reports in a timely fashion; such a report will be considered published and filed in a timely fashion if, not later than March 11, 1985, the report is published (after a public hearing following reasonable public notice) and a copy is submitted to the Commissioner. In addition, any report submitted not later than December 31, 1984, with respect to which an issuer in good faith attempted to satisfy the requirements of section 103A(j)(5) shall be treated as substantially satisfying the requirements of this paragraph. For example, with respect to a report submitted not later than December 31, 1984, an issuer shall not be treated as failing to satisfy the requirements of section 103A(j)(5) based on the fact that (A) the notice of public hearing failed to state the manner in which affected residents may obtain copies of the proposed report prior to the hearing, or (B) the proposed report was not available prior to or at the public hearing. With respect to reports required to be published and submitted to the Commissioner not later than December 31, 1986, the Commissioner has determined that there is reasonable cause for the failure to publish and file such reports in a timely fashion; such reports will be considered published and filed in a timely fashion if, not later than December 31, 1987, the report is published (after having a public hearing following reasonable public notice) and a copy is submitted to the Commissioner.

(2) *Definitions and special rules.*—(i) In the case of an issuer that issues qualified mortgage bonds on behalf of one or more governmental units, a single report may be filed provided that such report is signed (A) by the applicable elected representative of each governmental unit on whose behalf obligations have been issued during any preceding calendar year or (B) by the Governor of the State in which the issuer is located.

(ii) See section 103(k)(2)(E) and the regulations thereunder for the definition of the term "applicable elected representative".

(iii) In the case of qualified mortgage bonds issued by, or on behalf of, a governmental unit that did not reasonably expect during the preceding calendar year to issue (or have issued on its behalf by any other issuer) qualified mortgage bonds during the current calendar year, the requirements of this paragraph will be treated as met if the applicable governmental unit which is the issuer (or on behalf of which the issuing authority is empowered to issue qualified mortgage bonds) has published (after a public hearing following reasonable public notice) the report described in paragraph (l)(3) prior to the issuance of any qualified mortgage bonds and a copy of such report has been submitted to the Commissioner prior to such issuance.

(iv) For purposes of this paragraph a report will be considered to be "published" when the applicable elected representative of the governmental unit has made copies of the report available for distribution to the public. Reasonable public notice of the manner in which copies of the report may be obtained must be provided; such notice may be included as part of the public notice required by paragraph (l)(4).

(3) *Report.*—(i) A report is described in this paragraph (l)(3) if it contains the issuer's name, TIN, and the title "Policy Report Under Section 103A" stated on the cover page of the report and if it includes—

(A) A statement of the policies of the issuer with respect to housing, development, and low-income housing assistance which such issuer is to follow in issuing qualified mortgage bonds and mortgage credit certificates, and

(B) An assessment of the compliance of such issuer during the 1-year period preceding the date of the report with—

(1) The statement of policy on qualified mortgage bonds and mortgage credit certificates that was set forth in the previous report, if any, of the issuer, and

(2) The intent of Congress that State and local governments are expected to use their authority to issue qualified mortgage bonds and mortgage credit certificates to the greatest extent feasible (taking into account prevailing interest rates and conditions in the housing market) to assist lower income families to afford home ownership before assisting higher income families.

(ii) For example, a report described in this paragraph (l)(3) may (but is not required to) contain—

(A) A specific statement of the policies with respect to housing, development, and low-income housing assistance which the issuer is to follow in issuing qualified mortgage bonds and mortgage credit certificates, including, for example, a statement as to—

(1) With respect to housing policies, (i) whether the proceeds will be used to provide financing for the acquisition of residences, to provide qualified home improvement loans, or to provide qualified rehabilitation loans; (ii) whether all or a portion of the proceeds will be targeted to new, existing, or any other particular class or type of housing; (iii) how the existence of a need or absence of a need for such targeting has been determined; (iv) the method by which the proceeds will be targeted; (v) any other pertinent information relating to the issuer's housing policies; and (vi) how the housing policies relate to the issuer's development and low-income housing assistance policies;

(2) With respect to development policies, (i) whether all or a portion of the proceeds will be targeted to specific areas (including targeted areas as described in § 6a.103A-2(b)(3)); (ii) a description of the areas to which the proceeds will be targeted; (iii) the reasons for selecting such areas; (iv) whether proceeds targeted to each area are to be used to finance redevelopment of existing housing or new construction; (v) any other pertinent information relating to the issuer's development policies; and (vi) how the development policies relate to the issuer's low-income housing assistance policies; and

(3) With respect to low-income housing assistance policies, (i) whether all or a portion of the proceeds will be targeted to low-income (i.e., 80 percent of median income), moderate-income (i.e., 100 percent of median income), or any other class of borrowers; (ii) the method by which the proceeds will be targeted to such borrowers; and (iii) any other pertinent information relating to the issuer's low-income housing assistance policies;

(B) An assessment of the compliance of the governmental unit or issuing authority during the twelve-month period ending with the date of the report with the statement of housing, development, and low-income housing assistance policies with respect to qualified mortgage bonds and mortgage credit certificates that were set forth in the report, if any, published in the preceding year with respect to such governmental unit, including, for example, a statement as to whether the governmental unit or issuing authority successfully implemented its policies and, if not, an analysis of the reasons for such failure; and

(C) An assessment of the compliance of the governmental unit or issuing authority during the twelve-month period ending with the date of the report with the intent of Congress that State and local governments are expected to use their authority to issue qualified mortgage bonds and mortgage credit certificates to the greatest extent feasible (taking into account prevailing interest rates and conditions in the housing market) to assist lower income families to afford home ownership before assisting higher income families, including, for example, a description of (1) the method used by the governmental unit or issuing authority to distribute proceeds, (2) whether and how that method enabled the governmental unit or issuing authority to assist lower income families before higher income families, and (3) any income levels that have been defined and used by the governmental unit or issuing authority in connection with distribution of the proceeds (no specific definition of lower income and higher income is imposed on governmental units or issuing authorities).

(iii) For purposes of the assessments of compliance required by paragraph (l)(3)(i)(B) to be included in the report, the "date of the report" means June 30. For purposes of the report required to be filed prior to January 1, 1986, an issuer need not perform these assessments of compliance with respect to any period prior to January 1, 1985.

(iv) An issuer that fails to establish policies with respect to the criteria provided in paragraph (l)(3)(i) will not be treated as failing to satisfy the requirements of this paragraph. Thus, for example, an issuer may state in its report that none of the proceeds of the issue will be targeted to specific areas. Similarly, an issuer that fails to successfully implement its policies will not be treated as failing to satisfy the requirements of this paragraph.

(4) *Public hearing.*—The public hearing required by paragraph (l)(1) means a forum providing a reasonable opportunity for interested individuals to express their views, both orally and in writing, on the report that the applicable representative proposes to publish to satisfy the requirements of this paragraph (l). A public hearing held prior to January 1, 1985, will not fail to satisfy the requirements of this paragraph (l)(4) merely because the proposed policy statement was not available prior to the public hearing. In general, a governmental unit may select its own procedure for the hearing, provided that interested individuals have a reasonable opportunity to express their views. Thus, it may impose reasonable requirements on persons who wish to participate in the hearing, such as a requirement that persons desiring to speak at the hearing so request in writing at least 24 hours before the hearing or that they limit their oral remarks to 10 minutes. For purposes of this public hearing requirement, it is not

⟫⟫→ *Caution: Code Sec. 103A has been repealed. Similar exempt bond issue rules have been provided in Code Secs. 141-150.*

necessary that the applicable elected representative who will publish the report be present at the hearing, that a report on the hearing be submitted to that official, or that State administrative procedural requirements for public hearings in general be observed. However, compliance with such State procedural requirements (except those at variance with a specific requirement set forth in this paragraph) will generally assure that the hearing satisfies the requirements of this paragraph. The hearing may be conducted by any individual appointed or employed to perform such function by the governmental unit, its agencies, or by the issuer. Thus, for example, for a report to be issued by an issuing authority that acts on behalf of a county, the hearing may be conducted by the issuing authority, the county, or an appointee or employee of either.

(5) *Reasonable public notice.*—(i) The reasonable public notice required by paragraph (l)(1) means published notice which is reasonably designed to inform residents of the geographical area within the jurisdiction of the governmental unit that will publish the report. The notice must state the time and place for the hearing and contain the information required by paragraph (l)(5)(ii). Notice is presumed reasonable if published no fewer than 14 days before the hearing. Notice is presumed reasonably designed to inform affected residents only if published in one or more newspapers of general circulation available to residents of that locality or if announced by radio or television broadcast to those residents.

(ii) The notice of hearing described in this paragraph (l)(5) must state—

(A) The time and place for the hearing,

(B) Any applicable limitations regarding participation in the hearing,

(C) With respect to any notice of hearing published after December 31, 1984, the manner in which affected residents may obtain copies of the proposed report prior to the hearing, and

(D) With respect to any notice of hearing published after December 31, 1984, that the hearing will involve the issuer's policies with respect to housing, development, and low-income housing assistance which the issuer is to follow in issuing qualified mortgage bonds and mortgage credit certificates.

(6) *Procedure for public hearings of multiple jurisdiction issuers.*—In the case of an issuer that issues qualified mortgage bonds on behalf of two or more governmental units ("multiple jurisdiction issuer"), each governmental unit on whose behalf the issuer reasonably expects to issue qualified mortgage bonds during the succeeding calendar year must hold a public hearing following reasonable public notice prior to the publication of the report required by this paragraph. A multiple jurisdiction issuer may hold a combined hearing as long as the combined hearing is a joint undertaking that provides all residents of the participating governmental units (*i.e.*, each governmental unit on whose behalf qualified mortgage bonds were issued by the authority and each governmental unit on whose behalf the authority reasonably expects to issue qualified mortgage bonds during the succeeding calendar year) a reasonable opportunity to be heard. The location of any combined hearing is presumed to provide a reasonable opportunity for all affected residents to be heard if it is no farther than 100 miles from the seat of government of each participating governmental unit beyond whose geographic jurisdiction the hearing is conducted.

(7) *Place for filing.*—The report is to be filed with the Internal Revenue Service Center, Philadelphia, Pennsylvania 19255.

(m) *State certification requirements.*—(1) *In general.*—An issue meets the requirements of this paragraph only if the issuer in good faith attempted to meet the State certification requirements of this paragraph. The requirements of this paragraph apply to obligations issued after December 31, 1984; see section 149(e) and the regulations thereunder with respect to obligations issued after December 31, 1986.

(2) *Certification.*—(i) An issue satisfies the requirements of section 103A(j)(4) and this paragraph (m)(2) only if the State official designated by law (or, if there is no State official, the Governor) certifies on or before the later of the date of issue or October 3, 1985, following a request for such certification by the issuer, that, as of the date the certification is executed, the issue meets the requirements of section 103A(g) and the regulations thereunder (relating to volume limitation). In the case of any constitutional home rule city, the certification shall be made by the chief executive officer of the city. To the extent consistent with State and local law, the Governor (or the chief executive officer of any constitutional home rule city) may delegate the responsibility to execute the certification required by this paragraph.

(ii) The certifying official need not perform an independent investigation in order to determine whether the issue meets the requirements of section 103A(g). In determining the aggregate amount of qualified mortgage bonds previously issued by an issuer during a calendar year, the certifying official may rely on copies of the reports submitted, to date, by the issuer pursuant to section 103A(j)(3) for other issues of qualified mortgage bonds issued during that year and copies of any elections previously made pursuant to section 25(c)(2) not to issue qualified mortgage bonds, together with an affidavit executed by an officer of the issuer responsible for issuing the bonds stating that the issuer has not, to date during the calendar year, issued any other qualified mortgage bonds, the amount, if any, of the issuer's market limitation that it has, to date during the calendar year, surrendered to other issuing authorities, and that it has not, to date during the calendar year, made any other elections not to issue qualified mortgage bonds. If, based on such information, the certifying official determines that, as of the date the certification is executed, the issue will not exceed the issuer's market limitation for the year, the official may certify that the issue meets the requirements of section 103A(g).

(3) *Special rule.*—If 15 days elapse after the issuer files a proper request for the certification described in paragraph (m)(2) and the issuer has not received from the State official designated by law (or, if there is no State official, the Governor) certification that the issue meets the requirements of section 103A(g) and §6a.103A-2(g) or, in the alternative, a statement that the issue does not meet such requirements, the issuer may, instead, submit an affidavit executed by an officer of the issuer responsible for issuing the bonds stating that—

(i) The issue meets the requirements of section 103(A)(g) and §6a.103A-2(g),

(ii) At least 15 days before the execution of the affidavit the issuer filed a proper request for the certification described in paragraph (m)(2), and

(iii) The State official designated by law (or, if there is no State official, the Governor) has not provided the certification described in paragraph (m)(2).

In the case of obligations issued prior to October 4, 1985, the preceding sentence shall be applied by substituting "30 days" for "15 days". For purposes of this paragraph, a request for certification is proper if the request includes the reports and affidavits described in paragraph (m)(2)(ii).

(4) *Filing.*—The certification (or affidavit) required by this paragraph shall be filed with the Internal Revenue Service Center, Philadelphia, PA 19255. The certification (or affidavit) shall be submitted with the Form 8038 required to be filed by section 103A(j)(3) and paragraph (k) of this §1.103A-2. The Commissioner may grant an extension of time for filing the certification (or affidavit) if there is a reasonable cause for the failure to file such statement in a timely fashion.

(5) *Effect of certification.*—The fact that an issuer obtains the certification (or affidavit) described in this paragraph does not ensure that the requirements of paragraph (g) of this section are met. Obligations that do not meet the requirements of paragraph (g) are not described in section 103(a). [Reg. §1.103A-2.]

☐ [*T.D. 8049, 8-29-85. Amended by T.D. 8129, 3-10-87.*]

[Reg. §6a.103A-2]

§6a.103A-2. Qualified mortgage bond (Temporary).—(a) *In general.*—(1) *Qualified mortgage bond.*—A qualified mortgage bond shall not be treated as a mortgage subsidy bond, and the interest on a qualified mortgage bond will be exempt from Federal income taxation.

(2) *Termination date.*—No obligation issued after December 31, 1983, shall be treated as part of a qualified mortgage bond issue.

(b) *Definitions and special rules.*—For purposes of this section and §6a.103A-1, the following definitions apply:

(1) *Qualified mortgage bond.*—The term "qualified mortgage bond" means one or more obligations issued by a State or any political subdivision thereof (hereinafter referred to as "governmental unit") as part of an issue—

(i) All of the original proceeds of which, net of the costs of issuing the obligations and proceeds invested in a reasonably required reserve fund (such net amount hereinafter in this section referred to as "lendable proceeds"), are to be used to finance owner-occupied residences, and

(ii) Which meets each of the requirements of §6a.103A-1 and this section.

A qualified mortgage bond does not include any bond that is an industrial development bond under section 103(b).

⫸→ *Caution: Code Sec. 103A has been repealed. Similar exempt bond issue rules have been provided in Code Secs. 141–150.*

(2) *Constitutional home rule city.*—The term "constitutional home rule city" means, with respect to any calendar year, any political subdivision of a State which, under a State constitution which was adopted in 1970 and effective on July 1, 1971, had home rule powers on the 1st day of the calendar year.

(3) *Targeted area residence.*—The term "targeted area residence" means a residence in an area which is either—

(i) A qualified census tract, or

(ii) An area of chronic economic distress.

(4) *Qualified census tract.*—(i) The term "qualified census tract" means a census tract in which 70 percent or more of the families have an income which is 80 percent or less of the State-wide median family income.

(ii) The determination under subdivision (i) shall be made on the basis of the most recent decennial census for which data are available. With respect to any particular bond issue, such determination may be based upon the decennial census data available 3 months prior to the date of issuance and shall not be affected by official changes to such data during or after such 3-month period.

(iii) The term "census tract" means a census tract as defined by the Secretary of Commerce.

(5) *Areas of chronic economic distress.*—(i) The term "area of chronic economic distress" means an area designated by a State as meeting the standards established by that State for purposes of this subparagraph and approved by the Secretary and by the Secretary of Housing and Urban Development in accordance with the criteria set forth in (iii) of this subparagraph. A State may withdraw such designation at any time, with reasonable cause. Such withdrawal shall be effective upon notification by the State to the Assistant Secretary for Housing/Federal Housing Commissioner of the Department of Housing and Urban Development. Such withdrawal shall not affect the tax-exempt status of any outstanding issue of obligations.

(ii) For purposes of making a designation under this subparagraph, withdrawing a designation, or making any other submission, "State" means the governor of a State, or a State official commissioned by the governor or by State statute for such purposes.

(iii) The following criteria will be used in evaluating a proposed designation of an area of chronic economic distress:

(A) The condition of the housing stock, including the age of the housing and the number of abandoned and substandard residential units. Data pertinent to this criterion include the number and percentage of housing units that were constructed prior to 1940, the average age of the housing stock, the number and percentage of abandoned housing units, and the number and percentage of substandard residential units.

(B) The need of area residents for owner financing under a qualified mortgage bond issue as indicated by low per capita income, a high percentage of families in poverty, a high number of welfare recipients, and high unemployment rates. Data pertinent to this criterion include the per capita income of the population in the area, the number and percentage of families eligible to receive food stamps from a program pursuant to 7 U.S.C. 2011, the number and percentage of families eligible to receive payments under the Aid to Families with Dependent Children program, and the unemployment rate.

(C) The potential for use of owner financing under a qualified mortgage bond issue to improve housing conditions in the area. Data pertinent to this criterion include the number and percentage of owner-occupied homes that are substandard, the number and percentage of families that are low- or moderate-income renters, and the number and percentage of sub-standard units in the area that will be improved through the use of owner financing provided by the proceeds of a qualified mortgage bond issue.

(D) The existence of a housing assistance plan which provides a displacement program and a public improvements and services program (similar to the Housing Assistance Plan (HAP) required by the Department of Housing and Urban Development under the Community Development Block Grant program (42 U.S.C. section 5301 *et seq.*)).

This determination shall be based upon the most recent data available. The certification described in subdivision (iv)(C) shall satisfy the criteria set forth in subdivisions (C) and (D). A certification described in (iv)(D) shall satisfy the criteria set forth in subdivisions (A) and (B), provided that the majority of the households in the proposed area have incomes less than 80 percent of the median income for the standard metropolitan statistical area (SMSA) in which the proposed area is located or, if the proposed area is not within a SMSA, less than *80 percent of the median income for the State.*

(iv) A proposal by the State that an area be approved as an area of chronic economic distress shall contain the following information:

(A) A description of the proposed area by its geographical limits.

(B) Maps of the State and of areas within the State that are qualified census tracts and existing or proposed areas of chronic economic distress.

(C) Where applicable, a certification of the local Area Manager of the Department of Housing and Urban Development in which the proposed area is located that the proposed area is a Neighborhood Strategy Area (NSA) under 24 CFR 570.301(c) promulgated pursuant to the Community Development Block Grant program or an area comparable to a NSA which has been reviewed and approved by the Area Manager as meeting the standards for an NSA.

(D) Where applicable, a certification from the HUD Area Manager with jurisdiction over the proposed area that the proposed area is within a geographic area which has been declared eligible for grants under the Urban Development Action Grant Program, pursuant to 24 CFR 570.452, by the Secretary of Housing and Urban Development.

(E) Statistical and descriptive information pertinent to the criteria enumerated in subdivision (iii) of this section, and a succinct statement of how the information furnished satisfies those criteria. Such statistical information shall be based upon the most recent data available.

(F) If the State so desires, a written request for a conference prior to any adverse decision on the proposed designation.

(G) A certification by the Governor or designated official that the proposed designation conforms to these regulations.

(v) The proposed designation and the information furnished with it as required by subdivision (iv) shall be submitted in triplicate to the Assistant Secretary for Housing/Federal Housing Commissioner of the Department of Housing and Urban Development (Attention: Office of State Agency and Bond Financed Programs, Rm. 6138, 451 7th Street, S.W., Washington, D.C. 20410).

(vi) Only those areas of chronic economic distress that have been previously designated by the State and approved in accordance with this subparagraph at least 3 months prior to the date of issuance need to be taken into account for any particular bond issue. Residences located in areas designated as areas of chronic economic distress approved in accordance with this subparagraph within such 3-month period or after the date of issue, however, may be treated as targeted area residences. However, for purposes of paragraph (h) (2), relating to the specified portion of proceeds to be placed in targeted areas, and paragraph (i)(3)(ii)(A), relating to the $1\frac{1}{2}$ year temporary period, only areas approved as areas of chronic economic distress in accordance with this subparagraph at the time of issue may be taken into consideration.

(6) *Standard metropolitan statistical area.*—A standard metropolitan statistical area ("SMSA") is an area in and around a city of 50,000 inhabitants or more (or equivalent area) and defined by the Secretary of Commerce as an SMSA.

(7) *Statistical area.*—The term "statistical area" means—

(i) An SMSA,

(ii) Any county (or portion thereof) which is not within an SMSA, or

(iii) If there is insufficient recent statistical information with respect to a county (or portion thereof) described in subdivision (ii), such other area as may be designated by the Commissioner, upon proper application, as a substitute for such county (or portion thereof).

For purposes of subdivisions (ii) and (iii), in Alaska, the entire State, and in Louisiana, a parish, shall be treated in a manner similar to a county.

(8) *Acquisition cost.*—(i) The term "acquisition cost" means the cost of acquiring a residence from the seller as a completed residential unit. Acquisition cost includes the following:

(A) All amounts paid, either in cash or in kind, by the purchaser (or a related party or for the benefit of the purchaser) to the seller (or a related party or for the benefit of the seller) as consideration for the residence.

(B) If a residence is incomplete, the reasonable cost of completing the residence whether or not the cost of completing construction is to be financed with bond proceeds. For example, where a mortgagor purchases a building which is so incomplete that occupancy of the building is not permitted under local law, the acquisition cost includes the cost of completing the building so that occupancy of the building is permitted.

(C) Where a residence is purchased subject to a ground rent, the capitalized value of the ground rent. Such value shall be calculated using a discount rate equal to the yield on the issue (as defined in § 6a.103A-2(i)(2)(vi)).

»»→ *Caution: Code Sec. 103A has been repealed. Similar exempt bond issue rules have been provided in Code Secs. 141-150.*

(ii) The term "acquisition cost" does not include the following:

(A) The usual and reasonable settlement or financing costs. Settlement costs include titling and transfer costs, title insurance, survey fees, or other similar costs. Financing costs include credit reference fees, legal fees, appraisal expenses, "points" which are paid by the buyer (but not the seller, even though borne by the mortgagor through a higher purchase price) or other costs of financing the residence. However, such amounts will be excluded in determining acquisition cost only to the extent that the amounts do not exceed the usual and reasonable costs which would be paid by the buyer where financing is not provided through a qualified mortgage bond issue. For example, if the purchaser agrees to pay to the seller more than a pro rata share of property taxes, such excess shall be treated as part of the acquisition cost of a residence.

(B) The value of services performed by the mortgagor or members of the mortgagor's family in completing the residence. For purposes of the preceding sentence, the family of an individual shall include only the individual's brothers and sisters (whether by the whole or half blood), spouse, ancestors, and lineal descendants. For example, where the mortgagor builds a home alone or with the help of family members, the acquisition cost includes the cost of materials provided and work performed by subcontractors (whether or not related to the mortgagor) but does not include the imputed cost of any labor actually performed by the mortgagor or a member of the mortgagor's family in constructing the residence. Similarly, where the mortgagor purchases an incomplete residence, the acquisition cost includes the cost of material and labor paid by the mortgagor to complete the residence but does not include the imputed value of the mortgagor's labor or the labor of the mortgagor's family in completing the residence.

(C) The cost of land which has been owned by the mortgagor for at least 2 years prior to the date on which construction of the residence begins.

(iii) The following examples illustrate the provisions of subparagraph (8):

Example (1). A contracts with B, a builder of single-family residences, for the purchase of a residence. Under the terms of the contract, B will deliver a residential unit to A that contains an uncompleted recreation room and an unfinished third floor and which lacks a garage. Normally, a completed recreation room, a finished third floor and a garage are provided as part of the residence built by B. The contract price for the residence is $58,000. At the same time, A contracts with C, an affiliate of B, to complete the recreation room and third floor and to construct the garage for a contract price of $10,000. C will perform this work after A receives title to the unit from B. Under §6a.103A-2(b)(8)(i)(A), the acquisition cost of A's completed residential unit is $68,000, which represents the contract price of the residence plus the cost of completion of the recreation room and third floor and construction of the garage.

Example (2). E owns a single-family residence which E has listed for sale. D contracts to purchase E's residence, and the contract provides for a selling price of $30,000. D also agrees to pay an unsecured debt in the amount of $5,000, which E owes to X, a local bank. D further agrees to purchase from E the refrigerator, stove, washer, and dryer located in E's residence for $500. Such amount is equal to the fair market value of such personalty. D also agrees to purchase the light fixtures, curtain rods, and wall-to-wall carpeting for a fair market value price of $700. Under §6a.103A-2(b)(8)(i)(A), the acquisition cost of D's completed residential unit is $35,700. Such amount includes the $5,000 unsecured debt paid off by D. The $500 paid for the refrigerator, stove, washer, and dryer are not included because such items are not included within the definition of a residence under §6a.103A-2(d)(4). Such definition does include, however, the light fixtures, curtain rods, and wall-to-wall carpeting purchased by D.

Example (3). F contracts with G to purchase G's home for $40,000. After purchasing the residence, F pays a party unrelated to G $3,000 for painting, minor repairs, and refinishing the floors. Under §6a.103A-2(b)(8)(i)(A), the acquisition cost of the residence is $40,000. Such fix-up expenses are not treated as part of the acquisition costs. If G had incurred such fix-up expenses, however, F may not reduce his acquisition cost of the residence by such amounts.

(9) *Qualified home improvement loan.*—(i) The term "qualified home improvement loan" means the financing (whether or not secured by a mortgage), in an amount which does not exceed $15,000 with respect to any residence, of alterations, repairs, and improvements on, or in connection with, an existing single-family, owner-occupied residence by the owner thereof, but only if such items substantially protect or improve the basic livability or energy efficiency of the residence.

(ii) Alterations, repairs, or improvements that satisfy the requirement of subdivision (i) include the renovation of plumbing or electric systems, the installation of improved heating or air conditioning systems, the addition of living space, or the renovation of a kitchen area. Items that will not be considered to substantially protect or improve the basic livability of the residence include swimming pools, tennis courts, saunas, or other recreational or entertainment facilities.

(iii) If—

(A) Two or more qualified home improvement loans are provided for the same residence, whether or not by the same lender, and

(B) Any person who had a present ownership interest in such residence at the time the previous qualified home improvement loan or loans were made has a present ownership interest in the residence at the time the subsequent qualified home improvement loan is made,

then the allowable amount of the subsequent qualified home improvement loan shall be reduced by the amount, at origination, of any previous qualified home improvement loan, so that the sum of such loans does not exceed $15,000.

(iv) The following example illustrates the provisions of subparagraph (9):

Example. A and B jointly own a residence located in Town M. They obtain a qualified home improvement loan for $10,000 from Town M. A acquires B's interest in the residence. A applies to State X for a qualified home improvement loan. The maximum amount of a qualified home improvement loan which may be made by State X is $5,000, the amount that when added to the $10,000 previous loan from Town M does not exceed $15,000.

(10) *Qualified rehabilitation loans.*—(i) The term "qualified rehabilitation loan" means any owner financing provided in connection with—

(A) A qualified rehabilitation, or

(B) the acquisition of a residence with respect to which there has been a qualified rehabilitation,

but only if the mortgagor to whom such financing is provided is the first resident of the residence after completion of the rehabilitation. Where there are two or more mortgagors of a rehabilitation loan, the first residency requirement is met if any of the mortgagors meets the first residency requirement.

(ii) The term "qualified rehabilitation" means any rehabilitation of a residence if—

(A) There is a period of at least 20 years between the date on which the building was first used and the date on which physical work on such rehabilitation begins,

(B) 75 percent or more of the existing external walls of such building are retained in place as external walls in the rehabilitation process, and

(C) The expenditures for such rehabilitation are 25 percent or more of the mortgagor's adjusted basis in the residence (including the land on which the residence is located).

(iii) For purposes of (A) and (B), the rules applicable to the investment tax credit for qualified rehabilitated buildings under section 48(g)(1)(A)(iii) and (B) shall apply. However, unlike section 48(g)(1)(B), once a building meets the 20-year test, more than one rehabilitation of that building within a 20-year period may qualify as a qualified rehabilitation.

(iv) The adjusted basis to the mortgagor is the mortgagor's adjusted basis for purposes of determining gain or loss on the sale or exchange of a capital asset (as defined in section 1221). The mortgagor's adjusted basis shall be determined as of the date of completion of the rehabilitation, or, if later, the date the mortgagor acquires the residence, *i.e.*, the date on which the mortgagor includes in basis any amounts expended for rehabilitation that are expended for capital assets.

(v) The amounts expended by the mortgagor for rehabilitation include all amounts expended for rehabilitation regardless of whether the amounts expended were financed from the proceeds of the loan or from other sources, and regardless of whether the expenditure is a capital expenditure, so long as the expenditure is made during the rehabilitation of the residence and is reasonably related to the rehabilitation of the residence. The value of services performed by the mortgagor or members of the mortgagor's family (as used in §6a.103A-2(b)(8)(ii)(B)) in rehabilitating the residence will not be included in determining the rehabilitation expenditures for purposes of the 25-percent test.

(vi) Where a mortgagor purchases a residence that has been substantially rehabilitated, the 25-percent test is determined by comparing the total expenditures made by the seller for the rehabilitation of the residence with the acquisition cost of the residence to the mortgagor. The total expenditures made by the seller for rehabilita-

>>> *Caution: Code Sec. 103A has been repealed. Similar exempt bond issue rules have been provided in Code Secs. 141-150.*

tion do not include the cost of acquiring the building or land but do include all amounts directly expended by the seller in rehabilitating the building (excluding overhead and other indirect charges).

(c) *Good faith compliance efforts.*—(1) *Mortgage eligibility requirements.*—An issue of qualified mortgage bonds which fails to meet one or more of the requirements of paragraphs (d), (e), (f), and (i) shall be treated as meeting such requirements if each of the following provisions is met.

(i) The issue in good faith attempted to meet all such requirements before the mortgages were executed. Good faith requires that the trust indenture, participation agreements with loan originators, and other relevant instruments contain restrictions that permit the financing of mortgages only in accordance with such requirements. In addition, the issuer must establish reasonable procedures to ensure compliance with such requirements. Such procedures include reasonable investigations by the issuer or its agent to determine that the mortgages satisfy such requirements.

(ii) Ninety-five percent or more of the lendable proceeds (as defined in §6a.103A-2(b)(1)) that were devoted to owner financing were devoted to residences with respect to which, at the time the mortgages were executed or assumed, all such requirements were met. In determining whether the proceeds are devoted to owner financing which meets such requirements, the issuer may rely on an affidavit of the mortgagor that the property is located within the issuer's jurisdiction and an affidavit of the mortgagor and the seller that the requirements of §6a.103A-2(f) are met. The issuer may also rely on his own or his agent's examination of copies of income tax returns which were filed with the Internal Revenue Service and which are provided by the mortgagor or obtained by the issuer or loan originator in accordance with the procedures set forth in §301.6103(c)-1 which indicate that, during the preceding 3 years, the mortgagor did not claim deductions for taxes or interest on indebtedness with respect to real property constituting his principal residence, in addition to an affidavit of the mortgagor that the requirements of §6a.103A-2(e) are met. The mortgagor may also provide the issuer or his agent with an affidavit that the mortgagor was not required to file such return in accordance with section 6012 during one or all of the preceding 3 years. Where a particular mortgage fails to meet more than one of these requirements, the amount of the mortgage will be taken into account only once in determining whether the 95-percent requirement is met. However, all of the defects in the mortgage must be corrected pursuant to subdivision (iii).

(iii) Any failure to meet such requirements is corrected within a reasonable period after such failure is discovered. For example, where a mortgage fails to meet one or more of such requirements those failures can be corrected by calling the nonqualifying mortgage or by replacing the nonqualifying mortgage with a qualifying mortgage.

(iv) *Examples.*—The following examples illustrate the application of this subparagraph (1):

Example (1). State X issues obligations to be used to provide mortgages for owner-occupied residences. X contracts with bank M to originate and service the mortgages. The trust indenture and participation agreement require that the mortgages meet the mortgage eligibility requirements referred to in paragraph (c)(1). In addition, pursuant to procedures established by X, M obtains a signed affidavit from each applicant that the applicant intends to occupy the property as his or her principal residence within 60 days after the final closing and thereafter to maintain the property as his or her principal residence. Further, M obtains from each applicant copies certified by the Internal Revenue Service of the applicant's Federal tax returns for the preceding 3 years and examines each statement to determine whether the applicant has claimed a deduction for taxes on real property which was the applicant's principal residence pursuant to section 164(a)(1) or a deduction pursuant to section 163 for interest paid on a mortgage secured by real property which was the applicant's principal residence. Also in accordance with X's procedures, M obtains from each applicant a signed affidavit as to facts that are sufficient for M to determine whether the residence is located within X's jurisdiction and affidavits from the seller and the buyer that the purchase price and the new mortgage requirements have been met, and neither M nor X knows or has reason to believe that such affidavits are false. The mortgage instrument provides that the mortgage may not be assumed by another person unless X determines that the principal residence, 3-year, and purchase price requirements are met at the time of the assumption. These facts are sufficient evidence of the good faith of the issuer and meet the requirements of paragraph (c)(1)(i). Further, if 95 percent of the lendable proceeds are devoted to owner financing which according to these procedures meet the requirements of paragraphs (d), (e), (f), and (i), then the issue meets the requirements of paragraph (c)(1)(ii).

Example (2). State Y issues obligations to be used to provide mortgages for owner-occupied residences. Y contracts with bank N to originate and service the mortgages. The trust indenture and participation agreement require that the mortgagor certify compliance with the requirements referred to in paragraph (c)(1). By itself, this certification is not sufficient evidence of the good faith of the issuer to meet the requirements referred to in paragraph (c)(1).

Example (3). The facts are the same as in Example 1, except that M discovers through a verification procedure required by X that, at the time of closing, A fraudulently executed the residency affidavit. Instead of occupying the property as a principal residence, A leased the property to B for one year. A did not use the property as his residence during the lease term. Thus, at the time that A's mortgage was executed the residence failed to meet the requirements of paragraph (d) of this section.

More than 95 percent of the lendable proceeds of the issue were devoted to residences which met all the requirements referred to in paragraph (c)(1) at the time the mortgages were executed. Furthermore, pursuant to a provision in the mortgage instrument M called the loan. Any failures with respect to other mortgages are corrected by M. Based on these facts, the issue meets the requirements of subparagraph (c)(1).

Example (4). The facts are the same as in Example (1), except that the issuer requires copies of the applicant's signed tax returns that were filed with the Internal Revenue Service for the preceding 3 years but does not require that such returns be certified. If 95 percent of the lendable proceeds are devoted to owner financing which according to these procedures meet the requirements of paragraphs (d), (e), (f), and (i), then the issue meets the requirements of paragraph (c)(1)(ii).

(2) *Nonmortgage eligibility requirements.*—An issue of qualified mortgage bonds which fails to meet one or more of the requirements of paragraphs (g), (h), and (i) of this section and §6a.103A-1(a)(5) shall be treated as meeting such requirements if each of the following provisions is met.

(i) The issuer in good faith attempted to meet all such requirements. This good faith requirement will be met if all reasonable steps are taken by the issuer to ensure that the issue complies with these requirements.

(ii) Any failure to meet such requirements is due to inadvertent error, *e.g.*, mathematical error, after taking reasonable steps to comply with such requirements.

(iii) The following examples illustrate the application of this subparagraph (2):

Example (1). City X issues obligations to finance owner-occupied residences. However, despite taking all reasonable steps to determine accurately the size of the market share limitation, as provided in paragraph (g)(3), the limit is exceeded because the amount of the mortgages originated in the area during the past 3 years is incorrectly computed as a result of mathematical error. Such facts are sufficient evidence of the good faith of the issuer to meet the requirements of paragraph (c)(2).

Example (2). City Y issues $25 million of bonds to finance single-family, owner-occupied homes. Attorney A gives an opinion that the bonds satisfy the arbitrage requirements of §6a.103A-2(i) and §6a.103A-1(a)(3). In fact, however, the legal conclusion reached by A is erroneous, and the bonds do not meet the requirements of §6a.103A-2(i). The issue does not meet the requirements of subparagraph (c)(2) because the erroneous opinion does not constitute inadvertent error.

(d) *Residence requirements.*—(1) *In general.*—An issue meets the requirements of this paragraph only if all of the residences for which owner financing is provided under the issue meet the requirements of this paragraph. A residence meets the requirements of this paragraph only if—

(i) It is a single-family residence (as defined in §6a.103A-1(b)(6)) which, at the time the mortgage is executed or assumed, can reasonably be expected by the issuer to become the principal residence of the mortgagor within a reasonable time after the financing is provided; and

(ii) It is located within the jurisdiction of the authority issuing the obligation.

(2) *Affidavit.*—The requirements of subparagraph (1)(i) may normally be met if the mortgagor executes an affidavit of his intent to use the residence as his principal residence within a reasonable time (*e.g.*, 60 days) after the financing is provided.

(3) *Principal residence.*—Whether a residence is used as a principal residence depends upon all the facts and circumstances of each case, including the good faith of the mortgagor. A residence which is primarily intended to be used in a trade or business shall not satisfy

>>> Caution: *Code Sec. 103A has been repealed. Similar exempt bond issue rules have been provided in Code Secs. 141-150.*

the requirements of this subparagraph. For purposes of the preceding sentence, any use of a residence which does not qualify for a deduction allowable for certain expenses incurred in connection with the business use of a home under section 280A shall not be considered as a use in a trade or business. Except for certain owner-occupied residences described in paragraph (b)(6) of §6a.103A-1, a residence more than 15 percent of the total area of which is reasonably expected to be used primarily in a trade or business does not satisfy the requirements of this subparagraph. Further, a residence used as an investment property or a recreational home does not satisfy the requirements of this subparagraph.

(4) *Residence.*—(i) The term "residence" includes stock held by a tenant-stockholder in a cooperative housing corporation (as those terms are defined in section 216(b)(1) and (2)). It does not include property such as an appliance, a piece of furniture, a radio, etc., which, under applicable local law, is not a fixture. The term also includes factory-made housing which is permanently fixed to real property. The determination of whether factory-made housing is permanently fixed to real property shall be made on the basis of the facts and circumstances of each particular case.

(ii) *Land.*—Land appurtenant to a residence shall be considered as part of the residence only if such land reasonably maintains the basic livability of the residence and does not provide, other than incidentally, a source of income to the mortgagor.

(5) *Examples.*—The following examples illustrate the application of this paragraph (d):

Example (1). A contracts to purchase a new residence from B. Since B is unable to move from the residence until 1 month after the scheduled closing date, A agrees to lease the residence to B for 1 month at a rent equal to the fair rental value. A applies for a mortgage to be provided from the proceeds of a qualified mortgage bond. In light of all the facts and circumstances in the case, the fact that A temporarily leases the residence to B does not prevent the residence from being considered as property that can reasonably be expected to be used as A's principal residence within a reasonable period of time after financing is provided.

Example (2). C contracts to purchase a new residence located on 2 acres of land in city X. City X has a zoning regulation which prevents the subdividing of any lot in that part of the city for use as a private residence into parcels of less than 2 acres. In light of all the facts and circumstances in the case, the fact that the residence is located on 2 acres of land appurtenant to the residence does not prevent the entire property from being considered as property to be used by C as a residence.

Example (3). D contracts to purchase a new residence located on 40 acres of land that D intends to farm. Any financing provided for the purchase of that portion of the property intended to be farmed will not be considered as financing provided for an owner-occupied residence.

(e) *3-year requirement.*—(1) *In general.*—An issue meets the requirements of this paragraph only if each of the mortgagors to whom owner financing is provided under the issue meets the requirements of this paragraph. A mortgagor meets the requirements of this paragraph only if the mortgagor had no present ownership interest in a principal residence at any time during the 3-year period prior to the date on which the mortgage is executed. For purposes of the preceding sentence, the mortgagor's interest in the residence with respect to which the financing is being provided shall not be taken into account.

(2) *Exceptions.*—Subparagraph (1) shall not apply with respect to—

(i) Any financing provided with respect to a targeted area residence (as defined in §6a.103A-2(b)(3)),

(ii) Any qualified home improvement loan (as defined in §6a.103A-2(b)(9)), and

(iii) Any qualified rehabilitation loan (as defined in §6a.103A-2(b)(10)).

(3) *Multiple mortgagors.*—In the event that there is more than one mortgagor with respect to a particular residence, each of such mortgagors must meet the 3-year requirement. A person who is liable under a note secured by the mortgage but who does not have a present ownership interest in a residence subject to the mortgage need not meet the 3-year requirement. For example, where a parent of a home purchaser cosigns the note for a child but the parent takes no interest in the residence, it is not necessary that the parent meet the 3-year requirement since the parent is not a mortgagor of the residence.

(4) *Included interests.*—Examples of interests which constitute present ownership interests are the following:

(i) A fee simple interest;

(ii) A joint tenancy, a tenancy in common, or tenancy by the entirety;

(iii) The interest of a tenant-shareholder in a cooperative;

(iv) A life estate;

(v) A land contract (*i.e.*, a contract pursuant to which possession and the benefits and burdens of ownership are transferred although legal title is not transferred until some later time); and

(vi) An interest held in trust for the mortgagor (whether or not created by the mortgagor) that would constitute a present ownership interest if held directly by the mortgagor.

(5) *Excluded interests.*—Examples of interests which do not constitute present ownership interests are the following:

(i) A remainder interest;

(ii) A lease with or without an option to purchase;

(iii) A mere expectancy to inherit an interest in a principal residence;

(iv) The interest that a purchaser of a residence acquires on the execution of a purchase contract; and

(v) An interest in other than a principal residence during the previous 3 years.

(f) *Purchase price requirements.*—(1) *In general.*—An issue meets the requirements of this paragraph only if the acquisition cost (as defined in §6a.103A-2(b)(8)) of each residence, other than a targeted area residence, for which owner financing is provided does not exceed 90 percent of the average area purchase price applicable to such residence. In the case of a targeted area residence (as defined in §6a.103A-2(b)(3)), the acquisition cost may not exceed 110 percent of the average area purchase price applicable to such residence.

(2) *Exception.*—Paragraph (1) shall not apply with respect to any qualified home improvement loan (as defined in §6a.103A-2(b)(9)).

(3) *Average area purchase price.*—The term "average area purchase price" means, with respect to any residence, the average purchase price of all single-family residences in the statistical area (as defined in §6a.103A-2(b)(7)) in which the residence being financed is located for the most recent 12-month period for which sufficient statistical information is available. The determination whether a particular residence meets the purchase price requirement shall be made as of the date on which the commitment to provide the financing is made or, if earlier, the date of purchase of the residence.

(4) *Special rules.*—(i) In the case of a qualified rehabilitation loan, the requirements of this paragraph are met if the mortgagor's adjusted basis in the property as of the completion of the rehabilitation (including the cost of the rehabilitation) meets the requirements of paragraph (f)(1). For this purpose, a rehabilitated residence is to be treated as a residence which has been previously occupied.

(ii) The determination of average area purchase price shall be made separately with respect to—

(A) Residences which have not been previously occupied;

(B) Residences which have been previously occupied; and

(C) One-family, two-family, three-family, and four-family residences.

(5) *Safe harbor limitation.*—(i) For purposes of meeting the requirements of this paragraph, an issuer may rely upon average area purchase price limitations published by the Treasury Department for the statistical area in which a residence is located. These safe harbor limitations will be effective for the period stated at the time of publication. An issuer may use a limitation different from such safe harbor limitation for any statistical area (as defined in §6a.103A-2(b)(7)) for which the issuer has more accurate and comprehensive data.

(ii) The following example illustrates the application of subparagraph (5)(i):

Example. The average area purchase price safe harbor limitation for new single-family residences published by the Treasury Department for the second half of 1981 for the jurisdiction of governmental unit X is $41,500. However, on July 1, 1981, X determines that its average area purchase price for new single-family residences is actually $43,000. Such determination is based on a comprehensive survey of residential housing sales in the jurisdiction over the previous calendar year. The data accumulated are based on records maintained by the county clerk's office in X's jurisdiction, which enables X to compute average area purchase prices separately for new and used residences and for one-, two-, three-, and four-family residences. X cannot reasonably update such data more often than once a year. X may use average area purchase prices computed from these data for mortgages made from July 1, 1981, through June 30, 1982, rather than the safe harbor published by the Treasury Department.

»»→ Caution: Code Sec. 103A has been repealed. Similar exempt bond issue rules have been provided in Code Secs. 141-150.

(g) *Limitation on aggregate amount of qualified mortgage bonds issued during any calendar year.*—(1) *In general.*—An issue meets the requirements of this section only if the aggregate amount of bonds issued pursuant thereto, when added to the sum of (i) the aggregate amount of qualified mortgage bonds previously issued by the issuing authority during the calendar year and (ii) the amount of qualified mortgage bonds which the issuing authority previously elected not to issue under section 25(c)(2)(A)(ii) and the regulations thereunder during the calendar year, does not exceed the applicable limit ("market limitation") for such authority for such calendar year.

(2) *State housing finance agency.*—Except as provided in paragraph (g)(4), the market limitation for any State housing finance agency for any calendar year shall be 50 percent of the State ceiling for such year. For purposes of the preceding sentence, if any State has more than one housing finance agency all such agencies shall be treated as a single agency.

(3) *Other issuers.*—Except as provided in paragraph (g)(4), the market limitation for any issuing authority (other than a State housing finance agency) for any calendar year is an amount equal to that authority's proportionate share of 50 percent of the State ceiling amount for such calendar year. The proportionate share is an amount which bears the same ratio to 50 percent of the State ceiling for such year as—

(i) The average annual aggregate principal amount of mortgages executed during the immediately preceding 3 calendar years for single-family, owner-occupied residences located within the jurisdiction of such issuing authority bears to

(ii) An average determined in the same way for the entire State.

(4) *Constitutional home rule city.*—(i) In determining the market limitation for any constitutional home rule city (as defined in paragraph (b)(2)), subparagraph (3) shall be applied by substituting "100 percent" for "50 percent."

(ii) In a State with one or more constitutional home rule cities, in computing the market limitation for issuers other than constitutional home rule cities, the State ceiling amount for any calendar year shall be reduced by the aggregate market limitation for such year for all constitutional home rule cities in the State.

(5) *Overlapping jurisdictions.*—(i) For purposes of subparagraph (3), if an area is within the jurisdiction of two or more governmental units, such area shall be treated as only within the jurisdiction of the unit having jurisdiction over the smallest geographical area. However, the governmental unit with jurisdiction over the smallest geographical area may enter into a written agreement to allocate all or a designated portion of such overlapping area to the governmental unit having jurisdiction over the next smallest geographical area.

(ii) Where two governmental units have authority to issue mortgage subsidy bonds and both governmental units have jurisdiction over the identical geographical area, the aggregate principal amount of mortgages on residences located within that area shall be allocated to the governmental unit having broader sovereign powers.

(6) *State ceiling.*—(i) Except as provided in paragraph (g)(6)(v), the State ceiling applicable to any State for any calendar year shall be the greater of—

(A) 9 percent of the average annual aggregate principal amount of mortgages executed during the immediately preceding 3 calendar years for single-family, owner-occupied residences located within the jurisdiction of such State, or

(B) $200,000,000.

Only single-family owner-occupied residences (without regard to the definition of such term under §6a.103A-1(b)(6)) may be used in determining the market limitation regardless of whether or not residences with up to four family units are to be financed by the program. First and second mortgages or mortgages used to refinance an existing mortgage shall be used in making such determination. Liens, special assessments, and similar encumbrances may not be taken into consideration.

(ii) For mortgages on residences with more than one family unit, the full amount of the mortgage shall be applied toward the market limitation and not merely that portion allocable to the owner-occupied unit.

(iii) For purposes of determining the State ceiling amount applicable to any State for any calendar year an issuer may rely upon the State ceiling amount published by the Treasury Department for such calendar year. An issuer may rely on different State ceiling amount than such safe harbor limitation where the issuer has made a more accurate and comprehensive determination of such amount.

(iv) The following example illustrates the application of subparagraphs (3) and (6) of paragraph (g):

Example. Pursuant to the allocation rule provided in subparagraph (3), City Y determines that its maximum market limitation in 1981 is $15,000,000. This determination is based on records maintained by the county clerk's office from which data for the preceding 3 years have been accumulated by City Y as to the number of sales of single-family homes in City Y's jurisdiction, the purchase price in each such sales transaction, the number of such sales that were financed by mortgages and the volume of second mortgages and refinancing on previously purchased owner-occupied single-family residences. This information, combined with estimates made by City Y of the average mortgage-loan-to-purchase-price ratio and the ratio of sales of single-family, owner-occupied residences to all sales of single-family residences from a representative sample of sales transactions, enables Y to estimate the preceding 3 years' annual aggregate mortgage volume by using the following formula:

$$v = 1/3 \sum_{i=t-3}^{t-1} (u_i \cdot w_i \cdot x_i \cdot y_i \cdot z_i) + a_i,$$

where

v = the preceding 3 years' average annual aggregate volume of mortgages on single-family, owner-occupied residences in City Y,

u_i = number of sales of single-family residences,

w_i = average purchase price of all sales,

x_i = percent of all sales transactions that were financed with mortgages,

y_i = estimated average mortgage-loan-to-purchase-price ratio,

z_i = estimated percent of sales that were owner-occupied residences,

a_i = total volume of second mortgages and refinancing on previously purchased owner-occupied, single-family residences,

i = the annual period of calculation, and

t = the current year.

City Y determines its applicable limit for 1981 based on the following formula:

L	=	0.5 (v/s)r, where
L	=	market limitation for City Y for the current year,
s	=	the preceding 3 years' average annual aggregate volume of mortgages on single-family, owner-occupied residences in State X, and
r	=	ceiling for State X (*i.e.*, r = the greater of .09s or $200,000,000).

City Y may use the Treasury estimate of s which will be published with the mortgage volume safe harbor limitation. City Y may rely on its determination of its market limitation for obligations issued during 1981.

(v) *Reduction in State ceiling.*—If for any calendar year an issuer of mortgage credit certificates, as defined in section 25 and the regulations thereunder, fails to meet the requirements of section 25(d)(2) and the regulations thereunder, relating to the limit on the

>>>→ *Caution: Code Sec. 103A has been repealed. Similar exempt bond issue rules have been provided in Code Secs. 141-150.*

aggregate amount of mortgage credit certificates that may be issued, the applicable State ceiling under paragraph (g)(6)(i) of this section for the State in which that program operates will be reduced by 1.25 times the correction amount (as defined in section 25(f)(2) and the regulations thereunder) with respect to that failure for the calendar year following the calendar year in which the Commissioner determines the correction amount with respect to that failure.

(7) *Excess obligations.*—Where an issue of obligations when added to the aggregate amount of bonds issued by the same issuing authority in the same calendar year exceeds the market limitation determined in accordance with this paragraph (g), no portion of the issue will be treated as a qualified mortgage bond issue, and interest on such obligations shall be subject to Federal income taxation. However, previously issued qualified mortgage bond issues which met the market limitation at the time of their issuance will not cease to be qualified mortgage bond issues even though a subsequent issue causes the aggregate amount of obligations to exceed such limitation for a calendar year.

(8) *Transitional rule obligations.*—In applying this paragraph (g) to any calendar year, there shall not be taken into account any bond which, by reason of section 1104 of the Mortgage Subsidy Bond Tax Act of 1980 (94 Stat. 2670) (relating to transitional rules), receives the same tax treatment as bonds issued on or before April 24, 1979.

(9) *Procedure for providing a different allocation.*—(i) A State may, by law enacted after December 5, 1980, provide a different formula for allocating the State ceiling amount among the governmental units in such State (other than constitutional home rule jurisdictions) having authority to issue qualified mortgage bonds.

(ii) The governor of any State may proclaim a different formula than provided in subparagraphs (g)(2) and (g)(3) for allocating the State ceiling amount among the governmental units in such State having authority to issue qualified mortgage bonds. The authority of the governor to proclaim a different formula shall not apply after the earlier of—

(A) The 1st day of the 1st calendar year beginning after the 1st calendar year after 1980 during which the legislature of the State met in regular session, or

(B) The effective date of any State legislation dealing with such ceiling enacted after December 5, 1980.

If, on or before either date, the governor of any State exercises the authority to provide a different allocation, such allocation shall be effective until the date specified in (B).

(iii) Unless otherwise provided in a State constitutional amendment or by law changing the home rule provisions adopted in the manner provided by the State constitution, the allocation of that portion of the State ceiling which is allocated to any constitutional home rule city may not be changed by the governor or State legislature unless such city agrees to such different allocation.

(iv) Where a State elects to make a different allocation in accordance with subdivision (i) or (ii) of this subparagraph, the determination as to whether a particular bond issue meets the requirements of paragraph (g) will be based upon the allocation in effect at the time such bonds were issued. Moreover, the authority to provide for a different allocation may not be used directly or indirectly to increase the State ceiling amount.

(v) An issuing authority located in a State with one or more constitutional home rule cities may use an alternative method to those provided in subparagraphs (2), (3), and (4) for determining such issuing authority's market limitation if, prior to issuing any obligations for the calendar year, it demonstrates to the satisfaction of the Commissioner that—

(1) The use of the methods provided in subparagraph (2), (3), or (4) would impose an unreasonable hardship on the issuing authority, and

(2) Such alternative method is reasonable.

(h) *Portion of loans required to be placed in targeted areas.*—(1) *In general.*—An issue meets the requirements of this paragraph only if—

(i) The portion of the lendable proceeds (as defined in §6a.103A-2(b)(1)) of the issue specified in subparagraph (2) is made available for owner financing of targeted area residences (as defined in §6a.103A-2(b)(3)) for at least 1 year after the date on which owner financing is first made available with respect to targeted area residences, and

(ii) The issuer attempts with reasonable diligence to place such proceeds in qualified mortgages.

Proceeds are considered first made available with respect to targeted area residences on the date on which any financing of mortgages with the lendable proceeds of an issue first becomes available. Reasonable diligence requires that the issuer and the loan originators use reasonable efforts in trying to place mortgages in targeted areas, such as by advertising that mortgage funds are available for targeted areas. Reasonable diligence is not shown by merely providing in the governing instruments that the required amount be set aside for targeted areas.

(2) *Specified portion.*—The specified portion of lendable proceeds of an issue required to be made available in targeted areas is the lesser of—

(i) 20 percent of the lendable proceeds, or

(ii) 40 percent of the average annual aggregate principal amount of mortgages executed during the immediately preceding 3 calendar years for single-family, owner-occupied residences in targeted areas within the jurisdiction of the issuing authority.

(3) *Safe harbor.*—For purposes of computing the required portion of proceeds specified in subparagraph (2)(ii), where such provision is applicable, an issuer may rely upon the amount produced by the following formula:

$$P = .2\,(X/Y \times Z),$$

where

P	=	Required portion to be made available in targeted areas,
X	=	Average annual aggregate principal amount of mortgages executed during the immediately preceding 3 calendar years for single-family, owner-occupied residences within the State in which the issuing jurisdiction is located,
Y	=	The total population within the State, based on the most recent decennial census for which data are available, and
Z	=	The total population in the targeted areas located within the issuer's jurisdiction, based on the most recent decennial census for which data are available.

The issuing jurisdiction may use the Treasury Department estimate of X which will be published with the mortgage volume safe harbor limitation.

(4) *Minimum amount.*—(i) The specified portion required to be made available in targeted areas is a minimum amount. More than the minimum amount may be (but need not be) made available in targeted areas.

(ii) With respect to any proceeds not required to be made available in targeted areas, the requirements of this paragraph do not abrogate the requirement of the arbitrage rules that due diligence be used in placing lendable proceeds into mortgages.

(i) *Arbitrage and investment gain.*—(1) *In general.*—An issue meets the requirements of this paragraph only if such issue meets the requirements of subparagraphs (2), (3), and (4). For purposes of these requirements, all determinations of yield, effective interest rates, and amounts required to be paid or credited to mortgagors under subparagraph (i)(4)(i) shall be made on an actuarial basis taking into account the present value of money. The requirements of section 103A(i) and this paragraph are applicable in addition to the requirements of section 103(c) and §§1.103-13, 1.103-14, and 1.103-15.

(2) *Effective rate of mortgage interest not to exceed bond yield by more than 1 percentage point.*—(i) *Maximum yield.*—An issue of qualified mortgage bonds shall be treated as meeting the requirements of this subparagraph only if the excess of—

(A) The effective rate of interest on the mortgages financed by the issue, over

(B) The yield on the issue,

is not greater over the term of the issue than 1 percentage point.

(ii) *Effective rate of interest.*—(A) In determining the effective rate of interest on any mortgage for purposes of this subparagraph, there shall be taken into account all fees, charges, and other amounts borne by the mortgagor which are attributable to the mortgage or to the bond issue. Such amounts include points, commitment fees, origination fees, servicing fees, and prepayment penalties paid by the mortgagor.

(B) Items that shall be treated as borne by the mortgagor and shall be taken into account in calculating the effective rate of interest also include—

(1) All points, commitment fees, origination fees, or similar charges borne by the seller of the property;

Reg. §6a.103A-2(i)(2)(ii)(B)(1)

⟫⟫→ Caution: Code Sec. 103A has been repealed. Similar exempt bond issue rules have been provided in Code Secs. 141-150.

(2) The excess of any amounts received from any person other than the mortgagor by any person in connection with the acquisition of the mortgagor's interest in the property over the usual and reasonable costs incurred by a person acquiring like property where owner financing is not provided through the use of qualified mortgage bonds.

(C) The following items shall not be treated as borne by the mortgagor and shall not be taken into account in calculating the effective rate of interest:

(1) Any expected rebate of arbitrage profit (as required by §6a.103A-2(i)(4)).

(2) Any application fee, survey fee, credit report fee, insurance fee or similar settlement or financing cost to the extent such amount does not exceed amounts charged in such area in cases where owner financing is not provided through the use of qualified mortgage bonds. For example, amounts paid for FHA, VA, or similar private mortgage insurance on an individual's mortgage need not be taken into account so long as such amounts do not exceed the amounts charged in the area with respect to a similar mortgage that is not financed with qualified mortgage bonds. Premiums charged for pool mortgage insurance will be considered amounts in excess of the usual and reasonable amounts charged for insurance in cases where owner financing is not provided through the use of qualified mortgage bonds.

(D)(1) Where amounts other than those derived from the proceeds of a mortgage subsidy bond are used to finance single-family residences such amounts will not be treated as the proceeds of a qualified mortgage bond issue and will not be subject to the limitations set forth in subparagraphs (2), (3), and (4) of this paragraph (i). Such amounts may, however, be treated as proceeds for purposes of the requirements of section 103(c) and the regulations thereunder. Thus, the portion of the mortgage pool financed by the proceeds of a qualified mortgage bond issue will be subject to the limitations of subparagraphs (2), (3), and (4) of this paragraph (i), while the portion not provided with bond proceeds will not be subject to such limitations. The interest rate, points, origination fees, servicing fees, and other amounts charged with respect to that portion of a mortgage loan financed with non-bond amounts may not exceed the reasonable and customary amount which would be charged where financing is not provided through a qualified mortgage bond issue. Where the charge does exceed such reasonable and customary amount, any excess will be taken into account in computing the effective interest rate on the portion of the loan provided with the proceeds of the qualified mortgage bond issue. Furthermore, where such fees and other charges are less than the reasonable and customary charges, the issuer may not allocate that portion of the charges on the loan amounts made with bond proceeds which is equal to such differential to loan amounts made with non-bond proceeds.

(2) If any mortgage is allocated to two or more sources of funds, the receipt of amounts which are described in paragraph (i)(2)(ii)(A) and (B), repayments of principal, or payments of interest on such mortgage must be allocated to each source of funds.

(E) The effective rate of interest on any mortgage shall be determined in a manner consistent with actuarial methods and shall take into account the discounted value of all amounts from the time received to an amount equal to the "purchase price" of the mortgage. Such discount rate is the effective rate of interest on the mortgages. The "purchase price" of a mortgage means the net amount loaned to the mortgagor. For example, if a mortgage loan is in the amount of $30,000 and the mortgagor is charged one point ($300) as an origination fee which amount is deducted from loan proceeds available to the mortgagor, the purchase price is $29,700. If interest on an issue is paid semiannually, all regular monthly mortgage payments and prepayments of principal may be treated as being received at the end of each semiannual debt service period.

(1) If interest on an issue is paid semiannually, all regular monthly mortgage payments may be treated as being received at the end of each semiannual debt service period.

(2) Prepayments of principal shall be treated as being received on the last day of the month in which the issuer reasonably expects to receive such prepayments.

(F) The rate shall be determined on a composite basis for all mortgages financed by the issue.

(iii) *Example.*—The following example illustrates the provisions of subparagraph (2)(ii):

Example. Purchaser A contracts with seller B, who is represented by real estate agent C, for the purchase of B's residence for $65,000. A applies to County X for a mortgage provided by the proceeds of a qualified mortgage bond. County X requires that agent C provide it with a principal residence affidavit as well as verify the purchase price of the residence and the location of the purchaser's

previous residences. Due to the increased administrative burden imposed on agent C by County X, C charges B a real estate commission of 8 percent ($5,200), rather than 6 percent ($3,900). The normal real estate commission is 6 percent. Since the 8 percent commission charged by C and paid by B is in excess of the usual and reasonable real estate commission where owner financing is not provided through the use of qualified mortgage bonds, 2 percent ($1,300) shall be treated as borne by A and taken into account in calculating the effective rate of interest on the mortgage.

(iv) *Prepayment assumption.*—In determining the effective rate of interest on mortgages, it shall be assumed that the mortgage prepayment rate for mortgages made out of both original proceeds and mortgages that the issuer expects with reasonable certainty to be made out of prepayments of principal will be equal to 100 percent of the rate set forth in the most recent mortgage maturity experience table for mortgages having the same term insured under section 203 of the National Housing Act and published by the Federal Housing Administration in "Survivorship and Decrement Tables for HUD/FHA Home Mortgage Insurance Program" for the region, or, if available, the State in which the residence is located. For purposes of applying these tables, either the original balance method or the declining balance method of calculating mortgage loan prepayments may be used. For proceeds used to finance qualified home improvement loans or shorter term qualified rehabilitation loans for which there are no comparable FHA mortgage maturity experience tables, the assumption used by the issuer as to the rate of prepayment shall be based upon the reasonable expectations of the issuer, as reflected, where applicable, by the issuer's prior experience with such loans.

(v) *Net losses.*—The projected net losses on the mortgage pool (after foreclosure and payment of insurance proceeds), based on the most recent default experience for the area in which the residences are located, shall be taken into consideration in calculating the effective rate of interest on the mortgages. However, where mortgages provided under an issue are insured with FHA, VA, or private mortgage insurance, in conjunction with pool mortgage insurance, the expected net losses will be presumed to be zero. In the event that the actual losses on the mortgage pool exceed the projected net losses which were taken into consideration in calculating the effective rate of interest on the mortgages, investment proceeds earned from nonmortgage assets may be used to recover the excess losses and need not be paid or credited to the mortgagors under §6a.103A-2(i)(4).

(vi) *Yield on the issue.*—(A) The yield on an issue of qualified mortgage bonds shall be calculated on the basis of—

(1) The issue price, and

(2) An expected maturity for the bonds which is consistent with the prepayment assumption required under subparagraph (2)(iv). The expected maturity will be considered consistent with such prepayment assumption if all prepayments are assumed to be used to call bonds proportionately (*i.e.,* a "strip" call). The preceding sentence shall not apply to prepayments of mortgages provided from original proceeds to the extent such prepayments are used to provide mortgages.

(B) For purposes of (1) of this subdivision (vi), the term "issue price" shall have the same meaning as in section 1232(b)(2). Thus, in general, such term means the initial offering price to the public, not including bond houses and brokers, or similar persons or organizations acting in the capacity of underwriters or wholesalers, at which price a substantial amount of such obligations were sold or, if privately placed, the price paid by the first buyer of such obligations or the acquisition cost of the first buyer.

(3) *Nonmortgage investments.*—(i) *Maximum investment.*—Except as provided in (ii), an issue meets the requirements of this subparagraph only if—

(A) At no time during any bond year does the aggregate amount invested in nonmortgage investments, *e.g.,* reasonably required reserve funds, with a yield materially higher than the yield on the issue exceed 150 percent of the debt service on the issue for the current bond year, and

(B) Such aggregate amount invested in nonmortgage assets with a yield materially higher than the yield on the issue is promptly and appropriately reduced as mortgages are repaid.

The amount subject to the maximum investment rule in (i)(A) includes the original bond proceeds, investment proceeds and repayments of principal on the mortgages. For purposes of subdivision (B), the amount described in subdivision (A) shall be considered promptly and appropriately reduced if beginning in the first bond year after the expiration of the temporary period for original proceeds described in subdivision (ii)(A), such amount is reduced within 30 days of the beginning of each bond year by an amount equal to

>»→ *Caution: Code Sec. 103A has been repealed. Similar exempt bond issue rules have been provided in Code Secs. 141-150.*

the difference between the average scheduled monthly mortgage receipts for the bond year (excluding any receipts that were scheduled with respect to mortgages that were discharged in the preceding bond year) and the average scheduled monthly mortgage receipts for the preceding bond year.

(ii) *Temporary periods.* Subparagraph (3)(i) shall not apply to—

(A) Proceeds (including prepayments of principal designated to be used to acquire additional mortgages) of the issue invested for an initial temporary period not to exceed 1 year ($1^{1}/_{2}$ years for proceeds required to be set aside for placing mortgages in targeted areas) until such proceeds are needed for mortgages, and

(B) Repayments of principal and interest on mortgages that are contributed to a bona fide debt service fund (as defined in §1.103-13(b)(12)) and invested for a 13-month temporary period as provided in §1.103-14(b)(10).

(iii) *Debt service defined.*—For purposes of subparagraph (3)(i)(A), the debt service on the issue for any bond year is the scheduled amount of interest and amortization of principal payable for such year with respect to such issue. There shall not be taken into account amounts scheduled with respect to any bond which has been retired before the beginning of the bond year.

(iv) *Nonmortgage investments.*—A nonmortgage investment is any investment other than an investment in a qualified mortgage. For example, a mortgage-secured certificate or obligation is a nonmortgage investment. Investment earnings from participation fees (described in §6a.103A-1(b)(5)) are treated as investment proceeds on nonmortgage investments unless such fees are used to pay debt service or to finance owner occupied residences.

(v) *Bonds issued after June 30, 1993.*—Section 1.148-2(f)(2)(iv) applies to bonds issued after June 30, 1993, in lieu of this paragraph (i)(3).

(4) *Arbitrage and investment gains to be used to reduce costs of owner financing.*—(i) *Rebate requirement.*—An issue shall be treated as meeting the requirements of this subparagraph only if an amount equal to the sum of

(A) The excess of—

(1) The net amount earned on all nonmortgage investments pursuant to subparagraph (3)(i) and (ii) (other than investments attributable to an excess described in this subdivision (A)) over

(2) The amount which would have been earned if the investments were invested at a rate equal to the yield on the issue, plus

(B) Any income attributable to the excess described in subdivision (A),

shall be paid or credited to the mortgagors as rapidly as practicable. Such amount may be disproportionately distributed to the mortgagors if the larger portion of such amount is distributed to lower income mortgagors. The determination of the excess described in subdivision (A) shall take into account any reinvestment of nonmortgage investment receipts and any gain or loss realized on the disposition of nonmortgage investments. In addition, where nonmortgage investments are retained by the issuer after retirement of an issue, any unrealized gains or losses as of the date of retirement of such issue must be taken into account, in calculating the amount to be rebated to the mortgagors. The amount described in subdivision (A)(2) is the amount that would have been earned if the investments in nonmortgage obligations were invested at a rate equal to the yield on the issue calculated in the same manner as provided in §6a.103A-2(i)(2)(vi) and by using the same compounding method. For purposes of subdivision (B), any income attributable to the excess described in subdivision (A) shall be taken into account whether or not such income exceeds the yield on the bonds.

(ii) *Computation period.*—Whether earnings are amounts described in subdivision (i)(A) or (B) shall be determined by making computations on an annual basis. For example, if at the end of the first year the earnings on nonmortgage investments exceed the amount that could have been earned if such investments were invested at the bond yield, the amount of earnings equal to such difference constitutes an excess described in subdivision (i)(A). In the following year, investment proceeds earned on such excess must be taken into account, whether or not such earnings exceed the yield on the bonds, and may not be treated as "negative arbitrage".

(iii) *Paid or credited.*—For purposes of subdivision (i), amounts are paid or credited to mortgagors as rapidly as practicable if such amounts are paid or credited to such mortgagors at the time the mortgagor discharges the mortgage, for example, through prepayment of the entire principal amount or through making the last

regular payment on the mortgage. The amount paid or credited to the mortgagors must have a present value at least equal to the present value of the amount described in subdivision (i), using the yield on the bonds as the discount rate. In the case of prepayments, the cumulative amount required to be rebated under subparagraph (4)(i) may be determined as of a date before the actual prepayment but not more than 1 year earlier than the date of prepayment. Except as provided in subparagraph (2)(v) or subparagraph (4)(iv), such amount may not be subject to the claim of any party, *e.g.*, a bondholder, and may not be paid over to any party other than the mortgagor or the United States.

(iv) *Reduction where issuer does not use full 1 percentage point.*—(A) The amount required to be paid or credited to mortgagors under subparagraph (4)(i) shall be reduced by the amount which (if it were treated as an interest payment made by mortgagors) would result in the excess referred to in subparagraph (2)(i) being equal to 1 percentage point. Such amount shall be fixed and determined as of the yield determination date. This fixed dollar amount may be received by the issuer at any time but may not be adjusted for the time of payment. Such fixed dollar amount shall be equal to the difference between the purchase price of mortgages financed by the proceeds of the issue and the present value of expected payments of principal and interest on such mortgages, using a discount rate equal to the bond yield plus 1 percentage point.

(B) The following example illustrates the provisions of subparagraph (4)(iv)(A):

Example. In 1981, County X issues obligations to provide mortgages for owner-occupied residences. The yield paid on the obligations is 10 percent, and the effective rate of interest on the mortgages provided by the proceeds of such obligations is 9.75 percent. X maintains a reasonably required reserve fund which is invested at 15 percent and intends to recover that additional amount computed in the manner described in subparagraph (4)(iv) which could have been earned from investment of the proceeds in mortgages with an effective interest rate of 11 percent from the arbitrage earned from the reserve fund nonmortgage assets. X plans to recover such amount from the arbitrage over a period of 3 years; thus, X will not recover such amount until 1984. X may not adjust the amount to be received to account for the time when such amount will be received.

(v) *Election to pay United States.*—Subparagraph (4)(i) shall be satisfied with respect to any issue if the issuer elects in writing before issuing the obligations to pay over to the United States—

(A) Not less frequently than once each 5 years after the date of issue, an amount equal to 90 percent of the aggregate amount described in subdivision (i) earned during such period (and not theretofore paid to the United States), and

(B) Not later than 30 days after the redemption of the last obligation, 100 percent of such aggregate amount not theretofore paid to the United States.

(j) *New mortgages.*—(1) *In general.*—An issue meets the requirements of this paragraph only if no part of the proceeds of such issue is to be used to acquire or replace an existing mortgage. All of the lendable proceeds must be used to provide mortgage loans to persons who did not have a mortgage (whether or not paid off) on the residence securing the mortgage note at any time prior to the execution of the mortgage.

(2) *Exceptions.*—For purposes of this paragraph (j), the replacement of—

(i) Construction period loans,

(ii) Bridge loans or similar temporary initial financing, and

(iii) In the case of a qualified rehabilitation, an existing mortgage, shall not be treated as the acquisition or replacement of an existing mortgage. Generally, temporary initial financing is any financing which has a term of 24 months or less.

(3) *Assumptions.*—An issue meets the requirement of this paragraph only if a mortgage with respect to which owner financing has been provided under such issue may be assumed only if the requirements of paragraphs (d), (e), and (f) are met with respect to such assumption. The determination of whether these requirements are met is based upon the facts as they exist at the time of the assumption as if the loan were being made for the first time. For example, the purchase price requirement is to be determined by reference to the average area purchase price at the time of the assumption and not when the mortgage was originally placed. If the bond documents and relevant mortgage instruments provide that a mortgage may be assumed only if the issuer has determined that the conditions stated in this subparagraph are satisfied, the good faith and 95-percent requirements of paragraph (c)(1)(i) and (ii) will be considered satisfied with respect to the requirements of this subparagraph at the time

⟫⟫→ *Caution: Code Sec. 103A has been repealed. Similar exempt bond issue rules have been provided in Code Secs. 141-150.*

the mortgages were executed. However, any failure to meet the requirements of this subparagraph at the time a mortgage is assumed is subject to the remedy requirement in paragraph (c)(1)(iii).

(4) *Examples.*—The following examples illustrate the application of this paragraph (j):

Example (1). In June 1981 mortgagor A obtained a mortgage from a private lending institution in order to construct a house on land which A purchased without a mortgage in May 1981. In January 1982 A applies to obtain permanent financing on the residence from a program sponsored by State housing finance agency Y. Such program is funded with the proceeds of qualified mortgage bonds. If A meets the other requirements of this section, A qualifies for such permanent financing since the replacing of construction financing is not treated as the acquisition or replacement of an existing mortgage.

Example (2). In June 1981 mortgagor B purchased a new residence in a targeted area but was unable to sell his former residence. Therefore, B obtained temporary financing for his new residence until his former residence was sold. In October 1981 B applies to County Z to obtain financing from a program funded with proceeds of qualified mortgage bonds. Such financing is needed by B to replace the temporary financing for his new residence. If B meets the other requirements of this section, the mortgage qualifies for such permanent financing since the permanent financing replaces temporary initial financing.

Example (3). In 1979 mortgagor C purchased a residence but was unable to obtain financing from a program sponsored by County W because such program prohibited loans from the program which were in excess of 80 percent of the fair market value of the property. Therefore, in 1979 C obtained financing from a private lending institution with the intention of refinancing when he accumulated sufficient equity in the property. In 1981 C has accumulated sufficient equity in the property so as to comply with the requirements of the program. C applies to County W to refinance under the program, which is funded with the proceeds of qualified mortgage bonds. Even if C met the other requirements of this section, the mortgage would fail to meet the requirement of paragraph (j) since such a mortgage would replace an existing mortgage.

Example (4). In 1969 mortgagor D purchased a residence and obtained financing from a private lending institution. In 1981 D applies to County U for a loan for the rehabilitation of the property and for the refinancing of the existing mortgage. The program is funded with qualified mortgage bonds. If D meets the other requirements of this section the mortgage qualifies for such permanent financing since the replacement of the mortgage is not treated as the replacement or acquisition of an existing mortgage.

Example (5). In 1950 mortgagor E purchased a residence, obtaining a mortgage from a private lending institution to finance the purchase price. In 1980 E completed repaying the mortgage. In 1981 E applies for a loan from a program sponsored by State housing finance agency X and funded with the proceeds of qualified mortgage bonds. The mortgage does not meet the requirements of paragraph (j) since E had a previous mortgage on his residence, even though such mortgage was previously released.

(k) *Information reporting requirement.*—See § 1.103A-2(k) for rules relating to section 103A(j)(3).

(l) *Policy statement.*—See § 1.103A-2(l) for rules relating to section 103A(j)(5).

(m) *State certification.*—See § 1.103A-2(m) for rules relating to section 103A(j)(4). [Temporary Reg. § 6a.103A-2.]

☐ [*T.D. 7780, 6-29-81. Amended by T.D. 7794, 11-5-81; T.D. 7817, 5-19-82; T.D. 7819, 6-3-82; T.D. 7821, 6-24-82; T.D. 7995, 12-7-84; T.D. 8023, 5-3-85; T.D. 8049, 8-29-85 and T.D. 8476, 6-14-93.*]

[Reg. § 6a.103A-3]

§ 6a.103A-3. Qualified veteran's mortgage bonds (Temporary).— (a) *In general.*—A qualified veterans' mortgage bond shall not be treated as a mortgage subsidy bond, and the interest shall be exempt from Federal income taxation.

(b) *Qualified veterans' mortgage bond.*—(1) With respect to obligations issued prior to July 19, 1984, the term "qualified veterans' mortgage bond" means any issue of obligations—

(i) Which meets the requirements of § 6a.103A-1, § 6a.103A-2(j)(1) and (2), and this section;

(ii) Substantially all of the proceeds of which are to be used to provide financing for single-family, owner-occupied residences (which meet the requirements of § 6a.103A-1(b)(6) and § 6a.103A-2(d)) for veterans; and

(iii) Payment of the principal and interest on which is secured by a pledge of the full faith and credit of the issuing State.

A qualified veterans' mortgage bond does not include any bond that is an industrial development bond under section 103(b).

(2) With respect to obligations issued after July 18, 1984, the term "qualified veterans' mortgage bond" means any issue of obligations—

(i) Which meets the requirements of § 6a.103A-1, § 6a.103A-2(d) (relating to residence requirements), (j)(1) and (2) (relating to new mortgage requirement), and (k) (relating to information reporting requirement), and this section;

(ii) Substantially all of the proceeds of which are to be used to provide financing for qualified veterans; and

(iii) Payment of the principal and interest on which is secured by a pledge of the full faith and credit of the issuing State.

A qualified veterans' mortgage bond does not include any bond that is an industrial development bond under section 103(b).

(c) *Qualified veteran.*—(1) An issue meets the requirements of this paragraph only if each of the mortgagors to whom owner financing is provided is a qualified veteran.

(2) With respect to obligations issued prior to July 19, 1984, the term "qualified veteran" means any veteran.

(3) With respect to obligations issued after July 18, 1984, the term "qualified veteran" means any veteran who—

(i) Served on active duty at some time before January 1, 1977, and

(ii) Applied for financing before the later of—

(A) The date 30 years after the date on which such veteran left active service, or

(B) January 1, 1985.

(4) The term "veteran" shall have the same meaning as in 38 U.S.C. 101(2), that is, a person who served in the active military, naval, or air service, and who was discharged or released therefrom under conditions other than dishonorable.

(d) *Husband and wife.*—For purposes of this section, if a residence is to be owned by a husband and wife as joint tenants, as tenants by the entirety, or as community property, and if one spouse is a veteran, then both spouses shall be treated as satisfying the requirements of paragraph (c).

(e) *Substantially all.*—For purposes of this section, the term "substantially all" shall have the same meaning as in § 1.103-8.

(f) *Qualified home improvement loan.*—The term "qualified home improvement loan" means the financing (whether or not secured by a mortgage) of alterations, repairs, and improvements on, or in connection with, an existing single-family, owner-occupied residence by a veteran who is the owner thereof. The alterations, repairs, and improvements, however, must substantially protect or improve the basic livability or energy efficiency of the property, such as the renovation of plumbing or electric systems, the installation of improved heating or air conditioning systems, the addition of living space, or the renovation of a kitchen area. Items that will not be considered to substantially protect or improve the basic livability of the property include swimming pools, tennis courts, saunas, or other recreational or entertainment facilities.

(g) *Volume limitation.*—(1) *In general.*—In the case of obligations issued after June 22, 1984, an issue meets the requirements of this paragraph only if the aggregate amount of obligations issued pursuant thereto, when added to the aggregate amount of qualified veterans' mortgage bonds previously issued by the State during the calendar year, does not exceed the State veterans limit for such calendar year. In determining the aggregate amount of qualified veterans' mortgage bonds issued in calendar year 1984, obligations issued prior to June 23, 1984, shall not be taken into account.

(2) *State veterans limit.*—(i) The State veterans limit for any State is the amount equal to—

(A) The aggregate amount of qualified veterans' mortgage bonds issued by the State during the period beginning on January 1, 1979, and ending on June 22, 1984 (not including the amount of any qualified veterans' mortgage bonds actually issued during the calendar year, or the applicable portion of 1984, in such period for which the amount of such bonds was the lowest), divided by

(B) The number (not to exceed 5) of calendar years after 1978 and before 1985 during which the State issued qualified veterans' mortgage bonds.

In determining the number of calendar years after 1978 and before 1985 during which the State issued qualified veterans' mortgage bonds, any qualified veterans' mortgage bonds issued after June 22, 1984, shall not be taken into account. A State that did not issue qualified veterans' mortgage bonds during the period beginning on

>>>→ *Caution: Code Sec. 103A has been repealed. Similar exempt bond issue rules have been provided in Code Secs. 141-150.*

January 1, 1979, and ending on June 22, 1984, may not issue qualified veterans' mortgage bonds after June 22, 1984.

(ii) In the case of any obligation which has a term of 1 year or less and which was issued to provide financing for property taxes, the amount taken into account under this paragraph with respect to such obligation shall be 1/15 of its principal amount.

(3) *Examples.*—The following examples illustrate the provisions of this paragraph:

Example (1). State R issued the following issues of qualified veterans' mortgage bonds: a $200 million issue on March 31, 1979, a $150 million issue on May 1, 1980, a $75 million issue on September 1, 1981, a $200 million issue on June 5, 1982, a $125 million issue on March 1, 1983, a $60 million issue on April 1, 1984, and a $100 million issue on September 1, 1984. R issued no other issues of qualified veterans' mortgage bonds during the period beginning January 1, 1979, and ending on December 31, 1984. The aggregate amount of qualified veterans' mortgage bonds issued during the period January 1, 1984, through June 22, 1984 ($60 million), is not taken into account in determining R's State veterans limit because that is the lowest aggregate amount of qualified veterans' mortgage bonds issued during the calendar year or the applicable portion of 1984, in the period beginning on January 1, 1979, and ending on June 22, 1984. Thus, R's State veterans limit is $150 million ($750 million (which is the sum of $200 million, $150 million, $75 million, $200 million, and $125 million) divided by 5). The September 1, 1984, issue is not included in determining the State veterans limit because that issue was issued after June 22, 1984. The September 1, 1984, issue of qualified veterans' mortgage bonds meets the requirements of § 6a.103A-3(g) since the aggregate amount of qualified veterans' mortgage bonds issued in calendar year 1984 (not including obligations issued prior to June 23, 1984), does not exceed the State veterans limit.

Example (2). State S issued a $100 million issue of qualified veterans' mortgage bonds on March 31, 1984. S issued no other issues of qualified veterans' mortgage bonds during the period beginning on January 1, 1979, and ending on June 22, 1984. The aggregate amount of qualified veterans' mortgage bonds issued in the calendar year, or the applicable portion of 1984, in the period January 1, 1979, through June 22, 1984, for which the amount of bonds was the lowest is zero. Thus, the State veterans limit for S is $100 million ($100 million minus $0) divided by 1).

(h) *Good faith compliance efforts.*—(1) *Mortgage eligibility requirements.*—An issue of qualified veterans' mortgage bonds issued after July 18, 1984, which fails to meet the requirements of section 103A(o)(1), § 6a.103A-2(d) (relating to residence requirements), and § 6a.103A-2(j)(1) and (2) (relating to new mortgage requirement) shall be treated as meeting such requirements if each of the following provisions is complied with:

(i) The issuer in good faith attempted to meet all such requirements before the mortgages were executed. Good faith requires that the trust indenture, participation agreements with loan originators, and other relevant instruments contain restrictions that permit the financing of residences only in accordance with such requirements. In addition, the issuer must establish reasonable procedures to ensure compliance with such requirements. Such procedures include reasonable investigations by the issuer to satisfy such requirements.

(ii) Ninety-five percent or more of the lendable proceeds (as defined in § 6a.103A-2(b)(1)) that were devoted to owner-financing were devoted to residences with respect to which, at the time the mortgages were executed, all such requirements were met. In determining whether a person is a qualified veteran the issuer may rely on copies of the mortgagor's certificate of discharge indicating that the mortgagor served on active duty at some time before January 1, 1977, and stating the date on which the mortgagor left active service provided that neither the issuer nor its agent knows or has reason to believe that such affidavit is false. Where a particular mortgage fails to meet more than one of these requirements, the amount of the mortgage will be taken into account only once in determining whether the 95-percent requirement is met. However, all of the defects in the mortgage must be corrected pursuant to subdivision (iii).

(iii) Any failure to meet such requirements is corrected within a reasonable period after such failure is discovered. For example, failures can be corrected by calling the nonqualifying mortgage or by replacing the nonqualifying mortgage with a qualifying mortgage.

(2) *Nonmortgage eligibility requirements.*—An issue of qualified veterans' mortgage bonds issued after July 18, 1984, which fails to meet the requirements of paragraph (g) of this section shall be treated as meeting such requirements if each of the requirements of § 6a.103A-2(c)(2)(i) and (ii) is met. [Temporary Reg. § 6a.103A-3.]

☐ [T.D. 7780, 6-29-81. Amended by T.D. 7995, 12-7-84.]

[Reg. § 1.104-1]

§ 1.104-1. Compensation for injuries or sickness.—(a) *In general.*—Section 104(a) provides an exclusion from gross income with respect to certain amounts described in paragraphs (b), (c), (d) and (e) of this section, which are received for personal injuries or sickness, except to the extent that such amounts are attributable to (but not in excess of) deductions allowed under section 213 (relating to medical, etc., expenses) for any prior taxable year. See section 213 and the regulations thereunder.

(b) *Amounts received under workmen's compensation acts.*—Section 104(a)(1) excludes from gross income amounts which are received by an employee under a workmen's compensation act (such as the Longshoremen's and Harbor Workers' Compensation Act, 33 U.S.C., c. 18), or under a statute in the nature of a workmen's compensation act which provides compensation to employees for personal injuries or sickness incurred in the course of employment. Section 104(a)(1) also applies to compensation which is paid under a workmen's compensation act to the survivor or survivors of a deceased employee. However, section 104(a)(1) does not apply to a retirement pension or annuity to the extent that it is determined by reference to the employee's age or length of service, or the employee's prior contributions, even though the employee's retirement is occasioned by an occupational injury or sickness. Section 104(a)(1) also does not apply to amounts which are received as compensation for a nonoccupational injury or sickness nor to amounts received as compensation for an occupational injury or sickness to the extent that they are in excess of the amount provided in the applicable workmen's compensation act or acts. See, however, § § 1.105-1 through 1.105-5 for rules relating to exclusion of such amounts from gross income.

(c) *Damages received on account of personal physical injuries or physical sickness.*—(1) *In general.*—Section 104(a)(2) excludes from gross income the amount of any damages (other than punitive damages) received (whether by suit or agreement and whether as lump sums or as periodic payments) on account of personal physical injuries or physical sickness. Emotional distress is not considered a physical injury or physical sickness. However, damages for emotional distress attributable to a physical injury or physical sickness are excluded from income under section 104(a)(2). Section 104(a)(2) also excludes damages not in excess of the amount paid for medical care (described in section 213(d)(1)(A) or (B)) for emotional distress. For purposes of this paragraph (c), the term *damages* means an amount received (other than workers' compensation) through prosecution of a legal suit or action, or through a settlement agreement entered into in lieu of prosecution.

(2) *Cause of action and remedies.*—The section 104(a)(2) exclusion may apply to damages recovered for a personal physical injury or physical sickness under a statute, even if that statute does not provide for a broad range of remedies. The injury need not be defined as a tort under state or common law.

(3) *Effective/applicability date.*—This paragraph (c) applies to damages paid pursuant to a written binding agreement, court decree, or mediation award entered into or issued after September 13, 1995, and received after January 23, 2012. Taxpayers also may apply these final regulations to damages paid pursuant to a written binding agreement, court decree, or mediation award entered into or issued after September 13, 1995, and received after August 20, 1996. If applying these final regulations to damages received after August 20, 1996, results in an overpayment of tax, the taxpayer may file a claim for refund before the period of limitations under section 6511 expires. To qualify for a refund of tax on damages paid after August 20, 1996, under a written binding agreement, court decree, or mediation award entered into or issued after September 13, 1995, a taxpayer must meet the requirements of section 1605 of the Small Business Job Protection Act of 1996, Public Law 104-188 (110 Stat. 1838).

(d) *Accident or health insurance.*—Section 104(a)(3) excludes from gross income amounts received through accident or health insurance for personal injuries or sickness (other than amounts received by an employee, to the extent that such amounts (1) are attributable to contributions of the employer which were not includible in the gross income of the employee, or (2) are paid by the employer). Similar treatment is also accorded to amounts received under accident or health plans and amounts received from sickness or disability funds. See section 105(e) and § 1.105-5. If, therefore, an individual purchases a policy of accident or health insurance out of his own funds, amounts received thereunder for personal injuries or sickness are excludable from his gross income under section 104(a)(3). See, however, section 213 and the regulations thereunder as to the inclusion in gross income of amounts attributable to deductions allowed under section 213 for any prior taxable year. Section 104(a)(3) also applies to amounts received by an employee for personal injuries or sickness from a fund which is maintained exclusively by employee contributions. Conversely, if an employer is either the sole contributor to such a fund, or is the sole purchaser of a policy of accident or health insurance for his employees (on either a group or individual basis), the exclusion provided under section 104(a)(3) does not apply to any amounts received by his employees through such fund or insurance. If the employer and his employees contribute to a fund or purchase insurance which pays accident or health benefits to employees, section 104(a)(3) does not apply to amounts received thereunder by employees to the extent that such amounts are attributable to the employer's contributions. See §1.105-1 for rules relating to the determination of the amount attributable to employer contributions. Although amounts paid by or on behalf of an employer to an employee for personal injuries or sickness are not excludable from the employee's gross income under section 104(a)(3), they may be excludable therefrom under section 105. See §§1.105-1 through 1.105-5, inclusive. For treatment of accident or health benefits paid to or on behalf of a self-employed individual by a trust described in section 401(a) which is exempt under section 501(a) or under a plan described in section 403(a), see paragraph (g) of §1.72-15.

(e) *Amounts received as pensions, etc., for certain personal injuries or sickness.*—(1) Section 104(a)(4) excludes from gross income amounts which are received as a pension, annuity, or similar allowance for personal injuries or sickness resulting from active service in the armed forces of any country, or in the Coast and Geodetic Survey, or the Public Health Service. For purposes of this section, that part of the retired pay of a member of an armed force, computed under formula No. 1 or 2 of 10 U.S.C. 1401, or under 10 U.S.C. 1402(d), on the basis of years of service, which exceeds the retired pay that he would receive if it were computed on the basis of percentage of disability is not considered as a pension, annuity, or similar allowance for personal injury or sickness, resulting from active service in the armed forces of any country, or in the Coast and Geodetic Survey, or the Public Health Service (see 10 U.S.C. 1403 (formerly 37 U.S.C. 272(h), section 402(h) of the Career Compensation Act of 1949)). See paragraph (a)(3)(i)(a) of §1.105-4 for the treatment of retired pay in excess of the part computed on the basis of percentage of disability as amounts received through a wage continuation plan. For the rules relating to certain reduced uniformed services retirement pay, see paragraph (c)(2) of §1.122-1. For rules relating to a waiver by a member or former member of the uniformed services of a portion of disability retired pay in favor of a pension or compensation receivable under the laws administered by the Veterans Administration (38 U.S.C. 3105), see section 1.122-1(c)(3). For rules relating to a reduction of the disability retired pay of a member or former member of the uniformed services under the Dual Compensation Act of 1964 (5 U.S.C. 5531) by reason of Federal employment, see section 1.122-1(c)(4).

(2) Section 104(a)(4) excludes from gross income amounts which are received by a participant in the Foreign Service Retirement and Disability System in a taxable year of such participant ending after September 8, 1960, as a disability annuity payable under the provisions of section 831 of the Foreign Service Act of 1946, as amended (22 U.S.C. 1081; 60 Stat. 1021). However, if any amount is received by a survivor of a disabled or incapacitated participant, such amount is not excluded from gross income by reason of the provisions of section 104(a)(4).

(3) Section 104(a)(4) excludes from gross income amounts which are received by a participant in the Retired Serviceman's Family Protection Plan as a disability annuity payable under the provisions of 10 U.S.C. 1431. However, if any amount is received by a survivor of a disabled or incapacitated participant, such amount is not excluded from gross income by reason of the provisions of section 104(a)(4). [Reg. §1.104-1.]

☐ [*T.D.* 6169, 4-13-56. *Amended by T.D.* 6722, 4-13-64; *T.D.* 7043, 6-1-70 *and T.D.* 9573, 1-20-2012.]

[Reg. §1.105-1]

§1.105-1. Amounts attributable to employer contributions.—(a) *In general.*—Under section 105(a), amounts received by an employee through accident or health insurance for personal injuries or sickness must be included in his gross income to the extent that such amounts (1) are attributable to contributions of the employer which were not includible in the gross income of the employee, or (2) are paid by the employer, unless such amounts are excluded therefrom under section 105(b), (c), or (d). For purposes of this section, the term "amounts received by an employee through an accident or health plan" refers to any amounts received through accident or health insurance, and also to any amounts which, under section 105(e), are treated as being so received. See §1.105-5. In determining the extent to which amounts received for personal injuries or sickness by an employee through an accident or health plan are subject to the provisions of section 105(a), rather than section 104(a)(3), the provisions of paragraphs (b), (c), (d), and (e) of this section shall apply. A

self-employed individual is not an employee for purposes of section 105 and §§1.105-1 through 1.105-5. See paragraph (g) of §1.72-15. Thus, such an individual will not be treated as an employee with respect to benefits described in section 105 received from a plan in which he participates as an employee within the meaning of section 401(c)(1) at the time he, his spouse, or any of his dependents becomes entitled to receive such benefits.

(b) *Noncontributory plans.*—All amounts received by employees through an accident or health plan which is financed solely by their employer, either by payment of premiums on an accident or health insurance policy (whether on a group or individual basis), by contributions to a fund which pays accident or health benefits, or by direct payment of the benefits under the plan, are subject to the provisions of section 105(a), except to the extent that they are excludable under section 105(b), (c), or (d). This rule may be illustrated by the following examples:

Example (1). Employer A maintains a plan for his employees which provides that he will continue to pay regular wages to employees who are absent from work due to sickness or personal injuries. Employees make no contributions to the plan and all benefits are paid by the employer. Amounts received by employees under the plan are subject to section 105(a), and must be included in gross income unless excluded therefrom under section 150(b), (c), or (d).

Example (2). Pursuant to a State nonoccupational disability benefits law, employer B maintains an accident and health plan for his employees. Although under the State law B is authorized to withhold from his employees' wages a specified amount for employee contributions to the State fund, in actual practice B does not so withhold and makes all contributions out of his own funds. All amounts received by B's employees from the State fund are subject to section 105(a), and must be included in gross income unless excluded therefrom under section 105(b), (c), or (d).

(c) *Contributory plans.*—(1) In the case of amounts received by an employee through an accident or health plan which is financed partially by his employer and partially by contributions of the employee, section 105(a) applies to the extent that such amounts are attributable to contributions of the employer which were not includible in the employee's gross income. The portion of such amounts which is attributable to such contributions of the employer shall be determined in accordance with paragraph (d) of this section in the case of an insured plan, or paragraph (e) of this section in the case of a noninsured plan. As used in this section, the phrase "contributions of the employer" means employer contributions which are not includible in the gross income of the employee. See section 106 for the exclusion from an employee's gross income of employer contributions to accident or health plans.

(2) A separate determination of the portion of the amounts received under the accident or health plan which is attributable to the contributions of the employer shall be made with respect to each class of employees in any case where the plan provides that some classes of covered employees contribute but others do not, or that the employer will make different contributions for different classes of employees, or that different classes of employees will make different contributions, and where in any such case both the contributions of the employer on account of each such class of employees and the contributions of such class of employees can be ascertained. For example, if employees contribute during the first year of employment but not thereafter, there will have to be a separate determination for first-year employees, provided that the amount of the contributions of the employer on account of first-year employees and the contributions of such first-year employees can be ascertained for the required period to apply the rules of paragraph (d) or (e) of this section. If in such a case the contributions of the employer to the plan on account of first-year employees are not distinguishable from his other contributions to the plan, then the determination shall be made for all employees under the plan, and such determination shall be used by all employees under the plan.

(3) Except as provided in paragraph (c)(2) of §1.72-15, if the plan provides accident or health benefits as well as other benefits for the employees, and if the respective contributions made by the employer and the employees to provide the accident or health benefits cannot be ascertained, the determination of the portion of the accident or health benefits received under such plan which is attributable to the contributions of the employer shall be made in accordance with the rules of paragraph (d) or (e) of this section on the basis of the contributions of the employer and of the employees to the entire plan.

(4) A determination of the portion attributable to the contributions of the employer, once made in accordance with the rules of this section, shall as to such portion be used for all purposes. For example, if an employee receives amounts under a wage continuation plan during the month of January and terminates his services during February, the portion of such amounts which is attributable to the

contributions of the employer may be determined in order to provide the employee with such information at the time he is provided his Form W-2. The determination made for such purpose will also be used by the employee to report his income for his taxable year in which such amounts are received, without regard to the experience under the plan for the rest of the year.

(d) *Insured plans.*—(1) *Individual policies.*—If an amount is received from an insurance company by an employee under an individual policy of accident or health insurance purchased by contributions of the employer and the employee, the portion of the amount received which is attributable to the employer's contributions shall be an amount which bears the same ratio to the amount received as the portion of the premiums paid by the employer for the current policy year bears to the total premiums paid by the employer and the employee for that year. This rule may be illustrated by the following example:

Example. Employer A maintains a plan whereby he pays two-thirds of the annual premium cost on individual policies of accident and health insurance for his employees. The remainder of each employee's premium is paid by a payroll deduction from the wages of the employee. The annual premium for employee X is $24, of which $16 is paid by the employer. Thus, 16/24 or two-thirds of all amounts received by X under such insurance policy are attributable to the contributions of the employer and are subject to section 105(a), and the remaining one-third of such amounts is excludable from X's gross income under section 104(a)(3).

(2) *Group policies.*—If the accident or health coverage is provided under or is a part of a group insurance policy purchased by contributions of the employer and of the employees, and the net premiums for such coverage for a period of at least three policy years are known at the beginning of the calendar year, the portion of any amount received by an employee which is attributable to the contributions of the employer for such coverage shall be an amount which bears the same ratio to the amount received as the portion of the net premiums

$$\$7,000). \text{ Thus, } \frac{\$ 8,000}{\$24,000} \text{ or one-third, of the amounts received by an employee}$$

at any time during 1955 is attributable to contributions of the employer.

(e) *Noninsured plans.*—If the accident or health benefits are a part of a noninsured plan to which the employer and the employees contribute, and such plan has been in effect for at least three years before the beginning of the calendar year, the portion of the amount received which is attributable to the employer's contributions shall be an amount which bears the same ratio to the amount received as the contributions of the employer for the period of three calendar years next preceding the year of receipt bear to the total contributions of the employer and all the employees for such period. If, at the beginning of the calendar year of receipt, such plan has not been in effect for three years but has been in effect for at least one year, such determination shall be based upon the contributions made during the 1-year or 2-year period during which the plan has been in effect. If such plan has not been in effect for one full year at the beginning of the calendar year of receipt, such determination may be based upon the portion of the year of receipt preceding the time when the determination is made, or such determination may be made periodically (such as monthly or quarterly) and used throughout the succeeding period. For example, if an employee terminates his services on April 15, 1955, and 1955 is the first year the plan has been in effect, such determination may be based upon the contributions of the employer and the employees during the period beginning with January 1, and ending with April 15, or during the month of March, or during the quarter consisting of January, February, and March. [Reg. §1.105-1.]

☐ [T.D. 6169, 4-13-56. *Amended by T.D. 6485, 7-29-60 and T.D. 6722, 4-13-64.*]

[Reg. §1.105-2]

§1.105-2. Amounts expended for medical care.—Section 105(b) provides an exclusion from gross income with respect to the amounts referred to in section 105(a) (see §1.105-1) which are paid, directly or indirectly, to the taxpayer to reimburse him for expenses incurred for the medical care (as defined in section 213(e)) of the taxpayer, his spouse, and his dependents (as defined in section 152). However, the exclusion does not apply to amounts which are attributable to (and not in excess of) deductions allowed under section 213 (relating to medical, etc., expenses) for any prior taxable year. See section 213 and the regulations thereunder. Section 105(b) applies only to amounts which are paid specifically to reimburse the taxpayer for expenses incurred by him for the prescribed medical care. Thus, section 105(b) does not apply to amounts which the taxpayer would

contributed by the employer for the last three policy years which are known at the beginning of the calendar year bears to the total of the net premiums contributed by the employer and all employees for such policy years. If the net premiums for such coverage for a period of at least three policy years are not known at the beginning of the calendar year but are known for at least one policy year, such determination shall be made by using the net premiums for such coverage which are known at the beginning of the calendar year. If the net premiums for such coverage are not known at the beginning of the calendar year for even one policy year, such determination shall be made by using either (i) a reasonable estimate of the net premiums for the first policy year, or (ii) if the net premiums for a policy year are ascertained during the calendar year, by using such net premiums. These rules may be illustrated by the following example:

Example. An employer maintains a plan under which a portion of the cost of a group policy of accident and health insurance for his employees is paid through payroll deductions from wages of the employees. The remainder of the cost is borne by the employer. The policy year begins on November 1, and ends on October 31. The net premium for the policy year ended October 31, 1954, is not known on January 1, 1955, because retroactive premium adjustments, such as dividends and credits, are not determinable until after January 1. Therefore, for purposes of this computation the last three policy years are the policy years ended October 31, 1951, 1952, and 1953. The net premium for the policy year ended October 31, 1953, was $8,000, of which the employer contributed $3,000; the net premium for the policy year ended October 31, 1952, was $9,000, of which the employer contributed $3,500; and the net premium for the policy year ended October 31, 1951, was $7,000, of which the employer contributed $1,500. The portion of any amount received under the policy by an employee at any time during 1955 which is attributable to the contributions of the employer is to be determined by using the ratio of $8,000 ($3,000 plus $3,500 plus $1,500) to $24,000 ($8,000 plus $9,000 plus

be entitled to receive irrespective of whether or not he incurs expenses for medical care. For example, if under a wage continuation plan the taxpayer is entitled to regular wages during a period of absence from work due to sickness or injury, amounts received under such plan are not excludable from his gross income under section 105(b) even though the taxpayer may have incurred medical expenses during the period of illness. Such amounts may, however, be excludable from his gross income under section 105(d). See §1.105-4. If the amounts are paid to the taxpayer solely to reimburse him for expenses which he incurred for the prescribed medical care, section 105(b) is applicable even though such amounts are paid without proof of the amount of the actual expenses incurred by the taxpayer, but section 105(b) is not applicable to the extent that such amounts exceed the amount of the actual expenses for such medical care. If the taxpayer incurs an obligation for medical care, payment to the obligee in discharge of such obligation shall constitute indirect payment to the taxpayer as reimbursement for medical care. Similarly, payment to or on behalf of the taxpayer's spouse or dependents shall constitute indirect payment to the taxpayer. [Reg. §1.105-2.]

☐ [T.D. 6169, 4-13-56.]

[Reg. §1.105-3]

§1.105-3. Payments unrelated to absence from work.—Section 105(c) provides an exclusion from gross income with respect to the amounts referred to in section 105(a) to the extent that such amounts (a) constitute payments for the permanent loss or permanent loss of use of a member or function of the body, or the permanent disfigurement, of the taxpayer, his spouse, or a dependent (as defined in section 152), and (b) are computed with reference to the nature of the injury without regard to the period the employee is absent from work. Loss of use or disfigurement shall be considered permanent when it may reasonably be expected to continue for the life of the individual. For purposes of section 105(c), loss or loss of use of a member or function of the body includes the loss or loss of use of an appendage of the body, the loss of an eye, the loss of substantially all of the vision of an eye, and the loss of substantially all of the hearing in one or both ears. The term "disfigurement" shall be given a reasonable interpretation in the light of all the particular facts and circumstances. Section 105(c) does not apply if the amount of the benefits is determined by reference to the period the employee is absent from work. For example, if an employee is absent from work as a result of the loss of an arm, and under the accident and health plan established by his employer, he is to receive $125 a week so long as he is absent from work for a period not in excess of 52 weeks, section 105(c) is not applicable to such payments. See, however, section 105(d) and §1.105-4. However, for purposes of section 105(c), it is immaterial whether an amount is paid in a lump sum or in installments. Section 105(c) does not apply to amounts which are treated as workmen's compensation under paragraph (b) of §1.104-1, or to amounts paid by reason of the death of the employee (see section 101). [Reg. §1.105-3.]

☐ [T.D. 6169, 4-13-56.]

[Reg. §1.105-5]

§1.105-5. Accident and health plans.—(a) *In general.*—Sections 104(a)(3) and 105(b), (c), and (d) exclude from gross income certain amounts received through accident or health insurance. Section 105(e) provides that for purposes of sections 104 and 105 amounts received through an accident or health plan for employees, and amounts received from a sickness and disability fund for employees maintained under the law of a State, a Territory, or the District of Columbia, shall be treated as amounts received through accident or health insurance. In general, an accident or health plan is an arrangement for the payment of amounts to employees in the event of personal injuries or sickness. A plan may cover one or more employees, and there may be different plans for different employees or classes of employees. An accident or health plan may be either insured or noninsured, and it is not necessary that the plan be in writing or that the employee's rights to benefits under the plan be enforceable. However, if the employee's rights are not enforceable, an amount will be deemed to be received under a plan only if, on the date the employee became sick or injured, the employee was covered by a plan (or a program, policy, or custom having the effect of a plan) providing for the payment of amounts to the employee in the event of personal injuries or sickness, and notice or knowledge of such plan was reasonably available to the employee. It is immaterial who makes payment of the benefits provided by the plan. For example, payment may be made by the employer, a welfare fund, a State sickness or disability benefits fund, an association of employers or employees, or by an insurance company.

(b) *Self-employed individuals.*—Under section 105(g), a self-employed individual is not treated as an employee for purposes of section 105. Therefore, for example, benefits paid under an accident or health plan as referred to in section 105(e) to or on behalf of an individual who is self-employed in the business with respect to which the plan is established will not be treated as received through accident and health insurance for purposes of sections 104(a)(3) and 105. [Reg. §1.105-5.]

☐ [T.D. 6169, 4-13-56. *Amended by T.D. 6722, 4-13-64.*]

[Reg. §1.105-11]

§1.105-11. Self-insured medical reimbursement plan.—(a) *In general.*—Under section 105(a), amounts received by an employee through a self-insured medical reimbursement plan which are attributable to contributions of the employer, or are paid by the employer, are included in the employee's gross income unless such amounts are excludable under section 105(b). For amounts reimbursed to a highly compensated individual to be fully excludable from such individual's gross income under section 105(b), the plan must satisfy the requirements of section 105(h) and this section. Section 105(h) is not satisfied if the plan discriminates in favor of highly compensated individuals as to eligibility to participate or benefits. All or a portion of the reimbursements or payments on behalf of such individuals under a discriminatory plan are not excludable from gross income under section 105(b). However, benefits paid to participants who are not highly compensated individuals may be excluded from gross income if the requirements of section 105(b) are satisfied, even if the plan is discriminatory.

(b) *Self-insured medical reimbursement plan.*—(1) *General rule.*—(i) *Definition.*—A self-insured medical reimbursement plan is a separate written plan for the benefit of employees which provides for reimbursement of employee medical expenses referred to in section 105(b). A plan or arrangement is self-insured unless reimbursement is provided under an individual or group policy of accident or health insurance issued by a licensed insurance company or under an arrangement in the nature of a prepaid health care plan that is regulated under federal or state law in a manner similar to the regulation of insurance companies. Thus, for example, a plan of a health maintenance organization, established under the Health Maintenance Organization Act of 1973, would qualify as a prepaid health care plan. In addition, this section applies to a self-insured medical reimbursement plan, determined in accordance with the rules of this section, maintained by an employee organization described in section 501(c)(9).

(ii) *Shifting of risk.*—A plan underwritten by a policy of insurance or a prepaid health care plan that does not involve the shifting of risk to an unrelated third party is considered self-insured for

purposes of this section. Accordingly, a cost-plus policy or a policy which in effect merely provides administrative or bookkeeping services is considered self-insured for purposes of this section. However, a plan is not considered self-insured merely because one factor the insurer uses in determining the premium is the employer's prior claims experience.

(iii) *Captive insurance company.*—A plan underwritten by a policy of insurance issued by a captive insurance company is not considered self-insured for purposes of this section if for the plan year the premiums paid by companies unrelated to the captive insurance company equal or exceed 50 percent of the total premiums received and the policy of insurance is similar to policies sold to such unrelated companies.

(2) *Other rules.*—The rules of this section apply to a self-insured portion of an employer's medical plan or arrangement even if the plan is in part underwritten by insurance. For example, if an employer's medical plan reimburses employees for benefits not covered under the insured portion of an overall plan, or for deductible amounts under the insured portions, such reimbursement is subject to the rules of this section. However, a plan which reimburses employees for premiums paid under an insured plan is not subject to this section. In addition, medical expense reimbursements not described in the plan are not paid pursuant to a plan for the benefit of employees, and therefore are not excludable from gross income under section 105(b). Such reimbursements will not affect the determination of whether or not a plan is discriminatory.

(c) *Prohibited discrimination.*—(1) *In general.*—A self-insured medical reimbursement plan does not satisfy the requirements of section 105(h) and this paragraph for a plan year unless the plan satisfies subparagraphs (2) and (3) of this paragraph. However, a plan does not fail to satisfy the requirements of this paragraph merely because benefits under the plan are offset by benefits paid under a self-insured or insured plan of the employer or another employer, or by benefits paid under Medicare or other Federal or State law or similar foreign law. A self-insured plan may take into account the benefits provided under another plan only to the extent that the type of benefit subject to reimbursement is the same under both plans. For example, an amount reimbursed to an employee for a hospital expense under a medical plan maintained by the employer of the employee's spouse may be offset against the self-insured benefit where the self-insured plan covering the employee provides the same type of hospital benefit.

(2) *Eligibility to participate.*—(i) *Percentage test.*—A plan satisfies the requirements of this subparagraph if it benefits—

(A) Seventy percent or more of all employees, or

(B) Eighty percent or more of all the employees who are eligible to benefit under the plan if 70 percent or more of all employees are eligible to benefit under the plan.

(ii) *Classification test.*—A plan satisfies the requirements of this subparagraph if it benefits such employees as qualify under a classification of employees set up by the employer which is found by the Internal Revenue Service not to be discriminatory in favor of highly compensated individuals. In general, this determination will be made based upon the facts and circumstances of each case, applying the same standards as are applied under section 410(b)(1)(B) (relating to qualified pension, profit-sharing and stock bonus plans), without regard to the special rules in section 401(a)(5) concerning eligibility to participate.

(iii) *Exclusion of certain employees.*—Under section 105(h)(3), for purposes of this subparagraph (2), there may be excluded from consideration:

(A) Employees who have not completed 3 years of service prior to the beginning of the plan year. For purposes of this section years of service may be determined by any method that is reasonable and consistent. A determination made in the same manner as (and not requiring service in excess of how) a year of service is determined under section 410 (a)(3) shall be deemed to be reasonable. For purposes of the 3-year rule, all of an employee's years of service with the employer prior to a separation from service are not taken into account. For purposes of the 3-year rule, an employee's years of service prior to age 25, as a part-time or seasonal employee, as a member of a collective bargaining unit, or as a nonresident alien, as each is described in this subdivision, are not excluded by reason of being so described from counting towards satisfaction of the rule. In addition, if the employer is a predecessor employer (determined in a manner consistent with section 414(a)), service for such predecessor is treated as service for the employer.

(B) Employees who have not attained age 25 prior to the beginning of the plan year.

(C) Part-time employees whose customary weekly employment is less than 35 hours, if other employees in similar work with the same employer (or, if no employees of the employer are in similar work, in similar work in the same industry and location) have substantially more hours, and seasonal employees whose customary annual employment is less than 9 months, if other employees in similar work with the same employer (or, if no employees of the employer are in similar work, in similar work in the same industry and location) have substantially more months. Notwithstanding the preceding sentence, any employee whose customary weekly employment is less than 25 hours or any employee whose customary annual employment is less than 7 months may be considered as a part-time or seasonal employee.

(D) Employees who are included in a unit of employees covered by an agreement between employee representatives and one or more employers which the Commissioner finds to be a collective bargaining agreement, if accident and health benefits were the subject of good faith bargaining between such employee representatives and such employer or employers. For purposes of determining whether such bargaining occurred, it is not material that such employees are not covered by another medical plan or that the plan was not considered in such bargaining.

(E) Employees who are nonresident aliens and who receive no earned income (within the meaning of section 911(b) and the regulations thereunder) from the employer which constitutes income from sources within the United States (within the meaning of section 861(a)(3) and the regulations thereunder).

(3) *Nondiscriminatory benefits.*—(i) *In general.*—In general, benefits subject to reimbursement under a plan must not discriminate in favor of highly compensated individuals. Plan benefits will not satisfy the requirements of this subparagraph unless all the benefits provided for participants who are highly compensated individuals are provided for all other participants. In addition, all the benefits available for the dependents of employees who are highly compensated individuals must also be available on the same basis for the dependents of all other employees who are participants. A plan that provides optional benefits to participants will be treated as providing a single benefit with respect to the benefits covered by the option provided that (A) all eligible participants may elect any of the benefits covered by the option and (B) there are either no required employee contributions or the required employee contributions are the same amount. This test is applied to the benefits subject to reimbursement under the plan rather than the actual benefit payments of claims under the plan. The presence or absence of such discrimination will be determined by considering the type of benefit subject to reimbursement provided highly compensated individuals, as well as the amount of the benefit subject to reimbursement. A plan may establish a maximum limit for the amount of reimbursement which may be paid a participant for any single benefit, or combination of benefits. However, any maximum limit attributable to employer contributions must be uniform for all participants and for all dependents of employees who are participants and may not be modified by reason of a participant's age or years of service. In addition, if a plan covers employees who are highly compensated individuals, and the type or the amount of benefits subject to reimbursement under the plan are in proportion to employee compensation, the plan discriminates as to benefits.

(ii) *Discriminatory operation.*—Not only must a plan not discriminate on its face in providing benefits in favor of highly compensated individuals, the plan also must not discriminate in favor of such employees in actual operation. The determination of whether plan benefits discriminate in operation in favor of highly compensated individuals is made on the basis of the facts and circumstances of each case. A plan is not considered discriminatory merely because highly compensated individuals participating in the plan utilize a broad range of plan benefits to a greater extent than do other employees participating in the plan. In addition, if a plan (or a particular benefit provided by a plan) is terminated, the termination would cause the plan benefits to be discriminatory if the duration of the plan (or benefit) has the effect of discriminating in favor of highly compensated individuals. Accordingly, the prohibited discrimination may occur where the duration of a particular benefit coincides with the period during which a highly compensated individual utilizes the benefit.

(iii) *Retired employees.*—To the extent that an employer provides benefits under a self-insured medical reimbursement plan to a retired employee that would otherwise be excludible from gross income under section 105(b), determined without regard to section 105(h), such benefits shall not be considered a discriminatory benefit under this paragraph (c). The preceding sentence shall not apply to a retired employee who was a highly compensated individual unless the type, and the dollar limitations, of benefits provided retired employees who were highly compensated individuals are the same for all other retired participants. If this subdivision applies to a retired participant, that individual is not considered an employee for

purposes of determining the highest paid 25 percent of all employees under paragraph (d) of this section solely by reason of receiving such plan benefits.

(4) *Multiple plans, etc.*—(i) *General rule.*—An employer may designate two or more plans as constituting a single plan that is intended to satisfy the requirements of section 105(h)(2) and paragraph (c) of this section, in which case all plans so designated shall be considered as a single plan in determining whether the requirements of such section are satisfied by each of the separate plans. A determination that the combination of plans so designated does not satisfy such requirements does not preclude a determination that one or more of such plans, considered separately, satisfies such requirements. A single plan document may be utilized by an employer for two or more separate plans provided that the employer designates the plans that are to be considered separately and the applicable provisions of each separate plan.

(ii) *Other rules.*—If the designated combined plan discriminates as to eligibility to participate or benefits, the amount of the excess reimbursement will be determined under the rules of section 105(h)(7) and paragraph (e) of this section by taking into account all reimbursements made under the combined plan.

(iii) *H.M.O. participants.*—For purposes of section 105(h)(2)(A) and paragraph (c)(2) of this section, a self-insured plan will be deemed to benefit an employee who has enrolled in a health maintenance organization (HMO) that is offered on an optional basis by the employer in lieu of coverage under the self-insured plan if, with respect to that employee, the employer's contributions to the HMO plan equal or exceed those that would be made to the self-insured plan, and if the HMO plan is designated in accordance with subdivision (i) with the self-insured plan as a single plan. For purposes of section 105(h) and this section, except as provided in the preceding sentence, employees covered by, and benefits under, the HMO plan are not treated as part of the self-insured plan.

(d) *Highly compensated individuals defined.*—For purposes of section 105(h) and this section, the term "highly compensated individuals" means an individual who is—

(1) One of the 5 highest paid officers,

(2) A shareholder who owns (with the application of section 318) more than 10 percent in value of the stock of the employer, or

(3) Among the highest paid 25 percent of all employees (including the 5 highest paid officers, but not including employees excludable under paragraph (c)(2)(iii) of this section who are not participants in any self-insured medical reimbursement plan of the employer, whether or not designated as a single plan under paragraph (c)(4) of this section, or in a health maintenance organization plan).

The status of an employee as an officer or stockholder is determined with respect to a particular benefit on the basis of the employee's officer status or stock ownership at the time during the plan year at which the benefit is provided. In calculating the highest paid 25 percent of all employees, the number of employees included will be rounded to the next highest number. For example, if there are 5 employees, the top two are in the highest paid 25 percent. The level of an employee's compensation is determined on the basis of the employee's compensation for the plan year. For purposes of the preceding sentence, fiscal year plans may determine employee compensation on the basis of the calendar year ending within the plan year.

(e) *Excess reimbursement of highly compensated individual.*—(1) *In general.*—For purposes of section 105(h) and this section, a reimbursement paid to a highly compensated individual is an excess reimbursement if it is paid pursuant to a plan that fails to satisfy the requirements of paragraph (c)(2) or (c)(3) for the plan year. The amount reimbursed to a highly compensated individual which constitutes an excess reimbursement is not excludable from such individual's gross income under section 105(b).

(2) *Discriminatory benefit.*—In the case of a benefit available to highly compensated individuals but not to all other participants (or which otherwise discriminates in favor of highly compensated individuals as opposed to other participants), the amount of excess reimbursement equals the total amount reimbursed to the highly compensated individual with respect to the benefit.

(3) *Discriminatory coverage.*—In the case of benefits (other than discriminatory benefits described in subparagraph (2)) paid to a highly compensated individual under a plan which fails to satisfy the requirements of paragraph (c)(2) relating to nondiscrimination in eligibility to participate, the amount of excess reimbursement is determined by multiplying the total amount reimbursed to the individual by a fraction. The numerator of the fraction is the total amount reimbursed during that plan year to all highly compensated individuals. The denominator of the fraction is the total amount reimbursed

during that plan year to all participants. In computing the fraction and the total amount reimbursed to the individual, discriminatory benefits described in subparagraph (2) are not taken into account. Accordingly, any amount which is included in income by reason of the benefit's not being available to all other participants will not be taken into account.

(4) *Examples.*—The provisions of this paragraph are illustrated by the following examples:

Example (1). Corporation M maintains a self-insured medical reimbursement plan which covers all employees. The plan provides the following maximum limits on the amount of benefits subject to reimbursement: $5,000 for officers and $1,000 for all other participants. During a plan year Employee A, one of the 5 highest paid officers, received reimbursements in the amount of $4,000. Because the amount of benefits provided for highly compensated individuals is not provided for all other participants, the plan benefits are discriminatory. Accordingly, Employee A received an excess reimbursement of $3,000 ($4,000 – $1,000) which constitutes a benefit available to highly compensated individuals, but not to all other participants.

Example (2). Corporation N maintains a self-insured medical reimbursement plan which covers all employees. The plan provides a broad range of medical benefits subject to reimbursement for all participants. However, only the 5 highest paid officers are entitled to dental benefits. During the plan year Employee B, one of the 5 highest paid officers, received dental payments under the plan in the amount of $300. Because dental benefits are provided for highly compensated individuals, and not for all other participants, the plan discriminates as to benefits. Accordingly, Employee B received an excess reimbursement in the amount of $300.

Example (3). Corporation O maintains a self-insured medical reimbursement plan which discriminates as to eligibility by covering only the highest paid 40% of all employees. Benefits subject to reimbursement under the plan are the same for all participants. During a plan year Employee C, a highly compensated individual, received benefits in the amount of $1,000. The amount of excess reimbursement paid Employee C during the plan year will be calculated by multiplying the $1,000 by a fraction determined under subparagraph (3).

Example (4). Corporation P maintains a self-insured medical reimbursement plan for its employees. Benefits subject to reimbursement under the plan are the same for all plan participants. However, the plan fails the eligibility tests of section 105(h)(3)(A) and thereby discriminates as to eligibility. During the 1980 plan year Employee D, a highly compensated individual, was hospitalized for surgery and incurred medical expenses of $4,500 which were reimbursed to D under the plan. During that plan year the Corporation P medical plan paid $50,000 in benefits under the plan, $30,000 of which constituted benefits paid to highly compensated individuals. The amount of excess reimbursement not excludable by D under section 105(b) is $2,700

$$(\quad \$4,500 \times \dfrac{\$30,000}{\$50,000} \quad)$$

Example (5). Corporation Q maintains a self-insured medical reimbursement plan for its employees. The plan provides a broad range of medical benefits subject to reimbursement for participants. However, only the five highest paid officers are entitled to dental benefits. In addition, the plan fails the eligibility test of section 105(h)(3)(A) and thereby discriminates as to eligibility. During the calendar 1981 plan year, Employee E, a highly compensated individual, received dental benefits under the plan in the amount of $300, and no other employee received dental benefits. In addition, Employee E was hospitalized for surgery and incurred medical expenses, reimbursement for which was available to all participants, of $4,500 which were reimbursed to E under the plan. Because dental benefits are only provided for highly compensated individuals, Employee E received an excess reimbursement under paragraph (e)(2) above in the amount of $300. For the 1981 plan year, the Corporation Q medical plan paid $50,300 in total benefits under the plan, $30,300 of which constituted benefits paid to highly compensated individuals. In computing the fraction under paragraph (e)(3), discriminatory benefits described in paragraph (e)(2) are not taken into account. Therefore, the amount of excess reimbursement not excludable to Employee E with respect to the $4,500 of medical expenses incurred is $2,700,

$$(\quad \$4,500 \times \dfrac{\$30,000}{\$50,000} \quad)$$

and the total amount of excess reimbursements includable in E's income for 1981 is $3,000.

Example (6). (i) Corporation R maintains a calendar year self-insured medical reimbursement plan which covers all employees. The type of benefits subject to reimbursement under the plan include all medical care expenses as defined in section 213(e). The amount of reimbursement available to any employee for any calendar year is limited to 5 percent of the compensation paid to each employee during the calendar year. The amount of compensation and reimbursement paid to Employees A—F for the calendar year is as follows:

Employee	Compensation	Reimbursable Amount Paid
A	$100,000	$5,000
B	25,000	1,250
C	15,000	750
D	10,000	500
E	10,000	500
F	8,000	400
		$8,400

(ii) Because the amount of benefits subject to reimbursement under the plan is in proportion to employee compensation, the plan discriminates as to benefits. In addition, Employees A and B are highly compensated individuals. The amount of excess reimbursement paid Employees A and B during the year will be determined under paragraph (e)(2). Because benefits in excess of $400 (Employee F's maximum benefit) are provided for highly compensated individuals and not for all other participants, Employees A and B received, respectively, an excess reimbursement of $4,600 and $850.

(f) *Certain controlled groups.*—For purposes of applying the provisions of section 105(h) and this section, all employees who are treated as employed by a single employer under section 414(b) and (c), and the regulations thereunder (relating to special rules for qualified pension, profit-sharing and stock bonus plans), shall be treated as employed by a single employer.

(g) *Exception for medical diagnostic procedures.*—(1) *In general.*—For purposes of applying section 105(h) and this section, reimbursements paid under a plan for medical diagnostic procedures for an employee, but not a dependent, are not considered to be a part of a plan described in this section. The medical diagnostic procedures include routine medical examinations, blood tests, and X-rays. Such procedures do not include expenses incurred for the treatment, cure or testing of a known illness or disability, or treatment or testing for a physical injury, complaint or specific symptom of a bodily malfunction. For example, a routine dental examination with X-rays is a medical diagnostic procedure, but X-rays and treatment for a specific complaint are not. In addition, such procedures do not include any activity undertaken for exercise, fitness, nutrition, recreation, or the general improvement of health unless they are for medical care as defined in section 213(e). The diagnostic procedures must be performed at a facility which provides no services (directly or indirectly) other than medical, and ancillary, services. For purposes of the preceding sentence, physical proximity between a medical facility and nonmedical facilities will not for that reason alone cause the medical facility not to qualify. For example, an employee's annual physical examination conducted at the employee's personal physician's office is not considered a part of the medical reimbursement plan and therefore is not subject to the nondiscrimination requirements. Accordingly, the amount reimbursed may be excludable from the employee's income if the requirements of section 105(b) are satisfied.

(2) *Transportation, etc. expenses.*—Transportation expenses primarily for an allowable diagnostic procedure are included within the exception described in this paragraph, but only to the extent they are ordinary and necessary. Transportation undertaken merely for the general improvement of health, or in connection with a vacation, is not within the scope of this exception, nor are any incidental expenses for food or lodging; therefore, amounts reimbursed for such expenses may be excess reimbursements under paragraph (e).

(h) *Time of inclusion.*—Excess reimbursements (determined under paragraph (e)) paid to a highly compensated individual for a plan year will be considered as received in the taxable year of the individual in which (or with which) the plan year ends. The particular plan year to which reimbursements relate shall be determined under the plan provisions. In the absence of plan provisions reimbursements shall be attributed to the plan year in which payment is made. For example, under a calendar year plan an excess reimbursement paid to A in 1981 on account of an expense incurred and subject to reimbursement for the 1980 plan year under the terms of the plan will be considered as received in 1980 by A.

(i) *Self-insured contributory plan.*—A medical plan subject to this section may provide for employer and employee contributions. See §1.105-1(c). The tax treatment of reimbursements attributable to employee contributions is determined under section 104(a)(3). The tax treatment of reimbursements attributable to employer contributions is determined under section 105. The amount of reimbursements which are attributable to contributions of the employer shall be determined in accordance with § 1.105-1(e).

(j) *Effective date.*—Section 105(h) and this section are effective for taxable years beginning after December 31, 1979 and for amounts reimbursed after December 31, 1979. In determining plan discrimination and the taxability of excess reimbursements made for a plan year beginning in 1979 and ending in 1980, a plan's eligibility and benefit requirements as well as actual reimbursements made in the plan year during 1979, will not be taken into account. In addition, this section does not apply to expenses which are incurred in 1979 and paid in 1980.

(k) *Special rules.*—(1) *Relation to cafeteria plans.*—If a self-insured medical reimbursement plan is included in a cafeteria plan as described in section 125, the rules of this section will determine the status of a benefit as a taxable or nontaxable benefit, and the rules of section 125 will determine whether an employee is taxed as though he elected all available taxable benefits (including taxable benefits under a discriminatory medical reimbursement plan). This rule is illustrated by the following example:

Example. Corporation M maintains a cafeteria plan described in section 125. Under the plan an officer of the corporation may elect to receive medical benefits provided by a self-insured medical reimbursement plan which is subject to the rules of this section. However, the self-insured medical reimbursement plan fails the nondiscrimination rules under paragraph (c) of this section. Accordingly, the amount of excess reimbursement is taxable to the officer participating in the medical reimbursement plan pursuant to section 105(h) and this section. Therefore, the self-insured medical reimbursement plan will be considered a taxable benefit under section 125 and the regulations thereunder.

(2) *Benefit subject to reimbursement.*—For purposes of this section, a benefit subject to reimbursement is a benefit described in the plan under which a claim for reimbursement or for a payment directly to the health service provider may be filed by a plan participant. It does not refer to actual claims or benefit reimbursements paid under a plan. [Reg. § 1.105-11.]

☐ [*T.D. 7754, 1-13-81.*]

[Reg. § 1.106-1]

§ 1.106-1. Contributions by employer to accident and health plans.—(a) The gross income of an employee does not include the contributions that the employer makes to an accident or health plan for compensation (through insurance or otherwise) to the employee for personal injuries or sickness incurred by the employee, the employee's spouse, the employee's dependents (as defined in section 152 determined without regard to section 152(b)(1), (b)(2), or (d)(1)(B)), or any child (as defined in section 152(f)(1)) of the employee who as of the end of the taxable year has not attained age 27. The employer may contribute to an accident or health plan either by paying the premium (or a portion of the premium) on a policy of accident or health insurance covering one or more of his employees, or by contributing to a separate trust or fund (including a fund referred to in section 105(e)) which provides accident or health benefits directly or through insurance to one or more of his employees. However, if such insurance policy, trust, or fund provides other benefits in addition to accident or health benefits, section 106 applies only to the portion of the employer's contribution which is allocable to accident or health benefits. See paragraph (d) of § 1.104-1 and §§ 1.105-1 through 1.105-5, inclusive, for regulations relating to exclusion from an employee's gross income of amounts received through accident or health insurance and through accident or health plans. For the treatment of the payment of premiums for accident or health insurance from a qualified trust under section 401(a), see §§ 1.72-15 and 1.402(a)-1(e).

(b) *Effective/applicability date.*—The first and last sentences of paragraph (a) of this section apply for taxable years beginning on or after January 1, 2015. [Reg. § 1.106-1.]

☐ [*T.D. 6169, 4-13-56. Amended by T.D. 9665, 5-9-2014.*]

[Reg. § 1.107-1]

§ 1.107-1. Rental value of parsonages.—(a) In the case of a minister of the gospel, gross income does not include (1) the rental value of a home, including utilities, furnished to him as a part of his compensation, or (2) the rental allowance paid to him as part of his compensation to the extent such allowance is used by him to rent or otherwise provide a home. In order to qualify for the exclusion, the home or rental allowance must be provided as remuneration for services which are ordinarily the duties of a minister of the gospel. In general, the rules provided in § 1.1402(c)-5 will be applicable to such determination. Examples of specific services the performance of

which will be considered duties of a minister for purposes of section 107 include the performance of sacerdotal functions, the conduct of religious worship, the administration and maintenance of religious organizations and their integral agencies, and the performance of teaching and administrative duties at theological seminaries. Also, the service performed by a qualified minister as an employee of the United States (other than as a chaplain in the Armed Forces, whose service is considered to be that of a commissioned officer in his capacity as such, and not as a minister in the exercise of his ministry), or a State, Territory, or possession of the United States, or a political subdivision of any of the foregoing, or the District of Columbia, is in the exercise of his ministry provided the service performed includes such services as are ordinarily the duties of a minister.

(b) For purposes of section 107, the term "home" means a dwelling place (including furnishings) and the appurtenances thereto, such as a garage. The term "rental allowance" means an amount paid to a minister to rent or otherwise provide a home if such amount is designated as rental allowance pursuant to official action taken prior to January 1, 1958, by the employing church or other qualified organization, or if such amount is designated as rental allowance pursuant to official action taken in advance of such payment by the employing church or other qualified organization when paid after December 31, 1957. The designation of an amount as rental allowance may be evidenced in an employment contract, in minutes of or in a resolution by a church or other qualified organization or in its budget, or in any other appropriate instrument evidencing such official action. The designation referred to in this paragraph is a sufficient designation if it permits a payment or a part thereof to be identified as a payment of rental allowance as distinguished from salary or other remuneration.

(c) A rental allowance must be included in the minister's gross income in the taxable year in which it is received, to the extent that such allowance is not used by him during such taxable year to rent or otherwise provide a home. Circumstances under which a rental allowance will be deemed to have been used to rent or provide a home will include cases in which the allowance is expended (1) for rent of a home, (2) for purchase of a home, and (3) for expenses directly related to providing a home. Expenses for food and servants are not considered for this purpose to be directly related to providing a home. Where the minister rents, purchases, or owns a farm or other business property in addition to a home, the portion of the rental allowance expended in connection with the farm or business property shall not be excluded from his gross income. [Reg. § 1.107-1.]

☐ [*T.D. 6239, 6-14-57. Amended by T.D. 6691, 12-2-63.*]

[Reg. § 1.108-1]

§ 1.108-1. [Reserved.]

☐ [*T.D. 9304, 12-21-2006.*]

[Reg. § 1.108-2]

§ 1.108-2. Acquisition of indebtedness by a person related to the debtor.—(a) *General rules.*—The acquisition of outstanding indebtedness by a person related to the debtor from a person who is not related to the debtor results in the realization by the debtor of income from discharge of indebtedness (to the extent required by section 61(a)(12) and section 108) in an amount determined under paragraph (f) of this section. Income realized pursuant to the preceding sentence is excludible from gross income to the extent provided in section 108(a). The rules of this paragraph apply if indebtedness is acquired directly by a person related to the debtor in a direct acquisition (as defined in paragraph (b) of this section) or if a holder of indebtedness becomes related to the debtor in an indirect acquisition (as defined in paragraph (c) of this section).

(b) *Direct acquisition.*—An acquisition of outstanding indebtedness is a direct acquisition under this section if a person related to the debtor (or a person who becomes related to the debtor on the date the indebtedness is acquired) acquires the indebtedness from a person who is not related to the debtor. Notwithstanding the foregoing, the Commissioner may provide by Revenue Procedure or other published guidance that certain acquisitions of indebtedness described in the preceding sentence are not direct acquisitions for purposes of this section.

(c) *Indirect acquisition.*—(1) *In general.*—An indirect acquisition is a transaction in which a holder of outstanding indebtedness becomes related to the debtor, if the holder acquired the indebtedness in anticipation of becoming related to the debtor.

(2) *Proof of anticipation of relationship.*—In determining whether indebtedness was acquired by a holder in anticipation of becoming related to the debtor, all relevant facts and circumstances will be considered. Such facts and circumstances include, but are not limited to, the intent of the parties at the time of the acquisition, the nature of any contacts between the parties (or their respective affiliates) before

the acquisition, the period of time for which the holder held the indebtedness, and the significance of the indebtedness in proportion to the total assets of the holder group (as defined in paragraph (c)(5) of this section). For example, if a holder acquired the indebtedness in the ordinary course of its portfolio investment activities and the holder's acquisition of the indebtedness preceded any discussions concerning the acquisition of the holder by the debtor (or by a person related to the debtor) or the acquisition of the debtor by the holder (or by a person related to the holder), as the case may be, these facts, taken together, would ordinarily establish that the holder did not acquire the indebtedness in anticipation of becoming related to the debtor. The absence of discussions between the debtor and the holder (or their respective affiliates), however, does not by itself establish that the holder did not acquire the indebtedness in anticipation of becoming related to the debtor (if, for example, the facts and circumstances show that the holder was considering a potential acquisition of or by the debtor, or the relationship is created within a relatively short period of time of the acquisition, or the indebtedness constitutes a disproportionate portion of the holder group's assets).

(3) *Indebtedness acquired within 6 months of becoming related.*—Notwithstanding any other provision of this paragraph (c), a holder of indebtedness is treated as having acquired the indebtedness in anticipation of becoming related to the debtor if the holder acquired the indebtedness less than 6 months before the date the holder becomes related to the debtor.

(4) *Disclosure of potential indirect acquisition.*—(i) *In General.*—If a holder of outstanding indebtedness becomes related to the debtor under the circumstances described in paragraph (c)(4)(ii) or (iii) of this section, the debtor is required to attach the statement described in paragraph (c)(4)(iv) of this section to its tax return (or to a qualified amended return within the meaning of § 1.6664-2(c)(3)) for the taxable year in which the debtor becomes related to the holder, unless the debtor reports its income on the basis that the holder acquired the indebtedness in anticipation of becoming related to the debtor. Disclosure under this paragraph (c) (4) is in addition to, and is not in substitution for, any disclosure required to be made under section 6662, 6664 or 6694.

(ii) *Indebtedness represents more than 25 percent of holder group's assets.*—(A) *In general.*—Disclosure under this paragraph (c)(4) is required if, on the date the holder becomes related to the debtor, indebtedness of the debtor represents more than 25 percent of the fair market value of the total gross assets of the holder group (as defined in paragraph (c)(5) of this section).

(B) *Determination of total gross assets.*—In determining the total gross assets of the holder group, total gross assets do not include any cash, cash item, marketable stock or security, short-term indebtedness, option, futures contract, notional principal contract, or similar item (other than indebtedness of the debtor), nor do total gross assets include any asset in which the holder has substantially reduced its risk of loss. In addition, total gross assets do not include any ownership interest in or indebtedness of a member of the holder group.

(iii) *Indebtedness acquired within 6 to 24 months of becoming related.*—Disclosure under this paragraph (c)(4) is required if the holder acquired the indebtedness 6 months or more before the date the holder becomes related to the debtor, but less than 24 months before that date.

(iv) *Contents of statement.*—A statement under this paragraph (c)(4) must include the following—

(A) A caption identifying the statement as disclosure under § 1.108-2(c);

(B) An identification of the indebtedness with respect to which disclosure is made;

(C) The amount of such indebtedness and the amount of income from discharge of indebtedness if section 108(e)(4) were to apply;

(D) Whether paragraph (c)(4)(ii) or (iii) of this section applies to the transaction; and

(E) A statement describing the facts and circumstances supporting the debtor's position that the holder did not acquire the indebtedness in anticipation of becoming related to the debtor.

(v) *Failure to disclose.*—In addition to any other penalties that may apply, if a debtor fails to provide a statement required by this paragraph (c)(4), the holder is presumed to have acquired the indebtedness in anticipation of becoming related to the debtor unless the facts and circumstances clearly establish that the holder did not acquire the indebtedness in anticipation of becoming related to the debtor.

(5) *Holder group.*—For purposes of this paragraph (c), the holder group consists of the holder of the indebtedness and all persons who are both—

(i) Related to the holder before the holder becomes related to the debtor; and

(ii) Related to the debtor after the holder becomes related to the debtor.

(6) *Holding period.*—(i) *Suspensions.*—The running of the holding periods set forth in paragraphs (c)(3) and (c)(4)(iii) of this section is suspended during any period in which the holder or any person related to the holder is protected (directly or indirectly) against risk of loss by an option, a short sale, or any other device or transaction.

(ii) *Tacking.*—For purposes of paragraphs (c)(3) and (c)(4)(iii) of this section, the period for which a holder held the debtor's indebtedness includes—

(A) The period for which the indebtedness was held by a corporation to whose attributes the holder succeeded pursuant to section 381; and

(B) The period (ending on the date on which the holder becomes related to the debtor) for which the indebtedness was held continuously by members of the holder group (as defined in paragraph (c)(5) of this section).

(d) *Definitions.*—(1) *Acquisition date.*—For purposes of this section, the acquisition date is the date on which a direct acquisition of indebtedness or an indirect acquisition of indebtedness occurs.

(2) *Relationship.*—For purposes of this section, persons are considered related if they are related within the meaning of sections 267(b) or 707(b)(1). However—

(i) Sections 267(b) and 707(b)(1) are applied as if section 267(c)(4) provided that the family of an individual consists of the individual's spouse, the individual's children, grandchildren, and parents, and any spouse of the individual's children or grandchildren; and

(ii) Two entities that are treated as a single employer under subsection (b) or (c) of section 414 are treated as having a relationship to each other that is described in section 267(b).

(e) *Exceptions.*—(1) *Indebtedness retired within one year.*—This section does not apply to a direct or indirect acquisition of indebtedness with a stated maturity date on or before the date that is one year after the acquisition date, if the indebtedness is, in fact, retired on or before its stated maturity date.

(2) *Acquisitions by securities dealers.*—(i) This section does not apply to a direct acquisition or an indirect acquisition of indebtedness by a dealer that acquires and disposes of such indebtedness in the ordinary course of its business of dealing in securities if—

(A) The dealer accounts for the indebtedness as a security held primarily for sale to customers in the ordinary course of business;

(B) The dealer disposes of the indebtedness (or it matures while held by the dealer) within a period consistent with the holding of the indebtedness for sale to customers in the ordinary course of business, taking into account the terms of the indebtedness and the conditions and practices prevailing in the markets for similar indebtedness during the period in which it is held; and

(C) The dealer does not sell or otherwise transfer the indebtedness to a person related to the debtor (other than in a sale to a dealer that in turn meets the requirements of this paragraph (e)(2)).

(ii) A dealer will continue to satisfy the conditions of this paragraph (e)(2) with respect to indebtedness that is exchanged for successor indebtedness in a transaction in which unrelated holders also exchange indebtedness of the same issue, provided that the conditions of this paragraph (e)(2) are met with respect to the successor indebtedness.

(iii) For purposes of this paragraph (e)(2), if the period consistent with the holding of indebtedness for sale to customers in the ordinary course of business is 30 days or less, the dealer is considered to dispose of indebtedness within that period if the aggregate principal amount of indebtedness of that issue sold by the dealer to customers in the ordinary course of business (or that mature and are paid while held by the dealer) in the calendar month following the month in which the indebtedness is acquired equals or exceeds the aggregate principal amount of indebtedness of that issue held in the dealer's inventory at the close of the month in which the indebtedness is acquired. If the period consistent with the holding of indebtedness for sale to customers in the ordinary course of business is greater than 30 days, the dealer is considered to dispose of the indebtedness within that period if the aggregate principal amount of indebtedness of that issue sold by the dealer to customers in the ordinary course of business (or that mature and are paid while held by the dealer) within that period equals or exceeds the aggregate principal amount of indebtedness of that issue held in inventory at the close of the day on which the indebtedness was acquired.

(f) *Amount of discharge of indebtedness income realized.*—(1) *Holder acquired the indebtedness by purchase on or less than six months before the acquisition date.*—Except as otherwise provided in this paragraph (f), the amount of discharge of indebtedness income realized under paragraph (a) of this section is measured by reference to the adjusted basis of the related holder (or of the holder that becomes related to the debtor) in the indebtedness on the acquisition date if the holder acquired the indebtedness by purchase on or less than six months before the acquisition date. For purposes of this paragraph (f), indebtedness is acquired "by purchase" if the indebtedness in the hands of the holder is not substituted basis property within the meaning of section 7701(a)(42). However, indebtedness is also considered acquired by purchase within six months before the acquisition date if the holder acquired the indebtedness as transferred basis property (within the meaning of section 7701(a)(43)) from a person who acquired the indebtedness by purchase on or less than six months before the acquisition date.

(2) *Holder did not acquire the indebtedness by purchase on or less than six months before the acquisition date.*—Except as otherwise provided in this paragraph (f), the amount of discharge of indebtedness income realized under paragraph (a) of this section is measured by reference to the fair market value of the indebtedness on the acquisition date if the holder (or the transferor to the holder in a transferred basis transaction) did not acquire the indebtedness by purchase on or less than six months before the acquisition date.

(3) *Acquisitions of indebtedness in nonrecognition transactions.*— [Reserved]

(4) *Avoidance transactions.*—The amount of discharge of indebtedness income realized by the debtor under paragraph (a) of this section is measured by reference to the fair market value of the indebtedness on the acquisition date if the indebtedness is acquired in a direct or an indirect acquisition in which a principal purpose for the acquisition is the avoidance of federal income tax.

(g) *Correlative adjustments.*—(1) *Deemed issuance.*—For income tax purposes, if a debtor realizes income from discharge of its indebtedness in a direct or an indirect acquisition under this section (whether or not the income is excludible under section 108(a)), the debtor's indebtedness is treated as new indebtedness issued by the debtor to the related holder on the acquisition date (the deemed issuance). The new indebtedness is deemed issued with an issue price equal to the amount used under paragraph (f) of this section to compute the amount realized by the debtor under paragraph (a) of this section (*i.e.*, either the holder's adjusted basis or the fair market value of the indebtedness, as the case may be). Under section 1273(a)(1), the excess of the stated redemption price at maturity (as defined in section 1273(a)(2)) of the indebtedness over its issue price is original issue discount (OID) which, to the extent provided in sections 163 and 1272, is deductible by the debtor and includible in the gross income of the related holder. Notwithstanding the foregoing, the Commissioner may provide by Revenue Procedure or other published guidance that the indebtedness is not treated as newly issued indebtedness for purposes of designated provisions of the income tax laws.

(2) *Treatment of related holder.*—The related holder does not recognize any gain or loss on the deemed issuance described in paragraph (g)(1) of this section. The related holder's adjusted basis in the indebtedness remains the same as it was immediately before the deemed issuance. The deemed issuance is treated as a purchase of the indebtedness by the related holder for purposes of section 1272(a)(7) (pertaining to reduction of original issue discount where a subsequent holder pays acquisition premium) and section 1276 (pertaining to acquisitions of debt at a market discount).

(3) *Loss deferral on disposition of indebtedness acquired in certain exchanges.*—(i) Any loss otherwise allowable to a related holder on the disposition at any time of indebtedness acquired in a direct or indirect acquisition (whether or not any discharge of indebtedness income was realized under paragraph (a) of this section) is deferred until the date the debtor retires the indebtedness if—

(A) The related holder acquired the debtor's indebtedness in exchange for its own indebtedness; and

(B) The issue price of the related holder's indebtedness was not determined by reference to its fair market value (*e.g.*, the issue price was determined under section 1273(b)(4) or 1274(a) or any other provision of applicable law).

(ii) Any comparable tax benefit that would otherwise be available to the holder, debtor, or any person related to either, in any other transaction that directly or indirectly results in the disposition

of the indebtedness is also deferred until the date the debtor retires the indebtedness.

(4) *Examples.*—The following examples illustrate the application of this paragraph (g). In each example, all taxpayers are calendar-year taxpayers, no taxpayer is insolvent or under the jurisdiction of a court in a title 11 case and no indebtedness is qualified farm indebtedness described in section 108(g).

Example 1. (i) P, a domestic corporation, owns 70 percent of the single class of stock of S, a domestic corporation. S has outstanding indebtedness that has an issue price of $10,000,000 and provides for monthly interest payments of $80,000 payable at the end of each month and a payment at maturity of $10,000,000. The indebtedness has a stated maturity date of December 31, 1994. On January 1, 1992, P purchases S's indebtedness from I, an individual not related to S within the meaning of paragraph (d)(2) of this section, for cash in the amount of $9,000,000. S repays the indebtedness in full at maturity.

(ii) Under section 61(a)(12), section 108(e)(4), and paragraphs (a) and (f) of this section, S realizes $1,000,000 of income from discharge of indebtedness on January 1, 1992.

(iii) Under paragraph (g)(1) of this section, the indebtedness is treated as issued to P on January 1, 1992, with an issue price of $9,000,000. Under section 1273(a), the $1,000,000 excess of the stated redemption price at maturity of the indebtedness ($10,000,000) over its issue price ($9,000,000) is original issue discount, which is includible in gross income by P and deductible by S over the remaining term of the indebtedness under sections 163(e) and 1272(a).

(iv) Accordingly, S deducts and P includes in income original issue discount, in addition to stated interest, as follows: in 1992, $289,144.88; in 1993, $331,286.06; and in 1994, $379,569.06.

Example 2. The facts are the same as in *Example 1*, except that on January 1, 1993, P sells S's indebtedness to J, who is not related to S within the meaning of paragraph (d)(2) of this section, for $9,400,000 in cash. J holds S's indebtedness to maturity. On January 1, 1993, P's adjusted basis in S's indebtedness is $9,289,144.88. Accordingly, P realizes gain in the amount of $110,855.12 upon the disposition. S and J continue to deduct and include the original issue discount on the indebtedness in accordance with *Example 1*. The amount of original issue discount includible by J is reduced by the $110,855.12 acquisition premium as provided in section 1272(a)(7).

Example 3. The facts are the same as in *Example 1*, except that on February 1, 1992 (one month after P purchased S's indebtedness), S retires the indebtedness for an amount of cash equal to the fair market value of the indebtedness. Assume that the fair market value of the indebtedness is $9,022,621.41, which in this case equals the issue price of the indebtedness determined under paragraph (g)(1) of this section ($9,000,000) plus the accrued original issue discount through February 1 ($22,621.41). Section 1.61-12(c)(3) provides that if indebtedness is repurchased for a price that is exceeded by the issue price of the indebtedness plus the amount of discount already deducted, the excess is income from discharge of indebtedness. Therefore, S does not realize income from discharge of indebtedness. The result would be the same if P had contributed the indebtedness to the capital of S. Under section 108(e)(6), S would be treated as having satisfied the indebtedness with an amount of money equal to P's adjusted basis and, under section 1272(d)(2), P's adjusted basis is equal to $9,022,621.41.

Example 4. (i) P, a domestic corporation, owns 70 percent of the single class of stock of S, a domestic corporation. On January 1, 1986, P issued indebtedness that has an issue price of $5,000,000 and provides for no stated interest payments and a payment at maturity of $10,000,000. The indebtedness has a stated maturity date of December 31, 1995. On January 1, 1992, S purchases P's indebtedness from K, a partnership not related to P within the meaning of paragraph (d)(2) of this section, for cash in the amount of $6,000,000. The sum of the debt's issue price and previously deducted original issue discount is $7,578,582.83. P repays the indebtedness in full at maturity.

(ii) Under section 61(a)(12), section 108(e)(4), and paragraphs (a) and (f) of this section, P realizes $1,578,582.83 in income from discharge of indebtedness ($7,578,582.83 minus $6,000,000) on January 1, 1992.

(iii) Under paragraph (g)(1) of this section, the indebtedness is treated as issued to S on January 1, 1992, with an issue price of $6,000,000. Under section 1273(a), the $4,000,000 excess of the stated redemption price at maturity of the indebtedness ($10,000,000) over its issue price ($6,000,000) is original issue discount, which is includible in gross income by S and deductible by P over the remaining term of the indebtedness under sections 163(e) and 1272(a).

(iv) Accordingly, P deducts and S includes in income original issue discount as follows: in 1992, $817,316.20; in 1993, $928,650.49; in 1994, $1,055,150.67; and in 1995, $1,198,882.64.

(h) *Effective date.*—This section applies to any transaction described in paragraph (a) and in either paragraph (b) or (c) of this section with an acquisition date on or after March 21, 1991. Although this section does not apply to direct or indirect acquisitions occurring before March 21, 1991, section 108(e)(4) is effective for any transaction after December 31, 1980, subject to the rules of section 7 of the Bankruptcy Tax Act of 1980 (Pub. L. 96-589, 94 Stat. 3389, 3411). Taxpayers may use any reasonable method of determining the amount of discharge of indebtedness income realized and the treatment of correlative adjustments under section 108(e)(4) for acquisitions of indebtedness before March 21, 1991, if such method is applied consistently by both the debtor and related holder. [Reg. § 1.108-2.]

☐ [T.D. 8460, 12-28-92.]

[Reg. § 1.108-3]

§ 1.108-3. Intercompany losses and deductions.—(a) *General rule.*—This section applies to certain losses and deductions from the sale, exchange, or other transfer of property between corporations that are members of a consolidated group or a controlled group (an intercompany transaction). See section 267(f) (controlled groups) and § 1.1502-13 (consolidated groups) for applicable definitions. For purposes of determining the attributes to which section 108(b) applies, a loss or deduction not yet taken into account under section 267(f) or § 1.1502-13 (an intercompany loss or deduction) is treated as basis described in section 108(b) that the transferor retains in property. To the extent a loss not yet taken into account is reduced under this section, it cannot subsequently be taken into account under this section, it cannot subsequently be taken into account under 267(f) or § 1.1502-13. For example, if S and B are corporations filing a consolidated return, and S sells land with a $100 basis to B for $90 and the $10 loss is deferred under section 267(f) and § 1.1502-13, the deferred loss is treated for purposes of section 108(b) as $10 of basis that S has in land (even though S has no remaining interest in the land sold to B) and is subject to reduction under section 108(b)(2)(E). Similar principles apply, with appropriate adjustments, if S and B are members of a controlled group and S's loss is deferred only under Section 267(f).

(b) *Effective date.*—This section applies with respect to discharges of indebtedness occurring on or after September 11, 1995. [Reg. § 1.108-3.]

☐ [T.D. 8597, 7-12-95.]

[Reg. § 1.108-4]

§ 1.108-4. Election to reduce basis of depreciable property under section 108(b)(5) of the Internal Revenue Code.—(a) *Description.*—An election under section 108(b)(5) is available whenever a taxpayer excludes discharge of indebtedness income (COD income) from gross income under sections 108(a)(1)(A), (B), or (C) (concerning title 11 cases, insolvency, and qualified farm indebtedness, respectively). See sections 108(d)(2) and (3) for the definitions of *title 11 case* and *insolvent.* See section 108(g)(2) for the definition of *qualified farm indebtedness.*

(b) *Time and manner.*—To make an election under section 108(b)(5), a taxpayer must enter the appropriate information on Form 982, *Reduction of Tax Attributes Due to Discharge of Indebtedness (and Section 1082 Basis Adjustment),* and attach the form to the timely filed (including extensions) Federal income tax return for the taxable year in which the taxpayer has COD income that is excluded from gross income under section 108(a). An election under this section may be revoked only with the consent of the Commissioner.

(c) *Effective date.*—This section applies to elections concerning discharges of indebtedness occurring on or after October 22, 1998. [Reg. § 1.108-4.]

☐ [T.D. 8787, 10-21-98.]

[Reg. § 1.108-5]

§ 1.108-5. Time and manner for making election under the Omnibus Budget Reconciliation Act of 1993.—(a) *Description.*—Section 108(c)(3)(C), as added by section 13150 of the Omnibus Budget Reconciliation Act of 1993 (Public Law 103-66, 107 Stat. 446), allows certain noncorporate taxpayers to elect to treat certain indebtedness described in section 108(c)(3) that is discharged after December 31, 1992, as qualified real property business indebtedness. This discharged indebtedness is excluded from gross income to the extent allowed by section 108.

(b) *Time and manner for making election.*—The election described in this section must be made on the timely-filed (including extensions) Federal income tax return for the taxable year in which the taxpayer has discharge of indebtedness income that is excludible from gross income under section 108(a). The election is to be made on a completed Form 982, in accordance with that Form and its instructions.

(c) *Revocability of election.*—The election described in this section is revocable with the consent of the Commissioner.

(d) *Effective date.*—The rules set forth in this section are effective December 27, 1993. [Reg. § 1.108-5.]

☐ [T.D. 8688, 12-11-96. *Redesignated by T.D. 8787, 10-21-98.*]

[Reg. § 1.108-6]

§ 1.108-6. Limitations on the exclusion of income from the discharge of qualified real property business indebtedness.—(a) *Indebtedness in excess of value.*—With respect to any qualified real property business indebtedness that is discharged, the amount excluded from gross income under section 108(a)(1)(D) (concerning discharges of qualified real property business indebtedness) shall not exceed the excess, if any, of the outstanding principal amount of that indebtedness immediately before the discharge over the net fair market value of the qualifying real property, as defined in § 1.1017-1(c)(1), immediately before the discharge. For purposes of this section, *net fair market value* means the fair market value of the qualifying real property (notwithstanding section 7701(g)), reduced by the outstanding principal amount of any qualified real property business indebtedness (other than the discharged indebtedness) that is secured by such property immediately before and after the discharge. Also, for purposes of section 108(c)(2)(A) and this section, outstanding principal amount means the principal amount of indebtedness together with all additional amounts owed that, immediately before the discharge, are equivalent to principal, in that interest on such amounts would accrue and compound in the future, except that outstanding principal amount shall not include amounts that are subject to section 108(e)(2) and shall be adjusted to account for unamortized premium and discount consistent with section 108(e)(3).

(b) *Overall limitation.*—The amount excluded from gross income under section 108(a)(1)(D) shall not exceed the aggregate adjusted bases of all depreciable real property held by the taxpayer immediately before the discharge (other than depreciable real property acquired in contemplation of the discharge) reduced by the sum of any—

(1) Depreciation claimed for the taxable year the taxpayer excluded discharge of indebtedness from gross income under section 108(a)(1)(D); and

(2) Reductions to the adjusted bases of depreciable real property required under section 108(b) or section 108(g) for the same taxable year.

(c) *Effective date.*—This section applies to discharges of qualified real property business indebtedness occurring on or after, October 22, 1998. [Reg. § 1.108-6.]

☐ [T.D. 8787, 10-21-98.]

[Reg. § 1.108-7]

§ 1.108-7. Reduction of attributes.—(a) *In general.*—(1) If a taxpayer excludes discharge of indebtedness income (COD income) from gross income under section 108(a)(1)(A), (B), or (C), then the amount excluded shall be applied to reduce the following tax attributes of the taxpayer in the following order:

(i) Net operating losses.

(ii) General business credits.

(iii) Minimum tax credits.

(iv) Capital loss carryovers.

(v) Basis of property.

(vi) Passive activity loss and credit carryovers.

(vii) Foreign tax credit carryovers.

(2) The taxpayer may elect under section 108(b)(5), however, to apply any portion of the excluded COD income to reduce first the basis of depreciable property to the extent the excluded COD income is not so applied. The taxpayer must then reduce any remaining tax attributes in the order specified in section 108(b)(2). If the excluded COD income exceeds the sum of the taxpayer's tax attributes, the excess is permanently excluded from the taxpayer's gross income. For rules relating to basis reductions required by sections 108(b)(2)(E) and 108(b)(5), see section 1017 and § 1.1017-1. For rules relating to the time and manner for making an election under section 108(b)(5), see § 1.108-4.

(b) *Carryovers and carrybacks.*—The tax attributes subject to reduction under section 108(b)(2) and paragraph (a)(1) of this section that are carryovers to the taxable year of the discharge, or that may be carried back to taxable years preceding the year of the discharge, are taken into account by the taxpayer for the taxable year of the discharge or the preceding years, as the case may be, before such attributes are reduced pursuant to section 108(b)(2) and paragraph (a)(1) of this section.

(c) *Transactions to which section 381 applies.*—If a taxpayer realizes COD income that is excluded from gross income under section 108(a) either during or after a taxable year in which the taxpayer is the distributor or transferor of assets in a transaction described in section 381(a), any tax attributes to which the acquiring corporation succeeds, including the basis of property acquired by the acquiring corporation in the transaction, must reflect the reductions required by section 108(b). For this purpose, all attributes listed in section 108(b)(2) immediately prior to the transaction described in section 381(a), but after the determination of tax for the year of the distribution or transfer of assets, including basis of property, will be available for reduction under section 108(b)(2). However, the basis of stock or securities of the acquiring corporation, if any, received by the taxpayer in exchange for the transferred assets shall not be available for reduction under section 108(b)(2).

(d) *Special rules for S corporations.*—(1) *In general.*—If an S corporation excludes COD income from gross income under section 108(a)(1)(A), (B), or (C), the amount excluded shall be applied to reduce the S corporation's tax attributes under paragraph (a)(1) of this section. For purposes of paragraph (a)(1)(i) of this section, the aggregate amount of the shareholders' losses or deductions that are disallowed for the taxable year of the discharge under section 1366(d)(1), including disallowed losses or deductions of a shareholder that transfers all of the shareholder's stock in the S corporation during the taxable year of the discharge, is treated as the net operating loss tax attribute (deemed NOL) of the S corporation for the taxable year of the discharge.

(2) *Allocation of excess losses or deductions.*—(i) *In general.*—If the amount of an S corporation's deemed NOL exceeds the amount of the S corporation's COD income that is excluded from gross income under section 108(a)(1)(A), (B), or (C), the excess deemed NOL shall be allocated to the shareholder or shareholders of the S corporation as a loss or deduction that is disallowed under section 1366(d) for the taxable year of the discharge.

(ii) *Multiple shareholders.*—(A) *In general.*—If an S corporation has multiple shareholders, to determine the amount of the S corporation's excess deemed NOL to be allocated to each shareholder under paragraph (d)(2)(i) of this section, calculate with respect to each shareholder the shareholder's excess amount. The shareholder's excess amount is the amount (if any) by which the shareholder's losses or deductions disallowed under section 1366(d)(1) (before any reduction under paragraph (a)(1) of this section) exceed the amount of COD income that would have been taken into account by that shareholder under section 1366(a) had the COD income not been excluded under section 108(a).

(B) *Shareholders with a shareholder's excess amount.*—Each shareholder that has a shareholder's excess amount, as determined under paragraph (d)(2)(ii)(A) of this section, is allocated an amount equal to the S corporation's excess deemed NOL multiplied by a fraction, the numerator of which is the shareholder's excess amount and the denominator of which is the sum of all shareholders' excess amounts.

(C) *Shareholders with no shareholder's excess amount.*—If a shareholder does not have a shareholder's excess amount as determined in paragraph (d)(2)(ii)(A) of this section, none of the S corporation's excess deemed NOL shall be allocated to that shareholder.

(iii) *Terminating shareholder.*—Any amount of the S corporation's excess deemed NOL allocated under paragraph (d)(2) of this section to a shareholder that had transferred all of the shareholder's stock in the corporation during the taxable year of the discharge is permanently disallowed under §1.1366-2(a)(6), unless the transfer of stock is described in section 1041(a). If the transfer of stock is described in section 1041(a), the amount of the S corporation's excess deemed NOL allocated to the transferor under paragraph (d)(2) of this section shall be treated as a loss or deduction incurred by the corporation in the succeeding taxable year with respect to the transferee. See section 1366(d)(2)(B).

(3) *Character of excess losses or deductions allocated to a shareholder.*—The character of an S corporation's excess deemed NOL that is allocated to a shareholder under paragraph (d)(2) of this section consists of a proportionate amount of each item of the shareholder's loss or deduction that is disallowed for the taxable year of the discharge under section 1366(d)(1).

(4) *Information requirements.*—If an S corporation excludes COD income from gross income under section 108(a) for a taxable year, each shareholder of the S corporation during the taxable year of the discharge must report to the S corporation the amount of the shareholder's losses and deductions that are disallowed for the taxable year of the discharge under section 1366(d)(1), even if that amount is zero. If a shareholder fails to report the amount of the shareholder's

losses and deductions that are disallowed for the taxable year of the discharge under section 1366(d)(1) to the S corporation, or if the S corporation knows that the amount reported by the shareholder is inaccurate, or if the information, as reported, appears to be incomplete or incorrect, the S corporation may rely on its own books and records, as well as other information available to the S corporation, to determine the amount of the shareholder's losses and deductions that are disallowed for the taxable year of the discharge under section 1366(d)(1), provided that the S corporation knows or reasonably believes that its information presents an accurate reflection of the shareholder's disallowed losses and deductions under section 1366(d)(1). The S corporation must report to each shareholder the amount of the S corporation's excess deemed NOL that is allocated to that shareholder under paragraph (d)(2) of this section, even if that amount is zero, in accordance with applicable forms and instructions.

(e) *Examples.*—The following examples illustrate the application of this section:

Example 1. (i) *Facts.* In Year 4, X, a corporation in a title 11 case, is entitled under section 108(a)(1)(A) to exclude from gross income $100,000 of COD income. For Year 4, X has gross income in the amount of $50,000. In each of Years 1 and 2, X had no taxable income or loss. In Year 3, X had a net operating loss of $100,000, the use of which when carried over to Year 4 is not subject to any restrictions other than those of section 172.

(ii) *Analysis.* Pursuant to paragraph (b) of this section, X takes into account the net operating loss carryover from Year 3 in computing its taxable income for Year 4 before any portion of the COD income excluded under section 108(a)(1)(A) is applied to reduce tax attributes. Thus, the amount of the net operating loss carryover that is reduced under section 108(b)(2) and paragraph (a) of this section is $50,000.

Example 2. (i) *Facts.* The facts are the same as in *Example 1*, except that in Year 4 X sustains a net operating loss in the amount of $100,000. In addition, in each of Years 2 and 3, X reported taxable income in the amount of $25,000.

(ii) *Analysis.* Pursuant to paragraph (b) of this section and section 172, the net operating loss sustained in Year 4 is carried back to Years 2 and 3 before any portion of the COD income excluded under section 108(a)(1)(A) is applied to reduce tax attributes. Thus, the amount of the net operating loss that is reduced under section 108(b)(2) and paragraph (a) of this section is $50,000.

Example 3. (i) *Facts.* In Year 2, X, a corporation in a title 11 case, has outstanding debts of $200,000 and a depreciable asset that has an adjusted basis of $75,000 and a fair market value of $100,000. X has no other assets or liabilities. X has a net operating loss of $80,000 that is carried over to Year 2 but has no general business credit, minimum tax credit, or capital loss carryovers. Under a plan of reorganization, X transfers its asset to Corporation Y in exchange for Y stock with a value of $100,000. X distributes the Y stock to its creditors in exchange for release of their claims against X. X's shareholders receive nothing in the transaction. The transaction qualifies as a reorganization under section 368(a)(1)(G) that satisfies the requirements of section 354(b)(1)(A) and (B). For Year 2, X has gross income of $10,000 (without regard to any income from the discharge of indebtedness) and is allowed a depreciation deduction of $10,000 in respect of the asset. In addition, it generates no general business credits.

(ii) *Analysis.* On the distribution of Y stock to X's creditors, under section 108(a)(1)(A), X is entitled to exclude from gross income the debt discharge amount of $100,000. (Under section 108(e)(8), X is treated as satisfying $100,000 of the debt owed the creditors for $100,000, the fair market value of the Y stock transferred to those creditors.) In Year 2, X has no taxable income or loss because its gross income is exactly offset by the depreciation deduction. As a result of the depreciation deduction, X's basis in the asset is reduced by $10,000 to $65,000. Pursuant to paragraph (c) of this section, the amount of X's net operating loss to which Y succeeds pursuant to section 381 and the basis of X's property transferred to Y must take into account the reductions required by section 108(b). Pursuant to paragraph (a) of this section, X's net operating loss carryover in the amount of $80,000 is reduced by $80,000 of the COD income excluded under section 108(a)(1). In addition, X's basis in the asset is reduced by $20,000, the extent to which the COD income excluded under section 108(a)(1) did not reduce the net operating loss. Accordingly, as a result of the reorganization, there is no net operating loss to which Y succeeds under section 381. Pursuant to section 361, X recognizes no gain or loss on the transfer of its property to Y. Pursuant to section 362(b), Y's basis in the asset acquired from X is $45,000.

Example 4. (i) *Facts.* The facts are the same as in *Example 3*, except that X elects under section 108(b)(5) to reduce first the basis of its depreciable asset.

(ii) *Analysis.* As in *Example 3*, on the distribution of Y stock to X's creditors, under section 108(a)(1)(A), X is entitled to exclude from gross income the debt discharge amount of $100,000. In addition, in

Reg. §1.108-7(e)

Year 2, X has no taxable income or loss because its gross income is exactly offset by the depreciation deduction. As a result of the depreciation deduction, X's basis in the asset is reduced by $10,000 to $65,000. Pursuant to paragraph (c) of this section, the amount of X's net operating loss to which Y succeeds pursuant to section 381 and the basis of X's property transferred to Y must take into account the reductions required by section 108(b). As a result of the election under section 108(b)(5), X's basis in the asset is reduced by $65,000 to $0. In addition, X's net operating loss is reduced by $35,000, the extent to which the amount excluded from income under section 108(a)(1)(A) does not reduce X's asset basis. Accordingly, as a result of the reorganization, Y succeeds to X's net operating loss in the amount of $45,000 under section 381. Pursuant to section 361, X recognizes no gain or loss on the transfer of its property to Y. Pursuant to section 362(b), Y's basis in the asset acquired from X is $0.

Example 5. (i) *Facts.* During the entire calendar year 2009, A, B, and C each own equal shares of stock in X, a calendar year S corporation. As of December 31, 2009, A, B, and C each have a zero stock basis and X does not have any indebtedness to A, B, or C. For the 2009 taxable year, X excludes from gross income $45,000 of COD income under section 108(a)(1)(A). The COD income (had it not been excluded) would have been allocated $15,000 to A, $15,000 to B, and $15,000 to C under section 1366(a). For the 2009 taxable year, X has $30,000 of losses and deductions that X passes through pro rata to A, B, and C in the amount of $10,000 each. The losses and deductions that pass through to A, B, and C are disallowed under section 1366(d)(1). In addition, B has $10,000 of section 1366(d) losses from prior years and C has $20,000 of section 1366(d) losses from prior years. A's ($10,000), B's ($20,000) and C's ($30,000) combined $60,000 of disallowed losses and deductions for the taxable year of the discharge are treated as a current year net operating loss tax attribute of X under section 108(d)(7)(B) (deemed NOL) for purposes of the section 108(b) reduction of tax attributes.

(ii) *Allocation.* Under section 108(b)(2)(A), X's $45,000 of excluded COD income reduces the $60,000 deemed NOL to $15,000. Therefore, X has a $15,000 excess net operating loss (excess deemed NOL) to allocate to its shareholders. Under paragraph (d)(2)(ii)(C) of this section, none of the $15,000 excess deemed NOL is allocated to A because A's section 1366(d) losses and deductions immediately prior to the section 108(b)(2)(A) reduction ($10,000) do not exceed A's share of the excluded COD income for 2008 ($15,000). Thus, A has no shareholder's excess amount. Each of B's and C's respective section 1366(d) losses and deductions immediately prior to the section 108(b)(2)(A) reduction exceed each of B's and C's respective shares of the excluded COD income for 2008. B's excess amount is $5,000 ($20,000 - $15,000) and C's excess amount is $15,000 ($30,000 - $15,000). Therefore, the total of all shareholders' excess amounts is $20,000. Under paragraph (d)(2) of this section, X will allocate $3,750 of the $15,000 excess deemed NOL to B ($15,000 × $5,000 / $20,000) and $11,250 of the $15,000 excess deemed NOL to C ($15,000 × $15,000 / $20,000). These amounts are treated as losses and deductions disallowed under section 1366(d)(1) for the taxable year of the discharge. Accordingly, at the beginning of 2010, A has no section 1366(d)(2) carryovers, B has $3,750 of carryovers, and C has $11,250 of carryovers.

(iii) *Character.* Immediately prior to the section 108(b)(2)(A) reduction, B's $20,000 of section 1366(d) losses and deductions consisted of $8,000 of longterm capital losses, $7,000 of section 1231 losses, and $5,000 of ordinary losses. After the section 108(b)(2)(A) tax attribute reduction, X will allocate $3,750 of the excess deemed NOL to B. Under paragraph (d)(3) of this section, the $3,750 excess deemed NOL allocated to B consists of $1,500 of long-term capital losses (($8,000 / $20,000) × $3,750), $1,312.50 of section 1231 losses (($7,000 / $20,000) × $3,750), and $937.50 of ordinary losses (($5,000 / $20,000) × $3,750). As a result, at the beginning of 2010, B's $3,750 of section 1366(d)(2) carryovers consist of $1,500 of long-term capital losses, $1,312.50 of section 1231 losses, and $937.50 of ordinary losses.

Example 6. (i) A and B each own 50 percent of the shares of stock in X, a calendar year S corporation. On March 1, 2009, X realizes $12,000 of COD income and excludes this amount from gross income under section 108(a)(1)(A) for X's 2009 taxable year. On June 30, 2009, A sells all of her shares of stock in X to C in a transfer not described in section 1041(a). X does not make a terminating election under section 1377(a)(2). The COD income (had it not been excluded) would have been allocated $3,000 to A, $6,000 to B, and $3,000 to C under section 1366(a). Prior to the section 108(b)(2)(A) reduction, for the taxable year of the discharge the shareholders have disallowed losses and deductions under section 1366(d) (including disallowed losses carried over to the current year under section 1366(d)(2)) in the following amounts: A - $5,000, B - $13,000, and C - $2,000. The combined $20,000 of disallowed losses and deductions for the taxable year of the discharge are treated as a current year net operating loss tax attribute of X under section 108(d)(7)(B) (deemed NOL).

(ii) Under section 108(b)(2)(A), X's $12,000 of excluded COD income reduces the $20,000 deemed NOL to $8,000. Therefore, X has an $8,000 excess net operating loss (excess deemed NOL) to allocate to its shareholders. Under paragraph (d)(2)(ii)(C) of this section, none of the $8,000 excess deemed NOL is allocated to C because C's section 1366(d) losses and deductions immediately prior to the section 108(b)(2)(A) reduction ($2,000) do not exceed C's share of the excluded COD income for 2008 ($3,000). However, each of A's and B's respective section 1366(d) losses and deductions immediately prior to the section 108(b)(2)(A) reduction exceed each of A's and B's respective shares of the excluded COD income for 2009. A's excess amount is $2,000 ($5,000 - $3,000) and B's excess amount is $7,000 ($13,000 - $6,000). Therefore, the total of all shareholders' excess amounts is $9,000. Under paragraph (d)(2) of this section, X will allocate $1,777.78 of the $8,000 excess deemed NOL to A ($8,000 × $2,000 / $9,000) and $6,222.22 of the $8,000 excess deemed NOL to B ($8,000 × $7,000 / $9,000). However, because A transferred all of her shares of stock in X in a transaction not described in section 1041(a), A's $1,777.78 of section 1366(d) losses and deductions are permanently disallowed under paragraph (d)(2)(iii) of this section. Accordingly, at the beginning of 2010, B has $6,222.22 of section 1366(d)(2) carryovers and C has no section 1366(d)(2) carryovers.

Example 7. The facts are the same as in *Example 6,* except that X, with the consent of A and C, makes a terminating election under section 1377(a)(2) upon A's sale of her stock in X to C. Therefore, the COD income (had it not been excluded) would have been allocated $6,000 to A, $6,000 to B, and $0 to C. Under paragraph (d)(2)(ii)(C) of this section, none of the $8,000 excess deemed NOL is allocated to A because A's section 1366(d) losses and deductions immediately prior to the section 108(b)(2)(A) reduction ($5,000) do not exceed A's share of the excluded COD income for 2009 ($6,000). However, each of B's and C's respective section 1366(d) losses and deductions immediately prior to the section 108(b)(2)(A) reduction exceed each of B's and C's respective shares of the excluded COD income for 2009. B's excess amount is $7,000 ($13,000 - $6,000), C's excess amount is $2,000 ($2,000 - $0). Therefore, the total of all shareholders' excess amounts is $9,000. Under paragraph (d)(2) of this section, X will allocate $6,222.22 of the $8,000 excess deemed NOL to B ($8,000 × $7,000 / $9,000) and $1,777.78 of the $8,000 excess deemed NOL to C. Accordingly, at the beginning of 2010, B has $6,222.22 of section 1366(d)(2) carryovers and C has $1,777.78 of section 1366(d)(2) carryovers.

(f) *Effective date.*—(1) Paragraphs (a), (b), (c), and *Examples 1, 2, 3,* and 4 of paragraph (e) of this section apply to discharges of indebtedness occurring on or after May 10, 2004.

(2) Paragraph (d) and *Examples 5, 6,* and 7 of paragraph (e) of this section apply to discharges of indebtedness occurring on or after October 30, 2009. Paragraph (d)(2)(iii) of this section applies on and after July 23, 2014. For rules that apply before that date, see 26 CFR part 1 (revised as of April 1, 2014). [Reg. § 1.108-7.]

☐ [*T.D.* 9080, 7-17-2003 (*corrected* 8-21-2003 *and* 9-30-2003). *Redesignated and amended by T.D.* 9127, 5-10-2004. *Amended by T.D.* 9469, 10-29-2009 *and T.D.* 9682, 7-22-2014.]

[Reg. § 1.108-8]

§ 1.108-8. Indebtedness satisfied by partnership interest.—(a) *In general.*—For purposes of determining income of a debtor from discharge of indebtedness (COD income), if a debtor partnership transfers a capital or profits interest in the partnership to a creditor in satisfaction of its recourse or nonrecourse indebtedness (a debt-for-equity exchange), the partnership is treated as having satisfied the indebtedness with an amount of money equal to the fair market value of the partnership interest.

(b) *Determination of fair market value.*—(1) *In general.*—All the facts and circumstances are considered in determining the fair market value of a partnership interest transferred by a debtor partnership to a creditor in satisfaction of the debtor partnership's indebtedness (debt-for-equity interest) for purposes of paragraph (a) of this section. If the fair market value of the debt-for-equity interest does not equal the fair market value of the indebtedness exchanged, then general tax law principles shall apply to account for the difference.

(2) *Safe harbor.*—(i) *General rule.*—For purposes of paragraph (a) of this section, the fair market value of a debt-for-equity interest is deemed to be equal to the liquidation value of the debt-for-equity interest, as defined in paragraph (b)(2)(iii) of this section, if the following requirements are satisfied—

(A) The creditor, debtor partnership, and its partners treat the fair market value of the indebtedness as being equal to the liquidation value of the debt-for-equity interest for purposes of determining the tax consequences of the debt-for-equity exchange;

(B) If, as part of the same overall transaction, the debtor partnership transfers more than one debt-for-equity interest to one or more creditors, then each creditor, debtor partnership, and its partners treat the fair market value of each debt-for-equity interest transferred by the debtor partnership to such creditors as equal to its liquidation value;

(C) The debt-for-equity exchange is a transaction that has terms that are comparable to terms that would be agreed to by unrelated parties negotiating with adverse interests; and

(D) Subsequent to the debt-for-equity exchange, the debtor partnership does not redeem the debt-for-equity interest, and no person bearing a relationship to the debtor partnership or its partners that is specified in section 267(b) or section 707(b) purchases the debt-for-equity interest, as part of a plan at the time of the debt-for-equity exchange that has as a principal purpose the avoidance of COD income by the debtor partnership.

(ii) *Tiered-partnership rule.*—For purposes of this paragraph (b)(2), the liquidation value of a debt-for-equity interest in a partnership (upper-tier partnership) that directly or indirectly owns an interest in one or more partnerships (lower-tier partnership(s)) is determined by taking into account the liquidation value of such lower-tier partnership interests.

(iii) *Definition of liquidation value.*—For purposes of this paragraph (b)(2), the liquidation value of a debt-for-equity interest equals the amount of cash that the creditor would receive with respect to the debt-for-equity interest if, immediately after the debt-for-equity exchange, the partnership sold all of its assets (including goodwill, going concern value, and any other intangibles) for cash equal to the fair market value of those assets and then liquidated.

(c) *Example.*—The following example illustrates the provisions of this section:

Example. (i) AB partnership has $1,000 of outstanding indebtedness owed to C. C agrees to transfer to AB partnership the $1,000 indebtedness in a debt-for-equity exchange for a debt-for-equity interest in AB partnership. The liquidation value of C's debt-for-equity interest is $700, which is the amount of cash that C would receive with respect to that interest if, immediately after the debt-for-equity exchange, AB partnership sold all of its assets for cash equal to the fair market value of those assets and then liquidated. Each of the requirements of the liquidation value safe harbor described in paragraph (b)(2) of this section is satisfied.

(ii) Because the requirements in paragraph (b)(2) of this section are satisfied, the fair market value of C's debt-for-equity interest in AB partnership for purposes of determining AB partnership's COD income is the liquidation value of C's debt-for-equity interest, or $700. Accordingly, AB partnership is treated as satisfying the $1,000 indebtedness for $700 under section 108(e)(8).

(d) *Effective/applicability date.*—This section applies to debt-for-equity exchanges occurring on or after November 17, 2011. [Reg. §1.108-8.]

☐ [*T.D. 9557, 11-15-2011.*]

[Reg. §1.108-9]

§1.108-9. Application of the bankruptcy and the insolvency provisions of section 108 to grantor trusts and disregarded entities.— (a) *General rule.*—(1) *Owner is the taxpayer.*—For purposes of applying section 108(a)(1)(A) and (B) to discharge of indebtedness income of a grantor trust or a disregarded entity, neither the grantor trust nor the disregarded entity shall be considered to be the "taxpayer," as that term is used in section 108(a)(1) and (d)(1) through (3). Rather, for purposes of section 108(a)(1)(A) and (B) and (d)(1) through (3) and subject to section 108(d)(6), the owner of the grantor trust or the owner of the disregarded entity is the "taxpayer."

(2) *The bankruptcy exclusion.*—If indebtedness of a grantor trust or a disregarded entity is discharged in a title 11 case, section 108(a)(1)(A) applies to that discharged indebtedness only if the owner of the grantor trust or the owner of the disregarded entity is under the jurisdiction of the court in a title 11 case as the title 11 debtor. If the grantor trust or the disregarded entity is under the jurisdiction of the court in a title 11 case as the title 11 debtor, but the owner of the grantor trust or the owner of the disregarded entity is not, section 108(a)(1)(A) does not apply to the discharge of indebtedness income.

(3) *The insolvency exclusion.*—Section 108(a)(1)(B) applies to the discharged indebtedness of a grantor trust or a disregarded entity only to the extent the owner of the grantor trust or the owner of the disregarded entity is insolvent. If the grantor trust or the disregarded entity is insolvent, but the owner of the grantor trust or the owner of the disregarded entity is solvent, section 108(a)(1)(B) does not apply to the discharge of indebtedness income.

(b) *Application to partnerships.*—Under section 108(d)(6), in the case of a partnership, section 108(a)(1)(A) and (B) applies at the partner level. If a partnership holds an interest in a grantor trust or a disregarded entity, the applicability of section 108(a)(1)(A) and (B) to the discharge of indebtedness income is tested by looking to each partner to whom the income is allocable.

(c) *Definitions.*—(1) *Disregarded entity.*—For purposes of this section, a *disregarded entity* is an entity that is disregarded as an entity separate from its owner for Federal income tax purposes. See §301.7701-2(c)(2)(i) of this chapter, the Procedure and Administration Regulations. Examples of disregarded entities include a domestic single-member limited liability company that does not elect to be classified as a corporation for Federal income tax purposes pursuant to §301.7701-3 of this chapter, a corporation that is a qualified REIT subsidiary (within the meaning of section 856(i)(2)), and a corporation that is a qualified subchapter S subsidiary (within the meaning of section 1361(b)(3)(B)).

(2) *Grantor trust.*—For purposes of this section, a *grantor trust* is any portion of a trust that is treated under subpart E of part I of subchapter J of chapter 1 of subtitle A of title 26 of the United States Code as being owned by the grantor or another person.

(3) *Owner.*—Notwithstanding any other provision of this section to the contrary, neither a grantor trust nor a disregarded entity shall be considered an owner for purposes of this section.

(4) *Title 11 debtor.*—For purposes of this section, a *title 11 debtor* is a debtor in a case under title 11 of the United States Code, as defined in 11 U.S.C. 101(13).

(d) *Applicability date.*—The rules of this section apply to discharge of indebtedness income occurring on or after June 10, 2016. [Reg. §1.108-9.]

☐ [*T.D. 9771, 6-9-2016.*]

[Reg. §1.108(i)-0]

§1.108(i)-0. Definitions and effective/applicability dates.— (a) *Definitions.*—For purposes of regulations under section 108(i)—

(1) *Acquisition.*—An *acquisition,* with respect to any applicable debt instrument, includes an acquisition of the debt instrument for cash or other property, the exchange of the debt instrument for another debt instrument (including an exchange resulting from a modification of the debt instrument), the exchange of the debt instrument for corporate stock or a partnership interest, the contribution of the debt instrument to capital, the complete forgiveness of the indebtedness by the holder of the debt instrument, and a direct or an indirect acquisition within the meaning of §1.108-2.

(2) *Applicable debt instrument.*—An *applicable debt instrument* is a debt instrument that was issued by a C corporation or any other person in connection with the conduct of a trade or business by such person. In the case of an intercompany obligation (as defined in §1.1502-13(g)(2)(ii)), *applicable debt instrument* includes only an instrument for which COD income is realized upon the instrument's deemed satisfaction under §1.1502-13(g)(5).

(3) *C corporation issuer.*—*C corporation issuer* means a C corporation that issues a debt instrument with any deferred OID deduction.

(4) *C corporation partner.*—A *C corporation partner* is a C corporation that is a direct or indirect partner of an electing partnership or a related partnership.

(5) *COD income.*—*COD income* means income from the discharge of indebtedness, as determined under sections 61(a)(12) and 108(a) and the regulations under those sections.

(6) *COD income amount.*—A *COD income amount* is a partner's distributive share of COD income with respect to an applicable debt instrument of an electing partnership.

(7) *Debt instrument.*—*Debt instrument* means a bond, debenture, note, certificate, or any other instrument or contractual arrangement constituting indebtedness (within the meaning of section 1275(a)(1)).

(8) *Deferral period.*—For a reacquisition that occurs in 2009, *deferral period* means the taxable year of the reacquisition and the four taxable years following such taxable year. For a reacquisition that occurs in 2010, *deferral period* means the taxable year of the reacquisition and the three taxable years following such taxable year.

(9) *Deferred amount.*—A *deferred amount* is the portion of a partner's COD income amount with respect to an applicable debt instrument that is deferred under section 108(i).

(10) *Deferred COD income.*—*Deferred COD income* means COD income that is deferred under section 108(i).

(11) *Deferred item.*—A *deferred item* is any item of deferred COD income or deferred OID deduction that has not been previously taken into account under section 108(i).

(12) *Deferred OID deduction.*—A *deferred OID deduction* means an otherwise allowable deduction for OID that is deferred under section 108(i)(2) with respect to a debt instrument issued (or treated as issued under section 108(e)(4)) in a debt-for-debt exchange described in section 108(i)(2)(A) or a deemed debt-for-debt exchange described in §1.108(i)-3(a).

(13) *Deferred section 465 amount.*—A *deferred section 465 amount* is described in paragraph (d)(3) of §1.108(i)-2.

(14) *Deferred section 752 amount.*—A *deferred section 752 amount* is described in paragraph (b)(3) of §1.108(i)-2.

(15) *Direct partner.*—A *direct partner* is a person that owns a direct interest in a partnership.

(16) *Electing corporation.*—An *electing corporation* is a C corporation with deferred COD income by reason of a section 108(i) election.

(17) *Electing entity.*—An *electing entity* is an entity that is a taxpayer that makes an election under section 108(i).

(18) *Electing member.*—An *electing member* is an electing corporation that is a member of an affiliated group that files a consolidated return.

(19) *Electing partnership.*—An *electing partnership* is a partnership that makes an election under section 108(i).

(20) *Electing S corporation.*—An *electing S corporation* is an S corporation that makes an election under section 108(i).

(21) *Included amount.*—An *included amount* is the portion of a partner's COD income amount with respect to an applicable debt instrument that is not deferred under section 108(i) and is included in the partner's distributive share of partnership income for the taxable year of the partnership in which the reacquisition occurs.

(22) *Inclusion period.*—The *inclusion period* is the five taxable years following the last taxable year of the deferral period.

(23) *Indirect partner.*—An *indirect partner* is a person that owns an interest in a partnership through an S corporation and/or one or more partnerships.

(24) *Issuing entity.*—An *issuing entity* is any entity that is—

(i) A related partnership;

(ii) A related S corporation;

(iii) An electing partnership that issues a debt instrument (or is treated as issuing a debt instrument under section 108(e)(4)) in a debt-for-debt exchange described in section 108(i)(2)(A) or a deemed debt-for-debt exchange described in §1.108(i)-3(a); or

(iv) An electing S corporation that issues a debt instrument (or is treated as issuing a debt instrument under section 108(e)(4)) in a debt-for-debt exchange described in section 108(i)(2)(A) or a deemed debt-for-debt exchange described in §1.108(i)-3(a).

(25) *OID.*—*OID* means original issue discount, as determined under sections 1271 through 1275 (and the regulations under those sections). If the amount of OID with respect to a debt instrument is less than a de minimis amount as determined under §1.1273-1(d), the OID is treated as zero for purposes of section 108(i)(2).

(26) *Reacquisition.*—A *reacquisition*, with respect to any applicable debt instrument, is any event occurring after December 31, 2008 and before January 1, 2011, that causes COD income with respect to such applicable debt instrument, including any acquisition of the debt instrument by the debtor that issued (or is otherwise the obligor under) the debt instrument or a person related to such debtor (within the meaning of section 108(i)(5)(A)).

(27) *Related partnership.*—A *related partnership* is a partnership that is related to the electing entity (within the meaning of section 108(i)(5)(A)) and that issues a debt instrument in a debt-for-debt exchange described in section 108(i)(2)(A) or a deemed debt-for-debt exchange described in §1.108(i)-3(a).

(28) *Related S corporation.*—A *related S corporation* is an S corporation that is related to the electing entity (within the meaning of section 108(i)(5)(A)) and that issues a debt instrument in a debt-for-debt exchange described in section 108(i)(2)(A) or a deemed debt-for-debt exchange described in §1.108(i)-3(a).

(29) *Separate interest.*—A *separate interest* is a direct interest in an electing partnership or in a partnership or S corporation that is a direct or indirect partner of an electing partnership.

(30) *S corporation partner.*—An *S corporation partner* is an S corporation that is a direct or indirect partner of an electing partnership or a related partnership.

(b) *Effective/Applicability dates.*—(1) *In general.*—The rules of this section, §1.108(i)-1, and §1.108(i)-2, apply on or after July 2, 2013, to reacquisitions of applicable debt instruments in taxable years ending after December 31, 2008. In addition, the rules of §1.108(i)-3 apply on or after July 2, 2013, to debt instruments issued after December 31, 2008, in connection with reacquisitions of applicable debt instruments in taxable years ending after December 31, 2008.

(2) *Prior periods.*—For rules applying before July 2, 2013, see §1.108(i)-0T, §1.108(i)-1T, §1.108(i)-2T, and §1.108(i)-3T, as contained in 26 CFR part 1, revised April 1, 2013. [Reg. §1.108(i)-0]

☐ [T.D. 9622, 7-2-2013 (corrected 8-8-2013).]

[Reg. §1.108(i)-1]

§1.108(i)-1. Deferred discharge of indebtedness income and deferred original issue discount deductions of C corporations.— (a) *Overview.*—Section 108(i)(1) provides an election for the deferral of COD income arising in connection with the reacquisition of an applicable debt instrument. An electing corporation generally includes deferred COD income ratably over the inclusion period. Paragraph (b) of this section provides rules for the mandatory acceleration of an electing corporation's remaining deferred COD income, the mandatory acceleration of a C corporation issuer's deferred OID deductions, and for the elective acceleration of an electing member's (other than the common parent's) remaining deferred COD income. Paragraph (c) of this section provides examples illustrating the application of the mandatory and elective acceleration rules. Paragraph (d) of this section provides rules for the computation of an electing corporation's earnings and profits. Paragraph (e) of this section refers to the effective/applicability dates.

(b) *Acceleration events.*—(1) *Deferred COD income.*—Except as otherwise provided in paragraphs (b)(2) and (3) of this section, and §1.108(i)-2(b)(6) (in the case of a corporate partner), an electing corporation's deferred COD income is taken into account ratably over the inclusion period.

(2) *Mandatory acceleration events.*—An electing corporation takes into account all of its remaining deferred COD income, including its share of an electing partnership's deferred COD income, immediately before the occurrence of any one of the events described in this paragraph (b)(2) (mandatory acceleration events), regardless of whether the electing corporation is in a title 11 or similar case at the time the mandatory acceleration event occurs.

(i) *Changes in tax status.*—The electing corporation changes its tax status. For purposes of the preceding sentence, an electing corporation is treated as changing its tax status if it becomes one of the following entities:

(A) A tax-exempt entity as defined in §1.337(d)-4(c)(2).

(B) An S corporation as defined in section 1361(a)(1).

(C) A qualified subchapter S subsidiary as defined in section 1361(b)(3)(B).

(D) An entity operating on a cooperative basis within the meaning of section 1381.

(E) A regulated investment company (RIC) as defined in section 851 or a real estate investment trust (REIT) as defined in section 856.

(F) A qualified REIT subsidiary as defined in section 856(i), but only if the qualified REIT subsidiary was not a REIT immediately before it became a qualified REIT subsidiary.

(ii) *Cessation of corporate existence.*—(A) *In general.*—The electing corporation ceases to exist for Federal income tax purposes.

(B) *Exception for section 381(a) transactions.*—(1) *In general.*— The electing corporation is not treated as ceasing to exist and is not required to take into account its remaining deferred COD income solely because its assets are acquired in a transaction to which section 381(a) applies. In such a case, the acquiring corporation succeeds to the electing corporation's remaining deferred COD income and becomes subject to section 108(i) and the regulations thereunder, including all reporting requirements, as if the acquiring corporation were the electing corporation. A transaction is not treated as one to which section 381(a) applies for purposes of this paragraph (b)(2)(ii)(B) in the following circumstances—

(i) The acquisition of the assets of an electing corporation by an S corporation, if the acquisition is described in section 1374(d)(8);

(ii) The acquisition of the assets of an electing corporation by a RIC or REIT, if the acquisition is described in §1.337(d)-7(a)(2)(ii);

(iii) The acquisition of the assets of a domestic electing corporation by a foreign corporation;

(iv) The acquisition of the assets of a foreign electing corporation by a domestic corporation, if as a result of the transaction, one or more exchanging shareholders include in income as a deemed dividend the all earnings and profits amount with respect to stock in the foreign electing corporation pursuant to § 1.367(b)-3(b)(3);

(v) The acquisition of the assets of an electing corporation by a tax-exempt entity as defined in § 1.337(d)-4(c)(2); or

(vi) The acquisition of the assets of an electing corporation by an entity operating on a cooperative basis within the meaning of section 1381.

(2) Special rules for consolidated groups.—(i) Liquidations.— For purposes of paragraph (b)(2)(ii)(B) of this section, the acquisition of assets by distributee members of a consolidated group upon the liquidation of an electing corporation is not treated as a transaction to which section 381(a) applies, unless immediately prior to the liquidation, one of the distributee members owns stock in the electing corporation meeting the requirements of section 1504(a)(2) (without regard to § 1.1502-34). See § 1.1502-80(g).

*(ii) Taxable years.—*In the case of an intercompany transaction to which section 381(a) applies, the transaction does not cause the transferor or distributor to have a short taxable year for purposes of determining the taxable year of the deferral and inclusion period.

*(iii) Net value acceleration rule.—(A) In general.—*The electing corporation engages in an impairment transaction and, immediately after the transaction, the gross value of the electing corporation's assets (gross asset value) is less than one hundred and ten percent of the sum of its total liabilities and the tax on the net amount of its deferred items (the net value floor) (the net value acceleration rule). Impairment transactions are any transactions, however effected, that impair an electing corporation's ability to pay the amount of Federal income tax liability on its deferred COD income and include, for example, distributions (including section 381(a) transactions), redemptions, belowmarket sales, charitable contributions, and the incurrence of additional indebtedness without a corresponding increase in asset value. Value-for-value sales or exchanges (for example, an exchange to which section 351 or section 721 applies), or mere declines in the market value of the electing corporation's assets are not impairment transactions. In addition, an electing corporation's investments and expenditures in pursuance of its good faith business judgment are not impairment transactions. For purposes of determining an electing corporation's gross asset value, the amount of any distribution that is not treated as an impairment transaction under paragraph (b)(2)(iii)(D) of this section (distributions and charitable contributions consistent with historical practice) or under paragraph (b)(2)(iii)(E) of this section (special rules for RICs and REITs) is treated as an asset of the electing corporation. Solely for purposes of computing the amount of the net value floor, the tax on the deferred items is determined by applying the highest rate of tax specified in section 11(b) for the taxable year.

*(B) Transactions integrated.—*Any transaction that occurs before the reacquisition of an applicable debt instrument, but that occurs pursuant to the same plan as the reacquisition, is taken into account in determining whether the gross asset value of the electing corporation is less than the net value floor.

*(C) Corrective action to restore net value.—*An electing corporation is not required to take into account its deferred COD income under the net value acceleration rule of paragraph (b)(2)(iii)(A) of this section if, before the due date of the electing corporation's return (including extensions), value is restored in a transaction in an amount equal to the lesser of—

(1) The amount of value that was removed from the electing corporation in one or more impairment transactions (net of amounts previously restored under this paragraph (b)(2)(iii)(C)); or

(2) The amount by which the electing corporation's net value floor exceeds its gross asset value.

For example, assume an electing corporation incurs $50 of debt, distributes the $50 of proceeds to its shareholder, and immediately after the distribution, the electing corporation's gross asset value is below the net value floor by $25. The electing corporation may avoid the inclusion of its remaining deferred COD income if value of at least $25 is restored to it before the due date of the electing corporation's tax return (including extensions) for the taxable year that includes the distribution. The value that must be restored is determined at the time of the impairment transaction on a net value basis (for example, additional borrowings by an electing corporation do not restore value).

*(D) Exceptions for distributions and charitable contributions that are consistent with historical practice.—*An electing corporation's distri-

butions are not treated as impairment transactions (and are not taken into account as a reduction of the electing corporation's gross asset value when applying the net value acceleration rule to any impairment transaction), to the extent that the distributions are described in section 301(c) and the amount of these distributions, in the aggregate, for the applicable taxable year (applicable distribution amount) does not exceed the annual average amount of section 301(c) distributions over the preceding three taxable years (average distribution amount). If an electing corporation's applicable distribution amount exceeds its average distribution amount (excess amount), then the amount of the impairment transaction equals the excess amount. Appropriate adjustments must be made to take into account any issuances or redemptions of stock, or similar transactions, occurring during the taxable year of distribution or any of the preceding three taxable years. If the electing corporation has a short taxable year for the year of the distribution or for any of the preceding three taxable years, the amounts are determined on an annualized basis. If an electing corporation has been in existence for less than three years, the period during which the electing corporation has been in existence is substituted for the preceding three taxable years. For purposes of determining an electing corporation's average distribution amount, the electing corporation does not take into account the distribution history of a distributor or transferor in a transaction to which section 381(a) applies (other than a transaction described in section 368(a)(1)(F)). Rules similar to those prescribed in this paragraph (b)(2)(iii)(D) also apply to an electing corporation's charitable contributions (within the meaning of section 170(c)) that are consistent with its historical practice.

*(E) Special rules for RICs and REITs.—(1) Distributions.—*Notwithstanding paragraph (b)(2)(iii)(D) of this section, in the case of a RIC or REIT, any distribution with respect to stock that is treated as a dividend under section 852 or 857 is not treated as an impairment transaction (and is not taken into account as a reduction in gross asset value when applying the net value acceleration rule to any impairment transaction).

*(2) Redemptions by RICs.—*Any redemption of a redeemable security, as defined in 15 U.S.C. section 80a-2(a)(32), by a RIC in the ordinary course of business is not treated as an impairment transaction (and is not taken into account as a reduction in gross asset value when applying the net value acceleration rule to any impairment transaction).

*(F) Special rules for consolidated groups.—(1) Impairment transactions and net value acceleration rule.—*In the case of an electing member, the determination of whether the member has engaged in an impairment transaction is made on a groupwide basis. An electing member is treated as engaging in an impairment transaction if any member's transaction impairs the group's ability to pay the tax liability associated with all electing members' deferred COD income. Accordingly, intercompany transactions are not impairment transactions. Similarly, the net value acceleration rule is applied by reference to the gross asset value of all members (excluding stock of members whether or not described in section 1504(a)(4)), the liabilities of all members, and the tax on all members' deferred items. For example, assume P is the common parent of the P-S consolidated group, S has a section 108(i) election in effect, and S makes a $100 distribution to P which, on a separate entity basis, would reduce S's gross asset value below the net value floor. S's intercompany distribution to P is not an impairment transaction. However, if P makes a $100 distribution to its shareholder, P's distribution is an impairment transaction (unless the distribution is consistent with its historical practice under paragraph (b)(2)(iii)(D) of this section), and the net value acceleration rule is applied by reference to the assets, liabilities, and deferred items of the P-S group.

*(2) Departing member.—*If an electing member that previously engaged in one or more impairment transactions on a separate entity basis ceases to be a member of a consolidated group (departing member), the cessation is treated as an impairment transaction and the net value acceleration rule under paragraph (b)(2)(iii)(A) of this section is applied to the departing member on a separate entity basis immediately after ceasing to be a member (and taking into account the impairment transaction(s) that occurred on a separate entity basis). If the departing member's gross asset value is below the net value floor, the departing member's remaining deferred COD income is taken into account immediately before the departing member ceases to be a member (unless value is restored under paragraph (b)(2)(iii)(C) of this section). If the departing member's deferred COD income is not accelerated, the departing member is subject to the reporting requirements of section 108(i) on a separate entity basis. If the departing member becomes a member of another consolidated group, the cessation is treated as an impairment transaction and the net value acceleration rule under paragraph (b)(2)(iii)(A) of this section is applied by reference to the assets, liabilities, and the tax on

deferred items of the members of the acquiring group immediately after the transaction. If the acquiring group's gross asset value is below the net value floor, the departing member's remaining deferred COD income is taken into account immediately before the departing member ceases to be a member (unless value is restored under paragraph (b)(2)(iii)(C) of this section). If the departing member's remaining deferred COD income is not accelerated, the common parent of the acquiring group succeeds to the reporting requirements of section 108(i) with respect to the departing member.

(3) *Elective acceleration for certain consolidated group members.*—(i) *In general.*—An electing member (other than the common parent) of a consolidated group may elect at any time to accelerate in full (and not in part) the inclusion of its remaining deferred COD income with respect to all applicable debt instruments by filing a statement described in paragraph (b)(3)(ii) of this section. Once made, an election to accelerate deferred COD income under this paragraph (b)(3) is irrevocable.

(ii) *Time and manner for making election.*—(A) *In general.*—The election to accelerate the inclusion of an electing member's remaining deferred COD income with respect to all applicable debt instruments is made on a statement attached to a timely filed tax return (including extensions) for the year in which the deferred COD income is taken into account. The election is made by the common parent on behalf of the electing member. See § 1.1502-77(a).

(B) *Additional information.*—The statement must include—

(1) *Label.*—A label entitled "SECTION 1.108(i)-1 ELECTION AND INFORMATION STATEMENT BY [INSERT NAME AND EMPLOYER IDENTIFICATION NUMBER OF THE ELECTING MEMBER]"; and

(2) *Required Information.*—An identification of each applicable debt instrument to which an election under this paragraph (b)(3) applies and the corresponding amount of—

(i) Deferred COD income that is accelerated under this paragraph (b)(3); and

(ii) Deferred OID deductions that are accelerated under paragraph (b)(4) of this section.

(4) *Deferred OID deductions.*—(i) *In general.*—Except as otherwise provided in paragraph (b)(4)(ii) of this section and § 1.108(i)-2(b)(6) (in the case of a C corporation partner), a C corporation issuer's deferred OID deductions are taken into account ratably over the inclusion period.

(ii) *OID acceleration events.*—A C corporation issuer takes into account all of its remaining deferred OID deductions with respect to a debt instrument immediately before the occurrence of any one of the events described in this paragraph (b)(4)(ii), regardless of whether the C corporation issuer is in a title 11 or similar case.

(A) *Inclusion of deferred COD income.*—An electing entity or its owners take into account all of the remaining deferred COD income to which the C corporation issuer's deferred OID deductions relate. If, under § 1.108(i)-2(b) or (c), an electing entity or its owners take into account only a portion of the deferred COD income to which the deferred OID deductions relate, then the C corporation issuer takes into account a proportionate amount of the remaining deferred OID deductions.

(B) *Changes in tax status.*—The C corporation issuer changes its tax status within the meaning of paragraph (b)(2)(i) of this section.

(C) *Cessation of corporate existence.*—(1) *In general.*—The C corporation issuer ceases to exist for Federal income tax purposes.

(2) *Exception for section 381(a) transactions.*—(i) *In general.*—A C corporation issuer is not treated as ceasing to exist and does not take into account its remaining deferred OID deductions in a transaction to which section 381(a) applies, taking into account the application of § 1.1502-34, as appropriate. See § 1.1502-80(g). This exception does not apply to a transaction that is not treated as one to which section 381(a) applies under paragraph (b)(2)(iii)(B)(1) of this section.

(ii) *Taxable years.*—In the case of an intercompany transaction to which section 381(a) applies, the transaction does not cause the transferor or distributor to have a short taxable year for purposes of determining the taxable year of the deferral and inclusion period.

(c) *Examples.*—The application of this section is illustrated by the following examples. Unless otherwise stated, P, S, S1, and X are domestic C corporations, and each files a separate return on a calendar year basis:

Example 1. Net value acceleration rule. (i) *Facts.* On January 1, 2009, S reacquires its own note and realizes $400 of COD income. Pursuant to an election under section 108(i), S defers recognition of the entire $400 of COD income. Therefore, absent a mandatory acceleration event, S will take into account $80 of its deferred COD income in each year of the inclusion period. On December 31, 2010, S makes a $25 distribution to its sole shareholder, P, and this is the only distribution made by S in the past four years. Immediately following the distribution, S's gross asset value is $100, S has no liabilities, and the Federal income tax on S's $400 of deferred COD income is $140. Accordingly, S's net value floor is $154 (110% × $140).

(ii) *Analysis.* Under paragraph (b)(2)(iii)(A) of this section, S's distribution is an impairment transaction. Immediately following the distribution, S's gross asset value of $100 is less than the net value floor of $154. Accordingly, under the net value acceleration rule of paragraph (b)(2)(iii)(A) of this section, S takes into account its $400 of deferred COD income immediately before the distribution.

(iii) *Corrective action to restore value.* The facts are the same as in paragraph (i) of this *Example 1*, except that P contributes assets with a value of $25 to S before the due date of S's 2010 return (including extensions). Because P restores $25 of value to S (the lesser of the amount of value removed in the distribution ($25) or the amount by which S's net value floor exceeds its gross asset value ($54)), under paragraph (b)(2)(iii)(C) of this section, S does not take into account its $400 of deferred COD income.

Example 2. Distributions consistent with historical practice. (i) *Facts.* P, a publicly traded corporation, makes a valid section 108(i) election with respect to COD income realized in 2009. On December 31, 2009, P distributes $25 million on its 5 million shares of common stock outstanding. As of January 1, 2006, P has 10 million shares of common stock outstanding, and on March 31, 2006, P distributes $10 million on those 10 million shares. On September 15, 2006, P effects a 2:1 reverse stock split, and on December 31, 2006, P distributes $10 million on its 5 million shares of common stock outstanding. In each of 2007 and 2008, P distributes $5 million on its 5 million shares of common stock outstanding. All of the distributions are described in section 301(c).

(ii) *Amount of impairment transaction.* Under paragraph (b)(2)(iii)(D) of this section, P's 2009 distributions are not treated as impairment transactions (and are not taken into account as a reduction of P's gross asset value when applying the net value acceleration rule to any impairment transaction), to the extent that the aggregate amount distributed in 2009 (the applicable distribution amount) does not exceed the annual average amount of distributions (the average distribution amount) over the preceding three taxable years. Accordingly, P's applicable distribution amount for 2009 is $25 million, and its average distribution amount is $10 million ($20 million (2006) plus $5 million (2007) plus $5 million (2008) divided by 3). The reverse stock split in 2006 is not a transaction requiring an adjustment to the determination of the average distribution amount. Because P's applicable distribution amount of $25 million exceeds its average distribution amount of $10 million, under paragraph (b)(2)(iii)(D) of this section, the amount of P's 2009 distribution that is treated as an impairment transaction is $15 million. The balance of the 2009 distribution, $10 million, is not treated as an impairment transaction (and is not taken into account as a reduction in P's gross asset value when applying the net value acceleration rule to any impairment transaction).

(iii) *Distribution history.* The facts are the same as in paragraph (i) of this *Example 2*, except that in 2010, P merges into X in a transaction to which section 381(a) applies, with X succeeding to P's deferred COD income, and X makes a distribution to its shareholders. For purposes of determining whether X's distribution is consistent with its historical practice, the average distribution amount is determined solely with respect to X's distribution history.

Example 3. Cessation of corporate existence. (i) *Transaction to which section 381(a) applies.* P owns all of the stock of S. In 2009, S reacquires its own note and elects to defer recognition of its $400 of COD income under section 108(i). On December 31, 2010, S liquidates into P in a transaction that qualifies under section 332. Under paragraph (b)(2) of this section, S must take into account all of its remaining deferred COD income upon the occurrence of any one of the mandatory acceleration events. Although S ceases its corporate existence as a result of the liquidation, S is not required to take into account its remaining deferred COD income under the exception in paragraph (b)(2)(ii)(B) of this section because its assets are acquired in a transaction to which section 381(a) applies. However, under paragraph (b)(2)(iii)(A) of this section, S's distribution to P is an impairment transaction and the net value acceleration rule is applied with respect to the assets, liabilities, and deferred items of P (S's successor) immediately following the distribution. If S's deferred COD income is not taken into account under the net value acceleration rule of (b)(2)(iii) of this section, P succeeds to S's remaining deferred COD income and to S's reporting requirements as if P were the electing corporation.

(ii) *Debt-laden distributee.* The facts are the same as in paragraph (i) of this *Example 3,* except that in the liquidation, S distributes $100 of assets to P, a holding company whose only asset is its stock in S. Assume that immediately following the distribution, P's gross asset value is $100, P has $60 of liabilities, and the Federal income tax on the $400 of deferred COD income is $140. Under paragraph (b)(2) of this section, S must take into account all of its remaining deferred COD income upon the occurrence of any one of the mandatory acceleration events. Although S ceases its corporate existence as a result of the liquidation, S is not required to take into account its remaining deferred COD income under the exception in paragraph (b)(2)(ii)(B) of this section because its assets are acquired in a transaction to which section 381(a) applies. However, under paragraph (b)(2)(iii)(A) of this section, S's distribution to P is an impairment transaction and the net value acceleration rule is applied with respect to the assets, liabilities, and deferred items of P (S's successor). Immediately following the distribution, P's gross asset value of $100 is less than the net value floor of $220 [110% x ($60 + $140)]. Accordingly, under the net value acceleration rule of paragraph (b)(2)(iii)(A) of this section, S is required to take into account its $400 of deferred COD income immediately before the distribution, unless value is restored to P pursuant to paragraph (b)(2)(iii)(C) of this section.

(iii) *Foreign acquirer.* The facts are the same as in paragraph (i) of this *Example 3,* except that P is a foreign corporation. Although S's assets are acquired in a transaction to which section 381(a) applies, under paragraph (b)(2)(ii)(B)(*1*)(*iii*) of this section, the exception to accelerated inclusion does not apply and S takes into account its remaining deferred COD income immediately before the liquidation. See also section 367(e)(2) and the regulations thereunder.

(iv) *Section 338 transaction.* P, the common parent of a consolidated group (P group), owns all the stock of S1, one of the members of the P group. In 2009, S1 reacquires its own indebtedness and realizes $30 of COD income. Pursuant to an election under section 108(i), S1 defers recognition of the entire $30 of COD income. In 2010, P sells all the stock of S1 to X, an unrelated corporation, for $300, and P and X make a timely section 338(h)(10) election with respect to the sale. Under paragraph (b)(2)(ii)(A) of this section, an electing corporation takes into account its remaining deferred COD income when it ceases its existence for Federal income tax purposes unless the exception in paragraph (b)(2)(ii)(B) of this section applies. Pursuant to section 338(h)(10) and the regulations, S1 is treated as transferring all of its assets to an unrelated person in exchange for consideration that includes the discharge of its liabilities. This deemed value-for-value exchange is not an impairment transaction. Following the deemed sale, while S1 is still a member of the P group, S1 is treated as distributing all of its assets to P and as ceasing its existence. Under these facts, the distribution of all of S1's assets constitutes a deemed liquidation, and is a transaction to which sections 332 and 381(a) apply. Although S1 ceases its corporate existence as a result of the liquidation, S1 is not required to take into account its remaining deferred COD income under the exception in paragraph (b)(2)(ii)(B) of this section because its assets are acquired in a transaction to which section 381(a) applies. P succeeds to S1's remaining deferred COD income and to S1's reporting requirements as if P were the electing corporation. Under paragraph (b)(2)(iii)(F)(*1*) of this section, the intercompany distribution from S1 to P is not an impairment transaction.

(d) *Earnings and profits.*—(1) *In general.*—Deferred COD income increases earnings and profits in the taxable year that it is realized and not in the taxable year or years that the deferred COD income is includible in gross income. Deferred OID deductions decrease earnings and profits in the taxable year or years in which the deduction would be allowed without regard to section 108(i).

(2) *Exceptions.*—(i) *RICs and REITs.*—Notwithstanding paragraph (d)(1) of this section, deferred COD income increases earnings and profits of a RIC or REIT in the taxable year or years in which the deferred COD income is includible in gross income and not in the year that the deferred COD income is realized. Deferred OID deductions decrease earnings and profits of a RIC or REIT in the taxable year or years that the deferred OID deductions are deductible.

(ii) *Alternative minimum tax.*—For purposes of calculating alternative minimum taxable income, any items of deferred COD income or deferred OID deduction increase or decrease, respectively, adjusted current earnings under section 56(g)(4) in the taxable year or years that the item is includible or deductible.

(e) *Effective/applicability dates.*—For *effective/applicability dates,* see §1.108(i)-0(b). [Reg. §1.108(i)-1.]

☐ [*T.D. 9622, 7-2-2013 (corrected 8-8-2013).*]

[Reg. §1.108(i)-2]

§1.108(i)-2. Application of section 108(i) to partnerships and S corporations.—(a) *Overview.*—Under section 108(i), a partnership or an S corporation may elect to defer COD income arising in connection with a reacquisition of an applicable debt instrument for the deferral period. COD income deferred under section 108(i) is included in gross income ratably over the inclusion period, or earlier upon the occurrence of any acceleration event described in paragraph (b)(6) or (c)(3) of this section. If a debt instrument is issued (or treated as issued under section 108(e)(4)) in a debt-for-debt exchange described in section 108(i)(2)(A) or a deemed debt-for-debt exchange described in §1.108(i)-3(a), some or all of the deductions for OID with respect to such debt instrument must be deferred during the deferral period. The aggregate amount of OID deductions deferred during the deferral period is generally allowed as a deduction ratably over the inclusion period, or earlier upon the occurrence of any acceleration event described in paragraph (b)(6) or (c)(3) of this section. Paragraph (b) of this section provides rules that apply to partnerships. Paragraph (c) of this section provides rules that apply to S corporations. Paragraph (d) of this section provides general rules that apply to partnerships and S corporations. Paragraph (e) of this section provides election procedures and reporting requirements. Paragraph (f) of this section contains the effective/applicability date. See §1.108(i)-0(a) for definitions that apply to this section.

(b) *Specific rules applicable to partnerships.*—(1) *Allocation of COD income and partner's deferred amounts.*—An electing partnership that defers any portion of COD income realized from a reacquisition of an applicable debt instrument under section 108(i) must allocate all of the COD income with respect to the applicable debt instrument to its direct partners that are partners in the electing partnership immediately before the reacquisition in the manner in which the income would be included in the distributive shares of the partners under section 704 and the regulations under section 704, including §1.704-1(b)(2)(iii), without regard to section 108(i). The electing partnership may determine, in any manner, the portion, if any, of a partner's COD income amount with respect to an applicable debt instrument that is the deferred amount, and the portion, if any, that is the included amount. However, no partner's deferred amount with respect to an applicable debt instrument may exceed that partner's COD income amount with respect to such applicable debt instrument, and the aggregate amount of the partners' COD income amounts and deferred amounts with respect to each applicable debt instrument must equal the electing partnership's COD income amount and deferred amount, respectively, with respect to each such applicable debt instrument.

(2) *Basis adjustments and capital account maintenance.*—(i) *Basis adjustments.*—The adjusted basis of a partner's interest in a partnership is not increased under section 705(a)(1) by the partner's deferred amount in the taxable year of the reacquisition. The adjusted basis of a partner's interest in a partnership is not decreased under section 705(a)(2) by the partner's share of any deferred OID deduction in the taxable year in which the deferred OID accrues. The adjusted basis of a partner's interest in a partnership is adjusted under section 705(a) by the partner's share of the electing partnership's deferred items for the taxable year in which the partner takes into account such deferred items under this section.

(ii) *Capital account maintenance.*—For purposes of maintaining a partner's capital account under §1.704-1(b)(2)(iv) and notwithstanding §1.704-1(b)(2)(iv)(*n*), the capital account of a partner of a partnership is adjusted under §1.704-1(b)(2)(iv) for a partner's share of an electing partnership's deferred items as if no election under section 108(i) were made.

(3) *Deferred section 752 amount.*—(i) *In general.*—An electing partnership shall determine, for each of its direct partners with a deferred amount, the partner's deferred section 752 amount, if any, with respect to an applicable debt instrument. A partner's deferred section 752 amount with respect to an applicable debt instrument equals the decrease in the partner's share of a partnership liability under section 752(b) resulting from the reacquisition of the applicable debt instrument that is not treated as a current distribution of money under section 752(b) by reason of section 108(i)(6) (deferred section 752 amount). A partner's deferred section 752 amount is treated as a distribution of money by the partnership to the partner under section 752(b) at the same time and, to the extent remaining, in the same amount as the partner recognizes the deferred amount with respect to the applicable debt instrument.

(ii) *Electing partnership's computation of a partner's deferred section 752 amount.*—To compute a partner's deferred section 752 amount, the electing partnership must first determine the amount of gain that its direct partner would recognize in the taxable year of a reacquisition under section 731 as a result of the reacquisition of one or more applicable debt instruments during the taxable year absent the deferral provided in the second sentence of section 108(i)(6) (the section 108(i)(6) deferral). If a direct partner of an electing partnership would not recognize any gain under section 731 as a result of the reacquisition of one or more applicable debt instruments during the taxable year absent the section 108(i)(6) deferral, the partner will not have a deferred section 752 amount with respect to any applicable debt instrument that is reacquired during the taxable year. If a direct partner of an electing partnership would recognize gain under section 731 as a result of the reacquisition of one or more applicable debt instruments during the taxable year absent the section 108(i)(6) deferral, the partner's deferred section 752 amount for all applicable debt instruments that are reacquired during the taxable year is equal to the lesser of the partner's aggregate deferred amounts from the electing partnership for all applicable debt instruments reacquired during the taxable year, or the gain that the partner would recognize in the taxable year of the reacquisitions under section 731 as a result of the reacquisitions absent the section 108(i)(6) deferral. In determining the amount of gain that the direct partner would recognize in the taxable year of a reacquisition under section 731 as a result of the reacquisition of one or more applicable debt instruments during the taxable year absent the section 108(i)(6) deferral, the rule under §1.731-1(a)(1)(ii) applies to any deemed distribution of money under section 752(b) resulting from a decrease in the partner's share of a reacquired applicable debt instrument that is treated as an advance or drawing of money. The amount of any deemed distribution of money under section 752(b) resulting from a decrease in the partner's share of a reacquired applicable debt instrument that is treated as an advance or drawing of money under §1.731-1(a)(1)(ii) is determined as if no COD income resulting from the reacquisition of the applicable debt instrument is deferred under section 108(i).

(iii) *Multiple section 108(i) elections.*—If a direct partner of an electing partnership has a deferred section 752 amount under paragraph (b)(3)(ii) of this section for the taxable year of a reacquisition, and the partner has a deferred amount with respect to more than one applicable debt instrument from the electing partnership for which a section 108(i) election is made in that taxable year, the partner's deferred section 752 amount with respect to each such applicable debt instrument equals the partner's deferred section 752 amount as determined under paragraph (b)(3)(ii) of this section, multiplied by a ratio, the numerator of which is the partner's deferred amount with respect to such applicable debt instrument, and the denominator of which is the partner's aggregate deferred amounts from the electing partnership for all applicable debt instruments reacquired during the taxable year.

(iv) *Electing partnership's request for information.*—At the request of an electing partnership, each direct partner of the electing partnership that has a deferred amount with respect to such partnership must provide to the electing partnership a written statement containing information requested by the partnership that is necessary to determine the partner's deferred section 752 amount (such as the partner's adjusted basis in the partner's interest in the electing partnership). The written statement must be signed under penalties of perjury and provided to the requesting partnership within 30 days of the date of the request by the electing partnership.

(v) *Examples.*—The following examples illustrate the rules under paragraph (b)(3) of this section:

Example 1. (i) A and B each hold a 50 percent interest in Partnership, a calendar-year partnership. As of January 1, 2009, A and B each have an adjusted basis of $50 in their partnership interests. Partnership has two applicable debt instruments outstanding, debt one of $300 and debt two of $200. A and B share equally in the debt for section 752(b) purposes. On March 1, 2009, debt one is cancelled and Partnership realizes $300 of COD income. On December 1, 2009, debt two is cancelled and Partnership realizes $200 of COD income. The Partnership has no other income or loss items for 2009. A and B are each allocated $150 of COD income from debt one and $100 of COD income from debt two. Partnership makes an election under section 108(i) to defer $225 of the $300 of COD income realized from the reacquisition of debt one, $150 of which is A's deferred amount, and $75 of which is B's deferred amount. Partnership also makes an election under section 108(i) to defer $125 of the $200 of COD income realized from the reacquisition of debt two, $100 of which is A's deferred amount, and $25 of which is B's deferred amount. A has no included amount for either debt. B has an included amount of $75 with respect to debt one and an included amount of $75 with respect to debt two for 2009.

(ii) Under paragraph (b)(3)(ii) of this section, the amount of gain that A would *recognize* under *section 731* as a result of the reacquisitions absent the section 108(i)(6) deferral is $200. Thus, A's deferred section 752 amount with respect to debt one and debt two equals $200 (the lesser of A's aggregate deferred amounts with respect to debt one and debt two of $250, or gain that A would

recognize under section 731 in 2009, as a result of the reacquisitions absent the section 108(i)(6) deferral, of $200). Under paragraph (b)(3)(iii) of this section, $120 of A's $200 deferred section 752 amount relates to debt one ($200 × $150/$250) and $80 relates to debt two ($200 × $100/$250).

(iii) Under paragraph (b)(3)(ii) of this section, the amount of gain that B would recognize under section 731 as a result of the reacquisitions absent the section 108(i)(6) deferral is $50. Thus, B's deferred section 752 amount with respect to debt one and debt two equals $50 (the lesser of B's aggregate deferred amounts with respect to debt one and debt two of $100, or gain that B would recognize under section 731 in 2009, as a result of the reacquisitions absent the section 108(i)(6) deferral, of $50). Under paragraph (b)(3)(iii) of this section, $37.50 of B's $50 deferred section 752 amount relates to debt one ($50 × $75/$100) and $12.50 relates to debt two ($50 × $25/$100).

(iv) A will recognize $50 of deferred COD income ($30 with respect to debt one and $20 with respect to debt two) in each of the five taxable years of the inclusion period, provided there are no earlier acceleration events under paragraph (b)(6) of this section. Under paragraph (b)(3)(i) of this section, A will be treated as receiving a $30 deemed distribution under section 752(b) with respect to debt one and a $20 deemed distribution with respect to debt two in each of the first, second, third, and fourth taxable years of the inclusion period. A will not have any remaining deferred section 752 amounts in the fifth taxable year of the inclusion period.

(v) B will recognize $20 of deferred COD income ($15 with respect to debt one and $5 with respect to debt two) in each of the five taxable years of the inclusion period, provided there are no earlier acceleration events under paragraph (b)(6) of this section. Under paragraph (b)(3)(i) of this section, B will be treated as receiving a $15 deemed distribution under section 752(b) with respect to debt one and a $5 deemed distribution with respect to debt two in the first and second taxable year of the inclusion period, and a $7.50 deemed distribution under section 752(b) with respect to debt one ($10 x $15/$20) and a $2.50 deemed distribution with respect to debt two ($10 × $5/$20) in the third taxable year of the inclusion period. B will not have any remaining deferred section 752 amounts in the fourth and fifth taxable years of the inclusion period.

Example 2. (i) The facts are the same as in *Example 1*, except that Partnership has gross income for the year (including the $500 of COD income) of $700 and other separately stated losses of $500. A's and B's distributive share of each item is 50 percent.

(ii) In determining the amount of gain that A would recognize under section 731 as a result of the reacquisitions absent the section 108(i)(6) deferral, Partnership first increases A's $50 adjusted basis in his interest in Partnership by A's distributive share of Partnership income (other than the deferred amounts relating to debt one and debt two) of $100, and then decreases A's adjusted basis in Partnership by deemed distributions under section 752(b) of $250 and, thereafter, by A's distributive share of Partnership losses of $250, but only to the extent that A's basis is not reduced below zero. Under paragraph (b)(3)(ii) of this section, the amount of gain that A would recognize under section 731 as a result of the reacquisitions absent section 108(i)(6) deferral is $100. Thus, A's deferred section 752 amount with respect to debt one and debt two equals $100 (the lesser of A's aggregate deferred amounts with respect to debt one and debt two of $250, or gain that A would recognize under section 731 as a result of the reacquisitions absent the deferral section 108(i)(6) deferral of $100). Under paragraph (b)(3)(iii) of this section, A's deferred section 752 amount with respect to debt one is $60 ($100 × $150/$250), and A's deferred section 752 amount with respect to debt two is $40 ($100 × $100/$250). A's $250 of Partnership losses are suspended under section 704(d).

(iii) In determining the amount of gain that B would recognize under section 731 as a result of the reacquisitions absent the section 108(i)(6) deferral, Partnership first increases B's $50 adjusted basis in his interest in Partnership by B's distributive share of Partnership income (other than the deferred amounts relating to debt one and debt two) of $250 ($100 other income plus $150 included amount with respect to debt one and debt two), and then decreases B's adjusted basis in Partnership by deemed distributions under section 752(b) of $250 and, thereafter, by B's distributive share of Partnership losses of $250, but only to the extent that B's basis is not reduced below zero. Under paragraph (b)(3)(ii) of this section, B would not recognize any gain under section 731 as a result of the reacquisitions absent the section 108(i)(6) deferral. Thus, B has no deferred section 752 amount with respect to either debt one or debt two. B may deduct his distributive share of Partnership losses to the extent of $50, with the remaining $200 suspended under section 704(d).

(4) *Tiered partnerships.*—(i) *In general.*—If a partnership (upper-tier partnership) is a direct or indirect partner of an electing partnership and directly or indirectly receives an allocation of a COD income amount from the electing partnership, all or a portion of which is deferred under section 108(i), the upper-tier partnership must allo-

cate its COD income amount to its partners that are partners in the upper-tier partnership immediately before the reacquisition in the manner in which the income would be included in the distributive shares of the partners under section 704 and the regulations under section 704, including § 1.704-1(b)(2)(iii), without regard to section 108(i). The upper-tier partnership may determine, in any manner, the portion, if any, of a partner's COD income amount with respect to an applicable debt instrument that is the deferred amount, and the portion, if any, that is the included amount. However, no partner's deferred amount with respect to an applicable debt instrument may exceed that partner's COD income amount with respect to such applicable debt instrument, and the aggregate amount of the partners' COD income amounts and deferred amounts with respect to each applicable debt instrument must equal the upper-tier partnership's COD income amount and deferred amount, respectively, with respect to each such applicable debt instrument.

(ii) *Deferred section 752 amount.*—The computation of a partner's deferred section 752 amount, as described in paragraph (b)(3)(ii) of this section, is calculated only for direct partners of the electing partnership. An upper-tier partnership's deferred section 752 amount with respect to an applicable debt instrument of the electing partnership is allocated only to those partners of the upper-tier partnership that have a deferred amount with respect to that applicable debt instrument, and in proportion to such partners' share of the upper-tier partnership's deferred amount with respect to that applicable debt instrument. A partner's share of the upper-tier partnership's deferred section 752 amount with respect to an applicable debt instrument must not exceed that partner's share of the upper-tier partnership's deferred amount with respect to the applicable debt instrument to which the deferred section 752 amount relates. The deferred section 752 amount of a partner of an upper-tier partnership is treated as a distribution of money by the upper-tier partnership to the partner under section 752(b), at the same time and, to the extent remaining, in the same amount as the partner recognizes the deferred amount with respect to the applicable debt instrument.

(iii) *Examples.*—The following examples illustrate the rules under paragraph (b)(4) of this section:

Example 1. (i) PRS, a calendar-year partnership, has two equal partners, A, an individual, and XYZ, a partnership. As of January 1, 2009, A and XYZ each have an adjusted basis of $50 in their partnership interests. PRS has a $500 applicable debt instrument outstanding. On June 1, 2009, the creditor agrees to cancel the $500 indebtedness. PRS realizes $500 of COD income as a result of the reacquisition. PRS has no other income or loss items for 2009. PRS makes an election under section 108(i) to defer $200 of the $500 of COD income. PRS allocates the $500 of COD income equally between its partners ($250 each). PRS determines that, for each partner, $100 of the COD income amount is the deferred amount, and $150 is the included amount. For 2009, each of A's and XYZ's share of the decrease in PRS's reacquired applicable debt instrument is $250.

(ii) XYZ has two equal partners, individuals X and Y. X and Y share equally in XYZ's liabilities. XYZ allocates the $250 COD income amount from PRS equally between X and Y ($125 each). XYZ determines that X has a deferred amount of $100 and an included amount of $25. All $125 of Y's COD income amount is Y's included amount. For 2009, each of X's and Y's share of XYZ's $250 decrease in liability with respect to the reacquired applicable debt instrument of PRS is $125.

(iii) Under paragraph (b)(3)(ii) of this section, PRS determines that XYZ has a deferred section 752 amount of $50. Therefore, for 2009, of XYZ's $250 share of the decrease in PRS's reacquired applicable debt instrument, $200 is treated as a deemed distribution under section 752(b) and $50 is the deferred section 752 amount.

(iv) Under paragraph (b)(4)(ii) of this section, none of XYZ's $50 deferred section 752 amount is allocated to Y because Y does not have a deferred amount with respect to the reacquired applicable debt interest. XYZ's entire $50 of deferred section 752 amount is allocated to X. Therefore, of X's $125 share of the XYZ's decrease in liability with respect to the reacquired applicable debt instrument of PRS, $75 is treated as a deemed distribution under section 752(b) and $50 is X's deferred section 752 amount. Y's $125 share of XYZ's decrease in liability with respect to the reacquired applicable debt instrument of PRS is treated as a deemed distribution under section 752(b) and none is a deferred section 752 amount.

Example 2. (i) The facts are the same as in *Example 1*, except for the following: XYZ has three partners, X, Y, and Z. The profits and losses of XYZ are shared 25 percent by X, 25 percent by Y, and 50 percent by Z. XYZ allocates its $250 COD income amount from PRS $62.50 to each of X and Y, and $125 to Z. XYZ determines that X has a deferred amount of $50 and an included amount of $12.50, Y has a deferred amount of $0 and an included amount of $62.50, and Z has a deferred amount of $50 and an included amount of $75 with respect to the applicable debt instrument. X's, Y's, and Z's share of XYZ's

decrease in liability with respect to the reacquired applicable debt instrument of PRS is $62.50, $62.50 and $125, respectively.

(ii) Under paragraph (b)(4)(ii) of this section, none of XYZ's $50 deferred section 752 amount is allocated to Y because Y does not have a deferred amount with respect to the reacquired applicable debt instrument. XYZ's $50 deferred section 752 amount is allocated to X and Z in proportion to X's and Z's share of XYZ's deferred amount, or $25 each ($50 × ($50/$100)). Therefore, of X's $62.50 share of XYZ's decrease in liability with respect to the reacquired applicable debt instrument, $37.50 is treated as a deemed distribution under section 752(b) and $25 is X's deferred section 752 amount. All of Y's $62.50 share of XYZ's decrease in liability with respect to the reacquired applicable debt instrument is treated as a deemed distribution under section 752(b). Of Z's $125 share of XYZ's decrease in liability with respect to the reacquired applicable debt instrument, $100 is treated as a deemed distribution under section 752(b) and $25 is Z's deferred section 752 amount.

(5) *S corporation partner.*—(i) *In general.*—If an S corporation partner has a deferred amount with respect to an applicable debt instrument of an electing partnership, such deferred amount is shared pro rata only among those shareholders that are shareholders of the S corporation partner immediately before the reacquisition of the applicable debt instrument.

(ii) *Basis adjustments.*—The adjusted basis of a shareholder's stock in an S corporation partner is not increased under section 1367(a)(1) by the shareholder's share of the S corporation partner's deferred amount in the taxable year of the reacquisition. The adjusted basis of a shareholder's stock in an S corporation partner is not decreased under section 1367(a)(2) by the shareholder's share of the S corporation partner's deferred OID deduction in the taxable year in which the deferred OID accrues. The adjusted basis of a shareholder's stock in an S corporation partner is adjusted under section 1367(a) by the shareholder's share of the S corporation partner's share of the electing partnership's deferred items for the taxable year in which the shareholder takes into account its share of such deferred items under this section.

(iii) *Accumulated adjustments account.*—The accumulated adjustments account (AAA), as defined in section 1368(e)(1), of an S corporation partner that has a deferred amount with respect to an applicable debt instrument of an electing partnership is not increased by its deferred amount in the taxable year of the reacquisition. The AAA of an S corporation partner is not decreased by its share of any deferred OID deduction in the taxable year in which the deferred OID accrues. The AAA of an S corporation partner is adjusted under section 1368(e) by a shareholder's share of S corporation partner's share of the electing partnership's deferred items for the S period (as defined in section 1368(e)(2)) in which the shareholder of the S corporation partner takes into account its share of the deferred items under this section.

(6) *Acceleration of deferred items.*—(i) *Electing partnership-level events.*—(A) *General rules.*—Except as provided in paragraph (b)(6)(iii) of this section, a direct or indirect partner's share of an electing partnership's deferred items is accelerated and must be taken into account by such partner—

(1) In the taxable year in which the electing partnership liquidates;

(2) In the taxable year in which the electing partnership sells, exchanges, transfers (including contributions and distributions), or gifts substantially all of its assets;

(3) In the taxable year in which the electing partnership ceases doing business; or

(4) In the taxable year that includes the day before the day on which the electing partnership files a petition in a title 11 or similar case.

(B) *Substantially all requirement.*—For purposes of this paragraph (b)(6), substantially all of a partnership's assets means assets representing at least 90 percent of the fair market value of the net assets, and at least 70 percent of the fair market value of the gross assets, held by the partnership immediately prior to the sale, exchange, transfer, or gift. For purposes of applying the rule in paragraph (b)(6)(i)(A)(2) of this section a sale, exchange, transfer, or gift by any direct or indirect lower-tier partnership of the electing partnership (lower-tier partnership) of all or part of its assets is not treated as a sale, exchange, transfer, or gift of the assets of any partnership that holds, directly or indirectly, an interest in such lower-tier partnership. However, for purposes of applying the rule in paragraph (b)(6)(i)(A)(2) of this section, a sale, exchange, transfer, or gift of substantially all of the assets of a transferee partnership (as described in paragraph (b)(6)(iii)(A)(1) of this section), or of a lower-tier partnership that received assets of the electing partnership from a transferee partnership or another lower-tier partnership in a transaction governed all or in part by section 721, is treated as a sale, exchange, transfer, or gift by the holder of an interest in such transferee partnership or lower-tier partnership of its entire interest in that transferee partnership or lower-tier partnership.

(ii) *Direct or indirect partner-level events.*—(A) *General rules.*—Except as provided in paragraph (b)(6)(iii) of this section, a direct or indirect partner's share of an electing partnership's deferred items with respect to a separate interest is accelerated and must be taken into account by such partner in the taxable year in which—

(1) The partner dies or liquidates;

(2) The partner sells, exchanges (including redemptions treated as exchanges under section 302), transfers (including contributions and distributions), or gifts (including transfers treated as gifts under section 1041) all or a portion of its separate interest;

(3) The partner's separate interest is redeemed within the meaning of paragraph (b)(6)(ii)(B)(2) of this section; or

(4) The partner abandons its separate interest.

(B) *Meaning of terms; special rules.*—(1) *Partial transfers.*—For purposes of paragraph (b)(6)(ii)(A)(2) of this section, if a partner sells, exchanges (including redemptions treated as exchanges under section 302), transfers (including contributions and distributions), or gifts (including transfers treated as gifts under section 1041) a portion of its separate interest, such partner's share of the electing partnership's deferred items with respect to the separate interest proportionate to the separate interest sold, exchanged, transferred, or gifted is accelerated and must be taken into account by such partner.

(2) *Redemptions.*—For purposes of paragraph (b)(6)(ii)(A)(3) of this section, a partner's separate interest is redeemed if the partner receives a distribution of cash and/or property in complete liquidation of such separate interest.

(3) *S corporation partners.*—In addition to the rules in paragraphs (b)(6)(i) and (ii) of this section, an S corporation partner's share of the electing partnership's deferred items is accelerated and the shareholders of the S corporation partner must take into account their respective shares of the S corporation partner's share of the electing partnership's deferred items in the taxable year in which the S corporation partner's election under section 1362(a) terminates.

(4) *C corporation partners.*—In addition to the rules in paragraphs (b)(6)(i), (ii), and (iii) of this section, the acceleration rules in § 1.108(i)-1(b) and the earnings and profits rules in § 1.108(i)-1(d) apply to partners that are electing corporations.

(iii) *Events not constituting acceleration.*—Notwithstanding the rules in paragraphs (b)(6)(i) and (ii) of this section, a direct or indirect partner's share of an electing partnership's deferred items with respect to a separate interest is not accelerated by any of the events described in this paragraph (b)(6)(iii).

(A) *Section 721 contributions.*—(1) *Electing partnership contributions.*—A direct or indirect partner's share of an electing partnership's deferred items is not accelerated if the electing partnership contributes all or a portion of its assets in a transaction governed all or in part by section 721(a) to another partnership (transferee partnership) in exchange for an interest in the transferee partnership provided that the electing partnership does not terminate under section 708(b)(1)(A) or transfer its assets and liabilities in a transaction described in section 708(b)(2)(A) or section 708(b)(2)(B). See paragraph (b)(6)(iii)(D) of this section for transactions governed by section 708(b)(2)(A). Notwithstanding the rules in this paragraph (b)(6)(iii)(A)(1), the rules in paragraphs (b)(6)(i)(A) and (b)(6)(ii)(A) of this section apply to any part of the transaction to which section 721(a) does not apply.

(2) *Partner contributions.*—A direct or indirect partner's share of an electing partnership's deferred items with respect to a separate interest is not accelerated if the holder of such interest (contributing partner) contributes its entire separate interest (contributed separate interest) in a transaction governed all or in part by section 721(a) to another partnership (transferee partnership) in exchange for an interest in the transferee partnership provided that the partnership in which the separate interest is held does not terminate under section 708(b)(1)(A) or transfer its assets and liabilities in a transaction described in section 708(b)(2)(A) or section 708(b)(2)(B). See paragraph (b)(6)(iii)(D) of this section for transactions governed by section 708(b)(2)(A). The transferee partnership becomes subject to section 108(i), including all reporting requirements under this section, with respect to the contributing partner's share of the electing partnership's deferred items associated with the contributed separate interest. The transferee partnership must allocate and report the share of the electing partnership's deferred items that is associated with the contributed separate interest to the contributing partner to the same extent that such share of the electing partnership's deferred

items would have been allocated and reported to the contributing partner in the absence of such contribution. Notwithstanding the rules in this paragraph (b)(6)(iii)(A)(2), the rules in paragraph (b)(6)(ii)(A) of this section apply to any part of the transaction to which section 721(a) does not apply.

(B) *Section 1031 exchanges.*—A direct or indirect partner's share of the electing partnership's deferred items is not accelerated if the electing partnership transfers property held for productive use in a trade or business or for investment in exchange for property of like kind which is to be held either for productive use in a trade or business or for investment in a transaction to which section 1031(a)(1) applies. Notwithstanding the rules in this paragraph (b)(6)(iii)(B), to the extent the electing partnership receives money or other property which does not meet the requirements of section 1031(a) (boot) in the exchange, a proportionate amount of the property transferred by the electing partnership equal to the proportion of the boot to the total consideration received in the exchange shall be treated as sold for purposes of paragraph (b)(6)(i)(A)(2) of this section.

(C) *Section 708(b)(1)(B) terminations.*—A direct or indirect partner's share of the deferred items of an electing partnership with respect to a separate interest is not accelerated if the electing partnership or a partnership that is a direct or indirect partner of the electing partnership terminates under section 708(b)(1)(B). Notwithstanding the rules in this paragraph (b)(6)(iii)(C), the rules in paragraph (b)(6)(ii)(A) of this section apply to the event that causes the termination under section 708(b)(1)(B) to the extent not otherwise excepted under paragraph (b)(6)(iii) of this section.

(D) *Section 708(b)(2)(A) mergers or consolidations.*—A direct or indirect partner's share of the deferred items of an electing partnership with respect to a separate interest is not accelerated if the partnership in which the separate interest is held (the merger transaction partnership) merges into or consolidates with another partnership in a transaction to which section 708(b)(2)(A) applies. The resulting partnership or new partnership, as determined under § 1.708-1(c)(1), becomes subject to section 108(i), including all reporting requirements under this section, to the same extent that the merger transaction partnership was so subject prior to the transaction, and must allocate and report any merger transaction partnership's deferred items to the same extent and to the same partners that the merger transaction partnership allocated and reported such items prior to such transaction. Notwithstanding the rules in this paragraph (b)(6)(iii)(D), the rules in paragraphs (b)(6)(i)(A)(2) and (b)(6)(ii)(A)(2) of this section apply to that portion of the transaction that is treated as a sale, and the rules of (b)(6)(ii)(A)(3) apply if, as part of the transaction, the partner's separate interest is redeemed and the partner does not receive an interest in the resulting partnership with respect to such separate interest.

(E) *Certain distributions of separate interests.*—If a partnership (upper-tier partnership) that is a direct or indirect partner of an electing partnership distributes its entire separate interest (distributed separate interest) to one or more of its partners (distributee partners) that have a share of the electing partnership's deferred items from upper-tier partnership with respect to the distributed separate interest, the distributee partners' shares of the electing partnership's deferred items with respect to such distributed separate interest are not accelerated. The partnership, the separate interest in which was distributed, must allocate and report the share of the electing partnership's deferred items associated with the distributed separate interest only to such distributee partners that had a share of the electing partnership's deferred items from the upper-tier partnership with respect to the distributed separate interest prior to the distribution. This paragraph (b)(6)(iii)(E) does not apply if the electing partnership terminates under section 708(b)(1)(A).

(F) *Section 381 transactions.*—A C corporation partner's share of an electing partnership's deferred items is not accelerated if, as part of a transaction described in paragraph (b)(6)(ii)(A) of this section, the assets of the C corporation partner are acquired by another C corporation (acquiring C corporation) in a transaction that is treated, under § 1.108(i)-1(b)(2)(ii)(B), as a transaction to which section 381(a) applies. An S corporation partner's share of an electing partnership's deferred items is not accelerated if, as part of a transaction described in paragraph (b)(6)(ii)(A) of this section, the assets of the S corporation partner are acquired by another S corporation (acquiring S corporation) in a transaction to which section 381(a) applies. In such cases, the acquiring C corporation or acquiring S corporation, as the case may be, succeeds to the C corporation partner's or the S corporation partner's remaining share of the electing partnership's deferred items and becomes subject to section 108(i), including all reporting requirements under this section, as if the acquiring C corporation or acquiring S corporation were the C corporation partner or the S corporation partner, respectively. The acquiring S corporation must allocate and report the S corporation partner's deferred items to the same extent as the S corporation partner would have been required to allocate and report those deferred items, and only to those shareholders of the S corporation partner who had a share of the S corporation partner's deferred items from the electing partnership prior to the transaction. This paragraph (b)(6)(iii)(F) does not apply if the electing partnership terminates under section 708(b)(1)(A).

(G) *Intercompany transfers.*—A C corporation partner's share of an electing partnership's deferred items is not accelerated if, as part of a transaction described in paragraph (b)(6)(ii)(A) of this section, the C corporation partner transfers its entire separate interest in an intercompany transaction, as described in §1.1502-13(b)(1)(i), and the electing partnership does not terminate under section 708(b)(1)(A) as a result of the intercompany transaction.

(H) *Retirement of a debt instrument.*—See §1.108(i)-3(c)(1) for rules regarding the retirement of a debt instrument that is subject to section 108(i).

(I) *Other non-acceleration events.*—A direct or indirect partner's share of an electing partnership's deferred items is not accelerated with respect to any transaction if the Commissioner makes a determination by published guidance that such transaction is not an acceleration event under the rules of this paragraph (b)(6).

(iv) *Related partnerships.*—A direct or indirect partner's share of a related partnership's deferred OID deduction (as determined in paragraph (d)(2) of this section) that has not previously been taken into account is accelerated and taken into account by the direct or indirect partner in the taxable year in which, and to the extent that, the deferred COD income to which the related partnership's deferred OID deduction relates is taken into account by the electing entity or its owners.

(v) *Examples.*—The following examples illustrate the rules under this paragraph (b)(6):

Example 1. Meaning of "separate interest." (i) Electing partnership (EP) has three partners, MT1, MT2, and UT, each of which is a partnership. The partners of MT1 are X and UT. The partners of MT2 are Y, UT, and B. The partners of UT are A, B, and C. In addition to their interests in the partnerships noted, MT1, MT2, and UT own other assets.

(ii) Within the meaning of paragraph (a)(29) of §1.108(i)-0, A and C each hold one separate interest (their interests in UT), B holds two separate interests (its interests in UT and MT2), UT holds three separate interests (its interests in MT1, MT2, and EP), MT1 and MT2 each hold one separate interest (their interests in EP), and X and Y each hold one separate interest (their interests in MT1 and MT2, respectively) with respect to EP.

Example 2. Distributions of separate interests in an electing partnership. (i) The facts are the same as in *Example 1*, except that A, as a direct partner of UT, has a share of EP's deferred items with respect to UT's interests in MT1 and EP. A does not have a share of EP's deferred items with respect to UT's interest in MT2. B, as a direct partner of UT, has a share of EP's deferred items with respect to UT's interest in MT1 and MT2, but not with respect to UT's interest in EP. B also has a share of EP's deferred items with respect to its separate interest in MT2. C does not have any share of EP's deferred items with respect to UT's interest in MT1, MT2, or EP.

(ii) UT distributes 40 percent of its separate interest in MT1 to A in redemption of A's interest in UT. Under paragraphs (b)(6)(ii)(A)(2) and (b)(6)(ii)(B)(1) of this section, a portion of UT's interest in MT1 has been transferred and a corresponding portion (40 percent) of UT's share of EP's deferred items from MT1 is accelerated. Thus, 40 percent of A's and B's share of EP's deferred items from UT with respect to UT's interest in MT1 is accelerated. Further, because A's interest in UT is redeemed within the meaning of paragraph (b)(6)(ii)(B)(2) of this section, all of A's shares of EP's deferred items from UT are accelerated under paragraph (b)(6)(ii)(A)(3) of this section. UT continues to allocate and report to B its remaining share of EP's deferred items from its separate interest in MT1 that was not distributed to A.

(iii) UT distributes its entire separate interest in MT1 to B (other than in redemption of B's interest in UT). Under paragraph (b)(6)(ii)(A)(2) of this section, UT's share of EP's deferred items from MT1 would be accelerated. However, because UT distributes its entire separate interest in MT1 to B, B's share of EP's deferred items from UT with respect to UT's separate interest in MT1 is not accelerated under paragraph (b)(6)(iii)(E) of this section. MT1 allocates and reports to B B's share of EP's deferred items from UT's separate interest in MT1 that was distributed to B.

(iv) UT distributes its entire separate interest in MT1 to A and B (other than in redemption of their interests in UT). Under paragraph (b)(6)(iii)(E) of this section, none of A's or B's shares of EP's deferred items from UT with respect to UT's separate interest in MT1

is accelerated, and MT1 allocates and reports to A and B their respective share of EP's deferred items from UT's separate interest in MT1 that was distributed to A and B.

Example 3. Partial sale of interest by an indirect partner. (i) Individual A holds a 50 percent partnership interest in UTP, a partnership that holds a 50 percent interest in EP, a partnership that makes an election to defer COD income under section 108(i). A's share of UTP's deferred amount with respect to EP's election under section 108(i) is $100. During a taxable year within the deferral period, A sells 25 percent of his partnership interest in UTP to an unrelated third party.

(ii) Under paragraphs (b)(6)(ii)(A)(2) and (b)(6)(ii)(B)(1) of this section, 25 percent of A's $100 deferred amount is accelerated as a result of A's partial sale of his interest in UTP. Thus, A must recognize $25 of his deferred amount in the taxable year of the sale. A's remaining deferred amount is $75.

Example 4. Section 708(b)(1)(B) termination of electing partnership. (i) A and B are equal partners in partnership AB. On January 1, 2009, AB reacquires an applicable debt instrument and makes an election under section 108(i) to defer $400 of COD income. A and B each have a deferred amount with respect to the applicable debt instrument of $200. On January 1, 2010, A sells its entire 50 percent interest in AB to C in a transfer that terminates the partnership under section 708(b)(1)(B).

(ii) Under paragraph (b)(6)(iii)(C) of this section, the technical termination of AB under section 708(b)(1)(B) does not cause A's or B's shares of AB's deferred items to be accelerated. However, A's $200 deferred amount is accelerated under paragraph (b)(6)(ii)(A)(2) of this section as a result of the sale.

Example 5. Section 708(b)(2)(A) mergers. (i) A, B, and C are equal partners in partnership X, which has made an election under section 108(i) to defer $150 of COD income. The fair market value of each interest in partnership X is $100. A, B, and C each has a deferred amount of $50 with respect to partnership X's election under section 108(i). E, F, and G are partners in partnership Y. Partnership X and partnership Y merge in a taxable year during the deferral period of partnership X's election under section 108(i). Under section 708(b)(2)(A), the resulting partnership is considered a continuation of partnership Y and partnership X is considered terminated. Under state law, partnerships X and Y undertake the assets-over form of §1.708-1(c)(3)(i) to accomplish the merger. C does not want to become a partner in partnership Y, and partnership X does not have the resources to redeem C's interest before the merger. C, partnership X, and partnership Y enter into a merger agreement that satisfies the requirements of §1.708-1(c)(4) and specifies that partnership Y will purchase C's interest in partnership X for $100 before the merger, and as part of the agreement, C consents to treat the transaction in a manner that is consistent with the agreement. As part of the merger, partnership X receives from partnership Y $100 (which will be distributed to C immediately before the merger), $100 (which will be distributed equally to A and B ($50 each)), and interests in partnership Y with a value of $100 (which will be distributed equally to A and B) in exchange for partnership X's assets and liabilities.

(ii) Under the general rule of paragraph (b)(6)(iii)(D) of this section, and except as provided below, the deferred items of partnership X are not accelerated as a result of the merger with partnership Y. Partnership Y, the resulting partnership that is considered the continuation of partnership X, becomes subject to section 108(i), including all reporting requirements under section 108(i), to the same extent that partnership X was subject to such rules. Under paragraph (b)(6)(iii)(D) of this section, partnership Y must allocate and report partnership X's deferred items to A and B in the same manner as partnership X had prior to the merger transaction.

(iii) Under §1.708-1(c)(4), C is treated as selling its interest in partnership X immediately before the merger. As a result, C's $50 deferred amount is accelerated under paragraph (b)(6)(ii)(A)(2) of this section.

(iv) Under section 707(a)(2)(B), partnership X is deemed to have sold a portion of its assets to partnership Y. Because partnership X is not treated as selling substantially all of its assets under paragraph (b)(6)(i)(B) of this section, A's and B's deferred amounts are not accelerated under paragraph (b)(6)(i)(A)(2) of this section.

(v) Because A's and B's interests in partnership X are redeemed within the meaning of paragraph (b)(6)(ii)(B)(2) of this section, all of their shares of partnership X's deferred items would be accelerated under paragraph (b)(6)(ii)(A)(3). However, because they receive an interest in partnership Y in the merger, none of A's and B's share of partnership X's deferred items is accelerated.

(7) *Withholding under section 1446.*—See section 1446 regarding withholding by a partnership on a foreign partner's share of income effectively connected with a U.S. trade or business.

(c) *Specific rules applicable to S corporations.*—(1) *Deferred COD income.*—An electing S corporation's COD income deferred under section 108(i) (an S corporation's deferred COD income) is shared pro rata among those shareholders that are shareholders of the electing S corporation immediately before the reacquisition of the applicable debt instrument. Any COD income deferred under section 108(i) is taken into account under section 1366(a) by those shareholders in the inclusion period, or earlier upon the occurrence of an acceleration event described in paragraph (c)(3) of this section.

(2) *Basis adjustments and accumulated adjustments account.*— (i) *Basis adjustments.*—The adjusted basis of a shareholder's stock in an electing S corporation is not increased under section 1367(a)(1) by the shareholder's share of the S corporation's deferred COD income in the taxable year of the reacquisition. The adjusted basis of a shareholder's stock in an electing S corporation or a related S corporation is not decreased under section 1367(a)(2) by the shareholder's share of the S corporation's deferred OID deduction in the taxable year in which the deferred OID accrues. The adjusted basis of a shareholder's stock in an electing S corporation or a related S corporation is adjusted under section 1367(a) by the shareholder's share of the S corporation's deferred items for the taxable year in which the shareholder takes into account its share of the deferred items under this section.

(ii) *Accumulated adjustments account.*—The AAA of an electing S corporation is not increased by the S corporation's deferred COD income in the taxable year of a reacquisition. The AAA of an electing S corporation or a related S corporation is not decreased by the S corporation's deferred OID deduction in the taxable year in which the deferred OID accrues. The AAA of an electing S corporation or a related S corporation is adjusted under section 1368(e) by a shareholder's share of the S corporation's deferred items for the S period (as defined in section 1368(e)(2)) in which a shareholder of the S corporation takes into account its share of the deferred items under this section.

(3) *Acceleration of deferred items.*—(i) *Electing S corporation-level events.*—(A) *General rules.*—Except as provided in paragraph (c)(3)(iii) of this section, a shareholder's share of an electing S corporation's deferred items is accelerated and must be taken into account by such shareholder—

(1) In the taxable year in which the electing S corporation liquidates;

(2) In the taxable year in which the electing S corporation sells, exchanges, transfers (including contributions and distributions), or gifts substantially all of its assets;

(3) In the taxable year in which the electing S corporation ceases doing business;

(4) In the taxable year in which the electing S corporation's election under section 1362(a) terminates; or

(5) In the taxable year that includes the day before the day on which the electing S corporation files a petition in a title 11 or similar case.

(B) *Substantially all requirement.*—For purposes of this paragraph (c)(3), substantially all of an electing S corporation's or partnership's assets means assets representing at least 90 percent of the fair market value of the net assets, and at least 70 percent of the fair market value of the gross assets, held by the S corporation or partnership immediately prior to the sale, exchange, transfer, or gift. For purposes of applying the rule in paragraph (c)(3)(i)(A)(2) of this section, a sale, exchange, transfer, or gift by any direct or indirect lower-tier partnership of the electing S corporation (lower-tier partnership) of all or part of its assets is not treated as a sale, exchange, transfer, or gift of the assets of any person that holds, directly or indirectly, an interest in such lower-tier partnership. However, for purposes of applying the rule in paragraph (c)(3)(i)(A)(2) of this section, a sale, exchange, transfer, or gift of substantially all of the assets of a transferee partnership (as described in paragraph (c)(3)(iii)(A) of this section), or of a lower-tier partnership that received assets of the electing S corporation from a transferee partnership of the electing S corporation or another lower-tier partnership in a transaction governed all or in part by section 721, is treated as a sale, exchange, transfer, or gift by the holder of an interest in such transferee partnership or lower-tier partnership of its entire interest in that transferee partnership or lower-tier partnership.

(ii) *Shareholder events.*—(A) *General rules.*—Except as provided in paragraph (c)(3)(iii) of this section, a shareholder's share of an electing S corporation's deferred items is accelerated and must be taken into account by such shareholder in the taxable year in which—

(1) The shareholder dies;

(2) The shareholder sells, exchanges (including redemptions treated as exchanges under section 302), transfers (including contributions and distributions), or gifts (including transfers treated

as gifts under section 1041) all or a portion of its interest in the electing S corporation; or

(3) The shareholder abandons its interest in the electing S corporation.

(B) *Partial transfers.*—For purposes of paragraph (c)(3)(ii)(A)(2) of this section, if a shareholder of an electing S corporation sells, exchanges (including redemptions treated as exchanges under section 302), transfers (including contributions or distributions), or gifts (including transfers treated as gifts under section 1041) a portion of its interest in the electing S corporation, such shareholder's share of the electing S corporation's deferred items proportionate to the interest that was sold, exchanged, transferred, or gifted is accelerated and must be taken into account by such shareholder.

(iii) *Events not constituting acceleration.*—Notwithstanding the rules in paragraphs (c)(3)(i) and (ii) of this section, a shareholder's share of an electing S corporation's deferred items is not accelerated by any of the events described in this paragraph (c)(3)(iii).

(A) *Electing S corporation's contributions.*—A shareholder's share of an electing S corporation's deferred items is not accelerated if the electing S corporation contributes all or a portion of its assets in a transaction governed all or in part by section 721(a) to a partnership (transferee partnership) in exchange for an interest in the transferee partnership. Notwithstanding the rules in this paragraph (c)(3)(iii)(A), the rules in paragraph (c)(3)(i)(A) of this section apply to any part of the transaction to which section 721(a) does not apply.

(B) *Section 1031 exchanges.*—A shareholder's share of an electing S corporation's deferred items is not accelerated if the electing S corporation transfers property held for productive use in a trade or business or for investment in exchange for property of like kind which is to be held either for productive use in a trade or business or for investment in a transaction to which section 1031(a)(1) applies. Notwithstanding the rules in this paragraph (c)(3)(iii)(B), to the extent the electing S corporation receives money or other property which does not meet the requirements of section 1031(a) (boot) in the exchange, a proportionate amount of the property transferred by the electing S corporation equal to the proportion of the boot to the total consideration received in the exchange shall be treated as sold for purposes of paragraph (c)(3)(i)(A)(2) of this section.

(C) *Section 381 transactions.*—A shareholder's share of an electing S corporation's deferred items is not accelerated if, as part of a transaction described in paragraph (c)(3)(i)(A) of this section, the electing S corporation's assets are acquired by another S corporation (acquiring S corporation) in a transaction to which section 381(a) applies. In such a case, the acquiring S corporation succeeds to the electing S corporation's remaining deferred items and becomes subject to section 108(i), including all reporting requirements under this section, as if the acquiring S corporation were the electing S corporation. The acquiring S corporation must allocate and report the electing S corporation's deferred items to the same extent that the electing S corporation would have been required to allocate and report those deferred items, and only to those shareholders who had a share of the electing S corporation's deferred items prior to the transaction.

(D) *Retirement of a debt instrument.*—See § 1.108(i)-3(c)(1) for rules regarding the retirement of a debt instrument that is subject to section 108(i).

(E) *Other non-acceleration events.*—A shareholder's share of an electing S corporation's deferred items is not accelerated with respect to any transaction if the Commissioner makes a determination by published guidance that such transaction is not an acceleration event under the rules of this paragraph (c)(3).

(iv) *Related S corporations.*—A shareholder's share of a related S corporation's deferred OID deduction (as determined in paragraph (d)(2) of this section) that has not previously been taken into account is accelerated and taken into account by the shareholder in the taxable year in which, and to the extent that, deferred COD income to which the related S corporation's deferred OID deduction relates is taken into account by the electing entity or its owners.

(d) *General rules applicable to partnerships and S corporations.*— (1) *Applicable debt instrument (trade or business requirement).*—The determination of whether a debt instrument issued by a partnership or an S corporation is treated as a debt instrument issued in connection with the conduct of a trade or business by the partnership or S corporation for purposes of this section is based on all the facts and circumstances. However, a debt instrument issued by a partnership or an S corporation shall be treated as an applicable debt instrument for purposes of this section if the electing partnership or electing S corporation can establish that—

(i) The gross fair market value of the trade or business assets of the partnership or S corporation that issued the debt instrument represented at least 80 percent of the gross fair market value of that partnership's or S corporation's total assets on the date of issuance;

(ii) The trade or business expenditures of the partnership or S corporation that issued the debt instrument represented at least 80 percent of the partnership's or S corporation's total expenditures for the taxable year of issuance;

(iii) At least 95 percent of interest paid or accrued on the debt instrument issued by the partnership or S corporation was allocated to one or more trade or business expenditures under §1.163-8T for the taxable year of issuance;

(iv) At least 95 percent of the proceeds from the debt instrument issued by the partnership or S corporation were used by the partnership or S corporation to acquire one or more trades or businesses within six months from the date of issuance; or

(v) The partnership or S corporation issued the debt instrument to a seller of a trade or business to acquire the trade or business.

(2) *Deferral of OID at entity level.*—(i) *In general.*—For each taxable year during the deferral period, an issuing entity determines the amount of its deferred OID deduction with respect to a debt instrument, if any. An issuing entity's deferred OID deduction for a taxable year is the lesser of:

(A) The OID that accrues in a current taxable year during the deferral period with respect to the debt instrument (less any of such OID that is allowed as a deduction in the current taxable year as a result of an acceleration event), or

(B) The excess, if any, of the electing entity's deferred COD income (less the aggregate amount of such deferred COD income that has been included in income in the current taxable year and any previous taxable year during the deferral period) over the aggregate amount of OID that accrued in previous taxable years during the deferral period with respect to the debt instrument (less the aggregate amount of such OID that has been allowed as a deduction in the current taxable year and any previous taxable year during the deferral period).

(ii) *Excess deferred OID deduction.*—If, as a result of an acceleration event during a taxable year in the deferral period, an issuing entity's aggregate deferred OID deduction for previous taxable years with respect to a debt instrument (less the aggregate amount of such deferred OID deduction that has been allowed as a deduction in a previous taxable year during the deferral period) exceeds the amount of the electing entity's deferred COD income (less the aggregate amount of such deferred COD income that has been included in income in the current taxable year and any previous taxable year during the deferral period), the excess deferred OID deduction shall be allowed as a deduction in the taxable year in which the acceleration event occurs.

(iii) *Examples.*—The following examples illustrate the rules under paragraph (d)(2) of this section:

Example 1. Partner joins partnership during deferral period. (i) A and B each hold a 50 percent interest in AB partnership, a calendar-year partnership. On January 1, 2009, AB partnership issues a new debt instrument with OID and uses all of the proceeds to reacquire an outstanding applicable debt instrument of AB partnership, realizing $100 of COD income, and makes an election under section 108(i) to defer $50 of the COD income. During the deferral period, a total of $150 of OID accrues on the new debt instrument issued as part of the reacquisition. A and B each have a deferred amount of $25 with respect to the applicable debt instrument reacquired by AB partnership. For 2009, $28 of OID accrues on the new debt instrument and A and B are each allocated $14 of accrued OID with respect to the new debt instrument. On January 1, 2010, C contributes cash to AB partnership in exchange for a 1/3 partnership interest. For 2010, $29 of OID accrues on the new debt instrument, and A, B, and C are each allocated $9.67 of accrued OID.

(ii) Under paragraph (d)(2) of this section, AB partnership's deferred OID deduction for 2009 is the lesser of: $28 of OID that accrues on the new debt instrument in 2009, or the excess of AB partnership's deferred COD income of $50 over the aggregate amount of OID that accrued on the debt instrument in previous taxable years during the deferral period of $0, or $50. Thus, all $28 of the OID that accrues on the debt instrument in 2009 is deferred under section 108(i).

(iii) Under paragraph (d)(2) of this section, AB partnership's deferred OID deduction for 2010 is the lesser of: $29 of OID that accrues on the new debt instrument in 2010, or the excess of AB partnership's deferred COD income of $50 over the aggregate amount of OID that accrued on the debt instrument in previous taxable years during the deferral period of $28, or $22. Thus, $22 of the $29 of OID that accrues in 2010 is deferred under section 108(i). A, B, and C will each defer $7.33 of the $9.67 of accrued OID that was allocated to each of them.

Example 2. Acceleration of deferred items during deferral period. (i) On January 1, 2009, ABC partnership, a calendar-year partnership with three partners, issues a new debt instrument with OID and uses all of the proceeds to reacquire an outstanding applicable debt instrument of ABC partnership. ABC partnership realizes $150 of COD income and makes an election under section 108(i) to defer the $150 of COD income. A's deferred amount with respect to the applicable debt instrument is $75, while B and C each have a deferred amount of $37.50. In 2009, $28 of OID accrues on the new debt instrument and is allocated $7.00 to A and $10.50 to each of B and C. In 2010, $29 of OID accrues on the new debt instrument and is allocated $7.25 to A and $10.87 to each of B and C. In 2011, $30 of OID accrues on the new debt instrument and is allocated $7.50 to A and $11.25 to each of B and C. In 2012, $31 of OID accrues on the new debt instrument and is allocated $7.75 to A and $11.62 to each of B and C. On December 31, 2012, A's entire share of ABC partnership's deferred items is accelerated under paragraph (b)(6) of this section. For 2012, A includes $75 of COD income in income and is allowed a deduction of $21.75 for A's share of ABC partnership's deferred OID deduction for taxable years 2009 through 2011, and a deduction of $7.75 for A's share of ABC partnership's OID that accrues on the debt instrument in 2012.

(ii) Under paragraph (d)(2) of this section, ABC partnership's deferred OID deduction for 2012 is the lesser of: $23.25 ($31 of OID that accrues on the new debt instrument in 2012 less $7.75 of this OID that is allowed as a deduction to A in 2012) or $9.75 (the excess of $75 (ABC partnership's deferred COD income of $150 less A's share of ABC partnership's deferred COD income that is included in A's income for 2012 of $75) over $65.25 (the aggregate amount of OID that accrued in previous taxable years of $87 less the aggregate amount of such OID that has been allowed as a deduction by A in 2012 of $21.75)). Thus, of the $31 of OID that accrues in 2012, $9.75 is deferred under section 108(i).

(3) *Effect of an election under section 108(i) on recapture amounts under section 465(e).*—(i) *In general.*—To the extent that a decrease in a partner's or shareholder's amount at risk (as defined in section 465) in an activity as a result of a reacquisition of an applicable debt instrument would cause a partner with a deferred amount or a shareholder with a share of the S corporation's deferred COD income to have income under section 465(e) in the taxable year of the reacquisition, such decrease (not to exceed the partner's deferred amount or the shareholder's share of the S corporation's deferred COD income with respect to that applicable debt instrument) (deferred section 465 amount) shall not be taken into account for purposes of determining the partner's or shareholder's amount at risk in an activity under section 465 as of the close of the taxable year of the reacquisition. A partner's or shareholder's deferred section 465 amount is treated as a decrease in the partner's or shareholder's amount at risk in an activity at the same time, and to the extent remaining in the same amount, as the partner recognizes its deferred amount or the S corporation shareholder recognizes its share of the S corporation's deferred COD income.

(ii) *Example.*—The following example illustrates the rules in paragraph (d)(3) of this section:

Example. (i) PRS is a calendar-year partnership with two equal partners, individuals A and B. PRS is engaged in an activity described in section 465(c) (Activity). PRS has a $500 recourse applicable debt instrument outstanding. Each partner's amount at risk on January 1, 2009 is $50. On June 1, 2009, the creditor agrees to cancel the $500 indebtedness. PRS realizes $500 of COD income as a result of the reacquisition. The partners' share of the liabilities of PRS decreases by $500 under section 752(b), and each partner's amount at risk is decreased by $250. Other than the $500 of COD income, PRS's income and expenses for 2009 are equal. PRS makes an election under section 108(i) to defer $200 of the $500 COD income realized in connection with the reacquisition. PRS allocates the $500 of COD income equally between its partners, A and B. A and B each have a COD income amount of $250 with respect to the applicable debt instrument. PRS determines that for both partners A and B, $100 of the $250 COD income amount is the deferred amount, and $150 is the included amount. Beginning in each taxable year 2014 through 2018, A and B each include $20 of the deferred amount in gross income.

(ii) Under paragraph (d)(3)(i) of this section, $50 of the $250 decrease in A's and B's amount at risk in Activity is the deferred section 465 amount for each of A and B and is not taken into account for purposes of determining A's and B's amount at risk in Activity at the close of 2009. In taxable year 2014, A's and B's amount at risk in Activity is decreased by $20 (deferred section 465 amount that equals the deferred amount included in A's and B's gross income in 2014). In taxable year 2015, A's and B's amount at risk in Activity is decreased by $20 for the deferred section 465 amount that equals the deferred amount included in A's and B's gross income in 2015. In taxable year 2016, A's and B's amount at risk in Activity is decreased by $10 (the remaining amount of the deferred section 465 amount).

(e) *Election procedures and reporting requirements.*—(1) *Partnerships.*—(i) *In general.*—A partnership makes an election under section 108(i) by following procedures outlined in guidance and applicable forms and instructions issued by the Commissioner. An electing partnership (or its successor) must provide to its partners certain information as required by guidance and applicable forms and instructions issued by the Commissioner.

(ii) *Tiered passthrough entities.*—A partnership that is a direct or indirect partner of an electing partnership (or its successor) or a related partnership or an S corporation partner must provide to its partners or shareholders, as the case may be, certain information as required by guidance and applicable forms and instructions issued by the Commissioner.

(iii) *Related partnerships.*—A related partnership must provide to its partners certain information as required by guidance and applicable forms and instructions issued by the Commissioner.

(2) *S corporations.*—(i) *In general.*—An S corporation makes an election under section 108(i) by following procedures outlined in guidance and applicable forms and instructions issued by the Commissioner. An electing S corporation (or its successor) must provide to its shareholders certain information as required by guidance and applicable forms and instructions issued by the Commissioner.

(ii) *Related S corporations.*—A related S corporation must provide to its shareholders certain information as required by guidance and applicable forms and instructions issued by the Commissioner.

(f) *Effective/applicability dates.*—For the applicability dates of this section, see § 1.108(i)-0(b). [Reg. § 1.108(i)-2.]

☐ [T.D. 9623, 7-2-2013 (corrected 8-13-2013).]

[Reg. § 1.108(i)-3]

§ 1.108(i)-3. Rules for the deduction of OID.—(a) *Deemed debt-for-debt exchanges.*—(1) *In general.*—For purposes of section 108(i)(2) (relating to deferred OID deductions that arise in certain debt-for-debt exchanges involving the reacquisition of an applicable debt instrument), if the proceeds of any debt instrument are used directly or indirectly by the issuer or a person related to the issuer (within the meaning of section 108(i)(5)(A)) to reacquire an applicable debt instrument, the debt instrument shall be treated as issued for the applicable debt instrument being reacquired. Therefore, section 108(i)(2) may apply, for example, to a debt instrument issued by a corporation for cash in which some or all of the proceeds are used directly or indirectly by the corporation's related subsidiary in the reacquisition of the subsidiary's applicable debt instrument.

(2) *Directly or indirectly.*—Whether the proceeds of an issuance of a debt instrument are used directly or indirectly to reacquire an applicable debt instrument depends upon all of the facts and circumstances surrounding the issuance and the reacquisition. The proceeds of an issuance of a debt instrument will be treated as being used indirectly to reacquire an applicable debt instrument if—

(i) At the time of the issuance of the debt instrument, the issuer of the debt instrument anticipated that an applicable debt instrument of the issuer or a person related to the issuer would be reacquired by the issuer, and the debt instrument would not have been issued if the issuer had not so anticipated such reacquisition;

(ii) At the time of the issuance of the debt instrument, the issuer of the debt instrument or a person related to the issuer anticipated that an applicable debt instrument would be reacquired by a related person and the related person receives cash or property that it would not have received unless the reacquisition had been so anticipated; or

(iii) At the time of the reacquisition, the issuer or a person related to the issuer foresaw or reasonably should have foreseen that the issuer or a person related to the issuer would be required to issue a debt instrument, which it would not have otherwise been required to issue if the reacquisition had not occurred, in order to meet its future economic needs.

(b) *Proportional rule for accruals of OID.*—For purposes of section 108(i)(2), if only a portion of the proceeds from the issuance of a debt instrument are used directly or indirectly to reacquire an applicable debt instrument, the rules of section 108(i)(2)(A) will apply to the portion of OID on the debt instrument that is equal to the portion of the proceeds from such instrument used to reacquire the outstanding applicable debt instrument. Except as provided in the last sentence of section 108(i)(2)(A), the amount of deferred OID deduction that is subject to section 108(i)(2)(A) for a taxable year is equal to the product of the amount of OID that accrues in the taxable year under section 1272 or section 1275 (and the regulations under those sec-

tions), whichever section is applicable, and a fraction, the numerator of which is the portion of the total proceeds from the issuance of the debt instrument used directly or indirectly to reacquire the applicable debt instrument and the denominator of which is the total proceeds from the issuance of the debt instrument.

(c) *No acceleration.*—(1) *Retirement.*—Retirement of a debt instrument subject to section 108(i)(2) does not accelerate deferred OID deductions.

(2) *Cross-reference.*—See § 1.108(i)-1 and § 1.108(i)-2 for rules relating to the acceleration of deferred OID deductions.

(d) *Examples.*—The application of this section is illustrated by the following examples. Unless otherwise stated, all taxpayers in the following examples are calendar-year taxpayers, and P and S each file separate returns:

Example 1. (i) *Facts.* P, a domestic corporation, owns all of the stock of S, a domestic corporation. S has a debt instrument outstanding that has an adjusted issue price of $100,000. On January 1, 2010, P issues for $160,000 a four-year debt instrument that has an issue price of $160,000 and a stated redemption price at maturity of $200,000, resulting in $40,000 of OID. In P's discussion with potential lenders/holders, and as described in offering materials provided to potential lenders/holders, P disclosed that it planned to use all or a portion of the proceeds from the issuance of the debt instrument to reacquire outstanding debt of P and its affiliates. Following the issuance, P makes a $70,000 capital contribution to S. S then reacquires its debt instrument from X, a person not related to S within the meaning of section 108(i)(5)(A), for $70,000. At the time of the reacquisition, the adjusted issue price of S's debt instrument is $100,000. Under § 1.61-12(c), S realizes $30,000 of COD income. S makes a section 108(i) election for the $30,000 of COD income.

(ii) *Analysis.* Under the facts, at the time of P's issuance of its $160,000 debt instrument, P anticipated that the loan proceeds would be used to reacquire the debt of S, and P's debt instrument would not have been issued for an amount greater than $90,000 if P had not anticipated that S would use the proceeds to reacquire its debt. Pursuant to paragraph (a) of this section, the proceeds from P's issuance of its debt instrument are treated as being used indirectly to reacquire S's applicable debt instrument. Therefore, section 108(i)(2)(B) applies to P's debt instrument and P's OID deductions on its debt instrument are subject to deferral under section 108(i)(2)(A). However, because only a portion of the proceeds from P's debt instrument are used by S to reacquire its applicable debt instrument, only a portion of P's total OID deductions will be deferred under section 108(i)(2)(A). See section 108(i)(2)(B). Accordingly, a maximum of $17,500 ($40,000 x $70,000/$160,000) of P's $40,000 total OID deductions is subject to deferral under section 108(i)(2)(A). Under paragraph (b) of this section, the amount of P's deferred OID deduction each taxable year under section 108(i)(2)(A) is equal to the product of the amount of OID that accrues in the taxable year under section 1272 for the debt instrument and a fraction ($70,000/$160,000). As a result, P's deferred OID deductions are the following amounts: $4,015.99 for 2010 ($ 9,179.40 × $70,000/$160,000); $4,246.39 for 2011 ($9,706.04 × $70,000/$160,000); $4,490.01 for 2012 ($10,262.88 x $70,000/$160,000); and $4,747.61 for 2013 ($10,851.68 × $70,000/$160,000).

Example 2. (i) *Facts.* The facts are the same as in *Example 1,* except that S makes a section 108(i) election for only $10,000 of the $30,000 of COD income.

(ii) *Analysis.* The maximum amount of P's deferred OID deductions under section 108(i)(2)(A) is $10,000 rather than $17,500 because S made a section 108(i) election for only $10,000 of the $30,000 of COD income. Under section 108(i)(2)(A), because the amount of OID that accrues prior to 2014 attributable to the portion of the debt instrument issued to indirectly reacquire S's applicable debt instrument under paragraph (b) of this section ($17,500) exceeds the amount of deferred COD income under section 108(i) ($10,000), P's deferred OID deductions are the following amounts: $4,015.99 for 2010; $4,246.39 for 2011; $1,737.62 for 2012; and $0 for 2013.

Example 3. (i) *Facts.* The facts are the same as in *Example 1,* except that P pays $200,000 in cash to the lenders/holders on December 31, 2012, to retire the debt instrument. P did not directly or indirectly obtain the funds to retire the debt instrument from the issuance of another debt instrument with OID.

(ii) *Analysis.* Under paragraph (c)(1) of this section, the retirement of P's debt instrument is not an acceleration event for the deferred OID deductions of $4,015.99 for 2010, $4,246.39 for 2011, and $4,490.01 for 2012. Except as provided in § 1.108(i)-1(b)(4), these amounts will be taken into account during the inclusion period. P, however, paid a repurchase premium of $10,851.68 in 2012 ($200,000 minus the adjusted issue price of $189,148.32) to retire the debt instrument. If otherwise allowable, P may deduct this amount in 2012 under § 1.163-7(c).

(e) *Effective/applicability dates.*—For *effective/applicability dates*, see §1.108(i)-0(b). [Reg. §1.108(i)-3.]

☐ [T.D. 9622, 7-2-2013.]

[Reg. §1.109-1]

§1.109-1. Exclusion from gross income of lessor of real property of value of improvements erected by lessee.—(a) Income derived by a lessor of real property upon the termination, through forfeiture or otherwise, of the lease of such property and attributable to buildings erected or other improvements made by the lessee upon the leased property is excluded from gross income. However, where the facts disclose that such buildings or improvements represent in whole or in part a liquidation in kind of lease rentals, the exclusion from gross income shall not apply to the extent that such buildings or improvements represent such liquidation. The exclusion applies only with respect to the income realized by the lessor upon the termination of the lease and has no application to income, if any, in the form of rent, which may be derived by a lessor during the period of the lease and attributable to buildings erected or other improvements made by the lessee. It has no application to income which may be realized by the lessor upon the termination of the lease but not attributable to the value of such buildings or improvements. Neither does it apply to income derived by the lessor subsequent to the termination of the lease incident to the ownership of such buildings or improvements.

(b) The provisions of this section may be illustrated by the following example:

Example. The A Corporation leased in 1945 for a period of 50 years unimproved real property to the B Corporation under a lease providing that the B Corporation erect on the leased premises an office building costing $500,000, in addition to paying the A Corporation a lease rental of $10,000 per annum beginning on the date of completion of the improvements, the sum of $100,000 being placed in escrow for the payment of the rental. The building was completed on January 1, 1950. The lease provided that all improvements made by the lessee on the leased property would become the absolute property of the A Corporation on the termination of the lease by forfeiture or otherwise and that the lessor would become entitled on such termination to the remainder of the sum, if any, remaining in the escrow fund. The B Corporation forfeited its lease on January 1, 1955, when the improvements had a value of $100,000. Under the provisions of section 109, the $100,000 is excluded from gross income. The amount of $50,000 representing the remainder in the escrow fund is forfeited to the A Corporation and is included in the gross income of that taxpayer. As to the basis of the property in the hands of the A Corporation, see §1.1019-1. [Reg. §1.109-1.]

☐ [T.D. 6220, 12-28-56.]

[Reg. §1.110-1]

§1.110-1. Qualified lessee construction allowances.—(a) *Overview.*—Amounts provided to a lessee by a lessor for property to be constructed and used by the lessee pursuant to a lease are not includible in the lessee's gross income if the amount is a qualified lessee construction allowance under paragraph (b) of this section.

(b) *Qualified lessee construction allowance.*—(1) *In general.*—A qualified lessee construction allowance means any amount received in cash (or treated as a rent reduction) by a lessee from a lessor—

(i) Under a short-term lease of retail space;

(ii) For the purpose of constructing or improving qualified long-term real property for use in the lessee's trade or business at that retail space; and

(iii) To the extent the amount is expended by the lessee in the taxable year received on the construction or improvement of qualified long-term real property for use in the lessee's trade or business at that retail space.

(2) *Definitions.*—(i) *Qualified long-term real property* is nonresidential real property under section 168(e)(2)(B) that is part of, or otherwise present at, the retail space referred to in paragraph (b)(1)(i) of this section and which reverts to the lessor at the termination of the lease. Thus, qualified long-term real property does not include property qualifying as section 1245 property under section 1245(a)(3).

(ii) *Short-term lease* is a lease (or other agreement for occupancy or use) of retail space for 15 years or less (as determined pursuant to section 168(i)(3)).

(iii) *Retail space* is nonresidential real property under section 168(e)(2)(B) that is leased, occupied, or otherwise used by the lessee in its trade or business of selling tangible personal property or services to the general public. The term *retail space* includes not only the space where the retail sales are made, but also space where activities supporting the retail activity are performed (such as an administrative office, a storage area, and employee lounge). Examples of services typically sold to the general public include services provided by hair stylists, tailors, shoe repairmen, doctors, lawyers, accountants, insurance agents, stock brokers, securities dealers (including dealers who sell securities out of inventory), financial advisors and bankers. For purposes of this paragraph (b)(2)(iii), a taxpayer is selling to the general public if the products or services for sale are made available to the general public, even if the product or service is targeted to certain customers or clients.

(3) *Purpose requirement.*—An amount will meet the requirement in paragraph (b)(1)(ii) of this section only to the extent that the lease agreement for the retail space expressly provides that the construction allowance is for the purpose of constructing or improving qualified long-term real property for use in the lessee's trade or business at the retail space. An ancillary agreement between the lessor and the lessee providing for a construction allowance, executed contemporaneously with the lease or during the term of the lease, is considered a provision of the lease agreement for purposes of the preceding sentence, provided the agreement is executed before payment of the construction allowance.

(4) *Expenditure requirement.*—(i) *In general.*—Expenditures referred to in paragraph (b)(1)(iii) of this section may be treated as being made first from the lessee's construction allowance. Tracing of the construction allowance to the actual lessee expenditures for the construction or improvement of qualified long-term real property is not required. However, the lessee should maintain accurate records of the amount of the qualified lessee construction allowance received and the expenditures made for qualified long-term real property.

(ii) *Time when expenditures deemed made.*—For purposes of paragraph (b)(1)(iii) of this section, an amount is deemed to have been expended by a lessee in the taxable year in which the construction allowance was received by the lessee if—

(A) The amount is expended by the lessee within 8$\frac{1}{2}$months after the close of the taxable year in which the amount was received; or

(B) The amount is a reimbursement from the lessor for amounts expended by the lessee in a prior year and for which the lessee has not claimed any depreciation deductions.

(5) *Consistent treatment by lessor.*—Qualified long-term real property constructed or improved with any amount excluded from a lessee's gross income by reason of paragraph (a) of this section must be treated as nonresidential real property owned by the lessor (for purposes of depreciation under 168(e)(2)(B) and determining gain or loss under section 168(i)(8)(B)). For purposes of the preceding sentence, the lessor must treat the construction allowance as fully expended in the manner required by paragraph (b)(1)(iii) of this section unless the lessor is notified by the lessee in writing to the contrary. General tax principles apply for purposes of determining when the lessor may begin depreciation of its nonresidential real property. The lessee's exclusion from gross income under paragraph (a) of this section, however, is not dependent upon the lessor's treatment of the property as nonresidential real property.

(c) *Information required to be furnished.*—(1) *In general.*—The lessor and the lessee described in paragraph (b) of this section who are paying and receiving a qualified lessee construction allowance, respectively, must furnish the information described in paragraph (c)(3) of this section in the time and manner prescribed in paragraph (c)(2) of this section.

(2) *Time and manner for furnishing information.*—The requirement to furnish information under paragraph (c)(1) of this section is met by attaching a statement with the information described in paragraph (c)(3) of this section to the lessor's or the lessee's, as applicable, timely filed (including extensions) Federal income tax return for the taxable year in which the construction allowance was paid by the lessor or received by the lessee (either in cash or treated as a rent reduction), as applicable. A lessor or a lessee may report the required information for several qualified lessee construction allowances on a combined statement. However, a lessor's or a lessee's failure to provide information with respect to each lease will be treated as a separate failure to provide information for purposes of paragraph (c)(4) of this section.

(3) *Information required.*—(i) *Lessor.*—The statement provided by the lessor must contain the lessor's name (and, in the case of a consolidated group, the parent's name), employer identification number, taxable year and the following information for each lease:

(A) The lessee's name (in the case of a consolidated group, the parent's name).

(B) The address of the lessee.

(C) The employer identification number of the lessee.

(D) The location of the retail space (including mall or strip center name, if applicable, and store name).

(E) The amount of the construction allowance.

(F) The amount of the construction allowance treated by the lessor as nonresidential real property owned by the lessor.

(ii) *Lessee.*—The statement provided by the lessee must contain the lessee's name (and, in the case of a consolidated group, the parent's name), employer identification number, taxable year and the following information for each lease:

(A) The lessor's name (in the case of a consolidated group, the parent's name).

(B) The address of the lessor.

(C) The employer identification number of the lessor.

(D) The location of the retail space (including mall or strip center name, if applicable, and store name).

(E) The amount of the construction allowance.

(F) The amount of the construction allowance that is a qualified lessee construction allowance under paragraph (b) of this section.

(4) *Failure to furnish information.*—A lessor or a lessee that fails to furnish the information required in this paragraph (c) may be subject to a penalty under section 6721.

(d) *Effective date.*—This section is applicable to leases entered into on or after October 5, 2000. [Reg. §1.110-1.]

☐ [T.D. 8901, 9-1-2000.]

[Reg. §1.111-1]

§1.111-1. Recovery of certain items previously deducted or credited.—(a) *General.*—Section 111 provides that income attributable to the recovery during any taxable year of bad debts, prior taxes, and delinquency amounts shall be excluded from gross income to the extent of the "recovery exclusion" with respect to such items. The rule of exclusion so prescribed by statute applies equally with respect to all other losses, expenditures, and accruals made the basis of deductions from gross income for prior taxable years, including war losses referred to in section 127 of the Internal Revenue Code of 1939, but not including deductions with respect to depreciation, depletion, amortization, or amortizable bond premiums. The term "recovery exclusion" as used in this section means an amount equal to the portion of the bad debts, prior taxes, and delinquency amounts (the items specifically referred to in section 111), and of all other items subject to the rule of exclusion which, when deducted or credited for a prior taxable year, did not result in a reduction of any tax of the taxpayer under subtitle A (other than the accumulated earnings tax imposed by section 531 or the personal holding company tax imposed by section 541) of the Internal Revenue Code of 1954 or corresponding provisions of prior income tax laws (other than the World War II excess profits tax imposed under subchapter E of chapter 2 of the Internal Revenue Code of 1939.

(1) *Section 111 items.*—The term "section 111 items" as used in this section means bad debts, prior taxes, delinquency amounts, and all other items subject to the rule of exclusion, for which a deduction or credit was allowed for a prior taxable year. If a bad debt was previously charged against a reserve by a taxpayer on the reserve method of treating bad debts, it was not deducted, and it is, therefore, not considered a section 111 item. Bad debts, prior taxes, and delinquency amounts are defined in section 111(b)(1), (2), and (3), respectively. An example of a delinquency amount is interest on delinquent taxes. An example of the other items not expressly referred to in section 111 but nevertheless subject to the rule of exclusion is a loss sustained upon the sale of stock and later recovered, in whole or in part, through an action against the party from whom such stock had been purchased.

(2) *Definition of "recovery".*—Recoveries result from the receipt of amounts in respect of the previously deducted or credited section 111 items, such as from the collection or sale of a bad debt, refund or credit of taxes paid, or cancellation of taxes accrued. Care should be taken in the case of bad debts which were treated as only partially worthless in prior years to distinguish between the item described in section 111, that is, the part of such debt which was deducted, and the part not previously deducted, which is not a section 111 item and is considered the first part collected. The collection of the part not deducted is not considered a "recovery." Furthermore, the term "recovery" does not include the gain resulting from the receipt of an amount on account of a section 111 item which, together with previous such receipts, exceeds the deduction or credit previously allowed for such item. For instance, a $100 corporate bond purchased for $40 and later deducted as worthless is subsequently collected to the extent of $50. The $10 gain (excess of $50 collection over $40 cost) is not a recovery of a section 111 item. Such gain is in no case excluded from gross income under section 111, regardless of whether the $40 recovery is or is not included.

(3) *Treatment of debt deducted in more than one year by reason of partial worthlessness.*—In the case of a bad debt deducted in part for two or more prior years, each such deduction of a part of the debt is considered a separate section 111 item. A recovery with respect to such debt is considered first a recovery of those items (or portions thereof), resulting from such debt, for which there are recovery exclusions. If there are recovery exclusions for two or more items resulting from the same bad debt, such items are considered recovered in the order of the taxable years for which they were deducted, beginning with the latest. The recovery exclusion for any such item is determined by considering the recovery exclusion with respect to the prior year for which such item was deducted as being first used to offset all other applicable recoveries in the year in which the bad debt is recovered.

(4) *Special provisions as to worthless bonds, etc., which are treated as capital losses.*—Certain bad debts arising from the worthlessness of securities and certain nonbusiness bad debts are treated as losses from the sale or exchange of capital assets. See sections 165(g) and 166(d). The amounts of the deductions allowed for any year under section 1211 on account of such losses for such year are considered to be section 111 items. Any part of such losses which, under section 1211, is a deduction for a subsequent year through the capital loss carryover (any later receipt of an amount with respect to such deducted loss is a recovery) is considered a section 111 item for the year in which such loss was sustained.

(b) *Computation of recovery exclusion.*—(1) *Amount of recovery exclusion allowable for year of recovery.*—For the year of any recovery, the section 111 items which were deducted or credited for one prior year are considered as a group and the recovery thereon is considered separately from recoveries of any items which were deducted or credited for other years. This recovery is excluded from gross income to the extent of the recovery exclusion with respect to this group of items as (i) determined for the original year for which such items were deducted or credited (see subparagraph (2) of this paragraph) and (ii) reduced by the excludable recoveries in intervening years on account of all section 111 items for such original year. A taxpayer claiming a recovery exclusion shall submit, at the time the exclusion is claimed, the computation of the recovery exclusion claimed for the original year for which the items were deducted or credited, and computations showing the amount recovered in intervening years on account of the section 111 items deducted or credited for the original year.

(2) *Determination of recovery exclusion for original year for which items were deducted or credited.*—(i) The recovery exclusion for the taxable year for which section 111 items were deducted or credited (that is, the "original taxable year") is the portion of the aggregate amount of such deductions and credits which could be disallowed without causing an increase in any tax of the taxpayer imposed under subtitle A (other than the accumulated earnings tax imposed by section 531 or the personal holding company tax imposed by section 541) of the Internal Revenue Code of 1954 or corresponding provisions of prior income tax laws (other than the World War II excess profits tax imposed under subchapter E of chapter 2 of the Internal Revenue Code of 1939). For the purpose of such recovery exclusion, consideration must be given to the effect of net operating loss carryovers and carrybacks or capital loss carryovers.

(ii) This rule shall be applied by determining the recovery exclusion as the aggregate amount of the section 111 items for the original year for which such items were deducted or credited reduced by whichever of the following amounts is the greater:

(a) The difference between (1) the taxable income for such original year and (2) the taxable income computed without regard to the section 111 items for such original year.

(b) In the case of a taxpayer subject to any income tax in lieu of normal tax or surtax or both (except the alternative tax on capital gains imposed by section 1201, which is disregarded), the difference between (1) the income subject to such tax for such original year and (2) the income subject to such tax computed without regard to the section 111 items for such original year.

(Neither the amount determined under (1) nor the amount under (2) of (a) or (b) of this subdivision shall in any case be considered less than zero.) For this determination of the recovery exclusion, the aggregate of the section 111 items must be further decreased by the portion thereof which caused a reduction in tax in preceding or succeeding taxable years through any net operating loss carryovers or carrybacks or capital loss carryovers affected by such items. This decrease is the aggregate of the largest amount determined for each of such preceding and succeeding years under (a) and (b) of this subdivision, the computation of each carryover or carryback to the preceding or succeeding year being made under (1) of (a) and (b) of this subdivision with regard to the section 111 items for the original year and such computation being made under (2) of (a) and (b) of this subdivision without regard to such items. For the purpose of the preceding sentence, the computations under both (1) and (2) of (a) and (b) of this subdivision shall be made without regard to any section 111 items for such preceding or succeeding year and the carryovers and carrybacks to such year shall be determined without regard to any section 111 items for years subsequent to the original year.

(iii) The determination of the recovery exclusion for original taxable years subject to the provisions of the Internal Revenue Code of 1939 shall be made under 26 CFR (1939) 39.22(b)(12)-1(b)(2) of Regulations 118.

(3) *Example.*—The provisions of this paragraph may be illustrated by the following example:

Example. A single individual with no dependents has for his 1954 taxable year the following income and deductions:

	With deduction of section 111 items		Without deduction of section 111 items	
Gross income		$25,000		$25,000
Less deductions:				
Depreciation	$20,000		$20,000	
Business bad debts and taxes	6,300			
Personal exemption	600	26,900	600	20,600
Taxable income or (loss)		(1,900)		4,400
Adjustment under section 172(d)(3)		600		
Net operating loss		(1,300)		

The full amount of the net operating loss of $1,300 is carried back and allowed as a deduction for 1952. The aggregate of the section 111 items for 1954 is $6,300 (bad debts and taxes). The recovery exclusion on account of section 111 items for 1954 is $600, determined by reducing the $6,300 aggregate of the section 111 items by $5,700, i.e., the sum of (1) the difference between the amount of the taxable income for 1954 computed without regard to the section 111 items ($4,400) and the amount of the taxable income for 1954 (not less than zero) computed by taking such items into account, and (2) the amount of the net operating loss ($1,300) which caused the reduction in tax for 1952 by reason of the carryback provisions. If in 1956 the taxpayer recovers $400 of the bad debts, all of the recovery is excluded from the income by reason of the recovery exclusion of $600 determined for the original year 1954. If in 1957 the taxpayer recovers an additional $300 of the bad debts, only $200 is excluded from gross income. That is, the recovery exclusion of $600 determined for the original year 1954 is reduced by the $400 recovered in 1956, leaving a balance of $200 which is used in 1957. The balance of the amount recovered in 1957, $100 ($300 less $200), is included in gross income for 1957.

(c) *Provisions as to taxes imposed by section 531 (relating to the accumulated earnings tax) and section 541 (relating to the tax on personal holding companies).*—A recovery exclusion allowed for purposes of subtitle A (other than section 531 or section 541) of the Internal Revenue Code of 1954 shall also be allowed for the purpose of determining the accumulated earnings tax under section 531 or the personal holding company tax under section 541 regardless of whether or not the section 111 items on which such recovery exclusion is based resulted in a reduction of the tax under section 531 or section 541 of the Internal Revenue Code of 1954 (or corresponding provisions of prior income tax laws) for the prior taxable year. Furthermore, if there is recovery of a section 111 item which was not allowable as a deduction or credit for the prior taxable year for purposes of subtitle A (not including section 531 or section 541) or corresponding provisions of prior income tax laws (other than subchapter E of chapter 2 of the Internal Revenue Code of 1939, relating to World War II excess profits taxes), but was allowable for such prior taxable year in determining the tax under section 531 or section 541 (or corresponding provisions of prior income tax laws) then for the purpose of determining the tax under section 531 or section 541 a recovery exclusion shall be allowable with respect to such recovery if the section 111 item did not result in a reduction of the tax under section 531 or section 541 (or corresponding provisions of prior income tax laws). [Reg. § 1.111-1.]

☐ [T.D. 6220, 12-28-56.]

[Reg. §1.112-1]

§1.112-1. Combat zone compensation of members of the Armed Forces.—(a) *Combat zone compensation exclusion.*—(1) *Amount excluded.*—In addition to the exemptions and credits otherwise applicable, section 112 excludes from gross income the following compensation of members of the Armed Forces:

(i) *Enlisted personnel.*—Compensation received for active service as a member below the grade of commissioned officer in the Armed Forces of the United States for any month during any part of which the member served in a combat zone or was hospitalized at any place as a result of wounds, disease, or injury incurred while serving in the combat zone.

(ii) *Commissioned officers.*—Compensation not exceeding the monthly dollar limit received for active service as a commissioned officer in the Armed Forces of the United States for any month during any part of which the officer served in a combat zone or was hospitalized at any place as a result of wounds, disease, or injury incurred while serving in the combat zone. The monthly dollar limit is the monthly amount excludable from the officer's income under section 112(b) as amended. Beginning in 1966, the monthly dollar limit for periods of active service after 1965 became $500. As of September 10, 1993, the monthly dollar limit continues to be $500.

(2) *Time limits on exclusion during hospitalization.*—Compensation received for service for any month of hospitalization that begins more than 2 years after the date specified by the President in an Executive Order as the date of the termination of combatant activities in the combat zone cannot be excluded under section 112. Furthermore, compensation received while hospitalized after January 1978 for wounds, disease, or injury incurred in the Vietnam combat zone designated by Executive Order 11216 cannot be excluded under section 112.

(3) *Special terms.*—A commissioned warrant officer is not a *commissioned officer* under section 112(b) and is entitled to the exclusion allowed to enlisted personnel under section 112(a). *Compensation*, for the purpose of section 112, does not include pensions and retirement pay. *Armed Forces of the United States* is defined (and members of the Armed Forces are described) in section 7701(a)(15).

(4) *Military compensation only.*—Only compensation paid by the Armed Forces of the United States to members of the Armed Forces can be excluded under section 112, except for compensation paid by an agency or instrumentality of the United States or by an international organization to a member of the Armed Forces whose military active duty status continues during the member's assignment to the agency or instrumentality or organization on official detail. Compensation paid by other employers (whether private enterprises or governmental entities) to members of the Armed Forces cannot be excluded under section 112 even if the payment is made to supplement the member's military compensation or is labeled by the employer as compensation for active service in the Armed Forces of the United States. Compensation paid to civilian employees of the federal government, including civilian employees of the Armed Forces, cannot be excluded under section 112, except as provided in section 112(d)(2) (which extends the exclusion to compensation of civilian employees of the federal government in missing status due to the Vietnam conflict).

(b) *Service in combat zone.*—(1) *Active service.*—The exclusion under section 112 applies only if active service is performed in a combat zone. A member of the Armed Forces is in active service if the member is actually serving in the Armed Forces of the United States. Periods during which a member of the Armed Forces is absent from duty on account of sickness, wounds, leave, internment by the enemy, or other lawful cause are periods of active service. A member of the Armed Forces in active service in a combat zone who becomes a prisoner of war or missing in action in the combat zone is deemed, for the purpose of section 112, to continue in active service in the combat zone for the period for which the member is treated as a prisoner of war or as missing in action for military pay purposes.

(2) *Combat zone status.*—Except as provided in paragraphs (e) and (f) of this section, service is performed in a combat zone only if it is performed in an area which the President of the United States has designated by Executive Order, for the purpose of section 112, as an area in which Armed Forces of the United States are or have been engaged in combat, and only if it is performed on or after the date designated by the President by Executive Order as the date of the commencing of combatant activities in that zone and on or before the date designated by the President by Executive Order as the date of the termination of combatant activities in that zone.

(3) *Partial month service.*—If a member of the Armed Forces serves in a combat zone for any part of a month, the member is entitled to the exclusion for that month to the same extent as if the member has served in that zone for the entire month. If a member of the Armed Forces is hospitalized for a part of a month as a result of wounds, disease, or injury incurred while serving in that zone, the member is entitled to the exclusion for the entire month.

(4) *Payment time and place.*—The time and place of payment are irrelevant in considering whether compensation is excludable under section 112; rather, the time and place of the entitlement to compensation determine whether the compensation is excludable under section 112. Thus, compensation can be excluded under section 112 whether or not it is received outside a combat zone, or while the recipient is hospitalized, or in a year different from that in which the service was rendered for which the compensation is paid, provided that the member's entitlement to the compensation fully accrued in a month during which the member served in the combat zone or was hospitalized as a result of wounds, disease, or injury incurred while serving in the combat zone. For this purpose, entitlement to compensation fully accrues upon the completion of all actions required of the member to receive the compensation. Compensation received by a member of the Armed Forces for services rendered while in active service can be excluded under section 112 even though payment is received subsequent to discharge or release from active service. Compensation credited to a deceased member's account for a period subsequent to the established date of the member's death and received by the member's estate can be excluded from the gross income of the estate under section 112 to the same extent that it would have been excluded from the gross income of the member had the member lived and received the compensation.

(5) *Examples of combat zone compensation.*—The rules of this section are illustrated by the following examples:

Example 1. On January 5, outside of a combat zone, an enlisted member received basic pay for active duty services performed from the preceding December 1 through December 31. On December 4 (and no other date), the member performed services within a combat zone. The member may exclude from income the entire payment received on January 5, although the member served in the combat zone only one day during December, received the payment outside of the combat zone, and received the payment in a year other than the year in which the combat zone services were performed.

Example 2. From March through December, an enlisted member became entitled to 25 days of annual leave while serving in a combat zone. The member used all 25 days of leave in the following year. The member may exclude from income the compensation received for those 25 days, even if the member performs no services in the combat zone in the year the compensation is received.

Example 3. From March through December, a commissioned officer became entitled to 25 days of annual leave while serving in a combat zone. During that period the officer also received basic pay of $1,000 per month from which the officer excluded from income $500 per month (exhausting the monthly dollar limit under section 112 for that period). The officer used all 25 days of leave in the following year. The officer may not exclude from income any compensation received in the following year related to those 25 days of leave, since the officer had already excluded from income the maximum amount of combat zone compensation for the period in which the leave was earned.

Example 4. In November, while serving in a combat zone, an enlisted member competing for a cash award submitted an employee suggestion. After November, the member neither served in a combat zone nor was hospitalized for wounds incurred in the combat zone. In June of the following year, the member's suggestion was selected as the winner of the competition and the award was paid. The award can be excluded from income as combat zone compensation although granted and received outside of the combat zone, since the member completed the necessary action to win the award (submission of the suggestion) in a month during which the member served in the combat zone.

Example 5. In July, while serving in a combat zone, an enlisted member voluntarily reenlisted. After July, the member neither served in a combat zone nor was hospitalized for wounds incurred in the combat zone. In February of the following year, the member received a bonus as a result of the July reenlistment. The reenlistment bonus can be excluded from income as combat zone compensation although received outside of the combat zone, since the member completed the necessary action for entitlement to the reenlistment bonus in a month during which the member served in the combat zone.

Example 6. In July, while serving outside a combat zone, an enlisted member voluntarily reenlisted. In February of the following year, the member, while performing services in a combat zone, received a bonus as a result of the July reenlistment. The reenlistment bonus cannot be excluded from income as combat zone compensa-

tion although received while serving in the combat zone, since the member completed the necessary action for entitlement to the reenlistment bonus in a month during which the member had neither served in the combat zone nor was hospitalized for wounds incurred while serving in a combat zone.

(c) *Hospitalization.*—(1) *Presumption of combat zone injury.*—If an individual is hospitalized for [a]wound, disease, or injury while serving in a combat zone, the wound, disease, or injury will be presumed to have been incurred while serving in a combat zone, unless the contrary clearly appears. In certain cases, however, a wound, disease, or injury may have been incurred while serving in a combat zone even though the individual was not hospitalized for it while so serving. In exceptional cases, a wound, disease, or injury will not have been incurred while serving in a combat zone even though the individual was hospitalized for it while so serving.

(2) *Length of hospitalization.*—An individual is hospitalized only until the date the individual is discharged from the hospital.

(3) *Examples of combat zone injury.*—The rules of this paragraph (c) are illustrated by the following examples:

Example 1. An individual is hospitalized for a disease in the combat zone where the individual has been serving for three weeks. The incubation period of the disease is two to four weeks. The disease is incurred while serving in the combat zone.

Example 2. The facts are the same as in *Example 1* except that the incubation period of the disease is one year. The disease is not incurred while serving in the combat zone.

Example 3. A member of the Air Force, stationed outside the combat zone, is shot while participating in aerial combat over the combat zone, but is not hospitalized until returning to the home base. The injury is incurred while serving in a combat zone.

Example 4. An individual is hospitalized for a disease three weeks after having departed from a combat zone. The incubation period of the disease is two to four weeks. The disease is incurred while serving in a combat zone.

(d) *Married members.*—The exclusion under section 112 applies without regard to the marital status of the recipient of the compensation. If both spouses meet the requirements of the statute, then each spouse is entitled to the benefit of an exclusion. In the case of a husband and wife domiciled in a State recognized for Federal income tax purposes as a community property State, any exclusion from gross income under section 112 operates before apportionment of the gross income of the spouses under community property law. For example, a husband and wife are domiciled in a community property State and the member spouse is entitled, as a commissioned officer, to the benefit of the exclusion under section 112(b) of $500 for each month. The member receives $7,899 as compensation for active service for 3 months in a combat zone. Of that amount, $1,500 is excluded from gross income under section 112(b) and $6,399 is taken into account in determining the gross income of both spouses.

(e) *Service in area outside combat zone.*—(1) *Combat zone treatment.*—For purposes of section 112, a member of the Armed Forces who performs military service in an area outside the area designated by Executive Order as a combat zone is deemed to serve in that combat zone while the member's service is in direct support of military operations in that zone and qualifies the member for the special pay for duty subject to hostile fire or imminent danger authorized under section 310 of title 37 of the United States Code, as amended (37 U.S.C. 310) (hostile fire/imminent danger pay).

(2) *Examples of combat zone treatment.*—The examples in this paragraph (e)(2) are based on the following circumstances: Certain areas, airspace, and adjacent waters are designated as a combat zone for purposes of section 112 as of May 1. Some members of the Armed Forces are stationed in the combat zone; others are stationed in two foreign countries outside the combat zone, named Nearby Country and Destination Country.

Example 1. B is a member of an Armed Forces ground unit stationed in the combat zone. On May 31, B's unit crosses into Nearby Country. B performs military service in Nearby Country in direct support of the military operations in the combat zone from June 1 through June 8 that qualifies B for hostile fire/imminent danger pay. B does not return to the combat zone during June. B is deemed to serve in the combat zone from June 1 through June 8. Accordingly, B is entitled to the exclusion under section 112 for June. Of course, B is also entitled to the exclusion for any month (May, in this example) in which B actually served in the combat zone.

Example 2. B is a member of an Armed Forces ground unit stationed in the combat zone. On May 31, B's unit crosses into Nearby Country. On June 1, B is wounded while performing military service in Nearby Country in direct support of the military operations in the combat zone that qualifies B for hostile fire/imminent danger pay. On June 2, B is transferred for treatment to a hospital in the United States. B is hospitalized from June through October for those wounds. B is deemed to have incurred the wounds while serving in the combat zone on June 1. Accordingly, B is entitled to the exclusion under section 112 for June through October. Of course, B is also entitled to the exclusion for any month (May, in this example) in which B actually served in the combat zone.

Example 3. B is stationed in Nearby Country for the entire month of June as a member of a ground crew servicing combat aircraft operating in the combat zone. B's service in Nearby Country during June does not qualify B for hostile fire/imminent danger pay. Accordingly, B is not deemed to serve in the combat zone during June and is not entitled to the exclusion under section 112 for that month.

Example 4. B is assigned to an air unit stationed in Nearby Country for the entire month of June. In June, members of air units of the Armed Forces stationed in Nearby Country fly combat and supply missions into and over Destination Country in direct support of military operations in the combat zone. B flies combat missions over Destination Country from Nearby Country from June 1 through June 8. B's service qualifies B for hostile fire/imminent danger pay. Accordingly, B is deemed to serve in the combat zone during June and is entitled to the exclusion under section 112. The result would be the same if B were to fly supply missions into Destination Country from Nearby Country in direct support of operations in the combat zone qualifying B for hostile fire/imminent danger pay.

Example 5. Assigned to an air unit stationed in Nearby Country, B was killed in June when B's plane crashed on returning to the airbase in Nearby Country. B was performing military service in direct support of the military operations in the combat zone at the time of B's death. B's service also qualified B for hostile fire/imminent danger pay. B is deemed to have died while serving in the combat zone or to have died as a result of wounds, disease, or injury incurred while serving in the combat zone for purposes of section 692(a) and section 692(b) (providing relief from certain income taxes for members of the Armed Forces dying in a combat zone or as a result of wounds, disease, or injury incurred while serving in a combat zone) and section 2201 (providing relief from certain estate taxes for members of the Armed Forces dying in a combat zone or by reason of combat-zone-incurred wounds). The result would be the same if B's mission had been a supply mission instead of a combat mission.

Example 6. In June, B was killed as a result of an off-duty automobile accident while leaving the airbase in Nearby Country shortly after returning from a mission over Destination Country. At the time of B's death, B was not performing military duty qualifying B for hostile fire/imminent danger pay. B is not deemed to have died while serving in the combat zone or to have died as the result of wounds, disease, or injury incurred while serving in the combat zone. Accordingly, B does not qualify for the benefits of section 692(a), section 692(b), or section 2201.

Example 7. B performs military service in Nearby Country from June 1 through June 8 in direct support of the military operations in the combat zone. Nearby Country is designated as an area in which members of the Armed Forces qualify for hostile fire/imminent danger pay due to imminent danger, even though members in Nearby Country are not subject to hostile fire. B is deemed to serve in the combat zone from June 1 through June 8. Accordingly, B is entitled to the exclusion under section 112 for June.

(f) *Nonqualifying presence in combat zone.*—(1) *Inapplicability of exclusion.*—The following members of the Armed Forces are not deemed to serve in a combat zone within the meaning of section 112(a)(1) or section 112(b)(1) or to be hospitalized as a result of wounds, disease, or injury incurred while serving in a combat zone within the meaning of section 112(a)(2) or section 112(b)(2)—

(i) Members present in a combat zone while on leave from a duty station located outside a combat zone;

(ii) Members who pass over or through a combat zone during the course of a trip between two points both of which lie outside a combat zone; or

(iii) Members present in a combat zone solely for their own personal convenience.

(2) *Exceptions for temporary duty or special pay.*—Paragraph (f)(1) of this section does not apply to members of the Armed Forces who—

(i) Are assigned on official temporary duty to a combat zone (including official temporary duty to the airspace of a combat zone); or

(ii) Qualify for hostile fire/imminent danger pay.

(3) *Examples of nonqualifying presence and its exceptions.*—The examples in this paragraph (f)(3) are based on the following circumstances: Certain areas, airspace, and adjacent waters are designated as a combat zone for purposes of section 112 as of May 1. Some members of the Armed Forces are stationed in the combat zone;

others are stationed in two foreign countries outside the combat zone, named Nearby Country and Destination Country.

Example 1. B is a member of the Armed Forces assigned to a unit stationed in Nearby Country. On June 1, B voluntarily visits a city within the combat zone while on leave. B is not deemed to serve in a combat zone since B is present in a combat zone while on leave from a duty station located outside a combat zone.

Example 2. B is a member of the Armed Forces assigned to a unit stationed in Nearby Country. During June, B takes authorized leave and elects to spend the leave period by visiting a city in the combat zone. While on leave in the combat zone, B is subject to hostile fire qualifying B for hostile fire/imminent danger pay. Although B is present in the combat zone while on leave from a duty station outside the combat zone, B qualifies for the exclusion under section 112 because B qualifies for hostile fire/imminent danger pay while in the combat zone.

Example 3. B is a member of the Armed Forces assigned to a ground unit stationed in the combat zone. During June, B takes authorized leave and elects to spend the leave period in the combat zone. B is not on leave from a duty station located outside a combat zone, nor is B present in a combat zone solely for B's own personal convenience. Accordingly, B's combat zone tax benefits continue while B is on leave in the combat zone.

Example 4. B is assigned as a navigator to an air unit stationed in Nearby Country. On June 4, during the course of a flight between B's home base in Nearby Country and another base in Destination Country, the aircraft on which B serves as a navigator flies over the combat zone. B is not on official temporary duty to the airspace of the combat zone and does not qualify for hostile fire/imminent danger pay as a result of the flight. Accordingly, B is not deemed to serve in a combat zone since B passes over the combat zone during the course of a trip between two points both of which lie outside the combat zone without either being on official temporary duty to the combat zone or qualifying for hostile fire/imminent danger pay.

Example 5. B is a member of the Armed Forces assigned to a unit stationed in Nearby Country. B enters the combat zone on a 3-day pass. B is not on official temporary duty and does not qualify for hostile fire/imminent danger pay while present in the combat zone. Accordingly, B is not deemed to serve in a combat zone since B is present in the combat zone solely for B's own personal convenience.

Example 6. B, stationed in Nearby Country, is a military courier assigned on official temporary duty to deliver military pouches in the combat zone and in Destination Country. On June 1, B arrives in the combat zone from Nearby Country, and on June 2, B departs for Destination Country. Although B passes through the combat zone during the course of a trip between two points outside the combat zone, B is nevertheless deemed to serve in a combat zone while in the combat zone because B is assigned to the combat zone on official temporary duty.

Example 7. B is a member of an Armed Forces ground unit stationed in Nearby Country. On June 1, B took authorized leave and elected to spend the leave period by visiting a city in the combat zone. On June 2, while on leave in the combat zone, B was wounded by hostile fire qualifying B for hostile fire/imminent danger pay. On June 3, B was transferred for treatment to a hospital in the United States. B is hospitalized from June through October for those wounds. Although B was present in the combat zone while on leave from a duty station outside the combat zone, B is deemed to have incurred the wounds while serving in the combat zone on June 2, because B qualified for hostile fire/imminent danger pay while in the combat zone. Accordingly, B is entitled to the exclusion under section 112 for June through October.

Example 8. The facts are the same as in *Example 7* except that B dies on September 1 as a result of the wounds incurred in the combat zone. B is deemed to have died as a result of wounds, disease, or injury incurred while serving in the combat zone for purposes of section 692(a) and section 692(b) (providing relief from certain income taxes for members of the Armed Forces dying in a combat zone or as a result of wounds, disease, or injury incurred while serving in a combat zone) and section 2201 (providing relief from certain estate taxes for members of the Armed Forces dying in a combat zone or by reason of combat-zone-incurred wounds). [Reg. §1.112-1.]

☐ [T.D. 6220, 12-28-56. *Amended by* T.D. 6906, 12-28-66; T.D. 7066, 11-10-70 *and* T.D. 8489, 9-9-93.]

[Reg. §1.113-1]

§1.113-1. Mustering-out payments for members of the Armed Forces.—For the purposes of the exclusion from gross income under section 113 of mustering-out payments with respect to service in the Armed Forces, mustering-out payments are payments made to any recipients pursuant to the provisions of 38 U.S.C. 2105 (formerly section 5 of the Mustering-Out Payment Act of 1944 and section 505 of the Veterans Readjustment Assistance Act of 1952). [Reg. §1.113-1.]

☐ [T.D. 6220, 12-28-58.]

[Reg. §1.117-1]

§1.117-1. Exclusion of amounts received as a scholarship or fellowship grant.—(a) *In general.*—Any amount received by an individual as a scholarship at an educational institution or as a fellowship grant, including the value of contributed services and accommodations, shall be excluded from the gross income of the recipient, subject to the limitations set forth in section 117(b) and §1.117-2. The exclusion from gross income of an amount which is a scholarship or fellowship grant is controlled solely by section 117. Accordingly, to the extent that a scholarship or a fellowship grant exceeds the limitations of section 117(b) and §1.117-2, it is includible in the gross income of the recipient notwithstanding the provisions of section 102 relating to exclusion from gross income of gifts, or section 74(b) relating to exclusion from gross income of certain prizes and awards. For definitions, see §1.117-3.

(b) *Exclusion of amounts received to cover expenses.*—(1) Subject to the limitations provided in subparagraph (2) of this paragraph, any amount received by an individual to cover expenses for travel (including meals and lodging while traveling and an allowance for travel of the individual's family), research, clerical help, or equipment is excludable from gross income provided that such expenses are incident to a scholarship or fellowship grant which is excludable from gross income under section 117(a)(1). If, however, only a portion of a scholarship or fellowship grant is excludable from gross income under section 117(a)(1) because of the part-time employment limitation contained in section 117(b)(1) or because of the expiration of the 36-month period described in section 117(b)(2)(B), only the amount received to cover expenses incident to such excludable portion is excludable from gross income. The requirement that these expenses be incident to the scholarship or the fellowship grant means that the expenses of travel, research, clerical help, or equipment must be incurred by the individual in order to effectuate the purpose for which the scholarship or the fellowship grant was awarded.

(2)(i) In the case of a scholarship or fellowship grant which is awarded after July 28, 1956, the exclusion provided under subparagraph (1) of this paragraph is not applicable unless the amount received by the individual is specifically designated to cover expenses for travel, research, clerical help, or equipment.

(ii) In the case of a scholarship or fellowship grant awarded before July 29, 1956, the exclusion provided under subparagraph (1) of this paragraph is not applicable unless the recipient establishes, by competent evidence, that the amount was received to cover expenses for travel, research, clerical help, or equipment, but such amount need not be specifically designated. The fact that the recipient actually incurred expenses for travel, research, clerical help, or equipment is not sufficient to establish that the amount was received to cover such expenses.

(iii) The exclusion provided under subparagraph (1) of this paragraph is applicable only to the extent that the amount received for travel, research, clerical help, or equipment is actually expended for such expenses by the recipient during the term of the scholarship or fellowship grant and within a reasonable time before and after such term.

(3) The portion of any amount received to cover the expenses described in subparagraph (1) of this paragraph which is not actually expended for such expenses within the exclusion period described in subparagraph (2) of this paragraph shall, if not returned to the grantor within this period, be included in the gross income of the recipient for the taxable year in which such exclusion period expires. [Reg. §1.117-1.]

☐ [*T.D. 6186, 6-29-56. Amended by T.D. 6456, 3-22-60.*]

[Reg. §1.117-2]

§1.117-2. Limitations.—(a) *Individuals who are candidates for degrees.*—(1) *In general.*—Under the limitations provided by section 117(b)(1) in the case of an individual who is a candidate for a degree at an educational institution, the exclusion from gross income shall not apply (except as otherwise provided in subparagraph (2) of this paragraph) to that portion of any amount received as payment for teaching, research, or other services in the nature of part-time employment required as a condition to receiving a scholarship or fellowship grant. Payments for such part-time employment shall be included in the gross income of the recipient in an amount determined by reference to the rate of compensation ordinarily paid for similar services performed by an individual who is not the recipient of a scholarship or a fellowship grant. A typical example of employment under this subparagraph is the case of an individual who is required, as a condition to receiving the scholarship or the fellowship grant, to perform part-time teaching services. A requirement that the individual shall furnish periodic reports to the grantor of the scholarship or the fellowship grant for the purpose of keeping the grantor informed as to the general progress of the individual shall not be deemed to constitute the performance of services in the nature of part-time employment.

(2) *Exception.*—If teaching, research, or other services are required of all candidates (whether or not recipients of scholarships or fellowship grants) for a particular degree as a condition to receiving the degree, such teaching, research, or other services on the part of the recipient of a scholarship or fellowship grant who is a candidate for such degree shall not be regarded as part-time employment within the meaning of this paragraph. Thus, if all candidates for a particular education degree are required, as part of their regular course of study or curriculum, to perform part-time practice teaching services, such services are not to be regarded as part-time employment within the meaning of this paragraph.

(b) *Individuals who are not candidates for degrees.*—(1) *Conditions for exclusion.*—In the case of an individual who is not a candidate for a degree at an educational institution, the exclusion from gross income of an amount received as a scholarship or a fellowship grant shall apply (to the extent provided in subparagraph (2) of this paragraph) only if the grantor of the scholarship or fellowship grant is—

(i) An organization described in section 501(c)(3) which is exempt from tax under section 501(a),

(ii) The United States or an instrumentality or agency thereof, or a State, a territory, or a possession of the United States, or any political subdivision thereof, or the District of Columbia, or

(iii) For taxable years beginning after December 31, 1961, a foreign government, an international organization, or a binational or multinational educational and cultural foundation or commission created or continued pursuant to section 103 of the Mutual Educational and Cultural Exchange Act of 1961 (22 U.S.C. 2453).

(2) *Extent of exclusion.*—(i) In the case of an individual who is not a candidate for a degree, the amount received as a scholarship or a fellowship grant which is excludable from gross income under section 117(a)(1) shall not exceed an amount equal to $300 times the number of months for which the recipient received amounts under the scholarship or fellowship grant during the taxable year. In determining the number of months during the period for which the recipient received amounts under a scholarship or fellowship grant, computation shall be made on the basis of whole calendar months. A whole calendar month means a period of time terminating with the day of the succeeding month numerically corresponding to the day of the month of its beginning, less one, except that if there be no corresponding day of the succeeding month the period terminates with the last day of the succeeding month. For purposes of this computation a fractional part of a calendar month consisting of a period of time including 15 days or more shall be considered to be a whole calendar month and a fractional part of a calendar month consisting of a period of time including 14 days or less shall be disregarded. For example, if an individual receives a fellowship grant on September 13 which is to expire on June 12 of the following year, the grant shall be considered to have extended for a period of 9 months. If in the preceding example the grant expired on June 27, instead of June 12, the grant shall be considered to have extended for a period of 10 months.

(ii) No exclusion shall be allowed under section 117(a)(1) to an individual who is not a candidate for a degree after the recipient has, as an individual who is not a candidate for a degree, been entitled to an exclusion under that section for a period of 36 months. This limitation applies if the individual has received any amount which was either excluded or excludable from his gross income under section 117(a)(1) for any prior 36 months, whether or not consecutive. For example, if the individual received a fellowship grant of $7,200 for 3 years (which he elects to receive in 36 monthly installments of $200), his exclusion period would be exhausted even though he did not in any of the 36 months make use of the maximum exclusion. Accordingly, such individual would be entitled to no further exclusion from gross income with respect to any additional grants which he may receive as an individual who is not a candidate for a degree.

(iii) If an individual who is not a candidate for degree receives amounts from more than one scholarship or fellowship grant during the taxable year, the total amounts received in the taxable year shall be aggregated for the purpose of computing the amount which may be excludable from gross income for such taxable year. If amounts are received from more than one scholarship or fellowship grant during the same month or months within the taxable year, such month or months shall be counted only once for the purpose of determining the number of months for which the individual received such amounts under the scholarships or fellowship grants during the taxable year. For example, if an individual receives a fellowship grant from one source for the months of January to June of the taxable year and also receives a fellowship grant from another source for the months of March through December of the same taxable year, he shall be considered to have received amounts for 12 months of the taxable year. See example (4) in subparagraph (3) of this paragraph for further illustration.

(3) *Examples.*—The application of this paragraph may be further illustrated by the following examples, it being assumed that in each example the grantor is a grantor who is described in section 117(b)(2)(A) and subparagraph (1) of this paragraph.

Example (1). B, an individual who files his return on the calendar year basis, is awarded a post-doctorate fellowship grant in March 1955. The grant is to commence on September 1, 1955, and is to end on May 31, 1956, so that it will extend over a period of 9 months. The amount of the fellowship grant is $4,500 and B receives this amount in monthly installments of $500 on the first day of each month commencing September 1, 1955. During the taxable year 1955, B receives a total of $2,000 with respect to the 4-month period September through December, inclusive. He may exclude $1,200 from gross income in the taxable year 1955 ($300 × 4) and must include the remaining $800 in gross income for that year. For the year 1956, he will exclude $1,500 ($300 × 5) from gross income with respect to the $2,500 which he receives in that year and must include in gross income $1,000.

Example (2). Assume the same facts as in example (1) except that B receives the full amount of the grant ($4,500) on September 1, 1955. Since the amount received in the taxable year 1955 is for the full term of the fellowship grant (9 months), B may exclude $2,700 ($300 × 9) from gross income for the taxable year 1955. The remaining $1,800 must be included in gross income for that year.

Example (3). C, an individual who files his return on the calendar year basis, is awarded a post-doctorate fellowship grant in March 1955. The amount of the grant is $4,500 for a period commencing on September 1, 1955, and ending 24 months thereafter. C receives the full amount of the grant on September 1, 1955. C may exclude from gross income for the taxable year 1955, the full amount of the grant ($4,500) since this amount does not exceed an amount equal to $300 times the number of months (24) for which he received the amount of the grant during that taxable year.

Example (4). (i) F, an individual who files his return on the calendar year basis, is awarded a post-doctorate fellowship grant (Grant A) for two years commencing June 1, 1955, in the amount of $4,800. He elects to receive his grant in monthly installments of $200 commencing June 1, 1955. On March 1, 1956, F is awarded another post-doctorate fellowship grant (Grant B) for two years commencing September 1, 1956, in the amount of $7,200. He elects to receive this grant in monthly installments of $300 commencing September 1, 1956.

(ii) For the calendar year 1955, F receives $1,400 from Grant A which he is entitled to exclude from gross income since it does not exceed an amount equal to $300 times the number of months (7) for which he received amounts under the grant in the taxable year.

(iii) For the calendar year 1956, F receives $3,600 as the aggregate of amounts received under fellowship grants ($2,400 from Grant A and $1,200 from Grant B). F will be entitled to exclude the entire amount of $3,600 from gross income for the calendar year 1956 since such amount does not exceed an amount equal to $300 times the number of months (12) for which he received amounts under the grants in the taxable year.

(iv) For the calendar year 1957, F receives $4,600 as the aggregate of amounts received under fellowship grants ($1,000 from Grant A and $3,600 from Grant B). F will be entitled to exclude $3,600 ($300 × 12) from gross income for the calendar year 1957 and he will have to include $1,000 in gross income.

(v) For the calendar year 1958, F receives $2,400 from Grant B. F is entitled to exclude $1,500 ($300 × 5) from gross income for the calendar year 1958 and he will have to include $900 in gross income. While F receives amounts under fellowship Grant B for 8 months during the calendar year 1958, he is limited to an amount equal to $300 times 5 (months) because of the fact that he has already been entitled to exclude (and has in fact excluded) amounts received as a fellowship grant for a period of 31 months. Accordingly, he can only exclude amounts received under the fellowship grant for 5 months during the calendar year 1958, because of the 36-month limitation period. The fact that he was entitled to exclude only $1,400 ($200 a month for 7 months) instead of the maximum amount of $2,100 ($300 × 7) in 1955, is immaterial and the limitation period of 36 months is applicable.

(vi) The following chart illustrates the computation of the number of months for which F received amounts under the fellowship grants during the respective taxable years and the computation of the total amount received under the fellowship grants during each taxable year:

Period for which received and source	Number of months	Amounts received
1955:		
June 1 to December 31	7	
Grant A	...	$1,400
Grant B	...	None
Aggregate	7	1,400
1956:		
January 1 to August 31	8	
Grant A	...	$1,600
Grant B	...	None
September 1 to December 31	4	...
Grant A		800
Grant B	...	1,200
Aggregate	12	3,600
1957:		
January 1 to May 31	5	...
Grant A	...	1,000
Grant B	...	1,500
June 1 to December 31	7	
Grant A	...	None
Grant B	...	2,100
Aggregate	12	4,600
1958:		
January 1 to August 31	8	...
Grant A	...	None
Grant B	...	2,400
Aggregate	8	2,400

[Reg. §1.117-2.]

☐ [T.D. 6186, 6-29-56. Amended by T.D. 6782, 12-23-64.]

[Reg. §1.117-3]

§1.117-3. Definitions.—(a) *Scholarship.*—A scholarship generally means an amount paid or allowed to, or for the benefit of, a student, whether an undergraduate or a graduate, to aid such individual in pursuing his studies. The term includes the value of contributed services and accommodations (see paragraph (d) of this section) and the amount of tuition, matriculation, and other fees which are furnished or remitted to a student to aid him in pursuing his studies. The term also includes any amount received in the nature of a family allowance as a part of a scholarship. However, the term does not include any amount provided by an individual to aid a relative, friend, or other individual in pursuing his studies where the grantor is motivated by family or philanthropic considerations. If an educational institution maintains or participates in a plan whereby the tuition of a child of a faculty member of such institution is remitted by any other participating educational institution attended by such child, the amount of the tuition so remitted shall be considered to be an amount received as a scholarship.

(b) *Educational organization.*—For definition of "educational organization" paragraphs (a) and (b) of §117 adopt the definition of that term which is prescribed in section 151(e)(4). Accordingly, for purposes of section 117 the term "educational organization" means only an educational organization which normally maintains a regular faculty and curriculum and normally has a regularly organized body of students in attendance at the place where its educational activities are carried on. See section 151(e)(4) and regulations thereunder.

(c) *Fellowship grant.*—A fellowship grant generally means an amount paid or allowed to, or for the benefit of, an individual to aid him in the pursuit of study or research. The term includes the value of contributed services and accommodations (see paragraph (d) of this section) and the amount of tuition, matriculation, and other fees which are furnished or remitted to an individual to aid him in the pursuit of study or research. The term also includes any amount received in the nature of a family allowance as a part of a fellowship grant. However, the term does not include any amount provided by an individual to aid a relative, friend, or other individual in the pursuit of study or research where the grantor is motivated by family or philanthropic considerations.

(d) *Contributed services and accommodations.*—The term "contributed services and accommodations" means such services and accommodations as room, board, laundry service, and similar services or accommodations which are received by an individual as part of a scholarship or fellowship grant.

(e) *Candidate for a degree.*—The term "candidate for a degree" means an individual, whether an undergraduate or a graduate, who is pursuing studies or conducting research to meet the requirements for an academic or professional degree conferred by colleges or universities. It is not essential that such study or research be pursued or conducted at an educational institution which confers such degrees if the purpose thereof is to meet the requirements for a degree of a college or university which does confer such degrees. A student who receives a scholarship for study at a secondary school or other educational institution is considered to be a "candidate for a degree". [Reg. § 1.117-3.]

☐ [*T.D. 6186, 6-29-56. Amended by T.D. 8032, 7-1-85.*]

[Reg. § 1.117-4]

§ 1.117-4. Items not considered as scholarships or fellowship grants.—The following payments or allowances shall not be considered to be amounts received as a scholarship or a fellowship grant for the purpose of section 117:

(a) *Educational and training allowances to veterans.*—Educational and training allowances to a veteran pursuant to section 400 of the Servicemen's Readjustment Act of 1944 (58 Stat. 287) or pursuant to 38 U.S.C. 1631 (formerly section 231 of the Veterans Readjustment Assistance Act of 1952).

(b) *Allowances to members of the Armed Forces of the United States.*—Tuition and subsistence allowances to members of the Armed Forces of the United States who are students at an educational institution operated by the United States or approved by the United States for their education and training, such as the United States Naval Academy and the United States Military Academy.

(c) *Amounts paid as compensation for services or primarily for the benefit of the grantor.*

(1) Except as provided in paragraph (a) of § 1.117-2 and § 1.117-5, any amount paid or allowed to, or on behalf of, an individual to enable him to pursue studies or research, if such amount represents either compensation for past, present, or future employment services or represents payment for services which are subject to the direction or supervision of the grantor.

(2) Any amount paid or allowed to, or on behalf of, an individual to enable him to pursue studies or research primarily for the benefit of the grantor.

However, amounts paid or allowed to, or on behalf of, an individual to enable him to pursue studies or research are considered to be amounts received as a scholarship or fellowship grant for the purpose of section 117 if the primary purpose of the studies or research is to further the education and training of the recipient in his individual capacity and the amount provided by the grantor for such purpose does not represent compensation or payment for the services described in subparagraph (1) of this paragraph. Neither the fact that the recipient is required to furnish reports of his progress to the grantor, nor the fact that the results of his studies or research may be of some incidental benefit to the grantor shall, of itself, be considered to destroy the essential character of such amount as a scholarship or fellowship grant. [Reg. § 1.117-4.]

☐ [*T.D. 6186, 6-29-56. Amended by T.D. 8032, 7-1-85.*]

[Reg. § 1.117-5]

§ 1.117-5. Federal grants requiring future service as a federal employee.—(a) *In general.*—Under section 117(c), amounts received by an individual under a federal program as a scholarship or grant for qualified tuition and expenses at an institution of higher education are excluded from the gross income of the recipient even though the recipient is required to perform future service as a federal employee. See paragraph (c) of this section for the definitions of the terms "qualified tuition and expenses" and "institution of higher education."

(b) *Exception for uniformed services scholarship programs.*—The requirements of this section do not apply to amounts received before 1985 by a member of a uniformed service who entered training before 1981 under the Armed Forces Health Professions Scholarship Program, National Public Health Service Corps Scholarship Training Program, or other substantially similar federal programs requiring the recipient to work for a uniformed federal service after completion of studies. These awards are governed by section 4 of Pub. L. 93-483 as amended by Pub. L. 95-171, Pub. L. 95-600 and Pub. L. 96-167. See section 101(3) of title 37, United States Code for the definition of the term "uniformed service."

(c) *Definitions.*—(1) *Qualified tuition and related expenses.*—For purposes of section 117(c) and this section, qualified tuition and related expenses are those amounts which under the terms of the federal program are required to be used and in fact are used for payment of:

(i) Tuition and fees that are required for the recipient's enrollment or attendance at an institution of higher education; and

(ii) Those amounts used for payment of fees, books, supplies *and equipment required for courses of instruction at such an* institution.

Incidental expenses are not considered related expenses and thus are not excludable from gross income under section 117(c). Incidental expenses include room and board at an institution of

higher education, expenses for travel (including expenses for meals and lodging incurred during travel and allowances for travel of the recipient's family), research, clerical help, equipment and other expenses which are not required for enrollment at the institution or in a course of instruction at such institution.

(2) *Institution of higher education.*—To qualify as an institution of higher education under this section, the institution must be a public or other nonprofit institution in any state which—

(i) Admits as regular students only individuals who have a certificate of graduation from a high school or the recognized equivalent of such a certificate;

(ii) Is legally authorized within the state to provide a program of education beyond high school; and

(iii) Provides an education program for which it awards a bachelor's or higher degree or which is acceptable for full credit towards such a degree, or which trains and prepares students for gainful employment in a recognized health profession. For purposes of this section, recognized health professions are those health professions which are supervised or monitored by appropriate state or federal agencies or governing professional associations and which require members to be currently licensed or certified in order to practice.

(3) *Service as a federal employee.*—(i) *In general.*—Except as otherwise provided in paragraph (c)(3)(ii) of this section, service as a federal employee refers to employment of the recipient by the federal government to work directly for the federal government. Thus, federal grants or scholarships which do not require the recipient to work directly for the federal government are not governed by the rules of this section.

(ii) *Service in a health manpower shortage area.*—For purposes of this section an obligation under a grant for the recipient to serve in a health related field in a health manpower shortage area as designated by the Secretary of Health and Human Services according to the criteria of the Public Health Services Act (42 U.S.C. 254(e)) and the regulations promulgated thereunder (42 CFR 5.1-5.4) will be considered an obligation to serve as a federal employee.

(d) *Records required for exclusion from gross income.*—To exclude amounts received under federal programs requiring future services as a federal employee, the recipient must maintain records that establish that the amounts received under such programs were used for qualified tuition and related expenses as defined in paragraph (c)(1) of this section. Qualifying uses may be established by providing to the Service, upon request, copies of relevant bills, receipts, cancelled checks or other convenient documentation or records which clearly reflect the use of the money received under the grant. The recipient must also submit, upon request, documentation establishing receipt of the grant and setting out the terms and requirements of the particular grant.

(e) *Applicability of rules of § § 117(a) and 117(b).*—Except where a different rule has been expressly provided in this section, amounts received under federal grants requiring future service as a federal employee, and which meet the requirements for exclusion from gross income under this section, are subject to the rules, limitations and definitions specified in § § 117(a) and (b) of the Code and § § 1.117-1 through 1.117-4.

(f) *Effective date.*—Except as provided in paragraph (b) of this section, this section will apply to amounts received after December 31, 1980 under federal programs which meet the requirements of this section. [Reg. § 1.117-5.]

☐ [*T.D. 8032, 7-1-85.*]

[Reg. § 1.118-1]

§ 1.118-1. Contributions to the capital of a corporation.—In the case of a corporation, section 118 provides an exclusion from gross income with respect to any contribution of money or property to the capital of the taxpayer. Thus, if a corporation requires additional funds for conducting its business and obtains such funds through voluntary pro rata payments by its shareholders, the amounts so received being credited to its surplus account or to a special account, such amounts do not constitute income, although there is no increase in the outstanding shares of stock of the corporation. In such a case the payments are in the nature of assessments upon, and represent an additional price paid for, the shares of stock held by the individual shareholders, and will be treated as an addition to and as a part of the operating capital of the company. Section 118 also applies to contributions to capital made by persons other than shareholders. For example, the exclusion applies to the value of land or other property contributed to a corporation by a governmental unit or by a civic group for the purpose of inducing the corporation to locate its business in a particular community, or for the purpose of enabling the corporation to expand its operating facilities. However, the exclusion does not apply to any money or property transferred to the corporation in consideration for goods or services rendered, or to subsidies paid for the purpose of inducing the taxpayer to limit production. See section 362 for the basis of property acquired by a corporation through a contribution to its capital by its stockholders or by nonstockholders. [Reg. § 1.118-1.]

□ [T.D. 6220, 12-28-56.]

[Reg. § 1.118-2]

§1.118-2. Contribution in aid of construction.—(a) *Special rule for water and sewerage disposal utilities.*—(1) *In general.*—For purposes of section 118, the term *contribution to the capital of the taxpayer* includes any amount of money or other property received from any person (whether or not a shareholder) by a regulated public utility that provides water or sewerage disposal services if—

(i) The amount is a contribution in aid of construction under paragraph (b) of this section;

(ii) In the case of a contribution of property other than water or sewerage disposal facilities, the amount satisfies the expenditure rule under paragraph (c) of this section; and

(iii) The amount (or any property acquired or constructed with the amount) is not included in the taxpayer's rate base for ratemaking purposes.

(2) *Definitions.*—(i) *Regulated public utility* has the meaning given such term by section 7701(a)(33), except that such term does not include any utility which is not required to provide water or sewerage disposal services to members of the general public in its service area.

(ii) *Water or sewerage disposal facility* is defined as tangible property described in section 1231(b) that is used predominately (80% or more) in the trade or business of furnishing water or sewerage disposal services.

(b) *Contribution in aid of construction.*—(1) *In general.*—For purposes of section 118(c) and this section, the term *contribution in aid of construction* means any amount of money or other property contributed to a regulated public utility that provides water or sewerage disposal services to the extent that the purpose of the contribution is to provide for the expansion, improvement, or replacement of the utility's water or sewerage disposal facilities.

(2) *Advances.*—A contribution in aid of construction may include an amount of money or other property contributed to a regulated public utility for a water or sewerage disposal facility subject to a contingent obligation to repay the amount, in whole or in part, to the contributor (commonly referred to as an advance). For example, an amount received by a utility from a developer to construct a water facility pursuant to an agreement under which the utility will pay the developer a percentage of the receipts from the facility over a fixed period may constitute a contribution in aid of construction. Whether an advance is a contribution or a loan is determined under general principles of federal tax law based on all the facts and circumstances. For the treatment of any amount of a contribution in aid of construction that is repaid by the utility to the contributor, see paragraphs (c)(2)(ii) and (d)(2) of this section.

(3) *Customer connection fee.*—(i) *In general.*—Except as provided in paragraph (b)(3)(ii) of this section, a customer connection fee is not a contribution in aid of construction under this paragraph (b) and generally is includible in income. The term *customer connection fee* includes any amount of money or other property transferred to the utility representing the cost of installing a connection or service line (including the cost of meters and piping) from the utility's main water or sewer lines to the line owned by the customer or potential customer. A customer connection fee also includes any amount paid as a service charge for starting or stopping service.

(ii) *Exceptions.*—(A) *Multiple customers.*—Money or other property contributed for a connection or service line from the utility's main line to the customer's or the potential customer's line is not a customer connection fee if the connection or service line serves, or is designed to serve, more than one customer. For example, a contribution for a split service line that is designed to serve two customers is not a customer connection fee. On the other hand, if a water or sewerage disposal utility treats an apartment or office building as one utility customer, then the cost of installing a connection or service line from the utility's main water or sewer lines serving that single customer is a customer connection fee.

(B) *Fire protection services.*—Money or other property contributed for public and private fire protection services is not a customer connection fee.

(4) *Reimbursement for a facility previously placed in service.*—(i) *In general.*—If a water or sewerage disposal facility is placed in service by the utility before an amount is contributed to the utility, the contribution is not a contribution in aid of construction under this paragraph (b) with respect to the cost of the facility unless, no later than 8 1/2 months after the close of the taxable year in which the facility was placed in service, there is an agreement, binding under local law, that the utility is to receive the amount as reimbursement for the cost of acquiring or constructing the facility. An order or tariff, binding under local law, that is issued or approved by the applicable public utility commission requiring current or prospective utility customers to reimburse the utility for the cost of acquiring or constructing the facility, is a binding agreement for purposes of the preceding sentence. If an agreement exists, the basis of the facility must be reduced by the amount of the expected contributions. Appropriate adjustments must be made if actual contributions differ from expected contributions.

(ii) *Example.*—The application of paragraph (b)(4)(i) of this section is illustrated by the following example:

Example. M, a calendar year regulated public utility that provides water services, spent $1,000,000 for the construction of a water facility that can serve 200 customers. M placed the facility in service in 2000. In June 2001, the public utility commission that regulates M approves a tariff requiring new customers to reimburse M for the cost of constructing the facility by paying a service availability charge of $5,000 per lot. Pursuant to the tariff, M expects to receive reimbursements for the cost of the facility of $100,000 per year for the years 2001 through 2010. The reimbursements are contributions in aid of construction under paragraph (b) of this section because no later than 8 1/2 months after the close of the taxable year in which the facility was placed in service there was a tariff, binding under local law, approved by the public utility commission requiring new customers to reimburse the utility for the cost of constructing the facility. The basis of the $1,000,000 facility is zero because the expected contributions equal the cost of the facility.

(5) *Classification by ratemaking authority.*—The fact that the applicable ratemaking authority classifies any money or other property received by a utility as a contribution in aid of construction is not conclusive as to its treatment under this paragraph (b).

(c) *Expenditure rule.*—(1) *In general.*—An amount satisfies the expenditure rule of section 118(c)(2) if the amount is expended for the acquisition or construction of property described in section 118(c)(2)(A), the amount is paid or incurred before the end of the second taxable year after the taxable year in which the amount was received as required by section 118(c)(2)(B), and accurate records are kept of contributions and expenditures as provided in section 118(c)(2)(C).

(2) *Excess amount.*—(i) *Includible in the utility's income.*—An amount received by a utility as a contribution in aid of construction that is not expended for the acquisition or construction of water or sewerage disposal facilities as required by paragraph (c)(1) of this section (the excess amount) is not a contribution to the capital of the taxpayer under paragraph (a) of this section. Except as provided in paragraph (c)(2)(ii) of this section, such excess amount is includible in the utility's income in the taxable year in which the amount was received.

(ii) *Repayment of excess amount.*—If the excess amount described in paragraph (c)(2)(i) of this section is repaid, in whole or in part, either —

(A) Before the end of the time period described in paragraph (c)(1) of this section, the repayment amount is not includible in the utility's income; or

(B) After the end of the time period described in paragraph (c)(1) of this section, the repayment amount may be deducted by the utility in the taxable year in which it is paid or incurred to the extent such amount was included in income.

(3) *Example.*—The application of this paragraph (c) is illustrated by the following example:

Example. M, a calendar year regulated public utility that provides water services, received a $1,000,000 contribution in aid of construction in 2000 for the purpose of constructing a water facility. To the extent that the $1,000,000 exceeded the actual cost of the facility, the contribution was subject to being returned. In 2001, M built the facility at a cost of $700,000 and returned $200,000 to the contributor. As of the end of 2002, M had not returned the remaining $100,000. Assuming accurate records are kept, the requirement under section 118(c)(2) is satisfied for $700,000 of the contribution. Because $200,000 of the contribution was returned within the time period during which qualifying expenditures could be made, this amount is not includible in M's income. However, the remaining $100,000 is includible in M's income for its 2000 taxable year (the taxable year in which

Reg. § 1.118-2(c)(3)

the amount was received) because the amount was neither spent nor repaid during the prescribed time period. To the extent M repays the remaining $100,000 after year 2002, M would be entitled to a deduction in the year such repayment is paid or incurred.

(d) *Adjusted basis.*—(1) *Exclusion from basis.*—Except for a repayment described in paragraph (d)(2) of this section, to the extent that a water or sewerage disposal facility is acquired or constructed with an amount received as a contribution to the capital of the taxpayer under paragraph (a) of this section, the basis of the facility is reduced by the amount of the contribution. To the extent the water or sewerage disposal facility is acquired as a contribution to the capital of the taxpayer under paragraph (a) of this section, the basis of the contributed facility is zero.

(2) *Repayment of contribution.*—If a contribution to the capital of the taxpayer under paragraph (a) of this section is repaid to the contributor, either in whole or in part, then the repayment amount is a capital expenditure in the taxable year in which it is paid or incurred, resulting in an increase in the property's adjusted basis in such year. Capital expenditures allocated to depreciable property under paragraph (d)(3) of this section may be depreciated over the remaining recovery period for that property.

(3) *Allocation of contributions.*—An amount treated as a capital expenditure under this paragraph (d) is to be allocated proportionately to the adjusted basis of each property acquired or constructed with the contribution based on the relative cost of such property.

(4) *Example.*—The application of this paragraph (d) is illustrated by the following example:

Example. A, a calendar year regulated public utility that provides water services, received a $1,000,000 contribution in aid of construction in 2000 as an advance from B, a developer, for the purpose of constructing a water facility. To the extent that the $1,000,000 exceeds the actual cost of the facility, the contribution is subject to being returned. Under the terms of the advance, A agrees to pay to B a percentage of the receipts from the facility over a fixed period, but limited to the cost of the facility. In 2001, A builds the facility at a cost of $700,000 and returns $300,000 to B. In 2002, A pays $20,000 to B out of the receipts from the facility. Assuming accurate records are kept, the $700,000 advance is a contribution to the capital of A under paragraph (a) of this section and is excludable from A's income. The basis of the $700,000 facility constructed with this contribution to capital is zero. The $300,000 excess amount is not a contribution to the capital of A under paragraph (a) of this section because it does not meet the expenditure rule described in paragraph (c)(1) of this section. However, this excess amount is not includible in A's income pursuant to paragraph (c)(2)(ii) of this section since the amount is repaid to B within the required time period. The repayment of the $300,000 excess amount to B in 2001 is not treated as a capital expenditure by A. The $20,000 payment to B in 2002 is treated as a capital expenditure by A in 2002 resulting in an increase in the adjusted basis of the water facility from zero to $20,000.

(e) *Statute of limitations.*—(1) *Extension of statute of limitations.*— Under section 118(d)(1), the statutory period for assessment of any deficiency attributable to a contribution to capital under paragraph (a) of this section does not expire before the expiration of 3 years after the date the taxpayer notifies the Secretary in the time and manner prescribed in paragraph (e)(2) of this section.

(2) *Time and manner of notification.*—Notification is made by attaching a statement to the taxpayer's federal income tax return for the taxable year in which any of the reportable items in paragraphs (e)(2)(i) through (iii) of this section occur. The statement must contain the taxpayer's name, address, employer identification number, taxable year, and the following information with respect to contributions of property other than water or sewerage disposal facilities that are subject to the expenditure rule described in paragraph (c) of this section—

(i) The amount of contributions in aid of construction expended during the taxable year for property described in section 118(c)(2)(A) (qualified property) as required under paragraph (c)(1) of this section, identified by taxable year in which the contributions were received;

(ii) The amount of contributions in aid of construction that the taxpayer does not intend to expend for qualified property as required under paragraph (c)(1) of this section, identified by taxable year in which the contributions were received; and

(iii) The amount of contributions in aid of construction that the taxpayer failed to expend for qualified property as required under paragraph (c)(1) of this section, identified by taxable year in which the contributions were received.

(f) *Effective date.*—This section is applicable for any money or other property received by a regulated public utility that provides water or sewerage disposal services on or after January 11, 2001. [Reg. §1.118-2.]

☐ [T.D. 8936, 1-10-2001.]

[Reg. §1.119-1]

1.119-1. Meals and lodging furnished for the convenience of the employer.—(a) *Meals .*—(1) *In general .*—The value of meals furnished to an employee by his employer shall be excluded from the employee's gross income if two tests are met: (i) The meals are furnished on the business premises of the employer, and (ii) the meals are furnished for the convenience of the employer. The question of whether meals are furnished for the convenience of the employer is one of fact to be determined by analysis of all the facts and circumstances in each case. If the tests described in subdivisions (i) and (ii) of this subparagraph are met, the exclusion shall apply irrespective of whether under an employment contract or a statute fixing the terms of employment such meals are furnished as compensation.

(2) *Meals furnished without a charge .*—(i) Meals furnished by an employer without charge to the employee will be regarded as furnished for the convenience of the employer if such meals are furnished for a substantial noncompensatory business reason of the employer. If an employer furnishes meals as a means of providing additional compensation to his employee (and not for a substantial noncompensatory business reason of the employer), the meals so furnished will not be regarded as furnished for the convenience of the employer. Conversely, if the employer furnishes meals to his employee for a substantial noncompensatory business reason, the meals so furnished will be regarded as furnished for the convenience of the employer, even though such meals are also furnished for a compensatory reason. In determining the reason of an employer for furnishing meals, the mere declaration that meals are furnished for a noncompensatory business reason is not sufficient to prove that meals are furnished for the convenience of the employer, but such determination will be based upon an examination of all the surrounding facts and circumstances. In subdivision (ii) of this subparagraph, there are set forth some of the substantial noncompensatory business reasons which occur frequently and which justify the conclusion that meals furnished for such a reason are furnished for the convenience of the employer. In subdivision (iii) of this subparagraph, there are set forth some of the business reasons which are considered to be compensatory and which, in the absence of a substantial noncompensatory business reason, justify the conclusion that meals furnished for such a reason are not furnished for the convenience of the employer. Generally, meals furnished before or after the working hours of the employee will not be regarded as furnished for the convenience of the employer, but see subdivision (ii)(d) and (f) of this subparagraph for some exceptions to this general rule. Meals furnished on nonworking days do not qualify for the exclusion under section 119. If the employee is required to occupy living quarters on the business premises of his employer as a condition of his employment (as defined in paragraph (b) of this section), the exclusion applies to the value of any meal furnished without charge to the employee on such premises.

(ii)(a) Meals will be regarded as furnished for a substantial noncompensatory business reason of the employer when the meals are furnished to the employee during his working hours to have the employee available for emergency call during his meal period. In order to demonstrate that meals are furnished to the employee to have the employee available for emergency call during the meal period, it must be shown that emergencies have actually occurred, or can reasonably be expected to occur, in the employer's business which have resulted, or will result, in the employer calling on the employee to perform his job during his meal period.

(b) Meals will be regarded as furnished for a substantial noncompensatory business reason of the employer when the meals are furnished to the employee during his working hours because the employer's business is such that the employee must be restricted to a short meal period, such as 30 or 45 minutes, and because the employee could not be expected to eat elsewhere in such a short meal period. For example, meals may qualify under this subdivision when the employer is engaged in a business in which the peak workload occurs during the normal lunch hours. However, meals cannot qualify under this subdivision (b) when the reason for restricting the time of the meal period is so that the employee can be let off earlier in the day.

(c) Meals will be regarded as furnished for a substantial noncompensatory business reason of the employer when the meals are furnished to the employee during his working hours because the employee could not otherwise secure proper meals within a reasonable meal period. For example, meals may qualify under this subdivision (c) when there are insufficient eating facilities in the vicinity of the employer's premises.

(d) A meal furnished to a restaurant employee or other food service employee for each meal period in which the employee works will be regarded as furnished for a substantial noncompensatory business reason of the employer, irrespective of whether the meal is furnished during, immediately before, or immediately after the working hours of the employee.

(e) If the employer furnishes meals to employees at a place of business and the reason for furnishing the meals to each of substantially all of the employees who are furnished the meals is a substantial noncompensatory business reason of the employer, the meals furnished to each other employee will also be regarded as furnished for a substantial noncompensatory business reason of the employer.

(f) If an employer would have furnished a meal to an employee during his working hours for a substantial noncompensatory business reason, a meal furnished to such an employee immediately after his working hours because his duties prevented him from obtaining a meal during his working hours will be regarded as furnished for a substantial noncompensatory business reason.

(iii) Meals will be regarded as furnished for a compensatory business reason of the employer when the meals are furnished to the employee to promote the morale or goodwill of the employee, or to attract prospective employees.

(3) *Meals furnished with a charge* .—(i) If an employer provides meals which an employee may or may not purchase, the meals will not be regarded as furnished for the convenience of the employer. Thus, meals for which a charge is made by the employer will not be regarded as furnished for the convenience of the employer if the employee has a choice of accepting the meals and paying for them or of not paying for them and providing his meals in another manner.

(ii) If an employer furnishes an employee meals for which the employee is charged an unvarying amount (for example, by subtraction from his stated compensation) irrespective of whether he accepts the meals, the amount of such flat charge made by the employer for such meals is not, as such, part of the compensation includible in the gross income of the employee; whether the value of the meals so furnished is excludable under section 119 is determined by applying the rules of subparagraph (2) of this paragraph. If meals furnished for an unvarying amount are not furnished for the convenience of the employer in accordance with the rules of subparagraph (2) of this paragraph, the employee shall include in gross income the value of the meals regardless of whether the value exceeds or is less than the amount charged for such meals. In the absence of evidence to the contrary, the value of the meals may be deemed to be equal to the amount charged for them.

(b) *Lodging* .—The value of lodging furnished to an employee by the employer shall be excluded from the employee's gross income if three tests are met:

(1) The lodging is furnished on the business premises of the employer,

(2) The lodging is furnished for the convenience of the employer, and

(3) The employee is required to accept such lodging as a condition of his employment.

The requirement of subparagraph (3) of this paragraph that the employee is required to accept such lodging as a condition of his employment means that he be required to accept the lodging in order to enable him properly to perform the duties of his employment. Lodging will be regarded as furnished to enable the employee properly to perform the duties of his employment when, for example, the lodging is furnished because the employee is required to be available for duty at all times or because the employee could not perform the services required of him unless he is furnished such lodging. If the tests described in subparagraphs (1), (2), and (3) of this paragraph are met, the exclusion shall apply irrespective of whether a charge is made, or whether, under an employment contract or statute fixing the terms of employment, such lodging is furnished as compensation. If the employer furnishes the employee lodging for which the employee is charged an unvarying amount irrespective of whether he accepts the lodging, the amount of the charge made by the employer for such lodging is not, as such, part of the compensation includible in the gross income of the employee; whether the value of the lodging is excludable from gross income under section 119 is determined by applying the other rules of this paragraph. If the tests described in subparagraphs (1), (2), and (3) of this paragraph are not met, the employee shall include in gross income the value of the lodging regardless of whether it exceeds or is less than the amount charged. In the absence of evidence to the contrary, the value of the lodging may be deemed to be equal to the amount charged.

(c) *Business premises of the employer* .—(1) *In general* .—For purposes of this section, the term "business premises of the employer" generally means the place of employment of the employee. For example, meals and lodging furnished in the employer's home to a domestic servant would constitute meals and lodging furnished on the business premises of the employer. Similarly, meals furnished to cowhands while herding their employer's cattle on leased land would be regarded as furnished on the business premises of the employer.

(2) *Certain camps* .—For taxable years beginning after December 31, 1981, in the case of an individual who is furnished lodging by or on behalf of his employer in a camp (as defined in paragraph (d) of this section) in a foreign country (as defined in § 1.911-2(h)), the camp shall be considered to be part of the business premises of the employer.

(d) *Camp defined* .—(1) *In general* .—For the purposes of paragraph (c)(2) of this section, a camp is lodging that is all of the following:

(i) Provided by or on behalf of the employer for the convenience of the employer because the place at which the employee renders services is in a remote area where satisfactory housing is not available to the employee on the open market within a reasonable commuting distance of that place;

(ii) Located, as near as practicable, in the vicinity of the place at which the employee renders services; and

(iii) Furnished in a common area or enclave which is not available to the general public for lodging or accommodations and which normally accommodates ten or more employees.

(2) *Satisfactory housing* .—For purposes of paragraph (d)(1)(i) of this section, facts and circumstances that may be relevant in determining whether housing available to the employee is satisfactory include, but are not limited to, the size and condition of living space and the availability and quality of utilities such as water, sewers or other waste disposal facilities, electricity, or heat. The general environment in which housing is located (*e.g.* climate, prevalence of insects, etc.) does not of itself make housing unsatisfactory. The general environment is relevant, however, if housing is inadequate to protect the occupants from environmental conditions. The individual employee's income level is not relevant in determining whether housing is satisfactory; it may, however, be relevant in determining whether satisfactory housing is available to the employee (see paragraph (d)(3)(i)(B) of this section).

(3) *Availability of satisfactory housing* .—(i) *Facts and circumstances* .—For purposes of paragraph (d)(1)(i) of this section, facts and circumstances to be considered in determining whether satisfactory housing is available to the employee on the open market include but are not limited to:

(A) The number of housing units available on the open market in relation to the number of housing units required for the employer's employees;

(B) The cost of housing available on the open market;

(C) The quality of housing available on the open market; and

(D) The presence of warfare or civil insurrection within the area where housing would be available which would subject U.S. citizens to unusual risk of personal harm or property loss.

(ii) *Presumptions* .—Satisfactory housing will generally be considered to be unavailable to the employee on the open market if either of the following conditions is satisfied:

(A) The foreign government requires the employer to provide housing for its employees other than housing available on the open market; or

(B) An unrelated person awarding work to the employer requires that the employer's employees occupy housing specified by such unrelated person.

The condition of either paragraph (d)(3)(ii)(A) or (B) of this section is not satisfied if the requirement described therein and imposed either by a foreign government or unrelated person applies primarily to U.S. employers and not to a significant number of third country employers or applies primarily to employers of U.S. employees and not to a significant number of employers of third country employees.

(4) *Reasonable commuting distance* .—For purposes of paragraph (d)(1)(i) of this section, in determining whether a commuting distance is reasonable, the accessibility of the place at which the employee renders services due to geographic factors, the quality of the roads, the customarily available transportation, and the usual travel time (at the time of day such travel would be required) to the place at which the employee renders services shall be taken into account.

(5) *Common area or enclave* .—A cluster of housing units does not satisfy paragraph (d)(1)(iii) of this section if it is adjacent to or surrounded by substantially similar housing available to the general public. Two or more common areas or enclaves that house employees who work on the same project (for example, a highway project) are

Reg. 1.119-1(d)(5)

considered to be one common area or enclave in determining whether they normally accommodate ten or more employees.

(e) *Rules* .—The exclusion provided by section 119 applies only to meals and lodging furnished in kind by or on behalf of an employer to his employee. If the employee has an option to receive additional compensation in lieu of meals or lodging in kind, the value of such meals and lodging is not excludable from gross income under section 119. However, the mere fact that an employee, at his option, may decline to accept meals tendered in kind will not of itself require inclusion of the value thereof in gross income. Cash allowances for meals or lodging received by an employee are includible in gross income to the extent that such allowances constitute compensation.

(f) *Examples* .—The provisions of section 119 may be illustrated by the following examples:

Example (1). A waitress who works from 7 a.m. to 4 p.m. is furnished without charge two meals a work day. The employer encourages the waitress to have her breakfast on his business premises before starting work, but does not require her to have breakfast there. She is required, however, to have her lunch on such premises. Since the waitress is a food service employee and works during the normal breakfast and lunch periods, the waitress is permitted to exclude from her gross income both the value of the breakfast and the value of the lunch.

Example (2). The waitress in example (1) is allowed to have meals on the employer's premises without charge on her days off. The waitress is not permitted to exclude the value of such meals from her gross income.

Example (3). A bank teller who works from 9 a.m. to 5 p.m. is furnished his lunch without charge in a cafeteria which the bank maintains on its premises. The bank furnishes the teller such meals in order to limit his lunch period to 30 minutes since the bank's peak work load occurs during the normal lunch period. If the teller had to obtain his lunch elsewhere, it would take him considerably longer than 30 minutes for lunch, and the bank strictly enforces the 30-minute time limit. The bank teller may exclude from his gross income the value of such meals obtained in the bank cafeteria.

Example (4). Assume the same facts as in example (3), except that the bank charges the bank teller an unvarying rate per meal regardless of whether he eats in the cafeteria. The bank teller is not required to include in gross income such flat amount charged as part of his compensation, and he is entitled to exclude from his gross income the value of the meals he receives for such flat charge.

Example (5). A Civil Service employee of a State is employed at an institution and is required by his employer to be available for duty at all times. The employer furnishes the employee with meals and lodging at the institution without charge. Under the applicable State statute, his meals and lodging are regarded as part of the employee's compensation. The employee would nevertheless be entitled to exclude the value of such meals and lodging from his gross income.

Example (6). An employee of an institution is given the choice of residing at the institution free of charge, or of residing elsewhere and receiving a cash allowance in addition to his regular salary. If he elects to reside at the institution, the value to the employee of the lodging furnished by the employer will be includible in the employee's gross income because his residence at the institution is not required in order for him to perform properly the duties of his employment.

Example (7). A construction worker is employed at a construction project at a remote job site in Alaska. Due to the inaccessibility of facilities for the employees who are working at the job site to obtain food and lodging and the prevailing weather conditions, the employer is required to furnish meals and lodging to the employee at the camp site in order to carry on the construction project. The employee is required to pay $40 a week for the meals and lodging. The weekly charge of $40 is not, as such, part of the compensation includible in the gross income of the employee, and under paragraphs (a) and (b) of this section the value of the meals and lodging is excludable from his gross income.

Example (8). A manufacturing company provides a cafeteria on its premises at which its employees can purchase their lunch. There is no other eating facility located near the company's premises, but the employee can furnish his own meal by bringing his lunch. The amount of compensation which any employee is required to include in gross income is not reduced by the amount charged for the meals, and the meals are not considered to be furnished for the convenience of the employer.

Example (9). A hospital maintains a cafeteria on its premises where all of its 230 employees may obtain a meal during their working hours. No charge is made for these meals. The hospital furnishes such meals in order to have each of 210 of the employees available for any emergencies that may occur, and it is shown that each such employee is at times called upon to perform services during his meal period. Although the hospital does not require such employees to

remain on the premises during meal periods, they rarely leave the hospital during their meal period. Since the hospital furnishes meals to each of substantially all of its employees in order to have each of them available for emergency call during his meal period, all of the hospital employees who obtain their meals in the hospital cafeteria may exclude from their gross income the value of such meals. [Reg. § 1.119-1.]

☐ [T.D. 6220, 12-28-56. *Amended by T.D. 6745, 7-8-64 and T.D. 8006, 1-17-85.*]

[Reg. § 1.120-3]

§ 1.120-3. Notice of application for recognition of status of qualified group legal services plan.—(a) *In general.*—In order for a plan to be a qualified group legal services plan for purposes of the exclusion from gross income provided by section 120(a), the plan must give notice to the Internal Revenue Service that it is applying for recognition of its status as a qualified plan. Paragraph (b) of this section describes how the notice is to be filed for the plan. Paragraph (c) of this section describes the action that the Internal Revenue Service will take in response to the notice submitted for the plan. Paragraph (d) of this section describes the period of plan qualification.

(b) *Filing of notice.*—(1) *In general.*—A notice of application for recognition of the status of a qualified group legal services plan must be filed with the key district director of internal revenue as described in § 601.201(n). The notice must be filed on Form 1024, Application for Recognition of Exemption Under Section 501(a) or for Determination Under Section 120, with the accompanying Schedule L, and must contain the information required by the form and any accompanying instructions. The form may be filed by either the employer adopting the plan or the person administering the plan. No Form 1024 and Schedule L may be filed for a plan before an employer adopts the plan, or proposes to adopt the plan contingent only upon the recognition of the plan as a qualified plan.

(2) *Plans to which more than one employer contributes.*—In general, for purposes of section 120 the adoption of a plan by an employer constitutes the adoption of a separate plan to which that employer alone contributes, notwithstanding that, in form, the employer purports to adopt a plan with respect to which the employer is one of two or more contributing employers. Accordingly, a separate Schedule L must be filed pursuant to the instructions accompanying Form 1024 for each employer adopting a plan.

(3) *Certain collectively bargained plans.*—Notwithstanding subparagraph (2) of this paragraph, if a plan to which more than one employer contributes is a plan to which this subparagraph (3) applies, the plan is treated as a single plan for purposes of section 120. Accordingly, only one Form 1024 and Schedule L is required to be filed for the plan, regardless of the number of employers originally adopting the plan. In addition, once a Form 1024 and Schedule L is filed, no additional filing is required with respect to an employer who thereafter adopts the plan. In general, this subparagraph (3) applies to any plan that is maintained pursuant to a collective bargaining agreement between employee representatives and more than one employer who is required by the plan instrument or other agreement to contribute to the plan with respect to employees (or their spouses or dependents) participating in the plan. This subparagraph does not apply, however, if all employers required to contribute to the plan are corporations which are members of a controlled group of corporations within the meaning of section 1563(a), determined without regard to section 1563(e)(3)(C). If all employers required to contribute to the plan are corporations which are members of such a controlled group, the filing requirements described in subparagraph (2) of this paragraph apply, notwithstanding that the plan is maintained pursuant to a collective bargaining agreement.

(c) *Internal Revenue Service action on notice of application for recognition.*—The Internal Revenue Service will issue to the person submitting Form 1024 and Schedule L a ruling or determination letter stating that the plan is or is not a qualified group legal services plan. For general procedural rules, see § 601.201(a) through (n), as that section relates to rulings and determination letters.

(d) *Period of plan qualification.*—(1) *In general.*—In the case of a favorable determination, the plan will be considered a qualified group legal services plan. If a Form 1024 and Schedule L required to be filed by or on behalf of an employer is filed before—

(i) The end of the first plan year (as determined under the plan),

(ii) The end of the plan year within which the employer adopts the plan, or

(iii) July 29, 1980,

the period of plan qualification with respect to the employer will begin on the date the plan is adopted by the employer (or, if later,

January 1, 1977). If the form and schedule are not filed before the latest of the dates described in subdivisions (i), (ii) and (iii), the period of plan qualification with respect to the employer will begin on the date of filing. In any case in which either the Form 1024 or Schedule L filed by or on behalf of an employer is incomplete, the date of filing is the date on which the incomplete form or schedule is filed, if the necessary additional information is provided at the request of the Commissioner within the additional time period allowed by the Commissioner. If the additional information is not provided within the additional time period allowed, the date of filing is the date on which the additional information is filed. If no separate Form 1024 and Schedule L are required to be filed by or on behalf of an employer (see paragraph (b)(3) of this section), the period of plan qualification with respect to the employer will begin on the date the plan is adopted by the employer (or, if later, January 1, 1977). In any case in which a plan is materially modified to conform to the requirements of section 120, either before or after a Form 1024 and Schedule L are filed, the period of plan qualification will not include any period before the effective date of the modification.

(2) *Plans in existence on June 4, 1976.*—(i) Notwithstanding paragraph (d)(1) of this section, a written group legal services plan providing for employer contributions which was in existence on June 4, 1976, will be considered a qualified group legal services plan for the period January 1, 1977, through April 2, 1977. However, if the plan is maintained pursuant to one or more agreements which were in effect on October 4, 1976, and which the Secretary of Labor finds to be collective bargaining agreements, the period of deemed qualification will extend beyond April 2, 1977, and end on the date on which the last of the collective bargaining agreements relating to the plan terminates. Extensions of a bargaining agreement which are agreed to after October 4, 1976, are to be disregarded. The period of deemed qualification for a plan maintained pursuant to a collective bargaining agreement will not, however, extend beyond December 31, 1981.

(ii) A written group legal services plan will be considered to have been in existence on June 4, 1976, if on or before that date the plan was reduced to writing and adopted by one or more employers. No amounts need have been contributed under the plan as of June 4, 1976.

(iii) Notwithstanding that a plan is a qualified plan for the period of deemed qualification described in this paragraph (d)(2), the rules of paragraphs (c) and (d)(1) of this section still apply with respect to a Form 1024 and Schedule L filed for the plan. For example, if a Form 1024 and Schedule L filed by or on behalf of an employer are filed before the latest of the 3 dates described in paragraph (d)(1) of this section, in the case of a favorable determination the plan will be a qualified plan from the date the plan is adopted by the employer (or, if later, January 1, 1977), and any period of deemed qualification and the period of qualification based upon the favorable determination will overlap. However, in the case of a plan to which this paragraph (d)(2) applies, if a Form 1024 and Schedule L required to be filed by or on behalf of an employer is not filed before the latest of the 3 dates described in paragraph (d)(1) of this section, the following rules shall apply. In general, if Form 1024 and Schedule L are filed before the end of the plan year following the plan year with or within which the plan's period of deemed qualification expires, in the event of a favorable determination the plan will be a qualified plan with respect to the employer beginning on the earlier of the day following the date on which the period of deemed qualification expires or the date on which the Form 1024 and Schedule L are filed. The period of plan qualification with respect to an employer cannot, however, include any period before the employer adopts the plan. If the Form 1024 and Schedule L are not filed before the end of the plan year following the plan year with or within which the plan's period of deemed qualification expires, in the case of a favorable determination the plan will be a qualified plan with respect to an employer from the later of the date of filing or adoption of the plan by the employer. The rules described in paragraph (d)(1) of this section relating to incomplete filings and plan modifications apply with respect to a filing described in this paragraph (d)(2).

(e) *Effective date.*—This section is effective for notices of application for recognition of the status of a qualified group legal services plan filed after May 29, 1980. [Reg. § 1.120-3.]

☐ [T.D. 7696, 4-28-80.]

[Reg. § 1.121-1]

§ 1.121-1. Exclusion of gain from sale or exchange of a principal residence.—(a) *In general.*—Section 121 provides that, under certain circumstances, gross income does not include gain realized on the sale or exchange of property that was owned and used by a taxpayer as the taxpayer's principal residence. Subject to the other provisions of section 121, a taxpayer may exclude gain only if, during the 5-year period ending on the date of the sale or exchange, the taxpayer owned and used the property as the taxpayer's principal residence for periods aggregating 2 years or more.

(b) *Residence.*—(1) *In general.*—Whether property is used by the taxpayer as the taxpayer's residence depends upon all the facts and circumstances. A property used by the taxpayer as the taxpayer's residence may include a houseboat. a house trailer, or the house or apartment that the taxpayer is entitled to occupy as a tenant-stockholder in a cooperative housing corporation (as those terms are defined in section 216(b)(1) and (2)). Property used by the taxpayer as the taxpayer's residence does not include personal property that is not a fixture under local law.

(2) *Principal residence.*—In the case of a taxpayer using more than one property as a residence, whether property is used by the taxpayer as the taxpayer's principal residence depends upon all the facts and circumstances. If a taxpayer alternates between 2 properties, using each as a residence for successive periods of time, the property that the taxpayer uses a majority of the time during the year ordinarily will be considered the taxpayer's principal residence. In addition to the taxpayer's use of the property, relevant factors in determining a taxpayer's principal residence, include, but are not limited to—

(i) The taxpayer's place of employment;

(ii) The principal place of abode of the taxpayer's family members;

(iii) The address listed on the taxpayer's federal and state tax returns, driver's license, automobile registration, and voter registration card;

(iv) The taxpayer's mailing address for bills and correspondence;

(v) The location of the taxpayer's banks; and

(vi) The location of religious organizations and recreational clubs with which the taxpayer is affiliated.

(3) *Vacant land.*—(i) *In general.*—The sale or exchange of vacant land is not a sale or exchange of the taxpayer's principal residence unless—

(A) The vacant land is adjacent to land containing the dwelling unit of the taxpayer's principal residence;

(B) The taxpayer owned and used the vacant land as part of the taxpayer's principal residence;

(C) The taxpayer sells or exchanges the dwelling unit in a sale or exchange that meets the requirements of section 121 within 2 years before or 2 years after the date of the sale or exchange of the vacant land; and

(D) The requirements of section 121 have otherwise been met with respect to the vacant land.

(ii) *Limitations.*—(A) *Maximum limitation amount.*—For purposes of section 121(b)(1) and (2) (relating to the maximum limitation amount of the section 121 exclusion), the sale or exchange of the dwelling unit and the vacant land are treated as one sale or exchange. Therefore, only one maximum limitation amount of $250,000 ($500,000 for certain joint returns) applies to the combined sales or exchanges of vacant land and the dwelling unit. In applying the maximum limitation amount to sales or exchanges that occur in different taxable years, gain from the sale or exchange of the dwelling unit, up to the maximum limitation amount under section 121(b)(1) or (2), is excluded first and each spouse is treated as excluding one-half of the gain from a sale or exchange to which section 121(b)(2)(A) and § 1.121-2(a)(3)(i) (relating to the limitation for certain joint returns) apply.

(B) *Sale or exchange of more than one principal residence in 2-year period.*—If a dwelling unit and vacant land are sold or exchanged in separate transactions that qualify for the section 121 exclusion under this paragraph (b)(3), each of the transactions is disregarded in applying section 121(b)(3) (restricting the application of section 121 to only 1 sale or exchange every 2 years) to the other transactions but is taken into account as a sale or exchange of a principal residence on the date of the transaction in applying section 121(b)(3) to that transaction and the sale or exchange of any other principal residence.

(C) *Sale or exchange of vacant land before dwelling unit.*—If the sale or exchange of the dwelling unit occurs in a later taxable year than the sale or exchange of the vacant land and after the date prescribed by law (including extensions) for the filing of the return for the taxable year of the sale or exchange of the vacant land, any gain from the sale or exchange of the vacant land must be treated as taxable on the taxpayer's return for the taxable year of the sale or exchange of the vacant land. If the taxpayer has reported gain from the sale or exchange of the vacant land as taxable, after satisfying the requirements of this paragraph (b)(3) the taxpayer may claim the section 121 exclusion with regard to the sale or exchange of the vacant land (for any period for which the period of limitation under section 6511 has not expired) by filing an amended return.

(4) *Examples.*—The provisions of this paragraph (b) are illustrated by the following examples:

Example 1. Taxpayer A owns 2 residences, one in New York and one in Florida. From 1999 through 2004, he lives in the New York residence for 7 months and the Florida residence for 5 months of each year. In the absence of facts and circumstances indicating otherwise, the New York residence is A's principal residence. A would be eligible for the section 121 exclusion of gain from the sale or exchange of the New York residence, but not the Florida residence.

Example 2. Taxpayer B owns 2 residences, one in Virginia and one in Maine. During 1999 and 2000, she lives in the Virginia residence. During 2001 and 2002, she lives in the Maine residence. During 2003, she lives in the Virginia residence. B's principal residence during 1999, 2000, and 2003 is the Virginia residence. B's principal residence during 2001 and 2002 is the Maine residence. B would be eligible for the 121 exclusion of gain from the sale or exchange of either residence (but not both) during 2003.

Example 3. In 1991 Taxpayer C buys property consisting of a house and 10 acres that she uses as her principal residence. In May 2005 C sells 8 acres of the land and realizes a gain of $110,000. C does not sell the dwelling unit before the due date for filing C's 2005 return, therefore C is not eligible to exclude the $110,000 of gain. In March 2007 C sells the house and remaining 2 acres realizing a gain of $180,000 from the sale of the house. C may exclude the $180,000 of gain. Because the sale of the 8 acres occurred within 2 years from the date of the sale of the dwelling unit, the sale of the 8 acres is treated as a sale of the taxpayer's principal residence under paragraph (b)(3) of this section. C may file an amended return for 2005 to claim an exclusion for $70,000 ($250,000 – $180,000 gain previously excluded) of the $110,000 gain from the sale of the 8 acres.

Example 4. In 1998 Taxpayer D buys a house and 1 acre that he uses as his principal residence. In 1999 D buys 29 acres adjacent to his house and uses the vacant land as part of his principal residence. In 2003 D sells the house and 1 acre and the 29 acres in 2 separate transactions. D sells the house and 1 acre at a loss of $25,000. D realizes $270,000 of gain from the sale of the 29 acres. D may exclude the $245,000 gain from the 2 sales.

(c) *Ownership and use requirements.*—(1) *In general.*—The requirements of ownership and use for periods aggregating 2 years or more may be satisfied by establishing ownership and use for 24 full months or for 730 days (365 × 2). The requirements of ownership and use may be satisfied during nonconcurrent periods if both the ownership and use tests are met during the 5-year period ending on the date of the sale or exchange.

(2) *Use.*—(i) In establishing whether a taxpayer has satisfied the 2-year use requirement, occupancy of the residence is required. However, short temporary absences, such as for vacation or other seasonal absence (although accompanied with rental of the residence), are counted as periods of use.

(ii) *Determination of use during periods of out-of-residence care.*—If a taxpayer has become physically or mentally incapable of self-care and the taxpayer sells or exchanges property that the taxpayer owned and used as the taxpayer's principal residence for periods aggregating at least 1 year during the 5-year period preceding the sale or exchange, the taxpayer is treated as using the property as the taxpayer's principal residence for any period of time during the 5-year period in which the taxpayer owns the property and resides in any facility (including a nursing home) licensed by a State or political subdivision to care for an individual in the taxpayer's condition.

(3) *Ownership.*—(i) *Trusts.*—If a residence is owned by a trust, for the period that a taxpayer is treated under sections 671 through 679 (relating to the treatment of grantors and others as substantial owners) as the owner of the trust or the portion of the trust that includes the residence, the taxpayer will be treated as owning the residence for purposes of satisfying the 2-year ownership requirement of section 121, and the sale or exchange by the trust will be treated as if made by the taxpayer.

(ii) *Certain single owner entities.*—If a residence is owned by an eligible entity (within the meaning of § 301.7701-3(a) of this chapter) that has a single owner and is disregarded for federal tax purposes as an entity separate from its owner under § 301.7701-3 of this chapter, the owner will be treated as owning the residence for purposes of satisfying the 2-year ownership requirement of section 121, and the sale or exchange by the entity will be treated as if made by the owner.

(4) *Examples.*—The provisions of this paragraph (c) are illustrated by the following examples. The examples assume that § 1.121-3

(relating to the reduced maximum exclusion) does not apply to the sale of the property. The examples are as follows:

Example 1. Taxpayer A has owned and used his house as his principal residence since 1986. On January 31, 1998, A moves to another state. A rents his house to tenants from that date until April 18, 2000, when he sells it. A is eligible for the section 121 exclusion because he has owned and used the house as his principal residence for at least 2 of the 5 years preceding the sale.

Example 2. Taxpayer B owns and uses a house as her principal residence from 1986 to the end of 1997. On January 4, 1998, B moves to another state and ceases to use the house. B's son moves into the house in March 1999 and uses the residence until it is sold on July 1, 2001. B may not exclude gain from the sale under section 121 because she did not use the property as her principal residence for at least 2 years out of the 5 years preceding the sale.

Example 3. Taxpayer C lives in a townhouse that he rents from 1993 through 1996. On January 18, 1997, he purchases the townhouse. On February 1, 1998, C moves into his daughter's home. On May 25, 2000, while still living in his daughter's home, C sells his townhouse. The section 121 exclusion will apply to gain from the sale because C owned the townhouse for at least 2 years out of the 5 years preceding the sale (from January 19, 1997 until May 25, 2000) and he used the townhouse as his principal residence for at least 2 years during the 5-year period preceding the sale (from May 25, 1995 until February 1, 1998).

Example 4. Taxpayer D, a college professor, purchases and moves into a house on May 1, 1997. He uses the house as his principal residence continuously until September 1, 1998, when he goes abroad for a 1-year sabbatical leave. On October 1, 1999, 1 month after returning from the leave, D sells the house. Because his leave is not considered to be a short temporary absence under paragraph (c)(2) of this section, the period of the sabbatical leave may not be included in determining whether D used the house for periods aggregating 2 years during the 5-year period ending on the date of the sale. Consequently, D is not entitled to exclude gain under section 121 because he did not use the residence for the requisite period.

Example 5. Taxpayer E purchases a house on February 1, 1998, that he uses as his principal residence. During 1998 and 1999, E leaves his residence for a 2-month summer vacation. E sells the house on March 1, 2000. Although, in the 5-year period preceding the date of sale, the total time E used his residence is less than 2 years (21 months), the section 121 exclusion will apply to gain from the sale of the residence because, under paragraph (c)(2) of this section, the 2-month vacations are short temporary absences and are counted as periods of use in determining whether E used the residence for the requisite period.

(d) *Depreciation taken after May 6, 1997.*—(1) *In general.*—The section 121 exclusion does not apply to so much of the gain from the sale or exchange of property as does not exceed the portion of the depreciation adjustments (as defined in section 1250(b)(3)) attributable to the property for periods after May 6, 1997. Depreciation adjustments allocable to any portion of the property to which the section 121 exclusion does not apply under paragraph (e) of this section are not taken into account for this purpose.

(2) *Example.*—The provisions of this paragraph (d) are illustrated by the following example:

Example. On July 1, 1999, Taxpayer A moves into a house that he owns and had rented to tenants since July 1, 1997. A took depreciation deductions totaling $14,000 for the period that he rented the property. After using the residence as his principal residence for 2 full years, A sells the property on August 1, 2001. A's gain realized from the sale is $40,000. A has no other section 1231 or capital gains or losses for 2001. Only $26,000 ($40,000 gain realized – $14,000 depreciation deductions) may be excluded under section 121. Under section 121(d)(6) and paragraph (d)(1) of this section, A must recognize $14,000 of the gain as unrecaptured section 1250 gain within the meaning of section 1(h).

(e) *Property used in part as a principal residence.*—(1) *Allocation required.*—Section 121 will not apply to the gain allocable to any portion (separate from the dwelling unit) of property sold or exchanged with respect to which a taxpayer does not satisfy the use requirement. Thus, if a portion of the property was used for residential purposes and a portion of the property (separate from the dwelling unit) was used for non-residential purposes, only the gain allocable to the residential portion is excludable under section 121. No allocation is required if both the residential and non-residential portions of the property are within the same dwelling unit. However, section 121 does not apply to the gain allocable to the residential portion of the property to the extent provided by paragraph (d) of this section.

(2) *Dwelling unit.*—For purposes of this paragraph (e), the term *dwelling unit* has the same meaning as in section 280A(f)(1), but does not include appurtenant structures or other property.

(3) *Method of allocation.*—For purposes of determining the amount of gain allocable to the residential and non-residential portions of the property, the taxpayer must allocate the basis and the amount realized between the residential and the non-residential portions of the property using the same method of allocation that the taxpayer used to determine depreciation adjustments (as defined in section 1250(b)(3)), if applicable.

(4) *Examples.*—The provisions of this paragraph (e) are illustrated by the following examples:

Example 1. Non-residential use of property not within the dwelling unit. (i) Taxpayer A owns a property that consists of a house, a stable and 35 acres. A uses the stable and 28 acres for non-residential purposes for more than 3 years during the 5-year period preceding the sale. A uses the entire house and the remaining 7 acres as his principal residence for at least 2 years during the 5-year period preceding the sale. For periods after May 6, 1997, A claims depreciation deductions of $9,000 for the non-residential use of the stable. A sells the entire property in 2004, realizing a gain of $24,000. A has no other section 1231 or capital gains or losses for 2004.

(ii) Because the stable and the 28 acres used in the business are separate from the dwelling unit, the allocation rules under this paragraph (e) apply and A must allocate the basis and amount realized between the portion of the property that he used as his principal residence and the portion of the property that he used for non-residential purposes. A determines that $14,000 of the gain is allocable to the non-residential-use portion of the property and that $10,000 of the gain is allocable to the portion of the property used as his residence. A must recognize the $14,000 of gain allocable to the non-residential-use portion of the property ($9,000 of which is unrecaptured section 1250 gain within the meaning of section 1(h), and $5,000 of which is adjusted net capital gain). A may exclude $10,000 of the gain from the sale of the property.

Example 2. Non-residential use of property not within the dwelling unit and rental of the entire property. (i) In 1998 Taxpayer B buys a property that includes a house, a barn, and 2 acres. B uses the house and 2 acres as her principal residence and the barn for an antiques business. In 2002, B moves out of the house and rents it to tenants. B sells the property in 2004, realizing a gain of $21,000. Between 1998 and 2004 B claims depreciation deductions of $4,800 attributable to the antiques business. Between 2002 and 2004 B claims depreciation deductions of $3,000 attributable to the house. B has no other section 1231 or capital gains or losses for 2004.

(ii) Because the portion of the property used in the antiques business is separate from the dwelling unit, the allocation rules under this paragraph (e) apply. B must allocate basis and amount realized between the portion of the property that she used as her principal residence and the portion of the property that she used for non-residential purposes. B determines that $4,000 of the gain is allocable to the non-residential portion of the property and that $17,000 of the gain is allocable to the portion of the property that she used as her principal residence.

(iii) B must recognize the $4,000 of gain allocable to the non-residential portion of the property (all of which is unrecaptured section 1250 gain within the meaning of section 1(h)). In addition, the section 121 exclusion does not apply to the gain allocable to the residential portion of the property to the extent of the depreciation adjustments attributable to the residential portion of the property for periods after May 6, 1997 ($3,000). Therefore, B may exclude $14,000 of the gain from the sale of the property.

Example 3. Non-residential use of a separate dwelling unit. (i) In 2002 Taxpayer C buys a 3-story townhouse and converts the basement level, which has a separate entrance, into a separate apartment by installing a kitchen and bathroom and removing the interior stairway that leads from the basement to the upper floors. After the conversion, the property constitutes 2 dwelling units within the meaning of paragraph (e)(2) of this section. C uses the first and second floors of the townhouse as his principal residence and rents the basement level to tenants from 2003 to 2007. C claims depreciation deductions of $2,000 for that period with respect to the basement apartment. C *sells the entire property* in 2007, realizing gain of $18,000. C has no other section 1231 or capital gains or losses for 2007.

(ii) Because the basement apartment and the upper floors of the townhouse are separate dwelling units, C must allocate the gain between the portion of the property that he used as his principal residence and the portion of the property that he used for non-residential purposes under paragraph (e) of this section. After allocating the basis and the amount realized between the residential and non-residential portions of the property, C determines that $6,000 of the gain is allocable to the non-residential portion of the property and that $12,000 of the gain is allocable to the portion of the property

used as his residence. C must recognize the $6,000 of gain allocable to the non-residential portion of the property ($2,000 of which is unrecaptured section 1250 gain within the meaning of section 1(h), and $4,000 of which is adjusted net capital gain). C may exclude $12,000 of the gain from the sale of the property.

Example 4. Separate dwelling unit converted to residential use. The facts are the same as in *Example 3* except that in 2007 C incorporates the basement of the townhouse into his principal residence by eliminating the kitchen and building a new interior stairway to the upper floors. C uses all 3 floors of the townhouse as his principal residence for 2 full years and sells the townhouse in 2010, realizing a gain of $20,000. Under section 121(d)(6) and paragraph (d) of this section, C must recognize $2,000 of the gain as unrecaptured section 1250 gain within the meaning of section 1(h). Because C used the entire 3 floors of the townhouse as his principal residence for 2 of the 5 years preceding the sale of the property, C may exclude the remaining $18,000 of the gain from the sale of the house.

Example 5. Non-residential use within the dwelling unit, property depreciated. Taxpayer D, an attorney, buys a house in 2003. The house constitutes a single dwelling unit but D uses a portion of the house as a law office. D claims depreciation deductions of $2,000 during the period that she owns the house. D sells the house in 2006, realizing a gain of $13,000. D has no other section 1231 or capital gains or losses for 2006. Under section 121(d)(6) and paragraph (d) of this section, D must recognize $2,000 of the gain as unrecaptured section 1250 gain within the meaning of section 1(h). D may exclude the remaining $11,000 of the gain from the sale of her house because, under paragraph (e)(1) of this section, she is not required to allocate gain to the business use within the dwelling unit.

Example 6. Non-residential use within the dwelling unit, property not depreciated. The facts are the same as in *Example 5*, except that D is not entitled to claim any depreciation deductions with respect to her business use of the house. D may exclude $13,000 of the gain from the sale of her house because, under paragraph (e)(1) of this section, she is not required to allocate gain to the business use within the dwelling unit.

(f) *Effective date.*—This section is applicable for sales and exchanges on or after December 24, 2002. For rules on electing to apply the provisions of this section retroactively, see §1.121-4(j). [Reg. §1.121-1.]

☐ [T.D. 6856, 10-19-65. *Amended by* T.D. 7614, 4-26-79 *and* T.D. 9030, 12-23-2002.]

[Reg. §1.121-2]

§1.121-2. Limitations.—(a) *Dollar limitations.*—(1) *In general.*—A taxpayer may exclude from gross income up to $250,000 of gain from the sale or exchange of the taxpayer's principal residence. A taxpayer is eligible for only one maximum exclusion per principal residence.

(2) *Joint owners.*—If taxpayers jointly own a principal residence but file separate returns, each taxpayer may exclude from gross income up to $250,000 of gain that is attributable to each taxpayer's interest in the property, if the requirements of section 121 have otherwise been met.

(3) *Special rules for joint returns.*—(i) *In general.*—A husband and wife who make a joint return for the year of the sale or exchange of a principal residence may exclude up to $500,000 of gain if—

(A) Either spouse meets the 2-year ownership requirements of §1.121-1(a) and (c);

(B) Both spouses meet the 2-year use requirements of §1.121-1(a) and (c); and

(C) Neither spouse excluded gain from a prior sale or exchange of property under section 121 within the last 2 years (as determined under paragraph (b) of this section).

(ii) *Other joint returns.*—For taxpayers filing jointly, if either spouse fails to meet the requirements of paragraph (a)(3)(i) of this section, the maximum limitation amount to be claimed by the couple is the sum of each spouse's limitation amount determined on a separate basis as if they had not been married. For this purpose, each spouse is treated as owning the property during the period that either spouse owned the property.

(4) *Examples.*—The provisions of this paragraph (a) are illustrated by the following examples. The examples assume that §1.121-3 (relating to the reduced maximum exclusion) does not apply to the sale of the property. The examples are as follows:

Example 1. Unmarried Taxpayers A and B own a house as joint owners, each owning a 50 percent interest in the house. They sell the house after owning and using it as their principal residence for 2 full years. The gain realized from the sale is $256,000. A and B are each eligible to exclude $128,000 of gain because the amount of realized gain allocable to each of them from the sale does not exceed each taxpayer's available limitation amount of $250,000.

Example 2. The facts are the same as in *Example 1,* except that A and B are married taxpayers who file a joint return for the taxable year of the sale. A and B are eligible to exclude the entire amount of realized gain ($256,000) from gross income because the gain realized from the sale does not exceed the limitation amount of $500,000 available to A and B as taxpayers filing a joint return.

Example 3. During 1999, married Taxpayers H and W each sell a residence that each had separately owned and used as a principal residence before their marriage. Each spouse meets the ownership and use tests for his or her respective residence. Neither spouse meets the use requirement for the other spouse's residence. H and W file a joint return for the year of the sales. The gain realized from the sale of H's residence is $200,000. The gain realized from the sale of W's residence is $300,000. Because the ownership and use requirements are met for each residence by each respective spouse, H and W are each eligible to exclude up to $250,000 of gain from the sale of their individual residences. However, W may not use H's unused exclusion to exclude gain in excess of her limitation amount. Therefore, H and W must recognize $50,000 of the gain realized on the sale of W's residence.

Example 4. Married Taxpayers H and W sell their residence and file a joint return for the year of the sale. W, but not H, satisfies the requirements of section 121. They are eligible to exclude up to $250,000 of the gain from the sale of the residence because that is the sum of each spouse's dollar limitation amount determined on a separate basis as if they had not been married ($0 for H, $250,000 for W).

Example 5. Married Taxpayers H and W have owned and used their principal residence since 1998. On February 16, 2001, H dies. On September 24, 2001, W sells the residence and realizes a gain of $350,000. Pursuant to section 6013(a)(3), W and H's executor make a joint return for 2001. All $350,000 of the gain from the sale of the residence may be excluded.

Example 6. Assume the same facts as *Example 5,* except that W does not sell the residence until January 31, 2002. Because W's filing status for the taxable year of the sale is single, the special rules for joint returns under paragraph (a)(3) of this section do not apply and W may exclude only $250,000 of the gain.

(b) *Application of section 121 to only 1 sale or exchange every 2 years.*— (1) *In general.*—Except as otherwise provided in §1.121-3 (relating to the reduced maximum exclusion), a taxpayer may not exclude from gross income gain from the sale or exchange of a principal residence if, during the 2-year period ending on the date of the sale or exchange, the taxpayer sold or exchanged other property for which gain was excluded under section 121. For purposes of this paragraph (b)(1), any sale or exchange before May 7, 1997, is disregarded.

(2) *Example.*—The following example illustrates the rules of this paragraph (b). The example assumes that §1.121-3 (relating to the reduced maximum exclusion) does not apply to the sale of the property. The example is as follows:

Example. Taxpayer A owns a townhouse that he uses as his principal residence for 2 full years, 1998 and 1999. A buys a house in 2000 that he owns and uses as his principal residence. A sells the townhouse in 2002 and excludes gain realized on its sale under section 121. A sells the house in 2003. Although A meets the 2-year ownership and use requirements of section 121, A is not eligible to exclude gain from the sale of the house because A excluded gain within the last 2 years under section 121 from the sale of the townhouse.

(c) *Effective date.*—This section is applicable for sales and exchanges on or after December 24, 2002. For rules on electing to apply the provisions of this section retroactively, see §1.121-4(j). [Reg. §1.121-2.]

☐ [T.D. 6856, 10-19-65. *Amended by T.D. 7614, 4-26-79 and T.D. 9030,* 12-23-2002.]

[Reg. §1.121-3]

§1.121-3. Reduced maximum exclusion for taxpayers failing to meet certain requirements.—(a) *In general.*—In lieu of the limitation under section 121(b) and §1.121-2, a reduced maximum exclusion limitation may be available for a taxpayer who sells or exchanges property used as the taxpayer's principal residence but fails to satisfy the ownership and use requirements described in §1.121-1(a) and (c) or the 2-year limitation described in §1.121-2(b).

(b) *Primary reason for sale or exchange.*—In order for a taxpayer to claim a reduced maximum exclusion under section 121 (c), the sale or exchange must be by reason of a change in place of employment, health, or unforeseen circumstances. *If a safe harbor described in this section applies, a sale or exchange is deemed to be by reason of a change in place of employment, health, or unforeseen circumstances. If a safe harbor described in this section does not apply, a sale or*

exchange is by reason of a change in place of employment, health, or unforeseen circumstances only if the primary reason for the sale or exchange is a change in place of employment (within the meaning of paragraph (c) of this section), health (within the meaning of paragraph (d) of this section), or unforeseen circumstances (within the meaning of paragraph (e) of this section). Whether the requirements of this section are satisfied depends upon all the facts and circumstances. Factors that may be relevant in determining the taxpayer's primary reason for the sale or exchange include (but are not limited to) the extent to which—

(1) The sale or exchange and the circumstances giving rise to the sale or exchange are proximate in time;

(2) The suitability of the property as the taxpayer's principal residence materially changes;

(3) The taxpayer's financial ability to maintain the property is materially impaired;

(4) The taxpayer uses the property as the taxpayer's residence during the period of the taxpayer's ownership of the property;

(5) The circumstances giving rise to the sale or exchange are not reasonably foreseeable when the taxpayer begins using the property as the taxpayer's principal residence; and

(6) The circumstances giving rise to the sale or exchange occur during the period of the taxpayer's ownership and use of the property as the taxpayer's principal residence.

(c) *Sale or exchange by reason of a change in place of employment.*— (1) *In general.*—A sale or exchange is by reason of a change in place of employment if, in the case of a qualified individual described in paragraph (f) of this section, the primary reason for the sale or exchange is a change in the location of the individual's employment.

(2) *Distance safe harbor.*—A sale or exchange is deemed to be by reason of a change in place of employment (within the meaning of paragraph (c) (1) of this section) if—

(i) The change in place of employment occurs during the period of the taxpayer's ownership and use of the property as the taxpayer's principal residence; and

(ii) The qualified individual's new place of employment is at least 50 miles farther from the residence sold or exchanged than was the former place of employment, or, if there was no former place of employment, the distance between the qualified individual's new place of employment and the residence sold or exchanged is at least 50 miles.

(3) *Employment.*—For purposes of this paragraph (c), *employment* includes the commencement of employment with a new employer, the continuation of employment with the same employer, and the commencement or continuation of self-employment.

(4) *Examples.*—The following examples illustrate the rules of this paragraph (c):

Example 1. A is unemployed and owns a townhouse that she has owned and used as her principal residence since 2003. In 2004 A obtains a job that is 54 miles from her townhouse, and she sells the townhouse. Because the distance between A's new place of employment and the townhouse is at least 50 miles, the sale is within the safe harbor of paragraph (c) (2) of this section and A is entitled to claim a reduced maximum exclusion under section 121(c) (2).

Example 2. B is an officer in the United States Air Force stationed in Florida. B purchases a house in Florida in 2002. In May 2003 B moves out of his house to take a 3-year assignment in Germany. B sells his house in January 2004. Because B's new place of employment in Germany is at least 50 miles farther from the residence sold than is B's former place of employment in Florida, the sale is within the safe harbor of paragraph (c)(2) of this section and B is entitled to claim a reduced maximum exclusion under section 121(c)(2).

Example 3. C is employed by Employer R at R's Philadelphia office. C purchases a house in February 2002 that is 35 miles from R's Philadelphia office. In May 2003 C begins a temporary assignment at R's Wilmington office that is 72 miles from C's house, and moves out of the house. In June 2005 C is assigned to work in R's London office. C sells her house in August 2005 as a result of the assignment to London. The sale of the house is not within the safe harbor of paragraph (c)(2) of this section by reason of the change in place of employment from Philadelphia to Wilmington because the Wilmington office is not 50 miles farther from C's house than is the Philadelphia office. Furthermore, the sale is not within the safe harbor by reason of the change in place of employment to London because C is not using the house as her principal residence when she moves to London. However, C is entitled to claim a reduced maximum exclusion under section 121(c)(2) because, under the facts and circumstances, the primary reason for the sale is the change in C's place of employment.

Example 4. In July 2003 D, who works as an emergency medicine physician, buys a condominium that is 5 miles from her place of employment and uses it as her principal residence. In February 2004, D obtains a job that is located 51 miles from D's condominium. D may be called in to work unscheduled hours and, when called, must be able to arrive at work quickly. Because of the demands of the new job, D sells her condominium and buys a townhouse that is 4 miles from her new place of employment. Because D's new place of employment is only 46 miles farther from the condominium than is D's former place of employment, the sale is not within the safe harbor of paragraph (c)(2) of this section. However, D is entitled to claim a reduced maximum exclusion under section 121(c)(2) because, under the facts and circumstances, the primary reason for the sale is the change in D's place of employment.

(d) *Sale or exchange by reason of health.*—(1) *In general.*—A sale or exchange is by reason of health if the primary reason for the sale or exchange is to obtain, provide, or facilitate the diagnosis, cure, mitigation, or treatment of disease, illness, or injury of a qualified individual described in paragraph (f) of this section, or to obtain or provide medical or personal care for a qualified individual suffering from a disease, illness, or injury. A sale or exchange that is merely beneficial to the general health or well-being of an individual is not a sale or exchange by reason of health.

(2) *Physician's recommendation safe harbor.*—A sale or exchange is deemed to be by reason of health if a physician (as defined in section 213(d)(4)) recommends a change of residence for reasons of health (as defined in paragraph (d)(1) of this section).

(3) *Examples.*—The following examples illustrate the rules of this paragraph (d):

Example 1. In 2003 A buys a house that she uses as her principal residence. A is injured in an accident and is unable to care for herself. A sells her house in 2004 and moves in with her daughter so that the daughter can provide the care that A requires as a result of her injury. Because, under the facts and circumstances, the primary reason for the sale of A's house is A's health, A is entitled to claim a reduced maximum exclusion under section 121(c)(2).

Example 2. H's father has a chronic disease. In 2003 H and W purchase a house that they use as their principal residence. In 2004 H and W sell their house in order to move into the house of H's father so that they can provide the care he requires as a result of his disease. Because, under the facts and circumstances, the primary reason for the sale of their house is the health of H's father, H and W are entitled to claim a reduced maximum exclusion under section 121(c)(2).

Example 3. H and W purchase a house in 2003 that they use as their principal residence. Their son suffers from a chronic illness that requires regular medical care. Later that year their son begins a new treatment that is available at a hospital 100 miles away from their residence. In 2004 H and W sell their house so that they can be closer to the hospital to facilitate their son's treatment. Because, under the facts and circumstances, the primary reason for the sale is to facilitate the treatment of their son's chronic illness, H and W are entitled to claim a reduced maximum exclusion under section 121(c)(2).

Example 4. B, who has chronic asthma, purchases a house in Minnesota in 2003 that he uses as his principal residence. B's doctor tells B that moving to a warm, dry climate would mitigate B's asthma symptoms. In 2004 B sells his house and moves to Arizona to relieve his asthma symptoms. The sale is within the safe harbor of paragraph (d)(2) of this section and B is entitled to claim a reduced maximum exclusion under section 121(c)(2).

Example 5. In 2003 H and W purchase a house in Michigan that they use as their principal residence. H's doctor tells H that he should get more outdoor exercise, but H is not suffering from any disease that can be treated or mitigated by outdoor exercise. In 2004 H and W sell their house and move to Florida so that H can increase his general level of exercise by playing golf year-round. Because the sale of the house is merely beneficial to H's general health, the sale of the house is not by reason of H's health. H and W are not entitled to claim a reduced maximum exclusion under section 121(c)(2).

(e) *Sale or exchange by reason of unforeseen circumstances.*—(1) *In general.*—A sale or exchange is by reason of unforeseen circumstances if the primary reason for the sale or exchange is the occurrence of an event that the taxpayer could not reasonably have anticipated before purchasing and occupying the residence. A sale or exchange by reason of unforeseen circumstances (other than a sale or exchange deemed to be by reason of unforeseen circumstances under paragraph (e)(2) or (3) of this section) does not qualify for the reduced maximum exclusion if the primary reason for the sale or exchange is a preference for a different residence or an improvement in financial circumstances.

(2) *Specific event safe harbors.*—A sale or exchange is deemed to be by reason of unforeseen circumstances (within the meaning of paragraph (e)(1) of this section) if any of the events specified in

paragraphs (e)(2)(i) through (iii) of this section occur during the period of the taxpayer's ownership and use of the residence as the taxpayer's principal residence:

(i) The involuntary conversion of the residence.

(ii) Natural or man-made disasters or acts of war or terrorism resulting in a casualty to the residence (without regard to deductibility under section 165(h)).

(iii) In the case of a qualified individual described in paragraph (f) of this section—

(A) Death;

(B) The cessation of employment as a result of which the qualified individual is eligible for unemployment compensation (as defined in section 85(b));

(C) A change in employment or self-employment status that results in the taxpayer's inability to pay housing costs and reasonable basic living expenses for the taxpayer's household (including amounts for food, clothing, medical expenses, taxes, transportation, court-ordered payments, and expenses reasonably necessary to the production of income, but not for the maintenance of an affluent or luxurious standard of living);

(D) Divorce or legal separation under a decree of divorce or separate maintenance; or

(E) Multiple births resulting from the same pregnancy.

(3) *Designation of additional events as unforeseen circumstances.*—The Commissioner may designate other events or situations as unforeseen circumstances in published guidance of general applicability and may issue rulings addressed to specific taxpayers identifying other events or situations as unforeseen circumstances with regard to those taxpayers (see § 601.601(d)(2) of this chapter).

(4) *Examples.*—The following examples illustrate the rules of this paragraph (e):

Example 1. In 2003 A buys a house in California. After A begins to use the house as her principal residence, an earthquake causes damage to A's house. A sells the house in 2004. The sale is within the safe harbor of paragraph (e)(2)(ii) of this section and A is entitled to claim a reduced maximum exclusion under section 121(c)(2).

Example 2. H works as a teacher and W works as a pilot. In 2003 H and W buy a house that they use as their principal residence. Later that year W is furloughed from her job for six months. H and W are unable to pay their mortgage and reasonable basic living expenses for their household during the period W is furloughed. H and W sell their house in 2004. The sale is within the safe harbor of paragraph (e)(2)(iii)(C) of this section and H and W are entitled to claim a reduced maximum exclusion under section 121(c)(2).

Example 3. In 2003 H and W buy a two-bedroom condominium that they use as their principal residence. In 2004 W gives birth to twins and H and W sell their condominium and buy a four-bedroom house. The sale is within the safe harbor of paragraph (e)(2)(iii)(E) of this section, and H and W are entitled to claim a reduced maximum exclusion under section 121(c)(2).

Example 4. In 2003 B buys a condominium in a high-rise building and uses it as his principal residence. B's monthly condominium fee is $X. Three months after B moves into the condominium, the condominium association replaces the building's roof and heating system. Six months later, B's monthly condominium fee doubles in order to pay for the repairs. B sells the condominium in 2004 because he is unable to afford the new condominium fee along with a monthly mortgage payment. The safe harbors of paragraph (e)(2) of this section do not apply. However, under the facts and circumstances, the primary reason for the sale, the doubling of the condominium fee, is an unforeseen circumstance because B could not reasonably have anticipated that the condominium fee would double at the time he purchased and occupied the property. Consequently, the sale of the condominium is by reason of unforeseen circumstances and B is entitled to claim a reduced maximum exclusion under section 121(c)(2).

Example 5. In 2003 C buys a house that he uses as his principal residence. The property is located on a heavily traveled road. C sells the property in 2004 because C is disturbed by the traffic. The safe harbors of paragraph (e)(2) of this section do not apply. Under the facts and circumstances, the primary reason for the sale, the traffic, is not an unforeseen circumstance because C could reasonably have anticipated the traffic at the time he purchased and occupied the house. Consequently, the sale of the house is not by reason of unforeseen circumstances and C is not entitled to claim a reduced maximum exclusion under section 121(c)(2).

Example 6. In 2003 D and her fiancé E buy a house and live in it as their principal residence. In 2004 D and E cancel their wedding plans and E moves out of the house. Because D cannot afford to make the monthly mortgage payments alone, D and E sell the house in 2004. The safe harbors of paragraph (e)(2) of this section do not apply. However, under the facts and circumstances, the primary reason for the sale, the broken engagement, is an unforeseen circumstance because D and E could not reasonably have anticipated the broken engagement at the time they purchased and occupied the house. Consequently, the sale is by reason of unforeseen circumstances and D and E are each entitled to claim a reduced maximum exclusion under section 121(c)(2).

Example 7. In 2003 F buys a small condominium that she uses as her principal residence. In 2005 F receives a promotion and a large increase in her salary. F sells the condominium in 2004 and purchases a house because she can now afford the house. The safe harbors of paragraph (e)(2) of this section do not apply. Under the facts and circumstances, the primary reason for the sale of the house, F's salary increase, is an improvement in F's financial circumstances. Under paragraph (e)(1) of this section, an improvement in financial circumstances, even if the result of unforeseen circumstances, does not qualify for the reduced maximum exclusion by reason of unforeseen circumstances under section 121(c)(2).

Example 8. In April 2003 G buys a house that he uses as his principal residence. G sells his house in October 2004 because the house has greatly appreciated in value, mortgage rates have substantially decreased, and G can afford a bigger house. The safe harbors of paragraph (e)(2) of this section do not apply. Under the facts and circumstances, the primary reasons for the sale of the house, the changes in G's house value and in the mortgage rates, are an improvement in G's financial circumstances. Under paragraph (e)(1) of this section, an improvement in financial circumstances, even if the result of unforeseen circumstances, does not qualify for the reduced maximum exclusion by reason of unforeseen circumstances under section 121(c)(2).

Example 9. H works as a police officer for City X. In 2003 H buys a condominium that he uses as his principal residence. In 2004 H is assigned to City X's K-9 unit and is required to care for the police service dog at his home. Because H's condominium association does not permit H to have a dog in his condominium, in 2004 he sells the condominium and buys a house. The safe harbors of paragraph (e)(2) of this section do not apply. However, under the facts and circumstances, the primary reason for the sale, H's assignment to the K-9 unit, is an unforeseen circumstance because H could not reasonably have anticipated his assignment to the K-9 unit at the time he purchased and occupied the condominium. Consequently, the sale of the condominium is by reason of unforeseen circumstances and H is entitled to claim a reduced maximum exclusion under section 121(c)(2).

Example 10. In 2003, J buys a small house that she uses as her principal residence. After J wins the lottery, she sells the small house in 2004 and buys a bigger, more expensive house. The safe harbors of paragraph (e)(2) of this section do not apply. Under the facts and circumstances, the primary reason for the sale of the house, winning the lottery, is an improvement in J's financial circumstances. Under paragraph (e)(1) of this section, an improvement in financial circumstances, even if the result of unforeseen circumstances, does not qualify for the reduced maximum exclusion under section 121(c)(2).

(f) *Qualified individual.*—For purposes of this section, *qualified individual* means—

(1) The taxpayer;

(2) The taxpayer's spouse;

(3) A co-owner of the residence;

(4) A person whose principal place of abode is in the same household as the taxpayer; or

(5) For purposes of paragraph (d) of this section, a person bearing a relationship specified in sections 152(a)(1) through 152(a)(8) (without regard to qualification as a dependent) to a qualified individual described in paragraphs (f)(1) through (4) of this section, or a descendant of the taxpayer's grandparent.

(g) *Computation of reduced maximum exclusion.*—(1) The reduced maximum exclusion is computed by multiplying the maximum dollar limitation of $250,000 ($500,000 for certain joint filers) by a fraction. The numerator of the fraction is the shortest of the period of time that the taxpayer owned the property during the 5-year period ending on the date of the sale or exchange; the period of time that the taxpayer used the property as the taxpayer's principal residence during the 5-year period ending on the date of the sale or exchange; or the period of time between the date of a prior sale or exchange of property for which the taxpayer excluded gain under section 121 and the date of the current sale or exchange. The numerator of the fraction may be expressed in days or months. The denominator of the fraction is 730 days or 24 months (depending on the measure of time used in the numerator).

(2) *Examples.*—The following examples illustrate the rules of this paragraph (g):

Example 1. Taxpayer A purchases a house that she uses as her principal residence. Twelve months after the purchase, A sells the

house due to a change in place of her employment. A has not excluded gain under section 121 on a prior sale or exchange of property within the last 2 years. A is eligible to exclude up to $125,000 of the gain from the sale of her house (12/24 × $250,000).

Example 2. (i) Taxpayer H owns a house that he has used as his principal residence since 1996. On January 15, 1999, H and W marry and W begins to use H's house as her principal residence. On January 15, 2000, H sells the house due to a change in W's place of employment. Neither H nor W has excluded gain under section 121 on a prior sale or exchange of property within the last 2 years.

(ii) Because H and W have not each used the house as their principal residence for at least 2 years during the 5-year period preceding its sale, the maximum dollar limitation amount that may be claimed by H and W will not be $500,000, but the sum of each spouse's limitation amount determined on a separate basis as if they had not been married. (See § 1.121-2(a)(3)(ii).)

(iii) H is eligible to exclude up to $250,000 of gain because he meets the requirements of section 121. W is not eligible to exclude the maximum dollar limitation amount. Instead, because the sale of the house is due to a change in place of employment, W is eligible to claim a reduced maximum exclusion of up to $125,000 of the gain (365/730 × $250,000). Therefore, H and W are eligible to exclude up to $375,000 of gain ($250,000 + $125,000) from the sale of the house.

(h) *Effective dates.*—Paragraphs (a) and (g) of this section are applicable for sales and exchanges on or after December 24, 2002. Paragraphs (b) through (f) of this section are applicable for sales and exchanges on or after August 13, 2004. [Reg. § 1.121-3.]

□ [*T.D.* 6856, 10-19-65. *Amended by T.D.* 7614, 4-26-79; *T.D.* 9030, 12-23-2002 *and T.D.* 9152, 8-13-2004.]

[Reg. § 1.121-4]

§ 1.121-4. Special rules.—(a) *Property of deceased spouse.*—(1) *In general.*—For purposes of satisfying the ownership and use requirements of section 121, a taxpayer is treated as owning and using property as the taxpayer's principal residence during any period that the taxpayer's deceased spouse owned and used the property as a principal residence before death if—

(i) The taxpayer's spouse is deceased on the date of the sale or exchange of the property; and

(ii) The taxpayer has not remarried at the time of the sale or exchange of the property.

(2) *Example.*—The provisions of this paragraph (a) are illustrated by the following example. The example assumes that § 1.121-3 (relating to the reduced maximum exclusion) does not apply to the sale of the property. The example is as follows:

Example. Taxpayer H has owned and used a house as his principal residence since 1987. H and W marry on July 1, 1999 and from that date they use H's house as their principal residence. H dies on August 15, 2000, and W inherits the property. W sells the property on September 1, 2000, at which time she has not remarried. Although W has owned and used the house for less than 2 years, W will be considered to have satisfied the ownership and use requirements of section 121 because W's period of ownership and use includes the period that H owned and used the property before death.

(b) *Property owned by spouse or former spouse.*—(1) *Property transferred to individual from spouse or former spouse.*—If a taxpayer obtains property from a spouse or former spouse in a transaction described in section 1041(a), the period that the taxpayer owns the property will include the period that the spouse or former spouse owned the property.

(2) *Property used by spouse or former spouse.*—A taxpayer is treated as using property as the taxpayer's principal residence for any period that the taxpayer has an ownership interest in the property and the taxpayer's spouse or former spouse is granted use of the property under a divorce or separation instrument (as defined in section 71(b)(2)), provided that the spouse or former spouse uses the property as his or her principal residence.

(c) *Tenant-stockholder in cooperative housing corporation.*—A taxpayer who holds stock as a tenant-stockholder in a cooperative housing corporation (as those terms are defined in section 216(b)(1) and (2)) may be eligible to exclude gain under section 121 on the sale or exchange of the stock. In determining whether the taxpayer meets the requirements of section 121, the ownership requirements are applied to the holding of the stock and the use requirements are applied to the house or apartment that the taxpayer is entitled to occupy by reason of the taxpayer's stock ownership.

(d) *Involuntary conversions.*—(1) *In general.*—For purposes of section 121, the destruction, theft, seizure, requisition, or condemnation of property is treated as a sale of the property.

(2) *Application of section 1033.*—In applying section 1033 (relating to involuntary conversions), the amount realized from the sale or exchange of property used as the taxpayer's principal residence is treated as being the amount determined without regard to section 121, reduced by the amount of gain excluded from the taxpayer's gross income under section 121.

(3) *Property acquired after involuntary conversion.*—If the basis of the property acquired as a result of an involuntary conversion is determined (in whole or in part) under section 1033(b) (relating to the basis of property acquired through an involuntary conversion), then for purposes of satisfying the requirements of section 121, the taxpayer will be treated as owning and using the acquired property as the taxpayer's principal residence during any period of time that the taxpayer owned and used the converted property as the taxpayer's principal residence.

(4) *Example.*—The provisions of this paragraph (d) are illustrated by the following example:

Example. (i) On February 18, 1999, fire destroys Taxpayer A's house which has an adjusted basis of $80,000. A had owned and used this property as her principal residence for 20 years prior to its destruction. A's insurance company pays A $400,000 for the house. A realizes a gain of $320,000 ($400,000 – $80,000). On August 27, 1999, A purchases a new house at a cost of $100,000.

(ii) Because the destruction of the house is treated as a sale for purposes of section 121, A will exclude $250,000 of the realized gain from A's gross income. For purposes of section 1033, the amount realized is then treated as being $150,000 ($400,000 – $250,000) and the gain realized is $70,000 ($150,000 amount realized – $80,000 basis). A elects under section 1033 to recognize only $50,000 of the gain ($150,000 amount realized – $100,000 cost of new house). The remaining $20,000 of gain is deferred and A's basis in the new house is $80,000 ($100,000 cost – $20,000 gain not recognized).

(iii) A will be treated as owning and using the new house as A's principal residence during the 20-year period that A owned and used the destroyed house.

(e) *Sales or exchanges of partial interests.*—(1) *Partial interests other than remainder interests.*—(i) *In general.*—Except as provided in paragraph (e)(2) of this section (relating to sales or exchanges of remainder interests), a taxpayer may apply the section 121 exclusion to gain from the sale or exchange of an interest in the taxpayer's principal residence that is less than the taxpayer's entire interest if the interest sold or exchanged includes an interest in the dwelling unit. For rules relating to the sale or exchange of vacant land, see § 1.121-1(b)(3).

(ii) *Limitations.*—(A) *Maximum limitation amount.*—For purposes of section 121(b)(1) and (2) (relating to the maximum limitation amount of the section 121 exclusion), sales or exchanges of partial interests in the same principal residence are treated as one sale or exchange. Therefore, only one maximum limitation amount of $250,000 ($500,000 for certain joint returns) applies to the combined sales or exchanges of the partial interests. In applying the maximum limitation amount to sales or exchanges that occur in different taxable years, a taxpayer may exclude gain from the first sale or exchange of a partial interest up to the taxpayer's full maximum limitation amount and may exclude gain from the sale or exchange of any other partial interest in the same principal residence to the extent of any remaining maximum limitation amount, and each spouse is treated as excluding one-half of the gain from a sale or exchange to which section 121(b)(2)(A) and § 1.121-2(a)(3)(i) (relating to the limitation for certain joint returns) apply.

(B) *Sale or exchange of more than one principal residence in 2-year period.*—For purposes of applying section 121(b)(3) (restricting the application of section 121 to only 1 sale or exchange every 2 years), each sale or exchange of a partial interest is disregarded with respect to other sales or exchanges of partial interests in the same principal residence, but is taken into account as of the date of the sale or exchange in applying section 121(b)(3) to that sale or exchange and the sale or exchange of any other principal residence.

(2) *Sales or exchanges of remainder interests.*—(i) *In general.*—A taxpayer may elect to apply the section 121 exclusion to gain from the sale or exchange of a remainder interest in the taxpayer's principal residence.

(ii) *Limitations.*—(A) *Sale or exchange of any other interest.*—If a taxpayer elects to exclude gain from the sale or exchange of a remainder interest in the taxpayer's principal residence, the section 121 exclusion will not apply to a sale or exchange of any other interest in the residence that is sold or exchanged separately.

(B) *Sales or exchanges to related parties.*—This paragraph (e)(2) will not apply to a sale or exchange to any person that bears a

relationship to the taxpayer that is described in section 267(b) or 707(b).

(iii) *Election.*—The taxpayer makes the election under this paragraph (e)(2) by filing a return for the taxable year of the sale or exchange that does not include the gain from the sale or exchange of the remainder interest in the taxpayer's gross income. A taxpayer may make or revoke the election at any time before the expiration of a 3-year period beginning on the last date prescribed by law (determined without regard to extensions) for the filing of the return for the taxable year in which the sale or exchange occurred.

(3) *Example.*—The provisions of this paragraph (e) are illustrated by the following example:

Example. In 1991 Taxpayer A buys a house that A uses as his principal residence. In 2004 A's friend B moves into A's house and A sells B a 50% interest in the house realizing a gain of $136,000. A may exclude the $136,000 of gain. In 2005 A sells his remaining 50% interest in the home to B realizing a gain of $138,000. A may exclude $114,000 ($250,000 – $136,000 gain previously excluded) of the $138,000 gain from the sale of the remaining interest.

(f) *No exclusion for expatriates.*—The section 121 exclusion will not apply to any sale or exchange by an individual if the provisions of section 877(a) (relating to the treatment of expatriates) applies to the individual.

(g) *Election to have section not apply.*—A taxpayer may elect to have the section 121 exclusion not apply to a sale or exchange of property. The taxpayer makes the election by filing a return for the taxable year of the sale or exchange that includes the gain from the sale or exchange of the taxpayer's principal residence in the taxpayer's gross income. A taxpayer may make an election under this paragraph (g) to have section 121 not apply (or revoke an election to have section 121 not apply) at any time before the expiration of a 3-year period beginning on the last date prescribed by law (determined without regard to extensions) for the filing of the return for the taxable year in which the sale or exchange occurred.

(h) *Residences acquired in rollovers under section 1034.*—If a taxpayer acquires property in a transaction that qualifies under section 1034 (section 1034 property) for the nonrecognition of gain realized on the sale or exchange of another property and later sells or exchanges such property, in determining the period of the taxpayer's ownership and use of the property under section 121 the taxpayer may include the periods that the taxpayer owned and used the section 1034 property as the taxpayer's principal residence (and each prior residence taken into account under section 1223(7) in determining the holding period of the section 1034 property).

(i) [Reserved].

(j) *Election to apply regulations retroactively.*—Taxpayers who would otherwise qualify under §§ 1.121-1 through 1.121-4 to exclude gain from a sale or exchange of a principal residence before December 24, 2002 but on or after May 7, 1997, may elect to apply §§ 1.121-1 through 1.121-4 for any years for which the period of limitation under section 6511 has not expired. The taxpayer makes the election under this paragraph (j) by filing a return for the taxable year of the sale or exchange that does not include the gain from the sale or exchange of the taxpayer's principal residence in the taxpayer's gross income. Taxpayers who have filed a return for the taxable year of the sale or exchange may elect to apply the provisions of these regulations for any years for which the period of limitation under section 6511 has not expired by filing an amended return.

(k) *Audit protection.*—The Internal Revenue Service will not challenge a taxpayer's position that a sale or exchange of a principal residence occurring before December 24, 2002 but on or after May 7, 1997, qualifies for the section 121 exclusion if the taxpayer has made a reasonable, good faith effort to comply with the requirements of section 121. Compliance with the provisions of the regulations project under section 121 (REG-105235-99 (2000-2 C.B. 447)) generally will be considered a reasonable, good faith effort to comply with the requirements of section 121.

(l) *Effective date.*—This section is applicable for sales and exchanges on or after December 24, 2002. For rules on electing to apply the provisions retroactively, see paragraph (j) of this section. [Reg. § 1.121-4.]

☐ [*T.D. 6856, 10-19-65. Amended by T.D. 7614, 4-26-79; T.D. 7927, 12-15-83 and T.D. 9030, 12-23-2002 (corrected 2-6-2003).*]

[Reg. § 1.121-5]

§ 1.121-5. Suspension of 5-year period for certain members of the uniformed services and Foreign Service.—(a) *In general.*—Under section 121(d)(9), a taxpayer who is serving (or whose spouse is serving) on qualified official extended duty as a member of the uniformed services or Foreign Service of the United States may elect to suspend the running of the 5-year period of ownership and use during such service but for not more than 10 years. The election does not suspend the running of the 5-year period for any period during which the running of the 5-year period with respect to any other property of the taxpayer is suspended by an election under section 121(d)(9).

(b) *Manner of making election.*—The taxpayer makes the election under section 121(d)(9) and this section by filing a return for the taxable year of the sale or exchange of the taxpayer's principal residence that does not include the gain in the taxpayer's gross income.

(c) *Application of election to closed years.*—A taxpayer who would otherwise qualify under §§ 1.121-1 through 1.121-4 to exclude gain from a sale or exchange of a principal residence on or after May 7, 1997, may elect to apply section 121(d)(9) and this section for any years for which a claim for refund is barred by operation of any law or rule of law by filing an amended return before November 11, 2004.

(d) *Example.*—The provisions of this section are illustrated by the following example:

Example. B purchases a house in Virginia in 2003 that he uses as his principal residence for 3 years. For 8 years, from 2006 through 2014, B serves on qualified official extended duty as a member of the Foreign Service of the United States in Brazil. In 2015 B sells the house. B did not use the house as his principal residence for 2 of the 5 years preceding the sale. Under section 121(d)(9) and this section, however, B may elect to suspend the running of the 5-year period of ownership and use during his 8-year period of service with the Foreign Service in Brazil. If B makes the election, the 8-year period is not counted in determining whether B used the house for 2 of the 5 years preceding the sale. Therefore, B may exclude the gain from the sale of the house under section 121.

(e) *Effective date.*—This section is applicable for sales and exchanges on or after May 7, 1997. [Reg. § 1.121-5.]

□ [T.D. 9152, 8-13-2004.]

[Reg. § 1.122-1]

§ 1.122-1. Applicable rules relating to certain reduced uniformed services retirement pay.—(a) *Rule applicable prior to January 1, 1966.*—In the case of a member or former member of the uniformed services of the United States (as defined in 37 U. S. C. 101(3)) who has made an election under subchapter I of chapter 73 of title 10 of the United States Code (also referred to in this section as the Retired Serviceman's Family Protection Plan (10 U. S. C. 1431)) to receive a reduced amount of retired or retainer pay, gross income shall include the amount of any reduction made in his retired or retainer pay before January 1, 1966, by reason of such election, unless such reduction, or portion thereof, is otherwise excluded from gross income under part III of subchapter B of chapter 1 of the Internal Revenue Code of 1954 or any other provision of law.

(b) *Rule applicable after December 31, 1965.*—(1) In a case of a member or former member of the uniformed services of the United States (as defined in 37 U. S. C. 101(3)), gross income shall not include the amount of any reduction made in his or her retired or retainer pay after December 31, 1965, by reason of—

(i) An election made under the Retired Serviceman's Family Protection Plan (10 U. S. C. 1431), or

(ii) The provisions of subchapter II of chapter 73 of title 10 of the United States Code (also referred to in this section as the Survivor Benefit Plan (10 U. S. C. 1447)).

(2)(i) In a case where a member or former member of the uniformed services has, pursuant to the election described in paragraph (a) of this section, received before January 1, 1966, a reduced amount of retired or retainer pay, he shall, after December 31, 1965, exclude from gross income under section 122(b) and this subdivision all amounts received as uniformed services retired or retainer pay until there has been so excluded an amount of retired or retainer pay equal to the "consideration for the contract" (as described in subdivision (iii) of this subparagraph).

(ii) Upon the death of a member or former member of the uniformed services, where the "consideration for the contract" (as described in subdivision (iii) of this subparagraph) has not been excluded in whole or in part from gross income under section 122(b) and subdivision (i) of this subparagraph, the survivor of such member who is receiving an annuity under chapter 73 of title 10 of the United States Code shall, after December 31, 1965, exclude from gross income under section 72(o) and this subdivision such annuity payments received after December 31, 1965, until there has been so excluded annuity payments equalling the portion of the "consideration for the contract" not previously excluded under subdivision (i) of this subparagraph.

(iii) The term "consideration for the contract" as used in this subparagraph means—

(a) The total amount of the reductions, if any, before January 1, 1966, in retired or retainer pay by reason of an election under subchapter I of chapter 73 of title 10 of the United States Code, plus

(b) The total amount, if any, deposited by the serviceman at any time pursuant to the provisions of sections 1438 or 1452(d) of title 10 of the United States Code, plus

(c) The total amount, if any, excludable from income under section 101(b)(2)(D) and paragraph (a)(2) of § 1.101-2 with respect to a survivor annuity provided by such retired or retainer pay, minus

(d) The total amount, if any, excluded from income before January 1, 1966, pursuant to the provisions of section 72(b) and (d) with respect to a survivor annuity provided by such retired or retainer pay.

(iv) In determining whether there has been a recovery of the "consideration for the contract" under subdivision (i) of this subparagraph, the exclusion of retired pay from income after December 31, 1965, under sections 104(a)(4) and 105(d) shall not be considered as recovery of all or part of the "consideration for the contract."

(c) *Special rules.*—In any of the following situations, the computation of the excludable portion of disability retired pay received by the member or former member of the uniformed services shall be governed by the following rules:

(1) An exclusion under section 122(a) and paragraph (b)(1) of this section is applicable only in the taxable year in which a reduction in retired pay is made under the Retired Serviceman's Family Protection Plan (10 U. S. C. 1431) or the Survivor Benefit Plan (10 U. S. C. 1447).

(2) Where the member or former member of the uniformed services is entitled to exclude the whole or a portion of his retired pay under the provisions of section 104(a)(4) or section 105(d) and under section 122(a) and paragraph (b)(1) of this section, the exclusion under section 122(a) and paragraph (b)(1) of this section shall be applied prior to the exclusions under sections 104(a)(4) and 105(d).

(3) Where the member or former member of the uniformed services waives a portion of his disability retired pay, or such retired pay reduced under the Retired Serviceman's Family Protection Plan (10 U.S.C. 1431) or the Survivor Benefit Plan (10 U.S.C. 1447), in favor of a nontaxable pension or compensation receivable under laws administered by the Veterans Administration (38 U.S.C. 3105), the waived amount of such disability retired pay or reduced amount thereof, shall first be subtracted from any amounts which are excludable under the provisions of sections 104(a)(4) or 105(d) so as to reduce the amounts otherwise excludable under those sections.

(4) Where the member or former member of the uniformed services receives (before any forfeiture) disability retired pay (whether or not reduced under the Retired Serviceman's Family Protection Plan or Survivor Benefit Plan) which is partially excludable under section 104(a)(4), and also forfeits a portion of such disability retired pay under the Dual Compensation Act of 1964 (5 U.S.C. 5531 or any former corresponding provision of law), the amount of the forfeiture under such Act shall be applied against disability retired pay (before any forfeiture) in the same proportion that the excludable portion of such pay under section 104(a)(4) bears to the total amount of such pay after subtraction of any reduction under the Retired Serviceman's Family Protection Plan (10 U.S.C. 1431) or the Survivor Benefit Plan (10 U.S.C. 1447).

(5) The exclusion provided by section 122(b) and paragraph (b)(2)(i) of this section shall be available with respect to repayments made upon removal from the temporary disability retired list even though such repayments were previously excluded from gross income under section 104(a)(4) or 105(d).
However, the exclusion permitted by the prior sentence will apply only to the extent the repaid amount has not been previously excluded under section 122(b) and paragraph (b)(2)(i) of this section.

(d) *Examples with respect to the Retired Serviceman's Family Protection Plan.*—The rules discussed in this section relating to the Retired Serviceman's Family Protection Plan (10 U.S.C. 1431) may be illustrated by the following examples:

Example (1). A, a member of the uniformed services, retires on January 1, 1963, and receives nondisability retired pay computed to be 60 percent of his active duty pay of $10,000 per year, or $6,000 per year, based upon 24 years of service. He elects, under the Retired Serviceman's Family Protection Plan (10 U.S.C. 1431), to provide his survivor with an annuity equal to one-fourth of his reduced retired pay. His retired pay of $6,000 is reduced by $600, to $5,400, in order to provide a survivor annuity of $1,350 per year or $112.50 per month. For 1963, 1964, and 1965, A must include in gross income the unreduced amount of retired pay, or $6,000. For 1966 and subsequent years, he may exclude under section 122(a) and paragraph (b)(1) of this section the $600 total annual reductions to provide the survivor annuity, and may, for 1966, further exclude from gross income under section 122(b) and paragraph (b)(2)(i) of this section the $1,800 "consideration for the contract," *i.e.*, the total reductions which were made in 1963, 1964, and 1965, to provide the survivor annuity. Accordingly, A will include $3,600 of retired pay in gross income for 1966 ($6,000 minus the sum of $600 and $1,800).

Example (2). Assume the facts in Example (1) except that A retires on disability resulting from active service and his disability is rated at 40 percent. The entire amount of disability retirement pay, prior to and including 1966, is excludable from gross income under sections 104(a)(4) and 105(d), and in 1966, section 122(a). Assume further that A attains retirement age on December 31, 1966, dies on January 1, 1967, and his widow then begins receiving a survivor annuity under the Retired Serviceman's Family Protection Plan (10 U.S.C. 1431). A's widow may exclude from gross income in 1967 and 1968 under section 72(o) and paragraph (b)(2)(ii) of this section, the $1,800 of "consideration for the contract," *i.e.*, the reductions in 1963, 1964, and 1965 to provide the survivor annuity. Thus, A's widow will exclude all of the survivor annuity she receives in 1967 ($1,350) and $450 of the $1,350 annuity received in 1968. In addition, if A had not attained retirement age at the time of his death, his widow would, under section 101 and paragraph (a)(2) of § 1.101-2, exclude up to $5,000 subject to the limitations of paragraph (b)(2)(ii) of this section.

Example (3). Assume, in the previous example, that A dies on January 1, 1965, and his widow then begins receiving a survivor

annuity. Assume further that A's widow is entitled to exclude under section 72(b) $1,000 of the $1,350 she received in 1965. Under section 72(o) and paragraph (b)(2)(ii) of this section, A's widow for 1966 will exclude the $200 remaining consideration for the contract ($1,200 – $1,000) and will include $1,150 of the survivor annuity in gross income.

Example (4). B, a member of the uniformed services, retires on January 1, 1966, after 32 years of active military service, and receives disability retirement pay under section 1401 of title 10, limited to 75 percent of his active duty pay of $15,000 per year, or $11,250. His disability rating is 30 percent. B has not reached retirement age (as defined in § 1.79-2(b)(3)). He elects under the Retired Serviceman's Family Protection Plan (10 U.S.C. 1431) to provide his survivor with an annuity equal to one-half of his reduced retired pay and, for that purpose, his retired pay of $11,250 is reduced by $1,250 to provide an annuity of $5,000 per year. B also elects to waive retired pay in the amount of $1,000 in order to receive disability compensation in like amount under laws administered by the Veterans Administration. In addition, B is required to forfeit $4,088 of his retired pay under the Dual Compensation Act of 1964, 5 U.S.C. 5532 ($11,250 – $1,000 = $10,250 less one-half of excess thereof over $2,074) and by reason of his Federal employment is not entitled to an exclusion of his retired pay under section 105(d). B's taxable retired pay for 1966 is $3,002, computed as follows:

Gross retired pay		$11,250
Less: Section 122(a) exclusion		(1,250)
Reduced retired pay		$10,000
Less: Retired pay waived to receive V.A. compensation		(1,000)
Adjusted retired pay—		$ 9,000
Less:		
(i) Excludable retired pay computed under section 104(a)(4) as limited by 10 U.S.C. 1403	$4,500	
(ii) Less: Retired pay, not to exceed (i), waived to receive V.A. compensation	($1,000)	
(iii) Net disability exclusion		($3,500)
Taxable retired pay before adjustment for Dual Compensation forfeiture		$ 5,500
Less: Adjustment for Dual Compensation forfeiture of $4,088		
$\dfrac{5500}{9000} \times \$4,088 = \$2,498$ (rounded)		(2,498)
Net taxable retired pay		$3,002

Example (5). C, a member of the uniformed services retires on January 1, 1966, and receives disability retirement pay of $11,250 per year, which is reduced by $1,250 to provide a survivor annuity, and $1,000 of which is waived in order to receive disability compensation

in like amount under laws administered by the Veterans Administration. C has not reached retirement age for purposes of section 105(d) and is not employed by the Federal Government. C's taxable disability retirement pay for 1966 is $300 computed as follows:

Adjusted retired pay		$9,000
Less:		
(i) Excludable retired pay under section 104(a)(4) as limited by 10 U.S.C. 1403	$ 4,500	
(ii) Excludable retired pay under section 105(d)	5,200	
(iii) Total	$ 9,700	
(iv) Less: Retired pay, not to exceed (iii), waived to receive V.A. compensation	(1,000)	
(v) Net disability and "sick pay" exclusion		(8,700)
Net taxable retired pay		$300

Example (6). D, a member of the uniformed services, retires for physical disability resulting from active service on January 1, 1966, after 35 years of service and with a disability rated at 20 percent. His active duty pay is $4,000 per year and he attained retirement age prior to retirement. He had an election in effect under the Retired

Serviceman's Family Protection Plan to provide his survivor with an annuity and his retired pay is reduced therefor by $500 per year. He waives $1,300 of his retired pay in order to receive compensation from the Veterans Administration in like amount. His taxable retired pay for 1966 is $1,200 computed as follows:

Gross retired pay (75% × $4,000)		$3,000
Less: Section 122(a) exclusion		(500)
Reduced retired pay		$2,500
Less: V.A. waiver		(1,300)
Adjusted retired pay		$1,200
Less:		
(i) Section 104(a)(4) exclusion	$800	
(ii) Less: Retired pay, not to exceed (i), waived to receive V.A. compensation	(800)	
(iii) Net disability exclusion		0
Net taxable retired pay		$1,200

(e) *Principles applicable to the Survivor Benefit Plan.*—The principles illustrated by the examples set forth in paragraph (d) of this section apply to an annuity under the Survivor Benefit Plan (10 U.S.C. 1447). [Reg. § 1.122-1.]

☐ [*T.D.* 7043, 6-1-70. *Amended by T.D.* 7562, 8-30-78.]

[Reg. §1.123-1]

§1.123-1. Exclusion of insurance proceeds for reimbursement of certain living expenses.—(a) *In general.*—(1) Gross income does not include insurance proceeds received by an individual on or after January 1, 1969, pursuant to the terms of an insurance contract for indemnification of the temporary increase in living expenses resulting from the loss of use or occupancy of his principal residence, or a part thereof, due to damage or destruction by fire, storm, or other casualty. The term "other casualty" has the same meaning assigned to such term under section 165(c)(3). The exclusion also applies in the case of an individual who is denied access to his principal residence by governmental authorities because of the occurrence (or threat of occurrence) of such a casualty. The amount excludable under this section is subject to the limitation set forth in paragraph (b) of this section.

(2) This exclusion applies to amounts received as reimbursement or compensation for the reasonable and necessary increase in living expenses incurred by the insured and members of his household to maintain their customary standard of living during the loss period.

(3) This exclusion does not apply to an insurance recovery for the loss of rental income. Nor does the exclusion apply to any insurance recovery which compensates for the loss of, or damage to, real or personal property. See section 165(c)(3) relating to casualty losses; section 1231 relating to gain on an involuntary conversion of a capital asset held for more than 1 year (6 months for taxable years beginning before 1977; 9 months for taxable years beginning in 1977); and section 1033 relating to recognition of gain on an involuntary conversion. In the case of property used by an insured partially as a principal residence and partially for other purposes, the exclusion does not apply to the amount of insurance proceeds which compensates for the portion of increased expenses attributable to the nonresidential use of temporary replacement property during the loss period. In the case of denial of access to a principal residence by governmental authority, the exclusion provided by this section does not apply to an insurance recovery received by an individual as reimbursement for living expenses incurred by reason of a governmental condemnation or order not related to a casualty or the threat of a casualty.

(4)(i) Subject to the limitation set forth in paragraph (b), the amount excludable is the amount which is identified by the insurer as being paid exclusively for increased living expenses resulting from the loss of use or occupancy of the principal residence and pursuant to the terms of the insurance contract.

(ii) When a lump-sum insurance settlement includes, but does not specifically identify, compensation for property damage, loss of rental income, and increased living expenses, the amount of such settlement allocable to living expenses shall, in the case of uncontested claims, be that portion of the settlement which bears the same ratio to the total recovery as the amount of claimed increased living expense bears to the total amount of claimed losses and expenses, to the extent not in excess of the coverage limitations specified in the contract for such losses and expenses.

(iii) In the case of a lump-sum settlement involving contested claims, the insured shall establish the amount reasonably allocable to increased living expenses, consistent with the terms of the contract and other facts of the particular case.

(iv) In no event may the amount of a lump-sum settlement which is allocable to increased living expenses exceed the coverage limitation specified in the contract for increased living expenses. Where, however, a coverage limitation is applicable to the total amount payable for increased living expenses and, for example, loss of rental income, the amount of an unitemized settlement which is allocable to increased living expenses may not exceed the portion of the applicable coverage limitation which bears the same ratio to such limitation as the amount of increased living expenses bears to the sum of the amount of such increased living expenses and the amount, if any, of lost rental income.

(5) The portion of any insurance recovery for increased living expenses which exceeds the limitation set forth in paragraph (b) shall be included in gross income under section 61 of the Code.

(b) *Limitation.*—(1) *Amount excludable.*—The amount excludable under this section is limited to amounts received which are not in excess of the amount by which (i) total actual living expenses incurred by the insured and members of his household which result from the loss of use or occupancy of their residence exceed (ii) the total normal living expenses which would have been incurred during the loss period but are not incurred as a result of the loss of use or occupancy of the principal residence. Generally, the excludable amount represents such excess expenses acutally incurred by reason of a casualty, or threat thereof, for renting suitable housing and for

extraordinary expenses for transportation, food, utilities, and miscellaneous services during the period of repair or replacement of the damaged principal residence or denial of access by governmental authority.

(2) *Actual living expenses.*—For purposes of this section, actual living expenses are the reasonable and necessary expenses incurred as a result of the loss of use or occupancy of the principal residence to maintain the insured and members of his household in accordance with their customary standard of living. Actual living expenses must be of such a nature as to qualify as a reimbursable expense under the terms of the applicable insurance contract without regard to monetary limitations upon coverage. Generally, actual living expenses include the costs during the loss period of temporary housing, utilities furnished at the place of temporary housing, meals obtained at restaurants which customarily would have been prepared in the residence, transportation, and other miscellaneous services. To the extent that the loss of use or occupancy of the principal residence results merely in an increase in the amount expended for items of living expenses normally incurred, such as food and transportation, only the increase in such costs shall be considered as actual living expenses in computing the limitation.

(3) *Normal living expenses not incurred.*—Normal living expenses consist of the same categories of expenses comprising actual living expenses which would have been incurred but are not incurred as a result of the casualty or threat thereof. If the loss of use of the residence results in a decrease in the amount normally expended for a living expense item during the loss period, the item of normal living expense is considered not to have been incurred to the extent of the decrease for purposes of computing the limitation.

(4) *Examples.*—The application of this paragraph (b) may be illustrated by the following examples:

Example (1). On March 1, 1970, A's principal residence, a dwelling owned by A no part of which was rented to others or used for nonresidential purposes, was extensively damaged by fire. The damaged residence was under repair during the entire month of March making it necessary for A and his spouse to obtain temporary lodging and to take their meals at a restaurant. A and his spouse incur expenses of $200 for lodging at a motel, $180 for meals which customarily would have been prepared in his residence, and $25 for commercial laundry service which customarily would have been done by A's wife. A makes (directly or through mortgage insurance) or remains liable for, the required March payment of $190 on the mortgage note on his residence. The mortgage payment results from a contractual obligation having no causal relationship to the occurrence of the casualty and is not considered as an actual living expense resulting from the loss of use of the residence. A's customary commuting expense of $40 for bus fares to and from work is decreased by $20 for the month because of the motel's closer proximity to his place of employment. Other transportation expenses remain stable. Since there has been a decrease in the amount of A's customary bus fares, normal transportation expenses are considered not to have been incurred to the extent of the decrease. Finally, A does not incur customary expenses of $150 for food obtained for home preparation, $75 for utilities expenses, and $10 for laundry cleansers. The limitation upon the excludable amount of an insurance recovery for excess living expenses is $150, computed as follows:

	Actual resulting from casualty	Living Expenses Normal not incurred	Increase (decrease)
Housing	$200.00	$—	$200.00
Utilities	—	75.00	(75.00)
Meals	180.00	150.00	30.00
Transportation	—	20.00	(20.00)
Laundry	25.00	10.00	15.00
Total	$405.00	$255.00	$150.00

Example (2). Assume the same facts as in example (1) except that the damaged residence is not owned by A but is rented to him for $100 per month and that the risk of loss is upon the lessor. Since A would not have incurred the normal rental of $100 for March, the excludable amount is limited to $50 ($150 as in previous example less $100 normal rent not incurred).

(c) *Principal residence.*—Whether or not property is used by the insured taxpayer and members of his household as their principal residence depends upon all the facts and circumstances in each case. For purposes of this section a principal residence may be a dwelling or an apartment leased to the insured as well as a dwelling or apartment owned by the insured. [Reg. §1.123-1.]

☐ [*T.D.* 7118, 6-1-71. *Amended by T.D.* 7728, 10-31-80.]

[Reg. §1.125-3]

§1.125-3. **Effect of the Family and Medical Leave Act (FMLA) on the operation of cafeteria plans.**—The following questions and answers provide guidance on the effect of the Family and Medical Leave Act (FMLA), 29 U.S.C. 2601 et seq., on the operation of cafeteria plans:

Q-1: May an employee revoke coverage or cease payment of his or her share of group health plan premiums when taking unpaid FMLA, 29 U.S.C. 2601 et seq., leave?

A-1: Yes. An employer must either allow an employee on unpaid FMLA leave to revoke coverage, or continue coverage but allow the employee to discontinue payment of his or her share of the premium for group health plan coverage (including a health flexible spending arrangement (FSA)) under a cafeteria plan for the period of the FMLA leave. See 29 CFR 825.209(e). FMLA does not require that an employer allow an employee to revoke coverage if the employer pays the employee's share of premiums. As discussed in Q&A-3, if the employer continues coverage during an FMLA leave, the employer may recover the employee's share of the premiums when the employee returns to work. FMLA also provides the employee a right to be reinstated in the group health plan coverage (including a health FSA) provided under a cafeteria plan upon returning from FMLA leave if the employee's group health plan coverage terminated while on FMLA leave (either by revocation or due to nonpayment of premiums). Such an employee is entitled, to the extent required under FMLA, to be reinstated on the same terms as prior to taking FMLA leave (including family or dependent coverage), subject to any changes in benefit levels that may have taken place during the period of FMLA leave as provided in 29 CFR 825.209(d)(1). See 29 CFR 825.209(e) and 825.215(d). In addition, such an employee has the right to revoke or change elections under §1.125-4 (e.g., because of changes in status or cost or coverage changes as provided under §1.125-4) under the same terms and conditions as are available to employees participating in the cafeteria plan who are working and not on FMLA leave.

Q-2: Who is responsible for making premium payments under a cafeteria plan when an employee on FMLA leave continues group health plan coverage?

A-2: FMLA provides that an employee is entitled to continue group health plan coverage during FMLA leave whether or not that coverage is provided under a health FSA or other component of a cafeteria plan. See 29 CFR 825.209(b). FMLA permits an employer to require an employee who chooses to continue group health plan coverage while on FMLA leave to be responsible for the share of group health premiums that would be allocable to the employee if the employee were working, and, for this purpose, treats amounts paid pursuant to a pre-tax salary reduction agreement as amounts allocable to the employee. However, FMLA requires the employer to continue to contribute the share of the cost of the employee's coverage that the employer was paying before the employee commenced FMLA leave. See 29 CFR 825.100(b) and 825.210(a).

Q-3: What payment options are required or permitted to be offered under a cafeteria plan to an employee who continues group health plan coverage while on unpaid FMLA leave, and what is the tax treatment of these payments?

A-3: (a) *In general.* Subject to the limitations described in paragraph (b) of this Q&A-3, a cafeteria plan may offer one or more of the following payment options, or a combination of these options, to an employee who continues group health plan coverage (including a health FSA) while on unpaid FMLA leave; provided that the payment options for employees on FMLA leave are offered on terms at least as favorable as those offered to employees not on FMLA leave. These options are referred to in this section as pre-pay, pay-as-you-go, and catch-up. See also the FMLA notice requirements at 29 CFR 825.301(b)(1)(iv).

(1) *Pre-pay.* (i) Under the pre-pay option, a cafeteria plan may permit an employee to pay, prior to commencement of the FMLA leave period, the amounts due for the FMLA leave period. However, FMLA provides that the employer may not mandate that an employee pre-pay the amounts due for the leave period. See 29 CFR 825.210(c)(3) and (4).

(ii) Contributions under the pre-pay option may be made on a pre-tax salary reduction basis from any taxable compensation (including *from unused sick days or vacation days). However, see* Q&A-5 of this section regarding additional restrictions on pre-tax salary reduction contributions when an employee's FMLA leave spans two cafeteria plan years.

(iii) Contributions under the pre-pay option may also be made on an after-tax basis.

(2) *Pay-as-you-go.* (i) Under the pay-as-you-go option, employees may pay their share of the premium payments on the same schedule as payments would have been made if the employee were not on leave or under any other payment schedule permitted by the Labor Regulations at 29 CFR 825.210(c) (e.g., on the same schedule as

payments are made under section 4980B (relating to coverage under the Consolidated Omnibus Budget Reconciliation Act (COBRA), 26 U.S.C. 4980B), under the employer's existing rules for payment by employees on leave without pay, or under any other C6/ROP 10-12-01 system voluntarily agreed to between the employer and the employee that is not inconsistent with this section or with 29 CFR 825.210(c)).

(ii) Contributions under the pay-as-you-go option are generally made by the employee on an after-tax basis. However, contributions may be made on a pre-tax basis to the extent that the contributions are made from taxable compensation (e.g., from unused sick days or vacation days) that is due the employee during the leave period.

(iii) An employer is not required to continue the group health coverage of an employee who fails to make required premium payments while on FMLA leave, provided that the employer follows the notice procedures required under FMLA. See 29 CFR 825.212. However, if the employer chooses to continue the health coverage of an employee who fails to pay his or her share of the premium payments while on FMLA leave, FMLA permits the employer to recoup the premiums (to the extent of the employee's share). See 29 CFR 825.212(b). Such recoupment may be made as set forth in paragraphs (a)(3)(i) and (ii) of this Q&A-3. See also Q&A-6 of this section regarding coverage under a health FSA when an employee fails to make the required premium payments while on FMLA leave.

(3) *Catch-up.* (i) Under the catch-up option, the employer and the employee may agree in advance that the group coverage will continue during the period of unpaid FMLA leave, and that the employee will not pay premiums until the employee returns from the FMLA leave. Where an employee is electing to use the catch-up option, the employer and the employee must agree in advance of the coverage period that: the employee elects to continue health coverage while on unpaid FMLA leave; the employer assumes responsibility for advancing payment of the premiums on the employee's behalf during the FMLA leave; and these advance amounts are to be paid by the employee when the employee returns from FMLA leave.

(ii) When an employee fails to make required premium payments while on FMLA leave, an employer is permitted to utilize the catch-up option to recoup the employee's share of premium payments when the employee returns from FMLA leave. See, e.g., 29 CFR 825.212(b). If the employer chooses to continue group coverage under these circumstances, the prior agreement of the employee, as set forth in paragraph (a)(3)(i) of this Q&A-3, is not required.

(iii) Contributions under the catch-up option may be made on a pre-tax salary reduction basis from any available taxable compensation (including from unused sick days and vacation days) after the employee returns from FMLA leave. The cafeteria plan may provide for the catch-up option to apply on a pre-tax salary reduction basis if premiums have not been paid on any other basis (i.e., have not been paid under the pre-pay or pay-as-you-go options or on a catch-up after-tax basis).

(iv) Contributions under the catch-up option may also be made on an after-tax basis.

(b) *Exceptions.* Whatever payment options are offered to employees on non-FMLA leave must be offered to employees on FMLA leave. In accordance with 29 CFR 825.210(c), cafeteria plans may offer one or more of the payment options described in paragraph (a) of this Q&A-3, with the following exceptions:

(1) FMLA does not permit the pre-pay option to be the sole option offered to employees on FMLA leave. However, the cafeteria plan may include pre-payment as an option for employees on FMLA leave, even if such option is not offered to employees on non-FMLA leave-without-pay.

(2) FMLA allows the catch-up option to be the sole option offered to employees on FMLA leave if and only if the catch-up option is the sole option offered to employees on non-FMLA leave-without-pay.

(3) If the pay-as-you-go option is offered to employees on non-FMLA leave-without-pay, the option must also be offered to employees on FMLA leave. The employer may also offer employees on FMLA leave the pre-pay option and/or the catch-up option.

(c) *Voluntary waiver of employee payments.* In addition to the foregoing payment options, an employer may voluntarily waive, on a nondiscriminatory basis, the requirement that employees who elect to continue group health coverage while on FMLA leave pay the amounts the employees would otherwise be required to pay for the leave period.

(d) *Example.* The following example illustrates this Q&A-3:

Example. (i) Employer Y allows employees to pay premiums for group health coverage during an FMLA leave on an after-tax basis while the employee is on unpaid FMLA leave. Under the terms of Y's cafeteria plan, if an employee elects to continue health coverage during an unpaid FMLA leave and fails to pay one or more of the after-tax premium payments due for that coverage, the employee's salary after the employee returns from FMLA leave is reduced to cover unpaid premiums (i.e. the premiums that were to be paid by the employee on an after-tax basis during the FMLA leave, but were paid by the employer instead).

(ii) In this *Example*, Y's cafeteria plan satisfies the conditions in this Q&A-3. Y's cafeteria plan would also satisfy the conditions in this Q&A-3 if the plan provided for coverage to cease in the event the employee fails to make a premium payment when due during an unpaid FMLA leave.

Q-4: Do the special FMLA requirements concerning payment of premiums by an employee who continues group health plan coverage under a cafeteria plan apply if the employee is on paid FMLA leave?

A-4: No. The Labor Regulations provide that, if an employee's FMLA leave is paid leave as described at 29 CFR 825.207 and the employer mandates that the employee continue group health plan coverage while on FMLA leave, the employee's share of the premiums must be paid by the method normally used during any paid leave (e.g., by pre-tax salary reduction if the employee's share of premiums were paid by pre-tax salary reduction before the FMLA leave began). See 29 CFR 825.210(b).

Q-5: What restrictions apply to contributions when an employee's FMLA leave spans two cafeteria plan years?

A-5: (a) No amount will be included in an employee's gross income due to participation in a cafeteria plan during FMLA leave, provided that the plan complies with other generally applicable cafeteria plan requirements. Among other requirements, a plan may not operate in a manner that enables employees on FMLA leave to defer compensation from one cafeteria plan year to a subsequent cafeteria plan year. See section 125(d)(2).

(b) The following example illustrates this Q&A-5:

Example. (i) Employee A elects group health coverage under a calendar year cafeteria plan maintained by Employer X. Employee A's premium for health coverage is $100 per month throughout the 12-month period of coverage. Employee A takes FMLA leave for 12 weeks beginning on October 31 after making 10 months of premium payments totaling $1,000 (10 months × $100 = $1,000). Employee A elects to continue health coverage while on FMLA leave and utilizes the pre-pay option by applying his or her unused sick days in order to make the required premium payments due while he or she is on FMLA leave.

(ii) Because A cannot defer compensation from one plan year to a subsequent plan year, A may pre-pay the premiums due in November and December (i.e., $100 per month) on a pre-tax basis, but A cannot pre-pay the premium payment due in January on a pre-tax basis. If A participates in the cafeteria plan in the subsequent plan year, A must either pre-pay for January on an after-tax basis or use another option (e.g., pay-as-you-go, catch-up, reduction in unused sick days, etc.) to make the premium payment due in January.

Q-6: Are there special rules concerning employees taking FMLA leave who participate in health FSAs offered under a cafeteria plan?

A-6: (a) *In general.* (1) A group health plan that is a flexible spending arrangement (FSA) offered under a cafeteria plan must conform to the generally applicable rules in this section concerning employees who take FMLA leave. Thus, to the extent required by FMLA (see 29 CFR 825.209(b)), an employer must—

(i) Permit an employee taking FMLA leave to continue coverage under a health FSA while on FMLA leave; and

(ii) If an employee is on unpaid FMLA leave, either—

(A) Allow the employee to revoke coverage; or

(B) Continue coverage, but allow the employee to discontinue payment of his or her share of the premium for the health FSA under the cafeteria plan during the unpaid FMLA leave period.

(2) Under FMLA, the plan must permit the employee to be reinstated in health coverage upon return from FMLA leave on the same terms as if the employee had been working throughout the leave period, without a break in coverage. See 29 CFR 825.214(a) and 825.215(d)(1) and paragraph (b)(2) of this Q&A-6. In addition, under FMLA, a plan may require an employee to be reinstated in health coverage upon return from a period of unpaid FMLA leave, provided that employees who return from a period of unpaid leave not covered by the FMLA are also required to resume participation upon return from leave.

(b) *Coverage.* (1) Regardless of the payment option selected under Q&A-3 of this section, for so long as the employee continues health FSA coverage (or for so long as the employer continues the health FSA coverage of an employee who fails to make the required contributions as described in Q&A-3(a)(2)(iii) of this section), the full amount of the elected health FSA coverage, less any prior reimbursements, must be available to the employee at all times, including the FMLA leave period.

(2)(i) If an employee's coverage under the health FSA terminates while the employee is on FMLA leave, the employee is not entitled to receive reimbursements for claims incurred during the period when the coverage is terminated. If an employee subsequently elects or the employer requires the employee to be reinstated in the health FSA

upon return from FMLA leave for the remainder of the plan year, the employee may not retroactively elect health FSA coverage for claims incurred during the period when the coverage was terminated. Upon reinstatement into a health FSA upon return from FMLA leave (either because the employee elects reinstatement or because the employer requires reinstatement), the employee has the right under FMLA: to resume coverage at the level in effect before the FMLA leave and make up the unpaid premium payments, or to resume coverage at a level that is reduced and resume premium payments at the level in effect before the FMLA leave. If an employee chooses to resume health FSA coverage at a level that is reduced, the coverage is prorated for the period during the FMLA leave for which no premiums were paid. In both cases, the coverage level is reduced by prior reimbursements.

(ii) FMLA requires that an employee on FMLA leave have the right to revoke or change elections (because of events described in §1.125-4) under the same terms and conditions that apply to employees participating in the cafeteria plan who are not on FMLA leave. Thus, for example, if a group health plan offers an annual open enrollment period to active employees, then, under FMLA, an employee on FMLA leave when the open enrollment is offered must be offered the right to make election changes on the same basis as other employees. Similarly, if a group health plan decides to offer a new benefit package option and allows active employees to elect the new option, then, under FMLA, an employee on FMLA leave must be allowed to elect the new option on the same basis as other employees.

(3) The following examples illustrate the rules in this Q&A-6:

Example 1. (i) Employee B elects $1,200 worth of coverage under a calendar year health FSA provided under a cafeteria plan, with an annual premium of $1,200. Employee B is permitted to pay the $1,200 through pre-tax salary reduction amounts of $100 per month throughout the 12-month period of coverage. Employee B incurs no medical expenses prior to April 1. On April 1, B takes FMLA leave after making three months of contributions totaling $300 (3 months × $100 = $300). Employee B's coverage ceases during the FMLA leave. Consequently, B makes no premium payments for the months of April, May, and June, and B is not entitled to submit claims or receive reimbursements for expenses incurred during this period. Employee B returns from FMLA leave and elects to be reinstated in the health FSA on July 1.

(ii) Employee B must be given a choice of resuming coverage at the level in effect before the FMLA leave (i.e., $1,200) and making up the unpaid premium payments ($300), or resuming health FSA coverage at a level that is reduced on a prorata basis for the period during the FMLA leave for which no premiums were paid (i.e., reduced for 3 months or 1/4 of the plan year) less prior reimbursements (i.e., $0) with premium payments due in the same monthly amount payable before the leave (i.e., $100 per month). Consequently, if B chooses to resume coverage at the level in effect before the FMLA leave, B's coverage for the remainder of the plan year would equal $1,200 and B's monthly premiums would be increased to $150 per month for the remainder of the plan year, to make up the $300 in premiums missed ($100 per month plus $50 per month ($300 divided by the remaining 6 months)). If B chooses prorated coverage, B's coverage for the remainder of the plan year would equal $900, and B would resume making premium payments of $100 per month for the remainder of the plan year.

Example 2. (i) Assume the same facts as *Example 1* except that B incurred medical expenses totaling $200 in February and obtained reimbursement of these expenses.

(ii) The results are the same as in *Example 1*, except that if B chooses to resume coverage at the level in effect before the FMLA leave, B's coverage for the remainder of the year would equal $1,000 ($1,200 reduced by $200) and the monthly payments for the remainder of the year would still equal $150. If instead B chooses prorated coverage, B's coverage for the remainder of the plan year would equal $700 ($1,200 prorated for 3 months, and then reduced by $200) and the monthly payments for the remainder of the year would still equal $100.

Example 3. (i) Assume the same facts as *Example 1* except that, prior to taking FMLA leave, B elects to continue health FSA coverage during the FMLA leave. The plan permits B (and B elects) to use the catch-up payment option described in Q&A-3 of this section, and as further permitted under the plan, B chooses to repay the $300 in missed payments on a ratable basis over the remaining 6-month period of coverage (i.e., $50 per month).

(ii) Thus, B's monthly premium payments for the remainder of the plan year will be $150 ($100 + $50).

Q-7: Are employees entitled to non-health benefits while taking FMLA leave?

A-7: FMLA does not require an employer to maintain an employee's non-health benefits (e.g., life insurance) during FMLA leave. An employee's entitlement to benefits other than group health benefits under a cafeteria plan during a period of FMLA leave is to be determined by the employer's established policy for providing such benefits when the employee is on non-FMLA leave (paid or unpaid). See 29 CFR 825.209(h). Therefore, an employee who takes FMLA leave is entitled to revoke an election of non-health benefits under a cafeteria plan to the same extent as employees taking non-FMLA leave are permitted to revoke elections of non-health benefits under a cafeteria plan. For example, election changes are permitted due to changes of status or upon enrollment for a new plan year. See §1.125-4. However, FMLA provides that, in certain cases, an employer may continue an employee's non-health benefits under the employer's cafeteria plan while the employee is on FMLA leave in order to ensure that the employer can meet its responsibility to provide equivalent benefits to the employee upon return from unpaid FMLA. If the employer continues an employee's non-health benefits during FMLA leave, the employer is entitled to recoup the costs incurred for paying the employee's share of the premiums during the FMLA leave period. See 29 CFR 825.213(b). Such recoupment may be on a pre-tax basis. A cafeteria plan must, as required by FMLA, permit an employee whose coverage terminated while on FMLA leave (either by revocation or nonpayment of premiums) to be reinstated in the cafeteria plan on return from FMLA leave. See 29 CFR 825.214(a) and 825.215(d).

Q-8: What is the applicability date of the regulations in this section?

A-8: This section is applicable for cafeteria plan years beginning on or after January 1, 2002. [Reg. §1.125-3.]

☐ [T.D. 8966, 10-16-2001.]

[Reg. §1.125-4]

§1.125-4. Permitted election changes.—(a) *Election changes.*—A cafeteria plan may permit an employee to revoke an election during a period of coverage and to make a new election only as provided in paragraphs (b) through (g) of this section. Section 125 does not require a cafeteria plan to permit any of these changes. See paragraph (h) of this section for special provisions relating to qualified cash or deferred arrangements, and paragraph (i) of this section for special definitions used in this section.

(b) *Special enrollment rights.*—(1) *In general.*—A cafeteria plan may permit an employee to revoke an election for coverage under a group health plan during a period of coverage and make a new election that corresponds with the special enrollment rights provided in section 9801(f).

(2) *Examples.*—The following examples illustrate the application of this paragraph (b):

Example 1. (i) Employer M provides health coverage for its employees pursuant to a plan that is subject to section 9801(f). Under the plan, employees may elect either employee-only coverage or family coverage. M also maintains a calendar year cafeteria plan under which qualified benefits, including health coverage, are funded through salary reduction. M's employee, A, is married to B and they have a child, C. In accordance with M's cafeteria plan, Employee A elects employee-only health coverage before the beginning of the calendar year. During the year, A and B adopt a child, D. Within 30 days thereafter, A wants to revoke A's election for employee-only health coverage and obtain family health coverage for A's spouse, C, and D as of the date of D's adoption. Employee A satisfies the conditions for special enrollment of an employee with a new dependent under section 9801(f)(2), so that A may enroll in family coverage under M's accident or health plan in order to provide coverage effective as of the date of D's adoption.

(ii) M's cafeteria plan may permit A to change A's salary reduction election to family coverage for salary not yet currently available. The increased salary reduction is permitted to reflect the cost of family coverage from the date of adoption. (A's adoption of D is also a change in status, and the election of family coverage is consistent with that change in status. Thus, under paragraph (c) of this section, M's cafeteria plan could permit A to elect family coverage prospectively in order to cover B, C, and D for the remaining portion of the period of coverage.)

Example 2. (i) The employer plans and permissible coverage are the same as in *Example 1*. Before the beginning of the calendar year, Employee E elects employee-only health coverage under M's cafeteria plan. Employee E marries F during the plan year. F's employer, N, offers health coverage to N's employees, and, prior to the marriage, F had elected employee-only coverage. Employee E wants to revoke the election for employee-only coverage under M's cafeteria plan, and is considering electing family health coverage under M's plan or obtaining family health coverage under N's plan.

(ii) M's cafeteria plan may permit E to change E's salary reduction election to reflect the change to family coverage under M's accident or health plan because the marriage would result in special enrollment rights under section 9801(f), pursuant to which an elec-

tion of family coverage under M's accident or health plan would be required to be effective no later than the first day of the first calendar month beginning after the completed request for enrollment is received by the plan. Since no retroactive coverage is required in the event of marriage under section 9801(f), E's salary reduction election may only be changed on a prospective basis. (E's marriage to F is also a change in status under paragraph (c) of this section, as illustrated in *Example 1* of paragraph (c)(4) of this section.)

(c) *Changes in status.*—(1) *Change in status rule.*—A cafeteria plan may permit an employee to revoke an election during a period of coverage with respect to a qualified benefits plan (defined in paragraph (i)(8) of this section) to which this paragraph (c) applies and make a new election for the remaining portion of the period (referred to in this section as an election change) if, under the facts and circumstances—

(i) change in status described in paragraph (c)(2) of this section occurs; and

(ii) The election change satisfies the consistency rule of paragraph (c)(3) of this section.

(2) *Change in status events.*—The following events are changes in status for purposes of this paragraph (c):

(i) *Legal marital status.*—Events that change an employee's legal marital status, including the following: marriage; death of spouse; divorce; legal separation; and annulment.

(ii) *Number of dependents.*—Events that change an employee's number of dependents, including the following: birth; death; adoption; and placement for adoption.

(iii) *Employment status.*—Any of the following events that change the employment status of the employee, the employee's spouse, or the employee's dependent: a termination or commencement of employment; a strike or lockout; a commencement of or return from an unpaid leave of absence; and a change in worksite. In addition, if the eligibility conditions of the cafeteria plan or other employee benefit plan of the employer of the employee, spouse, or dependent depend on the employment status of that individual and there is a change in that individual's employment status with the consequence that the individual becomes (or ceases to be) eligible under the plan, then that change constitutes a change in employment under this paragraph (c) (e.g., if a plan only applies to salaried employees and an employee switches from salaried to hourly-paid with the consequence that the employee ceases to be eligible for the plan, then that change constitutes a change in employment status under this paragraph (c)(2)(iii)).

(iv) *Dependent satisfies or ceases to satisfy eligibility requirements.*—Events that cause an employee's dependent to satisfy or cease to satisfy eligibility requirements for coverage on account of attainment of age, student status, or any similar circumstance.

(v) *Residence.*—A change in the place of residence of the employee, spouse, or dependent.

(vi) *Adoption assistance.*—For purposes of adoption assistance provided through a cafeteria plan, the commencement or termination of an adoption proceeding.

(3) *Consistency rule.*—(i) *Application to accident or health coverage and group-term life insurance.*—An election change satisfies the requirements of this paragraph (c)(3) with respect to accident or health coverage or group-term life insurance only if the election change is on account of and corresponds with a change in status that affects eligibility for coverage under an employer's plan. A change in status that affects eligibility under an employer's plan includes a change in status that results in an increase or decrease in the number of an employee's family members or dependents who may benefit from coverage under the plan.

(ii) *Application to other qualified benefits.*—An election change satisfies the requirements of this paragraph (c)(3) with respect to other qualified benefits if the election change is on account of and corresponds with a change in status that affects eligibility for coverage under an employer's plan. An election change also satisfies the requirements of this paragraph (c)(3) if the election change is on account of and corresponds with a change in status that effects expenses described in section 129 (including employment-related expenses as defined in section 21(b)(2)) with respect to dependent care assistance, or expenses described in section 137 (including qualified adoption expenses as defined in section 137(d)) with respect to adoption assistance.

(iii) *Application of consistency rule.*—If the change in status is the employee's divorce, annulment or legal separation from a spouse, the death of a spouse or dependent, or a dependent ceasing to satisfy the eligibility requirements for coverage, an employee's election under the cafeteria plan to cancel accident or health insurance coverage for any individual other than the spouse involved in the divorce, annulment or legal separation, the deceased spouse or dependent, or the dependent that ceased to satisfy the eligibility requirements for coverage, respectively, fails to correspond with that change in status. Thus, if a dependent dies or ceases to satisfy the eligibility requirements for coverage, the employee's election to cancel accident or health coverage for any other dependent, for the employee, or for the employee's spouse fails to correspond with that change in status. In addition, if an employee, spouse, or dependent gains eligibility for coverage under a family member plan (as defined in paragraph (i)(5) of this section) as a result of a change in marital status under paragraph (c)(2)(i) of this section or a change in employment status under paragraph (c)(2)(iii) of this section, an employee's election under the cafeteria plan to cease or decrease coverage for that individual under the cafeteria plan corresponds with that change in status only if coverage for that individual becomes applicable or is increased under the family member plan. With respect to group-term life insurance and disability coverage (as defined in paragraph (i)(4) of this section), an election under a cafeteria plan to increase coverage (or an election to decrease coverage) in response to a change in status described in paragraph (c)(2) of this section is deemed to correspond with that change in status as required by paragraph (c)(3)(i) of this section.

(iv) *Exception for COBRA.*—If the employee, spouse, or dependent becomes eligible for continuation coverage under the group health plan of the employee's employer as provided in section 4980B or any similar state law, a cafeteria plan may permit the employee to elect to increase payments under the employer's cafeteria plan in order to pay for the continuation coverage.

(4) *Examples.*—The following examples illustrate the application of this paragraph (c):

Example 1. (i) Employer M provides health coverage (including a health FSA) for its employees through its cafeteria plan. Before the beginning of the calendar year, Employee A elects employee-only health coverage under M's cafeteria plan and elects salary reduction contributions to fund coverage under the health FSA. Employee A marries B during the year. Employee B's employer, N, offers health coverage to N's employees (but not including any health FSA), and, prior to the marriage, B had elected employee-only coverage. Employee A wants to revoke the election for employee-only coverage, and is considering electing family health coverage under M's plan or obtaining family health coverage under N's plan.

(ii) Employee A's marriage to B is a change in status under paragraph (c)(2)(i) of this section, pursuant to which B has become eligible for coverage under M's health plan under paragraph (c)(3)(i) of this section. Two possible election changes by A correspond with the change in status: Employee A may elect family health coverage under M's plan to cover A and B; or A may cancel coverage under M's plan, if B elects family health coverage under N's plan to cover A and B. Thus, M's cafeteria plan may permit A to make either election change.

(iii) Employee A may also increase salary reduction contributions to fund coverage for B under the health FSA.

Example 2. (i) Employee C, a single parent, elects family health coverage under a calendar year cafeteria plan maintained by Employer O. Employee C and C's 21-year old child, D, are covered under O's health plan. During the year, D graduates from college. Under the terms of the health plan, dependents over the age of 19 must be full-time students to receive coverage. Employee C wants to revoke C's election for family health coverage and obtain employee-only coverage under O's cafeteria plan.

(ii) D's loss of eligibility for coverage under the terms of the health plan is a change in status under paragraph (c)(2)(iv) of this section. A revocation of C's election for family coverage and new election for employee-only coverage corresponds with the change in status. Thus, O's cafeteria plan may permit C to elect employee-only coverage.

Example 3. (i) Employee E is married to F and they have one child, G. Employee E is employed by Employer P, and P maintains a calendar year cafeteria plan that allows employees to elect no health coverage, employee-only coverage, employee-plus-one-dependent coverage, or family coverage. Under the plan, before the beginning of the calendar year, E elects family health coverage for E, F, and G. E and F divorce during the year and F loses eligibility for coverage under P's plan. G does not lose eligibility for health coverage under P's plan upon the divorce. E now wants to revoke E's election under the cafeteria plan and elect no coverage.

(ii) The divorce is a change in status under paragraph (c)(2)(i). A change in the cafeteria plan election to cancel health coverage for F is consistent with that change in status. However, an election change to

cancel E's or G's health coverage does not satisfy the consistency rule under paragraph (c)(3)(iii) of this section regarding cancellation of coverage for an employee's other dependents in the event of divorce. Therefore, the cafeteria plan may not permit E to elect no coverage. However, an election to change to employee-plus-one-dependent health coverage would correspond with the change in status, and thus the cafeteria plan may permit E to elect employee-plus-one-dependent health coverage.

(iii) In addition, under paragraph (f)(4) of this section, if F makes an election change to cover G under F's employer's plan, then E may make a corresponding change to elect employee-only coverage under P's cafeteria plan.

Example 4. (i) Employer R maintains a calendar year cafeteria plan under which full-time employees may elect coverage under one of three benefit package options provided under an accident or health plan: an indemnity option or either of two HMO options for employees who work in the respective service areas of the two HMOs. Employee A, who works in the service area of HMO #1, elects the HMO #1 option. During the year, A is transferred to another work location which is outside the HMO #1 service area and inside the HMO #2 service area.

(ii) The transfer is a change in status under paragraph (c)(2)(iii) of this section (relating to a change in worksite), and, under the consistency rule in paragraph (c)(3) of this section, the cafeteria plan may permit A to make an election change to elect the indemnity option or HMO #2 or to cancel accident or health coverage.

(iii) The change in work location has no effect on A's eligibility under R's health FSA, so no change in A's health FSA is authorized under this paragraph (c).

Example 5. (i) Employer S maintains a calendar year cafeteria plan that allows employees to elect coverage under an accident or health plan providing indemnity coverage and coverage under a health FSA. Prior to the beginning of the calendar year, Employee B elects employee-only indemnity coverage, and elects salary reduction contributions of $600 during the year to fund coverage under the health FSA for up to $600 of reimbursements for the year. Employee B's spouse, C, has employee-only coverage under an accident or health plan maintained by C's employer. During the year, C terminates employment and loses coverage under that plan. B now wants to elect family coverage under S's accident or health plan and increase B's FSA election.

(ii) C's termination of employment is a change in status under paragraph (c)(2)(iii) of this section, and the election change satisfies the consistency rule of paragraph (c)(3) of this section. Therefore, the cafeteria plan may permit B to elect family coverage under S's accident or health plan and to increase B's FSA coverage.

Example 6. (i) Employer T provides group-term life insurance coverage as described under section 79. Under T's plan, an employee may elect life insurance coverage in an amount up to $50,000. T also maintains a calendar year cafeteria plan under which qualified benefits, including the group-term life insurance coverage, are funded through salary reduction. Employee D has a spouse and a child. Before the beginning of the year, D elects $10,000 of group-term life insurance coverage. During the year, D is divorced.

(ii) The divorce is a change in status under paragraph (c)(2)(i) of this section. Under paragraph (c)(3)(iii) of this section, either an increase or a decrease in coverage is consistent with this change in status. Thus, T's cafeteria plan may permit D to increase or to decrease D's group-term life insurance coverage.

Example 7. (i) Employee E is married to F and they have one child, G. Employee E's employer, U, maintains a cafeteria plan under which employees may elect no coverage, employee-only coverage, or family coverage under a group health plan maintained by U, and may make a separate vision coverage election under the plan. Before the beginning of the calendar year, E elects family health coverage and no vision coverage under U's cafeteria plan. Employee F's employer, V, maintains a cafeteria plan under which employees may elect no coverage, employee-only coverage, or family coverage under a group health plan maintained by V, and may make a separate vision coverage election under the plan. Before the beginning of the calendar year, F elects no health coverage and employee-only vision coverage under V's plan. During the year, F terminates employment with V and loses vision coverage under V's plan. Employee E now wants to elect family vision coverage under U's group health plan.

(ii) F's termination of employment is a change in status under paragraph (c)(2)(iii) of this section, and the election change satisfies the consistency rule of paragraph (c)(3) of this section. Therefore, U's cafeteria plan may permit E to elect family vision coverage (covering E and G as well as F) under U's group health plan.

Example 8. (i) Before the beginning of the year, Employee H elects to participate in a cafeteria plan maintained by H's employer, W. However, in order to change the election during the year so as to cancel coverage, and by prior understanding with W, H terminates employment and resumes employment one week later.

(ii) In this *Example 8*, under the facts and circumstances, a principal purpose of the termination of employment was to alter the election, and reinstatement of employment was understood at the time of termination. Accordingly, *H* does not have a change in status under paragraph (c)(2)(iii) of this section.

(iii) However, *H*'s termination of employment would constitute a change in status, permitting a cancellation of coverage during the period of unemployment, if *H*'s original cafeteria plan election for the period of coverage was reinstated upon resumption of employment (for example, if *W*'s cafeteria plan contains a provision requiring an employee who resumes employment within 30 days, without any other intervening event that would permit a change in election, to return to the election in effect prior to termination of employment).

(iv) If, instead, *H* terminates employment and cancels coverage during a period of unemployment, and then returns to work more than 30 days following termination of employment, the cafeteria plan may permit *H* the option of returning to the election in effect prior to termination of employment or making a new election under the plan. Alternatively, the cafeteria plan may prohibit *H* from returning to the plan during that plan year.

Example 9. (i) Employee *A* has one child, *B*. Employee *A*'s employer, *X*, maintains a calendar year cafeteria plan that allows employees to elect coverage under a dependent care FSA. Prior to the beginning of the calendar year, *A* elects salary reduction contributions of $4,000 during the year to fund coverage under the dependent care FSA for up to $4,000 of reimbursements for the year. During the year, *B* reaches the age of 13, and *A* wants to cancel coverage under the dependent care FSA.

(ii) When *B* turns 13, *B* ceases to satisfy the definition of qualifying individual under section 21(b)(1) of the Internal Revenue Code. Accordingly, *B*'s attainment of age 13 is a change in status under paragraph (c)(2)(iv) of this section that affects *A*'s employment-related expenses as defined in section 21(b)(2). Therefore, *A* may make a corresponding change under *X*'s cafeteria plan to cancel coverage under the dependent care FSA.

Example 10. (i) Employer *Y* maintains a calendar year cafeteria plan under which full-time employees may elect coverage under either an indemnity option or an HMO. Employee *C* elects the employee-only indemnity option. During the year, *C* marries *D*. *D* has two children from a previous marriage, and has family group health coverage in a cafeteria plan sponsored by *D*'s employer, *Z*. *C* wishes to change from employee-only indemnity coverage to HMO coverage for the family. *D* wishes to cease coverage in *Z*'s group health plan and certifies to *Z* that *D* will have family coverage under *C*'s plan (and *Z* has no reason to believe the certification is incorrect).

(ii) The marriage is a change in status under paragraph (c)(2)(i) of this section. Under the consistency rule in paragraph (c)(3) of this section, *Y*'s cafeteria plan may permit *C* to change his or her salary reduction contributions to reflect the change from employee-only indemnity to HMO family coverage, and *Z* may permit *D* to revoke coverage under *Z*'s cafeteria plan.

(d) *Judgment, decree, or order.*—(1) *Conforming election change.*—This paragraph (d) applies to a judgment, decree, or order (order) resulting from a divorce, legal separation, annulment, or change in legal custody (including a qualified medical child support order as defined in section 609 of the Employee Retirement Income Security Act of 1974 (Public Law 93-406 (88 Stat. 829))) that requires accident or health coverage for an employee's child or for a foster child who is a dependent of the employee. A cafeteria plan will not fail to satisfy section 125 if it—

(i) Changes the employee's election to provide coverage for the child if the order requires coverage for the child under the employee's plan; or

(ii) Permits the employee to make an election change to cancel coverage for the child if:

(A) The order requires the spouse, former spouse, or other individual to provide coverage for the child; and

(B) That coverage is, in fact, provided.

(2) *Example.*—The following example illustrates the application of this paragraph (d):

Example. (i) Employer *M* maintains a calendar year cafeteria plan that allows employees to elect no health coverage, employee-only coverage, employee-plus-one-dependent coverage, or family coverage. *M*'s employee, *A*, is married to *B* and they have one child, *C*. Before the beginning of the year, *A* elects employee-only health coverage. Employee *A* divorces *B* during the year and, pursuant to *A*'s divorce agreement with *B*, *M*'s health plan receives a qualified medical child support order (as defined in section 609 of the Employee Retirement Income Security Act of 1974) during the plan year. The order requires *M*'s health plan to cover *C*.

(ii) Under this paragraph (d), *M*'s cafeteria plan may change *A*'s election from employee-only health coverage to employee-plus-one-dependent coverage in order to cover *C*.

(e) *Entitlement to Medicare or Medicaid.*—If an employee, spouse, or dependent who is enrolled in an accident or health plan of the employer becomes entitled to coverage (i.e., becomes enrolled) under Part A or Part B of Title XVIII of the Social Security Act (Medicare) (Public Law 89-97 (79 Stat. 291)) or Title XIX of the Social Security Act (Medicaid) (Public Law 89-97 (79 Stat. 343)), other than coverage consisting solely of benefits under section 1928 of the Social Security Act (the program for distribution of pediatric vaccines), a cafeteria plan may permit the employee to make a prospective election change to cancel or reduce coverage of that employee, spouse, or dependent under the accident or health plan. In addition, if an employee, spouse, or dependent who has been entitled to such coverage under Medicare or Medicaid loses eligibility for such coverage, the cafeteria plan may permit the employee to make a prospective election to commence or increase coverage of that employee, spouse, or dependent under the accident or health plan.

(f) *Significant cost or coverage changes.*—(1) *In general.*—Paragraphs (f)(2) through (5) of this section set forth rules for election changes as a result of changes in cost or coverage. This paragraph (f) does not apply to an election change with respect to a health FSA (or on account of a change in cost or coverage under a health FSA).

(2) *Cost changes.*—(i) *Automatic changes.*—If the cost of a qualified benefits plan increases (or decreases) during a period of coverage and, under the terms of the plan, employees are required to make a corresponding change in their payments, the cafeteria plan may, on a reasonable and consistent basis, automatically make a prospective increase (or decrease) in affected employees' elective contributions for the plan.

(ii) *Significant cost changes.*—If the cost charged to an employee for a benefit package option (as defined in paragraph (i)(2) of this section) significantly increases or significantly decreases during a period of coverage, the cafeteria plan may permit the employee to make a corresponding change in election under the cafeteria plan. Changes that may be made include commencing participation in the cafeteria plan for the option with a decrease in cost, or, in the case of an increase in cost, revoking an election for that coverage and, in lieu thereof, either receiving on a prospective basis coverage under another benefit package option providing similar coverage or dropping coverage if no other benefit package option providing similar coverage is available. For example, if the cost of an indemnity option under an accident or health plan significantly increases during a period of coverage, employees who are covered by the indemnity option may make a corresponding prospective increase in their payments or may instead elect to revoke their election for the indemnity option and, in lieu thereof, elect coverage under another benefit package option including an HMO option (or drop coverage under the accident or health plan if no other benefit package option is offered).

(iii) *Application of cost changes.*—For purposes of paragraphs (f)(2)(i) and (ii) of this section, a cost increase or decrease refers to an increase or decrease in the amount of the elective contributions under the cafeteria plan, whether that increase or decrease results from an action taken by the employee (such as switching between full-time and part-time status) or from an action taken by an employer (such as reducing the amount of employer contributions for a class of employees).

(iv) *Application to dependent care.*—This paragraph (f)(2) applies in the case of a dependent care assistance plan only if the cost change is imposed by a dependent care provider who is not a relative of the employee. For this purpose, a relative is an individual who is related as described in section 152(a)(1) through (8), incorporating the rules of section 152(b)(1) and (2).

(3) *Coverage changes.*—(i) *Significant curtailment without loss of coverage.*—If an employee (or an employee's spouse or dependent) has a significant curtailment of coverage under a plan during a period of coverage that is not a loss of coverage as described in paragraph (f)(3)(ii) of this section (for example, there is a significant increase in the deductible, the copay, or the out-of-pocket cost sharing limit under an accident or health plan), the cafeteria plan may permit any employee who had been participating in the plan and receiving that coverage to revoke his or her election for that coverage and, in lieu thereof, to elect to receive on a prospective basis coverage under another benefit package option providing similar coverage. Coverage under a plan is significantly curtailed only if there is an overall reduction in coverage provided under the plan so as to constitute reduced coverage generally. Thus, in most cases, the loss of one particular physician in a network does not constitute a significant curtailment.

(ii) *Significant curtailment with loss of coverage.*—If an employee (or the employee's spouse or dependent) has a significant curtailment that is a loss of coverage, the plan may permit that employee to revoke his or her election under the Cafeteria plan and, in lieu thereof, to elect either to receive on a prospective basis coverage under another benefit package option providing similar coverage or to drop coverage if no similar benefit package option is available. For purposes of this paragraph (f)(3)(ii), a loss of coverage means a complete loss of coverage under the benefit package option or other coverage option (including the elimination of a benefits package option, an HMO ceasing to be available in the area where the individual resides, or the individual losing all coverage under the option by reason of an overall lifetime or annual limitation). In addition, the cafeteria plan may, in its discretion, treat the following as a loss of coverage—

(A) A substantial decrease in the medical care providers available under the option (such as a major hospital ceasing to be a member of a preferred provider network or a substantial decrease in the physicians participating in a preferred provider network or an HMO);

(B) A reduction in the benefits for a specific type of medical condition or treatment with respect to which the employee or the employee's spouse or dependent is currently in a course of treatment; or

(C) Any other similar fundamental loss of coverage.

(iii) *Addition or improvement of a benefit package option.*—If a plan adds a new benefit package option or other coverage option, or if coverage under an existing benefit package option or other coverage option is significantly improved during a period of coverage, the cafeteria plan may permit eligible employees (whether or not they have previously made an election under the cafeteria plan or have previously elected the benefit package option) to revoke their election under the cafeteria plan and, in lieu thereof, to make an election on a prospective basis for coverage under the new or improved benefit package option.

(4) *Change in coverage under another employer plan.*—A cafeteria plan may permit an employee to make a prospective election change that is on account of and corresponds with a change made under another employer plan (including a plan of the same employer or of another employer) if—

(i) The other cafeteria plan or qualified benefits plan permits participants to make an election change that would be permitted under paragraphs (b) through (g) of this section (disregarding this paragraph (f)(4)); or

(ii) The cafeteria plan permits participants to make an election for a period of coverage that is different from the period of coverage under the other cafeteria plan or qualified benefits plan.

(5) *Loss of coverage under other group health coverage.*—A cafeteria plan may permit an employee to make an election on a prospective basis to add coverage under a cafeteria plan for the employee, spouse, or dependent if the employee, spouse, or dependent loses coverage under any group health coverage sponsored by a governmental or educational institution, including the following—

(i) A State's children's health insurance program (SCHIP) under Title XXI of the Social Security Act;

(ii) A medical care program of an Indian Tribal government (as defined in section 7701(a)(40)), the Indian Health Service, or a tribal organization;

(iii) A State health benefits risk pool; or

(iv) A Foreign government group health plan.

(6) *Examples.*—The following examples illustrate the application of this paragraph (f):

Example 1. (i) A calendar year cafeteria plan is maintained pursuant to a collective bargaining agreement for the benefit of Employer *M*'s employees. The cafeteria plan offers various benefits, including indemnity health insurance and a health FSA. As a result of mid-year negotiations, premiums for the indemnity health insurance are reduced in the middle of the year, insurance co-payments for office visits are reduced under the indemnity plan by an amount which constitutes a significant benefit improvement, and an HMO option is added.

(ii) Under these facts, the reduction in health insurance premiums is a reduction in cost. Accordingly, under paragraph (f)(2)(i) of this section, the cafeteria plan may automatically decrease the amount of salary reduction contributions of affected participants by an amount that corresponds to the premium change. However, the plan may not permit employees to change their health FSA elections to reflect the mid-year change in copayments under the indemnity plan.

(iii) Also, the decrease in co-payments is a significant benefit improvement and the addition of the HMO option is an addition of a benefit package option. Accordingly, under paragraph (f)(3)(ii) of this section, the cafeteria plan may permit eligible employees to make

an election change to elect the indemnity plan or the new HMO option. However, the plan may not permit employees to change their health FSA elections to reflect differences in co-payments under the HMO option.

Example 2. (i) Employer *N* sponsors an accident or health plan under which employees may elect either employee-only coverage or family health coverage. The 12-month period of coverage under *N*'s cafeteria plan begins January 1, 2001. *N*'s employee, *A*, is married to *B*. Employee *A* elects employee-only coverage under *N*'s plan. *B*'s employer, *O*, offers health coverage to *O*'s employees under its accident or health plan under which employees may elect either employee-only coverage or family coverage. *O*'s plan has a 12-month period of coverage beginning September 1, 2001. *B* maintains individual coverage under *O*'s plan at the time *A* elects coverage under *N*'s plan, and wants to elect no coverage for the plan year beginning on September 1, 2001, which is the next period of coverage under *O*'s accident or health plan. *A* certifies to *N* that *B* will elect no coverage under *O*'s accident or health plan for the plan year beginning on September 1, 2001 and *N* has no reason to believe that *A*'s certification is incorrect.

(ii) Under paragraph (f)(4)(ii) of this section, *N*'s cafeteria plan may permit *A* to change *A*'s election prospectively to family coverage under that plan effective September 1, 2001.

Example 3. (i) Employer *P* sponsors a calendar year cafeteria plan under which employees may elect either employee-only or family health coverage. Before the beginning of the year, *P*'s employee, *C*, elects family coverage under *P*'s cafeteria plan. *C* also elects coverage under the health FSA for up to $200 of reimbursements for the year to be funded by salary reduction contributions of $200 during the year. *C* is married to *D*, who is employed by Employer *Q*. *Q* does not maintain a cafeteria plan, but does maintain an accident or health plan providing its employees with employee-only coverage. During the calendar year, *Q* adds family coverage as an option under its health plan. *D* elects family coverage under *Q*'s plan, and *C* wants to revoke *C*'s election for health coverage and elect no health coverage under *P*'s cafeteria plan for the remainder of the year.

(ii) *Q*'s addition of family coverage as an option under its health plan constitutes a new coverage option described in paragraph (f)(3)(ii) of this section. Accordingly, pursuant to paragraph (f)(4)(i) of this section, *P*'s cafeteria plan may permit *C* to revoke *C*'s health coverage election if *D* actually elects family health coverage under *Q*'s accident or health plan. Employer *P*'s plan may not permit *C* to change *C*'s health FSA election.

Example 4. (i) Employer *R* maintains a cafeteria plan under which employees may elect accident or health coverage under either an indemnity plan or an HMO. Before the beginning of the year, *R*'s employee, *E*, elects coverage under the HMO at a premium cost of $100 per month. During the year, *E* decides to switch to the indemnity plan, which charges a premium of $140 per month.

(ii) *E*'s change from the HMO to indemnity plan is not a change in cost or coverage under this paragraph (f), and none of the other election change rules under paragraphs (b) through (e) of this section apply.

(iii) Although *R*'s health plan may permit *E* to make the change from the HMO to the indemnity plan, *R*'s cafeteria plan may not permit *E* to make an election change to reflect the increased premium. Accordingly, if *E* switches from the HMO to the indemnity plan, *E* may pay the $40 per month additional cost on an after-tax basis.

Example 5. (i) Employee *A* is married to Employee *B* and they have one child, *C*. Employee *A*'s employer, *M*, maintains a calendar year cafeteria plan that allows employees to elect coverage under a dependent care FSA. Child *C* attends *X*'s on site child care center at an annual cost of $3,000. Prior to the beginning of the year, *A* elects salary reduction contributions of $3,000 during the year to fund coverage under the dependent care FSA for up to $3,000 of reimbursements for the year. Employee *A* now wants to revoke *A*'s election of coverage under the dependent care FSA, because A has found a new child care provider.

(ii) The availability of dependent care services from the new child care provider (whether the new provider is a household employee or family member of *A* or *B* or a person who is independent of *A* and *B*) is a significant change in coverage similar to a benefit package option becoming available. Because the FSA is a dependent care FSA rather than a health FSA, the coverage rules of this section apply and *M*'s cafeteria plan may permit *A* to elect to revoke *A*'s previous election of coverage under the dependent care FSA, and make a corresponding new election to reflect the cost of the new child care provider.

Example 6. (i) Employee *D* is married to Employee *E* and they have one child, *F*. Employee *D*'s employer, *N*, maintains a calendar year cafeteria plan that allows employees to elect coverage under a dependent care FSA. Child *F* is cared for by *Y*, *D*'s household employee, who provides child care services five days a week from 9 a.m. to 6 p.m. at an annual cost in excess of $5,000. Prior to the beginning of the year, D elects salary reduction contributions of $5,000 during the year to fund coverage under the dependent care FSA for up to $5,000 of reimbursements for the year. During the year, F begins school and, as a result, Y's regular hours of work are changed to five days a week from 3 p.m. to 6 p.m. Employee D now wants to revoke D's election under the dependent care FSA, and make a new election under the dependent care FSA to an annual cost of $4,000 to reflect a reduced cost of child care due to Y's reduced hours.

(ii) The change in the number of hours of work performed by Y is a change in coverage. Thus, N's cafeteria plan may permit D to reduce D's previous election under the dependent care FSA to $4,000.

Example 7. (i) Employee G is married to Employee H and they have one child, J. Employee G's employer, O, maintains a calendar year cafeteria plan that allows employees to elect coverage under a dependent care FSA. Child J is cared for by Z, G's household employee, who is not a relative of G and who provides child care services at an annual cost of $4,000. Prior to the beginning of the year, G elects salary reduction contributions of $4,000 during the year to fund coverage under the dependent care FSA for up to $4,000 of reimbursements for the year. During the year, G raises Z's salary. Employee G now wants to revoke G's election under the dependent care FSA, and make a new election under the dependent care FSA to an annual amount of $4,500 to reflect the raise.

(ii) The raise in Z's salary is a significant increase in cost under paragraph (f)(2)(ii) of this section, and an increase in election to reflect the raise corresponds with that change in status. Thus, O's cafeteria plan may permit G to elect to increase G's election under the dependent care FSA.

Example 8. (i) Employer P maintains a calendar year cafeteria plan that allows employees to elect employee-only, employee plus one dependent, or family coverage under an indemnity plan. During the middle of the year, Employer P gives its employees the option to select employee-only or family coverage from an HMO plan. P's employee, J, who had elected employee plus one dependent coverage under the indemnity plan, decides to switch to family coverage under the HMO plan.

(ii) Employer P's midyear addition of the HMO option is an addition of a benefit package option. Under paragraph (f) of this section, Employee J may change his or her salary reduction contributions to reflect the change from indemnity to HMO coverage, and also to reflect the change from employee plus one dependent to family coverage (however, an election of employee-only coverage under the new option would not correspond with the addition of a new option). Employer P may not permit J to change J's health FSA election.

(g) *Special requirements relating to the Family and Medical Leave Act.*—An employee taking leave under the Family and Medical Leave Act (FMLA) (Public Law 103-3 (107 Stat. 6)) may revoke an existing election of accident or health plan coverage and make such other election for the remaining portion of the period of coverage as may be provided for under the FMLA. See §1.125-3 for additional rules.

(h) *Elective contributions under a qualified cash or deferred arrangement.*—The provisions of this section do not apply with respect to elective contributions under a qualified cash or deferred arrangement (within the meaning of section 401(k)) or employee contributions subject to section 401(m). Thus, a cafeteria plan may permit an employee to modify or revoke elections in accordance with section 401(k) and (m) and the regulations thereunder.

(i) *Definitions.*—Unless otherwise provided, the definitions in paragraphs (i)(1) though (8) of this section apply for purposes of this section.

(1) *Accident or health coverage.*—Accident or health coverage means coverage under an accident or health plan as defined in regulations under section 105.

(2) *Benefit package option.*—A benefit package option means a qualified benefit under section 125(f) that is offered under a cafeteria plan, or an option for coverage under an underlying accident or health plan (such as an indemnity option, an HMO option, or a PPO option under an accident or health plan).

(3) *Dependent.*—A dependent means a dependent as defined in section 152, except that, for purposes of accident or health coverage, any child to whom section 152(e) applies is treated as a dependent of both parents, and, for purposes of dependent care assistance provided through a cafeteria plan, a dependent means a qualifying individual (as defined in section 21(b)(1)) with respect to the employee.

(4) *Disability coverage.*—Disability coverage means coverage under an accident or health plan that provides benefits due to personal injury or sickness, but does not reimburse expenses incurred for medical care (as defined in section 213(d)) of the employee or the employee's spouse and dependents. For purposes of this section, disability coverage includes payments described in section 105(c).

(5) *Family member plan.*—A family member plan means a cafeteria plan or qualified benefit plan sponsored by the employer of the employee's spouse or the employee's dependent.

(6) *FSA, health FSA.*—An FSA means a qualified benefits plan that is a flexible spending arrangement as defined in section 106(c)(2). A health FSA means a health or accident plan that is an FSA.

(7) *Placement for adoption.*—Placement for adoption means placement for adoption as defined in regulations under section 9801.

(8) *Qualified benefits plan.*—A qualified benefits plan means an employee benefit plan governing the provision of one or more benefits that are qualified benefits under section 125(f). A plan does not fail to be a qualified benefits plan merely because it includes an FSA, assuming that the FSA meets the requirements of section 125 and the regulations thereunder.

(9) *Similar coverage.*—Coverage for the same category of benefits for the same individuals (e.g., family to family or single to single). For example, two plans that provide coverage for major medical are considered to be similar coverage. For purposes of this definition, a health FSA is not similar coverage with respect to an accident or health plan that is not a health FSA. A plan may treat coverage by another employer, such as a spouse's or dependent's employer, as similar coverage.

(j) *Effective date.*—(1) *General rule.*—Except as provided in paragraph (j)(2) of this section, this section is applicable for cafeteria plan years beginning on or after January 1, 2001.

(2) *Delayed effective date for certain provisions.*—The following provisions are applicable for cafeteria plan years beginning on or after January 1, 2002: paragraph (c) of this section to the extent applicable to qualified benefits other than an accident or health plan or a group-term life insurance plan; paragraph (d)(1)(ii)(B) of this section (relating to a spouse, former spouse, or other individual obtaining accident or health coverage for an employee's child in response to a judgment, decree, or order); paragraph (f) of this section (rules for election changes as a result of cost or coverage changes); and paragraph (i)(9) of this section (defining similar coverage). [Reg. §1.125-4.]

☐ [T.D. 8878, 3-22-2000. Amended by T.D. 8921, 1-9-2001 (corrected 3-1-2001) and T.D. 8966, 10-16-2001.]

[Reg. §16A.126-0]

§16A.126-0. Effective dates (Temporary).—These temporary regulations shall apply to any payments received under the contract signed by the taxpayer and the appropriate agency after September 30, 1979. [Temporary Reg. §16A.126-0.]

☐ [T.D. 7778, 5-18-81.]

[Reg. §16A.126-1]

§16A.126-1. Certain cost sharing payments—In general (Temporary).—(a) *Introduction.*—In general, section 126 provides that recipients of payments made after September 30, 1979 under certain conservation, reclamation and restoration programs may exclude all or a portion of those payments from income if the payments do not substantially increase the annual income derived by the taxpayer from the affected property. For purposes of this section, the term "payment" as used in section 126 means payment of the economic benefit, if any, conferred upon the taxpayer upon receipt of the improvement. An increase in annual income is substantial if it exceeds the greater of 10 percent of the average annual income derived from the affected property prior to receipt of the improvement or an amount equal to $2.50 times the number of affected acres. The amount of gross income which a taxpayer realizes upon the receipt of a section 126 payment is the value of the section 126 improvement, reduced by the sum of the excludable portion and the taxpayer's share of the cost of the improvement (if any).

(b) *Definitions.*—For purposes of this section, the term:

(1) "Cost of the improvement" means the sum of amounts paid by a government and the taxpayer, whether or not with borrowed funds, for the improvement.

(2) "Section 126 cost" means the cost of the improvement less the sum of

(i) Any government payments under a program which is not listed in section 126(a),

(ii) Any portion of a government payment under a program which is listed in section 126(a) which the Secretary of Agriculture has not certified is primarily for purposes of conservation.

(iii) Any government payment to the taxpayer which is in the nature of rent or compensation for services.

(3) "Value of the section 126 improvement" means the fair market value of the improvement multiplied by a fraction, the numerator of which is the section 126 cost and the denominator of which is the cost of the improvement.

(4) "Affected acreage" means the acres affected by the improvement.

(5) "Excludable portion" means the present fair market value of the right to receive annual income from the affected acreage of the greater of 10 percent of the prior average annual income from the affected acreage or $2.50 times the number of affected acres.

(6) "Prior average annual income" means the average of the gross receipts from the affected acreage for the last three taxable years preceding the taxable year in which installation of the improvement is commenced.

(7) "Section 126 improvement" means the portion of the improvement equal to the percentage which government payments made to the taxpayer, which the Secretary of Agriculture has certified were made primarily for the purpose of conservation, bear to the cost of the improvement.

(c) *Income realized upon receipt of a section 126 improvement.*—(1) *Section 126 exclusion applied.*—Unless a taxpayer elects not to have section 126 apply, the amount of gross income realized on receipt of the section 126 improvement is the value of the section 126 improvement less the sum of the taxpayer's share of the cost of the improvement and the excludable portion.

(2) *Section 126 exclusion not applied.*—If a taxpayer elects under section 126(c) not to have section 126 apply in whole or in part, the amount realized on the receipt of the section 126 improvement is the value of the section 126 improvement less the sum of the taxpayer's share of the cost of the improvement and the excludable portion that applies, if any.

(d) *Payments under watershed programs.*—(1) *Programs within section 126(a)(9).*—Section 126(a)(9) covers certain programs affecting small watersheds. These programs must be administered by the Secretary of Agriculture and be determined by the Commissioner to be substantially similar to the type of program described in section 126(a)(1) through (8). The Commissioner has determined that section 126 improvements made in connection with small watersheds are within the scope of section 126(a)(9) if they are made under one of the following programs:

(A) The Watershed Protection and Flood Prevention Act, Pub. L. 566, 68 Stat. 666, as amended (16 U.S.C. 1001, et. seq.), as funded by the Act of November 9, 1979, Pub. L. 96-108, 93 Stat. 834.

(B) Flood Prevention Projects, Pub. L. 86-468, sec. 1, 74 Stat. 131, as amended (16 U.S.C. 1006a); Publ. L. 78-534, sec. 2, 58 Stat. 889 (33 U.S.C. 701a-1); Pub. L. 78-534, sec. 13, 58 Stat. 905;

(C) Emergency Watershed Protection, Pub. L. 81-516, sec. 216, 64 Stat. 184 (33 U.S.C. 701b-1), and

(D) Colorado River Basin Salinity Control Act, Pub. L. 93-320, 88 Stat. 266:

(1) Title 1—Programs downstream from Imperial Dam, and

(2) Title 2—Measures upstream from Imperial Dam.

(2) *Other programs.*—The Commissioner may announce further determinations under section 126(a)(9) from time to time in the Internal Revenue Bulletin.

(3) *Small watershed defined.*—A watershed is a "small watershed" under this paragraph and section 126(a)(9) if the watershed or sub-watershed does not exceed 250,000 acres and does not include any single structure providing more than 12,500 acre-feet of floodwater detention capacity, nor more than 25,000 acre-feet of total capacity.

(e) *Basis of property not increased by reason of excludable amounts.*—Notwithstanding any provision of section 1016 (relating to adjustments to basis) to the contrary, basis of any property does not include any amount which is excludable from gross income under section 126.

(f) *Cross reference.*—For rules relating to the recapture as ordinary income of the gain from the disposition (within 20 years of the date of receipt) of property for which an exclusion is claimed for a section 126 improvement, see section 1255 and the regulations thereunder.

(g) *Examples.*—The provisions of this section are illustrated by the following examples:

Example (1). In 1981, 100 acres of the taxpayer's land is reclaimed under a Rural Abandoned Mine Program contract with the Soil Conservation Service of the U.S. Department of Agriculture. The total cost of the improvement is $700,000. USDA pays $690,000, the taxpayer $10,000. The Secretary of Agriculture certifies that 95% of the $690,000 USDA payment was primarily for the purpose of conservation. Therefore, $34,500 ($690,000 × .05) is a nonsection 126 payment, $150,000 of USDA's payment is compensation for the taxpayer's service in the reclamation project and is includible in gross income as compensation for services. The taxpayer has $20,000 of allowable deductions in 1981, $15,500 of which are properly attributable to the USDA payment. Based on all the facts and circumstances, the value of the improvement is $21,000. The taxpayer elects not to have section 126 apply. The taxpayer computes the amount which is included in gross income as a result of receipt of the improvement as follows:

(1)

Cost of improvement	$700,000
Nonsection 126 payment	(34,500)
Compensation for services	(150,000)
Current deductions	(15,500)
Section 126 cost	500,000

(2)

Value of improvement	21,000
Multiplied by section 126 cost	× 500,000
Cost of improvement	700,000
Value of section 126 improvement	15,000

(3)

Value of section 126 improvement	15,000
Taxpayer's contribution	10,000
Amount included in gross income	5,000

Example (2). The facts are the same as example (1) except that section 126 applies. Based on all the facts and circumstances, the present fair market value of the right to receive annual income from the property of 10 percent of the prior average annual income of the affected acreage prior to the receipt of the improvement is $1,380 and the present fair market value of the right to receive $250 ($2.50 × 100 acres) is $1,550. The excludable portion is, therefore, $1,550. The taxpayer computes the amount included in gross income as follows:

value of section 126 improvement	$15,000
(taxpayer's contribution)	(10,000)
(excludable portion)	(1,550)
amount included in income	$3,450

Example (3). The facts are the same as example (2) except that the present value of 10 percent of the prior average annual income is $5,600. The taxpayer realizes no income as a result of receipt of the section 126 project.

value of section 126 improvement	$15,000
(taxpayer's contribution)	(10,000)
(excludable portion)	(5,600)
amount included in income	—0—

Example (4). In 1983, the taxpayer signs a contract under the water bank program under which he will maintain 20 acres of undistributed wetlands as a wildfowl preserve. In return he will receive $90 an acre as rent from the government. Although the payment is made under a program listed in section 126(a) and the Secretary of Agriculture has certified that the entire amount of payment was made primarily for the purpose of conservation, there is no income eligible for section 126 exclusion because the full payment is rent. The rent is included in full in gross income.

Example (5). In 1980, the taxpayer reforests 200 acres of nonindustrial private forest land by planting tree seedlings. The taxpayer pays the full cost of the reforestation, $15,000. Under the cost-sharing provisions of the forestry incentives program, the taxpayer receives a reimbursement from USDA of $12,000. The Secretary of Agriculture certifies that 100% of the USDA payment is primarily for the purpose of conservation. Assume that the excludable portion is $3,500 and that based on all the facts and circumstances, the value of the improvement is $15,000. The amount which is includible in income is the value of the section 126 improvement, reduced by the excludable portion and the taxpayer's share of the cost of the improvement. Therefore the taxpayer includes $8,500 in gross income as a result of the USDA payment, computed as follows:

value of section 126 improvement	$15,000
(excludable portion)	($3,500)

(taxpayer's contribution)	($5,000)
amount included in gross income	$ 8,500

[Temporary Reg. §16A.126-1.]

☐ [T.D. 7778, 5-18-81.]

[Reg. §16A.126-2]

§16A.126-2. Section 126 elections (temporary).—(a) *Election for section 126 not to apply in whole or in part.*—A taxpayer may elect under section 126(c) not to have section 126 apply to all or any part of an improvement described in section 126.

(b) *Application of the section 126 exclusion.*—To the extent the section 126 exclusion applies, the taxpayer should so indicate on an attachment to the tax return (or amended return) for the taxable year in which the taxpayer received the last payment made by a government for the improvement. The attachment should state the dollar amount of the section 126 cost funded by a government payment, the value of the section 126 improvement, and the amount that the taxpayer is excluding under section 126. [Temporary Reg. §16A.126-2.]

☐ [T.D. 7778, 5-18-81.]

[Reg. §1.127-1]

§1.127-1. Amounts received under a qualified educational assistance program.—(a) *Exclusion from gross income.*—The gross income of an employee does not include—

(1) Amounts paid to, or on behalf of the employee under a qualified educational assistance program described in §1.127-2, or

(2) The value of education provided to the employee under such a program.

(b) *Disallowance of excluded amounts as credit or deduction.*—Any amount excluded from the gross income of an employee under paragraph (a) of this section shall not be allowed as a credit or deduction to such employee under any other provision of this part.

(c) *Amounts received under a nonqualified program.*—Any amount received under an educational assistance program that is not a "qualified program" described in §1.127-2 will not be excluded from gross income under paragraph (a) of this section. All or part of the amounts received under such a non-qualified program may, however, be excluded under section 117 or deducted under section 162 or section 212 (as the case may be), if the requirements of such section are satisfied.

(d) *Definitions.*—For rules relating to the meaning of the terms "employee" and "employer", see paragraph (h) of §1.127-2.

(e) *Effective date.*—This section is effective for taxable years of the employee beginning after December 31, 1978, and before January 1, 1984. [Reg. §1.127-1.]

☐ [T.D. 7898, 7-5-83.]

[Reg. §1.127-2]

§1.127-2. Qualified educational assistance program.—(a) *In general.*—A qualified educational assistance program is a plan established and maintained by an employer under which the employer provides educational assistance to employees. To be a qualified program, the requirements described in paragraphs (b) through (g) of this section must be satisfied. It is not required that a program be funded or that the employer apply to the Internal Revenue Service for a determination that the plan is a qualified program. However, under §601.201 (relating to rulings and determination letters), an employer may request that the Service determine whether a plan is a qualified program.

(b) *Separate written plan.*—The program must be a separate written plan of the employer. This requirement means that the terms of the program must be set forth in a separate document or documents providing only educational assistance within the meaning of paragraph (c) of this section. The requirement for a separate plan does not, however, preclude an educational assistance program from being part of a more comprehensive employer plan that provides a choice of nontaxable benefits to employees.

(c) *Educational assistance.*—(1) *In general.*—The benefits provided under the program must consist solely of educational assistance. The term "educational assistance" means—

(i) The employer's payment of expenses incurred by or on behalf of an employee for education, or

(ii) The employer's provision of education to an employee.

(2) *Alternative benefits.*—Benefits will not be considered to consist solely of educational assistance if the program, in form or in actual operation, provides employees with a choice between educational assistance and other remuneration includible in the employee's gross income.

(3) *Certain benefits not considered educational assistance.*—The term "educational assistance" does not include the employer's payment for, or provision of—

(i) Tools or supplies (other than textbooks) that the employee may retain after completing a course of instruction,

(ii) Meals, lodging, or transportation, or

(iii) Education involving sports, games, or hobbies, unless such education involves the business of the employer or is required as part of a degree program. The phrase "sports, games, or hobbies" does not include education that instructs employees how to maintain and improve health so long as such education does not involve the use of athletic facilities or equipment and is not recreational in nature.

(4) *Education defined.*—As used in section 127, §1.127-1, and this section, the term "education" includes any form of instruction or training that improves or develops the capabilities of an individual. Education paid for or provided under a qualified program may be furnished directly by the employer, either alone or in conjunction with other employers, or through a third party such as an educational institution. Education is not limited to courses that are job related or part of a degree program.

(d) *Exclusive benefit.*—The program may benefit only the employees of the employer, including, at the employer's option, individuals who are employees within the meaning of paragraph (h)(1) of this section. A program that provides benefits to spouses or dependents of employees is not a qualified program within the meaning of this section.

(e) *Prohibited discrimination.*—(1) *Eligibility for benefits.*—The program must benefit the employer's employees generally. Among those benefited may be employees who are officers, shareholders, self-employed or highly compensated. A program is not for the benefit of employees generally, however, if the program discriminates in favor of employees described in the preceding sentence (or in favor of their spouses and dependents who are themselves employees) in requirements relating to eligibility for benefits. Thus, although a program need not provide benefits for all employees, it must benefit those employees who qualify under a classification of employees that does not discriminate in favor of the employees with respect to whom discrimination is prohibited. The classification of employees to be considered benefited will consist of that group of employees who are actually eligible for educational assistance under the program, taking into account the eligibility requirements set forth in the written plan, the eligibility requirements reflected in the types of educational assistance available under the program, and any other conditions that may affect the availability of benefits under the program. Thus, for example, if an employer's plan provides that all employees are eligible for educational assistance, yet limits that assistance to courses of study leading to post-graduate degrees in fields relating to the employer's business, then only those employees able to pursue such a course of study are considered actually eligible for educational assistance under the program. Whether any classification of employees discriminates in favor of employees with respect to whom discrimination is prohibited will generally be determined by applying the same standards as are applied under section 410(b)(1)(B) (relating to qualified pension, profit-sharing and stock bonus plans), without regard to section 401(a)(5). For purposes of making this determination, there shall be excluded from consideration employees not covered by the program who are included in a unit of employees covered by an agreement which the Secretary of Labor finds to be a collective bargaining agreement between employee representatives and one or more employers, if the Internal Revenue Service finds that educational assistance benefits were the subject of good faith bargaining between the employee representatives and the employer or employers. For purposes of determining whether such bargaining occurred, it is not material that the employees are not covered by another educational assistance program or that the employer's present program was not considered in the bargaining.

(2) *Factors not considered in determining the existence of prohibited discrimination.*—A program shall not be considered discriminatory under this paragraph (e) merely because—

(i) Different types of educational assistance available under the program are utilized to a greater degree by employees with respect to whom discrimination is prohibited than by other employees, or

(ii) With respect to a course of study for which benefits are otherwise available, successful completion of the course, attaining a particular course grade, or satisfying a reasonable condition subsequent (such as remaining employed for one year after completing the course) are required or considered in determining the availability of benefits.

(f) *Benefit limitation.*—(1) *In general.*—Under section 127(b)(3), a program is a qualified program for a program year only if no more than 5% of the amounts paid or incurred by the employer for educational assistance benefits during the year are provided to the limitation class described in subparagraph (2). For purposes of this paragraph (f), the program year must be specified in the written plan as either the calendar year or the taxable year of the employer.

(2) *Limitation class.*—The limitation class consists of—

(i) *Shareholders.*—Individuals who, on any day of the program year, own more than 5% of the total number of shares of outstanding stock of the employer, or

(ii) *Owners.*—In the case of an employer's trade or business which is not incorporated, individuals who, on any day of the program year, own more than 5% of the capital or profits interest in the employer, and

(iii) *Spouses or dependents.*—Individuals who are spouses or dependents of shareholders or owners described in subdivision (i) or (ii). For purposes of determining stock ownership, the attribution rules described in paragraph (h)(4) of this section apply. The regulations prescribed under section 414(c) are applicable in determining an individual's interest in the capital or profits of an unincorporated trade or business.

(g) *Notification of employees.*—A program is not a qualified program unless employees eligible to participate in the program are given reasonable notice of the terms and availability of the program.

(h) *Definitions.*—For purposes of this section and § 1.127-1—

(1) *Employee.*—The term "employee" includes—

(i) A retired, disabled or laid-off employee,

(ii) A present employee who is on leave, as, for example, in the Armed Forces of the United States, or

(iii) An individual who is self-employed within the meaning of section 401(c)(1).

(2) *Employer.*—An individual who owns the entire interest in an unincorporated trade or business shall be treated as his or her own employer. A partnership is treated as the employer of each partner who is an employee within the meaning of section 401(c)(1).

(3) *Officer.*—An officer is an individual who is an officer within the meaning of regulations prescribed under section 414(c).

(4) *Shareholder.*—The term "shareholder" includes an individual who is a shareholder as determined by the attribution rules under section 1563(d) and (e), without regard to section 1563(e)(3)(C).

(5) *Highly compensated.*—The term "highly compensated" has the same meaning as it does for purposes of section 410(b)(1)(B).

(i) *Substantiation.*—An employee receiving payments under a qualified educational assistance program must be prepared to provide substantiation to the employer such that it is reasonable to believe that payments or reimbursements made under the program constitute educational assistance within the meaning of paragraph (c) of this section. [Reg. § 1.127-2.]

☐ [*T.D.* 7898, 7-5-83.]

[Reg. § 1.132-0]

§ 1.132-0. Outline of regulations under section 132.—The following is an outline of regulations in this section relating to exclusions from gross income for certain fringe benefits:

§1.132-5(f) Safe harbor substantiation rule for vehicles not available to employees for personal use other than commuting.

§1.132-5(g) Safe harbor substantiation rule for vehicles used in connection with the business of farming that are available to employees for personal use.

    (1) In general.

    (2) Vehicles available to more than one individual.

    (3) Examples.

§1.132-5(h) Qualified nonpersonal use vehicles.

    (1) In general.

    (2) Shared usage of qualified nonpersonal use vehicles.

§1.132-5(i) [Reserved].

§1.132-5(j) Application of section 280F.

§1.132-5(k) Aircraft allocation rule.

§1.132-5(l) [Reserved].

§1.132-5(m) Employer-provided transportation for security concerns.

    (1) In general.

    (2) Demonstration of bona fide business-oriented security concerns.

    (3) Application of security rules to spouses and dependents.

    (4) Working condition safe harbor for travel on employer-provided aircraft.

    (5) Bodyguard/chauffeur provided for a bona fide business-oriented security concern.

    (6) Special valuation rule for government employees.

    (7) Government employer and employee defined.

    (8) Examples.

§1.132-5(n) Product testing.

    (1) In general.

    (2) Employer-imposed limits.

    (3) Discriminating classifications.

    (4) Factors that negate the existence of a product testing program.

    (5) Failure to meet the requirements of this paragraph (n).

    (6) Example.

§1.132-5(o) Qualified automobile demonstration use.

    (1) In general.

    (2) Full-time automobile salesman.

    (3) Demonstration automobile.

    (4) Substantial restrictions on personal use.

    (5) Sales area.

    (6) Applicability of substantiation requirements of sections 162 and 274(d).

    (7) Special valuation rules.

§1.132-5(p) Parking.

    (1) In general.

    (2) Reimbursement of parking expenses.

    (3) Parking on residential property.

    (4) Dates of applicability.

§1.132-5(q) Nonapplicability of nondiscrimination rules.

§1.132-5(r) Volunteers.

    (1) In general.

    (2) Limit on application of this paragraph.

    (3) Definitions.

    (4) Example.

§1.132-6. De minimis fringes.

§1.132-6(a) In general.

§1.132-6(b) Frequency.

    (1) Employee-measured frequency.

    (2) Employer-measured frequency.

§1.132-6(c) Administrability.

§1.132-6(d) Special rules.

    (1) Transit passes.

    (2) Occasional meal money or local transportation fare.

    (3) Use of special rules or examples to establish a general rule.

    (4) Benefits exceeding value and frequency limits.

§1.132-6(e) Examples.

    (1) Benefits excludable from income.

    (2) Benefits not excludable as de minimis fringes.

§1.132-6(f) Nonapplicability of nondiscrimination rules.

§1.132-7. Employer-operated eating facilities.

§1.132-7(a) In general.

    (1) Conditions for exclusion.

    (2) Employer-operated eating facility for employees.

    (3) Operation by the employer.

    (4) Example.

§1.132-7(b) Direct operating costs.

    (1) In general.

    (2) Multiple dining rooms or cafeterias.

    (3) Payment to operator of facility.

§1.132-7(c) Valuation of non-excluded meals provided at an employer-operated eating facility for employees.

§1.132-8. Fringe benefit nondiscrimination rules.

§1.132-8(a) Application of nondiscrimination rules.

    (1) General rule.

    (2) Consequences of discrimination.

    (3) Scope of the nondiscrimination rules provided in this section.

§1.132-8(b) Aggregation of employees.

    (1) Section 132(a)(1) and (2).

    (2) Section 132(e)(2).

    (3) Classes of employees who may be excluded.

§1.132-8(c) Availability on substantially the same terms.

    (1) General rule.

    (2) Certain terms relating to priority.

§1.132-8(d) Testing for discrimination.

    (1) Classification test.

    (2) Classifications that are per se discriminatory.

    (3) Former employees.

    (4) Restructuring of benefits.

    (5) Employer-operated eating facilities for employees.

§1.132-8(e) Cash bonuses or rebates.

§1.132-8(f) Highly compensated employee.

    (1) Government and non-government employees.

    (2) Former employees.

§1.132-9. Qualified transportation fringes.

§1.132-9(a) Table of contents.

§1.132-9(b) Questions and answers.

[Reg §1.132-0.]

☐ [*T.D. 8256, 7-5-89. Amended by T.D. 8457, 12-29-92 and T.D. 8933, 1-10-2001.*]

[Reg. §1.132-1]

§1.132-1. Exclusion from gross income for certain fringe benefits.—(a) *In general.*—Gross income does not include any fringe benefit which qualifies as a—

    (1) No-additional-cost service.

    (2) Qualified employee discount,

    (3) Working condition fringe, or

    (4) De minimis fringe.

Special rules apply with respect to certain on-premises gyms and other athletic facilities (§1.132-1(e)), demonstration use of employer-provided automobiles by full-time automobile salesmen (§1.132-5(o)), parking provided to an employee on or near the business premises of the employer (§1.132-5(p)), and on-premises eating facilities (§1.132-7).

    (b) *Definition of employee.*—(1) *No-additional-cost services and qualified employee discounts.*—For purposes of section 132(a)(1) (relating to no-additional-cost services) and section 132(a)(2) (relating to qualified employee discounts), the term "employee" (with respect to a line of business of an employer) means—

    (i) Any individual who is currently employed by the employer in the line of business,

    (ii) Any individual who was formerly employed by the employer in the line of business and who separated from service with the employer in the line of business by reason of retirement or disability, and

    (iii) Any widow or widower of an individual who died while employed by the employer in the line of business or who separated from service with the employer in the line of business by reason of retirement or disability.

For purposes of this paragraph (b)(1), any partner who performs services for a partnership is considered employed by the partnership. In addition, any use by the spouse or dependent child (as defined in paragraph (b)(5) of this section) of the employee will be treated as use by the employee. For purposes of section 132(a)(1) (relating to no-additional-cost services), any use of air transportation by a parent of an employee (determined without regard to section 132(f)(1)(B) and paragraph (b)(1)(iii) of this section) will be treated as use by the employee.

    (2) *Working condition fringes.*—For purposes of section 132(a)(3) (relating to working condition fringes), the term "employee" means—

    (i) Any individual who is currently employed by the employer,

    (ii) Any partner who performs services for the partnership,

    (iii) Any director of the employer, and

(iv) Any independent contractor who performs services for the employer.

Notwithstanding anything in this paragraph (b)(2) to the contrary, an independent contractor who performs services for the employer cannot exclude the value of parking or the use of consumer goods provided pursuant to a product testing program under §1.132-5(n); in addition, any director of the employer cannot exclude the value of the use of consumer goods provided pursuant to a product testing program under §1.132-5(n).

(3) *On-premises athletic facilities.*—For purposes of section 132(h)(5) (relating to on-premises athletic facilities), the term "employee" means—

(i) Any individual who is currently employed by the employer,

(ii) Any individual who was formerly employed by the employer and who separated from service with the employer by reason of retirement or disability, and

(iii) Any widow or widower of an individual who died while employed by the employer or who separated from service with the employer by reason of retirement or disability.

For purposes of this paragraph (b)(3), any partner who performs services for a partnership is considered employed by the partnership. In addition, any use by the spouse or dependent child (as defined in paragraph (b)(5) of this section) of the employee will be treated as use by the employee.

(4) *De minimis fringes.*—For purposes of section 132(a)(4) (relating to de minimis fringes), the term "employee" means any recipient of a fringe benefit.

(5) *Dependent child.*—The term "dependent child" means any son, stepson, daughter, or stepdaughter of the employee who is a dependent of the employee, or both of whose parents are deceased and who has not attained age 25. Any child to whom section 152(e) applies will be treated as the dependent of both parents.

(c) *Special rules for employers—Effect of section 414.*—All employees treated as employed by a single employer under section 414(b), (c), (m), or (o) will be treated as employed by a single employer for purposes of this section. Thus, employees of one corporation that is part of a controlled group of corporations may under certain circumstances be eligible to receive section 132 benefits from the other corporations that comprise the controlled group. However, the aggregation of employers described in this paragraph (c) does not change the other requirements for an exclusion, such as the line of business requirement. Thus, for example, if a controlled group of corporations consists of two corporations that operate in different lines of business, the corporations are not treated as operating in the same line of business even though the corporations are treated as one employer.

(d) *Customers not to include employees.*—For purposes of section 132 and the regulations thereunder, the term "customer" means any customer who is not an employee. However, the preceding sentence does not apply to section 132(c)(2) (relating to the gross profit percentage for determining a qualified employee discount). Thus, an employer that provides employee discounts cannot exclude sales made to employees in determining the aggregate sales to customers.

(e) *Treatment of on-premises athletic facilities.*—(1) *In general.*—Gross income does not include the value of any on-premises athletic facility provided by an employer to its employees. For purposes of section 132(h)(5) and this paragraph (e), the term "on-premises athletic facility" means any gym or other athletic facility (such as a pool, tennis court, or golf course)—

(i) Which is located on the premises of the employer,

(ii) Which is operated by the employer, and

(iii) Substantially all of the use of which during the calendar year is by employees of the employer, their spouses, and their dependent children.

For purposes of paragraph (e)(1)(iii) of this section, the term "dependent children" has the same meaning as the plural of the term "dependent child" in paragraph (b)(5) of this section. The exclusion of this paragraph (e) does not apply to any athletic facility if access to the facility is made available to the general public through the sale of memberships, the rental of the facility, or a similar arrangement.

(2) *Premises of the employer.*—The athletic facility need not be located on the employer's business premises. However, the athletic facility must be located on premises of the employer. The exclusion provided in this paragraph (e) applies whether the premises are owned or leased by the employer; in addition, the exclusion is available even if the employer is not a named lessee on the lease so long as the employer pays reasonable rent. The exclusion provided in this paragraph (e) does not apply to any athletic facility that is a facility for residential use. Thus, for example, a resort with accompanying athletic facilities (such as tennis courts, pool, and gym) would not qualify for the exclusion provided in this paragraph (e). An athletic facility is considered to be located on the employer's premises if the facility is located on the premises of a voluntary employees' beneficiary association funded by the employer.

(3) *Application of rules to membership in an athletic facility.*—The exclusion provided in this paragraph (e) does not apply to any membership in an athletic facility (including health clubs or country clubs) unless the facility is owned (or leased) and operated by the employer and substantially all the use of the facility is by employees of the employer, their spouses, and their dependent children. Therefore, membership in a health club or country club not meeting the rules provided in this paragraph (e) would not qualify for the exclusion.

(4) *Operation by the employer.*—An employer is considered to operate the athletic facility if the employer operates the facility through its own employees, or if the employer contracts out to another to operate the athletic facility. For example, if an employer hires an independent contractor to operate the athletic facility for the employer's employees, the facility is considered to be operated by the employer. In addition, if an athletic facility is operated by more than one employer, it is considered to be operated by each employer. For purposes of paragraph (e)(1)(iii) of this section, substantially all of the use of a facility that is operated by more than one employer must be by employees of the various employers, their spouses, and their dependent children. Where the facility is operated by more than one employer, an employer that pays rent either directly to the owner of the premises or to a sublessor of the premises is eligible for the exclusion. If an athletic facility is operated by a voluntary employees' beneficiary association funded by an employer, the employer is considered to operate the facility.

(5) *Nonapplicability of nondiscrimination rules.*—The nondiscrimination rules of section 132 and §1.132-8 do not apply to on-premises athletic facilities.

(f) *Nonapplicability of section 132 in certain cases.*—(1) *Tax treatment provided for in another section.*—If the tax treatment of a particular fringe benefit is expressly provided for in another section of Chapter 1 of the Internal Revenue Code of 1986, section 132 and the applicable regulations (except for section 132(e) and the regulations thereunder) do not apply to such fringe benefit. For example, because section 129 provides an exclusion from gross income for amounts paid or incurred by an employer for dependent care assistance for an employee, the exclusions under section 132 and this section do not apply to the provision by an employer to an employee of dependent care assistance. Similarly, because section 117(d) applies to tuition reductions, the exclusions under section 132 do not apply to free or discounted tuition provided to an employee by an organization operated by the employer, whether the tuition is for study at or below the graduate level. Of course, if the amounts paid by the employer are for education relating to the employee's trade or business of being an employee of the employer so that, if the employee paid for the education, the amount paid could be deducted under section 162, the costs of the education may be eligible for exclusion as a working condition fringe.

(2) *Limited statutory exclusions.*—If another section of Chapter 1 of the Internal Revenue Code of 1986 provides an exclusion from gross income based on the cost of the benefit provided to the employee and such exclusion is a limited amount, section 132 and the regulations thereunder may apply to the extent the cost of the benefit exceeds the statutory exclusion.

(g) *Effective date.*—Sections 1.132-0, 1.132-1, 1.132-2, 1.132-3, 1.132-4, 1.132-5, 1.132-6, 1.132-7 and 1.132-8 are effective as of January 1, 1989, except that §§1.132-1(b)(1) with respect to the use of air transportation by a parent of an employee and 1.132-4(d) are effective as of January 1, 1985. Furthermore, in §1.132-5, the eleventh sentence of paragraph (m)(1), *Examples 6* and *7* in paragraph (m)(8), and paragraphs (m)(2)(i), (m)(2)(v), (m)(3)(iv), (m)(6), (m)(7), and (r) are effective December 30, 1992; however, taxpayers may treat the rules as applicable to benefits provided on or after January 1, 1989. For the applicable rules relating to employer-provided transportation for security concerns prior to December 30, 1992, *see* §1.132-5(m) (as contained in 26 CFR part 1 (§§1.61 to 1.169) revised April 1, 1992). [Reg. §1.132-1.]

☐ [*T.D. 8256, 7-5-89. Amended by T.D. 8457, 12-29-92 and T.D. 9849, 3-11-2019.*]

[Reg. §1.132-2]

§1.132-2. No-additional-cost services.—(a) *In general.*—(1) *Definition.*—Gross income does not include the value of a no-additional-cost service. A "no-additional-cost service" is any service provided by an employer to an employee for the employee's personal use if—

(i) The service is offered for sale by the employer to its customers in the ordinary course of the line of business of the employer in which the employee performs substantial services, and

(ii) The employer incurs no substantial additional cost in providing the service to the employee (including foregone revenue and excluding any amount paid by or on behalf of the employee for the service).

For rules relating to the line of business limitation, see §1.132-4. For purposes of this section, a service will not be considered to be offered for sale by the employer to its customers if that service is primarily provided to employees and not to the employer's customers.

(2) *Excess capacity services.*—Services that are eligible for treatment as no-additional-cost services include excess capacity services such as hotel accommodations; transportation by aircraft, train, bus, subway, or cruise line; and telephone services. Services that are not eligible for treatment as no-additional-cost services are non-excess capacity services such as the facilitation by a stock brokerage firm of the purchase of stock. Employees who receive non-excess capacity services may, however, be eligible for a qualified employee discount of up to 20 percent of the value of the service provided. See §1.132-3.

(3) *Cash rebates.*—The exclusion for a no-additional-cost service applies whether the service is provided at no charge or at a reduced price. The exclusion also applies if the benefit is provided through a partial or total cash rebate of an amount paid for the service.

(4) *Applicability of nondiscrimination rules.*—The exclusion for a no-additional-cost service applies to highly compensated employees only if the service is available on substantially the same terms to each member of a group of employees that is defined under a reasonable classification set up by the employer that does not discriminate in favor of highly compensated employees. See §1.132-8.

(5) *No substantial additional cost.*—(i) *In general.*—The exclusion for a no-additional-cost service applies only if the employer does not incur substantial additional cost in providing the service to the employee. For purposes of the preceding sentence, the term "cost" includes revenue that is forgone because the service is provided to an employee rather than a nonemployee. (For purposes of determining whether any revenue is forgone, it is assumed that the employee would not have purchased the service unless it were available to the employee at the actual price charged to the employee.) Whether an employer incurs substantial additional cost must be determined without regard to any amount paid by the employee for the service. Thus, any reimbursement by the employee for the cost of providing the service does not affect the determination of whether the employer incurs substantial additional cost.

(ii) *Labor intensive services.*—An employer must include the cost of labor incurred in providing services to employees when determining whether the employer has incurred substantial additional cost. An employer incurs substantial additional cost, whether non-labor costs are incurred, if a substantial amount of time is spent by the employer or its employees in providing the service to employees. This would be the result whether the time spent by the employer or its employees in providing the services would have been "idle," or if the services were provided outside normal business hours. An employer generally incurs no substantial additional cost, however, if the services provided to the employee are merely incidental to the primary service being provided by the employer. For example, the in-flight services of a flight attendant and the cost of in-flight meals provided to airline employees traveling on a space-available basis are merely incidental to the primary service being provided (i.e., air transportation). Similarly, maid service provided to hotel employees renting hotel rooms on a space-available basis is merely incidental to the primary service being provided (i.e., hotel accommodations).

(6) *Payments for telephone service.*—Payment made by an entity subject to the modified final judgment (as defined in section 559(c)(5) of the Tax Reform Act of 1984) of all or part of the cost of local telephone service provided to an employee by a person other than an entity subject to the modified final judgment shall be treated as telephone service provided to the employee by the entity making the payment for purposes of this section. The preceding sentence also applies to a rebate of the amount paid by the employee for the service and a payment to the person providing the service. This paragraph (a)(6) applies only to services and employees described in §1.132-4(c). For a special line of business rule relating to such services and employees, see §1.132-4(c).

(b) *Reciprocal agreements.*—For purposes of the exclusion from gross income for a no-additional-cost service, an exclusion is available to an employee of one employer for a no-additional-cost service provided by an unrelated employer only if all of the following requirements are satisfied—

(1) The service provided to such employee by the unrelated employer is the same type of service generally provided to nonemployee customers by both the line of business in which the employee works and the line of business in which the service is provided to such employee (so that the employee would be permitted to exclude from gross income the value of the service if such service were provided directly by the employee's employer);

(2) Both employers are parties to a written reciprocal agreement under which a group of employees of each employer, all of whom perform substantial services in the same line of business, may receive no-additional-cost services from the other employer; and

(3) Neither employer incurs any substantial additional cost (including forgone revenue) in providing such service to the employees of the other employer, or pursuant to such agreement. If one employer receives a substantial payment from the other employer with respect to the reciprocal agreement, the paying employer will be considered to have incurred a substantial additional cost pursuant to the agreement, and consequently services performed under the reciprocal agreement will not qualify for exclusion as no-additional-cost services.

(c) *Example.*—The rules of this section are illustrated by the following example:

Example. Assume that a commercial airline permits its employees to take personal flights on the airline at no charge and receive reserved seating. Because the employer forgoes potential revenue by permitting the employees to reserve seats, employees receiving such free flights are not eligible for the no-additional-cost exclusion. [Reg. §1.132-2.]

☐ [T.D. 8256, 7-5-89.]

[Reg. §1.132-3]

§1.132-3. **Qualified employee discounts.**—(a) *In general.*—(1) *Definition.*—Gross income does not include the value of a qualified employee discount. A "qualified employee discount" is any employee discount with respect to qualified property or services provided by an employer to an employee for use by the employee to the extent the discount does not exceed—

(i) The gross profit percentage multiplied by the price at which the property is offered to customers in the ordinary course of the employer's line of business, for discounts on property, or

(ii) Twenty percent of the price at which the service is offered to customers, for discounts on services.

(2) *Qualified property or services.*—(i) *In general.*—The term "qualified property or services" means any property or services that are offered for sale to customers in the ordinary course of the line of business of the employer in which the employee performs substantial services. For rules relating to the line of business limitation, see §1.132-4.

(ii) *Exception for certain property.*—The term "qualified property" does not include real property and it does not include personal property (whether tangible or intangible) of a kind commonly held for investment. Thus, an employee may not exclude from gross income the amount of an employee discount provided on the purchase of securities, commodities, or currency, or of either residential or commercial real estate, whether or not the particular purchase is made for investment purposes.

(iii) *Property and services not offered in ordinary course of business.*—The term "qualified property or services" does not include any property or services of a kind that is not offered for sale to customers in the ordinary course of the line of business of the employer. For example, employee discounts provided on property or services that are offered for sale primarily to employees and their families (such as merchandise sold at an employee store or through an employer-provided catalog service) may not be excluded from gross income. For rules relating to employer-operated eating facilities, see §1.132-7, and for rules relating to employer-operated on-premises athletic facilities, see §1.132-1(e).

(3) *No reciprocal agreement exception.*—The exclusion for a qualified employee discount does not apply to property or services provided by another employer pursuant to a written reciprocal agreement that exists between employers to provide discounts on property and services to employees of the other employer.

(4) *Property or services provided without charge, at a reduced price, or by rebates.*—The exclusion for a qualified employee discount applies whether the property or service is provided at no charge (in which case only part of the discount may be excludable as a qualified employee discount) or at a reduced price. The exclusion also applies

Reg. §1.132-3(a)(4)

if the benefit is provided through a partial or total cash rebate of an amount paid for the property or service.

(5) *Property or services provided directly by the employer or indirectly through a third party.*—A qualified employee discount may be provided either directly by the employer or indirectly through a third party. For example, an employee of an appliance manufacturer may receive a qualified employee discount on the manufacturer's appliances purchased at a retail store that offers such appliances for sale to customers. The employee may exclude the amount of the qualified employee discount whether the employee is provided the appliance at no charge or purchases it at a reduced price, or whether the employee receives a partial or total cash rebate from either the employer-manufacturer or the retailer. If an employee receives additional rights associated with the property that are not provided by the employee's employer to customers in the ordinary course of the line of business in which the employee performs substantial services (such as the right to return or exchange the property or special warranty rights), the employee may only receive a qualified employee discount with respect to the property and not the additional rights. Receipt of such additional rights may occur, for example, when an employee of a manufacturer purchases property manufactured by the employee's employer at a retail outlet.

(6) *Applicability of nondiscrimination rules.*—The exclusion for a qualified employee discount applies to highly compensated employees only if the discount is available on substantially the same terms to each member of a group of employees that is defined under a reasonable classification set up by the employer that does not discriminate in favor of highly compensated employees. See § 1.132-8.

(b) *Employee discount.*—(1) *Definition.*—The term "employee discount" means the excess of—

(i) The price at which the property or service is being offered by the employer for sale to customers, over

(ii) The price at which the property or service is provided by the employer to an employee for use by the employee. A transfer of property by an employee without consideration is treated as use by the employee for purposes of this section. Thus, for example, if an employee receives a discount on property offered for sale by his employer to customers and the employee makes a gift of the property to his parent, the property will be considered to be provided for use by the employee; thus, the discount will be eligible for exclusion as a qualified employee discount.

(2) *Price to customers.*—(i) *Determined at time of sale.*—In determining the amount of an employee discount, the price at which the property or service is being offered to customers at the time of the employee's purchase is controlling. For example, assume that an employer offers a product to customers for $20 during the first six months of a calendar year, but at the time the employee purchases the product at a discount, the price at which the product is being offered to customers is $25. In this case, the price from which the employee discount is measured is $25. Assume instead that, at the time the employee purchases the product at a discount, the price at which the product is being offered to customers is $15 and the price charged the employee is $12. The employee discount is measured from $15, the price at which the product is offered for sale to customers at the time of the employee purchase. Thus, the employee discount is $15 – $12, or $3.

(ii) *Quantity discount not reflected.*—The price at which a property or service is being offered to customers cannot reflect any quantity discount unless the employee actually purchases the requisite quantity of the property or service.

(iii) *Price to employer's customers controls.*—In determining the amount of an employee discount, the price at which a property or service is offered to customers of the employee's employer is controlling. Thus, the price at which the property is sold to the wholesale customers of a manufacturer will generally be lower than the price at which the same property is sold to the customers of a retailer. However, see paragraph (a)(5) of this section regarding the effect of a wholesaler providing to its employees additional rights not provided to customers of the wholesaler in the ordinary course of its business.

(iv) *Discounts to discrete customer or consumer groups.*—Subject to paragraph (2)(ii) of this section, if an employer offers for sale property or services at one or more discounted prices to discrete customer or consumer groups, and sales at all such discounted prices comprise at least 35 percent of the employer's gross sales for a representative period, then in determining the amount of an employee discount, the price at which such property or service is being offered to customers for purposes of this section is a discounted price. The applicable discounted price is the current undiscounted price, reduced by the percentage discount at which the greatest percentage of the employer's discounted gross sales are made for

such representative period. If sales at different percentage discounts equal the same percentage of the employer's gross sales, the price at which the property or service is being provided to customers may be reduced by the average of the discounts offered to each of the two groups. For purposes of this section, a representative period is the taxable year of the employer immediately preceding the taxable year in which the property or service is provided to the employee at a discount. If more than one employer would be aggregated under section 414(b), (c), (m), or (o), and not all of the employers have the same taxable year, the employers required to be aggregated must designate the 12-month period to be used in determining gross sales for a representative period. The 12-month period designated, however, must be used on a consistent basis.

(v) *Examples.*—The rules provided in this paragraph (b)(2) are illustrated by the following examples:

Example (1). Assume that a wholesale employer offers property for sale to two discrete customer groups at differing prices. Assume further that during the prior taxable year of the employer, 70 percent of the employer's gross sales are made at a 15 percent discount and 30 percent at no discount. For purposes of this paragraph (b)(2), the current undiscounted price at which the property or service is being offered by the employer for sale to customers may be reduced by the 15 percent discount.

Example (2). Assume that a retail employer offers a 20 percent discount to members of the American Bar Association, a 15 percent discount to members of the American Medical Association, and a ten percent discount to employees of the Federal Government. Assume further that during the prior taxable year of the employer, sales to American Bar Association members equal 15 percent of the employer's gross sales, sales to American Medical Association members equal 20 percent of the employer's gross sales, and sales to Federal Government employees equal 25 percent of the employer's gross sales. For purposes of this paragraph (b)(2), the current undiscounted price at which the property or service is being offered by the employer for sale to customers may be reduced by the ten percent Federal Government discount.

(3) *Damaged, distressed, or returned goods.*—If an employee pays at least fair market value for damaged, distressed, or returned property, such employee will not have income attributable to such purchase.

(c) *Gross profit percentage.*—(1) *In general.*—(i) *General rule.*—An exclusion from gross income for an employee discount on qualified property is limited to the price at which the property is being offered to customers in the ordinary course of the employer's line of business, multiplied by the employer's gross profit percentage. The term "gross profit percentage" means the excess of the aggregate sales price of the property sold by the employer to customers (including employees) over the employer's aggregate cost of the property, then divided by the aggregate sales price.

(ii) *Calculation of gross profit percentage.*—The gross profit percentage must be calculated separately for each line of business based on the aggregate sales price and aggregate cost of property in that line of business for a representative period. For purposes of this section, a representative period is the taxable year of the employer immediately preceding the taxable year in which the discount is available. For example, if the aggregate amount of sales of property in an employer's line of business for the prior taxable year was $800,000, and the aggregate cost of the property for the year was $600,000, the gross profit percentage would be 25 percent ($800,000 minus $600,000, then divided by $800,000). If two or more employers are required to aggregate under section 414(b), (c), (m), or (o) (aggregated employer), and if all of the aggregated employers do not share the same taxable year, then the aggregated employers must designate the 12-month period to be used in determining the gross profit percentage. The 12-month period designated, however, must be used on a consistent basis. If an employee performs substantial services in more than one line of business, the gross profit percentage of the line of business in which the property is sold determines the amount of the excludable employee discount.

(iii) *Special rule for employers in their first year of existence.*—An employer in its first year of existence may estimate the gross profit percentage of a line of business based on its mark-up from cost. Alternatively, an employer in its first year of existence may determine the gross profit percentage by reference to an appropriate industry average.

(iv) *Redetermination of gross profit percentage.*—If substantial changes in an employer's business indicate at any time that it is inappropriate for the prior year's gross profit percentage to be used for the current year, the employer must, within a reasonable period, redetermine the gross profit percentage for the remaining portion of the current year as if such portion of the year were the first year of the employer's existence.

Reg. § 1.132-3(a)(5)

(2) *Line of business.*—In general, an employer must determine the gross profit percentage on the basis of all property offered to customers (including employees) in each separate line of business. An employer may instead select a classification of property that is narrower than the applicable line of business. However, the classification must be reasonable. For example, if an employer computes gross profit percentage according to the department in which products are sold, such classification is reasonable. Similarly, it is reasonable to compute gross profit percentage on the basis of the type of merchandise sold (such as high mark-up and low mark-up classifications). It is not reasonable, however, for an employer to classify certain low mark-up products preferred by certain employees (such as highly compensated employees) with high mark-up products or to classify certain high mark-up products preferred by other employees with low mark-up products.

(3) *Generally accepted accounting principles.*—In general, the aggregate sales price of property must be determined in accordance with generally accepted accounting principles. An employer must compute the aggregate cost of property in the same manner in which it is computed for the employer's Federal income tax liability; thus, for example, section 263A and the regulations thereunder apply in determining the cost of property.

(d) *Treatment of leased sections of department stores.*—(1) *In general.*—(i) *General rule.*—For purposes of determining whether employees of a leased section of a department store may receive qualified employee discounts at the department store and whether employees of the department store may receive qualified employee discounts at the leased section of the department store, the leased section is treated as part of the line of business of the person operating the department store, and employees of the leased section are treated as employees of the person operating the department store as well as employees of their employer. The term "leased section of a department store" means a section of a department store where substantially all of the gross receipts of the leased section are from over-the-counter sales of property made under a lease, license, or similar arrangement where it appears to the general public that individuals making such sales are employed by the department store. A leased section of a department store which, in connection with the offering of beautician services, customarily makes sales of beauty aids in the ordinary course of business is deemed to derive substantially all of its gross receipts from over-the-counter sales of property.

(ii) *Calculation of gross profit percentage.*—For purposes of paragraph (d) of this section, when calculating the gross profit percentage of property and services sold at a department store, sales of property and services sold at the department store, as well as sales of property and services sold at the leased section, are considered. The rule provided in the preceding sentence does not apply, however, if it is more reasonable to calculate the gross profit percentage for the department store and leased section separately, or if it would be inappropriate to combine them (such as where either the department store or the leased section but not both provides employee discounts).

(2) *Employees of the leased section.*—(i) *Definition.*—For purposes of this paragraph (d), "employees of the leased section" means all employees who perform substantial services at the leased section of the department store regardless of whether the employees engage in over-the-counter sales of property or services. The term "employee" has the same meaning as in section 132(f) and § 1.132-1(b)(1).

(ii) *Discounts offered to either department store employees or employees of the leased section.*—If the requirements of this paragraph (d) are satisfied, employees of the leased section may receive qualified employee discounts at the department store whether or not employees of the department store are offered discounts at the leased section. Similarly, employees of the department store may receive a qualified employee discount at the leased section whether or not employees of the leased section are offered discounts at the department store.

(e) *Excess discounts.*—Unless excludable under a provision of the Internal Revenue Code of 1986 other than section 132(a)(2), an employee discount provided on property is excludable to the extent of the gross profit percentage multiplied by the price at which the property is being offered for sale to customers. If an employee discount exceeds the gross profit percentage, the excess discount is includible in the employee's income. For example, if the discount on employer-purchased property is 30 percent and the employer's gross profit percentage for the period in the relevant line of business is 25 percent, then 5 percent of the price at which the property is being offered for sale to customers is includible in the employee's income. With respect to services, an employee discount of up to 20 percent may be excludable. If an employee discount exceeds 20 percent, the excess discount is includible in the employee's income. For example,

assume that a commercial airline provides a pass to each of its employees permitting the employees to obtain a free roundtrip coach ticket with a confirmed seat to any destination the airline services. Neither the exclusion of section 132(a)(1) (relating to no-additional-cost services) nor any other statutory exclusion applies to a flight taken primarily for personal purposes by an employee under this program. However, an employee discount of up to 20 percent may be excluded as a qualified employee discount. Thus, if the price charged to customers for the flight taken is $300 (under restrictions comparable to those actually placed on travel associated with the employee airline ticket), $60 is excludible from gross income as a qualified employee discount and $240 is includible in gross income. [Reg. § 1.132-3.]

□ [*T.D.* 8256, 7-5-89.]

[Reg. § 1.132-4]

§ 1.132-4. Line of business limitation.—(a) *In general.*—(1) *Applicability.*—(i) *General rule.*—A no-additional-cost service or a qualified employee discount provided to an employee is only available with respect to property or services that are offered for sale to customers in the ordinary course of the same line of business in which the employee receiving the property or service performs substantial services. Thus, an employee who does not perform substantial services in a particular line of business of the employer may not exclude from income under section 132(a)(1) or (a)(2) the value of services or employee discounts received on property or services in that line of business. For rules that relax the line of business requirement, see paragraphs (b) through (g) of this section.

(ii) *Property and services sold to employees rather than customers.*—Because the property or services must be offered for sale to customers in the ordinary course of the same line of business in which the employee performs substantial services, the line of business limitation is not satisfied if the employer's products or services are sold primarily to employees of the employer, rather than to customers. Thus, for example, an employer in the banking line of business is not considered in the variety store line of business if the employer establishes an employee store that offers variety store items for sale to the employer's employees. See § 1.132-7 for rules relating to employer-operated eating facilities, and see § 1.132-1(e) for rules relating to employer-operated on-premises athletic facilities.

(iii) *Performance of substantial services in more than one line of business.*—An employee who performs services in more than one of the employer's lines of business may only exclude no-additional-cost services and qualified employee discounts in the lines of business in which the employee performs substantial services.

(iv) *Performance of services that directly benefit more than one line of business.*—(A) *In general.*—An employee who performs substantial services that directly benefit more than one line of business of an employer is treated as performing substantial services in all such lines of business. For example, an employee who maintains accounting records for an employer's three lines of business may receive qualified employee discounts in all three lines of business. Similarly, if an employee of a minor line of business of an employer that is significantly interrelated with a major line of business of the employer performs substantial services that directly benefit both the major and the minor lines of business, the employee is treated as performing substantial services for both the major and the minor lines of business.

(B) *Examples.*—The rules provided in this paragraph (a)(1)(iv) are illustrated by the following examples:

Example (1). Assume that employees of units of an employer provide repair or financing services, or sell by catalog, with respect to retail merchandise sold by the employer. Such employees may be considered to perform substantial services for the retail merchandise line of business under paragraph (a)(1)(iv)(A) of this section.

Example (2). Assume that an employer operates a hospital and a laundry service. Assume further that some of the gross receipts of the laundry service line of business are from laundry services sold to customers other than the hospital employer. Only the employees of the laundry service who perform substantial services which directly benefit the hospital line of business (through the provision of laundry services to the hospital) will be treated as performing substantial services for the hospital line of business. Other employees of the laundry service line of business will not be treated as employees of the hospital line of business.

Example (3). Assume the same facts as in example (2), except that the employer also operates a chain of dry cleaning stores. Employees who perform substantial services which directly benefit the dry cleaning stores but who do not perform substantial services that directly benefit the hospital line of business will not be treated as performing substantial services for the hospital line of business.

(2) *Definition.*—(i) *In general.*—An employer's line of business is determined by reference to the Enterprise Standard Industrial Classification Manual (ESIC Manual) prepared by the Statistical Policy Division of the U.S. Office of Management and Budget. An employer is considered to have more than one line of business if the employer offers for sale to customers property or services in more than one two-digit code classification referred to in the ESIC Manual.

(ii) *Examples.*—Examples of two-digit classifications are general retail merchandise stores; hotels and other lodging places; auto repair, services, and garages; and food stores.

(3) *Aggregation of two-digit classifications.*—If, pursuant to paragraph (a)(2) of this section, an employer has more than one line of business, such lines of business will be treated as a single line of business where and to the extent that one or more of the following aggregation rules apply:

(i) If it is uncommon in the industry of the employer for any of the separate lines of business of the employer to be operated without the others, the separate lines of business are treated as one line of business.

(ii) If it is common for a substantial number of employees (other than those employees who work at the headquarters or main office of the employer) to perform substantial services for more than one line of business of the employer, so that determination of which employees perform substantial services for which line or lines of business would be difficult, then the separate lines of business of the employer in which such employees perform substantial services are treated as one line of business. For example, assume that an employer operates a delicatessen with an attached service counter at which food is sold for consumption on the premises. Assume further that most but not all employees work both at the delicatessen and at the service counter. Under the aggregation rule of this paragraph (a)(3)(ii), the delicatessen and the service counter are treated as one line of business.

(iii) If the retail operations of an employer that are located on the same premises are in separate lines of business but would be considered to be within one line of business under paragraph (a)(2) of this section if the merchandise offered for sale in such lines of business were offered for sale at a department store, then the operations are treated as one line of business. For example, assume that on the same premises an employer sells both women's apparel and jewelry. Because, if sold together at a department store, the operations would be part of the same line of business, the operations are treated as one line of business.

(b) *Grandfather rule for certain retail stores.*—(1) *In general.*—The line of business limitation may be relaxed under the special grandfather rule of this paragraph (b). Under this special grandfather rule, if—

(i) On October 5, 1983, at least 85 percent of the employees of one member of an affiliated group (as defined in section 1504 without regard to subsections (b)(2) and (b)(4) thereof) ("first member") were entitled to receive employee discounts at retail department stores operated by another member of the affiliated group ("second member"), and

(ii) More than 50 percent of the previous year's sales of the affiliated group are attributable to the operation of retail department stores,

then, for purposes of the exclusion from gross income of a qualified employee discount, the first member is treated as engaged in the same line of business as the second member (the operator of the retail department stores). Therefore, employees of the first member of the affiliated group may exclude from income qualified employee discounts received at the retail department stores operated by the second member. However, employees of the second member of the affiliated group may not under this paragraph (b)(1) exclude any discounts received on property or services offered for sale to customers by the first member of the affiliated group.

(2) *Taxable year of affiliated group.*—If not all of the members of an affiliated group have the same taxable year, the affiliated group must designate the 12-month period to be used in determining the "previous year's sales" (as referred to in the grandfather rule of this paragraph (b)). The 12-month period designated, however, must be used on a consistent basis.

(3) *Definition of "sales".*—For purposes of this paragraph (b), the term "sales" means the gross receipts of an affiliated group, based upon the accounting methods used by its members.

(4) *Retired and disabled employees.*—For purposes of this paragraph (b), an employee includes any individual who was, or whose spouse was, formerly employed by the first member of an affiliated group and who separated from service with the member by reason of retirement or disability if the second member of the group provided employee discounts to that individual on October 5, 1983.

(5) *Increase of employee discount.*—If, after October 5, 1983, the employee discount described in this paragraph (b) is increased, the grandfather rule of this paragraph (b) does not apply to the amount of the increase. For example, if on January 1, 1989, the employee discount is increased from ten percent to 15 percent, the grandfather rule will not apply to the additional five percent discount.

(c) *Grandfather rule for telephone service provided to predivestiture retirees.*—All entities subject to the modified final judgment (as defined in section 559(c)(5) of the Tax Reform Act of 1984) shall be treated as a single employer engaged in the same line of business for purposes of determining whether telephone service provided to certain employees is a no-additional-cost service. The preceding sentence applies only in the case of an employee who by reason of retirement or disability separated before January 1, 1984, from the service of an entity subject to the modified final judgment. This paragraph (c) only applies to services provided to such employees as of January 1, 1984. For a special no-additional-cost service rule relating to such employees and such services, see § 1.132-2(a)(6).

(d) *Special rule for certain affiliates of commercial airlines.*—(1) *General rule.*—If a qualified affiliate is a member of an airline affiliated group and employees of the qualified affiliate who are directly engaged in providing airline-related services are entitled to no-additional-cost service with respect to air transportation provided by such other member, then, for purposes of applying § 1.132-2 (relating to no-additional-cost services with respect to such air transportation), such qualified affiliate shall be treated as engaged in the same line of business as such other member.

(2) *"Airline affiliated group" defined.*—An "airline affiliated group" is an affiliated group (as defined in section 1504(a)) one of whose members operates a commercial airline that provides air transportation to customers on a per-seat basis.

(3) *"Qualified affiliate" defined.*—A "qualified affiliate" is any corporation that is predominantly engaged in providing airline-related services. The term "airline-related services" means any of the following services provided in connection with air transportation:

(i) Catering,

(ii) Baggage handling,

(iii) Ticketing and reservations,

(iv) Flight planning and weather analysis, and

(v) Restaurants and gift shops located at an airport.

(e) *Grandfather rule for affiliated groups operating airlines.*—The line of business limitation may be relaxed under the special grandfather rule of this paragraph (e). Under this special grandfather rule, if, as of September 12, 1984—

(1) An individual—

(i) Was an employee (within the meaning of § 1.132-1(b)) of one member of an affiliated group (as defined in section 1504(a)) ("first corporation"), and

(ii) Was eligible for no-additional-cost services in the form of air transportation provided by another member of such affiliated group ("second corporation"),

(2) At least 50 percent of the individuals performing services for the first corporation were, or had been employees of, or had previously performed services for, the second corporation, and

(3) The primary business of the affiliated group was air transportation of passengers,

then, for purposes of applying sections 132(a)(1) and (2), with respect to no-additional-cost services and qualified employee discounts provided after December 31, 1984, for that individual by the second corporation, the first corporation is treated as engaged in the same air transportation line of business as the second corporation. For purposes of the preceding sentence, an employee of the second corporation who is performing services for the first corporation is also treated as an employee of the first corporation.

(f) *Special rule for qualified air transportation organizations.*—A qualified air transportation organization is treated as engaged in the line of business of providing air transportation with respect to any individual who performs services for the organization if those services are performed primarily for persons engaged in providing air transportation, and are of a kind which (if performed on September 12, 1984) would qualify the individual for no-additional-cost services in the form of air transportation. The term "qualified air transportation organization" means any organization—

(1) If such organization (or a predecessor) was in existence on September 12, 1984,

(2) If such organization is—

(i) A tax-exempt organization under section 501(c)(6) whose membership is limited to entities engaged in the transportation by air of individuals or property for compensation or hire, or

(ii) Is a corporation all the stock of which is owned entirely by entities described in paragraph (f)(2)(i) of this section, and

(3) If such organization is operated in furtherance of the activities of its members or owners.

(g) *Relaxation of line of business requirement.*—The line of business requirement may be relaxed under an elective grandfather rule provided in section 4977. For rules relating to the section 4977 election, see § 54.4977-1T.

(h) *Line of business requirement does not expand benefits eligible for exclusion.*—The line of business requirement limits the benefits eligible for the no-additional-cost service and qualified employee discount exclusions to property or services provided by an employer to its customers in the ordinary course of the line of business of the employer in which the employee performs substantial services. The requirement is intended to ensure that employers do not offer, on a tax-free or reduced basis, property or services to employees that are not offered to the employer's customers, even if the property or services offered to the customers and the employees are within the same line of business (as defined in this section). [Reg. § 1.132-4.]

□ *[T.D. 8256, 7-5-89.]*

[Reg. § 1.132-5]

§ 1.132-5. Working condition fringes.—(a) *In general.*—(1) *Definition.*—Gross income does not include the value of a working condition fringe. A "working condition fringe" is any property or service provided to an employee of an employer to the extent that, if the employee paid for the property or service, the amount paid would be allowable as a deduction under section 162 or 167.

(i) A service or property offered by an employer in connection with a flexible spending account is not excludable from gross income as a working condition fringe. For purposes of the preceding sentence, a flexible spending account is an agreement (whether or not written) entered into between an employer and an employee that makes available to the employee over a time period a certain level of unspecified non-cash benefits with a pre-determined cash value.

(ii) If, under section 274 or any other section, certain substantiation requirements must be met in order for a deduction under section 162 or 167 to be allowable, then those substantiation requirements apply when determining whether a property or service is excludable as a working condition fringe.

(iii) An amount that would be deductible by the employee under a section other than section 162 or 167, such as section 212, is not a working condition fringe.

(iv) A physical examination program provided by the employer is not excludable as a working condition fringe even if the value of such program might be deductible to the employee under section 213. The previous sentence applies without regard to whether the employer makes the program mandatory to some or all employees.

(v) A cash payment made by an employer to an employee will not qualify as a working condition fringe unless the employer requires the employee to—

(A) Use the payment for expenses in connection with a specific or pre-arranged activity or undertaking for which a deduction is allowable under section 162 or 167,

(B) Verify that the payment is actually used for such expenses, and

(C) Return to the employer any part of the payment not so used.

(vi) The limitation of section 67(a) (relating to the two-percent floor on miscellaneous itemized deductions) is not considered when determining the amount of a working condition fringe. For example, assume that an employer provides a $1,000 cash advance to Employee A and that the conditions of paragraph (a)(1)(v) of this section are not satisfied. Even to the extent A uses the allowance for expenses for which a deduction is allowable under section 162 or 167, because such cash payment is not a working condition fringe, section 67(a) applies. The $1,000 payment is includible in A's gross income and subject to income and employment tax withholding. If, however, the conditions of paragraph (a)(1)(v) of this section are satisfied with respect to the payment, then the amount of A's working condition fringe is determined without regard to section 67(a). The $1,000 payment is excludible from A's gross income and not subject to income and employment tax reporting and withholding.

(2) *Trade or business of the employee.*—(i) *General.*—If the hypothetical payment for a property or service would be allowable as a deduction with respect to a trade or business of an employee other than the employee's trade or business of being an employee of the employer, it cannot be taken into account for purposes of determining the amount, if any, of the working condition fringe.

(ii) *Examples.*—The rule of paragraph (a)(2)(i) of this section may be illustrated by the following examples:

Example (1). Assume that, unrelated to company X's trade or business and unrelated to employee A's trade or business of being an employee of company X, A is a member of the board of directors of company Y. Assume further that company X provides A with air transportation to a company Y board of director's meeting. A may not exclude from gross income the value of the air transportation to the meeting as a working condition fringe. A may, however, deduct such amount under section 162 if the section 162 requirements are satisfied. The result would be the same whether the air transportation was provided in the form of a flight on a commercial airline or a seat on a company X airplane.

Example (2). Assume the same facts as in example (1) except that A serves on the board of directors of company Z and company Z regularly purchases a significant amount of goods and services from company X. Because of the relationship between Company Z and A's employer, A's membership on Company Z's board of directors is related to A's trade or business of being an employee of Company X. Thus, A may exclude from gross income the value of air transportation to board meetings as a working condition fringe.

Example (3). Assume the same facts as in example (1) except that A serves on the board of directors of a charitable organization. Assume further that the service by A on the charity's board is substantially related to company X's trade or business. In this case, A may exclude from gross income the value of air transportation to board meetings as a working condition fringe.

Example (4). Assume the same facts as in example (3) except that company X also provides A with the use of a company X conference room which A uses for monthly meetings relating to the charitable organization. Also assume that A uses company X's copy machine and word processor each month in connection with functions of the charitable organization. Because of the substantial business benefit that company X derives from A's service on the board of the charity, A may exclude as a working condition fringe the value of the use of company X property in connection with the charitable organization.

(b) *Vehicle allocation rules.*—(1) *In general.*—(i) *General rule.*—In general, with respect to an employer-provided vehicle, the amount excludable as a working condition fringe is the amount that would be allowable as a deduction under section 162 or 167 if the employee paid for the availability of the vehicle. For example, assume that the value of the availability of an employer-provided vehicle for a full year is $2,000, without regard to any working condition fringe (i.e., assuming all personal use). Assume further that the employee drives the vehicle 6,000 miles for his employer's business and 2,000 miles for reasons other than the employer's business. In this situation, the value of the working condition fringe is $2,000 multiplied by a fraction, the numerator of which is the business-use mileage (6,000 miles) and the denominator of which is the total mileage (8,000 miles). Thus, the value of the working condition fringe is $1,500. The total amount includible in the employee's gross income on account of the availability of the vehicle is $500 ($2,000 – $1,500). For purposes of this section, the term "vehicle" has the meaning given the term in § 1.61-21(e)(2). Generally, when determining the amount of an employee's working condition fringe, miles accumulated on the vehicle by all employees of the employer during the period in which the vehicle is available to the employee are considered. For example, assume that during the year in which the vehicle is available to the employee in the above example, other employees accumulate 2,000 additional miles on the vehicle (while the employee is not in the automobile). In this case, the value of the working condition fringe is $2,000 multiplied by a fraction, the numerator of which is the business-use mileage by the employee (including all mileage (business and personal) accumulated by other employees) (8,000 miles) and the denominator of which is the total mileage (including all mileage accumulated by other employees) (10,000 miles). Thus, the value of the working condition fringe is $1,600; the total amount includible in the employee's gross income on account of the availability of the vehicle is $400 ($2,000 – $1,600). If, however, substantially all of the use of the automobile by other employees in the employer's business is limited to a certain period, such as the last three months of the year, the miles driven by the other employees during that period would not be considered when determining the employee's working condition fringe exclusion. Similarly, miles driven by other employees are not considered if the pattern of use of the employer-provided automobiles is designed to reduce Federal taxes. For example, assume that an employer provides employees A and B each with the availability of an employer-provided automobile and that A uses the automobile assigned to him 80 percent for the employer's business and that B uses the automobile assigned to him 30 percent for the employer's business. If A and B alternate the use of their assigned automobiles each week in such a way as to achieve a reduction in federal taxes, then the employer may count only miles placed on the automobile by the employee to whom the automobile is assigned when determining each employee's working condition fringe.

(ii) *Use by an individual other than the employee.*—For purposes of this section, if the availability of a vehicle to an individual would be taxed to an employee, use of the vehicle by the individual is included in references to use by the employee.

(iii) *Provision of an expensive vehicle for personal use.*—If an employer provides an employee with a vehicle that an employee may use in part for personal purposes, there is no working condition fringe exclusion with respect to the personal miles driven by the employee; if the employee paid for the availability of the vehicle, he would not be entitled to deduct under section 162 or 167 any part of the payment attributable to personal miles. The amount of the inclusion is not affected by the fact that the employee would have chosen the availability of a less expensive vehicle. Moreover, the result is the same even though the decision to provide an expensive rather than an inexpensive vehicle is made by the employer for bona fide non-compensatory business reasons.

(iv) *Total value inclusion.*—In lieu of excluding the value of a working condition fringe with respect to an automobile, an employer using the automobile lease valuation rule of §1.61-21(d) may include in an employee's gross income the entire Annual Lease Value of the automobile. Any deduction allowable to the employee under section 162 or 167 with respect to the automobile may be taken on the employee's income tax return. The total inclusion rule of this paragraph (b)(1)(iv) is not available if the employer is valuing the use or availability of a vehicle under general valuation principles or a special valuation rule other than the automobile lease valuation rule. See §§1.162-25 and 1.162-25T for rules relating to the employee's deduction.

(v) *Shared usage.*—In calculating the working condition fringe benefit exclusion with respect to a vehicle provided for use by more than one employee, an employer shall compute the working condition fringe in a manner consistent with the allocation of the value of the vehicle under §1.61-21(c)(2)(ii)(B).

(2) *Use of different employer-provided vehicles.*—The working condition fringe exclusion must be applied on a vehicle-by-vehicle basis. For example, assume that automobile Y is available to employee D for 3 days in January and for 5 days in March, and automobile Z is available to D for a week in July. Assume further that the Daily Lease Value, as defined in §1.61-21(d)(4)(ii), of each automobile is $50. For the eight days of availability of Y in January and March, D uses Y 90 percent for business (by mileage). During July, D uses Z 60 percent for business (by mileage). The value of the working condition fringe is determined separately for each automobile. Therefore, the working condition fringe for Y is $360 ($400 × .90) leaving an income inclusion of $40. The working condition fringe for Z is $210 ($350 × .60), leaving an income inclusion of $140. If the value of the availability of an automobile is determined under the Annual Lease Value rule for one period and Daily Lease Value rule for a second period (see §1.61-21(d)), the working condition fringe exclusion must be calculated separately for the two periods.

(3) *Provision of a vehicle and chauffeur services.*—(i) *General rule.*—In general, with respect to the value of chauffeur services provided by an employer, the amount excludable as a working condition fringe is the amount that would be allowable as a deduction under section 162 or 167 if the employee paid for the chauffeur services. The working condition fringe with respect to a chauffeur is determined separately from the working condition fringe with respect to the vehicle. An employee may exclude from gross income the excess of the value of the chauffeur services over the value of the chauffeur services for personal purposes (such as commuting) as determined under §1.61-21(b)(5). See §1.61-21(b)(5) for additional rules and examples concerning the valuation of chauffeur services. See §1.132-5(m)(5) for rules relating to an exclusion from gross income for the value of bodyguard/chauffeur services. When determining whether miles placed on the vehicle are for the employer's business, miles placed on the vehicle by a chauffeur between the chauffeur's residence and the place at which the chauffeur picks up (or drops off) the employee are with respect to the employee (but not the chauffeur) considered to be miles placed on the vehicle for the employer's business and thus eligible for the working condition fringe exclusion. Thus, because miles placed on the vehicle by a chauffeur between the chauffeur's residence and the place at which the chauffeur picks up (or drops off) the employee are not considered business miles with respect to the chauffeur, the value of the availability of the vehicle for commuting is includible in the gross income of the chauffeur. For general and special rules concerning the valuation of the use of employer-provided vehicles, see paragraphs (b) through (f) of §1.61-21.

(ii) *Examples.*—The rules of paragraph (b)(3)(i) of this section are illustrated by the following examples:

Example (1). Assume that an employer makes available to an employee an automobile and a chauffeur. Assume further that the value of the chauffeur services determined in accordance with §1.61-21 is $30,000 and that the chauffeur spends 30 percent of each workday driving the employee for personal purposes. There may be excluded from the employee's income 70 percent of $30,000, or $21,000, leaving an income inclusion with respect to the chauffeur services of $9,000.

Example (2). Assume that the value of the availability of an employer-provided vehicle for a year is $4,850 and that the value of employer-provided chauffeur services with respect to the vehicle for the year is $20,000. Assume further that 40 percent of the miles placed on the vehicle are for the employer's business and that 60 percent are for other purposes. In addition, assume that the chauffeur spends 25 percent of each workday driving the employee for personal purposes (i.e., 2 hours). The value of the chauffeur services includible in the employee's income is 25 percent of $20,000, or $5,000. The excess of $20,000 over $5,000 or $15,000 is excluded from the employee's income as a working condition fringe. The amount excludable as a working condition fringe with respect to the vehicle is 40 percent of $4,850, or $1,940 and the amount includible is $4,850 – $1,940, or $2,910.

(c) *Applicability of substantiation requirements of sections 162 and 274 (d).*—(1) *In general.*—The value of property or services provided to an employee may not be excluded from the employee's gross income as a working condition fringe, by either the employer or the employee, unless the applicable substantiation requirements of either section 274 (d) or section 162 (whichever is applicable) and the regulations thereunder are satisfied. The substantiation requirements of section 274(d) apply to an employee even if the requirements of section 274 do not apply to the employee's employer for deduction purposes (such as when the employer is a tax-exempt organization or a governmental unit).

(2) *Section 274(d) requirements.*—The substantiation requirements of section 274(d) are satisfied by "adequate records or sufficient evidence corroborating the [employee's] own statement". Therefore, such records or evidence provided by the employee, and relied upon by the employer to the extent permitted by the regulations promulgated under section 274(d), will be sufficient to substantiate a working condition fringe exclusion.

(d) *Safe harbor substantiation rules.*—(1) *In general.*—Section 1.274-6T provides that the substantiation requirements of section 274(d) and the regulations thereunder may be satisfied, in certain circumstances, by using one or more of the safe harbor rules prescribed in §1.274-6T. If the employer uses one of the safe harbor rules prescribed in §1.274-6T during a period with respect to a vehicle (as defined in §1.61-21(e)(2)), that rule must be used by the employer to substantiate a working condition fringe exclusion with respect to that vehicle during the period. An employer that is exempt from Federal income tax may still use one of the safe harbor rules (if the requirements of that section are otherwise met during a period) to substantiate a working condition fringe exclusion with respect to a vehicle during the period. If the employer uses one of the methods prescribed in §1.274-6T during a period with respect to an employer-provided vehicle, that method may be used by an employee to substantiate a working condition fringe exclusion with respect to the same vehicle during the period, as long as the employee includes in gross income the amount allocated to the employee pursuant to §1.274-6T and this section. (See §1.61-21(c)(2) for other rules concerning when an employee must include in income the amount determined by the employer.) If, however, the employer uses the safe harbor rule prescribed in §1.274-6T(a)(2) or (3) and the employee without the employer's knowledge uses the vehicle for purposes other than de minimis personal use (in the case of the rule prescribed in §1.274-6T(a)(2)), or for purposes other than de minimis personal use and commuting (in the case of the rule prescribed in §1.274-6T(a)(3)), then the employee must include an additional amount in income for the unauthorized use of the vehicle.

(2) *Period for use of safe harbor rules.*—The rules prescribed in this paragraph (d) assume that the safe harbor rules prescribed in §1.274-6T are used for a one-year period. Accordingly, references to the value of the availability of a vehicle, amounts excluded as a working condition fringe, etc., are based on a one-year period. If the safe harbor rules prescribed in §1.274-6T are used for a period of less than a year, the amounts referred to in the previous sentence must be adjusted accordingly. For purposes of this section, the term "personal use" has the same meaning as prescribed in §1.274-6T(e)(5).

(e) *Safe harbor substantiation rule for vehicles not used for personal purposes.*—For a vehicle described in §1.274-6T(a)(2) (relating to certain vehicles not used for personal purposes), the working condition fringe exclusion is equal to the value of the availability of the vehicle if the employer uses the method prescribed in § 1.274-6T(a)(2).

(f) *Safe harbor substantiation rule for vehicles not available to employees for personal use other than commuting.*—For a vehicle described in § 1.274-6T(a)(3) (relating to certain vehicles not used for personal purposes other than commuting), the working condition fringe exclusion is equal to the value of the availability of the vehicle for purposes other than commuting if the employer uses the method prescribed in § 1.274-6T(a)(3). This rule applies only if the special rule for valuing commuting use, as prescribed in § 1.61-21(f), is used and the amount determined under the special rule is either included in the employee's income or reimbursed by the employee.

(g) *Safe harbor substantiation rule for vehicles used in connection with the business of farming that are available to employees for personal use.*— (1) *In general.*—For a vehicle described in § 1.274-6T(b) (relating to certain vehicles used in connection with the business of farming), the working condition fringe exclusion is calculated by multiplying the value of the availability of the vehicle by 75 percent.

(2) *Vehicles available to more than one individual.*—If the vehicle is available to more than one individual, the employer must allocate the gross income inclusion attributable to the vehicle (25 percent of the value of the availability of the vehicle) among the employees (and other individuals whose use would not be attributed to an employee) to whom the vehicle is available. This allocation must be done in a reasonable manner to reflect the personal use of the vehicle by the individuals. An amount that would be allocated to a sole proprietor reduces the amounts that may be allocated to employees but is otherwise to be disregarded for purposes of this paragraph (g). For purposes of this paragraph (g), the value of the availability of a vehicle may be calculated as if the vehicle were available to only one employee continuously and without regard to any working condition fringe exclusion.

(3) *Examples.*—The following examples illustrate a reasonable allocation of gross income with respect to an employer-provided vehicle between two employees:

Example (1). Assume that two farm employees share the use of a vehicle that for a calendar year is regularly used directly in connection with the business of farming and qualifies for use of the rule in § 1.274-6T(b). Employee A uses the vehicle in the morning directly in connection with the business of farming and employee B uses the vehicle in the afternoon directly in connection with the business of farming. Assume further that employee B takes the vehicle home in the evenings and on weekends. The employer should allocate all the income attributable to the availability of the vehicle to employee B.

Example (2). Assume that for a calendar year, farm employees C and D share the use of a vehicle that is regularly used directly in connection with the business of farming and qualifies for use of the rule in § 1.274-6T(b). Assume further that the employees alternate taking the vehicle home in the evening and alternate the availability of the vehicle for personal purposes on weekends. The employer should allocate the income attributable to the availability of the vehicle for personal use (25 percent of the value of the availability of the vehicle) equally between the two employees.

Example (3). Assume the same facts as in example (2) except that C is the sole proprietor of the farm. Based on these facts, C should allocate the same amount of income to D as was allocated to D in example (2). No other income attributable to the availability of the vehicle for personal use should be allocated.

(h) *Qualified nonpersonal use vehicles.*—(1) *In general.*—Except as provided in paragraph (h)(2) of this section, 100 percent of the value of the use of a qualified nonpersonal use vehicle (as described in § 1.274-5(k)) is excluded from gross income as a working condition fringe, provided that, in the case of a vehicle described in § 1.274-5(k)(3) through (8), the use of the vehicle conforms to the requirements of paragraphs (k)(3) through (8).

(2) *Shared usage of qualified nonpersonal use vehicles.*—In general, a working condition fringe under this paragraph (h) is available to the driver and all passengers of a qualified nonpersonal use vehicle. However, a working condition fringe under this paragraph (h) is available only with respect to the driver and not with respect to any passengers of a qualified nonpersonal use vehicle described in § 1.274-5(k)(2)(ii)(L) or (P).

(i) [Reserved.]

(j) *Application of section 280F.*—In determining the amount, if any, of an employee's working condition fringe, section 280F and the regulations thereunder do not apply. For example, assume that an employee has available for a calendar year an employer-provided automobile with a fair market value of $28,000. Assume further that

the special rule provided in § 1.61-21(d) is used yielding an Annual Lease Value, as defined in § 1.61-21(d), of $7,750, and that all of the employee's use of the automobile is for the employer's business. The employee would be entitled to exclude as a working condition fringe the entire Annual Lease Value, despite the fact that if the employee paid for the availability of the automobile, an income inclusion would be required under § 1.280F-6(d)(1). This paragraph (j) does not affect the applicability of section 280F to the employer with respect to such employer-provided automobile, nor does it affect the applicability of section 274 to either the employer or the employee. For rules concerning substantiation of an employee's working condition fringe, see paragraph (c) of this section.

(k) *Aircraft allocation rule.*—In general, with respect to a flight on an employer-provided aircraft, the amount excludable as a working condition fringe is the amount that would be allowable as a deduction under section 162 or 167 if the employee paid for the flight on the aircraft. For example, if employee P and P's spouse fly on P's employer's airplane primarily for business reasons of P's employer so that P could deduct the expenses relating to the trip to the extent of P's payments, the value of the flights is excludable from gross income as a working condition fringe. However, if P's children accompany P on the trip primarily for personal reasons, the value of the flights by P's children are includible in P's gross income. See § 1.61-21(g) for special rules for valuing personal flights on employer-provided aircraft.

(l) [Reserved.]

(m) *Employer-provided transportation for security concerns.*—(1) *In general.*—The amount of a working condition fringe exclusion with respect to employer-provided transportation is the amount that would be allowable as a deduction under section 162 or 167 if the employee paid for the transportation. Generally, if an employee pays for transportation taken for primarily personal purposes, the employee may not deduct any part of the amount paid. Thus, the employee may not generally exclude the value of employer-provided transportation as a working condition fringe if such transportation is primarily personal. If, however, for bona fide business-oriented security concerns, the employee purchases transportation that provides him or her with additional security, the employee may generally deduct the excess of the amount actually paid for the transportation over the amount the employee would have paid for the same mode of transportation absent the bona fide business-oriented security concerns. This is the case whether or not the employee would have taken the same mode of transportation absent the bona fide business-oriented security concerns. With respect to a vehicle, the phrase "the same mode of transportation" means use of the same vehicle without the additional security aspects, such as bulletproof glass. With respect to air transportation, the phrase "the same mode of transportation" means comparable air transportation. These same rules apply to the determination of an employee's working condition fringe exclusion. For example, if an employer provides an employee with a vehicle for commuting and, because of bona fide business-oriented security concerns, the vehicle is specially designed for security, then the employee may exclude from gross income the value of the special security design as a working condition fringe. The employee may not exclude the value of the commuting from income as a working condition fringe because commuting is a nondeductible personal expense. However, if an independent security study meeting the requirements of paragraph (m)(2)(v) of this section has been performed with respect to a government employee, the government employee may exclude the value of the personal use (other than commuting) of the employer-provided vehicle that the security study determines to be reasonable and necessary for local transportation. Similarly, if an employee travels on a personal trip in an employer-provided aircraft for bona fide business-oriented security concerns, the employee may exclude the excess, if any, of the value of the flight over the amount the employee would have paid for the same mode of transportation, but for the bona fide business-oriented security concerns. Because personal travel is a nondeductible expense, the employee may not exclude the total value of the trip as a working condition fringe.

(2) *Demonstration of bona fide business-oriented security concerns.*— (i) *In general.*—For purposes of this paragraph (m), a bona fide business-oriented security concern exists only if the facts and circumstances establish a specific basis for concern regarding the safety of the employee. A generalized concern for an employee's safety is not a bona fide business-oriented security concern. Once a bona fide business-oriented security concern is determined to exist with respect to a particular employee, the employer must periodically evaluate the situation for purposes of determining whether the bona fide business-oriented security concern still exists. Example[s] of factors indicating a specific basis for concern regarding the safety of an employee are—

(A) A threat of death or kidnapping of, or serious bodily harm to, the employee or a similarly situated employee because of either employee's status as an employee of the employer; or

(B) A recent history of violent terrorist activity (such as bombings) in the geographic area in which the transportation is provided, unless that activity is focused on a group of individuals which does not include the employee (or a similarly situated employee of an employer), or occurs to a significant degree only in a location within the geographic area where the employee does not travel.

(ii) *Establishment of overall security program.*—Notwithstanding anything in paragraph (m)(2)(i) of this section to the contrary, no bona fide business-oriented security concern will be deemed to exist unless the employee's employer establishes to the satisfaction of the Commissioner that an overall security program has been provided with respect to the employee involved. An overall security program is deemed to exist if the requirements of paragraph (m)(2)(iv) of this section are satisfied (relating to an independent security study).

(iii) *Overall security program.*—(A) *Defined.*—An overall security program is one in which security is provided to protect the employee on a 24-hour basis. The employee must be protected while at the employee's residence, while commuting to and from the employee's workplace, and while at the employee's workplace. In addition, the employee must be protected while traveling both at home and away from home, whether for business or personal purposes. An overall security program must include the provision of a bodyguard/chauffeur who is trained in evasive driving techniques; an automobile specially equipped for security; guards, metal detectors, alarms, or similar methods of controlling access to the employee's workplace and residence; and, in appropriate cases, flights on the employer's aircraft for business and personal reasons.

(B) *Application.*—There is no overall security program when, for example, security is provided at the employee's workplace but not at the employee's residence. In addition, the fact that an employer requires an employee to travel on the employer's aircraft, or in an employer-provided vehicle that contains special security features, does not alone constitute an overall security program. The preceding sentence applies regardless of the existence of a corporate or other resolution requiring the employee to travel in the employer's aircraft or vehicle for personal as well as business reasons.

(iv) *Effect of an independent security study.*—An overall security program with respect to an employee is deemed to exist if the conditions of this paragraph (m)(2)(iv) are satisfied:

(A) A security study is performed with respect to the employer and the employee (or a similarly situated employee of the employer) by an independent security consultant;

(B) The security study is based on an objective assessment of all facts and circumstances;

(C) The recommendation of the security study is that an overall security program (as defined in paragraph (m)(2)(iii) of this section) is not necessary and the recommendation is reasonable under the circumstances; and

(D) The employer applies the specific security recommendations contained in the security study to the employee on a consistent basis.
The value of transportation-related security provided pursuant to a security study that meets the requirements of this paragraph (m)(2)(iv) may be excluded from income if the security study conclusions are reasonable and, but for the bona fide business-oriented security concerns, the employee would not have had such security. No exclusion from income applies to security provided by the employer that is not recommended in the security study. Security study conclusions may be reasonable even if, for example, it is recommended that security be limited to certain geographic areas, as in the case in which air travel security is provided only in certain foreign countries.

(v) *Independent security study with respect to government employees.*—For purposes of establishing the existence of an overall security program under paragraph (m)(2)(ii) of this section with respect to a particular government employee, a security study conducted by the government employer (including an agency or instrumentality thereof) will be treated as a security study pursuant to paragraph (m)(2)(iv) of this section if, in lieu of the conditions of paragraphs (m)(2)(iv)(A) through (D) of this section, the following conditions are satisfied:

(A) The security study is conducted by a person expressly designated by the government employer as having the responsibility and independent authority to determine both the need for employer-provided security and the appropriate protective services in response to that determination;

(B) The security study is conducted in accordance with written internal procedures that require an independent and objective assessment of the facts and circumstances, such as the nature of the threat to the employee, the appropriate security response to that threat, an estimate of the length of time protective services will be necessary, and the extent to which employer-provided transportation may be necessary during the period of protection;

(C) With respect to employer-provided transportation, the security study evaluates the extent to which personal use, including commuting, by the employee and the employee's spouse and dependents may be necessary during the period of protection and makes a recommendation as to what would be considered reasonable personal use during that period; and

(D) The employer applies the specific security recommendations contained in the study to the employee on a consistent basis.

(3) *Application of security rules to spouses and dependents.*—(i) *In general.*—If a bona fide business-oriented security concern exists with respect to an employee (because, for example, threats are made on the life of an employee), the bona fide business-oriented security concern is deemed to exist with respect to the employee's spouse and dependents to the extent provided in this paragraph (m)(3).

(ii) *Certain transportation.*—If a working condition fringe exclusion is available under this paragraph (m) for transportation in a vehicle or aircraft provided for a bona fide business-oriented security concern with respect to an employee, the requirements of this paragraph (m) are deemed to be satisfied with respect to transportation in the same vehicle or aircraft provided at the same time to the employee's spouse and dependent children.

(iii) *Other.*—Except as provided in paragraph (m)(3)(ii) of this section, a bona fide business oriented security concern is deemed to exist for the spouse and dependent children of the employer only if the requirements of paragraph (m)(2)(iii) or (iv) of this section are applied independently to such spouse and dependent children.

(iv) *Spouses and dependents of government employees.*—The security rules of this paragraph (m)(3) apply to the spouse and dependents of a government employee. However, the value of local vehicle transportation provided to the government employee's spouse and dependents for personal purposes, other than commuting, during the period that a bona fide business-oriented security concern exists with respect to the government employee will not be included in the government employee's gross income if the personal use is determined to be reasonable and necessary by the security study described in paragraph (m)(2)(v) of this section.

(4) *Working condition safe harbor for travel on employer-provided aircraft.*—Under the safe harbor rule of this paragraph (m)(4), if, for a bona fide business-oriented security concern, the employer requires that an employee travel on an employer-provided aircraft for a personal trip, the employer and the employee may exclude from the employee's gross income, as a working condition fringe, the excess value of the aircraft trip over the safe harbor airfare without having to show what method of transportation the employee would have flown but for the bona fide business-oriented security concern. For purposes of the safe harbor rule of this paragraph (m)(4), the value of the safe harbor airfare is determined under the non-commercial flight valuation rule of §1.61-21(g) (regardless of whether the employer or employee elects to use such valuation rule) by multiplying an aircraft multiple of 200-percent by the applicable cents-per-mile rates and the number of miles in the flight and then adding the applicable terminal charge. The value of the safe harbor airfare determined under this paragraph (m)(4) must be included in the employee's income (to the extent not reimbursed by the employee) regardless of whether the employee or the employer uses the special valuation rule of §1.61-21(g). The excess of the value of the aircraft trip over this amount may be excluded from gross income as a working condition fringe. If, for a bona fide business-oriented security concern, the employer requires that an employee's spouse and dependents travel on an employer-provided aircraft for a personal trip, the special rule of this paragraph (m)(4) is available to exclude the excess value of the aircraft trips over the safe harbor airfares.

(5) *Bodyguard/chauffeur provided for a bona fide business-oriented security concern.*—If an employer provides an employee with vehicle transportation and a bodyguard/chauffeur for a bona fide business-oriented security concern, and but for the bona fide business-oriented security concern the employee would not have had a bodyguard or a chauffeur, then the entire value of the services of the bodyguard/chauffeur is excludable from gross income as a working condition fringe. For purposes of this section, a bodyguard/chauffeur must be trained in evasive driving techniques. An individual who performs services as a driver for an employee is not a bodyguard/chauffeur if the individual is not trained in evasive driving techniques. Thus, no part of the value of the services of such an individual is excludable

from gross income under this paragraph (m)(5). (See paragraph (b)(3) of this section for rules relating to the determination of the working condition fringe exclusion for chauffeur services.)

(6) *Special valuation rule for government employees.*—If transportation is provided to a government employee for commuting during the period that a bona fide business-oriented security concern under §1.132-5(m) exists, the commuting use may be valued by reference to the values set forth in §1.61-21(e)(1)(i) or (f)(3) (vehicle cents-per-mile or commuting valuation of $1.50 per one-way commute, respectively) without regard to the additional requirements contained in §1.61-21(e) or (f) and is deemed to have met the requirements of §1.61-21(c).

(7) *Government employer and employee defined.*—For purposes of this paragraph (m), "government employer" includes any Federal, state, or local government unit, and any agency or instrumentality thereof. A "government employee" is any individual who is employed by the government employer.

(8) *Examples.*—The provisions of this paragraph (m) may be illustrated by the following examples:

Example (1). Assume that in response to several death threats on the life of A, the president of X a multinational company, X establishes an overall security program for A, including an alarm system at A's home and guards at A's workplace, the use of a vehicle that is specially equipped with alarms, bulletproof glass, and armor plating, and a bodyguard/chauffeur. Assume further that A is driven for both personal and business reasons in the vehicle. Also, assume that but for the bona fide business-oriented security concerns, no part of the overall security program would have been provided to A. With respect to the transportation provided for security reasons, A may exclude as a working condition fringe the value of the special security features of the vehicle and the value attributable to the bodyguard/chauffeur. Thus, if the value of the specially equipped vehicle is $40,000, and the value of the vehicle without the security features is $25,000, A may determine A's inclusion in income attributable to the vehicle as if the vehicle were worth $25,000. A must include in income the value of the availability of the vehicle for personal use.

Example (2). Assume that B is the chief executive officer of Y, a multinational corporation. Assume further that there have been kidnapping attempts and other terrorist activities in the foreign countries in which B performs services and that at least some of such activities have been directed against B or similarly situated employees. In response to these activities, Y provides B with an overall security program, including an alarm system at B's home and bodyguards at B's workplace, a bodyguard/chauffeur, and a vehicle specially designed for security during B's overseas travels. In addition, assume that Y requires B to travel in Y's airplane for business and personal trips taken to, from, and within these foreign countries. Also, assume that but for bona fide business-oriented security concerns, no part of the overall security program would have been provided to B. B may exclude as a working condition fringe the value of the special security features of the automobile and the value attributable to the bodyguards and the bodyguard/chauffeur. B may also exclude the excess, if any, of the value of the flights over the amount A would have paid for the same mode of transportation but for the security concerns. As an alternative to the preceding sentence, B may use the working condition safe harbor described in paragraph (m)(4) of this section and exclude as a working condition fringe the excess, if any, of the value of personal flights in the Y airplane over the safe harbor airfare determined under the method described in paragraph (m)(4) of this section. If this alternative is used, B must include in income the value of the availability of the vehicle for personal use and the value of the safe harbor.

Example (3). Assume the same facts as in example (2) except that Y also requires B to travel in Y's airplane within the United States, and provides B with a chauffeur-driven limousine for business and personal travel in the United States. Assume further that Y also requires B's spouse and dependents to travel in Y's airplane for personal flights in the United States. If no bona fide business-oriented security concern exists with respect to travel in the United States, B may not exclude from income any portion of the value of the availability of the chauffeur or limousine for personal use in the United States. Thus, B must include in income the value of the availability of the vehicle and chauffeur for personal use. In addition, B may not exclude any portion of the value attributable to personal flights by B or B's spouse and dependents on Y's airplane. Thus, B must include in income the value attributable to the personal use of Y's airplane. See §1.61-21 for rules relating to the valuation of an employer-provided vehicle and chauffeur, and personal flights on employer-provided airplanes.

Example (4). Assume that company Z retains an independent security consultant to perform a security study with respect to its chief executive officer. Assume further that, based on an objective assessment of the facts and circumstances, the security consultant reasonably recommends that 24-hour protection is not necessary but that the employee be provided security at his workplace and for ground transportation, but not for air transportation. If company Z follows the recommendations on a consistent basis, an overall security program will be deemed to exist with respect to the workplace and ground transportation security only.

Example (5). Assume the same facts as in example (4) except that company Z only provides the employee security while commuting to and from work, but not for any other ground transportation. Because the recommendations of the independent security study are not applied on a consistent basis, an overall security program will not be deemed to exist. Thus, the value of commuting to and from work is not excludable from income. However, the value of a bodyguard with professional security training who does not provide chauffeur or other personal services to the employee or any member of the employee's family may be excludable as a working condition fringe if such expense would be otherwise allowable as a deduction by the employee under section 162 or 167.

Example (6). J is a United States District Judge. At the beginning of a 3-month criminal trial in J's court, a member of J's family receives death threats. M, the division (within government agency W) responsible for evaluating threats and providing protective services to the Federal judiciary, directs its threat analysis unit to conduct a security study with respect to J and J's family. The study is conducted pursuant to internal written procedures that require an independent and objective assessment of any threats to members of the federal judiciary and their families, a statement of the requisite security response, if any, to a particular threat (including the form of transportation to be furnished to the employee as part of the security program), and a description of the circumstances under which local transportation for the employee and the employee's spouse and dependents may be necessary for personal reasons during the time protective services are provided. M's study concludes that a bona fide business-oriented security concern exists with respect to J and J's family and determines that 24-hour protection of J and J's family is not necessary, but that protection is necessary during the course of the criminal trial whenever J or J's family is away from home. Consistent with that recommendation, J is transported every day in a government vehicle for both personal and business reasons and is accompanied by two bodyguard/chauffeurs who have been trained in evasive driving techniques. In addition, J's spouse is driven to and from work and J's children are driven to and from school and occasional school activities. Shortly after the trial is concluded, M's threat analysis unit determines that J and J's family no longer need special protection because the danger posed by the threat no longer exists and, accordingly, vehicle transportation is no longer provided. Because the security study conducted by M complies with the conditions of §1.132-5(m)(2)(v), M has satisfied the requirement for an independent security study and an overall security program with respect to J is deemed to exist. Thus, with respect to the transportation provided for security concerns, J may exclude as a working condition fringe the value of any special security features of the government vehicle and the value attributable to the two bodyguard/chauffeurs. *See Example (1)* of this paragraph (m)(8). The value of vehicle transportation provided to J and J's family for personal reasons, other than commuting, may also be excluded during the period of protection, because its provision was consistent with the recommendation of the security study.

Example (7). Assume the same facts as in *Example (6)* and that J's one-way commute between home and work is 10 miles. Under paragraph (m)(6) of this section, the Federal government may value transportation provided to J for commuting purposes pursuant to the value set forth in either the vehicle cents-per-mile rule of §1.61-21(e) or the commuting valuation rule of §1.61-21(f). Because the commuting valuation rule yields the least amount of taxable income to J under the circumstances, W values the transportation provided to J for commuting at $1.50 per one-way commute, even though J is a control employee within the meaning of §1.61-21(f)(6).

(n) *Product testing.*—(1) *In general.*—The fair market value of the use of consumer goods, which are manufactured for sale to nonemployees, for product testing and evaluation by an employee of the manufacturer outside the employee's workplace, is excludable from gross income as a working condition fringe if—

(i) Consumer testing and evaluation of the product is an ordinary and necessary business expense of the employer;

(ii) Business reasons necessitate that the testing and evaluation of the product be performed off the employer's business premises by employees (i.e., the testing and evaluation cannot be carried out adequately in the employer's office or in laboratory testing facilities);

(iii) The product is furnished to the employee for purposes of testing and evaluation;

(iv) The product is made available to the employee for no longer than necessary to test and evaluate its performance and (to the extent not exhausted) must be returned to the employer at completion of the testing and evaluation period;

(v) The employer imposes limits on the employee's use of the product that significantly reduce the value of any personal benefit to the employee; and

(vi) The employee must submit detailed reports to the employer on the testing and evaluation. The length of the testing and evaluation period must be reasonable in relation to the product being tested.

(2) *Employer-imposed limits.*—The requirement of paragraph (n)(1)(v) of this section is satisfied if—

(i) The employer places limits on the employee's ability to select among different models or varieties of the consumer product that is furnished for testing and evaluation purposes; and

(ii) The employer generally prohibits use of the product by persons other than the employee and, in appropriate cases, requires the employee, to purchase or lease at the employee's own expense the same type of product as that being tested (so that personal use by the employee's family will be limited). In addition, any charge by the employer for the personal use by an employee of a product being tested shall be taken into account in determining whether the requirement of paragraph (n)(1)(v) of this section is satisfied.

(3) *Discriminating classifications.*—If an employer furnishes products under a testing and evaluation program only, or presumably, to certain classes of employees (such as highly compensated employees, as defined in §1.132-8(g)), this fact may be relevant when determining whether the products are furnished for testing and evaluation purposes or for compensation purposes, unless the employer can show a business reason for the classification of employees to whom the products are furnished (e.g., that automobiles are furnished for testing and evaluation by an automobile manufacturer to its design engineers and supervisory mechanics).

(4) *Factors that negate the existence of a product testing program.*—If an employer fails to tabulate and examine the results of the detailed reports submitted by employees within a reasonable period of time after expiration of the testing period, the program will not be considered a product testing program for purposes of the exclusion of this paragraph (n). Existence of one or more of the following factors may also establish that the program is not a bona fide product testing program for purposes of the exclusion of this paragraph (n):

(i) The program is in essence a leasing program under which employees lease the consumer goods from the employer for a fee;

(ii) The nature of the product and other considerations are insufficient to justify the testing program; or

(iii) The expense of the program outweighs the benefits to be gained from testing and evaluation.

(5) *Failure to meet the requirements of this paragraph (n).*—The fair market value of the use of property for product testing and evaluation by an employee outside the employee's workplace, under a product testing program that does not meet all of the requirements of this paragraph (n), is not excludable from gross income as a working condition fringe under this paragraph (n).

(6) *Example.*—The rules of this paragraph (n) may be illustrated by the following example:

Example. Assume that an employer that manufactures automobiles establishes a product testing program under which 50 of its 5,000 employees test and evaluate the automobiles for 30 days. Assume further that the 50 employees represent a fair cross-section of all of the employees of the employer, such employees submit detailed reports to the employer on the testing and evaluation, the employer tabulates and examines the test results within a reasonable time, and the use of the automobiles is restricted to the employees. If the employer imposes the limits described in paragraph (n)(2) of this section, the employees may exclude the value of the use of the automobile during the testing and evaluation period.

(o) *Qualified automobile demonstration use.*—(1) *In general.*—The value of qualified automobile demonstration use is excludable from gross income as a working condition fringe. "Qualified automobile demonstration use" is any use of a demonstration automobile by a full-time automobile salesman in the sales area in which the automobile dealer's sales office is located if—

(i) Such use is provided primarily to facilitate the salesman's performance of services for the employer; and

(ii) There are substantial restrictions on the personal use of the automobile by the salesman.

(2) *Full-time automobile salesman.*—(i) *Defined.*—The term "full-time automobile salesman" means any individual who—

(A) Is employed by an automobile dealer;

(B) Customarily spends at least half of a normal business day performing the functions of a floor salesperson or sales manager;

(C) Directly engages in substantial promotion and negotiation of sales to customers;

(D) Customarily works a number of hours considered full-time in the industry (but at a rate not less than 1,000 hours per year); and

(E) Derives at least 25 percent of his or her gross income from the automobile dealership directly as a result of the activities described in paragraphs (o)(2)(i)(B) and (C) of this section.

For purposes of paragraph (o)(2)(i)(E) of this section, income is not considered to be derived directly as a result of activities described in paragraphs (o)(2)(i)(B) and (C) of this section to the extent that the income is attributable to an individual's ownership interest in the dealership. An individual will not be considered to engage in direct sales activities if the individual's sales-related activities are substantially limited to review of sales price offers from customers. An individual, such as the general manager of an automobile dealership, who receives a sales commission on the sale of an automobile is not a full-time automobile salesman unless the requirements of this paragraph (o)(2)(i) are met. The exclusion provided in this paragraph (o) is available to an individual who meets the definition of this paragraph (o)(2)(i) whether the individual performs services in addition to those described in this paragraph (o)(2)(i). For example, an individual who is an owner of the automobile dealership but who otherwise meets the requirements of this paragraph (o)(2)(i) may exclude from gross income the value of qualified automobile demonstration use. However, the exclusion of this paragraph (o) is not available to owners of large automobile dealerships who do not customarily engage in significant sales activities.

(ii) *Use by an individual other than a full-time automobile salesman.*—Personal use of a demonstration automobile by an individual other than a full-time automobile salesman is not treated as a working condition fringe. Therefore, any personal use, including commuting use, of a demonstration automobile by a part-time salesman, automobile mechanic, or other individual who is not a full-time automobile salesman is not "qualified automobile demonstration use" and thus not excludable from gross income. This is the case whether or not the personal use is within the sales area (as defined in paragraph (o)(5) of this section).

(3) *Demonstration automobile.*—The exclusion provided in this paragraph (o) applies only to qualified use of a demonstration automobile. A demonstration automobile is an automobile that is—

(i) Currently in the inventory of the automobile dealership; and

(ii) Available for test drives by customers during the normal business hours of the employee.

(4) *Substantial restrictions on personal use.*—Substantial restrictions on the personal use of a demonstration automobile exist when all of the following conditions are satisfied:

(i) Use by individuals other than the full-time automobile salesmen (e.g., the salesman's family) is prohibited;

(ii) Use for personal vacation trips is prohibited;

(iii) The storage of personal possessions in the automobile is prohibited; and

(iv) The total use by mileage of the automobile by the salesman outside the salesman's normal working hours is limited.

(5) *Sales area.*—(i) *In general.*—Qualified automobile demonstration use consists of use in the sales area in which the automobile dealer's sales office is located. The sales area is the geographic area surrounding the automobile dealer's sales office from which the office regularly derives customers.

(ii) *Sales area safe harbor.*—With respect to a particular full-time salesman, the automobile dealer's sales area may be treated as the area within a radius of the larger of—

(A) 75 miles or

(B) The one-way commuting distance (in miles) of the particular salesman from the dealer's sales office.

(6) *Applicability of substantiation requirements of sections 162 and 274 (d).*—Notwithstanding anything in this section to the contrary, the value of the use of a demonstration automobile may not be excluded from gross income as a working condition fringe, by either the employer or the employee, unless, with respect to the restrictions of paragraph (o)(4) of this section, the substantiation requirements of section 274(d) and the regulations thereunder are satisfied. See §1.132-5(c) for general and safe harbor rules relating to the applicability of the substantiation requirements of section 274(d).

(7) *Special valuation rules.*—See §1.61-21(d)(6)(ii) for special rules that may be used to value the availability of demonstration automobiles.

(p) *Parking.*—(1) *In general.*—The value of parking provided to an employee on or near the business premises of the employer is excludable from gross income as a working condition fringe under the special rule of this paragraph (p). If the rules of this paragraph (p) are satisfied, the value of parking is excludable from gross income whether the amount paid by the employee for parking would be deductible under section 162. The working condition fringe exclusion applies whether the employer owns or rents the parking facility or parking space.

(2) *Reimbursement of parking expenses.*—A reimbursement to the employee of the ordinary and necessary expenses of renting a parking space on or near the business premises of the employer is excludable from gross income as a working condition fringe, if, but for the parking expense, the employee would not have been entitled to receive and retain such amount from the employer. If, however an employee is entitled to retain a general transportation allowance or a similar benefit whether or not the employee has parking expenses, no portion of that allowance is excludable from gross income under this paragraph (p) even if it is used for parking expenses.

(3) *Parking on residential property.*—With respect to an employee, this paragraph (p) does not apply to any parking facility or space located on property owned or leased by the employee for residential purposes.

(4) *Dates of applicability.*—This paragraph (p) applies to benefits provided before January 1, 1993. For benefits provided after December 31, 1992, see §1.132-9.

(q) *Nonapplicability of nondiscrimination rules.*—Except to the extent provided in paragraph (n)(3) of this section (relating to discriminating classifications of a product testing program), the nondiscrimination rules of section 132(h)(1) and §1.132-8 do not apply in determining the amount, if any, of a working condition fringe.

(r) *Volunteers.*—(1) *In general.*—Solely for purposes of section 132(d) and paragraph (a)(1) of this section, a bona fide volunteer (including a director or officer) who performs services for an organization exempt from tax under section 501(a), or for a government employer (as defined in paragraph (m)(7) of this section), is deemed to have a profit motive under section 162.

(2) *Limit on application of this paragraph.*—This paragraph (r) shall not be used to support treatment of the bona fide volunteer as having a profit motive for purposes of any provision of the Internal Revenue Code of 1986 (Code) other than section 132(d). Nothing in this paragraph (r) shall be interpreted as determining the employment status of a bona fide volunteer for purposes of any section of the Code other than section 132(d).

(3) *Definitions.*—(i) *Bona fide volunteer.*—For purposes of this paragraph (r), an individual is considered a "bona fide volunteer" if the individual does not have a profit motive for purposes of section 162. For example, an individual is considered a "bona fide volunteer" if the total value of the benefits provided with respect to the volunteer services is substantially less than the total value of the volunteer services the individual provides to an exempt organization or government employer.

(ii) *Liability insurance coverage for a bona fide volunteer.*—For purposes of this paragraph (r), the receipt of liability insurance coverage by a volunteer, or an exempt organization or government employer's undertaking to indemnify the volunteer for liability, does not by itself confer a profit motive on the volunteer, provided the insurance coverage or indemnification relates to acts performed by the volunteer in the discharge of duties, or the performance of services, on behalf of the exempt organization or government employer.

(4) *Example.*—The following example illustrates the provisions of paragraph (r) of this section.

Example. A is a manager and full-time employee of P, a tax-exempt organization described in section 501(c)(3). B is a member of P's board of directors. Other than $25 to defray expenses for attending board meetings, B receives no compensation for serving as a director and does not have a profit motive. Therefore, B is a bona fide volunteer by application of paragraph (r)(3)(i) of this section and is deemed to have a profit motive under paragraph (r)(1) of this section for purposes of section 132(d). In order to provide liability insurance coverage, P purchases a policy that covers actions arising from A's and B's activities performed as part of their duties to P. The value of the policy and payments made to or on behalf of A under the policy are excludable from A's gross income as a working condition fringe,

because A has a profit motive under section 162 and would be able to deduct payments for liability insurance coverage had he paid for it himself. The receipt of liability insurance coverage by B does not confer a profit motive on B by application of paragraph (r)(3)(ii) of this section. Thus, the value of the policy and payments made to or on behalf of B under the policy are excludable from B's income as a working condition fringe. For the year in which the liability insurance coverage is provided to A and B, P may exclude the value of the benefit on the Form W-2 it issues to A or on any Form 1099 it might otherwise issue to B.

(s) *Application of section 274(a)(3).*—(1) *In general.*—If an employer's deduction under section 162(a) for dues paid or incurred for membership in any club organized for business, pleasure, recreation, or other social purpose is disallowed by section 274(a)(3), the amount, if any, of an employee's working condition fringe benefit relating to an employer-provided membership in the club is determined without regard to the application of section 274(a) to the employee. To be excludible as a working condition fringe benefit, however, the amount must otherwise qualify for deduction by the employee under section 162(a). If an employer treats the amount paid or incurred for membership in any club organized for business, pleasure, recreation, or other social purpose as compensation under section 274(e)(2), then the expense is deductible by the employer as compensation and no amount may be excluded from the employee's gross income as a working condition fringe benefit. See §1.274-2(f)(2)(iii)(A).

(2) *Treatment of tax-exempt employers.*—In the case of an employer exempt from taxation under subtitle A of the Internal Revenue Code, any reference in this paragraph (s) to a deduction disallowed by section 274(a)(3) shall be treated as a reference to the amount which would be disallowed as a deduction by section 274(a)(3) to the employer if the employer were not exempt from taxation under subtitle A of the Internal Revenue Code.

(3) *Examples.*—The following examples illustrate this paragraph (s):

Example 1. Assume that Company X provides Employee B with a country club membership for which it paid $20,000. B substantiates, within the meaning of paragraph (c) of this section, that the club was used 40 percent for business purposes. The business use of the club (40 percent) may be considered a working condition fringe benefit, notwithstanding that the employer's deduction for the dues allocable to the business use is disallowed by section 274(a)(3), if X does not treat the club membership as compensation under section 274(e)(2). Thus, B may exclude from gross income $8,000 (40 percent of the club dues, which reflects B's business use). X must report $12,000 as wages subject to withholding and payment of employment taxes (60 percent of the value of the club dues, which reflects B's personal use). B must include $12,000 in gross income. X may deduct as compensation the amount it paid for the club dues which reflects B's personal use provided the amount satisfies the other requirements for a salary or compensation deduction under section 162.

Example 2. Assume the same facts as *Example 1* except that Company X treats the $20,000 as compensation to B under section 274(e)(2). No portion of the $20,000 will be considered a working condition fringe benefit because the section 274(a)(3) disallowance will apply to B. Therefore, B must include $20,000 in gross income.

(t) *Application of section 274(m)(3).*—(1) *In general.*—If an employer's deduction under section 162(a) for amounts paid or incurred for the travel expenses of a spouse, dependent, or other individual accompanying an employee is disallowed by section 274(m)(3), the amount, if any, of the employee's working condition fringe benefit relating to the employer-provided travel is determined without regard to the application of section 274(m)(3). To be excludible as a working condition fringe benefit, however, the amount must otherwise qualify for deduction by the employee under section 162(a). The amount will qualify for deduction and for exclusion as a working condition benefit benefit if it can be adequately shown that the spouse's, dependent's, or other accompanying individual's presence on the employee's business trip has a bona fide business purpose and if the employee substantiates the travel within the meaning of paragraph (c) of this section. If the travel does not qualify as a working condition fringe benefit, the employee must include in gross income as a fringe benefit the value of the employer's payment of travel expenses with respect to a spouse, dependent, or other individual accompanying the employee on business travel. See §§1.61-21(a)(4) and 1.162-2(c). If an employer treats as compensation under section 274(e)(2) the amount paid or incurred for the travel expenses of a spouse, dependent, or other individual accompanying an employee, then the expense is deductible by the employer as compensation and no amount may be excluded from the employee's gross income as a working condition fringe benefit. See §1.274-2(f)(2)(iii)(A).

Reg. §1.132-5(t)(1)

(2) *Treatment of tax-exempt employers.*—In the case of an employer exempt from taxation under subtitle A of the Internal Revenue Code, any reference in this paragraph (t) to a deduction disallowed by section 274(m)(3) shall be treated as a reference to the amount which would be disallowed as a deduction by section 274 (m)(3) to the employer if the employer were not exempt from taxation under subtitle A of the Internal Revenue Code. [Reg. §1.132-5.]

  ☐ [*T.D.* 8256, 7-5-89. *Amended by T.D.* 8451, 12-4-92; *T.D.* 8457, 12-29-92; *T.D.* 8666, 5-29-96; *T.D.* 8933, 1-10-2001 *and T.D.* 9483, 5-18-2010.]

[Reg. §1.132-6]

§1.132-6. De minimis fringes.—(a) *In general.*—Gross income does not include the value of a de minimis fringe provided to an employee. The term "de minimis fringe" means any property or service the value of which is (after taking into account the frequency with which similar fringes are provided by the employer to the employer's employees) so small as to make accounting for it unreasonable or administratively impracticable.

(b) *Frequency.*—(1) *Employee-measured frequency.*—Generally, the frequency with which similar fringes are provided by the employer to the employer's employees is determined by reference to the frequency with which the employer provides the fringes to each individual employee. For example, if an employer provides a free meal in kind to one employee on a daily basis, but not to any other employee, the value of the meals is not de minimis with respect to that one employee even though with respect to the employer's entire workforce the meals are provided "infrequently."

(2) *Employer-measured frequency.*—Notwithstanding the rule of paragraph (b)(1) of this section, except for purposes of applying the special rules of paragraph (d)(2) of this section, where it would be administratively difficult to determine frequency with respect to individual employees, the frequency with which similar fringes are provided by the employer to the employer's employees is determined by reference to the frequency with which the employer provides the fringes to the workforce as a whole. Therefore, under this rule, the frequency with which any individual employee receives such a fringe benefit is not relevant and in some circumstances, the de minimis fringe exclusion may apply with respect to a benefit even though a particular employee receives the benefit frequently. For example, if an employer exercises sufficient control and imposes significant restrictions on the personal use of a company copying machine so that at least 85 percent of the use of the machine is for business purposes, any personal use of the copying machine by particular employees is considered to be a de minimis fringe.

(c) *Administrability.*—Unless excluded by a provision of chapter 1 of the Internal Revenue Code of 1986 other than section 132(a)(4), the value of any fringe benefit that would not be unreasonable or administratively impracticable to account for is includible in the employee's gross income. Thus, except as provided in paragraph (d)(2) of this section, the provision of any cash fringe benefit is never excludable under section 132(a) as a de minimis fringe benefit. Similarly except as otherwise provided in paragraph (d) of this section, a cash equivalent fringe benefit (such as a fringe benefit provided to an employee through the use of a gift certificate or charge or credit card) is generally not excludable under §132(a) even if the same property or service acquired (if provided in kind) would be excludable as a de minimis fringe benefit. For example, the provision of cash to an employee for a theatre ticket that would itself be excludable as a de minimis fringe (see paragraph (e)(1) of this section) is not excludable as a de minimis fringe.

(d) *Special rules.*—(1) *Transit passes.*—A public transit pass provided at a discount to defray an employee's commuting costs may be excluded from the employee's gross income as a de minimis fringe if such discount does not exceed $21 in any month. The exclusion provided in this paragraph (d)(1) also applies to the provision of tokens or fare cards that enable an individual to travel on the public transit system if the value of such tokens and fare cards in any month does not exceed by more than $21 the amount the employee paid for the tokens and fare cards for such month. Similarly, the exclusion of this paragraph (d)(1) applies to the provision of a voucher or similar instrument that is exchangeable solely for tokens, fare cards, or other instruments that enable the employee to use the public transit system if the value of such vouchers and other instruments in any month does not exceed $21. The exclusion of this paragraph (d)(1) also applies to reimbursements made by an employer to an employee after December 31, 1988, to cover the cost of commuting on a public transit system, provided the employee does not receive more than $21 in such reimbursements for commuting costs in any given month. The reimbursement must be made under a bona fide reimbursement arrangement. A reimbursement arrangement will be treated as bona fide if the employer establishes appropriate proce-

dures for verifying on a periodic basis that the employee's use of public transportation for commuting is consistent with the value of the benefit provided by the employer for that purpose. The amount of in-kind public transit commuting benefits and reimbursements provided during any month that are excludible under this paragraph (d)(1) is limited to $21. For months ending before July 1, 1991, the amount is $15 per month. The exclusion provided in this paragraph (d)(1) does not apply to the provision of any benefit to defray public transit expenses incurred for personal travel other than commuting.

(2) *Occasional meal money or local transportation fare.*—(i) *General rule.*—Meals, meal money or local transportation fare provided to an employee is excluded as a de minimis fringe benefit if the benefit provided is reasonable and is provided in a manner that satisfies the following three conditions:

(A) *Occasional basis.*—The meals, meal money or local transportation fare is provided to the employee on an occasional basis. Whether meal money or local transportation fare is provided to an employee on an occasional basis will depend upon the frequency i.e. the availability of the benefit and regularity with which the benefit is provided by the employer to the employee. Thus, meals, meal money, or local transportation fare or a combination of such benefits provided to an employee on a regular or routine basis is not provided on an occasional basis.

(B) *Overtime.*—The meals, meal money or local transportation fare is provided to an employee because overtime work necessitates an extension of the employee's normal work schedule. This condition does not fail to be satisfied merely because the circumstances giving rise to the need for overtime work are reasonably foreseeable.

(C) *Meal money.*—In the case of a meal or meal money, the meal or meal money is provided to enable the employee to work overtime. Thus, for example, meals provided on the employer's premises that are consumed during the period that the employee works overtime or meal money provided for meals consumed during such period satisfy this condition.

In no event shall meal money or local transportation fare calculated on the basis of the number of hours worked (e.g., $1.00 per hour for each hour over eight hours) be considered a de minimis fringe benefit.

(ii) *Applicability of other exclusions for certain meals and for transportation provided for security concerns.*—The value of meals furnished to an employee, an employee's spouse, or any of the employee's dependents by or on behalf of the employee's employer for the convenience of the employer is excluded from the employee's gross income if the meals are furnished on the business premises of the employer (see section 119). (For purposes of the exclusion under section 119, the definitions of an employee under §1.132-1(b) do not apply.) If, for a bona fide business-oriented security concern, an employer provides an employee vehicle transportation that is specially designed for security (for example, the vehicle is equipped with bulletproof glass and armor plating), and the conditions of §1.132-5(m) are satisfied, the value of the special security design is excludable from gross income as a working condition fringe if the employee would not have had such special security design but for the bona fide business-oriented security concern.

(iii) *Special rule for employer-provided transportation provided in certain circumstances.*—(A) *Partial exclusion of value.*—If an employer provides transportation (such as taxi fare) to an employee for use in commuting to and/or from work because of unusual circumstances and because, based on the facts and circumstances, it is unsafe for the employee to use other available means of transportation, the excess of the value of each one-way trip over $1.50 per one-way commute is excluded from gross income. The rule of this paragraph (d)(2)(iii) is not available to a control employee as defined in §1.61-21(f)(5) and (6).

(B) *"Unusual circumstances".*—Unusual circumstances are determined with respect to the employee receiving the transportation and are based on all facts and circumstances. An example of unusual circumstances would be when an employee is asked to work outside of his normal work hours (such as being called to the workplace at 1:00 am when the employee normally works from 8:00 am to 4:00 pm). Another example of unusual circumstances is a temporary change in the employee's work schedule (such as working from 12 midnight to 8:00 am rather than from 8:00 am to 4:00 pm for a two-week period).

(C) *"Unsafe conditions".*—Factors indicating whether it is unsafe for an employee to use other available means of transportation are the history of crime in the geographic area surrounding the employee's workplace or residence and the time of day during which the employee must commute.

(3) *Use of special rules or examples to establish a general rule.*—The special rules provided in this paragraph (d) or examples provided in paragraph (e) of this section may not be used to establish any general rule permitting exclusion as a de minimis fringe. For example, the fact that $252 (i.e., $21 per month for 12 months) worth of public transit passes can be excluded from gross income as a de minimis fringe in 1992 does not mean that any fringe benefit with a value equal to or less than $252 may be excluded as a de minimis fringe. As another example, the fact that the commuting use of an employer-provided vehicle more than one day a month is an example of a benefit not excludable as a de minimis fringe (see paragraph (e)(2) of this section) does not mean that the commuting use of a vehicle up to 12 times per year is excludable from gross income as a de minimis fringe.

(4) *Benefits exceeding value and frequency limits.*—If a benefit provided to an employee is not de minimis because either the value or frequency exceeds a limit provided in this paragraph (d), no amount of the benefit is considered to be a de minimis fringe. For example, if, in 1992, an employer provides a $50 monthly public transit pass, the entire $50 must be included in income, not just the excess value over $21.

(e) *Examples.*—(1) *Benefits excludable from income.*—Examples of de minimis fringe benefits are occasional typing of personal letters by a company secretary; occasional personal use of an employer's copying machine, provided that the employer exercises sufficient control and imposes significant restrictions on the personal use of the machine so that at least 85 percent of the use of the machine is for business purposes; occasional cocktail parties, group meals, or picnics for employees and their guests; traditional birthday or holiday gifts of property (not cash) with a low fair market value; occasional theater or sporting event tickets; coffee, doughnuts, and soft drinks; local telephone calls; and flowers, fruit, books, or similar property provided to employees under special circumstances (e.g., on account of illness, outstanding performance, or family crisis).

(2) *Benefits not excludable as de minimis fringes.*—Examples of fringe benefits that are not excludable from gross income as de minimis fringes are: season tickets to sporting or theatrical events; the commuting use of an employer-provided automobile or other vehicle more than one day a month; membership in a private country club or athletic facility, regardless of the frequency with which the employee uses the facility; employer-provided group-term life insurance on the life of the spouse or child of an employee; and use of employer-owned or leased facilities (such as an apartment, hunting lodge, boat, etc.) for a weekend. Some amount of the value of certain of these fringe benefits may be excluded from income under other statutory provisions, such as the exclusion for working condition fringes. See § 1.132-5.

(f) *Nonapplicability of nondiscrimination rules.*—Except to the extent provided in § 1.132-7, the nondiscrimination rules of section 132(h)(1) and § 1.132-8 do not apply in determining the amount, if any, of a de minimis fringe. Thus, a fringe benefit may be excludable as a de minimis fringe even if the benefit is provided exclusively to highly compensated employees of the employer. [Reg. § 1.132-6.]

☐ [*T.D. 8256, 7-5-89. Amended by T.D. 8389, 1-15-92.*]

[Reg. § 1.132-7]

§ 1.132-7. Employer-operated eating facilities.—(a) *In general.*—(1) *Condition for exclusion.*—(i) *General rule.*—The value of meals provided to employees at an employer-operated eating facility for employees is excludable from gross income as a de minimis fringe only if on an annual basis, the revenue from the facility equals or exceeds the direct operating costs of the facility.

(ii) *Additional condition for highly compensated employees.*—With respect to any highly compensated employee, an exclusion is available under this section only if the condition set out in paragraph (a)(1)(i) of this section is satisfied and access to the facility is available on substantially the same terms to each member of a group of employees that is defined under a reasonable classification set up by the employer that does not discriminate in favor of highly compensated employees. See § 1.132-8. For purposes of this paragraph (a)(1)(ii), each dining room or cafeteria in which meals are served is treated as a separate eating facility, whether each such dining room or cafeteria has its own kitchen or other food-preparation area.

(2) *Employer-operated eating facility for employees.*—An employer-operated eating facility for employees is a facility that meets all of the following conditions—

(i) The facility is owned or leased by the employer,

(ii) The facility is operated by the employer,

(iii) The facility is located on or near the business premises of the employer, and

(iv) The meals furnished at the facility are provided during, or immediately before or after, the employee's workday.

For purposes of this section, the term "meals" means food, beverages, and related services provided at the facility. If an employer can reasonably determine the number of meals that are excludable from income by the recipient employees under section 119, the employer may, in determining whether the requirement of paragraph (a)(1)(i) of this section is satisfied, disregard all costs and revenues attributable to such meals provided to such employees. If an employer can reasonably determine the number of meals received by volunteers who receive food and beverages at a hospital, free or at a discount, the employer may, in determining whether the requirement of paragraph (a)(1)(i) of this section is satisfied, disregard all costs and revenues attributable to such meals provided to such volunteers. If an employer charges nonemployees a greater amount than employees, in determining whether the requirement of paragraph (a)(1)(i) of this section is satisfied, the employer must disregard all costs and revenues attributable to such meals provided to such nonemployees.

(3) *Operation by the employer.*—If an employer contracts with another to operate an eating facility for its employees, the facility is considered to be operated by the employer for purposes of this section. If an eating facility is operated by more than one employer, it is considered to be operated by each employer.

(4) *Example.*—The provisions of this paragraph (a)(2) may be illustrated by the following example:

Example (1). Assume that a not-for-profit hospital system maintains cafeterias for the use of its employees and volunteers. Only the employees are charged for food service at the cafeteria and the policy of the hospital is to charge the employees only for the costs of food, beverage and labor directly attributable to the meal. Most of the cafeterias within the system furnish more free meals to volunteers than they serve paid meals to employees. For purposes of this paragraph, as long as the employer can accurately determine the number of meals received free or at a discount by volunteers, the employer may disregard all the costs and revenues attributable to such meals provided to volunteers. Therefore, for purposes of this paragraph, the costs of the hospital system for furnishing meals to employees who pay for them are the costs to be compared to determine if the revenues from the facility equal or exceed direct operating costs of the facility's service to employees.

(b) *Direct operating costs.*—(1) *In general.*—For purposes of this section, the direct operating costs of an eating facility are—

(i) The cost of food and beverages, and

(ii) The cost of labor for personnel whose services relating to the facility are performed primarily on the premises of the eating facility.

Direct operating costs do not include the labor cost attributable to personnel whose services relating to the facility are not performed primarily on the premises of the eating facility. Thus, for example, the labor costs attributable to cooks, waiters, and waitresses are included in direct operating costs, but the labor cost attributable to a manager of an eating facility whose services relating to the facility are not primarily performed on the premises of the eating facility is not included in direct operating costs. If an employee performs services relating to the facility both on and off the premises of the eating facility, only the portion of the total labor cost of the employee relating to the facility that bears the same proportion to such total labor cost as time spent on the premises bears to total time spent performing services relating to the facility is included in direct operating costs. For example, assume that 60 percent of the services of a cook in the above example are not related to the eating facility. Only 40 percent of the total labor cost of the cook is includible in direct operating costs. For purposes of this section, labor costs include all compensation required to be reported on a Form W-2 for income tax purposes and related employment taxes paid by the employer. In determining the direct operating costs of an eating facility, the employer may include as part of the facility, vending machines that are provided by the employer and located on the same premises as the other eating facilities operated by the employer.

(2) *Multiple dining rooms or cafeterias.*—The direct operating costs test may be applied separately for each dining room or cafeteria. Alternatively, the direct operating costs test may be applied with respect to all the eating facilities operated by the employer.

(3) *Payment to operator of facility.*—If an employer contracts with another to operate an eating facility for its employees, the direct operating costs of the facility consist both of direct operating costs, if any, incurred by the employer and the amount paid to the operator of the facility to the extent that such amount is attributable to what would be direct operating costs if the employer operated the facility directly.

(c) *Valuation of non-excluded meals provided at an employer-operated eating facility for employees.*—If the exclusion for meals provided at an employer-operated eating facility for employees is not available, the recipient of meals provided at such facility must include in income the amount by which the fair market value of the meals provided exceeds the sum of—

(1) the amount, if any, paid for the meals, and

(2) the amount, if any, specifically excluded by another section of chapter 1 of this subtitle.

For special valuation rules relating to such meals, see § 1.61-21(j). [Reg. § 1.132-7.]

□ [T.D. 8256, 7-5-89.]

[Reg. § 1.132-8]

§ 1.132-8. Fringe benefit nondiscrimination rules.— (a) *Application of nondiscrimination rules.*—(1) *General rule.*—A highly compensated employee who receives a no-additional cost service, a qualified employee discount or a meal provided at an employer-operated eating facility for employees shall not be permitted to exclude such benefit from his or her income unless the benefit is available on substantially the same terms to:

(i) All employees of the employer; or

(ii) A group of employees of the employer which is defined under a reasonable classification set up by the employer that does not discriminate in favor of highly compensated employees. See paragraph (f) of this section for the definition of a highly compensated employee.

(2) *Consequences of discrimination.*—(i) *In general.*—If an employer maintains more than one fringe benefit program, i.e., either different fringe benefits being provided to the same group of employees, or different classifications of employees or the same fringe benefit being provided to two or more classifications of employees, the nondiscrimination requirements of section 132 will generally be applied separately to each such program. Thus, a determination that one fringe benefit program discriminates in favor of highly compensated employees generally will not cause other fringe benefit programs covering the same highly compensated employees to be treated as discriminatory. If the fringe benefits provided to a highly compensated individual do not satisfy the nondiscrimination rules provided in this section, such individual shall be unable to exclude from gross income any portion of the benefit. For example, if an employer offers a 20 percent discount (which otherwise satisfies the requirements for a qualified employee discount) to all non-highly compensated employees and a 35 percent discount to all highly compensated employees, the entire value of the 35 percent discount (not just the excess over 20 percent) is includible in the gross income and wages of the highly compensated employees who make purchases at a discount.

(ii) *Exception.*—(A) *Related fringe benefit programs.*—If one of a group of fringe benefit programs discriminates in favor of highly compensated employees, no related fringe benefit provided to such highly compensated employees under any other fringe benefit program may be excluded from the gross income of such highly compensated employees. For example, assume a department store provides a 20 percent merchandise discount to all employees under one fringe benefit program. Assume further that under a second fringe benefit program, the department store provides an additional 15 percent merchandise discount to a group of employees defined under a classification which discriminates in favor of highly compensated employees. Because the second fringe benefit program is discriminatory, the 15 percent merchandise discount provided to the highly compensated employees is not a qualified employee discount. In addition, because the 20 percent merchandise discount provided under the first fringe benefit program is related to the fringe benefit provided under the second fringe benefit program, the 20 percent merchandise discount provided the highly compensated employees is not a qualified employee discount. Thus, the entire 35 percent merchandise discount provided to the highly compensated employees is includible in such employees' gross incomes.

(B) *Employer-operated eating facilities for employees.*—For purposes of paragraph (a)(2)(ii)(A) of this section, meals at different employer-operated eating facilities for employees are not related fringe benefits, so that a highly compensated employee may exclude from gross income the value of a meal at a nondiscriminatory facility even though any meals provided to him or her at a discriminatory facility cannot be excluded.

(3) *Scope of the nondiscrimination rules provided in this section.*—The nondiscrimination rules provided in this section apply only to fringe benefits provided pursuant to section 132(a)(1), (a)(2), and (e)(2). These rules have no application to any other employee benefit that may be subject to nondiscrimination requirements under any other section of the Code.

(b) *Aggregation of employees.*—(1) *Section 132(a)(1) and (2).*—For purposes of determining whether the exclusions for no-additional-cost services and qualified employee discounts are available to highly compensated employees, the nondiscrimination rules of this section are applied by aggregating the employees of all related employers (as defined in § 1.132-1(c)), except that employees in different lines of business (as defined in § 1.132-4) are not to be aggregated. Thus, in general, for purposes of this section, the term "employees of the employer" refers to all employees of the employer and any other entity that is a member of a group described in sections 414(b), (c), (m), or, (o) and that performs services within the same line of business as the employer which provides the particular fringe benefit. Employees in different lines of business will be aggregated, however, if the line of business limitation has been relaxed pursuant to paragraphs (b) through (g) of § 1.132-4.

(2) *Section 132(e)(2).*—For purposes of determining whether the exclusions for meals provided at employer-operated eating facilities are available to highly compensated employees, the nondiscrimination rules of this section are applied by aggregating the employees of all related employers (as defined in section § 1.132-1(c)) who regularly work at or near the premises on which the eating facility is located, except that employees in different lines of business (as defined in § 1.132-4) are not to be aggregated. The nondiscrimination rules of this section are applied separately to each eating facility. Each dining room or cafeteria in which meals are served is treated as a separate eating facility, regardless of whether each such dining room or cafeteria has its own kitchen or other food-preparation area.

(3) *Classes of employees who may be excluded.*—For purposes of applying the nondiscrimination rules of this section to a particular fringe benefit program, there may be excluded from consideration employees who may be excluded from consideration under section 89(h), as enacted by the Tax Reform Act of 1986, Public Law 99-514, 100 Stat. 2085 (1986) and amended by the Technical and Miscellaneous Revenue Act of 1988, Public Law 100-647, 102 Stat. 3342 (1988).

(c) *Availability on substantially the same terms.*—(1) *General rule.*—The determination of whether a benefit is available on substantially the same terms shall be made upon the basis of the facts and circumstances of each situation. In general, however, if any one of the terms or conditions governing the availability of a particular benefit to one or more employees varies from any one of the terms or conditions governing the availability of a benefit made available to one or more other employees, such benefit shall not be considered to be available on substantially the same terms except to the extent otherwise provided in paragraph (2) below. For example, if a department store provides a 20 percent qualified employee discount to all of its employees on all merchandise, then substantially the same terms requirement will be satisfied. Similarly, if the discount provided to all employees is 30 percent on certain merchandise (such as apparel), and 20 percent on all other merchandise, then substantially the same terms requirement will be satisfied. However, if a department store provides a 20 percent qualified employee discount to all employees, but as to the employees in certain departments, the discount is available upon hire, and as to the remaining departments, the discount is only available when an employee has completed a specified term of services, the 20 percent discount is not available on substantially the same terms to all of the employees of the employer. Similarly, if a greater discount is given to employees with more seniority, full-time work status, or a particular job description, such benefit (i.e., the discount) would not be available to all employees eligible for the discount on substantially the same terms, except to the extent otherwise provided in paragraph (2) below. These examples also apply to no-additional-cost services. Thus, if an employer charges non-highly compensated employees for a no-additional-cost service and does not charge highly compensated employees (or charges highly compensated employees a lesser amount), then substantially the same terms requirement will not be satisfied.

(2) *Certain terms relating to priority.*—Certain fringe benefits made available to employees are available only in limited quantities that may be insufficient to meet employee demand. This situation may occur either because of employer policy (such as where an employer determines that only a certain number of units of a specific product will be made available to employees each year) or because of the nature of the fringe benefit (such as where an employer provides a no-additional-cost transportation service that is limited to the number of seats available just before departure). Under these circumstances, an employer may find it necessary to establish some method of allocating the limited fringe benefits among the employees eligible to receive the fringe benefits. The employer may establish the priorities described below.

(i) *Priority on a first come, first served, or similar basis.*—A benefit shall not fail to be treated as available to a group of employees on substantially the same terms merely because the employer allocates the benefit among such employees on a "first come, first served" or lottery basis, provided that the same notice of the terms of availability is given to all employees in the group and the terms under which the benefit is provided to employees within the group are otherwise the same with respect to all employees. For purposes of the preceding sentence, a program that gives priority to employees who are the first to submit written requests for the benefit will constitute priority on a "first come, first served" basis. Similarly, if the employer regularly engages in the practice of allocating benefits on a priority basis to employees demonstrating a critical need, such benefit shall not fail to be treated as available on substantially the same terms to all of the employees with respect to whom such priority status is available as long as the determination is based upon uniform and objective criteria which have been communicated to all employees in the group of eligible employees. An example of a critical need would be priority transportation given to an employee in the event of a medical emergency involving the employee (or a member of the employee's immediate family) or a recent death in the employee's immediate family. Frustrated vacation plans or forfeited deposits would not be treated as giving rise to particularly critical needs.

(ii) *Priority on the basis of seniority.*—Solely for purposes of section 1.132-8, a benefit shall not fail to be treated as available to a group of employees of the employer on substantially the same terms merely because the employer allocates the benefit among such employees on a seniority basis provided that:

(A) the same notice of the terms of availability is given to all employees in the group; and

(B) the average value of the benefit provided for each nonhighly compensated employee is at least 75% of that provided for each highly compensated employee. For purposes of this test, the average value of the benefit provided for each nonhighly compensated (highly compensated) employee is determined by taking the sum of the fair market values of such benefit provided to all the nonhighly compensated (highly compensated) employees, determined in accordance with section 1.61-21, and then dividing that sum by the total number of nonhighly compensated (highly compensated) employees of the employer. For purposes of determining the average value of the benefit provided for each employee, all employees of the employer are counted, including those who are not eligible to receive the benefit from the employer.

(d) *Testing for discrimination.*—(1) *Classification test.*—In the event that a benefit described in section 132(a)(1), (a)(2) or (e)(2) is not available on substantially the same terms to all of the employees of the employer, no exclusion shall be available to a highly compensated employee for such benefit unless the program under which the benefit is provided satisfies the nondiscrimination standards set forth in this section. The nondiscrimination standard of this section will be satisfied only if the benefit is available on substantially the same terms to a group of employees of the employer which is defined under a reasonable classification established by the employer that does not discriminate in favor of highly compensated employees. The determination of whether a particular classification is discriminatory will generally depend upon the facts and circumstances involved, based upon principles similar to those applied for purposes of section 410(b)(2)(A)(i) or, for years commencing prior to January 1, 1988, section 410(b)(1)(B). Thus, in general, except as otherwise provided in this section, if a benefit is available on substantially the same terms to a group of employees which, when compared with all of the other employees of the employer, constitutes a nondiscriminatory classification under section 410(b)(2)(A)(i) (or, if applicable, section 410(b)(1)(B)), it shall be deemed to be nondiscriminatory.

(2) *Classifications that are per se discriminatory.*—A classification that, on its face, makes fringe benefits available principally to highly compensated employees is per se discriminatory. In addition, a classification that is based on either an amount or rate of compensation is per se discriminatory if it favors those with the higher amount or rate of compensation. On the other hand, a classification that is based on factors such as seniority, full-time vs. part-time employment, or job description is not per se discriminatory but may be discriminatory as applied to the workforce of a particular employer.

(3) *Former employees.*—When determining whether a classification is discriminatory, former employees shall be tested separately from other employees of the employer. Therefore, a classification is not discriminatory solely because the employer does not make fringe benefits available to any former employee. Whether a classification of former employees discriminates in favor of highly compensated employees will depend upon the particular facts and circumstances.

(4) *Restructuring of benefits.*—For purposes of testing whether a particular group of employees would constitute a discriminatory classification for purposes of this section, an employer may restructure its fringe benefit program as described in this paragraph. If a fringe benefit is provided to more than one group of employees, and one or more such groups would constitute a discriminatory classification if considered by itself, then for purposes of this section, the employer may restructure its fringe benefit program so that all or some of the members of such group may be aggregated with another group, provided that each member of the restructured group will have available to him or her the same benefit upon the same terms and conditions. For example, assume that all highly compensated employees of an employer have fewer than five years of service and all nonhighly compensated employees have over five years of service. If the employer provided a five percent discount to employees with under five years of service and a ten percent discount to employees with over five years of service, the discount program available to the highly compensated employees would not satisfy the nondiscriminatory classification test; however, as a result of the rule described in this paragraph (d)(4), the employer could structure the program to consist of a five percent discount for all employees and a five percent additional discount for nonhighly compensated employees.

(5) *Employer-operated eating facilities for employees.*—(i) *General rule.*—If access to an employer-operated eating facility for employees is available to a classification of employees that discriminates in favor of highly compensated employees, then the classification will not be treated as discriminating in favor of highly compensated employees unless the facility is used by one or more executive group employees more than a de minimis amount.

(ii) *Executive group employee.*—For purposes of this paragraph (d)(5), an employee is an "executive group employee" if the definition of paragraph (f)(1) of this section is satisfied. For purposes of identifying such employees, the phrase "top one percent of the employees" is substituted for the phrase "top ten percent of the employees" in section 414(q)(4) (relating to the definition of "top-paid group").

(e) *Cash bonuses or rebates.*—A cash bonus or rebate provided to an employee by an employer that is determined with reference to the value of employer-provided property or services purchased by the employee, is treated as an equivalent employee discount. For example, assume a department store provides a 20 percent merchandise discount to all employees under a fringe benefit program. In addition, assume that the department store provides cash bonuses to a group of employees defined under a classification which discriminates in favor of highly compensated employees. Assume further that such cash bonuses equal 15 percent of the value of merchandise purchased by each employee. This arrangement is substantially identical to the example described in paragraph (e)(2)(i) of this section concerning related fringe benefit programs. Thus, both the 20 percent merchandise discount and the 15 percent cash bonus provided to the highly compensated employees are includible in such employees' gross incomes.

(f) *Highly compensated employee.*—(1) *Government and nongovernment employees.*—A highly compensated employee of any employer is any employee who, during the year or the preceding year—

(i) Was a 5-percent owner,

(ii) Received compensation from the employer in excess of $75,000,

(iii) Received compensation from the employer in excess of $50,000 and was in the top-paid group of employees for such year, or

(iv) Was at any time an officer and received compensation greater than 150 percent of the amount in effect under section 415(c)(1)(A) for such year.

For purposes of determining whether an employee is a highly compensated employee, the rules of sections 414(q), (s), and (t) apply.

(2) *Former employees.*—A former employee shall be treated as a highly compensated employee if—

(i) The employee was a highly compensated employee when the employee separated from service, or

(ii) The employee was a highly compensated employee at any time after attaining age 55. [Reg. § 1.132-8.]

☐ [T.D. 8256, 7-5-89.]

[Reg. §1.132-9]

§1.132-9. Qualified transportation fringes.—(a) *Table of contents.*—This section contains a list of the questions and answers in §1.132-9.

(1) *General rules.*

Q-1. What is a qualified transportation fringe?

Q-2. What is transportation in a commuter highway vehicle?

Q-3. What are transit passes?

Q-4. What is qualified parking?

Q-5. May qualified transportation fringes be provided to individuals who are not employees?

Q-6. Must a qualified transportation fringe benefit plan be in writing?

(2) *Dollar limitations.*

Q-7. Is there a limit on the value of qualified transportation fringes that may be excluded from an employee's gross income?

Q-8. What amount is includible in an employee's wages for income and employment tax purposes if the value of the qualified transportation fringe exceeds the applicable statutory monthly limit?

Q-9. Are excludable qualified transportation fringes calculated on a monthly basis?

Q-10. May an employee receive qualified transportation fringes from more than one employer?

(3) *Compensation reduction.*

Q-11. May qualified transportation fringes be provided to employees pursuant to a compensation reduction agreement?

Q-12. What is a compensation reduction election for purposes of section 132(f)?

Q-13. Is there a limit to the amount of the compensation reduction?

Q-14. When must the employee have made a compensation reduction election and under what circumstances may the amount be paid in cash to the employee?

Q-15. May an employee whose qualified transportation fringe costs are less than the employee's compensation reduction carry over this excess amount to subsequent periods?

(4) *Expense reimbursements.*

Q-16. How does section 132(f) apply to expense reimbursements?

Q-17. May an employer provide nontaxable cash reimbursement under section 132(f) for periods longer than one month?

Q-18. What are the substantiation requirements if an employer distributes transit passes?

Q-19. May an employer choose to impose substantiation requirements in addition to those described in this regulation?

(5) *Special rules for parking and vanpools.*

Q-20. How is the value of parking determined?

Q-21. How do the qualified transportation fringe rules apply to van pools?

(6) *Reporting and employment taxes.*

Q-22. What are the reporting and employment tax requirements for qualified transportation fringes?

(7) *Interaction with other fringe benefits.*

Q-23. How does section 132(f) interact with other fringe benefit rules?

(8) *Application to individuals who are not employees.*

Q-24. May qualified transportation fringes be provided to individuals who are partners, 2-percent shareholders of S-corporations, or independent contractors?

(9) *Effective date.*

Q-25. What is the effective date of this section?

(b) *Questions and answers.*

Q-1. What is a qualified transportation fringe?

A-1. (a) The following benefits are qualified transportation fringe benefits:

(1) Transportation in a commuter highway vehicle.

(2) Transit passes.

(3) Qualified parking.

(b) An employer may simultaneously provide an employee with any one or more these three benefits.

Q-2. What is transportation in a commuter highway vehicle?

A-2. Transportation in a commuter highway vehicle is transportation provided by an employer to an employee in connection with travel between the employee's residence and place of employment. A commuter highway vehicle is a highway vehicle with a seating capacity of at least 6 adults (excluding the driver) and with respect to which at least 80 percent of the vehicle's mileage for a year is reasonably expected to be—

(a) For transporting employees in connection with travel between their residences and their place of employment; and

(b) On trips during which the number of employees transported for commuting is at least one-half of the adult seating capacity of the vehicle (excluding the driver).

Q-3. What are transit passes?

A-3. A transit pass is any pass, token, farecard, voucher, or similar item (including an item exchangeable for fare media) that entitles a person to transportation—

(a) On mass transit facilities (whether or not publicly owned); or

(b) Provided by any person in the business of transporting persons for compensation or hire in a highway vehicle with a seating capacity of at least 6 adults (excluding the driver).

Q-4. What is qualified parking?

A-4. (a) Qualified parking is parking provided to an employee by an employer—

(1) On or near the employer's business premises; or

(2) At a location from which the employee commutes to work (including commuting by carpool, commuter highway vehicle, mass transit facilities, or transportation provided by any person in the business of transporting persons for compensation or hire).

(b) For purposes of section 132(f), parking on or near the employer's business premises includes parking on or near a work location at which the employee provides services for the employer. However, qualified parking does not include—

(1) The value of parking provided to an employee that is excludable from gross income under section 132(a)(3) (as a working condition fringe), or

(2) Reimbursement paid to an employee for parking costs that is excludable from gross income as an amount treated as paid under an accountable plan. See § 1.62-2.

(c) However, parking on or near property used by the employee for residential purposes is not qualified parking.

(d) Parking is provided by an employer if—

(1) The parking is on property that the employer owns or leases;

(2) The employer pays for the parking; or

(3) The employer reimburses the employee for parking expenses (see Q/A-16 of this section for rules relating to cash reimbursements).

Q-5. May qualified transportation fringes be provided to individuals who are not employees?

A-5. An employer may provide qualified transportation fringes only to individuals who are currently employees of the employer at the time the qualified transportation fringe is provided. The term employee for purposes of qualified transportation fringes is defined in § 1.132-1(b)(2)(i). This term includes only common law employees and other statutory employees, such as officers of corporations. See Q/A-24 of this section for rules regarding partners, 2-percent shareholders, and independent contractors.

Q-6. Must a qualified transportation fringe benefit plan be in writing?

A-6. No. Section 132(f) does not require that a qualified transportation fringe benefit plan be in writing.

Q-7. Is there a limit on the value of qualified transportation fringes that may be excluded from an employee's gross income?

A-7. (a) *Transportation in a commuter highway vehicle and transit passes.* Before January 1, 2002, up to $65 per month is excludable from the gross income of an employee for transportation in a commuter highway vehicle and transit passes provided by an employer. On January 1, 2002, this amount is increased to $100 per month.

(b) *Parking.* Up to $175 per month is excludable from the gross income of an employee for qualified parking.

(c) *Combination.* An employer may provide qualified parking benefits in addition to transportation in a commuter highway vehicle and transit passes.

(d) *Cost-of-living adjustments.* The amounts in paragraphs (a) and (b) of this Q/A-7 are adjusted annually, beginning with 2000, to reflect cost-of-living. The adjusted figures are announced by the Service before the beginning of the year.

Q-8. What amount is includible in an employee's wages for income and employment tax purposes if the value of the qualified transportation fringe exceeds the applicable statutory monthly limit?

A-8. (a) Generally, an employee must include in gross income the amount by which the fair market value of the benefit exceeds the sum of the amount, if any, paid by the employee and any amount excluded from gross income under section 132(a)(5). Thus, assuming no other statutory exclusion applies, if an employer provides an employee with a qualified transportation fringe that exceeds the applicable statutory monthly limit and the employee does not make any payment, the value of the benefits provided in excess of the applicable statutory monthly limit is included in the employee's wages for income and employment tax purposes. See § 1.61-21(b)(1).

(b) The following examples illustrate the principles of this Q/A-8:

Example 1. (i) For each month in a year in which the statutory monthly transit pass limit is $100 (i.e., a year after 2001), Employer M provides a transit pass valued at $110 to Employee D, who does not pay any amount to Employer M for the transit pass.

(ii) In this *Example 1*, because the value of the monthly transit pass exceeds the statutory monthly limit by $10, $120 ($110 − $100, times 12 months) must be included in D's wages for income and employment tax purposes for the year with respect to the transit passes.

Example 2. (i) For each month in a year in which the statutory monthly qualified parking limit is $175, Employer M provides qualified parking valued at $195 to Employee E, who does not pay any amount to M for the parking.

(ii) In this *Example 2*, because the fair market value of the qualified parking exceeds the statutory monthly limit by $20, $240 ($195 – $175, times 12 months) must be included in Employee E's wages for income and employment tax purposes for the year with respect to the qualified parking.

Example 3. (i) For each month in a year in which the statutory monthly qualified parking limit is $175, Employer P provides qualified parking with a fair market value of $220 per month to its employees, but charges each employee $45 per month.

(ii) In this *Example 3*, because the sum of the amount paid by an employee ($45) plus the amount excludable for qualified parking ($175) is not less than the fair market value of the monthly benefit, no amount is includible in the employee's wages for income and employment tax purposes with respect to the qualified parking.

Q-9. Are excludable qualified transportation fringes calculated on a monthly basis?

A-9. (a) *In general.* Yes. The value of transportation in a commuter highway vehicle, transit passes, and qualified parking is calculated on a monthly basis to determine whether the value of the benefit has exceeded the applicable statutory monthly limit on qualified transportation fringes. Except in the case of a transit pass provided to an employee, the applicable statutory monthly limit applies to qualified transportation fringes used by the employee in a month. Monthly exclusion amounts are not combined to provide a qualified transportation fringe for any month exceeding the statutory limit. A month is a calendar month or a substantially equivalent period applied consistently.

(b) *Transit passes.* In the case of transit passes provided to an employee, the applicable statutory monthly limit applies to the transit passes provided by the employer to the employee in a month for that month or for any previous month in the calendar year. In addition, transit passes distributed in advance for more than one month, but not for more than twelve months, are qualified transportation fringes if the requirements in paragraph (c) of this Q/A-9 are met (relating to the income tax and employment tax treatment of advance transit passes). The applicable statutory monthly limit under section 132(f)(2) on the combined amount of transportation in a commuter highway vehicle and transit passes may be calculated by taking into account the monthly limits for all months for which the transit passes are distributed. In the case of a pass that is valid for more than one month, such as an annual pass, the value of the pass may be divided by the number of months for which it is valid for purposes of determining whether the value of the pass exceeds the statutory monthly limit.

(c) *Rule if employee's employment terminates—(1) income tax treatment.* The value of transit passes provided in advance to an employee with respect to a month in which the individual is not an employee is included in the employee's wages for income tax purposes.

(2) *Reporting and employment tax treatment.* Transit passes distributed in advance to an employee are excludable from wages for employment tax purposes under sections 3121, 3306, and 3401 (FICA, FUTA, and income tax withholding) if the employer distributes transit passes to the employee in advance for not more than three months and, at the time the transit passes are distributed, there is not an established date that the employee's employment will terminate (for example, if the employee has given notice of retirement) which will occur before the beginning of the last month of the period for which the transit passes are provided. If the employer distributes transit passes to an employee in advance for not more than three months and at the time the transit passes are distributed there is an established date that the employee's employment will terminate, and the employee's employment does terminate before the beginning of the last month of the period for which the transit passes are provided, the value of transit passes provided for months beginning after the date of termination during which the employee is not employed by the employer is included in the employee's wages for employment tax purposes. If transit passes are distributed in advance for more than three months, the value of transit passes provided for the months during which the employee is not employed by the employer is includible in the employee's wages for employment tax purposes *regardless* of whether at the time the transit passes were distributed there was an established date of termination of the employee's employment.

(d) *Examples.* The following examples illustrate the principles of this Q/A-9:

Example 1. (i) Employee E incurs $150 for qualified parking used during the month of June of a year in which the statutory monthly parking limit is $175, for which E is reimbursed $150 by Employer R. Employee E incurs $180 in expenses for qualified parking used during the month of July of that year, for which E is reimbursed $180 by Employer R.

(ii) In this *Example 1*, because monthly exclusion amounts may not be combined to provide a benefit in any month greater than the applicable statutory limit, the amount by which the amount reimbursed for July exceeds the applicable statutory monthly limit ($180 minus $175 equals $5) is includible in Employee E's wages for income and employment tax purposes.

Example 2. (i) Employee F receives transit passes from Employer G with a value of $195 in March of a year (for which the statutory monthly transit pass limit is $65) for January, February, and March of that year. F was hired during January and has not received any transit passes from G.

(ii) In this *Example 2*, the value of the transit passes (three months times $65 equals $195) is excludable from F's wages for income and employment tax purposes.

Example 3. (1) Employer S has a qualified transportation fringe benefit plan under which its employees receive transit passes near the beginning of each calendar quarter for that calendar quarter. All employees of Employer S receive transit passes from Employer S with a value of $195 on March 31 for the second calendar quarter covering the months April, May, and June (of a year in which the statutory monthly transit pass limit is $65).

(ii) In this *Example 3*, because the value of the transit passes may be calculated by taking into account the monthly limits for all months for which the transit passes are distributed, the value of the transit passes (three months times $65 equals $195) is excludable from the employees' wages for income and employment tax purposes.

Example 4. (i) Same facts as in *Example 3*, except that Employee T, an employee of Employer S, terminates employment with S on May 31. There was not an established date of termination for Employee T at the time the transit passes were distributed.

(ii) In this *Example 4*, because at the time the transit passes were distributed there was not an established date of termination for Employee T, the value of the transit passes provided for June ($65) is excludable from T's wages for employment tax purposes. However, the value of the transit passes distributed to Employee T for June ($65) is not excludable from T's wages for income tax purposes.

(iii) If Employee T's May 31 termination date was established at the time the transit passes were provided, the value of the transit passes provided for June ($65) is included in T's wages for both income and employment tax purposes.

Example 5. (i) Employer F has a qualified transportation fringe benefit plan under which its employees receive transit passes semiannually in advance of the months for which the transit passes are provided. All employees of Employer F, including Employee X, receive transit passes from F with a value of $390 on June 30 for the 6 months of July through December (of a year in which the statutory monthly transit pass limit is $65). Employee X's employment terminates and his last day of work is August 1. Employer F's other employees remain employed throughout the remainder of the year.

(ii) In this *Example 5*, the value of the transit passes provided to Employee X for the months September, October, November, and December ($65 times 4 months equals $260) of the year is included in X's wages for income and employment tax purposes. The value of the transit passes provided to Employer F's other employees is excludable from the employees' wages for income and employment tax purposes.

Example 6. (i) Each month during a year in which the statutory monthly transit pass limit is $65, Employer R distributes transit passes with a face amount of $70 to each of its employees. Transit passes with a face amount of $70 can be purchased from the transit system by any individual for $65.

(ii) In this *Example 6*, because the value of the transit passes distributed by Employer R does not exceed the applicable statutory monthly limit ($65), no portion of the value of the transit passes is included as wages for income and employment tax purposes.

Q-10. May an employee receive qualified transportation fringes from more than one employer?

A-10. (a) *General rule.* Yes. The statutory monthly limits described in Q/A-7 of this section apply to benefits provided by an employer to its employees. For this purpose, all employees treated as employed by a single employer under section 414(b), (c), (m), or (o) are treated as employed by a single employer. See section 414(t) and § 1.132-1(c). Thus, qualified transportation fringes paid by entities under common control under section 414(b), (c), (m), or (o) are combined for purposes of applying the applicable statutory monthly limit. In addition, an individual who is treated as a leased employee of the employer under section 414(n) is treated as an employee of that employer for purposes of section 132. See section 414(n)(3)(C).

(b) *Examples.* The following examples illustrate the principles of this Q/A-10:

Example 1. (i) During a year in which the statutory monthly qualified parking limit is $175, Employee E works for Employers M and N, who are unrelated and not treated as a single employer under section 414(b), (c), (m), or (o). Each month, M and N each provide qualified parking benefits to E with a value of $100.

(ii) In this *Example 1*, because M and N are unrelated employers, and the value of the monthly parking benefit provided by each is not more than the applicable statutory monthly limit, the parking benefits provided by each employer are excludable as qualified transportation fringes assuming that the other requirements of this section are satisfied.

Example 2. (i) Same facts as in Example 1, except that Employers M and N are treated as a single employer under section 414(b).

(ii) In this *Example 2*, because M and N are treated as a single employer, the value of the monthly parking benefit provided by M and N must be combined for purposes of determining whether the applicable statutory monthly limit has been exceeded. Thus, the amount by which the value of the parking benefit exceeds the monthly limit ($200 minus the monthly limit amount of $175 equals $25) for each month in the year is includible in E's wages for income and employment tax purposes.

Q-11. May qualified transportation fringes be provided to employees pursuant to a compensation reduction agreement?

A-11. Yes. An employer may offer employees a choice between cash compensation and any qualified transportation fringe. An employee who is offered this choice and who elects qualified transportation fringes is not required to include the cash compensation in income if—

(a) The election is pursuant to an arrangement described in Q/A-12 of this section;

(b) The amount of the reduction in cash compensation does not exceed the limitation in Q/A-13 of this section;

(c) The arrangement satisfies the timing and reimbursement rules in Q/A-14 and 16 of this section; and

(d) The related fringe benefit arrangement otherwise satisfies the requirements set forth elsewhere in this section.

Q-12. What is a compensation reduction election for purposes of section 132(f)?

A-12. (a) *Election requirements generally.* A compensation reduction arrangement is an arrangement under which the employer provides the employee with the right to elect whether the employee will receive either a fixed amount of cash compensation at a specified future date or a fixed amount of qualified transportation fringes to be provided for a specified future period (such as qualified parking to be used during a future calendar month). The employee's election must be in writing or another form, such as electronic, that includes, in a permanent and verifiable form, the information required to be in the election. The election must contain the date of the election, the amount of the compensation to be reduced, and the period for which the benefit will be provided. The election must relate to a fixed dollar amount or fixed percentage of compensation reduction. An election to reduce compensation for a period by a set amount for such period may be automatically renewed for subsequent periods.

(b) *Automatic election permitted.* An employer may provide under its qualified transportation fringe benefit plan that a compensation reduction election will be deemed to have been made if the employee does not elect to receive cash compensation in lieu of the qualified transportation fringe, provided that the employee receives adequate notice that a compensation reduction will be made and is given adequate opportunity to choose to receive the cash compensation instead of the qualified transportation fringe. See § 1.401(a)-21 of this chapter for rules permitting the use of electronic media to make participant elections with respect to employee benefit arrangements.

Q-13. Is there a limit to the amount of the compensation reduction?

A-13. Yes. Each month, the amount of the compensation reduction may not exceed the combined applicable statutory monthly limits for transportation in a commuter highway vehicle, transit passes, and qualified parking. For example, for a year in which the statutory monthly limit is $65 for transportation in a commuter highway vehicle and transit passes, and $175 for qualified parking, an employee could elect to reduce compensation for any month by no more than $240 ($65 plus $175) with respect to qualified transportation fringes. If an employee were to elect to reduce compensation by $250 for a month, the excess $10 ($250 minus $240) would be includible in the employee's wages for income and employment tax purposes.

Q-14. When must the employee have made a compensation reduction election and under what circumstances may the amount be paid in cash to the employee?

A-14. (a) The compensation reduction election must satisfy the requirements set forth under paragraphs (b), (c), and (d) of this Q/A-14.

(b) *Timing of election.* The compensation reduction election must be made before the employee is able currently to receive the cash or other taxable amount at the employee's discretion. The determination of whether the employee is able currently to receive the cash does not depend on whether it has been constructively received for purposes

of section 451. The election must specify that the period (such as a calendar month) for which the qualified transportation fringe will be provided must not begin before the election is made. Thus, a compensation reduction election must relate to qualified transportation fringes to be provided after the election. For this purpose, the date a qualified transportation fringe is provided is—

(1) The date the employee receives a voucher or similar item; or

(2) In any other case, the date the employee uses the qualified transportation fringe.

(c) *Revocability of elections.* The employee may not revoke a compensation reduction election after the employee is able currently to receive the cash or other taxable amount at the employee's discretion. In addition, the election may not be revoked after the beginning of the period for which the qualified transportation fringe will be provided.

(d) *Compensation reduction amounts not refundable.* Unless an election is revoked in a manner consistent with paragraph (c) of this Q/A-14, an employee may not subsequently receive the compensation (in cash or any form other than by payment of a qualified transportation fringe under the employer's plan). Thus, an employer's qualified transportation fringe benefit plan may not provide that an employee who ceases to participate in the employer's qualified transportation fringe benefit plan (such as in the case of termination of employment) is entitled to receive a refund of the amount by which the employee's compensation reductions exceed the actual qualified transportation fringes provided to the employee by the employer.

(e) *Examples.* The following examples illustrate the principles of this Q/A-14:

Example 1. (i) Employer P maintains a qualified transportation fringe benefit arrangement during a year in which the statutory monthly limit is $100 for transportation in a commuter highway vehicle and transit passes (2002 or later) and $180 for qualified parking. Employees of P are paid cash compensation twice per month, with the payroll dates being the first and the fifteenth day of the month. Under P's arrangement, an employee is permitted to elect at any time before the first day of a month to reduce his or her compensation payable during that month in an amount up to the applicable statutory monthly limit ($100 if the employee elects coverage for transportation in a commuter highway vehicle or a mass transit pass, or $180 if the employee chooses qualified parking) in return for the right to receive qualified transportation fringes up to the amount of the election. If such an election is made, P will provide a mass transit pass for that month with a value not exceeding the compensation reduction amount elected by the employee or will reimburse the cost of other qualified transportation fringes used by the employee on or after the first day of that month up to the compensation reduction amount elected by the employee. Any compensation reduction amount elected by the employee for the month that is not used for qualified transportation fringes is not refunded to the employee at any future date.

(ii) In this *Example 1*, the arrangement satisfies the requirements of this Q/A-14 because the election is made before the employee is able currently to receive the cash and the election specifies the future period for which the qualified transportation fringes will be provided. The arrangement would also satisfy the requirements of this Q/A-14 and Q/A-13 of this section if employees are allowed to elect to reduce compensation up to $280 per month ($100 plus $180).

(iii) The arrangement would also satisfy the requirements of this Q/A-14 (and Q/A-13 of this section) if employees are allowed to make an election at any time before the first or the fifteenth day of the month to reduce their compensation payable on that payroll date by an amount not in excess of one-half of the applicable statutory monthly limit (depending on the type of qualified transportation fringe elected by the employee) and P provides a mass transit pass on or after the applicable payroll date for the compensation reduction amount elected by the employee for the payroll date or reimburses the cost of other qualified transportation fringes used by the employee on or after the payroll date up to the compensation reduction amount elected by the employee for that payroll date.

Example 2. (i) Employee Q elects to reduce his compensation payable on March 1 of a year (for which the statutory monthly mass transit limit is $65) by $195 in exchange for a mass transit voucher to be provided in March. The election is made on the preceding February 27. Employee Q was hired in January of the year. On March 10 of the year, the employer of Employee Q delivers to Employee Q a mass transit voucher worth $195 for the months of January, February, and March.

(ii) In this *Example 2*, $65 is included in Employee Q's wages for income and employment tax purposes because the compensation reduction election fails to satisfy the requirement in this Q/A-14 and Q/A-12 of this section that the period for which the qualified transportation fringe will be provided not begin before the election is made to the extent the election relates to $65 worth of transit passes for January of the year. The $65 for February is not taxable because the election was for a future period that includes at least one day in February.

(iii) However, no amount would be included in Employee Q's wages as a result of the election if $195 worth of mass transit passes were instead provided to Q for the months of February, March, and April (because the compensation reduction would relate solely to fringes to be provided for a period not beginning before the date of the election and the amount provided does not exceed the aggregate limit for the period, i.e., the sum of $65 for each of February, March, and April). See Q/A-9 of this section for rules governing transit passes distributed in advance for more than one month.

Example 3. (i) Employee R elects to reduce his compensation payable on March 1 of a year (for which the statutory monthly parking limit is $175) by $185 in exchange for reimbursement by Employer T of parking expenses incurred by Employee R for parking on or near Employer T's business premises during the period beginning after the date of the election through March. The election is made on the preceding February 27, Employee R incurs $10 in parking expenses on February 28 of the year, and $175 in parking expenses during the month of March. On April 5 of the year, Employer T reimburses Employee R $185 for the parking expenses incurred on February 28, and during March, of the year.

(ii) In this *Example 3*, no amount would be includible in Employee R's wages for income and employment tax purposes because the compensation reduction related solely to parking on or near Employer R's business premises used during a period not beginning before the date of the election and the amount reimbursed for parking used in any one month does not exceed the statutory monthly limitation.

Q-15. May an employee whose qualified transportation fringe costs are less than the employee's compensation reduction carry over this excess amount to subsequent periods?

A-15. (a) Yes. An employee may carry over unused compensation reduction amounts to subsequent periods under the plan of the employee's employer.

(b) The following example illustrates the principles of this Q/A-15:

Example. (i) By an election made before November I of a year for which the statutory monthly mass transit limit is $65, Employee E elects to reduce compensation in the amount of $65 for the month of November. E incurs $50 in employee-operated commuter highway vehicle expenses during November for which E is reimbursed $50 by Employer R, E's employer. By an election made before December, E elects to reduce compensation by $65 for the month of December. E incurs $65 in employee-operated commuter highway vehicle expenses during December for which E is reimbursed $65 by R. Before the following January, E elects to reduce compensation by $50 for the month of January. E incurs $65 in employee-operated commuter highway vehicle expenses during January for which E is reimbursed $65 by R because R allows E to carry over to the next year the $15 amount by which the compensation reductions for November and December exceeded the employee-operated commuter highway vehicle expenses incurred during those months.

(ii) In this *Example*, because Employee E is reimbursed in an amount not exceeding the applicable statutory monthly limit, and the reimbursement does not exceed the amount of employee-operated commuter highway vehicle expenses incurred during the month of January, the amount reimbursed ($65) is excludable from E's wages for income and employment tax purposes.

Q-16. How does section 132(f) apply to expense reimbursements?

A-16. (a) *In general*. The term qualified transportation fringe includes cash reimbursement by an employer to an employee for expenses incurred or paid by an employee for transportation in a commuter highway vehicle or qualified parking. The term qualified transportation fringe also includes cash reimbursement for transit passes made under a bona fide reimbursement arrangement, but, in accordance with section 132(f)(3), only if permitted under paragraph (b) of this Q/A-16. The reimbursement must be made under a bona fide reimbursement arrangement which meets the rules of paragraph (c) of this Q/A-16. A payment made before the date an expense has been incurred or paid is not a reimbursement. In addition, a bona fide reimbursement arrangement does not include an arrangement that is dependent solely upon an employee certifying in advance that the employee will incur expenses at some future date.

(b) *Special rule for transit passes*—(1) *In general*. The term *qualified transportation fringe* includes cash reimbursement for transit passes made under a bona fide reimbursement arrangement, but, in accordance with section 132(f)(3), only if no voucher or similar item that may be exchanged only for a transit pass is readily available for direct distribution by the employer to employees. If a voucher is readily available, the requirement that a voucher be distributed in-kind by the employer is satisfied if the voucher is distributed by the employer or by another person on behalf of the employer (for example, if a transit operator credits amounts to the employee's fare card as a result of payments made to the operator by the employer).

(2) *Voucher or similar item*. For purposes of the special rule in paragraph (b) of this Q/A-16, a transit system voucher is an instrument that may be purchased by employers from a voucher provider that is accepted by one or more mass transit operators (e.g., train, subway, and bus) in an area as fare media or in exchange for fare media. Thus, for example, a transit pass that may be purchased by employers directly from a voucher provider is a transit system voucher.

(3) *Voucher provider*. The term voucher provider means any person in the trade or business of selling transit system vouchers to employers, or any transit system or transit operator that sells vouchers to employers for the purpose of direct distribution to employees. Thus, a transit operator might or might not be a voucher provider. A voucher provider is not, for example, a third-party employee benefits administrator that administers a transit pass benefit program for an employer using vouchers that the employer could obtain directly.

(4) *Readily available*. For purposes of this paragraph (b), a voucher or similar item is readily available for direct distribution by the employer to employees if and only if an employer can obtain it from a voucher provider that—

(i) does not impose fare media charges that cause vouchers to not be readily available as described in paragraph (b)(5) of this section; and

(ii) does not impose other restrictions that cause vouchers to not be readily available as described in paragraph (b)(6) of this section.

(5) *Fare media charges*. For purposes of paragraph (b)(4) of this section, fare media charges relate only to fees paid by the employer to voucher providers for vouchers. The determination of whether obtaining a voucher would result in fare media charges that cause vouchers to not be readily available as described in this paragraph (b) is made with respect to each transit system voucher. If more than one transit system voucher is available for direct distribution to employees, the employer must consider the fees imposed for the lowest cost monthly voucher for purposes of determining whether the fees imposed by the voucher provider satisfy this paragraph. However, if transit system vouchers for multiple transit systems are required in an area to meet the transit needs of the individual employees in that area, the employer has the option of averaging the costs applied to each transit system voucher for purposes of determining whether the fare media charges for transit system vouchers satisfy this paragraph. Fare media charges are described in this paragraph (b)(5), and therefore cause vouchers to not be readily available, if and only if the average annual fare media charges that the employer reasonably expects to incur for transit system vouchers purchased from the voucher provider (disregarding reasonable and customary delivery charges imposed by the voucher provider, e.g., not in excess of $15) are more than 1 percent of the average annual value of the vouchers for a transit system.

(6) *Other restrictions*. For purposes of paragraph (b)(4) of this section, restrictions that cause vouchers to not be readily available are restrictions imposed by the voucher provider other than fare media charges that effectively prevent the employer from obtaining vouchers appropriate for distribution to employees. Examples of such restrictions include—

(i) *Advance purchase requirements*. Advance purchase requirements cause vouchers to not be readily available only if the voucher provider does not offer vouchers at regular intervals or fails to provide the voucher within a reasonable period after receiving payment for the voucher. For example, a requirement that vouchers may be purchased only once per year may effectively prevent an employer from obtaining vouchers for distribution to employees. An advance purchase requirement that vouchers be purchased not more frequently than monthly does not effectively prevent the employer from obtaining vouchers for distribution to employees.

(ii) *Purchase quantity requirements*. Purchase quantity requirements cause vouchers to not be readily available if the voucher provider does not offer vouchers in quantities that are reasonably appropriate to the number of the employer's employees who use mass transportation (for example, the voucher provider requires a $1,000 minimum purchase and the employer seeks to purchase only $200 of vouchers).

(iii) *Limitations on denominations of vouchers that are available*. If the voucher provider does not offer vouchers in denominations appropriate for distribution to the employer's employees, vouchers are not readily available. For example, vouchers provided in $5 increments up to the monthly limit are appropriate for distribution to employees, while vouchers available only in a denomination equal to the monthly limit are not appropriate for distribution to employees if the amount of the benefit provided to the employer's employees each month is normally less than the monthly limit.

(7) *Example*. The following example illustrates the principles of this paragraph (b):

Example. (i) Company C in City X sells mass transit vouchers to employers in the metropolitan area of X in various denominations appropriate for distribution to employees. Employers can purchase vouchers monthly in reasonably appropriate quantities. Several different bus, rail, van pool, and ferry operators service X, and a number of the operators accept the vouchers either as fare media or in exchange for fare media. To cover its operating expenses, C imposes on each voucher a 50 cents charge, plus a reasonable and customary $15 charge for delivery of each order of vouchers. Employer M disburses vouchers purchased from C to its employees who use operators that accept the vouchers and M reasonably expects that $55 is the average value of the voucher it will purchase from C for the next calendar year.

(ii) In this *Example*, vouchers for X are readily available for direct distribution by the employer to employees because the expected cost of the vouchers disbursed to M's employees for the next calendar year is not more than 1 percent of the value of the vouchers (50 cents divided by $55 equals 0.91 percent), the delivery charges are disregarded because they are reasonable and customary, and there are no other restrictions that cause the vouchers to not be readily available. Thus, any reimbursement of mass transportation costs in X would not be a qualified transportation fringe.

(c) *Substantiation requirements.* Employers that make cash reimbursements must establish a bona fide reimbursement arrangement to establish that their employees have, in fact, incurred expenses for transportation in a commuter highway vehicle, transit passes, or qualified parking. For purposes of section 132(f), whether cash reimbursements are made under a bona fide reimbursement arrangement may vary depending on the facts and circumstances, including the method or methods of payment utilized within the mass transit system. The employer must implement reasonable procedures to ensure that an amount equal to the reimbursement was incurred for transportation in a commuter highway vehicle, transit passes, or qualified parking. The expense must be substantiated within a reasonable period of time. An expense substantiated to the payor within 180 days after it has been paid will be treated as having been substantiated within a reasonable period of time. An employee certification at the time of reimbursement in either written or electronic form may be a reasonable reimbursement procedure depending on the facts and circumstances. Examples of reasonable reimbursement procedures are set forth in paragraph (d) of this Q/A-16.

(d) *Illustrations of reasonable reimbursement procedures.* The following are examples of reasonable reimbursement procedures for purposes of paragraph (c) of this Q/A-16. In each case, the reimbursement is made at or within a reasonable period after the end of the events described in paragraphs (d)(1) through (d)(3) of this section.

(1) An employee presents to the employer a parking expense receipt for parking on or near the employer's business premises, the employee certifies that the parking was used by the employee, and the employer has no reason to doubt the employee's certification.

(2) An employee either submits a used time-sensitive transit pass (such as a monthly pass) to the employer and certifies that he or she purchased it or presents an unused or used transit pass to the employer and certifies that he or she purchased it and the employee certifies that he or she has not previously been reimbursed for the transit pass. In both cases, the employer has no reason to doubt the employee's certification.

(3) If a receipt is not provided in the ordinary course of business (e.g., if the employee uses metered parking or if used transit passes cannot be returned to the user), the employee certifies to the employer the type and the amount of expenses incurred, and the employer has no reason to doubt the employee's certification.

Q-17. May an employer provide nontaxable cash reimbursement under section 132(f) for periods longer than one month?

A-17. (a) *General rule.* Yes. Qualified transportation fringes include reimbursement to employees for costs incurred for transportation in more than one month, provided the reimbursement for each month in the period is calculated separately and does not exceed the applicable statutory monthly limit for any month in the period. See Q/A-8 and 9 of this section if the limit for a month is exceeded.

(b) *Example.* The following example illustrates the principles of this Q/A-17:

Example. (i) Employee R pays $100 per month for qualified parking used during the period from April 1 through June 30 of a year in which the statutory monthly qualified parking limit is $175. After receiving adequate substantiation from Employee R, R's employer reimburses R $300 in cash on June 30 of that year.

(ii) In this *Example*, because the value of the reimbursed expenses for each month did not exceed the applicable statutory monthly limit, the $300 reimbursement is excludable from R's wages for income and employment tax purposes as a qualified transportation fringe.

Q-18. What are the substantiation requirements if an employer distributes transit passes?

A-18. There are no substantiation requirements if the employer distributes transit passes. Thus, an employer may distribute a transit pass for each month with a value not more than the statutory

monthly limit without requiring any certification from the employee regarding the use of the transit pass.

Q-19. May an employer choose to impose substantiation requirements in addition those described in this regulation?

A-19. Yes.

Q-20. How is the value of parking determined?

A-20. Section 1.61-21(b)(2) applies for purposes of determining the value of parking.

Q-21. How do the qualified transportation fringe rules apply to van pools?

A-21. (a) *Van pools generally.* Employer and employee-operated van pools, as well as private or public transit-operated van pools, may qualify as qualified transportation fringes. The value of van pool benefits which are qualified transportation fringes may be excluded up to the applicable statutory monthly limit for transportation in a commuter highway vehicle and transit passes, less the value of any transit passes provided by the employer for the month.

(b) *Employer-operated van pools.* The value of van pool transportation provided by or for an employer to its employees is excludable as a qualified transportation fringe, provided the van qualifies as a commuter highway vehicle as defined in section 132(f)(5)(B) and Q/A-2 of this section. A van pool is operated by or for the employer if the employer purchases or leases vans to enable employees to commute together or the employer contracts with and pays a third party to provide the vans and some or all of the costs of operating the vans, including maintenance, liability insurance and other operating expenses.

(c) *Employee-operated van pools.* Cash reimbursement by an employer to employees for expenses incurred for transportation in a van pool operated by employees independent of their employer are excludable as qualified transportation fringes, provided that the van qualifies as a commuter highway vehicle as defined in section 132(f)(5)(B) and Q/A-2 of this section. See Q/A-16 of this section for the rules governing cash reimbursements.

(d) *Private or public transit-operated van pool transit passes.* The qualified transportation fringe exclusion for transit passes is available for travel in van pools owned and operated either by public transit authorities or by any person in the business of transporting persons for compensation or hire. In accordance with paragraph (b) of Q/A-3 of this section, the van must seat at least 6 adults (excluding the driver). See Q/A-16(b) and (c) of this section for a special rule for cash reimbursement for transit passes and the substantiation requirements for cash reimbursement.

(e) *Value of van pool transportation benefits.* Section 1.61-21(b)(2) provides that the fair market value of a fringe benefit is based on all the facts and circumstances. Alternatively, transportation in an employer-provided commuter highway vehicle may be valued under the automobile lease valuation rule in §1.61-21(d), the vehicle cents-per-mile rule in §1.61-21(e), or the commuting valuation rule in §11.61-21(f). If one of these special valuation rules is used, the employer must use the same valuation rule to value the use of the commuter highway vehicle by each employee who share the use. See §1.61-21(c)(2)(i)(B).

(f) *Qualified parking prime member.* If an employee obtains a qualified parking space as a result of membership in a car or van pool, the applicable statutory monthly limit for qualified parking applies to the individual to whom the parking space is assigned. This individual is the prime member. In determining the tax consequences to the prime member, the statutory monthly limit amounts of each car pool member may not be combined. If the employer provides access to the space and the space is not assigned to a particular individual, then the employer must designate one of its employees as the prime member who will bear the tax consequences. The employer may not designate more than one prime member for a car or van pool during a month. The employer of the prime member is responsible for including the value of the qualified parking in excess of the statutory monthly limit in the prime member's wages for income and employment tax purposes.

Q-22. What are the reporting and employment tax requirements for qualified transportation fringes?

A-22. (a) *Employment tax treatment generally.* Qualified transportation fringes not exceeding the applicable statutory monthly limit described in Q/A-7 of this section are not wages for purposes of the Federal Insurance Contributions Act (FICA), the Federal Unemployment Tax Act (FUTA), and federal income tax withholding. Any amount by which an employee elects to reduce compensation as provided in Q/A-11 of this section is not subject to the FICA, the FUTA, and federal income tax withholding. Qualified transportation fringes exceeding the applicable statutory monthly limit described in Q/A-7 of this section are wages for purposes of the FICA, the FUTA, and federal income tax withholding and are reported on the employee's Form W-2, Wage and Tax Statement.

(b) *Employment tax treatment of cash reimbursement exceeding monthly limits.* Cash reimbursement to employees (for example, cash reimbursement for qualified parking) in excess of the applicable statutory monthly limit under section 132(f) is treated as paid for employment tax purposes when actually or constructively paid. See §§ 31.3121(a)-2(a), 31.3301-4, 31.3402(a)-1(b) of this chapter. Employers must report and deposit the amounts withheld in addition to reporting and depositing other employment taxes. See Q/A-16 of this section for rules governing cash reimbursements.

(c) *Noncash fringe benefits exceeding monthly limits.* If the value of noncash qualified transportation fringes exceeds the applicable statutory monthly limit, the employer may elect, for purposes of the FICA, the FUTA, and federal income tax withholding, to treat the noncash taxable fringe benefits as paid on a pay period, quarterly, semiannual, annual, or other basis, provided that the benefits are treated as paid no less frequently than annually.

Q-23. How does section 132(f) interact with other fringe benefit rules?

A-23. For purposes of section 132, the terms working condition fringe and de minimis fringe do not include any qualified transportation fringe under section 132(f). If, however, an employer provides local transportation other than transit passes (without any direct or indirect compensation reduction election), the value of the benefit may be excludable, either totally or partially, under fringe benefit rules other than the qualified transportation fringe rules under section 132(f). See §§ 1.132-6(d)(2)(i) (occasional local transportation fare), 1.132-6(d)(2)(iii) (transportation provided under unusual circumstances), and 1.61-21(k) (valuation of local transportation provided to qualified employees). See also Q/A-4(b) of this section.

Q-24. May qualified transportation fringes be provided to individuals who are partners, 2-percent shareholders of S-corporations, or independent contractors?

A-24. (a) *General rule.* Section 132(f)(5)(E) states that self-employed individuals who are employees within the meaning of section 401(c)(1) are not employees for purposes of section 132(f). Therefore, individuals who are partners, sole proprietors, or other independent contractors are not employees for purposes of section 132(f). In addition, under section 1372(a), 2-percent shareholders of S corporations are treated as partners for fringe benefit purposes. Thus, an individual who is both a 2-percent shareholder of an S corporation and a common law employee of that S corporation is not considered an employee for purposes of section 132(f). However, while section 132(f) does not apply to individuals who are partners, 2-percent shareholders of S corporations, or independent contractors, other exclusions for working condition and de minimis fringes may be available as described in paragraphs (b) and (c) of this Q/A-24. See §§ 1.132-1(b)(2) and 1.132-1(b)(4).

(b) *Transit passes.* The working condition and de minimis fringe exclusions under section 132(a)(3) and (4) are available for transit passes provided to individuals who are partners, 2-percent shareholders, and independent contractors. For example, tokens or farecards provided by a partnership to an individual who is a partner that enable the partner to commute on a public transit system (not including privately-operated van pools) are excludable from the partner's gross income if the value of the tokens and farecards in any month does not exceed the dollar amount specified in § 1.132-6(d)(1). However, if the value of a pass provided in a month exceeds the dollar amount specified in § 1.132-6(d)(1), the full value of the benefit provided (not merely the amount in excess of the dollar amount specified in § 1.132-6(d)(1)) is includible in gross income.

(c) *Parking.* The working condition fringe rules under section 132(d) do not apply to commuter parking. See § 1.132-5(a)(1). However, the de minimis fringe rules under section 132(e) are available for parking provided to individuals who are partners, 2-percent shareholders, or independent contractors that qualifies under the de minimis rules. See § 1.132-6(a) and (b).

(d) *Example.* The following example illustrates the principles of this Q/A-24:

Example. (i) Individual G is a partner in partnership P. Individual G commutes to and from G's office every day and parks free of charge in P's lot.

(ii) In this *Example,* the value of the parking is not excluded under section 132(f), but may be excluded under section 132(e) if the parking is a de minimis fringe under § 1.132-6.

Q-25. What is the effective date of this section?

A-25. (a) Except as provided in paragraph (b) of this Q/A-25, this section is applicable for employee taxable years beginning after December 31, 2001. For this purpose, an employer may assume that the employee taxable year is the calendar year.

(b) The last sentence of paragraph (b)(5) of Q/A-16 of this section (relating to whether transit system vouchers for transit passes are readily available) is applicable for employee taxable years beginning after December 31, 2003. For this purpose, an employer may assume that the employee taxable year is the calendar year.

[Reg. § 1.132-9.]

☐ [T.D. 8933, 1-10-2001 (*corrected* 4-5-2001). *Amended by T.D. 9294,* 10-19-2006.]

[Reg. § 1.133-1T]

§ 1.133-1T. Questions and answers relating to interest on certain loans used to acquire employer securities (Temporary).

Q-1: What does section 133 provide?

A-1: In general, section 133 provides that certain commercial lenders may exclude from gross income fifty percent of the interest received with respect to securities acquisition loans. A securities acquisition loan is any loan to an employee stock ownership plan (ESOP) (as defined in section 4975(e)(7)) that qualifies as an exempt loan under § 54.4975-7 and -11 to the extent that the proceeds are used to acquire employer securities (within the meaning of section 409 (l)) for the ESOP. A loan made to a corporation sponsoring an ESOP (or to a person related to such corporation under section 133(b)(2)) may also qualify as a securities acquisition loan to the extent and for the period that the proceeds are (a) loaned to the corporation's ESOP under a loan that qualifies as an exempt loan under § 54.4975-7 and -11 and that has substantially similar terms as the loan from the commercial lender to the sponsoring corporation, and (b) used to acquire employer securities for the ESOP. The terms of the loan between the commercial lender and the sponsoring corporation (or a related corporation) and the loan between such corporation and the ESOP shall be treated as substantially similar only if the timing and rate at which employer securities would be released from encumbrance if the loan from the commercial lender were the exempt loan under the applicable rule of § 54.4975-7(b)(8) are substantially similar to the timing and rate at which employer securities will actually be released from encumbrance in accordance with such rule. For this purpose, if the loan from the commercial lender to the sponsoring corporation states a variable rate of interest and the loan between the corporation and the ESOP states a fixed rate of interest, whether the terms of the loans are substantially similar shall be determined at the time the obligations are initially issued by taking into account the adjustment interval on the variable rate loan and the maturity of the fixed rate loan. For example, if the rate on the loan from the commercial lender to the sponsoring corporation adjusts each six months and the loan from the corporation to the ESOP has a ten year term, the initial interest rate on the variable rate loan could be compared to the rate on the fixed rate loan by comparing the yields on 6 month and ten year Treasury obligations. Similarly, if the rates on the two loans are based on different compounding assumptions, whether the terms of the loans are substantially similar shall be determined by taking into account the different compounding assumptions. A securities acquisition loan may be evidenced by any note, bond, debenture, or certificate. Also, section 133(b)(2) provides that certain loans between related persons are not securities acquisition loans. In addition, a loan from a commercial lender to an ESOP or sponsoring corporation to purchase employer securities will not be treated as a securities acquisition loan to the extent that such loan is used, either directly or indirectly, to purchase employer securities from any other qualified plan, including any other ESOP, maintained by the employer or any other corporation which is a member of the same controlled group (as defined in section 409(l)(4).

Q-2: What lenders are eligible to receive the fifty percent interest exclusion?

A-2: Under section 133(a), a bank (within the meaning of section 581), an insurance company to which subchapter L applies, or a corporation (other than a subchapter S corporation) actively engaged in the business of lending money may exclude from gross income fifty percent of the interest received with respect to a securities acquisition loan (as defined in Q&A-1 of § 1.133-1T). For purposes of section 133(a)(3), a corporation is actively engaged in the business of lending money if it lends money to the public on a regular and continuing basis (other than in connection with the purchase by the public of goods and services from the lender or a related party). A corporation is not actively engaged in the business of lending money if a predominant share of the original value of the loans it makes to unrelated parties (other than in connection with the purchase by the public of goods and services from the lender or a related party) are securities acquisition loans.

Q-3: May loans which qualify for the fifty percent interest exclusion under section 133 be syndicated to other lending institutions?

A-3: Securities acquisition loans under section 133 may be syndicated to other lending institutions provided that such lending institutions are described in section 133(a)(1), (2) or (3) and the loan was originated by a qualified holder. Subsequent holders of the debt instrument may qualify for the partial interest exclusion of section 133 if such holders satisfy the requirements of section 133 and such loan does not fail to be a securities acquisition loan under section 133(b)(2).

Q-4: When is section 133 effective?

A-4: Section 133 applies to securities acquisition loans made after July 18, 1984, and used to acquire employer securities after July 18, 1984. The provision does not apply to loans made after July 18, 1984, to the extent that such loans are renegotiations, directly or indirectly, of loans outstanding on such date. A loan extended to an ESOP or sponsoring corporation after July 18, 1984, will be treated as a renegotiation of an outstanding loan if the loan proceeds are used to refinance acquisitions of employer securities made prior to July 19, 1984. For example, if an ESOP borrowed money prior to July 19, 1984,

to purchase employer securities and after July 18, 1984, borrows other funds from the same or a different commercial lender to repay the first loan, the second loan will be treated as a renegotiation of an outstanding loan to the extent of the repaid amount. Similarly, if, after July 18, 1984, an ESOP sells employer securities, uses the proceeds to retire a pre-July 19, 1984, loan and obtains a second loan to acquire replacement employer securities, the second loan will be treated as a renegotiation of an outstanding loan. [Temporary Reg. § 1.133-1T.]

☐ [*T.D. 8073, 1-29-86.*]

Tax Exemption Requirements for State and Local Bonds

[Reg. § 1.141-0]

§ 1.141-0. Table of contents.—This section lists the captioned paragraphs contained in §§ 1.141-1 through 1.141-16.

§1.141-16 Effective dates for qualified private activity bond provisions.
  (a) Scope.
  (b) Effective dates.
  (c) Permissive application.
  (d) Certain remedial actions.
    (1) General rule.
    (2) Special rule for allocations of nonqualified bonds.
[Reg. §1.141-0.]

☐ [*T.D. 8712, 1-10-97. Amended by T.D. 8757, 1-21-98; T.D. 8941,* 1-17-2001; *T.D. 9016, 9-19-2002; T.D. 9085, 8-1-2003; T.D. 9150,* 8-12-2004; *T.D. 9234, 12-16-2005, T.D. 9429, 10-20-2008, T.D. 9741,* 10-26-2015 *and T.D. 9777, 7-15-2016.*]

[Reg. §1.141-1]

§1.141-1. Definitions and rules of general application.—(a) *In general.*—For purposes of §§1.141-0 through 1.141-16, the following definitions and rules apply: the definitions in this section, the definitions in §1.150-1, the definition of placed in service in §1.150-2(c), the definition of reasonably required reserve or replacement fund in §1.148-2(f), and the definitions in §1.148-1 of bond year, commingled fund, fixed yield issue, higher yielding investments, investment, investment proceeds, issue price, issuer, nonpurpose investment, purpose investment, qualified guarantee, qualified hedge, reasonable expectations or reasonableness, rebate amount, replacement proceeds, sale proceeds, variable yield issue and yield.

(b) *Certain general definitions.*

Common areas means portions of a facility that are equally available to all users of a facility on the same basis for uses that are incidental to the primary use of the facility. For example, hallways and elevators generally are treated as common areas if they are used by the different lessees of a facility in connection with the primary use of that facility.

Consistently applied means applied uniformly to account for proceeds and other amounts.

Deliberate action is defined in §1.141-2(d)(3).

Discrete portion means a portion of a facility that consists of any separate and discrete portion of a facility to which use is limited, other than common areas. A floor of a building and a portion of a building separated by walls, partitions, or other physical barriers are examples of a discrete portion.

Disposition is defined in §1.141-12(c)(1).

Disposition proceeds is defined in §1.141-12(c)(1).

Essential governmental function is defined in §1.141-5(d)(4)(ii).

Financed means constructed, reconstructed, or acquired with proceeds of an issue.

Governmental bond has the same meaning as in §1.150-1(b), except that, for purposes of §1.141-13, governmental bond is defined in §1.141-13(b)(2)(iv).

Governmental person means a state or local governmental unit as defined in §1.103-1 or any instrumentality thereof. It does not include the United States or any agency or instrumentality thereof.

Hazardous waste remediation bonds is defined in §1.141-4(f)(1).

Measurement period is defined in §1.141-3(g)(2).

Nongovernmental person means a person other than a governmental person.

Output facility means electric and gas generation, transmission, distribution, and related facilities, and water collection, storage, and distribution facilities.

Private business tests means the private business use test and the private security or payment test of section 141(b).

Proceeds means the sale proceeds of an issue (other than those sale proceeds used to retire bonds of the issue that are not deposited in a reasonably required reserve or replacement fund). Proceeds also include any investment proceeds from investments that accrue during the project period (net of rebate amounts attributable to the project period). Disposition proceeds of an issue are treated as proceeds to the extent provided in §1.141-12. The Commissioner may treat any replaced amounts as proceeds.

Project period means the period beginning on the issue date and ending on the date that the project is placed in service. In the case of a multipurpose issue, the issuer may elect to treat the project period for the entire issue as ending on either the expiration of the temporary period described in §1.148-2(e)(2) or the end of the fifth bond year after the issue date.

Public utility property means public utility property as defined in section 168(i)(10).

Qualified bond means a qualified bond as defined in section 141(e).

Renewal option means a provision under which either party has a legally enforceable right to renew the contract. Thus, for example, a provision under which a contract is automatically renewed for 1-year periods absent cancellation by either party is not a renewal option (even if it is expected to be renewed).

Replaced amounts means replacement proceeds other than amounts that are treated as replacement proceeds solely because they are sinking funds or pledged funds.

Weighted average maturity is determined under section 147(b).

Weighted average reasonably expected economic life is determined under section 147(b). The reasonably expected economic life of property may be determined by reference to the class life of the property under section 168.

(c) *Elections.*—Elections must be made in writing on or before the issue date and retained as part of the bond documents, and, once made, may not be revoked without the permission of the Commissioner.

(d) *Related parties.*—Except as otherwise provided, all related parties are treated as one person and any reference to "person" includes any related party.

(e) *Partnerships.*—A partnership (as defined in section 7701(a)(2)) is treated as an aggregate of its partners, rather than as an entity. [Reg. §1.141-1.]

☐ [Reg. §1.141-1, issued under Code Sec. 141 as it existed prior to repeal by P.L. 95-30, was removed from the CFR, and Reg. §1.141-1, above, was adopted by *T.D. 8712, 1-10-97. Amended by T.D. 9234, 12-16-2005, T.D. 9741, 10-26-2015 and T.D. 9777, 7-15-2016.*]

[Reg. §1.141-2]

§1.141-2. Private activity bond tests.—(a) *Overview.*—Interest on a private activity bond is not excludable from gross income under section 103(a) unless the bond is a qualified bond. The purpose of the private activity bond tests of section 141 is to limit the volume of tax-exempt bonds that finance the activities of nongovernmental persons, without regard to whether a financing actually transfers benefits of tax-exempt financing to a nongovernmental person. The private activity bond tests serve to identify arrangements that have the potential to transfer the benefits of tax-exempt financing, as well as arrangements that actually transfer these benefits. The regulations under section 141 may not be applied in a manner that is inconsistent with these purposes.

(b) *Scope.*—Sections 1.141-0 through 1.141-16 apply generally for purposes of the private activity bond limitations under section 141.

(c) *General definition of private activity bond.*—Under section 141, bonds are private activity bonds if they meet either the private business use test and private security or payment test of section 141(b) or the private loan financing test of section 141(c). The private business use test and private security or payment tests are described in §§1.141-3 and 1.141-4. The private loan financing test is described in §1.141-5.

(d) *Reasonable expectations and deliberate actions.*—(1) *In general.*—An issue is an issue of private activity bonds if the issuer reasonably expects, as of the issue date, that the issue will meet either the private business tests or the private loan financing test. An issue is also an issue of private activity bonds if the issuer takes a deliberate action, subsequent to the issue date, that causes the conditions of either the private business tests or the private loan financing test to be met.

(2) *Reasonable expectations test.*—(i) *In general.*—In general, the reasonable expectations test must take into account reasonable expectations about events and actions over the entire stated term of an issue.

(ii) *Special rule for issues with mandatory redemption provisions.*—An action that is reasonably expected, as of the issue date, to occur after the issue date and to cause either the private business tests or the private loan financing test to be met may be disregarded for purposes of those tests if—

(A) The issuer reasonably expects, as of the issue date, that the financed property will be used for a governmental purpose for a substantial period before the action;

(B) The issuer is required to redeem all nonqualifying bonds (regardless of the amount of disposition proceeds actually received) within 6 months of the date of the action;

(C) The issuer does not enter into any arrangement with a nongovernmental person, as of the issue date, with respect to that specific action; and

(D) The mandatory redemption of bonds meets all of the conditions for remedial action under §1.141-12(a).

(3) *Deliberate action defined.*—(i) *In general.*—Except as otherwise provided in this paragraph (d)(3), a deliberate action is any action taken by the issuer that is within its control. An intent to violate the requirements of section 141 is not necessary for an action to be deliberate.

(ii) *Safe harbor exceptions.*—An action is not treated as a deliberate action if—

(A) It would be treated as an involuntary or compulsory conversion under section 1033; or

(B) It is taken in response to a regulatory directive made by the federal government. See §1.141-7(g)(4).

(4) *Special rule for dispositions of personal property in the ordinary course of an established governmental program.*—(i) *In general.*—Dispositions of personal property in the ordinary course of an established governmental program are not treated as deliberate actions if—

(A) The weighted average maturity of the bonds financing that personal property is not greater than 120 percent of the reasonably expected actual use of that property for governmental purposes;

(B) The issuer reasonably expects on the issue date that the fair market value of that property on the date of disposition will be not greater than 25 percent of its cost; and

(C) The property is no longer suitable for its governmental purposes on the date of disposition.

(ii) *Reasonable expectations test.*—The reasonable expectation that a disposition described in paragraph (d)(4)(i) of this section may occur in the ordinary course while the bonds are outstanding will not cause the issue to meet the private activity bond tests if the issuer is required to deposit amounts received from the disposition in a commingled fund with substantial tax or other governmental revenues and the issuer reasonably expects to spend the amounts on governmental programs within 6 months from the date of commingling.

(iii) *Separate issue treatment.*—An issuer may treat the bonds properly allocable to the personal property eligible for this exception as a separate issue under §1.150-1(c)(3).

(5) *Special rule for general obligation bond programs that finance a large number of separate purposes.*—The determination of whether bonds of an issue are private activity bonds may be based solely on the issuer's reasonable expectations as of the issue date if all of the requirements of paragraphs (d)(5)(i) through (vii) of this section are met.

(i) The issue is an issue of general obligation bonds of a general purpose governmental unit that finances at least 25 separate purposes (as defined in §1.150-1(c)(3)) and does not predominantly finance fewer than 4 separate purposes.

(ii) The issuer has adopted a fund method of accounting for its general governmental purposes that makes tracing the bond proceeds to specific expenditures unreasonably burdensome.

(iii) The issuer reasonably expects on the issue date to allocate all of the net proceeds of the issue to capital expenditures within 6 months of the issue date and adopts reasonable procedures to verify that net proceeds are in fact so expended. A program to randomly spot check that 10 percent of the net proceeds were so expended generally is a reasonable verification procedure for this purpose.

(iv) The issuer reasonably expects on the issue date to expend all of the net proceeds of the issue before expending proceeds of a subsequent issue of similar general obligation bonds.

(v) The issuer reasonably expects on the issue date that it will not make any loans to nongovernmental persons with the proceeds of the issue.

(vi) The issuer reasonably expects on the issue date that the capital expenditures that it could make during the 6-month period beginning on the issue date with the net proceeds of the issue that would not meet the private business tests are not less than 125 percent of the capital expenditures to be financed with the net proceeds of the issue.

(vii) The issuer reasonably expects on the issue date that the weighted average maturity of the issue is not greater than 120 percent of the weighted average reasonably expected economic life of the capital expenditures financed with the issue. To determine reasonably expected economic life for this purpose an issuer may use reasonable estimates based on the type of expenditures made from a fund.

(e) *When a deliberate action occurs.*—A deliberate action occurs on the date the issuer enters into a binding contract with a nongovernmental person for use of the financed property that is not subject to any material contingencies.

(f) *Certain remedial actions.*—See §1.141-12 for certain remedial actions that prevent a deliberate action with respect to property financed by an issue from causing that issue to meet the private business use test or the private loan financing test.

(g) *Examples.*—The following examples illustrate the application of this section:

Example 1. Involuntary action. City B issues bonds to finance the purchase of land. On the issue date, B reasonably expects that it will be the sole user of the land for the entire term of the bonds. Subsequently, the federal government acquires the land in a condemnation action. B sets aside the condemnation proceeds to pay debt service on the bonds but does not redeem them on their first call date. The bonds are not private activity bonds because B has not taken a deliberate action after the issue date. See, however, §1.141-14(b), *Example 2.*

Example 2. Reasonable expectations test—involuntary action. The facts are the same as in *Example 1*, except that, on the issue date, B reasonably expects that the federal government will acquire the land in a condemnation action during the term of the bonds. On the issue date, the present value of the amount that B reasonably expects to receive from the federal government is greater than 10 percent of the present value of the debt service on the bonds. The terms of the bonds do not require that the bonds be redeemed within 6 months of the acquisition by the federal government. The bonds are private activity bonds because the issuer expects as of the issue date that the private business tests will be met.

Example 3. Reasonable expectations test—mandatory redemption. City C issues bonds to rehabilitate an existing hospital that it currently owns. On the issue date of the bonds, C reasonably expects that the hospital will be used for a governmental purpose for a substantial period. On the issue date, C also plans to construct a new hospital, but the placed in service date of that new hospital is uncertain. C reasonably expects that, when the new hospital is placed in service, it will sell or lease the rehabilitated hospital to a private hospital corporation. The bond documents require that the bonds must be redeemed within 6 months of the sale or lease of the rehabilitated hospital (regardless of the amount actually received from the sale). The bonds meet the reasonable expectations requirement of the private activity bond tests if the mandatory redemption of bonds meets all of the conditions for a remedial action under §1.141-12(a).

Example 4. Dispositions in the ordinary course of an established governmental program. City D issues bonds with a weighted average maturity of 6 years for the acquisition of police cars. D reasonably expects on the issue date that the police cars will be used solely by its police department, except that, in the ordinary course of its police operations, D sells its police cars to a taxicab corporation after 5 years of use because they are no longer suitable for police use. Further, D reasonably expects that the value of the police cars when they are no longer suitable for police use will be no more than 25 percent of cost. D subsequently sells 20 percent of the police cars after only 3 years of actual use. At that time, D deposits the proceeds from the sale of the police cars in a commingled fund with substantial tax revenues and reasonably expects to spend the proceeds on governmental programs within 6 months of the date of deposit. D does not trace the actual use of these commingled amounts. The sale of the police cars does not cause the private activity bond tests to be met because the requirements of paragraph (d)(4) of this section are met.

[Reg. §1.141-2.]

☐ [*T.D. 8712, 1-10-97. Amended by T.D. 8757, 1-21-98 and T.D. 9016, 9-19-2002.*]

[Reg. §1.141-3]

§1.141-3. Definition of private business use.—(a) *General rule.*—(1) *In general.*—The private business use test relates to the use of the proceeds of an issue. The 10 percent private business use test of section 141(b)(1) is met if more than 10 percent of the proceeds of an issue is used in a trade or business of a nongovernmental person. For this purpose, the use of financed property is treated as the direct use of proceeds. Any activity carried on by a person other than a natural person is treated as a trade or business. Unless the context or a provision clearly requires otherwise, this section also applies to the private business use test under sections 141(b)(3) (unrelated or disproportionate use), 141(b)(4) ($15 million limitation for certain output facilities), and 141(b)(5) (the coordination with the volume cap where the nonqualified amount exceeds $15 million).

(2) *Indirect use.*—In determining whether an issue meets the private business use test, it is necessary to look to both the indirect and direct uses of proceeds. For example, a facility is treated as being used for a private business use if it is leased to a nongovernmental person and subleased to a governmental person or if it is leased to a governmental person and then subleased to a nongovernmental person, provided that in each case the nongovernmental person's use is in a trade or business. Similarly, the issuer's use of the proceeds to engage in a series of financing transactions for property to be used by nongovernmental persons in their trades or businesses may cause the private business use test to be met. In addition, proceeds are treated as used in the trade or business of a nongovernmental person if a nongovernmental person, as a result of a single transaction or a series of related transactions, uses property acquired with the proceeds of an issue.

(3) *Aggregation of private business use.*—The use of proceeds by all nongovernmental persons is aggregated to determine whether the private business use test is met.

(b) *Types of private business use arrangements.*—(1) *In general.*—Both actual and beneficial use by a nongovernmental person may be treated as private business use. In most cases, the private business use test is met only if a nongovernmental person has special legal entitlements to use the financed property under an arrangement with the issuer. In general, a nongovernmental person is treated as a private business user of proceeds and financed property as a result of ownership; actual or beneficial use of property pursuant to a lease, or a management or incentive payment contract; or certain other arrangements such as a take or pay or other output-type contract.

(2) *Ownership.*—Except as provided in paragraph (d)(1) or (d)(2) of this section, ownership by a nongovernmental person of financed property is private business use of that property. For this purpose, ownership refers to ownership for federal income tax purposes.

(3) *Leases.*—Except as provided in paragraph (d) of this section, the lease of financed property to a nongovernmental person is private business use of that property. For this purpose, any arrangement that is properly characterized as a lease for federal income tax purposes is treated as a lease. In determining whether a management contract is properly characterized as a lease, it is necessary to consider all of the facts and circumstances, including the following factors—

(i) The degree of control over the property that is exercised by a nongovernmental person; and

(ii) Whether a nongovernmental person bears risk of loss of the financed property.

(4) *Management contracts.*—(i) *Facts and circumstances test.*—Except as provided in paragraph (d) of this section, a management contract (within the meaning of paragraph (b)(4)(ii) of this section) with respect to financed property may result in private business use of that property, based on all of the facts and circumstances. A management contract with respect to financed property generally results in private business use of that property if the contract provides for compensation for services rendered with compensation based, in whole or in part, on a share of net profits from the operation of the facility.

(ii) *Management contract defined.*—For purposes of this section, a management contract is a management, service, or incentive payment contract between a governmental person and a service provider under which the service provider provides services involving all, a portion of, or any function of, a facility. For example, a contract for the provision of management services for an entire hospital, a contract for management services for a specific department of a hospital, and an incentive payment contract for physician services to patients of a hospital are each treated as a management contract.

(iii) *Arrangements generally not treated as management contracts.*—The arrangements described in paragraphs (b)(4)(iii)(A) through (D) of this section generally are not treated as management contracts that give rise to private business use.

(A) Contracts for services that are solely incidental to the primary governmental function or functions of a financed facility (for example, contracts for janitorial, office equipment repair, hospital billing, or similar services).

(B) The mere granting of admitting privileges by a hospital to a doctor, even if those privileges are conditioned on the provision of de minimis services, if those privileges are available to all qualified physicians in the area, consistent with the size and nature of its facilities.

(C) A contract to provide for the operation of a facility or system of facilities that consists predominantly of public utility property, if the only compensation is the reimbursement of actual and direct expenses of the service provider and reasonable administrative overhead expenses of the service provider.

(D) A contract to provide for services, if the only compensation is the reimbursement of the service provider for actual and direct expenses paid by the service provider to unrelated parties.

(iv) *Management contracts that are properly treated as other types of private business use.*—A management contract with respect to financed property results in private business use of that property if the service provider is treated as the lessee or owner of financed property for federal income tax purposes, unless an exception under paragraph (d) of this section applies to the arrangement.

(5) *Output contracts.*—See § 1.141-7 for special rules for contracts for the purchase of output of output facilities.

(6) *Research agreements.*—(i) *Facts and circumstances test.*—Except as provided in paragraph (d) of this section, an agreement by a nongovernmental person to sponsor research performed by a governmental person may result in private business use of the property used for the research, based on all of the facts and circumstances.

(ii) *Research agreements that are properly treated as other types of private business use.*—A research agreement with respect to financed property results in private business use of that property if the sponsor is treated as the lessee or owner of financed property for federal income tax purposes, unless an exception under paragraph (d) of this section applies to the arrangement.

(7) *Other actual or beneficial use.*—(i) *In general.*—Any other arrangement that conveys special legal entitlements for beneficial use of bond proceeds or of financed property that are comparable to special legal entitlements described in paragraphs (b)(2), (3), (4), (5), or (6) of this section results in private business use. For example, an arrangement that conveys priority rights to the use or capacity of a facility generally results in private business use.

(ii) *Special rule for facilities not used by the general public.*—In the case of financed property that is not available for use by the general public (within the meaning of paragraph (c) of this section), private business use may be established solely on the basis of a special economic benefit to one or more nongovernmental persons, even if those nongovernmental persons have no special legal entitlements to use of the property. In determining whether special economic benefit gives rise to private business use it is necessary to consider all of the facts and circumstances, including one or more of the following factors—

(A) Whether the financed property is functionally related or physically proximate to property used in the trade or business of a nongovernmental person;

(B) Whether only a small number of nongovernmental persons receive the special economic benefit; and

(C) Whether the cost of the financed property is treated as depreciable by any nongovernmental person.

(c) *Exception for general public use.*—(1) *In general.*—Use as a member of the general public (general public use) is not private business use. Use of financed property by nongovernmental persons in their trades or businesses is treated as general public use only if the property is intended to be available and in fact is reasonably available for use on the same basis by natural persons not engaged in a trade or business.

(2) *Use on the same basis.*—In general, use under an arrangement that conveys priority rights or other preferential benefits is not use on the same basis as the general public. Arrangements providing for use that is available to the general public at no charge or on the basis of rates that are generally applicable and uniformly applied do not convey priority rights or other preferential benefits. For this purpose, rates may be treated as generally applicable and uniformly applied even if—

(i) Different rates apply to different classes of users, such as volume purchasers, if the differences in rates are customary and reasonable; or

(ii) A specially negotiated rate arrangement is entered into, but only if the user is prohibited by federal law from paying the generally applicable rates, and the rates established are as comparable as reasonably possible to the generally applicable rates.

(3) *Long-term arrangements not treated as general public use.*—An arrangement is not treated as general public use if the term of the use under the arrangement, including all renewal options, is greater than 200 days. For this purpose, a right of first refusal to renew use under the arrangement is not treated as a renewal option if—

(i) The compensation for the use under the arrangement is redetermined at generally applicable, fair market value rates that are in effect at the time of renewal; and

(ii) The use of the financed property under the same or similar arrangements is predominantly by natural persons who are not engaged in a trade or business.

(4) *Relation to other use.*—Use of financed property by the general public does not prevent the proceeds from being used for a private business use because of other use under this section.

(d) *Other exceptions.*—(1) *Agents.*—Use of proceeds by nongovernmental persons solely in their capacity as agents of a governmental person is not private business use. For example, use by a nongovernmental person that issues obligations on behalf of a governmental person is not private business use to the extent the nongovernmental person's use of proceeds is in its capacity as an agent of the governmental person.

(2) *Use incidental to financing arrangements.*—Use by a nongovernmental person that is solely incidental to a financing arrangement

is not private business use. A use is solely incidental to a financing arrangement only if the nongovernmental person has no substantial rights to use bond proceeds or financed property other than as an agent of the bondholders. For example, a nongovernmental person that acts solely as an owner of title in a sale and leaseback financing transaction with a city generally is not a private business user of property leased to the city, provided that the nongovernmental person has assigned all of its rights to use the leased facility to the trustee for the bondholders upon default by the city. Similarly, bond trustees, servicers, and guarantors are generally not treated as private business users.

(3) *Exceptions for arrangements other than arrangements resulting in ownership of financed property by a nongovernmental person.*— (i) *Arrangements not available for use on the same basis by natural persons not engaged in a trade or business.*—Use by a nongovernmental person pursuant to an arrangement, other than an arrangement resulting in ownership of financed property by a nongovernmental person, is not private business use if—

(A) The term of the use under the arrangement, including all renewal options, is not longer than 100 days;

(B) The arrangement would be treated as general public use, except that it is not available for use on the same basis by natural persons not engaged in a trade or business because generally applicable and uniformly applied rates are not reasonably available to natural persons not engaged in a trade or business; and

(C) The property is not financed for a principal purpose of providing that property for use by that nongovernmental person.

(ii) *Negotiated arm's-length arrangements.*—Use by a nongovernmental person pursuant to an arrangement, other than an arrangement resulting in ownership of financed property by a nongovernmental person, is not private business use if—

(A) The term of the use under the arrangement, including all renewal options, is not longer than 50 days;

(B) The arrangement is a negotiated arm's-length arrangement, and compensation under the arrangement is at fair market value; and

(C) The property is not financed for a principal purpose of providing that property for use by that nongovernmental person.

(4) *Temporary use by developers.*—Use during an initial development period by a developer of an improvement that carries out an essential governmental function is not private business use if the issuer and the developer reasonably expect on the issue date to proceed with all reasonable speed to develop the improvement and property benefited by that improvement and to transfer the improvement to a governmental person, and if the improvement is in fact transferred to a governmental person promptly after the property benefited by the improvement is developed.

(5) *Incidental use.*—(i) *General rule.*—Incidental uses of a financed facility are disregarded, to the extent that those uses do not exceed 2.5 percent of the proceeds of the issue used to finance the facility. A use of a facility by a nongovernmental person is incidental if—

(A) Except for vending machines, pay telephones, kiosks, and similar uses, the use does not involve the transfer to the nongovernmental person of possession and control of space that is separated from other areas of the facility by walls, partitions, or other physical barriers, such as a night gate affixed to a structural component of a building (a nonpossessory use);

(B) The nonpossessory use is not functionally related to any other use of the facility by the same person (other than a different nonpossessory use); and

(C) All nonpossessory uses of the facility do not, in the aggregate, involve the use of more than 2.5 percent of the facility.

(ii) *Illustrations.*—Incidental uses may include pay telephones, vending machines, advertising displays, and use for television cameras, but incidental uses may not include output purchases.

(6) *Qualified improvements.*—Proceeds that provide a governmentally owned improvement to a governmentally owned building (including its structural components and land functionally related and subordinate to the building) are not used for a private business use if—

(i) The building was placed in service more than 1 year before the construction or acquisition of the improvement is begun;

(ii) The improvement is not an enlargement of the building or an improvement of interior space occupied exclusively for any private business use;

(iii) No portion of the improved building or any payments in respect of the improved building are taken into account under section 141(b)(2)(A) (the private security test); and

(iv) No more than 15 percent of the improved building is used for a private business use.

(e) *Special rule for tax assessment bonds.*—In the case of a tax assessment bond that satisfies the requirements of §1.141-5(d), the loan (or deemed loan) of the proceeds to the borrower paying the assessment is disregarded in determining whether the private business use test is met. However, the use of the loan proceeds is not disregarded in determining whether the private business use test is met.

(f) *Examples.*—The following examples illustrate the application of paragraphs (a) through (e) of this section. In each example, assume that the arrangements described are the only arrangements with nongovernmental persons for use of the financed property.

Example 1. Nongovernmental ownership. State A issues 20-year bonds to purchase land and equip and construct a factory. A then enters into an arrangement with Corporation X to sell the factory to X on an installment basis while the bonds are outstanding. The issue meets the private business use test because a nongovernmental person owns the financed facility. See also §1.141-2 (relating to the private activity bond tests), and §1.141-5 (relating to the private loan financing test).

Example 2. Lease to a nongovernmental person. (i) The facts are the same as in *Example 1*, except that A enters into an arrangement with X to lease the factory to X for 3 years rather than to sell it to X. The lease payments will be made annually and will be based on the tax-exempt interest rate on the bonds. The issue meets the private business use test because a nongovernmental person leases the financed facility. See also §1.141-14 (relating to anti-abuse rules).

(ii) The facts are the same as in *Example 2(i)*, except that the annual payments made by X will equal fair rental value of the facility and exceed the amount necessary to pay debt service on the bonds for the 3 years of the lease. The issue meets the private business use test because a nongovernmental person leases the financed facility and the test does not require that the benefits of tax-exempt financing be passed through to the nongovernmental person.

Example 3. Management contract in substance a lease. City L issues 30-year bonds to finance the construction of a city hospital. L enters into a 15-year contract with M, a nongovernmental person that operates a health maintenance organization relating to the treatment of M's members at L's hospital. The contract provides for reasonable fixed compensation to M for services rendered with no compensation based, in whole or in part, on a share of net profits from the operation of the hospital. However, the contract also provides that 30 percent of the capacity of the hospital will be exclusively available to M's members and M will bear the risk of loss of that portion of the capacity of the hospital so that, under all of the facts and circumstances, the contract is properly characterized as a lease for federal income tax purposes. The issue meets the private business use test because a nongovernmental person leases the financed facility.

Example 4. Ownership of title in substance a leasehold interest. Nonprofit corporation R issues bonds on behalf of City P to finance the construction of a hospital. R will own legal title to the hospital. In addition, R will operate the hospital, but R is not treated as an agent of P in its capacity as operator of the hospital. P has certain rights to the hospital that establish that it is properly treated as the owner of the property for federal income tax purposes. P does not have rights, however, to directly control operation of the hospital while R owns legal title to it and operates it. The issue meets the private business use test because the arrangement provides a nongovernmental person an interest in the financed facility that is comparable to a leasehold interest. See paragraphs (a)(2) and (b)(7)(i) of this section.

Example 5. Rights to control use of property treated as private business use—parking lot. Corporation C and City D enter into a plan to finance the construction of a parking lot adjacent to C's factory. Pursuant to the plan, C conveys the site for the parking lot to D for a nominal amount, subject to a covenant running with the land that the property be used only for a parking lot. In addition, D agrees that C will have the right to approve rates charged by D for use of the parking lot. D issues bonds to finance construction of the parking lot on the site. The parking lot will be available for use by the general public on the basis of rates that are generally applicable and uniformly applied. The issue meets the private business use test because a nongovernmental person has special legal entitlements for beneficial use of the financed facility that are comparable to an ownership interest. See paragraph (b)(7)(i) of this section.

Example 6. Other actual or beneficial use—hydroelectric enhancements. J, a political subdivision, owns and operates a hydroelectric generation plant and related facilities. Pursuant to a take or pay contract, J sells 15 percent of the output of the plant to Corporation K, an investor-owned utility. K is treated as a private business user of the plant. Under the license issued to J for operation of the plant, J is required by federal regulations to construct and operate various facilities for the preservation of fish and for public recreation. J issues its obligations to finance the fish preservation and public recreation facilities.

K has no special legal entitlements for beneficial use of the financed facilities. The fish preservation facilities are functionally related to the operation of the plant. The recreation facilities are available to natural persons on a short-term basis according to generally applicable and uniformly applied rates. Under paragraph (c) of this section, the recreation facilities are treated as used by the general public. Under paragraph (b)(7) of this section, K's use is not treated as private business use of the recreation facilities because K has no special legal entitlements for beneficial use of the recreation facilities. The fish preservation facilities are not of a type reasonably available for use on the same basis by natural persons not engaged in a trade or business. Under all of the facts and circumstances (including the functional relationship of the fish preservation facilities to property used in K's trade or business) under paragraph (b)(7)(ii) of this section, K derives a special economic benefit from the fish preservation facilities. Therefore, K's private business use may be established solely on the basis of that special economic benefit, and K's use of the fish preservation facilities is treated as private business use.

Example 7. Other actual or beneficial use—pollution control facilities. City B issues obligations to finance construction of a specialized pollution control facility on land that it owns adjacent to a factory owned by Corporation N. B will own and operate the pollution control facility, and N will have no special legal entitlements to use the facility. B, however, reasonably expects that N will be the only user of the facility. The facility will not be reasonably available for use on the same basis by natural persons not engaged in a trade or business. Under paragraph (b)(7)(ii) of this section, because under all of the facts and circumstances the facility is functionally related and is physically proximate to property used in N's trade or business, N derives a special economic benefit from the facility. Therefore, N's private business use may be established solely on the basis of that special economic benefit, and N's use is treated as private business use of the facility. See paragraph (b)(7)(ii) of this section.

Example 8. General public use—airport runway. (i) City I issues bonds and uses all of the proceeds to finance construction of a runway at a new city-owned airport. The runway will be available for take-off and landing by any operator of an aircraft desiring to use the airport, including general aviation operators who are natural persons not engaged in a trade or business. It is reasonably expected that most of the actual use of the runway will be by private air carriers (both charter airlines and commercial airlines) in connection with their use of the airport terminals leased by those carriers. These leases for the use of terminal space provide no priority rights or other preferential benefits to the air carriers for use of the runway. Moreover, under the leases the lease payments are determined without taking into account the revenues generated by runway landing fees (that is, the lease payments are not determined on a "residual" basis). Although the lessee air carriers receive a special economic benefit from the use of the runway, this economic benefit is not sufficient to cause the air carriers to be private business users, because the runway is available for general public use. The issue does not meet the private business use test. See paragraphs (b)(7)(ii) and (c) of this section.

(ii) The facts are the same as in *Example 8(i)*, except that the runway will be available for use only by private air carriers. The use by these private air carriers is not general public use, because the runway is not reasonably available for use on the same basis by natural persons not engaged in a trade or business. Depending on all of the facts and circumstances, including whether there are only a small number of lessee private air carriers, the issue may meet the private business use test solely because the private air carriers receive a special economic benefit from the runway. See paragraph (b)(7)(ii) of this section.

(iii) The facts are the same as in *Example 8(i)*, except that the lease payments under the leases with the private air carriers are determined on a residual basis by taking into account the net revenues generated by runway landing fees. These leases cause the private business use test to be met with respect to the runway because they are arrangements that convey special legal entitlements to the financed facility to nongovernmental persons. See paragraph (b)(7)(i) of this section.

Example 9. General public use—airport parking garage. City S issues bonds and uses all of the proceeds to finance construction of a city-owned parking garage at the city-owned airport. S reasonably expects that more than 10 percent of the actual use of the parking garage will be by employees of private air carriers (both charter airlines and commercial airlines) in connection with their use of the airport terminals leased by those carriers. The air carriers' use of the parking garage, however, will be on the same basis as passengers and other members of the general public using the airport. The leases for the use of the terminal space provide no priority rights to the air carriers for use of the parking garage, and the lease payments are determined without taking into account the revenues generated by the parking garage. Although the lessee air carriers receive a special economic benefit from the use of the parking garage, this economic benefit is not sufficient to cause the air carriers to be private business

users, because the parking garage is available for general public use. The issue does not meet the private business use test. See paragraphs (b)(7)(ii) and (c) of this section.

Example 10. Long-term arrangements not treated as general public use—insurance fund. Authority T deposits all of the proceeds of its bonds in its insurance fund and invests all of those proceeds in tax-exempt bonds. The insurance fund provides insurance to a large number of businesses and natural persons not engaged in a trade or business. Each participant receives insurance for a term of 1 year. The use by the participants, other than participants that are natural persons not engaged in a trade or business, is treated as private business use of the proceeds of the bonds because the participants have special legal entitlements to the use of bond proceeds, even though the contractual rights are not necessarily properly characterized as ownership, leasehold, or similar interests listed in paragraph (b) of this section. Use of the bond proceeds is not treated as general public use because the term of the insurance is greater than 200 days. See paragraphs (b)(7)(i) and (c)(3) of this section.

Example 11. General public use—port road. Highway Authority W uses all of the proceeds of its bonds to construct a 25-mile road to connect an industrial port owned by Corporation Y with existing roads owned and operated by W. Other than the port, the nearest residential or commercial development to the new road is 12 miles away. There is no reasonable expectation that development will occur in the area surrounding the new road. W and Y enter into no arrangement (either by contract or ordinance) that conveys special legal entitlements to Y for the use of the road. Use of the road will be available without restriction to all users, including natural persons who are not engaged in a trade or business. The issue does not meet the private business use test because the road is treated as used only by the general public.

Example 12. General public use of governmentally owned hotel. State Q issues bonds to purchase land and construct a hotel for use by the general public (that is, tourists, visitors, and business travelers). The bond documents provide that Q will own and operate the project for the term of the bonds. Q will not enter into a lease or license with any user for use of rooms for a period longer than 200 days (although users may actually use rooms for consecutive periods in excess of 200 days). Use of the hotel by hotel guests who are travelling in connection with trades or businesses of nongovernmental persons is not a private business use of the hotel by these persons because the hotel is intended to be available and in fact is reasonably available for use on the same basis by natural persons not engaged in a trade or business. See paragraph (c)(1) of this section.

Example 13. General public use with rights of first refusal. Authority V uses all of the proceeds of its bonds to construct a parking garage. At least 90 percent of the spaces in the garage will be available to the general public on a monthly first-come, first-served basis. V reasonably expects that the spaces will be predominantly leased to natural persons not engaged in a trade or business who have priority rights to renew their spaces at then current fair market value rates. More than 10 percent of the spaces will be leased to nongovernmental persons acting in a trade or business. These leases are not treated as arrangements with a term of use greater than 200 days. The rights to renew are not treated as renewal options because the compensation for the spaces is redetermined at generally applicable, fair market value rates that will be in effect at the time of renewal and the use of the spaces under similar arrangements is predominantly by natural persons who are not engaged in a trade or business. The issue does not meet the private business use test because at least 90 percent of the use of the parking garage is general public use. See paragraph (c)(3) of this section.

Example 14. General public use with a specially negotiated rate agreement with agency of United States. G, a sewage collection and treatment district, operates facilities that were financed with its bonds. F, an agency of the United States, has a base located within G. Approximately 20 percent of G's facilities are used to treat sewage produced by F under a specially negotiated rate agreement. Under the specially negotiated rate agreement, G uses its best efforts to charge F as closely as possible the same amount for its use of G's services as its other customers pay for the same amount of services, although those other customers pay for services based on standard district charges and tax levies. F is prohibited by federal law from paying for the services based on those standard district charges and tax levies. The use of G's facilities by F is on the same basis as the general public. See paragraph (c)(2)(ii) of this section.

Example 15. Arrangements not available for use by natural persons not engaged in a trade or business—federal use of prisons. Authority E uses all of the proceeds of its bonds to construct a prison. E contracts with federal agency F to house federal prisoners on a space-available, first-come, first-served basis, pursuant to which F will be charged approximately the same amount for each prisoner as other persons that enter into similar transfer agreements. It is reasonably expected that other persons will enter into similar agreements. The term of the use under the contract is not longer than 100 days, and F has no right to renew, although E reasonably expects to renew the contract indefinitely. The prison is not financed for a principal purpose of providing the prison for use by F. It is reasonably expected that during the term of the bonds, more than 10 percent of the prisoners at the prison will be federal prisoners. F's use of the facility is not general public use because this type of use (leasing space for prisoners) is not available for use on the same basis by natural persons not engaged in a trade or business. The issue does not meet the private business use test, however, because the leases satisfy the exception of paragraph (d)(3)(i) of this section.

Example 16. Negotiated arm's-length arrangements—auditorium reserved in advance. (i) City Z issues obligations to finance the construction of a municipal auditorium that it will own and operate. The use of the auditorium will be open to anyone who wishes to use it for a short period of time on a rate-scale basis. Z reasonably expects that the auditorium will be used by schools, church groups, sororities, and numerous commercial organizations. Corporation H, a nongovernmental person, enters into an arm's-length arrangement with Z to use the auditorium for 1 week for each year for a 10-year period (a total of 70 days), pursuant to which H will be charged a specific price reflecting fair market value. On the date the contract is entered into, Z has not established generally applicable rates for future years. Even though the auditorium is not financed for a principal purpose of providing use of the auditorium to H, H is not treated as using the auditorium as a member of the general public because its use is not on the same basis as the general public. Because the term of H's use of the auditorium is longer than 50 days, the arrangement does not meet the exception under paragraph (d)(3)(ii) of this section.

(ii) The facts are the same as in *Example 16(i)*, except that H will enter into an arm's-length arrangement with Z to use the auditorium for 1 week for each year for a 4-year period (a total of 28 days), pursuant to which H will be charged a specific price reflecting fair market value. H is not treated as a private business user of the auditorium because its contract satisfies the exception of paragraph (d)(3)(ii) of this section for negotiated arm's-length arrangements.

(g) *Measurement of private business use.*—(1) *In general.*—In general, the private business use of proceeds is allocated to property under §1.141-6. The amount of private business use of that property is determined according to the average percentage of private business use of that property during the measurement period.

(2) *Measurement period.*—(i) *General rule.*—Except as provided in this paragraph (g)(2), the measurement period of property financed by an issue begins on the later of the issue date of that issue or the date the property is placed in service and ends on the earlier of the last date of the reasonably expected economic life of the property or the latest maturity date of any bond of the issue financing the property (determined without regard to any optional redemption dates). In general, the period of reasonably expected economic life of the property for this purpose is based on reasonable expectations as of the issue date.

(ii) *Special rule for refundings of short-term obligations.*—For an issue of short-term obligations that the issuer reasonably expects to refund with a long-term financing (such as bond anticipation notes), the measurement period is based on the latest maturity date of any bond of the last refunding issue with respect to the financed property (determined without regard to any optional redemption dates).

(iii) *Special rule for reasonably expected mandatory redemptions.*—If an issuer reasonably expects on the issue date that an action will occur during the term of the bonds to cause either the private business tests or the private loan financing test to be met and is required to redeem bonds to meet the reasonable expectations test of §1.141-2(d)(2), the measurement period ends on the reasonably expected redemption date.

(iv) *Special rule for ownership by a nongovernmental person.*—The amount of private business use resulting from ownership by a nongovernmental person is the greatest percentage of private business use in any 1-year period.

(v) *Special rule for partners that are nongovernmental persons.*—(A) The amount of private business use by a nongovernmental person resulting from the use of property by a partnership in which that nongovernmental person is a partner is that nongovernmental partner's share of the amount of use of the property by the partnership. For this purpose, except as otherwise provided in paragraph (g)(2)(v)(B) of this section, a nongovernmental partner's share of the partnership's use of the property is the nongovernmental partner's greatest percentage share under section 704(b) of any partnership item of income, gain, loss, deduction, or credit attributable to the period that the partnership uses the property during the measurement period. For example, if a partnership has a nongovernmental partner and that partner's share of partnership items varies, with the

greatest share being 25 percent, then that nongovernmental partner's share of the partnership's use of property is 25 percent.

(B) An issuer may determine a nongovernmental partner's share of the partnership's use of the property under guidance published in the Internal Revenue Bulletin (see §601.601(d)(2)(ii)(b) of this chapter).

(vi) *Anti-abuse rule.*—If an issuer establishes the term of an issue for a period that is longer than is reasonably necessary for the governmental purposes of the issue for a principal purpose of increasing the permitted amount of private business use, the Commissioner may determine the amount of private business use according to the greatest percentage of private business use in any 1-year period.

(3) *Determining average percentage of private business use.*—The average percentage of private business use is the average of the percentages of private business use during the 1-year periods within the measurement period. Appropriate adjustments must be made for beginning and ending periods of less than 1 year.

(4) *Determining the average amount of private business use for a 1-year period.*—(i) *In general.*—The percentage of private business use of property for any 1-year period is the average private business use during that year. This average is determined by comparing the amount of private business use during the year to the total amount of private business use and use that is not private business use (government use) during that year. Paragraphs (g)(4)(ii) through (v) of this section apply to determine the average amount of private business use for a 1-year period.

(ii) *Uses at different times.*—For a facility in which actual government use and private business use occur at different times (for example, different days), the average amount of private business use generally is based on the amount of time that the facility is used for private business use as a percentage of the total time for all actual use. In determining the total amount of actual use, periods during which the facility is not in use are disregarded.

(iii) *Simultaneous use.*—In general, for a facility in which government use and private business use occur simultaneously, the entire facility is treated as having private business use. For example, a governmentally owned facility that is leased or managed by a nongovernmental person in a manner that results in private business use is treated as entirely used for a private business use. If, however, there is also private business use and actual government use on the same basis, the average amount of private business use may be determined on a reasonable basis that properly reflects the proportionate benefit to be derived by the various users of the facility (for example, reasonably expected fair market value of use). For example, the average amount of private business use of a garage with unassigned spaces that is used for government use and private business use is generally based on the number of spaces used for private business use as a percentage of the total number of spaces.

(iv) *Discrete portion.*—For purposes of this paragraph (g), measurement of the use of proceeds allocated to a discrete portion of a facility is determined by treating that discrete portion as a separate facility.

(v) *Relationship to fair market value.*—For purposes of paragraphs (g)(4)(ii) through (iv) of this section, if private business use is reasonably expected as of the issue date to have a significantly greater fair market value than government use, the average amount of private business use must be determined according to the relative reasonably expected fair market values of use rather than another measure, such as average time of use. This determination of relative fair market value may be made as of the date the property is acquired or placed in service if making this determination as of the issue date is not reasonably possible (for example, if the financed property is not identified on the issue date). In general, the relative reasonably expected fair market value for a period must be determined by taking into account the amount of reasonably expected payments for private business use for the period in a manner that properly reflects the proportionate benefit to be derived from the private business use.

(5) *Common areas.*—The amount of private business use of common areas within a facility is based on a reasonable method that properly reflects the proportionate benefit to be derived by the users of the facility. For example, in general, a method that is based on the average amount of private business use of the remainder of the entire facility reflects proportionate benefit.

(6) *Allocation of neutral costs.*—Proceeds that are used to pay costs of issuance, invested in a reserve or replacement fund, or paid as fees for a qualified guarantee or a qualified hedge must be allocated ratably among the other purposes for which the proceeds are used.

25,134

Tax Exempt. Requirements: State/Local Bonds
See p. 20,601 for regulations not amended to reflect law changes

(7) Commencement of measurement of private business use.—Generally, private business use commences on the first date on which there is a right to actual use by the nongovernmental person. However, if an issuer enters into an arrangement for private business use a substantial period before the right to actual private business use commences and the arrangement transfers ownership or is an arrangement for other long-term use (such as a lease for a significant portion of the remaining economic life of financed property), private business use commences on the date the arrangement is entered into, even if the right to actual use commences after the measurement period. For this purpose, 10 percent of the measurement period is generally treated as a substantial period.

(8) Examples.—The following examples illustrate the application of this paragraph (g):

Example 1. Research facility. University U, a state owned and operated university, owns and operates a research facility. U proposes to finance general improvements to the facility with the proceeds of an issue of bonds. U enters into sponsored research agreements with nongovernmental persons that result in private business use because the sponsors will own title to any patents resulting from the research. The governmental research conducted by U and the research U conducts for the sponsors take place simultaneously in all laboratories within the research facility. All laboratory equipment is available continuously for use by workers who perform both types of research. Because it is not possible to predict which research projects will be successful, it is not reasonably practicable to estimate the relative revenues expected to result from the governmental and nongovernmental research. U contributed 90 percent of the cost of the facility and the nongovernmental persons contributed 10 percent of the cost. Under this section, the nongovernmental persons are using the facility for a private business use on the same basis as the government use of the facility. The portions of the costs contributed by the various users of the facility provide a reasonable basis that properly reflects the proportionate benefit to be derived by the users of the facility. The nongovernmental persons are treated as using 10 percent of the proceeds of the issue.

Example 2. Stadium. (i) City L issues bonds and uses all of the proceeds to construct a stadium. L enters into a long-term contract with a professional sports team T under which T will use the stadium 20 times during each year. These uses will occur on nights and weekends. L reasonably expects that the stadium will be used more than 180 other times each year, none of which will give rise to private business use. This expectation is based on a feasibility study and historical use of the old stadium that is being replaced by the new stadium. There is no significant difference in the value of T's uses when compared to the other uses of the stadium, taking into account the payments that T is reasonably expected to make for its use. Assuming no other private business use, the issue does not meet the private business use test because not more than 10 percent of the use of the facility is for a private business use.

(ii) The facts are the same as in *Example 2(i)*, except that L reasonably expects that the stadium will be used not more than 60 other times each year, none of which will give rise to private business use. The issue meets the private business use test because 25 percent of the proceeds are used for a private business use.

Example 3. Airport terminal areas treated as common areas. City N issues bonds to finance the construction of an airport terminal. Eighty percent of the leasable space of the terminal will be leased to private air carriers. The remaining 20 percent of the leasable space will be used for the term of the bonds by N for its administrative purposes. The common areas of the terminal, including waiting areas, lobbies, and hallways are treated as 80 percent used by the air carriers for purposes of the private business use test.

[Reg. § 1.141-3.]

☐ [*T.D. 8712, 1-10-97. Amended by T.D. 8967, 11-19-2001 and T.D. 9741, 10-26-2015.*]

[Reg. § 1.141-4]

§ 1.141-4. Private security or payment test.—(a) *General rule.*—(1) *Private security or payment.*—The private security or payment test relates to the nature of the security for, and the source of, the payment of debt service on an issue. The private payment portion of the test takes into account the payment of the debt service on the issue that is directly or indirectly to be derived from payments (whether or not to the issuer or any related party) in respect of property, or borrowed money, used or to be used for a private business use. The private security portion of the test takes into account the payment of the debt service on the issue that is directly or indirectly secured by any interest in property used or to be used for a private business use or payments in respect of property used or to be used for a private business use. For additional rules for output facilities, see § 1.141-7.

(2) Aggregation of private payments and security.—For purposes of the private security or payment test, payments taken into account as private payments and payments or property taken into account as private security are aggregated. However, the same payments are not taken into account as both private security and private payments.

(3) Underlying arrangement.—The security for, and payment of debt service on, an issue is determined from both the terms of the bond documents and on the basis of any underlying arrangement. An underlying arrangement may result from separate agreements between the parties or may be determined on the basis of all of the facts and circumstances surrounding the issuance of the bonds. For example, if the payment of debt service on an issue is secured by both a pledge of the full faith and credit of a state or local governmental unit and any interest in property used or to be used in a private business use, the issue meets the private security or payment test.

(b) *Measurement of private payments and security.*—(1) *Scope.*—This paragraph (b) contains rules that apply to both private security and private payments.

(2) Present value measurement.—(i) *Use of present value.*—In determining whether an issue meets the private security or payment test, the present value of the payments or property taken into account is compared to the present value of the debt service to be paid over the term of the issue.

(ii) *Debt service.*—(A) *Debt service paid from proceeds.*—Debt service does not include any amount paid or to be paid from sale proceeds or investment proceeds. For example, debt service does not include payments of capitalized interest funded with proceeds.

(B) *Adjustments to debt service.*—Debt service is adjusted to take into account payments and receipts that adjust the yield on an issue for purposes of section 148(f). For example, debt service includes fees paid for qualified guarantees under § 1.148-4(f) and is adjusted to take into account payments and receipts on qualified hedges under § 1.148-4(h).

(iii) *Computation of present value.*—(A) *In general.*—Present values are determined by using the yield on the issue as the discount rate and by discounting all amounts to the issue date. See, however, § 1.141-13 for special rules for refunding bonds.

(B) *Fixed yield issues.*—For a fixed yield issue, yield is determined on the issue date and is not adjusted to take into account subsequent events.

(C) *Variable yield issues.*—The yield on a variable yield issue is determined over the term of the issue. To determine the reasonably expected yield as of any date, the issuer may assume that the future interest rate on a variable yield bond will be the then-current interest rate on the bonds determined under the formula prescribed in the bond documents. A deliberate action requires a recomputation of the yield on the variable yield issue to determine the present value of payments under that arrangement. In that case, the issuer must use the yield determined as of the date of the deliberate action for purposes of determining the present value of payments under the arrangement causing the deliberate action. See paragraph (g) of this section, *Example 3.*

(iv) *Application to private security.*—For purposes of determining the present value of debt service that is secured by property, the property is valued at fair market value as of the first date on which the property secures bonds of the issue.

(c) *Private payments.*—(1) *In general.*—This paragraph (c) contains rules that apply to private payments.

(2) Payments taken into account.—(i) *Payments for use.*—(A) *In general.*—Both direct and indirect payments made by any nongovernmental person that is treated as using proceeds of the issue are taken into account as private payments to the extent allocable to the proceeds used by that person. Payments are taken into account as private payments only to the extent that they are made for the period of time that proceeds are used for a private business use. Payments for a use of proceeds include payments (whether or not to the issuer) in respect of property financed (directly or indirectly) with those proceeds, even if not made by a private business user. Payments are not made in respect of financed property if those payments are directly allocable to other property being directly used by the person making the payment and those payments represent fair market value compensation for that other use. See paragraph (g) of this section, *Example 4* and *Example 5.* See also paragraph (c)(3) of this section for rules relating to allocation of payments to the source or sources of funding of property.

(B) *Payments not to exceed use.*—Payments with respect to proceeds that are used for a private business use are not taken into account to the extent that the present value of those payments exceeds the present value of debt service on those proceeds. Payments need not be directly derived from a private business user, however, to be taken into account. Thus, if 7 percent of the proceeds of an issue is used by a person over the measurement period, payments with respect to the property financed with those proceeds are taken into account as private payments only to the extent that the present value of those payments does not exceed the present value of 7 percent of the debt service on the issue.

(C) *Payments for operating expenses.*—Payments by a person for a use of proceeds do not include the portion of any payment that is properly allocable to the payment of ordinary and necessary expenses (as defined under section 162) directly attributable to the operation and maintenance of the financed property used by that person. For this purpose, general overhead and administrative expenses are not directly attributable to those operations and maintenance. For example, if an issuer receives $5,000 rent during the year for use of space in a financed facility and during the year pays $500 for ordinary and necessary expenses properly allocable to the operation and maintenance of that space and $400 for general overhead and general administrative expenses properly allocable to that space, $500 of the $5,000 received would not be considered a payment for the use of the proceeds allocable to that space (regardless of the manner in which that $500 is actually used).

(ii) *Refinanced debt service.*—Payments of debt service on an issue to be made from proceeds of a refunding issue are taken into account as private payments in the same proportion that the present value of the payments taken into account as private payments for the refunding issue bears to the present value of the debt service to be paid on the refunding issue. For example, if all the debt service on a note is paid with proceeds of a refunding issue, the note meets the private security or payment test if (and to the same extent that) the refunding issue meets the private security or payment test. This paragraph (c)(2)(ii) does not apply to payments that arise from deliberate actions that occur more than 3 years after the retirement of the prior issue that are not reasonably expected on the issue date of the refunding issue. For purposes of this paragraph (c)(2)(ii), whether an issue is a refunding issue is determined without regard to §1.150-1(d)(2)(i) (relating to certain payments of interest).

(3) *Allocation of payments.*—(i) *In general.*—Private payments for the use of property are allocated to the source or different sources of funding of property. The allocation to the source or different sources of funding is based on all of the facts and circumstances, including whether an allocation is consistent with the purposes of section 141. In general, a private payment for the use of property is allocated to a source of funding based upon the nexus between the payment and both the financed property and the source of funding. For this purpose, different sources of funding may include different tax-exempt issues, taxable issues, and amounts that are not derived from a borrowing, such as revenues of an issuer (equity).

(ii) *Payments for use of discrete property.*—Payments for the use of a discrete facility (or a discrete portion of a facility) are allocated to the source or different sources of funding of that discrete property.

(iii) *Allocations among two or more sources of funding.*—In general, except as provided in paragraphs (c)(3)(iv) and (v) of this section, if a payment is made for the use of property financed with two or more sources of funding (for example, equity and a tax-exempt issue), that payment must be allocated to those sources of funding in a manner that reasonably corresponds to the relative amounts of those sources of funding that are expended on that property. If an issuer has not retained records of amounts expended on the property (for example, records of costs of a building that was built 30 years before the allocation), an issuer may use reasonable estimates of those expenditures. For this purpose, costs of issuance and other similar neutral costs are allocated ratably among expenditures in the same manner as in §1.141-3(g)(6). A payment for the use of property may be allocated to two or more issues that finance property according to the relative amounts of debt service (both paid and accrued) on the issues during the annual period for which the payment is made, if that allocation reasonably reflects the economic substance of the arrangement. In general, allocations of payments according to relative debt service reasonably reflect the economic substance of the arrangement if the maturity of the bonds reasonably corresponds to the reasonably expected economic life of the property and debt service payments on the bonds are approximately level from year to year.

(iv) *Payments made under an arrangement entered into in connection with issuance of bonds.*—A private payment for the use of property made under an arrangement that is entered into in connection with the issuance of the issue that finances that property generally is allocated to that issue. Whether an arrangement is entered into in connection with the issuance of an issue is determined on the basis of all of the facts and circumstances. An arrangement is ordinarily treated as entered into in connection with the issuance of an issue if—

(A) The issuer enters into the arrangement during the 3-year period beginning 18 months before the issue date; and

(B) The amount of payments reflects all or a portion of debt service on the issue.

(v) *Allocations to equity.*—A private payment for the use of property may be allocated to equity before payments are allocated to an issue only if—

(A) Not later than 60 days after the date of the expenditure of those amounts, the issuer adopts an official intent (in a manner comparable to §1.150-2(e)) indicating that the issuer reasonably expects to be repaid for the expenditure from a specific arrangement; and

(B) The private payment is made not later than 18 months after the later of the date the expenditure is made or the date the project is placed in service.

(d) *Private security.*—(1) *In general.*—This paragraph (d) contains rules that relate to private security.

(2) *Security taken into account.*—The property that is the security for, or the source of, the payment of debt service on an issue need not be property financed with proceeds. For example, unimproved land or investment securities used, directly or indirectly, in a private business use that secures an issue provides private security. Private security (other than financed property and private payments) for an issue is taken into account under section 141(b), however, only to the extent it is provided, directly or indirectly, by a user of proceeds of the issue.

(3) *Pledge of unexpended proceeds.*—Proceeds qualifying for an initial temporary period under §1.148-2(e)(2) or (3) or deposited in a reasonably required reserve or replacement fund (as defined in §1.148-2(f)(2)(i)) are not taken into account under this paragraph (d) before the date on which those amounts are either expended or loaned by the issuer to an unrelated party.

(4) *Secured by any interest in property or payments.*—Property used or to be used for a private business use and payments in respect of that property are treated as private security if any interest in that property or payments secures the payment of debt service on the bonds. For this purpose, the phrase any interest in is to be interpreted broadly and includes, for example, any right, claim, title, or legal share in property or payments.

(5) *Payments in respect of property.*—The payments taken into account as private security are payments in respect of property used or to be used for a private business use. Except as otherwise provided in this paragraph (d)(5) and paragraph (d)(6) of this section, the rules in paragraphs (c)(2)(i)(A) and (B) and (c)(2)(ii) of this section apply to determine the amount of payments treated as payments in respect of property used or to be used for a private business use. Thus, payments made by members of the general public for use of a facility used for a private business use (for example, a facility that is the subject of a management contract that results in private business use) are taken into account as private security to the extent that they are made for the period of time that property is used by a private business user.

(6) *Allocation of security among issues.*—In general, property or payments from the disposition of that property that are taken into account as private security are allocated to each issue secured by the property or payments on a reasonable basis that takes into account bondholders' rights to the payments or property upon default.

(e) *Generally applicable taxes.*—(1) *General rule.*—For purposes of the private security or payment test, generally applicable taxes are not taken into account (that is, are not payments from a nongovernmental person and are not payments in respect of property used for a private business use).

(2) *Definition of generally applicable taxes.*—A generally applicable tax is an enforced contribution exacted pursuant to legislative authority in the exercise of the taxing power that is imposed and collected for the purpose of raising revenue to be used for governmental or public purposes. A generally applicable tax must have a uniform tax rate that is applied to all persons of the same classification in the appropriate jurisdiction and a generally applicable manner of determination and collection.

(3) *Special charges.*—A special charge (as defined in this paragraph (e)(3)) is not a generally applicable tax. For this purpose, a

Reg. §1.141-4(e)(3)

special charge means a payment for a special privilege granted or regulatory function (for example, a license fee), a service rendered (for example, a sanitation services fee), a use of property (for example, rent), or a payment in the nature of a special assessment to finance capital improvements that is imposed on a limited class of persons based on benefits received from the capital improvements financed with the assessment. Thus, a special assessment to finance infrastructure improvements in a new industrial park (such as sidewalks, streets, streetlights, and utility infrastructure improvements) that is imposed on a limited class of persons composed of property owners within the industrial park who benefit from those improvements is a special charge. By contrast, an otherwise qualified generally applicable tax (such as a generally applicable ad valorem tax on all real property within a governmental taxing jurisdiction) or an eligible PILOT under paragraph (e)(5) of this section that is based on such a generally applicable tax is not treated as a special charge merely because the taxes or PILOTs received are used for governmental or public purposes in a manner which benefits particular property owners.

(4) *Manner of determination and collection.*—(i) *In general.*—A tax does not have a generally applicable manner of determination and collection to the extent that one or more taxpayers make any impermissible agreements relating to payment of those taxes. An impermissible agreement relating to the payment of a tax is taken into account whether or not it is reasonably expected to result in any payments that would not otherwise have been made. For example, if an issuer uses proceeds to make a grant to a taxpayer to improve property, agreements that impose reasonable conditions on the use of the grant do not cause a tax on that property to fail to be a generally applicable tax. If an agreement by a taxpayer causes the tax imposed on that taxpayer not to be treated as a generally applicable tax, the entire tax paid by that taxpayer is treated as a special charge, unless the agreement is limited to a specific portion of the tax.

(ii) *Impermissible agreements.*—The following are examples of agreements that cause a tax to fail to have a generally applicable manner of determination and collection: an agreement to be personally liable on a tax that does not generally impose personal liability, to provide additional credit support such as a third party guarantee, or to pay unanticipated shortfalls; an agreement regarding the minimum market value of property subject to property tax; and an agreement not to challenge or seek deferral of the tax.

(iii) *Permissible agreements.*—The following are examples of agreements that do not cause a tax to fail to have a generally applicable manner of determination and collection: an agreement to use a grant for specified purposes (whether or not that agreement is secured); a representation regarding the expected value of the property following the improvement; an agreement to insure the property and, if damaged, to restore the property; a right of a grantor to rescind the grant if property taxes are not paid; and an agreement to reduce or limit the amount of taxes collected to further a bona fide governmental purpose. For example, an agreement to abate taxes to encourage a property owner to rehabilitate property in a distressed area is a permissible agreement.

(5) *Payments in lieu of taxes.*—A tax equivalency payment or other payment in lieu of a tax ("PILOT") is treated as a generally applicable tax if it meets the requirements of paragraphs (e)(5)(i) through (iv) of this section—

(i) *Maximum amount limited by underlying generally applicable tax.*—The PILOT is not greater than the amount imposed by a statute for a generally applicable tax in each year.

(ii) *Commensurate with a generally applicable tax.*—The PILOT is commensurate with the amount imposed by a statute for a generally applicable tax in each year under the commensurate standard set forth in this paragraph (e)(5)(ii). For this purpose, except as otherwise provided in this paragraph (e)(5)(ii), a PILOT is commensurate with a generally applicable tax only if it is equal to a fixed percentage of the generally applicable tax that would otherwise apply in each year or it reflects a fixed adjustment to the generally applicable tax that would otherwise apply in each year. A PILOT based on a property tax does not fail to be commensurate with the property tax as a result of changes in the level of the percentage of or adjustment to that property tax for a reasonable phase-in period ending when the subject property is placed in service (as defined in § 1.150-2(c)). A PILOT based on a property tax must take into account the current assessed value of the property for property tax purposes for each year in which the PILOT is paid and that assessed value must be determined in the same manner and with the same frequency as property subject to property tax. A PILOT is not commensurate with a generally applicable tax, however, if the PILOT is set at a fixed dollar amount (for example, fixed debt service on a bond issue) that

cannot vary with changes in the level of the generally applicable tax on which it is based.

(iii) *Use of PILOTs for governmental or public purposes.*—The PILOT is to be used for governmental or public purposes for which the generally applicable tax on which it is based may be used.

(iv) *No special charges.*—The PILOT is not a special charge under paragraph (e)(3) of this section.

(f) *Certain waste remediation bonds.*—(1) *Scope.*—This paragraph (f) applies to bonds issued to finance hazardous waste clean-up activities on privately owned land (hazardous waste remediation bonds).

(2) *Persons that are not private users.*—Payments from nongovernmental persons who are not (other than coincidentally) either users of the site being remediated or persons potentially responsible for disposing of hazardous waste on that site are not taken into account as private security. This paragraph (f)(2) applies to payments that secure (directly or indirectly) the payment of principal of, or interest on, the bonds under the terms of the bonds. This paragraph (f)(2) applies only if the payments are made pursuant to either a generally applicable state or local taxing statute or a state or local statute that regulates or restrains activities on an industry-wide basis of persons who are engaged in generating or handling hazardous waste, or in refining, producing, or transporting petroleum, provided that those payments do not represent, in substance, payment for the use of proceeds. For this purpose, a state or local statute that imposes payments that have substantially the same character as those described in Chapter 38 of the Code are treated as generally applicable taxes.

(3) *Persons that are private users.*—If payments from nongovernmental persons who are either users of the site being remediated or persons potentially responsible for disposing of hazardous waste on that site do not secure (directly or indirectly) the payment of principal of, or interest on, the bonds under the terms of the bonds, the payments are not taken into account as private payments. This paragraph (f)(3) applies only if at the time the bonds are issued the payments from those nongovernmental persons are not material to the security for the bonds. For this purpose, payments are not material to the security for the bonds if—

(i) The payments are not required for the payment of debt service on the bonds;

(ii) The amount and timing of the payments are not structured or designed to reflect the payment of debt service on the bonds;

(iii) The receipt or the amount of the payment is uncertain (for example, as of the issue date, no final judgment has been entered into against the nongovernmental person);

(iv) The payments from those nongovernmental persons, when and if received, are used either to redeem bonds of the issuer or to pay for costs of any hazardous waste remediation project; and

(v) In the case when a judgment (but not a final judgment) has been entered by the issue date against a nongovernmental person, there are, as of the issue date, costs of hazardous waste remediation other than those financed with the bonds that may be financed with the payments.

(g) *Examples.*—The following examples illustrate the application of this section:

Example 1. Aggregation of payments. State B issues bonds with proceeds of $10 million. B uses $9.7 million of the proceeds to construct a 10-story office building. B uses the remaining $300,000 of proceeds to make a loan to Corporation Y. In addition, Corporation X leases 1 floor of the building for the term of the bonds. Under all of the facts and circumstances, it is reasonable to allocate 10 percent of the proceeds to that 1 floor. As a percentage of the present value of the debt service on the bonds, the present value of Y's loan repayments is 3 percent and the present value of X's lease payments is 8 percent. The bonds meet the private security or payment test because the private payments taken into account are more than 10 percent of the present value of the debt service on the bonds.

Example 2. Indirect private payments. J, a political subdivision of a state, will issue several series of bonds from time to time and will use the proceeds to rehabilitate urban areas. Under all of the facts and circumstances, the private business use test will be met with respect to each issue that will be used for the rehabilitation and construction of buildings that will be leased or sold to nongovernmental persons for use in their trades or businesses. Nongovernmental persons will make payments for these sales and leases. There is no limitation either on the number of issues or the aggregate amount of bonds that may be outstanding. No group of bondholders has any legal claim prior to any other bondholders or creditors with respect to specific revenues of J, and there is no arrangement whereby revenues from a particular project are paid into a trust or constructive trust, or sinking fund, or are otherwise segregated or restricted for the benefit of any group of bondholders. There is, however, an unconditional obligation by J to pay the principal of, and the interest on, each issue. Although not directly pledged under the terms of the bond documents, the leases and sales are underlying arrangements. The payments relating to these leases and sales are taken into account as private payments to determine whether each issue of bonds meets the private security or payment test.

Example 3. Computation of payment in variable yield issues. (i) City M issues general obligation bonds with proceeds of $10 million to finance a 5-story office building. The bonds bear interest at a variable rate that is recomputed monthly according to an index that reflects current market yields. The yield that the interest index would produce on the issue date is 6 percent. M leases 1 floor of the office building to Corporation T, a nongovernmental person, for the term of the bonds. Under all of the facts and circumstances, T is treated as using more than 10 percent of the proceeds. Using the 6 percent yield as the discount rate, M reasonably expects on the issue date that the present value of lease payments to be made by T will be 8 percent of the present value of the total debt service on the bonds. After the issue date of the bonds, interest rates decline significantly, so that the yield on the bonds over their entire term is 4 percent. Using this actual 4 percent yield as the discount rate, the present value of lease payments made by T is 12 percent of the present value of the actual total debt service on the bonds. The bonds are not private activity bonds because M reasonably expected on the issue date that the bonds would not meet the private security or payment test and because M did not take any subsequent deliberate action to meet the private security or payment test.

(ii) The facts are the same as *Example 3(i),* except that 5 years after the issue date M leases a second floor to Corporation S, a nongovernmental person, under a long-term lease. Because M has taken a deliberate action, the present value of the lease payments must be computed. On the date this lease is entered into, M reasonably expects that the yield on the bonds over their entire term will be 5.5 percent, based on actual interest rates to date and the then-current rate on the variable yield bonds. M uses this 5.5 percent yield as the discount rate. Using this 5.5 percent yield as the discount rate, as a percentage of the present value of the debt service on the bonds, the present value of the lease payments made by S is 3 percent. The bonds are private activity bonds because the present value of the aggregate private payments is greater than 10 percent of the present value of debt service.

Example 4. Payments not in respect of financed property. In order to further public safety, City Y issues tax assessment bonds the proceeds of which are used to move existing electric utility lines underground. Although the utility lines are owned by a nongovernmental utility company, that company is under no obligation to move the lines. The debt service on the bonds will be paid using assessments levied by City Y on the customers of the utility. Although the utility lines are privately owned and the utility customers make payments to the utility company for the use of those lines, the assessments are payments in respect of the cost of relocating the utility line. Thus, the assessment payments are not made in respect of property used for a private business use. Any direct or indirect payments to Y by the utility company for the undergrounding are, however, taken into account as private payments.

Example 5. Payments from users of proceeds that are not private business users taken into account. City P issues general obligation bonds to finance the renovation of a hospital that it owns. The hospital is operated for P by D, a nongovernmental person, under a management contract that results in private business use under §1.141-3. P will use the revenues from the hospital (after the required payments to D and the payment of operation and maintenance expenses) to pay the debt service on the bonds. The bonds meet the private security or payment test because the revenues from the hospital are payments in respect of property used for a private business use.

Example 6. Limitation of amount of payments to amount of private business use not determined annually. City Q issues bonds with a term of 15 years and uses the proceeds to construct an office building. The debt service on the bonds is level throughout the 15-year term. Q enters into a 5-year lease with Corporation R under which R is treated as a user of 11 percent of the proceeds. R will make lease payments equal to 20 percent of the annual debt service on the bonds for each year of the lease. The present value of R's lease payments is equal to 12 percent of the present value of the debt service over the entire 15-year term of the bonds. If, however, the lease payments taken into account as private payments were limited to 11 percent of debt service paid in each year of the lease, the present value of these payments would be only 8 percent of the debt service on the bonds over the entire term of the bonds. The bonds meet the private security or payment test, because R's lease payments are taken into account as private payments in an amount not to exceed 11 percent of the debt service of the bonds.

Example 7. Allocation of payments to funds not derived from a borrowing. City Z purchases property for $1,250,000 using $1,000,000 of

proceeds of its tax increment bonds and $250,000 of other revenues that are in its redevelopment fund. Within 60 days of the date of purchase, Z declared its intent to sell the property pursuant to a redevelopment plan and to use that amount to reimburse its redevelopment fund. The bonds are secured only by the incremental property taxes attributable to the increase in value of the property from the planned redevelopment of the property. Within 18 months after the issue date, Z sells the financed property to Developer M for $250,000, which Z uses to reimburse the redevelopment fund. The property that M uses is financed both with the proceeds of the bonds and Z's redevelopment fund. The payments by M are properly allocable to the costs of property financed with the amounts in Z's redevelopment fund. See paragraphs (c)(3)(i) and (v) of this section.

Example 8. Allocation of payments to different sources of funding—improvements. In 1997, City L issues bonds with proceeds of $8 million to finance the acquisition of a building. In 2002, L spends $2 million of its general revenues to improve the heating system and roof of the building. At that time, L enters into a 10-year lease with Corporation M for the building providing for annual payments of $1 million to L. The lease payments are at fair market value, and the lease payments do not otherwise have a significant nexus to either the issue or to the expenditure of general revenues. Eighty percent of each lease payment is allocated to the issue and is taken into account under the private payment test because each lease payment is properly allocated to the sources of funding in a manner that reasonably corresponds to the relative amounts of the sources of funding that are expended on the building.

Example 9. Security not provided by users of proceeds not taken into account. County W issues certificates of participation in a lease of a building that W owns and covenants to appropriate annual payments for the lease. A portion of each payment is specified as interest. More than 10 percent of the building is used for private business use. None of the proceeds of the obligations are used with respect to the building. W uses the proceeds of the obligations to make a grant to Corporation Y for the construction of a factory that Y will own. Y makes no payments to W, directly or indirectly, for its use of proceeds, and Y has no relationship to the users of the leased building. If W defaults under the lease, the trustee for the holders of the certificates of participation has a limited right of repossession under which the trustee may not foreclose but may lease the property to a new tenant at fair market value. The obligations are secured by an interest in property used for a private business use. However, because the property is not provided by a private business user and is not financed property, the obligations do not meet the private security or payment test.

Example 10. Allocation of payments among issues. University L, a political subdivision, issued three separate series of revenue bonds during 1989, 1991, and 1993 under the same bond resolution. L used the proceeds to construct facilities exclusively for its own use. Bonds issued under the resolution are equally and ratably secured and payable solely from the income derived by L from rates, fees, and charges imposed by L for the use of the facilities. The bonds issued in 1989, 1991, and 1993 are not private activity bonds. In 1997, L issues another series of bonds under the resolution to finance additional facilities. L leases 20 percent of the new facilities for the term of the 1997 bonds to nongovernmental persons who will use the facilities in their trades or businesses. The present value of the lease payments from the nongovernmental users will equal 15 percent of the present value of the debt service on the 1997 bonds. L will commingle all of the revenues from all its bond-financed facilities in its revenue fund. The present value of the portion of the lease payments from nongovernmental lessees of the new facilities allocable to the 1997 bonds under paragraph (d) of this section is less than 10 percent of the present value of the debt service on the 1997 bonds because the bond documents provide that the bonds are equally and ratably secured. Accordingly, the 1997 bonds do not meet the private security test. The 1997 bonds meet the private payment test, however, because the private lease payments for the new facility are properly allocated to those bonds (that is, because none of the proceeds of the prior issues were used for the new facilities). See paragraph (c) of this section.

Example 11. Generally applicable tax. (i) Authority N issues bonds to finance the construction of a stadium. Under a long-term lease, Corporation X, a professional sports team, will use more than 10 percent of the stadium for this private business use. X will not, however, make any payments for this private business use. The security for the bonds will be a ticket tax imposed on each person purchasing a ticket for an event at the stadium. The portion of the ticket tax attributable to tickets purchased by persons attending X's events will, on a present value basis, exceed 10 percent of the present value of the debt service on N's bonds. The bonds meet the private security or payment test. The ticket tax is not a generally applicable tax and, to the extent that the tax receipts relate to X's events, the taxes are payments in respect of property used for a private business use.

(ii) The facts are the same as *Example 11(i),* except that the ticket tax is imposed by N on tickets purchased for events at a number of large

Reg. §1.141-4(g)

entertainment facilities within the N's jurisdiction (for example, other stadiums, arenas, and concert halls), some of which were not financed with tax-exempt bonds. The ticket tax is a generally applicable tax and therefore the revenues from this tax are not payments in respect of property used for a private business use. The receipt of the ticket tax does not cause the bonds to meet the private security or payment test.
[Reg. § 1.141-4.]

☐ [T.D. 8712, 1-10-97. Amended by T.D. 9429, 10-20-2008.]

[Reg. §1.141-5]

§1.141-5. Private loan financing test.—(a) *In general.*—Bonds of an issue are private activity bonds if more than the lesser of 5 percent or $5 million of the proceeds of the issue is to be used (directly or indirectly) to make or finance loans to persons other than governmental persons. Section 1.141-2(d) applies in determining whether the private loan financing test is met. In determining whether the proceeds of an issue are used to make or finance loans, indirect, as well as direct, use of the proceeds is taken into account.

(b) *Measurement of test.*—In determining whether the private loan financing test is met, the amount actually loaned to a nongovernmental person is not discounted to reflect the present value of the loan repayments.

(c) *Definition of private loan.*—(1) *In general.*—Any transaction that is generally characterized as a loan for federal income tax purposes is a loan for purposes of this section. In addition, a loan may arise from the direct lending of bond proceeds or may arise from transactions in which indirect benefits that are the economic equivalent of a loan are conveyed. Thus, the determination of whether a loan is made depends on the substance of a transaction rather than its form. For example, a lease or other contractual arrangement (for example, a management contract or an output contract) may in substance constitute a loan if the arrangement transfers tax ownership of the facility to a nongovernmental person. Similarly, an output contract or a management contract with respect to a financed facility generally is not treated as a loan of proceeds unless the agreement in substance shifts significant burdens and benefits of ownership to the nongovernmental purchaser or manager of the facility.

(2) *Application only to purpose investments.*—(i) *In general.*—A loan may be either a purpose investment or a nonpurpose investment. A loan that is a nonpurpose investment does not cause the private loan financing test to be met. For example, proceeds invested in loans, such as obligations of the United States, during a temporary period, as part of a reasonably required reserve or replacement fund, as part of a refunding escrow, or as part of a minor portion (as each of those terms are defined in §1.148-1 or §1.148-2) are generally not treated as loans under the private loan financing test.

(ii) *Certain prepayments treated as loans.*—Except as otherwise provided, a prepayment for property or services, including a prepayment for property or services that is made after the date that the contract to buy the property or services is entered into, is treated as a loan for purposes of the private loan financing test if a principal purpose for prepaying is to provide a benefit of tax-exempt financing to the seller. A prepayment is not treated as a loan for purposes of the private loan financing test if—

(A) Prepayments on substantially the same terms are made by a substantial percentage of persons who are similarly situated to the issuer but who are not beneficiaries of tax-exempt financing;

(B) The prepayment is made within 90 days of the reasonably expected date of delivery to the issuer of all of the property or services for which the prepayment is made; or

(C) The prepayment meets the requirements of §1.148-1(e)(2)(iii)(A) or (B) (relating to certain prepayments to acquire a supply of natural gas or electricity).

(iii) *Customary prepayments.*—The determination of whether a prepayment satisfies paragraph (c)(2)(ii)(A) of this section is generally made based on all the facts and circumstances. In addition, a prepayment is deemed to satisfy paragraph (c)(2)(ii)(A) of this section if—

(A) The prepayment is made for—

(1) Maintenance, repair, or an extended warranty with respect to personal property (for example, automobiles or electronic equipment); or

(2) Updates or maintenance or support services with respect to computer software; and

(B) The same maintenance, repair, extended warranty, updates or maintenance or support services, as applicable, are regularly provided to nongovernmental persons on the same terms.

(iv) *Additional prepayments as permitted by the Commissioner.*—The Commissioner may, by published guidance, set forth additional

circumstances in which a prepayment is not treated as a loan for purposes of the private loan financing test.

(3) *Grants.*—(i) *In general.*—A grant of proceeds is not a loan. Whether a transaction may be treated as a grant or a loan depends on all of the facts and circumstances.

(ii) *Tax increment financing.*—(A) *In general.*—Generally, a grant using proceeds of an issue that is secured by generally applicable taxes attributable to the improvements to be made with the grant is not treated as a loan, unless the grantee makes any impermissible agreements relating to the payment that results in the taxes imposed on that taxpayer not to be treated as generally applicable taxes under §1.141-4(e).

(B) *Amount of loan.*—If a grant is treated as a loan under this paragraph (c)(3), the entire grant is treated as a loan unless the impermissible agreement is limited to a specific portion of the tax. For this purpose, an arrangement with each unrelated grantee is treated as a separate grant.

(4) *Hazardous waste remediation bonds.*—In the case of an issue of hazardous waste remediation bonds, payments from nongovernmental persons that are either users of the site being remediated or persons potentially responsible for disposing of hazardous waste on that site do not establish that the transaction is a loan for purposes of this section. This paragraph (c)(4) applies only if those payments do not secure the payment of principal of, or interest on, the bonds (directly or indirectly), under the terms of the bonds and those payments are not taken into account under the private payment test pursuant to § 1.141-4(f)(3).

(d) *Tax assessment loan exception.*—(1) *General rule.*—For purposes of this section, a tax assessment loan that satisfies the requirements of this paragraph (d) is not a loan for purposes of the private loan financing test.

(2) *Tax assessment loan defined.*—A tax assessment loan is a loan that arises when a governmental person permits or requires property owners to finance any governmental tax or assessment of general application for an essential governmental function that satisfies each of the requirements of paragraphs (d)(3) through (5) of this section.

(3) *Mandatory tax or other assessment.*—The tax or assessment must be an enforced contribution that is imposed and collected for the purpose of raising revenue to be used for a specific purpose (that is, to defray the capital cost of an improvement). Taxes and assessments do not include fees for services. The tax or assessment must be imposed pursuant to a state law of general application that can be applied equally to natural persons not acting in a trade or business and persons acting in a trade or business. For this purpose, taxes and assessments that are imposed subject to protest procedures are treated as enforced contributions.

(4) *Specific essential governmental function.*—(i) *In general.*—A mandatory tax or assessment that gives rise to a tax assessment loan must be imposed for one or more specific, essential governmental functions.

(ii) *Essential governmental functions.*—For purposes of paragraph (d) of this section, improvements to utilities and systems that are owned by a governmental person and that are available for use by the general public (such as sidewalks; streets and street-lights; electric, telephone, and cable television systems; sewage treatment and disposal systems; and municipal water facilities) serve essential governmental functions. For other types of facilities, the extent to which the service provided by the facility is customarily performed (and financed with governmental bonds) by governments with general taxing powers is a primary factor in determining whether the facility serves an essential governmental function. For example, parks that are owned by a governmental person and that are available for use by the general public serve an essential governmental function. Except as otherwise provided in this paragraph (d)(4)(ii), commercial or industrial facilities and improvements to property owned by a nongovernmental person do not serve an essential governmental function. Permitting installment payments of property taxes or other taxes is not an essential governmental function.

(5) *Equal basis requirement.*—(i) *In general.*—Owners of both business and nonbusiness property benefiting from the financed improvements must be eligible, or required, to make deferred payments of the tax or assessment giving rise to a tax assessment loan on an equal basis (the equal basis requirement). A tax or assessment does not satisfy the equal basis requirement if the terms for payment of the tax or assessment are not the same for all taxed or assessed persons. For example, the equal basis requirement is not met if certain property owners are permitted to pay the tax or assessment over a period of years while others must pay the entire tax or assessment immedi-

ately or if only certain property owners are required to prepay the tax or assessment when the property is sold.

(ii) *General rule for guarantees.*—A guarantee of debt service on bonds, or of taxes or assessments, by a person that is treated as a borrower of bond proceeds violates the equal basis requirement if it is reasonable to expect on the date the guarantee is entered into that payments will be made under the guarantee.

(6) *Coordination with private business tests.*—See §§1.141-3 and 1.141-4 for rules for determining whether tax assessment loans cause the bonds financing those loans to be private activity bonds under the private business use and the private security or payment tests.

(e) *Examples.*—The following examples illustrate the application of this section:

Example 1. Turnkey contract not treated as a loan. State agency Z and federal agency H will each contribute to rehabilitate a project owned by Z. H can only provide its funds through a contribution to Z to be used to acquire the rehabilitated project on a turnkey basis from an approved developer. Under H's turnkey program, the developer must own the project while it is rehabilitated. Z issues its notes to provide funds for construction. A portion of the notes will be retired using the H contribution, and the balance of the notes will be retired through the issuance by Z of long-term bonds. Z lends the proceeds of its notes to Developer B as construction financing and transfers title to B for a nominal amount. The conveyance is made on condition that B rehabilitate the property and reconvey it upon completion, with Z retaining the right to force reconveyance if these conditions are not satisfied. B must name Z as an additional insured on all insurance. Upon completion, B must transfer title to the project back to Z at a set price, which price reflects B's costs and profit, not fair market value. Further, this price is adjusted downward to reflect any cost-underruns. For purposes of section 141(c), this transaction does not involve a private loan.

Example 2. Essential government function requirement not met. City D creates a special taxing district consisting of property owned by nongovernmental persons that requires environmental clean-up. D imposes a special tax on each parcel within the district in an amount that is related to the expected environmental clean-up costs of that parcel. The payment of the tax over a 20-year period is treated as a loan by the property owners for purposes of the private loan financing test. The special district issues bonds, acting on behalf of D, that are payable from the special tax levied within the district, and uses the proceeds to pay for the costs of environmental clean-up on the property within the district. The bonds meet the private loan financing test because more than 5 percent of the proceeds of the issue are loaned to nongovernmental persons. The issue does not meet the tax assessment loan exception because the improvements to property owned by a nongovernmental person are not an essential governmental function under section 141(c)(2). The issue also meets the private business tests of section 141(b).

[Reg. §1.141-5.]

☐ [*T.D. 8712, 1-10-97. Amended by T.D. 9085, 8-1-2003.*]

[Reg. §1.141-6]

§1.141-6. Allocation and accounting rules.—(a) *Allocations of proceeds to expenditures, projects, and uses in general.*—(1) *Allocations to expenditures.*—The allocations of proceeds and other sources of funds to expenditures under §1.148-6(d) apply for purposes of §§1.141-1 through 1.141-15.

(2) *Allocations of sources to a project and its uses.*—Except as provided in paragraph (b) of this section (regarding an eligible mixed-use project), if two or more sources of funding (including two or more tax-exempt issues) for a project (as defined in paragraph (a)(3) of this section) are allocated to capital expenditures (as defined in §1.150-1(b)) for a project (as defined in paragraph (a)(3) of this section), those sources are allocated throughout that project to the governmental use and private business use of the project in proportion to the relative amounts of those sources of funding spent on the project.

(3) *Definition of project.*—(i) *In general.*—For purposes of this section, *project* means one or more facilities or capital projects, including land, buildings, equipment, or other property, financed in whole or in part with proceeds of the issue.

(ii) *Output facilities.*—If an output facility has multiple undivided ownership interests (respectively owned by governmental persons or by both governmental and nongovernmental persons), each owner's interest in the facility is treated as a separate facility for purposes of this section, provided that all owners of the undivided ownership interests share the ownership and output in proportion to their contributions to the capital costs of the output facility.

(b) *Special allocation rules for eligible mixed-use projects.*—(1) *In general.*—The sources of funding allocated to capital expenditures for an eligible mixed-use project (as defined in paragraph (b)(2) of this section) are allocated to undivided portions of the eligible mixed-use project and the governmental use and private business use of the eligible mixed-use project in accordance with this paragraph (b). Qualified equity (as defined in paragraph (b)(3) of this section) is allocated first to the private business use of the eligible mixed-use project and then to governmental use, and proceeds are allocated first to the governmental use and then to private business use, using the percentages of the eligible mixed-use project financed with the respective sources and the percentages of the respective uses. Thus, if the percentage of the eligible mixed-use project financed with qualified equity is less than the percentage of private business use of the project, all of the qualified equity is allocated to the private business use. Proceeds are allocated to the balance of the private business use of the project. Similarly, if the percentage of the eligible mixed-use project financed with proceeds is less than the percentage of governmental use of the project, all of the proceeds are allocated to the governmental use, and qualified equity is allocated to the balance of the governmental use of the project. Further, if proceeds of more than one issue finance the eligible mixed-use project, proceeds of each issue are allocated ratably to the uses to which proceeds are allocated in proportion to the relative amounts of the proceeds of such issues allocated to the eligible mixed-use project. For private business use measured under §1.141-3(g), qualified equity and proceeds are allocated to the uses of the eligible mixed-use project in each one-year period under §1.141-3(g)(4). *See Example 1* of paragraph (f) of this section.

(2) *Definition of eligible mixed-use project.*—Eligible mixed-use project means a project (as defined in paragraph (a)(3) of this section) that is financed with proceeds of bonds that, when issued, purported to be governmental bonds (as defined in §1.150-1(b)) (the applicable bonds) and with qualified equity pursuant to the same plan of financing (within the meaning of §1.150-1(c)(1)(ii)). An eligible mixed-use project must be wholly owned by one or more governmental persons or by a partnership in which at least one governmental person is a partner.

(3) *Definition of qualified equity.*—For purposes of this section, *qualified equity* means proceeds of bonds that are not tax-advantaged bonds and funds that are not derived from proceeds of a borrowing that are spent on the same eligible mixed-use project as the proceeds of the applicable bonds. Qualified equity does not include equity interests in real property or tangible personal property. Further, qualified equity does not include funds used to redeem or repay governmental bonds. *See* §§1.141-2(d)(2)(ii) and 1.141-12(i) (regarding the effects of certain redemptions as remedial actions).

(4) *Same plan of financing.*—Qualified equity finances a project under the same plan of financing that includes the applicable bonds if the qualified equity pays for capital expenditures of the project on a date that is no earlier than a date on which such expenditures would be eligible for reimbursement by proceeds of the applicable bonds under §1.150-2(d)(2) (regardless of whether the applicable bonds are reimbursement bonds) and, except for a reasonable retainage (within the meaning of §1.148-7(h)), no later than the date on which the measurement period begins.

(c) *Allocations of private payments.*—Except as provided in this paragraph (c), private payments for a project are allocated in accordance with §1.141-4. Payments under an output contract that result in private business use of an eligible mixed-use project are allocated to the same source of funding (notwithstanding §1.141-4(c)(3)(v) (regarding certain allocations of private payments to equity)) allocated to the private business use from such contract under paragraph (b) of this section.

(d) *Allocations of proceeds to common costs of an issue.*—Proceeds used for expenditures for common costs (for example, issuance costs, qualified guarantee fees, or reasonably required reserve or replacement funds) are allocated in accordance with §1.141-3(g)(6). Proceeds, as allocated under §1.141-3(g)(6) to an eligible mixed-use project, are allocated to the uses of the project in the same proportions as the proceeds allocated to the uses under paragraph (b) of this section.

(e) *Allocations of proceeds to bonds.*—In general, proceeds are allocated to bonds in accordance with the rules for allocations of proceeds to bonds for separate purposes of multipurpose issues in §1.141-13(d). For an issue that is not a multipurpose issue (or is a multipurpose issue for which the issuer has not made a multipurpose allocation), proceeds are allocated to bonds ratably in a manner similar to the allocation of proceeds to projects under paragraph (a)(2) of this section.

(f) *Examples.*—The following examples illustrate the application of this section:

Example 1. Mixed-use project. City A issues $70x of bonds (the Bonds) and finances the construction of a 10-story office building costing $100x (the Project) with proceeds of the Bonds and $30x of qualified equity (the Qualified Equity). To the extent that the private business use of the Project does not exceed 30 percent in any particular year, the Qualified Equity is allocated to the private business use. If private business use of the Project were, for example, 44 percent in a year, the Qualified Equity would be allocated to 30 percent ($30x) private business use and proceeds of the Bonds would be allocated to the excess (that is, 14 percent or $14x), resulting in private business use of the Bonds in that year of 20 percent ($14x/$70x). Conversely, if private business use of the Project were 20 percent, Qualified Equity would be allocated to that 20 percent. The remaining Qualified Equity (that is, 10 percent or $10x) would be allocated to the governmental use in excess of the 70 percent to which the proceeds of the Bonds would be allocated.

Example 2. Mixed-use output facility. Authority A is a governmental person that owns and operates an electric transmission facility. Several years ago, Authority A used its equity to pay capital expenditures of $1000x for the facility. Authority A wants to make capital improvements to the facility in the amount of $100x (the Project). Authority A reasonably expects that, after completion of the Project, it will sell 46 percent of the available output of the facility, as determined under §1.141-7, under output contracts that result in private business use and it will sell 54 percent of the available output of the facility for governmental use. On January 1, 2017, Authority A issues $60x of bonds (the Bonds) and uses the proceeds of the Bonds and $40x of qualified equity (the Qualified Equity) to finance the Project. The Qualified Equity is allocated to 40 of the 46 percent private business use resulting from the output contracts. Proceeds of the Bonds are allocated to the 54 percent governmental use and thereafter to the remaining 6 percent private business use.

Example 3. Subsequent improvements and replacements. County A owns a hospital, which opened in 2001, that it financed entirely with proceeds of bonds it issued in 1998 (the 1998 Bonds). In 2017, County A finances the cost of an addition to the hospital with proceeds of bonds (the 2017 Bonds) and qualified equity (the 2017 Qualified Equity). The original hospital is a project (the 1998 Project) and the addition is a project (the 2017 Project). Proceeds of the 2017 Bonds and the 2017 Qualified Equity are allocated to the 2017 Project. The 2017 Qualified Equity is allocated first to the private business use of the 2017 Project and then to the governmental use of the 2017 Project. Proceeds of the 2017 Bonds are allocated first to the governmental use of the 2017 Project and then to the private business use of that project. Neither proceeds of the 2017 Bonds nor 2017 Qualified Equity is allocated to the uses of the 1998 Project. Proceeds of the 1998 Bonds are not allocated to uses of the 2017 Project. [Reg. §1.141-6.]

☐ [*T.D.* 8712, 1-10-97. Amended by *T.D.* 9741, 10-26-2015.]

[Reg. §1.141-7]

§1.141-7. Special rules for output facilities.—(a) *Overview.*—This section provides special rules to determine whether arrangements for the purchase of output from an output facility cause an issue of bonds to meet the private business tests. For this purpose, unless otherwise stated, water facilities are treated as output facilities. Sections 1.141-3 and 1.141-4 generally apply to determine whether other types of arrangements for use of an output facility cause an issue to meet the private business tests.

(b) *Definitions.*—For purposes of this section and §1.141-8, the following definitions and rules apply:

(1) *Available output.*—The available output of a facility financed by an issue is determined by multiplying the number of units produced or to be produced by the facility in one year by the number of years in the measurement period of that facility for that issue.

(i) *Generating facilities.*—The number of units produced or to be produced by a generating facility in one year is determined by reference to its nameplate capacity or the equivalent (or where there is no nameplate capacity or the equivalent, its maximum capacity), which is not reduced for reserves, maintenance or other unutilized capacity.

(ii) *Transmission and other output facilities.*—(A) *In general.*—For transmission, distribution, cogeneration, and other output facilities, available output must be measured in a reasonable manner to reflect capacity.

(B) *Electric transmission facilities.*—Measurement of the available output of all or a portion of electric transmission facilities may be determined in a manner consistent with the reporting rules and requirements for transmission networks promulgated by the Federal Energy Regulatory Commission (FERC). For example, for a transmission network, the use of aggregate load and load share ratios in a manner consistent with the requirements of the FERC may be

reasonable. In addition, depending on the facts and circumstances, measurement of the available output of transmission facilities using thermal capacity or transfer capacity may be reasonable.

(iii) *Special rule for facilities with significant unutilized capacity.*—If an issuer reasonably expects on the issue date that persons that are treated as private business users will purchase more than 30 percent of the actual output of the facility financed with the issue, the Commissioner may determine the number of units produced or to be produced by the facility in one year on a reasonable basis other than by reference to nameplate or other capacity, such as the average expected annual output of the facility. For example, the Commissioner may determine the available output of a financed peaking electric generating unit by reference to the reasonably expected annual output of that unit if the issuer reasonably expects, on the issue date of bonds that finance the unit, that an investor-owned utility will purchase more than 30 percent of the actual output of the facility during the measurement period under a take or pay contract, even if the amount of output purchased is less than 10 percent of the available output determined by reference to nameplate capacity. The reasonably expected annual output of the generating facility must be consistent with the capacity reported for prudent reliability purposes.

(iv) *Special rule for facilities with a limited source of supply.*—If a limited source of supply constrains the output of an output facility, the number of units produced or to be produced by the facility must be determined by reasonably taking into account those constraints. For this purpose, a limited source of supply shall include a physical limitation (for example, flow of water), but not an economic limitation (for example, cost of coal or gas). For example, the available output of a hydroelectric unit must be determined by reference to the reasonably expected annual flow of water through the unit.

(2) *Measurement period.*—The measurement period of an output facility financed by an issue is determined under §1.141-3(g).

(3) *Sale at wholesale.*—A sale at wholesale means a sale of output to any person for resale.

(4) *Take contract and take or pay contract.*—A *take contract* is an output contract under which a purchaser agrees to pay for the output under the contract if the output facility is capable of providing the output. A *take or pay contract* is an output contract under which a purchaser agrees to pay for the output under the contract, whether or not the output facility is capable of providing the output.

(5) *Requirements contract.*—A *requirements contract* is an output contract, other than a take contract or a take or pay contract, under which a nongovernmental person agrees to purchase all or part of its output requirements.

(6) *Nonqualified amount.*—The nonqualified amount with respect to an issue is determined under section 141(b)(8).

(c) *Output contracts.*—(1) *General rule.*—The purchase pursuant to a contract by a nongovernmental person of available output of an output facility (output contract) financed with proceeds of an issue is taken into account under the private business tests if the purchase has the effect of transferring the benefits of owning the facility and the burdens of paying the debt service on bonds used (directly or indirectly) to finance the facility (the benefits and burdens test). See paragraph (c)(4) of this section for the treatment of an output contract that is properly characterized as a lease for Federal income tax purposes. See paragraphs (d) and (e) of this section for rules regarding measuring the use of, and payments of debt service for, an output facility for determining whether the private business tests are met. See also §1.141-8 for rules for when an issue that finances an output facility (other than a water facility) meets the private business tests because the nonqualified amount of the issue exceeds $15 million.

(2) *Take contract or take or pay contract.*—The benefits and burdens test is met if a nongovernmental person agrees pursuant to a take contract or a take or pay contract to purchase available output of a facility.

(3) *Requirements contract.*—(i) *In general.*—A requirements contract may satisfy the benefits and burdens test under paragraph (c)(3)(ii) or (iii) of this section. See §1.141-15(f)(2) for special effective dates for the application of this paragraph (c)(3) to issues financing facilities subject to requirements contracts.

(ii) *Requirements contract similar to take contract or take or pay contract.*—A requirements contract generally meets the benefits and burdens test to the extent that it contains contractual terms that obligate the purchaser to make payments that are not contingent on the output requirements of the purchaser or that obligate the purchaser to have output requirements. For example, a requirements contract with an industrial purchaser meets the benefits and burdens test if the purchaser enters into additional contractual obligations with the issuer or another governmental unit not to cease operations. A requirements contract does not meet the benefits and burdens test, however, by reason of a provision that requires the purchaser to pay reasonable and customary damages (including liquidated damages) in the event of a default, or a provision that permits the purchaser to pay a specified amount to terminate the contract while the purchaser has requirements, in each case if the amount of the payment is reasonably related to the purchaser's obligation to buy requirements that is discharged by the payment.

(iii) *Wholesale requirements contract.*—(A) *In general.*—A requirements contract that is a sale at wholesale (a *wholesale requirements contract*) may satisfy the benefits and burdens test, depending on all the facts and circumstances.

(B) *Significant factors.*—Significant factors that tend to establish that a wholesale requirements contract meets the benefits and burdens test include, but are not limited to—

(1) The term of the contract is substantial relative to the term of the issue or issues that finance the facility; and

(2) The amount of output to be purchased under the contract represents a substantial portion of the available output of the facility.

(C) *Safe harbors.*—A wholesale requirements contract does not meet the benefits and burdens test if—

(1) The term of the contract, including all renewal options, does not exceed the lesser of 5 years or 30 percent of the term of the issue; or

(2) The amount of output to be purchased under the contract (and any other requirements contract with the same purchaser or a related party with respect to the facility) does not exceed 5 percent of the available output of the facility.

(iv) *Retail requirements contract.*—Except as otherwise provided in this paragraph (c)(3), a requirements contract that is not a sale at wholesale does not meet the benefits and burdens test.

(4) *Output contract properly characterized as a lease.*—Notwithstanding any other provision of this section, an output contract that is properly characterized as a lease for Federal income tax purposes shall be tested under the rules contained in §§ 1.141-3 and 1.141-4 to determine whether it is taken into account under the private business tests.

(d) *Measurement of private business use.*—If an output contract results in private business use under this section, the amount of private business use generally is the amount of output purchased under the contract.

(e) *Measurement of private security or payment.*—The measurement of payments made or to be made by nongovernmental persons under output contracts as a percent of the debt service of an issue is determined under the rules provided in § 1.141-4.

(f) *Exceptions for certain contracts.*—(1) *Small purchases of output.*—An output contract for the use of a facility is not taken into account under the private business tests if the average annual payments to be made under the contract do not exceed 1 percent of the average annual debt service on all outstanding tax-exempt bonds issued to finance the facility, determined as of the effective date of the contract.

(2) *Swapping and pooling arrangements.*—An agreement that provides for swapping or pooling of output by one or more governmental persons and one or more nongovernmental persons does not result in private business use of the output facility owned by the governmental person to the extent that—

(i) The swapped output is reasonably expected to be approximately equal in value (determined over periods of three years or less); and

(ii) The purpose of the agreement is to enable each of the parties to satisfy different peak load demands, to accommodate temporary outages, to diversify supply, or to enhance reliability in accordance with prudent reliability standards.

(3) *Short-term output contracts.*—An output contract with a nongovernmental person is not taken into account under the private business tests if—

(i) The term of the contract, including all renewal options, is not longer than 3 years;

(ii) The contract either is a negotiated, arm's-length arrangement that provides for compensation at fair market value, or is based on generally applicable and uniformly applied rates; and

(iii) The output facility is not financed for a principal purpose of providing that facility for use by that nongovernmental person.

(4) *Certain conduit parties disregarded.*—A nongovernmental person acting solely as a conduit for the exchange of output among

governmentally owned and operated utilities is disregarded in determining whether the private business tests are met with respect to financed facilities owned by a governmental person.

(g) *Special rules for electric output facilities used to provide open access.*—(1) *Operation of transmission facilities by nongovernmental persons.*—(i) *In general.*—The operation of an electric transmission facility by a nongovernmental person may result in private business use of the facility under § 1.141-3 and this section based on all the facts and circumstances. For example, a transmission facility is generally used for a private business use if a nongovernmental person enters into a contract to operate the facility and receives compensation based, in whole or in part, on a share of net profits from the operation of the facility.

(ii) *Certain use by independent transmission operators.*—A contract for the operation of an electric transmission facility by an independent entity, such as a regional transmission organization or an independent system operator (*independent transmission operator*), does not constitute private business use of the facility if—

(A) The facility is owned by a governmental person;

(B) The operation of the facility by the independent transmission operator is approved by the FERC under one or more provisions of the Federal Power Act (16 U.S.C. 791a through 825r) (or by a state authority under comparable provisions of state law);

(C) No portion of the compensation of the independent transmission operator is based on a share of net profits from the operation of the facility; and

(D) The independent transmission operator does not bear risk of loss of the facility.

(2) *Certain use by nongovernmental persons under output contracts.*—(i) *Transmission facilities.*—The use of an electric transmission facility by a nongovernmental person pursuant to an output contract does not constitute private business use of the facility if—

(A) The facility is owned by a governmental person;

(B) The facility is operated by an independent transmission operator in a manner that satisfies paragraph (g)(1)(ii) of this section; and

(C) The facility is not financed for a principal purpose of providing that facility for use by that nongovernmental person.

(ii) *Distribution facilities.*—The use of an electric distribution facility by a nongovernmental person pursuant to an output contract does not constitute private business use of the facility if—

(A) The facility is owned by a governmental person;

(B) The facility is available for use on a nondiscriminatory, open access basis by buyers and sellers of electricity in accordance with rates that are generally applicable and uniformly applied within the meaning of § 1.141-3(c)(2); and

(C) The facility is not financed for a principal purpose of providing that facility for use by that nongovernmental person (other than a retail end-user).

(3) *Ancillary services.*—The use of an electric output facility to provide ancillary services required to be offered as part of an open access transmission tariff under rules promulgated by the FERC under the Federal Power Act (16 U.S.C. 791a through 825r) (or by a state regulatory authority under comparable provisions of state law) does not result in private business use.

(4) *Exceptions to deliberate action rules.*—(i) *Mandated wheeling.*—Entering into a contract for the use of electric transmission or distribution facilities is not treated as a deliberate action under § 1.141-2(d) if—

(A) The contract is entered into in response to (or in anticipation of) an order by the United States under sections 211 and 212 of the Federal Power Act (16 U.S.C. 824j and 824k) (or a state regulatory authority under comparable provisions of state law); and

(B) The terms of the contract are bona fide and arm's-length, and the consideration paid is consistent with the provisions of section 212(a) of the Federal Power Act.

(ii) *Actions taken to implement non-discriminatory, open access.*—An action is not treated as a deliberate action under § 1.141-2(d) if it is taken to implement the offering of non-discriminatory, open access tariffs for the use of electric transmission or distribution facilities in a manner consistent with rules promulgated by the FERC under sections 205 and 206 of the Federal Power Act (16 U.S.C. 824d and 824e) (or comparable provisions of state law). This paragraph (g)(4)(ii) does not apply, however, to the sale, exchange, or other disposition (within the meaning of section 1001(a)) of transmission or distribution facilities to a nongovernmental person.

(iii) *Application of reasonable expectations test to certain current refunding bonds.*—An action taken or to be taken with respect to electric transmission or distribution facilities refinanced by an issue is

25,142

Tax Exempt. Requirements: State/Local Bonds
See p. 20,601 for regulations not amended to reflect law changes

not taken into account under the reasonable expectations test of §1.141-2(d) if—

(A) The action is described in paragraph (g)(4)(i) or (ii) of this section;

(B) The bonds of the issue are current refunding bonds that refund bonds originally issued before February 23, 1998; and

(C) The weighted average maturity of the refunding bonds is not greater than the remaining weighted average maturity of the prior bonds.

(5) *Additional transactions as permitted by the Commissioner.*—The Commissioner may, by published guidance, set forth additional circumstances in which the use of electric output facilities in a restructured electric industry does not constitute private business use.

(h) *Allocations of output facilities and systems.*—(1) *Facts and circumstances analysis.*—Whether output sold under an output contract is allocated to a particular facility (for example, a generating unit), to the entire system of the seller of that output (net of any uses of that system output allocated to a particular facility), or to a portion of a facility is based on all the facts and circumstances. Significant factors to be considered in determining the allocation of an output contract to financed property are the following:

(i) The extent to which it is physically possible to deliver output to or from a particular facility or system.

(ii) The terms of a contract relating to the delivery of output (such as delivery limitations and options or obligations to deliver power from additional sources).

(iii) Whether a contract is entered into as part of a common plan of financing for a facility.

(iv) The method of pricing output under the contract, such as the use of market rates rather than rates designed to pay debt service of tax-exempt bonds used to finance a particular facility.

(2) *Illustrations.*—The following illustrate the factors set forth in paragraph (h)(1) of this section:

(i) *Physical possibility.*—Output from a generating unit that is fed directly into a low voltage distribution system of the owner of that unit and that cannot physically leave that distribution system generally must be allocated to those receiving electricity through that distribution system. Output may be allocated without regard to physical limitations, however, if exchange or similar agreements provide output to a purchaser where, but for the exchange agreements, it would not be possible for the seller to provide output to that purchaser.

(ii) *Contract terms relating to performance.*—A contract to provide a specified amount of electricity from a system, but only when at least that amount of electricity is being generated by a particular unit, is allocated to that unit. For example, a contract to buy 20 MW of system power with a right to take up to 40 percent of the actual output of a specific 50 MW facility whenever total system output is insufficient to meet all of the seller's obligations generally is allocated to the specific facility rather than to the system.

(iii) *Common plan of financing.*—A contract entered into as part of a common plan of financing for a facility generally is allocated to the facility if debt service for the issue of bonds is reasonably expected to be paid, directly or indirectly, from payments under the contract.

(iv) *Pricing method.*—Pricing based on the capital and generating costs of a particular turbine tends to indicate that output under the contract is properly allocated to that turbine.

(3) *Transmission and distribution contracts.*—Whether use under an output contract for transmission or distribution is allocated to a particular facility or to a transmission or distribution network is based on all the facts and circumstances, in a manner similar to paragraphs (h)(1) and (2) of this section. In general, the method used to determine payments under a contract is a more significant contract term for this purpose than nominal contract path. In general, if reasonable and consistently applied, the determination of use of transmission or distribution facilities under an output contract may be based on a method used by third parties, such as reliability councils.

(4) *Allocation of payments.*—Payments for output provided by an output facility financed with two or more sources of funding are generally allocated under the rules in §1.141-4(c).

(i) *Examples.*—The following examples illustrate the application of this section:

Example 1. Joint ownership. Z, an investor-owned electric utility, and City H agree to construct an electric generating facility of a size sufficient to take advantage of the economies of scale. H will issue $50 million of its 24-year bonds, and Z will use $100 million of its

funds for construction of a facility they will jointly own as tenants in common. Each of the participants will share in the ownership, output, and operating expenses of the facility in proportion to its contribution to the cost of the facility, that is, one-third by H and two-thirds by Z. H's bonds will be secured by H's ownership interest in the facility and by revenues to be derived from its share of the annual output of the facility. H will need only 50 percent of its share of the annual output of the facility during the first 20 years of operations. It agrees to sell 10 percent of its share of the annual output to Z for a period of 20 years pursuant to a contract under which Z agrees to take that power if available. The facility will begin operation, and Z will begin to receive power, 4 years after the H bonds are issued. The measurement period for the property financed by the issue is 20 years. H also will sell the remaining 40 percent of its share of the annual output to numerous other private utilities under contracts of three years or less that satisfy the exception under paragraph (f)(3) of this section. No other contracts will be executed obligating any person to purchase any specified amount of the power for any specified period of time. No person (other than Z) will make payments that will result in a transfer of the burdens of paying debt service on bonds used directly or indirectly to provide H's share of the facilities. The bonds are not private activity bonds, because H's one-third interest in the facility is not treated as used by the other owners of the facility. Although 10 percent of H's share of the annual output of the facility will be used in the trade or business of Z, a nongovernmental person, under this section, that portion constitutes not more than 10 percent of the available output of H's ownership interest in the facility.

Example 2. Wholesale requirements contract. (i) City J issues 20-year bonds to acquire an electric generating facility having a reasonably expected economic life substantially greater than 20 years and a nameplate capacity of 100 MW. The available output of the facility under paragraph (b)(1) of this section is approximately 17,520,000 MWh (100 MW X 24 hours X 365 days X 20 years). On the issue date, J enters into a contract with T, an investor-owned utility, to provide T with all of its power requirements for a period of 10 years, commencing on the issue date. J reasonably expects that T will actually purchase an average of 30 MW over the 10-year period. The contract is taken into account under the private business tests pursuant to paragraph (c)(3) of this section because the term of the contract is substantial relative to the term of the issue and the amount of output to be purchased is a substantial portion of the available output.

(ii) Under paragraph (d) of this section, the amount of reasonably expected private business use under this contract is approximately 15 percent (30 MW X 24 hours X 365 days X 10 years, or 2,628,000 MWh) of the available output. Accordingly, the issue meets the private business use test. J reasonably expects that the amount to be paid for an average of 30 MW of power (less the operation and maintenance costs directly attributable to generating that 30 MW of power), will be more than 10 percent of debt service on the issue on a present-value basis. Accordingly, the issue meets the private security or payment test because J reasonably expects that payment of more than 10 percent of the debt service will be indirectly derived from payments by T. The bonds are private activity bonds under paragraph (c) of this section. Further, if 15 percent of the sale proceeds of the issue is greater than $15 million and the issue meets the private security or payment test with respect to the $15 million output limitation, the bonds are also private activity bonds under section 141(b)(4). See §1.141-8.

Example 3. Retail contracts. (i) State Agency M, a political subdivision, issues bonds in 2003 to finance the construction of a generating facility that will be used to furnish electricity to M's retail customers. In 2007, M enters into a 10-year contract with industrial corporation I. Under the contract, M agrees to supply I with all of its power requirements during the contract term, and I agrees to pay for that power at a negotiated price as it is delivered. The contract does not require I to pay for any power except to the extent I has requirements. In addition, the contract requires I to pay reasonable and customary liquidated damages in the event of a default by I, and permits I to terminate the contract while it has requirements by paying M a specified amount that is a reasonable and customary amount for terminating the contract. Any damages or termination payment by I will be reasonably related to I's obligation to buy requirements that is discharged by the payment. Under paragraph (c)(3) of this section, the contract does not meet the benefits and burdens test. Thus, it is not taken into account under the private business tests.

(ii) The facts are the same as in paragraph (i) of this *Example 3*, except that the contract requires I to make guaranteed minimum payments, regardless of I's requirements, in an amount such that the contract does not meet the exception for small purchases in paragraph (f)(1) of this section. Under paragraph (c)(3)(ii) of this section, the contract meets the benefits and burdens test because it obligates I to make payments that are not contingent on its output requirements. Thus, it is taken into account under the private business tests.

Example 4. Allocation of existing contracts to new facilities. Power Authority K, a political subdivision created by the legislature in State X to own and operate certain power generating facilities, sells all of the power from its existing facilities to four private utility systems under contracts executed in 1999, under which the four systems are required to take or pay for specified portions of the total power output until the year 2029. Existing facilities supply all of the present needs of the four utility systems, but their future power requirements are expected to increase substantially beyond the capacity of K's current generating system. K issues 20-year bonds in 2004 to construct a large generating facility. As part of the financing plan for the bonds, a fifth private utility system contracts with K to take or pay for 15 percent of the available output of the new facility. The balance of the output of the new facility will be available for sale as required, but initially it is not anticipated that there will be any need for that power. The revenues from the contract with the fifth private utility system will be sufficient to pay less than 10 percent of the debt service on the bonds (determined on a present value basis). The balance, which will exceed 10 percent of the debt service on the bonds, will be paid from revenues derived from the contracts with the four systems initially from sale of power produced by the old facilities. The output contracts with all the private utilities are allocated to K's entire generating system. See paragraphs (h)(1) and (2) of this section. Thus, the bonds meet the private business use test because more than 10 percent of the proceeds will be used in the trade or business of a nongovernmental person. In addition, the bonds meet the private security or payment test because payment of more than 10 percent of the debt service, pursuant to underlying arrangements, will be derived from payments in respect of property used for a private business use.

Example 5. Allocation to displaced resource. Municipal utility MU, a political subdivision, purchases all of the electricity required to meet the needs of its customers (1,000 MW) from B, an investor-owned utility that operates its own electric generating facilities, under a 50-year take or pay contract. MU does not anticipate that it will require additional electric resources, and any new resources would produce electricity at a higher cost to MU than its cost under its contract with B. Nevertheless, B encourages MU to construct a new generating plant sufficient to meet MU's requirements. MU issues obligations to construct facilities that will produce 1,000 MW of electricity. MU, B, and I, another investor-owned utility, enter into an agreement under which MU assigns to I its rights under MU's take or pay contract with B. Under this arrangement, I will pay MU, and MU will continue to pay B, for the 1,000 MW. I's payments to MU will at least equal the amounts required to pay debt service on MU's bonds. In addition, under paragraph (h)(1)(iii) of this section, the contract among MU, B, and I is entered into as part of a common plan of financing of the MU facilities. Under all the facts and circumstances, MU's assignment to I of its rights under the original take or pay contract is allocable to MU's new facilities under paragraph (h) of this section. Because I is a nongovernmental person, MU's bonds are private activity bonds.

Example 6. Operation of transmission facilities by regional transmission organization. (i) Public Power Agency D is a political subdivision that owns and operates electric generation, transmission and distribution facilities. In 2003, D transfers operating control of its transmission system to a regional transmission organization (RTO), a nongovernmental person, pursuant to an operating agreement that is approved by the FERC under sections 205 and 206 of the Federal Power Act. D retains ownership of its facilities. No portion of the RTO's compensation is based on a share of net profits from the operation of D's facilities, and the RTO does not bear any risk of loss of those facilities. Under paragraph (g)(1)(ii) of this section, the RTO's use of D's facilities does not constitute a private business use.

(ii) Company A is located in D's service territory. In 2004, Power Supplier E, a nongovernmental person, enters into a 10-year contract with A to supply A's electricity requirements. The electricity supplied by E to A will be transmitted over D's transmission and distribution facilities. D's distribution facilities are available for use on a nondiscriminatory, open access basis by buyers and sellers of electricity in accordance with rates that are generally applicable and uniformly applied within the meaning of § 1.141-3(c)(2). D's facilities are not financed for a principal purpose of providing the facilities for use by E. Under paragraph (g)(2) of this section, the contract between A and E does not result in private business use of D's facilities.

Example 7. Certain actions not treated as deliberate actions. The facts are the same as in *Example 6* of this paragraph (i), except that the RTO's compensation is based on a share of net profits from operating D's facilities. In addition, D had issued bonds in 1994 to finance improvements to its transmission system. At the time D transfers operating control of its transmission system to the RTO, D chooses to apply the private activity bond regulations of §§ 1.141 through 1.141-15 to the 1994 bonds. The operation of D's facilities by the RTO results in private business use under § 1.141-3 and paragraph (g)(1)(i) of this section. Under the special exception in paragraph (g)(4)(ii) of this section, however, the transfer of control is not treated as a deliberate action. Accordingly, the transfer of control does not cause the 1994 bonds to meet the private activity bond tests.

Example 8. Current refunding. The facts are the same as in *Example 7* of this paragraph (i), and in addition D issues bonds in 2004 to currently refund the 1994 bonds. The weighted average maturity of the 2004 bonds is not greater than the remaining weighted average maturity of the 1994 bonds. D chooses to apply the private activity bond regulations of §§ 1.141 through 1.141-15 to the refunding bonds. In general, reasonable expectations must be separately tested on the date that refunding bonds are issued under § 1.141-2(d). Under the special exception in paragraph (g)(4)(iii) of this section, however, the transfer of the financed facilities to the RTO need not be taken into account in applying the reasonable expectations test to the refunding bonds.

[Reg. § 1.141-7.]

☐ [*T.D.* 9016, 9-19-2002 (*corrected* 11-26-2002).]

[Reg. § 1.141-8]

§ 1.141-8. $15 million limitation for output facilities.—(a) *In general.*—(1) *General rule.*—Section 141(b)(4) provides a special private activity bond limitation (the $15 million output limitation) for issues 5 percent or more of the proceeds of which are to be used to finance output facilities (other than a facility for the furnishing of water). Under this rule, an issue consists of private activity bonds under the private business tests of section 141(b)(1) and (2) if the nonqualified amount with respect to output facilities financed by the proceeds of the issue exceeds $15 million. The $15 million output limitation applies in addition to the private business tests of section 141(b)(1) and (2). Under section 141(b)(4) and paragraph (a)(2) of this section, the $15 million output limitation is reduced in certain cases. Specifically, an issue meets the test in section 141(b)(4) if both of the following tests are met:

(i) More than $15 million of the proceeds of the issue to be used with respect to an output facility are to be used for a private business use. Investment proceeds are disregarded for this purpose if they are not allocated disproportionately to the private business use portion of the issue.

(ii) The payment of the principal of, or the interest on, more than $15 million of the sale proceeds of the portion of the issue used with respect to an output facility is (under the terms of the issue or any underlying arrangement) directly or indirectly—

(A) Secured by any interest in an output facility used or to be used for a private business use (or payments in respect of such an output facility); or

(B) To be derived from payments (whether or not to the issuer) in respect of an output facility used or to be used for a private business use.

(2) *Reduction in $15 million output limitation for outstanding issues.*—(i) *General rule.*—In determining whether an issue 5 percent or more of the proceeds of which are to be used with respect to an output facility consists of private activity bonds under the $15 million output limitation, the $15 million limitation on private business use and private security or payments is applied by taking into account the aggregate nonqualified amounts of any outstanding bonds of other issues 5 percent or more of the proceeds of which are or will be used with respect to that output facility or any other output facility that is part of the same project.

(ii) *Bonds taken into account.*—For purposes of this paragraph (a)(2), applying the $15 million output limitation to an issue (the later issue), a tax-exempt bond of another issue (the earlier issue) is taken into account if—

(A) That bond is outstanding on the issue date of the later issue;

(B) That bond will not be redeemed within 90 days of the issue date of the later issue in connection with the refunding of that bond by the later issue; and

(C) 5 percent or more of the sale proceeds of the earlier issue financed an output facility that is part of the same project as the output facility that is financed by 5 percent or more of the sale proceeds of the later issue.

(3) *Benefits and burdens test applicable.*—(i) *In general.*—In applying the $15 million output limitation, the benefits and burdens test of § 1.141-7 applies, except that "$15 million" is applied in place of "10 percent", or "5 percent" as appropriate.

(ii) *Earlier issues for the project.*—If bonds of an earlier issue are outstanding and must be taken into account under paragraph (a)(2) of this section, the nonqualified amount for that earlier issue is multiplied by a fraction, the numerator of which is the adjusted issue price of the earlier issue as of the issue date of the later issue, and the denominator of which is the issue price of the earlier issue. Pre-

25,144

Tax Exempt. Requirements: State/Local Bonds
See p. 20,601 for regulations not amended to reflect law changes

issuance accrued interest as defined in §1.148-1(b) is disregarded for this purpose.

(b) *Definition of project.*—(1) *General rule.*—For purposes of paragraph (a)(2) of this section, *project* has the meaning provided in this paragraph. Facilities that are functionally related and subordinate to a project are treated as part of that same project. Facilities having different purposes or serving different customer bases are not ordinarily part of the same project. For example, the following are generally not part of the same project—

(i) Generation, transmission and distribution facilities;

(ii) Separate facilities designed to serve wholesale customers and retail customers; and

(iii) A peaking unit and a baseload unit (regardless of the location of the units).

(2) *Separate ownership.*—Except as otherwise provided in this paragraph (b)(2), facilities that are not owned by the same person are not part of the same project. If different governmental persons act in concert to finance a project, however (for example as participants in a joint powers authority), their interests are aggregated with respect to that project to determine whether the $15 million output limitation is met. In the case of undivided ownership interests in a single output facility, property that is not owned by different persons is treated as separate projects only if the separate interests are financed—

(i) With bonds of different issuers; and

(ii) Without a principal purpose of avoiding the limitation in this section.

(3) *Generating property.*—(i) *Property on same site.*—In the case of generation and related facilities, *project* means property located at the same site.

(ii) *Special rule for generating units.*—Separate generating units are not part of the same project if one unit is reasonably expected, on the issue date of each issue that finances the units, to be placed in service more than 3 years before the other. Common facilities or property that will be functionally related to more than one generating unit must be allocated on a reasonable basis. If a generating unit already is constructed or is under construction (the first unit) and bonds are to be issued to finance an additional generating unit (the second unit), all costs for any common facilities paid or incurred before the earlier of the issue date of bonds to finance the second unit or the commencement of construction of the second unit are allocated to the first unit. At the time that bonds are issued to finance the second unit (or, if earlier, upon commencement of construction of that unit), any remaining costs of the common facilities may be allocated between the first and second units so that in the aggregate the allocation is reasonable.

(4) *Transmission and distribution.*—In the case of transmission or distribution facilities, *project* means functionally related or contiguous property. Separate transmission or distribution facilities are not part of the same project if one facility is reasonably expected, on the issue date of each issue that finances the facilities, to be placed in service more than 2 years before the other.

(5) *Subsequent improvements.*—(i) *In general.*—An improvement to generation, transmission or distribution facilities that is not part of the original design of those facilities (the original project) is not part of the same project as the original project if the construction, reconstruction, or acquisition of that improvement commences more than 3 years after the original project was placed in service and the bonds issued to finance that improvement are issued more than 3 years after the original project was placed in service.

(ii) *Special rule for transmission and distribution facilities.*—An improvement to transmission or distribution facilities that is not part of the original design of that property is not part of the same project as the original project if the issuer did not reasonably expect the need to make that improvement when it commenced construction of the original project and the construction, reconstruction, or acquisition of that improvement is mandated by the federal government or a state regulatory authority to accommodate requests for wheeling.

(6) *Replacement property.*—For purposes of this section, property that replaces existing property of an output facility is treated as part of the same project as the replaced property unless—

(i) The need to replace the property was not reasonably expected on the issue date or the need to replace the property occurred more than 3 years before the issuer reasonably expected (determined on the issue date of the bonds financing the property) that it would need to replace the property; and

(ii) The bonds that finance (and refinance) the output facility have a weighted average maturity that is not greater than 120 percent of the reasonably expected economic life of the facility.

(c) *Example.*—The application of the provisions of this section is illustrated by the following example:

Example: (i) Power Authority K, a political subdivision, intends to issue a single issue of tax-exempt bonds at par with a stated principal amount and sale proceeds of $500 million to finance the acquisition of an electric generating facility. No portion of the facility will be used for a private business use, except that L, an investor-owned utility, will purchase 10 percent of the output of the facility under a take contract and will pay 10 percent of the debt service on the bonds. The nonqualified amount with respect to the bonds is $50 million.

(ii) The maximum amount of tax-exempt bonds that may be issued for the acquisition of an interest in the facility in paragraph (i) of this *Example* is $465 million (that is, $450 million for the 90 percent of the facility that is governmentally owned and used plus a nonqualified amount of $15 million).

[Reg. §1.141-8.]

☐ [*T.D.* 9016, 9-19-2002.]

[Reg. §1.141-9]

§1.141-9. Unrelated or disproportionate use test.—(a) *General rules.*—(1) *Description of test.*—Under section 141(b)(3) (the unrelated or disproportionate use test), an issue meets the private business tests if the amount of private business use and private security or payments attributable to unrelated or disproportionate private business use exceeds 5 percent of the proceeds of the issue. For this purpose, the private business use test is applied by taking into account only use that is not related to any government use of proceeds of the issue (unrelated use) and use that is related but disproportionate to any government use of those proceeds (disproportionate use).

(2) *Application of unrelated or disproportionate use test.*—(i) *Order of application.*—The unrelated or disproportionate use test is applied by first determining whether a private business use is related to a government use. Next, private business use that relates to a government use is examined to determine whether it is disproportionate to that government use.

(ii) *Aggregation of unrelated and disproportionate use.*—All the unrelated use and disproportionate use financed with the proceeds of an issue are aggregated to determine compliance with the unrelated or disproportionate use test. The amount of permissible unrelated and disproportionate private business use is not reduced by the amount of private business use financed with the proceeds of an issue that is neither unrelated use nor disproportionate use.

(iii) *Deliberate actions.*—A deliberate action that occurs after the issue date does not result in unrelated or disproportionate use if the issue meets the conditions of §1.141-12(a).

(b) *Unrelated use.*—(1) *In general.*—Whether a private business use is related to a government use financed with the proceeds of an issue is determined on a case-by-case basis, emphasizing the operational relationship between the government use and the private business use. In general, a facility that is used for a related private business use must be located within, or adjacent to, the governmentally used facility.

(2) *Use for the same purpose as government use.*—Use of a facility by a nongovernmental person for the same purpose as use by a governmental person is not treated as unrelated use if the government use is not insignificant. Similarly, a use of a facility in the same manner both for private business use that is related use and private business use that is unrelated use does not result in unrelated use if the related use is not insignificant. For example, a privately owned pharmacy in a governmentally owned hospital does not ordinarily result in unrelated use solely because the pharmacy also serves individuals not using the hospital. In addition, use of parking spaces in a garage by a nongovernmental person is not treated as unrelated use if more than an insignificant portion of the parking spaces are used for a government use (or a private business use that is related to a government use), even though the use by the nongovernmental person is not directly related to that other use.

(c) *Disproportionate use.*—(1) *Definition of disproportionate use.*—A private business use is disproportionate to a related government use only to the extent that the amount of proceeds used for that private business use exceeds the amount of proceeds used for the related government use. For example, a private use of $100 of proceeds that is related to a government use of $70 of proceeds results in $30 of disproportionate use.

(2) *Aggregation of related uses.*—If two or more private business uses of the proceeds of an issue relate to a single government use of those proceeds, those private business uses are aggregated to apply the disproportionate use test.

(3) *Allocation rule.*—If a private business use relates to more than a single use of the proceeds of the issue (for example, two or more government uses of the proceeds of the issue or a government use and a private use), the amount of any disproportionate use may be determined by—

(i) Reasonably allocating the proceeds used for the private business use among the related uses;

(ii) Aggregating government uses that are directly related to each other; or

(iii) Allocating the private business use to the government use to which it is primarily related.

(d) *Maximum use taken into account.*—The determination of the amount of unrelated use or disproportionate use of a facility is based on the maximum amount of reasonably expected government use of a facility during the measurement period. Thus, no unrelated use or disproportionate use arises solely because a facility initially has excess capacity that is to be used by a nongovernmental person if the facility will be completely used by the issuer during the term of the issue for more than an insignificant period.

(e) *Examples.*—The following examples illustrate the application of this section:

Example 1. School and remote cafeteria. County X issues bonds with proceeds of $20 million and uses $18.1 million of the proceeds for construction of a new school building and $1.9 million of the proceeds for construction of a privately operated cafeteria in its administrative office building, which is located at a remote site. The bonds are secured, in part, by the cafeteria. The $1.9 million of proceeds is unrelated to the government use (that is, school construction) financed with the bonds and exceeds 5 percent of $20 million. Thus, the issue meets the private business tests.

Example 2. Public safety building and courthouse. City Y issues bonds with proceeds of $50 million for construction of a new public safety building ($32 million) and for improvements to an existing courthouse ($15 million). Y uses $3 million of the bond proceeds for renovations to an existing privately operated cafeteria located in the courthouse. The bonds are secured, in part, by the cafeteria. Y's use of the $3 million for the privately operated cafeteria does not meet the unrelated or disproportionate use test because these expenditures are neither unrelated use nor disproportionate use.

Example 3. Unrelated garage. City Y issues bonds with proceeds of $50 million for construction of a new public safety building ($30.5 million) and for improvements to an existing courthouse ($15 million). Y uses $3 million of the bond proceeds for renovations to an existing privately operated cafeteria located in the courthouse. The bonds are secured, in part, by the cafeteria. Y also uses $1.5 million of the proceeds to construct a privately operated parking garage adjacent to a private office building. The private business use of the parking garage is unrelated to any government use of proceeds of the issue. Since the proceeds used for unrelated uses and disproportionate uses do not exceed 5 percent of the proceeds, the unrelated or disproportionate use test is not met.

Example 4. Disproportionate use of garage. County Z issues bonds with proceeds of $20 million for construction of a hospital with no private business use ($17 million); renovation of an office building with no private business use ($1 million); and construction of a garage that is entirely used for a private business use ($2 million). The use of the garage is related to the use of the office building but not to the use of the hospital. The private business use of the garage results in $1 million of disproportionate use because the proceeds used for the garage ($2 million) exceed the proceeds used for the related government use ($1 million). The bonds are not private activity bonds, however, because the disproportionate use does not exceed 5 percent of the proceeds of the issue.

Example 5. Bonds for multiple projects. (i) County W issues bonds with proceeds of $80 million for the following purposes: (1) $72 million to construct a County-owned and operated waste incinerator; (2) $1 million for a County-owned and operated facility for the temporary storage of hazardous waste prior to final disposal; (3) $1 million to construct a privately owned recycling facility located at a remote site; and (4) $6 million to build a garage adjacent to the County-owned incinerator that will be leased to Company T to store and repair trucks that it owns and uses to haul County W refuse. Company T uses 75 percent of its trucks to haul materials to the incinerator and the remaining 25 percent of its trucks to haul materials to the temporary storage facility.

(ii) The $1 million of proceeds used for the recycling facility is used for an unrelated use. The garage is related use. In addition, 75 percent of the use of the $6 million of proceeds used for the garage is allocable to the government use of proceeds at the incinerator. The remaining 25 percent of the proceeds used for the garage ($1.5 million) relates to the government use of proceeds at the temporary storage facility. Thus, this portion of the proceeds used for the garage exceeds the proceeds used for the temporary storage facility by $0.5

million and this excess is disproportionate use (but not unrelated use). Thus, the aggregate amount of unrelated use and disproportionate use financed with the proceeds of the issue is $1.5 million. Alternatively, under paragraph (c)(3)(iii) of this section, the entire garage may be treated as related to the government use of the incinerator and, under that allocation, the garage is not disproportionate use. In either event, section 141(b)(3) limits the aggregate unrelated use and disproportionate use to $4 million. Therefore, the bonds are not private activity bonds under this section.

[Reg. § 1.141-9.]

☐ [T.D. 8712, 1-10-97.]

[Reg. § 1.141-10]

§ 1.141-10. Coordination with volume cap.—[Reserved.]

☐ [T.D. 8712, 1-10-97.]

[Reg. § 1.141-11]

§ 1.141-11. Acquisition of nongovernmental output property.—[Reserved.]

☐ [T.D. 8712, 1-10-97.]

[Reg. § 1.141-12]

§ 1.141-12. Remedial actions.—(a) *Conditions to taking remedial action.*—An action that causes an issue to meet the private business tests or the private loan financing test is not treated as a deliberate action if the issuer takes a remedial action described in paragraph (d), (e), or (f) of this section with respect to the nonqualified bonds and if all of the requirements in paragraphs (a)(1) through (5) of this section are met.

(1) *Reasonable expectations test met.*—The issuer reasonably expected on the issue date that the issue would meet neither the private business tests nor the private loan financing test for the entire term of the bonds. For this purpose, if the issuer reasonably expected on the issue date to take a deliberate action prior to the final maturity date of the issue that would cause either the private business tests or the private loan financing test to be met, the term of the bonds for this purpose may be determined by taking into account a redemption provision if the provisions of § 1.141-2(d)(2)(ii)(A) through (C) are met.

(2) *Maturity not unreasonably long.*—The term of the issue must not be longer than is reasonably necessary for the governmental purposes of the issue (within the meaning of § 1.148-1(c)(4)). Thus, this requirement is met if the weighted average maturity of the bonds of the issue is not greater than 120 percent of the average reasonably expected economic life of the property financed with the proceeds of the issue as of the issue date.

(3) *Fair market value consideration.*—Except as provided in paragraph (f) of this section, the terms of any arrangement that results in satisfaction of either the private business tests or the private loan financing test are bona fide and arm's-length, and the new user pays fair market value for the use of the financed property. Thus, for example, fair market value may be determined in a manner that takes into account restrictions on the use of the financed property that serve a bona fide governmental purpose.

(4) *Disposition proceeds treated as gross proceeds for arbitrage purposes.*—The issuer must treat any disposition proceeds as gross proceeds for purposes of section 148. For purposes of eligibility for temporary periods under section 148(c) and exemptions from the requirement of section 148(f) the issuer may treat the date of receipt of the disposition proceeds as the issue date of the bonds and disregard the receipt of disposition proceeds for exemptions based on expenditure of proceeds under § 1.148-7 that were met before the receipt of the disposition proceeds.

(5) *Proceeds expended on a governmental purpose.*—Except for a remedial action under paragraph (d) of this section, the proceeds of the issue that are affected by the deliberate action must have been expended on a governmental purpose before the date of the deliberate action.

(b) *Effect of a remedial action.*—1) *In general.*—The effect of a remedial action is to cure use of proceeds that causes the private business use test or the private loan financing test to be met. A remedial action does not affect application of the private security or payment test.

(2) *Effect on bonds that have been advance refunded.*—If proceeds of an issue were used to advance refund another bond, a remedial action taken with respect to the refunding bond proportionately reduces the amount of proceeds of the advance refunded bond that is taken into account under the private business use test or the private loan financing test.

(c) *Disposition proceeds.*—(1) *Definition.*—Disposition proceeds are any amounts (including property, such as an agreement to provide services) derived from the sale, exchange, or other disposition (disposition) of property (other than investments) financed with the proceeds of an issue.

(2) *Allocating disposition proceeds to an issue.*—In general, if the requirements of paragraph (a) of this section are met, after the date of the disposition, the proceeds of the issue allocable to the transferred property are treated as financing the disposition proceeds rather than the transferred property. If a disposition is made pursuant to an installment sale, the proceeds of the issue continue to be allocated to the transferred property. If an issue does not meet the requirements for remedial action in paragraph (a) of this section or the issuer does not take an appropriate remedial action, the proceeds of the issue are allocable to either the transferred property or the disposition proceeds, whichever allocation produces the greater amount of private business use and private security or payments.

(3) *Allocating disposition proceeds to different sources of funding.*—If property has been financed by different sources of funding, for purposes of this section, the disposition proceeds from that property are first allocated to the outstanding bonds that financed that property in proportion to the principal amounts of those outstanding bonds. In no event may disposition proceeds be allocated to bonds that are no longer outstanding or to a source of funding not derived from a borrowing (such as revenues of the issuer) if the disposition proceeds are not greater than the total principal amounts of the outstanding bonds that are allocable to that property. For purposes of this paragraph (c)(3), principal amount has the same meaning as in §1.148-9(b)(2) and outstanding bonds do not include advance refunded bonds.

(d) *Redemption or defeasance of nonqualified bonds.*—(1) *In general.*—The requirements of this paragraph (d) are met if all of the nonqualified bonds of the issue are redeemed. Proceeds of tax-exempt bonds must not be used for this purpose, unless the tax-exempt bonds are qualified bonds, taking into account the purchaser's use of the facility. Except as provided in paragraph (d)(3) of this section, if the bonds are not redeemed within 90 days of the date of the deliberate action, a defeasance escrow must be established for those bonds within 90 days of the deliberate action.

(2) *Special rule for dispositions for cash.*—If the consideration for the disposition of financed property is exclusively cash, the requirements of this paragraph (d) are met if the disposition proceeds are used to redeem a pro rata portion of the nonqualified bonds at the earliest call date after the deliberate action. If the bonds are not redeemed within 90 days of the date of the deliberate action, the disposition proceeds must be used to establish a defeasance escrow for those bonds within 90 days of the deliberate action.

(3) *Anticipatory remedial action.*—The requirements of paragraphs (d)(1) and (2) of this section for redemption or defeasance of the nonqualified bonds within 90 days of the deliberate action are met if the issuer declares its official intent to redeem or defease all of the bonds that would become nonqualified bonds in the event of a subsequent deliberate action that would cause the private business tests or the private loan financing test to be met and redeems or defeases such bonds prior to that deliberate action. The issuer must declare its official intent on or before the date on which it redeems or defeases such bonds, and the declaration of intent must identify the financed property or loan with respect to which the anticipatory remedial action is being taken and describe the deliberate action that potentially may result in the private business tests being met (for example, sale of financed property that the buyer may then lease to a nongovernmental person). Rules similar to those in §1.150-2(e) (regarding official intent for reimbursement bonds) apply to declarations of intent under this paragraph (d)(3), including deviations in the descriptions of the project or loan and deliberate action and the reasonableness of the official intent.

(4) *Notice of defeasance.*—The issuer must provide written notice to the Commissioner of the establishment of the defeasance escrow within 90 days of the date the defeasance escrow is established.

(5) *Special limitation.*—The establishment of a defeasance escrow does not satisfy the requirements of this paragraph (d) if the period between the issue date and the first call date of the bonds is more than 10 1/2 years.

(6) *Defeasance escrow defined.*—A defeasance escrow is an irrevocable escrow established to redeem bonds on their earliest call date in an amount that, together with investment earnings, is sufficient to pay all the principal of, and interest and call premium on, bonds from the date the escrow is established to the earliest call date. The escrow may not be invested in higher yielding investments or in any investment under which the obligor is a user of the proceeds of the bonds.

(e) *Alternative use of disposition proceeds.*—(1) *In general.*—The requirements of this paragraph (e) are met if—

(i) The deliberate action is a disposition for which the consideration is exclusively cash;

(ii) The issuer reasonably expects to expend the disposition proceeds within two years of the date of the deliberate action;

(iii) The disposition proceeds are treated as proceeds for purposes of section 141 and are used in a manner that does not cause the issue to meet either the private business tests or the private loan financing test, and the issuer does not take any action subsequent to the date of the deliberate action to cause either of these tests to be met; and

(iv) If the issuer does not use all of the disposition proceeds for an alternative use described in paragraph (e)(1)(iii) of this section, the issuer uses those remaining disposition proceeds for a remedial action that meets paragraph (d) of this section.

(2) *Special rule for use by 501(c)(3) organizations.*—If the disposition proceeds are to be used by a 501(c)(3) organization, the nonqualified bonds must in addition be treated as reissued for purposes of sections 141, 145, 147, 149, and 150 and, under this treatment, satisfy all of the applicable requirements for qualified 501(c)(3) bonds. Thus, beginning on the date of the deliberate action, nonqualified bonds that satisfy these requirements must be treated as qualified 501(c)(3) bonds for all purposes, including sections 145(b) and 150(b).

(f) *Alternative use of facility.*—The requirements of this paragraph (f) are met if—

(1) The facility with respect to which the deliberate action occurs is used in an alternative manner (for example, used for a qualifying purpose by a nongovernmental person or used by a 501(c)(3) organization rather than a governmental person);

(2) The nonqualified bonds are treated as reissued, as of the date of the deliberate action, for purposes of sections 55 through 59 and 141, 142, 144, 145, 146, 147, 149 and 150, and under this treatment, the nonqualified bonds satisfy all the applicable requirements for qualified bonds throughout the remaining term of the nonqualified bonds;

(3) The deliberate action does not involve a disposition to a purchaser that finances the acquisition with proceeds of another issue of tax-exempt bonds; and

(4) Any disposition proceeds other than those arising from an agreement to provide services (including disposition proceeds from an installment sale) resulting from the deliberate action are used to pay the debt service on the bonds on the next available payment date or, within 90 days of receipt, are deposited into an escrow that is restricted to the yield on the bonds to pay the debt service on the bonds on the next available payment date.

(g) *Rules for deemed reissuance.*—For purposes of determining whether bonds that are treated as reissued under paragraphs (e) and (f) of this section are qualified bonds—

(1) The provisions of the Code and regulations thereunder in effect as of the date of the deliberate action apply; and

(2) For purposes of paragraph (f) of this section, section 147(d) (relating to the acquisition of existing property) does not apply.

(h) *Authority of Commissioner to provide for additional remedial actions.*—The Commissioner may, by publication in the Federal Register or the Internal Revenue Bulletin, provide additional remedial actions, including making a remedial payment to the United States, under which a subsequent action will not be treated as a deliberate action for purposes of §1.141-2.

(i) *Effect of remedial action on continuing compliance.*—Solely for purposes of determining whether deliberate actions that are taken after a remedial action cause an issue to meet the private business tests or the private loan financing test—

(1) If a remedial action is taken under paragraph (d) of this section, the amount of private business use or private loans resulting from the deliberate action that is taken into account for purposes of determining whether the bonds are private activity bonds is that portion of the remaining bonds that is used for private business use or private loans (as calculated under paragraph (j) of this section);

(2) If a remedial action is taken under paragraph (e) or (f) of this section, the amount of private business use or private loans resulting from the deliberate action is not taken into account for purposes of determining whether the bonds are private activity bonds; and

(3) After a remedial action is taken, the amount of disposition proceeds is treated as equal to the proceeds of the issue that had been allocable to the transferred property immediately prior to the disposition. See paragraph (k) of this section, *Example 5.*

(j) *Nonqualified bonds.*—(1) *Amount of nonqualified bonds.*—The non-qualified bonds are a portion of the outstanding bonds in an amount that, if the remaining bonds were issued on the date on which the deliberate action occurs, the remaining bonds would not meet the private business use test or private loan financing test, as applicable. For this purpose, the amount of private business use is the greatest percentage of private business use in any one-year period commencing with the one-year period in which the deliberate action occurs.

(2) *Allocation of nonqualified bonds.*—Allocations of nonqualified bonds must be made on a pro rata basis, except that, for purposes of paragraph (d) of this section (relating to redemption or defeasance), an issuer may treat any bonds of an issue as the nonqualified bonds so long as—

(i) The remaining weighted average maturity of the issue, determined as of the date on which the nonqualified bonds are redeemed or defeased (determination date), and excluding from the determination the nonqualified bonds redeemed or defeased by the issuer in accordance with this section, is not greater than

(ii) The remaining weighted average maturity of the issue, determined as of the determination date, but without regard to the redemption or defeasance of any bonds (including the nonqualified bonds) occurring on the determination date.

(k) *Examples.*—The following examples illustrate the application of this section:

Example 1. Disposition proceeds less than outstanding bonds used to retire bonds. On June 1, 1997, City C issues 30-year bonds with an issue price of $10 million to finance the construction of a hospital building. The bonds have a weighted average maturity that does not exceed 120 percent of the reasonably expected economic life of the building. On the issue date, C reasonably expects that it will be the only user of the building for the entire term of the bonds. Six years after the issue date, C sells the building to Corporation P for $5 million. The sale price is the fair market value of the building, as verified by an independent appraiser. C uses all of the $5 million disposition proceeds to immediately retire a pro rata portion of the bonds. The sale does not cause the bonds to be private activity bonds because C has taken a remedial action described in paragraph (d) of this section so that P is not treated as a private business user of bond proceeds.

Example 2. Lease to nongovernmental person. The facts are the same as in *Example 1*, except that instead of selling the building, C, 6 years after the issue date, leases the building to P for 7 years and uses other funds to redeem all of the $10 million outstanding bonds within 90 days of the deliberate act. The bonds are not treated as private activity bonds because C has taken the remedial action described in paragraph (d) of this section.

Example 3. Sale for less than fair market value. The facts are the same as in *Example 1*, except that the fair market value of the building at the time of the sale to P is $6 million. Because the transfer was for less than fair market value, the bonds are ineligible for the remedial actions under this section. The bonds are private activity bonds because P is treated as a user of all of the proceeds and P makes a payment ($6 million) for this use that is greater than 10 percent of the debt service on the bonds, on a present value basis.

Example 4. Fair market value determined taking into account governmental restrictions. The facts are the same as in *Example 1*, except that the building was used by C only for hospital purposes and C determines to sell the building subject to a restriction that it be used only for hospital purposes. After conducting a public bidding procedure as required by state law, the best price that C is able to obtain for the building subject to this restriction is $4.5 million from P. C uses all of the $4.5 million disposition proceeds to immediately retire a pro rata portion of the bonds. The sale does not cause the bonds to be private activity bonds because C has taken a remedial action described in paragraph (d) of this section so that P is not treated as a private business user of bond proceeds.

Example 5. Alternative use of disposition proceeds. The facts are the same as in *Example 1*, except that C reasonably expects on the date of the deliberate action to use the $5 million disposition proceeds for another governmental purpose (construction of governmentally owned roads) within two years of receipt, rather than using the $5 million to redeem outstanding bonds. C treats these disposition proceeds as gross proceeds for purposes of section 148. The bonds are not private activity bonds because C has taken a remedial action described in paragraph (e) of this section. After the date of the deliberate action, the proceeds of all of the outstanding bonds are treated as used for the construction of the roads, even though only $5 million of disposition proceeds was actually used for the roads.

Example 6. Alternative use of financed property. The facts are the same as in *Example 1*, except that C determines to lease the hospital building to Q, an organization described in section 501(c)(3), for a term of 10 years rather than to sell the building to P. In order to induce Q to provide hospital services, C agrees to lease payments

that are less than fair market value. Before entering into the lease, an applicable elected representative of C approves the lease after a noticed public hearing. As of the date of the deliberate action, the issue meets all the requirements for qualified 501(c)(3) bonds, treating the bonds as reissued on that date. For example, the issue meets the two percent restriction on use of proceeds of finance issuance costs of section 147(g) because the issue pays no costs of issuance from disposition proceeds in connection with the deemed reissuance. C and Q treat the bonds as qualified 501(c)(3) bonds for all purposes commencing with the date of the deliberate action. The bonds are treated as qualified 501(c)(3) bonds commencing with the date of the deliberate action.

Example 7. Deliberate action before proceeds are expended on a governmental purpose. County J issues bonds with proceeds of $10 million that can be used only to finance a correctional facility. On the issue date of the bonds, J reasonably expects that it will be the sole user of the bonds for the useful life of the facility. The bonds have a weighted average maturity that does not exceed 120 percent of the reasonably expected economic life of the facility. After the issue date of the bonds, but before the facility is placed in service, J enters into a contract with the federal government pursuant to which the federal government will make a fair market value, lump sum payment equal to 25 percent of the cost of the facility. In exchange for this payment, J provides the federal government with priority rights to use of 25 percent of the facility. J uses the payment received from the federal government to defease the nonqualified bonds. The agreement does not cause the bonds to be private activity bonds because J has taken a remedial action described in paragraph (d) of this section. See paragraph (a)(5) of this section.

Example 8. Compliance after remedial action In 2007, City G issues bonds with proceeds of $10 million to finance a courthouse. The bonds have a weighted average maturity that does not exceed 120 percent of the reasonably expected economic life of the courthouse. City G enters into contracts with nongovernmental persons that result in private business use of 10 percent of the courthouse per year. More than 10 percent of the debt service on the issue is secured by private security or payments. In 2019, in a bona fide and arm's length arrangement, City G enters into a management contract with a nongovernmental person that results in private business use of an additional 40 percent of the courthouse per year during the remaining term of the bonds. City G immediately redeems the nonqualified bonds, or 44.44 percent of the outstanding bonds. This is the portion of the outstanding bonds that, if the remaining bonds were issued on the date on which the deliberate action occurs, the remaining bonds would not meet the private business use test, treating the amount of private business use as the greatest percentage of private business use in any one-year period commencing with the one-year period in which the deliberate action occurs (50 percent). This percentage is computed by dividing the percentage of the facility used for a government use (50 percent) by the minimum amount of government use required (90 percent), and subtracting the resulting percentage (55.56 percent) from 100 percent (44.44 percent). For purposes of subsequently applying section 141 to the issue, City G may continue to use all of the proceeds of the outstanding bonds in the same manner (that is, for the courthouse and the private business use) without causing the issue to meet the private business use test. The issue continues to meet the private security or payment test. The result would be the same if City G, instead of redeeming the bonds, established a defeasance escrow for those bonds, provided that the requirement of paragraph (d)(5) of this section is met. If City G takes a subsequent deliberate action that results in further private business use, it must take into account 10 percent of private business use in addition to that caused by the second deliberate act.

[Reg. §1.141-12.]

☐ [*T.D.* 8712, 1-10-97. Amended by *T.D.* 9741, 10-26-2015.]

[Reg. §1.141-13]

§1.141-13. Refunding issues.—(a) *In general.*—Except as provided in this section, a refunding issue and a prior issue are tested separately under section 141. Thus, the determination of whether a refunding issue consists of private activity bonds generally does not depend on whether the prior issue consists of private activity bonds.

(b) *Application of private business use test and private loan financing test.*—(1) *Allocation of proceeds.*—In applying the private business use test and the private loan financing test to a refunding issue, the proceeds of the refunding issue are allocated to the same expenditures and purpose investments as the proceeds of the prior issue.

(2) *Determination of amount of private business use.*—(i) *In general.*—Except as provided in paragraph (b)(2)(ii) of this section, the amount of private business use of a refunding issue is determined under §1.141-3(g), based on the measurement period for that issue (for example, without regard to any private business use that occurred prior to the issue date of the refunding issue).

25,148

Tax Exempt. Requirements: State/Local Bonds
See p. 20,601 for regulations not amended to reflect law changes

(ii) *Refundings of governmental bonds.*—In applying the private business use test to a refunding issue that refunds a prior issue of governmental bonds, the amount of private business use of the refunding issue is the amount of private business use—

(A) During the combined measurement period; or

(B) At the option of the issuer, during the period described in paragraph (b)(2)(i) of this section, but only if, without regard to the reasonable expectations test of §1.141-2(d), the prior issue does not satisfy the private business use test, based on a measurement period that begins on the first day of the combined measurement period and ends on the issue date of the refunding issue.

(iii) *Combined measurement period.*—(A) *In general.*—Except as provided in paragraph (b)(2)(iii)(B) of this section, the *combined measurement period* is the period that begins on the first day of the measurement period (as defined in §1.141-3(g)) for the prior issue (or, in the case of a series of refundings of governmental bonds, the first issue of governmental bonds in the series) and ends on the last day of the measurement period for the refunding issue.

(B) *Transition rule for refundings of bonds originally issued before May 16, 1997.*—If the prior issue (or, in the case of a series of refundings of governmental bonds, the first issue of governmental bonds in the series) was issued before May 16, 1997, then the issuer, at its option, may treat the combined measurement period as beginning on the date (the transition date) that is the earlier of December 19, 2005 or the first date on which the prior issue (or an earlier issue in the case of a series of refundings of governmental bonds) became subject to the 1997 regulations (as defined in §1.141-15(b)). If the issuer treats the combined measurement period as beginning on the transition date in accordance with this paragraph (b)(2)(iii)(B), then paragraph (c)(2) of this section shall be applied by treating the transition date as the issue date of the earliest issue, by treating the bonds as reissued on the transition date at an issue price equal to the value of the bonds (as determined under §1.148-4(e)) on that date, and by disregarding any private security or private payments before the transition date.

(iv) *Governmental bond.*—For purposes of this section, the term governmental bond means any bond that, when issued, purported to be a governmental bond, as defined in §1.150-1(b), or a qualified 501(c)(3) bond, as defined in section 145(a).

(v) *Special rule for refundings of qualified 501(c)(3) bonds with governmental bonds.*—For purposes of applying this paragraph (b)(2) to a refunding issue that refunds a qualified 501(c)(3) bond, any use of the property refinanced by the refunding issue before the issue date of the refunding issue by a 501(c)(3) organization with respect to its activities that do not constitute an unrelated trade or business under section 513(a) is treated as government use.

(c) *Application of private security or payment test.*—(1) *Separate issue treatment.*—If the amount of private business use of a refunding issue is determined based on the measurement period for that issue in accordance with paragraph (b)(2)(i) or (b)(2)(ii)(B) of this section, then the amount of private security and private payments allocable to the refunding issue is determined under §1.141-4 by treating the refunding issue as a separate issue.

(2) *Combined issue treatment.*—If the amount of private business use of a refunding issue is determined based on the combined measurement period for that issue in accordance with paragraph (b)(2)(ii)(A) of this section, then the amount of private security and private payments allocable to the refunding issue is determined under §1.141-4 by treating the refunding issue and all earlier issues taken into account in determining the combined measurement period as a combined issue. For this purpose, the present value of the private security and private payments is compared to the present value of the debt service on the combined issue (other than debt service paid with proceeds of any refunding bond). Present values are computed as of the issue date of the earliest issue taken into account in determining the combined measurement period (the earliest issue). Except as provided in paragraph (c)(3) of this section, present values are determined by using the yield on the combined issue as the discount rate. The yield on the combined issue is determined by taking into account payments on the refunding issue and all earlier issues taken into account in determining the combined measurement period (other than payments made with proceeds of any refunding bond), and based on the issue price of the earliest issue. In the case of a refunding of only a portion of the original principal amount of a prior issue, the refunded portion of the prior issue is treated as a separate issue and any private security or private payments with respect to the prior issue are allocated ratably between the combined issue and the unrefunded portion of the prior issue in a consistent manner based on relative debt service. See paragraph (b)(2)(iii)(B) of this section for special rules relating to

certain refundings of governmental bonds originally issued before May 16, 1997.

(3) *Special rule for arrangements not entered into in contemplation of the refunding issue.*—In applying the private security or payment test to a refunding issue that refunds a prior issue of governmental bonds, the issuer may use the yield on the prior issue to determine the present value of private security and private payments under arrangements that were not entered into in contemplation of the refunding issue. For this purpose, any arrangement that was entered into more than 1 year before the issue date of the refunding issue is treated as not entered into in contemplation of the refunding issue.

(d) *Multipurpose issue allocations.*—(1) *In general.*—For purposes of section 141, unless the context clearly requires otherwise, §1.148-9(h) applies to allocations of multipurpose issues (as defined in §1.148-1(b)), including allocations involving the refunding purposes of the issue. An allocation under this paragraph (d) may be made at any time, but once made, may not be changed. An allocation is not reasonable under this paragraph (d) if it achieves more favorable results under section 141 than could be achieved with actual separate issues. Each of the separate issues under the allocation must consist of one or more tax-exempt bonds. Allocations made under this paragraph (d) and §1.148-9(h) must be consistent for purposes of sections 141 and 148.

(2) *Exceptions.*—This paragraph (d) does not apply for purposes of sections 141(c)(1) and 141(d)(1).

(e) *Application of reasonable expectations test to certain refunding bonds.*—An action that would otherwise cause a refunding issue to satisfy the private business tests or the private loan financing test is not taken into account under the reasonable expectations test of §1.141-2(d) if—

(1) The action is not a deliberate action within the meaning of §1.141-2(d)(3); and

(2) The weighted average maturity of the refunding bonds is not greater than the weighted average reasonably expected economic life of the property financed by the prior bonds.

(f) *Special rule for refundings of certain general obligation bonds.*—Notwithstanding any other provision of this section, a refunding issue does not consist of private activity bonds if—

(1) The prior issue meets the requirements of §1.141-2(d)(5) (relating to certain general obligation bond programs that finance a large number of separate purposes); or

(2) The refunded portion of the prior issue is part of a series of refundings of all or a portion of an issue that meets the requirements of §1.141-2(d)(5).

(g) *Examples.*—The following examples illustrate the application of this section:

Example 1. Measuring private business use. In 2002, Authority A issues tax-exempt bonds that mature in 2032 to acquire an office building. The measurement period for the 2002 bonds under §1.141-3(g) is 30 years. At the time A acquires the building, it enters into a 10-year lease with a nongovernmental person under which the nongovernmental person will use 5 percent of the building in its trade or business during each year of the lease term. In 2007, A issues bonds to refund the 2002 bonds. The 2007 bonds mature on the same date as the 2002 bonds and have a measurement period of 25 years under §1.141-3(g). Under paragraph (b)(2)(ii)(A) of this section, the amount of private business use of the proceeds of the 2007 bonds is 1.67 percent, which equals the amount of private business use during the combined measurement period (5 percent of 1/3rd of the 30-year combined measurement period). In addition, the 2002 bonds do not satisfy the private business use test, based on a measurement period beginning on the first day of the measurement period for the 2002 bonds and ending on the issue date of the 2007 bonds, because only 5 percent of the proceeds of the 2002 bonds are used for a private business use during that period. Thus, under paragraph (b)(2)(ii)(B) of this section, A may treat the amount of private business use of the 2007 bonds as 1 percent (5 percent of 1/5th of the 25-year measurement period for the 2007 bonds). The 2007 bonds do not satisfy the private business use test.

Example 2. Combined issue yield computation. (i) On January 1, 2000, County B issues 20-year bonds to finance the acquisition of a municipal auditorium. The 2000 bonds have a yield of 7.7500 percent, compounded annually, and an issue price and par amount of $100 million. The debt service payments on the 2000 bonds are as follows:

Date	Debt Service
1/1/01	$9,996,470
1/1/02	9,996,470
1/1/03	9,996,470
1/1/04	9,996,470

Date	Debt Service
1/1/05	9,996,470
1/1/06	9,996,470
1/1/07	9,996,470
1/1/08	9,996,470
1/1/09	9,996,470
1/1/10	9,996,470
1/1/11	9,996,470
1/1/12	9,996,470
1/1/13	9,996,470
1/1/14	9,996,470
1/1/15	9,996,470
1/1/16	9,996,470
1/1/17	9,996,470
1/1/18	9,996,470
1/1/19	9,996,470
1/1/20	9,996,470
	$199,929,400

Date	Debt Service
1/1/06	$9,215,167
1/1/07	9,215,167
1/1/08	9,215,167
1/1/09	9,215,167
1/1/10	9,215,167
1/1/11	9,215,167
1/1/12	9,215,167
1/1/13	9,215,167
1/1/14	9,215,167
1/1/15	9,215,167
1/1/16	9,215,167
1/1/17	9,215,167
1/1/18	9,215,167
1/1/19	9,215,167
1/1/20	9,215,167
	$138,227,511

(ii) On January 1, 2005, B issues 15-year bonds to refund all of the outstanding 2000 bonds maturing after January 1, 2005 (in the aggregate principal amount of $86,500,000). The 2005 bonds have a yield of 6.0000 percent, compounded annually, and an issue price and par amount of $89,500,000. The debt service payments on the 2005 bonds are as follows:

(iii) In accordance with §1.141-15(h), B chooses to apply §1.141-13 (together with the other provisions set forth in §1.141-15(h)), to the 2005 bonds. For purposes of determining the amount of private security and private payments with respect to the 2005 bonds, the 2005 bonds and the refunded portion of the 2000 bonds are treated as a combined issue under paragraph (c)(2) of this section. The yield on the combined issue is determined in accordance with §§1.148-4, 1.141-4(b)(2)(iii) and 1.141-13(c)(2). Under this methodology, the yield on the combined issue is 7.1052 percent per year compounded annually, illustrated as follows:

Date	Previous Debt Service on Refunded Portion of Prior Issue	Refunding Debt Service	Total Debt Service	Present Value on 1/1/00
1/1/00				($86,500,000.00)
1/1/01	$6,689,793		$6,689,793	6,245,945.33
1/1/02	6,689,793		6,689,793	5,831,545.62
1/1/03	6,689,793		6,689,793	5,444,640.09
1/1/04	6,689,793		6,689,793	5,083,404.58
1/1/05	6,689,793		6,689,793	4,746,135.95
1/1/06		$9,215,167	9,215,167	6,104,023.84
1/1/07		9,215,167	9,215,167	5,699,040.20
1/1/08		9,215,167	9,215,167	5,320,926.00
1/1/09		9,215,167	9,215,167	4,967,898.55
1/1/10		9,215,167	9,215,167	4,638,293.40
1/1/11		9,215,167	9,215,167	4,330,556.57
1/1/12		9,215,167	9,215,167	4,043,237.15
1/1/13		9,215,167	9,215,167	3,774,980.51
1/1/14		9,215,167	9,215,167	3,524,521.90
1/1/15		9,215,167	9,215,167	3,290,680.46
1/1/16		9,215,167	9,215,167	3,072,353.70
1/1/17		9,215,167	9,215,167	2,868,512.26
1/1/18		9,215,167	9,215,167	2,678,195.09
1/1/19		9,215,167	9,215,167	2,500,504.89
1/1/20		9,215,167	9,215,167	2,334,603.90
	$33,448,965	$138,227,511	$171,676,476	0.00

Example 3. Determination of private payments allocable to combined issue. The facts are the same as in *Example 2.* In addition, on January 1, 2001, B enters into a contract with a nongovernmental person for the use of the auditorium. The contract results in a private payment in the amount of $500,000 on each January 1 beginning on January 1, 2001, and ending on January 1, 2020. Under paragraph (c)(2) of this

section, the amount of the private payments allocable to the combined issue is determined by treating the refunded portion of the 2000 bonds ($86,500,000 principal amount) as a separate issue, and by allocating the total private payments ratably between the combined issue and the unrefunded portion of the 2000 bonds ($13,500,000 principal amount) based on relative debt service, as follows:

Date	Private Payments	Debt Service on Unrefunded Portion of Prior Issue	Debt Service on Combined Issue	Percentage of Private Payments Allocable to Combined Issue	Amount of Private Payments Allocable to Combined Issue
1/1/01	$500,000	$3,306,677	$6,689,793	66.92%	$334,608
1/1/02	500,000	3,306,677	6,689,793	66.92	334,608
1/1/03	500,000	3,306,677	6,689,793	66.92	334,608
1/1/04	500,000	3,306,677	6,689,793	66.92	334,608
1/1/05	500,000	3,306,677	6,689,793	66.92	334,608
1/1/06	500,000		9,215,167	100.00	500,000
1/1/07	500,000		9,215,167	100.00	500,000
1/1/08	500,000		9,215,167	100.00	500,000
1/1/09	500,000		9,215,167	100.00	500,000
1/1/10	500,000		9,215,167	100.00	500,000
1/1/11	500,000		9,215,167	100.00	500,000
1/1/12	500,000		9,215,167	100.00	500,000
1/1/13	500,000		9,215,167	100.00	500,000
1/1/14	500,000		9,215,167	100.00	500,000

Date	Private Payments	Debt Service on Unrefunded Portion of Prior Issue	Debt Service on Combined Issue	Percentage of Private Payments Allocable to Combined Issue	Amount of Private Payments Allocable to Combined Issue
1/1/15	500,000		9,215,167	100.00	500,000
1/1/16	500,000		9,215,167	100.00	500,000
1/1/17	500,000		9,215,167	100.00	500,000
1/1/18	500,000		9,215,167	100.00	500,000
1/1/19	500,000		9,215,167	100.00	500,000
1/1/20	500,000		9,215,167	100.00	500,000
	$10,000,000	$16,533,385	$171,676,476		$9,173,039

Example 4. Refunding taxable bonds and qualified bonds. (i) In 1999, City C issues taxable bonds to finance the construction of a facility for the furnishing of water. The bonds are secured by revenues from the facility. The facility is managed pursuant to a management contract with a nongovernmental person that gives rise to private business use. In 2007, C terminates the management contract and takes over the operation of the facility. In 2009, C issues bonds to refund the 1999 bonds. On the issue date of the 2009 bonds, C reasonably expects that the facility will not be used for a private business use during the term of the 2009 bonds. In addition, during the term of the 2009 bonds, the facility is not used for a private business use. Under paragraph (b)(2)(i) of this section, the 2009 bonds do not satisfy the private business use test because the amount of private business use is based on the measurement period for those bonds and therefore does not take into account any private business use that occurred pursuant to the management contract.

(ii) The facts are the same as in paragraph (i) of this Example 4, except that the 1999 bonds are issued as exempt facility bonds under section 142(a)(4). The 2009 bonds do not satisfy the private business use test.

Example 5. Multipurpose issue. (i) In 2017, State D issues bonds to finance the construction of two office buildings, Building 1 and Building 2. D expends an equal amount of the proceeds on each building. D enters into arrangements that result in private business use of 8 percent of Building 1 and 12 percent of Building 2 during the measurement period under §1.141-3(g) and private payments of 4 percent of the 2017 bonds in respect of Building 1 and 6 percent of the 2017 bonds in respect of Building 2. These arrangements result in a total of 10 percent of the proceeds of the 2017 bonds being used for a private business use and total private payments of 10 percent. In 2022, D purports to make a multipurpose issue allocation under paragraph (d) of this section of the outstanding 2017 bonds, allocating the issue into two separate issues of equal amounts with one issue allocable to Building 1 and the second allocable to Building 2. An allocation is unreasonable under paragraph (d) of this section if it achieves more favorable results under section 141 than could be achieved with actual separate issues. D's allocation is unreasonable because, if permitted, it would allow more favorable results under section 141 for the 2017 bonds (that is, private business use and private payments that exceed 10 percent for the 2017 bonds allocable to Building 2) than could be achieved with actual separate issues. In addition, if D's purported allocation was intended to result in two separate issues of tax-exempt governmental bonds (versus tax-exempt private activity bonds), the allocation would violate paragraph (d) of this section in the first instance because the allocation to the separate issue for Building 2 would fail to qualify separately as an issue of tax-exempt governmental bonds as a result of its 12 percent of private business use and private payments.

(ii) The facts are the same as in paragraph (i) of this *Example 5*, except that D enters into arrangements only for Building 1, and it expects no private business use of Building 2. In 2022, D allocates an equal amount of the outstanding 2017 bonds to Building 1 and Building 2. D selects particular bonds for each separate issue such that the allocation does not achieve a more favorable result than could have been achieved by issuing actual separate issues. D uses the same allocation for purposes of both sections 141 and 148. D's allocation is reasonable.

(iii) The facts are the same as in paragraph (ii) of this *Example 5*, except that as part of the same issue, D issues bonds for a privately used airport. The airport bonds, if issued as a separate issue, would be qualified private activity bonds. The remaining bonds, if issued separately from the airport bonds, would be governmental bonds. Treated as one issue, however, the bonds are taxable private activity bonds. Therefore, D makes its allocation of the bonds under paragraph (d) of this section and §1.150-1(c)(3) into 3 separate issues on or before the issue date. Assuming all other applicable requirements are met, the bonds of the respective issues will be tax-exempt qualified private activity bonds or governmental bonds.

Example 6. Non-deliberate action. In 1998, City E issues bonds to finance the purchase of land and construction of a building (the prior bonds). On the issue date of the prior bonds, E reasonably expects that it will be the sole user of the financed property for the entire term of the bonds. In 2003, the federal government acquires the financed property in a condemnation action. In 2006, E issues bonds to refund the prior bonds (the refunding bonds). The weighted average maturity of the refunding bonds is not greater than the reasonably expected economic life of the financed property. In general, under §1.141-2(d) and this section, reasonable expectations must be separately tested on the issue date of a refunding issue. Under paragraph (e) of this section, however, the condemnation action is not taken into account in applying the reasonable expectations test to the refunding bonds because the condemnation action is not a deliberate action within the meaning of §1.141-2(d)(3) and the weighted average maturity of the refunding bonds is not greater than the weighted average reasonably expected economic life of the property financed by the prior bonds. Thus, the condemnation action does not cause the refunding bonds to be private activity bonds.

Example 7. Non-transitioned refunding of bonds subject to 1954 Code. In 1985, County F issues bonds to finance a court house. The 1985 bonds are subject to the provisions of the Internal Revenue Code of 1954. In 2006, F issues bonds to refund all of the outstanding 1985 bonds. The weighted average maturity of the 2006 bonds is longer than the remaining weighted average maturity of the 1985 bonds. In addition, the 2006 bonds do not satisfy any transitional rule for refundings in the Tax Reform Act of 1986, 100 Stat. 2085 (1986). Section 141 and this section apply to determine whether the 2006 bonds are private activity bonds including whether, for purposes of §1.141-13(b)(2)(ii)(B), the 1985 bonds satisfy the private business use test based on a measurement period that begins on the first day of the combined measurement period for the 2006 bonds and ends on the issue date of the 2006 bonds.]

[Reg. §1.141-13.]

☐ [*T.D.* 9234, 12-16-2005. Amended by *T.D.* 9741, 10-26-2015.]

[Reg. §1.141-14]

§1.141-14. Anti-abuse rules.—(a) *Authority of Commissioner to reflect substance of transactions.*—If an issuer enters into a transaction or series of transactions with respect to one or more issues with a principal purpose of transferring to nongovernmental persons (other than as members of the general public) significant benefits of tax-exempt financing in a manner that is inconsistent with the purposes of section 141, the Commissioner may take any action to reflect the substance of the transaction or series of transactions, including—

(1) Treating separate issues as a single issue for purposes of the private activity bond tests;

(2) Reallocating proceeds to expenditures, property, use, or bonds;

(3) Reallocating payments to use or proceeds;

(4) Measuring private business use on a basis that reasonably reflects the economic benefit in a manner different than as provided in §1.141-3(g); and

(5) Measuring private payments or security on a basis that reasonably reflects the economic substance in a manner different than as provided in §1.141-4.

(b) *Examples.*—The following examples illustrate the application of this section:

Example 1. Reallocating proceeds to indirect use. City C issues bonds with proceeds of $20 million for the stated purpose of financing improvements to roads that it owns. As a part of the same plan of financing, however, C also agrees to make a loan of $7 million to Corporation M from its general revenues that it otherwise would have used for the road improvements. The interest rate of the loan corresponds to the interest rate on a portion of the issue. A principal purpose of the financing arrangement is to transfer to M significant benefits of the tax-exempt financing. Although C actually allocates all of the proceeds of the bonds to the road improvements, the Commissioner may reallocate a portion of the proceeds of the bonds to the loan to M because a principal purpose of the financing arrangement is to transfer to M significant benefits of tax-exempt financing in a manner that is inconsistent with the purposes of section 141. The bonds are private activity bonds because the issue meets the private loan financing test. The bonds also meet the private business tests. See also §§1.141-3(a)(2), 1.141-4(a)(1), and 1.141-5(a), under which indirect use of proceeds and payments are taken into account.

Example 2. Taking into account use of amounts derived from proceeds that would be otherwise disregarded. County B issues bonds with proceeds of $10 million to finance the purchase of land. On the issue date, B reasonably expects that it will be the sole user of the land. Subsequently, the federal government acquires the land for $3 million in a condemnation action. B uses this amount to make a loan to Corporation M. In addition, the interest rate on the loan reflects the tax-exempt interest rate on the bonds and thus is substantially less than a current market rate. A principal purpose of the arrangement is to transfer to M significant benefits of the tax-exempt financing. Although the condemnation action is not a deliberate action, the Commissioner may treat the condemnation proceeds as proceeds of the issue because a principal purpose of the arrangement is to transfer to M significant benefits of tax-exempt financing in a manner inconsistent with the purposes of section 141. The bonds are private activity bonds.

Example 3. Measuring private business use on an alternative basis. City F issues bonds with a 30-year term to finance the acquisition of an industrial building having a reasonably expected useful economic life of more than 30 years. On the issue date, F leases the building to Corporation G for 3 years. F reasonably expects that it will be the sole user of the building for the remaining term of the bonds. Because of the local market conditions, it is reasonably expected that the fair rental value of the industrial building will be significantly greater during the early years of the term of the bonds than in the later years. The annual rental payments are significantly less than fair market value, reflecting the interest rate on the bonds. The present value of these rental payments (net of operation and maintenance expenses) as of the issue date, however, is approximately 25 percent of the present value of debt service on the issue. Under §1.141-3, the issue does not meet the private business tests, because only 10 percent of the proceeds are used in a trade or business by a nongovernmental person. A principal purpose of the issue is to transfer to G significant benefits of tax-exempt financing in a manner inconsistent with the purposes of section 141. The method of measuring private business use over the reasonably expected useful economic life of financed property is for the administrative convenience of issuers of state and local bonds. In cases where this method is used in a manner inconsistent with the purposes of section 141, the Commissioner may measure private business use on another basis that reasonably reflects economic benefit, such as in this case on an annual basis. If the Commissioner measures private business use on an annual basis, the bonds are private activity bonds because the private payment test is met and more than 10 percent of the proceeds are used in a trade or business by a nongovernmental person.

Example 4. Treating separate issues as a single issue. City D enters into a development agreement with Corporation T to induce T to locate its headquarters within D's city limits. Pursuant to the development agreement, in 1997 D will issue $20 million of its general obligation bonds (the 1997 bonds) to purchase land that it will grant to T. The development agreement also provides that, in 1998, D will issue $20 million of its tax increment bonds (the 1998 bonds), secured solely by the increase in property taxes in a special taxing district. Substantially all of the property within the special taxing district is owned by T or D. T will separately enter into an agreement to guarantee the payment of tax increment to D in an amount sufficient to retire the 1998 bonds. The proceeds of the 1998 bonds will be used to finance improvements owned and operated by D that will not give rise to private business use. Treated separately, the 1997 issue meets the private business use test, but not the private security or payment test; the 1998 issue meets the private security or payment test, but not the private business use test. A principal purpose of the financing plan including the two issues is to transfer significant benefits of tax-exempt financing to T for its headquarters. Thus, the 1997 issue and the 1998 issue may be treated by the Commissioner as a single issue for purposes of applying the private activity bond tests. Accordingly, the bonds of both the 1997 issue and the 1998 issue may be treated as private activity bonds.

Example 5. Reallocating proceeds. City E acquires an electric generating facility with a useful economic life of more than 40 years and enters into a 30-year take or pay contract to sell 30 percent of the available output to investor-owned utility M. E plans to use the remaining 70 percent of available output for its own governmental purposes. To finance the entire cost of the facility, E issues $30 million of its series A taxable bonds at taxable interest rates and $70 million series B bonds, which purport to be tax-exempt bonds, at tax-exempt interest rates. E allocates all of M's private business use to the proceeds of the series A bonds and all of its own government use to the proceeds of the series B bonds. The series A bonds have a weighted average maturity of 15 years, while the series B bonds have a weighted average maturity of 26 years. M's payments under the

take or pay contract are expressly determined by reference to 30 percent of M's total costs (that is, the sum of the debt service required to be paid on both the series A and the series B bonds and all other operating costs). The allocation of all of M's private business use to the series A bonds does not reflect economic substance because the series of transactions transfers to M significant benefits of the tax-exempt interest rates paid on the series B bonds. A principal purpose of the financing arrangement is to transfer to M significant benefits of the tax-exempt financing. Accordingly, the Commissioner may allocate M's private business use on a pro rata basis to both the series B bonds as well as the series A bonds, in which case the series B bonds are private activity bonds.

Example 6. Allocations respected. The facts are the same as in *Example 5*, except that the debt service component of M's payments under the take or pay contract is based exclusively on the amounts necessary to pay the debt service on the taxable series A bonds. E's allocation of all of M's private business use to the series A bonds is respected because the series of transactions does not actually transfer benefits of tax-exempt interest rates to M. Accordingly, the series B bonds are not private activity bonds. The result would be the same if M's payments under the take or pay contract were based exclusively on fair market value pricing, rather than the tax-exempt interest rates on E's bonds. The result also would be the same if the series A bonds and the series B bonds had substantially equivalent weighted average maturities and E and M had entered into a customary contract providing for payments based on a ratable share of total debt service. E would not be treated by the Commissioner in any of these cases as entering into the contract with a principal purpose of transferring the benefits of tax-exempt financing to M in a manner inconsistent with the purposes of section 141.

[Reg. §1.141-14.]

☐ [T.D. 8712, 1-10-97.]

[Reg. §1.141-15]

§1.141-15. Effective/applicability dates.—(a) *Scope.*—The effective dates of this section apply for purposes of §§1.141-1 through 1.141-14, 1.145-1 through 1.145-2, and 1.150-1(a)(3) and the definition of bond documents contained in §1.150-1(b).

(b) *Effective dates.*—(1) *In general.*—Except as otherwise provided in this section, §§1.141-0 through 1.141-6(a), 1.141-9 through 1.141-12, 1.141-14, 1.145-1 through 1.145-2(c), and the definition of bond documents contained in §1.150-1(b) (the 1997 regulations) apply to bonds issued on or after May 16, 1997, that are subject to section 1301 of the Tax Reform Act of 1986 (100 Stat. 2602).

(2) *Certain short-term arrangements.*—The provisions of §1.141-3 that refer to arrangements for 200 days, 100 days, or 50 days apply to any bond sold on or after November 20, 2001 and may be applied to any bond outstanding on November 20, 2001 to which §1.141-3 applies.

(3) *Certain prepayments.*—Except as provided in paragraph (c) of this section, paragraphs (c)(2)(ii), (c)(2)(iii) and (c)(2)(iv) of §1.141-5 apply to bonds sold on or after October 3, 2003. Issuers may apply paragraphs (c)(2)(ii), (c)(2)(iii) and (c)(2)(iv) of §1.141-5, in whole but not in part, to bonds sold before October 3, 2003, that are subject to §1.141-5.

(4) *Certain remedial actions.*—(i) *General rule.*—For bonds subject to §1.141-12, the provisions of §1.141-12(d)(3), (i), (j), and (k), *Example 8*, apply to deliberate actions that occur on or after January 25, 2016.

(ii) *Special rule for allocations of nonqualified bonds.*—For purposes of §1.141-12(j)(2), in addition to the allocation methods permitted in §1.141-12(j)(2), an issuer may treat bonds with the longest maturities (determined on a bond-by-bond basis) as the nonqualified bonds, but only for bonds sold before January 25, 2016.

(c) *Refunding bonds.*—Except as otherwise provided in this section, the 1997 regulations (defined in paragraph (b)(1) of this section) do not apply to any bonds issued on or after May 16, 1997, to refund a bond to which those regulations do not apply unless—

(1) The refunding bonds are subject to section 1301 of the Tax Reform Act of 1986 (100 Stat. 2602); and

(2)(i) The weighted average maturity of the refunding bonds is longer than-

(A) The weighted average maturity of the refunded bonds; or

(B) In the case of a short-term obligation that the issuer reasonably expects to refund with a long-term financing (such as a bond anticipation note), 120 percent of the weighted average reasonably expected economic life of the facilities financed; or

(ii) A principal purpose for the issuance of the refunding bonds is to make one or more new conduit loans.

25,152

Tax Exempt. Requirements: State/Local Bonds
See p. 20,601 for regulations not amended to reflect law changes

(d) *Permissive application of regulations.*—Except as provided in paragraph (e) of this section, the 1997 regulations (defined in paragraph (b)(1) of this section) may be applied in whole, but not in part, to actions taken before February 23, 1998, with respect to—

(1) Bonds that are outstanding on May 16, 1997, and subject to section 141; or

(2) Refunding bonds issued on or after May 16, 1997, that are subject to 141.

(e) *Permissive application of certain sections.*—(1) *In general.*—The following sections may each be applied by issuers to any bonds:

(i) Section 1.141-3(b)(4);

(ii) Section 1.141-3(b)(6); and

(iii) Section 1.141-12.

(2) *Transition rule for pre-effective date bonds.*—For purposes of paragraphs (e)(1) and (h) of this section, issuers may apply §1.141-12 to bonds issued before May 16, 1997, without regard to paragraph (d)(5) thereof with respect to deliberate actions that occur on or after April 21, 2003.

(f) *Effective dates for certain regulations relating to output facilities.*—(1) *General rule.*—Except as otherwise provided in this section, §§1.141-7 and 1.141-8 apply to bonds sold on or after November 22, 2002, that are subject to section 1301 of the Tax Reform Act of 1986 (100 Stat. 2602).

(2) *Transition rule for requirements contracts.*—For bonds otherwise subject to §§1.141-7 and 1.141-8, §1.141-7(c)(3) applies to output contracts entered into on or after September 19, 2002. An output contract is treated as entered into on or after that date if it is amended on or after that date, but only if the amendment results in a change in the parties to the contract or increases the amount of requirements covered by the contract by reason of an extension of the contract term or a change in the method for determining such requirements. For purposes of this paragraph (f)(2)—

(i) The extension of the term of a contract causes the contract to be treated as entered into on the first day of the additional term;

(ii) The exercise by a party of a legally enforceable right that was provided under a contract before September 19, 2002, on terms that were fixed and determinable before such date, is not treated as an amendment of the contract. For example, the exercise by a purchaser after September 19, 2002 of a renewal option that was provided under a contract before that date, on terms identical to the original contract, is not treated as an amendment of the contract; and

(iii) An amendment that increases the amount of requirements covered by the contract by reason of a change in the method for determining such requirements is treated as a separate contract that is entered into as of the effective date of the amendment, but only with respect to the increased output to be provided under the contract.

(g) *Refunding bonds for output facilities.*—Except as otherwise provided in paragraph (h) or (i) of this section, §§1.141-7 and 1.141-8 do not apply to any bonds sold on or after November 22, 2002, to refund a bond to which §§1.141-7 and 1.141-8 do not apply unless—

(1) The refunding bonds are subject to section 1301 of the Tax Reform Act of 1986 (100 Stat. 2602); and

(2)(i) The weighted average maturity of the refunding bonds is longer than—

(A) The weighted average maturity of the refunded bonds; or

(B) In the case of a short-term obligation that the issuer reasonably expects to refund with a long-term financing (such as a bond anticipation note), 120 percent of the weighted average reasonably expected economic life of the facilities financed; or

(ii) A principal purpose for the issuance of the refunding bonds is to make one or more new conduit loans.

(h) *Permissive retroactive application.*—Except as provided in paragraphs (d), (e) or (i) of this section, §§1.141-1 through 1.141-6(a), 1.141-7 through 1.141-14, 1.145-1 through 1.145-2, 1.149(d)-1(g), 1.150-1(a)(3), the definition of bond documents contained in §1.150-1(b) and §1.150-1(c)(3)(ii) may be applied by issuers in whole, but not in part, to—

(1) Outstanding bonds that are sold before February 17, 2006, and subject to section 141; or

(2) Refunding bonds that are sold on or after February 17, 2006, and subject to section 141.

(i) *Permissive application of certain regulations relating to output facilities.*—Issuers may apply each of the following sections to any bonds used to finance output facilities:

(1) Section 1.141-6;

(2) Section 1.141-7(f)(3); and

(3) Section 1.141-7(g).

(j) *Effective dates for certain regulations relating to refundings.*—Except as otherwise provided in this section, §§1.141-13, 1.145-2(d), 1.149(d)-1(g), 1.150-1(a)(3) and 1.150-1(c)(3)(ii) apply to bonds that are sold on or after February 17, 2006, and that are subject to the 1997 regulations (defined in paragraph (b)(1) of this section).

(k) *Effective/applicability dates for certain regulations relating to generally applicable taxes and payments in lieu of tax.*—(1) *In general.*—Except as otherwise provided in paragraphs (k)(2) and (k)(3) of this section, revised §§1.141-4(e)(2), 1.141-4(e)(3) and 1.141-4(e)(5) apply to bonds sold on or after October 24, 2008 that are otherwise subject to the 1997 Regulations (defined in paragraph (b)(1) of this section).

(2) *Transitional rule for certain refundings.*—Paragraph (k)(1) does not apply to bonds that are issued to refund bonds if—

(i) Either—

(A) The refunded bonds (or the original bonds in a series of refundings) were sold before October 24, 2008, or

(B) The refunded bonds (or the original bonds in a series of refundings) satisfied the transitional rule for projects substantially in progress under paragraph (k)(3) of this section; and

(ii) The weighted average maturity of the refunding bonds does not exceed the remaining weighted average maturity of the refunded bonds.

(3) *Transitional rule for certain projects substantially in progress.*—Paragraph (k)(1) of this section does not apply to bonds issued for projects for which all of the following requirements are met:

(i) A governmental person (as defined in §1.141-1) took official action evidencing its preliminary approval of the project before October 19, 2006, and the plan of finance for the project in place at that time contemplated financing the project with tax-exempt bonds to be paid or secured by PILOTs.

(ii) Before October 19, 2006, significant expenditures were paid or incurred with respect to the project or a contract was entered into to pay or incur significant expenditures with respect to the project.

(iii) The bonds for the project (excluding refunding bonds) are issued on or before December 31, 2009.

(l) *Applicability date for certain regulations relating to allocation and accounting.*—(1) *In general.*—Except as otherwise provided in this section, §§1.141-1(e), 1.141-3(g)(2)(v), 1.141-6, 1.141-13(d), and 1.145-2(b)(4), (b)(5), and (c)(2) apply to bonds that are sold on or after January 25, 2016 and to which the 1997 regulations (as defined in paragraph (b)(1) of this section) apply.

(2) *Refunding bonds.*—Except as otherwise provided in this section, §§1.141-1(e), 1.141-3(g)(2)(v), 1.141-6, and 1.145-2(b)(4), (b)(5), and (c)(2) do not apply to any bonds sold on or after January 25, 2016, to refund a bond to which these sections do not apply, provided that the weighted average maturity of the refunding bonds is no longer than—

(i) The remaining weighted average maturity of the refunded bonds; or

(ii) In the case of a short-term obligation that the issuer reasonably expects to refund with a long-term financing (such as a bond anticipation note), 120 percent of the weighted average reasonably expected economic life of the facilities financed.

(3) *Permissive application.*—Except as otherwise provided in this section, issuers may apply §§1.141-1(e), 1.141-3(g)(2)(v), 1.141-6, and 1.145-2(b)(4), (b)(5), and (c)(2), in whole but not in part, to bonds to which the 1997 regulations apply.

(m) *Permissive retroactive application of certain regulations.*—Issuers may apply §1.141-13(d) to bonds to which §1.141-13 applies.

(n) *Effective/applicability dates for certain regulations relating to certain definitions.*—§1.141-1(a) applies to bonds that are sold on or after October 17, 2016. [Reg. §1.141-15.]

☐ [*T.D. 8712, 1-10-97. Amended by T.D. 8757, 1-21-98; T.D. 8941, 1-17-2001; T.D. 8967, 11-19-2001; T.D. 9016, 9-19-2002; T.D. 9085, 8-1-2003; T.D. 9234, 12-16-2005 (corrected 1-11-2006), T.D. 9429, 10-20-2008, T.D. 9741, 10-26-2015 and T.D. 9777, 7-15-2016.*]

[Reg. §1.141-16]

§1.141-16. Effective dates for qualified private activity bond provisions.—(a) *Scope.*—The effective dates of this section apply for purposes of §§1.142-0 through 1.142-2, 1.144-0 through 1.144-2, 1.147-0 through 1.147-2, and 1.150-4.

(b) *Effective dates.*—Except as otherwise provided in this section, the regulations designated in paragraph (a) of this section apply to bonds issued on or after May 16, 1997, (the effective date).

(c) *Permissive application.*—The regulations designated in paragraph (a) of this section may be applied by issuers in whole, but not in part, to bonds outstanding on the effective date. For this purpose, issuers may apply §1.142-2 without regard to paragraph (c)(3) thereof to failures to properly use proceeds that occur on or after April 21, 2003.

(d) *Certain remedial actions.*—(1) *General rule.*—The provisions of §1.142-2(e) apply to failures to properly use proceeds that occur on or after August 13, 2004 and may be applied by issuers to failures to properly use proceeds that occur on or after May 14, 2004, provided that the bonds are subject to §1.142-2.

(2) *Special rule for allocations of nonqualified bonds.*—For purposes of §1.142-2(e)(2), in addition to the allocation methods permitted in §1.142-2(e)(2), an issuer may treat bonds with the longest maturities (determined on a bond-by-bond basis) as the nonqualified bonds, but only with respect to failures to properly use proceeds that occur on or after May 14, 2004 with respect to bonds sold before August 13, 2004. [Reg. §1.141-16.]

☐ [*T.D. 8712, 1-10-97. Amended by T.D. 9150, 8-12-2004.*]

[Reg. §1.142-0]

§1.142-0. Table of contents.—This section lists the captioned paragraphs contained in §§1.142-1 through 1.142-3.

§1.142-1 Exempt facility bonds.
  (a) Overview.
  (b) Scope.
  (c) Effective dates.

§1.142-2 Remedial actions.
  (a) General rule.
  (b) Reasonable expectations requirement.
  (c) Redemption or defeasance.
    (1) In general.
    (2) Notice of defeasance.
    (3) Special limitation.
    (4) Special rule for dispositions of personal property.
    (5) Definitions.
  (d) When a failure to properly use proceeds occurs.
    (1) Proceeds not spent.
    (2) Proceeds spent.
  (e) Nonqualified bonds.
    (1) Amount of nonqualified bonds.
    (2) Allocation of nonqualified bonds.

§1.142-3 Refunding issues.
[Reserved]
[Reg. §1.142-0.]

☐ [*T.D. 8712, 1-10-97. Amended by T.D. 9150, 8-12-2004.*]

[Reg. §1.142-1]

§1.142-1. Exempt facility bonds.—(a) *Overview.*—Interest on a private activity bond is not excludable from gross income under section 103(a) unless the bond is a qualified bond. Under section 141(e)(1)(A), an exempt facility bond issued under section 142 may be a qualified bond. Under section 142(a), an exempt facility bond is any bond issued as a part of an issue using 95 percent or more of the proceeds for certain exempt facilities.

(b) *Scope.*—Sections 1.142-0 through 1.142-3 apply for purposes of the rules for exempt facility bonds under section 142, except that, with respect to net proceeds that have been spent, §1.142-2 does not apply to bonds issued under section 142(d) (relating to bonds issued to provide qualified residential rental projects) and section 142(f)(2) and (4) (relating to bonds issued to provide local furnishing of electric energy or gas).

(c) *Effective dates.*—For effective dates of §§1.142-0 through 1.142-2, see §1.141-16. [Reg. §1.142-1.]

☐ [Reg. §1.142-1, issued under Code Sec. 142 as it existed prior to repeal by P.L. 95-30, was removed from the CFR, and Reg. §1.142-1, above, was adopted by *T.D. 8712, 1-10-97.*]

[Reg. §1.142-2]

§1.142-2. Remedial actions.—(a) *General rule.*—If less than 95 percent of the net proceeds of an exempt facility bond are actually used to provide an exempt facility, and for no other purpose, the issue will be treated as meeting the use of proceeds requirement of section 142(a) if the issue meets the condition of paragraph (b) of this section and the issuer takes the remedial action described in paragraph (c) of this section.

(b) *Reasonable expectations requirement.*—The issuer must have reasonably expected on the issue date that 95 percent of the net proceeds of the issue would be used to provide an exempt facility and for no other purpose for the entire term of the bonds (disregarding any redemption provisions). To meet this condition the amount of the issue must have been based on reasonable estimates about the cost of the facility.

(c) *Redemption or defeasance.*—(1) *In general.*—The requirements of this paragraph (c) are met if all of the nonqualified bonds of the issue are redeemed on the earliest call date after the date on which the failure to properly use the proceeds occurs under paragraph (d) of this section. Proceeds of tax-exempt bonds (other than those described in paragraph (d)(1) of this section) must not be used for this purpose. If the bonds are not redeemed within 90 days of the date on which the failure to properly use proceeds occurs, a defeasance escrow must be established for those bonds within 90 days of that date.

(2) *Notice of defeasance.*—The issuer must provide written notice to the Commissioner of the establishment of the defeasance escrow within 90 days of the date the escrow is established.

(3) *Special limitation.*—The establishment of a defeasance escrow does not satisfy the requirements of this paragraph (c) if the period between the issue date and the first call date is more than $10^1/_2$ years.

(4) *Special rule for dispositions of personal property.*—For dispositions of personal property exclusively for cash, the requirements of this paragraph (c) are met if the issuer expends the disposition proceeds within 6 months of the date of the disposition to acquire replacement property for the same qualifying purpose of the issue under section 142.

(5) *Definitions.*—For purposes of paragraph (c)(4) of this section, *disposition proceeds* means disposition proceeds as defined in §1.141-12(c).

(d) *When a failure to properly use proceeds occurs.*—(1) *Proceeds not spent.*—For net proceeds that are not spent, a failure to properly use proceeds occurs on the earlier of the date on which the issuer reasonably determines that the financed facility will not be completed or the date on which the financed facility is placed in service.

(2) *Proceeds spent.*—For net proceeds that are spent, a failure to properly use proceeds occurs on the date on which an action is taken that causes the bonds not to be used for the qualifying purpose for which the bonds were issued.

(e) *Nonqualified bonds.*—(1) *Amount of nonqualified bonds.*—For purposes of this section, the nonqualified bonds are a portion of the outstanding bonds in an amount that, if the remaining bonds were issued on the date on which the failure to properly use the proceeds occurs, at least 95 percent of the net proceeds of the remaining bonds would be used to provide an exempt facility. If no proceeds have been spent to provide an exempt facility, all of the outstanding bonds are nonqualified bonds.

(2) *Allocation of nonqualified bonds.*—Allocations of nonqualified bonds must be made on a pro rata basis, except that an issuer may treat any bonds of an issue as the nonqualified bonds so long as—

(i) The remaining weighted average maturity of the issue, determined as of the date on which the nonqualified bonds are redeemed or defeased (determination date), and excluding from the determination the nonqualified bonds redeemed or defeased by the issuer to meet the requirements of paragraph (c) of this section, is not greater than

(ii) The remaining weighted average maturity of the issue, determined as of the determination date, but without regard to the redemption or defeasance of any bonds (including the nonqualified bonds) occurring on the determination date. [Reg. §1.142-2.]

☐ [Reg. §1.142-2, issued under Code Sec. 142 as it existed prior to repeal by P.L. 95-30, was removed from the CFR, and Reg. §1.142-2, above, was adopted by *T.D. 8712, 1-10-97. Amended by T.D. 9150, 8-12-2004.*]

[Reg. §1.142-3]

§1.142-3. Refunding issues.—[Reserved.]

☐ [*T.D. 8712, 1-10-97.*]

[Reg. §1.142-4]

§1.142-4. Use of proceeds to provide a facility.—(a) *In general.*—[Reserved].

(b) *Reimbursement allocations.*—If an expenditure for a facility is paid before the issue date of the bonds to provide that facility, the facility is described in section 142(a) only if the expenditure meets the

25,154

Tax Exempt. Requirements: State/Local Bonds
See p. 20,601 for regulations not amended to reflect law changes

requirements of § 1.150-2 (relating to reimbursement allocations). For purposes of this paragraph (b), if the proceeds of an issue are used to pay principal of or interest on an obligation other than a State or local bond (for example, temporary construction financing of the conduit borrower), that issue is not a refunding issue, and, thus, § 1.150-2(g) does not apply.

(c) *Limitation on use of facilities by substantial users.*—(1) *In general.*—If the original use of a facility begins before the issue date of the bonds to provide the facility, the facility is not described in section 142(a) if any person that was a substantial user of the facility at any time during the 5-year period before the issue date or any related person to that user receives (directly or indirectly) 5 percent or more of the proceeds of the issue for the user's interest in the facility and is a substantial user of the facility at any time during the 5-year period after the issue date, unless—

(i) An official intent for the facility is adopted under § 1.150-2 within 60 days after the date on which acquisition, construction, or reconstruction of that facility commenced; and

(ii) For an acquisition, no person that is a substantial user or related person after the acquisition date was also a substantial user more than 60 days before the date on which the official intent was adopted.

(2) *Definitions.*—For purposes of paragraph (c)(1) of this section, *substantial user* has the meaning used in section 147(a)(1), *related person* has the meaning used in section 144(a)(3), and a user that is a governmental unit within the meaning of § 1.103-1 is disregarded.

(d) *Effective date.*—(1) *In general.*—This section applies to bonds sold on or after July 8, 1997. See § 1.103-8(a)(5) for rules applicable to bonds sold before that date.

(2) *Elective retroactive application.*—An issuer may apply this section to any bond sold before July 8, 1997. [Reg. § 1.142-4.]

□ [T.D. 8718, 5-8-97.]

[Reg. § 1.142(a)(5)-1]

§ 1.142(a)(5)-1. Exempt facility bonds: Sewage facilities.—(a) *In general.*—Under section 103(a), a private activity bond is a tax-exempt bond only if it is a qualified bond. A qualified bond includes an exempt facility bond, defined as any bond issued as part of an issue 95 percent or more of the net proceeds of which are used to provide a facility specified in section 142. One type of facility specified in section 142(a) is a sewage facility. This section defines the term sewage facility for purposes of section 142(a).

(b) *Definitions.*—(1) *Sewage facility defined.*—A sewage facility is property—

(i) Except as provided in paragraphs (b)(2) and (d) of this section, used for the secondary treatment of wastewater; however, for property treating wastewater reasonably expected to have an average daily raw wasteload concentration of biochemical oxygen demand (BOD) that exceeds 350 milligrams per liter as oxygen (measured at the time the influent enters the facility) (the *BOD limit*), this paragraph (b)(1)(i) applies only to the extent the treatment is for wastewater having an average daily raw wasteload concentration of BOD that does not exceed the BOD limit;

(ii) Used for the preliminary and/or primary treatment of wastewater but only to the extent used in connection with secondary treatment (without regard to the BOD limit described in paragraph (b)(1)(i) of this section);

(iii) Used for the advanced or tertiary treatment of wastewater but only to the extent used in connection with and after secondary treatment;

(iv) Used for the collection, storage, use, processing, or final disposal of—

(A) Wastewater, which property is necessary for such preliminary, primary, secondary, advanced, or tertiary treatment; or

(B) Sewage sludge removed during such preliminary, primary, secondary, advanced, or tertiary treatment (without regard to the BOD limit described in paragraph (b)(1)(i) of this section);

(v) Used for the treatment, collection, storage, use, processing, or final disposal of septage (without regard to the BOD limit described in paragraph (b)(1)(i) of this section); and

(vi) Functionally related and subordinate to property described in this paragraph (b)(1), such as sewage disinfection property.

(2) *Special rules and exceptions.*—(i) *Exception to BOD limit.*—A facility treating wastewater with an average daily raw wasteload concentration of BOD exceeding the BOD limit will not fail to qualify as a sewage facility described in paragraph (b)(1) of this section to the extent that the failure to satisfy the BOD limit results from the implementation of a federal, state, or local water conservation pro-

gram (for example, a program designed to promote water use efficiency that results in BOD concentrations beyond the BOD limit).

(ii) *Anti-abuse rule for BOD limit.*—A facility does not satisfy the BOD limit if there is any intentional manipulation of the BOD level to circumvent the BOD limit (for example, increasing the volume of water in the wastewater before the influent enters the facility with the intention of reducing the BOD level).

(iii) *Authority of Commissioner.*—In appropriate cases upon application to the Commissioner, the Commissioner may determine that facilities employing technologically advanced or innovative treatment processes qualify as sewage facilities if it is demonstrated that these facilities perform functions that are consistent with the definition of sewage facilities described in paragraph (b)(1) of this section.

(3) *Other applicable definitions.*—(i) *Advanced or tertiary treatment* means the treatment of wastewater after secondary treatment. Advanced or tertiary treatment ranges from biological treatment extensions to physical-chemical separation techniques such as denitrification, ammonia stripping, carbon adsorption, and chemical precipitation.

(ii) *Nonconventional pollutants* are any pollutants that are not listed in 40 CFR 401.15, 401.16, or app. A to part 423.

(iii) *Preliminary treatment* means treatment that removes large extraneous matter from incoming wastewater and renders the incoming wastewater more amenable to subsequent treatment and handling.

(iv) *Pretreatment* means a process that preconditions wastewater to neutralize or remove toxic, priority, or nonconventional pollutants that could adversely affect sewers or inhibit a preliminary, primary, secondary, advanced, or tertiary treatment operation.

(v) *Primary treatment* means treatment that removes material that floats or will settle, usually by screens or settling tanks.

(vi) *Priority pollutants* are those pollutants listed in app. A to 40 CFR part 423.

(vii) *Secondary treatment* means the stage in sewage treatment in which a bacterial process (or an equivalent process) consumes the organic parts of wastes, usually by trickling filters or an activated sludge process.

(viii) *Sewage sludge* is defined in 40 CFR 122.2 and includes septage.

(ix) *Toxic pollutants* are those pollutants listed in 40 CFR 401.15.

(c) *Other property not included in the definition of a sewage facility.*— Property other than property described in paragraph (b)(1) of this section is not a sewage facility. Thus, for example, property is not a sewage facility, or functionally related and subordinate property, if the property is used for pretreatment of wastewater (whether or not this treatment is necessary to perform preliminary, primary, secondary, advanced, or tertiary treatment), or the related collection, storage, use, processing, or final disposal of the wastewater. In addition, property used to treat, process, or use wastewater subsequent to the time the wastewater can be discharged into navigable waters, as defined in 33 U.S.C. 1362, is not a sewage facility.

(d) *Allocation of costs.*—In the case of property that has both a use described in paragraph (b)(1) of this section (a sewage treatment function) and a use other than sewage treatment, only the portion of the cost of the property allocable to the sewage treatment function is taken into account as an expenditure to provide sewage facilities. The portion of the cost of property allocable to the sewage treatment function is determined by allocating the cost of that property between the property's sewage treatment function and any other uses by any method which, based on all the facts and circumstances, reasonably reflects a separation of costs for each use of the property.

(e) *Effective date.*—(1) *In general.*—This section applies to issues of bonds issued after February 21, 1995.

(2) *Refundings.*—In the case of a refunding bond issued to refund a bond to which this section does not apply, the issuer need not apply this section to that refunding bond. This paragraph (e)(2) applies only if the weighted average maturity of the refunding bonds, as described in section 147(b), is not greater than the remaining weighted average maturity of the refunded bonds. [Reg. § 1.142(a)(5)-1.]

□ [T.D. 8576, 12-22-94.]

[Reg. § 1.142(a)(6)-1]

§ 1.142(a)(6)-1. Exempt facility bonds: solid waste disposal facilities.—(a) *In general.*—This section defines the term solid waste disposal facility for purposes of section 142(a)(6).

(b) *Solid waste disposal facility.*—The term *solid waste disposal facility* means a facility to the extent that the facility—

(1) Processes solid waste (as defined in paragraph (c) of this section) in a qualified solid waste disposal process (as defined in paragraph (d) of this section);

(2) Performs a preliminary function (as defined in paragraph (f) of this section); or

(3) Is functionally related and subordinate (within the meaning of §1.103-8(a)(3)) to a facility described in paragraph (b)(1) or (b)(2) of this section.

(c) *Solid waste.*—(1) *In general.*—Except to the extent excluded under paragraph (c)(2) of this section, for purposes of section 142(a)(6), the term *solid waste* means garbage, refuse, and other solid material derived from any agricultural, commercial, consumer, governmental, or industrial operation or activity if the material meets the requirements of both paragraph (c)(1)(i) and paragraph (c)(1)(ii) of this section. For purposes of this section, material is solid if it is solid at ambient temperature and pressure.

(i) *Used material or residual material.*—Material meets the requirements of this paragraph (c)(1)(i) if it is either used material (as defined in paragraph (c)(1)(i)(A)) of this section or residual material (as defined in paragraph (c)(1)(i)(B) of this section).

(A) *Used material.*—The term *used material* means any material that is a product of any agricultural, commercial, consumer, governmental, or industrial operation or activity, or a component of any such product or activity, and that has been used previously. Used material also includes animal waste produced by animals from a biological process.

(B) *Residual material.*—The term *residual material* means material that meets the requirements of this paragraph (c)(1)(i)(B). The material must be a residual byproduct or excess raw material that results from or remains after the completion of any agricultural, commercial, consumer, governmental, or industrial production process or activity or from the provision of any service. In the case of multiple processes constituting an integrated manufacturing or industrial process, the material must result from or remain after the completion of such integrated process. As of the issue date of the bonds used to finance the solid waste disposal facility, the material must be reasonably expected to have a fair market value that is lower than the value of all of the products made in that production process or lower than the value of the service that produces such residual material.

(ii) *Reasonably expected introduction into a qualified solid waste disposal process.*—Material meets the requirements of this paragraph (c)(1)(ii) if it is reasonably expected by the person who generates, purchases, or otherwise acquires it to be introduced within a reasonable time after such generation, purchase or acquisition into a qualified solid waste disposal process described in paragraph (d) of this section.

(2) *Exclusions from solid waste.*—The following materials do not constitute solid waste:

(i) *Virgin material.*—Except to the extent that virgin material constitutes an input to a final disposal process or residual material, solid waste excludes any virgin material. The term *virgin material* means material that has not been processed into an agricultural, commercial, consumer, governmental, or industrial product, or a component of any such product. Further, for this purpose, material continues to be virgin material after it has been grown, harvested, mined, or otherwise extracted from its naturally occurring location and cleaned, divided into component elements, modified, or enhanced, as long as further processing is required before it becomes an agricultural, commercial, consumer, or industrial product, or a component of any such product.

(ii) *Solids within liquids and liquid waste.*—Solid waste excludes any solid or dissolved material in domestic sewage or other significant pollutant in water resources, such as silt, dissolved or suspended solids in industrial waste water effluents, dissolved materials in irrigation return flows or other common water pollutants, and liquid or gaseous waste.

(iii) *Precious metals.*—Except to the extent that a precious metal constitutes an input to a final disposal process and/or an unrecoverable trace of the particular precious metal, solid waste excludes gold, silver, ruthenium, rhodium, palladium, osmium, iridium, platinum, gallium, rhenium, and any other precious metal material as may be identified by the Internal Revenue Service in future public administrative guidance.

(iv) *Hazardous material.*—Solid waste excludes any hazardous material that must be disposed of at a facility that is subject to final permit requirements under subtitle C of title II of the Solid Waste Disposal Act as in effect on the date of the enactment of the Tax Reform Act of 1986 (which is October 22, 1986). See section 142(h)(1) of the Internal Revenue Code for the definition of qualified hazardous waste facilities.

(v) *Radioactive material.*—Solid waste excludes any radioactive material subject to regulation under the Nuclear Regulatory Act (10 CFR 1.1 et seq.), as in effect on the issue date of the bonds.

(d) *Qualified solid waste disposal process.*—The term *qualified solid waste disposal process* means the processing of solid waste in a final disposal process (as defined in paragraph (d)(1) of this section), an energy conversion process (as defined in paragraph (d)(2) of this section), or a recycling process (as defined in paragraph (d)(3) of this section). Absent an express restriction to the contrary in this section, a qualified solid waste disposal process may employ any biological, engineering, industrial, or technological method.

(1) *Final disposal process.*—The term *final disposal process* means the placement of solid waste in a landfill (including, for this purpose, the spreading of solid waste over land in an environmentally compliant and safe manner with no intent to remove such solid waste), the incineration of solid waste without capturing any useful energy, or the containment of solid waste with a reasonable expectation as of the date of issue of the bonds that the containment will continue indefinitely and that the solid waste has no current or future beneficial use.

(2) *Energy conversion process.*—The term *energy conversion process* means a thermal, chemical, or other process that is applied to solid waste to create and capture synthesis gas, heat, hot water, steam, or other useful energy. The energy conversion process begins at the point of the first application of such process. The energy conversion process ends at the point at which the useful energy is first created, captured, or incorporated into the form of synthesis gas, heat, hot water, or other useful energy and before any transfer or distribution of such synthesis gas, heat, hot water or other useful energy, regardless of whether such synthesis gas, heat, hot water, or other useful energy constitutes a first useful product within the meaning of paragraph (e) of this section.

(3) *Recycling process.*—(i) *In general.*—The term *recycling process* means reconstituting, transforming, or otherwise processing solid waste into a useful product. The recycling process begins at the point of the first application of a process to reconstitute or transform the solid waste into a useful product, such as decontamination, melting, re-pulping, shredding, or other processing of the solid waste to accomplish this purpose. The recycling process ends at the point of completion of production of the first useful product from the solid waste.

(ii) *Refurbishment, repair, or similar activities.*—The term *recycling process* does not include refurbishment, repair, or similar activities. The term *refurbishment* means the breakdown and reassembly of a product if such activity is done on a product-by-product basis and if the finished product contains more than 30 percent of its original materials or components.

(e) *First useful product.*—The term *first useful product* means the first product produced from the processing of solid waste in a solid waste disposal process that is useful for consumption in agricultural, consumer, commercial, governmental, or industrial operation or activity and that could be sold for such use, whether or not actually sold. A useful product includes both a product useful to an individual consumer as an ultimate end-use consumer product and a product useful to an industrial user as a material or input for processing in some stage of a manufacturing or production process to produce a different end-use consumer product. The determination of whether a useful product has been produced may take into account operational constraints that affect the point in production when a useful product reasonably can be extracted or isolated and sold independently. For this purpose, the costs of extracting, isolating, storing, and transporting the product to a market may only be taken into account as operational constraints if the product is not to be used as part of an integrated manufacturing or industrial process in the same location as that in which the product is produced.

(f) *Preliminary function.*—A *preliminary function* is a function to collect, separate, sort, store, treat, process, disassemble, or handle solid waste that is preliminary to and directly related to a qualified solid waste disposal process.

(g) *Mixed-use facilities.*—(1) *In general.*—If a facility is used for both a qualified solid waste disposal function (including a qualified solid waste disposal process or a preliminary function) and a nonqualified function (a mixed-use facility), then the costs of the facility allocable to the qualified solid waste disposal function are determined using

Reg. §1.142(a)(6)-1(g)(1)

25,156

Tax Exempt. Requirements: State/Local Bonds
See p. 20,601 for regulations not amended to reflect law changes

any reasonable method, based on all the facts and circumstances. See §1.103-8(a)(1) for allocation rules on amounts properly allocable to an exempt facility. Facilities qualify as functionally related and subordinate to a qualified solid waste disposal function only to the extent that they are functionally related and subordinate to the portion of the mixed-use facility that is used for one or more qualified solid waste disposal functions (including a qualified solid waste disposal process or a preliminary function).

(2) *Mixed inputs.*—(i) *In general.*—Except as otherwise provided in paragraph (g)(2)(ii) of this section, for each facility (or a portion of a mixed-use facility) performing a qualified solid waste disposal process or a preliminary function, the percentage of the costs of the property used for such process that are allocable to a qualified solid waste disposal process or a preliminary function cannot exceed the average annual percentage of solid waste processed in that qualified solid waste disposal process or that preliminary function while the issue is outstanding. The annual percentage of solid waste processed in that qualified solid waste disposal process or preliminary function for any year is the percentage, by weight or volume, of the total materials processed in that qualified solid waste disposal process or preliminary function that constitute solid waste for that year.

(ii) *Special rule for mixed-input processes if at least 65 percent of the materials processed are solid waste.*—(A) *In general.*—Except as otherwise provided in paragraph (g)(2)(ii)(B) of this section, for each facility (or a portion of a mixed-use facility) performing a qualified solid waste disposal process or preliminary function, if the annual percentage of solid waste processed in that qualified solid waste disposal process or preliminary function for each year that the issue is outstanding (beginning with the date such facility is placed in service within the meaning of §1.150-2(c)) equals at least 65 percent of the materials processed in that qualified solid waste disposal process or preliminary function, then all of the costs of the property used for such process are treated as allocable to a qualified solid waste disposal process. The annual percentage of solid waste processed in such qualified solid waste disposal process or preliminary function for any year is the percentage, by weight or volume, of the total materials processed in that qualified solid waste disposal process or preliminary function that constitute solid waste for that year.

(B) *Special rule for extraordinary events.*—In the case of an extraordinary event that is beyond the control of the operator of a solid waste disposal facility (such as a natural disaster, strike, major utility disruption, or governmental intervention) and that causes a solid waste disposal facility to be unable to meet the 65 percent test under paragraph (g)(2)(ii)(A) of this section for a particular year, the percentage of solid waste processed for that year equals—

(1) The sum of the amount of solid waste processed in the solid waste disposal facility for the year affected by the extraordinary event and the amount of solid waste processed in the solid 18 waste disposal facility during the following two years in excess of the amount required to meet the general 65 percent threshold for the facility during each of such two years; divided by

(2) The total materials processed in the solid waste disposal facility during the year affected by the extraordinary event. If the resulting measure of solid waste processed for the year affected by the extraordinary event equals at least 65 percent, then the facility is treated as meeting the requirements of the 65 percent test under paragraph (g)(2)(ii)(A) of this section for such year.

(iii) *Facilities functionally related and subordinate to mixed-input facilities.*—Except to the extent that facilities are functionally related and subordinate to a mixed-input facility that meets the 65 percent test under paragraph (g)(2)(ii) of this section, facilities qualify as functionally related and subordinate to a mixed-input facility only to the extent that they are functionally related and subordinate to the qualified portion of the mixed-input facility that is used for one or more qualified solid waste disposal functions (including a qualified solid waste disposal process or a preliminary function).

(h) *Examples.*—The following examples illustrate the application of this section:

Example 1. Nonqualified Unused Material—Cloth. Company A takes wool and weaves it into cloth and then sells the cloth to a manufacturer to manufacture clothing. The cloth is material that has not been used previously as a product of or otherwise used in an agricultural, commercial, consumer, governmental, or industrial operation or activity, or as a component of any such product or activity. Accordingly, the cloth is not solid waste.

Example 2. Residual Material—Waste Coal. Company B mines coal. Some of the ore mined is a low quality byproduct of coal mining commonly known as waste coal, which cannot be converted to energy under a normal energy-production process because the BTU content is too low. Waste coal has the lowest fair market value of any product produced in Company B's coal mining process. Waste coal is solid waste because it is residual material within the meaning of paragraph (c)(1)(i)(B) of this section and Company B reasonably expects to introduce the waste coal into a solid waste disposal process.

Example 3. Virgin Material—Logs. Company C cuts down trees and sells the logs to another company, which further processes the logs into lumber. In order to facilitate shipping, Company C cuts the trees into uniform logs. The trees are not solid waste because they are virgin material within the meaning of paragraph (c)(2)(i) of this section that are not being introduced into a final disposal process within the meaning of paragraph (d)(1) of this section. The division of such trees into uniform logs does not change the status of the trees as virgin material.

Example 4. Qualified Solid Waste Disposal Process—Landfill. Company D plans to construct a landfill. The landfill will not be subject to the final permit requirements under subtitle C of title II of the Solid Waste Disposal Act (as in effect on the date of enactment of the Tax Reform Act of 1986). As of the issue date, Company D expects that the landfill will be filled entirely with material that will qualify as solid waste within the meaning of paragraph (c) of this section. Placing solid waste into a landfill is a qualified solid waste disposal process. The landfill is a qualified solid waste disposal facility.

Example 5. Qualified Solid Waste Disposal Process—Recycling Tires. Company E owns a facility that converts used tires into roadbed material. The used tires are used material within the meaning of paragraph (c)(1)(i)(A) of this section that qualifies as solid waste. Between the introduction of the old tires into the roadbed manufacturing process and the completion of the roadbed material, the facility does not create any interim useful products. The process for the manufacturing of the roadbed material from the old tires is a qualified solid waste disposal process as a recycling process and the facility that converts the tires into roadbed material is a qualified solid waste disposal facility. This conclusion would be the same if the recycling process took place at more than one plant.

Example 6. Qualified Solid Waste Disposal Process—Energy Conversion Process. Company F receives solid waste from a municipal garbage collector. Company F burns that solid waste in an incinerator to remove exhaust gas and to produce heat. Company F further processes the heat in a heat exchanger to produce steam. Company F further processes the steam to generate electricity. The energy conversion process ends with the production of steam. The facilities used to burn the solid waste and to capture the steam as useful energy are qualified solid waste disposal facilities because they process solid waste in an energy conversion process. The generating facilities used to process the steam further to generate electricity are not engaged in the energy conversion process and are not qualified solid waste disposal facilities.

Example 7. Nonqualified Refurbishment. Company G purchases used cars and restores them. This restoration process includes disassembly, cleaning, and repairing of the cars. Parts that cannot be repaired are replaced. The restored cars contain at least 30 percent of the original parts. While the cars are used material, the refurbishing process is not a qualified solid waste disposal process. Accordingly, Company G's facility is not a qualified solid waste disposal facility.

Example 8. Qualified Solid Waste Disposal Facility—First Useful Product Rule—Paper Recycling. (i) Company H employs an integrated process to re-pulp discarded magazines, clean the pulp, and produce retail paper towel products. Operational constraints on Company H's process do not allow for reasonable extraction, isolation, and sale of the cleaned paper pulp independently without degradation of the pulp. Company H further processes the paper pulp into large industrial-sized rolls of paper which are approximately 12 feet in diameter. At this point in the process, Company H could either sell such industrial-sized rolls of paper to another company for further processing to produce retail paper products or it could produce those retail products itself. In general, paper pulp is a useful product that is bought and sold on the market as a material for input into manufacturing or production processes. The discarded magazines are used material within the meaning of paragraph (c)(1)(i)(A) of this section. Company H's facility is engaged in a recycling process within the meaning of paragraph (d)(3) of this section to the extent that it repulps and cleans the discarded magazines generally and further to the extent that it produces industrial-sized rolls of paper under the particular circumstances here. Specifically, taking into account the operational constraints on Company H's facility that limit its ability reasonably to extract, isolate, and sell the paper pulp independently, the first useful products within the meaning of paragraph (e) of this section from Company H's recycling process are the industrial-sized rolls of paper. The portion of Company H's facility that processes the discarded magazines and produces industrial-sized rolls of paper is a qualified solid waste disposal facility, and the portion of Company H's facility that further processes the industrial-sized rolls of paper into retail paper towels is not a qualified solid waste facility.

(ii) The facts are the same as in paragraph (i) of this *Example 8*, except that Company H is able reasonably to extract the cleaned paper pulp from the process without degradation of the pulp and to sell the cleaned paper pulp at its dock for a price that exceeds its costs of extracting the pulp from the process. Therefore, the paper pulp is the first useful product within the meaning of paragraph (e) of this section. As a result, the portion of Company H's facility that processes the discarded magazines is a qualified solid waste disposal facility, and the portion of Company H's facility that produces industrial-sized rolls of paper is not a qualified solid waste disposal facility. If, however, the only reasonable way Company H could sell the pulp was to transport the pulp to a distant market, then the costs of storing and transporting the pulp to the market may be taken into account in determining whether the pulp is the first useful product.

Example 9. Preliminary Function—Energy Conversion Process. (i) Company I owns a paper mill. At the mill, logs from nearby timber operations are processed through a machine that removes bark. The stripped logs are used to manufacture paper. The stripped bark has the lowest fair market value of any product produced from the paper mill. The stripped bark falls onto a conveyor belt that transports the bark to a storage bin that is used to store the bark briefly until Company I feeds the bark into a boiler. The conveyor belt and storage bin are used only for these purposes. The boiler is used only to create steam by burning the bark, and the steam is used to generate electricity. The stripped bark is solid waste because it is residual material within the meaning of paragraph (c)(1)(i)(B) of this section and Company I expects to introduce the bark into an energy conversion process within a reasonable period of time. The creation of steam from the stripped bark is an energy conversion process that starts with the incineration of the stripped bark. The energy conversion process is a qualified solid waste disposal process. The conveyor belt performs a collection activity that is preliminary and that is directly related to the solid waste disposal function. The storage bin performs a storage function that is preliminary and that is directly related to the solid waste disposal function. Thus, the conveyor belt and storage bin are solid waste disposal facilities. The bark removal process is not a preliminary function because it is not directly related to the energy conversion process and it does not become so related merely because it results in material that is solid waste.

(ii) The facts are the same as in paragraph (i) of this *Example 9*, except that the stripped bark represents only 55 percent by weight and volume of the materials that are transported by the conveyor belt. The remaining 45 percent of the materials transported by the conveyor belt are not solid waste and these other materials are sorted from the conveyor belt by a sorting machine immediately before the stripped bark arrives at the storage bin. Fifty-five percent of the costs of the conveyor belt and the sorting machine are allocable to solid waste disposal functions.

Example 10. Preliminary Function—Final Disposal Process. Company J owns a waste transfer station and uses it to collect, sort, and process solid waste. Company J uses its trucks to haul the solid waste to the nearest landfill. At least 65 percent by weight and volume of the material brought to the transfer station is solid waste. The waste transfer station and the trucks perform functions that are preliminary and directly related to the solid waste disposal function of the landfill. Thus, the waste transfer station and the trucks qualify as solid waste disposal facilities.

Example 11. Mixed-Input Facility. Company K owns an incinerator financed by an issue and uses the incinerator exclusively to burn coal and other solid material to create steam. Each year while the issue is outstanding, 40 percent by volume and 45 percent by weight of the solid material that Company K processes in the conversion process is coal. The remainder of the solid material is either used material or residual material within the meaning of paragraph (c)(1)(i) of this section. Sixty percent of the costs of the property used to perform the energy conversion process are allocable to a solid waste disposal function.

(i) *Effective/Applicability Dates.*—(1) *In general.*—Except as otherwise provided in this paragraph (i), this section applies to bonds to which section 142 applies that are sold on or after October 18, 2011.

(2) *Elective retroactive application.*—Issuers may apply this section, in whole, but not in part, to outstanding bonds to which section 142 applies and which were sold before October 18, 2011.

(3) *Certain refunding bonds.*—An issuer need not apply this section to bonds that are issued in a current refunding to refund bonds to which this section does not apply if the weighted average maturity of the refunding bonds is no longer than the remaining weighted average maturity of the refunded bonds. [Reg. § 1.142(a)(6)-1.]

☐ [*T.D. 9546*, 8-18-2011 (*corrected* 9-6-2011).]

[Reg. § 1.142(f)(4)-1]

§ 1.142(f)(4)-1. Manner of making election to terminate tax-exempt bond financing.—(a) *Overview.*—Section 142(f)(4) permits a person engaged in the local furnishing of electric energy or gas (a local furnisher) that uses facilities financed with exempt facility bonds under section 142(a)(8) and that expands its service area in a manner inconsistent with the requirements of sections 142(a)(8) and (f) to make an election to ensure that those bonds will continue to be treated as exempt facility bonds. The election must meet the requirements of paragraphs (b) and (c) of this section.

(b) *Time for making election.*—(1) *In general.*—An election under section 142(f)(4)(B) must be filed with the Internal Revenue Service on or before 90 days after the date of the service area expansion that causes bonds to cease to meet the requirements of sections 142(a)(8) and (f).

(2) *Date of service area expansion.*—For the purposes of this section, the date of the service area expansion is the first date on which the local furnisher is authorized to collect revenue for the provision of service in the expanded area.

(c) *Manner of making election.*—An election under section 142(f)(4)(B) must be captioned "ELECTION TO TERMINATE TAX-EXEMPT BOND FINANCING", must be signed under penalties of perjury by a person who has authority to sign on behalf of the local furnisher, and must contain the following information—

(1) The name of the local furnisher;

(2) The tax identification number of the local furnisher;

(3) The complete address of the local furnisher;

(4) The date of the service area expansion;

(5) Identification of each bond issue subject to the election, including the complete name of each issue, the tax identification number of each issuer, the report number of the information return filed under section 149(e) for each issue, the issue date of each issue, the CUSIP number (if any) of the bond with the latest maturity of each issue, the issue price of each issue, the adjusted issue price of each issue as of the date of the election, the earliest date on which the bonds of each issue may be redeemed, and the principal amount of bonds of each issue to be redeemed on the earliest redemption date;

(6) A statement that the local furnisher making the election agrees to the conditions stated in section 142(f)(4)(B); and

(7) A statement that each issuer of the bonds subject to the election has received written notice of the election.

(d) *Effect on section 150(b).*—Except as provided in paragraph (e) of this section, if a local furnisher files an election within the period specified in paragraph (b) of this section, section 150(b) does not apply to bonds identified in the election during and after that period.

(e) *Effect of failure to meet agreements.*—If a local furnisher fails to meet any of the conditions stated in an election pursuant to paragraph (c)(6) of this section, the election is invalid.

(f) *Corresponding provisions of the Internal Revenue Code of 1954.*—Section 103(b)(4)(E) of the Internal Revenue Code of 1954 set forth corresponding requirements for the exclusion from gross income of the interest on bonds issued for facilities for the local furnishing of electric energy or gas. For the purposes of this section any reference to sections 142(a)(8) and (f) of the Internal Revenue Code of 1986 includes a reference to the corresponding portion of section 103(b)(4)(E) of the Internal Revenue Code of 1954.

(g) *Effective dates.*—This section applies to elections made on or after January 19, 2001. [Reg. § 1.142(f)(4)-1.]

☐ [*T.D. 8941*, 1-17-2001.]

[Reg. § 1.143(g)-1]

§ 1.143(g)-1. Requirements related to arbitrage.—(a) *In general.*—Under section 143, for an issue to be an issue of qualified mortgage bonds or qualified veterans' mortgage bonds (together, mortgage revenue bonds), the requirements of section 143(g) must be satisfied. An issue satisfies the requirements of section 143(g) only if such issue meets the requirements of paragraph (b) of this section and, in the case of an issue 95 percent or more of the net proceeds of which are to be used to provide residences for veterans, such issue also meets the requirements of paragraph (c) of this section. The requirements of section 143(g) and this section are applicable in addition to the requirements of section 148 and § § 1.148-0 through 1.148-11.

(b) *Effective rate of mortgage interest not to exceed bond yield by more than 1.125 percentage points.*—(1) *Maximum yield.*—An issue shall be treated as meeting the requirements of this paragraph (b) only if the excess of the effective rate of interest on the mortgages financed by the issue, over the yield on the issue, is not greater over the term of the issue than 1.125 percentage points.

(2) *Effective rate of interest.*—(i) In determining the effective rate of interest on any mortgage for purposes of this paragraph (b), there shall be taken into account all fees, charges, and other amounts borne by the mortgagor that are attributable to the mortgage or to the bond issue. Such amounts include points, commitment fees, origination fees, servicing fees, and prepayment penalties paid by the mortgagor.

(ii) Items that shall be treated as borne by the mortgagor and shall be taken into account in calculating the effective rate of interest also include—

(A) All points, commitment fees, origination fees, or similar charges borne by the seller of the property; and

(B) The excess of any amounts received from any person other than the mortgagor by any person in connection with the acquisition of the mortgagor's interest in the property over the usual and reasonable acquisition costs of a person acquiring like property when owner-financing is not provided through the use of mortgage revenue bonds.

(iii) The following items shall not be treated as borne by the mortgagor and shall not be taken into account in calculating the effective rate of interest—

(A) Any expected rebate of arbitrage profit under paragraph (c) of this section; and

(B) Any application fee, survey fee, credit report fee, insurance charge or similar settlement or financing cost to the extent such amount does not exceed amounts charged in the area in cases when owner-financing is not provided through the use of mortgage revenue bonds. For example, amounts paid for Federal Housing Administration, Veterans' Administration, or similar private mortgage insurance on an individual's mortgage, or amounts paid for pool mortgage insurance on a pool of mortgages, are not taken into account so long as such amounts do not exceed the amounts charged in the area with respect to a similar mortgage, or pool of mortgages, that is not financed with mortgage revenue bonds. For this purpose, amounts paid for pool mortgage insurance include amounts paid to an entity (for example, the Government National Mortgage Association, the Federal National Mortgage Association (FNMA), the Federal Home Loan Mortgage Corporation, or other mortgage insurer) to directly guarantee the pool of mortgages financed with the bonds, or to guarantee a pass-through security backed by the pool of mortgages financed with the bonds.

(C) The following example illustrates the provisions of this paragraph (b)(2)(iii):

Example. Housing Authority X issues bonds intended to be qualified mortgage bonds under section 143(a). At the time the bonds are issued, X enters into an agreement with a group of mortgage lending institutions (lenders) under which the lenders agree to originate and service mortgages that meet certain specified requirements. After originating a specified amount of mortgages, each lender issues a "pass-though security" (each, a PTS) backed by the mortgages and sells the PTS to X. Under the terms of the PTS, the lender pays X an amount equal to the regular monthly payments on the mortgages (less certain fees), whether or not received by the lender (plus any prepayments and liquidation proceeds in the event of a foreclosure or other disposition of any mortgages). FNMA guarantees the timely payment of principal and interest on each PTS. From the payments received from each mortgagor, the lender pays a fee to FNMA for its guarantee of the PTS. The amounts paid to FNMA do not exceed the amounts charged in the area with respect to a similar pool of mortgages that is not financed with mortgage revenue bonds. Under this paragraph (b)(2)(iii), the fees for the guarantee provided by FNMA are an insurance charge because the guarantee is pool mortgage insurance. Because the amounts charged for the guarantee do not exceed the amounts charged in the area with respect to a similar pool of mortgages that is not financed with mortgage revenue bonds, the amounts charged for the guarantee are not taken into account in computing the effective rate of interest on the mortgages financed with X's bonds.

(3) *Additional rules.*—To the extent not inconsistent with the Tax Reform Act of 1986, Public Law 99-514 (the 1986 Act), or subsequent law, § 6a.103A-2(i)(2) (other than paragraphs (i)(2)(i) and (i)(2)(ii)(A) through (C)) of this chapter applies to provide additional rules relating to compliance with the requirement that the effective rate of mortgage interest not exceed the bond yield by more than 1.125 percentage points.

(c) *Arbitrage and investment gains to be used to reduce costs of owner-financing.*—As provided in section 143(g)(3), certain earnings on nonpurpose investments must either be paid or credited to mortgagors, or paid to the United States, in certain circumstances. To the extent not inconsistent with the 1986 Act or subsequent law, § 6a.103A-2(i)(4) of this chapter applies to provide guidance relating to compliance with this requirement.

(d) *Effective dates.*—(1) *In general.*—Except as otherwise provided in this section, § 1.143(g)-1 applies to bonds sold on or after May 23, 2005, that are subject to section 143.

(2) *Permissive retroactive application in whole.*—Except as provided in paragraph (d)(4) of this section, issuers may apply § 1.143(g)-1, in whole, but not in part, to bonds sold before May 23, 2005, that are subject to section 143.

(3) *Bonds subject to the Internal Revenue Code of 1954.*—Except as provided in paragraph (d)(4) of this section and subject to the applicable effective dates for the corresponding statutory provisions, an issuer may apply § 1.143(g)-1, in whole, but not in part, to bonds that are subject to section 103A(i) of the Internal Revenue Code of 1954.

(4) *Special rule for pre-July 1, 1993 bonds.*—To the extent that an issuer applies this section to bonds issued before July 1, 1993, § 6a.103A-2(i)(3) of this chapter also applies to the bonds. [Reg. § 1.143(g)-1.]

☐ [*T.D.* 9204, 5-20-2005.]

[Reg. § 1.144-0]

§ 1.144-0. Table of contents.—This section lists the captioned paragraphs contained in §§ 1.144-1 and 1.144-2.

[Reg. § 1.144-0.]

☐ [*T.D.* 8712, 1-10-97.]

[Reg. § 1.144-1]

§ 1.144-1. Qualified small issue bonds, qualified student loan bonds, and qualified redevelopment bonds.—(a) *Overview.*—Interest on a private activity bond is not excludable from gross income under section 103(a) unless the bond is a qualified bond. Under section 141(e)(1)(D), a qualified small issue bond issued under section 144(a) may be a qualified bond. Under section 144(a), any qualified small issue bond is any bond issued as a part of an issue 95 percent or more of the proceeds of which are to be used to provide certain manufacturing facilities or certain depreciable farm property and which meets other requirements. Under section 141(e)(1)(F) a qualified redevelopment bond issued under section 144(c) is a qualified bond. Under section 144(c), a qualified redevelopment bond is any bond issued as a part of an issue 95 percent or more of the net proceeds of which are to be used for one or more redevelopment purposes and which meets certain other requirements.

(b) *Scope.*—Sections 1.144-0 through 1.144-2 apply for purposes of the rules for small issue bonds under section 144(a) and qualified redevelopment bonds under section 144(c), except that § 1.144-2 does not apply to the requirements for qualified small issue bonds under section 144(a)(4) (relating to the limitation on capital expenditures) or under section 144(a)(10) (relating to the aggregate limit of tax-exempt bonds per taxpayer).

(c) *Effective dates.*—For effective dates of §§ 1.144-0 through 1.144-2, see § 1.141-16. [Reg. § 1.144-1.]

☐ [Reg. § 1.144-1, issued under Code Sec. 144 as it existed prior to repeal by P.L. 95-30, was removed from the CFR, and Reg. § 1.144-1, above, was adopted by *T.D.* 8712, 1-10-97.]

[Reg. § 1.144-2]

§ 1.144-2. Remedial actions.—The remedial action rules of § 1.142-2 apply to qualified small issue bonds issued under section 144(a) and to qualified redevelopment bonds issued under section 144(c), for this purpose treating those bonds as exempt facility bonds and the qualifying purposes for those bonds as exempt facilities. [Reg. § 1.144-2.]

☐ [Reg. § 1.144-2, issued under Code Sec. 144 as it existed prior to repeal by P.L. 95-30, was removed from the CFR, and Reg. § 1.144-2, above, was adopted by *T.D.* 8712, 1-10-97.]

[Reg. § 1.145-0]

§ 1.145-0. Table of contents.—This section lists the captioned paragraphs contained in §§ 1.145-1 and 1.145-2.

§1.145-2 Application of private activity bond regulations.
(a) In general.
(b) Modification of private business tests.
(c) Exceptions.
(1) Certain provisions relating to governmental programs.
(2) Costs of issuance.
(d) Issuance costs financed by prior issue.
[Reg. §1.145-0.]

☐ [*T.D. 8712, 1-10-97. Amended by T.D. 9234, 12-16-2005.*]

[Reg. §1.145-1]

§1.145-1. Qualified 501(c)(3) bonds.—(a) *Overview.*—Interest on a private activity bond is not excludable from gross income under section 103(a) unless the bond is a qualified bond. Under section 141(e)(1)(G), a qualified 501(c)(3) bond issued under section 145 is a qualified bond. Under section 145, a qualified 501(c)(3) bond is any bond issued as a part of an issue that satisfies the requirements of sections 145(a) through (d).

(b) *Scope.*—Sections 1.145-0 through 1.145-2 apply for purposes of section 145(a).

(c) *Effective dates.*—For effective dates of §§1.145-0 through 1.145-2, see §1.141-15. [Reg. §1.145-1.]

☐ [*T.D. 8712, 1-10-97.*]

[Reg. §1.145-2]

§1.145-2. Application of private activity bond regulations.—(a) *In general.*—Except as provided in this section, §§1.141-0 through 1.141-15 apply to section 145(a). For example, under this section, §1.141-1, and §1.141-2, an issue ceases to be an issue of qualified 501(c)(3) bonds if the issuer or a conduit borrower 501(c)(3) organization takes a deliberate action, subsequent to the issue date, that causes the issue to fail to comply with the requirements of sections 141(e) and 145 (such as an action that results in revocation of exempt status of the 501(c)(3) organization).

(b) *Modification of private business tests.*—In applying §§1.141-0 through 1.141-15 to section 145(a)—

(1) References to governmental persons include 501(c)(3) organizations with respect to their activities that do not constitute unrelated trades or businesses under section 513(a);

(2) References to "10 percent" and "proceeds" in the context of the private business use test and the private security or payment test mean "5 percent" and "net proceeds"; and

(3) References to the private business use test in §§1.141-2 and 1.141-12 include the ownership test of section 145(a)(1).

(4) References to *governmental bonds* in §1.141-6 mean qualified 501(c)(3) bonds.

(5) References to *ownership by governmental persons* in §1.141-6 mean ownership by governmental persons or 501(c)(3) organizations.

(c) *Exceptions.*—(1) *Certain provisions relating to governmental programs.*—The following provisions do not apply to section 145: §1.141-2(d)(4) (relating to the special rule for dispositions of personal property in the ordinary course of an established governmental program) and §1.141-2(d)(5) (relating to the special rule for general obligation bond programs that finance a large number of separate purposes).

(2) *Costs of issuance.*—Sections 1.141-3(g)(6) and 1.141-6(d) do not apply to the extent costs of issuance are allocated among the other purposes for which the proceeds are used or to portions of a project. For purposes of section 145(a)(2), costs of issuance are treated as private business use.

(d) *Issuance costs financed by prior issue.*—Solely for purposes of applying the private business use test to a refunding issue under §1.141-13, the use of proceeds of the prior issue (or any earlier issue in a series of refundings) to pay issuance costs of the prior issue (or the earlier issue) is treated as a government use. [Reg. §1.145-2.]

☐ [*T.D. 8712, 1-10-97. Amended by T.D. 9234, 12-16-2005 and T.D. 9741, 10-26-2015.*]

[Reg. §1.147-0]

§1.147-0. Table of contents.—This section lists the captioned paragraphs contained in §§1.147-1 and 1.147-2.

§1.147-1 Other requirements applicable to certain private activity bonds.
(a) Overview.
(b) Scope.
(c) Effective dates.

§1.147-2 Remedial actions.
[Reg. §1.147-0.]

☐ [*T.D. 8712, 1-10-97.*]

[Reg. §1.147-1]

§1.147-1. Other requirements applicable to certain private activity bonds.—(a) *Overview.*—Interest on a private activity bond is not excludable from gross income under section 103(a) unless the bond is a qualified bond. Under section 147, certain requirements must be met for a private activity bond to qualify as a qualified bond.

(b) *Scope.*—Sections 1.147-0 through 1.147-2 apply for purposes of the rules in section 147 for qualified private activity bonds that permit use of proceeds to acquire land for environmental purposes (section 147(c)(3)), permit use of proceeds for certain rehabilitations (section 147(d)(2) and (3)), prohibit use of proceeds to finance skyboxes, airplanes, gambling establishments and similar facilities (section 147(e)), and require public approval (section 147(f)), but not for the rules limiting use of proceeds to acquire land or existing property under sections 147(c)(1) and (2), and (d)(1).

(c) *Effective dates.*—For effective dates of §§1.147-0 through 1.147-2, see §1.141-16. [Reg. §1.147-1.]

☐ [*T.D. 8712, 1-10-97.*]

[Reg. §1.147-2]

§1.147-2. Remedial actions.—The remedial action rules of §1.142-2 apply to the rules in section 147 for qualified private activity bonds that permit use of proceeds to acquire land for environmental purposes (section 147(c)(3)), permit use of proceeds for certain rehabilitations (section 147(d)(2) and (3)), prohibit use of proceeds to finance skyboxes, airplanes, gambling establishments and similar facilities (section 147(e)), and require public approval (section 147(f)), for this purpose treating those private activity bonds subject to the rules under section 147 as exempt facility bonds and the qualifying purposes for those bonds as exempt facilities. [Reg. §1.147-2.]

☐ [*T.D. 8712, 1-10-97.*]

[Reg. §1.147(b)-1]

§1.147(b)-1. Bond maturity limitation-treatment of working capital.—Section 147(b) does not apply to proceeds of a private activity bond issue used to finance working capital expenditures. [Reg. §1.147(b)-1.]

☐ [*T.D. 8476, 6-14-93.*]

[Reg. §1.147(f)-1]

§1.147(f)-1. Public approval of private activity bonds.—(a) *In general.*—Interest on a private activity bond is excludable from gross income under section 103(a) only if the bond meets the requirements for a qualified bond as defined in section 141(e) and other applicable requirements provided in section 103. In order to be a qualified bond as defined in section 141(e), among other requirements, a private activity bond must meet the requirements of section 147(f). A private activity bond meets the requirements of section 147(f) only if the bond is publicly approved pursuant to paragraph (b) of this section or the bond qualifies for the exception for refunding bonds in section 147(f)(2)(D).

(b) *Public approval requirement.*—(1) *In general.*—Except as otherwise provided in this section, a bond meets the requirements of section 147(f) if, before the issue date, the issue of which the bond is a part receives issuer approval and host approval (each a *public approval*) as defined in paragraphs (b)(2) and (3) of this section in accordance with the method and process set forth in paragraphs (c) through (f) of this section.

(2) *Issuer approval.*—Except as otherwise provided in this section, *issuer approval* means an approval that meets the requirements of this paragraph (b)(2). Either the governmental unit that issues the issue or the governmental unit on behalf of which the issue is issued must approve the issue. For this purpose, §1.103-1 applies to the determination of whether an issuer issues bonds on behalf of another governmental unit. If an issuer issues bonds on behalf of more than one governmental unit (for example, in the case of an authority that acts for two counties), any one of those governmental units may provide the issuer approval.

(3) *Host approval.*—Except as otherwise provided in this section, *host approval* means an approval that meets the requirements of this paragraph (b)(3). Each governmental unit the geographic jurisdiction of which contains the site of a project to be financed by the issue must approve the issue. If, however, the entire site of a project to be financed by the issue is within the geographic jurisdiction of more than one governmental unit within a State (counting the State as a governmental unit within such State), then any one of those governmental units may provide host approval for the issue for that project. For purposes of the host approval, if a project to be financed by the

25,160

Tax Exempt. Requirements: State/Local Bonds
See p. 20,601 for regulations not amended to reflect law changes

issue is located within the geographic jurisdiction of two or more governmental units but not entirely within any one of those governmental units, each portion of the project that is located entirely within the geographic jurisdiction of the respective governmental units may be treated as a separate project. The issuer approval provided pursuant to paragraph (b)(2) of this section may be treated as a host approval if the governmental unit providing the issuer approval is also a governmental unit eligible to provide the host approval pursuant to this section.

(4) *Special rule for host approval of airports or high-speed intercity rail facilities.*—Pursuant to a special rule in section 147(f)(3), if the proceeds of an issue are to be used to finance a project that consists of either facilities located at an airport (within the meaning of section 142(a)(1)) or high-speed intercity rail facilities (within the meaning of section 142(a)(11)) and the issuer of that issue is the owner or operator of the airport or high-speed intercity rail facilities, the issuer is the only governmental unit that is required to provide the host approval for that project.

(5) *Special rule for issuer approval of scholarship funding bond issues and volunteer fire department bond issues.*—In the case of a qualified scholarship funding bond as defined in section 150(d)(2), the governmental unit that made a request described in section 150(d)(2)(B) with respect to the issuer of the bond is the governmental unit on behalf of which the bond was issued for purposes of the issuer approval. If more than one governmental unit within a State made a request described in section 150(d)(2)(B), the State or any such requesting governmental unit may be treated as the governmental unit on behalf of which the bond was issued for purposes of the issuer approval. In the case of a bond of a volunteer fire department treated as a bond of a political subdivision of a State under section 150(e), the political subdivision described in section 150(e)(2)(B) with respect to that volunteer fire department is the governmental unit on behalf of which the bond is issued for purposes of the issuer approval.

(6) *Special rules for host approval of mortgage revenue bonds, student loan bonds, and certain qualified 501(c)(3) bonds.*—In the case of a mortgage revenue bond (as defined in paragraph (g)(5) of this section), a qualified student loan bond as defined in section 144(b), and the portion of an issue of qualified 501(c)(3) bonds as defined in section 145 that finances working capital expenditures, the issue or portion of the issue must receive an issuer approval but no host approval is necessary. See also paragraph (f)(5) of this section, providing certain optional alternative special rules for certain qualified 501(c)(3) bonds for pooled loan financings described in section 147(b)(4)(B).

(c) *Method of public approval.*—The method of public approval of an issue must satisfy either paragraph (c)(1) or (2) of this section. An approval may satisfy the requirements of this paragraph (c) without regard to the authority under State or local law for the acts constituting that approval.

(1) *Applicable elected representative.*—An applicable elected representative of the approving governmental unit approves the issue following a public hearing for which there was reasonable public notice.

(2) *Voter referendum.*—A voter referendum of the approving governmental unit approves the issue.

(d) *Public hearing and reasonable public notice.*—(1) *Public hearing.*—*Public hearing* means a forum providing a reasonable opportunity for interested individuals to express their views, orally or in writing, on the proposed issue of bonds and the location and nature of the proposed project to be financed.

(2) *Location of the public hearing.*—The public hearing must be held in a location that, based on the facts and circumstances, is convenient for residents of the approving governmental unit. The location of the public hearing is presumed convenient for residents of the unit if the public hearing is located in the approving governmental unit's capital or seat of government. If more than one governmental unit is required to hold a public hearing, the hearings may be combined as long as the combined hearing affords the residents of all of the participating governmental units a reasonable opportunity to be heard. The location of any combined hearing is presumed convenient for residents of each participating governmental unit if it is no farther than 100 miles from the seat of government of each participating governmental unit beyond whose geographic jurisdiction the hearing is conducted.

(3) *Procedures for conducting the public hearing.*—In general, a governmental unit may select its own procedure for a public hearing, provided that interested individuals have a reasonable opportunity to express their views. Thus, a governmental unit may impose reasonable requirements on persons who wish to participate in the hearing, such as a requirement that persons desiring to speak at the hearing make a written request to speak at least 24 hours before the hearing or that they limit their oral remarks to a prescribed time. For this purpose, it is unnecessary, for example, that the applicable elected representative of the approving governmental unit be present at the hearing, that a report on the hearing be submitted to that applicable elected representative, or that State administrative procedural requirements for public hearings be observed. Except to the extent State procedural requirements for public hearings are in conflict with a specific requirement of this section, a public hearing performed in compliance with State procedural requirements satisfies the requirements for a public hearing in this paragraph (d). A public hearing may be conducted by an individual appointed or employed to perform such function by the governmental unit or its agencies, or by the issuer. Thus, for example, for bonds to be issued by an authority that acts on behalf of a county, the hearing may be conducted by the authority, the county, or an appointee of either.

(4) *Reasonable public notice.*—*Reasonable public notice* means notice that is reasonably designed to inform residents of an approving governmental unit, including the issuing governmental unit and the governmental unit in whose geographic jurisdiction a project is to be located, of the proposed issue. The notice must state the time and place for the public hearing and contain the information required by paragraph (f)(2) of this section. Notice is presumed to be reasonably designed to inform residents of an approving governmental unit if it satisfies the requirements of this paragraph (d)(4) and is given no fewer than seven (7) calendar days before the public hearing in one or more of the ways set forth in paragraphs (d)(4)(i) through (iv) of this section.

(i) *Newspaper publication.*—Public notice may be given by publication in one or more newspapers of general circulation available to the residents of the governmental unit.

(ii) *Radio or television broadcast.*—Public notice may be given by radio or television broadcast to the residents of the governmental unit.

(iii) *Governmental unit Web site posting.*—Public notice may be given by electronic posting on the approving governmental unit's primary public Web site in an area of that Web site used to inform its residents about events affecting the residents (for example, notice of public meetings of the governmental unit). In the case of an issuer approval of an issue issued by an on-behalf-of issuer that acts on behalf of a governmental unit, such notice may be posted on the public Web site of the on-behalf-of issuer as an alternative to the public Web site of the approving governmental unit.

(iv) *Alternative State law public notice procedures.*—Public notice may be given in a way that is permitted under a general State law for public notices for public hearings for the approving governmental unit, provided that the public notice is reasonably accessible.

(e) *Applicable elected representative.*—(1) *In general.*—(i) *Definition of applicable elected representative.*—The *applicable elected representative* of a governmental unit means—

(A) The governmental unit's elected legislative body;

(B) The governmental unit's chief elected executive officer;

(C) In the case of a State, the chief elected legal officer of the State's executive branch of government; or

(D) Any official elected by the voters of the governmental unit and designated for purposes of this section by the governmental unit's chief elected executive officer or by State or local law to approve issues for the governmental unit.

(ii) *Elected officials.*—For purposes of paragraphs (e)(1)(i)(B), (C), and (D) of this section, an official is considered elected only if that official is popularly elected at-large by the voters of the governmental unit. If an official popularly elected at-large by the voters of a governmental unit is appointed or selected pursuant to State or local law to be the chief executive officer of the unit, that official is deemed to be an elected chief executive officer for purposes of this section but for no longer than the official's tenure as an official popularly elected at-large.

(iii) *Legislative bodies.*—In the case of a bicameral legislature that is popularly elected, both chambers together constitute an applicable elected representative. Absent designation under paragraph (e)(1)(i)(D) of this section, however, neither such chamber independently constitutes an applicable elected representative. If multiple elected legislative bodies of a governmental unit have independent legislative authority, the body with the more specific authority relating to the issue is the only legislative body that is treated as an elected legislative body under paragraph (e)(1)(i)(A) of this section.

(2) *Governmental unit with no applicable elected representative.*—(i) *In general.*—The applicable elected representatives of a govern-

mental unit with no applicable elected representative (but for this paragraph (e)(2) and section 147(f)(2)(E)(ii)) are the applicable elected representatives of the next higher governmental unit (with an applicable elected representative) from which the governmental unit derives its authority. Except as otherwise provided in this section, any governmental unit from which the governmental unit with no applicable elected representative derives its authority may be treated as the next higher governmental unit without regard to the relative status of such higher governmental unit under State law. A governmental unit derives its authority from another governmental unit that—

(A) Enacts a specific law (for example, a provision in a State constitution, charter, or statute) by or under which the governmental unit is created;

(B) Otherwise empowers or approves the creation of the governmental unit; or

(C) Appoints members to the governing body of the governmental unit.

(ii) *Host approval.*—For purposes of a host approval, a governmental unit may be treated as the next higher governmental unit only if the project is located within its geographic jurisdiction and eligible residents of the unit are entitled to vote for its applicable elected representatives.

(3) *On behalf of issuers.*—In the case of an issuer that issues bonds on behalf of a governmental unit, the applicable elected representative is any applicable elected representative of the governmental unit on behalf of which the bonds are issued.

(f) *Public approval process.*—(1) *In general.*—The public approval process for an issue, including scope, content, and timing of the public approval, must meet the requirements of this paragraph (f). A governmental unit must timely approve either each project to be financed with proceeds of the issue or a plan of financing for each project to be financed with proceeds of the issue.

(2) *General rule on information required for a reasonable public notice and public approval.*—Except as otherwise provided in this section, a project to be financed with proceeds of an issue is within the scope of a public approval under section 147(f) if the reasonable public notice of the public hearing, if applicable, and the public approval (together the notice and approval) include the information set forth in paragraphs (f)(2)(i) through (iv) of this section.

(i) *The project.*—The notice and approval must include a general functional description of the type and use of the project to be financed with the issue. For this purpose, a project description is sufficient if it identifies the project by reference to a particular category of exempt facility bond to be issued (for example, an exempt facility bond for an airport pursuant to section 142(a)(1)) or by reference to another general category of private activity bond together with information on the type and use of the project to be financed with the issue (for example, a qualified small issue bond as defined in section 144(a) for a manufacturing facility or a qualified 501(c)(3) bond as defined in section 145 for a hospital facility and working capital expenditures).

(ii) *The maximum stated principal amount of the issue.*—The notice and approval must include the maximum stated principal amount of the issue of private activity bonds to be issued to finance the project or projects. If an issue finances multiple projects (for example, facilities at different locations on non-proximate sites that are not treated as part of the same project), the notice and approval must specify separately the maximum stated principal amount of bonds to be issued to finance each separate project to be financed as part of the issue. The maximum stated principal amount of bonds to be issued to finance a project may be determined on any reasonable basis and may take into account contingencies, without regard to whether the occurrence of any such contingency is reasonably expected at the time of the notice.

(iii) *The name of the initial legal owner or principal user of the project.*—The notice and approval must include the name of either the expected initial legal owner or principal user (within the meaning of section 144(a)) of the project or, alternatively, the name of a significant true beneficial party of interest for such legal owner or user (for example, the name of a section 501(c)(3) organization that is the sole member of a limited liability company that is the legal owner or the name of a general partner of a partnership that owns the project).

(iv) *The location of the project.*—The notice and approval must include a general description of the prospective location of the project by street address, reference to boundary streets or other geographic boundaries, or other description of the specific geographic location that is reasonably designed to inform readers of the location. For a project involving multiple capital projects or facilities located on the same site, or on adjacent or reasonably proximate sites with similar uses, a consolidated description of the location of those capital projects or facilities provides a sufficient description of the location of the project. For example, a project for a section 501(c)(3) educational entity involving multiple buildings on the entity's main urban college campus may describe the location of the project by reference to the outside street boundaries of that campus with a reference to any noncontiguous features of that campus.

(3) *Special rule for mortgage revenue bonds.*—Mortgage loans financed by mortgage revenue bonds are within the scope of a public approval if the notice and approval state that the bonds are to be issued to finance residential mortgages, provide the maximum stated principal amount of mortgage revenue bonds expected to be issued, and provide a general description of the geographic jurisdiction in which the residences to be financed with the proceeds of the mortgage revenue bonds are expected to be located (for example, residences located throughout a State for an issuer with a statewide jurisdiction or residences within a particular local geographic jurisdiction, such as within a city or county, for a local issuer). For this purpose, in the case of mortgage revenue bonds, no information is required on specific names of mortgage loan borrowers or specific locations of individual residences to be financed.

(4) *Special rule for qualified student loan bonds.*—Qualified student loans financed by qualified student loan bonds as defined in section 144(b) are within the scope of a public approval if the notice and approval state that the bonds will be issued to finance student loans and state the maximum stated principal amount of qualified student loan bonds expected to be issued for qualified student loans. For this purpose, in the case of qualified student loan bonds, no information is required with respect to names of specific student loan borrowers.

(5) *Special rule for certain qualified 501(c)(3) bonds.*—Qualified 501(c)(3) bonds issued pursuant to section 145 for pooled loan financings that are described in section 147(b)(4)(B) (without regard to any election under section 147(b)(4)(A)) are within the scope of a public approval if the public approval either meets the general requirements of paragraph (b) of this section or, alternatively, at the issuer's option, meets the special requirements of paragraphs (f)(5)(i) and (ii) of this section.

(i) *Pre-issuance issuer approval.*—Within the time period required by paragraph (f)(7) of this section, an issuer approval is obtained after reasonable public notice of a public hearing is provided and a public hearing is held. For this purpose, a project is treated as described in the notice and approval if the notice and approval provide that the bonds will be qualified 501(c)(3) bonds to be used to finance loans described in section 147(b)(4)(B), state the maximum stated principal amount of bonds expected to be issued to finance loans to section 501(c)(3) organizations or governmental units as described in section 147(b)(4)(B), provide a general description of the type of project to be financed with such loans (for example, loans for hospital facilities or college facilities), and state that an additional public approval that includes specific project information will be obtained before any such loans are originated.

(ii) *Post-issuance public approval for specific loans.*—Before a loan described in section 147(b)(4)(B) is originated, a supplemental public approval, including issuer approval and host approval, for the bonds to be used to finance that loan is obtained that meets all the requirements of section 147(f) and the requirements for a public approval in paragraph (b) of this section. This post-issuance supplemental public approval requirement applies by treating the bonds to be used to finance such loan as if they were reissued for purposes of section 147(f) (without regard to paragraph (f)(5) of this section). For this purpose, proceeds to be used to finance such loan do not include the portion of the issue used to finance a common reserve fund or common costs of issuance.

(6) *Deviations in public approval information.*—(i) *In general.*—Except as otherwise provided in this section, a substantial deviation between the stated use or amount of proceeds of an issue included in the information required to be provided in the notice and approval (*public approval information*) and the actual use or amount of proceeds of the issue causes that issue to fail to meet the public approval requirement. Conversely, insubstantial deviations between the stated use or amount of proceeds of an issue included in the public approval information and the actual use or amount of proceeds of the issue do not cause such a failure. In general, the determination of whether a deviation is substantial is based on all the facts and circumstances. In all events, however, a change in the fundamental nature or type of a project is a substantial deviation.

(ii) *Certain insubstantial deviations in public approval information.*—The following deviations from the public approval information in the notice and approval are treated as insubstantial deviations:

25,162

Tax Exempt. Requirements: State/Local Bonds
See p. 20,601 for regulations not amended to reflect law changes

(A) *Size of bond issue and use of proceeds.*—A deviation between the maximum stated principal amount of a proposed issuance of bonds to finance a project that is specified in public approval information and the actual stated principal amount of bonds issued and used to finance that project is an insubstantial deviation if that actual stated principal amount is no more than ten percent (10%) greater than that maximum stated principal amount or is any amount less than that maximum stated principal amount. In addition, the use of proceeds to pay working capital expenditures directly associated with any project specified in the public approval information is an insubstantial deviation.

(B) *Initial legal owner or principal user.*—A deviation between the initial legal owner or principal user of the project named in the notice and approval and the actual initial legal owner or principal user of the project is an insubstantial deviation if such parties are related parties on the issue date of the issue.

(iii) *Supplemental public approval to cure certain substantial deviations in public approval information.*—A substantial deviation between the stated use or amount of proceeds of an issue included in the public approval information and the actual use or amount of the proceeds of the issue does not cause that issue to fail to meet the public approval requirement if all of the following requirements are met:

(A) *Original public approval and reasonable expectations.*—The issue met the requirements for a public approval in paragraph (b) of this section. In addition, on the issue date of the issue, the issuer reasonably expected there would be no substantial deviations between the stated use or amount of proceeds of an issue included in the public approval information and the actual use or amount of the proceeds of the issue.

(B) *Unexpected events or unforeseen changes in circumstances.*—As a result of unexpected events or unforeseen changes in circumstances that occur after the issue date of the issue, the issuer determines to use proceeds of the issue in a manner or amount not provided in a public approval.

(C) *Supplemental public approval.*—Before using proceeds of the bonds in a manner or amount not provided in a public approval, the issuer obtains a supplemental public approval for those bonds that meets the public approval requirement in paragraph (b) of this section. This supplemental public approval requirement applies by treating those bonds as if they were reissued for purposes of section 147(f).

(7) *Certain timing requirements.*—Public approval of an issue is timely only if the issuer obtains the public approval within one year before the issue date of the issue. Public approval of a plan of financing is timely only if the issuer obtains public approval for the plan of financing within one year before the issue date of the first issue issued under the plan of financing and the issuer issues all issues under the plan of financing within three years after the issue date of such first issue.

(g) *Definitions.*—The definitions in this paragraph (g) apply for purposes of this section. In addition, the general definitions in § 1.150-1 apply for purposes of this section.

(1) *Geographic jurisdiction* means the area encompassed by the boundaries prescribed by State or local law for a governmental unit or, if there are no such boundaries, the area in which a unit may exercise such sovereign powers that make that unit a governmental unit for purposes of § 1.103-1 and this section.

(2) *Governmental unit* has the meaning of "State or local governmental unit" as defined in § 1.103-1. Thus, a governmental unit is a State, territory, a possession of the United States, the District of Columbia, or any political subdivision thereof.

(3) *Host approval* is defined in paragraph (b)(3) of this section.

(4) *Issuer approval* is defined in paragraph (b)(2) of this section.

(5) *Mortgage revenue bonds* mean qualified mortgage bonds as defined in section 143(a), qualified veterans' mortgage bonds as defined in section 143(b), or refunding bonds issued to finance mortgages of owner-occupied residences pursuant to applicable law in effect prior to enactment of section 143(a) or section 143(b).

(6) *Proceeds* means "proceeds" as defined in § 1.141-1(b), except that it does not include disposition proceeds.

(7) *Project* generally means one or more capital projects or facilities, including land, buildings, equipment, and other property, to be financed with an issue, that are located on the same site, or adjacent or proximate sites used for similar purposes, and that are subject to the public approval requirement of section 147(f). Capital projects or facilities that are not located on the same site or adjacent or proximate sites may be treated as one project if those capital projects or facilities are used in an integrated operation. For an issue of mortgage revenue bonds or an issue of qualified student loan bonds as

defined in section 144(b), the term project means the mortgage loans or qualified student loans to be financed with the proceeds of the issue. For an issue of qualified 501(c)(3) bonds as defined in section 145, the term project means a project as defined in the first sentence of this definition, and also is deemed to include working capital expenditures to be financed with proceeds of the issue.

(8) *Public approval information* is defined in paragraph (f)(6)(i) of this section.

(9) *Public hearing* is defined in paragraph (d)(1) of this section.

(10) *Reasonable public notice* is defined in paragraph (d)(4) of this section.

(11) *Voter referendum* means a vote by the voters of the affected governmental unit conducted in the same manner and time as voter referenda on matters relating to governmental spending or bond issuances by the governmental unit under applicable State and local law.

(h) *Applicability date.*—This section applies to bonds issued pursuant to a public approval occurring on or after April 1, 2019. For bonds issued pursuant to a public approval occurring before April 1, 2019, see § 5f.103-2 as contained in 26 CFR part 5f, revised as of April 1, 2018. In addition, an issuer may apply the provisions of paragraph (f)(6) of this section in whole, but not in part, to bonds issued pursuant to a public approval occurring before April 1, 2019. [Reg. § 1.147(f)-1.]

☐ [T.D. 9845, 12-28-2018.]

[Reg. § 1.148-0]

§ 1.148-0. Scope and table of contents.—(a) *Overview.*—Under section 103(a), interest on certain obligations issued by States and local governments is excludable from the gross income of the owners. Section 148 was enacted to minimize the arbitrage benefits from investing gross proceeds of tax-exempt bonds in higher yielding investments and to remove the arbitrage incentives to issue more bonds, to issue bonds earlier, or to leave bonds outstanding longer than is otherwise reasonably necessary to accomplish the governmental purposes for which the bonds were issued. To accomplish these purposes, section 148 restricts the direct and indirect investment of bond proceeds in higher yielding investments and requires that certain earnings on higher yielding investments be rebated to the United States. Violation of these provisions causes the bonds in the issue to become *arbitrage bonds*, the interest on which is not excludable from the gross income of the owners under section 103(a). The regulations in §§ 1.148-1 through 1.148-11 apply in a manner consistent with these purposes.

(b) *Scope.*—Sections 1.148-1 through 1.148-11 apply generally for purposes of the arbitrage restrictions on State and local bonds under section 148.

(c) *Table of contents.*—This paragraph (c) lists the table of contents for §§ 1.148-1, 1.148-2, 1.148-3, 1.148-4, 1.148-5, 1.148-6, §§ 1.148-7, §§ 1.148-8, §§ 1.148-9, §§ 1.148-10 and §§ 1.148-11.

Reg. § 1.148-0

25,164

Tax Exempt. Requirements: State/Local Bonds
See p. 20,601 for regulations not amended to reflect law changes

☐ [*T.D.* 8418, 5-12-92. *Amended by T.D.* 8476, 6-14-93; *T.D.* 8538, 5-5-94; *T.D.* 8718, 5-8-97; *T.D.* 9085, 8-1-2003; *T.D.* 9097, 12-10-2003, *T.D.* 9701, 11-12-2014, *T.D.* 9777, 7-15-2016, *T.D.* 9801, 12-8-2016 *and T.D.* 9854, 4-8-2019.]

[Reg. § 1.148-1]

§1.148-1. Definitions and elections.—(a) *In general.*—The definitions in this section and the definitions under section 150 apply for purposes of section 148 and §§ 1.148-1 through 1.148-11.

(b) *Certain definitions.*—The following definitions apply:

Accounting method means both the overall method used to account for gross proceeds of an issue (e.g., the cash method or a modified accrual method) and the method used to account for or allocate any particular item within that overall accounting method (e.g., accounting for investments, expenditures, allocations to and from different sources, and particular items of the foregoing).

Annuity contract means annuity contract as defined in section 72.

Available amount means available amount as defined in § 1.148-6(d)(3)(iii).

Bona fide debt service fund means a fund, which may include proceeds of an issue, that—

(1) Is used primarily to achieve a proper matching of revenues with principal and interest payments within each bond year; and

(2) Is depleted at least once each bond year, except for a reasonable carryover amount not to exceed the greater of:

(i) the earnings on the fund for the immediately preceding bond year; or

(ii) one-twelfth of the principal and interest payments on the issue for the immediately preceding bond year.

Bond year means, in reference to an issue, each 1-year period that ends on the day selected by the issuer. The first and last bond years may be short periods. If no day is selected by the issuer before the earlier of the final maturity date of the issue or the date that is 5 years after the issue date, bond years end on each anniversary of the issue date and on the final maturity date.

Capital project or capital projects means all capital expenditures, plus related working capital expenditures to which the de minimis rule under § 1.148-6(d)(3)(ii)(A) applies, that carry out the governmental purposes of an issue. For example, a capital project may include capital expenditures for one or more buildings, plus related start-up operating costs.

Commingled fund means any fund or account containing both gross proceeds of an issue and amounts in excess of $25,000 that are not gross proceeds of that issue if the amounts in the fund or account are invested and accounted for collectively, without regard to the source of funds deposited in the fund or account. An open-end regulated investment company under section 851, however, is not a commingled fund.

Computation date means each date on which the rebate amount for an issue is computed under § 1.148-3(e).

Computation period means the period between computation dates. The first computation period begins on the issue date and ends on the first computation date. Each succeeding computation period begins on the date immediately following the computation date and ends on the next computation date.

Consistently applied means applied uniformly within a fiscal period and between fiscal periods to account for gross proceeds of an issue and any amounts that are in a commingled fund.

De minimis amount means—

(1) In reference to original issue discount (as defined in section 1273(a)(1)) or premium on an obligation—

(i) An amount that does not exceed 2 percent multiplied by the stated redemption price at maturity; plus

(ii) Any original issue premium that is attributable exclusively to reasonable underwriters' compensation; and

(2) In reference to market discount (as defined in section 1278(a)(2)(A)) or premium on an obligation, an amount that does not exceed 2 percent multiplied by the stated redemption price at maturity.

Economic accrual method (also known as the *constant interest method* or *actuarial method*) means the method of computing yield that is based on the compounding of interest at the end of each compounding period.

Fair market value means fair market value as defined in § 1.148-5(d)(6).

Fixed rate investment means any investment whose yield is fixed and determinable on the issue date.

Fixed yield bond means any bond whose yield is fixed and determinable on the issue date using the assumptions and rules provided in § 1.148-4(b).

Fixed yield issue means any issue if each bond that is part of the issue is a fixed yield bond.

Gross proceeds means any proceeds and replacement proceeds of an issue.

Guaranteed investment contract includes any nonpurpose investment that has specifically negotiated withdrawal or reinvestment provisions and a specifically negotiated interest rate, and also includes any agreement to supply investments on two or more future dates (e.g., a forward supply contract).

Higher yielding investments means higher yielding investments as defined in section 148(b)(1).

Investment means any investment property as defined in sections 148(b)(2) and 148(b)(3), and any other tax-exempt bond.

Investment proceeds means any amounts actually or constructively received from investing proceeds of an issue.

Investment-type property is defined in paragraph (e) of this section.

Caution: The definition of "Issue price", below, prior to amendment by T.D. 9801, applies to bond that are sold before June 7, 2017.

Issue price means, except as otherwise provided, issue price as defined in sections 1273 and 1274. Generally, the issue price of bonds that are publicly offered is the first price at which a substantial amount of the bonds is sold to the public. Ten percent is a substantial amount. The public does not include bond houses, brokers, or similar persons or organizations acting in the capacity of underwriters or wholesalers. The issue price does not change if part of the issue is later sold at a different price. The issue price of bonds that are not substantially identical is determined separately. The issue price of bonds for which a bona fide public offering is made is determined as of the sale date based on reasonable expectations regarding the initial public offering price. If a bond is issued for property, the applicable Federal tax-exempt rate is used in lieu of the Federal rate in determining the issue price under section 1274. The issue price of bonds may not exceed their fair market value as of the sale date.

Caution: The definition of "Issue price", below, as amended by T.D. 9801, applies to bond that are sold on or after June 7, 2017.

Issue price means issue price as defined in paragraph (f) of this section

Issuer generally means the entity that actually issues the issue, and, unless the context or a provision clearly requires otherwise, each conduit borrower of the issue. For example, rules imposed on issuers to account for gross proceeds of an issue apply to a conduit borrower to account for any gross proceeds received under a purpose investment. Provisions regarding elections, filings, liability for the rebate amount, and certifications of reasonable expectations apply only to the actual issuer.

Multipurpose issue means an issue the proceeds of which are used for two or more separate purposes determined in accordance with § 1.148-9(h).

Net sale proceeds means sale proceeds, less the portion of those sale proceeds invested in a reasonably required reserve or replacement fund under section 148(d) and as part of a minor portion under section 148(e).

Nonpurpose investment means any investment property, as defined in section 148(b), that is not a purpose investment.

Payment means a payment as defined in § 1.148-3(d) for purposes of computing the rebate amount, and a payment as defined in § 1.148-5(b) for purposes of computing the yield on an investment.

Plain par bond means a qualified tender bond or a bond—

(1) Issued with not more than a de minimis amount of original issue discount or premium;

(2) Issued for a price that does not include accrued interest other than pre-issuance accrued interest;

(3) That bears interest from the issue date at a single, stated, fixed rate or that is a variable rate debt instrument under section 1275, in each case with interest unconditionally payable at least annually; and

(4) That has a lowest stated redemption price that is not less than its outstanding stated principal amount.

Plain par investment means an investment that is an obligation—

(1) Issued with not more than a de minimis amount of original issue discount or premium, or, if acquired on a date other than the issue date, acquired with not more than a de minimis amount of market discount or premium;

(2) Issued for a price that does not include accrued interest other than pre-issuance accrued interest;

(3) That bears interest from the issue date at a single, stated, fixed rate or that is a variable rate debt instrument under section 1275, in each case with interest unconditionally payable at least annually; and

(4) That has a lowest stated redemption price that is not less than its outstanding stated principal amount.

Pre-issuance accrued interest means amounts representing interest that accrued on an obligation for a period not greater than one year before its issue date but only if those amounts are paid within one year after the issue date.

Proceeds means any sale proceeds, investment proceeds, and transferred proceeds of an issue. Proceeds do not include, however, amounts actually or constructively received with respect to a purpose investment that are properly allocable to the immaterially higher yield under § 1.148-2(d) or section 143(g) or to qualified administrative costs recoverable under § 1.148-5(e).

25,166

Tax Exempt. Requirements: State/Local Bonds
See p. 20,601 for regulations not amended to reflect law changes

Program investment means a purpose investment that is part of a governmental program in which—

(1) The program involves the origination or acquisition of purpose investments;

(2) At least 95 percent (90 percent for qualified student loans under section 144(b)(1)(A)) of the cost of the purpose investments acquired under the program represents one or more loans to a substantial number of persons representing the general public, States or political subdivisions, 501(c)(3) organizations, persons who provide housing and related facilities, or any combination of the foregoing;

(3) At least 95 percent of the receipts from the purpose investments are used to pay principal, interest, or redemption prices on issues that financed the program, to pay or reimburse administrative costs of those issues or of the program, to pay or reimburse anticipated future losses directly related to the program, to finance additional purpose investments for the same general purposes of the program, or to redeem and retire governmental obligations at the next earliest possible date of redemption;

(4) The program documents prohibit any obligor on a purpose investment financed by the program or any related party to that obligor from purchasing bonds of an issue that finance the program in an amount related to the amount of the purpose investment acquired from that obligor; and

(5) The issuer has not waived the right to treat the investment as a program investment.

Purpose investment means an investment that is acquired to carry out the governmental purpose of an issue.

Qualified administrative costs means qualified administrative costs as defined in § 1.148-5(e).

Qualified guarantee means a qualified guarantee as defined in § 1.148-4(f).

Qualified hedge means a qualified hedge as defined in § 1.148-4(h)(2).

Reasonable expectations or reasonableness. An issuer's expectations or actions are reasonable only if a prudent person in the same circumstances as the issuer would have those same expectations or take those same actions, based on all the objective facts and circumstances. Factors relevant to a determination of reasonableness include the issuer's history of conduct concerning stated expectations made in connection with the issuance of obligations, the level of inquiry by the issuer into factual matters, and the existence of covenants, enforceable by bondholders, that require implementation of specific expectations. For a conduit financing issue, factors relevant to a determination of reasonableness include the reasonable expectations of the conduit borrower, but only if, under the circumstances, it is reasonable and prudent for the issuer to rely on those expectations.

Rebate amount means 100 percent of the amount owed to the United States under section 148(f)(2), as further described in § 1.148-3.

Receipt means a receipt as defined in § 1.148-3(d) for purposes of computing the rebate amount, and a receipt as defined in § 1.148-5(b) for purposes of computing yield on an investment.

Refunding escrow means one or more funds established as part of a single transaction or a series of related transactions, containing proceeds of a refunding issue and any other amounts to provide for payment of principal or interest on one or more prior issues. For this purpose, funds are generally not so established solely because of—

(1) The deposit of proceeds of an issue and replacement proceeds of the prior issue in an escrow more than 6 months apart, or

(2) The deposit of proceeds of completely separate issues in an escrow.

Replacement proceeds is defined in paragraph (c) of this section.

Restricted working capital expenditures means working capital expenditures that are subject to the proceeds-spent-last rule in § 1.148-6(d)(3)(i) and are ineligible for any exception to that rule.

Sale proceeds means any amounts actually or constructively received from the sale of the issue, including amounts used to pay underwriters' discount or compensation and accrued interest other than pre-issuance accrued interest. Sale proceeds also include, but are not limited to, amounts derived from the sale of a right that is associated with a bond, and that is described in § 1.148(b)(4). See also § 1.148-4(h)(5) treating amounts received upon the termination of certain hedges as sale proceeds.

Stated redemption price means the redemption price of an obligation under the terms of that obligation, including any call premium.

Transferred proceeds means transferred proceeds as defined in § 1.148-9 (or the applicable corresponding provision of prior law).

Unconditionally payable means payable under terms in which—

(1) Late payment or nonpayment results in a significant penalty to the borrower or reasonable remedies to the lender, and

(2) It is reasonably certain on the issue date that the payment will actually be made.

Value means value determined under § 1.148-4(e) for a bond, and value determined under § 1.148-5(d) for an investment.

Variable yield bond means any bond that is not a fixed yield bond.

Variable yield issue means any issue that is not a fixed yield issue.

Yield means yield computed under § 1.148-4 for an issue, and yield computed under § 1.148-5 for an investment.

Yield restricted means required to be invested at a yield that is not materially higher than the yield on the issue under section 148(a) and § 1.148-2.

(c) *Definition of replacement proceeds.*—(1) *In general.*—Amounts are replacement proceeds of an issue if the amounts have a sufficiently direct nexus to the issue or to the governmental purpose of the issue to conclude that the amounts would have been used for that governmental purpose if the proceeds of the issue were not used or to be used for that governmental purpose. For this purpose, governmental purposes include the expected use of amounts for the payment of debt service on a particular date. The mere availability or preliminary earmarking of amounts for a governmental purpose, however, does not in itself establish a sufficient nexus to cause those amounts to be replacement proceeds. Replacement proceeds include, but are not limited to, sinking funds, pledged funds, and other replacement proceeds described in paragraph (c)(4) of this section, to the extent that those funds or amounts are held by or derived from a substantial beneficiary of the issue. A substantial beneficiary of an issue includes the issuer and any related party to the issuer, and, if the issuer is not a state, the state in which the issuer is located. A person is not a substantial beneficiary of an issue solely because it is a guarantor under a qualified guarantee.

(2) *Sinking fund.*—Sinking fund includes a debt service fund, redemption fund, reserve fund, replacement fund, or any similar fund, to the extent reasonably expected to be used directly or indirectly to pay principal or interest on the issue.

(3) *Pledged fund.*—(i) *In general.*—A *pledged fund* is any amount that is directly or indirectly pledged to pay principal or interest on the issue. A pledge need not be cast in any particular form but, in substance, must provide reasonable assurance that the amount will be available to pay principal or interest on the issue, even if the issuer encounters financial difficulties. A pledge to a guarantor of an issue is an indirect pledge to secure payment of principal or interest on the issue. A pledge of more than 50 percent of the outstanding stock of a corporation that is a conduit borrower of the issue is not treated as a pledge for this purpose, unless the corporation is formed or availed of to avoid the creation of replacement proceeds.

(ii) *Negative pledges.*—An amount is treated as pledged to pay principal or interest on an issue if it is held under an agreement to maintain the amount at a particular level for the direct or indirect benefit of the bondholders or a guarantor of the bonds. An amount is not treated as pledged under this paragraph (c)(3)(ii), however, if—

(A) The issuer or a substantial beneficiary may grant rights in the amount that are superior to the rights of the bondholders or the guarantor; or

(B) The amount does not exceed reasonable needs for which it is maintained, the required level is tested no more frequently than every 6 months, and the amount may be spent without any substantial restriction other than a requirement to replenish the amount by the next testing date.

(4) *Other replacement proceeds.*—(i) *Bonds outstanding longer than necessary.*—(A) *In general.*—Replacement proceeds arise to the extent that the issuer reasonably expects as of the issue date that—

(1) The term of an issue will be longer than is reasonably necessary for the governmental purposes of the issue, and

(2) There will be available amounts during the period that the issue remains outstanding longer than necessary. Whether an issue is outstanding longer than necessary is determined under § 1.148-10. Replacement proceeds are created under this paragraph (c)(4)(i)(A) at the beginning of each fiscal year during which an issue remains outstanding longer than necessary in an amount equal to available amounts of the issuer as of that date.

(B) *Safe harbor against creation of replacement proceeds.*—As a safe harbor, replacement proceeds do not arise under paragraph (c)(4)(i)(A) of this section—

(1) For the portion of an issue that is to be used to finance working capital expenditures, if that portion is not outstanding longer than the temporary period under § 1.148-2(e)(3) for which the proceeds qualify;

(2) For the portion of an issue (including a refunding issue) that is to be used to finance or refinance capital projects, if that portion has a weighted average maturity that does not exceed 120 percent of the average reasonably expected economic life of the financed capital projects, determined in the same manner as under section 147(b);

(3) For the portion of an issue that is a refunding issue, if that portion has a weighted average maturity that does not exceed the remaining weighted average maturity of the prior issue, and the issue of which the prior issue is a part satisfies paragraph (c)(4)(i)(B)(*1*) or (*2*) of this section; or

(4) For the portion of an issue (including a refunding issue) that is to be used to finance working capital expenditures, if that portion satisfies paragraph (c)(4)(ii) of this section.

(ii) *Safe harbor for longer-term working capital financings.*—A portion of an issue used to finance working capital expenditures satisfies this paragraph (c)(4)(ii) if the issuer meets the requirements of paragraphs (c)(4)(ii)(A) through (E) of this section.

(A) *Determine first testing year.*—On the issue date, the issuer must determine the first fiscal year following the applicable temporary period under §1.148-2(e) in which it reasonably expects to have available amounts (first testing year), but in no event can the first day of the first testing year be later than five years after the issue date.

(B) *Application of available amount to reduce burden on tax-exempt bond market.*—Beginning with the first testing year and for each subsequent fiscal year for which the portion of the issue that is the subject of this safe harbor remains outstanding, the issuer must determine the available amount as of the first day of each fiscal year. Then, except as provided in paragraph (c)(4)(ii)(D) of this section, within the first 90 days of that fiscal year, the issuer must apply that amount (or if less, the available amount on the date of the required redemption or investment) to redeem or to invest in eligible tax-exempt bonds (as defined in paragraph (c)(4)(ii)(E) of this section). For this purpose, available amounts in a bona fide debt service fund are not treated as available amounts.

(C) *Continuous investment requirement.*—Except as provided in this paragraph (c)(4)(ii)(C), any amounts invested in eligible tax-exempt bonds under paragraph (c)(4)(ii)(B) of this section must be invested continuously in such tax-exempt bonds to the extent provided in paragraph (c)(4)(ii)(D) of this section.

(1) Exception for reinvestment period.—Amounts previously invested in eligible tax-exempt bonds under paragraph (c)(4)(ii)(B) of this section that are held for not more than 30 days in a fiscal year pending reinvestment in eligible tax-exempt bonds are treated as invested in eligible tax-exempt bonds.

(2) Limited use of invested amounts.—An issuer may spend amounts previously invested in eligible tax-exempt bonds under paragraph (c)(4)(ii)(B) of this section within 30 days of the date on which they cease to be so invested to make expenditures for a governmental purpose on any date on which the issuer has no other available amounts for such purpose, or to redeem eligible tax-exempt bonds.

(D) *Cap on applied or invested amounts.*—The maximum amount that an issuer is required to apply under paragraph (c)(4)(ii)(B) of this section or to invest continuously under paragraph (c)(4)(ii)(C) of this section with respect to the portion of an issue that is the subject of this safe harbor is the outstanding principal amount of such portion. For purposes of this cap, an issuer receives credit towards its requirement to invest available amounts in eligible tax-exempt bonds for amounts previously invested under paragraph (c)(4)(ii)(B) of this section that remain continuously invested under paragraph (c)(4)(ii)(C) of this section.

(E) *Definition of eligible tax-exempt bonds.*—For purposes of paragraph (c)(4)(ii) of this section, *eligible tax-exempt bonds* means any of the following:

(1) A bond the interest on which is excludable from gross income under section 103 and that is not a specified private activity bond (as defined in section 57(a)(5)(C)) subject to the alternative minimum tax;

(2) An interest in a regulated investment company to the extent that at least 95 percent of the income to the holder of the interest is interest on a bond that is excludable from gross income under section 103 and that is not interest on a specified private activity bond (as defined in section 57(a)(5)(C)) subject to the alternative minimum tax; or

(3) A certificate of indebtedness issued by the United States Treasury pursuant to the Demand Deposit State and Local Government Series program described in 31 CFR part 344.

(d) *Elections.*—Except as otherwise provided, any required elections must be made in writing, and, once made, may not be revoked without the permission of the Commissioner.

(e) *Investment-type property.*—(1) *In general.*—Except as otherwise provided in this paragraph (e), investment-type property includes any property, other than property described in section 148(b)(2)(A), (B), (C), or (E), that is held principally as a passive vehicle for the production of income. For this purpose, production of income includes any benefit based on the time value of money.

(2) *Prepayments.*—(i) *In general.*—(A) *Generally.*—Except as otherwise provided in this paragraph (e)(2), a prepayment for property or services, including a prepayment for property or services that is made after the date that the contract to buy the property or services is entered into, also gives rise to investment-type property if a principal purpose for prepaying is to receive an investment return from the time the prepayment is made until the time payment otherwise would be made. A prepayment does not give rise to investment-type property if—

(1) Prepayments on substantially the same terms are made by a substantial percentage of persons who are similarly situated to the issuer but who are not beneficiaries of tax-exempt financing;

(2) The prepayment is made within 90 days of the reasonably expected date of delivery to the issuer of all of the property or services for which the prepayment is made; or

(3) The prepayment meets the requirements of paragraph (e)(2)(iii)(A) or (B) of this section.

(B) *Example.*—The following example illustrates an application of this paragraph (e)(2)(i):

Example. Prepayment after contract is executed. In 1998, City A enters into a ten-year contract with Company Y. Under the contract, Company Y is to provide services to City A over the term of the contract and in return City A will pay Company Y for its services as they are provided. In 2004, City A issues bonds to finance a lump sum payment to Company Y in satisfaction of City A's obligation to pay for Company Y's services to be provided over the remaining term of the contract. The use of bond proceeds to make the lump sum payment constitutes a prepayment for services under paragraph (e)(2)(i) of this section, even though the payment is made after the date that the contract is executed.

(ii) *Customary prepayments.*—The determination of whether a prepayment satisfies paragraph (e)(2)(i)(A)(*1*) of this section is generally made based on all the facts and circumstances. In addition, a prepayment is deemed to satisfy paragraph (e)(2)(i)(A)(*1*) of this section if—

(A) The prepayment is made for—

(1) Maintenance, repair, or an extended warranty with respect to personal property (for example, automobiles or electronic equipment); or

(2) Updates or maintenance or support services with respect to computer software; and

(B) The same maintenance, repair, extended warranty, updates or maintenance or support services, as applicable, are regularly provided to nongovernmental persons on the same terms.

(iii) *Certain prepayments to acquire a supply of natural gas or electricity.*—(A) *Natural gas prepayments.*—A prepayment meets the requirements of this paragraph (e)(2)(iii)(A) if—

(1) It is made by or for one or more utilities that are owned by a governmental person, as defined in §1.141-1(b) (each of which is referred to in this paragraph (e)(2)(iii)(A) as the issuing municipal utility), to purchase a supply of natural gas; and

(2) At least 90 percent of the prepaid natural gas financed by the issue is used for a qualifying use. Natural gas is used for a qualifying use if it is to be—

(i) Furnished to retail gas customers of the issuing municipal utility who are located in the natural gas service area of the issuing municipal utility, provided, however, that gas used to produce electricity for sale shall not be included under this paragraph (e)(2)(iii)(A)(*2*)(*i*);

(ii) Used by the issuing municipal utility to produce electricity that will be furnished to retail electric customers of the issuing municipal utility who are located in the electricity service area of the issuing municipal utility;

(iii) Used by the issuing municipal utility to produce electricity that will be sold to a utility that is owned by a governmental person and furnished to retail electric customers of the purchaser who are located in the electricity service area of the purchaser;

(iv) Sold to a utility that is owned by a governmental person if the requirements of paragraph (e)(2)(iii)(A)(*2*)(*i*), (*ii*) or (*iii*) of this section are satisfied by the purchaser (treating the purchaser as the issuing municipal utility); or

(v) Used to fuel the pipeline transportation of the prepaid gas supply acquired in accordance with this paragraph (e)(2)(iii)(A).

(B) *Electricity prepayments.*—A prepayment meets the requirements of this paragraph (e)(2)(iii)(B) if—

25,168

Tax Exempt. Requirements: State/Local Bonds
See p. 20,601 for regulations not amended to reflect law changes

(1) It is made by or for one or more utilities that are owned by a governmental person (each of which is referred to in this paragraph (e)(2)(iii)(B) as the issuing municipal utility) to purchase a supply of electricity; and

(2) At least 90 percent of the prepaid electricity financed by the issue is used for a qualifying use. Electricity is used for a qualifying use if it is to be—

(i) Furnished to retail electric customers of the issuing municipal utility who are located in the electricity service area of the issuing municipal utility; or

(ii) Sold to a utility that is owned by a governmental person and furnished to retail electric customers of the purchaser who are located in the electricity service area of the purchaser.

(C) Service area.—For purposes of this paragraph (e)(2)(iii), the service area of a utility owned by a governmental person consists of—

(1) Any area throughout which the utility provided, at all times during the 5-year period ending on the issue date—

(i) In the case of a natural gas utility, natural gas transmission or distribution service; and

(ii) In the case of an electric utility, electricity distribution service; and

(2) Any area recognized as the service area of the utility under state or Federal law.

(D) Retail customer.—For purposes of this paragraph (e)(2)(iii), a retail customer is a customer that purchases natural gas or electricity, as applicable, other than for resale.

(E) Commodity swaps.—A prepayment does not fail to meet the requirements of this paragraph (e)(2)(iii) by reason of any commodity swap contract that may be entered into between the issuer and an unrelated party (other than the gas or electricity supplier), or between the gas or electricity supplier and an unrelated party (other than the issuer), so long as each swap contract is an independent contract. A swap contract is an independent contract if the obligation of each party to perform under the swap contract is not dependent on performance by any person (other than the other party to the swap contract) under another contract (for example, a gas or electricity supply contract or another swap contract); provided, however, that a commodity swap contract will not fail to be an independent contract solely because the swap contract may terminate in the event of a failure of a gas or electricity supplier to deliver gas or electricity for which the swap contract is a hedge.

(F) Remedial action.—Issuers may apply principles similar to the rules of §1.141-12, including §1.141-12(d) (relating to redemption or defeasance of nonqualified bonds) and §1.141-12(e) (relating to alternative use of disposition proceeds), to cure a violation of paragraph (e)(2)(iii)(A)(2) or (e)(2)(iii)(B)(2) of this section. For this purpose, the amount of nonqualified bonds is determined in the same manner as for output contracts taken into account under the private business tests, including the principles of §1.141-7(d), treating nonqualified sales of gas or electricity under this paragraph (e)(2)(iii) as satisfying the benefits and burdens test under §1.141-7(c)(1).

(iv) Additional prepayments as permitted by the Commissioner.—The Commissioner may, by published guidance, set forth additional circumstances in which a prepayment does not give rise to investment-type property.

(3) Certain hedges.—Investment-type property also includes the investment element of a contract that is a hedge (within the meaning of §1.148-4(h)(2)(i)(A)) and that contains a significant investment element because a payment by the issuer relates to a conditional or unconditional obligation by the hedge provider to make a payment on a later date. See §1.148-4(h)(2)(ii) relating to hedges with a significant investment element.

(4) Exception for certain capital projects.—Investment-type property does not include real property or tangible personal property (for example, land, buildings, and equipment) that is used in furtherance of the public purposes for which the tax-exempt bonds are issued. For example, investment-type property does not include a courthouse financed with governmental bonds or an eligible exempt facility under section 142, such as a public road, financed with private activity bonds.

≫→ *Caution: Reg. §1.148-1(f), below, as added by T.D. 9801, applies to bond that are sold on or after June 7, 2017.*

(f) Definition of issue price.—*(1) In general.*—Except as otherwise provided in this paragraph (f), "issue price" is defined in sections 1273 and 1274 and the regulations under those sections.

(2) Bonds issued for money.—*(i) General rule.*—Except as otherwise provided in this paragraph (f)(2), the issue price of bonds issued for money is the first price at which a substantial amount of the bonds is sold to the public. If a bond is issued for money in a private placement to a single buyer that is not an underwriter or a related party (as defined in §1.150-1(b)) to an underwriter, the issue price of the bond is the price paid by that buyer. Issue price is not reduced by any issuance costs (as defined in §1.150-1(b)).

(ii) Special rule for use of initial offering price to the public.—The issuer may treat the initial offering price to the public as of the sale date as the issue price of the bonds if the requirements of paragraphs (f)(2)(ii)(A) and (B) of this section are met.

(A) The underwriters offered the bonds to the public for purchase at a specified initial offering price on or before the sale date, and the lead underwriter in the underwriting syndicate or selling group (or, if applicable, the sole underwriter) provides, on or before the issue date, a certification to that effect to the issuer, together with reasonable supporting documentation for that certification, such as a copy of the pricing wire or equivalent communication.

(B) Each underwriter agrees in writing that it will neither offer nor sell the bonds to any person at a price that is higher than the initial offering price to the public during the period starting on the sale date and ending on the earlier of the following:

(1) The close of the fifth (5th) business day after the sale date; or

(2) The date on which the underwriters have sold a substantial amount of the bonds to the public at a price that is no higher than the initial offering price to the public.

(iii) Special rule for competitive sales.—For bonds issued for money in a competitive sale, an issuer may treat the reasonably expected initial offering price to the public as of the sale date as the issue price of the bonds if the issuer obtains from the winning bidder a certification of the bonds' reasonably expected initial offering price to the public as of the sale date upon which the price in the winning bid is based.

(iv) Choice of rule for determining issue price.—If more than one rule for determining the issue price of the bonds is available under this paragraph (f)(2), at any time on or before the issue date, the issuer may select the rule it will use to determine the issue price of the bonds. On or before the issue date of the bonds, the issuer must identify the rule selected in its books and records maintained for the bonds.

(3) Definitions.—For purposes of this paragraph (f), the following definitions apply:

(i) Competitive sale means a sale of bonds by an issuer to an underwriter that is the winning bidder in a bidding process in which the issuer offers the bonds for sale to underwriters at specified written terms, if that process meets the following requirements:

(A) The issuer disseminates the notice of sale to potential underwriters in a manner that is reasonably designed to reach potential underwriters (for example, through electronic communication that is widely circulated to potential underwriters by a recognized publisher of municipal bond offering documents or by posting on an Internet-based website or other electronic medium that is regularly used for such purpose and is widely available to potential underwriters);

(B) All bidders have an equal opportunity to bid (within the meaning of §1.148-5(d)(6)(iii)(A)(6));

(C) The issuer receives bids from at least three underwriters of municipal bonds who have established industry reputations for underwriting new issuances of municipal bonds; and

(D) The issuer awards the sale to the bidder who submits a firm offer to purchase the bonds at the highest price (or lowest interest cost).

(ii) Public means any person (as defined in section 7701(a)(1)) other than an underwriter or a related party (as defined in §1.150-1(b)) to an underwriter.

(iii) Underwriter means:

(A) Any person (as defined in section 7701(a)(1)) that agrees pursuant to a written contract with the issuer (or with the lead underwriter to form an underwriting syndicate) to participate in the initial sale of the bonds to the public; and

(B) Any person that agrees pursuant to a written contract directly or indirectly with a person described in paragraph (f)(3)(iii)(A) of this section to participate in the initial sale of the bonds to the public (for example, a retail distribution agreement between a national lead underwriter and a regional firm under which the regional firm participates in the initial sale of the bonds to the public).

(4) Other special rules.—For purposes of this paragraph (f), the following special rules apply:

(i) *Separate determinations.*—The issue price of bonds in an issue that do not have the same credit and payment terms is determined separately. The issuer need not apply the same rule to determine issue price for all of the bonds in the issue.

(ii) *Substantial amount.*—Ten percent is a substantial amount.

(iii) *Bonds issued for property.*—If a bond is issued for property, the adjusted applicable Federal rate, as determined under section 1288 and §1.1288-1, is used in lieu of the applicable Federal rate to determine the bond's issue price under section 1274. [Reg. §1.148-1.]

☐ [*T.D.* 8418, 5-12-92. *Amended by T.D.* 8476, 6-14-93; *T.D.* 8538, 5-5-94; *T.D.* 8718, 5-8-97, *T.D.* 9085, 8-1-2003, *T.D.* 9777, 7-15-2016, *T.D.* 9801, 12-8-2016 *and T.D.* 9854, 4-8-2019.]

[Reg. §1.148-1A]

§1.148-1A. [Reserved].

☐ [*T.D.* 8538, 5-5-94. *Redesignated and amended by T.D.* 8718, 5-8-97. *Removed and reserved by T.D.* 9849, 3-11-2019.]

[Reg. §1.148-2]

§1.148-2. General arbitrage yield restriction rules.—(a) *In general.*—Under section 148(a), the direct or indirect investment of the gross proceeds of an issue in higher yielding investments causes the bonds of the issue to be arbitrage bonds. The investment of proceeds in higher yielding investments, however, during a temporary period described in paragraph (e) of this section, as part of a reasonably required reserve or replacement fund described in paragraph (f) of this section, or as part of a minor portion described in paragraph (g) of this section does not cause the bonds of the issue to be arbitrage bonds. Bonds are not arbitrage bonds under this section as a result of an inadvertent, insubstantial error.

(b) *Reasonable expectations.*—(1) *In general.*—Except as provided in paragraph (c) of this section, the determination of whether an issue consists of arbitrage bonds under section 148(a) is based on the issuer's reasonable expectations as of the issue date regarding the amount and use of the gross proceeds of the issue.

(2) *Certification of expectations.*—(i) *In general.*—An officer of the issuer responsible for issuing the bonds must, in good faith, certify the issuer's expectations as of the issue date. The certification must state the facts and estimates that form the basis for the issuer's expectations. The certification is evidence of the issuer's expectations, but does not establish any conclusions of law or any presumptions regarding either the issuer's actual expectations or their reasonableness.

(ii) *Exceptions to certification requirement.*—An issuer is not required to make a certification for an issue under paragraph (b)(2)(i) of this section if—

(A) The issuer reasonably expects as of the issue date that there will be no unspent gross proceeds after the issue date, other than gross proceeds in a bona fide debt service fund (e.g., equipment lease financings in which the issuer purchases equipment in exchange for an installment payment note); or

(B) The issue price of the issue does not exceed $1,000,000.

(c) *Intentional acts.*—The taking of any deliberate, intentional action by the issuer or person acting on its behalf after the issue date in order to earn arbitrage causes the bonds of the issue to be arbitrage bonds if that action, had it been expected on the issue date, would have caused the bonds to be arbitrage bonds. An intent to violate the requirements of section 148 is not necessary for an action to be intentional.

(d) *Materially higher yielding investments.*—(1) *In general.*—The yield on investments is materially higher than the yield on the issue to which the investments are allocated if the yield on the investments over the term of the issue exceeds the yield on the issue by an amount in excess of the applicable definition of *materially higher* set forth in paragraph (d)(2) of this section. If yield restricted investments in the same class are subject to different definitions of *materially higher*, the applicable definition of *materially higher* that produces the lowest permitted yield applies to all the investments in the class. The yield on the issue is determined under §1.148-4. The yield on investments is determined under §1.148-5.

(2) *Definitions of materially higher yield.*—(i) *General rule for purpose and nonpurpose investments.*—For investments that are not otherwise described in this paragraph (d)(2), materially higher means one-eighth of 1 percentage point.

(ii) *Refunding escrows and replacement proceeds.*—For investments in a refunding escrow or for investments allocable to replacement proceeds, materially higher means one-thousandth of 1 percentage point.

(iii) *Program investments.*—For program investments that are not described in paragraph (d)(2)(iv) of this section, materially higher means 1 and one-half percentage points.

(iv) *Student loans.*—For qualified student loans that are program investments, materially higher means 2 percentage points.

(v) *Tax-exempt investments.*—For investments that are tax-exempt bonds and are not investment property under section 148(b)(3), no yield limitation applies.

(3) *Mortgage loans.*—Qualified mortgage loans that satisfy the requirements of section 143(g) are treated as meeting the requirements of this paragraph (d).

(e) *Temporary periods.*—(1) *In general.*—During the temporary periods set forth in this paragraph (e), the proceeds and replacement proceeds of an issue may be invested in higher yielding investments without causing bonds in the issue to be arbitrage bonds. This paragraph (e) does not apply to refunding issues (see §1.148-9).

(2) *General 3-year temporary period for capital projects and qualified mortgage loans.*—(i) *In general.*—The net sale proceeds and investment proceeds of an issue reasonably expected to be allocated to expenditures for capital projects qualify for a temporary period of 3 years beginning on the issue date (the *3-year temporary period*). The 3-year temporary period also applies to the proceeds of qualified mortgage bonds and qualified veterans' mortgage bonds by substituting *qualified mortgage loans* in each place that *capital projects* appears in this paragraph (e)(2). The 3-year temporary period applies only if the issuer reasonably expects to satisfy the expenditure test, the time test, and the due diligence test. These rules apply separately to each conduit loan financed by an issue (other than qualified mortgage loans), with the expenditure and time tests measured from the issue date of the issue.

(A) *Expenditure test.*—The expenditure test is met if at least 85 percent of the net sale proceeds of the issue are allocated to expenditures on the capital projects by the end of the 3-year temporary period.

(B) *Time test.*—The time test is met if the issuer incurs within 6 months of the issue date a substantial binding obligation to a third party to expend at least 5 percent of the net sale proceeds of the issue on the capital projects. An obligation is not binding if it is subject to contingencies within the issuer's or a related party's control.

(C) *Due diligence test.*—The due diligence test is met if completion of the capital projects and the allocation of the net sale proceeds of the issue to expenditures proceed with due diligence.

(ii) *5-year temporary period.*—In the case of proceeds expected to be allocated to a capital project involving a substantial amount of construction expenditures (as defined in §1.148-7), a 5-year temporary period applies in lieu of the 3-year temporary period if the issuer satisfies the requirements of paragraph (e)(2)(i) of this section applied by substituting "5 years" in each place that "3 years" appears, and both the issuer and a licensed architect or engineer certify that the longer period is necessary to complete the capital project.

(3) *Temporary period for working capital expenditures.*—(i) *General rule.*—The proceeds of an issue that are reasonably expected to be allocated to working capital expenditures within 13 months after the issue date qualify for a temporary period of 13 months beginning on the issue date. Paragraph (e)(2) of this section contains additional temporary period rules for certain working capital expenditures that are treated as part of a capital project.

(ii) *Longer temporary period for certain tax anticipation issues.*—If an issuer reasonably expects to use tax revenues arising from tax levies for a single fiscal year to redeem or retire an issue, and the issue matures by the earlier of 2 years after the issue date or 60 days after the last date for payment of those taxes without interest or penalty, the temporary period under paragraph (e)(3)(i) of this section is extended until the maturity date of the issue.

(4) *Temporary period for pooled financings.*—(i) *In general.*—Proceeds of a pooled financing issue reasonably expected to be used to finance purpose investments qualify for a temporary period of 6 months while held by the issuer before being loaned to a conduit borrower. Any otherwise available temporary period for proceeds held by a conduit borrower, however, is reduced by the period of time during which those proceeds were held by the issuer before being loaned. For example, if the proceeds of a pooled financing issue loaned to a conduit borrower would qualify for a 3-year temporary period, and the proceeds are held by the issuer for 5 months before being loaned to the conduit borrower, the proceeds qualify for only an additional 31-month temporary period after being loaned to

25,170

Tax Exempt. Requirements: State/Local Bonds
See p. 20,601 for regulations not amended to reflect law changes

the conduit borrower. Except as provided in paragraph (e)(4)(iv) of this section, this paragraph (e)(4) does not apply to any qualified mortgage bond or qualified veterans' mortgage bond under section 143.

(ii) *Loan repayments.*—(A) *Amount held by the issuer.*—The temporary period under this paragraph (e)(4) for proceeds from the sale or repayment of any loan that are reasonably expected to be used to make or finance new loans is 3 months.

(B) *Amounts re-loaned to conduit borrowers.*—Any temporary period for proceeds held by a conduit borrower under a new loan from amounts described in paragraph (e)(4)(ii)(A) of this section is determined by treating the date the new loan is made as the issue date and by reducing the temporary period by the period the amounts were held by the issuer following the last repayment.

(iii) *Construction issues.*—If all or a portion of a pooled financing issue qualifies as a construction issue under §1.148-7(b)(6), paragraph (e)(4)(i) of this section is applied by substituting "2 years" for "6 months."

(iv) *Amounts re-loaned for qualified mortgage loans.*—The temporary period under this paragraph (e)(4) for proceeds from the sale, prepayment, or repayment of any qualified mortgage loan that are reasonably expected to be used to make or finance new qualified mortgage loans is 3 years.

(5) *Temporary period for replacement proceeds.*—(i) *In general.*—Except as otherwise provided, replacement proceeds qualify for a temporary period of 30 days beginning on the date that the amounts are first treated as replacement proceeds.

(ii) *Temporary period for bona fide debt service funds.*—Amounts in a bona fide debt service fund for an issue qualify for a temporary period of 13 months. If only a portion of a fund qualifies as a bona fide debt service fund, only that portion qualifies for this temporary period.

(6) *Temporary period for investment proceeds.*—Except as otherwise provided in this paragraph (e), investment proceeds qualify for a temporary period of 1 year beginning on the date of receipt.

(7) *Other amounts.*—Gross proceeds not otherwise eligible for a temporary period described in this paragraph (e) qualify for a temporary period of 30 days beginning on the date of receipt.

(f) *Reserve or replacement funds.*—(1) *General 10 percent limitation on funding with sale proceeds.*—An issue consists of arbitrage bonds if sale proceeds of the issue in excess of 10 percent of the stated principal amount of the issue are used to finance any reserve or replacement fund, without regard to whether those sale proceeds are invested in higher yielding investments. If an issue has more than a de minimis amount of original issue discount or premium, the issue price (net of pre-issuance accrued interest) is used to measure the 10-percent limitation in lieu of stated principal amount. This rule does not limit the use of amounts other than sale proceeds of an issue to fund a reserve or replacement fund.

(2) *Exception from yield restriction for reasonably required reserve or replacement funds.*—(i) *In general.*—The investment of amounts that are part of a reasonably required reserve or replacement fund in higher yielding investments will not cause an issue to consist of arbitrage bonds. A reasonably required reserve or replacement fund may consist of all or a portion of one or more funds, however labelled, derived from one or more sources. Amounts in a reserve or replacement fund in excess of the amount that is reasonably required are not part of a reasonably required reserve or replacement fund.

(ii) *Size limitation.*—The amount of gross proceeds of an issue that qualifies as a reasonably required reserve or replacement fund may not exceed an amount equal to the least of 10 percent of the stated principal amount of the issue, the maximum annual principal and interest requirements on the issue, or 125 percent of the average annual principal and interest requirements on the issue. If an issue has more than a de minimis amount of original issue discount or premium, the issue price of the issue (net of pre-issuance accrued interest) is used to measure the 10 percent limitation in lieu of its stated principal amount. For a reserve or replacement fund that secures more than one issue (e.g. a parity reserve fund), the size limitation may be measured on an aggregate basis.

(iii) *Valuation of investments.*—Investments in a reasonably required reserve or replacement fund may be valued in any reasonable, consistently applied manner that is permitted under §1.148-5.

(iv) *150 percent debt service limitation on investment in nonpurpose investments for certain private activity bonds.*—Section 148(d)(3) contains additional limits on the amount of gross proceeds of an

issue of private activity bonds, other than qualified 501(c)(3) bonds, that may be invested in higher yielding nonpurpose investments without causing the bonds to be arbitrage bonds. For purposes of these rules, *initial temporary period* means the temporary periods under paragraphs (e)(2), (e)(3), and (e)(4) of this section and under §1.148-9(d)(2)(i), (ii), and (iii).

(3) *Certain parity reserve funds.*—The limitation contained in paragraph (f)(1) of this section does not apply to an issue if the master legal document authorizing the issuance of the bonds (e.g., a master indenture) was adopted before August 16, 1986, and that document—

(i) Requires a reserve or replacement fund in excess of 10 percent of the sale proceeds, but not more than maximum annual principal and interest requirements;

(ii) Is not amended after August 31, 1986 (other than to permit the issuance of additional bonds as contemplated in the master legal document); and

(iii) Provides that bonds having a parity of security may not be issued by or on behalf of the issuer for the purposes provided under the document without satisfying the reserve fund requirements of the indenture.

(g) *Minor portion.*—Under section 148(e), a bond of an issue is not an arbitrage bond solely because of the investment in higher yielding investments of gross proceeds of the issue in an amount not exceeding the lesser of—

(1) 5 percent of the sale proceeds of the issue; or
(2) $100,000.

(h) *Certain waivers permitted.*—On or before the issue date, an issuer may elect to waive the right to invest in higher yielding investments during any temporary period under paragraph (e) of this section or as part of a reasonably required reserve or replacement fund under paragraph (f) of this section. At any time, an issuer may waive the right to invest in higher yielding investments as part of a minor portion under paragraph (g) of this section. [Reg. §1.148-2.]

☐ [*T.D. 8418, 5-12-92. Amended by T.D. 8476, 6-14-93; T.D. 8538, 5-5-94, T.D. 8718, 5-8-97 and T.D. 9777, 7-15-2016.*]

[Reg. §1.148-2A]

§1.148-2A. [Reserved].
☐ [*T.D. 8538, 5-5-94. Redesignated and amended by T.D. 8718, 5-8-97. Removed and reserved by T.D. 9849, 3-11-2019.*]

[Reg. §1.148-3]

§1.148-3. General arbitrage rebate rules.—(a) *In general.*—Section 148(f) requires that certain earnings on nonpurpose investments allocable to the gross proceeds of an issue be paid to the United States to prevent the bonds in the issue from being arbitrage bonds. The arbitrage that must be rebated is based on the difference between the amount actually earned on nonpurpose investments and the amount that would have been earned if those investments had a yield equal to the yield on the issue.

(b) *Definition of rebate amount.*—As of any date, the rebate amount for an issue is the excess of the future value, as of that date, of all receipts on nonpurpose investments over the future value, as of that date, of all payments on nonpurpose investments.

(c) *Computation of future value of a payment or receipt.*—The future value of a payment or receipt at the end of any period is determined using the economic accrual method and equals the value of that payment or receipt when it is paid or received (or treated as paid or received), plus interest assumed to be earned and compounded over the period at a rate equal to the yield on the issue, using the same compounding interval and financial conventions used to compute that yield.

(d) *Payments and receipts.*—(1) *Definition of payments.*—For purposes of this section, payments are—

(i) Amounts actually or constructively paid to acquire a nonpurpose investment (or treated as paid to a commingled fund);

(ii) For a nonpurpose investment that is first allocated to an issue on a date after it is actually acquired (e.g., an investment that becomes allocable to transferred proceeds or to replacement proceeds) or that becomes subject to the rebate requirement on a date after it is actually acquired (e.g., an investment allocated to a reasonably required reserve or replacement fund for a construction issue at the end of the 2-year spending period), the value of that investment on that date;

(iii) For a nonpurpose investment that was allocated to an issue at the end of the preceding computation period, the value of that investment at the beginning of the computation period;

(iv) On the last day of each bond year during which there are amounts allocated to gross proceeds of an issue that are subject to the rebate requirement, and on the final maturity date, a computation credit of $1,400 for any bond year ending in 2007 and, for bond years ending after 2007, a computation credit in the amount determined under paragraph (d)(4) of this section; and

(v) Yield reduction payments on nonpurpose investments made pursuant to § 1.148-5(c).

(2) *Definition of receipts.*—For purposes of this section, receipts are—

(i) Amounts actually or constructively received from a nonpurpose investment (including amounts treated as received from a commingled fund), such as earnings and return of principal;

(ii) For a nonpurpose investment that ceases to be allocated to an issue before its disposition or redemption date (e.g., an investment that becomes allocable to transferred proceeds of another issue or that ceases to be allocable to the issue pursuant to the universal cap under § 1.148-6) or that ceases to be subject to the rebate requirement on a date earlier than its disposition or redemption date (e.g., an investment allocated to a fund initially subject to the rebate requirement but that subsequently qualifies as a bona fide debt service fund), the value of that nonpurpose investment on that date; and

(iii) For a nonpurpose investment that is held at the end of a computation period, the value of that investment at the end of that period.

(3) *Special rules for commingled funds.*—Section 1.148-6(e) provides special rules to limit certain of the required determinations of payments and receipts for investments of a commingled fund.

(4) *Cost-of-living adjustment.*—For any calendar year after 2007, the $1,400 computation credit set forth in paragraph (d)(1)(iv) of this section shall be increased by an amount equal to such dollar amount multiplied by the cost-of-living adjustment determined under section 1(f)(3) for such year, as modified by this paragraph (d)(4). In applying section 1(f)(3) to determine this cost-of-living adjustment, the reference to "calendar year 1992" in section 1(f)(3)(B) shall be changed to "calendar year 2006." If any such increase determined under this paragraph (d)(4) is not a multiple of $10, such increase shall be rounded to the nearest multiple thereof.

(e) *Computation dates.*—(1) *In general.*—For a fixed yield issue, an issuer may treat any date as a computation date. For a variable yield issue, an issuer:

(i) May treat the last day of any bond year ending on or before the latest date on which the first rebate amount is required to be paid under paragraph (f) of this section (the *first required payment date*) as a computation date but may not change that treatment after the first payment date; and

(ii) After the first required payment date, must consistently treat either the end of each bond year or the end of each fifth bond year as computation dates and may not change these computation dates after the first required payment date.

(2) *Final computation date.*—The date that an issue is discharged is the final computation date. For an issue retired within 3 years of the issue date, however, the final computation date need not occur before the end of 8 months after the issue date or during the period in which the issuer reasonably expects that any of the spending exceptions under § 1.148-7 will apply to the issue.

(f) *Amount of required rebate installment payment.*—(1) *Amount of interim rebate payments.*—The first rebate installment payment must be made for a computation date that is not later than 5 years after the issue date. Subsequent rebate installment payments must be made for a computation date that is not later than 5 years after the previous computation date for which an installment payment was made. A rebate installment payment must be in an amount that, when added to the future value, as of the computation date, of previous rebate payments made for the issue, equals at least 90 percent of the rebate amount as of that date.

(2) *Amount of final rebate payment.*—For the final computation date, a final rebate payment must be paid in an amount that, when added to the future value of previous rebate payments made for the issue, equals 100 percent of the rebate amount as of that date.

(3) *Future value of rebate payments.*—The future value of a rebate payment is determined under paragraph (c) of this section. This value is computed by taking into account recoveries of overpayments.

(g) *Time and manner of payment.*—Each rebate payment must be paid no later than 60 days after the computation date to which the payment relates. Any rebate payment paid within this 60-day period may be treated as paid on the computation date to which it relates. A rebate payment is paid when it is filed with the Internal Revenue

Service at the place or places designated by the Commissioner. A payment must be accompanied by the form provided by the Commissioner for this purpose.

(h) *Penalty in lieu of loss of tax exemption.*—(1) *In general.*—The failure to pay the correct rebate amount when required will cause the bonds of the issue to be arbitrage bonds, unless the Commissioner determines that the failure was not caused by willful neglect and the issuer promptly pays a penalty to the United States. If no bond of the issue is a private activity bond (other than a qualified 501(c)(3) bond), the penalty equals 50 percent of the rebate amount not paid when required to be paid, plus interest on that amount. Otherwise, the penalty equals 100 percent of the rebate amount not paid when required to be paid, plus interest on that amount.

(2) *Interest on underpayments.*—Interest accrues at the underpayment rate under section 6621, beginning on the date the correct rebate amount is due and ending on the date 10 days before it is paid.

(3) *Waivers of the penalty.*—The penalty is automatically waived if the rebate amount that the issuer failed to pay plus interest is paid within 180 days after discovery of the failure, unless, the Commissioner determines that the failure was due to willful neglect, or the issue is under examination by the Commissioner at any time during the period beginning on the date the failure first occurred and ending on the date 90 days after the receipt of the rebate amount. Generally, extensions of this 180-day period and waivers of the penalty in other cases will be granted by the Commissioner only in unusual circumstances. See also § 1.148-3T(h)(3). For purposes of this paragraph (h)(3), willful neglect does not include a failure that is attributable solely to the permissible retroactive selection of a short first bond year if the rebate amount that the issuer failed to pay is paid within 60 days of the selection of that bond year.

(4) *Application to alternative penalty under § 1.148-7.*—Paragraphs (h)(1), (2), and (3) of this section apply to failures to pay penalty payments under § 1.148-7 (*alternative penalty amounts*) by substituting *alternative penalty amounts* for *rebate amount* and *the last day of each spending period* for *computation date.*

(i) *Recovery of overpayment of rebate.*—(1) *In general.*—An issuer may recover an overpayment for an issue of tax-exempt bonds by establishing to the satisfaction of the Commissioner that the overpayment occurred. An overpayment is the excess of the amount paid to the United States for an issue under section 148 over the sum of the rebate amount for the issue as of the most recent computation date and all amounts that are otherwise required to be paid under section 148 as of the date the recovery is requested.

(2) *Limitations on recovery.*—(i) An overpayment may be recovered only to the extent that a recovery on the date that it is first requested would not result in an additional rebate amount if that date were treated as a computation date.

(ii) Except for overpayments of penalty in lieu of rebate under section 148(f)(4)(C)(vii) and § 1.148-7(k), an overpayment of less than $5,000 may not be recovered before the final computation date.

(3) *Time and manner for requesting refund.*—(i) An issuer must request a refund of an overpayment (claim) no later than the date that is two years after the final computation date for the issue to which the overpayment relates (the filing deadline). The claim must be made using the form provided by the Commissioner for this purpose.

(ii) The Commissioner may request additional information to support a claim. The issuer must file the additional information by the date specified in the Commissioner's request, which date may be extended by the Commissioner if unusual circumstances warrant. An issuer will be given at least 21 calendar days to respond to a request for additional information.

(iii) A claim described in either paragraph (i)(3)(iii)(A) or (B) of this section that has been denied by the Commissioner may be appealed to the Office of Appeals under this paragraph (i)(3)(iii). Upon a determination in favor of the issuer, the Office of Appeals must return the undeveloped case to the Commissioner for further consideration of the substance of the claim.

(A) A claim is described in this paragraph (i)(3)(iii)(A) if the Commissioner asserts that the claim was filed after the filing deadline.

(B) A claim is described in this paragraph (i)(3)(iii)(B) if the Commissioner asserts that additional information to support the claim was not submitted within the time specified in the request for information or in any extension of such specified time period.

(j) *Examples.*—The provisions of this section may be illustrated by the following examples.

Example 1. Calculation and payment of rebate for a fixed yield issue. (i) *Facts.* On January 1, 1994, City A issues a fixed yield issue and invests

25,172

Tax Exempt. Requirements: State/Local Bonds
See p. 20,601 for regulations not amended to reflect law changes

all the sale proceeds of the issue ($49 million). There are no other gross proceeds. The issue has a yield of 7.0000 percent per year compounded semiannually (computed on a 30 day month/360 day

Date	
2/1/94	$3,000,000
5/1/94	5,000,000
1/1/95	5,000,000
9/1/95	20,000,000
3/1/96	22,000,000

(ii) *First computation date.* (A) City A chooses January 1, 1999, as its first computation date. This date is the latest date that may be used to compute the first required rebate installment payment. The rebate amount as of this date is computed by determining the future value of the receipts and the payments for the investment. The com-

Date	Receipts (Payments)	FV (7.0000 percent)
1/1/94	($49,000,000)	($69,119,339)
2/1/94	3,000,000	4,207,602
5/1/94	5,000,000	6,893,079
1/1/95	5,000,000	6,584,045
1/1/95	(1,000)	(1,317)
9/1/95	20,000,000	25,155,464
1/1/96	(1,000)	(1,229)
3/1/96	22,000,000	26,735,275
1/1/97	(1,000)	(1,148)
Rebate amount (1/01/99)		$452,432

(B) City A pays 90 percent of the rebate amount ($407,189) to the United States within 60 days of January 1, 1999.

Date	Receipts (Payments)	FV (7.0000 percent)
1/1/99	$452,432	$638,200
Rebate amount (1/01/04)		$638,200

(B) As of this computation date, the future value of the payment treated as made on January 1, 1999, is $574,380, which equals at least 90 percent of the rebate amount as of this computation date ($638,200 × 0.9), and thus no additional rebate payment is due as of this date.

Date	Receipts (Payments)	FV (7.0000 percent)
1/1/04	$638,200	$900,244
1/1/09	(1,000)	(1,000)
Rebate amount (1/01/09)		$899,244

(B) As of this computation date, the future value of the payment made on January 1, 1999, is $810,220 and thus an additional rebate payment of $89,024 is due. This payment reflects the future value of the 10 percent unpaid portion, and thus would not be owed had the issuer paid the full rebate amount as of any prior computation date.

Example 2. Calculation and payment of rebate for a variable yield issue. (i) *Facts.* On July 1, 1994, City B issues a variable yield issue and invests all of the sale proceeds of the issue ($30 million). There are no other gross proceeds. As of July 1, 1999, there are nonpurpose investments allocated to the issue. Prior to July 1, 1999, City B receives amounts from nonpurpose investments and immediately expends them for the governmental purpose of the issue as follows:

Date	Amount
8/1/1994	$5,000,000
7/1/1995	8,000,000

Date
7/1/1994
8/1/1994
7/1/1995
7/1/1995
12/1/1995
7/1/1996
7/1/1997
7/1/1998
7/1/1999
7/1/1999
7/1/1999
Rebate amount (7/01/1999)

(B) City B pays 90 percent of the rebate amount ($1,042,824.60) to the United States within 60 days of July 1, 1999.

(iii) *Next computation date.* (A) On July 1, 2004, City B redeems all of the bonds. Thus, the next computation date is July 1, 2004. On July 30, 1999, City B chose to compute rebate for periods following the

year basis). City A receives amounts from the investment and immediately expends them for the governmental purpose of the issue as follows:

	Amount
	$3,000,000
	5,000,000
	5,000,000
	20,000,000
	22,000,000

pounding interval is each 6-month (or shorter) period and the 30 day month/360 day year basis is used because these conventions were used to compute yield on the issue. The future value of these amounts, plus the computation credit, as of January 1, 1999, is:

(iii) *Second computation date.* (A) On the next required computation date, January 1, 2004, the future value of the payments and receipts is:

(iv) *Final computation date.* (A) On January 1, 2009, City A redeems all the bonds, and thus this date is the final computation date. The future value of the receipts and payments as of this date is:

Date	Amount
12/1/1995	17,000,000
7/1/1999	650,000

(ii) *First computation date.* (A) City B treats the last day of the fifth bond year (July 1, 1999) as a computation date. The yield on the variable yield issue during the first computation period (the period beginning on the issue date and ending on the first computation date) is 6.0000 percent per year compounded semiannually. The value of the nonpurpose investments allocated to the issue as of July 1, 1999, is $3 million. The rebate amount as of July 1, 1999, is computed by determining the future value of the receipts and the payments for the nonpurpose investments. The compounding interval is each 6-month (or shorter) period and the 30 day month/360 day year basis is used because these conventions were used to compute yield on the issue. The future value of these amounts and of the computation date credits as of July 1, 1999, is:

Receipts (Payments)	FV (6.0000 percent)
($30,000,000)	($40,317,491)
5,000,000	6,686,560
(1,000)	(1,267)
8,000,000	10,134,161
17,000,000	21,011,112
(1,000)	(1,194)
(1,000)	(1,126)
(1,000)	(1,061)
3,000,000	3,000,000
650,000	650,000
(1,000)	(1,000)
	$1,158,694

first computation period by treating the end of each fifth bond year as a computation date. The yield during the second computation period is 5.0000 percent per year compounded semiannually. The computation of the rebate amount as of this date reflects the value of the nonpurpose investments allocated to the issue at the end of the prior computation period. On July 1, 2004, City B sells those nonpurpose investments for $3,925,000 and expends that amount for the governmental purpose of the issue.

Date
7/1/1999
7/1/1999
7/1/2000
7/1/2001
7/1/2002
7/1/2003
7/1/2004
7/1/2004

(C) As of this computation date, the future value of the payment made on July 1, 1999, is $1,334,904 and thus an additional rebate payment of $226,535 is due.

(D) If the yield during the second computation period were, instead, 7.0000 percent, the rebate amount computed as of July 1, 2004, would be $1,320,891. The future value of the payment made on July 1, 1999, would be $1,471,007. Although the future value of the payment made on July 1, 1999 ($1,471,007), exceeds the rebate amount computed as of July 1, 2004 ($1,320,891), §1.148-3(i) limits the amount recoverable as a defined overpayment of rebate under section 148 to the excess of the total "amount paid" over the sum of the amount determined under the future value method to be the "rebate amount" as of the most recent computation date and all other amounts that are otherwise required to be paid under section 148 as of the date the recovery is requested. Because the total amount that the issuer paid on July 1, 1999 ($1,042,824.60), does not exceed the rebate amount as of July 1, 2004 ($1,320,891), the issuer would not be entitled to recover any overpayment of rebate in this case.

(k) *Bona fide debt service fund exception.*—Under section 148(f)(4)(A), the rebate requirement does not apply to amounts in certain bona fide debt service funds. An issue with an average annual debt service that is not in excess of $2,500,000 may be treated as satisfying the $100,000 limitation in section 148(f)(4)(A)(ii). [Reg. §1.148-3.]

☐ *[T.D. 8418, 5-12-92. Amended by T.D. 8476, 6-14-93; T.D. 8538, 5-5-94; T.D. 8718, 5-8-97, T.D. 9701, 11-12-2014 and T.D. 9777, 7-15-2016.]*

[Reg. §1.148-3A]

§1.148-3A. [Reserved].

☐ *[T.D. 8538, 5-5-94. Redesignated and amended by T.D. 8718, 5-8-97. Removed and reserved by T.D. 9849, 3-11-2019.]*

[Reg. §1.148-4]

§1.148-4. Yield on an issue of bonds.—(a) *In general.*—The yield on an issue of bonds is used to apply investment yield restrictions under section 148(a) and to compute rebate liability under section 148(f). Yield is computed under the economic accrual method using any consistently applied compounding interval of not more than one year. A short first compounding interval and a short last compounding interval may be used. Yield is expressed as an annual percentage rate that is calculated to at least four decimal places (for example, 5.2525 percent). Other reasonable, standard financial conventions, such as the 30 days per month/360 days per year convention, may be used in computing yield but must be consistently applied. The yield on an issue that would be a purpose investment (absent section 148(b)(3)(A)) is equal to the yield on the conduit financing issue that financed that purpose investment.

(b) *Computing yield on a fixed yield issue.*—(1) *In general.*—(i) *Yield on an issue.*—The yield on a fixed yield issue is the discount rate that, when used in computing the present value as of the issue date of all unconditionally payable payments of principal, interest, and fees for qualified guarantees on the issue and amounts reasonably expected to be paid as fees for qualified guarantees on the issue, produces an amount equal to the present value, using the same discount rate, of the aggregate issue price of bonds of the issue as of the issue date. Further, payments include certain amounts properly allocable to a qualified hedge. Yield on a fixed yield issue is computed as of the issue date and is not affected by subsequent unexpected events, except to the extent provided in paragraphs (b)(4) and (h)(3) of this section.

(ii) *Yield on a bond.*—Yield on a fixed yield bond is computed in the same manner as yield on a fixed yield issue.

(2) *Yield on certain fixed yield bonds subject to mandatory or contingent early redemption.*—(i) *In general.*—The yield on a fixed yield issue that includes a bond subject to mandatory early redemption or expected contingent redemption is computed by treating that bond as redeemed on its reasonably expected early redemption date for an

(B) As of July 1, 2004, the future value of the rebate amount computed as of July 1, 1999, and of all other payments and receipts is:

Receipts (Payments)	FV (5.0000 percent)
$1,158,694	$1,483,226
(3,000,000)	(3,840,254)
(1,000)	(1,218)
(1,000)	(1,160)
(1,000)	(1,104)
(1,000)	(1,051)
(2,000)	(2,000)
3,925,000	3,925,000
	$1,561,439

amount equal to its value on that date. Reasonable expectations are determined on the issue date. A bond is subject to mandatory early redemption if it is unconditionally payable in full before its final maturity date. A bond is subject to a contingent redemption if it must be, or is reasonably expected to be, redeemed prior to final maturity upon the occurrence of a contingency. A contingent redemption is taken into account only if the contingency is reasonably expected to occur, in which case the date of occurrence of the contingency must be reasonably estimated. For example, if bonds are reasonably expected to be redeemed early using excess revenues from general or special property taxes or benefit assessments or similar amounts, the reasonably expected redemption schedule is used to determine yield. For purposes of this paragraph (b)(2)(i), excess proceeds calls for issues for which the requirements of §1.148-2(e)(2) or (3) are satisfied, calamity calls, and refundings do not cause a bond to be subject to early redemption. The value of a bond is determined under paragraph (e) of this section.

(ii) *Substantially identical bonds subject to mandatory early redemption.*—If substantially identical bonds of an issue are subject to specified mandatory redemptions prior to final maturity (e.g., a mandatory sinking fund redemption requirement), yield on that issue is computed by treating those bonds as redeemed in accordance with the redemption schedule for an amount equal to their value. Generally, bonds are substantially identical if the stated interest rate, maturity, and payment dates are the same. In computing the yield on an issue containing bonds described in this paragraph (b)(2)(ii), each of those bonds must be treated as redeemed at its present value, unless the stated redemption price at maturity of the bond does not exceed the issue price of the bond by more than one-fourth of one percent multiplied by the product of the stated redemption price at maturity and the number of years to the weighted average maturity date of the substantially identical bonds, in which case each of those bonds must be treated as redeemed at its outstanding stated principal amount, plus accrued, unpaid interest. Weighted average maturity is determined by taking into account the mandatory redemption schedule.

(3) *Yield on certain fixed yield bonds subject to optional early redemption.*—(i) *In general.*—If a fixed yield bond is subject to optional early redemption and is described in paragraph (b)(3)(ii) of this section, the yield on the issue containing the bond is computed by treating the bond as redeemed at its stated redemption price on the optional redemption date that would produce the lowest yield on that bond.

(ii) *Fixed yield bonds subject to special yield calculation rule.*—A fixed yield bond is described in this paragraph (b)(3)(ii) only if it—

(A) Is subject to optional redemption within five years of the issue date, but only if the yield on the issue computed by assuming all bonds in the issue subject to redemption within 5 years of the issue date are redeemed at maturity is more than one-eighth of one percentage point higher than the yield on that issue computed by assuming all bonds subject to optional redemption within 5 years of the issue date are redeemed at the earliest date for their redemption;

(B) Is issued at an issue price that exceeds the stated redemption price at maturity by more than one-fourth of one percent multiplied by the product of the stated redemption price at maturity and the number of complete years to the first optional redemption date for the bond; or

(C) Bears interest at increasing interest rates (i.e., a *stepped coupon bond*).

(4) *Yield recomputed upon transfer of certain rights associated with the bond.*—For purposes of §1.148-3, as of the date of any transfer, waiver, modification, or similar transaction (collectively, a *transfer*) of any right that is part of the terms of a bond or is otherwise associated with a bond (e.g., a redemption right), in a transaction that is separate and apart from the original sale of the bond, the issue is treated as if it were retired and a new issue issued on the date of the transfer (*reissued*). The redemption price of the retired issue and the issue price of the new issue equal the aggregate values of all the bonds of the issue on the date of the transfer. In computing yield on the new

25,174

Tax Exempt. Requirements: State/Local Bonds
See p. 20,601 for regulations not amended to reflect law changes

issue, any amounts received by the issuer as consideration for the transfer are taken into account.

(5) *Special aggregation rule treating certain bonds as a single fixed yield bond.*—Two variable yield bonds of an issue are treated in the aggregate as a single fixed yield bond if—

(i) Aggregate treatment would result in the single bond being a fixed yield bond; and

(ii) The terms of the bonds do not contain any features that could distort the aggregate fixed yield from what the yield would be if a single fixed yield bond were issued. For example, if an issue contains a bond bearing interest at a floating rate and a related bond bearing interest at a rate equal to a fixed rate minus that floating rate, those two bonds are treated as a single fixed yield bond only if neither bond may be redeemed unless the other bond is also redeemed at the same time.

(6) *Examples.*—The provisions of this paragraph (b) may be illustrated by the following examples.

Example 1. No early call. (i) *Facts.* On January 1, 1994, City *A* issues an issue consisting of four identical fixed yield bonds. The stated final maturity date of each bond is January 1, 2004, and no bond is subject to redemption before this date. Interest is payable on January 1 of each year at a rate of 6.0000 percent per year on the outstanding principal amount. The total stated principal amount of the bonds is $20 million. The issue price of the bonds $20,060,000.

(ii) *Computation.* The yield on the issue is computed by treating the bonds as retired at the stated maturity under the general rule of § 1.148-4(b)(1). The bonds are treated as redeemed for their stated redemption prices. The yield on the issue is 5.8731 percent per year compounded semiannually, computed as follows:

Date	Payments	PV (5.8731 percent)
1/1/1995	$1,200,000	$1,132,510
1/1/1996	1,200,000	1,068,816
1/1/1997	1,200,000	1,008,704
1/1/1998	1,200,000	951,973
1/1/1999	1,200,000	898,433
1/1/2000	1,200,000	847,903
1/1/2001	1,200,000	800,216
1/1/2002	1,200,000	755,210
1/1/2003	1,200,000	712,736
1/1/2004	21,200,000	11,883,498
		$20,060,000

Example 2. Mandatory calls. (i) *Facts.* The facts are the same as in *Example 1.* In this case, however, the bonds are subject to mandatory sinking fund redemption on January 1 of each year, beginning January 1, 2001. On each sinking fund redemption date, one of the bonds is chosen by lottery and is required to be redeemed at par plus accrued interest.

(ii) *Computation.* Because the bonds are subject to specified redemptions, yield on the issue is computed by treating the bonds as redeemed in accordance with the redemption schedule under § 1.148-4(b)(2)(ii). Because the bonds are not sold at a discount, the bonds are treated as retired at their stated redemption prices. The yield on the issue is 5.8678 percent per year compounded semiannually, computed as follows:

Date	Payments	PV (5.8678 percent)
1/1/1995	$1,200,000	$1,132,569
1/1/1996	1,200,000	1,068,926
1/1/1997	1,200,000	1,008,860
1/1/1998	1,200,000	952,169
1/1/1999	1,200,000	898,664
1/1/2000	1,200,000	848,166
1/1/2001	6,200,000	4,135,942
1/1/2002	5,900,000	3,714,650
1/1/2003	5,600,000	3,327,647
1/1/2004	5,300,000	2,972,407
		$20,060,000

Example 3. Optional early call. (i) *Facts.* On January 1, 1994, City *C* issues an issue consisting of three bonds. Each bond has a stated principal amount of $10 million dollars and is issued for par. Bond *X* bears interest at 5 percent per year and matures on January 1, 1999. Bond *Y* bears interest at 6 percent per year and matures on January 1, 2002. Bond *Z* bears interest at 7 percent per year and matures on

January 1, 2004. Bonds *Y* and *Z* are callable by the issuer at par plus accrued interest after December 31, 1998.

(ii) *Computation.* (A) The yield on the issue computed as if each bond is outstanding to its maturity is 6.0834 percent per year compounded semiannually, computed as follows:

Date	Payments	PV (6.0834 percent)
1/1/1995	$1,800,000	$1,695,299
1/1/1996	1,800,000	1,596,689
1/1/1997	1,800,000	1,503,814
1/1/1998	1,800,000	1,416,342
1/1/1999	11,800,000	8,744,830
1/1/2000	1,300,000	907,374
1/1/2001	1,300,000	854,595
1/1/2002	11,300,000	6,996,316
1/1/2003	700,000	408,190
1/1/2004	10,700,000	5,876,551
		$30,000,000

(B) The yield on the issue computed as if all bonds are called at the earliest date for redemption is 5.9126 percent per year compounded semiannually, computed as follows:

Date	Payments	PV (5.9126 percent)
1/1/1995	$1,800,000	$1,698,113
1/1/1996	1,800,000	1,601,994
1/1/1997	1,800,000	1,511,315
1/1/1998	1,800,000	1,425,769

Date	Payments	PV
1/1/1999	31,800,000	(5.9126 percent)
		23,762,809
		$30,000,000

(C) Because the yield on the issue computed by assuming all bonds in the issue subject to redemption within 5 years of the issue date are redeemed at maturity is more than one-eighth of one percentage point higher than the yield on the issue computed by assuming all bonds subject to optional redemption within 5 years of the issue date are redeemed at the earliest date for their redemption, each bond is treated as redeemed on the date that would produce the lowest yield for the issue. The lowest yield on the issue would result from a redemption of all the bonds on January 1, 1999. Thus, the yield on the issue is 5.9126 percent per year compounded semiannually.

(c) *Computing yield on a variable yield issue.*—(1) *In general.*—The yield on a variable yield issue is computed separately for each computation period. The yield for each computation period is the discount rate that, when used in computing the present value as of the first day of the computation period of all the payments of principal and interest and fees for qualified guarantees that are attributable to the computation period, produces an amount equal to the present value, using the same discount rate, of the aggregate issue price (or deemed issue price, as determined in paragraph (c)(2)(iv) of this section) of the bonds of the issue as of the first day of the computation period. The yield on a variable yield bond is computed in the same manner as the yield on a variable yield issue. Except as provided in paragraph (c)(2) of this section, yield on any fixed yield bond in a variable yield issue is computed in the same manner as the yield on a fixed yield issue as provided in paragraph (b) of this section.

(2) *Payments on bonds included in yield for a computation period.*—(i) *Payments in general.*—The payments on a bond that are attributable to a computation period include any amounts actually paid during the period for principal on the bond. Payments also include any amounts paid during the current period both for interest accruing on the bond during the current period and for interest accruing during the prior period that was included in the deemed issue price of the bond as accrued unpaid interest at the start of the current period under this paragraph (c)(2). Further, payments include any amounts properly allocable to fees for a qualified guarantee of the bond for the period and to any amounts properly allocable to a qualified hedge for the period.

(ii) *Payments at actual redemption.*—If a bond is actually redeemed during a computation period, an amount equal to the greater of its value on the redemption date or the actual redemption price is a payment on the actual redemption date.

(iii) *Payments for bonds outstanding at end of computation period.*—If a bond is outstanding at the end of a computation period, a payment equal to the bond's value is taken into account on the last day of that period.

(iv) *Issue price for bonds outstanding at beginning of next computation period.*—A bond outstanding at the end of a computation period is treated as if it were immediately reissued on the next day for a deemed issue price equal to the value from the day before as determined under paragraph (c)(2)(iii) of this section.

(3) *Example.*—The provisions of this paragraph (c) may be illustrated by the following example.

Example. On January 1, 1994, City *A* issues an issue of identical plain par bonds in an aggregate principal amount of $1,000,000. The bonds pay interest at a variable rate on each June 1 throughout the term of the issue. The entire principal amount of the bonds plus accrued, unpaid interest is payable on the final maturity date of January 1, 2000. No bond year is selected. On June 1, 1994, 1995, 1996, 1997, and 1998, interest in the amounts of $30,000, $55,000, $57,000, $56,000, and $45,000 is paid on the bonds. From June 1, 1998, to January 1, 1999, $30,000 of interest accrues on the bonds. From January 1, 1999, to June 1, 1999, another $35,000 of interest accrues. On June 1, 1999, the issuer actually pays $65,000 of interest. On January 1, 2000, $1,000,000 of principal and $38,000 of accrued interest are paid. The payments for the computation period starting on the issue date and ending on January 1, 1999, include all annual interest payments paid from the issue date to June 1, 1998. Because the issue is outstanding on January 1, 1999, it is treated as redeemed on that date for [an] amount equal to its value ($1,000,000 plus accrued, unpaid interest of $30,000 under paragraph (e)(1) of this section). Thus, $1,030,000 is treated as paid on January 1, 1999. The issue is then treated as reissued on January 1, 1999, for $1,030,000. The payments for the next computation period starting on January 1,

1999, and ending on January 1, 2000, include the interest actually paid on the bonds during that period ($65,000 on June 1, 1999, plus $38,000 paid on January 1, 2000). Because the issue was actually redeemed on January 1, 2000, an amount equal to its stated redemption price is also treated as paid on January 1, 2000.

(d) *Conversion from variable yield issue to fixed yield issue.*—For purposes of determining yield under this section, as of the first day on which a variable yield issue would qualify as a fixed yield issue if it were newly issued on that date (a *conversion date*), that issue is treated as if it were reissued as a fixed yield issue on the conversion date. The redemption price of the variable yield issue and the issue price of the fixed yield issue equal the aggregate values of all the bonds on the conversion date. Thus, for example, for plain par bonds (e.g., tender bonds), the deemed issue price would be the outstanding principal amount, plus accrued unpaid interest. If the conversion date occurs on a date other than a computation date, the issuer may continue to treat the issue as a variable yield issue until the next computation date, at which time it must be treated as converted to a fixed yield issue.

(e) *Value of bonds.*—(1) *Plain par bonds.*—Except as otherwise provided, the value of a plain par bond is its outstanding stated principal amount, plus accrued unpaid interest. The value of a plain par bond that is actually redeemed or treated as redeemed is its stated redemption price on the redemption date, plus accrued, unpaid interest.

(2) *Other bonds.*—The value of a bond other than a plain par bond on a date is its present value on that date. The present value of a bond is computed under the economic accrual method taking into account all the unconditionally payable payments of principal, interest, and fees for a qualified guarantee to be paid on or after that date and using the yield on the bond as the discount rate, except that for purposes of § 1.148-6(b)(2) (relating to the universal cap), these values may be determined by consistently using the yield on the issue of which the bonds are a part. To determine yield on fixed yield bonds, see paragraph (b)(1) of this section. The rules contained in paragraphs (b)(2) and (b)(3) of this section apply for this purpose. In the case of bonds described in paragraph (b)(2)(ii) of this section, the present value of those bonds on any date is computed using the yield to the final maturity date of those bonds as the discount rate. In determining the present value of a variable yield bond under this paragraph (e)(2), the initial interest rate on the bond established by the interest index or other interest rate setting mechanism is used to determine the interest payments on that bond.

(f) *Qualified guarantees.*—(1) *In general.*—Fees properly allocable to payments for a qualified guarantee for an issue (as determined under paragraph (f)(6) of this section) are treated as additional interest on that issue under section 148. A guarantee is a qualified guarantee if it satisfies each of the requirements of paragraphs (f)(2) through (f)(4) of this section.

(2) *Interest savings.*—As of the date the guarantee is obtained, the issuer must reasonably expect that the present value of the fees for the guarantee will be less than the present value of the expected interest savings on the issue as a result of the guarantee. For this purpose, present value is computed using the yield on the issue, determined with regard to guarantee payments, as the discount rate.

(3) *Guarantee in substance.*—The arrangement must create a guarantee in substance. The arrangement must impose a secondary liability that unconditionally shifts substantially all of the credit risk for all or part of the payments, such as payments for principal and interest, redemption prices, or tender prices, on the guaranteed bonds. Reasonable procedural or administrative requirements of the guarantee do not cause the guarantee to be conditional. In the case of a guarantee against failure to remarket a qualified tender bond, commercially reasonable limitations based on credit risk, such as limitations on payment in the event of default by the primary obligor or the bankruptcy of a long-term credit guarantor, do not cause the guarantee to be conditional. The guarantee may be in any form. The guarantor may not be a co-obligor. Thus, the guarantor must not expect to make any payments other than under a direct-pay letter of credit or similar arrangement for which the guarantor will be reimbursed immediately. The guarantor and any related parties together must not use more than 10 percent of the proceeds of the portion of the issue allocable to the guaranteed bonds.

(4) *Reasonable charge.*—(i) *In general.*—Fees for a guarantee must not exceed a reasonable, arm's-length charge for the transfer of credit

25,176

Tax Exempt. Requirements: State/Local Bonds
See p. 20,601 for regulations not amended to reflect law changes

risk. In complying with this requirement, the issuer may not rely on the representations of the guarantor.

(ii) *Fees for services other than transfer of credit risk must be separately stated.*—A fee for a guarantee must not include any payment for any direct or indirect services other than the transfer of credit risk, unless the compensation for those other services is separately stated, reasonable, and excluded from the guarantee fee. Fees for the transfer of credit risk include fees for the guarantor's overhead and other costs relating to the transfer of credit risk. For example, a fee includes payment for services other than transfer of credit risk if—

(A) It includes payment for the cost of underwriting or remarketing bonds or for the cost of insurance for casualty to bond-financed property;

(B) It is refundable upon redemption of the guaranteed bond before the final maturity date and the amount of the refund would exceed the portion of the fee that had not been earned; or

(C) The requirements of § 1.148-2(e)(2) (relating to temporary periods for capital projects) are not satisfied, and the guarantor is not reasonably assured that the bonds will be repaid if the project to be financed is not completed.

(5) *Guarantee of purpose investments.*—Except for guarantees of qualified mortgage loans and qualified student loans, a guarantee of payments on a purpose investment is a qualified guarantee of the issue if all payments on the purpose investment reasonably coincide with payments on the related bonds and the payments on the purpose investment are unconditionally payable no more than 6 months before the corresponding interest payment and 12 months before the corresponding principal payments on the bonds. This paragraph (f)(5) only applies if, in addition to satisfying the other requirements of this paragraph (f), the guarantee is, in substance, a guarantee of the bonds allocable to that purpose investment and to no other bonds except for bonds that are equally and ratably secured by purpose investments of the same conduit borrower.

(6) *Allocation of qualified guarantee payments.*—(i) *In general.*—Payments for a qualified guarantee must be allocated to bonds and to computation periods in a manner that properly reflects the proportionate credit risk for which the guarantor is compensated. Proportionate credit risk for bonds that are not substantially identical may be determined using any reasonable, consistently applied method. For example, this risk may be based on the ratio of the total principal and interest paid and to be paid on a guaranteed bond to the total principal and interest paid and to be paid on all bonds of the guaranteed issue. An allocation method generally is not reasonable, for example, if a substantial portion of the fee is allocated to the construction portion of the issue and a correspondingly insubstantial portion is allocated to the later years covered by the guarantee. Reasonable letter of credit *set up* fees may be allocated ratably during the initial term of the letter of credit. Upon an early redemption of a variable yield bond, fees otherwise allocable to the period after the redemption are allocated to remaining outstanding bonds of the issue or, if none remain outstanding, to the period before the redemption.

(ii) *Safe harbor for allocation of qualified guarantee fees for variable yield issues.*—An allocation of non-level payments for a qualified guarantee for variable yield bonds is treated as meeting the requirements of paragraph (f)(6)(i) of this section if, for each bond year for which the guarantee is in effect, an equal amount (or for any short bond year, a proportionate amount of the equal amount) is treated as paid as of the beginning of that bond year. The present value of the annual amounts must equal the fee for the guarantee allocated to that bond, with present value computed as of the first day the guarantee is in effect by using as the discount rate the yield on the variable yield bonds covered by the guarantee, determined without regard to any fee allocated under this paragraph (f)(6)(ii).

(7) *Refund or reduction of guarantee payments.*—If as a result of an investment of proceeds of a refunding issue in a refunding escrow, there will be a reduction in, or refund of, payments for a guarantee (*savings*), the savings must be treated as a reduction in the payments on the refunding issue.

(g) *Yield on certain mortgage revenue and student loan bonds.*—For purposes of section 148 and this section, section 143(g)(2)(C)(ii) applies to the computation of yield on an issue of qualified mortgage bonds or qualified veterans' mortgage bonds. For purposes of applying section 148 and section 143(g) with respect to purpose investments allocable to a variable yield issue of qualified mortgage bonds, qualified veterans' mortgage bonds, or qualified student loan bonds *that is reasonably expected as of the issue date* to convert to a fixed yield issue, the yield may be computed over the term of the issue, and, if the yield is so computed, paragraph (d) of this section does not apply to the issue. As of any date, the yield over the term of the issue is based on—

(1) With respect to any bond of the issue that has not converted to a fixed and determinable yield on or before that date, the actual amounts paid or received to that date and the amounts that are reasonably expected (as of that date) to be paid or received with respect to that bond over the remaining term of the issue (taking into account prepayment assumptions under section 143(g)(2)(B)(iv), if applicable); and

(2) With respect to any bond of the issue that has converted to a fixed and determinable yield on or before that date, the actual amounts paid or received before that bond converted, if any, and the amount that was reasonably expected (on the date that bond converted) to be paid or received with respect to that bond over the remaining term of the issue (taking into account prepayment assumptions under section 143(g)(2)(B)(iv), if applicable).

(h) *Qualified hedging transactions.*—(1) *In general.*—Payments made or received by an issuer under a qualified hedge (as defined in paragraph (h)(2) of this section) relating to bonds of an issue are taken into account (as provided in paragraph (h)(3) of this section) to determine the yield on the issue. Except as provided in paragraphs (h)(4) and (h)(5)(ii)(E) of this section, the bonds to which a qualified hedge relates are treated as variable yield bonds from the issue date of the bonds. This paragraph (h) applies solely for purposes of sections 143(g), 148, and 149(d).

(2) *Qualified hedge defined.*—Except as provided in paragraph (h)(5) of this section, the term *qualified hedge* means a contract that satisfies each of the following requirements:

(i) *Hedge.*—(A) *In general.*—The contract is entered into primarily to modify the issuer's risk of interest rate changes with respect to a bond (a hedge). For example, the contract may be an interest rate swap, an interest rate cap, a futures contract, a forward contract, or an option.

(B) *Special rule for fixed rate issues.*—If the contract modifies the issuer's risk of interest rate changes with respect to a bond that is part of an issue that, absent the contract, would be a fixed rate issue, the contract must be entered into—

(1) No later than 15 days after the issue date (or the deemed issue date under paragraph (d) of this section) of the issue; or

(2) No later than the expiration of a qualified hedge with respect to bonds of that issue that satisfies paragraph (h)(2)(i)(B)(1) of this section; or

(3) No later than the expiration of a qualified hedge with respect to bonds of that issue that satisfies either paragraph (h)(2)(i)(B)(2) of this section or this paragraph (h)(2)(i)(B)(3).

(C) *Contracts with certain acquisition payments.*—If a hedge provider makes a single payment to the issuer (e.g., a payment for an off-market swap) in connection with the acquisition of a contract, the issuer may treat a portion of that contract as a hedge provided—

(1) The hedge provider's payment to the issuer and the issuer's payments under the contract in excess of those that it would make if the contract bore rates equal to the on-market rates for the contract (determined as of the date the parties enter into the contract) are separately identified in a certification of the hedge provider; and

(2) The payments described in paragraph (h)(2)(i)(C)(1) of this section are not treated as payments on the hedge.

(ii) *No significant investment element.*—(A) *In general.*—The contract does not contain a significant investment element. Except as provided in paragraph (h)(2)(ii)(B) of this section, a contract contains a significant investment element if a significant portion of any payment by one party relates to a conditional or unconditional obligation by the other party to make a payment on a different date. Examples of contracts that contain a significant investment element are a debt instrument held by the issuer; an interest rate swap requiring any payments other than periodic payments, within the meaning of § 1.446-3 (periodic payments) (e.g., a payment for an off-market swap or prepayment of part or all of one leg of a swap); and an interest rate cap requiring the issuer's premium for the cap to be paid in a single, up-front payment. Solely for purposes of determining if a hedge is a qualified hedge under this section, payments that an issuer receives pursuant to the terms of a hedge that are equal to the issuer's cost of funds are treated as periodic payments under § 1.446-3 without regard to whether the payments are calculated by reference to a "specified index" described in § 1.446-3(c)(2). Accordingly, a hedge does not have a significant investment element under this paragraph (h)(2)(ii)(A) solely because an issuer receives payments pursuant to the terms of a hedge that are computed to be equal to the issuer's cost of funds, such as the issuer's actual market-based tax-exempt variable interest rate on its bonds.

(B) *Special level payment rule for interest rate caps.*—An interest rate cap does not contain a significant investment element if—

(1) All payments to the issuer by the hedge provider are periodic payments;

(2) The issuer makes payments for the cap at the same time as periodic payments by the hedge provider must be made if the specified index (within the meaning of §1.446-3) of the cap is above the strike price of the cap; and

(3) Each payment by the issuer bears the same ratio to the notional principal amount (within the meaning of §1.446-3) that is used to compute the hedge provider's payment, if any, on that date.

(iii) Parties.—The contract is entered into between the issuer or the political subdivision on behalf of which the issuer issues the bonds (collectively referred to in this paragraph (h) as the *issuer*) and a provider that is not a related party (the *hedge provider*).

(iv) Hedged bonds.—The contract covers, in whole or in part, all of one or more groups of substantially identical bonds in the issue (i.e., all of the bonds having the same interest rate, maturity, and terms). Thus, for example, a qualified hedge may include a hedge of all or a pro rata portion of each interest payment on the variable rate bonds in an issue for the first 5 years following their issuance. For purposes of this paragraph (h), unless the context clearly requires otherwise, *hedged bonds* means the specific bonds or portions thereof covered by a hedge.

(v) Interest-based contract and size and scope of hedge.—The contract is primarily interest-based (for example, a hedge based on a debt index, including a tax-exempt debt index or a taxable debt index, rather than an equity index). In addition, the size and scope of the hedge under the contract is limited to that which is reasonably necessary to hedge the issuer's risk with respect to interest rate changes on the hedged bonds. For example, a contract is limited to hedging an issuer's risk with respect to interest rate changes on the hedged bonds if the hedge is based on the principal amount and the reasonably expected interest payments of the hedged bonds. For anticipatory hedges under paragraph (h)(5) of this section, the size and scope limitation applies based on the reasonably expected terms of the hedged bonds to be issued. A contract is not primarily interest based unless—

(A) The hedged bond, without regard to the contract, is either a fixed rate bond, a variable rate debt instrument within the meaning of §1.1275-5 provided the rate is not based on an objective rate other than a qualified inverse floating rate or a qualified inflation rate, a tax-exempt obligation described in §1.1275-4(d)(2), or an inflation-indexed debt instrument within the meaning of §1.1275-7; and

(B) As a result of treating all payments on (and receipts from) the contract as additional payments on (and receipts from) the hedged bond, the resulting bond would be substantially similar to either a fixed rate bond, a variable rate debt instrument within the meaning of §1.1275-5 provided the rate is not based on an objective rate other than a qualified inverse floating rate or a qualified inflation rate, a tax-exempt obligation described in §1.1275-4(d)(2), or an inflation-indexed debt instrument within the meaning of §1.1275-7. For this purpose, differences that would not prevent the resulting bond from being substantially similar to another type of bond include: a difference between the interest rate used to compute payments on the hedged bond and the interest rate used to compute payments on the hedge where one interest rate is substantially similar to the other; the difference resulting from the payment of a fixed premium for a cap (for example, payments for a cap that are made in other than level installments); and the difference resulting from the allocation of a termination payment where the termination was not expected as of the date the contract was entered into.

(vi) Payments closely correspond.—The payments received by the issuer from the hedge provider under the contract correspond closely in time to either the specific payments being hedged on the hedged bonds or specific payments required to be made pursuant to the bond documents, regardless of the hedge, to a sinking fund, debt service fund, or similar fund maintained for the issue of which the hedged bond is a part. For this purpose, such payments will be treated as corresponding closely in time under this paragraph (h)(2)(vi) if they are made within 90 calendar days of each other.

(vii) Source of payments.—Payments to the hedge provider are reasonably expected to be made from the same source of funds that, absent the hedge, would be reasonably expected to be used to pay principal and interest on the hedged bonds.

(viii) Identification.—(A) *In general.*—The actual issuer must identify the contract on its books and records maintained for the hedged bonds not later than 15 calendar days after the date on which there is a binding agreement to enter into a hedge contract (for example, the date of a hedge pricing confirmation, as distinguished from the closing date for the hedge or start date for payments on the hedge, if different). The identification must specify the name of the hedge provider, the terms of the contract, the hedged bonds, and include a hedge provider's certification as described in paragraph (h)(2)(viii)(B) of this section. The identification must contain sufficient detail to establish that the requirements of this paragraph (h)(2) and, if applicable, paragraph (h)(4) of this section are satisfied. In addition, the existence of the hedge must be noted on the first form relating to the issue of which the hedged bonds are a part that is filed with the Internal Revenue Service on or after the date on which the contract is identified pursuant to this paragraph (h)(2)(viii).

(B) *Hedge provider's certification.*—The hedge provider's certification must—

(1) Provide that the terms of the hedge were agreed to between a willing buyer and willing seller in a bona fide, arm's-length transaction;

(2) Provide that the hedge provider has not made, and does not expect to make, any payment to any third party for the benefit of the issuer in connection with the hedge, except for any such third-party payment that the hedge provider expressly identifies in the documents for the hedge;

(3) Provide that the amounts payable to the hedge provider pursuant to the hedge do not include any payments for underwriting or other services unrelated to the hedge provider's obligations under the hedge, except for any such payment that the hedge provider expressly identifies in the documents for the hedge; and

(4) Contain any other statements that the Commissioner may provide in guidance published in the Internal Revenue Bulletin. See §601.601(d)(2)(ii) of this chapter.

(3) Accounting for qualified hedges.—(i) *In general.*—Except as otherwise provided in paragraph (h)(4) of this section, payments made or received by the issuer under a qualified hedge are treated as payments made or received, as appropriate, on the hedged bonds that are taken into account in determining the yield on those bonds. These payments are reasonably allocated to the hedged bonds in the period to which the payments relate, as determined under paragraph (h)(3)(iii) of this section. Payments made or received by the issuer include payments deemed made or received when a contract is terminated or deemed terminated under this paragraph (h)(3). Payments reasonably allocable to the modification of risk of interest rate changes and to the hedge provider's overhead under this paragraph (h) are included as payments made or received under a qualified hedge.

(ii) Exclusions from hedge.—If any payment for services or other items under the contract is not expressly treated by paragraph (h)(3)(i) of this section as a payment under the qualified hedge, the payment is not a payment with respect to a qualified hedge.

(iii) Timing and allocation of payments.—Except as provided in paragraphs (h)(3)(iv) and (h)(5) of this section, payments made or received by the issuer under a qualified hedge are taken into account in the same period in which those amounts would be treated as income or deductions under §1.446-4 (without regard to §1.446-4(a)(2)(iv)) and are adjusted as necessary to reflect the end of a computation period and the start of a new computation period.

(iv) Accounting for modifications and terminations.—(A) *Modification defined.*—A modification of a qualified hedge includes, without limitation, a change in the terms of the hedge or an issuer's acquisition of another hedge with terms that have the effect of modifying an issuer's risk of interest rate changes or other terms of an existing qualified hedge. For example, if the issuer enters into a qualified hedge that is an interest rate swap under which it receives payments based on the Securities Industry and Financial Market Association (SIFMA) Municipal Swap Index and subsequently enters a second hedge (with the same or different provider) that limits the issuer's exposure under the existing qualified hedge to variations in the SIFMA Municipal Swap Index, the new hedge modifies the qualified hedge.

(B) *Termination defined.*—A termination means either an actual termination or a deemed termination of a qualified hedge. Except as otherwise provided, an actual termination of a qualified hedge occurs to the extent that the issuer sells, disposes of, or otherwise actually terminates all or a portion of the hedge. A deemed termination of a qualified hedge occurs if the hedge ceases to meet the requirements for a qualified hedge; the issuer makes a modification (as defined in paragraph (h)(3)(iv)(A) of this section) that is material either in kind or in extent and, therefore, results in a deemed exchange of the hedge and a realization event to the issuer under section 1001; or the issuer redeems all or a portion of the hedged bonds.

(C) *Special rules for certain modifications when the hedge remains qualified.*—A modification of a qualified hedge that otherwise would result in a deemed termination under paragraph (h)(3)(iv)(B) of this section does not result in such a termination if the modified hedge is re-tested for qualification as a qualified hedge as of the date of the modification, the modified hedge meets the requirements for a qualified hedge as of such date, and the modified hedge is treated as a qualified hedge prospectively in determining the yield on the hedged bonds. For purposes of this paragraph (h)(3)(iv)(C), when determining whether the modified hedge is qualified, the fact that the existing qualified hedge is off-market as of the date of the modification is disregarded and the identification requirement in paragraph (h)(2)(viii) of this section applies by measuring the time period for identification from the date of the modification and without regard to the requirement for a hedge provider's certification.

(D) *Continuations of certain qualified hedges in refundings.*—If hedged bonds are redeemed using proceeds of a refunding issue, the qualified hedge for the refunded bonds is not actually terminated, and the hedge meets the requirements for a qualified hedge for the refunding bonds as of the issue date of the refunding bonds, then no termination of the hedge occurs and the hedge instead is treated as a qualified hedge for the refunding bonds. For purposes of this paragraph (h)(3)(iv)(D), when determining whether the hedge is a qualified hedge for the refunding bonds, the fact that the hedge is off-market with respect to the refunding bonds as of the issue date of the refunding bonds is disregarded and the identification requirement in paragraph (h)(2)(viii) of this section applies by measuring the time period for identification from the issue date of the refunding bonds and without regard to the requirement for a hedge provider's certification.

(E) *General allocation rules for hedge termination payments.*— Except as otherwise provided in paragraphs (h)(3)(iv)(F), (G), and (H) of this section, a payment made or received by an issuer to terminate a qualified hedge, or a payment deemed made or received for a deemed termination, is treated as a payment made or received, as appropriate, on the hedged bonds. Upon an actual termination or a deemed termination of a qualified hedge, the amount that an issuer may treat as a termination payment made or received on the hedged bonds is the fair market value of the qualified hedge on its termination date, based on all of the facts and circumstances. Except as otherwise provided, a termination payment is reasonably allocated to the remaining periods originally covered by the terminated hedge in a manner that reflects the economic substance of the hedge.

(F) *Special rule for terminations when bonds are redeemed.*— Except as otherwise provided in this paragraph (h)(3)(iv)(F) and in paragraph (h)(3)(iv)(G) of this section, when a qualified hedge is deemed terminated because the hedged bonds are redeemed, the termination payment as determined under paragraph (h)(3)(iv)(E) of this section is treated as made or received on that date. When hedged bonds are redeemed, any payment received by the issuer on termination of a hedge, including a termination payment or a deemed termination payment, reduces, but not below zero, the interest payments made by the issuer on the hedged bonds in the computation period ending on the termination date. The remainder of the payment, if any, is reasonably allocated over the bond years in the immediately preceding computation period or periods to the extent necessary to eliminate the excess.

(G) *Special rules for refundings.*—When there is a termination of a qualified hedge because there is a refunding of the hedged bonds, to the extent that the hedged bonds are redeemed using the proceeds of a refunding issue, the termination payment is accounted for under paragraph (h)(3)(iv)(E) of this section by treating it as a payment on the refunding issue, rather than the hedged bonds. In addition, to the extent that the refunding issue is redeemed during the period to which the termination payment has been allocated to that issue, paragraph (h)(3)(iv)(F) of this section applies to the termination payment by treating it as a payment on the redeemed refunding issue.

(H) *Safe harbor for allocation of certain termination payments.*— A payment to terminate a qualified hedge does not result in that hedge failing to satisfy the applicable provisions of paragraph (h)(3)(iv)(E) of this section if that payment is allocated in accordance with this paragraph (h)(3)(iv)(H). For an issue that is a variable yield issue after termination of a qualified hedge, an amount must be allocated to each date on which the hedge provider's payment, if any, would have been made had the hedge not been terminated. The amounts allocated to each date must bear the same ratio to the notional principal amount (within the meaning of §1.446-3) that would have been used to compute the hedge provider's payment, if any, on that date, and the sum of the present values of those amounts must equal the present value of the termination payment. Present value is computed as of the day the qualified hedge is terminated, using the yield on the hedged bonds, determined without regard to

the termination payment. The yield used for this purpose is computed for the period beginning on the first date the qualified hedge is in effect and ending on the date the qualified hedge is terminated. On the other hand, for an issue that is a fixed yield issue after termination of a qualified hedge, the termination payment is taken into account as a single payment on the date it is paid.

(4) *Certain variable yield bonds treated as fixed yield bonds.*—(i) *In general.*—Except as otherwise provided in this paragraph (h)(4), if the issuer of variable yield bonds enters into a qualified hedge, the hedged bonds are treated as fixed yield bonds paying a fixed interest rate if:

(A) *Maturity.*—The term of the hedge is equal to the entire period during which the hedged bonds bear interest at variable interest rates, and the issuer does not reasonably expect that the hedge will be terminated before the end of that period.

(B) *Payments closely correspond.*—Payments to be received under the hedge correspond closely in time to the hedged portion of payments on the hedged bonds. Hedge payments received within 15 days of the related payments on the hedged bonds generally so correspond.

(C) *Aggregate payments fixed.*—Taking into account all payments made and received under the hedge and all payments on the hedged bonds (i.e., after netting all payments), the issuer's aggregate payments are fixed and determinable as of a date not later than 15 days after the issue date of the hedged bonds. Payments on bonds are treated as fixed for purposes of this paragraph (h)(4)(i)(C) if payments on the bonds are based, in whole or in part, on one interest rate, payments on the hedge are based, in whole or in part, on a second interest rate that is substantially the same as, but not identical to, the first interest rate and payments on the bonds would be fixed if the two rates were identical. Rates are treated as substantially the same if they are reasonably expected to be substantially the same throughout the term of the hedge. For example, an objective 30-day tax-exempt variable rate index or other objective index may be substantially the same as an issuer's individual 30-day interest rate. A hedge based on a taxable interest rate or taxable interest index cannot meet the requirements of this paragraph (h)(4)(i)(C) unless either—

(1) The hedge is an anticipatory hedge that is terminated or otherwise closed substantially contemporaneously with the issuance of the hedged bond in accordance with paragraph (h)(5)(ii) or (iii) of this section; or

(2) The issuer's payments on the hedged bonds and the hedge provider's payments on the hedge are based on identical interest rates.

(ii) *Accounting.*—Except as otherwise provided in this paragraph (h)(4)(ii), in determining yield on the hedged bonds, all the issuer's payments on the hedged bonds and all payments made and received on a hedge described in paragraph (h)(4)(i) of this section are taken into account. If payments on the bonds and payments on the hedge are based, in whole or in part, on variable interest rates that are substantially the same within the meaning of paragraph (h)(4)(i)(C) of this section (but not identical), yield on the issue is determined by treating the variable interest rates as identical. For example, if variable rate bonds bearing interest at a weekly rate equal to the rate necessary to remarket the bonds at par are hedged with an interest rate swap under which the issuer receives payments based on a short-term floating rate index that is substantially the same as, but not identical to, the weekly rate on the bonds, the interest payments on the bonds are treated as equal to the payments received by the issuer under the swap for purposes of computing the yield on the bonds.

(iii) *Effect of termination.*—(A) *In general.*—Except as otherwise provided in this paragraph (h)(4)(iii) and paragraph (h)(5) of this section, the issue of which the hedged bonds are a part is treated as if it were reissued as of the termination date of the qualified hedge covered by paragraph (h)(4)(i) of this section in determining yield on the hedged bonds for purposes of §1.148-3. The redemption price of the retired issue and the issue price of the new issue equal the aggregate values of all the bonds of the issue on the termination date. In computing the yield on the new issue for this purpose, any termination payment is accounted for under paragraph (h)(3)(iv) of this section, applied by treating the termination payment as made or received on the new issue under this paragraph (h)(4)(iii).

(B) *Effect of early termination.*—Except as otherwise provided in this paragraph (h)(4)(iii), the general rules of paragraph (h)(4)(i) of this section do not apply in determining the yield on the hedged bonds for purposes of §1.148-3 if the hedge is terminated or deemed terminated within 5 years after the issue date of the issue of which the hedged bonds are a part. Thus, the hedged bonds are treated as variable/yield bonds for purposes of §1.148-3 from the issue date.

(C) *Certain terminations disregarded.*—This paragraph (h)(4)(iii) does not apply to a termination if, based on the facts and circumstances (e.g., taking into account both the termination and any qualified hedge that immediately replaces the terminated hedge), there is no change in the yield.

(iv) *Consequences of certain modifications.*—The special rules under paragraph (h)(4)(iii) of this section regarding the effects of termination of a qualified hedge of fixed yield hedged bonds apply to a modification described in paragraph (h)(3)(iv)(C) of this section. Thus, such a modification is treated as a termination for purposes of paragraph (h)(4)(iii) of this section unless the rule in paragraph (h)(4)(iii)(C) applies.

(5) *Contracts entered into before issue date of hedged bond.*—(i) *In general.*—A contract does not fail to be a hedge under paragraph (h)(2)(i) of this section solely because it is entered into before the issue date of the hedged bond. However, that contract must be one to which either paragraph (h)(5)(ii) or (h)(5)(iii) of this section applies.

(ii) *Contracts expected to be closed substantially contemporaneously with the issue date of hedged bond.*—(A) *Application.*—This paragraph (h)(5)(ii) applies to a contract if, on the date the contract is identified, the issuer reasonably expects to terminate or otherwise close (terminate) the contract substantially contemporaneously with the issue date of the hedged bond.

(B) *Contract terminated.*—If a contract to which this paragraph (h)(5)(ii) applies is terminated substantially contemporaneously with the issue date of the hedged bond, the amount paid or received, or deemed to be paid or received, by the issuer in connection with the issuance of the hedged bond to terminate the contract is treated as an adjustment to the issue price of the hedged bond and as an adjustment to the sale proceeds of the hedged bond for purposes of section 148. Amounts paid or received, or deemed to be paid or received, before the issue date of the hedged bond are treated as paid or received on the issue date in an amount equal to the future value of the payment or receipt on that date. For this purpose, future value is computed using yield on the hedged bond without taking into account amounts paid or received (or deemed paid or received) on the contract.

(C) *Contract not terminated.*—If a contract to which this paragraph (h)(5)(ii) applies is not terminated substantially contemporaneously with the issue date of the hedged bond, the contract is deemed terminated for its fair market value as of the issue date of the hedged bond. Once a contract has been deemed terminated pursuant to this paragraph (h)(5)(ii)(C), payments on and receipts from the contract are no longer taken into account under this paragraph (h) for purposes of determining yield on the hedged bond.

(D) *Relation to other requirements of a qualified hedge.*—Payments made in connection with the issuance of a bond to terminate a contract to which this paragraph (h)(5)(ii) applies do not prevent the contract from satisfying the requirements of paragraph (h)(2)(vi) of this section.

(E) *Fixed yield treatment.*—A bond that is hedged with a contract to which this paragraph (h)(5)(ii) applies does not fail to be a fixed yield bond if, taking into account payments on the contract and the payments to be made on the bond, the bond satisfies the definition of fixed yield bond. See also paragraph (h)(4) of this section.

(iii) *Contracts expected not to be closed substantially contemporaneously with the issue date of hedged bond.*—(A) *Application.*—This paragraph (h)(5)(iii) applies to a contract if, on the date the contract is identified, the issuer does not reasonably expect to terminate the contract substantially contemporaneously with the issue date of the hedge bond.

(B) *Contract terminated.*—If a contract to which this paragraph (h)(5)(iii) applies is terminated in connection with the issuance of the hedged bond, the amount paid or received, or deemed to be paid or received, by the issuer to terminate the contract is treated as an adjustment to the issue price of the hedged bond and as an adjustment to the sale proceeds of the hedged bond for purposes of section 148.

(C) *Contract not terminated.*—If a contract to which this paragraph (h)(5)(iii) applies is not terminated substantially contemporaneously with the issue date of the hedged bond, no payments with respect to the hedge made by the issuer before the issue date of the hedged bond are taken into account under this section.

(iv) *Identification.*—The identification required under paragraph (h)(2)(viii) of this section must specify the reasonably expected governmental purpose, issue price, maturity, and issue date of the hedged bond, the manner in which interest is reasonably expected to be computed, and whether paragraph (h)(5)(ii) or (h)(5)(iii) of this

section applies to the contract. If an issuer identifies a contract under this paragraph (h)(5)(iv) that would be a qualified hedge with respect to the anticipated bond, but does not issue the anticipated bond on the identified issue date, the contract is taken into account as a qualified hedge of any bond of the issuer that is issued for the identified governmental purpose within a reasonable interval around the identified issue date of the anticipated bond.

(6) *Authority of the Commissioner.*—The Commissioner, by publication of a revenue ruling or revenue procedure (see § 601.601(d)(2) of this chapter), may specify contracts that, although they do not meet the requirements of paragraph (h)(2) of this section, are qualified hedges or, although they do not meet the requirements of paragraph (h)(4) of this section, cause the hedged bonds to be treated as fixed yield bonds. [Reg. § 1.148-4.]

☐ [T.D. 8418, 5-12-92. *Amended by T.D. 8476, 6-14-93; T.D. 8538, 5-5-94; T.D. 8718, 5-8-97, T.D. 8838, 9-3-99 and T.D. 9777, 7-15-2016 (corrected 4-2-2018).*]

[Reg. § 1.148-4A]

§ 1.148-4A. [Reserved].

☐ [T.D. 8538, 5-5-94. *Redesignated and amended by T.D. 8718, 5-8-97. Removed and reserved by T.D. 9849, 3-11-2019.*]

[Reg. § 1.148-5]

§ 1.148-5. Yield and valuation of investments.—(a) *In general.*—This section provides rules for computing the yield and value of investments allocated to an issue for various purposes under section 148.

(b) *Yield on an investment.*—(1) *In general.*—Except as otherwise provided, the yield on an investment allocated to an issue is computed under the economic accrual method, using the same compounding interval and financial conventions used to compute the yield on the issue. The yield on an investment allocated to an issue is the discount rate that, when used in computing the present value as of the date the investment is first allocated to the issue of all unconditionally payable receipts from the investment, produces an amount equal to the present value of all unconditionally payable payments for the investment. For this purpose, *payments* means amounts to be actually or constructively paid to acquire the investment, and *receipts* means amounts to be actually or constructively received from the investment, such as earnings and return of principal. The yield on a variable rate investment is determined in a manner comparable to the determination of the yield on a variable rate issue. For an issue of qualified mortgage bonds, qualified veterans' mortgage bonds, or qualified student loan bonds on which interest is paid semiannually, all regular monthly loan payments to be received during a semiannual debt service period may be treated as received at the end of that period. In addition, for any conduit financing issue, payments made by the conduit borrower are not treated as paid until the conduit borrower ceases to receive the benefit of earnings on those amounts.

(2) *Yield on a separate class of investments.*—(i) *In general.*—For purposes of the yield restriction rules of section 148(a) and § 1.148-2, yield is computed separately for each class of investments. For this purpose, in determining the yield on a separate class of investments, the yield on each individual investment within the class is blended with the yield on other individual investments within the class, whether or not held concurrently, by treating those investments as a single investment. The yields on investments that are not within the same class are not blended.

(ii) *Separate classes of investments.*—Each of the following is a separate class of investments—

(A) Each category of yield restricted purpose investment and program investment that is subject to a different definition of *materially higher* under § 1.148-2(d)(2);

(B) Yield-restricted nonpurpose investments; and

(C) All other nonpurpose investments;

(iii) *Permissive application of single investment rules to certain yield restricted investments for all purposes of section 148.*—For all purposes of section 148, if an issuer reasonably expects as of the issue date to establish and maintain a sinking fund solely to reduce the yield on the investments in a refunding escrow, then the issuer may treat all of the yield restricted nonpurpose investments in the refunding escrow and that sinking fund as a single investment having a single yield, determined under this paragraph (b)(2). Thus, an issuer may not treat the nonpurpose investments in a reasonably required reserve fund and a refunding escrow as a single investment having a single yield under this paragraph (b)(2)(iii).

(iv) *Mandatory application of single investment rules for refunding escrows for all purposes of section 148.*—For all purposes of section 148, in computing the yield on yield restricted investments allocable to proceeds (i.e., sale proceeds, investment proceeds, and transferred proceeds) of a refunding issue that are held in one or more refunding escrows, the individual investments are treated as a single investment having a single yield, whether or not held concurrently. For example, this single investment includes both the individual investments allocable to sale and investment proceeds of a refunding issue that are held in one refunding escrow for a prior issue and the investments allocable to transferred proceeds of that refunding issue that are held in another refunding escrow.

(3) *Investments to be held beyond issue's maturity or beyond temporary period.*—In computing the yield on investments allocable to an issue that are to be held beyond the reasonably expected redemption date of the issue, those investments are treated as sold for an amount equal to their value on that date. In computing the yield on investments that are held beyond an applicable temporary period under §1.148-2, for purposes of §1.148-2 those investments may be treated as purchased for an amount equal to their fair market value as of the end of the temporary period.

(4) *Consistent redemption assumptions on purpose investments.*—The yield on purpose investments allocable to an issue is computed using the same redemption assumptions used to compute the yield on the issue. Yield on purpose investments allocable to an issue of qualified mortgage bonds and qualified veterans' mortgage bonds must be determined in a manner that is consistent with, and using the assumptions required by, section 143(g)(2)(B).

(5) *Student loan special allowance payments included in yield.*—Except as provided in §1.148-11(e), the yield on qualified student loans is computed by including as receipts any special allowance payments made by the Secretary of Education pursuant to section 438 of the Higher Education Act of 1965.

(c) *Yield reduction payments to the United States.*—(1) *In general.*—In determining the yield on an investment to which this paragraph (c) applies, any amount paid to the United States in accordance with this paragraph (c), including a rebate amount, is treated as a payment for that investment that reduces the yield on that investment.

(2) *Manner of payment.*—(i) *In general.*—Except as otherwise provided in paragraph (c)(2)(ii) of this section, an amount is paid under this paragraph (c) if it is paid to the United States at the same time and in the same manner as rebate amounts are required to be paid or at such other time or in such manner as the Commissioner may prescribe. For example, yield reduction payments must be made on or before the date of required rebate installment payments as described in §§1.148-3(f), (g), and (h). The provisions of §1.148-3(i) apply to payments made under this paragraph (c).

(ii) *Special rule for purpose investments.*—For purpose investments allocable to an issue—

(A) No amounts are required to be paid to satisfy this paragraph (c) until the earlier of the end of the tenth bond year after the issue date of the issue or 60 days after the date on which the issue is no longer outstanding; and

(B) For payments made prior to the date on which the issue is retired, the issuer need not pay more than 75 percent of the amount otherwise required to be paid as of the date to which the payment relates.

(3) *Applicability of special yield reduction rule.*—Paragraph (c) applies only to investments that are described in at least one of paragraphs (c)(3)(i) through (ix) of this section and, except as otherwise expressly provided in paragraphs (c)(3)(i) through (ix) of this section, that are allocated to proceeds of an issue other than gross proceeds of an advance refunding issue.

(i) *Nonpurpose investments allocated to proceeds of an issue that qualified for certain temporary periods.*—Nonpurpose investments allocable to proceeds of an issue that qualified for one of the temporary periods available for capital projects, working capital expenditures, pooled financings, or investment proceeds under §1.148-2(e)(2), (3), (4), or (6), respectively.

(ii) *Investments allocable to certain variable yield issues.*—Investments allocable to a variable yield issue during any computation period in which at least 5 percent of the value of the issue is represented by variable yield bonds, unless the issue is an issue of hedge bonds (as defined in section 149(g)(3)(A)).

(iii) *Nonpurpose investments allocable to certain transferred proceeds.*—Nonpurpose investments allocable to transferred proceeds of—

(A) A current refunding issue to the extent necessary to reduce the yield on those investments to satisfy yield restrictions under section 148(a); or

(B) An advance refunding issue to the extent that investment of the refunding escrows allocable to the proceeds, other than transferred proceeds, of the refunding issue in zero-yielding nonpurpose investments is insufficient to satisfy yield restrictions under section 148(a).

(iv) *Purpose investments allocable to qualified student loans and qualified mortgage loans.*—Purpose investments allocable to qualified student loans and qualified mortgage loans.

(v) *Nonpurpose investments allocable to gross proceeds in certain reserve funds.*—Nonpurpose investments allocable to gross proceeds of an issue in a reasonably required reserve or replacement fund or a fund that, except for its failure to satisfy the size limitation in §1.148-2(f)(2)(ii), would qualify as a reasonably required reserve or replacement fund, but only to the extent the requirements in paragraphs (c)(3)(v)(A) or (B) of this section are met. This paragraph (c)(3)(v) includes nonpurpose investments described in this paragraph that are allocable to transferred proceeds of an advance refunding issue, but only to the extent necessary to satisfy yield restriction under section 148(a) on those proceeds treating all investments allocable to those proceeds as a separate class.

(A) The value of the nonpurpose investments in the fund is not greater than 15 percent of the stated principal amount of the issue, as computed under §1.148-2(f)(2)(ii).

(B) The amounts in the fund (other than investment earnings) are not reasonably expected to be used to pay debt service on the issue other than in connection with reductions in the amount required to be in that fund (for example, a reserve fund for a revolving fund loan program).

(vi) *Nonpurpose investments allocable to certain replacement proceeds of refunded issues.*—Nonpurpose investments allocated to replacement proceeds of a refunded issue, including a refunded issue that is an advance refunding issue, as a result of the application of the universal cap to amounts in a refunding escrow.

(vii) *Investments allocable to replacement proceeds under a certain transition rule.*—Investments described in §1.148-11(f).

(viii) *Nonpurpose investments allocable to proceeds when State and Local Government Series Securities are unavailable.*—Nonpurpose investments allocable to proceeds of an issue, including an advance refunding issue, that an issuer purchases if, on the date the issuer enters into the agreement to purchase such investments, the issuer is unable to subscribe for State and Local Government Series Securities because the U.S. Department of the Treasury, Bureau of the Fiscal Service, has suspended sales of those securities.

(ix) *Nonpurpose investments allocable to proceeds of certain variable yield advance refunding issues.*—Nonpurpose investments allocable to proceeds of the portion of a variable yield issue used for advance refunding purposes that are deposited in a yield restricted defeasance escrow if—

(A) The issuer has entered into a qualified hedge under §1.148-4(h)(2) with respect to all of the variable yield bonds of the issue allocable to the yield restricted defeasance escrow and that hedge is in the form of a variable-to-fixed interest rate swap under which the issuer pays the hedge provider a fixed interest rate and receives from the hedge provider a floating interest rate;

(B) Such qualified hedge covers a period beginning on the issue date of the hedged bonds and ending on or after the date on which the final payment is to be made from the yield restricted defeasance escrow; and

(C) The issuer restricts the yield on the yield restricted defeasance escrow to a yield that is not greater than the yield on the issue, determined by taking into account the issuer's fixed payments to be made under the hedge and by assuming that the issuer's variable yield payments to be paid on the hedged bonds are equal to the floating payments to be received by the issuer under the qualified hedge and are paid on the same dates (that is, such yield reduction payments can only be made to address basis risk differences between the variable yield payments on the hedged bonds and the floating payments received on the hedge).

(d) *Value of investments.*—(1) *In general.*—Except as otherwise provided, the value of an investment (including a payment or receipt on the investment) on a date must be determined using one of the following valuation methods consistently for all purposes of section 148 to that investment on that date:

(i) *Plain par investment—outstanding principal amount.*—A plain par investment may be valued at its outstanding stated principal amount, plus any accrued unpaid interest on that date.

(ii) *Fixed rate investment—present value.*—A fixed rate investment may be valued at its present value on that date.

(iii) *Any investment—fair market value.*—An investment may be valued at its fair market value on that date.

(2) *Mandatory valuation of certain yield restricted investments at present value.*—A purpose investment must be valued at present value, and except as otherwise provided in paragraphs (b)(3) and (d)(3) of this section, a yield restricted nonpurpose investment must be valued at present value.

(3) *Mandatory valuation of certain investments at fair market value.*—(i) *In general.*—Except as otherwise provided in paragraphs (d)(3)(ii) and (d)(4) of this section, a nonpurpose investment must be valued at fair market value on the date that it is first allocated to an issue or first ceases to be allocated to an issue as a consequence of a deemed acquisition or deemed disposition. For example, if an issuer deposits existing nonpurpose investments into a sinking fund for an issue, those investments must be valued at fair market value as of the date first deposited into the fund.

(ii) *Exception to fair market value requirement for transferred proceeds allocations, certain universal cap allocations, and commingled funds.*—Paragraph (d)(3)(i) of this section does not apply if the investment is allocated from one issue to another as a result of the transferred proceeds allocation rule under §1.148-9(b) or is deallocated from one issue as a result of the universal cap rule under §1.148-6(b)(2) and reallocated to another issue as a result of a preexisting pledge of the investment to secure that other issue, provided that, in either circumstance (that is, transferred proceeds allocations or universal cap deallocations), the issue from which the investment is allocated (that is, the first issue in an allocation from one issue to another issue) consists of tax-exempt bonds. In addition, paragraph (d)(3)(i) of this section does not apply to investments in a commingled fund (other than a bona fide debt service fund) unless it is an investment being initially deposited in or withdrawn from a commingled fund described in §1.148-6(e)(5)(iii).

(4) *Special transition rule for transferred proceeds.*—The value of a nonpurpose investment that is allocated to transferred proceeds of a refunding issue on a transfer date may not exceed the value of that investment on the transfer date used for purposes of applying the arbitrage restrictions to the refunded issue.

(5) *Definition of present value of an investment.*—Except as otherwise provided, present value of an investment is computed under the economic accrual method, using the same compounding interval and financial conventions used to compute the yield on the issue. The present value of an investment on a date is equal to the present value of all unconditionally payable receipts to be received from and payments to be paid for the investment after that date, using the yield on the investment as the discount rate.

(6) *Definition of fair market value.*—(i) *In general.*—The fair market value of an investment is the price at which a willing buyer would purchase the investment from a willing seller in a bona fide, arm's-length transaction. Fair market value generally is determined on the date on which a contract to purchase or sell the nonpurpose investment becomes binding (i.e., the trade date rather than the settlement date). On the purchase date, the fair market value of a United States Treasury obligation that is purchased directly from the United States Treasury, including a State and Local Government Series Security, is its purchase price. The fair market value of a State and Local Government Series Security on any date other than the purchase date is the redemption price for redemption on that date.

(ii) *Safe harbor for establishing fair market value for certificates of deposit.*—This paragraph (d)(6)(ii) applies to a certificate of deposit that has a fixed interest rate, a fixed payment schedule, and a substantial penalty for early withdrawal. The purchase price of such a certificate of deposit is treated as its fair market value on the purchase date if the yield on the certificate of deposit is not less than—

(A) The yield on reasonably comparable direct obligations of the United States; and

(B) The highest yield that is published or posted by the provider to be currently available from the provider on reasonably comparable certificates of deposit offered to the public.

(iii) *Safe harbor for establishing fair market value for guaranteed investment contracts and investments purchased for a yield restricted defeasance escrow.*—The purchase price of a guaranteed investment contract and the purchase price of an investment purchased for a yield restricted defeasance escrow will be treated as the fair market value of the investment on the purchase date if all of the following requirements are satisfied:

(A) The issuer makes a bona fide solicitation for the purchase of the investment. A bona fide solicitation is a solicitation that satisfies all of the following requirements:

(1) The bid specifications are in writing and are timely disseminated to potential providers. For purposes of this paragraph (d)(6)(iii)(A)(1), a writing may be in electronic form and may be disseminated by fax, email, an internet-based website, or other electronic medium that is similar to an internet-based website and regularly used to post bid specifications.

(2) The bid specifications include all material terms of the bid. A term is material if it may directly or indirectly affect the yield or the cost of the investment.

(3) The bid specifications include a statement notifying potential providers that submission of a bid is a representation that the potential provider did not consult with any other potential provider about its bid, that the bid was determined without regard to any other formal or informal agreement that the potential provider has with the issuer or any other person (whether or not in connection with the bond issue), and that the bid is not being submitted solely as a courtesy to the issuer or any other person for purposes of satisfying the requirements of paragraph (d)(6)(iii)(B)(1) or (2) of this section.

(4) The terms of the bid specifications are commercially reasonable. A term is commercially reasonable if there is a legitimate business purpose for the term other than to increase the purchase price or reduce the yield of the investment. For example, for solicitations of investments for a yield restricted defeasance escrow, the hold firm period must be no longer than the issuer reasonably requires.

(5) For purchases of guaranteed investment contracts only, the terms of the solicitation take into account the issuer's reasonably expected deposit and drawdown schedule for the amounts to be invested.

(6) All potential providers have an equal opportunity to bid. If the bidding process affords any opportunity for a potential provider to review other bids before providing a bid, then providers have an equal opportunity to bid only if all potential providers have an equal opportunity to review other bids. Thus, no potential provider may be given an opportunity to review other bids that is not equally given to all potential providers (that is, no exclusive "last look").

(7) At least three reasonably competitive providers are solicited for bids. A reasonably competitive provider is a provider that has an established industry reputation as a competitive provider of the type of investments being purchased.

(B) The bids received by the issuer meet all of the following requirements:

(1) The issuer receives at least three bids from providers that the issuer solicited under a bona fide solicitation meeting the requirements of paragraph (d)(6)(iii)(A) of this section and that do not have a material financial interest in the issue. A lead underwriter in a negotiated underwriting transaction is deemed to have a material financial interest in the issue until 15 days after the issue date of the issue. In addition, any entity acting as a financial advisor with respect to the purchase of the investment at the time the bid specifications are forwarded to potential providers has a material financial interest in the issue. A provider that is a related party to a provider that has a material financial interest in the issue is deemed to have a material financial interest in the issue.

(2) At least one of the three bids described in paragraph (d)(6)(iii)(B)(1) of this section is from a reasonably competitive provider, within the meaning of paragraph (d)(6)(iii)(A)(7) of this section.

(3) If the issuer uses an agent to conduct the bidding process, the agent did not bid to provide the investment.

(C) The winning bid meets the following requirements:

(1) *Guaranteed investment contracts.*—If the investment is a guaranteed investment contract, the winning bid is the highest yielding bona fide bid (determined net of any broker's fees).

(2) *Other investments.*—If the investment is not a guaranteed investment contract, the following requirements are met:

(i) The winning bid is the lowest cost bona fide bid (including any broker's fees). The lowest cost bid is either the lowest cost bid for the portfolio or, if the issuer compares the bids on an investment-by-investment basis, the aggregate cost of a portfolio comprised of the lowest cost bid for each investment. Any payment received by the issuer from a provider at the time a guaranteed investment contract is purchased (e.g., an escrow float contract) for a yield restricted defeasance escrow under a bidding procedure meeting the requirements of this paragraph (d)(6)(iii) is taken into account in determining the lowest cost bid.

(ii) The lowest cost bona fide bid (including any broker's fees) is not greater than the cost of the most efficient portfolio comprised exclusively of State and Local Government Series Securities from the United States Department of the Treasury, Bureau of Public Debt. The cost of the most efficient portfolio of State and Local Government Series Securities is to be determined at the time that bids are required to be submitted pursuant to the terms of the bid specifications.

(iii) If State and Local Government Series Securities from the United States Department of the Treasury, Bureau of Public Debt are not available for purchase on the day that bids are required to be submitted pursuant to terms of the bid specifications because sales of those securities have been suspended, the cost comparison of paragraph (d)(6)(iii) (C)(2)(ii) of this section is not required.

(D) The provider of the investments or the obligor on the guaranteed investment contract certifies the administrative costs that it pays (or expects to pay, if any) to third parties in connection with supplying the investment.

(E) The issuer retains the following records with the bond documents until three years after the last outstanding bond is redeemed:

(1) For purchases of guaranteed investment contracts, a copy of the contract, and for purchases of investments other than guaranteed investment contracts, the purchase agreement or confirmation.

(2) The receipt or other record of the amount actually paid by the issuer for the investments, including a record of any administrative costs paid by the issuer, and the certification under paragraph (d)(6)(iii)(D) of this section.

(3) For each bid that is submitted, the name of the person and entity submitting the bid, the time and date of the bid, and the bid results.

(4) The bid solicitation form and, if the terms of the purchase agreement or the guaranteed investment contract deviated from the bid solicitation form or a submitted bid is modified, a brief statement explaining the deviation and stating the purpose for the deviation. For example, if the issuer purchases a portfolio of investments for a yield restricted defeasance escrow and, in order to satisfy the yield restriction requirements of section 148, an investment in the winning bid is replaced with an investment with a lower yield, the issuer must retain a record of the substitution and how the price of the substitute investment was determined. If the issuer replaces an investment in the winning bid portfolio with another investment, the purchase price of the new investment is not covered by the safe harbor unless the investment is bid under a bidding procedure meeting the requirements of this paragraph (d)(6)(iii).

(5) For purchases of investments other than guaranteed investment contracts, the cost of the most efficient portfolio of State and Local Government Series Securities, determined at the time that the bids were required to be submitted pursuant to the terms of the bid specifications.

(e) Administrative costs of investments.—(1) *In general.*—Except as otherwise provided in this paragraph (e), an allocation of gross proceeds of an issue to a payment or a receipt on an investment is not adjusted to take into account any costs or expenses paid, directly or indirectly, to purchase, carry, sell, or retire the investment (*administrative costs*). Thus, these administrative costs generally do not increase the payments for, or reduce the receipts from, investments.

(2) Qualified administrative costs on nonpurpose investments.—(i) *In general.*—In determining payments and receipts on nonpurpose investments, qualified administrative costs are taken into account. Thus, qualified administrative costs increase the payments for, or decrease the receipts from, the investments. Qualified administrative costs are reasonable, direct administrative costs, other than carrying costs, such as separately stated brokerage or selling commissions, but not legal and accounting fees, recordkeeping, custody, and similar costs. General overhead costs and similar indirect costs of the issuer such as employee salaries and office expenses and costs associated with computing the rebate amount under section 148(f) are not qualified administrative costs. In general, administrative costs are not reasonable unless they are comparable to administrative costs that would be charged for the same investment or a reasonably comparable investment if acquired with a source of funds other than gross proceeds of tax-exempt bonds.

(ii) Special rule for administrative costs of nonpurpose investments in certain regulated investment companies and commingled funds.—Qualified administrative costs include all reasonable administrative costs, without regard to the limitation on indirect costs under paragraph (e)(2)(i) of this section, incurred by:

(A) Regulated investment companies.—A publicly offered regulated investment company (as defined in section 67(c)(2)(B)); and

(B) External commingled funds.—A widely held commingled fund in which no investor in the fund owns more than 10 percent of the beneficial interest in the fund. For purposes of this paragraph (e)(2)(ii)(B), a fund is treated as widely held only if, during the immediately preceding fixed, semiannual period chosen by the fund (for example, semiannual periods ending June 30 and December 31),

the fund had a daily average of more than 15 investors that were not related parties, and at least 16 of the unrelated investors each maintained a daily average amount invested in the fund that was not less than the lesser of $500,000 and one percent (1%) of the daily average of the total amount invested in the fund (with it being understood that additional smaller investors will not disqualify the fund). For purposes of this paragraph (e)(2)(ii)(B), an investor will be treated as owning not more than 10 percent of the beneficial interest in the fund if, on the date of each deposit by the investor into the fund, the total amount the investor and any related parties have on deposit in the fund is not more than 10 percent of the total amount that all investors have on deposit in the fund. For purposes of the preceding sentence, the total amount that all investors have on deposit in the fund is equal to the sum of all deposits made by the investor and any related parties on the date of those deposits and the closing balance in the fund on the day before those deposits. If any investor in the fund owns more than 10 percent of the beneficial interest in the fund, the fund does not qualify under this paragraph (e)(2)(ii)(B) until that investor makes sufficient withdrawals from the fund to reduce its beneficial interest in the fund to 10 percent or less.

(iii) Special rule for guaranteed investment contracts and investments purchased for a yield restricted defeasance escrow.—(A) *In general.*—An amount paid for a broker's commission or similar fee with respect to a guaranteed investment contract or investments purchased for a yield restricted defeasance escrow is a qualified administrative cost if the fee is reasonable within the meaning of paragraph (e)(2)(i) of this section.

(B) Safe harbor.—(1) *In general.*—A broker's commission or similar fee with respect to the acquisition of a guaranteed investment contract or investments purchased for a yield restricted defeasance escrow is reasonable within the meaning of paragraph (e)(2)(i) of this section to the extent that—

(i) The amount of the fee that the issuer treats as a qualified administrative cost does not exceed the lesser of:

(A) $30,000 and

(B) 0.2% of the computational base or, if more, $3,000; and

(ii) For any issue, the issuer does not treat as qualified administrative costs more than $85,000 in brokers' commissions or similar fees with respect to all guaranteed investment contracts and investments for yield restricted defeasance escrows purchased with gross proceeds of the issue.

(2) Computational base.—For purposes of paragraph (e)(2)(iii)(B)(1) of this section, computational base shall mean—

(i) For a guaranteed investment contract, the amount of gross proceeds the issuer reasonably expects, as of the date the contract is acquired, to be deposited in the guaranteed investment contract over the term of the contract, and

(ii) For investments (other than guaranteed investment contracts) to be deposited in a yield restricted defeasance escrow, the amount of gross proceeds initially invested in those investments.

(3) Cost-of-living adjustment.—In the case of a calendar year after 2004, each of the dollar amounts in paragraph (e)(2)(iii)(B)(1) of this section shall be increased by an amount equal to—

(i) Such dollar amount; multiplied by

(ii) The cost-of-living adjustment determined under section 1(f)(3) for such calendar year by using the language "calendar year 2003" instead of "calendar year 1992" in section 1(f)(3)(B).

(4) Rounding.—If any increase determined under paragraph (e)(2)(iii)(B)(3) of this section is not a multiple of $1,000, such increase shall be rounded to the nearest multiple thereof.

(5) Applicable year for cost-of-living adjustment.—The cost-of-living adjustments under paragraph (e)(2)(iii)(B)(3) of this section shall apply to the safe harbor amounts under paragraph (e)(2)(iii)(B)(1) of this section based on the year the guaranteed investment contract or the investments for the yield restricted defeasance escrow, as applicable, are acquired.

(6) Cost-of-living adjustment to determine remaining amount of per-issue safe harbor.—(i) *In general.*—This paragraph (e)(2)(iii)(B)(6) applies to determine the portion of the safe harbor amount under paragraph (e)(2)(iii)(B)(1)(ii) of this section, as modified by paragraph (e)(2)(iii)(B)(3) of this section (the per-issue safe harbor), that is available (the remaining amount) for any year (the determination year) if the per-issue safe harbor was partially used in one or more prior years.

(ii) Remaining amount of per-issue safe harbor.—The remaining amount of the per-issue safe harbor for any determination

year is equal to the per-issue safe harbor for that year, reduced by the portion of the per-issue safe harbor used in one or more prior years.

(iii) Portion of per-issue safe harbor used in prior years.— The portion of the per-issue safe harbor used in any prior year (the prior year) is equal to the total amount of broker's commissions or similar fees paid in connection with guaranteed investment contracts or investments for a yield restricted defeasance escrow acquired in the prior year that the issuer treated as qualified administrative costs for the issue, multiplied by a fraction the numerator of which is the per-issue safe harbor for the determination year and the denominator of which is the per-issue safe harbor for the prior year. See paragraph (e)(2)(iii)(C) *Example 2* of this section.

(C) *Examples.*—The following examples illustrate the application of the safe harbor in paragraph (e)(2)(iii)(B) of this section:

Example 1. Multipurpose issue. In 2003, the issuer of a multipurpose issue uses brokers to acquire the following investments with gross proceeds of the issue: a guaranteed investment contract for amounts to be deposited in a construction fund (construction GIC), Treasury securities to be deposited in a yield restricted defeasance escrow (Treasury investments) and a guaranteed investment contract that will be used to earn a return on what otherwise would be idle cash balances from maturing investments in the yield restricted defeasance escrow (the float GIC). The issuer deposits $22,000,000 into the construction GIC and reasonably expects that no further deposits will be made over its term. The issuer uses $8,040,000 of the proceeds to purchase the Treasury investments. The issuer reasonably expects that it will make aggregate deposits of $600,000 to the float GIC over its term. The brokers' fees are $30,000 for the construction GIC, $16,080 for the Treasury investments and $3,000 for the float GIC. The issuer has not previously treated any brokers' commissions or similar fees as qualified administrative costs. The issuer may claim all $49,080 in brokers' fees for these investments as qualified administrative costs because the fees do not exceed the safe harbors in paragraph (e)(2)(iii)(B) of this section. Specifically, each of the brokers' fees equals the lesser of $30,000 and 0.2% of the computational base (or, if more, $3,000) (*i.e.*, lesser of $30,000 and 0.2% × $22,000,000 for the construction GIC; lesser of $30,000 and 0.2% × $8,040,000 for the Treasury investments; and lesser of $30,000 and $3,000 for the float GIC). In addition, the total amount of brokers' fees claimed by the issuer as qualified administrative costs ($49,080) does not exceed the per-issue safe harbor of $85,000.

Example 2. Cost-of-living adjustment. In 2003, an issuer issues bonds and uses gross proceeds of the issue to acquire two guaranteed investment contracts. The issuer pays a total of $50,000 in brokers' fees for the two guaranteed investment contracts and treats these fees as qualified administrative costs. In a year subsequent to 2003 (Year Y), the issuer uses gross proceeds of the issue to acquire two additional guaranteed investment contracts, paying a total of $20,000 in broker's fees for the two guaranteed investment contracts, and treats those fees as qualified administrative costs. For Year Y, applying the cost-of-living adjustment under paragraph (e)(2)(iii)(B)(3) of this section, the safe harbor dollar limits under paragraph (e)(2)(iii)(B)(1) of this section are $3,000, $32,000 and $90,000. The remaining amount of the per-issue safe harbor for Year Y is $37,059 ($90,000-[$50,000 × $90,000/$85,000]). The broker's fees in Year Y do not exceed the per-issue safe harbor under paragraph (e)(2)(iii)(B)(1)(ii) (as modified by paragraph (e)(2)(iii)(B)(3) of this section because the broker's fees do not exceed the remaining amount of the per-issue safe harbor determined under paragraph (e)(2)(iii)(B)(6) of this section for Year Y. In a year subsequent to Year Y (Year Z), the issuer uses gross proceeds of the issue to acquire an additional guaranteed investment contract, pays a broker's fee of $15,000 for the guaranteed investment contract, and treats the broker's fee as a qualified administrative cost. For Year Z, applying the cost-of-living adjustment under paragraph (e)(2)(iii)(B)(3) of this section, the safe harbor dollar limits under paragraph (e)(2)(iii)(B)(1) of this section are $3,000, $33,000 and $93,000. The remaining amount of the per-issue safe harbor for Year Z is $17,627 ($93,000 − [($50,000 × $93,000/$85,000) + ($20,000 × $93,000/$90,000)]). The broker's fee incurred in Year Z does not exceed the per-issue safe harbor under paragraph (e)(2)(iii)(B)(1)(ii) (as modified by paragraph (e)(2)(iii)(B)(3) of this section because the broker's fee does not exceed the remaining amount of the per-issue safe harbor determined under paragraph (e)(2)(iii)(B)(6) of this section for Year Z. See paragraph (e)(2)(iii)(B)(6) of this section.

(3) *Qualified administrative costs on purpose investments.*—(i) *In general.*—In determining payments and receipts on purpose investments, qualified administrative costs described in this paragraph (e)(3) paid by the conduit borrower are taken into account. Thus, these costs increase the payments for, or decrease the receipts from, the purpose investments. This rule applies even if those payments merely reimburse the issuer. Although the actual payments by the conduit borrower may be made at any time, for this purpose, a pro rata portion of each payment made by a conduit borrower is treated

as a reimbursement of reasonable administrative costs, if the present value of those payments does not exceed the present value of the reasonable administrative costs paid by the issuer, using the yield on the issue as the discount rate.

(ii) *Definition of qualified administrative costs of purpose investments.*—(A) *In general.*—Except as otherwise provided in this paragraph (e)(3)(ii), qualified administrative costs of a purpose investment means—

(1) Costs or expenses paid, directly or indirectly, to purchase, carry, sell, or retire the investment; and

(2) Costs of issuing, carrying, or repaying the issue, and any underwriters' discount.

(B) *Limitation on program investments.*—For a program investment, qualified administrative costs include only those costs described in paragraph (e)(3)(ii)(A)(2) of this section. [Reg. § 1.148-5.]

☐ [T.D. 8418, 5-12-92. *Amended by T.D.* 8476, 6-14-93; T.D. 8538, 5-5-94; T.D. 8718, 5-8-97; T.D. 8801, 12-29-98, T.D. 9097, 12-10-2003 *and T.D.* 9777, 7-15-2016.]

[Reg. § 1.148-5A]

§ 1.148-5A. [Reserved].

☐ [T.D. 8538, 5-5-94. *Redesignated and amended by T.D.* 8718, 5-8-97. *Removed and reserved by T.D.* 9849, 3-11-2019.]

[Reg. § 1.148-6]

§ 1.148-6. General allocation and accounting rules.—(a) *In general.*—(1) *Reasonable accounting methods required.*—An issuer may use any reasonable, consistently applied accounting method to account for gross proceeds, investments, and expenditures of an issue.

(2) *Bona fide deviations from accounting method.*—An accounting method does not fail to be reasonable and consistently applied solely because a different accounting method is used for a bona fide governmental purpose to consistently account for a particular item. Bona fide governmental purposes may include special state law restrictions imposed on specific funds or actions to avoid grant forfeitures.

(3) *Absence of allocation and accounting methods.*—If an issuer fails to maintain books and records sufficient to establish the accounting method for an issue and the allocation of the proceeds of that issue, the rules of this section are applied using the specific tracing method. This paragraph (a)(3) applies to bonds issued on or after May 16, 1997.

(b) *Allocation of gross proceeds to an issue.*—(1) *One-issue rule and general ordering rules.*—Except as otherwise provided, amounts are allocable to only one issue at a time as gross proceeds, and if amounts simultaneously are proceeds of one issue and replacement proceeds of another issue, those amounts are allocable to the issue of which they are proceeds. Amounts cease to be allocated to an issue as proceeds only when those amounts are allocated to an expenditure for a governmental purpose, are allocated to transferred proceeds of another issue, or cease to be allocated to that issue at retirement of the issue or under the universal cap of paragraph (b)(2) of this section. Amounts cease to be allocated to an issue as replacement proceeds only when those amounts are allocated to an expenditure for a governmental purpose, are no longer used in a manner that causes those amounts to be replacement proceeds of that issue, or cease to be allocated to that issue because of the retirement of the issue or the application of the universal cap under paragraph (b)(2) of this section. Amounts that cease to be allocated to an issue as gross proceeds are eligible for allocation to another issue. Under § 1.148-10(a), however, the rules in this paragraph (b)(1) do not apply in certain cases involving abusive arbitrage devices.

(2) *Universal cap on value of nonpurpose investments allocated to an issue.*—(i) *Application.*—The rules in this paragraph (b)(2) provide an overall limitation on the amount of gross proceeds allocable to an issue. Although the universal cap generally may be applied at any time in the manner described in this paragraph (b)(2), it need not be applied on any otherwise required date of application if its application on that date would not result in a reduction or reallocation of gross proceeds of an issue. For this purpose, if an issuer reasonably expects as of the issue date that the universal cap will not reduce the amount of gross proceeds allocable to the issue during the term of the issue, the universal cap need not be applied on any date on which an issue actually has all of the following characteristics—

(A) No replacement proceeds are allocable to the issue, other than replacement proceeds in a bona fide debt service fund or a reasonably required reserve or replacement fund;

(B) The net sale proceeds of the issue—

(1) Qualified for one of the temporary periods available for capital projects, restricted working capital expenditures, or

pooled financings under §1.148-2(e)(2), (e)(3), or (e)(4), and those net sales proceeds were in fact allocated to expenditures prior to the expiration of the longest applicable temporary period; or

(2) were deposited in a refunding escrow and expended as originally expected;

(C) The issue does not refund a prior issue that, on any transfer date, has unspent proceeds allocable to it;

(D) None of the bonds are retired prior to the date on which those bonds are treated as retired in computing the yield on the issue; and

(E) No proceeds of the issue are invested in qualified student loans or qualified mortgage loans.

(ii) *General rule.*—Except as otherwise provided below, amounts that would otherwise be gross proceeds allocable to an issue are allocated (and remain allocated) to the issue only to the extent that the value of the nonpurpose investments allocable to those gross proceeds does not exceed the value of all outstanding bonds of the issue. For this purpose, gross proceeds allocable to cash, tax-exempt bonds that would be nonpurpose investments (absent section 148(b)(3)(A)), qualified student loans, and qualified mortgage loans are treated as nonpurpose investments. The values of bonds and investments are determined under §1.148-4(e) and §1.148-5(d), respectively. The value of all outstanding bonds of the issue is referred to as the *universal cap.* Thus, for example, the universal cap for an issue of plain par bonds is equal to the outstanding stated principal amount of those bonds plus accrued interest.

(iii) *Determination and application of the universal cap.*—Except as otherwise provided, beginning with the first bond year that commences after the second anniversary of the issue date, the amount of the universal cap and the value of the nonpurpose investments must be determined as of the first day of each bond year. For refunding and refunded issues, the cap and values must be determined as of each date that, but for this paragraph (b)(2), proceeds of the refunded issue would become transferred proceeds of the refunding issue, and need not otherwise be determined in the bond year in which that date occurs. All values are determined as of the close of business on each determination date, after giving effect to all payments on bonds and payments for and receipts on investments on that date.

(iv) *General ordering rule for allocations of amounts in excess of the universal cap.*—(A) *In general.*—If the value of all nonpurpose investments allocated to the gross proceeds of an issue exceeds the universal cap for that issue on a date as of which the cap is determined under paragraph (b)(2)(iii) of this section, nonpurpose investments allocable to gross proceeds necessary to eliminate that excess cease to be allocated to the issue, in the following order of priority—

(1) First, nonpurpose investments allocable to replacement proceeds;

(2) Second, nonpurpose investments allocable to transferred proceeds; and

(3) Third, nonpurpose investments allocable to sale proceeds and investment proceeds.

(B) *Re-allocation of certain amounts.*—Except as provided in §1.148-9(b)(3), amounts that cease to be allocated to an issue as a result of the application of the universal cap may only be allocated to another issue as replacement proceeds.

(C) *Allocations of portions of investments.*—Portions of investments to which this paragraph (b)(2)(iv) applies are allocated under either the ratable method or the representative method in the same manner as allocations of portions of investments to transferred proceeds under §1.148-9(c).

(v) *Nonpurpose investments in a bona fide debt service fund not counted.*—For purposes of this paragraph (b)(2), nonpurpose investments allocated to gross proceeds in a bona fide debt service fund for an issue are not taken into account in determining the value of the nonpurpose investments, and those nonpurpose investments remain allocated to the issue.

(c) *Fair market value limit on allocations to nonpurpose investments.*—Upon a purchase or sale of a nonpurpose investment, gross proceeds of an issue are not allocated to a payment for that nonpurpose investment in an amount greater than, or to a receipt from that nonpurpose investment in an amount less than, the fair market value of the nonpurpose investment as of the purchase or sale date. For purposes of this paragraph (c) only, the fair market value of a nonpurpose investment is adjusted to take into account qualified administrative costs allocable to the investment.

(d) *Allocation of gross proceeds to expenditures.*—(1) *Expenditures in general.*—(i) *General rule.*—Reasonable accounting methods for allocating funds from different sources to expenditures for the same governmental purpose include any of the following methods if con-

sistently applied: a specific tracing method; a gross proceeds spent first method; a first-in, first-out method; or a ratable allocation method.

(ii) *General limitation.*—An allocation of gross proceeds of an issue to an expenditure must involve a current outlay of cash for a governmental purpose of the issue. A *current outlay of cash* means an outlay reasonably expected to occur not later than 5 banking days after the date as of which the allocation of gross proceeds to the expenditure is made.

(iii) *Timing.*—An issuer must account for the allocation of proceeds to expenditures not later than 18 months after the later of the date the expenditure is paid or the date the project, if any, that is financed by the issue is placed in service. This allocation must be made in any event by the date 60 days after the fifth anniversary of the issue date or the date 60 days after the retirement of the issue, if earlier. This paragraph (d)(1)(iii) applies to bonds issued on or after May 16, 1997.

(2) *Treatment of gross proceeds invested in purpose investments.*—(i) *In general.*—Gross proceeds of an issue invested in a purpose investment are allocated to an expenditure on the date on which the conduit borrower under the purpose investment allocates the gross proceeds to an expenditure in accordance with this paragraph (d).

(ii) *Exception for qualified mortgage loans and qualified student loans.*—If gross proceeds of an issue are allocated to a purpose investment that is a qualified mortgage loan or a qualified student loan, those gross proceeds are allocated to an expenditure for the governmental purpose of the issue on the date on which the issuer allocates gross proceeds to that purpose investment.

(iii) *Continuing allocation of gross proceeds to purpose investments.*—Regardless of whether gross proceeds of a conduit financing issue invested in a purpose investment have been allocated to an expenditure under paragraph (d)(2)(i) or (ii) of this section, with respect to the actual issuer those gross proceeds continue to be allocated to the purpose investment until the sale, discharge, or other disposition of the purpose investment.

(3) *Expenditures for working capital purposes.*—(i) *In general.*—Except as otherwise provided in this paragraph (d)(3) or paragraph (d)(4) of this section, proceeds of an issue may only be allocated to working capital expenditures as of any date to the extent that those working capital expenditures exceed available amounts (as defined in paragraph (d)(3)(iii) of this section) as of that date (i.e., a "proceeds-spent-last" method). For this purpose, proceeds include replacement proceeds described in §1.148-1(c)(4).

(ii) *Exceptions.*—(A) *General de minimis exception.*—Paragraph (d)(3)(i) of this section does not apply to expenditures to pay—

(1) Any issuance costs of the issue or any qualified administrative costs within the meaning of §§1.148-5(e)(2)(i) or (ii), or §1.148-5(e)(3)(ii)(A);

(2) Fees for qualified guarantees of the issue or payments for a qualified hedge for the issue;

(3) Interest on the issue for a period commencing on the issue date and ending on the date that is the later of three years from the issue date or one year after the date on which the project is placed in service;

(4) Amounts paid to the United States under §§1.148-3, 1.148-5(c), or 1.148-7 for the issue;

(5) Costs, other than those described in paragraphs (d)(3)(ii)(A)(1) through (4) of this section, that do not exceed 5 percent of the sale proceeds of an issue and that are directly related to capital expenditures financed by the issue (e.g., initial operating expenses for a new capital project);

(6) Principal or interest on an issue paid from unexpected excess sale or investment proceeds; and

(7) Principal or interest on an issue paid from investment earnings on a reserve or replacement fund that are deposited in a bona fide debt service fund.

(B) *Exception for extraordinary items.*—Paragraph (d)(3)(i) of this section does not apply to expenditures for extraordinary, nonrecurring items that are not customarily payable from current revenues, such as casualty losses or extraordinary legal judgments in amounts in excess of reasonable insurance coverage. If, however, an issuer or a related party maintains a reserve for such items (e.g., a self-insurance fund) or has set aside other available amounts for such expenses, gross proceeds within that reserve must be allocated to expenditures only after all other available amounts in that reserve are expended.

(C) *Exception for payment of principal and interest on prior issues.*—Paragraph (d)(3)(i) of this section does not apply to expenditures for payment of principal, interest, or redemption prices on a prior issue and, for a crossover refunding issue, interest on that issue.

(D) *No exceptions if replacement proceeds created.*—The exceptions provided in this paragraph (d)(3)(ii) do not apply if the allocation merely substitutes gross proceeds for other amounts that would have been used to make those expenditures in a manner that gives rise to replacement proceeds. For example, if a purported reimbursement allocation of proceeds of a reimbursement bond does not result in an expenditure under §1.150-2, those proceeds may not be allocated to pay interest on an issue that, absent this allocation, would have been paid from the issuer's current revenues.

(iii) *Definition of available amount.*—(A) *In general.*—For purposes of this paragraph (d)(3), *available amount* means any amount that is available to an issuer for working capital expenditure purposes of the type financed by an issue. Except as otherwise provided, available amount excludes proceeds of any issue but includes cash, investments, and other amounts held in accounts or otherwise by the issuer or a related party if those amounts may be used by the issuer for working capital expenditures of the type being financed by an issue without legislative or judicial action and without a legislative, judicial, or contractual requirement that those amounts be reimbursed.

(B) *Reasonable working capital reserve treated as unavailable.*—A reasonable working capital reserve is treated as unavailable. Any working capital reserve is reasonable if it does not exceed 5 percent of the actual working capital expenditures of the issuer in the fiscal year before the year in which the determination of available amounts is made. For this purpose only, in determining the working capital expenditures of an issuer for a prior fiscal year, any expenditures (whether capital or working capital expenditures) that are paid out of current revenues may be treated as working capital expenditures.

(C) *Qualified endowment funds treated as unavailable.*—For a 501(c)(3) organization, a qualified endowment fund is treated as unavailable. A fund is a qualified endowment fund if—

(1) The fund is derived from gifts or bequests, or the income thereon, that were neither made nor reasonably expected to be used to pay working capital expenditures;

(2) Pursuant to reasonable, established practices of the organization, the governing body of the 501(c)(3) organization designates and consistently operates the fund as a permanent endowment fund or quasi-endowment fund restricted as to use; and

(3) There is an independent verification that the fund is reasonably necessary as part of the organization's permanent capital.

(D) *Application to statutory safe harbor for tax and revenue anticipation bonds.*—For purposes of section 148(f)(4)(B)(iii)(II), *available amount* has the same meaning as in paragraph (d)(3)(iii) of this section, except that the otherwise-permitted reasonable working capital reserve is treated as part of the available amount.

(4) *Expenditures for grants.*—(i) *In general.*—Gross proceeds of an issue that are used to make a grant are allocated to an expenditure on the date on which the grant is made.

(ii) *Characterization of repayments of grants.*—If any amount of a grant financed by gross proceeds of an issue is repaid to the grantor, the repaid amount is treated as unspent proceeds of the issue as of the repayment date unless expended within 60 days of repayment.

(5) *Expenditures for reimbursement purposes.*—In allocating gross proceeds of issues of reimbursement bonds (as defined in §1.150-2) to certain expenditures, §1.150-2 applies. In allocating gross proceeds to an expenditure to reimburse a previously paid working capital expenditure, paragraph (d)(3) of this section applies. Thus, if the expenditure is described in paragraph (d)(3)(ii) of this section or there are no available amounts on the date a working capital expenditure is made and there are no other available amounts on the date of the reimbursement of that expenditure, gross proceeds are allocated to the working capital expenditure as of the date of the reimbursement.

(6) *Expenditures of certain commingled investment proceeds of governmental issues.*—This paragraph (d)(6) applies to any issue of governmental bonds, any issue of private activity bonds issued to finance a facility that is required by section 142 to be owned by a governmental unit, and any portion of an issue that is not treated as consisting of private activity bonds under section 141(b)(9). Investment proceeds of the issue (other than investment proceeds held in a refunding escrow) are treated as allocated to expenditures for a governmental purpose when the amounts are deposited in a commingled fund with substantial tax or other revenues from governmental operations of the issuer and the amounts are reasonably expected to be spent for governmental purposes within 6 months

from the date of the commingling. In establishing these reasonable expectations, an issuer may use any reasonable accounting assumption and is not bound by the *proceeds-spent-last* assumption generally required for working capital expenditures under paragraph (d)(3) of this section.

(7) *Payments to related parties.*—Any payment of gross proceeds of the issue to a related party of the payor is not an expenditure of those gross proceeds.

(e) *Special rules for commingled funds.*—(1) *In general.*—An accounting method for gross proceeds of an issue in a commingled fund, other than a bona fide debt service fund, is reasonable only if it satisfies the requirements of paragraphs (e)(2) through (6) of this section in addition to the other requirements of this section.

(2) *Investments held by a commingled fund.*—(i) *Required ratable allocations.*—Not less frequently than as of the close of each fiscal period, all payments and receipts (including deemed payments and receipts) on investments held by a commingled fund must be allocated (but not necessarily distributed) among the different investors in the fund. This allocation must be based on a consistently applied, reasonable ratable allocation method.

(ii) *Safe harbors for ratable allocation methods.*—Reasonable ratable allocation methods include, without limitation, methods that allocate these items in proportion to either—

(A) The average daily balances of the amounts in the commingled fund from different investors during a fiscal period (as described in paragraph (e)(4) of this section); or

(B) The average of the beginning and ending balances of the amounts in the commingled fund from different investors for a fiscal period that does not exceed one month.

(iii) *Definition of investor.*—For purposes of this paragraph (e), the term *investor* means each different source of funds invested in a commingled fund. For example, if a city invests gross proceeds of an issue and tax revenues in a commingled fund, it is treated as two different investors.

(3) *Certain expenditures involving a commingled fund.*—If a ratable allocation method is used under paragraph (d) of this section to allocate expenditures from the commingled fund, the same ratable allocation method must be used to allocate payments and receipts on investments in the commingled fund under paragraph (e)(2) of this section.

(4) *Fiscal periods.*—The fiscal year of a commingled fund is the calendar year unless the fund adopts another fiscal year. A commingled fund may use any consistent fiscal period that does not exceed three months (e.g., a daily, weekly, monthly, or quarterly fiscal period).

(5) *Unrealized gains and losses on investments of a commingled fund.*—(i) *Mark-to-market requirement for internal commingled funds with longer-term investment portfolios.*—Except as otherwise provided in this paragraph (e), in the case of a commingled fund in which the issuer and any related party own more than 25 percent of the beneficial interests in the fund (an *internal commingled fund*), the fund must treat all its investments as if sold at fair market value either on the last day of the fiscal year or the last day of each fiscal period. The net gains or losses from these deemed sales of investments must be allocated to all investors of the commingled fund during the period since the last allocation.

(ii) *Exception for internal commingled funds with shorter-term investment portfolios.*—If the remaining weighted average maturity of all investments held by a commingled fund during a particular fiscal year does not exceed 18 months, and the investments held by the commingled fund during that fiscal year consist exclusively of obligations, the mark-to-market requirement of paragraph (e)(5)(i) of this section does not apply.

(iii) *Exception for commingled reserve funds and sinking funds.*—The mark-to-market requirement of paragraph (e)(5)(i) of this section does not apply to a commingled fund that operates exclusively as a reserve fund, sinking fund, or replacement fund for two or more issues of the same issuer.

(6) *Allocations of commingled funds serving as common reserve funds or sinking funds.*—(i) *Permitted ratable allocation methods.*—If a commingled fund serves as a common reserve fund, replacement fund, or sinking fund for two or more issues (a *commingled reserve*), after making reasonable adjustments to account for proceeds allocated under paragraph (b)(1) or (b)(2) of this section, investments held by that commingled fund must be allocated ratably among the issues served by the commingled fund in accordance with one of the following methods—

Reg. §1.148-6(e)(6)(i)

25,186

Tax Exempt. Requirements: State/Local Bonds
See p. 20,601 for regulations not amended to reflect law changes

(A) The relative values of the bonds of those issues under §1.148-4(e);

(B) The relative amounts of the remaining maximum annual debt service requirements on the outstanding principal amounts of those issues; or

(C) The relative original stated principal amounts of the outstanding issues.

(ii) *Frequency of allocations.*—An issuer must make any allocations required by this paragraph (e)(6) as of a date at least every 3 years and as of each date that an issue first becomes secured by the commingled reserve. If relative original principal amounts are used to allocate, allocations must also be made on the retirement of any issue secured by the commingled reserve. [Reg. §1.148-6.]

□ [T.D. 8418, 5-12-92. *Amended by* T.D. 8476, 6-14-93; T.D. 8538, 5-5-94; T.D. 8712, 1-10-97, T.D. 8718, 5-8-97 and T.D. 9777, 7-15-2016.]

[Reg. §1.148-6A]

§1.148-6A. [Reserved].

□ [T.D. 8538, 5-5-94. *Redesignated and amended by* T.D. 8718, 5-8-97. *Removed and reserved by* T.D. 9849, 3-11-2019.]

[Reg. §1.148-7]

§1.148-7. Spending exceptions to the rebate requirement.—(a) *Scope of section.*—(1) *In general.*—This section provides guidance on the spending exceptions to the arbitrage rebate requirement of section 148(f)(2). These exceptions are the 6-month exception in section 148(f)(4)(B) (the *6-month exception*), the 18-month exception under paragraph (d) of this section (the *18-month exception*), and the 2-year construction exception under section 148(f)(4)(C) (the *2-year exception*) (collectively, the *spending exceptions*).

(2) *Relationship of spending exceptions.*—Each of the spending exceptions is an independent exception to arbitrage rebate. For example, a construction issue may qualify for the 6-month exception or the 18-month exception even though the issuer makes one or more elections under the 2-year exception with respect to the issue.

(3) *Spending exceptions not mandatory.*—Use of the spending exceptions is not mandatory. An issuer may apply the arbitrage rebate requirement to an issue that otherwise satisfies a spending exception. If an issuer elects to pay penalty in lieu of rebate under the 2-year exception, however, the issuer must apply those penalty provisions.

(b) *Rules applicable for all spending exceptions.*—The provisions of this paragraph (b) apply for purposes of applying each of the spending exceptions.

(1) *Special transferred proceeds rules.*—(i) *Application to prior issues.*—For purposes of applying the spending exceptions to a prior issue only, proceeds of the prior issue that become transferred proceeds of the refunding issue continue to be treated as unspent proceeds of the prior issue. If the prior issue satisfies one of the spending exceptions, the proceeds of the prior issue that are excepted from rebate under that spending exception are not subject to rebate either as proceeds of the prior issue or as transferred proceeds of the refunding issue.

(ii) *Application to refunding issues.*—(A) *In general.*—The only spending exception applicable to refunding issues is the 6-month exception. For purposes of applying the 6-month exception to a refunding issue only, proceeds of the prior issue that become transferred proceeds of the refunding issue generally are not treated as proceeds of the refunding issue and need not be spent for the refunding issue to satisfy that spending exception. Even if the refunding issue qualifies for that spending exception, those transferred proceeds are subject to rebate as proceeds of the refunding issue unless an exception to rebate applied to those proceeds as proceeds of the prior issue.

(B) *Exception.*—For purposes of applying the 6-month exception to refunding issues, those transferred proceeds of the refunding issue issue excluded from the gross proceeds of the prior issue under the special definition of gross proceeds in paragraph (c)(3) of this section, and those that transferred from a prior taxable issue, are generally treated as gross proceeds of the refunding issue. Thus, for the refunding issue to qualify for the 6-month exception, those proceeds must be spent within 6 months of the issue date of the refunding issue, unless those amounts continue to be used in a manner that does not cause those amounts to be gross proceeds under paragraph (c)(3) of this section.

(2) *Application of multipurpose issue rules.*—Except as otherwise provided, if any portion of an issue is treated as a separate issue allocable to refunding purposes under §1.148-9(h) (relating to multi-

purpose issues), for purposes of this section, that portion is treated as a separate issue.

(3) *Expenditures for governmental purposes of the issue.*—For purposes of this section, expenditures for the governmental purpose of an issue include payments for interest, but not principal, on the issue, and for principal or interest on another issue of obligations. The preceding sentence does not apply for purposes of the 18-month and 2-year exceptions if those payments cause the issue to be a refunding issue.

(4) *De minimis rule.*—Any failure to satisfy the final spending requirement of the 18-month exception or the 2-year exception is disregarded if the issuer exercises due diligence to complete the project financed and the amount of the failure does not exceed the lesser of 3 percent of the issue price of the issue or $250,000.

(5) *Special definition of reasonably required reserve or replacement fund.*—For purposes of this section only, a reasonably required reserve or replacement fund also includes any fund to the extent described in §1.148-5(c)(3)(i)(E) or (G).

(6) *Pooled financing issue.*—(i) *In general.*—Except as otherwise provided in this paragraph (b)(6), the spending exceptions apply to a pooled financing issue as a whole, rather than to each loan separately.

(ii) *Election to apply spending exceptions separately to each loan.*—(A) *In general.*—At the election (made on or before the issue date) of the issuer of a pooled financing issue, the spending exceptions are applied separately to each conduit loan, and the applicable spending requirements for a loan begin on the earlier of the date the loan is made, or the first day following the 1-year period beginning on the issue date of the pooled financing issue. If this election is made, the rebate requirement applies to, and none of the spending exceptions are available for, gross proceeds of the pooled financing bonds before the date on which the spending requirements for those proceeds begin.

(B) *Application of spending exceptions.*—If the issuer makes the election under this paragraph (b)(6)(ii), the rebate requirement is satisfied for proceeds used to finance a particular conduit loan to the extent that the loan satisfies a spending exception or the small issuer exception under §1.148-8, regardless of whether any other conduit loans allocable to the issue satisfy such an exception. A pooled financing issue is an issue of arbitrage bonds, however, unless the entire issue satisfies the requirements of section 148. An issuer may pay rebate for some conduit loans and 1¹/₂ percent penalty for other conduit loans from the same pooled financing issue. The 1¹/₂ percent penalty is computed separately for each conduit loan.

(C) *Elections under 2-year exception.*—If the issuer makes the election under this paragraph (b)(6)(ii), the issuer may make all elections under the 2-year exception separately for each loan. Elections regarding a loan that otherwise must be made by the issuer on or before the issue date instead may be made on or before the date the loan is made (but not later than 1 year after the issue date).

(D) *Example.*—The operation of this paragraph (b)(6) is illustrated by the following example:

Example. Pooled financing issue. On January 1, 1994, Authority J issues bonds. As of the issue date, J reasonably expects to use the proceeds of the issue to make loans to City K, County L, and City M. J does not reasonably expect to use more than 75 percent of the available construction proceeds of the issue for construction expenditures. On or before the issue date, J elects to apply the spending exceptions separately for each loan, with spending requirements beginning on the earlier of the date the loan is made or the first day following the 1-year period beginning on the issue date. On February 1, 1994, J loans a portion of the proceeds to K, and K reasonably expects that 45 percent of those amounts will be used for construction expenditures. On the date this loan is made, J elects under paragraph (j) of this section to treat 60 percent of the amount loaned to K as a separate construction issue, and also elects the 1¹/₂ percent penalty under paragraph (k) of this section for the separate construction issue. On March 1, 1994, J loans a portion of the proceeds to L, and L reasonably expects that more than 75 percent of those amounts will be used for construction expenditures. On March 1, 1995, J loans the remainder of the proceeds to M, and none of those amounts will be used for construction expenditures. J must satisfy the rebate requirement for all gross proceeds before those amounts are loaned. For the loan to K, the spending periods begin on February 1, 1994, and the 1¹/₂ percent penalty must be paid for any failure to meet a spending requirement for the portion of the loan to K that is treated as a separate construction issue. Rebate must be paid on the remaining portion of the loan to K, unless that portion qualifies for the 6-month exception. For the loan to L, the spending periods begin on March 1, 1994, and the rebate requirement must be satisfied unless the 6-month, 18-month, or the 2-year exception is satisfied with respect to those amounts. For the loan to *M*, the spending periods begin on January 2, 1995, and the rebate requirement must be satisfied for those amounts unless the 6-month or 18-month exception is satisfied.

(c) *6-month exception.*—(1) *General rule.*—An issue is treated as meeting the rebate requirement if—

(i) The gross proceeds (as modified by paragraph (c)(3) of this section) of the issue are allocated to expenditures for the governmental purposes of the issue within the 6-month period beginning on the issue date (the *6-month spending period*); and

(ii) The rebate requirement is met for amounts not required to be spent within the 6-month spending period (excluding earnings on a bona fide debt service fund).

(2) *Additional period for certain bonds.*—The 6-month spending period is extended for an additional 6 months in certain circumstances specified under section 148(f)(4)(B)(ii).

(3) *Amounts not included in gross proceeds.*—For purposes of paragraph (c)(1)(i) of this section only, gross proceeds has the meaning used in § 1.148-1, except it does not include amounts—

(i) In a bona fide debt service fund;

(ii) In a reasonably required reserve or replacement fund (see § 1.148-7(b)(5));

(iii) That, as of the issue date, are not reasonably expected to be gross proceeds but that become gross proceeds after the end of the 6-month spending period;

(iv) Representing sale or investment proceeds derived from payments under any purpose investment of the issue; and

(v) Representing repayments of grants (as defined in § 1.150-1(f)) financed by the issue.

(4) *Series of refundings.*—If a principal purpose of a series of refunding issues is to exploit the difference between taxable and tax-exempt interest rates by investing proceeds during the temporary periods provided in § 1.148-9(d), the 6-month spending period for all issues in the series begins on the issue date of the first issue in the series.

(d) *18-month exception.*—(1) *General rule.*—An issue is treated as meeting the rebate requirement if all of the following requirements are satisfied—

(i) *18-month expenditure schedule met.*—The gross proceeds (as defined in paragraph (d)(3) of this section) are allocated to expenditures for a governmental purpose of the issue in accordance with the following schedule (the *18-month expenditure schedule*) measured from the issue date—

(A) At least 15 percent within 6 months (the *first spending period*);

(B) At least 60 percent within 12 months (the *second spending period*); and

(C) 100 percent within 18 months (the *third spending period*).

(ii) *Rebate requirement met for amounts not required to be spent.*—The rebate requirement is met for all amounts not required to be spent in accordance with the 18-month expenditure schedule (other than earnings on a bona fide debt service fund).

(iii) *Issue qualifies for initial temporary period.*—All of the gross proceeds (as defined in paragraph (d)(3)(i) of this section) of the issue qualify for the initial temporary period under § 1.148-2(e)(2).

(2) *Extension for reasonable retainage.*—An issue does not fail to satisfy the spending requirement for the third spending period as a result of a reasonable retainage if the reasonable retainage is allocated to expenditures within 30 months of the issue date. Reasonable retainage has the meaning under paragraph (h) of this section, as modified to refer to net sale proceeds on the date 18 months after the issue date.

(3) *Gross proceeds.*—(i) *Definition of gross proceeds.*—For purposes of paragraph (d)(1) of this section only, *gross proceeds* means gross proceeds as defined in paragraph (c)(3) of this section, as modified to refer to "18 months" in paragraph (c)(3)(iii) of this section in lieu of "6 months."

(ii) *Estimated earnings.*—For purposes of determining compliance with the first two spending periods under paragraph (d)(1)(i) of this section, the amount of investment proceeds included in gross proceeds of the issue is determined based on the issuer's reasonable expectations on the issue date.

(4) *Application to multipurpose issues.*—This paragraph (d) does not apply to an issue any portion of which is treated as meeting the

rebate requirement under paragraph (e) of this section (relating to the 2-year exception).

(e) *2-year exception.*—(1) *General rule.*—A construction issue is treated as meeting the rebate requirement for available construction proceeds if those proceeds are allocated to expenditures for governmental purposes of the issue in accordance with the following schedule (the *2-year expenditure schedule*), measured from the issue date—

(i) At least 10 percent within 6 months (the *first spending period*);

(ii) At least 45 percent within 1 year (the *second spending period*);

(iii) At least 75 percent within 18 months (the *third spending period*); and

(iv) 100 percent within 2 years (the *fourth spending period*).

(2) *Extension for reasonable retainage.*—An issue does not fail to satisfy the spending requirement for the fourth spending period as a result of unspent amounts for reasonable retainage (as defined in paragraph (h) of this section) if those amounts are allocated to expenditures within 3 years of the issue date.

(3) *Definitions.*—For purposes of the 2-year exception, the following definitions apply:

(i) *Real property* means land and improvements to land, such as buildings or other inherently permanent structures, including interests in real property. For example, real property includes wiring in a building, plumbing systems, central heating or air-conditioning systems, pipes or ducts, elevators, escalators installed in a building, paved parking areas, roads, wharves and docks, bridges, and sewage lines.

(ii) *Tangible personal property* means any tangible property other than real property, including interests in tangible personal property. For example, tangible personal property includes machinery that is not a structural component of a building, subway cars, fire trucks, automobiles, office equipment, testing equipment, and furnishings.

(iii) *Substantially completed.*—Construction may be treated as substantially completed when the issuer abandons construction or when at least 90 percent of the total costs of the construction reasonably expected, as of that date, to be financed with the available construction proceeds have been allocated to expenditures.

(f) *Construction issue.*—(1) *Definition.*—*Construction issue* means any issue that is not a refunding issue if—

(i) The issuer reasonably expects, as of the issue date, that at least 75 percent of the available construction proceeds of the issue will be allocated to construction expenditures (as defined in paragraph (g) of this section) for property owned by a governmental unit or a 501(c)(3) organization; and

(ii) Any private activity bonds that are part of the issue are qualified 501(c)(3) bonds or private activity bonds issued to finance property to be owned by a governmental unit or a 501(c)(3) organization.

(2) *Use of actual facts.*—For the provisions of paragraphs (e) through (m) of this section that apply based on the issuer's reasonable expectations, an issuer may elect on or before the issue date to apply all of those provisions based on actual facts, except that this election does not apply for purposes of determining whether an issue is a construction issue under paragraph (f)(1) of this section if the 1 and $^1/_2$ percent penalty election is made under paragraph (k) of this section.

(3) *Ownership requirement.*—(i) *In general.*—A governmental unit or 501(c)(3) organization is treated as the owner of property if it would be treated as the owner for Federal income tax purposes. For obligations issued on behalf of a State or local governmental unit, the entity that actually issues the bonds is treated as a governmental unit.

(ii) *Safe harbor for leases and management contracts.*—Property leased by a governmental unit or a 501(c)(3) organization is treated as owned by the governmental unit or 501(c)(3) organization if the lessee complies with the requirements of section 142(b)(1)(B). For a bond described in section 142(a)(6), the requirements of section 142(b)(1)(B) apply as modified by section 146(h)(2).

(g) *Construction expenditures.*—(1) *Definition.*—Except as otherwise provided, *construction expenditures* means capital expenditures (as defined in § 1.150-1) that are allocable to the cost of real property or constructed personal property (as defined in paragraph (g)(3) of this section). Except as provided in paragraph (g)(2) of this section, construction expenditures do not include expenditures for acquisitions of interests in land or other existing real property.

25,188

Tax Exempt. Requirements: State/Local Bonds
See p. 20,601 for regulations not amended to reflect law changes

(2) *Certain acquisitions under turnkey contracts treated as construction expenditures.*—Expenditures are not for the acquisition of an interest in existing real property other than land if the contract between the seller and the issuer requires the seller to build or install the property (e.g., a *turnkey contract*), but only to the extent that the property has not been built or installed at the time the parties enter into the contract.

(3) *Constructed personal property.*—*Constructed personal property* means tangible personal property (or, if acquired pursuant to a single acquisition contract, properties) or specially developed computer software if—

(i) A substantial portion of the property or properties is completed more than 6 months after the earlier of the date construction or rehabilitation commenced and the date the issuer entered into an acquisition contract;

(ii) Based on the reasonable expectations of the issuer, if any, or representations of the person constructing the property, with the exercise of due diligence, completion of construction or rehabilitation (and delivery to the issuer) could not have occurred within that 6-month period; and

(iii) If the issuer itself builds or rehabilitates the property, not more than 75 percent of the capitalizable cost is attributable to property acquired by the issuer (e.g., components, raw materials, and other supplies).

(4) *Specially developed computer software.*—*Specially developed computer software* means any programs or routines used to cause a computer to perform a desired task or set of tasks, and the documentation required to describe and maintain those programs, provided that the software is specially developed and is functionally related and subordinate to real property or other constructed personal property.

(5) *Examples.*—The operation of this paragraph (g) is illustrated by the following examples:

Example 1. Purchase of construction materials. City A issues bonds to finance a new office building. A uses proceeds of the bonds to purchase materials to be used in constructing the building, such as bricks, pipes, wires, lighting, carpeting, heating equipment, and similar materials. Expenditures by A for the construction materials are construction expenditures because those expenditures will be capitalizable to the cost of the building upon completion, even though they are not initially capitalizable to the cost of existing real property. This result would be the same if A hires a third-party to perform the construction, unless the office building is partially constructed at the time that A contracts to purchase the building.

Example 2. Turnkey contract. City B issues bonds to finance a new office building. B enters into a turnkey contract with developer D under which D agrees to provide B with a completed building on a specified completion date on land currently owned by D. Under the agreement, D holds title to the land and building and assumes any risk of loss until the completion date, at which time title to the land and the building will be transferred to B. No construction has been performed by the date that B and D enter into the agreement. All payments by B to D for construction of the building are construction expenditures because all the payments are properly capitalized to the cost of the building, but payments by B to D allocable to the acquisition of the land are not construction expenditures.

Example 3. Right-of-way. P, a public agency, issues bonds to finance the acquisition of a right-of-way and the construction of sewage lines through numerous parcels of land. The right-of-way is acquired primarily through P's exercise of its powers of eminent domain. As of the issue date, P reasonably expects that it will take approximately 2 years to acquire the entire right-of-way because of the time normally required for condemnation proceedings. No expenditures for the acquisition of the right-of-way are construction expenditures because they are costs incurred to acquire an interest in existing real property.

Example 4. Subway cars. City C issues bonds to finance new subway cars. C reasonably expects that it will take more than 6 months for the subway cars to be constructed to C's specifications. The subway cars are constructed personal property. Alternatively, if the builder of the subway cars informs C that it will only take 3 months to build the subway cars to C's specifications, no payments for the subway cars are construction expenditures.

Example 5. Fractional interest in property. U, a public agency, issues bonds to finance an undivided fractional interest in a newly constructed power-generating facility. U contributes its ratable share of the cost of building the new facility to the project manager for the facility. U's contributions are construction expenditures in the same proportion that the total expenditures for the facility qualify as construction expenditures.

Example 6. Park land. City D issues bonds to finance the purchase of unimproved land and the cost of subsequent improvements to the

land, such as grading and landscaping, necessary to transform it into a park. The costs of the improvements are properly capitalizable to the cost of the land, and therefore, are construction expenditures, but expenditures for the acquisition of the land are not.

(h) *Reasonable retainage definition.*—*Reasonable retainage* means an amount, not to exceed 5 percent of available construction proceeds as of the end of the fourth spending period, that is retained for reasonable business purposes relating to the property financed with the proceeds of the issue. For example, a reasonable retainage may include a retention to ensure or promote compliance with a construction contract in circumstances in which the retained amount is not yet payable, or in which the issuer reasonably determines that a dispute exists regarding completion or payment.

(i) *Available construction proceeds.*—(1) *Definition in general.*—*Available construction proceeds* has the meaning used in section 148(f)(4)(C)(vi). For purposes of this definition, earnings include earnings on any tax-exempt bond. Pre-issuance accrued interest and earnings thereon may be disregarded. Amounts that are not gross proceeds as a result of the application of the universal cap under § 1.148-6(b)(2) are not available construction proceeds.

(2) *Earnings on a reasonably required reserve or replacement fund.*—Earnings on any reasonably required reserve or replacement fund are available construction proceeds only to the extent that those earnings accrue before the earlier of the date construction is substantially completed or the date that is 2 years after the issue date. An issuer may elect on or before the issue date to exclude from available construction proceeds the earnings on such a fund. If the election is made, the rebate requirement applies to the excluded amounts from the issue date.

(3) *Reasonable expectations test for future earnings.*—For purposes of determining compliance with the spending requirements as of the end of each of the first three spending periods, available construction proceeds include the amount of future earnings that the issuer reasonably expected as of the issue date.

(4) *Issuance costs.*—Available construction proceeds do not include gross proceeds used to pay issuance costs financed by an issue, but do include earnings on such proceeds. Thus, an expenditure of gross proceeds of an issue for issuance costs does not count toward meeting the spending requirements. The expenditure of earnings on gross proceeds used to pay issuance costs does count toward meeting those requirements. If the spending requirements are met and the proceeds used to pay issuance costs are expended by the end of the fourth spending period, those proceeds and the earnings thereon are treated as having satisfied the rebate requirement.

(5) *One and one-half percent penalty in lieu of arbitrage rebate.*—For purposes of the spending requirements of paragraph (e) of this section, available construction proceeds as of the end of any spending period are reduced by the amount of penalty in lieu of arbitrage rebate (under paragraph (k) of this section) that the issuer has paid from available construction proceeds before the last day of the spending period.

(6) *Payments on purpose investments and repayments of grants.*—Available construction proceeds do not include—

(i) Sale or investment proceeds derived from payments under any purpose investment of the issue; or

(ii) Repayments of grants (as defined in § 1.150-1(f)) financed by the issue.

(7) *Examples.*—The operation of this paragraph (i) is illustrated by the following examples:

Example 1. Treatment of investment earnings. City F issues bonds having an issue price of $10,000,000. F deposits all of the proceeds of the issue into a construction fund to be used for expenditures other than costs of issuance. F estimates on the issue date that, based on reasonably expected expenditures and rates of investment, earnings on the construction fund will be $800,000. As of the issue date and the end of each of the first three spending periods, the amount of available construction proceeds is $10,800,000. To qualify as a construction issue, F must reasonably expect on the issue date that at least $8,100,000 (75 percent of $10,800,000) will be used for construction expenditures. In order to meet the 10 percent spending requirement at the end of the first spending period, F must spend at least $1,080,000. As of the end of the fourth spending period, F has received $1,100,000 in earnings. In order to meet the spending requirement at the end of the fourth spending period, however, F must spend all of the $11,100,000 of actual available construction proceeds (except for reasonable retainage not exceeding $555,000).

Example 2. Treatment of investment earnings without a reserve fund. City G issues bonds having an issue price of $11,200,000. G does not elect to exclude earnings on the reserve fund from available construction proceeds. *G* uses $200,000 of proceeds to pay issuance costs and deposits $1,000,000 of proceeds into a reasonably required reserve fund. *G* deposits the remaining $10,000,000 of proceeds into a construction fund to be used for construction expenditures. On the issue date, *G* reasonably expects that, based on the reasonably expected date of substantial completion and rates of investment, total earnings on the construction fund will be $800,000, and total earnings on the reserve fund to the date of substantial completion will be $150,000. *G* reasonably expects that substantial completion will occur during the fourth spending period. As of the issue date, the amount of available construction proceeds is $10,950,000 ($10,000,000 originally deposited into the construction fund plus $800,000 expected earnings on the construction fund and $150,000 expected earnings on the reserve fund). To qualify as a construction issue, *G* must reasonably expect on the issue date that at least $8,212,500 will be used for construction expenditures.

Example 3. Election to exclude earnings on a reserve fund. The facts are the same as *Example 2*, except that *G* elects on the issue date to exclude earnings on the reserve fund from available construction proceeds. The amount of available construction proceeds as of the issue date is $10,800,000.

(j) *Election to treat portion of issue used for construction as separate issue.*—(1) *In general.*—For purposes of paragraph (e) of this section, if any proceeds of an issue are to be used for construction expenditures, the issuer may elect on or before the issue date to treat the portion of the issue that is not a refunding issue as two, and only two, separate issues, if—

(i) One of the separate issues is a construction issue as defined in paragraph (f) of this section;

(ii) The issuer reasonably expects, as of the issue date, that this construction issue will finance all of the construction expenditures to be financed by the issue; and

(iii) The issuer makes an election to apportion the issue under this paragraph (j)(1) in which it identifies the amount of the issue price of the issue allocable to the construction issue.

(2) *Example.*—The operation of this paragraph (j) is illustrated by the following example.

Example. City *D* issues bonds having an issue price of $19,000,000. On the issue date, *D* reasonably expects to use $10,800,000 of bond proceeds (including investment earnings) for construction expenditures for the project being financed. *D* deposits $10,000,000 in a construction fund to be used for construction expenditures and $9,000,000 in an acquisition fund to be used for acquisition of equipment not qualifying as construction expenditures. *D* estimates on the issue date, based on reasonably expected expenditures and rates of investment, that total earnings on the construction fund will be $800,000 and total earnings on the acquisition fund will be $200,000. Because the total construction expenditures to be financed by the issue are expected to be $10,800,000, the maximum available construction proceeds for a construction issue is $14,400,000 ($10,800,000 divided by 0.75). To determine the maximum amount of the issue price allocable to a construction issue, the estimated investment earnings allocable to the construction issue are subtracted. The entire $800,000 of earnings on the construction fund are allocable to the construction issue. Only a portion of the $200,000 of earnings on the acquisition fund, however, are allocable to the construction issue. The total amount of the available construction proceeds that is expected to be used for acquisition is $3,600,000 ($14,400,000 − $10,800,000). The portion of earnings on the acquisition fund that is allocable to the construction issue is $78,261 ($200,000 × $3,600,000/$9,200,000). Accordingly, *D* may elect on or before the issue date to treat up to $13,521,739 of the issue price as a construction issue ($14,400,000 − $800,000 − $78,261). *D*'s election must specify the amount of the issue price treated as a construction issue. The balance of the issue price is treated as a separate nonconstruction issue that is subject to the rebate requirement unless it meets another exception to arbitrage rebate. Because the financing of a construction issue is a separate governmental purpose under §1.148-9(h), the election causes the issue to be a multipurpose issue under that section.

(k) *One and one-half percent penalty in lieu of arbitrage rebate.*—(1) *In general.*—Under section 148(f)(4)(C)(vii), an issuer of a construction issue may elect on or before the issue date to pay a penalty (the *1 ¹/₂ percent penalty*) to the United States in lieu of the obligation to pay the rebate amount on available construction proceeds upon failure to satisfy the spending requirements of paragraph (e) of this section. The 1 ¹/₂ percent penalty is calculated separately for each spending period, including each semiannual period after the end of the fourth spending period, and is equal to 1.5 percent times the underexpended proceeds as of the end of the spending period. For each spending period, underexpended proceeds equal the amount of available construction proceeds required to be spent by the end of the

spending period, less the amount actually allocated to expenditures for the governmental purposes of the issue by that date. The 1 ¹/₂ percent penalty must be paid to the United States no later than 90 days after the end of the spending period to which it relates. The 1 ¹/₂ percent penalty continues to apply at the end of each spending period and each semiannual period thereafter until the earliest of the following—

(i) The termination of the penalty under paragraph (l) of this section;

(ii) The expenditure of all of the available construction proceeds; or

(iii) The last stated final maturity date of bonds that are part of the issue and any bonds that refund those bonds.

(2) *Application to reasonable retainage.*—If an issue meets the exception for reasonable retainage except that all retainage is not spent within 3 years of the issue date, the issuer must pay the 1 ¹/₂ percent penalty to the United States for any reasonable retainage that was not so spent as of the close of the 3-year period and each later spending period.

(3) *Coordination with rebate requirement.*—The rebate requirement is treated as met with respect to available construction proceeds for a period if the 1 ¹/₂ percent penalty is paid in accordance with this section.

(l) *Termination of 1 ¹/₂ percent penalty.*—(1) *Termination after initial temporary period.*—The issuer may terminate the 1 ¹/₂ percent penalty after the initial temporary period (a *section 148(f)(4)(C)(viii) penalty termination*) if—

(i) Not later than 90 days after the earlier of the end of the initial temporary period or the date construction is substantially completed, the issuer elects to terminate the 1 ¹/₂ percent penalty; provided that solely for this purpose, the initial temporary period may be extended by the issuer to a date ending 5 years after the issue date;

(ii) Within 90 days after the end of the initial temporary period, the issuer pays a penalty equal to 3 percent of the unexpended available construction proceeds determined as of the end of the initial temporary period, multiplied by the number of years (including fractions of years computed to 2 decimal places) in the initial temporary period;

(iii) For the period beginning as of the close of the initial temporary period, the unexpended available construction proceeds are not invested in higher yielding investments; and

(iv) On the earliest date on which the bonds may be called or otherwise redeemed, with or without a call premium, the unexpended available construction proceeds as of that date (not including any amount earned after the date on which notice of the redemption was required to be given) must be used to redeem the bonds. Amounts used to pay any call premium are treated as used to redeem bonds. This redemption requirement may be met by purchases of bonds by the issuer on the open market at prices not exceeding fair market value. A portion of the annual principal payment due on serial bonds of a construction issue may be paid from the unexpended amount, but only in an amount no greater than the amount that bears the same ratio to the annual principal due that the total unexpended amount bears to the issue price of the construction issue.

(2) *Termination before end of initial temporary period.*—If the construction to be financed by the construction issue is substantially completed before the end of the initial temporary period, the issuer may elect to terminate the 1 ¹/₂ percent penalty before the end of the initial temporary period (a *section 148(f)(4)(C)(ix) penalty termination*) if—

(i) Before the close of the initial temporary period and not later than 90 days after the date the construction is substantially completed, the issuer elects to terminate the 1 ¹/₂ percent penalty;

(ii) The election identifies the amount of available construction proceeds that will not be spent for the governmental purposes of the issue; and

(iii) The issuer has met all of the conditions for a section 148(f)(4)(C)(viii) penalty termination, applied as if the initial temporary period ended as of the date the required election for a section 148(f)(4)(C)(ix) penalty termination is made. That penalty termination election satisfies the required election for a section 148(f)(4)(C)(viii) termination.

(3) *Application to reasonable retainage.*—Solely for purposes of determining whether the conditions for terminating the 1 ¹/₂ percent penalty are met, reasonable retainage may be treated as spent for a governmental purpose of the construction issue. Reasonable retainage that is so treated continues to be subject to the 1 ¹/₂ percent penalty.

Reg. §1.148-7(l)(3)

(4) *Example.*—The operation of this paragraph (l) is illustrated by the following example.

Example. City *I* issues a construction issue having a 20-year maturity and qualifying for a 3-year initial temporary period. The bonds are first subject to optional redemption 10 years after the issue date at a premium of 3 percent. *I* elects, on or before the issue date, to pay the 1 ¹/₂ percent penalty in lieu of arbitrage rebate. At the end of the 3-year temporary period, the project is not substantially completed, and $1,500,000 of available construction proceeds of the issue are unspent. At that time, *I* reasonably expects to need $500,000 to complete the project. *I* may terminate the 1 ¹/₂ percent penalty in lieu of arbitrage rebate with respect to the excess $1,500,000 by electing to terminate within 90 days of the end of the initial temporary period; paying a penalty to the United States of $135,000 (3 percent of $1,500,000 multiplied by 3 years); restricting the yield on the investment of unspent available construction proceeds for 7 years until the first call date, although any portion of these proceeds may still be spent on the project prior to that call date; and using the available construction proceeds that, as of the first call date, have not been allocated to expenditures for the governmental purposes of the issue to redeem bonds on that call date. If *I* fails to make the termination election, *I* is required to pay the 1 ¹/₂ percent penalty on unspent available construction proceeds every 6 months until the latest maturity date of bonds of the issue (or any bonds of another issue that refund such bonds).

(m) *Payment of penalties.*—Each penalty payment under this section must be paid in the manner provided in §1.148-3(g). See §1.148-3(h) for rules on failures to pay penalties under this section. [Reg. §1.148-7.]

☐ [*T.D. 8418, 5-12-92. Amended by T.D. 8476, 6-14-93 and T.D. 9777, 7-15-2016.*]

[Reg. §1.148-8]

§1.148-8. Small issuer exception to rebate requirement.—(a) *Scope.*—Under section 148(f)(4)(D), bonds issued to finance governmental activities of certain small issuers are treated as meeting the arbitrage rebate requirement of section 148(f)(2) (the "small issuer exception"). This section provides guidance on the small issuer exception.

(b) *General taxing powers.*—The small issuer exception generally applies only to bonds issued by governmental units with general taxing powers. A governmental unit has general taxing powers if it has the power to impose taxes (or to cause another entity to impose taxes) of general applicability which, when collected, may be used for the general purposes of the issuer. The taxing power may be limited to a specific type of tax, provided that the applicability of the tax is not limited to a small number of persons. The governmental unit's exercise of its taxing power may be subject to procedural limitations, such as voter approval requirements, but may not be contingent on approval by another governmental unit. See, also, section 148(f)(4)(D)(iv).

(c) *Size limitation.*—(1) *In general.*—An issue (other than a refunding issue) qualifies for the small issuer exception only if the issuer reasonably expects, as of the issue date, that the aggregate face amount of all tax-exempt bonds (other than private activity bonds) issued by it during that calendar year will not exceed $5,000,000; or the aggregate face amount of all tax-exempt bonds of the issuer (other than private activity bonds) actually issued during that calendar year does not exceed $5,000,000. For this purpose, if an issue has more than a de minimis amount of original issue discount or premium, *aggregate face amount* means the aggregate issue price of that issue (determined without regard to pre-issuance accrued interest).

(2) *Aggregation rules.*—The following aggregation rules apply for purposes of applying the $5,000,000 size limitation under paragraph (c)(1) of this section.

(i) *On-behalf-of issuers.*—An issuer and all entities (other than political subdivisions) that issue bonds on behalf of that issuer are treated as one issuer.

(ii) *Subordinate entities.*—(A) *In general.*—Except as otherwise provided in paragraph (d) of this section and section 148(f)(4)(D)(iv), all bonds issued by a subordinate entity are also treated as issued by each entity to which it is subordinate. An issuer is subordinate to another governmental entity if it is directly or indirectly controlled by the other entity within the meaning of §1.150-1(e).

(B) *Exception for allocations of size limitation.*—If an entity properly makes an allocation of a portion of its $5,000,000 size limitation to a subordinate entity (including an [entity] on behalf of issuer) under section 148(f)(4)(D)(iv), the portion of bonds issued by the subordinate entity under the allocation is treated as issued only by the allocating entity and not by any other entity to which the

issuing entity is subordinate. These allocations are irrevocable and must bear a reasonable relationship to the benefits received by the allocating unit from issues issued by the subordinate entity. The benefits to be considered include the manner in which—

(1) Proceeds are to be distributed;

(2) The debt service is to be paid;

(3) The facility financed is to be owned;

(4) The use or output of the facility is to be shared; and

(5) Costs of operation and maintenance are to be shared.

(iii) *Avoidance of size limitation.*—An entity formed or availed of to avoid the purposes of the $5,000,000 size limitation and all entities that would benefit from the avoidance are treated as one issuer. Situations in which an entity is formed or availed of to avoid the purposes of the $5,000,000 size limitation include those in which the issuer—

(A) Issues bonds which, but for the $5,000,000 size limitation, would have been issued by another entity; and

(B) Does not receive a substantial benefit from the project financed by the bonds.

(3) *Certain refunding bonds not taken into account.*—In applying the $5,000,000 size limitation, there is not taken into account the portion of an issue that is a current refunding issue to the extent that the stated principal amount of the refunding bond does not exceed the portion of the outstanding stated principal amount of the refunded bond paid with proceeds of the refunding bond. For this purpose, *principal amount* means, in reference to a plain par bond, its stated principal amount plus accrued unpaid interest, and in reference to any other bond, its present value.

(d) *Pooled financings—treatment of conduit borrowers.*—A loan to a conduit borrower in a pooled financing qualifies for the small issuer exception, regardless of the size of either the pooled financing or of any loan to other conduit borrowers, only if—

(1) The bonds of the pooled financing are not private activity bonds;

(2) None of the loans to conduit borrowers are private activity bonds; and

(3) The loan to the conduit borrower meets all the requirements of the small issuer exception.

(e) *Refunding issues.*—(1) *In general.*—Sections 148(f)(4)(D)(v) and (vi) provide restrictions on application of the small issuer exception to refunding issues.

(2) *Multipurpose issues.*—The multipurpose issue allocation rules of §1.148-9(h) apply for purposes of determining whether refunding bonds meet the requirements of section 148(f)(4)(D)(v). [Reg. §1.148-8.]

☐ [*T.D. 8418, 5-12-92. Amended by T.D. 8476, 6-14-93 and T.D. 9777, 7-15-2016.*]

[Reg. §1.148-9]

§1.148-9. Arbitrage rules for refunding issues.—(a) *Scope of application.*—This section contains special arbitrage rules for refunding issues. These rules apply for all purposes of section 148 and govern allocations of proceeds, bonds, and investments to determine transferred proceeds, temporary periods, reasonably required reserve or replacement funds, minor portions, and separate issue treatment of certain multipurpose issues.

(b) *Transferred proceeds allocation rule.*—(1) *In general.*—When proceeds of the refunding issue discharge any of the outstanding principal amount of the prior issue, proceeds of the prior issue become transferred proceeds of the refunding issue and cease to be proceeds of the prior issue. The amount of proceeds of the prior issue that becomes transferred proceeds of the refunding issue is an amount equal to the proceeds of the prior issue on the date of that discharge multiplied by a fraction—

(i) The numerator of which is the principal amount of the prior issue discharged with proceeds of the refunding issue on the date of that discharge; and

(ii) The denominator of which is the total outstanding principal amount of the prior issue on the date immediately before the date of that discharge.

(2) *Special definition of principal amount.*—For purposes of this section, *principal amount* means, in reference to a plain par bond, its stated principal amount, and in reference to any other bond, its present value.

(3) *Relation of transferred proceeds rule to universal cap rule.*—(i) *In general.*—Paragraphs (b)(1) and (c) of this section apply to allocate transferred proceeds and corresponding investments to a refunding issue on any date required by those paragraphs before the applica-

tion of the universal cap rule of §1.148-6(b)(2) to reallocate any of those amounts. To the extent nonpurpose investments allocable to proceeds of a refunding issue exceed the universal cap for the issue on the date that amounts become transferred proceeds of the refunding issue, those transferred proceeds and corresponding investments are reallocated back to the issue from which they transferred on that same date to the extent of the unused universal cap on that prior issue.

(ii) *Example.*—The following example illustrates the application of this paragraph of (b)(3):

Example. On January 1, 1995, $100,000 of nonpurpose investments allocable to proceeds of issue *A* become transferred proceeds of issue *B* under §1.148-9, but the unused portion of issue *B's* universal cap is $75,000 as of that date. On January 1, 1995, issue *A* has unused universal cap in excess of $25,000. Thus, $25,000 of nonpurpose investments representing the transferred proceeds are immediately reallocated back to issue *A* on January 1, 1995, and are proceeds of issue *A*. On the next transfer date under §1.148-9, the $25,000 receives no priority in determining transferred proceeds as of that date but is treated the same as all other proceeds of issue *A* subject to transfer.

(4) *Limitation on multi-generational transfers.*—This paragraph (b)(4) contains limitations on the manner in which proceeds of a first generation issue that is refunded by a refunding issue (a *second generation issue*) become transferred proceeds of a refunding issue (a *third generation issue*) that refunds the second generation issue. Proceeds of the first generation issue that become transferred proceeds of the third generation issue are treated as having a yield equal to the yield on the refunding escrow allocated to the second generation issue (i.e., as determined under §1.148-5(b)(2)(iv)). The determination of the transferred proceeds of the third generation issue does not affect compliance with the requirements of section 148, including the determination of the amount of arbitrage rebate with respect to or the yield on the refunding escrow, of the second generation issue.

(c) *Special allocation rules for refunding issues.*—(1) *Allocations of investments.*—(i) *In general.*—Except as otherwise provided in this paragraph (c), investments purchased with sale proceeds or investment proceeds of a refunding issue must be allocated to those proceeds, and investments not purchased with those proceeds may not be allocated to those proceeds (i.e., a *specific tracing method*).

(ii) *Allocations to transferred proceeds.*—When proceeds of a prior issue become transferred proceeds of a refunding issue, investments (and the related payments and receipts) of proceeds of the prior issue that are held in a refunding escrow for another issue are allocated to the transferred proceeds under the ratable allocation method described in paragraph (c)(1)(iii) of this section. Investments of proceeds of the prior issue that are not held in a refunding escrow for another issue are allocated to the transferred proceeds by application of the allocation methods described in paragraph (c)(1)(iii) or (iv) of this section, consistently applied to all investments on a transfer date.

(iii) *Ratable allocation method.*—Under the ratable allocation method, a ratable portion of each nonpurpose and purpose investment of proceeds of the prior issue is allocated to transferred proceeds of the refunding issue.

(iv) *Representative allocation method.*—(A) *In general.*—Under the representative allocation method, representative portions of the portfolio of nonpurpose investments and the portfolio of purpose investments of proceeds of the prior issue are allocated to transferred proceeds of the refunding issue. Unlike the ratable allocation method, this representative allocation method permits an allocation of particular whole investments. Whether a portion is representative is based on all the facts and circumstances, including, without limitation, whether the current yields, maturities, and current unrealized gains or losses on the particular allocated investments are reasonably comparable to those of the unallocated investments in the aggregate. In addition, if a portion of nonpurpose investments is otherwise representative, it is within the issuer's discretion to allocate the portion from whichever source of funds it deems appropriate, such as a reserve fund or a construction fund for a prior issue.

(B) *Mark-to-market safe harbor for representative allocation method.*—In addition to other representative allocations, a specific allocation of a particular nonpurpose investment to transferred proceeds (e.g., of lower yielding investments) is treated as satisfying the representative allocation method if that investment is valued at fair market value on the transfer date in determining the payments and receipts on that date, but only if the portion of the nonpurpose investments that transfers is based on the relative fair market value of all nonpurpose investments.

(2) *Allocations of mixed escrows to expenditures for principal, interest, and redemption prices on a prior issue.*—(i) *In general.*—Except for amounts required or permitted to be accounted for under paragraph (c)(2)(ii) of this section, proceeds of a refunding issue and other amounts that are not proceeds of a refunding issue that are deposited in a refunding escrow (a *mixed escrow*) must be accounted for under this paragraph (c)(2)(i). Those proceeds and other amounts must be allocated to expenditures for principal, interest, or stated redemption prices on the prior issue so that the expenditures of those proceeds do not occur faster than ratably with expenditures of the other amounts in the mixed escrow. During the period that the prior issue has unspent proceeds, however, these allocations must be ratable (with reasonable adjustments for rounding) both between sources for expenditures (i.e., proceeds and other amounts) and between uses (i.e., principal, interest, and stated redemption prices on the prior issue).

(ii) *Exceptions.*—(A) *Mandatory allocation of certain non-proceeds to earliest expenditures.*—If amounts other than proceeds of the refunding issue are deposited in a mixed escrow, but before the issue date of the refunding issue those amounts had been held in a bona fide debt service fund or a fund to carry out the governmental purpose of the prior issue (e.g., a construction fund), those amounts must be allocated to the earliest maturing investments in the mixed escrow.

(B) *Permissive allocation of non-proceeds to earliest expenditures.*—Excluding amounts covered by paragraph (c)(2)(ii)(A) of this section and subject to any required earlier expenditure of those amounts, any amounts in a mixed escrow that are not proceeds of a refunding issue may be allocated to the earliest maturing investments in the mixed escrow, provided that those investments mature and the proceeds thereof are expended before the date of any expenditure from the mixed escrow to pay any principal of the prior issue.

(d) *Temporary periods in refundings.*—(1) *In general.*—Proceeds of a refunding issue may be invested in higher yielding investments under section 148(c) only during the temporary periods described in paragraph (d)(2) of this section.

(2) *Types of temporary periods in refundings.*—The available temporary periods for proceeds of a refunding issue are as follows:

(i) *General temporary period for refunding issues.*—Except as otherwise provided in this paragraph (d)(2), the temporary period for proceeds (other than transferred proceeds) of a refunding issue is the period ending 30 days after the issue date of the refunding issue.

(ii) *Temporary periods for current refunding issues.*—(A) *In general.*—Except as otherwise provided in paragraph (d)(2)(ii)(B) of this section, the temporary period for proceeds (other than transferred proceeds) of a current refunding issue is 90 days.

(B) *Temporary period for short-term current refunding issues.*—The temporary period for proceeds (other than transferred proceeds) of a current refunding issue that has an original term to maturity of 270 days or less may not exceed 30 days. The aggregate temporary periods for proceeds (other than transferred proceeds) of all current refunding issues described in the preceding sentence that are part of the same series of refundings is 90 days. An issue is part of a series of refundings if it finances or refinances the same expenditures for a particular governmental purpose as another issue.

(iii) *Temporary periods for transferred proceeds.*—(A) *In general.*—Except as otherwise provided in paragraph (d)(2)(iii)(B) of this section, each available temporary period for transferred proceeds of a refunding issue begins on the date those amounts become transferred proceeds of the refunding issue and ends on the date that, without regard to the discharge of the prior issue, the available temporary period for those proceeds would have ended had those proceeds remained proceeds of the prior issue.

(B) *Termination of initial temporary period for prior issue in an advance refunding.*—The initial temporary period under §1.148-2(e)(2) and (3) for the proceeds of a prior issue that is refunded by an advance refunding issue (including transferred proceeds) terminates on the issue date of the advance refunding issue.

(iv) *Certain short-term gross proceeds.*—Except for proceeds of a refunding issue held in a refunding escrow, proceeds otherwise reasonably expected to be used to pay principal or interest on the prior issue, replacement proceeds not held in a bona fide debt service fund, and transferred proceeds, the temporary period for gross proceeds of a refunding issue is the 13-month period beginning on the date of receipt.

(e) *Reasonably required reserve or replacement funds in refundings.*—In addition to the requirements of §1.148-2(f), beginning on the issue date of a refunding issue, a reserve or replacement fund for a

25,192

Tax Exempt. Requirements: State/Local Bonds
See p. 20,601 for regulations not amended to reflect law changes

refunding issue or a prior issue is a reasonably required reserve or replacement fund under section 148(d) that may be invested in higher yielding investments only if the aggregate amount invested in higher yielding investments under this paragraph (e) for both the refunding issue and the prior issue does not exceed the size limitations under §1.148-2(f)(2) and (f)(3), measured by reference to the refunding issue only (regardless of whether proceeds of the prior issue have become transferred proceeds of the refunding issue).

(f) *Minor portions in refundings.*—Beginning on the issue date of the refunding issue, gross proceeds not in excess of a minor portion of the refunding issue qualify for investment in higher yielding investments under section 148(e), and gross proceeds not in excess of a minor portion of the prior issue qualify for investment in higher yielding investments under either section 148(e) or section 149(d)(3)(A)(v), whichever is applicable. *Minor portion* is defined in §1.148-2(g).

(g) *Certain waivers permitted.*—On or before the issue date, an issuer may waive the right to invest in higher yielding investments during any temporary period or as part of a reasonably required reserve or replacement fund. At any time, an issuer may waive the right to invest in higher yielding investments as part of a minor portion.

(h) *Multipurpose issue allocations.*—(1) *Application of multipurpose issue allocation rules.*—The portion of the bonds of a multipurpose issue reasonably allocated to any separate purpose under this paragraph (h) is treated as a separate issue for all purposes of section 148 except the following—

(i) *Arbitrage yield.*—Except to the extent that the proceeds of an issue are allocable to two or more conduit loans that are tax-exempt bonds, determining the yield on a multipurpose issue and the yield on investments for purposes of the arbitrage yield restrictions of section 148 and the arbitrage rebate requirement of section 148(f);

(ii) *Rebate amount.*—Except as provided in paragraph (h)(1)(i) of this section, determining the rebate amount for a multipurpose issue, including subsidiary matters with respect to that determination, such as the computation date credit under §1.148-3(d)(1), the due date for payments, and the $100,000 bona fide debt service fund exception under section 148(f)(4)(A)(ii);

(iii) *Minor portion.*—Determining the *minor portion* of an issue under section 148(e);

(iv) *Reasonably required reserve or replacement fund.*—Determining the portion of an issue eligible for investment in higher yielding investments as part of a reasonably required reserve or replacement fund under section 148(d); and

(v) *Effective date.*—Applying the provisions of §1.148-11(b) (relating to elective retroactive application of §§1.148-1 through 1.148-10 to certain issues).

(2) *Rules on allocations of multipurpose issues.*—(i) *In general.*—This paragraph (h) applies to allocations of multipurpose issues, including allocations involving the refunding purposes of the issue. Except as otherwise provided in this paragraph (h), proceeds, investments, and bonds of a multipurpose issue may be allocated among the various separate purposes of the issue using any reasonable, consistently applied allocation method. An allocation is not reasonable if it achieves more favorable results under section 148 or 149(d) than could be achieved with actual separate issues. An allocation under this paragraph (h) may be made at any time, but once made may not be changed.

(ii) *Allocations involving certain common costs.*—A ratable allocation of common costs (as described in paragraph (h)(3)(ii) of this section) among the separate purposes of the multipurpose issue is generally reasonable. If another allocation method more accurately reflects the extent to which any separate purpose of a multipurpose issue enjoys the economic benefit or bears the economic burden of certain common costs, that allocation method may be used.

(3) *Separate purposes of a multipurpose issue.*—(i) *In general.*—Separate purposes of a multipurpose issue include refunding a separate prior issue, financing a separate purpose investment, financing a construction issue (as defined in §1.148-7(f)), and any clearly discrete governmental purpose reasonably expected to be financed by that issue. In general, all integrated or functionally related capital projects that qualify for the same initial temporary period under §1.148-2(e)(2) are treated as having a single governmental purpose. The separate purposes of a refunding issue include the separate purposes of the prior issue, if any. Separate purposes may be treated as a single purpose if the proceeds used to finance those purposes are eligible for the same initial temporary period under section 148(c).

For example, the use of proceeds of a multipurpose issue to finance separate qualified mortgage loans may be treated as a single purpose.

(ii) *Financing common costs.*—Common costs of a multipurpose issue are not separate purposes. Common costs include issuance costs, accrued interest, capitalized interest on the issue, a reserve or replacement fund, qualified guarantee fees, and similar costs properly allocable to the separate purposes of the issue.

(iii) *Example.*—The following example illustrates the application of this paragraph (h)(3).

Example. On January 1, 1994, Housing Authority of State *A* issues a $10 million issue (the *1994 issue*) at an interest rate of 10 percent to finance qualified mortgage loans for owner-occupied residences under section 143. During 1994, *A* originates $5 million in qualified mortgage loans at an interest rate of 10 percent. In 1995, the market interest rates for housing loans falls to 8 percent and *A* is unable to originate further loans from the 1994 issue. On January 1, 1996, *A* issues a $5 million issue (the *1996 issue*) at an interest rate of 8 percent to refund partially the 1994 issue. Under paragraph (h) of this section, *A* treats the portion of the 1994 issue used to originate $5 million in loans as a separate issue comprised of that group of purpose investments. *A* allocates those purpose investments representing those loans to that separate unrefunded portion of the issue. In addition, *A* treats the unoriginated portion of the 1994 issue as a separate issue and allocates the nonpurpose investments representing the unoriginated proceeds of the 1994 issue to the refunded portion of the issue. Thus, when proceeds of the 1996 issue are used to pay principal on the refunded portion of the 1994 issue that is treated as a separate issue under paragraph (h) of this section, only the portion of the 1994 issue representing unoriginated loan funds invested in nonpurpose investments transfer to become transferred proceeds of the 1996 issue.

(4) *Allocations of bonds of a multipurpose issue.*—(i) *Reasonable allocation of bonds to portions of issue.*—After reasonable adjustment of the issue price of a multipurpose issue to account for common costs, the portion of the bonds of a multipurpose issue allocated to a separate purpose must have an issue price that bears the same ratio to the aggregate issue price of the multipurpose issue as the portion of the sale proceeds of the multipurpose issue used for that separate purpose bears to the aggregate sale proceeds of the multipurpose issue. For a refunding issue used to refund two or more prior issues, the portion of the sales proceeds allocated to the refunding of a separate prior issue is based on the present value of the refunded debt service on that prior issue, using the yield on investments in the refunding escrow allocable to the entire refunding issue as the discount rate.

(ii) *Safe harbor for pro rata allocation method for bonds.*—The use of the relative amount of sales proceeds used for each separate purpose to ratably allocate each bond or a ratable number of substantially identical whole bonds is a reasonable method for allocating bonds of a multipurpose issue.

(iii) *Safe harbor for allocations of bonds used to finance separate purpose investments.*—An allocation of a portion of the bonds of a multipurpose issue to a particular purpose investment is generally reasonable if that purpose investment has principal and interest payments that reasonably coincide in time and amount to principal and interest payments on the bonds allocated to that purpose investment.

(iv) *Rounding of bond allocations to next whole bond denomination permitted.*—An allocation that rounds each resulting fractional bond up or down to the next integral multiple of a permitted denomination of bonds of that issue not in excess of $100,000 does not prevent the allocation from satisfying this paragraph (h)(4).

(v) *Restrictions on allocations of bonds to refunding purposes.*—For each portion of a multipurpose issue that is used to refund a separate prior issue, a method of allocating bonds of that issue is reasonable under this paragraph (h) only if, in addition to the requirements of paragraphs (h)(1) and (h)(2) of this section, the portion of the bonds allocated to the refunding of that prior issue—

(A) Results from a pro rata allocation under paragraph (h)(4)(ii) of this section;

(B) Reflects aggregate principal and interest payable in each bond year that is less than, equal to, or proportionate to, the aggregate principal and interest payable on the prior issue in each bond year;

(C) Results from an allocation of all the bonds of the entire multipurpose issue in proportion to the remaining weighted average economic life of the capital projects financed or refinanced by the issue, determined in the same manner as under section 147(b); or

(D) Results from another reasonable allocation method, but only to the extent that the application of the allocation methods

Tax Exempt. Requirements: State/Local Bonds   **25,193**

See p. 20,601 for regulations not amended to reflect law changes

provided in this paragraph (h)(4)(v) is not permitted under state law restrictions applicable to the bonds, reasonable terms of bonds issued before, or subject to a master indenture that became effective prior to, July 1, 1993, or other similar restrictions or circumstances. This paragraph (h)(4)(v)(D) shall be strictly construed and is available only if it does not result in a greater burden on the market for tax-exempt bonds than would occur using one of the other allocation methods provided in this paragraph (h)(4)(v). (See also § 1.148-11(c)(2).)

(vi) *Exception for refundings of interim notes.*—Paragraph (h)(4)(v) of this section need not be applied to refunding bonds issued to provide permanent financing for one or more projects if the prior issue had a term of less than 3 years and was sold in anticipation of permanent financing, but only if the aggregate term of all prior issues sold in anticipation of permanent financing was less than 3 years.

(5) *Limitation on multi-generation allocations.*—This paragraph (h) does not apply to allocations of a multipurpose refunded issue unless that refunded issue is refunded directly by an issue to which this paragraph (h) applies. For example, if a 1994 issue refunds a 1984 multipurpose issue, which in turn refunded a 1980 multipurpose issue, this paragraph (h) applies to allocations of the 1984 issue for purposes of allocating the refunding purposes of the 1994 issue, but does not permit allocations of the 1980 issue.

(i) *Operating rules for separation of prior issue into refunded and unrefunded portions.*—(1) *In general.*—For purposes of paragraph (h)(3)(i) of this section, the separate purposes of a prior issue include the refunded and unrefunded portions of the prior issue. Thus, the refunded and unrefunded portions are treated as separate issues under paragraph (h)(1) of this section. Those separate issues must satisfy the requirements of paragraphs (h) and (i) of this section. The refunded portion of the bonds of a prior issue is based on a fraction the numerator of which is the principal amount of the prior issue to be paid with proceeds of the refunding issue and the denominator of which is the outstanding principal amount of the bonds of the prior issue, each determined as of the issue date of the refunding issue. (See also paragraph (b)(2) of this section.)

(2) *Allocations of proceeds and investments in a partial refunding.*—As of the issue date of a partial refunding issue under this paragraph (i), unspent proceeds of the prior issue are allocated ratably between the refunded and unrefunded portions of the prior issue and the investments allocable to those unspent proceeds are allocated in the manner required for the allocation of investments to transferred proceeds under paragraph (c)(1)(ii) of this section.

(3) *References to prior issue.*—If the refunded and unrefunded portions of a prior issue are treated as separate issues under this paragraph (i), then, except to the extent that the context clearly requires otherwise (e.g., references to the aggregate prior issue in the mixed escrow rule in paragraph (c)(2) of this section), all references in this section to a prior issue refer only to the refunded portion of that prior issue. [Reg. § 1.148-9.]

□ [*T.D. 8418, 5-12-92. Amended by T.D. 8476, 6-14-93; T.D. 8538, 5-5-94 and T.D. 8718, 5-8-97.*]

[Reg. § 1.148-9A]

§ 1.148-9A. [Reserved].

□ [*T.D. 8538, 5-5-94. Redesignated and amended by T.D. 8718, 5-8-97. Removed and reserved by T.D. 9849, 3-11-2019.*]

[Reg. § 1.148-10]

§ 1.148-10. Anti-abuse rules and authority of Commissioner.—(a) *Abusive arbitrage device.*—(1) *In general.*—Bonds of an issue are arbitrage bonds under section 148 if an abusive arbitrage device under paragraph (a)(2) of this section is used in connection with the issue. This paragraph (a) is to be applied and interpreted broadly to carry out the purposes of section 148, as further described in § 1.148-0. Except as otherwise provided in paragraph (c) of this section, any action that is expressly permitted by section 148 or §§ 1.148-1 through 1.148-11 is not an abusive arbitrage device (e.g., investment in higher yielding investments during a permitted temporary period under section 148(c)).

(2) *Abusive arbitrage device defined.*—Any action is an abusive arbitrage device if the action has the effect of—

(i) Enabling the issuer to exploit the difference between tax-exempt and taxable interest rates to obtain a material financial advantage; and

(ii) Overburdening the tax-exempt bond market.

(3) *Exploitation of tax-exempt interest rates.*—An action may exploit tax-exempt interest rates under paragraph (a)(2) of this section as a result of an investment of any portion of the gross proceeds of an issue over any period of time, notwithstanding that, in the aggregate, the gross proceeds of the issue are not invested in higher yielding investments over the term of the issue.

(4) *Overburdening the tax-exempt market.*—An action overburdens the tax-exempt bond market under paragraph (a)(2)(ii) of this section if it results in issuing more bonds, issuing bonds earlier, or allowing bonds to remain outstanding longer than is otherwise reasonably necessary to accomplish the governmental purposes of the bonds, based on all the facts and circumstances. Whether an action is reasonably necessary to accomplish the governmental purposes of the bonds depends on whether the primary purpose of the transaction is a bona fide governmental purpose (e.g., an issue of refunding bonds to achieve a debt service restructuring that would be issued independent of any arbitrage benefit). An important factor bearing on this determination is whether the action would reasonably be taken to accomplish the governmental purpose of the issue if the interest on the issue were not excludable from gross income under section 103(a) (assuming that the hypothetical taxable interest rate would be the same as the actual tax-exempt interest rate). Factors evidencing an overissuance include the issuance of an issue the proceeds of which are reasonably expected to exceed by more than a minor portion the amount necessary to accomplish the governmental purposes of the issue, or an issue the proceeds of which are, in fact, substantially in excess of the amount of sale proceeds allocated to expenditures for the governmental purposes of the issue. One factor evidencing an early issuance is the issuance of bonds that do not qualify for a temporary period under § 1.148-2(e)(2), (e)(3), or (e)(4). One factor evidencing that bonds may remain outstanding longer than necessary is a term that exceeds the safe harbors against the creation of replacement proceeds under § 1.148-1(c)(4)(i)(B). These factors may be outweighed by other factors, such as bona fide cost underruns, an issuer's bona fide need to finance extraordinary working capital items, or an issuer's long-term financial distress.

(b) *Consequences of overburdening the tax-exempt bond market.*—(1) *In general.*—An issue that overburdens the tax-exempt bond market (within the meaning of paragraph (a)(4) of this section) is subject to the following special limitations—

(i) *Special yield restriction.*—Investments are subject to the definition of *materially higher* yield under § 1.148-2(d) that is equal to one-thousandth of 1 percent. In addition, each investment is treated as a separate class of investments under § 1.148-5(b)(2)(ii), the yield on which may not be blended with that of other investments.

(ii) *Certain regulatory provisions inapplicable.*—The provisions of § 1.148-5(c) (relating to yield reduction payments) and § 1.148-5(e)(2) and (3) (relating to recovery of qualified administrative costs) do not apply.

(iii) *Restrictive expenditure rule.*—Proceeds are not allocated to expenditures unless the proceeds-spent-last rule under § 1.148-6(d)(3)(i) is satisfied, applied by treating those proceeds as proceeds to be used for restricted working capital expenditures. For this purpose, available amount includes a reasonable working capital reserve as defined in § 1.148-6(d)(3)(iii)(B).

(2) *Application.*—The provisions of this paragraph (b) only apply to the portion of an issue that, as a result of actions taken (or actions not taken) after the issue date, overburdens the market for tax-exempt bonds, except that for an issue that is reasonably expected as of the issue date to overburden the market, those provisions apply to all of the gross proceeds of the issue.

(c) *Anti-abuse rules on excess gross proceeds of advance refunding issues.*—(1) *In general.*—Except as otherwise provided in this paragraph (c), an abusive arbitrage device is used and bonds of an advance refunding issue are arbitrage bonds if the issue has excess gross proceeds.

(2) *Definition of excess gross proceeds.*—Excess gross proceeds means all gross proceeds of an advance refunding issue that exceed an amount equal to 1 percent of sale proceeds of the issue, other than gross proceeds allocable to—

(i) Payment of principal, interest, or call premium on the prior issue;

(ii) Payment of pre-issuance accrued interest on the refunding issue, and interest on the refunding issue that accrues for a period up to the completion date of any capital project for which the prior issue was issued, plus one year;

(iii) A reasonably required reserve or replacement fund for the refunding issue or investment proceeds of such a fund;

(iv) Payment of costs of issuance of the refunding issue;

25,194

Tax Exempt. Requirements: State/Local Bonds
See p. 20,601 for regulations not amended to reflect law changes

(v) Payment of administrative costs allocable to repaying the prior issue, carrying and repaying the refunding issue, or investments of the refunding issue;

(vi) Transferred proceeds that will be used or maintained for the governmental purpose of the prior issue;

(vii) Interest on purpose investments;

(viii) Replacement proceeds in a sinking fund for the refunding issue;

(ix) Qualified guarantee fees for the refunding issue or the prior issue; and

(x) Fees for a qualified hedge for the refunding issue.

(3) *Special treatment of transferred proceeds.*—For purposes of this paragraph (c), all unspent proceeds of the prior issue as of the issue date of the refunding issue are treated as transferred proceeds of the advance refunding issue.

(4) *Special rule for crossover refundings.*—An advance refunding issue is not an issue of arbitrage bonds under this paragraph (c) if all excess gross proceeds of the refunding issue are used to pay interest that accrues on the refunding issue before the prior issue is discharged, and no gross proceeds of any refunding issue are used to pay interest on the prior issue or to replace funds used directly or indirectly to pay such interest (other than transferred proceeds used to pay interest on the prior issue that accrues for a period up to the completion date of the project for which the prior issue was issued, plus one year, or proceeds used to pay principal that is attributable to accrued original issue discount).

(5) *Special rule for gross refundings.*—This paragraph (c)(5) applies if an advance refunding issue (the *series B issue*) is used together with one or more other advance refunding issues (the *series A issues*) in a gross refunding of a prior issue, but only if the use of a gross refunding method is required under bond documents that were effective prior to November 6, 1992. These advance refunding issues are not arbitrage bonds under this paragraph (c) if—

(i) All excess gross proceeds of the series B issue and each series A issue are investment proceeds used to pay principal and interest on the series B issue;

(ii) At least 99 percent of all principal and interest on the series B issue is paid with proceeds of the series B and series A issues or with the earnings on other amounts in the refunding escrow for the prior issue;

(iii) The series B issue is discharged not later than the prior issue; and

(iv) As of any date, the amount of gross proceeds of the series B issue allocated to expenditures does not exceed the aggregate amount of expenditures before that date for principal and interest on the series B issue, and administrative costs of carrying and repaying the series B issue, or of investments of the series B issue.

(d) *Examples.*—The provisions of this section are illustrated by the following examples:

Example 1. Mortgage sale. In 1982, City issued its revenue issue (the *1982 issue*) and lent the proceeds to Developer to finance a low-income housing project under former section 103(b)(4)(A) of the 1954 Code. In 1994, Developer encounters financial difficulties and negotiates with City to refund the 1982 issue. City issues $10 million in principal amount of its 8 percent bonds (the *1994 issue*). City lends the proceeds of the 1994 issue to Developer. To evidence Developer's obligation to repay that loan, Developer, as obligor, issues a note to City (the *City note*). Bank agrees to provide Developer with a direct-pay letter of credit pursuant to which Bank will make all payments to the trustee for the 1994 issue necessary to meet Developer's obligations under the City note. Developer pays Bank a fee for the issuance of the letter of credit and issues a note to Bank (the *Bank note*). The Bank note is secured by a mortgage on the housing project and is guaranteed by FHA. The Bank note and the 1994 issue have different prepayment terms. The City does not reasonably expect to treat prepayments of the Bank note as gross proceeds of the 1994 issue. At the same time or pursuant to a series of related transactions, Bank sells the Bank note to Investor for $9.5 million. Bank invests these monies together with its other funds. In substance, the transaction is a loan by City to Bank, under which Bank enters into a series of transactions that, in effect, result in Bank retaining $9.5 million in amounts treated as proceeds of the 1994 issue. Those amounts are invested in materially higher yielding investments that provide funds sufficient to equal or exceed the Bank's liability under the letter of credit. Alternatively, the letter of credit is investment property in a sinking fund for the 1994 issue provided by Developer, a substantial *beneficiary of the financing. Because, in substance,* Developer acquires the $10 million principal amount letter of credit for a fair market value purchase price of $9.5 million, the letter of credit is a materially higher yielding investment. Neither result would change if Developer's obligation under the Bank note is contingent on Bank

performing its obligation under the letter of credit. Each characterization causes the bonds to be arbitrage bonds.

Example 2. Bonds outstanding longer than necessary for yield-blending device. (i) *Longer bond maturity to create sinking fund.* In 1994, Authority issues an advance refunding issue (the *refunding issue*) to refund a 1982 prior issue (the *prior issue*). Under current market conditions, Authority will have to invest the refunding escrow at a yield significantly below the yield on the refunding issue. Authority issues its refunding issue with a longer weighted average maturity than otherwise necessary primarily for the purpose of creating a sinking fund for the refunding issue that will be invested in a guaranteed investment contract. The weighted average maturity of the refunding issue is less than 120 percent of the remaining average economic life of the facilities financed with the proceeds of the prior issue. The guaranteed investment contract has a yield that is higher than the yield on the refunding issue. The yield on the refunding escrow blended with the yield on the guaranteed investment contract does not exceed the yield on the issue. The refunding issue uses an abusive arbitrage device and the bonds of the issue are arbitrage bonds under section 148(a).

(ii) *Refunding of noncallable bonds.* The facts are the same as in paragraph (i) of this *Example 2* except that instead of structuring the refunding issue to enable it to take advantage of sinking fund investments, Authority will also refund other long-term, non-callable bonds in the same refunding issue. There are no savings attributable to the refunding of the non-callable bonds (e.g., a *low-to-high* refunding). The Authority invests the portion of the proceeds of the refunding issue allocable to the refunding of the non-callable bonds in the refunding escrow at a yield that is higher than the yield on the refunding issue, based on the relatively long escrow period for this portion of the refunding. The Authority invests the other portion of the proceeds of the refunding issue in the refunding escrow at a yield lower than the yield on the refunding issue. The blended yield on all the investments in the refunding escrow for the prior issues does not exceed the yield on the refunding issue. The portion of the refunding issue used to refund the noncallable bonds, however, was not otherwise necessary and was issued primarily to exploit the difference between taxable and tax-exempt rates for that long portion of the refunding escrow to minimize the effect of lower yielding investments in the other portion of the escrow. The refunding issue uses an abusive arbitrage device and the bonds of the issue are arbitrage bonds.

(iii) *Governmental purpose.* In paragraphs (i) and (ii) of this *Example 2,* the existence of a governmental purpose for the described financing structures would not change the conclusions unless Authority clearly established that the primary purpose for the use of the particular structure was a bona fide governmental purpose. The fact that each financing structure had the effect of eliminating significant amounts of negative arbitrage is strong evidence of a primary purpose that is not a bona fide governmental purpose. Moreover, in paragraph (i) of this *Example 2,* the structure of the refunding issue coupled with the acquisition of the guaranteed investment contract to lock in the investment yield associated with the structure is strong evidence of a primary purpose that is not a bona fide governmental purpose.

Example 3. Window refunding. (i) Authority issues its 1994 refunding issue to refund a portion of the principal and interest on its outstanding 1985 issue. The 1994 refunding issue is structured using zero-coupon bonds that pay no interest or principal for the 5-year period following the issue date. The proceeds of the 1994 refunding issue are deposited in a refunding escrow to be used to pay only the interest requirements of the refunded portion of the 1985 issue. Authority enters into a guaranteed investment contract with a financial institution, *G,* under which *G* agrees to provide a guaranteed yield on revenues invested by Authority during the 5-year period following the issue date. The guaranteed investment contract has a yield that is no higher than the yield on the refunding issue. The revenues to be invested under this guaranteed investment contract consist of the amounts that Authority otherwise would have used to pay principal and interest on the 1994 refunding issue. The guaranteed investment contract is structured to generate receipts at times and in amounts sufficient to pay the principal and redemption requirements of the refunded portion of the 1985 issue. A principal purpose of these transactions is to avoid transferred proceeds. Authority will continue to invest the unspent proceeds of the 1985 issue that are on deposit in a refunding escrow for its 1982 issue at a yield equal to the yield on the 1985 issue and will not otherwise treat those unspent proceeds as transferred proceeds of the 1994 refunding issue. The 1994 refunding issue is an issue of arbitrage bonds since these bonds involve a transaction or series of transactions that overburdens the market by leaving bonds outstanding longer than is necessary to obtain a material financial advantage based on arbitrage. Specifically, Authority has structured the 1994 refunding issue to make available for the refunding of the 1985 issue replacement proceeds rather than proceeds so that the unspent proceeds of the 1985 issue will not become transferred proceeds of the 1994 refunding issue.

(ii) The result would be the same in each of the following circumstances:

(A) The facts are the same as in paragraph (i) of this *Example 3* except that Authority does not enter into the guaranteed investment contract but instead, as of the issue date of the 1994 refunding issue, reasonably expects that the released revenues will be available for investment until used to pay principal and interest on the 1985 issue.

(B) The facts are the same as in paragraph (i) of this *Example 3* except that there are no unspent proceeds of the 1985 issue and Authority invests the released revenues at a yield materially higher than the yield on the 1994 issue.

(C) The facts are the same as in paragraph (i) of this *Example 3* except that Authority uses the proceeds of the 1994 issue for capital projects instead of to refund a portion of the 1985 issue.

Example 4. Sale of conduit loan. On January 1, 1994, Authority issues a conduit financing issue (the *1994 conduit financing issue*) and uses the proceeds to purchase from City, an unrelated party, a tax-exempt bond of City (the *City note*). The proceeds of the 1994 conduit financing issue are to be used to advance refund a prior conduit financing issue that was issued in 1988 and used to make a loan to City. The 1994 conduit financing issue and the City note each have a yield of 8 percent on January 1, 1994. On June 30, 1996, interest rates have decreased and Authority sells the City note to D, a person unrelated to either City or Authority. Based on the sale price of the City note and treating June 30, 1996 as the issue date of the City note, the City note has a 6 percent yield. Authority deposits the proceeds of the sale of the City note into an escrow to redeem the bonds of the 1994 conduit financing issue on January 1, 2001. The escrow is invested in nonpurpose investments having a yield of 8 percent. For purposes of section 149(d), City and Authority are related parties and, therefore, the issue date of the City note is treated as being June 30, 1996. Thus, the City note is an advance refunding of Authority's 1994 conduit financing issue. Interest on the City note is not exempt from Federal income tax from the date it is sold to D under section 149(d), because, by investing the escrow investments at a yield of 8 percent instead of a yield not materially higher than 6 percent, the sale of the City note employs a device to obtain a material financial advantage, based on arbitrage, apart from the savings attributable to lower interest rates. In addition, the City note is not a tax-exempt bond because the note is the second advance refunding of the original bond under section 149(d)(3). The City note also employs an abusive arbitrage device and is an arbitrage bond under section 148.

Example 5. Re-refunding. (i) On January 1, 1984, City issues a tax-exempt issue (the *1984 issue*) to finance the cost of constructing a prison. The 1984 issue has a 7 percent yield and a 30-year maturity. The 1984 issue is callable at any time on or after January 1, 1994. On January 1, 1990, City issues a refunding issue (the *1990 issue*) to advance refund the 1984 issue. The 1990 issue has an 8 percent yield and a 30-year maturity. The 1990 issue is callable at any time on or after January 1, 2000. The proceeds of the 1990 issue are invested at an 8 percent yield in a refunding escrow for the 1984 issue (the *original 1984 escrow*) in a manner sufficient to pay debt service on the 1984 issue until maturity (i.e., an escrow to maturity). On January 1, 1994, City issues a refunding issue (the *1994 issue*). The 1994 issue has a 6 percent yield and a 30-year maturity. City does not invest the proceeds of the 1994 issue in a refunding escrow for the 1990 issue in a manner sufficient to pay a portion of the debt service until, and redeem a portion of that issue on, January 1, 2000. Instead, City invests those proceeds at a 6 percent yield in a new refunding escrow for a portion of the 1984 issue (the *new 1984 escrow*) in a manner sufficient to pay debt service on a portion of the 1984 issue until maturity. City also liquidates the investments allocable to the proceeds of the 1990 issue held in the original 1984 escrow and reinvests those proceeds in an escrow to pay a portion of the debt service on the 1990 issue itself until, and redeem a portion of that issue on, January 1, 2000 (the *1990 escrow*). The 1994 bonds are arbitrage bonds and employ an abusive device under section 149(d)(4). Although, in form, the proceeds of the 1994 issue are used to pay principal on the 1984 issue, this accounting for the use of the proceeds of the 1994 issue is an unreasonable, inconsistent accounting method under § 1.148-6(a). Moreover, since the proceeds of the 1990 issue were set aside in an escrow to be used to retire the 1984 issue, the use of proceeds of the 1994 issue for that same purpose involves a replacement of funds invested in higher yielding investments under section 148(a)(2). Thus, using a reasonable, consistent accounting method and giving effect to the substance of the transaction, the proceeds of the 1994 issue are treated as used to refund the 1990 issue and are allocable to the 1990 escrow. The proceeds of the 1990 issue are treated as used to refund the 1984 issue and are allocable to the investments in the new 1984 escrow. The proceeds of the 1990 issue allocable to the nonpurpose investments in the new 1984 escrow become transferred proceeds of the 1994 issue as principal is paid on the 1990 issue from amounts on deposit in the 1990 escrow. As a result, the yield on nonpurpose investments allocable to the 1994 issue is materially higher than the yield on the 1994 issue, causing the bonds of the 1994 issue to be arbitrage bonds. In addition, the transaction employs a device under section 149(d)(4) to obtain a material financial advantage based on arbitrage, other than savings attributable to lower interest rates.

(ii) The following changes in the facts do not affect the conclusion that the 1994 issue consists of arbitrage bonds—

(1) The 1990 issue is a taxable issue;

(2) The original 1984 escrow is used to pay the 1994 issue (rather than the 1990 issue); or

(3) The 1994 issue is used to retire the 1984 issue within 90 days of January 1, 1994.

(e) *Authority of the Commissioner to prevent transactions that are inconsistent with the purpose of the arbitrage investment restrictions.*—If an issuer enters into a transaction for a principal purpose of obtaining a material financial advantage based on the difference between tax-exempt and taxable interest rates in a manner that is inconsistent with the purposes of section 148, the Commissioner may exercise the Commissioner's discretion to depart from the rules of § 1.148-1 through § 1.148-11 as necessary to reflect the economics of the transaction to prevent such financial advantage. For this purpose, the Commissioner may recompute yield on an issue or on investments, reallocate payments and receipts on investments, recompute the rebate amount on an issue, treat a hedge as either a qualified hedge or not a qualified hedge, or otherwise adjust any item whatsoever bearing upon the investments and expenditures of gross proceeds of an issue. For example, if the amount paid for a hedge is specifically based on the amount of arbitrage earned or expected to be earned on the hedged bonds, a principal purpose of entering into the contract is to obtain a material financial advantage based on the difference between tax-exempt and taxable interest rates in a manner that is inconsistent with the purposes of section 148.

(f) *Authority of the Commissioner to require an earlier date for payment of rebate.*—If the Commissioner determines that an issue is likely to fail to meet the requirements of § 1.148-3 and that a failure to serve a notice of demand for payment on the issuer will jeopardize the assessment or collection of tax on interest paid or to be paid on the issue, the date that the Commissioner serves notice on the issuer is treated as a required computation date for payment of rebate for that issue.

(g) *Authority of the Commissioner to waive regulatory limitations.*— Notwithstanding any specific provision in § § 1.148-1 through 1.148-11, the Commissioner may prescribe extensions of temporary periods, larger reasonably required reserve or replacement funds, or consequences of failures or remedial action under section 148 in lieu of or in addition to other consequences of those failures, or take other action, if the Commissioner finds that good faith or other similar circumstances so warrant, consistent with the purposes of section 148. [Reg. § 1.148-10.]

☐ [*T.D. 8284, 1-22-90. Amended by T.D. 8418, 5-12-92, T.D. 8476, 6-14-93; T.D. 8538, 5-5-94, T.D. 8713, 5-8-97 and T.D. 9777, 7-15-2016.*]

[Reg. § 1.148-10A]

§ 1.148-10A. [Reserved].

☐ [*T.D. 8538, 5-5-94. Redesignated and amended by T.D. 8718, 5-8-97. Removed and reserved by T.D. 9849, 3-11-2019.*]

[Reg. § 1.148-11]

§ 1.148-11. Effective/applicability dates.—(a) *In general.*—Except as otherwise provided in this section, § § 1.148-1 through 1.148-11 apply to bonds sold on or after July 8, 1997.

(b) *Elective retroactive application in whole.*—(1) *In general.*—Except as otherwise provided in this section, and subject to the applicable effective dates for the corresponding statutory provisions, an issuer may apply the provisions of § § 1.148-1 through 1.148-11 in whole, but not in part, to any issue that is outstanding on July 8, 1997, and is subject to section 148(f) or to sections 103(c)(6) or 103A(i) of the Internal Revenue Code of 1954, in lieu of otherwise applicable regulations under those sections.

(2) *No elective retroactive application for 18-month spending exception.*—The provisions of § 1.148-7(d) (relating to the 18-month spending exception) may not be applied to any issue issued on or before June 30, 1993.

(3) *No elective retroactive application for hedges of fixed rate issues.*— The provisions of § 1.148-4(h)(2)(i)(B) (relating to hedges of fixed rate issues) may not be applied to any bond sold on or before July 8, 1997.

(4) *No elective retroactive application for safe harbor for establishing fair market value for guaranteed investment contracts and investments*

25,196

Tax Exempt. Requirements: State/Local Bonds
See p. 20,601 for regulations not amended to reflect law changes

purchased for a yield restricted defeasance escrow.—The provisions of §§1.148-5(d)(6)(iii) (relating to the safe harbor for establishing fair market value of guaranteed investment contracts and yield restricted defeasance escrow investments) and 1.148-5(e)(2)(iv) (relating to a special rule for yield restricted defeasance escrow investments) may not be applied to any bond sold before December 30, 1998.

(c) *Elective retroactive application of certain provisions and special rules.*—(1) *Retroactive application of overpayment recovery provisions.*—An issuer may apply the provisions of §1.148-3(i) to any issue that is subject to section 148(f) or to sections 103(c)(6) or 103A(i) of the Internal Revenue Code of 1954.

(i) *Certain commingled funds.*—If paragraph (a) of this section applies to an issue, and that issue has a commingled fund to which the provisions of §1.148-6(e)(6) (relating to commingled reserves) apply, that provision may be applied to all issues secured by that commingled reserve.

(ii) *Certain applications of the universal cap.*—The provisions of §1.148-5(c)(3)(i)(F) (and related provisions) may be applied to satisfy the requirements of section 148 (or applicable prior law) if the application of the universal cap results in amounts in a refunding escrow becoming replacement proceeds of an issue issued on or before June 30, 1993.

(2) *Certain allocations of multipurpose issues.*—An allocation of bonds to a refunding purpose under §1.148-9(h) may be adjusted as necessary to reflect allocations made between May 18, 1992, and August 15, 1993, if the allocations satisfied the corresponding prior provision of §1.148-11(j)(4) under applicable prior regulations.

(3) *Special limitation.*—The provisions of §1.148-9 apply to issues issued before August 15, 1993, only if the issuer in good faith estimates the present value savings, if any, associated with the effect of the application of that section on refunding escrows, using any reasonable accounting method, and applies those savings, if any, to redeem outstanding tax-exempt bonds of the applicable issue at the earliest possible date on which those bonds may be redeemed or otherwise retired. These savings are not reduced to take into account any administrative costs associated with applying these provisions retroactively.

(d) *Transition rule excepting certain state guarantee funds from the definition of replacement proceeds.*—(1) *Certain perpetual trust funds.*—(i) A guarantee by a fund created and controlled by a State and established pursuant to its constitution does not cause the amounts in the fund to be pledged funds treated as replacement proceeds if—

(A) Substantially all of the corpus of the fund consists of nonfinancial assets, revenues derived from these assets, gifts, and bequests;

(B) The corpus of the guarantee fund may be invaded only to support specifically designated essential governmental functions (designated functions) carried on by political subdivisions with general taxing powers or public elementary and public secondary schools;

(C) Substantially all of the available income of the fund is required to be applied annually to support designated functions;

(D) The issue guaranteed consists of obligations that are not private activity bonds (other than qualified 501(c)(3) bonds) substantially all of the proceeds of which are to be used for designated functions;

(E) The fund satisfied each of the requirements of paragraphs (d)(1)(i) through (d)(1)(iii) of this section on August 16, 1986; and

(F) As of the sale date of the bonds to be guaranteed, the amount of the bonds to be guaranteed by the fund plus the then-outstanding amount of bonds previously guaranteed by the fund does not exceed a total amount equal to 500 percent of the total costs of the assets held by the fund as of December 16, 2009.

(ii) The Commissioner may, by published guidance, set forth additional circumstances under which guarantees by certain perpetual trust funds will not cause amounts in the fund to be treated as replacement proceeds.

(2) *Permanent University Fund.*—Replacement proceeds do not include amounts allocable to investments of the fund described in section 648 of Public Law 98-369.

(e) *Transition rule regarding special allowance payments.*—Section 1.148-5(b)(5) applies to any bond issued after January 5, 1990, except a bond issued exclusively to refund a bond issued before January 6, 1990, if the amount of the refunding bond does not exceed 101 percent of the amount of the refunded bond, and the maturity date of the refunding bond is not later than the date that is 17 years after the date on which the refunded bond was issued (or, in the case of a series of refundings, the date on which the original bond was issued),

but only if §1.148-2(d)(2)(iv) is applied by substituting 1 and one-half percentage points for 2 percentage points.

(f) *Transition rule regarding applicability of yield reduction rule.*—Section 1.148-5(c) applies to nonpurpose investments allocable to replacement proceeds of an issue that are held in a reserve or replacement fund to the extent that—

(1) Amounts must be paid into the fund under a constitutional provision, statute, or ordinance adopted before May 3, 1978;

(2) Under that provision, amounts paid into the fund (and investment earnings thereon) can be used only to pay debt service on the issues; and

(3) The size of the payments made into the fund is independent of the size of the outstanding issues or the debt service thereon.

(g) *Provisions applicable to certain bonds sold before effective date.*—Except for bonds to which paragraph (b)(1) of this section applies—

(1) Section 1.148-11A provides rules applicable to bonds sold after June 6, 1994, and before July 8, 1997; and

(2) Sections 1.148-1 through 1.148-11 as in effect on July 1, 1993 (see 26 CFR part 1 as revised April 1, 1994), and §1.148-11A(i) (relating to elective retroactive application of certain provisions) provide rules applicable to certain issues issued before June 7, 1994.

(h) *Safe harbor for establishing fair market value for guaranteed investment contracts and investments purchased for a yield restricted defeasance escrow.*—The provisions of §1.148-5(d)(6)(iii) are applicable to bonds sold on or after March 1, 1999. Issuers may apply these provisions to bonds sold on or after December 30, 1998, and before March 1, 1999.

(i) *Special rule for certain broker's commissions and similar fees.*—Section 1.148-5(e)(2)(iii) applies to bonds sold on or after February 9, 2004. In the case of bonds sold before February 9, 2004, that are subject to §1.148-5 (pre-effective date bonds), issuers may apply §1.148-5(e)(2)(iii), in whole but not in part, with respect to transactions entered into on or after December 11, 2003. If an issuer applies §1.148-5(e)(2)(iii) to pre-effective date bonds, the per-issue safe harbor in §1.148-5(e)(2)(iii)(B)(1)(ii) is applied by taking into account all brokers' commissions or similar fees with respect to guaranteed investment contracts and investments for yield restricted defeasance escrows that the issuer treats as qualified administrative costs for the issue, including all such commissions or fees paid before February 9, 2004. For purposes of §§1.148-5(e)(2)(iii)(B)(3) and 1.148-5(e)(2)(iii)(B)(6) (relating to cost-of-living adjustments), transactions entered into before 2003 are treated as entered into in 2003.

(j) *Certain prepayments.*—Section 1.148-1(e)(1) and (2) apply to bonds sold on or after October 3, 2003. Issuers may apply §1.148-1(e)(1) and (2), in whole but not in part, to bonds sold before October 3, 2003, that are subject to §1.148-1.

(k) *Certain arbitrage guidance updates.*—(1) *In general.*—Sections 1.148-1(c)(4)(i)(B)(1); 1.148-1(c)(4)(i)(B)(4); 1.148-1(c)(4)(ii); 1.148-2(e)(3)(i); 1.148-3(d)(1)(iv); 1.148-3(d)(4); 1.148-4(a); 1.148-4(b)(3)(i); 1.148-4(h)(2)(ii)(A); 1.148-4(h)(2)(v); 1.148-4(h)(2)(vi); 1.148(h)(4)(i)(C); 1.148-5(c)(3); 1.148-5(d)(2); 1.148-5(d)(3); 1.148-5(d)(6)(i); 1.148-5(d)(6)(iii)(A); 1.148-5(e)(2)(ii)(B); 1.148-6(d)(3)(iii)(A); 1.148-6(d)(4); 1.148-7(c)(3)(v); 1.148-7(i)(6)(iii); 1.148-10(a)(4); 1.148-10(e); 1.148-11(d)(1)(i)(B); 1.148-11(d)(1)(i)(D); 1.148-11(d)(1)(i)(F); and 1.148-11(d)(1)(ii) apply to bonds sold on or after October 17, 2016.

(2) *Valuation of investments in refunding transactions.*—Section 1.148-5(d)(3) also applies to bonds refunded by bonds sold on or after October 17, 2016.

(3) *Rebate overpayment recovery.*—(i) Section 1.148-3(i)(3)(i) applies to claims arising from an issue of bonds to which §1.148-3(i) applies and for which the final computation date is after June 24, 2008. For purposes of this paragraph (k)(3)(i), issues for which the actual final computation date is on or before June 24, 2008, are deemed to have a final computation date of July 1, 2008, for purposes of applying §1.148-3(i)(3)(i).

(ii) Section 1.148-3(i)(3)(ii) and (iii) apply to claims arising from an issue of bonds to which §1.148-3(i) applies and for which the final computation date is after September 16, 2013.

(iii) Section 1.148-3(j) applies to bonds subject to §1.148-3(i).

(4) *Hedge identification.*—Section 1.148-4(h)(2)(viii) applies to hedges that are entered into on or after October 17, 2016.

(5) *Hedge modifications and termination.*—Section 1.148-4(h)(3)(iv)(A) through (H) and (h)(4)(iv) apply to—

(i) Hedges that are entered into on or after October 17, 2016;

(ii) Qualified hedges that are modified on or after October 17, 2016 with respect to modifications on or after such date; and

(iii) Qualified hedges on bonds that are refunded on or after October 17, 2016 with respect to the refunding on or after such date.

Tax Exempt. Requirements: State/Local Bonds   **25,197**

See p. 20,601 for regulations not amended to reflect law changes

(6) *Small issuer exception to rebate requirement for conduit borrowers of pooled financings.*—Section 1.148-8(d) applies to bonds issued after May 17, 2006.

(l) *Permissive application of certain arbitrage updates.*—(1) *In general.*—Except as otherwise provided in this paragraph (l), issuers may apply the provisions described in paragraph (k)(1), (2), and (5) in whole, but not in part, to bonds sold before October 17, 2016.

(2) *Computation credit.*—Issuers may apply §1.148-3(d)(1)(iv) and (d)(4) for bond years ending on or after July 18, 2016.

(3) *Yield reduction payments.*—Issuers may apply §1.148-5(c)(3) for investments purchased on or after July 18, 2016.

(4) *External commingled funds.*—Issuers may apply §1.148-5(e)(2)(ii)(B) with respect to costs incurred on or after July 18, 2016.

(m) *Definition of issue price.*—The definition of issue price in §1.148-1(b) and (f) applies to bonds that are sold on or after June 7, 2017.

(n) *Investment-type property.*—Section 1.148-1(e)(1) and (4) apply to bonds sold on or after July 8, 2019. An issuer may apply the provisions of §1.148-1(e)(1) and (4) to bonds sold before July 8, 2019. [Reg. §1.148-11.]

☐ [*T.D. 8418, 5-12-92 (corrected 9-29-92). Amended by T.D. 8476, 6-14-93 (corrected 8-18-93 and 7-8-99); T.D. 8538, 5-5-94; T.D. 8718, 5-8-97; T.D. 9085, 8-1-2003; T.D. 9097, 12-10-2003, T.D. 9701, 11-12-2014, T.D. 9777, 7-15-2016 (corrected 8-22-2016), T.D. 9801, 12-8-2016 (corrected 8-11-2017) and T.D. 9854, 4-8-2019.*]

[Reg. §1.148-11A]

§1.148-11A. Effective dates.—(a) through (c)(3) [Reserved]. For guidance see §1.148-11.

(c)(4) *Retroactive application of overpayment recovery provisions.*—An issuer may apply the provisions of §1.148-3(i) to any issue that is subject to section 148(f) or to sections 103(c)(6) or 103A(i) of the Internal Revenue Code of 1954.

(d) through (h) [Reserved]. For guidance see §1.148-11.

(i) *Transition rules for certain amendments.*—(1) *In general.*—Section 1.103-8(a)(5), §§1.148-1, 1.148-2, 1.148-3, 1.148-4, 1.148-5, 1.148-6, 1.148-7, 1.148-8, 1.148-9, 1.148-10, 1.148-11, 1.149(d)-1, and 1.150-1 as in effect on June 7, 1994 (see 26 CFR part 1 as revised April 1, 1997), and §§1.148-1A through 1.148-11A, 1.149(d)-1A, and 1.150-1A apply, in whole, but not in part—

(i) To bonds sold after June 6, 1994, and before July 8, 1997;

(ii) To bonds issued before July 1, 1993, that are outstanding on June 7, 1994, if the first time the issuer applies §§1.148-1 through 1.148-11 as in effect on June 7, 1994 (see 26 CFR part 1 as revised April 1, 1997), to the bonds under §1.148-11(b) or (c) is after June 6, 1994, and before July 8, 1997;

(iii) At the option of the issuer, to bonds to which §§1.148-1 through 1.148-11, as in effect on July 1, 1993 (see 26 CFR part 1 as revised April 1, 1994), apply, if the bonds are outstanding on June 7, 1994, and the issuer applies §1.103-8(a)(5), §§1.148-1, 1.148-2, 1.148-3, 1.148-4, 1.148-5, 1.148-6, 1.148-7, 1.148-8, 1.148-10, 1.148-11, 1.149(d)-1, and 1.150-1 as in effect on June 7, 1994 (see 26 CFR part 1 as revised April 1, 1997), and §§1.148-1A through 1.148-11A, 1.149(d)-1A, and 1.150-1A to the bonds before July 8, 1997.

(2) *Special rule.*—For purposes of paragraph (i)(1) of this section, any reference to a particular paragraph of §§1.148-1T, 1.148-2T, 1.148-3T, 1.148-4T, 1.148-5T, 1.148-6T, 1.148-9T, 1.148-10T, 1.148-11T, 1.149(d)-1T, or 1.150-1T shall be applied as a reference to the corresponding paragraph of §§1.148-1A, 1.148-2A, 1.148-3A, 1.148-4A, 1.148-5A, 1.148-6A, 1.148-9A, 1.148-10A, 1.148-11A, 1.149(d)-1A, or 1.150-1A, respectively.

(3) *Identification of certain hedges.*—For any hedge entered into after June 18, 1993, and on or before June 6, 1994, that would be a qualified hedge within the meaning of §1.148-4(h)(2), as in effect on June 7, 1994 (see 26 CFR part 1 as revised April 1, 1997), except that the hedge does not meet the requirements of §1.148-4A(h)(2)(ix) because the issuer failed to identify the hedge not later than 3 days after which the issuer and the provider entered into the contract, the requirements of §1.148-4A(h)(2)(ix) are treated as met if the contract is identified by the actual issuer on its books and records maintained for the hedged bonds not later than July 8, 1997. [Reg. §1.148-11A.]

☐ [*T.D. 8538, 5-5-94. Redesignated and amended by T.D. 8718, 5-8-97.*]

[Reg. §1.149(b)-1]

§1.149(b)-1. Federally guaranteed bonds.—(a) *General rule.*—Under section 149(b) and this section, nothing in section 103(a) or in any other provision of law shall be construed to provide an exemption from Federal income tax for interest on any bond issued as part of an issue that is federally guaranteed.

(b) *Exceptions.*—Pursuant to section 149(b)(3)(B), section 149(b)(1) and paragraph (a) of this section do not apply to—

(1) Investments in obligations issued pursuant to §21B(d)(3) of the Federal Home Loan Bank Act, as amended by §511 of the Financial Institutions Reform, Recovery, and Enforcement Act of 1989, or any successor provision; or

(2) Any investments that are held in a refunding escrow (as defined in §1.148-1).

(c) *Effective date.*—This section applies to investments made after June 30, 1993. [Reg. §1.149(b)-1.]

☐ [*T.D. 8476, 6-14-93.*]

[Reg. §1.149(d)-1]

§1.149(d)-1. Limitations on advance refundings.—(a) *General rule.*—Under section 149(d) and this section, nothing in section 103(a) or in any other provision of law shall be construed to provide an exemption from Federal income tax for interest on any bond issued as part of an issue described in paragraphs (2), (3) or (4) of section 149(d).

(b) *Advance refunding issues that employ abusive devices.*—(1) *In general.*—An advance refunding issue employs an abusive device and is described in section 149(d)(4) if the issue violates any of the anti-abuse rules under §1.148-10.

(2) *Failure to pay required rebate.*—An advance refunding issue is described in section 149(d)(4) if the issue fails to meet the requirements of §1.148-3. This paragraph (b)(2) applies to any advance refunding issue issued after August 31, 1986.

(3) *Mixed escrows invested in tax-exempt bonds.*—An advance refunding issue is described in section 149(d)(4) if—

(i) Any of the proceeds of the issue are invested in a refunding escrow in which a portion of the proceeds are invested in tax-exempt bonds and a portion of the proceeds are invested in nonpurpose investments;

(ii) The yield on the tax-exempt bonds in the refunding escrow exceeds the yield on the issue

(iii) The yield on all the investments (including investment property and tax-exempt bonds) in the refunding escrow exceeds the yield on the issue; and

(iv) The weighted average maturity of the tax-exempt bonds in the refunding escrow is more than 25 percent greater or less than the weighted average maturity of the nonpurpose investments in the refunding escrow, and the weighted average maturity of nonpurpose investments in the refunding escrow is greater than 60 days.

(4) *Tax-exempt conduit loans.*—For purposes of applying section 149(d) to a conduit financing issue that finances any conduit loan that is a tax-exempt bond, the actual issuer of a conduit financing issue and the conduit borrower of that conduit financing issue are treated as related parties. Thus, the issue date of the conduit loan does not occur prior to the date on which the actual issuer of the conduit financing issue sells, exchanges, or otherwise disposes of that conduit loan, and the use of the proceeds of the disposition to pay debt service on the conduit financing issue causes the conduit loan to be a refunding issue. See §1.148-10(d), *Example 4.*

(c) *Unrefunded debt service remains eligible for future advance refunding.*—For purposes of section 149(d)(3)(A)(i), any principal or interest on a prior issue that has not been paid or provided for by any advance refunding issue is treated as not having been advance refunded.

(d) *Application of arbitrage regulations.*—(1) *Application of multipurpose issue rules.*—For purposes of sections 149(d)(2) and (3)(A)(i), (ii), and (iii), the provisions of the multipurpose issue rule in §1.148-9(h) apply, except that the limitation in §1.148-9(h)(5) is disregarded.

(2) *General mixed escrow rules.*—For purposes of section 149(d), the provisions of §1.148-9(c) (relating to mixed escrows) apply, except that those provisions do not apply for purposes of section 149(d)(2) and (d)(3)(A)(i) and (ii) to amounts that were not gross proceeds of the prior issue before the issue date of the refunding issue.

(3) *Temporary periods and minor portions.*—Section 1.148-9(d) and (f) contains rules applicable to temporary periods and minor portions for advance refunding issues.

(4) *Definitions.*—Section 1.148-1 applies for purposes of section 149(d).

25,198

Tax Exempt. Requirements: State/Local Bonds
See p. 20,601 for regulations not amended to reflect law changes

(e) *Taxable refundings.*—(1) *In general.*—Except as provided in paragraph (e)(2) of this section, for purposes of section 149(d)(3)(A)(i), an advance refunding issue the interest on which is not excludable from gross income under section 103(a) (i.e., a taxable advance refunding issue) is not taken into account. In addition, for this purpose, an advance refunding of a taxable issue is not taken into account unless the taxable issue is a conduit loan of a tax-exempt conduit financing issue.

(2) *Use to avoid section 149(d)(3)(A)(i).*—A taxable issue is taken into account under section 149(d)(3)(A)(i) if it is issued to avoid the limitations of that section. For example, in the case of a refunding of a tax-exempt issue with a taxable advance refunding issue that is, in turn, currently refunded with a tax-exempt issue, the taxable advance refunding issue is taken into account under section 149(d)(3)(A)(i) if the two tax-exempt issues are outstanding concurrently for more than 90 days.

(f) *Redemption at first call date.*—(1) *General rule.*—Under sections 149(d)(3)(A)(ii) and (iii) (the *first call requirement*), bonds refunded by an advance refunding must be redeemed on their first call date if the savings test under section 149(d)(3)(B)(i) (the *savings test*) is satisfied. The savings test is satisfied if the issuer may realize present value debt service savings (determined without regard to administrative expenses) in connection with the issue of which the refunding bond is a part.

(2) *First call date.*—*First call date* means the earliest date on which a bond may be redeemed (or, if issued before 1986, on the earliest date on which that bond may be redeemed at a redemption price not in excess of 103 percent of par). If, however, the savings test is not met with respect to the date described in the preceding sentence (i.e., there are no present value savings if the refunded bonds are retired on that date), the first call date is the first date thereafter on which the bonds can be redeemed and on which the savings test is met.

(3) *Application of savings test to multipurpose issues.*—Except as otherwise provided in this paragraph (f)(3), the multipurpose issue rules in § 1.148-9(h) apply for purposes of the savings test. If any separate issue in a multipurpose issue increases the aggregate present value debt service savings on the entire multipurpose issue or reduces the present value debt service losses on that entire multipurpose issue, that separate issue satisfies the savings test.

(g) *Limitation on advance refundings of private activity bonds.*—Under section 149(d)(2) and this section, interest on a bond is not excluded from gross income if any portion of the issue of which the bond is a part is issued to advance refund a private activity bond (other than a qualified 501(c)(3) bond). For this purpose, the term private activity bond—

(1) Includes a qualified bond described in section 141(e) (other than a qualified 501(c)(3) bond), regardless of whether the refunding issue consists of private activity bonds under § 1.141-13; and

(2) Does not include a taxable bond.

(h) *Effective dates.*—(1) *In general.*—Except as provided in this paragraph (h), this section applies to bonds issued after June 30, 1993, to which §§ 1.148-1 through 1.148-11 apply, including conduit loans that are treated as issued after June 30, 1993, under paragraph (b)(4) of this section. In addition, this section applies to any issue to which the election described in § 1.148-11(b)(1) is made.

(2) *Special effective date for paragraph (b)(3).*—Paragraph (b)(3) of this section applies to any advance refunding issue issued after May 28, 1991.

(3) *Special effective date for paragraph (f)(3).*—Paragraph (f)(3) of this section applies to bonds sold on or after July 8, 1997 and to any issue to which the election described in § 1.148-11(b)(1) is made. See § 1.148-11A(i) for rules relating to certain bonds sold before July 8, 1997.

(4) *Special effective date for paragraph (g).*—See § 1.141-15 for the applicability date of paragraph (g) of this section. [Reg. § 1.149(d)-1.]

☐ [*T.D. 8418, 5-12-92. Amended by T.D. 8476, 6-14-93; T.D. 8538, 5-5-94; T.D. 8718, 5-8-97 and T.D. 9234, 12-16-2005.*]

[Reg. § 1.149(e)-1]

§ 1.149(e)-1. Information reporting requirements for tax-exempt bonds.—(a) *General rule.*—Interest on a bond is included in gross income unless certain information with respect to the issue of which the bond is a part is reported to the Internal Revenue Service in accordance with the requirements of this section. This section applies to any bond if the issue of which the bond is a part is issued after December 31, 1986 (including any bond issued to refund a bond issued on or before December 31, 1986).

(b) *Requirements for private activity bonds.*—(1) *In general.*—If the issue of which the bond is a part is an issue of private activity bonds, the issuer must comply with the following requirements—

(i) Not later than the 15th day of the second calendar month after the close of the calendar quarter in which the issue is issued, the issuer must file with the Internal Revenue Service a completed information reporting form prescribed for this purpose;

(ii) If any bond that is part of the issue is taken into account under section 146 (relating to volume cap on private activity bonds), the state certification requirement of paragraph (b)(2) of this section must be satisfied; and

(iii) If any bond that is part of the issue is a qualified mortgage bond or qualified veterans' mortgage bond (within the meaning of section 143(a) or (b) or section 103A(c)(1) or (3) as in effect on the day before enactment of the Tax Reform Act of 1986), the issuer must submit the annual report containing information on the borrowers of the original proceeds of the issue as required under § 1.103A-2(k)(2)(ii) and (k)(3) through (k)(6).

(2) *State certification with respect to volume cap.*—(i) *In general.*—If an issue is subject to the volume cap under section 146, a state official designated by state law (if there is no such official, then the governor or the governor's delegate) must certify that the issue meets the requirements of section 146, and a copy of this certification must be attached to the information reporting form filed with respect to the issue. In the case of any constitutional home rule city (as defined in section 146(d)(3)(C)), the preceding sentence is applied by substituting "city" for "state" and "chief executive officer" for "governor."

(ii) *Certification.*—The certifying official need not perform an independent investigation in order to certify that the issue meets the requirements of section 146. For example, if the certifying official receives an affidavit that was executed by an officer of the issuer who is responsible for issuing the bonds and that sets forth, in brief and summary terms, the facts necessary to determine that the issue meets the requirements of section 146 and if the certifying official has compared the information in that affidavit to other readily available information with respect to that issuer (e.g., previous affidavits and certifications for other private activity bonds issued by that issuer), the certifying official may rely on the affidavit.

(c) *Requirements for governmental bonds.*—(1) *Issue price of $100,000 or more.*—If the issue of which the bond is a part has an issue price of $100,000 or more and is not an issue of private activity bonds, then, not later than the 15th day of the second calendar month after the close of the calendar quarter in which the issue is issued, the issuer must file with the Internal Revenue Service a completed information reporting form prescribed for this purpose.

(2) *Issue price of less than $100,000.*—(i) *In general.*—If the issue of which the bond is a part has an issue price of less than $100,000 and is not an issue of private activity bonds, the issuer must file with the Internal Revenue Service one of the following information reporting forms within the prescribed period—

(A) *Separate return.*—Not later than the 15th day of the second calendar month after the close of the calendar quarter in which the issue is issued, a completed information reporting form prescribed for this purpose with respect to that issue; or

(B) *Consolidated return.*—Not later than February 15 of the calendar year following the calendar year in which the issue is issued, a completed information form prescribed for this purpose with respect to all issues to which this paragraph (c)(2) applies that were issued by the issuer during the calendar year and for which information was not reported on a separate information return pursuant to paragraph (c)(2)(i)(A) of this section.

(ii) *Bond issues issued before January 1, 1992.*—Paragraph (c)(2)(i)(A) of this section does not apply if the issue of which the bond is a part is issued before January 1, 1992.

(iii) *Extended filing date for first and second calendar quarters of 1992.*—If the issue of which the bond is a part is issued during the first or second calendar quarter of 1992, the prescribed period for filing an information reporting form with respect to that issue pursuant to paragraph (c)(2)(i)(A) of this section is extended until November 16, 1992.

(d) *Filing of forms and special rules.*—(1) *Completed form.*—For purposes of this section—

(i) *Good faith effort.*—An information reporting form is treated as completed if the issuer (or a person acting on behalf of the issuer) has made a good faith effort to complete the form (taking into account the instructions to the form).

(ii) *Information.*—In general, information reporting forms filed pursuant to this section must be completed on the basis of available information and reasonable expectations as of the date the issue is issued. Forms that are filed on a consolidated basis pursuant to paragraph (c)(2)(i)(B) of this section, however, may be completed on the basis of information readily available to the issuer at the close of the calendar year to which the form relates, supplemented by estimates made in good faith.

(iii) *Certain information not required.*—An issuer need not report to the Internal Revenue Service any information specified in the first sentence of section 149(e)(2) that is not required to be reported to the Internal Revenue Service pursuant to the information reporting forms prescribed under that section and the instructions to those forms.

(2) *Manner of filing.*—(i) *Place for filing.*—The information reporting form must be filed with the Internal Revenue Service at the address specified on the form or in the instructions to the form.

(ii) *Extension of time.*—The Commissioner may grant an extension of time to file any form or attachment required under this section if the Commissioner determines that the failure to file in a timely manner was not due to willful neglect. The Commissioner may make this determination with respect to an issue or to a class of issues.

(e) *Definitions.*—For purposes of this section only—

(1) *Private activity bond.*—The term "private activity bond" has the meaning given that term in section 141(a) of the Internal Revenue Code, except that the term does not include any bond described in section 1312(c) of the Tax Reform Act of 1986 to which section 1312 or 1313 of the Tax Reform Act of 1986 applies.

(2) *Issue.*—(i) *In general.*—Except as otherwise provided in this paragraph (e)(2), bonds are treated as part of the same issue only if the bonds are issued—

(A) By the same issuer;

(B) On the same date; and

(C) Pursuant to a single transaction or to a series of related instructions.

(ii) *Draw-down loans, commercial paper, etc.*

(A) Bonds issued during the same calendar year may be treated as part of the same issue if the bonds are issued—

(1) Pursuant to a loan agreement under which amounts are to be advanced periodically ("draw-down loan"); or

(2) With a term not exceeding 270 days.

(B) In addition, the bonds must be equally and ratably secured under a single indenture or loan agreement and issued pursuant to a common financing arrangement (*e.g.,* pursuant to the same official statement that is periodically updated to reflect changing factual circumstances). In the case of bonds issued pursuant to a draw-down loan that meets the requirements of the preceding sentence, bonds issued during different calendar years may be treated as part of the same issue if all the amounts to be advanced pursuant to the draw-down loan are reasonably expected to be advanced within three years of the date of issue of the first bond.

(iii) *Leases and installment sales.*—Bonds other than private activity bonds may be treated as part of the same issue if—

(A) The bonds are issued pursuant to a single agreement that is in the form of a lease or installment sales agreement; and

(B) All of the property covered by that agreement is reasonably expected to be delivered within three years of the date of issue of the first bond.

(iv) *Qualified 501(c)(3) bonds.*—If an issuer elects under section 141(b)(9) to treat a portion of an issue as a qualified 501(c)(3) bond, that portion is treated as a separate issue.

(3) *Date of issue.*—(i) *Bond.*—The date of issue of a bond is determined under § 1.150-1.

(ii) *Issue.*—The date of issue of an issue of bonds is the date of issue of the first bond that is part of the issue. See paragraphs (e)(2)(ii) and (iii) of this section for rules relating to draw-down loans, commercial paper, *etc.,* and leases and installment sales.

(iii) *Bonds to which prior law applied.*—Notwithstanding the provisions of this paragraph (e)(3), an issue for which an information report was required to be filed under section 103(l) or section 103A(j)(3) is treated as issued prior to January 1, 1987.

(4) *Issue price.*—The term "issue price" has the same meaning given the term under § 1.148-1(b). [Reg. § 1.149(e)-1.]

☐ [*T.D.* 8425, 8-11-92.]

[Reg. § 1.149(g)-1]

§ 1.149(g)-1. Hedge bonds.—(a) *Certain definitions.*—Except as otherwise provided, the definitions set forth in § 1.148-1 apply for purposes of section 149(g) and this section. In addition, the following terms have the following meanings:

Reasonable expectations means reasonable expectations (as defined in § 1.148-1), as modified to take into account the provisions of section 149(f)(2)(B).

Spendable proceeds means net sale proceeds (as defined in § 1.148-1).

(b) *Applicability of arbitrage allocation and accounting rules.*—Section 1.148-6 applies for purposes of section 149(g), except that an expenditure that results in the creation of replacement proceeds (other than amounts in a bona fide debt service fund or a reasonably required reserve or replacement fund) is not an expenditure for purposes of section 149(g).

(c) *Refundings.*—(1) *Investment in tax-exempt bonds.*—A bond issued to refund a bond that is a tax-exempt bond by virtue of the rule in section 149(g)(3)(B) is not a tax-exempt bond unless the gross proceeds of that refunding bond (other than proceeds in a refunding escrow for the refunded bond) satisfy the requirements of section 149(g)(3)(B).

(2) *Anti-abuse rule.*—A refunding bond is treated as a hedge bond unless there is a significant governmental purpose for the issuance of that bond (e.g., an advance refunding bond issued to realize debt service savings or to relieve the issuer of significantly burdensome document provisions, but not to otherwise hedge against future increases in interest rates).

(d) *Effective date.*—This section applies to bonds issued after June 30, 1993 to which § § 1.148-1 through 1.148-11 apply. In addition, this section applies to any issue to which the election described in § 1.148-11(b)(1) is made. [Reg. § 1.149(g)-1.]

☐ [*T.D.* 8476, 6-14-93.]

[Reg. § 1.150-1]

§ 1.150-1. Definitions.—(a) *Scope and effective date.*—(1) *In general.*—Except as otherwise provided, the definitions in this section apply for all purposes of sections 103 and 141 through 150.

(2) *Effective/applicability date.*—(i) *In general.*—Except as otherwise provided in this paragraph (a)(2), this section applies to issues issued after June 30, 1993 to which § § 1.148-1 through 1.148-11 apply. In addition, this section (other than paragraph (c)(3) of this section) applies to any issue to which the election described in § 1.148-11(b)(1) is made.

(ii) *Special effective date for paragraphs (c)(1), (c)(4)(iii), and (c)(6).*—Paragraphs (c)(1), (c)(4)(iii), and (c)(6) of this section apply to bonds sold on or after July 8, 1997, and to any issue to which the election described in § 1.148-11(b)(1) is made. See § 1.148-11A(i) for rules relating to certain bonds sold before July 8, 1997.

(iii) *Special effective date for definitions of tax-advantaged bond, issue, and grant.*—The definition of tax-advantaged bond in paragraph (b) of this section, the revisions to the definition of issue in paragraph (c)(2) of this section, and the definition and rules regarding the treatment of grants in paragraph (f) of this section apply to bonds that are sold on or after October 17, 2016.

(3) *Exceptions to general effective date.*—See § 1.141-15 for the applicability date of the definition of bond documents contained in paragraph (b) of this section and the effective date of paragraph (c)(3)(ii) of this section.

(4) *Additional exception to the general applicability date.*—Section 1.150-1(b), *Issuance costs,* applies on and after July 6, 2011.

(b) *Certain general definitions.*—The following definitions apply:

Bond means any obligation of a State or political subdivision thereof under section 103(c)(1).

Bond documents means the bond indenture or resolution, transcript of proceedings, and any related documents.

Capital expenditure means any cost of a type that is properly chargeable to capital account (or would be so chargeable with a proper election or with the application of the definition of placed in service under § 1.150-2(c)) under general Federal income tax principles. For example, costs incurred to acquire, construct, or improve land, buildings, and equipment generally are capital expenditures. Whether an expenditure is a capital expenditure is determined at the time the expenditure is paid with respect to the property. Future changes in law do not affect whether an expenditure is a capital expenditure.

Conduit borrower means the obligor on a purpose investment (as defined in § 1.148-1). For example, if an issuer invests proceeds in a purpose investment in the form of a loan, lease, installment sale obligation, or similar obligation to another entity and the obligor uses the proceeds to carry out the governmental purpose of the issue, the obligor is a conduit borrower.

Conduit financing issue means an issue the proceeds of which are used or are reasonably expected to be used to finance at least one purpose investment representing at least one conduit loan to one conduit borrower.

Conduit loan means a purpose investment (as defined in § 1.148-1).

Governmental bond means any bond of an issue of tax-exempt bonds in which none of the bonds are private activity bonds.

Issuance costs means costs to the extent incurred in connection with, and allocable to, the issuance of an issue within the meaning of section 147(g). For example, issuance costs include the following costs but only to the extent incurred in connection with, and allocable to, the borrowing: underwriters' spread; counsel fees; financial advisory fees; fees paid to an organization to evaluate the credit quality of an issue; trustee fees; paying agent fees; bond registrar, certification, and authentication fees; accounting fees; printing costs for bonds and offering documents; public approval process costs; engineering and feasibility study costs; guarantee fees, other than for qualified guarantees (as defined in § 1.148-4(f)); and similar costs.

Issue date means, in reference to an issue, the first date on which the issuer receives the purchase price in exchange for delivery of the evidence of indebtedness representing any bond included in the issue. Issue date means, in reference to a bond, the date on which the issuer receives the purchase price in exchange for that bond. In no event is the issue date earlier than the first day on which interest begins to accrue on the bond or bonds for Federal income tax purposes.

Obligation means any valid evidence of indebtedness under general Federal income tax principles.

Pooled financing issue means an issue the proceeds of which are to be used to finance purpose investments representing conduit loans to two or more conduit borrowers, unless those conduit loans are to be used to finance a single capital project.

Private activity bond means a private activity bond (as defined in section 141).

Qualified mortgage loan means a mortgage loan with respect to an owner-occupied residence acquired with the proceeds of an obligation described in section 143(a)(1) or 143(b) (or applicable prior law).

Qualified student loan means a student loan acquired with the proceeds of an obligation described in section 144(b)(1).

Related party means, in reference to a governmental unit or a 501(c)(3) organization, any member of the same controlled group, and, in reference to any person that is not a governmental unit or 501(c)(3) organization, a related person (as defined in section 144(a)(3)).

Taxable bond means any obligation the interest on which is not excludable from gross income under section 103.

Tax-advantaged bond means a tax-exempt bond, a taxable bond that provides a federal tax credit to the investor with respect to the issuer's borrowing costs, a taxable bond that provides a refundable federal tax credit payable directly to the issuer of the bond for its borrowing costs under section 6431, or any future similar bond that provides a federal tax benefit that reduces an issuer's borrowing costs. Examples of tax-advantaged bonds include qualified tax credit bonds under section 54A(d)(1) and build America bonds under section 54AA.

Tax-exempt bond means any bond the interest on which is excludable from gross income under section 103(a). For purposes of section 148, tax-exempt bond includes:

(1) An interest in a regulated investment company to the extent that at least 95 percent of the income to the holder of the interest is interest that is excludable from gross income under section 103; and

(2) A certificate of indebtedness issued by the United States Treasury pursuant to the Demand Deposit State and Local Government Series program described in 31 CFR part 344.

Working capital expenditure means any cost that is not a capital expenditure. Generally, current operating expenses are working capital expenditures.

(c) *Definition of issue.*—(1) *In general.*—Except as otherwise provided in this paragraph (c), the term *issue* means two or more bonds that meet all of the following requirements:

(i) *Sold at substantially the same time.*—The bonds are sold at substantially the same time. Bonds are treated as sold at substantially the same time if they are sold less than 15 days apart.

(ii) *Sold pursuant to the same plan of financing.*—The bonds are sold pursuant to the same plan of financing. Factors material to the plan of financing include the purposes for the bonds and the structure of the financing. For example, generally—

(A) Bonds to finance a single facility or related facilities are part of the same plan of financing;

(B) Short-term bonds to finance working capital expenditures and long-term bonds to finance capital projects are not part of the same plan of financing; and

(C) Certificates of participation in a lease and general obligation bonds secured by tax revenues are not part of the same plan of financing.

(iii) *Payable from same source of funds.*—The bonds are reasonably expected to be paid from substantially the same source of funds, determined without regard to guarantees from parties unrelated to the obligor.

(2) *Exceptions for different types of tax-advantaged bonds and taxable bonds.*—Each type of tax-advantaged bond that has a different structure for delivery of the tax benefit that reduces the issuer's borrowing costs or different program eligibility requirements is treated as part of a different issue under this paragraph (c). Further, tax-advantaged bonds and bonds that are not tax-advantaged bonds are treated as part of different issues under this paragraph (c). The issuance of tax-advantaged bonds in a transaction with other bonds that are not tax-advantaged bonds must be tested under the arbitrage anti-abuse rules under § 1.148-10(a) and other applicable anti-abuse rules (for example, limitations against window maturity structures or unreasonable allocations of bonds).

(3) *Exception for certain bonds financing separate purposes.*—(i) *In general.*—Bonds may be treated as part of separate issues if the requirements of this paragraph (c)(3) are satisfied. Each of these separate issues must finance a separate purpose (e.g., refunding a separate prior issue, financing a separate purpose investment, financing integrated or functionally related capital projects, and financing any clearly discrete governmental purpose). Each of these separate issues independently must be a tax-exempt bond (e.g., a governmental bond or a qualified mortgage bond). The aggregate proceeds, investments, and bonds in such a transaction must be allocated between each of the separate issues using a reasonable, consistently applied allocation method. If any separate issue consists of refunding bonds, the allocation rules in § 1.148-9(h) must be satisfied. An allocation is not reasonable if it achieves more favorable results under sections 103 and 141 to 150 than could be achieved with actual separate issues. All allocations under this paragraph (c)(3) must be made in writing on or before the issue date.

(ii) *Exceptions.*—This paragraph (c)(3) does not apply for purposes of sections 141, 144(a), 148, 149(d) and 149(g).

(4) *Special rules for certain financings.*—(i) *Draw-down loans.*—Bonds issued pursuant to a draw-down loan are treated as part of a single issue. The issue date of that issue is the first date on which the aggregate draws under the loan exceed the lesser of $50,000 or 5 percent of the issue price.

(ii) *Commercial paper.*—(A) *In general.*—Short-term bonds having a maturity of 270 days or less (*commercial paper*) issued pursuant to the same commercial paper program may be treated as part of a single issue, the issue date of which is the first date the aggregate amount of commercial paper issued under the program exceeds the lesser of $50,000 or 5 percent of the aggregate issue price of the commercial paper in the program. A commercial paper program is a program to issue commercial paper to finance or refinance the same governmental purpose pursuant to a single master legal document. Commercial paper is not part of the same commercial paper program unless issued during an 18-month period, beginning on the deemed issue date. In addition, commercial paper issued after the end of this 18-month period may be treated as part of the program to the extent issued to refund commercial paper that is part of the program, but only to the extent that—

(1) There is no increase in the principal amount outstanding; and

(2) The program does not have a term in excess of—

(i) 30 years; or

(ii) The period reasonably necessary for the governmental purposes of the program.

(B) *Safe harbor.*—The requirement of paragraph (c)(4)(ii)(A)(2) of this section is treated as satisfied if the weighted average maturity of the issue does not exceed 120 percent of the weighted average expected economic life of the property financed by the issue.

(iii) *Certain general obligation bonds.*—Except as otherwise provided in paragraph (c)(2) of this section, bonds that are secured by a pledge of the issuer's full faith and credit (or a substantially similar pledge) and sold and issued on the same dates pursuant to a single offering document may be treated as part of the same issue if the issuer so elects on or before the issue date.

(5) *Anti-abuse rule.*—In order to prevent the avoidance of sections 103 and 141 through 150 and the general purposes thereof, the Commissioner may treat bonds as part of the same issue or as part of separate issues to clearly reflect the economic substance of a transaction.

(6) *Sale date.*—The sale date of a bond is the first day on which there is a binding contract in writing for the sale or exchange of the bond.

(d) *Definition of refunding issue and related definitions.*—(1) *General definition of refunding issue.*—Refunding issue means an issue of obligations the proceeds of which are used to pay principal, interest, or redemption price on another issue (a *prior issue*, as more particularly defined in paragraph (d)(5) of this section), including the issuance costs, accrued interest, capitalized interest on the refunding issue, a reserve or replacement fund, or similar costs, if any, properly allocable to that refunding issue.

(2) *Exceptions and special rules.*—For purposes of paragraph (d)(1) of this section, the following exceptions and special rules apply—

(i) *Payment of certain interest.*—An issue is not a refunding issue if the only principal and interest that is paid with proceeds of the issue (determined without regard to the multipurpose issue rules of §1.148-9(h)) is interest on another issue that—

(A) Accrues on the other issue during a one-year period including the issue date of the issue that finances the interest;

(B) Is a capital expenditure; or

(C) Is a working capital expenditure to which the de minimis rule of §1.148-6(d)(3)(ii)(A) applies.

(ii) *Certain issues with different obligors.*—(A) *In general.*—An issue is not a refunding issue to the extent that the obligor (as defined in paragraph (d)(2)(ii)(B) of this section) of one issue is neither the obligor of the other issue nor a related party with respect to the obligor of the other issue.

(B) *Definition of obligor.*—The *obligor* of an issue means the actual issuer of the issue, except that the obligor of the portion of an issue properly allocable to an investment in a purpose investment means the conduit borrower under that purpose investment. The obligor of an issue used to finance qualified mortgage loans, qualified student loans, or similar program investments (as defined in §1.148-1) does not include the ultimate recipient of the loan (e.g., the homeowner, the student).

(iii) *Certain special rules for purpose investments.*—For purposes of this paragraph (d), the following special rules apply:

(A) *Refunding of a conduit financing issue by a conduit loan refunding issue.*—Except as provided in paragraph (d)(2)(iii)(B) of this section, the use of the proceeds of an issue that is used to refund an obligation that is a purpose investment (a *conduit refunding issue*) by the actual issuer of the conduit financing issue determines whether the conduit refunding issue is a refunding of the conduit financing issue (in addition to a refunding of the obligation that is the purpose investment).

(B) *Recycling of certain payments under purpose investments.*—A conduit refunding issue is not a refunding of a conduit financing issue to the extent that the actual issuer of the conduit financing issue reasonably expects as of the date of receipt of the proceeds of the conduit refunding issue to use those amounts within 6 months (or, if greater, during the applicable temporary period for those amounts under section 148(c) or under applicable prior law) to acquire a new purpose investment. Any new purpose investment is treated as made from the proceeds of the conduit financing issue.

(C) *Application to tax-exempt loans.*—For purposes of this paragraph (d), obligations that would be purpose investments (absent section 148(b)(3)(A)) are treated as purpose investments.

(iv) *Substance of transaction controls.*—In the absence of other applicable controlling rules under this paragraph (d), the determination of whether an issue is a refunding issue is based on the substance of the transaction in light of all the facts and circumstances.

(v) *Certain integrated transactions in connection with asset acquisition not treated as refunding issues.*—If, within six months before or after a person assumes (including taking subject to) obligations of an unrelated party in connection with an asset acquisition (other than a transaction to which section 381(a) applies if the person assuming the obligation is the acquiring corporation within the meaning of section 381(a)), the assumed issue is refinanced, the refinancing issue is not treated as a refunding issue.

(3) *Current refunding issue.*—Current refunding issue means:

(i) Except as provided in paragraph (d)(3)(ii) of this section, a refunding issue that is issued not more than 90 days before the last expenditure of any proceeds of the refunding issue for the payment of principal or interest on the prior issue; and

(ii) In the case of a refunding issue issued before 1986—

(A) A refunding issue that is issued not more than 180 days before the last expenditure of any proceeds of the refunding issue for the payment of principal or interest on the prior issue; or

(B) A refunding issue if the prior issue had a term of less than 3 years and was sold in anticipation of permanent financing, but only if the aggregate term of all prior issues sold in anticipation of permanent financing was less than 3 years.

(4) *Advance refunding issue.*—Advance refunding issue means a refunding issue that is not a current refunding issue.

(5) *Prior issue.*—Prior issue means an issue of obligations all or a portion of the principal, interest, or call premium on which is paid or provided for with proceeds of a refunding issue. A prior issue may be issued before, at the same time as, or after a refunding issue. If the refunded and unrefunded portions of a prior issue are treated as separate issues under §1.148-9(i), for the purposes for which that section applies, except to the extent that the context clearly requires otherwise, references to a prior issue refer only to the refunded portion of that prior issue.

(e) *Controlled group.*—means a group of entities controlled directly or indirectly by the same entity or group of entities within the meaning of this paragraph (e).

(1) *Direct control.*—The determination of direct control is made on the basis of all the relevant facts and circumstances. One entity or group of entities (the *controlling entity*) generally controls another entity or group of entities (the *controlled entity*) for purposes of this paragraph if the controlling entity possesses either of the following rights or powers and the rights or powers are discretionary and non-ministerial—

(i) The right or power both to approve and to remove without cause a controlling portion of the governing body of the controlled entity; or

(ii) The right or power to require the use of funds or assets of the controlled entity for any purpose of the controlling entity.

(2) *Indirect control.*—If a controlling entity controls a controlled entity under the test in paragraph (e)(1) of this section, then the controlling entity also controls all entities controlled, directly or indirectly, by the controlled entity or entities.

(3) *Exception for general purpose governmental entities.*—An entity is not a controlled entity under this paragraph (e) if the entity possesses substantial taxing, eminent domain, and police powers. For example, a city possessing substantial amounts of each of these sovereign powers is not a controlled entity of the state.

(f) *Definition and treatment of grants.*—(1) *Definition.*—Grant means a transfer for a governmental purpose of money or property to a transferee that is not a related party to or an agent of the transferor. The transfer must not impose any obligation or condition to directly or indirectly repay any amount to the transferor or a related party. Obligations or conditions intended solely to assure expenditure of the transferred moneys in accordance with the governmental purpose of the transfer do not prevent a transfer from being a grant.

(2) *Treatment.*—Except as otherwise provided (for example, §1.148-6(d)(4), which treats proceeds used for grants as spent for arbitrage purposes when the grant is made), the character and nature of a grantee's use of proceeds are taken into account in determining which rules are applicable to the bond issue and whether the applicable requirements for the bond issue are met. For example, a grantee's use of proceeds generally determines whether the proceeds are used for capital projects or working capital expenditures under section 148 and whether the qualified purposes for the specific type of bond issue are met. [Reg. §1.150-1.]

☐ [*T.D.* 8394, 1-27-92. *Amended by T.D.* 8418, 5-12-92; *T.D.* 8476, 6-14-93; *T.D.* 8538, 5-5-94; *T.D.* 8712, 1-10-97; *T.D.* 8718, 5-8-97; *T.D.* 9234, 12-16-2005; *T.D.* 9533, 7-1-2011, *T.D.* 9637, 9-5-2013 *and T.D.* 9777, 7-15-2016.]

[Reg. §1.150-2]

§1.150-2. Proceeds of bonds used for reimbursement.—(a) *Table of contents.*—This table of contents contains a listing of the headings contained in §1.150-2.

    (a) Table of contents.

    (b) Scope.

    (c) Definitions.

    (d) General operating rules for reimbursement expenditures.

(1) Official intent.
(2) Reimbursement period.
(3) Nature of expenditure.
(e) Official intent rules.
(1) Form of official intent.
(2) Project description in official intent.
(3) Reasonableness of official intent.
(f) Exceptions to general operating rules.
(1) De minimis exception.
(2) Preliminary expenditures exception.
(g) Special rules on refundings.
(1) In general—once financed, not reimbursed.
(2) Certain proceeds of prior issue used for reimbursement treated as unspent.
(h) Anti-abuse rules.
(1) General rule.
(2) One-year step transaction rule.
(i) Authority of the Commissioner to prescribe rules.
(j) Effective date.
(1) In general.
(2) Transitional rules.
(3) Nature of expenditure.

(b) *Scope.*—This section applies to reimbursement bonds (as defined in paragraph (c) of this section) for all purposes of sections 103 and 141 to 150.

(c) *Definitions.*—The following definitions apply:
Issuer means—
(1) For any private activity bond (excluding a qualified 501(c)(3) bond, qualified student loan bond, qualified mortgage bond, or qualified veterans' mortgage bond), the entity that actually issues the reimbursement bond; and
(2) For any bond not described in paragraph (1) of this definition, either the entity that actually issues the reimbursement bond or, to the extent that the reimbursement bond proceeds are to be loaned to a conduit borrower, that conduit borrower.
Official intent means an issuer's declaration of intent to reimburse an original expenditure with proceeds of an obligation.
Original expenditure means an expenditure for a governmental purpose that is originally paid from a source other than a reimbursement bond.
Placed in service means, with respect to a facility, the date on which, based on all the facts and circumstances—
(1) The facility has reached a degree of completion which would permit its operation at substantially its design level; and
(2) The facility is, in fact, in operation at such level.
Reimbursement allocation means an allocation in writing that evidences an issuer's use of proceeds of a reimbursement bond to reimburse an original expenditure. An allocation made within 30 days after the issue date of a reimbursement bond may be treated as made on the issue date.
Reimbursement bond means the portion of an issue allocated to reimburse an original expenditure that was paid before the issue date.

(d) *General operating rules for reimbursement expenditures.*—Except as otherwise provided, a reimbursement allocation is treated as an expenditure of proceeds of a reimbursement bond for the governmental purpose of the original expenditure on the date of the reimbursement allocation only if:

(1) *Official intent.*—Not later than 60 days after payment of the original expenditure, the issuer adopts an official intent for the original expenditure that satisfies paragraph (e) of this section.

(2) *Reimbursement period.*—(i) *In general.*—The reimbursement allocation is made not later than 18 months after the later of—
    (A) The date the original expenditure is paid; or
    (B) The date the project is placed in service or abandoned, but in no event more than 3 years after the original expenditure is paid.

(ii) *Special rule for small issuers.*—In applying paragraph (d)(2)(i) of this section to an issue that satisfies section 148(f)(4)(D)(i)(I) through (IV), the "18 month" limitation is changed to "3 years" and the "3-year" maximum reimbursement period is disregarded.

(iii) *Special rule for long-term construction projects.*—In applying paragraph (d)(2)(i) to a construction project for which both the issuer and a licensed architect or engineer certify that at least 5 years is necessary to complete construction of the project, the maximum reimbursement period is changed from "3 years" to "5 years."

(3) *Nature of expenditure.*—The original expenditure is a capital expenditure, a cost of issuance for a bond, an expenditure described in § 1.148-6(d)(3)(ii)(B) (relating to certain extraordinary working capital items), a grant (as defined in § 1.150-1(f)), a qualified student loan, a qualified mortgage loan, or a qualified veterans' mortgage loan.

(e) *Official intent rules.*—An official intent satisfies this paragraph (e) if:

(1) *Form of official intent.*—The official intent is made in any reasonable form, including issuer resolution, action by an appropriate representative of the issuer (e.g., a person authorized or designated to declare official intent on behalf of the issuer), or specific legislative authorization for the issuance of obligations for a particular project.

(2) *Project description in official intent.*—(i) *In general.*—The official intent generally describes the project for which the original expenditure is paid and states the maximum principal amount of obligations expected to be issued for the project. A project includes any property, project, or program (e.g., *highway capital improvement program*, *hospital equipment acquisition*, or *school building renovation*).

(ii) *Fund accounting.*—A project description is sufficient if it identifies, by name and functional purpose, the fund or account from which the original expenditure is paid (e.g., *parks and recreation fund—recreational facility capital improvement program*).

(iii) *Reasonable deviations in project description.*—Deviations between a project described in an official intent and the actual project financed with reimbursement bonds do not invalidate the official intent to the extent that the actual project is reasonably related in function to the described project. For example, *hospital equipment* is a reasonable deviation from *hospital building improvements*. In contrast, a *city office building rehabilitation* is not a reasonable deviation from *highway improvements*.

(3) *Reasonableness of official intent.*—On the date of the declaration, the issuer must have a reasonable expectation (as defined in § 1.148-1(b)) that it will reimburse the original expenditure with proceeds of an obligation. Official intents declared as a matter of course or in amounts substantially in excess of the amounts expected to be necessary for the project (e.g., *blanket declarations*) are not reasonable. Similarly, a pattern of failure to reimburse actual original expenditures covered by official intents (other than in extraordinary circumstances) is evidence of unreasonableness. An official intent declared pursuant to a specific legislative authorization is rebuttably presumed to satisfy this paragraph (e)(3).

(f) *Exceptions to general operating rules.*—(1) *De minimis exception.*—Paragraphs (d)(1) and (d)(2) of this section do not apply to costs of issuance of any bond or to an amount not in excess of the lesser of $100,000 or 5 percent of the proceeds of the issue.

(2) *Preliminary expenditures exception.*—Paragraphs (d)(1) and (d)(2) of this section do not apply to any preliminary expenditures, up to an amount not in excess of 20 percent of the aggregate issue price of the issue or issues that finance or are reasonably expected by the issuer to finance the project for which the preliminary expenditures were incurred. Preliminary expenditures include architectural, engineering, surveying, soil testing, reimbursement bond issuance, and similar costs that are incurred prior to commencement of acquisition, construction, or rehabilitation of a project, other than land acquisition, site preparation, and similar costs incident to commencement of construction.

(g) *Special rules on refundings.*—(1) *In general—once financed, not reimbursed.*—Except as provided in paragraph (g)(2) of this section, paragraph (d) of this section does not apply to an allocation to pay principal or interest on an obligation or to reimburse an original expenditure paid by another obligation. Instead, such an allocation is analyzed under rules on refunding issues. See § 1.148-9.

(2) *Certain proceeds of prior issue used for reimbursement treated as unspent.*—In the case of a refunding issue (or series of refunding issues), proceeds of a prior issue purportedly used to reimburse original expenditures are treated as unspent proceeds of the prior issue unless the purported reimbursement was a valid expenditure under applicable law on reimbursement expenditures on the issue date of the prior issue.

(h) *Anti-abuse rules.*—(1) *General rule.*—A reimbursement allocation is not an expenditure of proceeds of an issue under this section if the allocation employs an abusive arbitrage device under § 1.148-10 to avoid the arbitrage restrictions or to avoid the restrictions under sections 142 through 147.

(2) *One-year step transaction rule.*—(i) *Creation of replacement proceeds.*—A purported reimbursement allocation is invalid and thus is not an expenditure of proceeds of an issue if, within 1 year after the allocation, funds corresponding to the proceeds of a reimbursement bond for which a reimbursement allocation was made are used in a manner that results in the creation of replacement proceeds (as defined in §1.148-1) of that issue or another issue. The preceding sentence does not apply to amounts deposited in a bona fide debt service fund (as defined in §1.148-1).

(ii) *Example.*—The provisions of paragraph (h)(2)(i) of this section are illustrated by the following example.

Example. On January 1, 1994, County *A* issues an issue of 7 percent tax-exempt bonds (the *1994 issue*) and makes a purported reimbursement allocation to reimburse an original expenditure for specified capital improvements. *A* immediately deposits funds corresponding to the proceeds subject to the reimbursement allocation in an escrow fund to provide for payment of principal and interest on its outstanding 1991 issue of 9 percent tax-exempt bonds (the *prior issue*). The use of amounts corresponding to the proceeds of the reimbursement bonds to create a sinking fund for another issue within 1 year after the purported reimbursement allocation invalidates the reimbursement allocation. The proceeds retain their character as unspent proceeds of the 7 percent issue upon deposit in the escrow fund. Accordingly, the proceeds are subject to the 7 percent yield restriction of the 1994 issue instead of the 9 percent yield restriction of the prior issue.

(i) *Authority of the Commissioner to prescribe rules.*—The Commissioner may by revenue ruling or revenue procedure (see §601.601(d)(2)(ii) (*b*) of this chapter) prescribe rules for the expenditure of proceeds of reimbursement bonds in circumstances that do not otherwise satisfy this section.

(j) *Effective date.*—(1) *In general.*—Except as otherwise provided, the provisions of this section apply to all allocations of proceeds of reimbursement bonds issued after June 30, 1993.

(2) *Transitional rules.*—(i) *Official intent.*—An official intent is treated as satisfying the official intent requirement of paragraph (d)(1) of this section if it—

(A) Satisfied the applicable provisions of §1.103-8(a)(5) as in effect prior to July 1, 1993, (as contained in 26 CFR part 1 revised as of April 1, 1993) and was made prior to that date, or

(B) Satisfied the applicable provisions of §1.103-18 as in effect between January 27, 1992, and June 30, 1993, (as contained in 26 CFR part 1 revised as of April 1, 1993) and was made during that period.

(ii) *Certain expenditures of private activity bonds.*—For any expenditure that was originally paid prior to August 15, 1993, and that would have qualified for expenditure by reimbursement from the proceeds of a private activity bond under T.D. 7199, section 1.103-8(a)(5), 1972-2 C.B. 45 (See §601.601(d)(2)(i)(*b*) of this chapter.), the requirements of that section may be applied in lieu of this section.

(3) *Nature of expenditure.*—Paragraph (d)(3) of this section applies to bonds that are sold on or after October 17, 2016. [Reg. §1.150-2.]

☐ [*T.D. 8476, 6-14-93. Amended by T.D. 9777, 7-15-2016.*]

[Reg. §1.150-4]

§1.150-4. Change in use of facilities financed with tax-exempt private activity bonds.—(a) *Scope.*—This section applies for pur-

poses of the rules for change of use of facilities financed with private activity bonds under sections 150(b)(3) (relating to qualified 501(c)(3) bonds), 150(b)(4) (relating to certain exempt facility bonds and small issue bonds), 150(b)(5) (relating to facilities required to be owned by governmental units or 501(c)(3) organizations), and 150(c).

(b) *Effect of remedial actions.*—(1) *In general.*—Except as provided in this section, the change of use provisions of sections 150(b)(3) through (5), and 150(c) apply even if the issuer takes a remedial action described in §§1.142-2, 1.144-2, or 1.145-2.

(2) *Exceptions.*—(i) *Redemption.*—If nonqualified bonds are redeemed within 90 days of a deliberate action under §1.145-2(a) or within 90 days of the date on which a failure to properly use proceeds occurs under §1.142-2 or §1.144-2, sections 150(b)(3) through (5) do not apply during the period between that date and the date on which the nonqualified bonds are redeemed.

(ii) *Alternative qualifying use of facility.*—If a bond-financed facility is used for an alternative qualifying use under §§1.145-2 and 1.141-12(f), sections 150(b)(3) and (5) do not apply because of the alternative use.

(iii) *Alternative use of disposition proceeds.*—If disposition proceeds are used for a qualifying purpose under §§1.145-2 and 1.141-12(e), 1.142-2(c)(4), or 1.144-2, sections 150(b)(3) through (5) do not apply because of the deliberate action that gave rise to the disposition proceeds after the date on which all of the disposition proceeds have been expended on the qualifying purpose. If all of the disposition proceeds are so expended within 90 days of the date of the deliberate action, however, sections 150(b)(3) through (5) do not apply because of the deliberate action.

(c) *Allocation rules.*—(1) *In general.*—If a change in use of a portion of the property financed with an issue of qualified private activity bonds causes section 150(b)(3), (b)(4), or (b)(5) to apply to an issue, the bonds of the issue allocable to that portion under section 150(c)(3) are the same as the nonqualified bonds determined for purposes of §§1.142-1, 1.144-1, and 1.145-1, except that bonds allocable to all common areas are also allocated to that portion.

(2) *Special rule when remedial action is taken.*—If an issuer takes a remedial action with respect to an issue of private activity bonds under §§1.142-2, 1.144-2, or 1.145-2, the bonds of the issue allocable to a portion of property are the same as the nonqualified bonds determined for purposes of those sections.

(d) *Effective dates.*—For effective dates of this section, see §1.141-16. [Reg. §1.150-4.]

☐ [*T.D. 8712, 1-10-97.*]

[Reg. §1.150-5]

§1.150-5. Filing notices and elections.—(a) *In general.*—Notices and elections under the following sections must be filed with the Internal Revenue Service, 1111 Constitution Avenue, NW, Attention: T:GE:TEB:O, Washington, DC 20224 or such other place designated by publication of a notice in the Internal Revenue Bulletin—

(1) Section 1.141-12(d)(4);

(2) Section 1.142(f)(4)-1; and

(3) Section 1.142-2(c)(2).

(b) *Effective dates.*—This section applies to notices and elections filed on or after January 19, 2001. [Reg. §1.150-5.]

☐ [*T.D. 8941, 1-17-2001. Amended by T.D. 9741, 10-26-2015.*]

Deductions for Personal Exemptions

[Reg. §1.151-1]

§1.151-1. Deductions for personal exemptions.—(a) *In general.*—(1) In computing taxable income, an individual is allowed a deduction for the exemptions specified in section 151. Such exemptions are: (i) The exemptions for an individual taxpayer and spouse (the so-called personal exemptions); (ii) the additional exemptions for a taxpayer attaining the age of 65 years and spouse attaining the age of 65 years (the so-called old-age exemptions); (iii) the additional exemptions for a blind taxpayer and a blind spouse; and (iv) the exemptions for dependents of the taxpayer.

(2) A nonresident alien individual who is a bona fide resident of Puerto Rico during the entire taxable year and subject to tax under section 1 or 1201(b) is allowed as deductions the exemptions specified in section 151, even though as to the United States such individual is a nonresident alien. See section 876 and the regulations thereunder, relating to alien residents of Puerto Rico.

(b) *Exemptions for individual taxpayer and spouse (so-called personal exemptions).*—Section 151(b) allows an exemption for the taxpayer and an additional exemption for the spouse of the taxpayer if a joint

return is not made by the taxpayer and his spouse, and if the spouse, for the calendar year in which the taxable year of the taxpayer begins, has no gross income and is not the dependent of another taxpayer. Thus, a husband is not entitled to an exemption for his wife on his separate return for the taxable year beginning in a calendar year during which she has any gross income (though insufficient to require her to file a return). Since, in the case of a joint return, there are two taxpayers (although under section 6013 there is only one income for the two taxpayers on such return, *i.e.*, their aggregate income), two exemptions are allowed on such return, one for each taxpayer spouse. If in any case a joint return is made by the taxpayer and his spouse, no other person is allowed an exemption for such spouse even though such other person would have been entitled to claim an exemption for such spouse as a dependent if such joint return had not been made.

(c) *Exemptions for taxpayer attaining age of 65 and spouse attaining the age of 65 (so-called old-age exemptions).*—(1) Section 151(c) provides an additional exemption for the taxpayer if he has attained the age of 65 before the close of his taxable year. An additional exemption is also allowed to the taxpayer for his spouse if a joint return is not made by the taxpayer and his spouse and if the spouse has attained the age of 65 before the close of the taxable year of the taxpayer and, for the calendar year in which the taxable year of the taxpayer begins, the spouse has no gross income and is not the dependent of another taxpayer. If a husband and wife make a joint return, an old-age exemption will be allowed as to each taxpayer spouse who has attained the age of 65 before the close of the taxable year for which the joint return is made. The exemptions under section 151(c) are in addition to the exemptions for the taxpayer and spouse under section 151(b).

(2) In determining the age of an individual for the purposes of the exemption for old age, the last day of the taxable year of the taxpayer is the controlling date. Thus, in the event of a separate return by a husband, no additional exemption for old age may be claimed for his spouse unless such spouse has attained the age of 65 on or before the close of the taxable year of the husband. In no event shall the additional exemption for old age be allowed with respect to a spouse who dies before attaining the age of 65 even though such spouse would have attained the age of 65 before the close of the taxable year of the taxpayer. For the purposes of the old-age exemption, an individual attains the age of 65 on the first moment of the day preceding his sixty-fifth birthday. Accordingly, an individual whose sixty-fifth birthday falls on January 1 in a given year attains the age of 65 on the last day of the calendar year immediately preceding.

(d) *Exemptions for the blind.*—(1) Section 151(d) provides an additional exemption for the taxpayer if he is blind at the close of his taxable year. An additional exemption is also allowed to the taxpayer for his spouse if the spouse is blind and, for the calendar year in which the taxable year of the taxpayer begins, has no gross income and is not the dependent of another taxpayer. The determination of whether the spouse is blind shall be made as of the close of the taxable year of the taxpayer, unless the spouse dies during such taxable year, in which case such determination shall be made as of the time of such death.

(2) The exemptions for the blind are in addition to the exemptions for the taxpayer and spouse under section 151(b) and are also in addition to the exemptions under section 151(c) for taxpayers and spouses attaining the age of 65 years. Thus, a single individual who has attained the age of 65 before the close of his taxable year and who is blind at the close of his taxable year is entitled, in addition to the so-called personal exemption, to two further exemptions, one by reason of his age and the other by reason of his blindness. If a husband and wife make a joint return, an exemption for the blind will be allowed as to each taxpayer spouse who is blind at the close of the taxable year for which the joint return is made.

(3) A taxpayer claiming an exemption allowed by section 151(d) for a blind taxpayer and a blind spouse shall, if the individual for whom the exemption is claimed is not totally blind as of the last day of the taxable year of the taxpayer (or in the case of a spouse who dies during such taxable year as of the time of such death), attach to his return a certificate from a physician skilled in the diseases of the eye or a registered optometrist stating that as of the applicable status determination date in the opinion of such physician or optometrist (i) the central visual acuity of the individual for whom the exemption is claimed did not exceed 20/200 in the better eye with correcting lenses or (ii) such individual's visual acuity was accompanied by a limitation in the fields of vision such that the widest diameter of the visual field subtends an angle no greater than 20 degrees. If such individual is totally blind as of the status determination date there shall be attached to the return a statement by the person or persons making the return setting forth such fact.

(4) Notwithstanding subparagraph (3) of this paragraph, this subparagraph may be applied where the individual for whom an exemption under section 151(d) is claimed is not totally blind, and in the certified opinion of an examining physician skilled in the diseases of the eye there is no reasonable probability that the individual's visual acuity will ever improve beyond the minimum standards described in subparagraph (3) of this paragraph. In this event, if the examination occurs during a taxable year for which the exemption is claimed, and the examining physician certifies that, in his opinion, the condition is irreversible, and a copy of this certification is filed with the return for that taxable year, then a statement described in subparagraph (3) of this paragraph need not be attached to such individual's return for subsequent taxable years so long as the condition remains irreversible. The taxpayer shall retain a copy of the certified opinion in his records, and a statement referring to such opinion shall be attached to future returns claiming the section 151(d) exemption. [Reg. §1.151-1.]

☐ [*T.D. 6231, 4-25-57. Amended by T.D. 7114, 5-17-71 and T.D. 7230, 12-21-72.*]

[Reg. §1.151-2]

§1.151-2. Additional exemptions for dependents.—(a) Section 151(e) allows to a taxpayer an exemption for each dependent (as defined in section 152) whose gross income (as defined in section 61) for the calendar year in which the taxable year of the taxpayer begins is less than the amount provided in section 151(e)(1)(A) applicable to the taxable year of the taxpayer, or who is a child of the taxpayer and who—

(1) Has not attained the age of 19 at the close of the calendar year in which the taxable year of the taxpayer begins, or

(2) Is a student, as defined in paragraph (b) of §1.151-3.

No exemption shall be allowed under section 151(e) for any dependent who has made a joint return with his spouse under section 6013 for the taxable year beginning in the calendar year in which the taxable year of the taxpayer begins. The amount provided in section 151(e)(1)(A) is $750 in the case of a taxable year beginning after December 31, 1972; $700 in the case of a taxable year beginning after December 31, 1971, and before January 1, 1973; $650 in the case of a taxable year beginning after December 31, 1970, and before January 1, 1972; $625 in the case of a taxable year beginning after December 31, 1969, and before January 1, 1971; and $600 in the case of a taxable year beginning before January 1, 1970. For special rules in the case of a taxpayer whose taxable year is a fiscal year ending after December 31, 1969, and beginning before January 1, 1973, see section 21(d) and the regulations thereunder.

(b) The only exemption allowed for a dependent of the taxpayer is that provided by section 151(e). The exemptions provided by section 151(c) (old-age exemptions) and section 151(d) (exemptions for the blind) are allowed only for the taxpayer or his spouse. For example, where a taxpayer provides the entire support for his father who meets all the requirements of a dependent, he is entitled to only one exemption for his father (section 151(e)), even though his father is over the age of 65. [Reg. §1.151-2.]

☐ [*T.D. 6231, 4-25-57. Amended by T.D. 7114, 5-17-71.*]

[Reg. §1.151-3]

§1.151-3. Definitions.—(a) *Child.*—For purposes of sections 151(e), 152, and the regulations thereunder, the term "child" means a son, stepson, daughter, stepdaughter, adopted son, adopted daughter, or for taxable years beginning after December 31, 1958, a child who is a member of an individual's household if the child was placed with the individual by an authorized placement agency for legal adoption pursuant to a formal application filed by the individual with the agency (see paragraph (c)(2) of §1.152-2), or, for taxable years beginning after December 31, 1969, a foster child (if such foster child satisfies the requirements set forth in paragraph (b) of §1.152-1 with respect to the taxpayer) of the taxpayer.

(b) *Student.*—For purposes of section 151(e) and section 152(d), and the regulations thereunder, the term "student" means an individual who during each of 5 calendar months during the calendar year in which the taxable year of the taxpayer begins is a full-time student at an educational institution or is pursuing a full-time course of institutional on-farm training under the supervision of an accredited agent of an educational insitution or of a State or political subdivision of a State. An example of "institutional on-farm training" is that authorized by 38 U. S. C. 1652 (formerly section 252 of the Veterans' Readjustment Assistance Act of 1952) as described in section 252 of such act. A full-time student is one who is enrolled for some part of 5 calendar months for the number of hours or courses which is considered to be full-time attendance. The 5 calendar months need not be consecutive. School attendance exclusively at night does not constitute full-time attendance. However, full-time attendance at an educational institution may include some attendance at night in connection with full-time course of study.

(c) *Educational institution.*—For purposes of sections 151(e) and 152, and the regulations thereunder, the term "educational institution" means a school maintaining a regular faculty and established curriculum, and having an organized body of students in attendance. It includes primary and secondary schools, colleges, universities, normal schools, technical schools, mechanical schools, and similar institutions, but does not include noneducational institutions, on-the-job training, correspondence schools, night schools, and so forth. [Reg. §1.151-3.]

☐ [*T.D. 6231, 4-25-57. Amended by T.D. 7051, 7-8-70.*]

[Reg. §1.151-4]

§1.151-4. Amount of deduction for each exemption under section 151.—The amount allowed as a deduction for each exemption under section 151 is (a) $750 in the case of a taxable year beginning after December 31, 1972; (b) $700 in the case of a taxable year beginning after December 31, 1971, and before January 1, 1973; (c) $650 in the case of a taxable year beginning after December 31, 1970, and before January 1, 1972; (d) $625 in the case of a taxable year beginning after December 31, 1969, and before January 1, 1971; and (e) $600 in the case of a taxable year beginning before January 1, 1970. For special rules in the case of a fiscal year ending after December 31, 1969, and beginning before January 1, 1973, see section 21(d) and the regulations thereunder. [Reg. § 1.151-4.]

☐ [T.D. 7114, 5-17-71.]

[Reg. § 1.9300-1]

§ 1.9300-1. Reduction in taxable income for housing displaced individuals.—(a) *In general.*—For a taxable year beginning in the applicable taxable year (as defined in paragraph (f)(1) of this section), a taxpayer who is a natural person may reduce taxable income by $500 for each displaced individual (as defined in paragraph (f)(2) of this section) to whom the taxpayer provides housing free of charge in, or on the site of, the taxpayer's principal residence for a period of at least 60 consecutive days. A taxpayer may claim the reduction in taxable income for any applicable taxable year in which a consecutive 60-day period ends. A taxpayer may not claim the reduction in taxable income unless the taxpayer includes the taxpayer identification number of the displaced individual on the taxpayer's income tax return.

(b) *Provision of housing.*—(1) *Principal residence.*—For purposes of this section, the term principal residence has the same meaning as in section 121 and the associated regulations. *See* § 1.121-1(b)(1) and (b)(2).

(2) *Legal interest required.*—A taxpayer is treated as providing housing for purposes of this section only if the taxpayer is an owner or lessee (including a co-owner or co-lessee) of the principal residence.

(3) *Compensation for providing housing.*—No reduction in taxable income is allowed under this section to a taxpayer who receives rent or any reimbursement or compensation (whether in cash, services, or property) from any source for providing housing to the displaced individual. For this purpose, lodging, utilities, and other similar items are treated as housing, but telephone calls, food, clothing, transportation, and other similar items are not treated as housing.

(c) *Limitations.*—(1) *Dollar limitation.*—(i) *In general.*—The reduction in taxable income under paragraph (a) of this section may not exceed the maximum dollar limitation, and must be reduced by the total amount of all reductions under this section for all prior taxable years (except as provided in paragraph (c)(5) of this section). The maximum dollar limitation is—

(A) $2,000 in the case of an unmarried individual; or

(B) $2,000 in the case of a husband and wife, whether the husband and wife file a joint income tax return or separate income tax returns; married taxpayers filing separate income tax returns may allocate this amount in $500 increments between their respective returns, provided that each spouse is otherwise eligible to claim that reduction in taxable income.

(ii) *Married individuals with separate principal residences.*—The limitation in paragraph (c)(1)(i)(B) of this section applies whether or not the married individuals occupy the same principal residence. A person is treated as married for purposes of this section if the individual is treated as married under section 7703.

(2) *Spouse or dependent of the taxpayer.*—No reduction of taxable income is allowed for a displaced individual who is the spouse or a dependent of the taxpayer.

(3) *One reduction per displaced individual.*—Except as provided in paragraph (c)(5) of this section, a taxpayer may not reduce taxable income under paragraph (a) of this section for a displaced individual for whom the taxpayer or any taxpayer residing in the same principal residence has reduced taxable income under this section for any prior taxable year.

(4) *Taxpayers occupying the same principal residence.*—Except as provided in paragraph (c)(5) of this section, for all taxable years, only one taxpayer occupying the same principal residence may reduce taxable income for a particular displaced individual.

(5) *Limitations applied separately to each disaster.*—The limitations of this paragraph (c) apply separately to each disaster area. Thus, a taxpayer may reduce taxable income by $2,000 for providing housing to Midwestern disaster displaced individuals even though the taxpayer reduced taxable income for providing housing to one or more Hurricane Katrina displaced individuals. For this purpose, all areas within the Midwestern disaster area are treated as one disaster area.

(d) *Substantiation.*—A taxpayer claiming a reduction of taxable income under this section must maintain records sufficient to show entitlement to the reduction as provided in forms, instructions, publications or other guidance published by the IRS.

(e) The Commissioner may apply this section in additional guidance of general applicability, see § 601.601(d)(2) of this chapter, to other disaster areas to which Congress extends relief under section 302 of the Katrina Emergency Tax Relief Act of 2005.

(f) *In general.*—The following definitions apply for all purposes of this section.

(1) *Applicable taxable year.*—The term *applicable taxable year* means—

(i) A taxable year beginning in 2005 or 2006, in the case of housing provided to a Hurricane Katrina displaced individual (as defined in paragraph (f)(2)(ii) of this section); and

(ii) A taxable year beginning in 2008 or 2009, in the case of housing provided to a Midwestern disaster displaced individual (as defined in paragraph (f)(2)(iii) of this section).

(2) *Displaced individual.*—(i) *Scope.*—The term *displaced individual* means a Hurricane Katrina displaced individual as defined in paragraph (f)(2)(ii) of this section and a Midwestern disaster displaced individual as defined in paragraph (f)(2)(iii) of this section.

(ii) *Hurricane Katrina displaced individual.*—The term *Hurricane Katrina displaced individual* means any natural person (other than the spouse or a dependent of the taxpayer) if the following requirements are met—

(A) The person's principal place of abode on August 28, 2005, was in the Hurricane Katrina disaster area (as defined in paragraph (f)(4)(ii) of this section);

(B) The person was displaced from that abode; and

(C) If the abode was located outside the Hurricane Katrina core disaster area (as defined in paragraph (f)(5)(ii) of this section)—

(1) The abode was damaged by Hurricane Katrina; or

(2) The person was evacuated from that abode by reason of Hurricane Katrina.

(iii) *Midwestern disaster displaced individual.*—The term *Midwestern disaster displaced individual* means any natural person (other than the spouse or a dependent of the taxpayer) if the following requirements are met—

(A) The person's principal place of abode on the Midwestern disaster date (as defined in paragraph (f)(3) of this section), was in any Midwestern disaster area (as defined in paragraph (f)(4)(iii) of this section);

(B) The person was displaced from that abode; and

(C) If the abode was located outside the Midwestern core disaster area (as defined in paragraph (f)(5)(iii) of this section)—

(1) The abode was damaged by any Midwestern disaster; or

(2) The person was evacuated from that abode by reason of any Midwestern disaster.

(3) *Midwestern disaster date.*—The term *Midwestern disaster date* means—

(i) In Arkansas, May 2 through May 12, 2008;

(ii) In Illinois, June 1 through July 22, 2008;

(iii) In Indiana, May 30 through June 27, 2008;

(iv) In Iowa, May 25 through August 13, 2008;

(v) In Kansas, May 22 through June 16, 2008;

(vi) In Michigan, June 6 through June 13, 2008;

(vii) In Minnesota, June 6 through June 12, 2008;

(viii) In Missouri, May 10 through May 11, 2008, and June 1 through August 13, 2008;

(ix) In Nebraska, April 23 through April 26, 2008, May 22 through June 24, 2008, and June 27, 2008; or

(x) In Wisconsin, June 5 through July 25, 2008.

(4) *Disaster area.*—(i) *Scope.*—The term *disaster area* means the Hurricane Katrina disaster area as defined in paragraph (f)(4)(ii) of this section and the Midwestern disaster area as defined in paragraph (f)(4)(iii) of this section.

(ii) *Hurricane Katrina disaster area.*—The term *Hurricane Katrina disaster area* means the states of Alabama, Florida, Louisiana, and Mississippi.

(iii) *Midwestern disaster area.*—The term *Midwestern disaster area* means an area for which the President declared a major disaster on or after May 20, 2008, and before August 1, 2008, under section 401 of the Robert T. Stafford Disaster Relief and Emergency Assistance Act (42 U.S.C. 5170) (Stafford Act) by reason of severe storms, tornados, or flooding occurring in any of the states of Arkansas,

Illinois, Indiana, Iowa, Kansas, Michigan, Minnesota, Missouri, Nebraska, and Wisconsin.

(5) *Core disaster area.*—(i) *Scope.*—The term *core disaster area* means the Hurricane Katrina core disaster area as defined in paragraph (f)(5)(ii) of this section and the Midwestern core disaster area as defined in paragraph (f)(5)(iii) of this section.

(ii) *Hurricane Katrina core disaster area.*—The term *Hurricane Katrina core disaster area* means the portion of the Hurricane Katrina disaster area designated by the President to warrant individual or individual and public assistance from the federal government under the Stafford Act.

(iii) *Midwestern core disaster area.*—The term *Midwestern core disaster area* means the portion of the Midwestern disaster area designated by the President to warrant individual or individual and public assistance from the federal government under the Stafford Act for damages attributable to the severe storms, tornados, or flooding in the Midwestern disaster area.

(g) *Examples.*—The provisions of this section are illustrated by the following examples. In each example, a taxpayer provides housing within the meaning of paragraph (b) of this section in, or on the site of, the taxpayer's principal residence for a period of at least 60 consecutive days (the 60th day being in the applicable taxable year) for each displaced individual, none of whom is a spouse or dependent of the taxpayer. The examples are as follows:

Example 1. Taxpayer A provides housing to N, a Hurricane Katrina displaced individual, from September 1, 2005, until March 10, 2006. Under paragraphs (a) and (c)(3) of this section, A may reduce A's taxable income by $500 on A's income tax return for calendar year 2005 or 2006 (but not both) for providing housing to N.

Example 2. The facts are the same as in *Example 1,* except that A and A's unmarried roommate B are co-lessees of their principal residence. Both A and B 12 provide housing to N. Under paragraphs (a) and (c)(4) of this section, either A or B, but not both, may reduce taxable income by $500 for 2005 or 2006 for providing housing to N. If A or B reduces taxable income for 2005 for providing housing to N, neither A nor B may reduce taxable income for 2006 for providing housing to N.

Example 3. The facts are the same as in *Example 2,* except that in 2009 A and B provide housing to N, who in 2009 is a Midwestern disaster displaced individual. Under paragraph (c)(5) of this section, the limitation of paragraph (c)(4) of this section applies separately to each disaster. Therefore, either A or B may reduce taxable income by $500 for 2009 for providing housing to N.

Example 4. During 2008, unmarried roommates and co-lessees C and D provide housing to eight Midwestern disaster displaced individuals. Under paragraphs (a) and (c)(1)(i)(A) of this section, C may reduce taxable income by $2,000 on C's 2008 income tax return for providing housing to any four of these displaced individuals and D may reduce taxable income by $2,000 on D's 2008 income tax return for providing housing to the other four displaced individuals.

Example 5. (i) In 2008, a married couple, H and W, provide housing to a Midwestern disaster displaced individual, O. H and W file their 2008 income tax return as married filing jointly. Under paragraphs (a) and (c)(4) of this section, H and W may reduce taxable income by $500 on their 2008 income tax return for providing housing to O.

(ii) In 2009, H and W provide housing to O and to another Midwestern disaster displaced individual, P. H and W file their 2009 income tax returns as married filing separately. Because H and W reduced their 2008 taxable income for providing housing to O, under paragraph (c)(3) of this section, neither H nor W may reduce taxable income on their 2009 income tax returns for providing housing to O. Under paragraphs (a) and (c)(4) of this section, either H or W but not both, may reduce taxable income by $500 on his or her 2009 income tax return for providing housing to P.

Example 6. The facts are the same as in *Example 5,* except that in 2009 H and W provide housing to five Midwestern disaster displaced individuals in addition to O. H and W together may reduce taxable income on their 2009 income tax returns by a total of $2,000 for the Midwestern disaster displaced individuals (other than O). Under paragraph (c)(1)(i)(B) of this section, H and W may allocate the $2,000 in increments of $500 between their separate returns. For example, either one may reduce taxable income by $500 and the other may reduce taxable income by $1,500, or H and W each may reduce taxable income by $1,000.

(h) *Effective/applicability date.*—This section applies for taxable years ending after December 11, 2006. [Reg. § 1.9300-1.]

☐ [*T.D. 9474,* 12-11-2009.]

[Reg. § 1.152-1]

§ 1.152-1. General definition of a dependent.—(a)(1) For purposes of the income taxes imposed on individuals by chapter 1 of the Code, the term "dependent" means any individual described in paragraphs (1) through (10) of section 152(a) over half of whose support, for the calendar year in which the taxable year of the taxpayer begins, was received from the taxpayer.

(2)(i) For purposes of determining whether or not an individual received, for a given calendar year, over half of his support from the taxpayer, there shall be taken into account the amount of support received from the taxpayer as compared to the entire amount of support which the individual received from all sources, including support which the individual himself supplied. The term "support" includes food, shelter, clothing, medical and dental care, education, and the like. Generally, the amount of an item of support will be the amount of expense incurred by the one furnishing such item. If the item of support furnished an individual is in the form of property or lodging, it will be necessary to measure the amount of such item of support in terms of its fair market value.

(ii) In computing the amount which is contributed for the support of an individual, there must be included any amount which is contributed by such individual for his own support, including income which is ordinarily excludable from gross income, such as benefits received under the Social Security Act. For example, a father receives $800 social security benefits, $400 interest, and $1,000 from his son during 1955, all of which sums represent his sole support during that year. The fact that the social security benefits of $800 are not includible in the father's gross income does not prevent such amount from entering into the computation of the total amount contributed for the father's support. Consequently, since the son's contribution of $1,000 was less than one-half of the father's support ($2,200) he may not claim his father as a dependent.

(iii)(a) For purposes of determining the amount of support furnished for a child (or children) by a taxpayer for a given calendar year, an arrearage payment made in a year subsequent to a calendar year for which there is an unpaid liability shall not be treated as paid either during that calendar year or in the year of payment, but no amount shall be treated as an arrearage payment to the extent that there is an unpaid liability (determined without regard to such payment) with respect to the support of a child for the taxable year of payment; and

(b) Similarly, payments made prior to any calendar year (whether or not made in the form of a lump sum payment in settlement of the parent's liability for support) shall not be treated as made during such calendar year, but payments made during any calendar year from amounts set aside in trust by a parent in a prior year, shall be treated as made during the calendar year in which paid.

(b) Section 152(a)(9) applies to any individual (other than an individual who at any time during the taxable year was the spouse, determined without regard to section 153, of the taxpayer) who lives with the taxpayer and is a member of the taxpayer's household during the entire taxable year of the taxpayer. An individual is not a member of the taxpayer's household if at any time during the taxable year of the taxpayer the relationship between such individual and the taxpayer is in violation of local law. It is not necessary under section 152(a)(9) that the dependent be related to the taxpayer. For example, foster children may qualify as dependents. It is necessary, however, that the taxpayer both maintain and occupy the household. The taxpayer and dependent will be considered as occupying the household for such entire taxable year notwithstanding temporary absences from the household due to special circumstances. A nonpermanent failure to occupy the common abode by reason of illness, education, business, vacation, military service, or a custody agreement under which the dependent is absent for less than six months in the taxable year of the taxpayer, shall be considered temporary absence due to special circumstances. The fact that the dependent dies during the year shall not deprive the taxpayer of the deduction if the dependent lived in the household for the entire part of the year preceding his death. Likewise, the period during the taxable year preceding the birth of an individual shall not prevent such individual from qualifying as a dependent under section 152(a)(9). Moreover, a child who actually becomes a member of the taxpayer's household during the taxable year shall not be prevented from being considered a member of such household for the entire taxable year, if the child is required to remain in a hospital for a period following its birth, and if such child would otherwise have been a member of the taxpayer's household during such period.

(c) In the case of a child of the taxpayer who is under 19 or who is a student, the taxpayer may claim the dependency exemption for such child provided he has furnished more than one-half of the support of such child for the calendar year in which the taxable year of the taxpayer begins, even though the income of the child for such calendar year may be equal to or in excess of the amount determined pursuant to § 1.151-2 applicable to such calendar year. In such a case, there may be two exemptions claimed for the child: One on the parent's (or stepparent's) return, and one on the child's return. In determining whether the taxpayer does in fact furnish more than one-half of the support of an individual who is a child, as defined in paragraph (a) of §1.151-3, of the taxpayer and who is a student, as defined in paragraph (b) of §1.151-3, a special rule regarding scholarships applies. Amounts received as scholarships, as defined in paragraph (a) of §1.117-3, for study at an educational institution shall not be considered in determining whether the taxpayer furnishes more than one-half the support of such individual. For example, A has a child who receives a $1,000 scholarship to the X college for 1 year. A contributes $500, which constitutes the balance of the child's support for that year. A may claim the child as a dependent, as the $1,000 scholarship is not counted in determining the support of the child. For purposes of this paragraph, amounts received for tuition payments and allowances by a veteran under the provisions of the Servicemen's Readjustment Act of 1944 (58 Stat. 284) or the Veterans' Readjustment Assistance Act of 1952 (38 U.S.C. ch. 38) are not amounts received as scholarships. See also §1.117-4. For definition of the terms "child," "student," and "educational institution," as used in this paragraph, see §1.151-3. [Reg. §1.152-1.]

☐ [*T.D.* 6231, 4-25-57. *Amended by T.D.* 6304, 8-22-58, *T.D.* 6441, 1-4-60, *T.D.* 6663, 7-10-63, *T.D.* 7099, 3-19-71 *and T.D.* 7114, 5-17-71.]

[Reg. §1.152-2]

§1.152-2. Rules relating to general definition of dependent.— (a)(1) Except as provided in subparagraph (2) of this paragraph, to qualify as a dependent an individual must be a citizen or resident of the United States or be a resident of the Canal Zone, the Republic of Panama, Canada, or Mexico, or, for taxable years beginning after December 31, 1971, a national of the United States, at some time during the calendar year in which the taxable year of the taxpayer begins. A resident of the Republic of the Philippines who was born to or legally adopted by the taxpayer in the Philippine Islands before January 1, 1956, at a time when the taxpayer was a member of the Armed Forces of the United States, may also be claimed as a dependent if such resident otherwise qualifies as a dependent. For definition of "Armed Forces of the United States," see section 7701(a)(15).

(2)(i) For any taxable year beginning after December 31, 1957, a taxpayer who is a citizen, or, for any taxable year beginning after December 31, 1971, a national of the United States is permitted under section 152(b)(3)(B) to treat as a dependent his legally adopted child who lives with him, as a member of his household, for the entire taxable year and who, but for the citizenship, nationality, or residence requirements of section 152(b)(3) and subparagraph (1) of this paragraph, would qualify as a dependent of the taxpayer for such taxable year.

(ii) Under section 152(b)(3)(B) and this subparagraph, it is necessary that the taxpayer both maintain and occupy the household. The taxpayer and his legally adopted child will be considered as occupying the household for the entire taxable year of the taxpayer notwithstanding temporary absences from the household due to special circumstances. A nonpermanent failure to occupy the common abode by reason of illness, education, business, vacation, military service, or a custody agreement under which the legally adopted child is absent for less than six months in the taxable year of the taxpayer shall be considered temporary absence due to special circumstances. The fact that a legally adopted child dies during the year shall not deprive the taxpayer of the deduction if the child lived in the household for the entire part of the year preceding his death. The period during the taxable year preceding the birth of a child shall not prevent such child from qualifying as a dependent under this subparagraph. Moreover, a legally adopted child who actually becomes a member of the taxpayer's household during the taxable year shall not be prevented from being considered a member of such household for the entire taxable year, if the child is required to remain in a hospital for a period following its birth and if such child would otherwise have been a member of the taxpayer's household during such period.

(iii) For purposes of section 152(b)(3)(B) and this subparagraph, any child whose legal adoption by the taxpayer (a citizen or national of the United States) becomes final at any time before the end of the taxable year of the taxpayer shall not be disqualified as a dependent of such taxpayer by reason of his citizenship, nationality, or residence, provided the child lived with the taxpayer and was a member of the taxpayer's household for the entire taxable year in which the legal adoption became final. For example, A, a citizen of the United States who makes his income tax returns on the basis of the calendar year, is employed in Brazil by an agency of the United States Government. In October 1958 he takes into his household C, a resident of Brazil who is not a citizen of the United States, for the purpose of initiating adoption proceedings. C lives with A and is a member of his household for the remainder of 1958 and for the entire calendar year 1959. On July 1, 1959, the adoption proceedings were completed and C became the legally adopted child of A. If C otherwise qualifies as a dependent, he may be claimed as a dependent by A for 1959.

(b)(1) A payment to a spouse (payee spouse) of alimony or separate maintenance is not treated as a payment by the payor spouse for the support of any dependent. Similarly, the distribution of income of an estate or trust to a divorced or legally separated payee spouse is not treated as a payment by the payor spouse for the support of any dependent. The preceding sentence will not apply, however, to the extent that such a distribution is in satisfaction of the amount or portion of income that, by the terms of a divorce decree, a written separation agreement, or the trust instrument is fixed as payable for the support of the minor children of the payor spouse.

(2) Paragraph (b)(1) of this section applies to taxable years beginning on or after October 13, 2020.

(c)(1) For purposes of determining the existence of any of the relationships specified in section 152(a) or (b)(1), a legally adopted child of an individual shall be treated as a child of such individual by blood.

(2) For any taxable year beginning after December 31, 1958, a child who is a member of an individual's household also shall be treated as a child of such individual by blood if the child was placed with the individual by an authorized placement agency for legal adoption pursuant to a formal application filed by the individual with the agency. For purposes of this subparagraph an authorized placement agency is any agency which is authorized by a State, the District of Columbia, a possession of the United States, a foreign country, or a political subdivision of any of the foregoing to place children for adoption. A taxpayer who claims as a dependent a child placed with him for adoption shall attach to his income tax return a statement setting forth the name of the child for whom the dependency deduction is claimed, the name and address of the authorized placement agency, and the date the formal application was filed with the agency.

(3) The application of this paragraph may be illustrated by the following example:

Example. On March 1, 1959, D. a resident of the United States, made formal application to an authorized child placement agency for the placement of E, a resident of the United States, with him for legal adoption. On June 1, 1959, E was placed with D for legal adoption. During the year 1959 E received over one-half of his support from D. D may claim E as a dependent for 1959. Since E was a resident of the United States, his qualification as a dependent is in no way based on the provisions of section 152(b)(3)(B). Therefore, it is immaterial that E was not a member of D's household during the entire taxable year.

(4) For purposes of determining the existence of any of the relationships specified in section 152(a) or (b)(1), a foster child of an individual (if such foster child satisfies the requirements set forth in paragraph (b) of §1.152-1 with respect to such individual) shall, for taxable years beginning after December 31, 1969, be treated as a child of such individual by blood. For purposes of this subparagraph, a foster child is a child who is in the care of a person or persons (other than the parents or adopted parents of the child) who care for the child as their own child. Status as a foster child is not dependent upon or affected by the circumstances under which the child became a member of the household.

(d) In the case of a joint return it is not necessary that the prescribed relationship exist between the person claimed as a dependent and the spouse who furnishes the support; it is sufficient if the prescribed relationship exists with respect to either spouse. Thus, a husband and wife making a joint return may claim as a dependent a daughter of the wife's brother (wife's niece) even though the husband is the one who furnishes the chief support. The relationship of affinity once existing will not terminate by divorce or the death of a spouse. For example, a widower may continue to claim his deceased wife's father (his father-in-law) as a dependent provided he meets the other requirements of section 151.

(e)(1) In defining a qualifying relative for taxable year 2018, the exemption amount in section 152(c)(1)(B) is $4,150. For taxable years 2019 through 2025, the exemption amount, as adjusted for inflation, is set forth in annual guidance published in the **Internal Revenue Bulletin**. *See* §601.601(d)(2) of this chapter.

(2) Paragraph (e)(1) of this section applies to taxable years ending after August 28, 2018. [Reg. §1.152-2.]

☐ [*T.D.* 6231, 4-25-57. *Amended by T.D.* 6441, 1-4-60, *T.D.* 6663, 7-10-63, *T.D.* 7051, 7-8-70, *T.D.* 7291, 12-3-73 *and T.D.* 9913, 10-9-2020.]

[Reg. §1.152-3]

§1.152-3. Multiple support agreements.—(a) Section 152(c) provides that a taxpayer shall be treated as having contributed over half of the support of an individual for the calendar year (in cases where two or more taxpayers contributed to the support of such individual) if:

(1) No one person contributed over half of the individual's support,

(2) Each member of the group which collectively contributed more than half of the support of the individual would have been

entitled to claim the individual as a dependent but for the fact that he did not contribute more than one-half of such support,

(3) The member of the group claiming the individual as a dependent contributed more than 10 percent of the individual's support, and

(4) Each other person in the group who contributed more than 10 percent of such support furnishes to the taxpayer claiming the dependent a written declaration that such other person will not claim the individual as a dependent for any taxable year beginning in such calendar year.

(b) *Examples.*—Application of the rule contained in paragraph (a) of this section may be illustrated by the following examples:

Example (1). During the taxable year, brothers A, B, C, and D contributed the entire support of their mother in the following percentages: A, 30 percent; B, 20 percent; C, 29 percent; and D, 21 percent. Any one of the brothers, except for the fact that he did not contribute more than half of her support, would have been entitled to claim his mother as a dependent. Consequently, any one of the brothers could claim a deduction for the exemption of the mother if he obtained a written declaration (as provided in paragraph (a)(4) of this section) from each of the other brothers. Even though A and D together contributed more than one-half the support of the mother, A, if he wished to claim his mother as a dependent, would be required to obtain written declarations from B, C, and D, since each of those three contributed more than 10 percent of the support and, but for the failure to contribute more than half of the mother's support, would have been entitled to claim his mother as a dependent.

Example (2). During the taxable year, E, an individual who resides with his son, S, received his entire support for that year as follows:

Source	Percentage of total
Social Security	25
N, an unrelated neighbor	11
B, a brother	14
D, a daughter	10
S, a son	40
Total received by E	100

B, D, and S are persons each of whom, but for the fact that none contributed more than half of E's support, could claim E as a dependent for the taxable year. The three together contributed 64 percent of E's support, and, thus, each is a member of the group to be considered for the purpose of section 152(c). B and S are the only members of such group who can meet all the requirements of section 152(c), and either one could claim E as a dependent for his taxable year if he obtained a written declaration (as provided in paragraph (a)(4) of this section) signed by the other, and furnished the other information required by the return with respect to all the contributions to E. Inasmuch as D did not contribute more than 10 percent of E's support, she is not entitled to claim E as a dependent for the taxable year nor is she required to furnish a written declaration with respect to her contributions to E. N contributed over 10 percent of the support of E, but, since he is an unrelated neighbor, he does not qualify as a member of the group for the purpose of the multiple support agreement under section 152(c).

(c)(1) The member of a group of contributors who claims an individual as a dependent for a taxable year beginning before January 1, 2002, under the multiple support agreement provisions of section 152(c) must attach to the member's income tax return for the year of the deduction a written declaration from each of the other persons who contributed more than 10 percent of the support of such individual and who, but for the failure to contribute more than half of the support of the individual, would have been entitled to claim the individual as a dependent.

(2) The taxpayer claiming an individual as a dependent for a taxable year beginning after December 31, 2001, under the multiple support agreement provisions of section 152(c) must provide with the income tax return for the year of the deduction—

(i) A statement identifying each of the other persons who contributed more than 10 percent of the support of the individual and who, but for the failure to contribute more than half of the support of the individual, would have been entitled to claim the individual as a dependent; and

(ii) A statement indicating that the taxpayer obtained a written declaration from each of the persons described in section 152(c)(2) waiving the right to claim the individual as a dependent.

(3) The taxpayer claiming the individual as a dependent for a *taxable year beginning after December 31, 2001,* must retain the waiver declarations and should be prepared to furnish the waiver declarations and any other information necessary to substantiate the claim, which may include a statement showing the names of all contributors (whether or not members of the group described in

section 152(c)(2)) and the amount contributed by each to the support of the claimed dependent. [Reg. § 1.152-3.]

☐ [T.D. 6231, 4-25-57. *Amended by* T.D. 6663, 7-10-63; T.D. 8989, 4-23-2002 *and* T.D. 9040, 1-30-2003.]

[Reg. § 1.152-4]

§ 1.152-4. Special rule for a child of divorced or separated parents or parents who live apart.—(a) *In general.*—A taxpayer may claim a dependency deduction for a child (as defined in section 152(f)(1)) only if the child is the qualifying child of the taxpayer under section 152(c) or the qualifying relative of the taxpayer under section 152(d). Section 152(c)(4)(B) provides that a child who is claimed as a qualifying child by parents who do not file a joint return together is treated as the qualifying child of the parent with whom the child resides for a longer period of time during the taxable year or, if the child resides with both parents for an equal period of time, of the parent with the higher adjusted gross income. However, a child is treated as the qualifying child or qualifying relative of the noncustodial parent if the custodial parent releases a claim to the exemption under section 152(e) and this section.

(b) *Release of claim by custodial parent.*—(1) *In general.*—Under section 152(e)(1), notwithstanding section 152(c)(1)(B), (c)(4), or (d)(1)(C), a child is treated as the qualifying child or qualifying relative of the noncustodial parent (as defined in paragraph (d) of this section) if the requirements of paragraphs (b)(2) and (b)(3) of this section are met.

(2) *Support, custody, and parental status.*—(i) *In general.*—The requirements of this paragraph (b)(2) are met if the parents of the child provide over one-half of the child's support for the calendar year, the child is in the custody of one or both parents for more than one-half of the calendar year, and the parents—

(A) Are divorced or legally separated under a decree of divorce or separate maintenance;

(B) Are separated under a written separation agreement; or

(C) Live apart at all times during the last 6 months of the calendar year whether or not they are or were married.

(ii) *Multiple support agreement.*—The requirements of this paragraph (b)(2) are not met if over one-half of the support of the child is treated as having been received from a taxpayer under section 152(d)(3).

(3) *Release of claim to child.*—The requirements of this paragraph (b)(3) are met for a calendar year if—

(i) The custodial parent signs a written declaration that the custodial parent will not claim the child as a dependent for any taxable year beginning in that calendar year and the noncustodial parent attaches the declaration to the noncustodial parent's return for the taxable year; or

(ii) A qualified pre-1985 instrument, as defined in section 152(e)(3)(B), applicable to the taxable year beginning in that calendar year, provides that the noncustodial parent is entitled to the dependency exemption for the child and the noncustodial parent provides at least $600 for the support of the child during the calendar year.

(c) *Custody.*—A child is in the custody of one or both parents for more than one-half of the calendar year if one or both parents have the right under state law to physical custody of the child for more than one-half of the calendar year.

(d) *Custodial parent.*—(1) *In general.*—The *custodial parent* is the parent with whom the child resides for the greater number of nights during the calendar year, and the *noncustodial parent* is the parent who is not the custodial parent. A child is treated as residing with neither parent if the child is emancipated under state law. For purposes of this section, a child resides with a parent for a night if the child sleeps—

(i) At the residence of that parent (whether or not the parent is present); or

(ii) In the company of the parent, when the child does not sleep at a parent's residence (for example, the parent and child are on vacation together).

(2) *Night straddling taxable years.*—A night that extends over two taxable years is allocated to the taxable year in which the night begins.

(3) *Absences.*—(i) Except as provided in paragraph (d)(3)(ii) of this section, for purposes of this paragraph (d), a child who does not reside (within the meaning of paragraph (d)(1) of this section) with a parent for a night is treated as residing with the parent with whom the child would have resided for the night but for the absence.

(ii) A child who does not reside (within the meaning of paragraph (d)(1) of this section) with a parent for a night is treated as not residing with either parent for that night if it cannot be determined with which parent the child would have resided or if the child would not have resided with either parent for the night.

(4) *Special rule for equal number of nights.*—If a child is in the custody of one or both parents for more than one-half of the calendar year and the child resides with each parent for an equal number of nights during the calendar year, the parent with the higher adjusted gross income for the calendar year is treated as the custodial parent.

(5) *Exception for a parent who works at night.*—If, in a calendar year, due to a parent's nighttime work schedule, a child resides for a greater number of days but not nights with the parent who works at night, that parent is treated as the custodial parent. On a school day, the child is treated as residing at the primary residence registered with the school.

(e) *Written declaration.*—(1) *Form of declaration.*—(i) *In general.*— The written declaration under paragraph (b)(3)(i) of this section must be an unconditional release of the custodial parent's claim to the child as a dependent for the year or years for which the declaration is effective. A declaration is not unconditional if the custodial parent's release of the right to claim the child as a dependent requires the satisfaction of any condition, including the noncustodial parent's meeting of an obligation such as the payment of support. A written declaration must name the noncustodial parent to whom the exemption is released. A written declaration must specify the year or years for which it is effective. A written declaration that specifies all future years is treated as specifying the first taxable year after the taxable year of execution and all subsequent taxable years.

(ii) *Form designated by IRS.*—A written declaration may be made on Form 8332, Release/Revocation of Release of Claim to Exemption for Child by Custodial Parent, or successor form designated by the IRS. A written declaration not on the form designated by the IRS must conform to the substance of that form and must be a document executed for the sole purpose of serving as a written declaration under this section. A court order or decree or a separation agreement may not serve as a written declaration.

(2) *Attachment to return.*—A noncustodial parent must attach a copy of the written declaration to the parent's return for each taxable year in which the child is claimed as a dependent.

(3) *Revocation of written declaration.*—(i) *In general.*—A parent may revoke a written declaration described in paragraph (e)(1) of this section by providing written notice of the revocation to the other parent. The parent revoking the written declaration must make reasonable efforts to provide actual notice to the other parent. The revocation may be effective no earlier than the taxable year that begins in the first calendar year after the calendar year in which the parent revoking the written declaration provides, or makes reasonable efforts to provide, the written notice.

(ii) *Form of revocation.*—The revocation may be made on Form 8332, Release/Revocation of Release of Claim to Exemption for Child by Custodial Parent, or successor form designated by the IRS whether or not the written declaration was made on a form designated by the IRS. A revocation not on that form must conform to the substance of the form and must be a document executed for the sole purpose of serving as a revocation under this section. The revocation must specify the year or years for which the revocation is effective. A revocation that specifies all future years is treated as specifying the first taxable year after the taxable year the revocation is executed and all subsequent taxable years.

(iii) *Attachment to return.*—The parent revoking the written declaration must attach a copy of the revocation to the parent's return for each taxable year for which the parent claims a child as a dependent as a result of the revocation. The parent revoking the written declaration must keep a copy of the revocation and evidence of delivery of the notice to the other parent, or of the reasonable efforts to provide actual notice.

(4) *Ineffective declaration or revocation.*—A written declaration or revocation that fails to satisfy the requirements of this paragraph (e) has no effect.

(5) *Written declaration executed in a taxable year beginning on or before July 2, 2008.*—A written declaration executed in a taxable year beginning on or before July 2, 2008, that satisfies the requirements for the form of a written declaration in effect at the time the written declaration is executed, will be treated as meeting the requirements of paragraph (e)(1) of this section. Paragraph (e)(3) of this section applies without regard to whether a custodial parent executed the written declaration in a taxable year beginning on or before July 2, 2008.

(f) *Coordination with other sections.*—If section 152(e) and this section apply, a child is treated as the dependent of both parents for purposes of sections 105(b), 132(h)(2)(B), and 213(d)(5).

(g) *Examples.*—The provisions of this section are illustrated by the following examples that assume, unless otherwise provided, that each taxpayer's taxable year is the calendar year, one or both of the child's parents provide over one-half of the child's support for the calendar year, one or both parents have the right under state law to physical custody of the child for more than one-half of the calendar year, and the child otherwise meets the requirements of a qualifying child under section 152(c) or a qualifying relative under section 152(d). In addition, in each of the examples, no qualified pre-1985 instrument or multiple support agreement is in effect. The examples are as follows:

Example 1. (i) B and C are the divorced parents of Child. In 2009, Child resides with B for 210 nights and with C for 155 nights. B executes a Form 8332 for 2009 releasing B's right to claim Child as a dependent for that year, which C attaches to C's 2009 return.

(ii) Under paragraph (d) of this section, B is the custodial parent of Child in 2009 because B is the parent with whom Child resides for the greater number of nights in 2009. Because the requirements of paragraphs (b)(2) and (3) of this section are met, C may claim Child as a dependent.

Example 2. The facts are the same as in *Example 1* except that B does not execute a Form 8332 or similar declaration for 2009. Therefore, section 152(e) and this section do not apply. Whether Child is the qualifying child or qualifying relative of B or C is determined under section 152(c) or (d).

Example 3. (i) D and E are the divorced parents of Child. Under a custody decree, Grandmother has the right under state law to physical custody of Child from January 1 to July 31, 2009.

(ii) Because D and E do not have the right under state law to physical custody of Child for over one-half of the 2009 calendar year, under paragraph (c) of this section, Child is not in the custody of one or both parents for over one-half of the calendar year. Therefore, section 152(e) and this section do not apply, and whether Child is the qualifying child or qualifying relative of D, E, or Grandmother is determined under section 152(c) or (d).

Example 4. (i) The facts are the same as in *Example 3,* except that Grandmother has the right to physical custody of Child from January 1 to March 31, 2009, and, as a result, Child resides with Grandmother during this period. D and E jointly have the right to physical custody of Child from April 1 to December 31, 2009. During this period, Child resides with D for 180 nights and with E for 95 nights. D executes a Form 8332 for 2009 releasing D's right to claim Child as a dependent for that year, which E attaches to E's 2009 return.

(ii) Under paragraph (c) of this section, Child is in the custody of D and E for over one-half of the calendar year, because D and E have the right under state law to physical custody of Child for over one-half of the calendar year.

(iii) Under paragraph (d)(3)(ii) of this section, the nights that Child resides with Grandmother are not allocated to either parent. Child resides with D for a greater number of nights than with E during the calendar year and, under paragraph (d)(1) of this section, D is the custodial parent.

(iv) Because the requirements of paragraphs (b)(2) and (3) of this section are met, section 152(e) and this section apply, and E may claim Child as a dependent.

Example 5. (i) The facts are the same as in *Example 4,* except that D is away on military service from April 10 to June 15, 2009, and September 6 to October 20, 2009. During these periods Child resides with Grandmother in Grandmother's residence. Child would have resided with D if D had not been away on military service. Grandmother claims Child as a dependent on Grandmother's 2009 return.

(ii) Under paragraph (d)(3)(i) of this section, Child is treated as residing with D for the nights that D is away on military service. Because the requirements of paragraphs (b)(2) and (3) of this section are met, section 152(e) and this section apply, and E, not Grandmother, may claim Child as a dependent.

Example 6. F and G are the divorced parents of Child. In May of 2009, Child turns age 18 and is emancipated under the law of the state where Child resides. Therefore, in 2009 and later years, F and G do not have the right under state law to physical custody of Child for over one-half of the calendar year, and Child is not in the custody of F and G for over one-half of the calendar year. Section 152(e) and this section do not apply, and whether Child is the qualifying child or qualifying relative of F or G is determined under section 152(c) or (d).

Example 7. (i) The facts are the same as in *Example 6,* except that Child turns age 18 and is emancipated under state law on August 1, 2009, resides with F from January 1, 2009, through May 31, 2009, and resides with G from June 1, 2009, through December 31, 2009. F executes a Form 8332 releasing F's right to claim Child as a dependent for 2009, which G attaches to G's 2009 return.

Reg. §1.152-4(g)

(ii) Under paragraph (c) of this section, Child is in the custody of F and G for over one-half of the calendar year.

(iii) Under paragraph (d)(1) of this section, Child is treated as not residing with either parent after Child's emancipation. Therefore, Child resides with F for 151 nights and with G for 61 nights. Because the requirements of paragraphs (b)(2) and (3) of this section are met, section 152(e) and this section apply, and G may claim Child as a dependent.

Example 8. H and J are the divorced parents of Child. Child generally resides with H during the week and with J every other weekend. Child resides with J in H's residence for 10 consecutive nights while H is hospitalized. Under paragraph (d)(1)(i) of this section, Child resides with H for the 10 nights.

Example 9. K and L, who are separated under a written separation agreement, are the parents of Child. In August 2009, K and Child spend 10 nights together in a hotel while on vacation. Under paragraph (d)(1)(ii) of this section, Child resides with K for the 10 nights that K and Child are on vacation.

Example 10. M and N are the divorced parents of Child. On December 31, 2009, Child attends a party at M's residence. After midnight on January 1, 2010, Child travels to N's residence, where Child sleeps. Under paragraph (d)(1) of this section, Child resides with N for the night of December 31, 2009, to January 1, 2010, because Child sleeps at N's residence that night. However, under paragraph (d)(2) of this section, the night of December 31, 2009, to January 1, 2010, is allocated to taxable year 2009 for purposes of determining whether Child resides with M or N for a greater number of nights in 2009.

Example 11. O and P, who never married, are the parents of Child. In 2009, Child spends alternate weeks residing with O and P. During a week that Child is residing with O, O gives Child permission to spend a night at the home of a friend. Under paragraph (d)(3)(i) of this section, the night Child spends at the friend's home is treated as a night that Child resides with O.

Example 12. The facts are the same as in *Example 11*, except that Child also resides at summer camp for 6 weeks. Because Child resides with each parent for alternate weeks, Child would have resided with O for 3 weeks and with P for 3 weeks of the period that Child is at camp. Under paragraph (d)(3)(i) of this section, Child is treated as residing with O for 3 weeks and with P for 3 weeks.

Example 13. The facts are the same as in *Example 12*, except that Child does not spend alternate weeks residing with O and P, and it cannot be determined whether Child would have resided with O or P for the period that Child is at camp. Under paragraph (d)(3)(ii) of this section, Child is treated as residing with neither parent for the 6 weeks.

Example 14. (i) Q and R are the divorced parents of Child. Q works from 11 PM to 7 AM Sunday through Thursday nights. Because of Q's nighttime work schedule, Child resides with R Sunday through Thursday nights and with Q Friday and Saturday nights. Therefore, in 2009, Child resides with R for 261 nights and with Q for 104 nights. Child spends all daytime hours when Child is not in school with Q and Q's address is registered with Child's school as Child's primary residence. Q executes a Form 8332 for 2009 releasing Q's right to claim Child as a dependent for that year, which R attaches to R's 2009 return.

(ii) Under paragraph (d) of this section, Q is the custodial parent of Child in 2009. Child resides with R for a greater number of nights than with Q due to Q's nighttime work schedule, and Child spends a greater number of days with Q. Therefore, paragraph (d)(5) of this section applies rather than paragraph (d)(1) of this section. Because the requirements of paragraphs (b)(2) and (3) of this section are met, R may claim Child as a dependent.

Example 15. (i) In 2009, S and T, the parents of Child, execute a written separation agreement. The agreement provides that Child will live with S and that T will make monthly child support payments to S. In 2009, Child resides with S for 335 nights and with T for 30 nights. S executes a letter declaring that S will not claim Child as a dependent in 2009 and in subsequent alternate years. The letter contains all the information requested on Form 8332, does not require the satisfaction of any condition such as T's payment of support, and has no purpose other than to serve as a written declaration under section 152(e) and this section. T attaches the letter to T's return for 2009 and 2011.

(ii) In 2010, T fails to provide support for Child, and S executes a Form 8332 revoking the release of S's right to claim Child as a dependent for 2011. S delivers a copy of the Form 8332 to T, attaches a copy of the Form 8332 to S's tax return for 2011, and keeps a copy of the Form 8332 and evidence of delivery of the written notice to T.

(iii) T may claim Child as a dependent for 2009 because S releases the right to claim Child as a dependent under paragraph (b)(3) of this section by executing the letter, which conforms to the requirements

of paragraph (e)(1) of this section, and T attaches the letter to T's return in accordance with paragraph (e)(2) of this section. In 2010, S revokes the release of the claim in accordance with paragraph (e)(3) of this section, and the revocation takes effect in 2011, the taxable year that begins in the first calendar year after S provides written notice of the revocation to T. Therefore, in 2011, section 152(e) and this section do not apply, and whether Child is the qualifying child or qualifying relative of S or T is determined under section 152(c) or (d).

Example 16. The facts are the same as *Example 15*, except that the letter expressly states that S releases the right to claim Child as a dependent only if T is current in the payment of support for Child at the end of the calendar year. The letter does not qualify as a written declaration under paragraph (b)(3) of this section because S's agreement not to claim Child as a dependent is conditioned on T's payment of support and, under paragraph (e)(1)(i) of this section, a written declaration must be unconditional. Therefore, section 152(e) and this section do not apply, and whether Child is the qualifying child or qualifying relative of S or T for 2009 as well as 2011 is determined under section 152(c) or (d).

Example 17. (i) U and V are the divorced parents of Child. Child resides with U for more nights than with V in 2009 through 2011. In 2009, U provides a written statement to V declaring that U will not claim Child as a dependent, but the statement does not specify the year or years it is effective. V attaches the statement to V's returns for 2009 through 2011.

(ii) Because the written statement does not specify a year or years, under paragraph (e)(1) of this section, it is not a written declaration that conforms to the substance of Form 8332. Under paragraph (e)(4) of this section, the statement has no effect. Section 152(e) and this section do not apply, and whether Child is the qualifying child or qualifying relative of U or V is determined under section 152(c) or (d).

Example 18. (i) W and X are the divorced parents of Child. In 2009, Child resides solely with W. The divorce decree requires X to pay child support to W and requires W to execute a Form 8332 releasing W's right to claim Child as a dependent. W fails to sign a Form 8332 for 2009, and X attaches an unsigned Form 8332 to X's return for 2009.

(ii) The order in the divorce decree requiring W to execute a Form 8332 is ineffective to allocate the right to claim Child as a dependent to X. Furthermore, under paragraph (e)(1) of this section, the unsigned Form 8332 does not conform to the substance of Form 8332, and under paragraph (e)(4) of this section, the Form 8332 has no effect. Therefore, section 152(e) and this section do not apply, and whether Child is the qualifying child or qualifying relative of W or X is determined under section 152(c) or (d).

(iii) If, however, W executes a Form 8332 for 2009, and X attaches the Form 8332 to X's return, then X may claim Child as a dependent in 2009.

Example 19. (i) Y and Z are the divorced parents of Child. In 2003, Y and Z enter into a separation agreement, which is incorporated into a divorce decree, under which Y, the custodial parent, releases Y's right to claim Child as a dependent for all future years. The separation agreement satisfies the requirements for the form of a written declaration in effect at the time it is executed. Z attaches a copy of the separation agreement to Z's returns for 2003 through 2009.

(ii) Under paragraph (e)(1)(ii) of this section, a separation agreement may not serve as a written declaration. However, under paragraph (e)(5) of this section, a written declaration executed in a taxable year beginning on or before July 2, 2008, that satisfies the requirements for the form of a written declaration in effect at the time the written declaration is executed, will be treated as meeting the requirements of paragraph (e)(1) of this section. Therefore, the separation agreement may serve as the written declaration required by paragraph (b)(3)(i) of this section for 2009, and Z may claim Child as a dependent in 2009 and later years.

Example 20. (i) The facts are the same as in *Example 19*, except that in 2009 Y executes a Form 8332 revoking the release of Y's right to claim Child as a dependent for 2010. Y complies with all the requirements of paragraph (e)(3) of this section.

(ii) Although Y executes the separation agreement releasing Y's right to claim Child as a dependent in a taxable year beginning on or before July 2, 2008, under paragraph (e)(5) of this section, Y's execution of the Form 8332 in 2009 is effective to revoke the release. Therefore, section 152(e) and this section do not apply in 2010, and whether Child is the qualifying child or qualifying relative of Y or Z is determined under section 152(c) or (d).

(h) *Effective/applicability date.*—This section applies to taxable years beginning after July 2, 2008. [Reg. § 1.152-4.]

□ [*T.D.* 7099, 3-19-71. *Amended by T.D.* 7145, 10-14-71; *T.D.* 7639, 8-17-79 *and T.D.* 9408, 7-1-2008.]

Itemized Deductions for Individuals and Corps.
See p. 20,601 for regulations not amended to reflect law changes

25,211

Itemized Deductions for Individuals and Corporations

[Reg. §1.161-1]

§1.161-1. Allowance of deductions.—Section 161 provides for the allowance as deductions, in computing taxable income under section 63(a), of the items specified in part VI (section 161 and following), subchapter B of chapter 1 of the Code, subject to the exceptions provided in part IX (section 261 and following), of such subchapter B, relating to the items not deductible. Double deductions are not permitted. Amounts deducted under one provision of the Internal Revenue Code of 1954 cannot again be deducted under any other provision thereof. See also section 7852(c), relating to the taking into account, both in computing a tax under subtitle A of the Internal Revenue Code of 1954 and a tax under chapter 1 or 2 of the Internal Revenue Code of 1939, of the same item of deduction. [Reg. §1.161-1.]

☐ [*T.D. 6291, 4-3-58.*]

[Reg. §1.162-1]

§1.162-1. Business expenses.—(a) *In general.*—Business expenses deductible from gross income include the ordinary and necessary expenditures directly connected with or pertaining to the taxpayer's trade or business, except items which are used as the basis for a deduction or a credit under provisions of law other than section 162. The cost of goods purchased for resale, with proper adjustment for opening and closing inventories, is deducted from gross sales in computing gross income. See paragraph (a) of §1.61-3. Among the items included in business expenses are management expenses, commissions (but see section 263 and the regulations thereunder), labor, supplies, incidental repairs, operating expenses of automobiles used in the trade or business, traveling expenses while away from home solely in the pursuit of a trade or business (see §1.162-2), advertising and other selling expenses, together with insurance premiums against fire, storm, theft, accident, or other similar losses in the case of a business, and rental for the use of business property. No such item shall be included in business expenses, however, to the extent that it is used by the taxpayer in computing the cost of property included in its inventory or used in determining the gain or loss basis of its plant, equipment, or other property. See section 1054 and the regulations thereunder. A deduction for an expense paid or incurred after December 30, 1969, which would otherwise be allowable under section 162 shall not be denied on the grounds that allowance of such deduction would frustrate a sharply defined public policy. See section 162(c), (f), and (g) and the regulations thereunder. The full amount of the allowable deduction for ordinary and necessary expenses in carrying on a business is deductible, even though such expenses exceed the gross income derived during the taxable year from such business. In the case of any sports program to which section 114 (relating to sports programs conducted for the American National Red Cross) applies, expenses described in section 114(a)(2) shall be allowable as deductions under section 162(a) only to the extent that such expenses exceed the amount excluded from gross income under section 114(a).

(b) *Cross references.*—(1) For charitable contributions by individuals and corporations not deductible under section 162, see §1.162-15.

(2) For items not deductible, see sections 261-276, inclusive, and the regulations thereunder.

(3) For research and experimental expenditures, see section 174 and regulations thereunder.

(4) For soil and water conservation expenditures, see section 175 and regulations thereunder.

(5) For expenditures attributable to grant or loan by United States for encouragement of exploration for, or development or mining of, critical and strategic minerals or metals, see section 621 and regulations thereunder.

(6) For treatment of certain rental payments with respect to public utility property, see section 167(1) and §1.167(1)-3.

(7) For limitations on the deductibility of miscellaneous itemized deductions, see section 67 and §§1.67-1T through 1.67-4T.

(8) For the timing of deductions with respect to notional principal contracts, see §1.446-3. [Reg. §1.162-1.]

☐ [*T.D. 6291, 4-3-58. Amended by T.D. 6690, 11-18-63; T.D. 6996, 1-17-69; T.D. 7315, 6-6-74; T.D. 7345, 2-19-75; T.D. 8189, 3-25-88 and T.D. 8491, 10-8-93.*]

[Reg. §1.162-2]

§1.162-2. Traveling expenses.—(a) Traveling expenses include travel fares, meals and lodging, and expenses incident to travel such as expenses for sample rooms, telephone and telegraph, public stenographers, etc. Only such traveling expenses as are reasonable and necessary in the conduct of the taxpayer's business and directly attributable to it may be deducted. If the trip is undertaken for other than business purposes, the travel fares and expenses incident to travel are personal expenses and the meals and lodging are living expenses. If the trip is solely on business, the reasonable and necessary traveling expenses, including travel fares, meals and lodging, and expenses incident to travel, are business expenses. For the allowance of traveling expenses as deductions in determining adjusted gross income, see section 62(2)(B) and the regulations thereunder.

(b)(1) If a taxpayer travels to a destination and while at such destination engages in both business and personal activities, traveling expenses to and from such destination are deductible only if the trip is related primarily to the taxpayer's trade or business. If the trip is primarily personal in nature, the traveling expenses to and from the destination are not deductible even though the taxpayer engages in business activities while at such destination. However, expenses while at the destination which are properly allocable to the taxpayer's trade or business are deductible even though the traveling expenses to and from the destination are not deductible.

(2) Whether a trip is related primarily to the taxpayer's trade or business or is primarily personal in nature depends on the facts and circumstances in each case. The amount of time during the period of the trip which is spent on personal activity compared to the amount of time spent on activities directly relating to the taxpayer's trade or business is an important factor in determining whether the trip is primarily personal. If, for example, a taxpayer spends one week while at a destination on activities which are directly related to his trade or business and subsequently spends an additional five weeks for vacation or other personal activities, the trip will be considered primarily personal in nature in the absence of a clear showing to the contrary.

(c) Where a taxpayer's wife accompanies him on a business trip, expenses attributable to her travel are not deductible unless it can be adequately shown that the wife's presence on the trip has a bona fide business purpose. The wife's performance of some incidental service does not cause her expenses to qualify as deductible business expenses. The same rules apply to any other members of the taxpayer's family who accompany him on such a trip.

(d) Expenses paid or incurred by a taxpayer in attending a convention or other meeting may constitute an ordinary and necessary business expense under section 162 depending upon the facts and circumstances of each case. No distinction will be made between self-employed persons and employees. The fact that an employee uses vacation or leave time or that his attendance at the convention is voluntary will not necessarily prohibit the allowance of the deduction. The allowance of deductions for such expenses will depend upon whether there is a sufficient relationship between the taxpayer's trade or business and his attendance at the convention or other meeting so that he is benefiting or advancing the interests of his trade or business by such attendance. If the convention is for political, social or other purposes unrelated to the taxpayer's trade or business, the expenses are not deductible.

(e) Commuters' fares are not considered as business expenses and are not deductible.

(f) For rules with respect to the reporting and substantiation of traveling and other business expenses of employees for taxable years beginning after December 31, 1957, see §1.162-17. [Reg. §1.162-2.]

☐ [*T.D. 6291, 4-3-58. Amended by T.D. 6306, 8-27-58.*]

>>→ *Caution: Reg. §1.162-3, below, as amended by T.D. 9636, generally applies to amounts paid or incurred in tax years beginning on or after January 1, 2014; see Reg. §1.162-3(j), below, for details and exceptions.*

[Reg. §1.162-3]

§1.162-3. Materials and supplies.—(a) *In general.*—(1) *Non-incidental materials and supplies.*—Except as provided in paragraphs (d), (e), and (f) of this section, amounts paid to acquire or produce materials and supplies (as defined in paragraph (c) of this section) are deductible in the taxable year in which the materials and supplies are first used in the taxpayer's operations or are consumed in the taxpayer's operations.

(2) *Incidental materials and supplies.*—Amounts paid to acquire or produce incidental materials and supplies (as defined in paragraph (c) of this section) that are carried on hand and for which no record of consumption is kept or of which physical inventories at the beginning and end of the taxable year are not taken, are deductible in the taxable year in which these amounts are paid, provided taxable income is clearly reflected.

>>>→ Caution: *Reg. §1.162-3, below, as amended by T.D. 9636, generally applies to amounts paid or incurred in tax years beginning on or after January 1, 2014; see Reg. §1.162-3(j), below, for details and exceptions.*

(3) *Use or consumption of rotable and temporary spare parts.*—Except as provided in paragraphs (d), (e), and (f) of this section, for purposes of paragraph (a)(1) of this section, rotable and temporary spare parts (defined under paragraph (c)(2) of this section) are first used in the taxpayer's operations or are consumed in the taxpayer's operations in the taxable year in which the taxpayer disposes of the parts.

(b) *Coordination with other provisions of the Internal Revenue Code.*—Nothing in this section changes the treatment of any amount that is specifically provided for under any provision of the Internal Revenue Code (Code) or regulations other than section 162(a) or section 212 and the regulations under those sections. For example, see §1.263(a)-3, which requires taxpayers to capitalize amounts paid to improve tangible property and section 263A and the regulations under section 263A, which require taxpayers to capitalize the direct and allocable indirect costs, including the cost of materials and supplies, of property produced by the taxpayer and property acquired for resale. See also §1.471-1, which requires taxpayers to include in inventory certain materials and supplies.

(c) *Definitions.*—(1) *Materials and supplies.*—For purposes of this section, *materials and supplies* means tangible property that is used or consumed in the taxpayer's operations that is not inventory and that—

(i) Is a component acquired to maintain, repair, or improve a unit of tangible property (as determined under §1.263(a)-3(e)) owned, leased, or serviced by the taxpayer and that is not acquired as part of any single unit of tangible property;

(ii) Consists of fuel, lubricants, water, and similar items, reasonably expected to be consumed in 12 months or less, beginning when used in the taxpayer's operations;

(iii) Is a unit of property as determined under §1.263(a)-3(e) that has an economic useful life of 12 months or less, beginning when the property is used or consumed in the taxpayer's operations;

(iv) Is a unit of property as determined under §1.263(a)-3(e) that has an acquisition cost or production cost (as determined under section 263A) of $200 or less (or other amount as identified in published guidance in the **Federal Register** or in the Internal Revenue Bulletin (see §601.601(d)(2)(ii)(*b*) of this chapter); or

(v) Is identified in published guidance in the **Federal Register** or in the Internal Revenue Bulletin (see §601.601(d)(2)(ii)(*b*) of this chapter) as materials and supplies for which treatment is permitted under this section.

(2) *Rotable and temporary spare parts.*—For purposes of this section, rotable spare parts are materials and supplies under paragraph (c)(1)(i) of this section that are acquired for installation on a unit of property, removable from that unit of property, generally repaired or improved, and either reinstalled on the same or other property or stored for later installation. Temporary spare parts are materials and supplies under paragraph (c)(1)(i) of this section that are used temporarily until a new or repaired part can be installed and then are removed and stored for later installation.

(3) *Standby emergency spare parts.*—Standby emergency spare parts are materials and supplies under paragraph (c)(1)(i) of this section that are—

(i) Acquired when particular machinery or equipment is acquired (or later acquired and set aside for use in particular machinery or equipment);

(ii) Set aside for use as replacements to avoid substantial operational time loss caused by emergencies due to particular machinery or equipment failure;

(iii) Located at or near the site of the installed related machinery or equipment so as to be readily available when needed;

(iv) Directly related to the particular machinery or piece of equipment they serve;

(v) Normally expensive;

(vi) Only available on special order and not readily available from a vendor or manufacturer;

(vii) Not subject to normal periodic replacement;

(viii) Not interchangeable in other machines or equipment;

(x) Not acquired in quantity (generally only one is on hand for each piece of machinery or equipment); and

(xi) Not repaired and reused.

(4) *Economic useful life.*—(i) *General rule.*—The economic useful life of a unit of property is not necessarily the useful life inherent in the property but is the period over which the property may reasonably be expected to be useful to the taxpayer or, if the taxpayer is engaged in a trade or business or an activity for the production of income, the period over which the property may reasonably be expected to be useful to the taxpayer in its trade or business or for the production of income, as applicable. The factors that must be considered in determining this period are provided under §1.167(a)-1(b).

(ii) *Taxpayers with an applicable financial statement.*—For taxpayers with an applicable financial statement (as defined in paragraph (c)(4)(iii) of this section), the economic useful life of a unit of property, solely for the purposes of applying the provisions of this paragraph (c), is the useful life initially used by the taxpayer for purposes of determining depreciation in its applicable financial statement, regardless of any salvage value of the property. If a taxpayer does not have an applicable financial statement for the taxable year in which a unit of property was originally acquired or produced, the economic useful life of the unit of property must be determined under paragraph (c)(4)(i) of this section. Further, if a taxpayer treats amounts paid for a unit of property as an expense in its applicable financial statement on a basis other than the useful life of the property or if a taxpayer does not depreciate the unit of property on its applicable financial statement, the economic useful life of the unit of property must be determined under paragraph (c)(4)(i) of this section. For example, if a taxpayer has a policy of treating as an expense on its applicable financial statement amounts paid for a unit of property costing less than a certain dollar amount, notwithstanding that the unit of property has a useful life of more than one year, the economic useful life of the unit of property must be determined under paragraph (c)(4)(i) of this section.

(iii) *Definition of applicable financial statement.*—The taxpayer's applicable financial statement is the taxpayer's financial statement listed in paragraphs (c)(4)(iii)(A) through (C) of this section that has the highest priority (including within paragraph (c)(4)(iii)(B) of this section). The financial statements are, in descending priority—

(A) A financial statement required to be filed with the Securities and Exchange Commission (SEC) (the 10-K or the Annual Statement to Shareholders);

(B) A certified audited financial statement that is accompanied by the report of an independent certified public accountant (or in the case of a foreign entity, by the report of a similarly qualified independent professional), that is used for—

(*1*) Credit purposes;

(*2*) Reporting to shareholders, partners, or similar persons; or

(*3*) Any other substantial non-tax purpose; or

(C) A financial statement (other than a tax return) required to be provided to the federal or a state government or any federal or state agency (other than the SEC or the Internal Revenue Service).

(5) *Amount paid.*—For purposes of this section, in the case of a taxpayer using an accrual method of accounting, the terms *amount paid* and *payment* mean a liability incurred (within the meaning of §1.446-1(c)(1)(ii)). A liability may not be taken into account under this section prior to the taxable year during which the liability is incurred.

(6) *Produce.*—For purposes of this section, *produce* means construct, build, install, manufacture, develop, create, raise, or grow. This definition is intended to have the same meaning as the definition used for purposes of section 263A(g)(1) and §1.263A-2(a)(1)(i), except that improvements are excluded from the definition in this paragraph (c)(6) and are separately defined and addressed in §1.263(a)-3. Amounts paid to produce materials and supplies are subject to section 263A.

(d) *Election to capitalize and depreciate certain materials and supplies.*—(1) *In general.*—A taxpayer may elect to treat as a capital expenditure and to treat as an asset subject to the allowance for depreciation the cost of any rotable spare part, temporary spare part, or standby emergency spare part as defined in paragraph (c)(2) or (c)(3) of this section. Except as specified in paragraph (d)(2) of this section, an election made under this paragraph (d) applies to amounts paid during the taxable year to acquire or produce any rotable, temporary, or standby emergency spare part to which paragraph (a) of this section would apply (but for the election under this paragraph (d)). Any property for which this election is made shall not be treated as a material or a supply.

(2) *Exceptions.*—A taxpayer may not elect to capitalize and depreciate under this paragraph (d) any amount paid to acquire or produce a rotable, temporary, or standby emergency spare part defined in paragraph (c)(2) or (c)(3) of this section if—

(i) The rotable, temporary, or standby emergency spare part is intended to be used as a component of a unit of property under paragraph (c)(1)(iii), (iv), or (v) of this section;

Itemized Deductions for Individuals and Corps.
See p. 20,601 for regulations not amended to reflect law changes
25,213

⮞⮞⮞ *Caution: Reg. §1.162-3, below, as amended by T.D. 9636, generally applies to amounts paid or incurred in tax years beginning on or after January 1, 2014; see Reg. §1.162-3(j), below, for details and exceptions.*

(ii) The rotable, temporary, or standby emergency spare part is intended to be used as a component of a property described in paragraph (c)(1)(i) and the taxpayer cannot or has not elected to capitalize and depreciate that property under this paragraph (d); or

(iii) The amount is paid to acquire or produce a rotable or temporary spare part and the taxpayer uses the optional method of accounting for rotable and temporary spare parts under paragraph (e) to of this section.

(3) *Manner of electing.*—A taxpayer makes the election under this paragraph (d) by capitalizing the amounts paid to acquire or produce a rotable, temporary, or standby emergency spare part in the taxable year the amounts are paid and by beginning to depreciate the costs when the asset is placed in service by the taxpayer for purposes of determining depreciation under the applicable provisions of the Internal Revenue Code and the Treasury Regulations. Section 1.263(a)-2 provides for the treatment of amounts paid to acquire or produce real or personal tangible property. A taxpayer must make the election under this paragraph (d) in its timely filed original Federal tax return (including extensions) for the taxable year the asset is placed in service by the taxpayer for purposes of determining depreciation. Sections 301.9100-1 through 301.9100-3 of this chapter provide the rules governing extensions of the time to make regulatory elections. In the case of an S corporation or a partnership, the election is made by the S corporation or partnership, and not by the shareholders or partners. A taxpayer may make an election for each rotable, temporary, or standby emergency spare part that qualifies for the election under this paragraph (d). This election does not apply to an asset or a portion thereof placed in service and disposed of in the same taxable year. A taxpayer may revoke an election made under this paragraph (d) or made under §1.162-3T(d), as contained in 26 CFR part 1, revised as of April 1, 2013, only by filing a request for a private letter ruling and obtaining the Commissioner's consent to revoke the election. The Commissioner may grant a request to revoke this election if the taxpayer acted reasonably and in good faith and the revocation will not prejudice the interests of the Government. See generally §301.9100-3 of this chapter. The manner of electing and revoking the election to capitalize under this paragraph (d) or under §1.162-3T(d), as contained in 26 CFR part 1, revised as of April 1, 2013, may be modified through guidance of general applicability (see §§601.601(d)(2) and 601.602 of this chapter). An election may not be made or revoked through the filing of an application for change in accounting method or, before obtaining the Commissioner's consent to make the late election or to revoke the election, by filing an amended Federal tax return.

(e) *Optional method of accounting for rotable and temporary spare parts.*—(1) *In general.*—This paragraph (e) provides an optional method of accounting for rotable and temporary spare parts (the optional method for rotable parts). A taxpayer may use the optional method for rotable parts, instead of the general rule under paragraph (a)(3) of this section, to account for its rotable and temporary spare parts as defined in paragraph (c)(2) of this section. A taxpayer that uses the optional method for rotable parts must use this method for all of its pools of rotable and temporary spare parts used in the same trade or business and for which it uses this method for its books and records. If a taxpayer uses the optional method for rotable parts for pools of rotable and temporary spare parts for which the taxpayer does not use the optional method for its books and records, then the taxpayer must use the optional method for all its pools in the same trade or business, whether rotable or temporary. The optional method for rotable parts is a method of accounting under section 446(a). Under the optional method for rotable parts, the taxpayer must apply the rules in this paragraph (e) to each rotable or temporary spare part (part) upon the taxpayer's initial installation, removal, repair, maintenance or improvement, reinstallation, and disposal of each part.

(2) *Description of optional method for rotable parts.*—(i) *Initial installation.*—The taxpayer must deduct the amount paid to acquire or produce the part in the taxable year that the part is first installed on a unit of property for use in the taxpayer's operations.

(ii) *Removal from unit of property.*—In each taxable year in which the part is removed from a unit of property to which it was initially or subsequently installed, the taxpayer must—

(A) Include in gross income the fair market value of the part; and

(B) Include in the basis of the part the fair market value of the part included in income under paragraph (e)(2)(ii)(A) of this section and the amount paid to remove the part from the unit of property.

(iii) *Repair, maintenance, or improvement of part.*—The taxpayer may not currently deduct and must include in the basis of the part any amounts paid to maintain, repair, or improve the part in the taxable year these amounts are paid.

(iv) *Reinstallation of part.*—The taxpayer must deduct the amounts paid to reinstall the part and those amounts included in the basis of the part under paragraphs (e)(2)(ii)(B) and (e)(2)(iii) of this section, to the extent that those amounts have not been previously deducted under this paragraph (e)(2)(iv), in the taxable year that the part is reinstalled on a unit of property.

(v) *Disposal of the part.*—The taxpayer must deduct the amounts included in the basis of the part under paragraphs (e)(2)(ii)(B) and (e)(2)(iii) of this section, to the extent that those amounts have not been previously deducted under paragraph (e)(2)(iv) of this section, in the taxable year in which the part is disposed of by the taxpayer.

(f) *Application of de minimis safe harbor.*—If a taxpayer elects to apply the de minimis safe harbor under §1.263(a)-1(f) to amounts paid for the production or acquisition of tangible property, then the taxpayer must apply the de minimis safe harbor to amounts paid for all materials and supplies that meet the requirements of §1.263(a)-1(f), except for those materials and supplies that the taxpayer elects to capitalize and depreciate under paragraph (d) of this section or for which the taxpayer properly uses the optional method of accounting for rotable and temporary spare parts under paragraph (e) of this section. If the taxpayer properly applies the de minimis safe harbor under §1.263(a)-1(f) to amounts paid for materials and supplies, then these amounts are not treated as amounts paid for materials and supplies under this section. See §1.263(a)-1(f)(5) for the time and manner of electing the de minimis safe harbor and §1.263(a)-1(f)(3)(iv) for the treatment of safe harbor amounts.

(g) *Sale or disposition of materials and supplies.*—Upon sale or other disposition, materials and supplies as defined in this section are not treated as a capital asset under section 1221 or as property used in the trade or business under section 1231. Any asset for which the taxpayer makes the election to capitalize and depreciate under paragraph (d) of this section shall not be treated as a material or supply, and the recognition and character of the gain or loss for such depreciable asset are determined under other applicable provisions of the Code.

(h) *Examples.*—The rules of this section are illustrated by the following examples, in which it is assumed, unless otherwise stated, that the property is not an incidental material or supply, that the taxpayer computes its income on a calendar year basis, that the taxpayer does not make the election to apply paragraph (d) of this section, or use the method of accounting described in paragraph (e) of this section, and that the taxpayer has not elected to apply the de minimis safe harbor under §1.263(a)-1(f). The following examples illustrate only the application of this section and, unless otherwise stated, do not address the treatment under other provisions of the Code (for example, section 263A).

Example 1. Non-rotable components. A owns a fleet of aircraft that it operates in its business. In Year 1, A purchases a stock of spare parts, which it uses to maintain and repair its aircraft. A keeps a record of consumption of these spare parts. In Year 2, A uses the spare parts for the repair and maintenance of one of its aircraft. Assume each aircraft is a unit of property under §1.263(a)-3(e) and that spare parts are not rotable or temporary spare parts under paragraph (c)(2) of this section. Assume these repair and maintenance activities do not improve the aircraft under §1.263(a)-3. These parts are materials and supplies under paragraph (c)(1)(i) of this section because they are components acquired and used to maintain and repair A's aircraft. Under paragraph (a)(1) of this section, the amounts that A paid for the spare parts in Year 1 are deductible in Year 2, the taxable year in which the spare parts are first used to repair and maintain the aircraft.

Example 2. Rotable spare parts; disposal method. B operates a fleet of specialized vehicles that it uses in its service business. Assume that each vehicle is a unit of property under §1.263(a)-3(e). At the time that it acquires a new type of vehicle, B also acquires a substantial number of rotable spare parts that it will keep on hand to quickly replace similar parts in B's vehicles as those parts break down or wear out. These rotable parts are removable from the vehicles and are repaired so that they can be reinstalled on the same or similar vehicles. In Year 1, B acquires several vehicles and a number of rotable spare parts to be used as replacement parts in these vehicles. In Year 2, B repairs several vehicles by using these rotable spare parts to replace worn or damaged parts. In Year 3, B removes these rotable spare parts from its vehicles, repairs the parts, and reinstalls them on

⋙→ *Caution: Reg. §1.162-3, below, as amended by T.D. 9636, generally applies to amounts paid or incurred in tax years beginning on or after January 1, 2014; see Reg. §1.162-3(j), below, for details and exceptions.*

other similar vehicles. In Year 5, B can no longer use the rotable parts it acquired in Year 1 and disposes of them as scrap. Assume that B does not improve any of the rotable spare parts under §1.263(a)-3. Under paragraph (c)(1)(i) of this section, the rotable spare parts acquired in Year 1 are materials and supplies. Under paragraph (a)(3) of this section, rotable spare parts are generally used or consumed in the taxable year in which the taxpayer disposes of the parts. Therefore, under paragraph (a)(1) of this section, the amounts that B paid for the rotable spare parts in Year 1 are deductible in Year 5, the taxable year in which B disposes of the parts.

Example 3. Rotable spare parts; application of optional method of accounting. C operates a fleet of specialized vehicles that it uses in its service business. Assume that each vehicle is a unit of property under §1.263(a)-3(e). At the time that it acquires a new type of vehicle, C also acquires a substantial number of rotable spare parts that it will keep on hand to replace similar parts in C's vehicles as those parts break down or wear out. These rotable parts are removable from the vehicles and are repaired so that they can be reinstalled on the same or similar vehicles. C uses the optional method of accounting for all its rotable and temporary spare parts under paragraph (e) of this section. In Year 1, C acquires several vehicles and a number of rotable spare parts (the "Year 1 rotable parts") to be used as replacement parts in these vehicles. In Year 2, C repairs several vehicles and uses the Year 1 rotable parts to replace worn or damaged parts. In Year 3, C pays amounts to remove these Year 1 rotable parts from its vehicles. In Year 4, C pays amounts to maintain, repair, or improve the Year 1 rotable parts. In Year 5, C pays amounts to reinstall the Year 1 rotable parts on other similar vehicles. In Year 8, C removes the Year 1 rotable parts from these vehicles and stores these parts for possible later use. In Year 9, C disposes of the Year 1 rotable parts. Under paragraph (e) of this section, C must deduct the amounts paid to acquire and install the Year 1 rotable parts in Year 2, the taxable year in which the rotable parts are first installed by C in C's vehicles. In Year 3, when C removes the Year 1 rotable parts from its vehicles, C must include in its gross income the fair market value of each part. Also, in Year 3, C must include in the basis of each Year 1 rotable part the fair market value of the rotable part and the amount paid to remove the rotable part from the vehicle. In Year 4, C must include in the basis of each Year 1 rotable part the amounts paid to maintain, repair, or improve each rotable part. In Year 5, the year that C reinstalls the Year 1 rotable parts (as repaired or improved) in other vehicles, C must deduct the reinstallation costs and the amounts previously included in the basis of each part. In Year 8, the year that C removes the Year 1 rotable parts from the vehicles, C must include in income the fair market value of each rotable part removed. In addition, in Year 8, C must include in the basis of each part the fair market value of that part and the amount paid to remove each rotable part from the vehicle. In Year 9, the year that C disposes of the Year 1 rotable parts, C may deduct the amounts remaining in the basis of each rotable part.

Example 4. Rotable part acquired as part of a single unit of property; not material or supply. D operates a fleet of aircraft. In Year 1, D acquires a new aircraft, which includes two new aircraft engines. The aircraft costs $500,000 and has an economic useful life of more than 12 months, beginning when it is placed in service. In Year 5, after the aircraft is operated for several years in D's business, D removes the engines from the aircraft, repairs or improves the engines, and either reinstalls the engines on a similar aircraft or stores the engines for later reinstallation. Assume the aircraft purchased in Year 1, including its two engines, is a unit of property under §1.263(a)-3(e). Because the engines were acquired as part of the aircraft, a single unit of property, the engines are not materials or supplies under paragraph (c)(1)(i) of this section nor rotable or temporary spare parts under paragraph (c)(2) of this section. Accordingly, D may not apply the rules of this section to the aircraft engines upon the original acquisition of the aircraft nor after the removal of the engines from the aircraft for use in the same or similar aircraft. Rather, D must apply the rules under §§1.263(a)-2 and 1.263(a)-3 to the aircraft, including its engines, to determine the treatment of amounts paid to acquire, produce, or improve the unit of property.

Example 5. Consumable property. E operates a fleet of aircraft that carries freight for its customers. E has several storage tanks on its premises, which hold jet fuel for its aircraft. Assume that once the jet fuel is placed in E's aircraft, the jet fuel is reasonably expected to be consumed within 12 months or less. On December 31, Year 1, E purchases a two-year supply of jet fuel. In Year 2, E uses a portion of the jet fuel purchased on *December 31, Year 1,* to fuel the aircraft used in its business. The jet fuel that E purchased in Year 1 is a material or supply under paragraph (c)(1)(ii) of this section because it is reasonably expected to be consumed within 12 months or less from the time it is placed in E's aircraft. Under paragraph (a)(1) of this section, E may deduct in Year 2 the amounts paid for the portion of jet fuel used in the operation of E's aircraft in Year 2.

Example 6. Unit of property that costs $200 or less. F operates a business that rents out a variety of small individual items to customers (rental items). F maintains a supply of rental items on hand. In Year 1, F purchases a large quantity of rental items to use in its rental business. Assume that each rental item is a unit of property under §1.263(a)-3(e) and costs $200 or less. In Year 2, F begins using all the rental items purchased in Year 1 by providing them to customers of its rental business. F does not sell or exchange these items on established retail markets at any time after the items are used in the rental business. The rental items are materials and supplies under paragraph (c)(1)(iv) of this section. Under paragraph (a)(1) of this section, the amounts that F paid for the rental items in Year 1 are deductible in Year 2, the taxable year in which the rental items are first used in F's business.

Example 7. Unit of property that costs $200 or less. G provides billing services to its customers. In Year 1, G pays amounts to purchase 50 scanners to be used by its employees. Assume each scanner is a unit of property under §1.263(a)-3(e) and costs less than $200. In Year 1, G's employees begin using 35 of the scanners, and F stores the remaining 15 scanners for use in a later taxable year. The scanners are materials and supplies under paragraph (c)(1)(iv) of this section. Under paragraph (a)(1) of this section, the amounts G paid for 35 of the scanners are deductible in Year 1, the taxable year in which G first uses each of those scanners. The amounts that G paid for each of the remaining 15 scanners are deductible in the taxable year in which each machine is first used in G's business.

Example 8. Materials and supplies that cost less than $200; de minimis safe harbor. Assume the same facts as in *Example 7* except that G's scanners qualify for the de minimis safe harbor under §1.263(a)-1(f), and G properly elects to apply the de minimis safe harbor under §1.263(a)-1(f) to amounts paid in Year 1. G must apply the de minimis safe harbor under §1.263(a)-1(f) to amounts paid for the scanners, rather than treat these amounts as costs of materials and supplies under this section. In accordance with §1.263(a)-1(f)(3)(iv), G may deduct the amounts paid for all 50 scanners under §1.162-1 in the taxable year the amounts are paid.

Example 9. Unit of property that costs $200 or less; bulk purchase. H provides consulting services to its customers. In Year 1, H pays $500 to purchase one box of 10 toner cartridges to use as needed for H's printers. Assume each toner cartridge is a unit of property under §1.263(a)-3(e). In Year 1, H's employees place 8 of the toner cartridges in printers in H's office, and store the remaining 2 cartridges for use in a later taxable year. The toner cartridges are materials and supplies under paragraph (c)(1)(iv) of this section because even though purchased in one box costing more than $200, the allocable cost of each unit of property equals $50. Therefore, under paragraph (a)(1) of this section, the $400 paid by H for 8 of the cartridges is deductible in Year 1, the taxable year in which H first uses each of those cartridges. The amounts paid by H for each of the remaining 2 cartridges ($50 each) are deductible in the taxable year in which each cartridge is first used in H's business.

Example 10. Materials and supplies used in improvements; coordination with §1.263(a)-3. J owns various machines that are used in its business. Assume that each machine is a unit of property under §1.263(a)-3(e). In Year 1, J purchases a supply of spare parts for its machines. J acquired the parts to use in the repair or maintenance of the machines under §1.162-4 or in the improvement of the machines under §1.263(a)-3. The spare parts are not rotable or temporary spare parts under paragraph (c)(2) of this section. In Year 2, J uses all of these spare parts in an activity that improves a machine under §1.263(a)-3. Under paragraph (c)(1)(i) of this section, the spare parts purchased by J in Year 1 are materials and supplies. Under paragraph (a)(1) of this section, the amounts paid for the spare parts are otherwise deductible as materials and supplies in Year 2, the taxable year in which J uses those parts. However, because these materials and supplies are used to improve J's machine, J is required to capitalize the amounts paid for those spare parts under §1.263(a)-3.

Example 11. Cost of producing materials and supplies; coordination with section 263A. K is a manufacturer that produces liquid waste as part of its operations. K determines that its current liquid waste disposal process is inadequate. To remedy the problem, in Year 1, K constructs a leaching pit to provide a draining area for the liquid waste. Assume the leaching pit is a unit of property under §1.263(a)-3(e) and has an economic useful life of 12 months or less, starting on the date that K begins to use the leaching pit as a draining area. At the end of this period, K's factory will be connected to the local sewer system. In Year 2, K starts using the leaching pit in its operations. The amounts paid to construct the leaching pit (including the direct and allocable indirect costs of property produced under section 263A) are amounts paid for a material or supply under paragraph (c)(1)(iii) of this

»»→ Caution: *Reg. §1.162-3, below, as amended by T.D. 9636, generally applies to amounts paid or incurred in tax years beginning on or after January 1, 2014; see Reg. §1.162-3(j), below, for details and exceptions.*

section. However, the amounts paid to construct the leaching pit may be subject to capitalization under section 263A if these amounts comprise the direct or allocable indirect costs of property produced by K.

Example 12. Costs of acquiring materials and supplies for production of property; coordination with section 263A. In Year 1, L purchases jigs, dies, molds, and patterns for use in the manufacture of L's products. Assume each jig, die, mold, and pattern is a unit of property under §1.263(a)-3(e). The economic useful life of each jig, die, mold, and pattern is 12 months or less, beginning when each item is used in the manufacturing process. The jigs, dies, molds, and patterns are not components acquired to maintain, repair, or improve any of L's equipment under paragraph (c)(1)(i) of this section. L begins using the jigs, dies, molds and patterns in Year 2 to manufacture its products. These items are materials and supplies under paragraph (c)(1)(iii) of this section. Under paragraph (a)(1) of this section, the amounts paid for the items are otherwise deductible in Year 2, the taxable year in which L first uses those items. However, the amounts paid for these materials and supplies may be subject to capitalization under section 263A if these amounts comprise the direct or allocable indirect costs of property produced by L.

Example 13. Election to capitalize and depreciate. M is in the mining business. M acquires certain temporary spare parts, which it keeps on hand to avoid operational time loss in the event it must make temporary repairs to a unit of property that is subject to depreciation. These parts are not used to improve property under §1.263(a)-3(d). These temporary spare parts are used until a new or repaired part can be installed and then are removed and stored for later temporary installation. M does not use the optional method of accounting for rotable and temporary spare parts in paragraph (e) of this section for any of its rotable or temporary spare parts. The temporary spare parts are materials and supplies under paragraph (c)(1)(i) of this section. Under paragraphs (a)(1) and (a)(3) of this section, the amounts paid for the temporary spare parts are deductible in the taxable year in which they are disposed of by M. However, because it is unlikely that the temporary spare parts will be disposed of in the near future, M would prefer to treat the amounts paid for the spare parts as capital expenditures subject to depreciation. M may elect under paragraph (d) of this section to treat the cost of each temporary spare part as a capital expenditure and as an asset subject to an allowance for depreciation. M makes this election by capitalizing the amounts paid for each spare part in the taxable year that M acquires the spare parts and by beginning to recover the costs of each part on its timely filed Federal tax return for the taxable year in which the part is placed in service for purposes of determining depreciation under the applicable provisions of the Internal Revenue Code and the Treasury Regulations. See §1.263(a)-2(g) for the treatment of capital expenditures.

Example 14. Election to apply de minimis safe harbor. (i) N provides consulting services to its customers. In Year 1, N pays amounts to purchase 50 laptop computers. Each laptop computer is a unit of property under §1.263(a)-3(e), costs $400, and has an economic useful life of more than 12 months. Also in Year 1, N purchases 50 office chairs to be used by its employees. Each office chair is a unit of property that costs $100. N has an applicable financial statement (as defined in §1.263(a)-1(f)(4)) and N has a written accounting policy at the beginning Year 1 to expense amounts paid for units of property costing $500 or less. N treats amounts paid for property costing $500 or less as an expense on its applicable financial statement in Year 1.

(ii) The laptop computers are not materials or supplies under paragraph (c) of this section. Therefore, the amounts N pays for the computers must generally be capitalized under §1.263(a)-2(d) as amounts paid for the acquisition of tangible property. The office chairs are materials and supplies under paragraph (c)(1)(iv) of this section. Thus, under paragraph (a)(1) of this section, the amounts paid for the office chairs are deductible in the taxable year in which they are first used in N's business. However, under paragraph (f) of this section, if N properly elects to apply the de minimis safe harbor under §1.263(a)-1(f) to amounts paid in Year 1, then N must apply the de minimis safe harbor under §1.263(a)-1(f) to amounts paid for

the computers and the office chairs, rather than treat the office chairs as the costs of materials and supplies under §1.162-3. Under the de minimis safe harbor, N may not capitalize the amounts paid for the computers under §1.263(a)-2 nor treat the office chairs as materials and supplies under §1.162-3. Instead, in accordance with §1.263(a)-1(f)(3)(iv), under §1.162-1, N may deduct the amounts paid for the computers and the office chairs in the taxable year paid.

(i) *Accounting method changes.*—Except as otherwise provided in this section, a change to comply with this section is a change in method of accounting to which the provisions of sections 446 and 481 and the accompanying regulations apply. A taxpayer seeking to change to a method of accounting permitted in this section must secure the consent of the Commissioner in accordance with §1.446-1(e) and follow the administrative procedures issued under §1.446-1(e)(3)(ii) for obtaining the Commissioner's consent to change its accounting method.

(j) *Effective/applicability date.*—(1) *In general.*—This section generally applies to amounts paid or incurred in taxable years beginning on or after January 1, 2014. However, a taxpayer may apply paragraph (e) of this section (the optional method of accounting for rotable and temporary spare parts) to taxable years beginning on or after January 1, 2014. Except as provided in paragraphs (j)(2) and (j)(3) of this section, §1.162-3 as contained in 26 CFR part 1 edition revised as of April 1, 2011, applies to taxable years beginning before January 1, 2014.

(2) *Early application of this section.*—(i) *In general.*—Except for paragraph (e) of this section, a taxpayer may choose to apply this section to amounts paid or incurred in taxable years beginning on or after January 1, 2012. A taxpayer may choose to apply paragraph (e) of this section (the optional method of accounting for rotable and temporary spare parts) to taxable years beginning on or after January 1, 2012.

(ii) *Transition rule for election to capitalize materials and supplies on 2012 and 2013 returns.*—If under paragraph (j)(2)(i) of this section, a taxpayer chooses to make the election to capitalize and depreciate certain materials and supplies under paragraph (d) of this section for its taxable year beginning on or after January 1, 2012, and ending on or before September 19, 2013 (applicable taxable year), and the taxpayer did not make the election specified in paragraph (d)(3) of this section on its timely filed original Federal tax return for the applicable taxable year, the taxpayer must make the election specified in paragraph (d)(3) of this section for the applicable taxable year by filing an amended Federal tax return for the applicable taxable year on or before 180 days from the due date including extensions of the taxpayer's Federal tax return for the applicable taxable year, notwithstanding that the taxpayer may not have extended the due date.

(3) *Optional application of TD 9564.*—Except for §1.162-3T(e), a taxpayer may choose to apply §1.162-3T as contained in TD 9564 (76 FR 81060) December 27, 2011, to amounts paid or incurred (to acquire or produce property) in taxable years beginning on or after January 1, 2012, and before January 1, 2014. In applying §1.162-3T(d)(3), as contained in 26 CFR part 1, revised as of April 1, 2013, a taxpayer makes the election under §1.162-3T(d) by capitalizing the amounts paid to acquire or produce a material or supply in the taxable year the amounts are paid and by beginning to depreciate the costs when the asset is placed in service by the taxpayer for purposes of determining depreciation under the applicable provisions of the Internal Revenue Code and the Treasury Regulations. The election under §1.162-3T(d), as contained in 26 CFR part 1, revised as of April 1, 2013, does not apply to an asset or a portion thereof placed in service and disposed of in the same taxable year. A taxpayer may choose to apply §1.162-3T(e) (the optional method of accounting for rotable and temporary spare parts) as contained in TD 9564 (76 FR 81060) December 27, 2011, to taxable years beginning on or after January 1, 2012, and before January 1, 2014. [Reg. §1.162-3.]

☐ [*T.D. 6291, 4-3-58. Amended by T.D. 9564, 12-23-2011 (corrected 3-27-2012) and T.D. 9636, 9-13-2013 (corrected 7-18-2014).*]

»»→ Caution: *Temporary Reg. §1.162-3T, below, was removed by T.D. 9636, but a taxpayer may choose to apply Temporary Reg. §1.162-3T to amounts paid or incurred in tax years beginning on or after January 1, 2012, and before January 1, 2014; for details and exceptions, see Reg. §1.162-3(j)(3).*

[Reg. §1.162-3T]

§1.162-3T. Materials and supplies (Temporary).—(a) *In general.*—(1) *Non-incidental materials and supplies.*—Amounts paid to acquire or produce materials and supplies are deductible in the taxable year in which the materials and supplies are used or consumed in the taxpayer's operations.

(2) *Incidental materials and supplies.*—Amounts paid to acquire or produce incidental materials and supplies that are carried on hand and for which no record of consumption is kept or of which physical inventories at the beginning and end of the taxable year are not taken, are deductible in the taxable year in which these amounts are paid, provided taxable income is clearly reflected.

>>>→ Caution: *Temporary Reg. §1.162-3T, below, was removed by T.D. 9636, but a taxpayer may choose to apply Temporary Reg. §1.162-3T to amounts paid or incurred in tax years beginning on or after January 1, 2012, and before January 1, 2014; for details and exceptions, see Reg. §1.162-3(j)(3).*

(3) *Use or consumption of rotable and temporary spare parts.*—Except as provided in paragraphs (d), (e), and (f) of this section, for purposes of paragraph (a)(1) of this section, rotable and temporary spare parts (defined under paragraph (c)(2) of this section) are used or consumed in the taxpayer's operations in the taxable year in which the taxpayer disposes of the parts.

(b) *Coordination with other provisions of the Internal Revenue Code.*—Nothing in this section changes the treatment of any amount that is specifically provided for under any provision of the Internal Revenue Code or regulations other than section 162(a) or section 212 and the regulations under those sections. For example, see section §1.263(a)-3T, which requires taxpayers to capitalize amounts paid to improve tangible property and section 263A and the regulations under section 263A, which require taxpayers to capitalize the direct and allocable indirect costs, including the cost of materials and supplies, to property produced or to property acquired for resale. See also §1.471-1, which requires taxpayers to include in inventory certain materials and supplies.

(c) *Definitions.*—(1) *Materials and supplies.*—For purposes of this section, *materials and supplies* means tangible property that is used or consumed in the taxpayer's operations that is not inventory and that—

(i) Is a component acquired to maintain, repair, or improve a unit of tangible property (as determined under §1.263(a)-3T(e)) owned, leased, or serviced by the taxpayer and that is not acquired as part of any single unit of tangible property;

(ii) Consists of fuel, lubricants, water, and similar items, that are reasonably expected to be consumed in 12 months or less, beginning when used in taxpayer's operations;

(iii) Is a unit of property as determined under §1.263(a)-3T(e) that has an economic useful life of 12 months or less, beginning when the property is used or consumed in the taxpayer's operations;

(iv) Is a unit of property as determined under §1.263(a)-3T(e) that has an acquisition cost or production cost (as determined under section 263A) of $100 or less (or other amount as identified in published guidance in the **Federal Register** or in the Internal Revenue Bulletin (see §601.601(d)(2)(ii)(*b*) of this chapter)); or

(v) Is identified in published guidance in the **Federal Register** or in the Internal Revenue Bulletin (see §601.601(d)(2)(ii)(*b*) of this chapter) as materials and supplies for which treatment under this section.

(2) *Rotable and temporary spare parts.*—For purposes of this section, rotable spare parts are materials and supplies under paragraph (c)(1)(i) of this section that are acquired for installation on a unit of property, removable from that unit of property, generally repaired or improved, and either reinstalled on the same or other property or stored for later installation. Temporary spare parts are materials and supplies under paragraph (c)(1)(i) of this section that are used temporarily until a new or repaired part can be installed and then are removed and stored for later (emergency or temporary) installation.

(3) *Economic useful life.*—(i) *General rule.*—The economic useful life of a unit of property is not necessarily the useful life inherent in the property but is the period over which the property may reasonably be expected to be useful to the taxpayer or, if the taxpayer is engaged in a trade or business or an activity for the production of income, the period over which the property may reasonably be expected to be useful to the taxpayer in its trade or business or for the production of income, as applicable. See §1.167(a)-1(b) for the factors to be considered in determining this period.

(ii) *Taxpayers with an applicable financial statement.*—For taxpayers with an applicable financial statement (as defined in paragraph (c)(3)(iii) of this section), the economic useful life of a unit of property, solely for the purposes of applying the provisions of paragraph (c)(1)(iii) of this section, is the useful life initially used by the taxpayer for purposes of determining depreciation in its applicable financial statement, regardless of any salvage value of the property. If a taxpayer does not have an applicable financial statement for the taxable year in which a unit of property was originally acquired or produced, the economic useful life of the unit of property must be determined under paragraph (c)(3)(i) of this section. Further, if a taxpayer treats amounts paid for a unit of property as an expense in its applicable financial statement on a basis other than the useful life of the property or if a taxpayer does not depreciate the unit of property on its applicable financial statement, the economic useful life of the unit of property must be determined under paragraph (c)(3)(i) of this section. For example, if a taxpayer has a policy of treating as an expense on its applicable financial statement amounts paid for a unit of property costing less than a certain dollar amount,

notwithstanding that the unit of property has a useful life of more than one year, the economic useful life of the unit of property must be determined under paragraph (c)(3)(i) of this section.

(iii) *Definition of applicable financial statement.*—The taxpayer's applicable financial statement is the taxpayer's financial statement listed in paragraphs (c)(3)(iii)(A) through (C) of this section that has the highest priority (including within paragraph (c)(3)(iii)(B) of this section). The financial statements are, in descending priority—

(A) A financial statement required to be filed with the Securities and Exchange Commission (SEC) (the 10-K or the Annual Statement to Shareholders);

(B) A certified audited financial statement that is accompanied by the report of an independent CPA (or in the case of a foreign entity, by the report of a similarly qualified independent professional), that is used for—

(*1*) Credit purposes;

(*2*) Reporting to shareholders, partners, or similar persons; or

(*3*) Any other substantial non-tax purpose; or

(C) A financial statement (other than a tax return) required to be provided to the Federal or a state government or any Federal or state agencies (other than the SEC or the Internal Revenue Service).

(4) *Amount paid.*—For purposes of this section, in the case of a taxpayer using an accrual method of accounting, the terms *amount paid* and *payment* mean a liability incurred (within the meaning of §1.446-1(c)(1)(ii)). A liability may not be taken into account under this section prior to the taxable year during which the liability is incurred.

(5) *Produce.*—For purposes of this section, *produce* means construct, build, install, manufacture, develop, create, raise, or grow. This definition is intended to have the same meaning as the definition used for purposes of section 263A(g)(1) and §1.263A-2(a)(1)(i), except that improvements are excluded from the definition in this paragraph (c)(5) and are separately defined and addressed in §1.263(a)-3T. Amounts paid to produce materials and supplies are subject to section 263A.

(d) *Election to capitalize and depreciate.*—(1) *In general.*—A taxpayer may elect to treat as a capital expenditure and to treat as an asset subject to the allowance for depreciation the cost of any material or supply as defined in paragraph (c)(1) of this section. Except as specified in paragraph (d)(2) of this section, an election made under this paragraph (d) applies to amounts paid during the taxable year to acquire or produce any material or supply to which paragraph (a) of this section would apply (but for the election under this paragraph (d)). Any asset for which this election is made shall not be treated as a material or a supply.

(2) *Exceptions.*—A taxpayer may not elect to capitalize and depreciate under paragraph (d) of this section—

(i) Any amount paid to acquire or produce a material or supply described in paragraph (c)(1)(i) of this section if—

(A) The material or supply is intended to be used as a component of a unit of property that is a material or supply under paragraph (c)(1)(iii), (iv), or (v) of this section; and

(B) The taxpayer has not elected to capitalize and depreciate that unit of property under this paragraph (d); or

(ii) Any amount paid to acquire or produce a rotable or temporary spare part if the taxpayer has applied the optional method of accounting for rotable and temporary spare parts under paragraph (e) of this section.

(3) *Manner of electing.*—A taxpayer makes the election under paragraph (d) of this section by capitalizing the amounts paid to acquire or produce a material or supply in the taxable year the amounts are paid and by beginning to recover the costs when the asset is placed in service by the taxpayer for the purposes of determining depreciation under the applicable provisions of Internal Revenue Code and regulations thereunder. A taxpayer must make this election in its timely filed original Federal income tax return (including extensions) for the taxable year the asset is placed in service by the taxpayer for purposes of determining depreciation. See §1.263(a)-2T for the treatment of amounts paid to acquire or produce real or personal tangible property. In the case of a pass-through entity, the election is made by the pass-through entity, and not by the shareholders or partners. A taxpayer may make an election for each material or supply that qualifies for the election under this paragraph (d). A taxpayer may revoke an election made under this paragraph (d) with respect to a material or supply only by filing a request for a private letter ruling and obtaining the Commissioner's consent to

>>>→ *Caution: Temporary Reg. §1.162-3T, below, was removed by T.D. 9636, but a taxpayer may choose to apply Temporary Reg. §1.162-3T to amounts paid or incurred in tax years beginning on or after January 1, 2012, and before January 1, 2014; for details and exceptions, see Reg. §1.162-3(j)(3).*

revoke the election. The Commissioner may grant a request to revoke this election if the taxpayer can demonstrate good cause for the revocation. An election may not be made or revoked through the filing of an application for change in accounting method or, before obtaining the Commissioner's consent to make the late election or to revoke the election, by filing an amended Federal income tax return.

(e) *Optional method of accounting for rotable and temporary spare parts.*—(1) *In general.*—This paragraph (e) provides an optional method of accounting for rotable and temporary spare parts (the optional method for rotables). A taxpayer may use the optional method for rotables, instead of the general rule under paragraph (a)(3) of this section, to account for its rotable and temporary spare parts as defined in paragraph (c)(2) of this section. A taxpayer that uses the optional method for rotables must use this method for all of its rotable and temporary spare parts in the same trade or business. The optional method for rotables is a method of accounting under section 446(a). Under the optional method for rotables, the taxpayer must apply the rules in this paragraph (e) to each rotable or temporary spare part (part) upon the taxpayer's initial installation, removal, repair, maintenance or improvement, reinstallation, and disposal of each part.

(2) *Description of optional method for rotables.*—(i) *Initial installation.*—The taxpayer must deduct the amount paid to acquire or produce the part in the taxable year that the part is first installed on a unit of property for use in the taxpayer's operations.

(ii) *Removal from unit of property.*—In each taxable year in which the part is removed from a unit of property to which it was initially or subsequently installed, the taxpayer must—

(A) Include in gross income the fair market value of the part; and

(B) Include in the basis of the part the fair market value of the part included in income under paragraph (e)(2)(ii)(A) of this section and the amount paid to remove the part from the unit of property.

(iii) *Repair, maintenance, or improvement of part.*—The taxpayer may not currently deduct and must include in the basis of the part any amounts paid to maintain, repair, or improve the part in the taxable year these amounts are paid.

(iv) *Reinstallation of part.*—The taxpayer must deduct the amounts paid to reinstall the part and those amounts included in the basis of the part under paragraphs (e)(2)(ii)(B) and (e)(2)(iii) of this section, to the extent that those amounts have not been previously deducted under this paragraph (e)(2)(iv), in the taxable year that the part is reinstalled on a unit of property.

(v) *Disposal of the part.*—The taxpayer must deduct the amounts included in the basis of the part under paragraphs (e)(2)(ii)(B) and (e)(2)(iii) of this section, to the extent that those amounts have not been previously deducted under paragraph (e)(2)(iv) of this section, in the taxable year in which the part is disposed of by the taxpayer.

(f) *Election to apply de minimis rule.*—(1) *In general.*—A taxpayer may elect to apply the de minimis rule under §1.263(a)-2T(g) to any material or supply defined in paragraph (c)(1) this section. Any material or supply to which the taxpayer elects to apply the de minimis rule under §1.263(a)-2T(g) is not treated as a material or supply under this section. *See* §1.263(a)-2T(g)(5).

(2) *Manner of electing.*—A taxpayer makes the election by deducting the amounts paid to acquire or produce a material or supply in the taxable year that the amounts are paid and by complying with the requirements set out in §1.263(a)-2T(g). A taxpayer must make this election in its timely filed original Federal income tax return (including extensions) for the taxable year that amounts are paid for the material or supply. In the case of a pass-through entity, the election is made by the pass-through entity and not by the shareholders or partners. A taxpayer may make an election for each material or supply that qualifies for the election under paragraph (f) of this section. A taxpayer may revoke an election made under paragraph (f) of this section with respect to a material or supply only by filing a request for a private letter ruling and obtaining the Commissioner's consent to revoke the election. The Commissioner may grant a request to revoke this election if the taxpayer can demonstrate good cause for the revocation. An election may not be made or revoked through the filing of an application for change in accounting method or, before obtaining the Commissioner's consent to make the late election or to revoke the election, by filing an amended Federal income tax return.

(g) *Sale or disposition of materials and supplies.*—Upon sale or other disposition, materials and supplies as defined in this section are not treated as a capital asset under section 1221 or as property used in the trade or business under section 1231. Any asset for which the taxpayer makes the election to capitalize and depreciate under paragraph (d) of this section shall not be treated as a material or supply.

(h) *Examples.*—The rules of this section are illustrated by the following examples, in which it is assumed (unless otherwise stated) that the property is not an incidental material or supply, that the taxpayer is a calendar year, accrual method taxpayer, and that the taxpayer has not elected to capitalize under paragraph (d) of this section or to apply the de minimis rule under paragraph (f) of this section.

Example 1. Non-rotable components. X owns a fleet of aircraft that it operates in its business. In Year 1, X purchases a stock of spare parts, which it uses to maintain and repair its aircraft. X keeps a record of consumption of these spare parts. In Year 2, X uses the spare parts for the repair and maintenance of one of its aircraft. Assume each aircraft is a unit of property under §1.263(a)-3T(e) and that spare parts are not rotable or temporary spare parts under paragraph (c)(2) of this section. Assume these repair and maintenance activities do not improve the aircraft under §1.263(a)-3T. These parts are materials and supplies under paragraph (c)(1)(i) of this section because they are components acquired and used to maintain and repair X's aircraft. Under paragraph (a)(1) of this section, the amounts that X paid for the spare parts in Year 1 are deductible in Year 2, the taxable year in which the spare parts are used to repair and maintain the aircraft.

Example 2. Rotable spare parts. X operates a fleet of specialized vehicles that it uses in its service business. Assume that each vehicle is a unit of property under §1.263(a)-3T(e). At the time that it acquires a new type of vehicle, X also acquires a substantial number of rotable spare parts that it will keep on hand to quickly replace similar parts in X's vehicles as those parts break down or wear out. These rotable parts are removable from the vehicles and are repaired so that they can be reinstalled on the same or similar vehicles. X does not use the optional method of accounting for rotable and temporary spare parts provided in paragraph (e) of this section. In Year 1, X acquires several vehicles and a number of rotable spare parts to be used as replacement parts in these vehicles. In Year 2, X repairs several vehicles by using these rotable spare parts to replace worn or damaged parts. In Year 3, X removes these rotable spare parts from its vehicles, repairs the parts, and reinstalls them on other similar vehicles. In Year 5, X can no longer use the rotable parts it acquired in Year 1 and disposes of them as scrap. Under paragraph (c)(1)(i) of this section, the rotable spare parts acquired in Year 1 are materials and supplies. Under paragraph (a)(3) of this section, rotable spare parts are generally used or consumed in the taxable year in which the taxpayer disposes of the parts. Therefore, under paragraph (a)(1) of this section, the amounts that X paid for the rotable spare parts in Year 1 are deductible in Year 5, the taxable year in which X disposes of the parts.

Example 3. Rotable spare parts; application of optional method of accounting. Assume the same facts as in *Example 2*, except X uses the optional method of accounting for all its rotable and temporary spare parts under paragraph (e) of this section. In Year 1, X acquires several vehicles and a number of rotable spare parts (the "Year 1 rotables") to be used as replacement parts in these vehicles. In Year 2, X repairs several vehicles and uses the Year 1 rotables to replace worn or damaged parts. In Year 3, X pays amounts to remove these Year 1 rotables from its vehicles. In Year 4, X pays amounts to maintain, repair, or improve the Year 1 rotables. In Year 5, X pays amounts to reinstall the Year 1 rotables on other similar vehicles. In Year 8, X removes the Year 1 rotables from these vehicles and stores these parts for possible later use. In Year 9, X disposes of the Year 1 rotables. Under paragraph (e) of this section, X must deduct the amounts paid to acquire and install the Year 1 rotables in Year 2, the taxable year in which the rotable spare parts are first installed by X in X's vehicles. In Year 3, when X removes the Year 1 rotables from its vehicles, X must include in its gross income the fair market value of each part. Also, in Year 3, X must include in the basis of each Year 1 rotable the fair market value of the rotable and the amount paid to remove the rotable from the vehicle. In Year 4, X must include in the basis of each Year 1 rotable the amounts paid to maintain, repair, or improve each rotable. In Year 5, the year that X reinstalls the Year 1 rotables (as repaired or improved) in other vehicles, X must deduct the reinstallation costs and the amounts previously included in the basis of each part. In Year 8, the year that X removes the Year 1 rotables from the vehicles, X must include in income the fair market value of each rotable part removed. In addition, in Year 8, X must include in the basis of each part the fair market value of that part and the amount paid to remove the each rotable from the vehicle. In Year 9, the year

»»→ Caution: *Temporary Reg. §1.162-3T, below, was removed by T.D. 9636, but a taxpayer may choose to apply Temporary Reg. §1.162-3T to amounts paid or incurred in tax years beginning on or after January 1, 2012, and before January 1, 2014; for details and exceptions, see Reg. §1.162-3(j)(3).*

that X disposes of the Year 1 rotables, X may deduct the amounts remaining in the basis of each rotable.

Example 4. Rotable part acquired as part of a single unit of property; not material or supply. X operates a fleet of aircraft. In Year 1, X acquires a new aircraft, which includes two new aircraft engines. The aircraft costs $500,000 and has an economic useful life of more than 12 months, beginning when it is placed in service. In Year 5, after the aircraft is operated for several years in X's business, X removes the engines from the aircraft, repairs or improves the engines, and either reinstalls the engines on a similar aircraft or stores the engines for later reinstallation. Assume the aircraft purchased in Year 1, including its two engines, is a unit of property under §1.263(a)-3T(e). Because the engines were acquired as part of the aircraft, a single unit of property, the engines are not materials or supplies under paragraph (c)(1)(i) of this section nor rotable or temporary spare parts under paragraph (c)(2) of this section. Accordingly, X may not apply the rules of this section to the aircraft engines upon the original acquisition of the aircraft nor after the removal of the engines from the aircraft for use in the same or similar aircraft. Rather, X must apply the rules under §§1.263(a)- 2T and 1.263(a)-3T to the aircraft, including its engines, to determine the treatment of amounts paid to acquire, produce, or improve the unit of property.

Example 5. Components of real property. X owns an apartment building that it leases in its business operation and discovers that a window in one of the apartments is broken. Assume that the building, including its windows, is a unit of property under §1.263(a)-3T(e) and the window is not a rotable or temporary spare part under paragraph (c)(2) of this section. X pays for the acquisition and delivery of a new window to replace the broken window. In the same taxable year, the new window is installed. Assume that the replacement of the window does not improve the property under §1.263(a)-3T and that X does not recognize gain or loss on the disposition of the broken window. The new window is a material or supply under paragraph (c)(1)(i) of this section because it is a component acquired and used to repair a unit of property owned by X and used in X's operations. Under paragraph (a)(1) of this section, the amounts X paid for the acquisition and delivery of the window are deductible in the taxable year in which the window is installed in the apartment building. See §1.168(i)-8T for the treatment of the disposition of the broken window.

Example 6. Consumable property. X operates a fleet of aircraft that carries freight for its customers. X has several storage tanks on its premises, which hold jet fuel for its aircraft. Assume that once the jet fuel is placed in X's aircraft, the jet fuel is reasonably expected to be consumed within 12 months or less. On December 31, Year 1, X purchases a two-year supply of jet fuel. In Year 2, X uses a portion of the jet fuel purchased on December 31, Year 1, to fuel the aircraft used in its business. The jet fuel that X purchased in Year 1 is a material or supply under paragraph (c)(1)(ii) of this section because it is reasonably expected to be consumed within 12 months or less from the time it is placed in X's aircraft. Under paragraph (a)(1) of this section, X may deduct in Year 2 the amounts paid for the portion of jet fuel used in the operation of X's aircraft in Year 2.

Example 7. Unit of property that costs $100 or less. X operates a business that rents out a variety of small individual items to customers (rental items). X maintains a supply of rental items on hand. In Year 1, X purchases a large quantity of rental items to use in its rental business. Assume that each rental item is a unit of property under §1.263(a)-3T(e) and costs $100 or less. In Year 2, X begins using all the rental items purchased in Year 1 by providing them to customers of its rental business. X does not sell or exchange these items on established retail markets at any time after the items are used in the rental business. The rental items are materials and supplies under paragraph (c)(1)(iv) of this section. Under paragraph (a)(1) of this section, the amounts that X paid for the rental items in Year 1 are deductible in Year 2, the taxable year in which the rental items are used in X's business.

Example 8. Unit of property that costs $100 or less. X provides billing services to its customers. In Year 1, X pays amounts to purchase 50 facsimile machines to be used by its employees. Assume each facsimile machine is a unit of property under §1.263(a)-3T(e) and costs less than $100. In Year 1, X's employees begin using 35 of the facsimile machines, and X stores the remaining 15 machines for use in a later taxable year. The facsimile machines are materials and supplies under paragraph (c)(1)(iv) of this section. Under paragraph (a)(1) of this section, the amounts X paid for 35 of the facsimile machines are deductible in Year 1, the taxable year in which X uses those machines. The amounts that X paid for each of the remaining 15 machines are deductible in the taxable year in which each machine is used.

Example 9. Materials and supplies used in improvements; coordination with §1.263(a)-3T. X owns various machines that are used in its business. Assume that each machine is a unit of property under §1.263(a)-3T(e). In Year 1, X purchases a supply of spare parts for its machines. X acquired the parts to use in the repair or maintenance of the machines under §1.162-4T or in the improvement of the machines under §1.263(a)-3T. The spare parts are not rotable or temporary spare parts under paragraph (c)(2) of this section. In Year 2, X uses all of these spare parts in an activity that improves a machine under §1.263(a)-3T. Under paragraph (c)(1)(i) of this section, the spare parts purchased by X in Year 1 are materials and supplies. Under paragraph (a)(1) of this section, the amounts paid for the spare parts are otherwise deductible as materials and supplies in Year 2, the taxable year in which X uses those parts. However, because these materials and supplies are used to improve X's machine, X is required to capitalize the amounts paid for those spare parts under §1.263(a)-3T. See also section 263A for the requirement to capitalize the direct and allocable indirect costs of property produced or property acquired for resale.

Example 10. Cost of producing materials and supplies; coordination with section 263A. X is a manufacturer that produces liquid waste as part of its operations. X determines that its current liquid waste disposal process is inadequate. To remedy the problem, in Year 1, X constructs a leaching pit to provide a draining area for the liquid waste. Assume the leaching pit is a unit of property under §1.263(a)-3T(e) and has an economic useful life 12 months or less, starting on the date that X begins to use the leaching pit as a draining area. At the end of this period, X's factory will be connected to the local sewer system. In Year 2, X starts using the leaching pit in its operations. The amounts paid to construct the leaching pit (including the direct and allocable indirect costs of property produced under section 263A) are amounts paid for a material or supply under paragraph (c)(1)(iii) of this section. Under paragraph (a)(1) of this section, the amounts paid for the leaching pit are otherwise deductible as materials and supplies in Year 2, the taxable year in which X uses the leaching pit. However, because the amounts paid to construct the leaching pit directly benefit or are incurred by reason of X's manufacturing operations, X must capitalize those costs under section 263A to the property produced. *See* §1.263A-1(e)(3)(ii)(E).

Example 11. Costs of acquiring materials and supplies for production of property; coordination with section 263A. In Year 1, X purchases jigs, dies, molds, and patterns for use in the manufacture of X's products. Assume each jig, die, mold, and pattern is a unit of property under §1.263(a)-3T(e). The economic useful life of each jig, die, mold, and pattern is 12 months or less, beginning when each item is used in the manufacturing process. The jigs, dies, molds, and patterns are not components acquired to maintain, repair, or improve any of X's equipment under paragraph (c)(1)(i) of this section. X begins using the jigs, dies, molds and patterns in Year 2 to manufacture its products. These items are materials and supplies under paragraph (c)(1)(iii) of this section. Under paragraph (a)(1) of this section, the amounts paid for the items are otherwise deductible in Year 2, the taxable year in which X uses those items. However, because the amounts paid for these materials and supplies directly benefit or are incurred by reason of X's manufacturing operations, X must capitalize the costs under section 263A to the property produced. *See* §1.263A-1(e)(3)(ii)(E).

Example 12. Election to capitalize and depreciate. X operates a rental business that rents out a variety of items (rental items) to its customers. Assume each rental item is a separate unit of property as determined under §1.263(a)-3T(e). X does not sell or exchange these items on established retail markets at any time after the items are used in the rental business. X purchases various rental items, each of which costs less than $100 or has an economic useful life of 12 months or less, beginning when the items are used or consumed. The rental items are materials and supplies under paragraph (c)(1)(iii) or (c)(1)(iv) of this section. Under paragraph (a)(1) of this section, the amount paid for each rental item is deductible in the taxable year in which the item is used in the rental business. However, X would prefer to treat the cost of each rental item as a capital expenditure subject to depreciation. Under paragraph (d) of this section, X may elect not to apply the rule contained in paragraph (a)(1) of this section to the rental items. X makes this election by capitalizing the amounts paid for each rental item in the taxable year that X purchases the item and by beginning to recover the costs of each item on its timely filed Federal income tax return for the taxable year that X places the item in service for purposes of determining depreciation under the applicable provisions of the Internal Revenue Code and the regulations thereunder. See §1.263(a)-2T(h) for the treatment of capital expenditures.

Example 13. Election to capitalize and depreciate. X is an electric utility. X acquires certain temporary spare parts, which it keeps on hand to avoid operational time loss in the event it must make emergency

>>>→ *Caution: Temporary Reg. §1.162-3T, below, was removed by T.D. 9636, but a taxpayer may choose to apply Temporary Reg. §1.162-3T to amounts paid or incurred in tax years beginning on or after January 1, 2012, and before January 1, 2014; for details and exceptions, see Reg. §1.162-3(j)(3).*

repairs to a unit of property that is subject to depreciation. These parts are not used to improve property under §1.263(a)-3T(d). These temporary spare parts are used until a new or repaired part can be installed and then are removed and stored for later emergency installation. X does not use the optional method of accounting for rotable and temporary spare parts in paragraph (e) of this section for any of its rotable or temporary spare parts. The temporary spare parts are materials and supplies under paragraph (c)(1)(i) of this section. Under paragraphs (a)(1) and (a)(3) of this section, the amounts paid for the temporary spare parts are deductible in the taxable year in which they are disposed of by the taxpayer. However, because it is unlikely that the temporary spare parts will be disposed of in the near future, X would prefer to treat the amounts paid for the spare parts as capital expenditures subject to depreciation. X may elect under paragraph (d) of this section not to apply the rule contained in paragraph (a)(1) of this section to each of its temporary spare parts. X makes this election by capitalizing the amounts paid for each spare part in the taxable year that X acquires the spare parts and by beginning to recover the costs of each part on its timely filed Federal income tax return for the taxable year in which the part is placed in service for purposes of determining depreciation under the applicable provisions of the Internal Revenue Code and the regulations thereunder. See §1.263(a)-2T(h) for the treatment of capital expenditures and section 263A for the requirement to capitalize the direct and allocable indirect costs of property produced or property acquired for resale.

Example 14. Election to apply de minimis rule. X provides consulting services to its customers. X purchases 50 office chairs to be used by its employees. Each office chair is a unit of property that costs $80. Also in the same taxable year, X pays amounts to purchase 50 customized briefcases. Assume each briefcase is a unit of property under §1.263(a)-3T(e), costs $120, and has an economic useful life of 12 months or less, beginning when used and consumed. X has an applicable financial statement (as defined in §1.263(a)-2T(g)(6)), and X has a written policy at the beginning of the taxable year to expense amounts paid for units of property costing less than $300. The briefcases and the office chairs are materials and supplies under paragraph (c)(1)(iii) and (c)(1)(iv), respectively, of this section. Under paragraph (a)(1) of this section, the amounts paid for the office chairs and briefcases are deductible in the taxable year in which they are used or consumed. However, assuming X meets all the requirements of §1.263(a)-2T(g), X may elect under paragraph (f) of this section to apply the de minimis rule under §1.263(a)-2T(g) to amounts paid for the office chairs and briefcases, rather than treat these amounts as the costs of materials and supplies under §1.162-3T.

(i) *Accounting method changes.*—Except as otherwise provided in this section, a change to comply with this section is a change in method of accounting to which the provisions of sections 446 and 481, and the regulations thereunder, apply. A taxpayer seeking to change to a method of accounting permitted in this section must secure the consent of the Commissioner in accordance with §1.446-1(e) and follow the administrative procedures issued under §1.446-1(e)(3)(ii) for obtaining the Commissioner's consent to change its accounting method.

(j) *Effective/applicability date.*—(1) *In general.*—This section generally applies to amounts paid or incurred (to acquire or produce property) in taxable years beginning on or after January 1, 2014. However, a taxpayer may apply paragraph (e) of this section (the optional method of accounting for rotable and temporary spare parts) to taxable years beginning on or after January 1, 2014. Section 1.162-3 as contained in 26 CFR part 1 edition revised as of April 1, 2011, applies to taxable years beginning before January 1, 2014.

(2) *Optional early application.*—Except for paragraph (e) of this section, a taxpayer may choose to apply this section to amounts paid or incurred (to acquire or produce property) in taxable years beginning on or after January 1, 2012. A taxpayer may choose to apply paragraph (e) of this section (the optional method of accounting for rotable and temporary spare parts) to taxable years beginning on or after January 1, 2012.

(k) *Expiration date.*—The applicability of this section expires on December 23, 2014. [Temporary Reg. §1.162-3T.]

☐ [T.D. 9564, 12-23-2011 (*corrected 3-27-2012 and 12-14-2012*). *Removed by T.D. 9636, 9-13-2013.*]

>>>→ *Caution: Reg. §1.162-4, below, as amended by T.D. 9636, generally applies to tax years beginning on or after January 1, 2014; see Reg. §1.162-4(c), below, for details and exceptions.*

[Reg. §1.162-4]

§1.162-4. Repairs.—(a) *In general.*—A taxpayer may deduct amounts paid for repairs and maintenance to tangible property if the amounts paid are not otherwise required to be capitalized. Optionally, §1.263(a)-3(n) provides an election to capitalize amounts paid for repair and maintenance consistent with the taxpayer's books and records.

(b) *Accounting method changes.*—A change to comply with this section is a change in method of accounting to which the provisions of sections 446 and 481 and the accompanying regulations apply. A taxpayer seeking to change to a method of accounting permitted in this section must secure the consent of the Commissioner in accordance with §1.446-1(e) and follow the administrative procedures issued under §1.446-1(e)(3)(ii) for obtaining the Commissioner's consent to change its accounting method.

(c) *Effective/applicability date.*—(1) *In general.*—This section applies to taxable years beginning on or after January 1, 2014. Except as provided in paragraphs (c)(2) and (c)(3) of this section, §1.162-4 as contained in 26 CFR part 1 edition revised as of April 1, 2011, applies to taxable years beginning before January 1, 2014.

(2) *Early application of this section.*—A taxpayer may choose to apply this section to taxable years beginning on or after January 1, 2012.

(3) *Optional application of TD 9564.*—A taxpayer may choose to apply §1.162-4T as contained in TD 9564 (76 FR 81060), December 27, 2011, to taxable years beginning on or after January 1, 2012, and before January 1, 2014. [Reg. §1.162-4.]

☐ [T.D. 6291, 4-3-58. *Amended by T.D. 9564, 12-23-2011 and T.D. 9636, 9-13-2013 (corrected 7-18-2014).*]

>>>→ *Caution: Temporary Reg. §1.162-4T, below, was removed by T.D. 9636, but a taxpayer may choose to apply Temporary Reg. §1.162-4T to tax years beginning on or after January 1, 2012, and before January 1, 2014.*

[Reg. §1.162-4T]

§1.162-4T. Repairs (Temporary).—(a) *In general.*—A taxpayer may deduct amounts paid for repairs and maintenance to tangible property if the amounts paid are not otherwise required to be capitalized.

(b) *Accounting method changes.*—Except as otherwise provided in this section, a change to comply with this section is a change in method of accounting to which the provisions of sections 446 and 481, and the regulations thereunder, apply. A taxpayer seeking to change to a method of accounting permitted in this section must secure the consent of the Commissioner in accordance with §1.446-1(e) and follow the administrative procedures issued under §1.446-1(e)(3)(ii) for obtaining the Commissioner's consent to change its accounting method.

(c) *Effective/applicability date.*—(1) *In general.*—This section applies to taxable years beginning on or after January 1, 2014. Section 1.162-4 as contained in 26 CFR part 1 edition revised as of April 1, 2011, applies to taxable years beginning before January 1, 2014.

(2) *Optional early application.*—A taxpayer may choose to apply this section to taxable years beginning on or after January 1, 2012.

(d) *Expiration date.*—The applicability of this section expires on December 23, 2014. [Temporary Reg. §1.162-4T.]

☐ [T.D. 9564, 12-23-2011 (*corrected 12-14-2012*). *Removed by T.D. 9636, 9-13-2013.*]

[Reg. §1.162-5]

§1.162-5. Expenses for education.—(a) *General rule.*—Expenditures made by an individual for education (including research undertaken as part of his educational program) which are not expenditures of a type described in paragraph (b)(2) or (3) of this section are deductible as ordinary and necessary business expenses (even though the education may lead to a degree) if the education—

(1) Maintains or improves skills required by the individual in his employment or other trade or business, or

(2) Meets the express requirements of the individual's employer, or the requirements of applicable law or regulations, imposed as a condition to the retention by the individual of an established employment relationship, status, or rate of compensation.

(b) *Nondeductible educational expenditures.*—(1) *In general.*—Educational expenditures described in subparagraphs (2) and (3) of this paragraph are personal expenditures or constitute an inseparable aggregate of personal and capital expenditures and, therefore, are not deductible as ordinary and necessary business expenses even though the education may maintain or improve skills required by the individual in his employment or other trade or business or may meet the express requirements of the individual's employer or of applicable law or regulations.

(2) *Minimum educational requirements.*—(i) The first category of nondeductible educational expenses within the scope of subparagraph (1) of this paragraph are expenditures made by an individual for education which is required of him in order to meet the minimum educational requirements for qualification in his employment or other trade or business. The minimum education necessary to qualify for a position or other trade or business must be determined from a consideration of such factors as the requirements of the employer, the applicable law and regulations, and the standards of the profession, trade, or business involved. The fact that an individual is already performing service in an employment status does not establish that he has met the minimum educational requirements for qualification in that employment. Once an individual has met the minimum educational requirements for qualification in his employment or other trade or business (as in effect when he enters the employment or trade or business), he shall be treated as continuing to meet those requirements even though they are changed.

(ii) The minimum educational requirements for qualification of a particular individual in a position in an educational institution is the minimum level of education (in terms of aggregate college hours or degree) which under the applicable laws or regulations, in effect at the time this individual is first employed in such position, is normally required of an individual initially being employed in such a position. If there are no normal requirements as to the minimum level of education required for a position in an educational institution, then an individual in such a position shall be considered to have met the minimum educational requirements for qualification in that position when he becomes a member of the faculty of the educational institution. The determination of whether an individual is a member of the faculty of an educational institution must be made on the basis of the particular practices of the institution. However, an individual will ordinarily be considered to be a member of the faculty of an institution if (*a*) he has tenure or his years of service are being counted toward obtaining tenure; (*b*) the institution is making contributions to a retirement plan (other than Social Security or a similar program) in respect of his employment; or (*c*) he has a vote in faculty affairs.

(iii) The application of this subparagraph may be illustrated by the following examples:

Example (1). General facts: State X requires a bachelor's degree for beginning secondary school teachers which must include 30 credit hours of professional educational courses. In addition, in order to retain his position, a secondary school teacher must complete a fifth year of preparation within 10 years after beginning his employment. If an employing school official certifies to the State Department of Education that applicants having a bachelor's degree and the required courses in professional education cannot be found, he may hire individuals as secondary school teachers if they have completed a minimum of 90 semester hours of college work. However, to be retained in his position, such an individual must obtain his bachelor's degree and complete the required professional educational courses within 3 years after his employment commences. Under these facts, a bachelor's degree, without regard to whether it includes 30 credit hours of professional educational courses, is considered to be the minimum educational requirement for qualification as a secondary school teacher in State X. This is the case notwithstanding the number of teachers who are actually hired without such a degree. The following are examples of the application of these facts in particular situations:

Situation 1. A, at the time he is employed as a secondary school teacher in State X, has a bachelor's degree including 30 credit hours of professional educational courses. After his employment, A completes a fifth college year of education and, as a result, is issued a standard certificate. The fifth college year of education undertaken by A is not education required to meet the minimum educational requirements for qualification as a secondary school teacher. Accordingly, the expenditures for such education are deductible unless the expenditures are for education which is part of a program of study being pursued by A which will lead to qualifying him in a new trade or business.

Situation 2. Because of a shortage of applicants meeting the stated requirements, B, who has a bachelor's degree, is employed as a secondary school teacher in State X even though he has only 20 credit hours of professional educational courses. After his employment, B takes an additional 10 credit hours of professional educational

courses. Since these courses do not constitute education required to meet the minimum educational requirements for qualification as a secondary school teacher which is a bachelor's degree and will not lead to qualifying B in a new trade or business, the expenditures for such courses are deductible.

Situation 3. Because of a shortage of applicants meeting the requirements, C is employed as a secondary school teacher in State X although he has only 90 semester hours of college work towards his bachelor's degree. After his employment, C undertakes courses leading to a bachelor's degree. These courses (including any courses in professional education) constitute education required to meet the minimum educational requirements for qualification as a secondary school teacher. Accordingly, the expenditures for such education are not deductible.

Situation 4. Subsequent to the employment of A, B, and C, but before they have completed a fifth college year of education, State X changes its requirements affecting secondary school teachers to provide that beginning teachers must have completed 5 college years of preparation. In the cases of A, B, and C, a fifth college year of education is not considered to be education undertaken to meet the minimum educational requirements for qualification as a secondary school teacher. Accordingly, expenditures for a fifth year of college will be deductible unless the expenditures are for education which is part of a program being pursued by A, B, or C which will lead to qualifying him in a new trade or business.

Example (2). D, who holds a bachelor's degree, obtains temporary employment as an instructor at University Y and undertakes graduate courses as a candidate for a graduate degree. D may become a faculty member only if he obtains a graduate degree and may continue to hold a position as instructor only so long as he shows satisfactory progress towards obtaining this graduate degree. The graduate courses taken by D constitute education required to meet the minimum educational requirements for qualification in D's trade or business and, thus, the expenditures for such courses are not deductible.

Example (3). E, who has completed 2 years of a normal 3-year law school course leading to a bachelor of laws degree (LL.B.), is hired by a law firm to do legal research and perform other functions on a full-time basis. As a condition to continued employment, E is required to obtain an LL.B. and pass the State bar examination. E completes his law school education by attending night law school, and he takes a bar review course in order to prepare for the State bar examination. The law courses and bar review course constitute education required to meet the minimum educational requirements for qualification in E's trade or business and, thus, the expenditures for such courses are not deductible.

(3) *Qualification for new trade or business.*—(i) The second category of nondeductible educational expenses within the scope of subparagraph (1) of this paragraph are expenditures made by an individual for education which is part of a program of study being pursued by him which will lead to qualifying him in a new trade or business. In the case of an employee, a change of duties does not constitute a new trade or business if the new duties involve the same general type of work as is involved in the individual's present employment. For this purpose, all teaching and related duties shall be considered to involve the same general type of work. The following are examples of changes in duties which do not constitute new trades or businesses:

(*a*) Elementary to secondary school classroom teacher.

(*b*) Classroom teacher in one subject (such as mathematics) to classroom teacher in another subject (such as science).

(*c*) Classroom teacher to guidance counselor.

(*d*) Classroom teacher to principal.

(ii) The application of this subparagraph to individuals other than teachers may be illustrated by the following examples:

Example (1). A, a self-employed individual practicing a profession other than law, for example, engineering, accounting, etc., attends law school at night and after completing his law school studies receives a bachelor of laws degree. The expenditures made by A in attending law school are nondeductible because this course of study qualifies him for a new trade or business.

Example (2). Assume the same facts as in example (1) except that A has the status of an employee rather than a self-employed individual, and that his employer requires him to obtain a bachelor of laws degree. A intends to continue practicing his nonlegal profession as an employee of such employer. Nevertheless, the expenditures made by A in attending law school are not deductible since this course of study qualifies him for a new trade or business.

Example (3). B, a general practitioner of medicine, takes a 2-week course reviewing new developments in several specialized fields of medicine. B's expenses for the course are deductible because the course maintains or improves skills required by him in his trade or business and does not qualify him for a new trade or business.

Example (4). C, while engaged in the private practice of psychiatry, undertakes a program of study and training at an accredited psychoanalytic institute which will lead to qualifying him to practice psychoanalysis. C's expenditures for such study and training are deductible because the study and training maintains or improves skills required by him in his trade or business and does not qualify him for a new trade or business.

(c) *Deductible educational expenditures.*—(1) *Maintaining or improving skills.*—The deduction under the category of expenditures for education which maintains or improves skills required by the individual in his employment or other trade or business includes refresher courses or courses dealing with current developments as well as academic or vocational courses provided the expenditures for the courses are not within either category of nondeductible expenditures described in paragraph (b) (2) or (3) of this section.

(2) *Meeting requirements of employer.*—An individual is considered to have undertaken education in order to meet the express requirements of his employer, or the requirements of applicable law or regulations, imposed as a condition to the retention by the taxpayer of his established employment relationship, status, or rate of compensation only if such requirements are imposed for a bona fide business purpose of the individual's employer. Only the minimum education necessary to the retention by the individual of his established employment relationship, status, or rate of compensation may be considered as undertaken to meet the express requirements of the taxpayer's employer. However, education in excess of such minimum education may qualify as education undertaken to maintain or improve the skills required by the taxpayer in his employment or other trade or business (see subparagraph (1) of this paragraph). In no event, however, is a deduction allowable for expenditures for education which, even though for education required by the employer or applicable law or regulations, are within one of the categories of nondeductible expenditures described in paragraph (b)(2) and (3) of this section.

(d) *Travel as a form of education.*—Subject to the provisions of paragraph (b) and (e) of this section, expenditures for travel (including travel while on sabbatical leave) as a form of education are deductible only to the extent such expenditures are attributable to a period of travel that is directly related to the duties of the individual in his employment or other trade or business. For this purpose, a period of travel shall be considered directly related to the duties of the individual in his employment or other trade or business only if the major portion of the activities during such period is of a nature which directly maintains or improves skills required by the individual in such employment or other trade or business. The approval of a travel program by an employer or the fact that travel is accepted by an employer in the fulfillment of its requirements for retention of rate of compensation, status or employment, is not determinative that the required relationship exists between the travel involved and the duties of the individual in his particular position.

(e) *Travel away from home.*—(1) If an individual travels away from home primarily to obtain education the expenses of which are deductible under this section, his expenditures for travel, meals, and lodging while away from home are deductible. However, if as an incident of such trip the individual engages in some personal activity such as sightseeing, social visiting, or entertaining, or other recreation, the portion of the expenses attributable to such personal activity constitutes nondeductible personal or living expenses and is not allowable as a deduction. If the individual's travel away from home is primarily personal, the individual's expenditures for travel, meals and lodging (other than meals and lodging during the time spent in participating in deductible educational pursuits) are not deductible. Whether a particular trip is primarily personal or primarily to obtain education the expenses of which are deductible under this section depends upon all the facts and circumstances of each case. An important factor to be taken into consideration in making the determination is the relative amount of time devoted to personal activity as compared with the time devoted to educational pursuits. The rules set forth in this paragraph are subject to the provisions of section 162(a)(2), relating to deductibility of certain traveling expenses, and section 274(c) and (d), relating to allocation of certain foreign travel expenses and substantiation required, respectively, and the regulations thereunder.

(2) *Examples.*—The application of this subsection may be illustrated by the following examples:

Example (1). A, a self-employed tax practitioner, decides to take a 1-week course in new developments in taxation, which is offered in City X, 500 miles away from his home. His primary purpose in going to X is to take the course, but he also takes a side trip to City Y (50 miles from X) for 1 day, takes a sightseeing trip while in X, and entertains some personal friends. A's transportation expenses to City X and return to his home are deductible but his transportation expenses to City Y are not deductible. A's expenses for meals and lodging while away from home will be allocated between his educational pursuits and his personal activities. Those expenses which are entirely personal, such as sightseeing and entertaining friends, are not deductible to any extent.

Example (2). The facts are the same as in example (1) except that A's primary purpose in going to City X is to take a vacation. This purpose is indicated by several factors, one of which is the fact that he spends only 1 week attending the tax course and devotes 5 weeks entirely to personal activities. None of A's transportation expenses are deductible and his expenses for meals and lodging while away from home are not deductible to the extent attributable to personal activities. His expenses for meals and lodging allocable to the week attending the tax course are, however, deductible.

Example (3). B, a high school mathematics teacher in New York City, in the summertime travels to a university in California in order to take a mathematics course the expense of which is deductible under this section. B pursues only one-fourth of a full course of study and the remainder of her time is devoted to personal activities the expense of which is not deductible. Absent a showing by B of a substantial nonpersonal reason for taking the course in the university in California, the trip is considered taken primarily for personal reasons and the cost of traveling from New York City to California and return would not be deductible. However, one-fourth of the cost of B's meals and lodging while attending the university in California may be considered properly allocable to deductible educational pursuits and, therefore, is deductible. [Reg. § 1.162-5.]

☐ [*T.D. 6291, 4-3-58. Amended by T.D. 6918, 5-1-67.*]

[Reg. § 1.162-7]

§ 1.162-7. Compensation for personal services.—(a) There may be included among the ordinary and necessary expenses paid or incurred in carrying on any trade or business a reasonable allowance for salaries or other compensation for personal services actually rendered. The test of deductibility in the case of compensation payments is whether they are reasonable and are in fact payments purely for services.

(b) The test set forth in paragraph (a) of this section and its practical application may be further stated and illustrated as follows:

(1) Any amount paid in the form of compensation, but not in fact as the purchase price of services is not deductible. An ostensible salary paid by a corporation may be a distribution of a dividend on stock. This is likely to occur in the case of a corporation having few shareholders, practically all of whom draw salaries. If in such a case the salaries are in excess of those ordinarily paid for similar services and the excessive payments correspond or bear a close relationship to the stockholdings of the officers or employees, it would seem likely that the salaries are not paid wholly for services rendered, but that the excessive payments are a distribution of earnings upon the stock. An ostensible salary may be in part payment for property. This may occur, for example, where a partnership sells out to a corporation, the former partners agreeing to continue in the service of the corporation. In such a case it may be found that the salaries of the former partners are not merely for services, but in part constitute payment for the transfer of their business.

(2) The form or method of fixing compensation is not decisive as to deductibility. While any form of contingent compensation invites scrutiny as a possible distribution of earnings of the enterprise, it does not follow that payments on a contingent basis are to be treated fundamentally on any basis different from that applying to compensation at a flat rate. Generally speaking, if contingent compensation is paid pursuant to a free bargain between the employer and the individual made before the services are rendered, not influenced by any consideration on the part of the employer other than that of securing on fair and advantageous terms the services of the individual, it should be allowed as a deduction even though in the actual working out of the contract it may prove to be greater than the amount which would ordinarily be paid.

(3) In any event the allowance for the compensation paid may not exceed what is reasonable under all the circumstances. It is, in general, just to assume that reasonable and true compensation is only such amount as would ordinarily be paid for like services by like enterprises under like circumstances. The circumstances to be taken into consideration are those existing at the date when the contract for services was made, not those existing at the date when the contract is questioned.

(4) For disallowance of deduction in the case of certain transfers of stock pursuant to employees stock options, see section 421 and the regulations thereunder. [Reg. § 1.162-7.]

☐ [*T.D. 6291, 4-3-58.*]

[Reg. §1.162-8]

§1.162-8. Treatment of excessive compensation.—The income tax liability of the recipient in respect of an amount ostensibly paid to him as compensation, but not allowed to be deducted as such by the payor, will depend upon the circumstances of each case. Thus, in the case of excessive payments by corporations, if such payments correspond or bear a close relationship to stockholders, and are found to be a distribution of earnings or profits, the excessive payments will be treated as a dividend. If such payments constitute payment for property, they should be treated by the payor as a capital expenditure and by the recipient as part of the purchase price. In the absence of evidence to justify other treatment, excessive payments for salaries or other compensation for personal services will be included in gross income of the recipient. [Reg. §1.162-8.]

☐ [T.D. 6291, 4-3-58.]

[Reg. §1.162-9]

§1.162-9. Bonuses to employees.—Bonuses to employees will constitute allowable deductions from gross income when such payments are made in good faith and as additional compensation for the services actually rendered by the employees, provided such payments, when added to the stipulated salaries, do not exceed a reasonable compensation for the services rendered. It is immaterial whether such bonuses are paid in cash or in kind or partly in cash and partly in kind. Donations made to employees and others, which do not have in them the element of compensation or which are in excess of reasonable compensation for services, are not deductible from gross income. [Reg. §1.162-9.]

☐ [T.D. 6291, 4-3-58.]

[Reg. §1.162-10]

§1.162-10. Certain employee benefits.—(a) *In general.*—Amounts paid or accrued by a taxpayer on account of injuries received by employees and lump-sum amounts paid or accrued as compensation for injuries are proper deductions as ordinary and necessary expenses. Such deductions are limited to the amount not compensated for by insurance or otherwise. Amounts paid or accrued within the taxable year for dismissal wages, unemployment benefits, guaranteed annual wages, vacations, or a sickness, accident, hospitalization, medical expense, recreational, welfare, or similar benefit plan, are deductible under section 162(a) if they are ordinary and necessary expenses of the trade or business. However, except as provided in paragraph (b) of this section, such amounts shall not be deductible under section 162(a) if, under any circumstances, they may be used to provide benefits under a stock bonus, pension, annuity, profit-sharing, or other deferred compensation plan of the type referred to in section 404(a). In such an event, the extent to which these amounts are deductible from gross income shall be governed by the provisions of section 404 and the regulations issued thereunder.

(b) *Certain negotiated plans.*—(1) Subject to the limitations set forth in subparagraphs (2) and (3) of this paragraph, contributions paid by an employer under a plan under which such contributions are held in a welfare trust for the purpose of paying (either from principal or income or both) for the benefit of employees, their families, and dependents, at least medical or hospital care, and pensions on retirement or death of employees, are deductible when paid as business expenses under section 162(a).

(2) For the purpose of subparagraph (1) of this paragraph, the word "plan" means any plan established prior to January 1, 1954, as a result of an agreement between employee representatives and the Government of the United States, during a period of Government operation, under seizure powers, of a major part of the productive facilities of the industry in which the employer claiming the deduction is engaged. The phrase "plan established prior to January 1, 1954, as a result of an agreement" is intended primarily to cover a trust established under the terms of such an agreement. It also includes a trust established under a plan of an employer, or group of employers, who, by reason of producing the same commodity, are in competition with the employers whose facilities were seized and who would therefore be expected to establish such a trust as a reasonable measure to maintain a sound position in the labor market producing the commodity. For example, if a trust was established under such an agreement in the bituminous coal industry, a similar trust established in the anthracite coal industry within a reasonable time, but before January 1, 1954, would qualify under subparagraph (1) of this paragraph.

(3) If any trust described in subparagraph (2) of this paragraph becomes qualified for exemption from tax under the provisions of section 501(a), the deductibility of contributions by an employer to such trust on or after any date of such qualification shall no longer be governed by the provisions of section 162, even though the trust may later lose its exemption from tax under section 501(a).

(c) *Other plans providing deferred compensation.*—For rules relating to the deduction of amounts paid to or under a stock bonus, pension, annuity, or profit-sharing plan or amounts paid or accrued under any other plan deferring the receipt of compensation, see section 404 and the regulations thereunder. [Reg. §1.162-10.]

☐ [T.D. 6291, 4-3-58.]

[Reg. §1.162-10T]

§1.162-10T. Questions and answers relating to the deduction of employee benefits under the Tax Reform Act of 1984; certain limits on amounts deductible (Temporary).—

Q-1: How does the amendment of section 404(b) by the Tax Reform Act of 1984 affect the deduction of employee benefits under section 162 of the Internal Revenue Code?

A-1: As amended by the Tax Reform Act of 1984, section 404(b) clarifies that section 404(a) and (d) (in the case of employees and nonemployees, respectively) shall govern the deduction of contributions paid or compensation paid or incurred under a plan, or method or arrangement, deferring the receipt of compensation or providing for deferred benefits. Section 404(a) and (d) requires that such a contribution or compensation be paid or incurred for purposes of section 162 or 212 and satisfy the requirements for deductibility under either of these sections. However, notwithstanding the above, section 404 does not apply to contributions paid or accrued with respect to a "welfare benefit fund" (as defined in section 419(e)) after July 18, 1984, in taxable years of employers (and payors) ending after that date. Also, section 463 shall govern the deduction of vacation pay by a taxpayer that has elected the application of such section. Section 404(b), as amended, generally applies to contributions paid and compensation paid or incurred after July 18, 1984, in taxable years of employers (and payors) ending after that date. See Q&A-3 of §1.404(b)-1T. For rules relating to the deduction of contributions attributable to the provision of deferred benefits, see section 404(a), (b) and (d) and §1.404(a)-1T, §1.404(b)-1T and §1.404(d)-1T. For rules relating to the deduction of contributions paid or accrued with respect to a welfare benefit fund, see section 419, §1.419-1T and §1.419A-2T. For rules relating to the deduction of vacation pay for which an election is made under section 463, see §301.9100-16T of this chapter and §1.463-1T.

Q-2: How does the enactment of section 419 by the Tax Reform Act of 1984 affect the deduction of employee benefits under section 162?

A-2: As enacted by the Tax Reform Act of 1984, section 419 shall govern the deduction of contributions paid or accrued by an employer (or a person receiving services under section 419(g)) with respect to a "welfare benefit fund" (within the meaning of section 419(e)) after December 31, 1985, in taxable years of the employer (or person receiving the services) ending after that date. Section 419(a) requires that such a contribution be paid or accrued for purposes of section 162 or 212 and satisfy the requirements for deductibility under either of those sections. Generally, subject to a binding contract exception (as described in section 511(e)(5) of the Tax Reform Act of 1984), section 419 shall also govern the deduction of the contribution of a facility (or other contribution used to acquire or improve a facility) to a welfare benefit fund after June 22, 1984. See Q&A-11 of §1.419-1T. In the case of a welfare benefit fund maintained pursuant to a collective bargaining agreement, section 419 applies to the extent provided under the special effective date rule described in Q&A-2 of §1.419-1T and the special rules of §1.419A-2T. For rules relating to the deduction of contributions paid or accrued with respect to a welfare benefit fund, see section 419 and §1.419-1T. [Temporary Reg. §1.162-10T.]

☐ [T.D. 8073, 1-29-86. *Amended by T.D.* 8435, 9-18-92.]

[Reg. §1.162-11]

§1.162-11. Rentals.—(a) *Acquisition of a leasehold.*—If a leasehold is acquired for business purposes for a specified sum, the purchaser may take as a deduction in his return an aliquot part of such sum each year, based on the number of years the lease has to run. Taxes paid by a tenant to or for a landlord for business property are additional rent and constitute a deductible item to the tenant and taxable income to the landlord, the amount of the tax being deductible by the latter. For disallowance of deduction for income taxes paid by a lessee corporation pursuant to a lease arrangement with the lessor corporation, see section 110 and the regulations thereunder. See section 178 and the regulations thereunder for rules governing the effect to be given renewal options in amortizing the costs incurred after July 28, 1958, of acquiring a lease. See §1.197-2 for rules governing the amortization of costs to acquire limited interests in section 197 intangibles.

(b) *Improvements by lessee on lessor's property.*—(1) *In general.*—The cost to a taxpayer of erecting buildings or making permanent improvements on property of which the taxpayer is a lessee is a capital expenditure. For the rules regarding improvements to leased prop-

Itemized Deductions for Individuals and Corps.
See p. 20,601 for regulations not amended to reflect law changes
25,223

erty when the improvements are tangible property, see §1.263(a)-3(f). For the rules regarding depreciation or amortization deductions for leasehold improvements, see §1.167(a)-4.

(2) *Effective/applicability date.*—(i) *In general.*—This paragraph (b) applies to taxable years beginning on or after January 1, 2014. Except as provided in paragraphs (b)(2)(ii) and (b)(2)(iii) of this section, §1.162-11(b) as contained in 26 CFR part 1 edition revised as of April 1, 2011, applies to taxable years beginning before January 1, 2014.

⟫→ *Caution: Temporary Reg. §1.162-11T, below, was removed by T.D. 9636, but a taxpayer may choose to apply Temporary Reg. §1.162-11T to tax years beginning on or after January 1, 2012, and before January 1, 2014.*

[Reg. §1.162-11T]

§1.162-11T. Rentals (Temporary).—(a) [Reserved]. For further guidance, see §1.162-11(a).

(b) *Improvements by lessee on lessor's property.*—The cost to a taxpayer of erecting buildings or making permanent improvements on property of which the taxpayer is a lessee is a capital expenditure and is not deductible as a business expense. For the rules regarding improvements to leased property where the improvements are tangible property, see §1.263(a)-3T(f)(1). For the rules regarding depreciation or amortization deductions for leasehold improvements, see §1.167(a)-4T.

(c) *Effective/applicability date.*—(1) *In general.*—This section applies to taxable years beginning on or after January 1, 2014. Section 1.162-11 as contained in 26 CFR part 1 edition revised as of April 1, 2011, applies to taxable years beginning before January 1, 2014.

(2) *Optional early application.*—A taxpayer may choose to apply this section to taxable years beginning on or after January 1, 2012.

(d) *Expiration date.*—The applicability of this section expires on December 23, 2014. [Temporary Reg. §1.162-11T.]

☐ [T.D. 9564, 12-23-2011 (corrected 12-14-2012). Removed by T.D. 9636, 9-13-2013.]

[Reg. §1.162-12]

§1.162-12. Expenses of farmers.—(a) *Farms engaged in for profit.*—A farmer who operates a farm for profit is entitled to deduct from gross income as necessary expenses all amounts actually expended in the carrying on of the business of farming. The cost of ordinary tools of short life or small cost, such as hand tools, including shovels, rakes, etc., may be deducted. The purchase of feed and other costs connected with raising livestock may be treated as expense deductions insofar as such costs represent actual outlay, but not including the value of farm produce grown upon the farm or the labor of the taxpayer. For rules regarding the capitalization of expenses of producing property in the trade or business of farming, see section 263A and the regulations thereunder. For taxable years beginning after July 12, 1972, where a farmer is engaged in producing crops and the process of gathering and disposal of such crops is not completed within the taxable year in which such crops were planted, expenses deducted may, with the consent of the Commissioner (see section 446 and the regulations thereunder), be determined upon the crop method, and such deductions must be taken in the taxable year in which the gross income from the crop has been realized. For taxable years beginning on or before July 12, 1972, where a farmer is engaged in producing crops which take more than a year from the time of planting to the process of gathering and disposal, expenses deducted may, with the consent of the Commissioner (see section 446 and the regulations thereunder), be determined upon the crop method, and such deductions must be taken in the taxable year in which the gross income from the crop has been realized. If a farmer does not compute income upon the crop method, the cost of seeds and young plants which are purchased for further development and cultivation prior to sale in later years may be deducted as an expense for the year of purchase, provided the farmer follows a consistent practice of deducting such costs as an expense from year to year. The preceding sentence does not apply to the cost of seeds and young plants connected with the planting of timber (see section 611 and the regulations thereunder). For rules regarding the capitalization of expenses of producing property in the trade or business of farming, see section 263A of the Internal Revenue Code and §1.263A-4. The cost of farm machinery, equipment, and farm buildings represents a capital investment and is not an allowable deduction as an item of expense. Amounts expended in the development of farms, orchards and ranches prior to the time when the productive state is reached may, at the election of the taxpayer, be regarded as investments of capital. For the treatment of soil and water conservation expenditures as expenses which are not chargeable to capital account, see section 175 and the regulations thereunder. For taxable years beginning after December 31, 1959, in the case of expenditures paid or incurred by

(ii) *Early application of this paragraph.*—A taxpayer may choose to apply this paragraph (b) to taxable years beginning on or after January 1, 2012.

(iii) *Optional application of TD 9564.*—A taxpayer may choose to apply §1.162-11T(b) as contained in TD 9564 (76 FR 81060) December 27, 2011, to taxable years beginning on or after January 1, 2012, and before January 1, 2014. [Reg. §1.162-11.]

☐ [T.D. 6291, 4-3-58. *Amended by* T.D. 6520, 12-30-60; T.D. 8865, 1-20-2000; T.D. 9564, 12-23-2011 *and* T.D. 9636, 9-13-2013.]

farmers for fertilizer, lime, etc., see section 180 and the regulations thereunder. Amounts expended in purchasing work, breeding, dairy, or sporting animals are regarded as investments of capital, and shall be depreciated unless such animals are included in an inventory in accordance with §1.61-4. The purchase price of an automobile, even when wholly used in carrying on farming operations, is not deductible, but is regarded as an investment of capital. The cost of gasoline, repairs, and upkeep of an automobile if used wholly in the business of farming is deductible as an expense; if used partly for business purposes and partly for the pleasure or convenience of the taxpayer or his family, such cost may be apportioned according to the extent of the use for purposes of business and pleasure or convenience, and only the proportion of such cost justly attributable to business purposes is deductible as a necessary expense.

(b) *Farms not engaged in for profit; taxable years beginning before January 1, 1970.*—(1) *In general.*—If a farm is operated for recreation or pleasure and not on a commercial basis, and if the expenses incurred in connection with the farm are in excess of the receipts therefrom, the entire receipts from the sale of farm products may be ignored in rendering a return of income, and the expenses incurred, being regarded as personal expenses, will not constitute allowable deductions.

(2) *Effective date.*—The provisions of this paragraph shall apply with respect to taxable years beginning before January 1, 1970.

(3) *Cross reference.*—For provisions relating to activities not engaged in for profit, applicable to taxable years beginning after December 31, 1969, see section 183 and the regulations thereunder. [Reg. §1.162-12.]

☐ [T.D. 6291, 4-3-58. *Amended by* T.D. 6548, 2-21-61; T.D. 7198, 7-12-72; T.D. 8729, 8-21-97 *and* T.D. 8897, 8-18-2000.]

[Reg. §1.162-13]

§1.162-13. Depositors' guaranty fund.—Banking corporations which pursuant to the laws of the State in which they are doing business are required to set apart, keep, and maintain in their banks the amount levied and assessed against them by the State authorities as a "Depositors' guaranty fund," may deduct from their gross income the amount so set apart each year to this fund provided that such fund, when set aside and carried to the credit of the State banking board or duly authorized State officer, ceases to be an asset of the bank and may be withdrawn in whole or in part upon demand by such board or State officer to meet the needs of these officers in reimbursing depositors in insolvent banks, and provided further that no portion of the amount thus set aside and credited is returnable under the laws of the State to the assets of the banking corporation. If, however, such amount is simply set up on the books of the bank as a reserve to meet a contingent liability and remains an asset of the bank, it will not be deductible except as it is actually paid out as required by law and upon demand of the proper State officers. [Reg. §1.162-13.]

☐ [T.D. 6291, 4-3-58.]

[Reg. §1.162-14]

§1.162-14. Expenditures for advertising or promotion of good will.—A corporation which has, for the purpose of computing its excess profits tax credit under subchapter E, chapter 2, or subchapter D, chapter 1 of the Internal Revenue Code of 1939, elected under section 733 or section 451 (applicable to the excess profits tax imposed by subchapter E of chapter 2, and subchapter D of chapter 1, respectively) to charge to capital account for taxable years in its base period expenditures for advertising or the promotion of good will which may be regarded as capital investments, may not deduct similar expenditures for the taxable year. See section 263(b). Such a taxpayer has the burden of proving that expenditures for advertising or the promotion of good will which it seeks to deduct in the taxable year may not be regarded as capital investments under the provisions of the regulations prescribed under section 733 or section 451 of the Internal Revenue Code of 1939. See 26 CFR, 1938 ed., §35.733-2 (Regulations 112) and 26 CFR (1939) §40.451-2 (Regulations 130). For the disallowance of deductions for the cost of advertising in programs of certain conventions of political parties, or in publications part of the proceeds of which directly of indirectly inures (or is intended to inure) to or for the use of a political party or political candidate, see §1.276-1. [Reg. §1.162-14.]

☐ [T.D. 6291, 4-3-58. Amended by T.D. 6996, 1-17-69.]

[Reg. §1.162-15]

§1.162-15. Contributions, dues, etc.—(a) *Payments and transfers to entities described in section 170(c).*—(1) *In general.*—A payment or transfer to or for the use of an entity described in section 170(c) that bears a direct relationship to the taxpayer's trade or business and that is made with a reasonable expectation of financial return commensurate with the amount of the payment or transfer may constitute an allowable deduction as a trade or business expense rather than a charitable contribution deduction under section 170. For payments or transfers in excess of the amount deductible under section 162(a), see §1.170A-1(h).

(2) *Examples.*—The following examples illustrate the rules of paragraph (a)(1) of this section:

(i) *Example 1.*—A, an individual, is a sole proprietor who manufactures musical instruments and sells them through a website. A makes a $1,000 payment to a local church (which is a charitable organization described in section 170(c)) for a half-page advertisement in the church's program for a concert. In the program, the church thanks its concert supporters, including A. A's advertisement includes the URL for the website through which A sells its instruments. A reasonably expects that the advertisement will attract new customers to A's website and will help A to sell more musical instruments. A may treat the $1,000 payment as an expense of carrying on a trade or business under section 162.

(ii) *Example 2.*—P, a partnership, operates a chain of supermarkets, some of which are located in State N. P operates a promotional program in which it sets aside the proceeds from one percent of its sales each year, which it pays to one or more charities described in section 170(c). The funds are earmarked for use in projects that improve conditions in State N. P makes the final determination on which charities receive payments. P advertises the program. P reasonably believes the program will generate a significant degree of name recognition and goodwill in the communities where it operates and thereby increase its revenue. As part of the program, P makes a $1,000 payment to a charity described in section 170(c). P may treat the $1,000 payment as an expense of carrying on a trade or business under section 162. This result is unchanged if, under State N's tax credit program, P expects to receive a $1,000 income tax credit on account of P's payment, and under State N law, the credit can be passed through to P's partners.

(3) *Safe harbors for C corporations and specified passthrough entities making payments in exchange for State or local tax credits.*—(i) *Safe harbor for C corporations.*—If a C corporation makes a payment to or for the use of an entity described in section 170(c) and receives or expects to receive in return a State or local tax credit that reduces a State or local tax imposed on the C corporation, the C corporation may treat such payment as meeting the requirements of an ordinary and necessary business expense for purposes of section 162(a) to the extent of the amount of the credit received or expected to be received.

(ii) *Safe harbor for specified passthrough entities.*—(A) *Definition of specified passthrough entity.*—For purposes of this paragraph (a)(3)(ii), an entity is a specified passthrough entity if each of the following requirements is satisfied—

(1) The entity is a business entity other than a C corporation and is regarded for all Federal income tax purposes as separate from its owners under §301.7701-3 of this chapter;

(2) The entity operates a trade or business within the meaning of section 162;

(3) The entity is subject to a State or local tax incurred in carrying on its trade or business that is imposed directly on the entity; and

(4) In return for a payment to an entity described in section 170(c), the entity described in paragraph (a)(3)(ii)(A)(1) of this section receives or expects to receive a State or local tax credit that the entity applies or expects to apply to offset a State or local tax described in paragraph (a)(3)(ii)(A)(3) of this section.

(B) *Safe harbor.*—Except as provided in paragraph (a)(3)(ii)(C) of this section, if a specified passthrough entity makes a payment to or for the use of an entity described in section 170(c), and receives or expects to receive in return a State or local tax credit that reduces a State or local tax described in paragraph (a)(3)(ii)(A)(3) of this section, the specified passthrough entity may treat such payment as an ordinary and necessary business expense for purposes of

section 162(a) to the extent of the amount of credit received or expected to be received.

(C) *Exception.*—The safe harbor described in this paragraph (a)(3)(ii) does not apply if the credit received or expected to be received reduces a State or local income tax.

(iii) *Definition of payment.*—For purposes of this paragraph (a)(3), payment is defined as a payment of cash or cash equivalent.

(iv) *Examples.*—The following examples illustrate the rules of paragraph (a)(3) of this section.

(A) *Example 1. C corporation that receives or expects to receive dollar-for-dollar State or local tax credit.*—A, a C corporation engaged in a trade or business, makes a payment of $1,000 to an entity described in section 170(c). In return for the payment, A expects to receive a dollar-for-dollar State tax credit to be applied to A's State corporate income tax liability. Under paragraph (a)(3)(i) of this section, A may treat the $1,000 payment as an expense of carrying on a trade or business under section 162.

(B) *Example 2. C corporation that receives or expects to receive percentage-based State or local tax credit.*—B, a C corporation engaged in a trade or business, makes a payment of $1,000 to an entity described in section 170(c). In return for the payment, B expects to receive a local tax credit equal to 80 percent of the amount of this payment ($800) to be applied to B's local real property tax liability. Under paragraph (a)(3)(i) of this section, B may treat $800 as an expense of carrying on a trade or business under section 162. The treatment of the remaining $200 will depend upon the facts and circumstances and is not affected by paragraph (a)(3)(i) of this section.

(C) *Example 3. Partnership that receives or expects to receive dollar-for-dollar State or local tax credit.*—P is a limited liability company classified as a partnership for Federal income tax purposes under §301.7701-3 of this chapter. P is engaged in a trade or business and makes a payment of $1,000 to an entity described in section 170(c). In return for the payment, P expects to receive a dollar-for-dollar State tax credit to be applied to P's State excise tax liability incurred by P in carrying on its trade or business. Under applicable State law, the State's excise tax is imposed at the entity level (not the owner level). Under paragraph (a)(3)(ii) of this section, P may treat the $1,000 as an expense of carrying on a trade or business under section 162.

(D) *Example 4. S corporation that receives or expects to receive percentage-based State or local tax credit.*—S is an S corporation engaged in a trade or business and is owned by individuals C and D. S makes a payment of $1,000 to an entity described in section 170(c). In return for the payment, S expects to receive a local tax credit equal to 80 percent of the amount of this payment ($800) to be applied to S's local real property tax liability incurred by S in carrying on its trade or business. Under applicable local law, the real property tax is imposed at the entity level (not the owner level). Under paragraph (a)(3)(ii) of this section, S may treat $800 of the payment as an expense of carrying on a trade or business under section 162. The treatment of the remaining $200 will depend upon the facts and circumstances and is not affected by paragraph (a)(3)(ii) of this section.

(v) *Applicability of section 170 to payments in exchange for State or local tax benefits.*—For rules regarding the availability of a charitable contribution deduction under section 170 where a taxpayer makes a payment or transfers property to or for the use of an entity described in section 170(c) and receives or expects to receive a State or local tax benefit in return for such payment, see §1.170A-1(h)(3).

(4) *Applicability dates.*—Paragraphs (a)(1) and (2) of this section, regarding the application of section 162 to taxpayers making payments or transfers to entities described in section 170(c), apply to payments or transfers made on or after December 17, 2019. Section 1.162-15(a), as it appeared in the April 1, 2020 edition of 26 CFR part 1, generally applies to payments or transfers made prior to December 17, 2019. However, taxpayers may choose to apply paragraphs (a)(1) and (2) of this section to payments and transfers made on or after January 1, 2018. Paragraph (a)(3) of this section, regarding the safe harbors for C corporations and specified passthrough entities making payments to section 170(c) entities in exchange for State or local tax credits, applies to payments made by these entities on or after December 17, 2019. However, taxpayers may choose to apply the safe harbors of paragraph (a)(3) to payments made on or after January 1, 2018.

(b) *Other contributions.*—Donations to organizations other than those described in section 170 which bear a direct relationship to the taxpayer's business and are made with a reasonable expectation of a financial return commensurate with the amount of the donation may constitute allowable deductions as business expenses, provided the donation is not made for a purpose for which a deduction is not allowable by reason of the provisions of paragraph (b)(1)(i) or (c) of §1.162-20. For example, a transit company may donate a sum of money to an organization (of a class not referred to in section 170) intending to hold a convention in the city in which it operates, with a reasonable expectation that the holding of such convention will augment its income through a greater number of people using its transportation facilities.

(c) *Dues.*—Dues and other payments to an organization, such as a labor union or a trade association, which otherwise meet the requirements of the regulations under section 162, are deductible in full. For limitations on the deductibility of dues and other payments, see paragraph (b) and (c) of §1.162-20.

(d) *Cross reference.*—For provisions dealing with expenditures for institutional or "good will" advertising, see §1.162-20(a)(2). [Reg. §1.162-15.]

☐ [T.D. 6291, 4-3-58. *Amended by* T.D. 6435, 12-28-59, T.D. 6819, 4-19-65 *and* T.D. 9907, 8-7-2020.]

[Reg. §1.162-16]

§1.162-16. **Cross reference.**—For special rules relating to expenses in connection with subdividing real property for sale, see section 1237 and the regulations thereunder. [Reg. §1.162-16.]

☐ [T.D. 6291, 4-3-58.]

[Reg. §1.162-17]

§1.162-17. **Reporting and substantiation of certain business expenses of employees.**—(a) *Introductory.*—The purpose of the regulations in this section is to provide rules for the reporting of information on income tax returns by taxpayers who pay or incur ordinary and necessary business expenses in connection with the performance of services as an employee and to furnish guidance as to the type of records which will be useful in compiling such information and in its substantiation, if required. The rules prescribed in this section do not apply to expenses paid or incurred for incidentals, such as office supplies for the employer or local transportation in connection with an errand. Employees incurring such incidental expenses are not required to provide substantiation for such amounts. The term "ordinary and necessary business expenses" means only those expenses which are ordinary and necessary in the conduct of the taxpayer's business and are directly attributable to such business. The term does not include nondeductible personal, living or family expenses.

(b) *Expenses for which the employee is required to account to his employer.*—(1) *Reimbursements equal to expenses.*—The employee need not report on his tax return (either itemized or in total amount) expenses for travel, transportation, entertainment, and similar purposes paid or incurred by him solely for the benefit of his employer for which he is required to account and does account to his employer and which are charged directly or indirectly to the employer (for example, through credit cards) or for which the employee is paid through advances, reimbursements, or otherwise, provided the total amount of such advances, reimbursements, and charges is equal to such expenses. In such a case the taxpayer need only state in his return that the total of amounts charged directly or indirectly to his employer through credit cards or otherwise and received from the employer as advances or reimbursements did not exceed the ordinary and necessary business expenses paid or incurred by the employee.

(2) *Reimbursements in excess of expenses.*—In case the total of amounts charged directly or indirectly to the employer and received from the employer as advances, reimbursements, or otherwise, exceeds the ordinary and necessary business expenses paid or incurred by the employee and the employee is required to and does account to his employer for such expenses, the taxpayer must include such excess in income and state on his return that he has done so.

(3) *Expenses in excess of reimbursements.*—If the employee's ordinary and necessary business expenses exceed the total of the amounts charged directly or indirectly to the employer and received from the employer as advances, reimbursements, or otherwise, and the employee is required to and does account to his employer for such expenses, the taxpayer may make the statement in his return required by subparagraph (1) of this paragraph unless he wishes to claim a deduction for such excess. If, however, he wishes to secure a deduction for such excess, he must submit a statement showing the following information as part of his tax return:

(i) The total of any charges paid or borne by the employer and of any other amounts received from the employer for payment of expenses, whether by means of advances, reimbursements or otherwise; and

(ii) The nature of his occupation, the number of days away from home on business, and the total amount of ordinary and necessary business expenses paid or incurred by him (including those charged directly or indirectly to the employer through credit cards or otherwise) broken down into such broad categories as transportation, meals and lodging while away from home overnight, entertainment expenses, and other business expenses.

(4) To "account" to his employer as used in this section means to submit an expense account or other required written statement to the employer showing the business nature and the amount of all the employee's expenses (including those charged directly or indirectly to the employer through credit cards or otherwise) broken down into such broad categories as transportation, meals and lodging while away from home overnight, entertainment expenses, and other business expenses. For this purpose, the Commissioner in his discretion may approve reasonable business practices under which mileage, per diem in lieu of subsistence, and similar allowances providing for ordinary and necessary business expenses in accordance with a fixed scale may be regarded as equivalent to an accounting to the employer.

(c) *Expenses for which the employee is not required to account to his employer.*—If the employee is not required to account to his employer for his ordinary and necessary business expenses, e.g., travel, transportation, entertainment, and similar items, or, though required, fails to account for such expenses, he must submit, as a part of his tax return, a statement showing the following information:

(1) The total of all amounts received as advances or reimbursements from his employer in connection with the ordinary and necessary business expenses of the employee, including amounts charged directly or indirectly to the employer through credit cards or otherwise; and

(2) The nature of his occupation, the number of days away from home on business, and the total amount of ordinary and necessary business expenses paid or incurred by him (including those charged directly or indirectly to the employer through credit cards or otherwise) broken down into such broad categories as transportation, meals and lodging while away from home overnight, entertainment expenses, and other business expenses.

(d) *Substantiation of items of expense.*—(1) Although the Commissioner may require any taxpayer to substantiate such information concerning expense accounts as may appear to be pertinent in determining tax liability, taxpayers ordinarily will not be called upon to substantiate expense account information except those in the following categories:

(i) A taxpayer who is not required to account to his employer, or who does not account;

(ii) A taxpayer whose expenses exceed the total of amounts charged to his employer and amounts received through advances, reimbursements or otherwise and who claims a deduction on his return for such excess;

(iii) A taxpayer who is related to his employer within the meaning of section 267(b); and

(iv) Other taxpayers in cases where it is determined that the accounting procedures used by the employer for the reporting and substantiation of expenses by employees are not adequate.

(2) The Code contemplates that taxpayers keep such records as will be sufficient to enable the Commissioner to correctly determine income tax liability. Accordingly, it is to the advantage of taxpayers who may be called upon to substantiate expense account information to maintain as adequate and detailed records of travel, transportation, entertainment, and similar business expenses as practical since the burden of proof is upon the taxpayer to show that such expenses were not only paid or incurred but also that they constitute ordinary and necessary business expenses. One method for substantiating expenses incurred by an employee in connection with his employment is through the preparation of a daily diary or record of expenditures, maintained in sufficient detail to enable him to readily identify the amount and nature of any expenditure, and the preservation of supporting documents, especially in connection with large or exceptional expenditures. Nevertheless, it is recognized that by reason of the nature of certain expenses or the circumstances under which they are incurred, it is often difficult for an employee to maintain detailed records or to preserve supporting documents for all his expenses. Detailed records of small expenditures incurred in traveling or for transportation, as for example, tips, will not be required.

(3) Where records are incomplete or documentary proof is unavailable, it may be possible to establish the amount of the expenditures by approximations based upon reliable secondary sources of information and collateral evidence. For example, in connection with an item of traveling expense a taxpayer might establish that he was in a travel status a certain number of days but that it was impractica-

ble for him to establish the details of all his various items of travel expense. In such a case rail fares or plane fares can usually be ascertained with exactness and automobile costs approximated on the basis of mileage covered. A reasonable approximation of meals and lodging might be based upon receipted hotel bills or upon average daily rates for such accommodations and meals prevailing in the particular community for comparable accommodations. Since detailed records of incidental items are not required, deductions for these items may be based upon a reasonable approximation. In cases where a taxpayer is called upon to substantiate expense account information, the burden is on the taxpayer to establish that the amounts claimed as a deduction are reasonably accurate and constitute ordinary and necessary business expenses paid or incurred by him in connection with his trade or business. In connection with the determination of factual matters of this type, due consideration will be given to the reasonableness of the stated expenditures for the claimed purposes in relation to the taxpayer's circumstances (such as his income and the nature of his occupation), to the reliability and accuracy of records in connection with other items more readily lending themselves to detailed record-keeping, and to all of the facts and circumstances in the particular case.

(e) *Applicability.*—(1) Except as provided in subparagraph (2) of this paragraph, the provisions of the regulations in this section are supplemental to existing regulations relating to information required to be submitted with income tax returns, and shall be applicable with respect to taxable years beginning after December 31, 1957, notwithstanding any existing regulation to the contrary.

(2) With respect to taxable years ending after December 31, 1962, but only in respect of periods after such date, the provisions of the regulations in this section are superseded by the regulations under section 274(d) to the extent inconsistent therewith. See § 1.274-5.

(3) For taxable years beginning on or after January 1, 1989, the provisions of this section are superseded by the regulations under section 62(c) to the extent this section is inconsistent with those regulations. See § 1.62-2. [Reg. § 1.162-17.]

☐ [T.D. 6306, 8-27-58. Amended by T.D. 6630, 12-27-62; T.D. 8276, 12-7-89 and T.D. 8324, 12-14-90.]

[Reg. § 1.162-18]

§ 1.162-18. Illegal bribes and kickbacks.—(a) *Illegal payments to government officials or employees.*—(1) *In general.*—No deduction shall be allowed under section 162(a) for any amount paid or incurred, directly or indirectly, to an official or employee of any government, or of any agency or other instrumentality of any government, if—

(i) In the case of a payment made to an official or employee of a government other than a foreign government described in subparagraph (3)(ii) or (iii) of this paragraph, the payment constitutes an illegal bribe or kickback, or

(ii) In the case of a payment made to an official or employee of a foreign government described in subparagraph (3)(ii) or (iii) of this paragraph, the making of the payment would be unlawful under the laws of the United States (if such laws were applicable to the payment and to the official or employee at the time the expenses were paid or incurred).

No deduction shall be allowed for an accrued expense if the eventual payment thereof would fall within the prohibition of this section. The place where the expenses are paid or incurred is immaterial. For purposes of subdivision (ii) of this subparagraph, lawfulness or unlawfulness of the payment under the laws of the foreign country is immaterial.

(2) *Indirect payment.*—For purposes of this paragraph, an indirect payment to an individual shall include any payment which inures to his benefit or promotes his interests, regardless of the medium in which the payment is made and regardless of the identity of the immediate recipient or payor. Thus, for example, payment made to an agent, relative, or independent contractor of an official or employee, or even directly into the general treasury of a foreign country of which the beneficiary is an official or employee, may be treated as an indirect payment to the official or employee, if in fact such payment inures or will inure to his benefit or promotes or will promote his financial or other interests. A payment made by an agent or independent contractor of the taxpayer which benefits the taxpayer shall be treated as an indirect payment by the taxpayer to the official or employee.

(3) *Official or employee of a government.*—Any individual officially connected with—

(i) The government of the United States, a State, a territory or possession of the United States, the District of Columbia, or the Commonwealth of Puerto Rico,

(ii) The government of a foreign country, or

(iii) A political subdivision of, or a corporation or other entity serving as an agency or instrumentality of, any of the above,

in whatever capacity, whether on a permanent or temporary basis, and whether or not serving for compensation, shall be included within the term "official or employee of a government", regardless of the place of residence or post of duty of such individual. An independent contractor would not ordinarily be considered to be an official or employee. For purposes of section 162(c) and this paragraph, the term "foreign country" shall include any foreign nation, whether or not such nation has been accorded diplomatic recognition by the United States. Individuals who purport to act on behalf of or as the government of a foreign nation, or an agency or instrumentality thereof, shall be treated under this section as officials or employees of a foreign government, whether or not such individuals in fact control such foreign nation, agency, or instrumentality, and whether or not such individuals are accorded diplomatic recognition. Accordingly, a group in rebellion against an established government ment shall be treated as officials or employees of a foreign government, as shall officials or employees of the government against which the group is in rebellion.

(4) *Laws of the United States.*—The term "laws of the United States", to which reference is made in paragraph (a)(1)(ii) of this section, shall be deemed to include only Federal statutes, including State laws which are assimilated into Federal law by Federal statute, and legislative and interpretative regulations thereunder. The term shall also be limited to statutes which prohibit some act or acts, for the violation of which there is a civil or criminal penalty.

(5) *Burden of proof.*—In any proceeding involving the issue of whether, for purposes of section 162(c)(1), a payment made to a government official or employee constitutes an illegal bribe or kickback (or would be unlawful under the laws of the United States) the burden of proof in respect of such issue shall be upon the Commissioner to the same extent as he bears the burden of proof in civil fraud cases under section 7454 (*i.e.*, he must prove the illegality of the payment by clear and convincing evidence).

(6) *Example.*—The application of this paragraph may be illustrated by the following example:

Example. X Corp. is in the business of selling hospital equipment in State Y. During 1970, X Corp. employed A who at the time was employed full time by State Y as Superintendent of Hospitals. The purpose of A's employment by X Corp. was to procure for it an improper advantage over other concerns in the making of sales to hospitals in respect of which A, as Superintendent, had authority. X Corp. paid A $5,000 during 1970. The making of this payment was illegal under the laws of State Y. Under section 162(c)(1), X Corp. is precluded from deducting as a trade or business expense the $5,000 paid to A.

(b) *Other illegal payments.*—(1) *In general.*—No deduction shall be allowed under section 162(a) for any payment (other than a payment described in paragraph (a) of this section) made, directly or indirectly, to any person, if the payment constitutes an illegal bribe, illegal kickback, or other illegal payment under the laws of the United States (as defined in paragraph (a)(4) of this section), or under any State law (but only if such State law is generally enforced), which subjects the payor to a criminal penalty or the loss (including a suspension) of license or privilege to engage in a trade or business (whether or not such penalty or loss is actually imposed upon the taxpayer). For purposes of this paragraph, a kickback includes a payment in consideration of the referral of a client, patient, or customer. This paragraph applies only to payments made after December 30, 1969.

(2) *State law.*—For purposes of this paragraph, State law means a statute of a State or the District of Columbia.

(3) *Generally enforced.*—For purposes of this paragraph, a State law shall be considered to be generally enforced unless it is never enforced or the only persons normally charged with violations thereof in the State (or the District of Columbia) enacting the law are infamous or those whose violations are extraordinarily flagrant. For example, a criminal statute of a State shall be considered to be generally enforced unless violations of the statute which are brought to the attention of appropriate enforcement authorities do not result in any enforcement action in the absence of unusual circumstances.

(4) *Burden of proof.*—In any proceeding involving the issue of whether, for purposes of section 162(c)(2), a payment constitutes an illegal bribe, illegal kickback, or other illegal payment the burden of proof in respect of such issue shall be upon the Commissioner to the same extent as he bears the burden of proof in civil fraud cases under section 7454 (*i.e.*, he must prove the illegality of the payment by clear and convincing evidence).

(5) *Example.*—The application of this paragraph may be illustrated by the following example:

Itemized Deductions for Individuals and Corps.
See p. 20,601 for regulations not amended to reflect law changes

25,227

Example. X Corp., a calendar-year taxpayer, is engaged in the ship repair business in State Y. During 1970, repairs on foreign ships accounted for a substantial part of its total business. It was X Corp.'s practice to kick back approximately 10 percent of the repair bill to the captain and chief engineer of all foreign-owned vessels, which kickbacks are illegal under a law of State Y (which is generally enforced) and potentially subject X Corp. to fines. During 1970, X Corp. paid $50,000 in such kickbacks. On X Corp.'s return for 1970, a deduction under section 162 was taken for the $50,000. The deduction of the $50,000 of illegal kickbacks during 1970 is disallowed under section 162(c)(2), whether or not X Corp. is prosecuted with respect to the kickbacks.

(c) *Kickbacks, rebates, and bribes under medicare and medicaid.*—No deduction shall be allowed under section 162(a) for any kickback, rebate, or bribe (whether or not illegal) made on or after December 10, 1971, by any provider of services, supplier, physician, or other person who furnishes items or services for which payment is or may be made under the Social Security Act, as amended, or in whole or in part out of Federal funds under a State plan approved under such Act, if such kickback, rebate, or bribe is made in connection with the furnishing of such items or services or the making or receipt of such payments. For purposes of this paragraph, a kickback includes a payment in consideration of the referral of a client, patient, or customer. [Reg. §1.162-18.]

☐ [*T.D.* 6448, 1-26-60. *Amended by T.D.* 7345, 2-19-75.]

[Reg. §1.162-19]

§1.162-19. Capital contributions to Federal National Mortgage Association.—(a) *In general.*—The initial holder of stock of the Federal National Mortgage Association (FNMA) which is issued pursuant to section 303(c) of the Federal National Mortgage Association Charter Act (12 U.S.C., sec. 1718) in a taxable year beginning after December 31, 1959, shall treat the excess, if any, of the issuance price (the amount of capital contributions evidenced by a share of stock) over the fair market value of the stock as of the issue date of such stock as an ordinary and necessary business expense paid or incurred during the year in which occurs the date of issuance of the stock. To the extent that a sale to FNMA of mortgage paper gives rise to the issuance of a share of FNMA stock during a taxable year beginning after December 31, 1959, such sale is to be treated in a manner consistent with the purpose for, and the legislative intent underlying the enactment of, the provisions of section 8, Act of September 14, 1960 (Public Law 86-779, 74 Stat. 1003). Thus, for the purpose of determining an initial holder's gain or loss from the sale to FNMA of mortgage paper, with respect to which a share of FNMA stock is issued in a taxable year beginning after December 31, 1959 (irrespective of when the sale is made), the amount realized by the initial holder from the sale of the mortgage paper is the amount of the "FNMA purchase price". The "FNMA purchase price" is the gross amount of the consideration agreed upon between FNMA and the initial holder for the purchase of the mortgage paper, without regard to any deduction therefrom as, for example, a deduction representing a capital contribution or a purchase or marketing fee. The date of issuance of the stock is the date which appears on the stock certificates of the initial holder as the date of issue. The initial holder is the original purchaser who is issued stock of the Federal National Mortgage Association pursuant to section 303(c) of the Act, and who appears on the books of FNMA as the initial holder. In determining the period for which the initial holder has held such stock, such period shall begin with the date of issuance.

(b) *Examples.*—The provisions of paragraph (a) of this section may be illustrated by the following examples:

Example (1). A, a banking institution which reports its income on a calendar year basis, sold mortgage paper with an outstanding principal balance of $12,500 to FNMA on October 17, 1960. The FNMA purchase price was $11,500. A's basis for the mortgage paper was $10,500. In accordance with the terms of the contract, FNMA deducted $375 ($250 representing capital contribution and $125 representing purchase and marketing fee) from the amount of the purchase price. FNMA credited A's account with the amount of the capital contribution. A stock certificate evidencing two shares of FNMA common stock of $100 par value was mailed to A and FNMA deducted $200 from A's account, leaving a net balance of $50 in such account. The stock certificate, bearing an issue date of November 1, 1960, was received by A on November 7, 1960. The fair market value of a share of FNMA stock on October 17, 1960, was $65, on November 1, 1960, was $67, and on November 7, 1960, was $68. A may deduct $66, the difference between the issuance price ($200) and the fair market value ($134) of the two shares of stock on the date of issuance (November 1, 1960), as a business expense for the taxable year 1960. The basis of each share of stock issued as of November 1, 1960 will be $67. See section 1054 and §1.1054-1. A's gain from the sale of the mortgage paper is $875 computed as follows:

Amount realized (FNMA purchase price)		$11,500
A's basis in mortgage paper	$10,500	
Purchase and marketing fee	125	10,625
Gain on sale		875

Example (2). Assume the same facts as in Example (1), and, in addition, that A sold to FNMA on December 15, 1960, additional mortgage paper having an outstanding principal balance of $12,500. FNMA deducted from the FNMA purchase price $250 representing capital contribution and credited A's account with this amount. A then had a total credit of $300 to his account consisting of the $50 balance from the transaction described in Example (1) and $250 from the December 15th transaction. A stock certificate evidencing three shares of FNMA common stock of $100 par value was mailed to A and FNMA deducted $300 from A's account. The stock certificate, bearing an issue date of January 1, 1961, was received by A on January 9, 1961. The fair market value of a share of FNMA stock on January 1, 1961, was $69. A may deduct $93, the difference between the issuance price ($300) and the fair market value ($207) of the three shares of stock on the date of issuance (January 1, 1961), as a business expense for the taxable year 1961. The gain or loss on the sale of mortgage paper on December 15, 1960, is reportable for the taxable year 1960. [Reg. §1.162-19.]

☐ [*T.D.* 6690, 11-18-63.]

[Reg. §1.162-20]

§1.162-20. Expenditures attributable to lobbying, political campaigns, attempts to influence legislation, etc., and certain advertising.—(a) *In general.*—(1) *Scope of section.*—This section contains rules governing the deductibility or non-deductibility of expenditures for lobbying purposes, for the promotion or defeat of legislation, for political campaign purposes (including the support of or opposition to any candidate for public office) or for carrying on propaganda (including advertising) related to any of the foregoing purposes. For rules applicable to such expenditures in respect of taxable years beginning before January 1, 1963, and for taxable years beginning after December 31, 1962, see paragraphs (b) and (c), respectively, of this section. This section also deals with expenditures for institutional or "good will" advertising.

(2) *Institutional or "good will" advertising.*—Expenditures for institutional or "good will" advertising which keeps the taxpayer's name before the public are generally deductible as ordinary and necessary business expenses provided the expenditures are related to the patronage the taxpayer might reasonably expect in the future. For example, a deduction will ordinarily be allowed for the cost of advertising which keeps the taxpayer's name before the public in connection with encouraging contributions to such organizations as the Red Cross, the purchase of United States Savings Bonds, or participation in similar causes. In like fashion, expenditures for advertising which presents views on economic, financial, social, or other subjects of a general nature, but which does not involve any of the activities specified in paragraph (b) or (c) of this section for which a deduction is not allowable, are deductible if they otherwise meet the requirements of the regulations under section 162.

(b) *Taxable years beginning before January 1, 1963.*—(1) *In general.*—(i) For taxable years beginning before January 1, 1963, expenditures for lobbying purposes, for the promotion or defeat of legislation, for political campaign purposes (including the support of or opposition to any candidate for public office), or for carrying on propaganda (including advertising) related to any of the foregoing purposes are not deductible from gross income. For example, the cost of advertising to promote or defeat legislation or to influence the public with respect to the desirability or undesirability of proposed legislation is not deductible as a business expense, even though the legislation may directly affect the taxpayer's business.

(ii) If a substantial part of the activities of an organization, such as a labor union or a trade association, consists of one or more of the activities specified in the first sentence of this subparagraph, deduction will be allowed only for such portion of the dues or other payments to the organization as the taxpayer can clearly establish is attributable to activities other than those so specified. The determination of whether such specified activities constitute a substantial part of an organization's activities shall be based on all the facts and circumstances. In no event shall special assessments or similar payments (including an increase in dues) made to any organization for any of such specified purposes be deductible. For other provisions relating to the deductibility of dues and other payments to an organization, such as a labor union or a trade association, see paragraph (c) of §1.162-15.

(2) *Expenditures for promotion or defeat of legislation.*—For purposes of this paragraph, expenditures for the promotion or the defeat of legislation include, but shall not be limited to, expenditures for the purpose of attempting to—

(i) Influence members of a legislative body directly, or indirectly by urging or encouraging the public to contact such members for the purpose of proposing, supporting, or opposing legislation, or

(ii) Influence the public to approve or reject a measure in a referendum, initiative, vote on a constitutional amendment, or similar procedure.

(c) *Taxable years beginning after December 31, 1962.*—(1) *In general.*—For taxable years beginning after December 31, 1962, certain types of expenses incurred with respect to legislative matters are deductible under section 162(a) if they otherwise meet the requirements of the regulations under section 162. These deductible expenses are described in subparagraph (2) of this paragraph. All other expenditures for lobbying purposes, for the promotion or defeat of legislation (see paragraph (b)(2) of this section), for political campaign purposes (including the support of or opposition to any candidate for public office), or for carrying on propaganda (including advertising) relating to any of the foregoing purposes are not deductible from gross income for such taxable years. For the disallowance of deductions for bad debts and worthless securities of a political party, see § 1.271-1. For the disallowance of deductions for certain indirect political contributions, such as the cost of certain advertising and the cost of admission to certain dinners, programs, and inaugural events, see § 1.276-1.

(2) *Appearances, etc., with respect to legislation.*—(i) *General rule.*—Pursuant to the provisions of section 162(e), expenses incurred with respect to legislative matters which may be deductible are those ordinary and necessary expenses (including, but not limited to, traveling expenses described in section 162(a)(2) and the cost of preparing testimony) paid or incurred by the taxpayer during a taxable year beginning after December 31, 1962, in carrying on any trade or business which are in direct connection with—

(a) appearances before, submission of statements to, or sending communications to, the committees, or individual members of Congress or of any legislative body of a State, a possession of the United States, or a political subdivision of any of the foregoing with respect to legislation or proposed legislation of direct interest to the taxpayer, or

(b) communication of information between the taxpayer and an organization of which he is a member with respect to legislation or proposed legislation of direct interest to the taxpayer and to such organization.

For provisions relating to dues paid or incurred with respect to an organization of which the taxpayer is a member, see subparagraph (3) of this paragraph.

(ii) *Legislation or proposed legislation of direct interest to the taxpayer.*—(a) *Legislation or proposed legislation.*—The term "legislation or proposed legislation" includes bills and resolutions introduced by a member of Congress or other legislative body referred to in subdivision (i)(a) of this subparagraph for consideration by such body as well as oral or written proposals for legislative action submitted to the legislative body or to a committee or member of such body.

(b) *Direct interest.*—(1) *In general.*—(i) Legislation or proposed legislation is of direct interest to a taxpayer if the legislation or proposed legislation is of such a nature that it will, or may reasonably be expected to, affect the trade or business of the taxpayer. It is immaterial whether the effect, or expected effect, on the trade or business will be beneficial or detrimental to the trade or business or whether it will be immediate. If legislation or proposed legislation has such a relationship to a trade or business that the expenses of any appearance or communication in connection with the legislation meets the ordinary and necessary test of section 162(a), then such legislation ordinarily meets the direct interest test of section 162(e). However, if the nature of the legislation or proposed legislation is such that the likelihood of its having an effect on the trade or business of the taxpayer is remote or speculative, the legislation or proposed legislation is not of direct interest to the taxpayer. Legislation or proposed legislation which will not affect the trade or business of the taxpayer is not of direct interest to the taxpayer even though such legislation will affect the personal, living, or family activities or expenses of the taxpayer. Legislation or proposed legislation is not of direct interest to a taxpayer merely because it may affect business in general; however, if the legislation or proposed legislation will, or may reasonably be expected to, affect the taxpayer's trade or business it will be of direct interest to the taxpayer even though it also will affect the trade or business of other taxpayers or business in general. To meet the direct interest test, it is not necessary that all provisions of the legislation or proposed legislation have an effect, or expected effect, on the taxpayer's trade or business. The test will be met if one of the provisions of the legislation has the specified effect. Legislation or proposed legislation will be considered to be of direct interest to a membership organization if it is of direct interest to the organization, as such, or if it is of direct interest to one or more of its members.

(ii) Legislation which would increase or decrease the taxes applicable to the trade or business, increase or decrease the operating costs or earnings of the trade or business, or increase or decrease the administrative burdens connected with the trade or business meets the direct interest test. Legislation which would increase the social security benefits or liberalize the right to such benefits meets the direct interest test because such changes in the social security benefits may reasonably be expected to affect the retirement benefits which the employer will be asked to provide his employees or to increase his taxes. Legislation which would impose a retailer's sales tax is of direct interest to a retailer because, although the tax may be passed on to his customers, collection of the tax will impose additional burdens on the retailer, and because the increased cost of his products to the consumer may reduce the demand for them. Legislation which would provide an income tax credit or exclusion for shareholders is of direct interest to a corporation, because those tax benefits may increase the sources of capital available to the corporation. Legislation which would favorably or adversely affect the business of a competitor so as to affect the taxpayer's competitive position is of direct interest to the taxpayer. Legislation which would improve the school system of a community is of direct interest to a membership organization comprised of employers in the community because the improved school system is likely to make the community more attractive to prospective employees of such employers. On the other hand, proposed legislation relating to Presidential succession in the event of the death of the President has only a remote and speculative effect on any trade or business and therefore does not meet the direct interest test. Similarly, if a corporation is represented before a congressional committee to oppose an appropriation bill merely because of a desire to bring increased Government economy with the hope that such economy will eventually cause a reduction in the Federal income tax, the legislation does not meet the direct interest test because any effect it may have upon the corporation's trade or business is highly speculative.

(2) *Appearances, etc., by expert witnesses.*—(i) An appearance or communication (of a type described in paragraph (c)(2)(i)(a) of this section) by an individual in connection with legislation or proposed legislation shall be considered to be with respect to legislation of direct interest to such individual if the legislation is in a field in which he specializes as an employee, if the appearance or communication is not on behalf of his employer, and if it is customary for individuals in his type of employment to publicly express their views in respect of matters in their field of competence. Expenses incurred by such an individual in connection with such an appearance or communication, including traveling expenses properly allocable thereto, represent ordinary and necessary business expenses and are, therefore, deductible under section 162. For example, if a university professor who teaches in the field of money and banking appears, on his own behalf, before a legislative committee to testify on proposed legislation regarding the banking system, his expenses incurred in connection with such appearance are deductible under section 162 since university professors customarily take an active part in the development of the law in their field of competence and publicly communicate the results of their work.

(ii) An appearance or communication (of a type described in paragraph (c)(2)(i)(a) of this section) by an employee or self-employed individual in connection with legislation or proposed legislation shall be considered to be with respect to legislation of direct interest to such person if the legislation is in the field in which he specializes in his business (or as an employee) and if the appearance or communication is made pursuant to an invitation extended to him individually for the purpose of receiving his expert testimony. Expenses incurred by an employee or self-employed individual in connection with such an appearance or communication, including traveling expenses properly allocable thereto, represent ordinary and necessary business expenses and are, therefore, deductible under section 162. For example, if a self-employed individual is personally invited by a congressional committee to testify on proposed legislation in the field in which he specializes in his business, his expenses incurred in connection with such appearance are deductible under section 162. If a self-employed individual makes an appearance, on his own behalf, before a legislative committee without having been extended an invitation his expenses will be deductible to the extent otherwise provided in this paragraph.

(3) *Nominations, etc.*—A taxpayer does not have a direct interest in matters such as nominations, appointments, or the operation of the legislative body.

(iii) *Allowable expenses.*—To be deductible under section 162(a), expenditures which meet the tests of deductibility under the provisions of this paragraph must also qualify as ordinary and necessary business expenses under section 162(a) and, in addition, be in direct connection with the carrying on of the activities specified in subdivision (i)(*a*) or (i) (*b*) of this subparagraph. For example, a taxpayer appearing before a committee of the Congress to present testimony concerning legislation or proposed legislation in which he has a direct interest may deduct the ordinary and necessary expenses directly connected with his appearance, such as traveling expenses described in section 162(a)(2), and the cost of preparing testimony.

(3) *Deductibility of dues and other payments to an organization.*—If a substantial part of the activities of an organization, such as a labor union or a trade association, consists of one or more of the activities to which this paragraph relates (legislative matters, political campaigns, etc.,) exclusive of any activity constituting an appearance or communication with respect to legislation or proposed legislation of direct interest to the organization (see subparagraph (2)(ii)(*b*)(*1*)), a deduction will be allowed only for such portion of the dues or other payments to the organization as the taxpayer can clearly establish is attributable to activities to which this paragraph does not relate and to any activity constituting an appearance or communication with respect to legislation or proposed legislation of direct interest to the organization. The determination of whether a substantial part of an organization's activities consists of one or more of the activities to which this paragraph relates (exclusive of appearance or communications with respect to legislation or proposed legislation of direct interest to the organization) shall be based on all the facts and circumstances. In no event shall a deduction be allowed for that portion of a special assessment or similar payment (including an increase in dues) made to any organization for any activity to which this paragraph relates if the activity does not constitute any appearance or communication with respect to legislation or proposed legislation of direct interest to the organization. If an organization pays or incurs expenses allocable to legislative activities which meet the tests of subdivisions (i) and (ii) of subparagraph (2) of this paragraph (appearances or communications with respect to legislation or proposed legislation of direct interest to the organization), on behalf of its members, the dues paid by a taxpayer are deductible to the extent used for such activities. Dues paid by a taxpayer will be considered to be used for such an activity, and thus deductible, although the legislation or proposed legislation involved is not of direct interest to the taxpayer, if, pursuant to the provisions of subparagraph (2)(ii)(*b*)(*1*) of this paragraph, the legislation or proposed legislation is of direct interest to the organization, as such, or is of direct interest to one or more members of the organization. For other provisions relating to the deductibility of dues and other payments to an organization, such as a labor union or a trade association, see paragraph (c) of §1.162-15.

(4) *Limitations.*—No deduction shall be allowed under section 162(a) for any amount paid or incurred (whether by way of contribution, gift, or otherwise) in connection with any attempt to influence the general public, or segments thereof, with respect to legislative matters, elections, or referendums. For example, no deduction shall be allowed for any expenses incurred in connection with "grassroot" campaigns or any other attempts to urge or encourage the public to contact members of a legislative body for the purpose of proposing, supporting, or opposing legislation.

(5) *Expenses paid or incurred after December 31, 1993, in connection with influencing legislation other than certain local legislation.*—The provisions of paragraphs (c)(1) through (3) of this section are superseded for expenses paid or incurred after December 31, 1993, in connection with influencing legislation (other than certain local legislation) to the extent inconsistent with section 162(e)(1)(A) (as limited by section 162(e)(2)) and §§1.162-20(d) and 1.162-29.

(d) *Dues allocable to expenditures after 1993.*—No deduction is allowed under section 162(a) for the portion of dues or other similar amounts paid by the taxpayer to an organization exempt from tax (other than an organization described in section 501(c)(3)) which the organization notifies the taxpayer under section 6033(e)(1)(A)(ii) is allocable to expenditures to which section 162(e)(1) applies. The first sentence of this paragraph (d) applies to dues or other similar amounts whether or not paid on or before December 31, 1993. Section 1.162-20(c)(3) is superseded to the extent inconsistent with this paragraph (d). [Reg. §1.162-20.]

☐ [T.D. 6819, 4-19-65. Amended by T.D. 6996, 1-17-69 and T.D. 8602, 7-20-95.]

[Reg. §1.162-21]

§1.162-21. Denial of deduction for certain fines, penalties, and other amounts.—(a) *Deduction Disallowed.*—Except as otherwise provided in this section, no deduction is allowed under chapter 1 of the Internal Revenue Code (Code) for any amount that is paid or incurred—

(1) By suit, settlement agreement (agreement), or otherwise, as defined in paragraph (e)(5) of this section;

(2) To, or at the direction of, a government, as defined in paragraph (e)(1) of this section, or a governmental entity, as defined in paragraph (e)(2) of this section; and

(3) In relation to the violation, or investigation or inquiry by such government or governmental entity into the potential violation, of any civil or criminal law.

(i) An amount that is paid or incurred in relation to the violation of any civil or criminal law includes a fine or penalty.

(ii) An investigation or inquiry into the potential violation of any law does not include routine investigations or inquiries, such as audits or inspections, of regulated businesses that are not related to any evidence of wrongdoing or suspected wrongdoing, but are conducted to ensure compliance with the rules and regulations applicable to those businesses.

(b) *Exception for restitution, remediation, and amounts paid to come into compliance with a law.*—(1) *In general.*—Paragraph (a) of this section does not apply to amounts paid or incurred for restitution (including remediation) or to come into compliance with a law, as defined in paragraphs (e)(4) of this section, provided that both the identification and the establishment requirements of paragraphs (b)(2) and (b)(3) of this section are met.

(2) *Identification requirement.*—(i) *In general.*—A court order (order) or an agreement, as defined in paragraph (e)(5) of this section, identifies a payment by stating the nature of, or purpose for, each payment each taxpayer is obligated to pay and the amount of each payment identified.

(ii) *Meeting the identification requirement.*—The identification requirement is met if an order or agreement specifically states the amount of the payment described in paragraph (b)(2)(i) of this section and that the payment constitutes restitution, remediation, or an amount paid to come into compliance with a law. If the order or agreement uses a different form of the required words (such as "remediate" or "comply with a law") and describes the purpose for which restitution or remediation will be paid or the law with which the taxpayer must comply, the order or agreement will be treated as stating that the payment constitutes restitution, remediation, or an amount paid to come into compliance with a law. Similarly, if an order or agreement specifically describes the damage done, harm suffered, or manner of noncompliance with a law and describes the action required of the taxpayer to provide restitution, remediation, or to come into compliance with any law, as defined in paragraph (e)(4) of this section, the order or agreement will be treated as stating that the payment constitutes restitution, remediation, or an amount paid to come into compliance with any law. Meeting the establishment requirement of paragraph (b)(3) of this section alone is not sufficient to meet the identification requirement of paragraph (b)(2) of this section.

(iii) *Payment amount not identified.*—(A) If the order or agreement identifies a payment as restitution, remediation, or to come into compliance with a law but does not identify some or all of the amount the taxpayer must pay or incur, the identification requirement may be met for any payment amount not identified if the order or agreement describes the damage done, harm suffered, or manner of noncompliance with a law, and describes the action required of the taxpayer, such as paying or incurring costs to provide services or to provide property.

(B) If the order or agreement identifies a lump-sum payment or multiple damages award as restitution, remediation, or to come into compliance with a law but does not allocate some or all of the amount the taxpayer must pay or incur among restitution, remediation, or to come into compliance with a law, or does not allocate the total payment amount among multiple taxpayers, the identification requirement may be met for any payment amount not specifically allocated if the order or agreement describes the damage done, harm suffered, or manner of noncompliance with a law, and describes the action required of the taxpayer, such as paying or incurring costs to provide services or to provide property.

(3) *Establishment requirement.*—(i) *Meeting the establishment requirement.*—The establishment requirement is met if the taxpayer, using documentary evidence, proves the taxpayer's legal obligation, pursuant to the order or agreement, to pay the amount identified as restitution, remediation, or to come into compliance with a law; the amount paid or incurred; the date the amount was paid or incurred; and that, based on the origin of the liability and the nature and purpose of the amount paid or incurred, the amount the taxpayer paid or incurred was for restitution or remediation, as defined in paragraph (e)(4)(i) of this section or to come into compliance with

any law, as defined in paragraph (e)(4)(ii) of this section. If the amount is paid or incurred to a segregated fund or account, as described in paragraphs (e)(4)(i)(A)(2) and (3), (e)(4)(i)(B), or (e)(4)(i)(C) of this section, the taxpayer may meet the establishment requirement even if each ultimate recipient, or each ultimate use, of the payment is not designated or is unknown. A taxpayer will not meet the establishment requirement if the taxpayer fails to prove that the taxpayer paid or incurred the amount identified as restitution, remediation, or to come into compliance with a law; the amount paid; the date the amount was paid or incurred; or that the amount the taxpayer paid or incurred was for the nature and purpose identified in the order or agreement as required by paragraph (b)(2)(i) of this section, or was made for the damage done, harm suffered, noncompliance, or to provide property or services as described in (b)(2)(iii) of this section. Meeting the identification requirement of paragraph (b)(2) of this section is not sufficient to meet the establishment requirement of paragraph (b)(3) of this section.

(ii) *Substantiating the establishment requirement.*—The documentary evidence described in paragraph (b)(3)(i) of this section includes, but is not limited to, receipts; the legal or regulatory provision related to the violation or potential violation of any law; documents issued by the government or governmental entity relating to the investigation or inquiry, including court pleadings filed by the government or governmental entity requesting restitution, remediation, or demanding that defendant take action to come into compliance with the law; judgment; decree; documents describing how the amount to be paid was determined; and correspondence exchanged between the taxpayer and the government or governmental entity before the order or agreement became binding under applicable law, determined without regard to whether all appeals have been exhausted or the time for filing an appeal has expired.

(c) *Other exceptions.*—(1) *Suits between private parties.*—Paragraph (a) of this section does not apply to any amount paid or incurred by reason of any order or agreement in a suit in which no government or governmental entity is a party or any order or agreement in a suit pursuant to which a government or governmental entity enforces its rights as a private party.

(2) *Taxes and related interest.*—Paragraph (a) of this section does not apply to amounts paid or incurred as otherwise deductible taxes or related interest. However, if penalties are imposed relating to such taxes, paragraph (a) of this section applies to disallow a deduction for such penalties and interest payments related to such penalties.

(3) *Failure to pay title 26 tax.*—In the case of any amount paid or incurred as restitution for failure to pay tax imposed under title 26 of the United States Code, paragraph (a) of this section does not disallow a deduction for title 26 taxes, such as excise and employment taxes, which are equal to or less than the deduction otherwise allowed under chapter 1 of the Code if the tax had been timely paid.

(d) *Application of general principles of Federal income tax law.*—(1) *Taxable year of deduction.*—If, under paragraph (b) or (c) of this section, the taxpayer is allowed a deduction for the amount paid or incurred pursuant to an order or agreement, the deduction is taken into account under the rules of section 461 and the related regulations, or under a provision specifically applicable to the allowed deduction, such as § 1.468B-3(c).

(2) *Tax benefit rule applies.*—If the deduction allowed under paragraphs (b) or (c) of this section results in a tax benefit to the taxpayer, the taxpayer must include in income, under sections 61 and 111, the recovery of any amount deducted in a prior taxable year to the extent the prior year's deduction reduced the taxpayer's tax liability.

(i) A tax benefit to the taxpayer includes a reduction in the taxpayer's tax liability for a prior taxable year or the creation of a net operating loss carryback or carryover.

(ii) A taxpayer's recovery of any amount deducted in a prior taxable year includes, but is not limited to—

(A) Receiving a refund, recoupment, rebate, reimbursement, or otherwise recovering some or all of the amount the taxpayer paid or incurred, or

(B) Being relieved of some or all of the payment liability under the order or agreement.

(e) *Definitions.*—For section 162(f) and § 1.162-21, the following definitions apply:

(1) *Government.*—A *government* means—

(i) The government of the United States, a State, or the District of Columbia;

(ii) The government of a territory of the United States, including American Samoa, Guam, the Northern Mariana Islands, Puerto Rico, or the U.S. Virgin Islands;

(iii) The government of a foreign country;

(iv) An Indian tribal government, as defined in section 7701(a)(40), or a subdivision of an Indian tribal government, as determined in accordance with section 7871(d); or

(v) A political subdivision (such as a local government unit) of a government described in paragraph (e)(1)(i), (ii), or (iii) of this section.

(2) *Governmental entity.*—A *governmental entity* means—

(i) A corporation or other entity serving as an agency or instrumentality of a government (as defined in paragraph (e)(1) of this section), or

(ii) A nongovernmental entity treated as a governmental entity as described in paragraph (e)(3) of this section.

(3) *Nongovernmental entity treated as a governmental entity.*—A *nongovernmental entity treated as a governmental entity* is an entity that—

(i) Exercises self-regulatory powers (including imposing sanctions) in connection with a qualified board or exchange, as defined in section 1256(g)(7); or

(ii) Exercises self-regulatory powers, including adopting, administering, or enforcing rules and imposing sanctions, as part of performing an essential governmental function.

(4) *Restitution, remediation of property, and amounts paid to come into compliance with a law.*—(i) *Amounts for restitution or remediation.*—An amount is paid or incurred for restitution or remediation pursuant to paragraph (b)(1) of this section if it is paid or incurred to restore, in whole or in part, the person, as defined in section 7701(a)(1); government; governmental entity; property; environment; wildlife; or natural resources harmed, injured, or damaged by the violation or potential violation of any law described in paragraph (a)(3) of this section to the same or substantially similar position or condition as existed prior to such harm, injury or damage.

(A) *Environment, wildlife, or natural resources.*—Restitution or remediation of the environment, wildlife, or natural resources includes amounts paid or incurred for the purpose of conserving soil, air, or water resources, protecting or restoring the environment or an ecosystem, improving forests, or providing a habitat for fish, wildlife, or plants. The amounts must be paid or incurred—

(1) To, or at the direction of, a government or governmental entity to be used exclusively for the restitution or remediation of a harm to the environment, wildlife, or natural resources;

(2) To a segregated fund or account established by a government or governmental entity and, pursuant to the order or agreement, the amounts are not disbursed to the general account of the government or governmental entity for general enforcement efforts or other discretionary purposes; or

(3) To a segregated fund or account established at the direction of a government or governmental entity.

(4) Paragraph (e)(4)(i)(A) of this section applies only if there is a strong nexus or connection between the purpose of the payment and the harm to the environment, natural resources, or wildlife that the taxpayer has caused or is alleged to have caused.

(B) *Disgorgement or forfeiture.*—Provided the identification and establishment requirements of paragraphs (b)(2) and (b)(3) of this section are met, restitution may include amounts paid or incurred as disgorgement or forfeiture, if paid or incurred at the direction of a government or governmental entity directly to the person, as defined in section 7701(a)(1), harmed by the violation or potential violation of any law or to, or at the direction of, the government or governmental entity, to establish a segregated fund or account for the benefit of such harmed person. This paragraph (e)(4)(i)(B) does not apply if the order or agreement identifies the payment amount as in excess of the taxpayer's net profits or, pursuant to the order or agreement, the amounts are disbursed to the general account of the government or governmental entity for general enforcement efforts or other discretionary purposes.

(C) *Segregated funds or accounts.*—Provided the identification and establishment requirements of paragraphs (b)(2) and (b)(3) of this section are met, restitution or remediation may include amounts paid or incurred, pursuant to an order or agreement, to a segregated fund or account to restore, in whole or in part, the person, as defined in section 7701(a)(1); government; governmental entity; property; environment; wildlife; or natural resources harmed, injured, or damaged by the violation or potential violation of any law described in paragraph (a)(3) of this section. This paragraph (e)(4)(i)(C) does not apply if, pursuant to the order or agreement, the amounts are disbursed to the general account of the government or governmental entity for general enforcement efforts or other discretionary purposes.

(ii) *Amounts to come into compliance with a law.*—An amount is paid or incurred to come into compliance with a law that the taxpayer has violated, or is alleged to have violated, by performing services; taking action, such as modifying equipment; providing property; or doing any combination thereof to come into compliance with that law.

(iii) *Amounts not included.*—Regardless of whether the order or agreement identifies them as such, restitution, remediation, and amounts paid to come into compliance with a law do not include any amount paid or incurred—

(A) As reimbursement to a government or governmental entity for investigation costs or litigation costs incurred in such government or governmental entity's investigation into, or litigation concerning, the violation or potential violation of any law; or

(B) At the taxpayer's election, in lieu of a fine or penalty.

(5) *Suit, agreement, or otherwise.*—A suit, agreement, or otherwise includes, but is not limited to, suits; settlement agreements; orders; non-prosecution agreements; deferred prosecution agreements; judicial proceedings; administrative adjudications; decisions issued by officials, committees, commissions, or boards of a government or governmental entity; and any legal actions or hearings which impose a liability on the taxpayer or pursuant to which the taxpayer assumes liability.

(f) *Examples.*—The application of this section is illustrated by the following examples.

(1) *Example 1.*—(i) *Facts.* Corp. A enters into an agreement with State Y's environmental enforcement agency (Agency) for violating state environmental laws. Pursuant to the agreement, Corp. A pays $40X to the Agency in civil penalties, $80X in restitution for the environmental harm that the taxpayer has caused, $50X for remediation of contaminated sites, and $60X to conduct comprehensive upgrades to Corp. A's operations to come into compliance with the state environmental laws.

(ii) *Analysis.* The identification requirement is satisfied for those amounts the agreement identifies as restitution, remediation, or to come into compliance with a law. If Corp. A meets the establishment requirement, as provided in paragraph (b)(3), paragraph (a) of this section will not disallow Corp. A's deduction for $80X in restitution and $50X for remediation. Under paragraph (a) of this section, Corp. A may not deduct the $40X in civil penalties. Paragraph (a) of this section will not disallow Corp. A's deduction for the $60X paid to come into compliance with the state environmental laws. See section 161, concerning items allowed as deductions, and section 261, concerning items for which no deduction is allowed, and the regulations related to sections 161 and 261.

(2) *Example 2.*—(i)*Facts.* Corp. A enters into an agreement with State T's securities agency (Agency) for violating a securities law by inducing B to make a $100X investment in Corp. C stock, which B lost when the Corp. C stock became worthless. As part of the agreement, Corp. A agrees to pay $100X to B as restitution for B's investment loss, incurred as a result of Corp. A's actions. The agreement specifically states that the $100X payment by Corp. A to B is restitution. The agreement also requires Corp. A to pay a $40X penalty for violating Agency law. Corp. A pays the $140X.

(ii) *Analysis.* Corp. A's $100X payment to B is identified in the agreement as restitution. If Corp. A establishes, as provided in paragraph (b)(3) of this section, that the amount paid was for that purpose, paragraph (a) of this section will not disallow Corp. A's deduction for the $100X payment. Under paragraph (a) of this section, Corp. A may not deduct its $40X payment to the Agency because it was paid for Corp. A's violation of Agency law.

(3) *Example 3.*—(i) *Facts.* Corp. B is under investigation by State X's environmental enforcement agency for a potential violation of State X's law governing emissions standards. Corp. B enters into an agreement with State X under which it agrees to upgrade the engines in a fleet of vehicles that Corp. B operates to come into compliance with State X's law. Although the agreement does not provide the specific amount Corp. B will incur to upgrade the engines to come into compliance with State X's law, it identifies that Corp. B must upgrade existing engines to lower certain emissions. Under the agreement, Corp. B also agrees to construct a nature center in a local park for the benefit of the community. Instead of paying $12X, to come into compliance with State X's law, Corp. B pays $15X to upgrade the engines to a standard higher than that which the law requires. Corp. B presents evidence to establish that it would cost $12X to upgrade the engines to come into compliance with State X's law.

(ii) *Analysis.* Because the agreement describes the specific action Corp. B must take to come into compliance with State X's law, and Corp. B provides evidence, as described in paragraph (b)(3)(ii) of this section, to establish that the agreement obligates it to incur costs to come into compliance with a law, paragraph (a) of this section will not disallow Corp. B's deduction for the $12X Corp. B incurs to come into compliance. Corp. B may also deduct the $3X if it is otherwise deductible under chapter 1 of the Code. However, Corp. B may not deduct the amounts paid to construct the nature center because no facts exist to establish that the amount was paid either to come into compliance with a law or as restitution or remediation.

(4) *Example 4.*—(i) *Facts.* Corp. D enters into an agreement with governmental entity, Trade Agency, for engaging in unfair trade practices in violation of Trade Agency laws. The agreement requires Corp. D to pay $80X to a Trade Agency fund, through disgorgement of net profits, to be used exclusively to pay restitution to the consumers harmed by Corp. D's violation of Trade Agency law. Corp. D pays $80X to Trade Agency fund and Trade Agency disburses all amounts in the restitution fund to the harmed consumers.

(ii) *Analysis.* The agreement identifies the $80X payment to the fund as restitution. Trade Agency uses the funds exclusively to provide restitution to the harmed consumers and does not use it for discretionary or general enforcement purposes. If Corp. D establishes, as provided in paragraph (b)(3) of this section, that the $80X constitutes restitution under paragraph (e)(4)(i)(B) of this section, paragraph (a) of this section does not apply.

(5) *Example 5.*—(i) *Facts.* B, a regulated banking institution, is subject to the supervision of, and annual examinations by governmental entity, R. In the ordinary course of its business, B is required to pay annual assessment fees to R, which fees are used to support R in supervising and examining banking institutions to ensure a safe and sound banking system. Following an annual examination conducted in the ordinary course of B's business, R issues a letter to B identifying concerns with B's internal compliance functions. B takes corrective action to address R's concerns by investing in its internal compliance functions. R does not conduct an investigation or inquiry into B's potential violation of any law.

(ii) *Analysis.* The payment of annual assessment fees by B to R in the ordinary course of business is not related to the violation of any law or the investigation or inquiry into the potential violation of any law. In addition, B's costs of taking the corrective action are not related to the violation of any law or the investigation or inquiry into the potential violation of any law as described in section 162(f)(1). Paragraph (a) of this section will not disallow the deduction of the annual assessment fees and the cost of the corrective actions.

(6) *Example 6.*—(i) *Facts.* B, a regulated banking institution, is subject to the supervision of, and annual examinations by governmental entity, R. Following an annual examination conducted in the ordinary course of B's business, R pursues an enforcement action against B for violation of banking laws. B and R enter a settlement agreement, pursuant to which B agrees to undertake certain improvements to come into compliance with banking laws and to pay R $20X for violation of banking laws. B pays the $20X.

(ii) *Analysis.* If the agreement meets the identification requirement of paragraph (b)(2) of this section and B meets the establishment requirement of paragraph (b)(3) of this section, paragraph (a) of this section will not disallow the deduction of the costs of the corrective actions to come into compliance with banking laws. However, B may not deduct the $20X paid to R because the amount was not paid to come into compliance with a law or as restitution or remediation.

(7) *Example 7.*—(i) *Facts.* Corp. C contracts with governmental entity, Q, to design and build a rail project within five years. Corp. C does not complete the project. Q sues Corp. C for breach of contract and damages of $10X. A jury finds Corp. C breached the contract and Corp. C pays $10X to Q.

(ii) *Analysis.* The suit arose out of a proprietary contract, wherein Q enforced its rights as a private party. Paragraph (a) of this section will not disallow Corp. C's deduction of the payment of $10X pursuant to this suit.

(8) *Example 8.*—(i) *Facts.* Corp. C contracts with governmental entity, Q, to design and build a rail project within five years. Site conditions cause construction delays and Corp. C asks Q to pay $50X in excess of the contracted amount to complete the project. After Q pays for the work, it learns that, at the time it entered the contract with Corp. C, Corp. C knew that certain conditions at the project site would make it challenging to complete the project within five years. Q sues Corp. C for withholding critical information during contract negotiations in violation of the False Claims Act (FCA). The court enters a judgment in favor of Q pursuant to which Corp. C will pay Q $50X in restitution and $150X in treble damages. Corp. C pays the $200X.

(ii) *Analysis.* The suit pertains to Corp. C's violation of the FCA. The order identifies the $50X Corp. C is required to pay as restitution, as described in paragraph (b)(2) of this section. If Corp. C establishes, as provided in paragraph (b)(3) of this section, that the amount paid was for restitution, paragraph (a) of this section will not disallow Corp. C's deduction for the $50X payment. Under paragraph (a) of this section, Corp. C may not deduct the $150X paid for the treble damages imposed for violation of the FCA because the order did not identify all or part of the payment as restitution.

(9) *Example 9.*—(i) *Facts.* Corp. T operates a truck fleet company incorporated in State A. State A requires that all vehicles registered in State A have a vehicle emissions test every two years. Corp. T's 40 trucks take the emissions test on March 1 for which it pays the $15 per vehicle. Under State A law, if a vehicle fails the emissions test, the vehicle owner has 30 days to certify to State A that the vehicle has been repaired and has passed the emissions test. State A imposes a $1X penalty per vehicle for failure to comply with this 30-day rule. Twenty trucks pass; twenty trucks fail. Corp. T does not submit the required certification to State A for the twenty trucks that failed the emissions test. State A imposes a $40X penalty against Corp. T. Corp. T pays the $40X.

(ii) *Analysis.* Emissions tests are conducted in the ordinary course of operating a truck fleet company and, therefore, paragraph (a) of this section does not apply to the $600 Corp. T pays for the emissions tests. However, Corp. T may not deduct the $40X penalty for failure to comply with State A requirements because the amount is required to be paid to a government in relation to the violation of a law.

(10) *Example 10.*—(i) *Facts.* Corp. G operates a chain of 20 grocery stores in County X. Under County X health and food safety code and regulations, Corp. G is subject to annual inspections for which Corp. G is required to pay an inspection fee of $40 per store. Pursuant to the annual inspection, the County X health inspector finds violations of County X's health and food safety code and regulations in three of Corp. G's 20 stores. County X bills Corp. G $800 for the annual inspection fees for the 20 stores and a $1,000 fine for each of the three stores, for a total fine of $3,000, for violations of the health and food safety code. Corp. G pays the fees and fines.

(ii) *Analysis.* Paragraph (a) of this section will not disallow Corp. G's deduction for the $800 inspection fees paid in the ordinary course of a regulated business. Under paragraph (a) of this section, Corp. G may not deduct the $3,000 fine for violation of the County X health code and food safety ordinances because it was paid to a government in relation to the violation of a law.

(11) *Example 11.*—(i) *Facts.* Corp. G operates a chain of grocery stores in County X. Under County X health and food safety code and regulations, Corp. G is subject to annual inspections. Pursuant to an annual inspection, the County X health inspector finds that the refrigeration system in one of Corp. G's stores does not keep food at the temperature required by the health and food safety code and regulations. The County X health inspector issues a warning letter instructing Corp. G to correct the violation and bring the refrigeration system into compliance with the law before a reinspection in 60 days or face the imposition of fines if it fails to comply. Corp. G pays $10,000 to bring its refrigeration system into compliance with the law.

(ii) *Analysis.* Provided the identification and establishment requirements of paragraphs (b)(2) and (b)(3), respectively, of this section are met, paragraph (a) of this section will not disallow Corp. G's deduction for the $10,000 it pays to bring its refrigeration system into compliance with the law.

(12) *Example 12.*—(i) *Facts.* Corp. G operates a chain of grocery stores in County X. Under County X health and food safety code and regulations, Corp. G is subject to annual inspections. Pursuant to an annual inspection, the County X health inspector finds that the refrigeration system in one of Corp. G's stores does not keep food at the temperature required by the health and food safety code and regulations. The County X health inspector issues a warning letter instructing Corp. G to correct the violation and bring the refrigeration system into compliance with the law before a reinspection in 60 days or face the imposition of fines if it fails to comply. The County X health inspector later reinspects the refrigeration system. Corp. G pays a reinspection fee of $80. During the reinspection, the health inspector finds that Corp. G did not bring its refrigeration system into compliance with the law. The health inspector issues a citation imposing a $250 fine on Corp. G. Corp. G pays the $250 fine.

(ii) *Analysis.* Paragraph (a) of this section will disallow Corp. G's deduction for the $80 inspection fee because it is paid in relation to the investigation or inquiry by County X into the potential violation of a law. Paragraph (a) of this section will also disallow Corp. G's deduction for the $250 fine paid for violation of the law.

(13) *Example 13.*—(i) *Facts.* Accounting Firm was convicted of embezzling $500X from Bank in violation of State X law. The court

issued an order requiring Accounting Firm to pay $100X in restitution to Bank. The court also issued an order of forfeiture and restitution for $400X, which was seized by the State X officials. Accounting Firm paid $100X to Bank. The $400X seized was deposited with Fund within the State X treasury and, at the discretion of the State X Attorney General, was used to support law enforcement programs.

(ii) *Analysis.* Although the order identified the amount forfeited as restitution, paragraph (a) of this section will disallow Accounting Firm's deduction for the $400X forfeited because, under paragraph (e)(4)(i)(B)(I) of this section, it does not constitute restitution. If Accounting Firm establishes, as provided in paragraph (b)(3) of this section, that the $100X constitutes restitution under paragraph (e)(4)(i), paragraph (a) of this section will not disallow Accounting Firm's deduction for the $100X paid, provided the $100X is otherwise deductible under chapter 1.

(g) *Applicability date.*—The rules of this section apply to taxable years beginning on or after January 19, 2021, except that such rules do not apply to amounts paid or incurred under any order or agreement pursuant to a suit, agreement, or otherwise, which became binding under applicable law before such date, determined without regard to whether all appeals have been exhausted or the time for filing appeals has expired. [Reg. § 1.162-21.]

☐ [*T.D. 7345, 2-19-75. Amended by T.D. 7366, 7-10-75 and T.D. 9946, 1-14-2021.*]

[Reg. § 1.162-22]

§ 1.162-22. **Treble damage payments under the antitrust laws.**— (a) *In general.*—In the case of a taxpayer who after December 31, 1969, either is convicted in a criminal action of a violation of the Federal antitrust laws or enters a plea of guilty or *nolo contendere* to an indictment or information charging such a violation, and whose conviction or plea does not occur in a new trial following an appeal of a conviction on or before such date, no deduction shall be allowed under section 162(a) for two-thirds of any amount paid or incurred after December 31, 1969, with respect to—

(1) Any judgment for damages entered against the taxpayer under section 4 of the Clayton Act (15 U.S.C. 15), as amended, on account of such violation or any related violation of the Federal antitrust laws, provided such related violation occurred prior to the date of the final judgment of such conviction, or

(2) Settlement of any action brought under such section 4 on account of such violation or related violation.

For purposes of this section, where a civil judgment has been entered or a settlement made with respect to a violation of the antitrust laws and a criminal proceeding is based upon the same violation, the criminal proceeding need not have been brought prior to the civil judgment or settlement. If, in his return for any taxable year, a taxpayer claims a deduction for an amount paid or incurred with respect to a judgment or settlement described in the first sentence of this paragraph and is subsequently convicted of a violation of the antitrust laws which makes a portion of such amount unallowable, then the taxpayer shall file an amended return for such taxable year on which the amount of the deduction is appropriately reduced. Attorney's fees, court costs, and other amounts paid or incurred in connection with a controversy under such section 4 which meet the requirements of section 162 are deductible under that section. For purposes of subparagraph (2) of this paragraph, the amount paid or incurred in settlement shall not include amounts attributable to the plaintiff's costs of suit and attorney's fees, to the extent that such costs or fees have actually been paid.

(b) *Conviction.*—For purposes of paragraph (a) of this section, a taxpayer is convicted of a violation of the antitrust laws if a judgment of conviction (whether or not a final judgment) with respect to such violation has been entered against him, provided a subsequent final judgment of acquittal has not been entered or criminal prosecution with respect to such violation terminated without a final judgment of conviction. During the pendency of an appeal or other action directly contesting a judgment of conviction, the taxpayer should file a protective claim for credit or refund to avoid being barred by the period of limitations on credit or refund under section 6511.

(c) *Related violation.*—For purposes of this section, a violation of the Federal antitrust laws is related to a subsequent violation if (1) with respect to the subsequent violation the United States obtains both a judgment in a criminal proceeding and an injunction against the taxpayer, and (2) the taxpayer's actions which constituted the prior violation would have contravened such injunction if such injunction were applicable at the time of the prior violation.

(d) *Settlement following a dismissal of an action or amendment of the complaint.*—For purposes of paragraph (a)(2) of this section, an amount may be considered as paid in settlement of an action even though the action is dismissed or otherwise disposed of prior to such

Itemized Deductions for Individuals and Corps.
See p. 20,601 for regulations not amended to reflect law changes
25,233

settlement or the complaint is amended to eliminate the claim with respect to the violation or related violation.

(e) *Antitrust laws.*—The term "antitrust laws" as used in section 162(g) and this section shall include the Federal acts enumerated in paragraph (1) of section 1 of the Clayton Act (15 U.S.C. 12), as amended.

(f) *Examples.*—The application of this section may be illustrated by the following examples:

Example (1). In 1970, the United States instituted a criminal prosecution against X Co., Y Co., A, the president of X Co., and B, the president of Y Co., under section 1 of the Sherman Anti-Trust Act, 15 U.S.C. 1. In the indictment, the defendants were charged with conspiring to fix and maintain prices of electrical transformers from 1965 to 1970. All defendants entered pleas of *nolo contendere* to these charges. These pleas were accepted and judgments of conviction entered. In a companion civil suit, the United States obtained an injunction prohibiting the defendants from conspiring to fix and maintain prices in the electrical transformer market. Thereafter, Z Co. sued X Co. and Y Co. for $300,000 in treble damages under section 4 of the Clayton Act. Z Co's complaint alleged that the criminal conspiracy between X Co. and Y Co. forced Z Co. to pay excessive prices for electrical transformers. X Co. and Y Co. each paid Z Co. $85,000 in full settlement of Z Co.'s action. Of each $85,000 paid, $10,000 was attributable to court costs and attorney's fees actually paid by Z Co. Under section 162(g), X Co. and Y Co. are each precluded from deducting as a trade or business expense more than $35,000 of the $85,000 paid to Z Co. in settlement.

$$(\quad \$10{,}000 + \frac{\$85{,}000 - \$10{,}000}{3} \quad)$$

Example (2). Assume the same facts as in example (1) except that Z Co.'s claim for treble damages was based on a conspiracy to fix and maintain prices in the sale of electrical transformers during 1963. Although the criminal prosecution of the defendants did not involve 1963 (a year barred by the applicable criminal statute of limitations when the prosecution was instituted), Z Co.'s pleadings alleged that the civil statute of limitations had been tolled by the defendants' fraudulent concealment of their conspiracy. Since the United States has obtained both a judgment in a criminal proceeding and an injunction against the defendants in connection with their activities from 1965 to 1970, and the alleged actions of the defendants in 1963 would have contravened such injunction if it were applicable in 1963, the alleged violation in 1963 is related to the violation from 1965 to 1970. Accordingly, the tax consequences to X Co. and Y Co. of the payments of $85,000 in settlement of Z Co.'s claim against X Co. and Y Co. are the same as in example (1).

Example (3). Assume the same facts as in example (1) except that Z Co.'s claim for treble damages was based on a conspiracy to fix and maintain prices with respect to electrical insulators for high-tension power poles. Since the civil action was not based on the same violation of the Federal antitrust laws as the criminal action, or on a related violation (a violation which would have contravened the injunction if it were applicable), X Co. and Y Co. are not precluded by section 162(g) from deducting as a trade or business expense the entire $85,000 paid by each in settlement of the civil action. [Reg. §1.162-22.]

☐ [T.D. 7217, 11-9-72.]

[Reg. §1.162-24]

§1.162-24. Travel expenses of state legislators.—(a) *In general.*—For purposes of section 162(a), in the case of any taxpayer who is a state legislator at any time during the taxable year and who makes an election under section 162(h) for the taxable year—

(1) The taxpayer's place of residence within the legislative district represented by the taxpayer is the taxpayer's home for that taxable year;

(2) The taxpayer is deemed to have expended for living expenses (in connection with the taxpayer's trade or business as a legislator) an amount determined by multiplying the number of legislative days of the taxpayer during the taxable year by the greater of—

(i) The amount generally allowable with respect to those days to employees of the state of which the taxpayer is a legislator for per diem while away from home, to the extent the amount does not exceed 110 percent of the amount described in paragraph (a)(2)(ii) of this section; or

(ii) The Federal per diem with respect to those days for the taxpayer's state capital; and

(3) The taxpayer is deemed to be away from home in the pursuit of a trade or business on each legislative day.

(b) *Legislative day.*—For purposes of section 162(h)(1) and this section, for any taxpayer who makes an election under section 162(h), a legislative day is any day on which the taxpayer is a state legislator and—

(1) The legislature is in session;

(2) The legislature is not in session for a period that is not longer than 4 consecutive days, without extension for Saturdays, Sundays, or holidays;

(3) The taxpayer's attendance at a meeting of a committee of the legislature is formally recorded; or

(4) The taxpayer's attendance at any session of the legislature that only a limited number of members are expected to attend (such as a *pro forma* session), on any day not described in paragraph (b)(1) or (b)(2) of this section, is formally recorded.

(c) *Fifty mile rule.*—Section 162(h) and this section do not apply to any taxpayer who is a state legislator and whose place of residence within the legislative district represented by the taxpayer is 50 or fewer miles from the capitol building of the state. For purposes of this paragraph (c), the distance between the taxpayer's place of residence within the legislative district represented by the taxpayer and the capitol building of the state is the shortest of the more commonly traveled routes between the two points.

(d) *Definitions and special rules.*—The following definitions apply for purposes of section 162(h) and this section.

(1) *State legislator.*—A taxpayer becomes a state legislator on the day the taxpayer is sworn into office and ceases to be a state legislator on the day following the day on which the taxpayer's term in office ends.

(2) *Living expenses.*—Living expenses include lodging, meals, and incidental expenses. *Incidental expenses* has the same meaning as in 41 CFR 300-3.1.

(3) *In session.*—(i) *In general.*—For purposes of this section, the legislature of which a taxpayer is a member is in session on any day if, at any time during that day, the members of the legislature are expected to attend and participate as an assembled body of the legislature.

(ii) *Examples.*—The following examples illustrate the rules of this paragraph (d)(3):

Example 1. B is a member of the legislature of State X. On Day 1, the State X legislature is convened and the members of the legislature are expected to attend and participate. On Day 1, the State X legislature is in session within the meaning of paragraph (d)(3)(i) of this section. B does not attend the session of the State X legislature on Day 1. However, Day 1 is a legislative day for B for purposes of section 162(h)(2)(A) and paragraph (b)(1) of this section.

Example 2. C, D, and E are members of the legislature of State X. On Day 2, the State X legislature is convened for a limited session in which not all members of the legislature are expected to attend and participate. Thus, on Day 2 the legislature is not in session within the meaning of paragraph (d)(3)(i) of this section, and Day 2 is not a legislative day under paragraph (b)(1) of this section. In addition, Day 2 is not a day described in paragraph (b)(2) of this section. C and D are the only members who are called to, and do, attend the limited session on Day 2, and their attendance at the session is formally recorded. E is not called and does not attend. Therefore, Day 2 is a legislative day as to C and D under section 162(h)(2)(B) and paragraph (b)(4) of this section. Day 2 is not a legislative day as to E.

(4) *Committee of the legislature.*—A committee of the legislature is any group that includes one or more legislators and that is charged with conducting business of the legislature. Committees of the legislature include, but are not limited to, committees to which the legislature refers bills for consideration, committees that the legislature has authorized to conduct inquiries into matters of public concern, and committees charged with the internal administration of the legislature. For purposes of this section, groups that are not considered committees of the legislature include, but are not limited to, groups that promote particular issues, raise campaign funds, or are caucuses of members of a political party.

(5) *Federal per diem.*—The Federal per diem for any city and day is the maximum amount allowable to employees of the executive branch of the Federal government for living expenses while away from home in pursuit of a trade or business in that city on that day. See 5 U.S.C. 5702 and the regulations under that section.

(e) *Election.*—(1) *Time for making election.*—A taxpayer's election under section 162(h) must be made for each taxable year for which the election is to be in effect and must be made no later than the due date (including extensions) of the taxpayer's Federal income tax return for the taxable year.

(2) *Manner of making election.*—A taxpayer makes an election under section 162(h) by attaching a statement to the taxpayer's income tax return for the taxable year for which the election is made. The statement must include—

   (i) The taxpayer's name, address, and taxpayer identification number;

   (ii) A statement that the taxpayer is making an election under section 162(h); and

   (iii) Information establishing that the taxpayer is a state legislator entitled to make the election, for example, a statement identifying the taxpayer's state and legislative district and representing that the taxpayer's place of residence in the legislative district is not 50 or fewer miles from the state capitol building.

(3) *Revocation of election.*—An election under section 162(h) may be revoked only with the consent of the Commissioner. An application for consent to revoke an election must be signed by the taxpayer and filed with the submission processing center with which the election was filed, and must include—

   (i) The taxpayer's name, address, and taxpayer identification number;

   (ii) A statement that the taxpayer is revoking an election under section 162(h) for a specified year; and

   (iii) A statement explaining why the taxpayer seeks to revoke the election.

(f) *Effect of election on otherwise deductible expenses for travel away from home.*—(1) *Legislative days.*—(i) *Living expenses.*—For any legislative day for which an election under section 162(h) and this section is in effect, the amount of an electing taxpayer's living expenses while away from home is the greater of the amount of the living expenses—

   (A) Specified in paragraph (a)(2) of this section in connection with the trade or business of being a legislator; or

   (B) Otherwise allowable under section 162(a)(2) in the pursuit of any trade or business of the taxpayer.

   (ii) *Other expenses.*—For any legislative day for which an election under section 162(h) and this section is in effect, the amount of an electing taxpayer's expenses (other than living expenses) for travel away from home is the sum of the substantiated expenses, such as expenses for travel fares, telephone calls, and local transportation, that are otherwise deductible under section 162(a)(2) in the pursuit of any trade or business of the taxpayer.

(2) *Non-legislative days.*—For any day that is not a legislative day, the amount of an electing taxpayer's expenses (including amounts for living expenses) for travel away from home is the sum of the substantiated expenses that are otherwise deductible under section 162(a)(2) in the pursuit of any trade or business of the taxpayer.

(g) *Cross references.*—See §1.62-1T(e)(4) for rules regarding allocation of unreimbursed expenses of state legislators and section 274(n) for limitations on the amount allowable as a deduction for expenses for or allocable to meals.

(h) *Effective/applicability date.*—This section applies to expenses paid or incurred, or deemed expended under section 162(h), in taxable years beginning after April 8, 2010. [Reg. §1.162-24.]

☐ [*T.D.* 9481, 4-7-2010.]

[Reg. §1.162-25]

§1.162-25. Deductions with respect to noncash fringe benefits.—(a) [Reserved]

(b) *Employee.*—If an employer provides the use of a vehicle (as defined in §1.61-21(e)(2)) to an employee as a noncash fringe benefit and includes the entire value of the benefit in the employee's gross income without taking into account any exclusion for a working condition fringe allowable under section 132 and the regulations thereunder, the employee may deduct that value multiplied by the percentage of the total use of the vehicle that is in connection with the employer's trade or business (business value). For taxable years beginning before January 1, 1990, the employee may deduct the business value from gross income in determining adjusted gross income. For taxable years beginning on or after January 1, 1990, the employee may deduct the business value only as a miscellaneous itemized deduction in determining taxable income, subject to the 2-percent floor provided in section 67. If the employer determines the value of the noncash fringe benefit under a special accounting rule that allows the employer to treat the value of benefits provided during the last two months of the calendar year or any shorter period as paid during the subsequent calendar year, then the employee must determine the deduction allowable under this paragraph (b)

without regard to any use of the benefit during those last two months or any shorter period. The employee may not use a cents-per-mile valuation method to determine the deduction allowable under this paragraph (b). [Reg. §1.162-25.]

☐ [*T.D.* 8451, 12-4-92.]

[Reg. §1.162-25T]

§1.162-25T. Deductions with respect to noncash fringe benefits (temporary).—(a) *Employer.*—If an employer includes the value of a noncash fringe benefit in an employee's gross income, the employer may not deduct this amount as compensation for services, but rather may deduct only the costs incurred by the employer in providing the benefit to the employee. The employer may be allowed a cost recovery deduction under section 168 or a deduction under section 179 for an expense not chargeable to capital account, or, if the noncash fringe benefit is property leased by the employer, a deduction for the ordinary and necessary business expense of leasing the property.

(b) [Reserved]

(c) *Examples.*—The following examples illustrate the provisions of this section.

(1) *Example (1).* On January 1, 1986, X Company owns and provides the use of an automobile with a fair market value of $20,000 to E, an employee, for the entire calendar year. Both X and E compute taxable income on the basis of the calendar year. Seventy percent of the use of the automobile by E is in connection with X's trade or business. If X uses the special rule provided in §1.61-21(d) for valuing the availability of the automobile and takes into account the amount excludable as a working condition fringe, X would include $1,680 ($5,600, the Annual Lease Value, less 70 percent of $5,600) in E's gross income for 1986. X may not deduct the amount included in E's income as compensation for services. X may, however, determine a cost recovery deduction under section 168, subject to the limitations under section 280F, for taxable year 1986.

(2) *Example (2).* The facts are the same as in *Example 1* of paragraph (c)(1) of this section, except that X includes $5,600 in E's gross income, the value of the noncash fringe benefit without taking into account the amount excludable as a working condition fringe. X may not deduct that amount as compensation for services, but may determine a cost recovery deduction under section 168, subject to the limitations under section 280F. For purposes of determining adjusted gross income, E may deduct $3,920 ($5,600 multiplied by the percent of business use). [Temporary Reg. §1.162-25T.]

☐ [*T.D.* 8004, 1-2-85. *Amended by T.D.* 8061, 11-1-85, *T.D.* 8063, 12-18-85, *T.D.* 8276, 12-7-89, *T.D.* 8451, 12-4-92 *and T.D.* 9849, 3-11-2019.]

[Reg. §1.162-27]

§1.162-27. Certain employee remuneration in excess of $1,000,000 not deductible for taxable years beginning on or after January 1, 1994, and for taxable years beginning prior to January 1, 2018.—(a) *Scope.*—This section provides rules for the application of the $1 million deduction limitation under section 162(m)(1) for taxable years beginning on or after January 1, 1994, and beginning prior to January 1, 2018, and, as provided in paragraph (j) of this section, for taxable years beginning after December 31, 2017. For rules concerning the applicability of section 162(m)(1) to taxable years beginning after December 31, 2017, see §1.162-33. Paragraph (b) of this section provides the general rule limiting deductions under section 162(m)(1). Paragraph (c) of this section provides definitions of generally applicable terms. Paragraph (d) of this section provides an exception from the deduction limitation for compensation payable on a commission basis. Paragraph (e) of this section provides an exception for qualified performance-based compensation. Paragraphs (f) and (g) of this section provide special rules for corporations that become publicly held corporations and payments that are subject to section 280G, respectively. Paragraph (h) of this section provides transition rules, including the rules for contracts that are grandfathered and not subject to section 162(m)(1). Paragraph (j) of this section contains the effective date provisions, which also specify when these rules apply to the deduction for compensation otherwise deductible in a taxable year beginning after December 31, 2017. For rules concerning the deductibility of compensation for services that are not covered by section 162(m)(1) and this section, see section 162(a)(1) and §1.162-7. This section is not determinative as to whether compensation meets the requirements of section 162(a)(1). For rules concerning the deduction limitation under section 162(m)(6) applicable to certain health insurance providers, see §1.162-31.

(b) *Limitation on deduction.*—Section 162(m) precludes a deduction under chapter 1 of the Internal Revenue Code by any publicly held corporation for compensation paid to any covered employee to the extent that the compensation for the taxable year exceeds $1,000,000.

(c) *Definitions.*—(1) *Publicly held corporation.*—(i) *General rule.*—A *publicly held corporation* means any corporation issuing any class of common equity securities required to be registered under section 12 of the Exchange Act. A corporation is not considered publicly held if the registration of its equity securities is voluntary. For purposes of this section, whether a corporation is publicly held is determined based solely on whether, as of the last day of its taxable year, the corporation is subject to the reporting obligations of section 12 of the Exchange Act.

(ii) *Affiliated groups.*—A publicly held corporation includes an affiliated group of corporations, as defined in section 1504 (determined without regard to section 1504(b)). For purposes of this section, however, an affiliated group of corporations does not include any subsidiary that is itself a publicly held corporation. Such a publicly held subsidiary, and its subsidiaries (if any), are separately subject to this section. If a covered employee is paid compensation in a taxable year by more than one member of an affiliated group, compensation paid by each member of the affiliated group is aggregated with compensation paid to the covered employee by all other members of the group. Any amount disallowed as a deduction by this section must be prorated among the payor corporations in proportion to the amount of compensation paid to the covered employee by each such corporation in the taxable year.

(2) *Covered employee.*—(i) *General rule.*—A *covered employee* means any individual who, on the last day of the taxable year, is—

(A) The chief executive officer of the corporation or is acting in such capacity; or

(B) Among the four highest compensated officers (other than the chief executive officer).

(ii) *Application of rules of the Securities and Exchange Commission.*—Whether an individual is the chief executive officer described in paragraph (c)(2)(i)(A) of this section or an officer described in paragraph (c)(2)(i)(B) of this section is determined pursuant to the executive compensation disclosure rules under the Exchange Act.

(3) *Compensation.*—(i) *In general.*—For purposes of the deduction limitation described in paragraph (b) of this section, *compensation* means the aggregate amount allowable as a deduction under chapter 1 of the Internal Revenue Code for the taxable year (determined without regard to section 162(m)) for remuneration for services performed by a covered employee, whether or not the services were performed during the taxable year.

(ii) *Exceptions.*—*Compensation* does not include—

(A) Remuneration covered in section 3121(a)(5)(A) through section 3121(a)(5)(D) (concerning remuneration that is not treated as *wages* for purposes of the Federal Insurance Contributions Act); and

(B) Remuneration consisting of any benefit provided to or on behalf of an employee if, at the time the benefit is provided, it is reasonable to believe that the employee will be able to exclude it from gross income. In addition, compensation does not include salary reduction contributions described in section 3121(v)(1).

(4) *Compensation Committee.*—The *compensation committee* means the committee of directors (including any subcommittee of directors) of the publicly held corporation that has the authority to establish and administer performance goals described in paragraph (e)(2) of this section, and to certify that performance goals are attained, as described in paragraph (e)(5) of this section. A committee of directors is not treated as failing to have the authority to establish performance goals merely because the goals are ratified by the board of directors of the publicly held corporation or, if applicable, any other committee of the board of directors. See paragraph (e)(3) of this section for rules concerning the composition of the compensation committee.

(5) *Exchange Act.*—The *Exchange Act* means the Securities Exchange Act of 1934.

(6) *Examples.*—This paragraph (c) may be illustrated by the following examples:

Example 1. Corporation X is a publicly held corporation with a July 1 to June 30 fiscal year. For Corporation X's taxable year ending on June 30, 1995, Corporation X pays compensation of $2,000,000 to A, an employee. However, A's compensation is not required to be reported to shareholders under the executive compensation disclosure rules of the Exchange Act because A is neither the chief executive officer nor one of the four highest compensated officers employed on the last day of the taxable year. A's compensation is not subject to the deduction limitation of paragraph (b) of this section.

Example 2. C, a covered employee, performs services and receives compensation from Corporations X, Y, and Z, members of an affiliated group of corporations. Corporation X, the parent corporation, is a publicly held corporation. The total compensation paid to C from all affiliated group members is $3,000,000 for the taxable year,

of which Corporation X pays $1,500,000; Corporation Y pays $900,000; and Corporation Z pays $600,000. Because the compensation paid by all affiliated group members is aggregated for purposes of section 162(m), $2,000,000 of the aggregate compensation paid is nondeductible. Corporations X, Y, and Z each are treated as paying a ratable portion of the nondeductible compensation. Thus, two thirds of each corporation's payment will be nondeductible. Corporation X has a nondeductible compensation expense of $1,000,000 ($1,500,000 x $2,000,000/$3,000,000). Corporation Y has a nondeductible compensation expense of $600,000 ($900,000 x $2,000,000/$3,000,000). Corporation Z has a nondeductible compensation expense of $400,000 ($600,000 x $2,000,000/$3,000,000).

Example 3. Corporation W, a calendar year taxpayer, has total assets equal to or exceeding $5 million and a class of equity security held of record by 500 or more persons on December 31, 1994. However, under the Exchange Act, Corporation W is not required to file a registration statement with respect to that security until April 30, 1995. Thus, Corporation W is not a publicly held corporation on December 31, 1994, but is a publicly held corporation on December 31, 1995.

Example 4. The facts are the same as in *Example 3*, except that on December 15, 1996, Corporation W files with the Securities and Exchange Commission to disclose that Corporation W is no longer required to be registered under section 12 of the Exchange Act and to terminate its registration of securities under that provision. Because Corporation W is no longer subject to Exchange Act reporting obligations as of December 31, 1996, Corporation W is not a publicly held corporation for taxable year 1996, even though the registration of Corporation W's securities does not terminate until 90 days after Corporation W files with the Securities and Exchange Commission.

(d) *Exception for compensation paid on a commission basis.*—The deduction limit in paragraph (b) of this section shall not apply to any compensation paid on a commission basis. For this purpose, compensation is paid on a commission basis if the facts and circumstances show that it is paid solely on account of income generated directly by the individual performance of the individual to whom the compensation is paid. Compensation does not fail to be attributable directly to the individual merely because support services, such as secretarial or research services, are utilized in generating the income. However, if compensation is paid on account of broader performance standards, such as income produced by a business unit of the corporation, the compensation does not qualify for the exception provided under this paragraph (d).

(e) *Exception for qualified performance-based compensation—*

(1) *In general.*—The deduction limit in paragraph (b) of this section does not apply to qualified performance-based compensation. Qualified performance-based compensation is compensation that meets all of the requirements of paragraphs (e)(2) through (e)(5) of this section.

(2) *Performance goal requirement.*—(i) *Preestablished goal.*—Qualified performance-based compensation must be paid solely on account of the attainment of one or more preestablished, objective performance goals. A performance goal is considered preestablished if it is established in writing by the compensation committee not later than 90 days after the commencement of the period of service to which the performance goal relates, provided that the outcome is substantially uncertain at the time the compensation committee actually establishes the goal. However, in no event will a performance goal be considered to be preestablished if it is established after 25 percent of the period of service (as scheduled in good faith at the time the goal is established) has elapsed. A performance goal is objective if a third party having knowledge of the relevant facts could determine whether the goal is met. Performance goals can be based on one or more business criteria that apply to the individual, a business unit, or the corporation as a whole. Such business criteria could include, for example, stock price, market share, sales, earnings per share, return on equity, or costs. A performance goal need not, however, be based upon an increase or positive result under a business criterion and could include, for example, maintaining the status quo or limiting economic losses (measured, in each case, by reference to a specific business criterion). A performance goal does not include the mere continued employment of the covered employee. Thus, a vesting provision based solely on continued employment would not constitute a performance goal. See paragraph (e)(2)(vi) of this section for rules on compensation that is based on an increase in the price of stock.

(ii) *Objective compensation formula.*—A preestablished performance goal must state, in terms of an objective formula or standard, the method for computing the amount of compensation payable to the employee if the goal is attained. A formula or standard is objective if a third party having knowledge of the relevant performance results could calculate the amount to be paid to the employee. In addition, a formula or standard must specify the individual employees or class of employees to which it applies.

(iii) *Discretion.*—(A) The terms of an objective formula or standard must preclude discretion to increase the amount of compensation payable that would otherwise be due upon attainment of the goal. A performance goal is not discretionary for purposes of this paragraph (e)(2)(iii) merely because the compensation committee reduces or eliminates the compensation or other economic benefit that was due upon attainment of the goal. However, the exercise of negative discretion with respect to one employee is not permitted to result in an increase in the amount payable to another employee. Thus, for example, in the case of a bonus pool, if the amount payable to each employee is stated in terms of a percentage of the pool, the sum of these individual percentages of the pool is not permitted to exceed 100 percent. If the terms of an objective formula or standard fail to preclude discretion to increase the amount of compensation merely because the amount of compensation to be paid upon attainment of the performance goal is based, in whole or in part, on a percentage of salary or base pay and the dollar amount of the salary or base pay is not fixed at the time the performance goal is established, then the objective formula or standard will not be considered discretionary for purposes of this paragraph (e)(2)(iii) if the maximum dollar amount to be paid is fixed at that time.

(B) If compensation is payable upon or after the attainment of a performance goal, and a change is made to accelerate the payment of compensation to an earlier date after the attainment of the goal, the change will be treated as an increase in the amount of compensation, unless the amount of compensation paid is discounted to reasonably reflect the time value of money. If compensation is payable upon or after the attainment of a performance goal, and a change is made to defer the payment of compensation to a later date, any amount paid in excess of the amount that was originally owed to the employee will not be treated as an increase in the amount of compensation if the additional amount is based either on a reasonable rate of interest or on one or more predetermined actual investments (whether or not assets associated with the amount originally owed are actually invested therein) such that the amount payable by the employer at the later date will be based on the actual rate of return of a specific investment (including any decrease as well as any increase in the value of an investment). If compensation is payable in the form of property, a change in the timing of the transfer of that property after the attainment of the goal will not be treated as an increase in the amount of compensation for purposes of this paragraph (e)(2)(iii). Thus, for example, if the terms of a stock grant provide for stock to be transferred after the attainment of a performance goal and the transfer of the stock also is subject to a vesting schedule, a change in the vesting schedule that either accelerates or defers the transfer of stock will not be treated as an increase in the amount of compensation payable under the performance goal.

(C) Compensation attributable to a stock option, stock appreciation right, or other stock-based compensation does not fail to satisfy the requirements of this paragraph (e)(2) to the extent that a change in the grant or award is made to reflect a change in corporate capitalization, such as a stock split or dividend, or a corporate transaction, such as any merger of a corporation into another corporation, any consolidation of two or more corporations into another corporation, any separation of a corporation (including a spinoff or other distribution of stock or property by a corporation), any reorganization of a corporation (whether or not such reorganization comes within the definition of such term in section 368), or any partial or complete liquidation by a corporation.

(iv) *Grant-by-grant determination.*—The determination of whether compensation satisfies the requirements of this paragraph (e)(2) generally shall be made on a grant-by-grant basis. Thus, for example, whether compensation attributable to a stock option grant satisfies the requirements of this paragraph (e)(2) generally is determined on the basis of the particular grant made and without regard to the terms of any other option grant, or other grant of compensation, to the same or another employee. As a further example, except as provided in paragraph (e)(2)(vi), whether a grant of restricted stock or other stock-based compensation satisfies the requirements of this paragraph (e)(2) is determined without regard to whether dividends, dividend equivalents, or other similar distributions with respect to stock, on such stock-based compensation are payable prior to the attainment of the performance goal. Dividends, dividend equivalents, or other similar distributions with respect to stock that are treated as separate grants under this paragraph (e)(2)(iv) are not performance-based compensation unless they separately satisfy the requirements of this paragraph (e)(2).

(v) *Compensation contingent upon attainment of performance goal.*—Compensation does not satisfy the requirements of this paragraph (e)(2) if the facts and circumstances indicate that the employee would receive all or part of the compensation regardless of whether the performance goal is attained. Thus, if the payment of compensation under a grant or award is only nominally or partially contingent on attaining a performance goal, none of the compensation payable under the grant or award will be considered performance-based. For example, if an employee is entitled to a bonus under either of two arrangements, where payment under a nonperformance-based arrangement is contingent upon the failure to attain the performance goals under an otherwise performance-based arrangement, then neither arrangement provides for compensation that satisfies the requirements of this paragraph (e)(2). Compensation does not fail to be qualified performance-based compensation merely because the plan allows the compensation to be payable upon death, disability, or change of ownership or control, although compensation actually paid on account of those events prior to the attainment of the performance goal would not satisfy the requirements of this paragraph (e)(2). As an exception to the general rule set forth in the first sentence of paragraph (e)(2)(iv) of this section, the facts-and-circumstances determination referred to in the first sentence of this paragraph (e)(2)(v) is made taking into account all plans, arrangements, and agreements that provide for compensation to the employee.

(vi) *Application of requirements to stock options and stock appreciation rights.*—(A) *In general.*—Compensation attributable to a stock option or a stock appreciation right is deemed to satisfy the requirements of this paragraph (e)(2) if the grant or award is made by the compensation committee; the plan under which the option or right is granted states the maximum number of shares with respect to which options or rights may be granted during a specified period to any individual employee; and, under the terms of the option or right, the amount of compensation the employee may receive is based solely on an increase in the value of the stock after the date of the grant or award. A plan may satisfy the requirement to provide a maximum number of shares with respect to which stock options and stock appreciation rights may be granted to any individual employee during a specified period if the plan specifies an aggregate maximum number of shares with respect to which stock options, stock appreciation rights, restricted stock, restricted stock units and other equity-based awards that may be granted to any individual employee during a specified period under a plan approved by shareholders in accordance with § 1.162-27(e)(4). If the amount of compensation the employee may receive under the grant or award is not based solely on an increase in the value of the stock after the date of grant or award (for example, in the case of restricted stock, or an option that is granted with an exercise price that is less than the fair market value of the stock as of the date of grant), none of the compensation attributable to the grant or award is qualified performance-based compensation under this paragraph (e)(2)(vi)(A). Whether a stock option grant is based solely on an increase in the value of the stock after the date of grant is determined without regard to any dividend equivalent that may be payable, provided that payment of the dividend equivalent is not made contingent on the exercise of the option. The rule that the compensation attributable to a stock option or stock appreciation right must be based solely on an increase in the value of the stock after the date of grant or award does not apply if the grant or award is made on account of, or if the vesting or exercisability of the grant or award is contingent on, the attainment of a performance goal that satisfies the requirements of this paragraph (e)(2).

(B) *Cancellation and repricing.*—Compensation attributable to a stock option or stock appreciation right does not satisfy the requirements of this paragraph (e)(2) to the extent that the number of options granted exceeds the maximum number of shares for which options may be granted to the employee as specified in the plan. If an option is canceled, the canceled option continues to be counted against the maximum number of shares for which options may be granted to the employee under the plan. If, after grant, the exercise price of an option is reduced, the transaction is treated as a cancellation of the option and a grant of a new option. In such case, both the option that is deemed to be canceled and the option that is deemed to be granted reduce the maximum number of shares for which options may be granted to the employee under the plan. This paragraph (e)(2)(vi)(B) also applies in the case of a stock appreciation right where, after the award is made, the base amount on which stock appreciation is calculated is reduced to reflect a reduction in the fair market value of stock.

(vii) *Examples.*—This paragraph (e)(2) may be illustrated by the following examples:

Example 1. No later than 90 days after the start of a fiscal year, but while the outcome is substantially uncertain, Corporation S establishes a bonus plan under which A, the chief executive officer, will receive a cash bonus of $500,000, if year-end corporate sales are increased by at least 5 percent. The compensation committee retains the right, if the performance goal is met, to reduce the bonus payment to A if, in its judgment, other subjective factors warrant a reduction. The bonus will meet the requirements of this paragraph (e)(2).

Example 2. The facts are the same as in *Example 1*, except that the bonus is based on a percentage of Corporation S's total sales for the fiscal year. Because Corporation S is virtually certain to have some sales for the fiscal year, the outcome of the performance goal is not substantially uncertain, and therefore the bonus does not meet the requirements of this paragraph (e)(2).

Example 3. The facts are the same as in *Example 1*, except that the bonus is based on a percentage of Corporation S's total profits for the fiscal year. Although some sales are virtually certain for virtually all public companies, it is substantially uncertain whether a company will have profits for a specified future period even if the company has a history of profitability. Therefore, the bonus will meet the requirements of this paragraph (e)(2).

Example 4. B is the general counsel of Corporation R, which is engaged in patent litigation with Corporation S. Representatives of Corporation S have informally indicated to Corporation R a willingness to settle the litigation for $50,000,000. Subsequently, the compensation committee of Corporation R agrees to pay B a bonus if B obtains a formal settlement for at least $50,000,000. The bonus to B does not meet the requirement of this paragraph (e)(2) because the performance goal was not established at a time when the outcome was substantially uncertain.

Example 5. Corporation S, a public utility, adopts a bonus plan for selected salaried employees that will pay a bonus at the end of a 3-year period of $750,000 each if, at the end of the 3 years, the price of S stock has increased by 10 percent. The plan also provides that the 10-percent goal will automatically adjust upward or downward by the percentage change in a published utilities index. Thus, for example, if the published utilities index shows a net increase of 5 percent over a 3-year period, then the salaried employees would receive a bonus only if Corporation S stock has increased by 15 percent. Conversely, if the published utilities index shows a net decrease of 5 percent over a 3-year period, then the salaried employees would receive a bonus if Corporation S stock has increased by 5 percent. Because these automatic adjustments in the performance goal are preestablished, the bonus meets the requirement of this paragraph (e)(2), notwithstanding the potential changes in the performance goal.

Example 6. The facts are the same as in *Example 5*, except that the bonus plan provides that, at the end of the 3-year period, a bonus of $750,000 will be paid to each salaried employee if either the price of Corporation S stock has increased by 10 percent or the earnings per share on Corporation S stock have increased by 5 percent. If both the earnings-per-share goal and the stock-price goal are preestablished, the compensation committee's discretion to choose to pay a bonus under either of the two goals does not cause any bonus paid under the plan to fail to meet the requirement of this paragraph (e)(2) because each goal independently meets the requirements of this paragraph (e)(2). The choice to pay under either of the two goals is tantamount to the discretion to choose not to pay under one of the goals, as provided in paragraph (e)(2)(iii) of this section.

Example 7. Corporation U establishes a bonus plan under which a specified class of employees will participate in a bonus pool if certain preestablished performance goals are attained. The amount of the bonus pool is determined under an objective formula. Under the terms of the bonus plan, the compensation committee retains the discretion to determine the fraction of the bonus pool that each employee may receive. The bonus plan does not satisfy the requirements of this paragraph (e)(2). Although the aggregate amount of the bonus plan is determined under an objective formula, a third party could not determine the amount that any individual could receive under the plan.

Example 8. The facts are the same as in *Example 7*, except that the bonus plan provides that a specified share of the bonus pool is payable to each employee, and the total of these shares does not exceed 100% of the pool. The bonus plan satisfies the requirements of this paragraph (e)(2). In addition, the bonus plan will satisfy the requirements of this paragraph (e)(2) even if the compensation committee retains the discretion to reduce the compensation payable to any individual employee, provided that a reduction in the amount of one employee's bonus does not result in an increase in the amount of any other employee's bonus.

Example 9. Corporation V establishes a stock option plan for salaried employees. The terms of the stock option plan specify that no individual salaried employee shall receive options for more than 100,000 shares over any 3-year period. The compensation committee grants options for 50,000 shares to each of several salaried employees. The exercise price of each option is equal to or greater than the fair market value of a share of V stock at the time of each grant. Compensation attributable to the exercise of the options satisfies the requirements of paragraph (e)(2)(vi) of this section. If, however, the terms of the options provide that the exercise price is less than fair market value of a share of V stock at the date of grant, no compensation attributable to the exercise of those options satisfies the requirements of this paragraph (e)(2) unless issuance or exercise of the options was contingent upon the attainment of a preestablished performance goal that satisfies this paragraph (e)(2). If, however, the terms of the plan also provide that Corporation V could grant options to purchase no more than 900,000 shares over any 3-year period, but did not provide a limitation on the number of shares that any individual employee could purchase, then no compensation attributable to the exercise of those options satisfies the requirements of paragraph (e)(2)(vi) of this section.

Example 10. The facts are the same as in *Example 9*, except that, within the same 3-year grant period the fair market value of Corporation V stock is significantly less than the exercise price of the options. The compensation committee reprices those options to that lower current fair market value of Corporation V stock. The repricing of the options for 50,000 shares held by each salaried employee is treated as the grant of new options for an additional 50,000 shares to each employee. Thus, each of the salaried employees is treated as having received grants for 100,000 shares. Consequently, if any additional options are granted to those employees during the 3-year period, compensation attributable to the exercise of those additional options would not satisfy the requirements of this paragraph (e)(2). The results would be the same if the compensation committee canceled the outstanding options and issued new options to the same employees that were exercisable at the fair market value of Corporation V stock on the date of reissue.

Example 11. Corporation W maintains a plan under which each participating employee may receive incentive stock options, nonqualified stock options, stock appreciation rights, or grants of restricted Corporation W stock. The plan specifies that each participating employee may receive options, stock appreciation rights, restricted stock, or any combination of each, for no more than 20,000 shares over the life of the plan. The plan provides that stock options may be granted with an exercise price of less than, equal to, or greater than fair market value on the date of grant. Options granted with an exercise price equal to, or greater than, fair market value on the date of grant do not fail to meet the requirements of this paragraph (e)(2) merely because the compensation committee has the discretion to determine the types of awards (i.e., options, rights, or restricted stock) to be granted to each employee or the discretion to issue options or make other compensation awards under the plan that would not meet the requirements of this paragraph (e)(2). Whether an option granted under the plan satisfies the requirements of this paragraph (e)(2) is determined on the basis of the specific terms of the option and without regard to other options or awards under the plan.

Example 12. Corporation X maintains a plan under which stock appreciation rights may be awarded to key employees. The plan permits the compensation committee to make awards under which the amount of compensation payable to the employee is equal to the increase in the stock price plus a percentage "gross up" intended to offset the tax liability of the employee. In addition, the plan permits the compensation committee to make awards under which the amount of compensation payable to the employee is equal to the increase in the stock price, based on the highest price, which is defined as the highest price paid for Corporation X stock (or offered in a tender offer or other arms-length offer) during the 90 days preceding exercise. Compensation attributable to awards under the plan satisfies the requirements of paragraph (e)(2)(vi) of this section, provided that the terms of the plan specify the maximum number of shares for which awards may be made.

Example 13. Corporation W adopts a plan under which a bonus will be paid to the CEO only if there is a 10% increase in earnings per share during the performance period. The plan provides that earnings per share will be calculated without regard to any change in accounting standards that may be required by the Financial Accounting Standards Board after the goal is established. After the goal is established, such a change in accounting standards occurs. Corporation W's reported earnings, for purposes of determining earnings per share under the plan, are adjusted pursuant to this plan provision to factor out this change in standards. This adjustment will not be considered an exercise of impermissible discretion because it is made pursuant to the plan provision.

Example 14. Corporation X adopts a performance-based incentive pay plan with a four-year performance period. Bonuses under the plan are scheduled to be paid in the first year after the end of the performance period (year 5). However, in the second year of the performance period, the compensation committee determines that any bonuses payable in year 5 will instead, for bona fide business reasons, be paid in year 10. The compensation committee also determines that any compensation that would have been payable in year 5 will be adjusted to reflect the delay in payment. The adjustment will be based on the greater of the future rate of return of a specified mutual fund that invests in blue chip stocks or of a specified venture capital investment over the five-year deferral period. Each of these investments, considered by itself, is a predetermined actual investment because it is based on the future rate of return of an actual investment. However, the adjustment in this case is not based on predetermined actual investments within the meaning of paragraph (e)(2)(iii)(B) of this section because the amount payable by Corporation X in year 10 will be based on the greater of the two investment returns and, thus, will not be based on the actual rate of return on either specific investment.

Example 15. The facts are the same as in *Example 14,* except that the increase will be based on Moody's Average Corporate Bond Yield over the five-year deferral period. Because this index reflects a reasonable rate of interest, the increase in the compensation payable that is based on the index's rate of return is not considered an impermissible increase in the amount of compensation payable under the formula.

Example 16. The facts are the same as in *Example 14,* except that the increase will be based on the rate of return for the Standard & Poor's 500 Index. This index does not measure interest rates and thus does not represent a reasonable rate of interest. In addition, this index does not represent an actual investment. Therefore, any additional compensation payable based on the rate of return of this index will result in an impermissible increase in the amount payable under the formula. If, in contrast, the increase were based on the rate of return of an existing mutual fund that is invested in a manner that seeks to approximate the Standard & Poor's 500 Index, the increase would be based on a predetermined actual investment within the meaning of paragraph (e)(2)(iii)(B) of this section and thus would not result in an impermissible increase in the amount payable under the formula.

(3) *Outside directors.*—(i) *General rule.*—The performance goal under which compensation is paid must be established by a compensation committee comprised solely of two or more outside directors. A director is an outside director if the director—

(A) Is not a current employee of the publicly held corporation;

(B) Is not a former employee of the publicly held corporation who receives compensation for prior services (other than benefits under a tax-qualified retirement plan) during the taxable year;

(C) Has not been an officer of the publicly held corporation; and

(D) Does not receive remuneration from the publicly held corporation, either directly or indirectly, in any capacity other than as a director. For this purpose, remuneration includes any payment in exchange for goods or services.

(ii) *Remuneration received.*—For purposes of this paragraph (e)(3), remuneration is received, directly or indirectly, by a director in each of the following circumstances:

(A) If remuneration is paid, directly or indirectly, to the director personally or to an entity in which the director has a beneficial ownership interest of greater than 50 percent. For this purpose, remuneration is considered paid when actually paid (and throughout the remainder of that taxable year of the corporation) and, if earlier, throughout the period when a contract or agreement to pay remuneration is outstanding.

(B) If remuneration, other than de minimis remuneration, was paid by the publicly held corporation in its preceding taxable year to an entity in which the director has a beneficial ownership interest of at least 5 percent but not more than 50 percent. For this purpose, remuneration is considered paid when actually paid or, if earlier, when the publicly held corporation becomes liable to pay it.

(C) If remuneration, other than de minimis remuneration, was paid by the publicly held corporation in its preceding taxable year to an entity by which the director is employed or self-employed other than as a director. For this purpose, remuneration is considered paid when actually paid or, if earlier, when the publicly held corporation becomes liable to pay it.

(iii) *De minimis remuneration.*—(A) *In general.*—For purposes of paragraphs (e)(3)(ii)(B) and (C) of this section, remuneration that was paid by the publicly held corporation in its preceding taxable year to an entity is de minimis if payments to the entity did not exceed 5 percent of the gross revenue of the entity for its taxable year ending with or within that preceding taxable year of the publicly held corporation.

(B) *Remuneration for personal services and substantial owners.*—Notwithstanding paragraph (e)(3)(iii)(A) of this section, remuneration in excess of $60,000 is not de minimis if the remuneration is paid to an entity described in paragraph (e)(3)(ii)(B) of this section, or is paid for personal services to an entity described in paragraph (e)(3)(ii)(C) of this section.

(iv) *Remuneration for personal services.*—For purposes of paragraph (e)(3)(iii)(B) of this section, remuneration from a publicly held corporation is for personal services if—

(A) The remuneration is paid to an entity for personal or professional services, consisting of legal, accounting, investment banking, and management consulting services (and other similar services that may be specified by the Commissioner in revenue rulings, notices, or other guidance published in the Internal Revenue Bulletin), performed for the publicly held corporation, and the remuneration is not for services that are incidental to the purchase of goods or to the purchase of services that are not personal services; and

(B) The director performs significant services (whether or not as an employee) for the corporation, division, or similar organization (within the entity) that actually provides the services described in paragraph (e)(3)(iv)(A) of this section to the publicly held corporation, or more than 50 percent of the entity's gross revenues (for the entity's preceding taxable year) are derived from that corporation, subsidiary, or similar organization.

(v) *Entity defined.*—For purposes of this paragraph (e)(3), entity means an organization that is a sole proprietorship, trust, estate, partnership, or corporation. The term also includes an affiliated group of corporations as defined in section 1504 (determined without regard to section 1504(b)) and a group of organizations that would be an affiliated group but for the fact that one or more of the organizations are not incorporated. However, the aggregation rules referred to in the preceding sentence do not apply for purposes of determining whether a director has a beneficial ownership interest of at least 5 percent or greater than 50 percent.

(vi) *Employees and former officers.*—Whether a director is an employee or a former officer is determined on the basis of the facts at the time that the individual is serving as a director on the compensation committee. Thus, a director is not precluded from being an outside director solely because the director is a former officer of a corporation that previously was an affiliated corporation of the publicly held corporation. For example, a director of a parent corporation of an affiliated group is not precluded from being an outside director solely because that director is a former officer of an affiliated subsidiary that was spun off or liquidated. However, an outside director would no longer be an outside director if a corporation in which the director was previously an officer became an affiliated corporation of the publicly held corporation.

(vii) *Officer.*—Solely for purposes of this paragraph (e)(3), *officer* means an administrative executive who is or was in regular and continued service. The term implies continuity of service and excludes those employed for a special and single transaction. An individual who merely has (or had) the title of officer but not the authority of an officer is not considered an officer. The determination of whether an individual is or was an officer is based on all the of facts and circumstances in the particular case, including without limitation the source of the individual's authority, the term for which the individual is elected or appointed, and the nature and extent of the individual's duties.

(viii) *Members of affiliated groups.*—For purposes of this paragraph (e)(3), the outside directors of the publicly held member of an affiliated group are treated as the outside directors of all members of the affiliated group.

(ix) *Examples.*—This paragraph (e)(3) may be illustrated by the following examples:

Example 1. Corporations X and Y are members of an affiliated group of corporations as defined in section 1504, until July 1, 1994, when Y is sold to another group. Prior to the sale, A served as an officer of Corporation Y. After July 1, 1994, A is not treated as a former officer of Corporation X by reason of having been an officer of Y.

Example 2. Corporation Z, a calendar-year taxpayer, uses the services of a law firm by which B is employed, but in which B has a less-than-5-percent ownership interest. The law firm reports income on a July 1 to June 30 basis. Corporation Z appoints B to serve on its compensation committee for calendar year 1998 after determining that, in calendar year 1997, it did not become liable to the law firm for remuneration exceeding the lesser of $60,000 or five percent of the law firm's gross revenue (calculated for the year ending June 30, 1997). On October 1, 1998, Corporation Z becomes liable to pay remuneration of $50,000 to the law firm on June 30, 1999. For the year ending June 30, 1998, the law firm's gross revenue was less than $1 million. Thus, in calendar year 1999, B is not an outside director. However, B may satisfy the requirements for an outside director in calendar year 2000, if, in calendar year 1999, Corporation Z does not become liable to the law firm for additional remuneration. This is because the remuneration actually paid on June 30, 1999 was considered paid on October 1, 1998 under paragraph (e)(3)(ii)(C) of this section.

Example 3. Corporation Z, a publicly held corporation, purchases goods from Corporation A. D, an executive and less-than-5-percent owner of Corporation A, sits on the board of directors of Corporation Z and on its compensation committee. For 1997, Corporation Z obtains representations to the effect that D is not eligible for any commission for D's sales to Corporation Z and that, for purposes of determining D's compensation for 1997, Corporation A's sales to Corporation Z are not otherwise treated differently than sales to other customers of Corporation A (including its affiliates, if any) or are irrelevant. In addition, Corporation Z has no reason to believe that these representations are inaccurate or that it is otherwise paying remuneration indirectly to D personally. Thus, in 1997, no remuneration is considered paid by Corporation Z indirectly to D personally under paragraph (e)(3)(ii)(A) of this section.

Example 4. (i) Corporation W, a publicly held corporation, purchases goods from Corporation T. C, an executive and less-than-5-percent owner of Corporation T, sits on the board of directors of Corporation W and on its compensation committee. Corporation T develops a new product and agrees on January 1, 1998 to pay C a bonus of $500,000 if Corporation W contracts to purchase the product. Even if Corporation W purchases the new product, sales to Corporation W will represent less than 5 percent of Corporation T's gross revenues. In 1999, Corporation W contracts to purchase the new product and, in 2000, C receives the $500,000 bonus from Corporation T. In 1998, 1999, and 2000, Corporation W does not obtain any representations relating to indirect remuneration to C personally (such as the representations described in *Example 3*).

(ii) Thus, in 1998, 1999, and 2000, remuneration is considered paid by Corporation W indirectly to C personally under paragraph (e)(3)(ii)(A) of this section. Accordingly, in 1998, 1999, and 2000, C is not an outside director of Corporation W. The result would have been the same if Corporation W had obtained appropriate representations but nevertheless had reason to believe that it was paying remuneration indirectly to C personally.

Example 5. Corporation R, a publicly held corporation, purchases utility service from Corporation Q, a public utility. The chief executive officer, and less-than-5-percent owner, of Corporation Q is a director of Corporation R. Corporation R pays Corporation Q more than $60,000 per year for the utility service, but less than 5 percent of Corporation Q's gross revenues. Because utility services are not personal services, the fees paid are not subject to the $60,000 *de minimis* rule for remuneration for personal services within the meaning of paragraph (e)(3)(iii)(B) of this section. Thus, the chief executive officer qualifies as an outside director of Corporation R, unless disqualified on some other basis.

Example 6. Corporation A, a publicly held corporation, purchases management consulting services from Division S of Conglomerate P. The chief financial officer of Division S is a director of Corporation A. Corporation A pays more than $60,000 per year for the management consulting services, but less than 5 percent of Conglomerate P's gross revenues. Because management consulting services are personal services within the meaning of paragraph (e)(3)(iv)(A) of this section, and the chief financial officer performs significant services for Division S, the fees paid are subject to the $60,000 *de minimis* rule as remuneration for personal services. Thus, the chief financial officer does not qualify as an outside director of Corporation A.

Example 7. The facts are the same as in *Example 6*, except that the chief executive officer, and less-than-5-percent owner, of the parent company of Conglomerate P is a director of Corporation A and does not perform significant services for Division S. If the gross revenues of Division S do not constitute more than 50 percent of the gross revenues of Conglomerate P for P's preceding taxable year, the chief executive officer will qualify as an outside director of Corporation A, unless disqualified on some other basis.

(4) *Shareholder approval requirement.*—(i) *General rule.*—The material terms of the performance goal under which the compensation is to be paid must be disclosed to and subsequently approved by the shareholders of the publicly held corporation before the compensation is paid. The requirements of this paragraph (e)(4) are not satisfied if the compensation would be paid regardless of whether the material terms are approved by shareholders. The material terms include the employees eligible to receive compensation; a description of the business criteria on which the performance goal is based; and either the maximum amount of compensation that could be paid to any employee or the formula used to calculate the amount of compensation to be paid to the employee if the performance goal is attained (except that, in the case of a formula based, in whole or in part, on a percentage of salary or base pay, the maximum dollar amount of compensation that could be paid to the employee must be disclosed).

(ii) *Eligible employees.*—Disclosure of the employees eligible to receive compensation need not be so specific as to identify the particular individuals by name. A general description of the class of eligible employees by title or class is sufficient, such as the chief executive officer and vice presidents, or all salaried employees, all executive officers, or all key employees.

(iii) *Description of business criteria.*—(A) *In general.*—Disclosure of the business criteria on which the performance goal is based need not include the specific targets that must be satisfied under the performance goal. For example, if a bonus plan provides that a bonus will be paid if earnings per share increase by 10 percent, the 10-percent figure is a target that need not be disclosed to shareholders. However, in that case, disclosure must be made that the bonus plan is based on an earnings-per-share business criterion. In the case of a plan under which employees may be granted stock options or stock appreciation rights, no specific description of the business criteria is required if the grants or awards are based on a stock price that is no less than current fair market value.

(B) *Disclosure of confidential information.*—The requirements of this paragraph (e)(4) may be satisfied even though information that otherwise would be a material term of a performance goal is not disclosed to shareholders, provided that the compensation committee determines that the information is confidential commercial or business information, the disclosure of which would have an adverse effect on the publicly held corporation. Whether disclosure would adversely affect the corporation is determined on the basis of the facts and circumstances. If the compensation committee makes such a determination, the disclosure to shareholders must state the compensation committee's belief that the information is confidential commercial or business information, the disclosure of which would adversely affect the company. In addition, the ability not to disclose confidential information does not eliminate the requirement that disclosure be made of the maximum amount of compensation that is payable to an individual under a performance goal. Confidential information does not include the identity of an executive or the class of executives to which a performance goal applies or the amount of compensation that is payable if the goal is satisfied.

(iv) *Description of compensation.*—Disclosure as to the compensation payable under a performance goal must be specific enough so that shareholders can determine the maximum amount of compensation that could be paid to any individual employee during a specified period. If the terms of the performance goal do not provide for a maximum dollar amount, the disclosure must include the formula under which the compensation would be calculated. Thus, if compensation attributable to the exercise of stock options is equal to the difference between the exercise price and the current value of the stock, then disclosure of the maximum number of shares for which grants may be made to any individual employee during a specified period and the exercise price of those options (for example, fair market value on date of grant) would satisfy the requirements of this paragraph (e)(4)(iv). In that case, shareholders could calculate the maximum amount of compensation that would be attributable to the exercise of options on the basis of their assumptions as to the future stock price.

(v) *Disclosure requirements of the Securities and Exchange Commission.*—To the extent not otherwise specifically provided in this paragraph (e)(4), whether the material terms of a performance goal are adequately disclosed to shareholders is determined under the same standards as apply under the Exchange Act.

(vi) *Frequency of disclosure.*—Once the material terms of a performance goal are disclosed to and approved by shareholders, no additional disclosure or approval is required unless the compensation committee changes the material terms of the performance goal. If, however, the compensation committee has authority to change the targets under a performance goal after shareholder approval of the goal, material terms of the performance goal must be disclosed to and reapproved by shareholders no later than the first shareholder meeting that occurs in the fifth year following the year in which shareholders previously approved the performance goal.

(vii) *Shareholder vote.*—For purposes of this paragraph (e)(4), the material terms of a performance goal are approved by shareholders if, in a separate vote, a majority of the votes cast on the issue (including abstentions to the extent abstentions are counted as voting under applicable state law) are cast in favor of approval.

(viii) *Members of affiliated group.*—For purposes of this paragraph (e)(4), the shareholders of the publicly held member of the affiliated group are treated as the shareholders of all members of the affiliated group.

(ix) *Examples.*—This paragraph (e)(4) may be illustrated by the following examples:

Example 1. Corporation X adopts a plan that will pay a specified class of its executives an annual cash bonus based on the overall increase in corporate sales during the year. Under the terms of the plan, the cash bonus of each executive equals $100,000 multiplied by the number of percentage points by which sales increase in the current year when compared to the prior year. Corporation X discloses to its shareholders prior to the vote both the class of executives eligible to receive awards and the annual formula of $100,000 multiplied by the percentage increase in sales. This disclosure meets the requirements of this paragraph (e)(4). Because the compensation committee does not have the authority to establish a different target under the plan, Corporation X need not redisclose to its shareholders and obtain their reapproval of the material terms of the plan until those material terms are changed.

Example 2. The facts are the same as in *Example 1* except that Corporation X discloses only that bonuses will be paid on the basis of the annual increase in sales. This disclosure does not meet the requirements of this paragraph (e)(4) because it does not include the formula for calculating the compensation or a maximum amount of compensation to be paid if the performance goal is satisfied.

Example 3. Corporation Y adopts an incentive compensation plan in 1995 that will pay a specified class of its executives a bonus every 3 years based on the following 3 factors: increases in earnings per share, reduction in costs for specified divisions, and increases in sales by specified divisions. The bonus is payable in cash or in Corporation Y stock, at the option of the executive. Under the terms of the plan, prior to the beginning of each 3-year period, the compensation committee determines the specific targets under each of the three factors (i.e., the amount of the increase in earnings per share, the reduction in costs, and the amount of sales) that must be met in order for the executives to receive a bonus. Under the terms of the plan, the compensation committee retains the discretion to determine whether a bonus will be paid under any one of the goals. The terms of the plan also specify that no executive may receive a bonus in excess of $1,500,000 for any 3-year period. To satisfy the requirements of this paragraph (e)(4), Corporation Y obtains shareholder approval of the plan at its 1995 annual shareholder meeting. In the proxy statement issued to shareholders, Corporation Y need not disclose to shareholders the specific targets that are set by the compensation committee. However, Corporation Y must disclose that bonuses are paid on the basis of earnings per share, reductions in costs, and increases in sales of specified divisions. Corporation Y also must disclose the maximum amount of compensation that any executive may receive under the plan is $1,500,000 per 3-year period. Unless changes in the material terms of the plan are made earlier, Corporation Y need not disclose the material terms of the plan to the shareholders and obtain their reapproval until the first shareholders' meeting held in 2000.

Example 4. The same facts as in *Example 3*, except that prior to the beginning of the second 3-year period, the compensation committee determines that different targets will be set under the plan for that period with regard to all three of the performance criteria (i.e., earnings per share, reductions in costs, and increases in sales). In addition, the compensation committee raises the maximum dollar amount that can be paid under the plan for a 3-year period to $2,000,000. The increase in the maximum dollar amount of compensation under the plan is a changed material term. Thus, to satisfy the requirements of this paragraph (e)(4), Corporation Y must disclose to and obtain approval by the shareholders of the plan as amended.

Example 5. In 1998, Corporation Z establishes a plan under which a specified group of executives will receive a cash bonus not to exceed $750,000 each if a new product that has been in development is completed and ready for sale to customers by January 1, 2000. Although the completion of the new product is a material term of the performance goal under this paragraph (e)(4), the compensation committee determines that the disclosure to shareholders of the performance goal would adversely affect Corporation Z because its competitors would be made aware of the existence and timing of its new product. In this case, the requirements of this paragraph (e)(4) are satisfied if all other material terms, including the maximum amount of compensation, are disclosed and the disclosure affirmatively states that the terms of the performance goal are not being disclosed because the compensation committee has determined that those terms include confidential information, the disclosure of which would adversely affect Corporation Z.

(5) *Compensation committee certification.*—The compensation committee must certify in writing prior to payment of the compensation that the performance goals and any other material terms were in fact satisfied. For this purpose, *approved minutes of the compensation committee meeting in which the certification is made are treated as a written certification.* Certification by the compensation committee is not required for compensation that is attributable solely to the increase in the value of the stock of the publicly held corporation.

(f) *Companies that become publicly held, spinoffs, and similar transactions.*—(1) *In general.*—In the case of a corporation that was not a publicly held corporation and then becomes a publicly held corporation, the deduction limit of paragraph (b) of this section does not apply to any remuneration paid pursuant to a compensation plan or agreement that existed during the period in which the corporation was not publicly held. However, in the case of such a corporation that becomes publicly held in connection with an initial public offering, this relief applies only to the extent that the prospectus accompanying the initial public offering disclosed information concerning those plans or agreements that satisfied all applicable securities laws then in effect. In accordance with paragraph (c)(1)(ii) of this section, a corporation that is a member of an affiliated group that includes a publicly held corporation is considered publicly held and, therefore, cannot rely on this paragraph (f)(1).

(2) *Reliance period.*—Paragraph (f)(1) of this section may be relied upon until the earliest of—

(i) The expiration of the plan or agreement;

(ii) The material modification of the plan or agreement, within the meaning of paragraph (h)(1)(iii) of this section;

(iii) The issuance of all employer stock and other compensation that has been allocated under the plan; or

(iv) The first meeting of shareholders at which directors are to be elected that occurs after the close of the third calendar year following the calendar year in which the initial public offering occurs or, in the case of a privately held corporation that becomes publicly held without an initial public offering, the first calendar year following the calendar year in which the corporation becomes publicly held.

(3) *Stock-based compensation.*—Paragraph (f)(1) of this section will apply to any compensation received pursuant to the exercise of a stock option or stock appreciation right, or the substantial vesting of restricted property, granted under a plan or agreement described in paragraph (f)(1) of this section if the grant occurs on or before the earliest of the events specified in paragraph (f)(2) of this section. This paragraph does not apply to any form of stock-based compensation other than the forms listed in the immediately preceding sentence. Thus, for example, compensation payable under a restricted stock unit arrangement or a phantom stock arrangement must be paid, rather than merely granted, on or before the occurrence of the earliest of the events specified in paragraph (f)(2) of this section in order for paragraph (f)(1) of this section to apply.

(4) *Subsidiaries that become separate publicly held corporations.*—(i) *In general.*—If a subsidiary that is a member of the affiliated group described in paragraph (c)(1)(ii) of this section becomes a separate publicly held corporation (whether by spinoff or otherwise), any remuneration paid to covered employees of the new publicly held corporation will satisfy the exception for performance-based compensation described in paragraph (e) of this section if the conditions in either paragraph (f)(4)(ii) or (f)(4)(iii) of this section are satisfied.

(ii) *Prior establishment and approval.*—Remuneration satisfies the requirements of this paragraph (f)(4)(ii) if the remuneration satisfies the requirements for performance-based compensation set forth in paragraphs (e)(2), (e)(3), and (e)(4) of this section (by application of paragraphs (e)(3)(viii) and (e)(4)(viii) of this section) before the corporation becomes a separate publicly held corporation, and the certification required by paragraph (e)(5) of this section is made by the compensation committee of the new publicly held corporation (but if the performance goals are attained before the corporation becomes a separate publicly held corporation, the certification may be made by the compensation committee referred to in paragraph (e)(3)(viii) of this section before it becomes a separate publicly held corporation). Thus, this paragraph (f)(4)(ii) requires that the outside directors and shareholders (within the meaning of paragraphs (e)(3)(viii) and (e)(4)(viii) of this section) of the corporation before it becomes a separate publicly held corporation establish and approve, respectively, the performance-based compensation for the covered employees of the new publicly held corporation in accordance with paragraphs (e)(3) and (e)(4) of this section.

(iii) *Transition period.*—Remuneration satisfies the requirements of this paragraph (f)(4)(iii) if the remuneration satisfies all of the requirements of paragraphs (e)(2), (e)(3), and (e)(5) of this section. The outside directors (within the meaning of paragraph (e)(3)(viii) of this section) of the corporation before it becomes a separate publicly held corporation, or the outside directors of the new publicly held corporation, may establish and administer the performance goals for the covered employees of the new publicly held corporation for purposes of satisfying the requirements of paragraphs (e)(2) and (e)(3) of this section. The certification required by paragraph (e)(5) of this section must be made by the compensation committee of the new publicly held corporation. However, a taxpayer may rely on this paragraph (f)(4)(iii) to satisfy the requirements of paragraph (e) of this section only for compensation paid, or stock options, stock appreciation rights, or restricted property granted, prior to the first regularly scheduled meeting of the shareholders of the new publicly held corporation that occurs more than 12 months after the date the corporation becomes a separate publicly held corporation. Compensation paid, or stock options, stock appreciation rights, or restricted property granted, on or after the date of that meeting of shareholders must satisfy all requirements of paragraph (e) of this section, including the shareholder approval requirement of paragraph (e)(4) of this section, in order to satisfy the requirements for performance-based compensation.

(5) *Example.*—The following example illustrates the application of paragraph (f)(4)(ii) of this section:

Example. Corporation P, which is publicly held, decides to spin off Corporation S, a wholly owned subsidiary of Corporation P. After the spinoff, Corporation S will be a separate publicly held corporation. Before the spinoff, the compensation committee of Corporation P, pursuant to paragraph (e)(3)(viii) of this section, establishes a bonus plan for the executives of Corporation S that provides for bonuses payable after the spinoff and that satisfies the requirements of paragraph (e)(2) of this section. If, pursuant to paragraph (e)(4)(viii) of this section, the shareholders of Corporation P approve the plan prior to the spinoff, that approval will satisfy the requirements of paragraph (e)(4) of this section with respect to compensation paid pursuant to the bonus plan after the spinoff. However, the compensation committee of Corporation S will be required to certify that the goals are satisfied prior to the payment of the bonuses in order for the bonuses to be considered performance-based compensation.

(g) *Coordination with disallowed excess parachute payments.*—The $1,000,000 limitation in paragraph (b) of this section is reduced (but not below zero) by the amount (if any) that would have been included in the compensation of the covered employee for the taxable year but for being disallowed by reason of section 280G. For example, assume that during a taxable year a corporation pays $1,500,000 to a covered employee and no portion satisfies the exception in paragraph (d) of this section for commissions or paragraph (e) of this section for qualified performance-based compensation. Of the $1,500,000, $600,000 is an excess parachute payment, as defined in section 280G(b)(1) and is disallowed by reason of that section. Because the excess parachute payment reduces the limitation of paragraph (b) of this section, the corporation can deduct $400,000, and $500,000 of the otherwise deductible amount is nondeductible by reason of section 162(m).

(h) *Transition rules.*—(1) *Compensation payable under a written binding contract which was in effect on February 17, 1993.*—(i) *General rule.*—The deduction limit of paragraph (b) of this section does not apply to any compensation payable under a written binding contract that was in effect on February 17, 1993. The preceding sentence does not apply unless, under applicable state law, the corporation is obligated to pay the compensation if the employee performs services. However, the deduction limit of paragraph (b) of this section does apply to a contract that is renewed after February 17, 1993. A written binding contract that is terminable or cancelable by the corporation after February 17, 1993, without the employee's consent is treated as a new contract as of the date that any such termination or cancellation, if made, would be effective. Thus, for example, if the terms of a contract provide that it will be automatically renewed as of a certain date unless either the corporation or the employee gives notice of termination of the contract at least 30 days before that date, the contract is treated as a new contract as of the date that termination would be effective if that notice were given. Similarly, for example, if the terms of a contract provide that the contract will be terminated or canceled as of a certain date unless either the corporation or the employee elects to renew within 30 days of that date, the contract is treated as renewed by the corporation as of that date. Alternatively, if the corporation will remain legally obligated by the terms of a contract beyond a certain date at the sole discretion of the employee, the contract will not be treated as a new contract as of that date if the employee exercises the discretion to keep the corporation bound to the contract. A contract is not treated as terminable or cancelable if it can be terminated or canceled only by terminating the employment relationship of the employee.

(ii) *Compensation payable under a plan or arrangement.*—If a compensation plan or arrangement meets the requirements of paragraph (h)(1)(i) of this section, the compensation paid to an employee pursuant to the plan or arrangement will not be subject to the deduction limit of paragraph (b) of this section even though the employee was not eligible to participate in the plan as of February 17, 1993. However, the preceding sentence does not apply unless the employee was employed on February 17, 1993, by the corporation

that maintained the plan or arrangement, or the employee had the right to participate in the plan or arrangement under a written binding contract as of that date.

(iii) *Material modifications.*—(A) Paragraph (h)(1)(i) of this section will not apply to any written binding contract that is materially modified. A material modification occurs when the contract is amended to increase the amount of compensation payable to the employee. If a binding written contract is materially modified, it is treated as a new contract entered into as of the date of the material modification. Thus, amounts received by an employee under the contract prior to a material modification are not affected, but amounts received subsequent to the material modification are not treated as paid under a binding, written contract described in paragraph (h)(1)(i) of this section.

(B) A modification of the contract that accelerates the payment of compensation will be treated as a material modification unless the amount of compensation paid is discounted to reasonably reflect the time value of money. If the contract is modified to defer the payment of compensation, any compensation paid in excess of the amount that was originally payable to the employee under the contract will not be treated as a material modification if the additional amount is based on either a reasonable rate of interest or one or more predetermined actual investments (whether or not assets associated with the amount originally owed are actually invested therein) such that the amount payable by the employer at the later date will be based on the actual rate of return of the specific investment (including any decrease as well as any increase in the value of the investment).

(C) The adoption of a supplemental contract or agreement that provides for increased compensation, or the payment of additional compensation, is a material modification of a binding, written contract where the facts and circumstances show that the additional compensation is paid on the basis of substantially the same elements or conditions as the compensation that is otherwise paid under the written binding contract. However, a material modification of a written binding contract does not include a supplemental payment that is equal to or less than a reasonable cost-of-living increase over the payment made in the preceding year under that written binding contract. In addition, a supplemental payment of compensation that satisfies the requirements of qualified performance-based compensation in paragraph (e) of this section will not be treated as a material modification.

(iv) *Examples.*—The following examples illustrate the exception of this paragraph (h)(1):

Example 1. Corporation X executed a 3-year compensation arrangement with C on February 15, 1993, that constitutes a written binding contract under applicable state law. The terms of the arrangement provide for automatic extension after the 3-year term for additional 1-year periods, unless the corporation exercises its option to terminate the arrangement within 30 days of the end of the 3-year term or, thereafter, within 30 days before each anniversary date. Termination of the compensation arrangement does not require the termination of C's employment relationship with Corporation X. Unless terminated, the arrangement is treated as renewed on February 15, 1996, and the deduction limit of paragraph (b) of this section applies to payments under the arrangement after that date.

Example 2. Corporation Y executed a 5-year employment agreement with B on January 1, 1992, providing for a salary of $900,000 per year. Assume that this agreement constitutes a written binding contract under applicable state law. In 1992 and 1993, B receives the salary of $900,000 per year. In 1994, Corporation Y increases B's salary with a payment of $20,000. The $20,000 supplemental payment does not constitute a material modification of the written binding contract because the $20,000 payment is less than or equal to a reasonable cost-of-living increase from 1993. However, the $20,000 supplemental payment is subject to the limitation in paragraph (b) of this section. On January 1, 1995, Corporation Y increases B's salary to $1,200,000. The $280,000 supplemental payment is a material modification of the written binding contract because the additional compensation is paid on the basis of substantially the same elements or conditions as the compensation that is otherwise paid under the written binding contract and it is greater than a reasonable, annual cost-of-living increase. Because the written binding contract is materially modified as of January 1, 1995, all compensation paid to B in 1995 and thereafter is subject to the deduction limitation of section 162(m).

Example 3. Assume the same facts as in *Example 2*, except that instead of an increase in salary, B receives a restricted stock grant subject to B's continued employment for the balance of the contract. The restricted stock grant is not a material modification of the binding written contract because any additional compensation paid to B under the grant is not paid on the basis of substantially the same elements and conditions as B's salary because it is based both on the stock price and B's continued service. However, compensation attributable to the restricted stock grant is subject to the deduction limitation of section 162(m).

(2) *Special transition rule for outside directors.*—A director who is a disinterested director is treated as satisfying the requirements of an outside director under paragraph (e)(3) of this section until the first meeting of shareholders at which directors are to be elected that occurs on or after January 1, 1996. For purposes of this paragraph (h)(2) and paragraph (h)(3) of this section, a director is a disinterested director if the director is disinterested within the meaning of Rule 16b-3(c)(2)(i), 17 CFR 240.16b-3(c)(2)(i), under the Exchange Act (including the provisions of Rule 16b-3(d)(3), as in effect on April 30, 1991).

(3) *Special transition rule for previously-approved plans.*—(i) *In general.*—Any compensation paid under a plan or agreement approved by shareholders before December 20, 1993, is treated as satisfying the requirements of paragraphs (e)(3) and (e)(4) of this section, provided that the directors administering the plan or agreement are disinterested directors and the plan was approved by shareholders in a manner consistent with Rule 16b-3(b), 17 CFR 240.16b-3(b), under the Exchange Act or Rule 16b-3(a), 17 CFR 240.16b-3(a) (as contained in 17 CFR part 240 revised April 1, 1990). In addition, for purposes of satisfying the requirements of paragraph (e)(2)(vi) of this section, a plan or agreement is treated as stating a maximum number of shares with respect to which an option or right may be granted to any employee if the plan or agreement that was approved by the shareholders provided for an aggregate limit, consistent with Rule 16b-3(b), 17 CFR 250.16b-3(b), on the shares of employer stock with respect to which awards may be made under the plan or agreement.

(ii) *Reliance period.*—The transition rule provided in this paragraph (h)(3) shall continue and may be relied upon until the earliest of—

(A) The expiration or material modification of the plan or agreement;

(B) The issuance of all employer stock and other compensation that has been allocated under the plan; or

(C) The first meeting of shareholders at which directors are to be elected that occurs after December 31, 1996.

(iii) *Stock-based compensation.*—This paragraph (h)(3) will apply to any compensation received pursuant to the exercise of a stock option or stock appreciation right, or the substantial vesting of restricted property, granted under a plan or agreement described in paragraph (h)(3)(i) of this section if the grant occurs on or before the earliest of the events specified in paragraph (h)(3)(ii) of this section.

(iv) *Example.*—The following example illustrates the application of this paragraph (h)(3):

Example. Corporation Z adopted a stock option plan in 1991. Pursuant to Rule 16b-3 under the Exchange Act, the stock option plan has been administered by disinterested directors and was approved by Corporation Z shareholders. Under the terms of the plan, shareholder approval is not required again until 2001. In addition, the terms of the stock option plan include an aggregate limit on the number of shares available under the plan. Option grants under the Corporation Z plan are made with an exercise price equal to or greater than the fair market value of Corporation Z stock. Compensation attributable to the exercise of options that are granted under the plan before the earliest of the dates specified in paragraph (h)(3)(ii) of this section will be treated as satisfying the requirements of paragraph (e) of this section for qualified performance-based compensation, regardless of when the options are exercised.

(i) (*Reserved*)

(j) *Effective date.*—(1) *In general.*—Section 162(m) and this section apply to the deduction for compensation that is otherwise deductible by the corporation in taxable years beginning on or after January 1, 1994, and beginning prior to January 1, 2018. Section 162(m) and this section also apply to compensation that is a grandfathered amount (as defined in §1.162-33(g)) at the time it is paid to the covered employee or otherwise deductible. For examples of the application of the rules of this section to grandfathered amounts paid during or otherwise deductible for taxable years beginning after December 31, 2017, see §1.162-33(g).

(2) *Delayed effective date for certain provisions.*—(i) *Date on which remuneration is considered paid.*—Notwithstanding paragraph (j)(1) of this section, the rules in the second sentence of each of paragraphs (e)(3)(ii)(A), (e)(3)(ii)(B), and (e)(3)(ii)(C) of this section for determining the date or dates on which remuneration is considered paid to a director are effective for taxable years beginning on or after January 1, 1995. Prior to those taxable years, taxpayers must follow the rules in paragraphs (e)(3)(ii)(A), (e)(3)(ii)(B), and (e)(3)(ii)(C) of this section or another reasonable, good faith interpretation of section 162(m)

with respect to the date or dates on which remuneration is considered paid to a director.

(ii) *Separate treatment of publicly held subsidiaries.*—Notwithstanding paragraph (j)(1) of this section, the rule in paragraph (c)(1)(ii) of this section that treats publicly held subsidiaries as separately subject to section 162(m) is effective as of the first regularly scheduled meeting of the shareholders of the publicly held subsidiary that occurs more than 12 months after December 2, 1994. The rule for stock-based compensation set forth in paragraph (f)(3) of this section will apply for this purpose, except that the grant must occur before the shareholder meeting specified in this paragraph (j)(2)(ii). Taxpayers may choose to rely on the rule referred to in the first sentence of this paragraph (j)(2)(ii) for the period prior to the effective date of the rule.

(iii) *Subsidiaries that become separate publicly held corporations.*—Notwithstanding paragraph (j)(1) of this section, if a subsidiary of a publicly held corporation becomes a separate publicly held corporation as described in paragraph (f)(4)(i) of this section, then, for the duration of the reliance period described in paragraph (f)(2) of this section, the rules of paragraph (f)(1) of this section are treated as applying (and the rules of paragraph (f)(4) of this section do not apply) to remuneration paid to covered employees of that new publicly held corporation pursuant to a plan or agreement that existed prior to December 2, 1994, provided that the treatment of that remuneration as performance-based is in accordance with a reasonable, good faith interpretation of section 162(m). However, if remuneration is paid to covered employees of that new publicly held corporation pursuant to a plan or agreement that existed prior to December 2, 1994, but that remuneration is not performance-based under a reasonable, good faith interpretation of section 162(m), the rules of paragraph (f)(1) of this section will be treated as applying only until the first regularly scheduled meeting of shareholders that occurs more than 12 months after December 2, 1994. The rules of paragraph (f)(4) of this section will apply as of that first regularly scheduled meeting. The rule for stock-based compensation set forth in paragraph (f)(3) of this section will apply for purposes of this paragraph (j)(2)(iii), except that the grant must occur before the shareholder meeting specified in the preceding sentence if the remuneration is not performance-based under a reasonable, good faith interpretation of section 162(m). Taxpayers may choose to rely on the rules of paragraph (f)(4) of this section for the period prior to the applicable effective date referred to in the first or second sentence of this paragraph (j)(2)(iii).

(iv) *Bonus Pools.*—Notwithstanding paragraph (j)(1) of this section, the rules in paragraph (e)(2)(iii)(A) that limit the sum of individual percentages of a bonus pool to 100 percent will not apply to remuneration paid before January 1, 2001, based on performance in any performance period that began prior to December 20, 1995.

(v) *Compensation based on a percentage of salary or base pay.*—Notwithstanding paragraph (j)(1) of this section, the requirement in paragraph (e)(4)(i) of this section that, in the case of certain formulas based on a percentage of salary or base pay, a corporation disclose to shareholders the maximum dollar amount of compensation that could be paid to the employee, will apply only to plans approved by shareholders after April 30, 1995.

(vi) The modifications to paragraphs (e)(2)(vi)(A), (e)(2)(vii) *Example 9*, and (e)(4)(iv) of this section concerning the maximum number of shares with respect to which a stock option or stock appreciation right that may be granted and the amount of compensation that may be paid to any individual employee apply to compensation attributable to stock options and stock appreciation rights that are granted on or after June 24, 2011. The last two sentences of §1.162-27(f)(3) apply to remuneration that is otherwise deductible resulting from a stock option, stock appreciation right, restricted stock (or other property), restricted stock unit, or any other form of equity-based remuneration that is granted on or after April 1, 2015. [Reg. §1.162-27.]

☐ [*T.D.* 8650, 12-19-95 *and T.D.* 9716, 3-30-15. *Amended by T.D.* 9932, 12-28-2020.]

[Reg. §1.162-28]

§1.162-28. Allocation of costs to lobbying activities.—(a) *Introduction.*—(1) *In general.*—Section 162(e)(1) denies a deduction for certain amounts paid or incurred in connection with activities described in section 162(e)(1)(A) and (D) (*lobbying activities*). To determine the nondeductible amount, a taxpayer must allocate costs to lobbying activities. This section describes costs that must be allocated to lobbying activities and prescribes rules permitting a taxpayer to use a reasonable method to allocate those costs. This section does not apply to taxpayers subject to section 162(e)(5)(A). In addition, this section does not apply for purposes of sections 4911 and 4945 and the regulations thereunder.

(2) *Recordkeeping.*—For recordkeeping requirements, see section 6001 and the regulations thereunder.

(b) *Reasonable method of allocating costs.*—(1) *In general.*—A taxpayer must use a reasonable method to allocate the costs described in paragraph (c) of this section to lobbying activities. A method is not reasonable unless it is applied consistently and is consistent with the special rules in paragraph (g) of this section. Except as provided in paragraph (b)(2) of this section, reasonable methods of allocating costs to lobbying activities include (but are not limited to)—

(i) The ratio method described in paragraph (d) of this section;

(ii) The gross-up method described in paragraph (e) of this section; and

(iii) A method that applies the principles of section 263A and the regulations thereunder (see paragraph (f) of this section).

(2) *Taxpayers not permitted to use certain methods.*—A taxpayer (other than one subject to section 6033(e)) that does not pay or incur reasonable labor costs for persons engaged in lobbying activities may not use the gross-up method. For example, a partnership or sole proprietorship in which the lobbying activities are performed by the owners who do not receive a salary or guaranteed payment for

$$\frac{\text{Lobbying labor hours}}{\text{Total labor hours}} \times \text{Total costs of operations.}$$

(2) *Lobbying labor hours.*—Lobbying labor hours are the hours that a taxpayer's personnel spend on lobbying activities during the taxable year. A taxpayer may use any reasonable method to determine the number of labor hours spent on lobbying activities and may use the the de minimis rule of paragraph (g)(1) of this section. A taxpayer may treat as zero the lobbying labor hours of personnel engaged in secretarial, clerical, support, and other administrative activities (as opposed to activities involving significant judgment with respect to lobbying activities). Thus, for example, the hours spent on lobbying activities by para-professionals and analysts may not be treated as zero.

(3) *Total labor hours.*—Total labor hours means the total number of hours that a taxpayer's personnel spend on a taxpayer's trade or business during the taxable year. A taxpayer may make reasonable assumptions concerning total hours spent by personnel on the taxpayer's trade or business. For example, it may be reasonable, based on all the facts and circumstances, to assume that all full-time personnel spend 1,800 hours per year on a taxpayer's trade or business. If, under paragraph (d)(2) of this section, a taxpayer treats as zero the lobbying labor hours of personnel engaged in secretarial, clerical, support, and other administrative activities, the taxpayer must also treat as zero the total labor hours of all personnel engaged in those activities.

services does not pay or incur reasonable labor costs for persons engaged in those activities and may not use the gross-up method.

(c) *Costs allocable to lobbying activities.*—(1) *In general.*—Costs properly allocable to lobbying activities include labor costs and general and administrative costs.

(2) *Labor costs.*—For each taxable year, labor costs include costs attributable to full-time, part-time, and contract employees. Labor costs include all elements of compensation, such as basic compensation, overtime pay, vacation pay, holiday pay, sick leave pay, payroll taxes, pension costs, employee benefits, and payments to a supplemental unemployment benefit plan.

(3) *General and administrative costs.*—For each taxable year, general and administrative costs include depreciation, rent, utilities, insurance, maintenance costs, security costs, and other administrative department costs (for example, payroll, personnel, and accounting).

(d) *Ratio method.*—(1) *In general.*—Under the ratio method described in this paragraph (d), a taxpayer allocates to lobbying activities the sum of its third-party costs (as defined in paragraph (d)(5) of this section) allocable to lobbying activities and the costs determined by using the following formula:

(4) *Total costs of operations.*—A taxpayer's total costs of operations means the total costs of the taxpayer's trade or business for a taxable year, excluding third-party costs (as defined in paragraph (d)(5) of this section).

(5) *Third-party costs.*—Third-party costs are amounts paid or incurred in whole or in part for lobbying activities conducted by third parties (such as amounts paid to taxpayers subject to section 162(e)(5)(A) or dues or other similar amounts that are not deductible in whole or in part under section 162(e)(3)) and amounts paid or incurred for travel (including meals and lodging while away from home) and entertainment relating in whole or in part to lobbying activities.

(6) *Example.*—The provisions of this paragraph (d) are illustrated by the following example.

Example. (i) In 1996, three full-time employees, A, B, and C, of Taxpayer W engage in both lobbying activities and nonlobbying activities. A spends 300 hours, B spends 1,700 hours, and C spends 1,000 hours on lobbying activities for W, for a total of 3,000 hours spent on lobbying activities for W. W reasonably assumes that each of its three employees spends 2,000 hours a year on W's business.

(ii) W's total costs of operations are $300,000. W has no third-party costs.

(iii) Under the ratio method, X allocates $150,000 to its lobbying activities for 1996, as follows:

$\dfrac{\text{Lobbying labor hours}}{\text{Total labor hours}}$	$\times$	Total costs of operations	$+$	Allocable third-party costs	$=$	Costs allocable to lobbying activities
$\dfrac{[300 + 1{,}700 + 1{,}000}{6{,}000}$	$\times$	$\$300{,}000]$	$+$	$[0]$	$=$	$\$150{,}000.$

(e) *Gross-up method.*—(1) *In general.*—Under the gross-up method described in this paragraph (e)(1), the taxpayer allocates to lobbying activities the sum of its third-party costs (as defined in paragraph (d)(5) of this section) allocable to lobbying activities and 175 percent of its basic lobbying labor costs (as defined in paragraph (e)(3) of this section) of all personnel.

(2) *Alternative gross-up method.*—Under the alternative gross-up method described in this paragraph (e)(2), the taxpayer allocates to lobbying activities the sum of its third-party costs (as defined in paragraph (d)(5) of this section) allocable to lobbying activities and 225 percent of its basic lobbying labor costs (as defined in paragraph (e)(3)), excluding the costs of personnel who engage in secretarial, clerical, support, and other administrative activities (as opposed to activities involving significant judgment with respect to lobbying activities).

(3) *Basic lobbying labor costs.*—For purposes of this paragraph (e), basic lobbying labor costs are the basic costs of lobbying labor hours (as defined in paragraph (d)(2) of this section) determined for the

appropriate personnel. For purposes of this paragraph (e), basic costs of lobbying labor hours are wages or other similar costs of labor, including, for example, guaranteed payments for services. Basic costs do not include pension, profit-sharing, employee benefits, and supplemental unemployment benefit plan costs, or other similar costs.

(4) *Example.*—The provisions of this paragraph (e) are illustrated by the following example.

Example. (i) In 1996, three employees, A, B, and C, of Taxpayer X engage in both lobbying activities and nonlobbying activities. A spends 300 hours, B spends 1,700 hours, and C spends 1,000 hours on lobbying activities.

(ii) X has no third-party costs.

(iii) For purposes of the gross-up method, X determines that its basic labor costs are $20 per hour for A, $30 per hour for B, and $25 per hour for C. Thus, its basic lobbying labor costs are ($20 × 300) + ($30 × 1,700) + ($25 × 1,000), or ($6,000 + $51,000 + $25,000), for total basic lobbying labor costs for 1996 of $82,000.

(iv) Under the gross-up method, X allocates $143,500 to its lobbying activities for 1996, as follows:

175%	×	Basic lobbying labor costs of all personnel	+	Allocable third-party costs	=	Costs allocable to lobbying activities
[175%	×	$82,000]	+	[0]	=	$143,500.

(f) *Section 263A cost allocation methods.*—(1) *In general.*—A taxpayer may allocate its costs to lobbying activities under the principles set forth in section 263A and the regulations thereunder, except to the extent inconsistent with paragraph (g) of this section. For this purpose, lobbying activities are considered a service department or function. Therefore, a taxpayer may allocate costs to lobbying activities by applying the methods provided in §§ 1.263A-1 through 1.263A-3. See § 1.263A-1(e)(4), which describes service costs generally; § 1.263A-1(f), which sets forth cost allocation methods available under section 263A; and § 1.263A-1(g)(4), which provides methods of allocating service costs.

(2) *Example.*—The provisions of this paragraph (f) are illustrated by the following example.

Example. (i) Three full-time employees, A, B, and C, work in the Washington office of Taxpayer Y, a manufacturing concern. They each engage in lobbying activities and nonlobbying activities. In 1996, A spends 75 hours, B spends 1,750 hours, and C spends 2,000 hours on lobbying activities. A's hours are not spent on direct contact lobbying as defined in paragraph (g)(2) of this section. All three work 2,000 hours during 1996. The Washington office also employs one secretary, D, who works exclusively for A, B, and C.

(ii) In addition, three departments in the corporate headquarters in Chicago benefit the Washington office: public affairs, human resources, and insurance.

(iii) Y is subject to section 263A and uses the step-allocation method to allocate its service costs. Prior to the amendments to section 162(e), the Washington office was treated as an overall management function for purposes of section 263A. As such, its costs were fully deductible and no further allocations were made under Y's step allocation. Following the amendments to section 162(e), Y adopts its 263A step-allocation methodology to allocate costs to lobbying activities. Y adds a lobbying department to its step-allocation program, which results in an allocation of costs to the lobbying department from both the Washington office and the Chicago office.

(iv) Y develops a labor ratio to allocate its Washington office costs between the newly defined lobbying department and the overall management department. To determine the hours allocable to lobbying activities, Y uses the de minimis rule of paragraph (g)(1) of this section. Under this rule, A's hours spent on lobbying activities are treated as zero because less than 5 percent of A's time is spent on lobbying (75/2,000 = 3.75%). In addition, because D works exclusively for personnel engaged in lobbying activities, D's hours are not used to develop the allocation ratio. Y assumes that D's allocation of time follows the average time of all the personnel engaged in lobbying activities. Thus, Y's labor ratio is determined as follows:

Departments

Employee	Lobbying Hours	Overall Management Hours	Total Hours
A	0	2,000	2,000
B	1,750	250	2,000
C	2,000	0	2,000
Totals	3,750	2,250	6,000

Lobbying Department Ratio	=	$\frac{3,750}{6,000}$	=	62.5%
Overall Management Department Ratio	=	$\frac{2,250}{6,000}$	=	37.5%

(v) In 1996, the Washington office has the following costs:

Account	Amount
Professional Salaries and Benefits	$660,000
Clerical Salaries and Benefits	50,000
Rent Expense	100,000
Depreciation on Furniture and Equip.	40,000
Utilities	15,000
Outside Payroll Service	5,000
Miscellaneous	10,000
Third-Party Lobbying (Law Firm)	90,000
Total Washington Costs	$970,000

(vi) In addition, $233,800 of costs from the public affairs department, $30,000 of costs from the insurance department, and $5,000 of costs from the human resources department are allocable to the Washington office from departments in Chicago. Therefore, the Washington office costs are allocated to the Lobbying and Overall Management departments as follows:

Total Washington department costs from above	$970,000
Plus Costs Allocated From Other Departments	268,800
Less third-party costs directly allocable to lobbying	(90,000)
Total Washington office costs	$1,148,800

	Lobbying Department	Overall Mgmt. Department
Department Allocation Ratios	62.5%	37.5%
× Washington Office Costs	$1,148,800	$1,148,800
= Costs Allocated To Departments	$718,000	$430,800

(vii) Y's step-allocation for its Lobbying Department is determined as follows:

Y's Step-Allocation	Lobbying Department
Washington Costs Allocated To Lobbying Department	$718,000
Plus Third-Party Costs	90,000
Total Costs of Lobbying Activities	$808,000

(g) *Special rules.*—The following rules apply to any reasonable method of allocating costs to lobbying activities.

(1) *De minimis rule for labor hours.*—Subject to the exception provided in paragraph (g)(2) of this section, a taxpayer may treat time spent by an individual on lobbying activities as zero if less than

five percent of the person's time is spent on lobbying activities. Reasonable methods must be used to determine if less than five percent of a person's time is spent on lobbying activities.

(2) *Direct contact lobbying labor hours.*—Notwithstanding paragraph (g)(1) of this section, a taxpayer must treat all hours spent by a person on direct contact lobbying (as well as the hours that person spends in connection with direct contact lobbying, including time spent traveling that is allocable to the direct contact lobbying) as labor hours allocable to lobbying activities. An activity is direct contact lobbying if it is a meeting, telephone conversation, letter, or other similar means of communication with a legislator (other than a local legislator) or covered executive branch official (as defined in section 162(e)(6)) and otherwise qualifies as a lobbying activity. A person who engages in research, preparation, and other background activities related to direct contact lobbying but who does not make direct contact with a legislator or covered executive branch official is not engaged in direct contact lobbying.

(3) *Taxpayer defined.*—For purposes of this section, a taxpayer includes a tax-exempt organization subject to section 6033(e).

(h) *Effective date.*—This section is effective for amounts paid or incurred on or after July 21, 1995. Taxpayers must adopt a reasonable interpretation of sections 162(e)(1)(A) and (D) for amounts paid or incurred before this date. [Reg. § 1.162-28.]

☐ [T.D. 8602, 7-20-95.]

[Reg. § 1.162-29]

§ 1.162-29. Influencing legislation.—(a) *Scope.*—This section provides rules for determining whether an activity is influencing legislation for purposes of section 162(e)(1)(A). This section does not apply for purposes of sections 4911 and 4945 and the regulations thereunder.

(b) *Definitions.*—For purposes of this section—

(1) *Influencing legislation.*—Influencing legislation means—

(i) Any attempt to influence any legislation through a lobbying communication; and

(ii) All activities, such as research, preparation, planning, and coordination, including deciding whether to make a lobbying communication, engaged in for a purpose of making or supporting a lobbying communication, even if not yet made. See paragraph (c) of this section for rules for determining the purposes for engaging in an activity.

(2) *Attempt to influence legislation.*—An attempt to influence any legislation through a lobbying communication is making the lobbying communication.

(3) *Lobbying communication.*—A lobbying communication is any communication (other than any communication compelled by subpoena, or otherwise compelled by Federal or State law) with any member or employee of a legislative body or any other government official or employee who may participate in the formulation of the legislation that—

(i) Refers to specific legislation and reflects a view on that legislation; or

(ii) Clarifies, amplifies, modifies, or provides support for views reflected in a prior lobbying communication.

(4) *Legislation.*—Legislation includes any action with respect to Acts, bills, resolutions, or other similar items by a legislative body. Legislation includes a proposed treaty required to be submitted by the President to the Senate for its advice and consent from the time the President's representative begins to negotiate its position with the prospective parties to the proposed treaty.

(5) *Specific legislation.*—Specific legislation includes a specific legislative proposal that has not been introduced in a legislative body.

(6) *Legislative bodies.*—Legislative bodies are Congress, state legislatures, and other similar governing bodies, excluding local councils (and similar governing bodies), and executive, judicial, or administrative bodies. For this purpose, administrative bodies include school boards, housing authorities, sewer and water districts, zoning boards, and other similar Federal, State, or local special purpose bodies, whether elective or appointive.

(7) *Examples.*—The provisions of this paragraph (b) are illustrated by the following examples.

Example 1. Taxpayer P's employee, A, is assigned to approach members of Congress to gain their support for a pending bill. A drafts and P prints a position letter on the bill. P distributes the letter to members of Congress. Additionally, A personally contacts several members of Congress or their staffs to seek support for P's position

on the bill. The letter and the personal contacts are lobbying communications. Therefore, P is influencing legislation.

Example 2. Taxpayer R is invited to provide testimony at a congressional oversight hearing concerning the implementation of The Financial Institutions Reform, Recovery, and Enforcement Act of 1989. Specifically, the hearing concerns a proposed regulation increasing the threshold value of commercial and residential real estate transactions for which an appraisal by a state licensed or certified appraiser is required. In its testimony, R states that it is in favor of the proposed regulation. Because R does not refer to any specific legislation or reflect a view on any such legislation, R has not made a lobbying communication. Therefore, R is not influencing legislation.

Example 3. State X enacts a statute that requires the licensing of all day-care providers. Agency B in State X is charged with writing rules to implement the statute. After the enactment of the statute, Taxpayer S sends a letter to Agency B providing detailed proposed rules that S recommends Agency B adopt to implement the statute on licensing of day-care providers. Because the letter to Agency B neither refers to nor reflects a view on any specific legislation, it is not a lobbying communication. Therefore, S is not influencing legislation.

Example 4. Taxpayer T proposes to a State Park Authority that it purchase a particular tract of land for a new park. Even if T's proposal would necessarily require the State Park Authority eventually to seek appropriations to acquire the land and develop the new park, T has not made a lobbying communication because there has been no reference to, nor any view reflected on, any specific legislation. Therefore, T's proposal is not influencing legislation.

Example 5. (i) Taxpayer U prepares a paper that asserts that lack of new capital is hurting State X's economy. The paper indicates that State X residents either should invest more in local businesses or increase their savings so that funds will be available to others interested in making investments. U forwards a summary of the unpublished paper to legislators in State X with a cover letter that states in part:

You must take action to improve the availability of new capital in the state.

(ii) Because neither the summary nor the cover letter refers to any specific legislative proposal and no other facts or circumstances indicate that they refer to an existing legislative proposal, forwarding the summary to legislators in State X is not a lobbying communication. Therefore, U is not influencing legislation.

(iii) Q, a member of the legislature of State X, calls U to request a copy of the unpublished paper from which the summary was prepared. U forwards the paper with a cover letter that simply refers to the enclosed materials. Because U's letter to Q and the unpublished paper do not refer to any specific legislation or reflect a view on any such legislation, the letter is not a lobbying communication. Therefore, U is not influencing legislation.

Example 6. (i) Taxpayer V prepares a paper that asserts that lack of new capital is hurting the national economy. The paper indicates that lowering the capital gains rate would increase the availability of capital and increase tax receipts from the capital gains tax. V forwards the paper to its representatives in Congress with a cover letter that says, in part:

I urge you to support a reduction in the capital gains tax rate.

(ii) V's communication is a lobbying communication because it refers to and reflects a view on a specific legislative proposal (i.e., lowering the capital gains rate). Therefore, V is influencing legislation.

Example 7. Taxpayer W, based in State A, notes in a letter to a legislator of State A that State X has passed a bill that accomplishes a stated purpose and then says that State A should pass such a bill. No such bill has been introduced into the State A legislature. The communication is a lobbying communication because it refers to and reflects a view on a specific legislative proposal. Therefore, W is influencing legislation.

Example 8. (i) Taxpayer Y represents citrus fruit growers. Y writes a letter to a United States senator discussing how pesticide O has benefited citrus fruit growers and disputing problems linked to its use. The letter discusses a bill pending in Congress and states in part:

This bill would prohibit the use of pesticide O. If citrus growers are unable to use this pesticide, their crop yields will be severely reduced, leading to higher prices for consumers and lower profits, even bankruptcy, for growers.

(ii) Y's views on the bill are reflected in this statement. Thus, the communication is a lobbying communication, and Y is influencing legislation.

Example 9. (i) B, the president of Taxpayer Z, an insurance company, meets with Q, who chairs the X state legislature's committee with jurisdiction over laws regulating insurance companies, to discuss the possibility of legislation to address current problems with surplus-line companies. B recommends that legislation be introduced that would create minimum capital and surplus requirements for surplus-line companies and create clearer guidelines concerning the risks that surplus-line companies can insure. B's discussion with Q is a lobbying communication because B refers to and reflects a view on a specific legislative proposal. Therefore, Z is influencing legislation.

(ii) Q is not convinced that the market for surplus-line companies is substantial enough to warrant such legislation and requests that B provide information on the amount and types of risks covered by surplus-line companies. After the meeting, B has employees of Z prepare estimates of the percentage of property and casualty insurance risks handled by surplus-line companies. B sends the estimates with a cover letter that simply refers to the enclosed materials. Although B's follow-up letter to Q does not refer to specific legislation or reflect a view on such legislation, B's letter supports the views reflected in the earlier communication. Therefore, the letter is a lobbying communication and Z is influencing legislation.

(c) *Purpose for engaging in an activity.*—(1) *In general.*—The purposes for engaging in an activity are determined based on all the facts and circumstances. Facts and circumstances include, but are not limited to—

(i) Whether the activity and the lobbying communication are proximate in time;

(ii) Whether the activity and the lobbying communication relate to similar subject matter;

(iii) Whether the activity is performed at the request of, under the direction of, or on behalf of a person making the lobbying communication;

(iv) Whether the results of the activity are also used for a nonlobbying purpose; and

(v) Whether, at the time the taxpayer engages in the activity, there is specific legislation to which the activity relates.

(2) *Multiple purposes.*—If a taxpayer engages in an activity both for the purpose of making or supporting a lobbying communication and for some nonlobbying purpose, the taxpayer must treat the activity as engaged in partially for a lobbying purpose and partially for a nonlobbying purpose. This division of the activity must result in a reasonable allocation of costs to influencing legislation. See § 1.162-28 (allocation rules for certain expenditures to which section 162(e)(1) applies). A taxpayer's treatment of these multiple-purpose activities will, in general, not result in a reasonable allocation if it allocates to influencing legislation—

(i) Only the incremental amount of costs that would not have been incurred but for the lobbying purpose; or

(ii) An amount based solely on the number of purposes for engaging in that activity without regard to the relative importance of those purposes.

(3) *Activities treated as having no purpose to influence legislation.*— A taxpayer that engages in any of the following activities is treated as having done so without a purpose of making or supporting a lobbying communication—

(i) Before evidencing a purpose to influence any specific legislation referred to in paragraph (c)(3)(i)(A) or (B) of this section (or similar legislation)—

(A) Determining the existence or procedural status of specific legislation, or the time, place, and subject of any hearing to be held by a legislative body with respect to specific legislation; or

(B) Preparing routine, brief summaries of the provisions of specific legislation;

(ii) Performing an activity for purposes of complying with the requirements of any law (for example, satisfying state or federal securities law filing requirements);

(iii) Reading any publications available to the general public or viewing or listening to other mass media communications; and

(iv) Merely attending a widely attended speech.

(4) *Examples.*—The provisions of this paragraph (c) are illustrated by the following examples.

Example 1. (i) *Facts.* In 1997, Agency F issues proposed regulations relating to the business of Taxpayer W. There is no specific legislation during 1997 that is similar to the regulatory proposal. W undertakes a study of the impact of the proposed regulations on its business. W incorporates the results of that study in comments sent to Agency F in 1997. In 1998, legislation is introduced in Congress that is similar to the regulatory proposal. Also in 1998, W writes a letter to Senator P stating that it opposes the proposed legislation. W encloses with the letter a copy of the comments it sent to Agency F.

(ii) *Analysis.* W's letter to Senator P refers to and reflects a view on specific legislation and *therefore is a* lobbying communication. Although W's study of the impact of the proposed regulations is proximate in time and similar in subject matter to its lobbying communication, W performed the study and incorporated the results in comments sent to Agency F when no legislation with a similar

subject matter was pending (a nonlobbying use). On these facts, W engaged in the study solely for a nonlobbying purpose.

Example 2. (i) *Facts.* The governor of State Q proposes a budget that includes a proposed sales tax on electricity. Using its records of electricity consumption, Taxpayer Y estimates the additional costs that the budget proposal would impose upon its business. In the same year, Y writes to members of the state legislature and explains that it opposes the proposed sales tax. In its letter, Y includes its estimate of the costs that the sales tax would impose on its business. Y does not demonstrate any other use of its estimates.

(ii) *Analysis.* The letter is a lobbying communication (because it refers to and reflects a view on specific legislation, the governor's proposed budget). Y's estimate of additional costs under the proposal supports the lobbying communication, is proximate in time and similar in subject matter to a specific legislative proposal then in existence, and is not used for a nonlobbying purpose. Based on these facts, Y estimated its additional costs under the budget proposal solely to support the lobbying communication.

Example 3. (i) *Facts.* A senator in the State Q legislature announces her intention to introduce legislation to require health insurers to cover a particular medical procedure in all policies sold in the state. Taxpayer Y has different policies for two groups of employees, one of which covers the procedure and one of which does not. After the bill is introduced, Y's legislative affairs staff asks Y's human resources staff to estimate the additional cost to cover the procedure for both groups of employees. Y's human resources staff prepares a study estimating Y's increased costs and forwards it to the legislative affairs staff. Y's legislative staff then writes to members of the state legislature and explains that it opposes the proposed change in insurance coverage based on the study. Y's legislative affairs staff thereafter forwards the study, prepared for its use in opposing the statutory proposal, to its labor relations staff for use in negotiations with employees scheduled to begin later in the year.

(ii) *Analysis.* The letter to legislators is a lobbying communication (because it refers to and reflects a view on specific legislation). The activity of estimating Y's additional costs under the proposed legislation relate to the same subject as the lobbying communication, occurs close in time to the lobbying communication, is conducted at the request of a person making a lobbying communication, and relates to specific legislation then in existence. Although Y used the study in its labor negotiations, mere use for that purpose does not establish that Y estimated its additional costs under the proposed legislation in part for a nonlobbying purpose. Thus, based on all the facts and circumstances, Y estimated the additional costs it would incur under the proposal solely to make or support the lobbying communication.

Example 4. (i) *Facts.* After several years of developmental work under various contracts, in 1996, Taxpayer A contracts with the Department of Defense (DOD) to produce a prototype of a new generation military aircraft. A is aware that DOD will be able to fund the contract only if Congress appropriates an amount for that purpose in the upcoming appropriations process. In 1997, A conducts simulation tests of the aircraft and revises the specifications of the aircraft's expected performance capabilities, as required under the contract. A submits the results of the tests and the revised specifications to DOD. In 1998, Congress considers legislation to appropriate funds for the contract. In that connection, A summarizes the results of the simulation tests and of the aircraft's expected performance capabilities, and submits the summary to interested members of Congress with a cover letter that encourages them to support appropriations of funds for the contract.

(ii) *Analysis.* The letter is a lobbying communication (because it refers to specific legislation (i.e., appropriations) and requests passage). The described activities in 1996, 1997, and 1998 relate to the same subject as the lobbying communication. The summary was prepared specifically for, and close in time to, that communication. Based on these facts, the summary was prepared solely for a lobbying purpose. In contrast, A conducted the tests and revised the specifications to comply with its production contract with DOD. A conducted the tests and revised the specifications solely for a nonlobbying purpose.

Example 5. (i) *Facts.* C, president of Taxpayer W, travels to the state capital to attend a two-day conference on new manufacturing processes. C plans to spend a third day in the capital meeting with state legislators to explain why W opposes a pending bill unrelated to the subject of the conference. At the meetings with the legislators, C makes lobbying communications by referring to and reflecting a view on the pending bill.

(ii) *Analysis.* C's traveling expenses (transportation and meals and lodging) are partially for the purpose of making or supporting the lobbying communications and partially for a nonlobbying purpose. As a result, under paragraph (c)(2) of this section, W must reasonably allocate C's traveling expenses between these two purposes. Allocating to influencing legislation only C's incremental transportation expenses (i.e., the taxi fare to meet with the state legislators) does not result in a reasonable allocation of traveling expenses.

Example 6. (i) *Facts.* On February 1, 1997, a bill is introduced in Congress that would affect Company E. Employees in E's legislative affairs department, as is customary, prepare a brief summary of the bill and periodically confirm the procedural status of the bill through conversations with employees and members of Congress. On March 31, 1997, the head of E's legislative affairs department meets with E's President to request that B, a chemist, temporarily help the legislative affairs department analyze the bill. The President agrees, and suggests that B also be assigned to draft a position letter in opposition to the bill. Employees of the legislative affairs department continue to confirm periodically the procedural status of the bill. On October 31, 1997, B's position letter in opposition to the bill is delivered to members of Congress.

(ii) *Analysis.* B's letter is a lobbying communication because it refers to and reflects a view on specific legislation. Under paragraph (c)(3)(i) of this section, the assignment of B to assist the legislative affairs department in analyzing the bill and in drafting a position letter in opposition to the bill evidences a purpose to influence legislation. Neither the activity of periodically confirming the procedural status of the bill nor the activity of preparing the routine, brief summary of the bill before March 31 constitutes influencing legislation. In contrast, periodically confirming the procedural status of the bill on or after March 31 relates to the same subject as, and is close in time to, the lobbying communication and is used for no nonlobbying purpose. Consequently, after March 31, E determined the procedural status of the bill for the purpose of supporting the lobbying communication by B.

(d) *Lobbying communication made by another.*—If a taxpayer engages in activities for a purpose of supporting a lobbying communication to be made by another person (or by a group of persons), the taxpayer's activities are treated under paragraph (b) of this section as influencing legislation. For example, if a taxpayer or an employee of the taxpayer (as a volunteer or otherwise) engages in an activity to assist a trade association in preparing its lobbying communication, the taxpayer's activities are influencing legislation even if the lobbying communication is made by the trade association and not the taxpayer. If, however, the taxpayer's employee, acting outside the employee's scope of employment, volunteers to engage in those activities, then the taxpayer is not influencing legislation.

(e) *No lobbying communication.*—Paragraph (e) of this section applies if a taxpayer engages in an activity for a purpose of making or supporting a lobbying communication, but no lobbying communication that the activity supports has yet been made.

(1) *Before the filing date.*—Under this paragraph (e)(1), if on the filing date of the return for any taxable year the taxpayer no longer expects, under any reasonably foreseeable circumstances, that a lobbying communication will be made that is supported by the activity, then the taxpayer will be treated as if it did not engage in the activity for a purpose of making or supporting a lobbying communication. Thus, the taxpayer need not treat any amount allocated to that activity for that year under § 1.162-28 as an amount to which section 162(e)(1)(A) applies. The filing date for purposes of paragraph (e) of this section is the earlier of the time the taxpayer files its timely return for the year or the due date of the timely return.

(2) *After the filing date.*—(i) *In general.*—If, at any time after the filing date, the taxpayer no longer expects, under any reasonably foreseeable circumstances, that a lobbying communication will be made that is supported by the activity, then any amount previously allocated under § 1.162-28 to the activity and disallowed under section 162(e)(1)(A) is treated as an amount that is not subject to section 162(e)(1)(A) and that is paid or incurred only at the time the taxpayer no longer expects that a lobbying communication will be made.

(ii) *Special rule for certain tax-exempt organizations.*—For a tax-exempt organization subject to section 6033(e), the amounts described in paragraph (e)(2)(i) of this section are treated as reducing (but not below zero) its expenditures to which section 162(e)(1) applies beginning with that year and continuing for subsequent years to the extent not treated in prior years as reducing those expenditures.

(f) *Anti-avoidance rule.*—If a taxpayer, alone or with others, structures its activities with a principal purpose of achieving results that are unreasonable in light of the purposes of section 162(e)(1)(A) and section 6033(e), the Commissioner can recast the taxpayer's activities for federal tax purposes as appropriate to achieve tax results that are consistent with the intent of section 162(e)(1)(A), section 6033(e) (if applicable), and this section, and the pertinent facts and circumstances.

(g) *Taxpayer defined.*—For purposes of this section, a taxpayer includes a tax-exempt organization subject to section 6033(e).

(h) *Effective date.*—This section is effective for amounts paid or incurred on or after July 21, 1995. Taxpayers must adopt a reasonable interpretation of section 162(e)(1)(A) for amounts paid or incurred before this date. [Reg. § 1.162-29.]

□ [T.D. 8602, 7-20-95.]

[Reg. § 1.162-31]

§ 1.162-31. The $500,000 deduction limitation for remuneration provided by certain health insurance providers.—(a) *Scope.*—This section sets forth rules regarding the deduction limitation under section 162(m)(6), which provides that a covered health insurance provider's deduction for applicable individual remuneration (AIR) and deferred deduction remuneration (DDR) attributable to services performed by an applicable individual in a disqualified taxable year is limited to $500,000. Paragraph (b) of this section sets forth definitions of the terms used in this section. Paragraph (c) of this section explains the general limitation on deductions under section 162(m)(6). Paragraph (d) of this section sets forth the methods that must be used to attribute AIR and DDR to services performed in one or more taxable years of a covered health insurance provider. Paragraph (e) of this section sets forth rules on how the deduction limit applies to AIR and DDR that is otherwise deductible under chapter 1 of the Internal Revenue Code (Code) but for the deduction limitation under section 162(m)(6) (referred to in this section as remuneration that is otherwise deductible). Paragraph (f) of this section sets forth additional rules for persons participating in certain corporate transactions. Paragraph (g) of this section explains the interaction of section 162(m)(6) with sections 162(m)(1) and 280G. Paragraph (h) of this section sets forth rules for determining the amounts of remuneration that are not subject to the deduction limitation under section 162(m)(6) due to the statutory effective date (referred to in this section as grandfathered amounts). Paragraph (i) of this section sets forth transition rules for DDR that is attributable to services performed in taxable years beginning after December 31, 2009 and before January 1, 2013. Paragraph (j) of this section sets forth the effective and applicability dates of the rules in this section.

(b) *Definitions.*—(1) *Health insurance issuer.*—For purposes of this section, a *health insurance issuer* is a health insurance issuer as defined in section 9832(b)(2).

(2) *Aggregated group.*—For purposes of this section, an *aggregated group* is a health insurance issuer and each other person that is treated as a single employer with the health insurance issuer at any time during the taxable year of the health insurance issuer under sections 414(b) (controlled groups of corporations), 414(c) (partnerships, proprietorships, etc. under common control), 414(m) (affiliated service groups), or 414(o), except that the rules in section 1563(a)(2) and (3) (with respect to corporations) and § 1.414(c)-2(c) and (d) (with respect to trades or businesses under common control) for brother-sister groups and combined groups are disregarded.

(3) *Parent entity.*—(i) *In general.*—For purposes of this section, a *parent entity* is either—

(A) the common parent of a parent-subsidiary controlled group of corporations (within the meaning of section 414(b)) or a parent-subsidiary group of trades or businesses under common control (within the meaning of section 414(c)) that includes a health insurance issuer, or

(B) the health insurance issuer in an aggregated group that is an affiliated service group (within the meaning of section 414(m)) or a group described in section 414(o).

(ii) *Certain aggregated groups with multiple health insurance issuers.*—(A) *In general.*—If two or more health insurance issuers are members of an aggregated group that is an affiliated service group (within the meaning of section 414(m)) or group described in section 414(o), the parent entity is the health insurance issuer in the aggregated group that is designated in writing by the other members of the aggregated group to act as the parent entity.

(B) *Successor parent entities.*—If a health insurance issuer that is the parent entity of an aggregated group pursuant to paragraph (b)(3)(ii)(A) of this section (a predecessor parent entity) ceases to be a member of the aggregated group (for example, as a result of a corporate transaction) and, after the predecessor parent entity ceases to be a member of the aggregated group, two or more health insurance issuers are members of the aggregated group, the new parent entity (the successor parent entity) is another member of the aggregated group designated in writing by the remaining members of the aggregated group. The successor parent entity must be a health insurance issuer in the aggregated group that has the same taxable year as the predecessor parent entity; provided, however, that if no health insurance issuer in the aggregated group has the same taxable year as the predecessor parent entity, the members of the aggregated group may designate in writing any other health insurance issuer in the aggregated group to be the parent entity.

(C) *Failure to designate a parent entity.*—If the members of an aggregated group that includes two or more health insurance issuers and that is an affiliated service group (within the meaning of section 414(m)) or a group described in section 414(o) fail to designate in writing a health insurance issuer to act as the parent entity of the aggregated group, the parent entity of the aggregated group for all taxable years is deemed to be an entity with a taxable year that is the calendar year (without regard to whether the aggregated group includes or has ever included an entity with a calendar year taxable year) for all purposes under this section for which a parent entity's taxable year is relevant.

(4) *Covered health insurance provider.*—(i) *In general.*—For purposes of this section and except as otherwise provided in this paragraph (b)(4), a *covered health insurance provider* is—

(A) a health insurance issuer for any of its taxable years beginning after December 31, 2012 in which at least 25 percent of the gross premiums it receives from providing health insurance coverage (as defined in section 9832(b)(1)) are from providing minimum essential coverage (as defined in section 5000A(f)),

(B) a health insurance issuer for any of its taxable years beginning after December 31, 2009 and before January 1, 2013 in which it receives premiums from providing health insurance coverage (as defined in section 9832(b)(1)),

(C) the parent entity of an aggregated group of which one or more health insurance issuers described in paragraphs (b)(4)(i)(A) or (B) of this section are members for the taxable year of the parent entity with which, or in which, ends the taxable year of any such health insurance issuer; however, if the parent entity of an aggregated group is a health insurance issuer described in paragraphs (b)(4)(i)(A) or (B) of this section, that health insurance issuer is a covered health insurance provider for any taxable year that it is otherwise a covered health insurance provider, without regard to whether the taxable year of any other health insurance issuer described in paragraphs (b)(4)(i)(A) or (B) of this section ends with or within its taxable year, and

(D) each other member of an aggregated group of which one or more health insurance issuers described in paragraphs (b)(4)(i)(A) or (B) of this section are members for the taxable year of the other member ending with, or within, the parent entity's taxable year.

(ii) *Parent entities with short taxable years.*—If for any reason a parent entity has a taxable year that is less than 12 months (for example, because the taxable year of a predecessor parent entity ends when it ceases to be a member of an aggregated group), then, for purposes of determining whether the parent entity and each other member of the aggregated group is a covered health insurance provider with respect to the parent entity's short taxable year (that is, for purposes of determining whether the taxable year of a health insurance issuer described in paragraph (b)(4)(i)(A) or (B) of this section ends with or within the short taxable year of the parent entity and for purposes of determining whether another member of the aggregated group has a taxable year ending with or within the short taxable year of the parent entity), the taxable year of the parent entity is treated as the 12-month period ending on the last day of the short taxable year. Accordingly, a parent entity is a covered health insurance provider for its short taxable year if it is a health insurance issuer described in paragraph (b)(4)(i)(A) or (B) of this section or if the taxable year of a health insurance issuer described in paragraph (b)(4)(i)(A) or (B) of this section in an aggregated group with the parent entity ends with or within the 12-month period ending on the last day of the parent entity's short taxable year. Similarly, each other member of the parent entity's aggregated group is a covered health insurance provider for its taxable year ending with or within the 12-month period ending on the last day of the parent entity's short taxable year.

(iii) *Predecessor and successor parent entities.*—If the parent entity of an aggregated group changes, the members of the aggregated group may be covered health insurance providers based on their relationship to either or both parent entities with respect to the taxable years of the parent entities in which the change occurs.

(iv) *Self-insured plans.*—For purposes of this section, a person is not a covered health insurance provider solely because it maintains a self-insured medical reimbursement plan. For this purpose, a self-insured medical *reimbursement plan is a separate written plan for the benefit of employees* (including former employees) that provides for reimbursement of medical expenses referred to in section 105(b) and does not provide for reimbursement under an individual or group policy of accident or health insurance issued by a licensed insurance company or under an arrangement in the nature of a prepaid health care plan that is regulated under federal or state law in a manner similar to the regulation of insurance companies, and may include a plan maintained by an employee organization described in section 501(c)(9).

(v) *De minimis exception.*—(A) *In general.*—A health insurance issuer and any member of its aggregated group that would otherwise be a covered health insurance provider under paragraph (b)(4)(i), (ii), or (iii) of this section for a taxable year beginning after December 31, 2012 is not a covered health insurance provider under this section for that taxable year if the premiums received by the health insurance issuer and any other health insurance issuers in its aggregated group from providing health insurance coverage (as defined in section 9832(b)(1)) that constitutes minimum essential coverage (as defined in section 5000A(f)) are less than two percent of the gross revenues of the health insurance issuer and all other members of its aggregated group for that taxable year. A health insurance issuer and any member of its aggregated group that would otherwise be a covered health insurance provider under paragraph (b)(4)(i), (ii), or (iii) of this section for a taxable year beginning after December 31, 2009 and before January 1, 2013 is not a covered health insurance provider for purposes of this section for that taxable year if the premiums received by the health insurance issuer and any other health insurance issuers in its aggregated group from providing health insurance coverage (as defined in section 9832(b)(1)) are less than two percent of the gross revenues of the health insurance issuer and all other members of its aggregated group for that taxable year. In determining whether premiums constitute less than two percent of gross revenues, the amount of gross revenues must be determined in accordance with generally accepted accounting principles. For the definition of the term *premiums*, see paragraph (b)(5) of this section. A person that would be a covered health insurance provider for a taxable year in an aggregated group with a predecessor parent entity and that would also be a covered health insurance provider for that taxable year in an aggregated group with a successor parent entity is not a covered health insurance provider under the *de minimis* exception only if the aggregated groups of which the person is a member meet the requirements of the *de minimis* exception based on both the taxable year of the predecessor parent entity and the taxable year of the successor parent entity.

(B) *One-year de minimis exception transition period.*—If a health insurance issuer or a member of an aggregated group is not a covered health insurance provider for a taxable year solely by reason of the *de minimis* exception described in paragraph (b)(4)(v)(A) of this section, but fails to meet the requirements of the *de minimis* exception described in paragraph (b)(4)(v)(A) of this section for the immediately following taxable year, that health insurance issuer or member of an aggregated group will not be a covered health insurance provider for that immediately following taxable year.

(vi) *Examples.*—The following examples illustrate the principles of this paragraph (b)(4). For purposes of these examples, each corporation has a taxable year that is the calendar year, unless the example provides otherwise.

Example 1. (i) Corporations Y and Z are members of an aggregated group under paragraph (b)(2) of this section. Y is a health insurance issuer that is a covered health insurance provider pursuant to paragraph (b)(4)(i)(A) of this section and receives premiums from providing health insurance coverage that is minimum essential coverage during its 2015 taxable year in an amount that is less than two percent of the combined gross revenues of Y and Z for their 2015 taxable years. Z is not a health insurance issuer.

(ii) Y and Z are not covered health insurance providers under paragraph (b)(4) of this section for their 2015 taxable years because they meet the requirements of the *de minimis* exception under paragraph (b)(4)(v)(A) of this section.

Example 2. (i) Corporations V, W, and X are members of an aggregated group under paragraph (b)(2) of this section. V is a health insurance issuer that is a covered health insurance provider pursuant to paragraph (b)(4)(i)(A) of this section, but neither W nor X is a health insurance issuer. W is the parent entity of the aggregated group. V's taxable year ends on December 31, W's taxable year ends on June 30, and X's taxable year ends on September 30. For its taxable year ending December 31, 2016, V receives $3x of premiums from providing minimum essential coverage and has no other revenue. For its taxable year ending June 30, 2017, W has $100x in gross revenue. For its taxable year ending September 30, 2016, X has $60x in gross revenue.

(ii) But for the *de minimis* exception, V (the health insurance issuer) would be a covered health insurance provider for its taxable year ending December 31, 2016; W (the parent entity) would be a covered health insurance provider for its taxable year ending June 30, 2017 (its taxable year with which, or within which, ends the taxable year of the health insurance issuer); and X (the other member of the aggregated group) would be a covered health insurance provider for its taxable year ending on September 30, 2016 (its taxable year ending with, or within, the taxable year of the parent entity). However, the premiums received by V (the health insurance issuer) from providing minimum essential coverage during the taxable year that it would otherwise be a covered health insurance provider under paragraph (b)(4)(i)(A) of this section are less than two percent of the combined gross revenues of V, W, and X for the related taxable years that they would otherwise be covered health insurance providers under paragraph (b)(4)(i) of this section ($3x is less than $3.26x (two percent of $163x)). Therefore, the *de minimis* exception of paragraph (b)(4)(v)(A) of this section applies, and V, W, and X are not covered health insurance providers for these taxable years.

Example 3. (i) The facts are the same as *Example 2*, except that V receives $4x of premiums for providing minimum essential coverage for its taxable year ending December 31, 2016. In addition, the members of the VWX aggregated group were not covered health insurance providers for their taxable years ending December 31, 2015, June 30, 2016, and September 30, 2015, respectively (their immediately preceding taxable years) solely by reason of the *de minimis* exception of paragraph (b)(4)(v)(A) of this section.

(ii) Although the premiums received by the members of the aggregated group from providing minimum essential coverage are more than two percent of the gross revenues of the aggregated group for the taxable years during which the members would otherwise be treated as covered health insurance providers under paragraph (b)(4)(i) of this section ($4x is greater than $3.28x (two percent of $164x)), they were not covered health insurance providers for their immediately preceding taxable years solely because of the *de minimis* exception of paragraph (b)(4)(v)(A) of this section. Therefore, V, W, and X are not covered health insurance providers for their taxable years ending on December 31, 2016, June 30, 2017, and September 30, 2016, respectively, because of the one-year transition period under paragraph (b)(4)(v)(B) of this section. However, the members of the VWX aggregated group will be covered health insurance providers for their subsequent taxable years if they would otherwise be covered health insurance providers for those taxable years under paragraph (b)(4) of this section.

Example 4. (i) Corporations W, X, Y, and Z are members of a controlled group described in section 414(b)) that is an aggregated group under paragraph (b)(2) of this section. W and X are health insurance issuers. Y and Z are not health insurance issuers. W is the parent entity of the aggregated group. W's and Y's taxable years end on December 31; X's taxable year ends on March 31; and Z's taxable year ends on June 30. As a result of a corporate transaction, W is no longer a member of the WXYZ aggregated group as of September 30, 2016, and W's taxable year ends on that date. Following the corporate transaction, X becomes the parent entity of the XYZ aggregated group.

(ii) Because W's taxable year is treated as the 12-month period ending on September 30, 2016, W is the parent entity for X's taxable year ending March 31, 2016, Z's taxable year ending June 30, 2016, and Y's taxable year ending December 31, 2015. Because X's taxable year begins on April 1, 2016 and ends on March 31, 2017, for purposes of paragraph (b)(4) of this section, X is the parent entity for Z's taxable year ending June 30, 2016, Y's taxable year ending December 31, 2016, and W's taxable year ending September 30, 2016.

Example 5. (i) The facts are the same as *Example 4*. In addition, W receives $4x of premiums for providing minimum essential coverage and no other revenue for its taxable year beginning January 1, 2016 and ending September 30, 2016. X receives $2x of premiums for providing minimum essential coverage and has no other revenue for its taxable year ending March 31, 2016. X receives $1x of premiums for providing minimum essential coverage and no other revenue for its taxable year ending March 31, 2017. For its taxable year ending December 31, 2015, Y has $100x in gross revenue. For its taxable year ending December 31, 2016, Y has $200x in gross revenue. For its taxable year ending June 30, 2016, Z has $120x in gross revenue (none of which constitute premiums for providing health insurance coverage that constitutes minimum essential coverage (as defined in section 5000A(f)). W, X, Y, and Z did not qualify for the *de minimis* exception in any prior taxable years.

(ii) For its taxable year ending June 30, 2016, Z does not meet the requirements for the *de minimis* exception described in paragraph (b)(4)(v)(A). Even though Z meets the requirements for the *de minimis* exception with respect to the taxable year of parent entity X ending March 31, 2017 ($5x is less than two percent of $325x), Z does not meet the requirements for the *de minimis* exception based on the premiums and gross revenues of the taxable years of its aggregated group members ending with or within the deemed 12-month taxable year of parent entity W ending September 30, 2016 ($6x is more than two percent of $226x). Therefore, Z is a covered health insurance provider for its June 30, 2016 taxable year.

(iii) For its taxable year ending December 31, 2015, Y does not meet the requirements for the *de minimis* exception described in paragraph (b)(4)(v)(A) ($6x is more than two percent of $226x). For its taxable year ending December 31, 2016, Y meets the requirements for the *de minimis* exception described in paragraph (b)(4)(v)(A) ($5x is less than two percent of $325x). Therefore, Y is a covered health insurance provider for its December 31, 2015 taxable year, but is not a covered health insurance provider for its December 31, 2016 taxable year.

(iv) For its taxable year ending September 30, 2016, W does not meet the requirements for the *de minimis* exception described in paragraph (b)(4)(v)(A). Even though W meets the requirements for the *de minimis* exception with respect to X's taxable year ending March 31, 2017 ($5x is less than two percent of $325x), W does not meet the requirements for the *de minimis* exception with respect its taxable year ending September 30, 2016 ($6x is more than two percent of $226x). Therefore, W is a covered health insurance provider for its September 30, 2016 taxable year.

(v) For its taxable year ending March 31, 2016, X does not meet the requirements for the *de minimis* exception ($6x is more than two percent of $226x). For its taxable year ending March, 31 2017, X meets the requirements for the *de minimis* exception ($5x is less than two percent of $325x). Therefore, X is a covered health insurance provider for its March 31, 2016 taxable year, but is not a covered health insurance provider for its March 31 2017 taxable year.

(5) *Premiums.*—(i) For purposes of this section, the term *premiums* means premiums written (including premiums written for assumption reinsurance, but reduced by assumption reinsurance ceded (as described in paragraph (b)(5)(ii) of this section), excluding indemnity reinsurance written (as described in paragraph (b)(5)(iii) of this section) and direct service payments (as described in paragraph (b)(5)(iv) of this section), but without reduction for ceding commissions or medical loss ratio rebates, determined in a manner consistent with the requirements for reporting under the Supplemental Health Care Exhibit published by the National Association of Insurance Commissioners or the MLR Annual Reporting Form filed with the Center for Medicare & Medicaid Services' Center for Consumer Information and Insurance Oversight of the U.S. Department of Health and Human Services (or any successor or replacement exhibits or forms).

(ii) *Assumption reinsurance.*—For purposes of this paragraph (b)(5), the term *assumption reinsurance* means reinsurance for which there is a novation and the reinsurer takes over the entire risk of loss pursuant to a new contract.

(iii) *Indemnity reinsurance.*—For purposes of this paragraph (b)(5), the term *indemnity reinsurance* means reinsurance provided pursuant to an agreement between a health insurance issuer and a reinsuring company under which the reinsuring company agrees to indemnify the health insurance issuer for all or part of the risk of loss under policies specified in the agreement, and the health insurance issuer retains its liability to provide health insurance coverage (as defined in section 9832(b)(1)) to, and its contractual relationship with, the insured.

(iv) *Direct service payments.*—For purposes of this paragraph (b)(5), the term *direct service payment* means a capitated, prepaid, periodic, or other payment made by a health insurance issuer or another entity that receives premiums from providing health insurance coverage (as defined in section 9832(b)(1)) to another organization as compensation for providing, managing, or arranging for the provision of healthcare services by physicians, hospitals, or other healthcare providers, regardless of whether the organization that receives the compensation is subject to healthcare provider, health insurance, health plan licensing, financial solvency, or other similar regulatory requirements under state insurance law.

(6) *Disqualified taxable year.*—For purposes of this section, the term *disqualified taxable year* means, with respect to any person, any taxable year for which the person is a covered health insurance provider.

(7) *Applicable individual.*—(i) *In general.*—For purposes of this section, except as provided in paragraph (b)(7)(ii) of this section, the term *applicable individual* means, with respect to any covered health insurance provider for any disqualified taxable year, any individual (or any other person described in guidance of general applicability published in the Internal Revenue Bulletin)—

(A) who is an officer, director, or employee in that taxable year, or

(B) who provides services for or on behalf of the covered health insurance provider during that taxable year.

(ii) *Independent contractors.*—Remuneration for services performed by an independent contractor for a covered health insurance provider is subject to the deduction limitation under section 162(m)(6). However, an independent contractor is not an applicable individual with respect to a covered health insurance provider for a disqualified taxable year if each of the following requirements is satisfied:

(A) The independent contractor is actively engaged in the trade or business of providing services to recipients, other than as an employee or as a member of the board of directors of a corporation (or similar position with respect to an entity that is not a corporation);

(B) The independent contractor provides significant services (as defined in § 1.409A-1(f)(2)(iii)) to two or more persons to which the independent contractor is not related and that are not related to one another (as defined in § 1.409A-1(f)(2)(ii)); and

(C) The independent contractor is not related to the covered health insurance provider or any member of its aggregated group, applying the definition of related person contained in § 1.409A-1(f)(2)(ii), subject to the modification that for purposes of applying the references to sections 267(b) and 707(b)(1), the language "20 percent" is not used instead of "50 percent" each place "50 percent" appears in sections 267(b) and 707(b)(1).

(8) *Service provider.*—For purposes of this section, the term *service provider* means, with respect to a covered health insurance provider for any period, an individual who is an officer, director, or employee, or who provides services for, or on behalf of, the covered health insurance provider or any member of its aggregated group.

(9) *Remuneration.*—(i) *In general.*—For purposes of this section, except as provided in paragraph (b)(9)(ii) of this section, the term *remuneration* has the same meaning as the term *applicable employee remuneration,* as defined in section 162(m)(4), but without regard to the exceptions under section 162(m)(4)(B) (remuneration payable on a commission basis), section 162(m)(4)(C) (performance-based compensation), and section 162(m)(4)(D) (existing binding contracts), and the regulations under those sections.

(ii) *Exceptions.*—For purposes of this section, remuneration does not include—

(A) A payment made to, or for the benefit of, an applicable individual from or to a trust described in section 401(a) within the meaning of section 3121(a)(5)(A),

(B) A payment made under an annuity plan described in section 403(a) within the meaning of section 3121(a)(5)(B),

(C) A payment made under a simplified employee pension plan described in section 408(k)(1) within the meaning of section 3121(a)(5)(C),

(D) A payment made under an annuity contract described in section 403(b) within the meaning of section 3121(a)(5)(D),

(E) Salary reduction contributions described in section 3121(v)(1), and

(F) Remuneration consisting of any benefit provided to, or on behalf of, an employee if, at the time the benefit is provided, it is reasonable to believe that the employee will be able to exclude the value of the benefit from gross income.

(10) *Applicable Individual Remuneration or AIR.*—For purposes of this section, the term *applicable individual remuneration* or *AIR* means, with respect to any applicable individual for any disqualified taxable year, the aggregate amount allowable as a deduction under this chapter for that taxable year (determined without regard to section 162(m)) for remuneration for services performed by that applicable individual (whether or not in that taxable year). AIR does not include any DDR with respect to services performed during any taxable year. AIR for a disqualified taxable year may include remuneration for services performed in a taxable year before the taxable year in which the deduction for the remuneration is allowable. For example, a discretionary bonus granted and paid to an applicable individual in a disqualified taxable year in recognition of services performed in prior taxable years is AIR for the disqualified taxable year in which the bonus is granted and paid. In addition, a grant of restricted stock in a disqualified taxable year with respect to which an applicable individual makes an election under section 83(b) is AIR for the disqualified taxable year of the covered health insurance provider in which the grant of the restricted stock is made. See paragraph (b)(9)(ii) of this section for certain remuneration that is not treated as AIR for purposes of this section.

(11) *Deferred Deduction Remuneration or DDR.*—For purposes of this section, the term *deferred deduction remuneration* or *DDR* means remuneration that would be AIR for services performed in a disqualified taxable year but for the fact that the deduction (determined without regard to section 162(m)(6)) for the remuneration is allowable in a subsequent taxable year. Whether remuneration is DDR is determined without regard to when the remuneration is paid, except to the extent that the timing of the payment affects the taxable year in which the remuneration is otherwise deductible. For example, payments that are otherwise deductible by a covered health insurance provider in an initial taxable year, but are paid to an applicable individual by the 15th day of the third month of the immediately subsequent taxable year of the covered health insurance provider (as described in § 1.404(b)-1T, Q&A-2(b)(1)), are AIR for the initial taxable year (and not DDR) because the deduction for the payments is allowable in the initial taxable year, and not a subsequent taxable year. Except as otherwise provided in paragraph (i) of this section (regarding transition rules for certain DDR attributable to services performed in taxable years beginning before January 1, 2013), DDR that is attributable to services performed in a disqualified taxable year of a covered health insurance provider is subject to the section 162(m)(6) deduction limitation even if the taxable year in which the remuneration is otherwise deductible is not a disqualified taxable year. Similarly, DDR is subject to the section 162(m)(6) deduction limitation regardless of whether an applicable individual is a service provider of the covered health insurance provider in the taxable year in which the DDR is otherwise deductible. However, remuneration that is attributable to services performed in a taxable year that is not a disqualified taxable year is not DDR even if the remuneration is otherwise deductible in a disqualified taxable year. See also paragraph (b)(9)(ii) of this section for certain remuneration that is not treated as DDR for purposes of this section.

(12) *Substantial risk of forfeiture.*—For purposes of this section, the term *substantial risk of forfeiture* has the same meaning as provided in § 1.409A-1(d).

(13) *In-service payment.*—An *in-service payment* is any amount that is paid with respect to an applicable individual from an account balance plan described in § 1.409A- 1(c)(2)(i)(A) or (B) or a nonaccount balance plan described in § 1.409A-1(c)(2)(i)(C) in a taxable year of a covered health insurance provider during which at any time the applicable individual is a service provider (including amounts that became otherwise deductible, but were not paid, in a previous taxable year of a covered health insurance provider). Amounts that are paid in the last year that an applicable individual is a service provider (for example, amounts paid at separation from service) are in-service payments if the applicable individual is a service provider at any time during the taxable year of the covered health insurance provider in which the payment is made.

(14) *Payment year.*—For purposes of this section, the term *payment year* means the taxable year of a covered health insurance provider for which remuneration becomes otherwise deductible.

(15) *Measurement date.*—For purposes of this section, the term *measurement date* means the last day of the taxable year of a covered health insurance provider.

(c) *Deduction Limitation.*—(1) *AIR.*—For any disqualified taxable year beginning after December 31, 2012, no deduction is allowed under this chapter for AIR that is attributable to services performed by an applicable individual in that taxable year to the extent that the amount of that remuneration exceeds $500,000.

(2) *DDR.*—For any taxable year beginning after December 31, 2012, no deduction is allowed under this chapter for DDR that is attributable to services performed by an applicable individual in any disqualified taxable year beginning after December 31, 2009, to the extent that the amount of such remuneration exceeds $500,000 reduced (but not below zero) by the sum of:

(i) The AIR for that applicable individual for that disqualified taxable year; and

(ii) The portion of the DDR for those services that was subject to the deduction limitation under section 162(m)(6)(A)(ii) and this paragraph (c)(2) in a preceding taxable year, or would have been subject to the deduction limitation under section 162(m)(6)(A)(ii) and this paragraph (c)(2) in a preceding taxable year if section 162(m)(6) was effective for taxable years beginning after December 31, 2009 and before January 1, 2013.

(d) *Services to which remuneration is attributable.*—(1) *Attribution to a taxable year.*—(i) *In general.*—The deduction limitation under section 162(m)(6) applies to AIR and DDR attributable to services performed by an applicable individual in a disqualified taxable year of a covered health insurance provider. When an amount of AIR or DDR becomes otherwise deductible (and not before that time), that remuneration must be attributed to services performed by an applicable individual in a taxable year of the covered health insurance provider in accordance with the rules of this paragraph (d). After the remuneration has been attributed to services performed by an applicable individual in a taxable year of a covered health insurance provider, the rules of paragraph (e) of this section are then applied to determine whether the deduction with respect to the remuneration is limited by section 162(m)(6).

(ii) Overview.—Paragraphs (d)(1)(iii) through (v) of this section, and paragraph (d)(2) of this section, set forth rules of general applicability for attributing remuneration to services performed by an applicable individual in a taxable year of a covered health insurance provider. Paragraph (d)(3) sets forth two methods for attributing remuneration provided under an account balance plan—the account balance ratio method (described in paragraph (d)(3)(ii) of this section) and the principal additions method (described in paragraph (d)(3)(iii) of this section). Paragraph (d)(4) of this section sets forth two methods for attributing remuneration provided under a nonaccount balance plan—the present value ratio method (described in paragraph (d)(4)(ii) of this section) and the formula benefit ratio method (described in paragraph (d)(4)(iii) of this section). Paragraph (d)(5) of this section sets forth rules for attributing remuneration resulting from equity-based remuneration (such as stock options, stock appreciation rights, restricted stock, and restricted stock units). Paragraph (d)(6) of this section sets forth rules for attributing remuneration that is involuntary separation pay. Paragraph (d)(7) of this section sets forth rules for attributing remuneration that is received under a reimbursement arrangement, and paragraph (d)(8) of this section sets forth rules for attributing remuneration that results from a split-dollar life insurance arrangement.

(iii) No attribution to taxable years during which no services are performed or before a legally binding right arises.—(A) *In general.*—For purposes of this section, remuneration is not attributable—

    (1) To a taxable year of a covered health insurance provider ending before the later of the date the applicable individual begins providing services to the covered health insurance provider (or any member of its aggregated group) and the date the applicable individual obtains a legally binding right to the remuneration, or

    (2) To any other taxable year of a covered health insurance provider during which the applicable individual is not a service provider.

    (B) *Attribution of remuneration before the commencement of services or a legally binding right arises.*—To the extent that remuneration would otherwise be attributable in accordance with paragraphs (d)(2) through (11) of this section to a taxable year ending before the later of the date an applicable individual begins providing services to a covered health insurance provider (or any member of its aggregated group) and the date the applicable individual obtains a legally binding right to the remuneration, the remuneration is attributed to services performed in the taxable year in which the later of these dates occurs. For example, if an applicable individual obtains a contractual right to remuneration in a taxable year of a covered health insurance provider and the remuneration would otherwise be attributable to that taxable year pursuant to paragraph (d)(2) of this section, but the applicable individual does not begin providing services to the covered health insurance provider until the next taxable year, the remuneration is attributable to the taxable year in which the applicable individual begins providing services.

    (iv) Attribution to 12-month periods.—To the extent that a covered health insurance provider is required to attribute remuneration on a daily *pro rata* basis under this paragraph (d), it may treat any 12-month period as having 365 days (and so may ignore the extra day in leap years).

    (v) Remuneration subject to nonlapse restriction or similar formula.—For purposes of this section, if stock or other property is subject to a nonlapse restriction (as defined in § 1.83-3(h)), or if the remuneration payable to an applicable individual is determined under a formula that, if applied to stock or other property, would be a nonlapse restriction, the amount of the remuneration and the attribution of that remuneration to taxable years must be determined based upon application of the nonlapse restriction or formula. For example, if the earnings or losses on an account under an account balance plan are determined based upon the performance of company stock, the valuation of which is based on a formula that if applied to the stock would be a nonlapse restriction, then that formula must be used consistently for purposes of determining the amount of the remuneration credited to that account balance in taxable years and the attribution of that remuneration to taxable years.

(2) *Legally binding right.*—Unless attributable to services performed in a different taxable year pursuant to paragraphs (d)(3) through (11) of this section, remuneration is attributable to services performed in the taxable year of a covered health insurance provider in which an applicable individual obtains a legally binding right to the remuneration. An applicable individual does not have a legally binding right to remuneration if the remuneration may be reduced unilaterally or eliminated by a covered health insurance provider or other person after the services creating the right to the remuneration have been performed. However, if the facts and circumstances indicate that the discretion to reduce or eliminate the remuneration is available or exercisable only upon a condition, or the discretion to reduce or eliminate the remuneration lacks substantive significance, an applicable individual will be considered to have a legally binding right to the remuneration. For this purpose, remuneration is not considered to be subject to unilateral reduction or elimination merely because it may be reduced or eliminated by operation of the objective terms of a plan, such as the application of a nondiscretionary, objective provision creating a substantial risk of forfeiture.

(3) *Account balance plans.*—(i) *In general.*—When remuneration for services performed by an applicable individual for a covered health insurance provider becomes otherwise deductible (for example, because the amount was paid or made available during that taxable year) from a plan described in § 1.409A-1(c)(2)(i)(A) or (B) (an *account balance plan*), that remuneration must be attributed to services performed by the applicable individual in a taxable year of the covered health insurance provider in accordance with an attribution method described in either paragraph (d)(3)(ii) or (d)(3)(iii) of this section. However, except as provided in paragraphs (d)(3)(ii)(D) and (f)(3) of this section, the covered health insurance provider and all members of its aggregated group must apply the same attribution method under this paragraph (d)(3) consistently for all taxable years beginning after September 23, 2014 for all amounts that become otherwise deductible under all account balance plans.

    (ii) *Account balance ratio method.*—(A) *In general.*—Under this method, remuneration for services performed by an applicable individual for a covered health insurance provider that becomes otherwise deductible under an account balance plan must be attributed to services performed by the applicable individual in each taxable year of the covered health insurance provider ending with or before the payment year during which the applicable individual was a service provider and for which the account balance of the applicable individual increased (determined in accordance with paragraph (d)(3)(ii)(B) and (C) of this section). The amount attributed to each such taxable year is equal to the amount of remuneration that becomes otherwise deductible multiplied by a fraction, the numerator of which is the increase in the applicable individual's account balance under the plan for the taxable year, and the denominator of which is the sum of all such increases for all taxable years during which the applicable individual was a service provider. Thus, remuneration that becomes otherwise deductible under a plan is attributed to a taxable year of the covered health insurance provider in proportion to the increase in the applicable individual's account balance for that taxable year.

    (B) *Increase in the account balance.*—For purposes of this paragraph (d)(3)(ii), an increase in an account balance under an account balance plan occurs for a taxable year if the account balance as of the measurement date in that taxable year is greater than the account balance as of the measurement date in every earlier taxable year. In that case, the amount of the increase for that taxable year is equal to the excess of the applicable individual's account balance as of the measurement date for that taxable year over the greatest of the applicable individual's account balances under the plan as of the measurement date in every earlier taxable year. If the applicable individual's account balance as of the measurement date in a taxable year is less than or equal to the applicable individual's account balance as of the measurement date in any earlier taxable year, there is no increase in the account balance for that later taxable year.

    (C) *Certain account balance adjustments.*—For purposes of determining the account balance on a measurement date under paragraph (d)(3)(ii)(B) of this section, the account balance is adjusted as provided in this paragraph (d)(3)(ii)(C).

    (1) In-service payments.—If an in-service payment is made from the account of an applicable individual under an account balance plan in any taxable year of a covered health insurance provider, then the rules of this paragraph (d)(3)(ii)(C)(1) apply.

    (i) Solely for purposes of determining the increase in the applicable individual's account balance as of the measurement date in the payment year (and not for purposes of attributing any amount that becomes otherwise deductible in any later taxable year), the account balance as of the measurement date for that taxable year is increased by the amount of all in-service payments made from the plan during that taxable year.

    (ii) For purposes of attributing any amount that becomes otherwise deductible under the plan in any taxable year after the payment year of the in-service payment —

    (A) the account balance as of the measurement date in each taxable year that ends before the taxable year to which the in-service payment is attributed pursuant to this paragraph (d)(3)(ii) is reduced by the sum of the amount of the in-service payment that is attributed to that taxable year and the amount of the in-service

payment that is attributed to each taxable year that ends before that taxable year, if any, and

(B) to the extent that the in-service payment includes an amount that was deductible by the covered health insurance provider in a previous taxable year and, therefore, was previously attributable to services performed by the applicable individual in one or more taxable years of the covered health insurance provider (for example, because the amount was made available in a previous taxable year but was not paid at that time), the account balance as of the measurement date for each taxable year that ends before the taxable year to which the in-service payment is attributed pursuant to this paragraph (d)(3)(ii) is reduced by the sum of the amount of the in-service payment previously attributable to that taxable year and the amount of the in-service payment previously attributable to each taxable year that ends before that taxable year, if any.

(2) Certain increases after ceasing to be a service provider.— Any addition (other than income or earnings) to an account balance plan made in a taxable year that begins after an applicable individual ceases to be a service provider (and that ends before the applicable individual becomes a service provider again, if applicable) is added to the account balance of the applicable individual as of the measurement date of the first preceding taxable year in which the applicable individual was a service provider.

(3) Account balance adjustments for grandfathered amounts.— If a covered health insurance provider uses the principal additions method for determining grandfathered amounts for an applicable individual under paragraph (h) of this section, then, for purposes of determining the increase in the applicable individual's account balance, the account balance as of any measurement date is reduced by the amount of any grandfathered amounts otherwise included in the account balance.

(D) *Transition rule for amounts attributed before the applicability date of the final regulations.*—Amounts that become otherwise deductible in taxable years beginning before September 23, 2014 may be attributed to services performed in taxable years of a covered health insurance provider under the rules set forth in the proposed regulations. If a covered health insurance provider attributes an amount paid to an applicable individual pursuant to a method permitted under the proposed regulations and then chooses to use the account balance ratio method to attribute amounts that subsequently become otherwise deductible with respect to that applicable individual, then, for purposes of applying the account balance ratio method to attribute any amount that becomes otherwise deductible under the plan after the taxable year in which the last payment was made that was attributed pursuant to the proposed regulations, the account balance as of the measurement date for each taxable year that ends before the taxable year in which the last payment that was attributed pursuant to the proposed regulations is reduced by the sum of the amount previously attributed to that taxable year under the proposed regulations and the amount previously attributable to each taxable year that ends prior to that taxable year under the proposed regulations, if any.

(iii) *Principal additions method.*—(A) *In general.*—Under this method, remuneration that becomes otherwise deductible under an account balance plan during a payment year must be attributed to services performed by the applicable individual in the taxable year of the covered health insurance provider during which the applicable individual was a service provider and in which the principal addition to which the amount relates is credited under the plan (determined in accordance with paragraph (d)(3)(iii)(B) and (C) of this section). An amount relates to a principal addition if the amount is a payment of the principal addition or earnings on the principal addition, based on a separate accounting of these amounts. The principal additions method described in this paragraph may be used to attribute amounts that become otherwise deductible under an account balance plan only if the covered health insurance provider separately accounts for each principal addition to the plan (and any earnings thereon) and traces each amount that becomes otherwise deductible under the plan to a principal addition made in a taxable year of the covered health insurance provider.

(B) *Principal addition.*—(1) For purposes of this paragraph (d)(3)(iii), the excess (if any) of the sum of the account balance of an applicable individual in an account balance plan as of the last day of a taxable year and any payments made during the taxable year over the account balance as of the last day of the immediately preceding taxable year, that is not due to earnings or losses (as described in paragraph (d)(3)(iii)(C) of this section), is treated as a principal addition that is credited to the plan in that taxable year if the applicable individual was a service provider during that taxable year. If the applicable individual was not a service provider during that taxable year, the excess described in the preceding sentence is treated

as a principal addition that is credited to the plan in accordance with paragraph (d)(3)(iii)(B)(2) of this section.

(2) Principal additions after termination of employment.— Any principal addition to an account balance plan made in a taxable year that begins after an applicable individual ceases to be a service provider (and that ends before the applicable individual becomes a service provider again, if applicable) is treated as a principal addition that is credited in the first preceding taxable year in which the applicable individual was a service provider.

(C) *Earnings.*—Whether remuneration constitutes earnings on a principal addition is determined under the principles defining income attributable to an amount taken into account under §31.3121(v)(2)-1(d)(2). Therefore, for an account balance plan, earnings on an amount deferred generally include an amount credited on behalf of an applicable individual under the terms of the arrangement that reflects a rate of return that does not exceed either the rate of return on a predetermined actual investment (as defined in §31.3121(v)(2)-1(d)(2)(i)(B)), or, if the income does not reflect the rate of return on a predetermined actual investment, a rate of return that reflects a reasonable rate of interest (as defined in §31.3121(v)(2)-1(d)(2)(i)(C)). For purposes of this paragraph (d)(3)(iii), the use of a rate of return that is not based on a predetermined actual investment or a reasonable rate of interest generally will result in the treatment of some or all of the remuneration as a principal addition that is attributable to services performed by an applicable individual in a taxable year of a covered health insurance provider in accordance with this paragraph (d)(3)(iii) of this section.

(4) *Nonaccount balance plans.*—(i) *In general.*—When remuneration for services performed by an applicable individual for a covered health insurance provider becomes otherwise deductible under a plan described in §1.409A-1(c)(2)(i)(C) (a nonaccount balance plan), that remuneration must be attributed to services performed by the applicable individual in a taxable year of the covered health insurance provider in accordance with the attribution method described in either paragraph (d)(4)(ii) or (d)(4)(iii) of this section. However, except as provided in paragraphs (d)(4)(ii)(D) and (d)(4)(iii)(D) and (f)(3) of this section, the covered health insurance provider and all members of its aggregated group must apply the same attribution method under this paragraph (d)(4) consistently for all taxable years beginning after September 23, 2014 for all amounts that become deductible under all nonaccount balance plans.

(ii) *Present value ratio attribution method.*—(A) *In general.*— Under this method, remuneration for services performed by an applicable individual for a covered health insurance provider that becomes otherwise deductible under a nonaccount balance plan must be attributed to services performed by the applicable individual in each taxable year of the covered health insurance provider ending with or before the payment year during which the applicable individual was a service provider for which the present value of the future payment(s) to be made to or on behalf of the applicable individual under the plan increased (determined in accordance with paragraph (d)(3)(ii)(B) and (C) of this section). The amount attributed to each such taxable year is equal to the amount of remuneration that becomes otherwise deductible under the plan multiplied by a fraction, the numerator of which is the increase in the present value of the future payment(s) to which the applicable individual has a legally binding right under the plan for the taxable year, and the denominator of which is the sum of all such increases for all taxable years during which the applicable individual was a service provider. Thus, remuneration that becomes otherwise deductible under a plan is attributed to a taxable year of the covered health insurance provider in proportion to the increase in the present value of the future payment(s) under the plan for that taxable year.

(B) *Increase in present value of future payments.*—For purposes of this paragraph (d)(4)(ii), for a taxable year of a covered health insurance provider, an increase in the present value of the future payment(s) to which an applicable individual has a legally binding right under a nonaccount balance plan occurs if the present value of the future payment(s) as of the measurement date in the taxable year is greater than the present value of the future payment(s) as of the measurement date in every earlier taxable year. In that case, the amount of the increase for that taxable year is equal to the excess of the present value of the future payment(s) to which the applicable individual has a legally binding right under the plan as of the measurement date for that taxable year over the greatest present value of the future payment(s) to which the applicable individual had a legally binding right under the plan as of the measurement date in every earlier taxable year. If the present value of the future payment(s) as of a measurement date in a taxable year is less than or equal to the present value of the future payment(s) as of the measurement date in any earlier taxable year, then there is no increase in the present value of the future payment(s) to which the applicable indi-

Itemized Deductions for Individuals and Corps.
See p. 20,601 for regulations not amended to reflect law changes
25,253

vidual has a legally binding right under the plan for that later taxable year. For purposes of determining the increase (or decrease) in the present value of a future payment(s) under a nonaccount balance plan, the rules of §31.3121(v)(2)-1(c)(2) apply (including the requirement that reasonable actuarial assumptions and methods be used).

(C) *Certain present value adjustments.*—For purposes of determining the present value of the future payment(s) to which an applicable individual has a legally binding right to receive as of a measurement date under paragraph (d)(4)(ii)(B) of this section, the present value is adjusted as provided in this paragraph (d)(3)(iii)(C).

(1) In-service payments.—If an in-service payment is made to or on behalf of an applicable individual under a nonaccount balance plan in any taxable year of a covered health insurance provider, then the rules of this paragraph (d)(3)(iii)(C)(1) apply.

(i) Solely for purposes of determining the increase in the present value of the future payment(s) under the plan for the payment year (and not for purposes of attributing any amount that becomes otherwise deductible in any later taxable year), the present value of the future payment(s) under the plan as of the measurement date in the payment year is increased by the amount of any reduction in the present value of the future payment(s) resulting from the in-service payment made from the plan during that taxable year.

(ii) For purposes of attributing any amount that becomes otherwise deductible under the plan in any taxable year after the payment year of the in-service payment, the present value of the future payment(s) as of the measurement date for each taxable year that ends before the payment year is reduced by the present value of the future payment to which the applicable individual had a legally binding right to be paid on the date of the in-service payment (determined as of the measurement date based upon all of the applicable factors under the plan as of the measurement date, such as compensation and years of service on that date).

(2) Increases in the present value of future payments after ceasing to be a service provider.—Any increase in the present value of the future payment(s) under a plan in a taxable year that begins after an applicable individual ceases to be a service provider (and that ends before the applicable individual becomes a service provider again, if applicable) that is not due merely to the passage of time or a change in the reasonable actuarial assumptions used to determine the present value of the future payment(s) is added to the present value of the future payment(s) for the applicable individual as of the measurement date of the most recent preceding taxable year in which the applicable individual was a service provider.

(D) *Transition rule for amounts attributed before the effective date of the final regulations.*—Amounts that become otherwise deductible in taxable years beginning before September 23, 2014 may be attributed under the rules set forth in the proposed regulations. If a covered health insurance provider attributes an amount paid to an applicable individual pursuant to the proposed regulations and then chooses to use the present value ratio method to attribute amounts that subsequently become otherwise deductible with respect to that applicable individual, then, for purposes of applying the present value ratio method to attribute any amount that becomes otherwise deductible under the plan in any taxable year after the taxable year in which the last payment was made that was attributed pursuant to the proposed regulations, the present value of the future payment(s) as of the measurement date for each taxable year that ends before the taxable year in which the last payment that was attributed pursuant to the proposed regulations is reduced by the present value of each future payment to which the applicable individual had a legally binding right to be paid that was attributed pursuant to the proposed regulations (determined as of the measurement date based upon all of the applicable factors under the plan as of the measurement date, such as compensation and years of service on that date), with no adjustment for an amount that became otherwise deductible, but was not paid.

(iii) Formula benefit ratio method.—(A) *In general.*—Under this method, remuneration that becomes otherwise deductible under a nonaccount balance plan on a date (referred to for these purposes as *the date of payment*) must be attributed to services performed by the applicable individual in each taxable year of the covered health insurance provider ending with or before the payment year during which the applicable individual was a service provider and for which the formula benefit of the applicable individual under the plan increased (determined in accordance with paragraph (d)(3)(iii)(B), (C) and (D) of this section. The amount attributed to each such taxable year is equal to the amount of remuneration that becomes otherwise deductible under the plan on the date of payment multiplied by a fraction, the numerator of which is the increase in the applicable individual's formula benefit under the plan for the taxable year and the denominator of which is the sum of all such increases for all

taxable years during which the applicable individual was a service provider (which will generally be the amount that becomes otherwise deductible under the plan on the date of payment). Thus, remuneration that becomes otherwise deductible under a plan is attributed to a taxable year of the covered health insurance provider in proportion to the increase in the applicable individual's formula benefit under the plan in that taxable year.

(B) *Formula benefit.*—For purposes of this paragraph (d)(4)(iii), an applicable individual's formula benefit as of any date is the benefit (or portion thereof) to which the applicable individual has a legally binding right under a nonaccount balance plan as of that date determined based upon all of the applicable factors under the plan (for example, compensation and years of service as of that date), disregarding any substantial risk of forfeiture and assuming that the applicable individual meets any applicable eligibility requirements for the benefit as of that date. For this purpose, the formula benefit is expressed in the form that it has become otherwise deductible. For example, if an applicable individual's benefit under a plan is paid in the form of a single lump sum, then the applicable individual's formula benefit under the plan is expressed in the form of a single lump sum for all purposes under this paragraph (d)(4)(iii). If the amount that becomes otherwise deductible is payable in more than one form of payment (for example, 50 percent of the benefit is paid in the form of a lump sum and 50 percent is paid in the form of a life annuity), then each separate form of payment is treated as a separate formula benefit to which this paragraph (d)(4)(iii) is applied separately.

(C) *Increase in formula benefit.*—For purposes of this paragraph (d)(4)(iii), an increase in an applicable individual's formula benefit under a nonaccount balance plan occurs for a taxable year of a covered health insurance provider if the formula benefit as of the measurement date in that taxable year is greater than the formula benefit as of the measurement date in every earlier taxable year. In that case, the amount of the increase for that taxable year is equal to excess of the formula benefit as of the measurement date in that taxable year over the greatest formula benefit as of any measurement date in any earlier taxable year. If the applicable individual's formula benefit as of a measurement date in a taxable year is less than or equal to the applicable individual's formula benefit as of the measurement date in any earlier taxable year, there is no increase in the formula benefit to which the applicable individual has a legally binding right under the plan for that later taxable year.

(D) *Certain adjustments.*—For purposes of determining the increase in the formula benefit as of a date of payment under paragraph (d)(4)(iii)(C) of this section, the rules of this paragraph (d)(3)(iii)(D) apply—

(1) Attribution to payment year.—Solely for purposes of attributing a payment under this paragraph (d)(4)(iii) (including an in-service payment), the date of payment is substituted for the measurement date in the payment year to determine whether an increase in the formula benefit occurs in the payment year and the amount of any such increase.

(2) Amounts not paid.—If an amount becomes otherwise deductible under a nonaccount balance plan, but is not paid, the formula benefit for that amount must be determined using the form in which it will be paid, if that form is known, or any form in which it may be paid, if the actual form of payment is unknown.

(3) Increases in the formula benefit after ceasing to be a service provider.—Any increase in the formula benefit with respect to an applicable individual resulting from a legally binding right arising in a taxable year that begins after the applicable individual ceases to be a service provider (and that ends before the applicable individual becomes a service provider again, if applicable) is added to the formula benefit with respect to the applicable individual as of the measurement date of the first preceding taxable year in which the applicable individual was a service provider. However, any increase in the formula benefit resulting from a legally binding right arising in a taxable year that begins before the applicable individual ceases to be a service provider is added to the formula benefit with respect to the applicable individual as of the measurement date of the taxable year in which the legally binding right arises, even if the increase is not reflected until after the applicable individual ceases to be a service provider (such as in the case of a cost of living adjustment).

(5) Equity-based remuneration.—(i) *Stock options and stock appreciation rights.*—(A) *In general.*—Except as provided in paragraph (d)(5)(i)(B) of this section, remuneration resulting from the exercise of a stock option (including compensation income arising at the time of a disqualifying disposition of an incentive stock option described in section 422 or an option under an employee stock purchase plan described in section 423) or a stock appreciation right (SAR) is

attributable to services performed by an applicable individual for a covered health insurance provider on a daily *pro rata* basis over the period beginning on the date of grant (within the meaning of §1.409A- 1(b)(5)(vi)(B)) of the stock option or SAR and ending on the date that the stock option or SAR is exercised, excluding any days on which the applicable individual is not a service provider.

(B) *Stock options or SARs subject to a substantial risk of forfeiture.*—If a stock option or SAR is subject to a substantial risk of forfeiture, a covered health insurance provider may attribute remuneration resulting from the exercise of the stock option or SAR to services performed by an applicable individual in a taxable year on a daily *pro rata* basis over the period beginning on the date of grant (within the meaning of §1.409A-1(b)(5)(vi)(B)) of the stock option or SAR and ending on the first date that the stock option or SAR is no longer subject to a substantial risk of forfeiture, but only if the covered health insurance provider uses this attribution method consistently for all stock options or SARs exercised in taxable years of a covered health insurance provider beginning after September 23, 2014 except as provided in paragraph (f)(3) of this section.

(ii) *Restricted stock.*—Remuneration resulting from restricted stock, for which an election under section 83(b) has not been made, that becomes substantially vested or transferred is attributed on a daily *pro rata* basis to services performed by an applicable individual for a covered health insurance provider over the period, excluding any days on which the applicable individual is not a service provider, beginning on the date the applicable individual obtains a legally binding right to the restricted stock and ending on the earliest of—

(A) The date the restricted stock becomes substantially vested, or

(B) The date the restricted stock is transferred by the applicable individual.

(iii) *Restricted stock units.*—Remuneration resulting from a restricted stock unit (*RSU*) is attributed on a daily pro rata basis to services performed by an applicable individual for a covered health insurance provider over the period beginning on the date the applicable individual obtains a legally binding right to the RSU and ending on the date the remuneration is paid or made available, excluding any days on which the applicable individual is not a service provider.

(iv) *Partnership interests and other equity.*—[Reserved]

(6) *Involuntary separation pay.*—Involuntary separation pay is attributable to services performed by an applicable individual for a covered health insurance provider in the taxable year in which the involuntary separation from service occurs. Alternatively, the covered health insurance provider may attribute involuntary separation pay to services performed by an applicable individual on a daily *pro rata* basis beginning on the date that the applicable individual obtains a legally binding right to the involuntary separation pay and ending on the date of the involuntary separation from service. Involuntary separation pay to different individuals may be attributed using different methods; however, if involuntary separation payments are made to the same individual over multiple taxable years, all the payments must be attributed using the same method. For purposes of this section, the term *involuntary separation pay* means remuneration to which an applicable individual has a right to payment solely as a result of the individual's involuntary separation from service (within the meaning of §1.409A-1(n)). To the extent that involuntary separation pay is attributed to services performed in two or more taxable years of a covered health insurance provider as permitted under this paragraph, any amount of involuntary separation pay that is paid or made available must be attributed to services performed in all of those taxable years in the same proportion that the total involuntary separation pay is attributed to taxable years of the covered health insurance provider.

(7) *Reimbursements.*—Remuneration that is provided in the form of a reimbursement or benefit provided in-kind (other than cash) is attributable to services performed by an applicable individual in the taxable year of a covered health insurance provider in which the applicable individual makes a payment for which the applicable individual has a right to reimbursement or receives an in-kind benefit, except that remuneration provided in the form of a reimbursement or in-kind benefit during a taxable year of a covered health insurance provider in which an applicable individual is not a service provider is attributable to services performed in the most recent preceding taxable year of the covered health insurance provider in which the applicable individual is a service provider.

(8) *Split-dollar life insurance.*—Remuneration resulting from a split-dollar life insurance arrangement (as defined in §1.61-22(b)) under which an applicable individual has a legally binding right to

economic benefits described in §1.61-22(d)(2)(ii) (policy cash value to which the non-owner has current access within the meaning of §1.61-22(d)(4)(ii)) or §1.61-22(d)(2)(iii) (any other economic benefits provided to the nonowner) is attributable to services performed in the taxable year of the covered health insurance provider in which the legally binding right arises. Split-dollar life insurance arrangements under which payments are treated as split-dollar loans under §1.7872-15 generally will not give rise to DDR within the meaning of paragraph (b)(11) of this section, although they may give rise to AIR. However, in certain situations, this type of arrangement may give rise to DDR for purposes of section 162(m)(6), for example, if amounts due on a split-dollar loan are waived, cancelled, or forgiven.

(9) *Examples.*—The following examples illustrate the principles of paragraphs (d)(1) through (8) of this section. For purposes of these examples, each corporation has a taxable year that is the calendar year and is a covered health insurance provider for all relevant taxable years, DDR is otherwise deductible in the taxable year in which it is paid, and amounts payable under nonaccount balance plans are not forfeitable upon the death of the applicable individual. For purposes of these examples, the interest rates used in these examples are assumed to be reasonable.

Example 1 (Account balance plan - account balance ratio method with earnings and a single payment). (i) B is an applicable individual of corporation Y for all relevant taxable years. On January 1, 2016, B begins participating in a nonqualified deferred compensation plan of Y that is an account balance plan. Under the terms of the plan, all amounts are fully vested at all times, and Y will pay B's entire account balance on January 1, 2019. B's account earns five percent interest per year, compounded annually. Y credits $10,000 to B under the plan annually on January 1 for three years beginning on January 1, 2016. Thus, B's account balance is $10,500 ($10,000 + ($10,000 × 5%)) on December 31, 2016; $21,525 ($10,500 + $10,000 + ($20,500 × 5%)) on December 31, 2017; and $33,101 ($21,525 + $10,000 + ($31,525 × 5%)) on December 31, 2018. On January 1, 2019, Y pays B $33,101, the entire account balance. Y attributes payments under its account balance plans using the account balance ratio method described in paragraph (d)(3)(i) of this section.

(ii) The increase in B's account balance during 2016 is $10,500 ($10,500 - zero); the increase in B's account balance for 2017 is $11,025 ($21,525 - $10,500); and the increase in B's account balance for 2018 is $11,576 ($33,101 - $21,525). The sum of all the increases is $33,101 ($10,500 + $11,025 + $11,576). Accordingly, for Y's 2016 taxable year, the attribution fraction is .3172 ($10,500 / $33,101); for Y's 2017 taxable year, the attribution fraction is .3331 ($11,025 / $33,101); and for Y's 2018 taxable year, the attribution fraction is .3497 ($11,576 / $33,101).

(iii) With respect to the $33,301 payment made on January 1, 2019, $10,500 ($33,101 × .3172) of DDR is attributable to services performed by B in Y's 2016 taxable year; $11,026 ($33,101 × .3331) of DDR is attributable to services performed by B in Y's 2017 taxable year; and $11,575 ($33,101 × .3497) of DDR is attributable to services performed by B in Y's 2018 taxable year.

Example 2 (Account balance plan - principal additions method with earnings and a single payment. (i) The facts are the same as in *Example 1*, except that Y attributes remuneration using the principal additions method described in paragraph (d)(3)(ii) of this section.

(ii) The $10,000 principal addition made on January 1, 2016 and $1,576 of earnings thereon (interest on the 2016 $10,000 principal addition at five percent for three years compounded annually) are attributable to services performed by B in Y's 2016 taxable year; the principal addition of $10,000 on January 1, 2017 and $1,025 of earnings thereon (interest on the 2017 $10,000 principal addition at five percent for two years compounded annually) are attributable to services performed by B in Y's 2017 taxable year; and the principal addition of $10,000 to B's account on January 1, 2018 and $500 of earnings thereon (interest on the 2018 $10,000 principal addition at five percent for one year compounded annually) are attributable to services performed by B in Y's 2018 taxable year. Accordingly, with respect to the $33,301 payment made on January 1, 2019, $11,576 ($10,000 + $1,576) is attributable to services performed by B in Y's 2016 taxable year; $11,025 ($10,000 + $1,025) is attributable to services performed in Y's 2017 taxable year; and $10,500 ($10,000 + $500) is attributable to services performed by B in Y's 2018 taxable year.

Example 3 (Account balance plan - account balance ratio method with earnings and losses). (i) J is an applicable individual of corporation Z for all relevant taxable years. On January 1, 2016, J begins participating in a nonqualified deferred compensation plan of Z that is an account balance plan. Under the terms of the plan, all amounts are fully vested at all times, and Z will pay J's entire account balance on January 1, 2019. Z credits $10,000 to J under the plan on January 1, 2016 and January 1, 2018. Earnings under the terms of the plan are based on a predetermined actual investment (as defined in §31.3121(v)(2)-1(e)(2)(i)(B)), which results in J's account balance increasing by five percent in the 2016 taxable year, decreasing by five percent in the 2017 taxable year, and increasing again by five percent in the 2018 taxable year. Therefore, on December 31, 2016, J's account balance is $10,500 ($10,000 + ($10,000 x 5%)); on December 31, 2017, J's account balance is $9,975 ($10,500 - ($10,500 × 5%)); and on December 31, 2018, J's account balance is $20,974 ($9,975 + $10,000 + ($19,975 × 5%)). On January 1, 2019, Z pays J the entire account balance of $20,974.

(ii) The increase in J's account balance for 2016 is $10,500 ($10,500 - zero); the increase in J's account balance for 2017 is zero (because J's account balance decreased by $525 ($9,975 - $10,500)); the increase in J's account balance for 2018 is $10,474 ($20,974 - $10,500, which is the highest account balance in any prior taxable year). The sum of all the increases is $20,974 ($10,500 + $10,474). Thus, for Z's 2016 taxable year the attribution fraction is .5006 ($10,500 / $20,974); for Z's 2017 taxable year the attribution fraction is zero because there was a decrease in the account balance for the year; and for Z's 2018 taxable year the attribution fraction is .4994 ($10,474 / $20,974).

(iii) Accordingly, with respect to the $20,974 payment made on January 1, 2019, $10,499 ($20,974 × .5006) of DDR is attributable to services performed by J in Z's 2016 taxable year, and $10,474 ($20,973.75 × .4994) of DDR is attributable to services performed by J in Z's 2018 taxable year. No amount is attributable to services performed by J in Z's 2017 taxable year because there was no increase in the account balance for that taxable year.

Example 4 (Account balance plan — principal additions method with earnings and losses). (i) The facts are the same as in *Example 3*, except that Z attributes remuneration using the principal additions method described in paragraph (d)(3)(ii) of this section.

(ii) The $10,000 principal addition made on January 1, 2016 and the $474 of net earnings thereon ($500 of earnings for 2016, $525 of losses for 2017, and $499 of earnings for 2018) are attributable to services performed by J in Z's 2016 taxable year; and the $10,000 principal addition made on January 1, 2018 and the $500 of earnings thereon are attributable to services performed by J in Z's 2018 taxable year. Accordingly, with respect to the $20,974 payment made on January 1, 2019, $10,474 ($10,000 + $474) of DDR is attributable to services performed by J in Z's 2016 taxable year, and $10,500 ($10,000 + $500) of DDR is attributable to services performed by J in Z's 2018 taxable year.

Example 5 (Account balance plan - account balance ratio method with losses and an in-service payment). (i) N is an applicable individual of corporation M for all relevant taxable years. On January 1, 2016, N begins participating in a nonqualified deferred compensation plan sponsored by M that is an account balance plan. Under the plan, all amounts are fully vested at all times. The balances in N's account are $110,000 on December 31, 2016; $90,000 on December 31, 2017; $250,000 on December 31, 2018; and $240,000 on December 31, 2019. N ceases providing services to N on December 31, 2019. In accordance with the plan terms, M pays to N $10,000 on September 30, 2017, $150,000 on January 1, 2021, and $100,000 on January 1, 2022. M attributes payments under its account balance plans using the account balance ratio method described in paragraph (d)(3)(i) of this section.

(ii) For purposes of attributing the $10,000 payment made on September 30, 2017 to taxable years, the increase in N's account balance for 2016 is $110,000 ($110,000 - zero). N's account balance for 2017 is treated as $100,000 ($90,000 + $10,000 payment on September 30, 2017), but, because the account balance of $100,000 is less than the account balance in an earlier year, the increase in N's account balance for 2017 is zero. The sum of all the increases in N's account balance is $110,000 ($110,000 + $0). Thus, the attribution fraction for 2016 is 1 ($110,000 / $110,000), and the attribution fraction for 2017 is zero ($0 / $110,000). Accordingly, with respect to the $10,000 payment made on September 30, 2017, the entire $10,000 is attributable to services performed by N in M's 2016 taxable year, and no amount is attributable to services performed by N in M's 2017 taxable year.

(iii) After attributing the September 30, 2017 payment of $10,000 to 2016, N's account balance for 2016 is treated as being $100,000 ($110,000 - $10,000), and the increase for 2016 is likewise treated as $100,000; N's account balance for 2017 decreased; the increase in N's account balance for 2018 is $150,000 ($250,000 - $100,000); and N's account balance for 2018 decreased. The sum of all the increases is $250,000 ($100,000 + $150,000). Thus, the attribution fraction for 2016 is .40 ($100,000 / $250,000); *the attribution fraction for 2017 is zero ($0 / $250,000); the attribution fraction for 2018 is .60 ($150,000 / $250,000); and the attribution fraction for 2019 is zero ($0 / $250,000).*

(iv) Accordingly, with respect to the $150,000 payment made on January 1, 2021, $60,000 ($150,000 × .40) is attributable to services performed by N in M's 2016 taxable year, and $90,000 ($150,000 × .60) is attributable to services performed by N in M's 2018 taxable year. With respect to the $100,000 payment made on January 1, 2022, $40,000 ($100,000 × .40) is attributable to services performed by N in M's 2016 taxable year, and $60,000 ($100,000 × .60) is attributable to services performed by N in M's 2018 taxable year. No amount is

attributable to services performed by N in M's 2017 and 2019 taxable years.

Example 6 (Account balance plan - principal additions method with multiple payments). (i) O is an applicable individual of corporation L for all relevant taxable years. On January 1, 2016, O begins participating in a nonqualified deferred compensation plan sponsored by L that is an account balance plan. Under the plan, all amounts are fully vested at all times. L credits principal additions to O's account each year, and credits earnings based on a predetermined actual investment within the meaning of §31.3121(v)(2)-1(d)(2)(i)(B). L makes principal additions of $90,000 on June 30, 2016; $140,000 on June 30, 2017; and $180,000 on June 30, 2018. The predetermined actual investment earns five percent for 2016, seven percent for 2017; eight percent for 2018; and nine percent for 2019 Thus, as of December 31, 2018, the earnings with respect to the $90,000 principal addition made on June 30, 2016 are $16,605, for a total of $106,605; and the earnings with respect to the $140,000 principal addition made on June 30, 2017 are $16,492, for a total of $156,492. As of January 1, 2020, the earnings with respect to the $180,000 principal addition made on June 30, 2018 are $24,048, for a total of $204,048. Under the terms of the plan, the principal addition (and earnings thereon) made on June 30, 2016 and June 30, 2017 are payable on December 31, 2018, and the principal addition (and earnings thereon) made on June 30, 2018 is payable on January 1, 2020. On December 31, 2018, L pays O $263,097 in accordance with the plan terms. On January 1, 2020, L pays O the remaining account balance of $204,048 in accordance with the plan terms.

(ii) The $263,097 payment made on December 31, 2018 is attributed to services performed by O in the 2016 and 2017 taxable years. Of the $263,097 payment, $106,605 is attributable to services performed by O in L's 2016 taxable year because this amount represents the $90,000 principal addition made on June 30, 2016 and earnings thereon. The remaining $156,492 is attributable to services performed by O in L's 2017 taxable year because this amount represents the $140,000 principal addition made on June 30, 2017 and earnings thereon. The $204,048 payment made on January 1, 2020 is attributable to services performed by O in L's 2018 taxable year because this amount represents the $180,000 principal addition made on June 30, 2018 and earnings thereon.

Example 7 (Account balance plan - account balance ratio method with an employer contribution after the applicable individual ceases to be a service provider). (i) A is an applicable individual of corporation Z for all relevant taxable years. On January 1, 2016, A begins participating in a nonqualified deferred compensation plan of Z that is an account balance plan. Under the terms of the plan, all amounts are fully vested at all times. The balances in A's account (including employer contributions and earnings) are $20,000 on December 31, 2016, and $60,000 on December 31, 2017. On December 31, 2017, A ceases providing services to Z. On January 1, 2019, Z makes a discretionary contribution of $30,000 to A's account balance plan. On December 31, 2019, in accordance with the plan terms, Z pays $120,000 to A, which is N's entire account balance. Z attributes payments under its account balance plans using the account balance ratio method described in paragraph (d)(3)(i) of this section.

(ii) The increase in A's account balance for 2016 is $20,000; the increase in A's account balance for 2017 is $40,000. The discretionary contribution made on January 1, 2019 of $30,000 is added to the account balance for 2017. Thus, the discretionary contribution of $30,000 on January 1, 2019, is treated as increasing A's account balance for 2017 by $30,000. The increase in A's account balance for 2016 is $20,000, and the increase in A's account balance for 2017 is $70,000 ($40,000 + $30,000). The sum of all the increases is $90,000 ($20,000+$70,000).

(iii) Thus, the attribution fraction for 2016 is .2222 ($20,000 / $90,000); and the attribution fraction for 2017 is .7778 ($70,000 / $90,000). Accordingly, with respect to the $120,000 payment made on January 1, 2019, $26,664 ($120,000 × .2222) is attributable to services performed by A in Z's 2016 taxable year, and $93,336 ($120,000 × .7778) is attributable to services performed by A in Z's 2017 taxable year.

Example 8 (Account balance plan - principal additions method with a principal addition after the applicable individual ceases to be a service provider). (i) C is an applicable individual of corporation X for all relevant taxable years. On January 1, 2016, C begins participating in a nonqualified deferred compensation plan of X that is an account balance plan. Earnings under the terms of the plan are based on a predetermined actual investment (as defined in §31.3121(v)(2)-1(e)(2)(i)(B)). Under the terms of the plan, all amounts are fully vested at all times. X credits a $10,000 principal addition to C under the plan on April 1, 2016, and a $20,000 principal addition to C on April 1, 2017. C ceases providing services to X on December 31, 2017. On January 1, 2019, X credits $30,000 to C's account in recognition of C's past services. The $10,000 principal addition made on April 1, 2016 increases to $15,000 as of December 31, 2018, as a result of earnings. The $20,000 principal addition made on April 1, 2017, increases to $28,000 as of December 31, 2019 as a result of earnings.

The January 1, 2019, contribution of $30,000 increases to $33,000 as of December 31, 2019, as a result of earnings. On December 31, 2019, in accordance with the plan terms, X pays C's entire account balance of $76,000. X attributes payments under its account balance plans using the principal additions method described in paragraph (d)(3)(ii) of this section.

(ii) When the $76,000 payment is made to C on December 31, 2019, the remuneration becomes attributable to service performed by C in prior taxable years. The $10,000 principal addition in 2016 plus earnings thereon of $5,000 are attributable to services performed by C in X's 2016 taxable year, and the $20,000 principal addition in 2017 (plus earnings thereon of $8,000) are attributable to services performed by C in X's 2017 taxable year. The principal addition of $30,000 plus earnings thereon of $3,000 ($33,000) are also attributable to services performed by C in X's 2017 taxable year. Thus, $16,500 of the $33,000 is attributed to services performed by C in X's 2017 taxable year.

(iii) Accordingly, with respect to the $76,000 payment by X to C on December 31, 2019, $15,000 ($10,000 + $5,000) is attributed to services performed by C in X's 2016 taxable year, and $61,000 ($20,000 + $8,000 + $33,000) is attributed to services performed by C in X's 2017 taxable year.

Example 9 (Nonaccount balance plan - present value ratio method with a single payment). (i) C is an applicable individual of corporation X for all relevant taxable years. On January 1, 2015, X grants C a vested right to a $100,000 payment on January 1, 2020. C ceases providing services on December 31, 2019. The payment of $100,000 is made on January 1, 2020. X determines the present value of the payment using an interest rate of five percent for all years.

(ii) The present value of $100,000 payable on January 1, 2020, determined using a five percent interest rate, is $82,270 as of December 31, 2015; $86,384 as of December 31, 2016; $90,703 as of December 31, 2017; $95,238 as of December 31, 2018, and $100,000 as of December 31, 2019. Accordingly, $82,270 is the amount of the increase in the present value of the future payment of $100,000 for X's 2015 taxable year ($82,270 - $0); $4,114 ($86,384 - $82,270) is the increase in the present value of the future payment for X's 2016 taxable year; $4,319 ($90,703 - $86,384) is the increase in the present value of the future payment for X's 2017 taxable year; $4,535 ($95,238 - $90,703) is the increase in the present value of the future payment for X's 2018 taxable year; and $4,762 ($100,000 - $95,238) is the increase in the present value of the future payment for X's 2019 taxable year. The sum of all the increases is $100,000 ($82,270 + $4,114 + $4,319 + $4,535 + $4,762). Thus, the attribution fraction for 2015 is .8227 ($82,270 / $100,000); the attribution fraction for 2016 is .0411 ($4,114 / $100,000); the attribution fraction for 2017 is .0432 ($4,319 / $100,000); the attribution fraction for 2018 is .0454 ($4,535 / $100,000); and the attribution fraction for 2019 is .0476 ($4,762 / $100,000).

(iii) The $100,000 payment made on January 1, 2020 is multiplied by the attribution fraction for each taxable year, and the result is the amount that is attributable to service performed by C for that taxable year. Accordingly, $82,270 ($100,000 × .8227) is attributable to services performed by C in X's 2015 taxable year; $4,114 ($100,000 × .0411) is attributable to services performed by C in X's 2016 taxable year; $4,319 ($100,000 × .0432) is attributable to services performed by C in X's 2017 taxable year; $4,535 ($100,000 × .0454) is attributable to services performed by C in X's 2018 taxable year; and $4,762 ($100,000 × .0476) is attributable to services performed by C in X's 2019 taxable year.

Example 10. (Nonaccount balance plan - present value ratio method with an in-service payment). (i) The facts are the same as *Example 9*, except that X grants C a vested right to a $40,000 payment on June 30, 2018 and a vested right to a $60,000 payment on January 1, 2020.

(ii) The present value of the future payments ($40,000 payable on June 30, 2018 and $60,000 payable on January 1, 2020), determined using a five percent interest rate, is $84,758 as of December 31, 2015; $88,996 as of December 31, 2016; $93,446 as of December 31, 2017; and $57,143 as of December 31, 2018. However, for purposes of determining the increase in the present value of the future payments during 2018 (the year of the in-service payment), $57,143 must be increased by $40,000, the amount of the in-service payment, resulting in a present value of future payments as of December 31, 2018, of $97,143 solely for purposes of attributing the $40,000 in-service payment. Accordingly, $84,758 is the amount of the increase in the present value of the future payments for X's 2015 taxable year, $4,238 ($88,896 - $84,758) is the increase in the present value of the future payments for X's 2016 taxable year, $4,450 ($93,446 - $88,996) is the increase in the present value of the future payments for X's 2017 taxable year, and $3,697 ($97,143 - $93,446) is the increase in the present value of the future payments for X's 2018 taxable year. The sum of all the increases is $97,143 ($84,758 + $4,238 + $4,450 + $3,697). Thus, the attribution fraction for 2015 is .8725 ($84,758 / $97,143); the attribution fraction for 2016 is .0436 ($4,238 / $97,143); the attribution

fraction for 2017 is .0458 ($4,450 / $97,143); and the attribution fraction for 2018 is .0381 ($3,697 / $97,143).

(iii) Accordingly, with respect to the $40,000 payment made on June 30, 2018, $34,900 ($40,000 × .8725) is attributable to services performed by C in X's 2015 taxable year; $1,744 ($40,000 × .0436) is attributable to services performed by C in X's 2016 taxable year; $1,832 ($40,000 × .0458) is attributable to services performed by C in X's 2017 taxable year; and $1,524 ($40,000 × .0381) is attributable to services performed by C in X's 2018 taxable year.

(iv) For purposes of attributing the $60,000 payment made on January 1, 2020, the present value of the future payments for each taxable year that ends prior to the taxable year in which the $40,000 in-service payment is paid is reduced by the present value of the future payment to which the applicable individual had a legally binding right to be paid on the date the $40,000 in-service is paid (based on the applicable factors and plan provisions as of the measurement date in each such taxable year). The present value of that future payment is $35,396 as of December 31, 2015; $37,166 as of December 31, 2016; and $39,024 as of December 31, 2017. Therefore, for purposes of attributing the $60,000 payment on January 1, 2020, the present value of future payments as of December 31, 2015, is $49,362 ($84,758 - $35,396); the present value of future payments as of December 31, 2016, is $51,830 ($88,996 - $37,166); the present value of future payments as of December 31, 2017, is $54,422 ($93,446 - $39,024). The present value of future payments as of December 31, 2018, is $57,143. Accordingly, $49,362 is the increase in the present value of the future payment of $60,000 for X's 2015 taxable year; $2,468 ($51,830 - $49,362) is the increase in the present value of the future payment for X's 2016 taxable year; $2,592 ($54,422 - $51,830) is the increase in the future value of the payment for X's 2017 taxable year; $2,721 ($57,143 - $54,422) is the increase in the future value of the payments for X's 2018 taxable year; and $2,857 ($60,000 - $57,143) is the increase in the future value of the payment for X's 2019 taxable year. The sum of all the increases is $60,000 ($49,362 + $2,468 + $2,592 + $2,721 + $2,857). Thus, the attribution fraction for 2015 is .8227 ($49,362 / $60,000); the attribution fraction for 2016 is .0411 ($2,468 / $60,000); the attribution fraction for 2017 is .0432 ($2,592 / $60,000); the attribution fraction for 2018 is .0454 ($2,721 / $60,000); and the attribution fraction for 2019 is .0476 ($2,857 / $60,000).

(v) Accordingly, with respect to the $60,000 payment made on January 1, 2020, $49,362 ($60,000 × .8227) is attributable to services performed by C in X's 2015 taxable year; $2,468 ($60,000 × .0411) is attributable to services performed by C in X's 2016 taxable year; $2,592 ($60,000 × .0432) is attributable to services performed by C in X's 2017 taxable year; $2,721 ($60,000 × .0454) is attributable to services performed by C in X's 2018 taxable year; and $2,857 ($60,000 × .0476) is attributable to services performed by C in X's 2019 taxable year.

Example 11 (Nonaccount balance plan - formula benefit ratio method with losses and multiple payments). (i) D is an applicable individual of W for all relevant taxable years. D becomes a participant in a nonaccount balance plan sponsored by R on January 1, 2018. The plan provides W with the vested right to receive a five annual installments each equal to $20,000 times the full years of service that D completes. The first payment is to be made on the later of December 31, 2027, or on the December 31 of the first year in which D is no longer a service provider. D has a break in service in 2020 and does not accrue an additional benefit during 2020. D ceases to be a service provider on December 31, 2022, after having completed four years of service, entitling D to five annual payments equal to $80,000 per year commencing on December 31, 2027. W determines the present value of amounts to be paid under the plan using an interest rate of five percent for 2018 and 2019, and seven percent for 2021, 2022, and 2023. W uses the formula benefit ratio method described in paragraph (d)(4)(ii) of this section.

(ii) Under the plan formula, in 2018, E accrued the right to a $20,000 annual payment for five years, and E accrued an additional $20,000 in annual payments in 2019, 2021, and 2022, resulting in the right to receive an annual payment of $80,000 commencing on December 31, 2027. Thus, the attribution fraction is .25 for 2018 ($20,000 / $80,000), .25 for 2019 ($20,000 / $80,000), .25 for 2021 ($20,000 / $80,000), and .25 for 2022 ($20,000 / $80,000). The attribution fraction for 2020 is zero because no additional formula benefit accrued during that year.

(iii) The attribution fraction for each disqualified taxable year is multiplied by each payment and the result is attributed to that taxable year. Accordingly, with respect to each $80,000 payment, $20,000 ($80,000 × .25) is attributable to services performed by D in W's 2018 taxable year; $20,000 ($80,000 × .25) is attributable to services performed by D in W's 2019 taxable year; $20,000 ($80,000 × .25) is attributable to services performed by D in W's 2021 taxable year; and $20,000 ($80,000 × .25) is attributable to services performed by D in W's 2022 taxable year. No amount is attributable to services performed by D in W's 2020 taxable year.

Example 12 (Stock option). (i) E is an applicable individual of corporation V for all relevant taxable years. On January 1, 2016, V grants E an option to purchase 100 shares of V common stock at an exercise price of $50 per share (the fair market value of V common stock on the date of grant). The stock option is not subject to a substantial risk of forfeiture. On December 31, 2017, E ceases to be a service provider of V or any member of V's aggregated group. On January 1, 2019, E resumes providing services for V and again becomes both a service provider and an applicable individual of V. On December 31, 2020, when the fair market value of V common stock is $196 per share, E exercises the stock option. The remuneration resulting from the stock option exercise is $14,600 (($196 - $50) × 100).

(ii) The $14,600 is attributed *pro rata* over the 1,460 days from January 1, 2016 to December 31, 2017 and from January 1, 2019 to December 31, 2020 (365 days per year for the 2016, 2017, 2019, and 2020 taxable years), so that $10 ($14,600 divided by 1,460) is attributed to each calendar day in this period, and $3,650 (365 days × $10) of remuneration is attributed to services performed by E in each of V's 2016, 2017, 2019, and 2020 taxable years.

Example 13 (Stock option subject to a substantial risk of forfeiture). (i) The facts are the same as *Example 14*, except that the stock option is subject to a substantial risk of forfeiture that lapses on December 31, 2017, and is not transferable until that date, and V chooses to attribute remuneration resulting from the exercise of stock options that are subject to a substantial risk of forfeiture over the period beginning on the date of grant and ending on the date the substantial risk of forfeiture lapses, as permitted under paragraph (d)(5)(i)(B) of this section.

(ii) The $14,600 is attributed *pro rata* over the 730 days from January 1, 2016 to December 31, 2017 (365 days per year for the 2016 and 2017 taxable years), so that $20 ($14,600 divided by 730) is attributed to each calendar day in this period, and $7,300 (365 days × $20) is attributed to services performed by E in each of V's 2016 and 2017 taxable years.

Example 14 (Restricted stock). (i) F is an applicable individual of corporation U for all relevant taxable years. On January 1, 2017, U grants to F 1000 shares of restricted U common stock. Under the terms of the grant, the shares will be forfeited if F voluntarily terminates employment before December 31, 2019 (so that the shares are subject to a substantial risk of forfeiture through that date) and are nontransferable until the substantial risk of forfeiture lapses. F does not make an election under section 83(b) and continues in employment with U through December 31, 2019, at which time F's rights in the stock become substantially vested within the meaning of § 1.83-3(b) and the fair market value of a share of the stock is $109.50. The remuneration resulting from the vesting of the restricted stock is $109,500 ($109.50 × 1000).

(ii) The $109,500 of remuneration is attributed to services performed by F over the 1,095 days between January 1, 2017 and December 31, 2019 (365 days per year for the 2017, 2018, and 2019 taxable years), so that $100 ($109,500 divided by 1,095) is attributed to each calendar day in this period, and remuneration of $36,500 (365 days × $100) is attributed to services performed by F in each of U's 2017, 2018, and 2019 taxable years.

Example 15 (RSUs). (i) G is an applicable individual of corporation T for all relevant taxable years. On January 1, 2018, T grants to G 1000 RSUs. Under the terms of the grant, T will pay G an amount on December 31, 2020 equal to the fair market value of 1000 shares of T common stock on that date, but only if G continues to provide substantial services to T (so that the RSU is subject to a substantial risk of forfeiture) through December 31, 2020. G remains employed by T through December 31, 2020, at which time the fair market value of a share of the stock is $219, and T pays G $219,000 ($219 × 1000).

(ii) The $219,000 in remuneration is attributed to services performed by G over the 1,095 days beginning on January 1, 2018 and ending on December 31, 2020 (365 days per year for the 2018, 2019, and 2020 taxable years), so that $200 ($219,000 / 1,095) is attributed to each calendar day in this period, and $73,000 (365 days × $200) is attributed to service performed by G in each of T's 2018, 2019, and 2020 taxable years.

Example 16 (Involuntary separation pay). (i) H is an applicable individual of corporation S. On January 1, 2015, H and S enter into an employment contract providing that S will make two payments of $150,000 each to H if H has an involuntary separation from service. Under the terms of the contract, the first payment is due on January 1 following the involuntary separation from service, and the second payment is due on January 1 of the following year. On December 31, 2016, H has an involuntary separation from service. S pays H $150,000 on January 1, 2017 and $150,000 on January 1, 2018.

(ii) Pursuant to paragraph (d)(6) of this section, involuntary separation pay may be attributed to services performed by H in the taxable year of S in which the involuntary separation from service occurs. Alternatively, involuntary separation pay may be attributed

to services performed by H on a daily *pro rata* basis beginning on the date H obtains a legally binding right to the involuntary separation pay and ending on the date of the involuntary separation from service. The entire $300,000 amount, including both $150,000 payments, must be attributed using the same method. Therefore, the entire $300,000 amount (comprised of two $150,000 payments) may be attributed to services performed by H in S's 2016 taxable year, which is the taxable year in which the involuntary separation from service occurs. Alternatively, each $150,000 payment may be attributed on a daily *pro rata* basis to the period beginning on January 1, 2015 and ending December 31, 2016. so that $410.96 (($150,000 × 2) / (365 × 2)) is attributed to each day of S's 2015 and 2016 taxable years. Accordingly, $150,000 is attributed to services performed by H in each of S's 2015 and 2016 taxable years.

Example 17 (Reimbursement after termination of services). (i) I is an applicable individual of corporation R. On January 1, 2018, I enters into an agreement with R under which R will reimburse I's country club dues for two years following I's separation from service. On December 31, 2020, I ceases to be a service provider of R. I pays $50,000 in country club dues on January 1, 2021 and $50,000 on January 2, 2022. Pursuant to the agreement, R reimburses I $50,000 for the country club dues in 2021 and $50,000 in 2022.

(ii) $100,000 is attributed to services performed in R's 2020 taxable year, the taxable year in which I ceases to be a service provider.

(10) *Certain remuneration subject to a substantial risk of forfeiture.*— If remuneration is attributable in accordance with paragraphs (d)(2) (legally binding right), (d)(3) (account balance plan), or (d)(4) (nonaccount balance plan) of this section to services performed in a period that includes two or more taxable years of a covered health insurance provider during which the remuneration is subject to a substantial risk of forfeiture, that remuneration must be attributed using a two-step process. First, the remuneration must be attributed to the taxable years of the covered health insurance provider in accordance with paragraph (d)(2), (3), or (4) of this section, as applicable. Second, the remuneration attributed to the period during which the remuneration is subject to a substantial risk of forfeiture (the vesting period) must be reattributed on a daily *pro rata* basis over that period beginning on the date that the applicable individual obtains a legally binding right to the remuneration and ending on the date that the substantial risk of forfeiture lapses. If a vesting period begins on a day other than the first day of a covered health insurance provider's taxable year or ends on a day other than the last day of the covered health insurance provider's taxable year, the remuneration attributable to that taxable year under the first step of the attribution process is divided between the portion of the taxable year that includes the vesting period and the portion of the taxable year that does not include the vesting period. The amount attributed to the portion of the taxable year that includes the vesting period is equal to the total amount of remuneration that would be attributable to the taxable year under the first step of the attribution process, multiplied by a fraction, the numerator of which is the number of days during the taxable year that the amount is subject to a substantial risk of forfeiture and the denominator of which is the number of days in such taxable year. The remaining amount is attributed to the portion of the taxable year that does not include the vesting period and, therefore, is not reattributed under the second step of the attribution process.

(11) *Example.*—The following example illustrates the principles of paragraph (d)(10) of this section. For purposes of this example, the corporation has a taxable year that is the calendar year and is a covered health insurance provider for all relevant taxable years, DDR is otherwise deductible in the taxable year in which it is paid, and amounts payable under nonaccount balance plans are not forfeitable upon the death of the applicable individual.

Example (Account balance plan subject to a substantial risk of forfeiture using the principal additions method). (i) J is an applicable individual of corporation Q for all relevant taxable years. On January 1, 2016, J begins participating in a nonqualified deferred compensation plan that is an account balance plan. Under the terms of the plan, Q will pay J's account balance on January 1, 2021, but only if J continues to provide substantial services to Q through December 31, 2018 (so that the amount credited to J's account is subject to a substantial risk of forfeiture through that date). Q credits $10,000 to J's account annually for five years on January 1 of each year beginning on January 1, 2016. The account earns interest at a fixed rate of five percent per year, compounded annually, which solely for the purposes of this example, is assumed to be a reasonable rate of interest. Q attributes increases in account balances under the plan using the principal additions method described in paragraph (d)(3)(ii) of this section.

(ii) Earnings on a principal addition are attributed to the same disqualified taxable year of Q to which the principal addition is attributed; therefore, the amount initially attributable to Q's 2016 taxable year is $12,763 (the $10,000 principal addition in 2016 at five percent interest for five years); the amount initially attributable to Q's 2017 taxable year is $12,155 (the $10,000 principal addition in 2017 at five percent interest for four years); the amount initially attributable to Q's 2018 taxable year is $11,576 (the $10,000 principal addition in 2018 at five percent interest for three years); the amount attributable to Q's 2019 taxable year is $11,025 (the $10,000 principal addition in 2019 at five percent interest for two years); and the amount attributable to Q's 2020 taxable year is $10,500 (the $10,000 principal addition in 2020 at five percent interest for one year).

(iii) Remuneration that is attributable to two or more taxable years of Q during which it is subject to a substantial risk of forfeiture must be reattributed on a daily *pro rata* basis to the period beginning on the date that J obtains a legally binding right to the remuneration and ending on the date that the substantial risk of forfeiture lapses. Therefore, $36,494 ($12,763 + $12,155 + $11,576) is reattributed on a daily *pro rata* basis over the period beginning on January 1, 2016, and ending on December 31, 2018. Thus, $12,165 is attributed to services performed by J in each of Q's 2016, 2017, and 2018 taxable years.

(e) *Application of the deduction limitation.*—(1) *Application to aggregate amounts.*—The $500,000 deduction limitation is applied to the aggregate amount of AIR and DDR attributable to services performed by an applicable individual in a disqualified taxable year. The aggregate amount of AIR and DDR attributable to services performed by an applicable individual in a disqualified taxable year that exceeds the $500,000 deduction limit is not allowed as a deduction in any taxable year. Therefore, for example, if an applicable individual has more than $500,000 of AIR attributable to services performed for a covered health insurance provider in a disqualified taxable year, the amount of that AIR that exceeds $500,000 is not deductible in any taxable year, and no DDR attributable to services performed by the applicable individual in that disqualified taxable year is deductible in any taxable year. However, if an applicable individual has AIR for a disqualified taxable year that is $500,000 or less and DDR attributable to services performed in the same disqualified taxable year that, when combined with the AIR for the year, exceeds $500,000, all of the AIR is deductible in that disqualified taxable year, but the amount of DDR attributable to that taxable year that is deductible in future taxable years is limited to an amount equal to $500,000 less the amount of the AIR for that taxable year.

(2) *Order of application and calculation of deduction limitation.*—(i) *In general.*—The deduction limitation with respect to any applicable individual for any disqualified taxable year is applied to AIR and DDR attributable to services performed by that applicable individual in that disqualified taxable year at the time that the remuneration becomes otherwise deductible, and each time the deduction limitation is applied to an amount that is otherwise deductible, the deduction limit is reduced (but not below zero) by the amount against which it is applied. Accordingly, the deduction limitation is applied first to an applicable individual's AIR attributable to services performed in a disqualified taxable year and is reduced (but not below zero) by the amount of the AIR to which the deduction limit is applied. If the applicable individual also has an amount of DDR attributable to services performed in that disqualified taxable year that becomes otherwise deductible in a subsequent taxable year, the deduction limit, as reduced, is applied to that amount of DDR in the first taxable in which the DDR becomes otherwise deductible. The deduction limit is then further reduced (but not below zero) by the amount of the DDR to which the deduction limit is applied. If the applicable individual has an additional amount of DDR attributable to services performed in the original disqualified taxable year that becomes otherwise deductible in a subsequent taxable year, the deduction limit, as further reduced, is applied to that amount of DDR in the taxable year in which it is otherwise deductible. This process continues for future taxable years in which DDR attributable to services performed by the applicable individual in the original disqualified taxable year is otherwise deductible. No deduction is allowed in any taxable year for any AIR or DDR attributable to services performed by an applicable individual in a disqualified taxable year for the excess of those amounts over the deduction limit (as reduced, if applicable) for that disqualified taxable year at the time the deduction limitation is applied to the remuneration.

(ii) *Application to payments.*—(A) *In general.*—Any payment of remuneration may include amounts that are attributable to services performed by an applicable individual in one or more taxable years of a covered health insurance provider pursuant to paragraphs (d)(2) through (11) of this section. In that case, a separate deduction limitation applies to each portion of the payment *that is attributed to services performed in a different disqualified taxable year.* Any portion of a payment that is attributed to a taxable year that is a disqualified taxable year is deductible only to the extent that it does not exceed the deduction limit that applies with respect to the

applicable individual for that disqualified taxable year, as reduced by the amount, if any, of AIR and DDR attributable to services performed in that disqualified taxable year that was deductible in an earlier taxable year.

(3) *Examples.*—The following examples illustrate the rules of paragraphs (e)(1) and (2) of this section. For purposes of these examples, each corporation has a taxable year that is the calendar year and is a covered health insurance provider for all relevant taxable years; DDR is otherwise deductible in the taxable year in which it is paid; and amounts payable under nonaccount balance plans are not forfeitable upon the death of the applicable individual.

Example 1 (Lump-sum payment of DDR attributable to a single taxable year). (i) L is an applicable individual of corporation O. During O's 2015 taxable year, O pays L $550,000 in salary, which is AIR, and grants L a right to $50,000 of DDR payable upon L's separation from service from O. L has a separation from service in 2020, at which time O pays L the $50,000 of DDR attributable to services performed by L in O's 2015 taxable year.

(ii) The $500,000 deduction limitation for 2015 is applied first to L's $550,000 of AIR for 2015. Because the $550,000 of AIR in 2015 is greater than the deduction limit, O may deduct only $500,000 of the AIR for 2015, and $50,000 of the $550,000 of AIR is not deductible for any taxable year. The deduction limit for remuneration attributable to services provided by L in O's 2015 taxable year is then reduced to zero. Because the $50,000 in DDR attributable to services performed by L in 2015 exceeds the reduced deduction limit of zero, that $50,000 is not deductible for any taxable year.

Example 2 (Installment payments of DDR attributable to a single taxable year). (i) M is an applicable individual of corporation N. During N's 2016 taxable year, N pays M $300,000 in salary, which is AIR, and grants M a right to $220,000 of DDR payable on a fixed schedule beginning upon M's separation from service. The $220,000 is attributable to services provided by M in N's 2016 taxable year. M ceases providing services on December 31, 2016. In 2020, N pays M $120,000 of DDR that is attributable to services performed in N's 2016 taxable year. In 2021, N pays M the remaining $100,000 of DDR attributable to services performed by M in N's 2016 taxable year.

(ii) The $500,000 deduction limitation for 2016 is applied first to M's $300,000 of AIR for 2016. Because the deduction limit is greater than the AIR, N may deduct the entire $300,000 of AIR paid in 2016. The $500,000 deduction limit is then reduced to $200,000 because the limitation is reduced by the amount of AIR ($500,000 - $300,000). The reduced deduction limit is then applied to M's $120,000 of DDR attributable to services performed by M in N's 2016 taxable year that is paid in 2020. Because the reduced deduction limit of $200,000 is greater than the $120,000 of DDR, N may deduct the entire $120,000 of DDR paid in 2020. The $200,000 deduction limit is reduced to $80,000 by the $120,000 in DDR because the limit is reduced by the amount of DDR to which the deduction limit applied ($200,000 - $120,000). The reduced deduction limit of $80,000 is then applied to the remaining $100,000 payment of DDR attributable to services performed by M in N's 2016 taxable year. Because the $100,000 payment by N for 2021 exceeds the reduced deduction limit of $80,000, N may deduct only $80,000 of the payment for the 2021 taxable year, and $20,000 of the $100,000 payment is not deductible by N for any taxable year.

Example 3 (Lump-sum payment attributable to multiple years from an account balance plan using the account balance ratio method). (i) N is an applicable individual of corporation M for all relevant taxable years. On January 1, 2015, N begins participating in a nonqualified deferred compensation plan sponsored by M that is an account balance plan. Under the plan, all amounts are fully vested at all times. The balances in N's account (including earnings) are $50,000 on December 31, 2015, $100,000 on December 31, 2016, and $200,000 on December 31, 2017. N's AIR from M is $425,000 for 2015, $450,000 for 2016, and $500,000 for 2017. On January 1, 2018, in accordance with the plan terms, M pays $200,000 to N, which is a payment of N's entire account balance under the plan. M uses the account balance ratio method to attribute amounts to services performed in taxable years.

(ii) To determine the extent to which M is entitled to a deduction for any portion of the $200,000 payment under the plan, the payment must first be attributed to services performed by N in M's taxable years in accordance with the attribution rules set forth in paragraph (d) of this section. The increase in N's account balance during 2015 is $50,000 ($50,000 - zero); the increase in N's account balance for 2016 is $50,000 ($100,000 - $50,000); and the increase in N's account balance for 2017 is $100,000 ($200,000 - $100,000). The sum of all the increases is $200,000 ($50,000 + $50,000 + $100,000). Accordingly, for N's 2015 taxable year, the attribution fraction is .25 ($50,000 / $200,000); for N's 2016, taxable year, the attribution fraction is .25 ($50,000 / $200,000); and for N's 2017 taxable year, the attribution fraction is .50 ($100,000 / $200,000).

(iii) With respect to the $200,000 payment made on January 1, 2018, $50,000 ($200,000 × .25) of DDR is attributable to services performed by N in M's 2015 taxable year; $50,000 ($200,000 × .25) of DDR is attributable to services performed by N in M's 2016 taxable year; and $100,000 ($200,000 × .50) of DDR is attributable to services performed by N in M's 2017 taxable year.

(iv) The $500,000 deduction limitation for 2015 is applied first to N's $425,000 of AIR for 2015. Because the deduction limit is greater than the AIR, M may deduct the entire $425,000 of AIR paid in 2015. The $500,000 deduction limit is then reduced to $75,000 by the amount of AIR against which it is applied ($500,000 - $425,000). The reduced deduction limit is then applied to N's $50,000 of DDR attributable to services performed by N in M's 2015 taxable year that is paid in 2018. Because $50,000 does not exceed the reduced deduction limit of $75,000, all $50,000 of the DDR attributable to services performed by N in M's 2015 taxable year is deductible for 2018, the year of payment. The deduction limit for remuneration attributable to services performed by N in 2015 is then reduced to $25,000 ($75,000 - $50,000), and this reduced limit is applied to any future payment of DDR attributable to services performed by N in 2015. With respect to M's 2016 taxable year, the $500,000 deduction limit for 2016 is applied first to N's $450,000 of AIR for 2016. Because the deduction limit is greater than the AIR, M may deduct the entire $450,000 of AIR paid in 2016. The $500,000 deduction limit is then reduced to $50,000 by the AIR ($500,000 - $450,000). The reduced deduction limit is then applied to N's $50,000 of DDR attributable to services performed by N in M's 2016 taxable year that is paid in 2018. Because $50,000 does not exceed the reduced deduction limit of $50,000, all $50,000 of the DDR attributed to M's 2016 taxable year is deductible for 2018, the year of payment. The deduction limit for remuneration attributable to services performed by N in 2016 is then reduced to zero, and this reduced limit is applied to any future payment of DDR attributable to services performed by N in 2016. With respect to M's 2017 taxable year, the $500,000 deduction limit for 2017 is applied first to N's $500,000 of AIR for 2017. Because the deduction limit is not greater than the AIR, M may deduct the entire $500,000 of AIR paid in 2017. The $500,000 deduction limit is then reduced to zero by the amount of the AIR against which it is applied ($500,000 - $500,000). The reduced deduction limit is applied to N's $100,000 of DDR attributable to services performed by N in M's 2017 taxable year that is paid in 2018. Because $100,000 exceeds the reduced deduction limit of zero, the $100,000 of the DDR attributed to services performed by N in M's 2017 taxable year is not deductible for the year of payment (or any other taxable year). As a result, $100,000 of the $200,000 payment ($50,000 + $50,000 + $0) is deductible by M for M's 2018 taxable year, and the remaining $100,000 is not deductible by M for any taxable year.

Example 4 (Installment payments and in-service payment attributable to multiple taxable years from an account balance plan using the account balance ratio method). (i) O is an applicable individual of corporation L for all relevant taxable years. On January 1, 2016, O begins participating in a nonqualified deferred compensation plan sponsored by L that is an account balance plan. Under the plan, all amounts are fully vested at all times. L makes contributions to O's account each year and credits earnings based on a predetermined actual investment within the meaning of §31.3121(v)(2)-1(d)(2)(i)(B). The closing balances in O's account (including contributions, earnings, and distributions made during the year) are $100,000 on December 31, 2016, $250,000 on December 31, 2017, and $50,000 on December 31, 2018. O's AIR from L is $500,000 for 2016, $300,000 for 2017, and $450,000 for 2018. On December 31, 2018, L pays O $400,000 in accordance with the plan terms. On December 31, 2019, O's account balance is $200,000, reflecting additional credits of $125,000 made during the year and earnings on the account. O's AIR from L is $200,000 for 2019. O ceases providing services to L on December 31, 2019. On January 1, 2020, L pays O $200,000 in accordance with the plan terms. L uses the account balance ratio method to attribute amounts to services performed in taxable years.

(ii) To determine the extent to which L is entitled to a deduction for any portion of the payments under the plan, O's payments under the plan must first be attributed to services performed by O in L's taxable years in accordance with the attribution rules set forth in paragraph (d) of this section. For purposes of attributing the $400,000 payment made on December 31, 2018 to a taxable year, the increase in O's account balance during 2016 is $100,000 ($100,000 - zero); the increase in O's account balance for 2017 is $150,000 ($250,000 - $100,000); and the increase in O's account balance for 2018 is $200,000 ($50,000 - $250,000 + $400,000 (payment on December 31, 2018)). The sum of all the increases is $450,000 ($100,000 + $150,000 + $200,000). Thus, for L's 2016 taxable year, the attribution fraction is .2222 ($100,000 / $450,000); for L's 2017 taxable year, the attribution fraction is .3333 ($150,000 / $450,000); and for L's 2018 taxable year, the attribution fraction is .4444 ($200,000 / $450,000). Accordingly, with respect to the $400,000 payment made on December 31, 2019, $88,889 ($400,000 × .2222) is attributable to services performed by O in L's 2016 taxable year; $133,333 ($400,000 × .3333) is attributable to services performed by O in L's 2017 taxable year; and $177,778

($400,000 × .4444) is attributable to services performed by O in L's 2018 taxable year.

(iii) The portion of the $400,000 payment attributed to services performed in a disqualified taxable year under paragraph (d) of this section that exceeds the deduction limit for that disqualified taxable year, as reduced through the date of payment, is not deductible in any taxable year. The $500,000 deduction limit for 2016 is applied first to O's $500,000 of AIR for 2016. Because the deduction limit is equal to the $500,000 of AIR, L may deduct the entire $500,000 of AIR paid in 2016. The $500,000 deduction limit is then reduced to zero by the amount of the AIR ($500,000 - $500,000). The reduced deduction limit is applied to O's $88,889 of DDR attributable to services performed by O in L's 2016 taxable year that is paid in 2018. Because $88,889 exceeds the reduced deduction limit of zero, the $88,889 of DDR attributed to 2016 is not deductible for L's 2018 taxable year or any other taxable year. With respect to L's 2017 taxable year, the $500,000 deduction limitation for 2017 is applied first to O's $300,000 of AIR for 2017. Because the $500,000 deduction limit is greater than the $300,000 of AIR, L may deduct the entire $300,000 of AIR paid in 2017. The $500,000 deduction limit is reduced to $200,000 by the amount of the AIR ($500,000 - $300,000). The reduced deduction limit is then applied to O's $133,333 of DDR attributable to services performed by O in L's 2017 taxable year that is paid in 2018. Because $133,333 does not exceed that reduced deduction limit of $200,000, the $133,333 is deductible for 2018. The deduction limit for remuneration attributable to services performed by O in 2017 is then reduced to $66,667 ($200,000 - $133,333), and this reduced limit is applied to any future payment of DDR attributable to services performed by O in 2017. With respect to L's 2018 taxable year, the $500,000 deduction limit for 2018 is applied first to O's $450,000 of AIR for 2018. Because the deduction limit is greater than the AIR, L may deduct the entire $450,000 of AIR paid in 2017. The $500,000 deduction limit is reduced to $50,000 by the amount of the AIR ($500,000 - $450,000). The reduced deduction limit is applied to O's $177,778 attributable to services performed by O in L's 2018 taxable year that is paid in 2018. Because the $177,778 exceeds the reduced deduction limit of $50,000, $50,000 of DDR is deductible for L's 2018 taxable year, and $127,778 of the $177,778 is not deductible for L's 2018 taxable year or any other taxable year. As a result, $183,333 of the $400,000 payment ($0 + $133,333 + $50,000) is deductible by L for L's 2018 taxable year, and the remaining $216,667 is not deductible by L for any taxable year.

(iv) For purposes of attributing amounts paid or made available from the plan in future taxable years, the following adjustments are made to O's account balances to reflect the in-service payment of $400,000 in 2018. O's account balance as of December 31, 2016 is reduced by the $88,889 attributable to 2016; and for 2017 is reduced by the sum of the $133,333 attributable to 2017 and the $88,889 attributable to 2016. Therefore, after attributing the $400,000 payment, O's adjusted closing account balance as of December 31, 2016, is $11,111 ($100,000 - $88,889), and as of December 31, 2017, is $27,778 ($250,000 - $133,333 - $88,889).

(v) For purposes of attributing the $200,000 payment made on January 1, 2020, to services performed in the taxable years of S, the increase in O's account balance during 2016 is $11,111 ($11,111 - $0); the increase in O's account balance for 2017 is $16,667 ($27,778 - $11,111); the increase in O's account balance for 2018 is $22,222 ($50,000 - $27,778), and the increase in O's account balance for 2019 is $150,000 ($200,000 - $50,000). The sum of all such increases is $200,000 ($11,111 + $16,667 + $22,222 + $150,000). Thus, for O's 2016 taxable year, the attribution fraction is .0556 ($11,111 / $200,000); for O's 2017, taxable year, the attribution fraction is .0833 ($16,667 / $200,000); for O's 2018 taxable year, the attribution fraction is .1111 ($22,222 / $200,000); for O's 2019 taxable year, the attribution fraction is .7500 ($150,000 / $200,000). Accordingly, with respect to the $200,000 payment made on January 1, 2020, $11,111 ($200,000 × .0556) of DDR is attributable to services performed by O in L's 2016 taxable year; $16,667 ($200,000 × .0833) of DDR is attributable to services performed by O in L's 2017 taxable year; $22,222 ($200,000 × .1111) of DDR is attributable to services performed by O in L's 2018 taxable year; and $150,000 ($200,000 × .7500) of DDR is attributable to services performed by O in L's 2019 taxable year.

(vi) The portion of the DDR attributed to a disqualified taxable year under paragraph (d) of this section that exceeds the deduction limit for that disqualified taxable year, as reduced, is not deductible for any taxable year. For L's 2016 taxable year, the deduction limit is reduced to zero by the $500,000 of AIR for that year. Because $11,111 exceeds the reduced deduction limit of zero, $11,111 of the DDR is not deductible for L's 2020 taxable year or any other taxable year. For L's 2017 taxable year, the deduction limit is reduced to $200,000 by the $300,000 of AIR for that year and further reduced to $66,667 by the $133,333 of DDR previously attributed to 2017. Because $16,667 does not exceed the $66,667 deduction limit, the $16,667 of DDR is deductible for L's 2020 taxable year, the year of payment. The deduction limit for remuneration attributable to services performed by O in 2017 is then reduced to $50,000 ($66,667 - $16,667), and this reduced limit is applied to any future payment attributable to services performed by O in 2017. For L's 2018 taxable year, the deduction limit is reduced to zero by the $450,000 of AIR for that year and the $50,000 of DDR previously attributed to 2018. Because $22,222 exceeds the reduced deduction limit of zero for 2018, the $22,222 of DDR is not deductible for L's 2020 taxable year or any other taxable year. For L's 2019 taxable year, the $500,000 deduction limit for 2019 is applied first to O's $200,000 of AIR for 2019. Because the deduction limit is greater than the AIR, L may deduct the entire $200,000 of AIR paid in 2019. The $500,000 deduction limit is reduced to $300,000 by the amount of the AIR ($500,000 - $200,000). The reduced deduction limit is applied to O's $150,000 of DDR attributable to services performed by O in L's 2019 taxable year that is paid in 2020. Because $150,000 does not exceed the $300,000 limit, the $150,000 of DDR is deductible for L's 2020 taxable year, the year of payment. The deduction limit for remuneration attributable to services performed by O in 2019 is then reduced to $150,000 ($500,000 - $200,000 - $150,000), and this reduced limit is applied to any future payment attributable to services performed by O in 2019. As a result, $166,667 of the $200,000 payment ($0 + $16,667 + $0 + $150,000) is deductible by L for L's 2020 taxable year, the year of payment, and the remaining $33,333 is not deductible by L for any taxable year.

Example 5 (Installment payments and in-service payment attributable to multiple taxable years from an account balance plan using the principal additions method). (i) The facts are the same as set forth in *Example 4,* paragraph (i), except that L uses the principal additions method for attributing remuneration from an account balance plan; principal additions under the plan are $100,000 in 2016, $125,000 in 2017, $150,000 in 2018, and $125,000 in 2019; as of the December 31, 2018 initial date of payment, earnings on the 2016, 2017, and 2018 principal additions are $40,000, $30,000, and $5,000 respectively. Under the terms of the plan, the $400,000 payment made on December 31, 2018, is from principal additions in 2016, 2017, and 2018, and earnings thereon, and the $200,000 payment made on January 1, 2020, is from principal additions in 2018 and 2019, and earnings thereon.

(ii) To determine the extent to which L is entitled to a deduction for any portion of either payment under the plan, the payments to O under the plan must first be attributed to services performed by O's taxable years in accordance with the attribution rules set forth in paragraph (d) of this section. Under the rules in paragraph (d)(3)(ii) of this section, the $400,000 payment on January 1, 2019, is attributed to services performed by O in the taxable year to which the payment relates under the terms of the plan. DDR including principal additions and earnings thereon are attributed to services performed by O in a taxable year of L when the $400,000 payment is made to O on December 31, 2018. Under the terms of the plan, the $400,000 payment made on December 31, 2018 is attributed to services performed by O in L's 2016 taxable year in the amount of $140,000, and is attributed to services performed by O in L's 2017 taxable year in the amount of $155,000, and the remaining $105,000 ($400,000 - $140,000 - $155,000) is attributed to services performed by O in L's 2018 taxable year.

(iii) The portion of the DDR attributable to services performed in a disqualified taxable year under paragraph (d) of this section that exceeds the deduction limit for that disqualified taxable year, as reduced, is not deductible for any taxable year. The $500,000 deduction limitation for 2016 is applied first to O's $500,000 of AIR for 2016. Because the deduction limit is equal to the $500,000 of AIR, L may deduct the entire $500,000 of AIR paid in 2016. The $500,000 deduction limit is then reduced to zero by the amount of the AIR ($500,000 - $500,000). The reduced deduction limit is applied to O's $140,000 of DDR attributable to services performed by O in L's 2016 taxable year that is paid in 2018. Because $140,000 exceeds the reduced deduction limit of zero, the $140,000 is not deductible for L's 2018 taxable year (the year of payment), or any other taxable year. For L's 2017 taxable year, the $500,000 deduction limit for 2017 is applied first to O's $300,000 of AIR for 2017. Because the deduction limit is greater than the AIR, L may deduct the entire $300,000 of AIR paid in 2017. The $500,000 deduction limit is then reduced to $200,000 by the amount of the AIR ($500,000 - $300,000). The reduced deduction limit is applied to O's $155,000 of DDR attributable to services performed by O in L's 2017 taxable year that is paid in 2018. Because $155,000 does not exceed the reduced deduction limit of $200,000, the $155,000 payment is deductible for 2018. For L's 2018 taxable year, the $500,000 deduction limitation for 2018 is applied first to O's $450,000 of AIR for 2018. Because the deduction limit is greater than the AIR, L may deduct the entire $450,000 of AIR paid in 2018. The $500,000 deduction limit is then reduced to $50,000 by the amount of the AIR ($500,000 - $450,000). The reduced deduction limit is applied to O's $105,000 of DDR attributable to services performed by O in L's 2018 taxable year that is paid in 2018. Because $105,000 exceeds the reduced deduction limit of $50,000, $55,000 of the $105,000 attributable to L's 2018 taxable year is not deductible for 2018 (the year of payment), or any other taxable year. As a result, $205,000 of the $400,000 payment ($0 + $155,000 + $50,000) is deductible by L for L's

2018 taxable year (the year of payment) and the remaining $195,000 is not deductible by L for any taxable year.

(iv) Earnings through January 1, 2020 on the principal addition for L's 2018 taxable year ($50,000) that was not paid as part of the December 31, 2018 payment are $5,000. Earnings through January 1, 2020 on the $125,000 credited to O's account on January 1, 2019 are $20,000. On December 31, 2018, after the $400,000 payment is applied to 2016, 2017, and 2018, the account balance for 2016 and 2017 is reduced to zero, and the account balance for 2018 is reduced to $50,000 ($150,000 + $5,000 (earnings) - $105,000). Under the terms of the plan, the $200,000 payment made on January 1, 2020, is attributable to services performed by O in L's 2018 and 2019 taxable years. Therefore, the $200,000 payment on January 1, 2020 is attributed to services performed by O in L's taxable years as follows: $55,000 ($50,000 + $5,000) to 2018 and $145,000 ($125,000 + $20,000) to 2019.

(v) The portion of the DDR attributed to a disqualified taxable year under paragraph (d) of this section that exceeds the deduction limit for that disqualified taxable year, as reduced, is not deductible for any taxable year. For L's 2018 taxable year, the deduction limit is reduced to zero by the $450,000 of AIR for that year and the payment of $50,000 of DDR attributable to that year. Because $55,000 exceeds the reduced deduction limit of zero, the $55,000 is not deductible for 2020, the year of payment (or any other taxable year). With respect to L's 2019 taxable year, the $500,000 deduction limit for 2019 is applied first to O's $200,000 of AIR for 2019. Because the deduction limit is greater than the AIR, L may deduct the entire $200,000 of AIR paid in 2019. The $500,000 deduction limit is then reduced to $300,000 by the amount of the AIR ($500,000 - $200,000). The reduced deduction limit is applied to O's $145,000 of DDR attributable to services performed by O in L's 2019 taxable year that is paid in 2020. Because $145,000 does not exceed the $300,000 reduced limit, the $145,000 is deductible for 2020 (the year of payment). As a result, $145,000 of the $200,000 payment ($0 + $145,000) is deductible for L's 2020 taxable year, and the remaining $55,000 is not deductible by L for any taxable year.

(4) *Application of deduction limitation to aggregated groups of covered health insurance providers.*—(i) *In general.*—The total combined deduction for AIR and DDR attributable to services performed by an applicable individual in a disqualified taxable year allowed for all members of an aggregated group that are covered health insurance providers for any taxable year is limited to $500,000. Therefore, if two or more members of an aggregated group that are covered health insurance providers may otherwise deduct AIR or DDR attributable to services performed by an applicable individual in a disqualified taxable year, the AIR and DDR otherwise deductible by all members of the aggregated group is combined, and the deduction limitation is applied to the total amount.

(ii) *Proration of deduction limitation.*—If the total amount of AIR or DDR attributable to services performed by an applicable individual in a disqualified taxable year that is otherwise deductible by two or more members of an aggregated group in any taxable year exceeds the $500,000 deduction limit (as reduced by previously deductible AIR or DDR, if applicable), the deduction limit is prorated based on the AIR or DDR otherwise deductible by the members of the aggregated group in the taxable year and allocated to each member of the aggregated group. The deduction limit allocated to each member of the aggregated group is determined by multiplying the deduction limit for the disqualified taxable year (as previously reduced, if applicable) by a fraction, the numerator of which is the AIR or DDR otherwise deductible by that member in that taxable year that is attributable to services performed by the applicable individual in the disqualified taxable year, and the denominator of which is the total AIR or DDR otherwise deductible by all members of the aggregated group in that taxable year that is attributable to services performed by the applicable individual in the disqualified taxable year. The amount of AIR or DDR otherwise deductible by a member of the aggregated group in excess of the portion of the deduction limit allocated to that member is not deductible in any taxable year. If a covered health insurance provider is a member of more than one aggregated group, the deduction limit for that covered health insurance provider under section 162(m)(6) may in no event exceed $500,000 for AIR and DDR attributable to services performed by an applicable individual in a disqualified taxable year.

(5) *Examples.*—The following examples illustrate the rules of paragraph (e)(4) of this section. For purposes of these examples, each corporation has a taxable year that is the calendar year and is a covered health insurance provider for all relevant taxable years, and DDR is otherwise deductible by the covered health insurance provider in the taxable year in which it is paid.

Example 1. (i) Corporations I, J, and K are members of the same aggregated group under paragraph (b)(3) of this section. At separate times during 2016, C is an employee of, and performs services for, I, J, and K. C's total AIR for 2016 is $1,500,000, which consists of

Itemized Deductions for Individuals and Corps.
See p. 20,601 for regulations not amended to reflect law changes
25,261

$750,000 of AIR for services performed to K; $450,000 of AIR for services provided to J; and $300,000 of AIR for services to I.

(ii) Because I, J, and K are members of the same aggregated group, the AIR otherwise deductible by them is aggregated for purposes of applying the deduction limitation. Further, because the aggregate AIR otherwise deductible by I, J, and K for 2016 exceeds the deduction limitation for C for that taxable year, the deduction limit is prorated and allocated to the members of the aggregated group in proportion to the AIR otherwise deductible by each member of the aggregated group for that taxable year. Therefore, the deduction limit that applies to the AIR otherwise deductible by K is $250,000 ($500,000 × ($750,000 / $1,500,000)); the deduction limit that applies to the AIR otherwise deductible by J is $150,000 ($500,000 x ($450,000 / $1,500,000)); and the deduction limit that applies to AIR otherwise deductible by I is $100,000 ($500,000 × ($300,000 / $1,500,000)). For the 2016 taxable year, K may not deduct $500,000 of the $750,000 of AIR paid to C ($750,000 - $250,000); J may not deduct $300,000 of the $450,000 of AIR paid to C ($450,000 - $150,000); and I may not deduct $200,000 of the $300,000 of AIR paid to C ($300,000 - $100,000).

Example 2. (i) The facts are the same as *Example 1*, except that C's total AIR for 2016 is $400,000, which consists of $75,000 for services provided to K; $150,000 for services provided to J; and $175,000 for services provided to I. In addition, C becomes entitled to $60,000 of DDR attributable to services provided to K in 2016, which is payable (and paid) on April 1, 2018, and $75,000 of DDR attributable to services provided to J in 2016, which is payable (and paid) on April 1, 2019.

(ii) Because C's total AIR of $400,000 for 2016 for services provided to K, J, and I do not exceed the $500,000 limitation, K, J, and I may deduct $75,000, $150,000, and $175,000, respectively, for 2016. The deduction limit is then reduced to $100,000 by the total AIR deductible by all members of the aggregated group ($500,000 - $400,000). The deduction limit, as reduced, is then applied to any DDR attributable to services provided by C in 2016 in the first subsequent taxable year that DDR becomes deductible. The first year that DDR for 2016 becomes deductible is 2018, due to the $60,000 payment made on April 1, 2018. Because the $60,000 of DDR otherwise deductible by K does not exceed the 2016 $100,000 deduction limit, K may deduct the entire $60,000 for its 2018 taxable year. The $100,000 deduction limit is then reduced by the $60,000 of DDR deductible by K for 2018, and the reduced deduction limit of $40,000 ($100,000 - $60,000) is applied to the $75,000 of DDR that is otherwise deductible for 2019. Because the DDR of $75,000 otherwise deductible by J exceeds the reduced deduction limit of $40,000, J may deduct only $40,000, and the remaining $35,000 ($75,000 - $40,000) is not deductible by J for that taxable year or any other taxable year.

Example 3. (i) The facts are the same as *Example 2*, except that C's DDR of $75,000 attributable to services performed by C in J's 2016 taxable year is payable (and paid) on July 1, 2018.

(ii) The results are the same as *Example 2*, except that the reduced deduction limit of $100,000 is prorated between K and J in proportion to the DDR otherwise deductible by them for 2018. Accordingly, $44,444 of the remaining deduction limit is allocated to K ($100,000 × ($60,000 / $135,000)), and $55,556 of the remaining deduction limit is allocated to J ($100,000 × ($75,000 / $135,000)). Because the $60,000 of DDR otherwise deductible by K exceeds the $44,444 deduction limit applied to that remuneration, K may deduct only $44,444 of the $60,000 payment, and $15,556 may not be deducted by K for the 2018 taxable year or any other taxable year. Similarly, because the $75,000 of DDR otherwise deductible by J exceeds the $55,556 deduction limit applied to that remuneration, J may deduct only $55,556 of the $75,000 payment, and $19,444 may not be deducted by J for that taxable year or any other taxable year.

(f) *Corporate transactions.*—(1) *Treatment as a covered health insurance provider in connection with a corporate transaction.*—Except as otherwise provided in this paragraph (f), a person that participates in a corporate transaction is a covered health insurance provider for the taxable year in which the corporate transaction occurs (and any other taxable year) if it would otherwise be a covered health insurance provider under paragraph (b)(4) of this section for that taxable year. For example, if a member of an aggregated group that did not previously include a health insurance issuer purchases a health insurance issuer that is a covered health insurance provider (so that the health insurance issuer becomes a member of the aggregated group), each member of the acquiring aggregated group will be a covered health insurance provider for its full taxable year in which the corporate transaction occurs and each subsequent taxable year in which the health insurance issuer continues to be a member of the group, if it would otherwise be a covered health insurance provider under paragraph (b)(4), except as otherwise provided in this paragraph (f). For purposes of this section, the term *corporate transaction* means a merger, acquisition or disposition of assets or stock, reorganization,

consolidation, separation, or any other transaction resulting in a change in the composition of an aggregated group.

(2) *Transition period relief for a person becoming a covered health insurance provider solely as a result of a corporate transaction.*—(i) *In general.*—Except as provided in paragraph (f)(2)(ii) of this section, a person that is not a covered health insurance provider before a corporate transaction, but would (except for application of this paragraph (f)(2)(i)) become a covered health insurance provider solely because it becomes a member of an aggregated group with another person that is a health insurance issuer as a result of the corporate transaction, is not a covered health insurance provider subject to the deduction limitation of section 162(m)(6) for the taxable year of that person in which the corporate transaction occurs (the *transition period relief*).

(ii) *Certain applicable individuals.*—The transition period relief described in paragraph (f)(2)(i) of this section does not apply with respect to the remuneration of any individual who is an applicable individual of a person that would have been a covered health insurance provider for the taxable year in which the corporate transaction occurred without regard to the occurrence of the corporate transaction (for example, the applicable individuals of a health insurance issuer and the members of its affiliated group that were covered health insurance issuers before the occurrence of a corporate transaction). This exception to the transition period relief applies even with respect to remuneration attributable to services performed by the applicable individual for a person that is eligible for the transition period relief described in paragraph (f)(1)(ii)(A) of this section. Accordingly, each member of an acquiring aggregated group that would become a covered health insurance provider solely as a result of a corporate transaction, but is not a covered health insurance provider under the transition period relief described in paragraph (f)(1)(ii)(A) of this section, is subject to the deduction limitation of section 162(m)(6) for its taxable year in which the corporate transaction occurs with respect to AIR and DDR attributable to services performed by any individual who is an applicable individual of the acquired health insurance issuer and any member of its aggregated group that would have been a covered health insurance provider in the taxable year in which the corporate transaction occurred, even if the corporate transaction had not occurred.

(3) *Transition relief from the attribution consistency requirements.*—(i) *In general.*—Paragraphs (d)(3)(i), (d)(4)(i) and (d)(5)(i)(B) of this section require a covered health insurance provider and all members of its aggregated group to use the same method for attributing remuneration to services performed by applicable individuals consistently for all taxable years (*attribution consistency requirements*). As a result of a corporate transaction, however, a covered health insurance provider that uses an attribution method for its account balance plans, nonaccount balance plans, or stock options or SARs may become a member of an aggregated group with another covered health insurance provider that uses a different attribution method for those types of plans or arrangements. In that case, neither member of the aggregated group will be treated as violating the attribution consistency requirements merely because it uses an attribution method that is different from the attribution method used by another member of its aggregated group to attribute remuneration that becomes otherwise deductible in the taxable year in which the corporate transaction occurs. However, the attribution consistency requirements apply with respect to remuneration that becomes otherwise deductible in all subsequent taxable years. Following the date of the corporate transaction, any member of the aggregated group may change the attribution method that it used before the date of the corporate transaction to attribute remuneration under its account balance plans, nonaccount balance plans, or stock options or SARs to make its method consistent with the method used by any other member of the aggregated group. Notwithstanding the foregoing, the Secretary may subject this change in attribution method to limitations, or may otherwise modify the attribution consistency requirements, pursuant to a notice, revenue ruling, or other guidance of general applicability published in the Internal Revenue Bulletin.

(ii) *Exception for certain applicable individuals.*—Notwithstanding the transition relief described in paragraphs (f)(2)(A) of this section, if a covered health insurance provider has attributed remuneration under a method described in paragraphs (d)(3), (d)(4), or (d)(5) of this section with respect to an applicable individual before a corporate transaction, the covered health insurance provider must continue at all times to use that attribution method for all other remuneration that becomes otherwise deductible under the same type of plan (that is, an account balance plan, a nonaccount balance plan, or a stock option or SAR) to which the applicable individual has a legally binding right as of the corporate transaction.

(4) *Deduction limitation not prorated for short taxable years.*—If a corporate transaction results in a short taxable year for a covered

Reg. § 1.162-31(f)(4)

health insurance provider, the $500,000 deduction limit for the short taxable year is neither prorated nor reduced. For example, if a corporate transaction results in a short taxable year of three months, the deduction limit under section 162(m)(6) for that short taxable year is $500,000 (and is not reduced to $125,000).

(5) *Effect of a corporate transaction on the application of the de minimis exception.*—If a person becomes or ceases to be a member of an aggregated group, only the premiums and gross revenues of that person for the portion of its taxable year during which it is a member of the aggregated group are taken into account for purposes of determining whether the *de minimis* exception applies.

(6) *Examples.*—The following examples illustrate the principles of this paragraph (f). For purposes of these examples, each corporation has a taxable year that is the calendar year unless stated otherwise, and none of the corporations qualify for the *de minimis* exception under paragraph (b)(4)(v) of this section.

Example 1. (i) Corporation J merges with and into corporation H on June 30, 2015, such that H is the surviving entity. As a result of the merger, J's taxable year ends on June 30, 2015. For its taxable year ending June 30, 2015, J is a health insurance issuer that is a covered health insurance provider. For all taxable years before the taxable year of the merger, H is not a covered health insurance provider.

(ii) Corporation J is a covered health insurance provider for its short taxable year ending June 30, 2015. As a result of the merger, H becomes a covered health insurance provider for its 2015 taxable year, but Corporation H is not a covered health insurance provider for its 2015 taxable year by reason of the transition period relief in paragraph (f)(1)(ii)(A) of this section. However, applicable individuals of J continue to be subject to the deduction limit under section 162(m)(6) for amounts that become otherwise deductible in the 2015 taxable year and DDR that is attributable to services performed by applicable individuals of J, and H is a covered health insurance provider for all subsequent taxable years for which it is a covered health insurance provider under paragraph (b)(4) of this section.

Example 2. (i) On January 1, 2016, corporations D, E, and F are members of a controlled group within the meaning of section 414(b). F is a health insurance issuer that is a covered health insurance provider under paragraph (b)(4)(i)(A) of this section. D and E are not health insurance issuers (but are covered health insurance providers pursuant to paragraphs (b)(4)(i)(C) and (D) of this section). D is the parent entity of the DEF aggregated group. F's taxable year ends on September 30. P is an applicable individual of F for all taxable years. On May 1, 2016, a controlled group within the meaning of section 414(b) consisting of corporations C and B purchases all of the stock of corporation F, resulting in a controlled group within the meaning of section 414(b) consisting of corporations C, B, and F. The amount of premiums received by F from providing minimum essential coverage during the portion of its taxable year when it was a member of the DEF aggregated group constitute more than two percent of the gross revenues of the aggregated group for the taxable year of D (the parent entity) ending on December 31, 2016, and the taxable years of E and F ending with or within D's taxable year (December 31, 2016 and May 1, 2016 respectively). C and B are not health insurance issuers. C is the parent entity of the CBF aggregated group. The CBF aggregated group is also a consolidated group within the meaning of § 1.1502-1(h). Thus, F's taxable year ends on May 1, 2016 by reason of § 1.1502-76(b)(1)(ii)(A)(1), and F becomes part of the CBF consolidated group for the taxable year ending December 31, 2016.

(ii) D and E are covered health insurance providers for the taxable year ending December 31, 2016, and the de minimis exception does not apply because the amount of premiums received by F from providing minimum essential coverage during the short taxable year that it was a member of the DEF aggregated group are more than two percent of the gross revenues of the aggregated group for the taxable years during which the members would otherwise be a covered health insurance providers under paragraph (b)(4)(i) of this section. Accordingly, D and E are subject to the deduction limitation under section 162(m)(6) for their taxable years ending December 31, 2016. C and B are not covered health insurance providers for their taxable year ending December 31, 2016, by reason of the transition period relief of paragraph (f)(1)(ii)(A) of this section.

(iii) As a result of leaving the aggregated group, F has a new taxable year beginning on May 2, 2016 and ending on December 31, 2016. F is a covered health insurance provider within the meaning of paragraph (b)(4) of this section for its new taxable year ending on December 31, 2016 (even though C and B are not covered health insurance providers for their taxable years ending December 31, 2016) unless the CBF aggregated group qualifies for the *de minimis* exception for that taxable year.

(iv) P is an applicable individual whose remuneration from F is subject to the deduction limitation under section 162(m)(6) for F's short taxable year ending May 1, 2016 and F's taxable year ending December 31, 2016. In addition, any remuneration provided to P by C

or B at any time for services provided by P from May 1, 2016 to December 31, 2016 is also subject to the deduction limitation under section 162(m)(6), even though C and B are not covered health insurance providers for their taxable years ending December 31, 2016 by reason of the transition period relief of paragraph (f)(1)(ii)(A) of this section. Remuneration to which P had the legally binding right on or before the date of the transaction is subject to the deduction limitation when that remuneration becomes otherwise deductible.

Example 3. (i) The same facts as *Example 2*, except that E is a health insurance issuer that is a covered health insurance provider under paragraph (b)(4) of this section and thus receives premiums from providing minimum essential coverage (instead of F), and F is not a health insurance issuer.

(ii) F is a covered health insurance provider for its short taxable year ending May 1, 2016. However, because F is not a health insurance issuer that is a covered health insurance provider and there are no other health insurance issuers in the BCF aggregated group, F is not a covered health insurance provider for its short, postacquisition taxable year ending December 31, 2016.

(iii) With respect to P, remuneration to which P had the legally binding right on or before the date of the transaction is subject to the deduction limitation. However, remuneration to which P obtains the legally binding right after the date of the corporate transaction is not subject to the deduction limitation.

Example 4. (i) Corporations N, O, and P are members of an aggregated group as described in paragraph (b)(2) of this section. N is a health insurance issuer that is a covered health insurance provider pursuant to paragraph (b)(4)(i)(A) of this section, but neither O nor P is a health insurance issuer. P is the parent entity of the aggregated group. On April 1, 2016, O ceases to be a member of the NOP aggregated group as the result of a corporate transaction. O's taxable year does not end as a result of the corporate transaction.

(ii) Because O was a member of the NOP aggregated group during a portion of its taxable year, O is a covered health insurance provider for its taxable year ending December 31, 2016.

Example 5. (i) Corporations V, W, and X are members of an aggregated group as described in paragraph (b)(2) of this section. V is a health insurance issuer that is a covered health insurance provider pursuant to paragraph (b)(4)(i)(A) of this section, but neither W nor X is a health insurance issuer. W is the parent entity of the aggregated group. V's taxable year ends on December 31; W's taxable year ends on June 30; and X's taxable year ends on September 30. For its taxable year ending June 30, 2017, W has $100x in gross revenue. For its taxable year ending September 30, 2016, X has $60x in gross revenue. For its taxable year ending December 31, 2016, V receives $4x of premiums from providing minimum essential coverage and has no other revenue. As of September 30, 2016, V ceases to be a member of the VWX aggregated group. V's taxable year does not end on September 30, 2016 as a result of the transaction. Of the $4x that that V receives for providing minimum essential coverage during its taxable year ending December 31, 2016, $3x is received during the period from January 1, 2016 through September 30, 2016. As a result of the corporate transaction, V's taxable year ends on September 30, 2016. The *de minimis* exception of paragraph (b)(4)(v)(A) of this section did not apply to the members of the VWX aggregated group for their immediately preceding taxable years ending December 31, 2015, June 30, 2016, and September 30, 2015, respectively.

(ii) For purposes of applying the *de minimis* exception to an aggregated group for a taxable year during which a person leaves or joins the aggregated group, only the premiums and revenues of the person for the portion of its taxable year during which it was a member of the aggregated group are taken into account. The premiums from providing minimum essential coverage received by the VWX aggregated group for W's taxable year ending June 30, 2017 are $3x. The revenues of the V, W, and X aggregated group for W's taxable year ending June 30, 2017 are $163x. Accordingly, the premiums received by the members of the aggregated group from providing minimum essential coverage are less than two percent of the gross revenues of the aggregated group ($3x is less than $3.26x (two percent of $163x)). Therefore, V, W and X are not covered health insurance providers for their taxable years ending December 31, 2016, June 30, 2017, and September 30, 2016, respectively.

Example 6. (i) The facts are the same as *Example 5*, except that F received $4x of premiums during the period from January 1, 2016 to September 30, 2016, and the members of the VWX aggregated group were not covered health insurance providers for their taxable years ending December 31, 2015, June 30, 2016, and September 30, 2015, respectively (their immediately preceding taxable years) solely by reason of the *de minimis* exception of paragraph (b)(4)(v)(A) of this section.

(ii) The premiums from providing minimum essential coverage received by the VWX aggregated group for W's taxable year ending June 30, 2017 are $4x. The revenues of the VWX aggregated group for W's taxable year ending June 30, 2017 are $164x. Accordingly, the

Itemized Deductions for Individuals and Corps.
See p. 20,601 for regulations not amended to reflect law changes
25,263

premiums received by the members of the aggregated group from providing minimum essential coverage are greater than two percent of the gross revenues of the aggregated group ($4x is greater than $3.28x (two percent of $164x)). Therefore, V, W, and X do not qualify for the *de minimis* exception for their taxable years ending December 31, 2016, June 30, 2017, and September 30, 2016, respectively. However, V, W, and X are not covered health insurance providers for these taxable years by reason of the *de minimis* exception one year transition period described in paragraph (b)(4)(v)(B) of this section.

Example 7. (i) Corporation N is a health insurance issuer that is a covered health insurance provider. Corporation O is also a health insurance issuer that is a covered health insurance provider. Both N and O have taxable years ending December 31. N uses the account balance ratio method to attribute remuneration that becomes otherwise deductible under its account balance plans. O uses the principal additions method to attribute amounts that become otherwise deductible under its account balance plans. On June 30, 2016, O purchases all of the stock of N.

(ii) For the taxable year of N and O ending December 31, 2016, N may continue to attribute amounts that become deductible under its account balance plans using the account balance ratio method, and O can continue to attribute amounts that become otherwise deductible under its account balance plan using the principal additions method, even though they are members of the same aggregated group, pursuant to the transition period relief described in paragraph (f)(2) of this section. In all subsequent taxable years, N and O must use the same method to attribute amounts that become otherwise deductible under their account balance plans. Either N or O may change the method that it uses to attribute amounts under its account balance plans to be consistent with the attribution method used by the other.

Example 8. (i) The facts are the same as *Example 7.* In addition, B is an applicable individual of N before the corporate transaction and is a participant in an account balance plan of N. On December 31, 2015, N made a payment to B, and N used the account balance ratio method described in paragraph (d)(3)(ii) of this section to attribute the payment to services performed by B in taxable years of N.

(ii) Because N used the account balance ratio method described in paragraph (d)(3)(ii) of this section to attribute an amount that became otherwise deductible under the plan before the corporate transaction, N must continue to use the account balance ratio method for attributing amounts to which B had a legally binding right as of the corporate transaction, whenever those amounts become otherwise deductible

(g) *Coordination.*—(1) *Coordination with section 162(m)(1).*—If section 162(m)(1) and section 162(m)(6) both otherwise would apply with respect to the remuneration of an applicable individual, the deduction limitation under section 162(m)(6) applies without regard to section 162(m)(1). For example, if an applicable individual is both a covered employee of a publicly held corporation (see sections 162(m)(2) and (3); § 1.162-27) and an applicable individual within the meaning of paragraph (b)(7) of this section, remuneration earned by the applicable individual that is attributable to a disqualified taxable year of a covered health insurance provider is subject to the $500,000 deduction limitation under section 162(m)(6) with respect to such disqualified taxable year, without regard to section 162(m)(1).

(2) *Coordination with disallowed excess parachute payments.*—(i) *In general.*—The $500,000 deduction limitation of section 162(m)(6) is reduced (but not below zero) by the amount (if any) that would have been included in the AIR or DDR of the applicable individual for a taxable year but for the deduction for the AIR or DDR being disallowed by reason of section 280G.

(ii) *Example.*—The following example illustrates the rule of this paragraph (g)(2).

Example. Corporation A, a covered health insurance provider, pays $750,000 of AIR to P, an applicable individual, during A's disqualified taxable year ending December 31, 2016. Of the $750,000, $300,000 is an excess parachute payment as defined in section 280G(b)(1), the deduction for which is disallowed by reason of that section. The excess parachute payment reduces the $500,000 deduction limit to $200,000 ($500,000 - $300,000). Therefore, A may deduct only $200,000 of the $750,000 in AIR, and $250,000 of the payment is not deductible by reason of section 162(m)(6).

(h) *Grandfathered amounts attributable to services performed in taxable years beginning before January 1, 2010.*—(1) *In general.*—The section 162(m)(6) deduction limitation does not apply to remuneration attributable to services performed in taxable years of a covered health insurance provider beginning before January 1, 2010 (*grandfathered amounts*). For purposes of this paragraph (h), whether remuneration is attributable to services performed in a taxable year beginning before January 1, 2010, is determined by applying an attribution method described in paragraph (h)(2) of this section.

(2) *Identification of services performed in taxable years beginning before January 1, 2010.*—(i) *In general.*—DDR described in paragraphs (d)(2) (legally binding right), (d)(3) (account balance plans), (d)(4) (nonaccount balance plans), (d)(6) (involuntary separation pay), (d)(7) (reimbursements), and (d)(8) (split dollar life insurance) of this section is attributable to services performed in a taxable year beginning before January 1, 2010 if it is attributable to services performed before that date under the rules of these paragraphs, without regard to whether that remuneration is subject to a substantial risk of forfeiture on or after that date. Notwithstanding the requirement under paragraph (d)(3)(i) of this section that a covered health insurance provider must use the same attribution method for its account balance plans for all taxable years, a covered health insurance provider that uses the account balance ratio method described in paragraph (d)(3)(i) of this section to attribute remuneration to services performed in taxable years beginning after December 31, 2009 may use the principal additions method described in paragraph (d)(3)(ii) of this section to attribute remuneration under an account balance plan to services performed in a taxable year beginning before January 1, 2010 for purposes of determining grandfathered amounts under the plan. (See paragraph (d)(3)(ii)(C)(3) of this section for required account balance adjustments if a covered health insurance provider generally uses the account balance ratio method to attribute amounts otherwise deductible under its account balance plans but uses the principal additions method to attribute remuneration to services performed in taxable years beginning before January 1, 2010.)

(ii) *Equity-based remuneration.*—For purposes of this section, all remuneration resulting from a stock option, stock appreciation right, restricted stock, or restricted stock unit and the right to any associated dividends or dividend equivalents (together, referred to as *equity-based remuneration*) granted before the first day of the taxable year of the covered health insurance provider beginning on or after January 1, 2010, is attributable to services performed in taxable years beginning before January 1, 2010, regardless of the date on which the equity-based remuneration is exercised (in the case of a stock option or SAR), the date on which the amounts due under the equity-based remuneration are paid or includible in income, or whether the equity-based remuneration is subject to a substantial risk of forfeiture on or after the first day of the taxable year of the covered health insurance provider beginning on or after January 1, 2010. For example, appreciation in the value of restricted shares granted before the first day of the taxable year beginning on or after January 1, 2010 is treated as remuneration that is attributable to services performed in taxable years beginning before January 1, 2010, regardless of whether the shares are vested at that time.

(i) *Transition rules for certain DDR.*—(1) *Transition rule for DDR attributable to services performed in taxable years of the covered health insurance provider beginning after December 31, 2009 and before January 1, 2013.*—The deduction limitation under section 162(m)(6) applies to DDR attributable to services performed in a disqualified taxable year of a covered health insurance provider beginning after December 31, 2009 and before January 1, 2013, only if that remuneration is otherwise deductible in a disqualified taxable year of the covered health insurance provider beginning after December 31, 2012. However, if the deduction limitation applies to DDR attributable to services performed by an applicable individual in a disqualified taxable year of a covered health insurance provider beginning after December 31, 2009 and before January 1, 2013, the deduction limitation is calculated as if it had been applied to the applicable individual's AIR and DDR deductible in those taxable years.

(2) *Examples.*—The following examples illustrate the principles of this paragraph (i). For purposes of these examples, each corporation has a taxable year that is the calendar year, and DDR is otherwise deductible by the covered health insurance provider in the taxable year in which it is paid.

Example 1. (i) Q is an applicable individual of corporation Z. Z's 2010, 2011, and 2012 taxable years are disqualified taxable years. Z's 2013, 2014, and 2015 taxable years are not disqualified taxable years. However, Z's 2016 taxable year and all subsequent taxable years are disqualified taxable years. Q receives $200,000 of AIR from Z for 2012, and becomes entitled to $800,000 of DDR that is attributable to services performed by Q in 2012. Z pays Q $350,000 of the DDR in 2015, and the remaining $450,000 of the DDR in 2016. These payments are otherwise deductible by Z in 2015 and 2016, respectively.

(ii) DDR attributable to services performed by Q in Z's 2010, 2011, and 2012 taxable years that is otherwise deductible in Z's 2013, 2014, or 2015 taxable years is not subject to the deduction limitation under section 162(m)(6) by reason of the transition rule under paragraph (i)(1) of this section. However, DDR attributable to services performed in Z's 2010, 2011, and 2012 taxable years that is otherwise deductible in a later taxable year that is a disqualified taxable year (in this case, Z's 2016 and subsequent taxable years) is subject to the deduction limitation under section 162(m)(6). Accordingly, the deduction limitation with respect to AIR and DDR attributable to services performed by Q in 2012 is determined by reducing the $500,000 deduction limit by the $200,000 of AIR paid to Q by Z for 2012 ($500,000 - $200,000). Under the transition rule of paragraph (i)(1) of this section, no portion of the reduced deduction limit of $300,000 for the 2012 taxable year is applied against the $350,000 payment made in 2015, and accordingly, the deduction limit is not reduced by the amount of that payment. The reduced deduction limit is then applied to Q's $450,000 of DDR attributable to services performed by Q in 2012 that is paid to Q and becomes otherwise deductible in 2016. Because the reduced deduction limit of $300,000 is less than the $450,000 otherwise deductible by Z in 2016, Z may deduct only $300,000 of the DDR, and $150,000 of the $450,000 payment is not deductible by Z in that taxable year or any taxable year.

Example 2. (i) R is an applicable individual of corporation Y, which is a covered health insurance provider for all relevant taxable years. During 2010, Y pays R $400,000 in salary and grants R a right to $200,000 in DDR payable on a fixed schedule in 2011, 2012, and 2013. Pursuant to the fixed schedule, Y pays R $50,000 of DDR in 2011, $50,000 of DDR in 2012, and the remaining $100,000 of DDR in 2013.

(ii) Because the deduction limitation for DDR under section 162(m)(6)(A)(ii) is effective for DDR that is attributable to services performed by an applicable individual during any disqualified taxable year beginning after December 31, 2009 that would otherwise be deductible in a taxable year beginning after December 31, 2012, only the DDR paid by Y in 2013 is subject to the deduction limitation. However, the limitation is applied as if section 162(m)(6) and paragraph (c)(2) of this section were effective for taxable years beginning after December 31, 2009 and before January 1, 2013. Accordingly, the deduction limitation with respect to remuneration for services performed by R in 2010 is determined by reducing the $500,000 deduction limit by the $400,000 of AIR paid to R for 2010 ($500,000 - $400,000). The reduced deduction limit of $100,000 is further reduced to zero by the $50,000 of DDR attributable to services performed by R in Y's 2010 taxable year that is deductible in each of 2011 and 2012 (($100,000 - $50,000 - $50,000). Because the deduction limit is reduced to zero, none of the $100,000 of DDR attributable to services performed by R in Y's 2010 taxable year and paid to R in 2013 is deductible.

(j) *Effective/applicability dates.*—These regulations are effective on September 23, 2014. The regulations apply to taxable years beginning on or after September 23, 2014. [Reg. § 1.162-31.]

☐ [T.D. 9694, 9-18-2014.]

[Reg. § 1.162-32]

§ 1.162-32. Expenses paid or incurred for lodging when not traveling away from home.—(a) *In general.*—Expenses paid or incurred for lodging of an individual who is not traveling away from home (local lodging) generally are personal, living, or family expenses that are nondeductible by the individual under section 262(a). Under certain circumstances, however, local lodging expenses may be deductible under section 162(a) as ordinary and necessary expenses paid or incurred in connection with carrying on a taxpayer's trade or business, including a trade or business as an employee. Whether local lodging expenses are paid or incurred in carrying on a taxpayer's trade or business is determined under all the facts and circumstances. One factor is whether the taxpayer incurs an expense because of a bona fide condition or requirement of employment imposed by the taxpayer's employer. Expenses paid or incurred for local lodging that is lavish or extravagant under the circumstances or that primarily provides an individual with a social or personal benefit are not incurred in carrying on a taxpayer's trade or business.

(b) *Safe harbor for local lodging at business meetings and conferences.*— An individual's local lodging expenses will be treated as ordinary and necessary business expenses if—

(1) The lodging is necessary for the individual to participate fully in or be available for a bona fide business meeting, conference, training activity, or other business function;

(2) The lodging is for a period that does not exceed five calendar days and does not recur more frequently than once per calendar quarter;

(3) If the individual is an employee, the employee's employer requires the employee to remain at the activity or function overnight; and

(4) The lodging is not lavish or extravagant under the circumstances and does not provide *any significant element of personal pleasure, recreation, or benefit.*

(c) *Examples.*—The provisions of the facts and circumstances test of paragraph (a) of this section are illustrated by the following exam-

ples. In each example the employer and the employees meet all other requirements (such as substantiation) for deductibility of the expense and for exclusion from income of the value of the lodging as a working condition fringe or of reimbursements under an accountable plan.

Example 1. (i) Employer conducts a seven-day training session for its employees at a hotel near Employer's main office. The training is directly connected with Employer's trade or business. Some employees attending the training are traveling away from home and some employees are not traveling away from home. Employer requires all employees attending the training to remain at the hotel overnight for the bona fide purpose of facilitating the training. Employer pays the costs of the lodging at the hotel directly to the hotel and does not treat the value as compensation to the employees.

(ii) Because the training is longer than five calendar days, the safe harbor in paragraph (b) of this section does not apply. However, the value of the lodging may be excluded from income if the facts and circumstances test in paragraph (a) of this section is satisfied.

(iii) The training is a bona fide condition or requirement of employment and Employer has a noncompensatory business purpose for paying the lodging expenses. Employer is not paying the expenses primarily to provide a social or personal benefit to the employees, and the lodging Employer provides is not lavish or extravagant. If the employees who are not traveling away from home had paid for their own lodging, the expenses would have been deductible by the employees under section 162(a) as ordinary and necessary business expenses. Therefore, the value of the lodging is excluded from the employees' income as a working condition fringe under section 132(a) and (d).

(iv) Employer may deduct the lodging expenses, including lodging for employees who are not traveling away from home, as ordinary and necessary business expenses under section 162(a).

Example 2. (i) The facts are the same as in *Example 1,* except that the employees pay the cost of their lodging at the hotel directly to the hotel, Employer reimburses the employees for the cost of the lodging, and Employer does not treat the reimbursement as compensation to the employees.

(ii) Because the training is longer than five calendar days, the safe harbor in paragraph (b) of this section does not apply. However, the reimbursement of the expenses for the lodging may be excluded from income if the facts and circumstances test in paragraph (a) of this section is satisfied.

(iii) The training is a bona fide condition or requirement of employment and Employer is reimbursing the lodging expenses for a noncompensatory business purpose and not primarily to provide a social or personal benefit to the employees and the lodging Employer provides is not lavish or extravagant. The employees incur the expenses in performing services for the employer. If Employer had not reimbursed the employees who are not traveling away from home for the cost of the lodging, the expenses would have been deductible by the employees under section 162(a) as ordinary and necessary business expenses. Therefore, the reimbursements to the employees are made under an accountable plan and are excluded from the employees' gross income.

(iv) Employer may deduct the lodging expense reimbursements, including reimbursements for employees who are not traveling away from home, as ordinary and necessary business expenses under section 162(a).

Example 3. (i) Employer is a professional sports team. Employer requires its employees (for example, players and coaches) to stay at a local hotel the night before a home game to conduct last minute training and ensure the physical preparedness of the players. Employer pays the lodging expenses directly to the hotel and does not treat the value as compensation to the employees.

(ii) Because the overnight stays occur more than once per calendar quarter, the safe harbor in paragraph (b) of this section does not apply. However, the value of the lodging may be excluded from income if the facts and circumstances test in paragraph (a) of this section is satisfied.

(iii) The overnight stays are a bona fide condition or requirement of employment and Employer has a noncompensatory business purpose for paying the lodging expenses. Employer is not paying the lodging expenses primarily to provide a social or personal benefit to the employees and the lodging Employer provides is not lavish or extravagant. If the employees had paid for their own lodging, the expenses would have been deductible by the employees under section 162(a) as ordinary and necessary business expenses. Therefore, the value of the lodging is excluded from the employees' income as a working condition fringe.

(iv) Employer may deduct the expenses for lodging the employees at the hotel as ordinary and necessary business expenses under section 162(a).

Example 4. (i) Employer hires Employee, who currently resides 500 miles from Employer's business premises. Employer pays for tempo-

Itemized Deductions for Individuals and Corps.
See p. 20,601 for regulations not amended to reflect law changes
25,265

rary lodging for Employee near Employer's business premises while Employee searches for a residence.

(ii) Employer is paying the temporary lodging expense primarily to provide a personal benefit to Employee by providing housing while Employee searches for a residence. Employer incurs the expense only as additional compensation and not for a noncompensatory business purpose. If Employee paid the temporary lodging expense, the expense would not be an ordinary and necessary employee business expense under section 162(a) because the lodging primarily provides a personal benefit to Employee. Therefore, the value of the lodging is includible in Employee's gross income as additional compensation.

(iii) Employer may deduct the lodging expenses as ordinary and necessary business expenses under section 162(a) and §1.162-25T.

Example 5. (i) Employee normally travels two hours each way between her home and her office. Employee is working on a project that requires Employee to work late hours. Employer provides Employee with lodging at a hotel near the office.

(ii) Employer is paying the temporary lodging expense primarily to provide a personal benefit to Employee by relieving her of the daily commute to her residence. Employer incurs the expense only as additional compensation and not for a noncompensatory business purpose. If Employee paid the temporary lodging expense, the expense would not be an ordinary and necessary business expense under section 162(a) because the lodging primarily provides a personal benefit to Employee. Therefore, the value of the lodging is includible in Employee's gross income as additional compensation.

(iii) Employer may deduct the lodging expenses as ordinary and necessary business expenses under section 162(a) and §1.162-25T.

Example 6. (i) Employer requires an employee to be "on duty" each night to respond quickly to emergencies that may occur outside of normal working hours. Employees who work daytime hours each serve a "duty shift" once each month in addition to their normal work schedule. Emergencies that require the duty shift employee to respond occur regularly. Employer has no sleeping facilities on its business premises and pays for a hotel room nearby where the duty shift employee stays until called to respond to an emergency.

(ii) Because an employee's expenses for lodging while on the duty shift occur more frequently than once per calendar quarter, the safe harbor in paragraph (b) of this section does not apply. However, the value of the lodging may be excluded from income if the facts and circumstances test in paragraph (a) of this section is satisfied.

(iii) The duty shift is a bona fide condition or requirement of employment and Employer has a noncompensatory business purpose for paying the lodging expenses. Employer is not providing the lodging to duty shift employees primarily to provide a social or personal benefit to the employees and the lodging Employer provides is not lavish or extravagant. If the employees had paid for their lodging, the expenses would have been deductible by the employees under section 162(a) as ordinary and necessary business expenses. Therefore, the value of the lodging is excluded from the employees' income as a working condition fringe.

(iv) Employer may deduct the lodging expenses as ordinary and necessary business expenses under section 162(a).

(d) *Effective/applicability date.*—This section applies to expenses paid or incurred on or after October 1, 2014. However, taxpayers may apply these regulations to local lodging expenses that are paid or incurred in taxable years for which the period of limitation on credit or refund under section 6511 has not expired. [Reg. §1.162-32.]

☐ [T.D. 9696, 9-30-2014.]

[Reg. §1.162-33]

§1.162-33. Certain employee remuneration in excess of $1,000,000 not deductible for taxable years beginning after December 31, 2017.—(a) *Scope.*—This section provides rules for the application of the $1 million deduction limitation under section 162(m)(1) for taxable years beginning after December 31, 2017. For rules concerning the applicability of section 162(m)(1) to taxable years beginning on or after January 1, 1994, and prior to January 1, 2018, see §1.162-27. Paragraph (b) of this section provides the general rule limiting deductions under section 162(m)(1). Paragraph (c) of this section provides definitions of generally applicable terms. Paragraph (d) of this section provides rules for determining when a corporation becomes a publicly held corporation. Paragraph (e) of this section provides rules for payments that are subject to section 280G (golden parachute payments). Paragraph (f) of this section provides a special rule for coordination with section 4985 (stock compensation of insiders in expatriated corporations). Paragraph (g) of this section provides transition rules addressing the amendments made by Public Law 115-97, including the rules for contracts that are grandfathered. Paragraph (h) of this section sets forth the effective date provisions. For rules concerning the deductibility of compensation for services that are not covered by section 162(m)(1) and this section, see section

162(a)(1) and §1.162-7. This section is not determinative as to whether compensation meets the requirements of section 162(a)(1). For rules concerning the deduction limitation under section 162(m)(6) applicable to certain health insurance providers, see §1.162-31. For purposes of this section, references to an amount being paid to an employee refer to the event that otherwise would result in the availability of a deduction to the employer with respect to such amount, whether that results from an actual payment in cash, transfer of property, or other event.

(b) *Limitation on deduction.*—Section 162(m)(1) precludes a deduction under chapter 1 of the Internal Revenue Code by any publicly held corporation for compensation paid to any covered employee to the extent that the compensation for the taxable year exceeds $1,000,000.

(c) *Definitions.*—(1) *Publicly held corporation.*—(i) *General rule.*—A publicly held corporation means any corporation that issues securities required to be registered under section 12 of the Exchange Act or that is required to file reports under section 15(d) of the Exchange Act. In addition, a publicly held corporation means any S corporation (as defined in section 1361(a)(1)) that issues securities that are required to be registered under section 12(b) of the Exchange Act, or that is required to file reports under section 15(d) of the Exchange Act. For purposes of this section, whether a corporation is publicly held is determined based solely on whether, as of the last day of its taxable year, the securities issued by the corporation are required to be registered under section 12 of the Exchange Act or the corporation is required to file reports under section 15(d) of the Exchange Act. Whether registration under the Exchange Act is required by rules other than those of the Exchange Act is irrelevant to this determination. A publicly traded partnership that is treated as a corporation under section 7704 (or otherwise) is a publicly held corporation if, as of the last day of its taxable year, its securities are required to be registered under section 12 of the Exchange Act or it is required to file reports under section 15(d) of the Exchange Act.

(ii) *Affiliated groups.*—(A) *In general.*—A publicly held corporation includes an affiliated group of corporations (affiliated group), as defined in section 1504 (determined without regard to section 1504(b)), that includes one or more publicly held corporations (as defined in paragraph (c)(1)(i) of this section). In the case of an affiliated group that includes two or more publicly held corporations as defined in paragraph (c)(1)(i) of this section, each member of the affiliated group that is a publicly held corporation as defined in paragraph (c)(1)(i) of this section is separately subject to this section, and, due to having at least one member that is a publicly held corporation, the affiliated group as a whole is subject to this section. Thus, for example, assume that a publicly held corporation (as defined in paragraph (c)(1)(i) of this section) is a wholly-owned subsidiary of another publicly held corporation (as defined in paragraph (c)(1)(i) of this section), which is a wholly-owned subsidiary of a privately held corporation. In this case, the two subsidiaries are separately subject to this section, and all three corporations are members of an affiliated group that is subject to this section. If an individual is a covered employee of both subsidiaries, each subsidiary has its own $1 million deduction limitation with respect to that covered employee. Furthermore, each subsidiary has its own set of covered employees as defined in paragraphs (c)(2)(i) through (iv) of this section (although the same individual may be a covered employee of both subsidiaries).

(B) *Proration of amount disallowed as a deduction.*—If, in a taxable year, a covered employee (as defined in paragraphs (c)(2)(i) through (v) of this section) of one member of an affiliated group is paid compensation by more than one member of the affiliated group, compensation paid by each member of the affiliated group is aggregated with compensation paid to the covered employee by all other members of the affiliated group (excluding compensation paid by any other publicly held corporation in the affiliated group, as defined in paragraph (c)(1)(i) of this section, of which the individual is also a covered employee as defined in paragraphs (c)(2)(i) through (v) of this section). In the event that, in a taxable year, a covered employee (as defined in paragraphs (c)(2)(i) through (v) of this section) is paid compensation by more than one publicly held corporation in an affiliated group and is also a covered employee of more than one publicly held payor corporation (as defined in paragraph (c)(1)(i) of this section) in the affiliated group, the amount disallowed as a deduction is determined separately with respect to each publicly held corporation of which the individual is a covered employee. Any amount disallowed as a deduction by this section must be prorated among the payor corporations (excluding any other publicly held payor corporation of which the individual is also a covered employee) in proportion to the amount of compensation paid to the covered employee (as defined in paragraphs (c)(2)(i) through (v) of this section) by each such corporation in the taxable year. For purposes of this paragraph (c)(1)(ii)(B), the amount of compensation treated as paid by a payor corporation that is not a publicly held corporation (as defined in paragraph (c)(1)(i) of this section) is determined by prorating the amount actually paid by that payor corporation in proportion to the total amount paid by all of the publicly held corporations of which the individual is a covered employee (as defined in paragraph (c)(2)(i) through (v) of this section). This process is repeated for each publicly held payor corporation of which the individual is a covered employee.

(iii) *Disregarded entities.*—For purposes of paragraph (c)(1) of this section, a publicly held corporation includes a corporation that owns an entity that is disregarded as an entity separate from its owner within the meaning of § 301.7701-2(c)(2)(i) of this chapter if the disregarded entity issues securities required to be registered under section 12(b) of the Exchange Act, or is required to file reports under section 15(d) of the Exchange Act.

(iv) *Qualified subchapter S subsidiaries.*—For purposes of paragraph (c)(1) of this section, a publicly held corporation includes an S corporation that owns a qualified subchapter S subsidiary as defined in section 1361(b)(3)(B) (QSub) if the QSub issues securities required to be registered under section 12(b) of the Exchange Act, or is required to file reports under section 15(d) of the Exchange Act.

(v) *Qualified real estate investment trust subsidiaries.*—For purposes of paragraph (c)(1) of this section, a publicly held corporation includes a real estate investment trust as defined in section 856(a) that owns a qualified real estate investment trust subsidiary as defined in section 856(i)(2) (QRS), if the QRS issues securities required to be registered under section 12(b) of the Exchange Act or is required to file reports under section 15(d) of the Exchange Act.

(vi) *Examples.*—The following examples illustrate the provisions of this paragraph (c)(1). For each example, assume that no corporation is a predecessor of a publicly held corporation within the meaning of paragraph (c)(2)(ii) of this section. Furthermore, for each example, unless provided otherwise, a reference to a publicly held corporation means a publicly held corporation as defined in paragraph (c)(1)(i) of this section. Additionally, for each example, assume that the corporation is a calendar-year taxpayer and has a fiscal year ending December 31 for reporting purposes under the Exchange Act. The examples in this paragraph (c)(1)(vi) are not intended to provide guidance on the legal requirements of the Securities Act and Exchange Act and the rules thereunder (17 CFR part 240).

(A) *Example 1 (Corporation required to file reports under section 15(d) of the Exchange Act).*—(1) *Facts.* Corporation Z plans to issue debt securities in a public offering registered under the Securities Act. Corporation Z is not required to file reports under section 15(d) of the Exchange Act for any other class of securities and does not have another class of securities required to be registered under section 12 of the Exchange Act. On April 1, 2021, the SEC declares effective the Securities Act registration statement for Corporation Z's debt securities. As a result, Corporation Z is required to file reports under section 15(d) of the Exchange Act, and this requirement continues to apply as of December 31, 2021.

(2) *Conclusion.* Corporation Z is a publicly held corporation for its 2021 taxable year because it is required to file reports under section 15(d) of the Exchange Act as of the last day of its taxable year.

(B) *Example 2 (Corporation not required to file reports under section 15(d) of the Exchange Act).*—(1) *Facts.* The facts are the same as in paragraph (c)(1)(vi)(A) of this section (*Example 1*), except that, on January 1, 2022, pursuant to section 15(d) of the Exchange Act, Corporation Z's obligation to file reports under section 15(d) is automatically suspended for the fiscal year ending December 31, 2022, because Corporation Z meets the statutory requirements for an automatic suspension. As of December 31, 2022, Corporation Z is not required to file reports under section 15(d) of the Exchange Act.

(2) *Conclusion.* Corporation Z is not a publicly held corporation for its 2022 taxable year because it is not required to file reports under section 15(d) of the Exchange Act as of as of the last day of its taxable year.

(C) *Example 3 (Corporation not required to file reports under section 15(d) of the Exchange Act).*—(1) *Facts.* The facts are the same as in paragraph (c)(1)(vi)(B) of this section (*Example 2*), except that, on January 1, 2022, pursuant to section 15(d) of the Exchange Act, Corporation Z's obligation to file reports under section 15(d) is not automatically suspended for the fiscal year ending December 31, 2022. Instead, on May 2, 2022, Corporation Z is eligible to suspend its section 15(d) reporting obligation under 17 CFR 240.12h-3 (Rule 12h-3 under the Exchange Act) and files Form 15, Certification and Notice of Termination of Registration under Section 12(g) of the Securities Exchange Act of 1934 or Suspension of Duty to File Reports under Sections 13 and 15(d) of the Securities Exchange Act of

1934, (or its successor) to suspend its section 15(d) reporting obligation for its fiscal year ending December 31, 2022. As of December 31, 2022, Corporation Z is not required to file reports under section 15(d) of the Exchange Act.

(2) *Conclusion.* Corporation Z is not a publicly held corporation for its 2022 taxable year because it is not required to file reports under section 15(d) of the Exchange Act as of the last day of its taxable year. If Corporation Z had not utilized Rule 12h-3 to suspend its section 15(d) reporting obligation, Corporation Z would be a publicly held corporation for its 2022 taxable year because it would have been required to file reports under section 15(d) of the Exchange Act as of the last day of its taxable year.

(D) *Example 4 (Corporation required to file reports under section 15(d) of the Exchange Act).*—(1) *Facts.* Corporation Y is a wholly-owned subsidiary of Corporation X, which is required to file reports under the Exchange Act. Corporation Y issued a class of debt securities in a public offering registered under the Securities Act, and therefore is required to file reports under section 15(d) of the Exchange Act for its fiscal year ending December 31, 2020. Corporation Y has no other class of securities registered under the Exchange Act. In its Form 10-K, Annual Report Pursuant to section 13 or section 15(d) of the Securities Exchange Act of 1934, (or its successor) for the 2020 fiscal year, Corporation Y may omit Item 11, Executive Compensation (required by Part III of Form 10-K), which requires disclosure of compensation of certain executive officers, because it is wholly-owned by Corporation X and the other conditions of General Instruction I to Form 10-K are satisfied.

(2) *Conclusion.* Corporation Y is a publicly held corporation for its 2020 taxable year because it is required to file reports under section 15(d) of the Exchange Act as of the last day of its taxable year.

(E) *Example 5 (Corporation not required to file reports under section 15(d) of the Exchange Act and not required to register securities under section 12 of the Exchange Act).*—(1) *Facts.* Corporation A has a class of securities registered under section 12(g) of the Exchange Act. For its 2020 taxable year, Corporation A is a publicly held corporation. On September 30, 2021, Corporation A is eligible to terminate the registration of its securities under section 12(g) of the Exchange Act pursuant to 17 CFR 240.12g-4(a)(2) (Rule 12g-4(a)(2) under the Exchange Act), but does not terminate the registration of its securities prior to December 31, 2021. Because Corporation A did not issue securities in a public offering registered under the Securities Act, Corporation A is not required to file reports under section 15(d) of the Exchange Act.

(2) *Conclusion.* Corporation A is not a publicly held corporation for its 2021 taxable year because, as of the last day of its taxable year, the securities issued by Corporation A are not required to be registered under section 12 of the Exchange Act and Corporation A is not required to file reports under section 15(d) of the Exchange Act.

(F) *Example 6 (Corporation required to file reports under section 15(d) of the Exchange Act).*—(1) *Facts.* The facts are the same as in paragraph (c)(1)(vi)(E) of this section (*Example 5*), except that Corporation A previously issued a class of securities in a public offering registered under the Securities Act. Furthermore, on October 1, 2021, Corporation A terminates the registration of its securities under section 12(g) of the Exchange Act. Because Corporation A issued a class of securities in a public offering registered under the Securities Act and is not eligible to suspend its reporting obligation under section 15(d) of the Exchange Act, as of December 31, 2021, Corporation A is required to file reports under section 15(d) of the Exchange Act.

(2) *Conclusion.* Corporation A is a publicly held corporation for its 2021 taxable year because it is required to file reports under section 15(d) of the Exchange Act as of the last day of its taxable year.

(G) *Example 7 (Corporation not required to file reports under section 15(d) of the Exchange Act and not required to register securities under section 12 of the Exchange Act).*—(1) *Facts.* On November 1, 2021, Corporation B is an issuer with only one class of equity securities. On November 5, 2021, Corporation B files a registration statement for its equity securities under section 12(g) of the Exchange Act. Corporation B's filing of its registration statement is voluntary because the Exchange Act does not require Corporation B to register its class of securities under section 12(g) of the Exchange Act based on the number and composition of its record holders. On December 1, 2021, the SEC declares effective the Exchange Act registration statement for Corporation B's securities. As of December 31, 2021, Corporation B continues to have its class of equity securities registered voluntarily under section 12 of the Exchange Act. Corporation B is not required to file reports under section 15(d) of the Exchange Act because it did not register any class of securities in a public offering under the Securities Act.

(2) *Conclusion.* Corporation B is not a publicly held corporation for its 2021 taxable year because, as of the last day of that taxable

Itemized Deductions for Individuals and Corps.
See p. 20,601 for regulations not amended to reflect law changes
25,267

year, the securities issued by Corporation B are not required to be registered under section 12 of the Exchange Act and Corporation B is not required to file reports under section 15(d) of the Exchange Act.

(H) *Example 8 (Corporation not required to file reports under section 15(d) of the Exchange Act and not required to register securities under section 12 of the Exchange Act).*—(1) *Facts.* The facts are the same as in paragraph (c)(1)(vi)(G) of this section (*Example 7*), except that, on December 31, 2022, because of a change in circumstances, Corporation B must register its class of equity securities under section 12(g) of the Exchange Act within 120 days of December 31, 2022. On February 1, 2023, the SEC declares effective the Exchange Act registration statement for Corporation B's securities.

(2) *Conclusion.* Corporation B is not a publicly held corporation for its 2022 taxable year because, as of the last day of that taxable year, Corporation B is not required to file reports under section 15(d) of the Exchange Act and the class of equity securities issued by Corporation B is not yet required to be registered under section 12 of the Exchange Act.

(I) *Example 9 (Securities of foreign private issuer in the form of ADRs traded in the over-the-counter market).*—(1) *Facts.* For its fiscal and taxable years ending December 31, 2021, Corporation W is a foreign private issuer. Because Corporation W has not registered an offer or sale of securities under the Securities Act, it is not required to file reports under section 15(d) of the Exchange Act. Corporation W qualifies for an exemption from registration of its securities under section 12(g) of the Exchange Act pursuant to 17 CFR 240.12g3-2(b) (Rule 12g3-2(b) under the Exchange Act). Corporation W wishes to have its securities traded in the U.S. in the over-the-counter market in the form of ADRs. Because Corporation W qualifies for an exemption pursuant to Rule 12g3-2(b), Corporation W is not required to register its securities underlying the ADRs under section 12 of the Exchange Act; however, the depositary bank is required to register the ADRs under the Securities Act. Even though the depositary bank is required to register the ADRs under the Securities Act, the registration of the ADRs does not result in either the depositary bank or Corporation W being required to file reports under section 15(d) of the Exchange Act. On February 3, 2021, the SEC declares effective the Securities Act registration statement for the ADRs. On February 4, 2021, Corporation W's ADRs begin trading in the over-the-counter market. On December 31, 2021, the securities of Corporation W are not required to be registered under section 12 of the Exchange Act because Corporation W qualifies for an exemption pursuant to Rule 240.12g3-2(b). Furthermore, on December 31, 2021, Corporation W is not required to file reports under section 15(d) of the Exchange Act.

(2) *Conclusion.* Corporation W is not a publicly held corporation for its 2021 taxable year because, as of the last day of that taxable year, the securities underlying the ADRs are not required to be registered under section 12 of the Exchange Act and Corporation W is not required to file reports under section 15(d) of the Exchange Act. The result would be the same if Corporation W had its securities traded in the over-the-counter market other than in the form of ADRs.

(J) *Example 10 (Securities of foreign private issuer in the form of ADRs quoted on Over the Counter Bulletin Board).*—(1) *Facts.* The facts are the same as in paragraph (c)(1)(vi)(I) of this section (*Example 9*), except that Corporation W has its securities quoted on the Over the Counter Bulletin Board (OTCBB) in the form of ADRs. Because Corporation W qualifies for an exemption pursuant to 17 CFR 240.12g3-2(b) (Rule 12g3-2(b) under the Exchange Act), Corporation W is not required to register its securities underlying the ADRs under section 12 of the Exchange Act. However, the depositary bank is required to register the ADRs under the Securities Act. In addition, section 6530(b)(1) of the OTCBB Rules requires that a foreign equity security may be quoted on the OTCBB only if the security is registered with the SEC pursuant to section 12 of the Exchange Act and the issuer of the security is current in its reporting obligations. To comply with the OTCBB Rules, on February 5, 2021, Corporation W files a registration statement for its class of securities underlying the ADRs under section 12(g) of the Exchange Act. On February 26, 2021, the SEC declares effective the Exchange Act registration statement for Corporation W's securities. As of December 31, 2021, Corporation W is subject to the reporting obligations under section 12 of the Exchange Act as a result of the section 12 registration.

(2) *Conclusion.* Corporation W is not a publicly held corporation for its 2021 taxable year because, as of the last day of that taxable year, its ADRs and the securities underlying the ADRs are not required by the Exchange Act to be registered under section 12 and Corporation W is not required to file reports under section 15(d) of the Exchange Act. The Securities Act requirement applicable to the bank pursuant to the OTCBB Rules is irrelevant. The result would be the same if Corporation W had its securities traded on the OTCBB other than in the form of ADRs.

(K) *Example 11 (Securities of foreign private issuer in the form of ADRs listed on a national securities exchange without a capital raising transaction).*—(1) *Facts.* For its fiscal and taxable years ending December 31, 2021, Corporation V is a foreign private issuer. Corporation V wishes to list its securities on the New York Stock Exchange (NYSE) in the form of ADRs without a capital raising transaction. Under the Exchange Act, Corporation V is required to register its securities underlying the ADRs under section 12(b) of the Exchange Act. Because the ADRs and the deposited securities are separate securities, the depositary bank is required to register the ADRs under the Securities Act. On February 2, 2021, the SEC declares effective Corporation V's registration statement under section 12(b) of the Exchange Act in connection with the underlying securities, and the depositary bank's registration statement under the Securities Act in connection with the ADRs. On March 1, 2021, Corporation V's securities begin trading on the NYSE in the form of ADRs. As of December 31, 2021, Corporation V is not required to file reports under section 15(d) of the Exchange Act; however, the securities underlying the ADRs are required to be registered under section 12(b) of the Exchange Act.

(2) *Conclusion.* Corporation V is a publicly held corporation for its 2021 taxable year because, as of the last day of that taxable year, the securities underlying the ADRs are required to be registered under section 12 of the Exchange Act. The result would be the same if Corporation V had its securities listed on the NYSE other than in the form of ADRs. The result also would be the same if Corporation V had wished to raised capital during its 2021 taxable year and been required to register the offer of securities underlying the ADRs under the Securities Act and to register the class of those securities under section 12(b) of the Exchange Act, and the depositary bank was required to register the ADRs under the Securities Act.

(L) *Example 12 (Foreign private issuer incorporates subsidiary in the United States to issue debt securities and subsequently issues a guarantee).*—(1) *Facts.* For its fiscal and taxable years ending December 31, 2021, Corporation T is a foreign private issuer. Corporation T wishes to access the U.S. capital markets. Corporation T incorporates Corporation U, a wholly-owned subsidiary, in the U.S. to issue debt securities. On January 15, 2021, the SEC declares effective Corporation U's Securities Act registration statement. To enhance Corporation U's credit and the marketability of Corporation U's debt securities, Corporation T issues a guarantee of Corporation U's securities and, as required, registers the guarantee under the Securities Act on Corporation U's registration statement. On December 31, 2021, Corporations T and U are required to file reports under section 15(d) of the Exchange Act.

(2) *Conclusion.* Corporations T and U are publicly held corporations for their 2021 taxable years because they are required to file reports under section 15(d) of the Exchange Act as of the last day of their taxable years.

(M) *Example 13 (Affiliated group comprised of two corporations, one of which is a publicly held corporation).*—(1) *Facts.* Employee D, a covered employee of Corporation N, receives compensation from, Corporations N and O, members of an affiliated group. Corporation N, the parent corporation, is a publicly held corporation. Corporation O is a direct subsidiary of Corporation N and is a privately held corporation. The total compensation paid to Employee D from the affiliated group members is $3,000,000 for the taxable year, of which Corporation N pays $2,100,000 and Corporation O pays $900,000.

(2) *Conclusion.* Because the compensation paid by all affiliated group members is aggregated for purposes of section 162(m)(1), $2,000,000 of the aggregate compensation paid is nondeductible. Corporations N and O each are treated as paying a ratable portion of the nondeductible compensation. Thus, two thirds of each corporation's payment will be nondeductible. Corporation N has a nondeductible compensation expense of $1,400,000 ($2,100,000 x $2,000,000/$3,000,000). Corporation O has a nondeductible compensation expense of $600,000 ($900,000 x $2,000,000/$3,000,000).

(N) *Example 14 (Affiliated group comprised of two corporations, one of which is a publicly held corporation).*—(1) *Facts.* The facts are the same as in paragraph (c)(1)(vi)(M) of this section (*Example 13*), except that Corporation O is a publicly held corporation, Corporation N is a privately held corporation, and Employee D is a covered employee of Corporation O (instead of Corporation N).

(2) *Conclusion.* The result is the same as in paragraph (c)(1)(vi)(M) of this section (*Example 13*). Even though subsidiary Corporation O is the publicly held corporation, Corporations N and O still comprise an affiliated group. Accordingly, $2,000,000 of the aggregate compensation paid is nondeductible, and Corporations N and O each are treated as paying a ratable portion of the nondeductible compensation.

(O) *Example 15 (Affiliated group comprised of two publicly held corporations).*—(1) *Facts.* The facts are the same as in paragraph (c)(1)(vi)(M) of this section (*Example 13*), except that Corporation O is a publicly held corporation. As in paragraph (c)(1)(vi)(M) of this section (Example 13), Employee D is not a covered employee of Corporation O.

(2) *Conclusion.* The result is the same as in paragraph (c)(1)(vi)(M) of this section (Example 13). Even though Corporations N and O each are publicly held corporations, Corporations N and O comprise an affiliated group for purposes of prorating the amount disallowed as a deduction. Accordingly, $2,000,000 of the aggregate compensation paid is nondeductible, and Corporations N and O each are treated as paying a ratable portion of the nondeductible compensation.

(P) *Example 16 (Affiliated group comprised of two publicly held corporations).*—(1) *Facts.* The facts are the same as in paragraph (c)(1)(vi)(O) of this section (Example 15), except that Employee D also is a covered employee of Corporation O.

(2) *Conclusion.* Corporations N and O each are publicly held corporations and separately subject to this section, but also comprise an affiliated group. Because Employee D is a covered employee of both Corporations N and O, each of which is a separate publicly held corporation, the determination of the amount disallowed as a deduction is made separately for each publicly held corporation. Corporation N has a nondeductible compensation expense of $1,100,000 (the excess of $2,100,000 over $1,000,000), and Corporation O has no nondeductible compensation expense because the amount it paid to Employee D did not exceed $1,000,000.

(Q) *Example 17 (Affiliated group comprised of three corporations, one of which is a publicly held corporation).*—(1) *Facts.* Employee C, a covered employee of publicly held parent Corporation P, receives compensation from Corporations P, Q, and R, members of an affiliated group. Corporation Q is a direct subsidiary of Corporation P, and Corporation R is a direct subsidiary of Corporation Q. Corporations Q and R both are privately held. The total compensation paid to Employee C from the affiliated group members is $3,000,000 for the taxable year, of which Corporation P pays $1,500,000, Corporation Q pays $900,000, and Corporation R pays $600,000.

(2) *Conclusion.* Because the compensation paid by affiliated group members is aggregated for purposes of section 162(m)(1), $2,000,000 of the aggregate compensation paid is nondeductible. Corporations P, Q, and R each are treated as paying a ratable portion of the nondeductible compensation. Thus, two thirds of each corporation's payment will be nondeductible. The nondeductible compensation expense for Corporation P is $1,000,000 ($1,500,000 x $2,000,000/$3,000,000); for Corporation Q is $600,000 ($900,000 x $2,000,000/$3,000,000); and for Corporation R is $400,000 ($600,000 x $2,000,000/$3,000,000).

(R) *Example 18 (Affiliated group comprised of three corporations, one of which is a publicly held corporation).*—(1) *Facts.* The facts are the same as in paragraph (c)(1)(vi)(Q) of this section (Example 17), except that Corporation Q is a publicly held corporation and Corporation P is a privately held corporation, and Employee C is a covered employee of Corporation Q (instead of Corporation P).

(2) *Conclusion.* The result is the same as in paragraph (c)(1)(vi)(Q) of this section (Example 17). Even though Corporation Q, the subsidiary, is the publicly held corporation, Corporations P, Q, and R comprise an affiliated group. Accordingly, $2,000,000 of the aggregate compensation paid is nondeductible, and Corporations P, Q, and R each are treated as paying a ratable portion of the nondeductible compensation.

(S) *Example 19 (Affiliated group comprised of three corporations, two of which are publicly held corporations).*—(1) *Facts.* The facts are the same as in paragraph (c)(1)(vi)(R) of this section (Example 18), except that Corporation R also is a publicly held corporation. As in paragraph (c)(1)(vi)(R) of this section (Example 18), Corporation Q is a publicly held corporation, Corporation P is a privately held corporation, and Employee C is a covered employee of Corporation Q but not a covered employee of Corporation R.

(2) *Conclusion.* The result is the same as in paragraph (c)(1)(vi)(R) of this section (Example 18). Even though Corporation R also is a publicly held corporation, Corporations P, Q, and R comprise an affiliated group. Accordingly, $2,000,000 of the aggregate compensation paid is nondeductible, and Corporations P, Q, and R each are treated as paying a ratable portion of the nondeductible compensation.

(T) *Example 20 (Affiliated group comprised of three publicly held corporations).*—(1) *Facts.* The facts are the same as in paragraph (c)(1)(vi)(Q) of this section (Example 17), except that Corporations Q and R also are publicly held corporations, and Employee C is a covered employee of both Corporations P and Q but is not a covered employee of Corporation R.

(2) *Conclusion.* Even though Corporations P, Q, and R each are publicly held corporations, they comprise an affiliated group.

Because Employee C is a covered employee of both Corporations P and Q, the determination of the amount disallowed as a deduction is separately prorated among Corporations P and R and among Corporations Q and R. For each separate calculation of the total amount of the disallowed deduction and the proration of the disallowed deduction, the amount paid by Corporation R is taken into account in proportion to the total compensation paid by Corporations P and Q. With respect to Corporations P and R, $875,000 of the aggregate compensation is nondeductible (the excess of $1,875,000 (the sum of the compensation paid by Corporation P ($1,500,000) and the portion of compensation paid by Corporation R that is treated as allocable to Employee C being a covered employee of Corporation P ($600,000 x $1,500,000/($1,500,000 + $900,000) = $375,000) over the $1,000,000 deduction limitation). Corporations P and R each are treated as paying a ratable portion of the nondeductible compensation. Corporation P has a nondeductible compensation expense of $700,000 ($1,500,000 x $875,000/$1,875,000), and Corporation R has a nondeductible compensation expense of $175,000 ($375,000 x $875,000/$1,875,000). For Corporations Q and R, $125,000 of the aggregate compensation is nondeductible (the excess of $1,125,000 (the sum of the compensation paid by Corporation Q ($900,000) and the portion of compensation paid by Corporation R that is treated as allocable to Employee C being a covered employee of Corporation Q ($600,000 x $900,000/($1,500,000 + $900,000) = $225,000) over the $1,000,000 deduction limitation). Corporation Q has a nondeductible compensation expense of $100,000 ($900,000 x $125,000/$1,125,000), and Corporation R has a nondeductible compensation expense of $25,000 ($225,000 x $125,000/$1,125,000). The total nondeductible compensation expense for Corporation R is $200,000.

(U) *Example 21 (Affiliated group comprised of three publicly held corporations).*—(1) *Facts.* The facts are the same as in paragraph (c)(1)(vi)(T) of this section (Example 20), except that Employee C does not receive any compensation from Corporation R.

(2) *Conclusion.* Even though Corporations P, Q, and R each are publicly held corporations and separately subject to this section, they comprise an affiliated group. Because Employee C is a covered employee of, and receives compensation from, both Corporations P and Q, each of which is a separate publicly held corporation, the determination of the amount disallowed as a deduction is made separately for Corporations P and Q. Corporation P has a nondeductible compensation expense of $500,000 (the excess of $1,500,000 over $1,000,000), and Corporation Q has no nondeductible compensation expense because the amount it paid to Employee C was below $1,000,000.

(V) *Example 22 (Affiliated group comprised of three corporations, one of which is a publicly held corporation).*—(1) *Facts.* The facts are the same as in paragraph (c)(1)(vi)(Q) of this section (Example 17), except that Corporation R is a direct subsidiary of Corporation P (and not a direct subsidiary of Corporation Q).

(2) *Conclusion.* The result is the same as in paragraph (c)(1)(vi)(Q) of this section (Example 17). Corporations P, Q, and R comprise an affiliated group. Accordingly, $2,000,000 of the aggregate compensation paid is nondeductible, and Corporations P, Q, and R each are treated as paying a ratable portion of the nondeductible compensation.

(W) *Example 23 (Affiliated group comprised of three publicly held corporations).*—(1) *Facts.* The facts are the same as in paragraph (c)(1)(vi)(V) of this section (Example 22), except that Corporations Q and R also are publicly held corporations, and Employee C is a covered employee of both Corporations P and Q but not of Corporation R.

(2) *Conclusion.* The result is the same as in paragraph (c)(1)(vi)(V) of this section (Example 22). Even though Corporations P, Q, and R each are publicly held corporations, they comprise an affiliated group. Because Employee C is a covered employee of both Corporations P and Q, the amount disallowed as a deduction is prorated separately among Corporations P and R and among Corporations Q and R.

(X) *Example 24 (Disregarded entity).*—(1) *Facts.* Corporation G is privately held for its 2020 taxable year. Entity H, a limited liability company, is wholly-owned by Corporation G and is disregarded as an entity separate from its owner under § 301.7701-2(c)(2)(i) of this chapter. As of December 31, 2020, Entity H is required to file reports under section 15(d) of the Exchange Act.

(2) *Conclusion.* Because Entity H is required to file reports under section 15(d) of the Exchange Act and is disregarded as an entity separate from its owner, Corporation G is a publicly held corporation for its 2020 taxable year. The result would be the same if Corporation G was a REIT under section 856(a) and Entity H was a QRS under section 856(i)(2).

Itemized Deductions for Individuals and Corps.
See p. 20,601 for regulations not amended to reflect law changes
25,269

(2) *Covered employee.*—(i) *General rule.*—Except as provided in paragraph (c)(2)(vi) of this section, with respect to a publicly held corporation as defined in paragraph (c)(1) of this section (without regard to paragraph (c)(1)(ii) of this section), for the publicly held corporation's taxable year, a covered employee means any of the following—

(A) The principal executive officer (PEO) or principal financial officer (PFO) of the publicly held corporation serving at any time during the taxable year, including individuals acting in either such capacity.

(B) The three highest compensated executive officers of the publicly held corporation for the taxable year (other than the principal executive officer or principal financial officer, or an individual acting in such capacity), regardless of whether the executive officer is serving at the end of the publicly held corporation's taxable year, and regardless of whether the executive officer's compensation is subject to disclosure for the last completed fiscal year under the executive compensation disclosure rules under the Exchange Act. For purposes of this paragraph (c)(2)(i)(B), the term "executive officer" means an executive officer as defined in 17 CFR 240.3b-7. The amount of compensation used to identify the three most highly compensated executive officers for the taxable year is determined pursuant to the executive compensation disclosure rules under the Exchange Act (using the taxable year as the fiscal year for purposes of making the determination), regardless of whether the corporation's fiscal year and taxable year end on the same date.

(C) Any individual who was a covered employee of the publicly held corporation (or any predecessor of the publicly held corporation, within the meaning of paragraph (c)(2)(ii) of this section) for any preceding taxable year beginning after December 31, 2016. For taxable years beginning prior to January 1, 2018, covered employees are identified in accordance with the rules in §1.162-27(c)(2).

(ii) *Predecessor of a publicly held corporation.*—(A) *Publicly held corporations that become privately held.*—For purposes of this paragraph (c)(2)(ii), a predecessor of a publicly held corporation includes a publicly held corporation that, after becoming a privately held corporation, again becomes a publicly held corporation for a taxable year ending before the 36-month anniversary of the due date for the corporation's U.S. Federal income tax return (disregarding any extensions) for the last taxable year for which the corporation was previously publicly held.

(B) *Corporate reorganizations.*—A predecessor of a publicly held corporation includes a publicly held corporation the stock or assets of which are acquired in a corporate reorganization (as defined in section 368(a)(1)).

(C) *Corporate divisions.*—A predecessor of a publicly held corporation includes a publicly held corporation that is a distributing corporation (within the meaning of section 355(a)(1)(A)) that distributes the stock of a controlled corporation (within the meaning of section 355(a)(1)(A)) to its shareholders in a distribution or exchange qualifying under section 355(a)(1) (corporate division). The rule of this paragraph (c)(2)(ii)(C) applies only with respect to covered employees of the distributing corporation who begin performing services for the controlled corporation (or for a corporation affiliated with the controlled corporation that receives stock of the controlled corporation in the corporate division) within the period beginning 12 months before and ending 12 months after the distribution.

(D) *Affiliated groups.*—A predecessor of a publicly held corporation includes any other publicly held corporation that becomes a member of its affiliated group (as defined in paragraph (c)(1)(ii) of this section).

(E) *Asset acquisitions.*—If a publicly held corporation, including one or more members of an affiliated group as defined in paragraph (c)(1)(ii) of this section (acquiror), acquires at least 80% of the gross operating assets (determined by fair market value on the date of acquisition) of another publicly held corporation (target), then the target is a predecessor of the acquiror. For an acquisition of assets that occurs over time, only assets acquired within a 12-month period are taken into account to determine whether at least 80% of the target's gross operating assets were acquired. However, this 12-month period is extended to include any continuous period that ends on, or begins on, any day during which the acquiror has an arrangement to purchase, directly or indirectly, assets of the target. A shareholder's additions to the assets of target made as part of a plan or arrangement to avoid the application of this subsection to acquiror's purchase of target's assets are disregarded in applying this paragraph (c)(2)(ii)(E). This paragraph (c)(2)(ii)(E) applies only with respect to the target's covered employees who begin performing services for the acquiror (or a corporation affiliated with the acquiror) within the period beginning 12 months before and ending 12 months

after the date of the transaction as defined in paragraph (c)(2)(ii)(I) of this section (incorporating any extensions to the 12-month period made pursuant to this paragraph).

(F) *Predecessor of a predecessor.*—For purposes of this paragraph (c)(2)(ii), a predecessor of a corporation includes each predecessor of the corporation and the predecessor or predecessors of any prior predecessor or predecessors.

(G) *Corporations that are not publicly held at the time of the transaction and sequential transactions.*—(1) *Predecessor corporation is not publicly held at the time of the transaction.*—This paragraph (c)(2)(ii)(G)(1) applies if a corporation that was previously publicly held (the first corporation) would be a predecessor to another corporation (the second corporation) under the rules of this paragraph (c)(2)(ii) but for the fact that the first corporation is not a publicly held corporation at the time of the relevant transaction (or transactions). If this paragraph (c)(2)(ii)(G)(1) applies, the first corporation is a predecessor of a publicly held corporation if the second corporation is a publicly held corporation at the time of the relevant transaction (or transactions) and the relevant transaction (or transactions) take place during a taxable year ending before the 36-month anniversary of the due date for the first corporation's U.S. Federal income tax return (excluding any extensions) for the last taxable year for which the first corporation was previously publicly held.

(2) *Second corporation is not publicly held at the time of the transaction.*—This paragraph (c)(2)(ii)(G)(2) applies if a corporation that is publicly held (the first corporation) at the time of the relevant transaction (or transactions) would be a predecessor to another corporation (the second corporation) under the rules of this paragraph (c)(2)(ii) but for the fact that the second corporation is not a publicly held corporation at the time of the relevant transaction (or transactions). If this paragraph (c)(2)(ii)(G)(2) applies, the first corporation is a predecessor of a publicly held corporation if the second corporation becomes a publicly held corporation for a taxable year ending before the 36-month anniversary of the due date for the first corporation's U.S. Federal income tax return (excluding any extensions) for the first corporation's last taxable year in which the transaction is taken into account.

(3) *Neither corporation is publicly held at the time of the transaction.*—This paragraph (c)(2)(ii)(G)(3) applies if a corporation that was previously publicly held (the first corporation) would be a predecessor to another corporation (the second corporation) under the rules of this paragraph (c)(2)(ii) but for the fact that neither the first corporation nor the second corporation is a publicly held corporation at the time of the relevant transaction (or transactions). If this paragraph (c)(2)(ii)(G)(3) applies, the first corporation is a predecessor of a publicly held corporation if the second corporation becomes a publicly held corporation for a taxable year ending before the 36-month anniversary of the due date for the first corporation's U.S. Federal income tax return (excluding any extensions) for the last taxable year for which the first corporation was previously publicly held.

(4) *Sequential transactions.*—If a corporation that was previously publicly held (the first corporation) would be a predecessor to another corporation (the second corporation) under the rules of this paragraph (c)(2)(ii) but for the fact that the first corporation is (or its assets are) transferred to one or more intervening corporations prior to being transferred to the second corporation, and if each intervening corporation would be a predecessor of a publicly held corporation with respect to the second corporation if the intervening corporation or corporations were publicly held corporations, then paragraphs (c)(2)(ii)(G)(1) through (3) of this section also apply without regard to the intervening corporations.

(H) *Elections under sections 336(e) and 338.*—For purposes of this paragraph (c)(2), if a corporation makes an election to treat as an asset purchase either the sale, exchange, or distribution of stock pursuant to regulations under section 336(e) (§§1.336-1 through 1.336-5) or the purchase of stock pursuant to regulations under section 338 (§§1.338-1 through 1.338-11, 1.338(h)(10)-1, and 1.338(i)-1), the corporation that issued the stock is treated as the same corporation both before and after such transaction.

(I) *Date of transaction.*—For purposes of this paragraph (c)(2)(ii), the date that a transaction is treated as having occurred is the date on which all events necessary for the transaction to be described in the relevant provision in this paragraph (c)(2)(ii) have occurred.

(J) *Publicly traded partnership.*—For purposes of applying this paragraph (c)(2)(ii), a publicly traded partnership is a predecessor of a publicly held corporation if under the same facts and circumstances a corporation substituted for the publicly traded partnership would be a predecessor of the publicly held corporation, and at the time of the transaction the publicly traded partnership is treated as a publicly held corporation as defined in paragraph (c)(1)(i) of this section. In making this determination, the rules in paragraphs (c)(2)(ii)(A) through (I) of this section apply by analogy to publicly traded partnerships.

(iii) *Disregarded entities.*—If a publicly held corporation under paragraph (c)(1) of this section owns an entity that is disregarded as an entity separate from its owner under § 301.7701-2(c)(2)(i) of this chapter, then the covered employees of the publicly held corporation are determined pursuant to paragraphs (c)(2)(i) and (ii) of this section. The executive officers of the entity that is disregarded as an entity separate from its corporate owner under § 301.7701-2(c)(2)(i) of this chapter are neither covered employees of the entity nor of the publicly held corporation unless they meet the definition of covered employee in paragraphs (c)(2)(i) and (ii) of this section with respect to the publicly held corporation, in which case they are covered employees for its taxable year.

(iv) *Qualified subchapter S subsidiaries.*—If a publicly held corporation under paragraph (c)(1) of this section owns an entity that is a QSub under section 1361(b)(3)(B), then the covered employees of the publicly held corporation are determined pursuant to paragraphs (c)(2)(i) and (ii) of this section. The executive officers of the QSub are neither covered employees of the QSub nor of the publicly held corporation unless they meet the definition of covered employee in paragraphs (c)(2)(i) and (ii) of this section with respect to the publicly held corporation, in which case they are covered employees for the taxable year of the publicly held corporation.

(v) *Qualified real estate investment trust subsidiaries.*—If a publicly held corporation under paragraph (c)(1) of this section owns an entity that is a QRS under section 856(i)(2), then the covered employees of the publicly held corporation are determined pursuant to paragraphs (c)(2)(i) and (ii) of this section. The executive officers of the QRS are neither covered employees of the QRS nor of the publicly held corporation unless they meet the definition of covered employee in paragraphs (c)(2)(i) and (ii) of this section with respect to the publicly held corporation, in which case they are covered employees for the taxable year of the publicly held corporation.

(vi) *Covered employee of an affiliated group.*—A person who is identified as a covered employee in paragraphs (c)(2)(i) through (v) of this section for a publicly held corporation's taxable year is also a covered employee for the taxable year of an affiliated group treated as a publicly held corporation pursuant to paragraph (c)(1)(ii) of this section (treatment of an affiliated group).

(vii) *Examples.*—The following examples illustrate the provisions of this paragraph (c)(2). For each example, assume that the corporation has a taxable year that is a calendar year and has a fiscal year ending December 31 for reporting purposes under the Exchange Act. Also, for each example, unless provided otherwise, assume that none of the employees were covered employees for any taxable year preceding the first taxable year set forth in that example (since being a covered employee for a preceding taxable year would provide a separate, independent basis for classifying that employee as a covered employee for a subsequent taxable year).

(A) *Example 1 (Covered employees of members of an affiliated group).*—(1) *Facts.* Corporations A, B, and C are direct wholly-owned subsidiaries of Corporation D. Corporations D and A are each publicly held corporations as of December 31, 2020. Corporations B and C are not publicly held corporations for their 2020 taxable years. Employee E served as the PEO of Corporation D from January 1, 2020, to March 31, 2020. Employee F served as the PEO of Corporation D from April 1, 2020, to December 31, 2020. Employee G served as the PEO of Corporation A for its entire 2020 taxable year. Employee H served as the PEO of Corporation B for its entire 2020 taxable year. Employee I served as the PEO of Corporation C for its entire 2020 taxable year. From April 1, 2020, through September 30, 2020, Employee E served as an advisor (not as a PEO) to Employee I and received compensation from Corporation C for these services. In 2020, all four corporations paid compensation to their respective PEOs.

(2) *Conclusion (Employees E and F).* Because both Employees E and F served as the PEO of Corporation D during its 2020 taxable year, both Employees E and F are covered employees of Corporation D for its 2020 and subsequent taxable years.

(3) *Conclusion (Employee G).* Because Employee G served as the PEO of Corporation A, Employee G is a covered employee of Corporation A for its 2020 and subsequent taxable years.

(4) *Conclusion (Employee H).* Even though Employee H served as the PEO of Corporation B, Employee H is not a covered employee of Corporation B for its 2020 taxable year, because Corporation B is considered a publicly held corporation solely by reason of

being a member of an affiliated group as defined in paragraph (c)(1)(ii) of this section.

(5) *Conclusion (Employee I).* Even though Employee I served as the PEO of Corporation C, Employee I is not a covered employee of Corporation C for its 2020 taxable year, because Corporation C is considered a publicly held corporation solely by reason of being a member of an affiliated group as defined in paragraph (c)(1)(ii) of this section.

(B) *Example 2 (Covered employees of a publicly held corporation).*—(1) *Facts.* Corporation J is a publicly held corporation. Corporation J is not a smaller reporting company or emerging growth company for purposes of reporting under the Exchange Act. For 2020, Employee K served as the sole PEO of Corporation J and Employees L and M both served as the PFO of Corporation J at separate times during the year. Employees N, O, and P were, respectively, the first, second, and third highest compensated executive officers of Corporation J for 2020 other than the PEO and PFO, and all three retired before December 31, 2020. Employees Q, R, and S were, respectively, Corporation J's fourth, fifth, and sixth highest compensated executive officers other than the PEO and PFO for 2020, and all three were serving on December 31, 2020. On March 1, 2021, Corporation J filed its Form 10-K, Annual Report Pursuant to Section 13 or 15(d) of the Securities Exchange Act of 1934 with the SEC. With respect to Item 11, Executive Compensation (as required by Part III of Form 10-K, or its successor), Corporation J disclosed the compensation of Employee K for serving as the PEO, Employees L and M for serving as the PFO, and Employees Q, R, and S pursuant to 17 CFR 229.402(a)(3)(iii) (Item 402 of Regulation S-K). Corporation J also disclosed the compensation of Employees N and O pursuant to 17 CFR 229.402(a)(3)(iv) (Item 402 of Regulation S-K).

(2) *Conclusion (Employee K).* Because Employee K served as the PEO during 2020, Employee K is a covered employee for Corporation J's 2020 taxable year.

(3) *Conclusion (Employees L and M).* Because Employees L and M served as the PFO during 2020, Employees L and M are covered employees for Corporation J's 2020 taxable year.

(4) *Conclusion (Employees N, O, P, Q, R and S).* Even though the executive compensation disclosure rules under the Exchange Act require Corporation J to disclose the compensation of Employees N, O, Q, R, and S for 2020, Corporation J's three highest compensated executive officers who are covered employees for its 2020 taxable year are Employees N, O, and P, because these are the three highest compensated executive officers other than the PEO and PFO for 2020.

(C) *Example 3 (Covered employees of a smaller reporting company).*—(1) *Facts.* The facts are the same as in paragraph (c)(2)(vii)(B) of this section (*Example 2*), except that Corporation J is a smaller reporting company or emerging growth company for purposes of reporting under the Exchange Act. With respect to Item 11, Executive Compensation, Corporation J disclosed the compensation of Employee K for serving as the PEO, Employees Q and R pursuant to 17 CFR 229.402(m)(2)(ii) (Item 402(m) of Regulation S-K), and Employees N and O pursuant to 17 CFR 229.402(m)(2)(iii) (Item 402(m) of Regulation S-K).

(2) *Conclusion.* The result is the same as in paragraph (c)(2)(vii)(L) of this section (*Example 2*). For purposes of identifying a corporation's covered employees, it is irrelevant whether the reporting obligation under the Exchange Act for smaller reporting companies and emerging growth companies apply to the corporation, and it is irrelevant whether the specific executive officers' compensation must be disclosed pursuant to the disclosure rules under the Exchange Act applicable to the corporation.

(D) *Example 4 (Covered employees of a publicly held corporation that is not required to file a Form 10-K).*—(1) *Facts.* The facts are the same as in paragraph (c)(2)(vii)(B) of this section (*Example 2*), except that on February 4, 2021, Corporation J files Form 15, Certification and Notice of Termination of Registration under Section 12(g) of the Securities Exchange Act of 1934 or Suspension of Duty to File Reports under Sections 13 and 15(d) of the Securities Exchange Act of 1934, (or its successor) to terminate the registration of its securities. Corporation J's duty to file reports under Section 13(a) of the Exchange Act is suspended upon the filing of the Form 15 and, as a result, Corporation J is not required to file a Form 10-K and disclose the compensation of its executive officers for 2020.

(2) *Conclusion.* The result is the same as in paragraph (c)(2)(vii)(B) of this section (*Example 2*). Covered employees include executive officers of a publicly held corporation even if the corporation is not required to disclose the compensation of its executive officers under the Exchange Act. Therefore, Employees K, L, M, N, O, and P are covered employees for 2020. The result would be different if Corporation J filed Form 15 to terminate the registration of its securities prior to December 31, 2020. In that case, Corporation J would not be a publicly held corporation for its 2020 taxable year,

and, therefore, Employees K, L, M, N, O, and P would not be covered employees for Corporation J's 2020 taxable year.

(E) *Example 5 (Covered employees of two publicly held corporations after a corporate transaction).*—(1) *Facts.* Corporation T is a publicly held corporation for its 2019 taxable year. Corporation U is a privately held corporation for its 2019 and 2020 taxable years. On July 31, 2020, Corporation U acquires for cash 80% of the only class of outstanding stock of Corporation T. The affiliated group (comprised of Corporations U and T) elects to file a consolidated Federal income tax return. As a result of this election, Corporation T has a short taxable year ending on July 31, 2020. Corporation T does not change its fiscal year for reporting purposes under the Exchange Act to correspond to the short taxable year. Corporation T remains a publicly held corporation for its short taxable year ending on July 31, 2020, and its subsequent taxable year ending on December 31, 2020, for which it files a consolidated Federal income tax return with Corporation U. For Corporation T's taxable year ending July 31, 2020, Employee V serves as the only PEO, and Employee W serves as the only PFO. Employees X, Y, and Z are the three most highly compensated executive officers of Corporation T for the taxable year ending July 31, 2020, other than the PEO and PFO. As a result of the acquisition, effective July 31, 2020, Employee V ceases to serve as the PEO of Corporation T. Instead, Employee AA starts serving as the PEO of Corporation T on August 1, 2020. Employee V continues to provide services for Corporation T but never serves as PEO again (or as an individual acting in such capacity). For Corporation T's taxable year ending December 31, 2020, Employee AA serves as the only PEO, and Employee W serves as the only PFO. Employees X, Y, and Z continue to serve as executive officers of Corporation T during the taxable year ending December 31, 2020. Employees BB, CC, and DD are the three most highly compensated executive officers of Corporation T, other than the PEO and PFO, for the taxable year ending December 31, 2020.

(2) *Conclusion (Employee V).* Because Employee V served as the PEO during Corporation T's short taxable year ending July 31, 2020, Employee V is a covered employee for Corporation T's short taxable year ending July 31, 2020, even though Employee V's compensation is required to be disclosed pursuant to the executive compensation disclosure rules under the Exchange Act only for the fiscal year ending December 31, 2020. Because Employee V was a covered employee for Corporation T's short taxable year ending July 31, 2020, Employee V is also a covered employee for Corporation T's short taxable year ending December 31, 2020.

(3) *Conclusion (Employee W).* Because Employee W served as the PFO during Corporation T's short taxable years ending July 31, 2020, and December 31, 2020, Employee W is a covered employee for both taxable years, even though Employee W's compensation is required to be disclosed pursuant to the executive compensation disclosure rules under the Exchange Act only for the fiscal year ending December 31, 2020. Because Employee W was a covered employee for Corporation T's short taxable year ending July 31, 2020, Employee W would be a covered employee for Corporation T's short taxable year ending December 31, 2020, even if Employee W did not serve as the PFO during this taxable year.

(4) *Conclusion (Employee AA).* Because Employee AA served as the PEO during Corporation T's short taxable year ending December 31, 2020, Employee AA is a covered employee for that short taxable year.

(5) *Conclusion (Employees X, Y, and Z).* Employees X, Y, and Z are covered employees for Corporation T's short taxable years ending July 31, 2020, and December 31, 2020. Employees X, Y, and Z are covered employees for Corporation T's short taxable year ending July 31, 2020, because those employees are the three highest compensated executive officers for that short taxable year. Because they were covered employees for Corporation T's short taxable year ending July 31, 2020, Employees X, Y, and Z are covered employees for Corporation T's short taxable year ending December 31, 2020 and would be covered employees for that later short taxable year even if their compensation would not be required to be disclosed pursuant to the executive compensation disclosure rules under the Exchange Act.

(6) *Conclusion (Employees BB, CC, and DD).* Employees BB, CC, and DD are covered employees for Corporation T's short taxable year ending December 31, 2020, because those employees are the three highest compensated executive officers for that short taxable year.

(F) *Example 6 (Predecessor of a publicly held corporation).*—(1) *Facts.* Corporation EE is a publicly held corporation for its 2021 taxable year. Corporation EE is a privately held corporation for its 2022 and 2023 taxable years. For its 2024 taxable year, Corporation EE is a publicly held corporation.

(2) *Conclusion.* For its 2024 taxable year, Corporation EE is a predecessor of a publicly held corporation within the meaning of paragraph (c)(2)(ii)(A) of this section because, after ceasing to be a publicly held corporation, it again became a publicly held corporation for a taxable year ending prior to April 15, 2025. Therefore, for Corporation EE's 2024 taxable year, the covered employees of Corporation EE include the covered employees of Corporation EE for its 2021 taxable year and any additional covered employees determined pursuant to this paragraph (c)(2).

(G) *Example 7 (Predecessor of a publicly held corporation).*—(1) *Facts.* The facts are the same as in paragraph (c)(2)(vii)(F) of this section *(Example 6)*, except that Corporation EE remains a privately held corporation until it becomes a publicly held corporation for its 2027 taxable year.

(2) *Conclusion.* Corporation EE is not a predecessor of a publicly held corporation within the meaning of paragraph (c)(2)(ii)(A) of this section because it became a publicly held corporation for a taxable year ending after April 15, 2025. Therefore, any covered employee of Corporation EE for its 2021 taxable year is not a covered employee of Corporation EE for its 2027 taxable year due to that individual's status as a covered employee of Corporation EE for a preceding taxable year (beginning after December 31, 2016) but may be a covered employee due to that individual's status during the 2027 taxable year.

(H) *Example 8 (Predecessor of a publicly held corporation that is party to a merger).*—(1) *Facts.* On June 30, 2021, Corporation FF (a publicly held corporation) merged into Corporation GG (a publicly held corporation) in a transaction that qualifies as a reorganization under section 368(a)(1)(A), with Corporation GG as the surviving corporation. As a result of the merger, Corporation FF has a short taxable year ending June 30, 2021. Corporation FF is a publicly held corporation for this short taxable year. Corporation GG does not have a short taxable year and is a publicly held corporation for its 2021 taxable year.

(2) *Conclusion.* Corporation FF is a predecessor of a publicly held corporation within the meaning of paragraph (c)(2)(ii)(B) of this section. Therefore, any covered employee of Corporation FF for its short taxable year ending June 30, 2021, is a covered employee of Corporation GG for its 2021 taxable year. For Corporation GG's 2021 and subsequent taxable years, the covered employees of Corporation GG include the covered employees of Corporation FF (for a preceding taxable year beginning after December 31, 2016) and any additional covered employees determined pursuant to this paragraph (c)(2).

(I) *Example 9 (Predecessor of a publicly held corporation that is party to a merger).*—(1) *Facts.* The facts are the same as in paragraph (c)(2)(vii)(H) of this section *(Example 8)*, except that, after the merger, Corporation GG is a privately held corporation for its 2021 taxable year.

(2) *Conclusion.* Because Corporation GG is a privately held corporation for its 2021 taxable year, it is not subject to section 162(m)(1) for this taxable year.

(J) *Example 10 (Predecessor of a publicly held corporation that is party to a merger).*—(1) *Facts.* The facts are the same as in paragraph (c)(2)(vii)(I) of this section *(Example 9)*, except that Corporation GG, becomes a publicly held corporation (as defined in paragraph (c)(1)(i) of this section) on June 30, 2023, and is a publicly held corporation for its 2023 taxable year.

(2) *Conclusion.* Because Corporation GG became a publicly held corporation for a taxable year ending prior to April 15, 2025, Corporation FF is a predecessor of a publicly held corporation within the meaning of paragraph (c)(2)(ii)(G) of this section. For Corporation GG's 2023 and subsequent taxable years, the covered employees of Corporation GG include the covered employees of Corporation FF (for a preceding taxable year beginning after December 31, 2016) and any additional covered employees determined pursuant to this paragraph (c)(2).

(K) *Example 11 (Predecessor of a publicly held corporation that is party to a merger).*—(1) *Facts.* The facts are the same as in paragraph (c)(2)(vii)(J) of this section *(Example 10)*, except that Corporation FF is a privately held corporation for its taxable year ending June 30, 2021, but was a publicly held corporation for its 2020 taxable year.

(2) *Conclusion.* Even though Corporation FF was a privately held corporation when it merged with Corporation GG on June 30, 2021, Corporation FF will be a predecessor corporation if Corporation GG becomes a publicly held corporation within a taxable year ending prior to April 15, 2024. Because Corporation GG became a publicly held corporation for its taxable year ending December 31, 2023, Corporation FF is a predecessor of a publicly held corporation within the meaning of paragraph (c)(2)(ii)(G) of this section. For Corporation GG's 2023 and subsequent taxable years, the covered employees of Corporation GG include the covered employees of Corporation FF (for a preceding taxable year beginning after Decem-

ber 31, 2016) and any additional covered employees determined pursuant to this paragraph (c)(2).

(L) *Example 12 (Predecessor of a publicly held corporation that is party to a merger and subsequently becomes member of an affiliated group).*—(1) *Facts.* The facts are the same as in paragraph (c)(2)(vii)(J) of this section *(Example 10)*, except that, on June 30, 2022, Corporation GG becomes a publicly held corporation by becoming a member of an affiliated group (as defined in paragraph (c)(1)(ii) of this section). Corporation II is the parent corporation of the group and is a publicly held corporation. Employee HH was a covered employee of Corporation FF for its taxable year ending June 30, 2021. On July 1, 2022, Employee HH becomes an employee of Corporation II.

(2) *Conclusion.* By becoming a member of an affiliated group (as defined in paragraph (c)(1)(ii) of this section) on June 30, 2022, Corporation GG became a publicly held corporation for a taxable year ending prior to April 15, 2025. Therefore, Corporation FF is a predecessor of a publicly held corporation (Corporation GG) within the meaning of paragraph (c)(2)(ii)(G) of this section. Furthermore, Corporation FF is also a predecessor of Corporation II, a publicly held corporation within the meaning of paragraph (c)(2)(ii)(G) of this section. For Corporation II's 2022 and subsequent taxable years, Employee HH is a covered employee of the affiliated group that includes Corporation II because Employee HH was a covered employee of Corporation FF for its taxable year ending June 30, 2021.

(M) *Example 13 (Predecessor of a publicly held corporation that is party to a merger and subsequently becomes member of an affiliated group).*—(1) *Facts.* The facts are the same as in paragraph (c)(2)(vii)(L) of this section *(Example 12)*, except that Corporation FF was a privately held corporation for its taxable year ending June 30, 2021, and Employee HH was a covered employee of Corporation FF for its taxable year ending December 31, 2020.

(2) *Conclusion.* Even though Corporation FF was a privately held corporation when it merged with Corporation GG on June 30, 2021, Corporation FF will be a predecessor corporation if Corporation GG becomes a publicly held corporation for a taxable year ending prior to April 15, 2024. Because Corporation GG became a publicly held corporation for its 2022 taxable year by becoming a member of an affiliated group (as defined in paragraph (c)(1)(ii) of this section), Corporation FF is a predecessor of a publicly held corporation (Corporation GG) within the meaning of paragraph (c)(2)(ii)(G) of this section. Furthermore, Corporation FF is also a predecessor of Corporation II, a publicly held corporation within the meaning of paragraph (c)(2)(ii)(G) of this section. Therefore, any covered employee of Corporation FF for its 2020 taxable year is a covered employee of the affiliated group that includes Corporation II for its 2022 and subsequent taxable years. For Corporation II's 2022 taxable year, Employee HH is a covered employee of the affiliated group that includes Corporation II because Employee HH was a covered employee of Corporation FF for its 2020 taxable year.

(N) *Example 14 (Predecessor of a publicly held corporation that is a party to a merger).*—(1) *Facts.* Corporation JJ is a publicly held corporation for its 2019 taxable year and is incorporated in State KK. On June 1, 2019, Corporation JJ formed a wholly-owned subsidiary, Corporation LL. Corporation LL is a publicly held corporation incorporated in State MM. On June 30, 2021, Corporation JJ merged into Corporation LL under State MM law in a transaction that qualifies as a reorganization under section 368(a)(1)(A), with Corporation LL as the surviving corporation. As a result of the merger, Corporation JJ has a short taxable year ending June 30, 2021. Corporation JJ is a publicly held corporation for this short taxable year.

(2) *Conclusion.* Corporation JJ is a predecessor of a publicly held corporation within the meaning of paragraph (c)(2)(ii)(B) of this section. For Corporation LL's taxable years ending after June 30, 2021, the covered employees of Corporation LL include the covered employees of Corporation JJ for its short taxable year ending June 30, 2021 (as well as preceding taxable years beginning after December 31, 2016) and any additional covered employees determined pursuant to this paragraph (c)(2).

(O) *Example 15 (Predecessor of a publicly held corporation becomes member of an affiliated group).*—(1) *Facts.* On June 30, 2021, Corporation OO acquires for cash 100% of the only class of outstanding stock of Corporation NN. The affiliated group (comprised of Corporations NN and OO) elects to file a consolidated Federal income tax return. As a result of this election, Corporation NN has a short taxable year ending on June 30, 2021. Corporation NN is a publicly held corporation for its taxable year ending June 30, 2021, and a privately held corporation for subsequent taxable years. On June 30, 2022, Corporation OO completely liquidates Corporation NN. Corporation OO is a publicly held corporation for its 2021 and 2022 taxable years.

(2) *Conclusion.* After Corporation OO acquired Corporation NN, Corporations NN and OO comprise an affiliated group as defined in paragraph (c)(1)(ii) of this section. Thus, Corporation NN is a predecessor of a publicly held corporation within the meaning of paragraph (c)(2)(ii)(D) of this section. For Corporation OO's taxable years ending after June 30, 2021, the covered employees of Corporation OO include the covered employees of Corporation NN for its short taxable year ending June 30, 2021 (as well as preceding taxable years beginning after December 31, 2016) and any additional covered employees determined pursuant to this paragraph (c)(2).

(P) *Example 16 (Predecessor of a publicly held corporation becomes member of an affiliated group).*—(1) *Facts.* The facts are the same as in paragraph (c)(2)(vii)(O) of this section *(Example 15)*, except that Corporation OO is a privately held corporation on June 30, 2021, and for its 2021 and 2022 taxable years.

(2) *Conclusion.* Because Corporation OO is a privately held corporation for its 2021 and 2022 taxable years, it is not subject to section 162(m)(1) for these taxable years.

(Q) *Example 17 (Predecessor of a publicly held corporation becomes member of an affiliated group).*—(1) *Facts.* The facts are the same as in paragraph (c)(2)(vii)(P) of this section *(Example 16)*, except that, on October 1, 2022, the SEC declares effective Corporation OO's Securities Act registration statement in connection with its initial public offering, and Corporation OO is a publicly held corporation for its 2022 taxable year.

(2) *Conclusion (Taxable Year Ending December 31, 2021).* Because Corporation OO is a privately held corporation for its 2021 taxable year, it is not subject to section 162(m)(1) for this taxable year.

(3) *Conclusion (Taxable Year Ending December 31, 2022).* For the 2022 taxable year, Corporations NN and OO comprise an affiliated group as defined in paragraph (c)(1)(ii) of this section. Corporation NN is a predecessor of a publicly held corporation within the meaning of paragraph (c)(2)(ii)(D) and (G) of this section because Corporation OO became a publicly held corporation for a taxable year ending prior to April 15, 2025. For Corporation OO's 2022 and subsequent taxable years, the covered employees of Corporation OO include the covered employees of Corporation NN for its short taxable year ending June 30, 2021 (as well as preceding taxable years beginning after December 31, 2016) and any additional covered employees determined pursuant to this paragraph (c)(2).

(R) *Example 18 (Predecessor of a publicly held corporation and asset acquisition).*—(1) *Facts.* Corporations VV, WW, and XX are publicly held corporations for their 2020 and 2021 taxable years. Corporations VV and WW are members of an affiliated group. Corporation WW is a direct subsidiary of Corporation VV. On June 30, 2021, Corporation VV acquires for cash 40% of the gross operating assets (determined by fair market value as of January 31, 2022) of Corporation XX. On January 31, 2022, Corporation WW acquires an additional 40% of the gross operating assets (determined by fair market value as of January 31, 2022) of Corporation XX. Employees EB, EC, and EA are covered employees for Corporation XX's 2020 taxable year. Employees ED and EF are also covered employees for Corporation XX's 2021 taxable year. On January 15, 2021, Employee EA started performing services as an employee of Corporation WW. On July 1, 2021, Employee EB started performing services as an employee of Corporation WW. On February 1, 2022, Employees EC and ED started performing services as employees of Corporation WW. On June 30, 2023, Employee EF started performing services as an employee of Corporation WW.

(2) *Conclusion.* Because an affiliated group, comprised of Corporations VV and WW, acquired 80% of Corporation XX's gross operating assets (determined by fair market value) within a twelve-month period, Corporation XX is a predecessor of a publicly held corporation within the meaning of paragraph (c)(2)(ii)(E) of this section. Therefore, any covered employee of Corporation XX for its 2020 and 2021 taxable years (who started performing services as an employee of Corporation WW within the period beginning 12 months before and ending 12 months after the date of the January 31, 2022, acquisition (determined under paragraph (c)(2)(ii)(I) of this section) is a covered employee of Corporation WW for its 2021, 2022, and subsequent taxable years. For Corporation WW's 2021 and subsequent taxable years, the covered employees of Corporation WW include Employee EB and any additional covered employees determined pursuant to paragraph (c)(2)(i) of this section. For Corporation WW's 2022 and subsequent taxable years, the covered employees of Corporation WW include Employees EB, EC, and ED, and any additional covered employees determined pursuant to this paragraph (c)(2). Because Employee EA started performing services as an employee of Corporation WW before January 31, 2021, Employee EA is not a covered employee of Corporation WW for its 2021 taxable year and subsequent taxable years by reason of paragraph (c)(2)(ii)(E) of this section, but may be a covered employee of Corporation WW by application of other rules in this paragraph (c)(2). Because Employee EF started performing services as an employee of Corporation WW after January 31, 2023, Employee EF is not a covered employee of

Corporation WW for its 2023 taxable year by reason of paragraph (c)(2)(ii)(E) of this section, but may be a covered employee of Corporation WW by application of other rules in this paragraph (c)(2).

(S) *Example 19 (Predecessor of a publicly held corporation and asset acquisition).*—(1) *Facts.* The facts are the same as in paragraph (c)(2)(vii)(R) of this section (*Example 18*), except that Corporations VV and WW are not publicly held corporations on June 30, 2021, or for their 2021 taxable years.

(2) *Conclusion.* Because Corporations VV and WW are not publicly held corporations for their 2021 taxable years, they are not subject to section 162(m)(1) for their 2021 taxable years.

(T) *Example 20 (Predecessor of a publicly held corporation and asset acquisition).*—(1) *Facts.* The facts are the same as in paragraph (c)(2)(vii)(R) of this section (*Example 18*), except that, on October 1, 2022, the SEC declares effective Corporation VV's Securities Act registration statement in connection with its initial public offering, and Corporation VV is a publicly held corporation for its 2022 taxable year.

(2) *Conclusion (2021 taxable year).* Because Corporations VV and WW are not publicly held corporations for their 2021 taxable years, they are not subject to section 162(m)(1) for their 2021 taxable years.

(3) *Conclusion (2022 taxable year).* Corporation XX is a predecessor of a publicly held corporation within the meaning of paragraphs (c)(2)(ii)(E) and (G) of this section because a member of the affiliated group comprised of Corporations VV and WW acquired 80% of Corporation XX's gross operating assets (determined by fair market value) within a twelve-month period ending on January 31, 2022, and the parent of the affiliated group, Corporation VV, subsequently became a publicly held corporation for a taxable year ending prior to April 15, 2024. Therefore, any covered employee of Corporation XX for its 2020 and 2021 taxable years (who started performing services as an employee of Corporation WW within the period beginning 12 months before and ending 12 months after the acquisition) is a covered employee of the affiliated group comprised of Corporations VV and WW for its 2022 and subsequent taxable years. For Corporation WW's 2022 and subsequent taxable years, the covered employees of Corporation WW include Employees EB, EC, and ED, and any additional covered employees determined pursuant to this paragraph (c)(2).

(U) *Example 21 (Predecessor of a publicly held corporation and a division).*—(1) *Facts.* Corporation CA is a publicly held corporation for its 2021 and 2022 taxable years. On March 2, 2021, Corporation DDD forms a wholly-owned subsidiary, Corporation CB, and transfers assets to it. On April 1, 2022, Corporation CA distributes all shares of Corporation CB to its shareholders in a transaction described in section 355(a)(1). On April 1, 2022, the SEC declares effective Corporation CB's Securities Act registration statement in connection with its initial public offering. Corporation CB is a publicly held corporation for its 2022 taxable year. Employee EG serves as the PFO of Corporation CA from January 1, 2022, to March 31, 2022. On April 2, 2022, Employee EG starts performing services as an employee of Corporation CB advising the PFO of Corporation CB. After March 31, 2022, Employee EG ceases to provide services for Corporation CA.

(2) *Conclusion.* Because the distribution of the stock of Corporation CB is a transaction described under section 355(a)(1), Corporation CA is a predecessor of Corporation CB within the meaning of paragraph (c)(2)(ii)(C) of this section. Because Employee EG was a covered employee of Corporation CA for its 2022 taxable year, Employee ED is a covered employee of Corporation CB for its 2022 taxable year. The result is the same whether Employee EG performs services as an advisor for Corporation CB as an employee or an independent contractor.

(V) *Example 22 (Predecessor of a publicly held corporation and a division).*—(1) *Facts.* The facts are the same as in paragraph (c)(2)(vii)(U) of this section (*Example 21*), except that Corporation CA distributes 100% of the shares of Corporation CB to Corporation CD in exchange for all of Corporation CD's stock in Corporation CA in a transaction described in section 355(a)(1) and Corporation CB does not register any class of securities with the SEC. Also, Employee EG performs services as an employee of Corporation CD instead of as an employee of Corporation CB. Corporation CD is a privately held corporation for its 2022 taxable year. On October 1, 2023, the SEC declares effective Corporation CD's Securities Act registration statement in connection with its initial public offering. Corporation CD is a publicly held corporation for its 2023 taxable year. On January 1, 2028, Employee EG starts performing services as an employee of Corporation CA. Corporation CA is a publicly held corporation for its 2028 taxable year.

(2) *Conclusion (2022 taxable year).* Because Corporation CD is a privately held corporation for its 2022 taxable year, it is not subject to section 162(m)(1) for this taxable year.

(3) *Conclusion (2023 taxable year).* Because the exchange of the stock of Corporation CB for the stock of Corporation CA is a transaction described in section 355(a)(1), Corporations CB and CD are an affiliated group, and Corporation CD became a publicly held corporation for a taxable year ending prior to April 15, 2026, Corporation CA is a predecessor of Corporation CD within the meaning of paragraphs (c)(2)(ii)(D) and (G) of this section. Employee EG was a covered employee of Corporation CA for its 2022 taxable year, and started performing services as an employee of Corporation CD following April 1, 2021, and before April 1, 2023. Therefore, Employee ED is a covered employee of Corporation CD for its 2023 taxable year.

(4) *Conclusion (2028 taxable year).* Because Employee EG served as the PFO of Corporation CA from January 1, 2022, to March 31, 2022, Employee EG was a covered employee of Corporation CA for its 2022 taxable year. Because an individual who is a covered employee for a taxable year remains a covered employee for all subsequent taxable years (even after the individual has separated from service), Employee EG is a covered employee of Corporation CA for its 2028 taxable year.

(W) *Example 23 (Predecessor of a publicly held corporation and a division).*—(1) *Facts.* The facts are the same as in paragraph (c)(2)(vii)(V) of this section (*Example 22*), except that Employee EG starts performing services as an employee of Corporation CD on June 30, 2023, instead of on April 2, 2022, and never performs services for Corporation CA after June 30, 2023. Furthermore, on June 30, 2023, Employee EH, a covered employee of Corporation CB for all of its taxable years, starts performing services for Corporation EF as an independent contractor advising its PEO but not serving as a PEO.

(2) *Conclusion (2023 taxable year).* Because the exchange of the stock of Corporation CB for the stock of Corporation CA is a transaction described in section 355(a)(1) and Corporation CD became a publicly held corporation for a taxable year ending before April 15, 2026, Corporation CA is a predecessor of Corporation CD within the meaning of paragraphs (c)(2)(ii)(D) and (G) of this section. Even though Employee EG was a covered employee of Corporation CA for its 2022 taxable year, because Employee EG started performing services as an employee of Corporation CD after April 1, 2023, Employee EG is not a covered employee of Corporation CD for its 2023 taxable year under paragraph (c)(2)(ii)(C) of this section. However, Employee EG may be a covered employee of Corporation CD by application of other rules in this paragraph (c)(2). Because Employee EH was a covered employee of Corporation CB for its 2022 taxable year, Employee EH is a covered employee of Corporation CD for its 2023 taxable year.

(X) *Example 24 (Predecessor of a publicly held corporation and election under section 338(h)(10)).*—(1) *Facts.* Corporation CE is the common parent of a group of corporations filing consolidated returns that includes Corporation CF as a member. Corporation CE wholly-owns Corporation CF, a publicly held corporation within the meaning of paragraph (c)(1)(i) of this section. On June 30, 2021, Corporation CG purchases Corporation CF from Corporation CE. Corporation CE and Corporation CG make a timely election under section 338(h)(10) with respect to the purchase of Corporation CF stock. For its taxable year ending December 31, 2021, Corporation CF continues to be a publicly held corporation within the meaning of paragraph (c)(1)(i) of this section.

(2) *Conclusion.* As provided in paragraph (c)(2)(ii)(H) of this section, Corporation CF is treated as the same corporation after the section 338(h)(10) transaction as before the transaction for purposes for purposes of this paragraph (c)(2). Any covered employee of Corporation CF for its short taxable year ending June 30, 2021, is a covered employee of Corporation CF for its short taxable year ending on December 31, 2021, and subsequent taxable years.

(Y) *Example 25 (Disregarded entity).*—(1) *Facts.* Corporation CH is a privately held corporation for its 2020 taxable year. Entity CI is a wholly-owned limited liability company and is disregarded as an entity separate from its owner, Corporation CH, under § 301.7701-2(c)(2)(i) of this chapter. As of December 31, 2020, Entity CI is required to file reports under section 15(d) of the Exchange Act. For the 2020 taxable year, Employee EI is the PEO and Employee EJ is the PFO of Corporation CH. Employees EK, EL, and EM, are the three most highly compensated executive officers of Corporation CH (other than Employees EI and EJ). Employee EN is the PFO of Entity CI and does not perform any policy making functions for Corporation CH. Entity CI has no other executive officers.

(2) *Conclusion.* Because Entity CI is disregarded as an entity separate from its owner, Corporation CH, and is required to file reports under section 15(d) of the Exchange Act, Corporation CH is a publicly held corporation under paragraph (c)(1)(iii) of this section

for its 2020 taxable year. Even though Employee EN is a PFO of Entity CI, Employee EN is not considered a PFO of Corporation CH under paragraph (c)(2)(iii) of this section. As PEO and PFO, Employees EI and EJ are covered employees of Corporation CH under paragraph (c)(2)(i) of this section. Additionally, as the three most highly compensated executive officers of Corporation CH (other than Employees EI and EJ), Employees EK, EL, and EM also are covered employees of Corporation CH under paragraph (c)(2)(i) of this section for Corporation CH's 2020 taxable year. The result would be the same if Entity CI was not required to file reports under section 15(d) of the Exchange Act and Corporation CH was a publicly held corporation pursuant to paragraph (c)(1)(i) instead of paragraph (c)(1)(iii) of this section.

(Z) *Example 26 (Disregarded entity).*—(1) *Facts.* The facts are the same as in paragraph (c)(2)(vii)(Y) of this section (*Example 25*), except that Employee EN performs a policy making function for Corporation CH. If Corporation CH were subject to the SEC executive compensation disclosure rules, then Employee EN would be treated as an executive officer of Corporation CH pursuant to 17 CFR 240.3b-7 for purposes of determining the three highest compensated executive officers for Corporation CH's 2020 taxable year. Employee EN is compensated more than Employee EK, but less than Employees EL and EM.

(2) *Conclusion.* Because Entity CI is disregarded as an entity separate from its owner, Corporation CH, and is required to file reports under section 15(d) of the Exchange Act, Corporation CH is a publicly held corporation under paragraph (c)(1)(iii) of this section for its 2020 taxable year. As PEO and PFO, Employees EI and EJ are covered employees of Corporation CH under paragraph (c)(2)(i) of this section. Employee EN is one of the three highest compensated executive officers for Corporation CH's taxable year. Because Employees EN, EL, and EM are the three most highly compensated executive officers of Corporation CH (other than Employees EI and EJ), they are covered employees of Corporation CH under paragraph (c)(2)(i) of this section for Corporation CH's 2020 taxable year. The result would be the same if Entity CI was not required to file reports under section 15(d) of the Exchange Act and Corporation CH was a publicly held corporation pursuant to paragraph (c)(1)(i) instead of paragraph (c)(1)(iii) of this section.

(AA) *Example 27 (Individual as covered employee of a publicly held corporation that includes the affiliated group).*—(1) *Facts.* Corporations CJ and CK are publicly held corporations for their 2020, 2021, and 2022 taxable years. Corporation CK is a direct subsidiary of Corporation CJ. Employee EO is an employee, but not a covered employee (as defined in paragraph (c)(2)(i) of this section), of Corporation CJ for its 2020, 2021, and 2022 taxable years. From April 1, 2020, to September 30, 2020, Employee EO serves as the PFO of Corporation CK. Employee EO does not perform any services for Corporation CK for its 2021 and 2022 taxable years, however, employee EO is a covered employee (as defined in paragraph (c)(2)(i) of this section) of Corporation CK for its 2020, 2021, and 2022 taxable years. For the 2020 taxable year, Employee EO receives compensation of $1,500,000 for services provided to Corporations CJ and CK. Employee EO receives $2,000,000 from Corporation CJ for performing services for Corporation CJ during each of its 2021 and 2022 taxable years. On June 30, 2022, Corporation CK pays $500,000 to Employee EO from a nonqualified deferred compensation plan that complies with section 409A.

(2) *Conclusion (2020 taxable year).* Because Employee EO is a covered employee of Corporation CK and because the affiliated group (comprised of Corporations CJ and CK) is a publicly held corporation, Employee EO is a covered employee of the publicly held corporation that is the affiliated group pursuant to paragraph (c)(2)(vi) of this section. Compensation paid by Corporations CJ and CK is aggregated for purposes of section 162(m)(1) and, as a result, $500,000 of the aggregate compensation paid is nondeductible. The result would be the same if Corporation CJ was a privately held corporation for its 2020 taxable year.

(3) *Conclusion (2021 taxable year).* Because Employee EO is a covered employee of Corporation CK pursuant to paragraph (c)(2)(i)(C) of this section and because the affiliated group (comprised of Corporations CJ and CK) is a publicly held corporation, Employee EO is a covered employee of the publicly held corporation that is the affiliated group pursuant to paragraph (c)(2)(vi) of this section. Compensation paid by Corporations CJ and CK is aggregated for purposes of section 162(m)(1) and, as a result, $1,000,000 of the aggregate compensation paid is nondeductible. The result would be the same if Corporation CJ was a privately held corporation for its 2021 taxable year.

(4) *Conclusion (2022 taxable year).* Because Employee EO is a covered employee of Corporation CK pursuant to paragraph (c)(2)(i)(C) of this section and because the affiliated group (comprised of Corporations CJ and CK) is a publicly held corporation, Employee

EO is a covered employee of the publicly held corporation that is the affiliated group pursuant to paragraph (c)(2)(vi) of this section. Compensation paid by Corporations CJ and CK is aggregated for purposes of section 162(m)(1) and, as a result, $1,500,000 of the aggregate compensation paid is nondeductible. The result would be the same if Corporation CJ was a privately held corporation for its 2022 taxable year.

(BB) *Example 28 (Individual as covered employee of a publicly held corporation that includes the affiliated group).*—(1) *Facts.* Corporation CL is a publicly held corporation for its 2020 through 2023 taxable years. Corporations CM and CN are direct subsidiaries of Corporation CL and are privately held corporations for their 2020 through 2022 taxable years. Employee EP serves as the PFO of Corporation CL from January 1, 2020 to December 31, 2020, when Employee EP terminates employment from Corporation CL. On January 1, 2021, Employee EP starts performing services as an employee of Corporation CM. In 2021, Employee EP receives compensation from Corporation CM in excess of $1,000,000. On April 1, 2022, Employee EP starts performing services as an employee of Corporation CN. On September 30, 2022, Employee EP terminates employment from Corporations CM and CN. In 2022, Employee EP receives compensation from Corporations CM and CN in excess of $1,000,000. For the 2021 and 2022 taxable years, Employee EP does not serve as either the PEO or PFO of Corporations CM and CN, and is not one of the three highest compensated executive officers (other than the PEO or PFO) of Corporations CM and CN. On April 1, 2023, Corporation CL distributes all the shares of Corporation CM to its shareholders in a transaction described in section 355(a)(1). On April 1, 2023, the SEC declares effective Corporation CM's Securities Act registration statement in connection with its initial public offering. Corporation CM is a publicly held corporation for its 2023 taxable year. On April 2, 2023, Employee EP starts performing services as an employee of Corporation CM but is not an executive officer of Corporation CM.

(2) *Conclusion (2021 taxable year).* Employee EP is a covered employee of Corporation CL for the 2020 and subsequent taxable years. Because Employee EP is a covered employee of Corporation CL and because the affiliated group (comprised of Corporations CL, CM, and CN) is a publicly held corporation, Employee EP is a covered employee of the publicly held corporation that is the affiliated group pursuant to paragraph (c)(2)(vi) of this section for the 2020 and subsequent taxable years. Therefore, Corporation CM's deduction for compensation paid to Employee EP for the 2021 taxable year is subject to section 162(m)(1). The result would be the same if Corporation CM was a publicly held corporation as defined in paragraph (c)(1)(i) of this section.

(3) *Conclusion (2022 taxable year).* Because Employee EP is a covered employee of Corporation CL and because the affiliated group (comprised of Corporations CL, CM, and CN) is a publicly held corporation, Employee EP is a covered employee of the publicly held corporation that is the affiliated group pursuant to paragraph (c)(2)(vi) of this section. Therefore, Corporation CM's and CN's deduction for compensation paid to Employee EP for the 2022 taxable year is subject to section 162(m)(1). Because the compensation paid by all affiliated group members is aggregated for purposes of section 162(m)(1), $1,000,000 of the aggregate compensation paid is nondeductible. Corporations CM and CN are each treated as paying a ratable portion of the nondeductible compensation. The result would be the same if either Corporation CM or CN (or both) was a publicly held corporation as defined in paragraph (c)(1)(i) of this section.

(4) *Conclusion (2023 taxable year).* Because the distribution of the stock of Corporation CM is a transaction described in section 355(a)(1), Corporation CL is a predecessor of Corporation CM within the meaning of paragraph (c)(2)(ii)(C) of this section. However, because Employee EP started performing services as an employee of Corporation CM on January 1, 2021, and the distribution of stock of Corporation CM did not occur until April 1, 2023, Employee EP is not a covered employee of Corporation CM for its 2023 taxable year.

(3) *Compensation.*—(i) *In general.*—For purposes of the deduction limitation described in paragraph (b) of this section, compensation means the aggregate amount allowable as a deduction to the publicly held corporation under chapter 1 of the Internal Revenue Code for the taxable year (determined without regard to section 162(m)(1)) for remuneration for services performed by a covered employee in any capacity, whether or not the services were performed during the taxable year. Compensation includes an amount that is includible in the income of, or paid to, a person other than the covered employee (including a beneficiary after the death of the covered employee) for services performed by the covered employee.

(ii) *Compensation paid by a partnership.*—For purposes of paragraph (c)(3)(i) of this section, compensation includes an amount equal to a publicly held corporation's distributive share of a partnership's deduction for compensation expense attributable to the remuneration paid by the partnership to a covered employee of the publicly held corporation for services performed by the covered employee, including a payment for services under section 707(a) or under section 707(c).

(iii) *Exceptions.*—Compensation does not include—

(A) Remuneration covered in section 3121(a)(5)(A) through (D) (concerning remuneration that is not treated as wages for purposes of the Federal Insurance Contributions Act);

(B) Remuneration consisting of any benefit provided to or on behalf of an employee if, at the time the benefit is provided, it is reasonable to believe that the employee will be able to exclude it from gross income; or

(C) Salary reduction contributions described in section 3121(v)(1).

(iv) *Examples.*—The following examples illustrate the provisions of this paragraph (c)(3). For each example, assume that the corporation is a calendar year taxpayer.

(A) *Example 1.*—(1) *Facts.* Corporation Z is a publicly held corporation for its 2020 taxable year, during which Employee A serves as the PEO of Corporation Z and also serves on the board of directors of Corporation Z. In 2020, Corporation Z paid $1,200,000 to Employee A plus a $50,000 fee for serving as a director of Corporation Z. These amounts are otherwise deductible for Corporation Z's 2020 taxable year.

(2) *Conclusion.* The $1,200,000 paid to Employee A in 2020 plus the $50,000 director's fee paid to Employee A in 2020 are compensation within the meaning of this paragraph (c)(3). Therefore, Corporation Z's $1,250,000 deduction for the 2020 taxable year is subject to the section 162(m)(1) limit.

(B) *Example 2.*—(1) *Facts.* Corporation X is a publicly held corporation for its 2020 and all subsequent taxable years. Employee B serves as the PEO of Corporation X for its 2020 taxable year and is a participant in the Corporation X nonqualified retirement plan that meets the requirements of section 409A. The plan provides for the distribution of benefits over a three-year period beginning after a participant separates from service. Employee B terminates employment in 2021. In 2022, Employee B receives a $75,000 fee for services as a director and $1,500,000 as the first payment under the retirement plan. Employee B continues to serve on the board of directors until 2023 when Employee B dies before receiving the retirement benefit for 2023 and before becoming entitled to any director's fees for 2023. In 2023 and 2024, Corporation X pays the $1,500,000 annual retirement benefits to Person C, a beneficiary of Employee B.

(2) *Conclusion (2022 Taxable Year).* In 2022, Corporation X paid Employee B $1,575,000, including $1,500,000 under the retirement plan and $75,000 in director's fees. The retirement benefit and the director's fees are compensation within the meaning of this paragraph (c)(3). Therefore, Corporation X's $1,575,000 deduction for the 2022 taxable year is subject to the section 162(m)(1) limit.

(3) *Conclusion (2023 and 2024 Taxable Years).* In 2023 and 2024, Corporation X made payments to Person C of $1,500,000 under the retirement plan. The retirement benefits are compensation within the meaning of this paragraph (c)(3). Therefore, Corporation X's deduction for each annual payment of $1,500,000 for the 2023 and 2024 taxable years is subject to the section 162(m)(1) limit.

(C) *Example 3.*—(1) *Facts.* Corporation T is a publicly held corporation for its 2021 taxable year. Corporation S is a privately held corporation for its 2021 taxable year. On January 2, 2021, Corporations S and T form a general partnership. Under the partnership agreement, Corporations S and T each have a 50% distributive share of the partnership's income, gain, loss, and deductions. For the taxable year ending December 31, 2021, Employee D, a covered employee of Corporation T, performs services for the partnership, and the partnership pays $800,000 to Employee D for these services, the deduction of $400,000 of which is allocated to Corporation T. Corporation T's $400,000 distributive share of the partnership's deduction is reported separately to Corporation T pursuant to § 1.702-1(a)(8)(iii).

(2) *Conclusion.* Because Corporation T's $400,000 distributive share of the partnership's deduction is attributable to the compensation *paid by the partnership for services* performed by Employee D, a covered employee of Corporation T, the $400,000 is compensation within the meaning of this paragraph (c)(3) and Corporation T's deduction for this expense for its 2021 taxable year is subject to the section 162(m)(1) limit. Corporation T's $400,000 allocation of the partnership's deduction is aggregated with Corporation T's deduction for compensation paid to Employee D, if any, in determining the amount allowable as a deduction to Corporation T for compensation paid to Employee D for Corporation T's 2021 taxable year. The result is the same whether Employee D performs services for the partnership as a common law employee, an independent contractor, or a

partner, and whether the payment to Employee D is a payment under section 707(a) or section 707(c).

(4) *Securities Act.*—The Securities Act means the Securities Act of 1933.

(5) *Exchange Act.*—The Exchange Act means the Securities Exchange Act of 1934.

(6) *SEC.*—The SEC means the United States Securities and Exchange Commission.

(7) *Foreign Private Issuer.*—A foreign private issuer means an issuer as defined in 17 CFR 240.3b-4(c).

(8) *American Depositary Receipt (ADR).*—An American Depositary Receipt or ADR means a negotiable certificate that evidences ownership of a specified number (or fraction) of a foreign private issuer's securities held by a depositary (typically, a U.S. bank).

(9) *Privately held corporation.*—A privately held corporation is a corporation that is not a publicly held corporation as defined in paragraph (c)(1) of this section (without regard to paragraph (c)(1)(ii) of this section).

(d) *Corporations that become publicly held.*—(1) *In general.*—In the case of a corporation that was a privately held corporation and then becomes a publicly held corporation, the deduction limitation of paragraph (b) of this section applies to any compensation that is otherwise deductible for the taxable year ending on or after the date that the corporation becomes a publicly held corporation. A corporation is considered to become publicly held on the date that its registration statement becomes effective either under the Securities Act or the Exchange Act. The rules in this section apply to a partnership that becomes a publicly traded partnership that is a publicly held corporation within the meaning of paragraph (c)(1)(i) of this section.

(2) *Example.*—The following example illustrates the provision of this paragraph (d).

(i) *Facts.* In 2021, Corporation E plans to issue debt securities in a public offering registered under the Securities Act. Corporation E is not required to file reports under section 15(d) of the Exchange Act with respect to any other class of securities and does not have another class of securities required to be registered under section 12 of the Exchange Act. On December 18, 2021, the SEC declares effective the Securities Act registration statement for Corporation E's debt securities.

(ii) *Conclusion.* Corporation E becomes a publicly held corporation on December 18, 2021 because it is then required to file reports under section 15(d) of the Exchange Act. The deduction limitation of paragraph (b) of this section applies to any compensation that is otherwise deductible for Corporation E's taxable year ending on or after December 18, 2021.

(e) *Coordination with disallowed excess parachute payments under section 280G.*—The $1,000,000 limitation in paragraph (b) of this section is reduced (but not below zero) by the amount (if any) that would have been included in the compensation of the covered employee for the taxable year but for being disallowed by reason of section 280G. For example, assume that during a taxable year a corporation pays $1,500,000 to a covered employee, of which $600,000 is an excess parachute payment, as defined in section 280G(b)(1), and a deduction for that excess parachute payment is disallowed by reason of section 280G(a). Because the $1,000,000 limitation in paragraph (b) of this section is reduced by the amount of the excess parachute payment, the corporation may deduct $400,000 ($1,000,000 - $600,000), and $500,000 of the otherwise deductible amount is nondeductible by reason of section 162(m)(1). Thus $1,100,000 (of the total $1,500,000 payment) is non-deductible, reflecting the disallowance related to the excess parachute payment under section 280G and the application of section 162(m)(1).

(f) *Coordination with excise tax on specified stock compensation.*—The $1,000,000 limitation in paragraph (b) of this section is reduced (but not below zero) by the amount (if any) of any payment (with respect to such employee) of the tax imposed by section 4985 directly or indirectly by the expatriated corporation (as defined in section 4985(e)(2)) or by any member of the expanded affiliated group (as defined in section 4985(e)(4)) that includes such corporation.

(g) *Transition rules.*—(1) *Amount of compensation payable under a written binding contract that was in effect on November 2, 2017.*—(i) *General rule.*—This section does not apply to the deduction for compensation payable under a written binding contract that was in effect on November 2, 2017, and that is not modified in any material respect on or after that date (a grandfathered amount). Instead, section 162(m), as in effect prior to its amendment by Public Law

115-97, applies to limit the deduction for that compensation. Because §1.162-27 implemented section 162(m) as in effect prior to its amendment by Public Law 115-97, the rules of §1.162-27 determine the applicability of the deduction limitation under section 162(m) with respect to the payment of a grandfathered amount (including the potential application of the separate grandfathering rules contained in §1.162-27(h)). Compensation is a grandfathered amount only to the extent that as of November 2, 2017, the corporation was and remains obligated under applicable law (for example, state contract law) to pay the compensation under the contract if the employee performs services or satisfies the applicable vesting conditions. This section applies to the deduction for any amount of compensation that exceeds the grandfathered amount. If a grandfathered amount and non-grandfathered amount are otherwise deductible for the same taxable year and, under the rules of §1.162-27, the deduction of some or all of the grandfathered amount may be limited (for example, the grandfathered amount does not satisfy the requirements of §1.162-27(e)(2) through (5) as qualified performance-based compensation), then the grandfathered amount is aggregated with the non-grandfathered amount to determine the deduction disallowance for the taxable year under section 162(m)(1) (so that the deduction limit applies to the excess of the aggregated amount over $1 million).

(ii) *Contracts that are terminable or cancelable.*—If a written binding contract is renewed after November 2, 2017, this section (and not §1.162-27) applies to any payments made after the renewal. A written binding contract that is terminable or cancelable by the corporation without the employee's consent after November 2, 2017, is treated as renewed as of the earliest date that any such termination or cancellation, if made, would be effective. Thus, for example, if the terms of a contract provide that it will be automatically renewed or extended as of a certain date unless either the corporation or the employee provides notice of termination of the contract at least 30 days before that date, the contract is treated as renewed as of the date that termination would be effective if that notice were given. Similarly, for example, if the terms of a contract provide that the contract will be terminated or canceled as of a certain date unless either the corporation or the employee elects to renew within 30 days of that date, the contract is treated as renewed by the corporation as of that date (unless the contract is renewed before that date, in which case, it is treated as renewed on the earlier date). Alternatively, if the corporation will remain legally obligated by the terms of a contract beyond a certain date at the sole discretion of the employee, the contract will not be treated as renewed as of that date if the employee exercises the discretion to keep the corporation bound to the contract. A contract is not treated as terminable or cancelable if it can be terminated or canceled only by terminating the employment relationship of the employee. A contract is not treated as renewed if upon termination or cancellation of the contract the employment relationship continues but would no longer be covered by the contract. However, if the employment continues after the termination or cancellation, payments with respect to the post-termination or post-cancellation employment are not made pursuant to the contract (and, therefore, are not grandfathered amounts).

(iii) *Compensation payable under a plan or arrangement.*—If a compensation plan or arrangement is a written binding contract in effect on November 2, 2017, the deduction for the amount that the corporation is obligated to pay to an employee pursuant to the plan or arrangement is not subject to this section solely because the employee was not eligible to participate in the plan or arrangement as of November 2, 2017, provided the employee was employed on November 2, 2017, by the corporation that maintained the plan or arrangement, or the employee had the right to participate in the plan or arrangement under a written binding contract as of that date.

(iv) *Compensation subject to recovery by corporation.*—If the corporation is obligated or has discretion to recover compensation paid in a taxable year only upon the future occurrence of a condition that is objectively outside of the corporation's control, then the corporation's right to recovery is disregarded for purposes of determining the grandfathered amount for the taxable year. Whether or not the corporation exercises its discretion to recover any compensation does not affect the amount of compensation that the corporation remains obligated to pay under applicable law.

(v) *Compensation payable from an account balance plan.*—(A) *In general.*—Except as otherwise provided in this paragraph (g), the grandfathered amount of payments from an account balance plan (as defined in §1.409A-1(c)(2)(i)(A)) that is a written binding contract in effect as of November 2, 2017, is the amount that the corporation is obligated to pay pursuant to the terms of the account balance plan in effect as of that date, as determined under applicable law. If under the terms of the plan, the corporation is obligated to pay the employee the account balance that is credited with earnings and losses and has no right to terminate or materially amend the plan, then the

grandfathered amount would be the account balance as of November 2, 2017, plus any additional contributions and earnings and losses that the corporation is obligated to credit to the account balance in accordance with the terms of the plan as of November 2, 2017, through the date of payment.

(B) *Account balance plan providing right to terminate.*—If under the terms of the account balance plan in effect as of November 2, 2017, the corporation may terminate the contract and distribute the account balance to the employee, then the grandfathered amount would be the account balance determined as if the corporation had terminated the plan on November 2, 2017 or, if later, the earliest possible date the plan could be terminated in accordance with the terms of the plan (termination date). Whether additional contributions and earnings and losses credited to the account balance after the termination date, through the earliest possible date the account balance could have been distributed to the employee in accordance with the terms of the plan, are grandfathered depends on whether the terms of the plan require the corporation to make those contributions or credit those earnings and losses through that distribution date. Notwithstanding the foregoing, the corporation may treat the account balance as of the termination date as the grandfathered amount regardless of when the amount is paid and regardless of whether it has been credited with additional contributions or earnings or losses prior to payment.

(C) *Account balance plan providing right to discontinue future contributions.*—If under the terms of the account balance plan in effect as of November 2, 2017, the corporation has no right to terminate the plan, but may discontinue future contributions and distribute the account balance in accordance with the terms of the plan, then the grandfathered amount would be the account balance determined as if the corporation had exercised the right to discontinue contributions on November 2, 2017, or, if later, the earliest permissible date the corporation could exercise that right in accordance with the terms of the plan (the freeze date). If, after the freeze date, the plan requires the crediting of earnings and losses on the account balance through the payment date, then the earnings and losses credited to the grandfathered account balance would also be grandfathered. Notwithstanding the foregoing, the corporation may treat the account balance as of the freeze date as the grandfathered amount regardless of when the amount is paid and regardless of whether it has been credited with earnings or losses prior to payment.

(vi) *Compensation payable from a nonaccount balance plan.*—(A) *In general.*—Except as otherwise provided in this paragraph (g), the grandfathered amount of payments from a nonaccount balance plan (as defined in §1.409A-1(c)(2)(i)(C)) that is a written binding contract in effect as of November 2, 2017, is the amount that the corporation is obligated to pay pursuant to the terms of the nonaccount balance plan in effect as of that date, as determined under applicable law. If under the terms of the plan, the corporation is obligated to pay the employee the benefit under the plan and has no right to terminate or materially amend the plan, then the grandfathered amount would be the benefit under the plan as of November 2, 2017, plus any additional accrued benefits that the corporation is obligated to pay in accordance with the terms of the plan as of November 2, 2017, through the date of payment.

(B) *Nonaccount balance plan providing right to terminate.*—If under the terms of the nonaccount balance plan in effect as of November 2, 2017, the corporation may terminate the plan and distribute the total benefit to the employee, then the grandfathered amount would be the present value of the total benefit (lump sum value) determined as if the corporation had terminated the plan on November 2, 2017 or, if later, the earliest possible date the plan could be terminated in accordance with the terms of the plan (termination date). Whether an increase or decrease in the lump sum value after the termination date, through the earliest possible date the lump sum value could have been distributed to the employee, is grandfathered depends on whether the terms of the plan require the corporation to increase or decrease the lump sum value through the distribution date. For example, if the plan did not require the corporation to make further service or compensation credits, then any increase in the lump sum value for these credits after the termination date is not grandfathered. Notwithstanding the foregoing, the corporation may treat the lump sum value as of the termination date as the grandfathered amount regardless of when the amount is paid and regardless of whether it has increased or decreased prior to payment. For purposes of this paragraph (g)(1)(vi)(B), the lump sum value is determined based on the actuarial methods and assumptions provided in the plan in effect on November 2, 2017, if the assumptions are reasonable, or any reasonable actuarial assumptions if the plan does not provide for applicable actuarial methods and assumptions or the terms of the plan were not reasonable. The determination of the lump sum value may not take into account the likelihood that payments will not be made (or will be reduced) because of the unfunded status of the plan, the risk that the employer, the trustee, or another party will be unwilling or unable to pay, the possibility of future plan amendments, the possibility of a future change in the law, or similar risks or contingencies. If the benefit provided under the plan in effect on November 2, 2017, is paid as a life annuity or other form of benefit that is not a single lump sum payment, the application of the grandfathered amount to the payments of the benefit is determined in accordance with the ordering rule of paragraph (g)(1)(viii) of this section.

(C) *Nonaccount balance plan providing right to discontinue future accrual of benefits.*—If under the terms of the nonaccount balance plan in effect as of November 2, 2017, the corporation has no right to terminate the plan, but may discontinue future accruals of benefits and distribute the benefit in accordance with the terms of the plan, then the grandfathered amount would be the lump sum value of the total benefit (lump sum value) determined as if the corporation had exercised the right to discontinue the future accrual of benefits on November 2, 2017, or, if later, the earliest permissible date the corporation could exercise such right in accordance with the terms of the plan (the freeze date). If, after the freeze date, the plan required the corporation to increase or decrease the lump sum value through the payment date, then any increase to the grandfathered lump sum would also be grandfathered. Notwithstanding the foregoing, the corporation may treat the lump sum value determined as of the freeze date as the grandfathered amount regardless of when the amount is paid and regardless of whether it has been increased or decreased prior to payment. For purposes of this paragraph (g)(1)(vi)(C), the lump sum value is determined based on the actuarial methods and assumptions provided in the plan in effect on November 2, 2017, if the assumptions are reasonable, or any reasonable actuarial assumptions if the plan does not provide for applicable actuarial methods and assumptions or the terms of the plan were not reasonable. The determination of the lump sum value may not take into account the likelihood that payments will not be made (or will be reduced) because of the unfunded status of the plan, the risk that the employer, the trustee, or another party will be unwilling or unable to pay, the possibility of future plan amendments, the possibility of a future change in the law, or similar risks or contingencies. If the benefit paid under the plan in effect on November 2, 2017, is paid as a life annuity or other form of benefit that is not a single lump sum payment, the application of the grandfathered amount to the payments of the benefit is determined in accordance with the ordering rule of paragraph (g)(1)(viii) of this section.

(vii) *Grandfathered amount limited to a particular plan or arrangement.*—The grandfathered amount under a plan or arrangement applies solely to the amounts paid under that plan or arrangement, so that regardless of whether all of the grandfathered amount is paid to the participant (for example, regardless of whether some or all of the grandfathered amount under the plan is forfeited under the terms of the plan), no portion of that grandfathered amount may be treated as a grandfathered amount under any other separate plan or arrangement in which the employee is a participant.

(viii) *Ordering rule.*—If a portion of the amount payable under a plan or arrangement is a grandfathered amount and a portion is subject to this section, and payment under the plan or arrangement is made in a series of payments (including payments as a life annuity), the grandfathered amount is allocated to the first payment of an amount under the plan or arrangement that is otherwise deductible. If the grandfathered amount exceeds the initial payment, the excess is allocated to the next payment of an amount under the plan or arrangement that is otherwise deductible, and this process is repeated until the entire grandfathered amount has been paid. Notwithstanding the foregoing, for amounts otherwise deductible for taxable years ending before December 20, 2019, the grandfathered amount may be allocated to each payment on a pro rata basis or to the last otherwise deductible payment. If one of these two methods was used for taxable years ending before December 20, 2019, then, for taxable years ending on or after December 20, 2019, the method must be changed to allocate any remaining grandfathered amount to the first payment for the remaining payments (treating as the first payment the first otherwise deductible amount for taxable years ending on or after December 20, 2019).

(2) *Material modifications.*—(i) If a written binding contract is modified on or after November 2, 2017, this section (and not § 1.162-27) applies to any payments made after the modification. A material modification occurs when the contract is amended to increase the amount of compensation payable to the employee. If a written binding contract is materially modified, it is treated as a new contract entered into as of the date of the material modification. Thus, amounts received by an employee under the contract before a material modification are not affected, but amounts received subse-

quent to the material modification are treated as paid pursuant to a new contract, rather than as paid pursuant to a written binding contract in effect on November 2, 2017.

(ii) A modification of the contract that accelerates the payment of compensation is a material modification unless the amount of compensation paid is discounted to reasonably reflect the time value of money. If the contract is modified to defer the payment of compensation, any compensation paid or to be paid that is in excess of the amount that was originally payable to the employee under the contract will not be treated as resulting in a material modification if the additional amount is based on applying to the amount originally payable either a reasonable rate of interest or the rate of return on a predetermined actual investment as defined in § 31.3121(v)(2)-1(d)(2)(i)(B) of this chapter (whether or not assets associated with the amount originally owed are actually invested therein) such that the amount payable by the employer at the later date will be based on the reasonable rate of interest or the actual rate of return on the predetermined actual investment (including any decrease, as well as any increase, in the value of the investment). For an arrangement under which the grandfathered amounts are subject to increase or decrease based on the performance of a predetermined actual investment, the addition or substitution of a predetermined actual investment or reasonable interest rate as an investment alternative for amounts deferred is not treated as a material modification. However, a modification of a contract to defer payment of a grandfathered amount that results in payment of additional amounts (such as additional earnings) does not necessarily mean that the additional amounts are grandfathered amounts; for rules concerning the determination of grandfathered amounts see paragraph (g) of this section. Notwithstanding the foregoing, if compensation attributable to an option to purchase stock (other than an incentive stock option described in section 422 or a stock option granted under an employee stock purchase plan described in section 423) or a stock appreciation right is grandfathered, an extension of the exercise period that is extended in compliance with § 1.409A-1(b)(5)(v)(C)(1) will not be treated as a material modification and the amount of compensation paid upon the exercise of the stock option or stock appreciation right will be grandfathered.

(iii) The adoption of a supplemental contract or agreement that provides for increased compensation, or the payment of additional compensation, is a material modification of a written binding contract if the facts and circumstances demonstrate that the additional compensation to be paid is based on substantially the same elements or conditions as the compensation that is otherwise paid pursuant to the written binding contract. However, a material modification of a written binding contract does not include a supplemental payment that is equal to or less than a reasonable cost-of-living increase over the payment made in the preceding year under that written binding contract. In addition, the failure, in whole or in part, to exercise negative discretion under a contract does not result in the material modification of that contract (although the existence of the negative discretion under the contract may impact the initial determination of whether amounts under the contract are grandfathered amounts).

(iv) If a grandfathered amount is subject to a substantial risk of forfeiture (as defined in § 1.409A-1(d)), then a modification of the contract that results in a lapse of the substantial risk of forfeiture is not considered a material modification. Furthermore, for compensation received pursuant to the substantial vesting of restricted property, or the exercise of a stock option or stock appreciation right that does not provide for a deferral of compensation (as defined in § 1.409A-1(b)(5)(i) and (ii)), a modification of a written binding contract in effect on November 2, 2017, that results in a lapse of the substantial risk of forfeiture (as defined § 1.83-3(c)) is not considered a material modification.

(3) *Examples.*—The following examples illustrate the provisions of this paragraph (g). For each example, assume for all relevant years that the corporation is a publicly held corporation within the meaning of paragraph (c)(1) of this section and is a calendar year taxpayer, and is not a "smaller reporting company" or "emerging growth company" for purposes of reporting under the Exchange Act. Furthermore, assume that, for each example, if any arrangement is subject to section 409A, then the arrangement complies with section 409A, and that no arrangement is subject to section 457A.

(i) *Example 1 (Multi-year agreement for annual salary).*—(A) *Facts.* On October 2, 2017, Corporation X executed a three-year employment agreement with Employee A for an annual salary of $2,000,000 beginning on January 1, 2018. Employee A serves as the PFO of Corporation X for the 2017 through 2020 taxable years. The agreement provides for automatic extensions after the three-year term for additional one-year periods, unless the corporation exercises its option to terminate the agreement within 30 days before the end of the three-year term or, thereafter, within 30 days before each anniversary date. Termination of the employment agreement does not require the termination of Employee A's employment with Corporation X. Under applicable law, the agreement for annual salary constitutes a written binding contract in effect on November 2, 2017, to pay $2,000,000 of annual salary to Employee A for three years through December 31, 2020.

(B) *Conclusion.* If this section applies, Employee A is a covered employee for Corporation X's 2018 through 2020 taxable years. Because the October 2, 2017, employment agreement is a written binding contract to pay Employee A an annual salary of $2,000,000, this section does not apply (and § 1.162-27 does apply) to the deduction for Employee A's annual salary. Pursuant to § 1.162-27(c)(2), Employee A is not a covered employee for Corporation X's 2018 through 2020 taxable years. The deduction for Employee A's annual salary for the 2018 through 2020 taxable years is not subject to section 162(m)(1). However, the employment agreement is treated as renewed on January 1, 2021, unless it is previously terminated, and the deduction limit of this § 1.162-33 (and not § 1.162-27) will apply to the deduction for any payments made under the employment agreement on or after that date.

(ii) *Example 2 (Agreement for severance based on annual salary and discretionary bonus).*—(A) *Facts.* The facts are the same as in paragraph (g)(3)(i) of this section (*Example 1*), except that the employment agreement also requires Corporation X to pay Employee A severance if Corporation X terminates the employment relationship without cause during the term of the agreement. The amount of severance is equal to the sum of two times Employee A's annual salary plus two times Employee A's discretionary bonus (if any) paid within 24 months preceding termination. Under applicable law, the agreement for severance constitutes a written binding contract in effect on November 2, 2017, to pay $4,000,000 (two times Employee A's $2,000,000 annual salary) if Corporation X terminates Employee A's employment without cause during the term of the agreement.

(B) *Conclusion.* If this section applies, Employee A is a covered employee for Corporation X's 2018 through 2020 taxable years. Because the October 2, 2017, employment agreement is a written binding contract to pay Employee A $4,000,000 if Employee A is terminated without cause prior to December 31, 2020, this section does not apply (and § 1.162-27 does apply) to the deduction for $4,000,000 of Employee A's severance. Pursuant to § 1.162-27(c)(2), Employee A is not a covered employee for Corporation X's 2018 through 2020 taxable years. The deduction for $4,000,000 of Employee A's severance is not subject to section 162(m)(1). However, the employment agreement is treated as renewed on January 1, 2021, unless it is previously terminated, and this § 1.162-33 (and not § 1.162-27) will apply to the deduction for any payments made under the employment agreement, including for severance, on or after that date.

(iii) *Example 3 (Effect of discretionary bonus payment on agreement for severance based on annual salary and discretionary bonus).*—(A) *Facts.* The facts are the same as in paragraph (g)(3)(ii) of this section (*Example 2*), except that, on October 31, 2017, Corporation X paid Employee A a discretionary bonus of $100,000, on May 14, 2018, Corporation X paid Employee A a discretionary bonus of $600,000, and on April 30, 2019, terminated Employee A's employment without cause. Pursuant to the terms of the employment agreement for severance, on May 1, 2019, Corporation X paid to Employee A a $5,400,000 severance payment (the sum of two times the $2,000,000 annual salary, two times the $100,000 discretionary bonus, and two times the $600,000 discretionary bonus).

(B) *Conclusion.* If this section applies, Employee A is a covered employee for Corporation X's 2019 taxable year. Because the October 2, 2017, agreement is a written binding contract to pay Employee A $4,000,000 if Employee A is terminated without cause prior to December 31, 2020, and $200,000 if Corporation X terminates Employee A's employment without cause prior to October 31, 2019, this section does not apply (and § 1.162-27 does apply) to the deduction for $4,200,000 of Employee A's severance payment. The deduction for $4,200,000 of Employee A's severance payment is not subject to section 162(m)(1). Because the October 2, 2017, agreement is not a written binding contract to pay Employee A's $600,000 discretionary bonus (since, as of November 2, 2017, Corporation X was not obligated under applicable law to make the bonus payment), the deduction for $1,200,000 of the $5,400,000 payment is subject to this section (and not § 1.162-27).

(iv) *Example 4 (Effect of adjustment to annual salary on severance).*—(A) *Facts.* The facts are the same as in paragraph (g)(3)(ii) of this section (*Example 2*), except that the employment agreement provides for discretionary increases in salary and, on January 1, 2019, Corporation X increased Employee A's annual salary from $2,000,000 to $2,050,000, an increase that was less than a reasonable, cost-of-living adjustment.

(B) *Conclusion (Annual salary).* If this section applies, Employee A is a covered employee for Corporation X's 2018 through 2020 taxable years. Because the October 2, 2017, agreement is a written binding contract to pay Employee A an annual salary of $2,000,000, this section does not apply (and § 1.162-27 does apply) to the deduction for Employee A's annual salary unless the change in the salary is a material modification. Even though the $50,000 increase is paid on the basis of substantially the same elements or conditions as the salary that is otherwise paid under the contract, the $50,000 increase does not constitute a material modification because it is less than or equal to a reasonable cost-of-living increase to the $2,000,000 annual salary Corporation X is required to pay under applicable law as of November 2, 2017. However, the deduction for the $50,000 increase is subject to this section (and not § 1.162-27).

(C) *Conclusion (Severance payment).* Because the October 2, 2017, agreement is a written binding contract to pay Employee A severance of $4,000,000, this section would not apply (and § 1.162-27 would apply) to the deduction for this amount of severance unless the change in the employment agreement is a material modification. Even though the $100,000 increase in severance (two times the $50,000 increase in salary) would be paid on the basis of substantially the same elements or conditions as the severance that would otherwise be paid pursuant to the written binding contract, the $50,000 increase in salary on which it is based does not constitute a material modification of the written binding contract since it is less than or equal to a reasonable cost-of-living increase. However, the deduction for the $100,000 increase in severance is subject to this section (and not § 1.162-27).

(v) *Example 5 (Effect of adjustment to annual salary on severance).*—(A) *Facts.* The facts are the same as in paragraph (g)(3)(iv) of this section (*Example 4*), except that, on January 1, 2019, Corporation X increased Employee A's annual salary from $2,000,000 to $3,000,000, an increase that exceeds a reasonable, cost-of-living adjustment.

(B) *Conclusion (Annual salary).* If this section applies, Employee A is a covered employee for Corporation X's 2018 through 2020 taxable years. Because the October 2, 2017, agreement is a written binding contract to pay Employee A an annual salary of $2,000,000, this section does not apply (and § 1.162-27 does apply) to the deduction for Employee A's annual salary unless the change in the employment agreement is a material modification. The $1,000,000 increase is a material modification of the written binding contract because the additional compensation is paid on the basis of substantially the same elements or conditions as the compensation that is otherwise paid pursuant to the written binding contract, and it exceeds a reasonable, annual cost-of-living increase from the $2,000,000 annual salary for 2018 that Corporation X is required to pay under applicable law as of November 2, 2017. Because the written binding contract is materially modified as of January 1, 2019, the deduction for all annual salary paid to Employee A in 2019 and thereafter is subject to this section (and not § 1.162-27).

(C) *Conclusion (Severance payment).* Because the October 2, 2017, agreement is a written binding contract to pay Employee A severance of $4,000,000, this section would not apply (and § 1.162-27 would apply) to the deduction for this amount of severance unless the change in the employment agreement is a material modification. The additional $2,000,000 severance payment (two times the $1,000,000 increase in annual salary) constitutes a material modification of the written binding contract because the $1,000,000 increase in salary on which it is based constitutes a material modification of the written binding contract since it exceeds a reasonable cost-of-living increase from the $2,000,000 annual salary for 2018 that Corporation X is required to pay under applicable law as of November 2, 2017. Because the agreement is materially modified as of January 1, 2019, the deduction for any amount of severance paid to Employee A under the agreement is subject to this section (and not § 1.162-27).

(vi) *Example 6 (Elective deferral of an amount that corporation was obligated to pay under applicable law).*—(A) *Facts.* The facts are the same as in paragraph (g)(3)(i) of this section (*Example 1*), except that, on December 15, 2018, Employee A makes a deferral election under a nonqualified deferred compensation (NQDC) plan to defer $200,000 of annual salary earned and payable in 2019. Pursuant to the NQDC plan, the $200,000, including earnings, is to be paid in a lump sum on the date six months following Employee A's separation from service. The earnings are based on the Standard & Poor's 500 Index. Under applicable law, pursuant to the written binding contract in effect on November 2, 2017, (and absent the deferral agreement) Corporation X would have been obligated to pay $200,000 to Employee A in 2019, but is not obligated to pay any earnings on the $200,000 deferred pursuant to the deferral election Employee A makes on December 15, 2018. Employee A separates from service on December 15, 2020. On June 15, 2021, Corporation X pays $250,000 (the deferred $200,000 of salary plus $50,000 in earnings).

(B) *Conclusion*. If this section applies, Employee A is a covered employee for Corporation X's 2021 taxable year. Employee A's NQDC plan is not a material modification of the written binding contract in effect on November 2, 2017, because the earnings to be paid under the NQDC plan are based on a predetermined actual investment (as defined in §31.3121(v)(2)-1(d)(2)(i)(B) of this chapter). The deduction for the $50,000 of earnings to be paid that exceed the amount originally payable to Employee A under the written binding contract ($200,000 of salary) are subject to this section (and not §1.162-27). This section does not apply (and §1.162-27 does apply) to the deduction for the $200,000 portion of the $250,000 payment that Corporation X was obligated under applicable law to pay as of November 2, 2017. Pursuant to §1.162-27(c)(2), Employee A is not a covered employee for Corporation X's 2021 taxable year; thus, the deduction for the $200,000 payment is not subject to section 162(m)(1).

(vii) *Example 7 (Compensation subject to discretionary recovery by corporation)*.—(A) *Facts*. Employee B serves as the PFO of Corporation Z for its 2017 through 2019 taxable years. On October 2, 2017, Corporation Z executed a bonus agreement with Employee B that requires Corporation Z to pay Employee B a performance bonus of $3,000,000 on May 1, 2019, if Corporation Z's net earnings increase by at least 10% for its 2018 taxable year based on the financial statements filed with the SEC. The agreement does not permit Corporation Z to reduce the amount of the bonus payment for any reason if the Corporation Z attains the net earnings performance target. However, the agreement provides that, if the bonus is paid and subsequently the financial statements are restated to show that the net earnings did not increase by at least 10%, then Corporation Z may, in its discretion, recover the $3,000,000 from Employee B within six months of the restatement. Under applicable law, the agreement for the performance bonus constitutes a written binding contract in effect on November 2, 2017, to pay $3,000,000 to Employee B if Corporation Z's net earnings increase by at least 10% for its 2018 taxable year based on the financial statements filed with the SEC. On May 1, 2019, Corporation Z pays $3,000,000 to Employee B because its net earnings increased by at least 10% of its 2018 taxable year.

(B) *Conclusion*. If this section applies, Employee B is a covered employee for Corporation Z's 2019 taxable year. Because the October 2, 2017, agreement is a written binding contract to pay Employee B $3,000,000 if the applicable conditions are met, this section does not apply (and §1.162-27 does apply) to the deduction for the $3,000,000 regardless of whether Corporation Z's financial statements are restated to show that its net earnings did not increase by at least 10%, and regardless of whether Corporation Z exercises its discretion to recover the bonus if Corporation Z's financial statements are restated to show that its net earnings did not increase by at least 10%.

(viii) *Example 8 (Performance bonus plan with negative discretion)*.—(A) *Facts*. Employee E serves as the PEO of Corporation V for the 2017 and 2018 taxable years. On February 1, 2017, Corporation V establishes a bonus plan, under which Employee E will receive a cash bonus of $1,500,000 if a specified performance goal is satisfied. The compensation committee retains the right, if the performance goal is met, to reduce the bonus payment to no less than $400,000 if, in its judgment, other subjective factors warrant a reduction. On November 2, 2017, under applicable law, which takes into account the employer's ability to exercise negative discretion, the bonus plan established on February 1, 2017, constitutes a written binding contract to pay $400,000. On March 1, 2018, the compensation committee certifies that the performance goal was satisfied, but exercises its discretion to reduce the award to $500,000. On April 1, 2018, Corporation V pays $500,000 to Employee E. The payment satisfies the requirements of §1.162-27(e)(2) through (5) as qualified performance-based compensation.

(B) *Conclusion*. If this section applies, Employee E is a covered employee for Corporation V's 2018 taxable year. Because the February 1, 2017, plan is a written binding contract to pay Employee E $400,000 if the performance goal is satisfied, this section does not apply (and §1.162-27 does apply) to the deduction for the $400,000 portion of the $500,000 payment. Furthermore, pursuant to paragraph (g)(2)(iii) of this section, the failure of the compensation committee to exercise its discretion to reduce the award further to $400,000, instead of $500,000, does not result in a material modification of the contract. Pursuant to §1.162-27(e)(1), the deduction for the $400,000 payment is not subject to section 162(m)(1) because the payment satisfies the requirements of §1.162-27(e)(2) through (5) as qualified performance-based compensation. The deduction for the remaining $100,000 of the $500,000 payment is subject to this section (and not §1.162-27) and therefore the status as qualified performance-based compensation is irrelevant to the application of section 162(m)(1) to this remaining amount.

(ix) *Example 9 (Equity-based compensation with underlying grants made prior to November 2, 2017)*.—(A) *Facts*. On January 2, 2017,

Corporation T executed a 4-year employment agreement with Employee G to serve as its PEO, and Employee G serves as the PEO for the four-year term. Pursuant to the employment agreement, on January 2, 2017, Corporation T executed a grant agreement and granted to Employee G nonqualified stock options to purchase 1,000 shares of Corporation T stock, stock appreciation rights (SARs) on 1,000 shares, and 1,000 shares of Corporation T restricted stock. On the date of grant, the stock options had no readily ascertainable fair market value as defined in §1.83-7(b), and neither the stock options nor the SARs provided for a deferral of compensation under §1.409A-1(b)(5)(i)(A) and (B). The stock options, SARs, and shares of restricted stock are subject to a substantial risk of forfeiture and all substantially vest on January 2, 2020. Employee G may exercise the stock options and the SARs at any time from January 2, 2020, through January 2, 2027. On January 2, 2020, Employee G exercises the stock options and the SARs, and the 1,000 shares of restricted stock become substantially vested (as defined in §1.83-3(b)). The grant agreement pursuant to which grants of the stock options, SARs, and shares of restricted stock are made constitutes a written binding contract under applicable law. The compensation attributable to the stock options and the SARs satisfy the requirements of §1.162-27(e)(2) through (5) as qualified performance-based compensation.

(B) *Conclusion*. If this section applies, Employee G is a covered employee for Corporation T's 2020 taxable year. Because the January 2, 2017, grant agreement constitutes a written binding contract, this section does not apply (and §1.162-27 does apply) to the deduction for compensation received pursuant to the exercise of the stock options and the SARs, or the restricted stock becoming substantially vested (as defined in §1.83-3(b)). Pursuant to §1.162-27(e)(1), the deduction attributable to the stock options and the SARs is not subject to section 162(m)(1) because the compensation satisfies the requirements of §1.162-27(e)(2) through (5) as qualified performance-based compensation. However, the deduction attributable to the restricted stock is subject to section 162(m)(1) because the compensation does not satisfy the requirements of §1.162-27(e)(2) through (5) as qualified performance-based compensation.

(x) *Example 10 (Plan in which an employee is not a participant on November 2, 2017)*.—(A) *Facts*. On October 2, 2017, Employee H executes an employment agreement with Corporation Y to serve as its PFO, and begins employment with Corporation Y. The employment agreement, which is a written binding contract under applicable law, provides that if Employee H continues in his position through April 1, 2018, Employee H will become a participant in the NQDC plan of Corporation Y and that Employee H's benefit accumulated on that date will be $3,000,000. On April 1, 2021, Employee H receives a payment of $4,500,000 (the increase from $3,000,000 to $4,500,000 is not a result of a material modification as defined in paragraph (g)(2) of this section), which is the entire benefit accumulated under the plan through the date of payment.

(B) *Conclusion*. If this section applies, Employee H is a covered employee for Corporation Y's 2021 taxable year. Even though Employee H was not eligible to participate in the NQDC plan on November 2, 2017, Employee H had the right to participate in the plan under a written binding contract as of that date. Because the amount required to be paid pursuant to the written binding contract is $3,000,000, this section does not apply (and §1.162-27 does apply) to the deduction for the $3,000,000 portion of the $4,500,000. Pursuant to §1.162-27(c)(2), Employee H is not a covered employee of Corporation Y for the 2021 taxable year. The deduction for the $3,000,000 portion of the $4,500,000 is not subject to section 162(m)(1). The deduction for the remaining $1,500,000 portion of the payment is subject to this section (and not §1.162-27).

(xi) *Example 11 (Material modification of annual salary)*.—(A) *Facts*. On January 2, 2017, Corporation R executed a 5-year employment agreement with Employee I to serve as Corporation R's PFO, providing for an annual salary of $1,800,000. The agreement constitutes a written binding contract under applicable law. In 2017 and 2018, Employee I receives the salary of $1,800,000 per year. In 2019, Corporation R increases Employee I's salary by $40,000, which is less than a reasonable cost-of-living increase from $1,800,000. On January 1, 2020, Corporation R increases Employee I's salary to $2,400,000. The $560,000 increase exceeds a reasonable, annual cost-of-living increase from $1,840,000.

(B) *Conclusion ($1,840,000 Payment in 2019)*. If this section applies, Employee I is a covered employee for Corporation R's 2018 through 2020 taxable years. Because the January 1, 2017, agreement is a written binding contract to pay Employee I an annual salary of $1,800,000, this section does not apply (and §1.162-27 does apply) to the deduction for Employee I's annual salary unless the change in the employment agreement is a material modification. Pursuant to §1.162-27(c)(2), Employee I is not a covered employee of Corporation R for the 2019 taxable year, so the deduction for the $1,800,000 salary is not subject to section 162(m)(1). Even though the $40,000 increase is made on the basis of substantially the same elements or conditions as the salary, the $40,000 increase does not constitute a material modification of the written binding contract because the $40,000 is less than or equal to a reasonable cost-of-living increase. However, the deduction for the $40,000 increase is subject to this section (and not § 1.162-27).

(C) *Conclusion (Salary increase to $2,400,000 in 2020).* The $560,000 increase in salary in 2020 is a material modification of the written binding contract because the additional compensation is paid on the basis of substantially the same elements or conditions as the salary, and it exceeds a reasonable, annual cost-of-living increase from $1,840,000. Because the written binding contract is materially modified as of January 1, 2020, the deduction for all salary paid to Employee I on and after January 1, 2020, is subject is subject to this section (and not § 1.162-27).

(xii) *Example 12 (Additional payment not considered a material modification).*—(A) *Facts.* The facts are the same as in paragraph (g)(3)(xi) of this section (*Example 11*), except that instead of an increase in salary, in 2020 Employee I receives a restricted stock grant subject to Employee I's continued employment for the balance of the contract.

(B) *Conclusion.* The restricted stock grant is not a material modification of the written binding contract because any additional compensation paid to Employee I under the grant is not paid on the basis of substantially the same elements and conditions as Employee I's salary. However, the deduction attributable to the restricted stock grant is subject to this section (and not § 1.162-27).

(h) *Effective/Applicability dates.*—(1) *Effective date.*—This section is effective on December 30, 2020.

(2) *Applicability dates.*—(i) *General applicability date.*—Except as otherwise provided in paragraph (h)(2)(ii) of this section, this section applies to taxable years beginning on or after December 30, 2020. Taxpayers may choose to apply this section for taxable years beginning after December 31, 2017, and before December 30, 2020 provided the taxpayer applies this section in its entirety and in a consistent manner.

(ii) *Special applicability dates.*—(A) *Definition of covered employee.*—The definition of covered employee in paragraph (c)(2)(i) of this section applies to taxable years ending on or after September 10, 2018. However, for a corporation whose fiscal year and taxable year do not end on the same date, the rule in paragraph (c)(2)(i)(B) of this section requiring the determination of the three most highly compensated executive officers to be made pursuant to the rules under the Exchange Act applies to taxable years ending on or after December 20, 2019.

(B) *Definition of predecessor of a publicly held corporation.*—(1) *Publicly held corporations that become privately held.*—The definition of predecessor of a publicly held corporation in paragraph (c)(2)(ii)(A) of this section applies to any publicly held corporation that becomes a privately held corporation for a taxable year beginning after December 31, 2017, and, subsequently, again becomes a publicly held corporation on or after December 30, 2020 The definition of predecessor of a publicly held corporation in paragraph (c)(2)(ii)(A) of this section does not apply to any publicly held corporation that became a privately held corporation for a taxable year beginning before January 1, 2018, with respect to the earlier period as a publicly held corporation; or a publicly held corporation that becomes a privately held corporation for a taxable year beginning after December 31, 2017, and, subsequently, again becomes a publicly held corporation before December 30, 2020.

(2) *Corporate transactions.*—The definition of predecessor of a publicly held corporation in paragraphs (c)(2)(ii)(B) through (H) of this section applies to corporate transactions that occur (as provided in the transaction timing rule of paragraph (c)(2)(ii)(I) of this section) on or after December 30, 2020. With respect to any of the following corporate transactions occurring after December 20, 2019, and before December 30, 2020, excluding target corporations from the definition of the term "predecessor" is not a reasonable good faith interpretation of the statute:

(i) A publicly held target corporation the stock or assets of which are acquired by another publicly held corporation in a transaction to which section 381(a) applies.

(ii) A publicly held target corporation, at least 80% of the total voting power of the stock of which, and at least 80% of the total value of the stock of which, are acquired by a publicly held acquiring corporation (including an affiliated group).

(C) *Definition of compensation.*—The definition of compensation provided in paragraph (c)(3)(ii) of this section (relating to distributive share of partnership deductions for compensation paid) applies to any deduction for compensation that is paid after Decem-

ber 18, 2020. The definition of compensation in paragraph (c)(3)(ii) does not apply to compensation paid pursuant to a written binding contract that is in effect on December 20, 2019, and that is not materially modified after that date. For purposes of this paragraph (h)(3), written binding contract and material modification have the same meanings as provided in paragraphs (g)(1) and (2) of this section.

(D) *Corporations that become publicly held.*—The rule in paragraph (d) of this section (providing that the deduction limitation of paragraph (b) of this section applies to a deduction for any compensation that is otherwise deductible for the taxable year ending on or after the date that a privately held corporation becomes a publicly held corporation) applies to corporations that become publicly held after December 20, 2019. A privately held corporation that becomes a publicly held corporation on or before December 20, 2019, may rely on the transition rules provided in § 1.162-27(f)(1) until the earliest of the events provided in § 1.162-27(f)(2). A subsidiary that is a member of an affiliated group (as defined in § 1.162-27(c)(1)(ii)) may rely on transition relief provided in § 1.162-27(f)(4) if it becomes a separate publicly held corporation (whether in a spin-off transaction or otherwise) on or before December 20, 2019.

(E) *Transition rules.*—Except for the transition rules in paragraphs (g)(1)(v) through (vii) of this section, the transition rules in paragraphs (g)(1) and (2) of this section (providing that this section does not apply to compensation payable under a written binding contract which was in effect on November 2, 2017, and which is not modified in any material respect on or after such date) apply to taxable years ending on or after September 10, 2018. [Reg. § 1.162-33.]

☐ [*T.D. 9932, 12-28-2020.*]

[Reg. § 1.162(k)-1]

§ 1.162(k)-1. Disallowance of deduction for reacquisition payments.—(a) *In general.*—Except as provided in paragraph (b) of this section, no deduction otherwise allowable is allowed under Chapter 1 of the Internal Revenue Code for any amount paid or incurred by a corporation in connection with the reacquisition of its stock or the stock of any related person (as defined in section 465(b)(3)(C)). Amounts paid or incurred in connection with the reacquisition of stock include amounts paid by a corporation to reacquire its stock from an ESOP that are used in a manner described in section 404(k)(2)(A). See § 1.404(k)-3.

(b) *Exceptions.*—Paragraph (a) of this section does not apply to any—

(1) Deduction allowable under section 163 (relating to interest);

(2) Deduction for amounts that are properly allocable to indebtedness and amortized over the term of such indebtedness;

(3) Deduction for dividends paid (within the meaning of section 561); or

(4) Amount paid or incurred in connection with the redemption of any stock in a regulated investment company that issues only stock which is redeemable upon the demand of the shareholder.

(c) *Effective date.*—This section applies with respect to amounts paid or incurred on or after August 30, 2006. [Reg. § 1.162(k)-1.]

☐ [*T.D. 9282, 8-29-2006.*]

[Reg. § 1.162(l)-0]

§ 1.162(l)-0. Table of Contents.—This section lists the table of contents for § 1.162(l)-1.

§ 1.162(l)-1 Deduction for health insurance costs of self-employed individuals.

(a) Coordination of section 162(l) deduction for taxpayers subject to section 36B.

(1) In general.

(2) Specified premiums.

(3) Specified premiums not paid through advance credit payments.

(b) Additional guidance.

(c) Applicability date. [Reg. § 1.162(l)-0.]

☐ [*T.D. 9822, 7-24-2017.*]

[Reg. § 1.162(l)-1]

§ 1.162(l)-1. Deduction for health insurance costs of self-employed individual.—(a) *Coordination of section 162(l) deduction for taxpayers subject to section 36B.*—(1) *In general.*—A taxpayer is allowed a deduction under section 162(l) for specified premiums, as defined in paragraph (a)(2) of this section, not to exceed an amount equal to the lesser of—

(i) The specified premiums less the premium tax credit attributable to the specified premiums; and

Itemized Deductions for Individuals and Corps.
See p. 20,601 for regulations not amended to reflect law changes
25,281

(ii) The sum of the specified premiums not paid through advance credit payments, as described in paragraph (a)(3) of this section and the additional tax (if any) imposed under section 36B(f)(2)(A) and § 1.36B-4(a)(1) with respect to the specified premiums after application of the limitation on additional tax in section 36B(f)(2)(B) and § 1.36B-4(a)(3).

(2) *Specified premiums.*—For purposes of paragraph (a)(1) of this section, specified premiums' means premiums for a specified qualified health plan or plans for which the taxpayer may otherwise claim a deduction under section 162(l). For purposes of this paragraph (a)(2), a specified qualified health plan is a qualified health plan, as defined in § 1.36B-1(c), covering the taxpayer, the taxpayer's spouse, or a dependent of the taxpayer (enrolled family member) for a month that is a coverage month within the meaning of § 1.36B-3(c) for the enrolled family member. If a specified qualified health plan covers individuals other than enrolled family members, the specified premiums include only the portion of the premiums for the specified qualified health plan that is allocable to the enrolled family members under rules similar to § 1.36B-3(h), which provides rules for determining the amount under § 1.36B-3(d)(1) when two families are enrolled in the same qualified health plan.

(3) *Specified premiums not paid through advance credit payments.*—For purposes of paragraph (a)(1)(ii) of this section, specified premiums not paid through advance credit payments equal the amount of the specified premiums minus the advance credit payments attributable to the specified premiums.

(b) *Additional guidance.*—The Secretary may provide by publication in the **Federal Register** or in the Internal Revenue Bulletin (see § 601.601(d)(2) of this chapter) additional guidance on coordinating the deduction allowed under section 162(l) and the credit provided under section 36B.

(c) *Applicability date.*—This section applies for taxable years beginning after December 31, 2013. [Reg. § 1.162(l)-1.]

☐ [*T.D.* 9822, 7-24-2017.]

[Reg. § 1.163-1]

§ 1.163-1. Interest deduction in general.—(a) Except as otherwise provided in sections 264 to 267, inclusive, interest paid or accrued within the taxable year on indebtedness shall be allowed as a deduction in computing taxable income. For rules relating to interest on certain deferred payments, see section 483 and the regulations thereunder.

(b) Interest paid by the taxpayer on a mortgage upon real estate of which he is the legal or equitable owner, even though the taxpayer is not directly liable upon the bond or note secured by such mortgage, may be deducted as interest on his indebtedness. Pursuant to the provisions of section 163(c), any annual or periodic rental payment made by a taxpayer on or after January 1, 1962, under a redeemable ground rent, as defined in section 1055(c) and paragraph (b) of § 1.1055-1, is required to be treated as interest on an indebtedness secured by a mortgage and, accordingly, may be deducted by the taxpayer as interest on his indebtedness. Section 163(c) has no application in respect of any annual or periodic rental payment made prior to January 1, 1962, or pursuant to an arrangement which does not constitute a "redeemable ground rent" as defined in section 1055(c) and paragraph (b) of § 1.1055-1. Accordingly, annual or periodic payments of Pennsylvania ground rents made before, on, or after January 1, 1962, are deductible as interest if the ground rent is redeemable. An annual or periodic rental payment under a Maryland redeemable ground rent made prior to January 1, 1962, is deductible in accordance with the rules and regulations applicable at the time such payment was made. Any annual or periodic rental payment under a Maryland redeemable ground rent made by the taxpayer on or after January 1, 1962, is, pursuant to the provisions of section 163(c), treated as interest on an indebtedness secured by a mortgage and, accordingly, is deductible by the taxpayer as interest on his indebtedness. In any case where the ground rent is irredeemable, any annual or periodic ground rent payment shall be treated as rent and shall be deductible only to the extent that the payment constitutes a proper business expense. Amounts paid in redemption of a ground rent shall not be treated as interest. For treatment of redeemable ground rents and *real property held subject to liabilities* under redeemable ground rents, see section 1055 and the regulations thereunder.

(c) Interest calculated for costkeeping or other purposes on account of capital or surplus invested in the business which does not represent a charge arising under an interest-bearing obligation, is not an allowable deduction from gross income. Interest paid by a corporation on scrip dividends is an allowable deduction. So-called interest on preferred stock, which is in reality a dividend thereon, cannot be deducted in computing taxable income. (See, however, section 583). In case of banks and loan or trust companies, interest paid

within the year on deposits, such as interest paid on moneys received for investment and secured by interest-bearing certificates of indebtedness issued by such bank or loan or trust company, may be deducted from gross income.

(d) To the extent of assistance payments made in respect of an indebtedness of the taxpayer during the taxable year by the Department of Housing and Urban Development under section 235 of the National Housing Act (12 U.S.C. § 1715z), as amended, no deduction shall be allowed under section 163 and this section for interest paid or accrued with respect to such indebtedness. However, such payments shall not affect the amount of any deduction under any section of the Code other than section 163. The provisions of this paragraph shall apply to taxable years beginning after December 31, 1974. [Reg. § 1.163-1.]

☐ [*T.D.* 6223, 1-23-57. *Amended by T.D.* 6593, 2-28-62, *T.D.* 6821, 5-3-65, *T.D.* 6873, 1-24-66, *and T.D.* 7408, 3-4-76.]

[Reg. § 5f.163-1]

§ 5f.163-1. Denial of interest deduction on certain obligations issued after December 31, 1982, unless issued in registered form (temporary).—(a) *Denial of deduction generally.*—Interest paid or accrued on a registration-required obligation (as defined in paragraph (b) of this section) shall not be allowed as a deduction under section 163 or any other provision of law unless such obligation is issued in registered form (as defined in § 5f.103-1(c)).

(b) *Registration-required obligation.*—For purposes of this section, the term "registration-required obligation" means any obligation except any one of the following:

(1) An obligation issued by a natural person.

(2) An obligation not of a type offered to the public. The determination as to whether an obligation is not of a type offered to the public shall be based on whether similar obligations are in fact publicly offered or traded.

(3) An obligation that has a maturity at the date of issue of not more than 1 year.

(4) An obligation issued before January 1, 1983. An obligation first issued before January 1, 1983, shall not be considered to have been issued on or after such date merely as a result of the existence of a right on the part of the holder of such obligation to convert such obligation from registered form into bearer form, or as a result of the exercise of such a right.

(5) An obligation described in subparagraph (1) of paragraph (c) (relating to certain obligations issued to foreign persons).

(c) [Reserved.]

(d) *Effective date.*—The provisions of this section shall apply to obligations issued after December 31, 1982, unless issued on an exercise of a warrant for the conversion of a convertible obligation if such warrant or obligation was offered or sold outside the United States without registration under the Securities Act of 1933 and was issued before August 10, 1982.

(e) *Obligations first issued after December 31, 1982, where the right exists for the holder to convert such obligation from registered form into bearer form.*—[Reserved]

(f) *Examples.*—The application of this section may be illustrated by the following examples:

Example (1). All of the shares of Corporation X are owned by two individuals, A and B. X desires to sell all of its assets to Corporation Y, all of the shares of which are owned by individual C. Following the sale, Corporation X will be completely liquidated. As partial consideration for the Corporation X assets, Corporation Y delivers a promissory note to X, secured by a security interest and mortgage on the acquired assets. The note given by Y to X is not of a type offered to the public.

Example (2). Corporation 2 has a credit agreement with Bank M pursuant to which Corporation Z may borrow amounts not exceeding $10X upon delivery of Z's note to Bank M. The note Z delivers to M is not of a type offered to the public.

Example (3). Individuals D and E operate a retail business through partnership DE. D wishes to loan partnership DE $5X. DE's note evidencing the loan from D is not of a type offered to the public.

Example (4). Individual F owns one-third of the shares of Corporation W. F makes a cash advance to W. W's note evidencing F's cash advance is not of a type offered to the public.

Example (5). Closely-held Corporation R places its convertible debentures with 30 individuals who are United States persons. The offering is not required to be registered under the Securities Act of 1933. Similar debentures are publicly offered and traded. The obligations are not considered of a type not offered to the public.

Example (6). In 1980, Corporation V issued its bonds due in 1986 through an offering registered with the Securities and Exchange Commission. Although the bonds were initially issued in registered form, the terms of the bonds permit a holder, at his option, to convert a bond into bearer form at any time prior to maturity. Similarly, a person who holds a bond in bearer form may, at any time, have the bond converted into registered form.

(i) Assume G bought one of Corporation V's bonds upon the original issuance in 1980. In 1983, G requests that V convert the bond into bearer form. Except for the change from registered to bearer form, the terms of the bond are unchanged. The bond held by G is not considered issued after December 31, 1982, under §5f.163-1(b)(4).

(ii) Assume H buys one of Corporation V's bonds in the secondary market in 1983. The bond H receives is in registered form, but H requests that V convert the obligation into bearer form. There is no other change in the terms of the instrument. The bond held by H is not considered issued after December 31, 1982, under §5f.163-1(b)(4).

(iii) Assume the same facts as in (ii) except that in 1984 I purchases H's V Corporation bond, which is in bearer form. I requests V to convert the bond into registered form. There is no other change in the terms of the instrument. In 1985, I requests V to convert the bond bank into bearer form. Again, there is no other change in the terms of the instrument. The bond purchased by I is not considered issued after December 31, 1982, under §5f.163-1(b)(4).

Example (7). Corporation U wishes to make a public offering of its debentures to United States persons. U issues a master note to Bank N. The terms of the note require that any person who acquires an interest in the note must have such interest reflected in a book entry. Bank N offers for sale interests in the Corporation U note. Ownership interests in the note are reflected on the books of Bank N. Corporation U's debenture is considered issued in registered form.

Example (8). Issuer S wishes to make a public offering of its debt obligations to United States persons. The obligations will have a maturity in excess of one year. On November 1, 1982, the closing on the debt offering occurs. At the closing, the net cash proceeds of the offering are delivered to S, and S delivers a master note to the underwriter of the offering. On January 2, 1983, S delivers the debt obligations to the purchasers, in definitive form and the master note is cancelled. The obligations are not registration-required because they are considered issued before January 1, 1983.

Example (9). In July 1983, Corporation T sells an issue of debt obligations maturing in 1985 to the public in the United States. Three of the obligations of the issue are issued to J in bearer form. The balance of the obligations of the issue are issued in registered form. The terms of the registered and bearer obligations are identical. The obligations issued to J are of a type offered to the public and are registration-required obligations. Since the three obligations are issued in bearer form, T is subject to the tax imposed under section 4701 with respect to the three bearer obligations. In addition, interest paid or accrued on the three bearer obligations is not deductible by T. Moreover, since the issuance of the three bearer obligations is subject to tax under section 4701, J is not prohibited from deducting losses on the obligations under section 165(j) or from treating gain on the obligations as capital gain under section 1232(d). The balance of the obligations in the issue do not give rise to liability for the tax under section 4701, and the deductibility of interest on such obligations is not affected by section 163(f).

Example (10). Broker K acquires a bond issued in 1980 by the United States Treasury through the Bureau of Public Debt. Broker K sells interests in the bond to the public after December 31, 1982. A purchaser may acquire an interest in any interest payment falling due under the bond or an interest in the principal of the bond. The bond is held by Custodian L for the benefit of the persons acquiring these interests. On receipt of interest and principal payments under the bond, Custodian L transfers the amount received to the person whose ownership interest corresponds to the bond component giving rise to the payment. Under section 1232B, each bond component is treated as an obligation issued with original issue discount equal to the excess of the stated redemption price at maturity over the purchase price of the bond component. The interests sold by K are obligations of a type offered to the public. Further, the interests are, in accordance with section 1232B, considered issued after December 31, 1982. Accordingly, the interests are registration-required obligations under §5f.163-1(b). [Temporary Reg. §5f.163-1.]

☐ [*T.D.* 7852, 11-9-82. Amended by T.D. 7965, 8-17-84.]

[Reg. §1.163-2]

§1.163-2. Installment purchases where interest charge is not separately stated.—(a) *In general.*—(1) Whenever there is a contract with a seller for the purchase of personal property providing for payment of part or all of the purchase price in installments and there *is a separately stated carrying charge (including a finance charge, service charge, and the like)* but the actual interest charge cannot be ascertained, a portion of the payments made during the taxable year under the contract shall be treated as interest and is deductible under section 163 and this section. Section 163(b) contains a formula, de-

scribed in paragraph (b) of this section, in accordance with which the amount of interest deductible in the taxable year must be computed. This formula is designed to operate automatically in the case of any installment purchase, without regard to whether payments under the contract are made when due or are in default. For applicable limitations when an obligation to pay is terminated, see paragraph (c) of this section.

(2) Whenever there is a contract with an educational institution for the purchase of educational services providing for payment of part or all of the purchase price in installments and there is a separately stated carrying charge (including a finance charge, service charge, and the like) but the actual interest charge cannot be ascertained, a portion of the payments made during the taxable year under the contract shall be treated as interest and is deductible under section 163 and this section. See paragraphs (b) and (c) of this section for the applicable computation and limitations rules. For purposes of section 163(b) and this section, the term "educational services" means any service (including lodging), which is purchased from an educational institution (as defined in section 151(e)(4) and paragraph (c) of §1.151-3) and which is provided for a student of such institution.

(3) Section 163(b) and this section do not apply to a contract for the loan of money, even if the loan is to be repaid in installments and even if the borrowed amount is used to purchase personal property or educational services. In cases to which the preceding sentence applies, the portion of the installment payment which constitutes interest (as distinguished from payments of principal and charges such as payments for credit life insurance) is deductible under section 163(a) and §1.163-1.

(b) *Computation.*—The portion of any such payments to be treated as interest shall be equal to 6 percent of the average unpaid balance under the contract during the taxable year. For purposes of this computation, the average unpaid balance under the contract is the sum of the unpaid balance outstanding on the first day of each month beginning during the taxable year, divided by 12.

(c) *Limitations.*—The amount treated as interest under section 163(b) and this section for any taxable year shall not exceed the amount of the payments made under the contract during the taxable year nor the aggregate carrying charges properly attributable to each contract for such taxable year. In computing the amount to be treated as interest if the obligation to pay is terminated as, for example, in the case of a repossession of the property, the unpaid balance on the first day of the month during which the obligation is terminated shall be zero.

(d) *Illustrations.*—The provisions of this section may be illustrated by the following examples:

Example (1). On January 20, 1955, A purchased a television set for $400, including a stated carrying charge of $25. The down payment was $50, and the balance was paid in 14 monthly installments of $25 each, on the 20th day of each month commencing with February. Assuming that A is a cash method, calendar year taxpayer and that no other installment purchases were made, the amount to be treated as interest in 1955 is $12.38, computed as follows:

Year 1955

First day of:	Unpaid balance outstanding
January	$0
February	350
March	325
April	300
May	275
June	250
July	225
August	200
September	175
October	150
November	125
December	100
	$2,475

Sum of unpaid balances $2,475 ÷ 12 = $206.25;
6 percent thereof = $12.38.

Example (2). On November 20, 1955, B purchased a furniture set for $1,250, including a stated carrying charge of $48. The down payment was $50 and the balance was payable in 12 monthly installments of $100 each, on the first day of each month commencing with December 1955. Assume that B is a cash method, calendar year taxpayer and that no other installment purchases were made. Assume further that B made the first payment when due, but made only one other payment on June 1, 1956. The amount to be treated as interest in 1955 is $4, and the amount to be treated as interest in 1956 is $33, computed as follows:

Year 1955

First day of:	Unpaid balance outstanding
December	$1,200

Sum of unpaid balances $1200 ÷ 12 = $100;
6 percent thereof = $6.
Carrying charges attributable to 1955 = $4.

Year 1956

First day of:	Unpaid balance outstanding
January	$1,100
February	1,000
March	900
April	800
May	700
June	600
July	500
August	400
September	300
October	200
November	100
	$6,600

Sum of unpaid balances $6,600 ÷ 12 = $550;
6 percent thereof = $33.
Carrying charges attributable to 1956 = $44. ($4 × 11).

Example (3). Assume the same facts as in example (2), except that the furniture was repossessed and B's obligation to pay terminated as of July 15, 1956. The amount to be treated as interest in 1955 is $4, computed as in example (2) above. The amount to be treated as interest in 1956 is $25.50, computed as follows:

Year 1956

First day of:	Unpaid balance outstanding
January	$1,100
February	1,000
March	900
April	800
May	700
June	600
July—November	0
	$5,100

Sum of unpaid balances $5,100 ÷ 12 = $425;
6 percent thereof = $25.50.
Carrying charges attributable to 1956 = $44 ($4 × 11).

Example (4). (i) On September 15, 1968, C registered at X University for the 1968-69 academic year. C entered into an agreement with the X University for the purchase during such academic year of educational services (including lodging and tuition) for a total fee of $1,000, including a separately stated carrying charge of $50. Under the terms of the agreement, an initial payment of $200 was to be made by C on September 15, 1968, and the balance was to be paid in 8 monthly installments of $100 each, on the 15th day of each month commencing with October 1968. C made all of the required 1968 payments. Assuming that C is a cash method, calendar year taxpayer and that no other installment purchases of services or property were made, the amount to be treated as interest in 1968 is $10.50, computed as follows:

Year 1968

First day of:	Unpaid balance outstanding
January—September	$0
October	800
November	700
December	600
	$2,100

The sum of unpaid balances ($2,100) divided by 12 is $175; 6 percent thereof is $10.50. The carrying charges attributable to 1968 are $18.75 (i.e., the total carrying charges ($50), divided by the total number of payments (8), multiplied by the number of payments made in 1968 (3)). Since the amount to be treated as interest in 1968 ($10.50) does not exceed the carrying charges attributable to 1968 ($18.75), the limitation set forth in paragraph (c) of this section is not applicable.

(ii) The result in this example would be the same even if the X University assigned the agreement to a bank or other financial institution and C made his payments directly to the bank or other financial institution.

Example (5). On September 15, 1968, D registered at Y University for the 1968-69 academic year. The tuition for such year was $1,500. In order to pay his tuition, D borrowed $1,500 from the M Corporation, a lending institution, and remitted that sum to the Y University. The loan agreement between M Corporation and D provided that D was to repay the loan, plus a service charge, in 10 equal monthly installments, on the first day of each month commencing with October 1968. The service charge consisted of interest and the cost of credit life insurance on D's life. Since section 163(b) and this section do not apply to a contract for the loan of money, D is not entitled to compute his interest deduction with respect to his loan from M Corporation under such sections. D may deduct that portion of each installment payment which constitutes interest (as distinguished from payments of principal and the charge for credit life insurance) under section 163(a) and § 1.163-1, provided that the amount of such interest can be ascertained.

(e) *Effective date.*—Except in the case of payments made under a contract for educational services, the rule provided in section 163(b) and this section applies to payments made during taxable years beginning after December 31, 1953, and ending after August 16, 1954, regardless of when the contract of sale was made. In the case of payments made under a contract for educational services, the rule provided in section 163(b) and this section applies to payments made during taxable years beginning after December 31, 1963, regardless of when the contract for educational services was made. [Reg. § 1.163-2.]

☐ [T.D. 6223, 1-23-57. Amended by T.D. 6991, 1-16-69.]

[Reg. § 1.163-3]

§ 1.163-3. **Deduction for discount on bond issued on or before May 27, 1969.**—(a) *Discount upon issuance.*—(1) If bonds are issued by a corporation at a discount, the net amount of such discount is deductible and should be prorated or amortized over the life of the bonds. For purposes of this section, the amortizable bond discount equals the excess of the amount payable at maturity (or, in the case of a callable bond, at the earlier call date) over the issue price of the bond (as defined in paragraph (b)(2) of § 1.1232-3).

(2) In the case of a bond issued by a corporation after December 31, 1954, as part of an investment unit consisting of an obligation and an option, the issue price of the bond is determined by allocating the amount received for the investment unit to the individual elements of the unit in the manner set forth in subdivision (ii)(a) of § 1.1232-3(b)(2). Discount with respect to bonds issued by a corporation as part of investment units consisting of obligations and options after December 31, 1954, and before December 24, 1968—

(i) Increased by any amount treated as bond premium which has been included in gross income with respect to such bonds prior to December 24, 1968, or

(ii) Decreased by any amount which has been deducted by the issuer as discount attributable to such bonds prior to December 24, 1968, and

(iii) Decreased by any amount which has been deducted by the issuer prior to December 24, 1968, upon the exercise or sale by investors of options issued in investment units with such bonds, should be amortized, starting with the first taxable year ending on or after December 24, 1968, over the remaining life of such bonds.

(b) *Examples.*—The rules in paragraph (a) of this section are illustrated by the following examples:

Example (1). M Corporation, on January 1, 1960, the beginning of its taxable year, issued for $95,000, 3 percent bonds, maturing 10 years from the date of issue, with a stated redemption price at maturity of $100,000. M Corporation should treat $5,000 ($100,000 − $95,000) as the total amount to be amortized over the life of the bonds.

Example (2). Assume the same facts as example (1), except that the bonds are convertible into common stock of M Corporation. Since the issue price of the bonds includes any amount attributable to the conversion privilege, the result is the same as in example (1).

Example (3). Assume the same facts as example (1), except that the bonds are issued as part of an investment unit consisting of an obligation and an option. Assume further that the issue price of the bonds as determined under the rules of allocation set forth in subdivision (ii)(a) of § 1.1232-3(b)(2) is $94,000. Accordingly, M Corporation should treat $6,000 ($100,000 − $94,000) as the total amount to be amortized over the life of the bonds.

Example (4). Assume in example (3), that prior to December 24, 1968, M Corporation had only treated $5,000 as the bond discount to be amortized and deducted only $4,000 of this amount. Starting with the first taxable year ending on or after December 24, 1968, M Corporation should amortize $2,000 ($6,000 discount, less $4,000 previously deducted) over the remaining life of the bonds.

Example (5). N Corporation, on January 1, 1956, for a consideration of $102,000, issued 20-year bonds in the face amount of $100,000, together with options to purchase stock of N Corporation. The issue price of the bonds as determined under the rules of allocation set forth in subdivision (ii)(a) of §1.1232-3(b)(2) is $99,000. Until December 24, 1968, N Corporation has treated as bond premium, $2,000, representing the excess of the consideration received for the bond-option investment units over the maturity value of the bonds, and has accordingly prorated and included in income $1,200 of such amount. Starting with the first taxable year beginning on or after December 24, 1968, N Corporation may amortize as a deduction over the remaining life of the bonds the amount of $2,200 ($1,000 discount, plus $1,200 previously included in income).

Example (6). O Corporation, on January 1, 1956, for a consideration of $100,000, issued 20-year bonds with a $100,000 face value, together with options to purchase stock of O Corporation, which could be exercised at any time up to 5 years from the date of issue. The issue price of the bonds as determined under the rules of allocation set forth in subdivision (ii)(a) of §1.1232-3(b)(2) is $98,000. O Corporation, upon the exercise of the options prior to December 24, 1968, had deducted from income their fair market value at the time of exercise, which is assumed for purposes of this example to have been $3,000. Even though the bonds are considered to have been issued at a discount under paragraph (a)(1) of this section, O Corporation would have no deduction over the remaining life of the bonds, inasmuch as O Corporation, in computing the amount of such deduction, is required under paragraph (a)(2)(iii) of this section to reduce the amount which would otherwise be treated as bond discount, $2,000 ($100,000 – $98,000), by the amount deducted from income upon the exercise of the options, in this case, $3,000.

(c) *Deduction upon repurchase.*—(1) Except as provided in subparagraphs (2) and (3) of this paragraph, if bonds are issued by a corporation and are subsequently repurchased by the corporation at a price in excess of the issue price plus any amount of discount deducted prior to repurchase, or (in the case of bonds issued subsequent to Feb. 28, 1913) minus any amount of premium returned as income prior to repurchase, the excess of the purchase price over the issue price adjusted for amortized premium or discount is a deductible expense for the taxable year.

(2) In the case of a convertible bond (except a bond which the corporation, before September 5, 1968, has obligated itself to repurchase at a specified price), the deduction allowable under subparagraph (1) of this paragraph may not exceed an amount equal to one year's interest at the rate specified in the bond, except to the extent that the corporation can demonstrate to the satisfaction of the Commissioner or his delegate that an amount in excess of one year's interest does not include any amount attributable to the conversion feature.

(3) No deduction shall be allowed under subparagragh (1) of this paragraph to the extent a deduction is disallowed under subparagraph (2) of this paragraph or to the extent a deduction is disallowed by section 249 (relating to limitation on deduction of bond premium on repurchase of convertible obligation) and the regulations thereunder. See paragraph (f) of §1.249-1 for effective date limitation on section 249.

(d) *Definition.*—For purposes of this section, a debenture, note, certificate or other evidence of indebtedness, issued by a corporation and bearing interest shall be given the same treatment as a bond.

(e) *Effective date.*—The provisions of this section shall not apply in respect of a bond issued after May 27, 1969, unless issued pursuant to a written commitment which was binding on that date and at all times thereafter. [Reg. §1.163-3.]

☐ [*T.D. 6984, 12-23-68. Amended by T.D. 7154, 12-27-71 and T.D. 7259, 2-9-73.*]

[Reg. §1.163-4]

§1.163-4. Deduction for original issue discount on certain obligations issued after May 27, 1969.—(a) *In general.*—(1) If an obligation is issued by a corporation with original issue discount, the amount of such discount is deductible as interest and shall be prorated or amortized over the life of the obligation. For purposes of this section the term "obligation" shall have the same meaning as in §1.1232-1 (without regard to whether the obligation is a capital asset in the hands of the holder) and the term "original issue discount" shall have the same meaning as in section 1232(b)(1) (without regard to the one-fourth-of-1-percent limitation in the second sentence thereof). Thus, in general, the amount of original issue discount equals the excess of the amount payable at maturity over the issue price of the bond (as defined in paragraph (b)(2) of §1.1232-3), regardless of whether that amount is less than one-fourth of 1 percent of the redemption price at maturity multiplied by the number of *complete years to maturity. For the rule as to whether there is original issue discount in the case of an obligation issued in an exchange for property other than money, and the amount thereof, see* paragraph (b)(2)(iii) of §1.1232-3. In any case in which original issue discount is carried over from one corporation to another corporation

under section 381(c)(9) or from an obligation exchanged to an obligation received in any exchange under paragraph (b)(1)(iv) of §1.1232-3, such discount shall be carried over for purposes of this section. The amount of original issue discount carried over in an exchange of obligations under the preceding sentence shall be prorated or amortized over the life of the obligation issued in such exchange. For computation of issue price and the amount of original issue discount in the case of serial obligations, see paragraph (b)(2)(iv) of §1.1232-3.

(2) In the case of an obligation issued by a corporation as part of an investment unit (as defined in paragraph (b)(2)(ii)(a) of §1.1232-3) consisting of an obligation and other property, the issue price of the obligation is determined by allocating the amount received for the investment unit to the individual elements of the unit in the manner set forth in paragraph (b)(2)(ii) of §1.1232-3.

(3) *Recovery or retention of amounts previously deducted.*—In any taxable year in which an amount of original issue discount which was deducted as interest under this section is retained or recovered by the taxpayer, such as, for example, by reason of a fine, penalty, forfeiture, or other withdrawal fee, such amount shall be includible in the gross income of such taxpayer for such taxable year.

(b) *Examples.*—The rules in paragraph (a) of this section are illustrated by the following examples:

Example (1). N Corporation, which uses the calendar year as its taxable year, on January 1, 1970, issued for $99,000, 9 percent bonds maturing 10 years from the date of issue, with a stated redemption price at maturity of $100,000. The original issue discount on each bond (as determined under section 1232(b)(1) without regard to the one-fourth-of-1-percent limitation in the second sentence thereof) is $1,000, *i.e.,* redemption price, $100,000, minus issue price, $99,000. N shall treat $1,000 as the total amount to be amortized over the life of the bonds.

Example (2). Assume the same facts as example (1), except that the bonds are convertible into common stock of N Corporation. Since the issue price of the bonds includes any amount attributable to the conversion privilege, the result is the same as in example (1).

Example (3). Assume the same facts as example (1), except that the bonds are issued as part of an investment unit consisting of an obligation and an option. Assume further that the issue price of the bonds as determined under the rules of allocation set forth in paragraph (b)(2)(ii) of §1.1232-3 is $94,000. The original issue discount on the bond (as determined under section 1232(b)(1) without regard to the one-fourth-of-1-percent limitation in the second sentence thereof) is $6,000, *i.e.,* redemption price, $100,000, minus issue price, $94,000. N shall treat $6,000 as the total amount to be amortized over the life of the bonds.

Example (4). On January 1, 1971, a commercial bank which uses the calendar year as its taxable year, issued a certificate of deposit for $10,000. The certificate of deposit is not redeemable until December 31, 1975, except in an emergency as defined in, and subject to the qualifications provided by, Regulations Q of the Board of Governors of the Federal Reserve. See 12 CFR §217.4(d). The stated redemption price at maturity is $13,382.26. The certificate is an obligation to which section 1232(a)(3)(A) applies (see paragraph (d) of §1.1232-1), and the original issue discount with respect to the certificate (as determined under section 1232(b)(1) without regard to the one-fourth-of-1-percent limitation in the second sentence thereof) is $3,382.26 (*i.e.,* redemption price, $13,382.26, minus issue price, $10,000). Y shall treat $3,382.26 as the total amount to be amortized over the life of the certificate.

(c) *Deduction upon repurchase..*—(1) Except as provided in subparagraph (2) of this paragraph, if bonds are issued by a corporation and are subsequently repurchased by the corporation at a price in excess of the issue price plus any amount of original issue discount deducted prior to repurchase, or minus any amount of premium returned as income prior to repurchase, the excess of the repurchase price over the issue price adjusted for amortized premium or deducted discount is deductible as interest for the taxable year.

(2) The provisions of subparagraph (1) of this paragraph shall not apply to the extent a deduction is disallowed by section 249 (relating to limitation on deduction of bond premium or repurchase of convertible obligation) and the regulations thereunder.

(d) *Effective date.*—The provisions of this section shall apply in respect of obligations issued after May 27, 1969, other than—

(1) Obligations issued pursuant to a written commitment which was binding on May 27, 1969, and at all times thereafter, and

(2) Deposits made before January 1, 1971, in the case of certificates of deposit, time deposits, bonus plans, and other deposit arrangements with banks, domestic building and loan associations, and similar financial institutions. [Reg. §1.163-4.]

☐ [*T.D. 7154, 12-27-71. Amended by T.D. 7213, 10-17-72 and T.D. 7259, 2-9-73.*]

[Reg. §1.163-5]

§1.163-5. Denial of interest deduction on certain obligations issued after December 31, 1982, unless issued in registered form.—

(a) [Reserved]

(b) [Reserved]

(c) *Obligations issued to foreign persons after September 21, 1984.—* (1) *In general.—*A determination of whether an obligation satisfies each of the requirements of this paragraph shall be made on an obligation-by-obligation basis. An obligation issued directly (or through affiliated entities) in bearer form by, or guaranteed by, a United States Government-owned agency or a United States Government-sponsored enterprise, such as the Federal National Mortgage Association, the Federal Home Loan Banks, the Federal Loan Mortgage Corporation, the Farm Credit Administration, and the Student Loan Marketing Association, may not satisfy this paragraph (c). An obligation issued after September 21, 1984 is described in this paragraph if—

(i) There are arrangements reasonably designed to ensure that such obligation will be sold (or resold in connection with its original issuance) only to a person who is not a United States person or who is a United States person that is a financial institution (as defined in §1.165-12 (c)(1)(v)) purchasing for its own account or for the account of a customer and that agrees to comply with the requirements of section 165(j)(3)(A), (B), or (C) and the regulations thereunder, and

(ii) In the case of an obligation which is not in registered form—

(A) Interest on such obligation is payable only outside the United States and its possessions, and

(B) Unless the obligation is described in subparagraph (2)(i)(C) of this paragraph or is a temporary global security, the following statement in English either appears on the face of the obligation and on any interest coupons which may be detached therefrom or, if the obligation is evidenced by a book entry, appears in the book or record in which the book entry is made: "Any United States person who holds this obligation will be subject to limitations under the United States income tax laws, including the limitations provided in sections 165(j) and 1287(a) of the Internal Revenue Code." For purposes of this paragraph, the term "temporary global security" means a security which is held for the benefit of the purchasers of the obligations of the issuer and interests in which are exchangeable for securities in definitive registered or bearer form prior to its stated maturity.

(2) *Rules for the application of this paragraph.—(i) Arrangements reasonably designed to ensure sale to non-United States persons.—*An obligation will be considered to satisfy paragraph (c)(1)(i) of this section if the conditions of paragraph (c)(2)(i)(A), (B), (C) or (D) of this section are met in connection with the original issuance of the obligation. An exchange of one obligation for another is considered an original issuance if and only if the exchange constitutes a disposition of property for purposes of section 1001 of the Code. However, an exchange of one obligation for another will not be considered a new issuance if the obligation received is identical in all respects to the obligation surrendered in exchange therefor, except that the obligor of the obligation received need not be the same obligor as the obligor of the obligation surrendered. Obligations that meet the conditions of paragraph (c)(2)(i)(A), (B), (C) or (D) of this section may be issued in a single public offering. The preceding sentence does not apply to certificates of deposit issued under the conditions of paragraph (c)(2)(i)(C) of this section by a United States person or by a controlled foreign corporation within the meaning of section 957(a) that is engaged in the active conduct of a banking business within the meaning of section 954(c)(3)(B) as in effect prior to the Tax Reform Act of 1986, and the regulations thereunder. A temporary global security need not satisfy the conditions of paragraph (c)(2)(i)(A), (B) or (C) of this section, but must satisfy the applicable requirements of paragraph (c)(2)(i)(D) of this section.

(A) In connection with the original issuance of an obligation, the obligation is offered for sale or resale only outside of the United States and its possessions, is delivered only outside the United States and its possessions and is not registered under the Securities Act of 1933 because it is intended for distribution to persons who are not United States persons. An obligation will not be considered to be required to be registered under the Securities Act of 1933 if the issuer, in reliance on the written opinion of counsel received prior to the issuance thereof, determines in good faith that the obligation need not be registered under the Securities Act of 1933 for the reason that it is intended for distribution to persons who are not United States persons. Solely for purposes of this subdivision (i)(A), the term "United States person" has the same meaning as it has for purposes of determining whether an obligation is intended for distribution to persons under the Securities Act of 1933. Except as

provided in paragraph (c)(3) of this section, this paragraph (c)(2)(i)(A) applies only to obligations issued on or before September 7, 1990.

(B) The obligation is registered under the Securities Act of 1933, is exempt from registration by reason of section 3 or section 4 of such Act, or does not qualify as a security under the Securities Act of 1933; all of the conditions set forth in paragraph (c)(2)(i)(B)(1), (2), (3), (4), and (5) of this section are met with respect to such obligations; and, except as provided in paragraph (c)(3) of this section, the obligation is issued on or before September 7, 1990.

(1) In connection with the original issuance of an obligation in bearer form, the obligation is offered for sale or resale only outside the United States and its possessions.

(2) The issuer does not, and each underwriter and each member of the selling group, if any, covenants that it will not, in connection with the original issuance of the obligation, offer to sell or resell the obligation in bearer form to any person inside the United States or to a United States person unless such United States person is a financial institution as defined in §1.165-12(c)(v) purchasing for its own account or for the account of a customer, which financial institution, as a condition of the purchase, agrees to provide on delivery of the obligation (or on issuance, if the obligation is not in definitive form) the certificate required under paragraph (c)(2)(i)(B)(4).

(3) In connection with its sale or resale during the original issuance of the obligation in bearer form, each underwriter and each member of the selling group, if any, or the issuer, if there is no underwriter or selling group, sends a confirmation to the purchaser of the bearer obligation stating that the purchaser represents that it is not a United States person or, if it is a United States person, it is a financial institution as defined in §1.165-12(c)(v) purchasing for its own account or for the account of a customer and that the financial institution will comply with the requirements of section 165(j)(3)(A), (B), or (C) and the regulations thereunder. The confirmation must also state that, if the purchaser is a dealer, it will send similar confirmations to whomever purchases from it.

(4) In connection with the original issuance of the obligation in bearer form it is delivered in definitive form (or issued, if the obligation is not in definitive form) to the person entitled to physical delivery thereof only outside the United States and its possessions and only upon presentation of a certificate signed by such person to the issuer, underwriter, or member of the selling group, which certificate states that the obligation is not being acquired by or on behalf of a United States person, or for offer to resell or for resale to a United States person or any person inside the United States, or, if a beneficial interest in the obligation is being acquired by a United States person, that such person is a financial institution as defined in §1.165-12(c)(1)(v) or is acquiring through a financial institution and that the obligation is held by a financial institution that has agreed to comply with the requirements of section 165(j)(3)(A), (B), or (C) and the regulations thereunder and that is not purchasing for offer to resell or for resale inside the United States. When a certificate is provided by a clearing organization, it must be based on statements provided to it by its member organizations. A clearing organization is an entity which is in the business of holding obligations for member organizations and transferring obligations among such members by credit or debit to the account of a member without the necessity of physical delivery of the obligation. For purposes of paragraph (c)(2)(i)(B), the term "delivery" does not include the delivery of an obligation to an underwriter or member of the selling group, if any.

(5) The issuer, underwriter, or member of the selling group does not have actual knowledge that the certificate described in paragraph (c)(2)(i)(B)(4) of this section is false. The issuer, underwriter, or member of the selling group shall be deemed to have actual knowledge that the certificate described in paragraph (c)(2)(i)(B)(4) of this section is false if the issuer, underwriter, or member of the selling group has a United States address for the beneficial owner (other than a financial institution as defined in §1.165-12(c)(v) that represents that it will comply with the requirements of section 165(j)(3)(A), (B), or (C) and the regulations thereunder) and does not have documentary evidence as described in §1.6049-5(c)(1) that the beneficial owner is not a United States person.

(C) The obligation is issued only outside the United States and its possessions by an issuer that does not significantly engage in interstate commerce with respect to the issuance of such obligation either directly or through its agent, an underwriter, or a member of the selling group. In the case of an issuer that is a United States person, such issuer may only satisfy the test set forth in this paragraph (c)(2)(i)(C) if—

(1) It is engaged through a branch in the active conduct of a banking business, within the meaning of section 954(c)(3)(B) as in

effect before the Tax Reform Act of 1986, and the regulations thereunder, outside the United States;

(2) The obligation is issued outside of the United States by the branch in connection with that trade or business;

(3) The obligation that is so issued is sold directly to the public and is not issued as a part of a larger issuance made by means of a public offering; and

(4) The issuer either maintains documentary evidence as described in subdivision (iii) of A-5 of 35a.9999-4T that the purchaser is not a United States person (provided that the issuer has no actual knowledge that the documentary evidence is false) or on delivery of the obligation the issuer receives a statement signed by the person entitled to physical delivery thereof and stating either that the obligation is not being acquired by or on behalf of a United States person or that, if a beneficial interest in the obligation is being acquired by a United States person, such person is a financial institution as defined in § 1.165-12(c)(v) or is acquiring through a financial institution and the obligation is held by a financial institution that has agreed to comply with the requirements of 165 (j)(3)(A), (B), or (C) and the regulations thereunder and that it is not purchasing for offer to resell or for resale inside the United States (provided that the issuer has no actual knowledge that the statement is false).

In addition, an issuer that is a controlled foreign corporation within the meaning of section 957(a) that is engaged in the active conduct of a banking business outside the United States within the meaning of section 954(c)(3)(B) as in effect before the Tax Reform Act of 1986, and the regulations thereunder, can only satisfy the provisions of this paragraph (c)(2)(i)(C), if it meets the requirements of this paragraph (c)(2)(i)(C)(2), (3) and (4).

(D) The obligation is issued after September 7, 1990, and all of the conditions set forth in this paragraph (c)(2)(i)(D) are met with respect to such obligation.

(1) *Offers and sales.—(i) Issuer.*—The issuer does not offer or sell the obligation during the restricted period to a person who is within the United States or its possessions or to a United States person.

(ii) *Distributors.—(A)* The distributor of the obligation does not offer or sell the obligation during the restricted period to a person who is within the United States or its possessions or to a United States person.

(B) The distributor of the obligation will be deemed to satisfy the requirements of paragraph (c)(2)(i)(D)(1)(ii)(A) of this section if the distributor of the obligation covenants that it will not offer or sell the obligation during the restricted period to a person who is within the United States or its possessions or to a United States person; and the distributor of the obligation has in effect, in connection with the offer and sale of the obligation during the restricted period, procedures reasonably designed to ensure that its employees or agents who are directly engaged in selling the obligation are aware that the obligation cannot be offered or sold during the restricted period to a person who is within the United States or its possessions or is a United States person.

(iii) *Certain rules.*—For purposes of paragraph (c)(2)(i)(D)(1)(i) and (ii) of this section:

(A) An offer or sale will be considered to be made to a person who is within the United States or its possessions if the offeror or seller of the obligation has an address within the United States or its possessions for the offeree or buyer of the obligation with respect to the offer or sale.

(B) An offer or sale of an obligation will not be treated as made to a person within the United States or its possessions or to a United States person if the person to whom the offer or sale is made is: An exempt distributor, as defined in paragraph (c)(2)(i)(D)(5) of this section; An international organization as defined in section 7701(a)(18) and the regulations thereunder, or a foreign central bank as defined in section 895 and the regulations thereunder, or the foreign branch of a United States financial institution as described in paragraph (c)(2)(i)(D)(6)(i) of this section. Paragraph (c)(2)(i)(D)(1)(iii)(B) regarding an exempt distributor will only apply to an offer to the United States office of an exempt distributor, and paragraph (c)(2)(i)(D)(1)(iii)(B) regarding an international organization or foreign central bank will only apply to an offer to an international organization or foreign central bank, if such offer is made directly and specifically to the United States office, organization or bank.

(C) A sale of an obligation will not be treated as made to a person within the United States or its possessions or to a *United States person if the person to whom the sale is made is a* person described in paragraph (c)(2)(i)(D)(6)(ii) of this section.

(2) *Delivery.*—In connection with the sale of the obligation during the restricted period, neither the issuer nor any distribu-

tor delivers the obligation in definitive form within the United States or its possessions.

(3) *Certification.—(i) In general.*—On the earlier of the date of the first actual payment of interest by the issuer on the obligation or the date of delivery by the issuer of the obligation in definitive form, a certificate is provided to the issuer of the obligation stating that on such date:

(A) The obligation is owned by a person that is not a United States person;

(B) The obligation is owned by a United States person described in paragraph (c)(2)(i)(D)(6) of this section; or

(C) The obligation is owned by a financial institution for purposes of resale during the restricted period, and such financial institution certifies in addition that it has not acquired the obligation for purposes of resale directly or indirectly to a United States person or to a person within the United States or its possessions.

A certificate described in paragraph (c)(2)(i)(D)(3)(i)(A) or (B) of this section may not be given with respect to an obligation that is owned by a financial institution for purposes of resale during the restricted period. For purposes of paragraph (c)(2)(i)(D)(2) and (3) of this section, a temporary global security (as defined in § 1.163-5(c)(1)(ii)(B)) is not considered to be an obligation in definitive form. If the issuer does not make the obligation available for delivery in definitive form within a reasonable period of time after the end of the restricted period, then the obligation shall be treated as not satisfying the requirements of this paragraph (c)(2)(i)(D)(3). The certificate must be signed (or sent, as provided in paragraph (c)(2)(i)(D)(3)(ii) of this section) either by the owner of the obligation or by a financial institution or clearing organization through which the owner holds the obligation, directly or indirectly. For purposes of this paragraph (c)(2)(i)(D)(3), the term "financial institution" means a financial institution described in § 1.165-12(c)(1)(v). When a certificate is provided by a clearing organization, the certificate must be based on statements provided to it by its member organizations. The requirement of this paragraph (c)(1)(D)(3) shall be deemed not to be satisfied with respect to an obligation if the issuer knows or has reason to know that the certificate with respect to such obligation is false. The certificate must be retained by the issuer (and statements by member organizations must be retained by the clearing organization, in the case of certificates based on such statements) for a period of four calendar years following the year in which the certificate is received.

(ii) *Electronic certification.*—The certificate required by paragraph (c)(2)(i)(D)(3)(i) of this section (including a statement provided to a clearing organization by a member organization) may be provided electronically, but only if the person receiving such electronic certificate maintains adequate records, for the retention period described in paragraph (c)(2)(i)(D)(3)(i) of this section, establishing that such certificate was received in respect of the subject obligation, and only if there is a written agreement entered into prior to the time of certification (including the written membership rules of a clearing organization) to which the sender and recipient are subject, providing that the electronic certificate shall have the effect of a signed certificate described in paragraph (c)(2)(i)(D)(3)(i) of this section.

(iii) *Exception for certain obligations.*—This paragraph (c)(2)(i)(D)(3) shall not apply, and no certificate shall be required, in the case of an obligation that is sold during the restricted period and that satisfies all of the following requirements:

(A) The interest and principal with respect to the obligation are denominated only in the currency of a single foreign country.

(B) The interest and principal with respect to the obligation are payable only within that foreign country (according to rules similar to those set forth in § 1.163-5(c)(2)(v)).

(C) The obligation is offered and sold in accordance with practices and documentation customary in that foreign country.

(D) The distributor covenants to use reasonable efforts to sell the obligation within that foreign country.

(E) The obligation is not listed, or the subject of an application for listing, on an exchange located outside that foreign country.

(F) The Commissioner has designated that foreign country as a foreign country in which certification under paragraph (c)(2)(i)(D)(3)(i) of this section is not permissible.

(G) The issuance of the obligation is subject to guidelines or restrictions imposed by governmental, banking or securities authorities in that foreign country.

(H) More than 80 percent by value of the obligations included in the offering of which the obligation is a part are offered and sold to non-distributors by distributors maintaining an office located in that foreign country. Foreign currency denominated obligations that are convertible into U.S. dollar denominated obligations

Itemized Deductions for Individuals and Corps.
See p. 20,601 for regulations not amended to reflect law changes
25,287

or that by their terms are linked to the U.S. dollar in a way which effectively converts the obligations to U.S. dollar denominated obligations do not satisfy the requirements of this paragraph (c)(2)(i)(D)(3)(iii). A foreign currency denominated obligation will not be treated as linked, by its terms, to the U.S. dollar solely because the obligation is the subject of a swap transaction.

(4) *Distributor.*—For purposes of this paragraph (c)(2)(i)(D), the term "distributor" means:

(i) a person that offers or sells the obligation during the restricted period pursuant to a written contract with the issuer;

(ii) any person that offers or sells the obligation during the restricted period pursuant to a written contract with a person described in paragraph (c)(2)(i)(D)(4)(i); and

(iii) any affiliate that acquires the obligation from another member of its affiliated group for the purpose of offering or selling the obligation during the restricted period, but only if the transferor member of the group is the issuer or a person described in paragraph (c)(2)(i)(D)(4)(i) or (ii) of this section. The terms "affiliate" and "affiliated group" have the same meanings as in section 1504(a) of the Code, but without regard to the exceptions contained in section 1504(b) and substituting "50 percent" for "80 percent" each time it appears.

For purposes of this paragraph (c)(2)(i)(D)(4), a written contract does not include a confirmation or other notice of the transaction.

(5) *Exempt distributor.*—For purposes of this paragraph (c)(2)(i)(D), the term "exempt distributor" means a distributor that covenants in its contract with the issuer or with a distributor described in paragraph (c)(2)(i)(D)(4)(i) that it is buying the obligation for the purpose of resale in connection with the original issuance of the obligation, and that if it retains the obligation for its own account, it will only do so in accordance with the requirements of paragraph (c)(2)(i)(D)(6) of this section. In the latter case, the covenant will constitute the certificate required under paragraph (c)(2)(i)(D)(6). The provisions of paragraph (c)(2)(i)(D)(7) governing the restricted period for unsold allotments or subscriptions shall apply to any obligation retained for investment by an exempt distributor.

(6) *Certain United States persons.*—A person is described in this paragraph (c)(2)(i)(D)(6) if the requirements of this paragraph are satisfied and the person is:

(i) The foreign branch of a United States financial institution purchasing for its own account or for resale, or

(ii) A United States person who acquired the obligation through the foreign branch of a United States financial institution and who, for purposes of the certification required in paragraph (c)(2)(i)(D)(3) of this section, holds the obligation through such financial institution on the date of certification.

For purposes of paragraph (c)(2)(i)(D)(6)(ii) of this section, a United States person will be considered to acquire and hold an obligation through the foreign branch of a United States financial institution if the United States person has an account with the United States office of a financial institution, and the transaction is executed by a foreign office of that financial institution, or by the foreign office of another financial institution acting on behalf of that financial institution. This paragraph (c)(2)(i)(D)(6) will apply, however, only if the United States financial institution (or the United States office of a foreign financial institution) holding the obligation provides a certificate to the issuer or distributor selling the obligation within a reasonable time stating that it agrees to comply with the requirements of section 165(j)(3)(A), (B), or (C) and the regulations thereunder. For purposes of this paragraph (c)(2)(i)(D)(6), the term "financial institution" means a financial institution as defined in §1.165-12(c)(1)(v). As an alternative to the certification required above, a financial institution may provide a blanket certificate to the issuer or distributor selling the obligation stating that the financial institution will comply with the requirements of section 165(j)(3)(A), (B) or (C) and the regulations thereunder. A blanket certificate must be received by the issuer or the distributor in the year of the issuance of the obligation or in either of the preceding two calendar years, and must be retained by the issuer or distributor for at least four years after the end of the last calendar year to which it relates.

(7) *Restricted period.*—For purposes of this paragraph (c)(2)(i)(D), the restricted period with respect to an obligation begins on the earlier of the closing date (or the date on which the issuer receives the loan proceeds, if there is no closing with respect to the obligation), or the first date on which the obligation is offered to persons other than a distributor. The restricted period with respect to an obligation ends on the expiration of the forty day period beginning on the closing date (or the date on which the issuer receives the loan proceeds, if there is no closing with respect to the obligation). Notwithstanding the preceding sentence, any offer or sale of the obligation by the issuer or a distributor shall be deemed to be during the restricted period if the issuer or distributor holds the obligation as part of an unsold allotment or subscription.

(8) *Clearing organization.*—For purposes of this paragraph (c)(2)(i)(D), a "clearing organization" is an entity which is in the business of holding obligations for member organizations and transferring obligations among such members by credit or debit to the account of a member without the necessity of physical delivery of the obligation.

(ii) *Special rules.*—An obligation shall not be considered to be described in paragraph (c)(2)(i)(C) of this section if it is—

(A) Guaranteed by a United States shareholder of the issuer;

(B) Convertible into a debt or equity interest in a United States shareholder of the issuer; or

(C) Substantially identical to an obligation issued by a United States shareholder of the issuer.

For purposes of this paragraph (c)(2)(ii), the term "United States shareholder" is defined as it is defined in section 951(b) and the regulations thereunder. For purposes of this paragraph (c)(2)(ii)(C), obligations are substantially identical if the face amount, interest rate, term of the issue, due dates for payments, and maturity date of each is substantially identical to the other.

(iii) *Interstate commerce.*—For purposes of this paragraph, the term "interstate commerce" means trade or commerce in obligations or any transportation or communication relating thereto between any foreign country and the United States or its possessions.

(A) An issuer will not be considered to engage significantly in interstate commerce with respect to the issuance of an obligation if the only activities with respect to which the issuer uses the means or instrumentalities of interstate commerce are activities of a preparatory or auxiliary character that do not involve communication between a prospective purchaser and an issuer, its agent, an underwriter, or member of the selling group if either is inside the United States or its possessions. Activities of a preparatory or auxiliary character include, but are not limited to, the following activities:

(1) Establishment or participation in establishment of policies concerning the issuance of obligations and the allocation of funding by a United States shareholder with respect to obligations issued by a foreign corporation or by a United States office with respect to obligations issued by a foreign branch;

(2) Negotiation between the issuer and underwriters as to the terms and pricing of an issue

(3) Transfer of funds to an office of an issuer in the United States or its possessions by a foreign branch or to a United States shareholder by a foreign corporation;

(4) Consultation by an issuer with accountants and lawyers or other financial advisors in the United States or its possessions regarding the issuance of an obligation;

(5) Document drafting and printing; and

(6) Provision of payment or delivery instructions to members of the selling group by an issuer's office or agent that is located in the United States or its possessions.

(B) Activities that will not be considered to be of a preparatory or auxiliary character include, but are not limited to, any of the following activities:

(1) Negotiation or communication between a prospective purchaser and an issuer, its agent, an underwriter, or a member of the selling group concerning the sale of an obligation if either is inside the United States or its possessions;

(2) Involvement of an issuer's office, its agent, an underwriter, or a member of the selling group in the United States or its possessions in the offer or sale of a particular obligation, either directly with the prospective purchaser, or through the issuer in a foreign country;

(3) Delivery of an obligation in the United States or its possessions; or

(4) Advertising or otherwise promoting an obligation in the United States or its possessions.

(C) The following examples illustrate the application of this subdivision (iii) of §1.163-5(c)(2).

Example (1). Foreign corporation A, a corporation organized in and doing business in foreign country Z, and not a controlled foreign corporation within the meaning of section 957(a) that is engaged in the conduct of a banking business within the meaning of section 954(c)(3)(B) as in effect before the Tax Reform Act of 1986, issues its debentures outside the United States. The debentures are not guaranteed by a United States shareholder of A, nor are they convertible into a debt or equity interest of a United States shareholder of A, nor are they substantially identical to an obligation issued by a United States shareholder of A. A consults its accountants and lawyers in the United States for certain securities and tax advice regarding the debt offering. The underwriting and selling group in respect of A's offering is composed entirely of foreign securities firms, some of which are foreign subsidiaries of United States securities firms. A U.S. affiliate of the foreign underwriter communicates payment and delivery instruction to the selling group. All offering circulars for the offering are mailed and delivered outside the United States and its possessions. All debentures are delivered and paid for outside the United States and its possessions. No office located in the United States or in a United States possession is involved in the sale of debentures. Interest on the debentures is payable only outside the United States and its possessions. A is not significantly engaged in interstate commerce with respect to the offering.

Example (2). B, a United States bank, does business in foreign country X through a branch located in X. The branch is a staffed and operating unit engaged in the active conduct of a banking business consisting of one or more of the activities set forth in §1.954-2(d)(2)(ii). As part of its ongoing business, the branch in X issues negotiable certificates of deposit with a maturity in excess of one year to customers upon request. The certificates of deposit are not guaranteed by a United States shareholder of B, nor are they convertible into a debt or equity interest of a United States shareholder of B, nor are they substantially identical to an obligation issued by a United States shareholder of B. Policies regarding the issuance of negotiable certificates of deposit and funding allocations for foreign branches are set in the United States at B's main office. Branch personnel decide whether to issue a negotiable certificate of deposit based on the guidelines established by the United States offices of B, but without communicating with the United States offices of B with respect to the issuance of a particular obligation. Negotiable certificates of deposits are delivered and paid for outside the United States and its possessions. Interest on the negotiable certificates of deposit is payable only outside the United States and its possessions. B maintains documentary evidence described in §1.163-5(c)(2)(i)(C)(4). After the issuance of negotiable certificates of deposit by the foreign branch of B, the foreign branch sends the funds to a United States branch of B for use in domestic operations. B is not significantly engaged in interstate commerce with respect to the issuance of such obligation.

Example (3). The facts in Example (2) apply except that the foreign branch of B consulted, by telephone, the main office in the United States to request approval of the issuance of the certificate of deposit at a particular rate of interest. The main office granted permission to issue the negotiable certificate of deposit to the customer by a telex sent from the main office of B to the branch in X. B is significantly engaged in interstate commerce with respect to the issuance of the obligation as a result of the involvement of B's United States office in the issuance of the obligation.

Example (4). The facts in Example (2) apply with the additional fact that a customer contacted the foreign branch of B through a telex originating in the United States or its possessions. Subsequent to the telex, the foreign branch issued the negotiable certificate of deposit and recorded it on the books. B is significantly engaged in interstate commerce with respect to the issuance of the obligation as a result of its communication by telex with a customer in the United States.

(iv) *Possessions.*—For purposes of this section, the term "possessions" includes Puerto Rico, the U.S. Virgin Islands, Guam, American Samoa, Wake Island, and Northern Mariana Islands.

(v) *Interest payable outside of the United States.*—Interest will be considered payable only outside the United States and its possessions if payment of such interest can be made only upon presentation of a coupon, or upon making of any other demand for payment, outside of the United States and its possessions to the issuer or a paying agent. The fact that payment is made by a draft drawn on a United States bank account or by a wire or other electronic transfer from a United States account does not affect this result. Interest payments will be considered to be made within the United States if the payments are made by a transfer of funds into an account maintained by the payee in the United States or mailed to an address in the United States, if—

(A) The interest is paid on an obligation issued by either a United States person, a controlled foreign corporation as defined in section 957(a), or a foreign corporation if 50 percent or more of the gross income of the foreign corporation from all sources of the 3-year period ending with the close of its taxable year preceding the original issuance of the obligation (or for such part of the period that the foreign corporation has been in existence) was effectively connected *with the conduct of a trade or business within the United States; and*

(B) The interest is paid to a person other than—

(1) A person who may satisfy the requirements of section 165(j)(3)(A), (B), or (C) and the regulations thereunder; and

(2) A financial institution as a step in the clearance of funds and such interest is promptly credited to an account maintained outside the United States for such financial institution or for persons for which the financial institution has collected such interest.

Interest is considered to be paid within the United States and its possessions if a coupon is presented, or a demand for payment is otherwise made, to the issuer or a paying agent (whether a United States or foreign person) in the United States and its possessions even if the funds paid are credited to an account maintained by the payee outside the United States and its possessions. Interest will be considered payable only outside the United States and its possessions notwithstanding that such interest may become payable at the office of the issuer or its United States paying agent under the following conditions: the issuer has appointed paying agents located outside the United States and its possessions with the reasonable expectation that such paying agents will be able to pay the interest in United States dollars, and the full amount of such payment at the offices of all such paying agents is illegal or effectively precluded because of the imposition of exchange controls or other similar restrictions on the full payment or receipt of interest in United States dollars. A lawsuit brought in the United States or its possessions for payment of the obligation or interest thereon as a result of a default shall not be considered to be a demand for payment. For purposes of this subdivision (v), interest includes original issue discount as defined in section 1273(a). Therefore, an amount equal to the original issue discount as defined in section 1273(a) is payable only outside the United States and its possessions. The amount of market discount as defined in section 1278(a) does not affect the amount of interest to be considered payable only outside the United States and its possessions.

(vi) *Rules relating to obligations issued after December 31, 1982 and on or before September 21, 1984.*—Whether an obligation originally issued after December 31, 1982 and on or before September 21, 1984, or an obligation originally issued after September 21, 1984 pursuant to the exercise of a warrant or the conversion of a convertible obligation, which warrant or obligation (including conversion privilege) was issued after December 31, 1982 and on or before September 21, 1984, is described in section 163(f)(2)(B) shall be determined under the rules provided in §5f.163-1(c) as in effect prior to its removal. Notwithstanding the preceding sentence, an issuer will be considered to satisfy the requirements of section 163(f)(2)(B) with respect to an obligation issued after December 31, 1982 and on or before September 21, 1984 or after September 21, 1984 pursuant to the exercise of a warrant or the conversion of a convertible obligation, which warrant or obligation (including conversion privilege) was issued after December 31, 1982 and on or before September 21, 1984, if the issuer substantially complied with the proposed regulations provided in §1.163-5(c), which were published in the Federal Register on September 2, 1983 (48 FR 39953) and superseded by temporary regulations published in the Federal Register on August 22, 1984 (49 FR 33228).

(3) *Effective date.*—(i) *In general.*—These regulations apply generally to obligations issued after January 20, 1987. A taxpayer may choose to apply the rules of §1.163-5(c) with respect to an obligation issued after December 31, 1982 and on or before January 20, 1987. If this choice is made, the rules of §1.163-5(c) will apply in lieu of §1.163-5T(c) except that the legend requirement under §1.163-5(c)(1)(ii)(B) does not apply with respect to a bearer obligation evidenced exclusively by a book entry and that the certification requirement under §1.163-5T(c)(2)(i)(B)(4) applies in lieu of the certification under §1.163-5(c)(2)(i)(B)(4).

(ii) *Special rules.*—If an obligation is originally issued after September 7, 1990 pursuant to the exercise of a warrant or the conversion of a convertible obligation, which warrant or obligation (including conversion privilege) was issued on or before May 10, 1990, then the issuer may choose to apply either the rules of §1.163-5(c)(2)(i)(A) or §1.163-5(c)(2)(i)(B), or the rules of §1.163-5(c)(2)(i)(D). The issuer of an obligation may choose to apply either the rules of §1.163-5(c)(2)(i)(A) or (B), or the rules of §1.163-5(c)(2)(i)(D), to an obligation that is originally issued after May 10, 1990, and on or before September 7, 1990. However, any issuer choosing to apply the rules of §1.163-5(c)(2)(i)(A) must apply the definition of United States person used for such purposes on December 31, 1989, and must obtain any certificates that would have been required under applicable law on December 31, 1989. [Reg. §1.163-5.]

☐ [T.D. 8110, 12-16-86. *Amended by* T.D. 8203, 5-19-88; T.D. 8300, 5-9-90 *and* T.D. 8734, 10-6-97 (T.D. 8804 delayed the effective date of T.D. 8734 from January 1, 1999, to January 1, 2000; T.D. 8856 further delayed the effective date of T.D. 8734 until January 1, 2001).]

Itemized Deductions for Individuals and Corps.
See p. 20,601 for regulations not amended to reflect law changes

25,289

[Reg. §1.163-5T]

§1.163-5T. Denial of interest deduction on certain obligations issued after December 31, 1982, unless issued in registered form (Temporary).—

(a) [Reserved]

(b) [Reserved]

(c) [Reserved]

(d) *Pass-through certificates.*—(1) A pass-through or participation certificate evidencing an interest in a pool of mortgage loans which under Subpart E of Subchapter J of the Code is treated as a trust of which the grantor is the owner (or similar evidence of interest in a similar pooled fund or pooled trust treated as a grantor trust) ("pass-through certificate") is considered to be a "registration-required obligation" under section 163(f)(2)(A) and §1.163-5(c) if the pass-through certificate is described in section 163(f)(2)(A) and §1.163-5(c) without regard to whether any obligation held by the fund or trust to which the pass-through certificate relates is described in section 163(f)(2)(A) and §1.163-5(c). A pass-through certificate is considered to be described in section 163(f)(2)(B) and §1.163-5(c) if the pass-through certificate is described in section 163(f)(2)(B) and §1.163-5(c) without regard to whether any obligation held by the fund or trust to which the pass-through certificate relates is described in section 163(f)(2)(B) and §1.163-5(c).

(2) An obligation held by a fund or trust in which ownership interests are represented by pass-through certificates is considered to be in registered form under section 149(a) and the regulations thereunder or to be described in section 163(f)(2)(A) or (B), if the obligation held by the fund or trust is in registered form under section 149(a) and the regulations thereunder or is described in section 163(f)(2)(A) or (B), respectively, without regard to whether the pass-through certificates are so considered.

(3) For purposes of section 4701, a pass-through certificate is considered to be issued solely by the recipient of the proceeds from the issuance of the pass-through certificate (hereinafter the "sponsor"). The sponsor is therefore liable for any excise tax under section 4701 that may be imposed with reference to the principal amount of the pass-through certificate.

(4) In order to implement the purpose of section 163, §1.163-5(c) and this section, the Commissioner may characterize a certificate or other evidence of interest in a fund or trust which under Subpart E of Subchapter J of the Code is treated as a trust of which the grantor is the owner and any obligation held by such fund or trust in accordance with the substance of the arrangement they represent and may impose the penalties provided under section 163(f)(1) and 4701 in the appropriate amounts and on the appropriate persons. This provision may be applied, for example, where a corporation issues obligations purportedly in registered form, contributes them to a grantor trust as its only assets, and arranges for the sale to investors of bearer certificates of interest in the trust which do not meet the requirements of section 163(f)(2)(B). If this provision is applied, the obligations held by the fund or trust will not be considered to be issued in registered form or to meet the requirements of section 163(f)(2)(B). The corporation will not be allowed a deduction for the payment of interest on the obligations held by the trust, and the excise tax under section 4701, calculated with reference to the principal amount of the obligations held by the trust will be imposed on the corporation may be collected from the corporation and its agents. This paragraph (d)(4) will not be applied so as to alter the tax consequences of transactions as to which rulings have been issued by the Internal Revenue Service prior to September 19, 1985.

(5) The rules set forth in this paragraph (d) apply solely for purposes of sections 4701, 163(f)(2)(A), 163(f)(2)(B), §1.163-5(c), and any other section that refers to this section for the definition of the term "registration-required obligation" (such as the regulations under sections 871(h) and 881(c)). The treatment of obligations described in this paragraph (d) for purposes of section 163(f)(2)(A) and (B) does not affect the determination of whether bearer obligations that are issued or guaranteed by the United States Government, a United States Government-owned agency, a United States Government sponsored enterprise (within the meaning of §1.163-5(c)(1)) or that are backed (as described in the Treasury Department News *Release R-2835* of September 10, 1984 and Treasury Department News *Release R-2847 of September 14, 1984*) by obligations issued by the United States Government, a United States Government-owned agency, or a United States Government sponsored enterprise comply with the requirements of section 163(f)(2)(B) and the regulations thereunder.

(6) The provisions of this paragraph (d)(1) through (5) may be illustrated by the following example:

Commercial Bank K forms a pool of 1000 residential mortgage loans, each made to a different individual homeowner, by assigning them to Commercial Bank L, an unrelated entity serving as trustee of the pool. Commercial Bank L immediately sells in a public offering certificates of interest in the trust of a maturity of 10 years in registered form. Commercial Bank L transfers the cash proceeds of the offering to Commercial Bank K. The certificates of interest in the trust are of a type offered to the public and are not described in section 163(f)(2)(B). Pursuant to paragraph (d)(1), the certificates of interest in the pool are registration-required obligations without regard to the fact that the obligations held by the trust are not registration-required obligations.

(e) *Regular interests in REMICs.*—(1) A regular interest in a REMIC, as defined in sections 860D and 860G and the regulations thereunder, is considered to be a "registration-required obligation" under section 163(f)(2)(A) and §1.163-5(c) if the regular interest is described in section 163(f)(2)(A) and §1.163-5(c), without regard to whether any obligation held by the REMIC to which the regular interest relates is described in section 163(f)(2)(A) and §1.163-5(c). A regular interest in a REMIC is considered to be described in section 163(f)(2)(B) and §1.163-5(c), if the regular interest is described in section 163(f)(2)(B) and §1.163(c), without regard to whether any obligation held by the REMIC to which the regular interest relates is described in section 163(f)(2)(B) and §1.163-5(c).

(2) An obligation held by a REMIC is considered to be described in section 163(f)(2)(A) or (B) if such obligation is described in section 163(f)(2)(A) or (B), respectively, without regard to whether the regular interests in the REMIC are so considered.

(3) For purposes of section 4701, a regular interest is considered to be issued solely by the recipient of the proceeds from the issuance of the regular interest (hereinafter the "sponsor"). The sponsor is therefore liable for any excise tax under section 4701 that may be imposed with reference to the principal amount of the regular interest.

(4) In order to implement the purpose of section 163, §1.163-5(c), and this section, the Commissioner may characterize a regular interest in a REMIC and any obligation held by such REMIC in accordance with the substance of the arrangement they represent and may impose the penalties provided under sections 163(f)(1) and 4701 in the appropriate amounts and on the appropriate persons. This provision may be applied, for example, where a corporation issues an obligation that is purportedly in registered form and that will qualify as a "qualified mortgage" within the meaning of section 860G(a)(3) in the hands of a REMIC, contributes the obligation to a REMIC as its only asset, and arranges for the sale to investors of regular interests in the REMIC in bearer form that do not meet the requirements of section 163(f)(2)(B). If this provision is applied, the obligation held by the REMIC will not be considered to be issued in registered form or to meet the requirements of section 163(f)(2)(B). The corporation will not be allowed a deduction for the payment of interest on the obligation held by the REMIC, and the excise tax under section 4701, calculated with reference to the principal amount of the obligation held by the REMIC, will be imposed on the corporation and may be collected from the corporation and its agents. [Temporary Reg. §1.163-5T.]

☐ [*T.D.* 8202, 5-18-88. *Amended by T.D.* 8300, 5-9-90.]

[Reg. §1.163-6T]

§1.163-6T. Reduction of deduction where section 25 credit taken (Temporary).—(a) *In general.*—The amount of the deduction under section 163 for interest paid or accrued during any taxable year on a certified indebtedness amount with respect to a mortgage credit certificate which has been issued under section 25 shall be reduced by the amount of the credit allowable with respect to such interest under section 25 (determined without regard to section 26).

(b) *Cross reference.*—See §§1.25-1T through 1.25-8T with respect to rules relating to mortgage credit certificates. [Temporary Reg. §1.163-6T.]

☐ [*T.D.* 8023, 5-3-85.]

[Reg. §1.163-7]

§1.163-7. Deduction for OID on certain debt instruments.—(a) *General rule.*—Except as otherwise provided in paragraph (b) of this section, an issuer (including a transferee) determines the amount of OID that is deductible each year under section 163(e)(1) by using the constant yield method described in §1.1272-1(b). This determination, however, is made without regard to section 1272(a)(7) (relating to acquisition premium) and §1.1273-1(d) (relating to de minimis OID). An issuer is permitted a deduction under section 163(e)(1) only to the extent the issuer is primarily liable on the debt instrument. For certain limitations on the deductibility of OID, see sections 163(e) and 1275(b)(2). To determine the amount of interest (OID) that is deductible each year on a debt instrument that provides for contingent payments, see §1.1275-4.

(b) *Special rules for de minimis OID.*—(1) *Stated interest.*—If a debt instrument has a de minimis amount of OID (within the meaning of

§ 1.1273-1(d)), the issuer treats all stated interest on the debt instrument as qualified stated interest. See §§ 1.446-2(b) and 1.461-1 for the treatment of qualified stated interest.

(2) *Deduction of de minimis OID on other than a constant yield basis.*—In lieu of deducting de minimis OID under the general rule of paragraph (a) of this section, an issuer of a debt instrument with a de minimis amount of OID (other than a de minimis amount treated as qualified stated interest under paragraph (b)(1) of this section) may choose to deduct the OID at maturity, on a straight-line basis over the term of the debt instrument, or in proportion to stated interest payments. The issuer makes this choice by reporting the de minimis OID in a manner consistent with the method chosen on the issuer's timely filed Federal income tax return for the taxable year in which the debt instrument is issued.

(c) *Deduction upon repurchase.*—Except to the extent disallowed by any other section of the Internal Revenue Code (e.g., section 249) or this paragraph (c), if a debt instrument is repurchased by the issuer for a price in excess of its adjusted issue price (as defined in § 1.1275-1(b)), the excess (repurchase premium) is deductible as interest for the taxable year in which the repurchase occurs. If the issuer repurchases a debt instrument in a debt-for-debt exchange, the repurchase price is the issue price of the newly issued debt instrument (reduced by any unstated interest within the meaning of section 483). However, if the issue price of the newly issued debt instrument is determined under either section 1273(b)(4) or section 1274, any repurchase premium is not deductible in the year of the repurchase, but is amortized over the term of the newly issued debt instrument in the same manner as if it were OID.

(d) *Choice of accrual periods to determine whether a debt instrument is an applicable high yield discount obligation (AHYDO).*—Section 163(e)(5) affects an issuer's OID deductions for certain high yield debt instruments that have significant OID. For purposes of section 163(i)(2), which defines significant OID, the issuer's choice of accrual periods to determine OID accruals is used to determine whether a debt instrument has significant OID. See § 1.1275-2(e) for rules relating to the issuer's obligation to disclose certain information to holders.

(e) *Qualified reopening.*—(1) *In general.*—In a qualified reopening of an issue of debt instruments, if a holder pays more or less than the adjusted issue price of the original debt instruments to acquire an additional debt instrument, the issuer treats this difference as an adjustment to the issuer's interest expense for the original and additional debt instruments. As provided by paragraphs (e)(2) through (5) of this section, the adjustment is taken into account over the term of the instrument using constant yield principles.

(2) *Positive adjustment.*—If the difference is positive (that is, the holder pays more than the adjusted issue price of the original debt instrument), then, with respect to the issuer but not the holder, the difference increases the aggregate adjusted issue prices of all of the debt instruments in the issue, both original and additional.

(3) *Negative adjustment.*—If the difference is negative (that is, the holder pays less than the adjusted issue price of the original debt instrument), then, with respect to the issuer but not the holder, the difference reduces the aggregate adjusted issue prices of all of the debt instruments in the issue, both original and additional.

(4) *Determination of issuer's interest accruals.*—As of the reopening date, the issuer must redetermine the yield of the debt instruments in the issue for purposes of applying the constant yield method described in § 1.1272-1(b) to determine the issuer's accruals of interest expense over the remaining term of the debt instruments in the issue. This redetermined yield is based on the aggregate adjusted issue prices of the debt instruments in the issue (as determined under this paragraph (e)) and the remaining payment schedule of the debt instruments in the issue. If the aggregate adjusted issue prices of the debt instruments in the issue (as determined under this paragraph (e)) are less than the aggregate stated redemption price at maturity of the instruments (determined as of the reopening date) by a de minimis amount (within the meaning of § 1.1273-1(d)), the issuer may use the rules in paragraph (b) of this section to determine the issuer's accruals of interest expense.

(5) *Effect of adjustments on issuer's adjusted issue price.*—The adjustments made under this paragraph (e) are taken into account for purposes of determining the issuer's adjusted issue price under § 1.1275-1(b).

(6) *Definitions.*—The terms *additional debt instrument, original debt instrument, qualified reopening,* and *reopening date* have the same meanings as in § 1.1275-2(k).

(f) *Effective dates.*—This section (other than paragraph (e) of this section) applies to debt instruments issued on or after April 4, 1994.

Taxpayers, however, may rely on this section (other than paragraph (e) of this section) for debt instruments issued after December 21, 1992, and before April 4, 1994. Paragraph (e) of this section applies to qualified reopenings where the reopening date is on or after March 13, 2001. [Reg. § 1.163-7.]

☐ [*T.D. 8517, 1-27-94. Amended by T.D. 8674, 6-11-96 and T.D. 8934, 1-11-2001.*]

[Reg. § 1.163-8T]

§ 1.163-8T. Allocation of interest expense among expenditures (temporary).—(a) *In general.*—(1) *Application.*—This section prescribes rules for allocating interest expense for purposes of applying sections 469 (the "passive loss limitation") and 163(d) and (h) (the "nonbusiness interest limitations").

(2) *Cross-references.*—This paragraph provides an overview of the manner in which interest expense is allocated for the purposes of applying the passive loss limitation and nonbusiness interest limitations and the manner in which interest expense allocated under this section is treated. See paragraph (b) of this section for definitions of certain terms, paragraph (c) for the rules for allocating debt and interest expense among expenditures, paragraphs (d) and (e) for the treatment of debt repayments and refinancings, paragraph (j) for the rules for reallocating debt upon the occurrence of certain events, paragraph (m) for the coordination of the rules in this section with other limitations on the deductibility of interest expense, and paragraph (n) of this section for effective date and transitional rules.

(3) *Manner of allocation.*—In general, interest expense on a debt is allocated in the same manner as the debt to which such interest expense relates is allocated. Debt is allocated by tracing disbursements of the debt proceeds to specific expenditures. This section prescribes rules for tracing debt proceeds to specific expenditures.

(4) *Treatment of interest expense.*—(i) *General rule.*—Except as otherwise provided in paragraph (m) of this section (relating to limitations on interest expense other than the passive loss and nonbusiness interest limitations), interest expense allocated under the rules of this section is treated in the following manner:

(A) Interest expense allocated to a trade or business expenditure (as defined in paragraph (b)(7) of this section) is taken into account under section 163(h)(2)(A);

(B) Interest expense allocated to a passive activity expenditure (as defined in paragraph (b)(4) of this section) or a former passive activity expenditure (as defined in paragraph (b)(2) of this section) is taken into account for purposes of section 469 in determining the income or loss from the activity to which such expenditure relates;

(C) Interest expense allocated to an investment expenditure (as defined in paragraph (b)(3) of this section) is treated for purposes of section 163(d) as investment interest;

(D) Interest expense allocated to a personal expenditure (as defined in paragraph (b)(5) of this section) is treated for purposes of section 163(h) as personal interest; and

(E) Interest expense allocated to a portfolio expenditure (as defined in paragraph (b)(6) of this section) is treated for purposes of section 469(e)(2)(B)(ii) as interest expense described in section 469(e)(1)(A)(i)(III).

(ii) *Examples.*—The following examples illustrate the application of this paragraph (a)(4):

Example (1). Taxpayer A, an individual, incurs interest expense allocated under the rules of this section to the following expenditures:

$6,000	Passive activity expenditure
$4,000	Personal expenditure

The $6,000 interest expense allocated to the passive activity expenditure is taken into account for purposes of section 469 in computing A's income or loss from the activity to which such interest relates. Pursuant to section 163(h), A may not deduct the $4,000 interest expense allocated to the personal expenditure (except to the extent such interest is qualified residence interest, within the meaning of section 163(h)(3)).

Example (2). (i) Corporation M, a closely held C corporation (within the meaning of section 469(j)(1)) has $10,000 of interest expense for a taxable year. Under the rules of this section, M's interest expense is allocated to the following expenditures:

$2,000	Passive activity expenditure
$3,000	Portfolio expenditure
$5,000	Other expenditures

(ii) Under section 163(d)(3)(D) and this paragraph (a)(4), the $2,000 interest expense allocated to the passive activity expenditure is taken into account in computing M's passive activity loss for the taxable year, but, pursuant to section 469(e)(1) and this paragraph (a)(4), the interest expense allocated to the portfolio expenditure and the other expenditures is not taken into account for such purposes.

(iii) Since M is a closely held C corporation, its passive activity loss is allowable under section 469(e)(2)(A) as a deduction from net active income. Under section 469(e)(2)(B) and this paragraph (a)(4), the $5,000 interest expense allocated to other expenditures is taken into account in computing M's net active income, but the interest expense allocated to the passive activity expenditure and the portfolio expenditure is not taken into account for such purposes.

(iv) Since M is a corporation, the $3,000 interest expense allocated to the portfolio expenditure is allowable without regard to section 163(d). If M were an individual, however, the interest expense allocated to the portfolio expenditure would be treated as investment interest for purposes of applying the limitation of section 163(d).

(b) *Definitions.*—For purposes of this section—

(1) "Former passive activity" means an activity described in section 469(f)(3), but only if an unused deduction or credit (within the meaning of section 469(f)(1)(A) or (B)) is allocable to the activity under section 469(b) for the taxable year.

(2) "Former passive activity expenditure" means an expenditure that is taken into account under section 469 in computing the income or loss from a former passive activity of the taxpayer or an expenditure (including an expenditure properly chargeable to capital account) that would be so taken into account if such expenditure were otherwise deductible.

(3) "Investment expenditure" means an expenditure (other than a passive activity expenditure) properly chargeable to capital account with respect to property held for investment (within the meaning of section 163(d)(5)(A)) or an expenditure in connection with the holding of such property.

(4) "Passive activity expenditure" means an expenditure that is taken into account under section 469 in computing income or loss from a passive activity of the taxpayer or an expenditure (including an expenditure properly chargeable to capital account) that would be so taken into account if such expenditure were otherwise deductible. For purposes of this section, the term passive activity expenditure does not include any expenditure with respect to any low-income housing project in any taxable year in which any benefit is allowed with respect to such project under section 502 of the Tax Reform Act of 1986.

(5) "Personal expenditure" means an expenditure that is not a trade or business expenditure, a passive activity expenditure, or an investment expenditure.

(6) "Portfolio expenditure" means an investment expenditure properly chargeable to capital account with respect to property producing income of a type described in section 469(e)(1)(A) or an investment expenditure for an expense clearly and directly allocable to such income.

(7) "Trade or business expenditure" means an expenditure (other than a passive activity expenditure or an investment expenditure) in connection with the conduct of any trade or business other than the trade or business of performing service as an employee.

(c) *Allocation of debt and interest expense.*—(1) *Allocation in accordance with use of proceeds.*—Debt is allocated to expenditures in accordance with the use of the debt proceeds and, except as provided in paragraph (m) of this section, interest expense accruing on a debt during any period is allocated to expenditures in the same manner as the debt is allocated from time to time during such period. Except as provided in paragraph (m) of this section, debt proceeds and related interest expense are allocated solely by reference to the use of such proceeds, and the allocation is not affected by the use of an interest in any property to secure the repayment of such debt or interest. The following example illustrates the principles of this paragraph (c)(1):

Example. Taxpayer A, an individual, pledges corporate stock held for investment as security for a loan and uses the debt proceeds to purchase an automobile for personal use. Interest expense accruing on the debt is allocated to the personal expenditure to purchase the automobile even though the debt is secured by investment property.

(2) *Allocation period.*—(i) *Allocation of debt.*—Debt is allocated to an expenditure for the period beginning on the date the proceeds of the debt are used or treated as used under the rules of this section to make the expenditure and ending on the earlier of—

(A) The date the debt is repaid; or

(B) The date the debt is reallocated in accordance with the rules in paragraphs (c)(4) and (j) of this section.

(ii) *Allocation of interest expense.*—(A) *In general.*—Except as otherwise provided in paragraph (m) of this section, interest expense accruing on a debt for any period is allocated in the same manner as the debt is allocated from time to time, regardless of when the interest is paid.

(B) *Effect of compounding.*—Accrued interest is treated as a debt until it is paid and any interest accruing on unpaid interest is allocated in the same manner as the unpaid interest is allocated. For the taxable year in which a debt is reallocated under the rules in paragraphs (c)(4) and (j) of this section, however, compound interest accruing on such debt (other than compound interest accruing on interest that accrued before the beginning of the year) may be allocated between the original expenditure and the new expenditure on a straight-line basis (i.e., by allocating an equal amount of such interest expense to each day during the taxable year). In addition, a taxpayer may treat a year as consisting of 12 30-day months for purposes of allocating interest on a straight-line basis.

(C) *Accrual of interest expense.*—For purposes of this paragraph (c)(2)(ii), the amount of interest expense that accrues during any period is determined by taking into account relevant provisions of the loan agreement and any applicable law such as sections 163(e), 483, and 1271 through 1275.

(iii) *Examples.*—The following examples illustrate the principles of this paragraph (c)(2):

Example (1). (i) On January 1, taxpayer B, a calendar year taxpayer, borrows $1,000 at an interest rate of 11 percent, compounded semiannually. B immediately uses the debt proceeds to purchase an investment security. On July 1, B sells the investment security for $1,000 and uses the sales proceeds to make a passive activity expenditure. On December 31, B pays accrued interest on the $1,000 debt for the entire year.

(ii) Under this paragraph (c)(2) and paragraph (j) of this section, the $1,000 debt is allocated to the investment expenditure for the period from January 1 through June 30, and to the passive activity expenditure from July 1 through December 31. Interest expense accruing on the $1,000 debt is allocated in accordance with the allocation of the debt from time to time during the year even though the debt was allocated to the passive activity expenditure on the date the interest was paid. Thus, the $55 interest expense for the period from January 1 through June 30 is allocated to the investment expenditure. In addition, during the period from July 1 through December 31, the interest expense allocated to the investment expenditure is a debt, the proceeds of which are treated as used to make an investment expenditure. Accordingly, an additional $3 of interest expense for the period from July 1 through December 31 ($55 × .055) is allocated to the investment expenditure. The remaining $55 of interest expense for the period from July 1 through December 31 ($1,000 × .055) is allocated to the passive activity expenditure.

(iii) Alternatively, under the rule in paragraph (c)(2)(ii)(B) of this section, B may allocate the interest expense on a straight-line basis and may also treat the year as consisting of 12 30-day months for this purpose. In that case, $56.50 of interest expense (180/360 × $113) would be allocated to the investment expenditure and the remaining $56.50 of interest expense would be allocated to the passive activity expenditure.

Example (2). On January 1, 1988, taxpayer C borrows $10,000 at an interest rate of 11 percent, compounded annually. All interest and principal on the debt is payable in a lump sum on December 31, 1992. C immediately uses the debt proceeds to make a passive activity expenditure. C materially participates in the activity in 1990, 1991, and 1992. Therefore, under paragraphs (c)(2)(i) and (j) of this section, the debt is allocated to a passive activity expenditure from January 1, 1988, through December 31, 1989, and to a former passive activity expenditure from January 1, 1990, through December 31, 1992. In accordance with the loan agreement (and consistent with § 1.1272-1(d)(1) of the proposed regulations), interest expense accruing during any period is determined on the basis of annual compounding. Accordingly, the interest expense on the debt is allocated as follows:

Year	Amount		Expenditure
1988	$10,000 × .11	$1,100	Passive activity
1989	11,100 × .11	1,221	Passive activity
1990	12,321 × .11 = 1,355		
	1,355 × 2,321/12,321	255	Passive activity
			Former passive
	1,355 × 10,000/12,321	1,100	activity
		1,355	

Year	Amount		Expenditure
1991	$13,676 \times .11 = 1,504$		
	$1,504 \times 2,576/13,676$	283	Passive activity
			Former passive
	$1,504 \times 11,100/13,676$	1,221	activity
		1,504	
1992	$15,180 \times .11 = 1,670$		
	$1,670 \times 2,859/15,180$	315	Passive activity
			Former passive
	$1,670 \times 12,321/15,180$	1,355	activity
		1,670	

(3) *Allocation of debt; proceeds not disbursed to borrower.*—(i) *Third-party financing.*—If a lender disburses debt proceeds to a person other than the borrower in consideration for the sale or use of property, for services, or for any other purpose, the debt is treated for purposes of this section as if the borrower used an amount of the debt proceeds equal to such disbursement to make an expenditure for such property, services, or other purpose.

(ii) *Debt assumptions not involving cash disbursements.*—If a taxpayer incurs or assumes a debt in consideration for the sale or use of property, for services, or for any other purpose, or takes property subject to a debt, and no debt proceeds are disbursed to the taxpayer, the debt is treated for purposes of this section as if the taxpayer used an amount of the debt proceeds equal to the balance of the debt outstanding at such time to make an expenditure for such property, services, or other purpose.

(4) *Allocation of debt; proceeds deposited in borrower's account.*—(i) *Treatment of deposit.*—For purposes of this section, a deposit of debt proceeds in an account is treated as an investment expenditure, and amounts held in an account (whether or not interest bearing) are treated as property held for investment. Debt allocated to an account under this paragraph (c)(4)(i) must be reallocated as required by paragraph (j) of this section whenever debt proceeds held in the account are used for another expenditure. This paragraph (c)(4) provides rules for determining when debt proceeds are expended from the account. The following example illustrates the principles of this paragraph (c)(4)(i):

Example. Taxpayer C, a calendar year taxpayer, borrows $100,000 on January 1 and immediately uses the proceeds to open a noninterest-bearing checking account. No other amounts are deposited in the account during the year, and no portion of the principal amount of the debt is repaid during the year. On April 1, C uses $20,000 of the debt proceeds held in the account for a passive activity expenditure. On September 1, C uses an additional $40,000 of the debt proceeds held in the account for a personal expenditure. Under this paragraph (c)(4)(i), from January 1 through March 31 the entire $100,000 debt is allocated to an investment expenditure for the account. From April 1 through August 31, $20,000 of the debt is allocated to the passive activity expenditure, and $80,000 of the debt is allocated to the investment expenditure for the account. From September 1 through December 31, $40,000 of the debt is allocated to the personal expenditure, $20,000 is allocated to the passive activity expenditure, and $40,000 is allocated to an investment expenditure for the account.

(ii) *Expenditures from account; general ordering rule.*—Except as provided in paragraph (c)(4)(iii)(B) or (C) of this section, debt proceeds deposited in an account are treated as expended before—

(A) Any unborrowed amounts held in the account at the time such debt proceeds are deposited; and

(B) Any amounts (borrowed or unborrowed) that are deposited in the account after such debt proceeds are deposited.

The following example illustrates the application of this paragraph (c)(4)(ii):

Example. On January 10, taxpayer E opens a checking account, depositing $500 of proceeds of Debt A and $1,000 of unborrowed funds. The following chart summarizes the transactions which occur during the year with respect to the account:

Date		Transaction
January 10	$500	proceeds of Debt A and $1,000 unborrowed funds deposited
January 11	$500	proceeds of Debt B deposited
February 17	$800	personal expenditure
February 26	$700	passive activity expenditure
June 21	$1,000	proceeds of Debt C deposited
November 24	$800	investment expenditure
December 20	$600	*personal expenditure*

The $800 personal expenditure is treated as made from the $500 proceeds of Debt A and $300 of the proceeds of Debt B. The $700 passive activity expenditure is treated as made from the remaining $200 proceeds of Debt B and $500 of unborrowed funds. The $800

investment expenditure is treated as made entirely from the proceeds of Debt C. The $600 personal expenditure is treated as made from the remaining $200 proceeds of Debt C and $400 of unborrowed funds. Under paragraph (c)(4)(i) of this section, debt is allocated to an investment expenditure for periods during which debt proceeds are held in the account.

(iii) *Expenditures from account; supplemental ordering rules.*—(A) *Checking or similar accounts.*—Except as otherwise provided in this paragraph (c)(4)(iii), an expenditure from a checking or similar account is treated as made at the time the check is written on the account, provided the check is delivered or mailed to the payee within a reasonable period after the writing of the check. For this purpose, the taxpayer may treat checks written on the same day as written in any order. In the absence of evidence to the contrary, a check is presumed to be written on the date appearing on the check and to be delivered or mailed to the payee within a reasonable period thereafter. Evidence to the contrary may include the fact that a check does not clear within a reasonable period after the date appearing on the check.

(B) *Expenditures within 15 days after deposit of borrowed funds.*—The taxpayer may treat any expenditure made from an account within 15 days after debt proceeds are deposited in such account as made from such proceeds to the extent thereof even if under paragraph (c)(4)(ii) of this section the debt proceeds would be treated as used to make one or more other expenditures. Any such expenditures and the debt proceeds from which such expenditures are treated as made are disregarded in applying paragraph (c)(4)(ii) of this section. The following examples illustrate the application of this paragraph (c)(4)(iii)(B):

Example (1). Taxpayer D incurs a $1,000 debt on June 5 and immediately deposits the proceeds in an account ("Account A"). On June 17, D transfers $2,000 from Account A to another account ("Account B"). On June 30, D writes a $1,500 check on Account B for a passive activity expenditure. In addition, numerous deposits of borrowed and unborrowed amounts and expenditures occur with respect to both accounts throughout the month of June. Notwithstanding these other transactions, D may treat $1,000 of the deposit to Account B on June 17 as an expenditure from the debt proceeds deposited in Account A on June 5. In addition, D may similarly treat $1,000 of the passive activity expenditure on June 30 as made from debt proceeds treated as deposited in Account B on June 17.

Example (2). The facts are the same as in the example in paragraph (c)(4)(ii) of this section, except that the proceeds of Debt B are deposited on February 11 rather than on January 11. Since the $700 passive activity expenditure occurs within 15 days after the proceeds of Debt B are deposited in the account, E may treat such expenditure as being made from the proceeds of Debt B to the extent thereof. If E treats the passive activity expenditure in this manner, the expenditures from the account are treated as follows: The $800 personal expenditure is treated as made from the $500 proceeds of Debt A and $300 of unborrowed funds. The $700 passive activity expenditure is treated as made from the $500 proceeds of Debt B and $200 of unborrowed funds. The remaining expenditures are treated as in the example in paragraph (c)(4)(ii) of this section.

(C) *Interest on segregated account.*—In the case of an account consisting solely of the proceeds of a debt and interest earned on such account, the taxpayer may treat any expenditure from such account as made first from amounts constituting interest (rather than debt proceeds) to the extent of the balance of such interest in the account at the time of the expenditure, determined by applying the rules in this paragraph (c)(4). To the extent any expenditure is treated as made from interest under this paragraph (c)(4)(iii)(C), the expenditure is disregarded in applying paragraph (c)(4)(ii) of this section.

(iv) *Optional method for determining date of reallocation.*—Solely for the purpose of determining the date on which debt allocated to an account under paragraph (c)(4)(i) of this section is reallocated, the taxpayer may treat all expenditures made during any calendar month from debt proceeds in the account as occurring on the later of the first day of such month or the date on which such debt proceeds are deposited in the account. This paragraph (c)(4)(iv) applies only if

Itemized Deductions for Individuals and Corps.
See p. 20,601 for regulations not amended to reflect law changes
25,293

all expenditures from an account during the same calendar month are similarly treated. The following example illustrates the application of this paragraph (c)(4)(iv):

Example. On January 10, taxpayer G opens a checking account, depositing $500 of proceeds of Debt A and $1,000 of unborrowed funds. The following chart summarizes the transactions which occur during the year with respect to the account (note that these facts are the same as the facts of the example in paragraph (c)(4)(ii) of this section):

Date		Transaction
January 10	$500	proceeds of Debt A and $1,000 unborrowed funds deposited
January 11	$500	proceeds of Debt B deposited
February 17	$800	personal expenditure
February 26	$700	passive activity expenditure
June 21	$1,000	proceeds of Debt C deposited
November 24	$800	investment expenditure
December 20	$600	personal expenditure

Assume that G chooses to apply the optional rule of this paragraph (c)(4)(iv) to all expenditures. For purposes of determining the date on which debt is allocated to the $800 personal expenditure made on February 17, the $500 treated as made from the proceeds of Debt A and the $300 treated as made from the proceeds of Debt B are treated as expenditures occurring on February 1. Accordingly, Debt A is allocated to an investment expenditure for the account from January 10 through January 31 and to the personal expenditure from February 1 through December 31, and $300 of Debt B is allocated to an investment expenditure for the account from January 11 through January 31 and to the personal expenditure from February 1 through December 31. The remaining $200 of Debt B is allocated to an investment expenditure for the account from January 11 through January 31 and to the passive activity expenditure from February 1 through December 31. The $800 of Debt C used to make the investment expenditure on November 24 is allocated to an investment expenditure for the account from June 21 through October 31 and to an investment expenditure from November 1 through December 31. The remaining $200 of Debt C is allocated to an investment expenditure for the account from June 21 through November 30 and to a personal expenditure from December 1 through December 31.

(v) *Simultaneous deposits.*—(A) *In general.*—If the proceeds of two or more debts are deposited in an account simultaneously, such proceeds are treated for purposes of this paragraph (c)(4) as deposited in the order in which the debts were incurred.

(B) *Order in which debts incurred.*—If two or more debts are incurred simultaneously or are treated under applicable law as incurred simultaneously, the debts are treated for purposes of this paragraph (c)(4)(v) as incurred in any order the taxpayer selects.

(C) *Borrowings on which interest accrues at different rates.*—If interest does not accrue at the same fixed or variable rate on the entire amount of a borrowing, each portion of the borrowing on which interest accrues at a different fixed or variable rate is treated as a separate debt for purposes of this paragraph (c)(4)(v).

(vi) *Multiple accounts.*—The rules in this paragraph (c)(4) apply separately to each account of a taxpayer.

(5) *Allocation of debt; proceeds received in cash.*—(i) *Expenditure within 15 days of receiving debt proceeds.*—If a taxpayer receives the proceeds of a debt in cash, the taxpayer may treat any cash expenditure made within 15 days after receiving the cash as made from such debt proceeds to the extent thereof and may treat such expenditure as made on the date the taxpayer received the cash. The following example illustrates the rule in this paragraph (c)(5)(i):

Example. Taxpayer F incurs a $1,000 debt on August 4 and receives the debt proceeds in cash. F deposits $1,500 cash in an account on August 15 and on August 27 writes a check on the account for a passive activity expenditure. In addition, F engages in numerous other cash transactions throughout the month of August, and numerous deposits of borrowed and unborrowed amounts and expenditures occur with respect to the account during the same period. Notwithstanding these other transactions, F may treat $1,000 of the deposit on August 15 as an expenditure made from the debt proceeds on August 4. In addition, under the rule in paragraph (c)(4)(v)(B) of this section, F may treat the passive activity expenditure on August 27 as made from the $1,000 debt proceeds treated as deposited in the account.

(ii) *Other expenditures.*—Except as provided in paragraphs (c)(5)(i) and (iii) of this section, any debt proceeds a taxpayer (other

than a corporation) receives in cash are treated as used to make personal expenditures. For purposes of this paragraph (c)(5), debt proceeds are received in cash if, for example, a withdrawal of cash from an account is treated under the rules of this section as an expenditure of debt proceeds.

(iii) *Special rules for certain taxpayers.*—[Reserved.]

(6) *Special rules.*—(i) *Qualified residence debt.*—[Reserved.]

(ii) *Debt used to pay interest.*—To the extent proceeds of a debt are used to pay interest, such debt is allocated in the same manner as the debt on which such interest accrued is allocated from time to time. The following example illustrates the application of this paragraph (c)(6)(ii):

Example. On January 1, taxpayer H incurs a debt of $1,000, bearing interest at an annual rate of 10 percent, compounded annually, payable at the end of each year ("Debt A"). H immediately opens a checking account, in which H deposits the proceeds of Debt A. No other amounts are deposited in the account during the year. On April 1, H writes a check for a personal expenditure in the amount of $1,000. On December 31, H borrows $100 ("Debt B") and immediately uses the proceeds of Debt B to pay the accrued interest of $100 on Debt A. From January 1 through March 31, Debt A is allocated, under the rule in paragraph (c)(4)(i) of this section, to the investment expenditure for the account. From April 1 through December 31, Debt A is allocated to the personal expenditure. Under the rule in paragraph (c)(2)(ii) of this section, $25 of the interest on Debt A for the year is allocated to the investment expenditure, and $75 of the interest on Debt A for the year is allocated to the personal expenditure. Accordingly, for the purpose of allocating the interest on Debt B for all periods until Debt B is repaid, $25 of Debt B is allocated to the investment expenditure, and $75 of Debt B is allocated to the personal expenditure.

(iii) *Debt used to pay borrowing costs.*—(A) *Borrowing costs with respect to different debt.*—To the extent the proceeds of a debt (the "ancillary debt") are used to pay borrowing costs (other than interest) with respect to another debt (the "primary debt"), the ancillary debt is allocated in the same manner as the primary debt is allocated from time to time. To the extent the primary debt is repaid, the ancillary debt will continue to be allocated in the same manner as the primary debt was allocated immediately before its repayment. The following example illustrates the rule in this paragraph (c)(6)(iii)(A):

Example. Taxpayer I incurs debts of $60,000 ("Debt A") and $10,000 ("Debt B"). I immediately uses $30,000 of the proceeds of Debt A to make a trade or business expenditure, $20,000 to make a passive activity expenditure, and $10,000 to make an investment expenditure. I immediately uses $3,000 of the proceeds of Debt B to pay borrowing costs (other than interest) with respect to Debt A (such as loan origination, loan commitment, abstract, and recording fees) and deposits the remaining $7,000 in an account. Under the rule in this paragraph (c)(6)(iii)(A), the $3,000 of Debt B used to pay expenses of incurring Debt A is allocated $1,500 to the trade or business expenditure ($3,000 × $30,000/$60,000), $1,000 to the passive activity expenditure ($3,000 × $20,000/$60,000), and $500 ($3,000 × $10,000/$60,000) to the investment expenditure. The manner in which the $3,000 of Debt B used to pay expenses of incurring Debt A is allocated may change if the allocation of Debt A changes, but such allocation will be unaffected by any repayment of Debt A. The remaining $7,000 of Debt B is allocated to an investment expenditure for the account until such time, if any, as this amount is used for a different expenditure.

(B) *Borrowing costs with respect to same debt.*—To the extent the proceeds of a debt are used to pay borrowing costs (other than interest) with respect to such debt, such debt is allocated in the same manner as the remaining debt is allocated from time to time. The remaining debt for this purpose is the portion of the debt that is not used to pay borrowing costs (other than interest) with respect to such debt. Any repayment of the debt is treated as a repayment of the debt allocated under this paragraph (c)(6)(iii)(B) and the remaining debt in the same proportion as such amounts bear to each other. The following example illustrates the application of this paragraph (c)(6)(iii)(B):

Example. (i) Taxpayer J borrows $85,000. The lender disburses $80,000 of this amount to J, retaining $5,000 for borrowing costs (other than interest) with respect to the loan. J immediately uses $40,000 of the debt proceeds to make a personal expenditure, $20,000 to make a passive activity expenditure, and $20,000 to make an investment expenditure. Under the rule in this paragraph (c)(6)(iii)(B), the $5,000 used to pay borrowing costs is allocated $2,500 ($5,000 × $40,000/$80,000) to the personal expenditure, $1,250 ($5,000 × $20,000/$80,000) to the passive activity expenditure, and $1,250 ($5,000 × $20,000/$80,000) to the investment expenditure. The manner in which this $5,000 is allocated may change if the allocation of the remaining $80,000 of debt is changed.

(ii) Assume that J repays $50,000 of the debt. The repayment is treated as a repayment of $2,941 ($50,000 × $5,000/$85,000) of the debt used to pay borrowing costs and a repayment of $47,059 ($50,000 × $80,000/$85,000) of the remaining debt. Under paragraph (d) of this section, J is treated as repaying the $42,500 of debt allocated to the personal expenditure ($2,500 of debt used to pay borrowing costs and $40,000 of remaining debt). In addition, assuming that under paragraph (d)(2) J chooses to treat the allocation to the passive activity expenditure as having occurred before the allocation to the investment expenditure, J is treated as repaying $7,500 of debt allocated to the passive activity expenditure ($441 of debt used to pay borrowing costs and $7,059 of remaining debt).

(iv) *Allocation of debt before actual receipt of debt proceeds.*—If interest properly accrues on a debt during any period before the debt proceeds are actually received or used to make an expenditure, the debt is allocated to an investment expenditure for such period.

(7) *Antiabuse rules.*—[Reserved.]

(d) *Debt repayments.*—(1) *General ordering rule.*—If, at the time any portion of a debt is repaid, such debt is allocated to more than one expenditure, the debt is treated for purposes of this section as repaid in the following order:

(i) Amounts allocated to personal expenditures;

(ii) Amounts allocated to investment expenditures and passive activity expenditures (other than passive activity expenditures described in paragraph (d)(1)(iii) of this section);

(iii) Amounts allocated to passive activity expenditures in connection with a rental real estate activity with respect to which the taxpayer actively participates (within the meaning of section 469(i));

(iv) Amounts allocated to former passive activity expenditures; and

(v) Amounts allocated to trade or business expenditures and to expenditures described in the last sentence of paragraph (b)(4) of this section.

(2) *Supplemental ordering rules for expenditures in same class.*—Amounts allocated to two or more expenditures that are described in the same subdivision of paragraph (d)(1) of this section (e.g., amounts allocated to different personal expenditures) are treated as repaid in the order in which the amounts were allocated (or reallocated) to such expenditures. For purposes of this paragraph (d)(2), the taxpayer may treat allocations and reallocations that occur on the same day as occurring in any order (without regard to the order in which expenditures are treated as made under paragraph (c)(4)(iii)(A) of this section).

(3) *Continuous borrowings.*—In the case of borrowings pursuant to a line of credit or similar account or arrangement that allows a taxpayer to borrow funds periodically under a single loan agreement—

(i) All borrowings on which interest accrues at the same fixed or variable rate are treated as a single debt; and

(ii) Borrowings or portions of borrowings on which interest accrues at different fixed or variable rates are treated as different debts, and such debts are treated as repaid for purposes of this paragraph (d) in the order in which such debts are treated as repaid under the loan agreement.

(4) *Examples.*—The following examples illustrate the application of this paragraph (d):

Example (1). Taxpayer B borrows $100,000 ("Debt A") on July 12, immediately deposits the proceeds in an account, and uses the debt proceeds to make the following expenditures on the following dates:

August 31	$40,000 passive activity expenditure #1
October 5	$20,000 passive activity expenditure #2
December 24	$40,000 personal expenditure

On January 19 of the following year, B repays $90,000 of Debt A (leaving $10,000 of Debt A outstanding). The $40,000 of Debt A allocated to the personal expenditure, the $40,000 allocated to passive activity expenditure # 1, and $10,000 of the $20,000 allocated to passive activity expenditure # 2 are treated as repaid.

Example (2). (i) Taxpayer A obtains a line of credit. Interest on any borrowing on the line of credit accrues at the lender's "prime lending rate" on the date of the borrowing plus two percentage points. The loan documents provide that borrowings on the line of credit are treated as repaid in the order the borrowings were made. A borrows $30,000 ("Borrowing # 1") on the line of credit and immediately uses $20,000 of the debt proceeds to make a personal expenditure ("personal expenditure # 1") and $10,000 to make a trade or business expenditure ("trade or business expenditure # 1"). A subsequently borrows another $20,000 ("Borrowing # 2") on the line of credit and immediately uses $15,000 of the debt proceeds to make a personal expenditure ("personal expenditure # 2") and $5,000 to

make a trade or business expenditure ("trade or business expenditure # 2"). A then repays $40,000 of the borrowings.

(ii) If the prime lending rate plus two percentage points was the same on both the date of Borrowing # 1 and the date of Borrowing # 2, the borrowings are treated for purposes of this paragraph (d) as a single debt, and A is treated as having repaid $35,000 of debt allocated to personal expenditure # 1 and personal expenditure # 2, and $5,000 of debt allocated to trade or business expenditure # 1.

(iii) If the prime lending rate plus two percentage points was different on the date of Borrowing # 1 and Borrowing # 2, the borrowings are treated as two debts, and, in accordance with the loan agreement, the $40,000 repaid amount is treated as a repayment of Borrowing # 1 and $10,000 of Borrowing # 2. Accordingly, A is treated as having repaid $20,000 of debt allocated to personal expenditure # 1, $10,000 of debt allocated to trade or business expenditure # 1, and $10,000 of debt allocated to personal expenditure # 2.

(e) *Debt refinancings.*—(1) *In general.*—To the extent proceeds of any debt (the "replacement debt") are used to repay any portion of a debt, the replacement debt is allocated to the expenditures to which the repaid debt was allocated. The amount of replacement debt allocated to any such expenditure is equal to the amount of debt allocated to such expenditure that was repaid with proceeds of the replacement debt. To the extent proceeds of the replacement debt are used for expenditures other than repayment of a debt, the replacement debt is allocated to expenditures in accordance with the rules of this section.

(2) *Example.*—The following example illustrates the application of this paragraph (e):

Example. Taxpayer C borrows $100,000 ("Debt A") on July 12, immediately deposits the debt proceeds in an account, and uses the proceeds to make the following expenditures on the following dates (note that the facts of this example are the same as the facts of example (1) in paragraph (d)(4) of this section):

August 31	$40,000 passive activity expenditure #1
October 5	$20,000 passive activity expenditure #2
December 24	$40,000 personal expenditure #1

On January 19 of the following year, C borrows $120,000 ("Debt B") and uses $90,000 of the proceeds to repay $90,000 of Debt A (leaving $10,000 of Debt A outstanding). In addition, C uses $30,000 of the proceeds of Debt B to make a personal expenditure ("personal expenditure # 2"). Debt B is allocated $40,000 to personal expenditure # 1, $40,000 to passive activity expenditure # 1, $10,000 to passive activity expenditure # 2, and $30,000 to personal expenditure # 2. Under paragraph (d)(1) of this section, Debt B will be treated as repaid in the following order: (1) amounts allocated to personal expenditure # 1, (2) amounts allocated to personal expenditure # 2, (3) amounts allocated to passive activity expenditure # 1, and (4) amounts allocated to passive activity expenditure # 2.

(f) *Debt allocated to distributions by passthrough entities.*—[Reserved.]

(g) *Repayment of passthrough entity debt.*—[Reserved.]

(h) *Debt allocated to expenditures for interests in passthrough entities.*—[Reserved.]

(i) *Allocation of debt to loans between passthrough entities and interest holders.*—[Reserved.]

(j) *Reallocation of debt.*—(1) *Debt allocated to capital expenditures.*—(i) *Time of reallocation.*—Except as provided in paragraph (j)(2) of this section, debt allocated to an expenditure properly chargeable to capital account with respect to an asset (the "first expenditure") is reallocated to another expenditure on the earlier of—

(A) The date on which proceeds from a disposition of such asset are used for another expenditure; or

(B) The date on which the character of the first expenditure changes (e.g., from a passive activity expenditure to an expenditure that is not a passive activity expenditure) by reason of a change in the use of the asset with respect to which the first expenditure was capitalized.

(ii) *Limitation on amount reallocated.*—The amount of debt reallocated under paragraph (j)(1)(i)(A) of this section may not exceed the proceeds from the disposition of the asset. The amount of debt reallocated under paragraph (j)(1)(i)(B) of this section may not exceed the fair market value of the asset on the date of the change in use. In applying this paragraph (j)(1)(ii) with respect to a debt in any case in which two or more debts are allocable to expenditures properly chargeable to capital account with respect to the same asset, only a ratable portion (determined with respect to any such debt by dividing the amount of such debt by the aggregate amount of all such debts) of the fair market value or proceeds from the disposition of such asset shall be taken into account.

Reg. § 1.163-8T(c)(6)(iv)

(iii) *Treatment of loans made by the taxpayer.*—Except as provided in paragraph (j)(1)(iv) of this section, an expenditure to make a loan is treated as an expenditure properly chargeable to capital account with respect to an asset, and for purposes of paragraph (j)(1)(i)(A) of this section any repayment of the loan is treated as a disposition of the asset. Paragraph (j)(3) of this section applies to any repayment of a loan in installments.

(iv) *Treatment of accounts.*—Debt allocated to an account under paragraph (c)(4)(i) of this section is treated as allocated to an expenditure properly chargeable to capital account with respect to an asset, and any expenditure from the account is treated as a disposition of the asset. See paragraph (c)(4) of this section for rules under which debt proceeds allocated to an account are treated as used for another expenditure.

(2) *Disposition proceeds in excess of debt.*—If the proceeds from the disposition of an asset exceed the amount of debt reallocated by reason of such disposition, or two or more debts are reallocated by reason of the disposition of an asset, the proceeds of the disposition are treated as an account to which the rules in paragraph (c)(4) of this section apply.

(3) *Special rule for deferred payment sales.*—If any portion of the proceeds of a disposition of an asset are received subsequent to the disposition—

(i) The portion of the proceeds to be received subsequent to the disposition is treated for periods prior to the receipt as used to make an investment expenditure; and

(ii) Debt reallocated by reason of the disposition is allocated to such investment expenditure to the extent such debt exceeds the proceeds of the disposition previously received (other than proceeds used to repay such debt).

(4) *Examples.*—The following examples illustrate the application of this paragraph (j):

Example (1). On January 1, 1988, taxpayer D sells an asset for $25,000. Immediately before the sale, the amount of debt allocated to expenditures properly chargeable to capital account with respect to the asset was $15,000. The proceeds of the disposition are treated as an account consisting of $15,000 of debt proceeds and $10,000 of unborrowed funds to which paragraph (c)(4) of this section applies. Thus, if D immediately makes a $10,000 personal expenditure from the proceeds and within 15 days deposits the remaining proceeds in an account, D may, pursuant to paragraph (c)(4)(iii)(B) of this section, treat the entire $15,000 deposited in the account as proceeds of a debt.

Example (2). The facts are the same as in example (1) except that, instead of receiving all $25,000 of the sale proceeds on January 1, 1988, D receives $5,000 on that date, $10,000 on January 1, 1989, and $10,000 on January 1, 1990. D does not use any portion of the sale proceeds to repay the debt. Between January 1, 1988, and December 31, 1988, D is treated under paragraph (j)(3) of this section as making an investment expenditure of $20,000 to which $10,000 of debt is allocated. In addition, the remaining $5,000 of debt is reallocated on January 1, 1988, in accordance with D's use of the sales proceeds received on that date. Between January 1, 1989, and December 31, 1989, D is treated as making an investment expenditure of $10,000 to which no debt is allocated. In addition, as of January 1, 1989, $10,000 of debt is reallocated in accordance with D's use of the sales proceeds received on that date.

Example (3). The facts are the same as in example (2), except that D immediately uses the $5,000 sale proceeds received on January 1, 1988, to repay $5,000 of the $15,000 debt. Between January 1, 1988, and December 31, 1988, D is treated as making an investment expenditure of $20,000 to which the remaining balance ($10,000) of the debt is reallocated. The results in 1989 are as described in example (2).

(k) *Modification of rules in the case of interest expense allocated to foreign source income.*—[Reserved.]

(l) *Reserved.*

(m) *Coordination with other provisions.*—(1) *Effect of other limitations.*—(i) *In general.*—All debt is allocated among expenditures pursuant to the rules in this section, without regard to any limitations on the deductibility of interest expense on such debt. The applicability of the passive loss and nonbusiness interest limitations to interest on such debt, however, may be affected by other limitations on the deductibility of interest expense.

(ii) *Disallowance provisions.*—Interest expense that is not allowable as a deduction by reason of a disallowance provision (within the meaning of paragraph (m)(7)(ii) of this section) is not taken into account for any taxable year for purposes of applying the passive loss and nonbusiness interest limitations.

(iii) *Deferral provisions.*—Interest expense that is not allowable as a deduction for the taxable year in which paid or accrued by reason of a deferral provision (within the meaning of paragraph (m)(7)(iii) of this section) is allocated in the same manner as the debt giving rise to the interest expense is allocated for such taxable year. Such interest expense is taken into account for purposes of applying the passive loss and nonbusiness interest limitations for the taxable year in which such interest expense is allowable under such deferral provision.

(iv) *Capitalization provisions.*—Interest expense that is capitalized pursuant to a capitalization provision (within the meaning of paragraph (m)(7)(i) of this section) is not taken into account as interest for any taxable year for purposes of applying the passive loss and nonbusiness interest limitations.

(2) *Effect on other limitations.*—(i) *General rule.*—Except as provided in paragraph (m)(2)(ii) of this section, any limitation on the deductibility of an item (other than the passive loss and nonbusiness interest limitations) applies without regard to the manner in which debt is allocated under this section. Thus, for example, interest expense treated under section 265(a)(2) as interest on indebtedness incurred or continued to purchase or carry obligations the interest on which is wholly exempt from Federal income tax is not deductible regardless of the expenditure to which the underlying debt is allocated under this section.

(ii) *Exception.*—Capitalization provisions (within the meaning of paragraph (m)(7)(i) of this section) do not apply to interest expense allocated to any personal expenditure under the rules of this section.

(3) *Qualified residence interest.*—Qualified residence interest (within the meaning of section 163 (h)(3)) is allowable as a deduction without regard to the manner in which such interest expense is allocated under the rules of this section. In addition, qualified residence interest is not taken into account in determining the income or loss from any activity for purposes of section 469 or in determining the amount of investment interest for purposes of section 163(d). The following example illustrates the rule in this paragraph (m)(3):

Example. Taxpayer E, an individual, incurs a $20,000 debt secured by a residence and immediately uses the proceeds to purchase an automobile exclusively for E's personal use. Under the rules in this section, the debt and interest expense on the debt are allocated to a personal expenditure. If, however, the interest on the debt is qualified residence interest within the meaning of section 163(h)(3), the interest is not treated as personal interest for purposes of section 163(h).

(4) *Interest described in section 163(h)(2)(E).*—Interest described in section 163(h)(2)(E) is allowable as a deduction without regard to the rules of this section.

(5) *Interest on deemed distributee debt.*—[Reserved.]

(6) *Examples.*—The following examples illustrate the relationship between the passive loss and nonbusiness interest limitations and other limitations on the deductibility of interest expense:

Example (1). Debt is allocated pursuant to the rules in this section to an investment expenditure for the purchase of taxable investment securities. Pursuant to section 265(a)(2), the debt is treated as indebtedness incurred or continued to purchase or carry obligations the interest on which is wholly exempt from Federal income tax, and, accordingly, interest on the debt is disallowed. If section 265(a)(2) subsequently ceases to apply (because, for example, the taxpayer ceases to hold any tax-exempt obligations), and the debt at such time continues to be allocated to an investment expenditure, interest on the debt that accrues after such time is subject to section 163(d).

Example (2). An accrual method taxpayer incurs a debt payable to a cash method lender who is related to the taxpayer within the meaning of section 267(b). During the period in which interest on the debt is not deductible by reason of section 267(a)(2), the debt is allocated to a passive activity expenditure. Thus, interest that accrues on the debt for such period is also allocated to the passive activity expenditure. When such interest expense becomes deductible under section 267(a)(2), it will be allocated to the passive activity expenditure, regardless of how the debt is allocated at such time.

Example (3). A taxpayer incurs debt that is allocated under the rules of this section to an investment expenditure. Under section 263A(f), however, interest expense on such debt is capitalized during the production period (within the meaning of section 263A(f)(4)(B)) of property used in a passive activity of the taxpayer. The capitalized interest expense is not allocated to the investment expenditure, and depreciation deductions attributable to the capitalized interest expense are subject to the passive loss limitation as long as the property is used in a passive activity. However, interest expense on the debt for periods after the production period is allocated to the investment expenditure as long as the debt remains allocated to the investment expenditure.

(7) Other limitations on interest expense.—(i) *Capitalization provisions.*—A capitalization provision is any provision that requires or allows interest expense to be capitalized. Capitalization provisions include sections 263(g), 263A(f), and 266.

(ii) Disallowance provisions.—A disallowance provision is any provision (other than the passive loss and nonbusiness interest limitations) that disallows a deduction for interest expense for all taxable years and is not a capitalization provision. Disallowance provisions include sections 163(f)(2), 264(a)(2), 264(a)(4), 265(a)(2), 265(b)(2), 279(a), 291(e)(1)(B)(ii), 805(b)(1), and 834(c)(5).

(iii) Deferral provisions.—A deferral provision is any provision (other than the passive loss and nonbusiness interest limitations) that disallows a deduction for interest expense for any taxable year and is not a capitalization or disallowance provision. Deferral provisions include sections 267(a)(2), 465, 1277, and 1282.

(n) Effective date.—(1) *In general.*—This section applies to interest expense paid or accrued in taxable years beginning after December 31, 1986.

(2) Transitional rule for certain expenditures.—For purposes of determining whether debt is allocated to expenditures made on or before August 3, 1987, paragraphs (c)(4)(iii)(B) and (c)(5)(i) of this section are applied by substituting "90 days" for "15 days."

(3) Transitional rule for certain debt.—(i) *General rule.*—Except as provided in paragraph (n)(3)(ii) of this section, any debt outstanding on December 31, 1986, that is properly attributable to a business or rental activity is treated for purposes of this section as debt allocated to expenditures properly chargeable to capital account with respect to the assets held for use or for sale to customers in such business or rental activity. Debt is properly attributable to a business or rental activity for purposes of this section (regardless of whether such debt otherwise would be allocable under this section to expenditures in connection with such activity) if the taxpayer has properly and consistently deducted interest expense (including interest subject to limitation under section 163(d) as in effect prior to the Tax Reform Act of 1986) on such debt on Schedule C, E, or F of Form 1040 in computing income or loss from such business or rental activity for taxable years beginning before January 1, 1987. For purposes of this paragraph (n)(3), amended returns filed after July 2, 1987, are disregarded in determining whether a taxpayer has consistently deducted interest expense on Schedule C, E, or F of Form 1040 in computing income or loss from a business or rental activity.

(ii) Exceptions.—(A) *Debt financed distributions by pass-through entities.*—[Reserved.]

(B) Election out.—This paragraph (n)(3) does not apply with respect to debt of a taxpayer who elects under paragraph (n)(3)(viii) of this section to allocate debt outstanding on December 31, 1986, in accordance with the provisions of this section other than this paragraph (n)(3) (i.e., in accordance with the use of the debt proceeds).

(iii) Business or rental activity.—For purposes of this paragraph (n)(3), a business or rental activity is any trade or business or rental activity of the taxpayer. For this purpose—

(A) A trade or business includes a business or profession the income and deductions of which (or, in the case of a partner or S corporation shareholder, the taxpayer's share thereof) are properly reported on Schedule C, E, or F of Form 1040; and

(B) A rental activity includes an activity of renting property the income and deductions of which (or, in the case of a partner or S corporation shareholder, the taxpayer's share thereof) are properly reported on Schedule E of Form 1040.

(iv) Example.—The following example illustrates the circumstances in which debt is properly attributable to a business or rental activity:

Example. Taxpayer H incurred a debt in 1979 and properly deducted the interest expense on the debt on Schedule C of Form 1040 for each year from 1979 through 1986. Under this paragraph (n)(3), the debt is properly attributable to the business the results of which are reported on Schedule C.

(v) Allocation requirement.—(A) *In general.*—Debt outstanding on December 31, 1986, that is properly attributable (within the meaning of paragraph (n)(3)(i) of this section) to a business or rental activity must be allocated in a reasonable and consistent manner among the assets held for use or for sale to customers in such activity on the last day of the taxable year that includes December 31, 1986. The taxpayer shall specify the manner in which such debt is allocated *by filing a statement in accordance with paragraph (n)(3)(vii) of this section.* If the taxpayer does not file such a statement or fails to allocate such debt in a reasonable and consistent manner, the Commissioner shall allocate the debt.

(B) Reasonable and consistent manner—examples of improper allocation.—For purposes of this paragraph (n)(3)(v), debt is not treated as allocated in a reasonable and consistent manner if—

(1) The amount of debt allocated to goodwill exceeds the basis of the goodwill; or

(2) The amount of debt allocated to an asset exceeds the fair market value of the asset, and the amount of debt allocated to any other asset is less than the fair market value (lesser of basis or fair market value in the case of goodwill) of such other asset.

(vi) Coordination with other provisions.—The effect of any events occurring after the last day of the taxable year that includes December 31, 1986, shall be determined under the rules of this section, applied by treating the debt allocated to an asset under paragraph (n)(3)(v) of this section as if proceeds of such debt were used to make an expenditure properly chargeable to capital account with respect to such asset on the last day of the taxable year that includes December 31, 1986. Thus, debt that is allocated to an asset in accordance with this paragraph (n)(3) must be reallocated in accordance with paragraph (j) of this section upon the occurrence with respect to such asset of any event described in such paragraph (j). Similarly, such debt is treated as repaid in the order prescribed in paragraph (d) of this section. In addition, a replacement debt (within the meaning of paragraph (e) of this section) is allocated to an expenditure properly chargeable to capital account with respect to an asset to the extent the proceeds of such debt are used to repay the portion of a debt allocated to such asset under this paragraph (n)(3).

(vii) Form for allocation of debt.—A taxpayer shall allocate debt for purposes of this paragraph (n)(3) by attaching to the taxpayer's return for the first taxable year beginning after December 31, 1986, a statement that is prominently identified as a TRANSITIONAL ALLOCATION STATEMENT UNDER § 1.163-8T(n)(3) and includes the following information:

(A) A description of the business or rental activity to which the debt is properly attributable;

(B) The amount of debt allocated;

(C) The assets among which the debt is allocated;

(D) The manner in which the debt is allocated;

(E) The amount of debt allocated to each asset; and

(F) Such other information as the Commissioner may require.

(viii) Form for election out.—A taxpayer shall elect to allocate debt outstanding on December 31, 1986, in accordance with the provisions of this section other than this paragraph (n)(3) by attaching to the taxpayer's return (or amended return) for the first taxable year beginning after December 31, 1986, a statement to that effect, prominently identified as an ELECTION OUT UNDER § 1.163-8T(n)(3).

(ix) Special rule for partnerships and S corporations.—For purposes of paragraph (n)(3)(ii)(B), (v), (vii) and (viii) of this section (relating to the allocation of debt and election out), a partnership or S corporation shall be treated as the taxpayer with respect to the debt of the partnership or S corporation.

(x) Irrevocability.—An allocation or election filed in accordance with paragraph (n)(3)(vii) or (viii) of this section may not be revoked or modified except with the consent of the Commissioner. [Temporary Reg. § 1.163-8T.]

☐ [T.D. 8145, 7-1-87.]

[Reg. § 1.163-9T]

§ 1.163-9T. Personal interest (temporary).—(a) *In general.*—No deduction under any provision of Chapter 1 of the Internal Revenue Code shall be allowed for personal interest paid or accrued during the taxable year by a taxpayer other than a corporation.

(b) *Personal interest.*—(1) *Definition.*—For purposes of this section, personal interest is any interest expense other than—

(i) Interest paid or accrued on indebtedness properly allocable (within the meaning of § 1.163-8T) to the conduct of a trade or business (other than the trade or business of performing services as an employee),

(ii) Any investment interest (within the meaning of section 163(d)(3)),

(iii) Any interest that is taken into account under section 469 in computing income or loss from a passive activity of the taxpayer,

(iv) Any qualified residence interest (within the meaning of section 163(h)(3) and § 1.163-10T), and

(v) Any interest payable under section 6601 with respect to the unpaid portion of the tax imposed by section 2001 for the period during which an extension of time for payment of such tax is in effect under section 6163, 6166, or 6166A (as in effect before its repeal by the Economic Recovery Tax Act of 1981).

(2) *Interest relating to taxes.*—(i) *In general.*—Except as provided in paragraph (b)(2)(iii) of this section, personal interest includes interest—

(A) Paid on underpayments of individual Federal, State or local income taxes and on indebtedness used to pay such taxes (within the meaning of §1.163-8T), regardless of the source of the income generating the tax liability;

(B) Paid under section 453C(e)(4)(B) (interest on deferred tax resulting from certain installment sales) and section 1291(c) (interest on deferred tax attributable to passive foreign investment companies); or

(C) Paid by a trust, S corporation, or other pass-through entity on underpayments of State or local income taxes and on indebtedness used to pay such taxes.

(ii) *Example.*—A, an individual, owns stock of an S corporation. On its return for 1987, the corporation underreports its taxable income. Consequently, A underreports A's share of that income on A's tax return. In 1989, A pays the resulting deficiency plus interest to the Internal Revenue Service. The interest paid by A in 1989 on the tax deficiency is personal interest, notwithstanding the fact that the additional tax liability may have arisen out of income from a trade or business. The result would be the same if A's business had been operated as a sole proprietorship.

(iii) *Certain other taxes.*—Personal interest does not include interest—

(A) Paid with respect to sales, excise and similar taxes that are incurred in connection with a trade or business or an investment activity;

(B) Paid by an S corporation with respect to an underpayment of income tax from a year in which the S corporation was a C corporation or with respect to an underpayment of the taxes imposed by sections 1374 or 1375, or similar provision of State law; or

(C) Paid by a transferee under section 6901 (tax liability resulting from transferred assets), or a similar provision of State law, with respect to a C corporation's underpayment of income tax.

(3) *Cross references.*—See §1.163-8T for rules for determining the allocation of interest expense to various activities. See §1.163-10T for rules concerning qualified residence interest.

(c) *Effective date.*—(1) *In general.*—The provisions of this section are effective for taxable years beginning after December 31, 1986. In the case of any taxable year beginning in calendar years 1987 through 1990, the amount of personal interest that is nondeductible under this section is limited to the applicable percentage of such amount.

(2) *Applicable percentage.*—The applicable percentages for taxable years beginning in 1987 through 1990 are as follows:

1987: 35 percent
1988: 60 percent
1989: 80 percent
1990: 90 percent [Temporary Reg. §1.163-9T.]

☐ [*T.D. 8168, 12-21-87 (corrected 3-18-2003).*]

[Reg. §1.163-10T]

§1.163-10T. Qualified residence interest (temporary).—(a) *Table of contents.*—This paragraph (a) lists the major paragraphs that appear in this section 1.163-10T.

(a) Table of contents.
(b) Treatment of qualified residence interest.
(c) Determination of qualified residence interest when secured debt does not exceed the adjusted purchase price.
  (1) In general.
  (2) Examples.
(d) Determination of qualified residence interest when secured debt exceeds adjusted purchase price—Simplified method.
  (1) In general.
  (2) Treatment of interest paid or accrued on secured debt that is not qualified residence interest.
  (3) Example.
(e) Determination of qualified residence interest when secured debt exceeds adjusted purchase price—Exact method.
  (1) In general.
  (2) Determination of applicable debt limit.
  (3) Example.
  (4) Treatment of interest paid or accrued with respect to secured debt that is not qualified residence interest.
    (i) In general.
    (ii) Example.

    (iii) Special rule if debt is allocated to more than one expenditure.
    (iv) Example.
(f) Special rules.
  (1) Special rules for personal property.
    (i) In general.
    (ii) Example.
  (2) Special rule for real property.
    (i) In general.
    (ii) Example.
(g) Selection of method.
(h) Average balance.
  (1) Average balance defined
  (2) Average balance reported by lender.
  (3) Average balance computed on a daily basis.
    (i) In general.
    (ii) Example.
  (4) Average balance computed using the interest rate.
    (i) In general.
    (ii) Points and prepaid interest.
    (iii) Examples.
  (5) Average balance computed using average of beginning and ending balance.
    (i) In general.
    (ii) Example.
  (6) Highest principal balance.
  (7) Other methods provided by the Commissioner.
  (8) Anti-abuse rule.
(i) [Reserved.]
(j) Determination of interest paid or accrued during the taxable year.
  (1) In general.
  (2) Special rules for cash-basis taxpayers.
    (i) Points deductible in year paid under section 461(g)(2).
    (ii) Points and other prepaid interest described in section 461(g)(1).
  (3) Examples.
(k) Determination of adjusted purchase price and fair market value.
  (1) Adjusted purchase price.
    (i) In general.
    (ii) Adjusted purchase price of a qualified residence acquired incident to divorce.
    (iii) Examples.
  (2) Fair market value.
    (i) In general.
    (ii) Examples.
  (3) Allocation of adjusted purchase price and fair market value.
(l) [Reserved].
(m) Grandfathered amount.
  (1) Substitution for adjusted purchase price.
  (2) Determination of grandfathered amount.
    (i) In general.
    (ii) Special rule for lines of credit and certain other debt.
    (iii) Fair market value limitation.
    (iv) Examples.
  (3) Refinancing of grandfathered debt.
    (i) In general.
    (ii) Determination of grandfathered amount.
  (4) Limitation on term of grandfathered debt.
    (i) In general.
    (ii) Special rule for nonamortizing debt.
    (iii) Example.
(n) Qualified indebtedness (secured debt used for medical and educational purposes).
  (1) In general.
    (i) Treatment of qualified indebtedness.
    (ii) Determination of amount of qualified indebtedness.
    (iii) Determination of amount of qualified indebtedness for mixed-use debt.
    (iv) Example.
    (v) Prevention of double counting in year of refinancing.
    (vi) Special rule for principal payments in excess of qualified expenses.
  (2) Debt used to pay for qualified medical or educational expenses.
    (i) In general.
    (ii) Special rule for refinancing.
    (iii) Other special rules.

(iv) Examples.

(3) Qualified medical expenses.

(4) Qualified educational expenses.

(o) Secured debt.

(1) In general.

(2) Special rule for debt in certain States.

(3) Time at which debt is treated as secured.

(4) Partially secured debt.

  (i) In general.

  (ii) Example.

(5) Election to treat debt as not secured by a qualified residence.

  (i) In general.

  (ii) Example.

  (iii) Allocation of debt secured by two qualified residences.

(p) Definition of qualified residence.

(1) In general.

(2) Principal residence.

(3) Second residence.

  (i) In general.

  (ii) Definition of residence.

  (iii) Use as a residence.

  (iv) Election of second residence.

(4) Allocations between residence and other property.

  (i) In general.

  (ii) Special rule for rental of residence.

  (iii) Examples.

(5) Residence under construction.

  (i) In general.

  (ii) Example.

(6) Special rule for the time-sharing arrangements.

(q) Special rules for tenant-stockholders in cooperative housing corporations.

(1) In general.

(2) Special rule where stock may not be used to secure debt.

(3) Treatment of interest expense of the cooperative described in section 216(a)(2).

(4) Special rule to prevent tax avoidance.

(5) Other definitions.

(r) Effective date.

(b) *Treatment of qualified residence interest.*—Except as provided below, qualified residence interest is deductible under section 163(a). Qualified residence interest is not subject to limitation or otherwise taken into account under section 163(d) (limitation on investment interest), section 163(h)(1) (disallowance of deduction for personal interest), section 263A (capitalization and inclusion in inventory costs of certain expenses) or section 469 (limitations on losses from passive activities). Qualified residence interest is subject to the limitation imposed by section 263(g) (certain interest in the case of straddles), section 264(a)(2) and (4) (interest paid in connection with certain insurance), section 265(a)(2) (interest relating to tax-exempt income), section 266 (carrying charges), section 267(a)(2) (interest with respect to transactions between related taxpayers), section 465 (deductions limited to amount at risk), section 1277 (deferral of interest deduction allocable to accrued market discount), and section 1282 (deferral of interest deduction allocable to accrued discount).

(c) *Determination of qualified residence interest when secured debt does not exceed adjusted purchase price.*—(1) *In general.*—If the sum of the average balances for the taxable year of all secured debts on a qualified residence does not exceed the adjusted purchase price (determined as of the end of the taxable year) of the qualified residence, all of the interest paid or accrued during the taxable year with respect to the secured debts is qualified residence interest. If the sum of the average balances for the taxable year of all secured debts exceeds the adjusted purchase price of the qualified residences (determined as of the end of the taxable year), the taxpayer must use either the simplified method (see paragraph (d) of this section) or the exact method (see paragraph (e) of this section) to determine the amount of interest that is qualified residence interest.

(2) *Examples.*

Example (1). T purchases a qualified residence in 1987 for $65,000. T pays $6,500 in cash and finances the remainder of the purchase with a mortgage of $58,500. In 1988, the average balance of the mortgage is $58,000. Because the average balance of the mortgage is less than the adjusted purchase price of the residence ($65,000), all of the interest paid or accrued during 1988 on the mortgage is qualified residence interest.

Example (2). The facts are the same as in example (1), except that T incurs a second mortgage on January 1, 1988, with an initial principal balance of $2,000. The average balance of the second mort-

gage in 1988 is $1,900. Because the sum of the average balance of the first and second mortgages ($59,900) is less than the adjusted purchase price of the residence ($65,000), all of the interest paid or accrued during 1988 on both the first and second mortgages is qualified residence interest.

Example (3). P borrows $50,000 on January 1, 1988 and secures the debt by a qualified residence. P pays the interest on the debt monthly, but makes no principal payments in 1988. There are no other debts secured by the residence during 1988. On December 31, 1988, the adjusted purchase price of the residence is $40,000. The average balance of the debt in 1988 is $50,000. Because the average balance of the debt exceeds the adjusted purchase price ($10,000), some of the interest on the debt is not qualified residence interest. The portion of the total interest that is qualified residence interest must be determined in accordance with the rules of paragraph (d) or paragraph (e) of this section.

(d) *Determination of qualified residence interest when secured debt exceeds adjusted purchase price—Simplified method.*—(1) *In general.*—Under the simplified method, the amount of qualified residence interest for the taxable year is equal to the total interest paid or accrued during the taxable year with respect to all secured debts multiplied by a fraction (not in excess of one), the numerator of which is the adjusted purchase price (determined as of the end of the taxable year) of the qualified residence and the denominator of which is the sum of the average balances of all secured debts.

(2) *Treatment of interest paid or accrued on secured debt that is not qualified residence interest.*—Under the simplified method, the excess of the total interest paid or accrued during the taxable year with respect to all secured debts over the amount of qualified residence interest is personal interest.

(3) *Example.*—R's principal residence has an adjusted purchase price on December 31, 1988, of $105,000. R has two debts secured by the residence, with the following average balances and interest payments:

Debt	Date Secured	Average Balance	Interest
Debt 1	June 1983	$80,000	$8,000
Debt 2	May 1987	$40,000	$4,800
Total		$120,000	$12,800

The amount of qualified residence interest is determined under the simplified method by multiplying the total interest ($12,800) by a fraction (expressed as a decimal amount) equal to the adjusted purchase price ($105,000) of the residence divided by the combined average balances ($120,000). For 1988, this fraction is equal to 0.875 ($105,000/$120,000). Therefore, $11,200 ($12,800 × 0.875) of the total interest is qualified residence interest. The remaining $1,600 in interest ($12,800 − $11,200) is personal interest, even if (under the rules of §1.163-8T) such remaining interest would be allocated to some other category of interest.

(e) *Determination of qualified residence interest when secured debt exceeds adjusted purchase price—Exact method.*—(1) *In general.*—Under the exact method, the amount of qualified residence interest for the taxable year is determined on a debt-by-debt basis by computing the applicable debt limit for each secured debt and comparing each such applicable debt limit to the average balance of the corresponding debt. If, for the taxable year, the average balance of a secured debt does not exceed the applicable debt limit for that debt, all of the interest paid or accrued during the taxable year with respect to the debt is qualified residence interest. If the average balance of the secured debt exceeds the applicable debt limit for that debt, the amount of qualified residence interest with respect to the debt is determined by multiplying the interest paid or accrued with respect to the debt by a fraction, the numerator of which is the applicable debt limit for that debt and the denominator of which is the average balance of the debt.

(2) *Determination of applicable debt limit.*—For each secured debt, the applicable debt limit for the taxable year is equal to

(i) The lesser of—

(A) The fair market value of the qualified residence as of the date the debt is first secured, and

(B) The adjusted purchase price of the qualified residence as of the end of the taxable year,

(ii) Reduced by the average balance of each debt previously secured by the qualified residence.

For purposes of paragraph (e)(2)(ii) of this section, the average balance of a debt shall be treated as not exceeding the applicable debt limit of such debt. See paragraph (n)(1)(i) of this section for the rule that increases the adjusted purchase price in paragraph (e)(2)(i)(B) of this section by the amount of any qualified indebtedness (certain medical and educational debt). See paragraph (f) of this section for special rules relating to the determination of the fair market value of the qualified residence.

(3) *Example.—(i)* R's principal residence has an adjusted purchase price on December 31, 1988, of $105,000. R has two debts secured by the residence. The average balances and interest payments on each debt during 1988 and fair market value of the residence on the date each debt was secured are as follows:

Debt	Date Secured	Fair Market Value	Average Balance	Interest
Debt 1	June 1983	$100,000	$80,000	$8,000
Debt 2	May 1987	$140,000	$40,000	$4,800
Total			$120,000	$12,800

(ii) The amount of qualified residence interest for 1988 under the exact method is determined as follows. Because there are no debts previously secured by the residence, the applicable debt limit for Debt 1 is $100,000 (the lesser of the adjusted purchase price as of the end of the taxable year and the fair market value of the residence at the time the debt was secured). Because the average balance of Debt 1 ($80,000) does not exceed its applicable debt limit ($100,000), all of the interest paid on the debt during 1988 ($8,000) is qualified residence interest.

(iii) The applicable debt limit for Debt 2 is $25,000 ($105,000 (the lesser of $140,000 fair market value and $105,000 adjusted purchase price) reduced by $80,000 (the average balance of Debt 1)). Because the average balance of Debt 2 ($40,000) exceeds its applicable debt limit, the amount of qualified residence interest on Debt 2 is determined by multiplying the amount of interest paid on the debt during the year ($4,800) by a fraction equal to its applicable debt limit divided by its average balance ($25,000/$40,000 = 0.625). Accordingly, $3,000 ($4,800 × 0.625) of the interest paid in 1988 on Debt 2 is qualified residence interest. The character of the remaining $1,800 of interest paid on Debt 2 is determined under the rules of paragraph (e)(4) of this section.

(4) *Treatment of interest paid or accrued with respect to secured debt that is not qualified residence interest.—(i) In general.*—Under the exact method, the excess of the interest paid or accrued during the taxable year with respect to a secured debt over the amount of qualified residence interest with respect to the debt is allocated under the rules of § 1.163-8T.

(ii) *Example.*—T borrows $20,000 and the entire proceeds of the debt are disbursed by the lender to T's broker to purchase securities held for investment. T secures the debt with T's principal residence. In 1990, T pays $2,000 of interest on the debt. Assume that under the rules of paragraph (e) of this section, $1,500 of the interest is qualified residence interest. The remaining $500 in interest expense would be allocated under the rules of § 1.163-8T. Section 1.163-8T generally allocates debt (and the associated interest expense) by tracing disbursements of the debt proceeds to specific expenditures. Accordingly, the $500 interest expense on the debt that is not qualified residence interest is investment interest subject to section 163(d).

(iii) *Special rule if debt is allocated to more than one expenditure.*—If—

(A) The average balance of a secured debt exceeds the applicable debt limit for that debt, and

(B) Under the rules of § 1.163-8T, interest paid or accrued with respect to such debt is allocated to more than one expenditure, the interest expense that is not qualified residence interest may be allocated among such expenditures, to the extent of such expenditures, in any manner selected by the taxpayer.

(iv) *Example.—(i)* C borrows $60,000 secured by a qualified residence. C uses (within the meaning of § 1.163-8T) $20,000 of the proceeds in C's trade or business, $20,000 to purchase stock held for investment and $20,000 for personal purposes. In 1990, C pays $6,000 in interest on the debt and, under the rules of § 1.163-8T, $2,000 in interest is allocable to trade or business expenses, $2,000 to investment expenses and $2,000 to personal expenses. Assume that under paragraph (e) of this section, $2,500 of the interest is qualified residence interest and $3,500 of the interest is not qualified residence interest.

(ii) Under paragraph (e)(4)(iii) of this section, C may allocate up to $2,000 of the interest that is not qualified residence interest to any of the three categories of expenditures up to a total of $3,500 for all three categories. Therefore, for example, C may allocate $2,000 of such interest to C's trade or business and $1,500 of such interest to the purchase of stock.

(f) *Special rules.*—(1) *Special rules for personal property.—(i) In general.*—If a qualified residence is personal property under State law (*e.g.*, a boat or motorized vehicle)—

(A) For purposes of paragraphs (c)(1) and (d)(1) of this section, if the fair market value of the residence as of the date that any secured debt (outstanding during the taxable year) is first secured by the residence is less than the adjusted purchase price as of the end of the taxable year, the lowest such fair market value shall be substituted for the adjusted purchase price.

(B) For purposes of paragraphs (e)(2)(i)(A) and (f)(1)(i)(A) of this section, the fair market value of the residence as of the date the debt is first secured by the residence shall not exceed the fair market value as of any date on which the taxpayer borrows any additional amount with respect to the debt.

(ii) *Example.*—D owns a recreational vehicle that is a qualified residence under paragraph (p)(4) of this section. The adjusted purchase price and fair market value of the recreational vehicle is $20,000 in 1989. In 1989, D establishes a line of credit secured by the recreational vehicle. As of June 1, 1992, the fair market value of the vehicle has decreased to $10,000. On that day, D borrows an additional amount on the debt by using the line of credit. Although under paragraphs (e)(2)(i) and (f)(1)(i)(A) of this section, fair market value is determined at the time the debt is first secured, under paragraph (f)(1)(i)(B) of this section, the fair market value is the lesser of that amount or the fair market value on the most recent date that D borrows any additional amount with respect to the line of credit. Therefore, the fair market value with respect to the debt is $10,000.

(2) *Special rule for real property.—(i) In general.*—For purposes of paragraph (e)(2)(i)(A) of this section, the fair market value of a qualified residence that is real property under State law is presumed irrebuttably to be not less than the adjusted purchase price of the residence as of the last day of the taxable year.

(ii) *Example.—(i)* C purchases a residence on August 11, 1987, for $50,000, incurring a first mortgage. The residence is real property under State law. During 1987, C makes $10,000 in home improvements. Accordingly, the adjusted purchase price of the residence as of December 31, 1988, is $60,000. C incurs a second mortgage on May 19, 1988, as of which time the fair market value of the residence is $55,000.

(ii) For purposes of determining the applicable debt limit for each debt, the fair market value of the residence is generally determined as of the time the debt is first secured. Accordingly, the fair market value would be $50,000 and $55,000 with respect to the first and second mortgage, respectively. Under the special rule of paragraph (f)(2)(i) of this section, however, the fair market value with respect to both debts in 1988 is $60,000, the adjusted purchase price on December 31, 1988.

(g) *Selection of method.*—For any taxable year, a taxpayer may use the simplified method (described in paragraph (d) of this section) or the exact method (described in paragraph (e) of this section) by completing the appropriate portion of Form 8598. A taxpayer with two qualified residences may use the simplified method for one residence and the exact method for the other residence.

(h) *Average balance.*—(1) *Average balance defined.*—For purposes of this section, the term "average balance" means the amount determined under this paragraph (h). A taxpayer is not required to use the same method to determine the average balance of all secured debts during a taxable year or of any particular secured debt from one year to the next.

(2) *Average balance reported by lender.*—If a lender that is subject to section 6050H (returns relating to mortgage interest received in trade or business from individuals) reports the average balance of a secured debt on Form 1098, the taxpayer may use the average balance so reported.

(3) *Average balance computed on a daily basis.—(i) In general.*—The average balance may be determined by—

(A) Adding the outstanding balance of a debt on each day during the taxable year that the debt is secured by a qualified residence, and

(B) Dividing the sum by the number of days during the taxable year that the residence is a qualified residence.

(ii) *Example.*—Taxpayer A incurs a debt of $10,000 on September 1, 1989, securing the debt with A's principal residence. The residence is A's principal residence during the entire taxable year. A pays current interest on the debt monthly, but makes no principal payments. The debt is, therefore, outstanding for 122 days with a balance each day of $10,000. The residence is a qualified residence for 365 days. The average balance of the debt for 1989 is $3,342 (122 × $10,000/365).

(4) *Average balance computed using the interest rate.*—(i) *In general.*—If all accrued interest on a secured debt is paid at least monthly, the average balance of the secured debt may be determined by dividing the interest paid or accrued during the taxable year while the debt is secured by a qualified residence by the annual interest rate on the debt. If the interest rate on a debt varies during the taxable year, the lowest annual interest rate that applies to the debt during the taxable year must be used for purposes of this paragraph (h)(4). If the residence securing the debt is a qualified residence for less than the entire taxable year, the average balance of any secured debt may be determined by dividing the average balance determined under the preceding sentence by the percentage of the taxable year that the debt is secured by a qualified residence.

(ii) *Points and prepaid interest.*—For purposes of paragraph (h)(4)(i) of this section, the amount of interest paid during the taxable year does not include any amount paid as points and includes prepaid interest only in the year accrued.

(iii) *Examples.*—*Example (1).* B has a line of credit secured by a qualified residence for the entire taxable year. The interest rate on the debt is 10 percent throughout the taxable year. The principal balance on the debt changes throughout the year. B pays the accrued interest on the debt monthly. B pays $2,500 in interest on the debt during the taxable year. The average balance of the debt ($25,000) may be computed by dividing the total interest paid by the interest rate ($25,000 = $2,500/0.10).

Example (2). Assume the same facts as in example 1, except that the residence is a qualified residence, and the debt is outstanding, for only one-half of the taxable year and B pays only $1,250 in interest on the debt during the taxable year. The average balance of the debt may be computed by first dividing the total interest paid by the interest rate ($12,500 = $1,250/0.10). Second, because the residence is not a qualified residence for the entire taxable year, the average balance must be determined by dividing this amount ($12,500) by the portion of the year that the residence is qualified (0.50). The average balance is therefore $25,000 ($12,500/0.50).

(5) *Average balance computed using average of beginning and ending balances.*—(i) *In general.*—If—

(A) A debt requires level payments at fixed equal intervals (*e.g.*, monthly, quarterly) no less often than semi-annually during the taxable year,

(B) The taxpayer prepays no more than one month's principal on the debt during the taxable year, and

(C) No new amounts are borrowed on the debt during the taxable year,

the average balance of the debt may be determined by adding the principal balance as of the first day of the taxable year that the debt is secured by the qualified residence and the principal balance as of the last day of the taxable year that the debt is secured by the qualified residence and dividing the sum by 2. If the debt is secured by a qualified residence for less than the entire period during the taxable year that the residence is a qualified residence, the average balance may be determined by multiplying the average balance determined under the preceding sentence by a fraction, the numerator of which is the number of days during the taxable year that the debt is secured by the qualified residence and the denominator of which is the number of days during the taxable year that the residence is a qualified residence. For purposes of this paragraph (h)(5)(i), the determination of whether payments are level shall disregard the fact that the amount of the payments may be adjusted from time to time to take into account changes in the applicable interest rate.

(ii) *Example.*—C borrows $10,000 in 1988, securing the debt with a second mortgage on a principal residence. The terms of the loan require C to make equal monthly payments of principal and interest so as to amortize the entire loan balance over 20 years. The balance of the debt is $9,652 on January 1, 1990, and is $9,450 on December 31, 1990. The average balance of the debt during 1990 may be computed as follows:

Balance on first day of the year		$9,652
Balance on last day of the year		$9,450
Average balance . . . $\dfrac{\$9,652 + \$9,450}{2}$	=	$9,551

(6) *Highest principal balance.*—The average balance of a debt may be determined by taking the highest principal balance of the debt during the taxable year.

(7) *Other methods provided by the Commissioner.*—The average balance may be determined using any other method provided by the Commissioner by form, publication, revenue ruling, or revenue procedure. Such methods may include methods similar to (but with restrictions different from) those provided in paragraph (h) of this section.

(8) *Anti-abuse rule.*—If, as a result of the determination of the average balance of a debt using any of the methods specified in paragraphs (h)(4), (5), or (6) of this section, there is a significant overstatement of the amount of qualified residence interest and a principal purpose of the pattern of payments and borrowing on the debt is to cause the amount of such qualified residence interest to be overstated, the district director may redetermine the average balance using the method specified under paragraph (h)(3) of this section.

(i) [Reserved.]

(j) *Determination of interest paid or accrued during the taxable year.*—(1) *In general.*—For purposes of determining the amount of qualified residence interest with respect to a secured debt, the amount of interest paid or accrued during the taxable year includes only interest paid or accrued while the debt is secured by a qualified residence.

(2) *Special rules for cash-basis taxpayers.*—(i) *Points deductible in year paid under section 461(g)(2).*—If points described in section 461(g)(2) (certain points paid in respect of debt incurred in connection with the purchase or improvement of a principal residence) are paid with respect to a debt, the amount of such points is qualified residence interest.

(ii) *Points and other prepaid interest described in section 461(g)(1).*—The amount of points or other prepaid interest charged to capital account under section 461(g)(1) (prepaid interest) that is qualified residence interest shall be determined under the rules of paragraphs (c) through (e) of this section in the same manner as any other interest paid with respect to the debt in the taxable year to which such payments are allocable under section 461(g)(1).

(3) *Examples.*

Example (1). T designates a vacation home as a qualified residence as of October 1, 1987. The home is encumbered by a mortgage during the entire taxable year. For purposes of determining the amount of qualified residence interest for 1987, T may take into account the interest paid or accrued on the secured debt from October 1, 1987, through December 31, 1987.

Example (2). R purchases a principal residence on June 17, 1987. As part of the purchase price, R obtains a conventional 30-year mortgage, secured by the residence. At closing, R pays $2\frac{1}{2}$ points on the mortgage and interest on the mortgage for the period June 17, 1987 through June 30, 1987. The points are actually paid by R and are not merely withheld from the loan proceeds. R incurs no additional secured debt during 1987. Assuming that the points satisfy the requirements of section 461(g)(2), the entire amount of points and the interest paid at closing are qualified residence interest.

Example (3). (i) On July 1, 1987, W borrows $120,000 to purchase a residence to use as a vacation home. W secures the debt with the residence. W pays 2 points, or $2,400. The debt has a term of 10 years and requires monthly payments of principal and interest. W is permitted to amortize the points at the rate of $20 per month over 120 months. W elects to treat the residence as a second residence. W has no other debt secured by the residence. The average balance of the debt in each taxable year is less than the adjusted purchase price of the residence. W sells the residence on June 30, 1990, and pays off the remaining balance of the debt.

(ii) W is entitled to treat the following amounts of the points as interest paid on a debt secured by a qualified residence—

1987	$120	= $20 × 6 months;
1988	$240	= $20 × 12 months;
1989	$120	= $20 × 6 months.
TOTAL	$480	

All of the interest paid on the debt, including the allocable points, is qualified residence interest. Upon repaying the debt, the remaining $1,920 ($2,400 – $480) in unamortized points is treated as interest paid in 1990 and, because the average balance of the secured debt in 1990 is less than the adjusted purchase price, is also qualified residence interest.

(k) *Determination of adjusted purchase price and fair market value.*—(1) *Adjusted purchase price.*—(i) *In general.*—For purposes of this section, the adjusted purchase price of a qualified residence is equal to the taxpayer's basis in the residence as initially determined under section 1012 or other applicable sections of the Internal Revenue Code, increased by the cost of any improvements to the residence that have been added to the taxpayer's basis in the residence under section 1016(a)(1). Any other adjustments to basis, including those required under section 1033(b) (involuntary conversions), and 1034(e) (rollover of gain on sale of principal residence) are disregarded in determining the taxpayer's adjusted purchase price. If, for example, a taxpayer's second residence is rented for a portion of the year and its basis is reduced by depreciation allowed in connection with the rental use of the property, the amount of the taxpayer's adjusted purchase price in the residence is not reduced. See paragraph (m) of this section for a rule that treats the sum of the grandfathered amounts of all secured debts as the adjusted purchase price of the residence.

(ii) *Adjusted purchase price of a qualified residence acquired incident to divorce.*—[Reserved.]

(iii) *Examples.*—*Example (1).* X purchases a residence for $120,000. X's basis, as determined under section 1012, is the cost of the property, or $120,000. Accordingly, the adjusted purchase price of the residence is initially $120,000.

Example (2). Y owns a principal residence that has a basis of $30,000. Y sells the residence for $100,000 and purchases a new principal residence for a $120,000. Under section 1034, Y does not recognize gain on the sale of the former residence. Under section 1034(e), Y's basis in the new residence is reduced by the amount of gain not recognized. Therefore, under section 1034(e), Y's basis in the new residence is $50,000 ($120,000 – $70,000). For purposes of section 163(h), however, the adjusted purchase price of the residence is not adjusted under section 1034(e). Therefore, the adjusted purchase price of the residence is initially $120,000.

Example (3). Z acquires a residence by gift. The donor's basis in the residence was $30,000. Z's basis in the residence, determined under section 1015, is $30,000. Accordingly, the adjusted purchase price of the residence is initially $30,000.

(2) *Fair market value.*—(i) *In general.*—For purposes of this section, the fair market value of a qualified residence on any date is the fair market value of the taxpayer's interest in the residence on such date. In addition, the fair market value determined under this paragraph (k)(2)(i) shall be determined by taking into account the cost of improvements to the residence reasonably expected to be made with the proceeds of the debt.

(ii) *Example.*—In 1988, the adjusted purchase price of P's second residence is $65,000 and the fair market value of the residence is $70,000. At that time, P incurs an additional debt of $10,000, the proceeds of which P reasonably expects to use to add two bedrooms to the residence. Because the fair market value is determined by taking into account the cost of improvements to the residence that are reasonably expected to be made with the proceeds of the debt, the fair market value of the residence with respect to the debt incurred in 1988 is $80,000 ($70,000 + $10,000).

(3) *Allocation of adjusted purchase price and fair market value.*—If a property includes both a qualified residence and other property, the adjusted purchase price and the fair market value of such property must be allocated between the qualified residence and the other property. See paragraph (p)(4) of this section for rules governing such an allocation.

(l) [Reserved].

(m) *Grandfathered amount.*—(1) *Substitution for adjusted purchase price.*—If, for the taxable year, the sum of the grandfathered amounts, if any, of all secured debts exceeds the adjusted purchase price of the qualified residence, such sum may be treated as the adjusted purchase price of the residence under paragraphs (c), (d) and (e) of this section.

(2) *Determination of grandfathered amount.*—(i) *In general.*—For any taxable year, the grandfathered amount of any secured debt that was incurred on or before August 16, 1986, and was secured by the residence continuously from August 16, 1986, through the end of the taxable year, is the average balance of the debt for the taxable year. A secured debt that was not incurred and secured on or before August 16, 1986, has no grandfathered amount.

(ii) *Special rule for lines of credit and certain other debt.*—If, with respect to a debt described in paragraph (m)(2)(i) of this section, a taxpayer has borrowed any additional amounts after August 16, 1986, the grandfathered amount of such debt is equal to the lesser of—

(A) The average balance of the debt for the taxable year, or

(B) The principal balance of the debt as of August 16, 1986, reduced (but not below zero) by all principal payments after August 16, 1986, and before the first day of the current taxable year. For purposes of this paragraph (m)(2)(ii), a taxpayer shall not be considered to have borrowed any additional amount with respect to a debt merely because accrued interest is added to the principal

balance of the debt, so long as such accrued interest is paid by the taxpayer no less often than quarterly.

(iii) *Fair market value limitation.*—The grandfathered amount of any debt for any taxable year may not exceed the fair market value of the residence on August 16, 1986, reduced by the principal balance on that day of all previously secured debt.

(iv) *Examples.*—*Example (1).* As of August 16, 1986, T has one debt secured by T's principal residence. The debt is a conventional self-amortizing mortgage and, on August 16, 1986, it has an outstanding principal balance of $75,000. In 1987, the average balance of the mortgage is $73,000. The adjusted purchase price of the residence as of the end of 1987 is $50,000. Because the mortgage was incurred and secured on or before August 16, 1986 and T has not borrowed any additional amounts with respect to the mortgage, the grandfathered amount is the average balance, $73,000. Because the grandfathered amount exceeds the adjusted purchase price ($50,000), T may treat the grandfathered amount as the adjusted purchase price in determining the amount of qualified residence interest.

Example (2). (i) The facts are the same as in example (1), except that in May 1986, T also obtains a home equity line of credit that, on August 16, 1986, has a principal balance of $40,000. In November 1986, T borrows an additional $10,000 on the home equity line, increasing the balance to $50,000. In December 1986, T repays $5,000 of principal on the home equity line. The average balance of the home equity line in 1987 is $45,000.

(ii) Because T has borrowed additional amounts on the line of credit after August 16, 1986, the grandfathered amount for that debt must be determined under the rules of paragraph (m)(2)(ii) of this section. Accordingly, the grandfathered amount for the line of credit is equal to the lesser of $45,000, the average balance of the debt in 1987, and $35,000, the principal balance on August 16, 1986, reduced by all principal payments between August 17, 1986, and December 31, 1986 ($40,000 – $5,000). The sum of the grandfathered amounts with respect to the residence is $108,000 ($73,000 + $35,000). Because the sum of the grandfathered amounts exceeds the adjusted purchase price ($50,000), T may treat the sum as the adjusted purchase price in determining the qualified residence interest for 1987.

(3) *Refinancing of grandfathered debt.*—(i) *In general.*—A debt incurred and secured on or before August 16, 1986, is refinanced if some or all of the outstanding balance of such a debt (the "original debt") is repaid out of the proceeds of a second debt secured by the same qualified residence (the "replacement debt"). In the case of a refinancing, the replacement debt is treated as a debt incurred and secured on or before August 16, 1986, and the grandfathered amount of such debt is the amount (but not less than zero) determined pursuant to paragraph (m)(3)(ii) of this section.

(ii) *Determination of grandfathered amount.*—(A) *Exact refinancing.*—If—

(1) The entire proceeds of a replacement debt are used to refinance one or more original debts, and

(2) The taxpayer has not borrowed any additional amounts after August 16, 1986, with respect to the original debt or debts,

the grandfathered amount of the replacement debt is the average balance of the replacement debt. For purposes of the preceding sentence, the fact that proceeds of a replacement debt are used to pay costs of obtaining the replacement debt (including points or other closing costs) shall be disregarded in determining whether the entire proceeds of the replacement debt have been used to refinance one or more original debts.

(B) *Refinancing other than exact refinancings.*—(1) *Year of refinancing.*—In the taxable year in which an original debt is refinanced, the grandfathered amount of the original and replacement debts is equal to the lesser of—

(i) The sum of the average balances of the original debt and the replacement debt, and

(ii) The principal balance of the original debt as of August 16, 1986, reduced by all principal payments on the original debt after August 16, 1986, and before the first day of the current taxable year.

(2) *In subsequent years.*—In any taxable year after the taxable year in which an original debt is refinanced, the grandfathered amount of the replacement debt is equal to the least of—

(i) The average balance of the replacement debt for the taxable year,

(ii) The amount of the replacement debt used to repay the principal balance of the original debt, reduced by all principal payments on the replacement debt after the date of the refinancing and before the first day of the current taxable year, or *(iii)* The principal balance of the original debt on August 16, 1986, reduced by all principal payments on the original debt after August 16, 1986, and before the date of the refinancing, and further reduced by all principal payments on the replacement debt after the date of the refinancing and before the first day of the current taxable year.

*(C) Example.—(i) Facts.—*On August 16, 1986, T has a single debt secured by a principal residence with a balance of $150,000. On July 1, 1988, T refinances the debt, which still has a principal balance of $150,000, with a new secured debt. The principal balance of the replacement debt throughout 1988 and 1989 is $150,000. The adjusted purchase price of the residence is $100,000 throughout 1987, 1988 and 1989. The average balance of the original debt was $150,000 in 1987 and $75,000 in 1988. The average balance of the replacement debt is $75,000 in 1988 and $150,000 in 1989.

*(ii) Grandfathered amount in 1987.—*The original debt was incurred and secured on or before August 16, 1986 and T has not borrowed any additional amounts with respect to the debt. Therefore, its grandfathered amount in 1987 is its average balance ($150,000). This amount is treated as the adjusted purchase price for 1987 and all of the interest paid on the debt is qualified residence interest.

*(iii) Grandfathered amount in 1988.—*Because the replacement debt was used to refinance a debt incurred and secured on or before August 16, 1986, the replacement debt is treated as a grandfathered debt. Because all of the proceeds of the replacement debt were used in the refinancing and because no amounts have been borrowed after August 16, 1986, on the original debt, the grandfathered amount for the original debt is its average balance ($75,000) and the grandfathered amount for the replacement debt is its average balance ($75,000). Since the sum of the grandfathered amounts ($150,000) exceeds the adjusted purchase price of the residence, the sum of the grandfathered amounts may be substituted for the adjusted purchase price for 1988 and all of the interest paid on the debt is qualified residence interest.

*(iv) Grandfathered amount in 1989.—*The grandfathered amount for the replacement debt is its average balance ($150,000). This amount is treated as the adjusted purchase price for 1989 and all of the interest paid on the mortgage is qualified residence interest.

*(4) Limitation on term of grandfathered debt.—(i) In general.—*An original debt or replacement debt shall not have any grandfathered amount in any taxable year that begins after the date, as determined on August 16, 1986, that the original debt was required to be repaid in full (the "maturity date"). If a replacement debt is used to refinance more than one original debt, the maturity date is determined by reference to the original debt that, as of August 16, 1986, had the latest maturity date.

*(ii) Special rule for nonamortizing debt.—*If an original debt was actually incurred and secured on or before August 16, 1986, and if as of such date the terms of such debt did not require the amortization of its principal over its original term, the maturity date of the replacement debt is the earlier of the maturity date of the replacement debt or the date 30 years after the date the original debt is first refinanced.

*(iii) Example.—*C incurs a debt on May 10, 1986, the final payment of which is due May 1, 2006. C incurs a second debt on August 11, 1990, with a term of 20 years and uses the proceeds of the second debt to refinance the first debt. Because, under paragraph (m)(4)(i) of this section, a replacement debt will not have any grandfathered amount in any taxable year that begins after the maturity date of the original debt (May 1, 2006), the second debt has no grandfathered amount in any taxable year after 2006.

*(n) Qualified indebtedness (secured debt used for medical and educational purposes).—(1) In general.—(i) Treatment of qualified indebtedness.—*The amount of any qualified indebtedness resulting from a secured debt may be added to the adjusted purchase price under paragraph (e)(2)(i)(B) of this section to determine the applicable debt limit for that secured debt and any other debt subsequently secured by the qualified residence.

*(ii) Determination of amount of qualified indebtedness.—*If, as of the end of the taxable year (or the last day in the taxable year that the debt is secured), at least 90 percent of the proceeds of a secured debt are used *(within the meaning of paragraph (n)(2) of this section)* to pay for qualified medical and educational expenses *(within the meaning of paragraphs (n)(3) and (n)(4) of this section)*, the amount of qualified indebtedness resulting from that debt for the taxable year is equal to the average balance of such debt for the taxable year.

*(iii) Determination of amount of qualified indebtedness for mixed-use debt.—*If, as of the end of the taxable year (or the last day in the taxable year that the debt is secured), more than ten percent of the proceeds of a secured debt are used to pay for expenses other than qualified medical and educational expenses, the amount of qualified indebtedness resulting from that debt for the taxable year shall equal the lesser of—

(A) The average balance of the debt, or

(B) The amount of the proceeds of the debt used to pay for qualified medical and educational expenses through the end of the taxable year, reduced by any principal payments on the debt before the first day of the current taxable year.

(iv) Example.—(i) C incurs a $10,000 debt on April 20, 1987, which is secured on that date by C's principal residence. C immediately uses (within the meaning of paragraph (n)(2) of this section) $4,000 of the proceeds of the debt to pay for a qualified medical expense. C makes no principal payments on the debt during 1987. During 1988 and 1989, C makes principal payments of $1,000 per year. The average balance of the debt during 1988 is $9,500 and the average balance during 1989 is $8,500.

(ii) Under paragraph (n)(1)(iii) of this section, C determines the amount of qualified indebtedness for 1988 as follows:

Average balance		$9,500
Amount of debt used to pay for qualified medical expenses	$4,000	
Less payments of principal before 1988		
. . . .	$0	
Net qualified expenses		$4,000

The amount of qualified indebtedness for 1988 is, therefore, $4,000 (lesser of $9,500 average balance or $4,000 net qualified expenses). This amount may be added to the adjusted purchase price of C's principal residence under paragraph (e)(2)(i)(B) of this section for purposes of computing the applicable debt limit for this debt and any other debt subsequently secured by the principal residence.

(iii) C determines the amount of qualified indebtedness for 1989 as follows:

Average balance		$8,500
Amount of debt used to pay qualified medical expenses	$4,000	
Less payments of principal before 1989		
. . . .	$1,000	
Net qualified expenses		$3,000

The amount of qualified indebtedness for 1989 is, therefore, $3,000 (lesser of $8,500 average balance or $3,000 net qualified expense).

*(v) Prevention of double counting in year of refinancing.—(A) In general.—*A debt used to pay for qualified medical or educational expenses is refinanced if some or all of the outstanding balance of the debt (the "original debt") is repaid out of the proceeds of a second debt (the "replacement debt"). If, in the year of a refinancing, the combined qualified indebtedness of the original debt and the replacement debt exceeds the combined qualified expenses of such debts, the amount of qualified indebtedness for each such debt shall be determined by multiplying the amount of qualified indebtedness for each such debt by a fraction, the numerator of which is the combined qualified expenses and the denominator of which is the combined qualified indebtedness.

*(B) Definitions.—*For purposes of paragraph (n)(1)(v)(A) of this section—

(1) The term "combined qualified indebtedness" means the sum of the qualified indebtedness (determined without regard to paragraph (n)(1)(v) of this section) for the original debt and the replacement debt.

(2) The term "combined qualified expenses" means the amount of the proceeds of the original debt used to pay for qualified medical and educational expenses through the end of the current taxable year, reduced by any principal payments on the debt before the first day of the current taxable year, and increased by the amount, if any, of the proceeds of the replacement debt used to pay such expenses through the end of the current taxable year other than as part of the refinancing.

(C) Example.—(i) On August 11, 1987, C incurs a $8,000 debt secured by a principal residence. C uses (within the meaning of paragraph (n)(2)(i) of this section) $5,000 of the proceeds of the debt to pay for qualified educational expenses. C makes no principal payments on the debt. On July 1, 1988, C incurs a new debt in the amount of $8,000 secured by C's principal residence and uses all of the proceeds of the new debt to repay the original debt. Under paragraph (n)(2)(ii) of this section $5,000 of the new debt is treated as being used to pay for qualified educational expenses. C makes no

principal payments (other than the refinancing) during 1987 or 1988 on either debt and pays all accrued interest monthly. The average balance of each debt in 1988 is $4,000.

(ii) Under paragraph (n)(1)(iii) of this section, the amount of qualified indebtedness for 1988 with respect to the original debt is $4,000 (the lesser of its average balance ($4,000) and the amount of the debt used to pay for qualified medical and educational expenses ($5,000)). Similarly, the amount of qualified indebtedness for 1988 with respect to the replacement debt is also $4,000. Both debts, however, are subject in 1988 to the limitation in paragraph (n)(1)(v)(A) of this section. The combined qualified indebtedness, determined without regard to the limitation, is $8,000 ($4,000 of qualified indebtedness from each debt). The combined qualified expenses are $5,000 ($5,000 from the original debt and $0 from the replacement debt). The amount of qualified indebtedness from each debt must, therefore, be reduced by a fraction, the numerator of which is $5,000 (the combined qualified expenses) and the denominator of which is $8,000 (the combined qualified indebtedness). After application of the limitation, the amount of qualified indebtedness for the original debt is $2,500 ($4,000 × $^5/_8$). Similarly, the amount of qualified indebtedness for the replacement debt is $2,500. Note that the total qualified indebtedness for both the original and the replacement debt is $5,000 ($2,500 + $2,500). Therefore, C is entitled to the same amount of qualified indebtedness as C would have been entitled to if C had not refinanced the debt.

(vi) *Special rule for principal payments in excess of qualified expenses.*—For purposes of paragraph (n)(1)(iii)(B), (n)(1)(v)(B)(2) and (n)(2)(ii) of this section, a principal payment is taken into account only to the extent that the payment, when added to all prior payments, does not exceed the amount used on or before the date of the payment to pay for qualified medical and educational expenses.

(2) *Debt used to pay for qualified medical or educational expenses.*— (i) *In general.*—For purposes of this section, the proceeds of a debt are used to pay for qualified medical or educational expenses to the extent that—

(A) The taxpayer pays qualified medical or educational expenses within 90 days before or after the date that amounts are actually borrowed with respect to the debt, the proceeds of the debt are not directly allocable to another expense under § 1.163-8T(c)(3) (allocation of debt; proceeds not disbursed to borrower) and the proceeds of any other debt are not allocable to the medical or educational expenses under § 1.163-8T(c)(3), or

(B) The proceeds of the debt are otherwise allocated to such expenditures under § 1.163-8T.

(ii) *Special rule for refinancings.*—For purposes of this section, the proceeds of a debt are used to pay for qualified medical and educational expenses to the extent that the proceeds of the debt are allocated under § 1.163-8T to the repayment of another debt (the "original debt"), but only to the extent of the amount of the original debt used to pay for qualified medical and educational expenses, reduced by any principal payments on such debt up to the time of the refinancing.

(iii) *Other special rules.*—The following special rules apply for purposes of this section.

(A) Proceeds of a debt are used to pay for qualified medical or educational expenses as of the later of the taxable year in which such proceeds are borrowed or the taxable year in which such expenses are paid.

(B) The amount of debt which may be treated as being used to pay for qualified medical or educational expenses may not exceed the amount of such expenses.

(C) Proceeds of a debt may not be treated as being used to pay for qualified medical or educational expenses to the extent that:

(1) The proceeds have been repaid as of the time the expense is paid;

(2) The proceeds are actually borrowed before August 17, 1986; or

(3) The medical or educational expenses are paid before August 17, 1986.

(iv) *Examples.*—*Example (1).* A pays a $5,000 qualified educational expense from a checking account that A maintains at Bank 1 on November 9, 1987. On January 1, 1988, A incurs a $20,000 debt that is secured by A's residence and places the proceeds of the debt in a savings account that A also maintains at Bank 1. A pays another $5,000 qualified educational expense on March 15 from a checking account that A maintains at Bank 2. Under paragraph (n)(2) of this section, the debt proceeds are used to pay for both educational expenses, regardless of other deposits to, or expenditures from, the accounts, because both expenditures are made within 90 days before or after the debt was incurred.

Example (2). B pays a $5,000 qualified educational expense from a checking account on November 1, 1987. On November 30, 1987, B incurs a debt secured by B's residence, and the lender disburses the debt proceeds directly to a person who sells B a new car. Although the educational expense is paid within 90 days of the date the debt is incurred, the proceeds of the debt are not used to pay for the educational expense because the proceeds are directly allocable to the purchase of the new car under § 1.163-8T(c)(3).

Example (3). On November 1, 1987, C borrows $5,000 from C's college. The proceeds of this debt are not disbursed to C, but rather are used to pay tuition fees for C's attendance at the college. On November 30, 1987, C incurs a second debt and secures the debt by C's residence. Although the $5,000 educational expense is paid within 90 days before the second debt is incurred, the proceeds of the second debt are not used to pay for the educational expense, because the proceeds of the first debt are directly allocable to the educational expense under § 1.163-8T(c)(3).

Example (4). On January 1, 1988, D incurs a $20,000 debt secured by a qualified residence. D places the proceeds of the debt in a separate account (*i.e.,* the proceeds of the debt are the only deposit in the account). D makes payments of $5,000 each for qualified educational expenses on September 1, 1988, September 1, 1989, September 1, 1990, and September 1, 1991. Because the debt proceeds are allocated to educational expenses as of the date the expenses are paid, under the rules of § 1.163-8T(c)(4), the following amounts of the debt proceeds are used to pay for qualified educational expenses as of the end of each year:

1988:	$ 5,000
1989:	$10,000
1990:	$15,000
1991:	$20,000

Example (5). During 1987 E incurs a $10,000 debt secured by a principle [sic] residence. E uses (within the meaning of paragraph (n)(2)(i) of this section) all of the proceeds of the debt to pay for qualified educational expenses. On August 20, 1988, at which time the balance of the debt is $9,500, E incurs a new debt in the amount of $9,500 secured by E's principal residence and uses all of the proceeds of the new debt to repay the original debt. Under paragraph (n)(2)(ii) of this section, all of the proceeds of the new debt are used to pay for qualified educational expenses.

(3) *Qualified medical expenses.*—Qualified medical expenses are amounts that are paid for medical care (within the meaning of section 213(d)(1)(A) and (B)) for the taxpayer, the taxpayer's spouse, or a dependent of the taxpayer (within the meaning of section 152), and that are not compensated for by insurance or otherwise.

(4) *Qualified educational expenses.*—Qualified educational expenses are amounts that are paid for tuition, fees, books, supplies and equipment required for enrollment, attendance or courses of instruction at an educational organization described in section 170(b)(1)(A)(ii) and for any reasonable living expenses while away from home while in attendance at such an institution, for the taxpayer, the taxpayer's spouse or a dependent of the taxpayer (within the meaning of section 152) and that are not reimbursed by scholarship or otherwise.

(o) *Secured debt.*—(1) *In general.*—For purposes of this section, the term "secured debt" means a debt that is on the security of any instrument (such as a mortgage, deed of trust, or land contract)—

(i) That makes the interest of the debtor in the qualified residence specific security for the payment of the debt,

(ii) Under which, in the event of default, the residence could be subjected to the satisfaction of the debt with the same priority as a mortgage or deed of trust in the jurisdiction in which the property is situated, and

(iii) That is recorded, where permitted, or is otherwise perfected in accordance with applicable State law.

A debt will not be considered to be secured by a qualified residence if it is secured solely by virtue of a lien upon the general assets of the taxpayer or by a security interest, such as a mechanic's lien or judgment lien, that attaches to the property without the consent of the debtor.

(2) *Special rule for debt in certain States.*—Debt will not fail to be treated as secured solely because, under an applicable State or local homestead law or other debtor protection law in effect on August 16, 1986, the security interest is ineffective or the enforceability of the security interest is restricted.

(3) *Time at which debt is treated as secured.*—For purposes of this section, a debt is treated as secured as of the date on which each of the requirements of paragraph (o)(1) of this section are satisfied, regardless of when amounts are actually borrowed with respect to the debt. For purposes of this paragraph (o)(3), if the instrument is

recorded within a commercially reasonable time after the security interest is granted, the instrument will be treated as recorded on the date that the security interest was granted.

(4) *Partially secured debt.*—(i) *In general.*—If the security interest is limited to a prescribed maximum amount or portion of the residence, and the average balance of the debt exceeds such amount or the value of such portion, such excess shall not be treated as secured debt for purposes of this section.

(ii) *Example.*—T borrows $80,000 on January 1, 1991. T secures the debt with a principal residence. The security in the residence for the debt, however, is limited to $20,000. T pays $8,000 in interest on the debt in 1991 and the average balance of the debt in that year is $80,000. Because the average balance of the debt exceeds the maximum amount of the security interest, such excess is not treated as secured debt. Therefore, for purposes of applying the limitation on qualified residence interest, the average balance of the secured debt is $20,000 (the maximum amount of the security interest) and the interest paid or accrued on the secured debt is $2,000 (the total interest paid on the debt multiplied by the ratio of the average balance of the secured debt ($20,000) and the average balance of the total debt ($80,000)).

(5) *Election to treat debt as not secured by a qualified residence.*—(i) *In general.*—For purposes of this section, a taxpayer may elect to treat any debt that is secured by a qualified residence as not secured by the qualified residence. An election made under this paragraph shall be effective for the taxable year for which the election is made and for all subsequent taxable years unless revoked with the consent of the Commissioner.

(ii) *Example.*—T owns a principal residence with a fair market value of $75,000 and an adjusted purchase price of $40,000. In 1988, debt A, the proceeds of which were used to purchase the residence, has an average balance of $15,000. The proceeds of debt B, which is secured by a second mortgage on the property, are allocable to T's trade or business under § 1.163-8T and has an average balance of $25,000. In 1988, T incurs debt C, which is also secured by T's principal residence and which has an average balance in 1988 of $5,000. In the absence of an election to treat debt B as unsecured, the applicable debt limit for debt C in 1988 under paragraph (e) of this section would be zero dollars ($40,000 − $15,000 − $25,000) and none of the interest paid on debt C would be qualified residence interest. If, however, T makes or has previously made an election pursuant to paragraph (o)(5)(i) of this section to treat debt B as not secured by the residence, the applicable debt limit for debt C would be $25,000 ($40,000 − $15,000), and all of the interest paid on debt C during the taxable year would be qualified residence interest. Since the proceeds of debt B are allocable to T's trade or business under § 1.163-8T, interest on debt B may be deductible under other sections of the Internal Revenue Code.

(iii) *Allocation of debt secured by two qualified residences.*—[Reserved.]

(p) *Definition of qualified residence.*—(1) *In general.*—The term "qualified residence" means the taxpayer's principal residence (as defined in paragraph (p)(2) of this section), or the taxpayer's second residence (as defined in paragraph (p)(3) of this section).

(2) *Principal residence.*—The term "principal residence" means the taxpayer's principal residence within the meaning of section 1034. For purposes of this section, a taxpayer cannot have more than one principal residence at any one time.

(3) *Second residence.*—(i) *In general.*—The term "second residence" means—

(A) A residence within the meaning of paragraph (p)(3)(ii) of this section,

(B) That the taxpayer uses as a residence within the meaning of paragraph (p)(3)(iii) of this section, and

(C) That the taxpayer elects to treat as a second residence pursuant to paragraph (p)(3)(iv) of this section.

A taxpayer cannot have more than one second residence at any time.

(ii) *Definition of residence.*—Whether property is a residence shall be determined based on all the facts and circumstances, including the good faith of the taxpayer. A residence generally includes a house, condominium, mobile home, boat, or house trailer, that contains sleeping space and toilet and cooking facilities. A residence does not include personal property, such as furniture or a television, that, in accordance with the applicable local law, is not a fixture.

(iii) *Use as a residence.*—If a residence is rented at any time during the taxable year, it is considered to be used as a residence only if the taxpayer uses it during the taxable year as a residence within the meaning of section 280A(d). If a residence is not rented at any time during the taxable year, it shall be considered to be used as a residence. For purposes of the preceding sentence, a residence will be deemed to be rented during any period that the taxpayer holds the residence out for rental or resale or repairs or renovates the residence with the intention of holding it out for rental or resale.

(iv) *Election of second residence.*—A taxpayer may elect a different residence (other than the taxpayer's principal residence) to be the taxpayer's second residence for each taxable year. A taxpayer may not elect different residences as second residences at different times of the same taxable year except as provided below—

(A) If the taxpayer acquires a new residence during the taxable year, the taxpayer may elect the new residence as the taxpayer's second residence as of the date acquired;

(B) If property that was the taxpayer's principal residence during the taxable year ceases to qualify as the taxpayer's principal residence, the taxpayer may elect that property as the taxpayer's second residence as of the date that the property ceases to be the taxpayer's principal residence; or

(C) If property that was the taxpayer's second residence is sold during the taxable year or becomes the taxpayer's principal residence, the taxpayer may elect a new second residence as of such day.

(4) *Allocations between residence and other property.*—(i) *In general.*—For purposes of this section, the adjusted purchase price and fair market value of property must be allocated between the portion of the property that is a qualified residence and the portion that is not a qualified residence. Neither the average balance of the secured debt nor the interest paid or accrued on secured debt is so allocated. Property that is not used for residential purposes does not qualify as a residence. For example, if a portion of the property is used as an office in the taxpayer's trade or business, that portion of the property does not qualify as a residence.

(ii) *Special rule for rental of residence.*—If a taxpayer rents a portion of his or her principal or second residence to another person (a "tenant"), such portion may be treated as used by the taxpayer for residential purposes if, but only if—

(A) Such rented portion is used by the tenant primarily for residential purposes,

(B) The rented portion is not a self-contained residential unit containing separate sleeping space and toilet and cooking facilities, and

(C) The total number of tenants renting (directly or by sublease) the same or different portions of the residence at any time during the taxable year does not exceed two. For this purpose, if two persons (and the dependents, as defined by section 152, of either of them) share the same sleeping quarters, they shall be treated as a single tenant.

(iii) *Examples.—Example (1).* D, a dentist, uses a room in D's principal residence as an office which qualifies under section 280A(c)(1)(B) as a portion of the dwelling unit used exclusively on a regular basis as a place of business for meeting with patients in the normal course of D's trade or business. D's adjusted purchase price of the property is $65,000; $10,000 of which is allocable under paragraph (o)(4)(i) of this section to the room used as an office. For purposes of this section, D's residence does not include the room used as an office. The adjusted purchase price of the residence is, accordingly, $55,000. Similarly, the fair market value of D's residence must be allocated between the office and the remainder of the property.

Example (2). J rents out the basement of property that is otherwise used as J's principal residence. The basement is a self-contained residential unit, with sleeping space and toilet and cooking facilities. The adjusted purchase price of the property is $100,000; $15,000 of which is allocable under paragraph (o)(4)(i) of this section to the basement. For purposes of this section, J's residence does not include the basement and the adjusted purchase price of the residence is $85,000. Similarly, the fair market value of the residence must be allocated between the basement unit and the remainder of the property.

(5) *Residence under construction.*—(i) *In general.*—A taxpayer may treat a residence under construction as a qualified residence for a period of up to 24 months, but only if the residence becomes a qualified residence, without regard to this paragraph (p)(5)(i), as of the time that the residence is ready for occupancy.

(ii) *Example.*—X owns a residential lot suitable for the construction of a vacation home. On April 20, 1987, X obtains a mortgage secured by the lot and any property to be constructed on the lot. On August 9, 1987, X begins construction of a residence on the lot. The residence is ready for occupancy on November 9, 1989. The residence is used as a residence within the meaning of paragraph (p)(3)(iii) of this section during 1989 and X elects to treat the residence as his second residence for the period November 9, 1989, through December 31, 1989. Since the residence under construction is a qualified residence as of the first day that the residence is ready for occupancy (November 9, 1987), X may treat the residence as his second residence under paragraph (p)(5)(i) of this section for up to 24 months of the period during which the residence is under construction, commencing on or after the date that construction is begun (August 9, 1987). If X treats the residence under construction as X's second residence beginning on August 9, 1987, the residence under construction would cease to qualify as a qualified residence under paragraph (p)(5)(i) on August 8, 1989. The residence's status as a qualified residence for future periods would be determined without regard to paragraph (p)(5)(i) of this section.

(6) *Special rule for time-sharing arrangements.*—Property that is otherwise a qualified residence will not fail to qualify as such solely because the taxpayer's interest in or right to use the property is restricted by an arrangement whereby two or more persons with interests in the property agree to exercise control over the property for different periods during the taxable year. For purposes of determining the use of a residence under paragraph (p)(3)(iii) of this section, a taxpayer will not be considered to have used or rented a residence during any period that the taxpayer does not have the right to use the property or to receive any benefits from the rental of the property.

(q) *Special rules for tenant-stockholders in cooperative housing corporations.*—(1) *In general.*—For purposes of this section, a residence includes stock in a cooperative housing corporation owned by a tenant-stockholder if the house or apartment which the tenant-stockholder is entitled to occupy by virtue of owning such stock is a residence within the meaning of paragraph (p)(3)(ii) of this section.

(2) *Special rule where stock may not be used to secure debt.*—For purposes of this section, if stock described in paragraph (q)(1) of this section may not be used to secure debt because of restrictions under local or State law or because of restrictions in the cooperative agreement (other than restrictions the principal purpose of which is to permit the tenant-stockholder to treat unsecured debt as secured debt under this paragraph (q)(2)), debt may be treated as secured by such stock to the extent that the proceeds of the debt are allocated to the purchase of the stock under the rules of §1.163-8T. For purposes of this paragraph (q)(2), proceeds of debt incurred prior to January 1, 1987, may be treated as allocated to the purchase of such stock to the extent that the tenant-stockholder has properly and consistently deducted interest expense on such debt as home mortgage interest attributable to such stock on Schedule A of Form 1040 in determining his taxable income for taxable years beginning before January 1, 1987. For purposes of this paragraph (q)(2), amended returns filed after December 22, 1987 are disregarded.

(3) *Treatment of interest expense of the cooperative described in section 216(a)(2).*—For purposes of section 163(h) and §1.163-9T (disallowance of deduction for personal interest) and section 163(d) (limitation on investment interest), any amount allowable as a deduction to a tenant-stockholder under section 216(a)(2) shall be treated as interest paid or accrued by the tenant-stockholder. If a tenant-stockholder's stock in a cooperative housing corporation is a qualified residence of the tenant-shareholder, any amount allowable as a deduction to the tenant-stockholder under section 216(a)(2) is qualified residence interest.

(4) *Special rule to prevent tax avoidance.*—If the amount treated as qualified residence interest under this section exceeds the amount which would be so treated if the tenant-stockholder were treated as directly owning his proportionate share of the assets and liabilities of the cooperative and one of the principal purposes of the cooperative arrangement is to permit the tenant-stockholder to increase the amount of qualified residence interest, the district director may determine that such excess is not qualified residence interest.

(5) *Other definitions.*—For purpose of this section, the terms "tenant-stockholder," "cooperative housing corporation" and "proportionate share" shall have the meaning given by section 216 and the regulations thereunder.

(r) *Effective date.*—The provisions of this section are effective for taxable years beginning after December 31, 1986. [Temporary Reg. §1.163-10T.]

☐ [T.D. 8168, 12-21-87.]

[Reg. §1.163-11]

§1.163-11. Allocation of certain prepaid qualified mortgage insurance premiums.—(a) *Allocation.*—(1) *In general.*—As provided in section 163(h)(3)(E), premiums paid or accrued for qualified mortgage insurance during the taxable year in connection with acquisition indebtedness with respect to a qualified residence (as defined in section 163(h)(4)(A)) of the taxpayer shall be treated as qualified residence interest (as defined in section 163(h)(3)(A)). If an individual taxpayer pays such a premium that is properly allocable to a mortgage the payment of which extends to periods beyond the close of the taxable year in which the premium is paid, the taxpayer must allocate the premium to determine the amount treated as qualified residence interest for each taxable year. The premium must be allocated ratably over the shorter of—

(i) The stated term of the mortgage; or

(ii) A period of 84 months, beginning with the month in which the insurance was obtained.

(2) *Limitation.*—If a mortgage is satisfied before the end of its stated term, no deduction as qualified residence interest shall be allowed for any amount of the premium that is allocable to periods after the mortgage is satisfied.

(b) *Scope.*—The allocation requirement in paragraph (a) of this section applies only to mortgage insurance provided by the Federal Housing Administration or private mortgage insurance (as defined by section 2 of the Homeowners Protection Act of 1998 (12 U.S.C. 4901) as in effect on December 20, 2006). It does not apply to mortgage insurance provided by the Department of Veterans Affairs or the Rural Housing Service. Paragraph (a) of this section applies whether the qualified mortgage insurance premiums are paid in cash or are financed, without regard to source.

(c) *Limitation on the treatment of mortgage insurance premiums as interest.*—This section applies to prepaid qualified mortgage insurance premiums described in paragraph (a) of this section that are paid or accrued on or after January 1, 2011, and during periods to which section 163(h)(3)(E) is applicable. This section does not apply to any amount of prepaid qualified mortgage insurance premiums that are allocable to any periods to which section 163(h)(3)(E) is not applicable.

(d) *Effective/applicability date.*—This section is applicable on and after January 1, 2011. For regulations applicable before January 1, 2011, see §1.163-11T in effect prior to January 1, 2011 (§1.163-11T as contained in 26 CFR part 1 edition revised as of April 1, 2011). [Reg. §1.163-11.]

☐ [T.D. 9588, 5-4-2012.]

[Reg. §1.163-12]

§1.163-12. Deduction of original issue discount on instrument held by related foreign person.—(a) *General rules.*—(1) *Deferral of deduction.*—Except as provided in paragraph (b) of this section, section 163(e)(3) requires a taxpayer to use the cash method of accounting with respect to the deduction of original issue discount owed to a related foreign person. A deduction for an otherwise deductible portion of original issue discount with respect to a debt instrument will not be allowable as a deduction to the issuer until paid if, at the close of the issuer's taxable year in which such amount would otherwise be deductible, the person holding the debt instrument is a related foreign person. For purposes of this section, a related foreign person is any person that is not a United States person within the meaning of section 7701(a)(30), and that is related (within the meaning of section 267(b)) to the issuer at the close of the taxable year in which the amount incurred by the taxpayer would otherwise be deductible. Section 267(f) defines "controlled group" for purposes of section 267(b) without regard to the limitations of section 1563(b). An amount is treated as paid for purposes of this section if the amount is considered paid for purposes of section 1441 or section 1442 (including an amount taken into account pursuant to section 871(a)(1)(C), section 881(a)(3), or section 884(f)). The rules of this paragraph (a) apply even if the original issue discount is not subject to United States tax, or is subject to a reduced rate of tax, pursuant to a provision of the Internal Revenue Code or a treaty obligation of the United States. For purposes of this section, original issue discount is an amount described in section 1273, whether from sources inside or outside the United States.

(2) *Change in method of accounting.*—A taxpayer that uses a method of accounting other than that required by the rules of this section must change its method of accounting to conform its method to the rules of this section. The taxpayer's change in method must be made pursuant to the rules of section 446(e), the regulations thereunder, and any applicable administrative procedures prescribed by the Commissioner. Because the rules of this section prescribe a method of accounting, these rules apply in the determination of a taxpayer's earnings and profits pursuant to §1.312-6(a).

(b) *Exceptions and special rules.*—(1) *Effectively connected income.*—The provisions of section 267(a)(2) and the regulations thereunder, and not the provisions of paragraph (a) of this section, apply to an amount of original issue discount that is income of the related foreign person that is effectively connected with the conduct of a United States trade or business of such related foreign person. An amount described in this paragraph (b)(1) thus is allowable as a deduction as of the day on which the amount is includible in the gross income of the related foreign person as effectively connected income under sections 872(a)(2) or 882(b) (or, if later, as of the day on which the deduction would be so allowable but for section 267(a)(2)). However, this paragraph (b)(1) does not apply if the related foreign person is exempt from United States income tax on the amount owed, or is subject to a reduced rate of tax, pursuant to a treaty obligation of the United States (such as under an article relating to the taxation of business profits).

(2) *Certain obligations issued by natural persons.*—This section does not apply to any debt instrument described in section 163(e)(4) (relating to obligations issued by natural persons before March 2, 1984, and to loans between natural persons).

(3) *Amounts owed to a foreign personal holding company, controlled foreign corporation, or passive foreign investment company.*—(i) *Foreign personal holding companies.*—If an amount to which paragraph (a) of this section otherwise applies is owed to a related foreign person that is a foreign personal holding company within the meaning of section 552, then the amount is allowable as a deduction as of the day on which the amount is includible in the income of the foreign personal holding company. The day on which the amount is includible in income is determined with reference to the method of accounting under which the foreign personal holding company computes its taxable income and earnings and profits for purposes of sections 551 through 558. See section 551(c) and the regulations thereunder for the reporting requirements of the foreign personal holding company provisions (sections 551 through 558).

(ii) *Controlled foreign corporations.*—If an amount to which paragraph (a) of this section otherwise applies is owed to a related foreign person that is a controlled foreign corporation within the meaning of section 957, then the amount is allowable as a deduction as of the day on which the amount is includible in the income of the controlled foreign corporation. The day on which the amount is includible in income is determined with reference to the method of accounting under which the controlled foreign corporation computes its taxable income and earnings and profits for purposes of sections 951 through 964. See section 6038 and the regulations thereunder for the reporting requirements of the controlled foreign corporation provisions (sections 951 through 964).

(iii) *Passive foreign investment companies.*—If an amount to which paragraph (a) of this section otherwise applies is owed to a related foreign person that is a passive foreign investment company within the meaning of section 1296, then the amount is allowable as a deduction as of the day on which [the] amount is includible in the income of the passive foreign investment company. The day on which the amount is includible in income is determined with reference to the method of accounting under which the earnings and profits of the passive foreign investment company are computed for purposes of sections 1291 through 1297. See sections 1291 through 1297 and the regulations thereunder for the reporting requirements of the passive foreign investment company provisions. This exception shall apply, however, only if the person that owes the amount at issue has made and has in effect an election pursuant to section 1295 with respect to the passive foreign investment company to which the amount at issue is owed.

(c) *Application of section 267.*—Except as limited in paragraph (b)(1) of this section, the provisions of section 267 and the regulations thereunder shall apply to any amount of original issue discount to which the provisions of this section do not apply.

(d) *Effective date.*—The rules of this section are effective with respect to all original issue discount on debt instruments issued after June 9, 1984. [Reg. § 1.163-12.]

☐ [T.D. 8465, 12-31-92.]

[Reg. § 1.163-13]

§ **1.163-13. Treatment of bond issuance premium.**—(a) *General rule.*—If a debt instrument is issued with bond issuance premium, this section limits the amount of the issuer's interest deduction otherwise allowable under section 163(a). In general, the issuer determines its interest deduction by offsetting the interest allocable to an accrual period with the bond issuance premium allocable to that period. Bond issuance premium is allocable to an accrual period based on a constant yield. The use of a constant yield to amortize bond issuance premium is intended to generally conform the treatment of debt instruments having bond issuance premium with those having original issue discount. Unless otherwise provided, the terms

used in this section have the same meaning as those terms in section 163(e), sections 1271 through 1275, and the corresponding regulations. Moreover, unless otherwise provided, the provisions of this section apply in a manner consistent with those of section 163(e), sections 1271 through 1275, and the corresponding regulations. In addition, the anti-abuse rule in § 1.1275-2(g) applies for purposes of this section. For rules dealing with the treatment of bond premium by a holder, see § § 1.171-1 through 1.171-5.

(b) *Exceptions.*—This section does not apply to—

(1) A debt instrument described in section 1272(a)(6)(C) (regular interests in a REMIC, qualified mortgages held by a REMIC, and certain other debt instruments, or pools of debt instruments, with payments subject to acceleration); or

(2) A debt instrument to which § 1.1275-4 applies (relating to certain debt instruments that provide for contingent payments).

(c) *Bond issuance premium.*—Bond issuance premium is the excess, if any, of the issue price of a debt instrument over its stated redemption price at maturity. For purposes of this section, the issue price of a convertible bond (as defined in § 1.171-1(e)(1)(iii)(C)) does not include an amount equal to the value of the conversion option (as determined under § 1.171-1(e)(1)(iii)(A)).

(d) *Offsetting qualified stated interest with bond issuance premium.*—(1) *In general.*—An issuer amortizes bond issuance premium by offsetting the qualified stated interest allocable to an accrual period with the bond issuance premium allocable to the accrual period. This offset occurs when the issuer takes the qualified stated interest into account under its regular method of accounting.

(2) *Qualified stated interest allocable to an accrual period.*—See § 1.446-2(b) to determine the accrual period to which qualified stated interest is allocable and to determine the accrual of qualified stated interest within an accrual period.

(3) *Bond issuance premium allocable to an accrual period.*—The bond issuance premium allocable to an accrual period is determined under this paragraph (d)(3). Within an accrual period, the bond issuance premium allocable to the period accrues ratably.

(i) *Step one: Determine the debt instrument's yield to maturity.*—The yield to maturity of a debt instrument is determined under the rules of § 1.1272-1(b)(1)(i).

(ii) *Step two: Determine the accrual periods.*—The accrual periods are determined under the rules of § 1.1272-1(b)(1)(ii).

(iii) *Step three: Determine the bond issuance premium allocable to the accrual period.*—The bond issuance premium allocable to an accrual period is the excess of the qualified stated interest allocable to the accrual period over the product of the adjusted issue price at the beginning of the accrual period and the yield. In performing this calculation, the yield must be stated appropriately taking into account the length of the particular accrual period. Principles similar to those in § 1.1272-1(b)(4) apply in determining the bond issuance premium allocable to an accrual period.

(4) *Bond issuance premium in excess of qualified stated interest.*—(i) *Ordinary income.*—If the bond issuance premium allocable to an accrual period exceeds the qualified stated interest allocable to the accrual period, the excess is treated as ordinary income by the issuer for the accrual period. However, the amount treated as ordinary income is limited to the amount by which the issuer's total interest deductions on the debt instrument in prior accrual periods exceed the total amount treated by the issuer as ordinary income on the debt instrument in prior accrual periods.

(ii) *Carryforward.*—If the bond issuance premium allocable to an accrual period exceeds the sum of the qualified stated interest allocable to the accrual period and the amount treated as ordinary income for the accrual period under paragraph (d)(4)(i) of this section, the excess is carried forward to the next accrual period and is treated as bond issuance premium allocable to that period. If a carryforward exists on the date the debt instrument is retired, the carryforward is treated as ordinary income on that date.

(e) *Special rules.*—(1) *Variable rate debt instruments.*—An issuer determines bond issuance premium on a variable rate debt instrument by reference to the stated redemption price at maturity of the equivalent fixed rate debt instrument constructed for the variable rate debt instrument. The issuer also allocates any bond issuance premium among the accrual periods by reference to the equivalent fixed rate debt instrument. The issuer constructs the equivalent fixed rate debt instrument, as of the issue date, by using the principles of § 1.1275-5(e).

(2) *Inflation-indexed debt instruments.*—An issuer determines bond issuance premium on an inflation-indexed debt instrument by

assuming that there will be no inflation or deflation over the term of the instrument. The issuer also allocates any bond issuance premium among the accrual periods by assuming that there will be no inflation or deflation over the term of the instrument. The bond issuance premium allocable to an accrual period offsets qualified stated interest allocable to the period. Notwithstanding paragraph (d)(4) of this section, if the bond issuance premium allocable to an accrual period exceeds the qualified stated interest allocable to the period, the excess is treated as a deflation adjustment under §1.1275-7(f)(1)(ii). See §1.1275-7 for other rules relating to inflation-indexed debt instruments.

(3) *Certain debt instruments subject to contingencies.*—(i) *In general.*—Except as provided in paragraph (e)(3)(ii) of this section, the rules of §1.1272-1(c) apply to determine a debt instrument's payment schedule for purposes of this section. For example, an issuer uses the payment schedule determined under §1.1272-1(c) to determine the amount, if any, of bond issuance premium on the debt instrument, the yield and maturity of the debt instrument, and the allocation of bond issuance premium to an accrual period.

(ii) *Mandatory sinking fund provision.*—Notwithstanding paragraph (e)(3)(i) of this section, if a debt instrument is subject to a mandatory sinking fund provision described in §1.1272-1(c)(3), the issuer must determine the payment schedule by assuming that a pro rata portion of the debt instrument will be called under the sinking fund provision.

(4) *Remote and incidental contingencies.*—For purposes of determining the amount of bond issuance premium and allocating bond issuance premium among accrual periods, if a bond provides for a contingency that is remote or incidental (within the meaning of §1.1275-2(h)), the issuer takes the contingency into account under the rules for remote and incidental contingencies in §1.1275-2(h).

(f) *Example.*—The following example illustrates the rules of this section:

Example—(i) *Facts.* On February 1, 1999, X issues for $110,000 a debt instrument maturing on February 1, 2006, with a stated principal amount of $100,000, payable at maturity. The debt instrument provides for unconditional payments of interest of $10,000, payable on February 1 of each year. X uses the calendar year as its taxable year, X uses the cash receipts and disbursements method of accounting, and X decides to use annual accrual periods ending on February 1 of each year. X's calculations assume a 30-day month and 360-day year.

(ii) *Amount of bond issuance premium.* The issue price of the debt instrument is $110,000. Because the interest payments on the debt instrument are qualified stated interest, the stated redemption price at maturity of the debt instrument is $100,000. Therefore, the amount of bond issuance premium is $10,000 ($110,000 – $100,000).

(iii) *Bond issuance premium allocable to the first accrual period.* Based on the payment schedule and the issue price of the debt instrument, the yield of the debt instrument is 8.07 percent, compounded annually. (Although, for purposes of simplicity, the yield as stated is rounded to two decimal places, the computations do not reflect this rounding convention.) The bond issuance premium allocable to the accrual period ending on February 1, 2000, is the excess of the qualified stated interest allocable to the period ($10,000) over the product of the adjusted issue price at the beginning of the period ($110,000) and the yield (8.07 percent, compounded annually). Therefore, the bond issuance premium allocable to the accrual period is $1,118.17 ($10,000 – $8,881.83).

(iv) *Premium used to offset interest.* Although X makes an interest payment of $10,000 on February 1, 2000, X only deducts interest of $8,881.83, the qualified stated interest allocable to the period ($10,000) offset with the bond issuance premium allocable to the period ($1,118.17).

(g) *Effective date.*—This section applies to debt instruments issued on or after March 2, 1998.

(h) *Accounting method changes.*—(1) *Consent to change.*—An issuer required to change its method of accounting for bond issuance premium to comply with this section must secure the consent of the Commissioner in accordance with the requirements of §1.446-1(e). Paragraph (h)(2) of this section provides the Commissioner's automatic consent for certain changes.

(2) *Automatic consent.*—The Commissioner grants consent for an issuer to change its method of accounting for bond issuance premium on debt instruments issued on or after March 2, 1998. Because this change is made on a cut-off basis, no items of income or deduction are omitted or duplicated and, therefore, no adjustment under section 481 is allowed. The consent granted by this paragraph (h)(2) applies provided—

(i) The change is made to comply with this section;

(ii) The change is made for the first taxable year for which the issuer must account for a debt instrument under this section; and

(iii) The issuer attaches to its federal income tax return for the taxable year containing the change a statement that it has changed its method of accounting under this section. [Reg. §1.163-13.]

☐ [*T.D. 8746, 12-30-97. Amended by T.D. 8838, 9-3-99.*]

[Reg. §1.163-15]

§1.163-15. Debt Proceeds Distributed from Any Taxpayer Account or from Cash.—(a) *In general.*—Regardless of paragraphs (c)(4) and (5) of §1.163-8T, in the case of debt proceeds deposited in an account, a taxpayer that is applying §1.163-8T or §1.163-14 may treat any expenditure made from any account of the taxpayer, or from cash, within 30 days before or 30 days after debt proceeds are deposited in any account of the taxpayer as made from such proceeds to the extent thereof. Similarly, in the case of debt proceeds received in cash, a taxpayer that is applying §1.163-8T or §1.163-14 may treat any expenditure made from any account of the taxpayer, or from cash, within 30 days before or 30 days after debt proceeds are received in cash as made from such proceeds to the extent thereof. For purposes of this section, terms used have the same meaning as in §1.163-8T(c)(4) and (5).

(b) *Applicability date.*—This section applies to taxable years beginning on or after March 22, 2021. However, taxpayers and their related parties, within the meaning of sections 267(b) (determined without regard to section 267(c)(3)) and 707(b)(1), may choose to apply the rules in this section to a taxable year beginning after December 31, 2017, and before March 22, 2021, provided that those taxpayers and their related parties consistently apply all of the rules in this section to that taxable year and each subsequent taxable year. [Reg. §1.163-15.]

☐ [*T.D. 9943, 1-13-2021.*]

[Reg. §1.163(d)-1]

§1.163(d)-1. Time and manner for making election under the Omnibus Budget Reconciliation Act of 1993 and the Jobs and Growth Tax Relief Reconciliation Act of 2003.—(a) *Description.*—Section 163(d)(4)(B)(iii), as added by section 13206(d) of the Omnibus Budget Reconciliation Act of 1993 (Public Law 103-66, 107 Stat. 467), allows an electing taxpayer to take all or a portion of certain net capital gain attributable to dispositions of property held for investment into account as investment income. Section 163(d)(4)(B), as amended by section 302(b) of the Jobs and Growth Tax Relief Reconciliation Act of 2003 (Public Law 108-27, 117 Stat. 762), allows an electing taxpayer to take all or a portion of qualified dividend income, as defined in section 1(h)(11)(B), into account as investment income. As a consequence, the net capital gain and qualified dividend income taken into account as investment income under these elections are not eligible to be taxed at the capital gains rates. An election may be made for net capital gain recognized by noncorporate taxpayers during any taxable year beginning after December 31, 1992. An election may be made for qualified dividend income received by noncorporate taxpayers during any taxable year beginning after December 31, 2002, but before January 1, 2009.

(b) *Time and manner for making the elections.*—The elections for net capital gain and qualified dividend income must be made on or before the due date (including extensions) of the income tax return for the taxable year in which the net capital gain is recognized or the qualified dividend income is received. The elections are to be made on Form 4952, "Investment Interest Expense Deduction," in accordance with the form and its instructions.

(c) *Revocability of elections.*—The elections described in this section are revocable with the consent of the Commissioner.

(d) *Effective date.*—The rules set forth in this section regarding the net capital gain election apply beginning December 12, 1996. The rules set forth in this section regarding the qualified dividend income election apply to any taxable year beginning after December 31, 2002, but before January 1, 2009. [Reg. §1.163(d)-1.]

☐ [*T.D. 8688, 12-11-96. Amended by T.D. 9147, 8-4-2004 and T.D. 9191, 3-17-2005.*]

[Reg. §1.163(j)-0]

§1.163(j)-0. Table of contents.—This section lists the table of contents for §§1.163(j)-1 through 1.163(j)-11.

(iii) Depreciation, amortization, or depletion capitalized under section 263A.

(iv) Application of § 1.163(j)-1(b)(1)(ii)(C), (D), and (E).

(A) Sale or other disposition.

    (1) In general.

    (2) Intercompany transactions.

    (3) Deconsolidations.

    (4) Nonrecognition transactions.

(B) Deductions by members of a consolidated group.

    (1) In general.

    (2) Application of the alternative computation method.

(C) Successor rules.

    (1) Successor assets.

    (2) Successor entities.

(D) Anti-duplication rule.

    (1) In general.

    (2) Adjustments following deconsolidation.

(E) Alternative computation method.

    (1) Alternative computation method for property dispositions.

    (2) Alternative computation method for dispositions of member stock.

    (3) Alternative computation method for dispositions of partnership interests.

(F) Cap on negative adjustments.

    (1) In general.

    (2) Example.

(G) Treatment of depreciation, amortization, or depletion capitalized under section 263A.

(v) Other adjustments.

(vi) Additional rules relating to adjusted taxable income in other sections.

(vii) ATI cannot be less than zero.

(viii) Examples.

(2) Applicable CFC.

(3) Business interest expense.

(i) In general.

(ii) Special rules.

(4) Business interest income.

(i) In general.

(ii) Special rules.

(5) C corporation.

(6) Cleared swap.

(7) Consolidated group.

(8) Consolidated return year.

(9) Current-year business interest expense.

(10) Disallowed business interest expense.

(11) Disallowed business interest expense carryforward.

(12) Disallowed disqualified interest.

(13) Electing farming business.

(14) Electing real property trade or business.

(15) Excepted regulated utility trade or business.

(i) In general.

(A) Automatically excepted regulated utility trades or businesses.

(B) Electing regulated utility trades or businesses.

(C) Designated excepted regulated utility trades or businesses.

(ii) Depreciation and excepted and non-excepted utility trades or businesses.

(A) Depreciation.

(B) Allocation of items.

(iii) Election to be an excepted regulated utility trade or business.

(A) In general.

(B) Scope and effect of election.

    (1) In general.

    (2) Irrevocability.

(C) Time and manner of making election.

    (1) In general.

    (2) Election statement contents.

    (3) Consolidated group's or partnership's trade or business.

    (4) Termination of election.

    (5) Additional guidance.

(16) Excess business interest expense.

(17) Excess taxable income.

(18) Floor plan financing indebtedness.

(19) Floor plan financing interest expense.

(20) Group.

(21) Intercompany transaction.

(22) Interest.

(i) In general.

(ii) Swaps with significant nonperiodic payments.

(A) In general.

(B) Exception for cleared swaps.

(C) Exception for non-cleared swaps subject to margin or collateral requirements.

(iii) Other amounts treated as interest.

(A) Treatment of premium.

    (1) Issuer.

    (2) Holder.

(B) Treatment of ordinary income or loss on certain debt instruments.

(C) Substitute interest payments.

(D) Section 1258 gain.

(E) Factoring income.

(F) Section 163(j) interest dividends.

    (1) In general.

    (2) Limitation on amount treated as interest income.

    (3) Conduit amounts.

    (4) Holding period.

    (5) Exception to holding period requirement for money market funds and certain regularly declared dividends.

(iv) Anti-avoidance rules.

(A) Principal purpose to reduce interest expense.

    (1) Treatment as interest expense.

    (2) Corresponding treatment of amounts as interest income.

(B) Interest income artificially increased.

(C) Principal purpose.

(D) Coordination with anti-avoidance rule in § 1.163(j)-2(j).

(v) Examples.

(23) Interest expense.

(24) Interest income.

(25) Member.

(26) Motor vehicle.

(27) Old section 163(j).

(28) Ownership change.

(29) Ownership date.

(30) Real estate investment trust.

(31) Real property.

(32) Regulated investment company.

(33) Relevant foreign corporation.

(34) S corporation.

(35) Section 163(j) interest dividend.

(i) In general.

(ii) Reduction in the case of excess reported amounts.

(iii) Allocation of excess reported amount.

(A) In general.

(B) Special rule for noncalendar year RICs.

(iv) Definitions.

(A) Reported section 163(j) interest dividend amount.

(B) Excess reported amount.

(C) Aggregate reported amount.

(D) Post-December reported amount.

(E) Excess section 163(j) interest income.

(v) Example.

(36) Section 163(j) limitation.

(37) Section 163(j) regulations.

(38) Separate return limitation year.

(39) Separate return year.

(40) Separate tentative taxable income.

(41) Tax-exempt corporation.

(42) Tax-exempt organization.

(43) Tentative taxable income.

(i) In general.

(ii) [Reserved]

(iii) Special rules for defining tentative taxable income.

(44) Trade or business.

(i) In general.

(ii) Excepted trade or business.

(iii) Non-excepted trade or business.

(45) Unadjusted basis.

(46) United States shareholder.

(c) Applicability date.

(1) In general.

(2) Anti-avoidance rules.

(3) Swaps with significant nonperiodic payments.

Itemized Deductions for Individuals and Corps.
See p. 20,601 for regulations not amended to reflect law changes
25,309

(1) Section 163(j) items.
(2) Partner basis items.
(3) Remedial items.
(4) Excess business interest income.
(5) Deductible business interest expense.
(6) Section 163(j) excess items.
(7) Non-excepted assets.
(8) Excepted assets.
  (c) Business interest income and business interest expense of the partnership.
(1) Modification of business interest income for partnerships.
(2) Modification of business interest expense for partnerships.
(3) Transition rule.
(4) Character of business interest expense.
  (d) Adjusted taxable income of a partnership.
(1) Tentative taxable income of a partnership.
(2) Section 734(b), partner basis items, and remedial items.
(3) Section 743(b) adjustments and publicly traded partnerships.
(4) Modification of adjusted taxable income for partnerships.
(5) Election to use 2019 adjusted taxable income for taxable years beginning in 2020.
  (e) Adjusted taxable income and business interest income of partners.
(1) Modification of adjusted taxable income for partners.
(2) Partner basis items and remedial items.
(3) Disposition of partnership interests.
(4) Double counting of business interest income and floor plan financing interest expense prohibited.
(5) Partner basis items, remedial items, and publicly traded partnerships.
(6) [Reserved].
  (f) Allocation and determination of section 163(j) excess items made in the same manner as nonseparately stated taxable income or loss of the partnership.
(1) Overview.
    (i) In general.
    (ii) Relevance solely for purposes of section 163(j).
    (iii) Exception applicable to publicly traded partnerships.
(2) Steps for allocating deductible business interest expense and section 163(j) excess items.
    (i) Partnership-level calculation required by section 163(j)(4)(A).
    (ii) Determination of each partner's relevant section 163(j) items.
    (iii) Partner-level comparison of business interest income and business interest expense.
    (iv) Matching partnership and aggregate partner excess business interest income.
    (v) Remaining business interest expense determination.
    (vi) Determination of final allocable ATI.
      (A) Positive allocable ATI.
      (B) Negative allocable ATI.
      (C) Final allocable ATI.
    (vii) Partner-level comparison of 30 percent of adjusted taxable income and remaining business interest expense.
    (viii) Partner priority right to ATI capacity excess determination.
    (ix) Matching partnership and aggregate partner excess taxable income.
    (x) Matching partnership and aggregate partner excess business interest expense.
    (xi) Final section 163(j) excess item and deductible business interest expense allocation.
  (g) Carryforwards.
(1) In general.
(2) Treatment of excess business interest expense allocated to partners.
(3) Excess taxable income and excess business interest income ordering rule.
(4) Special rule for taxable years beginning in 2019 and 2020.
  (h) Basis adjustments.
(1) Section 704(d) ordering.
(2) Excess business interest expense basis adjustments.
(3) Partner basis adjustment upon disposition of partnership interest.
    (4)-(5) [Reserved]
  (i)-(j) [Reserved]
  (k) Investment items and certain other items.
  (l) S corporations.
(1) In general.
    (i) Corporate level limitation.

    (ii) Short taxable periods.
(2) Character of deductible business interest expense.
(3) Adjusted taxable income of an S corporation.
(4) Adjusted taxable income and business interest income of S corporation shareholders.
    (i) Adjusted taxable income of S corporation shareholders.
    (ii) Disposition of S corporation stock.
    (iii) Double counting of business interest income and floor plan financing interest expense prohibited.
    (iv) [Reserved].
(5) Carryforwards.
(6) Basis adjustments and disallowed business interest expense carryforwards.
(7) Accumulated adjustment accounts.
(8) Termination of qualified subchapter S subsidiary election.
(9) Investment items.
(10) Application of section 382.
  (m) Partnerships and S corporations not subject to section 163(j).
(1) Exempt partnerships and S corporations.
(2) Partnerships and S corporations engaged in excepted trades or businesses.
(3) Treatment of excess business interest expense from partnerships that are exempt entities in a succeeding taxable year.
(4) S corporations with disallowed business interest expense carryforwards prior to becoming exempt entities.
  (n) Treatment of self-charged lending transactions between partnerships and partners.
  (o) Examples.
  (p) Applicability dates.
(1) In general.
(2) Paragraphs (c)(1) and (2), (d)(3) through (5), (e)(5), (f)(1)(iii), (g)(4), (n), and (o)(24) through (29), and (34) through (36).
§1.163(j)-7 Application of the section 163(j) limitation to foreign corporations and United States shareholders.
  (a) Overview.
  (b) General rule regarding the application of section 163(j) to relevant foreign corporations.
  (c) Application of section 163(j) to CFC group members of a CFC group.
(1) Scope.
(2) Calculation of section 163(j) limitation for a CFC group for a specified period.
    (i) In general.
    (ii) Certain transactions between CFC group members disregarded.
    (iii) [Reserved]
    (iv) [Reserved]
(3) Deduction of business interest expense.
    (i) CFC group business interest expense.
      (A) In general.
      (B) Modifications to relevant terms.
    (ii) Carryforwards treated as attributable to the same taxable year.
    (iii) Multiple specified taxable years of a CFC group member with respect to a specified period.
    (iv) Limitation on pre-group disallowed business interest expense carryforward.
      (A) General rule.
        (1) CFC group member pre-group disallowed business interest expense carryforward.
        (2) Subgrouping.
        (3) Transition rule.
      (B) Deduction of pre-group disallowed business interest expense carryforwards.
(4) Currency translation.
(5) Special rule for specified periods beginning in 2019 or 2020.
    (i) 50 percent ATI limitation applies to a specified period of a CFC group.
    (ii) Election to use 2019 ATI applies to a specified period of a CFC group.
      (A) In general.
      (B) Specified taxable years that do not begin in 2020.
  (d) Determination of a specified group and specified group members.
(1) Scope.
(2) Rules for determining a specified group.
    (i) Definition of a specified group.
    (ii) Indirect ownership.
    (iii) Specified group parent.
    (iv) Qualified U.S. person.
    (v) Stock.

(1) In general.
  (i) Purposes.
  (ii) Application of section.
(2) Coordination with other rules.
  (i) In general.
  (ii) Treatment of investment interest, investment income, investment expenses, and certain other tax items of a partnership with a C corporation or tax-exempt corporation as a partner.
(3) Application of allocation rules to foreign corporations and foreign partnerships.
(4) Application of allocation rules to members of a consolidated group.
  (i) In general.
  (ii) Application of excepted business percentage to members of a consolidated group.
  (iii) Basis in assets transferred in an intercompany transaction.
(5) Tax-exempt organizations.
(6) Application of allocation rules to disallowed disqualified interest.
(7) Examples.
(b) Allocation of tax items other than interest expense and interest income.
(1) In general.
(2) Gross income other than dividends and interest income.
(3) Dividends.
  (i) Look-through rule.
  (ii) Inapplicability of the look-through rule.
(4) Gain or loss from the disposition of non-consolidated C corporation stock, partnership interests, or S corporation stock.
  (i) Non-consolidated C corporations.
  (ii) Partnerships and S corporations.
(5) Expenses, losses, and other deductions.
  (i) Expenses, losses, and other deductions that are definitely related to a trade or business.
  (ii) Other deductions.
(6) Treatment of investment items and certain other items of a partnership with a C corporation partner.
(7) Examples: Allocation of income and expense.
(c) Allocating interest expense and interest income that is properly allocable to a trade or business.
(1) General rule.
  (i) In general.
  (ii) De minimis exception.
(2) Example.
(3) Asset used in more than one trade or business.
  (i) General rule.
  (ii) Permissible methodologies for allocating asset basis between or among two or more trades or businesses.
  (iii) Special rules.
    (A) Consistent allocation methodologies.
     (1) In general.
     (2) Consent to change allocation methodology.
    (B) De minimis exception.
    (C) Allocations of excepted regulated utility trades or businesses.
     (1) In general.
     (2) Permissible method for allocating asset basis for utility trades or businesses.
     (3) De minimis rule for excepted utility trades or businesses.
     (4) Example.
    (D) Special allocation rule for real property trades or business subject to special anti-abuse rule.
     (1) In general.
     (2) Allocation methodology for real property.
     (3) Example.
(4) Disallowed business interest expense carryforwards; floor plan financing interest expense.
(5) Additional rules relating to basis.
  (i) Calculation of adjusted basis.
    (A) Non-depreciable property other than land.
    (B) Depreciable property other than inherently permanent structures.
    (C) Special rule for land and inherently permanent structures.
    (D) Depreciable or amortizable *intangible* property and depreciable income forecast method property.
    (E) Assets not yet used in a trade or business.
    (F) Trusts established to fund specific liabilities.
    (G) Inherently permanent structure.

  (ii) Partnership interests; stock in non-consolidated C corporations.
    (A) Partnership interests.
     (1) Calculation of asset basis.
     (2) Allocation of asset basis.
      (i) In general.
      (ii) De minimis rule.
      (iii) Partnership assets not properly allocable to a trade or business.
      (iv) Inapplicability of partnership look-through rule.
    (B) Stock in domestic non-consolidated corporations.
     (1) In general.
     (2) Domestic non-consolidated C corporations.
      (i) Allocation of asset basis.
      (ii) De minimis rule.
      (iii) Inapplicability of corporate look-through rule.
      (iv) Use of inside basis for purposes of C corporation look-through rule.
     (3) S corporations.
      (i) Calculation of asset basis.
      (ii) Allocation of asset basis.
      (iii) De minimis rule.
      (iv) Inapplicability of S corporation look-through rule.
    (C) Stock in relevant foreign corporations.
     (1) In general.
     (2) Special rule for CFC utilities.
    (D) Limitations on application of look-through rules.
     (1) Inapplicability of look-through rule to partnerships or non-consolidated C corporations to which the small business exemption applies.
     (2) Limitation on application of look-through rule to C corporations.
    (E) Tiered entities.
  (iii) Cash and cash equivalents and customer receivables.
  (iv) Deemed asset sale.
  (v) Other adjustments.
(6) Determination dates; determination periods; reporting requirements.
  (i) Determination dates and determination periods.
    (A) Quarterly determination periods.
    (B) Annual determination periods.
  (ii) Application of look-through rules.
  (iii) Reporting requirements.
    (A) Books and records.
    (B) Information statement.
  (iv) Failure to file statement.
(7) Ownership threshold for look-through rules.
  (i) Corporations.
    (A) Asset basis.
    (B) Dividends.
  (ii) Partnerships.
  (iii) Inapplicability of look-through rule.
(8) Anti-abuse rule.
(d) Direct allocations.
(1) In general.
(2) Qualified nonrecourse indebtedness.
(3) Assets used in more than one trade or business.
(4) Adjustments to basis of assets to account for direct allocations.
(5) Example: Direct allocation of interest expense.
(e) Examples.
(f) Applicability dates.
(1) In general.
(2) Paragraph (c)(5)(ii)(D)(2).
§ 1.163(j)-11 Transition rules.
(a) Overview.
(b) Application of section 163(j) limitation if a corporation joins a consolidated group during a taxable year of the group beginning before January 1, 2018.
(1) In general.
(2) Example
(c) Treatment of disallowed disqualified interest.
(1) In general.
(2) Earnings and profits.
(3) Disallowed disqualified interest of members of an affiliated group.
  (i) Scope.
  (ii) Allocation of disallowed disqualified interest to members of the affiliated group.
    (A) In general.

(B) Definitions.

(1) Allocable share of the affiliated group's disallowed disqualified interest.

(2) Disallowed disqualified interest ratio.

(3) Exempt related person interest expense.

(iii) Treatment of carryforwards.

(4) Application of section 382.

(i) Ownership change occurring before November 13, 2020.

(A) Pre-change loss.

(B) Loss corporation.

(ii) Ownership change occurring on or after November 13, 2020.

(A) Pre-change loss.

(B) Loss corporation.

(5) Treatment of excess limitation from taxable years beginning before January 1, 2018.

(6) Example: Members of an affiliated group.

(d) Applicability date.

[Reg. §1.163(j)-0.]

☐ [*T.D. 9905, 9-3-2020. Amended by T.D. 9943, 1-13-2021.*]

[Reg. §1.163(j)-1]

§1.163(j)-1. Definitions.—(a) *In general.*—The definitions provided in this section apply for purposes of the section 163(j) regulations. For purposes of the rules set forth in §§1.163(j)-2 through 1.163(j)-11, additional definitions for certain terms are provided in those sections.

(b) *Definitions.*—(1) *Adjusted taxable income.*—The term *adjusted taxable income* (ATI) means the tentative taxable income of the taxpayer for the taxable year, with the adjustments in this paragraph (b)(1).

(i) *Additions.*—The amounts of the following items that were included in the computation of the taxpayer's tentative taxable income (if any) are added to tentative taxable income to determine ATI—

(A) Any business interest expense, other than disallowed business interest expense carryforwards;

(B) Any net operating loss deduction under section 172;

(C) Any deduction under section 199A;

(D) Subject to paragraph (b)(1)(iii) of this section, for taxable years beginning before January 1, 2022, any depreciation under section 167, section 168, or section 168 of the Internal Revenue Code (Code) of 1954 (former section 168);

(E) Subject to paragraph (b)(1)(iii) of this section, for taxable years beginning before January 1, 2022, any amortization of intangibles (for example, under section 167 or 197) and other amortized expenditures (for example, under section 174(b), 195(b)(1)(B), 248, or 1245(a)(2)(C));

(F) Subject to paragraph (b)(1)(iii) of this section, for taxable years beginning before January 1, 2022, any depletion under section 611;

(G) Any deduction for a capital loss carryback or carryover; and

(H) Any deduction or loss that is not properly allocable to a non-excepted trade or business (for rules governing the allocation of items to an excepted trade or business, see §§1.163(j)-1(b)(44) and 1.163(j)-10).

(ii) *Subtractions.*—The amounts of the following items (if any) are subtracted from the taxpayer's tentative taxable income to determine ATI—

(A) Any business interest income that was included in the computation of the taxpayer's tentative taxable income;

(B) Any floor plan financing interest expense for the taxable year that was included in the computation of the taxpayer's tentative taxable income;

(C) With respect to the sale or other disposition of property, the greater of the allowed or allowable depreciation, amortization, or depletion of the property, as provided under section 1016(a)(2), for the taxpayer (or, if the taxpayer is a member of a consolidated group, the consolidated group) *for the taxable years beginning after* December 31, 2017, and before January 1, 2022, with respect to such property;

(D) With respect to the sale or other disposition of stock of a member of a consolidated group by another member, the investment adjustments under §1.1502-32 with respect to such stock that are attributable to deductions described in paragraph (b)(1)(ii)(C) of this section;

(E) With respect to the sale or other disposition of an interest in a partnership, the taxpayer's distributive share of deductions described in paragraph (b)(1)(ii)(C) of this section with respect to

property held by the partnership at the time of such sale or other disposition to the extent such deductions were allowable under section 704(d);

(F) Any income or gain that is not properly allocable to a non-excepted trade or business (for rules governing the allocation of items to an excepted trade or business, see §§1.163(j)-1(b)(44) and 1.163(j)-10)) and that was included in the computation of the taxpayer's tentative taxable income; and

(G) An amount equal to the sum of any specified deemed inclusions that were included in the computation of the taxpayer's tentative taxable income, reduced by the portion of the deduction allowed under section 250(a) by reason of the specified deemed inclusions. For this purpose, a *specified deemed inclusion* is the inclusion of an amount by a United States shareholder (as defined in section 951(b)) in gross income under section 78, 951(a), or 951A(a) with respect to an applicable CFC (as defined in §1.163(j)-1(b)(2)) that is properly allocable to a non-excepted trade or business. Furthermore, a specified deemed inclusion includes any amounts included in a domestic partnership's gross income under section 951(a) or 951A(a) with respect to an applicable CFC to the extent such amounts are attributable to investment income of the partnership and are allocated to a domestic C corporation (that is a direct (or indirect) partner) and treated as properly allocable to a non-excepted trade or business of the domestic C corporation under §§1.163(j)-4(b)(3) and 1.163(j)-10. To determine the amount of a specified deemed inclusion described in this paragraph (b)(1)(ii)(G), the portion of a United States shareholder's inclusion under section 951A(a) treated as being with respect to an applicable CFC is determined under section 951A(f)(2) and §1.951A-6(b)(2).

(iii) *Depreciation, amortization, or depletion capitalized under section 263A.*—For purposes of paragraph (b)(1)(i) of this section, amounts of depreciation, amortization, or depletion that are capitalized under section 263A during the taxable year are deemed to be included in the computation of the taxpayer's tentative taxable income for such taxable year, regardless of the period in which the capitalized amount is recovered. See *Example 3* in §1.163(j)-2(h)(3).

(iv) *Application of §1.163(j)-1(b)(1)(ii)(C), (D), and (E).*—(A) *Sale or other disposition.*—(1) *In general.*—For purposes of paragraphs (b)(1)(ii)(C), (D), and (E) and paragraphs (b)(1)(iv)(B) and (E) of this section, except as otherwise provided in this paragraph (b)(1)(iv)(A), the term *sale or other disposition* does not include a transfer of an asset to an acquiring corporation in a transaction to which section 381(a) applies.

(2) *Intercompany transactions.*—For purposes of paragraphs (b)(1)(ii)(C) and (D) and paragraphs (b)(1)(iv)(B) and (b)(1)(iv)(E)(1) and (2) of this section, the term *sale or other disposition* excludes all intercompany transactions, within the meaning of §1.1502-13(b)(1)(i), to the extent necessary to achieve single-entity taxation of the consolidated group.

(3) *Deconsolidations.*—Notwithstanding any other rule in this paragraph (b)(1)(iv)(A), any transaction in which a member (S) leaves a consolidated group (selling group), including a section 381(a) transaction described in paragraph (b)(1)(iv)(A)(1) of this section, is treated as a taxable disposition of all S stock held by any member of the selling group for purposes of paragraphs (b)(1)(ii)(C) and (D) and paragraphs (b)(1)(iv)(B) and (b)(1)(iv)(E)(1) and (2) of this section, unless the transaction is described in §1.1502-13(j)(5)(i). Following S's deconsolidation, any subsequent sales or dispositions of S stock by the selling group do not trigger further adjustments under paragraphs (b)(1)(ii)(C) and (D) and paragraphs (b)(1)(iv)(B) and (b)(1)(iv)(E)(1) and (2) of this section. If a transaction is described in §1.1502-13(j)(5)(i), the transaction is not treated as a sale or other disposition for purposes of paragraphs (b)(1)(ii)(C) and (D) and paragraphs (b)(1)(iv)(B) and (b)(1)(iv)(E)(1) and (2) of this section. See also the successor rules in paragraph (b)(1)(iv)(C) of this section.

(4) *Nonrecognition transactions.*—The disposition of property, member stock (other than in a deconsolidation described in paragraph (b)(1)(iv)(A)(3) of this section), or partnership interests in a nonrecognition transaction, other than a section 381(a) transaction described in paragraph (b)(1)(iv)(A)(1) of this section, is treated as a taxable disposition of the property, member stock, or partnership interest disposed of for purposes of paragraph (b)(1)(iv)(E)(1)(i), (b)(1)(iv)(E)(2)(i), and (b)(1)(iv)(E)(3)(i) of this section, respectively. For example, if a taxpayer transfers property to a wholly owned, non-consolidated subsidiary, the transfer of the property is treated as a taxable disposition for purposes of paragraph (b)(1)(iv)(E)(1)(i) of this section notwithstanding the application of section 351.

(B) *Deductions by members of a consolidated group.*—(1) *In general.*—If paragraph (b)(1)(ii)(C), (D), or (E) of this section applies to adjust the tentative taxable income of a consolidated group, and if the consolidated group does not use the alternative computation method in paragraph (b)(1)(iv)(E) of this section, the amount of the adjustment under paragraph (b)(1)(ii)(C) of this section equals the greater of the allowed or allowable depreciation, amortization, or depletion of the property, as provided under section 1016(a)(2), for the consolidated group for the taxable years beginning after December 31, 2017, and before January 1, 2022, with respect to such property.

(2) *Application of the alternative computation method.*—If paragraph (b)(1)(ii)(C), paragraph (b)(1)(ii)(D), or paragraph (b)(1)(ii)(E) of this section applies to adjust the tentative taxable income of a consolidated group, and if the consolidated group uses the alternative computation method in paragraph (b)(1)(iv)(E) of this section, the amount of the adjustment computed under paragraph (b)(1)(iv)(E)(*1*)(*i*), paragraph (b)(1)(iv)(E)(*2*)(*i*), or paragraph (b)(1)(iv)(E)(*3*)(*i*) of this section must take into account the net gain that would be taken into account by the consolidated group, including from intercompany transactions, determined by treating the sale or other disposition as a taxable transaction (see paragraphs (b)(1)(iv)(A)(*3*) and (4) of this section regarding deconsolidations and certain nonrecognition transactions, respectively).

(C) *Successor rules.*—(1) *Successor assets.*—This paragraph (b)(1)(iv)(C)(*1*) applies if deductions described in paragraph (b)(1)(ii)(C) of this section are allowed or allowable to a consolidated group member (S) and either the depreciable property or S's stock is subsequently transferred to another member (S1) in an intercompany transaction in which the transferor receives S1 stock. If this paragraph (b)(1)(iv)(C)(*1*) applies, and if the transferor's basis in the S1 stock received in the intercompany transaction is determined, in whole or in part, by reference to its basis in the depreciable property or the S stock, the S1 stock received in the intercompany transaction is treated as a successor asset for purposes of paragraph (b)(1)(ii)(D) and (b)(1)(iv)(E)(2) of this section. Thus, except as otherwise provided in paragraph (b)(1)(iv)(D) of this section, the subsequent disposition of either the S1 stock or the S stock (or both) may require the application of the adjustment rules of paragraph (b)(1)(ii)(D) or paragraph (b)(1)(iv)(E)(2) of this section.

(2) *Successor entities.*—The acquiring corporation in a section 381(a) transaction to which the exception in paragraph (b)(1)(iv)(A)(*1*) of this section applies is treated as a successor to the distributor or transferor corporation for purposes of paragraphs (b)(1)(ii)(C) through (E) and (b)(1)(iv)(B) and (E) of this section. Therefore, for example, in applying paragraphs (b)(1)(ii)(C) through (E) and (b)(1)(iv)(B) and (E) of this section, the acquiring corporation is treated as succeeding to the allowed or allowable items of the distributor or transferor corporation. Similarly, the surviving group in a transaction described in § 1.1502-13(j)(5)(i) to which the exception in paragraph (b)(1)(iv)(A)(3) of this section applies is treated as a successor to the terminating group for purposes of paragraphs (b)(1)(ii)(C) through (E) and (b)(1)(iv)(B) and (E) of this section.

(D) *Anti-duplication rule.*—(1) *In general.*—The aggregate of the subtractions from tentative taxable income of a consolidated group under paragraphs (b)(1)(ii)(C) through (E) or paragraphs (b)(1)(iv)(E)(*1*) through (3) of this section with respect to an item of property (including with regard to dispositions of successor assets described in paragraph (b)(1)(iv)(C)(*1*) of this section) cannot exceed the aggregate amount of the consolidated group members' deductions described in paragraph (b)(1)(ii)(C) of this section with respect to such item of property. In addition, once an item of property is no longer held by any member of a consolidated group (whether or not an adjustment to the tentative taxable income of the group is made under paragraph (b)(1)(ii)(C) of this section with respect to the direct or indirect disposition of that property), no further adjustment to the group's tentative taxable income is made under paragraph (b)(1)(ii)(D) or paragraph (b)(1)(iv)(E)(2) of this section in relation to the same property with respect to any subsequent stock disposition.

(2) *Adjustments following deconsolidation.*—If a corporation (S) leaves a consolidated group (Group 1) in a transaction that requires an adjustment under paragraph (b)(1)(ii)(D) or paragraph (b)(1)(iv)(E)(2) of this section, no further adjustment is required under paragraph (b)(1)(ii)(C) or (E) or paragraph (b)(1)(iv)(E) of this section in a separate return year (as defined in § 1.1502-1(e)) of S with respect to depreciation, amortization, or depletion deductions allowed or allowable to Group 1. See paragraph (b)(1)(iv)(A) of this section for special rules regarding the meaning of the term "sale or other disposition" for purposes of the adjustments required under paragraphs (b)(1)(ii)(C) through (E) and paragraphs (b)(1)(iv)(B) and (E) of this section. For example, assume that S deconsolidates from Group 1 in a transaction *not described* in *§ 1.1502-13(j)(5)(i)* after *holding property for which* depreciation, amortization, or depletion deductions were allowed or allowable in Group 1. On the deconsolidation, S and Group 1 would adjust tentative taxable income with regard to that property. See paragraphs (b)(1)(iv)(A)(3), (b)(1)(ii)(D),

and (b)(1)(iv)(E)(2) of this section. If, following the deconsolidation, S sells the property referred to in the previous sentence, no subtraction from tentative taxable income is made under paragraph (b)(1)(ii)(C) or paragraph (b)(1)(iv)(E)(*1*) of this section during S's separate return year with regard to the amounts included in Group 1. See paragraphs (b)(1)(iv)(A)(3), (b)(1)(ii)(D), and (b)(1)(iv)(E)(2) of this section.

(E) *Alternative computation method.*—If paragraph (b)(1)(ii)(C), (D), or (E) of this section applies to adjust the tentative taxable income of a taxpayer, the taxpayer may compute the amount of the adjustments required by such paragraph using the formulas in paragraph (b)(1)(iv)(E)(*1*), (2), and (3) of this section, respectively, provided that the taxpayer applies such formulas to all dispositions for which an adjustment is required under paragraph (b)(1)(ii)(C), (D), or (E) of this section. For special rules regarding the treatment of deconsolidating transactions and nonrecognition transactions, see paragraph (b)(1)(iv)(A)(3) and (4) of this section, respectively. For special rules regarding the application of the formulas in paragraph (b)(1)(iv)(E)(*1*), (2), and (3) of this section by consolidated groups, see paragraph (b)(1)(iv)(B)(2) of this section.

(1) *Alternative computation method for property dispositions.*—With respect to the sale or other disposition of property, the lesser of:

(i) Any gain recognized on the sale or other disposition of such property by the taxpayer (or, if the taxpayer is a member of a consolidated group, the consolidated group); and

(ii) The greater of the allowed or allowable depreciation, amortization, or depletion of the property, as provided under section 1016(a)(2), for the taxpayer (or, if the taxpayer is a member of a consolidated group, the consolidated group) for the taxable years beginning after December 31, 2017, and before January 1, 2022, with respect to such property.

(2) *Alternative computation method for dispositions of member stock.*—With respect to the sale or other disposition by a member of a consolidated group of stock of another member for whom depreciation, amortization, or depletion was allowed or allowable with regard to an item of property (or stock of any successor to that member), the lesser of:

(i) Any gain recognized on the sale or other disposition of such stock; and

(ii) The investment adjustments under § 1.1502-32 with respect to such stock that are attributable to deductions described in paragraph (b)(1)(ii)(C) of this section. The investment adjustments referred to in this paragraph (b)(1)(iv)(E)(2)(ii) include investment adjustments replicated in stock of members that are successor entities.

(3) *Alternative computation method for dispositions of partnership interests.*—With respect to the sale or other disposition of an interest in a partnership, the lesser of:

(i) Any gain recognized on the sale or other disposition of such interest; and

(ii) The taxpayer's (or, if the taxpayer is a consolidated group, the consolidated group's) distributive share of deductions described in paragraph (b)(1)(ii)(C) of this section with respect to property held by the partnership at the time of such sale or other disposition to the extent such deductions were allowable under section 704(d).

(F) *Cap on negative adjustments.*—(1) *In general.*—A subtraction from (or negative adjustment to) tentative taxable income that is required under paragraph (b)(1)(ii)(C), (D), or (E) or paragraph (b)(1)(iv)(B) or (E) of this section is reduced to the extent the taxpayer establishes that the positive adjustments to tentative taxable income under paragraphs (b)(1)(i)(D) through (F) of this section in a prior taxable year did not result in an increase in the amount allowed as a deduction for business interest expense for such year. The extent to which the positive adjustments under paragraphs (b)(1)(i)(D) through (F) of this section resulted in an increase in the amount allowed as a deduction for business interest expense in a prior taxable year (such amount of positive adjustments, the *negative adjustment cap*) is determined after taking into account all other adjustments to tentative taxable income under paragraph (b)(1)(i) and (ii) of this section for that year, as established through books and records. The amount of the negative adjustment cap for a prior taxable year is reduced in future taxable years to the extent of negative adjustments under paragraphs (b)(1)(ii)(C) through (E) and paragraphs (b)(1)(iv)(B) and (E) of this section with respect to the prior taxable year.

(2) *Example.*—A is a calendar-year individual taxpayer engaged in a trade or business that is neither an excepted trade or business nor eligible for the small business exemption. A has no disallowed business interest expense carryforwards. In 2021, A has $100x of business interest expense, no business interest income or

Itemized Deductions for Individuals and Corps.
See p. 20,601 for regulations not amended to reflect law changes
25,315

floor plan financing interest expense, and $400x of tentative taxable income. After taking into account the adjustments to tentative taxable income under paragraph (b)(1)(i) and (ii) of this section other than positive adjustments under paragraphs (b)(1)(i)(D) through (F) of this section, A has tentative taxable income of $450x. A increases its tentative taxable income by $30x (from $450x to $480x) under paragraph (b)(1)(i)(D) of this section to reflect $30x of depreciation deductions with respect to Asset Y in 2021. Thus, for 2021, A would have a section 163(j) limitation of $135x ($450x x 30 percent) without regard to adjustments under paragraphs (b)(1)(i)(D) through (F) of this section. After the application of paragraph (b)(1)(i)(D) of this section, A has a section 163(j) limitation of $144x ($480x x 30 percent). In 2022, A sells Asset Y at a gain of $50x. Under paragraph (b)(1)(iv)(F)(1) of this section, A is not required to reduce its tentative taxable income in 2022 under paragraph (b)(1)(ii)(C) through (E) or paragraph (b)(1)(iv)(E) of this section. As established by A, the $30x addition to tentative taxable income under paragraph (b)(1)(i)(D) of this section resulted in no increase in the amount allowed as a deduction for business interest expense in 2021.

(G) *Treatment of depreciation, amortization, or depletion capitalized under section 263A.*—Paragraphs (b)(1)(ii)(C) through (E) of this section and this paragraph (b)(1)(iv) apply with respect to the sale or other disposition of property to which paragraph (b)(1)(iii) of this section applies. For example, if a taxpayer with depreciable machinery capitalizes the depreciation into inventory under section 263A, paragraph (b)(1)(ii)(C) or paragraph (b)(1)(iv)(E) of this section (and, if the taxpayer is a consolidated group, paragraph (b)(1)(iv)(B) of this section) applies upon the disposition of the machinery, subject to the cap in paragraph (b)(1)(iv)(F) of this section. Similarly, the successor asset rules in paragraph (b)(1)(iv)(C)(1) of this section would apply if the depreciable machinery subsequently were transferred to another member (S1) in an intercompany transaction in which the transferor received S1 stock.

(v) *Other adjustments.*—ATI is computed with the other adjustments provided in §§ 1.163(j)-2 through 1.163(j)-11.

(vi) *Additional rules relating to adjusted taxable income in other sections.*—(A) For rules governing the ATI of C corporations, see §§ 1.163(j)-4(b)(2) and (3) and 1.163(j)-10(a)(2)(ii).

(B) For rules governing the ATI of RICs and REITs, see § 1.163(j)-4(b)(4).

(C) For rules governing the ATI of tax-exempt corporations, see § 1.163(j)-4(b)(5).

(D) For rules governing the ATI of consolidated groups, see § 1.163(j)-4(d)(2)(iv) and (v).

(E) For rules governing the ATI of partnerships, see § 1.163(j)-6(d).

(F) For rules governing the ATI of partners, see §§ 1.163(j)-6(e) and 1.163(j)-6(m)(1) and (2).

(G) For rules governing partnership basis adjustments affecting ATI, see § 1.163(j)-6(h)(2).

(H) For rules governing the ATI of S corporations, see § 1.163(j)-6(l)(3).

(I) For rules governing the ATI of S corporation shareholders, see § 1.163(j)-6(l)(4).

(J) For rules governing the ATI of certain beneficiaries of trusts and estates, see § 1.163(j)-2(f).

(vii) *ATI cannot be less than zero.*—If the ATI of a taxpayer would be less than zero, the ATI of the taxpayer is zero.

(viii) *Examples.*—The examples in this paragraph (b)(1)(viii) illustrate the application of paragraphs (b)(1)(ii), (iii), and (iv) of this section. Unless otherwise indicated, A, B, P, S, and T are calendar-year domestic C corporations; P is the parent of a consolidated group of which S and T are members; the exemption for certain small businesses in § 1.163(j)-2(d) does not apply; no entity is engaged in an excepted trade or business; no entity has business interest income or floor plan financing interest expense; and all amounts of interest expense are deductible except for the potential application of section 163(j).

(A) *Example 1.*—(1) *Facts.* In 2021, A purchases a depreciable asset (Asset X) for $30x and fully depreciates *Asset X* under section 168(k). For the 2021 taxable year, A establishes that its ATI before adding back depreciation deductions with respect to Asset X under paragraph (b)(1)(i)(D) of this section is $130x, and that its ATI after adding back depreciation deductions with respect to Asset X under paragraph (b)(1)(i)(D) of this section is $160x. A incurs $45x of business interest expense in 2021. In 2024, A sells Asset X to an unrelated third party for $25x.

(2) *Analysis.* A's section 163(j) limitation for 2021 is $48x ($160x × 30 percent). Thus, all $45x of A's business interest expense incurred in 2021 is deductible in that year. Under paragraph

(b)(1)(ii)(C) of this section, A must subtract $30x from its tentative taxable income in computing its ATI for its 2024 taxable year. Alternatively, under paragraph (b)(1)(iv)(E)(1) of this section, A must subtract $25x (the lesser of $30x or $25x ($25x - $0x)) from its tentative taxable income in computing its ATI for its 2024 taxable year. However, the negative adjustments under paragraphs (b)(1)(ii)(C) and (b)(1)(iv)(E)(1) of this section are both subject to the negative adjustment cap in paragraph (b)(1)(iv)(F) of this section. Under that paragraph, A's negative adjustment under either paragraph (b)(1)(ii)(C) or paragraph (b)(1)(iv)(E)(1) of this section is capped at $20x, or $150x (the amount of ATI that A needed in order to deduct all $45x of business interest expense in 2021) minus $130x (the amount of A's tentative taxable income in 2021 before adding back any amounts under paragraph (b)(1)(i)(D) through (F) of this section). As established by A, the additional $10x ($30x - $20x) of depreciation deductions that were added back to tentative taxable income in 2021 under paragraph (b)(1)(i)(D) of this section did not increase A's business interest expense deduction for that year.

(3) *Transfer of assets in a nonrecognition transaction to which section 381 applies.* The facts are the same as in paragraph (b)(1)(viii)(A)(1) of this section, except that, rather than sell Asset X to an unrelated third party in 2024, A merges with and into an unrelated third party in 2024 in a transaction described in section 368(a)(1)(A) in which no gain is recognized. As provided in paragraph (b)(1)(iv)(A)(1) of this section, the merger transaction is not treated as a "sale or other disposition" for purposes of paragraph (b)(1)(ii)(C) or paragraph (b)(1)(iv)(E)(1) of this section. Thus, no adjustment to tentative taxable income is required in 2024 under paragraph (b)(1)(ii)(C) or paragraph (b)(1)(iv)(E)(1) of this section.

(4) *Transfer of assets in a nonrecognition transaction to which section 351 applies.* The facts are the same as in paragraph (b)(1)(viii)(A)(1) of this section, except that, rather than sell Asset X to an unrelated third party in 2024, A transfers Asset X to B (A's wholly owned subsidiary) in 2024 in a transaction to which section 351 applies. The section 351 transaction is treated as a "sale or other disposition" for purposes of paragraphs (b)(1)(ii)(C) and (b)(1)(iv)(E)(1) of this section, and it is treated as a taxable disposition for purposes of paragraph (b)(1)(iv)(E)(1) of this section. See paragraph (b)(1)(iv)(A)(1) and (4) of this section. However, the negative adjustments under paragraphs (b)(1)(ii)(C) and (b)(1)(iv)(E)(1) of this section are both subject to the negative adjustment cap in paragraph (b)(1)(iv)(F) of this section. Thus, A must subtract $20x from its tentative taxable income in computing its ATI for its 2024 taxable year.

(B) *Example 2.*—(1) *Facts.* In 2021, S purchases a depreciable asset (Asset Y) for $30x and fully depreciates Asset Y under section 168(k). P reduces its basis in its S stock by $30x under § 1.1502-32 to reflect S's depreciation deductions with respect to Asset Y. For the 2021 taxable year, the P group establishes that its ATI before adding back S's depreciation deductions with respect to Asset Y under paragraph (b)(1)(i)(D) of this section is $130x, and that its ATI after adding back S's depreciation deductions with respect to Asset Y under paragraph (b)(1)(i)(D) of this section is $160x. The P group incurs $45x of business interest expense in 2021. In 2024, P sells all of its S stock to an unrelated third party at a gain of $25x.

(2) *Analysis.* The P group's section 163(j) limitation for 2021 is $48x ($160x × 30 percent). Thus, all $45x of the P group's business interest expense incurred in 2021 is deductible in that year. Under paragraph (b)(1)(ii)(D) of this section, the P group must subtract $30x from its tentative taxable income in computing its ATI for its 2024 taxable year. Alternatively, under paragraph (b)(1)(iv)(E)(2) of this section, the P group must subtract $25x (the lesser of $30x or $25x) from its tentative taxable income in computing its ATI for its 2024 taxable year. However, the negative adjustments under paragraphs (b)(1)(ii)(D) and (b)(1)(iv)(E)(2) of this section are both subject to the negative adjustment cap in paragraph (b)(1)(iv)(F) of this section. Under that paragraph, the P group's negative adjustment under either paragraph (b)(1)(ii)(D) or paragraph (b)(1)(iv)(E)(2) of this section is capped at $20x, or $150x (the amount of ATI the P group needed in order to deduct all $45x of business interest expense in 2021) minus $130x (the amount of the P group's tentative taxable income in 2021 before adding back any amounts under paragraph (b)(1)(i)(D) through (F) of this section). As established by the P group, the additional $10x ($30x - $20x) of depreciation deductions that were added back to tentative taxable income in 2021 under paragraph (b)(1)(i)(D) of this section did not increase the P group's business interest expense deduction for that year.

(3) *Disposition of less than all member stock.* The facts are the same as in paragraph (b)(1)(viii)(B)(1) of this section, except that, in 2024, P sells half of its S stock to an unrelated third party. The results are the same as in paragraph (b)(1)(viii)(B)(2) of this section. See paragraph (b)(1)(iv)(A)(3) of this section. Thus, the P group must subtract $20x from its tentative taxable income in computing its ATI for its 2024 taxable year. No further adjustment under paragraphs

(b)(1)(ii)(C) and (D) or paragraphs (b)(1)(iv)(E)(1) and (2) of this section is required if P subsequently sells its remaining S stock or if S subsequently disposes of Asset Y. See paragraphs (b)(1)(iv)(A)(3) and (b)(1)(iv)(D) of this section.

(4) *Intercompany transfer; disposition of successor assets*—(i) *Adjustments in 2024.* The facts are the same as in paragraph (b)(1)(viii)(B)(1) of this section, except that, rather than sell all of its S stock to an unrelated third party in 2024, P transfers all of its S stock to T in 2024 in a transaction to which section 351 applies and, in 2025, P sells all of its T stock to an unrelated third party at a gain of $40x. As provided in paragraph (b)(1)(iv)(A)(2) of this section, P's intercompany transfer of its S stock to T is not a "sale or other disposition" for purposes of paragraph (b)(1)(ii)(D) or paragraph (b)(1)(iv)(E)(2) of this section. Thus, no adjustment to tentative taxable income is required in 2024 under paragraph (b)(1)(ii)(D) or paragraph (b)(1)(iv)(E)(2) of this section.

(ii) *Adjustments in 2025.* Pursuant to paragraph (b)(1)(iv)(C)(1) of this section, P's stock in T is treated as a successor asset for purposes of paragraph (b)(1)(ii)(D) and (b)(1)(iv)(E)(2) of this section. Moreover, P's sale of its T stock causes both T and S to deconsolidate. Thus, under paragraph (b)(1)(iv)(A)(3) of this section, the transaction is treated as a taxable disposition of all of the T stock and all of the S stock held by all members of the P group. Under the anti-duplication rule in paragraph (b)(1)(iv)(D) of this section, the total amount of gain recognized for purposes of paragraph (b)(1)(iv)(E)(2)(i) of this section is $40x, the greater of the gain on the disposition of the T stock ($40x) or on the disposition of the S stock ($25x). However, the negative adjustments under paragraph (b)(1)(iv)(E)(2) of this section are subject to the negative adjustment cap in paragraph (b)(1)(iv)(F) of this section. Thus, the P group must subtract $20x from its tentative taxable income in computing its ATI for its 2025 taxable year.

(5) *Alternative computation and non-deconsolidating disposition of member stock.* The facts are the same as in paragraph (b)(1)(viii)(B)(1) of this section, except that, in 2024, P sells just ten percent of its S stock to an unrelated third party at a gain of $2.5x. Under paragraph (b)(1)(iv)(E)(2) of this section, the lesser of P's gain recognized on the sale of the S stock ($2.5x) and the investment adjustments under §1.1502-32 with respect to the S stock P sold ($3x) is $2.5x, an amount less than the $20x limitation under paragraph (b)(1)(iv)(F) of this section. Thus, the P group must subtract $2.5x from its tentative taxable income in computing its ATI for its 2024 taxable year.

(6) *Non-deconsolidating disposition of member stock followed by asset disposition.* The facts are the same as in paragraph (b)(1)(viii)(B)(5) of this section, except that, in 2025, S sells Asset Y to an unrelated third party for a gain of $20x. Under paragraph (b)(1)(iv)(E)(1) of this section, the amount of the adjustment in 2025 is the lesser of two amounts. The first amount is the amount of S's gain recognized on the sale of Asset Y ($20x). See paragraph (b)(1)(iv)(E)(1)(i) of this section. The second amount is the amount of depreciation with respect to Asset Y (see paragraph (b)(1)(iv)(E)(1)(ii) of this section), reduced by the amount of depreciation previously taken into account in the computation under paragraph (b)(1)(iv)(E)(2)(ii) of this section ($30x - $3x, or $27x). See paragraph (b)(1)(iv)(D)(1) of this section. Thus, the amount of the adjustment under paragraphs (b)(1)(iv)(D) and (b)(1)(iv)(E)(1) of this section is $20x. In turn, this amount is subject to the negative adjustment cap under paragraph (b)(1)(iv)(F), which, after accounting for the negative adjustment on the earlier sale of S stock in 2024, is $17.5x ($20x - $2.5x). Accordingly, the P group must subtract $17.5x from its tentative taxable income in computing its ATI for its 2025 taxable year.

(C) *Example 3.*—(1) *Facts.* The facts are the same as in paragraph (b)(1)(viii)(B)(1) of this section, except that, in 2024, S sells Asset Y to an unrelated third party for $25x and, in 2025, P sells all of its S stock to an unrelated third party at a gain of $25x.

(2) *Analysis.* The results are the same as in paragraph (b)(1)(viii)(B)(2) of this section. Thus, the P group must subtract $20x from its tentative taxable income in computing its ATI for its 2024 taxable year. P's sale of all of its S stock in 2025 is a "sale or other disposition" for purposes of paragraph (b)(1)(ii)(D) and (b)(1)(iv)(E)(2) of this section. However, pursuant to paragraph (b)(1)(iv)(D)(1) of this section, no further adjustment to the P group's tentative taxable income is required in 2025 under paragraph (b)(1)(ii)(D) or paragraph (b)(1)(iv)(E)(2) of this section.

(3) *Disposition of S stock prior to S's asset disposition.* The facts are the same as in paragraph (b)(1)(viii)(C)(1) of this section, except that, in 2024, P sells all of its S stock to an unrelated third party at a gain of $25x and, in 2025, S sells Asset Y to an unrelated third party for $25x. The results are the same as in paragraph (b)(1)(viii)(B)(2) of this section. Thus, the P group must subtract $20x from its tentative taxable income in computing its ATI for its 2024 taxable year. Pursuant to paragraph (b)(1)(iv)(D)(2) of this section, no adjustment to the

acquiring group's tentative taxable income is required in 2025 under paragraph (b)(1)(ii)(C) or paragraph (b)(1)(iv)(E)(1) of this section.

(4) *Deconsolidation of S in nonrecognition transaction.* The facts are the same as in paragraph (b)(1)(viii)(C)(3) of this section, except that, rather than sell all of its S stock to an unrelated third party, P causes S to merge with and into an unrelated third party in a transaction described in section 368(a)(1)(A). As provided in paragraph (b)(1)(iv)(A)(3) of this section, the merger transaction is treated as a taxable disposition of all of P's stock in S for purposes of paragraphs (b)(1)(ii)(D) and (b)(1)(iv)(E)(2) of this section because S leaves the P group. Thus, the results are the same as in paragraph (b)(1)(viii)(C)(3) of this section.

(D) *Example 4.*—(1) *Facts.* P wholly owns T, which wholly owns S. In 2021, S purchases a depreciable asset (Asset Z) for $30x and fully depreciates Asset Z under section 168(k). T reduces its basis in its S stock, and P reduces its basis in its T stock, by $30x under §1.1502-32 to reflect S's depreciation deductions with respect to Asset Z. For the 2021 taxable year, the P group establishes that its ATI before adding back S's depreciation deductions with respect to Asset Z under paragraph (b)(1)(i)(D) of this section is $130x, and that its ATI after adding back S's depreciation deductions with respect to Asset Z under paragraph (b)(1)(i)(D) of this section is $160x. The P group incurs $45x of business interest expense in 2021. In 2024, T sells all of its S stock to an unrelated third party at a gain of $25x. In 2025, P sells all of its T stock to an unrelated third party at a gain of $40x.

(2) *Analysis.* The results are the same as in paragraph (b)(1)(viii)(3)(2) of this section. Thus, the P group must subtract $20x from its tentative taxable income in computing its ATI for its 2024 taxable year. Pursuant to paragraph (b)(1)(iv)(D)(1) of this section, no negative adjustment to the P group's tentative taxable income is required in 2025 under paragraph (b)(1)(ii)(D) or paragraph (b)(1)(iv)(E)(2) of this section.

(3) *Disposition of T stock in 2024.* The facts are the same as in paragraph (b)(1)(viii)(D)(1) of this section, except that, in 2024, P sells all of its T stock to another consolidated group at a gain of $40x and, in 2025, T sells all of its S stock to an unrelated party at a gain of $25x. Whereas the transaction described in paragraph (b)(1)(viii)(B)(4) of this section is treated as a taxable disposition of both the T stock and the S stock, only the actual disposition of the T stock in the transaction described in this paragraph (b)(1)(viii)(D)(3) is treated as a taxable disposition for purposes of paragraphs (b)(1)(ii)(D) and (b)(1)(iv)(E)(2) of this section. See paragraph (b)(1)(iv)(A)(3) of this section. However, the results are the same as in paragraph (b)(1)(viii)(B)(2) and (b)(1)(viii)(B)(4) of this section because of the negative adjustment cap in paragraph (b)(1)(iv)(F) of this section. Thus, the P group must subtract $20x from its tentative taxable income in computing its ATI for its 2024 taxable year. Pursuant to paragraph (b)(1)(iv)(D) of this section, no negative adjustment to the acquiring group's tentative taxable income is required in 2025 under paragraph (b)(1)(ii)(D) or paragraph (b)(1)(iv)(E)(2) of this section.

(E) *Example 5.*—(1) *Facts.* In 2021, A purchases Assets X and Y for $30x and $80x, respectively, and fully depreciates each asset under section 168(k). For the 2021 taxable year, A establishes that its ATI before adding back depreciation deductions with respect to Assets X and Y under paragraph (b)(1)(i)(D) of this section is $150x, and that its ATI after adding back depreciation deductions with respect to Assets X and Y under paragraph (b)(1)(i)(D) of this section is $260x. A incurs $75x of business interest expense in 2021. In 2024, A sells Assets X and Y to an unrelated third party for $40x and $90x, respectively.

(2) *Analysis.* A's section 163(j) limitation for 2021 is $78x ($260x × 30 percent). Thus, all $75x of A's business interest expense incurred in 2021 is deductible in that year. Under paragraph (b)(1)(ii)(C) of this section, A must subtract $110x ($30x + $80x) from its tentative taxable income in computing its ATI for its 2024 taxable year. Alternatively, under paragraph (b)(1)(iv)(E)(1) of this section, A must subtract $30x with respect to Asset X (the lesser of $30x or $40x ($40x - $0x)), and $80x with respect to Asset Y (the lesser of $80x or $90x ($90x - $0x)), from its tentative taxable income in computing its ATI for its 2024 taxable year. However, the negative adjustments under paragraphs (b)(1)(ii)(C) and (b)(1)(iv)(E)(1) of this section are both subject to the negative adjustment cap in paragraph (b)(1)(iv)(F) of this section. Under that paragraph, A's negative adjustment in 2024 under either paragraph (b)(1)(ii)(C) ($110x) or paragraph (b)(1)(iv)(E)(1) (also $110x) of this section is limited to $100x. This amount equals $250x (the amount of ATI that A needed in order to deduct all $75x of business interest expense in 2021) minus $150x (the amount of A's tentative taxable income in 2021 before adding back any amounts under paragraph (b)(1)(i)(D) through (F) of this section). As established by A, the additional $10x ($110x - $100x) of depreciation deductions that were added back to tentative taxable income in 2021 under paragraph (b)(1)(i)(D) of this section did not increase A's business interest expense deduction for that year.

(3) Sale of assets in different taxable years. The facts are the same as in paragraph (b)(1)(viii)(E)(*1*) of this section, except that A sells Asset Y to an unrelated third party for $90x in 2025. Under paragraph (b)(1)(ii)(C) of this section, A must subtract $30x from its tentative taxable income in computing its ATI for its 2024 taxable year. Alternatively, under paragraph (b)(1)(iv)(E)(*1*) of this section, A must subtract $30x (the lesser of $30x or $40x ($40x - $0x)) from its tentative taxable income in computing its ATI for its 2024 taxable year. Because A's negative adjustment cap for its 2021 taxable year is $100x (see paragraph (b)(1)(viii)(E)(*2*) of this section), A's negative adjustment in 2024 of $30x is not reduced under paragraph (b)(1)(iv)(F) of this section. In 2025, A must subtract $80x from its tentative taxable income under paragraph (b)(1)(ii)(C) of this section in computing its ATI. Alternatively, under paragraph (b)(1)(iv)(E)(*1*) of this section, A must subtract $80x (the lesser of $80x or $90x ($90x - $0x)) from its tentative taxable income in computing its ATI for its 2025 taxable year. However, the negative adjustments under paragraphs (b)(1)(ii)(C) and (b)(1)(iv)(E)(*1*) of this section are both subject to the negative adjustment cap in paragraph (b)(1)(iv)(F) of this section. Moreover, A's negative adjustment cap for its 2021 taxable year is reduced from $100x to $70x to reflect A's $30x negative adjustment in 2024. See paragraph (b)(1)(iv)(F) of this section. Thus, A's negative adjustment for 2025 under either paragraph (b)(1)(ii)(C) or paragraph (b)(1)(iv)(E)(*1*) of this section is reduced from $80x to $70x. As established by A, the additional $10x ($110x - $100x) of depreciation deductions that were added back to tentative taxable income in 2021 under paragraph (b)(1)(i)(D) of this section did not increase A's business interest expense deduction for that year.

(2) *Applicable CFC.*—The term *applicable CFC* means a foreign corporation described in section 957, but only if the foreign corporation has at least one United States shareholder that owns, within the meaning of section 958(a), stock of the foreign corporation.

(3) *Business interest expense.*—(i) *In general.*—The term *business interest expense* means interest expense that is properly allocable to a non-excepted trade or business or that is floor plan financing interest expense. Business interest expense also includes disallowed business interest expense carryforwards (as defined in paragraph (b)(11) of this section). However, business interest expense does not include amounts of interest expense carried forward to the taxable year from a prior taxable year due to the application of section 465 or section 469, which apply after the application of section 163(j). For the treatment of investment interest, see section 163(d); and for the treatment of personal interest, see section 163(h).

(ii) *Special rules.*—For special rules for defining business interest expense in certain circumstances, see §§ 1.163(j)-3(b)(2) (regarding disallowed interest expense), 1.163(j)-4(b) (regarding C corporations) and 1.163(j)-4(d)(2)(iii) (regarding consolidated groups), 1.163(j)-1(b)(9)(regarding current-year business interest expense), and 1.163(j)-6(c) (regarding partnerships and S corporations).

(4) *Business interest income.*—(i) *In general.*—The term *business interest income* means interest income includible in the gross income of a taxpayer for the taxable year which is properly allocable to a non-excepted trade or business. For the treatment of investment income, see section 163(d).

(ii) *Special rules.*—For special rules defining business interest income in certain circumstances, see §§ 1.163(j)-4(b) (regarding C corporations), 1.163(j)-4(d)(2)(iii) (regarding consolidated groups), and 1.163(j)-6(c) (regarding partnerships and S corporations).

(5) *C corporation.*—The term *C corporation* has the meaning provided in section 1361(a)(2).

(6) *Cleared swap.*—The term *cleared swap* means a swap that is cleared by a derivatives clearing organization, as such term is defined in section 1a of the Commodity Exchange Act (7 U.S.C. 1a), or by a clearing agency, as such term is defined in section 3 of the Securities Exchange Act of 1934 (15 U.S.C. 78c), that is registered as a derivatives clearing organization under the Commodity Exchange Act or as a clearing agency under the Securities Exchange Act of 1934, respectively, if the derivatives clearing organization or clearing agency requires the parties to the swap to post and collect margin or collateral.

(7) *Consolidated group.*—The term *consolidated group* has the meaning provided in § 1.1502-1(h).

(8) *Consolidated return year.*—The term *consolidated return year* has the meaning provided in § 1.1502-1(d).

(9) *Current-year business interest expense.*—The term *current-year business interest expense* means business interest expense that would be deductible in the current taxable year without regard to section

163(j) and that is not a disallowed business interest expense carryforward from a prior taxable year.

(10) *Disallowed business interest expense.*—The term *disallowed business interest expense* means the amount of business interest expense for a taxable year in excess of the amount allowed as a deduction for the taxable year under section 163(j)(1) and § 1.163(j)-2(b). For purposes of section 163(j) and the regulations in this part under section 163(j) of the Internal Revenue Code (Code) disallowed business interest expense is treated as "paid or accrued" in the taxable year in which the expense is deductible for Federal income tax purposes (without regard to section 163(j)) or in the taxable year in which a deduction for the business interest expense is permitted under section 163(j), as the context may require.

(11) *Disallowed business interest expense carryforward.*—The term *disallowed business interest expense carryforward* means any business interest expense described in § 1.163(j)-2(c).

(12) *Disallowed disqualified interest.*—The term *disallowed disqualified interest* means interest expense, including carryforwards, for which a deduction was disallowed under old section 163(j) (as defined in paragraph (b)(27) of this section) in the taxpayer's last taxable year beginning before January 1, 2018, and that was carried forward pursuant to old section 163(j).

(13) *Electing farming business.*—The term *electing farming business* means a trade or business that makes an election as provided in § 1.163(j)-9 or other published guidance and that is—

(i) A farming business, as defined in section 263A(e)(4) or § 1.263A-4(a)(4);

(ii) Any trade or business of a specified agricultural or horticultural cooperative, as defined in section 199A(g)(4); or

(iii) Specifically designated by the Secretary in guidance published in the Federal Register or the Internal Revenue Bulletin (see § 601.601(d) of this chapter) as a farming business for purposes of section 163(j).

(14) *Electing real property trade or business.*—The term *electing real property trade or business* means a trade or business that makes an election as provided in § 1.163(j)-9 or other published guidance and that is—

(i) A real property trade or business described in section 469(c)(7)(C) and § 1.469-9(b)(2); or

(ii) A REIT that qualifies for the safe harbor described in § 1.163(j)-9(h); or

(iii) A trade or business specifically designated by the Secretary in guidance published in the Federal Register or the Internal Revenue Bulletin (see § 601.601(d) of this chapter) as a real property trade or business for purposes of section 163(j).

(15) *Excepted regulated utility trade or business.*—(i) *In general.*—The term *excepted regulated utility trade or business* means:

(A) *Automatically excepted regulated utility trades or businesses.*—A trade or business—

(1) That furnishes or sells—

(i) Electrical energy, water, or sewage disposal services;

(ii) Gas or steam through a local distribution system; or

(iii) Transportation of gas or steam by pipeline; but only

(2) To the extent that the rates for the furnishing or sale of the items in paragraph (b)(15)(i)(A)(*1*) of this section—

(i) Have been established or approved by a State or political subdivision thereof, by any agency or instrumentality of the United States, or by a public service or public utility commission or other similar body of any State or political subdivision thereof and are determined on a cost of service and rate of return basis; or

(ii) Have been established or approved by the governing or ratemaking body of an electric cooperative; or

(B) *Electing regulated utility trades or businesses.*—A trade or business that makes a valid election under paragraph (b)(15)(iii) of this section; or

(C) *Designated excepted regulated utility trades or businesses.*—A trade or business that is specifically designated by the Secretary in guidance published in the Federal Register or the Internal Revenue Bulletin as an excepted regulated utility trade or business (see § 601.601(d) of this chapter) for section 163(j) purposes.

(ii) *Depreciation and excepted and non-excepted utility trades or businesses.*—(A) *Depreciation.*—Taxpayers engaged in an excepted trade or business described in paragraph (b)(15)(i) of this section cannot claim the additional first-year depreciation deduction under section 168(k) for any property that is primarily used in the excepted regulated utility trade or business.

(B) *Allocation of items.*—If a taxpayer is engaged in one or more excepted trades or businesses, as described in paragraph (b)(15)(i) of this section, and one or more non-excepted trades or businesses, the taxpayer must allocate items between the excepted and non-excepted utility trades or businesses. See §§ 1.163(j)-1(b)(44) and 1.163(j)-10(c)(3)(iii)(C). Some trades or businesses with de minimis furnishing or sales of items described in paragraph (b)(15)(i)(A)(1) of this section that are not sold pursuant to rates that are determined on a cost of service and rate of return basis or established or approved by the governing or ratemaking body of an electric cooperative, and are not subject to an election in paragraph (b)(15)(iii), are treated as excepted trades or businesses. See § 1.163(j)-10(c)(3)(iii)(C)(3). For look-through rules applicable to certain CFCs that furnish or sell items described in paragraph (b)(15)(i)(A)(1) of this section that are not sold pursuant to rates that are determined on a cost of service and rate of return basis or established or approved by the governing or ratemaking body of an electric cooperative as described in paragraph (b)(15)(i)(A)(2) of this section, see § 1.163(j)-10(c)(5)(ii)(C).

(iii) *Election to be an excepted regulated utility trade or business.*—(A) *In general.*—A trade or business that is not an excepted regulated utility trade or business described in paragraph (b)(15)(i)(A) or (C) of this section and that furnishes or sells items described in paragraph (b)(15)(i)(A)(1) of this section is eligible to make an election to be an excepted regulated utility trade or business to the extent that the rates for furnishing or selling the items described in paragraph (b)(15)(i)(A)(1) of this section have been established or approved by a regulatory body described in paragraph (b)(15)(i)(A)(2)(i) of this section.

(B) *Scope and effect of election.*—(1) *In general.*—An election under paragraph (b)(15)(iii) of this section is made with respect to each eligible trade or business of the taxpayer and applies only to the trade or business for which the election is made. An election under paragraph (b)(15)(iii) of this section applies to the taxable year in which the election is made and to all subsequent taxable years.

(2) *Irrevocability.*—An election under paragraph (b)(15)(iii) of this section is irrevocable.

(C) *Time and manner of making election.*—(1) *In general.*— Subject to paragraph (b)(15)(iii)(C)(5) of this section, a taxpayer makes an election under paragraph (b)(15)(iii) by attaching an election statement to the taxpayer's timely filed original Federal income tax return, including extensions. A taxpayer may make elections for multiple trades or businesses on a single election statement.

(2) *Election statement contents.*—The election statement should be titled "Section 1.163(j)-1(b)(15)(iii) Election" and must contain the following information for each trade or business:

(i) The taxpayer's name;

(ii) The taxpayer's address;

(iii) The taxpayer's social security number (SSN) or employer identification number (EIN);

(iv) A description of the taxpayer's electing trade or business sufficient to demonstrate qualification for an election under this section, including the principal business activity code; and

(v) A statement that the taxpayer is making an election under section 1.163(j)-1(b)(15)(iii).

(3) *Consolidated group's or partnership's trade or business.*— The rules in § 1.163(j)-9(d)(3) and (4) apply with respect to an election under paragraph (b)(15)(iii) of this section for a consolidated group's or partnership's trade or business.

(4) *Termination of election.*—The rules in § 1.163(j)-9(e) apply to determine when an election under paragraph (b)(15)(iii) of this section terminates.

(5) *Additional guidance.*—The rules and procedures regarding the time and manner of making an election under paragraph (b)(15)(iii) of this section and the election statement contents in paragraph (b)(15)(iii)(C)(2) of this section may be modified through other guidance (see §§ 601.601(d) and 601.602 of this chapter). Additional situations in which an election may terminate under paragraph (b)(15)(iii)(C)(4) of this section may be provided through guidance published in the Federal Register or in the Internal Revenue Bulletin (see § 601.601(d) of this chapter).

(16) *Excess business interest expense.*—For any partnership, the term *excess business interest expense* means the amount of disallowed business interest expense of the partnership for a taxable year under section § 1.163(j)-2(b). With respect to a partner, see § 1.163(j)-6(g) and (h).

(17) *Excess taxable income.*—With respect to any partnership or S corporation, the term *excess taxable income* means the amount which bears the same ratio to the partnership's ATI as—

(i) The excess (if any) of—

(A) The amount determined for the partnership or S corporation under section 163(j)(1)(B); over

(B) The amount (if any) by which the business interest expense of the partnership, reduced by the floor plan financing interest expense, exceeds the business interest income of the partnership or S corporation; bears to

(ii) The amount determined for the partnership or S corporation under section 163(j)(1)(B).

(18) *Floor plan financing indebtedness.*—The term floor plan financing indebtedness means indebtedness—

(i) Used to finance the acquisition of motor vehicles held for sale or lease; and

(ii) Secured by the motor vehicles so acquired.

(19) *Floor plan financing interest expense.*—The term *floor plan financing interest expense* means interest paid or accrued on floor plan financing indebtedness. For purposes of the section 163(j) regulations, all floor plan financing interest expense is treated as business interest expense. See paragraph (b)(3) of this section.

(20) *Group.*—The term *group* has the meaning provided in § 1.1502-1(a).

(21) *Intercompany transaction.*—The term *intercompany transaction* has the meaning provided in § 1.1502-13(b)(1)(i).

(22) *Interest.*—The term *interest* means any amount described in paragraph (b)(22)(i), (ii), (iii), or (iv) of this section.

(i) *In general.*—Interest is an amount paid, received, or accrued as compensation for the use or forbearance of money under the terms of an instrument or contractual arrangement, including a series of transactions, that is treated as a debt instrument for purposes of section 1275(a) and § 1.1275-1(d), and not treated as stock under § 1.385-3, or an amount that is treated as interest under other provisions of the Code or the Income Tax Regulations. Thus, interest includes, but is not limited to, the following:

(A) Original issue discount (OID), as adjusted by the holder for any acquisition premium or amortizable bond premium;

(B) Qualified stated interest, as adjusted by the holder for any amortizable bond premium or by the issuer for any bond issuance premium;

(C) Acquisition discount;

(D) Amounts treated as taxable OID under section 1286 (relating to stripped bonds and stripped coupons);

(E) Accrued market discount on a market discount bond to the extent includible in income by the holder under either section 1276(a) or 1278(b);

(F) OID includible in income by a holder that has made an election under § 1.1272-3 to treat all interest on a debt instrument as OID;

(G) OID on a synthetic debt instrument arising from an integrated transaction under § 1.1275-6;

(H) Repurchase premium to the extent deductible by the issuer under § 1.163-7(c) (determined without regard to section 163(j));

(I) Deferred payments treated as interest under section 483;

(J) Amounts treated as interest under a section 467 rental agreement;

(K) Amounts treated as interest under section 988;

(L) Forgone interest under section 7872;

(M) De minimis OID taken into account by the issuer;

(N) Amounts paid or received in connection with a sale-repurchase agreement treated as indebtedness under Federal tax principles; however, in the case of a sale-repurchase agreement relating to tax-exempt bonds, the amount is not tax-exempt interest;

(O) Redeemable ground rent treated as interest under section 163(c); and

(P) Amounts treated as interest under section 636.

(ii) *Swaps with significant nonperiodic payments.*—(A) *In general.*—Except as provided in paragraphs (b)(22)(ii)(B) and (C) of this section, a swap with significant nonperiodic payments is treated as two separate transactions consisting of an on-market, level payment swap and a loan. The loan must be accounted for by the parties to the contract independently of the swap. The time value component associated with the loan, determined in accordance with § 1.446-3(f)(2)(iii)(A), is recognized as interest expense to the payor and interest income to the recipient.

Itemized Deductions for Individuals and Corps.
See p. 20,601 for regulations not amended to reflect law changes
25,319

(B) *Exception for cleared swaps.*—Paragraph (b)(22)(ii)(A) of this section does not apply to a cleared swap (as defined in paragraph (b)(6) of this section).

(C) *Exception for non-cleared swaps subject to margin or collateral requirements.*—Paragraph (b)(22)(ii)(A) of this section does not apply to a non-cleared swap that requires the parties to meet the margin or collateral requirements of a federal regulator or that provides for margin or collateral requirements that are substantially similar to a cleared swap or a non-cleared swap subject to the margin or collateral requirements of a federal regulator. For purposes of this paragraph (b)(22)(ii)(C), the term *federal regulator* means the Securities and Exchange Commission (SEC), the Commodity Futures Trading Commission (CFTC), or a prudential regulator, as defined in section 1a(39) of the Commodity Exchange Act (7 U.S.C. 1a), as amended by section 721 of the Dodd-Frank Wall Street Reform and Consumer Protection Act of 2010, Public Law No. 111-203, 124 Stat. 1376, Title VII.

(iii) *Other amounts treated as interest.*—(A) *Treatment of premium.*—(1) *Issuer.*—If a debt instrument is issued at a premium within the meaning of §1.163-13, any ordinary income under §1.163-13(d)(4) is treated as interest income of the issuer.

(2) *Holder.*—If a taxable debt instrument is acquired at a premium within the meaning of §1.171-1 and the holder elects to amortize the premium, any amount deductible as a bond premium deduction under section 171(a)(1) and §1.171-2(a)(4)(i)(A) or (C) is treated as interest expense of the holder.

(B) *Treatment of ordinary income or loss on certain debt instruments.*—If an issuer of a contingent payment debt instrument subject to §1.1275-4(b), a nonfunctional currency contingent payment debt instrument subject to §1.988-6, or an inflation-indexed debt instrument subject to §1.1275-7 recognizes ordinary income on the debt instrument in accordance with the rules in §1.1275-4(b), §1.988-6(b)(2), or §1.1275-7(f), whichever is applicable, the ordinary income is treated as interest income of the issuer. If a holder of a contingent payment debt instrument subject to §1.1275-4(b), a nonfunctional currency contingent payment debt instrument subject to §1.988-6, or an inflation-indexed debt instrument subject to §1.1275-7 recognizes an ordinary loss on the debt instrument in accordance with the rules in §1.1275-4(b), §1.988-6(b)(2), or §1.1275-7(f), whichever is applicable, the ordinary loss is treated as interest expense of the holder.

(C) *Substitute interest payments.*—A substitute interest payment described in §1.861-2(a)(7) is treated as interest expense to the payor only if the payment relates to a sale-repurchase agreement or a securities lending transaction that is not entered into by the payor in the ordinary course of the payor's business. A substitute interest payment described in §1.861-2(a)(7) is treated as interest income to the recipient only if the payment relates to a sale-repurchase agreement or a securities lending transaction that is not entered into by the recipient in the ordinary course of the recipient's business; however, in the case of a sale-repurchase agreement or a securities lending transaction relating to tax-exempt bonds, the recipient of a substitute payment does not receive tax-exempt interest income. This paragraph (b)(22)(iii)(C) does not apply to an amount described in paragraph (b)(22)(i)(N) of this section.

(D) *Section 1258 gain.*—Any gain treated as ordinary gain under section 1258 is treated as interest income.

(E) *Factoring income.*—The excess of the amount that a taxpayer collects on a factored receivable (or realizes upon the sale or other disposition of the factored receivable) over the amount paid for the factored receivable by the taxpayer is treated as interest income. For purposes of this paragraph (b)(22)(iii)(E), the term *factored receivable* includes any account receivable or other evidence of indebtedness, whether or not issued at a discount and whether or not bearing stated interest, arising out of the disposition of property or the performance of services by any person, if such account receivable or evidence of indebtedness is acquired by a person other than the person who disposed of the property or provided the services that gave rise to the account receivable or evidence of indebtedness. This paragraph (b)(22)(iii)(E) does not apply to an amount described in paragraph (b)(22)(i)(C) or (E) of this section.

(F) *Section 163(j) interest dividends.*—(1) *In general.*—Except as otherwise provided in this paragraph (b)(22)(iii)(F), a section 163(j) interest dividend is treated as interest income.

(2) *Limitation on amount treated as interest income.*—A shareholder may not treat any part of a section 163(j) interest dividend as interest income to the extent the amount of the section 163(j) interest dividend exceeds the excess of the amount of the entire dividend that includes the section 163(j) interest dividend over the sum of the conduit amounts other than interest-related dividends under section 871(k)(1)(C) and section 163(j) interest dividends that affect the shareholder's treatment of that dividend.

(3) *Conduit amounts.*—For purposes of paragraph (b)(22)(iii)(F)(2) of this section, the term *conduit amounts* means, with respect to any category of income (including tax-exempt interest) earned by a RIC for a taxable year, the amounts identified by the RIC (generally in a designation or written report) in connection with dividends of the RIC for that taxable year that are subject to a limit determined by reference to that category of income. For example, a RIC's conduit amount with respect to its net capital gain is the amount of the RIC's capital gain dividends under section 852(b)(3)(C).

(4) *Holding period.*—Except as provided in paragraph (b)(22)(iii)(F)(5) of this section, no dividend is treated as interest income under paragraph (b)(22)(iii)(F)(1) of this section if the dividend is received with respect to a share of RIC stock—

(i) That is held by the shareholder for 180 days or less (taking into account the principles of section 246(c)(3) and (4)) during the 361-day period beginning on the date which is 180 days before the date on which the share becomes ex-dividend with respect to such dividend; or

(ii) To the extent that the shareholder is under an obligation (whether pursuant to a short sale or otherwise) to make related payments with respect to positions in substantially similar or related property.

(5) *Exception to holding period requirement for money market funds and certain regularly declared dividends.*—Paragraph (b)(22)(iii)(F)(4)(i) of this section does not apply to dividends distributed by any RIC regulated as a money market fund under 17 CFR 270.2a-7 (Rule 2a-7 under the 1940 Act) or to regular dividends paid by a RIC that declares section 163(j) interest dividends on a daily basis in an amount equal to at least 90 percent of its excess section 163(j) interest income, as defined in paragraph (b)(35)(iv)(E) of this section, and distributes such dividends on a monthly or more frequent basis.

(iv) *Anti-avoidance rules.*—(A) *Principal purpose to reduce interest expense.*—(1) *Treatment as interest expense.*—Any expense or loss economically equivalent to interest is treated as interest expense if a principal purpose of structuring the transaction(s) is to reduce an amount incurred by the taxpayer that otherwise would have been described in paragraph (b)(22)(i), (ii), or (iii) of this section. For this purpose, the fact that the taxpayer has a business purpose for obtaining the use of funds does not affect the determination of whether the manner in which the taxpayer structures the transaction(s) is with a principal purpose of reducing the taxpayer's interest expense. In addition, the fact that the taxpayer has obtained funds at a lower pre-tax cost based on the structure of the transaction(s) does not affect the determination of whether the manner in which the taxpayer structures the transaction(s) is with a principal purpose of reducing the taxpayer's interest expense. For purposes of this paragraph (b)(22)(iv)(A)(1), any expense or loss is economically equivalent to interest to the extent that the expense or loss is—

(i) Deductible by the taxpayer;

(ii) Incurred by the taxpayer in a transaction or series of integrated or related transactions in which the taxpayer secures the use of funds for a period of time;

(iii) Substantially incurred in consideration of the time value of money; and

(iv) Not described in paragraph (b)(22)(i), (ii), or (iii) of this section.

(2) *Corresponding treatment of amounts as interest income.*—If a taxpayer knows that an expense or loss is treated by the payor as interest expense under paragraph (b)(22)(iv)(A)(1) of this section, the taxpayer provides the use of funds for a period of time in the transaction(s) subject to paragraph (b)(22)(iv)(A)(1) of this section, the taxpayer earns income or gain with respect to the transaction(s), and such income or gain is substantially earned in consideration of the time value of money provided by the taxpayer, such income or gain is treated as interest income to the extent of the expense or loss treated by the payor as interest expense under paragraph (b)(22)(iv)(A)(1) of this section.

(B) *Interest income artificially increased.*—Notwithstanding paragraphs (b)(22)(i) through (iii) of this section, any income realized by a taxpayer in a transaction or series of integrated or related transactions is not treated as interest income of the taxpayer if and to the extent that a principal purpose for structuring the transaction(s) is to artificially increase the taxpayer's business interest income. For this purpose, the fact that the taxpayer has a business purpose for holding interest generating assets does not affect the determination of whether the manner in which the taxpayer structures the transaction(s) is with a principal purpose of artificially increasing the taxpayer's business interest income.

(C) *Principal purpose.*—Whether a transaction or a series of integrated or related transactions is entered into with a principal purpose described in paragraph (b)(22)(iv)(A) or (B) of this section depends on all the facts and circumstances related to the transaction(s), except for those facts described in paragraph (b)(22)(iv)(A) or (B) of this section. A purpose may be a principal purpose even though it is outweighed by other purposes (taken together or separately). Factors to be taken into account in determining whether one of the taxpayer's principal purposes for entering into the transaction(s) include the taxpayer's normal borrowing rate in the taxpayer's functional currency, whether the taxpayer would enter into the transaction(s) in the ordinary course of the taxpayer's trade or business, whether the parties to the transaction(s) are related persons (within the meaning of section 267(b) or section 707(b)), whether there is a significant and bona fide business purpose for the structure of the transaction(s), whether the transactions are transitory, for example, due to a circular flow of cash or other property, and the substance of the transaction(s).

(D) *Coordination with anti-avoidance rule in §1.163(j)-2(j).*—The anti-avoidance rules in paragraphs (b)(22)(iv)(A) through (C) of this section, rather than the anti-avoidance rules in §1.163(j)-2(j), apply to determine whether an item is treated as interest expense or interest income.

(v) *Examples.*—The examples in this paragraph (b)(22)(v) illustrate the application of paragraph (b)(22)(iv) of this section. Unless otherwise indicated, A, B, C, D, and Bank are domestic C corporations that are publicly traded; the exemption for certain small businesses in §1.163(j)-2(d) does not apply; A is not engaged in an excepted trade or business; and all amounts of interest expense are deductible except for the potential application of section 163(j).

(A) *Example 1.*—(1) *Facts.* A is engaged in a manufacturing business and uses the calendar year as its annual accounting period. A's functional currency is the U.S. dollar and A conducts virtually all of its business in the U.S. dollar. A has no connection to Japan or the Japanese yen in the ordinary course of business. A projects that it will have business interest expense of $100x on an existing loan obligation with a stated principal amount of $2,000x (Loan 1) and no business interest income in its taxable year ending December 31, 2021. In early 2021, A enters into the following transactions, which A would not have entered into in the ordinary course of A's trade or business:

(i)A enters into a loan obligation in which A borrows Japanese yen from Bank in an amount equivalent to $2,000x with an interest rate of 1 percent (Loan 2) (at the time of the loan, the U.S. dollar equivalent interest rate on a loan of $2,000x is 5 percent);

(ii)A enters into a foreign currency swap transaction (FX Swap) with Bank with a notional principal amount of $2,000x under which A receives Japanese yen at 1 percent multiplied by the amount of Japanese yen borrowed from Bank (which for 2021 equals $20x) and pays U.S. dollars at 5 percent multiplied by a notional amount of $2,000x ($100x per year);

(iii) The FX Swap is not integrated with Loan 2 under §1.988-5; and

(iv) A enters into a spot transaction with Bank to convert the proceeds of Loan 2 into $2,000x U.S. dollars and A uses the U.S. dollars to repay Loan 1.

(2) *Analysis.* A principal purpose of A entering into the transactions with Bank was to try to reduce the amount incurred by A that otherwise would be interest expense; in effect, A sought to alter A's cost of borrowing by converting a substantial portion of its interest expense deductions on Loan 1 into section 165 deductions on the FX Swap ($100x interest expense related to Loan 1 compared to $20x interest expense related to Loan 2 and $80x section 165 deduction). A's functional currency is the U.S. dollar and A conducts virtually all of its business in the U.S. dollar. A has no connection to Japan or the Japanese yen and would not have entered into the transactions in the ordinary course of A's trade or business. The section 165 deductions related to the FX Swap were incurred by A in a series of transactions in which A secured the use of funds for a period of time and were substantially incurred in consideration of the time value of money. As a result, under paragraph (b)(22)(iv)(A)(1) of this section, for purposes of section 163(j), the $80x paid by A to Bank on the FX Swap is treated by A as interest expense.

(B) *Example 2.*—(1) *Facts.* A is engaged in a manufacturing business and uses the calendar year as its annual accounting period. A does not use gold in its manufacturing business. In 2021, A expects to borrow $1,000x for six months. In January 2021, A borrows from B two ounces of gold at a time when the spot price for gold is $500x per ounce. A agrees to return the two ounces of gold in six months. A sells the two ounces of gold to C for $1,000x. A then enters into a

contract with D to purchase two ounces of gold six months in the future for $1,013x. In exchange for the use of $1,000x in cash for six months, A has sustained a loss of $13x in connection with these related transactions. A would not have entered into the gold transactions in the ordinary course of A's trade or business.

(2) *Analysis.* In a series of related transactions, A has obtained the use of $1,000x for six months and created a loss of $13x substantially incurred in consideration of the time value of money. A would not have entered into the gold transactions in the ordinary course of A's trade or business. A entered into the transactions with a principal purpose of structuring the transactions to reduce its interest expense (in effect, A sought to convert what otherwise would be interest expense into a loss through the transactions). As a result, under paragraph (b)(22)(iv)(A)(1) of this section, for purposes of section 163(j), the loss of $13x is treated by A as interest expense.

(C) *Example 3.*—(1) *Facts.* A is engaged in a manufacturing business and uses the calendar year as its annual accounting period. A's functional currency is the U.S. dollar and A conducts virtually all of its business in the U.S. dollar. A has no connection to Argentina or the Argentine peso as part of its ordinary course of business. As of January 1, 2021, A expects to have adjusted taxable income (as defined in paragraph (b)(1) of this section) of $200x in the taxable year ending December 31, 2021. A also projects that it will have business interest expense of $70x on an existing loan in 2021. A has cash equivalents of $100x on which A expects to earn $5x of business interest income. In early 2021, A enters into the following transactions, which A would not have entered into in the ordinary course of A's trade or business:

(i)A enters into a spot transaction with Bank to convert the $100x of cash equivalents into an amount in Argentine pesos equivalent to $100x and A uses the Argentine pesos to purchase an Argentine peso note (Note) issued by a subsidiary of Bank for the Argentine peso equivalent of $100x; the Note pays interest at a 10 percent rate; and

(ii) A enters into a foreign currency swap transaction (FX Swap) with Bank with a notional principal amount of $100x under which A pays Argentine pesos at 10 percent multiplied by the amount of Argentine peso principal amount on the Note (which for 2021 equals $10x) and receives U.S. dollars at 5 percent multiplied by a notional amount of $100x ($5x per year).

(2) *Analysis.* A principal purpose of A entering into the transactions was to increase the amount of business interest income received by A; in effect, A increased its business interest income by separately accounting for its net deduction of $5x per year on the FX Swap. A's functional currency is the U.S. dollar and A conducts virtually all of its business in the U.S. dollar. A has no connection to Argentina or the Argentine peso and would not have entered into the transactions in the ordinary course of A's trade or business. The FX Swap was incurred by A as a part of a transaction that A entered into with a principal purpose of artificially increasing its business interest income. As a result, under paragraph (b)(22)(iv)(B) of this section, for purposes of section 163(j), the $10x business interest income earned on the Note by A is reduced by $5x (the net $5x paid by A on the FX Swap).

(D) *Example 4.*—(1) *Facts.* A is wholly owned by FC, a foreign corporation organized in foreign country X. A uses the calendar year for its annual accounting period. FC has a better credit rating than A. A needs to borrow $2,000x in the taxable year ending December 31, 2021, to fund its business operations. A also projects that, if it borrows $2,000x on January 1, 2021, and pays a market rate of interest, it will have business interest expense of $100x in its taxable year ending December 31, 2021. In early 2021, A enters into the following transactions:

(i) A enters into a loan obligation in which A borrows $2,000x from Bank with an interest rate of 3 percent (Loan 1);

(ii) FC and Bank enter into a guarantee arrangement (Guarantee) under which FC agrees to guarantee Bank that Bank will be timely paid all of the amounts due on Loan 1; and

(iii) A enters into a guarantee fee agreement with FC (Guarantee Fee Agreement) under which A agrees to pay FC $40x in return for FC entering into the Guarantee, which was not an agreement that A would have entered into in the ordinary course of A's trade or business.

(2) *Analysis.* A principal purpose of A entering into the transactions was to reduce the amount incurred by A that otherwise would be interest expense; in effect, A sought to convert a substantial portion of its interest expense deductions on Loan 1 into section 162 deductions on the Guarantee Fee Agreement ($100x interest expense had A borrowed without the Guarantee compared to $60x interest expense related to Loan 1 and $40x section 162 deduction). A would not have entered into the Guarantee Fee Agreement in the ordinary course of A's trade or business. The $40x section 162 deductions related to the Guarantee Fee Agreement were incurred by A in a

Itemized Deductions for Individuals and Corps.
See p. 20,601 for regulations not amended to reflect law changes
25,321

series of transactions in which A secured the use of funds for a period of time and were substantially incurred in consideration of the time value of money. As a result, under paragraph (b)(22)(iv)(A)(1) of this section, for purposes of section 163(j), the $40x paid by A to FC on the Guarantee Fee Agreement is treated by A as interest expense.

(E) *Example 5.*—(1) *Facts.* A, B, and C are equal partners in ABC partnership. ABC is considering acquiring an additional loan from a third-party lender to expand its business operations. However, ABC already has significant debt and interest expense. For the purpose of reducing the amount of additional interest expense ABC would have otherwise incurred by borrowing, A agrees to make an additional contribution to ABC for use in its business operations in exchange for a guaranteed payment for the use of capital under section 707(c).

(2) *Analysis.* The guaranteed payment is deductible by ABC, incurred by ABC in a transaction in which ABC secures the use of funds for a period of time, substantially incurred in consideration of the time value of money, and not described in paragraph (b)(22)(i), (ii), or (iii) of this section. As a result, the guaranteed payment to A is economically equivalent to the interest that ABC would have incurred on an additional loan from a third-party lender. A principal purpose of A making a contribution in exchange for a guaranteed payment for the use of capital was to reduce the amount incurred by ABC that otherwise would be interest expense. As a result, under paragraph (b)(22)(iv)(A)(1) of this section, for purposes of section 163(j), such guaranteed payment is treated as interest expense of ABC for purposes of section 163(j). In addition, under paragraph (b)(22)(iv)(A)(2) of this section, if A knows that the guaranteed payment is treated as interest expense of ABC, because A provides the use of funds for a period of time in a transaction subject to paragraph (b)(22)(iv)(A)(1) of this section, A earns income or gain with respect to the transaction, and such income or gain is substantially earned in consideration of the time value of money provided by A, the guaranteed payment is treated as interest income of A for purposes of section 163(j).

(23) *Interest expense.*—The term *interest expense* means interest that is paid or accrued, or treated as paid or accrued, for the taxable year.

(24) *Interest income.*—The term *interest income* means interest that is included in gross income for the taxable year.

(25) *Member.*—The term *member* has the meaning provided in § 1.1502-1(b).

(26) *Motor vehicle.*—The term *motor vehicle* means a motor vehicle as defined in section 163(j)(9)(C).

(27) *Old section 163(j).*—The term *old section 163(j)* means section 163(j) immediately prior to its amendment by Public Law No. 115-97, 131 Stat. 2054 (2017).

(28) *Ownership change.*—The term *ownership change* has the meaning provided in section 382 and the regulations in this part under section 382 of the Code.

(29) *Ownership date.*—The term *ownership date* has the meaning provided in section 382 and the regulations in this part under section 382 of the Code.

(30) *Real estate investment trust.*—The term *real estate investment trust* (REIT) has the meaning provided in section 856.

(31) *Real property.*—The term *real property* includes—

(i) Real property as defined in § 1.469-9(b)(2); and

(ii) Any direct or indirect right, including a license or other contractual right, to share in the appreciation in value of, or the gross or net proceeds or profits generated by, an interest in real property, including net proceeds or profits associated with tolls, rents or other similar fees.

(32) *Regulated investment company.*—The term *regulated investment company* (RIC) has the meaning provided in section 851.

(33) *Relevant foreign corporation.*—The term *relevant foreign corporation* means any foreign corporation whose classification is relevant under § 301.7701-3(d)(1) for a taxable year, other than solely pursuant to section 881 or 882.

(34) *S corporation.*—The term *S corporation* has the meaning provided in section 1361(a)(1).

(35) *Section 163(j) interest dividend.*—The term *section 163(j) interest dividend* means a dividend paid by a RIC for a taxable year for which section 852(b) applies to the RIC, to the extent described in paragraph (b)(35)(i) or (ii) of this section, as applicable.

(i) *In general.*—Except as provided in paragraph (b)(35)(ii) of this section, a section 163(j) interest dividend is any dividend, or part of a dividend, that is reported by the RIC as a section 163(j) interest dividend in written statements furnished to its shareholders.

(ii) *Reduction in the case of excess reported amounts.*—If the aggregate reported amount with respect to the RIC for the taxable year exceeds the excess section 163(j) interest income of the RIC for such taxable year, the section 163(j) interest dividend is—

(A) The reported section 163(j) interest dividend amount; reduced by

(B) The excess reported amount that is allocable to that reported section 163(j) interest dividend amount.

(iii) *Allocation of excess reported amount.*—(A) *In general.*—Except as provided in paragraph (b)(35)(iii)(B) of this section, the excess reported amount, if any, that is allocable to the reported section 163(j) interest dividend amount is that portion of the excess reported amount that bears the same ratio to the excess reported amount as the reported section 163(j) interest dividend amount bears to the aggregate reported amount.

(B) *Special rule for noncalendar year RICs.*—In the case of any taxable year that does not begin and end in the same calendar year, if the post-December reported amount equals or exceeds the excess reported amount for that taxable year, paragraph (b)(35)(iii)(A) of this section is applied by substituting "post-December reported amount" for "aggregate reported amount," and no excess reported amount is allocated to any dividend paid on or before December 31 of such taxable year.

(iv) *Definitions.*—The following definitions apply for purposes of this paragraph (b)(35):

(A) *Reported section 163(j) interest dividend amount.*—The term *reported section 163(j) interest dividend amount* means the amount of a dividend distribution reported to the RIC's shareholders under paragraph (b)(35)(i) of this section as a section 163(j) interest dividend.

(B) *Excess reported amount.*—The term *excess reported amount* means the excess of the aggregate reported amount over the RIC's excess section 163(j) interest income for the taxable year.

(C) *Aggregate reported amount.*—The term *aggregate reported amount* means the aggregate amount of dividends reported by the RIC under paragraph (b)(35)(i) of this section as section 163(j) interest dividends for the taxable year (including section 163(j) interest dividends paid after the close of the taxable year described in section 855).

(D) *Post-December reported amount.*—The term *post-December reported amount* means the aggregate reported amount determined by taking into account only dividends paid after December 31 of the taxable year.

(E) *Excess section 163(j) interest income.*—The term *excess section 163(j) interest income* means, with respect to a taxable year of a RIC, the excess of the RIC's business interest income for the taxable year over the sum of the RIC's business interest expense for the taxable year and the RIC's other deductions for the taxable year that are properly allocable to the RIC's business interest income.

(v) *Example.*—(A) *Facts.* X is a domestic C corporation that has elected to be a RIC. For its taxable year ending December 31, 2021, X has $100x of business interest income (all of which is qualified interest income for purposes of section 871(k)(1)(E)) and $10x of dividend income (all of which is qualified dividend income within the meaning of section 1(h)(11) and would be eligible for the dividends received deduction under section 243, determined as described in section 854(b)(3)). X has $10x of business interest expense and $20x of other deductions. X has no other items for the taxable year. On December 31, 2021, X pays a dividend of $80x to its shareholders, and reports, in written statements to its shareholders, $71.82x as a section 163(j) interest dividend; $10x as dividends that may be treated as qualified dividend income or as dividends eligible for the dividends received deduction; and $72.73x as interest-related dividends under section 871(k)(1)(C). Shareholder A, a domestic C corporation, meets the holding period requirements in paragraph (b)(22)(iii)(F)(4) of this section with respect to the stock of X, and receives a dividend of $8x from X on December 31, 2021.

(B) *Analysis.* X determines that $18.18x of other deductions are properly allocable to X's business interest income. X's excess section 163(j) interest income under paragraph (b)(35)(iv)(E) of this section is $71.82x ($100x business interest income – ($10x business interest expense + $18.18x other deductions allocated) = $71.82x). Thus, X may report up to $71.82x of its dividends paid on December 31, 2021, as section 163(j) interest dividends to its shareholders. X may also report up to $10x of its dividends paid on December 31, 2021, as dividends that may be treated as qualified dividend income or as dividends that are eligible for the dividends received deduction. X determines that $9.09x of interest expense and $18.18x of other deductions are properly allocable to X's qualified interest income. Therefore, X may report up to $72.73x of its dividends paid on December 31, 2021, as interest-related dividends under section 871(k)(1)(C) ($100x qualified interest income - $27.27x deductions allocated = $72.73x). A treats $1x of its $8x dividend as a dividend eligible for the dividends received deduction and no part of the dividend as an interest-related dividend under section 871(k)(1)(C). Therefore, under paragraph (b)(22)(iii)(F)(2) of this section, A may treat $7x of the section 163(j) interest dividend as interest income for purposes of section 163(j) ($8x dividend - $1x conduit amount = $7x limitation).

(36) *Section 163(j) limitation.*—The term *section 163(j) limitation* means the limit on the amount of business interest expense that a taxpayer may deduct in a taxable year under section 163(j) and § 1.163(j)-2(b).

(37) *Section 163(j) regulations.*—The term *section 163(j) regulations* means this section and §§ 1.163(j)-2 through 1.163(j)-11.

(38) *Separate return limitation year.*—The term *separate return limitation year* (SRLY) has the meaning provided in § 1.1502-1(f).

(39) *Separate return year.*—The term *separate return year* has the meaning provided in § 1.1502-1(e).

(40) *Separate tentative taxable income.*—The term *separate tentative taxable income* with respect to a taxpayer and a taxable year has the meaning provided in § 1.1502-12, but for this purpose computed without regard to the application of the section 163(j) limitation and with the addition of the adjustments made in paragraph (b)(43)(ii) of this section and § 1.163(j)-4(d)(2)(iv).

(41) *Tax-exempt corporation.*—The term *tax-exempt corporation* means any tax-exempt organization that is organized as a corporation.

(42) *Tax-exempt organization.*—The term *tax-exempt organization* means any entity subject to tax under section 511.

(43) *Tentative taxable income.*—(i) *In general.*—The term *tentative taxable income*, with respect to a taxpayer and a taxable year, generally is determined in the same manner as taxable income under section 63 but for this purpose computed without regard to the application of the section 163(j) limitation. Tentative taxable income is computed without regard to any disallowed business interest expense carryforwards.

(ii) [Reserved]

(iii) *Special rules for defining tentative taxable income.*—(A) For special rules defining the tentative taxable income of a RIC or REIT, see § 1.163(j)-4(b)(4)(ii).

(B) For special rules defining the tentative taxable income of consolidated groups, see § 1.163(j)-4(d)(2)(iv).

(C) For special rules defining the tentative taxable income of a partnership, see § 1.163(j)-6(d)(1).

(D) For special rules defining the tentative taxable income of an S corporation, see § 1.163(j)-6(l)(3).

(E) For special rules clarifying that tentative taxable income takes sections 461(l), 465, and 469 into account, see § 1.163(j)-3(b)(4).

(F) For special rules clarifying that tentative taxable income takes sections 461(l), 465, and 469 into account, see § 1.163(j)-3(b)(4).

(G) For special rules clarifying that tentative taxable income takes sections 461(l), 465, and 469 into account, see § 1.163(j)-3(b)(4).

(44) *Trade or business.*—(i) *In general.*—The term *trade or business* means a trade or business within the meaning of section 162.

(ii) *Excepted trade or business.*—The term *excepted trade or business* means the trade or business of performing services as an employee, an electing real property trade or business, an electing farming business, or an excepted regulated utility trade or business. For additional rules related to excepted trades or businesses, including elections made under section 163(j)(7)(B) and (C), see § 1.163(j)-9.

(iii) *Non-excepted trade or business.*—The term *non-excepted trade or business* means any trade or business that is not an excepted trade or business.

(45) *Unadjusted basis.*—The term *unadjusted basis* means the basis as determined under *section 1012 or other applicable sections of chapter 1 of subtitle A of the Code*, including subchapters O (relating to gain or loss on dispositions of property), C (relating to corporate distributions and adjustments), K (relating to partners and partnerships), and P (relating to capital gains and losses) of the Code.

Unadjusted basis is determined without regard to any adjustments described in section 1016(a)(2) or (3), any adjustments for tax credits claimed by the taxpayer (for example, under section 50(c)), or any adjustments for any portion of the basis that the taxpayer has elected to treat as an expense (for example, under section 179, 179B, or 179C).

(46) *United States shareholder.*—The term *United States shareholder* has the meaning provided in section 951(b).

(c) *Applicability date.*—(1) *In general.*—Except as provided in paragraphs (c)(2), (3), and (4) of this section, this section applies to taxable years beginning on or after November 13, 2020. However, taxpayers and their related parties, within the meaning of sections 267(b) and 707(b)(1), may choose to apply the rules of this section to a taxable year beginning after December 31, 2017, and before November 13, 2020 so long as the taxpayers and their related parties consistently apply the rules of the section 163(j) regulations, and, if applicable, §§ 1.263A-9, 1.263A-15, 1.381(c)(20)-1, 1.382-1, 1.382-2, 1.382-5, 1.382-6, 1.383-0, 1.383-1, 1.469-9, 1.469-11, 1.704-1, 1.882-5, 1.1362-3, 1.1368-1, 1.1377-1, 1.1502-13, 1.1502-21, 1.1502-36, 1.1502-79, 1.1502-91 through 1.1502-99 (to the extent they effectuate the rules of §§ 1.382-2, 1.382-5, 1.382-6, and 1.383-1), and 1.1504-4, to that taxable year. Additionally, taxpayers and their related parties within the meaning of sections 267(b) and 707(b)(1), otherwise relying on the notice of proposed rulemaking that was published on December 28, 2018, in the Federal Register (83 FR 67490) in its entirety under § 1.163(j)-1(c), may alternatively choose to follow § 1.163(j)-1(b)(1)(iii), rather than proposed § 1.163(j)-1(b)(1)(iii).

(2) *Anti-avoidance rules.*—The anti-avoidance rules in paragraph (b)(22)(iv) of this section apply to transactions entered into on or after September 14, 2020.

(3) *Swaps with significant nonperiodic payments.*—(i) *In general.*—Except as provided in paragraph (c)(3)(ii) of this section, the rules provided in paragraph (b)(22)(ii) of this section apply to notional principal contracts entered into on or after September 14, 2021. However, taxpayers may choose to apply the rules provided in paragraph (b)(22)(ii) of this section to notional principal contracts entered into before September 14, 2021.

(ii) *Anti-avoidance rule.*—The anti-avoidance rules in paragraph (b)(22)(iv) of this section (applied without regard to the references to paragraph (b)(22)(ii) of this section) apply to a notional principal contract entered into on or after September 14, 2020.

(4) *Paragraphs (b)(1)(iv)(A)(2) through (4), (B) through (G), (b)(22)(iii)(F), and (b)(35).*—Paragraphs (b)(1)(iv)(A)(2) through (4), (b)(1)(iv)(B) through (G), (b)(22)(iii)(F), and (b)(35) of this section apply to taxable years beginning on or after March 22, 2021. Taxpayers and their related parties, within the meaning of sections 267(b) (determined without regard to section 267(c)(3)) and 707(b)(1), may choose to apply the rules in paragraphs (b)(1)(iv)(A)(2) through (4), (b)(1)(iv) (B) through (G), (b)(22)(iii)(F), and (b)(35) of this section to a taxable year beginning after December 31, 2017, and before March 22, 2021, provided that those taxpayers and their related parties consistently apply all of the rules in the section 163(j) regulations contained in T.D. 9905, (§§ 1.163(j)-0 through 1.163(j)-11, effective November 13, 2020) as modified by T.D. 9943 (effective January 13, 2021), and, if applicable, §§ 1.263A-9, 1.263A-15, 1.381(c)(20)-1, 1.382-1, 1.382-2, 1.382-5, 1.382-6, 1.382-7, 1.383-0, 1.383-1, 1.469-9, 1.469-11, 1.704-1, 1.882-5, 1.1362-3, 1.1368-1, 1.1377-1, 1.1502-13, 1.1502-21, 1.1502-36, 1.1502-79, 1.1502-91 through 1.1502-99 (to the extent they effectuate the rules of §§ 1.382-2, 1.382-5, 1.382-6, and 1.383-1), and 1.1504-4 contained in T.D. 9905 as modified by T.D. 9943, to that taxable year and all subsequent taxable years. [Reg. § 1.163(j)-1.]

☐ [T.D. 9905, 9-3-2020. Amended by T.D. 9943, 1-13-2021.]

[Reg. § 1.163(j)-2]

§ 1.163(j)-2. Deduction for business interest expense limited.—(a) *Overview.*—This section provides general rules regarding the section 163(j) limitation. Paragraph (b) of this section provides rules regarding the basic computation of the section 163(j) limitation. Paragraph (c) of this section provides rules for disallowed business interest expense carryforwards. Paragraph (d) of this section provides rules regarding the small business exemption from the section 163(j) limitation. Paragraph (e) of this section that is part of provides rules regarding real estate mortgage investment conduits (REMICs). Paragraph (f) of this section provides rules regarding the calculation of ATI with respect to certain beneficiaries. Paragraph (g) of this section provides rules regarding tax-exempt organizations. Paragraph (h) of this section provides examples illustrating the application of this section. Paragraph (i) of this section is reserved. Paragraph (j) of this section provides an anti-avoidance rule.

(b) *General rule.*—(1) *In general.*—Except as otherwise provided in this section or in §§ 1.163(j)-3 through 1.163(j)-11, the amount allowed as a deduction for business interest expense for the taxable year cannot exceed the sum of—

(i) The taxpayer's business interest income for the taxable year;

(ii) 30 percent of the taxpayer's ATI for the taxable year, or zero if the taxpayer's ATI for the taxable year is less than zero; and

(iii) The taxpayer's floor plan financing interest expense for the taxable year.

(2) *50 percent ATI limitation for taxable years beginning in 2019 or 2020.*—(i) *In general.*—Except as otherwise provided in section 163(j)(10) and paragraph (b)(2) of this section, for any taxable year beginning in 2019 or 2020, paragraph (b)(1)(ii) of this section is applied by substituting 50 percent for 30 percent. The 50 percent ATI limitation does not apply to partnerships for taxable years beginning in 2019. Further, for a partnership taxable year beginning in 2020 for which an election out of section 163(j)(10)(A)(i) has not been made, §1.163(j)-6(f)(2)(xi) is applied by substituting two for ten-thirds when grossing up each partner's final ATI capacity excess amount.

(ii) *Election out of the 50 percent ATI limitation.*—A taxpayer may elect to not have paragraph (b)(2)(i) of this section apply for any taxable year beginning in 2019 or 2020. In the case of a partnership, the election must be made by the partnership and may be made only for taxable years beginning in 2020.

(3) *Election to use 2019 ATI in 2020.*—(i) *In general.*—Subject to paragraph (b)(3)(ii), a taxpayer may elect to use the taxpayer's ATI for the last taxable year beginning in 2019 (2019 ATI) as the ATI for any taxable year beginning in 2020.

(ii) *Short taxable years.*—If an election is made under paragraph (b)(3)(i) of this section for a taxable year beginning in 2020 that is a short taxable year, the ATI for such taxable year is equal to the amount that bears the same ratio to 2019 ATI as the number of months in the short taxable year bears to 12.

(iii) *Transactions to which section 381 applies.*—For purposes of the election described in paragraph (b)(3)(i) of this section, and subject to the limitation in paragraph (b)(3)(ii) of this section, the 2019 ATI of the acquiring corporation in a transaction to which section 381 applies equals the amount of the acquiring corporation's ATI for its last taxable year beginning in 2019.

(iv) *Consolidated groups.*—For purposes of the election described in paragraph (b)(3)(i) of this section, and subject to the limitation in paragraph (b)(3)(ii) of this section, the 2019 ATI of a consolidated group equals the amount of the consolidated group's ATI for its last taxable year beginning in 2019.

(4) *Time and manner of making or revoking the elections.*—The rules and procedures regarding the time and manner of making, or revoking, an election under paragraphs (b)(2) and (3) of this section are provided in Revenue Procedure 2020-22, 2020-18 I.R.B. 745, or in other guidance that may be issued (see §§601.601(d) and 601.602 of this chapter).

(c) *Disallowed business interest expense carryforward.*—(1) *In general.*—Any business interest expense disallowed under paragraph (b) of this section, or any disallowed disqualified interest that is properly allocable to a non-excepted trade or business under §1.163(j)-10, is carried forward to the succeeding taxable year as a disallowed business interest expense carryforward, and is therefore business interest expense that is subject to paragraph (b) of this section in such succeeding taxable year. Disallowed business interest expense carryforwards are not re-allocated between non-excepted and excepted trades or businesses in a succeeding taxable year. Instead, the carryforwards continue to be treated as allocable to a non-excepted trade or business. See §1.163(j)-10(c)(4).

(2) *Coordination with small business exemption.*—If disallowed business interest expense is carried forward under the rules of paragraph (c)(1) of this section to a taxable year in which the small business exemption in paragraph (d) of this section applies to the taxpayer, then the general rule in paragraph (b) of this section does not apply to limit the deduction of the disallowed business interest expense carryforward of the taxpayer in that taxable year. See §1.163(j)-6(m)(3) for rules applicable to the treatment of excess business interest expense from a partnership that is not subject to section 163(j) in a succeeding taxable year, and see §1.163(j)-6(m)(4) for rules applicable to S corporations with disallowed business interest expense carryforwards that are not subject to section 163(j) in a succeeding taxable year.

(3) *Cross-references.*—(i) For special rules regarding disallowed business interest expense carryforwards for taxpayers that are C corporations, including members of a consolidated group, see §1.163(j)-5.

(ii) For special rules regarding disallowed business interest expense carryforwards of S corporations, see §§1.163(j)-5(b)(2) and 1.163(j)-6(l)(5).

(iii) For special rules regarding disallowed business interest expense carryforwards from partnerships, see §1.163(j)-6.

(iv)-(v) [Reserved]

(d) *Small business exemption.*—(1) *Exemption.*—The general rule in paragraph (b) of this section does not apply to any taxpayer, other than a tax shelter as defined in section 448(d)(3), in any taxable year in which the taxpayer meets the gross receipts test of section 448(c) and the regulations in this part under section 448 of the Code for the taxable year. See §1.163(j)-9(b) for elections available under section 163(j)(7)(B) and 163(j)(7)(C) for real property trades or businesses or farming businesses that also may be exempt small businesses. See §1.163(j)-6(m) for rules applicable to partnerships and S corporations not subject to section 163(j).

(2) *Application of the gross receipts test.*—(i) *In general.*—In the case of any taxpayer that is not a corporation or a partnership, and except as provided in paragraphs (d)(2)(ii), (iii), and (iv) of this section, the gross receipts test of section 448(c) and the regulations in this part under section 448 of the Code are applied in the same manner as if such taxpayer were a corporation or partnership.

(ii) *Gross receipts of individuals.*—Except as provided in paragraph (d)(2)(iii) of this section (regarding partnership and S corporation interests), an individual taxpayer's gross receipts include all items specified as gross receipts in regulations under section 448(c), whether or not derived in the ordinary course of the taxpayer's trade or business. For purposes of section 163(j), an individual taxpayer's gross receipts do not include inherently personal amounts, including, but not limited to, personal injury awards or settlements with respect to an injury of the individual taxpayer, disability benefits, Social Security benefits received by the taxpayer during the taxable year, and wages received as an employee that are reported on Form W-2.

(iii) *Partners and S corporation shareholders.*—Except when the aggregation rules of section 448(c) apply, each partner in a partnership includes a share of partnership gross receipts in proportion to such partner's distributive share (as determined under section 704) of items of gross income that were taken into account by the partnership under section 703. Additionally, each shareholder in an S corporation includes a pro rata share of S corporation gross receipts.

(iv) *Tax-exempt organizations.*—For purposes of section 163(j), the gross receipts of a tax-exempt organization include only gross receipts taken into account in determining its unrelated business taxable income.

(3) *Determining a syndicate's loss amount.*—For purposes of section 163(j), losses allocated under section 1256(e)(3)(B) and §1.448-1T(b)(3) are determined without regard to section 163(j). See also §1.1256(e)-2(b).

(e) *REMICs.*—For the treatment of interest expense by a REMIC as defined in section 860D, see §1.860C-2(b)(2)(ii).

(f) *Trusts.*—(i) *Calculation of ATI with respect to certain trusts and estates.*—The ATI of a trust or a decedent's estate taxable under section 641 is computed without regard to deductions under sections 642(c), 651, and 661.

(ii) *Calculation of ATI with respect to certain beneficiaries.*—The ATI of a beneficiary (including a tax-exempt beneficiary) of a trust or a decedent's estate is reduced by any income (including any distributable net income) received from the trust or estate by the beneficiary to the extent such income was necessary to permit a deduction under section 163(j)(1)(B) and §1.163(j)-2(b) for any business interest expense of the trust or estate that was in excess of any business interest income of the trust or estate.

(g) *Tax-exempt organizations.*—Except as provided in paragraph (d) of this section, the section 163(j) limitation applies to tax-exempt organizations for purposes of computing their unrelated business taxable income under section 512. For rules on determining the gross receipts of a tax-exempt organization for purposes of the small business exemption, see paragraph (d)(2)(iv) of this section. For special rules applicable to tax-exempt beneficiaries of a trust or a decedent's estate, see §1.163(j)-2(f). For special rules applicable to tax-exempt corporations, see §1.163(j)-4. For special allocation rules applicable to tax-exempt organizations, see §1.163(j)-10(a)(5).

(h) *Examples.*—The examples in this paragraph (h) illustrate the application of section 163(j) and the provisions of this section. Unless otherwise indicated, X and Y are domestic C corporations; C and D are U.S. resident individuals not subject to any foreign income tax; PRS is a domestic partnership with partners who are all individuals;

all taxpayers use a calendar taxable year; the exemption for certain small businesses in section 163(j)(3) and paragraph (d) of this section does not apply; and the interest expense would be deductible but for section 163(j).

(1) *Example 1: Limitation on business interest expense deduction.*—(i) *Facts.* During its taxable year ending December 31, 2021, X has ATI of $100x. X has business interest expense of $50x, which includes $10x of floor plan financing interest expense, and business interest income of $20x.

(ii) *Analysis.* For the 2021 taxable year, X's section 163(j) limitation is $60x, which is the sum of its business interest income ($20x), plus 30 percent of its ATI ($100x x 30 percent = $30x), plus its floor plan financing interest expense ($10x). See § 1.163(j)-2(b). Because X's business interest expense ($50x) does not exceed X's section 163(j) limitation ($60x), X can deduct all $50x of its business interest expense for the 2021 taxable year.

(2) *Example 2: Carryforward of business interest expense.*—(i) *Facts.* The facts are the same as in *Example 1* in paragraph (h)(1)(i) of this section, except that X has $80x of business interest expense, which includes $10x of floor plan financing interest expense.

(ii) *Analysis.* As in *Example 1* in paragraph (h)(1)(ii) of this section, X's section 163(j) limitation is $60x. Because X's business interest expense ($80x) exceeds X's section 163(j) limitation ($60x), X may only deduct $60x of its business interest expense for the 2021 taxable year, and the remaining $20x of its business interest expense will be carried forward to the succeeding taxable year as a disallowed business interest expense carryforward. See § 1.163(j)-2(c).

(3) *Example 3: ATI computation.*—(i) *Facts.* During the 2020 taxable year, Y has tentative taxable income of $30x, which is determined without regard to the application of the section 163(j) limitation on business interest expense. Y's tentative taxable income includes the following: $20x of business interest income; $50x of business interest expense, which includes $10x of floor plan financing interest expense; $25x of net operating loss deduction under section 172; and $15x of depreciation under section 167, of which $10x is capitalized to inventory under section 263A. Of the $10x capitalized to inventory, only $7x is recovered through cost of goods sold during the 2020 taxable year and $3x remains in ending inventory at the end of the 2020 taxable year. The $3x of ending inventory is recovered through cost of goods sold during the 2021 taxable year. Y also has a disallowed business interest expense carryforward from the prior year of $8x.

(ii) *Analysis.* (A) For purposes of determining the section 163(j) limitation for 2020, Y's disallowed business interest expense carryforward is not taken into account in determining tentative taxable income or ATI. Y's ATI is $90x, calculated as follows:

Table 1 to paragraph (h)(3)(ii)(A)

Tentative taxable income:	$30x
Less:	
Floor plan financing interest	10x
Business interest income	*20x*
	0x

(B) Plus:

Table 2 to paragraph (h)(3)(ii)(B)

Business interest expense	$50x
Net operating loss deduction	25x
Depreciation	*15x*
ATI	$90x

(C) For Y's 2021 taxable year, the $3x of ending inventory that is recovered through cost of goods sold in 2021 is not added back to tentative taxable income (TTI) in determining ATI because it was already included as an addback in ATI in Y's 2020 taxable year. See § 1.163(j)-1(b)(1)(iii).

(4) *Example 4: Floor plan financing interest expense.*—(i) *Facts.* C is the sole proprietor of an automobile dealership that uses a cash method of accounting. In the 2021 taxable year, C paid $30x of interest on a loan that was obtained to purchase sedans for sale by the dealership. The indebtedness is secured by the sedans purchased with the loan proceeds. In addition, C paid $20x of interest on a loan, secured by the dealership's office equipment, which C obtained to purchase convertibles for sale by the dealership.

(ii) *Analysis.* For the purpose of calculating C's section 163(j) limitation, only the $30x of interest paid on the loan to purchase the sedans is floor plan financing interest expense. The $20x paid on the loan to purchase the convertibles is not floor plan financing interest expense for purposes of section 163(j) because the indebtedness was not secured by the inventory of convertibles. However, because under § 1.163(j)-10 the interest paid on the loan to purchase the convertibles is properly allocable to C's dealership trade or business, and because floor plan financing interest expense is also business

interest expense, C has $50x of business interest expense for the 2021 taxable year.

(5) *Example 5: Interest not properly allocable to non-excepted trade or business.*—(i) *Facts.* The facts are the same as in *Example 4* in paragraph (h)(4)(i) of this section, except that the $20x of interest C pays is on acquisition indebtedness obtained to purchase C's personal residence and not to purchase convertibles for C's dealership trade or business.

(ii) *Analysis.* Because the $20x of interest expense is not properly allocable to a non-excepted trade or business, and therefore is not business interest expense, C's only business interest expense is the $30x that C pays on the loan used to purchase sedans for sale in C's dealership trade or business. C deducts the $20x of interest related to his residence under the rules of section 163(h), without regard to section 163(j).

(6) *Example 6: Small business exemption.*—(i) *Facts.* During the 2021 taxable year, D, the sole proprietor of a trade or business reported on Schedule C, has interest expense properly allocable to that trade or business. D does not conduct an electing real property trade or business or an electing farming business. D also earns gross income from providing services as an employee that is reported on a Form W-2. Under section 448(c) and the regulations in this part under section 448, D has average annual gross receipts of $21 million, including $1 million of wages in each of the three prior taxable years and $2 million of income from investments not related to a trade or business in each of the three prior taxable years. Also, in each of the three prior taxable years, D received $5 million in periodic payments of compensatory damages awarded in a personal injury lawsuit.

(ii) *Analysis.* Section 163(j) does not apply to D for the taxable year, because D qualifies for the small business exemption under § 1.163(j)-2(d). The wages that D receives as an employee and the compensatory damages that D received from D's personal injury lawsuit are not gross receipts, as provided in § 1.163(j)-2(d)(2)(ii). D may deduct all of its business interest expense for the 2021 taxable year without regard to section 163(j).

(7) *Example 7: Partnership with excess business interest expense qualifies for the small business exemption in a succeeding taxable year.*—(i) *Facts.* X and Y are equal partners in partnership PRS. In addition to being partners in PRS, X and Y each operate their own sole proprietorships. For the taxable year ending December 31, 2021, PRS is subject to section 163(j) and has excess business interest expense of $10x. For the taxable year ending December 31, 2022, PRS has $40x of business interest expense, and X and Y have $20x of business interest expense from their respective sole proprietorships. For the taxable year ending December 31, 2022, PRS and Y qualify for the small business exemption under § 1.163(j)-2(d), while X is subject to section 163(j) and has a section 163(j) limitation of $22x.

(ii) *Partnership-level analysis.* For the 2021 taxable year, PRS allocates the $10x of excess business interest expense equally to X and Y ($5x each). See § 1.163(j)-6(f)(2). For the 2022 taxable year, section 163(j) does not apply to PRS because PRS qualifies for the small business exemption. As a result, none of PRS's $40x of business interest expense for the 2022 taxable year is subject to the section 163(j) limitation at the partnership level.

(iii) *Partner-level analysis.* For the 2022 taxable year, each partner treats its $5x of excess business interest expense from PRS as paid or accrued in that year. See § 1.163(j)-6(m)(3). This amount becomes business interest expense that each partner must subject to its own section 163(j) limitation, if any. With this $5x, each partner has $25x of business interest expense for the 2022 taxable year ($20x from its sole proprietorship, plus $5x of excess business interest expense treated as paid or accrued in the 2020 taxable year). X deducts $22x of its business interest expense pursuant to its section 163(j) limitation and carries forward the remainder ($3x) as a disallowed business interest expense carryforward to the taxable year ending December 31, 2023. Y is not subject to section 163(j) because Y qualifies for the small business exemption. Y therefore deducts all $25x of its business interest expense for the 2022 taxable year.

(8) *Example 8: Aggregation of gross receipts.*—(i) *Facts.* X and Y are domestic C corporations under common control, within the meaning of section 52(a) and § 1.52-1(b). X's only trade or business is a farming business described in § 1.263A-4(a)(4). During the taxable year ending December 31, 2020, X has average annual gross receipts under section 448(c) of $6 million. During the same taxable year, Y has average annual gross receipts under section 448(c) of $21 million.

(ii) *Analysis.* Because X and Y are under common control, they must aggregate gross receipts for purposes of section 448(c) and the small business exemption in § 1.163(j)-2(d). See section 448(c)(2). Therefore, X and Y are both considered to have $27 million in average annual gross receipts for 2020. X and Y must separately apply section 163(j) to determine any limitation on the deduction for business interest expense. Assuming X otherwise meets the requirements in § 1.163(j)-9 in 2020, X may elect for its farming business to be an excepted trade or business.

(i) [Reserved]

(j) *Anti-avoidance rule.*—(1) *In general.*—Arrangements entered into with a principal purpose of avoiding the rules of section 163(j) or the section 163(j) regulations, including the use of multiple entities to avoid the gross receipts test of section 448(c), may be disregarded or recharacterized by the Commissioner of the IRS to the extent necessary to carry out the purposes of section 163(j).

(2) *Examples.*—The examples in this paragraph (j)(2) illustrate the application of this section.

(i) *Example 1.*—(A) *Facts.* Individual A operates an excepted trade or business (Business X) and a non-excepted trade or business (Business Y). With a principal purpose of avoiding the rules of section 163(j) or the regulations in this part under section 163(j) of the Code, A contributes Business X to newly-formed C corporation B in exchange for stock; A then causes B to borrow funds from a third party and distributes a portion of the borrowed funds to A for use in Business Y. B takes the position that its interest payments on the debt are not subject to the section 163(j) limitation because B is engaged solely in an excepted trade or business.

(B) *Analysis.* A has entered into an arrangement with a principal purpose of avoiding the rules of section 163(j) or the regulations in this part under section 163(j). Thus, under paragraph (j)(1) of this section, the Commissioner of the IRS may disregard or recharacterize this transaction to the extent necessary to carry out the purposes of section 163(j). In this case, payments of interest on the debt may be recharacterized as payments of interest properly allocable to a non-excepted trade or business subject to the section 163(j) limitation.

(ii) *Example 2.*—(A) *Facts.* Partnership UTP has two non-excepted trades or businesses. Business A has gross income of $1000x and gross deductions of $200x. Business B has gross income of $100x and gross deductions of $600x. With a principal purpose of avoiding the rules in section 163(j) or the regulations in this part under section 163(j), UTP and a partner of UTP form partnership LTP and UTP contributes Business B to LTP prior to borrowing funds. UTP takes the position that it does not take its share of LTP gross deductions into account when computing its ATI.

(B) *Analysis.* UTP has entered into an arrangement with a principal purpose of avoiding the rules of section 163(j) or the regulations in this part under section 163(j). Thus, under paragraph (j)(1) of this section, the Commissioner of the IRS may disregard or recharacterize this transaction to the extent necessary to carry out the purposes of section 163(j). In this case, UTP's share of gross deductions from LTP may be recharacterized as gross deductions incurred directly by UTP solely for purposes of computing UTP's ATI.

(k) *Applicability dates.*—(1) *In general.*—This section applies to taxable years beginning on or after November 13, 2020. However, taxpayers and their related parties, within the meaning of sections 267(b) and 707(b)(1), may choose to apply the rules of this section to a taxable year beginning after December 31, 2017, so long as the taxpayers and their related parties consistently apply the rules of the section 163(j) regulations, and, if applicable, §§ 1.263A-9, 1.263A-15, 1.381(c)(20)-1, 1.382-1, 1.382-2, 1.382-5, 1.382-6, 1.382-7, 1.383-0, 1.383-1, 1.469-9, 1.469-11, 1.704-1, 1.882-5, 1.1362-3, 1.1368-1, 1.1377-1, 1.1502-13, 1.1502-21, 1.1502-36, 1.1502-79, 1.1502-91 through 1.1502-99 (to the extent they effectuate the rules of §§ 1.382-2, 1.382-5, 1.382-6, and 1.383-1), and 1.1504-4, to that taxable year.

(2) *Paragraphs (b)(3)(iii), (b)(3)(iv), and (d)(3).*—Paragraphs (b)(3)(iii) and (iv) and (d)(3) of this section apply to taxable years beginning on or after March 22, 2021. However, taxpayers and their related parties, within the meaning of sections 267(b) (determined without regard to section 267(c)(3)) and 707(b)(1), may choose to apply the rules in paragraphs (b)(3)(iii), (b)(3)(iv), and (d)(3) of this section to a taxable year beginning after December 31, 2017, and before March 22, 2021, provided that those taxpayers and their related parties consistently apply all of the rules in paragraphs (b)(3)(iii) and (iv) of this section and the rules in the section 163(j) regulations contained in T.D. 9905 (§§ 1.163(j)-0 through 1.163(j)-11, effective November 13, 2020) as modified by T.D. 9943, (effective January 13, 2021), and, if applicable, §§ 1.263A-9, 1.263A-15, 1.381(c)(20)-1, 1.382-1, 1.382-2, 1.382-5, 1.382-6, 1.383-0, 1.383-1, 1.469-9, 1.469-11, 1.704-1, 1.882-5, 1.1362-3, 1.1368-1, 1.1377-1, 1.1502-13, 1.1502-21, 1.1502-36, 1.1502-79, 1.1502-91 through 1.1502-99 (to the extent they effectuate the rules of §§ 1.382-2, 1.382-5, 1.382-6, and 1.383-1), and 1.1504-4 contained in T.D. 9905 as modified by T.D. 9943, for that taxable year and for each subsequent taxable year. [Reg. § 1.163(j)-2.]

☐ [*T.D. 9905, 9-3-2020. Amended by T.D. 9943, 1-13-2021.*]

[Reg. § 1.163(j)-3]

§ 1.163(j)-3. Relationship of the section 163(j) limitation to other provisions affecting interest.—(a) *Overview.*—This section contains rules regarding the relationship between section 163(j) and certain other provisions of the Code. Paragraph (b) of this section provides the general rules concerning the relationship between section 163(j) and certain other provisions of the Code. Paragraph (c) of this section provides examples illustrating the application of this section. For rules regarding the relationship between sections 163(j) and 704(d), see § 1.163(j)-6(h)(1) and (2).

(b) *Coordination of section 163(j) with certain other provisions.*—(1) *In general.*—Section 163(j) and the regulations in this part under section 163(j) of the Code generally apply only to business interest expense that would be deductible in the current taxable year without regard to section 163(j). Thus, for example, a taxpayer must apply § 1.163-8T, if applicable, to determine which items of interest expense are investment interest under section 163(d) before applying the rules in this section to interest expense. Except as otherwise provided in this section, section 163(j) applies after the application of provisions that subject interest expense to disallowance, deferral, capitalization, or other limitation. For the rules that must be applied in determining whether excess business interest is paid or accrued by a partner, see section 163(j)(4)(B)(ii) and § 1.163(j)-6.

(2) *Disallowed interest provisions.*—For purposes of section 163(j), business interest expense does not include interest expense that is permanently disallowed as a deduction under another provision of the Code, such as in section 163(e)(5)(A)(i), (f), (l), or (m), or section 264(a), 265, 267A, or 279.

(3) *Deferred interest provisions.*—Other than sections 461(l), 465, and 469, Code provisions that defer the deductibility of interest expense, such as section 163(e)(3) and (e)(5)(A)(ii), 267(a)(2) and (3), 1277, or 1282, apply before the application of section 163(j).

(4) *At risk rules, passive activity loss provisions, and limitation on excess business losses of noncorporate taxpayers.*—Section 163(j) generally applies to limit the deduction for business interest expense before the application of sections 461(l), 465, and 469. However, in determining tentative taxable income for purposes of computing ATI, sections 461(l), 465, and 469 are taken into account.

(5) *Capitalized interest expenses.*—Section 163(j) applies after the application of provisions that require the capitalization of interest, such as sections 263A and 263(g). Capitalized interest expense under those sections is not treated as business interest expense for purposes of section 163(j). For ordering rules that determine whether interest expense is capitalized under section 263A(f), see the regulations under section 263A(f), including § 1.263A-9(g).

(6) *Reductions under section 246A.*—Section 246A applies before section 163(j). Any reduction in the dividends received deduction under section 246A reduces the amount of interest expense taken into account under section 163(j).

(7) *Section 381.*—Disallowed business interest expense carryforwards are items to which an acquiring corporation succeeds under section 381(a). See section 381(c)(20) and §§ 1.163(j)-5(c) and 1.381(c)(20)-1.

(8) *Section 382.*—For rules governing the interaction of sections 163(j) and 382, see section 382(d)(3) and (k)(1), §§ 1.163(j)-5(e) and 1.163(j)-11(c), the regulations in this part under sections 382 and 383 of the Code, and §§ 1.1502-91 through 1.1502-99.

(c) *Examples.*—The examples in this paragraph (c) illustrate the application of section 163(j) and the provisions of this section. Unless otherwise indicated, X and Y are calendar-year domestic C corporations; D is a U.S. resident individual not subject to any foreign income tax; none of the taxpayers have floor plan financing interest expense; and the exemption for certain small businesses in § 1.163(j)-2(d) does not apply.

(1) *Example 1: Disallowed interest expense.*—(i) *Facts.* In 2021, X has $30x of interest expense. Of X's interest expense, $10x is permanently disallowed under section 265. X's business interest income is $3x and X's ATI is $90x.

(ii) *Analysis.* Under paragraph (b)(2) of this section, the $10x interest expense that is permanently disallowed under section 265 cannot be taken into consideration for purposes of section 163(j) in the 2021 taxable year. X's section 163(j) limitation, or the amount of business interest expense that X may deduct is limited to $30x under § 1.163(j)-2(b), by adding X's business interest income ($3x) and 30 percent of X's 2019 ATI ($27x). Therefore, in the 2021 taxable year, none of the $20x of X's deduction for its business interest expense is disallowed under section 163(j).

(2) *Example 2: Deferred interest expense.*—(i) *Facts.* In 2021, Y has no business interest income, $120x of ATI, and $70x of interest expense. Of Y's interest expense, $30x is not currently deductible under section 267(a)(2). The $30x expense is allowed as a deduction under section 267(a)(2) in 2022.

(ii) *Analysis.* Under paragraph (b)(3) of this section, section 267(a)(2) is applied before section 163(j). Accordingly, $30x of Y's interest expense cannot be taken into consideration for purposes of section 163(j) in 2021 because it is not currently deductible under section 267(a)(2). Accordingly, in 2021, if the interest expense is properly allocable to a non-excepted trade or business, Y will have $4x of disallowed business interest expense because the $40x of business interest expense in 2021 ($70x - $30x) exceeds 30 percent of its ATI for the taxable year ($36x). The $30x of interest expense not allowed as a deduction in the 2021 taxable year under section 267(a)(2) will be taken into account in determining the business interest expense deduction under section 163(j) in 2022, the taxable year in which it is allowed as a deduction under section 267(a)(2), if it is allocable to a trade or business. Additionally, the $4x of disallowed business interest expense in 2021 will be carried forward to 2022 as a disallowed business interest expense carryforward. See § 1.163(j)-2(c).

(3) *Example 3: Passive activity loss.*—(i) *Facts.* D is engaged in a rental activity treated as a passive activity within the meaning of section 469. For the 2021 taxable year, D receives $200x of rental income and incurs $300x of expenses all properly allocable to the rental activity, consisting of $150x of interest expense, $60x of maintenance expenses, and $90x of depreciation expense. D's ATI is $400x.

(ii) *Analysis.* Under paragraph (b)(4) of this section, section 163(j) is applied before the section 469 passive loss rules apply, except that section 469 is taken into account in the determination of tentative taxable income for purposes of computing ATI. D's section 163(j) limitation is $120x, determined by adding to D's business interest income ($0), floor plan financing ($0), and 30 percent of D's ATI ($120x). See § 1.163(j)-2(b). Because D's business interest expense of $150x exceeds D's section 163(j) limitation for 2021, $30x of D's business interest expense is disallowed under section 163(j) and will be carried forward as a disallowed business interest expense carryforward. See § 1.163(j)-2(c). Because the section 163(j) limitation is applied before the limitation under section 469, only $120x of the business interest expense allowable under section 163(j) is included in determining D's passive activity loss limitation for the 2021 tax year under section 469. The $30x of disallowed business interest expense is not an allowable deduction under section 163(j) and, therefore, is not a deduction under section 469 in the current taxable year. See § 1.469-2(d)(8).

(4) *Example 4: Passive activity loss by taxpayer that also participates in a non-passive activity.*—(i) *Facts.* For 2021, D has no business interest income and ATI of $1,000x, entirely attributable to a passive activity within the meaning of section 469. D has business interest expense of $1,000x, $900x of which is properly allocable to a passive activity and $100x of which is properly allocable to a non-passive activity in which D materially participates. D has other business deductions that are not subject to section 469 of $600x, and a section 469 passive loss from the previous year of $250x.

(ii) *Analysis.* Under paragraph (b)(4) of this section, section 163(j) is applied before the section 469 passive loss rules apply. D's section 163(j) limitation is $300x, determined by adding D's business interest income ($0), floor plan financing ($0), and 30 percent of D's ATI ($300x)). Next, applying the limitation under section 469 to the $300x business interest expense deduction allowable under section 163(a) and (j), $270x (a proportionate amount of the $300x (0.90 x $300x)) is business interest expense included in determining D's passive activity loss limitation under section 469, and $30x (a proportionate amount of the $300x (0.10 x $300)) is business interest expense not included in determining D's passive activity loss limitation under section 469. Because D's interest expense of $1,000x exceeds 30 percent of its ATI for 2021, $700x of D's interest expense is disallowed under section 163(j) and will be carried forward as a disallowed business interest expense carryforward. Section 469 does not apply to any portion of the $700x disallowed business interest expense because that business interest expense is not an allowable deduction under section 163(j) and, therefore, is not an allowable deduction under section 469 in the current taxable year. See § 1.469-2(d)(8).

(5) *Example 5: ATI calculation with passive activity loss.*—(i) *Facts.* D is an individual who engages in a trade or business, V, as a sole proprietorship. D relies on employees to *perform most of the work* and, as a result, D does not materially participate in V. Therefore, V is a passive activity of D. V is not an excepted trade or business. In Year 1, V generates $500x of passive income, $400x of business interest expense, and $600x of ordinary and necessary expenses deductible

under section 162 (not including any interest described in § 1.163(j)-1(b)(22)). No disallowed business interest expense carryforward has been carried to Year 1 from a prior year, and no amounts have been carried over to Year 1 from a prior year under either section 465(a)(2) or section 469(b).

(ii) *Tentative taxable income.* Under § 1.163(j)-1(b)(43), tentative taxable income is determined as though all business interest expense was not subject to the section 163(j) limitation. Sections 461(l), 465, and 469 apply in the determination of tentative taxable income. For year 1, D has $500x of allowable deductions and a $500x tentative passive activity loss under section 469, because D's $1000x of passive expenses exceeds D's $500x of passive income from V. The tentative disallowance of $500x is generally allocated pro rata between D's passive expenses under § 1.469-1T(f)(2)(ii)(A). In this case, fifty percent ($500x of passive activity loss divided by $1000x of total passive expenses) of each category of passive expense is tentatively disallowed: $200x of business interest expense and $300x of section 162 expense. D's tentative taxable income is $0 (zero), which is determined by reducing $500x of gross income by the remaining $200x of business interest expense and $300x of section 162 expense ($500x - $200x - $300x).

(iii) *ATI.* Under section § 1.163(j)-1(b)(1), to determine ATI, D must add business interest expense to tentative taxable income, but only to the extent that the business interest expense reduced tentative taxable income, or $200x. The $200x of business interest expense that was tentatively disallowed under section 469 is not added to tentative taxable income to determine ATI. D's ATI is $200x, which is determined by adding the $200x of business interest expense that reduced tentative taxable income to D's tentative taxable income, or $0 (0 + $200x).

(iv) *Section 163(j) limitation.* D's section 163(j) limitation in Year 1 is D's business interest income, or $0, plus 30 percent of ATI, or $60x (30 percent x $200x ATI), plus D's floor plan financing, or $0, for a total of $60x ($0 + $60x + $0). Before the application of section 469, D has $60x of deductible business interest expense and $340x of disallowed business interest expense carryforward under § 1.163(j)-2(c).

(v) *Passive activity loss.* Because D's passive deductions exceed the passive income from V, and D does not have any passive income from other sources, section 469 applies to limit D's passive loss from V. Having first applied section 163(j), D has $660x of passive expenses, determined by adding D's $60x of business interest expense that is allowed by section 163(j) as a deduction and $600x of section 162 expense ($60x + $600x). D offsets $500x of the passive expenses against $500x of passive income; therefore, D has a passive activity loss of $160x in Year 1, determined as the excess of D's total passive expenses over D's passive income ($660x – $500x). The amount of D's loss from the passive activity that is disallowed under section 469 ($160x) is generally ratably allocated to each of D's passive activity deductions under § 1.469-1T(f)(2)(ii)(A). As a general rule, each deduction is multiplied by the ratio of the total passive loss to total passive expenses (160x / 660x). Of D's $60x business interest expense, $14.55x (($160x / $660x) x $60x) is disallowed in Year 1. Additionally, of D's $600x section 162 expense, $145.45x (($160x / $660x) x $600x) is disallowed. The amounts disallowed under section 469(a)(1) and § 1.469-2T(f)(2) are carried over to the succeeding taxable year under section 469(b) and § 1.469-1(f)(4).

(6) *Example 6: Effect of passive activity loss carryforwards.*—(i) *Facts.* The facts are the same as in *Example 5* in paragraph (c)(5)(i) of this section. In Year 2, V generates $500x of passive income, $100x of business interest expense, and $0 (zero) of other deductible expenses. D is not engaged in any other trade or business activities. A disallowed business interest expense carryforward of $340x has been carried to Year 2 from Year 1. Under section 469, D has a suspended loss from Year 1 that includes $14.55x of business interest expense and $145.45x of section 162 expense. These amounts are treated as passive activity deductions in Year 2.

(ii) *Tentative taxable income.* To determine D's tentative taxable income, D must first determine D's allowable deductions. In year 2, D has $260x of allowable deductions, which includes $100x of business interest expense generated Year 2, $14.55x of business interest expense disallowed in Year 1 by section 469, and $145.45x of section 162 expense disallowed in Year 1 by section 469 ($100x + $14.55x + $145.45x)). D's disallowed business interest expense carryforward from Year 1 is not taken into account in determining tentative taxable income. See § 1.163(j)-1(b)(43). Additionally, the $14.55x of business interest expense disallowed in Year 1 by section 469 is not business interest expense in Year 2 because it was deductible after the application of section 163(j) (but before the application of section 469) in Year 1. D does not have a tentative passive activity loss in Year 2, because D's $500x of passive income from V exceeds D's $260x of tentative passive expenses. Therefore, D's tentative taxable income in Year 2 is $240x, which is determined by subtracting D's allowable deductions other than disallowed business interest expense carryforwards, or $260x, from D's gross income, or $500x ($500x - $260x).

Itemized Deductions for Individuals and Corps.
See p. 20,601 for regulations not amended to reflect law changes
25,327

(iii) *ATI*. D's ATI in Year 2 is $340x, which is determined by adding D's business interest expense, or $100x, to D's tentative taxable income, or $240x ($240x + $100x). Because disallowed business interest expense carryforwards are not taken into account in determining tentative taxable income, there is no corresponding adjustment for disallowed business interest expense carryforwards in calculating ATI. Therefore, there is no adjustment for D's $340x of disallowed business interest expense carryforward in calculating D's ATI. D has no other adjustments to determine ATI.

(iv) *Section 163(j) limitation*. D's section 163(j) limitation in Year 2 is $102x, which is determined by adding D's business interest income, or $0, 30 percent of D's ATI for year 2, $102 ($340x x 30 percent), and D's floor plan financing for Year 2, or $0 ($0 + ($102x) + $0). Accordingly, before the application of section 469 in Year 2, $102x of D's $440x of total business interest expense (determined by adding $340x of disallowed business interest expense carryforward from Year 1 and $100x of business interest expense in Year 2) is deductible. D has $338x of disallowed business interest expense carryforward that will carry forward to subsequent taxable years under §1.163(j)-2(c), determined by subtracting D's deductible business interest expense in Year 2, or $102x, from D's total business interest expense in Year 2, or $440x ($440x - $102x).

(v) *Section 469*. After applying the section 163(j) limitation, D applies section 469 to determine if any amount of D's expense is a disallowed passive activity loss. For Year 2, D has $262x of passive expenses, determined by adding D's business interest expense deduction allowed by section 163(j) ($102x), D's section 162 expense carried forward from Year 1 under section 469 ($145.45x), and D's interest expense carried forward from Year 1 under section 469 which is not business interest expense in Year 2, or $14.55x ($102x + $145.45x + $14.55x). Therefore, D has $238x of net passive income in Year 2, determined by reducing D's total passive income in Year 2 ($500x), by D's disallowed passive activity loss, or $262x ($500x - $262x). D does not have a passive activity loss in Year 2, and no part of D's $262x of passive expenses is disallowed in Year 2 under section 469.

(7) *Example 7: Capitalized interest expense.*—(i) *Facts*. In 2020, X has $50x of interest expense. Of X's interest expense, $10x is required to be capitalized under section 263A. X capitalizes this interest expense to a depreciable asset. X's business interest income is $9x and X's ATI is $80x. X makes the election in §1.163(j)-2(b)(2)(ii) to use 30 percent, rather than 50 percent, of ATI in determining X's section 163(j) limitation for the 2020 taxable year.

(ii) *Analysis*. Under paragraph (b)(5) of this section, section 263A is applied before section 163(j). Accordingly, $10x of X's interest expense cannot be taken into consideration for purposes of section 163(j) in 2020. Additionally, under paragraph (b)(5) of this section, X's $10 of capitalized interest expense is not business interest expense for purposes of section 163(j). As a result, when X recovers its capitalized interest expense through depreciation deductions, such capitalized interest expense will not be taken into account as business interest expense in determining X's section 163(j) limitation. X's section 163(j) limitation in 2020, or the amount of business interest expense that X may deduct, is limited to $33x under §1.163(j)-2(b), determined by adding X's business interest income ($9x) and 30 percent of X's 2020 ATI ($24x). X therefore has $7x of disallowed business interest expense in 2020 that will be carried forward to 2021 as a disallowed business interest expense carryforward.

(d) *Applicability date.*—This section applies to taxable years beginning on or after November 13, 2020. However, taxpayers and their related parties, within the meaning of sections 267(b) and 707(b)(1), may choose to apply the rules of this section to a taxable year beginning after December 31, 2017, so long as the taxpayers and their related parties consistently apply the rules of the section 163(j) regulations, and, if applicable, §§1.263A-9, 1.263A-15, 1.381(c)(20)-1, 1.382-1, 1.382-2, 1.382-5, 1.382-6, 1.382-7, 1.383-0, 1.383-1, 1.469-9, 1.469-11, 1.704-1, 1.882-5, 1.1362-3, 1.1368-1, 1.1377-1, 1.1502-13, 1.1502-21, 1.1502-36, 1.1502-79, 1.1502-91 through 1.1502-99 (to the extent they effectuate the rules of §§1.382-2, 1.382-5, 1.382-6, and 1.383-1), and 1.1504-4, to that taxable year. [Reg. §1.163(j)-3.]

☐ [T.D. 9905, 9-3-2020.]

[Reg. §1.163(j)-4]

§1.163(j)-4. General rules applicable to C corporations (including REITs, RICs, and members of consolidated groups) and tax-exempt corporations.—(a) *Scope.*—This section provides rules regarding the computation of items of income and expense under section 163(j) for taxpayers that are C corporations, including, for example, members of a consolidated group, REITs, RICs, tax-exempt corporations, and cooperatives. Paragraph (b) of this section provides rules regarding the characterization of items of income, gain, deduction, or loss. Paragraph (c) of this section provides rules regarding

adjustments to earnings and profits. Paragraph (d) of this section provides rules applicable to members of a consolidated group. Paragraph (e) of this section provides rules governing the ownership of partnership interests by members of a consolidated group. Paragraph (f) of this section provides cross-references to other rules within the 163(j) regulations that may be applicable to C corporations.

(b) *Characterization of items of income, gain, deduction, or loss.*—(1) *Interest expense and interest income.*—Solely for purposes of section 163(j), all interest expense of a taxpayer that is a C corporation is treated as properly allocable to a trade or business. Similarly, solely for purposes of section 163(j), all interest income of a taxpayer that is a C corporation is treated as properly allocable to a trade or business. For rules governing the allocation of interest expense and interest income between excepted and non-excepted trades or businesses, see §1.163(j)-10.

(2) *Adjusted taxable income.*—Solely for purposes of section 163(j), all items of income, gain, deduction, or loss of a taxpayer that is a C corporation are treated as properly allocable to a trade or business. For rules governing the allocation of tax items between excepted and non-excepted trades or businesses, see §1.163(j)-10.

(3) *Investment interest, investment income, investment expenses, and certain other tax items of a partnership with a C corporation partner.*—(i) *Characterization as expense or income properly allocable to a trade or business.*—For purposes of section 163(j), any investment interest, investment income, or investment expense (within the meaning of section 163(d)) that a partnership pays, receives, or accrues and that is allocated to a C corporation partner as a separately stated item is treated by the C corporation partner as properly allocable to a trade or business of that partner. Similarly, for purposes of section 163(j), any other tax items of a partnership that are neither properly allocable to a trade or business of the partnership nor described in section 163(d) and that are allocated to a C corporation partner as separately stated items are treated as properly allocable to a trade or business of that partner.

(ii) *Effect of characterization on partnership.*—The characterization of a partner's tax items pursuant to paragraph (b)(3)(i) of this section does not affect the characterization of these items at the partnership level.

(iii) *Separately stated interest expense and interest income of a partnership not treated as excess business interest expense or excess taxable income of a C corporation partner.*—Investment interest expense and other interest expense of a partnership that is treated as business interest expense by a C corporation partner under paragraph (b)(3)(i) of this section is not treated as excess business interest expense of the partnership. Investment interest income and other interest income of a partnership that is treated as business interest income by a C corporation partner under paragraph (b)(3)(i) of this section is not treated as excess taxable income of the partnership. For rules governing excess business interest expense and excess taxable income, see §1.163(j)-6.

(iv) *Treatment of deemed inclusions of a domestic partnership that are not allocable to any trade or business.*—If a United States shareholder that is a domestic partnership includes amounts in gross income under sections 951(a) or 951A(a) that are not properly allocable to a trade or business of the domestic partnership, then, notwithstanding paragraph (b)(3)(i) of this section, to the extent a C corporation partner, including an indirect partner in the case of tiered partnerships, takes such amounts into account as a distributive share in accordance with section 702 and §1.702-1(a)(8)(ii), the C corporation partner may not treat such amounts as properly allocable to a trade or business of the C corporation partner.

(4) *Application to RICs and REITs.*—(i) *In general.*—Except as otherwise provided in paragraphs (b)(4)(ii) and (iii) of this section, the rules in this paragraph (b) apply to RICs and REITs.

(ii) *Tentative taxable income of RICs and REITs.*—The tentative taxable income of a RIC or REIT for purposes of calculating ATI is the tentative taxable income of the corporation, without any adjustment that would be made under section 852(b)(2) or 857(b)(2) to compute investment company taxable income or real estate investment trust taxable income, respectively. For example, the tentative taxable income of a RIC or REIT is not reduced by the deduction for dividends paid, but is reduced by the dividends received deduction (DRD) and the other deductions described in sections 852(b)(2)(C) and 857(b)(2)(A). See paragraph (b)(4)(iii) of this section for an adjustment to ATI in respect of these items.

(iii) *Other adjustments to adjusted taxable income for RICs and REITs.*—In the case of a taxpayer that, for a taxable year, is a RIC to which section 852(b) applies or a REIT to which section 857(b) applies, the taxpayer's ATI for the taxable year is increased by the amounts of any deductions described in section 852(b)(2)(C) or 857(b)(2)(A).

(5) *Application to tax-exempt corporations.*—The rules in this paragraph (b) apply to a tax-exempt corporation only with respect to that corporation's items of income, gain, deduction, or loss that are taken into account in computing the corporation's unrelated business taxable income, as defined in section 512.

(6) *Adjusted taxable income of cooperatives.*—Solely for purposes of computing the ATI of a cooperative under § 1.163(j)-1(b)(1), tentative taxable income is not reduced by the amount of any patronage dividend under section 1382(b)(1) or by any amount paid in redemption of nonqualified written notices of allocation distributed as patronage dividends under section 1382(b)(2) (for cooperatives subject to taxation under sections 1381 through 1388), any amount described in section 1382(c) (for cooperatives described in section 1381(a)(1) and section 521), or any equivalent amount deducted by an organization that operates on a cooperative basis but is not subject to taxation under sections 1381 through 1388.

(7) *Examples.*—The principles of this paragraph (b) are illustrated by the following examples. For purposes of the examples in this paragraph (b)(7) of this section, T is a taxable domestic C corporation whose taxable year ends on December 31; T is neither a consolidated group member nor a RIC or a REIT; neither T nor PS1, a domestic partnership, owns at least 80 percent of the stock of any corporation; neither T nor PS1 qualifies for the small business exemption in § 1.163(j)-2(d) or is engaged in an excepted trade or business; T has no floor plan financing expense; all interest expense is deductible except for the potential application of section 163(j); and the facts set forth the only corporate or partnership activity.

(i) *Example 1: C corporation items properly allocable to a trade or business.*—(A) *Facts.* In taxable year 2021, T's tentative taxable income (without regard to the application of section 163(j)) is $320x. This amount is comprised of the following tax items: $1,000x of revenue from inventory sales; $500x of ordinary and necessary business expenses (excluding interest and depreciation); $200x of interest expense; $50x of interest income; $50x of depreciation deductions under section 168; and a $20x gain on the sale of stock.

(B)*Analysis.* For purposes of section 163(j), each of T's tax items is treated as properly allocable to a trade or business. Thus, T's ATI for the 2021 taxable year is $520x ($320x of tentative taxable income + $200x business interest expense - $50x business interest income + $50x depreciation deductions = $520x), and its section 163(j) limitation for the 2021 taxable year is $206x ($50x of business interest income + 30 percent of its ATI (30 percent x $520x) = $206x). As a result, all $200x of T's interest expense is deductible in the 2021 taxable year under section 163(j).

(C) *Taxable year beginning in 2022.* The facts are the same as in *Example 1* in paragraph (b)(7)(i)(A) of this section, except that the taxable year begins in 2022 and therefore depreciation deductions are not added back to ATI under § 1.163(j)-1(b)(1)(i)(E). As a result, T's ATI for 2022 is $470x ($320x of tentative taxable income + $200x business interest expense - $50x business interest income = $470x), and its section 163(j) limitation for the 2022 taxable year is $191x ($50x of business interest income + 30 percent of its ATI (30 percent x $470x) = $191x). As a result, T may only deduct $191x of its business interest expense for the taxable year, and the remaining $9x is carried forward to the 2023 taxable year as a disallowed business interest expense carryforward. See § 1.163(j)-2(c).

(ii) *Example 2: C corporation partner.*—(A) *Facts.* T and individual A each own a 50 percent interest in PS1, a general partnership. PS1 borrows funds from a third party (Loan 1) and uses those funds to buy stock in publicly-traded corporation X. PS1's only activities are holding X stock (and receiving dividends) and making payments on Loan 1. In the 2021 taxable year, PS1 receives $150x in dividends and pays $100x in interest on Loan 1.

(B) *Analysis.* For purposes of section 163(d) and (j), PS1 has investment interest expense of $100x and investment income of $150x, and PS1 has no interest expense or interest income that is properly allocable to a trade or business. PS1 allocates its investment interest expense and investment income equally to its two partners pursuant to § 1.163(j)-6(k). Pursuant to paragraph (b)(3) of this section, T's allocable share of PS1's investment interest expense is treated as a business interest expense of T, and T's allocable share of PS1's investment income is treated as properly allocable to a trade or business of T. This business interest expense is not treated as excess business interest *expense, and this income is not treated as excess taxable income.* See paragraph (b)(3)(iii) of this section. T's treatment of its allocable share of PS1's investment interest expense and investment income as business interest expense and income properly allocable to a trade or business, respectively, does not affect the character

of these items at the PS1 level and does not affect the character of A's allocable share of PS1's investment interest and investment income.

(C) *Partnership engaged in a trade or business.* The facts are the same as in *Example 2* in paragraph (b)(7)(ii)(A) of this section, except that PS1 also is engaged in Business 1, and PS1 borrows funds from a third party to finance Business 1 (Loan 2). In 2021, Business 1 earns $150x of net income (excluding interest expense and depreciation), and PS1 pays $100x of interest on Loan 2. For purposes of section 163(d) and (j), PS1 treats the interest paid on Loan 2 as properly allocable to a trade or business. As a result, PS1 has investment interest expense of $100x (attributable to Loan 1), business interest expense of $100x (attributable to Loan 2), $150x of investment income, and $150x of income from Business 1. PS1's ATI is $150x (its net income from Business 1 excluding interest and depreciation), and its section 163(j) limitation is $45x (30 percent x $150x). Pursuant to § 1.163(j)-6, PS1 has $55x of excess business interest expense ($100x - $45x), half of which ($27.5x) is allocable to T. Additionally, pursuant to paragraph (b)(3)(i) of this section, T's allocable share of PS1's investment interest expense ($50x) is treated as a business interest expense of T for purposes of section 163(j), and T's allocable share of PS1's investment income ($75x) is treated as properly allocable to a trade or business of T. Therefore, with respect to T's interest in PS1, T is treated as having $50x of business interest expense that is not treated as excess business interest expense, $75x of income that is properly allocable to a trade or business, and $27.5x of excess business interest expense.

(c) *Effect on earnings and profits.*—(1) *In general.*—In the case of a taxpayer that is a domestic C corporation, except as otherwise provided in paragraph (c)(2) of this section, the disallowance and carryforward under § 1.163(j)-2 (and § 1.163(j)-5, in the case of a taxpayer that is a consolidated group member) of a deduction for business interest expense of the taxpayer or of a partnership in which the taxpayer is a partner does not affect whether or when the business interest expense reduces the taxpayer's earnings and profits. In the case of a foreign corporation, the disallowance and carryforward of a deduction for the corporation's business interest expense under § 1.163(j)-2 does not affect whether and when such business interest expense reduces the corporation's earnings and profits. Thus, for example, if a United States person has elected under section 1295 to treat a passive foreign investment company (as defined in section 1297) (PFIC) as a qualified electing fund, then the disallowance and carryforward of a deduction for the PFIC's business interest expense under § 1.163(j)-2 does not affect whether or when such business interest expense reduces the PFIC's earnings and profits.

(2) *Special rule for RICs and REITs.*—In the case of a taxpayer that is a RIC or a REIT for the taxable year in which a deduction for the taxpayer's business interest expense is disallowed under § 1.163(j)-2(b), or in which the RIC or REIT is allocated any excess business interest expense from a partnership under section 163(j)(4)(B)(i) and § 1.163(j)-6, the taxpayer's earnings and profits are adjusted in the taxable year or years in which the business interest expense is deductible or, if earlier, in the first taxable year for which the taxpayer no longer is a RIC or a REIT.

(3) *Special rule for partners that are C corporations.*—If a taxpayer that is a C corporation is allocated any excess business interest expense from a partnership, and if all or a portion of the excess business interest expense has not yet been treated as business interest expense by the taxpayer at the time of the taxpayer's disposition of all or a portion of its interest in the partnership, the taxpayer must increase its earnings and profits immediately prior to the disposition by an amount equal to the amount of the basis adjustment required under section 163(j)(4)(B)(iii)(II) and § 1.163(j)-6(h)(3).

(4) *Examples.*—The principles of this paragraph (c) are illustrated by the following examples. For purposes of the examples in this paragraph (c)(4), except as otherwise provided in the examples, X is a taxable domestic C corporation whose taxable year ends on December 31; X is not a member of a consolidated group; X does not qualify for the small business exemption under § 1.163(j)-2(d); X is not engaged in an excepted trade or business; X has no floor plan financing indebtedness; all interest expense is deductible except for the potential application of section 163(j); X has no accumulated earnings and profits at the beginning of the 2021 taxable year; and the facts set forth the only corporate activity.

(i) *Example 1: Earnings and profits of a taxable domestic C corporation other than a RIC or a REIT.*—(A) *Facts.* X is a corporation that does not intend to qualify as a RIC or a REIT for its 2021 taxable year. In that year, X has tentative taxable income (without regard to the application of section 163(j)) of $0, which includes $100x of gross income and $100x of interest expense on a loan from an unrelated third party. X also makes a $100x distribution to its shareholders that year.

(B) *Analysis.* The $100x of interest expense is business interest expense for purposes of section 163(j) (see paragraph (b)(1) of this section). X's ATI in the 2021 taxable year is $100x ($0 of tentative taxable income computed without regard to $100x of business interest expense). Thus, X may deduct $30x of its $100x of business interest expense in the 2021 taxable year under §1.163(j)-2(b) (30 percent x $100x), and X may carry forward the remainder ($70x) to X's 2022 taxable year as a disallowed business interest expense carryforward under §1.163(j)-2(c). Although X may not currently deduct all $100x of its business interest expense in the 2021 taxable year, X must reduce its earnings and profits in that taxable year by the full amount of its business interest expense ($100x) in that taxable year. As a result, no portion of X's distribution of $100x to its shareholders in the 2021 taxable year is a dividend within the meaning of section 316(a).

(ii) *Example 2: RIC adjusted taxable income and earnings and profits.*—(A) *Facts.* X is a corporation that intends to qualify as a RIC for its 2021 taxable year. In that taxable year, X's only items are $100x of interest income, $50x of dividend income from C corporations that only issue common stock and in which X has less than a twenty percent interest (by vote and value), $10x of net capital gain, and $125x of interest expense. None of the dividends are received on debt financed portfolio stock under section 246A. The DRD determined under section 243(a) with respect to X's $50x of dividend income is $25x. X pays $42x in dividends to its shareholders, meeting the requirements of section 562 during X's 2021 taxable year, including $10x that X reports as capital gain dividends in written statements furnished to X's shareholders.

(B) *Analysis.* (1) Under paragraph (b) of this section, all of X's interest expense is considered business interest expense, all of X's interest income is considered business interest income, and all of X's other income is considered to be properly allocable to a trade or business. Under paragraph (b)(4)(ii) of this section, prior to the application of section 163(j), X's tentative taxable income is $10x ($100x business interest income + $50x dividend income + $10x net capital gain - $125x business interest expense - $25x DRD = $10x). Under paragraph (b)(4)(iii) of this section, X's ATI is increased by the DRD. As such, X's ATI for the 2021 taxable year is $60x ($10x tentative taxable income + $125x business interest expense - $100x business interest income + $25x DRD = $60x).

(2) X may deduct $118x of its $125x of business interest expense in the 2021 taxable year under section 163(j)(1) ($100x business interest income + (30 percent x $60x of ATI) = $118x), and X may carry forward the remainder ($7x) to X's 2022 taxable year. See §1.163(j)-2(b) and (c).

(3) After the application of section 163(j), X has taxable income of $17x ($100x interest income + $50x dividend income + $10x capital gain - $25x DRD - $118x allowable interest expense = $17x) for the 2021 taxable year. X will have investment company taxable income (ICTI) in the amount of $0 ($17x taxable income - $10x capital gain + $25x DRD - $32x dividends paid deduction for ordinary dividends = $0). The excess of X's net capital gain ($10x) over X's dividends paid deduction determined with reference to capital gain dividends ($10x) is also $0.

(4) Under paragraph (c)(2) of this section, X will not reduce its earnings and profits by the amount of interest expense disallowed as a deduction in the 2021 taxable year under section 163(j). Thus, X has current earnings and profits in the amount of $42x ($100x interest income + $50x dividend income + $10x capital gain - $118x allowable business interest expense = $42x) before giving effect to dividends paid during the 2021 taxable year.

(iii) *Example 3: Carryforward of disallowed interest expense.*—(A) *Facts.* The facts are the same as the facts in *Example 2* in paragraph (c)(4)(ii)(A) of this section for the 2021 taxable year. In addition, X has $50x of interest income and $20x of interest expense for the 2022 taxable year.

(B) *Analysis.* Under paragraph (b) of this section, all of X's interest expense is considered business interest expense, all of X's interest income is considered business interest income, and all of X's other income is considered to be properly allocable to a trade or business. Because X's $50x of business interest income exceeds the $20x of business interest expense from the 2022 taxable year and the $7x of disallowed business interest expense carryforward from the 2021 taxable year, X may deduct $27x of business interest expense in the 2022 taxable year. Under paragraph (c)(2) of this section, X must reduce its current earnings and profits for the 2022 taxable year by the full amount of the deductible business interest expense ($27x).

(iv) *Example 4: REIT adjusted taxable income and earnings and profits.*—(A) *Facts.* X is a corporation that intends to qualify as a REIT for its 2021 taxable year. X is not engaged in an excepted trade or business and is not engaged in a trade or business that is eligible to make any election under section 163(j)(7). In that year, X's only items

are $100x of mortgage interest income, $30x of dividend income from C corporations that only issue common stock and in which X has less than a ten percent interest (by vote and value), $10x of net capital gain from the sale of mortgages on real property that is not property described in section 1221(a)(1), and $125x of interest expense. None of the dividends are received on debt financed portfolio stock under section 246A. The DRD determined under section 243(a) with respect to X's $30x of dividend income is $15x. X pays $28x in dividends meeting the requirements of section 562 during X's 2021 taxable year, including $10x that X properly designates as capital gain dividends under section 857(b)(3)(B).

(B) *Analysis.* (1) Under paragraph (b) of this section, all of X's interest expense is considered business interest expense, all of X's interest income is considered business interest income, and all of X's other income is considered to be properly allocable to a trade or business. Under paragraph (b)(4)(ii) of this section, prior to the application of section 163(j), X's tentative taxable income is $0 ($100x business interest income + $30x dividend income + $10x net capital gain - $125x business interest expense - $15x DRD = $0). Under paragraph (b)(4)(iii) of this section, X's ATI is increased by the DRD. As such, X's ATI for the 2021 taxable year is $40x ($0 tentative taxable income + $125x business interest expense - $100x business interest income + $15x DRD = $40x).

(2) X may deduct $112x of its $125x of business interest expense in the 2021 taxable year under section 163(j)(1) ($100x business interest income + (30 percent x $40x of ATI) = $112x), and X may carry forward the remainder of its business interest expense ($13x) to X's 2022 taxable year.

(3) After the application of section 163(j), X has taxable income of $13x ($100x business interest income + $30x dividend income + $10x capital gain - $15x DRD - $112x allowable business interest expense = $13x) for the 2021 taxable year. X will have real estate investment trust taxable income (REITTI) in the amount of $0 ($13x taxable income + $15x of DRD - $28x dividends paid deduction = $0).

(4) Under paragraph (c)(2) of this section, X will not reduce earnings and profits by the amount of business interest expense disallowed as a deduction in the 2021 taxable year. Thus, X has current earnings and profits in the amount of $28x ($100x business interest income + $30x dividend income + $10x capital gain - $112x allowable business interest expense = $28x) before giving effect to dividends paid during X's 2021 taxable year.

(v) *Example 5: Carryforward of disallowed interest expense.*—(A) *Facts.* The facts are the same as in *Example 4* in paragraph (c)(4)(iv)(A) of this section for the 2021 taxable year. In addition, X has $50x of mortgage interest income and $20x of interest expense for the 2022 taxable year. X has no other tax items for the 2022 taxable year.

(B) *Analysis.* Because X's $50x of business interest income exceeds the $20x of business interest expense from the 2022 taxable year and the $13x of disallowed business interest expense carryforwards from the 2021 taxable year, X may deduct $33x of business interest expense in 2022. Under paragraph (c)(2) of this section, X must reduce its current earnings and profits for 2022 by the full amount of the deductible interest expense ($33x).

(d) *Special rules for consolidated groups.*—(1) *Scope.*—This paragraph (d) provides rules applicable to members of a consolidated group. For all members of a consolidated group for a consolidated return year, the computations required by section 163(j) and the regulations in this part under section 163(j) are made in accordance with the rules of this paragraph (d) unless otherwise provided elsewhere in the section 163(j) regulations. For rules governing the ownership of partnership interests by members of a consolidated group, see paragraph (e) of this section.

(2) *Calculation of the section 163(j) limitation for members of a consolidated group.*—(i) *In general.*—A consolidated group has a single section 163(j) limitation, the absorption of which is governed by §1.163(j)-5(b)(3)(ii).

(ii) *Interest.*—For purposes of determining whether amounts, other than amounts in respect of intercompany obligations (as defined in §1.1502-13(g)(2)(ii)), intercompany items (as defined in §1.1502-13(b)(2)), or corresponding items (as defined in §1.1502-13(b)(3)), are treated as interest within the meaning of §1.163(j)-1(b)(22), all members of a consolidated group are treated as a single taxpayer.

(iii) *Calculation of business interest expense and business interest income for a consolidated group.*—For purposes of calculating the section 163(j) limitation for a consolidated group, the consolidated group's current-year business interest expense and business interest income, respectively, are the sum of each member's current-year business interest expense and business interest income, including amounts treated as business interest expense and business interest income under paragraph (b)(3) of this section.

(iv) Calculation of adjusted taxable income.—For purposes of calculating the ATI for a consolidated group, the tentative taxable income is the consolidated group's consolidated taxable income, determined under §1.1502-11 but without regard to any carryforwards or disallowances under section 163(j). Further, for purposes of calculating the ATI of the group, intercompany items and corresponding items are disregarded to the extent that they offset in amount. Thus, for example, certain portions of the intercompany items and corresponding items of a group member engaged in a non-excepted trade or business will not be included in ATI to the extent that the counterparties to the relevant intercompany transactions are engaged in one or more excepted trades or businesses.

(v) Treatment of intercompany obligations.—(A) *In general.*—Except as otherwise provided in paragraph (d)(2)(v)(B) of this section, for purposes of determining a member's business interest expense and business interest income, and for purposes of calculating the consolidated group's ATI, all intercompany obligations, as defined in §1.1502-13(g)(2)(ii), are disregarded. Therefore, except as otherwise provided in paragraph (d)(2)(v)(B) of this section, interest expense and interest income from intercompany obligations are not treated as business interest expense and business interest income.

(B) *Repurchase premium.*—This paragraph (d)(2)(v)(B) applies if a member of a consolidated group purchases an obligation of another member of the same consolidated group in a transaction to which §1.1502-13(g)(5) applies. Notwithstanding the general rule of paragraph (d)(2)(v)(A) of this section, if, as a result of the deemed satisfaction of the obligation under §1.1502-13(g)(5)(ii), the debtor member has repurchase premium that is deductible under §1.163-7(c), such repurchase premium is treated as interest that is subject to the section 163(j) limitation. See §1.163(j)-1(b)(22)(i)(H).

(3) *Investment adjustments.*—For rules governing investment adjustments within a consolidated group, see §1.1502-32(b).

(4) *Examples.*—The principles in this paragraph (d) are illustrated by the following examples. For purposes of the examples in this paragraph (d)(4), S is a member of the calendar-year consolidated group of which P is the common parent; the P group does not qualify for the small business exemption in §1.163(j)-2(d); no member of the P group is engaged in an excepted trade or business; all interest expense is deductible except for the potential application of section 163(j); and the facts set forth the only corporate activity.

(i) *Example 1: Calculation of the section 163(j) limitation.*—(A) *Facts.* In the 2021 taxable year, P has $50x of separate tentative taxable income after taking into account $65x of interest paid on a loan from a third party (without regard to any disallowance under section 163(j)) and $35x of depreciation deductions under section 168. In turn, S has $40x of separate tentative taxable income in the 2021 taxable year after taking into account $10x of depreciation deductions under section 168. S has no interest expense in the 2021 taxable year. The P group's tentative taxable income the 2021 taxable year is $90x, determined under §1.1502-11 without regard to any disallowance under section 163(j).

(B) *Analysis.* As provided in paragraph (b)(1) of this section, P's interest expense is treated as business interest expense for purposes of section 163(j). If P and S were to apply the section 163(j) limitation on a separate-entity basis, then P's ATI would be $150x ($50x + $65x + $35x = $150x), its section 163(j) limitation would be $45x (30 percent x $150x = $45x), and a deduction for $20x of its $65x of business interest expense would be disallowed in the 2021 taxable year under section 163(j). However, as provided in paragraph (d)(2) of this section, the P group computes a single section 163(j) limitation, and that computation begins with the P group's tentative taxable income (as determined prior to the application of section 163(j)), or $90x. The P group's ATI is $200x ($50x + $40x + $65x + $35x + $10x = $200x). Thus, the P group's section 163(j) limitation for the 2021 taxable year is $60x (30 percent x $200x = $60x). As a result, all but $5x of the P group's business interest expense is deductible in the 2021 taxable year. P carries over the $5x of disallowed business interest expense to the succeeding taxable year.

(ii) *Example 2: Intercompany obligations.*—(A) *Facts.* On January 1, 2021, G, a corporation unrelated to P and S, lends P $100x in exchange for a note that accrues interest at a 10 percent annual rate. A month later, P lends $100x to S in exchange for a note that accrues interest at a 12 percent annual rate. In 2021, P accrues and pays $10x of interest to G on P's note, and S accrues and pays $12x of interest to P on S's note. For that year, the P group's only other items of income, gain, deduction, and loss are $40x of income earned by S from the sale of inventory, and a $30x deductible expense arising from P's payment of tort liability claims.

(B) *Analysis.* As provided in paragraph (d)(2)(v) of this section, the intercompany obligation between P and S is disregarded in determining P and S's business interest expense and business interest

income and in determining the P group's ATI. For purposes of section 163(j), P has $10x of business interest expense and a $30x deduction for the payment of tort liability claims, and S has $40x of income. The P group's ATI is $10x ($40x - $30x = $10x), and its section 163(j) limitation is $3x (30 percent x $10x = $3x). The P group may deduct $3x of its business interest expense in the 2021 taxable year. A deduction for P's remaining $7x of business interest expense is disallowed in the 2021 taxable year, and this amount is carried forward to the 2022 taxable year.

(e) *Ownership of partnership interests by members of a consolidated group.*—(1) [Reserved]

(2) *Change in status of a member.*—A change in status of a member (that is, becoming or ceasing to be a member of the group) is not treated as a disposition for purposes of section 163(j)(4)(B)(iii)(II) and §1.163(j)-6(h)(3).

(3) *Basis adjustments under §1.1502-32.*—A member's allocation of excess business interest expense from a partnership and the resulting decrease in basis in the partnership interest under section 163(j)(4)(B)(iii)(I) is not a noncapital, nondeductible expense for purposes of §1.1502-32(b)(3)(iii). Additionally, an increase in a member's basis in a partnership interest under section 163(j)(4)(B)(iii)(II) to reflect excess business interest expense not deducted by the consolidated group is not tax-exempt income for purposes of §1.1502-32(b)(3)(ii). Investment adjustments are made under §1.1502-32(b)(3)(i) when the excess business interest expense from the partnership is converted into business interest expense, deducted, and absorbed by the consolidated group. See §1.1502-32(b).

(4) *Excess business interest expense and §1.1502-36.*—Excess business interest expense is a Category D asset within the meaning of §1.1502-36(d)(4)(i).

(f) *Cross-references.*—For rules governing the treatment of disallowed business interest expense carryforwards for C corporations, including rules governing the treatment of disallowed business interest expense carryforwards when members enter or leave a consolidated group, see §1.163(j)-5. For rules governing the application of section 163(j) to a C corporation or a consolidated group engaged in both excepted and non-excepted trades or businesses, see §1.163(j)-10.

(g) *Applicability date.*—(1) *In general.*—This section applies to taxable years beginning on or after November 13, 2020. However, taxpayers and their related parties, within the meaning of sections 267(b) and 707(b)(1), may choose to apply the rules of this section to a taxable year beginning after December 31, 2017, so long as the taxpayers and their related parties consistently apply the rules of the section 163(j) regulations, and, if applicable, §§1.263A-9, 1.263A-15, 1.381(c)(20)-1, 1.382-1, 1.382-2, 1.382-5, 1.382-6, 1.382-7, 1.383-0, 1.383-1, 1.469-9, 1.469-11, 1.704-1, 1.882-5, 1.1362-3, 1.1368-1, 1.1377-1, 1.1502-13, 1.1502-21, 1.1502-36, 1.1502-79, 1.1502-91 through 1.1502-99 (to the extent they effectuate the rules of §§1.382-2, 1.382-5, 1.382-6, and 1.383-1), and 1.1504-4, to that taxable year.

(2) [Reserved] [Reg. §1.163(j)-4.]

☐ [*T.D.* 9905, 9-3-2020.]

[Reg. §1.163(j)-5]

§1.163(j)-5. General rules governing disallowed business interest expense carryforwards for C corporations.—(a) *Scope and definitions.*—(1) *Scope.*—This section provides rules regarding disallowed business interest expense carryforwards for taxpayers that are C corporations, including members of a consolidated group. Paragraph (b) of this section provides rules regarding the treatment of disallowed business interest expense carryforwards. Paragraph (c) of this section provides a cross-reference to other rules regarding disallowed business interest expense carryforwards in transactions to which section 381(a) applies. Paragraph (d) of this section provides rules regarding limitations on disallowed business interest expense carryforwards from separate return limitation years (SRLYs). Paragraph (e) of this section provides cross-references to other rules regarding the application of section 382 to disallowed business interest expense carryforwards. Paragraph (f) of this section provides a cross-reference to other rules regarding the overlap of the SRLY limitation with section 382. Paragraph (g) of this section references additional rules that may limit the deductibility of interest or the use of disallowed business interest expense carryforwards.

(2) *Definitions.*—(i) *Allocable share of the consolidated group's remaining section 163(j) limitation.*—The term allocable share of the consolidated group's remaining section 163(j) limitation means, with respect to any member of a consolidated group, the product of the consolidated group's remaining section 163(j) limitation and the member's remaining current-year interest ratio.

(ii) *Consolidated group's remaining section 163(j) limitation.*—The term *consolidated group's remaining section 163(j) limitation* means the amount of the consolidated group's section 163(j) limitation calculated pursuant to §1.163(j)-4(d)(2), reduced by the amount of interest deducted by members of the consolidated group pursuant to paragraph (b)(3)(ii)(C)(2) of this section.

(iii) *Remaining current-year interest ratio.*—The term *remaining current-year interest ratio* means, with respect to any member of a consolidated group for a particular taxable year, the ratio of the remaining current-year business interest expense of the member after applying the rule in paragraph (b)(3)(ii)(C)(2) of this section, to the sum of the amounts of remaining current-year business interest expense for all members of the consolidated group after applying the rule in paragraph (b)(3)(ii)(C)(2) of this section.

(b) *Treatment of disallowed business interest expense carryforwards.*— (1) *In general.*—The amount of any business interest expense of a C corporation not allowed as a deduction for any taxable year as a result of the section 163(j) limitation is carried forward to the succeeding taxable year as a disallowed business interest expense carryforward under section 163(j)(2) and §1.163(j)-2(c).

(2) *Deduction of business interest expense.*—For a taxpayer that is a C corporation, current-year business interest expense is deducted in the current taxable year before any disallowed business interest expense carryforwards from a prior taxable year are deducted in that year. Disallowed business interest expense carryforwards are deducted in the order of the taxable years in which they arose, beginning with the earliest taxable year, subject to certain limitations (for example, the limitation under section 382). For purposes of section 163(j), disallowed disqualified interest is treated as carried forward from the taxable year in which a deduction was disallowed under old section 163(j).

(3) *Consolidated groups.*—(i) *In general.*—A consolidated group's disallowed business interest expense carryforwards for the current consolidated return year (the current year) are the carryforwards from the group's prior consolidated return years plus any carryforwards from separate return years.

(ii) *Deduction of business interest expense.*—(A) *General rule.*—All current-year business interest expense of members of a consolidated group is deducted in the current year before any disallowed business interest expense carryforwards from prior taxable years are deducted in the current year. Disallowed business interest expense carryforwards from prior taxable years are deducted in the order of the taxable years in which they arose, beginning with the earliest taxable year, subject to the limitations described in this section.

(B) *Section 163(j) limitation equals or exceeds the current-year business interest expense and disallowed business interest expense carryforwards from prior taxable years.*—If a consolidated group's section 163(j) limitation for the current year equals or exceeds the aggregate amount of its members' current-year business interest expense and disallowed business interest expense carryforwards from prior taxable years that are available for deduction, then none of the current-year business interest expense or disallowed business interest expense carryforwards is subject to disallowance in the current year under section 163(j). However, a deduction for the members' business interest expense may be subject to limitation under other provisions of the Code or the Income Tax Regulations (see, for example, paragraphs (c), (d), (e), and (f) of this section).

(C) *Current-year business interest expense and disallowed business interest expense carryforwards exceed section 163(j) limitation.*—If the aggregate amount of members' current-year business interest expense and disallowed business interest expense carryforwards from prior taxable years exceeds the consolidated group's section 163(j) limitation for the current year, then the following rules apply in the order provided:

(1) The group first determines whether its section 163(j) limitation for the current year equals or exceeds the aggregate amount of the members' current-year business interest expense.

(i) If the group's section 163(j) limitation for the current year equals or exceeds the aggregate amount of the members' current-year business interest expense, then no amount of the group's current-year business interest expense is subject to disallowance in the current year under section 163(j). Once the group has taken into account its members' current-year business interest expense, the group applies the rules of paragraph (b)(3)(ii)(C)(4) of this section.

(ii) If the aggregate amount of members' current-year business interest expense exceeds the group's section 163(j) limitation for the current year, then the group applies the rule in paragraph (b)(3)(ii)(C)(2) of this section.

(2) If this paragraph (b)(3)(ii)(C)(2) applies (see paragraph (b)(3)(ii)(C)(1)(ii) of this section), then each member with current-year business interest expense and with current-year business interest income or floor plan financing interest expense deducts current-year business interest expense in an amount that does not exceed the sum of the member's business interest income and floor plan financing interest expense for the current year.

(3) After applying the rule in paragraph (b)(3)(ii)(C)(2) of this section, if the group has any section 163(j) limitation remaining for the current year, then each member with remaining current-year business interest expense deducts a portion of its expense based on its allocable share of the consolidated group's remaining section 163(j) limitation.

(4) If this paragraph (b)(3)(ii)(C)(4) applies (see paragraph (b)(3)(ii)(C)(1)(i) of this section), and if the group has any section 163(j) limitation remaining for the current year after applying the rules in paragraph (b)(3)(ii)(C)(1) of this section, then disallowed business interest expense carryforwards permitted to be deducted (including under paragraph (d)(1)(A) of this section) in the current year are to be deducted in the order of the taxable years in which they arose, beginning with the earliest taxable year. Disallowed business interest expense carryforwards from taxable years ending on the same date that are available to offset tentative taxable income for the current year generally are to be deducted on a pro rata basis under the principles of paragraph (b)(3)(ii)(C)(3) of this section. For example, assume that P and S are the only members of a consolidated group with a section 163(j) limitation for the current year (Year 2) of $200x; the amount of current-year business interest expense deducted in Year 2 is $100x; and P and S, respectively, have $140x and $60x of disallowed business interest expense carryforwards from Year 1 that are not subject to limitation under paragraph (c), (d), or (e) of this section. Under these facts, P would be allowed to deduct $70x of its carryforwards from Year 1 ($100x x ($140x / ($60x + $140x)) = $70x), and S would be allowed to deduct $30x of its carryforwards from Year 1 ($100x x ($60x / ($60x + $140x)) = $30x). But see §1.383-1(d)(1)(ii), providing that, if losses subject to and not subject to the section 382 limitation are carried from the same taxable year, losses subject to the limitation are deducted before losses not subject to the limitation.

(5) Each member with remaining business interest expense after applying the rules of this paragraph (b)(3)(ii), taking into account the limitations in paragraphs (c), (d), (e), and (f) of this section, carries the expense forward to the succeeding taxable year as a disallowed business interest expense carryforward under section 163(j)(2) and §1.163(j)-2(c).

(iii) *Departure from group.*—If a corporation ceases to be a member during a consolidated return year, the corporation's current-year business interest expense from the taxable period ending on the day of the corporation's change in status as a member, as well as the corporation's disallowed business interest expense carryforwards from prior taxable years that are available to offset tentative taxable income in the consolidated return year, are first made available for deduction during that consolidated return year. See §1.1502-76(b)(1)(i); see also §1.1502-36(d) (regarding reductions of deferred deductions on the transfer of loss shares of subsidiary stock). Only the amount that is neither deducted by the group in that consolidated return year nor otherwise reduced under the Code or regulations may be carried to the corporation's first separate return year after its change in status.

(iv) *Example: Deduction of interest expense.*—(A) *Facts.* (1) P wholly owns A, which is a member of the consolidated group of which P is the common parent. P and A each borrow money from Z, an unrelated third party. The business interest expense of P and A in Years 1, 2, and 3, and the P group's section 163(j) limitation for those years, are as follows:

Table 1 to paragraph (b)(3)(iv)(A)(1)

Year	P's business interest expense	A's business interest expense	P group's section 163(j) limitation
1	$150x	$50x	$100x
2	60x	90x	120x
3	25x	50x	185x

(2) P and A have neither business interest income nor floor plan financing interest expense in Years 1, 2, and 3. Additionally, the P group is neither eligible for the small business exemption in §1.163(j)-2(d) nor engaged in an excepted trade or business.

(B) Analysis—(1) Year 1. In Year 1, the aggregate amount of the P group members' current-year business interest expense ($150x + $50x) exceeds the P group's section 163(j) limitation ($100x). As a result, the rules of paragraph (b)(3)(ii)(C) of this section apply. Because the P group members' current-year business interest expense exceeds the group's section 163(j) limitation for Year 1, P and A must apply the rule in paragraph (b)(3)(ii)(C)(2) of this section. Pursuant to paragraph (b)(3)(ii)(C)(2) of this section, each of P and A must deduct its current-year business interest expense to the extent of its business interest income and floor plan financing interest expense. Neither P nor A has business interest income or floor plan financing interest expense in Year 1. Next, pursuant to paragraph (b)(3)(ii)(C)(3) of this section, each of P and A must deduct a portion of its current-year business interest expense based on its allocable share of the consolidated group's remaining section 163(j) limitation ($100x). P's allocable share is $75x ($100x x ($150x / $200x) = $75x), and A's allocable share is $25x ($100x x ($50x / $200x) = $25x). Accordingly, in Year 1, P deducts $75x of its current-year business interest expense, and A deducts $25x of its current-year business interest expense. P has a disallowed business interest expense carryforward from Year 1 of $75x ($150x - $75x = $75x), and A has a disallowed business interest expense carryforward from Year 1 of $25x ($50x - $25x = $25x).

(2) Year 2. In Year 2, the aggregate amount of the P group members' current-year business interest expense ($60x + $90x) and disallowed business interest expense carryforwards ($75x + $25x) exceeds the P group's section 163(j) limitation ($120x). As a result, the rules of paragraph (b)(3)(ii)(C) of this section apply. Because the P group members' current-year business interest expense exceeds the group's section 163(j) limitation for Year 2, P and A must apply the rule in paragraph (b)(3)(ii)(C)(2) of this section. Pursuant to paragraph (b)(3)(ii)(C)(2) of this section, each of P and A must deduct its current-year business interest expense to the extent of its business interest income and floor plan financing interest expense. Neither P nor A has business interest income or floor plan financing interest expense in Year 2. Next, pursuant to paragraph (b)(3)(ii)(C)(3) of this section, each of P and A must deduct a portion of its current-year business interest expense based on its allocable share of the consolidated group's remaining section 163(j) limitation ($120x). P's allocable share is $48x (($120x x ($60x / $150x)) = $48x), and A's allocable share is $72x (($120x x ($90x / $150x)) = $72x). Accordingly, in Year 2, P deducts $48x of current-year business interest expense, and A deducts $72x of current-year business interest expense. P has a disallowed business interest expense carryforward from Year 2 of $12x ($60x - $48x = $12x), and A has a disallowed business interest expense carryforward from Year 2 of $18x ($90x - $72x = $18x). Additionally, because the P group has no section 163(j) limitation remaining after deducting current-year business interest expense in Year 2, the full amount of P and A's disallowed business interest expense carryforwards from Year 1 ($75x and $25x, respectively) also are carried forward to Year 3. As a result, at the beginning of Year 3, P and A's respective disallowed business interest expense carryforwards are as follows:

Table 2 to paragraph (b)(3)(iv)(B)(2)

	Year 1 disallowed business interest expense carryforwards	Year 2 disallowed business interest expense carryforwards	Total disallowed business interest expense carryforwards
P	$75x	$12x	$87x
A	25x	18x	43x
Total	100x	30x	130x

(3) Year 3. In Year 3, the aggregate amount of the P group members' current-year business interest expense ($25x + $50x = $75x) and disallowed business interest expense carryforwards ($130x) exceeds the P group's section 163(j) limitation ($185x). As a result, the rules of paragraph (b)(3)(ii)(C) of this section apply. Because the P group's section 163(j) limitation for Year 3 equals or exceeds the P group members' current-year business interest expense, no amount of the members' current-year business interest expense is subject to disallowance under section 163(j) (see paragraph (b)(3)(ii)(C)(1) of this section). After each of P and A deducts its current-year business interest expense, the P group has $110x of section 163(j) limitation remaining for Year 3 ($185x - $25x - $50x = $110x). Next, pursuant to paragraph (b)(3)(ii)(C)(4) of this section, $110x of disallowed business interest expense carryforwards are deducted on a pro rata basis, beginning with carryforwards from Year 1. Because the total amount of carryforwards from Year 1 ($100x) is less than the section 163(j) limitation remaining after the deduction of Year 3 business interest expense ($110x), all of the Year 1 carryforwards are deducted in Year 3. After current-year business interest expense and Year 1 carryforwards are deducted, the P group's remaining section 163(j) limitation in Year 3 is $10x. Because the Year 2 carryforwards ($30x) exceed the remaining section 163(j) limitation ($10x), under paragraph (b)(3)(ii)(C)(4) of this section, each of P and A will deduct a portion of its Year 2 carryforwards based on its allocable share of the consolidated group's remaining section 163(j) limitation. P's allocable share is $4x (($10x x ($12x / $30x)) = $4x), and A's allocable share is $6x (($10x x ($18x / $30x)) = $6x). Accordingly, P and A may deduct $4x and $6x, respectively, of their Year 2 carryforwards. For Year 4, P and A have $8x and $12x of disallowed business interest expense carryforwards from Year 2, respectively.

(c) Disallowed business interest expense carryforwards in transactions to which section 381(a) applies.—For rules governing the application of section 381(c)(20) to disallowed business interest expense carryforwards, including limitations on an acquiring corporation's use of the disallowed business interest expense carryforwards of the transferor or distributor corporation in the acquiring corporation's first taxable year ending after the date of distribution or transfer, see §1.381(c)(20)-1.

(d) Limitations on disallowed business interest expense carryforwards from separate return limitation years.—(1) *General rule.*— (A) *Cumulative section 163(j) SRLY limitation.*—This paragraph (d) applies to disallowed business interest expense carryforwards of a member arising in a SRLY (see §1.1502-1(f)) or treated as arising in a SRLY under the principles of §1.1502-21(c) and (g). The amount of the carryforwards described in the preceding sentence that are included in the consolidated group's business interest expense deduc-

tion for any taxable year under paragraph (b) of this section may not exceed the aggregate section 163(j) limitation for all consolidated return years of the group, determined by reference only to the member's items of income, gain, deduction, and loss, and reduced (including below zero) by the member's business interest expense (including disallowed business interest expense carryforwards) absorbed by the group in all consolidated return years (cumulative section 163(j) SRLY limitation). For purposes of computing the member's cumulative section 163(j) SRLY limitation, intercompany items referred to in §1.163(j)-4(d)(2)(iv) are included, with the exception of interest items with regard to intercompany obligations. See §1.163(j)-4(d)(2)(v). Thus, for purposes of this paragraph (d), income and expense items arising from intercompany transactions (other than interest income and expense with regard to intercompany obligations) are included in the calculation of the cumulative section 163(j) SRLY limitation. In addition, items of interest expense with regard to intercompany obligations are not characterized as business interest expense for purposes of the reduction described in the second sentence of this paragraph (d)(1)(A).

(B) *Subgrouping.*—For purposes of this paragraph (d), the SRLY subgroup principles of §1.1502-21(c)(2)(i) (with regard to carryovers of SRLY losses) apply with appropriate adjustments.

(2) *Deduction of disallowed business interest expense carryforwards arising in a SRLY.*—Notwithstanding paragraph (d)(1) of this section, disallowed business interest expense carryforwards of a member arising in a SRLY are available for deduction by the consolidated group in the current year only to the extent the group has remaining section 163(j) limitation for the current year after the deduction of current-year business interest expense and disallowed business interest expense carryforwards from earlier taxable years that are permitted to be deducted in the current year (see paragraph (b)(3)(ii)(A) of this section). SRLY-limited disallowed business interest expense carryforwards are deducted on a pro rata basis (under the principles of paragraph (b)(3)(ii)(C)(3) of this section) with non-SRLY limited disallowed business interest expense carryforwards from taxable years ending on the same date. See also §1.1502-21(b)(1).

(3) *Examples.*—The principles of this paragraph (d) are illustrated by the following examples. For purposes of the examples in this paragraph (d)(3), unless otherwise stated, P, R, S, and T are taxable domestic C corporations that are not RICs or REITs and that file their tax returns on a calendar-year basis; none of P, R, S, or T qualifies for the small business exemption under section 163(j)(3) or is engaged in an excepted trade or business; all interest expense is deductible except for the potential application of section 163(j); and the facts set forth the only corporate activity.

Itemized Deductions for Individuals and Corps.
See p. 20,601 for regulations not amended to reflect law changes
25,333

(i) *Example 1: Determination of SRLY limitation.*—(A) *Facts.* Individual A owns P. In 2021, A forms T, which pays or accrues a $100x business interest expense for which a deduction is disallowed under section 163(j) and that is carried forward to 2022. P does not pay or accrue business interest expense in 2021, and P has no disallowed business interest expense carryforwards from prior taxable years. At the close of 2021, A acquires all of the stock of T, which joins with P in filing a consolidated return beginning in 2022. Neither P nor T pays or accrues business interest expense in 2022, and the P group has a section 163(j) limitation of $300x in that year. This limitation would be $70x if determined by reference solely to T's items for all consolidated return years of the P group.

(B) *Analysis.* T's $100x of disallowed business interest expense carryforwards from 2021 arose in a SRLY. P's acquisition of T was not an ownership change as defined by section 382(g); thus, T's disallowed business interest expense carryforwards are subject to the SRLY limitation in paragraph (d)(1) of this section. T's cumulative section 163(j) SRLY limitation for 2022 is the P group's section 163(j) limitation, determined by reference solely to T's items for all consolidated return years of the P group ($70x). See paragraph (d)(1) of this section. Thus, $70x of T's disallowed business interest expense carryforwards are available to be deducted by the P group in 2022, and the remaining $30x of T's disallowed business interest expense carryforwards are carried forward to 2023. After the P group deducts $70x of T's disallowed business interest expense carryforwards, T's cumulative section 163(j) SRLY limitation is reduced by $70x to $0.

(C) *Cumulative section 163(j) SRLY limitation of $0.* The facts are the same as in *Example 1* in paragraph (d)(3)(i)(A) of this section, except that T's cumulative section 163(j) SRLY limitation for 2022 is $0. Because the amount of T's disallowed business interest expense carryforwards that may be deducted by the P group in 2022 may not exceed T's cumulative section 163(j) SRLY limitation, none of T's carryforwards from 2021 may be deducted by the P group in 2022. Because none of T's disallowed business interest expense carryforwards are absorbed by the P group in 2022, T's cumulative section 163(j) SRLY limitation remains at $0 entering 2023.

(ii) *Example 2: Cumulative section 163(j) SRLY limitation less than zero.*—(A) *Facts.* P and S are the only members of a consolidated group. P has neither current-year business interest expense nor disallowed business interest expense carryforwards. For the current year, the P group has a section 163(j) limitation of $150x, $25x of which is attributable to P, and $125x of which is attributable to S. S has $100x of disallowed business interest expense carryforwards that arose in a SRLY and $150x of current-year business interest expense. S's cumulative section 163(j) SRLY limitation entering the current year (computed by reference solely to S's items for all consolidated return years of the P group) is $0.

(B) *Analysis.* Under paragraph (d)(1) of this section, S's cumulative section 163(j) SRLY limitation is increased by $125x to reflect S's tax items for the current year. The P group's section 163(j) limitation permits the P group to deduct all $150x of S's current-year business interest expense. S's cumulative section 163(j) SRLY limitation is reduced by the $150x of S's business interest expense absorbed by the P group in the current year, which results in a -$25x balance. Thus, none of S's SRLY'd disallowed business interest expense carryforwards may be deducted by the P group in the current year. Entering the subsequent year, S's cumulative section 163(j) SRLY limitation remains -$25x.

(iii) *Example 3: Pro rata absorption of SRLY-limited disallowed business interest expense carryforwards.*—(A) *Facts.* P, R, and S are the only members of a consolidated group, and no member has floor plan financing or business interest income. P has $60x of current-year business interest expense and $40x of disallowed business interest expense carryforwards from the previous year, which was not a separate return year. R has $120x of current-year business interest expense and $80x of disallowed business interest expense carryforwards from the previous year, which was not a separate return year. S has $70x of current-year business interest expense and $30x of disallowed business interest expense carryforwards from the previous year, which was a separate return year. The P group has a section 163(j) limitation of $300x, $50x of which is attributable to P, $90x to R, and $160x to S. S's cumulative section 163(j) SRLY limitation entering the current year (computed by reference solely to S's items for all consolidated return years of the P group) is $0.

Table 3 to paragraph (d)(3)(iii)(A)			
	Current-year business interest expense	Disallowed business interest expense carryforwards from prior taxable year	Section 163(j) limitation
P	$60x	$40x	$50x
R	$120x	$80x	$90x
S	$70x	(SRLY) $30x	$160x
Total	$250x	$150x	$300x

(B) *Analysis.* Under paragraph (d)(1) of this section, S's cumulative section 163(j) SRLY limitation is increased in the current year by $160x. The P group's section 163(j) limitation permits the P group to deduct all $70x of S's current-year business interest expense (and all $180x of P and R's current-year business interest expense). S's cumulative section 163(j) SRLY limitation is reduced by the $70x of S's business interest expense absorbed by the P group in the current year, resulting in a $90x balance. Because the P group has $50x of section 163(j) limitation remaining after the absorption of current-year business interest expense, the P group can absorb $50x of its members' disallowed business interest expense carryforwards. Under paragraph (d)(2) of this section, SRLY-limited disallowed business interest expense carryforwards are deducted on a pro rata basis with other disallowed business interest expense carryforwards from the same taxable year. Accordingly, the P group can deduct $10x ($50x x ($30x / $150x)) of S's SRLY-limited disallowed business interest expense carryforwards. S's cumulative section 163(j) SRLY limitation is reduced (to $80x) by the $10x of SRLY-limited disallowed business interest carryforwards absorbed by the P group in the current year.

(C) *Cumulative section 163(j) SRLY limitation of -$75x.* The facts are the same as in *Example 3* in paragraph (d)(3)(iii)(A) of this section, except that S's cumulative section 163(j) SRLY limitation entering the current year is -$75x. After adjusting for S's tax items for the current year ($160x) and the P group's absorption of S's current-year business interest expense ($70x), S's cumulative section 163(j) SRLY limitation is $15x (-$75x + $160x - $70x). Because S's cumulative section 163(j) SRLY limitation ($15x) is less than the amount of S's SRLY-limited disallowed business interest expense carryforwards ($30x), the pro rata calculation under paragraph (d)(2) of this section is applied to $15x (rather than $30x) of S's carryforwards. Accordingly, the P group can deduct $5.56x ($50x x ($15x / $135x)) of S's SRLY-limited disallowed business interest expense carryforwards. S's cu-

mulative section 163(j) SRLY limitation is reduced (to $9.44x) by the $5.56x of SRLY-limited disallowed business interest carryforwards absorbed by the P group in the current year.

(e) *Application of section 382.*—(1) *Pre-change loss.*—For rules governing the treatment of a disallowed business interest expense as a pre-change loss for purposes of section 382, see §§ 1.382-2(a) and 1.382-6. For rules governing the application of section 382 to disallowed disqualified interest carryforwards, see § 1.163(j)-11(c)(4).

(2) *Loss corporation.*—For rules governing when a disallowed business interest expense causes a corporation to be a loss corporation within the meaning of section 382(k)(1), see § 1.382-2(a). For the application of section 382 to disallowed disqualified interest carryforwards, see § 1.163(j)-11(c)(4).

(3) *Ordering rules for utilization of pre-change losses and for absorption of the section 382 limitation.*—For ordering rules for the utilization of disallowed business interest expense, net operating losses, and other pre-change losses, and for the absorption of the section 382 limitation, see § 1.383-1(d).

(4) *Disallowed business interest expense from the pre-change period in the year of a testing date.*—For rules governing the treatment of disallowed business interest expense from the pre-change period (within the meaning of § 1.382-6(g)(2)) in the year of a testing date, see § 1.382-2.

(5) *Recognized built-in loss.*—For a rule providing that a section 382 disallowed business interest carryforward (as defined in § 1.382-2(a)(7)) is not treated as a recognized built-in loss for purposes of section 382, see § 1.382-7(d)(5).

(f) *Overlap of SRLY limitation with section 382.*—For rules governing the overlap of the application of section 382 and the application of the SRLY rules, see § 1.1502-21(g).

(g) *Additional limitations.*—Additional rules provided under the Code or regulations also apply to limit the use of disallowed business interest expense carryforwards. For rules governing the relationship between section 163(j) and other provisions affecting the deductibility of interest, see § 1.163(j)-3.

(h) *Applicability date.*—This section applies to taxable years beginning on or after November 13, 2020. However, taxpayers and their related parties, within the meaning of sections 267(b) and 707(b)(1), may choose to apply the rules of this section to a taxable year beginning after December 31, 2017, so long as the taxpayers and their related parties consistently apply the rules of the section 163(j) regulations, and, if applicable, §§ 1.263A-9, 1.263A-15, 1.381(c)(20)-1, 1.382-1, 1.382-2, 1.382-5, 1.382-6, 1.382-7, 1.383-0, 1.383-1, 1.469-9, 1.469-11, 1.704-1, 1.882-5, 1.1362-3, 1.1368-1, 1.1377-1, 1.1502-13, 1.1502-21, 1.1502-36, 1.1502-79, 1.1502-91 through 1.1502-99 (to the extent they effectuate the rules of §§ 1.382-2, 1.382-5, 1.382-6, and 1.383-1), and 1.1504-4, to that taxable year. [Reg. § 1.163(j)-5.]

☐ [*T.D.* 9905, 9-3-2020.]

[Reg. § 1.163(j)-6]

§ 1.163(j)-6. Application of the section 163(j) limitation to partnerships and subchapter S corporations.—(a) *Overview.*—If a deduction for business interest expense of a partnership or an S corporation is subject to the section 163(j) limitation, section 163(j)(4) provides that the section 163(j) limitation applies at the partnership or S corporation level and any deduction for business interest expense is taken into account in determining the nonseparately stated taxable income or loss of the partnership or S corporation. Once a partnership or an S corporation determines its business interest expense, business interest income, ATI, and floor plan financing interest expense, the partnership or S corporation calculates its section 163(j) limitation by applying the rules of § 1.163(j)-2(b) and this section. Paragraph (b) of this section provides definitions used in this section. Paragraph (c) of this section provides rules regarding the character of a partnership's deductible business interest expense and excess business interest expense. Paragraph (d) of this section provides rules regarding the calculation of a partnership's ATI and floor plan financing interest expense. Paragraph (e) of this section provides rules regarding a partner's ATI and business interest income. Paragraph (f) of this section provides an eleven-step computation necessary for properly allocating a partnership's deductible business interest expense and section 163(j) excess items to its partners. Paragraph (g) of this section applies carryforward rules at the partner level if a partnership has excess business interest expense. Paragraph (h) of this section provides basis adjustment rules, and paragraph (k) of this section provides rules regarding investment items of a partnership. Paragraph (l) of this section provides rules regarding S corporations. Paragraph (m) of this section provides rules for partnerships and S corporations not subject to section 163(j). Paragraph (o) of this section provides examples illustrating the rules of this section.

(b) *Definitions.*—In addition to the definitions contained in § 1.163(j)-1, the following definitions apply for purposes of this section.

(1) *Section 163(j) items.*—The term *section 163(j) items* means the partnership or S corporation's business interest expense, business interest income, and items comprising ATI.

(2) *Partner basis items.*—The term *partner basis items* means any items of income, gain, loss, or deduction resulting from either an adjustment to the basis of partnership property used in a non-excepted trade or business made pursuant to section 743(b) or the operation of section 704(c)(1)(C)(i) with respect to such property. Partner basis items also include section 743(b) basis adjustments used to increase or decrease a partner's share of partnership gain or loss on the sale of partnership property used in a non-excepted trade or business (as described in § 1.743-1(j)(3)(i)) and amounts resulting from the operation of section 704(c)(1)(C)(i) used to decrease a partner's share of partnership gain or increase a partner's share of partnership loss on the sale of such property.

(3) *Remedial items.*—The term *remedial items* means any allocation to a partner of remedial items of income, gain, loss, or deduction pursuant to section 704(c) and § 1.704-3(d).

(4) *Excess business interest income.*—The term *excess business interest income* means the amount by which a partnership's or S corporation's business interest income exceeds its business interest expense in a taxable year.

(5) *Deductible business interest expense.*—The term *deductible business interest expense* means the amount of a partnership's or S corporation's business interest expense that is deductible under section 163(j) in the current taxable year following the application of the limitation contained in § 1.163(j)-2(b).

(6) *Section 163(j) excess items.*—The term *section 163(j) excess items* means the partnership's excess business interest expense, excess taxable income, and excess business interest income.

(7) *Non-excepted assets.*—The term *non-excepted assets* means assets from a non-excepted trade or business.

(8) *Excepted assets.*—The term *excepted assets* means assets from an excepted trade or business.

(c) *Business interest income and business interest expense of a partnership.*—(1) *Modification of business interest income for partnerships.*—The business interest income of a partnership generally is determined in accordance with § 1.163(j)-1(b)(4). However, to the extent that interest income of a partnership that is properly allocable to trades or businesses that are per se non-passive activities is allocated to partners that do not materially participate (within the meaning of section 469), as described in § 1.469-1T(e)(6) and subject to section 163(d)(5)(A)(ii), such interest income shall not be considered business interest income for purposes of determining the section 163(j) limitation of a partnership pursuant to § 1.163(j)-2(b). A per se non-passive activity is an activity that is not treated as a passive activity for purposes of section 469 regardless of whether the owners of the activity materially participate in the activity.

(2) *Modification of business interest expense for partnerships.*—The business interest expense of a partnership generally is determined in accordance with § 1.163(j)-1(b)(3). However, to the extent that interest expense of a partnership that is properly allocable to trades or businesses that are per se non-passive activities is allocated to partners that do not materially participate (within the meaning of section 469), as described in § 1.469-1T(e)(6) and subject to section 163(d)(5)(A)(ii), such interest expense shall not be considered business interest expense for purposes of determining the section 163(j) limitation of a partnership pursuant to § 1.163(j)-2(b).

(3) *Transition rule.*—With respect to a partner in a partnership engaged in a trade or business described in § 1.469-1T(e)(6) and subject to section 163(d)(5)(A)(ii), if such partner had been allocated EBIE from the partnership with respect to the trade or business described in § 1.469-1T(e)(6) and subject to section 163(d)(5)(A)(ii) in any prior taxable year in which the partner did not materially participate, such partner may treat such excess business interest expense not previously treated as paid or accrued under § 1.163(j)-6(g)(2) as paid or accrued by the partner in the first taxable year ending on or after the effective date of the final regulations in accordance with § 1.163(j)-6(g)(2)(i) without regard to the amount of excess taxable income or excess business interest income that may be allocated by the partnership from the partnership to the partner in the first taxable year ending on or after the effective date of these regulations.

(4) *Character of business interest expense.*—If a partnership has deductible business interest expense, such deductible business interest expense is not subject to any additional application of section 163(j) at the partner-level because it is taken into account in determining the nonseparately stated taxable income or loss of the partnership. However, for all other purposes of the Code, deductible business interest expense and excess business interest expense retain their character as business interest expense at the partner-level. For example, for purposes of section 469, such business interest expense retains its character as either passive or non-passive in the hands of the partner. Additionally, for purposes of section 469, deductible business interest expense and excess business interest expense from a partnership remain interest derived from a trade or business in the hands of a partner even if the partner does not materially participate in the partnership's trade or business activity. For additional rules regarding the interaction between sections 465, 469, and 163(j), see § 1.163(j)-3.

(d) *Adjusted taxable income of a partnership.*—(1) *Tentative taxable income of a partnership.*—For purposes of computing a partnership's ATI under § 1.163(j)-1(b)(1), the tentative taxable income of a partnership is the partnership's taxable income determined under section 703(a), but computed without regard to the application of the section 163(j) limitation.

(2) *Section 734(b), partner basis items, and remedial items.*—A partnership takes into account items resulting from adjustments made to the basis of its property pursuant to section 734(b) for purposes of calculating its ATI pursuant to § 1.163(j)-1(b)(1). However, partner basis items and remedial items are not taken into account in determining a partnership's ATI under § 1.163(j)-1(b)(1). Instead, partner basis items and remedial items are taken into account by the partner in determining the partner's ATI pursuant to § 1.163(j)-1(b)(1). See *Example 6* in paragraph (o)(6) of this section.

(3) *Section 743(b) adjustments and publicly traded partnerships.*—Solely for purposes of § 1.163(j)-6, a publicly traded partnership, as

defined in §1.7704-1, shall treat the amount of any section 743(b) adjustment of a purchaser of a partnership unit that relates to a remedial item that the purchaser inherits from the seller as an offset to the related section 704(c) remedial item. For this purpose, §1.163(j)-6(e)(2)(ii) applies. See *Example 25* in paragraph (o)(25) of this section.

(4) *Modification of adjusted taxable income for partnerships.*—The adjusted taxable income of a partnership generally is determined in accordance with §1.163(j)-1(b)(1). However, to the extent that the items comprising the adjusted taxable income of a partnership that are properly allocable to trades or businesses that are per se non-passive activities are allocated to partners that do not materially participate (within the meaning of section 469), as described in section 163(d)(5)(A)(ii), such partnership items shall not be considered adjusted taxable income for purposes of determining the section 163(j) limitation of a partnership pursuant to §1.163(j)-2(b).

(5) *Election to use 2019 adjusted taxable income for taxable years beginning in 2020.*—In the case of any taxable year beginning in 2020, a partnership may elect to apply this section by substituting its adjusted taxable income for the last taxable year beginning in 2019 for the adjusted taxable income for such taxable year (post-election ATI or 2019 ATI). See §1.163(j)-2(b)(4) for the time and manner of making or revoking this election. An electing partnership determines each partner's allocable ATI (as defined in paragraph (f)(2)(ii) of this section) by using the partnership's 2019 section 704 income, gain, loss, and deduction as though such amounts were recognized by the partnership in 2020. See *Example 34* in paragraph (o)(34) of this section.

(e) *Adjusted taxable income and business interest income of partners.*—(1) *Modification of adjusted taxable income for partners.*—The ATI of a partner in a partnership generally is determined in accordance with §1.163(j)-1(b)(1), without regard to such partner's distributive share of any items of income, gain, deduction, or loss of such partnership, except as provided for in paragraph (m) of this section, and is increased by such partner's distributive share of such partnership's excess taxable income determined under paragraph (f) of this section. For rules regarding corporate partners, see §1.163(j)-4(b)(3).

(2) *Partner basis items and remedial items.*—Partner basis items and remedial items are taken into account as items derived directly by the partner in determining the partner's ATI for purposes of the partner's section 163(j) limitation. If a partner is allocated remedial items, such partner's ATI is increased or decreased by the amount of such items. Additionally, to the extent a partner is allocated partner basis items, such partner's ATI is increased or decreased by the amount of such items. See *Example 6* in paragraph (o)(6) of this section.

(3) *Disposition of partnership interests.*—If a partner recognizes gain or loss upon the disposition of interests in a partnership, and the partnership in which the interest is being disposed owns only non-excepted trade or business assets, the gain or loss on the disposition of the partnership interest is included in the partner's ATI. See §1.163(j)-10(b)(4)(ii) for dispositions of interests in partnerships that own—

(i) Non-excepted assets and excepted assets; or

(ii) Investment assets; or

(iii) Both.

(4) *Double counting of business interest income and floor plan financing interest expense prohibited.*—For purposes of calculating a partner's section 163(j) limitation, the partner does not include—

(i) Business interest income from a partnership that is subject to section 163(j), except to the extent the partner is allocated excess business interest income from that partnership pursuant to paragraph (f)(2) of this section; and

(ii) The partner's allocable share of the partnership's floor plan financing interest expense, because such floor plan financing interest expense already has been taken into account by the partnership in determining its nonseparately stated taxable income or loss for purposes of section 163(j).

(5) *Partner basis items, remedial items, and publicly traded partnerships.*—Solely for purposes of §1.163(j)-6, a publicly traded partnership, as defined in §1.7704-1, shall either allocate gain that would otherwise be allocated under section 704(c) based on a partner's section 704(b) sharing ratios, or, for purposes of allocating cost recovery deductions under section 704(c), determine a partner's remedial items, as defined in §1.163(j)-6(b)(3), based on an allocation of the partnership's asset basis (inside basis) items among its partners in proportion to their share of corresponding section 704(b) items (rather than applying the traditional method, described in §1.704-3(b)). See *Example 24* in paragraph (o)(24) of this section.

(f) *Allocation and determination of section 163(j) excess items made in the same manner as nonseparately stated taxable income or loss of the partnership.*—(1) *Overview.*—(i) *In general.*—The purpose of this paragraph is to provide guidance regarding how a partnership must allocate its deductible business interest expense and section 163(j) excess items, if any, among its partners. For purposes of section 163(j)(4) and this section, allocations and determinations of deductible business interest expense and section 163(j) excess items are considered made in the same manner as the nonseparately stated taxable income or loss of the partnership if, and only if, such allocations and determinations are made in accordance with the eleven-step computation set forth in paragraphs (f)(2)(i) through (xi) of this section. A partnership first determines its section 163(j) limitation, total amount of deductible business interest expense, and section 163(j) excess items under paragraph (f)(2)(i) of this section. The partnership then applies paragraphs (f)(2)(ii) through (xi) of this section, in that order, to determine how those items of the partnership are allocated among its partners. At the conclusion of the eleven-step computation set forth in paragraphs (f)(2)(i) through (xi) of this section, the total amount of deductible business interest expense and section 163(j) excess items allocated to each partner will equal the partnership's total amount of deductible business interest expense and section 163(j) excess items.

(ii) *Relevance solely for purposes of section 163(j).*—No rule set forth in paragraph (f)(2) of this section prohibits a partnership from making an allocation to a partner of any item of partnership income, gain, loss, or deduction that is otherwise permitted under section 704 and the regulations under section 704 of the Code. Accordingly, any calculations in paragraphs (f)(2)(i) through (xi) of this section are solely for the purpose of determining each partner's deductible business interest expense and section 163(j) excess items and do not otherwise affect any other provision under the Code, such as section 704(b). Additionally, floor plan financing interest expense is not allocated in accordance with paragraph (f)(2) of this section. Instead, floor plan financing interest expense of a partnership is allocated to its partners under section 704(b) and is taken into account as a nonseparately stated item of loss for purposes of section 163(j).

(iii) *Exception applicable to publicly traded partnerships.*—Publicly traded partnerships, as defined in §1.7704-1, do not apply the rules in paragraph (f)(2) of this section to determine a partner's share of section 163(j) excess items. Rather, publicly traded partnerships determine a partner's share of section 163(j) excess items by applying the same percentage used to determine the partner's share of the corresponding section 704(b) items that comprise ATI.

(2) *Steps for allocating deductible business interest expense and section 163(j) excess items.*—(i) *Partnership-level calculation required by section 163(j)(4)(A).*—First, a partnership must determine its section 163(j) limitation pursuant to §1.163(j)-2(b). This calculation determines a partnership's total amounts of excess business interest income, excess taxable income, excess business interest expense (that is, the partnership's section 163(j) excess items), and deductible business interest expense under section 163(j) for a taxable year.

(ii) *Determination of each partner's relevant section 163(j) items.*—Second, a partnership must determine each partner's allocable share of each section 163(j) item under section 704(b) and the regulations under section 704 of the Code, including any allocations under section 704(c), other than remedial items. Only section 163(j) items that were actually taken into account in the partnership's section 163(j) calculation under paragraph (f)(2)(i) of this section are taken into account for purposes of this paragraph (f)(2)(ii). Partner basis items, allocations of investment income and expense, remedial items, and amounts determined for the partner under §1.163-8T are not taken into account for purposes of this paragraph (f)(2)(ii). For purposes of paragraphs (f)(2)(ii) through (xi) of this section, the term *allocable ATI* means a partner's distributive share of the partnership's ATI (that is, a partner's distributive share of gross income and gain items comprising ATI less such partner's distributive share of gross loss and deduction items comprising ATI), the term *allocable business interest income* means a partner's distributive share of the partnership's business interest income, and the term *allocable business interest expense* means a partner's distributive share of the partnership's business interest expense that is not floor plan financing interest expense. If the partnership determines that each partner has a pro rata share of allocable ATI, allocable business interest income, and allocable business interest expense, then the partnership may bypass paragraphs (f)(2)(iii) through (xi) of this section and allocate its section 163(j) excess items in the same proportion. See *Example 1* through *Example 16* in paragraphs (o)(1) through (16), respectively. This pro-rata exception does not result in allocations of section 163(j) excess items that vary from the array of allocations of section 163(j) excess items that would have resulted had paragraphs (f)(2)(iii) through (xi) been applied.

(iii) *Partner-level comparison of business interest income and business interest expense.*—Third, a partnership must compare each partner's allocable business interest income to such partner's allocable business interest expense. Paragraphs (f)(2)(iii) through (v) of this section determine how a partnership must allocate its excess business interest income among its partners, as well as the amount of each partner's allocable business interest expense that is not deductible business interest expense after taking the partnership's business interest income into account. To the extent a partner's allocable business interest income exceeds its allocable business interest expense, the partner has an *allocable business interest income excess*. The aggregate of all the partners' allocable business interest income excess amounts is the *total allocable business interest income excess*. To the extent a partner's allocable business interest expense exceeds its allocable business interest income, the partner has an *allocable business interest income deficit*. The aggregate of all the partners' allocable business interest income deficit amounts is the *total allocable business interest income deficit*. These amounts are required to perform calculations in paragraphs (f)(2)(iv) and (v) of this section, which appropriately reallocate allocable business interest income excess to partners with allocable business interest income deficits in order to reconcile the partner-level calculation under paragraph (f)(2)(iii) of this section with the partnership-level result under paragraph (f)(2)(i) of this section.

(iv) *Matching partnership and aggregate partner excess business interest income.*—Fourth, a partnership must determine each partner's final allocable business interest income excess. A partner's *final allocable business interest income excess* is determined by reducing, but not below zero, such partner's allocable business interest income excess (if any) by the partner's step four adjustment amount. A partner's *step four adjustment amount* is the product of the total allocable business interest income deficit and the ratio of such partner's allocable business interest income excess to the total allocable business interest income excess. The rules of this paragraph (f)(2)(iv) ensure that, following the application of paragraph (f)(2)(xi) of this section, the aggregate of all the partners' allocations of excess business interest income equals the total amount of the partnership's excess business interest income as determined in paragraph (f)(2)(i) of this section.

(v) *Remaining business interest expense determination.*—Fifth, a partnership must determine each partner's remaining business interest expense. A partner's *remaining business interest expense* is determined by reducing, but not below zero, such partner's allocable business interest income deficit (if any) by such partner's step five adjustment amount. A partner's *step five adjustment amount* is the product of the total allocable business interest income excess and the ratio of such partner's allocable business interest income deficit to the total allocable business interest income deficit. Generally, a partner's remaining business interest expense is a partner's allocable business interest income deficit adjusted to reflect a reallocation of allocable business interest income excess from other partners. Determining a partner's remaining business interest expense is necessary to perform an ATI calculation that begins in paragraph (f)(2)(vii) of this section.

(vi) *Determination of final allocable ATI.*—Sixth, a partnership must determine each partner's final allocable ATI. Paragraphs (f)(2)(vi) through (x) of this section determine how a partnership must allocate its excess taxable income and excess business interest expense among its partners.

(A) *Positive allocable ATI.*—To the extent a partner's income and gain items comprising its allocable ATI exceed its deduction and loss items comprising its allocable ATI, the partner has *positive allocable ATI*. The aggregate of all the partners' positive allocable ATI amounts is the *total positive allocable ATI*.

(B) *Negative allocable ATI.*—To the extent a partner's deduction and loss items comprising its allocable ATI exceed its income and gain items comprising its allocable ATI, the partner has negative allocable ATI. The aggregate of all the partners' negative allocable ATI amounts is the *total negative allocable ATI*.

(C) *Final allocable ATI.*—Any partner with a negative allocable ATI, or an allocable ATI of $0, has a positive allocable ATI of $0. Any partner with a positive allocable ATI of $0 has a final allocable ATI of $0. The final allocable ATI of any partner with a positive allocable ATI greater than $0 is such partner's positive allocable ATI reduced, but not below zero, by the partner's step six adjustment amount. A partner's *step six adjustment amount* is the product of the total negative allocable ATI and the ratio of such partner's positive allocable ATI to the total positive allocable ATI. The total of the partners' final allocable ATI amounts must equal the partnership's ATI amount used to compute its section 163(j) limitation pursuant to §1.163(j)-2(b).

(vii) *Partner-level comparison of 30 percent of adjusted taxable income and remaining business interest expense.*—Seventh, a partnership must compare each partner's ATI capacity to such partner's remaining business interest expense as determined under paragraph (f)(2)(v) of this section. A partner's *ATI capacity* is the amount that is 30 percent of such partner's final allocable ATI as determined under paragraph (f)(2)(vi) of this section. A partner's final allocable ATI is grossed down to 30 percent prior to being compared to its remaining business interest expense in this calculation to parallel the partnership's adjustment to its ATI under section 163(j)(1)(B). To the extent a partner's ATI capacity exceeds its remaining business interest expense, the partner has an *ATI capacity excess*. The aggregate of all the partners' ATI capacity excess amounts is the *total ATI capacity excess*. To the extent a partner's remaining business interest expense exceeds its ATI capacity, the partner has an *ATI capacity deficit*. The aggregate of all the partners' ATI capacity deficit amounts is the *total ATI capacity deficit*. These amounts (which may be subject to adjustment under paragraph (f)(2)(viii) of this section) are required to perform calculations in paragraphs (f)(2)(ix) and (x) of this section, which appropriately reallocate ATI capacity excess to partners with ATI capacity deficits in order to reconcile the partner-level calculation under paragraph (f)(2)(vii) of this section with the partnership-level result under paragraph (f)(2)(i) of this section.

(viii) *Partner priority right to ATI capacity excess determination.*—(A) Eighth, the partnership must determine whether it is required to make any adjustments described in this paragraph (f)(2)(viii) and, if it is, make such adjustments. The rules of this paragraph (f)(2)(viii) are necessary to account for adjustments made to a partner's allocable ATI in paragraph (f)(2)(vi) of this section to ensure that the partners who had a negative allocable ATI do not inappropriately benefit under the rules of paragraphs (f)(2)(ix) through (xi) of this section to the detriment of the partners who had positive allocable ATI. The partnership must perform the calculations and make the necessary adjustments described under paragraphs (f)(2)(viii)(B) and (C) or paragraph (f)(2)(viii)(D) of this section if, and only if, there is—

(1) An excess business interest expense amount greater than $0 under paragraph (f)(2)(i) of this section;

(2) A total negative allocable ATI amount greater than $0 under paragraph (f)(2)(vi) of this section; and

(3) A total ATI capacity excess amount greater than $0 under paragraph (f)(2)(vii) of this section.

(B) A partnership must determine each partner's priority amount and usable priority amount. A partner's *priority amount* is 30 percent of the amount by which a partner's positive allocable ATI under paragraph (f)(2)(vi)(A) of this section exceeds such partner's final allocable ATI under paragraph (f)(2)(vi)(C) of this section. However, only partners with an ATI capacity deficit as determined under paragraph (f)(2)(vii) of this section can have a priority amount greater than $0. The aggregate of all the partners' priority amounts is the *total priority amount*. A partner's *usable priority amount* is the lesser of such partner's priority amount or such partner's ATI capacity deficit as determined under paragraph (f)(2)(vii) of this section. The aggregate of all the partners' usable priority amounts is the *total usable priority amount*. If the total ATI capacity excess amount, as determined under paragraph (f)(2)(vii) of this section, is greater than or equal to the total usable priority amount, then the partnership must perform the adjustments described in paragraph (f)(2)(viii)(C) of this section. If the total usable priority amount is greater than the total ATI capacity excess amount, as determined under paragraph (f)(2)(vii) of this section, then the partnership must perform the adjustments described in paragraph (f)(2)(viii)(D) of this section.

(C) For purposes of paragraph (f)(2)(ix) of this section, each partner's final ATI capacity excess amount is $0. For purposes of paragraph (f)(2)(x) of this section, the following terms have the following meanings for each partner:

(1) Each partner's *ATI capacity deficit* is such partner's ATI capacity deficit as determined under paragraph (f)(2)(vii) of this section, reduced by such partner's usable priority amount.

(2) The *total ATI capacity deficit* is the total ATI capacity deficit as determined under paragraph (f)(2)(vii) of this section, reduced by the total usable priority amount.

(3) The *total ATI capacity excess* is the total ATI capacity excess as determined under paragraph (f)(2)(vii) of this section, reduced by the total usable priority amount.

(D) Any partner with a priority amount greater than $0 is a *priority partner*. Any partner that is not a priority partner is a *non-priority partner*. For purposes of paragraph (f)(2)(ix) of this section, each partner's final ATI capacity excess amount is $0. For purposes of paragraph (f)(2)(x) of this section, each non-priority partner's final ATI capacity deficit amount is such partner's ATI capacity deficit as determined under paragraph (f)(2)(vii) of this section. For purposes of paragraph (f)(2)(x) of this section, the following terms have the following meanings for priority partners.

Itemized Deductions for Individuals and Corps.
See p. 20,601 for regulations not amended to reflect law changes
25,337

(1) Each priority partner must determine its step eight excess share. A partner's *step eight excess share* is the product of the total ATI capacity excess as determined under paragraph (f)(2)(vii) of this section and the ratio of the partner's priority amount to the total priority amount.

(2) To the extent a priority partner's step eight excess share exceeds its ATI capacity deficit as determined under paragraph (f)(2)(vii) of this section, such excess amount is the priority partner's *ATI capacity excess* for purposes of paragraph (f)(2)(x) of this section. The *total ATI capacity excess* is the aggregate of the priority partners' ATI capacity excess amounts as determined under this paragraph (f)(2)(viii)(D)(2).

(3) To the extent a priority partner's ATI capacity deficit as determined under paragraph (f)(2)(vii) of this section exceeds its step eight excess share, such excess amount is the priority partner's *ATI capacity deficit* for purposes of paragraph (f)(2)(x) of this section. The *total ATI capacity deficit* is the aggregate of the priority partners' ATI capacity deficit amounts as determined under this paragraph (f)(2)(viii)(D)(3).

(ix) *Matching partnership and aggregate partner excess taxable income.*—Ninth, a partnership must determine each partner's final ATI capacity excess. A partner's *final ATI capacity excess* amount is determined by reducing, but not below zero, such partner's ATI capacity excess (if any) by the partner's step nine adjustment amount. A partner's *step nine adjustment amount* is the product of the total ATI capacity deficit and the ratio of such partner's ATI capacity excess to the total ATI capacity excess. The rules of this paragraph (f)(2)(ix) ensure that, following the application of paragraph (f)(2)(xi) of this section, the aggregate of all the partners' allocations of excess taxable income equals the total amount of the partnership's excess taxable income as determined in paragraph (f)(2)(i) of this section.

(x) *Matching partnership and aggregate partner excess business interest expense.*—Tenth, a partnership must determine each partner's final ATI capacity deficit. A partner's *final ATI capacity deficit* amount is determined by reducing, but not below zero, such partner's ATI capacity deficit (if any) by the partner's step ten adjustment amount. A partner's *step ten adjustment amount* is the product of the total ATI capacity excess and the ratio of such partner's ATI capacity deficit to the total ATI capacity deficit. Generally, a partner's final ATI capacity deficit is a partner's ATI capacity deficit adjusted to reflect a reallocation of ATI capacity excess from other partners. The rules of this paragraph (f)(2)(x) ensure that, following the application of paragraph (f)(2)(xi) of this section, the aggregate of all the partners' allocations of excess business interest expense equals the total amount of the partnership's excess business interest expense as determined in paragraph (f)(2)(i) of this section.

(xi) *Final section 163(j) excess item and deductible business interest expense allocation.*—Eleventh, a partnership must allocate section 163(j) excess items and deductible business interest expense to its partners. Excess business interest income calculated under paragraph (f)(2)(i) of this section, if any, is allocated dollar for dollar by the partnership to its partners with final allocable business interest income excess amounts. Excess business interest expense calculated under paragraph (f)(2)(i) of this section, if any, is allocated dollar for dollar to partners with final ATI capacity deficit amounts. After grossing up each partner's final ATI capacity excess amount by ten-thirds, excess taxable income calculated under paragraph (f)(2)(i) of this section, if any, is allocated dollar for dollar to partners with final ATI capacity excess amounts. A partner's allocable business interest expense is deductible business interest expense to the extent it exceeds such partner's share of excess business interest expense. See *Example 17* through *Example 21* in paragraphs (o)(17) through (21) of this section, respectively.

(g) *Carryforwards.*—(1) *In general.*—The amount of any business interest expense not allowed as a deduction to a partnership by reason of § 1.163(j)-2(b) and paragraph (f)(2) of this section for any taxable year is—

(i) Not treated as business interest expense of the partnership in the succeeding taxable year; and

(ii) Subject to paragraph (g)(2) of this section, treated as excess *business interest expense,* which is allocated to each partner pursuant to paragraph (f)(2) of this section.

(2) *Treatment of excess business interest expense allocated to partners.*—If a partner is allocated excess business interest expense from a partnership under paragraph (f)(2) of this section for any taxable year and the excess business interest expense is treated as such under paragraph (h)(2) of this section—

(i) Solely for purposes of section 163(j), such excess business interest expense is treated as business interest expense paid or accrued by the partner in the next succeeding taxable year in which the partner is allocated excess taxable income or excess business interest

income from such partnership, but only to the extent of such excess taxable income or excess business interest income; and

(ii) Any portion of such excess business interest expense remaining after the application of paragraph (g)(2)(i) of this section is excess business interest expense that is subject to the limitations of paragraph (g)(2)(i) of this section in succeeding taxable years, unless paragraph (m)(3) of this section applies. See *Example 1* through *Example 16* in paragraphs (o)(1) through (16) of this section, respectively.

(3) *Excess taxable income and excess business interest income ordering rule.*—In the event a partner has excess business interest expense from a prior taxable year and is allocated excess taxable income or excess business interest income from the same partnership in a succeeding taxable year, the partner must treat, for purposes of section 163(j), the excess business interest expense as business interest expense paid or accrued by the partner in an amount equal to the partner's share of the partnership's excess taxable income or excess business interest income in such succeeding taxable year. See *Example 2* through *Example 16* in paragraphs (o)(2) through (16) of this section, respectively.

(4) *Special rule for taxable years beginning in 2019 and 2020.*—In the case of any excess business interest expense of a partnership for any taxable year beginning in 2019 that is allocated to a partner under paragraph (f)(2) of this section, 50 percent of such excess business interest expense (§ 1.163(j)-6(g)(4) business interest expense) is treated as business interest expense that, notwithstanding paragraph (g)(2) of this section, is paid or accrued by the partner in the partner's first taxable year beginning in 2020. Additionally, § 1.163(j)-6(g)(4) business interest expense is not subject to the section 163(j) limitation at the level of the partner. For purposes of paragraph (h)(1) of this section, any § 1.163(j)-6(g)(4) business interest expense is, similar to deductible business interest expense, taken into account before any excess business interest expense. This paragraph applies after paragraph (n) of this section. If a partner disposes of a partnership interest in the partnership's 2019 or 2020 taxable year, § 1.163(j)-6(g)(4) business interest expense is deductible by the partner (to the extent that the partner has basis to deduct such expense under section 704(d) immediately prior to the disposition) and thus does not result in a basis increase under paragraph (h)(3) of this section. See *Example 35* and *Example 36* in paragraphs (o)(35) and (o)(36), respectively, of this section. A partner may elect to not have this provision apply with respect to each partnership interest held by the partner on an interest by interest basis. The rules and procedures regarding the time and manner of making, or revoking, such an election are provided in Revenue Procedure 2020-22, 2020-18 I.R.B. 745, and may be further modified through other guidance (see § § 601.601(d) and 601.602 of this chapter).

(h) *Basis adjustments.*—(1) *Section 704(d) ordering.*—Deductible business interest expense and excess business interest expense are subject to section 704(d). If a partner is subject to a limitation on loss under section 704(d) and a partner is allocated losses from a partnership in a taxable year, § 1.704-1(d)(2) requires that the limitation on losses under section 704(d) be apportioned amongst these losses based on the character of each loss (each grouping of losses based on character being a *section 704(d) loss class*). If there are multiple section 704(d) loss classes in a given year, § 1.704-1(d)(2) requires the partner to apportion the limitation on losses under section 704(d) to each section 704(d) loss class proportionately. For purposes of applying this proportionate rule, any deductible business interest expense and business interest expense of an exempt entity (whether allocated to the partner in the current taxable year or suspended under section 704(d) in a prior taxable year), any excess business interest expense allocated to the partner in the current taxable year, and any excess business interest expense from a prior taxable year that was suspended under section 704(d) (negative section 163(j) expense) shall comprise the same section 704(d) loss class. Once the partner determines the amount of limitation on losses apportioned to this section 704(d) loss class, any deductible business interest expense is taken into account before any excess business interest expense or negative section 163(j) expense. See *Example 7* in paragraph (o)(7) of this section.

(2) *Excess business interest expense basis adjustments.*—The adjusted basis of a partner in a partnership interest is reduced, but not below zero, by the amount of excess business interest expense allocated to the partner pursuant to paragraph (f)(2) of this section. Negative section 163(j) expense is not treated as excess business interest expense in any subsequent year until such negative section 163(j) expense is no longer suspended under section 704(d). Therefore, negative section 163(j) expense does not affect, and is not affected by, any allocation of excess taxable income to the partner. Accordingly, any excess taxable income allocated to a partner from a partnership while the partner still has negative section 163(j) expense

will be included in the partner's ATI. However, once the negative section 163(j) expense is no longer suspended under section 704(d), it becomes excess business interest expense, which is subject to the general rules in paragraph (g) of this section. See *Example 8* in paragraph (o)(8) of this section.

(3) *Partner basis adjustment upon disposition of partnership interest.*—If a partner (transferor) disposes of an interest in a partnership, the adjusted basis of the partnership interest being disposed of (transferred interest) is increased immediately before the disposition by the amount of the excess (if any) of the amount of the basis reduction under paragraph (h)(2) of this section over the portion of any excess business interest expense allocated to the transferor under paragraph (f)(2) of this section which has previously been treated under paragraph (g) of this section as business interest expense paid or accrued by the transferor, multiplied by the ratio of the fair market value of the transferred interest to the total fair market value of the transferor's partnership interest immediately prior to the disposition. Therefore, the adjusted basis of the transferred interest is not increased immediately before the disposition by any allocation of excess business interest expense from the partnership that did not reduce the transferor's adjusted basis in its partnership interest pursuant to paragraph (h) of this section prior to the disposition, or by any excess business interest expense that was treated under paragraph (g) of this section as business interest expense paid or accrued by the transferor prior to the disposition. If the transferor disposes of all of its partnership interest, no deduction under section 163(j) is allowed to the transferor or transferee under chapter 1 of subtitle A of the Code for any excess business interest expense or negative section 163(j) expense. If the transferor disposes of a portion of its partnership interest, no deduction under section 163(j) is allowed to the transferor or transferee under chapter 1 of subtitle A of the Code for the amount of excess business interest expense proportionate to the transferred interest. The amount of excess business interest expense proportionate to the partnership interest retained by the transferor shall remain as excess business interest expense of the transferor until such time as such excess business interest expense is treated as business interest expense paid or accrued by the transferor pursuant to paragraph (g) of this section. Further, if the transferor disposes of a portion of its partnership interest, any negative section 163(j) expense shall remain negative section 163(j) expense of the transferor partner until such negative section 163(j) expense is no longer suspended under section 704(d). For purposes of this paragraph, a disposition includes a distribution of money or other property by the partnership to a partner in complete liquidation of its interest in the partnership. Further, solely for purposes of this section, each partner is considered to have disposed of its partnership interest if the partnership terminates under section 708(b)(1). See *Example 9* and *Example 10* in paragraphs (o)(9) and (o)(10) of this section, respectively.

(i)-(j) [Reserved]

(k) *Investment items and certain other items.*—Any item of a partnership's income, gain, deduction, or loss that is investment interest income or expense pursuant to §1.163-8T, and any other tax item of a partnership that is neither properly allocable to a trade or business of the partnership nor described in section 163(d), is allocated to each partner in accordance with section 704(b) and the regulations under section 704 of the Code, and the effect of such allocation for purposes of section 163 is determined at the partner-level. See §1.163(j)-4(b)(3), section 163(d), and §1.163-8T.

(l) *S corporations.*—(1) *In general.*—(i) *Corporate level limitation.*—In the case of any S corporation, the section 163(j) limitation is applied at the S corporation level, and any deduction allowed for business interest expense is taken into account in determining the nonseparately stated taxable income or loss of the S corporation. An S corporation determines its section 163(j) limitation in the same manner as set forth in §1.163(j)-2(b). Allocations of excess taxable income and excess business interest income are made in accordance with the shareholders' pro rata interests in the S corporation pursuant to section 1366(a)(1) after determining the S corporation's section 163(j) limitation pursuant to §1.163(j)-2(b). See *Example 22* and *Example 23* in paragraphs (o)(22) and (23) of this section, respectively.

(ii) *Short taxable periods.*—For rules on applying the section 163(j) limitation where an S corporation has a two short taxable periods or where its taxable year consists of two separate taxable years see §§1.1362-3(c), 1.1368-1(g), and 1.1377-1(b).

(2) *Character of deductible business interest expense.*—If an S corporation has deductible business interest expense, such deductible business interest expense is not subject to any additional application of section 163(j) at the shareholder-level because such deductible business interest expense is taken into account in determining the nonseparately stated taxable income or loss of the S corporation. However, for all other purposes of the Code, deductible business

interest expense retains its character as business interest expense at the shareholder-level. For example, for purposes of section 469, such deductible business interest expense retains its character as either passive or non-passive in the hands of the shareholder. Additionally, for purposes of section 469, deductible business interest expense from an S corporation remains interest derived from a trade or business in the hands of a shareholder even if the shareholder does not materially participate in the S corporation's trade or business activity. For additional rules regarding the interaction between sections 465, 469, and 163(j), see §1.163(j)-3.

(3) *Adjusted taxable income of an S corporation.*—The ATI of an S corporation generally is determined in accordance with §1.163(j)-1(b)(1). For purposes of computing the S corporation's ATI, the tentative taxable income of the S corporation is determined under section 1363(b) and includes—

(i) Any item described in section 1363(b)(1); and

(ii) Any item described in §1.163(j)-1(b)(1), to the extent such item is consistent with subchapter S of the Code.

(4) *Adjusted taxable income and business interest income of S corporation shareholders.*—(i) *Adjusted taxable income of S corporation shareholders.*—The ATI of an S corporation shareholder is determined in accordance with §1.163(j)-1(b)(1) without regard to such shareholder's distributive share of any items of income, gain, deduction, or loss of such S corporation, except as provided in paragraph (m), and is increased by such shareholder's distributive share of such S corporation's excess taxable income.

(ii) *Disposition of S corporation stock.*—If a shareholder of an S corporation recognizes gain or loss upon the disposition of stock of the S corporation, and the corporation the stock of which is being disposed of only owns non-excepted trade or business assets, the gain or loss on the disposition of the stock is included in the shareholder's ATI. See §1.163(j)-10(b)(4)(ii) for dispositions of stock of S corporations that own—

(A) Non-excepted assets and excepted assets; or

(B) Investment assets; or

(C) Both.

(iii) *Double counting of business interest income and floor plan financing interest expense prohibited.*—For purposes of calculating an S corporation shareholder's section 163(j) limitation, the shareholder does not include—

(A) Business interest income from an S corporation that is subject to section 163(j), except to the extent the shareholder is allocated excess business interest income from that S corporation pursuant to paragraph (l)(1) of this section; and

(B) The shareholder's share of the S corporation's floor plan financing interest expense, because such floor plan financing interest expense already has been taken into account by the S corporation in determining its nonseparately stated taxable income or loss for purposes of section 163(j).

(5) *Carryforwards.*—The amount of any business interest expense not allowed as a deduction for any taxable year by reason of the limitation contained in §1.163(j)-2(b) is carried forward in the succeeding taxable year as a disallowed business interest expense carryforward under the rules set forth in §1.163(j)-2(c) (whether to an S corporation taxable year or a C corporation taxable year). For purposes of applying section 163(j), S corporations are subject to the same ordering rules as a C corporation that is not a member of a consolidated group. See §1.163(j)-5(b)(2).

(6) *Basis adjustments and disallowed business interest expense carryforwards.*—An S corporation shareholder's adjusted basis in its S corporation stock is reduced, but not below zero, when a disallowed business interest expense carryforward becomes deductible under section 163(j).

(7) *Accumulated adjustment accounts.*—The accumulated adjustment account of an S corporation is adjusted to take into account business interest expense in the year in which the S corporation treats such business interest expense as deductible under the section 163(j) limitation. See section 1368(e)(1).

(8) *Termination of qualified subchapter S subsidiary election.*—If a corporation's qualified subchapter S subsidiary election terminates and any disallowed business interest expense carryforward is attributable to the activities of the qualified subchapter S subsidiary at the time of termination, such disallowed business interest expense carryforward remains with the parent S corporation, and no portion of these items is allocable to the former qualified subchapter S subsidiary.

(9) *Investment items.*—Any item of an S corporation's income, gain, deduction, or loss that is investment interest income or expense

pursuant to §1.163-8T is allocated to each shareholder in accordance with the shareholders' pro rata interests in the S corporation pursuant to section 1366(a)(1). See section 163(d) and §1.163-8T.

(10) *Application of section 382.*—In the event of an ownership change, within the meaning of section 382(g), the S corporation's business interest expense is subject to section 382. Therefore, the allocation of the S corporation's business interest expense between the pre-change period (as defined in §1.382-6(g)(2)) and the post-change period (as defined in §1.382-6(g)(3)), and the determination of the amount that is deducted and carried forward, is determined pursuant to §1.382-6. If the date of the ownership change is also the date of a qualifying disposition (as defined in §1.1368-1(g)(2)) or the date for a termination of shareholder interest (as defined in §1.1377-1(b)(4)), then—

(i) The rules of this paragraph govern the S corporation's business interest expense;

(ii) The S corporation must make an election under §1.382-6(b) with respect to such date if it also makes an election under §1.1368-1(g)(2) or a shareholder termination election to apply normal tax accounting rules, as applicable, with respect to such date; and

(iii) The S corporation may not make an election under §1.382-6(b) with respect to such date if it does not make an election under §1.1368-1(g)(2) or a termination election under §1.1377-1(b)(1), as applicable, with respect to such date.

(m) *Partnerships and S corporations not subject to section 163(j).*— (1) *Exempt partnerships and S corporations.*—If the small business exemption in §1.163(j)-2(d) applies to a partnership or an S corporation in a taxable year (exempt entity), the general rule in §1.163(j)-2 and this section does not apply to limit the deduction for business interest expense of the exempt entity in that taxable year. Additionally, if a partner or S corporation shareholder is allocated business interest expense from an exempt entity, such business interest expense is not subject to the section 163(j) limitation at the partner's or S corporation shareholder's level. However, see paragraph (h)(1) of this section. Further, a partner or S corporation shareholder of an exempt entity includes its share of non-excepted trade or business items of income, gain, loss, and deduction (including business interest expense and business interest income) of such exempt entity when calculating its ATI. However, if a partner's or S corporation shareholder's allocations of non-excepted trade or business items of loss and deduction from an exempt entity exceed its allocations of non-excepted trade or business items of income and gain from such exempt entity (net loss allocation), then such net loss allocation will not reduce a partner's or S corporation shareholder's ATI. See *Example 11* and *Example 12* in paragraphs (o)(11) and (12) of this section, respectively.

(2) *Partnerships and S corporations engaged in excepted trades or businesses.*—To the extent a partnership or an S corporation is engaged in an excepted trade or business, the general rule in §1.163(j)-2 and this section does not apply to limit the deduction for business interest expense that is allocable to such excepted trade or business. If a partner or S corporation shareholder is allocated any section 163(j) item that is allocable to an excepted trade or business of the partnership or S corporation (excepted 163(j) items), such excepted 163(j) items are excluded from the partner's or shareholder's section 163(j) deduction calculation. See §1.163(j)-10(c) (regarding the allocation of items between excepted and non-excepted trades or businesses). See also *Example 13* in paragraph (o)(13) of this section.

(3) *Treatment of excess business interest expense from partnerships that are exempt entities in a succeeding taxable year.*—If a partner is allocated excess business interest expense from a partnership and, in a succeeding taxable year, such partnership is an exempt entity, then the partner shall treat any of its excess business interest expense that was previously allocated from such partnership as business interest expense paid or accrued by the partner in such succeeding taxable year, which is potentially subject to limitation at the partner level under section 163(j). However, if a partner is allocated excess business interest expense from a partnership and, in a succeeding taxable year, such partnership engages in excepted trades or businesses, then the partner shall not treat any of its excess business interest expense that was previously allocated from such partnership as business interest expense paid or accrued by the partner in such succeeding taxable year by reason of the partnership engaging in excepted trades or businesses. See *Example 14* through *Example 16* in paragraphs (o)(14) through (o)(16) of this section, respectively. For rules regarding the treatment of excess business interest expense from a partnership that terminates under section 708(b)(1), see paragraph (h)(3) of this section.

(4) *S corporations with disallowed business interest expense carryforwards prior to becoming exempt entities.*—If an S corporation has a disallowed business interest expense carryforward for a taxable year

and, in a succeeding taxable year, such S corporation is an exempt entity, then such disallowed business interest expense carryforward—

(i) Continues to be carried forward at the S corporation level;

(ii) Is no longer subject to the section 163(j) limitation; and

(iii) Is taken into account in determining the nonseparately stated taxable income or loss of the S corporation.

(n) *Treatment of self-charged lending transactions between partnerships and partners.*—In the case of a lending transaction between a partner (lending partner) and partnership (borrowing partnership) in which the lending partner owns a direct interest (self-charged lending transaction), any business interest expense of the borrowing partnership attributable to the self-charged lending transaction is business interest expense of the borrowing partnership for purposes of this section. If in a given taxable year the lending partner is allocated excess business interest expense from the borrowing partnership and has interest income attributable to the self-charged lending transaction (interest income), the lending partner is deemed to receive an allocation of excess business interest income from the borrowing partnership in such taxable year. The amount of the lending partner's deemed allocation of excess business interest income is the lesser of such lending partner's allocation of excess business interest expense from the borrowing partnership in such taxable year or the interest income attributable to the self-charged lending transaction in such taxable year. To prevent the double counting of business interest income, the lending partner includes interest income that was treated as excess business interest income pursuant to this paragraph (n) only once when calculating its own section 163(j) limitation. To the extent an amount of interest income received by a lending partner is attributable to a self-charged lending transaction, and is deemed to be an allocation of excess business interest income from the borrowing partnership pursuant to this paragraph (n), such an amount of interest income will not be treated as investment income for purposes of section 163(d). In cases where the lending partner is not a C corporation, to the extent that any interest income exceeds the lending partner's allocation of excess business interest expense from the borrowing partnership for the taxable year, and such interest income otherwise would be properly treated as investment income of the lending partner for purposes of section 163(d) for that year, such excess amount of interest income will continue to be treated as investment income of the lending partner for that year for purposes of section 163(d). See *Example 26* in paragraph (o)(26) of this section.

(o) *Examples.*—The examples in this paragraph illustrate the provisions of section 163(j) as applied to partnerships and subchapter S corporations. For purposes of these examples, unless stated otherwise, each partnership and S corporation is subject to the provisions of section 163(j), is only engaged in non-excepted trades or businesses, was created or organized in the United States, and uses the calendar year for its annual accounting period. Unless stated otherwise, all partners and shareholders are subject to the provisions of section 163(j), are not subject to a limitation under section 704(d) or 1366(d), have no tax items other than those listed in the example, are U.S. citizens, and use the calendar year for their annual accounting period. The phrase "section 163(j) limit" shall equal the maximum potential deduction allowed under section 163(j)(1). Unless stated otherwise, business interest expense means business interest expense that is not floor plan financing interest expense. With respect to partnerships, all allocations are in accordance with section 704(b) and the regulations in this part under section 704 of the Code.

(1) *Example 1.*—(i) *Facts.* X and Y are equal partners in partnership PRS. In Year 1, PRS has $100 of ATI and $40 of business interest expense. PRS allocates the items comprising its $100 of ATI $50 to X and $50 to Y. PRS allocates its $40 of business interest expense $20 to X and $20 to Y. X has $100 of ATI and $20 of business interest expense from its sole proprietorship. Y has $0 of ATI and $20 of business interest expense from its sole proprietorship.

(ii) *Partnership-level.* In Year 1, PRS's section 163(j) limit is 30 percent of its ATI, or $30 ($100 x 30 percent). Thus, PRS has $30 of deductible business interest expense and $10 of excess business interest expense. Such $30 of deductible business interest expense is includable in PRS's nonseparately stated income or loss, and is not subject to further limitation under section 163(j) at the partners' level.

(iii) *Partner-level allocations.* Pursuant to §1.163(j)-6(f)(2), X and Y are each allocated $15 of deductible business interest expense and $5 of excess business interest expense. At the end of Year 1, X and Y each have $5 of excess business interest expense from PRS, which is not treated as paid or accrued by the partner until such partner is allocated excess taxable income or excess business interest income from PRS in a succeeding taxable year. Pursuant to §1.163(j)-6(e)(1), X and Y, in computing their limit under section 163(j), do not increase any of their section 163(j) items by any of PRS's section 163(j) items. X and Y each increase their outside basis in PRS by $30 ($50 - $20).

(iv) *Partner-level computations.* X, in computing its limit under section 163(j), has $100 of ATI and $20 of business interest expense from its sole proprietorship. X's section 163(j) limit is $30 ($100 x 30 percent). Thus, X's $20 of business interest expense is deductible business interest expense. Y, in computing its limit under section 163(j), has $20 of business interest expense from its sole proprietorship. Y's section 163(j) limit is $0 ($0 x 30 percent). Thus, Y's $20 of business interest expense is not allowed as a deduction and is treated as business interest expense paid or accrued by Y in Year 2.

(2) *Example 2.*—(i) *Facts.* The facts are the same as in *Example 1* in paragraph (o)(1)(i) of this section. In Year 2, PRS has $200 of ATI, $0 of business interest income, and $30 of business interest expense. PRS allocates the items comprising its $200 of ATI $100 to X and $100 to Y. PRS allocates its $30 of business interest expense $15 to X and $15 to Y. X has $100 of ATI and $20 of business interest expense from its sole proprietorship. Y has $0 of ATI and $20 of business interest expense from its sole proprietorship.

(ii) *Partnership-level.* In Year 2, PRS's section 163(j) limit is 30 percent of its ATI plus its business interest income, or $60 ($200 x 30 percent). Thus, PRS has $100 of excess taxable income, $30 of deductible business interest expense, and $0 of excess business interest expense. Such $30 of deductible business interest expense is includable in PRS's nonseparately stated income or loss, and is not subject to further limitation under section 163(j) at the partners' level.

(iii) *Partner-level allocations.* Pursuant to § 1.163(j)-6(f)(2), X and Y are each allocated $50 of excess taxable income, $15 of deductible business interest expense, and $0 of excess business interest expense. As a result, X and Y each increase their ATI by $50. Because X and Y are each allocated $50 of excess taxable income from PRS, and excess business interest expense from a partnership is treated as paid or accrued by a partner to the extent excess taxable income and excess business interest income are allocated from such partnership to a partner, X and Y each treat $5 of excess business interest expense (the carryforward from Year 1) as paid or accrued in Year 2. X and Y each increase their outside basis in PRS by $85 ($100 - $15).

(iv) *Partner-level computations.* X, in computing its limit under section 163(j), has $150 of ATI ($100 from its sole proprietorship, plus $50 excess taxable income) and $25 of business interest expense ($20 from its sole proprietorship, plus $5 excess business interest expense treated as paid or accrued in Year 2). X's section 163(j) limit is $45 ($150 x 30 percent). Thus, X's $25 of business interest expense is deductible business interest expense. At the end of Year 2, X has $0 of excess business interest expense from PRS ($5 from Year 1, less $5 treated as paid or accrued in Year 2). Y, in computing its limit under section 163(j), has $50 of ATI ($0 from its sole proprietorship, plus $50 excess taxable income) and $45 of business interest expense ($20 from its sole proprietorship, plus $20 disallowed business interest expense from Year 1, plus $5 excess business interest expense treated as paid or accrued in Year 2). Y's section 163(j) limit is $15 ($50 x 30 percent). Thus, $15 of Y's business interest expense is deductible business interest expense. The $30 of Y's business interest expense not allowed as a deduction ($45 business interest expense, less $15 section 163(j) limit) is treated as business interest expense paid or accrued by Y in Year 3. At the end of Year 2, Y has $0 of excess business interest expense from PRS ($5 from Year 1, less $5 treated as paid or accrued in Year 2).

(3) *Example 3.*—(i) *Facts.* The facts are the same as in *Example 1* in paragraph (o)(1)(i) of this section. In Year 2, PRS has $0 of ATI, $60 of business interest income, and $40 of business interest expense. PRS allocates its $60 of business interest income $30 to X and $30 to Y. PRS allocates its $40 of business interest expense $20 to X and $20 to Y. X has $100 of ATI and $20 of business interest expense from its sole proprietorship. Y has $0 of ATI and $20 of business interest expense from its sole proprietorship.

(ii) *Partnership-level.* In Year 2, PRS's section 163(j) limit is 30 percent of its ATI plus its business interest income, or $60 (($0 x 30 percent) + $60). Thus, PRS has $20 of excess business interest income, $0 of excess taxable income, $40 of deductible business interest expense, and $0 of excess business interest expense. Such $40 of deductible business interest expense is includable in PRS's nonseparately stated income or loss, and is not subject to further limitation under section 163(j) at the partners' level.

(iii) *Partner-level allocations.* Pursuant to § 1.163(j)-6(f)(2), X and Y are each allocated $10 of excess business interest income, and $20 of deductible business interest expense. As a result, X and Y each increase their business interest income by $10. Because X and Y are each allocated $10 of excess business interest income from PRS, and excess business interest expense from a partnership is treated as paid or accrued by a partner to the extent excess taxable income and excess business interest income are allocated from such partnership to a partner, X and Y each treat $5 of excess business interest expense (the carryforward from Year 1) as paid or accrued in Year 2. X and Y each increase their outside basis in PRS by $10 ($30 - $20).

(iv) *Partner-level computations.* X, in computing its limit under section 163(j), has $100 of ATI (from its sole proprietorship), $10 of business interest income (from the allocation of $10 of excess business interest income from PRS), and $25 of business interest expense ($20 from its sole proprietorship, plus $5 excess business interest expense treated as paid or accrued in Year 2). X's section 163(j) limit is $40 (($100 x 30 percent) + $10). Thus, X's $25 of business interest expense is deductible business interest expense. At the end of Year 2, X has $0 of excess business interest expense from PRS ($5 from Year 1, less $5 treated as paid or accrued in Year 2). Y, in computing its limit under section 163(j), has $0 of ATI (from its sole proprietorship), $10 of business interest income, and $45 of business interest expense ($20 from its sole proprietorship, plus $20 disallowed business interest expense from Year 1, plus $5 excess business interest expense treated as paid or accrued in Year 2). Y's section 163(j) limit is $10 (($0 x 30 percent) + $10). Thus, $10 of Y's business interest expense is deductible business interest expense. The $35 of Y's business interest expense not allowed as a deduction ($45 business interest expense, less $10 section 163(j) limit) is treated as business interest expense paid or accrued by Y in Year 3. At the end of Year 2, Y has $0 of excess business interest expense from PRS ($5 from Year 1, less $5 treated as paid or accrued in Year 2).

(4) *Example 4.*—(i) *Facts.* The facts are the same as in *Example 1* in paragraph (o)(1)(i) of this section. In Year 2, PRS has $100 of ATI, $60 of business interest income, and $40 of business interest expense. PRS allocates the items comprising its $100 of ATI $50 to X and $50 to Y. PRS allocates its $60 of business interest income $30 to X and $30 to Y. PRS allocates its $40 of business interest expense $20 to X and $20 to Y. X has $100 of ATI and $20 of business interest expense from its sole proprietorship. Y has $0 of ATI and $20 of business interest expense from its sole proprietorship.

(ii) *Partnership-level.* In Year 2, PRS's section 163(j) limit is 30 percent of its ATI plus its business interest income, or $90 (($100 x 30 percent)) + $60). Thus, PRS has $20 of excess business interest income, $100 of excess taxable income, $40 of deductible business interest expense, and $0 of excess business interest expense. Such $40 of deductible business interest expense is includable in PRS's nonseparately stated income or loss, and is not subject to further limitation under section 163(j) at the partners' level.

(iii) *Partner-level allocations.* Pursuant to § 1.163(j)-6(f)(2), X and Y are each allocated $10 of excess business interest income, $50 of excess taxable income, and $20 of deductible business interest expense. As a result, X and Y each increase their business interest income by $10 and ATI by $50. Because X and Y are each allocated $10 of excess business interest income and $50 of excess taxable income from PRS, and excess business interest expense from a partnership is treated as paid or accrued by a partner to the extent excess taxable income and excess business interest income are allocated from such partnership to a partner, X and Y each treat $5 of excess business interest expense (the carryforward from Year 1) as paid or accrued in Year 2. X and Y each increase their outside basis in PRS by $60 ($80 - $20).

(iv) *Partner-level computations.* X, in computing its limit under section 163(j), has $150 of ATI ($100 from its sole proprietorship, plus $50 excess taxable income), $10 of business interest income, and $25 of business interest expense ($20 from its sole proprietorship, plus $5 excess business interest expense treated as paid or accrued in Year 2). X's section 163(j) limit is $55 (($150 x 30 percent) + $10). Thus, $25 of X's business interest expense is deductible business interest expense. At the end of Year 2, X has $0 of excess business interest expense from PRS ($5 from Year 1, less $5 treated as paid or accrued in Year 2). Y, in computing its limit under section 163(j), has $50 of ATI ($0 from its sole proprietorship, plus $50 excess taxable income), $10 of business interest income, and $45 of business interest expense ($20 from its sole proprietorship, plus $20 disallowed business interest expense from Year 1, plus $5 excess business interest expense treated as paid or accrued in Year 2). Y's section 163(j) limit is $25 (($50 x 30 percent) + $10). Thus, $25 of Y's business interest expense is deductible business interest expense. Y's $20 of business interest expense not allowed as a deduction ($45 business interest expense, less $25 section 163(j) limit) is treated as business interest expense paid or accrued by Y in Year 3. At the end of Year 2, Y has $0 of excess business interest expense from PRS ($5 from Year 1, less $5 treated as paid or accrued in Year 2).

(5) *Example 5.*—(i) *Facts.* The facts are the same as in *Example 1* in paragraph (o)(1)(i) of this section. In Year 2, PRS has $100 of ATI, $11.20 of business interest income, and $40 of business interest expense. PRS allocates the items comprising its $100 of ATI $50 to X and $50 to Y. PRS allocates its $11.20 of business interest income $5.60 to X and $5.60 to Y. PRS allocates its $40 of business interest expense $20 to X and $20 to Y. X has $100 of ATI and $20 of business interest expense from its sole proprietorship. Y has $0 of ATI and $20 of business interest expense from its sole proprietorship.

(ii) *Partnership-level*. In Year 2, PRS's section 163(j) limit is 30 percent of its ATI plus its business interest income, or $41.20 (($100 x 30 percent) + $11.20). Thus, PRS has $0 of excess business interest income, $4 of excess taxable income, and $40 of deductible business interest expense. Such $40 of deductible business interest expense is includable in PRS's nonseparately stated income or loss, and is not subject to further limitation under section 163(j) at the partners' level.

(iii) *Partner-level allocations*. Pursuant to §1.163(j)-6(f)(2), X and Y are each allocated $2 of excess taxable income, $20 of deductible business interest expense, and $0 of excess business interest expense. As a result, X and Y each increase their ATI by $2. Because X and Y are each allocated $2 of excess taxable income from PRS, and excess business interest expense from a partnership is treated as paid or accrued by a partner to the extent excess taxable income and excess business interest expense are allocated from such partnership to a partner, X and Y each treat $2 of excess business interest expense (a portion of the carryforward from Year 1) as paid or accrued in Year 2. X and Y each increase their outside basis in PRS by $35.60 ($55.60 - $20).

(iv) *Partner-level computations*. X, in computing its limit under section 163(j), has $102 of ATI ($100 from its sole proprietorship, plus $2 excess taxable income), $0 of business interest income, and $22 of business interest expense ($20 from its sole proprietorship, plus $2 excess business interest expense treated as paid or accrued). X's section 163(j) limit is $30.60 ($102 x 30 percent). Thus, X's $22 of business interest expense is deductible business interest expense. At the end of Year 2, X has $3 of excess business interest expense from PRS ($5 from Year 1, less $2 treated as paid or accrued in Year 2). Y, in computing its limit under section 163(j), has $2 of ATI ($0 from its sole proprietorship, plus $2 excess taxable income), $0 of business interest income, and $42 of business interest expense ($20 from its sole proprietorship, plus $20 disallowed business interest expense from Year 1, plus $2 excess business interest expense treated as paid or accrued in Year 2). Y's section 163(j) limit is $0.60 ($2 x 30 percent). Thus, $0.60 of Y's business interest expense is deductible business interest expense. Y's $41.40 of business interest expense not allowed as a deduction ($42 business interest expense, less $0.60 section 163(j) limit) is treated as business interest expense paid or accrued by Y in Year 3. At the end of Year 2, Y has $3 of excess business interest expense from PRS ($5 from Year 1, less $2 treated as paid or accrued in Year 2).

(6) *Example 6.*—(i) *Facts*. In Year 1, X, Y, and Z formed partnership PRS. Upon formation, X and Y each contributed $100, and Z contributed non-excepted and non-depreciable trade or business property with a basis of $0 and fair market value of $100 (Blackacre). PRS allocates all items pro rata between its partners. Immediately after the formation of PRS, Z sold all of its interest in PRS to A for $100 (assume the interest sale is respected for U.S. Federal income tax purposes). In connection with the interest transfer, PRS made a valid election under section 754. Therefore, after the interest sale, A had a $100 positive section 743(b) adjustment in Blackacre. In Year 1, PRS had $0 of ATI, $15 of business interest expense, and $0 of business interest income. Pursuant to §1.163(j)-6(f)(2), PRS allocated each of the partners $5 of excess business interest expense. In Year 2, PRS sells Blackacre for $100 which generated $100 of ATI. The sale of Blackacre was PRS's only item of income in Year 2. In accordance with section 704(c), PRS allocates all $100 of gain resulting from the sale of Blackacre to A. Additionally, PRS has $15 of business interest expense, all of which it allocates to X. A has $50 of ATI and $20 of business interest expense from its sole proprietorship.

(ii) *Partnership-level*. In Year 2, PRS's section 163(j) limit is 30 percent of its ATI, or $30 ($100 x 30 percent). Thus, PRS has $15 of deductible business interest expense and $50 of excess taxable income. Such $15 of deductible business interest expense is includable in PRS's nonseparately stated income or loss, and is not subject to further limitation under section 163(j) at X's level.

(iii) *Partner-level allocations*. Pursuant to §1.163(j)-6(f)(2), X is allocated $15 of deductible business interest expense and X's outside basis in PRS is reduced by $15. A is allocated $50 of excess taxable income and, as a result, A increases its ATI by $50. Because A is allocated $50 of excess taxable income, and excess business interest expense from a partnership is treated as paid or accrued by a partner to the extent excess taxable income and excess business interest income are allocated from such partnership to a partner, A treats $5 of excess business interest expense (the carryforward from Year 1) as paid or accrued in Year 2. PRS's $100 of gain allocated to A in Year 2 is fully reduced by A's $100 section 743(b) adjustment. Therefore, at the end of Year 2, there is no change to A's outside basis in PRS.

(iv) *Partner-level*. A, in computing its limit under section 163(j), has $0 of ATI ($50 from its sole proprietorship, plus $50 excess taxable income, less $100 ATI reduction as a result of A's section 743(b) adjustment under §1.163(j)-6(e)(2)) and $25 of business interest expense ($20 from its sole proprietorship, plus $5 excess business interest expense treated as paid or accrued in Year 2). A's section

163(j) limit is $0 ($0 x 30 percent). Thus, all $25 of A's business interest expense is not allowed as a deduction and is treated as business interest expense paid or accrued by A in Year 3.

(7) *Example 7.*—(i) *Facts*. X and Y are equal partners in partnership PRS. At the beginning of Year 1, X and Y each have an outside basis in PRS of $5. In Year 1, PRS has $0 of ATI, $20 of business interest income, and $40 of business interest expense. PRS allocates its $20 of business interest income $10 to X and $10 to Y. PRS allocates $40 of business interest expense $20 to X and $20 to Y. X has $100 of ATI and $20 of business interest expense from its sole proprietorship. Y has $0 of ATI and $20 of business interest expense from its sole proprietorship.

(ii) *Partnership-level*. In Year 1, PRS's section 163(j) limit is 30 percent of its ATI plus its business interest income, or $20 (($0 x 30 percent) + $20). Thus, PRS has $0 of excess business interest income, $0 of excess taxable income, $20 of deductible business interest expense, and $20 of excess business interest expense. Such $20 of deductible business interest expense is includable in nonseparately stated income or loss of PRS, and not subject to further limitation under section 163(j) by the partners.

(iii) *Partner-level allocations*. Pursuant to §1.163(j)-6(f)(2), X and Y are each allocated $10 of deductible business interest expense and $10 of excess business interest expense. After adjusting each partner's respective basis for business interest income under section 705(a)(1)(A), pursuant to §1.163(j)-6(h)(1), X and Y each take their $10 of deductible business interest expense into account when reducing their outside basis in PRS before taking the $10 of excess business interest expense into account. Following each partner's reduction in outside basis due to the $10 of deductible business interest expense, each partner has $5 of outside basis remaining in PRS. Pursuant to §1.163(j)-6(h)(2), each partner has $5 of excess business interest expense and $5 of negative section 163(j) expense. In sum, at the end of Year 1, X and Y each have $5 of excess business interest expense from PRS which reduces each partner's outside basis to $0 (and is not treated as paid or accrued by the partners until such partner is allocated excess taxable income or excess business interest income from PRS in a succeeding taxable year), and $5 of negative section 163(j) expense (which is suspended under section 704(d) and not treated as excess business interest expense of the partners until such time as the negative section 163(j) expense is no longer subject to a limitation under section 704(d)).

(iv) *Partner-level computations*. X, in computing its limit under section 163(j), has $100 of ATI (from its sole proprietorship) and $20 of business interest expense (from its sole proprietorship). X's section 163(j) limit is $30 ($100 x 30 percent). Thus, $20 of X's business interest expense is deductible business interest expense. Y, in computing its limit under section 163(j), has $20 of business interest expense (from its sole proprietorship). Y's section 163(j) limit is $0 ($0 x 30 percent). Thus, $20 of Y's business interest expense is not allowed as a deduction in Year 1, and is treated as business interest expense paid or accrued by Y in Year 2.

(8) *Example 8.*—(i) *Facts*. The facts are the same as in *Example 7* in paragraph (o)(7)(i) of this section. In Year 2, PRS has $20 of gross income that is taken into account in determining PRS's ATI (in other words, properly allocable to a trade or business), $30 of gross deductions from an investment activity, and $0 of business interest expense. PRS allocates the items comprising its $20 of ATI $10 to X and $10 to Y. PRS allocates the items comprising its $30 of gross deductions $15 to X and $15 to Y. X has $100 of ATI and $20 of business interest expense from its sole proprietorship. Y has $0 of ATI and $20 of business interest expense from its sole proprietorship.

(ii) *Partnership-level*. In Year 2, PRS's section 163(j) limit is 30 percent of its ATI plus its business interest income, or $6 ($20 x 30 percent). Because PRS has no business interest expense, all $20 of its ATI is excess taxable income.

(iii) *Partner-level allocations*. Pursuant to §1.163(j)-6(f)(2), X and Y are each allocated $10 of excess taxable income. Because X and Y are each allocated $10 of excess taxable income from PRS, X and Y each increase their ATI by $10. Pursuant to §1.704-1(d)(2), each partner's limitation on losses under section 704(d) must be allocated to its distributive share of each such loss. Thus, each partner reduces its adjusted basis of $10 (attributable to the allocation of items comprising PRS's ATI in Year 2) by $7.50 of gross deductions from Year 2 ($10 x ($15 of total gross deductions from Year 2 / $20 of total losses disallowed)), and $2.50 of excess business interest expense that was carried over as negative section 163(j) expense from Year 1 ($10 x ($5 of negative section 163(j) expense treated as excess business interest expense solely for the purposes of section 704(d) / $20 of total losses disallowed)). Following the application of section 704(d), each partner has $7.50 of excess business interest expense from PRS ($5 excess business interest expense from Year 1, plus $2.50 of excess business interest expense that was formerly negative section 163(j) expense carried over from Year 1). Excess business interest expense from a partnership is treated as paid or accrued by a partner to the extent excess taxable income and excess business interest income are allocated from such partnership to the partner. As a result, X and Y each treat $7.50 of excess business interest expense as paid or accrued in Year 2.

(iv) *Partner-level computations.* X, in computing its limit under section 163(j), has $110 of ATI ($100 from its sole proprietorship, plus $10 excess taxable income) and $27.50 of business interest expense ($20 from its sole proprietorship, plus $7.50 excess business interest expense treated as paid or accrued in Year 2). X's section 163(j) limit is $33 ($110 x 30 percent). Thus, $27.50 of X's business interest expense is deductible business interest expense. At the end of Year 2, X has $0 of excess business interest expense from PRS ($5 from Year 1, plus $2.50 treated as excess business interest expense in Year 2, less $7.50 treated as paid or accrued in Year 2), and $2.50 of negative section 163(j) expense from PRS. Y, in computing its limit under section 163(j), has $10 of ATI ($0 from its sole proprietorship, plus $10 excess taxable income) and $47.50 of business interest expense ($20 from its sole proprietorship, plus $20 disallowed business interest expense from Year 1, plus $7.50 excess business interest expense treated as paid or accrued in Year 2). Y's section 163(j) limit is $3 ($10 x 30 percent). Thus, $3 of Y's business interest expense is deductible business interest expense. The $44.50 of Y's business interest expense not allowed as a deduction ($47.50 business interest expense, less $3 section 163(j) limit) is treated as business interest expense paid or accrued by Y in Year 3. At the end of Year 2, Y has $0 of excess business interest expense from PRS ($5 from Year 1, plus $2.50 treated as excess business interest expense in Year 2, less $7.50 treated as paid or accrued in Year 2), and $2.50 of negative section 163(j) expense from PRS.

(9) *Example 9.*—(i) *Facts.* X and Y are equal partners in partnership PRS, and are not members of a consolidated group. At the beginning of Year 1, X and Y each have $120 of outside basis in PRS. Neither X nor Y's share of partnership liabilities exceeds the adjusted basis of its entire interest. In Year 1, X is allocated $20 of excess business interest expense, which reduces its outside basis from $120 to $100. In Year 2, X sells 80 percent of its interest in PRS to Z for $160. Immediately prior to the sale, X's entire PRS interest had a fair market value of $200 and the transferred portion of the interest had a fair market value of $160.

(ii) *Basis adjustment.* Immediately before the sale to Z, X increases its basis in the portion of the interest sold by 80 percent of the amount of the excess of the amount of the basis reduction under paragraph (h)(2) of this section ($20) over the portion of any excess business interest expense allocated the partner under paragraph (f)(2) of this section that has previously been treated under paragraph (g) of this section as business interest expense paid or accrued by X ($0). Therefore, X's basis in the portion of its interest sold is $96 (($100 x 80%) + ($20 x 80%)), and X's gain is $64 ($160 - $96). Following the sale, X has $20 of outside basis in its remaining partnership interest and $4 of excess business interest expense.

(10) *Example 10.*—(i) *Facts.* X and Y are equal partners in partnership PRS, and are not members of a consolidated group. At the beginning of Year 1, X and Y each have an outside basis in PRS of $10. Neither X nor Y's share of partnership liabilities exceeds the adjusted basis of its entire interest. In Year 1, X is allocated $8 of excess business interest expense and $12 of loss from PRS. As a result, X has $4 of excess business interest expense, $4 of negative section 163(j) expense, $6 of allowable loss, $6 of loss suspended under section 704(d), and $0 of outside basis in PRS at the end of Year 1. In Year 2, X sells 50 percent of its interest in PRS to Z for $20. Immediately prior to the sale, X's entire partnership interest had a fair market value of $40 and the transferred portion of the interest had a fair market value of $20.

(ii) *Basis adjustment.* Immediately before the sale to Z, X increases its basis in the portion of the interest sold by 50 percent of the amount of the excess of the amount of the basis reduction under paragraph (h)(2) of this section ($4) over the portion of any excess business interest expense allocated the partner under paragraph (f)(2) of this section that has previously been treated under paragraph (g) of this section as business interest expense paid or accrued by X ($0). Therefore, X's basis in the portion of its interest sold is $2 (($0 x 50%) + $2), and X's gain is $18 ($20 - $2). Following the sale, X has $0 of outside basis in its remaining partnership interest, $2 of excess business interest expense, $4 of negative section 163(j) expense, and $6 of loss suspended under section 704(d).

(11) *Example 11.*—(i) *Facts.* X (a corporation), Y (an individual), and Z (an individual) are equal partners in partnership PRS. X, Y, and Z are subject to *section 163(j). PRS is not subject to section 163(j) under section 163(j)(3). In 2021, PRS* has $150 of trade or business income (not taking into account business interest income or business interest expense), $30 of business interest income, and $45 of business interest expense. PRS also has $75 of investment income and $60 of

investment interest expense. PRS allocates its items of income, gain, loss, and deduction equally among its partners. X, Y, and Z each have $10 of business interest expense from their respective businesses.

(ii) *Partnership-level.* PRS is not subject to section 163(j) by reason of section 163(j)(3). As a result, none of PRS's $45 of business interest expense is subject to the section 163(j) limitation.

(iii) *Partner-level allocations.* Because PRS is not subject to section 163(j) by reason of section 163(j)(3), PRS's $45 of business interest expense does not retain its character as business interest expense for purposes of section 163(j). As a result, such business interest expense is not subject to the section 163(j) limitation at the level of either the partnership or partner. Additionally, pursuant to §1.163(j)-6(m)(1), each partner includes its share of non-excepted trade or business items of income, gain, loss, and deduction (including business interest expense and business interest income) of PRS when calculating its ATI. As a result, each partner increases its ATI by $45 (one third of $150 + $30 - $45). Also, X increases its ATI by an additional $25 because its items of investment income and loss from PRS are recharacterized as non-excepted trade or business income and loss at its level pursuant to §§1.163(j)-4(b)(3)(i) and 1.163(j)-10(b)(6). Further, X increases its business interest expense by its $20 allocation of investment interest expense from PRS pursuant to §§1.163(j)-4(b)(3)(i) and 1.163(j)-10(b)(6).

(iv) *Partner-level computations.* X, in computing its limit under section 163(j), has $70 of ATI and $30 of business interest expense. X's section 163(j) limit is $21 ($70 x 30 percent). Thus, X has $21 of deductible business interest expense. X's $9 of business interest expense not allowed as a deduction is treated as business interest expense paid or accrued by X in 2020. Y and Z, in computing their respective limits under section 163(j), each have $45 of ATI and $10 of business interest expense. Y and Z each have a section 163(j) limit of $13.50 ($45 x 30 percent). Thus, Y and Z each have $10 of deductible business interest expense.

(12) *Example 12.*—(i) *Facts.* The facts are the same as in *Example 11* in paragraph (o)(11)(i) of this section, except PRS has $200 of depreciation deductions in addition to its other items of income, gain, loss, and deduction.

(ii) *Partnership-level.* Same analysis as *Example 11* in paragraph (o)(11)(ii) of this section.

(iii) *Partner-level allocations.* Because PRS is not subject to section 163(j) by reason of section 163(j)(3), PRS's $45 of business interest expense does not retain its character as business interest expense for purposes of section 163(j). As a result, such business interest expense is not subject to the section 163(j) limitation at the level of either the partnership or partner. Additionally, pursuant to §1.163(j)-6(m)(1), each partner includes its share of non-excepted trade or business items of income, gain, loss, and deduction (including business interest expense and business interest income) of PRS when calculating its ATI; however, a net loss allocation of trade or business items from an exempt entity does not reduce a partner's ATI. Because each of the partners has a net loss allocation of trade or business items from PRS, none of the partners adjust their ATI for the trade or business items of PRS. X, the corporate partner, increases its ATI by $25 because its items of investment income and loss from PRS are recharacterized as trade or business income and loss at its level pursuant to §§1.163(j)-4(b)(3)(i) and 1.163(j)-10(b)(6). Further, X increases its business interest expense by its $20 allocation of investment interest expense from PRS pursuant to §§1.163(j)-4(b)(3)(i) and 1.163(j)-10(b)(6).

(iv) *Partner-level computations.* In computing its limit under section 163(j), each partner has $0 of ATI and $10 of business interest expense. Each partner's section 163(j) limit is $0 ($0 x 30 percent). Thus, each partner's $10 of business interest expense is not allowed as a deduction and is treated as business interest expense paid or accrued by the partner in 2020. X, in computing its limit under section 163(j), has $25 of ATI and $30 of business interest expense. X's section 163(j) limit is $7.50 ($25 x 30 percent). Thus, X has $7.50 of deductible business interest expense. X's $22.50 of business interest expense not allowed as a deduction is treated as business interest expense paid or accrued by X in 2020. Y and Z, in computing their respective limits under section 163(j), each have $0 of ATI and $10 of business interest expense. Thus, Y and Z each have $10 of business interest expense not allowed as a deduction that is treated as business interest expense paid or accrued in 2020.

(13) *Example 13.*—(i) *Facts.* X, Y, and Z are equal partners in partnership PRS. X, Y, and Z are each individuals subject to section 163(j). PRS is not subject to section 163(j) under section 163(j)(3). PRS has one excepted and one non-excepted trade or business. In Year 1, PRS has $200 of income and $10 of business interest expense from its excepted trade or business, and $60 of business interest income and $30 of business interest expense from its non-excepted trade or business. PRS allocates its items of income, gain, loss, and deduction

equally among its partners. X, Y, and Z each have $10 of business interest expense from their respective businesses.

(ii) *Partnership-level*. PRS is not subject to section 163(j) by reason of section 163(j)(3). As a result, none of PRS's business interest expense is subject to the section 163(j) limitation.

(iii) *Partner-level allocations*. Because PRS's business interest expense is not subject to the section 163(j) limitation, such business interest expense is not subject to the section 163(j) limitation at the level of either the partnership or partner. Additionally, pursuant to §1.163(j)-6(m)(1), each partner includes its share of non-excepted trade or business items of income, gain, loss, and deduction (including business interest expense and business interest income) of PRS when calculating its ATI. Therefore, each partner increases its ATI by $10 (each partner's share of $20 of non-excepted income less each partner's share of $10 of non-excepted loss).

(iv) *Partner-level computations*. In computing its limit under section 163(j), each partner has $10 of ATI and $10 of business interest expense. Each partner's section 163(j) limit is $3 ($10 x 30 percent). Thus, each partner has $3 of deductible business interest expense. Each partner has $7 of business interest expense not allowed as a deduction that is treated as business interest expense paid or accrued by the partner in Year 2.

(14) *Example 14*.—(i) *Facts*. The facts are the same as in *Example 5* in paragraph (o)(5)(i) of this section, except in Year 2 Y is not subject to section 163(j) under section 163(j)(3).

(ii) *Partnership-level*. Same analysis as *Example 5* in paragraph (o)(5)(ii) of this section.

(iii) *Partner-level allocations*. Same analysis as *Example 5* in paragraph (o)(5)(iii) of this section.

(iv) *Partner-level computations*. For X, same analysis as *Example 5* in paragraph (o)(5)(iv) of this section. Y is not subject to section 163(j) under section 163(j)(3). Thus, all $42 of business interest expense ($20 from its sole proprietorship, plus $20 disallowed business interest expense from Year 1, plus $2 excess business interest expense treated as paid or accrued in Year 2) is not subject to limitation under §1.163(j)-2(d). At the end of Year 2, Y has $3 of excess business interest expense from PRS ($5 from Year 1, less $2 treated as paid or accrued in Year 2).

(15) *Example 15*.—(i) *Facts*. The facts are the same as in *Example 5* in paragraph (o)(5)(i) of this section, except in Year 2 PRS and Y become not subject to section 163(j) by reason of section 163(j)(3).

(ii) *Partnership-level*. In Year 2, PRS is not subject to section 163(j) by reason of section 163(j)(3). As a result, none of PRS's $40 of business interest expense is subject to the section 163(j) limitation at the level of either the partnership or partner.

(iii) *Partner-level allocations*. Because PRS is not subject to section 163(j) by reason of section 163(j)(3), PRS's $40 of business interest expense does not retain its character as business interest expense for purposes of section 163(j). As a result, such business interest expense is not subject to the section 163(j) limitation at the level of either the partnership or partner. Additionally, pursuant to §1.163(j)-6(m)(1), each partner includes its share of non-excepted trade or business items of income, gain, loss, and deduction (including business interest expense and business interest income) of PRS when calculating its ATI. As a result, X and Y each increase their ATI by $35.60. Further, because PRS is not subject to section 163(j) by reason of section 163(j)(3), the excess business interest expense from Year 1 is treated as paid or accrued by the partners pursuant to §1.163(j)-6(m)(3). As a result, X and Y each treat their $5 of excess business interest expense from Year 1 as paid or accrued in Year 2, and increase their business interest expense by $5.

(iv) *Partner-level computations*. X, in computing its limit under section 163(j), has $135.60 of ATI ($100 from its sole proprietorship, plus $35.60 ATI from PRS) and $25 of business interest expense ($20 from its sole proprietorship, plus $5 of excess business interest expense treated as paid or accrued in Year 2). X's section 163(j) limit is $40.68 ($135.60 x 30 percent). Thus, $25 of X's business interest expense is deductible business interest expense. Y is not subject to section 163(j) under section 163(j)(3). As a result, Y's business interest expense is not subject to the section 163(j) limitation. Thus, all $45 of Y's business interest expense ($20 from its sole proprietorship, plus

$20 disallowed from year 1, plus $5 of excess business interest expense treated as paid or accrued in Year 2) is not subject to the section 163(j) limitation.

(16) *Example 16*.—(i) *Facts*. The facts are the same as in *Example 1* in paragraph (o)(1)(i) of this section, except that PRS's only trade or business is a real property trade or business for which PRS does not make the election provided for in section 163(j)(7)(B). In Year 2, when PRS's only trade or business is still its real property trade or business, PRS makes the election provided for in section 163(j)(7)(B). Further, in Year 2, PRS has $100 of income and $40 of business interest expense. PRS allocates its items of income, gain, deduction, and loss equally between X and Y. X has $100 of ATI and $20 of business interest expense from its sole proprietorship. Y has $0 of ATI and $20 of business interest expense from its sole proprietorship.

(ii) *Partnership-level*. In Year 2, PRS is not subject to section 163(j) because its only trade or business is an excepted trade or business. As a result, none of PRS's $40 of business interest expense is subject to the section 163(j) limitation at the level of either the partnership or partner.

(iii) *Partner-level allocations*. Because PRS is not subject to section 163(j), PRS's $40 of business interest expense does not retain its character as business interest expense for purposes of section 163(j). As a result, such business interest expense is not subject to the section 163(j) limitation at the partners' level. Pursuant to §1.163(j)-6(m)(1), the partners do not include their respective $50 shares of income from PRS when calculating their own ATI because such $50 is excepted trade or business income.

(iv) *Partner-level computations*. X, in computing its limit under section 163(j), has $100 of ATI ($100 from its sole proprietorship) and $20 of business interest expense ($20 from its sole proprietorship). X's section 163(j) limit is $30 ($100 x 30 percent). Thus, $20 of X's business interest expense is deductible business interest expense. At the end of Year 2, X has $5 of excess business interest expense from PRS ($5 from Year 1). Y, in computing its limit under section 163(j), has $0 of ATI and $40 of business interest expense ($20 from its sole proprietorship, plus $20 disallowed business interest expense from Year 1). Y's section 163(j) limit is $0. Thus, Y's $40 of business interest expense not allowed as a deduction is treated as business interest expense paid or accrued by Y in Year 3. At the end of Year 2, Y has $5 of excess business interest expense from PRS ($5 from Year 1).

(17) *Example 17: Facts*.—A (an individual) and B (a corporation) own all of the interests in partnership PRS. At the beginning of Year 1, A and B each have $100 section 704(b) capital account and $100 of basis in PRS. In Year 1, PRS has $100 of ATI, $10 of investment interest income, $20 of business interest income (BII), $60 of business interest expense (BIE), and $10 of floor plan financing interest expense. PRS's ATI consists of $100 of gross income and $0 of gross deductions. PRS allocates its items comprising ATI $100 to A and $0 to B. PRS allocates its business interest income $10 to A and $10 to B. PRS allocates its business interest expense $30 to A and $30 to B. PRS allocates all $10 of its investment interest income and all $10 of its floor plan financing interest income to B. A has ATI from a sole proprietorship, unrelated to PRS, in the amount of $300.

(i) First, PRS determines its limitation pursuant to §1.163(j)-2. PRS's section 163(j) limit is 30 percent of its ATI plus its business interest income, or $50 (($100 x 30 percent) + $20). Thus, PRS has $0 of excess business interest income (EBII), $0 of excess taxable income, $50 of deductible business interest expense, and $10 of excess business interest expense. PRS takes its $10 of floor plan financing into account in determining its nonseparately stated taxable income or loss.

(ii) Second, PRS determines each partner's allocable share of section 163(j) items used in its own section 163(j) calculation. B's $10 of investment interest income is not included in B's allocable business interest income amount because the $10 of investment interest income was not taken into account in PRS's section 163(j) calculation. B's $10 of floor plan financing interest expense is not included in B's allocable business interest expense. The $300 of ATI from A's sole proprietorship is not included in A's allocable ATI amount because the $300 was not taken into account in PRS's section 163(j) calculation.

Table 1 to paragraph (o)(17)(ii)			
	A	B	Total
Allocable ATI	$100	$0	$100
Allocable BII	$10	$10	$20
Allocable BIE	$30	$30	$60

(iii) Third, PRS compares each partner's allocable business interest income to such partner's allocable business interest expense. Because each partner's allocable business interest expense exceeds its

allocable business interest income by $20 ($30 - $10), each partner has an allocable business interest income deficit of $20. Thus, the total allocable business interest income deficit is $40 ($20 + $20). No partner has allocable business interest income excess because no partner has allocable business interest income in excess of its alloca-

ble business interest expense. Thus, the total allocable business interest income excess is $0.

Table 2 to paragraph (o)(17)(iii)	A	B	Total
Allocable BII	$10	$10	N/A
Allocable BIE	$30	$30	N/A
If allocable BII exceeds allocable BIE, then such amount = Allocable BII excess	$0	$0	$0
If allocable BIE exceeds allocable BII, then such amount = Allocable BII deficit	$20	$20	$40

(iv) Fourth, PRS determines each partner's final allocable business interest income excess. Because no partner had any allocable business interest income excess, each partner has final allocable business interest income excess of $0.

(v) Fifth, PRS determines each partner's remaining business interest expense. PRS determines A's remaining business interest expense by reducing, but not below $0, A's allocable business interest income deficit ($20) by the product of the total allocable business interest income excess ($0) and the ratio of A's allocable business interest income deficit to the total business interest income deficit

($20/$40). Therefore, A's allocable business interest income deficit of $20 is reduced by $0 ($0 x 50 percent). As a result, A's remaining business interest expense is $20. PRS determines B's remaining business interest expense by reducing, but not below $0, B's allocable business interest income deficit ($20) by the product of the total allocable business interest income excess ($0) and the ratio of B's allocable business interest income deficit to the total business interest income deficit ($20/$40). Therefore, B's allocable business interest income deficit of $20 is reduced by $0 ($0 x 50 percent). As a result, B's remaining business interest expense is $20.

Table 3 to paragraph (o)(17)(v)	A	B	Total
Allocable BII deficit	$20	$20	$40
Less: (Total allocable BII excess) x (Allocable BII deficit / Total allocable BII deficit)	$0	$0	N/A
= Remaining BIE	$20	$20	$40

(vi) Sixth, PRS determines each partner's final allocable ATI. Any partner with a negative allocable ATI, or an allocable ATI of $0, has a positive allocable ATI of $0. Therefore, B has a positive allocable ATI of $0. Because A's allocable ATI is comprised of $100 of income and gain and $0 of deduction and loss, A has positive allocable ATI of $100. Thus, the total positive allocable ATI is $100 ($100 + $0). PRS determines A's final allocable ATI by reducing, but not below $0, A's

positive allocable ATI ($100) by the product of total negative allocable ATI ($0) and the ratio of A's positive allocable ATI to the total positive allocable ATI ($100/$100). Therefore, A's positive allocable ATI is reduced by $0 ($0 x 100 percent). As a result, A's final allocable ATI is $100. Because B has a positive allocable ATI of $0, B's final allocable ATI is $0.

Table 4 to paragraph (o)(17)(vi)	A	B	Total
Allocable ATI	$100	$0	$100
If deduction and loss items comprising allocable ATI exceed income and gain items comprising allocable ATI, then such excess amount = Negative allocable ATI	$0	$0	$0
If income and gain items comprising allocable ATI equal or exceed deduction and loss items comprising allocable ATI, then such amount = Positive allocable ATI	$100	$0	$100

Table 5 to paragraph (o)(17)(vi)	A	B	Total
Positive allocable ATI	$100	$0	$100
Less: (Total negative allocable ATI) x (Positive allocable ATI / Total positive allocable ATI)	$0	$0	N/A
= Final allocable ATI	$100	$0	$100

(vii) Seventh, PRS compares each partner's ATI capacity (ATIC) amount to such partner's remaining business interest expense. A's ATIC amount is $30 ($100 x 30 percent) and B's ATIC amount is $0 ($0 x 30 percent). Because A's ATIC amount exceeds its remaining business interest expense by $10 ($30 - $20), A has an ATIC excess of

$10. B does not have any ATIC excess. Thus, the total ATIC excess is $10 ($10 + $0). A does not have any ATIC deficit. Because B's remaining business interest expense exceeds its ATIC amount by $20 ($20 - $0), B has an ATIC deficit of $20. Thus, the total ATIC deficit is $20 ($0 + $20).

Table 6 to paragraph (o)(17)(vii)	A	B	Total
ATIC (Final allocable ATI x 30 percent)	$30	$0	N/A
Remaining BIE	$20	$20	N/A
If ATIC exceeds remaining BIE, then such excess = ATIC excess	$10	$0	$10
If remaining BIE exceeds ATIC, then such excess = ATIC deficit	$0	$20	$20

(viii)(A) Eighth, PRS must perform the calculations and make the necessary adjustments described under paragraph (f)(2)(viii) of this section if, and only if, PRS has—

(1) An excess business interest expense greater than $0 under paragraph (f)(2)(i) of this section;

Reg. §1.163(j)-6(o)(17)

(2) A total negative allocable ATI greater than $0 under paragraph (f)(2)(vi) of this section; and

(3) A total ATIC excess amount greater than $0 under paragraph (f)(2)(vii) of this section.

(B) Because PRS does not meet all three requirements in paragraph (o)(17)(viii)(A) of this section, PRS does not perform the calculations or adjustments described in paragraph (f)(2)(viii) of this section. In sum, the correct amounts to be used in paragraphs (o)(17)(ix) and (x) of this section are as follows.

Table 7 to paragraph (o)(17)(viii)(B)

	A	B	Total
ATIC excess	$10	$0	$10
ATIC deficit	$0	$20	$20

(ix) Ninth, PRS determines each partner's final ATIC excess amount. Because A has an ATIC excess, PRS must determine A's final ATIC excess amount. A's final ATIC excess amount is A's ATIC excess ($10), reduced, but not below $0, by the product of the total ATIC deficit ($20) and the ratio of A's ATIC excess to the total ATIC excess ($10/$10). Therefore, A has $0 of final ATIC excess ($10 – ($20 x 100 percent)).

Table 8 to paragraph (o)(17)(ix)

	A	B	Total
ATIC excess	$10	$0	N/A
Less: (Total ATIC deficit) x (ATIC excess / Total ATIC excess)	$20	$0	N/A
= Final ATIC excess	$0	$0	$0

(x) Tenth, PRS determines each partner's final ATIC deficit amount. Because B has an ATIC deficit, PRS must determine B's final ATIC deficit amount. B's final ATIC deficit amount is B's ATIC deficit ($20), reduced, but not below $0, by the product of the total ATIC excess ($10) and the ratio of B's ATIC deficit to the total ATIC deficit ($20/$20). Therefore, B has $10 of final ATIC deficit ($20 – ($10 x 100 percent)).

Table 9 to paragraph (o)(17)(x)

	A	B	Total
ATIC deficit	$0	$20	N/A
Less: (Total ATIC excess) x (ATIC deficit / Total ATIC deficit)	$0	$10	N/A
= Final ATIC deficit	$0	$10	$10

(xi) Eleventh, PRS allocates deductible business interest expense and section 163(j) excess items to the partners. Pursuant to paragraph (f)(2)(i) of this section, PRS has $10 of excess business interest expense. PRS allocates the excess business interest expense dollar for dollar to the partners with final ATIC deficits amounts. Thus, PRS allocates all $10 of its excess business interest expense to B. A partner's allocable business interest expense is deductible business interest expense to the extent it exceeds such partner's share of excess business interest expense. Therefore, A has deductible business interest expense of $30 ($30 - $0) and B has deductible business interest expense of $20 ($30 - $10). As a result of its allocations from PRS, A increases its section 704(b) capital account and basis in PRS by $80 to $180. As a result of its allocations from PRS, B decreases its capital account and basis in PRS by $20 to $80.

Table 10 to paragraph (o)(17)(xi)

	A	B	Total
Deductible BIE	$30	$20	$50
EBIE allocated	$0	$10	$10
ETI allocated	$0	$0	$0
EBII allocated	$0	$0	$0

(18) *Example 18: Facts.*—A, B, and C own all of the interests in partnership PRS. In Year 1, PRS has $150 of ATI, $10 of business interest income, and $40 of business interest expense. PRS's ATI consists of $200 of gross income and $50 of gross deductions. PRS allocates its items comprising ATI ($50) to A, $200 to B, and $0 to C. PRS allocates its business interest income $0 to A, $0 to B, and $10 to C. PRS allocates its business interest expense $30 to A, $10 to B, and $0 to C.

(i) First, PRS determines its limitation pursuant to § 1.163(j)-2. PRS's section 163(j) limit is 30 percent of its ATI plus its business interest income, or $55 (($150 x 30 percent) + $10). Thus, PRS has $0 of excess business interest income, $50 of excess taxable income, $40 of deductible business interest expense, and $0 of excess business interest expense.

(ii) Second, PRS determines each partner's allocable share of section 163(j) items used in its own section 163(j) calculation.

Table 11 to paragraph (o)(18)(ii)

	A	B	C	Total
Allocable ATI	($50)	$200	$0	$150
Allocable BII	$0	$0	$10	$10
Allocable BIE	$30	$10	$0	$40

(iii) Third, PRS compares each partner's allocable business interest income to such partner's *allocable business interest expense*. Because A's allocable business interest expense exceeds its allocable business interest income by $30 ($30 - $0), A has an allocable business interest income deficit of $30. Because B's allocable business interest expense exceeds its allocable business interest income by $10 ($10 - $0), B has an allocable business interest income deficit of $10. C does not have any allocable business interest income deficit. Thus, the total allocable business interest income deficit is $40 ($30 + $10 + $0). A and B do not have any allocable business interest income excess. Because C's allocable business interest income exceeds its allocable business interest expense by $10 ($10 - $0), C has an allocable business interest income excess of $10. Thus, the total allocable business interest income excess is $10 ($0 + $0 + $10).

Table 12 to paragraph (o)(18)(iii)

	A	B	C	Total
Allocable BII	$0	$0	$10	N/A
Allocable BIE	$30	$10	$0	N/A
If allocable BII exceeds allocable BIE, then such amount = Allocable BII excess	$0	$0	$10	$10
If allocable BIE exceeds allocable BII, then such amount = Allocable BII deficit	$30	$10	$0	$40

(iv) Fourth, PRS determines each partner's final allocable business interest income excess. Because A and B do not have any allocable business interest income excess, each partner has final allocable business interest income excess of $0. PRS determines C's final allocable business interest income excess by reducing, but not below $0, C's allocable business interest income excess ($10) by the product of the total allocable business interest income deficit ($40) and the ratio of C's allocable business interest income excess to the total allocable business interest income excess ($10/$10). Therefore, C's allocable business interest income excess of $10 is reduced by $10 ($40 x 100 percent). As a result, C's allocable business interest income excess is $0.

Table 13 to paragraph (o)(18)(iv)

	A	B	C	Total
Allocable BII excess	$0	$0	$10	N/A
Less: (Total allocable BII deficit) x (Allocable BII excess / Total allocable BII excess)	$0	$0	$40	N/A
= Final Allocable BII Excess	$0	$0	$0	$10

(v) Fifth, PRS determines each partner's remaining business interest expense. PRS determines A's remaining business interest expense by reducing, but not below $0, A's allocable business interest income deficit ($30) by the product of the total allocable business interest income excess ($10) and the ratio of A's allocable business interest income deficit to the total business interest income deficit ($30/$40). Therefore, A's allocable business interest income deficit of $30 is reduced by $7.50 ($10 x 75 percent). As a result, A's remaining business interest expense is $22.50. PRS determines B's remaining business interest expense by reducing, but not below $0, B's allocable business interest income deficit ($10) by the product of the total allocable business interest income excess ($10) and the ratio of B's allocable business interest income deficit to the total business interest income deficit ($10/$40). Therefore, B's allocable business interest income deficit of $10 is reduced by $2.50 ($10 x 25 percent). As a result, B's remaining business interest expense is $7.50. Because C does not have any allocable business interest income deficit, C's remaining business interest expense is $0.

Table 14 to paragraph (o)(18)(v)

	A	B	C	Total
Allocable BII deficit	$30	$10	$0	$40
Less: (Total allocable BII excess) x (Allocable BII deficit / Total allocable BII deficit)	$7.50	$2.50	$0	N/A
= Remaining BIE	$22.50	$7.50	$0	N/A

(vi) Sixth, PRS determines each partner's final allocable ATI. Because A's allocable ATI is comprised of $50 of items of deduction and loss and $0 of income and gain, A has negative allocable ATI of $50. A is the only partner with negative allocable ATI. Thus, the total negative allocable ATI amount is $50. Any partner with a negative allocable ATI, or an allocable ATI of $0, has a positive allocable ATI of $0. Therefore, A and C have a positive allocable ATI of $0. Because B's allocable ATI is comprised of $200 of items of income and gain and $0 of deduction and loss, B has positive allocable ATI of $200. Thus, the total positive allocable ATI is $200 ($0 + $200 + $0). PRS determines B's final allocable ATI by reducing, but not below $0, B's positive allocable ATI ($200) by the product of total negative allocable ATI ($50) and the ratio of B's positive allocable ATI to the total positive allocable ATI ($200/$200). Therefore, B's positive allocable ATI is reduced by $50 ($50 x 100 percent). As a result, B's final allocable ATI is $150.

Table 15 to paragraph (o)(18)(vi)

	A	B	C	Total
Allocable ATI	($50)	$200	$0	$150
If deduction and loss items comprising allocable ATI exceed income and gain items comprising allocable ATI, then such excess amount = Negative allocable ATI	$50	$0	$0	$50
If income and gain items comprising allocable ATI equal or exceed deduction and loss items comprising allocable ATI, then such amount = Positive allocable ATI	$0	$200	$0	$200

Table 16 to paragraph (o)(18)(vi)

	A	B	C	Total
Positive allocable ATI	$0	$200	$0	$200
Less: (Total negative allocable ATI) x (Positive allocable ATI / Total positive allocable ATI)	$0	$50	$0	N/A
= Final allocable ATI	$0	$150	$0	$150

(vii) Seventh, PRS compares each partner's ATI capacity (ATIC) amount to such partner's remaining business interest expense. A's ATIC amount is $0 ($0 x 30 percent), B's ATIC amount is $45 ($150 x 30 percent), and C's ATIC amount is $0 ($0 x 30 percent). A does not have any ATIC excess. Because B's ATIC amount exceeds its remaining business interest expense by $37.50 ($45 - $7.50), B has an ATIC excess amount of $37.50. C does not have any ATIC excess. Thus, the total ATIC excess amount is $37.50 ($0 + $37.50 + $0). Because A's remaining business interest expense exceeds its ATIC amount by $22.50 ($22.50 - $0), A has an ATIC deficit of $22.50. B and C do not have any ATIC deficit. Thus, the total ATIC deficit is $22.50 ($22.50 + $0 + $0).

Table 17 to paragraph (o)(18)(vii)

	A	B	C	Total
ATIC (Final allocable ATI x 30 percent)	$0	$45	$0	N/A
Remaining BIE	$22.50	$7.50	$0	N/A
If ATIC exceeds remaining BIE, then such excess = ATIC excess	$0	$37.50	$0	$37.50
If remaining BIE exceeds ATIC, then such excess = ATIC deficit	$22.50	$0	$0	$22.50

(viii)(A) Eighth, PRS must perform the calculations and make the necessary adjustments described under paragraph (f)(2)(viii) of this section if, and only if, PRS has—

(1) An excess business interest expense greater than $0 under paragraph (f)(2)(i) of this section;

(2) A total negative allocable ATI greater than $0 under paragraph (f)(2)(vi) of this section; and

(3) A total ATIC excess amount greater than $0 under paragraph (f)(2)(vii) of this section.

(B) Because PRS does not meet all three requirements in paragraph (o)(18)(viii)(A) of this section, PRS does not perform the calculations or adjustments described in paragraph (f)(2)(viii) of this section. In sum, the correct amounts to be used in paragraphs (o)(18)(ix) and (x) of this section are as follows.

Table 18 to paragraph (o)(18)(viii)(B)

	A	B	C	Total
ATIC excess	$0	$37.50	$0	$37.50
ATIC deficit	$22.50	$0	$0	$22.50

(ix) Ninth, PRS determines each partner's final ATIC excess amount. Because B has ATIC excess, PRS must determine B's final ATIC excess amount. B's final ATIC excess amount is B's ATIC excess ($37.50), reduced, but not below $0, by the product of the total ATIC deficit ($22.50) and the ratio of B's ATIC excess to the total ATIC excess ($37.50/$37.50). Therefore, B has $15 of final ATIC excess ($37.50 – ($22.50 x 100 percent)).

Table 19 to paragraph (o)(18)(ix)

	A	B	C	Total
ATIC excess	$0	$37.50	$0	N/A
Less: (Total ATIC deficit) x (ATIC excess / Total ATIC excess)	$0	$22.50	$0	N/A
= Final ATIC excess	$0	$15	$0	$15

(x) Tenth, PRS determines each partner's final ATIC deficit amount. Because A has an ATIC deficit, PRS must determine A's final ATIC deficit amount. A's final ATIC deficit amount is A's ATIC deficit ($22.50), reduced, but not below $0, by the product of the total ATIC excess ($37.50) and the ratio of A's ATIC deficit to the total ATIC deficit ($22.50/$22.50). Therefore, A has $0 of final ATIC deficit ($22.50 – ($37.50 x 100 percent)).

Table 20 to paragraph (o)(18)(x)

	A	B	C	Total
ATIC deficit	$22.50	$0	$0	N/A
Less: (Total ATIC excess) x (ATIC deficit / Total ATIC deficit)	$37.50	$0	$0	N/A
= Final ATIC deficit	$0	$0	$0	$0

(xi) Eleventh, PRS allocates deductible business interest expense and section 163(j) excess items to the partners. Pursuant to paragraph (f)(2)(i) of this section, PRS has $50 of excess taxable income and $40 of deductible business interest expense. After grossing up each partner's final ATIC excess amounts by ten-thirds, excess taxable income is allocated dollar for dollar to partners with final ATIC excess amounts. Thus, PRS allocates its excess taxable income $50 to B. A partner's allocable business interest expense to the extent it exceeds such partner's share of excess business interest expense is deductible business interest expense. Therefore, A has deductible business interest expense of $30 ($30 - $0), B has deductible business interest expense of $10 ($10 - $0), and C has deductible business interest expense of $0 ($0 - $0).

Table 21 to paragraph (o)(18)(xi)

	A	B	C	Total
Deductible BIE	$30	$10	$0	$40
EBIE allocated	$0	$0	$0	$0
ETI allocated	$0	$50	$0	$50
EBII allocated	$0	$0	$0	$0

(19) *Example 19: Facts.*—A, B, and C own all of the interests in partnership PRS. In Year 1, PRS has $100 of ATI, $0 of business interest income, and $50 of business interest expense. PRS's ATI consists of $200 of gross income and $100 of gross deductions. PRS allocates its items comprising ATI $100 to A, $100 to B, and ($100) to C. PRS allocates its business interest expense $0 to A, $25 to B, and $25 to C.

(i) First, PRS determines its limitation pursuant to § 1.163(j)-2. PRS's section 163(j) limit is 30 percent of its ATI plus its business interest income, or $30 ($100 x 30 percent). Thus, PRS has $30 of deductible business interest expense and $20 of excess business interest expense.

(ii) Second, PRS determines each partner's allocable share of section 163(j) items used in its own section 163(j) calculation.

Table 22 to paragraph (o)(19)(ii)

	A	B	C	Total
Allocable ATI	$100	$100	($100)	$100
Allocable BII	$0	$0	$0	$0
Allocable BIE	$0	$25	$25	$50

(iii) Third, PRS compares each partner's allocable business interest income to such partner's allocable business interest expense. No partner has allocable business interest income. Consequently, each partner's allocable business interest income deficit is equal to such partner's allocable business interest expense. Thus, A's allocable business interest income deficit is $0, B's allocable business interest income deficit is $25, and C's allocable business interest income deficit is $25. The total allocable business interest income deficit is $50 ($0 + $25 + $25). No partner has allocable business interest income excess because no partner has allocable business interest income in excess of its allocable business interest expense. Thus, the total allocable business interest income excess is $0.

Table 23 to paragraph (o)(19)(iii)

	A	B	C	Total
Allocable BII	$0	$0	$0	N/A
Allocable BIE	$0	$25	$25	N/A
If allocable BII exceeds allocable BIE, then such amount = Allocable BII excess	$0	$0	$0	$0
If allocable BIE exceeds allocable BII, then such amount = Allocable BII deficit	$0	$25	$25	$50

(iv) Fourth, PRS determines each partner's final allocable business interest income excess. Because no partner had any allocable business interest income excess, each partner has final allocable business interest income excess of $0.

(v) Fifth, PRS determines each partner's remaining business interest expense. Because no partner has any allocable business interest income excess, each partner's remaining business interest expense equals its allocable business interest income deficit. Thus, A's remaining business interest expense is $0, B's remaining business interest expense is $25, and C's remaining business interest expense is $25.

Table 24 to paragraph (o)(19)(v)

	A	B	C	Total
Allocable BII deficit	$0	$25	$25	$50
Less: (Total allocable BII excess) x (Allocable BII deficit / Total allocable BII deficit)	$0	$0	$0	N/A
= Remaining BIE	$0	$25	$25	N/A

(vi) Sixth, PRS determines each partner's final allocable ATI. Because C's allocable ATI is comprised of $100 of items of deduction and loss and $0 of income and gain, C has negative allocable ATI of $100. C is the only partner with negative allocable ATI. Thus, the total negative allocable ATI amount is $100. Any partner with a negative allocable ATI, or an allocable ATI of $0, has a positive allocable ATI of $0. Therefore, C has a positive allocable ATI of $0. Because A's allocable ATI is comprised of $100 of items of income and gain and $0 of deduction and loss, A has positive allocable ATI of $100. Because B's allocable ATI is comprised of $100 of items of income and gain and $0 of deduction and loss, B has positive allocable ATI of $100. Thus, the total positive allocable ATI is $200 ($100 + $100 + $0). PRS determines A's final allocable ATI by reduc-

ing, but not below $0, A's positive allocable ATI ($100) by the product of total negative allocable ATI ($100) and the ratio of A's positive allocable ATI to the total positive allocable ATI ($100/$200). Therefore, A's positive allocable ATI is reduced by $50 ($100 x 50 percent). As a result, A's final allocable ATI is $50. PRS determines B's final allocable ATI by reducing, but not below $0, B's positive allocable ATI ($100) by the product of total negative allocable ATI ($100) and the ratio of B's positive allocable ATI to the total positive allocable ATI ($100/$200). Therefore, B's positive allocable ATI is reduced by $50 ($100 x 50 percent). As a result, B's final allocable ATI is $50. Because C has a positive allocable ATI of $0, C's final allocable ATI is $0.

Table 25 to paragraph (o)(19)(vi)

	A	B	C	Total
Allocable ATI	$100	$100	($100)	$100
If deduction and loss items comprising allocable ATI exceed income and gain items comprising allocable ATI, then such excess amount = Negative allocable ATI	$0	$0	$100	$100
If income and gain items comprising allocable ATI equal or exceed deduction and loss items comprising allocable ATI, then such amount = Positive allocable ATI	$100	$100	$0	$200

Table 26 to paragraph (o)(19)(vi)

	A	B	C	Total
Positive allocable ATI	$100	$100	$0	$200
Less: (Total negative allocable ATI) x (Positive allocable ATI / Total positive allocable ATI)	$50	$50	$0	N/A
= Final allocable ATI	$50	$50	$0	$100

(vii) Seventh, PRS compares each partner's ATI capacity (ATIC) amount to such partner's remaining business interest expense. A's ATIC amount is $15 ($50 x 30 percent), B's ATIC amount is $15 ($50 x 30 percent), and C's ATIC amount is $0 ($0 x 30 percent). Because A's ATIC amount exceeds its remaining business interest expense by $15 ($15 - $0), A has an ATIC excess of $15. B and C do not have any

ATIC excess. Thus, the total ATIC excess is $15 ($15 + $0 + $0). A does not have any ATIC deficit. Because B's remaining business interest expense exceeds its ATIC amount by $10 ($25 - $15), B has an ATIC deficit of $10. Because C's remaining business interest expense exceeds its ATIC amount by $25 ($25 - $0), C has an ATIC deficit of $25. Thus, the total ATIC deficit is $35 ($0 + $10 + $25).

Table 27 to paragraph (o)(19)(vii)	A	B	C	Total
ATIC (Final allocable ATI x 30 percent)	$15	$15	$0	N/A
Remaining BIE	$0	$25	$25	N/A
If ATIC exceeds remaining BIE, then such excess = ATIC excess	$15	$0	$0	$15
If remaining BIE exceeds ATIC, then such excess = ATIC deficit	$0	$10	$25	$35

(viii)(A) Eighth, PRS must perform the calculations and make the necessary adjustments described under paragraph (f)(2)(viii) of this section if, and only if, PRS has—

(1) An excess business interest expense greater than $0 under paragraph (f)(2)(i) of this section;

(2) A total negative allocable ATI greater than $0 under paragraph (f)(2)(vi) of this section; and

(3) A total ATIC excess greater than $0 under paragraph (f)(2)(vii) of this section. Because PRS satisfies each of these three requirements, PRS must perform the calculations and make the necessary adjustments described under paragraphs (f)(2)(viii)(B) and (C) or (D) of this section.

(B) PRS must determine each partner's priority amount and usable priority amount. Only partners with an ATIC deficit under paragraph (f)(2)(vii) of this section can have a priority amount greater than $0. Thus, only partners B and C can have a priority amount greater than $0. PRS determines a partner's priority amount as 30 percent of the amount by which such partner's allocable positive ATI exceeds its final allocable ATI. Therefore, A's priority amount is $0, B's priority amount is $15 (($100 - $50) x 30 percent), and C's priority amount is $0 (($0 - $0) x 30 percent). Thus, the total priority amount is $15 ($0 + $15 + $0). Next, PRS must determine each partner's usable priority amount. Each partner's usable priority amount is the lesser of such partner's priority amount or ATIC deficit. Thus, A has a usable priority amount of $0, B has a usable priority amount of $10, and C has a usable priority amount of $0. As a result, the total usable priority amount is $10 ($0 + $10 + $0). Because the total ATIC excess under paragraph (f)(2)(vii) of this section ($15) is greater than the total usable priority amount ($10), PRS must perform the adjustments described in paragraph (f)(2)(viii)(C) of this section.

Table 28 to paragraph (o)(19)(viii)(B)	A	B	C	Total
(Positive allocable ATI - Final allocable ATI)	$0	$50	$0	N/A
Multiplied by 30 percent	30%	30%	30%	N/A
= Priority amount	$0	$15	$0	$15

Table 29 to paragraph (o)(19)(viii)(B)	A	B	C	Total
Priority amount	$0	$15	$0	N/A
ATIC deficit	$0	$10	$25	N/A
Lesser of priority amount or ATIC deficit = Usable priority amount	$0	$10	$0	$10

(C) For purposes of paragraph (f)(2)(ix) of this section, each partner's final ATIC excess is $0. For purposes of paragraph (f)(2)(x) of this section, the following terms have the following meanings. Each partner's ATIC deficit is such partner's ATIC deficit as determined pursuant to paragraph (f)(2)(vii) of this section reduced by such partner's usable priority amount. Thus, A's ATIC deficit is $0 ($0 - $0), B's ATIC deficit is $0 ($10 - $10), and C's ATIC deficit is $25 ($25 - $0). The total ATIC deficit is the total ATIC deficit determined pursuant to paragraph (f)(2)(vii) ($35) reduced by the total usable priority amount ($10). Thus, the total ATIC deficit is $25 ($35 - $10). The total ATIC excess is the total ATIC excess determined pursuant to paragraph (f)(2)(vii) of this section ($15) reduced by the total usable priority amount ($10). Thus, the total ATIC excess is $5 ($15 - $5).

Table 30 to paragraph (o)(19)(viii)(C)	A	B	C	Total
ATIC deficit	$0	$10	$25	N/A
Less: Usable priority amount	$0	$10	$0	N/A
= ATIC deficit for purposes of paragraph (f)(2)(x) of this section	$0	$0	$25	$25

(D)(1) In light of the fact that the total ATIC excess was greater than the total usable priority amount under paragraph (f)(2)(viii)(B) of this section, paragraph (f)(2)(viii)(D) of this section does not apply.

(2) In sum, the correct amounts to be used in paragraphs (o)(19)(ix) and (x) of this section are as follows.

Table 31 to paragraph (o)(19)(viii)(D)(2)	A	B	C	Total
ATIC excess	$5	$0	$0	$5
ATIC deficit	$0	$0	$25	$25

(ix) Ninth, PRS determines each partner's final ATIC excess amount. Pursuant to paragraph (f)(2)(viii)(C) of this section, each partner's final ATIC excess amount is $0.

(x) Tenth, PRS determines each partner's final ATIC deficit amount. Because C has an ATIC deficit, PRS must determine C's final ATIC deficit amount. C's final ATIC deficit amount is C's ATIC deficit ($25), reduced, but not below $0, by the product of the total ATIC excess ($5) and the ratio of C's ATIC deficit to the total ATIC deficit ($25/$25). Therefore, C has $20 of final ATIC deficit ($25 – ($5 x 100 percent)).

Table 32 to paragraph (o)(19)(x)	A	B	C	Total
ATIC deficit	$0	$0	$25	N/A

Table 32 to paragraph (o)(19)(x)

	A	B	C	Total
Less: (Total ATIC excess) x (ATIC deficit / Total ATIC deficit)	$0	$0	$5	N/A
= Final ATIC deficit	$0	$0	$20	$20

(ix) Eleventh, PRS allocates deductible business interest expense and section 163(j) excess items to the partners. Pursuant to paragraph (f)(2)(i) of this section, PRS has $20 of excess business interest expense. PRS allocates the excess business interest expense dollar for dollar to the partners with final ATIC deficits. Thus, PRS allocates its excess business interest expense $20 to C. A partner's allocable business interest expense is deductible business interest expense to the extent it exceeds such partner's share of excess business interest expense. Therefore, A has deductible business interest expense of $0 ($0 - $0), B has deductible business interest expense of $25 ($25 - $0), and C has deductible business interest expense of $5 ($25 - $20).

Table 33 to paragraph (o)(19)(xi)

	A	B	C	Total
Deductible BIE	$0	$25	$5	$30
EBIE allocated	$0	$0	$20	$20
ETI allocated	$0	$0	$0	$0
EBII allocated	$0	$0	$0	$0

(20) *Example 20: Facts.*—A, B, C, and D own all of the interests in partnership PRS. In Year 1, PRS has $200 of ATI, $0 of business interest income, and $140 of business interest expense. PRS's ATI consists of $600 of gross income and $400 of gross deductions. PRS allocates its items comprising ATI $100 to A, $100 to B, $400 to C, and ($400) to D. PRS allocates its business interest expense $0 to A, $40 to B, $60 to C, and $40 to D.

(i) First, PRS determines its limitation pursuant to §1.163(j)-2. PRS's section 163(j) limit is 30 percent of its ATI plus its business interest income, or $60 ($200 x 30 percent). Thus, PRS has $60 of deductible business interest expense and $80 of excess business interest expense.

(ii) Second, PRS determines each partner's allocable share of section 163(j) items used in its own section 163(j) calculation.

Table 34 to paragraph (o)(20)(ii)

	A	B	C	D	Total
Allocable ATI	$100	$100	$400	($400)	$200
Allocable BII	$0	$0	$0	$0	$0
Allocable BIE	$0	$40	$60	$40	$140

(iii) Third, PRS compares each partner's allocable business interest income to such partner's allocable business interest expense. No partner has allocable business interest income. Consequently, each partner's allocable business interest income deficit is equal to such partner's allocable business interest expense. Thus, A's allocable business interest income deficit is $0, B's allocable business interest income deficit is $40, C's allocable business interest income deficit is $60, and D's allocable business interest income deficit is $40. The total allocable business interest income deficit is $140 ($0 + $40 + $60 + $40). No partner has allocable business interest income excess because no partner has allocable business interest income in excess of its allocable business interest expense. Thus, the total allocable business interest income excess is $0.

Table 35 to paragraph (o)(20)(iii)

	A	B	C	D	Total
Allocable BII	$0	$0	$0	$0	N/A
Allocable BIE	$0	$40	$60	$40	N/A
If allocable BII exceeds allocable BIE, then such amount = Allocable BII excess	$0	$0	$0	$0	$0
If allocable BIE exceeds allocable BII, then such amount = Allocable BII deficit	$0	$40	$60	$40	$140

(iv) Fourth, PRS determines each partner's final allocable business interest income excess. Because no partner has any allocable business interest income excess, each partner has final allocable business interest income excess of $0.

(v) Fifth, PRS determines each partner's remaining business interest expense. Because no partner has any allocable business interest income excess, each partner's remaining business interest expense equals its allocable business interest income deficit. Thus, A's remaining business interest expense is $0, B's remaining business interest expense is $40, C's remaining business interest expense is $60, and D's remaining business interest expense is $40.

Table 36 to paragraph (o)(20)(v)

	A	B	C	D	Total
Allocable BII deficit	$0	$40	$60	$40	$140
Less: (Total allocable BII excess) x (Allocable BII deficit / Total allocable BII deficit)	$0	$0	$0	$0	N/A
= Remaining BIE	$0	$40	$60	$40	N/A

(vi) Sixth, PRS determines each partner's final allocable ATI. Because D's allocable ATI is comprised of $400 of items of deduction and loss and $0 of income and gain, D has negative allocable ATI of $400. D is the only partner with negative allocable ATI. Thus, the total negative allocable ATI amount is $400. Any partner with a negative allocable ATI, or an allocable ATI of $0, has a positive allocable ATI of $0. *Therefore, D has a positive allocable ATI of $0. PRS determines A's final allocable ATI by reducing, but not below $0, A's positive allocable ATI ($100) by the product of total negative allocable ATI ($400) and the ratio of A's positive allocable ATI to the total positive allocable ATI ($100/$600). Therefore, A's positive allo-* cable ATI is reduced by $66.67 ($400 x 16.67 percent). As a result, A's final allocable ATI is $33.33. PRS determines B's final allocable ATI by reducing, but not below $0, B's positive allocable ATI ($100) by the product of total negative allocable ATI ($400) and the ratio of B's positive allocable ATI to the total positive allocable ATI ($100/$600). Therefore, B's positive allocable ATI is reduced by $66.67 ($400 x 16.67 percent). As a result, B's final allocable ATI is $33.33. PRS determines C's final allocable ATI by reducing, but not below $0, C's positive allocable ATI ($400) by the product of total negative allocable ATI ($400) and the ratio of C's positive allocable ATI to the total positive allocable ATI ($400/$600). Therefore, C's positive allocable

ATI is reduced by $266.67 ($400 x 66.67 percent). As a result, C's final allocable ATI is $133.33. Because D has a positive allocable ATI of $0, D's final allocable ATI is $0.

Table 37 to paragraph (o)(20)(vi)	A	B	C	D	Total
Allocable ATI	$100	$100	$400	($400)	$200
If deduction and loss items comprising allocable ATI exceed income and gain items comprising allocable ATI, then such excess amount = Negative allocable ATI	$0	$0	$0	$400	$400
If income and gain items comprising allocable ATI equal or exceed deduction and loss items comprising allocable ATI, then such amount = Positive allocable ATI	$100	$100	$400	$0	$600

Table 38 to paragraph (o)(20)(vi)	A	B	C	D	Total
Positive allocable ATI	$100	$100	$400	$0	$600
Less: (Total negative allocable ATI) x (Positive allocable ATI / Total positive allocable ATI)	$66.67	$66.67	$266.67	$0	N/A
= Final allocable ATI	$33.33	$33.33	$133.33	$0	$200

(vii) Seventh, PRS compares each partner's ATI capacity (ATIC) amount to such partner's remaining business interest expense. A's ATIC amount is $10 ($33.33 x 30 percent), B's ATIC amount is $10 ($33.33 x 30 percent), C's ATIC amount is $40 ($133.33 x 30 percent), and D's ATIC amount is $0 ($0 x 30 percent). Because A's ATIC amount exceeds its remaining business interest expense by $10 ($10 - $0), A has an ATIC excess of $10. B, C, and D do not have any ATIC excess. Thus, the total ATIC excess is $10 ($10 + $0 + $0 + $0). A does not have any ATIC deficit. Because B's remaining business interest expense exceeds its ATIC amount by $30 ($40 - $10), B has an ATIC deficit of $30. Because C's remaining business interest expense exceeds its ATIC amount by $20 ($60 - $40), C has an ATIC deficit of $20. Because D's remaining business interest expense exceeds its ATIC amount by $40 ($40 - $0), D has an ATIC deficit of $40. Thus, the total ATIC deficit is $90 ($0 + $30 + $20 + $40).

Table 39 to paragraph (o)(20)(vii)	A	B	C	D	Total
ATIC (Final allocable ATI x 30 percent)	$10	$10	$40	$0	N/A
Remaining BIE	$0	$40	$60	$40	N/A
If ATIC exceeds remaining BIE, then such excess = ATIC excess	$10	$0	$0	$0	$10
If remaining BIE exceeds ATIC, then such excess = ATIC deficit	$0	$30	$20	$40	$90

(viii)(A) Eighth, PRS must perform the calculations and make the necessary adjustments described under paragraph (f)(2)(viii) of this section if, and only if, PRS has (1) an excess business interest expense greater than $0 under paragraph (f)(2)(i) of this section, (2) a total negative allocable ATI greater than $0 under paragraph (f)(2)(vi) of this section, and (3) a total ATIC excess amount greater than $0 under paragraph (f)(2)(vii) of this section. Because PRS satisfies each of these three requirements, PRS must perform the calculations and make the necessary adjustments described under paragraphs (f)(2)(viii)(B) and (C) or paragraph (f)(2)(viii)(D) of this section.

(B) PRS must determine each partner's priority amount and usable priority amount. Only partners with an ATIC deficit under paragraph (f)(2)(vii) of this section can have a priority amount greater than $0. Thus, only partners B, C, and D can have a priority amount greater than $0. PRS determines a partner's priority amount as 30 percent of the amount by which such partner's allocable positive ATI exceeds its final allocable ATI. Therefore, B's priority amount is $20 (($100 - $33.33) x 30 percent), C's priority amount is $80 (($400 - $133.33) x 30 percent), and D's priority amount is $0 (($0 - $0) x 30 percent). Thus, the total priority amount is $100 ($0 + $20 + $80 + $0). Next, PRS must determine each partner's usable priority amount. Each partner's usable priority amount is the lesser of such partner's priority amount or ATIC deficit. Thus, A has a usable priority amount of $0, B has a usable priority amount of $20, C has a usable priority amount of $20, and D has a usable priority amount of $0. As a result, the total usable priority amount is $40 ($0 + $20 + $20 + $0). Because the total usable priority amount ($40) is greater than the total ATIC excess under paragraph (f)(2)(vii) of this section ($10), PRS must perform the adjustments described in paragraph (f)(2)(viii)(D) of this section.

Table 40 to paragraph (o)(20)(viii)(B)	A	B	C	D	Total
(Positive allocable ATI - Final allocable ATI)	$0	$66.67	$266.67	$0	N/A
Multiplied by 30 percent	30%	30%	30%	30%	N/A
= Priority amount	$0	$20	$80	$0	$100

Table 41 to paragraph (o)(20)(viii)(B)	A	B	C	D	Total
Priority amount	$0	$20	$80	$0	N/A
ATIC deficit	$0	$30	$20	$40	N/A
Lesser of priority amount or ATIC deficit = Usable priority amount	$0	$20	$20	$0	$40

(C) In light of the fact that the total usable priority amount is greater than the total ATIC excess under paragraph (f)(2)(viii)(B) of this section, paragraph (f)(2)(viii)(C) of this section does not apply.

(D)(1) Because B and C are the only partners with priority amounts greater than $0, B and C are priority partners, while A and D are non-priority partners. For purposes of paragraph (f)(2)(ix) of this section, each partner's final ATIC excess amount is $0. For purposes of paragraph (f)(2)(x) of this section, each non-priority partner's final ATIC deficit amount is such partner's ATIC deficit determined pursuant to paragraph (f)(2)(vii) of this section. Therefore, A has a final ATIC deficit of $0 and D has a final ATIC deficit of $40. Additionally, for purposes of paragraph (f)(2)(x) of this section, PRS must determine each priority partner's step eight excess share. A priority partner's step eight excess share is the product of the total

ATIC excess and the ratio of the partner's priority amount to the total priority amount. Thus, B's step eight excess share is $2 ($10 x ($20/$100)) and C's step eight excess share is $8 ($10 x ($80/$100)). To the extent a priority partner's step eight excess share exceeds its ATIC deficit, the excess will be the partner's ATIC excess for purposes of paragraph (f)(2)(x) of this section. Thus, B and C each have an ATIC excess of $0, resulting in a total ATIC excess is $0. To the extent a priority partner's ATIC deficit exceeds its step eight excess

share, the excess will be the partner's ATIC deficit for purposes of paragraph (f)(2)(x) of this section. Because B's ATIC deficit ($30) exceeds its step eight excess share ($2), B's ATIC deficit for purposes of paragraph (f)(2)(x) of this section is $28 ($30 - $2). Because C's ATIC deficit ($20) exceeds its step eight excess share ($8), C's ATIC deficit for purposes of paragraph (f)(2)(x) of this section is $12 ($20 - $8). Thus, the total ATIC deficit is $40 ($28 + $12).

Table 42 to paragraph (o)(20)(viii)(D)(1)

	A	B	C	D	Total
Non-priority partners ATIC deficit in paragraph (f)(2)(vii) = Final ATIC deficit for purposes of paragraph (f)(2)(x) of this section	$0	N/A	N/A	$40	N/A

Table 43 to paragraph (o)(20)(viii)(D)(1)

	A	B	C	D	Total
Priority partners step eight excess share = (Total ATIC excess) x (Priority / Total priority)	N/A	$2	$8	N/A	N/A
ATIC deficit	N/A	$30	$20	N/A	N/A
If step eight excess share exceeds ATIC deficit, then such excess = ATIC excess for purposes of paragraph (f)(2)(x) of this section	N/A	$0	$0	N/A	$0
If ATIC deficit exceeds step eight excess share, then such excess = ATIC deficit for purposes of paragraph (f)(2)(x) of this section	N/A	$28	$12	N/A	$40

(2) In sum, the correct amounts to be used in paragraphs (o)(20)(ix) and (x) of this section are as follows.

Table 44 to paragraph (o)(20)(viii)(D)(2)

	A	B	C	D	Total
ATIC excess	$0	$0	$0	$0	$0
ATIC deficit	$0	$28	$12	$0	$40
Non-priority partner final ATIC deficit	$0	$0	$0	$40	N/A

(ix) Ninth, PRS determines each partner's final ATIC excess amount. Pursuant to paragraph (f)(2)(viii)(D) of this section, each priority and non-priority partner's final ATIC excess amount is $0.

(x) Tenth, PRS determines each partner's final ATIC deficit amount. Because B has an ATIC deficit, PRS must determine B's final ATIC deficit amount. B's final ATIC deficit amount is B's ATIC deficit ($28), reduced, but not below $0, by the product of the total ATIC excess ($0) and the ratio of B's ATIC deficit to the total ATIC deficit

($28/$40). Therefore, B has $28 of final ATIC deficit ($28 – ($0 x 70 percent)). Because C has an ATIC deficit, PRS must determine C's final ATIC deficit amount. C's final ATIC deficit amount is C's ATIC deficit ($12), reduced, but not below $0, by the product of the total ATIC excess ($0) and the ratio of C's ATIC deficit to the total ATIC deficit ($12/$40). Therefore, C has $12 of final ATIC deficit ($12 – ($0 x 30 percent)). Pursuant to paragraph (f)(2)(viii)(D) of this section, D's final ATIC deficit amount is $40.

Table 45 to paragraph (o)(20)(x)

	A	B	C	D	Total
ATIC deficit	N/A	$28	$12	N/A	N/A
Less: (Total ATIC excess) x (ATIC deficit / Total ATIC deficit)	N/A	$0	$0	N/A	N/A
= Final ATIC deficit	$0	$28	$12	$40	$80

(xi) Eleventh, PRS allocates deductible business interest expense and section 163(j) excess items to the partners. Pursuant to paragraph (f)(2)(i) of this section, PRS has $80 of excess business interest expense. PRS allocates the excess business interest expense dollar for dollar to the partners with final ATIC deficits. Thus, PRS allocates its excess business interest expense $28 to B, $12 to C, and $40 to D. A partner's allocable business interest expense is deductible business

interest expense to the extent it exceeds such partner's share of excess business interest expense. Therefore, A has deductible business interest expense of $0 ($0 - $0), B has deductible business interest expense of $12 ($40 - $28), C has deductible business interest expense of $48 ($60 - $12), and D has deductible business interest expense of $0 ($40 - $40).

Table 46 to paragraph (o)(20)(xi)

	A	B	C	D	Total
Deductible BIE	$0	$12	$48	$0	$60
EBIE allocated	$0	$28	$12	$40	$80
ETI allocated	$0	$0	$0	$0	$0
EBII allocated	$0	$0	$0	$0	$0

(21) *Example 21: Facts.*—A, B, C, and D own all of the interests in partnership PRS. In Year 1, PRS has $200 of ATI, $0 of business interest income, and $150 of business interest expense. PRS's ATI consists of $500 of gross income and $300 of gross deductions. PRS allocates its items comprising ATI $50 to A, $50 to B, $400 to C, and ($300) to D. PRS allocates its business interest expense $0 to A, $50 to B, $50 to C, and $50 to D.

(i) First, PRS determines its limitation pursuant to §1.163(j)-2. PRS's section 163(j) limit is 30 percent of its ATI plus its business interest income, or $60 ($200 x 30 percent). Thus, PRS has $60 of deductible business interest expense, and $90 of excess business interest expense.

(ii) Second, PRS determines each partner's allocable share of section 163(j) items used in its own section 163(j) calculation.

Table 47 to paragraph (o)(21)(ii)	A	B	C	D	Total
Allocable ATI	$50	$50	$400	($300)	$200
Allocable BII	$0	$0	$0	$0	$0
Allocable BIE	$0	$50	$50	$50	$150

(iii) Third, PRS compares each partner's allocable business interest income to such partner's allocable business interest expense. No partner has allocable business interest income. Consequently, each partner's allocable business interest income deficit is equal to such partner's allocable business interest expense. Thus, A's allocable business interest income deficit is $0, B's allocable business interest income deficit is $50, C's allocable business interest income deficit is $50, and D's allocable business interest income deficit is $50. The total allocable business interest income deficit is $150 ($0 + $50 + $50 + $50). No partner has allocable business interest income excess because no partner has allocable business interest income in excess of its allocable business interest expense. Thus, the total allocable business interest income excess is $0.

Table 48 to paragraph (o)(21)(iii)	A	B	C	D	Total
Allocable BII	$0	$0	$0	$0	N/A
Allocable BIE	$0	$50	$50	$50	N/A
If allocable BII exceeds allocable BIE, then such amount = Allocable BII excess	$0	$0	$0	$0	$0
If allocable BIE exceeds allocable BII, then such amount = Allocable BII deficit	$0	$50	$50	$50	$150

(iv) Fourth, PRS determines each partner's final allocable business interest income excess. Because no partner has any allocable business interest income excess, each partner has final allocable business interest income excess of $0.

(v) Fifth, PRS determines each partner's remaining business interest expense. Because no partner has any allocable business interest income excess, each partner's remaining business interest expense equals its allocable business interest income deficit. Thus, A's remaining business interest expense is $0, B's remaining business interest expense is $50, C's remaining business interest expense is $50, and D's remaining business interest expense is $50.

Table 49 to paragraph (o)(21)(v)	A	B	C	D	Total
Allocable BII deficit	$0	$50	$50	$50	$150
Less: (Total allocable BII excess) x (Allocable BII deficit / Total allocable BII deficit)	$0	$0	$0	$0	N/A
= Remaining BIE	$0	$50	$50	$50	N/A

(vi) Sixth, PRS determines each partner's final allocable ATI. Because D's allocable ATI is comprised of $300 of items of deduction and loss and $0 of income and gain, D has allocable ATI of $300. D is the only partner with negative allocable ATI. Thus, the total negative allocable ATI amount is $300. Any partner with a negative allocable ATI, or an allocable ATI of $0, has a positive allocable ATI of $0. Therefore, D has a positive allocable ATI of $0. PRS determines A's final allocable ATI by reducing, but not below $0, A's positive allocable ATI ($50) by the product of total negative allocable ATI ($300) and the ratio of A's positive allocable ATI to the total positive allocable ATI ($50/$500). Therefore, A's positive allocable ATI is reduced by $30 ($300 x 10 percent). As a result, A's final allocable ATI is $20. PRS determines B's final allocable ATI by reducing, but not below $0, B's positive allocable ATI ($50) by the product of total negative allocable ATI ($300) and the ratio of B's positive allocable ATI to the total positive allocable ATI ($50/$500). Therefore, B's positive allocable ATI is reduced by $30 ($300 x 10 percent). As a result, B's final allocable ATI is $20. PRS determines C's final allocable ATI by reducing, but not below $0, C's positive allocable ATI ($400) by the product of total negative allocable ATI ($300) and the ratio of C's positive allocable ATI to the total positive allocable ATI ($400/$500). Therefore, C's positive allocable ATI is reduced by $240 ($300 x 80 percent). As a result, C's final allocable ATI is $160. Because D has a positive allocable ATI of $0, D's final allocable ATI is $0.

Table 50 to paragraph (o)(21)(vi)	A	B	C	D	Total
Allocable ATI	$50	$50	$400	($300)	$200
If deduction and loss items comprising allocable ATI exceed income and gain items comprising allocable ATI, then such excess amount = Negative allocable ATI	$0	$0	$0	$300	$300
If income and gain items comprising allocable ATI equal or exceed deduction and loss items comprising allocable ATI, then such amount = Positive allocable ATI	$50	$50	$400	$0	$500

Table 51 to paragraph (o)(21)(vi)	A	B	C	D	Total
Positive allocable ATI	$50	$50	$400	$0	$500
Less: (Total negative allocable ATI) x (Positive allocable ATI / Total positive allocable ATI)	$30	$30	$240	$0	N/A
= Final allocable ATI	$20	$20	$160	$0	$200

(vii) Seventh, PRS compares each partner's ATI capacity (ATIC) amount to such partner's remaining business interest expense. A's ATIC amount is $6 ($20 x 30 percent), B's ATIC amount is $6 ($20 x 30 percent), C's ATIC amount is $48 ($160 x 30 percent), and D's ATIC amount is $0 ($0 x 30 percent). Because A's ATIC amount exceeds its remaining business interest expense by $6 ($6 - $0), A has an ATIC excess of $6. B, C, and D do not have any ATIC excess. Thus, the total ATIC excess amount is $6 ($6 + $0 + $0 + $0). A does not have any ATIC deficit. Because B's remaining business interest expense exceeds its ATIC amount by $44 ($50 - $6), B has an ATIC deficit of $44. Because C's remaining business interest expense exceeds its ATIC amount by $2 ($50 - $48), C has an ATIC deficit of $2. Because D's remaining business interest expense exceeds its ATIC amount by $50 ($50 - $0), D has an ATIC deficit of $50. Thus, the total ATIC deficit is $96 ($0 + $44 + $2 + $50).

Table 52 to paragraph (o)(21)(vii)	A	B	C	D	Total
ATIC (Final allocable ATI x 30 percent)	$6	$6	$48	$0	N/A
Remaining BIE	$0	$50	$50	$50	N/A
If ATIC exceeds remaining BIE, then such excess = ATIC excess	$6	$0	$0	$0	$6
If remaining BIE exceeds ATIC, then such excess = ATIC deficit	$0	$44	$2	$50	$96

(viii)(A) Eighth, PRS must perform the calculations and make the necessary adjustments described under paragraph (f)(2)(viii) of this section if, and only if, PRS has—

(1)An excess business interest expense greater than $0 under paragraph (f)(2)(i) of this section;

(2)A total negative allocable ATI greater than $0 under paragraph (f)(2)(vi) of this section; and

(3)A total ATIC excess amount greater than $0 under paragraph (f)(2)(vii) of this section. Because PRS satisfies each of these three requirements, PRS must perform the calculations and make the necessary adjustments described under paragraph (f)(2)(viii) of this section.

(B)PRS must determine each partner's priority amount and usable priority amount. Only partners with an ATIC deficit under paragraph (f)(2)(vii) of this section of this section can have a priority

amount greater than $0. Thus, only partners B, C, and D can have a priority amount greater than $0. PRS determines a partner's priority amount as 30 percent of the amount by which such partner's allocable positive ATI exceeds its final allocable ATI. Therefore, B's priority amount is $9 (($50 - $20) x 30 percent), C's priority amount is $72 (($400 - $160) x 30 percent), and D's priority amount is $0 (($0 - $0) x 30 percent). Thus, the total priority amount is $81 ($0 + $9 + $72 + $0). Next, PRS must determine each partner's usable priority amount. Each partner's usable priority amount is the lesser of such partner's priority amount or ATIC deficit. Thus, B has a usable priority amount of $9, C has a usable priority amount of $2, and D has a usable priority amount of $0. As a result, the total usable priority amount is $11 ($0 + $9 + $2 + $0). Because the total usable priority amount ($11) is greater than the total ATIC excess ($6) under paragraph (f)(2)(vii) of this section, PRS must perform the adjustments described in paragraph (f)(2)(viii)(D) of this section.

Table 53 to paragraph (o)(21)(viii)(B)	A	B	C	D	Total
(Positive allocable ATI - Final allocable ATI)	$0	$30	$240	$0	N/A
Multiplied by 30 percent	30%	30%	30%	30%	N/A
= Priority amount	$0	$9	$72	$0	$81

Table 54 to paragraph (o)(21)(viii)(B)	A	B	C	D	Total
Priority amount	$0	$9	$72	$0	N/A
ATIC deficit	$0	$44	$2	$50	N/A
Lesser of priority amount or ATIC deficit = Usable priority amount	$0	$9	$2	$0	$11

(C) In light of the fact that the total usable priority amount is greater than the total ATIC excess under paragraph (f)(2)(viii)(B) of this section, paragraph (f)(2)(viii)(C) of this section does not apply.

(D)(1) Because B and C are the only partners with priority amounts greater than $0, B and C are priority partners, while A and D are non-priority partners. For purposes of paragraph (f)(2)(ix) of this section, each partner's final ATIC excess amount is $0. For purposes of paragraph (f)(2)(x) of this section, each non-priority partner's final ATIC deficit amount is such partner's ATIC deficit determined pursuant to paragraph (f)(2)(vii) of this section. Therefore, A has a final ATIC deficit of $0 and D has a final ATIC deficit of $50. Additionally, for purposes of paragraph (f)(2)(x) of this section, PRS must determine each priority partner's step eight excess share. A priority partner's step eight excess share is the product of the total ATIC excess and the ratio of the partner's priority amount to the total priority amount. Thus, B's step eight excess share is $0.67 ($6 x

($9/$81)) and C's step eight excess share is $5.33 ($6 x ($72/$81)). To the extent a priority partner's step eight excess share exceeds its ATIC deficit, the excess will be the partner's ATIC excess for purposes of paragraph (f)(2)(x) of this section. B's step eight excess share does not exceed its ATIC deficit. Because C's step eight excess share ($5.33) exceeds its ATIC deficit ($2), C's ATIC excess for purposes of paragraph (f)(2)(x) of this section is $3.33 ($5.33 - $2). Thus, the total ATIC excess for purposes of paragraph (f)(2)(x) of this section is $3.33 ($0 + $3.33). To the extent a priority partner's ATIC deficit exceeds its step eight excess share, the excess will be the partner's ATIC deficit for purposes of paragraph (f)(2)(x) of this section. Because B's ATIC deficit ($44) exceeds its step eight excess share ($0.67), B's ATIC deficit for purposes of paragraph (f)(2)(x) of this section is $43.33 ($44 - $0.67). C's ATIC deficit does not exceed its step eight excess share. Thus, the total ATIC deficit for purposes of paragraph (f)(2)(x) of this section is $43.33 ($43.33 + $0).

Table 55 to paragraph (o)(21)(viii)(D)(1)	A	B	C	D	Total
Non-priority partners ATIC deficit in paragraph (f)(2)(vii) = Final ATIC deficit for purposes of paragraph (f)(2)(x) of this section	$0	N/A	N/A	$50	N/A

Table 56 to paragraph (o)(21)(viii)(D)(1)	A	B	C	D	Total
Priority partners step eight excess share = (Total ATIC excess) x (Priority / Total priority)	N/A	$0.67	$5.33	N/A	N/A
ATIC deficit	N/A	$44	$2	N/A	N/A
If step eight excess share exceeds ATIC deficit, then such excess = ATIC excess for purposes of paragraph (f)(2)(x) of this section	N/A	$0	$3.33	N/A	$3.33
If ATIC deficit exceeds step eight excess share, then such excess = ATIC deficit for purposes of paragraph (f)(2)(x) of this section	N/A	$43.33	$0	N/A	$43.33

(2) In sum, the correct amounts to be used in paragraphs (o)(21)(ix) and (x) of this section are as follows.

Table 57 to paragraph (o)(21)(viii)(D)(2)					
	A	B	C	D	Total
ATIC excess	$0	$0	$3.33	$0	$3.33
ATIC deficit	$0	$43.33	$0	$0	$43.33
Non-priority partner final ATIC deficit	$0	$0	$0	$50	N/A

(ix) Ninth, PRS determines each partner's final ATIC excess amount. Pursuant to paragraph (f)(2)(viii)(D) of this section, each priority and non-priority partner's final ATIC excess amount is $0.

(x) Tenth, PRS determines each partner's final ATIC deficit amount. Because B has an ATIC deficit, PRS must determine B's final ATIC deficit amount. B's final ATIC deficit amount is B's ATIC deficit ($43.33), reduced, but not below $0, by the product of the total ATIC excess ($3.33) and the ratio of B's ATIC deficit to the total ATIC deficit ($43.33/$43.33). Therefore, B has $40 of final ATIC deficit ($43.33 – ($3.33 x 100 percent)). Pursuant to paragraph (f)(2)(viii)(D) of this section, D's final ATIC deficit amount is $40.

Table 58 to paragraph (o)(21)(x)					
	A	B	C	D	Total
ATIC deficit	$0	$43.33	$0	N/A	N/A
Less: (Total ATIC excess) x (ATIC deficit / Total ATIC deficit)	$0	$3.33	$0	N/A	N/A
= Final ATIC deficit	$0	$40	$0	$50	$90

(xi) Eleventh, PRS allocates deductible business interest expense and section 163(j) excess items to the partners. Pursuant to paragraph (f)(2)(i) of this section, PRS has $90 of excess business interest expense. PRS allocates the excess business interest expense dollar for dollar to the partners with final ATIC deficits. Thus, PRS allocates its excess business interest expense $40 to B and $50 to D. A partner's allocable business interest expense is deductible business interest expense to the extent it exceeds such partner's share of excess business interest expense. Therefore, A has deductible business interest expense of $0 ($0 - $0), B has deductible business interest expense of $10 ($50 - $40), C has deductible business interest expense of $50 ($50 - $0), and D has deductible business interest expense of $0 ($50 - $50).

Table 59 to paragraph (o)(21)(xi)					
	A	B	C	D	Total
Deductible BIE	$0	$10	$50	$0	$60
EBIE allocated	$0	$40	$0	$50	$90
ETI allocated	$0	$0	$0	$0	$0
EBII allocated	$0	$0	$0	$0	$0

(22) *Example 22.*—(i) *Facts.* A and B are equal shareholders in X, a subchapter S corporation. In Year 1, X has $100 of ATI and $40 of business interest expense. A has $100 of ATI and $20 of business interest expense from its sole proprietorship. B has $0 of ATI and $20 of business interest expense from its sole proprietorship.

(ii) *S corporation-level.* In Year 1, X's section 163(j) limit is 30 percent of its ATI, or $30 ($100 x 30 percent). Thus, X has $30 of deductible business interest expense and $10 of disallowed business interest expense. Such $30 of deductible business interest expense is includable in X's nonseparately stated income or loss, and is not subject to further limitation under section 163(j). X carries forward the $10 of disallowed business interest expense to Year 2 as a disallowed business interest expense carryforward under § 1.163(j)-2(c). X may not currently deduct all $40 of its business interest expense in Year 1. X only reduces its accumulated adjustments account in Year 1 by the $30 of deductible business interest expense in Year 1 under § 1.163(j)-6(l)(7).

(iii) *Shareholder allocations.* A and B are each allocated $35 of nonseparately stated taxable income ($50 items of income or gain, less $15 of deductible business interest expense) from X. A and B do not reduce their basis in X by the $10 of disallowed business interest expense.

(iv) *Shareholder-level computations.* A, in computing its limit under section 163(j), has $100 of ATI and $20 of business interest expense from its sole proprietorship. A's section 163(j) limit is $30 ($100 x 30 percent). Thus, A's $20 of business interest expense is deductible business interest expense. B, in computing its limit under section 163(j), has $20 of business interest expense from its sole proprietorship. B's section 163(j) limit is $0 ($0 x 30 percent). Thus, B's $20 of business interest expense is not allowed as a deduction and is treated as business interest expense paid or accrued by B in Year 2.

(23) *Example 23.*—(i) *Facts.* The facts are the same as in *Example 22* in paragraph (o)(22)(i) of this section. In Year 2, X has $233.33 of ATI, $0 of business interest income, and $30 of business interest expense. A has $100 of ATI and $20 of business interest expense from its sole proprietorship. B has $0 of ATI and $20 of business interest expense from its sole proprietorship.

(ii) *S corporation-level.* In Year 2, X's section 163(j) limit is 30 percent of its ATI plus its business interest income, or $70 ($233.33 x 30 percent). Because X's section 163(j) limit exceeds X's $40 of business interest expense ($30 from Year 2, plus the $10 disallowed business interest expense carryforwards from Year 1), X may deduct all $40 of business interest expense in Year 2. Such $40 of deductible business interest expense is includable in X's nonseparately stated income or loss, and is not subject to further limitation under section 163(j). Pursuant to § 1.163(j)-6(l)(7), X must reduce its accumulated adjustments account by $40. Additionally, X has $100 of excess taxable income under § 1.163(j)-1(b)(17).

(iii) *Shareholder allocations.* A and B are each allocated $96.67 of nonseparately stated taxable income ($116.67 items of income or gain, less $20 of deductible business interest expense) from X. Additionally, A and B are each allocated $50 of excess taxable income under § 1.163(j)-6(l)(4). As a result, A and B each increase their ATI by $50.

(iv) *Shareholder-level computations.* A, in computing its limit under section 163(j), has $150 of ATI ($100 from its sole proprietorship, plus $50 excess taxable income) and $20 of business interest expense (from its sole proprietorship). A's section 163(j) limit is $45 ($150 x 30 percent). Thus, A's $20 of business interest expense is deductible business interest expense. B, in computing its limit under section 163(j), has $50 of ATI ($0 from its sole proprietorship, plus $50 excess taxable income) and $40 of business interest expense ($20 from its sole proprietorship, plus $20 disallowed business interest expense from its sole proprietorship in Year 1). B's section 163(j) limit is $15 ($50 x 30 percent). Thus, $15 of B's business interest expense is deductible business interest expense. The $25 of B's business interest expense not allowed as a deduction ($40 business interest expense, less $15 section 163(j) limit) is treated as business interest expense paid or accrued by B in Year 3.

(24) *Example 24.*—(i) *Facts.* On January 1, 2020, L and M form LM, a publicly traded partnership (as defined in § 1.7704-1), and agree that each will be allocated a 50 percent share of all LM items. The partnership agreement provides that LM will make allocations under section 704(c) using the remedial allocation method under § 1.704-3(d). L contributes depreciable property with an adjusted tax basis of $4,000 and a fair market value of $10,000. The property is depreciated using the straight-line method with a 10-year recovery period and has 4 years remaining on its recovery period. M contributes $10,000 in cash, which LM uses to purchase land. Except for the depreciation deductions, LM's expenses equal its income in each year

of the 10 years commencing with the year LM is formed. LM has a valid section 754 election in effect.

(ii) *Section 163(j) remedial items and partner basis items.* LM sells the asset contributed by L in a fully taxable transaction at a time when the adjusted basis of the property is $4,000. Under §1.163(j)-6(e)(2)(ii), solely for purposes of §1.163(j)-6, the tax gain of $6,000 is allocated equally between L and M ($3,000 each). To avoid shifting built-in gain to the non-contributing partner (M) in a manner consistent with the rule in section 704(c), a remedial deduction of $3,000 is allocated to M (leaving M with no net tax gain), and remedial income of $3,000 is allocated to L (leaving L with total tax gain of $6,000).

(25) *Example 25.*—(i) *Facts.* The facts are the same as *Example 24* in paragraph (o)(24) of this section except the property contributed by L had an adjusted tax basis of zero. For each of the 10 years following the contribution, there would be $500 of section 704(c) remedial income allocated to L and $500 of remedial deductions allocated to M with respect to the contributed asset. A buyer of M's units would step into M's shoes with respect to the $500 of annual remedial deductions. A buyer of L's units would step into L's shoes with respect to the $500 of annual remedial income and would have an annual section 743(b) deduction of $1,000 (net $500 of deductions).

(ii) *Analysis.* Pursuant to §1.163(j)-6(d)(2)(ii), solely for purposes of §1.163(j)-6, a buyer of L's units immediately after formation of LM would offset its $500 annual section 704(c) remedial income allocation with $500 of annual section 743(b) adjustment (leaving the buyer with net $500 of section 743(b) deduction). As a result, such buyer would be in the same position as a buyer of M's units. Each buyer would have net deductions of $500 per year, which would not affect ATI before 2022.

(26) *Example 26.*—(i) *Facts.* X and Y are partners in partnership PRS. In Year 1, PRS had $200 of excess business interest expense. Pursuant to §1.163(j)-6(f)(2), PRS allocated $100 of such excess business interest expense to each of its partners. In Year 2, X lends $10,000 to PRS and receives $1,000 of interest income for the taxable year (self-charged lending transaction). X is not in the trade or business of lending money. The $1,000 of interest expense resulting from this loan is allocable to PRS's trade or business assets. As a result, such $1,000 of interest expense is business interest expense of PRS. X and Y are each allocated $500 of such business interest expense as their distributive share of PRS's business interest expense for the taxable year. Additionally, in Year 2, PRS has $3,000 of ATI. PRS allocates the items comprising its $3,000 of ATI $0 to X and $3,000 to Y.

(ii) *Partnership-level.* In Year 2, PRS's section 163(j) limit is 30 percent of its ATI plus its business interest income, or $900 ($3,000 x 30 percent). Thus, PRS has $900 of deductible business interest expense, $100 of excess business interest expense, $0 of excess taxable income, and $0 of excess business interest income. Pursuant to §1.163(j)-6(f)(2), $400 of X's allocation of business interest expense is treated as deductible business interest expense, $100 of X's allocation of business interest expense is treated as excess business interest expense, and $500 of Y's allocation of business interest expense is treated as deductible business interest expense.

(iii) *Lending partner.* Pursuant to §1.163(j)-6(n), X treats $100 of its $1,000 of interest income as excess business interest income allocated from PRS in Year 2. Because X is deemed to have been allocated $100 of excess business interest income from PRS, and excess business interest expense from a partnership is treated as paid or accrued by a partner to the extent excess business interest income is allocated from such partnership to a partner, X treats its $100 allocation of excess business interest expense from PRS in Year 2 as business interest expense paid or accrued in Year 2. X, in computing its limit under section 163(j), has $100 of business interest income ($100 deemed allocation of excess business interest income from PRS in Year 2) and $100 of business interest expense ($100 allocation of excess business interest expense treated as paid or accrued in Year 2). Thus, X's $100 of business interest expense is deductible business interest expense. At the end of Year 2, X has $100 of excess business interest expense from PRS ($100 from Year 1). X treats $900 of its $1,000 of interest income as investment income for purposes of section 163(d).

(27)-(33) [Reserved].

(34) *Example 34.*—(i) *Facts.* X and Y are equal partners in partnership PRS. Further, X and Y share the profits of PRS equally. In 2019, PRS had ATI of $100. Additionally, in 2019, PRS had $100 of section 704(b) income which was allocated $50 to X and $50 to Y (PRS did not have any section 704(c) income in 2019). In 2020, PRS's only items of income, gain, loss or deduction was $1 of trade or business income, which it allocated to X pursuant to section 704(c).

(ii) *Partnership-level.* In 2020, PRS makes the election described in §1.163(j)-6(d)(5) to use its 2019 ATI in 2020. As a result, PRS has $100

of ATI in 2020. PRS does not have any business interest expense. Therefore, PRS has $100 of excess taxable income in 2020.

(iii) *Partner-level allocations.* PRS allocates its $100 of excess taxable income to X and Y pursuant to §1.163(j)-6(f)(2). To determine each partner's share of the $100 of excess taxable income, PRS must determine each partner's allocable ATI (as defined in §1.163(j)-6(f)(2)(ii)). Because PRS made the election described in §1.163(j)-6(d)(5), PRS must determine the allocable ATI of each of its partners pursuant to paragraph (d)(5). Specifically, PRS determines each partner's share of allocable ATI based on PRS's 2019 section 704 income, gain, loss, and deduction. PRS had $100 of section 704(b) income in 2019 which was allocated $50 to X and $50 to Y. Therefore, in 2020, X and Y are both allocated $50 of excess taxable income (50% x $100).

(35) *Example 35.*—(i) *Facts.* X, a partner in partnership PRS, was allocated $20 of excess business interest expense from PRS in 2018 and $10 of excess business interest expense from PRS in 2019. In 2020, PRS allocated $16 of excess taxable income to X.

(ii) *Analysis.* X treats 50 percent of its $10 of excess business interest expense allocated from PRS in 2019 as §1.163(j)-6(g)(4) business interest expense. Thus, $5 of §1.163(j)-6(g)(4) business interest expense is treated as paid or accrued by X in 2020 and is not subject to the section 163(j) limitation at X's level. Because X was allocated $16 of excess taxable income from PRS in 2020, X treats $16 of its $25 of excess business interest expense as business interest expense paid or accrued pursuant to §1.163(j)-6(g)(2). X, in computing its limit under section 163(j) in 2020, has $16 of ATI (as a result of its allocation of $16 of excess taxable income from PRS), $0 of business interest income, and $16 of business interest expense ($16 of excess business interest expense treated as paid or accrued in 2020). Pursuant to §1.163(j)-2(b)(2)(i), X's section 163(j) limit in 2020 is $8 ($16 x 50 percent). Thus, X has $8 of business interest expense that is deductible under section 163(j). The $8 of X's business interest expense not allowed as a deduction ($16 business interest expense subject to section 163(j), less $8 section 163(j) limit) is treated as business interest expense paid or accrued by X in 2021. At the end of 2020, X has $9 of excess business interest expense from PRS ($20 from 2018, plus $10 from 2019, less $5 treated as paid or accrued pursuant to §1.163(j)-6(g)(4), less $16 treated as paid or accrued pursuant to §1.163(j)-6(g)(2)).

(36) *Example 36.*—(i) *Facts.* X is a partner in partnership PRS. At the beginning of 2018, X's outside basis in PRS was $100. X was allocated $20 of excess business interest expense from PRS in 2018 and $10 of excess business interest expense from PRS in 2019. X sold its PRS interest in 2019 for $70.

(ii) *Analysis.* X treats 50 percent of its $10 of excess business interest expense allocated from PRS in 2019 as §1.163(j)-6(g)(4) business interest expense. Thus, $5 of §1.163(j)-6(g)(4) business interest expense is treated as paid or accrued by X in 2020 and is not subject to the section 163(j) limitation at X's level. Pursuant to paragraph (h)(3) of this section, immediately before the disposition, X increases the basis of its PRS interest from $70 to $95 (add back of $20 of EBIE from 2018 and $5 of remaining EBIE from 2019). Thus, X has a $25 section 741 loss recognized on the sale ($70 - $95).

(p) *Applicability dates.*—(1) *In general.*—This section applies to taxable years beginning on or after November 13, 2020. However, taxpayers and their related parties, within the meaning of sections 267(b) and 707(b)(1), may choose to apply the rules of this section to a taxable year beginning after December 31, 2017, so long as the taxpayers and their related parties consistently apply the rules of the section 163(j) regulations, and, if applicable, §§1.263A-9, 1.263A-15, 1.381(c)(20)-1, 1.382-1, 1.382-2, 1.382-5, 1.382-6, 1.382-7, 1.383-0, 1.383-1, 1.469-9, 1.469-11, 1.704-1, 1.882-5, 1.1362-3, 1.1368-1, 1.1377-1, 1.1502-13, 1.1502-21, 1.1502-36, 1.1502-79, 1.1502-91 through 1.1502-99 (to the extent they effectuate the rules of §§1.382-2, 1.382-5, 1.382-6, and 1.383-1), and 1.1504-4, to that taxable year.

(2) *Paragraphs (c)(1) and (2), (d)(3) through (5), (e)(5), (f)(1)(iii), (g)(4), (n), and (o)(24) through (29), and (34) through (36).*—Paragraphs (c)(1) and (2), (d)(3) through (5), (e)(5), (f)(1)(iii), (g)(4), (n), and (o)(24) through (29), and (34) through (36) of this section apply to taxable years beginning on or after March 22, 2021. However, taxpayers and their related parties, within the meaning of sections 267(b) (determined without regard to section 267(c)(3)) and 707(b)(1), may choose to apply the rules in paragraphs (c)(1) and (2), (d)(3) through (5), (e)(5), (f)(1)(iii), (g)(4), (n), and (o)(24) through (29), and (34) through (36) to a taxable year beginning after December 31, 2017, and before March 22, 2021, provided that those taxpayers and their related parties consistently apply all of the rules in T.D. 9905 (§§1.163(j)-0 through 1.163(j)-11, effective November 13, 2020) as

modified by T.D. 9943 (effective January 13, 2021), and, if applicable, §§ 1.263A-9, 1.263A-15, 1.381(c)(20)-1, 1.382-1, 1.382-2, 1.382-5, 1.382-6, 1.382-7, 1.383-0, 1.383-1, 1.469-9, 1.469-11, 1.704-1, 1.882-5, 1.1362-3, 1.1368-1, 1.1377-1, 1.1502-13, 1.1502-21, 1.1502-36, 1.1502-79, 1.1502-91 through 1.1502-99 (to the extent they effectuate the rules of §§ 1.382-2, 1.382-5, 1.382-6, and 1.383-1), and 1.1504-4 contained in T.D. 9905 as modified by T.D. 9943, for that taxable year and for each subsequent taxable year. [Reg. § 1.163(j)-6.]

☐ [*T.D. 9905, 9-3-2020. Amended by T.D. 9943, 1-13-2021.*]

[Reg. § 1.163(j)-7]

§ 1.163(j)-7. Application of the section 163(j) limitation to foreign corporations and United States shareholders.—(a) *Overview.*—This section provides rules for the application of section 163(j) to relevant foreign corporations and United States shareholders of relevant foreign corporations. Paragraph (b) of this section provides the general rule regarding the application of section 163(j) to a relevant foreign corporation. Paragraph (c) of this section provides rules for applying section 163(j) to CFC group members of a CFC group. Paragraph (d) of this section provides rules for determining a specified group and specified group members. Paragraph (e) of this section provides rules and procedures for treating a specified group member as a CFC group member and for determining a CFC group. Paragraph (f) of this section provides rules regarding the treatment of a CFC group member that has ECI. Paragraph (g) of this section provides rules concerning the computation of ATI of an applicable CFC. Paragraph (h) of this section provides a safe harbor that exempts certain stand-alone applicable CFCs and CFC groups from the application of section 163(j) for a taxable year. Paragraphs (i) and (j) of this section are reserved. Paragraph (k) of this section provides definitions that apply for purposes of this section (see also § 1.163(j)-1 for additional definitions). Paragraph (l) of this section provides examples illustrating the application of this section.

(b) *General rule regarding the application of section 163(j) to relevant foreign corporations.*—Except as otherwise provided in this section, section 163(j) and the section 163(j) regulations apply to determine the deductibility of a relevant foreign corporation's business interest expense for purposes of computing its taxable income for U.S. income tax purposes (if any) in the same manner as those provisions apply to determine the deductibility of a domestic C corporation's business interest expense for purposes of computing its taxable income. See also § 1.952-2. If a relevant foreign corporation is a direct or indirect partner in a partnership, see § 1.163(j)-6 (concerning the application of section 163(j) to partnerships).

(c) *Application of section 163(j) to CFC group members of a CFC group.*—(1) *Scope.*—This paragraph (c) provides rules for applying section 163(j) to a CFC group and a CFC group member. Paragraph (c)(2) of this section provides rules for computing a single section 163(j) limitation for a specified period of a CFC group. Paragraph (c)(3) of this section provides rules for allocating a CFC group's section 163(j) limitation to CFC group members for specified taxable years. Paragraph (c)(4) of this section provides currency translation rules. Paragraph (c)(5) of this section provides special rules for specified periods beginning in 2019 or 2020.

(2) *Calculation of section 163(j) limitation for a CFC group for a specified period.*—(i) *In general.*—A single section 163(j) limitation is computed for a specified period of a CFC group. For purposes of applying section 163(j) and the section 163(j) regulations, the current-year business interest expense, disallowed business interest expense carryforwards, business interest income, floor plan financing interest expense, and ATI of a CFC group for a specified period equal the sums of each CFC group member's respective amounts for its specified taxable year with respect to the specified period. A CFC group member's current-year business interest expense, business interest income, floor plan financing interest expense, and ATI for a specified taxable year are generally determined on a separate-company basis. For purposes of determining the ATI of a CFC group, § 1.163(j)-1(b)(1)(vii) (providing that ATI cannot be less than zero) applies with respect to the ATI of the CFC group but not the ATI of any CFC group member.

(ii) *Certain transactions between CFC group members disregarded.*—Any transaction between CFC group members of a CFC group that is entered into with a principal purpose of affecting a CFC group or a CFC group member's section 163(j) limitation by increasing or decreasing a CFC group or a CFC group member's ATI or business interest income for a specified taxable year is disregarded for purposes of applying section 163(j) and the section 163(j) regulations.

(3) *Deduction of business interest expense.*—(i) *CFC group business interest expense.*—(A) *In general.*—The extent to which a CFC group member's current-year business interest expense and disallowed business interest expense carryforwards for a specified taxable year that ends with or within a specified period may be deducted under section 163(j) is determined under the rules and principles of § 1.163(j)-5(a)(2) and (b)(3)(ii), subject to the modifications described in paragraph (c)(3)(i)(B) of this section.

(B) *Modifications to relevant terms.*—For purposes of paragraph (c)(3)(i)(A) of this section, the rules and principles of § 1.163(j)-5(b)(3)(ii) are applied by—

(1) Replacing "§ 1.163(j)-4(d)(2)" in § 1.163(j)-5(a)(2)(ii) with "§ 1.163(j)-7(c)(2)(i)";

(2) Replacing the term "allocable share of the consolidated group's remaining section 163(j) limitation" with "allocable share of the CFC group's remaining section 163(j) limitation";

(3) Replacing the terms "consolidated group" and "group" with "CFC group";

(4) Replacing the term "consolidated group's remaining section 163(j) limitation" with "CFC group's remaining section 163(j) limitation";

(5) Replacing the term "consolidated return year" with "specified period";

(6) Replacing the term "current year" or "current-year" with "current specified period" or "specified taxable year with respect to the current specified period," as the context requires;

(7) Replacing the term "member" with "CFC group member"; and

(8) Replacing the term "taxable year" with "specified taxable year with respect to a specified period."

(ii) *Carryforwards treated as attributable to the same taxable year.*—For purposes of applying the principles of § 1.163(j)-5(b)(3)(ii), as required under paragraph (c)(3)(i) of this section, CFC group members' disallowed business interest expense carryforwards that arose in specified taxable years with respect to the same specified period are treated as disallowed business interest expense carryforwards from taxable years ending on the same date and are deducted on a pro rata basis, under the principles of § 1.163(j)-5(b)(3)(ii)(C)(3), pursuant to paragraph (c)(3)(i) of this section.

(iii) *Multiple specified taxable years of a CFC group member with respect to a specified period.*—If a CFC group member has more than one specified taxable year (each year, an *applicable specified taxable year*) with respect to a single specified period of a CFC group, then all the applicable specified taxable years are taken into account for purposes of applying the principles of § 1.163(j)-5(b)(3)(ii), as required under paragraph (c)(3)(i) of this section, with respect to the specified period. The portion of the section 163(j) limitation allocable to disallowed business interest expense carryforwards of the CFC group member that arose in taxable years before the first applicable specified taxable year is prorated among the applicable specified taxable years in proportion to the number of days in each applicable specified taxable year.

(iv) *Limitation on pre-group disallowed business interest expense carryforward.*—(A) *General rule.*—(1) *CFC group member pre-group disallowed business interest expense carryforward.*—This paragraph (c)(3)(iv) applies to pre-group disallowed business interest expense carryforwards of a CFC group member. The amount of the pre-group disallowed business interest expense carryforwards described in the preceding sentence that may be included in any CFC group member's business interest expense deduction for any specified taxable year under this paragraph (c)(3) may not exceed the aggregate section 163(j) limitation for all specified periods of the CFC group, determined by reference only to the CFC group member's items of income, gain, deduction, and loss, and reduced (including below zero) by the CFC group member's business interest expense (including disallowed business interest expense carryforwards) taken into account as a deduction by the CFC group member in all specified taxable years in which the CFC group member has continuously been a CFC group member of the CFC group (*cumulative section 163(j) pre-group carryforward limitation*).

(2) *Subgrouping.*—In the case of a pre-group disallowed business interest expense carryforward, a pre-group subgroup is composed of the CFC group member with the pre-group disallowed business interest expense carryforward (the *loss member*) and each other CFC group member of the loss member's CFC group (the *current group*) that was a member of the CFC group in which the pre-group disallowed business interest expense carryforward arose and joined the specified group of the current group at the same time as

the loss member. A CFC group member that is a member of a pre-group subgroup remains a member of the pre-group subgroup until its first taxable year during which it ceases to be a member of the same specified group as the loss member. For purposes of this paragraph (c), the rules and principles of §1.163(j)-5(d)(1)(B) apply to a pre-group subgroup as if the pre-group subgroup were a SRLY subgroup.

(3) *Transition rule.*—Solely for purposes of paragraph (c)(3)(iv)(A)(2) of this section, a CFC group includes a group of applicable CFCs for which a CFC group election was made under guidance under section 163(j) published on December 28, 2018. Therefore, if the requirements of paragraph (c)(3)(iv)(A)(2) of this section are satisfied, a group of applicable CFCs described in the preceding sentence may be treated as a pre-group subgroup.

(B) *Deduction of pre-group disallowed business interest expense carryforwards.*—Notwithstanding paragraph (c)(3)(iv)(A)(1) of this section, pre-group disallowed business interest expense carryforwards are available for deduction by a CFC group member in its specified taxable year only to the extent the CFC group has remaining section 163(j) limitation for the specified period after the deduction of current-year business interest expense and disallowed business interest expense carryforwards from earlier taxable years that are permitted to be deducted in specified taxable years of CFC group members with respect to the specified period. See paragraph (c)(3)(i) of this section and §1.163(j)-5(b)(3)(ii)(A). Pre-group disallowed business interest expense carryforwards are deducted on a pro rata basis (under the principles of paragraph (c)(3)(i) of this section and §1.163(j)-5(b)(3)(ii)(C)(4)) with other disallowed business interest expense carryforwards from taxable years ending on the same date.

(4) *Currency translation.*—For purposes of applying this paragraph (c), items of a CFC group member are translated into a single currency for the CFC group and back to the functional currency of the CFC group member using the average exchange rate for the CFC group member's specified taxable year. The single currency for the CFC group may be the U.S. dollar or the functional currency of a plurality of the CFC group members.

(5) *Special rule for specified periods beginning in 2019 or 2020.*—(i) *50 percent ATI limitation applies to a specified period of a CFC group.*—In the case of a CFC group, §1.163(j)-2(b)(2) (including the election under §1.163(j)-2(b)(2)(ii)) applies to a specified period of the CFC group beginning in 2019 or 2020, rather than to a specified taxable year of a CFC group member. An election under §1.163(j)-2(b)(2)(ii) for a specified period of a CFC group is not effective unless made by each designated U.S. person. Except as otherwise provided in this paragraph (c)(5)(i), the election is made in accordance with Revenue Procedure 2020-22, 2020-18 I.R.B. 745. For purposes of applying §1.964-1(c), the election is treated as if made for each CFC group member.

(ii) *Election to use 2019 ATI applies to a specified period of a CFC group.*—(A) *In general.*—In the case of a CFC group, for purposes of applying paragraph (c)(2) of this section, an election under §1.163(j)-2(b)(3)(i) is made for a specified period of a CFC group beginning in 2020 and applies to the specified taxable years of each CFC group member with respect to such specified period, taking into account the application of paragraph (c)(5)(ii)(B) of this section. The election under §1.163(j)-2(b)(3)(i) does not apply to any specified taxable year of a CFC group member other than those described in the preceding sentence. An election under §1.163(j)-2(b)(3)(i) for a specified period of a CFC group is not effective unless made by each designated U.S. person. Except as otherwise provided in this paragraph (c)(5)(ii)(A), the election is made in accordance with Revenue Procedure 2020-22, 2020-18 I.R.B. 745. For purposes of applying §1.964-1(c), the election is treated as if made for each CFC group member.

(B) *Specified taxable years that do not begin in 2020.*—If a specified taxable year of a CFC group member with respect to the specified period described in paragraph (c)(5)(ii)(A) of this section begins in 2019, then, for purposes of applying paragraph (c)(2) of this section, §1.163(j)-2(b)(3) is applied to such specified taxable year by substituting "2018" for "2019" and "2019" for "2020." If a specified taxable year of a CFC group member with respect to the specified period described in paragraph (c)(5)(ii)(A) of this section begins in 2021, then, for purposes of applying paragraph (c)(2) of this section, §1.163(j)-2(b)(3) is applied to such specified taxable year by substituting "2020" for "2019" and "2021" for "2020."

(d) *Determination of a specified group and specified group members.*—(1) *Scope.*—This paragraph (d) provides rules for determining a specified group and specified group members. Paragraph (d)(2) of this section provides rules for determining a specified group. Paragraph

(d)(3) of this section provides rules for determining specified group members.

(2) *Rules for determining a specified group.*—(i) *Definition of a specified group.*—Subject to paragraph (d)(2)(ii) of this section, the term *specified group* means one or more applicable CFCs or chains of applicable CFCs connected through stock ownership with a specified group parent (which is included in the specified group only if it is an applicable CFC), but only if—

(A) The specified group parent owns directly or indirectly stock meeting the requirements of section 1504(a)(2)(B) in at least one applicable CFC; and

(B) Stock meeting the requirements of section 1504(a)(2)(B) in each of the applicable CFCs (except the specified group parent) is owned directly or indirectly by one or more of the other applicable CFCs or the specified group parent.

(ii) *Indirect ownership.*—For purposes of applying paragraph (d)(2)(i) of this section, stock is owned indirectly only if it is owned under section 318(a)(2)(A) through a partnership or under section 318(a)(2)(A) or (B) through an estate or trust not described in section 7701(a)(30).

(iii) *Specified group parent.*—The term *specified group parent* means a qualified U.S. person or an applicable CFC.

(iv) *Qualified U.S. person.*—The term *qualified U.S. person* means a United States person described in section 7701(a)(30)(A) or (C). For purposes of this paragraph (d), members of a consolidated group that file (or that are required to file) a consolidated U.S. Federal income tax return are treated as a single qualified U.S person and individuals described in section 7701(a)(30)(A) whose filing status is married filing jointly are treated as a single qualified U.S. person.

(v) *Stock.*—For purposes of this paragraph (d)(2), the term *stock* has the same meaning as "stock" in section 1504 (without regard to §1.1504-4, except as provided in paragraph (d)(2)(vi) of this section) and all shares of stock within a single class are considered to have the same value. Thus, control premiums and minority and blockage discounts within a single class are not taken into account.

(vi) *Options treated as exercised.*—For purposes of this paragraph (d)(2), options that are reasonably certain to be exercised, as determined under §1.1504-4(g), are treated as exercised. For purposes of this paragraph (d)(2)(vi), options include call options, warrants, convertible obligations, put options, and any other instrument treated as an option under §1.1504-4(d), determined by replacing the term "a principal purpose of avoiding the application of section 1504 and this section" with "a principal purpose of avoiding the application of section 163(j)."

(vii) *When a specified group ceases to exist.*—The principles of §1.1502-75(d)(1), (d)(2)(i) and (ii), and (d)(3)(i) through (iv), apply for purposes of determining when a specified group ceases to exist. Solely for purposes of applying these principles, references to the common parent are treated as references to the specified group parent and each applicable CFC that is treated as a specified group member for a taxable year with respect to a specified period is treated as affiliated with the specified group parent from the beginning to the end of the specified period, without regard to the beginning or end of its taxable year.

(3) *Rules for determining a specified group member.*—If two or more applicable CFCs are included in a specified group on the last day of a taxable year of each applicable CFC that ends with or within a specified period, then each applicable CFC is a *specified group member* with respect to the specified period for its entire taxable year ending with or within the specified period. If only one applicable CFC is included in a specified group on the last day of its taxable year that ends with or within the specified period, it is not a specified group member. If an applicable CFC has multiple taxable years that end with or within a specified period, this paragraph (d)(3) is applied separately to each taxable year to determine if the applicable CFC is a specified group member for such taxable year.

(e) *Rules and procedures for treating a specified group as a CFC group.*—(1) *Scope.*—This paragraph (e) provides rules and procedures for treating a specified group member as a CFC group member and for determining a CFC group for purposes of applying section 163(j) and the section 163(j) regulations.

(2) *CFC group and CFC group member.*—(i) *CFC group.*—The term *CFC group* means, with respect to a specified period, all CFC group members for their specified taxable years.

(ii) *CFC group member.*—The term *CFC group member* means, with respect to a specified taxable year and a specified period, a specified group member of a specified group for which a CFC group election is in effect. However, notwithstanding the prior sentence, a specified group member is not treated as a CFC group member for a taxable year of the specified group member beginning before January 1, 2018.

(3) *Duration of a CFC group.*—A CFC group continues until the CFC group election is revoked, or there is no longer a specified period with respect to the specified group. A failure to provide the information described in paragraph (e)(6) of this section does not terminate a CFC group election.

(4) *Joining or leaving a CFC group.*—If an applicable CFC becomes a specified group member for a specified taxable year with respect to a specified period of a specified group for which a CFC group election is in effect, the CFC group election applies to the applicable CFC and the applicable CFC becomes a CFC group member. If an applicable CFC ceases to be a specified group member for a specified taxable year with respect to a specified period of a specified group for which a CFC group election is in effect, the CFC group election terminates solely with respect to the applicable CFC.

(5) *Manner of making or revoking a CFC group election.*—(i) *In general.*—An election is made or revoked under this paragraph (e)(5) (*CFC group election*) with respect to a specified period of a specified group. A CFC group election remains in effect for each specified period of the specified group until revoked. A CFC group election that is in effect with respect to a specified period of a specified group applies to each specified group member for its specified taxable year that ends with or within the specified period. The making or revoking of a CFC group election is not effective unless made or revoked by each designated U.S. person.

(ii) *Revocation by election.*—A CFC group election cannot be revoked with respect to any specified period beginning before 60 months following the last day of the specified period for which the election was made. Once a CFC group election has been revoked, a new CFC group election cannot be made with respect to any specified period beginning before 60 months following the last day of the specified period for which the election was revoked.

(iii) *Timing.*—A CFC group election must be made or revoked with respect to a specified period of a specified group no later than the due date (taking into account extensions, if any) of the original Federal income tax return for the taxable year of each designated U.S. person in which or with which the specified period ends.

(iv) *Election statement.*—To make or revoke a CFC group election for a specified period of a specified group, each designated U.S. person must attach a statement to its relevant Federal income tax or information return in accordance with publications, forms, instructions, or other guidance. The statement must include the name and taxpayer identification number of all designated U.S. persons, a statement that the CFC group election is being made or revoked, as applicable, the specified period for which the CFC group election is being made or revoked, and the name of each CFC group member and its specified taxable year with respect to the specified period. The statement must be filed in the manner prescribed in publications, forms, instructions, or other guidance.

(v) *Effect of prior CFC group election.*—A CFC group election is made solely pursuant to the provisions of this paragraph (e)(5), without regard to whether a CFC group election described in guidance under section 163(j) published on December 28, 2018, was in effect.

(6) *Annual information reporting.*—Each designated U.S. person must attach a statement to its relevant Federal income tax or information return for each taxable year in which a CFC group election is in effect that contains information concerning the computation of the CFC group's section 163(j) limitation and the application of paragraph (c)(3) of this section to the CFC group in accordance with publications, forms, instructions, or other guidance.

(f) *Treatment of a CFC group member that has ECI.*—(1) *In general.*—If a CFC group member has ECI in its specified taxable year, then for purposes of section 163(j) and the section 163(j) regulations—

(i) The items, disallowed business interest expense carryforwards, and other attributes of the CFC group member that are ECI are treated as items, disallowed business interest expense carryforwards, and attributes of a separate applicable CFC (such deemed corporation, an *ECI deemed corporation*) that has the same taxable year and shareholders as the applicable CFC; and

(ii) The ECI deemed corporation is not treated as a specified group member for the specified taxable year.

(2) [Reserved].

(g) *Rules concerning the computation of adjusted taxable income of a relevant foreign corporation.*—(1) *Tentative taxable income.*—For purposes of computing the tentative taxable income of a relevant foreign corporation for a taxable year, the relevant foreign corporation's gross income and allowable deductions are determined under the principles of §1.952-2 or under the rules of section 882 for determining income that is, or deductions that are allocable to, effectively connected income, as applicable.

(2) *Treatment of certain dividends.*—For purposes of computing the ATI of a relevant foreign corporation for a taxable year, any dividend included in gross income that is received from a related person, within the meaning of section 954(d)(3), with respect to the distributee is subtracted from tentative taxable income.

(3) *Treatment of certain foreign income taxes.*—For purposes of computing the ATI of a relevant foreign corporation for a taxable year, no deduction is taken into account for any foreign income tax (as defined in §1.960-1(b), but substituting the phrase "relevant foreign corporation" for the phrase "controlled foreign corporation").

(4) *Anti-abuse rule.*—(i) *In general.*—If a specified group member of a specified group or an applicable partnership (*specified lender*) includes an amount (*payment amount*) in income and such amount is attributable to business interest expense incurred by another specified group member or an applicable partnership of the specified group (*specified borrower*) during its taxable year, then the ATI of the specified borrower for the taxable year is increased by the ATI adjustment amount if—

(A) The business interest expense is incurred with a principal purpose of reducing the Federal income tax liability of any United States shareholder of a specified group member (including over other taxable years);

(B) Absent the application of this paragraph (g)(4), the effect of the specified borrower treating all or part of the payment amount as disallowed business interest expense would be to reduce the Federal income tax liability of any United States shareholder of a specified group member; and

(C) Either no CFC group election is in effect with respect to the specified group or the specified borrower is an applicable partnership.

(ii) *ATI adjustment amount.*—(A) *In general.*—For purposes of this paragraph (g)(4), the term *ATI adjustment amount* means, with respect to a specified borrower and a taxable year, the product of 3 1/3 and the lesser of the payment amount or the disallowed business interest expense, computed without regard to this paragraph (g)(4).

(B) *Special rule for taxable years or specified periods beginning in 2019 or 2020.*—For any taxable year of an applicable CFC or specified taxable year of a CFC group member with respect to a specified period for which the section 163(j) limitation is determined based, in part, on 50 percent of ATI, in accordance with §1.163(j)-2(b)(2), paragraph (g)(4)(ii)(A) of this section is applied by substituting "2" for "3 1/3."

(iii) *Applicable partnership.*—For purposes of this paragraph (g)(4), the term *applicable partnership* means, with respect to a specified group, a partnership in which at least 80 percent of the interests in profits or capital is owned, directly or indirectly through one or more other partnerships, by specified group members of the specified group. For purposes of this paragraph (g)(4)(iii), a partner's interest in the profits of a partnership is determined in accordance with the rules and principles of §1.706-1(b)(4)(ii) and a partner's interest in the capital of a partnership is determined in accordance with the rules and principles of §1.706-1(b)(4)(iii).

(h) *Election to apply safe-harbor.*—(1) *In general.*—If an election to apply this paragraph (h)(1) (*safe-harbor election*) is in effect with respect to a taxable year of a stand-alone applicable CFC or a specified taxable year of a CFC group member, as applicable, then, for such year, no portion of the applicable CFC's business interest expense is disallowed under the section 163(j) limitation. This paragraph (h) does not apply to excess business interest expense, as described in §1.163(j)-6(f)(2), until the taxable year in which it is treated as paid or accrued by an applicable CFC under §1.163(j)-6(g)(2)(i). Furthermore, excess business interest expense is not taken into account for purposes of determining whether the safe-harbor election is available for a stand-alone applicable CFC or a CFC group until the taxable year in which it is treated as paid or accrued by an applicable CFC under §1.163(j)-6(g)(2)(i).

(2) *Eligibility for safe-harbor election.*—(i) *Stand-alone applicable CFC.*—The safe-harbor election may be made for the taxable year of a stand-alone applicable CFC only if, for the taxable year, the business interest expense of the applicable CFC is less than or equal to either—

(A) The business interest income of the applicable CFC; or

(B) 30 percent of the lesser of the eligible amount or the qualified tentative taxable income of the applicable CFC.

(ii) *CFC group.*—The safe-harbor election may be made for the specified period of a CFC group only if, for the specified period, no CFC group member has any pre-group disallowed business interest expense carryforward and the business interest expense of the CFC group for the specified period is less than or equal to either—

(A) The business interest income of the CFC group; or

(B) 30 percent of the lesser of the eligible amount or the qualified tentative taxable income of the CFC group.

(iii) *Currency translation.*—For purposes of applying this paragraph (h), BII, BIE, and qualified tentative taxable income of a stand-alone applicable CFC or a CFC group must be determined using the U.S. dollar. If BII, BIE, or any items of income, gain, deduction, or loss that are taken into account in computing qualified tentative taxable income are maintained in a currency other than the U.S. dollar, then those items must be translated into the U.S. dollar using the average exchange rate for the taxable year or the specified taxable year, as applicable.

(3) *Eligible amount.*—(i) *Stand-alone applicable CFC.*—The *eligible amount* of a stand-alone applicable CFC for a taxable year is the sum of the amounts a domestic corporation would include in gross income under sections 951(a)(1)(A) and 951A(a), reduced by any deductions that would be allowed under section 245A (by reason of section 964(e)(4)) or section 250(a)(1)(B)(i), determined as if the domestic corporation has a taxable year that ends on the last date of the taxable year of the stand-alone applicable CFC, it wholly owns the stand-alone applicable CFC throughout the CFC's taxable year, it does not own any assets other than stock in the stand-alone applicable CFC, and it has no other items of income, gain, deduction, or loss.

(ii) *CFC group.*—The *eligible amount* of a CFC group for a specified period is the sum of the amounts a domestic corporation would include in gross income under sections 951(a)(1)(A) and 951A(a), reduced by any deductions that would be allowed under section 245A (by reason of section 964(e)(4)) or section 250(a)(1)(B)(i), determined as if the domestic corporation has a taxable year that is the specified period, it wholly owns each CFC group member throughout the CFC group member's specified taxable year, it does not own any assets other than stock in the CFC group members, and it has no other items of income, gain, deduction, or loss.

(iii) *Additional rules for determining an eligible amount.*—For purposes of paragraphs (h)(3)(i) and (ii) of this section, the amounts that would be included in gross income of a United States shareholder under sections 951(a)(1)(A) and 951A(a), and any corresponding deductions that would be allowed under section 245A (by reason of section 964(e)(4)) or section 250(a)(1)(B)(i), are determined by taking into account any elections that are made with respect to the applicable CFC(s), including under § 1.954-1(d)(5) (relating to the subpart F high-tax exception) and § 1.951A-2(c)(7)(viii) (relating to the GILTI high-tax exclusion). These amounts are also determined without regard to any section 163(j) limitation on business interest expense and without regard to any disallowed business interest expense carryovers. In addition, those amounts are determined by only taking in account items of the applicable CFC(s) that are properly allocable to a non-excepted trade or business under § 1.163(j)-10.

(4) *Qualified tentative taxable income.*—The term *qualified tentative taxable income* means, with respect to a taxable year of a stand-alone applicable CFC, the applicable CFC's tentative taxable income, and with respect to a specified period of a CFC group, the sum of each CFC group member's tentative taxable income for the specified taxable year; provided that for purposes of this paragraph (h)(4), tentative taxable income is determined by taking into account only items properly allocable to a non-excepted trade or business under § 1.163(j)-10.

(5) *Manner of making a safe-harbor election.*—(i) *In general.*—A safe-harbor election is an annual election made under this paragraph (h)(5) with respect to a taxable year of a stand-alone applicable CFC or with respect to a specified period of a CFC group. A safe-harbor election that is made with respect to a specified period of a CFC group is effective with respect to each CFC group member for its specified taxable year. A safe-harbor election is only effective if made by each designated U.S. person with respect to a stand-alone applicable CFC or a CFC group. A safe-harbor election is made with respect to a taxable year of a stand-alone applicable CFC, or a specified period of a CFC group, no later than the due date (taking into account extensions, if any) of the original Federal income tax return for the taxable year of each designated U.S. person, respectively, in which or with which the taxable year of the stand-alone applicable CFC ends or the specified period of the CFC group ends.

(ii) *Election statement.*—To make a safe-harbor election, each designated U.S. person must attach to its relevant Federal income tax return or information return a statement that includes the name and taxpayer identification number of all designated U.S. persons, a statement that a safe-harbor election is being made pursuant to § 1.163(j)-7(h) and a calculation that substantiates that the requirements for making the election are satisfied, and the taxable year of the stand-alone applicable CFC or the specified period of the CFC group, as applicable, for which the safe-harbor election is being made in accordance with publications, forms, instructions, or other guidance. In the case of a CFC group, the statement must also include the name of each CFC group member and its specified taxable year that ends with or within the specified period for which the safe-harbor election is being made. The statement must be filed in the manner prescribed in publications, forms, instructions, or other guidance.

(6) *Special rule for taxable years or specified periods beginning in 2019 or 2020.*—In the case of a stand-alone applicable CFC, for any taxable year beginning in 2019 or 2020, paragraph (h)(2)(i) of this section is applied by substituting "50 percent" for "30 percent." In the case of a CFC group, for any specified period beginning in 2019 or 2020, paragraph (h)(2)(ii)(A) of this section is applied by substituting "50 percent" for "30 percent."

(i)-(j) [Reserved]

(k) *Definitions.*—The following definitions apply for purposes of this section.

(1) *Applicable partnership.*—The term *applicable partnership* has the meaning provided in paragraph (g)(4)(iii) of this section.

(2) *Applicable specified taxable year.*—The term *applicable specified taxable year* has the meaning provided in paragraph (c)(3)(iii) of this section.

(3) *ATI adjustment amount.*—The term *ATI adjustment amount* has the meaning provided in paragraph (g)(4)(ii) of this section.

(4)-(5) [Reserved].

(6) *CFC group.*—The term *CFC group* has the meaning provided in paragraph (e)(2)(i) of this section.

(7) *CFC group election.*—The term *CFC group election* means the election described in paragraph (e)(5) of this section.

(8) *CFC group member.*—The term *CFC group member* has the meaning provided in paragraph (e)(2)(ii) of this section.

(9) [Reserved].

(10) *Cumulative section 163(j) pre-group carryforward limitation.*—The term *cumulative section 163(j) pre-group carryforward limitation* has the meaning provided in paragraph (c)(3)(iv)(A)(1) of this section.

(11) *Current group.*—The term *current group* has the meaning provided in paragraph (c)(3)(iv)(A)(2) of this section.

(12) *Designated U.S. person.*—The term *designated U.S. person* means—

(i) With respect to a stand-alone applicable CFC, each controlling domestic shareholder, as defined in § 1.964-1(c)(5)(i) of the applicable CFC; or

(ii) With respect to a specified group, the specified group parent, if the specified group parent is a qualified U.S. person, or each controlling domestic shareholder, as defined in § 1.964-1(c)(5)(i), of the specified group parent, if the specified group parent is an applicable CFC.

(13) *ECI deemed corporation.*—The term *ECI deemed corporation* has the meaning provided in paragraph (f)(1)(i) of this section.

(14) *Effectively connected income.*—The term *effectively connected income* (or *ECI*) means income or gain that is ECI, as defined in § 1.884-1(d)(1)(iii), and deduction or loss that is allocable to, ECI, as defined in § 1.884-1(d)(1)(iii).

(15) *Eligible amount.*—The term *eligible amount* has the meaning provided in paragraph (h)(3)(i) of this section.

(16) *Former group.*—The term *former group* has the meaning provided in paragraph (c)(3)(iv)(A)(2) of this section.

(17) *Loss member.*—The term *loss member* has the meaning provided in paragraph (c)(3)(iv)(A)(2) of this section.

(18) *Payment amount.*—The term *payment amount* has the meaning provided in paragraph (g)(4)(i) of this section.

(19) *Pre-group disallowed business interest expense carryforward.*—The term *pre-group disallowed business interest expense carryforward* means, with respect to a CFC group member and a specified taxable

year, any disallowed business interest expense carryforward of the CFC group member that arose in a taxable year during which the CFC group member (or its predecessor) was not a CFC group member of the CFC group.

(20) *Qualified tentative taxable income.*—The term *qualified tentative taxable income* has the meaning provided in paragraph (h)(4) of this section.

(21) *Qualified U.S. person.*—The term *qualified U.S. person* has the meaning provided in paragraph (d)(2)(iv) of this section.

(22) *Relevant period.*—The term *relevant period* has the meaning provided in paragraph (c)(3)(iv)(A)(2) of this section.

(23) *Safe-harbor election.*—The term *safe-harbor election* has the meaning provided in paragraph (h)(1) of this section.

(24) *Specified borrower.*—The term *specified borrower* has the meaning provided in paragraph (g)(4)(i) of this section.

(25) *Specified group.*—The term *specified group* has the meaning provided in paragraph (d)(2)(i) of this section.

(26) *Specified group member.*—The term *specified group member* has the meaning provided in paragraph (d)(3) of this section.

(27) *Specified group parent.*—The term *specified group parent* has the meaning provided in paragraph (d)(2)(iii) of this section.

(28) *Specified lender.*—The term *specified lender* has the meaning provided in paragraph (g)(4)(i) of this section.

(29) *Specified period.*—(i) *In general.*—Except as otherwise provided in paragraph (k)(29)(ii) of this section, the term *specified period* means, with respect to a specified group—

(A) If the specified group parent is a qualified U.S. person, the period ending on the last day of the taxable year of the specified group parent and beginning on the first day after the last day of the specified group's immediately preceding specified period; or

(B) If the specified group parent is an applicable CFC, the period ending on the last day of the specified group parent's required year described in section 898(c)(1), without regard to section 898(c)(2), and beginning on the first day after the last day of the specified group's immediately preceding specified period.

(ii) *Short specified period.*—A specified period begins no earlier than the first date on which a specified group exists. A specified period ends on the date a specified group ceases to exist under paragraph (d)(2)(vii) of this section. If the last day of a specified period, as determined under paragraph (k)(29)(i) of this section, changes, and, but for this paragraph (k)(29)(ii), the change in the last day of the specified period would result in the specified period being longer than 12 months, the specified period ends on the date on which the specified period would have ended had the change not occurred.

(30) *Specified taxable year.*—The term *specified taxable year* means, with respect to an applicable CFC that is a specified group member of a specified group and a specified period, a taxable year of the applicable CFC that ends with or within the specified period.

(31) *Stand-alone applicable CFC.*—The term *stand-alone applicable CFC* means any applicable CFC that is not a specified group member.

(32) *Stock.*—The term *stock* has the meaning provided in paragraph (d)(2)(v) of this section.

(l) *Examples.*—The following examples illustrate the application of this section. For each example, unless otherwise stated, no exemptions from the application of section 163(j) are available, no foreign corporation has ECI, and all relevant taxable years and specified periods begin after December 31, 2020.

(1) *Example 1. Specified taxable years included in specified period of a specified group.*—(i) *Facts.* As of June 30, Year 1, USP, a domestic corporation, owns 60 percent of the common stock of FP, which owns all of the stock of FC1, FC2, and FC3. The remaining 40 percent of the common stock of FP is owned by an unrelated foreign corporation. FP has a single class of stock. FP acquired the stock of FC3 from an unrelated person on March 22, Year 1. The acquisition did not result in a change in FC3's taxable year or a close of its taxable year. USP's interest in FP and FP's interest in FC1 and FC2 has been the same for several years. USP has a taxable year ending June 30, Year 1, which is not a short taxable year. Each of FP, FC1, FC2, and FC3 are applicable CFCs. Pursuant to section 898(c)(2), FP and FC1 have taxable years ending May 31, Year 1. Pursuant to section 898(c)(1), FC2 and FC3 have taxable years ending June 30, Year 1.

(ii) *Analysis*—(A) *Determining a specified group and specified period of the specified group.* Pursuant to paragraph (d) of this section, FP,

FC1, FC2, and FC3 are members of a specified group, and FP is the specified group parent. Because the specified group parent, FP, is an applicable CFC, the specified period of the specified group is the period ending on June 30, Year 1, which is the last day of FP's required year described in section 898(c)(1), without regard to section 898(c)(2), and beginning on July 1, Year 0, which is the first day following the last day of the specified group's immediately preceding specified period (June 30, Year 0). See paragraph (k)(29)(i)(B) of this section.

(B) *Determining the specified taxable years with respect to the specified period.* Pursuant to paragraph (d)(3) of this section, because each of FP and FC1 are included in the specified group on the last day of their taxable years ending May 31, Year 1, and such taxable years end with or within the specified period ending June 30, Year 1, FP and FC1 are specified group members with respect to the specified period ending June 30, Year 1, for their entire taxable years ending May 31, Year 1, and those taxable years are specified taxable years. Similarly, because each of FC2 and FC3 are included in the specified group on the last day of their taxable years ending June 30, Year 1, and such taxable years end with or within the specified period ending June 30, Year 1, FC2 and FC3 are specified group members with respect to the specified period ending June 30, Year 1, for their entire taxable years ending June 30, Year 1, and those taxable years are specified taxable years. The fact that FC3 was acquired on March 22, Year 1, does not prevent FC3 from being a specified group member with respect to the specified period for the portion of its specified taxable year before March 22, Year 1.

(2) *Example 2. CFC groups.*—(i) *Facts.* The facts are the same as in *Example 1* in paragraph (l)(1)(i) of this section except that, in addition, a CFC group election is in place with respect to the specified period ending June 30, Year 1.

(ii) *Analysis.* Because a CFC group election is in place for the specified period ending June 30, Year 1, pursuant to paragraph (e)(2)(ii) of this section, each specified group member is a CFC group member with respect to its specified taxable year ending with or within the specified period. Accordingly, FP, FC1, FC2, and FC3 are CFC group members with respect to the specified period ending June 30, Year 1, for their specified taxable years ending May 31, Year 1, and June 30, Year 1, respectively. Pursuant to paragraph (e)(2)(i) of this section, the CFC group for the specified period ending June 30, Year 1, consists of FP, FC1, FC2, and FC3 for their specified taxable years ending May 31, Year 1, and June 30, Year 1, respectively. Pursuant to paragraph (c)(2) of this section, a single section 163(j) limitation is computed for the specified period ending June 30, Year 1. That section 163(j) calculation will include FP and FC1's specified taxable years ending May 31, Year 1, and FC2 and FC3's specified taxable years ending June 30, Year 1.

(3) *Example 3. Application of anti-abuse rule.*—(i) *Facts.* USP, a domestic corporation, owns all of the stock of CFC1 and CFC2. Thus, USP is the specified group parent of a specified group, the specified group members of which are CFC1 and CFC2. USP has a calendar year taxable year. All specified group members also have a calendar year taxable year and a functional currency of the U.S. dollar. CFC1 is organized in, and a tax resident of, a jurisdiction that imposes no tax on certain types of income, including interest income. With respect to Year 1, USP expects to pay no residual U.S. tax on its income inclusion under section 951A(a) (GILTI inclusion amount) and expects to have unused foreign tax credits in the category described in section 904(d)(1)(A). A CFC group election is not in effect for Year 1. With a principal purpose of reducing USP's Federal income tax liability in subsequent taxable years, on January 1, Year 1, CFC1 loans $100x to CFC2. On December 31, Year 1, CFC2 pays interest of $10x to CFC1 and repays the principal of $100x. Absent the application of paragraph (g)(4)(i) of this section, all $10x of CFC2's interest expense would be disallowed business interest expense and, therefore, CFC2 would have $10x of disallowed business interest expense carryforward to Year 2. In Year 2, CFC2 disposes of one of its businesses at a substantial gain that gives rise to tested income (within the meaning of section 951A(c)(2)(A) and § 1.951A-2(b)(1)). As a result of the gain being included in the ATI of CFC2, absent the application of paragraph (g)(4)(i) of this section, CFC2 would be allowed to deduct the entire $10x of disallowed business interest expense carryforward and therefore reduce the amount of its tested income. Also, USP would pay residual U.S. tax on its GILTI inclusion amount in Year 2, without regard to the application of paragraph (g)(4)(i) of this section.

(ii) *Analysis.* The $10x of business interest expense paid in Year 1 is a payment amount described in paragraph (g)(4)(i) of this section because it is between specified group members, CFC1 and CFC2. Furthermore, the requirements of paragraphs (g)(4)(i)(A), (B), and (C) of this section are satisfied because the $10x of business interest expense is incurred with a principal purpose of reducing USP's Federal income tax liability; absent the application of paragraph (g)(4)(i) of this section, the effect of CFC2 treating the $10x of business interest expense as disallowed business interest expense in Year 1 would be to reduce USP's Federal income tax liability in Year 2; and no CFC group election is in effect with respect to the specified group in Year 1. Because the requirements of paragraphs (g)(4)(i)(A), (B), and (C) of this section are satisfied, CFC2's ATI for Year 1 is increased by the ATI adjustment amount, or $33.33x, which is the amount equal to 3 1/3 multiplied by $10x (the lesser of the payment amount of $10x and the disallowed business interest expense of $10x). As a result, the $10x of business interest expense is not disallowed business interest expense of CFC2 in Year 1, and therefore does not give rise to a disallowed business interest expense carryforward to Year 2.

(m) *Applicability dates.*—(1) *General applicability date.*—Except as provided in paragraph (m)(2) of this section, this section applies for a taxable year of a foreign corporation beginning on or after November 13, 2020.

(2) *Exception.*—Paragraphs (a), (c)(1), (2)(i) and (ii), and (3) through (5), (d), (e), (f)(1), (g)(3) and (4), (h), and (k)(1) through (3), (6) through (8), and (10) through (32) of this section apply for a taxable year of a foreign corporation beginning on or after March 22, 2021.

(3) *Early application.*—(i) *Rules for paragraphs (b) and (g)(1) and (2) of this section.*—Taxpayers and their related parties, within the meaning of sections 267(b) (determined without regard to section 267(c)(3)) and 707(b)(1), may choose to apply the rules in paragraphs (b) and (g)(1) and (2) of this section for a taxable year beginning after December 31, 2017, and before November 13, 2020, provided that those taxpayers and their related parties consistently apply all of those rules and the rules described in paragraph (m)(4) of this section for that taxable year. If a taxpayer and its related parties apply the rules described in paragraph (m)(4) of this section, as contained in T.D. 9905 (§§1.163(j)-0 through 1.163(j)-11, effective November 13, 2020), they will be considered as applying the rules described in paragraph (m)(4) of this section for purposes of this paragraph (m)(3)(i).

(ii) *Rules for certain other paragraphs in this section.*—Taxpayers and their related parties, within the meaning of sections 267(b) (determined without regard to section 267(c)(3)) and 707(b)(1), may choose to apply the rules in paragraphs (a), (c)(1), (2)(i) and (ii), and (3) through (5), (d), (e), (f)(1), (g)(3) and (4), (h), and (k)(1) through (3), (6) through (8), and (10) through (32) of this section for a taxable year beginning after December 31, 2017, and before March 22, 2021, provided that those taxpayers and their related parties consistently apply all of those rules and the rules described in paragraph (m)(4) of this section for that taxable year and for each subsequent taxable year. If a taxpayer and its related parties apply the rules described in paragraph (m)(4) of this section, as contained in T.D. 9905 (§§1.163(j)-0 through 1.163(j)-11, effective November 13, 2020) as modified by T.D. 9943, (effective January 13, 2021), they will be considered as applying the rules described in paragraph (m)(4) of this section for purposes of this paragraph (m)(3)(ii).

(4) *Additional rules that must be applied consistently.*—The rules described in this paragraph (m)(4) are the section 163(j) regulations and, if applicable, §§1.263A-9, 1.263A-15, 1.381(c)(20)-1, 1.382-1, 1.382-2, 1.382-5, 1.382-6, 1.382-7, 1.383-0, 1.383-1, 1.469-9, 1.469-11, 1.704-1, 1.882-5, 1.1362-3, 1.1368-1, 1.1377-1, 1.1502-13, 1.1502-21, 1.1502-36, 1.1502-79, 1.1502-91 through 1.1502-99 (to the extent they effectuate the rules of §§1.382-2, 1.382-5, 1.382-6, and 1.383-1), and 1.1504-4.

(5) *Election for prior taxable years and specified periods.*—Notwithstanding paragraph (e)(5)(iii) or (h)(5)(i) of this section, in the case of a specified period of a specified group or a taxable year of a standalone applicable CFC that ends with or within a taxable year of a designated U.S. person ending before November 13, 2020, a CFC group election or a safe-harbor election may be made on an amended Federal income tax return filed on or before the due date (taking into account extensions, if any) of the original Federal income tax return for the first taxable year of each designated U.S. person ending on or after November 13, 2020. [Reg. §1.163(j)-7.]

☐ [*T.D. 9905, 9-3-2020. Amended by T.D. 9943, 1-13-2021.*]

[Reg. §1.163(j)-8]

§1.163(j)-8. [Reserved].
☐ [*T.D. 9905, 9-3-2020.*]

[Reg. §1.163(j)-9]

§1.163(j)-9. Elections for excepted trades or businesses; safe harbor for certain REITs.—(a) *Overview.*—The limitation in section 163(j) applies to business interest, which is defined under section 163(j)(5) as interest properly allocable to a trade or business. The term trade or business does not include any electing real property trade or business or any electing farming business. See section 163(j)(7). This section provides the rules and procedures for taxpayers to follow in making an election under section 163(j)(7)(B) for a trade or business to be an electing real property trade or business and an election under section 163(j)(7)(C) for a trade or business to be an electing farming business.

(b) *Availability of election.*—(1) *In general.*—An election under section 163(j)(7)(B) for a real property trade or business to be an electing real property trade or business is available to any trade or business that is described in §1.163(j)-1(b)(14)(i), (ii), or (iii), and an election under section 163(j)(7)(C) for a farming business to be an electing farming business is available to any trade or business that is described in §1.163(j)-1(b)(13)(i), (ii), or (iii).

(2) *Special rules.*—(i) *Exempt small businesses.*—An election described in paragraph (b)(1) of this section is available regardless of whether the real property trade or business or farming business making the election also meets the requirements of the small business exemption in section 163(j)(3) and §1.163(j)-2(d). See paragraph (c)(2) of this section for the effect of the election relating to depreciation.

(ii) *Section 162 trade or business not required for electing real property trade or business.*—An election described in paragraph (b)(1) of this section to be an electing real property trade or business is available regardless of whether the trade or business with respect to which the election is made is a trade or business under section 162. For example, a taxpayer engaged in activities described in section 469(c)(7)(C) and §1.469-9(b)(2), as required in §1.163(j)-1(b)(14)(i), may make an election for a trade or business to be an electing real property trade or business, regardless of whether its activities rise to the level of a section 162 trade or business.

(c) *Scope and effect of election.*—(1) *In general.*—An election under this section is made with respect to each eligible trade or business of the taxpayer and applies only to such trade or business for which the election is made. An election under this section applies to the taxable year in which the election is made and to all subsequent taxable years. See paragraph (e) of this section for terminations of elections.

(2) *Irrevocability.*—An election under this section is irrevocable.

(3) *Depreciation.*—Taxpayers making an election under this section are required to use the alternative depreciation system for certain types of property under section 163(j)(11) and cannot claim the additional first-year depreciation deduction under section 168(k) for those types of property.

(d) *Time and manner of making election.*—(1) *In general.*—Subject to paragraph (f) of this section, a taxpayer makes an election under this section by attaching an election statement to the taxpayer's timely filed original Federal income tax return, including extensions. A taxpayer may make elections for multiple trades or businesses on a single election statement.

(2) *Election statement contents.*—The election statement should be titled "Section 1.163(j)-9 Election" and must contain the following information for each trade or business:

(i) The taxpayer's name;

(ii) The taxpayer's address;

(iii) The taxpayer's social security number (SSN) or employer identification number (EIN);

(iv) A description of the taxpayer's electing trade or business sufficient to demonstrate qualification for an election under this section, including the principal business activity code; and

(v) A statement that the taxpayer is making an election under section 163(j)(7)(B) or (C), as applicable.

(3) *Consolidated group's trade or business.*—For a consolidated group's trade or business, the election under this section is made by the agent for the group, as defined in §1.1502-77, on behalf of itself and members of the consolidated group. Only the name and taxpayer identification number (TIN) of the agent for the group, as defined in §1.1502-77, must be provided on the election statement.

(4) *Partnership's trade or business.*—An election for a partnership must be made on the partnership's return for a trade or business that the partnership conducts. An election by a partnership does not apply to a trade or business conducted by a partner outside the partnership.

(e) *Termination of election.*—(1) *In general.*—An election under this section automatically terminates if a taxpayer ceases to engage in the electing trade or business. A taxpayer is considered to cease to engage in an electing trade or business if the taxpayer sells or transfers substantially all of the assets of the electing trade or business to an acquirer that is not a related party in a taxable asset transfer. A taxpayer is also considered to cease to engage in an electing trade or business if the taxpayer terminates its existence for Federal income tax purposes or ceases operation of the electing trade or business, except to the extent that such termination or cessation results in the sale or transfer of substantially all of the assets of the electing trade or business to an acquirer that is a related party, or in a transaction that is not a taxable asset transfer.

(2) *Taxable asset transfer defined.*—For purposes of this paragraph (e), the term *taxable asset transfer* means a transfer in which the acquirer's basis or adjusted basis in the assets is not determined, directly or indirectly, in whole or in part, by reference to the transferor's basis in the assets.

(3) *Related party defined.*—For purposes of this paragraph (e), the term *related party* means any person who bears a relationship to the taxpayer which is described in section 267(b) or 707(b)(1).

(4) *Anti-abuse rule.*—If, within 60 months of a sale or transfer of assets described in paragraph (e)(1) of this section, the taxpayer or a related party reacquires substantially all of the assets that were used in the taxpayer's prior electing trade or business, or substantially similar assets, and resumes conducting such prior electing trade or business, the taxpayer's previously terminated election under this section is reinstated and is effective on the date the prior electing trade or business is reacquired.

(f) *Additional guidance.*—The rules and procedures regarding the time and manner of making an election under this section and the election statement contents in paragraph (d) of this section may be modified through other guidance (see §§ 601.601(d) and 601.602 of this chapter). Additional situations in which an election may terminate under paragraph (e) of this section may be provided through guidance published in the Federal Register or in the Internal Revenue Bulletin (see § 601.601(d) of this chapter).

(g) *Examples.*—The examples in this paragraph (g) illustrate the application of this section. Unless otherwise indicated, X and Y are domestic C corporations; D and E are U.S. resident individuals not subject to any foreign income tax; and the exemption for certain small businesses in § 1.163(j)-2(d) does not apply.

(1) *Example 1: Scope of election.*—(i) *Facts.* For the taxable year ending December 31, 2021, D, a sole proprietor, owned and operated a dairy farm and an orchard as separate farming businesses described in section 263A(e)(4). D filed an original Federal income tax return for the 2021 taxable year on August 1, 2022, and included with the return an election statement meeting the requirements of paragraph (d)(2) of this section. The election statement identified D's dairy farm business as an electing trade or business under this section. On March 1, 2023, D sold some but not all or substantially all of the assets from D's dairy farm business to D's neighbor, E, who is unrelated to D. After the sale, D continued to operate the dairy farm trade or business.

(ii) *Analysis.* D's election under this section was properly made and is effective for the 2021 taxable year and subsequent years. D's dairy farm business is an excepted trade or business because D made the election with D's timely filed Federal income tax return. D's orchard business is a non-excepted trade or business, because D did not make an election for the orchard business to be an excepted trade or business. The sale of some but not all or substantially all of the assets from D's dairy farm business does not affect D's election under this section.

(2) *Example 2: Availability of election.*—(i) *Facts.* E, an individual, operates a dairy business that is a farming business under section 263A and also owns real property that is not part of E's dairy business that E leases to an unrelated party through a triple net lease. E's average gross receipts, excluding inherently personal amounts, for the three years prior to 2021 are approximately $25 million, but E is unsure of the exact amount.

(ii) *Analysis.* Under paragraph (b)(2)(i) of this section, E may make an election under this section for the dairy business to be an electing farming business, even though E is unsure whether the small business exemption of § 1.163(j)-2(d) applies. Additionally, under paragraph (b)(2)(ii) of this section, assuming the requirements of section 163(j)(7)(C) and this section are otherwise satisfied, E may make an election under this section for its triple net lease property to be an electing real property trade or business, even though E may not be engaged in a trade or business under section 162 with respect to the real property.

(3) *Example 3: Cessation of entire trade or business.*—(i) *Facts.* X has a real property trade or business for which X made an election under this section by attaching an election statement to A's 2021 Federal income tax return. On March 1, 2022, X sold all of the assets used in its real property trade or business to Y, an unrelated party, and ceased to engage in the electing trade or business. On June 1, 2027, X

started a new real property trade or business that was substantially similar to X's prior electing trade or business.

(ii) *Analysis.* X's election under this section terminated on March 1, 2022, under paragraph (e)(1) of this section. X may choose whether to make an election under this section for X's new real property trade or business that A started in 2027.

(4) *Example 4: Anti-abuse rule.*—(i) *Facts.* The facts are the same as in *Example* 3 in paragraph (g)(3)(i) of this section, except that X restarted its previous real property trade or business on February 1, 2023, when X reacquired substantially all of the assets that X had sold on March 1, 2022.

(ii) *Analysis.* X's election under this section terminated on March, 1, 2022, under paragraph (e)(1) of this section. On February 1, 2023, X's election was reinstated under paragraph (e)(4) of this section. X's new real property trade or business is treated as a resumption of X's prior electing trade or business and is therefore treated as an electing real property trade or business.

(5) *Example 5: Trade or business continuing after acquisition.*—(i) *Facts.* X has a farming business for which X made an election under this section by attaching an election statement to X's timely filed 2021 Federal income tax return. Y, unrelated to X, also has a farming business, but Y has not made an election under this section. On July 1, 2022, X transferred all of its assets to Y in a transaction described in section 368(a)(1)(D). After the transfer, Y continues to operate the farming trade or business acquired from X.

(ii) *Analysis.* Under paragraph (e)(1) of this section, Y is subject to X's election under this section for the trade or business that uses X's assets because the sale or transfer was not in a taxable transaction. Y cannot revoke X's election, but X's election has no effect on Y's existing farming business for which Y has not made an election under this section.

(6) *Example 6: Trade or business merged after acquisition.*—(i) *Facts.* The facts are the same as in *Example* 5 in paragraph (g)(5)(i) of this section, except that Y uses the assets acquired from X in a trade or business that is neither a farming business (as defined in section 263A(e)(4) or § 1.263A-4(a)(4)) nor a trade or business of a specified agricultural or horticultural cooperative (as defined in section 199A(g)(4)).

(ii) *Analysis.* Y is not subject to X's election for Y's farming business because the farming trade or business ceased to exist after the acquisition.

(h) *Safe harbor for REITs.*—(1) *In general.*—If a REIT holds real property, as defined in § 1.856-10, interests in one or more partnerships directly or indirectly holding real property (through interests in other partnerships or shares in other REITs), as defined in § 1.856-10, or shares in one or more other REITs directly or indirectly holding real property (through interests in partnerships or shares in other REITs), as defined in § 1.856-10, the REIT is eligible to make the election described in paragraph (b)(1) of this section to be an electing real property trade or business for purposes of sections 163(j)(7)(B) and 168(g)(1)(F) for all or part of its assets. The portion of the REIT's assets eligible for this election is determined under paragraph (h)(2) or (3) of this section.

(2) *REITs that do not significantly invest in real property financing assets.*—If a REIT makes the election under paragraph (h)(1) of this section and the value of the REIT's real property financing assets, as defined in paragraphs (h)(5) and (6) of this section, at the close of the taxable year is 10 percent or less of the value of the REIT's total assets at the close of the taxable year, as determined under section 856(c)(4)(A), then all of the REIT's assets are treated as assets of an excepted trade or business.

(3) *REITs that significantly invest in real property financing assets.*—If a REIT makes the election under paragraph (h)(1) of this section and the value of the REIT's real property financing assets, as defined in paragraphs (h)(5) and (6) of this section, at the close of the taxable year is more than 10 percent of the value of the REIT's total assets at the close of the taxable year, as determined under section 856(c)(4)(A), then for the allocation of interest expense, interest income, and other items of expense and gross income to excepted and non-excepted trades or businesses, the REIT must apply the rules set forth in § 1.163(j)-10 as modified by paragraph (h)(4) of this section.

(4) *REIT real property assets, interests in partnerships, and shares in other REITs.*—(i) *Real property assets.*—Assets held by a REIT described in paragraph (h)(3) of this section that meet the definition of real property under § 1.856-10 are treated as assets of an excepted trade or business.

(ii) *Partnership interests.*—If a REIT described in paragraph (h)(3) of this section holds an interest in a partnership, in applying the partnership look-through rule described in

§ 1.163(j)-10(c)(5)(ii)(A)(2), the REIT treats assets of the partnership that meet the definition of real property under § 1.856-10 as assets of an excepted trade or business. This application of the definition of real property under § 1.856-10 does not affect the characterization of the partnership's assets at the partnership level or for any non-REIT partner. However, no portion of the adjusted basis of the REIT's interest in the partnership is allocated to a non-excepted trade or business if the partnership makes an election under paragraph (h)(7) of this section and if all of the partnership's assets are treated as assets of an excepted trade or business under paragraph (h)(2) of this section.

(iii) *Shares in other REITs.*—(A) *In general.*—If a REIT (shareholder REIT) described in paragraph (h)(3) of this section holds an interest in another REIT, then for purposes of applying the allocation rules in § 1.163(j)-10, the partnership look-through rule described in § 1.163(j)-10(c)(5)(ii)(A)(2), as modified by paragraph (h)(4)(ii) of this section, applies to the assets of the other REIT (as if the other REIT were a partnership) in determining the portion of shareholder REIT's adjusted basis in the shares of the other REIT that is allocable to an excepted or non-excepted trade or business of shareholder REIT. However, no portion of the adjusted basis of shareholder REIT's shares in the other REIT is allocated to a non-excepted trade or business if all of the other REIT's assets are treated as assets of an excepted trade or business under paragraph (h)(2) of this section.

(B) *Information necessary.*—If shareholder REIT does not receive, either directly from the other REIT or indirectly through the analysis of an applicable financial statement (within the meaning of section 451(b)(3)) of the other REIT, the information necessary to determine whether and to what extent the assets of the other REIT are investments in real property financing assets, then shareholder REIT's shares in the other REIT are treated as assets of a non-excepted trade or business under § 1.163(j)-10(c).

(iv) *Tiered entities.*—In applying § 1.163(j)-10(c)(5)(ii)(E), the rules in paragraphs (h)(4)(ii) and (h)(4)(iii)(A) and (B) of this section apply to any partnerships and other REITs within the tier.

(5) *Value of shares in other REITs.*—(i) *In general.*—If a REIT (shareholder REIT) holds shares in another REIT, then solely for purposes of applying the value tests under paragraphs (h)(2) and (3) of this section, the value of shareholder REIT's real property financing assets includes the portion of the value of shareholder REIT's shares in the other REIT that is attributable to the other REIT's investments in real property financing assets. However, no portion of the value of shareholder REIT's shares in the other REIT is included in the value of shareholder REIT's real property financing assets if all of the other REIT's assets are treated as assets of an excepted trade or business under paragraph (h)(2) of this section.

(ii) *Information necessary.*—If shareholder REIT does not receive, either directly from the other REIT or indirectly through the analysis of an applicable financial statement (within the meaning of section 451(b)(3)) of the other REIT, the information necessary to determine whether and to what extent the assets of the other REIT are investments in real property financing assets, then shareholder REIT's shares in the other REIT are treated as real property financing assets for purposes of paragraphs (h)(2) and (3) of this section.

(iii) *Tiered REITs.*—The rules in paragraphs (h)(5)(i) and (ii) of this section apply successively to the extent that the other REIT, and any other REIT in the tier, holds shares in another REIT.

(6) *Real property financing assets.*—For purposes of this paragraph (h), *real property financing assets* include interests, including participation interests, in the following: mortgages, deeds of trust, and installment land contracts; mortgage pass-through certificates guaranteed by Government National Mortgage Association (GNMA), Federal National Mortgage Association (FNMA), Federal Home Loan Mortgage Corporation (FHLMC), or Canada Mortgage and Housing Corporation (CMHC); REMIC regular interests; other interests in investment trusts classified as trusts under § 301.7701-4(c) of this chapter that represent undivided beneficial ownership in a pool of obligations principally secured by interests in real property and related assets that would be permitted investments if the investment trust were a REMIC; obligations secured by manufactured housing treated as single family residences under section 25(e)(10), without regard to the treatment of the obligations or the properties under state law; and debt instruments issued by publicly offered REITs.

(7) *Application of safe harbor for partnerships controlled by REITs.*—A partnership is eligible to make the election under paragraph (h)(1) of this section if one or more REITs own directly or indirectly at least 50 percent of the partnership's capital and profits, the partnership meets the requirements of section 856(c)(2), (3), and (4) as if the partnership were a REIT, and the partnership satisfies the require-

ments described in paragraph (h)(1) of this section as if the partnership were a REIT. The portion of the partnership's assets eligible for this election is determined under paragraph (h)(2) or (3) of this section, treating the partnership as if it were a REIT.

(8) *REITs or partnerships controlled by REITs that do not apply the safe harbor.*—A REIT or a partnership that is eligible but chooses not to apply the safe harbor provisions of paragraph (h)(1) or (7) of this section, respectively, may still elect, under paragraph (b)(1) of this section, for one or more of its trades or businesses to be an electing real property trade or business, provided that such trade or business is otherwise eligible to elect under paragraph (b)(1) of this section. A REIT or partnership that makes the election under paragraph (b)(1) of this section without utilizing the safe harbor provisions of paragraph (h) of this section may not rely on any portion of paragraphs (h)(1) through (7) of this section.

(i) [Reserved]

(j) *Special anti-abuse rule for certain real property trades or businesses.*—(1) *In general.*—Except as provided in paragraph (j)(2) of this section, a trade or business (lessor) does not constitute a trade or business eligible for an election described in paragraph (b)(1) of this section to be an electing real property trade or business if at least 80 percent, determined by fair market rental value, of the real property used in the business is leased to a trade or business (lessee) under common control with the lessor, regardless of whether the arrangement is pursuant to a written lease or pursuant to a service contract or another agreement that is not denominated as a lease. For purposes of this paragraph (j), fair market rental value is the amount of rent that a prospective lessee that is unrelated to the lessor would be willing to pay for a rental interest in real property, taking into account the geographic location, size, and type of the real property. For purposes of this paragraph (j), two trades or businesses are under common control if 50 percent of the direct and indirect ownership of both businesses are held by related parties within the meaning of sections 267(b) and 707(b).

(2) *Exceptions.*—(i) *De minimis exception.*—The limitation in paragraph (j)(1) of this section does not apply, and the lessor is eligible to make an election under paragraph (b)(1) of this section, if the lessor leases, regardless of whether the arrangement is pursuant to a written lease or pursuant to a service contract or another agreement that is not denominated as a lease, at least 90 percent of the lessor's real property, determined by fair market rental value, to one or more of the following:

(A) A party not under common control with the lessor or lessee;

(B) A party under common control with the lessor or lessee that has made an election described in paragraph (b)(1) of this section for a trade or business to be an electing real property trade or business or electing farming business, but only to the extent that the real property is used as part of its electing real property trade or business or electing farming business; or

(C) A party under common control with the lessor or lessee that is an excepted regulated utility trade or business, but only to the extent that the real property is used as part of its excepted regulated utility trade or business.

(ii) *Look-through exception.*—If the de minimis exception in paragraph (j)(2)(i) of this section does not apply because less than 90 percent of the lessor's real property is leased to parties described in paragraphs (j)(2)(i)(A), (B), and (C), the lessor is eligible to make the election under paragraph (b)(1) of this section to the extent that the lessor leases the real property to parties described in paragraph (j)(2)(A), (B), or (C), and to the extent that the lessee subleases (or lessees ultimately sublease) the real property to:

(A) A party not under common control with the lessor or lessee;

(B) A party under common control with the lessor or lessee that has made an election described in paragraph (b)(1) of this section for a trade or business to be an electing real property trade or business or electing farming business to the extent that the real property is used as part of its electing real property trade or business or electing farming business; or

(C) A party under common control with the lessor or lessee that is an excepted regulated utility trade or business to the extent that the real property is used as part of its excepted regulated utility trade or business.

(iii) *Inapplicability of exceptions to consolidated groups.*—The exceptions in paragraphs (j)(2)(i) and (ii) of this section do not apply when the lessor and lessee are members of the same consolidated group.

(iv) *Exception for certain REITs.*—The special anti-abuse rule in paragraph (j)(1) of this section does not apply to REITs or to partnerships making an election under paragraph (h)(7) of this section that lease qualified lodging facilities, as defined in section 856(d)(9)(D), and qualified health care properties, as defined in section 856(e)(6)(D).

(3) *Allocations.*—See §1.163(j)-10(c)(3)(iii)(D) for rules related to the allocation of the basis of assets used in lessor trades or businesses described in paragraphs (j)(1) and (j)(2)(i) of this section.

(4) *Examples.*—The examples in this paragraph (j)(4) illustrate the application of paragraphs (j)(1), (2), and (3) of this section. Unless otherwise indicated, the parties are all domestic entities and are not members of a single consolidated group within the meaning of §1.1502-1(h).

(i) *Example 1: Related party lease of hotel.*—(A) *Facts.* X and Y are under common control, as defined in paragraph (j)(1) of this section. X owns one piece of real property, a hotel, that X leases to Y. Y operates the hotel and provides hotel rooms and associated amenities to third party guests of the hotel. The form of the arrangement with third party hotel guests is a license to use rooms in the hotel and associated amenities. Y is a real property trade or business that has made an election under paragraph (b)(1) of this section.

(B) *Analysis.* Because X leases at least 80 percent of X's real property to a party under common control, X is subject to the anti-abuse rule in paragraph (j)(1) of this section. However, under the de minimis exception under paragraph (j)(2)(i) of this section, 100 percent of the fair market rental value of the building is leased to a party under common control that has made an election to be an electing real property trade or business. Accordingly, X is eligible to make the election described in paragraph (b)(1) of this section for its entire trade or business.

(ii) *Example 2.*—(A) *Facts.* The facts are the same as in *Example 1* in paragraph (j)(4)(i)(A) of this section, except that Y has not made an election under paragraph (b)(1) of this section, and is not otherwise using the real property in an excepted trade or business.

(B) *Analysis.* Because X leases at least 80 percent of X's real property, determined by fair market rental value, to Y, a party under common control, X is subject to the anti-abuse rule in paragraph (j)(1) of this section. X is not eligible for the de minimis exception under paragraph (j)(2)(i) of this section because X does not lease at least 90 percent of its real property to a party under common control, as defined in paragraph (j)(1) of this section, such as Y, and Y is not using the property in an otherwise excepted trade or business. However, X is eligible for the look-through exception under paragraph (j)(2)(ii) of this section because X leases 100 percent of its real property to Y, a party that is under common control, and Y subleases 100 percent of the real property to parties that are not under common control with X or Y. The fact that the license provided to hotel guests is not denominated as a lease does not prevent these licenses from being treated as a lease for purposes of paragraph (j) of this section. Accordingly, under the look-through exception under paragraph (j)(2)(ii) of this section, X is eligible to make the election described in paragraph (b)(1) of this section with regard to its entire trade or business.

(iii) *Example 3: Sublease to related party and unrelated third party.*—(A) *Facts.* X owns one piece of real property that X leases to Y, a party under common control, as defined in paragraph (j)(1) of this section. Y does not operate an excepted trade or business. Y subleases 80 percent of the real property, determined by the fair market rental value, to a party under common control with Y that does not operate an excepted trade or business and 20 percent of the real property, determined by the fair market rental value, to an unrelated third party.

(B) *Analysis.* Because X leases at least 80 percent of X's real property, determined by fair market rental value, to a party under common control, X is subject to the anti-abuse rule in paragraph (j)(1) of this section. X is not eligible for the de minimis exception in paragraph (j)(2)(i) of this section because X is not leasing at least 90 percent of the real property, determined by fair market rental value, to a party under common control that operates an excepted trade or business and/or unrelated parties. Under the look-through exception under paragraph (j)(2)(ii) of this section, X is eligible to make the election described in paragraph (b)(1) of this section with respect to the 20 percent of the fair market rental value of the real property subleased to an unrelated party because X is treated as directly leasing this portion to an unrelated party. X is not eligible to make the election described in paragraph (b)(1) of this section with respect to the 80 percent of the building subleased to a party under common control because X is still treated as directly leasing this portion to a related party. Under §1.163(j)-10(c)(3)(iii)(D), X must allocate 80 percent of the basis in the real property as a non-excepted trade or business and 20 percent of the basis in the real property as an excepted trade or business.

(iv) *Example 4: Multiple subleases.*—(A) *Facts.* X owns a building that X leases to Y, a party under common control as defined in paragraph (j)(1) of this section. Y does not operate an excepted trade or business. Y subleases 80 percent of the building, determined by fair market rental value, to Z, a party under common control with both X and Y. Y subleases the remaining 20 percent of the building, determined by fair market rental value, to unrelated parties. Z subleases 50 percent of its leasehold interest, determined by fair market rental value, to parties unrelated to X, Y and Z, and uses the remaining leasehold interest in its retail business. Z does not operate an excepted trade or business.

(B) *Analysis.* Because X leases at least 80 percent of X's real property, determined by fair market rental value, to a party under common control, X is subject to the anti-abuse rule in paragraph (j)(1) of this section. X is not eligible for the de minimis exception in paragraph (j)(2)(i) because X is not leasing at least 90 percent of the building, determined by fair market rental value, to a party under common control that operates an excepted trade or business and/or unrelated parties. Under the look-through exception under paragraph (j)(2)(ii) of this section, X is eligible to make the election described in paragraph (b)(1) of this section with respect to the 60 percent of the building that is subleased to unrelated parties, determined by adding 40 percent (50 percent of the 80 percent leasehold interest) from Z's sublease to an unrelated party and 20 percent from Y's sublease to unrelated parties (40 + 20). X is not eligible to make the election described in paragraph (b)(1) of this section with respect to the 40 percent of the building subleased to Z, because Z is a related party that does not operate an excepted trade or business.

(v) *Example 5: Lessee's Trade or Business.*—(A) *Facts.* X owns a building that X leases to W, a party under common control as defined in paragraph (j)(1) of this section. W operates the building as a widget manufacturing plant and does not sublease any portion of the building.

(B) *Analysis.* X is not eligible to make the election described in paragraph (b)(1) of this section because X leases the entire building to a party under common control. X is not eligible for the de minimis exception in paragraph (j)(2)(i) of this section because X is not leasing at least 90 percent of the real property to a party under common control that operates an excepted trade or business and/or unrelated parties. W's trade or business cannot be an electing real property trade or business. X is not eligible for the look-through exception under paragraph (j)(2)(ii) of this section because W is not subleasing any part of the building.

(k) *Applicability date.*—This section applies to taxable years beginning on or after November 13, 2020. However, taxpayers and their related parties, within the meaning of sections 267(b) and 707(b)(1), may choose to apply the rules of this section to a taxable year beginning after December 31, 2017, so long as the taxpayers and their related parties consistently apply the rules of the section 163(j) regulations, and, if applicable, §§1.263A-9, 1.263A-15, 1.381(c)(20)-1, 1.382-1, 1.382-2, 1.382-5, 1.382-6, 1.382-7, 1.383-0, 1.383-1, 1.469-9, 1.469-11, 1.704-1, 1.882-5, 1.1362-3, 1.1368-1, 1.1377-1, 1.1502-13, 1.1502-21, 1.1502-36, 1.1502-79, 1.1502-91 through 1.1502-99 (to the extent they effectuate the rules of §§1.382-2, 1.382-5, 1.382-6, and 1.383-1), and 1.1504-4, to that taxable year. [Reg. §1.163(j)-9.]

□ [T.D. 9905, 9-3-2020.]

[Reg. §1.163(j)-10]

§1.163(j)-10. Allocation of interest expense, interest income, and other items of expense and gross income to an excepted trade or business.—(a) *Overview.*—(1) *In general.*—(i) *Purposes.*—Except as provided in §1.163(j)-6(m) or §1.163(j)-9(h), this section provides the exclusive rules for allocating tax items that are properly allocable to a trade or business between excepted trades or businesses and non-excepted trades or businesses for purposes of section 163(j). The amount of a taxpayer's interest expense that is properly allocable to excepted trades or businesses is not subject to the section 163(j) limitation. The amount of a taxpayer's other items of income, gain, deduction, or loss, including interest income, that is properly allocable to excepted trades or businesses is excluded from the calculation of the taxpayer's section 163(j) limitation. See section 163(j)(6) and (j)(8)(A)(i); see also §1.163(j)-1(b)(1)(i)(H), (b)(1)(ii)(F), and (b)(3). The general method of allocation set forth in paragraph (c) of this section is based on the approach that money is fungible and that interest expense is attributable to all activities and property, regardless of any specific purpose for incurring an obligation on which interest is paid. In no event may the amount of interest expense allocated under this section exceed the amount of interest paid or accrued, or treated as paid or accrued, by the taxpayer within the taxable year.

(ii) *Application of section.*—The amount of a taxpayer's tax items properly allocable to a trade or business, other than interest expense and interest income, that is properly allocable to excepted trades or businesses for purposes of section 163(j) is determined as set forth in paragraph (b) of this section. The amount of a taxpayer's interest expense and interest income that is properly allocable to excepted trades or businesses for purposes of section 163(j) generally is determined as set forth in paragraph (c) of this section, except as otherwise provided in paragraph (d) of this section. For purposes of this section, a taxpayer's activities are not treated as a separate trade or business to the extent those activities involve the provision of real property, goods, or services to a trade or business of the taxpayer (or, if the taxpayer is a member of a consolidated group, the consolidated group). For example, if a taxpayer engaged in a manufacturing trade or business has in-house legal personnel that provide legal services solely with respect to the taxpayer's manufacturing business, the taxpayer is not treated as also engaged in the trade or business of providing legal services. Similarly, if the taxpayer described in the previous sentence constructs or acquires real property solely for use by the taxpayer's manufacturing business, the taxpayer is not treated as also engaged in a real property trade or business.

(2) *Coordination with other rules.*—(i) *In general.*—The rules of this section apply after a taxpayer has determined whether any interest expense or interest income paid, received, or accrued is properly allocable to a trade or business. Similarly, the rules of this section apply to other tax items after a taxpayer has determined whether those items are properly allocable to a trade or business. For instance, a taxpayer must apply § 1.163-8T, if applicable, to determine which items of interest expense are investment interest under section 163(d) before applying the rules in paragraph (c) of this section to allocate interest expense between excepted and non-excepted trades or businesses. After determining whether its tax items are properly allocable to a trade or business, a taxpayer that is engaged in both excepted and non-excepted trades or businesses must apply the rules of this section to determine the amount of interest expense that is business interest expense subject to the section 163(j) limitation and to determine which items are included or excluded in computing its section 163(j) limitation.

(ii) *Treatment of investment interest, investment income, investment expenses, and certain other tax items of a partnership with a C corporation or tax-exempt corporation as a partner.*—For rules governing the treatment of investment interest, investment income, investment expenses, and certain other separately stated tax items of a partnership with a C corporation or tax-exempt corporation as a partner, see §§ 1.163(j)-4(b)(3) and 1.163(j)-6(k).

(3) *Application of allocation rules to foreign corporations and foreign partnerships.*—The rules of this section apply to foreign corporations and foreign partnerships.

(4) *Application of allocation rules to members of a consolidated group.*—(i) *In general.*—As provided in § 1.163(j)-4(d), the computations required by section 163(j) and the regulations in this part under section 163(j) of the Code generally are made for a consolidated group on a consolidated basis. In this regard, for purposes of applying the allocation rules of this section, all members of a consolidated group are treated as one corporation. Therefore, the rules of this section apply to the activities conducted by the group as if those activities were conducted by a single corporation. For example, the group (rather than a particular member) is treated as engaged in excepted or non-excepted trades or businesses. In the case of intercompany obligations, within the meaning of § 1.1502-13(g)(2)(ii), for purposes of allocating asset basis between excepted and non-excepted trades or businesses, the obligation of the member borrower is not considered an asset of the creditor member. Similarly, intercompany transactions, within the meaning of § 1.1502-13(b)(1)(i), are disregarded for purposes of this section, as are the resulting offsetting items, and property is allocated to a trade or business based on the activities of the group as if the members of the group were divisions of a single corporation. Further, stock of a group member that is owned by another member of the same group is not treated as an asset for purposes of this section, and the transfer of any amount of member stock to a non-member is treated by the group as a transfer of the member's assets proportionate to the amount of member stock transferred. Additionally, stock of a corporation that is not a group member is treated as owned by the group.

(ii) *Application of excepted business percentage to members of a consolidated group.*—After a consolidated group has determined the percentage of the group's interest expense allocable to excepted trades or businesses for the taxable year (and thus not subject to the section 163(j) limitation), this exempt percentage is applied to the interest paid or accrued by each member during the taxable year to any lender that is not a group member. Therefore, except to the extent paragraph (d) of this section (providing rules for certain qualified nonrecourse indebtedness) applies, an identical percentage of the interest paid or accrued by each member of the group to any

lender that is not a group member is treated as allocable to excepted trades or businesses, regardless of whether any particular member actually engaged in an excepted trade or business.

(iii) *Basis in assets transferred in an intercompany transaction.*—For purposes of allocating interest expense and interest income under paragraph (c) of this section, the basis of property does not include any gain or loss realized with respect to the property by another member in an intercompany transaction, as defined in § 1.1502-13(b), whether or not the gain or loss is deferred.

(5) *Tax-exempt organizations.*—For tax-exempt organizations, section 512 and the regulations in this part under section 512 of the Code determine the rules for allocating all income and expenses among multiple trades or businesses.

(6) *Application of allocation rules to disallowed disqualified interest.*—A taxpayer may apply the allocation rules of this section to disallowed disqualified interest by either:

(i) Applying the allocation rules of this section to all of the taxpayer's disallowed disqualified interest in the taxable year(s) in which the disallowed disqualified interest was paid or accrued (the historical approach); or

(ii) Treating all of the taxpayer's disallowed disqualified interest as if it were paid or accrued in the taxpayer's first taxable year beginning after December 31, 2017 (the effective date approach).

(7) *Examples.*—The following examples illustrate the principles of this paragraph (a).

(i) *Example 1: Items properly allocable to a trade or business.*—(A) *Facts.* Individual T operates Business X, a non-excepted trade or business, as a sole proprietor. In Year 1, T pays or accrues $40x of interest expense and receives $100x of gross income with respect to Business X that is not eligible for a section 199A deduction. T borrows money to buy a car for personal use, and T pays or accrues $20x of interest expense with respect to the car loan. T also invests in corporate bonds, and, in Year 1, T receives $50x of interest income on those bonds.

(B) *Analysis.* Under paragraphs (a)(1) and (2) of this section, T must determine which items of income and expense, including items of interest income and interest expense, are properly allocable to a trade or business. T's $100x of gross income and T's $40x of interest expense with respect to Business X are properly allocable to a trade or business. However, the interest expense on T's car loan is personal interest within the meaning of section 163(h)(2) rather than interest properly allocable to a trade or business. Similarly, T's interest income from corporate bonds is not properly allocable to a trade or business because it is interest from investment activity. See section 163(d)(4)(B).

(ii) *Example 2: Intercompany transaction.*—(A) *Facts.* S is a member of a consolidated group of which P is the common parent. P conducts an electing real property trade or business (Business X), and S conducts a non-excepted trade or business (Business Y). P leases Building V (which P owns) to S for use in Business Y.

(B) *Analysis.* Under paragraph (a)(4)(i) of this section, a consolidated group is treated as a single corporation for purposes of applying the allocation rules of this section, and the consolidated group (rather than a particular member of the group) is treated as engaged in excepted and non-excepted trades or businesses. Thus, intercompany transactions are disregarded for purposes of this section. As a result, the lease of Building V by P to S is disregarded. Moreover, because Building V is used in Business Y, basis in this asset is allocated to Business Y rather than Business X for purposes of these allocation rules, regardless of which member (P or S) owns the building.

(iii) *Example 3: Intercompany sale of natural gas.*—(A) *Facts.* S is a member of a consolidated group of which P is the common parent. S drills for natural gas and is not an excepted regulated utility trade or business. S sells most of its natural gas production to P, which produces electricity at its natural gas-fired power plants, and S sells the rest of its natural gas production to third parties at market rates. P is an excepted regulated utility trade or business to the extent that it is engaged in a trade or business described in § 1.163(j)-1(b)(15)(i).

(B) *Analysis.* Intercompany transactions are disregarded for purposes of this section. As a result, the intercompany sales of natural gas by S to P are disregarded. Moreover, the assets of S and P are allocated between the excepted and non-excepted trades or businesses of the P group based on the assets used in each trade or business. Assets of S may be allocated to the P group's excepted trade or business to the extent those assets are used in the trade or business of the furnishing or sale of electrical energy. Likewise, assets of P may be allocated to the P group's non-excepted trade or business to the extent those assets are used in the trade or business of natural gas production.

(iv) *Example 4: Disallowed disqualified interest.*—(A) *Facts.* S is a member of a consolidated group of which P is the common parent. P and S are the only members of an affiliated group under old section 163(j)(6)(C). S operates a farm equipment leasing business (Business X) that is not an excepted trade or business. P is engaged in an electing farming business (Business Y). Entering its first taxable year beginning after December 31, 2017, the P group has disallowed disqualified interest of $120x, all of which the P group paid or accrued in earlier taxable years in which it only operated Business X. The P group also incurs $100x of interest expense during its 2018 taxable year, of which $25x (25 percent of $100x) is business interest expense properly allocable to Business X and $75x (75 percent of $100x) is properly allocable to Business Y under paragraph (c) of this section.

(B) *Analysis.* Under paragraph (a)(6) of this section, the P group may allocate disallowed disqualified interest to Business X and Business Y by either applying the allocation rules of this section in the taxable years in which the disallowed disqualified interest was paid or accrued (the historical approach) or by treating such interest as though it were paid or accrued in the P group's first taxable year beginning after December 31, 2017 (the effective date approach). Accordingly, if the P group chooses to rely on the historical approach, it allocates all $120x of disallowed disqualified interest to Business X (a non-excepted trade or business), and all $120x of disallowed disqualified interest is subject to the section 163(j) limitation. If, instead, the P group chooses to rely on the effective date approach, it allocates its $120x of disallowed disqualified interest in the same proportion as its $100x of business interest expense that was paid or accrued in its 2018 taxable year. Of the $120x of disallowed disqualified interest, $30x (25 percent of $120x) is allocated to Business X and $90x (75 percent of $120x) is allocated to Business Y. The $90x of disallowed disqualified interest that is properly allocable to Business Y (an excepted trade or business) is not subject to the section 163(j) limitation.

(b) *Allocation of tax items other than interest expense and interest income.*—(1) *In general.*—Except as otherwise provided in §1.163(j)-6(m) or §1.163(j)-9(h), for purposes of calculating ATI, tax items other than interest expense and interest income are allocated to a particular trade or business in the manner described in this paragraph (b). It is not necessary to allocate items under this paragraph (b) for purposes of calculating ATI if all of the taxpayer's items subject to allocation under this paragraph (b) are allocable to excepted trades or businesses, or if all of those items are allocable to non-excepted trades or businesses.

(2) *Gross income other than dividends and interest income.*—A taxpayer's gross income other than dividends and interest income is allocated to the trade or business that generated the gross income.

(3) *Dividends.*—(i) *Look-through rule.*—If a taxpayer receives a dividend, within the meaning of section 316, that is not investment income, within the meaning of section 163(d), and if the taxpayer satisfies the minimum ownership threshold in paragraph (c)(7) of this section, then, solely for purposes of allocating amounts received as a dividend during the taxable year to excepted or non-excepted trades or businesses under this paragraph (b), the dividend income is treated as allocable to excepted or non-excepted trades or businesses based upon the relative amounts of the payor corporation's adjusted basis in its assets used in its trades or businesses, determined pursuant to paragraph (c) of this section. If at least 90 percent of the payor corporation's adjusted basis in its assets during the taxable year, determined pursuant to paragraph (c) of this section, is allocable to either excepted trades or businesses or to non-excepted trades or businesses, all of the taxpayer's dividend income from the payor corporation for the taxable year is treated as allocable to either excepted or non-excepted trades or businesses, respectively.

(ii) *Inapplicability of the look-through rule.*—If a taxpayer receives a dividend that is not investment income, within the meaning of section 163(d), and if the taxpayer does not satisfy the minimum ownership threshold in paragraph (c)(7) of this section, then the taxpayer must treat the dividend as allocable to a non-excepted trade or business.

(4) *Gain or loss from the disposition of non-consolidated C corporation stock, partnership interests, or S corporation stock.*—(i) *Non-consolidated C corporations.*—(A) If a taxpayer recognizes gain or loss upon the disposition of stock in a non-consolidated C corporation that is not property held for investment, within the meaning of section 163(d)(5), and if the taxpayer looks through to the assets of the C corporation under paragraph (c)(5)(ii) of this section for the taxable year, then the taxpayer must allocate gain or loss from the disposition of stock to excepted or non-excepted trades or businesses based upon the relative amounts of the C corporation's adjusted basis in the assets used in its trades or businesses, determined pursuant to paragraph (c) of this section. If at least 90 percent of the C corporation's

adjusted basis in its assets during the taxable year, determined pursuant to paragraph (c) of this section, is allocable to either excepted trades or businesses or to non-excepted trades or businesses, all of the taxpayer's gain or loss from the disposition is treated as allocable to either excepted or non-excepted trades or businesses, respectively.

(B) If a taxpayer recognizes gain or loss upon the disposition of stock in a non-consolidated C corporation that is not property held for investment, within the meaning of section 163(d)(5), and if the taxpayer does not look through to the assets of the C corporation under paragraph (c)(5)(ii) of this section for the taxable year, then the taxpayer must treat the gain or loss from the disposition of stock as allocable to a non-excepted trade or business.

(C) For rules governing the transfer of stock of a member of a consolidated group, see paragraph (a)(4)(i) of this section.

(ii) *Partnerships and S corporations.*—(A) If a taxpayer recognizes gain or loss upon the disposition of interests in a partnership or stock in an S corporation that owns—

(1) Non-excepted assets and excepted assets;

(2) Investment assets; or

(3) Both;

(B) The taxpayer determines a proportionate share of the amount properly allocable to a non-excepted trade or business in accordance with the allocation rules set forth in paragraph (c)(5)(ii)(A) or (c)(5)(ii)(B)(3) of this section, as appropriate, and includes such proportionate share of gain or loss in the taxpayer's ATI. However, if at least 90 percent of the partnership's or S corporation's adjusted basis in its assets during the taxable year, determined pursuant to paragraph (c) of this section, is allocable to either excepted trades or businesses or to non-excepted trades or businesses, all of the taxpayer's gain or loss from the disposition is treated as allocable to either excepted or non-excepted trades or businesses, respectively. This rule also applies to tiered passthrough entities by looking through each passthrough entity tier (for example, an S corporation that is the partner of the highest-tier partnership would look through each lower-tier partnership), subject to paragraph (c)(5)(ii)(D) of this section. With respect to a partner that is a C corporation or tax-exempt corporation, a partnership's investment assets are taken into account and treated as non-excepted trade or business assets. For purposes of this paragraph, a passthrough entity means a partnership, S corporation, or any other entity (domestic or foreign) that is not a corporation if all items of income and deduction of the entity are included in the income of its owners or beneficiaries.

(5) *Expenses, losses, and other deductions.*—(i) *Expenses, losses, and other deductions that are definitely related to a trade or business.*—Expenses (other than interest expense), losses, and other deductions (collectively, *deductions* for purposes of this paragraph (b)(5)) that are definitely related to a trade or business are allocable to the trade or business to which they relate. A deduction is considered definitely related to a trade or business if the item giving rise to the deduction is incurred as a result of, or incident to, an activity of the trade or business or in connection with property used in the trade or business (see §1.861-8(b)(2)). If a deduction is definitely related to one or more excepted trades or businesses and one or more non-excepted trades or businesses, the deduction is apportioned between the excepted and non-excepted trades or businesses based upon the relative amounts of the taxpayer's adjusted basis in the assets used in those trades or businesses, as determined under paragraph (c) of this section.

(ii) *Other deductions.*—Deductions that are not described in paragraph (b)(5)(i) of this section are ratably apportioned based on the gross income of each trade or business.

(6) *Treatment of investment items and certain other items of a partnership with a C corporation partner.*—Any investment income, investment expense, or other item that a partnership receives, pays, or accrues and that is treated as properly allocable to a trade or business of a C corporation partner under §1.163(j)-4(b)(3)(i) is treated as properly allocable to a non-excepted trade or business of the C corporation partner, except that any item with respect to property or activities for which an election has been made by the partnership under §1.163(j)-9(b) is treated as properly allocable to an excepted trade or business. See, for example, an election for activities described in §1.163(j)-9(b)(2)(ii) or an election under §1.163(j)-9(h).

(7) *Examples: Allocation of income and expense.*—The following examples illustrate the principles of this paragraph (b):

(i) *Example 1: Allocation of income and expense between excepted and non-excepted trades or businesses.*—(A) *Facts.* T conducts an electing real property trade or business (Business Y), which is an excepted trade or business. T also operates a lumber yard (Business Z), which is a non-excepted trade or business. In Year 1, T receives $100x of gross rental income from real property leasing activities. T also pays or accrues $60x of expenses in connection with its real property leasing activities and $20x of legal services performed on behalf of both Business Y and Business Z. T receives $60x of gross income from lumber yard customers and pays or accrues $50x of expenses related to the lumber yard business. For purposes of expense allocations under paragraphs (b) and (c) of this section, T has $240x of adjusted basis in its Business Y assets and $80x of adjusted basis in its Business Z assets.

(B) *Analysis.* Under paragraph (b)(2) of this section, for Year 1, $100x of rental income is allocated to Business Y, and $60x of income from lumber yard customers is allocated to Business Z. Under paragraph (b)(5)(i) of this section, $60x of expenses paid or accrued in connection with real property leasing activities are allocated to Business Y, and $50x of expenses related to the lumber yard are allocated to Business Z. The $20x of remaining expenses for legal services performed on behalf of both Business Y and Business Z are allocated according to the relative amounts of T's basis in the assets used in each business. The total amount of T's basis in the assets used in Businesses Y and Z is $320x, of which 75 percent ($240x / $320x) is used in Business Y and 25 percent ($80x / $320x) is used in Business Z. Accordingly, $15x of the expenses for legal services are allocated to Business Y and $5x are allocated to Business Z.

(ii) *Example 2: Allocation of partnership items from investment activity.*—(A) *Facts.* U, a domestic C corporation, directly conducts an electing real property trade or business. U also has an interest in PRS, a partnership that holds real property for investment. PRS's investment in real property is not a trade or business under section 162 or a real property trade or business under section 469. During the taxable year, PRS sells some of its real property to third parties and allocates $80x of income to U from these sales. In addition, PRS incurs deductible expenses related to its investment in real property and allocates $9x of these deductible expenses to U.

(B) *Analysis.* Under paragraph (b)(6) of this section, any investment income or investment expense that a partnership receives, pays, or accrues and that is treated as properly allocable to a trade or business of a C corporation partner is treated as properly allocable to a non-excepted trade or business of the C corporation partner. Because PRS generates its income and expense from investment activity that is not a trade or business under section 162 or a real property trade or business under section 469, U's allocation of $80x of income and $9x of deductible expense from PRS is treated as properly allocable to a non-excepted trade or business.

(c) *Allocating interest expense and interest income that is properly allocable to a trade or business.*—(1) *General rule.*—(i) *In general.*—Except as otherwise provided in this section, § 1.163(j)-6(m), or § 1.163(j)-9(h), the amount of a taxpayer's interest expense and interest income that is properly allocable to a trade or business is allocated to the taxpayer's excepted or non-excepted trades or businesses for purposes of section 163(j) based upon the relative amounts of the taxpayer's adjusted basis in the assets, as determined under paragraph (c)(5) of this section, used in its excepted or non-excepted trades or businesses. The taxpayer must determine the adjusted basis in its assets as of the close of each determination date, as defined in paragraph (c)(6) of this section, in the taxable year and average those amounts to determine the relative amounts of asset basis for its excepted and non-excepted trades or businesses for that year. It is not necessary to allocate interest expense or interest income under this paragraph (c) for purposes of determining a taxpayer's business interest expense and business interest income if all of the taxpayer's interest income and expense is allocable to excepted trades or businesses (in which case the taxpayer is not subject to the section 163(j) limitation) or if all of the taxpayer's interest income and expense is allocable to non-excepted trades or businesses.

(ii) *De minimis exception.*—If at least 90 percent of the taxpayer's basis in its assets for the taxable year is allocable to either excepted or non-excepted trades or businesses pursuant to this paragraph (c), then all of the taxpayer's interest expense and interest income for that year that is properly allocable to a trade or business is treated as allocable to either excepted or non-excepted trades or businesses, respectively.

(2) *Example.*—The following example illustrates the principles of paragraph (c)(1) of this section:

(i) *Facts.* T is a calendar-year C corporation engaged in an electing real property trade or business, the business of selling wine, and the business of selling hand-carved wooden furniture. In Year 1, T has $100x of interest expense that is deductible except for the potential application of section 163(j). Based upon determinations made on the determination dates in Year 1, T's average adjusted basis in the assets used in the electing real property trade or business (an excepted trade or business) in Year 1 is $800x, and T's total average adjusted basis in the assets used in the other two businesses (which are non-excepted trades or businesses) in Year 1 is $200x.

(ii) *Analysis.* $80x (($800x / ($800x + $200x)) x $100x) of T's interest expense for Year 1 is allocable to T's electing real property trade or business and is not business interest expense subject to the section 163(j) limitation. The remaining $20x of T's interest expense is business interest expense for Year 1 that is subject to the section 163(j) limitation.

(3) *Asset used in more than one trade or business.*—(i) *General rule.*—If an asset is used in more than one trade or business during a determination period, as defined in paragraph (c)(6) of this section, the taxpayer's adjusted basis in the asset is allocated to each trade or business using the permissible methodology under this paragraph (c)(3) that most reasonably reflects the use of the asset in each trade or business during that determination period. An allocation methodology most reasonably reflects the use of the asset in each trade or business if it most properly reflects the proportionate benefit derived from the use of the asset in each trade or business. A taxpayer is not required to use the same allocation methodology for each type of asset used in a trade a business. Instead, a taxpayer may use different allocation methodologies for different types of assets used in a trade or business. If none of the permissible methodologies set forth in paragraph (c)(3)(ii) of this section reasonably reflects the use of the asset in each trade or business, the taxpayer's basis in the asset is not taken into account for purposes of this paragraph (c).

(ii) *Permissible methodologies for allocating asset basis between or among two or more trades or businesses.*—Subject to the special rules in paragraphs (c)(3)(iii) and (c)(5) of this section, a taxpayer's basis in an asset used in two or more trades or businesses during a determination period may be allocated to those trades or businesses based upon—

(A) The relative amounts of gross income that an asset generates, has generated, or may reasonably be expected to generate, within the meaning of § 1.861-9T(g)(3), with respect to the trades or businesses;

(B) If the asset is land or an inherently permanent structure, the relative amounts of physical space used by the trades or businesses; or

(C) If the trades or businesses generate the same unit of output, the relative amounts of output of those trades or businesses (for example, if an asset is used in two trades or businesses, one of which is an excepted regulated utility trade or business, and the other of which is a non-excepted regulated utility trade or business, the taxpayer may allocate basis in the asset based upon the relative amounts of kilowatt-hours generated by each trade or business).

(iii) *Special rules.*—(A) *Consistent allocation methodologies.*—(1) *In general.*—Except as otherwise provided in paragraph (c)(3)(iii)(A)(2) of this section, a taxpayer must maintain the same allocation methodology for a period of at least five taxable years.

(2) *Consent to change allocation methodology.*—If a taxpayer has used the same allocation methodology for at least five taxable years, the taxpayers may change its method of allocation under paragraphs (c)(3)(i) and (ii) of this section without the consent of the Commissioner. If a taxpayer has used the same allocation methodology for less than five taxable years, and if the taxpayer determines that a different allocation methodology properly reflects the proportionate benefit derived from the use of assets in its trades or businesses, the taxpayer may change its method of allocation under paragraphs (c)(3)(i) and (ii) of this section only with the consent of the Commissioner. To obtain consent, a taxpayer must submit a request for a letter ruling under the applicable administrative procedures, and consent will be granted only in extraordinary circumstances.

(B) *De minimis exception.*—If at least 90 percent of the taxpayer's basis in an asset would be allocated to either excepted trades or businesses or non-excepted trades or businesses during a determination period pursuant to this paragraph (c)(3), the taxpayer's entire basis in the asset for the determination period must be allocated to either excepted or non-excepted trades or businesses, respectively. This rule applies before the application of paragraph (c)(1)(ii) of this section.

(C) *Allocations of excepted regulated utility trades or businesses.*—(1) *In general.*—Except as provided in the de minimis rule in paragraph (c)(3)(iii)(C)(3) of this section, a taxpayer is engaged in an excepted regulated utility trade or business only to the extent that the taxpayer is engaged in an excepted regulated utility trade or business described in § 1.163(j)-1(b)(15)(i)(A), (B), or (C), and any remaining utility trade or business is a non-excepted trade or business. Thus, for example, electricity sold by a utility trade or business at rates not established or approved by an entity described in § 1.163(j)-1(b)(15)(i)(A)(2) and not subject to an election under § 1.163(j)-1(b)(15)(iii) must be treated as electricity sold by a non-excepted regulated utility trade or business. The taxpayer must allocate under this paragraph (c) the basis of assets used in the utility trade or business between its excepted and non-excepted trades or businesses.

(2) Permissible method for allocating asset basis for utility trades or businesses.—In the case of a utility trade or business described in paragraph (c)(3)(iii)(C)(*1*) of this section, and except as provided in the de minimis rule in paragraph (c)(3)(iii)(C)(*3*) of this section, the method described in paragraph (c)(3)(iii)(C) of this section is the only permissible method under this paragraph (c)(3) for allocating the taxpayer's basis in assets used in both the excepted and non-excepted trades or businesses of selling or furnishing the items described in §1.163(j)-1(b)(15)(i)(A)(1).

(3) De minimis rule for excepted utility trades or businesses.— If a taxpayer is engaged in a utility trade or business described in paragraph (c)(3)(iii)(C)(*1*) of this section, and if at least 90 percent of the items described in §1.163(j)-1(b)(15)(i)(A)(*1*) are furnished or sold by trades or businesses described in §1.163(j)-1(b)(15)(i)(A), (B) or (C), the taxpayer's entire trade or business is an excepted regulated utility trade or business, and paragraph (c)(3)(iii)(C)(2) of this section does not apply. This rule applies before the application of paragraph (c)(3)(iii)(B) of this section.

(4) Example.—The following example illustrates the principles of this paragraph (c)(3)(iii)(C):

(i) Facts. X, a C corporation, is engaged in the trade or business of generating electrical energy. During each determination period in the taxable year, 80 percent of the megawatt-hours generated in the electricity generation trade or business is sold at rates negotiated with the purchaser, and with respect to which X filed a schedule of rates with a public utility commission. The public utility commission has the authority to take action on the filed schedule of rates, but if no action is taken, the rules governing the public utility commission explicitly state that the public utility commission is deemed to have approved the rates. The public utility has taken no action with respect to the negotiated rate. The remaining 20 percent of the megawatt-hours is sold on the wholesale market at rates not established or subject to approval by a regulator described in §1.163(j)-1(b)(15)(i)(A)(2). X has not made an election under §1.163(j)-1(b)(15)(iii). None of the assets used in X's utility generation trade or business are used in any other trade or business.

(ii) Analysis. For purposes of section 163(j), under paragraph (c)(3)(iii)(C)(*1*) of this section, 80 percent of X's electricity generation business is an excepted regulated utility trade or business, because the rate for the sale of the electricity was subject to approval by a regulator described in §1.163(j)-1(b)(15)(i)(A)(2). The remaining 20 percent of X's business is a non-excepted utility trade or business. Under paragraph (c)(3)(iii)(C)(2) of this section, X must allocate 80 percent of the basis of the assets used in its utility business to excepted trades or business and the remaining 20 percent of the basis in the assets to non-excepted trades or businesses.

(D) Special allocation rule for real property trades or businesses subject to special anti-abuse rule.—*(1) In general.*—In the case of a trade or business that leases real property subject to an arrangement described in §1.163(j)-9(j)(1), including trades or businesses to which the look-through exception in §1.163(j)-9(j)(2)(ii) applies, the taxpayer must allocate under this paragraph (c)(3) the basis of property used in both the excepted and non-excepted portions of its trade or business, as determined under §1.163(j)-9(j)(3).

(2) Allocation methodology for real property.—For purposes of this paragraph (c)(3)(iii)(D), a taxpayer must allocate the basis of real property leased under an arrangement described in §1.163(j)-9(j)(1) or (j)(2)(i) between the excepted and non-excepted portions of the real property trade or business based on the relative fair market rental value of the real property that is attributable to the excepted and non-excepted portions of the trade or business, respectively.

(3) Example.—The following example illustrates the principles of this paragraph (c)(3)(iii)(D):

(i) Facts. X and Y are domestic C corporations under common control within the meaning of section 267(b), but neither X nor Y are members of a consolidated group. The small business exemption in §1.163(j)-2(d) does not apply to X or Y. X owns an office building and leases the entire building to Y. Y subleases 80 percent of the office building, measured by fair market rental value, to a related party. Y subleases the remaining 20 percent of the building to unrelated third parties. X also owns depreciable scaffolding equipment, which it uses to clean all of the building's windows as part of its leasing arrangement with Y.

(ii) Analysis. Under §1.163(j)-9(j)(2)(ii), X is eligible to make an election for 20 percent of its business of leasing the office building to be an electing real property trade or business. Assuming X makes such an election, X must allocate the basis of assets used in

both the excepted and non-excepted portions of its leasing trade or business under this paragraph (c). Under paragraph (c)(3)(iii)(D)(2) of this section, X must allocate the basis of the office building based on the relative fair market value attributable to the excepted and non-excepted portions of its leasing business. Therefore, X must allocate 20 percent of the basis of the building to the excepted portion of its leasing business, and it must allocate the remaining 80 percent of the building to the non-excepted portion of its leasing business. Under paragraph (c)(3)(iii)(D)(2) of this section, X may use one of the allocation methods described in paragraph (c)(3)(iii) of this section to allocate the basis of its scaffolding equipment between the excepted and non-excepted portions of its leasing trade or business.

(4) Disallowed business interest expense carryforwards; floor plan financing interest expense.—Disallowed business interest expense carryforwards (which were treated as allocable to a non-excepted trade or business in a prior taxable year) are not re-allocated between non-excepted and excepted trades or businesses in a succeeding taxable year. Instead, the carryforwards continue to be treated as allocable to a non-excepted trade or business. Floor plan financing interest expense also is not subject to allocation between excepted and non-excepted trades or businesses (see §1.163(j)-1(b)(19)) and is always treated as allocable to non-excepted trades or businesses.

(5) Additional rules relating to basis.—(i) *Calculation of adjusted basis.*—(A) *Non-depreciable property other than land.*—Except as otherwise provided in paragraph (c)(5)(i)(E) of this section, for purposes of this section, the adjusted basis of an asset other than land with respect to which no deduction is allowable under section 167, former section 168, or section 197, as applicable, is the adjusted basis of the asset for determining gain or loss from the sale or other disposition of that asset as provided in §1.1011-1. Self-created intangible assets are not taken into account for purposes of this paragraph (c).

(B) Depreciable property other than inherently permanent structures.—For purposes of this section, the adjusted basis of any tangible asset with respect to which a deduction is allowable under section 167, other than inherently permanent structures, is determined by using the alternative depreciation system under section 168(g) before any application of the additional first-year depreciation deduction (for example, under section 168(k) or (m)), and the adjusted basis of any tangible asset with respect to which a deduction is allowable under former section 168, other than inherently permanent structures, is determined by using the taxpayer's method of computing depreciation for the asset under former section 168. The depreciation deduction with respect to the property described in this paragraph (c)(5)(i)(B) is allocated ratably to each day during the period in the taxable year to which the depreciation relates. A change to the alternative depreciation system should be determined in a manner similar to that in §1.168(i)-4(d)(4) or (d)(5)(ii)(B), as applicable.

(C) Special rule for land and inherently permanent structures.— Except as otherwise provided in paragraph (c)(5)(i)(E) of this section, for purposes of this section, the adjusted basis of any asset that is land, including nondepreciable improvements to land, or an inherently permanent structure is its unadjusted basis.

(D) Depreciable or amortizable intangible property and depreciable income forecast method property.—For purposes of this section, the adjusted basis of any intangible asset with respect to which a deduction is allowable under section 167 or 197, as applicable, is determined in accordance with section 167 or 197, as applicable, and the adjusted basis of any asset described in section 167(g)(6) for which a deduction is allowable under section 167 is determined in accordance with section 167(g). The adjusted basis of any intangible asset under this paragraph (c)(5)(i)(D) is determined before any application of the additional first-year depreciation deduction. The depreciation or amortization deduction with respect to the property described in this paragraph (c)(5)(i)(D) is allocated ratably to each day during the period in the taxable year to which the depreciation or amortization relates.

(E) Assets not yet used in a trade or business.—Assets that have been acquired or that are under development but that are not yet used in a trade or business are not taken into account for purposes of this paragraph (c). For example, construction works in progress (such as buildings, airplanes, or ships) are not taken into account for purposes of this paragraph (c). Similarly, land acquired by a taxpayer for construction of a building by the taxpayer to be used in a trade or business is not taken into account for purposes of under this paragraph (c) until the building is placed in service. This rule does not apply to interests in a partnership or stock in a corporation.

(F) Trusts established to fund specific liabilities.—Trusts required to fund specific liabilities (for example, pension trusts, and nuclear decommissioning funds (including, but not limited to, those

funds for which an election is made under section 468A)) are not taken into account for purposes of this paragraph (c).

(G) *Inherently permanent structure.*—For purposes of this section, the term *inherently permanent structure* has the meaning provided in § 1.856-10(d)(2).

(ii) *Partnership interests; stock in non-consolidated C corporations.*—(A) *Partnership interests.*—(1) *Calculation of asset basis.*—For purposes of this section, a partner's interest in a partnership is treated as an asset of the partner. For these purposes, the partner's adjusted basis in a partnership interest is reduced, but not below zero, by the partner's share of partnership liabilities, as determined under section 752, and is further reduced as provided in paragraph (c)(5)(ii)(A)(2)(*iii*) of this section. If a partner elects or is required to apply the rules in this paragraph (c)(5)(ii)(A) to look through to a partnership's basis in the partnership's assets, the partner's basis in the partnership interest is adjusted to the extent of the partner's share of any adjustments to the basis of the partnership's assets required pursuant to the rules in paragraph (c)(5)(i) of this section.

(2) *Allocation of asset basis*—

(i) *In general.*—For purposes of determining the extent to which a partner's adjusted basis in its partnership interest is allocable to an excepted or non-excepted trade or business, the partner may look through to such partner's share of the partnership's basis in the partnership's assets, taking into account any adjustments under sections 734(b) and 743(b), and adjusted to the extent required under paragraph (d)(4) of this section, except as otherwise provided in paragraph (c)(5)(ii)(D) of this section. For purposes of the preceding sentence, such partner's share of partnership assets is determined using a reasonable method taking into account special allocations under section 704(b). Notwithstanding paragraph (c)(7) of this section, if a partner's direct and indirect interest in a partnership is greater than or equal to 80 percent of the partnership's capital or profits, the partner must apply the rules in this paragraph (c)(5)(ii)(A)(2) to look through to the partnership's basis in the partnership's assets. If a partner elects or is required to apply the rules in this paragraph (c)(5)(ii)(A)(2) to look through to a partnership's basis in the partnership's assets, the partner allocates the basis of its partnership interest between excepted and non-excepted trades or businesses based on the ratio in which the partner's share of the partnership's adjusted tax basis in its trade or business assets is allocated between excepted and non-excepted trade or business assets.

(ii) *De minimis rule.*—If, after applying paragraph (c)(5)(ii)(A)(2)(*iii*) of this section, at least 90 percent of a partner's share of a partnership's basis in its assets (including adjustments under sections 734(b) and 743(b)) is allocable to either excepted trades or businesses or non-excepted trades or businesses, without regard to assets not properly allocable to a trade or business, the partner's entire basis in its partnership interest is treated as allocable to either excepted or non-excepted trades or businesses, respectively. For purposes of the preceding sentence, such partner's share of partnership assets is determined using a reasonable method taking into account special allocations under section 704(b).

(iii) *Partnership assets not properly allocable to a trade or business.*—For purposes of applying paragraphs (c)(5)(ii)(A)(2)(*i*) and (*ii*) of this section to a partner that is a C corporation or tax-exempt corporation, such partner's share of a partnership's assets that are not properly allocable to a trade or business is treated as properly allocable to a non-excepted trade or business of such partner. However, if the partnership made an election under § 1.163(j)-9(b) or § 1.163(j)-9(h) with respect to an asset or activity, the assets (or assets related to such activities) are treated as properly allocable to an excepted trade or business of such partner. See, for example, an election under § 1.163(j)-9(h) for an asset or an election under § 1.163(j)-9(b) with respect to activities described in § 1.163(j)-9(b)(2)(ii). For a partner other than a C corporation or tax-exempt corporation, a partnership's assets that are not properly allocable to a trade or business are treated as neither excepted nor non-excepted trade or business assets; instead, such partner's adjusted basis in its partnership interest is decreased by that partner's share of the excess of the partnership's basis in those assets over the partnership's debt that is traced to such assets in accordance with § 1.163-8T, and it is increased by that partner's share of the excess of the partnership's debt that is traced to such assets in accordance with § 1.163-8T over the partnership's basis in those assets. For purposes of the preceding sentence, the partnership's asset basis in property not allocable to a trade or business is adjusted pursuant to the rules in paragraph (c)(5)(i) of this section. For purposes of this paragraph (c)(5)(ii)(A)(2)(*iii*), such partner's share of a partnership's assets is determined under a reasonable method taking into account special allocations under section 704(b).

(iv) *Inapplicability of partnership look-through rule.*—If a partner, other than a C corporation or a tax-exempt corporation, chooses not to look through to the partnership's basis in the partnership's assets under paragraph (c)(5)(ii)(A)(2)(*i*) of this section or is precluded by paragraph (c)(5)(ii)(D) of this section from applying such partnership look-through rule, the partner generally will treat its basis in the partnership interest as either an asset held for investment or a non-excepted trade or business asset as determined under section 163(d). If a partner that is a C corporation or a tax-exempt corporation chooses not to look through to the partnership's basis in the partnership's assets under paragraph (c)(5)(ii)(A)(2)(*i*) of this section or is precluded by paragraph (c)(5)(ii)(D) of this section from applying such partnership look-through rule, the taxpayer must treat its entire basis in the partnership interest as allocable to a non-excepted trade or business.

(B) *Stock in domestic non-consolidated corporations.*—(1) *In general.*—For purposes of this section, if a taxpayer owns stock in a domestic C corporation that is not a member of the taxpayer's consolidated group, or if the taxpayer owns stock in an S corporation, the stock is treated as an asset of the taxpayer.

(2) *Domestic non-consolidated C corporations*—

(i) *Allocation of asset basis.*—If a shareholder satisfies the minimum ownership threshold in paragraph (c)(7) of this section for stock in a domestic non-consolidated C corporation, and if dividends paid on such stock would not be included in the shareholder's investment income under section 163(d)(4)(B), then, for purposes of determining the extent to which the shareholder's basis in the stock is allocable to an excepted or non-excepted trade or business, the shareholder must look through to the corporation's basis in the corporation's assets, adjusted to the extent required under paragraph (d)(4) of this section, except as otherwise provided in paragraph (c)(5)(ii)(D) of this section. If a shareholder does not satisfy the minimum ownership threshold in paragraph (c)(7) of this section for stock in a domestic non-consolidated C corporation, but the shareholder's direct and indirect interest in such corporation is greater than or equal to 80 percent by value, and if dividends paid on such stock would not be included in the shareholder's investment income under section 163(d)(4)(B), then, for purposes of determining the extent to which the shareholder's basis in the stock is allocable to an excepted or non-excepted trade or business, the shareholder may look through to the corporation's basis in the corporation's assets, adjusted to the extent required under paragraph (d)(4) of this section, except as otherwise provided in paragraph (c)(5)(ii)(D) of this section. For purposes of the preceding sentence, indirect stock ownership is determined by applying the constructive ownership rules of section 318(a).

(ii) *De minimis rule.*—If at least 90 percent of the domestic non-consolidated C corporation's basis in the corporation's assets is allocable to either excepted trades or businesses or non-excepted trades or businesses, the shareholder's entire interest in the corporation's stock is treated as allocable to either excepted or non-excepted trades or businesses, respectively.

(iii) *Inapplicability of corporate look-through rule.*—If a shareholder other than a C corporation or a tax-exempt corporation is ineligible to look through or chooses not to look through to a corporation's basis in its assets under paragraph (c)(5)(ii)(B)(2)(*i*) of this section, the shareholder generally will treat its entire basis in the corporation's stock as an asset held for investment. If a shareholder that is a C corporation or a tax-exempt corporation is ineligible to look through or chooses not to look through to a corporation's basis in its assets under paragraph (c)(5)(ii)(B)(2)(*i*) of this section, the shareholder must treat its entire basis in the corporation's stock as allocable to a non-excepted trade or business.

(iv) *Use of inside basis for purposes of C corporation look-through rule.*—This paragraph (c)(5)(ii)(B)(2)(*iv*) applies if a shareholder meets the requirements to look through the stock of a domestic non-consolidated C corporation under paragraph (c)(5)(ii)(B)(2)(*i*) of this section, determined without applying the constructive ownership rules of section 318(a). If this paragraph (c)(5)(ii)(B)(2)(*iv*) applies, then solely for purposes of allocating asset basis under paragraph (c)(5)(ii)(B)(2)(*i*) of this section, and except as otherwise provided in paragraph (c)(5)(ii)(D) of this section, the shareholder may look through to such shareholder's pro rata share of the C corporation's basis in its assets, taking into account the modifications in paragraph (c)(5)(i) of this section with respect to the C corporation's assets, and adjusted to the extent required under paragraph (d)(4) of this section (asset basis look-through approach). If a shareholder applies the asset basis look-through approach, it must do so for all domestic non-consolidated C corporations for which the shareholder is eligible to use this approach, and it must report its use of this approach on the information statement described in paragraph (c)(6)(iii) of this section. The shareholder also must continue to use

Itemized Deductions for Individuals and Corps.
See p. 20,601 for regulations not amended to reflect law changes
25,371

the asset basis look-through approach in all future taxable years in which the shareholder is eligible to use this approach.

(3) *S corporations.*—(i) *Calculation of asset basis.*—For purposes of this section, a shareholder's share of stock in an S corporation is treated as an asset of the shareholder. Additionally, for these purposes, the shareholder's adjusted basis in a share of S corporation stock is adjusted to take into account the modifications in paragraph (c)(5)(i) of this section with respect to the assets of the S corporation (for example, a shareholder's adjusted basis in its S corporation stock is increased by the shareholder's share of depreciation with respect to an inherently permanent structure owned by the S corporation).

(ii) *Allocation of asset basis.*—For purposes of determining the extent to which a shareholder's basis in its stock of an S corporation is allocable to an excepted or non-excepted trade or business, the shareholder may look through to such shareholder's share of the S corporation's basis in the S corporation's assets, allocated on a pro rata basis, adjusted to the extent required under paragraph (d)(4) of this section, except as otherwise provided in paragraph (c)(5)(ii)(D) of this section. Notwithstanding paragraph (c)(7) of this section, if a shareholder's direct and indirect interest in an S corporation is greater than or equal to 80 percent of the S corporation's stock by vote and value, the shareholder must apply the rules in this paragraph (c)(5)(ii)(B)(3) to look through to the S corporation's basis in the S corporation's assets. For these purposes, indirect stock ownership is determined by applying the constructive ownership rules of section 318(a).

(iii) *De minimis rule.*—If at least 90 percent of a shareholder's share of an S corporation's basis in its assets is allocable to either excepted trades or businesses or non-excepted trades or businesses, the shareholder's entire basis in its S corporation stock is treated as allocable to either excepted or non-excepted trades or businesses, respectively.

(iv) *Inapplicability of S corporation look-through rule.*—If a shareholder chooses not to look through to the S corporation's basis in the S corporation's assets under paragraph (c)(5)(ii)(B)(3)(ii) of this section or is precluded by paragraph (c)(5)(ii)(D) of this section from applying such S corporation look-through rule, the shareholder will treat its basis in the S corporation stock as either an asset held for investment or a non-excepted trade or business asset as determined under section 163(d).

(C) *Stock in relevant foreign corporations.*—(1) *In general.*—The rules applicable to domestic non-consolidated C corporations in paragraph (c)(5)(ii)(B) of this section also apply to relevant foreign corporations (as defined in § 1.163(j)-1(b)(33)).

(2) *Special rule for CFC utilities.*—Solely for purposes of applying the rules in paragraph (c)(5)(ii)(B) of this section, a utility trade or business conducted by an applicable CFC is treated as an excepted regulated utility trade or business, but only to the extent that the applicable CFC sells or furnishes the items described in § 1.163(j)-1(b)(15)(i)(A)(1) pursuant to rates established or approved by an entity described in § 1.163(j)-1-b(15)(i)(A)(2), a foreign government, a public service or public utility commission or other similar body of any foreign government, or the governing or ratemaking body of a foreign electric cooperative. For purposes of this paragraph (c)(5)(ii)(C)(2), the term *foreign government* means any foreign government, any political subdivision of a foreign government, or any wholly owned agency or instrumentality of any one of the foregoing within the meaning of § 1.1471-6(b).

(D) *Limitations on application of look-through rules.*—(1) *Inapplicability of look-through rule to partnerships or non-consolidated C corporations to which the small business exemption applies.*—A taxpayer may not apply the look-through rules in paragraphs (b)(3) and (c)(5)(ii)(A), (B), and (C) of this section to a partnership, S corporation, or non-consolidated C corporation that is eligible for the small business exemption under section 163(j)(3) and § 1.163(j)-2(d)(1), unless the partnership, S corporation, or non-consolidated C corporation elects under § 1.163(j)-9 for a trade or business to be an electing real property trade or business or an electing farming business.

(2) *Limitation on application of look-through rule to C corporations.*—Except as provided in § 1.163(j)-9(h)(4)(iii) and (iv) (for a REIT or a partnership making the election under § 1.163(j)-9(h)(1) or (7), respectively), for purposes of applying the look-through rules in paragraph (c)(5)(ii)(B) and (C) of this section to a non-consolidated C corporation (upper-tier entity), that upper-tier entity may not apply these look-through rules to a lower-tier non-consolidated C corporation if a principal purpose for borrowing funds at the upper-tier entity level or adding an upper-tier or lower-tier entity to the ownership structure is increasing the amount of the taxpayer's basis allocable to excepted trades or businesses. For example, P wholly and directly owns S1 (the upper-tier entity), which wholly and directly

owns S2. Each of S1 and S2 is a non-consolidated C corporation to which the small business exemption does not apply, and S2 is engaged in an excepted trade or business. With a principal purpose of increasing the amount of basis allocable to its excepted trades or businesses, P has S1 (rather than S2) borrow funds from a third party. S1 may not look through the stock of S2 (and may not apply the asset basis look-through rule described in paragraph (c)(5)(ii)(B)(2)(iv) of this section) for purposes of P's allocation of its basis in its S1 stock between excepted and non-excepted trades or businesses; instead, S1 must treat its stock in S2 as an asset used in a non-excepted trade or business for that purpose. However, S1 may look through the stock of S2 for purposes of S1's allocation of its basis in its S2 stock between excepted and non-excepted trades or businesses.

(E) *Tiered entities.*—If a taxpayer applies the look-through rules of this paragraph (c)(5)(ii), the taxpayer must do so for all lower-tier entities with respect to which the taxpayer satisfies, directly or indirectly, the minimum ownership threshold in paragraph (c)(7) of this section, subject to the limitation in paragraph (c)(5)(ii)(D) of this section, beginning with the lowest-tier entity.

(iii) *Cash and cash equivalents and customer receivables.*—Except as otherwise provided in the last sentence of this paragraph (c)(5)(iii), a taxpayer's basis in its cash and cash equivalents and customer receivables is not taken into account for purposes of this paragraph (c). This rule also applies to a lower-tier entity if a taxpayer looks through to the assets of that entity under paragraph (c)(5)(ii) of this section. For purposes of this paragraph (c)(5)(iii), the term *cash and cash equivalents* includes cash, foreign currency, commercial paper, any interest in an investment company registered under the Investment Company Act of 1940 (1940 Act) and regulated as a money market fund under 17 CFR 270.2a-7 (Rule 2a-7 under the 1940 Act), any obligation of a government, and any derivative that is substantially secured by an obligation of a government, or any similar asset. For purposes of this paragraph (c)(5)(iii), a *derivative* is a derivative described in section 59A(h)(4)(A), without regard to section 59A(h)(4)(C). For purposes of this paragraph (c)(5)(iii), the term *government* means the United States or any agency or instrumentality of the United States; a State, a territory, a possession of the United States, the District of Columbia, or any political subdivision thereof within the meaning of section 103 and § 1.103-1; or any foreign government, any political subdivision of a foreign government, or any wholly owned agency or instrumentality of any one of the foregoing within the meaning of § 1.1471-6(b). This paragraph (c)(5)(iii) does not apply to an entity that qualifies as a financial services entity as described in § 1.904-4(e)(3).

(iv) *Deemed asset sale.*—Solely for purposes of determining the amount of basis allocable to excepted and non-excepted trades or businesses under this section, an election under section 336, 338, or 754, as applicable, is deemed to have been made for any acquisition of corporate stock or partnership interests with respect to which the taxpayer demonstrates, in the information statement required by paragraph (c)(6)(iii)(B) of this section, that the acquisition qualified for such an election and that, immediately before the acquisition, the acquired entity had a regulatory liability for deferred taxes recorded on its books with respect to property predominantly used in an excepted regulated utility trade or business. Any additional basis taken into account under this rule is reduced ratably over a 15-year period beginning with the month of the acquisition and is not subject to the anti-abuse rule in paragraph (c)(8) of this section.

(v) *Other adjustments.*—The Commissioner may make appropriate adjustments to prevent a taxpayer from intentionally and artificially increasing its basis in assets attributable to an excepted trade or business.

(6) *Determination dates; determination periods; reporting requirements.*—(i) *Determination dates and determination periods.*—(A) *Quarterly determination periods.*—For purposes of this section, and except as otherwise provided in paragraph (c)(6)(i)(B) of this section, the term *determination date* means the last day of each quarter of the taxpayer's taxable year (and the last day of the taxpayer's taxable year, if the taxpayer has a short taxable year), and the term *determination period* means the period beginning the day after one determination date and ending on the next determination date.

(B) *Annual determination periods.*—If a taxpayer satisfies the requirements of the last sentence of this paragraph (c)(6)(i)(B), the taxpayer may allocate asset basis for a taxable year based on the average of adjusted asset basis at the beginning of the year and the end of the year (annual determination method). For these purposes, the term *determination date* means the last day of the taxpayer's taxable year, and the term *determination period* has the same meaning as provided in paragraph (c)(6)(i)(A) of this section. A taxpayer may use the annual determination method for a taxable year only if the taxpayer demonstrates that its total adjusted basis (as determined under paragraph (c)(5) of this section) at the end of the year in its assets used in its excepted trades or businesses, as a percentage of the taxpayer's total adjusted basis at the end of such year in all of its assets used in a trade or business, does not differ by more than 20 percent from such percentage at the beginning of the year.

(ii) *Application of look-through rules.*—If a taxpayer that applies the look-through rules of paragraph (c)(5)(ii) of this section has a different taxable year than the partnership or non-consolidated C corporation to which the taxpayer is applying those rules, then, for purposes of this paragraph (c)(6), the taxpayer must use the most recent asset basis figures from the partnership or non-consolidated C corporation. For example, assume that PS1 is a partnership with a May 31 taxable year, and that C (a calendar-year C corporation that is ineligible to use the annual determination method for the taxable year) is a partner in PS1. PS1's determination dates are February 28, May 31, August 31, and November 30. In turn, C's determination dates are March 31, June 30, September 30, and December 31. If C looks through to PS1's basis in its assets under paragraph (c)(5)(ii) of this section, then, for purposes of determining the amount of C's asset basis that is attributable to its excepted and non-excepted businesses on March 31, C must use PS1's asset basis calculations for February 28.

(iii) *Reporting requirements.*—(A) *Books and records.*—A taxpayer must maintain books of account and other records and data as necessary to substantiate the taxpayer's use of an asset in an excepted trade or business and to substantiate any adjustments to asset basis for purposes of applying this paragraph (c). One indication that a particular asset is used in a particular trade or business is if the taxpayer maintains separate books and records for all of its excepted and non-excepted trades or businesses and can show the asset in the books and records of a particular excepted or non-excepted trade or business. For rules governing record retention, see § 1.6001-1.

(B) *Information statement.*—Except as otherwise provided in publications, forms, instructions, or other guidance, each taxpayer that is making an allocation under this paragraph (c), including any taxpayer that satisfies the de minimis rule in paragraph (c)(1)(ii) of this section, must prepare a statement titled "Section 163(j) Asset Basis Calculations" containing the information described in paragraphs (c)(6)(iii)(B)(*1*) through (*7*) of this section and must attach the statement to its timely filed Federal income tax return for the taxable year:

(*1*) The taxpayer's adjusted basis in the assets used in its excepted and non-excepted businesses, determined as set forth in this section, including detailed information for the different groups of assets identified in paragraphs (c)(5)(i) and (ii) and (d) of this section;

(*2*) The determination dates on which asset basis was measured during the taxable year;

(*3*) The names and taxpayer identification numbers (TINs) of all entities for which basis information is being provided, including partnerships and corporations if the taxpayer that owns an interest in a partnership or corporation looks through to the partnership's or corporation's basis in the partnership's or corporation's assets under paragraph (c)(5)(ii) of this section. If the taxpayer is a member of a consolidated group, the name and TIN of the agent for the group, as defined in § 1.1502-77, must be provided, but the taxpayer need not provide the names and TINs of all other consolidated group members;

(*4*) Asset basis information for corporations or partnerships if the taxpayer looks through to the corporation's or partnership's basis in the corporation's or partnership's assets under paragraph (c)(5)(ii) of this section;

(*5*) A summary of the method or methods used to determine asset basis in property used in both excepted and non-excepted businesses, as well as information regarding any deemed sale under paragraph (c)(5)(iv) of this section;

(*6*) Whether the taxpayer used the historical approach or the effective date approach for all of its disallowed disqualified interest; and

(*7*) If the taxpayer changed its methodology for allocating asset basis between or among two or more trades or businesses under paragraph (c)(3)(ii) of this section, a statement that the taxpayer has changed the allocation methodology and a description of the new methodology or, if the taxpayer is required to request consent for the allocation methodology change under paragraph (c)(3)(iii)(A)(*2*) of this section, a statement that the request has been or will be filed and a description of the methodology change.

(iv) *Failure to file statement.*—If a taxpayer fails to file the statement described in paragraph (c)(6)(iii) of this section or files a statement that does not comply with the requirements of paragraph (c)(6)(iii) of this section, the Commissioner may treat the taxpayer as

if all of its interest expense is properly allocable to a non-excepted trade or business, unless the taxpayer shows that there was reasonable cause for failing to comply with, and the taxpayer acted in good faith with respect to, the requirements of paragraph (c)(6)(iii) of this section, taking into account all pertinent facts and circumstances.

(7) *Ownership threshold for look-through rules.*—(i) *Corporations.*—(A) *Asset basis.*—For purposes of this section, a shareholder must look through to the assets of a domestic non-consolidated C corporation or a relevant foreign corporation under paragraph (c)(5)(ii) of this section if the shareholder's direct and indirect interest in the corporation satisfies the ownership requirements of section 1504(a)(2). For purposes of this paragraph (c)(7)(i)(A), indirect stock ownership is determined by applying the constructive ownership rules of section 318(a). A shareholder may look through to the assets of an S corporation under paragraph (c)(5)(ii) of this section for purposes of allocating the shareholder's basis in its stock in the S corporation between excepted and non-excepted trades or businesses regardless of the shareholder's direct and indirect interest in the S corporation.

(B) *Dividends.*—A shareholder must look through to the activities of a domestic non-consolidated C corporation or a relevant foreign corporation under paragraph (b)(3) of this section if the shareholder's direct interest in the corporation satisfies the ownership requirements of section 1504(a)(2). A shareholder may look through to the activities of a domestic non-consolidated C corporation or an applicable CFC under paragraph (b)(3) of this section if the shareholder's direct interest in the corporation is greater than or equal to 80 percent by value. A shareholder may look through to the activities of an S corporation under paragraph (b)(3) of this section regardless of the shareholder's direct interest in the S corporation.

(ii) *Partnerships.*—A partner may look through to the assets of a partnership under paragraph (c)(5)(ii) of this section for purposes of allocating the partner's basis in its partnership interest between excepted and non-excepted trades or businesses regardless of the partner's direct and indirect interest in the partnership.

(iii) *Inapplicability of look-through rule.*—For circumstances in which a taxpayer that satisfies the ownership threshold in this paragraph (c)(7) may not apply the look-through rules in paragraphs (b)(3) and (c)(5)(ii) of this section, see paragraph (c)(5)(ii)(D) of this section.

(8) *Anti-abuse rule.*—If a principal purpose for the acquisition, disposition, or change in use of an asset was to artificially shift the amount of basis allocable to excepted or non-excepted trades or businesses on a determination date, the additional basis or change in use will not be taken into account for purposes of this section. For example, if an asset is used in a non-excepted trade or business for most of the taxable year, and if the taxpayer begins using the asset in an excepted trade or business towards the end of the year with a principal purpose of shifting the amount of basis in the asset that is allocable to the excepted trade or business, the change in use is disregarded for purposes of this section. A purpose may be a principal purpose even though it is outweighed by other purposes (taken together or separately). In determining whether a taxpayer has a principal purpose described in this paragraph (c)(8), factors to be considered include, for example, the following: the business purpose for the acquisition, disposition, or change in use; the length of time the asset was used in a trade or business; whether the asset was acquired from a related person; and whether the taxpayer's aggregate basis in its assets increased or decreased temporarily on or around a determination date. A principal purpose is presumed to be present in any case in which the acquisition, disposition, or change in use lacks a substantial business purpose and increases the taxpayer's basis in assets used in its excepted trades or businesses by more than 10 percent during the taxable year.

(d) *Direct allocations.*—(1) *In general.*—It is not necessary to allocate interest expense under this paragraph (d) if all of the taxpayer's interest expense is allocable to excepted trades or businesses or if all of the taxpayer's interest expense is allocable to non-excepted trades or businesses.

(2) *Qualified nonrecourse indebtedness.*—For purposes of this section, a taxpayer with qualified nonrecourse indebtedness must directly allocate interest expense from the indebtedness to the taxpayer's assets in the manner and to the extent provided in § 1.861-10T(b). For purposes of this paragraph (d)(2), the term *qualified nonrecourse indebtedness* has the meaning provided in § 1.861-10T(b), except that the term *cash flow from the property* (within the meaning of § 1.861-10T(b)(3)(i)) includes revenue derived from the sale or lease of inventory or similar property with respect to an excepted regulated utility trade or business or a non-excepted regulated utility trade or business.

(3) *Assets used in more than one trade or business.*—If an asset is used in more than one trade or business, the taxpayer must apply the rules in paragraph (c)(3) of this section to determine the extent to which interest that is directly allocated under this paragraph (d) is allocable to excepted or non-excepted trades or businesses.

(4) *Adjustments to basis of assets to account for direct allocations.*—In determining the amount of a taxpayer's basis in the assets used in its excepted and non-excepted trades or businesses for purposes of paragraph (c) of this section, adjustments must be made to reflect direct allocations under this paragraph (d). These adjustments consist of reductions in the taxpayer's basis in its assets for purposes of paragraph (c) of this section to reflect assets to which interest expense is directly allocated under this paragraph (d). The amount of the taxpayer's basis in these assets must be reduced, but not below zero, by the amount of qualified nonrecourse indebtedness secured by these assets. These adjustments must be made before the taxpayer averages the adjusted basis in its assets as determined on each determination date during the taxable year.

(5) *Example: Direct allocation of interest expense.*—(i) *Facts.* T conducts an electing real property trade or business (Business X) and operates a retail store that is a non-excepted trade or business (Business Y). In Year 1, T issues Note A to a third party in exchange for $1,000x for the purpose of acquiring Building B. Note A is qualified nonrecourse indebtedness (within the meaning of §1.861-10T(b)) secured by Building B. T then uses those funds to acquire Building B for $1,200x, and T uses Building B in Business X. During Year 1, T pays $500x of interest, of which $100x is interest payments on Note A. For Year 1, T's basis in its assets used in Business X (as determined under paragraph (c) of this section) is $3,600x (excluding cash and cash equivalents), and T's basis in its assets used in Business Y (as determined under paragraph (c) of this section) is $800x (excluding cash and cash equivalents). Each of Business X and Business Y also has $100x of cash and cash equivalents.

(ii) *Analysis.* Because Note A is qualified nonrecourse indebtedness that is secured by Building B, in allocating interest expense between Businesses X and Y, T first must directly allocate the $100x of interest expense it paid with respect to Note A to Business X in accordance with paragraph (d)(2) of this section. Thereafter, T must allocate the remaining $400x of interest expense between Businesses X and Y under paragraph (c) of this section. After excluding $1,000x of T's basis in Building B to reflect the amount of Note A (see paragraph (d)(4) of this section), and without regard to T's $200x of cash and cash equivalents (see paragraph (c)(5)(iii) of this section), T's basis in its assets used in Businesses X and Y is $2,600x and $800x (76.5 percent and 23.5 percent), respectively. Thus, $306x of the remaining $400x of interest expense would be allocated to Business X, and $94x would be allocated to Business Y.

(e) *Examples.*—The examples in this paragraph (e) illustrate the principles of this section. For purposes of these examples, no taxpayer is eligible for the small business exemption under section 163(j)(3) and §1.163(j)-2(d), no taxpayer has floor plan financing interest expense, and no taxpayer has qualified nonrecourse indebtedness within the meaning of §1.861-10T(b).

(1) *Example 1: Interest allocation within a consolidated group.*—(i) *Facts.* S is a member of a consolidated group of which P is the common parent. P conducts an electing real property trade or business (Business X), and S conducts a non-excepted trade or business (Business Y). In Year 1, P pays or accrues (without regard to section 163(j)) $35x of interest expense and receives $10x of interest income, and S pays or accrues (without regard to section 163(j)) $115x of interest expense and receives $5x of interest income (for a total of $150x of interest expense and $15x of interest income). For purposes of this example, assume that, pursuant to paragraph (c) of this section, $30x of the P group's interest expense and $3x of the P group's interest income is allocable to Business X, and the remaining $120x of interest expense and $12x of interest income is allocable to Business Y.

(ii) *Analysis.* Under paragraph (a)(4) of this section, 20 percent of the P group's Year 1 interest expense ($30x / $150x) and interest income ($3x / $15x) is allocable to an excepted trade or business. Thus, $7x ($35x x 20 percent) of P's interest expense and $2x ($10x x 20 percent) of P's interest income is allocable to an excepted trade or business. The remaining $28x of P's interest expense is business interest expense subject to the section 163(j) limitation, and the remaining $8x of P's interest income is business interest income that increases the group's section 163(j) limitation. In turn, $23x ($115x x 20 percent) of S's interest expense and $1x ($5x x 20 percent) of S's interest income is allocable to an excepted trade or business. The remaining $92x of S's interest expense is business interest expense subject to the section 163(j) limitation, and the remaining $4x of S's interest income is business interest income that increases the group's section 163(j) limitation.

(2) *Example 2: Interest allocation within a consolidated group with assets used in more than one trade or business.*—(i) *Facts.* S is a member of a consolidated group of which P is the common parent. P conducts an electing real property trade or business (Business X), and S conducts a non-excepted trade or business (Business Y). In Year 1, P pays or accrues (without regard to section 163(j)) $50x of interest expense, and S pays or accrues $100x of interest expense (without regard to section 163(j)). P leases 40 percent of space in Building V (which P owns) to S for use in Business Y, and P leases the remaining 60 percent of space in Building V to third parties. For purposes of allocating interest expense under paragraph (c) of this section, the P group's basis in its assets (excluding Building V) used in Businesses X and Y is $180x and $620x, respectively. The P group's basis in Building V for purposes of allocating interest expense under paragraph (c) of this section is $200x.

(ii) *Analysis.* Under paragraph (c)(3)(ii) of this section, the P group's basis in Building V ($200x) is allocated to excepted and non-excepted trades or businesses in accordance with the use of space by Business Y (40 percent) and Business X (the remainder, or 60 percent). Accordingly, $120x of the basis in Building V is allocated to excepted trades or businesses (60 percent x $200x), and $80x is allocated to non-excepted trades or businesses (40 percent x $200x). After allocating the basis in Building V, the P group's total basis in the assets used in excepted and non-excepted trades or businesses is $300x and $700x, respectively. Under paragraphs (a)(4) and (c) of this section, 30 percent ($300x / $1,000x) of the P group's Year 1 interest expense is properly allocable to an excepted trade or business. Thus, $15x ($50x x 30 percent) of P's interest expense is properly allocable to an excepted trade or business, and the remaining $35x of P's interest expense is business interest expense subject to the section 163(j) limitation. In turn, $30x ($100x x 30 percent) of S's interest expense is properly allocable to an excepted trade or business, and the remaining $70x of S's interest expense is business interest expense subject to the section 163(j) limitation.

(3) *Example 3: Application of look-through rules.*—(i) *Facts.* A) Each of Corp A, Corp B, Corp C, and Corp D is a domestic calendar-year corporation that is not a member of a consolidated group. Corp A owns 100 percent of the stock of Corp C; the basis of Corp A's stock in Corp C is $500x. Corp C owns 10 percent of the interests in PS1 (a domestic partnership), and Corp B owns the remaining 90 percent. Corp C's basis in its PS1 interests is $25x; Corp B's basis in its PS1 interests is $225x. PS1 owns 100 percent of the stock of Corp D; the basis of PS1's stock in Corp D is $1,000x. Corp A and Corp B are owned by unrelated, non-overlapping shareholders.

(B) In 2021, Corp C was engaged solely in a non-excepted trade or business. That same year, PS1's only activity was holding Corp D stock. In turn, Corp D was engaged in both an electing farming business and a non-excepted trade or business. Under the allocation rules in paragraph (c) of this section, 50 percent of Corp D's asset basis in 2021 was allocable to the electing farming business, and the remaining 50 percent was allocable to the non-excepted trade or business.

(C) Corp A and Corp B each paid or accrued (without regard to section 163(j)) $150x of interest expense allocable to a trade or business. Corp A's trade or business was an excepted trade or business, and Corp B's trade or business was a non-excepted trade or business. Corp A's basis in the assets used in its trade or business was $100x, and Corp B's basis in the assets used in its trade or business was $112.5x.

(ii) *Analysis.* (A) As provided in paragraph (c)(5)(ii)(E) of this section, if a taxpayer applies the look-through rules of paragraph (c)(5)(ii) of this section, the taxpayer must begin with the lowest-tier entity to which it is eligible to apply the look-through rules. Corp A directly owns 100 percent of the stock of Corp C; thus, Corp A satisfies the 80 percent minimum ownership threshold with respect to Corp C. Corp A also owns 10 percent of the interests in PS1. There is no minimum ownership threshold for partnerships; thus, Corp A may apply the look-through rules to PS1. However, Corp A does not directly or indirectly own at least 80 percent of the stock of Corp D; thus, Corp A cannot look through its indirect interest in Corp D. In turn, Corp B directly owns 90 percent of the interests in PS1, and Corp B indirectly owns at least 80 percent of the stock of Corp D. Thus, Corp B must apply the look-through rules to PS1 and Corp D.

(B) From Corp A's perspective, PS1 is not engaged in a trade or business for purposes of section 163(j); instead, PS1 is merely holding its Corp D stock as an investment. Under paragraph (c)(5)(ii)(A)(2) of this section, if a partnership is not engaged in a trade or business, then its C corporation partner must treat its entire basis in the partnership interest as allocable to a non-excepted trade or business. Thus, for purposes of Corp A's application of the look-through rules, Corp C's entire basis in its PS1 interest ($25x) is allocable to a non-excepted trade or business. Corp C's basis in its other assets also is allocable to a non-excepted trade or business (the only trade or business in which Corp C is engaged). Thus, under paragraph (c) of this section, Corp A's $500x basis in its Corp C stock is allocable entirely to a non-excepted trade or business. Corp A's $100x basis in its other business assets is allocable to an excepted trade or business. Thus, 5/6 (or $125x) of Corp A's $150x of interest expense is properly allocable to a non-excepted trade or business and is business interest expense subject to the section 163(j) limitation, and the remaining $25x of Corp A's $150x of interest expense is allocable to an excepted trade or business and is not subject to the section 163(j) limitation.

(C) From Corp B's perspective, PS1 must look through its stock in Corp D to determine the extent to which PS1's basis in the stock is allocable to an excepted or non-excepted trade or business. Half of Corp D's basis in its assets is allocable to an excepted trade or business, and the other half is allocable to a non-excepted trade or business. Thus, from Corp B's perspective, $500x of PS1's basis in its Corp D stock (PS1's only asset) is allocable to an excepted trade or business, and the other half is allocable to a non-excepted trade or business. Corp B's basis in its PS1 interests is $225x. Applying the look-through rules to Corp B's PS1 interests, $112.5x of Corp B's basis in its PS1 interests is allocable to an excepted trade or business, and $112.5x of Corp B's basis in its PS1 interests is allocable to a non-excepted trade or business. Since Corp B's basis in the assets used in its non-excepted trade or business also was $112.5x, two-thirds of Corp B's interest expense ($100x) is properly allocable to a non-excepted trade or business and is business interest expense subject to the section 163(j) limitation, and one-third of Corp B's interest expense ($50x) is allocable to an excepted trade or business and is not subject to the section 163(j) limitation.

(4) *Example 4: Excepted and non-excepted trades or businesses in a consolidated group.*—(i) *Facts.* P is the common parent of a consolidated group of which A and B are the only other members. A conducts an electing real property trade or business (Business X), and B conducts a non-excepted trade or business (Business Y). In Year 1, A pays or accrues (without regard to section 163(j)) $50x of interest expense and earns $70x of gross income in the conduct of Business X, and B pays or accrues (without regard to section 163(j)) $100x of interest expense and earns $150x of gross income in the conduct of Business Y. B owns Building V, which it uses in Business Y. For purposes of allocating the P group's Year 1 business interest expense between excepted and non-excepted trades or businesses under paragraph (c) of this section, the P group's basis in its assets (other than Building V) used in Businesses X and Y is $180x and $620x, respectively, and the P group's basis in Building V is $200x. At the end of Year 1, B sells Building V to a third party and realizes a gain of $60x in addition to the $150x of gross income B earned that year from the conduct of Business Y.

(ii) *Analysis.* (A) Under paragraphs (a)(4) and (c) of this section, the P group's basis in its assets used in its trades or businesses is allocated between the P group's excepted trade or business (Business X) and its non-excepted trade or business (Business Y) as though these trades or businesses were conducted by a single corporation. Under paragraph (c) of this section, the P group's basis in its assets used in Businesses X and Y is $180x and $820x, respectively. Accordingly, 18 percent ($180x / $1,000x) of the P group's total interest expense ($150x) is properly allocable to an excepted trade or business ($27x), and the remaining 82 percent of the P group's total interest expense is business interest expense properly allocable to a non-excepted trade or business ($123x).

(B) To determine the P group's section 163(j) limitation, paragraph (a) of this section requires that certain items of income and deduction be allocated to the excepted and non-excepted trades or businesses of the P group as though these trades or businesses were conducted by a single corporation. In Year 1, the P group's excepted trade or business (Business X) has gross income of $70x, and the P group's non-excepted trade or business (Business Y) has gross income of $150x. Because Building V was used exclusively in Business Y, the $60x of gain from the sale of Building V in Year 1 is attributed to Business Y under paragraph (b)(2) of this section. The P group's section 163(j) limitation is $63x (30 percent x $210x), which allows the P group to deduct $63x of its $123x of business interest expense allocated to the P group's non-excepted trades or businesses. The group's $27x of interest expense that is allocable to excepted trades or businesses may be deducted without limitation under section 163(j).

(iii) *Intercompany transaction.* The facts are the same as in *Example 4* in paragraph (e)(4)(i) of this section, except that A owns Building V and leases it to B in Year 1 for $20x for use in Business Y, and A sells Building V to a third party for a $60 gain at the end of Year 1. Under paragraphs (a)(4) and (c) of this section, all members of the P group are treated as a single corporation. As a result, the P group's basis in its assets used in its trades or businesses is allocated between the P group's excepted trade or business (Business X) and its non-excepted trade or business (Business Y) as though these trades or businesses were conducted by a single corporation. A lease between two divisions of a single corporation would produce no rental income or expense. Thus, the $20x of rent paid by B to A does not affect the P

group's ATI. Moreover, under paragraph (c) of this section, Building V is an asset used in the P group's non-excepted trade or business (Business Y). Accordingly, although A owns Building V, the basis in Building V is added to the P group's basis in assets used in Business Y for purposes of allocating interest expense under paragraph (c) of this section. In the same vein, when A sells Building V to a third party at a gain of $60x, the gain is included in the P group's ATI because Building V was used in a non-excepted trade or business of the P group (Business Y) prior to its sale.

(5) *Example 5: Captive activities.*—(i) *Facts.* S and T are members of a consolidated group of which P is the common parent. P conducts an electing real property trade or business (Business X), S conducts a non-excepted trade or business (Business Y), and T provides transportation services to Businesses X and Y but does not have any customers outside of the P group. For Year 1, T provides transportation services using a single bus with a basis of $120x.

(ii) *Analysis.* Under paragraph (a)(4) of this section, activities conducted by a consolidated group are treated as though those activities were conducted by a single corporation. Because the activities of T are limited to providing intercompany transportation services, T does not conduct a trade or business for purposes of section 163(j). Under paragraph (c)(3) of this section, business interest expense is allocated to excepted and non-excepted trades or businesses based on the relative basis of the assets used in those businesses. The basis in T's only asset, a bus, is therefore allocated between Business X and Business Y according to the use of T's bus by these businesses. Business X uses one-third of T's services, and Business Y uses two-thirds of T's services. Thus, $40x of the basis of T's bus is allocated to Business X, and $80x of the basis of T's bus is allocated to Business Y.

(6) *Example 6: Constructive ownership.*—(i) *Facts.* P, S, T, and U are domestic C corporations that are not members of a consolidated group. P directly owns 80 percent of the stock of each of S and T as measured by total voting power and value; an unrelated third party, X, owns the remaining 20 percent. In turn, S and T directly own 15 percent and 80 percent, respectively, of the stock of U as measured by total voting power and value; P directly owns the remaining 5 percent. P conducts both excepted and non-excepted trades or businesses. S and T conduct only non-excepted trades or businesses, and U conducts both excepted and non-excepted trades or businesses.

(ii) *Analysis.* Under paragraph (c)(7)(i)(A) of this section, a shareholder must look through to the assets of a domestic non-consolidated C corporation for purposes of allocating the shareholder's basis in its stock in the corporation between excepted and non-excepted trades or businesses if the shareholder's direct and indirect interest in the corporation satisfies the ownership requirements of section 1504(a)(2). For purposes of paragraph (c)(7)(i)(A) of this section, a shareholder's stock ownership is determined by applying the constructive ownership rules of section 318(a). P directly owns 80 percent of each of S and T as measured by total voting power and value; thus, P must look through to the assets of S and T when allocating the basis in its stock of S and T. P directly owns 5 percent of the stock of U as measured by total voting power and value, and P constructively owns the other 95 percent; thus, P also must look through to U's assets when allocating the basis in its U stock. S directly owns 15 percent of the stock of U, and S constructively owns only 5 percent through P; thus, S cannot look through to U's assets when allocating the basis in its U stock. T directly owns 80 percent of the stock of U, and T constructively owns an additional 5 percent; thus, T must look through to U's assets when allocating the basis in its U stock.

(iii) *Dividend.* The facts are the same as in paragraph (e)(6)(i) of this section, except that U distributes a $160x dividend pro rata to its shareholders. Thus, P receives $8x (5 percent of $160x) of the U dividend, S receives $24x (15 percent of $160x), and T receives $128x (80 percent of $160x). Under paragraph (c)(7)(i)(B) of this section, if a shareholder's direct interest in a corporation satisfies the ownership requirements of section 1504(a)(2), the shareholder must look through to the activities of a domestic non-consolidated C corporation in determining whether dividend income is from an excepted or non-excepted trade or business. The constructive ownership rules do not apply in allocating dividends under paragraph (c)(7)(i)(B) of this section. P directly owns 5 percent of the stock of U as measured by vote and value, and S directly owns 15 percent of the stock of U as measured by vote and value; thus, neither P nor S is required to apply the look-through rules in allocating its dividend income from U, and all such income is allocable to non-excepted trades or businesses. T directly owns 80 percent of the stock of U as measured by vote and value; thus, T must allocate its U dividend in accordance with the activities of U's excepted and non-excepted trades or businesses.

(7) *Example 7: Dispositions with a principal purpose of shifting basis.*—(i) *Facts.* U and V are members of a consolidated group of which P is the common parent. U conducts an electing farming business

(Business F), and V conducts a farm equipment leasing business (Business L) that is a non-excepted trade or business. After the end of a farming season, the P group, with a principal purpose of shifting basis from Business L to Business F, has V sell to U all off-lease farming equipment that previously was leased out as part of Business L. Immediately before the start of the next season, U sells the farming equipment back to V for use in Business L.

(ii) *Analysis.* Under paragraph (c)(8) of this section, in the case of a disposition of assets undertaken with a principal purpose of artificially shifting the amount of basis allocable to excepted or non-excepted trades or businesses on a determination date, the additional basis or change in use will not be taken into account. Because V's sale of farming equipment to U for storage in Business F's facilities is undertaken with a principal purpose of shifting basis from Business L to Business F, the additional basis Business F receives from these transactions will not be taken into account for purposes of this section. Instead, the basis of the farming equipment will be allocated as though the farming equipment continued to be used in Business L.

(f) *Applicability dates.*—(1) *In general.*—This section applies to taxable years beginning on or after November 13, 2020. However, taxpayers and their related parties, within the meaning of sections 267(b) and 707(b)(1), may choose to apply the rules of this section to a taxable year beginning after December 31, 2017, so long as the taxpayers and their related parties consistently apply the rules of the section 163(j) regulations, and, if applicable, §§1.263A-9, 1.263A-15, 1.381(c)(20)-1, 1.382-1, 1.382-2, 1.382-5, 1.382-6, 1.382-7, 1.383-0, 1.383-1, 1.469-9, 1.469-11, 1.704-1, 1.882-5, 1.1362-3, 1.1368-1, 1.1377-1, 1.1502-13, 1.1502-21, 1.1502-36, 1.1502-79, 1.1502-91 through 1.1502-99 (to the extent they effectuate the rules of §§1.382-2, 1.382-5, 1.382-6, and 1.383-1), and 1.1504-4, to that taxable year. Accordingly, for purposes of §1.163(j)-10(c)(5), taxpayers make any change to the alternative depreciation system as of November 13, 2020, or if relying on the provisions of §1.163(j)-10 in regulation project REG-106089-18 (83 FR 67490), as of December 28, 2018.

(2) *Paragraph (c)(5)(ii)(D)(2).*—The rules contained in paragraph (c)(5)(ii)(D)(2) of this section apply for taxable years beginning on or after March 22, 2021. However, taxpayers may choose to apply the rules in paragraph (c)(5)(ii)(D)(2) of this section to a taxable year beginning after December 31, 2017, and before March 22, 2021, provided that those taxpayers and their related parties consistently apply all of the rules in the section 163(j) regulations as contained in T.D. 9905 (§§1.163(j)-0 through 1.163(j)-11, effective November 13, 2020) as modified by T.D. 9943, (effective January 13, 2021), and, if applicable, §§1.263A-9, 1.263A-15, 1.381(c)(20)-1, 1.382-1, 1.382-2, 1.382-5, 1.382-6, 1.383-0, 1.383-1, 1.469-9, 1.704-1, 1.882-5, 1.1362-3, 1.1368-1, 1.1377-1, 1.1502-13, 1.1502-21, 1.1502-79, 1.1502-91 through 1.1502-99 (to the extent they effectuate the rules of §§1.382-2, 1.382-5, 1.382-6, and 1.383-1), and 1.1504-4 contained in T.D. 9905 as modified by T.D. 9943, to that taxable year and each subsequent taxable year. [Reg. §1.163(j)-10.]

☐ [*T.D. 9905, 9-3-2020. Amended by T.D. 9943, 1-13-2021.*]

[Reg. §1.163(j)-11]

§1.163(j)-11. Transition rules.—(a) *Overview.*—This section provides transition rules regarding the section 163(j) limitation. Paragraph (b) of this section provides rules regarding the application of the section 163(j) limitation to a corporation that joins a consolidated group during a taxable year of the group beginning before January 1, 2018 and is subject to the section 163(j) limitation at the time of its change in status. Paragraph (c) of this section provides rules regarding the treatment of carryforwards of disallowed disqualified interest.

(b) *Application of section 163(j) limitation if a corporation joins a consolidated group during a taxable year of the group beginning before January 1, 2018.*—(1) *In general.*—If a corporation (S) joins a consolidated group during a taxable year of the group beginning before January 1, 2018, and if S is subject to the section 163(j) limitation at the time of its change in status, then section 163(j) will apply to S's short taxable year that ends on the day of S's change in status, but section 163(j) will not apply to S's short taxable year that begins the next day (when S is a member of the acquiring consolidated group). Any business interest expense paid or accrued (without regard to section 163(j)) by S in its short taxable year ending on the day of S's change in status for which a deduction is disallowed under section 163(j) will be carried forward to the acquiring group's first taxable year beginning after December 31, 2017. Those disallowed business interest expense carryforwards may be subject to limitation under other provisions of these regulations (see, for example, §1.163(j)-5(c), (d), (e), and (f)).

(2) *Example.*—Acquiring Group is a consolidated group with a fiscal year end of November 30; Target is a stand-alone calendar-year C corporation. On May 31, 2018, Acquiring Group acquires Target in a transaction that is not an ownership change for purposes of section 382. Acquiring Group is not subject to the section 163(j) limitation during its taxable year beginning December 1, 2017. As a result of the acquisition, Target has a short taxable year beginning January 1, 2018 and ending May 31, 2018. Target is subject to the section 163(j) limitation during this short taxable year. However, Target (as a member of Acquiring Group) is not subject to the section 163(j) limitation during Acquiring Group's taxable year ending November 30, 2018. Any disallowed business interest expense carryforwards from Target's taxable year ending May 31, 2018, will not be available for use in Acquiring Group's taxable year ending November 30, 2018. However, that disallowed business interest expense is carried forward to Acquiring Group's taxable year beginning December 1, 2018, and can be deducted by the group, subject to the separate return limitation year (SRLY) limitation. See §1.163(j)-5(d).

(c) *Treatment of disallowed disqualified interest.*—(1) *In general.*—Disallowed disqualified interest is carried forward to the taxpayer's first taxable year beginning after December 31, 2017. Disallowed disqualified interest is subject to disallowance as a disallowed business interest expense carryforward under section 163(j) and §1.163(j)-2 to the extent the interest is properly allocable to a non-excepted trade or business under §1.163(j)-10. Disallowed disqualified interest that is properly allocable to an excepted trade or business is not subject to the section 163(j) limitation. See §1.163(j)-10(a)(6) for rules governing the allocation of disallowed disqualified interest between excepted and non-excepted trades or businesses.

(2) *Earnings and profits.*—A taxpayer may not reduce its earnings and profits in a taxable year beginning after December 31, 2017, to reflect any disallowed disqualified interest carryforwards to the extent the payment or accrual of the disallowed disqualified interest reduced the earnings and profits of the taxpayer in a prior taxable year.

(3) *Disallowed disqualified interest of members of an affiliated group.*—(i) *Scope.*—This paragraph (c)(3)(i) applies to corporations that were treated as a single taxpayer under old section 163(j)(6)(C) and that had disallowed disqualified interest.

(ii) *Allocation of disallowed disqualified interest to members of the affiliated group.*—(A) *In general.*—Each member of the affiliated group is allocated its allocable share of the affiliated group's disallowed disqualified interest as provided in paragraph (c)(3)(ii)(B) of this section.

(B) *Definitions.*—The following definitions apply for purposes of paragraph (c)(3)(ii) of this section.

(1) *Allocable share of the affiliated group's disallowed disqualified interest.*—The term *allocable share of the affiliated group's disallowed disqualified interest* means, with respect to any member of an affiliated group for the member's last taxable year beginning before January 1, 2018, the product of the total amount of the disallowed disqualified interest of all members of the affiliated group under old section 163(j)(6)(C) and the member's disallowed disqualified interest ratio.

(2) *Disallowed disqualified interest ratio.*—The term *disallowed disqualified interest ratio* means, with respect to any member of an affiliated group for the member's last taxable year beginning before January 1, 2018, the ratio of the exempt related person interest expense of the member for the last taxable year beginning before January 1, 2018, to the sum of the amounts of exempt related person interest expense for all members of the affiliated group.

(3) *Exempt related person interest expense.*—The term *exempt related person interest expense* means interest expense that is, or is treated as, paid or accrued by a domestic C corporation, or by a foreign corporation with income, gain, or loss that is effectively connected, or treated as effectively connected, with the conduct of a trade or business in the United States, to—

(i) Any person related to the taxpayer, within the meaning of sections 267(b) or 707(b)(1), applying the constructive ownership and attribution rules of section 267(c), if no U.S. tax is imposed with respect to the interest under subtitle A of the Code, determined without regard to net operating losses or net operating loss carryovers, and taking into account any applicable treaty obligation of the United States. For this purpose, interest that is subject to a reduced rate of tax under any treaty obligation of the United States applicable to the recipient is treated as, in part, subject to the statutory tax rate under sections 871 or 881 and, in part, not subject to tax, based on the proportion that the rate of tax under the treaty bears to the statutory tax rate. Thus, for purposes of section 163(j), if the statutory tax rate is 30 percent, and pursuant to a treaty U.S. tax is instead limited to a rate of 10 percent, two-thirds of the interest is considered interest not subject to U.S. tax under subtitle A of the Code;

(ii) A person that is not related to the taxpayer, within the meaning of section 267(b) or 707(b)(1), applying the constructive ownership and attribution rules of section 267(c), with respect to indebtedness on which there is a disqualified guarantee, within the meaning of paragraph (6)(D) of old section 163(j), of such indebtedness, and no gross basis U.S. tax is imposed with respect to the interest. For purposes of this paragraph (c)(3)(ii)(B)(3)(ii), a *gross basis U.S. tax* means any tax imposed by this subtitle A of the Code that is determined by reference to the gross amount of any item of income without any reduction for any deduction allowed by subtitle A of the Code. Interest that is subject to a gross basis U.S. tax that is eligible for a reduced rate of tax under any treaty obligation of the United States applicable to the recipient is treated as, in part, subject to the statutory tax rate under section 871 or 881 and, in part, not subject to a gross basis U.S. tax, based on the proportion that the rate of tax under the treaty bears to the statutory tax rate. Thus, for purposes of section 163(j), if the statutory tax rate is 30 percent, and pursuant to a treaty U.S. tax is instead limited to a rate of 10 percent, two-thirds of the interest is considered interest not subject to a gross basis U.S. tax under subtitle A of the Code; or

(iii) A REIT, directly or indirectly, to the extent that the domestic C corporation, or a foreign corporation with income, gain, or loss that is effectively connected, or treated as effectively connected, with the conduct of a trade or business in the United States, is a taxable REIT subsidiary, as defined in section 856(l), with respect to the REIT.

(iii) *Treatment of carryforwards.*—The amount of disallowed disqualified interest allocated to a taxpayer pursuant to paragraph (c)(3)(ii) of this section is treated in the same manner as described in paragraph (c)(1) of this section.

(4) *Application of section 382.*—(i) *Ownership change occurring before* November 13, 2020—

(A) *Pre-change loss.*—For purposes of section 382(d)(3), unless the rules of § 1.382-2(a)(7) apply, disallowed disqualified interest is not a pre-change loss under § 1.382-2(a) subject to a section 382 limitation with regard to an ownership change on a change date occurring before November 13, 2020. But see section 382(h)(6)(B) (regarding built-in deduction items).

(B) *Loss corporation.*—For purposes of section 382(k)(1), unless the rules of § 1.382-2(a)(7) apply, disallowed disqualified interest is not a carryforward of disallowed interest described in section 381(c)(20) with regard to an ownership change on a change date occurring before November 13, 2020. But see section 382(h)(6) (regarding built-in deductions).

(ii) *Ownership change occurring on or after* November 13, 2020—

(A) *Pre-change loss.*—For rules governing the treatment of disallowed disqualified interest as a pre-change loss for purposes of section 382 with regard to an ownership change on a change date occurring on or after November 13, 2020, see § § 1.382-2(a)(2) and 1.382-6(c)(3).

(B) *Loss corporation.*—For rules governing when disallowed disqualified interest causes a corporation to be a loss corporation with regard to an ownership change occurring on or after November 13, 2020, see § 1.382-2(a)(1)(i)(A).

(5) *Treatment of excess limitation from taxable years beginning before January 1, 2018.*—No amount of excess limitation under old section 163(j)(2)(B) may be carried forward to taxable years beginning after December 31, 2017.

(6) *Example: Members of an affiliated group.*—(i) *Facts.* A, B, and C are calendar-year domestic C corporations that are members of an affiliated group (within the meaning of section 1504(a)) that was treated as a single taxpayer under old section 163(j)(6)(C) and the proposed regulations in this part under old section 163(j) (see formerly proposed § 1.163(j)-5). For the taxable year ending December 31, 2017, the separately determined amounts of exempt related person interest expense of A, B, and C were $0, $600x, and $150x, respectively (for a total of $750x). The affiliated group has $200x of disallowed disqualified interest in that year.

(ii) *Analysis.* The affiliated group's disallowed disqualified interest expense for the 2017 taxable year ($200x) is allocated among A, B, and C based on the ratio of each member's exempt related person interest expense to the group's exempt related person interest expense. Because A has no exempt related person interest expense, no disallowed disqualified interest is allocated to A. Disallowed disqualified interest of $160x is allocated to B (($600x / $750x) x $200x), and disallowed disqualified interest of $40x is allocated to C (($150x / $750x) x $200x). Thus, B and C have $160x and $40x, respectively, of disallowed disqualified interest that is carried forward to the first taxable year beginning after December 31, 2017. No excess limitation

that was allocated to A, B, or C under old section 163(j) will carry forward to a taxable year beginning after December 31, 2017.

(iii) *Carryforward of disallowed disqualified interest to 2018 taxable year.* The facts are the same as in the *Example* in paragraph (c)(7)(i) of this section, except that, for the taxable year ending December 31, 2018, A, B, and C are members of a consolidated group that has a section 163(j) limitation of $140x, current-year business interest expense (as defined in § 1.163(j)-1(b)(9)) of $80x, and no excepted trade or business. Under paragraph (c)(1) of this section, disallowed disqualified interest is carried to the taxpayer's first taxable year beginning after December 31, 2017, and is subject to disallowance under section 163(j) and § 1.163(j)-2. Under § 1.163(j)-5(b)(3)(ii)(D)(1), a consolidated group that has section 163(j) limitation remaining for the current year after deducting all current-year business interest expense deducts each member's disallowed disqualified interest carryforwards from prior taxable years, starting with the earliest taxable year, on a pro rata basis (subject to certain limitations). In accordance with paragraph (c)(1) of this section, the rule in § 1.163(j)-5(b)(3)(ii)(D)(1) applies to disallowed disqualified interest carried forward to the taxpayer's first taxable year beginning after December 31, 2017. Accordingly, after deducting $80x of current-year business interest expense in 2018, the group may deduct $60x of its $200x disallowed disqualified interest carryforwards. Under paragraph (c)(3) of this section, B has $160x of disallowed disqualified interest carryforwards, and C has $40x of disallowed disqualified interest carryforwards. Thus, $48x (($160x / $200x) x $60x) of B's disallowed disqualified interest carryforwards, and $12x (($40x / $200x) x $60x) of C's disallowed disqualified interest carryforwards, are deducted by the consolidated group in the 2018 taxable year.

(d) *Applicability date.*—This section applies to taxable years beginning on or after November 13, 2020. However, taxpayers and their related parties, within the meaning of sections 267(b) and 707(b)(1), may choose to apply the rules of this section to a taxable year beginning after December 31, 2017, so long as the taxpayers and their related parties consistently apply the rules of the section 163(j) regulations, and, if applicable, § § 1.263A-9, 1.263A-15, 1.381(c)(20)-1, 1.382-1, 1.382-2, 1.382-5, 1.382-6, 1.382-7, 1.383-0, 1.383-1, 1.469-9, 1.469-11, 1.704-1, 1.882-5, 1.1362-3, 1.1368-1, 1.1377-1, 1.1502-13, 1.1502-21, 1.1502-36, 1.1502-79, 1.1502-91 through 1.1502-99 (to the extent they effectuate the rules of § § 1.382-2, 1.382-5, 1.382-6, and 1.383-1), and 1.1504-4, to that taxable year. [Reg. § 1.163(j)-11.]

☐ [T.D. 9905, 9-3-2020.]

[Reg. §1.164-1]

§1.164-1. Deduction for taxes.—(a) *In general.*—Only the following taxes shall be allowed as a deduction under this section for the taxable year within which paid or accrued, according to the method of accounting used in computing taxable income:

(1) State and local, and foreign, real property taxes.
(2) State and local personal property taxes.
(3) State and local, and foreign, income, war profits, and excess profits taxes.
(4) State and local general sales taxes.
(5) State and local taxes on the sale of gasoline, diesel fuel, and other motor fuels.

In addition, there shall be allowed as a deduction under this section State and local, and foreign, taxes not described in subparagraphs (1) through (5) of this paragraph which are paid or accrued within the taxable year in carrying on a trade or business or an activity described in section 212 (relating to expenses for production of income). For example, dealers or investors in securities and dealers or investors in real estate may deduct State stock transfer and real estate transfer taxes, respectively, under section 164, to the extent they are expenses incurred in carrying on a trade or business or an activity for the production of income. In general, taxes are deductible only by the person upon whom they are imposed. However, see § 1.164-5 in the case of certain taxes paid by the consumer. Also, in the case of a qualified State individual income tax (as defined in section 6362 and the regulations thereunder) which is determined by reference to a percentage of the Federal income tax (pursuant to section 6362(c)), an accrual method taxpayer shall use the cash receipts and disbursements method to compute the amount of his deduction therefor. Thus, the deduction under section 164 is in the amount actually paid with respect to the qualified tax, rather than the amount accrued with respect thereto, during the taxable year even though the taxpayer uses the accrual method of accounting for other purposes. In addition, see paragraph (f)(1) of § 301.6361-1 of this chapter (Regulations on Procedure and Administration) with respect to rules relating to allocation and reallocation of amounts collected on account of the Federal income tax and qualified taxes.

(b) *Taxable years beginning before January 1, 1964.*—For taxable years beginning before January 1, 1964, except as otherwise provided in § § 1.164-2 through 1.164-8, inclusive, taxes imposed by the United

States, any State, territory, possession of the United States, or a political subdivision of any of the foregoing, or by any foreign country, are deductible from gross income for the taxable year in which paid or accrued, according to the method of accounting used in computing taxable income. For this purpose, postage is not a tax and automobile license or registration fees are ordinarily taxes.

(c) *Cross references.*—For the definition of the term "real property taxes", see paragraph (b) of §1.164-3. For the definition of the term "foreign taxes", see paragraph (d) of §1.164-3. For the definition of the term "general sales taxes", see paragraph (f) of §1.164-3. For the treatment of gasoline, diesel fuel, and other motor fuel taxes, see §1.164-5. For apportionment of taxes on real property between seller and purchaser, see section 164(d) and §1.164-6. For the general rule for taxable year of deduction, see section 461. For provisions disallowing any deduction for the tax paid at the source on interest from tax-free covenant bonds, see section 1451(f). [Reg. §1.164-1.]

☐ [*T.D. 6256*, 10-7-57. *Amended by T.D. 6406*, 8-14-59, *T.D. 6780*, 12-21-64 *and T.D. 7577*, 12-19-78.]

[Reg. §1.164-2]

§1.164-2. Deduction denied in case of certain taxes.—This section and §1.275 describe certain taxes for which no deduction is allowed. In the case of taxable years beginning before January 1, 1964, the denial is provided for by section 164(b) (prior to being amended by section 207 of the Revenue Act of 1964 (78 Stat. 40)). In the case of taxable years beginning after December 31, 1963, the denial is governed by sections 164 and 275. No deduction is allowed for the following taxes:

(a) *Federal income taxes.*—Federal income taxes, including the taxes imposed by section 3101, relating to the tax on employees under the Federal Insurance Contributions Act (chapter 21 of the Code); sections 3201 and 3211, relating to the taxes on railroad employees and railroad employee representatives; section 3402, relating to the tax withheld at source on wages; and by corresponding provisions of prior internal revenue laws.

(b) *Federal war profits and excess profits taxes.*—Federal war profits and excess profits taxes including those imposed by Title II of the Revenue Act of 1917 (39 Stat. 1000), Title III of the Revenue Act of 1918 (40 Stat. 1088), Title III of the Revenue Act of 1921 (42 Stat. 271), section 216 of the National Industrial Recovery Act (48 Stat. 208), section 702 of the Revenue Act of 1934 (48 Stat. 770), subchapter D, chapter 1 of the Internal Revenue Code of 1939, and subchapter E, chapter 2 of the Internal Revenue Code of 1939.

(c) *Estate and gift taxes.*—Estate, inheritance, legacy, succession, and gift taxes.

(d) *Foreign income taxes.*—Except as provided in §1.901-1(c)(2) and (3), foreign income taxes, as defined in §1.901-2(a), paid or accrued (as the case may be, depending on the taxpayer's method of accounting for such taxes) in a taxable year, if the taxpayer chooses to take to any extent the benefits of section 901, relating to the credit for taxes of foreign countries and possessions of the United States, for taxes that are paid or accrued (according to the taxpayer's method of accounting for such taxes) in such taxable year.

(e) *Real property taxes.*—Taxes on real property, to the extent that section 164(d) and §1.164-6 require such taxes to be treated as imposed on another taxpayer.

(f) *Federal duties and excise taxes.*—Federal import or tariff duties, business, license, privilege, excise, and stamp taxes (not described in paragraphs (a), (b), (c) or (h) of this section, of §1.164-4) paid or accrued within the taxable year. The fact that any such tax is not deductible as a tax under section 164 does not prevent (1) its deduction under section 162 or section 212, provided it represents an ordinary and necessary expense paid or incurred during the taxable year by a corporation or an individual in the conduct of any trade or business or, in the case of an individual for the production or collection of income, for the management, conservation, or maintenance of property held for the production of income, or in connection with the determination, collection, or refund of any tax, or (2) its being taken into account during the taxable year by a corporation or an individual as a part of the cost of acquiring or producing property in the trade or business or, in the case of an individual, as a part of the cost of property held for the production of income with respect to which it relates.

(g) *Taxes for local benefits.*—Except as provided in §1.164-4, taxes assessed against local benefits of a kind tending to increase the value of the property assessed.

(h) *Excise tax on real estate investment trusts.*—The excise tax imposed on certain real estate investment trusts by section 4981.

(i) *Applicability dates.*—Paragraph (d) of this section applies to foreign taxes paid or accrued in taxable years beginning on or after December 28, 2021. [Reg. §1.164-2.]

☐ [*T.D. 6256*, 10-7-57. *Amended by T.D. 6780*, 12-21-64, *T.D. 7767*, 2-3-81 *and T.D. 9959*, 12-28-2021.]

[Reg. §1.164-3]

§1.164-3. Definitions and special rules.—For purposes of section 164 and §1.164-1 to §1.164-8, inclusive—

(a) *State or local taxes.*—A State or local tax includes only a tax imposed by a State, a possession of the United States, or a political subdivision of any of the foregoing, or by the District of Columbia.

(b) *Real property taxes.*—The term "real property taxes" means taxes imposed on interests in real property and levied for the general public welfare, but it does not include taxes assessed against local benefits. See §1.164-4.

(c) *Personal property taxes.*—The term "personal property tax" means an ad valorem tax which is imposed on an annual basis in respect of personal property. To qualify as a personal property tax, a tax must meet the following three tests:

(1) The tax must be ad valorem—that is, substantially in proportion to the value of the personal property. A tax which is based on criteria other than value does not qualify as ad valorem. For example, a motor vehicle tax based on weight, model year, and horsepower, or any of these characteristics is not an ad valorem tax. However, a tax which is partly based on value and partly based on other criteria may qualify in part. For example, in the case of a motor vehicle tax of 1 per cent of value plus 40 cents per hundredweight, the part of the tax equal to 1 percent of value qualifies as an ad valorem tax and the balance does not qualify.

(2) The tax must be imposed on an annual basis, even if collected more frequently or less frequently.

(3) The tax must be imposed in respect of personal property. A tax may be considered to be imposed in respect of personal property even if in form it is imposed on the exercise of a privilege. Thus, for taxable years beginning after December 31, 1963, State and local taxes on the registration or licensing of highway motor vehicles are not deductible as personal property taxes unless and to the extent that the tests prescribed in this subparagraph are met. For example, an annual ad valorem tax qualifies as a personal property tax although it is denominated a registration fee imposed for the privilege of registering motor vehicles or of using them on the highways.

(d) *Foreign taxes.*—The term "foreign tax" includes only a tax imposed by the authority of a foreign country. A tax imposed by a political subdivision of a foreign country is considered to be imposed by the authority of that foreign country.

(e) *Sales tax.*—(1) The term "sales tax" means a tax imposed upon persons engaged in selling tangible personal property, or upon the consumers of such property, including persons selling gasoline or other motor vehicle fuels at wholesale or retail, which is a stated sum per unit of property sold or which is measured by the gross sales price or the gross receipts from the sale. The term also includes a tax imposed upon persons engaged in furnishing services which is measured by the gross receipts for furnishing such services.

(2) In general, the term "consumer" means the ultimate user or purchaser; it does not include a purchaser such as a retailer, who acquires the property for resale.

(f) *General sales tax.*—A "general sales tax" is a sales tax which is imposed at one rate in respect of the sale at retail of a broad range of classes of items. No foreign sales tax is deductible under section 164(a) and paragraph (a)(4) of §1.164-1. To qualify as a general sales tax, a tax must meet the following two tests:

(1) The tax must be a tax in respect of sales at retail. This may include a tax imposed on persons engaged in selling property at retail or furnishing services at retail, for example, if the tax is measured by gross sales price or by gross receipts from sales or services. Rentals qualify as sales at retail if so treated under applicable State sales tax laws.

(2) The tax must be general—that is, it must be imposed at one rate in respect of the retail sales of a broad range of classes of items. A sales tax is considered to be general although imposed on sales of various classes of items at more than one rate provided that one rate applies to the retail sales of a broad range of classes of items. The term "items" includes both commodities and services.

(g) *Special rules relating to general sales taxes.*—(1) A sales tax which is general is usually imposed at one rate in respect of the retail sales of all tangible personal property (with exception and additions). However, a sales tax which is selective—that is, a tax which applies at one rate with respect to retail sales of specified classes of items also qualifies as general if the specified classes represent a broad range of classes of items. A selective sales tax which does not apply at one rate to the retail sales of a broad range of classes of items is not general. For example, a tax which applies only to sales of alcoholic beverages, tobacco, admissions, luxury items, and a few other items is not general. Similarly, a tax imposed solely on services is not general. However a selective sales tax may be deemed to be part of the general sales tax and hence may be deductible, even if imposed by a separate Title, etc., of the State or local law, if imposed at the same rate as the general rate of tax (as defined in subparagraph (4) of this paragraph) which qualifies a tax in the taxing jurisdiction as a general sales tax. For example, if a State has a 5 percent general sales tax and a separate selective sales tax of 5 percent on transient accommodations, the tax on transient accommodations is deductible.

(2) A tax is imposed at one rate only if it is imposed at that rate on generally the same base for all items subject to tax. For example, a sales tax imposed at a 3 percent rate on 100 percent of the sales price of some classes of items and at a 3 percent rate on 50 percent of the sales price of other classes of items would not be imposed at one rate with respect to all such classes. However, a tax is considered to be imposed at one rate although it allows dollar exemptions, if the exemptions are designed to exclude all sales under a certain dollar amount. For example, a tax may be imposed at one rate although it applies to all sales of tangible personal property but applies only to sales amounting to more than 10 cents.

(3) The fact that a sales tax exempts food, clothing, medical supplies, and motor vehicles, or any of them, shall not be taken into account in determining whether the tax applies to a broad range of classes of items. The fact that a sales tax applies to food, clothing, medical supplies, and motor vehicles, or any of them, at a rate which is lower than the general rate of tax (as defined in subparagraph (4) of this paragraph) is not taken into account in determining whether the tax is imposed at one rate on the retail sales of a broad range of classes of items. For purposes of this section, the term "food" means food for human consumption off the premises where sold, and the term "medical supplies" includes drugs, medicines, and medical devices.

(4) Except in the case of a lower rate of tax applicable in respect of food, clothing, medical supplies, and motor vehicles, or any of them, no deduction is allowed for a general sales tax in respect of any item if the tax is imposed on such item at a rate other than the general rate of tax. The general rate of tax is the one rate which qualifies a tax in a taxing jurisdiction as a general sales tax because the tax is imposed at such one rate on a broad range of classes of items. There can be only one general rate of tax in any one taxing jurisdiction. However, a general sales tax imposed at a lower rate or rates on food, clothing, motor vehicles, and medical supplies, or any of them, may nonetheless be deductible with respect to such items. For example, a sales tax which is imposed at 1 percent with respect to food, imposed at 3 percent with respect to a broad range of classes of tangible personal property, and imposed at 4 percent with respect to transient accommodations would qualify as a general sales tax. Taxes paid at the 1 percent and the 3 percent rates are deductible, but tax paid at the 4 percent rate is not deductible. The fact that a sales tax provides for the adjustment of the general rate of tax to reflect the sales tax rate in another taxing jurisdiction shall not be taken into account in determining whether the tax is imposed at one rate on the retail sales of a broad range of classes of items. Moreover, a general sales tax imposed at a lower rate with respect to an item in order to reflect the tax rate in another jurisdiction is also deductible at such lower rate. For example, State E imposes a general sales tax whose general rate is 3 percent. The State E sales tax law provides that in areas bordering on States with general sales taxes, selective sales taxes, or special excise taxes, the rate applied in the adjoining State will be used if such rate is under 3 percent. State F imposes a 2 percent sales tax. The 2 percent sales tax paid by residents of State E in areas bordering on State F is deductible.

(h) *Compensating use taxes.*—A compensating use tax in respect of any item is treated as a general sales tax. The term "compensating use tax" means, in respect of any item, a tax which is imposed on the use, storage, or consumption of such item and which is complementary to a general sales tax which is deductible with respect to sales of similar items.

(i) *Special rules relating to compensating use taxes.*—(1) In general, a use tax on an item is complementary to a general sales tax on similar items if the use tax is imposed on an item which was not subject to such general sales tax but which would have been subject to such general sales tax if the sale of the item had taken place within the jurisdiction imposing the use tax. For example, a tax imposed by State A on the use of a motor vehicle purchased in State B is complementary to the general sales tax of State A on similar items, if the latter tax applies to motor vehicles sold in State A.

(2) Since a compensating use tax is treated as a general sales tax, it is subject to the rule of subparagraph (C) of section 164(b)(2) and paragraph (g)(4) of this section that no deduction is allowed for a general sales tax imposed in respect of an item at a rate other than the general rate of tax (except in the case of lower rates on the sale of food, clothing, medical supplies, and motor vehicles). The fact that a compensating use tax in respect of any item provides for an adjustment in the rate of the compensating use tax or the amount of such tax to be paid on account of a sales tax on such item imposed by another taxing jurisdiction is not taken into account in determining whether the compensating use tax is imposed in respect of the item at a rate other than the general rate of tax. For example, a compensating use tax imposed by State C on the use of an item purchased in State D is considered to be imposed at the general rate of tax even though the tax imposed by State C allows a credit for any sales tax paid on such item in State D, or the rate of such compensating use tax is adjusted to reflect the rate of sales tax imposed by State D.

(j) *Safe harbor for payments made by individuals in exchange for State or local tax credits.*—(1) *In general.*—An individual who itemizes deductions and who makes a payment to or for the use of an entity described in section 170(c) in consideration for a State or local tax credit may treat as a payment of State or local tax for purposes of section 164 the portion of such payment for which a charitable contribution deduction under section 170 is disallowed under §1.170A-1(h)(3). This treatment as payment of a State or local tax is allowed in the taxable year in which the payment is made to the extent that the resulting credit is applied, consistent with applicable State or local law, to offset the individual's State or local tax liability for such taxable year or the preceding taxable year.

(2) *Credits carried forward.*—To the extent that a State or local tax credit described in paragraph (j)(1) of this section is not applied to offset the individual's applicable State or local tax liability for the taxable year of the payment or the preceding taxable year, any excess State or local tax credit permitted to be carried forward may be treated as a payment of State or local tax under section 164(a) in the taxable year or years for which the carryover credit is applied in accordance with State or local law.

(3) *Limitation on individual deductions.*—Nothing in this paragraph (j) may be construed as permitting a taxpayer who applies this safe harbor to avoid the limitation of section 164(b)(6) for any amount paid as a tax or treated under this paragraph (j) as a payment of tax.

(4) *No safe harbor for transfers of property.*—The safe harbor provided in this paragraph (j) applies only to a payment of cash or cash equivalent.

(5) *Coordination with other deductions.*—An individual who deducts a payment under section 164 may not also deduct the same payment under any other Code section.

(6) *Examples.*—In the following examples, the taxpayer is an individual who itemizes deductions for Federal income tax purposes.

(i) *Example 1.*—In year 1, Taxpayer *A* makes a payment of $500 to an entity described in section 170(c). In return for the payment, *A* receives a dollar-for-dollar State income tax credit. Prior to application of the credit, *A*'s State income tax liability for year 1 was more than $500. *A* applies the $500 credit to *A*'s year 1 State income tax liability. Under paragraph (j)(1) of this section, *A* treats the $500 payment as a payment of State income tax in year 1. To determine *A*'s deduction amount, *A* must apply the provisions of section 164 applicable to payments of State and local taxes, including the limitation in section 164(b)(6). See paragraph (j)(3) of this section.

(ii) *Example 2.*—In year 1, Taxpayer *B* makes a payment of $7,000 to an entity described in section 170(c). In return for the payment, *B* receives a dollar-for-dollar State income tax credit, which under State law may be carried forward for three taxable years. Prior to application of the credit, *B*'s State income tax liability for year 1 was $5,000; *B* applies $5,000 of the $7,000 credit to *B*'s year 1 State income tax liability. Under paragraph (j)(1) of this section, *B* treats $5,000 of the $7,000 payment as a payment of State income tax in year 1. Prior to application of the remaining credit, *B*'s State income tax liability for year 2 exceeds $2,000. *B* applies the excess credit of $2,000 to *B*'s year 2 State income tax liability. For year 2, under paragraph (j)(2) of this section, *B* treats the $2,000 as a payment of State income tax under section 164. To determine *B*'s deduction amounts in years 1 and 2, *B* must apply the provisions of section 164 applicable to payments of State and local taxes, including the limitation under section 164(b)(6). See paragraph (j)(3) of this section.

(iii) *Example 3.*—In year 1, Taxpayer *C* makes a payment of $7,000 to an entity described in section 170(c). In return for the payment, *C* receives a local real property tax credit equal to 25 percent of the amount of this payment ($1,750). Prior to application of the credit, C's local real property tax liability in year 1 was more than $1,750. C applies the $1,750 credit to C's year 1 local real property tax liability. Under paragraph (j)(1) of this section, for year 1, C treats $1,750 of the $7,000 payment as a payment of local real property tax for purposes of section 164. To determine C's deduction amount, C must apply the provisions of section 164 applicable to payments of State and local taxes, including the limitation under section 164(b)(6). See paragraph (j)(3) of this section.

(7) *Applicability date.*—This paragraph (j) applies to payments made to section 170(c) entities on or after June 11, 2019. However, a taxpayer may choose to apply this paragraph (j) to payments made to section 170(c) entities after August 27, 2018. [Reg. §1.164-3.]

☐ [*T.D. 6256, 10-7-57. Amended by T.D. 6780, 12-21-64 and T.D. 9907, 8-7-2020.*]

[Reg. §1.164-4]

§1.164-4. Taxes for local benefits.—(a) So-called taxes for local benefits referred to in paragraph (g) of §1.164-2 more properly assessments, paid for local benefits such as street, sidewalks, and other like improvements, imposed because of and measured by some benefit inuring directly to the property against which the assessment is levied are not deductible as taxes. A tax is considered assessed against local benefits when the property subject to the tax is limited to property benefited. Special assessments are not deductible, even though an incidental benefit may inure to the public welfare. The real property taxes deductible are those levied for the general public welfare by the proper taxing authorities at a like rate against all property in the territory over which such authorities have jurisdiction. Assessments under the statutes of California relating to irrigation, and of Iowa relating to drainage, and under certain statutes of Tennessee relating to levees, are limited to property benefited, and if the assessments are so limited, the amounts paid thereunder are not deductible as taxes. For treatment of assessments for local benefits as adjustments to the basis of property, see section 1016(a)(1) and the regulations thereunder.

(b)(1) Insofar as assessments against local benefits are made for the purpose of maintenance or repair or for the purpose of meeting interest charges with respect to such benefits, they are deductible. In such cases, the burden is on the taxpayer to show the allocation of the amounts assessed to the different purposes. If the allocation cannot be made, none of the amount so paid is deductible.

(2) Taxes levied by a special taxing district which was in existence on December 31, 1963, for the purpose of retiring indebtedness existing on such date, are deductible, to the extent levied for such purpose, if (i) the district covers the whole of at least one county, (ii) if at least 1,000 persons are subject to the taxes levied by the district, and (iii) if the district levies its assessments annually at a uniform rate on the same assessed value of real property, including improvements, as is used for purposes of the real property tax generally. [Reg. §1.164-4.]

☐ [*T.D. 6256, 10-7-57. Amended by T.D. 6780, 12-21-64.*]

[Reg. §1.164-5]

§1.164-5. Certain retail sales taxes and gasoline taxes.—For taxable years beginning before January 1, 1964, any amount representing a State or local sales tax paid by a consumer of services or tangible personal property is deductible by such consumer as a tax, provided it is separately stated and not paid in connection with his trade or business. For taxable years beginning after December 31, 1963, only the amount of any separately stated State and local general sales tax (as defined in paragraph (g) of §1.164-3) and tax on the sale of gasoline, diesel fuel or other motor fuel paid by the consumer (other than in connection with his trade or business) is deductible by the consumer as tax. The fact that, under the law imposing the tax, the incidence of such State or local tax does not fall on the consumer is immaterial. The requirement that the amount of tax must be separately stated will be deemed complied with where it clearly appears that at the time of sale to the consumer, the tax was added to the sales price and collected or charged as a separate item. It is not necessary, for the purpose of this section, that the consumer be furnished with a sales slip, bill, invoice, or other statement on which the tax is separately stated. For example, where the law imposing the State or local tax for which the taxpayer seeks a deduction contains a prohibition against the seller absorbing the tax, or a provision requiring a posted notice stating that the tax will be added to the quoted price, or a requirement that the tax be separately shown in advertisements or separately stated on all bills and invoices, it is presumed that the amount of the State or local tax was separately stated at the time paid by the consumer; except that such presumption shall have no application to a tax on the sale of gasoline, diesel fuel or other motor fuel imposed upon a wholesaler unless such provisions of law apply with respect to both the sale at wholesale and the sale at retail. [Reg. §1.164-5.]

☐ [*T.D. 6256, 10-7-57. Amended by T.D. 6780, 12-21-64.*]

[Reg. §1.164-6]

§1.164-6. Apportionment of taxes on real property between seller and purchaser.—(a) *Scope.*—Except as provided otherwise in section 164(f) and §1.164-8, when real property is sold, section 164(d)(1) governs the deduction by the seller and the purchaser of current real property taxes. Section 164(d)(1) performs two functions: (1) It provides a method by which a portion of the taxes for the real property tax year in which the property is sold may be deducted by the seller and a portion by the purchaser; and (2) it limits the deduction of the seller and the purchaser to the portion of the taxes corresponding to the part of the real property tax year during which each was the owner of the property. These functions are accomplished by treating a portion of the taxes for the real property tax year in which the property is sold as imposed on the seller and a portion as imposed on the purchaser. To the extent that the taxes are treated as imposed on the seller and the purchaser, each shall be allowed a deduction, under section 164(a), in the taxable year such tax is paid or accrued, or treated as paid or accrued under section 164(d)(2)(A) or (D) and this section. No deduction is allowed for taxes on real property to the extent that they are imposed on another taxpayer, or are treated as imposed on another taxpayer under section 164(d). For the election to accrue real property taxes ratably see section 461(c) and the regulations thereunder.

(b) *Application of rule of apportionment.*—(1)(i) For purposes of the deduction provided by section 164(a), if real property is sold during any real property tax year, the portion of the real property tax properly allocable to that part of the real property tax year which ends on the day before the date of the sale shall be treated as a tax imposed on the seller, and the portion of such tax properly allocable to that part of such real property tax year which begins on the date of the sale shall be treated as a tax imposed on the purchaser. For definition of "real property tax year" see paragraph (c) of this section. This rule shall apply whether or not the seller and the purchaser apportion such tax. The rule of apportionment contained in section 164(d)(1) applies even though the same real property is sold more than once during the real property tax year. (See paragraph (d)(5) of this section for rule requiring inclusion in gross income of excess deductions.)

(ii) Where the real property tax becomes a personal liability or a lien before the beginning of the real property tax year to which it relates and the real property is sold subsequent to the time the tax becomes a personal liability or a lien but prior to the beginning of the related real property tax year—

(a) The seller may not deduct any amount for real property taxes for the related real property tax year, and

(b) To the extent that he holds the property for such real property tax year, the purchaser may deduct the amount of such taxes for the taxable year they are paid (or amounts representing such taxes are paid to the seller, mortgagee, trustee or other person having an interest in the property as security) or accrued by him according to his method of accounting.

(iii) Similarly, where the real property tax becomes a personal liability or a lien after the end of the real property tax year to which it relates and the real property is sold prior to the time the tax becomes a personal liability or a lien but after the end of the related real property tax year—

(a) The purchaser may not deduct any amount for real property taxes for the related real property tax year, and

(b) To the extent that he holds the property for such real property tax year, the seller may deduct the amount of such taxes for the taxable year they are paid (or amounts representing such taxes are paid to the purchaser, mortgagee, trustee, or other person having an interest in the property as security) or accrued by him according to his method of accounting.

(iv) Where the real property is sold (or purchased) during the related real property tax year the real property taxes for such year are apportioned between the parties to such sale and may be deducted by such parties in accordance with the provisions of paragraph (d) of this section.

(2) Section 164(d) does not apply to delinquent real property taxes for any real property tax year prior to the real property tax year in which the property is sold.

(3) The provisions of this paragraph may be illustrated by the following examples:

Example (1). The real property tax year in County R is April 1 to March 31. A, the owner on April 1, 1954, of real property located in County R sells the real property to B on June 30, 1954. B owns the real property from June 30, 1954, through March 31, 1955. The real property tax for the real property tax year April 1, 1954-March 31, 1955 is

$365. For purposes of section 164(a), $90 (90/365 × $365, April 1, 1954-June 29, 1954) of the real property tax is treated as imposed on A, the seller, and $275 (275/365 × $365, June 30, 1954-March 31, 1955) of such real property tax is treated as imposed on B, the purchaser.

Example (2). In County S the real property tax year is the calendar year. The real property tax becomes a lien on June 1 and is payable on July 1 of the current real property tax year, but there is no personal liability for such tax. On April 30, 1955, C, the owner of real property in County S on January 1, 1955, sells the real property to D. On July 1, 1955, D pays the 1955 real property tax. On August 31, 1955, D sells the same real property to E. C, D, and E use the cash receipts and disbursements method of accounting. Under the provisions of section 164(d)(1), 119/365 (January 1-April 29, 1955) of the real property tax payable on July 1, 1955, for the 1955 real property tax year is treated as imposed on C, and, under the provisions of section 164(d)(2)(A), such portion is treated as having been paid by him on the date of sale. Under the provisions of section 164(d)(1), 123/365 (April 30-August 30, 1955) of the real property tax paid July 1, 1955, for the 1955 real property tax year is treated as imposed on D and may be deducted by him. Under the provisions of section 164(d)(1), 123/365 (August 31-December 31, 1955) of the real property tax due and paid on July 1, 1955, for the 1955 real property tax year is treated as imposed on E and, under the provisions of section 164(d)(2)(A) such portion is treated as having been paid by him on the date of sale.

Example (3). In State X the real property tax year is the calendar year. The real property tax becomes a lien on November 1 of the preceding calendar year. On November 15, 1955, F sells real property in State X to G. G owns the real property through December 31, 1956. Under section 164(d)(1), the real property tax (which became a lien on November 1, 1954) for the 1955 real property tax year is apportioned between F and G. No part of the real property tax for the 1956 real property tax year may be deducted by F. The entire real property tax for the 1956 real property tax year may be deducted by G when paid or accrued, depending upon the method of accounting used by him. See subparagraph (6) of paragraph (d) and section 461(c) and the regulations thereunder.

(c) *Real property tax year.*—As used in section 164(d), the term "real property tax year" refers to the period which, under the law imposing the tax, is regarded as the period to which the tax imposed relates. Where the State and one or more local governmental units each imposes a tax on real property, the real property tax year for each tax must be determined for purposes of applying the rule of apportionment of section 164(d)(1) to each tax. The time when the tax rate is determined, the time when the assessment is made, the time when the tax becomes a lien, or the time when the tax becomes due or delinquent does not necessarily determine the real property tax year. The real property tax year may or may not correspond to the fiscal year of the governmental unit imposing the tax. In each case the State or local law determines what constitutes the real property tax year. Although the seller and the purchaser may or may not make an allocation of real property taxes, the meaning of "real property tax year" in section 164(d) and the application of section 164(d) do not depend upon what real property taxes were allocated nor the method of allocation used by the parties.

(d) *Special rules.*—(1) *Seller using cash receipts and disbursements method of accounting.*—Under the provisions of section 164(d), if the seller by reason of his method of accounting may not deduct any amount for taxes unless paid, and—

(i) The purchaser (under the law imposing the real property tax) is liable for the real property tax for the real property tax year, or

(ii) The seller (under the law imposing the real property tax) is liable for the real property tax for the real property tax year and the tax is not payable until after the date of sale,

then the portion of the tax treated under section 164(d)(1) as imposed upon the seller (whether or not actually paid by him in the taxable year in which the sale occurs) shall be considered as having been paid by him in such taxable year. Such portion may be deducted by him for the taxable year in which the sale occurs, or, if at a later time, for the taxable year (which would be proper under the taxpayer's method of accounting) in which the tax is actually paid, or an amount representing such tax is paid to the purchaser, mortgagee, trustee, or other person having an interest in the property as security.

(2) *Purchasers using the cash receipts and disbursements method of accounting.*—Under the provisions of section 164(d), if the purchaser by reason of his method of accounting may not deduct any amount for taxes unless paid and the seller (under the law imposing the real property tax) is liable for the real property tax for the real property tax year, the portion of the tax treated under section 164(d)(1) as imposed upon the purchaser (whether or not actually paid by him in the taxable year in which the sale occurs) shall be considered as having been paid by him in such taxable year. Such portion may be deducted by him for the taxable year in which the sale occurs, or if at

a later time, for the taxable year (which would be proper under the taxpayer's method of accounting) in which the tax is actually paid, or an amount representing such tax is paid to the seller, mortgagee, trustee, or other person having an interest in the property as security.

(3) *Persons considered liable for tax.*—Where the tax is not a liability of any person, the person who holds the property at the time the tax becomes a lien on the property shall be considered liable for the tax. As to a particular sale, in determining:

(i) Whether the other party to the sale is liable for the tax or,

(ii) The person who holds the property at the time the tax becomes a lien on the property (where the tax is not a liability of any person),

prior or subsequent sales of the property during the real property tax year shall be disregarded.

(4) *Examples.*—The provisions of subparagraphs (1), (2), and (3) of this paragraph may be illustrated as follows:

Example (1). In County X the real property tax year is the calendar year. The real property tax is a personal liability of the owner of the real property on June 30 of the current real property tax year, but is not payable until February 28 of the following real property tax year. A, the owner of real property in County X on January 1, 1955, uses the cash receipts and disbursements method of accounting. On May 30, 1955, A sells the real property to B, who also uses the cash receipts and disbursements method of accounting. B retains ownership of the real property for the balance of the 1955 calendar year. Under the provisions of section 164(d)(1), 149/365 (January 1-May 29, 1955) of the real property tax payable on February 28, 1956, for the 1955 real property tax year is treated as imposed on A, the seller, and under the provisions of section 164(d)(2)(A) such portion is treated as having been paid by him on the date of sale and may be deducted by him for his taxable year in which the sale occurs (whether or not such portion is actually paid by him in that year) or for his taxable year in which the tax is actually paid or an amount representing such tax is paid. Under the provisions of section 164(d)(1), 216/365 (May 30-December 31, 1955) of the real property tax payable on February 28, 1956, for the 1955 real property tax year is treated as imposed on B, the purchaser, and may be deducted by him for his taxable year in which the tax is actually paid, or an amount representing such tax is paid.

Example (2). In County Y, the real property tax year is the calendar year. The real property tax becomes a lien on January 1, 1955, and is payable on April 30, 1955. There is no personal liability for the real property tax imposed by County Y. On April 30, 1955, C, the owner of real property in County Y on January 1, 1955, pays the real property tax for the 1955 real property tax year. On May 1, 1955, C sells the real property to D. On September 1, 1955, D sells the real property to E. C, D, and E use the cash receipts and disbursements method of accounting. Under the provisions of section 164(d)(1), 120/365 (January 1-April 30, 1955) of the real property tax is treated as imposed upon C and may be deducted by him for his taxable year in which the tax is actually paid. Under section 164(d)(1), 123/365 (May 1-August 31, 1955) of the real property tax is treated as imposed upon D and, under the provisions of section 164(d)(2)(A), is treated as having been paid by him on May 1, 1955, and may be deducted by D for his taxable year in which the sale from C to him occurs (whether or not such portion is actually paid by him in that year), or for his taxable year in which an amount representing such tax is paid. Since, according to paragraph (d)(3) of this section, the prior sale by C to D is disregarded, under the provisions of section 164(d)(1), 122/365 (September 1-December 31, 1955) of the real property tax is treated as imposed on E and, under the provisions of section 164(d)(2)(A), is treated as having been paid by him on September 1, 1955, and may be deducted by E for his taxable year in which the sale from D to him occurs (whether or not such portion is actually paid by him in that year), or for his taxable year in which an amount representing such tax is paid.

Example (3). In County X the real property tax year is the calendar year and the real property taxes are assessed and become a lien on June 30 of the current real property tax year, but are not payable until September 1 of that year. There is no personal liability for the real property tax imposed by County X. A, the owner on January 1, 1955, of real property in County X, uses the cash receipts and disbursements method of accounting. On July 15, 1955, A sells the real property to B. Under the provisions of section 164(d)(1), 195/365 (January 1-July 14, 1955) of the real property tax payable on September 1, 1955, for the 1955 real property tax year is treated as imposed on A, and may be deducted by him for his taxable year in which the sale occurs (whether or not such portion is actually paid by him in that year) or for his taxable year in which the tax is actually paid or an amount representing such tax is paid. Under the provisions of section 164(d)(1), 170/365 (July 15-December 31, 1955) of the real property tax is treated as imposed on B and may be deducted by him for his taxable year in which the sale occurs (whether or not such portion is actually paid by him in that year), or for his taxable year in which the tax is actually paid or an amount representing such tax is paid.

(5) *Treatment of excess deduction.*—If, for a taxable year prior to the taxable year of sale of real property, a taxpayer has deducted an amount for real property tax in excess of the portion of such real property tax treated as imposed on him under the provisions of section 164(d), the excess of the amount deducted over the portion treated as imposed on him shall be included in his gross income for the taxable year of the sale, subject to the provisions of section 111, relating to the recovery of bad debts, prior taxes, and delinquency amounts. The provisions of this subparagraph may be illustrated as follows:

Example (1). In Borough Y the real property tax is due and payable on November 30 for the succeeding calendar year, which is also the real property tax year. On November 30, 1954, taxpayer A, who reports his income on a calendar year under the cash receipts and disbursements method of accounting, pays the real property tax on real property owned by him in Borough Y for the 1955 real property tax year. On June 30, 1955, A sells the real property. Under the provisions of section 164(d), only 180/365 (January 1-June 29, 1955) of the real property tax for the 1955 real property tax year is treated as imposed on A, and the excess of the amount of real property tax for 1955 deducted by A, on his 1954 income tax return, over the 180/365 portion of such tax treated as imposed on him under section 164(d), must be included in gross income in A's 1955 income tax return, subject to the provisions of section 111.

Example (2). In County Z the real property tax year is the calendar year. The real property tax becomes a personal liability of the owner of real property on January 1 of the current real property tax year, and is payable on July 1 of the current real property tax year. On May 1, 1955, A, the owner of real property in County Z on January 1, 1955, sells the real property to B. On November 1, 1955, B sells the same real property to C. B uses the cash receipts and disbursements method of accounting and reports his income on the basis of a fiscal year ending July 31. B, on July 1, 1955, pays the entire real property tax for the real property tax year ending December 31, 1955. Under the provisions of section 164(d), only 184/365 (May 1-October 31, 1955) of the real property tax for the 1955 real property tax year is treated as imposed on B, and the excess of the amount of real property tax for 1955 deducted by B on his income tax return for the fiscal year ending July 31, 1955, over the 184/365 portion of such tax treated as imposed on him under section 164(d), must be included in gross income in B's income tax return for his fiscal year ending July 31, 1956, subject to the provisions of section 111.

(6) *Persons using an accrual method of accounting.*—Where real property is sold and the seller or the purchaser computes his taxable income (for the taxable year during which the sale occurs) on an accrual method of accounting, then, if the seller or the purchaser has not made the election provided in section 461(c) (relating to the accrual of real property taxes), the portion of any real property tax which is treated as imposed on him and which may not be deducted by him for any taxable year by reason of his method of accounting shall be treated as having accrued on the date of sale. The provisions of this subparagraph may be illustrated as follows:

Example. In County X the real property tax becomes a lien on property and is assessed on November 30 for the current calendar year, which is also the real property tax year. There is no personal liability for the real property tax imposed by County X. A owns, on January 1, 1955, real property in County X. A uses an accrual method of accounting and has not made any election under section 461(c) to accrue ratably real property taxes. A sells real property on June 30, 1955. By reason of A's method of accounting, he could not deduct any part of the real property tax for 1955 on the real property since he sold the real property prior to November 30, 1955, the accrual date. Under section 164(d)(1), 180/365 (January 1-June 29, 1955) of the real property tax for the 1955 real property tax year is treated as imposed on A, and under section 164(d)(2)(D) that portion is treated as having accrued on June 30, 1955, and may be deducted by A for his taxable year in which such date falls. B, the purchaser from A, who uses an accrual method of accounting, has likewise not made an election under section 461(c) to accrue real property taxes ratably. Under section 164(d)(1), 185/365 of the real property taxes may be accrued by B on November 30, 1955, and deducted for his taxable year in which such date falls.

(7) *Cross references.*—For determination of amount realized on a sale of real property, see section 1001(b) and the regulations thereunder. For determination of basis of real property acquired by purchase, see section 1012 and the regulations thereunder.

(8) *Effective dates.*—Section 164(d) applies to taxable years ending after December 31, 1953, but only in the case of sales made after December 31, 1953. However, section 164(d) does not apply to any real property tax to the extent that such tax was allowable as a deduction under the Internal Revenue Code of 1939 to the seller for any taxable year which ended before January 1, 1954. [Reg. § 1.164-6.]

☐ [*T.D. 6256, 10-7-57. Amended by T.D. 6293, 5-20-58 and T.D. 6406, 8-14-59.*]

[Reg. § 1.164-7]

§ 1.164-7. Taxes of shareholder paid by corporation.—Banks and other corporations paying taxes assessed against their shareholders on account of their ownership of the shares of stock issued by such corporations without reimbursement from such shareholders may deduct the amount of taxes so paid. In such cases no deduction shall be allowed to the shareholders for such taxes. The amount so paid should not be included in the gross income of the shareholder. [Reg. § 1.164-7.]

☐ [*T.D. 6256, 10-7-57.*]

[Reg. § 1.164-8]

§ 1.164-8. Payments for municipal services in atomic energy communities.—(a) *General.*—For taxable years beginning after December 31, 1957, amounts paid or accrued by any owner of real property within any community (as defined in section 21b of the Atomic Energy Community Act of 1955 (42 U.S.C. 2304)) to compensate the Atomic Energy Commission for municipal-type services (or any agent or contractor authorized by the Atomic Energy Commission to charge for such services) shall be treated as State real property taxes paid or accrued for purposes of section 164. Such amounts shall be deductible as taxes to the extent provided in section 164, §§ 1.164-1 through 1.164-7, and this section. See paragraph (b) of this section for definition of the term "Atomic Energy Commission"; paragraph (c) of this section for the definition of the term "municipal-type services"; and paragraph (d) of this section for the definition of the term "owner."

(b) *Atomic Energy Commission.*—For purposes of paragraph (a) of this section, the term "Atomic Energy Commission" shall mean—

(1) The Atomic Energy Commission, and

(2) Any other agency of the United States Government to which the duties and responsibilities of providing municipal-type services are delegated under the authority of section 101 of the Atomic Energy Community Act of 1955 (42 U.S.C. 2313).

(c) *Municipal-type services.*—For purposes of paragraph (a) of this section, the term "municipal-type services" includes services usually rendered by a municipality and usually paid for by taxes. Examples of municipal-type services are police protection, fire protection, public recreational facilities, public libraries, public schools, public health, public welfare, and the maintenance of roads and streets. The term shall include sewage and refuse disposal which are maintained out of revenues derived from a general charge for municipal-type services; however, the term shall not include sewage and refuse disposal if a separate charge for such services is made. Charges assessed against local benefits of a kind tending to increase the value of the property assessed are not charges for municipal-type services. See section 164(c)(1) and § 1.164-4.

(d) *Owner.*—For purposes of paragraph (a) of this section, the term "owner" includes a person who holds the real property under a leasehold of 40 or more years from the Atomic Energy Commission (or any agency of the United States Government to which the duties and responsibilities of leasing real property are delegated under section 101 of the Atomic Energy Community Act of 1955), and a person who has entered into a contract to purchase under section 61 of the Atomic Energy Community Act of 1955 (42 U.S.C. 2361). An assignee (either immediate or more remote) of a lessee referred to in the preceding sentence will also qualify as an owner for purposes of paragraph (a) of this section.

(e) *Nonapplication of section 164(d).*—Section 164(d) and § 1.164-6, relating to apportionment of taxes on real property between seller and purchaser, do not apply to a sale by the United States or any of its agencies of real property to which section 164(f) and this section apply. Thus, amounts paid or accrued which qualify under paragraph (a) of this section will continue to be deductible as taxes to the extent provided in this section, even in the taxable year in which the owner actually purchases the real property from the United States or any of its agencies. However, the provisions of section 164(d) and § 1.164-6 shall apply to a sale of real property to which section 164(f) and this section apply, if the seller is other than the United States or any of its agencies. [Reg. § 1.164-8.]

☐ [*T.D. 6406, 8-14-59. Amended by T.D. 6780, 12-21-64*]

[Reg. §1.165-1]

§1.165-1. Losses.—(a) *Allowance of deduction.*—Section 165(a) provides that, in computing taxable income under section 63, any loss actually sustained during the taxable year and not made good by insurance or some other form of compensation shall be allowed as a deduction subject to any provision of the internal revenue laws which prohibits or limits the amount of the deduction. This deduction for losses sustained shall be taken in accordance with section 165 and the regulations thereunder. For the disallowance of deductions for worthless securities issued by a political party, see §1.271-1.

(b) *Nature of loss allowable.*—To be allowable as a deduction under section 165(a), a loss must be evidenced by closed and completed transactions, fixed by identifiable events, and, except as otherwise provided in section 165(h) and §1.165-11, relating to disaster losses, actually sustained during the taxable year. Only a bona fide loss is allowable. Substance and not mere form shall govern in determining a deductible loss.

(c) *Amount deductible.*—(1) The amount of loss allowable as a deduction under section 165(a) shall not exceed the amount prescribed by §1.1011-1 as the adjusted basis for determining the loss from the sale or other disposition of the property involved. In the case of each such deduction claimed, therefore, the basis of the property must be properly adjusted as prescribed by §1.1011-1 for such items as expenditures, receipts, or losses, properly chargeable to capital account, and for such items as depreciation, obsolescence, amortization, and depletion, in order to determine the amount of loss allowable as a deduction. To determine the allowable loss in the case of property acquired before March 1, 1913, see also paragraph (b) of §1.1053-1.

(2) The amount of loss recognized upon the sale or exchange of property shall be determined for purposes of section 165(a) in accordance with §1.1002-1.

(3) A loss from the sale or exchange of a capital asset shall be allowed as a deduction under section 165(a) but only to the extent allowed in section 1211 (relating to limitation on capital losses) and section 1212 (relating to capital loss carrybacks and carryovers), and in the regulations under those sections.

(4) In determining the amount of loss actually sustained for purposes of section 165(a), proper adjustment shall be made for any salvage value and for any insurance or other compensation received.

(d) *Year of deduction.*—(1) A loss shall be allowed as a deduction under section 165(a) only for the taxable year in which the loss is sustained. For this purpose, a loss shall be treated as sustained during the taxable year in which the loss occurs as evidenced by closed and completed transactions and as fixed by identifiable events occurring in such taxable year. For provisions relating to situations where a loss attributable to a disaster will be treated as sustained in the taxable year immediately preceding the taxable year in which the disaster actually occurred, see section 165(h) and §1.165-11.

(2)(i) If a casualty or other event occurs which may result in a loss and, in the year of such casualty or event, there exists a claim for reimbursement with respect to which there is a reasonable prospect of recovery, no portion of the loss with respect to which reimbursement may be received is sustained, for purposes of section 165, until it can be ascertained with reasonable certainty whether or not such reimbursement will be received. Whether a reasonable prospect of recovery exists with respect to a claim for reimbursement of a loss is a question of fact to be determined upon an examination of all facts and circumstances. Whether or not such reimbursement will be received may be ascertained with reasonable certainty, for example, by a settlement of the claim, by an adjudication of the claim, or by an abandonment of the claim. When a taxpayer claims that the taxable year in which a loss is sustained is fixed by his abandonment of the claim for reimbursement, he must be able to produce objective evidence of his having abandoned the claim, such as the execution of a release.

(ii) If in the year of the casualty or other event a portion of the loss is not covered by a claim for reimbursement with respect to which there is a reasonable prospect of recovery, then such portion of the loss is sustained during the taxable year in which the casualty or other event occurs. For example, if property having an adjusted basis of $10,000 is completely destroyed by fire in 1961, and if the taxpayer's only claim for reimbursement consists of an insurance claim for $8,000 which is settled in 1962, the taxpayer sustains a loss of $2,000 in 1961. However, if the taxpayer's automobile is completely destroyed in 1961 as a result of the negligence of another person and there exists a reasonable prospect of recovery on a claim for the full value of the automobile against such person, the taxpayer does not sustain any loss until the taxable year in which the claim is adjudicated or otherwise settled. If the automobile had an adjusted basis of $5,000 and the taxpayer secures a judgment of $4,000 in 1962, $1,000 is deductible for the taxable year 1962. If in 1963 it becomes reasona-

bly certain that only $3,500 can ever be collected on such judgment, $500 is deductible for the taxable year 1963.

(iii) If the taxpayer deducted a loss in accordance with the provisions of this paragraph and in a subsequent taxable year receives reimbursement for such loss, he does not recompute the tax for the taxable year in which the deduction was taken but includes the amount of such reimbursement in his gross income for the taxable year in which received, subject to the provisions of section 111, relating to recovery of amounts previously deducted.

(3) Any loss arising from theft shall be treated as sustained during the taxable year in which the taxpayer discovers the loss (see §1.165-8, relating to theft losses). However, if in the year of discovery there exists a claim for reimbursement with respect to which there is a reasonable prospect of recovery, no portion of the loss with respect to which reimbursement may be received is sustained, for purposes of section 165, until the taxable year in which it can be ascertained with reasonable certainty whether or not such reimbursement will be received.

(4) The rules of this paragraph are applicable with respect to a casualty or other event which may result in a loss and which occurs after January 16, 1960. If the casualty or other event occurs on or before such date, a taxpayer may treat any loss resulting therefrom in accordance with the rules then applicable, or, if he so desires, in accordance with the provisions of this paragraph; but no provision of this paragraph shall be construed to permit a deduction of the same loss or any part thereof in more than one taxable year or to extend the period of limitations within which a claim for credit or refund may be filed under section 6511.

(e) *Limitation on losses of individuals.*—In the case of an individual, the deduction for losses granted by section 165(a) shall, subject to the provisions of section 165(c) and paragraph (a) of this section, be limited to:

(1) Losses incurred in a trade or business;

(2) Losses incurred in any transaction entered into for profit, though not connected with a trade or business; and

(3) Losses of property not connected with a trade or business and not incurred in any transaction entered into for profit, if such losses arise from fire, storm, shipwreck, or other casualty, or from theft, and if the loss involved has not been allowed for estate tax purposes in the estate tax return. For additional provisions pertaining to the allowance of casualty and theft losses, see §§1.165-7 and 1.165-8, respectively. For special rules relating to an election by a taxpayer to deduct disaster losses in the taxable year immediately preceding the taxable year in which the disaster occurred, see section 165(h) and §1.165-11. [Reg. §1.165-1.]

☐ [*T.D. 6445, 1-15-60. Amended by T.D. 6753, 5-18-64, T.D. 6996, 1-17-69, T.D. 7301, 1-3-74 and T.D. 7522, 12-15-77.*]

[Reg. §1.165-2]

§1.165-2. Obsolescence of nondepreciable property.—(a) *Allowance of deduction.*—A loss incurred in a business or in a transaction entered into for profit and arising from the sudden termination of the usefulness in such business or transaction of any nondepreciable property, in a case where such business or transaction is discontinued or where such property is permanently discarded from use therein, shall be allowed as a deduction under section 165(a) for the taxable year in which the loss is actually sustained. For this purpose, the taxable year in which the loss is sustained is not necessarily the taxable year in which the overt act of abandonment, or the loss of title to the property, occurs.

(b) *Exceptions.*—This section does not apply to losses sustained upon the sale or exchange of property, losses sustained upon the obsolescence or worthlessness of depreciable property, casualty losses, or losses reflected in inventories required to be taken under section 471. The limitations contained in sections 1211 and 1212 upon losses from the sale or exchange of capital assets do not apply to losses allowable under this section.

(c) *Cross references.*—For the allowance under section 165(a) of losses arising from the permanent withdrawal of depreciable property from use in the trade or business or in the production of income, see §1.167(a)-8, §1.168(i)-1, or §1.168(i)-8, as applicable. For provisions respecting the obsolescence of depreciable property for which depreciation is determined under section 167 (but not under section 168, section 1400I, section 1400L(c), section 168 prior to its amendment by the Tax Reform Act of 1986, Public Law 99-514 (100 Stat. 2121 (1986)), or under an additional first year depreciation deduction provision of the Internal Revenue Code (for example, section 168(k) through (n), 1400L(b), or 1400N(d))), see §1.167(a)-9. For the allowance of casualty losses, see §1.165-7.

(d) *Effective/applicability date.*—(1) *In general.*—This section applies to taxable years beginning on or after January 1, 2014. Except as provided in paragraphs (d)(2) and (d)(3) of this section, §1.165-2 as contained in 26 CFR part 1 edition revised as of April 1, 2011, applies to taxable years beginning before January 1, 2014.

(2) *Early application of §1.165-2(c).*—A taxpayer may choose to apply paragraph (c) of this section to taxable years beginning on or after January 1, 2012.

» **Caution: Temporary Reg. §1.165-2T, below, was removed by T.D. 9636, but a taxpayer may choose to apply Temporary Reg. §1.165-2T to tax years beginning on or after January 1, 2012, and before January 1, 2014.**

[Reg. §1.165-2T]

§1.165-2T. Obsolescence of nondepreciable property (Temporary).—(a) and (b) [Reserved]. For further guidance, see §1.165-2(a) and (b).

(c) *Cross references.*—For the allowance under section 165(a) of losses arising from the permanent withdrawal of depreciable property from use in the trade or business or in the production of income, see §1.167(a)-8T, §1.168(i)-1T, or §1.168(i)-8T, as applicable. For provisions respecting the obsolescence of depreciable property for which depreciation is determined under section 167 (but not under section 168, section 1400I, section 1400L(c), section 168 prior to its amendment by the Tax Reform Act of 1986 (100 Stat. 2121), or under an additional first year depreciation deduction provision of the Internal Revenue Code (for example, section 168(k) through (n), 1400L(b), or 1400N(d))), see §1.167(a)-9. For the allowance of casualty losses, see §1.165-7.

(d) *Effective/applicability date.*—(1) *In general.*—This section applies to taxable years beginning on or after January 1, 2014. Section 1.165-2 as contained in 26 CFR part 1 edition revised as of April 1, 2011, applies to taxable years beginning before January 1, 2014.

(2) *Optional early application.*—A taxpayer may choose to apply this section to taxable years beginning on or after January 1, 2012.

(e) *Expiration date.*—The applicability of this section expires on December 23, 2014. [Temporary Reg. §1.165-2T.]

□ [*T.D. 9564, 12-23-2011 (corrected 12-14-2012). Removed by T.D. 9636, 9-13-2013.*]

[Reg. §1.165-3]

§1.165-3. Demolition of buildings.—(a) *Intent to demolish formed at time of purchase.*—(1) Except as provided in subparagraph (2) of this paragraph, the following rule shall apply when, in the course of a trade or business or in a transaction entered into for profit, real property is purchased with the intention of demolishing either immediately or subsequently the buildings situated thereon: No deduction shall be allowed under section 165(a) on account of the demolition of the old buildings even though any demolition originally planned is subsequently deferred or abandoned. The entire basis of the property so purchased shall, notwithstanding the provisions of §1.167(a)-5, be allocated to the land only. Such basis shall be increased by the net cost of demolition or decreased by the net proceeds from demolition.

(2)(i) If the property is purchased with the intention of demolishing the buildings and the buildings are used in a trade or business or held for the production of income before their demolition, a portion of the basis of the property may be allocated to such buildings and depreciated over the period during which they are so used or held. The fact that the taxpayer intends to demolish the buildings shall be taken into account in making the apportionment of basis between the land and buildings under §1.167(a)-5. In any event, the portion of the purchase price which may be allocated to the buildings shall not exceed the present value of the right to receive rentals from the buildings over the period of their intended use. The present value of such right shall be determined at the time that the buildings are first used in the trade or business or first held for the production of income. If the taxpayer does not rent the buildings, but uses them in his own trade or business or in the production of his income, the present value of such right shall be determined by reference to the rentals which could be realized during such period of intended use. The fact that the taxpayer intends to rent or use the buildings for a limited period before their demolition shall also be taken into account in computing the useful life in accordance with paragraph (b) of §1.167(a)-1.

(ii) Any portion of the purchase price which is allocated to the buildings in accordance with this subparagraph shall not be included in the basis of the land computed under subparagraph (1) of this paragraph, and any portion of the basis of the buildings which has not been recovered through depreciation or otherwise at the time of the demolition of the buildings is allowable as a deduction under section 165.

(iii) The application of this subparagraph may be illustrated by the following example:

(3) *Optional application of TD 9564.*—A taxpayer may choose to apply §1.165-2T as contained in TD 9564 (76 FR 81060) December 27, 2011, to taxable years beginning on or after January 1, 2012, and before January 1, 2014. [Reg. §1.165-2.]

□ [*T.D. 6445, 1-15-60. Amended by T.D. 9564, 12-23-2011; T.D. 9636, 9-13-2013 and T.D. 9689, 8-14-2014.*]

Example. In January 1958, A purchased land and a building for $60,000 with the intention of demolishing the building. In the following April, A concludes that he will be unable to commence the construction of a proposed new building for a period of more than 3 years. Accordingly, on June 1, 1958, he leased the building for a period of 3 years at an annual rental of $1,200. A intends to demolish the building upon expiration of the lease. A may allocate a portion of the $60,000 basis of the property to the building to be depreciated over the 3-year period. That portion is equal to the present value of the right to receive $3,600 (3 times $1,200). Assuming that the present value of that right determined as of June 1, 1958, is $2,850, A may allocate that amount to the building and, if A files his return on the basis of a taxable year ending May 31, 1959, A may take a depreciation deduction with respect to such building of $950 for such taxable year. The basis of the land to A as determined under subparagraph (1) of this paragraph is reduced by $2,850. If on June 1, 1960, A ceases to rent the building and demolishes it, the balance of the undepreciated portion allocated to the buildings, $950, may be deducted from gross income under section 165.

(3) The basis of any building acquired in replacement of the old buildings shall not include any part of the basis of the property originally purchased even though such part was, at the time of purchase, allocated to the buildings to be demolished for purposes of determining allowable depreciation for the period before demolition.

(b) *Intent to demolish formed subsequent to the time of acquisition.*—(1) Except as provided in subparagraph (2) of this paragraph, the loss incurred in a trade or business or in a transaction entered into for profit and arising from a demolition of old buildings shall be allowed as a deduction under section 165(a) if the demolition occurs as a result of a plan formed subsequent to the acquisition of the buildings demolished. The amount of the loss shall be the adjusted basis of the buildings demolished increased by the net cost of demolition or decreased by the net proceeds from demolition. See paragraph (c) of §1.165-1 relating to amount deductible under section 165. The basis of any building acquired in replacement of the old buildings shall not include any part of the basis of the property demolished.

(2) If a lessor or lessee of real property demolishes the buildings situated thereon pursuant to a lease or an agreement which resulted in a lease, under which either the lessor was required or the lessee was required or permitted to demolish such buildings, no deduction shall be allowed to the lessor under section 165(a) on account of the demolition of the old buildings. However, the adjusted basis of the demolished buildings, increased by the net cost of demolition or decreased by the net proceeds from demolition, shall be considered as a part of the cost of the lease to be amortized over the remaining term thereof.

(c) *Evidence of intention.*—(1) Whether real property has been purchased with the intention of demolishing the buildings thereon or whether the demolition of the buildings occurs as a result of a plan formed subsequent to their acquisition is a question of fact, and the answer depends upon an examination of all the surrounding facts and circumstances. The answer to the question does not depend solely upon the statements of the taxpayer at the time he acquired the property or demolished the buildings, but such statements, if made, are relevant and will be considered. Certain other relevant facts and circumstances that exist in some cases and the inferences that might reasonably be drawn from them are described in subparagraphs (2) and (3) of this paragraph. The question as to the taxpayer's intention is not answered by any inference that is drawn from any one fact or circumstance but can be answered only by a consideration of all relevant facts and circumstances and the reasonable inferences to be drawn therefrom.

(2) An intention at the time of acquisition to demolish may be suggested by:

(i) A short delay between the date of acquisition and the date of demolition;

(ii) Evidence of prohibitive remodeling costs determined at the time of acquisition;

(iii) Existence of municipal regulations at the time of acquisition which would prohibit the continued use of the buildings for profit purposes;

(iv) Unsuitability of the buildings for the taxpayer's trade or business at the time of acquisition; or

(v) Inability at the time of acquisition to realize a reasonable income from the buildings.

(3) The fact that the demolition occurred pursuant to a plan formed subsequent to the acquisition of the property may be suggested by:

(i) Substantial improvement of the buildings immediately after their acquisition;

(ii) Prolonged use of the buildings for business purposes after their acquisition;

(iii) Suitability of the buildings for investment purposes at the time of acquisition;

(iv) Substantial change in economic or business conditions after the date of acquisition;

(v) Loss of useful value occurring after the date of acquisition;

(vi) Substantial damage to the buildings occurring after their acquisition;

(vii) Discovery of latent structural defects in the buildings after their acquisition;

(viii) Decline in the taxpayer's business after the date of acquisition;

(ix) Condemnation of the property by municipal authorities after the date of acquisition; or

(x) Inability after acquisition to obtain building material necessary for the improvement of the property. [Reg. § 1.165-3.]

☐ *[T.D. 6445, 1-15-60. Amended by T.D. 7447, 12-21-76.]*

[Reg. § 1.165-4]

§ 1.165-4. Decline in value of stock.—(a) *Deduction disallowed.*—No deduction shall be allowed under section 165(a) solely on account of a decline in the value of stock owned by the taxpayer when the decline is due to a fluctuation in the market price of the stock or to other similar cause. A mere shrinkage in the value of stock owned by the taxpayer, even though extensive, does not give rise to a deduction under section 165(a) if the stock has any recognizable value on the date claimed as the date of loss. No loss for a decline in the value of stock owned by the taxpayer shall be allowed as a deduction under section 165(a) except insofar as the loss is recognized under § 1.1002-1 upon the sale or exchange of the stock and except as otherwise provided in § 1.165-5 with respect to stock which becomes worthless during the taxable year.

(b) *Stock owned by banks.*—(1) In the regulation of banks and certain other corporations, Federal and State authorities may require that stock owned by such organizations be charged off as worthless or written down to a nominal value. If, in any such case, this requirement is premised upon the worthlessness of the stock, the charging off or writing down will be considered prima facie evidence of worthlessness for purposes of section 165(a); but, if the charging off or writing down is due to a fluctuation in the market price of the stock or if no reasonable attempt to determine the worthlessness of the stock has been made, then no deduction shall be allowed under section 165(a) for the amount so charged off or written down.

(2) This paragraph shall not be construed, however, to permit a deduction under section 165(a) unless the stock owned by the bank or other corporation actually becomes worthless in the taxable year. Such a taxpayer owning stock which becomes worthless during the taxable year is not precluded from deducting the loss under section 165(a) merely because, in obedience to the specific orders or general policy of such supervisory authorities, the value of the stock is written down to a nominal amount instead of being charged off completely.

(c) *Application to inventories.*—This section does not apply to a decline in the value of corporate stock reflected in inventories required to be taken by a dealer in securities under section 471. See § 1.471-5.

(d) *Definition.*—As used in this section, the term "stock" means a share of stock in a corporation or a right to subscribe for, or to receive, a share of stock in a corporation. [Reg. § 1.165-4.]

☐ *[T.D. 6445, 1-15-60.]*

[Reg. § 1.165-5]

§ 1.165-5. Worthless securities.—(a) *Definition of security.*—As used in section 165(g) and this section, the term "security" means:

(1) A share of stock in a corporation;

(2) A right to subscribe for, or to receive, a share of stock in a corporation; or

(3) A bond, debenture, note, or certificate, or other evidence of indebtedness to pay a fixed or determinable sum of money, which has been issued with interest coupons or in registered form by a domestic or foreign corporation or by any government or political subdivision thereof.

(b) *Ordinary loss.*—If any security which is not a capital asset becomes wholly worthless during the taxable year, the loss resulting therefrom may be deducted under section 165(a) as an ordinary loss.

(c) *Capital loss.*—If any security which is a capital asset becomes wholly worthless at any time during the taxable year, the loss resulting therefrom may be deducted under section 165(a) but only as though it were a loss from a sale or exchange, on the last day of the taxable year, of a capital asset. See section 165(g)(1). The amount so allowed as a deduction shall be subject to the limitations upon capital losses described in paragraph (c)(3) of § 1.165-1.

(d) *Loss on worthless securities of an affiliated corporation.*—(1) *Deductible as an ordinary loss.*—If a taxpayer which is a domestic corporation owns any security of a domestic or foreign corporation which is affiliated with the taxpayer within the meaning of subparagraph (2) of this paragraph and such security becomes wholly worthless during the taxable year, the loss resulting therefrom may be deducted under section 165(a) as an ordinary loss in accordance with paragraph (b) of this section. The fact that the security is in fact a capital asset of the taxpayer is immaterial for this purpose, since section 165(g)(3) provides that such security shall be treated as though it were not a capital asset for the purposes of section 165(g)(1). A debt which becomes wholly worthless during the taxable year shall be allowed as an ordinary loss in accordance with the provisions of this subparagraph, to the extent that such debt is a security within the meaning of paragraph (a)(3) of this section.

(2) *Affiliated corporation defined.*—For purposes of this paragraph, a corporation shall be treated as affiliated with the taxpayer owning the security if—

(i)(a) In the case of a taxable year beginning on or after January 1, 1970, the taxpayer owns directly—

(1) Stock possessing at least 80 percent of the voting power of all classes of such corporation's stock, and

(2) At least 80 percent of each class of such corporation's nonvoting stock

excluding for purposes of this subdivision (i)(a) nonvoting stock which is limited and preferred as to dividends (see section 1504(a)), or

(b) In the case of a taxable year beginning before January 1, 1970, the taxpayer owns directly at least 95 percent of each class of the stock of such corporation;

(ii) None of the stock of such corporation was acquired by the taxpayer solely for the purpose of converting a capital loss sustained by reason of the worthlessness of any such stock into an ordinary loss under section 165(g)(3), and

(iii) More than 90 percent of the aggregate of the gross receipts of such corporation for all the taxable years during which it has been in existence has been from sources other than royalties, rents (except rents derived from rental of properties to employees of such corporation in the ordinary course of its operating business), dividends, interest (except interest received on the deferred purchase price of operating assets sold), annuities and gains from sales or exchanges of stocks and securities. For this purpose, the term "gross receipts" means total receipts determined without any deduction for cost of goods sold, and gross receipts from sales or exchanges of stocks and securities shall be taken into account only to the extent of gains from such sales or exchanges.

(e) *Bonds issued by an insolvent corporation.*—A bond of an insolvent corporation secured only by a mortgage from which nothing is realized for the bondholders on foreclosure shall be regarded as having become worthless not later than the year of the foreclosure sale, and no deduction in respect of the loss shall be allowed under section 165(a) in computing a bondholder's taxable income for a subsequent year. See also paragraph (d) of § 1.165-1.

(f) *Decline in market value.*—A taxpayer possessing a security to which this section relates shall not be allowed any deduction under section 165(a) on account of mere market fluctuation in the value of such security. See also § 1.165-4.

(g) *Application to inventories.*—This section does not apply to any loss upon the worthlessness of any security reflected in inventories required to be taken by a dealer in securities under section 471. See § 1.471-5.

(h) *Special rules for banks.*—For special rules applicable under this section to worthless securities of a bank, including securities issued by an affiliated bank, see § 1.582-1.

(i) *Abandonment of securities.*—(1) *In general.*—For purposes of section 165 and this section, a security that becomes wholly worthless includes a security described in paragraph (a) of this section that is abandoned and otherwise satisfies the requirements for a deductible loss under section 165. If the abandoned security is a capital asset and is not described in section 165(g)(3) and paragraph (d) of this section (concerning worthless securities of certain affiliated corporations), the resulting loss is treated as a loss from the sale or exchange, on the last day of the taxable year, of a capital asset. See section 165(g)(1) and paragraph (c) of this section. To abandon a security, a taxpayer must permanently surrender and relinquish all rights in the security and receive no consideration in exchange for the security. For purposes of this section, all the facts and circumstances determine whether the transaction is properly characterized as an abandonment or other type of transaction, such as an actual sale or exchange, contribution to capital, dividend, or gift.

(2) *Effective/applicability date.*—*This paragraph (i) applies to any abandonment of* stock or other securities after March 12, 2008.

(j) *Examples.*—The provisions of this section may be illustrated by the following examples:

Example (1). (i) X Corporation, a domestic manufacturing corporation which makes its return on the basis of the calendar year, owns 100 percent of each class of the stock of Y Corporation; and, in addition, 19 percent of the common stock (the only class of stock) of Z Corporation, which it acquired in 1948. Y Corporation, a domestic manufacturing corporation which makes its return on the basis of the calendar year, owns 81 percent of the common stock of Z Corporation, which it acquired in 1946. It is established that the stock of Z Corporation, which has from its inception derived all its gross receipts from manufacturing operations, became worthless during 1971.

(ii) Since the stock of Z Corporation which is owned by X Corporation is a capital asset and since X Corporation does not directly own at least 80 percent of the stock of Z Corporation, any loss sustained by X Corporation upon the worthlessness of such stock shall be deducted under section 165(g)(1) and paragraph (c) of this section as a loss from a sale or exchange on December 31, 1971, of a capital asset. The loss so sustained by X Corporation shall be considered a long-term capital loss under the provisions of section 1222(4), since the stock was held by that corporation for more than 6 months.

(iii) Since Z Corporation is considered to be affiliated with Y Corporation under the provisions of paragraph (d)(2) of this section, any loss sustained by Y Corporation upon the worthlessness of the stock of Z Corporation shall be deducted in 1971 under section 165(g)(3) and paragraph (d)(1) of this section as an ordinary loss.

Example (2). (i) On January 1, 1971, X Corporation, a domestic manufacturing corporation which makes its return on the basis of the calendar year, owns 60 percent of each class of the stock of Y Corporation, a foreign corporation, which it acquired in 1950. Y Corporation has, from the date of its incorporation, derived all of its gross receipts from manufacturing operations. It is established that the stock of Y Corporation became worthless on June 30, 1971. On August 1, 1971, X Corporation acquires the balance of the stock of Y Corporation for the purpose of obtaining the benefit of section 165(g)(3) with respect to the loss it has sustained on the worthlessness of the stock of Y Corporation.

(ii) Since the stock of Y Corporation which is owned by X Corporation is a capital asset and since Y Corporation is not to be treated as affiliated with X Corporation under the provisions of paragraph (d)(2) of this section, notwithstanding the fact that, at the close of 1971, X Corporation owns 100 percent of each class of stock of Y Corporation, any loss sustained by X Corporation upon the worthlessness of such stock shall be deducted under the provisions of section 165(g)(1) and paragraph (c) of this section as a loss from a sale or exchange on December 31, 1971, of a capital asset.

Example (3). (i) X Corporation, a domestic manufacturing corporation which makes its return on the basis of the calendar year, owns 80 percent of each class of the stock of Y Corporation, which from its inception has derived all of its gross receipts from manufacturing operations. As one of its capital assets, X Corporation owns $100,000 in registered bonds issued by Y Corporation payable at maturity on December 31, 1974. It is established that these bonds became worthless during 1971.

(ii) Since Y Corporation is considered to be affiliated with X Corporation under the provisions of paragraph (d)(2) of this section, any loss sustained by X Corporation upon the worthlessness of these bonds may be deducted in 1971 under section 165(g)(3) and paragraph (d)(1) of this section as an ordinary loss. The loss may not be deducted under section 166 as a bad debt. See section 166(e). [Reg. §1.165-5.]

□ [T.D. 6445, 1-15-60. *Amended by T.D. 7224, 12-5-72 and T.D. 9386,* 3-11-2008.]

[Reg. §1.165-6]

§1.165-6. Farming losses.—(a) *Allowance of losses.*—(1) Except as otherwise provided in this section, any loss incurred in the operation of a farm as a trade or business shall be allowed as a deduction under section 165(a) or as a net operating loss deduction in accordance with the provisions of section 172. See §1.172-1.

(2) If the taxpayer owns and operates a farm for profit in addition to being engaged in another trade or business, but sustains a loss from the operation of the farming business, then the amount of loss sustained in the operation of the farm may be deducted from gross income, if any, from all other sources.

(3) Loss incurred in the operation of a farm for recreation or pleasure shall not be allowed as a deduction from gross income. See §1.162-12.

(b) *Loss from shrinkage.*—If, in the course of the business of farming, farm products are held for a favorable market, no deduction shall be allowed under section 165(a) in respect of such products merely because of shrinkage in weight, decline in value, or deterioration in storage.

(c) *Loss of prospective crop.*—The total loss by frost, storm, flood, or fire of a prospective crop being grown in the business of farming shall not be allowed as a deduction under section 165(a).

(d) *Loss of livestock.*—(1) *Raised stock.*—A taxpayer engaged in the business of raising and selling livestock, such as cattle, sheep, or horses, may not deduct as a loss under section 165(a) the value of animals that perish from among those which were raised on the farm.

(2) *Purchased stock.*—The loss sustained upon the death by disease, exposure, or injury of any livestock purchased and used in the trade or business of farming shall be allowed as a deduction under section 165(a). See, also, paragraph (e) of this section.

(e) *Loss due to compliance with orders of governmental authority.*—The loss sustained upon the destruction by order of the United States, a State, or any other governmental authority, of any livestock, or other property, purchased and used in the trade or business of farming shall be allowed as a deduction under section 165(a).

(f) *Amount deductible.*—(1) *Expenses of operation.*—The cost of any feed, pasture, or care which is allowed under section 162 as an expense of operating a farm for profit shall not be included as a part of the cost of livestock for purposes of determining the amount of loss deductible under section 165(a) and this section. For the deduction of farming expenses, see §1.162-12.

(2) *Losses reflected in inventories.*—If inventories are taken into account in determining the income from the trade or business of farming, no deduction shall be allowed under this section for losses sustained during the taxable year upon livestock or other products, whether purchased for resale or produced on the farm, to the extent such losses are reflected in the inventory on hand at the close of the taxable year. Nothing in this section shall be construed to disallow the deduction of any loss reflected in the inventories of the taxpayer. For provisions relating to inventories of farmers, see section 471 and the regulations thereunder.

(3) *Other limitations.*—For other provisions relating to the amount deductible under this section, see paragraph (c) of §1.165-1, relating to the amount deductible under section 165(a); §1.165-7, relating to casualty losses; and §1.1231-1, relating to gains and losses from the sale or exchange of certain property used in the trade or business.

(g) *Other provisions applicable to farmers.*—For other provisions relating to farmers, see §1.61-4, relating to gross income of farmers; paragraph (b) of §1.167(a)-6, relating to depreciation in the case of farmers; and §1.175-1, relating to soil and water conservation expenditures. [Reg. §1.165-6.]

□ [T.D. 6445, 1-15-60.]

[Reg. §1.165-7]

§1.165-7. Casualty losses.—(a) *In general.*—(1) *Allowance of deduction.*—Except as otherwise provided in paragraphs (b)(4) and (c) of this section, any loss arising from fire, storm, shipwreck, or other casualty is allowable as a deduction under section 165(a) for the taxable year in which the loss is sustained. However, see §1.165-6, relating to farming losses, and §1.165-11, relating to an election by a taxpayer to deduct disaster losses in the taxable year immediately preceding the taxable year in which the disaster occurred. The manner of determining the amount of a casualty loss allowable as a deduction in computing taxable income under section 63 is the same whether the loss has been incurred in a trade or business or in any transaction entered into for profit, or whether it has been a loss of property not connected with a trade or business and not incurred in any transaction entered into for profit. The amount of a casualty loss shall be determined in accordance with paragraph (b) of this section.

For other rules relating to the treatment of deductible casualty losses, see § 1.1231-1, relating to the involuntary conversion of property.

(2) *Method of valuation.*—(i) In determining the amount of loss deductible under this section, the fair market value of the property immediately before and immediately after the casualty shall generally be ascertained by competent appraisal. This appraisal must recognize the effects of any general market decline affecting undamaged as well as damaged property which may occur simultaneously with the casualty, in order that any deduction under this section shall be limited to the actual loss resulting from damage to the property.

(ii) The cost of repairs to the property damaged is acceptable as evidence of the loss of value if the taxpayer shows that (*a*) the repairs are necessary to restore the property to its condition immediately before the casualty, (*b*) the amount spent for such repairs is not excessive, (*c*) the repairs do not care for more than the damage suffered, and (*d*) the value of the property after the repairs does not as a result of the repairs exceed the value of the property immediately before the casualty.

(3) *Damage to automobiles.*—An automobile owned by the taxpayer, whether used for business purposes or maintained for recreation or pleasure, may be the subject of a casualty loss, including those losses specifically referred to in subparagraph (1) of this paragraph. In addition, a casualty loss occurs when an automobile owned by the taxpayer is damaged and when:

(i) The damage results from the faulty driving of the taxpayer or other person operating the automobile but is not due to the willful act or willful negligence of the taxpayer or of one acting in his behalf, or

(ii) The damage results from the faulty driving of the operator of the vehicle with which the automobile of the taxpayer collides.

(4) *Application to inventories.*—This section does not apply to a casualty loss reflected in the inventories of the taxpayer. For provisions relating to inventories, see section 471 and the regulations thereunder.

(5) *Property converted from personal use.*—In the case of property which originally was not used in the trade or business or for income-producing purposes and which is thereafter converted to either of such uses, the fair market value of the property on the date of conversion, if less than the adjusted basis of the property at such time, shall be used, after making proper adjustments in respect of basis, as the basis for determining the amount of loss under paragraph (b)(1) of this section. See paragraph (b) of § 1.165-9, and § 1.167(g)-1.

(6) *Theft losses.*—A loss which arises from theft is not considered a casualty loss for purposes of this section. See § 1.165-8, relating to theft losses.

(b) *Amount deductible.*—(1) *General rule.*—In the case of any casualty loss whether or not incurred in a trade or business or in any transaction entered into for profit, the amount of loss to be taken into account for purposes of section 165(a) shall be the lesser of either—

(i) The amount which is equal to the fair market value of the property immediately before the casualty reduced by the fair market value of the property immediately after the casualty; or

(ii) The amount of the adjusted basis prescribed in § 1.1011-1 for determining the loss from the sale or other disposition of the property involved. However, if the property used in a trade or business or held for the production of income is totally destroyed by casualty, and if the fair market value of such property immediately before the casualty is less than the adjusted basis of such property, the amount of the adjusted basis of such property shall be treated as the amount of the loss for purposes of section 165(a).

(2) *Aggregation of property for computing loss.*—(i) A loss incurred in a trade or business or in any transaction entered into for profit shall be determined under subparagraph (1) of this paragraph by reference to the single, identifiable property damaged or destroyed. Thus, for example, in determining the fair market value of the property before and after the casualty in a case where damage by casualty has occurred to a building and ornamental or fruit trees used in a trade or business, the decrease in value shall be measured by taking the building and trees into account separately, and not together as an integral part of the realty, and separate losses shall be determined for such building and trees.

(ii) In determining a casualty loss involving real property and improvements thereon not used in a trade or business or in any transaction entered into for profit, the improvements (such as buildings and ornamental trees and shrubbery) to the property damaged or destroyed shall be considered an integral part of the property, for purposes of subparagraph (1) of this paragraph, and no separate basis need by apportioned to such improvements.

(3) *Examples.*—The application of this paragraph may be illustrated by the following examples:

Example (1). In 1956 B purchases for $3,600 an automobile which he uses for nonbusiness purposes. In 1959 the automobile is damaged in an accidental collision with another automobile. The fair market value of B's automobile is $2,000 immediately before the collision and $1,500 immediately after the collision. B receives insurance proceeds of $300 to cover the loss. The amount of the deduction allowable under section 165(a) for the taxable year 1959 is $200, computed as follows:

Value of automobile immediately before casualty	$2,000
Less: Value of automobile immediately after casualty	1,500
Value of property actually destroyed	500
Loss to be taken into account for purposes of section 165(a): Lesser amount of property actually destroyed ($500) or adjusted basis of property ($3,600)	$500
Less: Insurance received	300
Deduction allowable	200

Example (2). In 1958 A purchases land containing an office building for the lump sum of $90,000. The purchase price is allocated between the land ($18,000) and the building ($72,000) for purposes of determining basis. After the purchase A planted trees and ornamental shrubs on the grounds surrounding the building. In 1961 the land, building, trees, and shrubs are damaged by hurricane. At the time of the casualty the adjusted basis of the land is $18,000 and the adjusted basis of the building is $66,000. At that time the trees and shrubs have an adjusted basis of $1,200. The fair market value of the land and building immediately before the casualty is $18,000 and $70,000, respectively, and immediately after the casualty is $18,000 and $52,000, respectively. The fair market value of the trees and shrubs immediately before the casualty is $2,000 and immediately after the casualty is $400. In 1961 insurance of $5,000 is received to cover the loss to the building. A has no other gains or losses in 1961 subject to section 1231 and § 1.1231-1. The amount of the deduction allowable under section 165(a) with respect to the building for the taxable year 1961 is $13,000, computed as follows:

Value of property immediately before casualty	$70,000
Less: Value of property immediately after casualty	52,000
Value of property actually destroyed	18,000
Loss to be taken into account for purposes of section 165(a): Lesser amount of property actually destroyed ($18,000) or adjusted basis of property ($66,000)	$18,000
Less: Insurance received	5,000
Deduction allowable	13,000

The amount of the deduction allowable under section 165(a) with respect to the trees and shrubs for the taxable year 1961 is $1,200, computed as follows:

Value of property immediately before casualty	$2,000
Less: Value of property immediately after casualty	400
Value of property actually destroyed	1,600
Loss to be taken into account for purposes of section 165(a): Lesser amount of property actually destroyed ($1,600) or adjusted basis of property ($1,200)	$1,200

Example (3). Assume the same facts as in example (2) except that A purchases land containing a house instead of an office building. The house is used as his private residence. Since the property is used for personal purposes, no allocation of the purchase price is necessary for the land and house. Likewise, no individual determination of the fair market values of the land, house, trees, and shrubs is necessary. The amount of the deduction allowable under section 165(a) with respect to the land, house, trees, and shrubs for the taxable year 1961 is $14,600, computed as follows:

Value of property immediately before casualty	$90,000
Less: Value of property immediately after casualty	70,400
Value of property actually destroyed	$19,600
Loss to be taken into account for purposes of section 165(a): Lesser amount of property actually destroyed ($19,600) or adjusted basis of property ($91,200)	$19,600
Less: Insurance received	5,000
Deduction allowable	14,600

(4) *Limitation on certain losses sustained by individuals after December 31, 1963.*—(i) Pursuant to section 165(c)(3), the deduction allowable under section 165(a) in respect of a loss sustained—

(a) After December 31, 1963, in a taxable year ending after such date,

(b) In respect of property not used in a trade or business or for income producing purposes, and

(c) From a single casualty

shall be limited to that portion of the loss which is in excess of $100. The nondeductibility of the first $100 of loss applies to a loss sustained after December 31, 1963, without regard to when the casualty occurred. Thus, if property not used in a trade or business or for income producing purposes is damaged or destroyed by a casualty which occurred prior to January 1, 1964, and loss resulting therefrom is sustained after December 31, 1963, the $100 limitation applies.

(ii) The $100 limitation applies separately in respect of each casualty and applies to the entire loss sustained from each casualty. Thus, if as a result of a particular casualty occurring in 1964, a taxpayer sustains in 1964 a loss of $40 and in 1965 a loss of $250, no deduction is allowable for the loss sustained in 1964 and the loss sustained in 1965 must be reduced by $60 ($100–$40). The determination of whether damage to, or destruction of, property resulted from a single casualty or from two or more separate casualties will be made upon the basis of the particular facts of each case. However, events which are closely related in origin generally give rise to a single casualty. For example, if a storm damages a taxpayer's residence and his automobile parked in his driveway, any loss sustained results from a single casualty. Similarly, if a hurricane causes high waves, all wind and flood damage to a taxpayer's property caused by the hurricane and the waves results from a single casualty.

(iii) Except as otherwise provided in this subdivision, the $100 limitation applies separately to each individual taxpayer who sustains a loss even though the property damaged or destroyed is owned by two or more individuals. Thus, if a house occupied by two sisters and jointly owned by them is damaged or destroyed, the $100 limitation applies separately to each sister in respect of any loss sustained by her. However, for purposes of applying the $100 limitation, a husband and wife who file a joint return for the first taxable year in which the loss is allowable as a deduction are treated as one individual taxpayer. Accordingly, if property jointly owned by a husband and wife, or property separately owned by the husband or by the wife, is damaged or destroyed by a single casualty in 1964, and a loss is sustained in that year by either or both the husband or wife, only one $100 limitation applies if a joint return is filed for 1964. If, however, the husband and wife file separate returns for 1964, the $100 limitation applies separately in respect of any loss sustained by the husband and in respect of any loss sustained by the wife. Where losses from a single casualty are sustained in two or more separate tax years, the husband and wife shall, for purposes of applying the $100 limitation to such losses, be treated as one individual for all such years if they file a joint return for the first year in which a loss is sustained from the casualty; they shall be treated as separate individuals for all such years if they file separate returns for the first such year. If a joint return is filed in the first loss year but separate returns are filed in a subsequent year, any unused portion of the $100 limitation shall be allocated equally between the husband and wife in the latter year.

(iv) If a loss is sustained in respect of property used partially for business and partially for nonbusiness purposes, the $100 limitation applies only to that portion of the loss properly attributable to the nonbusiness use. For example, if a taxpayer sustains a $1,000 loss in respect of an automobile which he uses 60 percent for business and 40 percent for nonbusiness, the loss is allocated 60 percent to business use and 40 percent to nonbusiness use. The $100 limitation applies to the portion of the loss allocable to the nonbusiness loss.

(c) *Loss sustained by an estate.*—A casualty loss of property not connected with a trade or business and not incurred in any transaction entered into for profit which is sustained during the settlement of an estate shall be allowed as a deduction under sections 165(a) and 641(b) in computing the taxable income of the estate if the loss has not been allowed under section 2054 in computing the taxable estate of the decedent and if the statement has been filed in accordance with § 1.642(g)-1. See section 165(c)(3).

(d) *Loss treated as though attributable to a trade or business.*—For the rule treating a casualty loss not connected with a trade or business as though it were a deduction attributable to a trade or business for purposes of computing a net operating loss, see paragraph (a)(3)(iii) of § 1.172-3.

(e) *Effective date.*—The rules of this section are applicable to any taxable year beginning after January 16, 1960. If, for any taxable year beginning on or before such date, a taxpayer computed the amount of any casualty loss in accordance with the rules then applicable, such taxpayer is not required to change the amount of the casualty loss allowable for any such prior taxable year. On the other hand, the taxpayer may, if he so desires, amend his income tax return for such year to compute the amount of a casualty loss in accordance with the provisions of this section, but no provision in this section shall be construed as extending the period of limitations within which a claim for credit or refund may be filed under section 6511. [Reg. § 1.165-7.]

☐ [*T.D. 6445, 1-15-60. Amended by T.D. 6712, 3-23-64, T.D. 6735, 5-18-64, T.D. 6786, 12-28-64 and T.D. 7522, 12-15-77.*]

[Reg. § 1.165-8]

§ 1.165-8. Theft losses.—(a) *Allowance of deduction.*—(1) Except as otherwise provided in paragraphs (b) and (c) of this section, any loss arising from theft is allowable as a deduction under section 165(a) for the taxable year in which the loss is sustained. See section 165(c)(3).

(2) A loss arising from theft shall be treated under section 165(a) as sustained during the taxable year in which the taxpayer discovers the loss. See section 165(e). Thus, a theft loss is not deductible under section 165(a) for the taxable year in which the theft actually occurs unless that is also the year in which the taxpayer discovers the loss. However, if in the year of discovery there exists a claim for reimbursement with respect to which there is a reasonable prospect of recovery, see paragraph (d) of § 1.165-1.

(3) The same theft loss shall not be taken into account both in computing a tax under chapter 1, relating to the income tax, or chapter 2, relating to additional income taxes, of the Internal Revenue Code of 1939 and in computing the income tax under the Internal Revenue Code of 1954. See section 7852(c), relating to items not to be twice deducted from income.

(b) *Loss sustained by an estate.*—A theft loss of property not connected with a trade or business and not incurred in any transaction entered into for profit which is discovered during the settlement of an estate, even though the theft actually occurred during a taxable year of the decedent, shall be allowed as a deduction under sections 165(a) and 641(b) in computing the taxable income of the estate if the loss has not been allowed under section 2054 in computing the taxable estate of the decedent and if the statement has been filed in accordance with § 1.642(g)-1. See section 165(c)(3). For purposes of determining the year of deduction, see paragraph (a)(2) of this section.

(c) *Amount deductible.*—The amount deductible under this section in respect of a theft loss shall be determined consistently with the manner prescribed in § 1.165-7 for determining the amount of casualty loss allowable as a deduction under section 165(a). In applying the provisions of paragraph (b) of § 1.165-7 for this purpose, the fair market value of the property immediately after the theft shall be considered to be zero. In the case of a loss sustained after December

31, 1963, in a taxable year ending after such date, in respect of property not used in a trade or business or for income producing purposes, the amount deductible shall be limited to that portion of the loss which is in excess of $100. For rules applicable in applying the $100 limitation, see subparagraph (b)(4) of § 1.165-7. For other rules relating to the treatment of deductible theft losses, see § 1.1231-1, relating to the involuntary conversion of property.

(d) *Definition.*—For purposes of this section the term "theft" shall be deemed to include, but shall not necessarily be limited to, larceny, embezzlement, and robbery.

(e) *Application to inventories.*—This section does not apply to a theft loss reflected in the inventories of the taxpayer. For provisions relating to inventories, see section 471 and the regulations thereunder.

(f) *Example.*—The application of this section may be illustrated by the following example:

Example. In 1955 B, who makes her return on the basis of the calendar year, purchases for personal use a diamond brooch costing $4,000. On November 30, 1961, at which time it has a fair market value of $3,500, the brooch is stolen; but B does not discover the loss until January 1962. The brooch was fully insured against theft. A controversy develops with the insurance company over its liability in respect of the loss. However, in 1962, B has a reasonable prospect of recovery of the fair market value of the brooch from the insurance company. The controversy is settled in March 1963, at which time B receives $2,000 in insurance proceeds to cover the loss from theft. No deduction for the loss is allowable for 1961 or 1962; but the amount of the deduction allowable under section 165(a) for the taxable year 1963 is $1,500, computed as follows:

Value of property immediately before theft	$3,500
Less: Value of property immediately after the theft	0
Balance	$3,500

Loss to be taken into account for purposes of section 165(a):

($3,500 but not to exceed adjusted basis of $4,000 at time of theft)	$3,500
Less: Insurance received in 1963	2,000
Deduction allowable for 1963	$1,500

[Reg. § 1.165-8.]

☐ [*T.D. 6445, 1-15-60. Amended by T.D. 6786, 12-28-64.*]

[Reg. § 1.165-9]

§ 1.165-9. Sale of residential property.—(a) *Losses not allowed.*—A loss sustained on the sale of residential property purchased or constructed by the taxpayer for use as his personal residence and so used by him up to the time of the sale is not deductible under section 165(a).

(b) *Property converted from personal use.*—(1) If property purchased or constructed by the taxpayer for use as his personal residence is, prior to its sale, rented or otherwise appropriated to income-producing purposes and is used for such purposes up to the time of its sale, a loss sustained on the sale of the property shall be allowed as a deduction under section 165(a).

(2) The loss allowed under this paragraph upon the sale of the property shall be the excess of the adjusted basis prescribed in § 1.1011-1 for determining loss over the amount realized from the sale. For this purpose, the adjusted basis for determining loss shall be the lesser of either of the following amounts, adjusted as prescribed in § 1.1011-1 for the period subsequent to the conversion of the property to income-producing purposes:

(i) The fair market value of the property at the time of conversion, or

(ii) The adjusted basis for loss, at the time of conversion, determined under § 1.1011-1 but without reference to the fair market value.

(3) For rules relating to casualty losses of property converted from personal use, see paragraph (a)(5) of § 1.165-7. To determine the basis for depreciation in the case of such property, see § 1.167(g)-1. For limitations on the loss from the sale of a capital asset, see paragraph (c)(3) of § 1.165-1.

(c) *Examples.*—The application of paragraph (b) of this section may be illustrated by the following examples:

Example (1). Residential property is purchased by the taxpayer in 1943 for use as his personal residence at a cost of $25,000, of which $15,000 is allocable to the building. The taxpayer uses the property as his personal residence until January 1, 1952, at which time its fair market value is $22,000, of which $12,000 is allocable to the building. The taxpayer rents the property from January 1, 1952, until January 1, 1955, at which time it is sold for $16,000. On January 1, 1952, the

building has an estimated useful life of 20 years. It is assumed that the building has no estimated salvage value and that there are no adjustments in respect of basis other than depreciation, which is computed on the straight-line method. The loss to be taken into account for purposes of section 165(a) for the taxable year 1955 is $4,200, computed as follows:

Basis of property at time of conversion for purposes of this section (that is, the lesser of $25,000 cost or $22,000 fair market value)	$22,000
Less: Depreciation allowable from January 1, 1952, to January 1, 1955 (3 years at 5 percent based on $12,000, the value of the building at time of conversion, as prescribed by § 1.167(g)-1)	$1,800
Adjusted basis prescribed in § 1.1011-1 for determining loss on sale of the property	$20,200
Less: Amount realized on sale	16,000
Loss to be taken into account for purposes of section 165(a)	$4,200

In this example the value of the building at the time of conversion is used as the basis for computing depreciation. See example (2) of this paragraph wherein the adjusted basis of the building is required to be used for such purpose.

Example (2). Residential property is purchased by the taxpayer in 1940 for use as his personal residence at a cost of $23,000, of which $10,000 is allocable to the building. The taxpayer uses the property as his personal residence until January 1, 1953, at which time its fair market value is $20,000, of which $12,000 is allocable to the building. The taxpayer rents the property from January 1, 1953, until January 1, 1957, at which time it is sold for $17,000. On January 1, 1953, the building has an estimated useful life of 20 years. It is assumed that the building has no estimated salvage value and that there are no adjustments in respect of basis other than depreciation, which is computed on the straight-line method. The loss to be taken into account for purposes of section 165(a) for the taxable year 1957 is $1,000, computed as follows:

Basis of property at time of conversion for purposes of this section (that is, the lesser of $23,000 cost or $20,000 fair market value)	$20,000
Less: Depreciation allowable from January 1, 1953, to January 1, 1957 (4 years at 5% based on $10,000, the cost of the building, as prescribed by § 1.167(g)-1)	2,000
Adjusted basis prescribed in § 1.1011-1 for determining loss on sale of the property	$18,000
Less: Amount realized on sale	17,000
Loss to be taken into account for purposes of section 165(a)	$1,000

[Reg. § 1.165-9.]

☐ [*T.D. 6445, 1-15-60. Amended by T.D. 6712, 3-23-64.*]

[Reg. § 1.165-10]

§ 1.165-10. Wagering losses.—Losses sustained during the taxable year on wagering transactions shall be allowed as a deduction but only to the extent of the gains during the taxable year from such transactions. In the case of a husband and wife making a joint return for the taxable year, the combined losses of the spouses from wagering transactions shall be allowed to the extent of the combined gains of the spouses from wagering transactions. [Reg. § 1.165-10.]

☐ [*T.D. 6445, 1-15-60.*]

[Reg. § 1.165-11]

§ 1.165-11. Election to take disaster loss deduction for preceding year.—(a) *In general.*—Section 165(i) allows a taxpayer who has sustained a loss attributable to a federally declared disaster in a taxable year to elect to deduct that disaster loss in the preceding year. This section provides rules and procedures for making and revoking an election to claim a disaster loss in the preceding year.

(b) *Definitions.*—The following definitions apply for purposes of this section:

(1) A *federally declared disaster* means any disaster subsequently determined by the President of the United States to warrant assistance by the Federal Government under the Robert T. Stafford Disaster Relief and Emergency Assistance Act (Stafford Act). A federally declared disaster includes both a major disaster declared under section 401 of the Stafford Act and an emergency declared under section 501 of the Stafford Act.

(2) A *federally declared disaster area* is the area determined to be eligible for assistance pursuant to the Presidential declaration in paragraph (b)(1) of this section.

(3) A *disaster loss* is a loss occurring in a federally declared disaster area that is attributable to a federally declared disaster and

that is otherwise allowable as a deduction for the disaster year under section 165(a) and §§ 1.165-1 through 1.165-10.

(4) The *disaster year* is the taxable year in which a taxpayer sustains a loss attributable to a federally declared disaster.

(5) The *preceding year* is the taxable year immediately prior to the disaster year.

(c) *Scope and effect of election.*—An election made pursuant to section 165(i) for a disaster loss attributable to a particular disaster applies to the entire loss sustained by the taxpayer from that disaster during the disaster year. If the taxpayer makes a section 165(i) election with respect to a particular disaster occurring during the disaster year, the disaster to which the election relates is deemed to have occurred, and the disaster loss to which the election applies is deemed to have been sustained, in the preceding year.

(d) *Requirement to file consistent returns.*—A taxpayer may not make a section 165(i) election for a disaster loss if the taxpayer claims a deduction (as a loss, as cost of goods sold, or otherwise) for the same loss for the disaster year. If a taxpayer has claimed a deduction for a disaster loss for the disaster year and the taxpayer wants to make a section 165(i) election with respect to that loss, the taxpayer must file an amended Federal income tax return to remove the previously deducted loss on or before the date that the taxpayer makes the section 165(i) election for the loss. Similarly, if a taxpayer has claimed a deduction for a disaster loss for the preceding year based on a section 165(i) election and the taxpayer wants to revoke that election, the taxpayer must file an amended Federal income tax return to remove the loss for the preceding year on or before the date the taxpayer files the Federal income tax return or amended Federal income tax return for the disaster year that includes the loss.

(e) *Manner of making election.*—An election under section 165(i) to deduct a disaster loss for the preceding year is made either on an original Federal income tax return for the preceding year or an amended Federal income tax return for the preceding year in the manner specified by guidance issued pursuant to this section.

(f) *Due date for making election.*—The due date for making the section 165(i) election is six months after the due date for filing the taxpayer's Federal income tax return for the disaster year (determined without regard to any extension of time to file).

(g) *Revocation.*—Subject to the requirements in paragraph (d) of this section, a section 165(i) election may be revoked on or before the date that is ninety (90) days after the due date for making the election.

(h) *Applicability dates.*—(1) *In general.*—Except as provided in paragraph (h)(2) of this section, this section applies to elections and revocations that are made on or after October 16, 2019.

(2) *Paragraph (b)(1) of this section.*—The second sentence of paragraph (b)(1) of this section applies to elections and revocations that are made on or after June 11, 2021. [Reg. § 1.165-11.]

☐ [T.D. 6735, 5-18-64. *Amended by T.D. 7224,* 12-5-72, T.D. 7522, 12-15-77, T.D. 9789, 10-13-2016, T.D. 9878, 10-11-2019 *and T.D. 9950,* 6-10-2021.]

[Reg. § 1.165-12]

§ 1.165-12. Denial of deduction for losses on registration-required obligations not in registered form.—(a) *In general.*—Except as provided in paragraph (c) of this section, nothing in section 165(a) and the regulations thereunder, or in any other provision of law, shall be construed to provide a deduction for any loss sustained on any registration-required obligation held after December 31, 1982, unless the obligation is in registered form or the issuance of the obligation was subject to tax under section 4701. The term "registration-required obligation" has the meaning given to that term in section 163(f)(2), except that clause (iv) of subparagraph (A) thereof shall not apply. Therefore, although an obligation that is not in registered form is described in § 1.163-5(c)(1), the holder of such an obligation shall not be allowed a deduction of any loss sustained on such obligation unless paragraph (c) of this section applies. The term "holder" means the person that would be denied a loss deduction under section 165(j)(1) or denied capital gain treatment under section 1287(a). For purposes of this section, the term *United States* means the United States and its possessions within the meaning of § 1.163-5(c)(2)(iv).

(b) *Registered form.*—(1) *Obligations issued after September 21, 1984.*—With respect to any obligation originally issued after September 21, 1984, the term "registered form" has the meaning given that term in section 103(j)(3) and the regulations thereunder. Therefore, an obligation that would otherwise be in registered form is not considered to be in registered form if it can be transferred at that time or at any time until its maturity by any means not described in

§ 5f.103-1(c). An obligation that, as of a particular time, is not considered to be in registered form because it can be transferred by any means not described in § 5f.103-1(c) is considered to be in registered form at all times during the period beginning with a later time and ending with the maturity of the obligation in which the obligation can be transferred only by a means described in § 5f.103-1(c).

(2) *Obligations issued after December 31, 1982 and on or before September 21, 1984.*—With respect to any obligation originally issued after December 31, 1982 and on or before September 21, 1984 or an obligation originally issued after September 21, 1984 pursuant to the exercise of a warrant or the conversion of a convertible obligation, which warrant or obligation (including conversion privilege) was issued after December 31, 1982 and on or before September 21, 1984, that obligation will be considered in registered form if it satisfied § 5f.163-1 or the proposed regulations provided in § 1.163-5(c) and published in the Federal Register on September 2, 1983 (48 FR 39953).

(c) *Registration-required obligations not in registered form which are not subject to section 165(j)(1).*—Notwithstanding the fact that an obligation is a registration-required obligation that is not in registered form, the holder will not be subject to section 165(j)(1) if the holder meets the conditions of any one of the following subparagraphs (1), (2), (3), or (4) of this paragraph (c).

(1) *Persons permitted to hold in connection with the conduct of a trade or business..*—(i) The holder is an underwriter, broker, dealer, bank, or other financial institution (defined in paragraph (c)(1)(iv)) that holds such obligation in connection with its trade or business conducted outside the United States; or the holder is a broker-dealer (registered under Federal or State law or exempted from registration by the provisions of such law because it is a bank) that holds such obligation for sale to customers in the ordinary course of its trade or business.

(ii) The holder must offer to sell, sell and deliver the obligation in bearer form only outside of the United States except that a holder that is a registered broker-dealer as described in paragraph (c)(1)(i) of this section may offer to sell and sell the obligation in bearer form inside the United States to a financial institution as defined in paragraph (c)(1)(iv) of this section for its own account or for the account of another financial institution or of an exempt organization as defined in section 501(c)(3).

(iii) The holder may deliver an obligation in bearer form that is offered or sold inside the United States only if the holder delivers it to a financial institution that is purchasing for its own account, or for the account of another financial institution or of an exempt organization, and the financial institution or organization that purchases the obligation for its own account or for whose account the obligation is purchased represents that it will comply with the requirements of section 165(j)(3)(A), (B), or (C). Absent actual knowledge that the representation is false, the holder may rely on a written statement provided by the financial institution or exempt organization, including a statement that is delivered in electronic form. The holder may deliver a registration-required obligation in bearer form that is offered and sold outside the United States to a person other than a financial institution only if the holder has evidence in its records that such person is not a U.S. citizen or resident and does not have actual knowledge that such evidence is false. Such evidence may include a written statement by that person, including a statement that is delivered electronically. For purposes of this paragraph (c), the term *deliver* includes a transfer of an obligation evidenced by a book entry including a book entry notation by a clearing organization evidencing transfer of the obligation from one member of the organization to another member. For purposes of this paragraph (c), the term *deliver* does not include a transfer of an obligation to the issuer or its agent for cancellation or extinguishment. The record-retention provisions in § 1.1441-1(e)(4)(iii) shall apply to any statement that a holder receives pursuant to this paragraph (c)(1)(iii).

(iv) For purposes of paragraph (c) of this section, the term "financial institution" means a person which itself is, or more than 50 percent of the total combined voting power of all classes of whose stock entitled to vote is owned by a person which is—

(A) Engaged in the conduct of a banking, financing, or similar business within the meaning of section 954(c)(3)(B) as in effect before the Tax Reform Act of 1986, and the regulations thereunder;

(B) Engaged in business as a broker or dealer in securities;

(C) An insurance company;

(D) A person that provides pensions or other similar benefits to retired employees;

(E) Primarily engaged in the business of rendering investment advice;

(F) A regulated investment company or other mutual fund; or

(G) A finance corporation a substantial part of the business of which consists of making loans (including the acquisition of obligations under a lease which is entered into primarily as a financing transaction), acquiring accounts receivable, notes or installment obligations arising out of the sale of tangible personal property or the performing of services, or servicing debt obligations.

(2) *Persons permitted to hold obligations for their own investment account.*—The holder is a financial institution holding the obligation for its own investment account that satisfies the conditions set forth in subdivisions (i), (ii), (iii), and (iv) of this paragraph (c)(2).

(i) The holder reports on its Federal income tax return for the taxable year any interest payments received (including original issue discount includable in gross income for such taxable year) with respect to such obligation and gain or loss on the sale or other disposition of such obligation;

(ii) The holder indicates on its Federal income tax return that income, gain or loss described in paragraph (c)(2)(i) is attributable to registration-required obligations held in bearer form for its own account;

(iii) The holder of a bearer obligation that resells the obligation inside the United States resells the obligation only to another financial institution for its own account or for the account of another financial institution or exempt organization; and

(iv) The holder delivers such obligation in bearer form to any other person in accordance with paragraph (c)(1)(ii) and (iii) of this section.

(3) *Persons permitted to hold through financial institutions.*—The holder is any person that purchases and holds a registration-required obligation in bearer form through a financial institution with which the holder maintains a customer, custodial or nominee relationship and such institution agrees to satisfy, and does in fact satisfy, the conditions set forth in subdivisions (i), (ii), (iii), (iv) and (v) of this paragraph (c)(3).

(i) The financial institution makes a return of information to the Internal Revenue Service with respect to any interest payments received. The financial institution must report original issue discount includable in the holder's gross income for the taxable year on any obligation so held, but only if the obligation appears in an Internal Revenue Service publication of obligations issued at an original issue discount and only in an amount determined in accordance with information contained in that publication. An information return for any interest payment shall be made on a Form 1099 for the calendar year. It shall indicate the aggregate amount of the payment received, the name, address and taxpayer identification number of the holder, and such other information as is required by the form. No return of information is required under this subdivision if the financial institution reports payments under section 6041 or 6049.

(ii) The financial institution makes a return of information on Form 1099B with respect to any disposition by the holder of such obligation. The return shall show the name, address, and taxpayer identification number of the holder of the obligation, Committee on Uniform Security Information Procedures (CUSIP), gross proceeds, sale date, and such other information as may be required by the form. No return of information is required under this subdivision if such financial institution reports with respect to the disposition under section 6045.

(iii) In the case of a bearer obligation offered for resale or resold in the United States, the financial institution may resell the obligation only to another financial institution for its own account or for the account of an exempt organization.

(iv) The financial institution covenants with the holder that the financial institution will deliver the obligation in bearer form in accordance with the requirements set forth in paragraph (c)(1)(ii) and (iii).

(v) The financial institution delivers the obligation in bearer form in accordance with paragraph (c)(1)(ii) and (iv) as if the financial institution delivering the obligation were the holder referred to in such paragraph.

(4) *Conversion of obligations into registered form.*—The holder is not a person described in paragraph (c)(1), (2), or (3) of this section, and within thirty days of the date when the seller or other transferor is reasonably able to make the bearer obligation available to the holder, the holder surrenders the obligation to a transfer agent or the issuer for conversion of the obligation into registered form. If such obligation is not registered within such 30 day period, the holder shall be subject to sections 165(j) and 1287(a).

(d) *Effective date.*—These regulations apply generally to obligations issued after January 20, 1987. However, a taxpayer may choose to apply the rules of §1.165-12 with respect to an obligation issued after December 31, 1982 and on or before January 20, 1987, which obligation is held after January 20, 1987. [Reg. §1.165-12.]

□ [*T.D. 8110*, 12-16-86. *Amended by T.D. 8734*, 10-6-97 (T.D. 8804 delayed the effective date of T.D. 8734 from January 1, 1999, to

January 1, 2000; T.D. 8856 further delayed the effective date of T.D. 8734 until January 1, 2001).]

[Reg. §1.166-1]

§1.166-1. Bad debts.—(a) *Allowance of deduction.*—Section 166 provides that, in computing taxable income under section 63, a deduction shall be allowed in respect of bad debts owed to the taxpayer. For this purpose, bad debts shall, subject to the provisions of section 166 and the regulations thereunder, be taken into account either as—

(1) A deduction in respect of debts which become worthless in whole or in part; or as

(2) A deduction for a reasonable addition to a reserve for bad debts.

(b) *Manner of selecting method.*—(1) A taxpayer filing a return of income for the first taxable year for which he is entitled to a bad debt deduction may select either of the two methods prescribed by paragraph (a) of this section for treating bad debts, but such selection is subject to the approval of the district director upon examination of the return. If the method so selected is approved, it shall be used in returns for all subsequent taxable years unless the Commissioner grants permission to use the other method. A statement of facts substantiating any deduction claimed under section 166 on account of bad debts shall accompany each return of income.

(2) Taxpayers who have properly selected one of the two methods for treating bad debts under provisions of prior law corresponding to section 166 shall continue to use that method for all subsequent taxable years unless the Commissioner grants permission to use the other method.

(3)(i) For taxable years beginning after December 31, 1959, application for permission to change the method of treating bad debts shall be made in accordance with section 446(e) and paragraph (e)(3) of §1.446-1.

(ii) For taxable years beginning before January 1, 1960, application for permission to change the method of treating bad debts shall be made at least 30 days before the close of the taxable year for which the change is effective.

(4) Notwithstanding paragraph (b) (1), (2), and (3) of this section, a dealer in property currently employing the accrual method of accounting and currently maintaining a reserve for bad debts under section 166(c) (which may have included guaranteed debt obligations described in section 166(f)(1)(A)) may establish a reserve for section 166(f)(1)(A) guaranteed debt obligations for a taxable year ending after October 21, 1965 under section 166(f) and §1.166-10 by filing on or before April 17, 1986, an amended return indicating that such a reserve has been established. The establishment of such a reserve will not be considered a change in method of accounting for purposes of section 446(e). However, an election by a taxpayer to establish a reserve for bad debts under section 166(c) shall be treated as a change in method of accounting. See also §1.166-4, relating to reserve for bad debts, and §1.166-10, relating to reserve for guaranteed debt obligations.

(c) *Bona fide debt required.*—Only a bona fide debt qualifies for purposes of section 166. A bona fide debt is a debt which arises from a debtor-creditor relationship based upon a valid and enforceable obligation to pay a fixed or determinable sum of money. A debt arising out of the receivables of an accrual method taxpayer is deemed to be an enforceable obligation for purposes of the preceding sentence to the extent that the income such debt represents has been included in the return of income for the year for which the deduction as a bad debt is claimed or for a prior taxable year. For example, a debt arising out of gambling receivables that are unenforceable under state or local law, which an accrual method taxpayer includes in income under section 61, is an enforceable obligation for purposes of this paragraph. A gift or contribution to capital shall not be considered a debt for purposes of section 166. The fact that a bad debt is not due at the time of deduction shall not of itself prevent its allowance under section 166. For the disallowance of deductions for bad debts owed by a political party, see §1.271-1.

(d) *Amount deductible.*—(1) *General rule.*—Except in the case of a deduction for a reasonable addition to a reserve for bad debts, the basis for determining the amount of deduction under section 166 in respect of a bad debt shall be the same as the adjusted basis prescribed by §1.1011-1 for determining the loss from the sale or other disposition of property. To determine the allowable deduction in the case of obligations acquired before March 1, 1913, see also paragraph (b) of §1.1053-1.

(2) *Specific cases.*—Subject to any provision of section 166 and the regulations thereunder which provides to the contrary, the following amounts are deductible as bad debts:

(i) *Notes or accounts receivable.*—(a) If, in computing taxable income, a taxpayer values his notes or accounts receivable at their fair market value when received, the amount deductible as a bad debt under section 166 in respect of such receivables shall be limited to such fair market value even though it is less than their face value.

(b) A purchaser of accounts receivable which become worthless during the taxable year shall be entitled under section 166 to a deduction which is based upon the price he paid for such receivables but not upon their face value.

(ii) *Bankruptcy claim.*—Only the difference between the amount received in distribution of the assets of a bankrupt and the amount of the claim may be deducted under section 166 as a bad debt.

(iii) *Claim against decedent's estate.*—The excess of the amount of the claim over the amount received by a creditor of a decedent in distribution of the assets of the decedent's estate may be considered a worthless debt under section 166.

(e) *Prior inclusion in income required.*—Worthless debts arising from unpaid wages, salaries, fees, rents, and similar items of taxable income shall not be allowed as a deduction under section 166 unless the income such items represent has been included in the return of income for the year for which the deduction as a bad debt is claimed or for a prior taxable year.

(f) *Recovery of bad debts.*—Any amount attributable to the recovery during the taxable year of a bad debt, or of a part of a bad debt, which was allowed as a deduction from gross income in a prior taxable year shall be included in gross income for the taxable year of recovery, except to the extent that the recovery is excluded from gross income under the provisions of §1.111-1, relating to the recovery of certain items previously deducted or credited. This paragraph shall not apply, however, to a bad debt which was previously charged against a reserve by a taxpayer on the reserve method of treating bad debts.

(g) *Worthless securities.*—(1) Section 166 and the regulations thereunder do not apply to a debt which is evidenced by a bond, debenture, note, or certificate, or other evidence of indebtedness, issued by a corporation, or by a government or political subdivision thereof, with interest coupons or in registered form. See section 166(e). For provisions allowing the deduction of a loss resulting from the worthlessness of such a debt, see §1.165-5.

(2) The provisions of subparagraph (1) of this paragraph do not apply to any loss sustained by a bank and resulting from the worthlessness of a security described in section 165(g)(2)(C). See paragraph (a) of §1.582-1. [Reg. §1.166-1.]

☐ [T.D. 6403, 7-30-59. *Amended by T.D. 6996, 1-17-69, T.D. 7902, 7-20-83 and T.D. 8071, 1-17-86.*]

[Reg. §1.166-2]

§1.166-2. Evidence of worthlessness.—(a) *General rule.*—In determining whether a debt is worthless in whole or in part the district director will consider all pertinent evidence, including the value of the collateral, if any, securing the debt and the financial condition of the debtor.

(b) *Legal action not required.*—Where the surrounding circumstances indicate that a debt is worthless and uncollectible and that legal action to enforce payment would in all probability not result in the satisfaction of execution on a judgment, a showing of these facts will be sufficient evidence of the worthlessness of the debt for purposes of the deduction under section 166.

(c) *Bankruptcy.*—(1) *General rule.*—Bankruptcy is generally an indication of the worthlessness of at least a part of an unsecured and unpreferred debt.

(2) *Year of deduction.*—In bankruptcy cases a debt may become worthless before settlement in some instances; and in others, only when a settlement in bankruptcy has been reached. In either case, the mere fact that bankruptcy proceedings instituted against the debtor are terminated in a later year, thereby confirming the conclusion that the debt is worthless, shall not authorize the shifting of the deduction under section 166 to such later year.

(d) *Banks and other regulated corporations.*—(1) *Worthlessness presumed in year of charge-off.*—If a bank or other corporation which is subject to supervision by Federal authorities, or by State authorities maintaining substantially equivalent standards, charges off a debt in whole or in part, either—

(i) In obedience to the specific orders of such authorities, or

(ii) In accordance with established policies of such authorities, and, upon their first audit of the bank or other corporation subsequent to the charge-off, such authorities confirm in writing that the charge-off would have been subject to such specific orders if the audit had been made on the date of the charge-off,

then the debt shall, to the extent charged off during the taxable year, be conclusively presumed to have become worthless, or worthless only in part, as the case may be, during such taxable year. But no such debt shall be so conclusively presumed to be worthless, or worthless only in part, as the case may be, if the amount so charged off is not claimed as a deduction by the taxpayer at the time of filing the return for the taxable year in which the charge-off takes place.

(2) *Evidence of worthlessness in later taxable year.*—If such a bank or other corporation does not claim a deduction for such a totally or partially worthless debt in its return for the taxable year in which the charge-off takes place, but claims the deduction for a later taxable year, then the charge-off in the prior taxable year shall be deemed to have been involuntary and the deduction under section 166 shall be allowed for the taxable year for which claimed, provided that the taxpayer produces sufficient evidence to show that—

(i) The debt became wholly worthless in the later taxable year, or became recoverable only in part subsequent to the taxable year of the involuntary charge-off, as the case may be; and,

(ii) To the extent that the deduction claimed in the later taxable year for a debt partially worthless was not involuntarily charged off in prior taxable years, it was charged off in the later taxable year.

(3) *Conformity election.*—(i) *Eligibility for election.*—In lieu of applying paragraphs (d)(1) and (2) of this section, a bank (as defined in paragraph (d)(4)(i) of this section) that is subject to supervision by Federal authorities, or by state authorities maintaining substantially equivalent standards, may elect under this paragraph (d)(3) to use a method of accounting that establishes a conclusive presumption of worthlessness for debts, provided that the bank meets the express determination requirement of paragraph (d)(3)(iii)(D) of this section for the taxable year of the election.

(ii) *Conclusive presumption.*—(A) *In general.*—If a bank satisfies the express determination requirement of paragraph (d)(3)(iii)(D) of this section and elects to use the method of accounting under this paragraph (d)(3)—

(1) Debts charged off, in whole or in part, for regulatory purposes during a taxable year are conclusively presumed to have become worthless, or worthless only in part, as the case may be, during that year, but only if the charge-off results from a specific order of the bank's supervisory authority or corresponds to the bank's classification of the debt, in whole or in part, as a loss asset, as described in paragraph (d)(3)(ii)(C) of this section; and

(2) A bad debt deduction for a debt that is subject to regulatory loss classification standards is allowed for a taxable year only to the extent that the debt is conclusively presumed to have become worthless under paragraph (d)(3)(ii)(A)(1) of this section during that year.

(B) *Charge-off should have been made in earlier year.*—The conclusive presumption that a debt is worthless in the year that it is charged off for regulatory purposes applies even if the bank's supervisory authority determines in a subsequent year that the charge-off should have been made in an earlier year. A pattern of charge-offs in the wrong year, however, may result in revocation of the bank's election by the Commissioner pursuant to paragraph (d)(3)(iv)(D) of this section.

(C) *Loss asset defined.*—A debt is classified as a loss asset by a bank if the bank assigns the debt to a class that corresponds to a loss asset classification under the standards set forth in the "Uniform Agreement on the Classification of Assets and Securities Held by Banks" (See Attachment to Comptroller of the Currency Banking Circular No. 127, Rev. 4-26-91, Comptroller of the Currency, Communications Department, Washington, DC 20219) or similar guidance issued by the Office of the Comptroller of the Currency, the Federal Deposit Insurance Corporation, the Board of Governors of the Federal Reserve, or the Farm Credit Administration; or for institutions under the supervision of the Office of Thrift Supervision, 12 CFR 563.160(b)(3).

(iii) *Election.*—(A) *In general.*—An election under this paragraph (d)(3) is to be made on a bank-by-bank basis and constitutes either the adoption of or a change in method of accounting, depending on the particular bank's facts. A change in method of accounting that results from the making of an election under this paragraph (d)(3) has the effects described in paragraph (d)(3)(iii)(B) of this section.

(B) *Effect of change in method of accounting.*—A change in method of accounting resulting from an election under this paragraph (d)(3) does not require or permit an adjustment under section 481(a). Under this cut-off approach—

(1) There is no change in the §1.1011-1 adjusted basis of the bank's existing debts (as determined under the bank's former

method of accounting for bad debts) as a result of the change in method of accounting;

(2) With respect to debts that are subject to regulatory loss classification standards and are held by the bank at the beginning of the year of change (to the extent they have not been charged off for regulatory purposes), and with respect to debts subject to regulatory loss classification standards that are originated or acquired subsequent to the beginning of the year of change, bad debt deductions in the year of change and thereafter are determined under the method of accounting for bad debts prescribed by this paragraph (d)(3);

(3) With respect to debts that are not subject to regulatory loss classification standards or that have been totally charged off prior to the year of change, bad debt deductions are determined under the general rules of section 166; and

(4) If there was any partial charge-off of a debt in a pre-change year, any portion of which was not claimed as a deduction, the deduction reflecting that partial charge-off must be taken in the first year in which there is any further charge-off of the debt for regulatory purposes.

(C) Procedures.—(1) In general.—A new bank adopts the method of accounting under this paragraph (d)(3) for any taxable year ending on or after December 31, 1991 (and for all subsequent taxable years) when it adopts its overall method of accounting for bad debts, by attaching a statement to this effect to its income tax return for that year. Any other bank makes an election for any taxable year ending on or after December 31, 1991 (and for all subsequent taxable years) by filing a completed Form 3115 (Application for Change in Accounting Method) in accordance with the rules of paragraph (d)(3)(iii)(C)(2) or (3) of this section. The statement or Form 3115 must include the name, address, and taxpayer identification number of the electing bank and contain a declaration that the express determination requirement of paragraph (d)(3)(iii)(D) of this section is satisfied for the taxable year of the election. When a Form 3115 is used, the declaration must be made in the space provided on the form for "Other changes in method of accounting." The words "ELECTION UNDER §1.166-2(d)(3)" must be typed or legibly printed at the top of the statement or page 1 of the Form 3115.

(2) First election.—The first time a bank makes this election, the statement or Form 3115 must be attached to the bank's timely filed return (taking into account extensions of time to file) for the first taxable year covered by the election. The consent of the Commissioner to make a change in method of accounting under this paragraph (d)(3) is granted, pursuant to section 446(e), to any bank that makes the election in accordance with this paragraph (d)(3)(iii)(C), provided the bank has not made a prior election under this paragraph (d)(3).

(3) Subsequent elections.—The advance consent of the Commissioner is required to make any election under this paragraph (d)(3) after a previous election has been revoked pursuant to paragraph (d)(3)(iv) of this section. This consent must be requested under the procedures, terms, and conditions prescribed under the authority of section 446(e) and §1.446-1(e) for requesting a change in method of accounting.

(D) Express determination requirement.—In connection with its most recent examination involving the bank's loan review process, the bank's supervisory authority must have made an express determination (in accordance with any applicable administrative procedure prescribed hereunder) that the bank maintains and applies loan loss classification standards that are consistent with the regulatory standards of that supervisory authority. For purposes of this paragraph (d)(3)(iii)(D), the supervisory authority of a bank is the *appropriate Federal banking agency* for the bank, as that term is defined in 12 U.S.C. 1813(q), or, in the case of an institution in the Farm Credit System, the Farm Credit Administration.

(E) Transition period election.—For taxable years ending before completion of the first examination of the bank by its supervisory authority (as defined in paragraph (d)(3)(iii)(D) of this section) that is after October 1, 1992, and that involves the bank's loan review process, the statement or Form 3115 filed by the bank must include a declaration that the bank maintains and applies loan loss classification standards that are consistent with the regulatory standards of that supervisory authority. A bank that makes this declaration is deemed to satisfy the express determination requirement of paragraph (d)(3)(iii)(D) of this section for those years, even though an express determination has not yet been made.

(iv) Revocation of Election.—(A) In general.—Revocation of an election under this paragraph (d)(3) constitutes a change in method of accounting that has the effects described in paragraph (d)(3)(iv)(B) of this section. If an election under this paragraph (d)(3) has been

revoked, a bank may make a subsequent election only under the provisions of paragraph (d)(3)(iii)(C)(3) of this section.

(B) Effect of change in method of accounting.—A change in method of accounting resulting from revocation of an election under this paragraph (d)(3) does not require or permit an adjustment under section 481(a). Under this cut-off approach—

(1) There is no change in the §1.1011-1 adjusted basis of the bank's existing debts (as determined under this paragraph (d)(3) method or any other former method of accounting used by the bank with respect to its bad debts) as a result of the change in method of accounting; and

(2) Bad debt deductions in the year of change and thereafter with respect to all debts held by the bank, whether in existence at the beginning of the year of change or subsequently originated or acquired, are determined under the new method of accounting.

(C) Automatic revocation.—(1) In general.—A bank's election under this paragraph (d)(3) is revoked automatically if, in connection with any examination involving the bank's loan review process by the bank's supervisory authority as defined in paragraph (d)(3)(iii)(D) of this section, the bank does not obtain the express determination required by that paragraph.

(2) Year of revocation.—If a bank makes the conformity election under the transition rules of paragraph (d)(3)(iii)(E) of this section and does not obtain the express determination in connection with the first examination involving the bank's loan review process that is after October 1, 1992, the election is revoked as of the beginning of the taxable year of the election or, if later, the earliest taxable year for which tax may be assessed. In other cases in which a bank does not obtain an express determination in connection with an examination of its loan review process, the election is revoked as of the beginning of the taxable year that includes the date as of which the supervisory authority conducts the examination even if the examination is completed in the following taxable year.

(3) Consent granted.—Under the Commissioner's authority in section 446(e) and §1.446-1(e), the bank is directed to and is granted consent to change from this paragraph (d)(3) method as of the year of revocation (year of change) prescribed by paragraph (d)(3)(iv)(C)(2) of this section.

(4) Requirements.—A bank changing its method of accounting under the automatic revocation rules of this paragraph (d)(3)(iv)(C) must attach a completed Form 3115 to its income tax return for the year of revocation prescribed by paragraph (d)(3)(iv)(C)(2) of this section. The words "REVOCATION OF §1.166-2(d)(3) ELECTION" must be typed or legibly printed at the top of page 1 of the Form 3115. If the year of revocation is a year for which the bank has already filed its income tax return, the bank must file an amended return for that year reflecting its change in method of accounting and must attach the completed Form 3115 to that amended return. The bank also must file amended returns reflecting the new method of accounting for all subsequent taxable years for which returns have been filed and tax may be assessed.

(D) Revocation by Commissioner.—An election under this paragraph (d)(3) may be revoked by the Commissioner as of the beginning of any taxable year for which a bank fails to follow the method of accounting prescribed by this paragraph. In addition, the Commissioner may revoke an election as of the beginning of any taxable year for which the Commissioner determines that a bank has taken charge-offs and deductions that, under all facts and circumstances existing at the time, were substantially in excess of those warranted by the exercise of reasonable business judgment in applying the regulatory standards of the bank's supervisory authority as defined in paragraph (d)(3)(iii)(D) of this section.

(E) Voluntary revocation.—A bank may apply for revocation of its election made under this paragraph (d)(3) by timely filing a completed Form 3115 for the appropriate year and obtaining the consent of the Commissioner in accordance with section 446(e) and §1.446-1(e) (including any applicable administrative procedures prescribed thereunder). The words "REVOCATION OF §1.166-2(d)(3) ELECTION" must be typed or legibly printed at the top of page 1 of the Form 3115. If any bank has had its election automatically revoked pursuant to paragraph (d)(3)(iv)(C) of this section and has not changed its method of accounting in accordance with the requirements of that paragraph, the Commissioner will require that any voluntary change in method of accounting under this paragraph (d)(3)(iv)(E) be implemented retroactively pursuant to the same amended return terms and conditions as are prescribed by paragraph (d)(3)(iv)(C) of this section.

(4) Definitions.—For purposes of this paragraph (d)—

(i) *Bank.*—The term "bank" has the meaning assigned to it by section 581. The term "bank" also includes any corporation that would be a bank within the meaning of section 581 except for the fact that it is a foreign corporation, but this paragraph (d) applies only with respect to loans the interest on which is effectively connected with the conduct of a banking business within the United States. In addition, the term "bank" includes a Farm Credit System institution that is subject to supervision by the Farm Credit Administration.

(ii) *Charge-off.*—For banks regulated by the Office of Thrift Supervision, the term "charge-off" includes the establishment of specific allowances for loan losses in the amount of 100 percent of the portion of the debt classified as loss. [Reg. § 1.166-2.]

☐ [*T.D. 6403, 7-30-59. Amended by T.D. 7254, 1-24-73; T.D. 8396, 2-21-92; T.D. 8441, 10-1-92 and T.D. 8492, 10-15-93.*]

[Reg. § 1.166-3]

§ 1.166-3. Partial or total worthlessness.—(a) *Partial worthlessness.*—(1) *Applicable to specific debts only.*—A deduction under section 166 (a)(2) on account of partially worthless debts shall be allowed with respect to specific debts only.

(2) *Charge-off required.*—(i) If, from all the surrounding and attending circumstances, the district director is satisfied that a debt is partially worthless, the amount which has become worthless shall be allowed as a deduction under section 166(a)(2) but only to the extent charged off during the taxable year.

(ii) If a taxpayer claims a deduction for a part of a debt for the taxable year within which that part of the debt is charged off and the deduction is disallowed for that taxable year, then, in a case where the debt becomes partially worthless after the close of that taxable year, a deduction under section 166(a)(2) shall be allowed for a subsequent taxable year but not in excess of the amount charged off in the prior taxable year plus any amount charged off in the subsequent taxable year. In such instance, the charge-off in the prior taxable year shall, if consistently maintained as such, be sufficient to that extent to meet the charge-off requirement of section 166(a)(2) with respect to the subsequent taxable year.

(iii) Before a taxpayer may deduct a debt in part, he must be able to demonstrate to the satisfaction of the district director the amount thereof which is worthless and the part thereof which has been charged off.

(3) *Significantly modified debt.*—(i) *Deemed charge-off.*—If a significant modification of a debt instrument (within the meaning of § 1.1001-3) during a taxable year results in the recognition of gain by a taxpayer under § 1.1001-1(a), and if the requirements of paragraph (a)(3)(ii) of this section are met, there is a deemed charge-off of the debt during that taxable year in the amount specified in paragraph (a)(3)(iii) of this section.

(ii) *Requirements for deemed charge-off.*—A debt is deemed to have been charged off only if—

(A) The taxpayer (or, in the case of a debt that constitutes transferred basis property within the meaning of section 7701(a)(43), a transferor taxpayer) has claimed a deduction for partial worthlessness of the debt in any prior taxable year; and

(B) Each prior charge-off and deduction for partial worthlessness satisfied the requirements of paragraphs (a)(1) and (2) of this section.

(iii) *Amount of deemed charge-off.*—The amount of the deemed charge-off, if any, is the amount by which the tax basis of the debt exceeds the greater of the fair market value of the debt or the amount of the debt recorded on the taxpayer's books and records reduced as appropriate for a specific allowance for loan losses. The amount of the deemed charge-off, however, may not exceed the amount of recognized gain described in paragraph (a)(3)(i) of this section.

(iv) *Effective date.*—This paragraph (a)(3) applies to significant modifications of debt instruments occurring on or after September 23, 1996.

(b) *Total worthlessness.*—If a debt becomes wholly worthless during the taxable year, the amount thereof which has not been allowed as a deduction from gross income for any prior taxable year shall be allowed as a deduction for the current taxable year. [Reg. § 1.166-3.]

☐ [*T.D. 6403, 7-30-59. Amended by T.D. 8763, 1-28-98.*]

[Reg. § 1.166-4]

§ 1.166-4. Reserve for bad debts.—(a) *Allowance of deduction.*—A taxpayer who has established the reserve method of treating bad debts and has maintained proper reserve accounts for bad debts or who, in accordance with paragraph (b) of § 1.166-1, adopts the reserve method of treating bad debts may deduct from gross income a reasonable addition to a reserve for bad debts in lieu of deducting specific bad debt items. This paragraph applies both to bad debts owed to the taxpayer and to bad debts arising out of section 166(f)(1)(A) guaranteed debt obligations. If a reserve is maintained for bad debts arising out of section 166(f)(1)(A) guaranteed debt obligations, then a separate reserve must also be maintained for all other debt obligations of the taxpayer in the same trade or business, if any. A taxpayer may not maintain a reserve for bad debts arising out of section 166(f)(1)(A) guaranteed debt obligations if with respect to direct debt obligations in the same trade or business the taxpayer takes deductions when the debts become worthless in whole or in part rather than maintaining a reserve for such obligations. See § 1.166-10 for rules concerning section 166(f)(1)(A) guaranteed debt obligations.

(b) *Reasonableness of addition to reserve.*—(1) *Relevant factors.*—What constitutes a reasonable addition to a reserve for bad debts shall be determined in the light of the facts existing at the close of the taxable year of the proposed addition. The reasonableness of the addition will vary as between classes of business and with conditions of business prosperity. It will depend primarily upon the total amount of debts outstanding as of the close of the taxable year, including those arising currently as well as those arising in prior taxable years, and the total amount of the existing reserve.

(2) *Correction of errors in prior estimates.*—In the event that subsequent realizations upon outstanding debts prove to be more or less than estimated at the time of the creation of the existing reserve, the amount of the excess or inadequacy in the existing reserve shall be reflected in the determination of the reasonable addition necessary in the current taxable year.

(c) *Statement required.*—A taxpayer using the reserve method shall file with his return a statement showing—

(1) The volume of his charge sales or other business transactions for the taxable year and the percentage of the reserve to such amount;

(2) The total amount of notes and accounts receivable at the beginning and close of the taxable year;

(3) The amount of the debts which have become wholly or partially worthless and have been charged against the reserve account; and

(4) The computation of the addition to the reserve for bad debts.

(d) *Special rules applicable to financial institutions.*—For special rules for the addition to the bad debt reserves of certain banks, see §§ 1.585-1 through 1.585-3. [Reg. § 1.166-4.]

☐ [*T.D. 6403, 7-30-59. Amended by T.D. 6728, 5-4-64, T.D. 7444, 12-6-76, T.D. 8071, 1-17-86 and T.D. 9849, 3-11-2019.*]

[Reg. § 1.166-5]

§ 1.166-5. Nonbusiness debts.—(a) *Allowance of deduction as capital loss.*—(1) The loss resulting from any nonbusiness debt's becoming partially or wholly worthless within the taxable year shall not be allowed as a deduction under either section 166(a) or section 166(c) in determining the taxable income of a taxpayer other than a corporation. See section 166(d)(1)(A).

(2) If, in the case of a taxpayer other than a corporation, a nonbusiness debt becomes wholly worthless within the taxable year, the loss resulting therefrom shall be treated as a loss from the sale or exchange, during the taxable year, of a capital asset held for not more than 1 year (6 months for taxable years beginning before 1977; 9 months for taxable years beginning in 1977). Such a loss is subject to the limitations provided in section 1211, relating to the limitation on capital losses, and section 1212, relating to the capital loss carryover, and in the regulations under those sections. A loss on a nonbusiness debt shall be treated as sustained only if and when the debt has become totally worthless, and no deduction shall be allowed for a nonbusiness debt which is recoverable in part during the taxable year.

(b) *Nonbusiness debt defined.*—For purposes of section 166 and this section, a nonbusiness debt is any debt other than —

(1) A debt which is created, or acquired, in the course of a trade or business of the taxpayer, determined without regard to the relationship of the debt to a trade or business of the taxpayer at the time when the debt becomes worthless; or

(2) A debt the loss from the worthlessness of which is incurred in the taxpayer's trade or business.

The question whether a debt is a nonbusiness debt is a question of fact in each particular case. The determination of whether the loss on a debt's becoming worthless has been incurred in a trade or business of the taxpayer shall, for this purpose, be made in substantially the same manner for determining whether a loss has been incurred in a trade or business for purposes of section 165(c)(1). For purposes of subparagraph (2) of this paragraph, the character of the debt is to be determined by the relation which the loss resulting from the debt's becoming worthless bears to the trade or business of the taxpayer. If that relation is a proximate one in the conduct of the trade or business in which the taxpayer is engaged at the time the debt becomes worthless, the debt comes within the exception provided by that subparagraph. The use to which the borrowed funds are put by the debtor is of no consequence in making a determination under this paragraph. For purposes of section 166 and this section, a nonbusiness debt does not include a debt described in section 165(g)(2)(C). See §1.165-5, relating to losses on worthless securities.

(c) *Guaranty of obligations.*—For provisions treating a loss sustained by a guarantor of obligations as a loss resulting from the worthlessness of a debt, see §§1.166-8 and 1.166-9.

(d) *Examples.*—The application of this section may be illustrated by the following examples involving a case where A, an individual who is engaged in the grocery business and who makes his return on the basis of the calendar year, extends credit to B in 1955 on an open account:

Example (1). In 1956 A sells the business but retains the claim against B. The claim becomes worthless in A's hands in 1957. A's loss is not controlled by the nonbusiness debt provisions, since the original consideration has been advanced by A in his trade or business.

Example (2). In 1956 A sells the business to C but sells the claim against B to the taxpayer, D. The claim becomes worthless in D's hands in 1957. During 1956 and 1957, D is not engaged in any trade or business. D's loss is controlled by the nonbusiness debt provisions even though the original consideration has been advanced by A in his trade or business, since the debt has not been created or acquired in connection with a trade or business of D and since in 1957 D is not engaged in a trade or business incident to the conduct of which a loss from the worthlessness of such claims is a proximate result.

Example (3). In 1956 A dies, leaving the business, including the accounts receivable, to his son, C, the taxpayer. The claim against B becomes worthless in C's hands in 1957. C's loss is not controlled by the nonbusiness debt provisions. While C does not advance any consideration for the claim, or create or acquire it in connection with his trade or business, the loss is sustained as a proximate incident to the conduct of the trade or business in which he is engaged at the time the debt becomes worthless.

Example (4). In 1956 A dies, leaving the business to his son, C, but leaving the claim against B to his son, D, the taxpayer. The claim against B becomes worthless in D's hands in 1957. During 1956 and 1957, D is not engaged in any trade or business. D's loss is controlled by the nonbusiness debt provisions even though the original consideration has been advanced by A in his trade or business, since the debt has not been created or acquired in connection with a trade or business of D and since in 1957 D is not engaged in a trade or business incident to the conduct of which a loss from the worthlessness of such claims is a proximate result.

Example (5). In 1956 A dies, and, while his executor, C, is carrying on the business, the claim against B becomes worthless in 1957. The loss sustained by A's estate is not controlled by the nonbusiness debt provisions. While C does not advance any consideration for the claim on behalf of the estate, or create or acquire it in connection with a trade or business in which the estate is engaged, the loss is sustained as a proximate incident to the conduct of the trade or business in which the estate is engaged at the time the debt becomes worthless.

Example (6). In 1956, A, in liquidating the business, attempts to collect the claim against B but finds that it has become worthless. A's loss is not controlled by the nonbusiness debt provisions, since the original consideration has been advanced by A in his trade or business and since a loss incurred in liquidating a trade or business is a proximate incident to the conduct thereof. [Reg. §1.166-5.]

☐ [T.D. 6403, 7-23-59. Amended by T.D. 7657, 11-28-79 and T.D. 7728, 10-31-80.]

[Reg. §1.166-6]

§1.166-6. Sale of mortgaged or pledged property.—(a) *Deficiency deductible as bad debts.*—(1) *Principal amount.*—If mortgaged or pledged property is lawfully sold (whether to the creditor or another purchaser) for less than the amount of the debt, and the portion of the indebtedness remaining unsatisfied after the sale is wholly or partially uncollectible, the mortgagee or pledgee may deduct such amount under section 166(a) (to the extent that it constitutes capital or represents an item the income from which has been returned by him) as a bad debt for the taxable year in which it becomes wholly worthless or is charged off as partially worthless. See §1.166-3.

(2) *Accrued interest.*—Accrued interest may be included as part of the deduction allowable under this paragraph, but only if it has previously been returned as income.

(b) *Realization of gain or loss.*—(1) *Determination of amount.*—If, in the case of a sale described in paragraph (a) of this section, the creditor buys in the mortgaged or pledged property, loss or gain is also realized, measured by the difference between the amount of those obligations of the debtor which are applied to the purchase or bid price of the property (to the extent that such obligations constitute capital or represent an item the income from which has been returned by the creditor) and the fair market value of the property.

(2) *Fair market value defined.*—The fair market value of the property for this purpose shall, in the absence of clear and convincing proof to the contrary, be presumed to be the amount for which it is bid in by the taxpayer.

(c) *Basis of property purchased.*—If the creditor subsequently sells the property so acquired, the basis for determining gain or loss upon the subsequent sale is the fair market value of the property at the date of its acquisition by the creditor.

(d) *Special rules applicable to certain banking organizations.*—For special rules relating to the treatment of mortgaged or pledged property by certain mutual savings banks, domestic building and loan associations, and cooperative banks, see section 595 and the regulations thereunder.

(e) *Special rules applicable to certain reacquisitions of real property.*—Notwithstanding this section, special rules apply for taxable years beginning after September 2, 1964 (and for certain taxable years beginning after December 31, 1957), to the gain or loss on certain reacquisitions of real property, to indebtedness remaining unsatisfied as a result of such reacquisitions, and to the basis of the reacquired real property. See §§1.1038 through 1.1038-3. [Reg. §1.166-6.]

☐ [T.D. 6403, 7-30-59. Amended by T.D. 6814, 4-6-65 and T.D. 6916, 4-12-67.]

[Reg. §1.166-7]

§1.166-7. Worthless bonds issued by an individual.—(a) *Allowance of deduction.*—A bond or other similar obligation issued by an individual, if it becomes worthless in whole or in part, is subject to the bad debt provisions of section 166. The loss from the worthlessness of any such bond or obligation is deductible in accordance with section 166(a), unless such bond or obligation is a nonbusiness debt as defined in section 166(d)(2). If the bond or obligation is a nonbusiness debt, it is subject to section 166(d) and §1.166-5.

(b) *Decline in market value.*—A taxpayer possessing debts evidenced by bonds or other similar obligations issued by an individual shall not be allowed any deduction under section 166 on account of mere market fluctuation in the value of such obligations.

(c) *Worthless bonds issued by corporation.*—For provisions allowing the deduction under section 165(a) of the loss sustained upon the worthlessness of any bond or similar obligation issued by a corporation or a government, see §1.165-5.

(d) *Application to inventories.*—This section does not apply to any loss upon the worthlessness of any bond or similar obligation reflected in inventories required to be taken by a dealer in securities under section 471. See §1.471-5. [Reg. §1.166-7.]

☐ [T.D. 6403, 7-30-59.]

[Reg. §1.166-8]

§1.166-8. Losses of guarantors, endorsers, and indemnitors.—(a) *Noncorporate obligations.*—(1) *Deductible as bad debt.*—A payment during the taxable year by a taxpayer other than a corporation in discharge of part or all of his obligation as a guarantor, endorser, or indemnitor of an obligation issued by a person other than a corporation shall, for purposes of section 166 and the regulations thereunder, be treated as a debt's becoming worthless within the taxable year, if—

(i) The proceeds of the obligation so issued have been used in the trade or business of the borrower, and

(ii) The borrower's obligation to the person to whom the taxpayer's payment is made is worthless at the time of payment except for the existence of the guaranty, endorsement, or indemnity, whether or not such obligation has in fact become worthless within the taxable year in which payment is made.

(2) *Nonbusiness debt rule not applicable.*—If a payment is treated as a loss in accordance with the provisions of subparagraph (1) of this paragraph, section 166(d), relating to the special rule for losses sustained on the worthlessness of a nonbusiness debt, shall not apply. Accordingly, in each instance the loss shall be deducted under section 166(a)(1) as a wholly worthless debt even though there has been a discharge of only a part of the taxpayer's obligation. Thus, if the taxpayer makes a payment during the taxable year in discharge of only part of his obligation as a guarantor, endorser, or indemnitor, he may treat such payment under section 166(a)(1) as a debt's becoming

wholly worthless within the taxable year, provided that he can establish that such part of the borrower's obligation to the person to whom the taxpayer's payment is made is worthless at the time of payment and the conditions of subparagraph (1) of this paragraph have otherwise been satisfied.

(3) *Other applicable provisions.*—Other provisions of the internal revenue laws relating to bad debts, such as section 111, relating to the recovery of bad debts, shall be deemed to apply to any payment which, under the provisions of this paragraph, is treated as a bad debt. If the requirements of section 166(f) are not met, any loss sustained by a guarantor, endorser, or indemnitor upon the worthlessness of the debtor's obligation shall be treated under the provisions of law applicable thereto. See, for example, paragraph (b) of this section.

(b) *Corporate obligations.*—The loss sustained during the taxable year by a taxpayer other than a corporation in discharge of all of his obligation as a guarantor of an obligation issued by a corporation shall be treated, in accordance with section 166(d) and the regulations thereunder, as a loss sustained on the worthlessness of a nonbusiness debt if the debt created in the guarantor's favor as a result of the payment does not come within the exceptions prescribed by section 166(d)(2)(A) or (B). See paragraph (a)(2) of § 1.166-5.

(c) *Examples.*—The application of this section may be illustrated by the following examples:

Example (1). During 1955, A, an individual who makes his return on the basis of the calendar year, guarantees payment of an obligation of B, an individual, to the X Bank, the proceeds of the obligation being used in B's business. B defaults on his obligation in 1956. A makes payment to the X Bank during 1957 in discharge of his entire obligation as a guarantor, the obligation of B to the X Bank being wholly worthless. For his taxable year 1957, A is entitled to a deduction under section 166(a)(1) as a result of his payment during that year.

Example (2). During 1955, A, an individual who makes his return on the basis of the calendar year, guarantees payment of an obligation of B, an individual, to the X Bank, the proceeds of the obligation being used in B's business. In 1956, B pays a part of his obligation to the X Bank but defaults on the remaining part. In 1957, A makes payment to the X Bank, in discharge of part of his obligation as a guarantor, of the remaining unpaid part of B's obligation to the bank, such part of B's obligation then being worthless. For his taxable year 1957, A is entitled to a deduction under section 166(a)(1) as a result of his payment of the remaining unpaid part of B's obligation.

Example (3). During 1955, A, an individual who makes his return on the basis of the calendar year, guarantees payment of an obligation of B, an individual, to the X Bank, the proceeds of the obligation being used for B's personal use. B defaults on his obligation in 1956. A makes payment to the X Bank during 1957 in discharge of his entire obligation as a guarantor, the obligation of B to X Bank being wholly worthless. A may not apply the benefit of section 166(f) to his loss, since the proceeds of B's obligation have not been used in B's trade or business.

Example (4). During 1955, A, an individual who makes his return on the basis of the calendar year, guarantees payment of an obligation of Y Corporation to the X Bank, the proceeds of the obligation being used in Y Corporation's business. Y Corporation defaults on its obligation in 1956. A makes payment to the X Bank during 1957 in discharge of his entire obligation as a guarantor, the obligation of Y Corporation to the X Bank being wholly worthless. At no time during 1955 or 1957 is A engaged in a trade or business. For his taxable year 1957, A is entitled to deduct a capital loss in accordance with the provisions of section 166(d) and paragraph (a)(2) of § 1.166-5. He may not apply the benefit of section 166(f) to his loss, since his payment is in discharge of an obligation issued by a corporation.

(d) *Effective date.*—This section applies only to losses, regardless of the taxable year in which incurred, on agreements made before January 1, 1976. [Reg. § 1.166-8.]

☐ [*T.D. 6403, 7-30-59. Amended by T.D. 7657, 11-28-79.*]

[Reg. § 1.166-9]

§ 1.166-9. Losses of guarantors, endorsers, and indemnitors incurred, on agreements made after December 31, 1975, in taxable years beginning after such date.—(a) *Payment treated as worthless business debt.*—This paragraph applies to taxpayers who, after December 31, 1975, enter into an agreement in the course of their trade or business to act as (or in a manner essentially equivalent to) a guarantor, endorser, or indemnitor of (or other secondary obligor upon) a debt obligation. Subject to the provisions of paragraphs (c), (d), and (e) of this section, a payment of principal or interest made during a taxable year beginning after December 31, 1975, by the taxpayer in discharge of part or all of the taxpayer's obligation as a guarantor, endorser, or indemnitor is treated as a business debt becoming worthless in the taxable year in which the payment is made or in the taxable year described in paragraph (e)(2) of this section. Neither section 163 (relating to interest) nor section 165 (relating to losses) shall apply with respect to such a payment.

(b) *Payment treated as worthless nonbusiness debt.*—This paragraph applies to taxpayers (other than corporations) who, after December 31, 1975, enter into a transaction for profit, but not in the course of their trade or business, to act as (or in a manner essentially equivalent to) a guarantor, endorser, or indemnitor of (or other secondary obligor upon) a debt obligation. Subject to the provisions of paragraphs (c), (d), and (e) of this section, a payment of principal or interest made during a taxable year beginning after December 31, 1975, by the taxpayer in discharge of part or all of the taxpayer's obligation as a guarantor, endorser, or indemnitor is treated as a worthless nonbusiness debt in the taxable year in which the payment is made or in the taxable year described in paragraph (e)(2) of this section. Neither section 163 nor section 165 shall apply with respect to such a payment.

(c) *Obligations issued by corporations.*—No treatment as a worthless debt is allowed with respect to a payment made by the taxpayer in discharge of part or all of the taxpayer's obligation as a guarantor, endorser, or indemnitor of an obligation issued by a corporation if, on the basis of the facts and circumstances at the time the obligation was entered into, the payment constitutes a contribution to capital by a shareholder. The rule of this paragraph (c) applies to payments whenever made (see paragraph (f) of this section).

(d) *Certain payments treated as worthless debts.*—A payment in discharge of part or all of taxpayer's agreement to act as guarantor, endorser, or indemnitor of an obligation is to be treated as a worthless debt only if—

(1) The agreement was entered into in the course of the taxpayer's trade or business or a transaction for profit;

(2) There was an enforceable legal duty upon the taxpayer to make the payment (except that legal action need not have been brought against the taxpayer); and

(3) The agreement was entered into before the obligation became worthless (or partially worthless in the case of an agreement entered into in the course of the taxpayer's trade or business). See §§ 1.166-2 and 1.166-3 for rules on worthless and partially worthless debts. For purposes of this paragraph (d)(3), an agreement is considered as entered into before the obligation became worthless (or partially worthless) if there was a reasonable expectation on the part of the taxpayer at the time the agreement was entered into that the taxpayer would not be called upon to pay the debt (subject to such agreement) without full reimbursement from the issuer of the obligation.

(e) *Special rules.*—(1) *Reasonable consideration required.*—Treatment as a worthless debt of a payment made by a taxpayer in discharge of part or all of the taxpayer's agreement to act as a guarantor, endorser, or indemnitor of an obligation is allowed only if the taxpayer demonstrates that reasonable consideration was received for entering into the agreement. For purposes of this paragraph (e)(1), reasonable consideration is not limited to direct consideration in the form of cash or property. Thus, where a taxpayer can demonstrate that the agreement was given without direct consideration in the form of cash or property but in accordance with normal business practice or for a good faith business purpose, worthless debt treatment is allowed with respect to a payment in discharge of part or all of the agreement if the conditions of this section are met. However, consideration received from a taxpayer's spouse or any individual listed in section 152(a) must be direct consideration in the form of cash or property.

(2) *Right of subrogation.*—With respect to a payment made by a taxpayer in discharge of part or all of the taxpayer's agreement to act as a guarantor, endorser, or indemnitor where the agreement provides for a right of subrogation or other similar right against the issuer, treatment as a worthless debt is not allowed until the taxable year in which the right of subrogation or other similar right becomes totally worthless (or partially worthless in the case of an agreement which arose in the course of the taxpayer's trade or business).

(3) *Other applicable provisions.*—Unless inconsistent with this section, other Internal Revenue laws concerning worthless debts, such as section 111 relating to the recovery of bad debts, apply to any payment which, under the provisions of this section, is treated as giving rise to a worthless debt.

(4) *Taxpayer defined.*—For purposes of this section, except as otherwise provided, the term "taxpayer" means any taxpayer and includes individuals, corporations, partnerships, trusts and estates.

(f) *Effective date.*—This section applies to losses incurred on agreements made after December 31, 1975, in taxable years beginning after such date. However, paragraph (c) of this section also applies to payments, regardless of the taxable year in which made, under agreements made before January 1, 1976. [Reg. §1.166-9.]

□ [T.D. 7657, 11-28-79. *Amended by T.D. 7747,* 12-29-80 *and T.D. 7920,* 11-2-83.]

[Reg. §1.166-10]

§1.166-10. Reserve for guaranteed debt obligations.—(a) *Definitions.*—The following provisions apply for purposes of this section and section 166(f):

(1) *Dealer in property.*—A dealer in property is a person who regularly sells property in the ordinary course of the person's trade or business.

(2) *Guaranteed debt obligation.*—A guaranteed debt obligation is a legal duty of one person as a guarantor, endorser or indemnitor of a second person to pay a third person. It does not include duties based solely on moral or good public relations considerations that are not legally binding. A guaranteed debt obligation typically arises where a seller receives in payment for property or services the debt obligation of a purchaser and sells that obligation to a third party with recourse. However, a guaranteed debt obligation also may arise out of a sale in respect of which there is no direct debtor-creditor relationship between the debtor purchaser and the seller. For example, it arises where a purchaser borrows money from a third party to make payment to the seller and the seller guarantees the payment of the purchaser's debt. Generally, debt obligations which are sold without recourse do not result in any obligation of the seller as a guarantor, endorser, or indemnitor. However, there are certain without-recourse transactions which may give rise to a seller's liability as a guarantor or indemnitor. For example, such a liability may arise where a holder of a debt obligation holds money or other property of a seller which the holder may apply, without seeking permission of the seller, against any uncollectible debt obligations transferred to the holder by the seller without recourse, or where the seller is under a legal obligation to reacquire the real or tangible personal property from the holder of the debt obligation who repossessed property in satisfaction of the debt obligations.

(3) *Real or tangible personal property.*—Real or tangible personal property generally does not include other forms of property, such as securities. However, if the sale of other property is related to the sale of actual real or tangible personal property, the other property will be considered to be real or tangible personal property. In order for the sale of other property to be related, it must be—

(i) Incidental to the sale of the actual real or tangible personal property; and

(ii) Made under an agreement, entered into at the same time as the sale of actual real or tangible personal property, between the dealer in that property and the customer with respect to that property.

The other property may be charged for as a part of, or in addition to, the sales price of the actual real or tangible personal property. If the value of the other property is not greater than 20 percent of the total sales price, including the value of all related services other than financing services, the sale of the other property is related to the sale of actual real or tangible personal property.

(4) *Related services.*—In the case of a sale of both property and services a determination must be made as to whether the services are related to the property. Related services include only those services which are—

(i) Incidental to the sale of the real or tangible personal property; and

(ii) To be performed under an agreement, entered into at the same time as the sale of the property, between the dealer in property and the customer with respect to the property.

Delivery, financing, installation, maintenance, repair, or instructional services generally qualify as related services. The services may be charged for as a part of, or in addition to, the sales price of the property. Where the value of all services other than financing services is not greater than 20 percent of the total of the sales price of the property, including the value of all the services other than financing services, all of the services are considered to be incidental to the sale of the property. Where the value of the services is greater than 20 percent, the determination as to whether a service is a related service in a particular case is to be made on the basis of all relevant facts and circumstances.

(5) *Examples.*—The following examples apply to paragraph (a)(4) of this section:

Example (1). A, a dealer in television sets, sells a television set to B, his customer. If at the time of the sale A, for a separate charge

which is added to the sales price of the set and which is not greater than 20 percent of the total sales price, provides a 3-year service contract on only that television set, the service contract is a related service agreement. However, if A does not sell the service contract to B contemporaneously with the sale of the television set, as would be the case if the service agreement were entered into after the sale of the set were completed, or if the service contract includes services for a television set in addition to the one then sold by A to B, the service contract is not an agreement for a related service.

Example (2). C, an automobile dealer, at the time of the sale by C of an automobile to D, agrees to make available to D driving instructions furnished by the M driving school, the cost of which is included in the sale price of the automobile and is not greater than 20 percent of the total sales price. C also agrees to pay M for the driving instructions furnished to D. Since C's agreement with D to make available driving instructions is incidental to the sale of the automobile, is made contemporaneously with the sale, and is charged for as part of the sales price of the automobile, it is an agreement for a related service. In contrast, however, because M's agreement with C is not an agreement between the dealer in property and the customer, M's agreement with C to provide driving instructions to C's customers is not an agreement for a related service.

(b) *Incorporation by reference of section 166(c) rules.*—A reserve for section 166(f)(1)(A) guaranteed debt obligations must be established and maintained under the rules applicable to the reserve for bad debts under section 166(c) (with the exception of the statement requirement under §1.166-4(c)). For example, the rules in §1.166-4(b), relating to what constitutes a reasonable addition to a reserve for bad debts and to correction of errors in prior estimates, apply to a reserve for section 166(f)(1)(A) guaranteed debt obligations as well.

(c) *Special requirements.*—Any reserve for section 166(f)(1)(A) guaranteed debt obligations must be established and maintained separately from any reserve for other debt obligations. In addition, a taxpayer who charges off direct debts when they become worthless in whole or in part rather than maintaining a reserve for such obligations may not maintain a reserve for section 166(f)(1)(A) guaranteed debt obligations in the same trade or business.

(d) *Requirement of statement.*—A taxpayer who uses the reserve method of treating section 166(f)(1)(A) guaranteed debt obligations must attach to his return for each taxable year, returns for which are filed after April 17, 1986, and for each trade or business for which the reserve is maintained a statement showing—

(1) The total amount of these obligations at the beginning of the taxable year;

(2) The total amount of these obligations incurred during the taxable year;

(3) The amount of the initial balance of the suspense account, if any, established with respect to these obligations;

(4) The balance of the suspense account, if any, at the beginning of the taxable year;

(5) The adjustment, if any, to that account;

(6) The adjusted balance, if any, at the close of the taxable year;

(7) The reconciliation of the beginning and closing balances of the reserve for these obligations and the computation of the addition to the reserve; and

(8) The taxable year for which the reserve for these obligations was established.

(e) *Computation of opening balance.*—(1) *In general.*—The opening balance of a reserve for section 166(f)(1)(A) guaranteed debt obligations established for the first taxable year for which a taxpayer maintains such a reserve shall be determined as if the taxpayer had maintained such a reserve for the taxable years preceding that taxable year. The amount of the opening balance may be determined under the following formula:

$$OB = CG \times \frac{SNL}{SG}$$

where—

OB = the opening balance at the beginning of the first taxable year

CG = the amount of these obligations at the close of the last preceding taxable year

SG = the sum of the amounts of these obligations at the close of the five preceding taxable years

SNL = the sum of the amounts of net losses arising from these obligations for the five preceding taxable years

(2) *Example.*—The following example applies to paragraph (e)(1) of this section.

Example. For 1977, A, a dealer in automobiles who uses the calendar year as the taxable year, adopts in accordance with this section the reserve method of treating section 166(f)(1)(A) guaranteed

Year	Obligations outstanding at close of year
1972	$0
1973	780,000
1974	795,000
1975	850,000
1976	820,000
Totals	$3,245,000

The opening balance for 1977 of A's reserve for these obligations is $8,200, determined as follows:

$$\$8,200 = \$820,000 \times \frac{\$32,450}{\$3,245,000}$$

(3) *More appropriate balance.*—A taxpayer may select a balance other than the one produced under paragraph (e)(1) of this section if it is more appropriate, based upon the taxpayer's actual experience, and in the event the taxpayer's return is examined, if the balance is approved by the district director.

(4) *No losses in the five preceding taxable years.*—If a taxpayer is in the taxpayer's first taxable year of a particular trade or business, or if the taxpayer has no losses arising from section 166(f)(1)(A) guaranteed debt obligations in a particular trade or business for any other reason in the five preceding taxable years, then the taxpayer's opening balance is zero for that particular trade or business.

(5) *Where reserve method was used before October 22, 1965.*—If for a taxable year ending before October 22, 1965, the taxpayer maintained a reserve for bad debts under section 166(c) which included guaranteed debt obligations described in section 166(f)(1)(A), and if the taxpayer is allowed a deduction referred to in paragraph (g)(2) of this section on account of those obligations, the amount of the opening

(1)	Taxable year	1977
(2)	Closing reserve account balance	$8,400
(3)	Opening suspense account balance	$8,200
(4)	Line (2) less line (3)	$200
(5)	Adjustment to suspense account balance	0
(6)	Closing suspense account balance (line 3 plus line 5)	$8,200

(g) *Effective date.*—(1) *In general.*—This section is generally effective for taxable years ending after October 21, 1965.

(2) *Transitional rule.*—Section 2(b) of the Act of November 2, 1966 (Pub. L. 89-722, 80 Stat. 1151) allows additions to section 166(c) bad debt reserves in earlier taxable years on account of section 166(f)(1)(A) guaranteed debt obligations to be deducted for those earlier taxable years. Paragraphs (c), (d), (e), and (f) of this section do not apply in determining whether a deduction is allowed under section 2(b) of the Act. See Rev. Rul. 68-313 (1968-1 C.B. 75) for rules relating to that deduction. [Reg. § 1.166-10.]

□ [*T.D. 8071*, 1-17-86.]

[Reg. § 1.167(a)-1]

§ 1.167(a)-1. Depreciation in general.—(a) *Reasonable allowance.*—Section 167(a) provides that a reasonable allowance for the exhaustion, wear and tear, and obsolescence of property used in the trade or business or of property held by the taxpayer for the production of income shall be allowed as a depreciation deduction. The allowance is that amount which should be set aside for the taxable year in accordance with a reasonably consistent plan (not necessarily at a uniform rate), so that the aggregate of the amounts set aside, plus the salvage value, will, at the end of the estimated useful life of the depreciable property, equal the cost or other basis of the property as provided in section 167(g) and § 1.167(g)-1. An asset shall not be depreciated below a reasonable salvage value under any method of computing depreciation. However, see section 167(f) and § 1.167(f)-1 for rules which permit a reduction in the amount of salvage value to be taken into account for certain personal property acquired after October 16, 1962. See also paragraph (c) of this section for definition of salvage. The allowance shall not reflect amounts representing a

debt obligations. A's first year in business as an automobile dealer is 1973. For 1972, 1973, 1974, 1975, and 1976, A's records disclose the following information with respect to these obligations:

Gross losses from these obligations	Recoveries from these obligations	Net losses from these obligations
$0	$0	$0
9,700	1,000	8,700
8,900	1,050	7,850
8,850	850	8,000
9,300	1,400	7,900
$36,750	$4,300	$32,450

balance of the reserve for section 166(f)(1)(A) guaranteed debt obligations for the taxpayer's first taxable year ending after October 21, 1965, shall be an amount equal to that portion of the section 166(c) reserve at the close of the last taxable year which is attributable to those debt obligations. The amount of the balance of the section 166(c) reserve for the taxable year shall be reduced by the amount of the opening balance of the reserve for those guaranteed debt obligations.

(f) *Suspense account.*—(1) *Zero opening balance cases.*—No suspense account shall be maintained if the opening balance of the reserve for section 166(f)(1)(A) guaranteed debt obligations under section 166(f)(3) is zero.

(2) *Example.*—The following example applies to section 166(f)(4)(B), relating to adjustments to the suspense account:

Example. In 1977, A, an individual who operates an appliance store and uses the calendar year as the taxable year, adopts the reserve method of treating section 166(f)(1)(A) guaranteed debt obligations. The initial balance of A's suspense account is $8,200. At the close of 1977, 1978, 1979, and 1980, the balance of A's reserve for these obligations is $8,400, $8,250, $8,150, and $8,175, respectively, after making the addition to the reserve for each year. The adjustments under section 166(f)(4)(B) to the suspense account at the close of each of the years involved are as follows:

1978	1979	1980
$8,250	$8,150	$8,175
$8,200	$8,200	$8,150
$50	$(50)	$25
0	$(50)	$25
$8,200	$8,150	$8,175

mere reduction in market value. See section 179 and § 1.179-1 for a further description of the term "reasonable allowance."

(b) *Useful life.*—For the purpose of section 167 the estimated useful life of an asset is not necessarily the useful life inherent in the asset but is the period over which the asset may reasonably be expected to be useful to the taxpayer in his trade or business or in the production of his income. This period shall be determined by reference to his experience with similar property taking into account present conditions and probable future developments. Some of the factors to be considered in determining this period are (1) wear and tear and decay or decline from natural causes, (2) the normal progress of the art, economic changes, inventions, and current developments within the industry and the taxpayer's trade or business, (3) the climatic and other local conditions peculiar to the taxpayer's trade or business, and (4) the taxpayer's policy as to repairs, renewals, and replacements. Salvage value is not a factor for the purpose of determining useful life. If the taxpayer's experience is inadequate, the general experience in the industry may be used until such time as the taxpayer's own experience forms an adequate basis for making the determination. The estimated remaining useful life may be subject to modification by reason of conditions known to exist at the end of the taxable year and shall be redetermined when necessary regardless of the method of computing depreciation. However, estimated remaining useful life shall be redetermined only when the change in the useful life is significant and there is a clear and convincing basis for the redetermination. For rules covering agreements with respect to useful life, see section 167(d) and § 1.167(d)-1. If a taxpayer claims an investment credit with respect to an asset for a taxable year preceding the taxable year in which the asset is considered as placed in service under § 1.167(a)-10(b) or § 1.167(a)-11(e), the useful life of the

(c) *Salvage.*—(1) Salvage value is the amount (determined at the time of acquisition) which is estimated will be realizable upon sale or other disposition of an asset when it is no longer useful in the taxpayer's trade or business or in the production of his income and is to be retired from service by the taxpayer. Salvage value shall not be changed at any time after the determination made at the time of acquisition merely because of changes in price levels. However, if there is a redetermination of useful life under the rules of paragraph (b) of this section, salvage value may be redetermined based upon facts known at the time of such redetermination of useful life. Salvage, when reduced by the cost of removal, is referred to as net salvage. The time at which an asset is retired from service may vary according to the policy of the taxpayer. If the taxpayer's policy is to dispose of assets which are still in good operating condition, the salvage value may represent a relatively large proportion of the original basis of the asset. However, if the taxpayer customarily uses an asset until its inherent useful life has been substantially exhausted, salvage value may represent no more than junk value. Salvage value must be taken into account in determining the depreciation deduction either by a reduction of the amount subject to depreciation or by a reduction in the rate of depreciation, but in no event shall an asset (or an account) be depreciated below a reasonable salvage value. See, however, paragraph (a) of §1.167(b)-2 for the treatment of salvage under the declining balance method, and §1.179-1 for the treatment of salvage in computing the additional first-year depreciation allowance. The taxpayer may use either salvage or net salvage in determining depreciation allowances but such practice must be consistently followed and the treatment of the costs of removal must be consistent with the practice adopted. For specific treatment of salvage value, see §§1.167(b)-1, 1.167(b)-2, and 1.167(b)-3. When an asset is retired or disposed of, appropriate adjustments shall be made in the asset and depreciation reserve accounts. For example, the amount of the salvage adjusted for the costs of removal may be credited to the depreciation reserve.

(2) For taxable years beginning after December 31, 1961, and ending after October 16, 1962, see section 167(f) and §1.167(f)-1 for rules applicable to the reduction of salvage value taken into account for certain personal property acquired after October 16, 1962. [Reg. §1.167(a)-1.]

☐ [*T.D. 6182, 6-11-56. Amended by T.D. 6507, 12-1-60, T.D. 6712, 3-23-64 and T.D. 7203, 8-24-72.*]

[Reg. §1.167(a)-2]

§1.167(a)-2. Tangible property.—The depreciation allowance in the case of tangible property applies only to that part of the property which is subject to wear and tear, to decay or decline from natural causes, to exhaustion, and to obsolescence. The allowance does not apply to inventories or stock in trade, or to land apart from the improvements of physical development added to it. The allowance does not apply to natural resources which are subject to the allowance for depletion provided in section 611. No deduction for depreciation shall be allowed on automobiles or other vehicles used solely for pleasure, on a building used by the taxpayer solely as his residence, or on furniture or furnishings therein, personal effects, or clothing; but properties and costumes used exclusively in a business, such as a theatrical business, may be depreciated. [Reg. §1.167(a)-2.]

☐ [*T.D. 6182, 6-11-56.*]

⟫→ Caution: Reg. §1.167(a)-4, below, as amended by T.D. 9636, generally applies to tax years beginning on or after January 1, 2014; see Reg. §1.167(a)-4(b), below, for details and exceptions.

[Reg. §1.167(a)-4]

§1.167(a)-4. Leased property.—(a) *In general.*—Capital expenditures made by either a lessee or lessor for the erection of a building or for other permanent improvements on leased property are recovered by the lessee or lessor under the provisions of the Internal Revenue Code (Code) applicable to the cost recovery of the building or improvements, if subject to depreciation or amortization, without regard to the period of the lease. For example, if the building or improvement is property to which section 168 applies, the lessee or lessor determines the depreciation deduction for the building or improvement under section 168. See section 168(i)(8)(A). If the improvement is property to which section 167 or section 197 applies, the lessee or lessor determines the depreciation or amortization deduction for the improvement under section 167 or section 197, as applicable.

(b) *Effective/applicability date.*—(1) *In general.*—Except as provided in paragraph (b)(2) or (b)(3) of this section, this section applies to taxable years beginning on or after January 1, 2014.

[Reg. §1.167(a)-3]

§1.167(a)-3. Intangibles.—(a) *In general.*—If an intangible asset is known from experience or other factors to be of use in the business or in the production of income for only a limited period, the length of which can be estimated with reasonable accuracy, such an intangible asset may be the subject of a depreciation allowance. Examples are patents and copyrights. An intangible asset, the useful life of which is not limited, is not subject to the allowance for depreciation. No allowance will be permitted merely because, in the unsupported opinion of the taxpayer, the intangible asset has a limited useful life. No deduction for depreciation is allowable with respect to good will. For rules with respect to organizational expenditures, see section 248 and the regulations thereunder. For rules with respect to trademark and trade name expenditures, see section 177 and the regulations thereunder. See sections 197 and 167(f) and, to the extent applicable, §§1.197-2 and 1.167(a)-14 for amortization of goodwill and certain other intangibles acquired after August 10, 1993, or after July 25, 1991, if a valid retroactive election under §1.197-1T has been made.

(b) *Safe harbor amortization for certain intangible assets.*—(1) *Useful life.*—Solely for purposes of determining the depreciation allowance referred to in paragraph (a) of this section, a taxpayer may treat an intangible asset as having a useful life equal to 15 years unless—

(i) An amortization period or useful life for the intangible asset is specifically prescribed or prohibited by the Internal Revenue Code, the regulations thereunder (other than by this paragraph (b)), or other published guidance in the Internal Revenue Bulletin (see §601.601(d)(2) of this chapter);

(ii) The intangible asset is described in §1.263(a)-4(c) (relating to intangibles acquired from another person) or §1.263(a)-4(d)(2) (relating to created financial interests);

(iii) The intangible asset has a useful life the length of which can be estimated with reasonable accuracy; or

(iv) The intangible asset is described in §1.263(a)-4(d)(8) (relating to certain benefits arising from the provision, production, or improvement of real property), in which case the taxpayer may treat the intangible asset as having a useful life equal to 25 years solely for purposes of determining the depreciation allowance referred to in paragraph (a) of this section.

(2) *Applicability to acquisitions of a trade or business, changes in the capital structure of a business entity, and certain other transactions.*—The safe harbor useful life provided by paragraph (b)(1) of this section does not apply to an amount required to be capitalized by §1.263(a)-5 (relating to amounts paid to facilitate an acquisition of a trade or business, a change in the capital structure of a business entity, and certain other transactions).

(3) *Depreciation method.*—A taxpayer that determines its depreciation allowance for an intangible asset using the 15-year useful life prescribed by paragraph (b)(1) of this section (or the 25-year useful life in the case of an intangible asset described in §1.263(a)-4(d)(8)) must determine the allowance by amortizing the basis of the intangible asset (as determined under section 167(c) and without regard to salvage value) ratably over the useful life beginning on the first day of the month in which the intangible asset is placed in service by the taxpayer. The intangible asset is not eligible for amortization in the month of disposition.

(4) *Effective date.*—This paragraph (b) applies to intangible assets created on or after December 31, 2003. [Reg. §1.167(a)-3.]

☐ [*T.D. 6182, 6-11-56. Amended by T.D. 6452, 2-3-60; T.D. 8865, 1-20-2000 and T.D. 9107, 12-31-2003.*]

(2) *Application of this section to leasehold improvements placed in service after December 31, 1986, in taxable years beginning before January 1, 2014.*—For leasehold improvements placed in service after December 31, 1986, in taxable years beginning before January 1, 2014, a taxpayer may—

(i) Apply the provisions of this section; or

(ii) Depreciate any leasehold improvement to which section 168 applies under the provisions of section 168 and depreciate or amortize any leasehold improvement to which section 168 does not apply under the provisions of the Code that are applicable to the cost recovery of that leasehold improvement, without regard to the period of the lease.

(3) *Application of this section to leasehold improvements placed in service before January 1, 1987.*—Section 1.167(a)-4 as contained in 26 CFR part 1 edition revised as of April 1, 2011, applies to leasehold improvements placed in service before January 1, 1987.

(4) *Change in method of accounting.*—Except as provided in §1.446-1(e)(2)(ii)(d)(3)(i), a change to comply with this section for

Itemized Deductions for Individuals and Corps.
See p. 20,601 for regulations not amended to reflect law changes
25,399

>>> *Caution: Reg. §1.167(a)-4, below, as amended by T.D. 9636, generally applies to tax years beginning on or after January 1, 2014; see Reg. §1.167(a)-4(b), below, for details and exceptions.*

depreciable assets placed in service in a taxable year ending on or after December 30, 2003, is a change in method of accounting to which the provisions of section 446(e) and the regulations under section 446(e) apply. Except as provided in § 1.446-1(e)(2)(ii)(*d*)(3)(*i*), a taxpayer also may treat a change to comply with this section for depreciable assets placed in service in a taxable year ending before December 30, 2003, as a change in method of accounting to which the provisions of section 446(e) and the regulations under section 446(e) apply. [Reg. § 1.167(a)-4.]

□ [*T.D. 6182, 6-11-56. Amended by T.D. 6520, 12-23-60; T.D. 9564, 12-23-2011 and T.D. 9636, 9-13-2013.*]

[Reg. § 1.167(a)-5]

§ 1.167(a)-5. Apportionment of basis.—In the case of the acquisition on or after March 1, 1913, of a combination of depreciable and nondepreciable property for a lump sum, as for example, buildings and land, the basis for depreciation cannot exceed an amount which bears the same proportion to the lump sum as the value of the depreciable property at the time of acquisition bears to the value of the entire property at that time. In the case of property which is subject to both the allowance for depreciation and amortization, depreciation is allowable only with respect to the portion of the depreciable property which is not subject to the allowance for amortization and may be taken concurrently with the allowance for amortization. After the close of the amortization period or after amortization deductions have been discontinued with respect to any such property, the unrecovered cost or other basis of the depreciable portion of such property will be subject to depreciation. For adjustments to basis, see section 1016 and other applicable provisions of law. For the adjustment to the basis of a structure in the case of a donation of a qualified conservation contribution under section 170(h), see § 1.170A-14(h)(3)(iii). [Reg. § 1.167(a)-5.]

□ [*T.D. 6182, 6-11-56. Amended by T.D. 8069, 1-13-86.*]

[Reg. § 1.167(a)-5T]

§ 1.167(a)-5T. Application of section 1060 to section 167 (temporary).—In the case of an acquisition of a combination of depreciable and nondepreciable property for a lump sum in an applicable asset acquisition to which section 1060 applies, the basis for depreciation of the depreciable property cannot exceed the amount of consideration allocated to that property under section 1060 and § 1.1060-1T. [Temporary Reg. § 1.167(a)-5T.]

□ [*T.D. 8215, 7-15-88.*]

[Reg. § 1.167(a)-6]

§ 1.167(a)-6. Depreciation in special cases.—(a) *Depreciation of patents or copyrights.*—The cost or other basis of a patent or copyright shall be depreciated over its remaining useful life. Its cost to the patentee includes the various Government fees, cost of drawings, models, attorneys' fees, and similar expenditures. For rules applicable to research and experimental expenditures, see sections 174 and 1016 and the regulations thereunder. If a patent or copyright becomes valueless in any year before its expiration the unrecovered cost or other basis may be deducted in that year. See § 1.167(a)-14(c)(4) for depreciation of a separately acquired interest in a patent or copyright described in section 167(f)(2) acquired after January 25, 2000. See § 1.197-2 for amortization of interests in patents and copyrights that constitute amortizable section 197 intangibles.

(b) *Depreciation in case of farmers.*—A reasonable allowance for depreciation may be claimed on farm buildings (except a dwelling occupied by the owner), farm machinery, and other physical property but not including land. Livestock acquired for work, breeding, or dairy purposes may be depreciated unless included in an inventory used to determine profits in accordance with section 61 and the regulations thereunder. Such depreciation should be determined with reference to the cost or other basis, salvage value, and the estimated useful life of the livestock. See also section 162 and the regulations thereunder relating to trade or business expenses, section 165 and the regulations thereunder relating to losses of farmers, and section 175 and the regulations thereunder relating to soil or water conservation expenditures. [Reg. § 1.167(a)-6.]

□ [*T.D. 6182, 6-11-56. Amended by T.D. 8865, 1-20-2000.*]

[Reg. § 1.167(a)-7]

§ 1.167(a)-7. Accounting for depreciable property.—(a) Depreciable property may be accounted for by treating each individual item as an account, or by combining two or more assets in a single account. Assets may be grouped in an account in a variety of ways. For example, assets similar in kind with approximately the same useful lives may be grouped together. Such an account is commonly known as a group account. Another appropriate grouping might consist of assets segregated according to use without regard to useful life, for example, machinery and equipment, furniture and fixtures, or transportation equipment. Such an account is commonly known as a classified account. A broader grouping, where assets are included in the same account regardless of their character or useful lives, is commonly referred to as a composite account. For example, all the assets used in a business may be included in a single account. Group, classified, or composite accounts may be further broken down on the basis of location, dates of acquisition, cost, character, use, etc.

(b) When group, classified, or composite accounts are used with average useful lives and a normal retirement occurs, the full cost or other basis of the asset retired, unadjusted for depreciation or salvage, shall be removed from the asset account and shall be charged to the depreciation reserve. Amounts representing salvage ordinarily are credited to the depreciation reserve. Where an asset is disposed of for reasons other than normal retirement, the full cost or other basis of the asset shall be removed from the asset account, and the depreciation reserve shall be charged with the depreciation applicable to the retired asset. For rules with respect to losses on normal retirements, see § 1.167(a)-8.

(c) A taxpayer may establish as many accounts for depreciable property as he desires. Depreciation allowances shall be computed separately for each account. Such depreciation preferably should be recorded in a depreciation reserve account; however, in appropriate cases it may be recorded directly in the asset account. Where depreciation reserves are maintained, a separate reserve account shall be maintained for each asset account. The regular books of account or permanent auxiliary records shall show for each account the basis of the property, including adjustments necessary to conform to the requirements of section 1016 and other provisions of law relating to adjustments to basis, and the depreciation allowances for tax purposes. In the event that reserves for book purposes do not correspond with reserves maintained for tax purposes, permanent auxiliary records shall be maintained with the regular books of account reconciling the differences in depreciation for tax and book purposes because of different methods of depreciation, bases, rates, salvage, or other factors. Depreciation schedules filed with the income tax return shall show the accumulated reserves computed in accordance with the allowances for income tax purposes.

(d) In classified or composite accounts, the average useful life and rate shall be redetermined whenever additions, retirements, or replacements substantially alter the relative proportion of types of assets in the accounts. See example (2) in paragraph (b) of § 1.167(b)-1 for a method of determining the depreciation rate for a classified or composite account.

(e) *Applicability.*—Paragraphs (a), (b), and (d) of this section apply to property for which depreciation is determined under section 167 (but not under section 168, section 1400I, section 1400L(c), section 168 prior to its amendment by the Tax Reform Act of 1986, Public Law 99-514 (100 Stat. 2121 (1986)), or under an additional first year depreciation deduction provision of the Internal Revenue Code (for example, section 168(k) through (n), 1400L(b), or 1400N(d))). Paragraph (c) of this section does not apply to general asset accounts as provided by section 168(i)(4), § 1.168(i)-1, § 1.168(i)-1T and Prop. Reg. § 1.168(i)-1 (September 19, 2013).

(f) *Effective/applicability date.*—(1) *In general.*—This section applies to taxable years beginning on or after January 1, 2014. Except as provided in paragraphs (f)(2) and (f)(3) of this section, § 1.167(a)-7 as contained in 26 CFR part 1 edition revised as of April 1, 2011, applies to taxable years beginning before January 1, 2014.

(2) *Early application of § 1.167(a)-7(e).*—A taxpayer may choose to apply paragraph (e) of this section to taxable years beginning on or after January 1, 2012.

(3) *Optional application of TD 9564.*—A taxpayer may choose to apply § 1.167(a)-7T as contained in TD 9564 (76 FR 81060) December 27, 2011, to taxable years beginning on or after January 1, 2012, and before January 1, 2014. [Reg. § 1.167(a)-7.]

□ [*T.D. 6182, 6-11-56. Amended by T.D. 9564, 12-23-2011 and T.D. 9636, 9-13-2013.*]

>>> *Caution: Temporary Reg. §1.167(a)-7T, below, was removed by T.D. 9636, but a taxpayer may choose to apply Temporary Reg. §1.167(a)-7T to tax years beginning on or after January 1, 2012, and before January 1, 2014.*

[Reg. §1.167(a)-7T]

§1.167(a)-7T. Accounting for depreciable property (Temporary).—(a) through (d) [Reserved]. For further guidance, see §1.167(a)-7(a) through (d).

(e) *Applicability.*—Paragraphs (a), (b), and (d) of this section apply to property for which depreciation is determined under section 167 (but not under section 168, section 1400L, section 1400L(c), section 168 prior to its amendment by the Tax Reform Act of 1986 (100 Stat. 2121), or under an additional first year depreciation deduction provision of the Internal Revenue Code (for example, section 168(k) through (n), 1400L(b), or 1400N(d))). Paragraph (c) of this section does not apply to general asset accounts as provided by section 168(i)(4) and §1.168(i)-1T.

(f) *Effective/applicability date.*—(1) *In general.*—This section applies to taxable years beginning on or after January 1, 2014. Section 1.167(a)-7 as contained in 26 CFR part 1 edition revised as of April 1, 2011, applies to taxable years beginning before January 1, 2014.

(2) *Optional early application.*—A taxpayer may choose to apply this section to taxable years beginning on or after January 1, 2012.

(g) *Expiration date.*—The applicability of this section expires on December 23, 2014. [Temporary Reg. §1.167(a)-7T.]

☐ [T.D. 9564, 12-23-2011 (corrected 12-14-2012). Removed by T.D. 9636, 9-13-2013.]

[Reg. §1.167(a)-8]

§1.167(a)-8. Retirements.—(a) *Gains and losses on retirements.*—For the purposes of this section the term "retirement" means the permanent withdrawal of depreciable property from use in the trade or business or in the production of income. The withdrawal may be made in one of several ways. For example, the withdrawal may be made by selling or exchanging the asset, or by actual abandonment. In addition, the asset may be withdrawn from such productive use without disposition as, for example, by being placed in a supplies or scrap account. The tax consequences of a retirement depend upon the form of the transaction, the reason therefor, the timing of the retirement, the estimated useful life used in computing depreciation, and whether the asset is accounted for in a separate or multiple asset account. Upon the retirement of assets, the rules in this section apply in determining whether gain or loss will be recognized, the amount of such gain or loss, and the basis for determining gain or loss:

(1) Where an asset is retired by sale at arm's length, recognition of gain or loss will be subject to the provisions of sections 1002, 1231, and other applicable provisions of law.

(2) Where an asset is retired by exchange, the recognition of gain or loss will be subject to the provisions of sections 1002, 1031, 1231, and other applicable provisions of law.

(3) Where an asset is permanently retired from use in the trade or business or in the production of income but is not disposed of by the taxpayer or physically abandoned (as, for example, when the asset is transferred to a supplies or scrap account), gain will not be recognized. In such a case loss will be recognized measured by the excess of the adjusted basis of the asset at the time of retirement over the estimated salvage value or over the fair market value at the time of such retirement if greater, but only if—

(i) The retirement is an abnormal retirement, or

(ii) The retirement is a normal retirement from a single asset account (but see paragraph (d) of this section for special rule for item accounts), or

(iii) The retirement is a normal retirement from a multiple asset account in which the depreciation rate was based on the maximum expected life of the longest lived asset contained in the account.

(4) Where an asset is retired by actual physical abandonment (as, for example, in the case of a building condemned as unfit for further occupancy or other use), loss will be recognized measured by the amount of the adjusted basis of the asset abandoned at the time of such abandonment. In order to qualify for the recognition of loss from physical abandonment, the intent of the taxpayer must be irrevocably to discard the asset so that it will neither be used again by him nor retrieved by him for sale, exchange, or other disposition. Experience with assets which have attained an exceptional or unusual age shall, with respect to similar assets, be disregarded in determining the maximum expected useful life of the longest lived asset in a multiple asset account. For example, if a manufacturer establishes a proper multiple asset account for 50 assets which are expected to have an average life of 30 years but which will remain useful to him for varying periods between 20 and 40 years, the maximum expected useful life will be 40 years, even though an occasional asset of this kind may last 60 years.

(b) *Definition of normal and abnormal retirements.*—For the purpose of this section the determination of whether a retirement is normal or abnormal shall be made in the light of all the facts and circumstances. In general, a retirement shall be considered a normal retirement unless the taxpayer can show that the withdrawal of the asset was due to a cause not contemplated in setting the applicable depreciation rate. For example, a retirement is considered normal if made within the range of years taken into consideration in fixing the depreciation rate and if the asset has reached a condition at which, in the normal course of events, the taxpayer customarily retires similar assets from use in his business. On the other hand, a retirement may be abnormal if the asset is withdrawn at an earlier time or under other circumstances, as, for example, when the asset has been damaged by casualty or has lost its usefulness suddenly as the result of extraordinary obsolescence.

(c) *Basis of assets retired.*—The basis of an asset at the time of retirement for computing gain or loss shall be its adjusted basis for determining gain or loss upon a sale or other disposition as determined in accordance with the provisions of section 1011 and the following rules:

(1) In the case of a normal retirement of an asset from a multiple asset account where the depreciation rate is based on average expected useful life, the term "adjusted basis" means the salvage value estimated in determining the depreciation deduction in accordance with the provisions in paragraph (c) of §1.167(a)-1.

(2) In the case of a normal retirement of an asset from a multiple asset account in which the depreciation rate was based on the maximum expected life of the longest lived asset in the account, the adjustment for depreciation allowed or allowable shall be made at the rate which would have been proper if the asset had been depreciated in a single asset account (under the method of depreciation used for the multiple asset account) using a rate based upon the maximum expected useful life of that asset, and

(3) In the case of an abnormal retirement from a multiple asset account the adjustment for depreciation allowed or allowable shall be made at the rate which would have been proper had the asset been depreciated in a single asset account (under the method of depreciation used for the multiple asset account) and using a rate based upon either the average expected useful life or the maximum expected useful life of the asset, depending upon the method of determining the rate of depreciation used in connection with the multiple asset account.

(d) *Special rule for item accounts.*—(1) As indicated in paragraphs (a)(3)(ii) and (iii) of this section, a loss is recognized upon the normal retirement of an asset from a single asset account but a loss on the normal retirement of an asset in a multiple asset account is not allowable where the depreciation rate is based upon the average useful life of the assets in the account. Where a taxpayer with more than one depreciable asset chooses to set up a separate account for each such asset and the depreciation rate is based on the average useful life of such assets (so that he uses the same life for each account), the question arises whether his depreciation deductions in substance are the equivalent of those which would result from the use of multiple asset accounts and, therefore, he should be subject to the rules governing losses on retirements of assets from multiple asset accounts. Where a taxpayer has only a few depreciable assets which he chooses to account for in single asset accounts, particularly where such assets cover a relatively narrow range of lives, it cannot be said in the usual case that the allowance of losses on retirements from such accounts clearly will distort income. This results from the fact that where a taxpayer has only a few depreciable assets it is usually not possible clearly to determine that the depreciation rate is based upon the average useful life of such assets. Accordingly, it cannot be said that the taxpayer is in effect clearly operating with a multiple asset account using an average life rate so that losses should not be allowed on normal retirements. Therefore, losses normally will be allowed upon retirement of assets from single asset accounts where the taxpayer has only a few depreciable assets. On the other hand, when a taxpayer who has only a few depreciable assets chooses to account for them in single asset accounts, using for each account a depreciation rate based on the average useful life of such assets, and the assets cover a wide range of lives, the likelihood that income will be distorted is greater than where the group of assets covers a relatively narrow range of lives. In those cases where the allowance of losses would distort income, the rules with respect to the allowance of losses on normal retirement shall be applied to such assets in the same manner as though the assets had been accounted for in multiple asset accounts using a rate based upon average expected useful life.

(2) Where a taxpayer has a large number of depreciable assets and depreciation is based on the average useful life of such assets,

Itemized Deductions for Individuals and Corps.
See p. 20,601 for regulations not amended to reflect law changes
25,401

then, whether such assets are similar or dissimilar and regardless of whether they are accounted for in individual asset accounts or multiple asset accounts the allowance of losses on the normal retirement of such assets would distort income. Such distortion would result from the fact that the use of average useful life (and, accordingly, average rate) assumes that while some assets normally will be retired before the expiration of the average life, others normally will be retired after expiration of the average life. Accordingly, if instead of accounting for a large number of similar or dissimilar depreciable assets in multiple asset accounts, the taxpayer chooses to account separately for such assets, using a rate based upon the average life of such assets, the rules with respect to the allowances of losses on normal retirements will be applied to such assets in the same manner as though the assets were accounted for in multiple asset accounts using a rate based upon average expected useful life.

(3) Where a taxpayer who does not have a large number of depreciable assets (and who therefore is not subject to subparagraph (2) of this paragraph) chooses to set up a separate account for each such asset, and has sought to compute an average life for such assets on which to base his depreciation deductions (so that he uses the same life for each account), the allowance of losses on normal retirements from such accounts may in some situations substantially distort income. Such distortion would result from the fact that the use of average useful life (and, accordingly, average rate) assumes that while some assets normally will be retired before expiration of the average life, others normally will be retired after expiration of the average life. Accordingly, where a taxpayer chooses to account separately for such assets instead of accounting for them in multiple asset accounts, and the result is to substantially distort his income, the rules with respect to the allowance of losses on normal retirements shall be applied to such assets in the same manner as though the assets had been accounted for in multiple asset accounts using a rate based upon average expected useful life.

(4) Whenever a taxpayer is treated under this paragraph as though his assets were accounted for in a multiple asset account using an average life rate, and, therefore, he is denied a loss on retirements, the unrecovered cost less salvage of each asset which was accounted for separately may be amortized in accordance with the regulation stated in paragraph (e)(1)(ii) of this section.

(e) *Accounting treatment of asset retirements.*—(1) In the case of a normal retirement where under the foregoing rules no loss is recognized and where the asset is retired without disposition or abandonment, (i) if the asset was contained in a multiple asset account, the full cost of such asset, reduced by estimated salvage, shall be charged to the depreciation reserve, or (ii) if the asset was accounted for separately, the unrecovered cost or other basis, less salvage, of the

asset may be amortized through annual deductions from gross income in amounts equal to the unrecovered cost or other basis of such asset, divided by the average expected useful life (not the remaining useful life) applicable to the asset at the time of retirement. For example, if an asset is retired after six years of use and at the time of retirement depreciation was being claimed on the basis of an average expected useful life of ten years, the unrecovered cost or other basis less salvage would be amortized through equal annual deductions over a period of ten years from the time of retirement.

(2) Where multiple asset accounts are used and acquisitions and retirements are numerous, if a taxpayer, in order to avoid unnecessarily detailed accounting for individual retirements, consistently follows the practice of charging the reserve with the full cost or other basis of assets retired and of crediting it with all receipts from salvage, the practice may be continued so long as, in the opinion of the Commissioner, it clearly reflects income. Conversely, where the taxpayer customarily follows a practice of reporting all receipts from salvage as ordinary taxable income such practice may be continued so long as, in the opinion of the Commissioner, it clearly reflects income.

(f) *Cross reference.*—For special rules in connection with the retirement of the last asset of a given year's acquisitions under the declining balance method, see example (2) in paragraph (b) of § 1.167(b)-2.

(g) *Applicability.*—This section applies to property for which depreciation is determined under section 167 (but not under section 168, section 1400I, section 1400L(c), section 168 prior to its amendment by the Tax Reform Act of 1986, Public Law 99-514 (100 Stat. 2121(1986)), or under an additional first year depreciation deduction provision of the Internal Revenue Code (for example, section 168(k) through (n), 1400L(b), or 1400N(d))).

(h) *Effective/applicability date.*—(1) *In general.*—This section applies to taxable years beginning on or after January 1, 2014. Except as provided in paragraphs (h)(2) and (h)(3) of this section, § 1.167(a)-8 as contained in 26 CFR part 1 edition revised as of April 1, 2011, applies to taxable years beginning before January 1, 2014.

(2) *Early application of § 1.167(a)-8(g).*—A taxpayer may choose to apply paragraph (g) of this section to taxable years beginning on or after January 1, 2012.

(3) *Optional application of TD 9564.*—A taxpayer may choose to apply § 1.167(a)-8T as contained in TD 9564 (76 FR 81060) December 27, 2011, to taxable years beginning on or after January 1, 2012, and before January 1, 2014. [Reg. § 1.167(a)-8.]

☐ [T.D. 6182, 6-11-56. *Amended by T.D.* 9564, 12-23-2011 *and T.D.* 9636, 9-13-2013.]

⟫⟫→ *Caution: Temporary Reg. §1.167(a)-8T, below, was removed by T.D. 9636, but a taxpayer may choose to apply Temporary Reg. §1.167(a)-8T to tax years beginning on or after January 1, 2012, and before January 1, 2014.*

[Reg. § 1.167(a)-8T]

§ 1.167(a)-8T. Retirements (Temporary).—(a) through (f) [Reserved]. For further guidance, see § 1.167(a)-8(a) through (f).

(g) *Applicability.*—This section applies to property for which depreciation is determined under section 167 (but not under section 168, section 1400I, section 1400L(c), section 168 prior to its amendment by the Tax Reform Act of 1986 (100 Stat. 2121), or under an additional first year depreciation deduction provision of the Internal Revenue Code (for example, section 168(k) through (n), 1400L(b), or 1400N(d))).

(h) *Effective/applicability date.*—(1) *In general.*—This section applies to taxable years beginning on or after January 1, 2014. Section 1.167(a)-8 as contained in 26 CFR part 1 edition revised as of April 1, 2011, applies to taxable years beginning before January 1, 2014.

(2) *Optional early application.*—A taxpayer may choose to apply this section to taxable years beginning on or after January 1, 2012.

(i) *Expiration date.*—The applicability of this section expires on December 23, 2014. [Temporary Reg. § 1.167(a)-8T.]

☐ [T.D. 9564, 12-23-2011 (corrected 12-14-2012). *Removed by T.D.* 9636, 9-13-2013.]

[Reg. § 1.167(a)-9]

§ 1.167(a)-9. Obsolescence.—The depreciation allowance includes an allowance for normal obsolescence which should be taken into account to the extent that the expected useful life of property will be shortened by reason thereof. Obsolescence may render an asset economically useless to the taxpayer regardless of its physical condition. Obsolescence is attributable to many causes, including technological improvements and reasonably foreseeable economic changes. Among these causes are normal progress of the arts and sciences, supersession or inadequacy brought about by developments in the industry,

products, methods, markets, sources of supply, and other like changes, and legislative or regulatory action. In any case in which the taxpayer shows that the estimated useful life previously used should be shortened by reason of obsolescence greater than had been assumed in computing such estimated useful life, a change to a new and shorter estimated useful life computed in accordance with such showing will be permitted. No such change will be permitted merely because in the unsupported opinion of the taxpayer the property may become obsolete. For rules governing the allowance of a loss when the usefulness of depreciable property is suddenly terminated, see § 1.167(a)-8. If the estimated useful life and the depreciation rates have been the subject of a previous agreement, see section 167(d) and § 1.167(d)-1. [Reg. § 1.167(a)-9.]

☐ [T.D. 6182, 6-11-56. *Amended by T.D.* 6445, 1-15-60.]

[Reg. § 1.167(a)-10]

§ 1.167(a)-10. When depreciation deduction is allowable.—(a) A taxpayer should deduct the proper depreciation allowance each year and may not increase his depreciation allowances in later years by reason of his failure to deduct any depreciation allowance or of his action in deducting an allowance plainly inadequate under the known facts in prior years. The inadequacy of the depreciation allowance for property in prior years shall be determined on the basis of the allowable method of depreciation used by the taxpayer for such property or under the straight line method if no allowance has ever been claimed for such property. The preceding sentence shall not be construed as precluding application of any method provided in section 167 (b) if taxpayer's failure to claim any allowance for depreciation was due solely to erroneously treating as a deductible expense an item properly chargeable to capital account. For rules relating to adjustments to basis, see section 1016 and the regulations thereunder.

(b) The period for depreciation of an asset shall begin when the asset is placed in service and shall end when the asset is retired from service. A proportionate part of one year's depreciation is allowable for that part of the first and last year during which the asset was in service. However, in the case of a multiple asset account, the amount of depreciation may be determined by using what is commonly described as an "averaging convention" that is, by using an assumed timing of additions and retirements. For example, it might be assumed that all additions and retirements to the asset account occur uniformly throughout the taxable year, in which case depreciation is computed on the average of the beginning and ending balances of the asset account for the taxable year. See example (3) under paragraph (b) of §1.167(b)-1. Among still other averaging conventions which may be used is the one under which it is assumed that all additions and retirements during the first half of a given year were made on the first day of that year and that all additions and retirements during the second half of the year were made on the first day of the following year. Thus, a full year's depreciation would be taken on additions in the first half of the year and no depreciation would be taken on additions in the second half. Moreover, under this convention, no depreciation would be taken on retirements in the first half of the year and a full year's depreciation would be taken on the retirements in the second half. An averaging convention, if used, must be consistently followed as to the account or accounts for which it is adopted, and must be applied to both additions and retirements. In any year in which an averaging convention substantially distorts the depreciation allowance for the taxable year, it may not be used. [Reg. §1.167(a)-10.]

☐ [T.D. 6182, 6-11-56.]

[Reg. §1.167(a)-11]

§1.167(a)-11. Depreciation based on class lives and asset depreciation ranges for property placed in service after December 31, 1970.—(a) *In general.*—(1) *Summary.*—This section provides an asset depreciation range and class life system for determining the reasonable allowance for depreciation of designated classes of assets placed in service after December 31, 1970. The system is designed to minimize disputes between taxpayers and the Internal Revenue Service as to the useful life of property, and as to salvage value, repairs, and other matters. The system is optional with the taxpayer. The taxpayer has an annual election. Generally, an election for a taxable year must apply to all additions of eligible property during the taxable year of election, but does not apply to additions of eligible property in any other taxable year. The taxpayer's election, made with the return for the taxable year, may not be revoked or modified for any property included in the election. Generally, the taxpayer must establish vintage accounts for all eligible property included in the election, must determine the allowance for depreciation of such property in the taxable year of election, and in subsequent taxable years, on the basis of the asset depreciation period selected, and must apply the first-year convention specified in the election to determine the allowance for depreciation of such property. This section also contains special provisions for the treatment of salvage value, retirements, and the costs of the repair, maintenance, rehabilitation or improvement of property. In general, a taxpayer may not apply any provision of this section unless he makes an election and thereby consents to, and agrees to apply, all the provisions of this section. A taxpayer who elects to apply this section does, however, have certain options as to the application of specified provisions of this section. A taxpayer may elect to apply this section for a taxable year only if for such taxable year he complies with the requirements of paragraph (f)(4) of this section.

(2) *Definitions.*—For the meaning of certain terms used in this section, see paragraphs (b)(2) ("eligible property"), (b)(3) ("vintage account" and "vintage"), (b)(4) ("asset depreciation range", "asset guideline class", "asset guideline period", and "asset depreciation period"), (b)(5)(iii)(c) ("used property"), (b)(6)(i) ("public utility property"), (c)(1)(iv) ("original use"), (c)(1)(v) ("unadjusted basis" and "adjusted basis"), (c)(2)(ii) ("modified half-year convention"), (c)(2)(iii) ("half-year convention"), (d)(1)(i) ("gross salvage value"), (d)(1)(ii) ("salvage value"), (d)(2)(iii) ("repair allowance", "repair allowance percentage", and "repair allowance property"), (d)(2)(vi) ("excluded addition"), (d)(2)(vii) ("property improvement"), (d)(3)(ii) ("ordinary retirement" and "extraordinary retirement"), (d)(3)(vi) ("special basis vintage account"), and (e)(1) ("first placed in service") of this section.

(b) *Reasonable allowance using asset depreciation ranges.*—(1) *In general.*—The allowance for depreciation of eligible property (as defined in subparagraph (2) of this paragraph) to which the taxpayer elects to apply this section shall be determined as provided in paragraph (c) of this section and shall constitute the reasonable allowance for depreciation of such property under section 167(a).

(2) *Definition of eligible property.*—For purposes of this section, the term "eligible property" means tangible property which is subject

to the allowance for depreciation provided by section 167(a) but only if—

    (i) An asset guideline class and asset guideline period are in effect for such property for the taxable year of election (see subparagraph (4) of this paragraph);

    (ii) The property is first placed in service (as described in paragraph (e)(1) of this section) by the taxpayer after December 31, 1970 (but see subparagraph (7) of this paragraph for special rule where there is a mere change in the form of conducting a trade or business); and

    (iii) The property is either—

        (a) Section 1245 property as defined in section 1245(a)(3), or

        (b) Section 1250 property as defined in section 1250(c).

See, however, subparagraph (6) of this paragraph for special rule for certain public utility property as defined in section 167(1)(3)(A). Property which meets the requirements of this subparagraph is eligible property even if depreciation with respect to such property, determined in accordance with this section, is allocated to or otherwise required to be reflected in the cost of a capitalized item. The term "eligible property" includes any property which meets the requirements of this subparagraph, whether such property is new property, "used property" (as described in subparagraph (5)(iii)(c) of this paragraph), a "property improvement" (as described in paragraph (d)(2)(vii) of this section), or an "excluded addition" (as described in paragraph (d)(2)(vi) of this section). For the treatment of expenditures for the repair, maintenance, rehabilitation or improvement of certain property, see paragraph (d)(2) of this section.

(3) *Requirement of vintage accounts.*—(i) *In general.*—For purposes of this section, a "vintage account" is a closed-end depreciation account containing eligible property to which the taxpayer elects to apply this section, first placed in service by the taxpayer during the taxable year of election. The "vintage" of an account refers to the taxable year during which the eligible property in the account is first placed in service by the taxpayer. Such an account will consist of an asset, or a group of assets, within a single asset guideline class established pursuant to subparagraph (4) of this paragraph and may contain only eligible property. Each item of eligible property to which the taxpayer elects to apply this section, first placed in service by the taxpayer during the taxable year of election (determined without regard to a convention described in paragraph (c)(2) of this section) shall be placed in a vintage account of the taxable year of election. For rule regarding "special basis vintage accounts" for certain property improvements, see paragraph (d)(2)(viii) and (3)(vi) of this section. Any number of vintage accounts of a taxable year may be established. More than one account of the same vintage may be established for different assets of the same asset guideline class. See paragraph (d)(3)(xi) of this section for special rule for treatment of certain multiple asset and item accounts.

    (ii) *Special rule.*—Section 1245 property may not be placed in a vintage account with section 1250 property. Property the original use of which does not commence with the taxpayer may not be placed in a vintage account with property the original use of which commences with the taxpayer. Property described in section 167(f)(2) may not be placed in a vintage account with property not described in section 167(f)(2). Property described in section 179(d)(1) for which the taxpayer elects the allowance for the first taxable year in accordance with section 179(c) may not be placed in a vintage account with property not described in section 179(d)(1) or for which the taxpayer does not elect such allowance for the first taxable year. For special rule for property acquired in a transaction to which section 381(a) applies, see paragraph (e)(3)(i) of this section. For additional rules with respect to accounting for eligible property, see paragraph (e) of this section.

(4) *Asset depreciation ranges and periods.*—(i) *Selection of asset depreciation period.*—The taxpayer's books and records must specify for each vintage account of the taxable year of election—

    (a) In the case of a vintage account for property in an asset guideline class for which no asset depreciation range is in effect for the taxable year, the asset depreciation period (which shall be equal to the asset guideline period for the assets in such account), or

    (b) In the case of a vintage account for property in an asset guideline class for which an asset depreciation range is in effect for the taxable year, the asset depreciation period selected by the taxpayer from the asset depreciation range for the assets in such account.

Unless otherwise expressly provided in the establishment thereof, for purposes of this section, the term "asset guideline class" means a category of assets (including "subsidiary assets") for which a separate asset guideline period is in effect for the taxable year as provided in subdivision (ii) of this subparagraph. The "asset depreciation range" is a period of years which extends from 80 percent of the asset guideline period to 120 percent of such period, determined in each case by rounding any fractional part of a year to the nearer of the nearest whole or half year. Except as provided in paragraph (e)(3)(iv) of this section, in the case of an asset guideline class for which an asset depreciation range is in effect, any period within the asset depreciation range which is a whole number of years or a whole number of years plus a half year, may be selected. The term "asset depreciation period" means the period selected from the asset depreciation range, or if no asset depreciation range is in effect for the class, the asset guideline period. The "asset guideline period" is established in accordance with subdivision (ii) of this subparagraph and is the class life under section 167(m). See Revenue Procedure 72-10 [superseded by Rev. Proc. 77-10, which was superseded by Rev. Proc. 83-35, which was obsoleted by Rev. Proc. 87-56; see ¶310A.01, 310B.01 and 310D.01] for special rules for section 1250 property and property predominately used outside the United States. In general, an asset guideline period, but no asset depreciation range, is in effect for such property.

(ii) *Establishment of asset guideline classes and periods.*—The asset guideline classes and the asset guideline periods, and the asset depreciation ranges determined from such periods, in effect for taxable years ending before the effective date of the first supplemental asset guideline classes, asset guideline periods, and asset depreciation ranges, established pursuant to this section are set forth in Revenue Procedure 72-10 [superseded by Rev. Proc. 77-10, which was superseded by Rev. Proc. 83-35, which was obsoleted by Rev. Proc. 87-56; see ¶310A.01, 310B.01 and 310D.01]. Asset guideline classes and periods, and asset depreciation ranges, will from time to time be established, supplemented, and revised with express reference to this section, and will be published in the Internal Revenue Bulletin. The asset guideline classes, the asset guideline periods, and the asset depreciation ranges determined from such periods in effect as of the last day of a taxable year of election shall apply to all vintage accounts of such taxable year, except that neither the asset guideline period nor the lower limit of the asset depreciation range for any such account shall be longer than the asset guideline period or the lower limit of the asset depreciation range, as the case may be, for such account in effect as of the first day of the taxable year (or as of such later time in such year as an asset guideline class first established during such year becomes effective). Generally, the reasonable allowance for depreciation of property for any taxable year in a vintage account shall not be changed to reflect any supplement or revision of the asset guideline classes or periods, and asset depreciation ranges, for the taxable year in which the account is established, which occurs after the end of such taxable year. However, if expressly provided in such a supplement or revision, the taxpayer may, at his option in the manner specified therein, apply the revised or supplemented asset guideline classes or periods and asset depreciation ranges to such property for such taxable year and succeeding taxable years.

(iii) *Applicable guideline classes and periods in special situations.*—(a) An electric or gas utility which would in accordance with Revenue Procedure 64-21 be entitled to use a composite guideline class basis for applying Revenue Procedure 62-21 may, solely with respect to property for which an asset depreciation range is in effect for the taxable year, elect to apply this section on the basis of a composite asset guideline class and asset guideline period determined by applying the provisions of Revenue Procedure 64-21 to such property. The asset depreciation range for such a composite asset guideline class shall be determined by reference to the composite asset guideline period at the beginning of the first taxable year to which the taxpayer elects to apply this section and shall not be changed until such time as major variations in the asset mix or the asset guideline classes or periods justify some other composite asset guideline period. Except as provided in paragraph (d)(2)(iii) of this section with respect to buildings and other structures, for the purposes of this section, all property in the composite asset guideline class shall be treated as included in a single asset guideline class. If the taxpayer elects to apply this subdivision, the election shall be made on the tax return filed for the first taxable year for which the taxpayer elects to apply this section. An election to apply this subdivision for any taxable year shall apply to all succeeding taxable years to which the taxpayer elects to apply this section, except to the extent the election to apply this subdivision is with the consent of the Commissioner terminated with respect to a succeeding taxable year and all taxable years thereafter.

(b) For purposes of this section, property shall be included in the asset guideline class for the activity in which the property is primarily used. See paragraph (e)(3)(iii) of this section for rule for leased property. Property shall be classified according to primary use even though the activity in which such property is primarily used is insubstantial in relation to all the taxpayer's activities. No change in the classification of property shall be made because of a change in primary use after the end of the taxable year in which property is

first placed in service, including a change in use which results in section 1250 property becoming section 1245 property.

(c) An incorrect classification or characterization by the taxpayer of property for the purposes of this section (such as under (b) of this subdivision or under subparagraph (2) or (3)(ii) of this paragraph) shall not cause or permit a revocation of the election to apply this section for the taxable year in which such property was first placed in service. The classification or characterization of such property shall be corrected. All adjustments necessary to the correction shall be made, including adjustments of unadjusted basis, adjusted basis, salvage value, the reserve for depreciation of all vintage accounts affected, and the amount of depreciation allowable for all taxable years for which the period for assessment of tax prescribed in section 6501 has not expired. If because of incorrect classification or characterization property included in an election to apply this section was not placed in a vintage account and no asset depreciation period was selected for the property or the property was placed in a vintage account but an asset depreciation period was selected from an incorrect asset depreciation range, the taxpayer shall place the property in a vintage account and select an asset depreciation period for the account from the correct asset depreciation range.

(d) Generally, except as provided in subparagraph (5)(v)(a) of this paragraph, a taxpayer may not compute depreciation for eligible property first placed in service during the taxable year under a method of depreciation not described in section 167(b)(1), (2), or (3). (If the taxpayer computes depreciation with respect to such property under section 167(k), or amortizes such property, the property must be excluded from the election to apply this section.) (See subparagraph (5)(v)(b) of this paragraph.) However, if the taxpayer establishes to the satisfaction of the Commissioner that a method of depreciation not described in section 167(b)(1), (2), (3), or (k) was adopted for property in the asset guideline class on the basis of a good faith mistake as to the proper asset guideline class for the property, then, unless the requirements of subparagraph (5)(v)(a) of this paragraph are met, the taxpayer must terminate (as of the beginning of the taxable year) such method of depreciation with respect to all eligible property in the asset guideline class which was first placed in service during the taxable year. In such event, the taxpayer's election to apply this section shall include eligible property in the asset guideline class without regard to subparagraph (5)(v)(a) of this paragraph. The provisions of (c) of this subdivision shall apply to the correction in the classification of the property.

(e) If the provisions of section 167(j) apply to require a change in the method of depreciation with respect to an item of section 1250 property in a multiple asset vintage account, the asset shall be removed from the account and placed in a separate item vintage account. The unadjusted basis of the asset shall be removed from the unadjusted basis of the vintage account as of the first day of the taxable year in which the change in method of depreciation is required and the depreciation reserve established for the account shall be reduced by the depreciation allowable for the property computed in the manner prescribed in paragraph (c)(1)(v)(b) of this section for determination of the adjusted basis of property. See paragraph (d)(3)(vii)(e) of this section for treatment of salvage value when property is removed from a vintage account.

(iv) *Examples.*—The principles of this subparagraph may be illustrated by the following examples:

Example (1). Corporation X purchases a bulldozer for use in its construction business. The bulldozer is first placed in service in 1972. Since the bulldozer is tangible property for which an asset guideline class and period have been established, the bulldozer is eligible property. The bulldozer is in asset guideline class 15.1 of Revenue Procedure 72-10, and the asset depreciation range is 4-6 years.

Example (2). In 1972, corporation Y first places in service a factory building. Since the factory building is tangible property for which an asset guideline class and period have been established, it is eligible property. The factory building is in asset guideline class 65.11 of Revenue Procedure 72-10. Since no asset depreciation range is in effect for the asset guideline class, the asset depreciation period is the asset guideline period of 45 years. (See subparagraph (5)(vi) of this paragraph for election to exclude certain section 1250 property during transition period.)

Example (3). In January of 1971, corporation Y, a calendar year taxpayer, pays or incurs $2,000 for the rehabilitation and improvement of machine A which was first placed in service in 1969. On January 1, 1971, corporation Y first placed in service machines B and C, each with an unadjusted basis of $10,000. Machines B and C are eligible property. Machine A would be eligible property but for the fact it was first placed in service prior to January 1, 1971 (that is, machine A is eligible property determined without regard to subparagraph (2)(ii) of this paragraph). Corporation Y elects to apply this section for the taxable year, and adopts the modified half-year convention described in paragraph (c)(2)(ii) of this section, but does not elect to apply the asset guideline class repair allowance described in paragraph (d)(2)(iii) of this section. Machines A, B, and C are in asset guideline class 24.4 under Revenue Procedure 72-10 for which the asset depreciation range is 8 to 12 years. The $2,000 expended on machine A substantially increases its capacity and is a capital expenditure under sections 162 and 263. The $2,000 is a property improvement (as defined in paragraph (d)(2)(vii)(*b*) of this section) which is

	Dec. 31, 1972, reserve for depreciation	Dec. 31, 1972, adjusted basis
Vintage account for machine B, with an asset depreciation period of 5 years and an unadjusted basis of $10,000 for which corporation Y adopts the straight line method	$4,000	$6,000
Vintage account for machine C, with an asset depreciation period of 8 years and an unadjusted basis of $10,000 for which corporation Y adopts the straight line method	2,500	7,500

After audit in 1973 of corporation Y's taxable years 1971 and 1972, it is determined that the $2,000 paid in 1971 for the rehabilitation and improvement of machine A is a capital expenditure and that machine B is in asset guideline class 24.4. The incorrect classification is corrected. Corporation Y places machine B and the property improvement in a vintage account of 1971 and on its tax return filed for 1973 selects an asset depreciation period of 8 years for that account. Giving effect to the correction in classification of the property in accordance with subdivision (iii)(*c*) of this subparagraph, at the end of 1972 the unadjusted basis, reserve for depreciation, and adjusted basis of the vintage account for machine B and the property improvement with respect to machine A are $12,000, $3,000 and $9,000, respectively. Corporation Y's deduction of the $2,000 property improvement in 1971 as a repair expense under section 162 was disallowed. For 1971 and 1972 depreciation deductions are disallowed in the amount of $500 each year (that is, $750 excess annual depreciation on machine B minus $250 annual depreciation on the property improvement).

Example (4). (*a*) In 1971, Corporation X, a calendar year taxpayer, first places in service machines A through M, all of which are eligible property. All the machines except machine A are in asset guideline class 24.3 under Revenue Procedure 72-10. Machine A is in asset guideline class 24.4 under Revenue Procedure 72-10. Machine B has an unadjusted basis equal to 80 percent of the total unadjusted basis of machines B through M. By good faith mistake as to proper classification, corporation X includes both machine A and machine B in asset guideline class 24.4. Corporation X consistently uses the machine hour method of depreciation on all property in asset guideline class 24.4, and for 1971 computes depreciation for machines A and B under that method. Corporation X elects to apply this section for 1971 on the assumption that the election includes machines C through M which are in asset guideline class 24.3. In 1973, upon audit of corporation X's taxable years 1971 and 1972, it is determined that machine B is included in asset guideline class 24.3 and that since for 1971 corporation X computed depreciation on machine B under the machine hour method, in accordance with subparagraph (5)(v)(*a*) of this paragraph, all property in asset guideline class 24.3 (machines B through M) is excluded from corporation X's election to apply this section for 1971. Although corporation X has consistently used the machine hour method for asset guideline class 24.4, corporation X has not in the past used the machine hour method for machines of the type and function of machines C through M which are in asset guideline class 24.3. Both machine A and machine B are used in connection with the manufacture of wood products. There is reasonable basis for corporation X having assumed that machine B is in asset guideline 24.4 along with machine A to which it is similar. Corporation X establishes to the satisfaction of the Commissioner that it used the machine hour method for machine B on the basis of a good faith mistake as to the proper classification of the machine. Corporation X may, at its option (see subparagraph (5)(v) of this paragraph), terminate the machine hour method of depreciation for machine B as of the beginning of 1971, and in that event corporation X's election to apply this section for 1971 will apply to machines B through M without regard to subparagraph (5)(v)(*a*) of this paragraph. The adjustments provided in subdivision (iii)(*c*) of this subparagraph will be made as a result of the correction in classification of property. If corporation X does not terminate the machine hour method with respect to machine B, machines B through M must be excluded from the election to apply this section (see subparagraph (5)(v) of this paragraph.)

(*b*) The facts are the same as in (*a*) of this example except that machine B has an unadjusted basis equal to only 65 percent of the total unadjusted basis of machines B through M. In this case, corporation X must either terminate the machine hour method of depreciation with respect to asset B (since the provisions of subparagraph (5)(v) of this paragraph do *not permit the exclusion of the property from the election to apply this section*) or otherwise comply with the provisions of subparagraph (5)(v) of this paragraph.

(See paragraph (c)(1)(iv) for limitation on methods which may be adopted for property included in the election to apply this section.)

eligible property. However, corporation Y by mistake treats the property improvement of $2,000 as a deductible repair. Also by mistake, corporation Y includes machine B in asset guideline class 24.3 under Revenue Procedure 72-10 for which the asset depreciation range is 5 to 7 years. Corporation Y establishes vintage accounts for 1971, and computes depreciation for 1971 and 1972 as follows:

(5) *Requirements of election.*—(i) *In general.*—Except as otherwise provided in paragraph (d)(2) of this section dealing with expenditures for the repair, maintenance, rehabilitation or improvement of certain property, no provision of this section shall apply to any property other than eligible property to which the taxpayer elects in accordance with this section, to apply this section. For the time and manner of election, and certain conditions to an election, see paragraph (f) of this section. Except as otherwise provided in subparagraph (4)(iii) of this paragraph, subdivision (v) of this subparagraph, and in subparagraph (6)(iii) of this paragraph, a taxpayer's election to apply this section may not be revoked or modified after the last day prescribed for filing the election. Thus, for example, after such day, a taxpayer may not cease to apply this section to property included in the election, establish different vintage accounts for the taxable year of election, select a different period from the asset depreciation range for any such account, or adopt a different first-year convention for any such account.

(ii) *Property required to be included in election.*—Except as otherwise provided in subdivision (iii) of this subparagraph dealing with certain "used property", in subdivision (iv) of this subparagraph dealing with "section 38 property", in subdivision (v) of this subparagraph dealing with property subject to special depreciation or amortization, in subdivision (vi) of this subparagraph dealing with certain section 1250 property, in subdivision (vii) of this subparagraph dealing with certain subsidiary assets, and in paragraph (e)(3)(i) and (iv) of this section dealing with transactions to which section 381(a) applies, if the taxpayer elects to apply this section to any eligible property first placed in service by the taxpayer during the taxable year of election, the election shall apply to all such eligible property, whether placed in service in a trade or business or held for production of income.

(iii) *Special 10 percent used property rule.*—(*a*) If (*1*) the unadjusted basis of eligible used section 1245 property (as defined in (*c*) of this subdivision) first placed in service by the taxpayer during the taxable year of election, for which no specific used property asset guideline class (as defined in (*c*) of this subdivision) is in effect for the taxable year, exceeds (*2*) 10 percent of the unadjusted basis of all eligible section 1245 property first placed in service during the taxable year of election, the taxpayer may exclude all (but not less than all) the property described in (*a*)(*1*) of this subdivision from the election to apply this section.

(*b*) If (*1*) the unadjusted basis of eligible used section 1250 property first placed in service by the taxpayer during the taxable year of election, for which no specific used property asset guideline class is in effect for the taxable year, exceeds (*2*) 10 percent of the unadjusted basis of all eligible section 1250 property first placed in service during the taxable year of election, the taxpayer may exclude all (but not less than all) the property described in (*b*)(*1*) of this subdivision from the election to apply this section.

(*c*) For the purposes of this section, the term "used property" means property the original use of which does not commence with the taxpayer. Solely for the purpose of determining whether the 10 percent rule of this subdivision is satisfied, (*1*) eligible used property first placed in service during the taxable year and excluded from the election to apply this section pursuant to subdivision (v)(*a*) of this subparagraph and (*2*) eligible property acquired during the taxable year in a transaction to which section 381(a) applies, shall all be treated as used property regardless of whether such property would be treated as new property under section 167(c) and the regulations thereunder. The term "specific used property asset guideline class" means a class established in accordance with subparagraph (4) of this paragraph solely for used property primarily used in connection with the activity to which the class relates.

(iv) *Property subject to investment tax credit.*—The taxpayer may exclude from an election to apply this section all, or less than all, units of eligible property first placed in service during the taxable year which is—

Itemized Deductions for Individuals and Corps.
See p. 20,601 for regulations not amended to reflect law changes
25,405

(a) "Section 38 property" as defined in section 48(a) which meets the requirements of section 49 and which is not property described in section 50, or

(b) Property to which section 47(a)(5)(B) applies which would be section 38 property but for section 49 which is placed in service to replace section 38 property (other than property described in section 50) disposed of prior to August 15, 1971.

(v) *Property subject to special method of depreciation or amortization.*—(a) In the case of eligible property first placed in service in a taxable year of election (and not otherwise properly excluded from an election to apply this section) the taxpayer may not compute depreciation for any of such property in the asset guideline class under a method not described in section 167(b)(1), (2), (3) or (k) unless he (1) computes depreciation under a method or methods not so described for eligible property first placed in service in the taxable year in the asset guideline class with an unadjusted basis at least equal to 75 percent of the unadjusted basis of all eligible property first placed in service in the taxable year in the asset guideline class and (2) agrees to continue to depreciate such property under such method or methods until the consent of the Commissioner is obtained to a change in method. The consent of the Commissioner must be obtained by filing Form 3115 with the Commissioner of Internal Revenue, Washington, D.C. 20224, within the first 180 days of the taxable year for which the change is desired. If for the taxable year of election the taxpayer computes depreciation under any method not described in section 167(b)(1), (2), (3) or (k) for any eligible property (other than property otherwise properly excluded from an election to apply this section) first placed in service during the taxable year, an election to apply this section for the taxable year shall not include such property or any other eligible property in the same asset guideline class as such property. With respect to a taxable year beginning before January 1, 1973, if the taxpayer has adopted a method of depreciation which is not permitted under this subdivision, the taxpayer may under this section adopt a method of depreciation permitted under this subdivision or otherwise comply with the provisions of this subdivision.

(b) An election to apply this section shall not include eligible property for which, for the taxable year of election, the taxpayer computes depreciation under section 167(k), or computes amortization under section 169, 184, 185, 187, 188 or paragraph (b) or § 1.162-11. If the taxpayer has elected to apply this section to eligible property described in section 167(k), 169, 184, 185, or 187 and the taxpayer thereafter computes depreciation or amortization for such property for any taxable year in accordance with section 167(k), 169, 184,185, or 187, then the election to apply this section to such property shall terminate as of the beginning of the taxable year for which depreciation or amortization is computed under such section. Application of this section to the property for any period prior to the termination date will not be affected by the termination. The unadjusted basis of the property shall be removed as of the termination date from the unadjusted basis of the vintage account. The depreciation reserve established for the account shall be reduced by the depreciation allowable for the property, computed in the manner prescribed in paragraph (c)(1)(v)(b) of this section for determination of the adjusted basis of the property. See paragraph (d)(3)(vii)(e) of this section for treatment of salvage value when property is removed from a vintage account.

(vi) *Certain section 1250 property.*—(a) The taxpayer may exclude from an election to apply this section all, or less than all, items of eligible section 1250 property first placed in service during the taxable year of election provided that—

(1) The item is first placed in service before the earlier of the effective date of the first supplemental asset guideline class including such property established in accordance with subparagraph (4)(ii) of this paragraph, or January 1, 1974, and

(2) The taxpayer establishes that a useful life shorter than the asset guideline period in effect on January 1, 1971, for such item of property is justified for such taxable year.

A useful life shorter than the asset guideline period in effect on January 1, 1971, will be considered justified only if such life is justified in accordance with the provisions of Revenue Procedure 62-21 (including all modifications, amendments or supplements thereto as of January 1, 1971), determined without application of the minimal adjustment rule in section 4, Part II, of Revenue Procedure 65-13. If an item of section 1250 property is excluded from an election to apply this section pursuant to this subdivision, any elevator or escalator which is a part of such item shall also be excluded from the election.

(b) If the taxpayer excludes an item of section 1250 property from an election to apply this section in accordance with this subdivision, the useful life justified under Revenue Procedure 62-21 in accordance with this subdivision for the taxable year of exclusion will be treated as justified for such item of section 1250 property for the taxable year of the exclusion and all subsequent taxable years.

(vii) *Subsidiary assets.*—The taxpayer may exclude from an election to apply this section all (but not less than all) subsidiary assets first placed in service during the taxable year of election in an asset guideline class, provided that—

(a) the unadjusted basis of eligible subsidiary assets first placed in service during the taxable year in the class is as much as 3 percent of the unadjusted basis of all eligible property first placed in service during the taxable year in the class, and

(b) such subsidiary assets are first placed in service by the taxpayer before the earlier of (1) the effective date of the first supplemental asset guideline class including such subsidiary assets established in accordance with subparagraph (4)(ii) of this paragraph, or (2) January 1, 1974. For purposes of this subdivision the term "subsidiary assets" includes jigs, dies, molds, returnable containers, glassware, silverware, textile mill cam assemblies, and other equipment included in Group One, Class 5, of Revenue Procedure 62-21 which is usually and properly accounted for separately from other property and under a method of depreciation not expressed in terms of years.

(6) *Special rule for certain public utility property.*—(i) *Requirement of normalization in certain cases.*—Under section 167(l), in the case of public utility property (as defined in section 167(l)(3)(A)), if the taxpayer—

(a) Is entitled to use a method of depreciation other than a "subsection (1) method" of depreciation (as defined in section 167(l)(3)(F)) only if it uses the "normalization method of accounting" (as defined in section 167(l)(3)(G)) with respect to such property, or

(b) Is entitled for the taxable year to use only a "subsection (1) method" of depreciation,
such property shall be eligible property (as defined in subparagraph (2) of this paragraph) only if the taxpayer normalizes the tax deferral resulting from the election to apply this section.

(ii) *Normalization.*—The taxpayer will be considered to normalize the tax deferral resulting from the election to apply this section only if it computes its tax expense for purposes of establishing its cost of service for rate-making purposes and for reflecting operating results in its regulated books of account using a period for depreciation no less than the lesser of—

(a) 100% of the asset guideline period in effect in accordance with subparagraph (4)(ii) of this paragraph for the first taxable year to which this section applies, or

(b) The period for computing its depreciation expense for rate-making purposes and for reflecting operating results in its regulated books of account,
and makes adjustments to a reserve to reflect the deferral of taxes resulting from the use of a period for depreciation under section 167 in accordance with an election to apply this section different from the lesser of the periods described in (a) and (b) of this subdivision. In the case of public utility property described in section 167(l)(3)(A)(iii) for which no guideline life was prescribed in Revenue Procedure 62-21 (or for which reference was made in Revenue Procedure 62-21 to lives or rates established by governmental regulatory agencies), for the purpose of (a) of this subdivision, the asset guideline period shall be deemed to be the period for computing the taxpayer's depreciation expense for rate-making purposes and for reflecting operating results in its regulated books of account instead of the asset guideline period in effect in accordance with subparagraph (4)(ii) of this paragraph for the first taxable year to which this section applies. A determination whether the taxpayer is considered to normalize under this subdivision the tax deferral resulting from the election to apply this section shall be made in a manner consistent with the principles for determining whether a taxpayer is using the "normalization" method of accounting (within the meaning of section 167(l)(3)(G)). See § 1.167(l)-1(h).

(iii) *Failure to normalize.*—If a taxpayer, which has elected to apply this section to any eligible public utility property and is required under subdivision (i) of this subparagraph to normalize the tax deferral resulting from the election to apply this section to such property, fails to normalize such tax deferral, the election to apply this section to such property shall terminate as of the beginning of the taxable year for which the taxpayer fails to normalize such tax deferral. Application of this section to such property for any period prior to the termination date will not be affected by the termination. The unadjusted basis of the property shall be removed as of the termination date from the unadjusted basis of the vintage account. The depreciation reserve established for the account shall be reduced by the depreciation allowable for the property, computed in the manner prescribed in paragraph (c)(1)(v)(b) of this section for determination of the adjusted basis of the property. See paragraph (d)(3)(vii)(e) of this section for treatment of salvage value when property is removed from a vintage account.

(iv) *Examples.*—The principles of this subparagraph may be illustrated by the following examples:

Example (1). Corporation A is a gas pipeline company, subject to the jurisdiction of the Federal Power Commission, which is entitled under section 167(l) to use a method of depreciation other than a "subsection (l) method" of depreciation (as defined in section 167(l)(3)(F)) only if it uses the "normalization method of accounting" (as defined in section 167 (l)(3)(G)). Corporation A elects to apply this section for 1972 with respect to all eligible property. In 1972, corporation A places in service eligible property with an unadjusted basis of $2 million. One hundred percent of the asset guideline period for such property is 22 years and the asset depreciation range is from 17.5 years to 26.5 years. The taxpayer uses the double declining balance method of depreciation, selects an asset depreciation period of 17.5 years and applies the half-year convention (described in paragraph (c)(2)(iii) of this section). The depreciation allowable under this section with respect to such property in 1972 is $114,285. The taxpayer will be considered to normalize the tax deferral resulting from the election to apply this section and to use the "normalization method of accounting" (within the meaning of section 167(l)(3)(G)) if it computes its tax expense for purposes of determining its cost of service for rate making purposes and for reflecting operating results in its regulated books of account using a "subsection (l) method" of depreciation, such as the straight line method, determined by using a depreciation period of 22 years (that is, 100 percent of the asset guideline period). A depreciation allowance computed in this manner is $45,454. The difference in the amount determined under this section ($114,285) and the amount used in computing its tax expense for purposes of estimating its cost of service for rate making purposes and for reflecting operating results in its regulated books of account ($45,454) is $68,831. Assuming a tax rate of 48 percent, the deferral of taxes resulting from an election to apply this section and using a different method of depreciation for tax purposes from that used for establishing its cost of service for rate making purposes and for reflecting operating results in its regulated books of account is 48 percent of $68,831, or $33,039, which amount should be added to a reserve to reflect the deferral of taxes resulting from the election to apply this section and from the use of a different method of depreciation in computing the allowance for depreciation under section 167 from that used in computing its depreciation expense for purposes of establishing its cost of service for rate making purposes and for reflecting operating results in its regulated books of account.

Example (2). Corporation B, a telephone company subject to the jurisdiction of the Federal Communications Commission used a "flow-through method of accounting" (as defined in section 167(l)(3)(H)) for its "July 1969 accounting period" (as defined in section 167(l)(3)(I)) with respect to all of its pre-1970 public utility property and did not make an election under section 167(l)(4)(A). Thus, corporation B is entitled under section 167(l) to use a method of depreciation other than a "subsection (l) method" with respect to certain property without using the "normalization method of accounting." In 1972, corporation B makes an election to apply this section with respect to all eligible property. Corporation B is not required to normalize the tax deferral resulting from the election to apply this section in the case of property for which it is not required to use the "normalization method of accounting" under section 167(l).

Example (3). Assume the same facts as in example (2) except that corporation B made a timely election under section 167(l)(4)(A) that section 167(l)(2)(C) not apply with respect to property which increases the productive or operational capacity of the taxpayer. Corporation B must normalize the tax deferral resulting from the election to apply this section with respect to such property.

(7) *Mere change in form of conducting a trade or business.*—Property which was first placed in service by the transferor before January 1, 1971, shall not be eligible property if such property is first placed in service by the transferee after December 31, 1970, by reason of a mere change in the form of conducting a trade or business in which such property is used. A mere change in the form of conducting a trade or business in which such property is used will be considered to have occurred if—

(i) The transferor (or in a case where the transferor is a partnership, estate, trust, or corporation, the partners, beneficiaries, or shareholders) of such property retains a substantial interest in such trade or business, or

(ii) The basis of such property in the hands of the transferee is determined in whole or in part by reference to the basis of such property in the hands of the transferor.

For purposes of this subparagraph, a transferor (or in a case where the transferor is a partnership, estate, trust, or corporation, the partners, beneficiaries, or shareholders) shall be considered as having retained a substantial interest in the trade or business only if, after the change in form, his (or their) interest in such trade or business is

substantial in relation to the total interest of all persons in such trade or business. This subparagraph shall apply to property first placed in service prior to January 1, 1971, held for the production of income (within the meaning of section 167(a)(2)) as well as to property used in a trade or business. The principles of this subdivision may be illustrated by the following examples:

Example (1). Corporation X and corporation Y are includible corporations in an affiliated group as defined in section 1504(a). In 1971 corporation X sells property to corporation Y for cash. The property would meet the requirements of subparagraph (2) of this paragraph for eligible property except that it was first placed in service by corporation X in 1970. After the transfer, the property is first placed in service by corporation Y in 1971. The property is not eligible property because of the mere change in the form of conducting a trade or business.

Example (2). In 1971, in a transaction to which section 351 applies, taxpayer B transfers to corporation W property which would meet the requirements of subparagraph (2) of this paragraph for eligible property except that the property was first placed in service by B in 1969. Corporation W first places the property in service in 1971. The property is not eligible property because of the mere change in the form of conducting a trade or business.

(c) *Manner of determining allowance.*—(1) *In general.*—(i) *Computation of allowance.*—(a) The allowance for depreciation of property in a vintage account shall be determined in the manner specified in this paragraph by using the method of depreciation adopted by the taxpayer for the account and a rate based upon the asset depreciation period for the account. (For limitations on methods of depreciation permitted with respect to property, see section 167(c) and (j) and subdivision (iv) of this subparagraph.) In applying the method of depreciation adopted by the taxpayer, the annual allowance for depreciation of a vintage account shall be determined without adjustment for the salvage value of the property in such account except that no account may be depreciated below the reasonable salvage value of the account. (For rules regarding estimation and treatment of salvage value, see paragraph (d)(1) and (3) (vii) and (viii) of this section.) Regardless of the method of depreciation adopted by the taxpayer, the depreciation allowable for a taxable year with respect to a vintage account may not exceed the amount by which (as of the beginning of the taxable year) the unadjusted basis of the account exceeds (1) the reserve for depreciation established for the account plus (2) the salvage value of the account. The unadjusted basis of a vintage account is defined in subdivision (v) of this subparagraph. The adjustments to the depreciation reserve are described in subdivision (ii) of this subparagraph.

(b) The annual allowance for depreciation of a vintage account using the straight line method of depreciation shall be determined by dividing the unadjusted basis of the vintage account (without reduction for salvage value) by the number of the years in the asset depreciation period selected for the account. See subdivision (iii)(b) of this subparagraph for the manner of computing the depreciation allowance following a change from the declining balance method or the sum of the years-digits method to the straight line method.

(c) In the case of the sum of the years-digits method, the annual allowance for depreciation of a vintage account shall be computed by multiplying the unadjusted basis of the vintage account (without reduction for salvage value) by a fraction, the numerator of which changes each year to a number which corresponds to the years remaining in the asset depreciation period for the account (including the year for which the allowance is being computed) and the denominator of which is the sum of all the year's digits corresponding to the asset depreciation period for the account. See subdivision (iii)(c) of this subparagraph for the manner of computing the depreciation allowance following a change from the declining balance method to the sum of the years-digits method.

(d) The annual allowance for depreciation of a vintage account using a declining balance method is determined by applying a uniform rate to the excess of the unadjusted basis of the vintage account over the depreciation reserve established for that account. The rate under the declining balance method may not exceed twice the straight line rate based upon the asset depreciation period for the vintage account.

(e) The allowance for depreciation under this paragraph shall constitute the amount of depreciation allowable under section 167. See section 179 for additional first-year allowance for certain property.

(ii) *Establishment of depreciation reserve.*—The taxpayer must establish a depreciation reserve for each vintage account. The amount of the reserve for a guideline class must be stated on each income tax return on which depreciation with respect to such class is determined under this section. The depreciation reserve for a vintage account consists of the accumulated depreciation allowable under this section

Itemized Deductions for Individuals and Corps.
See p. 20,601 for regulations not amended to reflect law changes
25,407

with respect to the vintage account, increased by the adjustments for ordinary retirements prescribed by paragraph (d)(3)(iii) of this section, by the adjustments for reduction of the salvage value of a vintage account prescribed by paragraph (d)(3)(vii)(d) of this section, and by the adjustments for transfers to supplies or scrap prescribed by paragraph (d)(3)(viii)(b) of this section, and decreased by the adjustments for extraordinary retirements and certain special retirements as prescribed by paragraph (d)(3)(iv) and (v) of this section, by the adjustments for the amount of the reserve in excess of the unadjusted basis of a vintage account prescribed by paragraph (d)(3)(ix)(a) of this section, and by the adjustments for property removed from a vintage account prescribed by paragraph (b)(4)(iii)(e), (5)(v)(b) and (6)(iii) of this section. The adjustments to the depreciation reserve for ordinary retirements during the taxable year shall be made as of the beginning of the taxable year. The adjustments to the depreciation reserve for extraordinary retirements shall be made as of the date the retirement is treated as having occurred in accordance with the first-year convention (described in subparagraph (2) of this paragraph) adopted by the taxpayer for the vintage account. The adjustment to the depreciation reserve for reduction of salvage value and for transfers to supplies or scrap shall, in the case of an ordinary retirement, be made as of the beginning of the taxable year, and in the case of an extraordinary retirement the adjustment for reduction of salvage value shall be made as of the date the retirement is treated as having occurred in accordance with the first-year convention (described in subparagraph (2) of this paragraph) adopted by the taxpayer for the vintage account. The adjustment to the depreciation reserve for property removed from a vintage account in accordance with paragraph (b)(4)(iii)(e), (5)(v)(b) and (6)(iii) of this section shall be made as of the beginning of the taxable year. The depreciation reserve of a vintage account may not be decreased below zero.

(iii) *Consent to change in method of depreciation.*—(a) During the asset depreciation period for a vintage account, the taxpayer is permitted to change under this section from a declining balance method of depreciation to the sum of the years-digits method of depreciation and from a declining balance method of depreciation or the sum of the years-digits method of depreciation to the straight line method of depreciation with respect to such account. Except as provided in section 167(j)(2) and (l) and paragraph (e)(3)(i) of this section, no other changes in the method of depreciation adopted for a vintage account will be permitted. The provisions of §1.167(e)-1 shall not apply to any change in depreciation method permitted under this section. The change in method applies to all property in the vintage account and must be adhered to for the entire taxable year of the change.

(b) When a change is made to the straight line method of depreciation, the annual allowance for depreciation of the vintage account shall be determined by dividing the adjusted basis of the vintage account (without reduction for salvage value) by the number of years remaining (at the time as of which the change is made) in the asset depreciation period selected for the account. However, the depreciation allowable for any taxable year following a change to the straight line method may not exceed an amount determined by dividing the unadjusted basis of the vintage account (without reduction for salvage value) by the number of years in the asset depreciation period selected for the account.

(c) When a change is made from the declining balance method of depreciation to the sum of the years-digits method of depreciation, the annual allowance for depreciation of a vintage account shall be determined by multiplying the adjusted basis of the account (without reduction for salvage value) at the time as of which the change is made by a fraction, the numerator of which changes each year to a number which corresponds to the number of years remaining in the asset depreciation period selected for the account (including the year for which the allowance is being computed), and the denominator of which is the sum of all the year's digits corresponding to the number of years remaining in the asset depreciation period at the time as of which the change is made.

(d) The number of years remaining in the asset depreciation period selected for an account is equal to the asset depreciation period less the number of years of depreciation previously allowed. For this purpose, regardless of the first year convention adopted by the taxpayer, it will be assumed that depreciation was allowed for one-half of a year in the first year.

(e) The taxpayer shall furnish a statement setting forth the vintage accounts for which the change is made with the income tax return filed for the taxable year of the change.

(f) The principles of this subdivision may be illustrated by the following examples:

Example (1). A, calendar year taxpayer, places new section 1245 property in service in a trade or business as follows:

Asset	Placed in service	Unadjusted basis	Estimated salvage
X	March 15, 1971	$400	$20
Y	June 13, 1971	$500	50
Z	July 30, 1971	$100	0

The property is eligible property and is properly included in a single vintage account. The asset depreciation range for such property is 5 to 7 years and the taxpayer selects an asset depreciation period of 5½ years and adopts the 200-percent declining balance method of depreciation. The taxpayer adopts the half-year convention described in subparagraph (2)(iii) of this paragraph. After 3 years, A changes from the 200-percent declining balance method to the straight line method of depreciation. Depreciation allowances would be as follows:

Year	Unadjusted basis	Rate	Depreciation	Reserve	Adjusted basis
1971	$1,000.00	.18182	$181.82	$181.82	$818.18
1972	1,000.00	.36363	297.52	479.34	520.66
1973	1,000.00	.36363	189.33	668.67	331.33
1974	1,000.00	.33333 [1]	110.44	779.11	220.89
1975	1,000.00	.33333	110.44	889.56	110.44
1976	1,000.00	.33333	40.44 [2]	930.00	70.00

[1] Rate applied to adjusted basis of the account (without reduction by salvage) at the time as of which the change is made to the straight line method.
[2] The allowable depreciation is limited by estimated salvage.

Example (2). The facts are the same as in example (1) except that A elects to use the modified half-year convention described in subparagraph (2)(ii) of this paragraph. The depreciation allowances would be as follows:

Year	Unadjusted basis	Rate	Depreciation	Reserve	Adjusted basis
1971	$1,000.00	.36363 [1]	$327.27	$327.27	$672.73
1972	1,000.00	.36363	244.63	571.90	428.10
1973	1,000.00	.36363	155.67	727.57	272.43
1974	1,000.00	.33333	90.81	818.38	181.62
1975	1,000.00	.33333	90.81	909.19	90.81
1976	1,000.00	.33333	20.81 [2]	930.00	70.00

[1] Rate applied to $900.00, the amount of assets placed in service during the first half of the taxable year.
[2] The allowable depreciation is limited by estimated salvage.

Example (3). The facts are the same as in example (1) except that A adopted the sum of the years-digits method of depreciation and does not change to the straight-line method of depreciation. The depreciation allowances would be as follows:

Reg. §1.167(a)-11(c)(1)(iii)(f)

Year	Unadjusted basis	Rate	Depreciation	Reserve	Adjusted basis
1971	$1,000.00	2.75/18 [1]	$152.78	$152.78	$847.22
1972	1,000.00	5/18	277.78	430.56	569.44
1973	1,000.00	4/18	222.22	652.78	347.22
1974	1,000.00	3/18	166.67	819.45	180.55
1975	1,000.00	2/18	110.55 [2]	930.00	70.00
1976	1,000.00	1/18	0.00	930.00	70.00
1977	1,000.00	0.25/18	0.00	930.00	70.00

[1] Rate is equal to one-half of 5.5/18. The denominator is equal to 5.5 + 4.5 + 3.5 + 2.5 + 1.5 + .5.
[2] The allowable depreciation is limited by estimated salvage.

Example (4). The facts are the same as in example (3) except that A elects to use the modified half-year convention described in subparagraph (2)(ii) of this paragraph. The depreciation allowances would be as follows:

Year	Unadjusted basis	Rate	Depreciation	Reserve	Adjusted basis
1971	$1,000.00	5.5/18 [1]	$275.00	$275.00	$725.00
1972	1,000.00	5/18	277.78	552.78	447.22
1973	1,000.00	4/18	222.22	775.00	225.00
1974	1,000.00	3/18	155.00 [2]	930.00	70.00
1975	1,000.00	2/18	0.00	930.00	70.00
1976	1,000.00	1/18	0.00	930.00	70.00
1977	1,000.00	0.25/18	0.00	930.00	70.00

[1] Rate applied to $900.00, the amount of assets placed in service during the first half of the taxable year.
[2] The allowable depreciation is limited by estimated salvage.

Example (5). The facts are the same as in example (2) except that after 2 years A changes from the 200-percent declining balance method to the sum of the years-digits method of depreciation. The depreciation allowances would be as follows:

Year	Unadjusted basis	Rate	Depreciation	Reserve	Adjusted basis
1971	$1,000.00	.36363	$327.27	$327.27	$672.73
1972	1,000.00	.36363	244.63	571.90	428.10
1973	1,000.00	4/10	171.24	743.14	256.86
1974	1,000.00	3/10	128.43	871.57	128.43
1975	1,000.00	2/10	58.43 [1]	930.00	70.00
1976	1,000.00	1/10	0.00	930.00	70.00

[1] The allowable depreciation is limited by estimated salvage.

(iv) *Limitation on methods.*—(a) The same method of depreciation must be adopted for all property in a single vintage account. Generally, the method of depreciation which may be adopted is subject to the limitations contained in section 167(c), (j) and (l).

(b) Except as otherwise provided in section 167(j) with respect to certain eligible section 1250 property—

(1) In the case of a vintage account for which the taxpayer has selected an asset depreciation period of 3 years or more and which only contains property the original use of which commences with the taxpayer, any method of depreciation described in section 167(b)(1), (2), or (3) may be adopted, but if the vintage account contains property the original use of which does not commence with the taxpayer, or if the asset depreciation period for the account is less than 3 years, a method of depreciation described in section 167(b)(2) or (3) may not be adopted for the account, and

(2) The declining balance method using a rate not in excess of 150 percent of the straight line rate based upon the asset depreciation period for the vintage account may be adopted for the account even if the original use of the property does not commence with the taxpayer provided the asset depreciation period for the account is at least 3 years.

(c) The term "original use" means the first use to which the property is put, whether or not such use corresponds to the use of such property by the taxpayer. (See § 1.167(c)-1).

(v) *Unadjusted and adjusted basis.*—(a) For purposes of this section, the unadjusted basis of an asset (including an "excluded addition" and a "property improvement" as described, respectively, in paragraph (d)(2)(vi) and (vii) of this section) is its cost or other basis without any adjustment for depreciation or amortization (other than depreciation under section 179) but with other adjustments required under section 1016 or other applicable provisions of law. The unadjusted basis of a vintage account is the total of the unadjusted bases of all the assets in the account. The unadjusted basis of a "special basis vintage account" as described in paragraph (d)(3)(vi) of this section is the amount of the property improvement determined in paragraph (d)(2)(vii)(a) of this section.

(b) The adjusted basis of a vintage account is the amount by which the unadjusted basis of the account exceeds the reserve for depreciation for the account. The adjusted basis of an asset in a vintage account is the amount by which the unadjusted basis of the asset exceeds the *amount of depreciation allowable for the asset under this section computed by using the method of depreciation and the rate applicable to the account.* For purposes of this subdivision, the depreciation allowable for an asset shall include, to the extent identifiable, the amount of proceeds previously added to the depreciation reserve in accordance with paragraph (d)(3)(iii) of this section upon the retirement of any portion of such asset. (See paragraph (d)(3)(vi) of this section for election under certain circumstances to allocate adjusted basis of an amount of property improvement determined under paragraph (d)(2)(vii) (a) of this section.)

(2) *Conventions applied to additions and retirements.*—(i) *In general.*—The allowance for depreciation of a vintage account (whether an item account or a multiple asset account) shall be determined by applying one of the conventions described in subdivisions (ii) and (iii) of this subparagraph. (For the manner of applying a convention in the case of taxable years beginning before and ending after December 31, 1970, see subparagraph (3) of this paragraph.) The same convention must be adopted for all vintage accounts of a taxable year, but the same convention need not be adopted for the vintage accounts of another taxable year. An election to apply this section must specify the convention adopted. (See paragraph (f) of this section for information required in making the election.) The convention adopted by the taxpayer is a method of accounting for purposes of section 446, but the consent of the Commissioner will be deemed granted to make an annual adoption of either of the conventions described in subdivisions (ii) and (iii) of this subparagraph.

(ii) *Modified half-year convention.*—The depreciation allowance for a vintage account for which the taxpayer adopts the "modified half-year convention" shall be determined by treating: (a) all property in such account which is placed in service during the first half of the taxable year as placed in service on the first day of the taxable year; and (b) all property in such account which is placed in service during the second half of the taxable year as placed in service on the first day of the succeeding taxable year. The depreciation allowance for a vintage account for a taxable year in which there is an extraordinary retirement (as defined in paragraph (d)(3)(ii) of this section) of property first placed in service during the first half of the taxable year is determined by treating all such retirements from such account during the first half of the taxable year as occurring on the first day of the taxable year and all such retirements from such account during the second half of the taxable year as occurring on the first day of the second half of the taxable year. The depreciation allowance for a vintage account for a taxable year in which there is an extraordinary retirement (as defined in paragraph (d)(3)(ii) of this section) of property first placed in service during the second half of the taxable year is determined by treating all such retirements from such account during the first half of the taxable year as occurring on the first day of the second half of the taxable year and all such retirements in the second half of the taxable year as occurring on the first day of the succeeding taxable year.

(iii) *Half-year convention.*—The depreciation allowance for a vintage account for which the taxpayer adopts the "half-year convention" shall be determined by treating all property in the account as placed in service on the first day of the second half of the taxable year and by treating all extraordinary retirements (as defined in paragraph (d)(3)(ii) of this section) from the account as occurring on the first day of the second half of the taxable year.

(iv) *Rules of application.*—(a) The first-year convention adopted for a vintage account must be consistently applied to all additions to and all extraordinary retirements from such account. See paragraph (d)(3)(ii) and (iii) of this section for definition and treatment of ordinary retirements.

(b) If the actual number of months in a taxable year is other than 12 full calendar months, depreciation is allowed only for such actual number months and the term "taxable year", for purposes of this subparagraph, shall mean only such number of months. In such event, the first half of such taxable year shall be deemed to expire at the close of the last day of a calendar month which is the closest such last day to the middle of such taxable year and the second half of such taxable year shall be deemed to begin the day after the expiration of the first half of such taxable year. If a taxable year consists of a period which includes only one calendar month, the first half of the taxable year shall be deemed to expire on the first day which is nearest to the midpoint of the month, and the second half of the taxable year shall begin the day after the expiration of the first half of the month.

(c) For purposes of this subparagraph, for property placed in service after November 14, 1979, other than depreciable property described in paragraph (c)(2)(iv)(e) of this section, the taxable year of the person placing such property in service does not include any month before the month in which the person begins engaging in a trade or business or holding depreciable property for the production of income.

(d) For purposes of paragraph (c)(2)(iv)(c) of this section—

(1) For property placed in service after February 21, 1981, an employee is not considered engaged in a trade or business by virtue of employment.

(2) If a person engages in a small amount of trade or business activity after February 21, 1981, for the purpose of obtaining a disproportionately large depreciation deduction for assets for the taxable year in which they are placed in service, and placing those assets in service represents a substantial increase in the person's level of business activity, then for purposes of depreciating those assets the person will not be treated as beginning a trade or business until the increased amount of business activity begins. For property held for the production of income, the principle of the preceding sentence applies.

(3) A person may elect to apply the rules of § 1.167(a)-11(c)(2)(iv)(d) as set forth in T.D. 7763 ("(d) rules in T.D. 7763"). This election shall be made by reflecting it under paragraph (f)(4) of this section in the books and records. If necessary, amended returns shall be filed.

(4) If an averaging convention was adopted in reliance on or in anticipation of the (d) rules in T.D. 7763, that convention may be changed without regard to paragraph (f)(3) of this section. Similarly, if an election is made under paragraph (c)(2)(iv)(d) (3) of this section to apply the (d) rules in T.D. 7763, the averaging convention adopted for the taxable years for which the election is made may be changed. The change shall be made by filing a timely amended return for the taxable year for which the convention was adopted. Notwithstanding the three preceding sentences, if an averaging convention was adopted in reliance on or in anticipation of the (d) rules in T.D. 7763, and if an election is made to apply those rules, the averaging convention adopted cannot be changed except as provided in paragraph (f) of this section.

(e) The rules in paragraph (c)(2)(iv)(c) of this section do not apply to depreciable property placed in service after November 14, 1979, and the rules in paragraph (c)(2)(iv)(d) of this section do not

apply to depreciable property placed in service after February 21, 1981, with respect to which substantial expenditures were paid or incurred prior to November 15, 1979. For purposes of the preceding sentence, expenditures will not be considered substantial unless they exceed the lesser of 30 percent of the final cost of the property or $10 million. Expenditures that are not includible in the basis of the depreciable property will be considered expenditures with respect to property if they are directly related to a specific project involving such property. For purposes of determining whether expenditures were paid or incurred prior to November 15, 1979, expenditures made by a person (transferor) other than the person placing the property in service (transferee) will be taken into account only if the basis of the property in the hands of the transferee is determined in whole or in part by reference to the basis in the hands of the transferor. The principle of the preceding sentence also applies if there are multiple transfers.

(v) *Mass assets.*—In the case of mass assets, if extraordinary retirements of such assets in a guideline class during the first half of the taxable year are allocated to a particular vintage year for which the taxpayer applied the modified half-year convention, then that portion of the mass assets so allocated which bears the same ratio to the total number of mass assets so allocated as the mass assets in the same vintage and asset guideline class placed in service during the first half of that vintage year bear to the total mass assets in the same vintage and asset guideline class shall be treated as retired on the first day of the taxable year. The remaining mass assets which are subject to extraordinary retirement during the first half of the taxable year and which are allocated to that vintage year and asset guideline class shall be treated as retired on the first day of the second half of the taxable year. If extraordinary retirements of mass assets in a guideline class occur in the second half of the taxable year and are allocated to a particular vintage year for which the taxpayer applied the modified half-year convention, then that portion of the mass assets so allocated which bears the same ratio to the total number of mass assets so allocated as the mass assets in the same vintage and asset guideline class first placed in service during the first half of that vintage year bear to the total mass assets in the same vintage and asset guideline class shall be treated as retired on the first day of the second half of the taxable year. The remaining mass assets which are subject to extraordinary retirements during the second half of the taxable year and which are allocated to that same vintage and asset guideline class shall be treated as retired on the first day of the succeeding taxable year. If the taxpayer has applied the half-year convention for the vintage year to which the extraordinary retirements are allocated, the mass assets shall be treated as retired on the first day of the second half of the taxable year.

(3) *Taxable years beginning before and ending after December 31, 1970.*—In the case of a taxable year which begins before January 1, 1971, and ends after December 31, 1970, property first placed in service after December 31, 1970, but treated as first placed in service before January 1, 1971, by application of a convention described in subparagraph (2) of this paragraph shall be treated as provided in this subparagraph. The depreciation allowed (or allowable) for the taxable year shall consist of the depreciation allowed (or allowable) for the period before January 1, 1971, determined without regard to this section plus the amount allowable for the period after December 31, 1970, determined under this section. However, neither the modified half-year convention described in subparagraph (2)(ii) of this paragraph, nor the half-year convention described in subparagraph (2)(iii) of this paragraph may for any such taxable year be applied with respect to property placed in service after December 31, 1970, to allow depreciation for any period prior to January 1, 1971, unless such convention is consistent with the convention applied by the taxpayer with respect to property placed in service in such taxable year prior to January 1, 1971.

(4) *Examples.*—The principles of this paragraph may be illustrated by the following examples:

Example (1). Taxpayer A, a calendar year taxpayer, places new property in service in a trade or business as follows:

Asset	Placed in Service	Unadjusted Basis
W	April 1, 1971	$5,000
X	June 30, 1971	8,000
Y	July 15, 1971	12,000

Taxpayer A adopts the modified half-year convention described in subparagraph (2)(ii) of this paragraph. Assets W, X, and Y are placed in a multiple asset account for which the asset depreciation range is 8 to 12 years. A selects 8 years, the minimum asset depreciation period with respect to such assets, and adopts the declining balance method of depreciation using a rate twice the straight line rate (computed without reduction for salvage). The annual rate under this method using a period of 8 years is 25 percent. The depreciation allowance

for assets W and X for 1971 is $3,250, a full year's depreciation under the modified half-year convention (that is, basis of $13,000 (unreduced by salvage) multiplied by 25 percent). The depreciation allowance for asset Y for 1971 is zero under the modified half-year convention.

Example (2). The facts are the same as in example (1), except that the taxpayer adopts the half-year convention described in subparagraph (2)(iii) of this paragraph. The depreciation allowance with respect to asset Y is $1,500 (that is the basis of $12,000 multiplied by 25 percent, then multiplied by 1/2). Assets W and X are also entitled to a depreciation allowance for only a half year. Thus, the depreciation allowance for assets W and X for 1971 is $1,625 (that is, 1/2 of the $3,250 allowance computed in example (1)).

Example (3). Asset Z is placed in service by a calendar year taxpayer on December 1, 1971. The taxpayer places asset Z in an item account and adopts the sum of the years-digits method and the half-year convention described in subparagraph (2)(iii) of this paragraph. The asset depreciation range for such asset is 4 to 6 years and the taxpayer selects an asset depreciation period of 5 years. The depreciation allowance for asset Z in 1971 is $10,000 (that is, basis of $60,000

Asset	Placed in Service	Unadjusted Basis
A	April 30, 1970	$10,000
B	December 15, 1970	10,000
C	January 1, 1971	10,000

The taxpayer adopted a convention under §1.167(a)-10(b) with respect to assets placed in service prior to January 1, 1971, which treats assets placed in service during the first half of the year as placed in service on the first day of such year and assets placed in service in the second half of the year as placed in service on the first day of the following year. If the taxpayer selects the half-year convention described in subparagraph (2)(iii) of this paragraph, one year's depreciation is allowable on asset A determined without regard to this section. No depreciation is allowable for asset B. No depreciation is allowable for asset C for the period prior to January 1, 1971. One-

Asset	
A	August 1, 1970
B	January 15, 1971
C	June 30, 1971

The taxpayer adopted a convention under §1.167(a)-10(b) with respect to assets placed in service prior to January 1, 1971, which treats all assets as placed in service at the mid-point of the taxable year. If the taxpayer selects the half-year convention described in subparagraph (2)(iii) of this paragraph, one-half year's depreciation is allowable for asset A determined without regard to this section. One-half year's depreciation is allowable for assets B and C determined under this section.

Example (7). X, a calendar year corporation, is incorporated on July 1, 1978, and begins engaging in a trade or business in September 1979. X purchases asset A and places it in service on November 20, 1979. Substantial expenditures were not paid or incurred by X with respect to asset A prior to November 15, 1979. For purposes of applying the conventions under this section to determine depreciation for asset A, the 1979 taxable year is treated as consisting of 4 months. The first half of the taxable year ends on October 31, 1979, and the second half begins on November 1, 1979. X adopts the half-year convention. Asset A is treated as placed in service on November 1, 1979.

Example (8). On January 20, 1982, A, B, and C enter an agreement to form partnership P for the purpose of purchasing and leasing a ship to a third party, Z. P uses the calendar year as its taxable year. On December 15, 1982, P acquires the ship and leases it to Z. For purposes of applying the conventions, P begins its leasing business in December 1982, and its taxable year begins on December 1, 1982. Assuming that P elects to apply this section and adopts the modified half-year convention, P depreciates the ship placed in service in 1982 for the 1-month period beginning December 1, 1982, and ending December 31, 1982.

Example (9). A and B form partnership P on December 15, 1981, to conduct a business of leasing small aircraft. P uses the calendar year as its taxable year. On January 15, 1982, P acquires and places in service a $25,000 aircraft. P begins engaging in business with only one aircraft for the purpose of obtaining a disproportionately large depreciation deduction for aircraft that P plans to acquire at the end of the year. On December 10, 1982, P acquires and places in service 4 aircraft, the total purchase price of which is $250,000. For purposes of applying the conventions to the aircraft acquired in December, P begins its leasing business in December 1982, and P's taxable year begins December 1, 1982, and ends December 31, 1982. Assuming that P elects to apply this section and adopts the modified half-year convention, P depreciates the aircraft placed in service in December 1982, for the 1-month period beginning December 1, 1982, and ending December 31, 1982. P depreciates the aircraft placed in service in January 1982, for the 12-month period beginning January 1, 1982, and ending December 31, 1982.

(d) *Special rules for salvage, repairs and retirements.*—(1) *Salvage value.*—(i) *Definition of gross salvage value.*—"Gross salvage" value is the amount which is estimated will be realized upon a sale or other disposition of the property in the vintage account when it is no

(unreduced by salvage) multiplied by 5/15, the appropriate fraction using the sum of the years-digits method then multiplied by 1/2, since only one half year's depreciation is allowable under the convention).

Example (4). A is a calendar year taxpayer. All taxpayer A's assets are placed in service in the first half of 1971. If the taxpayer selects the modified half-year convention described in subparagraph (2)(ii) of this paragraph, a full year's depreciation is allowable for all assets.

Example (5). (i) The taxpayer during his taxable year which begins April 1, 1970, and ends March 31, 1971, places new property in service in a trade or business as follows:

fourth year's depreciation is allowable on asset C determined under this section.

(ii) The facts are the same as in (i) of this example except that the taxpayer adopts the modified half-year convention described in subparagraph (2)(ii) of this paragraph for 1971. No depreciation is allowable for assets B and C which were placed in service in the second half of the taxable year.

Example (6). The taxpayer during his taxable year which begins August 1, 1970, and ends July 31, 1971, places new property in service in a trade or business as follows:

longer useful in the taxpayer's trade or business or in the production of his income and is to be retired from service, without reduction for the cost of removal, dismantling, demolition or similar operations. If a taxpayer customarily sells or otherwise disposes of property at a time when such property is still in good operating condition, the gross salvage value of such property is the amount expected to be realized upon such sale or disposition, and under certain circumstances, as where such property is customarily sold at a time when it is still relatively new, the gross salvage value may constitute a relatively large proportion of the unadjusted basis of such property.

(ii) *Definition of salvage value.*—"Salvage value" means gross salvage value less the amount, if any, by which the gross salvage value is reduced by application of section 167(f). Generally, as provided in section 167(f), a taxpayer may reduce the amount of gross salvage value of a vintage account by an amount which does not exceed 10 percent of the unadjusted basis of the personal property (as defined in section 167(f)(2)) in the account. See paragraph (b)(3)(ii) of this section for requirement of separate vintage accounts for personal property described in section 167(f)(2).

(iii) *Estimation of salvage value.*—The salvage value of each vintage account of the taxable year shall be estimated by the taxpayer at the time the election to apply this section is made, upon the basis of all the facts and circumstances existing at the close of the taxable year in which the account is established. The taxpayer shall specify the amount, if any, by which gross salvage value taken into account is reduced by application of section 167(f). The salvage value estimated by the taxpayer will not be redetermined merely as a result of fluctuations in price levels or as a result of other facts and circumstances occurring after the close of the taxable year of election. Salvage value for a vintage account need not be established or increased as a result of a property improvement as described in subparagraph (2)(vii) of this paragraph. The taxpayer shall maintain records reasonably sufficient to determine facts and circumstances taken into account in estimating salvage value.

(iv) *Salvage as limitation on depreciation.*—In no case may a vintage account be depreciated below a reasonable salvage value after taking into account any reduction in gross salvage value permitted by section 167(f).

(v) *Limitation on adjustment of reasonable salvage value.*—The salvage value established by the taxpayer for a vintage account will not be redetermined if it is reasonable. Since the determination of salvage value is a matter of estimation, minimal adjustments will not be made. The salvage value established by the taxpayer will be deemed to be reasonable unless there is sufficient basis in the facts and circumstances existing at the close of the taxable year in which the account is established for a determination of an amount of salvage value for the account which exceeds the salvage value established by the taxpayer for the account by an amount greater than 10 percent of the unadjusted basis of the account at the close of the taxable year in which the account is established. If the salvage value established by the taxpayer for the account is not within the 10 percent range, or if the taxpayer follows the practice of understating his estimates of gross salvage value to take advantage of this subdivision, and if there is a determination of an amount of salvage value for the account which exceeds the salvage value established by the taxpayer for the account, an adjustment will be made by increasing the salvage value established by the taxpayer for the account by an amount equal to the difference between the salvage value as determined and the salvage value established by the taxpayer for the account. For the purposes of this subdivision, a determination of salvage value shall include all determinations at all levels of audit and appellate proceedings, and as well as all final determinations within the meaning of section 1313(a)(1). This subdivision shall apply to each such determination. (See example (3) of subdivision (vi) of this subparagraph.)

(vi) *Examples.*—The principles of this subparagraph may be illustrated by the following examples in which it is assumed that the taxpayer has not followed a practice of understating his estimates of gross salvage value:

Example (1). Taxpayer B elects to apply this section to assets Y and Z, which are placed in a multiple asset vintage account of 1971 for which the taxpayer selects an asset depreciation period of 8 years. The unadjusted basis of asset Y is $50,000 and the unadjusted basis of asset Z is $30,000. B estimates a gross salvage value of $55,000. The property qualifies under section 167(f)(2) and B reduces the amount of salvage taken into account by $8,000 (that is, 10 percent of $80,000 under section 167(f)). Thus, B establishes a salvage value of $47,000 for the account. Assume that there is not sufficient basis for determining a salvage value for the account greater than $52,000 (that is, $60,000 minus the $8,000 reduction under section 167(f)). Since the salvage value of $47,000 established by B for the account is within the 10 percent range, it is reasonable. Salvage value for the account will not be redetermined.

Example (2). The facts are the same as in example (1) except that B estimates a gross salvage value of $50,000 and establishes a salvage value of $42,000 for the account (that is, $50,000 minus the $8,000 reduction under section 167(f)). There is sufficient basis for determining an amount of salvage value greater than $50,000 (that is, $58,000 minus the $8,000 reduction under section 167(f)). The salvage value of $42,000 established by B for the account can be redetermined without regard to the limitation in subdivision (v) of this subparagraph, since it is not within the 10 percent range. Upon audit of B's tax return for a taxable year for which the redetermination would affect the amount of depreciation allowable for the account, salvage value is determined to be $52,000 after taking into account the reduction under section 167(f). Salvage value for the account will be adjusted to $52,000.

Example (3). The facts are the same as in example (1) except that upon audit of B's tax return for a taxable year the examining officer determines the salvage value to be $58,000 (that is, $66,000 minus the $8,000 reduction under section 167(f)), and proposes to adjust salvage value for the vintage account to $58,000 which will result in disallowing an amount of depreciation for the taxable year. B does not agree with the finding of the examining officer. After receipt of a "30-day letter", B waives a district conference and initiates proceedings before the Appellate Division. In consideration of the case by the Appellate Division it is concluded that there is not sufficient basis for determining an amount of salvage value for the account in excess of $55,000 (that is, $63,000 minus the $8,000 reduction under section 167(f)). Since the salvage of $47,000 established by B for the account is within the 10 percent range, it is reasonable. Salvage value for the account will not be redetermined.

Example (4). Taxpayer C elects to apply this section to factory building X which is placed in an item vintage account of 1971. The unadjusted basis of factory building X is $90,000. C estimates a gross salvage value for the account of $10,000. The property does not qualify under section 167(f)(2). C establishes a salvage value of $10,000 for the account. Assume that there is not sufficient basis for determining a salvage value for the account greater than $18,000. Since the salvage value of $10,000 established by B for the account is within the 10 percent range, it is reasonable. Salvage value for the account will not be redetermined.

(2) *Treatment of repairs.*—(i) *In general.*—(a) Sections 162, 212, and 263 provide general rules for the treatment of certain expenditures for the repair, maintenance, rehabilitation or improvement of property. In general, under those sections, expenditures which substantially prolong the life of an asset, or are made to increase its value or adapt it to a different use are capital expenditures. If an expenditure is treated as a capital expenditure under section 162, 212, or 263, it is subject to the allowance for depreciation. On the other hand, in general, expenditures which do not substantially prolong the life of

an asset or materially increase its value or adapt it for a substantially different use may be deducted as an expense in the taxable year in which paid or incurred. Expenditures, or a series of expenditures, may have characteristics both of deductible expenses and capital expenditures. Other expenditures may have the characteristics of capital expenditures, as in the case of an "excluded addition" (as defined in subdivision (vi) of this subparagraph). This subparagraph provides a simplified procedure for determining whether expenditures with respect to certain property are to be treated as deductible expenses or capital expenditures.

(b) [Reserved]

(ii) *Election of repair allowance.*—In the case of an asset guideline class which consists of "repair allowance property" as defined in subdivision (iii) of this subparagraph, subject to the provisions of subdivision (v) of this subparagraph, the taxpayer may elect to apply the asset guideline class repair allowance described in subdivision (iii) of this subparagraph for any taxable year ending after December 31, 1970, for which the taxpayer elects to apply this section.

(iii) *Repair allowance for an asset guideline class.*—For a taxable year for which the taxpayer elects to apply this section, the "repair allowance" for an asset guideline class which consists of "repair allowance property" is an amount equal to—

(a) The average of (1) the unadjusted basis of all "repair allowance property" in the asset guideline class at the beginning of the taxable year, less in the case of such property in a vintage account the unadjusted basis of all such property retired in an ordinary retirement (as described in subparagraph (3)(ii) of this paragraph) in prior taxable years, and (2) the unadjusted basis of all "repair allowance property" in the asset guideline class at the end of the taxable year, less in the case of such property in a vintage account the unadjusted basis of all such property retired in an ordinary retirement (including ordinary retirements during the taxable year), multiplied by—

(b) The repair allowance percentage in effect for the asset guideline class for the taxable year.

In applying the asset guideline class repair allowance to buildings which are section 1250 property, for the purpose of this subparagraph each building shall be treated as in a separate guideline class. If two or more buildings are in the same asset guideline class determined without regard to the preceding sentence, and are operated as an integrated unit (as evidenced by their actual operation, management, financing, and accounting), they shall be treated as a single building for this purpose. The "repair allowance percentages" in effect for taxable years ending before the effective date of the first supplemental repair allowance percentages established pursuant to this section are set forth in Revenue Procedure 72-10 [superseded by Rev. Proc. 77-10; see ¶ 1732D.08]. Repair allowance percentages will from time to time be established, supplemented and revised with express reference to this section. These repair allowance percentages will be published in the Internal Revenue Bulletin. The repair allowance percentages in effect on the last day of the taxable year of election shall apply for the taxable year, except that the repair allowance percentage for a particular taxable year shall not be less than the repair allowance percentage in effect on the first day of such taxable year (or as of such later time in such year as a repair allowance percentage first established during such year becomes effective). Generally, the repair allowance percentages for a taxable year shall not be changed to reflect any supplement or revision of the repair allowance percentages after the end of such taxable year. However, if expressly provided in such a supplement or revision of the repair allowance percentages, the taxpayer may, at his option in the manner specified therein, apply the revised or supplemented repair allowance percentages for such taxable year and succeeding taxable years. For the purposes of this section, "repair allowance property" means eligible property determined without regard to paragraph (b)(2)(ii) of this section (that is, without regard to whether such property was first placed in service by the taxpayer before or after December 31, 1970) in an asset guideline class for which a repair allowance percentage is in effect for the taxable year. The determination whether property is repair allowance property shall be made without regard to whether such property is excluded, under paragraph (b)(5) of this section, from an election to apply this section. Property in an asset guideline class for which the taxpayer elects to apply the asset guideline class repair allowance described in this subdivision, which results from expenditures in the taxable year of election for the repair, maintenance, rehabilitation, or improvement of property in an asset guideline class shall not be "repair allowance property" for such taxable year but shall be for each succeeding taxable year provided such property is a property improvement as described in subdivision (vii)(a) of this subparagraph and is in an asset guideline class for which a repair allowance percentage is in effect for such succeeding taxable year.

(iv) *Application of asset guideline class repair allowance.*—In accordance with the principles of sections 162, 212, and 263, if the taxpayer pays or incurs any expenditures during the taxable year for the repair, maintenance, rehabilitation or improvement of eligible property (determined without regard to paragraph (b)(2)(ii) of this section), the taxpayer must either—

(a) If such property is repair allowance property and if the taxpayer elects to apply the repair allowance for the asset guideline class, treat an amount of all such expenditures in such taxable year with respect to all such property in the asset guideline class which does not exceed in total the repair allowance for that asset guideline class as deductible repairs, and treat the excess of all such expenditures with respect to all such property in the asset guideline class in the manner described for a property improvement in subdivision (viii) of this subparagraph, or

(b) If such property is not repair allowance property or if the taxpayer does not elect to apply the repair allowance for the asset guideline class, treat each of such expenditures in such taxable year with respect to all such property in the asset guideline class as either a capital expenditure or as a deductible repair in accordance with the principles of sections 162, 212, and 263 (without regard to (a) of this subdivision), and treat the expenditures which are required to be capitalized under sections 162, 212, and 263 (without regard to (a) of this subdivision) in the manner described for a property improvement in subdivision (viii) of this subparagraph.

For the purposes of (a) of this subdivision expenditures for the repair, maintenance, rehabilitation or improvement of property do not include expenditures for an excluded addition or for which a deduction is allowed under section 167(k). (See subdivision (viii) of this subparagraph for treatment of an excluded addition.) The taxpayer shall elect each taxable year whether to apply the repair allowance and treat expenditures under (a) of this subdivision, or to treat expenditures under (b) of this subdivision. The treatment of expenditures under this subdivision for a taxable year for all asset guideline classes shall be specified in the books and records of the taxpayer for the taxable year. The taxpayer may treat expenditures under (a) of this subdivision with respect to property in one asset guideline class and treat expenditures under (b) of this subdivision with respect to property in some other asset guideline class. In addition, the taxpayer may treat expenditures with respect to property in an asset guideline class under (a) of this subdivision in one taxable year, and treat expenditures with respect to property in that asset guideline class under (b) of this subdivision in another taxable year.

(v) *Special rules for repair allowance.*—(a) The asset guideline class repair allowance described in subdivision (iii) of this subparagraph shall apply only to expenditures for the repair, maintenance, rehabilitation or improvement of repair allowance property (as described in subdivision (iii) of this subparagraph). The taxpayer may apply the asset guideline class repair allowance for the taxable year only if he maintains books and records reasonably sufficient to determine:

(1) The amount of expenditures paid or incurred during the taxable year for the repair, maintenance, rehabilitation or improvement of repair allowance property in the asset guideline class, and

(2) The expenditures (and the amount thereof) with respect to such property which are for excluded additions (such as whether the expenditure is for an additional identifiable unit of property, or substantially increases the productivity or capacity of an existing identifiable unit of property or adapts it for a substantially different use).

In general, such books and records shall be sufficient to identify the amount and nature of expenditures with respect to specific items of repair allowance property or groups of similar properties in the same asset guideline class. However, in the case of such expenditures with respect to property, part of which is in one asset guideline class and part in another, or part of which is repair allowance property and part of which is not, and in comparable circumstances involving property in the same asset guideline class, to the extent books and records are not maintained identifying such expenditures with specific items of property or groups of similar properties and it is not practicable to do so, the total amount of such expenditures which is not specifically identified may be allocated by any reasonable method consistently applied. In any case, the cost or repair, maintenance, rehabilitation or improvement of property performed by production personnel may be allocated by any reasonable method consistently applied and, if performed incidental to production and not substantial in amount, no allocation to repair, maintenance, rehabilitation or improvement need be made. The types of expenditures for which *specific identification would ordinarily be made* include: substantial expenditures such as for major parts or major structural materials for which a work order is or would customarily be written; expenditures for work performed by an outside contractor; or expenditures under a specific down time program. Types of expendi-

tures for which specific identification would ordinarily be impractical include: general maintenance costs of machinery, equipment, and plant in the case of a taxpayer having assets in more than one class (or different types of assets in the same class) which are located together and generally maintained by the same work crew; small supplies which are used with respect to various classes or types of property; labor costs of personnel who work on property in different classes, or different types of property in the same class, if the work is performed on a routine, as needed, basis and the only identification of the property repaired is by the personnel. Factors which will be taken into account in determining the reasonableness of the taxpayer's allocation of expenditures include prior experience of the taxpayer; relative bases of the assets in the guideline class; types of assets involved; and relationship to specifically identified expenditures.

(b) If for the taxable year the taxpayer elects to deduct under section 263(e) expenditures with respect to repair allowance property consisting of railroad rolling stock (other than a locomotive) in a particular asset guideline class, the taxpayer may not, for such taxable year, use the asset guideline class repair allowance described in subdivision (iii) of this subparagraph for any property in such asset guideline class.

(c)(1) If the taxpayer repairs, rehabilitates or improves property for sale or resale to customers, the asset guideline class repair allowance described in subdivision (iii) of this subparagraph shall not apply to expenditures for the repair, maintenance, rehabilitation or improvement of such property, or

(2) if a taxpayer follows the practice of acquiring for his own use property (in need of repair, rehabilitation or improvement to be suitable for the use intended by the taxpayer) and of making expenditures to repair, rehabilitate or improve such property in order to take advantage of this subparagraph, the asset guideline class repair allowance described in subdivision (iii) of this subparagraph shall not apply to such expenditures. In either event, such property shall not be "repair allowance property" as described in subdivision (iii) of this subparagraph.

(vi) *Definition of excluded addition.*—The term "excluded addition" means—

(a) An expenditure which substantially increases the productivity of an existing identifiable unit of property over its productivity when first acquired by the taxpayer;

(b) An expenditure which substantially increases the capacity of an existing identifiable unit of property over its capacity when first acquired by the taxpayer;

(c) An expenditure which modifies an existing identifiable unit of property for a substantially different use;

(d) An expenditure for an identifiable unit of property if (1) such expenditure is for an additional identifiable unit of property or (2) such expenditure (other than an expenditure described in (e) of this subdivision) is for replacement of an identifiable unit of property which was retired;

(e) An expenditure for replacement of a part in or a component or portion of an existing identifiable unit of property (whether or not such part, component or portion is also an identifiable unit of property) if such part, component or portion is for replacement of a part, component or portion which was retired in a retirement upon which gain or loss is recognized (or would be recognized but for a special nonrecognition provision of the Code or § 1.1502-13).

(f) In the case of a building or other structure (in addition to (b), (c), (d) and (e) of this subdivision which also apply to such property), an expenditure for additional cubic or linear space; and

(g) In the case of those units of property of pipelines, electric utilities, telephone companies, and telegraph companies consisting of lines, cables and poles (in addition to (a) through (e) of this subdivision which also apply to such property), an expenditure for replacement of a material portion of the unit of property.

Except as provided in (d) and (e) of this subdivision, notwithstanding any other provision of this subdivision, the term "excluded addition" does not include any expenditure in connection with the repair, maintenance, rehabilitation or improvement of an identifiable unit of property which does not exceed $100. For this purpose all related expenditures with respect to the unit of property shall be treated as a single expenditure. For the purposes of (a) and (b) of this subdivision, an increase in productivity or capacity is substantial only if the increase is more than 25 percent. An expenditure which merely extends the productive life of an identifiable unit of property is not an increase in productivity within the meaning of (a) of this subdivision. Under (g) of this subdivision a replacement is material only if the portion replaced exceeds 5 percent of the unit of property with respect to which the replacement is made. For the purposes of this subdivision, a unit of property generally consists of each operating unit (that is, each separate machine or piece of equipment) which performs a discrete function and which the taxpayer customarily acquires for original installation and retires as a unit. The taxpayer's accounting classification of units of property will generally be accepted for purposes of this subdivision provided the classifications are reasonably consistent with the preceding sentence and are consistently applied. In the case of a building the unit of property generally consists of the building as well as its structural components; except that each building service system (such as an elevator, an escalator, the electrical system, or the heating and cooling system) is an identifiable unit for the purpose of (a), (b), (c), and (d) of this subdivision. However, both in the case of machinery and equipment and in the case of a building, for the purpose of applying (d)(1) of this subdivision a unit of property may consist of a part in or a component or portion of a larger unit of property. In the case of property described in (g) of this subdivision (such as a pipeline), a unit of property generally consists of each segment which performs a discreet function either as to capacity, service, transmission or distribution between identifiable points. Thus, for example, under this subdivision in the case of a vintage account of five automobiles each automobile is an identifiable unit of property which is not merely a part in or a component or portion of larger unit of property within the meaning of (e) of this subdivision). Accordingly, the replacement of one of the automobiles (which is retired) with another automobile is an excluded addition under (d)(2) of this subdivision. Also the purchase of a sixth automobile is an expenditure for an additional identifiable unit of property and is an excluded addition under (d)(1) of this subdivision. An automobile air conditioner is also an identifiable unit of property for the purposes of (d)(1) of this subdivision, but not for the purposes of (d)(2) of this subdivision. Accordingly, the addition of an air conditioner to an automobile is an excluded addition under (d)(1) of this subdivision, but the replacement of an existing air conditioner in an automobile is not an excluded addition under (d)(2) of this subdivision (since it is merely the replacement of a part in an existing identifiable unit of property). The replacement of the air conditioner may, however, be an excluded addition under (e) of this subdivision, if the air conditioner replaced was retired in a retirement upon which gain or loss was recognized. The principles of this subdivision may be further illustrated by the following examples in which it is assumed (unless otherwise stated) that (e) of this subdivision does not apply.

Example (1). For the taxable year, B pays or incurs only the following expenditures: (1) $5,000 for general maintenance of repair allowance property (as described in subdivision (iii) of this subparagraph) such as inspection, oiling, machine adjustments, cleaning, and painting; (2) $175 for replacement of the bearings and gears in an existing lathe; (3) $125 for replacement of an electric starter (of the same capacity) and certain electrical wiring in an automatic drill press; (4) $300 for modification of a metal fabricating machine (including replacement of certain parts) which substantially increases its capacity; (5) $175 for repair of the same metal fabricating machine which does not substantially increase its capacity; (6) $800 for the replacement of an existing lathe with a new lathe; and (7) $65 for the repair of a drill press. Expenditures (1) through (3) are expenditures for the repair, maintenance, rehabilitation or improvement of property to which B can elect to apply the asset guideline class repair allowance described in subdivision (iii) of this subparagraph. Expenditure (4) is an excluded addition under (b) of this subdivision. Expenditure (5) is not an excluded addition. Expenditure (6) is an excluded addition under (d)(2) of this subdivision. Without regard to (a), (b) and (c) of this subdivision, expenditure (7) is not an excluded addition, since the expenditure does not exceed $100.

Example (2). Corporation M operates a steel plant which produces rails, blooms, billets, special bar sections, reinforcing bars, and large diameter line pipe. During the taxable year, corporation M: (1) relines an open-hearth furnace; (2) places in service 20 new ingot molds; (3) replaces one reversing roll in the blooming mill; (4) overhauls the rail and billet mill with no increase in capacity; (5) replaces a roll stand in the 20-inch bar mill; and (6) overhauls the 11-inch bar mill and reducing stands increasing billet speed from 1800 feet per minute to 2300 feet per minute. Assume that each expenditure exceeds $100. Expenditure (1) is not an excluded addition. Expenditure (2) is an excluded addition under (d)(1) of this subdivision. Expenditure (3) is not an excluded addition since the expenditure for the reversing roll merely replaces a part in an existing identifiable unit of property. Expenditure (4) is not an excluded addition. Expenditure (5) is an excluded addition under (d)(2) of this subdivision since the roll stand is not merely a part of an existing identifiable unit of property. Expenditure (6) is an excluded addition under (a) of this subdivision since it increases the billet speed by more than 25 percent.

Example (3). For the taxable year, corporation X pays or incurs the following expenditures: (1) $1,000 for two new temporary partition walls in the company's offices; (2) $1,400 for repainting the exterior of a terminal building; (3) $300 for repair of the roof of a warehouse; (4) $150 for replacement of two window frames and panes in the warehouse; and (5) $100 for plumbing repair. Expendi-

ture (1) is an excluded addition under (d)(1) of this subdivision. None of the other expenditures are excluded additions.

Example (4). For the taxable year, corporation Y pays or incurs the following expenditures: (1) $10,000 for expansion of a loading dock from 600 square feet to 750 square feet; (2) $600 for replacement of two roof girders in a factory building; and (3) $9,500 for replacement of columns and girders supporting the floor of a second story loft storage area within the factory building in order to permit storage of supplies with a gross weight 50 percent greater than the previous capacity of the loft. Expenditure (1) is an excluded addition under (f) of this subdivision. Expenditure (2) is not an excluded addition. Expenditure (3) is an excluded addition under (b) of this subdivision.

Example (5). Corporation A has an office building with an unadjusted basis of $10,000,000. The building has 10 elevators, five of which are manually operated and five of which are automatic. During 1971, corporation A:

(1) replaces the five manually operated elevators with high-speed automatic elevators at a cost of $400,000;

(2) replaces the cable in one of the existing automatic elevators at a cost of $1,700.

The replacements of the elevators are excluded additions under (d)(2) of this subdivision. The replacement of the cable is not an excluded addition.

Example (6). Taxpayer W, a cement manufacturer, engages in the following modification and maintenance activities during the taxable year: (1) replaces eccentric-bearing, spindle, and wearing surface in a gyratory crusher; (2) places in service a new apron feeder and hammer mill; (3) replaces four buckets on a chain bucket elevator; (4) relines refractory surface in the burning zone of a rotary kiln; (5) installs additional new dust collectors; and (6) replaces two 16-inch x 90-foot belts on his conveyor system. Assume that there is no increase in productivity or capacity and that each expenditure exceeds $100. Expenditure (1) is not an excluded addition. Expenditure (2) [is] an excluded addition under (d)(1) of this subdivision. Expenditures (3) and (4) are not excluded additions. Expenditure (5) is an excluded addition under (d)(1) of this subdivision. Expenditure (6) is not an excluded addition.

Example (7). Corporation X, a gas pipeline company, has, in addition to others, the following units of property: (1) a gathering pipeline for a field consisting of 25 gas wells; (2) the main transmission line between compressor stations (that is, in the case of a 500 mile main transmission line with a compressor station every 100 miles, each one hundred miles section between compressor stations is a separate unit of property); (3) a lateral transmission line from the main transmission line to a city border station; (4) a medium pressure distribution line to the northern portion of the city; and (5) a low pressure distribution line serving a group of approximately 200 residential customers off the medium pressure distribution line. In 1971, corporation X pays or incurs the following expenditures in connection with the repair, maintenance, rehabilitation or improvement of repair allowance property; (1) replaces a meter on a gas well; (2) in connection with the repair and rehabilitation of a unit of property consisting of a two-mile gathering pipeline, replaces a 3,000-foot section of the gathering line; (3) in connection with the repair of leaks in a unit of property consisting of a 100-mile gas transmission line (that is, the 100 miles between compressor stations), replaces a 2,000-foot section of pipeline at one point; and (4) at another point replaces a 7-mile section of the same 100-mile gas transmission line. Assume that none of these expenditures substantially increases capacity and that each expenditure exceeds $100. Expenditure (1) is an excluded addition under (d) of this subdivision. Expenditure (2) is an excluded addition under (g) of this subdivision since the portion replaced is more than 5 percent of the unit of property. Expenditure (3) is not an excluded addition. Expenditure (4) is an excluded addition under (g) of this subdivision.

Example (8). Taxpayer Y, an electric utility company, has in addition to others, the following units of property: (1) a high voltage transmission circuit from the switching station (at the generating station) to the transmission station; (2) a series of 100 poles (fully dressed) supporting the circuit in (1); (3) a high voltage circuit from the transmission station to the distribution substation; (4) a high voltage distribution circuit (either radial or looped) from the distribution substation; (5) a transformer on a distribution pole; (6) a circuit breaker on a distribution pole; and (7) all 220 (and lower) volt circuit (including customer service connections) off the distribution circuit in (4). In 1971, taxpayer Y pays or incurs the following expenditures for the repair, maintenance, rehabilitation or improvement of repair allowance property: (1) replaces 25 adjacent poles in a unit of property consisting of the 300 poles supporting a radial distribution circuit from a distribution substation; (2) replaces a transformer on one of the poles in (1); (3) replaces a cross-arm on one of the poles in (1); (4) replaces a 200-foot section of a 2-mile radial distribution circuit serving 100 residential customers; and (5) replaces a 2,000-foot

Reg. §1.167(a)-11(d)(2)(vi)(g)

section on a 10-mile high voltage circuit from a transmission station to a distribution substation which was destroyed by a casualty which taxpayer Y treated as an extraordinary retirement under paragraph (d)(3)(ii) of this section. Expenditure (1) is an excluded addition under (g) of this subdivision. Expenditure (2) is an excluded addition under (d)(2) of this subdivision. Expenditures (3) and (4) are not excluded additions. Expenditure (5) is an excluded addition under (e) of this subdivision.

Example (9). Corporation Z, a telephone company, has in addition to others, the following units of property: (1) a buried feeder cable 3 miles in length off a local switching station; (2) a buried sub-feeder cable one mile in length off the feeder cable in (1); (3) all the distribution cable (and customer service drops) off the sub-feeder cable in (2); (4) the 300 poles (fully dressed) supporting the distribution cable in (3); (5) a 10-mile local trunk cable which interconnects two local tandem switching stations; (6) a toll connecting trunk cable from a local tandem switching station to a long distance tandem switching station; (7) a toll trunk cable 50 miles in length from the access point at one city to the access point at another city. In 1971, corporation Z pays or incurs the following expenditures in connection with the repair, maintenance, rehabilitation or improvement of repair allowance property: (1) replaces 100 feet of distribution cable in a unit of property consisting of 8 miles of local distribution cable (plus customer service drops); (2) replaces an amplifier in the distribution system; and (3) replaces 10 miles of a unit of property consisting of a toll trunk cable 50 miles in length.

Expenditure (1) is not an excluded addition. Expenditure (2) is an excluded addition under (d)(2) of this subdivision. Expenditure (3) is an excluded addition under (g) of this subdivision.

(vii) *Definition of property improvement.*—The term "property improvement" means—

(a) If the taxpayer treats expenditures for the asset guideline class under subdivision (iv)(a) of this subparagraph, the amount of all expenditures paid or incurred during the taxable year for the repair, maintenance, rehabilitation or improvement of repair allowance property in the asset guideline class, which exceeds the asset guideline class repair allowance for the taxable year; and

(b) If the taxpayer treats expenditures for the asset guideline class under subdivision (iv)(b) of this subparagraph, the amount of each expenditure paid or incurred during the taxable year for the repair, maintenance, rehabilitation or improvements of property which is treated under sections 162, 212 and 263 as a capital expenditure.

The term "property improvement" does not include any expenditure for an excluded addition.

(viii) *Treatment of property improvements and excluded additions.*—If for the taxable year there is a property improvement as described in subdivision (vii) of this subparagraph or an excluded addition as described in subdivision (vi) of this subparagraph, the following rules shall apply—

(a) The total amount of any property improvement for the asset guideline class determined under subdivision (vii)(a) of this subparagraph shall be capitalized in a single "special basis vintage account" of the taxable year in accordance with the taxpayer's election to apply this section for the taxable year (applied without regard to paragraph (b)(5)(v)(a) of this section). See subparagraph (3)(vi) of this paragraph for definition and treatment of a "special basis vintage account".

(b) Each property improvement determined under subdivision (vii)(b) of this subparagraph, if it is eligible property, shall be capitalized in a vintage account of the taxable year in accordance with the taxpayer's election to apply this section for the taxable year (applied without regard to paragraph (b)(5)(v)(a) of this section).

(c) Each excluded addition, if it is eligible property, shall be capitalized in a vintage account of the taxable year in accordance with the taxpayer's election to apply this section for the taxable year. For rule as to date on which a property improvement or an excluded addition is first placed in service, see paragraph (e)(1)(iii) and (iv) of this section.

(ix) *Examples.*—The principles of this subparagraph may be illustrated by the following examples:

Example (1). For the taxable year 1972, B elects to apply this section. B has repair allowance property (as described in subdivision (iii) of this subparagraph) in asset guideline class 20.2 under Revenue Procedure 72-10 with an average unadjusted basis determined as provided in subdivision (iii)(a) of this subparagraph of $100,000 and repair allowance property in asset guideline class 24.4 with an average unadjusted basis of $300,000. The repair allowance percentage for asset guideline class 20.2 is 4.5 percent and for asset guideline class 24.4 is 6.5 percent. The two asset guideline class repair allowances for 1972 are $4,500 and $19,500, respectively, determined as follows:

Asset Guideline Class 20.2

$100,000 average unadjusted basis multiplied by 4.5 percent	$4,500

Asset Guideline Class 24.4

$300,000 average unadjusted basis multiplied by 6.5 percent	$19,500

Example (2). The facts are the same as in example (1). During the taxable year 1972, B pays or incurs the following expenditures for the repair, maintenance, rehabilitation or improvement of repair allowance property in asset guideline class 20.2.

General maintenance (including primarily labor costs)	$3,000
Replacement of parts in several machines (including labor costs of $1,650)	$4,000
	$7,000

In addition, in connection with the rehabilitation and improvement of two other machines B pays or incurs $6,000 (including labor costs of $2,000) which is treated as an excluded addition because the capacity of the machines was substantially increased. For 1972, B elects to apply this section and to apply the asset guideline class repair allowance to asset guideline class 20.2. Since the asset guideline class repair allowance is $4,500, B can deduct $4,500 in accordance with subdivision (iv)(a) of this subparagraph. B must capitalize $2,500 in a special basis vintage account in accordance with subdivisions (vii)(a) and (viii)(a) of this subparagraph. Since the excluded addition is a capital item and is eligible property, B must also capitalize $6,000 in a vintage account in accordance with subdivision (viii)(c) of this subparagraph. B selects from the asset depreciation range an asset depreciation period of 17 years for the special basis vintage account. B includes the excluded addition in a vintage account of 1972 for which he also selects an asset depreciation period of 17 years.

(3) *Treatment of retirements.*—(i) *In general.*—The rules of this subparagraph specify the treatment of all retirements from vintage accounts. The rules of § 1.167(a)-8 shall not apply to any retirement from a vintage account. An asset in a vintage account is retired when such asset is permanently withdrawn from use in a trade or business or in the production of income by the taxpayer. A retirement may occur as a result of a sale or exchange, by other act of the taxpayer amounting to a permanent disposition of an asset, or by physical abandonment of an asset. A retirement may also occur by transfer of an asset to supplies or scrap.

(ii) *Definitions of ordinary and extraordinary retirements.*—The term "ordinary retirement" means any retirement of section 1245 property from a vintage account which is not treated as an "extraordinary retirement" under this subparagraph. The retirement of an asset from a vintage account in a taxable year is an "extraordinary retirement" if—

(a) The asset is section 1250 property;

(b) The asset is section 1245 property which is retired as the direct result of fire, storm, shipwreck, or other casualty and the taxpayer, at his option consistently applied (taking into account type, frequency and the size of such casualties) treats such retirements as extraordinary; or

(c) (1) The asset is section 1245 property which is retired (other than by transfer to supplies or scrap) in a taxable year as the direct result of a cessation, termination, curtailment, or disposition of a business, manufacturing, or other income producing process, operation, facility or unit, and (2) the unadjusted basis (determined without regard to subdivision (vi) of this subparagraph) of all such assets so retired in such taxable year from such account as a direct result of the event described in (c)(1) of this subdivision exceeds 20 percent of the unadjusted basis of such account immediately prior to such event.

(d) The asset is section 1245 property which is retired after December 30, 1980, by a charitable contribution for which a deduction is allowable under section 170.

For the purposes of (c) of this subdivision, all accounts (other than a special basis vintage account as described in subdivision (vi) of this subparagraph) containing section 1245 property of the same vintage in the same asset guideline class, and from which a retirement as a direct result of such event occurs within the taxable year, shall be treated as a single vintage account. See subdivision (xi) of this subparagraph for special rule for item accounts. The principles of this subdivision may be illustrated by the following examples:

Example (1). Taxpayer A is a processor and distributor of dairy products. Part of taxpayer A's operation is a bottle washing facility consisting of machines X, Y, and Z, each of which is in an item vintage account of 1971. Each item vintage account has an unadjusted basis of $1,000. Taxpayer A also has a 1971 multiple asset vintage account consisting of machines E, S, and C. Machines E and S, used in processing butter, each as an unadjusted basis of $10,000. Machine C used in capping bottles has an unadjusted basis of $1,000. In 1975, taxpayer A changes to the use of paper milk cartons and disposes of all bottle washing machines (X, Y, and Z) as well as machine C which was used in capping bottles. The sales of machines C, X, Y, and Z are the direct result of the termination of a manufacturing process. However, since the total unadjusted basis of the eligible section 1245 property retired as a direct result of such event is only $4,000 (which is less than 20 percent of the total unadjusted basis of machines E, S, C, X, Y, and Z, $24,000) the sales are ordinary retirements. All the assets are in the same asset guideline class and are of the same vintage. Accordingly, machines E, S, C, X, Y, and Z are for this purpose treated as being in a single vintage account.

Example (2). The facts are the same as in example (1) except that in 1976, taxpayer A sells six of his 12 milk delivery trucks as a direct result of eliminating home deliveries to customers in the suburbs. Deliveries within the city require only six trucks. Each of the trucks has an unadjusted basis of $3,000. Six of the taxpayer's delivery trucks are in a multiple asset vintage account of 1974 and six are in a multiple asset vintage account of 1972. Neither account contains any other property. Four trucks are retired from the 1972 vintage account and two trucks are retired from the 1974 vintage account. The sales result from the curtailment of taxpayer A's home delivery operation. The unadjusted basis of the four trucks retired from the 1972 vintage exceeds 20 percent of the total unadjusted basis of the affected account. The same is true for the two trucks retired from the 1974 vintage account. The sales of the trucks are extraordinary retirements.

(iii) *Treatment of ordinary retirements.*—No loss shall be recognized upon an ordinary retirement. Gain shall be recognized only to the extent specified in this subparagraph. All proceeds from ordinary retirements shall be added to the depreciation reserve of the vintage account from which the retirement occurs. See subdivision (vi) of this subparagraph for optional allocation of basis in the case of a special basis vintage account. See subdivision (ix) of this subparagraph for recognition of gain when the depreciation reserve exceeds the unadjusted basis of the vintage account. The amount of salvage value for a vintage account shall be reduced (but not below zero) as of the beginning of the taxable year by the excess of *(a)* the depreciation reserve for the account, after adjustment for depreciation allowable for such taxable year and all other adjustments prescribed by this section (other than the adjustment prescribed by subdivision (ix) of this subparagraph), over *(b)* the unadjusted basis of the account less the amount of salvage value for the account before such reduction. Thus, in the case of a vintage account with an unadjusted basis of $1,000 and a salvage value of $100, to the extent that proceeds from ordinary retirements increase the depreciation reserve above $900, the salvage value is reduced. If the proceeds increase the depreciation reserve for the account to $1,000, the salvage value is reduced to zero. The unadjusted basis of the asset retired in an ordinary retirement is not removed from the account and the depreciation reserve for the account is not reduced by the depreciation allowable for the retired asset. The previously unrecovered basis of the retired asset will be recovered through the allowance for depreciation with respect to the vintage account. See subdivision (v)(*a*) of this subparagraph for treatment of retirements on which gain or loss is not recognized in whole or in part. See subdivision (v)(*b*) of this subparagraph for treatment of retirements by disposition to a member of an affiliated group as defined in section 1504(a). See subdivision (v)(*c*) of this subparagraph for treatment of transfers between members of an affiliated group of corporations or other related parties as extraordinary retirements.

(iv) *Treatment of extraordinary retirements.*—(a) Unless the transaction is governed by a special nonrecognition section of the Code such as 1031 or 337 or is one to which subdivision (v)(*b*) of this subparagraph applies, gain or loss shall be recognized upon an extraordinary retirement in the taxable year in which such retirement occurs subject to section 1231, section 165, and all other applicable provisions of law such as sections 1245 and 1250. If the asset which is retired in an extraordinary retirement is the only or last asset in the account, the account shall terminate and no longer be an account to which this section applies. In all other cases, the unadjusted basis of the retired asset shall be removed from the unadjusted basis of the

vintage account, and the depreciation reserve established for the account shall be reduced by the depreciation allowable for the retired asset computed in the manner prescribed in paragraph (c)(1)(v)(*b*) of this section for determination of the adjusted basis of the asset. See subdivision (ix) of this subparagraph for recognition of gain in the case of an account containing section 1245 property when the depreciation reserve exceeds the unadjusted basis of the vintage account. See subdivision (iii) of this subparagraph for reduction of salvage value for such an account when the depreciation reserve exceeds the unadjusted basis of the account minus salvage value. See subdivision (v)(*b*) of this subparagraph for treatment of retirements by disposition to a member of an affiliated group as defined in section 1504(a).

(b) The principles of this subdivision may be illustrated by the following examples:

Example (1). Corporation X has a multiple asset vintage account of 1971 consisting of assets K, R, A and P all of which are section 1245 property. The unadjusted basis of the account is $40,000. The unadjusted basis of asset A is $10,000. When the reserve for depreciation for the account is $20,000, asset A is sold in an extraordinary retirement for $8,000 in cash. The $10,000 unadjusted basis of asset A is removed from the account and the $5,000 depreciation allowable for asset A is removed from the reserve for depreciation. Gain in the amount of $3,000 (to which section 1245 applies) is recognized upon the sale of asset A.

Example (2). Corporation X has an item vintage account of 1972 consisting of residential apartment unit A. Unit A is section 1250 property. It is residential rental property and meets the requirements of section 167(j)(2). Corporation X adopts the declining balance method of depreciation using a rate twice the straight line rate. The asset depreciation period is 40 years. Unit A has an unadjusted basis of $200,000. On June 30, 1974, when the reserve for depreciation for the account is $19,500, unit A is sold for $220,000. Since unit A is section 1250 property, the sale is an extraordinary retirement in accordance with subdivision (ii)(*c*) of this subparagraph (without regard to subdivision (ii)(*b*) or (c) of this subparagraph). The adjusted basis of unit A is $180,500. Gain in the amount of $39,500 is recognized. The "additional depreciation" (as defined in section 1250(b)) for unit A is $9,500. Accordingly, $9,500 is in accordance with section 1250 treated as gain from the sale or exchange of an asset which is neither a capital asset nor property described in section 1231. The $30,000 balance of the gain from the sale of unit A may be gain to which section 1231 applies.

(v) *Special rule for certain retirements.*—(a) In the case of an ordinary retirement on which gain or loss is in whole or in part not recognized because of a special nonrecognition section of the Code, such as 1031 or 337, no part of the proceeds from such retirement shall be added to the depreciation reserve of the vintage account in accordance with subdivision (iii) of this subparagraph. Instead, such retirement shall for all purposes of this section be treated as an extraordinary retirement.

(b) The provisions of § 1.1502-13 shall apply to a retirement. In the case of an ordinary retirement to which the provisions of § 1.1502-13 apply, no part of the proceeds from such retirement shall be added to the depreciation reserve of the vintage account in accordance with subdivision (iii) of this subparagraph. Instead, such retirement shall for all purposes of this section be treated as an extraordinary retirement.

(c) In a case in which property is transferred, in a transaction which would without regard to this subdivision be treated as an ordinary retirement, during the taxable year in which first placed in service to a person who bears a relationship described in section 179(d)(2)(A) or (B), such transfer shall for all purposes of this section be treated as an extraordinary retirement.

(d)(1) If, in the case of mass assets, it is impracticable for the taxpayer to maintain records from which he can establish the vintage of such assets as retirements occur, and if he adopts other reasonable recordkeeping practices, then the vintage of mass asset retirements may be determined by use of an appropriate mortality dispersion table. Such a mortality dispersion table may be based upon an acceptable sampling of the taxpayer's actual experience or other acceptable statistical or engineering techniques. Alternatively, the taxpayer may use a standard mortality dispersion table prescribed by the Commissioner for this purpose. If the taxpayer uses such standard mortality dispersion table for any taxable year of election, it must be used for all subsequent taxable years of election unless the taxpayer obtains the consent of the Commissioner to change to another dispersion table or to actual identification of retirements. For information requirements regarding mass assets, see paragraph (f)(5) of this section.

(2) For purposes of this section, the term "mass assets" has the same meaning as when used in paragraph (e)(4) of § 1.47-1.

(e) The principles of this subdivision may be illustrated by the following examples:

Example (1). Corporation X has a vintage account of 1971 consisting of machines A, B and C, each with an unadjusted basis of $1,000. The unadjusted basis of the account is $3,000 and at the end of 1977 the reserve for depreciation is $2,100. On January 1, 1978, machine A is transferred to corporation Y solely for stock in the amount of $1,400 in a transaction to which section 351 applies. Since the adjusted basis of machine A is $300, a gain of $1,100 is realized, but no gain is recognized under section 351. Even though machine A was transferred in an ordinary retirement in accordance with (a) of this subdivision, the rules for an extraordinary retirement are applied. The proceeds are not added to the reserve for depreciation for the account. Machine A is removed from the account, the unadjusted basis of the account is reduced by $1,000, and the reserve for depreciation for the account is reduced by $700.

Example (2). The facts are the same as in example (1) except that the consideration received for machine A is stock of corporation Y in the amount of $1,200 and cash in the amount of $200. The result is the same as in example (1) except that gain is recognized in the amount of $200 all of which is gain to which section 1245 applies.

Example (3). The facts are the same as in example (1) except that machine A is sold for $1,400 cash in an ordinary retirement and corporation X and corporation Y are includible corporations in an affiliated group as defined in section 1504(a) which files a consolidated return for 1978. Accordingly, (b) of this subdivision applies. The retirement is treated as an extraordinary retirement. Machine A is removed from the account, the unadjusted basis of the account is reduced by $1,000, and the reserve for depreciation for the account is reduced by $700. The gain of $1,100 is deferred gain to which § 1.1502-13 applies.

(vi) *Treatment of special basis vintage accounts.*—A "special basis vintage account" is a vintage account for an amount of property improvement determined under subparagraph (2)(vii)(a) of this paragraph. In general, reference in this section to a "vintage account" shall include a special basis vintage account. The unadjusted basis of a special basis vintage account shall be recovered through the allowance for depreciation in accordance with this section over the asset depreciation period for the account. Except as provided in this subdivision, the unadjusted basis, adjusted basis and reserve for depreciation of such account shall not be allocated to any specific asset in the asset guideline class, and the provisions of this subparagraph shall not apply to such account. However, in the event of a sale, exchange or other disposition of "repair allowance property" (as described in subparagraph (2)(iii) of this paragraph) in an extraordinary retirement as described in subdivision (ii) of this subparagraph (or if the asset is not in a vintage account, in an abnormal retirement as described in § 1.167(a)-8, the taxpayer may, if consistently applied to all such retirements in the taxable year and adequately identified in the taxpayer's books and records, elect to allocate the adjusted basis (as of the end of the taxable year) of all special basis vintage accounts for the asset guideline class to each such retired asset in the proportion that the adjusted basis of the retired asset (as of the beginning of the taxable year) bears to the adjusted basis of all repair allowance property in the asset guideline class at the beginning of the taxable year. The election to allocate basis in accordance with this subdivision shall be made on the tax return filed for the taxable year. The principles of this subdivision may be illustrated by the following example:

Example. In addition to other property, the taxpayer has machines A, B, and C all in the same asset guideline class and each with an adjusted basis on January 1, 1977, of $10,000. The adjusted basis on January 1, 1977, of all repair allowance property (as described in subparagraph (2)(iii) of this paragraph) in the asset guideline class is $90,000. The machines are sold in an extraordinary retirement in 1977. The taxpayer is entitled to and does elect to allocate basis in accordance with this subdivision. There is also a 1972 special basis vintage account for the asset guideline class, as follows:

	Unadjusted Basis	Reserve for Depreciation	Dec. 31, 1977, Adjusted Basis
1972 special basis vintage account, for which the taxpayer selected an asset depreciation period of 10 years, adopted the straight line method, and used the half-year convention	$2,000	$1,100	$900

By application of this subdivision, the adjusted basis of machines A, B, and C is increased to $10,100 each (that is, $10,000/$90,000× $900=$100). The unadjusted basis, reserve for depreciation and adjusted basis of the special basis vintage account are reduced, respectively, by 1/3 (that is, $300/$900 = 1/3) in order to reflect the allocation of basis from the special basis vintage account.

(vii) *Reduction in the salvage value of a vintage account.*—(a) A taxpayer may apply this section without reducing the salvage value for a vintage account in accordance with this subdivision or in accordance with subdivision (viii) of this subparagraph (relating to transfers to supplies or scrap). See subdivision (iii) of this subparagraph for reduction of salvage value in certain circumstances in the amount of proceeds from ordinary retirements.

(b) However, the taxpayer may, at his option, follow the consistent practice of reducing, as retirements occur, the salvage value for a vintage account by the amount of salvage value attributable to the retired asset, or the taxpayer may consistently follow the practice of so reducing the salvage value for a vintage account as extraordinary retirements occur while not reducing the salvage value for the account as ordinary retirements occur. If the taxpayer does not reduce the salvage value for a vintage account as ordinary retirements occur, the taxpayer may be entitled to a deduction in the taxable year in which the last asset is retired from the account in accordance with subdivision (ix) (b) of this subparagraph.

(c) For purposes of this subdivision, the portion of the salvage value for a vintage account attributable to a retired asset may be determined by multiplying the salvage value for the account by a fraction, the numerator of which is the unadjusted basis of the retired asset and the denominator of which is the unadjusted basis of the account, or any other method consistently applied which reasonably reflects that portion of the salvage value for the account originally attributable to the retired asset.

(d) In the case of ordinary retirements the taxpayer may—

(1) In the case of retirements (other than by transfer to supplies or scrap) follow the consistent practice of reducing the salvage value for the account by the amount of salvage value attributable to the retired asset and not adding the same amount to the depreciation reserve for the account, and

(2) In the case of retirements by transfer to supplies or scrap, follow the consistent practice of reducing the salvage value for the account by the amount of salvage value attributable to the retired asset and not adding the same amount to the depreciation reserve for the account (in which case the basis in the supplies or scrap account of the retired asset will be zero) or follow the consistent practice of reducing the salvage value for the account by the amount of salvage value attributable to the retired asset and adding the same amount to the depreciation reserve for the account (up to an amount which does not increase the depreciation reserve to an amount in excess of the unadjusted basis of the account) in which case the basis in the supplies or scrap account of the retired asset will be the amount added to the depreciation reserve for the account.

Thus, for example, in the case of an ordinary retirement by transfer of an asset to supplies or scrap, the basis of the asset in the supplies or scrap account would either be zero or the amount added to the depreciation reserve of the vintage account from which the retirement occurred. When the depreciation reserve for the account equals the unadjusted basis of the account no further adjustment to salvage value for the account will be made. See subdivision (viii) of this subparagraph for special optional rule for reduction of salvage value in the case of an ordinary retirement by transfer of an asset to supplies or scrap.

(e) In the event of a removal of property from a vintage account in accordance with paragraph (b)(4)(iii)(e), (5)(v)(b) or (6)(iii) of this section the salvage value for the account may be reduced by the amount of salvage value attributable to the asset removed determined as provided in (c) of this subdivision.

(viii) *Special optional adjustments for transfers to supplies or scrap.*—If the taxpayer does not follow the consistent practice of reducing, as ordinary retirements occur, the salvage value for a vintage account in accordance with subdivision (vii) of this subparagraph, the taxpayer may (in lieu of the method described in subdivision (vii)(c) and (d) of this subparagraph) follow the consistent practice of reducing salvage value as ordinary retirements occur by transfer of assets to supplies or scrap and of determining the basis (in the supplies or scrap account) as assets retired in an ordinary retirement by transfer to supplies or scrap, in the following manner—

(a) The taxpayer may determine the value of the asset (not to exceed its unadjusted basis) by any reasonable method consistently applied (such as average cost, conditioned cost, or fair market value) if such method is adequately identified in the taxpayer's books and records.

(b) The value attributable to the asset determined in accordance with (a) of this subdivision shall be subtracted from the salvage value for the account (to the extent thereof) and the greater of (1) the amount subtracted from the salvage value for the vintage account and (2) the value of the asset determined in accordance with

Itemized Deductions for Individuals and Corps.
See p. 20,601 for regulations not amended to reflect law changes
25,417

(*a*) of this subdivision, shall be added to the reserve for depreciation of the vintage account.

(*c*) The amount added to the reserve for depreciation of the vintage account in accordance with (*b*) of this subdivision shall be treated as the basis of the retired asset in the supplies or scrap account. If the taxpayer makes the adjustments in accordance with this subdivision, the reserve for depreciation of the vintage account may exceed the unadjusted basis of the account, and in that event gain will be recognized in accordance with subdivision (ix) of this subparagraph.

(ix) *Recognition of gain or loss in certain situations.*—(*a*) In the case of a vintage account for section 1245 property, if at the end of any taxable year after adjustment for depreciation allowable for such taxable year and all other adjustments prescribed by this section, the depreciation reserve established for such account exceeds the unadjusted basis of the account, the entire amount of such excess shall be recognized as gain in such taxable year. Such gain—

(*1*) Shall constitute gain to which section 1245 applies to the extent that it does not exceed the total amount of depreciation allowances in the depreciation reserve at the end of such taxable year, reduced by gain recognized pursuant to this subdivision with respect to the account previously treated as gain to which section 1245 applies, and

(*2*) May constitute gain to which section 1231 applies to the extent that it exceeds such total amount as so reduced.

In such event, the depreciation reserve shall be reduced by the amount of gain recognized, so that after such reduction the amount of the depreciation reserve is equal to the unadjusted basis of the account.

(*b*) In the case of an account for section 1245 property, if at the time the last asset in the vintage account is retired the unadjusted basis of the account exceeds the depreciation reserve for the account (after all adjustments prescribed by this section), the entire amount of such excess shall be recognized in such taxable year as a loss under section 165 or as a deduction for depreciation under section 167. If the retirement of such asset occurs by sale or exchange on which gain or loss is recognized, the amount of such excess may constitute a loss subject to section 1231. Upon retirement of the last asset in a vintage account, the account shall terminate and no longer be an account to which this section applies. See subdivision (xi) of this subparagraph for treatment of certain multiple asset and item accounts.

(*c*) The principles of this subdivision may be illustrated by the following example:

Example. The taxpayer has a vintage account for section 1245 property with an unadjusted basis of $1,000 and a depreciation reserve of $700 (of which $600 represents depreciation allowances and $100 represents the proceeds of ordinary retirements from the account). If $500 is realized during the taxable year from ordinary retirements of assets from the account, the reserve is increased to $1,200, gain is recognized to the extent of $200 (the amount by which the depreciation reserve before further adjustment exceeds $1,000) and the depreciation reserve is then decreased to $1,000. The $200 of gain constitutes gain to which section 1245 applies. If the amount realized from ordinary retirements during the year had been $1,100 instead of $500, the gain of $800 would have consisted of $600 of gain to which section 1245 applies and $200 of gain to which section 1231 may apply.

(x) *Dismantling cost.*—The cost of dismantling, demolishing, or removing an asset in the process of a retirement from the vintage account shall be treated as an expense deductible in the year paid or incurred, and such cost shall not be subtracted from the depreciation reserve for the account.

(xi) *Special rule for treatment of multiple asset and item accounts.*—For the purposes of subdivision (ix)(*b*) of this subparagraph, all accounts (other than a special basis vintage account as described in subdivision (vi) of this subparagraph) of the same vintage in the same asset guideline class for which the taxpayer has selected the same asset depreciation period and adopted the same method of depreciation, and which contain only section 1245 property permitted by paragraph (b)(3)(ii) of this section to be included in the same vintage account, shall be treated as a single multiple asset vintage account.

(4) *Examples.*—The principles of this paragraph may be illustrated by the following examples:

Example (1). (*a*) Taxpayer A has a multiple asset vintage account for section 1245 property with an unadjusted basis of $1,000. All the assets were first placed in service by A on January 15, 1971. This account contains all of A's assets in a single asset guideline class. A elects to apply this section for 1971 and adopts the modified half-year convention. A estimates a salvage value for the account of $100 and this estimate is determined to be reasonable. (See subparagraph (1)(v) of this paragraph for limitation on adjustment of reasonable salvage

value.) A adopts the straight line method of depreciation with respect to the account and selects a 10-year asset depreciation period. A does not follow a practice of reducing the salvage value for the account in the amount of salvage value attributable to each retired asset in accordance with subparagraph (3)(vii) of this paragraph. The depreciation allowance for each of the first 4 years is $100, that is 1/10 multiplied by the unadjusted basis of $1,000, without reduction for salvage.

(*b*) In the fifth year of the asset depreciation period, three assets are sold in an ordinary retirement for $300. Under paragraph (c)(1)(ii) of this section and subparagraph (3)(iii) of this paragraph, the proceeds of the retirement are added to the depreciation reserve as of the beginning of the fifth year. Accordingly, the reserve as of the beginning of the fifth year is $700, that is, $400 of depreciation as of the beginning of the year plus $300 proceeds from ordinary retirements. The depreciation allowance for the fifth year is $100, that is 1/10 multiplied by the unadjusted basis of $1,000, without reduction for salvage. Accordingly, the depreciation reserve at the end of the fifth year is $800.

(*c*) In the sixth year, asset X is sold in an extraordinary retirement for $30 and gain or loss is recognized. Under the first-year convention used by the taxpayer, the unadjusted basis of X, $300, is removed from the unadjusted basis of the vintage account as of the beginning of the sixth year and the depreciation reserve as of the beginning of such year is reduced to $650 by removing the depreciation applicable to asset X, $150 (see subparagraph (3)(iv) of this paragraph). Since the depreciation reserve ($650) exceeds the unadjusted basis of the account ($700) minus salvage value ($100) by $50, under subparagraph (3)(iii) of this paragraph, salvage value is reduced by $50. No depreciation is allowable for the sixth year.

(*d*) In the seventh year, an asset is sold in an ordinary retirement for $110. This would increase the reserve as of the beginning of the seventh year to $760 and under subparagraph (3)(iii) of this paragraph the salvage value is reduced to zero. Under subparagraph (3)(ix)(*a*) of this paragraph the depreciation reserve is then decreased to $700 (the unadjusted basis of the account) and $60 is reported as gain, without regard to the adjusted basis of the asset. No depreciation is allowable for the seventh year since the depreciation reserve ($700) equals the unadjusted basis of the account ($700).

(*e*)(1) In the eighth year, A elects to apply this section and to treat expenditures during the year for repair, maintenance, rehabilitation or improvement under subparagraph (2)(iii) and (iv)(*a*) of this paragraph (the "guideline class repair allowance"). This results in the treatment of $300 as a property improvement for the asset guideline class. (See subparagraph (2)(vii) of this paragraph for definition of a property improvement.) The property improvement is capitalized in a special basis vintage account of the eighth taxable year (see subparagraph (2)(viii)(*a*) of this paragraph). A selects an asset depreciation period of 10 years and adopts the straight line method for the special basis vintage account. A adopts the modified half-year convention for the eighth year.

(2) In the eighth year, A sells asset Y in an ordinary retirement for $175. Under paragraph (c)(1)(ii) of this section and subparagraph (3)(iii) of this paragraph, $175 is added to the depreciation reserve for the account as of the beginning of the taxable year. Since the depreciation reserve for the account ($875) exceeds the unadjusted basis of the account ($700) by $175, that amount of gain is recognized under subparagraph (3)(ix) of this paragraph. Upon recognition of gain in the amount of $175, the depreciation reserve for the account is reduced to $700.

(3) No depreciation is allowable in the eighth year for the vintage account since the depreciation reserve ($700) equals the unadjusted basis of the account ($700). The depreciation allowable in the eighth year for the special basis vintage account is $15, that is, unadjusted basis of $300, multiplied by 1/10, the asset depreciation period selected for the special basis vintage account, but limited to $15 under the modified half-year convention. (See paragraph (e)(1)(iv) of this section for treatment of $150 of the property improvement as first placed in service in the first half of the taxable year and $150 of the property improvement as first placed in service in the last half of the taxable year.)

Example (2). Taxpayer B has a 1971 multiple asset vintage account for section 1245 property with an unadjusted basis of $100,000. B selects from the asset depreciation range an asset depreciation period of 10 years and adopts the straight line method of depreciation and the modified half-year convention. B establishes a salvage value for the account of $10,000. All the assets in the account are first placed in service on January 15, 1971. B follows the practice of reducing salvage value for the account as ordinary retirements occur in accordance with subparagraph (3)(vii) of this paragraph, but does not follow the optional practice of determining the basis of assets transferred to supplies or scrap in accordance with subparagraph (3)(viii) of this paragraph. No retirements occur during the first five years. The depreciation reserve at the beginning of the sixth year is

$50,000. In the sixth year an asset with an unadjusted basis of $20,000 is transferred to supplies in an ordinary retirement. By application of subparagraph (3)(vii)(c) and (d)(2) of this paragraph B determines the reduction in salvage value for the account attributable to such asset to be $2,000 (that is, $20,000/$100,000 × $10,000 = $2,000).

B reduces the salvage value for the account by $2,000 and adds $2,000 to the depreciation reserve for the account. The basis of the retired asset in the supplies account is $2,000. The depreciation allowable for the account for the sixth year is $10,000. The depreciation reserve for the account at the beginning of the seventh year is $62,000. At the mid-point of the seventh year all the remaining assets in the account are sold in an ordinary retirement for $20,000, which is added to the depreciation reserve as of the beginning of the seventh year, thus increasing the reserve to $82,000. The $5,000 depreciation allowable for the account for the seventh year (one-half of a full-year's depreciation of $10,000) increases the depreciation reserve to $87,000. Under subparagraph (3)(ix)(b) of this paragraph, a loss of $13,000 subject to section 1231 is realized in the seventh year (that is, the excess of the unadjusted basis of $100,000 over the depreciation reserve of $87,000). No depreciation is allowable for the account after the mid-point of the seventh year since all the assets are retired and the account has terminated.

(e) *Accounting for eligible property.*—(1) *Definition of first placed in service.*—(i) *In general.*—The term "first placed in service" refers to the time the property is first placed in service by the taxpayer, not to the first time the property is placed in service. Property is first placed in service when first placed in a condition or state of readiness and availability for a specifically assigned function, whether in a trade or business, in the production of income, in a tax-exempt activity, or in a personal activity. In general, the provisions of paragraph (d)(1)(ii) and (2) of § 1.46-3 shall apply for the purpose of determining the date on which property is placed in service, but see subdivision (ii) of this subparagraph for special rule for certain replacement parts. In the case of a building which is intended to house machinery and equipment and which is constructed, reconstructed, or erected by or for the taxpayer and for the taxpayer's use, the building will ordinarily be placed in service on the date such construction, reconstruction, or erection is substantially complete and the building is in a condition or state of readiness and availability. Thus, for example, in the case of a factory building, such readiness and availability shall be determined without regard to whether the machinery or equipment which the building houses, or is intended to house, has been placed in service. However, in an appropriate case, as for example where the building is essentially an item of machinery or equipment, or the use of the building is so closely related to the use of the machinery or equipment that it clearly can be expected to be replaced or retired when the property it initially houses is replaced or retired, the determination of readiness or availability of the building shall be made by taking into account the readiness and availability of such machinery or equipment. The date on which depreciation begins under a convention used by the taxpayer or under a particular method of depreciation, such as the unit of production method or the retirement method, shall not determine the date on which the property is first placed in service. See paragraph (c)(2) of this section for application of a first-year convention to determine the allowance for depreciation of property in a vintage account.

(ii) *Certain replacement parts.*—Property (such as replacement parts) the cost or other basis of which is deducted as a repair expense in accordance with the asset guideline repair allowance described in paragraph (d)(2)(iii) of this section shall not be treated as placed in service.

(iii) *Property improvements and excluded additions.*—(a) Except as provided in (b) of this subdivision, a property improvement determined under paragraph (d)(2)(vii)(b) of this section, and an excluded addition (other than an excluded addition referred to in the succeeding sentence) is first placed in service when its cost is paid or incurred. The general rule in subdivision (i) of this subparagraph applies to an excluded addition described in paragraph (d)(2)(vi)(d), (e), (f) or (g) of this section.

(b) If a property improvement or an excluded addition to which the first sentence of (a) of this subdivision applies is paid or incurred in part in one taxable year and in part in the succeeding taxable year (or in part in the first half of a taxable year and in part in the last half of the taxable year) the taxpayer may at his option consistently treat such property improvements and excluded additions under the general rule in subdivision (i) of this subparagraph.

(iv) *Certain property improvements.*—In the case of an amount of property improvement determined under paragraph (d)(2)(vii)(a) of this section, one-half of such amount is first placed in service in the first half of the taxable year in which the cost is paid or incurred and one-half is first placed in service in the last half of such taxable year.

(v) *Special rules for clearing accounts.*—In the case of public utilities which consistently account for certain property through "clearing accounts", the date on which such property is first placed in service shall be determined in accordance with rules to be prescribed by the Commissioner.

(2) *Special rules for transferred property.*—If eligible property is first placed in service by the taxpayer during a taxable year of election, and the property is disposed of before the end of the taxable year, the election for such taxable year shall include such property unless such property is excluded in accordance with paragraph (b)(5)(iii), (iv), (v), (vi) or (vii) of this section.

(3) *Special rules in the case of certain transfers.*—(i) *Transaction to which section 381(a) applies.*—(a) In general the acquiring corporation in a transaction to which section 381(a) applies is for the purposes of this section treated as if it were the distributor or transferor corporation.

(b) If the distributor or transferor corporation (including any distributor or transferor corporation of any distributor or transferor corporation) has made an election to apply this section to eligible property transferred in a transaction to which section 381(a) applies, the acquiring corporation must segregate such eligible property (to which the distributor or transferor corporation elected to apply this section) into vintage accounts as nearly coextensive as possible with the vintage accounts created by the distributor or transferor corporation identified by reference to the year the property was first placed in service by the distributor or transferor corporation. The asset depreciation period for the vintage account in the hands of the distributor or transferor corporation must be used by the acquiring corporation. The method of depreciation adopted by the distributor or transferor corporation, shall be used by the acquiring corporation unless such corporation obtains the consent of the Commissioner to use another method of depreciation in accordance with paragraph (e) of § 1.446-1 or changes the method of depreciation under paragraph (c)(1)(iii) of this section.

(c) The acquiring corporation may apply this section to the property so acquired only if the distributor or transferor corporation elected to apply this section to such property.

(d) See paragraph (b)(7) of this section for special rule for certain property where there is a mere change in the form of conducting a trade or business.

(ii) *Partnerships, trusts, estates, donees, and corporations.*—Except as provided in subdivision (i) of this subparagraph with respect to transactions to which section 381(a) applies, and subdivision (iv) of this subparagraph with respect to certain transfers between members of an affiliated group of corporations or other related parties, if eligible property is placed in service by an individual, trust, estate, partnership, or corporation, the election to apply this section shall be made by the individual, trust, estate, partnership, or corporation placing such property in service. For example, if a partnership places in service property contributed to the partnership by a partner, the partnership may elect to apply this section to such property. If the partnership does not make the election, this section will not apply to such property. See paragraph (b)(7) of this section for special rule for certain property where there is mere change in the form of conducting a trade or business.

(iii) *Leased property.*—The asset depreciation range and the asset depreciation period for eligible property subject to a lease shall be determined without regard to the period for which such property is leased, including any extensions or renewals of such period. See paragraph (b)(5)(v) of this section for exclusion of property amortized under paragraph (b) of § 1.162-11 from an election to apply this section. In the case of a lessor of property, unless there is an asset guideline class in effect for lessors of such property, the asset guideline class for such property shall be determined as if the property were owned by the lessee. However, in the case of an asset guideline class based upon the type of property (such as trucks or railroad cars) as distinguished from the activity in which used, the property shall be classified without regard to the activity of the lessee. Notwithstanding the preceding sentence, if a lease with respect to property, which would be includible in an asset guideline class based upon the type of property under the preceding sentence (such as trucks or railroad cars), is entered into after March 12, 1971, and before April 23, 1973, or a written contract to execute such a lease is entered into during such period and such contract is binding on April 23, 1973, and at all times thereafter, and if the rent or rate of return is based on a classification of such property as if it were owned by the lessee, then such property shall be classified as if it were owned by the lessee. However, the preceding sentence shall not apply if pursuant to the terms or conditions of the lease or binding contract the rent or rate of return may be adjusted to take account of a change in the period for depreciation with respect to the property resulting from inclusion of the property in an asset guideline class based upon the

Itemized Deductions for Individuals and Corps.
See p. 20,601 for regulations not amended to reflect law changes
25,419

type of property rather than in an asset guideline class based upon the activity of the lessee. Similarly, where the terms of such a lease or contract provide that the obligation of the taxpayer to enter into the lease is subject to a condition that the property be included in an asset guideline class based upon the activity of the lessee, the contract or lease will not be considered as binding upon the taxpayer, for purposes of this subdivision. See paragraph (b)(4)(iii)(b) of this section for general rule for classification of property according to primary use.

(iv) *Treatment of certain transfers between members of affiliated groups or other related persons.*—If section 38 property in an asset guideline class (determined without regard to whether the taxpayer elects to apply this section) is transferred by the taxpayer to a person who bears a relationship described in section 179(d)(2)(A) or (B), such property is in the same asset guideline class in the hands of transferee, and the transfer is neither described in section 381(a) nor treated as a disposition or cessation within the meaning of section 47, then the asset guideline period for such property selected by the taxpayer under this section shall not be shorter than the period used for computing the qualified investment with respect to the property under section 46(c). In a case in which the asset depreciation range for the asset guideline class which includes such property does not include the period for depreciation used by the transferor in computing the qualified investment with respect to such property, the transferee will not be permitted to include such property in an election under this section. However, in such a case, the transferor of the property may recompute the qualified investment for the year the property was placed in service using a period for depreciation which falls within the asset depreciation range.

(f) *Election with respect to eligible property.*—(1) *Time and manner of election.*—(i) *In general.*—An election to apply this section to eligible property shall be made with the income tax return filed for the taxable year in which the property is first placed in service (see paragraph (e)(1) of this section) by the taxpayer. In the case of an affiliated group of corporations (as defined in section 1504(a)) which makes a consolidated return with respect to income tax in accordance with section 1502 and the regulations thereunder, each corporation which joins in the making of such return may elect to apply this section for a taxable year. An election to compute the allowance for depreciation under this section is a method of accounting but the consent of the Commissioner will be deemed granted to make an annual election. For election by a partnership see section 703(b) and paragraph (e)(3)(ii) of this section. If the taxpayer does not file a timely return (taking into account extensions of the time for filing) for the taxable year in which the property is first placed in service, the election shall be filed at the time the taxpayer files his first return for that year. The election may be made with an amended return filed within the time prescribed by law (including extensions) for filing the original return for the taxable year of election. If an election is not made within the time and in the manner prescribed in this paragraph, no election may be made for such taxable year (by the filing of an amended return or in any other manner) with respect to any eligible property placed in service in the taxable year.

(ii) *Other elections under this section.*—All other elections under this section may be made only within the time and in the manner prescribed by subdivision (i) of this subparagraph with respect to an election to apply this section.

(iii) *Effective date.*—See paragraph (f)(6) of this section for the effective date of this paragraph.

(2) *Information required.*—A taxpayer who elects to apply this section must specify in the election:

(i) That the taxpayer makes such election and consents to, and agrees to apply, all the provisions of this section;

(ii) The asset guideline class for each vintage account of the taxable year;

(iii) The first-year convention adopted by the taxpayer for the taxable year of election;

(iv) Whether the special 10 percent used property rule described in paragraph (b)(5)(iii) of this section has been applied to exclude used property from the election;

(v) Whether the taxpayer elects to apply the asset guideline class repair allowance described in paragraph (d)(2)(iii) of this section;

(vi) Whether the taxpayer elects for the taxable year to allocate the adjusted basis of a special basis vintage account in accordance with paragraph (d)(3)(vi) of this section;

(vii) Whether any eligible property for which the taxpayer was not required or permitted to make an election was excluded because of the special rules of paragraph (b)(5)(v) or (6), or paragraph (e)(3)(i) or (iv) of this section;

(viii) Whether any "section 38 property" was excluded under paragraph (b)(5)(iv) of this section from the election to apply this section;

(ix) If the taxpayer is an electric or gas utility, whether the taxpayer elects to apply this section on the basis of a composite asset guideline class in accordance with paragraph (b)(4)(iii)(a) of this section; and

(x) Such other information as may reasonably be required. The information required under this subparagraph may be provided in accordance with rules prescribed by the Commissioner for reasonable grouping of assets or accounts. Form 4832 is provided for making an election and for submission of the information required. An election may be made and the information submitted only in accordance with Form 4832. An election to apply this section will not be rendered invalid under this subparagraph so long as there is substantial compliance, in good faith, with the requirements of this subparagraph.

(3) *Irrevocable election.*—An election to apply this section to eligible property for any taxable year may not be revoked or changed after the time for filing the election prescribed under subparagraph (1) of this paragraph has expired. No other election under this section may be revoked or changed after such time unless expressly provided for under this section. (See paragraph (b)(5)(v)(b) of this section for special rule.)

(4) *Special conditions to election to apply this section.*—(i) *Maintenance of books and records.*—The taxpayer may not elect to apply this section for a taxable year unless the taxpayer maintains the books and records required under this section. In addition to any other information required under this section, the taxpayer's books and records must specify—

(a) The asset depreciation period selected by the taxpayer for each vintage account;

(b) If the taxpayer applies the modified half-year convention, the total cost or other basis of all eligible property first placed in service in the first half of the taxable year and the total cost or other basis of all eligible property first placed in service in the last half of the taxable year;

(c) The unadjusted basis and salvage value for each vintage account, and the amount, if any, by which gross salvage value was decreased under section 167(f);

(d) Each asset guideline class for which the taxpayer elects to apply the asset guideline class repair allowance described in paragraph (d)(2)(iii) of this section;

(e) The amount of property improvement, determined under paragraph (d)(2)(vii)(a) of this section, for each asset guideline class for which the taxpayer elects to apply the asset guideline class repair allowance;

(f) A reasonable description of property excluded from an election to apply this section and the basis for the exclusion;

(g) The total unadjusted basis of all assets retired during the taxable year from each asset guideline class, and the proceeds realized during the taxable year from such retirements; and

(h) The vintage (that is, the taxable year in which established) of the assets retired during the year from each asset guideline class.

For purposes of paragraph (f)(4)(i)(g) and (h) of this section, all accounts of the same vintage and asset guideline class may be treated as a single account. The taxpayer must specify the information required under paragraph (f)(4)(i)(g) and (h) without regard to the retirement of an asset by transfer to a supplies account for reuse.

(ii) *Response to survey.*—Taxpayers who elect to apply this section must respond to infrequent data surveys conducted by the Treasury Department. These periodic surveys, which will be conducted on the basis of scientifically sound sampling methods, are designed to obtain data (including industry asset acquisitions and retirements) used to keep the asset guideline classes and periods up to date.

(iii) *Effect of noncompliance.*—An election to apply this section will not be rendered invalid under this subparagraph so long as there is substantial compliance, in good faith, with the requirements of this subparagraph.

(5) *Mass assets.*—In the case of mass assets, if the taxpayer assigns retirements to vintage accounts in the manner provided in paragraph (d)(3)(v)(c) of this section, the following information must be supplied with Form 4832:

(i) Whether the taxpayer used the standard mortality dispersion curve or a curve based upon his own experience, and

(ii) Such other reasonable information as may be required by the Commissioner.

Reg. §1.167(a)-11(f)(5)(ii)

(6) *Effective date.*—The rules in this paragraph apply to elections for taxable years ending on or after December 31, 1978. In the case of an election for a taxable year ending before December 31, 1978, the rules in paragraph (f) of this section, in effect before the amendments made by T.D. 7593, approved January 11, 1979, shall apply. See 26 C.F.R. § 1.167(a)-11(f) (1977) for paragraph (f) of this section as it appeared before the amendments made by T.D. 7593.

(g) *Relationship to other provisions.*—(1) *Useful life.*—(i) *In general.*—Except as provided in subdivision (ii) of this subparagraph, an election to apply this section to eligible property constitutes an agreement under section 167(d) and this section to treat the asset depreciation period for each vintage account as the useful life of the property in such account for all purposes of the Code, including sections 46, 47, 48, 57, 163(d), 167(c), 167(f)(2), 179, 312(m), 514(a), and 4940(c). For example, since section 167(c) requires a useful life of at least 3 years and the asset depreciation period selected is treated as the useful life for purposes of section 167(c), the taxpayer may adopt a method of depreciation described in section 167(b)(2) or (3) for an account only if the asset depreciation period selected for the account is at least 3 years.

(ii) *Special rules.*—(a) For the purposes of paragraph (d) of this section, the anticipated period of use (estimated at the close of the taxable year in which the asset is first placed in service) on the basis of which salvage value is estimated, shall be determined without regard to the asset depreciation period for the property.

(b) For the purposes of sections 162 and 263 and the regulations thereunder, whether an expenditure prolongs the life of an asset shall be determined on the basis of the anticipated period of use of the asset (estimated at the close of the taxable year in which the asset is first placed in service) without regard to the asset depreciation period for such asset.

(c) The determination whether a transaction with respect to qualified property constitutes a sale or a lease of such property shall be made without regard to the asset depreciation period for the property.

(d) The principles of this subdivision may be illustrated by the following example:

Example: Corporation X has assets in the asset guideline class 32.3 which are used in the manufacture of stone and clay products. The asset depreciation range for assets in asset guideline class 32.3 is from 12 to 18 years. Assume that corporation X selects 14 years as the asset depreciation period for all assets in asset guideline class 32.3. Under paragraph (d)(1)(i) of this section, corporation X must estimate salvage value on the basis of the anticipated period of use of the property (determined as of the close of the taxable year in which the property is first placed in service). The anticipated period of use must also be used for purposes of sections 162 and 263 in determining whether an expenditure materially prolongs the useful life of an asset. The anticipated period of use of an asset is determined without regard to the asset depreciation period of 14 years. Corporation X has, among other assets in the asset guideline class, machines A, B, and C. Corporation X estimates the anticipated period of use of machines A, B, and C as 8 years, 14 years, and 22 years, respectively. These estimates are reasonable and will be used for estimating salvage value and for purposes of sections 162 and 263.

(2) *Section 167 (d) agreements.*—If the taxpayer has, prior to January 1, 1971, entered into a section 167(d) agreement which applies to any eligible property, the taxpayer will be permitted to withdraw the eligible property from the agreement provided that an election is made to apply this section to such property. The statement of intent to withdraw eligible property from such an agreement must be made in an election filed for the taxable year in which the property is first placed in service. The withdrawal, in accordance with this subparagraph, of any eligible property from a section 167(d) agreement shall not affect any other property covered by such an agreement.

(3) *Relationship to the straight line method.*—(i) *In general.*—For purposes of determining the amount of depreciation which would be allowable under the straight line method of depreciation, such amount shall be computed with respect to any property in a vintage account using the straight line method in the manner described in paragraph (c)(1)(i) of this section and a rate based upon the period for the vintage account selected from the asset depreciation range. Thus, for example, section 57(a)(3) requires a taxpayer to compute an amount using the straight line method of depreciation if the taxpayer uses an accelerated method of depreciation. For purposes of section 57(a)(3), the amount for property in a vintage account shall be computed using the asset depreciation period for the vintage account selected from the asset depreciation range. In the case of property to which the taxpayer does not elect to apply this section, such amount computed by using the straight line method shall be determined under § 1.167(b)-1 without regard to this section.

(ii) *Examples.*—The principles of this subparagraph may be illustrated by the following example:

Example. (a) Corporation X places a new asset in service to which it elects to apply this section. The cost of the asset is $200,000 and the estimated salvage value is zero. The taxpayer selects 9 years from the applicable asset depreciation range of 8 to 12 years. Corporation X adopts the double declining balance method of depreciation and thus the rate of depreciation is 22.2 percent (twice the applicable straight line rate). The depreciation allowance in the first year would be $44,400, that is, 22.2 percent of $200,000.

(b) Assume that the provisions of section 57(a)(3) apply to the property. The amount of the tax preference would be $22,200, that is, the excess of the depreciation allowed under this section ($44,400) over the depreciation which would have been allowable if the taxpayer had used the period selected from the asset depreciation range and the straight line rate ($22,200). [Reg. § 1.167(a)-11.]

☐ [*T.D. 7128,* 6-22-71. *Amended by T.D. 7272,* 4-20-73; *T.D. 7315,* 6-6-74; *T.D. 7593,* 1-25-79; *T.D. 7763,* 1-19-81; *T.D. 7828,* 8-31-82; *T.D. 7831,* 9-8-82 *and T.D. 8597,* 7-12-95.]

[Reg. § 1.167(a)-12]

§ 1.167(a)-12. Depreciation based on class lives for property first placed in service before January 1, 1971.—(a) *In general.*—(1) *Summary.*—This section provides an elective class life system for determining the reasonable allowance for depreciation of certain classes of assets for taxable years ending after December 31, 1970. The system applies only to assets placed in service before January 1, 1971. Depreciation for such assets during periods prior to January 1, 1971, may have been determined in accordance with Revenue Procedure 62-21. Accordingly, rules are provided which permit taxpayers to apply the system in taxable years ending after December 31, 1970, to such assets without the necessity of changing or regrouping their depreciation accounts other than as previously required by Revenue Procedure 62-21. The system is designed to minimize disputes between taxpayers and the Internal Revenue Service as to the useful life of assets, salvage value, and repairs. See § 1.167(a)-11 for a similar system for property placed in service after December 31, 1970. See paragraph (d)(2) of § 1.167(a)-11 for treatment of expenditures for the repair, maintenance, rehabilitation or improvement of certain property. The system provided by this section is optional with the taxpayer. An election under this section applies only to qualified property in an asset guideline class for which an election is made and only for the taxable year of election. The taxpayer's election is made with the income tax return for the taxable year. This section also revokes the reserve ratio test for taxable years ending after December 31, 1970, and provides transitional rules for taxpayers who after January 11, 1971, adopt Revenue Procedure 62-21 for a taxable year ending prior to January 1, 1971.

(2) *Revocation of reserve ratio test and other matters.*—Except as otherwise expressly provided in this section and in paragraph (b)(5)(vi) of § 1.167(a)-11, the provisions of Revenue Procedure 62-21 shall not apply to any property for any taxable year ending after December 31, 1970, whether or not the taxpayer elects to apply this section to any property. See paragraph (f) of this section for rules for the adoption of Revenue Procedure 62-21 for taxable years ending prior to January 1, 1971.

(3) *Definition of qualified property.*—The term "qualified property" means tangible property which is subject to the allowance for depreciation provided by section 167(a), but only if—

(i) An asset guideline class and asset guideline period are in effect for such property for the taxable year, and

(ii) The property is first placed in service by the taxpayer before January 1, 1971.

(iii) The property is placed in service before January 1, 1971, but first placed in service by the taxpayer after December 31, 1970, and is not includible in an election under § 1.167(a)-11 by reason of § 1.167(a)-11(b)(7) (property acquired as a result of a mere change in form) or § 1.167(a)-11(e)(3)(i) (certain property acquired in a transaction to which section 381(a) applies), or

(iv) The property is acquired and first placed in service by the taxpayer after December 31, 1970, pursuant to a binding written contract entered into prior to January 1, 1971, and is excluded in accordance with paragraph (b)(5)(iv) of § 1.167(a)-11 from an election to apply § 1.167(a)-11. The provisions of paragraph (e)(1) of § 1.167(a)-11 apply in determining whether property is first placed in service before January 1, 1971. See subparagraph (4)(ii) of this paragraph for special rules for the exclusion of property from the definition of qualified property.

(4) *Requirements of election.*—(i) *In general.*—An election to apply this section to qualified property must be made within the time and in the manner specified in paragraph (e) of this section. The election must specify that the taxpayer consents to and agrees to apply all the

provisions of this section. The election may be made separately for each asset guideline class. Thus, a taxpayer may for the taxable year elect to apply this section to one, more than one, or all asset guideline classes in which he has qualified property. An election to apply this section for a taxable year must include all qualified property in the asset guideline class for which the election is made.

(ii) *Special rules for exclusion of property from application of this section.*—(a) If for the taxable year of election, the taxpayer computes depreciation under section 167(k) or computes amortization under section 169, 185, 186, 187, 188, or paragraph (b) of §1.162-11 with respect to property, such property is not qualified property for such taxable year. If for the taxable year of election, the taxpayer computes depreciation under any method of depreciation (other than a method described in the preceding sentence) not permitted by subparagraph (5) (v) of this paragraph for any property in an asset guideline class (other than subsidiary assets excluded from an election under (b) of this subdivision), no property in such asset guideline class is qualified property for such taxable year.

(b) The taxpayer may exclude from an election to apply this section all (but not less than all) subsidiary assets. Subsidiary assets so excluded are not qualified property for such taxable year. For purposes of this subdivision the term "subsidiary assets" includes jigs, dies, molds, returnable containers, glassware, silverware, textile mill cam assemblies, and other equipment includable in Group One, Class 5, of Revenue Procedure 62-21 which is usually and properly accounted for separately from other property and under a method of depreciation not expressed in terms of years.

(iii) *Special rule for certain public utility property.*—(a) In the case of public utility property described in section 167(1)(3)(A)(iii) for which no guideline life was prescribed in Revenue Procedure 62-21 (or for which reference was made in Revenue Procedure 62-21 to lives or rates established by governmental regulatory agencies) of a taxpayer which—

(1) Is entitled to use a method of depreciation other than a "subsection (l) method" of depreciation (as defined in section 167(1)(3)(F)) only if it uses the "normalization method of accounting" (as defined in section 167(1)(3)(G)) with respect to such property, or

(2) Is entitled for the taxable year to use only a "subsection (l) method" of depreciation,

such property shall be qualified property (as defined in subparagraph (3) of this paragraph) only if the taxpayer normalizes the tax deferral resulting from the election to apply this section.

(b) The taxpayer will be considered to normalize the tax deferral resulting from the election to apply this section only if it computes its tax expense for purposes of establishing its cost of service for ratemaking purposes and for reflecting operating results in its regulated books of account using a period for depreciation no less than the period used for computing its depreciation expense for ratemaking purposes and for reflecting operating results in its regulated books of account for the taxable year, and the taxpayer makes adjustments to a reserve to reflect the deferral of taxes resulting from the use of a period for depreciation under section 167 in accordance with an election to apply this section different from the period used for computing its depreciation expense for ratemaking purposes and for reflecting operating results in its regulated books of account for the taxable year. A determination whether the taxpayer is considered to normalize under this subdivision the tax deferral resulting from the election to apply this section shall be made in a manner consistent with the principles for determining whether a taxpayer is using the "normalization method of accounting" (within the meaning of section 167(1)(3)(G)). See §1.167(l)-1(h).

(c) If a taxpayer, which has elected to apply this section to any qualified public utility property and is required under (a) of this subdivision to normalize the tax deferral resulting from the election to apply this section to such property, fails to normalize such tax deferral, the election to apply this section to such property shall terminate as of the beginning of the taxable year for which the taxpayer fails to normalize such tax deferral. Application of this section to such property for any period prior to the termination date will not be affected by this termination.

(5) *Determination of reasonable allowance for depreciation.*—(i) *In general.*—The allowance for depreciation of qualified property to which the taxpayer elects to apply this section shall be determined in accordance with this section. The annual allowance for depreciation is determined by using the method of depreciation adopted by the taxpayer and rate based on a life permitted by this section. In the case of the straight-line method of depreciation, the rate of depreciation shall be based upon the class life (or individual life if the taxpayer assigns individual depreciable lives in accordance with subdivision (iii) of this subparagraph) used by the taxpayer with respect to the assets in the asset guideline class. Such rate will be applied to the unadjusted basis of the asset guideline class (individual assets or depreciation accounts if the taxpayer assigns individual depreciable

lives). In the case of the sum of the years-digits method of depreciation, the rate of depreciation will be determined based upon the remaining life of the class (or individual remaining lives if the taxpayer assigns such lives in accordance with subdivision (iii) of this subparagraph) and is applied to the adjusted basis of the class (or individual accounts or asset) as of the beginning of the taxable year of election. The remaining life of a depreciation account is determined by dividing the unrecovered cost or other basis of the account, as computed by straight-line depreciation, by the gross cost or unadjusted basis of the account, and multiplying the result by the class life used with respect to the account. In the case of the declining balance method of depreciation, the rate of depreciation for the asset guideline class shall be based upon the class life (or individual life if the taxpayer assigns such lives in accordance with subdivision (iii) of this subparagraph). Such rate is applied to the adjusted basis of the class (or individual accounts or assets) as of the beginning of the taxable year of election.

(ii) *Reasonable allowance by reference to class lives.*—The amount of depreciation for all qualified property in an asset guideline class to which the taxpayer elects to apply this section will constitute the reasonable allowance provided by section 167(a) and the depreciation for the asset guideline class will not be adjusted if—

(a) The taxpayer's qualified property is accounted for in one or more depreciation accounts which conform to the asset guideline class, and the depreciation for each such account is determined by using a rate based upon a life not less than the class life, or

(b) The taxpayer's qualified property is accounted for in one or more depreciation accounts (whether or not conforming to the asset guideline class) for which depreciation is determined at a rate based upon the taxpayer's estimate of the lives of the assets (instead of the class life) and the total amount of depreciation so determined for the asset guideline class for the taxable year of election is not more than would be permitted under (a) of this subdivision for such year using the method of depreciation adopted by the taxpayer for the property.

See subdivision (vii) of this subparagraph for determination of reasonable allowance if depreciation exceeds the amount permitted by this subdivision. See paragraph (b) of this section for rules regarding the determination of "class life". For rules for regrouping depreciation accounts to conform to the asset guideline class, see subdivision (iv) of this subparagraph.

(iii) *Consistency when individual lives are used.*—If the taxpayer assigns individual depreciable lives to assets in accordance with subdivision (ii)(b) of this subparagraph, even though the total amount of depreciation for the asset guideline class will not be adjusted, the lives assigned to the various assets in the asset guideline class must be reasonably in proportion to their relative expected periods of use in the taxpayer's business. Thus, although the taxpayer who uses individual asset lives normally has latitude in thereby allocating the depreciation for the asset guideline class among the assets, if the lives are grossly disproportionate (as where a short life is assigned to one asset and a long life to another even though the expected periods of use are the same), the taxpayer's allocation of depreciation to particular assets or depreciation accounts may be adjusted. For example, the taxpayer's allocation may be adjusted for purposes of determining adjusted basis under section 1016(a) or in allocating depreciation to the 50-percent limitation on percentage depletion provided by section 613(a). See paragraph (d) of this section for rules regarding the use of individual asset lives for purposes of classifying retirements as normal or abnormal.

(iv) *Regrouping depreciation accounts.*—Without the consent of the Commissioner, the taxpayer may for any taxable year for which he elects to apply this section to an asset guideline class, regroup his accounts for that and all succeeding taxable years to conform to the asset guideline class. Other changes in accounting, including a change from item accounts to multiple-asset accounting, may be made with the consent of the Commissioner. No depreciation accounts for which the straight line or sum of the years-digits method of depreciation is adopted may be combined under this section which would not be permitted to be combined under part III of Revenue Procedure 65-13, as in effect on January 1, 1971. Accordingly, whether or not the taxpayer adopted the guideline system of Revenue Procedure 62-21 for a taxable year to which Part III of Revenue Procedure 65-13 is applicable, the depreciation allowance for any taxable year of election under this section may not exceed that amount which would have been allowed for such year if the taxpayer had used item accounts or year of acquisition accounts. Thus, for example, if a calendar year taxpayer acquired a $90 asset on the first day of each year from 1966 through 1970, placed such assets in a single multiple asset account, adopted the sum of the years-digits method of depreciation and used a 5-year depreciable life for such assets, and in 1971 uses the 5-year class life determined under paragraph (b) of this section, the depreciation allowance for such assets in 1971 under this section may not exceed $60, that is, the amount which would be allowed if the taxpayer had used year of acquisition accounts for the assets for the years 1966 through 1970. For purposes of this subparagraph, a taxpayer's depreciation accounts conform to the asset guideline class if each depreciation account includes only assets of the same asset guideline class.

(v) *Method of depreciation.*—The same method of depreciation must be applied to all property in a single depreciation account. The method of depreciation is subject to the limitations of section 167(c), (j) and (l). Except as otherwise provided in this subdivision, the taxpayer must apply a method of depreciation described in section 167(b)(1), (2), or (3) for qualified property to which the taxpayer elects to apply this section. A method of depreciation permitted under section 167(b)(4) may be used under this section if the method was used by the taxpayer with respect to the property for his last taxable year ending before January 1, 1971, the method is expressed in terms of years, the taxpayer establishes to the satisfaction of the Commissioner that the method is both a reasonable and consistent method, and if the taxpayer applies paragraph (b)(2) of this section (relating to class lives in special situations) to determine a class life, that the method of determining such class life is consistent with the principles of Revenue Procedure 62-21 as applied to such a method. If the taxpayer has applied a method of depreciation with respect to the property which is not described in section 167(b)(1), (2), (3), or (4) (as permitted under the preceding sentence), he must change under this section to a method of depreciation described in section 167(b)(1), (2), or (3) for the first taxable year for which an election is made under this section. Other changes in depreciation method may be made with the consent of the Commissioner (see section 446 and the regulations thereunder). (See also section 167(e).)

(vi) *Salvage value.*—In applying the method of depreciation adopted by the taxpayer, the annual allowance for depreciation is determined without adjustment for the salvage value of the property, except that no depreciation account may be depreciated below a reasonable salvage value for the account. See paragraph (c) of this section for definition and treatment of salvage value.

(vii) *Reasonable allowance when depreciation exceeds amount based on class life.*—In the event that the total amount of depreciation claimed by the taxpayer on his income tax return, in a claim for refund, or otherwise, for an asset guideline class with respect to which an election is made under this section for the taxable year, exceeds the maximum amount permitted under subdivision (ii)() of this subparagraph—

(a) If the excess is established to the satisfaction of the Commissioner to be the result of a good faith mistake by the taxpayer in determining the maximum amount permitted under subdivision (ii)(a) of this subparagraph, the taxpayer's election to apply this section will be treated as valid and only such excess will be disallowed, and

(b) In all other cases, the taxpayers' election to apply this section to the asset guideline class for the taxable year is invalid and the reasonable allowance for depreciation will be determined without regard to this section. (See §1.167(a)-1(b) for rules regarding the estimated useful life of property.)

(b) *Determination of class lives.*—(1) *Class lives in general.*—The class life determined under this paragraph (without regard to any range or variance permitted with respect to class lives under §1.167(a)-11) will be applied for purposes of determining whether the allowance for depreciation for qualified property included in an election under this section is subject to adjustment. The taxpayer is not required to use the class life determined under this paragraph for purposes of determining the allowance for depreciation. Except as provided in subparagraph (2) of this paragraph, the class life of qualified property to which the taxpayer elects to apply this section is the shorter of—

(i) The asset guideline period for the asset guideline class as set forth in Revenue Procedure 72-10 as in effect on March 1, 1972 (applied without regard to any special provision therein with respect to property predominantly used outside the United States), or

(ii) The asset guideline period for the asset guideline class as set forth in any supplement or revision of Revenue Procedure 72-10, but only if and to the extent by express reference in such supplement or revision made applicable for the purpose of changing the asset guideline period or classification of qualified property to which this section applies. See paragraph (e)(3)(iii) of this section for requirement that the election for the taxable year specify the class life for each asset guideline class. Generally, the applicable asset guideline class and asset guideline period for qualified property to which the taxpayer has elected to apply this section will not be changed for the taxable year of election to reflect any supplement or revision thereof after the taxable year. However, if expressly provided in such a supplement or revision, the taxpayer may, at his option in the manner specified therein, apply the revised or supplemented asset guide-

line classes or periods to such property for such taxable year and succeeding taxable years. The principles of this subparagraph may be illustrated by the following example:

Example. (i) Corporation X, a calendar year taxpayer, has assets in asset guideline class 20.4 of Revenue Procedure 72-10 which were placed in service by corporation X in 1967, 1968, and 1970. Corporation X also has assets in asset guideline class 22.1 of Revenue Procedure 72-10 which were placed in service at various times prior to 1971. Corporation X has no other qualified property. Corporation X elects to apply this section for 1971 to both classes. Assume that the class lives are determined under this subparagraph and not under subparagraph (2) of this paragraph.

(ii) The class lives for asset guideline classes 20.4 and 22.1 are their respective asset guideline periods of 12 years and 9 years in Revenue Procedure 72-10.

(iii) Accordingly, in the election for the taxable year, in accordance with paragraph (e)(3)(iii) of this section, corporation X specifies a class life of 12 years for asset guideline class 20.4 and a class life of 9 years for asset guideline class 22.1.

(2) *Class lives in special situations.*—Notwithstanding subparagraph (1) of this paragraph, for the purposes of this section the class life for the asset guideline class determined under this subparagraph shall be used if such class life is shorter than the class life determined under subparagraph (1) of this paragraph. If property described in paragraph (a)(2)(iii) of this section in an asset guideline class is acquired by the taxpayer in a transaction to which section 381(a) applies, for purposes of this subparagraph such property shall be segregated from other property in the class and treated as in a separate asset guideline class, and the class life for that asset guideline class under this subparagraph shall be the shortest class life the transferor was entitled to use under this section for such property on the date of such transfer. In all other cases, the class life for the asset guideline class for purposes of this subparagraph shall be the shortest class life (within the meaning of section 4, Part II, of Revenue Procedure 62-21) which can be justified by application of section 3.02(a), 3.03(a) or 3.05, Part II, of Revenue Procedure 62-21 (other than the portion of such section 3.05 dealing with justification of a class life by reference to facts and circumstances) for the taxpayer's last taxable year ending prior to January 1, 1971. A class life justified by application of section 3.03(a), Part II, of Revenue Procedure 62-21 shall not be shorter than can be justified under the Adjustment Table for Class Lives in Part III of such Revenue Procedure. For purposes of this subparagraph and paragraph (f)(1)(iii) of this section, the reserve ratio test is met only if the taxpayer's reserve ratio does not exceed the upper limit of the appropriate reserve ratio range or in the alternative during the transitional period there provided does not exceed the appropriate "transitional upper limit" in section 3, Part II, of Revenue Procedure 65-13. References to Revenue Procedure 62-21 include all modifications, amendments, and supplements thereto as of January 1, 1971. The guideline form of the reserve ratio test, as described in Revenue Procedure 65-13, may be applied for purposes of this subparagraph in a manner consistent with the rules contained in section 7, Part II, of Revenue Procedure 65-13 and sections 3.02, 3.03, and 3.05, Part II, of Revenue Procedure 62-21. The principles of this subparagraph may be illustrated by the following examples:

Example (1). Corporation X, a calendar year taxpayer, has all its assets in asset guideline class 20.4 of Revenue Procedure 72-10 which were placed in service by corporation X prior to 1971. Corporation X elects to apply this section for 1971. For taxable years 1967 through 1969, corporation X had used a class life (within the meaning of section 4, Part II, of Revenue Procedure 62-21) for asset guideline class 20.4 of 12 years. The asset guideline period in Revenue Procedure 72-10 in effect for 1971 is also 12 years. Assume that for 1969 corporation X's reserve ratio was below that appropriate reserve ratio lower limit. However, corporation X could not justify a class life shorter than the asset guideline period of 12 years for 1970 since corporation X had not used the 12-year class life for a period at least equal to one-half of 12 years. (See section 3.03(a), Part II, of Revenue Procedure 62-21.) Accordingly, the class life for asset guideline class 20.4 in 1971 is the asset guideline period of 12 years in accordance with subparagraph (1) or this paragraph.

Example (2). The facts are the same as in example (1) except that corporation X had used a class life of 10 years for guideline class 20.4 since 1967. Corporation X had not used the class life of 10 years for a period at least equal to one-half of 10 years. However, in 1968 corporation X's 10-year class life was accepted on audit by the Internal Revenue Service and corporation X met the reserve ratio test in 1970 for guideline class 20.4 using a test life of 10 years. (See section 3.05, Part II, of Revenue Procedure 62-21.) Accordingly, the class life of 10 years is justified for 1970 and the class life for 1971 is 10 years in accordance with this subparagraph. If the taxpayer's class life had not been audited and accepted for 1968, and in the absence of other circumstances, the taxpayer could not justify a class life shorter than the asset guideline period of 12 years since it had not used the

10-year class life for a period at least equal to one-half of 10 years. (See section 3.02, Part II, of Revenue Procedure 62-21.)

Example (3). Corporation Y, a calendar year taxpayer, has all its assets in asset guideline class 13.3 of Revenue Procedure 72-10 which were placed in service from 1960 through 1970. Corporation Y elects to apply this section for 1971. The asset guideline period in Revenue Procedure 72-10 in effect for 1971 is 16 years. Since 1963 corporation Y had used a class life of 16 years for asset guideline 13.3. At the end of 1969 corporation Y's reserve ratio for guideline class 13.3 was 36 percent. With a growth rate of 8 percent and a test life of 16 years the appropriate reserve ratio lower limit was 37 percent. Corporation Y's reserve ratio of 36 percent was below the lower limit of the appropriate reserve ration range. Corporation Y had used the 16-year class life for at least eight years. A class life of 13.5 years for 1970 was justified by application of section 3.03(a), Part II, of Revenue Procedure 62-21 and the Adjustment Table for Class Lives in Part III, of Revenue Procedure 62-21. The class life for 1971 is 13.5 years in accordance with this subparagraph.

(3) *Classification of property.*—(i) *In general.*—Property to which this section applies shall be included in the asset guideline class for the activity in which the property is primarily used in the taxable year of election. See paragraph (d)(5) of this section for rule regarding the classification of leased property.

(ii) *Insubstantial activity.*—The provisions of Revenue Procedure 62-21 with respect to classification of assets used in an activity which is insubstantial may be applied under this section.

(iii) *Special rule for certain public utilities.*—An electric or gas utility which in accordance with Revenue Procedure 64-21 used a composite guideline class basis for applying Revenue Procedure 64-21 for its last taxable year prior to January 1, 1971, may apply Revenue Procedure 72-10 and this section on the basis of such composite asset guideline class determined as provided in Revenue Procedure 64-21. For the purposes of this section all property in the composite guideline class shall be treated as included in a single asset guideline class.

(c) *Salvage value.*—(1) *In general.*—(i) *Definition of gross salvage value.*—"Gross salvage" value is the amount (determined at or as of the time of acquisition but without regard to the application of Revenue Procedure 62-21) which is estimated will be realized upon a sale or other disposition of qualified property when it is no longer useful in the taxpayer's trade or business or in the production of his income and is to be retired from service, without reduction for the cost of removal, dismantling, demolition, or similar operations. "Net salvage" is gross salvage reduced by the cost of removal, dismantling, demolition, or similar operations. If a taxpayer customarily sells or otherwise disposes of property at a time when such property is still in good operating condition, the gross salvage value of such property is the amount expected to be realized upon such sale or disposition, and under certain circumstances, as where such property is customarily sold at a time when it is still relatively new, the gross salvage value may constitute a relatively large proportion of the unadjusted basis of such property.

(ii) *Definition of salvage value.*—"Salvage value" for purposes of this section means gross or net salvage value less the amount, if any, by which reduced by application of section 167(f). Generally, as provided in section 167(f), a taxpayer may reduce the gross or net salvage value for an account by an amount which does not exceed 10 percent of the unadjusted basis of the personal property (as defined in section 167(f)(2)) in the account.

(2) *Estimation of salvage value.*—(i) *In general.*—For the first taxable year for which he elects to apply this section, the taxpayer must (in accordance with paragraph (e)(3)(iv)(c) of this section) establish salvage value for all qualified property to which the election applies. The taxpayer may (in accordance with subparagraph (1) of this paragraph) determine either gross or net salvage, but an election under this section does not constitute permission to change the manner of estimating salvage. Permission to change the manner of estimating salvage must be obtained by filing Form 3115 with the Commissioner of Internal Revenue, Washington, D.C. 20224, within the time otherwise permitted for the taxable year or before September 6, 1973. Salvage value in succeeding taxable years of election will be determined by adjustments of such initial salvage value for the account, as retirements occur. This salvage value established by the taxpayer for the first taxable year of election will not be redetermined merely as a result of fluctuations in price levels or as a result of other circumstances occurring after the close of such taxable year. See paragraph (e)(3)(iv) of this section for requirements that the taxpayer specify in his election the aggregate amount of salvage value for an asset guideline class and that the taxpayer maintain records reasonably sufficient to identify the salvage value established for each depreciation account in the class.

(ii) *Salvage as limitation on depreciation.*—In no case may an account be depreciated under this section below a reasonable salvage value, after taking into account any reduction in gross or net salvage value permitted by section 167(f). For example, if the salvage value of an account for 1971 is $75, the unadjusted basis of the account is $500, and the depreciation reserve is $425, no depreciation is allowable for 1971.

(iii) *Special rule for first taxable year.*—If for a taxable year ending prior to January 1, 1971, the taxpayer had adopted Revenue Procedure 62-21 prior to January 12, 1971 (see paragraph (f)(2) of this section), no adjustment in the amount of depreciation allowable for any taxable year ending prior to January 1, 1971, shall be made solely by reason of establishing salvage value under this paragraph for any taxable year ending after December 31, 1970. The principles of this subdivision may be illustrated by the following example:

Example: Taxpayer A had adopted Revenue Procedure 62-21 prior to January 12, 1971, for taxable years prior to 1971. Taxpayer A had not taken into account any salvage value for account No. 1 which is one of four depreciation accounts A has in the class. The reserve ratio test has been met for all years prior to 1971 and in accordance with Revenue Procedure 62-21 no adjustments in depreciable lives or salvage values were made. At the end of A's taxable year 1970, the unadjusted basis of account No. 1 was $10,000 and the reserve for depreciation was $9,800. Pursuant to this paragraph, A establishes a salvage value of $400 for account No. 1 (determined at or as of the time of acquisition). This salvage value is determined to be correct. No depreciation is allowable for account No. 1 in 1971. No depreciation is disallowed for any taxable year prior to 1971, solely by reason of establishing salvage value under this paragraph.

(3) *Limitation on adjustment of reasonable salvage value.*—The salvage value established by the taxpayer for a depreciation account will not be redetermined if it is reasonable. Since the determination of salvage value is a matter of estimation, minimal adjustments will not be made. The salvage value established by the taxpayer will be deemed to be reasonable unless there is sufficient basis for a determination of an amount of salvage value for the account which exceeds the salvage value established by the taxpayer for the account by an amount greater than 10 percent of the unadjusted basis of the account at the close of such taxable year. If the salvage value established by the taxpayer for the account is not within the 10 percent range or if the taxpayer follows the practice of understating his estimates of salvage to take advantage of this subdivision, and if there is a determination of an amount of salvage value for the account for the taxable year which exceeds the salvage value established by the taxpayer for the account for such taxable year, an adjustment will be made by increasing the salvage value established by the taxpayer for the account by an amount equal to the difference between the salvage value as determined and the salvage value established by the taxpayer for the account. For the purposes of this subdivision, a determination of salvage value shall include all determinations at all levels of audit and appellate proceedings, as well as all final determinations within the meaning of section 1313(a)(1). This subparagraph shall apply to each such determination.

(4) *Examples.*—The principles of this paragraph may be illustrated by the following examples in which it is assumed that the taxpayer has established salvage value in accordance with this paragraph and has not followed a practice of understating his estimates of salvage value:

Example (1). Taxpayer B elects to apply this section for 1971. Assets Y and Z are the only assets in a multiple asset account of 1967, the year in which the assets were acquired. The unadjusted basis of asset Y is $50,000 and the unadjusted basis of asset Z is $30,000. B estimated a gross salvage value of $55,000 at the time of acquisition. The property qualified under section 167(f)(2) and B reduced the amount of salvage taken into account by $8,000 (that is, 10 percent of $80,000, under section 167(f)). Thus, in accordance with this paragraph and paragraph (e)(3)(iv)(c) of this section, B establishes a salvage value of $47,000 for the account for 1971. Assume that there is not sufficient basis for determining a salvage value for the account greater than $52,000 (that is $60,000 minus the $8,000 reduction under section 167(f)). Since the salvage value of $47,000 established by B for the account is within the 10 percent range, it is reasonable. Salvage for the account will not be redetermined.

Example (2). The facts are the same as in example (1) except that B estimated a gross salvage value of $50,000 and establishes a salvage value of $42,000 for the account (that is $50,000 minus the $8,000 reduction under section 167(f)). There is sufficient basis for determining an amount of salvage value greater than $50,000 (that is, $58,000 minus the $8,000 reduction under section 167(f)). The salvage value of $42,000 established by B for the account can be redetermined without regard to the limitation in subparagraph (3) of this paragraph, since it is not within the 10 percent range. Upon audit of B's tax return for 1971 (a year in which the redetermination would affect the amount of depreciation allowable for the account), salvage value is determined to be $52,000 after taking into account the reduction under section 167(f). Salvage value for the account will be adjusted to $52,000.

Example (3). The facts are the same as in example (1) except that upon audit of B's tax return for 1971 the examining officer determines the salvage value to be $58,000 (that is $66,000 minus the $8,000 reduction under section 167(f)), and proposes to adjust salvage value for the account to $58,000 which will result in disallowing an amount of depreciation for the taxable year. B does not agree with the finding of the examining officer. After receipt of a "30-day letter," B waives a district conference and initiates proceedings before the Appellate Division. In consideration of the case by the Appellate Division it is concluded that there is not sufficient basis for determining an amount of salvage value for the account in excess of $55,000 (that is, $63,000 minus the $8,000 reduction under section 167(f)). Since the salvage value of $47,000 established by B for the account is within the 10 percent range, it is reasaonable. Salvage value for the account will not be redetermined.

Example (4). For 1971, taxpayer C elects to apply this section to factory building X which is in an item account of 1965, the year in which the building was acquired. The unadjusted basis of factory building X is $90,000. C estimated a gross salvage value for the account of $10,000. The property did not qualify under section 167(f)(2). Thus, C establishes a salvage value of $10,000 for the account for 1971. Assume that there is not sufficient basis for determining a salvage value for the account greater than $14,000. Since the salvage value of $10,000 established by C for the account is within the 10 percent range, it is reasonable. Salvage value for the account will not be redetermined.

(d) *Accounting for qualified property.*—(1) *In general.*—Qualified property for which the taxpayer elects to apply this section may be accounted for in any number of item or multiple asset accounts.

(2) *Retirements of qualified property.*—(i) *In general.*—The provisions of this subparagraph and § 1.167(a)-8 apply to retirements of qualified property to which the taxpayer elects to apply this section for the taxable year. See subdivision (iii) of this subparagraph for special rule for normal retirements.

(ii) *Adjusted basis of assets retired.*—In the case of a taxpayer who depreciates qualified property in a multiple asset account conforming to the asset guideline class at a rate based on the class life in accordance with paragraph (a)(5)(ii)(*a*) of this section, § 1.167(a)-8(c) (relating to basis of assets retired) shall be applied by assuming that the class life is the average expected useful life of the assets in the account. See § 1.167(a)-8, generally, for the basis of assets retired.

(iii) *Definition of normal retirements.*—Notwithstanding § 1.167 (a)-8(b), the determination whether a retirement of qualified property is normal or abnormal shall be made in light of all facts and circumstances, primarily with reference to the expected period of use of the asset in the taxpayer's business without regard to paragraph (a)(5)(ii) of this section. A retirement is not abnormal unless the taxpayer can show that the withdrawal of the asset was not due to a cause which would customarily be contemplated (in light of the taxpayer's practice and experience) in setting a depreciation rate for the assets without regard to paragraph (a)(5)(ii) of this section. Thus, for example, a retirement is normal if made within the range of years which would customarily be taken into account in setting such depreciation rate and if the asset has reached a condition at which, in the normal course of events, the taxpayer customarily retires similar assets from use in his business. A retirement may be abnormal if the asset is withdrawn at an earlier time or under other circumstances, as, for example, when the asset has been damaged by casualty or has lost its usefulness suddenly as the result of extraordinary obsolescence.

(3) *Special rules.*—(i) *In general.*—The provisions of this subparagraph shall apply to qualified property in a taxable year for which an election to apply this section is made.

(ii) *Repairs.*—For the purpose of sections 162 and 263 and the regulations thereunder, whether an expenditure prolongs the life of an asset shall be determined by reference to the expected period of use of the asset in the taxpayer's business without regard to paragraph (a)(5)(ii) of this section.

(iii) *Sale and lease.*—For the purpose of comparison with the term of a lease of such property, the remaining life of qualified property shall be determined by reference to the expected period of use of the asset in the taxpayer's business without regard to paragraph (a)(5)(ii) of this section.

(4) *Expected period of use.*—For the purposes of subparagraphs (2) and (3) of this paragraph, the determination of the expected period of use of an asset shall be made in light of all the facts and circum-

stances. The expected period of use of a particular asset will not necessarily coincide with the class life used for depreciation (or with the individual asset life for depreciation under the alternative method in paragraph (a)(5)(ii)(*b*) of this section for applying the class life). Thus, for example, if the question is whether an asset has been leased for a period less than, equal to or greater than its remaining life, the determination shall be based on the remaining expected period of use of the individual asset without regard to the fact that the asset is depreciated at a rate based on the class life in accordance with paragraph (a)(5)(ii)(*a*) of this section.

(5) *Leased property.*—In the case of a lessor of qualified property, unless there is an asset guideline class in effect for such lessors, the asset guideline class for such property shall be determined by reference to the activity in which such property is primarily used by the lessee. See paragraph (b)(3) of this section for general rule for classification of qualified property according to primary use. However, in the case of an asset guideline class based upon the type of property (such as trucks or railroad cars), as distinguished from the activity in which used, the property shall be classified without regard to the activity of the lessee.

(e) *Election under this section.*—(1) *Consent to change in method of accounting.*—An election to apply this section for a taxable year ending after December 31, 1970, is a method of accounting but the consent of the Commissioner will be deemed granted to make an annual election.

(2) *Election for taxable years ending after December 31, 1976.*—For taxable years ending after December 31, 1976, the election to apply this section for a taxable year shall be made by attaching to the income tax return a statement that an election under this section is being made. If the taxpayer does not file a timely return (taking into account extensions of time for filing) for the taxable year, the election shall be made at the time the taxpayer files his first return for the taxable year. The election may be made with an amended return only if such amended return is filed no later than the time prescribed by law (including extensions thereof) for filing the return for the taxable year. A taxpayer who makes an election under this subparagraph must maintain books and records reflecting the information described in paragraph (e)(3)(ii) and (iii) of this section.

(3) *Election for taxable years ending on or before December 31, 1976.*—(i) For taxable years ending on or before December 31, 1976, the election to apply this section for a taxable year may be made by filing Form 5006 with the income tax return for the taxable year. If the taxpayer does not file a timely return (taking into account extensions of time for filing) for the taxable year, the election shall be filed at the time the taxpayer files his first return for the taxable year. The election may be made with an amended return only if such amended return is filed no later than the later of (*a*) the time prescribed by law (including extensions thereof) for filing the return for the taxable year, or (*b*) November 5, 1973.

(ii) The election to apply this section for a taxable year ending on or before December 31, 1976, will be deemed to be made if the tax return (filed within the periods referred to in paragraph (e)(3)(i) of this section) contains information sufficient to establish the following:

(*a*) Each asset guideline class for which the election is intended to apply;

(*b*) The class life for each such asset guideline class and whether the class life is determined under paragraph (b)(1) or (2) of this section;

(*c*) For each asset guideline class, as of the end of the taxable year of election, (*1*) the total unadjusted basis of all qualified property, (*2*) the aggregate of the reserves for depreciation of all accounts in the asset guideline class, and (*3*) the aggregate of the salvage value established for all accounts in the asset guideline class; and

(*d*) Whether the taxpayer is an electric or gas utility using a composite asset guideline class basis in accordance with paragraph (b)(3)(iii) of this section.

If an election is deemed to be made under this subdivision (ii), the taxpayer will be deemed to have consented to apply all provisions of this section.

(iii) A taxpayer to whom the election applies shall maintain books and records for each asset guideline class reasonably sufficient to identify the unadjusted basis, reserve for depreciation and salvage value established for each depreciation account in such assset guideline class.

(f) *Depreciation for taxable years ending before January 1, 1971.*—(1) *Adoption of Revenue Procedure 62-21.*—(i) *In general.*—Except as provided in subdivision (ii) of this subparagraph, a taxpayer may elect to be examined under the provisions of Revenue Procedure 62-21 for a taxable year ending before January 1, 1971, only in accordance with the rules of this paragraph. The election must specify:

(a) That the taxpayer makes such election and consents to, and agrees to apply, all the provisions of this paragraph;

(b) Each guideline class and taxable year for which the taxpayer elects to be examined under Revenue Procedure 62-21;

(c) The class life claimed for each such guideline class;

(d) The class life and the total amount of the depreciation for the guideline class claimed on the last income tax return for such taxable year filed prior to January 12, 1971 (or in case no income tax return was filed prior to January 12, 1971, on the first income tax return filed for such taxable year);

(e) The class life claimed and the total amount of depreciation for the guideline class under the election to apply Revenue Procedure 62-21, in accordance with this paragraph, for the taxable year; and

(f) If the class life or total amount of depreciation for the guideline class is different in (d) and (e) of this subdivision, a reasonable description of the computation of the class life in (e) of this subdivision, the amount of difference in tax liability resulting therefrom, and the amount of any refund or reduction in any deficiency in tax.

The election shall be made in an amended tax return or claim for refund (or by a supplement to the tax return or claim) for the taxable year, and if the class life or total amount of depreciation for the guideline class is different in accordance with (f) of this subdivision, such difference shall be reflected in the amended tax return or claim for refund. Forms may be provided for making the election and submission of the information. In the case of an election made after issuance of such Forms and more than 30 days after publication of notice thereof in the Internal Revenue Bulletin, the election may be made and the information submitted only in accordance with such forms. An election will not otherwise be invalid under this paragraph so long as there is substantial compliance, in good faith, with the requirements of this paragraph.

(ii) *Special rule.*—The provisions of this subparagraph shall not apply to a guideline class in any taxable year for which the taxpayer has prior to January 12, 1971, adopted Revenue Procedure 62-21 for such class. See subparagraph (2) of this paragraph for determination of adoption of Revenue Procedure 62-21 prior to January 12, 1971.

(iii) *Justification of class life claimed and limitations on refunds.*—If the taxpayer elects for a taxable year to be examined under the provisions of Revenue Procedure 62-21 in accordance with subdivision (i) of this subparagraph, any of the provisions of Revenue Procedure 62-21 may be applied to justify a class life claimed on the income tax return filed for such year or to offset an increase in tax liability for such year. Unless it meets the reserve ratio test, no class life will be accepted on audit which (after all other adjustments in tax liability for such year) results in a reduction (or further reduction) in the amount of tax liability shown on the income tax return (specified in subdivision (i)(d) of this subparagraph) for such taxable year, or results in an amount of loss carryback or carryover to any taxable year, but if it is justified under Revenue Procedure 62-21 and meets the reserve ratio test, a class life will be accepted on audit without regard to the foregoing limitations and, for example, may produce a refund or credit against tax. For example, if a class life of 9 years is otherwise justified under Revenue Procedure 62-21 for 1969, but the taxpayer does not meet the reserve ratio test for 1969 using a test life of 9 years, a class life of 9 years (or any class life justified under Revenue Procedure 62-21) will be accepted on audit under Revenue Procedure 62-21 pursuant to an election in accordance with this paragraph provided it does not result in the reduction or further reduction in tax liability or in an amount of loss carryback or carryover as described in the preceding sentence. On the other hand, for example, if a class life of 10 years is justified under Revenue Procedure 62-21 for 1969 and the taxpayer meets the reserve ratio test for 1969 using a test life of 10 years, a class life of 10 years will be accepted on audit under Revenue Procedure 62-21 pursuant to an election in accordance with this paragraph even though it results in a reduction or further reduction in tax liability or in an amount of loss carryback or carryover as described above and produces a refund of tax. For purposes of this section, the term "audit" includes examination of claims for refund or credit against tax.

(iv) *Definitions.*—For purposes of this paragraph, the determination whether the reserve ratio test is met shall be made in accordance with that portion of paragraph (b)(2) of this section which is by express reference therein made applicable to this paragraph. In addition, the guideline form of the reserve ratio test, as described in Revenue Procedure 65-13, may be applied.

For purposes of this paragraph, references to Revenue Procedure 62-21 include all modifications, amendments, and supplements

thereto as of January 11, 1971. The terms "class life" and "guideline class" have the same meaning as in Revenue Procedure 62-21.

(2) *Determination whether Revenue Procedure 62-21 adopted prior to January 12, 1971.*—(i) *In general.*—For the purposes of this paragraph, a taxpayer will be treated as having adopted prior to January 12, 1971, Revenue Procedure 62-21 for a guideline class for a taxable year ending before January 1, 1971, only if—

(a) For the guideline class and taxable year, the taxpayer adopted Revenue Procedure 62-21 by expressly so indicating on the income tax return filed for such taxable year prior to January 12, 1971;

(b) For the guideline class and taxable year, the taxpayer adopted Revenue Procedure 62-21 prior to January 12, 1971, by expressly so indicating in a proceeding before the Internal Revenue Service (such as upon examination of the income tax return for such taxable year) and there is reasonable evidence to that effect; or

(c) There is other reasonable evidence that prior to January 12, 1971, the taxpayer adopted Revenue Procedure 62-21 for the guideline class and taxable year.

If not treated under (b) or (c) of this subdivision as having done so for the last taxable year ending before January 1, 1971, and if the taxpayer files his first income tax return for such taxable year after January 11, 1971, the taxpayer will be treated as having adopted Revenue Procedure 62-21 prior to January 12, 1971, for a guideline class for such taxable year if he expressly so indicated on that return, or is treated under this subparagraph as having adopted Revenue Procedure 62-21 prior to January 12, 1971, for that guideline class for the immediately preceeding taxable year.

(ii) *Examples.*—The principles of this subparagraph may be illustrated by the following examples:

Example (1). Taxpayer A, an individual who uses the calendar year as his taxable year, has property in Group Three, Class 16(a), of Revenue Procedure 62-21. On A's income tax return for 1968, filed prior to January 12, 1971, he adopted Revenue Procedure 62-21 for the guideline class by so indicating under "Summary of Depreciation" in the appropriate schedule of Form 1040 for 1968. Under subdivision (i)(a) of this subparagraph, A is treated as having adopted Revenue Procedure 62-21 for the guideline class for 1968 prior to January 12, 1971.

Example (2). Taxpayer B, an individual who uses the calendar year as his taxable year, has property in Group Two, Class 5, of Revenue Procedure 62-21. B filed timely income tax returns for 1966 through 1968 but did not adopt Revenue Procedure 62-21 on any of such returns. In 1969 upon audit of B's taxable years 1966 through 1968, B exercised his option to be examined under the provisions of Revenue Procedure 62-21. The Revenue Agent's report shows that B was examined under Revenue Procedure 62-21 for taxable years 1966 through 1968. B will be treated under subdivision (ii)(b) of this subparagraph as having adopted Revenue Procedure 62-21 for such years prior to January 12, 1971.

Example (3). The facts are the same as in example (2) except that B did not upon examination by the Revenue Agent in 1969 exercise his option to be examined under Revenue Procedure 62-21. B has six accounts in the guideline class, Nos. 1 through 6. The Revenue Agent proposed to lengthen the depreciable lives on accounts Nos. 2 and 3 from 8 years to 12 years. In proceedings before the Appellate Division in 1970, B exercised his option to be examined under the provisions of Revenue Procedure 62-21. This is shown by correspondence between B and the Appellate Conferee as well as by other documents in the case before the Appellate Division. The case was settled on that basis before the Appellate Division without adjustment of the depreciable lives for B's accounts Nos. 2 and 3. B will be treated under subdivision (ii)(b) of this subparagraph as having adopted Revenue Procedure 62-21 for taxable years 1966 through 1968 prior to January 12, 1971.

Example (4). Corporation X uses the calendar year as its taxable year and has assets in Group Two, Class 5, of Revenue Procedure 62-21. Beginning in 1964, corporation X used the guideline life of 10 years as the depreciable life for all assets in the guideline class. In 1967, corporation X's taxable years 1964 through 1966 were examined and corporation X exercised its option to be examined under the provisions of Revenue Procedure 62-21. Corporation X did not adopt Revenue Procedure 62-21 on any of its income tax returns, for the years 1964 through 1970. Corporation X has not been examined since 1967, but has continued to use the guideline life of 10 years for all property in the guideline class including additions since 1966. Corporation X will be treated under subdivision (ii)(c) and (d) of this subparagraph as having adopted Revenue Procedure 62-21 prior to January 12, 1971 for taxable years 1964 through 1970.

Example (5). Corporation Y uses the calendar year as its taxable year and has assets in Group Two, Class 5, of Revenue Procedure 62-21. Since 1964, corporation Y has used various depreciable lives, based on the facts and circumstances, for different accounts in the guideline class. Corporation Y was examined in 1968 for taxable years 1965 through 1967. Corporation Y was also examined in 1970 for taxable years 1968 and 1969. Corporation Y did not exercise its option to be examined under the provisions of Revenue Procedure 62-21. Corporation Y has not adopted Revenue Procedure 62-21 on any income tax return. For taxable years 1964 through 1970, corporation Y's class life (within the meaning of section 4, Part II, of Revenue Procedure 62-21) was between 12 and 14 years. In August of 1971, corporation Y filed amended income tax returns for 1968 and 1969, and an income tax return for 1970, using a depreciable life of 10 years (equal to the guideline life) for all assets in the guideline class. Corporation Y will not be treated as having adopted Revenue Procedure 62-21 prior to January 12, 1971.

Example (6). Corporation Z uses the calendar year as its taxable year and has assets in Group Two, Class 5, of Revenue Procedure 62-21. Corporation Z adopted Revenue Procedure 62-21 for this guideline class by expressly so indicating on its tax return for 1966, which was filed before January 12, 1971. Corporation Z computed its allowable depreciation for 1966 as if it adopted Rev. Proc. 62-21 for this guideline class for its taxable years 1962 through 1965, although it had earlier filed its tax returns for those years without regard to Rev. Proc. 62-21. The depreciation thus claimed in 1966 was less than what would have been allowed if corporation Z first adopted Rev. Proc. 62-21 in 1966. This was the result of certain accounts becoming fully depreciated through use of Rev. Proc. 62-21 in computing depreciation for 1962 through 1965. In addition, in deferred tax accounting procedures employed before January 12, 1971, for financial reporting purposes, corporation Z calculated its tax deferrals on the basis that it had adopted Rev. Proc. 62-21 for the years 1962 through 1965. Corporation Z will be treated under subdivision (i)(c) of this subparagraph as having adopted Rev. Proc. 62-21 for taxable years 1962 through 1965 prior to January 12, 1971. [Reg. § 1.167(a)-12.]

☐ [*T.D. 7278, 6-6-73. Amended by T.D. 7315, 6-6-74 and T.D. 7517,* 11-11-77.]

[Reg. § 1.167(a)-13T]

§ 1.167(a)-13T. Certain elections for intangible property (temporary).—For rules applying the elections under section 13261(g)(2) and (3) of the Omnibus Budget Reconciliation Act of 1993 to intangible property described in section 167(f), see § 1.197-1T. [Temporary Reg. § 1.167(a)-13T.]

☐ [*T.D. 8528, 3-10-94.*]

[Reg. § 1.167(a)-14]

§ 1.167(a)-14. Treatment of certain intangible property excluded from section 197.—(a) *Overview.*—This section provides rules for the amortization of certain intangibles that are excluded from section 197 (relating to the amortization of goodwill and certain other intangibles). These excluded intangibles are specifically described in § 1.197-2(c)(4), (6), (7), (11), and (13) and include certain computer software and certain other separately acquired rights, such as rights to receive tangible property or services, patents and copyrights, certain mortgage servicing rights, and rights of fixed duration or amount. Intangibles for which an amortization amount is determined under section 167(f) and intangibles otherwise excluded from section 197 are amortizable only if they qualify as property subject to the allowance for depreciation under section 167(a).

(b) *Computer software.*—(1) *In general.*—The amount of the deduction for computer software described in section 167(f)(1) and § 1.197-2(c)(4) is determined by amortizing the cost or other basis of the computer software using the straight line method described in § 1.167(b)-1 (except that its salvage value is treated as zero) and an amortization period of 36 months beginning on the first day of the month that the computer software is placed in service. Before determining the amortization deduction allowable under this paragraph (b), the cost or other basis of computer software that is section 179 property, as defined in section 179(d)(1)(A)(ii), must be reduced for any portion of the basis the taxpayer properly elects to treat as an expense under section 179. In addition, the cost or other basis of computer software that is qualified property under section 168(k)(2) and § 1.168(k)-1 or § 1.168(k)-2, as applicable, 50-percent bonus depreciation property under section 168(k)(4) or § 1.168(k)-1, or qualified New York Liberty Zone property under section 1400L(b) or § 1.1400L(b)-1, must be reduced by the amount of the additional first year depreciation deduction allowed or allowable, whichever is greater, under section 168(k) or section 1400L(b) for the computer software. If costs for developing computer software that the taxpayer *properly elects to defer under section 174(b)* result in the development of property subject to the allowance for depreciation under section 167, the rules of this paragraph (b) will apply to the unrecovered costs. In addition, this paragraph (b) applies to the cost of

separately acquired computer software if the cost to acquire the software is separately stated and the cost is required to be capitalized under section 263(a).

(2) *Exceptions.*—Paragraph (b)(1) of this section does not apply to the cost of computer software properly and consistently taken into account under § 1.162-11. The cost of acquiring an interest in computer software that is included, without being separately stated, in the cost of the hardware or other tangible property is treated as part of the cost of the hardware or other tangible property that is capitalized and depreciated under other applicable sections of the Internal Revenue Code.

(3) *Additional rules.*—Rules similar to those in § 1.197-2(f)(1)(iii), (f)(1)(iv), and (f)(2) (relating to the computation of amortization deductions and the treatment of contingent amounts) apply for purposes of this paragraph (b).

(c) *Certain interests or rights not acquired as part of a purchase of a trade or business.*—(1) *Certain rights to receive tangible property or services.*—The amount of the deduction for a right (other than a right acquired as part of a purchase of a trade or business) to receive tangible property or services under a contract or from a governmental unit (as specified in section 167(f)(2) and § 1.197-2(c)(6)) is determined as follows:

(i) *Amortization of fixed amounts.*—The basis of a right to receive a fixed amount of tangible property or services is amortized for each taxable year by multiplying the basis of the right by a fraction, the numerator of which is the amount of tangible property or services received during the taxable year and the denominator of which is the total amount of tangible property or services received or to be received under the terms of the contract or governmental grant. For example, if a taxpayer acquires a favorable contract right to receive a fixed amount of raw materials during an unspecified period, the taxpayer must amortize the cost of acquiring the contract right by multiplying the total cost by a fraction, the numerator of which is the amount of raw materials received under the contract during the taxable year and the denominator of which is the total amount of raw materials received or to be received under the contract.

(ii) *Amortization of unspecified amount over fixed period.*—The cost or other basis of a right to receive an unspecified amount of tangible property or services over a fixed period is amortized ratably over the period of the right. (See paragraph (c)(3) of this section regarding renewals).

(iii) *Amortization in other cases.*—[Reserved]

(2) *Rights of fixed duration or amount.*—The amount of the deduction for a right (other than a right acquired as part of a trade or business) of fixed duration or amount received under a contract or granted by a governmental unit (specified in section 167(f)(2) and § 1.197-2(c)(13)) and not covered by paragraph (c)(1) of this section is determined as follows:

(i) *Rights to a fixed amount.*—The basis of a right to a fixed amount is amortized for each taxable year by multiplying the basis by a fraction, the numerator of which is the amount received during the taxable year and the denominator of which is the total amount received or to be received under the terms of the contract or governmental grant.

(ii) *Rights to an unspecified amount over fixed duration of less than 15 years.*—The basis of a right to an unspecified amount over a fixed duration of less than 15 years is amortized ratably over the period of the right.

(3) *Application of renewals.*—(i) For purposes of paragraphs (c)(1) and (2) of this section, the duration of a right under a contract (or granted by a governmental unit) includes any renewal period if, based on all of the facts and circumstances in existence at any time during the taxable year in which the right is acquired, the facts clearly indicate a reasonable expectancy of renewal.

(ii) The mere fact that a taxpayer will have the opportunity to renew a contract right or other right on the same terms as are available to others, in a competitive auction or similar process that is designed to reflect fair market value and in which the taxpayer is not contractually advantaged, will generally not be taken into account in determining the duration of such right provided that the bidding produces a fair market value price comparable to the price that would be obtained if the rights were purchased immediately after renewal from a person (other than the person granting the renewal) in an arm's-length transaction.

(iii) The cost of a renewal not included in the terms of the contract or governmental grant is treated as the acquisition of a separate intangible asset.

(4) *Patents and copyrights.*—If the purchase price of a interest (other than an interest acquired as part of a purchase of a trade or business) in a patent or copyright described in section 167(f)(2) and §1.197-2(c)(7) is payable on at least an annual basis as either a fixed amount per use or a fixed percentage of the revenue derived from the use of the patent or copyright, the depreciation deduction for a taxable year is equal to the amount of the purchase price paid or incurred during the year. Otherwise, the basis of such patent or copyright (or an interest therein) is depreciated either ratably over its remaining useful life or under section 167(g) (income forecast method). If a patent or copyright becomes valueless in any year before its legal expiration, the adjusted basis may be deducted in that year.

(5) *Additional rules.*—The period of amortization under paragraphs (c)(1) through (4) of this section begins when the intangible is placed in service, and rules similar to those in §1.197-2(f)(2) apply for purposes of this paragraph (c).

(d) *Mortgage servicing rights.*—(1) *In general.*—The amount of the deduction for mortgage servicing rights described in section 167(f)(3) and §1.197-2(c)(11) is determined by using the straight line method described in §1.167(b)-1 (except that the salvage value is treated as zero) and an amortization period of 108 months beginning on the first day of the month that the rights are placed in service. Mortgage servicing rights are not depreciable to the extent the rights are stripped coupons under section 1286.

(2) *Treatment of rights acquired as a pool.*—(i) *In general.*—Except as provided in paragraph (d)(2)(ii) of this section, all mortgage servicing rights acquired in the same transaction or in a series of related transactions are treated as a single asset (the pool) for purposes of determining the depreciation deduction under this paragraph (d) and any gain or loss from the sale, exchange, or other disposition of the rights. Thus, if some (but not all) of the rights in a pool become worthless as a result of prepayments, no loss is recognized by reason of the prepayment and the adjusted basis of the pool is not affected by the unrecognized loss. Similarly, any amount realized from the sale or exchange of some (but not all) of the mortgage servicing rights is included in income and the adjusted basis of the pool is not affected by the realization.

(ii) *Multiple accounts.*—If the taxpayer establishes multiple accounts within a pool at the time of its acquisition, gain or loss is recognized on the sale or exchange of all mortgage servicing rights within any such account.

(3) *Additional rules.*—Rules similar to those in §1.197-2(f)(1)(iii), (f)(1)(iv), and (f)(2) (relating to the computation of amortization deductions and the treatment of contingent amounts) apply for purposes of this paragraph (d).

(e) *Effective dates.*—(1) *In general.*—This section applies to property acquired after January 25, 2000, except that §1.167(a)-14(c)(2) (depreciation of the cost of certain separately acquired rights) and so much of §1.167(a)-14(c)(3) as relates to §1.167(a)-14(c)(2) apply to property acquired after August 10, 1993 (or July 25, 1991, if a valid retroactive election has been made under §1.197-1T).

(2) *Change in method of accounting.*—See §1.197-2(l)(4) for rules relating to changes in method of accounting for property to which §1.167(a)-14 applies. However, see §1.168(k)-1(g)(4) or 1.1400L(b)-1(g)(4) for rules relating to changes in method of accounting for computer software to which the third sentence in §1.167(a)-14(b)(1) applies.

(3) *Qualified property, 50-percent bonus depreciation property, qualified New York Liberty Zone property, or section 179 property.*—This section also applies to computer software that is qualified property under section 168(k)(2) or qualified New York Liberty Zone property under section 1400L(b) acquired by a taxpayer after September 10, 2001, and to computer software that is 50-percent bonus depreciation property under section 168(k)(4) acquired by a taxpayer after May 5, 2003. This section also applies to computer software that is section 179 property placed in service by a taxpayer in a taxable year beginning after 2002. The language "or §1.168(k)-2, as applicable," in the third sentence in paragraph (b)(1) of this section applies to computer software that is qualified property under section 168(k)(2) and placed in service by a taxpayer during or after the taxpayer's taxable year that includes September 24, 2019. However, a taxpayer may choose to apply the language "or §1.168(k)-2, as applicable," in

the third sentence in paragraph (b)(1) of this section for computer software that is qualified property under section 168(k)(2) and acquired and placed in service after September 27, 2017, by the taxpayer during taxable years ending on or after September 28, 2017. A taxpayer may rely on the language "or §1.168(k)-2, as applicable," in the third sentence in paragraph (b)(1) of this section in regulation project REG-104397-18 (2018-41 I.R.B. 558) (see §601.601(d)(2)(ii)(b) of this chapter) for computer software that is qualified property under section 168(k)(2) and acquired and placed in service after September 27, 2017, by the taxpayer during taxable years ending on or after September 28, 2017, and ending before the taxpayer's taxable year that includes September 24, 2019. [Reg. §1.167(a)-14.]

☐ [*T.D.* 8865, 1-20-2000. *Amended by T.D.* 9091, 9-5-2003, *T.D.* 9283, 8-28-2006 *and T.D.* 9874, 9-17-2019.]

[Reg. §1.167(b)-0]

§1.167(b)-0. Methods of computing depreciation.—(a) *In general.*—Any reasonable and consistently applied method of computing depreciation may be used or continued in use under section 167. Regardless of the method used in computing depreciation, deductions for depreciation shall not exceed such amounts as may be necessary to recover the unrecovered cost or other basis less salvage during the remaining useful life of the property. The reasonableness of any claim for depreciation shall be determined upon the basis of conditions known to exist at the end of the period for which the return is made. It is the responsibility of the taxpayer to establish the reasonableness of the deduction for depreciation claimed. Generally, depreciation deductions so claimed will be changed only where there is a clear and convincing basis for a change.

(b) *Certain methods.*—Methods previously found adequate to produce a reasonable allowance under the Internal Revenue Code of 1939 or prior revenue laws will, if used consistently by the taxpayer, continue to be acceptable under section 167(a). Examples of such methods which continue to be acceptable are the straight line method, the declining balance method with the rate limited to 150 percent of the applicable straight line rate, and under appropriate circumstances, the unit of production method. The methods described in section 167(b) and §§1.167(b)-1, 1.167(b)-2, 1.167(b)-3, and 1.167(b)-4 shall be deemed to produce a reasonable allowance for depreciation except as limited under section 167(c) and §1.167(c)-1. See also §1.167(e)-1 for rules relating to change in method of computing depreciation.

(c) *Application of methods.*—In the case of item accounts, any method which results in a reasonable allowance for depreciation may be selected for each item of property, but such method must thereafter be applied consistently to that particular item. In the case of group, classified, or composite accounts, any method may be selected for each account. Such method must be applied to that particular account consistently thereafter but need not necessarily be applied to acquisitions of similar property in the same or subsequent years, provided such acquisitions are set up in separate accounts. See, however, §1.167(e)-1 and section 446 and the regulations thereunder, for rules relating to changes in the method of computing depreciation, and §1.167(c)-1 for restriction on the use of certain methods. See also §1.167(a)-7 for definition of account. [Reg. §1.167(b)-0.]

☐ [*T.D.* 6182, 6-11-56.]

[Reg. §1.167(b)-1]

§1.167(b)-1. Straight line method.—(a) *Application of method.*—Under the straight line method the cost or other basis of the property less its estimated salvage value is deductible in equal annual amounts over the period of the estimated useful life of the property. The allowance for depreciation for the taxable year is determined by dividing the adjusted basis of the property at the beginning of the taxable year, less salvage value, by the remaining useful life of the property at such time. For convenience, the allowance so determined may be reduced to a percentage or fraction. The straight line method may be used in determining a reasonable allowance for depreciation for any property which is subject to depreciation under section 167 and it shall be used in all cases where the taxpayer has not adopted a different acceptable method with respect to such property.

(b) *Illustrations.*—The straight line method is illustrated by the following examples:

Example (1). Under the straight line method items may be depreciated separately:

Year 1954	Item	Cost or other basis less salvage	Useful life Years	Depreciation allowable 1954	1955	1954
	Asset A	$1,600	4	$200 [1]	$400	$400
	Asset B	12,000	40	150 [1]	300	300

[1] In this example it is assumed that the assets were placed in service on July 1, 1954.

Example (2). In group, classified, or composite accounting, a number of assets with the same or different useful lives may be combined into one account, and a single rate of depreciation, i.e., the group, classified, or composite rate used for the entire account. In the case of group accounts, i.e., accounts containing assets which are similar in kind and which have approximately the same estimated useful lives, the group rate is determined from the average of the useful lives of the assets. In the case of classified or composite accounts, the classi-fied or composite rate is generally computed by determining the amount of one year's depreciation for each item or each group of similar items, and by dividing the total depreciation thus obtained by the total cost or other basis of the assets. The average rate so obtained is to be used as long as subsequent additions, retirements, or replacements do not substantially alter the relative proportions of different types of assets in the account. An example of the computation of a classified or composite rate follows:

Cost or other basis	Estimated useful life Years	Annual depreciation
$10,000	5	$2,000
10,000	15	667
20,000		2,667

Average rate is 13.33 percent ($2,667 ÷ $20,000) unadjusted for salvage. Assuming the estimated salvage value is 10 percent of the cost or other basis, the rate adjusted for salvage will be 13.33 percent minus 10 percent of 13.33 percent (13.33% — 1.33%), or 12 percent.

Example (3). The use of the straight line method for group, classified, or composite accounts is illustrated by the following example: A taxpayer filing his returns on a calendar year basis maintains an asset account for which a group rate of 20 percent has been determined, before adjustment for salvage. Estimated salvage is determined to be 6 $2/3$ percent, resulting in an adjusted rate of 18.67 percent. During the years illustrated, the initial investment, additions, retirements, and salvage recoveries, which were determined not to change the composition of the group sufficiently to require a change in rate, were assumed to have been made as follows:

    1954—Initial investment of $12,000
    1957—Retirement $2,000, salvage realized $200
    1958—Retirement $2,000, salvage realized $200
    1959—Retirements $4,000, salvage realized $400
    1959—Additions $10,000
    1960—Retirement $2,000, no salvage realized
    1961—Retirement $2,000, no salvage realized

Depreciable Asset Account and Depreciation Computation on Average Balances

Year	Asset balance Jan. 1	Current additions	Current retire-ments	Asset balance Dec. 31	Average balance	Rate (percent)	Allowable depreciation
1954	—	$12,000	—	$12,000	$6,000	18.67	$1,120
1955	$12,000	—	—	12,000	12,000	18.67	2,240
1956	12,000	—	—	12,000	12,000	18.67	2,240
1957	12,000	—	$2,000	10,000	11,000	18.67	2,054
1958	10,000	—	2,000	8,000	9,000	18.67	1,680
1959	8,000	10,000	4,000	14,000	11,000	18.67	2,054
1960	14,000	—	2,000	12,000	13,000	18.67	2,427
1961	12,000	—	2,000	10,000	11,000	18.67	2,054

Corresponding Depreciation Reserve Account

Year	Depreciation reserve Jan. 1	Depreciation allowable	Current retirements	Salvage realized	Depreciation reserve Dec. 31
1954	—	$1,120	—	—	$1,120
1955	$1,120	2,240	—	—	3,360
1956	3,360	2,240	—	—	5,600
1957	5,600	2,054	$2,000	$200	5,854
1958	5,854	1,680	2,000	200	5,734
1959	5,734	2,054	4,000	400	4,188
1960	4,188	2,427	2,000	—	4,615
1961	4,615	2,054	2,000	—	4,669

[Reg. § 1.167(b)-1.]

☐ [*T.D. 6182,* 6-11-56.]

[Reg. §1.167(b)-2]

§1.167(b)-2. Declining balance method.—(a) *Application of method.*—Under the declining balance method a uniform rate is applied each year to the unrecovered cost or other basis of the property. The unrecovered cost or other basis is the basis provided by section 167(g), adjusted for depreciation previously allowed or allowable, and for all other adjustments provided by section 1016 and other applicable provisions of law. The declining balance rate may be determined without resort to formula. Such rate determined under section 167(b)(2) shall not exceed twice the appropriate straight line rate computed without adjustment for salvage. While salvage is not taken into account in determining the annual allowances under this method, in no event shall an asset (or an account) be depreciated below a reasonable salvage value. However, see section 167(f) and §1.167(f)-1 for rules which permit a reduction in the amount of salvage value to be taken into account for certain personal property acquired after October 16, 1962. Also, see section 167(c) and §1.167(c)-1 for restrictions on the use of the declining balance method.

(b) *Illustrations.*—The declining balance method is illustrated by the following examples:

Example (1). A new asset having an estimated useful life of 20 years was purchased on January 1, 1954, for $1,000. The normal straight line rate (without adjustment for salvage) is 5 percent, and the declining balance rate at twice the normal straight line rate is 10 percent. The annual depreciation allowances for 1954, 1955, and 1956 are as follows:

Year	Basis	Declining balance rate (percent)	Depreciation allowance
1954	$1,000	10	$100
1955	900	10	90
1956	810	10	81

Example (2). A taxpayer filing his returns on a calendar year basis maintains a group account to which a 5 year life and a 40 percent declining balance rate are applicable. Original investment, additions, retirements, and salvage recoveries are the same as those set forth in example (3) of paragraph (b) of §1.167(b)-1. Although salvage value is not taken into consideration in computing a declining balance rate, it must be recognized and accounted for when assets are retired.

Depreciable Asset Account and Depreciation Computation Using Average Asset and Reserve Balances

Year	Asset balance Jan. 1	Current additions	Current retirements	Asset balance Dec. 31	Average balance	Average reserve before depreciation	Net depreciable balance	Rate (percent)	Allowable depreciation
1954		$12,000	—	$12,000	$6,000	—	$6,000	40	$2,400
1955	$12,000	—	—	12,000	12,000	$2,400	9,600	40	3,840
1956	12,000	—	—	12,000	12,000	6,240	5,760	40	2,304
1957	12,000	—	$2,000	10,000	11,000	7,644	3,356	40	1,342
1958	10,000	—	2,000	8,000	9,000	7,186	1,814	40	726
1959	8,000	10,000	4,000	14,000	11,000	5,212	5,788	40	2,315
1960	14,000	—	2,000	12,000	13,000	4,727	8,273	40	3,309
1961	12,000	—	2,000	10,000	11,000	6,036	4,964	40	1,986

Depreciation Reserve

Year	Reserve Jan. 1	Current retirements	Salvage realized	Reserve Dec. 31, before depreciation	Average reserve before depreciation	Allowable depreciation	Reserve Dec. 31, after depreciation
1954	—	—	—	—	—	$2,400	$2,400
1955	$2,400	—	—	$2,400	$2,400	3,840	6,240
1956	6,240	—	—	6,240	6,240	2,304	8,544
1957	8,544	$2,000	$200	6,744	7,644	1,342	8,086
1958	8,086	2,000	200	6,286	7,186	726	7,012
1959	7,012	4,000	400	3,412	5,212	2,315	5,727
1960	5,727	2,000	—	3,727	4,727	3,309	7,036
1961	7,036	2,000	—	5,036	6,036	1,986	7,022

Where separate depreciation accounts are maintained by year of acquisition and there is an unrecovered balance at the time of the last retirement, such unrecovered balance may be deducted as part of the depreciation allowance for the year of such retirement. Thus, if the taxpayer had kept separate depreciation accounts by year of acquisition and all the retirements shown in the example above were from 1954 acquisitions, depreciation would be computed on the 1954 and 1959 acquisitions as follows:

1954 ACQUISITIONS

Year	Asset balance Jan. 1	Acquisitions	Current retirements	Asset balance Dec. 31	Average balance	Average reserve before depreciation	Net depreciable balance	Rate (percent)	Allowable depreciation
1954	—	$12,000	—	$12,000	$6,000	—	$6,000	40	$2,400
1955	$12,000	—	—	12,000	12,000	$2,400	9,600	40	3,840
1956	12,000	—	—	12,000	12,000	6,240	5,760	40	2,304
1957	12,000	—	$2,000	10,000	11,000	7,644	3,356	40	1,342
1958	10,000	—	2,000	8,000	9,000	7,186	1,814	40	726
1959	8,000	—	4,000	4,000	6,000	5,212	788	40	315
1960	4,000	—	2,000	2,000	3,000	2,727	273	40	109
1961	2,000	—	2,000	—	1,000	836	164	40	164 [1]

[1] Balance allowable as depreciation in the year of retirement of the last survivor of the 1954 acquisitions.

Depreciation Reserve for 1954 Acquisitions

Year	Reserve Jan. 1	Current retirements	Salvage realized	Reserve Dec. 31, before depreciation	Average reserve before depreciation	Allowable depreciation	Reserve Dec. 31, after depreciation
1954	—	—	—	—	—	$2,400	$2,400
1955	$2,400	—	—	$2,400	$2,400	3,840	6,240
1956	6,240	—	—	6,240	6,240	2,304	8,544
1957	8,544	$2,000	$200	6,744	7,644	1,342	8,086
1958	8,086	2,000	200	6,286	7,186	726	7,012
1959	7,012	4,000	400	3,412	5,212	315	3,727
1960	3,727	2,000	—	1,727	2,727	109	1,836
1961	1,836	2,000	—	(164)	836	164	—

1959 ACQUISITIONS

Year	Asset balance Jan.1	Acquisitions	Current retirements	Asset balance Dec. 31	Average balance	Reserve Dec. 31, before depreciation	Net depreciable balance	Rate (percent)	Allowable depreciation	Reserve Dec. 31, after depreciation
1959	—	$10,000	—	$10,000	$5,000	None	$5,000	40	$2,000	$2,000
1960	$10,000	—	—	10,000	10,000	$2,000	8,000	40	3,200	5,200
1961	10,000	—	—	10,000	10,000	5,200	4,800	40	1,920	7,120

In the above example, the allowable depreciation on the 1954 acquisitions totals $11,200. This amount when increased by salvage realized in the amount of $800, equals the entire cost or other basis of the 1954 acquisitions ($12,000).

(c) *Change in estimated useful life.*—In the declining balance method when a change is justified in the useful life estimated for an account, subsequent computations shall be made as though the revised useful life had been originally estimated. For example, assume that an account has an estimated useful life of ten years and that a declining balance rate of 20 percent is applicable. If, at the end of the sixth year, it is determined that the remaining useful life of the account is six years, computations shall be made as though the estimated useful life was originally determined as twelve years. Accordingly, the applicable depreciation rate will be 162/3 percent. This rate is thereafter applied to the unrecovered cost or other basis. [Reg. § 1.167(b)-2.]

☐ [*T.D. 6182, 6-11-56. Amended by T.D. 6712, 3-23-64.*]

[Reg. § 1.167(b)-3]

§ 1.167(b)-3. Sum of the years-digits method.—(a) *Applied to a single asset.*—(1) *General rule.*—Under the sum of the years-digits method annual allowances for depreciation are computed by applying changing fractions to the cost or other basis of the property reduced by estimated salvage. The numerator of the fraction changes each year to a number which corresponds to the remaining useful life of the asset (including the year for which the allowance is being computed), and the denominator which remains constant is the sum of all the years digits corresponding to the estimated useful life of the asset. See section 167(c) and § 1.167(c)-1 for restrictions on the use of the sum of the years-digits method.

(i) *Illustrations.*—Computation of depreciation allowances on a single asset under the sum of the years-digits method is illustrated by the following examples:

Example (1). A new asset having an estimated useful life of five years was acquired on January 1, 1954, for $1,750. The estimated salvage is $250. For a taxpayer filing his returns on a calendar year basis, the annual depreciation allowances are as follows:

Year	Cost or other basis less salvage	Fraction[1]	Allowable depreciation	Depreciation reserve
1954	$1,500	5/15	$500	$500
1955	1,500	4/15	400	900
1956	1,500	3/15	300	1,200
1957	1,500	2/15	200	1,400
1958	1,500	1/15	100	1,500
Uncovered value (salvage)				250

[1] The denominator of the fraction is the sum of the digits representing the years of useful life, i.e., 5, 4, 3, 2, and 1, or 15.

Example (2). Assume in connection with an asset acquired in 1954 that 3/4 of a year's depreciation is allowable in that year. The following illustrates a reasonable method of allocating depreciation:

	Depreciation for 12 months		1954		1955		1956
1st year	$500	(3/4)	$375	(1/4)	$125		
2nd year	400			(3/4)	300	(1/4)	$100
3rd year	300					(3/4)	225
			375		425		325

(ii) *Change in useful life.*—Where in the case of a single asset, a change is justified in the useful life, subsequent computations shall be made as though the remaining useful life at the beginning of the taxable year of change were the useful life of a new asset acquired at such time and with a basis equal to the unrecovered cost or other basis of the asset at that time. For example, assume that a new asset with an estimated useful life of ten years is purchased in 1954. At the time of making out his return for 1959, the taxpayer finds that the asset has a remaining useful life of seven years from January 1, 1959. Depreciation for 1959 should then be computed as though 1959 were the first year of the life on an asset estimated to have a useful life of seven years, and the allowance for 1959 would be 7/28 of the unrecovered cost or other basis of the asset after adjustment for salvage.

(2) *Remaining life.*—(i) *Application.*—Under the sum of the years-digits method, annual allowances for depreciation may also be computed by applying changing fractions to the unrecovered cost or other basis of the asset reduced by estimated salvage. The numerator of the fraction changes each year to a number which corresponds to the remaining useful life of the asset (including the year for which the allowance is being computed), and the denominator changes each year to a number which represents the sum of the digits corresponding to the years of estimated remaining useful life of the asset. For decimal equivalents of such fractions, see Table I of subdivision (ii) of this subparagraph. For example, a new asset with an estimated useful life of 10 years is purchased January 1, 1954, for $6,000. Assuming a salvage value of $500, the depreciation allowance for 1954 is $1,000 ($5,500 × 0.1818, the applicable rate from Table I). For 1955, the unrecovered balance is $4,500, and the remaining life is 9 years. The depreciation allowance for 1955 would then be $900 ($4,500 × .2000, the applicable rate from Table I).

(ii) *Table I.*—This table shows decimal equivalents of sum of the years digits fractions corresponding to remaining lives from 1 to 100 years.

TABLE I—DECIMAL EQUIVALENTS FOR USE OF SUM OF THE YEARS-DIGITS METHOD, BASED ON REMAINING LIFE

Remaining life (years)	Decimal equivalent	Remaining life (years)	Decimal equivalent	Remaining life (years)	Decimal equivalent
100.0	.0198	98.1	.0202	96.2	.0206
99.9	.0198	98.0	.0202	96.1	.0206
99.8	.0198	97.9	.0202	96.0	.0206
99.7	.0199	97.8	.0202	95.9	.0206
99.6	.0199	97.7	.0203	95.8	.0207
99.5	.0199	97.6	.0203	95.7	.0207
99.4	.0199	97.5	.0203	95.6	.0207
99.3	.0199	97.4	.0203	95.5	.0207
99.2	.0200	97.3	.0203	95.4	.0207
99.1	.0200	97.2	.0204	95.3	.0208
99.0	.0200	97.1	.0204	95.2	.0208
98.9	.0200	97.0	.0204	95.1	.0208
98.8	.0200	96.9	.0204	95.0	.0208
98.7	.0201	96.8	.0204	94.9	.0209
98.6	.0201	96.7	.0205	94.8	.0209
98.5	.0201	96.6	.0205	94.7	.0209
98.4	.0201	96.5	.0205	94.6	.0209
98.3	.0201	96.4	.0205	94.5	.0209
98.2	.0202	96.3	.0206	94.4	.0210

Remaining life (years)	Decimal equivalent	Remaining life (years)	Decimal equivalent	Remaining life (years)	Decimal equivalent
94.3	.0210	85.9	.0230	77.5	.0255
94.2	.0210	85.8	.0230	77.4	.0255
94.1	.0210	85.7	.0231	77.3	.0255
94.0	.0211	85.6	.0231	77.2	.0256
93.9	.0211	85.5	.0231	77.1	.0256
93.8	.0211	85.4	.0231	77.0	.0256
93.7	.0211	85.3	.0232	76.9	.0257
93.6	.0211	85.2	.0232	76.8	.0257
93.5	.0212	85.1	.0232	76.7	.0257
93.4	.0212	85.0	.0233	76.6	.0258
93.3	.0212	84.9	.0233	76.5	.0258
93.2	.0212	84.8	.0233	76.4	.0258
93.1	.0213	84.7	.0233	76.3	.0259
93.0	.0213	84.6	.0234	76.2	.0259
92.9	.0213	84.5	.0234	76.1	.0259
92.8	.0213	84.4	.0234	76.0	.0260
92.7	.0213	84.3	.0234	75.9	.0260
92.6	.0214	84.2	.0235	75.8	.0260
92.5	.0214	84.1	.0235	75.7	.0261
92.4	.0214	84.0	.0235	75.6	.0261
92.3	.0214	83.9	.0236	75.5	.0261
92.2	.0215	83.8	.0236	75.4	.0262
92.1	.0215	83.7	.0236	75.3	.0262
92.0	.0215	83.6	.0236	75.2	.0262
91.9	.0215	83.5	.0237	75.1	.0263
91.8	.0216	83.4	.0237	75.0	.0263
91.7	.0216	83.3	.0237	74.9	.0264
91.6	.0216	83.2	.0238	74.8	.0264
91.5	.0216	83.1	.0238	74.7	.0264
91.4	.0216	83.0	.0238	74.6	.0265
91.3	.0217	82.9	.0238	74.5	.0265
91.2	.0217	82.8	.0239	74.4	.0265
91.1	.0217	82.7	.0239	74.3	.0266
91.0	.0217	82.6	.0239	74.2	.0266
90.9	.0218	82.5	.0240	74.1	.0266
90.8	.0218	82.4	.0240	74.0	.0267
90.7	.0218	82.3	.0240	73.9	.0267
90.6	.0218	82.2	.0240	73.8	.0267
90.5	.0219	82.1	.0241	73.7	.0268
90.4	.0219	82.0	.0241	73.6	.0268
90.3	.0219	81.9	.0241	73.5	.0268
90.2	.0219	81.8	.0242	73.4	.0269
90.1	.0220	81.7	.0242	73.3	.0269
90.0	.0220	81.6	.0242	73.2	.0270
89.9	.0220	81.5	.0242	73.1	.0270
89.8	.0220	81.4	.0243	73.0	.0270
89.7	.0221	81.3	.0243	72.9	.0271
89.6	.0221	81.2	.0243	72.8	.0271
89.5	.0221	81.1	.0244	72.7	.0271
89.4	.0221	81.0	.0244	72.6	.0272
89.3	.0221	80.9	.0244	72.5	.0272
89.2	.0222	80.8	.0244	72.4	.0272
89.1	.0222	80.7	.0245	72.3	.0273
89.0	.0222	80.6	.0245	72.2	.0273
88.9	.0222	80.5	.0245	72.1	.0274
88.8	.0223	80.4	.0246	72.0	.0274
88.7	.0223	80.3	.0246	71.9	.0274
88.6	.0223	80.2	.0246	71.8	.0275
88.5	.0223	80.1	.0247	71.7	.0275
88.4	.0224	80.0	.0247	71.6	.0275
88.3	.0224	79.9	.0247	71.5	.0276
88.2	.0224	79.8	.0248	71.4	.0276
88.1	.0224	79.7	.0248	71.3	.0277
88.0	.0225	79.6	.0248	71.2	.0277
87.9	.0225	79.5	.0248	71.1	.0277
87.8	.0225	79.4	.0249	71.0	.0278
87.7	.0225	79.3	.0249	70.9	.0278
87.6	.0226	79.2	.0249	70.8	.0279
87.5	.0226	79.1	.0250	70.7	.0279
87.4	.0226	79.0	.0250	70.6	.0279
87.3	.0226	78.9	.0250	70.5	.0280
87.2	.0227	78.8	.0251	70.4	.0280
87.1	.0227	78.7	.0251	70.3	.0280
87.0	.0227	78.6	.0251	70.2	.0281
86.9	.0228	78.5	.0252	70.1	.0281
86.8	.0228	78.4	.0252	70.0	.0282
86.7	.0228	78.3	.0252	69.9	.0282
86.6	.0228	78.2	.0253	69.8	.0282
86.5	.0229	78.1	.0253	69.7	.0283
86.4	.0229	78.0	.0253	69.6	.0283
86.3	.0229	77.9	.0253	69.5	.0284
86.2	.0229	77.8	.0254	69.4	.0284
86.1	.0230	77.7	.0254	69.3	.0284
86.0	.0230	77.6	.0254	69.2	.0285

Reg. §1.167(b)-3(a)(2)(ii)

Remaining life (years)	Decimal equivalent	Remaining life (years)	Decimal equivalent	Remaining life (years)	Decimal equivalent
69.1	.0285	60.7	.0324	52.1	.0377
69.0	.0286	60.6	.0325	52.0	.0377
68.9	.0286	60.5	.0325	51.9	.0378
68.8	.0287	60.4	.0326	51.8	.0379
68.7	.0287	60.3	.0326	51.7	.0379
68.6	.0287	60.2	.0327	51.6	.0380
68.5	.0288	60.1	.0327	51.5	.0381
68.4	.0288	60.0	.0328	51.4	.0382
68.3	.0289	59.9	.0328	51.3	.0382
68.2	.0289	59.8	.0329	51.2	.0383
68.1	.0289	59.7	.0329	51.1	.0384
68.0	.0290	59.6	.0330	51.0	.0385
67.9	.0290	59.5	.0331	50.9	.0385
67.8	.0291	59.4	.0331	50.8	.0386
67.7	.0291	59.3	.0332	50.7	.0387
67.6	.0292	59.2	.0332	50.6	.0388
67.5	.0292	59.1	.0333	50.5	.0388
67.4	.0292	58.8	.0334	50.4	.0389
67.3	.0293	58.7	.0335	50.3	.0390
67.2	.0293	58.6	.0336	50.2	.0391
67.1	.0294	58.5	.0336	50.1	.0391
67.0	.0294	58.4	.0337	50.0	.0392
66.9	.0295	58.3	.0337	49.9	.0393
66.8	.0295	58.2	.0338	49.8	.0394
66.7	.0295	58.1	.0338	49.7	.0394
66.6	.0296	58.0	.0339	49.6	.0395
66.5	.0296	57.9	.0340	49.5	.0396
66.4	.0297	57.8	.0340	49.4	.0397
66.3	.0297	57.7	.0341	49.3	.0398
66.2	.0298	57.6	.0341	49.2	.0398
66.1	.0298	57.5	.0342	49.1	.0399
66.0	.0299	57.4	.0342	49.0	.0400
65.9	.0299	57.3	.0343	48.9	.0401
65.8	.0299	57.2	.0344	48.8	.0402
65.7	.0300	57.1	.0344	48.7	.0402
65.6	.0300	57.0	.0345	48.6	.0403
65.5	.0301	56.9	.0345	48.5	.0404
65.4	.0301	56.8	.0346	48.4	.0405
65.3	.0302	56.7	.0347	48.3	.0406
65.2	.0302	56.6	.0347	48.2	.0406
65.1	.0303	56.5	.0348	48.1	.0407
65.0	.0303	56.4	.0348	48.0	.0408
64.9	.0303	56.3	.0349	47.9	.0409
64.8	.0304	56.2	.0350	47.8	.0410
64.7	.0304	56.1	.0350	47.7	.0411
64.6	.0305	56.0	.0351	47.6	.0411
64.5	.0305	55.9	.0351	47.5	.0412
64.4	.0306	55.8	.0352	47.4	.0413
64.3	.0306	55.7	.0353	47.3	.0414
64.2	.0307	55.6	.0353	47.2	.0415
64.1	.0307	55.5	.0354	47.1	.0416
64.0	.0308	55.4	.0355	47.0	.0417
63.9	.0308	55.3	.0355	46.9	.0418
63.8	.0309	55.2	.0356	46.8	.0418
63.7	.0309	55.1	.0356	46.7	.0419
63.6	.0310	55.0	.0357	46.6	.0420
63.5	.0310	54.9	.0358	46.5	.0421
63.4	.0311	54.8	.0358	46.4	.0422
63.3	.0311	54.7	.0359	46.3	.0423
63.2	.0312	54.6	.0360	46.2	.0424
63.1	.0312	54.5	.0360	46.1	.0425
63.0	.0313	54.4	.0361	46.0	.0426
62.9	.0313	54.3	.0362	45.9	.0426
62.8	.0313	54.2	.0362	45.8	.0427
62.7	.0314	54.1	.0363	45.7	.0428
62.6	.0314	54.0	.0364	45.6	.0429
62.5	.0315	53.9	.0364	45.5	.0430
62.4	.0315	53.8	.0365	45.4	.0431
62.3	.0316	53.7	.0366	45.3	.0432
62.2	.0316	53.6	.0366	45.2	.0433
62.1	.0317	53.5	.0367	45.1	.0434
62.0	.0317	53.4	.0368	45.0	.0435
61.9	.0318	53.3	.0368	44.9	.0436
61.8	.0318	53.2	.0369	44.8	.0437
61.7	.0319	53.1	.0370	44.7	.0438
61.6	.0319	53.0	.0370	44.6	.0439
61.5	.0320	52.9	.0371	44.5	.0440
61.4	.0320	52.8	.0372	44.4	.0440
61.3	.0321	52.7	.0372	44.3	.0441
61.2	.0322	52.6	.0373	44.2	.0442
61.1	.0322	52.5	.0374	44.1	.0443
61.0	.0323	52.4	.0374	44.0	.0444
60.9	.0323	52.3	.0375	43.9	.0445
60.8	.0324	52.2	.0376	43.8	.0446

Reg. §1.167(b)-3(a)(2)(ii)

Remaining life (years)	Decimal equivalent	Remaining life (years)	Decimal equivalent	Remaining life (years)	Decimal equivalent
43.7	.0447	35.3	.0551	26.9	.0717
43.6	.0448	35.2	.0552	26.8	.0719
43.5	.0449	35.1	.0554	26.7	.0722
43.4	.0450	35.0	.0556	26.6	.0724
43.3	.0451	34.9	.0557	26.5	.0727
43.2	.0452	34.8	.0559	26.4	.0730
43.1	.0453	34.7	.0560	26.3	.0732
43.0	.0455	34.6	.0562	26.2	.0735
42.9	.0456	34.5	.0563	26.1	.0738
42.8	.0457	34.4	.0565	26.0	.0741
42.7	.0458	34.3	.0566	25.9	.0743
42.6	.0459	34.2	.0568	25.8	.0746
42.5	.0460	34.1	.0570	25.7	.0749
42.4	.0461	34.0	.0571	25.6	.0752
42.3	.0462	33.9	.0573	25.5	.0754
42.2	.0463	33.8	.0575	25.4	.0757
42.1	.0464	33.7	.0576	25.3	.0760
42.0	.0465	33.6	.0578	25.2	.0763
41.9	.0466	33.5	.0580	25.1	.0766
41.8	.0467	33.4	.0581	25.0	.0769
41.7	.0468	33.3	.0583	24.9	.0772
41.6	.0469	33.2	.0585	24.8	.0775
41.5	.0471	33.1	.0586	24.7	.0778
41.4	.0472	33.0	.0588	24.6	.0781
41.3	.0473	32.9	.0590	24.5	.0784
41.2	.0474	32.8	.0592	24.4	.0787
41.1	.0475	32.7	.0593	24.3	.0790
41.0	.0476	32.6	.0595	24.2	.0793
40.9	.0477	32.5	.0597	24.1	.0797
40.8	.0478	32.4	.0599	24.0	.0800
40.7	.0480	32.3	.0600	23.9	.0803
40.6	.0481	32.2	.0602	23.8	.0806
40.5	.0482	32.1	.0604	23.7	.0809
40.4	.0483	32.0	.0606	23.6	.0813
40.3	.0484	31.9	.0608	23.5	.0816
40.2	.0485	31.8	.0610	23.4	.0819
40.1	.0487	31.7	.0611	23.3	.0823
40.0	.0488	31.6	.0613	23.2	.0826
39.9	.0489	31.5	.0615	23.1	.0830
39.8	.0490	31.4	.0617	23.0	.0833
39.7	.0491	31.3	.0619	22.9	.0837
39.6	.0493	31.2	.0621	22.8	.0840
39.5	.0494	31.1	.0623	22.7	.0844
39.4	.0495	31.0	.0625	22.6	.0847
39.3	.0496	30.9	.0627	22.5	.0851
39.2	.0497	30.8	.0629	22.4	.0854
39.1	.0499	30.7	.0631	22.3	.0858
39.0	.0500	30.6	.0633	22.2	.0862
38.9	.0501	30.5	.0635	22.1	.0866
38.8	.0502	30.4	.0637	22.0	.0870
38.7	.0504	30.3	.0639	21.9	.0873
38.6	.0505	30.2	.0641	21.8	.0877
38.5	.0506	30.1	.0643	21.7	.0881
38.4	.0508	30.0	.0645	21.6	.0885
38.3	.0509	29.9	.0647	21.5	.0888
38.2	.0510	29.8	.0649	21.4	.0892
38.1	.0511	29.7	.0651	21.3	.0896
58.0	.0513	29.6	.0653	21.2	.0901
37.9	.0514	29.5	.0656	21.1	.0905
37.8	.0515	29.4	.0658	21.0	.0909
37.7	.0517	29.3	.0660	20.9	.0913
37.6	.0518	29.2	.0662	20.8	.0917
37.5	.0519	29.1	.0664	20.7	.0921
37.4	.0521	29.0	.0667	20.6	.0925
37.3	.0522	28.9	.0669	20.5	.0930
37.2	.0524	28.8	.0671	20.4	.0934
37.1	.0525	28.7	.0673	20.3	.0939
37.0	.0526	28.6	.0675	20.2	.0943
36.9	.0528	28.5	.0678	20.1	.0948
36.8	.0529	28.4	.0680	20.0	.0952
36.7	.0530	28.3	.0682	19.9	.0957
36.6	.0532	28.2	.0685	19.8	.0961
36.5	.0533	28.1	.0687	19.7	.0966
36.4	.0535	28.0	.0690	19.6	.0970
36.3	.0536	27.9	.0692	19.5	.0975
36.2	.0538	27.8	.0694	19.4	.0980
36.1	.0539	27.7	.0697	19.3	.0985
36.0	.0541	27.6	.0699	19.2	.0990
35.9	.0542	27.5	.0702	19.1	.0995
35.8	.0543	27.4	.0704	19.0	.1000
35.7	.0545	27.3	.0707	18.9	.1005
35.6	.0546	27.2	.0709	18.8	.1010
35.5	.0548	27.1	.0712	18.7	.1015
35.4	.0549	27.0	.0714	18.6	.1020

Reg. §1.167(b)-3(a)(2)(ii)

Itemized Deductions for Individuals and Corps.
See p. 20,601 for regulations not amended to reflect law changes

25,435

Remaining life (years)	Decimal equivalent	Remaining life (years)	Decimal equivalent	Remaining life (years)	Decimal equivalent
18.5	.1025	12.6	.1469	6.7	.2587
18.4	.1030	12.5	.1479	6.6	.2619
18.3	.1036	12.4	.1490	6.5	.2653
18.2	.1041	12.3	.1502	6.4	.2689
18.1	.1047	12.2	.1514	6.3	.2727
18.0	.1053	12.1	.1526	6.2	.2768
17.9	.1058	12.0	.1538	6.1	.2811
17.8	.1063	11.9	.1549	6.0	.2857
17.7	.1069	11.8	.1561	5.9	.2892
17.6	.1074	11.7	.1573	5.8	.2929
17.5	.1080	11.6	.1585	5.7	.2969
17.4	.1086	11.5	.1597	5.6	.3011
17.3	.1092	11.4	.1610	5.5	.3056
17.2	.1098	11.3	.1624	5.4	.3103
17.1	.1105	11.2	.1637	5.3	.3155
17.0	.1111	11.1	.1652	5.2	.3210
16.9	.1117	11.0	.1667	5.1	.3269
16.8	.1123	10.9	.1680	5.0	.3333
16.7	.1129	10.8	.1693	4.9	.3379
16.6	.1135	10.7	.1707	4.8	.3429
16.5	.1142	10.6	.1721	4.7	.3481
16.4	.1148	10.5	.1736	4.6	.3538
16.3	.1155	10.4	.1751	4.5	.3600
16.2	.1162	10.3	.1767	4.4	.3667
16.1	.1169	10.2	.1783	4.3	.3739
16.0	.1176	10.1	.1800	4.2	.3818
15.9	.1183	10.0	.1818	4.1	.3905
15.8	.1190	9.9	.1833	4.0	.4000
15.7	.1197	9.8	.1849	3.9	.4063
15.6	.1204	9.7	.1865	3.8	.4130
15.5	.1211	9.6	.1882	3.7	.4205
15.4	.1218	9.5	.1900	3.6	.4286
15.3	.1226	9.4	.1918	3.5	.4375
15.2	.1234	9.3	.1938	3.4	.4474
15.1	.1242	9.2	.1957	3.3	.4583
15.0	.1250	9.1	.1978	3.2	.4706
14.9	.1257	9.0	.2000	3.1	.4844
14.8	.1265	8.9	.2018	3.0	.5000
14.7	.1273	8.8	.2037	2.9	.5088
14.6	.1281	8.7	.2057	2.8	.5185
14.5	.1289	8.6	.2077	2.7	.5294
14.4	.1297	8.5	.2099	2.6	.5417
14.3	.1306	8.4	.2121	2.5	.5556
14.2	.1315	8.3	.2145	2.4	.5714
14.1	.1324	8.2	.2169	2.3	.5897
14.0	.1333	8.1	.2195	2.2	.6111
13.9	.1342	8.0	.2222	2.1	.6364
13.8	.1350	7.9	.2244	2.0	.6667
13.7	.1359	7.8	.2267	1.9	.6786
13.6	.1368	7.7	.2292	1.8	.6923
13.5	.1378	7.6	.2317	1.7	.7083
13.4	.1387	7.5	.2344	1.6	.7273
13.3	.1397	7.4	.2372	1.5	.7500
13.2	.1407	7.3	.2401	1.4	.7778
13.1	.1418	7.2	.2432	1.3	.8125
13.0	.1429	7.1	.2465	1.2	.8571
12.9	.1438	7.0	.2500	1.1	.9167
12.8	.1448	6.9	.2527	1.0	1.0000
12.7	.1458	6.8	.2556		

Note: For determination of decimal equivalents of remaining lives falling between those shown in the above table, the taxpayer may use the next longest life shown in the table, interpolate from the table, or use the following formula from which the table was derived.

$$D = \frac{2R}{(W + 2F)(W + 1)}$$

where
D = Decimal equivalent
R = Remaining life
W = Whole number of years in remaining life
F = Fractional part of year in remaining life

If the taxpayer desires to carry his calculations of decimal equivalents to a greater number of decimal places than is provided in the table, he may use the formula. The procedure adopted must be consistently followed thereafter.

(b) *Applied to group, classified, or composite accounts.*—(1) *General rule.*—The sum of the years-digits method may be applied to group, classified, or composite accounts in accordance with the plan described in subparagraph (2) of this paragraph or in accordance with other plans as explained in subparagraph (3) of this paragraph.

(2) *Remaining life plan.*—The remaining life plan as applied to a single asset is described in paragraph (a)(2) of this section. This plan may also be applied to group, classified, or composite accounts. Under this plan the allowance for depreciation is computed by applying changing fractions to the unrecovered cost or other basis of the account reduced by estimated salvage. The numerator of the fraction changes each year to a number which corresponds to the remaining useful life of the account (including the year for which the allowance is being computed), and the denominator changes each year to a number which represents the sum of the years digits

corresponding to the years of estimated remaining useful life of the account. Decimal equivalents of such fractions can be obtained by use of Table I under paragraph (a)(2)(ii) of this section. The proper application of this method requires that the estimated remaining useful life of the account be determined each year. This determination, of course, may be made each year by analysis, i.e., by determining the remaining lives for each of the components in the account, and averaging them. The estimated remaining life of any account, however, may also be determined arithmetically. For example, it may

$$\frac{\$12,600 - \$9,450}{\$12,600} \text{ times 10 years equals 2.50 years.}$$

Example. The use of the sum of the years-digits method with group, classified, or composite accounts under the remaining life plan is illustrated by the following example: A calendar year taxpayer maintains a group account to which a five-year life is applica-

be computed by dividing the unrecovered cost or other basis of the account, as computed by straight line depreciation, by the gross cost or other basis of the account, and multiplying the result by the average life of the assets in the account. Salvage value is not a factor for the purpose of determining remaining life. Thus, if a group account with an average life of ten years had at January 1, 1958, a gross asset balance of $12,600 and a depreciation reserve computed on the straight line method of $9,450, the remaining life of the account at January 1, 1958, would be computed as follows:

ble. Original investment, additions, retirements, and salvage recoveries are the same as those set forth in example (3) of paragraph (b) of §1.167(b)-1.

DEPRECIATION COMPUTATIONS ON A GROUP ACCOUNT UNDER REMAINING LIFE PLAN

Year	1 Asset balance Jan. 1	2 Current additions	3 Current retirements	4 Average asset balance	5 Straight line amount Col. (4) ÷ life	6 Straight line reserve Col. (5) − Col. (3) accumulated Jan. 1	7 Remaining life [Col. (6) ÷ Col. (1)] [Col. (1) ÷ average service life]	8 Asset balance reduced by salvage Col. (1) × (100% − 6.67%)	9 Current additions reduced by salvage Col. (2) × (100% − 6.67%)	10 Salvage realized	11 Accumulated reserve Jan. 1 Prior reserve + Col. (14) + Col. (10) − Col. (3)	12 Unrecovered Jan. 1 Col. (8) − Col. (11)	13 Rate based on Col. (7) from Table 1	14 Allowable depreciation Col. (12) × Col. (13) + ½ × Col. (9) × F²
1954	...	$12,000	...	$6,000	$1,200 [1]	...	5.00	−	$11,200	...	...	...	.3333	$1,866
1955	$12,000	...	...	12,000	2,400	$1,200	4.50	$11,200	...	...	$1,866	$9,334	.360	3,360
1956	12,000	...	...	12,000	2,400	3,600	3.50	11,200	...	...	5,226	5,974	.4375	2,614
1957	12,000	...	$2,000	11,000	2,200	6,000	2.50	11,200	...	$200	7,840	3,360	.5556	1,867
1958	10,000	...	2,000	9,000	1,800	6,200	1.90	9,333	...	200	7,907	1,426	.6786	968
1959	8,000	10,000	4,000	11,000	2,200	6,000	1.25	7,466	9,333	400	7,075	391	.8125	1,874
1960	14,000	...	2,000	13,000	2,600	4,200	3.50	13,066	...	...	5,349	7,717	.4375	3,376
1961	12,000	...	2,000	11,000	2,200	4,800	3.00	11,200	...	...	6,725	4,475	.5000	2,238
1962	...	...	...	...	...	5,000	...	...	...	...	6,963	...	...	...

[1] ½ year's amount.
[2] F = Rate based on average service life (.3333 in this example).

(3) *Other plans for application of the sum of the years-digits method.*—Taxpayers who wish to use the sum of the years-digits method in computing depreciation for group, classified, or composite accounts in accordance with a sum of the years digits plan other than the remaining life plan described herein may do so only with the consent of the Commissioner. Request for permission to use plans other than that described shall be addressed to the Commissioner of Internal Revenue, Washington 25, D.C. [Reg. § 1.167(b)-3.]

☐ *[T.D. 6182, 6-11-56.]*

[Reg. § 1.167(b)-4]

§ 1.167(b)-4. Other methods.—(a) Under section 167(b)(4) a taxpayer may use any consistent method of computing depreciation, such as the sinking fund method, provided depreciation allowances computed in accordance with such method do not result in accumulated allowances at the end of any taxable year greater than the total of the accumulated allowances which could have resulted from the use of the declining balance method described in section 167(b)(2). This limitation applies only during the first two-thirds of the useful life of the property. For example, an asset costing $1,000 having a useful life of six years may be depreciated under the declining balance method in accordance with § 1.167(b)-2, at a rate of 33⅓ percent. During the first four years or ⅔ of its useful life, maximum depreciation allowances under the declining balance method would be as follows:

	Current depreciation	Accumulated depreciation	Balance
Cost of asset		$1,000	
First year	$333	$ 333	$667
Second year	222	555	445
Third year	148	703	297
Fourth year	99	802	198

An annual allowance computed by any other method under section 167(b)(4) could not exceed $333 for the first year, and at the end of the second year the total allowances for the two years could not exceed $555. Likewise, the total allowances for the three years could not exceed $703 and for the four years could not exceed $802. This limitation would not apply in the fifth and sixth years. See section 167(c) and § 1.167(c)-1 for restrictions on the use of certain methods.

(b) It shall be the responsibility of the taxpayer to establish to the satisfaction of the Commissioner that a method of depreciation under section 167(b)(4) is both a reasonable and consistent method and that it does not produce depreciation allowances in excess of the amount permitted under the limitations provided in such section. [Reg. § 1.167(b)-4.]

☐ *[T.D. 6182, 6-11-56.]*

[Reg. § 1.167(c)-1]

§ 1.167(c)-1. Limitations on methods of computing depreciation under section 167(b)(2), (3), and (4).—(a) *In general.*—(1) Section 167(c) provides limitations on the use of the declining balance method described in section 167(b)(2), the sum of the years-digits method described in section 167(b)(3), and certain other methods authorized by section 167(b)(4). These methods are applicable only to tangible property having a useful life of three years or more. If construction, reconstruction, or erection by the taxpayer began before January 1, 1954, and was completed after December 31, 1953, these methods apply only to that portion of the basis of the property which is properly attributable to such construction, reconstruction, or erection after December 31, 1953. Property is considered as constructed, reconstructed, or erected by the taxpayer if the work is done for him in accordance with his specifications. The portion of the basis of such property attributable to construction, reconstruction, or erection after December 31, 1953, consists of all costs of the property allocable to the period after December 31, 1953, including the cost or other basis of materials entering into such work. It is not necessary that such materials be acquired after December 31, 1953, or that they be new in use. If construction or erection by the taxpayer began after December 31, 1953, the entire cost or other basis of such construction or erection qualifies for these methods of depreciation. In the case of reconstruction of property, these methods do not apply to any part of the adjusted basis of such property on December 31, 1953. For purposes of this section, construction, reconstruction, or erection by the taxpayer begins when physical work is started on such construction, reconstruction, or erection.

(2) If the property was not constructed, reconstructed, or erected by the taxpayer, these methods apply only if it was acquired after December 31, 1953, and if the original use of the property commences with the taxpayer and commences after December 31, 1953. For the purpose of the preceding sentence, property shall be deemed to be acquired when reduced to physical possession, or control. The term "original use" means the first use to which the property is put, whether or not such use corresponds to the use of such property by the taxpayer. For example, a reconditioned or rebuilt machine acquired after December 31, 1953, will not be treated as being put to original use by the taxpayer even though it is put to a different use, nor will a horse acquired for breeding purposes be treated as being put to original use by the taxpayer if prior to the purchase the horse was used for racing purposes. See § § 1.167(b)-2, 1.167(b)-3, and 1.167(b)-4 for application of the various methods.

(3) Assets having an estimated average useful life of less than three years shall not be included in a group, classified, or composite account to which the methods described in § § 1.167(b)-2, 1.167(b)-3, and 1.167(b)-4 are applicable. However, an incidental retirement of an asset from such an account prior to the expiration of a useful life of three years will not prevent the application of these methods to such an account.

(4) See section 381(c)(6) and the regulations thereunder for rules covering the use of depreciation methods by acquiring corporations in the case of certain corporate acquisitions.

(5) See § § 1.1502-12(g) and 1.1502-13 for provisions dealing with depreciation of property received by a member of an affiliated group from another member of the group during a consolidated return period.

(6) Except in the cases described in subparagraphs (4) and (5) of this paragraph, the methods of depreciation described in § § 1.167(b)-2, 1.167(b)-3, and 1.167(b)-4 are not applicable to property in the hands of a distributee, vendee, transferee, donee, or grantee unless the original use of the property begins with such person and the conditions required by section 167(c) and this section are otherwise met. For example, these methods of depreciation may not be used by a corporation with respect to property which it acquires from an individual or partnership in exchange for its stock. Similarly, if an individual or partnership receives property in a distribution upon dissolution of a corporation, these methods of depreciation may not be used with respect to property so acquired by such individual or partnership. As a further example, these methods of depreciation may not be used by a partnership with respect to contributed property, nor by a partner with respect to partnership property distributed to him. Moreover, where a partnership is entitled to use these depreciation methods, and the optional adjustment to basis of partnership property provided by section 743 is applicable, (i) in the case of an increase in the adjusted basis of the partnership property under such section, the transferee partner with respect to whom such adjustment is applicable shall not be entitled to use such methods with respect to such increase, and (ii) in the case of a decrease in the adjusted basis of the partnership property under such section, the transferee partner with respect to whom such adjustment is applicable shall include in his income an amount equal to the portion of the depreciation deducted by the partnership which is attributable to such decrease.

(b) *Illustrations.*—(1) The application of these methods to property constructed, reconstructed, or erected by the taxpayer after December 31, 1953, may be illustrated by the following examples:

Example (1). If a building with a total cost of $100,000 is completed after December 31, 1953, and the portion attributable to construction after December 31, 1953, is determined by engineering estimates or by cost accounting records to be $30,000, the methods referred to in paragraph (a)(1) of this section, are applicable only to the $30,000 portion of the total.

Example (2). In 1954, a taxpayer has an old machine with an unrecovered cost of $1,000. If he contracts to have it reconditioned, or reconditions it himself, at a cost of an additional $5,000, only the $5,000 may be depreciated under the methods referred to in paragraph (a)(1) of this section, whether or not the materials used for reconditioning are new in use.

Example (3). A taxpayer who acquired a building in 1940 makes major maintenance or repair expenditures in 1954 of a type which must be capitalized. For these expenditures the taxpayer may use a method of depreciation different from that used on the building (for example, the methods referred to in paragraph (a)(1) of this section) only if he accounts for such expenditures separately from the account which contained the original building. In such case, the unadjusted basis on any parts replaced shall be removed from the asset account and shall be charged to the appropriate depreciation reserve account. In the alternative he may capitalize such expenditures by charging them to the depreciation reserve account for the building.

(2) The application of these methods to property which was not constructed, reconstructed, or erected by the taxpayer but which was acquired after December 31, 1953, may be illustrated by the following examples:

Example (1). A taxpayer contracted in 1953 to purchase a new machine which he acquired in 1954 and put into first use in that year. He may use the methods referred to in paragraph (a)(1) of this section, in recovering the cost of the new machine.

Example (2). A taxpayer instead of reconditioning his old machine buys a "factory reconditioned" machine in 1954 to replace it.

He cannot apply the methods referred to in paragraph (a)(1) of this section, to any part of the cost of the reconditioned machine since he is not the first user of the machine.

Example (3). In 1954, a taxpayer buys a house for $20,000 which had been used as a personal residence and thus had not been subject to depreciation allowances. He makes a capital addition of $5,000 and rents the property to another. The taxpayer may use the methods referred to in paragraph (a)(1) of this section, only with respect to the $5,000 cost of the addition.

(c) *Election to use methods.*—Subject to the limitations set forth in paragraph (a) of this section, the methods of computing the allowance for depreciation specified in section 167(b)(2), (3), and (4) may be adopted without permission and no formal election is required. In order for a taxpayer to elect to use these methods for any property described in paragraph (a) of this section, he need only compute depreciation thereon under any of these methods for any taxable year ending after December 31, 1953, in which the property may first be depreciated by him. The election with respect to any property shall not be binding with respect to acquisitions of similar property in the same year or subsequent year which are set up in separate accounts. If a taxpayer has filed his return for a taxable year ending after December 31, 1953, for which the return is required to be filed on or before September 15, 1956, an election to compute the depreciation allowance under any of the methods specified in section 167(b) or a change in such an election may be made in an amended return or claim for refund filed on or before September 15, 1956. [Reg. §1.167(c)-1.]

☐ [*T.D. 6182, 6-11-56. Amended by T.D. 7244, 12-29-72; T.D. 8560, 8-12-94 and T.D. 8597, 7-12-95.*]

[Reg. §1.167(d)-1]

§1.167(d)-1. Agreement as to useful life and rates of depreciation.—After August 16, 1954, a taxpayer may, for taxable years ending after December 31, 1953, enter into an agreement with respect to the estimated useful life, method and rate of depreciation, and treatment of salvage of any property which is subject to the allowance for depreciation. An application for such agreement may be made to the district director for the internal revenue district in which the taxpayer's return is required to be filed. Such application shall be filed in quadruplicate and shall contain in such detail as may be practical the following information:

(a) The character and location of the property.

(b) The original cost or other basis and date of acquisition.

(c) Proper adjustments to the basis including depreciation accumulated to the first taxable year to be covered by the agreement.

(d) Estimated useful life and estimated salvage value.

(e) Method and rate of depreciation.

(f) Any other facts and circumstances pertinent to making a reasonable estimate of the useful life of the property and its salvage value.

The agreement must be in writing and must be signed by the taxpayer and by the district director. The agreement must be signed in quadruplicate, and two of the signed copies will be returned to the taxpayer. The agreement shall set forth its effective date, the estimated remaining useful life, the estimated salvage value, and rate and method of depreciation of the property and the facts and circumstances taken into consideration in adoption of the agreement, and shall relate only to depreciation allowances for such property on and after the effective date of the agreement. Such an agreement shall be binding on both parties until such time as facts and circumstances which were not taken into account in making the agreement are shown to exist. The party wishing to modify or change the agreement shall have the responsibility of establishing the existence of such facts and circumstances. Any change in the useful life or rate specified in such agreement shall be effective only prospectively, that is, it shall be effective beginning with the taxable year in which notice of the intention to change, including facts and circumstances warranting the adjustment of useful life and rate, is sent by the party proposing the change to the other party and is sent by registered mail, if such notice is mailed before September 3, 1958, or is sent by certified mail or registered mail, if such notice is mailed after September 2, 1958. A copy of the agreement (and any modification thereof) shall be filed with the taxpayer's return for the first taxable year which is affected by the agreement (or any modification thereof). A signed copy should be retained with the permanent records of the taxpayer. For rules relating to changes in method of depreciation, see §1.167(e)-1 and section 446 and the regulations thereunder. [Reg. §1.167(d)-1.]

☐ [*T.D. 6182, 6-11-56. Amended by T.D. 6426, 11-30-59.*]

[Reg. §1.167(e)-1]

§1.167(e)-1. Change in method.—(a) *In general.*—(1) Any change in the method of computing the depreciation allowances with respect to a particular account (other than a change in method permitted or required by reason of the operation of former section 167(j)(2) and §1.167(j)-3(c)) is a change in method of accounting, and such a change will be permitted only with the consent of the Commissioner, except that certain changes to the straight line method of depreciation will be permitted without consent as provided in former section 167(e)(1), (2), and (3). Except as provided in paragraphs (c) and (d) of this section, a change in method of computing depreciation will be permitted only with respect to all the assets contained in a particular account as defined in §1.167(a)-7. Any change in the percentage of the current straight line rate under the declining balance method, for example, from 200 percent of the straight line rate to any other percent of the straight line rate, or any change in the interest factor used in connection with a compound interest or sinking fund method, will constitute a change in method of depreciation. Any request for a change in method of depreciation shall be made in accordance with section 446(e) and the regulations under section 446(e). For rules covering the use of depreciation methods by acquiring corporations in the case of certain corporate acquisitions, see section 381(c)(6) and the regulations under section 381(c)(6).

(2) Paragraphs (b), (c), and (d) of this section apply to property for which depreciation is determined under section 167 (other than under section 168, section 14001, section 1400L(c), under section 168 prior to its amendment by the Tax Reform Act of 1986 (100 Stat. 2121), or under an additional first year depreciation deduction provision (for example, section 168(k), 1400L(b), or 1400N(d))) of the Internal Revenue Code.

(b) *Declining balance to straight line.*—In the case of an account to which the method described in section 167(b)(2) is applicable, a taxpayer may change without the consent of the Commissioner from the declining balance method of depreciation to the straight line method at any time during the useful life of the property under the following conditions. Such a change may not be made if a provision prohibiting such a change is contained in an agreement under section 167(d). When the change is made, the unrecovered cost or other basis (less a reasonable estimate for salvage) shall be recovered through annual allowances over the estimated remaining useful life determined in accordance with the circumstances existing at the time. With respect to any account, this change will be permitted only if applied to all the assets in the account as defined in section 1.167(a)-7. If the method of depreciation described in section 167(b)(2) (the declining balance method of depreciation using a rate not exceeding 200 percent of the straight line rate) is an acceptable method of depreciation with respect to a particular account, the taxpayer may elect under this paragraph to change to the straight line method of depreciation, even if with respect to that particular account, the declining balance method is permitted under a provision other than section 167(b)(2). Thus, for example, in the case of section 1250 property to which section 167(j)(1) is applicable, section 167(b) does not apply, but the declining balance method of depreciation using 150 percent of the straight line rate is an acceptable method of depreciation under section 167(j)(1)(B). Accordingly, the taxpayer may elect under this paragraph to change to the straight line method of depreciation with respect to such property. Similarly, if the taxpayer acquired used property before July 25, 1969, and adopted the 150 percent declining balance method of depreciation permitted with respect to such property under §1.167(b)-0(b), the taxpayer may elect under this paragraph to change to the straight line method of depreciation with respect to such property. The taxpayer shall furnish a statement with respect to the property which is the subject of the change showing the date of acquisition, cost or other basis, amounts recovered through depreciation and other allowances, the estimated salvage value, the character of the property, the remaining useful life of the property, and such other information as may be required. The statement shall be attached to the taxpayer's return for the taxable year in which the change is made. A change to the straight line method must be adhered to for the entire taxable year of the change and for all subsequent taxable years unless, with the consent of the Commissioner, a change to another method is permitted.

(c) *Change with respect to section 1245 property.*—(1) In respect of his first taxable year beginning after December 31, 1962, a taxpayer may elect, without the consent of the Commissioner, to change the method of depreciation of section 1245 property (as defined in section 1245(a)(3)) from any declining balance method or sum of the years-digits method to the straight line method. With respect to any account (as defined in §1.167(a)-7), this change may be made notwithstanding any provision to the contrary in an agreement under section 167(d), but such change shall constitute (as of the first day of such taxable year) a termination of such agreement as to all property in such account. With respect to any account, this change will be permitted only if applied to all the section 1245 property in the account. The election shall be made by a statement on, or attached to, the return for such taxable year filed on or before the last day prescribed by law, including any extensions thereof, for filing such return.

(2) When an election under this paragraph is made in respect of section 1245 property in an account, the unrecovered cost or other basis (less a reasonable estimate for salvage) of all the section 1245 property in the account shall be recovered through annual allowances over the estimated remaining useful life determined in accordance with the circumstances existing at that time. If there is other property in such account, the other property shall be placed in a separate account and depreciated by using the same method as was used before the change permitted by this paragraph, but the estimated useful life of such property shall be redetermined in accordance with §1.167(b)-2 or 1.167(b)-3, whichever is applicable. The taxpayer shall maintain records which permit specific identification of the section 1245 property in the account with respect to which the election is made, and any other property in such account. The records shall also show for all the property in the account the date of acquisition, cost or other basis, amounts recovered through depreciation and other allowances, the estimated salvage value, the character of the property, and the remaining useful life of the property. A change to the straight line method under this paragraph must be adhered to for the entire taxable year of the change and for all subsequent taxable years unless, with the consent of the Commissioner, a change to another method is permitted.

(d) *Change with respect to section 1250 property.*—(1) In respect of his first taxable year beginning after July 24, 1969, a taxpayer may elect, without the consent of the Commissioner, to change the method of depreciation of section 1250 property (as defined in section 1250(c)) from any declining balance method or sum of the years-digits method to the straight line method. With respect to any account (as defined in §1.167(a)-7) this change may be made notwithstanding any provision to the contrary in an agreement under section 167(d), but such change will constitute (as of the first day of such taxable year) a termination of such agreement as to all property in such account. With respect to any account, this change will be permitted only if applied to all the section 1250 property in the account. The election shall be made by a statement on, or attached to, the return for such taxable year filed on or before the last day prescribed by law, including extensions thereof, for filing such return.

(2) When an election under this paragraph is made in respect of section 1250 property in an account, the unrecovered cost or other basis (less a reasonable estimate for salvage) of all the section 1250 property in the account shall be recovered through annual allowances over the estimated remaining useful life determined in accordance with the circumstances existing at that time. If there is other property in such account, the other property shall be placed in a separate account and depreciated by using the same method as was used before the change permitted by this paragraph, but the estimated useful life of such property shall be redetermined in accordance with §1.167(b)-2 or §1.167(b)-3, whichever is applicable. The taxpayer shall maintain records which permit specific identification of the section 1250 property in the account with respect to which the election is made and any other property in such account. The records shall also show for all the property in the account the date of acquisition, cost or other basis, amounts recovered through depreciation and other allowances, the estimated salvage value, the character of the property, and the estimated remaining useful life of the property. A change to the straight line method under this paragraph must be adhered to for the entire taxable year of the change and for all subsequent taxable years unless, with the consent of the Commissioner, a change to another method is permitted.

(e) *Effective date.*—This section applies on or after December 30, 2003. For the applicability of regulations before December 30, 2003, see §1.167(e)-1 in effect prior to December 30, 2003 (§1.167(e)-1 as contained in 26 CFR part 1 edition revised as of April 1, 2003). [Reg. §1.167(e)-1.]

☐ [*T.D.* 6182, 6-11-56. *Amended by T.D.* 6832, 7-6-65; *T.D.* 7166, 3-10-72; *T.D.* 9105, 12-30-2003 *and T.D.* 9307, 12-22-2006.]

[Reg. §1.167(f)-1]

§1.167(f)-1. Reduction of salvage value taken into account for certain personal property.—(a) *In general.*—For taxable years beginning after December 31, 1961, and ending after October 16, 1962, a taxpayer may reduce the amount taken into account as salvage value in computing the allowance for depreciation under section 167(a) with respect to "personal property" as defined in section 167(f)(2) and paragraph (b) of this section. The reduction may be made in an amount which does not exceed 10 percent of the basis of the property for determining depreciation, as of the time as of which salvage value is required to be determined (or when salvage value is redetermined), taking into account all adjustments under section 1016 other than (1) the adjustment under section 1016(a)(2) for depreciation allowed or allowable to the taxpayer, and (2) the adjustment under section 1016(a)(19) for a credit earned by the taxpayer under section 38, to the extent such adjustment is reflected in the basis for deprecia-

tion. See paragraph (c) of §1.167(a)-1 for the definition of salvage value, the time for making the determination, the redetermination of salvage value, and the general rules with respect to the treatment of salvage value. See also section 167(g) and §1.167(g)-1 for basis for depreciation. A reduction of the amount taken into account as salvage value with respect to any property shall not be binding with respect to other property. In no event shall an asset (or an account) be depreciated below a reasonable salvage value after taking into account the reduction in salvage value permitted by section 167(f) and this section.

(b) *Definitions and special rules.*—The following definitions and special rules apply for purposes of section 167(f) and this section.

(1) *Personal property.*—The term "personal property" shall include only depreciable—

(i) Tangible personal property (as defined in section 48 and the regulations thereunder) and

(ii) Intangible personal property

which has an estimated useful life (determined at the time of acquisition) of 3 years or more and which is acquired after October 16, 1962. Such term shall not include livestock. The term "livestock" includes horses, cattle, hogs, sheep, goats, and mink and other fur-bearing animals, irrespective of the use to which they are put or the purpose for which they are held. The original use of the property need not commence with the taxpayer so long as he acquired it after October 16, 1962; thus, the property may be new or used. For purposes of determining the estimated useful life, the provisions of paragraph (b) of §1.167(a)-1 shall be applied. For rules determining when property is acquired, see subparagraph (2) of this paragraph. For purposes of determining the types of intangible personal property which are subject to the allowance for depreciation, see §1.167(a)-3.

(2) *Acquired.*—In determining whether property is acquired after October 16, 1962, property shall be deemed to be acquired when reduced to physical possession, or control. Property which has not been used in the taxpayer's trade or business or held for the production of income and which is thereafter converted by the taxpayer to such use shall be deemed to be acquired on the date of such conversion. In addition, property shall be deemed to be acquired if constructed, reconstructed, or erected by the taxpayer. If construction, reconstruction, or erection by the taxpayer began before October 17, 1962, and was completed after October 16, 1962, section 167(f) and this section apply only to that portion of the basis of the property which is properly attributable to such construction, reconstruction, or erection after October 16, 1962. Property is considered as constructed, reconstructed, or erected by the taxpayer if the work is done for him in accordance with his specifications. The portion of the basis of such property attributable to construction, reconstruction, or erection after October 16, 1962, consists of all costs of the property allocable to the period after October 16, 1962, including the cost or other basis of materials entering into such work. It is not necessary that such materials be acquired after October 16, 1962, or that they be new in use. If construction or erection by the taxpayer began after October 16, 1962, the entire cost or other basis of such construction or erection qualifies for the reduction provided for by section 167(f) and this section. In the case of reconstruction of property, section 167(f) and this section do not apply to any part of the adjusted basis of such property on October 16, 1962. For purposes of this section, construction, reconstruction, or erection by the taxpayer begins when physical work is started on such construction, reconstruction, or erection.

(c) *Illustrations.*—The provisions of paragraphs (a) and (b) of this section may be illustrated by the following examples:

Example (1). Taxpayer A purchases a new asset for use in his business on January 1, 1963, for $10,000. The asset qualifies for the investment credit under section 38 and for the additional first-year depreciation allowance under section 179. A is entitled to an investment credit of $700 (7% × $10,000) and elects to take an additional first-year depreciation allowance of $2,000 (20% × $10,000). The basis for depreciation (determined in accordance with the provisions of section 167(g) and §1.167(g)-1) is computed as follows:

Purchase price		$10,000
Less: Adjustment required for taxable years beginning before Jan. 1, 1964, under section 1016(a) (19) for the investment credit	$700	
Adjustment required under section 1016(a)(2) for the additional first-year depreciation allowance	2,000	2,700
Basis for depreciation for the taxable year 1963		$7,300

However, the basis of the property for determining depreciation as of the time as of which salvage value is required to be determined is $10,000, the purchase price of the property. A files his income tax returns on a calendar year basis and uses the straight line method of depreciation. A estimates that he will use the asset in his business for 10 years after which it will have a salvage value of $500, which is less than $1,000 (10% × $10,000, the basis of the property for determining depreciation as of the time as of which salvage value is required to be determined). For the taxable year 1963 A may deduct $730 as the depreciation allowance. As of January 1, 1964, the basis of the asset is increased by $700 in accordance with paragraph (d) of §1.48-7. In computing his total depreciation allowance on the asset, A may reduce the amount taken into account as salvage value to zero and may claim depreciation deductions (including the additional first-year depreciation allowance) totaling $10,000. See paragraph (d) of §1.48-7 for the computation of depreciation for taxable years beginning after December 31, 1963, where there is an increase in basis of property subject to the investment credit.

Example (2). Assume the same facts as in example (1) except that A in a subsequent taxable year redetermines the estimate of the useful life of the asset and at the same time also redetermines the estimate of salvage value. Assume also that at such time the only reductions reflected in the basis are for depreciation allowed or allowable. Accordingly, the reduction under section 167(f) and this section will be computed with regard to the purchase price and not the unrecovered basis for depreciation at the time of the redetermination.

Example (3). Assume the same facts as in example (1) except that A estimates that the asset will have a salvage value of $1,200 at the end of its useful life. In computing his depreciation for the asset, A may reduce the amount to be taken into account as salvage value to $200 ($1,200 – $1,000). Accordingly, A may claim depreciation deductions (including the additional first-year depreciation allowance) totaling $9,800, i.e., the purchase price of the property ($10,000) less the amount taken into account as salvage value ($200).

Example (4). Assume the same facts as in example (1) except that the taxpayer had taken into account salvage value of only $200 but that the estimated salvage value had actually been $700. The amount of salvage value taken into account by the taxpayer is permissible since the reduction of salvage value by $500 ($700 – $200) would be within the limit provided for in section 167(f), i.e., $1,000 (10% × $10,000).

Example (5). On January 1, 1963, taxpayer B, a taxicab operator, traded his old taxicab plus cash for a new one, which had an estimated useful life of three years, in a transaction qualifying as a nontaxable exchange. The old taxicab had an adjusted basis of $2,500. B was allowed $3,000 for his old taxicab and paid $1,000 in cash. The basis of the new taxicab for determining depreciation (as determined under section 167(g) and §1.167(g)-1) is the adjusted basis of the old taxicab at the time of trade-in ($2,500) plus the additional cash paid out ($1,000), or $3,500. In computing his depreciation allowance on the new taxicab, B may reduce the amount taken into account as salvage value by $350 (10% of $3,500).

Example (6). Taxpayer C purchases a new asset for use in his business on January 1, 1963, for $10,000. At the time of purchase, the asset has an estimated useful life of 10 years and an estimated salvage value of $1,500. C elects to compute his depreciation allowance for the asset by the declining balance method of depreciation, using a rate of 20% which is twice the normal straight line rate of 10% (without adjustment for salvage value). C files his income tax returns on a calendar year basis. In computing his depreciation allowance for the year 1966, C changes his method of determining the depreciation allowance for the asset from the declining balance method to the straight line method (in which salvage value is accounted for in determining the annual depreciation allowances) in accordance with the provisions of section 167(e) and paragraph (b) of §1.167(e)-1. He also wishes to reduce the amount of salvage value taken into account in accordance with the provisions of section 167(f) and this section. At the close of the year 1966, the only reductions reflected in the basis of the asset are for depreciation allowances. Thus, C may reduce the amount of salvage value taken into account by $1,000 (10% × $10,000, the basis of the asset when it was acquired), and, therefore, will account for salvage value of only $500 in computing his depreciation allowance for the asset in 1966 and subsequent years.

Example (7). Taxpayer D purchases a station wagon for his personal use on January 1, 1962, for $4,500. On January 1, 1963, D converts the use of the station wagon to his business, and at that time it has an estimated useful life of 4 years, an estimated salvage value of $500, and a basis of $3,000 (as determined under section 167(g) and §1.167(g)-1). Thus, for purposes of section 167(f) and this section, D is deemed to have acquired the station wagon on January 1, 1963. D elects the straight line method of depreciation in computing the depreciation allowance for the station wagon and also wishes to reduce the amount of salvage value taken into account in accordance with the provisions of section 167(f) and this section. Accordingly, D may reduce the amount of salvage value taken into account by $300 (10% of $3,000). D files his income tax returns on a calendar year

basis. His depreciation allowance for the year 1963 would be computed as follows:

Basis for depreciation			$3,000
Less: Salvage value	$500		
Reduction permitted by section 167(f)	300		200
Amount to be depreciated over the useful life			2,800

D's depreciation allowance on the station wagon for the year 1963 would be $700 ($2,800 divided by 4, the remaining useful life). [Reg. §1.167(f)-1.]

☐ [*T.D. 6712, 3-23-64. Amended by T.D. 6838, 7-19-65.*]

[Reg. §1.167(g)-1]

§1.167(g)-1. Basis for depreciation.—The basis upon which the allowance for depreciation is to be computed with respect to any property shall be the adjusted basis provided in section 1011 for the purpose of determining gain on the sale or other disposition of such property. In the case of property which has not been used in the trade or business or held for the production of income and which is thereafter converted to such use, the fair market value on the date of such conversion, if less than the adjusted basis of the property at that time, is the basis for computing depreciation. [Reg. §1.167(g)-1.]

☐ [*T.D. 6182, 6-11-56. Amended by T.D. 6712, 3-23-64.*]

[Reg. §1.167(h)-1]

§1.167(h)-1. Life tenants and beneficiaries of trusts and estates.—(a) *Life tenants.*—In the case of property held by one person for life with remainder to another person, the deduction for depreciation shall be computed as if the life tenant were the absolute owner of the property so that he will be entitled to the deduction during his life, and thereafter the deduction, if any, shall be allowed to the remainderman.

(b) *Trusts.*—If property is held in trust, the allowable deduction is to be apportioned between the income beneficiaries and the trustee on the basis of the trust income allocable to each, unless the governing instrument (or local law) requires or permits the trustee to maintain a reserve for depreciation in any amount. In the latter case, the deduction is first allocated to the trustee to the extent that income is set aside for a depreciation reserve, and any part of the deduction in excess of the income set aside for the reserve shall be apportioned between the income beneficiaries and the trustee on the basis of the trust income (in excess of the income set aside for the reserve) allocable to each. For example:

(1) If under the trust instrument or local law the income of a trust computed without regard to depreciation is to be distributed to a named beneficiary, the beneficiary is entitled to the deduction to the exclusion of the trustee.

(2) If under the trust instrument or local law the income of a trust is to be distributed to a named beneficiary, but the trustee is directed to maintain a reserve for depreciation in any amount, the deduction is allowed to the trustee (except to the extent that income set aside for the reserve is less than the allowable deduction). The same result would follow if the trustee sets aside income for a depreciation reserve pursuant to discretionary authority to do so in the governing instrument.

No effect shall be given to any allocation of the depreciation deduction which gives any beneficiary or the trustee a share of such deduction greater than his pro rata share of the trust income, irrespective of any provisions in the trust instrument, except as otherwise provided in this paragraph when the trust instrument or local law requires or permits the trustee to maintain a reserve for depreciation.

(c) *Estates.*—In the case of an estate, the allowable deduction shall be apportioned between the estate and the heirs, legatees, and devisees on the basis of income of the estate which is allocable to each. [Reg. §1.167(h)-1.]

☐ [*T.D. 6182, 6-11-56. Amended by T.D. 6712, 3-23-64.*]

[Reg. §1.167(i)-1]

§1.167(i)-1. Depreciation of improvements in the case of mines, etc.—Property used in the trade or business or held for the production of income which is subject to the allowance for depreciation provided in section 611 shall be treated for all purposes of the Code as if it were property subject to the allowance for depreciation under section 167. The preceding sentence shall not limit the allowance for depreciation otherwise allowable under section 611. [Reg. §1.167(i)-1.]

☐ [*T.D. 6182, 6-11-56. Amended by T.D. 6712, 3-23-64.*]

[Reg. § 1.167(l)-1]

§ 1.167(l)-1. Limitations on reasonable allowance in case of property of certain public utilities.—(a) *In general.*—(1) *Scope.*—Section 167(l) in general provides limitations on the use of certain methods of computing a reasonable allowance for depreciation under section 167(a) with respect to "public utility property" (see paragraph (b) of this section) for all taxable years for which a Federal income tax return was not filed before August 1, 1969. The limitations are set forth in paragraph (c) of this section for "pre-1970 public utility property" and in paragraph (d) of this section for "post-1969 public utility property." Under section 167(l), a taxpayer may always use a straight line method (or other "subsection (l) method" as defined in paragraph (f) of this section). In general, the use of a method of depreciation other than a subsection (l) method is not prohibited by section 167(l) for any taxpayer if the taxpayer uses a "normalization method of regulated accounting" (described in paragraph (h) of this section). In certain cases, the use of a method of depreciation other than a subsection (l) method is not prohibited by section 167(l) if the taxpayer used a "flow-through method of regulated accounting" (described in paragraph (i) of this section) for its "July 1969 regulated accounting period" (described in paragraph (g) of this section) whether or not the taxpayer uses either a normalization or a flow-through method of regulated accounting after its July 1969 regulated accounting period. However, in no event may a method of depreciation other than a subsection (l) method be used in the case of pre-1970 public utility property unless such method of depreciation is the "applicable 1968 method" (within the meaning of paragraph (e) of this section). The normalization requirements of section 167(l) with respect to public utility property defined in section 167(l)(3)(A) pertain only to the deferral of Federal income tax liability resulting from the use of an accelerated method of depreciation for computing the allowance for depreciation under section 167 and the use of straight line depreciation for computing tax expense and depreciation expense for purposes of establishing cost of services and for reflecting operating results in regulated books of account. Regulations under section 167(l) do not pertain to other book-tax timing differences with respect to State income taxes, F.I.C.A. taxes, construction costs, or any other taxes and items. The rules provided in paragraph (h)(6) of this section are to insure that the same time period is used to determine the deferred tax reserve amount resulting from the use of an accelerated method of depreciation for cost of service purposes and the reserve amount that may be excluded from the rate base or included in no-cost capital in determining such cost of services. The formula provided in paragraph (h)(6)(ii) of this section is to be used in conjunction with the method of accounting for the reserve for deferred taxes (otherwise proper under paragraph (h)(2) of this section) in accordance with the accounting requirements prescribed or approved, if applicable, by the regulatory body having jurisdiction over the taxpayer's regulated books of account. The formula provides a method to determine the period of time during which the taxpayer will be treated as having received amounts credited or charged to the reserve account so that the disallowance of earnings with respect to such amounts through rate base exclusion or treatment as no-cost capital will take into account the factor of time for which such amounts are held by the taxpayer. The formula serves to limit the amount of such disallowance.

(2) *Methods of depreciation.*—For purposes of section 167(l), in the case of declining balance method each different uniform rate applied to the unrecovered cost or other basis of the property is a different method of depreciation. For purposes of section 167(l), a change in a uniform rate of depreciation due to a change in the useful life of the property or a change in the taxpayer's unrecovered cost or other basis for the property is not a change in the method of depreciation. The use of "guideline lives" or "class lives" for Federal income tax purposes and different lives on the taxpayer's regulated books of account is generally not treated for purposes of section 167(l) as a different method of depreciation. Further, the use of an unrecovered cost or other basis or salvage value for Federal income tax purposes different from the basis or salvage value used on the taxpayer's regulated books of account is not treated as a different method of depreciation.

(3) *Application of certain other provisions to public utility property.*—For rules with respect to application of the investment credit to public utility property, see section 46(e). For rules with respect to the application of the class life asset depreciation range system, including the treatment of the use of "class lives" for Federal income tax purposes and different lives on the taxpayer's regulated books of account, see § 1.167(a)-11 and § 1.167(a)-12.

(4) *Effect on agreements under section 167(d).*—If the taxpayer has entered into an agreement under section 167(d) as to any public utility property and such agreement requires the use of a method of depreciation prohibited by section 167(l), such agreement shall terminate as to such property. The termination, in accordance with this subparagraph, shall not affect any other property (whether or not public utility property) covered by the agreement.

(5) *Effect of change in method of depreciation.*—If, because the method of depreciation used by the taxpayer with respect to public utility property is prohibited by section 167(l), the taxpayer changes to a method of depreciation not prohibited by section 167(l), then when the change is made the unrecovered cost or other basis shall be recovered through annual allowances over the estimated remaining useful life determined in accordance with the circumstances existing at that time.

(b) *Public utility property.*—(1) *In general.*—Under section 167(l)(3)(A), property is "public utility property" during any period in which it is used predominantly in a "section 167(l) public utility activity." The term "section 167(l) public utility activity" means the trade or business of the furnishing or sale of—

(i) Electrical energy, water, or sewage disposal services,

(ii) Gas or steam through a local distribution system,

(iii) Telephone services,

(iv) Other communication services (whether or not telephone services) if furnished or sold by the Communications Satellite Corporation for purposes authorized by the Communications Satellite Act of 1962 (47 U.S.C. 701), or

(v) Transportation of gas or steam by pipeline,

if the rates for such furnishing or sale, as the case may be, are regulated, i.e., have been established or approved by a regulatory body described in section 167(l)(3)(A). The term "regulatory body described in section 167(l)(3)(A)" means a State (including the District of Columbia) or political subdivision thereof, any agency or instrumentality of the United States, or a public service or public utility commission or other body of any State or political subdivision thereof similar to such a commission. The term "established or approved" includes the filing of a schedule of rates with a regulatory body which has the power to approve such rates, even though such body has taken no action on the filed schedule or generally leaves undisturbed rates filed by the taxpayer involved.

(2) *Classification of property.*—If property is not used solely in a section 167(l) public utility activity, such property shall be public utility property if its predominant use is in a section 167(l) public utility activity. The predominant use of property for any period shall be determined by reference to the proper accounts to which expenditures for such property are chargeable under the system of regulated accounts required to be used for the period for which the determination is made and in accordance with the principles of § 1.46-3(g)(4) (relating to credit for investment in certain depreciable property). Thus, for example, for purposes of determining whether property is used predominantly in the trade or business of the furnishing or sale of transportation of gas by pipeline, or furnishing or sale of gas through a local distribution system, or both, the rules prescribed in § 1.46-3(g)(4) apply, except that accounts 365 through 371, inclusive (Transmission Plant), shall be added to the accounts enumerated in subdivision (i) of such paragraph (g)(4).

(c) *Pre-1970 public utility property.*—(1) *Definition.*—(i) Under section 167(l)(3)(B), the term "pre-1970 public utility property" means property which was public utility property at any time before January 1, 1970. If a taxpayer acquires pre-1970 public utility property, such property shall be pre-1970 public utility property in the hands of the taxpayer even though such property may have been acquired by the taxpayer in an arm's-length cash sale at fair market value or in a tax-free exchange. Thus, for example, if corporation X which is a member of the same controlled group of corporations (within the meaning of section 1563(a)) as corporation Y sells pre-1970 public utility property to Y, such property is pre-1970 public utility property in the hands of Y. The result would be the same if X and Y were not members of the same controlled group of corporations.

(ii) If the basis of public utility property acquired by the taxpayer in a transaction is determined in whole or in part by reference to the basis of any of the taxpayer's pre-1970 public utility property by reason of the application of any provision of the code, and if immediately after the transaction the adjusted basis of the property acquired is less than 200 percent of the adjusted basis of such pre-1970 public utility property immediately before the transaction, the property acquired is pre-1970 public utility property.

(2) *Methods of depreciation not prohibited.*—Under section 167(l)(1), in the case of pre-1970 public utility property, the term "reasonable allowance" as used in section 167(a) means, for a taxable year for which a Federal income tax return was not filed before August 1, 1969, and in which such property is public utility property, an allowance (allowable without regard to section 167(l)) computed under—

(i) A subsection (l) method, or

(ii) The applicable 1968 method (other than a subsection (l) method) used by the taxpayer for such property, but only if—

(a) The taxpayer uses in respect of such taxable year a normalization method of regulated accounting for such property.

(b) The taxpayer used a flow-through method of regulated accounting for such property for its July 1969 regulated accounting period, or

(c) The taxpayer's first regulated accounting period with respect to such property is after the taxpayer's July 1969 regulated accounting period and the taxpayer used a flow-through method of regulated accounting for its July 1969 regulated accounting period for public utility property of the same kind (or if there is no property of the same kind, property of the most similar kind) most recently placed in service. See paragraph (e)(5) of this section for determination of same (or similar) kind.

(3) *Flow-through method of regulated accounting in certain cases.*— See paragraph (e)(6) of this section for treatment of certain taxpayers with pending applications for change in method of accounting as being deemed to have used a flow-through method of regulated accounting for the July 1969 regulated accounting period.

(4) *Examples.*—The provisions of this paragraph may be illustrated by the following examples:

Example (1). Corporation X, a calendar-year taxpayer subject to the jurisdiction of a regulatory body described in section 167(l)(3)(A), used the straight line method of depreciation (a subsection (l) method) for all of its public utility property for which depreciation was allowable on its Federal income tax return for 1967 (the latest taxable year for which X, prior to August 1, 1969, filed a return). Assume that under paragraph (e) of this section, X's applicable 1968 method is a subsection (l) method with respect to all of its public utility property. Thus, with respect to its pre-1970 public utility property, X may only use a straight line method (or any other subsection (l) method) of depreciation for all taxable years after 1967.

Example (2). Corporation Y, a calendar-year taxpayer subject to the jurisdiction of the Federal Power Commission, is engaged exclusively in the transportation of gas by pipeline. On its Federal income tax return for 1967 (the latest taxable year for which Y, prior to August 1, 1969, filed a return), Y used the declining balance method of depreciation using a rate of 150 percent of the straight line rate for all of its nonsection 1250 public utility property with respect to which depreciation was allowable. Assume that with respect to all of such property, Y's applicable 1968 method under paragraph (e) of this section is such 150 percent declining balance method. Assume that Y used a normalization method of regulated accounting for all relevant regulated accounting periods. If Y continues to use a normalization method of regulated accounting, Y may compute its reasonable allowance for purposes of section 167(a) using such 150 percent declining balance method for its non-section 1250 pre-1970 public utility property for all taxable years beginning with 1968, provided the use of such method is allowable without regard to section 167(l). Y may also use a subsection (l) method for any of such pre-1970 public utility property for all taxable years beginning after 1967. However, because each different uniform rate applied to the basis of the property is a different method of depreciation, Y may not use a declining balance method of depreciation using a rate of twice the straight line rate for any of such pre-1970 public utility property for any taxable year beginning after 1967.

Example (3). Assume the same facts as in example (2) except that with respect to all of its nonsection 1250 pre-1970 public utility property accounted for in its July 1969 regulated accounting period Y used a flow-through method of regulated accounting for such period. Assume further that such property is the property on the basis of which the applicable 1968 method is established for pre-1970 public utility property of the same kind, but having a first regulated accounting period after the taxpayer's July 1969 regulated accounting period. Beginning with 1968, with respect to such property Y may compute its reasonable allowance for purposes of section 167(a) using the declining balance method of depreciation and a rate of 150 percent of the straight line rate, whether it uses a normalization or flow-through method of regulated accounting after its July 1969 regulated accounting period, provided the use of such method is allowable without regard to section 167(l).

(d) *Post-1969 public utility property.*—(1) *In general.*—Under section 167(l)(3)(C), the term "post-1969 public utility property" means any public utility property which is not pre-1970 public utility property.

(2) *Methods of depreciation not prohibited.*—Under section 167(l)(2), in the case of post-1969 public utility property, the term "reasonable allowance" as used in section 167(a) means, for a taxable year, an allowance (allowable without regard to section 167(l)) computed under—

(i) A subsection (l) method,

(ii) A method of depreciation otherwise allowable under section 167 if, with respect to the property, the taxpayer uses in respect of such taxable year a normalization method of regulated accounting, or

(iii) The taxpayer's applicable 1968 method (other than a subsection (l) method) with respect to the property in question, if the taxpayer used a flow-through method of regulated accounting for its July 1969 regulated accounting period for the property of the same (or similar) kind most recently placed in service, provided that the property in question is not property to which an election under section 167(l)(4)(A) applies. See §1.167(l)-2 for rules with respect to an election under section 167(l)(4)(A). See paragraph (e)(5) of this section for definition of same (or similar) kind.

(3) *Examples.*—The provisions of this paragraph may be illustrated by the following examples:

Example (1). Corporation X is engaged exclusively in the trade or business of the transportation of gas by pipeline and is subject to the jurisdiction of the Federal Power Commission. With respect to all its public utility property, X's applicable 1968 method (as determined under paragraph (e) of this section) is the straight line method of depreciation. X may determine its reasonable allowance for depreciation under section 167(a) with respect to its post-1969 public utility property under a straight line method (or other subsection (l) method) or, if X uses a normalization method of regulated accounting, any other method of depreciation, provided that the use of such other method is allowable under section 167 without regard to section 167(l).

Example (2). Assume the same facts as in example (1) except that with respect to all of X's post-1969 public utility property the applicable 1968 method (as determined under paragraph (e) of this section) is the declining balance method using a rate of 150 percent of the straight line rate. Assume further that all of X's pre-1970 public utility property was accounted for in its July 1969 regulated accounting period, and that X used a flow-through method of regulated accounting for such period. X may determine its reasonable allowance for depreciation under section 167 with respect to its post-1969 public utility property by using the straight-line method of depreciation (or any other subsection (l) method), by using any method otherwise allowable under section 167 (such as a declining balance method) if X uses a normalization method of regulated accounting, or, by using the declining balance method using a rate of 150 percent of the straight line rate, whether or not X uses a normalization or a flow-through method of regulated accounting.

(e) *Applicable 1968 method.*—1) *In general.*—Under section 167(l)(3)(D), except as provided in subparagraphs (3) and (4) of this paragraph, the term "applicable 1968 method" means with respect to any public utility property—

(i) The method of depreciation properly used by the taxpayer in its Federal income tax return with respect to such property for the latest taxable year for which a return was filed before August 1, 1969,

(ii) If subdivision (i) of this subparagraph does not apply, the method of depreciation properly used by the taxpayer in its Federal income tax return for the latest taxable year for which a return was filed before August 1, 1969, with respect to public utility property of the same kind (or if there is no property of the same kind, property of the most similar kind) most recently placed in service before the end of such latest taxable year, or

(iii) If neither subdivision (i) nor (ii) of this subparagraph applies, a subsection (l) method.

If, on or after August 1, 1969, the taxpayer files an amended return for the taxable year referred to in subdivisions (i) and (ii) of this subparagraph, such amended return shall not be taken into consideration in determining the applicable 1968 method. The term "applicable 1968 method" also means with respect to any public utility property, for the year of change and subsequent years, a method of depreciation otherwise allowable under section 167 to which the taxpayer changes from an applicable 1968 method, if such new method results in a lesser allowance for depreciation for such property under section 167 in the year of change and the taxpayer secures the Commissioner's consent to the change in accordance with the procedures of section 446(e) and §1.446-1.

(2) *Placed in service.*—For purposes of this section, property is placed in service on the date on which the period for depreciation begins under section 167. See, for example, §1.167(a)-10(b) and proposed §1.167(a)-11(c)(2). If under an averaging convention, property which is placed in service (as defined in §1.46-3(d)(ii)) by the taxpayer on different dates is treated as placed in service on the same date, then for purposes of section 167(l) the property shall be treated as having been placed in service on the date the period for depreciation with respect to such property would begin under section 167 absent such averaging convention. Thus, for example, if, except for the fact that the averaging convention used assumes that all addi-

tions and retirements made during the first half of the year were made on the first day of the year, the period of depreciation for two items of public utility property would begin on January 10 and March 15, respectively, then for purposes of determining the property of the same (or similar) kind most recently placed in service, such items of property shall be treated as placed in service on January 10 and March 15, respectively.

(3) *Certain section 1250 property.*—If a taxpayer is required under section 167(j) to use a method of depreciation other than its applicable 1968 method with respect to any section 1250 property, the term "applicable 1968 method" means the method of depreciation allowable under section 167(j) which is the most nearly comparable method to the applicable 1968 method determined under subparagraph (1) of this paragraph. For example, if the applicable 1968 method on new section 1250 property is the declining balance method using 200 percent of the straight line rate, the most nearly comparable method allowable for new section 1250 property under section 167(j) would be the declining balance method using 150 percent of the straight line rate. If the applicable 1968 method determined under subparagraph (1) of this paragraph is the sum of the years-digits method, the term "most nearly comparable method" refers to any method of depreciation allowable under section 167(j).

(4) *Applicable 1968 method in certain cases.*—(i)(a) Under section 167(l)(3)(E), if the taxpayer evidenced within the time and manner specified in (b) of this subdivision (i) the intent to use a method of depreciation under section 167 (other than its applicable 1968 method as determined under subparagraph (1) or (3) of this paragraph or a subsection (l) method) with respect to any public utility property, such method of depreciation shall be deemed to be the taxpayer's applicable 1968 method with respect to such public utility property and public utility property of the same (or most similar) kind subsequently placed in service.

(b) Under this subdivision (i), the intent to use a method of depreciation under section 167 is evidenced—

(1) By a timely application for permission for a change in method of accounting filed by the taxpayer before August 1, 1969, or

(2) By the use of such method of depreciation in the computation by the taxpayer of its tax expense for purposes of reflecting operating results in its regulated books of account for its July 1969 regulated accounting period, as established in the manner prescribed in subparagraph (g)(1)(i), (ii), or (iii) of this section.

(ii)(a) If public utility property is acquired in a transaction in which its basis in the hands of the transferee is determined in whole or in part by reference to its basis in the hands of the transferor by reason of the application of any provision of the Code, or in a transfer (including any purchase for cash or in exchange) from a related person, then in the hands of the transferee the applicable 1968 method with respect to such property shall be determined by reference to the treatment in respect of such property in the hands of the transferor.

(b) For purposes of this subdivision (ii), the term "related person" means a person who is related to another person if either immediately before or after the transfer—

(1) The relationship between such persons would result in a disallowance of losses under section 267 (relating to disallowance of losses, etc., between related taxpayers) or section 707(b) (relating to losses disallowed, etc., between partners and controlled partnerships) and the regulations thereunder, or

(2) Such persons are members of the same controlled group of corporations, as defined in section 1563(a) (relating to definition of controlled group of corporations), except that "more than 50 percent" shall be substituted for "at least 80 percent" each place it appears in section 1563(a) and the regulations thereunder.

(5) *Same or similar.*—The classification of property as being of the same (or similar) kind shall be made by reference to the function of the public utility to which the primary use of the property relates. Property which performs the identical function in the identical manner shall be treated as property of the same kind. The determination that property is of a similar kind shall be made by reference to the proper account to which expenditures for the property are chargeable under the system of regulated accounts required to be used by the taxpayer for the period in which the property in question was acquired. Property, the expenditure for which is chargeable to the same account, is property of the most similar kind. Property, the expenditure for which is chargeable to an account for property which serves the same general function, is property of a similar kind. Thus, for example, if corporation X, a natural gas company, subject to the jurisdiction of the Federal Power Commission, had property properly chargeable to account 366 (relating to transmission plant structures and improvements) acquired an additional structure properly chargeable to account 366, under the uniform system of accounts prescribed for natural gas companies (class A and class B) by the

Federal Power Commission, effective September 1, 1968, the addition would constitute property of the same kind if it performed the identical function in the identical manner. If, however, the addition did not perform the identical function in the identical manner, it would be property of the most similar kind.

(6) *Regulated method of accounting in certain cases.*—Under section 167(l)(4)(B), if with respect to any pre-1970 public utility property the taxpayer filed a timely application for change in method of accounting referred to in subparagraph (4)(i)(b)(1) of this paragraph and with respect to property of the same (or similar) kind most recently placed in service the taxpayer used a flow-through method of regulated accounting for its July 1969 regulated accounting period, then for purposes of section 167(l)(1)(B) and paragraph (c) of this section the taxpayer shall be deemed to have used a flow-through method of regulated accounting with respect to such pre-1970 public utility property.

(7) *Examples.*—The provisions of this paragraph may be illustrated by the following examples:

Example (1). Corporation X is a calendar-year taxpayer. On its Federal income tax return for 1967 (the latest taxable year for which X, prior to August 1, 1969, filed a return) X used a straight line method of depreciation with respect to certain public utility property placed in service before 1965 and used the declining balance method of depreciation using 200 percent of the straight line rate (double declining balance) with respect to the same kind of public utility property placed in service after 1964. In 1968 and 1970, X placed in service additional public utility property of the same kind. The applicable 1968 method with respect to the above described public utility property is shown in the following chart:

Property held in 1970	Placed in service	Method on 1967 return	Applicable 1968 method
Group 1	Before 1965	Straight line	Straight line
Group 2	After 1964 and before 1968.	Double declining balance.	Double declining balance.
Group 3	After 1967 and before 1969.	. . . .	Do.
Group 4	After 1968	. . . .	Do.

Example (2). Corporation Y is a calendar-year taxpayer engaged exclusively in the trade or business of the furnishing of electrical energy. In 1954, Y placed in service hydroelectric generators and for all purposes Y has taken straight line depreciation with respect to such generators. In 1960, Y placed in service fossil fuel generators and for all purposes since 1960 has used the declining balance method of depreciation using a rate of 150 percent of the straight line rate (computed without reduction for salvage) with respect to such generators. After 1960 and before 1970 Y did not place in service any generators. In 1970, Y placed in service additional hydroelectric generators. The applicable 1968 method with respect to the hydroelectric generators placed in service in 1970 would be the straight line method because it was the method used by Y on its return for the latest taxable year for which Y filed a return before August 1, 1969, with respect to property of the same kind (i.e., hydroelectric generators) most recently placed in service.

Example (3). Assume the same facts as in example (2), except that the generators placed in service in 1970 were nuclear generators. The applicable 1968 method with respect to such generators is the declining balance method using a rate of 150 percent of the straight line rate because, with respect to property of the most similar kind (fossil fuel generators) most recently placed in service, Y used such declining balance method on its return for the latest taxable year for which it filed a return before August 1, 1969.

(f) *Subsection (l) method.*—Under section 167(l)(3)(F), the term "subsection (l) method" means a reasonable and consistently applied ratable method of computing depreciation which is allowable under section 167(a), such as, for example, the straight-line method or a unit of production method or machine-hour method. The term "subsection (l) method" does not include any declining balance method (regardless of the uniform rate applied), sum of the years-digits method, or method of depreciation which is allowable solely by reason of section 167(b)(4) or (j)(1)(C).

(g) *July 1969 regulated accounting period.*—(1) *In general.*—Under section 167(l)(3)(I), the term "July 1969 regulated accounting period" means the taxpayer's latest accounting period ending before August 1, 1969, for which the taxpayer regularly computed, before January 1, 1970, its tax expense for purposes of reflecting operating results in its regulated books of account. The computation by the taxpayer of such tax expense may be established by reference to the following:

(i) The most recent periodic report of a period ending before August 1, 1969, required by a regulatory body described in section 167(l)(3)(A) having jurisdiction over the taxpayer's regulated books

Reg. § 1.167(l)-1(e)(3)

of account which was filed with such body before January 1, 1970 (whether or not such body has jurisdiction over rates).

(ii) If subdivision (i) of the subparagraph does not apply, the taxpayer's most recent report to its shareholders for a period ending before August 1, 1969, but only if such report was distributed to the shareholders before January 1, 1970, and if the taxpayer's stocks or securities are traded in an established securities market during such period. For purposes of this subdivision, the term "established securities market" has the meaning assigned to such term in § 1.453-3(d)(4).

(iii) If subdivisions (i) and (ii) of this subparagraph do not apply, entries made to the satisfaction of the district director before January 1, 1970, in its regulated books of account for its most recent accounting period ending before August 1, 1969.

(2) *July 1969 method of regulated accounting in certain acquisitions.*—If public utility property is acquired in a transaction in which its basis in the hands of the transferee is determined in whole or in part by reference to its basis in the hands of the transferor by reason of the application of any provision of the Code, or in a transfer (including any purchase for cash or in exchange) from a related person, then in the hands of the transferee the method of regulated accounting for such property's July 1969 regulated accounting period shall be determined by reference to the treatment in respect of such property in the hands of the transferor. See paragraph (e)(4)(ii) of this section for definition of "related person."

(3) *Determination date.*—For purposes of section 167(l), any reference to a method of depreciation under section 167(a), or a method of regulated accounting, taken into account by the taxpayer in computing its tax expense for its July 1969 regulated accounting period shall be a reference to such tax expense as shown on the periodic report or report to shareholders to which subparagraph (l)(i) or (ii) of this paragraph applies or the entries made on the taxpayer's regulated books of account to which subparagraph (l)(iii) of this paragraph applies. Thus, for example, assume that regulatory body A having jurisdiction over public utility property with respect to X's regulated books of account requires X to reflect its tax expense in such books using the same method of depreciation which regulatory body B uses for determining X's cost of service for ratemaking purposes. If in 1971, in the course of approving a rate change for X, B retroactively determines X's cost of service for ratemaking purposes for X's July 1969 regulated accounting period using a method of depreciation different from the method reflected in X's regulated books of account as of January 1, 1970, the method of depreciation used by X for its July 1969 regulated accounting period would be determined without reference to the method retroactively used by B in 1971.

(h) *Normalization method of accounting.*—(1) *In general.*—(i) Under section 167(l), a taxpayer uses a normalization method of regulated accounting with respect to public utility property—

(*a*) If the same method of depreciation (whether or not a subsection (l) method) is used to compute both its tax expense and its depreciation expense for purposes of establishing cost of service for ratemaking purposes and for reflecting operating results in its regulated books of account, and

(*b*) If to compute its allowance for depreciation under section 167 it uses a method of depreciation other than the method it used for purposes described in (*a*) of this subdivision, the taxpayer makes adjustments consistent with subparagraph (2) of this paragraph to a reserve to reflect the total amount of the deferral of Federal income tax liability resulting from the use with respect to all of its public utility property of such different methods of depreciation.

(ii) In the case of a taxpayer described in section 167(l) (1)(B) or (2)(C), the reference in subdivision (i) of this subparagraph shall be a reference only to such taxpayer's "qualified public utility property." See § 1.167(l)-2(b) for definition of "qualified public utility property."

(iii) Except as provided in this subparagraph, the amount of Federal income tax liability deferred as a result of the use of different method of depreciation under subdivision (i) of this subparagraph is the excess (computed without regard to credits) of the amount the tax liability would have been had a subsection (l) method been used over the amount of the actual tax liability. *Such amount* shall be taken into account for the taxable year in which such different methods of depreciation are used. If, however, in respect of any taxable year the use of a method of depreciation other than a subsection (l) method for purposes of determining the taxpayer's reasonable allowance under section 167(a) results in a net operating loss carryover (as determined under section 172) to a year succeeding such taxable year which would not have arisen (or an increase in such carryover which would not have arisen) had the taxpayer determined his reasonable allowance under section 167(a) using a subsection (l) method, then the amount and time of the deferral of tax liability shall be taken into account in such appropriate time and manner as is satisfactory to the district director.

(2) *Adjustments to reserve.*—(i) The taxpayer must credit the amount of deferred Federal income tax determined under subparagraph (l)(i) of this paragraph for any taxable year to a reserve for deferred taxes, a depreciation reserve, or other reserve account. The taxpayer need not establish a separate reserve account for such amount but the amount of deferred tax determined under subparagraph (l)(i) of this paragraph must be accounted for in such a manner so as to be readily identifiable. With respect to any account, the aggregate amount allocable to deferred tax under section 167(l) shall not be reduced except to reflect the amount for any taxable year by which Federal income taxes are greater by reason of the prior use of different methods of depreciation under subparagraph (l)(i) of this paragraph. An additional exception is that the aggregate amount allocable to deferred tax under section 167(l) may be properly adjusted to reflect asset retirements or the expiration of the period for depreciation used in determining the allowance for depreciation under section 167(a).

(ii) The provisions of this subparagraph may be illustrated by the following examples:

Example (1). Corporation X is exclusively engaged in the transportation of gas by pipeline subject to the jurisdiction of the Federal Power Commission. With respect to its post-1969 public utility property, X is entitled under section 167(l)(2)(B) to use a method of depreciation other than a subsection (l) method if it uses a normalization method of regulated accounting. With respect to such property, X has not made any election under § 1.167(a)-11 (relating to depreciation based on class lives and asset depreciation ranges). In 1972, X places in service public utility property with an unadjusted basis of $2 million, and an estimated useful life of 20 years. X uses the declining-balance method of depreciation with a rate twice the straight line rate. If X uses a normalization method of regulated accounting, the amount of depreciation allowable under section 167(a) with respect to such property for 1972 computed under the double declining balance method would be $200,000. X computes its tax expense and depreciation expense for purposes of determining its cost of service for ratemaking purposes and for reflecting operating results in its regulated books of account using the straight line method of depreciation (a subsection (l) method). A depreciation allowance computed in this manner is $100,000. The excess of the depreciation allowance determined under the double declining balance method ($200,000) over the depreciation expense computed using the straight line method ($100,000) is $100,000. Thus, assuming a tax rate of 48 percent, X used a normalization method of regulated accounting for 1972 with respect to property placed in service that year if for 1972 it added to a reserve $48,000 as taxes deferred as a result of the use by X of a method of depreciation for Federal income tax purposes different from that used for establishing its cost of service for ratemaking purposes and for reflecting operating results in its regulated books of account.

Example (2). Assume the same facts as in example (l), except that X elects to apply § 1.167(a)-11 with respect to all eligible property placed in service in 1972. Assume further that all property X placed in service in 1972 is eligible property. One hundred percent of the asset guideline period for such property is 22 years and the asset depreciation range is from 17.5 years to 26.5 years. X uses the double declining balance method of depreciation, selects an asset depreciation period of 17.5 years, and applies the half-year convention (described in § 1.167(a)-11(c)(2)(iii)). In 1972, the depreciation allowable under section 167(a) with respect to property placed in service in 1972 is $114,285 (determined without regard to the normalization requirements in § 1.167(a)-11(b)(6) and in section 167(l)). X computes its tax expense for purposes of determining its cost of service for ratemaking purposes and for reflecting operating results in its regulated books of account using the straight-line method of depreciation (a subsection (l) method), an estimated useful life of 22 years (that is, 100 percent of the asset guideline period), and the half-year convention. A depreciation allowance computed in this manner is $45,454. Assuming a tax rate of 48 percent, the amount that X must add to a reserve for 1972 with respect to property placed in service that year in order to qualify as using a normalization method of regulated accounting under section 167(l)(3)(G) is $27,429 and the amount in order to satisfy the normalization requirements of proposed § 1.167(a)-11(b)(6) is $5,610. X determined such amounts as follows:

(1)	Depreciation allowance on tax return (determined without regard to section 167(l) and § 1.167(a)-11(b)(6))	$114,285
(2)	Line (1), recomputed using a straight line method	57,142
(3)	Difference in depreciation allowance attributable to different methods (line (1) minus line (2)) . .	$57,143

Reg. § 1.167(l)-1(h)(2)(ii)

(4)   Amount to add to reserve under this paragraph
(48 percent of line (3)) $27,429

(5)   Amount in line (2) $57,142

(6)   Line (5), recomputed by using an estimated
useful life of 22 years and the half-year
convention 45,454

(7)   Difference in depreciation allowance attributable
to difference in depreciation periods $11,688

(8)   Amount to add to reserve under
§ 1.167(a)-11(b)(6)(ii) (48 percent of line (7)) . . . 5,610

If, for its depreciation expense for purposes of determining its cost of service for ratemaking purposes and for reflecting operating results in its regulated books of account, X had used a period in excess of the asset guideline period of 22 years, the total amount in lines (4) and (8) in this example would not be changed.

Example (3). Corporation Y, a calendar-year taxpayer which is engaged in furnishing electrical energy, made the election provided by section 167(l)(4)(a) with respect to its "qualified public utility property" (as defined in § 1.167(l)-2(b)). In 1971, Y placed in service qualified public utility property which had an adjusted basis of $2 million, estimated useful life of 20 years, and no salvage value. With respect to property of the same kind most recently placed in service, Y used a flow-through method of regulated accounting for its July 1969 regulated accounting period and the applicable 1968 method is the declining balance method of depreciation using 200 percent of the straight line rate. The amount of depreciation allowable under the double declining balance method with respect to the qualified public utility property would be $200,000. Y computes its tax expense and depreciation expense for purposes of determining its cost of service for ratemaking purposes and for reflecting operating results in its regulated books of account using the straight line method of depreciation. A depreciation allowance with respect to the qualified public utility property determined in this manner is $100,000. The excess of the depreciation allowance determined under the double declining balance method ($200,000) over the depreciation expense computed using the straight line method ($100,000) is $100,000. Thus, assuming a tax rate of 48 percent, Y used a normalization method of regulated accounting for 1971 if for 1971 it added to a reserve $48,000 as tax deferred as a result of the use by Y of a method of depreciation for Federal income tax purposes with respect to its qualified public utility property which method was different from that used for establishing its cost of service for ratemaking purposes and for reflecting operating results in its regulated books of account for such property.

Example (4). Corporation Z, exclusively engaged in a public utility activity did not use a flow-through method of regulated accounting for its July 1969 regulated accounting period. In 1971, a regulatory body having jurisdiction over all of Z's property issued an order applicable to all years beginning with 1968 which provided, in effect, that Z use an accelerated method of depreciation for purposes of section 167 and for determining its tax expenses for purposes of reflecting operating results in its regulated books of account. The order further provided that Z normalize 50 percent of the tax deferral resulting from the use of the accelerated method of depreciation and that Z flow-through 50 percent of the tax deferral resulting therefrom. Under section 167(l), the method of accounting provided in the order would not be a normalization method of regulated accounting because Z would not be permitted to normalize 100 percent of the tax deferral resulting from the use of an accelerated method of depreciation. Thus, with respect to its public utility property for purposes of section 167, Z may only use a subsection (l) method of depreciation.

Example (5). Assume the same facts as in example (4) except that the order of the regulatory body provided, in effect, that Z normalize 100 percent of the tax deferral with respect to 50 percent of its public utility property and flow-through the tax savings with respect to the other 50 percent of its property. Because the effect of such an order would allow Z to flow-through a portion of the tax savings resulting from the use of an accelerated method of depreciation, Z would not be using a normalization method of regulated accounting with respect to any of its properties. Thus, with respect to its public utility property for purposes of section 167, Z may only use a subsection (l) method of depreciation.

(3) *Establishing compliance with normalization requirements in respect of operating books of account.*—The taxpayer may establish compliance with the requirement in subparagraph (l)(i) of this paragraph in respect of reflecting operating results, and adjustments to a reserve, in its operating books of account by reference to the following:

(i) The most recent *periodic report for a period beginning* before the end of the taxable year, required by a regulatory body described in section 167(l)(3)(A) having jurisdiction over the taxpayer's regulated operating books of account which was filed with such body before the due date (determined with regard to exten-

sions) of the taxpayer's Federal income tax return for such taxable year (whether or not such body has jurisdiction over rates).

(ii) If subdivision (i) of this subparagraph does not apply, the taxpayer's most recent report to its shareholders for the taxable year but only if (a) such report was distributed to the shareholders before the due date (determined with regard to extensions) of the taxpayer's Federal income tax return for the taxable year and (b) the taxpayer's stocks or securities are traded in an established securities market during such taxable year. For purposes of this subdivision, the term "established securities market" has the meaning assigned to such term in § 1.453-3(d)(4).

(iii) If neither subdivision (i) nor (ii) of this subparagraph applies, entries made to the satisfaction of the district director before the due date (determined with regard to extensions) of the taxpayer's Federal income tax return for the taxable year in its regulated books of account for its most recent period beginning before the end of such taxable year.

(4) *Establishing compliance with normalization requirements in computing cost of service for ratemaking purposes.*—(i) In the case of a taxpayer which used a flow-through method of regulated accounting for its July 1969 regulated accounting period or thereafter, with respect to all or a portion if its pre-1970 public utility property, if a regulatory body having jurisdiction to establish the rates of such taxpayer as to such property (or a court which has jurisdiction over such body) issues an order of general application (or an order of specific application to the taxpayer) which states that such regulatory body (or court) will permit a class of taxpayers of which such taxpayer is a member (or such taxpayer) to use the normalization method of regulated accounting to establish cost of service for ratemaking purposes with respect to all or a portion of its public utility property, the taxpayer will be presumed to be using the same method of depreciation to compute both its tax expense and its depreciation expense for purposes of establishing its cost of service for ratemaking purposes with respect to the public utility property to which such order applies. In the event that such order is in any way conditional, the preceding sentence shall not apply until all of the conditions contained in such order which are applicable to the taxpayer have been fulfilled. The taxpayer shall establish to the satisfaction of the Commissioner or his delegate that such conditions have been fulfilled.

(ii) In the case of a taxpayer which did not use the flow-through method of regulated accounting for its July 1969 regulated accounting period or thereafter (including a taxpayer which used a subsection (l) method of depreciation to compute its allowance for depreciation under section 167(a) and to compute its tax expense for purposes of reflecting operating results in its regulated books of account), with respect to any of its public utility property, it will be presumed that such taxpayer is using the same method of depreciation to compute both its tax expense and its depreciation expense for purposes of establishing its cost of service for ratemaking purposes with respect to its post-1969 public utility property. The presumption described in the preceding sentence shall not apply in any case where there is (a) an expression of intent (regardless of the manner in which such expression of intent is indicated) by the regulatory body (or bodies), having jurisdiction to establish the rates of such taxpayer, which indicates that the policy of such regulatory body is in any way inconsistent with the use of the normalization method of regulated accounting by such taxpayer or by a class of taxpayers of which such taxpayer is a member, or (b) a decision by a court having jurisdiction over such regulatory body which decision is any way inconsistent with the use of the normalization method of regulated accounting by such taxpayer or a class of taxpayers of which such taxpayer is a member. The presumption shall be applicable on January 1, 1970, and shall, unless rebutted, be effective until an inconsistent expression of intent is indicated by such regulatory body or by such court. An example of such an inconsistent expression of intent is the case of a regulatory body which has, after the July 1969 regulated accounting period and before January 1, 1970, directed public utilities subject to its ratemaking jurisdiction to use a flow-through method of regulated accounting, or has issued an order of general application which states that such agency will direct a class of public utilities of which the taxpayer is a member to use a flow-through method of regulated accounting. The presumption described in this subdivision may be rebutted by evidence that the flow-through method of regulated accounting is being used by the taxpayer with respect to such property.

(iii) The provisions of this subparagraph may be illustrated by the following examples:

Example (1). Corporation X is a calendar-year taxpayer and its "applicable 1968 method" is a straight line method of depreciation. Effective January 1, 1970, X began collecting rates which were based on a sum of the years-digits method of depreciation and a normalization method of regulated accounting which rates had been approved by a regulatory body having jurisdiction over X. On October 1, 1971, a court of proper jurisdiction annulled the rate order prospectively, which annulment was not appealed, on the basis that the regulatory body had abused its discretion by determining the rates on the basis of a normalization method of regulated accounting. As there was no inconsistent expression of intent during 1970 or prior to the due date of X's return for 1970, X's use of the sum of the years-digits method of depreciation for purposes of section 167 on such return was proper. For 1971, the presumption is in effect through September 30. During 1971, X may use the sum of the years-digits method of depreciation for purposes of section 167 from January 1 through September 30, 1971. After September 30, 1971, and for taxable years after 1971, X must use a straight line method of depreciation until the inconsistent court decision is on longer in effect.

Example (2). Assume the same facts as in example (1), except that pursuant to the order of annulment, X was required to refund the portion of the rates attributable to the use of the normalization method of regulated accounting. As there was no inconsistent expression of intent during 1970 or prior to the due date of X's return for 1970, X has the benefit of the presumption with respect to its use of the sum of the years-digits method of depreciation for purposes of section 167, but because of the retroactive nature of the rate order X must file an amended return for 1970 using a straight line method of depreciation. As the inconsistent decision by the court was handed down prior to the due date of X's Federal income tax return for 1971, for 1971 and thereafter the presumption of subdivision (ii) of this subparagraph does not apply. X must file its Federal income tax returns for such years using a straight line method of depreciation.

Example (3). Assume the same facts as in example (2), except that the annulment order was stayed pending appeal of the decision to a court of proper appellate jurisdiction. X has the benefit of the presumption as described in example (2) for the year 1970, but for 1971 and thereafter the presumption of subdivision (ii) of this subparagraph does not apply. Further, X must file an amended return for 1970 using a straight line method of depreciation and for 1971 and thereafter X must file its returns using a straight line method of depreciation unless X and the district director have consented in writing to extend the time for assessment of tax for 1970 and thereafter with respect to the issue of normalization method of regulated accounting for as long as may be necessary to allow for resolution of the appeal with respect to the annulment of the rate order.

(5) *Change in method of regulated accounting.*—The taxpayer shall notify the district director of a change in its method of regulated accounting, an order by a regulatory body or court that such method be changed, or an interim or final rate determination by a regulatory body which determination is inconsistent with the method of regulated accounting used by the taxpayer immediately prior to the effective date of such rate determination. Such notification shall be made within 90 days of the date that the change in method, the order, or the determination is effective. In the case of a change in the method of regulated accounting, the taxpayer shall recompute its tax liability for any affected taxable year and such recomputation shall be made in the form of an amended return where necessary unless the taxpayer and the district director have consented in writing to extend the time for assessment of tax with respect to the issue of normalization method of regulated accounting.

(6) *Exclusion of normalization reserve from rate base.*— (i) Notwithstanding the provisions of subparagraph (1) of this paragraph, a taxpayer does not use a normalization method of regulated accounting if, for ratemaking purposes, the amount of the reserve for deferred taxes under section 167(l) which is excluded from the base to which the taxpayer's rate of return is applied, or which is treated as no-cost capital in those rate cases in which the rate of return is based upon the cost of capital, exceeds the amount of such reserve for deferred taxes for the period used in determining the taxpayer's tax expense in computing cost of service in such ratemaking.

(ii) For the purpose of determining the maximum amount of the reserve to be excluded from the rate base (or to be included as no-cost capital) under subdivision (i) of this subparagraph, if solely an historical period is used to determine depreciation for Federal income tax expense for ratemaking purposes, then the amount of the reserve account for the period is the amount of the reserve (determined under subparagraph (2) of this paragraph) at the end of the historical period. If solely a future period is used for such determination, the amount of the reserve account for the period is the amount of the reserve at the beginning of the period and a pro rata portion of the amount of any projected increase to be credited or decrease to be charged to the account during such period. If such determination is made by reference both to an historical portion and to a future portion of a period, the amount of the reserve account for the period is the amount of the reserve at the end of the historical portion of the period and a pro rata portion of the amount of any projected increase to be credited or decrease to be charged to the account during the future portion of the period. The pro rata portion of any increase to be credited or decrease to be charged during a future period (or the future portion of a part-historical and part-future period) shall be determined by multiplying any such increase or decrease by a fraction, the numerator of which is the number of days remaining in the period at the time such increase or decrease is to be accrued, and the denominator of which is the total number of days in the period (or future portion).

(iii) The provisions of subdivision (i) of this subparagraph shall not apply in the case of a final determination of a rate case entered on or before May 31, 1973. For this purpose, a determination is final if all rights to request a review, a rehearing, or a redetermination by the regulatory body which makes such determination have been exhausted or have lapsed. The provisions of subdivision (ii) of this subparagraph shall not apply in the case of a rate case filed prior to June 7, 1974, for which a rate order is entered by a regulatory body having jurisdiction to establish the rates of the taxpayer prior to September 5, 1974, whether or not such order is final, appealable, or subject to further review or reconsideration.

(iv) The provisions of this subparagraph may be illustrated by the following examples:

Example (1). Corporation X is exclusively engaged in the transportation of gas by pipeline subject to the jurisdiction of the Z Power Commission. With respect to its post-1969 public utility property, X is entitled under section 167(l)(2)(B) to use a method of depreciation other than a subsection (l) method if it uses a normalization method of regulated accounting. With respect to X the Z Power Commission for purposes of establishing cost of service uses a recent consecutive 12-month period ending not more than 4 months prior to the date of filing a rate case adjusted for certain known changes occurring within a 9-month period subsequent to the base period. X's rate case is filed on January 1, 1975. The year 1974 is the recorded test period for X's rate case and is the period used in determining X's tax expense in computing cost of service. The rates are contemplated to be in effect for the years 1975, 1976, and 1977. The adjustments for known changes relate only to wages and salaries. X's rate base at the end of 1974 is $145,000,000. The amount of the reserve for deferred taxes under section 167(l) at the end of 1974 is $1,300,000, and the reserve is projected to be $4,400,000 at the end of 1975, $6,500,000 at the end of 1976, and $9,800,000 at the end of 1977. X does not use a normalization method of regulated accounting if the Z Power Commission excludes more than $1,300,000 from the rate base to which X's rate of return is applied. Similarly, X does not use a normalization method of regulated accounting if, instead of the above, the Z Power Commission, in determining X's rate of return which is applied to the rate base, assigns to no-cost capital an amount that represents the reserve account for deferred tax that is greater than $1,300,000.

Example (2). Assume the same facts as in example (1) except that the adjustments for known changes in cost of service made by the Z Power Commission include an additional depreciation expense that reflects the installation of new equipment put into service on January 1, 1975. Assume further that the reserve for deferred taxes under section 167(l) at the end of 1974 is $1,300,000 and that the monthly net increases for the first 9 months of 1975 are projected to be

January	1–31	....	$310,000
February	1–28	....	300,000
March	1–31	....	300,000
April	1–30	....	280,000
May	1–31	....	270,000
June	1–30	....	260,000
July	1–31	....	260,000
August	1–31	....	250,000
Sept.	1–30	....	240,000
			$2,470,000

For its regulated books of account X accrues such increases as of the last day of the month but as a matter of convenience credits increases or charges decreases to the reserve account on the 15th day of the month following the whole month for which such increase or decrease is accrued. The maximum amount that may be excluded from the rate base is $2,470,879 (the amount in the reserve at the end of the historical portion of the period ($1,300,000) and a pro rata portion of the amount of any projected increase for the future portion of the period to be credited to the reserve ($1,170,879)). Such pro rata portion is computed (without regard to the date such increase will actually be posted to the account) as follows:

$310,000	×	243/273	=	$275,934
300,000	×	215/273	=	236,264
300,000	×	184/273	=	202,198
280,000	×	154/273	=	157,949
270,000	×	123/273	=	121,648
260,000	×	93/273	=	88,571
260,000	×	62/273	=	59,048
250,000	×	31/273	=	28,388
240,000	×	1/273	=	879
				$1,170,879

Reg. §1.167(l)-1(h)(6)(iv)

Example (3). Assume the same facts as in example (1) except that for purposes of establishing cost of service the Z Power Commission uses a future test year (1975). The rates are contemplated to be in effect for 1975, 1976, and 1977. Assume further that plant additions, depreciation expense, and taxes are projected to the end of 1975 and that the reserve for deferred taxes under section 167(l) is $1,300,000 for 1974 and is projected to be $4,400,000 at the end of 1975. Assume also that the Z Power Commission applies the rate of return to X's 1974 rate base of $145,000,000. X and the Z Power Commission through negotiation arrive at the level of approved rates. X uses a normalization method of regulated accounting only if the settlement agreement, the rate order, or record of the proceedings of the Z Power Commission indicates that the Z Power Commission did not exclude an amount representing the reserve for deferred taxes from X's rate base ($145,000,000) greater than $1,300,000 plus a pro rata portion of the projected increases and decreases that are to be credited or charged to the reserve account for 1975. Assume that for 1975 quarterly net increases are projected to be

1st quarter	$910,000
2nd quarter	810,000
3rd quarter	750,000
4th quarter	630,000
Total	$3,100,000

For its regulated books of account X will accrue such increases as of the last day of the quarter but as a matter of convenience will credit increases or charge decreases to the reserve account on the 15th day of the month following the last month of the quarter for which suce reserve account on the 15th day of the month following the last month of the quarter for which such increase or decrease will be accrued. The maximum amount that may be excluded from the rate base is $2,591,480 (the amount of the reserve at the beginning of the period ($1,300,000) plus a pro rata portion ($1,291,480) of the $3,100,000 projected increase to be credited to the reserve during the period). Such portion is computed (without regard to the date such increase will actually be posted to the account) as follows:

$910,000	×	276/365	=	$688,110
810,000	×	185/365	=	410,548
750,000	×	93/365	=	191,096
630,000	×	1/365	=	1,726
				$1,291,480

(i) *Flow-through method of regulated accounting.*—Under section 167(l)(3)(H), a taxpayer uses a flow-through method of regulated accounting with respect to public utility property if it uses the same method of depreciation (other than a subsection (l) method) to compute its allowance for depreciation under section 167 and to compute its tax expense for purposes of reflecting operating results in its regulated books of account unless such method is the same method used by the taxpayer to determine its depreciation expense for purposes of reflecting operating results in its regulated books of account. Except as provided in the preceding sentence, the method of depreciation used by a taxpayer with respect to public utility property for purposes of determining cost of service for ratemaking purposes or rate base for ratemaking purposes shall not be considered in determining whether the taxpayer used a flow-through method of regulated accounting. A taxpayer may establish use of a flow-through method of regulated accounting in the same manner that compliance with normalization requirements in respect of operating books of account may be established under paragraph (h)(4) of this section. [Reg. § 1.167(l)-1.]

☐ [*T.D. 7315, 6-6-74.*]

[Reg. § 1.167(l)-2]

§1.167(l)-2. Public utility property; election as to post-1969 property representing growth in capacity.—(a) *In general.*—Section 167(l)(2) prescribes the methods of depreciation which may be used by a taxpayer with respect to its post-1969 public utility property. Under section 167(l)(2)(A) and (B) the taxpayer may use a subsection (l) method of depreciation (as defined in section 167(l)(3)(F)) or any other method of depreciation which is otherwise allowable under section 167 if, in conjunction with the use of such other method, such taxpayer uses the normalization method of accounting (as defined in section 167(l)(3)(G)). Paragraph (2)(C) of section 167(l) permits a taxpayer which used the flow-through method of accounting for its July 1969 accounting period (as these terms are defined in section 167(l)(3)(H) and (I), respectively) to use its applicable 1968 method of depreciation with respect to certain property. Section 167(l)(3)(D) describes the term "applicable 1968 method." Accordingly, a regulatory agency is not precluded by section 167(l) from requiring such a taxpayer subject to its jurisdiction to continue to use the flow-through method of accounting unless the taxpayer makes the election

pursuant to section 167(l)(4)(A) and this section. Whether or not the election is made, if such regulatory agency permits the taxpayer to change from the flow-through method of accounting, subsection (l)(2)(A) or (B) would apply and such taxpayer could, subject to the provisions of section 167(e) and the regulations thereunder (relating to change in method), use a subsection (l) method of depreciation or, if the taxpayer uses the normalization method of accounting, any other method of depreciation otherwise allowable under section 167.

(1) *Election.*—Under subparagraph (A) of section 167(l)(4), if the taxpayer so elects, the provisions of paragraph (2)(C) of section 167(l) shall not apply to its qualified public utility property (as such term is described in paragraph (b) of this section). In such case the taxpayer making the election shall use a method of depreciation prescribed by section 167(l)(2)(A) or (B) with respect to such property.

(2) *Property to which election shall apply.*—(i) Except as provided in subdivision (ii) of this subparagraph the election provided by section 167(l)(4)(A) shall apply to all of the qualified public utility property of the taxpayer.

(ii) In the event that the taxpayer wishes the election provided by section 167(l)(4)(A) to apply to only a portion of its qualified public utility property, it must clearly identify the property to be subject to the election in the statement of election described in paragraph (e) of this section. Where all property which performs a certain function is included within the election, the election shall apply to all future acquisitions of qualified public utility property which performs the same function. Where only certain property within a functional group of property is included within the election, the election shall apply only to property which is of the same kind as the included property.

(iii) The provisions of subdivision (ii) of this subparagraph may be illustrated by the following examples:

Example (1). Corporation A, an electric utility company, wishes to have the election provided by section 167(l)(4)(A) apply only with respect to its production plant. A statement that the election shall apply only with respect to production plant will be sufficient to include within the election all of the taxpayer's qualified production plant of any kind. All public utility property of the taxpayer other than production plant will not be subject to the election.

Example (2). Corporation B, an electric utility company, wishes to have the election provided by section 167(l)(4)(A) apply only with respect to nuclear production plant. A statement which clearly indicates that only nuclear production plant will be included in the election will be sufficient to exclude from the election all public utility property other than nuclear production plant.

(b) *Qualified public utility property.*—(1) *Definition.*—For purposes of this section the term "qualified public utility property" means post-1969 public utility property to which section 167(l)(2)(C) applies, or would apply if the election described in section 167(l)(4)(A) had not been made, to the extent that such property constitutes property which increases the productive or operational capacity of the taxpayer with respect to the goods or services described in section 167(l)(3)(A) and does not represent the replacement of existing capacity. In the event that particular assets which are post-1969 public utility property both replace existing public utility property and increase the productive or operational capacity of the taxpayer, only that portion of each such asset which is properly allocable, pursuant to the provisions of subparagraph (3)(v) of this paragraph or paragraph (c)(2) of this section (as the case may be), to increasing the productive or operational capacity of the taxpayer shall be qualified public utility property.

(2) *Limitation on use of formula method.*—A taxpayer which makes the election with respect to all of its post-1969 public utility property may determine the amount of its qualified public utility property by using the formula method described in paragraph (c) of this section or, where the taxpayer so chooses, it may use any other method based on engineering data which is satisfactory to the Commissioner. A taxpayer which chooses to include only a portion of its post-1969 public utility property in the election described in paragraph (a)(1) of this section shall, in a manner satisfactory to the Commissioner and consistent with the provisions of subparagraph (3) of this paragraph, use a method based on engineering data. If the taxpayer uses the formula method described in paragraph (c) of this section, it must continue to use such method with respect to additions made in subsequent taxable years. The taxpayer may change from an engineering method to the formula method described in paragraph (c) of this section if it could have used such formula method for the prior taxable year.

(3) *Measuring capacity under an engineering method in the case of a general election.*—(i) The provisions of this subparagraph apply in the

case of an election made with respect to all of the post-1969 public utility property of the taxpayer.

(ii) A taxpayer which uses a method based on engineering data to determine the portion of its additions for a taxable year which constitutes qualified public utility property shall make such determination with reference to its "adjusted capacity" as of the first day of the taxable year during which such additions are placed in service. For purposes of this subparagraph, the term "adjusted capacity" means the taxpayer's capacity as of January 1, 1970, adjusted upward in the manner described in subdivision (iii) of this subparagraph for each taxpayer year ending after December 31, 1969, and before the first day of the taxable year during which the additions described in the preceding sentence are placed in service.

(iii) The adjustment described in this subdivision for each taxable year shall be equal to the number of units of capacity by which additions for the taxable year of public utility property with respect to which the election had been made exceed the number of units of capacity of retirements for such taxable year of public utility property with respect to which the flow-through method of accounting was being used at the time of their retirement. If for any taxable year the computation in the preceding sentence results in a negative amount, such negative amount shall be taken into account as a reduction in the amount of the adjustment (computed without regard to this sentence) in succeeding taxable years.

(iv) The provisions of this subparagraph may be illustrated by the following table which assumes that the taxpayer's adjusted capacity as of January 1, 1970, was 5,000 units:

1 Year	2 Additions	3 Flow-through Retirements	4 Net Additions	5 Adjusted Capacity[1]	6 Actual Capacity	7 Units of Qualified Additions[2]
1970	1000	700	300	5000	5300	300
1971	300	500	(200)	5300	5100	...
1972	500	200	300	5300	5400	100
1973	400	800	(400)	5400	5000	...
1974	600	400	200	5400	5200	...
1975	800	300	500	5400	5700	300

[1] Capacity as of January 1, 1970 plus amounts in column 7 for years prior to the year for which determination is being made.
[2] Column 6 minus column 5.

(v) The qualified portion of the basis for depreciation (as defined in section 167(g)) of each asset or group of assets (if group or composite accounting is used by the taxpayer) subject to the election shall be determined using the following ratio:

$$\frac{\text{Qualified portion of basis of asset}}{\text{Total basis of asset}} = \frac{\text{Units of qualified additions computed in column 7 on chart}}{\text{Units of capacity of additions computed in column 2 on chart}}$$

(c) *Formula method of determining amount of property subject to election.*—(1) *In general.*—The following formula method may be used to determine the amount of qualified public utility property:

Step 1. Find the total cost (within the meaning of section 1012) to the taxpayer of additions during the taxable year of all post-1969 public utility property with respect to which section 167(l)(2)(C) would apply if the election had not been made.

Step 2. Aggregate the cost (within the meaning of section 1012) to the taxpayer of all retirements during the taxable year of public utility property with respect to which the flow-through method of accounting was being used at the time of their retirement.

Step 3. Subtract the figure reached in step 2 from the figure reached in step 1.

$$\frac{\text{Amount of qualified additions computed in step 3}}{\text{Amount of total additions computed in step 1}} =$$

In the event that the figure reached in step 2 exceeds the figure reached in step 1 such excess shall be carried forward to the next taxable year and shall be aggregated with the cost (within the meaning of section 1012) to the taxpayer of all retirements referred to in step 2 for such next taxable year.

(2) *Allocation of bases.*—The amount of qualified public utility property as determined in accordance with the formula method described in subparagraph (1) of this paragraph shall be allocated to the basis for depreciation (as defined in section 167(g)) of each asset or group of assets (if group or composite accounting is used by the taxpayer) subject to the election using the following ratio:

$$\frac{\text{Qualified portion of basis of asset}}{\text{Total basis of asset}} =$$

(d) *Examples.*—The provisions of this section may be illustrated by the following examples:

Example (1). Corporation A, a telephone company subject to the jurisdiction of the Federal Communications Commission, elected, pursuant to the provisions of section 167(l)(4)(A) and this section, with respect to all of its qualified post-1969 public utility property, to have the provisions of paragraph (2)(C) of section 167(l) not apply. In 1971 the Corporation added new underground cable with a cost (within the meaning of section 1012) to it of $4.0 million to its underground cable account. In the same year it retired public utility property with a cost (within the meaning of section 1012) to Corporation A of $1.5 million. The flow-through method of accounting was being used with respect to all of the retired property at the time of retirement. Using the formula method described in paragraph (c) of

this section, the amount of qualified underground cable would be determined as follows:

Step 1.	Aggregate cost of flow-through additions	$4.0 million
Step 2.	Cost of all flow-through retirements	1.5 million
Step 3.	Figure reached in step 1 less figure reached in step 2	$2.5 million

The amount of qualified public utility property to which section 167(l)(2)(C) will not apply is $2.5 million. Pursuant to the provisions of paragraph (c)(2) of this section, the amount of qualified public utility property would be allocated to the basis for depreciation (as defined in section 167(g)) of an asset with a total basis for depreciation of $2 million as follows:

$$\frac{\text{Qualified portion of basis of asset}}{\$2 \text{ million}}$$

$$\frac{\$2.5 \text{ million (figure in step 3)}}{\$4 \text{ million (figure in step 1)}} =$$
Qualified portion of basis of asset = $1.25 million

Example (2). In 1972 Corporation A (the corporation described in example (1)) added underground cable with a cost (within the meaning of section 1012) to it of $1.0 million. In the same year the cost (within the meaning of section 1012) to the corporation of retirements of public utility property with respect to which the flow-through method of accounting was being used was $3.0 million. There were no other additions or retirements. The amount of qualified public utility property would be determined as follows:

Step 1.	Aggregate cost of flow-through additions	$1.0 million
Step 2.	Cost of all flow-through retirements	3.0 million
Step 3.	Figure reached in step 1 less figure reached in step 2	($2.0 million)

Since retirements of flow-through public utility property for the year 1972 exceeded additions made during such year, the excess retirements, $2.0 million, must be carried forward to be aggregated with retirements for 1973.

Example (3). Corporation *B*, a gas pipeline company subject to the jurisdiction of the Federal Power Commission, made the election provided by section 167(l)(4)(A) and this section with respect to all of its post-1969 public utility property. Corporation *B* chose to use an engineering data method of determining which property was subject to the election provided by this section. In 1970, the corporation replaced a portion of its pipeline with respect to which the flow-through method of accounting was being used at the time of its retirement which had a peak capacity on January 1, 1970 of 100,000 thousand cubic feet (MCF) per day at a pressure of 14.73 pounds per square inch absolute (PSIA) with pipe with a capacity of 125.000 MCF per day at 14.73 PSIA. Assuming that there were no other additions or retirements, using an engineering data method one-fifth of the new pipeline would be property subject to the election of this section effective for its taxable year beginning on January 1, 1971.

Example (4). In 1970 Corporation *C* (with the same characteristics as the corporation described in example (3)) extended its pipeline five miles further than it extended on January 1, 1970. Assuming that there were no other additions or retirements, the entire extension would be property subject to the election provided by this section effective for its taxable year beginning on January 1, 1971.

Example (5). As a result of a change of service areas between two corporations, in 1970 Corporation *D* (with the same characteristics as the corporation described in example (3)) retired a pipeline running north and south and replaced it with a pipeline of equal length and capacity running east and west. No part of the pipeline running east and west is property subject to the election.

(e) *Manner of making election.*—The election described in paragraph (a) of this section shall be made by filing, in duplicate, with the Commissioner of Internal Revenue, Washington, D.C. 20224, Attention, T:I:E, a statement of such election.

(f) *Content of statement.*—The statement described in paragraph (e) of this section shall indicate that an election is being made under section 167(l) of the Internal Revenue Code of 1954, and it shall contain the following information:

(1) The name, address, and taxpayer identification number of the taxpayer,

(2) Whether the taxpayer will use the formula method of determining the amount of its qualified public utility property described in paragraph (c) of this section, or an engineering method, and

(3) Where the taxpayer wishes to include only a portion of its public utility property in the election pursuant to the provisions of paragraph (a)(2) of this section, a description sufficient to clearly identify the property to be included.

(g) *Time for making election.*—The election permitted by this section shall be made by filing the statement described in paragraph (e) of this section not later than Monday, June 29, 1970.

(h) *Change of method of determining amount of qualified property.*—Where a taxpayer which has elected pursuant to the provisions of section 167(l)(4)(A) wishes to change, pursuant to the provisions of paragraph (b)(2) of this section, from an engineering data method of determining which of its property is qualified public utility property to the formula method described in paragraph (c) of this section, it may do so by filing a statement to that effect at the time that it files its income tax return, with the district director or director of the regional service center, with whom the taxpayer's income tax return is required to be filed.

(i) *Revocability of election.*—An election made under section 167(l) shall be irrevocable.

(j) *Effective date.*—The election prescribed by section 167(l)(4)(A) and this section shall be effective for taxable years beginning after December 31, 1970. [Reg. § 1.167(l)-2.]

☐ [*T.D. 7045, 6-5-70. Amended by T.D. 7315, 6-6-74.*]

[Reg. § 1.167(l)-3]

§ 1.167(l)-3. Multiple regulation, asset acquisitions, reorganizations, etc.—(a) *Property not entirely subject to jurisdiction of one regulatory body.*—(1) *In general.*—If a taxpayer which uses a method of depreciation other than a subsection (l) method of depreciation is required by regulatory body having jurisdiction over less than all of its property to use, or not to use, a method of regulated accounting (i.e., normalization or flow-through), such taxpayer shall be considered as using, or not using, such method of regulated accounting only with respect to property subject to the jurisdiction of such regulatory body. In the case of property which is contained in a multiple asset account, the provisions of § 1.167(a)-7(c) and § 1.167(a)-11(c)(1)(iv) apply to prohibit depreciating a single account by two or more different methods.

(2) *Jurisdiction of regulatory body.*—For purposes of this paragraph, a regulatory body is considered to have jurisdiction over

property of a taxpayer if expenses with respect to the property area included in cost of service as determined by the regulatory body for ratemaking purposes or for reflecting operating results in its regulated books of account. For example, if regulatory body A, having jurisdiction over 60 percent of an item of X corporation's public utility property, required X to use the flow-through method of regulated accounting in circumstances which would bar X from using a method of depreciation under section 167(a) other than a subsection (l) method, and if regulatory body B, having jurisdiction over the remaining 40 percent of such item of property does not so require X to use the flow-through method of regulated accounting (or if the remaining 40 percent is not subject to the jurisdiction of any regulatory body), then with respect to 60 percent of the adjusted basis of the property X is prohibited from using a method of depreciation for purposes of section 167(a) other than a subsection (l) method. If in such example, A, having jurisdiction over 60 percent of X's public utility property, had jurisdiction over 100 percent of a particular generator, then with respect to the generator X would be prohibited from using a method of depreciation other than a subsection (l) method.

(3) *Public utility property subject to more than one regulatory body.*—If a regulatory body having jurisdiction over public utility property with respect to the taxpayer's regulated books of account requires the taxpayer to reflect its tax expense in such books in the manner used by the regulatory body having jurisdiction over the public utility property for purposes of determining the taxpayer's cost of service for ratemaking purposes, the rules of subparagraphs (1) and (2) of this paragraph shall apply.

(b) *Leasing transactions.*—(1) *Leased property.*—Public utility property as defined in paragraph (b) of § 1.167(l)-1 includes property which is leased by a taxpayer where the leasing of such property is part of the lessor's section 167(l) public utility activity. Thus, such leased property qualifies as public utility property even though the predominant use of such property by the lessee is in other than a section 167(l) public utility activity. Further, leased property qualifies as public utility property under section 167(l) even though the leasing is not part of the lessor's public utility activity if the predominant use of such property by the lessee or any sublessee is in a section 167(l) public utility activity. However, the limitations of section 167(l) apply to a taxpayer only if such taxpayer is subject to the jurisdiction of a regulatory body described in section 167(l)(3)(A). For example, if a financial institution purchases property which it then leases to a lessee which uses such property predominantly in a section 167(l) public utility activity, the property qualifies as public utility property. However, because the financial institution's rates for leasing the property are not subject to the jurisdiction of a regulatory body described in section 167(l)(3)(A), the provisions of section 167(l) do not apply to the depreciation deductions taken with respect to the property by the financial institution. For possible application of section 167(l) to the lessee, see subparagraph (2) of this paragraph.

(2) *Certain rental payments.*—Under section 167(l)(5), if a taxpayer leases property which is public utility property and the regulatory body having jurisdiction over such property for purposes of determining the taxpayer's operating results in its regulated books of account or for ratemaking purposes allows only an amount of such lessee's expenses with respect to the lease which is less than the amount which the taxpayer deducts for purposes of its Federal income tax liablity, then a portion of the difference between such amounts shall not be allowed as a deduction by the taxpayer for purposes of its Federal income tax liability in such manner and time as the Commissioner or his delegate may determine consistent with the principles of § 1.167(l)-1 and this section applicable as to when a method of depreciation other than a subsection (l) method may be used for purposes of section 167(a).

(c) *Certain partnership arrangements.*—Under section 167(l)(5), if property held by a partnership is not public utility property in the hands of the partnership but would be public utility property if an election was made under section 761 to be excluded from partnership treatment, then section 167(l) shall be applied by treating the partners as directly owning the property in proportion to their partnership interests.

(d) *Cross reference.*—See § 1.167(l)-1(c)(1) for treatment of certain property as "pre-1970 public utility property" and § 1.167(l)-1(e)(4)(ii) for applicable 1968 method in the case of property acquired in certain transactions. [Reg. § 1.167(l)-3.]

☐ [*T.D. 7315, 6-6-74.*]

[Reg. § 1.167(l)-4]

§ 1.167(l)-4. Public utility property; election to use asset depreciation range system.—(a) *Application of section 167(l) to certain property subject to asset depreciation range system.*—If the taxpayer elects to compute depreciation under the asset depreciation range system

Itemized Deductions for Individuals and Corps.
See p. 20,601 for regulations not amended to reflect law changes
25,451

described in §1.167(a)-11 with respect to certain public utility property placed in service after December 31, 1970, see §1.167(a)-11(b)(6). [Reg. §1.167(l)-4.]

☐ [*T.D. 7128, 6-22-71. Amended by T.D. 7315, 6-6-74.*]

[Reg. §1.167(m)-1]

§1.167(m)-1. Class lives.—(a) For rules regarding the election to use the class life system authorized by section 167(m), see the provisions of §1.167(a)-11. [Reg. §1.167(m)-1.]

☐ [*T.D. 7272, 4-20-73.*]

If the recovery year is:	1981	And the year the property is placed in service is:		
		1982	1983	1984
		The applicable percentage is:		
1	100	50	33	25
2		50	45	38
3			22	25
4				12

(ii) The provisions of paragraph (a)(1)(i) of this section do not apply to any taxpayer who did not use the RRB method of depreciation under section 167 as of December 31, 1980. In such case, RRB replacement property placed in service by the taxpayer after December 31, 1980, shall be treated as other 5-year recovery property under section 168.

(2) *RRB replacement property placed in service after December 31, 1984.*—RRB replacement property placed in service after December 31, 1984, is treated as other 5-year recovery property under section 168.

(3) *RRB replacement property defined.*—RRB replacement property, for purposes of section 168, means replacement track material (including rail, ties, other track material, and ballast) installed by a railroad (including a railroad switching or terminal company) if—

(i) The replacement is made pursuant to a scheduled program for replacement,

(ii) The replacement is made pursuant to observations by maintenance-of-way personnel of specific track material needing replacement,

(iii) The replacement is made pursuant to the detection by a rail-test car of specific track material needing replacement, or

(iv) The replacement is made as a result of a casualty.

Replacements made as a result of a casualty shall be RRB replacement property only to the extent that, in the case of each casualty, the replacement cost with respect to the replacement track material exceeds $50,000.

(4) *Recovery of adjusted basis of RRB property as of December 31, 1980.*—The taxpayer shall recover the adjusted basis of RRB property (as defined in section 168(g)(6)) as of December 31, 1980, over a period of not less than 5 years and not more than 50 years, using a rate of recovery consistent with any method described in section 167(b), including the method described in section 167(b)(2), switching to the method described in section 167(b)(3) at a time to maximize the deduction. For purposes of determining the recovery allowance under this subparagraph, salvage value shall be disregarded and, in the case of a taxpayer that depreciated RRB property placed in service before January 1, 1981, using the RRB method consistently for all periods after February 28, 1913, the adjusted basis of RRB property is the adjusted basis for purposes of determining the deduction for retirements under the RRB method, with no adjustment for depreciation sustained prior to March 1, 1913.

(5) *RRB property (which is not RRB replacement property) placed in service after December 31, 1980.*—Property placed in service by the taxpayer after December 31, 1980, which is not RRB replacement property and which, under the taxpayer's method of depreciation as of December 31, 1980, would have been depreciated by the taxpayer under the RRB method, is treated as other property under section 168.

(b)-(f) [Reserved]
[Reg. §1.168-5.]

☐ [*T.D. 8116, 12-23-86.*]

[Reg. §1.168(a)-1]

§1.168(a)-1. Modified accelerated cost recovery system.—(a) Section 168 determines the depreciation allowance for tangible property that is of a character subject to the allowance for deprecia-

[Reg. §1.168-5]

§1.168-5. Special rules.—(a) *Retirement-replacement-betterment (RRB) property.*—(1) *RRB replacement property placed in service before January 1, 1985.*—(i) Except as provided in paragraph (a)(1)(ii) of this section, the recovery deduction for the taxable year for retirement-replacement-betterment (RRB) replacement property (as defined in paragraph (a)(3) of this section) placed in service before January 1, 1985, shall be (in lieu of the amount determined under section 168(b)) an amount determined by applying to the unadjusted basis (as defined in section 168(d)(1) and regulations thereunder) of such property the applicable percentage determined in accordance with the following table:

tion provided in section 167(a) and that is placed in service after December 31, 1986 (or after July 31, 1986, if the taxpayer made an election under section 203(a)(1)(B) of the Tax Reform Act of 1986; 100 Stat. 2143). Except for property excluded from the application of section 168 as a result of section 168(f) or as a result of a transitional rule, the provisions of section 168 are mandatory for all eligible property. The allowance for depreciation under section 168 constitutes the amount of depreciation allowable under section 167(a). The determination of whether tangible property is property of a character subject to the allowance for depreciation is made under section 167 and the regulations under section 167.

(b) This section is applicable on and after February 27, 2004. [Reg. §1.168(a)-1.]

☐ [*T.D. 9314, 2-26-2007.*]

[Reg. §1.168(b)-1]

§1.168(b)-1. Definitions.—(a) *Definitions.*—For purposes of section 168 and the regulations under section 168, the following definitions apply:

(1) *Depreciable property* is property that is of a character subject to the allowance for depreciation as determined under section 167 and the regulations under section 167.

(2) *MACRS property* is tangible, depreciable property that is placed in service after December 31, 1986 (or after July 31, 1986, if the taxpayer made an election under section 203(a)(1)(B) of the Tax Reform Act of 1986; 100 Stat. 2143) and subject to section 168, except for property excluded from the application of section 168 as a result of section 168(f) or as a result of a transitional rule.

(3) *Unadjusted depreciable basis* is the basis of property for purposes of section 1011 without regard to any adjustments described in section 1016(a)(2) and (3). This basis reflects the reduction in basis for the percentage of the taxpayer's use of property for the taxable year other than in the taxpayer's trade or business (or for the production of income), for any portion of the basis the taxpayer properly elects to treat as an expense under section 179, section 179C, section 181, or any similar provision, and for any adjustments to basis provided by other provisions of the Internal Revenue Code and the regulations under the Code (other than section 1016(a)(2) and (3)) (for example, a reduction in basis by the amount of the disabled access credit pursuant to section 44(d)(7)). For property subject to a lease, see section 167(c)(2).

(4) *Adjusted depreciable basis* is the unadjusted depreciable basis of the property, as defined in §1.168(b)-1(a)(3), less the adjustments described in section 1016(a)(2) and (3).

(5) *Qualified improvement property.*—(i) Is any improvement that is section 1250 property to an interior portion of a building, as defined in §1.48-1(e)(1), that is nonresidential real property, as defined in section 168(e)(2)(B), if the improvement is placed in service by the taxpayer after the date the building was first placed in service by any person and if—

(A) For purposes of section 168(e)(6), the improvement is made by the taxpayer and is placed in service by the taxpayer after December 31, 2017;

(B) For purposes of section 168(k)(3) as in effect on the day before amendment by section 13204(a)(4)(B) of the Tax Cuts and Jobs Act, Public Law 115-97 (131 Stat. 2054 (December 22, 2017)) ("Act"), the improvement is acquired by the taxpayer before September 28, 2017, the improvement is placed in service by the taxpayer before January 1, 2018, and the improvement meets the original use requirement in section 168(k)(2)(A)(ii) as in effect on the day before amendment by section 13201(c)(1) of the Act; or

(C) For purposes of section 168(k)(3) as in effect on the day before amendment by section 13204(a)(4)(B) of the Act, the improvement is acquired by the taxpayer after September 27, 2017; the improvement is placed in service by the taxpayer after September 27, 2017, and before January 1, 2018; and the improvement meets the requirements in section 168(k)(2)(A)(ii) as amended by section 13201(c)(1) of the Act; and

(ii) Does not include any qualified improvement for which an expenditure is attributable to—

(A) The enlargement, as defined in §1.48-12(c)(10), of the building;

(B) Any elevator or escalator, as defined in §1.48-1(m)(2); or

(C) The internal structural framework, as defined in §1.48-12(b)(3)(iii), of the building.

(b) *Applicability date.*—(1) *In general.*—Except as provided in paragraph (b)(2) of this section, this section is applicable on or after February 27, 2004.

(2) *Application of paragraph (a)(5) of this section and addition of "section 181" in paragraph (a)(3) of this section.*—(i) *In general.*—Except as provided in paragraphs (b)(2)(ii) through (iv) of this section, paragraph (a)(5) of this section and the language "section 181," in the second sentence in paragraph (a)(3) of this section are applicable on or after September 24, 2019.

(ii) *Early application of paragraph (a)(5) of this section and addition of "section 181" in paragraph (a)(3) of this section.*—A taxpayer may choose to apply paragraph (a)(5) of this section and the language "section 181," in the second sentence in paragraph (a)(3) of this section for the taxpayer's taxable years ending on or after September 28, 2017.

(iii) *Early application of regulation project REG-104397-18.*—A taxpayer may rely on the provisions of paragraph (a)(5) of this section in regulation project REG-104397-18 (2018-41 I.R.B 558) (see §601.601(d)(2)(ii)(*b*) of this chapter) for the taxpayer's taxable years ending on or after September 28, 2017, and ending before the taxpayer's taxable year that includes September 24, 2019.

(iv) *Addition of language in paragraph (a)(5)(i)(A) of this section.*—The language "is made by the taxpayer and" in paragraph (a)(5)(i)(A) of this section applies to property placed in service by the taxpayer after December 31, 2017. [Reg. §1.168(b)-1.]

☐ [*T.D. 9314, 2-26-2007. Amended by T.D. 9874, 9-17-2019 and T.D. 9916, 11-5-2020.*]

[Reg. §1.168(d)-0]

§1.168(d)-0. Table of contents for the applicable convention rules.—This section lists the major paragraphs in §1.168(d)-1.

☐ [*T.D. 8444, 10-28-92.*]

[Reg. §1.168(d)-1]

§1.168(d)-1. Applicable conventions—half-year and mid-quarter conventions.—(a) *In general.*—Under section 168(d), the half-year convention applies to depreciable property (other than certain real property described in section 168(d)(2)) placed in service during a taxable year, unless the mid-quarter convention applies to the property. Under section 168(d)(3)(A), the mid-quarter convention applies to *depreciable property* (other than certain real property described in section 168(d)(2)) placed in service during a taxable year if the aggregate basis of property placed in service during the last three months of the taxable year exceeds 40 percent of the aggregate basis of property placed in service during the taxable year ("the 40-percent

test"). Thus, if the depreciable property is placed in service during a taxable year that consists of three months or less, the mid-quarter convention applies to the property. Under section 168(d)(3)(B)(i), the depreciable basis of nonresidential real property, residential rental property, and any railroad grading or tunnel bore is disregarded in applying the 40-percent test. For rules regarding property that is placed in service and disposed of in the same taxable year, see paragraph (b)(3) of this section. For the definition of "aggregate basis of property," see paragraph (b)(4) of this section.

(b) *Additional rules for determining whether the mid-quarter convention applies and for applying the applicable convention.*—(1) *Property described in section 168(f).*—In determining whether the 40-percent test is satisfied for a taxable year, the depreciable basis of property described in section 168(f) (property to which section 168 does not apply) is not taken into account.

(2) *Listed property.*—The depreciable basis of listed property (as defined in section 280F(d)(4) and the regulations thereunder) placed in service during a taxable year is taken into account (unless otherwise excluded) in applying the 40-percent test.

(3) *Property placed in service and disposed of in the same taxable year.*—(i) Under section 168(d)(3)(B)(ii), the depreciable basis of property placed in service and disposed of in the same taxable year is not taken into account in determining whether the 40-percent test is satisfied. However, the depreciable basis of property placed in service, disposed of, subsequently reacquired, and again placed in service, by the taxpayer in the same taxable year must be taken into account in applying the 40-percent test, but the basis of the property is only taken into account on the later of the dates that the property is placed in service by the taxpayer during the taxable year. Further, see §§1.168(i)-6(c)(4)(v)(B) and 1.168(i)-6(f) for rules relating to property placed in service and exchanged or involuntarily converted during the same taxable year.

(ii) The applicable convention, as determined under this section, applies to all depreciable property (except nonresidential real property, residential rental property, and any railroad grading or tunnel bore) placed in service by the taxpayer during the taxable year, excluding property placed in service and disposed of in the same taxable year. However, see §§1.168(i)-6(c)(4)(v)(A) and 1.168(i)-6(f) for rules relating to MACRS property that has a basis determined under section 1031(d) or section 1033(b). No depreciation deduction is allowed for property placed in service and disposed of during the same taxable year. However, see §1.168(k)-1(f)(1) for rules relating to qualified property or 50-percent bonus depreciation property, and §1.1400L(b)-1(f)(1) for rules relating to qualified New York Liberty Zone property, that is placed in service by the taxpayer in the same taxable year in which either a partnership is terminated as a result of a technical termination under section 708(b)(1)(B) or the property is transferred in a transaction described in section 168(i)(7). Further, see §1.168(k)-2(g)(1) for rules relating to qualified property under section 168(k), as amended by the Tax Cuts and Jobs Act, Public Law 115-97 (131 Stat. 2054 (December 22, 2017)), that is placed in service by the taxpayer in the same taxable year in which either a partnership is terminated as a result of a technical termination under section 708(b)(1)(B) or the property is transferred in a transaction described in section 168(i)(7).

(4) *Aggregate basis of property.*—For purposes of the 40-percent test, the term "aggregate basis of property" means the sum of the depreciable bases of all items of depreciable property that are taken into account in applying the 40-percent test. "Depreciable basis" means the basis of depreciable property for purposes of determining gain under sections 1011 through 1024. The depreciable basis for the taxable year the property is placed in service reflects the reduction in basis for—

(i) Any portion of the basis the taxpayer properly elects to treat as an expense under section 179;

(ii) Any adjustment to basis under section 48(q); and

(iii) The percentage of the taxpayer's use of property for the taxable year other than in the taxpayer's trade or business (or for the production of income), but is determined before any reduction for depreciation under section 167(a) for that taxable year.

(5) *Special rules for affiliated groups.*—(i) In the case of a consolidated group (as defined in §1.1502-1(h)), all members of the group that are included on the consolidated return are treated as one taxpayer for purposes of applying the 40-percent test. Thus, the depreciable bases of all property placed in service by members of a consolidated group during a consolidated return year are taken into account (unless otherwise excluded) in applying the 40-percent test to determine whether the mid-quarter convention applies to property placed in service by the members during the consolidated return year. The 40-percent test is applied separately to the depreciable bases of property placed in service by any member of an affiliated

group that is not included in a consolidated return for the taxable year in which the property is placed in service.

(ii) In the case of a corporation formed by a member or members of a consolidated group and that is itself a member of the consolidated group ("newly-formed subsidiary"), the depreciable bases of property placed in service by the newly-formed subsidiary in the consolidated return year in which it is formed is included with the depreciable bases of property placed in service during the consolidated return year by the other members of the consolidated group in applying the 40-percent test. If depreciable property is placed in service by a newly-formed subsidiary during the consolidated return year in which it was formed, the newly-formed subsidiary is considered as being in existence for the entire consolidated return year for purposes of applying the applicable convention to determine when the recovery period begins.

(iii) The provisions of paragraph (b)(5)(ii) of this section are illustrated by the following example.

Example. Assume a member of a consolidated group that files its return on a calendar-year basis forms a subsidiary on August 1. The subsidiary places depreciable property in service on August 5. If the mid-quarter convention applies to property placed in service by the members of the consolidated group (including the newly-formed subsidiary), the property placed in service by the subsidiary on August 5 is deemed placed in service on the mid-point of the third quarter of the consolidated return year (*i.e.*, August 15). If the mid-quarter convention does not apply, the property is deemed placed in service on the mid-point of the consolidated return year (*i.e.*, July 1).

(iv) In the case of a corporation that joins or leaves a consolidated group, the depreciable bases of property placed in service by the corporation joining or leaving the group during the portion of the consolidated return year that the corporation is a member of the consolidated group is included with the depreciable bases of property placed in service during the consolidated return year by the other members in applying the 40-percent test. The depreciable bases of property placed in service by the joining or leaving member in the taxable year before it joins or after it leaves the consolidated group is not taken into account by the consolidated group in applying the 40-percent test for the consolidated return year. If a corporation leaves a consolidated group and joins another consolidated group, each consolidated group takes into account, in applying the 40-percent test, the depreciable bases of property placed in service by the corporation while a member of the group.

(v) The provisions of paragraph (b)(5)(iv) of this section are illustrated by the following example.

Example. Assume Corporations A and B file a consolidated return on a calendar-year basis. Corporation C, also a calendar-year taxpayer, enters the consolidated group on July 1 and is included on the consolidated return for that taxable year. The depreciable bases of property placed in service by C during the period of July 1 to December 31 is included with the depreciable bases of property placed in service by A and B during the entire consolidated return year in applying the 40-percent test. The depreciable bases of property placed in service by C from January 1 to June 30 is not taken into account by the consolidated group in applying the 40-percent test. If C was a member of another consolidated group during the period from January 1 to June 30, that consolidated group would include the depreciable bases of property placed in service by C during that period.

(vi) A corporation that joins or leaves a consolidated group during a consolidated year is considered as being a member of the consolidated group for the entire consolidated return year for purposes of applying the applicable convention to determine when the recovery period begins for depreciable property placed in service by the corporation during the portion of the consolidated return year that the corporation is a member of the group.

(vii) If depreciable property is placed in service by a corporation in the taxable year ending immediately before it joins a consolidated group or beginning immediately after it leaves a consolidated group, the applicable convention is applied to the property under either the full taxable year rules or the short taxable year rules, as applicable.

(viii) The provisions of paragraphs (d)(5)(vi) and (vii) of this section are illustrated by the following example.

Example. Assume that on July 1, C, a calendar-year corporation, joins a consolidated group that files a return on a calendar-year basis. The short taxable year rules apply to C for the period of January 1 to June 30. However, in applying the applicable convention to determine when the recovery period begins for depreciable property placed in service for the period of July 1 to December 31, C is considered as being a member of the consolidated group for the entire consolidated return year. Thus, if the half-year convention applies to depreciable property placed in service by the consolidated group (taking into account the depreciable bases of property placed in service by C after June 30), the property is deemed placed in service on the mid-point of the consolidated return year (*i.e.*, July 1, if the group did not have a short taxable year).

(ix) In the case of a transfer of depreciable property between members of a consolidated group, the following special rules apply for purposes of applying the 40-percent test. Property that is placed in service by one member of a consolidated group and transferred to another member of the same group is considered as placed in service on the date that it is placed in service by the transferor member, and the date it is placed in service by the transferee member is disregarded. In the case of multiple transfers of property between members of a consolidated group, the property is considered as placed in service on the date that the first member places the property in service, and the dates it is placed in service by other members are disregarded. The depreciable basis of the transferred property that is taken into account in applying the 40-percent test is the depreciable basis of the property in the hands of the transferor member (as determined under paragraph (b)(4) of this section), or, in the case of multiple transfers of property between members, the depreciable basis in the hands of the first member that placed the property in service.

(x) The provisions of paragraph (b)(5)(ix) of this section are illustrated by the following example.

Example. Assume the ABC consolidated group files its return on a calendar-year basis. A, a member of the consolidated group, purchases depreciable property costing $50,000 and places the property in service on January 5, 1991. On December 1, 1991, the property is transferred for $75,000 to B, another member of the consolidated group. In applying the 40-percent test to the members of the consolidated group for 1991, the property is considered as placed in service on January 5, the date that A placed the property in service, and the depreciable basis of the property that is taken into account is $50,000.

(6) *Special rule for partnerships and S corporations.*—In the case of property placed in service by a partnership or an S corporation, the 40-percent test is generally applied at the partnership or corporate level. However, if a partnership or an S corporation is formed or availed of for the principal purpose of either avoiding the application of the mid-quarter convention or having the mid-quarter convention apply where it otherwise would not, the 40-percent test is applied at the partner, shareholder, or other appropriate level.

(7) *Certain nonrecognition transactions.*—(i) Except as provided in paragraph (b)(6) of this section, if depreciable property is transferred in a transaction described in section 168(i)(7)(B)(i) (other than in a transaction between members of a consolidated group) in the same taxable year that the property is placed in service by the transferor, the 40-percent test is applied by treating the transferred property as placed in service by the transferee on the date of transfer. Thus, if the aggregate basis of property (including the transferred property) placed in service by the transferee during the last three months of its taxable year exceeds 40 percent of the aggregate basis of property (including the transferred property) placed in service by the transferee during the taxable year, the mid-quarter convention applies to the transferee's depreciable property, including the transferred property. The depreciable basis of the transferred property is not taken into account by the transferor in applying the 40-percent test for the taxable year that the transferor placed the property in service.

(ii) In applying the applicable convention to determine when the recovery period for the transferred property begins, the date on which the transferor placed the property in service must be used. Thus, for example, if the mid-quarter convention applies, the recovery period for the transferred property begins on the mid-point of the quarter of the taxable year that the transferor placed the property in service. If the transferor placed the transferred property in service in a short taxable year, then for purposes of applying the applicable convention and allocating the depreciation deduction between the transferor and the transferee, the transferor is treated as having a full 12-month taxable year commencing on the first day of the short taxable year. The depreciation deduction for the transferor's taxable year in which the property was placed in service is allocated between the transferor and the transferee based on the number of months in the transferor's taxable year that each party held the property in service. For purposes of allocating the depreciation deduction, the transferor takes into account the month in which the property was placed in service but does not take into account the month in which the property was transferred. The transferee is allocated the remaining portion of the depreciation deduction for the transferor's taxable year in which the property was transferred. For the remainder of the transferee's current taxable year (if the transferee has a different taxable year than the transferor) and for subsequent taxable years, the depreciation deduction for the transferee is calculated by allocating to the transferee's taxable year the depreciation attributable to each recovery year, or portion thereof, that falls within the transferee's taxable year. However, see §1.168(k)-2(g)(1)(iii) for a special rule regarding the allocation of the additional first year depreciation deduction in the case of certain contributions of property to a partnership under section 721.

(iii) If the applicable convention for the transferred property has not been determined by the time the transferor files its income tax return for the year of transfer because the transferee's taxable year has not ended, the transferor may use either the mid-quarter or the half-year convention in determining the depreciation deduction for the property. However, the transferor must specify on the depreciation form filed for the taxable year that the applicable convention has not been determined for the property. If the transferee determines that a different convention applies to the transferred property, the transferor should redetermine the depreciation deduction on the property, and, within the period of limitation, should file an amended income tax return for the taxable year and pay any additional tax due plus interest.

(iv) The provisions of this paragraph (b)(7) are illustrated by the following example.

Example. (i) During 1991, C, a calendar-year taxpayer, purchases satellite equipment costing $100,000, and computer equipment costing $15,000. The satellite equipment is placed in service in January, and the computer equipment in February. On October 1, C transfers the computer equipment to Z Partnership in a transaction described in section 721. During 1991, Z, a calendar-year partnership, purchases 30 office desks for a total of $15,000. The desks are placed in service in June. These are the only items of depreciable property placed in service by C and Z during 1991.

(ii) In applying the 40-percent test, because C transferred the computer equipment in a transaction described in section 168(i)(7)(B)(i) in the same taxable year that C placed it in service, the computer equipment is treated as placed in service by the transferee, Z, on the date of transfer, October 1. The 40-percent test is satisfied with respect to Z, because the computer equipment is placed in service during the last three months of Z's taxable year and its basis ($15,000) exceeds 40 percent of the aggregate basis of property placed in service by Z during the taxable year (desks and computer equipment with an aggregate basis of $30,000).

(iii) In applying the mid-quarter convention to determine when the computer equipment is deemed to be placed in service, the date on which C placed the property in service is used. Accordingly, because C placed the computer equipment in service during the first quarter of its taxable year, the computer equipment is deemed placed in service on February 15, 1991, the mid-point of the first quarter of C's taxable year. The depreciation deduction allowable for C's 1991 taxable year, $5,250 ($15,000 × 40 percent × 10.5/12), is allocated between C and Z based on the number of months in C's taxable year that C and Z held the property in service. Thus, because the property was in service for 11 months during C's 1991 taxable year and C held it for 8 of those 11 months, C is allocated $3,818 ($8/11 × $5,250). Z is allocated $1,432, the remaining $3/11$ of the $5,250 depreciation deduction for C's 1991 taxable year. For 1992, Z's depreciation deduction for the computer equipment is $3,900, the sum of the remaining 1.5 months of depreciation deduction for the first recovery year and 10.5 months of depreciation deduction for the second recovery year (($15,000 × 40 percent × $^{1.5}$/12) + ($9,000 × 40 percent × $^{10.5}$/12)).

(c) *Disposition of property subject to the half-year or mid-quarter convention.*—(1) *In general.*—If depreciable property is subject to the half-year (or mid-quarter) convention in the taxable year in which it is placed in service, it also is subject to the half-year (or mid-quarter) convention in the taxable year in which it is disposed of.

(2) *Example.*—The provisions of paragraph (c)(1) of this section are illustrated by the following example.

Example. In October 1991, B, a calendar-year taxpayer, purchases and places in service a light general purpose truck costing $10,000. B does not elect to expense any part of the cost of the truck, and this is the only item of depreciable property placed in service by B during 1991. The 40-percent test is satisfied and the mid-quarter convention applies, because the truck is placed in service during the last three months of the taxable year and no other assets are placed in service in that year. In April 1993 (prior to the end of the truck's recovery period), B sells the truck. The mid-quarter convention applies in determining the depreciation deduction for the truck in 1993, the year of disposition.

(d) *Effective dates.*—(1) *In general.*—This section applies to depreciable property placed in service in taxable years ending after January 30, 1991. For depreciable property placed in service after December 31, 1986, in taxable years ending on or before January 30, 1991, a taxpayer may use a method other than the method provided in this section in applying the 40-percent test and the applicable convention, provided the method is reasonable and is consistently applied to the taxpayer's property.

(2) *Qualified property, 50-percent bonus depreciation property, or qualified New York Liberty Zone property.*—This section also applies to

qualified property under section 168(k)(2) or qualified New York Liberty Zone property under section 1400L(b) acquired by a taxpayer after September 10, 2001, and to 50-percent percent bonus depreciation property under section 168(k)(4) acquired by a taxpayer after May 5, 2003. The last sentences in paragraphs (b)(3)(ii) and (b)(7)(ii) of this section apply to qualified property under section 168(k)(2) placed in service by a taxpayer during or after the taxpayer's taxable year that includes September 24, 2019. However, a taxpayer may choose to apply the last sentences in paragraphs (b)(3)(ii) and (b)(7)(ii) of this section to qualified property under section 168(k)(2) acquired and placed in service after September 27, 2017, by the taxpayer during taxable years ending on or after September 28, 2017. A taxpayer may rely on the last sentences in paragraphs (b)(3)(ii) and (b)(7)(ii) of this section in regulation project REG-104397-18 (2018-41 I.R.B. 558) (see §601.601(d)(2)(ii)(b) of this chapter) for qualified property under section 168(k)(2) acquired and placed in service after September 27, 2017, by the taxpayer during taxable years ending on or after September 28, 2017, and ending before the taxpayer's taxable year that includes September 24, 2019.

(3) *Like-kind exchanges and involuntary conversions.*—The last sentence in paragraph (b)(3)(i) and the second sentence in paragraph (b)(3)(ii) of this section apply to exchanges to which section 1031 applies, and involuntary conversions to which section 1033 applies, of MACRS property for which the time of disposition and the time of replacement both occur after February 27, 2004. [Reg. §1.168(d)-1.]

☐ [T.D. 8444, 10-28-92. *Amended by* T.D. 9091, 9-5-2003; T.D. 9115, 2-27-2004; T.D. 9283, 8-28-2006, T.D. 9314, 2-26-2007 *and* T.D. 9874, 9-17-2019.]

[Reg. §1.168(h)-1]

§1.168(h)-1. Like-kind exchanges involving tax-exempt use property.—(a) *Scope.*—(1) This section applies with respect to a direct or indirect transfer of property among related persons, including transfers made through a qualified intermediary (as defined in §1.1031(k)-1(g)(4)) or other unrelated person, (a transfer) if—

(i) Section 1031 applies to any party to the transfer or to any related transaction; and

(ii) A principal purpose of the transfer or any related transaction is to avoid or limit the application of the alternative depreciation system (within the meaning of section 168(g)).

(2) For purposes of this section, a person is related to another person if they bear a relationship specified in section 267(b) or section 707(b)(1).

(b) *Allowable depreciation deduction for property subject to this section.*—(1) *In general.*—Property (tainted property) transferred directly or indirectly to a taxpayer by a related person (related party) as part of, or in connection with, a transaction in which the related party receives tax-exempt use property (related tax-exempt use property) will, if the tainted property is subject to an allowance for depreciation, be treated in the same manner as the related tax-exempt use property for purposes of determining the allowable depreciation deduction under section 167(a). Under this paragraph (b), the tainted property is depreciated by the taxpayer over the remaining recovery period of, and using the same depreciation method and convention as that of, the related tax-exempt use property.

(2) *Limitations.*—(i) *Taxpayer's basis in related tax-exempt use property.*—The rules of this paragraph (b) apply only with respect to so much of the taxpayer's basis in the tainted property as does not exceed the taxpayer's adjusted basis in the related tax-exempt use property prior to the transfer. Any excess of the taxpayer's basis in the tainted property over its adjusted basis in the related tax-exempt use property prior to the transfer is treated as property to which this section does not apply. This paragraph (b)(2)(i) does not apply if the related tax-exempt use property is not acquired from the taxpayer (e.g., if the taxpayer acquires the tainted property for cash but section 1031 nevertheless applies to the related party because the transfer involves a qualified intermediary).

(ii) *Application of section 168(i)(7).*—This section does not apply to so much of the taxpayer's basis in the tainted property as is subject to section 168(i)(7).

(c) *Related tax-exempt use property.*—(1) For purposes of paragraph (b) of this section, related tax-exempt use property includes—

(i) Property that is tax-exempt use property (as defined in section 168(h)) at the time of the transfer; and

(ii) Property that does not become tax-exempt use property until after the transfer if, at the time of the transfer, it was intended that the property become tax-exempt use property.

(2) For purposes of determining the remaining recovery period of the related tax-exempt use property in the circumstances described in paragraph (c)(1)(ii) of this section, the related tax-exempt use property will be treated as having, prior to the transfer, a lease term

equal to the term of any lease that causes such property to become tax-exempt use property.

(d) *Examples.*—The following examples illustrate the application of this section. The examples do not address common law doctrines or other authorities that may apply to recharacterize or alter the effects of the transactions described therein. Unless otherwise indicated, parties to the transactions are not related to one another.

Example 1. (i) X owns all of the stock of two subsidiaries, B and Z. X, B and Z do not file a consolidated federal income tax return. On May 5, 1995, B purchases an aircraft (*FA*) for $1 million and leases it to a foreign airline whose income is not subject to United States taxation and which is a tax-exempt entity as defined in section 168(h)(2). On the same date, Z owns an aircraft (*DA*) with a fair market value of $1 million, which has been, and continues to be, leased to an airline that is a United States taxpayer. Z's adjusted basis in DA is $0. The next day, at a time when each aircraft is still worth $1 million, B transfers FA to Z (subject to the lease to the foreign airline) in exchange for DA (subject to the lease to the airline that is a United States taxpayer). Z realizes gain of $1 million on the exchange, but that gain is not recognized pursuant to section 1031(a) because the exchange is of like-kind properties. Assume that a principal purpose of the transfer of DA to B or of FA to Z is to avoid the application of the alternative depreciation system. Following the exchange, Z has a $0 basis in FA pursuant to section 1031(d). B has a $1 million basis in DA.

(ii) B has acquired property from Z, a related person; Z's gain is not recognized pursuant to section 1031(a); Z has received tax-exempt use property as part of the transaction; and a principal purpose of the transfer of DA to B or of FA to Z is to avoid the application of the alternative depreciation system. Accordingly, the transaction is within the scope of this section. Pursuant to paragraph (b) of this section, B must recover its $1 million basis in DA over the remaining recovery period of, and using the same depreciation method and convention as that of, FA, the related tax-exempt use property.

(iii) If FA did not become tax-exempt use property until after the exchange, it would still be related tax-exempt use property and paragraph (b) of this section would apply if, at the time of the exchange, it was intended that FA become tax-exempt use property.

Example 2. (i) X owns all of the stock of two subsidiaries, B and Z. X, B and Z do not file a consolidated federal income tax return. B and Z each own identical aircraft. B's aircraft (*FA*) is leased to a tax-exempt entity as defined in section 168(h)(2) and has a fair market value of $1 million and an adjusted basis of $500,000. Z's aircraft (DA) is leased to a United States taxpayer and has a fair market value of $1 million and an adjusted basis of $10,000. On May 1, 1995, B and Z exchange aircraft, subject to their respective leases. B realizes gain of $500,000 and Z realizes gain of $990,000, but neither person recognizes gain because of the operation of section 1031(a). Moreover, assume that a principal purpose of the transfer of DA to B or of FA to Z is to avoid the application of the alternative depreciation system.

(ii) As in *Example 1*, B has acquired property from Z, a related person; Z's gain is not recognized pursuant to section 1031(a); Z has received tax-exempt use property as part of the transaction; and a principal purpose of the transfer of DA to B or of FA to Z is to avoid the application of the alternative depreciation system. Thus, the transaction is within the scope of this section even though B has held tax-exempt use property for a period of time and, during that time, has used the alternative depreciation system with respect to such property. Pursuant to paragraph (b) of this section, B, which has a substituted basis determined pursuant to section 1031(d) of $500,000 in DA, must depreciate the aircraft over the remaining recovery period of FA, using the same depreciation method and convention. Z holds tax-exempt use property with a basis of $10,000, which must be depreciated under the alternative depreciation system.

(iii) Assume the same facts as in paragraph (i) of this *Example 2*, except that B and Z are members of an affiliated group that files a consolidated federal income tax return. Of B's $500,000 basis in DA, $10,000 is subject to section 168(i)(7) and therefore not subject to this section. The remaining $490,000 of basis is subject to this section. But see §1.1502-80(f) making section 1031 inapplicable to intercompany transactions occurring in consolidated return years beginning on or after July 12, 1995.

(e) *Effective date.*—This section applies to transfers made on or after April 20, 1995. [Reg. §1.168(h)-1.]

☐ [T.D. 8667, 4-26-96.]

[Reg. §1.168(i)-0]

§1.168(i)-0. Table of contents for the general asset account rules.—This section lists the major paragraphs contained in §1.168(i)-1.

☐ [T.D. 8566, 10-7-94. *Amended by* T.D. 9115, 2-27-2004; T.D. 9132, 6-16-2004; T.D. 9314, 2-26-2007; T.D. 9564, 12-23-2011 (*corrected* 12-18-2012) *and* T.D. 9689, 8-14-2014.]

[Reg. § 1.168(i)-1]

§ 1.168(i)-1. General asset accounts.—(a) *Scope.*—This section provides rules for general asset accounts under section 168(i)(4). The provisions of this section apply only to assets for which an election has been made under paragraph (l) of this section.

(b) *Definitions.*—For purposes of this section, the following definitions apply:

(1) *Unadjusted depreciable basis* has the same meaning given such term in § 1.168(b)-1(a)(3).

(2) *Unadjusted depreciable basis of the general asset account* is the sum of the unadjusted depreciable bases of all assets included in the general asset account.

(3) *Adjusted depreciable basis of the general asset account* is the unadjusted depreciable basis of the general asset account less the adjustments to basis described in section 1016(a)(2) and (3).

(4) *Building* has the same meaning as that term is defined in § 1.48-1(e)(1).

(5) *Expensed cost* is the amount of any allowable credit or deduction treated as a deduction allowable for depreciation or amortization for purposes of section 1245 (for example, a credit allowable under section 30 or a deduction allowable under section 179, section 179A, or section 190). Expensed cost does not include any additional first year depreciation deduction.

(6) *Mass assets* is a mass or group of individual items of depreciable assets—

(i) That are not necessarily homogenous;

(ii) Each of which is minor in value relative to the total value of the mass or group;

(iii) Numerous in quantity;

(iv) Usually accounted for only on a total dollar or quantity basis;

(v) With respect to which separate identification is impracticable; and

(vi) Placed in service in the same taxable year.

(7) *Portion of an asset* is any part of an asset that is less than the entire asset as determined under paragraph (e)(2)(viii) of this section.

(8) *Remaining adjusted depreciable basis of the general asset account* is the unadjusted depreciable basis of the general asset account less the amount of the additional first year depreciation deduction allowed or allowable, whichever is greater, for the general asset account.

(9) *Structural component* has the same meaning as that term is defined in § 1.48-1(e)(2).

(c) *Establishment of general asset accounts.*—(1) *Assets eligible for general asset accounts.*—(i) *General rules.*—Assets that are subject to either the general depreciation system of section 168(a) or the alternative depreciation system of section 168(g) may be accounted for in one or more general asset accounts. An asset is included in a general asset account only to the extent of the asset's unadjusted depreciable basis. However, an asset is not to be included in a general asset account if the asset is used both in a trade or business or for the production of income and in a personal activity at any time during the taxable year in which the asset is placed in service by the taxpayer or if the asset is placed in service and disposed of during the same taxable year.

(ii) *Special rules for assets generating foreign source income.*—(A) Assets that generate foreign source income, both United States and foreign source income, or combined gross income of a foreign sales corporation (as defined in former section 922), domestic international sales corporation (as defined in section 992(a)), or possession corporation (as defined in section 936) and its related supplier may be included in a general asset account if the requirements of paragraph (c)(2)(i) of this section are satisfied. If, however, the inclusion of these assets in a general asset account results in a substantial distortion of income, the Commissioner may disregard the general asset account election and make any reallocations of income or expense necessary to clearly reflect income.

(B) A general asset account shall be treated as a single asset for purposes of applying the rules in § 1.861-9T(g)(3) (relating to allocation and apportionment of interest expense under the asset method). A general asset account that generates income in more than one grouping of income (statutory and residual) is a multiple category asset (as defined in § 1.861-9T(g)(3)(ii)), and the income yield from the general asset account must be determined by applying the rules for multiple category assets as if the general asset account were a single asset.

(2) *Grouping assets in general asset accounts.*—(i) *General rules.*—If a taxpayer makes the election under paragraph (l) of this section, assets that are subject to the election are grouped into one or more general asset accounts. Assets that are eligible to be grouped into a single general asset account may be divided into more than one

general asset account. Each general asset account must include only assets that—

(A) Have the same applicable depreciation method;

(B) Have the same applicable recovery period;

(C) Have the same applicable convention; and

(D) Are placed in service by the taxpayer in the same taxable year.

(ii) *Special rules.*—In addition to the general rules in paragraph (c)(2)(i) of this section, the following rules apply when establishing general asset accounts—

(A) Assets subject to the mid-quarter convention may only be grouped into a general asset account with assets that are placed in service in the same quarter of the taxable year;

(B) Assets subject to the mid-month convention may only be grouped into a general asset account with assets that are placed in service in the same month of the taxable year;

(C) Passenger automobiles for which the depreciation allowance is limited under section 280F(a) must be grouped into a separate general asset account;

(D) Assets not eligible for any additional first year depreciation deduction, including assets for which the taxpayer elected not to deduct the additional first year depreciation, provided by, for example, section 168(k), section 168(l), section 168(m), section 168(n), section 1400L(b), or section 1400N(d), must be grouped into a separate general asset account;

(E) Assets eligible for the additional first year depreciation deduction may only be grouped into a general asset account with assets for which the taxpayer claimed the same percentage of the additional first year depreciation (for example, 30 percent, 50 percent, or 100 percent);

(F) Except for passenger automobiles described in paragraph (c)(2)(ii)(C) of this section, listed property (as defined in section 280F(d)(4)) must be grouped into a separate general asset account;

(G) Assets for which the depreciation allowance for the placed-in-service year is not determined by using an optional depreciation table (for further guidance, see section 8 of Rev. Proc. 87-57, 1987-2 CB 687, 693 (see § 601.601(d)(2) of this chapter)) must be grouped into a separate general asset account;

(H) Mass assets that are or will be subject to paragraph (j)(2)(i)(D) of this section (disposed of or converted mass asset is identified by a mortality dispersion table) must be grouped into a separate general asset account; and

(I) Assets subject to paragraph (h)(2)(iii)(A) of this section (change in use results in a shorter recovery period or a more accelerated depreciation method) for which the depreciation allowance for the year of change (as defined in § 1.168(i)-4(a)) is not determined by using an optional depreciation table must be grouped into a separate general asset account.

(3) *Examples.*—The following examples illustrate the application of this paragraph (c):

Example 1. In 2014, J, a proprietorship with a calendar year-end, purchases and places in service one item of equipment that costs $550,000. This equipment is section 179 property and also is 5-year property under section 168(e). On its Federal tax return for 2014, J makes an election under section 179 to expense $25,000 of the equipment's cost and makes an election under paragraph (l) of this section to include the equipment in a general asset account. As a result, the unadjusted depreciable basis of the equipment is $525,000. In accordance with paragraph (c)(1) of this section, J must include only $525,000 of the equipment's cost in the general asset account.

Example 2. In 2014, K, a proprietorship with a calendar year-end, purchases and places in service 100 items of equipment. All of these items are 5-year property under section 168(e), are not listed property, and are not eligible for any additional first year depreciation deduction. On its Federal tax return for 2014, K does not make an election under section 179 to expense the cost of any of the 100 items of equipment and does make an election under paragraph (l) of this section to include the 100 items of equipment in a general asset account. K depreciates its 5-year property placed in service in 2014 using the optional depreciation table that corresponds with the general depreciation system, the 200-percent declining balance method, a 5-year recovery period, and the half-year convention. In accordance with paragraph (c)(2) of this section, K includes all of the 100 items of equipment in one general asset account.

Example 3. The facts are the same as in *Example 2*, except that K decides not to include all of the 100 items of equipment in one general asset account. Instead and in accordance with paragraph (c)(2) of this section, K establishes 100 general asset accounts and includes one item of equipment in each general asset account.

Example 4. L, a calendar-year corporation, is a wholesale distributer. In 2014, L places in service the following properties for use in its wholesale distribution business: computers, automobiles, and fork-lifts. On its Federal tax return for 2014, L does not make an election under section 179 to expense the cost of any of these items of equipment and does make an election under paragraph (l) of this section to include all of these items of equipment in a general asset account. All of these items are 5-year property under section 168(e) and are not eligible for any additional first year depreciation deduction. The computers are listed property, and the automobiles are listed property and are subject to section 280F(a). L depreciates its 5-year property placed in service in 2014 using the optional deprecia-tion table that corresponds with the general depreciation system, the 200-percent declining balance method, a 5-year recovery period, and the half-year convention. Although the computers, automobiles, and forklifts are 5-year property, L cannot include all of them in one general asset account because the computers and automobiles are listed property. Further, even though the computers and automobiles are listed property, L cannot include them in one general asset account because the automobiles also are subject to section 280F(a). In accordance with paragraph (c)(2) of this section, L establishes three general asset accounts: one for the computers, one for the automo-biles, and one for the forklifts.

Example 5. M, a fiscal-year corporation with a taxable year end-ing June 30, purchases and places in service ten items of new equip-ment in October 2014, and purchases and places in service five other items of new equipment in February 2015. On its Federal tax return for the taxable year ending June 30, 2015, M does not make an election under section 179 to expense the cost of any of these items of equipment and does make an election under paragraph (l) of this section to include all of these items of equipment in a general asset account. All of these items of equipment are 7-year property under section 168(e), are not listed property, and are property described in section 168(k)(2)(B). All of the ten items of equipment placed in service in October 2014 are eligible for the 50-percent additional first year depreciation deduction provided by section 168(k)(1). All of the five items of equipment placed in service in February 2015 are not eligible for any additional first year depreciation deduction. M depre-ciates its 7-year property placed in service for the taxable year ending June 30, 2015, using the optional depreciation table that corresponds with the general depreciation system, the 200-percent declining bal-ance method, a 7-year recovery period, and the half-year convention. Although the 15 items of equipment are depreciated using the same depreciation method, recovery period, and convention, M cannot include all of them in one general asset account because some of items of equipment are not eligible for any additional first year depreciation deduction. In accordance with paragraph (c)(2) of this section, M establishes two general asset accounts: one for the ten items of equipment eligible for the 50-percent additional first year depreciation deduction and one for the five items of equipment not eligible for any additional first year depreciation deduction.

(d) *Determination of depreciation allowance.*—(1) *In general.*—Depre-ciation allowances are determined for each general asset account. The depreciation allowances must be recorded in a depreciation reserve account for each general asset account. The allowance for deprecia-tion under this section constitutes the amount of depreciation allowa-ble under section 167(a).

(2) *Assets in general asset account are eligible for additional first year depreciation deduction.*—If all the assets in a general asset account are eligible for the additional first year depreciation deduction, the tax-payer first must determine the allowable additional first year depre-ciation deduction for the general asset account for the placed-in-service year and then must determine the amount otherwise allowa-ble as a depreciation deduction for the general asset account for the placed-in-service year and any subsequent taxable year. The allowa-ble additional first year depreciation deduction for the general asset account for the placed-in-service year is determined by multiplying the unadjusted depreciable basis of the general asset account by the additional first year depreciation deduction percentage applicable to the assets in the account (for example, 30 percent, 50 percent, or 100 percent). The remaining adjusted depreciable basis of the general asset account then is depreciated using the applicable depreciation method, recovery period, and convention for the assets in the account.

(3) *No assets in general asset account are eligible for additional first year depreciation deduction.*—If none of the assets in a general asset account are eligible for the additional first year depreciation deduc-tion, the taxpayer must determine the allowable depreciation deduc-tion for the general asset account for the placed-in-service year and any subsequent taxable year by using the applicable depreciation method, recovery period, and convention for the assets in the account.

(4) *Special rule for passenger automobiles.*—For purposes of apply-ing section 280F(a), the depreciation allowance for a general asset account established for passenger automobiles is limited for each taxable year to the amount prescribed in section 280F(a) multiplied by the excess of the number of automobiles originally included in the account over the number of automobiles disposed of during the taxable year or in any prior taxable year in a transaction described in paragraph (e)(3)(iii) (disposition of an asset in a qualifying disposi-tion), paragraph (e)(3)(iv) (transactions subject to section 168(i)(7)), paragraph (e)(3)(v) (transactions subject to section 1031 or section 1033), paragraph (e)(3)(vi) (technical termination of a partnership), paragraph (e)(3)(vii) (anti-abuse rule), paragraph (g) (assets subject to recapture), or paragraph (h)(1) (conversion to any personal use) of this section.

(e) *Dispositions from a general asset account.*—(1) *Scope and defini-tion.*—(i) *In general.*—This paragraph (e) provides rules applicable to dispositions of assets included in a general asset account. For pur-poses of this paragraph (e), an asset in a general asset account is disposed of when ownership of the asset is transferred or when the asset is permanently withdrawn from use either in the taxpayer's trade or business or in the production of income. A disposition includes the sale, exchange, retirement, physical abandonment, or destruction of an asset. A disposition also occurs when an asset is transferred to a supplies, scrap, or similar account, or when a portion of an asset is disposed of as described in paragraph (e)(1)(ii) of this section. If a structural component, or a portion thereof, of a building is disposed of in a disposition described in paragraph (e)(1)(ii) of this section, a disposition also includes the disposition of such structural component or such portion thereof.

(ii) *Disposition of a portion of an asset.*—For purposes of apply-ing paragraph (e) of this section, a disposition includes a disposition of a portion of an asset in a general asset account as a result of a casualty event described in section 165, a disposition of a portion of an asset in a general asset account for which gain, determined without regard to section 1245 or section 1250, is not recognized in whole or in part under section 1031 or section 1033, a transfer of a portion of an asset in a general asset account in a transaction de-scribed in section 168(i)(7)(B), a sale of a portion of an asset in a general asset account, or a disposition of a portion of an asset in a general asset account in a transaction described in paragraph (e)(3)(vii)(B) of this section. For other transactions, a disposition includes a disposition of a portion of an asset in a general asset account only if the taxpayer makes the election under paragraph (e)(3)(ii) of this section to terminate the general asset account in which that disposed portion is included or makes the election under paragraph (e)(3)(iii) of this section for that disposed portion.

(2) *General rules for a disposition.*—(i) *No immediate recovery of basis.*—Except as provided in paragraph (e)(3) of this section, imme-diately before a disposition of any asset in a general asset account or a disposition of a portion of such asset as described in paragraph (e)(1)(ii) of this section, the asset or the portion of the asset, as applicable, is treated as having an adjusted depreciable basis (as defined in § 1.168(b)-1(a)(4)) of zero for purposes of section 1011. Therefore, no loss is realized upon the disposition of an asset from the general asset account or upon the disposition of a portion of such asset as described in paragraph (e)(1)(ii) of this section. Similarly, where an asset or a portion of an asset, as applicable, is disposed of by transfer to a supplies, scrap, or similar account, the basis of the asset or the portion of the asset, as applicable, in the supplies, scrap, or similar account will be zero.

(ii) *Treatment of amount realized.*—Any amount realized on a disposition is recognized as ordinary income, notwithstanding any other provision of subtitle A of the Internal Revenue Code (Code), to the extent the sum of the unadjusted depreciable basis of the general asset account and any expensed cost (as defined in paragraph (b)(5) of this section) for assets in the account exceeds any amounts previ-ously recognized as ordinary income upon the disposition of other assets in the account or upon the disposition of portions of such assets as described in paragraph (e)(1)(ii) of this section. The recogni-tion and character of any excess amount realized are determined under other applicable provisions of the Code other than sections 1245 and 1250 or provisions of the Code that treat gain on a disposi-tion as subject to section 1245 or section 1250.

(iii) *Effect of disposition on a general asset account.*—Except as provided in paragraph (e)(3) of this section, the unadjusted deprecia-ble basis and the depreciation reserve of the general asset account are not affected as a result of a disposition of an asset from the general asset account or of a disposition of a portion of such asset as de-scribed in paragraph (e)(1)(ii) of this section.

(iv) *Coordination with nonrecognition provisions.*—For purposes of determining the basis of an asset or a portion of an asset, as applicable, acquired in a transaction, other than a transaction de-scribed in paragraph (e)(3)(iv) (pertaining to transactions subject to section 168(i)(7)), paragraph (e)(3)(v) (pertaining to transactions subject to section 1031 or section 1033), and paragraph (e)(3)(vi) (pertaining to technical terminations of partnerships) of this section, to which a nonrecognition section of the Code applies, determined without regard to this section, the amount of ordinary income recognized under this paragraph (e)(2) is treated as the amount of gain recognized on the disposition.

(v) *Manner of disposition.*—The manner of disposition (for example, normal retirement, abnormal retirement, ordinary retirement, or extraordinary retirement) is not taken into account in determining whether a disposition occurs or gain or loss is recognized.

(vi) *Disposition by transfer to a supplies account.*—If a taxpayer made an election under § 1.162-3(d) to treat the cost of any rotable spare part, temporary spare part, or standby emergency spare part (as defined in § 1.162-3(c)) as a capital expenditure subject to the allowance for depreciation and also made an election under paragraph (l) of this section to include that rotable, temporary, or standby emergency spare part in a general asset account, the taxpayer can dispose of the rotable, temporary, or standby emergency spare part by transferring it to a supplies account only if the taxpayer has obtained the consent of the Commissioner to revoke the § 1.162-3(d) election. If a taxpayer made an election under § 1.162-3T(d) to treat the cost of any material and supply (as defined in § 1.162-3T(c)(1)) as a capital expenditure subject to the allowance for depreciation and also made an election under paragraph (l) of this section to include that material and supply in a general asset account, the taxpayer can dispose of the material and supply by transferring it to a supplies account only if the taxpayer has obtained the consent of the Commissioner to revoke the § 1.162-3T(d) election. See § 1.162-3(d)(3) for the procedures for revoking a § 1.162-3(d) or a § 1.162-3T(d) election.

(vii) *Leasehold improvements.*—The rules of paragraph (e) of this section also apply to—

(A) A lessor of leased property that made an improvement to that property for the lessee of the property, has a depreciable basis in the improvement, made an election under paragraph (l) of this section to include the improvement in a general asset account, and disposes of the improvement, or disposes of a portion of the improvement as described in paragraph (e)(1)(ii) of this section, before or upon the termination of the lease with the lessee. See section 168(i)(8)(B); and

(B) A lessee of leased property that made an improvement to that property, has a depreciable basis in the improvement, made an election under paragraph (l) of this section to include the improvement in a general asset account, and disposes of the improvement, or disposes of a portion of the improvement as described in paragraph (e)(1)(ii) of this section, before or upon the termination of the lease.

(viii) *Determination of asset disposed of.*—(A) *General rules.*—For purposes of applying paragraph (e) of this section to the disposition of an asset in a general asset account, instead of the disposition of the general asset account, the facts and circumstances of each disposition are considered in determining what is the appropriate asset disposed of. The asset for disposition purposes may not consist of items placed in service by the taxpayer on different dates, without taking into account the applicable convention. For purposes of determining what is the appropriate asset disposed of, the unit of property determination under § 1.263(a)-3(e) or in published guidance in the Internal Revenue Bulletin under section 263(a) (see § 601.601(d)(2) of this chapter) and the distinct asset determination under § 1.1031(a)-3(a)(4) do not apply.

(B) *Special rules.*—In addition to the general rules in paragraph (e)(2)(viii)(A) of this section, the following rules apply for purposes of applying paragraph (e) of this section to the disposition of an asset in a general asset account instead of the disposition of the general asset account:

(1) Each building, including its structural components, is the asset, except as provided in § 1.1250-1(a)(2)(ii) or in paragraph (e)(2)(viii)(B)(2) or (4) of this section.

(2) If a building has two or more condominium or cooperative units, each condominium or cooperative unit, including its structural components, is the asset, except as provided in § 1.1250-1(a)(2)(ii) or in paragraph (e)(2)(viii)(B)(4) of this section.

(3) If a taxpayer properly includes an item in one of the asset classes 00.11 through 00.4 of Rev. Proc. 87-56 (1987-2 CB 674) (see § 601.601(d)(2) of this chapter) or properly classifies an item in one of the categories under section 168(e)(3), except for a category that includes buildings or structural components (for example, retail motor fuels outlet, qualified leasehold improvement property, qualified restaurant property, and qualified retail improvement property), each item is the asset, provided that paragraph (e)(2)(viii)(B)(4) of this section does not apply to the item. For example, each desk is the

asset, each computer is the asset, and each qualified smart electric meter is the asset.

(4) If the taxpayer places in service an improvement or addition to an asset after the taxpayer placed the asset in service, the improvement or addition and, if applicable, its structural components are a separate asset.

(ix) *Examples.*—The following examples illustrate the application of this paragraph (e)(2):

Example 1. A, a calendar-year partnership, maintains one general asset account for one office building that cost $10 million. A discovers a leak in the roof of the building and decides to replace the entire roof. The roof is a structural component of the building. In accordance with paragraph (e)(2)(viii)(B)(1) of this section, the office building, including its structural components, is the asset for disposition purposes. The retirement of the replaced roof is not a disposition of a portion of an asset as described in paragraph (e)(1)(ii) of this section. Thus, the retirement of the replaced roof is not a disposition under paragraph (e)(1) of this section. As a result, A continues to depreciate the $10 million cost of the general asset account. If A must capitalize the amount paid for the replacement roof pursuant to § 1.263(a)-3, the replacement roof is a separate asset for disposition purposes pursuant to paragraph (e)(2)(viii)(B)(4) of this section and for depreciation purposes pursuant to section 168(i)(6).

Example 2. B, a calendar-year commercial airline company, maintains one general asset account for five aircraft that cost a total of $500 million. These aircraft are described in asset class 45.0 of Rev. Proc. 87-56. B replaces the existing engines on one of the aircraft with new engines. Assume each aircraft is a unit of property as determined under § 1.263(a)-3(e)(3) and each engine of an aircraft is a major component or substantial structural part of the aircraft as determined under § 1.263(a)-3(k)(6). Assume also that B treats each aircraft as the asset for disposition purposes in accordance with paragraph (e)(2)(viii) of this section. The retirement of the replaced engines is not a disposition of a portion of an asset as described in paragraph (e)(1)(ii) of this section. Thus, the retirement of the replaced engines is not a disposition under paragraph (e)(1) of this section. As a result, B continues to depreciate the $500 million cost of the general asset account. If B must capitalize the amount paid for the replacement engines pursuant to § 1.263(a)-3, the replacement engines are a separate asset for disposition purposes pursuant to paragraph (e)(2)(viii)(B)(4) of this section and for depreciation purposes pursuant to section 168(i)(6).

Example 3. (i) R, a calendar-year corporation, maintains one general asset account for ten machines. The machines cost a total of $10,000 and are placed in service in June 2014. Of the ten machines, one machine costs $8,200 and nine machines cost a total of $1,800. Assume R depreciates this general asset account using the optional depreciation table that corresponds with the general depreciation system, the 200-percent declining balance method, a 5-year recovery period, and a half-year convention. R does not make a section 179 election for any of the machines, and all of the machines are not eligible for any additional first year depreciation deduction. As of January 1, 2015, the depreciation reserve of the account is $2,000 ($10,000 × 20%).

(ii) On February 8, 2015, R sells the machine that cost $8,200 to an unrelated party for $9,000. Under paragraph (e)(2)(i) of this section, this machine has an adjusted depreciable basis of zero.

(iii) On its 2015 tax return, R recognizes the amount realized of $9,000 as ordinary income because such amount does not exceed the unadjusted depreciable basis of the general asset account ($10,000), plus any expensed cost for assets in the account ($0), less amounts previously recognized as ordinary income ($0). Moreover, the unadjusted depreciable basis and depreciation reserve of the account are not affected by the disposition of the machine. Thus, the depreciation allowance for the account in 2015 is $3,200 ($10,000 × 32%).

Example 4. (i) The facts are the same as in *Example 3*. In addition, on June 4, 2016, R sells seven machines to an unrelated party for a total of $1,100. In accordance with paragraph (e)(2)(i) of this section, these machines have an adjusted depreciable basis of zero.

(ii) On its 2016 tax return, R recognizes $1,000 as ordinary income (the unadjusted depreciable basis of $10,000, plus the expensed cost of $0, less the amount of $9,000 previously recognized as ordinary income). The recognition and character of the excess amount realized of $100 ($1,100-$1,000) are determined under applicable provisions of the Code other than section 1245 (such as section 1231). Moreover, the unadjusted depreciable basis and depreciation reserve of the account are not affected by the disposition of the machines. Thus, the depreciation allowance for the account in 2016 is $1,920 ($10,000 × 19.2%).

(3) *Special rules.*—(i) *In general.*—This paragraph (e)(3) provides the rules for terminating general asset account treatment upon certain dispositions. While the rules under paragraphs (e)(3)(ii) and (iii)

of this section are optional rules, the rules under paragraphs (e)(3)(iv), (v), (vi), and (vii) of this section are mandatory rules. A taxpayer elects to apply paragraph (e)(3)(ii) or (iii) of this section by reporting the gain, loss, or other deduction on the taxpayer's timely filed original Federal tax return, including extensions, for the taxable year in which the disposition occurs. However, if the loss is on account of the demolition of a structure to which section 280B and §1.280B-1 apply, a taxpayer elects to apply paragraph (e)(3)(ii) or (iii) of this section by ending depreciation for the structure at the time of the disposition of the structure, taking into account the convention applicable to the general asset account in which the demolished structure was included, and reporting the amount of depreciation for that structure for the taxable year in which the disposition occurs on the taxpayer's timely filed original Federal tax return, including extensions, for that taxable year. A taxpayer may revoke the election to apply paragraph (e)(3)(ii) or (iii) of this section only by filing a request for a private letter ruling and obtaining the Commissioner's consent to revoke the election. The Commissioner may grant a request to revoke this election if the taxpayer acted reasonably and in good faith, and the revocation will not prejudice the interests of the Government. See generally §301.9100-3 of this chapter. The election to apply paragraph (e)(3)(ii) or (iii) of this section may not be made or revoked through the filing of an application for change in accounting method. For purposes of applying paragraphs (e)(3)(iii) through (vii) of this section, see paragraph (j) of this section for identifying an asset disposed of and its unadjusted depreciable basis. Solely for purposes of applying paragraphs (e)(3)(iii), (e)(3)(iv)(C), (e)(3)(v)(B), and (e)(3)(vii) of this section, the term *asset* is:

(A) The asset as determined under paragraph (e)(2)(viii) of this section; or

(B) The portion of such asset that is disposed of in a disposition described in paragraph (e)(1)(ii) of this section.

(ii) *Disposition of all assets remaining in a general asset account.*— (A) *Optional termination of a general asset account.*—Upon the disposition of all of the assets, the last asset, or the remaining portion of the last asset in a general asset account, a taxpayer may apply this paragraph (e)(3)(ii) to recover the adjusted depreciable basis of the general asset account rather than having paragraph (e)(2) of this section apply. Under this paragraph (e)(3)(ii), the general asset account terminates and the amount of gain or loss for the general asset account is determined under section 1001(a) by taking into account the adjusted depreciable basis of the general asset account at the time of the disposition, as determined under the applicable convention for the general asset account. Whether and to what extent gain or loss is recognized is determined under other applicable provisions of the Code, including section 280B and §1.280B-1. The character of the gain or loss is determined under other applicable provisions of the Code, except that the amount of gain subject to section 1245 is limited to the excess of the depreciation allowed or allowable for the general asset account, including any expensed cost, over any amounts previously recognized as ordinary income under paragraph (e)(2) of this section, and the amount of gain subject to section 1250 is limited to the excess of the additional depreciation allowed or allowable for the general asset account, over any amounts previously recognized as ordinary income under paragraph (e)(2) of this section.

(B) *Examples.*—The following examples illustrate the application of this paragraph (e)(3)(ii):

Example 1. (i) T, a calendar-year corporation, maintains a general asset account for 1,000 calculators. The calculators cost a total of $60,000 and are placed in service in 2014. Assume T depreciates this general asset account using the optional depreciation table that corresponds with the general depreciation system, the 200-percent declining balance method, a 5-year recovery period, and a half-year convention. T does not make a section 179 election for any of the calculators, and all of the calculators are not eligible for any additional first year depreciation deduction. In 2015, T sells 200 of the calculators to an unrelated party for a total of $10,000 and recognizes the $10,000 as ordinary income in accordance with paragraph (e)(2) of this section.

(ii) On March 26, 2016, T sells the remaining calculators in the general asset account to an unrelated party for $35,000. T elects to apply paragraph (e)(3)(ii) of this section. As a result, the account terminates and gain or loss is determined for the account.

(iii) On the date of disposition, the adjusted depreciable basis of the account is $23,040 (unadjusted depreciable basis of $60,000 less the depreciation allowed or allowable of $36,960). Thus, in 2016, T recognizes gain of $11,960 (amount realized of $35,000 less the adjusted depreciable basis of $23,040). The gain of $11,960 is subject to section 1245 to the extent of the depreciation allowed or allowable for the account, plus the expensed cost for assets in the account, less the amounts previously recognized as ordinary income ($36,960 + $0 - $10,000 = $26,960). As a result, the entire gain of $11,960 is subject to section 1245.

Example 2. (i) J, a calendar-year corporation, maintains a general asset account for one item of equipment. This equipment costs $2,000 and is placed in service in 2014. Assume J depreciates this general asset account using the optional depreciation table that corresponds with the general depreciation system, the 200-percent declining balance method, a 5-year recovery period, and a half-year convention. J does not make a section 179 election for the equipment, and it is not eligible for any additional first year depreciation deduction. In June 2016, J sells the equipment to an unrelated party for $1,000. J elects to apply paragraph (e)(3)(ii) of this section. As a result, the account terminates and gain or loss is determined for the account.

(ii) On the date of disposition, the adjusted depreciable basis of the account is $768 (unadjusted depreciable basis of $2,000 less the depreciation allowed or allowable of $1,232). Thus, in 2016, J recognizes gain of $232 (amount realized of $1,000 less the adjusted depreciable basis of $768). The gain of $232 is subject to section 1245 to the extent of the depreciation allowed or allowable for the account, plus the expensed cost for assets in the account, less the amounts previously recognized as ordinary income ($1,232 + $0 - $0 = $1,232). As a result, the entire gain of $232 is subject to section 1245.

(iii) *Disposition of an asset in a qualifying disposition.*— (A) *Optional determination of the amount of gain, loss, or other deduction.*—In the case of a qualifying disposition (described in paragraph (e)(3)(iii)(B) of this section) of an asset, a taxpayer may elect to apply this paragraph (e)(3)(iii) rather than having paragraph (e)(2) of this section apply. Under this paragraph (e)(3)(iii), general asset account treatment for the asset terminates as of the first day of the taxable year in which the qualifying disposition occurs, and the amount of gain, loss, or other deduction for the asset is determined under §1.168(i)-8 by taking into account the asset's adjusted depreciable basis at the time of the disposition. The adjusted depreciable basis of the asset at the time of the disposition, as determined under the applicable convention for the general asset account in which the asset was included, equals the unadjusted depreciable basis of the asset less the greater of the depreciation allowed or allowable for the asset. The allowable depreciation is computed by using the depreciation method, recovery period, and convention applicable to the general asset account in which the asset was included and by including the portion of the additional first year depreciation deduction claimed for the general asset account that is attributable to the asset disposed of. Whether and to what extent gain, loss, or other deduction is recognized is determined under other applicable provisions of the Code, including section 280B and §1.280B-1. The character of the gain, loss, or other deduction is determined under other applicable provisions of the Code, except that the amount of gain subject to section 1245 or section 1250 is limited to the lesser of—

(1) The depreciation allowed or allowable for the asset, including any expensed cost or, in the case of section 1250 property, the additional depreciation allowed or allowable for the asset; or

(2) The excess of—

(i) The original unadjusted depreciable basis of the general asset account plus, in the case of section 1245 property originally included in the general asset account, any expensed cost; over

(ii) The cumulative amounts of gain previously recognized as ordinary income under either paragraph (e)(2) of this section or section 1245 or section 1250.

(B) *Qualifying dispositions.*—A *qualifying disposition* is a disposition that does not involve all the assets, the last asset, or the remaining portion of the last asset remaining in a general asset account and that is—

(1) A direct result of a fire, storm, shipwreck, or other casualty, or from theft;

(2) A charitable contribution for which a deduction is allowable under section 170;

(3) A direct result of a cessation, termination, or disposition of a business, manufacturing or other income producing process, operation, facility, plant, or other unit, other than by transfer to a supplies, scrap, or similar account; or

(4) A transaction, other than a transaction described in paragraph (e)(3)(iv) (pertaining to transactions subject to section 168(i)(7)), paragraph (e)(3)(v) (pertaining to transactions subject to section 1031 or section 1033), paragraph (e)(3)(vi) (pertaining to technical terminations of partnerships), or paragraph (e)(3)(vii) (anti-abuse rule) of this section, to which a nonrecognition section of the Internal Revenue Code applies (determined without regard to this section).

(C) *Effect of a qualifying disposition on a general asset account.*—If the taxpayer elects to apply this paragraph (e)(3)(iii) to a qualifying disposition of an asset, then—

(1) The asset is removed from the general asset account as of the first day of the taxable year in which the qualifying disposition

occurs. For that taxable year, the taxpayer accounts for the asset in a single asset account in accordance with the rules under § 1.168(i)-7(b);

(2) The unadjusted depreciable basis of the general asset account is reduced by the unadjusted depreciable basis of the asset as of the first day of the taxable year in which the disposition occurs;

(3) The depreciation reserve of the general asset account is reduced by the greater of the depreciation allowed or allowable for the asset as of the end of the taxable year immediately preceding the year of disposition. The allowable depreciation is computed by using the depreciation method, recovery period, and convention applicable to the general asset account in which the asset was included and by including the portion of the additional first year depreciation deduction claimed for the general asset account that is attributable to the asset disposed of; and

(4) For purposes of determining the amount of gain realized on subsequent dispositions that is subject to ordinary income treatment under paragraph (e)(2)(ii) of this section, the amount of any expensed cost with respect to the asset is disregarded.

(D) *Examples.*—The following examples illustrate the application of this paragraph (e)(3)(iii):

Example 1. (i) Z, a calendar-year corporation, maintains one general asset account for 12 machines. Each machine costs $15,000 and is placed in service in 2014. Of the 12 machines, nine machines that cost a total of $135,000 are used in Z's Kentucky plant, and three machines that cost a total of $45,000 are used in Z's Ohio plant. Assume Z depreciates this general asset account using the optional depreciation table that corresponds with the general depreciation system, the 200-percent declining balance method, a 5-year recovery period, and the half-year convention. Z does not make a section 179 election for any of the machines, and all of the machines are not eligible for any additional first year depreciation deduction. As of December 31, 2015, the depreciation reserve for the account is $93,600.

(ii) On May 27, 2016, Z sells its entire manufacturing plant in Ohio to an unrelated party. The sales proceeds allocated to each of the three machines at the Ohio plant is $5,000. This transaction is a qualifying disposition under paragraph (e)(3)(iii)(B)(3) of this section, and Z elects to apply paragraph (e)(3)(iii) of this section.

(iii) For Z's 2016 return, the depreciation allowance for the account is computed as follows. As of December 31, 2015, the depreciation allowed or allowable for the three machines at the Ohio plant is $23,400. Thus, as of January 1, 2016, the unadjusted depreciable basis of the account is reduced from $180,000 to $135,000 ($180,000 less the unadjusted depreciable basis of $45,000 for the three machines), and, as of December 31, 2015, the depreciation reserve of the account is decreased from $93,600 to $70,200 ($93,600 less the depreciation allowed or allowable of $23,400 for the three machines as of December 31, 2015). Consequently, the depreciation allowance for the account in 2016 is $25,920 ($135,000 × 19.2%).

(iv) For Z's 2016 return, gain or loss for each of the three machines at the Ohio plant is determined as follows. The depreciation allowed or allowable in 2016 for each machine is $1,440 (($15,000 × 19.2%)/ 2). Thus, the adjusted depreciable basis of each machine under section 1011 is $5,760 (the adjusted depreciable basis of $7,200 removed from the account less the depreciation allowed or allowable of $1,440 in 2016). As a result, the loss recognized in 2016 for each machine is $760 ($5,000 - $5,760), which is subject to section 1231.

Example 2. (i) A, a calendar-year partnership, maintains one general asset account for one office building that cost $20 million and was placed in service in July 2011. A depreciates this general asset account using the optional depreciation table that corresponds with the general depreciation system, the straight-line method, a 39-year recovery period, and the mid-month convention. As of January 1, 2014, the depreciation reserve for the account is $1,261,000.

(ii) In May 2014, a tornado occurs where the building is located and damages the roof of the building. A decides to replace the entire roof. The roof is replaced in June 2014. The roof is a structural component of the building. Because the roof was damaged as a result of a casualty event described in section 165, the partial disposition rule provided under paragraph (e)(1)(ii) of this section applies to the roof. Although the office building, including its structural components, is the asset for disposition purposes, the partial disposition rule provides that the retirement of the replaced roof is a disposition under paragraph (e)(1) of this section. This retirement is a qualifying disposition under paragraph (e)(3)(iii)(B)(1) of this section, and A elects to apply paragraph (e)(3)(iii) of this section for the retirement of the damaged roof.

(iii) Of the $20 million cost of the office building, assume $1 million is the cost of the retired roof.

(iv) For A's 2014 return, the depreciation allowance for the account is computed as follows. As of December 31, 2013, the depreciation allowed or allowable for the retired roof is $63,050. Thus, as of January 1, 2014, the unadjusted depreciable basis of the account is

reduced from $20,000,000 to $19,000,000 ($20,000,000 less the unadjusted depreciable basis of $1,000,000 for the retired roof), and the depreciation reserve of the account is decreased from $1,261,000 to $1,197,950 ($1,261,000 less the depreciation allowed or allowable of $63,050 for the retired roof as of December 31, 2013). Consequently, the depreciation allowance for the account in 2014 is $487,160 ($19,000,000 × 2.564%).

(v) For A's 2014 return, gain or loss for the retired roof is determined as follows. The depreciation allowed or allowable in 2014 for the retired roof is $11,752 (($1,000,000 × 2.564%) × 5.5/12). Thus, the adjusted depreciable basis of the retired roof under section 1011 is $925,198 (the adjusted depreciable basis of $936,950 removed from the account less the depreciation allowed or allowable of $11,752 in 2014). As a result, the loss recognized in 2014 for the retired roof is $925,198, which is subject to section 1231.

(vi) If A must capitalize the amount paid for the replacement roof under § 1.263(a)-3, the replacement roof is a separate asset for depreciation purposes pursuant to section 168(i)(6). If A includes the replacement roof in a general asset account, the replacement roof is a separate asset for disposition purposes pursuant to paragraph (e)(2)(viii)(B)(4) of this section. If A includes the replacement roof in a single asset account or a multiple asset account under § 1.168(i)-7, the replacement roof is a separate asset for disposition purposes pursuant to § 1.168(i)-8(c)(4)(ii)(D).

(iv) *Transactions subject to section 168(i)(7).*—(A) *In general.*—If a taxpayer transfers one or more assets, or a portion of such asset, in a general asset account in a transaction described in section 168(i)(7)(B) (pertaining to treatment of transferees in certain nonrecognition transactions), the taxpayer (the transferor) and the transferee must apply this paragraph (e)(3)(iv) to the asset or the portion of such asset, instead of applying paragraph (e)(2), (e)(3)(ii), or (e)(3)(iii) of this section. The transferee is bound by the transferor's election under paragraph (l) of this section for the portion of the transferee's basis in the asset or the portion of such asset that does not exceed the transferor's adjusted depreciable basis of the general asset account or the asset or the portion of such asset, as applicable, as determined under paragraph (e)(3)(iv)(B)(2) or (C)(2) of this section, as applicable.

(B) *All assets remaining in general asset account are transferred.*—If a taxpayer transfers all the assets, the last asset, or the remaining portion of the last asset in a general asset account in a transaction described in section 168(i)(7)(B)—

(1) The taxpayer (the transferor) must terminate the general asset account on the date of the transfer. The allowable depreciation deduction for the general asset account for the transferor's taxable year in which the section 168(i)(7)(B) transaction occurs is computed by using the depreciation method, recovery period, and convention applicable to the general asset account. This allowable depreciation deduction is allocated between the transferor and the transferee on a monthly basis. This allocation is made in accordance with the rules in § 1.168(d)-1(b)(7)(ii) for allocating the depreciation deduction between the transferor and the transferee;

(2) The transferee must establish a new general asset account for all the assets, the last asset, or the remaining portion of the last asset, in the taxable year in which the section 168(i)(7)(B) transaction occurs for the portion of its basis in the assets that does not exceed the transferor's adjusted depreciable basis of the general asset account in which all the assets, the last asset, or the remaining portion of the last asset, were included. The transferor's adjusted depreciable basis of this general asset account is equal to the adjusted depreciable basis of that account as of the beginning of the transferor's taxable year in which the transaction occurs, decreased by the amount of depreciation allocable to the transferor for the year of the transfer, as determined under paragraph (e)(3)(iv)(B)(1) of this section. The transferee is treated as the transferor for purposes of computing the allowable depreciation deduction for the new general asset account under section 168. The new general asset account must be established in accordance with the rules in paragraph (c) of this section, except that the unadjusted depreciable bases of all the assets, the last asset, or the remaining portion of the last asset, and the greater of the depreciation allowed or allowable for all the assets, the last asset, or the remaining portion of the last asset, including the amount of depreciation for the transferred assets that is allocable to the transferor for the year of the transfer, are included in the newly established general asset account. Consequently, this general asset account in the year of the transfer will have a beginning balance for both the unadjusted depreciable basis and the depreciation reserve of the general asset account; and

(3) For purposes of section 168 and this section, the transferee treats the portion of its basis in the assets that exceeds the transferor's adjusted depreciable basis of the general asset account in which all the assets, the last asset, or the remaining portion of the last asset, were included, as determined under paragraph (e)(3)(iv)(B)(2)

of this section, as a separate asset that the transferee placed in service on the date of the transfer. The transferee accounts for this asset under §1.168(i)-7 or may make an election under paragraph (l) of this section to include the asset in a general asset account.

(C) *Not all assets remaining in general asset account are transferred.*—If a taxpayer transfers an asset in a general asset account in a transaction described in section 168(i)(7)(B) and if paragraph (e)(3)(iv)(B) of this section does not apply to this asset—

(1) The taxpayer (the transferor) must remove the transferred asset from the general asset account in which the asset is included, as of the first day of the taxable year in which the section 168(i)(7)(B) transaction occurs. In addition, the adjustments to the general asset account described in paragraphs (e)(3)(iii)(C)(2) through (4) of this section must be made. The allowable depreciation deduction for the asset for the transferor's taxable year in which the section 168(i)(7)(B) transaction occurs is computed by using the depreciation method, recovery period, and convention applicable to the general asset account in which the asset was included. This allowable depreciation deduction is allocated between the transferor and the transferee on a monthly basis. This allocation is made in accordance with the rules in §1.168(d)-1(b)(7)(ii) for allocating the depreciation deduction between the transferor and the transferee;

(2) The transferee must establish a new general asset account for the asset in the taxable year in which the section 168(i)(7)(B) transaction occurs for the portion of its basis in the asset that does not exceed the transferor's adjusted depreciable basis of the asset. The transferee's adjusted depreciable basis of this asset is equal to the adjusted depreciable basis of the asset as of the beginning of the transferor's taxable year in which the transaction occurs, decreased by the amount of depreciation allocable to the transferor for the year of the transfer, as determined under paragraph (e)(3)(iv)(C)(1) of this section. The transferee is treated as the transferor for purposes of computing the allowable depreciation deduction for the new general asset account under section 168. The new general asset account must be established in accordance with the rules in paragraph (c) of this section, except that the unadjusted depreciable basis of the asset, and the greater of the depreciation allowed or allowable for the asset, including the amount of depreciation for the transferred asset that is allocable to the transferor for the year of the transfer, are included in the newly established general asset account. Consequently, this general asset account in the year of the transfer will have a beginning balance for both the unadjusted depreciable basis and the depreciation reserve of the general asset account; and

(3) For purposes of section 168 and this section, the transferee treats the portion of its basis in the asset that exceeds the transferor's adjusted depreciable basis of the asset, as determined under paragraph (e)(3)(iv)(C)(2) of this section, as a separate asset that the transferee placed in service on the date of the transfer. The transferee accounts for this asset under §1.168(i)-7 or may make an election under paragraph (l) of this section to include the asset in a general asset account.

(v) *Transactions subject to section 1031 or section 1033.*—(A) *Like-kind exchange or involuntary conversion of all assets remaining in a general asset account.*—If all the assets, the last asset, or the remaining portion of the last asset in a general asset account are transferred by a taxpayer in a like-kind exchange (as defined under §1.168-6(b)(11)) or in an involuntary conversion (as defined under §1.168-6(b)(12)), the taxpayer must apply this paragraph (e)(3)(v)(A) instead of applying paragraph (e)(2), (e)(3)(ii), or (e)(3)(iii) of this section. Under this paragraph (e)(3)(v)(A), the general asset account terminates as of the first day of the year of disposition (as defined in §1.168(i)-6(b)(5)) and—

(1) The amount of gain or loss for the general asset account is determined under section 1001(a) by taking into account the adjusted depreciable basis of the general asset account at the time of disposition (as defined in §1.168(i)-6(b)(3)). The depreciation allowance for the general asset account in the year of disposition is determined in the same manner as the depreciation allowance for the relinquished MACRS property (as defined in §1.168(i)-6(b)(2)) in the year of disposition is determined under §1.168(i)-6. The recognition and character of gain or loss are determined in accordance with paragraph (e)(3)(ii)(A) of this section, notwithstanding that paragraph (e)(3)(ii) of this section is an optional rule; and

(2) The adjusted depreciable basis of the general asset account at the time of disposition is treated as the adjusted depreciable basis of the relinquished MACRS property.

(B) *Like-kind exchange or involuntary conversion of less than all assets remaining in a general asset account.*—If an asset in a general asset account is transferred by a taxpayer in a like-kind exchange or in an involuntary conversion and if paragraph (e)(3)(v)(A) of this section does not apply to this asset, the taxpayer must apply this

paragraph (e)(3)(v)(B) instead of applying paragraph (e)(2), (e)(3)(ii), or (e)(3)(iii) of this section. Under this paragraph (e)(3)(v)(B), general asset account treatment for the asset terminates as of the first day of the year of disposition (as defined in §1.168(i)-6(b)(5)), and—

(1) The adjusted depreciable basis of the asset at the time of disposition equals the unadjusted depreciable basis of the asset less the greater of the depreciation allowed or allowable for the asset. The allowable depreciation is computed by using the depreciation method, recovery period, and convention applicable to the general asset account in which the asset was included and by including the portion of the additional first year depreciation deduction claimed for the general asset account that is attributable to the relinquished asset.

(2) As of the first day of the year of disposition, the taxpayer must remove the relinquished asset from the general asset account and make the adjustments to the general asset account described in paragraphs (e)(3)(iii)(C)(2) through (4) of this section.

(vi) *Technical termination of a partnership.*—In the case of a technical termination of a partnership under section 708(b)(1)(B), the terminated partnership must apply this paragraph (e)(3)(vi) instead of applying paragraph (e)(2), (e)(3)(ii), or (e)(3)(iii) of this section. Under this paragraph (e)(3)(vi), all of the terminated partnership's general asset accounts terminate as of the date of its termination under section 708(b)(1)(B). The terminated partnership computes the allowable depreciation deduction for each of its general asset accounts for the taxable year in which the technical termination occurs by using the depreciation method, recovery period, and convention applicable to the general asset account. The new partnership is not bound by the terminated partnership's election under paragraph (l) of this section.

(vii) *Anti-abuse rule.*—(A) *In general.*—If an asset in a general asset account is disposed of by a taxpayer in a transaction described in paragraph (e)(3)(vii)(B) of this section, general asset account treatment for the asset terminates as of the first day of the taxable year in which the disposition occurs. Consequently, the taxpayer must determine the amount of gain, loss, or other deduction attributable to the disposition in the manner described in paragraph (e)(3)(iii)(A) of this section, notwithstanding that paragraph (e)(3)(iii)(A) of this section is an optional rule, and must make the adjustments to the general asset account described in paragraphs (e)(3)(iii)(C)(1) through (4) of this section.

(B) *Abusive transactions.*—A transaction is described in this paragraph (e)(3)(vii)(B) if the transaction is not described in paragraph (e)(3)(iv), (e)(3)(v), or (e)(3)(vi) of this section, and if the transaction is entered into, or made, with a principal purpose of achieving a tax benefit or result that would not be available absent an election under this section. Examples of these types of transactions include—

(1) A transaction entered into with a principal purpose of shifting income or deductions among taxpayers in a manner that would not be possible absent an election under this section to take advantage of differing effective tax rates among the taxpayers; or

(2) An election made under this section with a principal purpose of disposing of an asset from a general asset account to utilize an expiring net operating loss or credit if the transaction is not a bona fide disposition. The fact that a taxpayer with a net operating loss carryover or a credit carryover transfers an asset to a related person or transfers an asset pursuant to an arrangement where the asset continues to be used or is available for use by the taxpayer pursuant to a lease or otherwise indicates, absent strong evidence to the contrary, that the transaction is described in this paragraph (e)(3)(vii)(B).

(f) *Assets generating foreign source income.*—(1) *In general.*—This paragraph (f) provides the rules for determining the source of any income, gain, or loss recognized, and the appropriate section 904(d) separate limitation category or categories for any foreign source income, gain, or loss recognized on a disposition (within the meaning of paragraph (e)(1) of this section) of an asset in a general asset account that consists of assets generating both United States and foreign source income. These rules apply only to a disposition to which paragraph (e)(2) (general disposition rules), paragraph (e)(3)(ii) (disposition of all assets remaining in a general asset account), paragraph (e)(3)(iii) (disposition of an asset in a qualifying disposition), paragraph (e)(3)(v) (transactions subject to section 1031 or section 1033), or paragraph (e)(3)(vii) (anti-abuse rule) of this section applies. Solely for purposes of applying this paragraph (f), the term *asset* is:

(i) The asset as determined under paragraph (e)(2)(viii) of this section; or

(ii) The portion of such asset that is disposed of in a disposition described in paragraph (e)(1)(ii) of this section.

(2) *Source of ordinary income, gain, or loss.*—(i) *Source determined by allocation and apportionment of depreciation allowed.*—The amount of any ordinary income, gain, or loss that is recognized on the disposition of an asset in a general asset account must be apportioned between United States and foreign sources based on the allocation and apportionment of the—

(A) Depreciation allowed for the general asset account as of the end of the taxable year in which the disposition occurs if paragraph (e)(2) of this section applies to the disposition;

(B) Depreciation allowed for the general asset account as of the time of disposition if the taxpayer applies paragraph (e)(3)(ii) of this section to the disposition of all assets, the last asset, or the remaining portion of the last asset, in the general asset account, or if all the assets, the last asset, or the remaining portion of the last asset, in the general asset account are disposed of in a transaction described in paragraph (e)(3)(v)(A) of this section; or

| Foreign Source Income, Gain, or Loss from The Disposition of an Asset | = | Total Ordinary Income, Gain, or Loss from the Disposition of an Asset | X | Allowed Depreciation Deductions Allocated and Apportioned to Foreign Source Income/Total Allowed Depreciation Deductions for the General Asset Account or for the Asset Disposed of (as applicable) |

(3) *Section 904(d) separate categories.*—If the assets in the general asset account generate foreign source income in more than one separate category under section 904(d)(1) or another section of the Code (for example, income treated as foreign source income under section 904(g)(10)), or under a United States income tax treaty that requires the foreign tax credit limitation to be determined separately for specified types of income, the amount of foreign source income,

| Foreign Source Income, Gain, or Loss in a Separate Category | = | Foreign Source Income, Gain, or Loss from The Disposition of an Asset | X | Allowed Depreciation Deductions Allocated and Apportioned to a Separate Category/Total Allowed Depreciation Deductions and Apportioned to Foreign Source Income |

(g) *Assets subject to recapture.*—If the basis of an asset in a general asset account is increased as a result of the recapture of any allowable credit or deduction (for example, the basis adjustment for the recapture amount under section 30(e)(5), 50(c)(2), 168(l)(6), 168(n)(4), 179(d)(10), 179A(e)(4), or 1400N(d)(5)), general asset account treatment for the asset terminates as of the first day of the taxable year in which the recapture event occurs. Consequently, the taxpayer must remove the asset from the general asset account as of that day and must make the adjustments to the general asset account described in paragraphs (e)(3)(iii)(C)(2) through (4) of this section.

(h) *Changes in use.*—(1) *Conversion to any personal use.*—An asset in a general asset account becomes ineligible for general asset account treatment if a taxpayer uses the asset in any personal activity during a taxable year. Upon a conversion to any personal use, the taxpayer must remove the asset from the general asset account as of the first day of the taxable year in which the change in use occurs (the year of change) and must make the adjustments to the general asset account described in paragraphs (e)(3)(iii)(C)(2) through (4) of this section.

(2) *Change in use results in a different recovery period and/or depreciation method.*—(i) *No effect on general asset account election.*—A change in the use described in §1.168(i)-4(d) (change in use results in a different recovery period or depreciation method) of an asset in a general asset account shall not cause or permit the revocation of the election made under this section.

(ii) *Asset is removed from the general asset account.*—Upon a change in the use described in §1.168(i)-4(d), the taxpayer must remove the asset from the general asset account as of the first day of the year of change (as defined in §1.168(i)-4(a)) and must make the adjustments to the general asset account described in paragraphs (e)(3)(iii)(C)(2) through (4) of this section. If, however, the result of the change in use is described in §1.168(i)-4(d)(3) (change in use results in a shorter recovery period or a more accelerated depreciation method) and the taxpayer elects to treat the asset as though the change in use had not occurred pursuant to §1.168(i)-4(d)(3)(ii), no adjustment is made to the general asset account upon the change in use.

(iii) *New general asset account is established.*—(A) *Change in use results in a shorter recovery period or a more accelerated depreciation method.*—If the result of the change in use is described in §1.168(i)-4(d)(3) (change in use results in a shorter recovery period or a more accelerated depreciation method) and adjustments to the

(C) Depreciation allowed for the asset disposed of for only the taxable year in which the disposition occurs if the taxpayer applies paragraph (e)(3)(iii) of this section to the disposition of the asset in a qualifying disposition, if the asset is disposed of in a transaction described in paragraph (e)(3)(v)(B) of this section (like-kind exchange or involuntary conversion), or if the asset is disposed of in a transaction described in paragraph (e)(3)(vii) of this section (anti-abuse rule).

(ii) *Formula for determining foreign source income, gain, or loss.*—The amount of ordinary income, gain, or loss recognized on the disposition that shall be treated as foreign source income, gain, or loss must be determined under the formula in this paragraph (f)(2)(ii). For purposes of this formula, the allowed depreciation deductions are determined for the applicable time period provided in paragraph (f)(2)(i) of this section. The formula is:

gain, or loss from the disposition of an asset, as determined under the formula in paragraph (f)(2)(ii) of this section, must be allocated and apportioned to the applicable separate category or categories under the formula in this paragraph (f)(3). For purposes of this formula, the allowed depreciation deductions are determined for the applicable time period provided in paragraph (f)(2)(i) of this section. The formula is:

general asset account are made pursuant to paragraph (h)(2)(ii) of this section, the taxpayer must establish a new general asset account for the asset in the year of change in accordance with the rules in paragraph (c) of this section, except that the adjusted depreciable basis of the asset as of the first day of the year of change is included in the general asset account. For purposes of paragraph (c)(2) of this section, the applicable depreciation method, recovery period, and convention are determined under §1.168(i)-4(d)(3)(i).

(B) *Change in use results in a longer recovery period or a slower depreciation method.*—If the result of the change in use is described in §1.168(i)-4(d)(4) (change in use results in a longer recovery period or a slower depreciation method), the taxpayer must establish a separate general asset account for the asset in the year of change in accordance with the rules in paragraph (c) of this section, except that the unadjusted depreciable basis of the asset, and the greater of the depreciation of the asset allowed or allowable in accordance with section 1016(a)(2), as of the first day of the year of change are included in the newly established general asset account. Consequently, this general asset account as of the first day of the year of change will have a beginning balance for both the unadjusted depreciable basis and the depreciation reserve of the general asset account. For purposes of paragraph (c)(2) of this section, the applicable depreciation method, recovery period, and convention are determined under §1.168(i)-4(d)(4)(ii).

(i) *Redetermination of basis.*—If, after the placed-in-service year, the unadjusted depreciable basis of an asset in a general asset account is redetermined due to a transaction other than that described in paragraph (g) of this section (for example, due to contingent purchase price or discharge of indebtedness), the taxpayer's election under paragraph (l) of this section for the asset also applies to the increase or decrease in basis resulting from the redetermination. For the taxable year in which the increase or decrease in basis occurs, the taxpayer must establish a new general asset account for the amount of the increase or decrease in basis in accordance with the rules in paragraph (c) of this section. For purposes of paragraph (c)(2) of this section, the applicable recovery period for the increase or decrease in basis is the recovery period of the asset remaining as of the beginning of the taxable year in which the increase or decrease in basis occurs, the applicable depreciation method and applicable convention for the increase or decrease in basis are the same depreciation method and convention applicable to the asset that applies for the taxable year in which the increase or decrease in basis occurs, and the increase or decrease in basis is deemed to be placed in service in the same taxable year as the asset.

(j) *Identification of disposed or converted asset.*—(1) *In general.*—The rules of this paragraph (j) apply when an asset in a general asset account is disposed of or converted in a transaction described in paragraph (e)(3)(iii) (disposition of an asset in a qualifying disposition), paragraph (e)(3)(iv)(B) (transactions subject to section 168(i)(7)), paragraph (e)(3)(v)(B) (transactions subject to section 1031 or section 1033), paragraph (e)(3)(vii) (anti-abuse rule), paragraph (g) (assets subject to recapture), or paragraph (h)(1) (conversion to any personal use) of this section.

(2) *Identifying which asset is disposed of or converted.*—(i) *In general.*—For purposes of identifying which asset in a general asset account is disposed of or converted, a taxpayer must identify the disposed of or converted asset by using—

(A) The specific identification method of accounting. Under this method of accounting, the taxpayer can determine the particular taxable year in which the disposed of or converted asset was placed in service by the taxpayer;

(B) A first-in, first-out method of accounting if the taxpayer can readily determine from its records the total dispositions of assets with the same recovery period during the taxable year but the taxpayer cannot readily determine from its records the unadjusted depreciable basis of the disposed of or converted asset. Under this method of accounting, the taxpayer identifies the general asset account with the earliest placed-in-service year that has the same recovery period as the disposed of or converted asset and that has assets at the beginning of the taxable year of the disposition or conversion, and the taxpayer treats the disposed of or converted asset as being from that general asset account. To determine which general asset account has assets at the beginning of the taxable year of the disposition or conversion, the taxpayer reduces the number of assets originally included in the account by the number of assets disposed of or converted in any prior taxable year in a transaction to which this paragraph (j) applies;

(C) A modified first-in, first-out method of accounting if the taxpayer can readily determine from its records the total dispositions of assets with the same recovery period during the taxable year and the unadjusted depreciable basis of the disposed of or converted asset. Under this method of accounting, the taxpayer identifies the general asset account with the earliest placed-in-service year that has the same recovery period as the disposed of or converted asset and that has assets at the beginning of the taxable year of the disposition or conversion with the same unadjusted depreciable basis as the disposed of or converted asset, and the taxpayer treats the disposed of or converted asset as being from that general asset account. To determine which general asset account has assets at the beginning of the taxable year of the disposition or conversion, the taxpayer reduces the number of assets originally included in the account by the number of assets disposed of or converted in any prior taxable year in a transaction to which this paragraph (j) applies;

(D) A mortality dispersion table if the asset is a mass asset accounted for in a separate general asset account in accordance with paragraph (c)(2)(ii)(H) of this section and if the taxpayer can readily determine from its records the total dispositions of assets with the same recovery period during the taxable year. The mortality dispersion table must be based upon an acceptable sampling of the taxpayer's actual disposition and conversion experience for mass assets or other acceptable statistical or engineering techniques. To use a mortality dispersion table, the taxpayer must adopt recordkeeping practices consistent with the taxpayer's prior practices and consonant with good accounting and engineering practices; or

(E) Any other method as the Secretary may designate by publication in the **Federal Register** or in the Internal Revenue Bulletin (see § 601.601(d)(2) of this chapter) on or after September 19, 2013. See paragraph (j)(2)(iii) of this section regarding the last-in, first-out method of accounting.

(ii) *Disposition of a portion of an asset.*—If a taxpayer disposes of a portion of an asset and paragraph (e)(1)(ii) of this section applies to that disposition, the taxpayer may identify the asset by using any applicable method provided in paragraph (j)(2)(i) of this section, after taking into account paragraph (j)(2)(iii) of this section.

(iii) *Last-in, first-out method of accounting.*—For purposes of paragraph (j)(2) of this section, a last-in, first-out method of accounting may not be used. Examples of a last-in, first-out method of accounting include the taxpayer identifying the general asset account with the most recent placed-in-service year that has the same recovery period as the disposed of or converted asset and that has assets at the beginning of the taxable year of the disposition or conversion, and the taxpayer treating the disposed of or converted asset as being from that general asset account, or the taxpayer treating the disposed portion of an asset as being from the general asset account with the

most recent placed-in-service year that has assets that are the same as the asset of which the disposed portion is a part.

(3) *Basis of disposed of or converted asset.*—(i) Solely for purposes of this paragraph (j)(3), the term *asset* is the asset as determined under paragraph (e)(2)(viii) of this section or the portion of such asset that is disposed of in a disposition described in paragraph (e)(1)(ii) of this section. After identifying which asset in a general asset account is disposed of or converted, the taxpayer must determine the unadjusted depreciable basis of, and the depreciation allowed or allowable for, the disposed of or converted asset. If it is impracticable from the taxpayer's records to determine the unadjusted depreciable basis of the disposed of or converted asset, the taxpayer may use any reasonable method that is consistently applied to all assets in the same general asset account for purposes of determining the unadjusted depreciable basis of the disposed of or converted asset in that general asset account. Examples of a reasonable method include, but are not limited to, the following:

(A) If the replacement asset is a restoration (as defined in § 1.263(a)-3(k)), and is not a betterment (as defined in § 1.263(a)-3(j)) or an adaptation to a new or different use (as defined in § 1.263(a)-3(l)), discounting the cost of the replacement asset to its placed-in-service year cost using the Producer Price Index for Finished Goods or its successor, the Producer Price Index for Final Demand, or any other index designated by guidance in the Internal Revenue Bulletin (see § 601.601(d)(2) of this chapter) for purposes of this paragraph (j)(3);

(B) A pro rata allocation of the unadjusted depreciable basis of the general asset account based on the replacement cost of the disposed asset and the replacement cost of all of the assets in the general asset account; and

(C) A study allocating the cost of the asset to its individual components.

(ii) The depreciation allowable for the disposed of or converted asset is computed by using the depreciation method, recovery period, and convention applicable to the general asset account in which the disposed of or converted asset was included and by including the additional first year depreciation deduction claimed for the disposed of or converted asset.

(k) *Effect of adjustments on prior dispositions.*—The adjustments to a general asset account under paragraph (e)(3)(iii), (e)(3)(iv), (e)(3)(v), (e)(3)(vii), (g), or (h) of this section have no effect on the recognition and character of prior dispositions subject to paragraph (e)(2) of this section.

(l) *Election.*—(1) *Irrevocable election.*—If a taxpayer makes an election under this paragraph (l), the taxpayer consents to, and agrees to apply, all of the provisions of this section to the assets included in a general asset account. Except as provided in paragraph (c)(1)(ii)(A), (e)(3), (g), or (h) of this section or except as otherwise expressly provided by other guidance published in the Internal Revenue Bulletin (see § 601.601(d)(2) of this chapter), an election made under this section is irrevocable and will be binding on the taxpayer for computing taxable income for the taxable year for which the election is made and for all subsequent taxable years. An election under this paragraph (l) is made separately by each person owning an asset to which this section applies (for example, by each member of a consolidated group, at the partnership level and not by the partner separately, or at the S corporation level and not by the shareholder separately).

(2) *Time for making election.*—The election to apply this section shall be made on the taxpayer's timely filed (including extensions) income tax return for the taxable year in which the assets included in the general asset account are placed in service by the taxpayer.

(3) *Manner of making election.*—In the year of election, a taxpayer makes the election under this section by typing or legibly printing at the top of the Form 4562, "GENERAL ASSET ACCOUNT ELECTION MADE UNDER SECTION 168(i)(4)," or in the manner provided for on Form 4562 and its instructions. The taxpayer shall maintain records (for example, "General Asset Account #1—all 1995 additions in asset class 00.11 for Salt Lake City, Utah facility") that identify the assets included in each general asset account, that establish the unadjusted depreciable basis and depreciation reserve of the general asset account, and that reflect the amount realized during the taxable year upon dispositions from each general asset account. (But see section 179(c) and § 1.179-5 for the recordkeeping requirements for section 179 property.) The taxpayer's recordkeeping practices should be consistently applied to the general asset accounts. If Form 4562 is revised or renumbered, any reference in this section to that form shall be treated as a reference to the revised or renumbered form.

(m) *Effective/applicability dates.*—(1) *In general.*—Except as provided in paragraph (m)(5) of this section, this section applies to taxable years beginning on or after January 1, 2014. Except as provided in paragraphs (m)(2), (m)(3), and (m)(4) of this section, §1.168(i)-1 as contained in 26 CFR part 1 edition revised as of April 1, 2011, applies to taxable years beginning before January 1, 2014.

(2) *Early application of this section.*—A taxpayer may choose to apply the provisions of this section to taxable years beginning on or after January 1, 2012.

(3) *Early application of regulation project REG-110732-13.*—A taxpayer may rely on the provisions of this section in regulation project REG-110732-13 (2013-43 IRB 404) (see §601.601(d)(2) of this chapter) for taxable years beginning on or after January 1, 2012. However, a taxpayer may not rely on the provisions of this section in regulation project REG-110732-13 for taxable years beginning on or after January 1, 2014.

(4) *Optional application of TD 9564.*—A taxpayer may choose to apply §1.168(i)-1T as contained in 26 CFR part 1 edition revised as of April 1, 2014, to taxable years beginning on or after January 1, 2012. However, a taxpayer may not apply §1.168(i)-1T as contained in 26 CFR part 1 edition revised as of April 1, 2014, to taxable years beginning on or after January 1, 2014.

(5) *Application of paragraph (e)(2)(viii)(A).*—The language "and the distinct asset determination under §1.1031(a)-3(a)(4) do not apply." in the last sentence of paragraph (e)(2)(viii)(A) of this section applies on or after December 2, 2020. Paragraph (e)(2)(viii)(A) of this section as contained in 26 CFR part 1 edition revised as of April 1, 2020, applies before December 2, 2020.

(6) *Change in method of accounting.*—A change to comply with this section for depreciable assets placed in service in a taxable year ending on or after December 30, 2003, is a change in method of accounting to which the provisions of section 446(e) and the regulations under section 446(e) apply. A taxpayer also may treat a change to comply with this section for depreciable assets placed in service in a taxable year ending before December 30, 2003, as a change in method of accounting to which the provisions of section 446(e) and the regulations under section 446(e) apply. This paragraph (m)(5) does not apply to a change to comply with paragraph (e)(3)(ii), (e)(3)(iii), or (l) of this section, except as otherwise expressly provided by other guidance published in the Internal Revenue Bulletin (see §601.601(d)(2) of this chapter). [Reg. §1.168(i)-1.]

☐ [T.D. 8566, 10-7-94. *Amended by T.D. 9115, 2-27-2004; T.D. 9132, 6-16-2004; T.D. 9314, 2-26-2007; T.D. 9564, 12-23-2011 (corrected 12-18-2012), T.D. 9689, 8-14-2014 (corrected 12-30-2014) and T.D. 9935, 11-30-2020.]*

[Reg. §1.168(i)-2]

§1.168(i)-2. Lease term.—(a) *In general.*—For purposes of section 168, a lease term is determined under all the facts and circumstances. Paragraph (b) of this section and §1.168(j)-1T, Q&A 17, describe certain circumstances that will result in a period of time not included in the stated duration of an original lease (additional period) nevertheless being included in the lease term. These rules do not prevent the inclusion of an additional period in the lease term in other circumstances.

(b) *Lessee retains financial obligation.*—(1) *In general.*—An additional period of time during which a lessee may not continue to be the lessee will nevertheless be included in the lease term if the lessee (or a related person)—

(i) Has agreed that one or both of them will or could be obligated to make a payment of rent or a payment in the nature of rent with respect to such period; or

(ii) Has assumed or retained any risk of loss with respect to the property for such period (including, for example, by holding a note secured by the property).

(2) *Payments in the nature of rent.*—For purposes of paragraph (b)(1)(i) of this section, a payment in the nature of rent includes a payment intended to substitute for rent or to fund or supplement the rental payments of another. For example, a payment in the nature of rent includes a payment of any kind (whether denominated as supplemental rent, as liquidated damages, or otherwise) that is required to be made in the event that—

(i) The leased property is not leased for the additional period;

(ii) The leased property is leased for the additional period under terms that do not satisfy specified terms and conditions;

(iii) There is a failure to make a payment of rent with respect to such additional period; or

(iv) Circumstances similar to those described in paragraph (b)(2)(i), (ii), or (iii) of this section occur.

(3) *De minimis rule.*—For the purposes of this paragraph (b), obligations to make de minimis payments will be disregarded.

(c) *Multiple leases or subleases.*—If property is subject to more than one lease (including any sublease) entered into as part of a single transaction (or a series of related transactions), the lease term includes all periods described in one or more of such leases. For example, if one taxable corporation leases property to another taxable corporation for a 20-year term and, as part of the same transaction, the lessee subleases the property to a tax-exempt entity for a 10-year term, then the lease term of the property for purposes of section 168 is 20 years. During the period of tax-exempt use, the property must be depreciated under the alternative depreciation system using the straight line method over the greater of its class life or 25 years (125 percent of the 20-year lease term).

(d) *Related person.*—For purposes of paragraph (b) of this section, a person is related to the lessee if such person is described in section 168(h)(4).

(e) *Changes in status.*—Section 168(i)(5) (changes in status) applies if an additional period is included in a lease term under this section and the leased property ceases to be tax-exempt use property for such additional period.

(f) *Example.*—The following example illustrates the principles of this section. The example does not address common law doctrines or other authorities that may apply to cause an additional period to be included in the lease term or to recharacterize a lease as a conditional sale or otherwise for federal income tax purposes. Unless otherwise indicated, parties to the transactions are not related to one another.

Example. Financial obligation with respect to an additional period—(i) *Facts.* X, a taxable corporation, and Y, a foreign airline whose income is not subject to United States taxation, enter into a lease agreement under which X agrees to lease an aircraft to Y for a period of 10 years. The lease agreement provides that, at the end of the lease period, Y is obligated to find a subsequent lessee (replacement lessee) to enter into a subsequent lease (replacement lease) of the aircraft from X for an additional 10-year period. The provisions of the lease agreement require that any replacement lessee be unrelated to Y and that it not be a tax-exempt entity as defined in section 168(h)(2). The provisions of the lease agreement also set forth the basic terms and conditions of the replacement lease, including its duration and the required rental payments. In the event Y fails to secure a replacement lease, the lease agreement requires Y to make a payment to X in an amount determined under the lease agreement.

(ii) *Application of this section.* The lease agreement between X and Y obligates Y to make a payment in the event the aircraft is not leased for the period commencing after the initial 10-year lease period and ending on the date the replacement lease is scheduled to end. Accordingly, pursuant to paragraph (b) of this section, the term of the lease between X and Y includes such additional period, and the lease term is 20 years for purposes of section 168.

(iii) *Facts modified.* Assume the same facts as in paragraph (i) of this *Example*, except that Y is required to guarantee the payment of rentals under the 10-year replacement lease and to make a payment to X equal to the present value of any excess of the replacement lease rental payments specified in the lease agreement between X and Y, over the rental payments actually agreed to be paid by the replacement lessee. Pursuant to paragraph (b) of this section, the term of the lease between X and Y includes the additional period, and the lease term is 20 years for purposes of section 168.

(iv) *Changes in status.* If, upon the conclusion of the stated duration of the lease between X and Y, the aircraft either is returned to X or leased to a replacement lessee that is not a tax-exempt entity as defined in section 168(h)(2), the subsequent method of depreciation will be determined pursuant to section 168(i)(5).

(g) *Effective date.*—(1) *In general.*—Except as provided in paragraph (g)(2) of this section, this section applies to leases entered into on or after April 20, 1995.

(2) *Special rules.*—Paragraphs (b)(1)(ii) and (c) of this section apply to leases entered into after April 26, 1996. [Reg. §1.168(i)-2.]

☐ [T.D. 8667, 4-26-96.]

[Reg. §1.168(i)-3]

§1.168(i)-3. Treatment of excess deferred income tax reserve upon disposition of deregulated public utility property.—(a) *Scope.*—(1) *In general.*—This section provides rules for the application of section 203(e) of the Tax Reform Act of 1986, Public Law 99-514 (100 Stat. 2146) to a taxpayer with respect to public utility property (within the meaning of section 168(i)(10)) that ceases, whether by disposition, deregulation, or otherwise, to be public utility property with respect to the taxpayer and that is not described in paragraph (a)(2) of this section (deregulated public utility property).

(2) *Exceptions.*—This section does not apply to the following property:

(i) Property that ceases to be public utility property with respect to the taxpayer on account of an ordinary retirement within the meaning of § 1.167(a)-11(d)(3)(ii).

(ii) Property transferred by the taxpayer if after the transfer the property is public utility property of the transferee and the taxpayer's excess tax reserve with respect to the property (within the meaning of section 203(e) of the Tax Reform Act of 1986) is treated as an excess tax reserve of the transferee with respect to the property.

(b) *Amount of reduction.*—If public utility property of a taxpayer becomes deregulated public utility property to which this section applies, the reduction in the taxpayer(s excess tax reserve permitted under section 203(e) of the Tax Reform Act of 1986 is equal to the amount by which the reserve could be reduced under that provision if all such property had remained public utility property of the taxpayer and the taxpayer had continued use of its normalization method of accounting with respect to such property.

(c) *Cross reference.*—See § 1.46-6(k) for rules relating to the treatment of accumulated deferred investment tax credits when utilities dispose of regulated public utility property.

(d) *Effective/applicability dates.*—(1) *In general.*—Except as provided in paragraph (d)(2) of this section, this section applies to public utility property that becomes deregulated public utility property after December 21, 2005.

(2) *Property that becomes public utility property of the transferee.*—This section does not apply to property that becomes deregulated public utility property with respect to a taxpayer an account of a transfer on or before March 20, 2008, if after the transfer the property is public utility property of the transferee.

(3) *Application of regulation project (REG-104385-01).*—A reduction in the taxpayer's excess deferred income tax reserve will be treated as ratable if it is consistent with the proposed rules in regulation project (REG-104385-01) (68 FR 10190) March 4, 2003, and occurs during the period beginning on March 5, 2003, and ending on the earlier of—

(i) The last date on which the utility's rates are determined under the rate order in effect on December 21, 2005; or

(ii) December 21, 2007. [Reg. § 1.168(i)-3.]

□ [*T.D.* 9387, 3-19-2008.]

[Reg. § 1.168(i)-4]

§ 1.168(i)-4. Changes in use.—(a) *Scope.*—This section provides the rules for determining the depreciation allowance for MACRS property (as defined in § 1.168(b)-1T(a)(2)) for which the use changes in the hands of the same taxpayer (change in the use). The allowance for depreciation under this section constitutes the amount of depreciation allowable under section 167(a) for the year of change and any subsequent taxable year. For purposes of this section, the year of change is the taxable year in which a change in the use occurs.

(b) *Conversion to business or income-producing use.*—(1) *Depreciation deduction allowable.*—This paragraph (b) applies to property that is converted from personal use to use in a taxpayer's trade or business, or for the production of income, during a taxable year. This conversion includes property that was previously used by the taxpayer for personal purposes, including real property (other than land) that is acquired before 1987 and converted from personal use to business or income-producing use after 1986, and depreciable property that was previously used by a tax-exempt entity before the entity changed to a taxable entity. Except as otherwise provided by the Internal Revenue Code or regulations under the Internal Revenue Code, upon a conversion to business or income-producing use, the depreciation allowance for the year of change and any subsequent taxable year is determined as though the property is placed in service by the taxpayer on the date on which the conversion occurs. Thus, except as otherwise provided by the Internal Revenue Code or regulations under the Internal Revenue Code, the taxpayer must use any applicable depreciation method, recovery period, and convention prescribed under section 168 for the property in the year of change, consistent with any election made under section 168 by the taxpayer for that year (see, for example, section 168(b)(5)). See § 1.168(k)-1(f)(6)(iii) or 1.168(k)-2(g)(6)(iii), as applicable, and § 1.1400L(b)-1(f)(6) for the additional first year depreciation deduction rules applicable to a conversion to business or income-producing use. The depreciable basis of the property for the year of change is the lesser of its fair market value or its adjusted depreciable basis (as defined in § 1.168(b)-1T(a)(4)), as applicable, at the time of the conversion to business or income-producing use.

(2) *Example.*—The application of this paragraph (b) is illustrated by the following example:

Example. A, a calendar-year taxpayer, purchases a house in 1985 that she occupies as her principal residence. In February 2004, A ceases to occupy the house and converts it to residential rental property. At the time of the conversion to residential rental property, the house's fair market value (excluding land) is $130,000 and adjusted depreciable basis attributable to the house (excluding land) is $150,000. Pursuant to this paragraph (b), A is considered to have placed in service residential rental property in February 2004 with a depreciable basis of $130,000. A depreciates the residential rental property under the general depreciation system by using the straight-line method, a 27.5-year recovery period, and the mid-month convention. Pursuant to § § 1.168(k)-1T(f)(6)(iii)(B) or 1.1400L(b)-1T(f)(6), this property is not eligible for the additional first year depreciation deduction provided by section 168(k) or section 1400L(b). Thus, the depreciation allowance for the house for 2004 is $4,137, after taking into account the mid-month convention (($130,000 adjusted depreciable basis multiplied by the applicable depreciation rate of 3.636% (1/27.5)) multiplied by the mid-month convention fraction of 10.5/12). The amount of depreciation computed under section 168, however, may be limited under other provisions of the Internal Revenue Code, such as, section 280A.

(c) *Conversion to personal use.*—The conversion of MACRS property from business or income-producing use to personal use during a taxable year is treated as a disposition of the property in that taxable year. The depreciation allowance for MACRS property for the year of change in which the property is treated as being disposed of is determined by first multiplying the adjusted depreciable basis of the property as of the first day of the year of change by the applicable depreciation rate for that taxable year (for further guidance, for example, see section 6 of Rev. Proc. 87-57 (1987-2 C. B. 687, 692) (see § 601.601(d)(2)(ii)(*b*) of this chapter)). This amount is then multiplied by a fraction, the numerator of which is the number of months (including fractions of months) the property is deemed to be placed in service during the year of change (taking into account the applicable convention) and the denominator of which is 12. No depreciation deduction is allowable for MACRS property placed in service and disposed of in the same taxable year. See § 1.168(k)-1(f)(6)(ii) or 1.168(k)-2(g)(6)(ii), as applicable, and § 1.1400L(b)-1(f)(6) for the additional first year depreciation deduction rules applicable to property placed in service and converted to personal use in the same taxable year. Upon the conversion to personal use, no gain, loss, or depreciation recapture under section 1245 or section 1250 is recognized. However, the provisions of section 1245 or section 1250 apply to any disposition of the converted property by the taxpayer at a later date. For listed property (as defined in section 280F(d)(4)), see section 280F(b)(2) for the recapture of excess depreciation upon the conversion to personal use.

(d) *Change in the use results in a different recovery period and/or depreciation method.*—(1) *In general.*—This paragraph (d) applies to a change in the use of MACRS property during a taxable year subsequent to the placed-in-service year, if the property continues to be MACRS property owned by the same taxpayer and, as a result of the change in the use, has a different recovery period, a different depreciation method, or both. For example, this paragraph (d) applies to MACRS property that—

(i) Begins or ceases to be used predominantly outside the United States;

(ii) Results in a reclassification of the property under section 168(e) due to a change in the use of the property; or

(iii) Begins or ceases to be tax-exempt use property (as defined in section 168(h)).

(2) *Determination of change in the use.*—(i) *In general.*—Except as provided in paragraph (d)(2)(ii) of this section, a change in the use of MACRS property occurs when the primary use of the MACRS property in the taxable year is different from its primary use in the immediately preceding taxable year. The primary use of MACRS property may be determined in any reasonable manner that is consistently applied to the taxpayer's MACRS property.

(ii) *Alternative depreciation system property.*—(A) *Property used within or outside the United States.*—A change in the use of MACRS property occurs when a taxpayer begins or ceases to use MACRS property predominantly outside the United States during the taxable year. The determination of whether MACRS property is used predominantly outside the United States is made in accordance with the test in § 1.48-1(g)(1)(i) for determining predominant use.

(B) *Tax-exempt bond financed property.*—A change in the use of MACRS property occurs when the property changes to tax-exempt bond financed property, as described in section 168(g)(1)(C) and (g)(5), during the taxable year. For purposes of this paragraph (d),

MACRS property changes to tax-exempt bond financed property when a tax-exempt bond is first issued after the MACRS property is placed in service. MACRS property continues to be tax-exempt bond financed property in the hands of the taxpayer even if the tax-exempt bond (including any refunding issue) is no longer outstanding or is redeemed.

(C) *Other mandatory alternative depreciation system property.*— A change in the use of MACRS property occurs when the property changes to, or changes from, property described in section 168(g)(1)(B) (tax-exempt use property) or (D) (imported property covered by an Executive order) during the taxable year.

(iii) *Change in the use deemed to occur on first day of the year of change.*—If a change in the use of MACRS property occurs under this paragraph (d)(2), the depreciation allowance for that MACRS property for the year of change is determined as though the use of the MACRS property changed on the first day of the year of change.

(3) *Change in the use results in a shorter recovery period and/or a more accelerated depreciation method.*—(i) *Treated as placed in service in the year of change.*—(A) *In general.*—If a change in the use results in the MACRS property changing to a shorter recovery period and/or a depreciation method that is more accelerated than the method used for the MACRS property before the change in the use, the depreciation allowances beginning in the year of change are determined as though the MACRS property is placed in service by the taxpayer in the year of change.

(B) *Computation of depreciation allowance.*—The depreciation allowances for the MACRS property for any 12-month taxable year beginning with the year of change are determined by multiplying the adjusted depreciable basis of the MACRS property as of the first day of each taxable year by the applicable depreciation rate for each taxable year. In determining the applicable depreciation rate for the year of change and subsequent taxable years, the taxpayer must use any applicable depreciation method and recovery period prescribed under section 168 for the MACRS property in the year of change, consistent with any election made under section 168 by the taxpayer for that year (see, for example, section 168(b)(5)). If there is a change in the use of MACRS property, the applicable convention that applies to the MACRS property is the same as the convention that applied before the change in the use of the MACRS property. However, the depreciation allowance for the year of change for the MACRS property is determined without applying the applicable convention, unless the MACRS property is disposed of during the year of change. See paragraph (d)(5) of this section for the rules relating to the computation of the depreciation allowance under the optional depreciation tables. If the year of change or any subsequent taxable year is less than 12 months, the depreciation allowance determined under this paragraph (d)(3)(i) must be adjusted for a short taxable year (for further guidance, for example, see Rev. Proc. 89-15 (1989-1 C.B. 816) (see § 601.601(d)(2)(ii)(*b*) of this chapter)).

(C) *Special rules.*—MACRS property affected by this paragraph (d)(3)(i) is not eligible in the year of change for the election provided under section 168(f)(1), 179, or 1400L(f), or for the additional first year depreciation deduction provided in section 168(k) or 1400L(b). See § 1.168(k)-1(f)(6)(iv) or 1.168(k)-2(g)(6)(iv), as applicable, and § 1.400(b)-1(f)(6) for other additional first year depreciation deduction rules applicable to a change in the use of MACRS property subsequent to its placed-in-service year. For purposes of determining whether the mid-quarter convention applies to other MACRS property placed in service during the year of change, the unadjusted depreciable basis (as defined in § 1.168(b)-1T(a)(3)) or the adjusted depreciable basis of MACRS property affected by this paragraph (d)(3)(i) is not taken into account.

(ii) *Option to disregard the change in the use.*—In lieu of applying paragraph (d)(3)(i) of this section, the taxpayer may elect to determine the depreciation allowance as though the change in the use had not occurred. The taxpayer elects this option by claiming on the taxpayer's timely filed (including extensions) Federal income tax return for the year of change the depreciation allowance for the property as though the change in the use had not occurred. See paragraph (g)(2) of this section for the manner for revoking this election.

(4) *Change in the use results in a longer recovery period and/or a slower depreciation method.*—(i) *Treated as originally placed in service with longer recovery period and/or slower depreciation method.*—If a change in the use results in a longer recovery period and/or a depreciation method for the MACRS property that is less accelerated than the method used for the MACRS property before the change in the use, the depreciation allowances beginning with the year of change are determined as though the MACRS property had been originally placed in service by the taxpayer with the longer recovery period and/or the slower depreciation method. MACRS property affected by this paragraph (d)(4) is not eligible in the year of change for the election provided under section 168(f)(1), 179, or 1400L(f), or for the additional first year depreciation deduction provided in section 168(k) or 1400L(b). See § 1.168(k)-1(f)(6)(iv) or 1.168(k)-2(g)(6)(iv), as applicable, and § 1.400L(b)-1(f)(6) for other additional first year depreciation deduction rules applicable to a change in the use of MACRS property subsequent to its placed-in-service year.

(ii) *Computation of the depreciation allowance.*—The depreciation allowances for the MACRS property for any 12-month taxable year beginning with the year of change are determined by multiplying the adjusted depreciable basis of the MACRS property as of the first day of each taxable year by the applicable depreciation rate for each taxable year. If there is a change in the use of MACRS property, the applicable convention that applies to the MACRS property is the same as the convention that applied before the change in the use of the MACRS property. If the year of change or any subsequent taxable year is less than 12 months, the depreciation allowance determined under this paragraph (d)(4)(ii) must be adjusted for a short taxable year (for further guidance, for example, see Rev. Proc. 89-15 (1989-1 C.B. 816) (see § 601.601(d)(2)(ii)(*b*) of this chapter)). See paragraph (d)(5) of this section for the rules relating to the computation of the depreciation allowance under the optional depreciation tables. In determining the applicable depreciation rate for the year of change and any subsequent taxable year—

(A) The applicable depreciation method is the depreciation method that would apply in the year of change and any subsequent taxable year for the MACRS property had the taxpayer used the longer recovery period and/or the slower depreciation method in the placed-in-service year of the property. If the 200- or 150-percent declining balance method would have applied in the placed-in-service year but the method would have switched to the straight line method in the year of change or any prior taxable year, the applicable depreciation method beginning with the year of change is the straight line method; and

(B) The applicable recovery period is either—

(1) The longer recovery period resulting from the change in the use if the applicable depreciation method is the 200- or 150-percent declining balance method (as determined under paragraph (d)(4)(ii)(A) of this section) unless the recovery period did not change as a result of the change in the use, in which case the applicable recovery period is the same recovery period that applied before the change in the use; or

(2) The number of years remaining as of the beginning of each taxable year (taking into account the applicable convention) had the taxpayer used the longer recovery period in the placed-in-service year of the property if the applicable depreciation method is the straight line method (as determined under paragraph (d)(4)(ii)(A) of this section) unless the recovery period did not change as a result of the change in the use, in which case the applicable recovery period is the number of years remaining as of the beginning of each taxable year (taking into account the applicable convention) based on the recovery period that applied before the change in the use.

(5) *Using optional depreciation tables.*—(i) *Taxpayer not bound by prior use of table.*—If a taxpayer used an optional depreciation table for the MACRS property before a change in the use, the taxpayer is not bound to use the appropriate new table for that MACRS property beginning in the year of change (for further guidance, for example, see section 8 of Rev. Proc. 87-57 (1987-2 C.B. 687, 693) (see § 601.601(d)(2)(ii)(*b*) of this chapter)). If a taxpayer did not use an optional depreciation table for MACRS property before a change in the use and the change in the use results in a shorter recovery period and/or a more accelerated depreciation method (as described in paragraph (d)(3)(i) of this section), the taxpayer may use the appropriate new table for that MACRS property beginning in the year of change. If a taxpayer chooses not to use the optional depreciation table, the depreciation allowances for the MACRS property beginning in the year of change are determined under paragraph (d)(3)(i) or (4) of this section, as applicable.

(ii) *Taxpayer chooses to use optional depreciation table after a change in the use.*—If a taxpayer chooses to use an optional depreciation table for the MACRS property after a change in the use, the depreciation allowances for the MACRS property for any 12-month taxable year beginning with the year of change are determined as follows:

(A) *Change in the use results in a shorter recovery period and/or a more accelerated depreciation method.*—If a change in the use results in a shorter recovery period and/or a more accelerated depreciation method (as described in paragraph (d)(3)(i) of this section), the depreciation allowances for the MACRS property for any 12-month taxable year beginning with the year of change are determined by multiplying the adjusted depreciable basis of the MACRS property as of the first day of the year of change by the annual depreciation rate for each recovery year (expressed as a decimal equivalent) specified in the appropriate optional depreciation table. The appropriate optional depreciation table for the MACRS property is based on the depreciation system, depreciation method, recovery period, and convention applicable to the MACRS property in the year of change as determined under paragraph (d)(3)(i) of this section. The depreciation allowance for the year of change for the MACRS property is determined by taking into account the applicable convention (which is already factored into the optional depreciation tables). If the year of change or any subsequent taxable year is less than 12 months, the depreciation allowance determined under this paragraph (d)(5)(ii)(A) must be adjusted for a short taxable year (for further guidance, for example, see Rev. Proc. 89-15 (1989-1 C.B. 816) (see § 601.601(d)(2)(ii)(b) of this chapter)).

(B) *Change in the use results in a longer recovery period and/or a slower depreciation method.*—(1) *Determination of the appropriate optional depreciation table.*—If a change in the use results in a longer recovery period and/or a slower depreciation method (as described in paragraph (d)(4)(i) of this section), the depreciation allowances for the MACRS property for any 12-month taxable year beginning with the year of change are determined by choosing the optional depreciation table that corresponds to the depreciation system, depreciation method, recovery period, and convention that would have applied to the MACRS property in the placed-in-service year had that property been originally placed in service by the taxpayer with the longer recovery period and/or the slower depreciation method. If there is a change in the use of MACRS property, the applicable convention that applies to the MACRS property is the same as the convention that applied before the change in the use of the MACRS property. If the year of change or any subsequent taxable year is less than 12 months, the depreciation allowance determined under this paragraph (d)(5)(ii)(B) must be adjusted for a short taxable year (for further guidance, for example, see Rev. Proc. 89-15 (1989-1 C.B. 816) (see § 601.601(d)(2)(ii)(b) of this chapter)).

(2) *Computation of the depreciation allowance.*—The depreciation allowances for the MACRS property for any 12-month taxable year beginning with the year of change are computed by first determining the appropriate recovery year in the table identified under paragraph (d)(5)(ii)(B)(1) of this section. The appropriate recovery year for the year of change is the year that corresponds to the year of change. For example, if the recovery year for the year of change would have been Year 4 in the table that applied before the change in the use of the MACRS property, then the recovery year for the year of change is Year 4 in the table identified under paragraph (d)(5)(ii)(B)(1) of this section. Next, the annual depreciation rate (expressed as a decimal equivalent) for each recovery year is multiplied by a transaction coefficient. The transaction coefficient is the formula (1 / (1 - x)) where x equals the sum of the annual depreciation rates from the table identified under paragraph (d)(5)(ii)(B)(1) of this section (expressed as a decimal equivalent) for the taxable years beginning with the placed-in-service year of the MACRS property through the taxable year immediately prior to the year of change. The product of the annual depreciation rate and the transaction coefficient is multiplied by the adjusted depreciable basis of the MACRS property as of the beginning of the year of change.

(6) *Examples.*—The application of this paragraph (d) is illustrated by the following examples:

Example 1. Change in the use results in a shorter recovery period and/ or a more accelerated depreciation method and optional depreciation table is not used—(i) X, a calendar-year corporation, places in service in 1999 equipment at a cost of $100,000 and uses this equipment from 1999 through 2003 primarily in its *A* business. X depreciates the equipment for 1999 through 2003 under the general depreciation system as 7-year property by using the 200-percent declining balance method (which switched to the straight-line method in 2003), a 7-year recovery period, and a half-year convention. Beginning in 2004, X primarily uses the equipment in its *B* business. As a result, the classification of the equipment under section 168(e) changes from 7-year property to 5-year property and the recovery period of the equipment under the general depreciation system changes from 7 years to 5 years. The depreciation method does not change. On January 1, 2004, the adjusted depreciable basis of the equipment is $22,311. X depreciates its 5-year recovery property placed in service in 2004 under the general depreciation system by using the 200-percent declining balance method and a 5-year recovery period. X does not use the optional depreciation tables.

(ii) Under paragraph (d)(3)(i) of this section, X's allowable depreciation deduction for the equipment for 2004 and subsequent taxable years is determined as though X placed the equipment in service in 2004 for use primarily in its *B* business. The depreciable basis of the equipment as of January 1, 2004, is $22,311 (the adjusted depreciable basis at January 1, 2004). Because X does not use the optional depreciation tables, the depreciation allowance for 2004 (the deemed placed-in-service year) for this equipment only is computed without taking into account the half-year convention. Pursuant to paragraph (d)(3)(i)(C) of this section, this equipment is not eligible for the additional first year depreciation deduction provided by section 168(k) or section 1400L(b). Thus, X's allowable depreciation deduction for the equipment for 2004 is $8,924 ($22,311 adjusted depreciable basis at January 1, 2004, multiplied by the applicable depreciation rate of 40% (200/5)). X's allowable depreciation deduction for the equipment for 2005 is $5,355 ($13,387 adjusted depreciable basis at January 1, 2005, multiplied by the applicable depreciation rate of 40% (200/5)).

(iii) Alternatively, under paragraph (d)(3)(ii) of this section, X may elect to disregard the change in the use and, as a result, may continue to treat the equipment as though it is used primarily in its *A* business. If the election is made, X's allowable depreciation deduction for the equipment for 2004 is $8,924 ($22,311 adjusted depreciable basis at January 1, 2004, multiplied by the applicable depreciation rate of 40% (1/2.5 years remaining at January 1, 2004)). X's allowable depreciation deduction for the equipment for 2005 is $8,925 ($13,387 adjusted depreciable basis at January 1, 2005, multiplied by the applicable depreciation rate of 66.67% (1/1.5 years remaining at January 1, 2005)).

Example 2. Change in the use results in a shorter recovery period and/ or a more accelerated depreciation method and optional depreciation table is used—(i) Same facts as in *Example 1*, except that X used the optional depreciation tables for computing depreciation for 1999 through 2003. Pursuant to paragraph (d)(5) of this section, X chooses to continue to use the optional depreciation table for the equipment. X does not make the election provided in paragraph (d)(3)(ii) of this section to disregard the change in use.

(ii) In accordance with paragraph (d)(5)(ii)(A) of this section, X must first identify the appropriate optional depreciation table for the equipment. This table is table 1 in Rev. Proc. 87-57 because the equipment will be depreciated in the year of change (2004) under the general depreciation system using the 200-percent declining balance method, a 5-year recovery period, and the half-year convention (which is the convention that applied to the equipment in 1999). Pursuant to paragraph (d)(3)(i)(C) of this section, this equipment is not eligible for the additional first year depreciation deduction provided by section 168(k) or section 1400L(b). For 2004, X multiplies its adjusted depreciable basis in the equipment as of January 1, 2004, of $22,311, by the annual depreciation rate in table 1 for recovery year 1 for a 5-year recovery period (.20), to determine the depreciation allowance of $4,462. For 2005, X multiplies its adjusted depreciable basis in the equipment as of January 1, 2004, of $22,311, by the annual depreciation rate in table 1 for recovery year 2 for a 5-year recovery period (.32), to determine the depreciation allowance of $7,140.

Example 3. Change in the use results in a longer recovery period and/or a slower depreciation method—(i) Y, a calendar-year corporation, places in service in January 2002, equipment at a cost of $100,000 and uses this equipment in 2002 and 2003 only within the United States. Y elects to deduct the additional first year depreciation under section 168(k). Y depreciates the equipment for 2002 and 2003 under the general depreciation system by using the 200-percent declining balance method, a 5-year recovery period, and a half-year convention. Beginning in 2004, Y uses the equipment predominantly outside the United States. As a result of this change in the use, the equipment is subject to the alternative depreciation system beginning in 2004. Under the alternative depreciation system, the equipment is depreciated by using the straight line method and a 9-year recovery period. The adjusted depreciable basis of the equipment at January 1, 2004, is $48,000.

(ii) Pursuant to paragraph (d)(4) of this section, Y's allowable depreciation deduction for 2004 and subsequent taxable years is determined as though the equipment had been placed in service in January 2002, as property used predominantly outside the United States. Further, pursuant to paragraph (d)(4)(i) of this section, the equipment is not eligible in 2004 for the additional first year depreciation deduction provided by section 168(k) or section 1400L(b). In determining the applicable depreciation rate for 2004, the applicable depreciation method is the straight line method and the applicable recovery period is 7.5 years, which is the number of years remaining at January 1, 2004, for property placed in service in 2002 with a 9-year recovery period (taking into account the half-year convention). Thus, the depreciation allowance for 2004 is $6,398 ($48,000 adjusted depreciable basis at January 1, 2004, multiplied by the applicable depreciation rate of 13.33% (1/7.5 years)). The depreciation allowance for 2005 is $6,398 ($41,602 adjusted depreciable basis at January 1, 2005, multiplied by the applicable depreciation rate of 15.38% (1/6.5 years remaining at January 1, 2005)).

Example 4. Change in the use results in a longer recovery period and/or a slower depreciation method and optional depreciation table is used—(i) Same facts as in *Example 3*, except that Y used the optional depreciation tables for computing depreciation in 2002 and 2003. Pursuant to paragraph (d)(5) of this section, Y chooses to continue to use the optional depreciation table for the equipment. Further, pursuant to paragraph (d)(4)(i) of this section, the equipment is not eligible in 2004 for the additional first year depreciation deduction provided by section 168(k) or section 1400L(b).

(ii) In accordance with paragraph (d)(5)(ii)(B) of this section, Y must first determine the appropriate optional depreciation table for the equipment pursuant to paragraph (d)(5)(ii)(B)(*1*) of this section. This table is table 8 in Rev. Proc. 87-57, which corresponds to the alternative depreciation system, the straight line method, a 9-year recovery period, and the half-year convention (because Y depreciated 5-year property in 2002 using a half-year convention). Next, Y must determine the appropriate recovery year in table 8. Because the year of change is 2004, the depreciation allowance for the equipment for 2004 is determined using recovery year 3 of table 8. For 2004, Y multiplies its adjusted depreciable basis in the equipment as of January 1, 2004, of $48,000, by the product of the annual depreciation rate in table 8 for recovery year 3 for a 9-year recovery period (.1111) and the transaction coefficient of 1.200 [1´/(1-(.0556 (table 8 for recovery year 1 for a 9-year recovery period) +.1111 (table 8 for recovery year 2 for a 9-year recovery period)))], to determine the depreciation allowance of $6,399. For 2005, Y multiplies its adjusted depreciable basis in the equipment as of January 1, 2004, of $48,000, by the product of the annual depreciation rate in table 8 for recovery year 4 for a 9-year recovery period (.1111) and the transaction coefficient (1.200), to determine the depreciation allowance of $6,399.

(e) *Change in the use of MACRS property during the placed-in-service year.*—(1) *In general.*—Except as provided in paragraph (e)(2) of this section, if a change in the use of MACRS property occurs during the placed-in-service year and the property continues to be MACRS property owned by the same taxpayer, the depreciation allowance for that property for the placed-in-service year is determined by its primary use during that year. The primary use of MACRS property may be determined in any reasonable manner that is consistently applied to the taxpayer's MACRS property. For purposes of this paragraph (e), the determination of whether the mid-quarter convention applies to any MACRS property placed in service during the year of change is made in accordance with § 1.168(d)-1.

(2) *Alternative depreciation system property.*—(i) *Property used within and outside the United States.*—The depreciation allowance for the placed-in-service year for MACRS property that is used within and outside the United States is determined by its predominant use during that year. The determination of whether MACRS property is used predominantly outside the United States during the placed-in-service year shall be made in accordance with the test in § 1.48-1(g)(1)(i) for determining predominant use.

(ii) *Tax-exempt bond financed property.*—The depreciation allowance for the placed-in-service year for MACRS property that changes to tax-exempt bond financed property, as described in section 168(g)(1)(C) and (g)(5), during that taxable year is determined under the alternative depreciation system. For purposes of this paragraph (e), MACRS property changes to tax-exempt bond financed property when a tax-exempt bond is first issued after the MACRS property is placed in service. MACRS property continues to be tax-exempt bond financed property in the hands of the taxpayer even if the tax-exempt bond (including any refunding issue) is not outstanding at, or is redeemed by, the end of the placed-in-service year.

(iii) *Other mandatory alternative depreciation system property.*— The depreciation allowance for the placed-in-service year for MACRS property that changes to, or changes from, property described in section 168(g)(1)(B) (tax-exempt use property) or (D) (imported property covered by an Executive order) during that taxable year is determined under—

(A) The alternative depreciation system if the MACRS property is described in section 168(g)(1)(B) or (D) at the end of the placed-in-service year; or

(B) The general depreciation system if the MACRS property is not described in section 168(g)(1)(B) or (D) at the end of the placed-in-service year, unless other provisions of the Internal Revenue Code or regulations under the Internal Revenue Code require the depreciation allowance for that MACRS property to be determined under the alternative depreciation system (for example, section 168(g)(7)).

(3) *Examples.*—The application of this paragraph (e) is illustrated by the following examples:

Example 1. (i) Z, a utility and calendar-year corporation, acquires and places in service on January 1, 2004, equipment at a cost of $100,000. Z uses this equipment in its combustion turbine production plant for 4 months and then uses the equipment in its steam production plant for the remainder of 2004. Z's combustion turbine production plant assets are classified as 15-year property and are depreciated by Z under the general depreciation system using a 15-year recovery period and the 150-percent declining balance method of depreciation. Z's steam production plant assets are classified as 20-year property and are depreciated by Z under the general depreciation system using a 20-year recovery period and the 150-percent declining balance method of depreciation. Z uses the optional depreciation tables. The equipment is 50-percent bonus depreciation property for purposes of section 168(k).

(ii) Pursuant to this paragraph (e), Z must determine depreciation based on the primary use of the equipment during the placed-in-service year. Z has consistently determined the primary use of all of its MACRS properties by comparing the number of full months in the taxable year during which a MACRS property is used in one manner with the number of full months in that taxable year during which that MACRS property is used in another manner. Applying this approach, Z determines the depreciation allowance for the equipment for 2004 is based on the equipment being classified as 20-year property because the equipment was used by Z in its steam production plant for 8 months in 2004. If the half-year convention applies in 2004, the appropriate optional depreciation table is table 1 in Rev. Proc. 87-57, which is the table for MACRS property subject to the general depreciation system, the 150-percent declining balance method, a 20-year recovery period, and the half-year convention. Thus, the depreciation allowance for the equipment for 2004 is $51,875, which is the total of $50,000 for the 50-percent additional first year depreciation deduction allowable (the unadjusted depreciable basis of $100,000 multiplied by .50), plus $1,875 for the 2004 depreciation allowance on the remaining adjusted depreciable basis of $50,000 [(the unadjusted depreciable basis of $100,000 less the additional first year depreciation deduction of $50,000) multiplied by the annual depreciation rate of .0375 in table 1 for recovery year 1 for a 20-year recovery period].

Example 2. T, a calendar year corporation, places in service on January 1, 2004, several computers at a total cost of $100,000. T uses these computers within the United States for 3 months in 2004 and then moves and uses the computers outside the United States for the remainder of 2004. Pursuant to § 1.48-1(g)(1)(i), the computers are considered as used predominantly outside the United States in 2004. As a result, for 2004, the computers are required to be depreciated under the alternative depreciation system of section 168(g) with a recovery period of 5 years pursuant to section 168(g)(3)(C). T uses the optional depreciation tables. If the half-year convention applies in 2004, the appropriate optional depreciation table is table 8 in Rev. Proc. 87-57, which is the table for MACRS property subject to the alternative depreciation system, the straight line method, a 5-year recovery period, and the half-year convention. Thus, the depreciation allowance for the computers for 2004 is $10,000, which is equal to the unadjusted depreciable basis of $100,000 multiplied by the annual depreciation rate of .10 in table 8 for recovery year 1 for a 5-year recovery period. Because the computers are required to be depreciated under the alternative depreciation system in their placed-in-service year, pursuant to section 168(k)(2)(C)(i) and § 1.168(k)-1T(b)(2)(ii), the computers are not eligible for the additional first year depreciation deduction provided by section 168(k).

(f) *No change in accounting method.*—A change in computing the depreciation allowance in the year of change for property subject to this section is not a change in method of accounting under section 446(e). See § 1.446-1(e)(2)(ii)(*d*)(3)(*ii*).

(g) *Effective dates.*—(1) *In general.*—Except as provided in paragraph (g)(2) of this section, this section applies to any change in the use of MACRS property in a taxable year ending on or after June 17, 2004. For any change in the use of MACRS property after December 31, 1986, in a taxable year ending before June 17, 2004, the Internal Revenue Service will allow any reasonable method of depreciating the property under section 168 in the year of change and the subsequent taxable years that is consistently applied to any property for which the use changes in the hands of the same taxpayer or the taxpayer may choose, on a property-by-property basis, to apply the provisions of this section.

(2) *Qualified property under section 168(k) acquired and placed in service after September 27, 2017.*—(i) *In general.*—The language "or § 1.168(k)-2(g)(6)(iii), as applicable" in paragraph (b)(1) of this section, the language "or § 1.168(k)-2(g)(6)(ii), as applicable" in paragraph (c) of this section, and the language "or § 1.168(k)-2(g)(6)(iv), as applicable" in paragraphs (d)(3)(i)(C) and (d)(4)(i) of this section applies to any change in use of MACRS property, which is qualified property under section 168(k)(2), by a taxpayer during or after the taxpayer's taxable year that includes September 24, 2019.

(ii) *Early application.*—A taxpayer may choose to apply the language "or § 1.168(k)-2(g)(6)(iii), as applicable" in paragraph (b)(1) of this section, the language "or § 1.168(k)-2(g)(6)(ii), as applicable" in paragraph (c) of this section, and the language "or

§ 1.168(k)-2(g)(6)(iv), as applicable" in paragraphs (d)(3)(i)(C) and (d)(4)(i) of this section for any change in use of MACRS property, which is qualified property under section 168(k)(2) and acquired and placed in service after September 27, 2017, by the taxpayer during taxable years ending on or after September 28, 2017.

(iii) *Early application of regulation project REG-104397-18.*—A taxpayer may rely on the language "or § 1.168(k)-2(f)(6)(iii), as applicable" in paragraph (b)(1) of this section, the language "or § 1.168(k)-2(f)(6)(ii), as applicable" in paragraph (c) of this section, and the language "or § 1.168(k)-2(f)(6)(iv), as applicable" in paragraphs (d)(3)(i)(C) and (d)(4)(i) of this section in regulation project REG-104397-18 (2018-41 I.R.B. 558) (see § 601.601(d)(2)(ii)(*b*) of this chapter) for any change in use of MACRS property, which is qualified property under section 168(k)(2) and acquired and placed in service after September 27, 2017, by the taxpayer during taxable years ending on or after September 28, 2017, and ending before the taxpayer's taxable year that includes September 24, 2019.

(3) *Change in method of accounting.*—(i) *In general.*—If a taxpayer adopted a method of accounting for depreciation due to a change in the use of MACRS property in a taxable year ending on or after December 30, 2003, and the method adopted is not in accordance with the method of accounting for depreciation provided in this section, a change to the method of accounting for depreciation provided in this section is a change in method of accounting to which the provisions of sections 446(e) and 481 and the regulations under sections 446(e) and 481 apply. Also, a revocation of the election provided in paragraph (d)(3)(ii) of this section to disregard a change in the use is a change in method of accounting to which the provisions of sections 446(e) and 481 and the regulations under sections 446(e) and 481 apply. However, if a taxpayer adopted a method of accounting for depreciation due to a change in the use of MACRS property after December 31, 1986, in a taxable year ending before December 30, 2003, and the method adopted is not in accordance with the method of accounting for depreciation provided in this section, the taxpayer may treat the change to the method of accounting for depreciation provided in this section as a change in method of accounting to which the provisions of sections 446(e) and 481 and the regulations under sections 446(e) and 481 apply.

(ii) *Automatic consent to change method of accounting.*—A taxpayer changing its method of accounting in accordance with this paragraph (g)(2) must follow the applicable administrative procedures issued under § 1.446-1(e)(3)(ii) for obtaining the Commissioner's automatic consent to a change in method of accounting (for further guidance, for example, see Rev. Proc. 2002-9 (2002-1 C.B. 327), (see § 601.601(d)(2)(ii)(*b*) of this chapter)). Any change in method of accounting made under this paragraph (g)(2) must be made using an adjustment under section 481(a). For purposes of Form 3115, *Application for Change in Accounting Method*, the designated number for the automatic accounting method change authorized by this paragraph (g)(2) is "88." If Form 3115 is revised or renumbered, any reference in this section to that form is treated as a reference to the revised or renumbered form. [Reg. § 1.168(i)-4.]

☐ [*T.D. 9132, 6-16-2004. Amended by T.D. 9307, 12-22-2006 and T.D. 9874, 9-17-2019.*]

[Reg. § 1.168(i)-5]

§ 1.168(i)-5. Table of contents.—This section lists the major paragraphs contained in § 1.168(i)-6.

(3) Like-kind exchanges and involuntary conversions where the taxpayer made the election under section 168(f)(1) for the relinquished property.
[Reg. § 1.168(i)-5.]

☐ [*T.D. 9314,* 2-26-2007.]

[Reg. § 1.168(i)-6]

§ 1.168(i)-6. Like-kind exchanges and involuntary conversions.—
(a) *Scope.*—This section provides the rules for determining the depreciation allowance for MACRS property acquired in a like-kind exchange or an involuntary conversion, including a like-kind exchange or an involuntary conversion of MACRS property that is exchanged or replaced with other MACRS property in a transaction between members of the same affiliated group. The allowance for depreciation under this section constitutes the amount of depreciation allowable under section 167(a) for the year of replacement and any subsequent taxable year for the replacement MACRS property and for the year of disposition of the relinquished MACRS property. The provisions of this section apply only to MACRS property to which § 1.168(h)-1 (like-kind exchanges of tax-exempt use property) does not apply. Additionally, paragraphs (c) through (f) of this section apply only to MACRS property for which an election under paragraph (i) of this section has not been made.

(b) *Definitions.*—For purposes of this section, the following definitions apply:

(1) *Replacement MACRS property* is MACRS property (as defined in § 1.168(b)-1(a)(2)) in the hands of the acquiring taxpayer that is acquired for other MACRS property in a like-kind exchange or an involuntary conversion.

(2) *Relinquished MACRS property* is MACRS property that is transferred by the taxpayer in a like-kind exchange, or in an involuntary conversion.

(3) *Time of disposition* is when the disposition of the relinquished MACRS property takes place under the convention, as determined under § 1.168(d)-1, that applies to the relinquished MACRS property.

(4) *Time of replacement* is the later of—

(i) When the replacement MACRS property is placed in service under the convention, as determined under this section, that applies to the replacement MACRS property; or

(ii) The time of disposition of the exchanged or involuntarily converted property.

(5) *Year of disposition* is the taxable year that includes the time of disposition.

(6) *Year of replacement* is the taxable year that includes the time of replacement.

(7) *Exchanged basis* is determined after the depreciation deductions for the year of disposition are determined under paragraph (c)(5)(i) of this section and is the lesser of—

(i) The basis in the replacement MACRS property, as determined under section 1031(d) and the regulations under section 1031(d) or section 1033(b) and the regulations under section 1033(b); or

(ii) The adjusted depreciable basis (as defined in § 1.168(b)-1(a)(4)) of the relinquished MACRS property.

(8) *Excess basis* is any excess of the basis in the replacement MACRS property, as determined under section 1031(d) and the regulations under section 1031(d) or section 1033(b) and the regulations under section 1033(b), over the exchanged basis as determined under paragraph (b)(7) of this section.

(9) *Depreciable exchanged basis* is the exchanged basis as determined under paragraph (b)(7) of this section reduced by—

(i) The percentage of such basis attributable to the taxpayer's use of property for the taxable year other than in the taxpayer's trade or business (or for the production of income); and

(ii) Any adjustments to basis provided by other provisions of the Internal Revenue Code (Code) and the regulations under the Code (including section 1016(a)(2) and (3), for example, depreciation deductions in the year of replacement allowable under section 168(k) or 1400L(b)).

(10) *Depreciable excess basis* is the excess basis as determined under paragraph (b)(8) of this section reduced by—

(i) The percentage of such basis attributable to the taxpayer's use of property for the taxable year other than in the taxpayer's trade or business (or for the production of income);

(ii) Any portion of the basis the taxpayer properly elects to treat as an expense under section 179; and

(iii) Any adjustments to basis provided by other provisions of the Code and the regulations under the Code (including section 1016(a)(2) and (3), for example, depreciation deductions in the year of replacement allowable under section 168(k) or 1400L(b)).

(11) *Like-kind exchange* is an exchange of property in a transaction to which section 1031(a)(1), (b), or (c) applies.

(12) *Involuntary conversion* is a transaction described in section 1033(a)(1) or (2) that resulted in the nonrecognition of any part of the gain realized as the result of the conversion.

(c) *Determination of depreciation allowance.*—(1) *Computation of the depreciation allowance for depreciable exchanged basis beginning in the year of replacement.*—(i) *In general.*—This paragraph (c) provides rules for determining the applicable recovery period, the applicable depreciation method, and the applicable convention used to determine the depreciation allowances for the depreciable exchanged basis beginning in the year of replacement. See paragraph (c)(5) of this section for rules relating to the computation of the depreciation allowance for the year of disposition and for the year of replacement. See paragraph (d)(1) of this section for rules relating to the computation of the depreciation allowance for depreciable excess basis. See paragraph (d)(4) of this section if the replacement MACRS property is acquired before disposition of the relinquished MACRS property in a transaction to which section 1033 applies. See paragraph (e) of this section for rules relating to the computation of the depreciation allowance using the optional depreciation tables.

(ii) *Applicable recovery period, depreciation method, and convention.*—The recovery period, depreciation method, and convention determined under this paragraph (c) are the only permissible methods of accounting for MACRS property within the scope of this section unless the taxpayer makes the election under paragraph (i) of this section not to apply this section.

(2) *Effect of depreciation treatment of the replacement MACRS property by previous owners of the acquired property.*—If replacement MACRS property is acquired by a taxpayer in a like-kind exchange or an involuntary conversion, the depreciation treatment of the replacement MACRS property by previous owners has no effect on the determination of depreciation allowances for the replacement MACRS property in the hands of the acquiring taxpayer. For example, a taxpayer exchanging, in a like-kind exchange, MACRS property for property that was depreciated under section 168 of the Internal Revenue Code of 1954 (ACRS) by the previous owner must use this section because the replacement property will become MACRS property in the hands of the acquiring taxpayer. In addition, elections made by previous owners in determining depreciation allowances for the replacement MACRS property have no effect on the acquiring taxpayer. For example, a taxpayer exchanging, in a like-kind exchange, MACRS property that the taxpayer depreciates under the general depreciation system of section 168(a) for other MACRS property that the previous owner elected to depreciate under the alternative depreciation system pursuant to section 168(g)(7) does not have to continue using the alternative depreciation system for the replacement MACRS property.

(3) *Recovery period and/or depreciation method of the properties are the same, or both are not the same.*—(i) *In general.*—For purposes of paragraphs (c)(3) and (c)(4) of this section in determining whether the recovery period and the depreciation method prescribed under section 168 for the replacement MACRS property are the same as the recovery period and the depreciation method prescribed under section 168 for the relinquished MACRS property, the recovery period and the depreciation method for the replacement MACRS property are considered to be the recovery period and the depreciation method that would have applied under section 168, taking into account any elections made by the acquiring taxpayer under section 168(b)(5) or 168(g)(7), had the replacement MACRS property been placed in service by the acquiring taxpayer at the same time as the relinquished MACRS property.

(ii) *Both the recovery period and the depreciation method are the same.*—If both the recovery period and the depreciation method prescribed under section 168 for the replacement MACRS property are the same as the recovery period and the depreciation method prescribed under section 168 for the relinquished MACRS property, the depreciation allowances for the replacement MACRS property beginning in the year of replacement are determined by using the same recovery period and depreciation method that were used for the relinquished MACRS property. Thus, the replacement MACRS property is depreciated over the remaining recovery period (taking into account the applicable convention), and by using the depreciation method, of the relinquished MACRS property. Except as provided in paragraph (c)(5) of this section, the depreciation allowances for the depreciable exchanged basis for any 12-month taxable year beginning with the year of replacement are determined by multiplying the depreciable exchanged basis by the applicable depreciation rate for each taxable year (for further guidance, for example, see section 6 of Rev. Proc. 87-57 (1987-2 CB 687, 692) and § 601.601(d)(2)(ii)(b) of this chapter).

(iii) *Either the recovery period or the depreciation method is the same, or both are not the same.*—If either the recovery period or the depreciation method prescribed under section 168 for the replacement MACRS property is the same as the recovery period or the depreciation method prescribed under section 168 for the relinquished MACRS property, the depreciation allowances for the depreciable exchanged basis beginning in the year of replacement are determined using the recovery period or the depreciation method that is the same as the relinquished MACRS property. See paragraph (c)(4) of this section to determine the depreciation allowances when the recovery period or the depreciation method of the replacement MACRS property is not the same as that of the relinquished MACRS property.

(4) *Recovery period or depreciation method of the properties is not the same.*—If the recovery period prescribed under section 168 for the replacement MACRS property (as determined under paragraph (c)(3)(i) of this section) is not the same as the recovery period prescribed under section 168 for the relinquished MACRS property, the depreciation allowances for the depreciable exchanged basis beginning in the year of replacement are determined under this paragraph (c)(4). Similarly, if the depreciation method prescribed under section 168 for the replacement MACRS property (as determined under paragraph (c)(3)(i) of this section) is not the same as the depreciation method prescribed under section 168 for the relinquished MACRS property, the depreciation method used to determine the depreciation allowances for the depreciable exchanged basis beginning in the year of replacement is determined under this paragraph (c)(4).

(i) *Longer recovery period.*—If the recovery period prescribed under section 168 for the replacement MACRS property (as determined under paragraph (c)(3)(i) of this section) is longer than that prescribed for the relinquished MACRS property, the depreciation allowances for the depreciable exchanged basis beginning in the year of replacement are determined as though the replacement MACRS property had originally been placed in service by the acquiring taxpayer in the same taxable year the relinquished MACRS property was placed in service by the acquiring taxpayer, but using the longer recovery period of the replacement MACRS property (as determined under paragraph (c)(3)(i) of this section) and the convention determined under paragraph (c)(4)(v) of this section. Thus, the depreciable exchanged basis is depreciated over the remaining recovery period (taking into account the applicable convention) of the replacement MACRS property.

(ii) *Shorter recovery period.*—If the recovery period prescribed under section 168 for the replacement MACRS property (as determined under paragraph (c)(3)(i) of this section) is shorter than that of the relinquished MACRS property, the depreciation allowances for the depreciable exchanged basis beginning in the year of replacement are determined using the same recovery period as that of the relinquished MACRS property. Thus, the depreciable exchanged basis is depreciated over the remaining recovery period (taking into account the applicable convention) of the relinquished MACRS property.

(iii) *Less accelerated depreciation method.*—(A) If the depreciation method prescribed under section 168 for the replacement MACRS property (as determined under paragraph (c)(3)(i) of this section) is less accelerated than that of the relinquished MACRS property at the time of disposition, the depreciation allowances for the depreciable exchanged basis beginning in the year of replacement are determined as though the replacement MACRS property had originally been placed in service by the acquiring taxpayer at the same time the relinquished MACRS property was placed in service by the acquiring taxpayer, but using the less accelerated depreciation method. Thus, the depreciable exchanged basis is depreciated using the less accelerated depreciation method.

(B) Except as provided in paragraph (c)(5) of this section, the depreciation allowances for the depreciable exchanged basis for any 12-month taxable year beginning in the year of replacement are determined by multiplying the adjusted depreciable basis by the applicable depreciation rate for each taxable year. If, for example, the depreciation method of the replacement MACRS property in the year of replacement is the 150-percent declining balance method and the depreciation method of the relinquished MACRS property in the year of replacement is the 200-percent declining balance method, and neither method had been switched to the straight line method in the year of replacement or any prior taxable year, the applicable depreciation rate for the year of replacement and subsequent taxable years is determined by using the depreciation rate of the replacement MACRS property as if the replacement MACRS property was placed in service by the acquiring taxpayer at the same time the relinquished MACRS property was placed in service by the acquiring taxpayer, until the 150-percent declining balance method has been switched to the straight line method. If, for example, the depreciation method of the replacement MACRS property is the straight line method, the applicable depreciation rate for the year of replacement is determined by using the remaining recovery period at the beginning of

the year of disposition (as determined under this paragraph (c)(4) and taking into account the applicable convention).

(iv) *More accelerated depreciation method.*—(A) If the depreciation method prescribed under section 168 for the replacement MACRS property (as determined under paragraph (c)(3)(i) of this section) is more accelerated than that of the relinquished MACRS property at the time of disposition, the depreciation allowances for the replacement MACRS property beginning in the year of replacement are determined using the same depreciation method as the relinquished MACRS property.

(B) Except as provided in paragraph (c)(5) of this section, the depreciation allowances for the depreciable exchanged basis for any 12-month taxable year beginning in the year of replacement are determined by multiplying the adjusted depreciable basis by the applicable depreciation rate for each taxable year. If, for example, the depreciation method of the relinquished MACRS property in the year of replacement is the 150-percent declining balance method and the depreciation method of the replacement MACRS property in the year of replacement is the 200-percent declining balance method, and neither method had been switched to the straight line method in the year of replacement or any prior taxable year, the applicable depreciation rate for the year of replacement and subsequent taxable years is the same depreciation rate that applied to the relinquished MACRS property in the year of replacement, until the 150-percent declining balance method has been switched to the straight line method. If, for example, the depreciation method is the straight line method, the applicable depreciation rate for the year of replacement is determined by using the remaining recovery period at the beginning of the year of disposition (as determined under this paragraph (c)(4) and taking into account the applicable convention).

(v) *Convention.*—The applicable convention for the exchanged basis is determined under this paragraph (c)(4)(v).

(A) *Either the relinquished MACRS property or the replacement MACRS property is mid-month property.*—If either the relinquished MACRS property or the replacement MACRS property is property for which the applicable convention (as determined under section 168(d)) is the mid-month convention, the exchanged basis must be depreciated using the mid-month convention.

(B) *Neither the relinquished MACRS property nor the replacement MACRS property is mid-month property.*—If neither the relinquished MACRS property nor the replacement MACRS property is property for which the applicable convention (as determined under section 168(d)) is the mid-month convention, the applicable convention for the exchanged basis is the same convention that applied to the relinquished MACRS property. If the relinquished MACRS property is placed in service in the year of disposition, and the time of replacement is also in the year of disposition, the convention that applies to the relinquished MACRS property is determined under paragraph (f)(1)(i) of this section. If, however, relinquished MACRS property was placed in service in the year of disposition and the time of replacement is in a taxable year subsequent to the year of disposition, the convention that applies to the exchanged basis is the convention that applies in that subsequent taxable year (see paragraph (f)(1)(ii) of this section).

(5) *Year of disposition and year of replacement.*—No depreciation deduction is allowable for MACRS property disposed of by a taxpayer in a like-kind exchange or involuntary conversion in the same taxable year that such property was placed in service by the taxpayer. If replacement MACRS property is disposed of by a taxpayer during the same taxable year that the relinquished MACRS property is placed in service by the taxpayer, no depreciation deduction is allowable for either MACRS property. Otherwise, the depreciation allowances for the year of disposition and for the year of replacement are determined as follows:

(i) *Relinquished MACRS property.*—(A) *General rule.*—Except as provided in paragraphs (c)(5)(i)(B), (c)(5)(iii), (e), and (i) of this section, the depreciation allowance in the year of disposition for the relinquished MACRS property is computed by multiplying the allowable depreciation deduction for the property for that year by a fraction, the numerator of which is the number of months (including fractions of months) the property is deemed to be placed in service during the year of disposition (taking into account the applicable convention of the relinquished MACRS property), and the denominator of which is 12. In the case of termination under § 1.168(i)-1(e)(3)(v) of general asset account treatment of an asset, or of all the assets remaining, in a general asset account, the allowable depreciation deduction in the year of disposition for the asset or assets for which general asset account treatment is terminated is determined using the depreciation method, recovery period, and convention of the general asset account. This allowable depreciation deduction is adjusted to account for the period the asset or assets is deemed to be in service in accordance with this paragraph (c)(5)(i).

(B) *Special rule.*—If, at the beginning of the year of disposition, the remaining recovery period of the relinquished MACRS property, taking into account the applicable convention of such property, is less than the period between the beginning of the year of disposition and the time of disposition, the depreciation deduction for the relinquished MACRS property for the year of disposition is equal to the adjusted depreciable basis of the relinquished MACRS property at the beginning of the year of disposition. If this paragraph applies, the exchanged basis is zero and no depreciation is allowable for the exchanged basis in the replacement MACRS property.

(ii) *Replacement MACRS property.*—(A) *Remaining recovery period of the replacement MACRS property.*—The replacement MACRS property is treated as placed in service at the time of replacement under the convention that applies to the replacement MACRS property as determined under this paragraph (c)(5)(ii). The remaining recovery period of the replacement MACRS property at the time of replacement is the excess of the recovery period for the replacement MACRS property, as determined under paragraph (c) of this section, over the period of time that the replacement MACRS property would have been in service if it had been placed in service when the relinquished MACRS property was placed in service and removed from service at the time of disposition of the relinquished MACRS property. This period is determined by using the convention that applied to the relinquished MACRS property to determine the date that the relinquished MACRS property is deemed to have been placed in service and the date that it is deemed to have been disposed of. The length of time the replacement MACRS property would have been in service is determined by using these dates and the convention that applies to the replacement MACRS property.

(B) *Year of replacement is 12 months.*—Except as provided in paragraphs (c)(5)(iii), (e), and (i) of this section, the depreciation allowance in the year of replacement for the depreciable exchanged basis is determined by—

(1) Calculating the applicable depreciation rate for the replacement MACRS property as of the beginning of the year of replacement taking into account the depreciation method prescribed for the replacement MACRS property under paragraph (c)(3) of this section and the remaining recovery period of the replacement MACRS property as of the beginning of the year of disposition as determined under this paragraph (c)(5)(ii);

(2) Calculating the depreciable exchanged basis of the replacement MACRS property, and adding to that amount the amount determined under paragraph (c)(5)(i) of this section for the year of disposition; and

(3) Multiplying the product of the amounts determined under paragraphs (c)(5)(ii)(B)(*1*) and (B)(2) of this section by a fraction, the numerator of which is the number of months (including fractions of months) the property is deemed to be in service during the year of replacement (in the year of replacement the replacement MACRS property is deemed to be placed in service by the acquiring taxpayer at the time of replacement under the convention determined under paragraph (c)(4)(v) of this section), and the denominator of which is 12.

(iii) *Year of disposition or year of replacement is less than 12 months.*—If the year of disposition or the year of replacement is less than 12 months, the depreciation allowance determined under paragraph (c)(5)(ii)(A) of this section must be adjusted for a short taxable year (for further guidance, for example, see Rev. Proc. 89-15 (1989-1 CB 816) and § 601.601(d)(2)(ii)(*b*) of this chapter).

(iv) *Deferred transactions.*—(A) *In general.*—If the replacement MACRS property is not acquired until after the disposition of the relinquished MACRS property, taking into account the applicable convention of the relinquished MACRS property and replacement MACRS property, depreciation is not allowable during the period between the disposition of the relinquished MACRS property and the acquisition of the replacement MACRS property. The recovery period for the replacement MACRS property is suspended during this period. For purposes of paragraph (c)(5)(ii) of this section, only the depreciable exchanged basis of the replacement MACRS property is taken into account for calculating the amount in paragraph (c)(5)(ii)(B)(2) of this section if the year of replacement is a taxable year subsequent to the year of disposition.

(B) *Allowable depreciation for a qualified intermediary.*—[Reserved].

(v) *Remaining recovery period.*—The remaining recovery period of the replacement MACRS property is determined as of the beginning of the year of disposition of the relinquished MACRS property. For purposes of determining the remaining recovery period of the

replacement MACRS property, the replacement MACRS property is deemed to have been originally placed in service under the convention determined under paragraph (c)(4)(v) of this section but at the time the relinquished MACRS property was deemed to be placed in service under the convention that applied to it when it was placed in service.

(6) *Examples.*—The application of this paragraph (c) is illustrated by the following examples:

Example 1. A1, a calendar-year taxpayer, exchanges Building M, an office building, for Building N, a warehouse in a like-kind exchange. Building M is relinquished in July 2004 and Building N is acquired and placed in service in October 2004. A1 did not make any elections under section 168 for either Building M or Building N. The unadjusted depreciable basis of Building M was $4,680,000 when placed in service in July 1997. Since the recovery period and depreciation method prescribed under section 168 for Building N (39 years, straight line method) are the same as the recovery period and depreciation method prescribed under section 168 for Building M (39 years, straight line method), Building N is depreciated over the remaining recovery period of, and using the same depreciation method and convention as that of, Building M. Applying the applicable convention, Building M is deemed disposed of on July 15, 2004, and Building N is placed in service on October 15, 2004. Thus, Building N will be depreciated using the straight line method over a remaining recovery period of 32 years beginning in October 2004 (the remaining recovery period of 32 years and 6.5 months at the beginning of 2004, less the 6.5 months of depreciation taken prior to the disposition of the exchanged MACRS property (Building M) in 2004). For 2004, the year in which the transaction takes place, the depreciation allowance for Building M is ($120,000)(6.5/12) which equals $65,000. The depreciation allowance for Building N for 2004 is ($120,000)(2.5/12) which equals $25,000. For 2005 and subsequent years, Building N is depreciated over the remaining recovery period of, and using the same depreciation method and convention as that of, Building M. Thus, the depreciation allowance for Building N is the same as Building M, namely $10,000 per month.

Example 2. B, a calendar-year taxpayer, placed in service Bridge P in January 1998. Bridge P is depreciated using the half-year convention. In January 2004, B exchanges Bridge P for Building Q, an apartment building, in a like-kind exchange. Pursuant to paragraph (k)(2)(i) of this section, B decided to apply § 1.168(i)-6 to the exchange of Bridge P for Building Q, the replacement MACRS property. B did not make any elections under section 168 for either Bridge P or Building Q. Since the recovery period prescribed under section 168 for Building Q (27.5 years) is longer than that of Bridge P (15 years), Building Q is depreciated as if it had originally been placed in service in July 1998 and disposed of in July 2004 using a 27.5 year recovery period. Additionally, since the depreciation method prescribed under section 168 for Building Q (straight line method) is less accelerated than that of Bridge P (150-percent declining balance method), then the depreciation allowance for Building Q is computed using the straight line method. Thus, when Building Q is acquired and placed in service in 2004, its basis is depreciated over the remaining 21.5 year recovery period using the straight line method of depreciation and the mid-month convention beginning in July 2004.

Example 3. C, a calendar-year taxpayer, placed in service Building R, a restaurant, in January 1996. In January 2004, C exchanges Building R for Tower S, a radio transmitting tower, in a like-kind exchange. Pursuant to paragraph (k)(2)(i) of this section, C decided to apply § 1.168(i)-6 to the exchange of Building R for Tower S, the replacement MACRS property. C did not make any elections under section 168 for either Building R or Tower S. Since the recovery period prescribed under section 168 for Tower S (15 years) is shorter than that of Building R (39 years), Tower S is depreciated over the remaining recovery period of Building R. Additionally, since the depreciation method prescribed under section 168 for Tower S (150% declining balance method) is more accelerated than that of Building R (straight line method), then the depreciation allowance for Tower S is also computed using the same depreciation method as Building R. Thus, Tower S is depreciated over the remaining 31 year recovery period of Building R using the straight line method of depreciation and the mid-month convention. Alternatively, C may elect under paragraph (i) of this section to treat Tower S as though it is placed in service in January 2004. In such case, C uses the applicable recovery period, depreciation method, and convention prescribed under section 168 for Tower S.

Example 4. (i) In February 2002, D, a calendar-year taxpayer and manufacturer of rubber products, acquired for $60,000 and placed in service Asset T (a special tool) and depreciated Asset T using the straight line method election under section 168(b)(5) and the mid-quarter convention over its 3-year recovery period. D elected not to deduct the additional first year depreciation for 3-year property placed in service in 2002. In June 2004, D exchanges Asset T for Asset U (not a special tool) in a like-kind exchange. D elected not to deduct the additional first year depreciation for 7-year property placed in service in 2004. Since the recovery period prescribed under section 168 for Asset U (7 years) is longer than that of Asset T (3 years), Asset U is depreciated as if it had originally been placed in service in February 2002 using a 7-year recovery period. Additionally, since the depreciation method prescribed under section 168 for Asset U (200-percent declining balance method) is more accelerated than that of Asset T (straight line method) at the time of disposition, the depreciation allowance for Asset U is computed using the straight line method. Asset U is depreciated over its remaining recovery period of 4.75 years using the straight line method of depreciation and the mid-quarter convention.

(ii) The 2004 depreciation allowance for Asset T is $7,500 ($20,000 allowable depreciation deduction for 2004) × 4.5 months ÷ 12).

(iii) The depreciation rate in 2004 for Asset U is 0.1951 (1 ÷ 5.125 years (the length of the applicable recovery period remaining as of the beginning of 2004)). Therefore, the depreciation allowance for Asset U in 2004 is $2,744 (0.1951 × $22,500 (the sum of the $15,000 depreciable exchanged basis of Asset U ($22,500 adjusted depreciable basis at the beginning of 2004 for Asset T, less the $7,500 depreciation allowable for Asset T for 2004) and the $7,500 depreciation allowable for Asset T for 2004) × 7.5 months ÷ 12).

Example 5. The facts are the same as in *Example 4* except that D exchanges Asset T for Asset U in June 2005, in a like-kind exchange. Under these facts, the remaining recovery period of Asset T at the beginning of 2005 is 1.5 months and, as a result, is less than the 5-month period between the beginning of 2005 (year of disposition) and June 2005 (time of disposition). Accordingly, pursuant to paragraph (c)(5)(i)(B) of this section, the 2005 depreciation allowance for Asset T is $2,500 ($2,500 adjusted depreciable basis at the beginning of 2005 ($60,000 original basis minus $17,500 depreciation deduction for 2002 minus $20,000 depreciation deduction for 2003 minus $20,000 depreciation deduction for 2004)). Because the exchanged basis of asset U is $0.00 no depreciation is allowable for asset U.

Example 6. On January 1, 2004, E, a calendar-year taxpayer, acquired and placed in service Canopy V, a gas station canopy. The purchase price of Canopy V was $60,000. On August 1, 2004, Canopy V was destroyed in a hurricane and was therefore no longer usable in E's business. On October 1, 2004, as part of the involuntary conversion, E acquired and placed in service new Canopy W with the insurance proceeds E received due to the loss of Canopy V. E elected not to deduct the additional first year depreciation for 5-year property placed in service in 2004. E depreciates both canopies under the general depreciation system of section 168(a) by using the 200-percent declining balance method of depreciation, a 5-year recovery period, and the half-year convention. No depreciation deduction is allowable for Canopy V. The depreciation deduction allowable for Canopy W for 2004 is $12,000 ($60,000 × the annual depreciation rate of .40 × 1/2 year). For 2005, the depreciation deduction for Canopy W is $19,200 ($48,000 adjusted basis × the annual depreciation rate of .40).

Example 7. The facts are the same as in *Example 6*, except that E did not make the election out of the additional first year depreciation for 5-year property placed in service in 2004. E depreciates both canopies under the general depreciation system of section 168(a) by using the 200-percent declining balance method of depreciation, a 5-year recovery period, and the half-year convention. No depreciation deduction is allowable for Canopy V. For 2004, E is allowed a 50-percent additional first year depreciation deduction of $30,000 for Canopy W (the unadjusted depreciable basis of $60,000 multiplied by .50), and a regular MACRS depreciation deduction of $6,000 for Canopy W (the depreciable exchanged basis of $30,000 multiplied by the annual depreciation rate of .40 × 1/2 year). For 2005, E is allowed a regular MACRS depreciation deduction of $9,600 for Canopy W (the depreciable exchanged basis of $24,000 ($30,000 minus regular 2003 depreciation of $6,000) multiplied by the annual depreciation rate of .40).

Example 8. In January 2001, F, a calendar-year taxpayer, places in service a paved parking lot, Lot W, and begins depreciating Lot W over its 15-year recovery period. F's unadjusted depreciable basis in Lot W is $1,000x. On April 1, 2004, F disposes of Lot W in a like-kind exchange for Building X, which is nonresidential real property. Lot W is depreciated using the 150 percent declining balance method and the half-year convention. Building X is depreciated using the straight-line method with a 39-year recovery period and using the mid-month convention. Both Lot W and Building X were in service at the time of the exchange. Because Lot W was depreciated using the half-year convention, it is deemed to have been placed in service on July 1, 2001, the first day of the second half of 2001, and to have been disposed of on July 1, 2004, the first day of the second half of 2004. To determine the remaining recovery period of Building X at the time of replacement, Building X is deemed to have been placed in service on July 1, 2001, and removed from service on July 1, 2004. Thus, Build-

ing X is deemed to have been in service, at the time of replacement, for 3 years (36 months = 5.5 months in 2001 + 12 months in 2002 + 12 months in 2003 + 6.5 months in 2004) and its remaining recovery period is 36 years (39 – 3). Because Building X is deemed to be placed in service at the time of replacement, July 1, 2004, the first day of the second half of 2004, Building X is depreciated for 5.5 months in 2004. However, at the beginning of the year of replacement the remaining recovery period for Building X is 36 years and 6.5 months (39 years – 2 years and 5.5 months (5.5 months in 2001 + 12 months in 2002 + 12 months in 2003)). The depreciation rate for building X for 2004 is 0.02737 (= 1/(39 – 2 – 5.5/12)). For 2005, the depreciation rate for Building X is 0.02814 (= 1/(39 – 3 – 5.5/12)).

Example 9. The facts are the same as in *Example 8*. F did not make the election under paragraph (i) of this section for Building Y in the initial exchange. In January 2006, F exchanges Building Y for Building Z, an office building, in a like-kind exchange. F did not make any elections under section 168 for either Building Y or Building Z. Since the recovery period prescribed for Building Y as a result of the initial exchange (39 years) is longer than that of Building Z (27.5 years), Building Z is depreciated over the remaining 33 years of the recovery period of Building Y. The depreciation methods are the same for both Building Y and Building Z so F's exchanged basis in Building Z is depreciated over 33 years, using the straight-line method and the mid-month convention, beginning in January 2006. Alternatively, F could have made the election under paragraph (i) of this section. If F makes such election, Building Z is treated as placed in service by F when acquired in January 2006 and F would recover its exchanged basis in Building Z over 27.5 years, using the straight line method and the mid-month convention, beginning in January 2006.

(d) *Special rules for determining depreciation allowances.*—(1) *Excess basis.*—(i) *In general.*—Any excess basis in the replacement MACRS property is treated as property that is placed in service by the acquiring taxpayer in the year of replacement. Thus, the depreciation allowances for the depreciable excess basis are determined by using the applicable recovery period, depreciation method, and convention prescribed under section 168 for the property at the time of replacement. However, if replacement MACRS property is disposed of during the same taxable year the relinquished MACRS property is placed in service by the acquiring taxpayer, no depreciation deduction is allowable for either MACRS property. See paragraph (g) of this section regarding the application of section 179. See paragraph (h) of this section regarding the application of section 168(k) or 1400L(b).

(ii) *Example.*—The application of this paragraph (d)(1) is illustrated by the following example:

Example. In 1989, G placed in service a hospital. On January 16, 2004, G exchanges this hospital plus $2,000,000 cash for an office building in a like-kind exchange. On January 16, 2004, the hospital has an adjusted depreciable basis of $1,500,000. After the exchange, the basis of the office building is $3,500,000. Pursuant to paragraph (k)(2)(i) of this section, G decided to apply §1.168(i)-6 to the exchange of the hospital for the office building, the replacement MACRS property. The depreciable exchanged basis of the office building is depreciated in accordance with paragraph (c) of this section. The depreciable excess basis of $2,000,000 is treated as being placed in service by G in 2004 and, as a result, is depreciated using the applicable depreciation method, recovery period, and convention prescribed for the office building under section 168 at the time of replacement.

(2) *Depreciable and nondepreciable property.*—(i) If land or other nondepreciable property is acquired in a like-kind exchange for, or as a result of an involuntary conversion of, depreciable property, the land or other nondepreciable property is not depreciated. If both MACRS and nondepreciable property are acquired in a like-kind exchange for, or as part of an involuntary conversion of, MACRS property, the basis allocated to the nondepreciable property (as determined under section 1031(d) and the regulations under section 1031(d) or section 1033(b) and the regulations under section 1033(b)) is not depreciated and the basis allocated to the replacement MACRS property (as determined under section 1031(d) and the regulations under section 1031(d) or section 1033(b) and the regulations under section 1033(b)) is depreciated in accordance with this section.

(ii) If MACRS property is acquired, or if both MACRS and nondepreciable property are acquired, in a like-kind exchange for, or as part of an involuntary conversion of, land or other nondepreciable property, the basis in the replacement MACRS property that is attributable to the relinquished nondepreciable property is treated as though the replacement MACRS property is placed in service by the acquiring taxpayer in the year of replacement. Thus, the depreciation allowances for the replacement MACRS property are determined by using the applicable recovery period, depreciation method, and convention prescribed under section 168 for the replacement MACRS property at the time of replacement. See paragraph (g) of this section

Reg. §1.168(i)-6(d)(2)(ii)

regarding the application of section 179. See paragraph (h) of this section regarding the application of section 168(k) or 1400L(b).

(3) *Depreciation limitations for automobiles.*—(i) *In general.*—Depreciation allowances under section 179 and section 167 (including allowances under sections 168 and 1400L(b)) for a passenger automobile, as defined in section 280F(d)(5), are subject to the limitations of section 280F(a). The depreciation allowances for a passenger automobile that is replacement MACRS property (replacement MACRS passenger automobile) generally are limited in any taxable year to the replacement automobile section 280F limit for the taxable year. The taxpayer's basis in the replacement MACRS passenger automobile is treated as being comprised of two separate components. The first component is the exchanged basis and the second component is the excess basis, if any. The depreciation allowances for a passenger automobile that is relinquished MACRS property (relinquished MACRS passenger automobile) for the taxable year generally are limited to the relinquished automobile section 280F limit for that taxable year. In the year of disposition the sum of the depreciation deductions for the relinquished MACRS passenger automobile and the replacement MACRS passenger automobile may not exceed the replacement automobile section 280F limit unless the taxpayer makes the election under §1.168(i)-6(i). 6(i). For purposes of this paragraph (d)(3), the following definitions apply:

(A) *Replacement automobile section 280F limit* is the limit on depreciation deductions under section 280F(a) for the taxable year based on the time of replacement of the replacement MACRS passenger automobile (including the effect of any elections under section 168(k) or section 1400L(b), as applicable).

(B) *Relinquished automobile section 280F limit* is the limit on depreciation deductions under section 280F(a) for the taxable year based on when the relinquished MACRS passenger automobile was placed in service by the taxpayer.

(ii) *Order in which limitations on depreciation under section 280F(a) are applied.*—Generally, depreciation deductions allowable under section 280F(a) reduce the basis in the relinquished MACRS passenger automobile and the exchanged basis of the replacement MACRS passenger automobile, before the excess basis of the replacement MACRS passenger automobile is reduced. The depreciation deductions for the relinquished MACRS passenger automobile in the year of disposition and the replacement MACRS passenger automobile in the year of replacement and each subsequent taxable year are allowable in the following order:

(A) The depreciation deduction allowable for the relinquished MACRS passenger automobile as determined under paragraph (c)(5)(i) of this section for the year of disposition to the extent of the smaller of the replacement automobile section 280F limit and the relinquished automobile section 280F limit, if the year of disposition is the year of replacement. If the year of replacement is a taxable year subsequent to the year of disposition, the depreciation deduction allowable for the relinquished MACRS passenger automobile for the year of disposition is limited to the relinquished automobile section 280F limit.

(B) The additional first year depreciation allowable on the remaining exchanged basis (remaining carryover basis as determined under §1.168(k)-1(f)(5), §1.168(k)-2(g)(5), or §1.1400L(b)-1(f)(5), as applicable) of the replacement MACRS passenger automobile, as determined under §1.168(k)-1(f)(5), §1.168(k)-2(g)(5), or §1.1400L(b)-1(f)(5), as applicable, to the extent of the excess of the replacement automobile section 280F limit over the amount allowable under paragraph (d)(3)(ii)(A) of this section.

(C) The depreciation deduction allowable for the taxable year on the depreciable exchanged basis of the replacement MACRS passenger automobile determined under paragraph (c) of this section to the extent of any excess over the sum of the amounts allowable under paragraphs (d)(3)(ii)(A) and (B) of this section of the smaller of the replacement automobile section 280F limit and the relinquished automobile section 280F limit.

(D) Any section 179 deduction allowable in the year of replacement on the excess basis of the replacement MACRS passenger automobile to the extent of the excess of the replacement automobile section 280F limit over the sum of the amounts allowable under paragraphs (d)(3)(ii)(A), (B), and (C) of this section.

(E) The additional first year depreciation allowable on the remaining excess basis of the replacement MACRS passenger automobile, as determined under §1.168(k)-1(f)(5), §1.168(k)-2(g)(5), or §1.1400L(b)-1(f)(5), as applicable, to the extent of the excess of the replacement automobile section 280F limit over the sum of the amounts allowable under paragraphs (d)(3)(ii)(A), (B), (C), and (D) of this section.

(F) The depreciation deduction allowable under paragraph (d) of this section for the depreciable excess basis of the replacement MACRS passenger automobile to the extent of the excess of the replacement automobile section 280F limit over the sum of the

amounts allowable under paragraphs (d)(3)(ii)(A), (B), (C), (D), and (E) of this section.

(iii) *Examples.*—The application of this paragraph (d)(3) is illustrated by the following examples:

Example 1. H, a calendar-year taxpayer, acquired and placed in service Automobile X in January 2000 for $30,000 to be used solely for H's business. In December 2003, H exchanges, in a like-kind exchange, Automobile X plus $15,000 cash for new Automobile Y that will also be used solely in H's business. Automobile Y is 50-percent bonus depreciation property for purposes of section 168(k)(4). Both automobiles are depreciated using the double declining balance method, the half-year convention, and a 5-year recovery period. Pursuant to §1.168(k)-1(g)(3)(ii) and paragraph (k)(2)(i) of this section, H decided to apply §1.168(i)-6 to the exchange of Automobile X for Automobile Y, the replacement MACRS property. The relinquished automobile section 280F limit for 2003 for Automobile X is $1,775. The replacement automobile section 280F limit for Automobile Y is $10,710. The exchanged basis for Automobile Y is $17,315 ($30,000 less total depreciation allowable of $12,685 (($3,060 for 2000, $4,900 for 2001, $2,950 for 2002, and $1,775 for 2003)). Without taking section 280F into account, the additional first year depreciation deduction for the remaining exchanged 99basis is $8,658 ($17,315 × 0.5). Because this amount is less than $8,935 ($10,710 (the replacement automobile section 280F limit for 2003 for Automobile Y) − $1,775 (the depreciation allowable for Automobile X for 2003)), the additional first year depreciation deduction for the exchanged basis is $8,658. No depreciation deduction is allowable in 2003 for the depreciable exchanged basis because the depreciation deductions taken for Automobile X and the remaining exchanged basis exceed the exchanged automobile section 280F limit. An additional first year depreciation deduction of $277 is allowable for the excess basis of $15,000 in Automobile Y. Thus, at the end of 2003 the adjusted depreciable basis in Automobile Y is $23,379 comprised of adjusted depreciable exchanged basis of $8,657 ($17,315 (exchanged basis) − $8,658 (additional first year depreciation for exchanged basis)) and of an adjusted depreciable excess basis of $14,723 ($15,000 (excess basis) − $277 (additional first year depreciation for 2003)).

Example 2. The facts are the same as in *Example 1*, except that H used Automobile X only 75 percent for business use. As such, the total allowable depreciation for Automobile X is reduced to reflect that the automobile is only used 75 percent for business. The total allowable depreciation of Automobile X is $9,513.75 ($2,295 for 2000 ($3,060 limit × .75), $3,675 for 2001 ($4,900 limit × .75), $2,212.50 for 2002 ($2,950 limit × .75), and $1,331.25 for 2003 ($1,775 limit × .75). However, under §1.280F-2T(g)(2)(ii)(A), the exchanged basis is reduced by the excess (if any) of the depreciation that would have been allowable if the exchanged automobile had been used solely for business over the depreciation that was allowable in those years. Thus, the exchanged basis, for purposes of computing depreciation, for Automobile Y is $17,315.

Example 3. The facts are the same as in *Example 1*, except that H placed in service Automobile X in January 2002, and H elected not to claim the additional first year depreciation deduction for 5-year property placed in service in 2002 and 2003. The relinquished automobile section 280F limit for Automobile X for 2003 is $4,900. Because the replacement automobile section 280F limit for 2003 for Automobile Y ($3,060) is less than the relinquished automobile section 280F limit for Automobile X for 2003 and is less than $5,388 (($30,000 (cost) − $3,060 (depreciation allowable for 2002)) × 0.4 × 6/12), the depreciation that would be allowable for Automobile X (determined without regard to section 280F) in the year of disposition, the depreciation for Automobile X in the year of disposition is limited to $3,060. For 2003 no depreciation is allowable for the excess basis and the exchanged basis in Automobile Y.

Example 4. AB, a calendar-year taxpayer, purchased and placed in service Automobile X1 in February 2000 for $10,000. X1 is a passenger automobile subject to section 280F(a) and is used solely for AB's business. AB depreciated X1 using a 5-year recovery period, the double declining balance method, and the half-year convention. As of January 1, 2003, the adjusted depreciable basis of X1 was $2,880 ($10,000 original cost minus $2,000 depreciation deduction for 2000, minus $3,200 depreciation deduction for 2001, and $1,920 depreciation deduction for 2002). In November 2003, AB exchanges, in a like-kind exchange, Automobile X1 plus $14,000 cash for new Automobile Y1 that will be used solely in AB's business. Automobile Y1 is 50-percent bonus depreciation property for purposes of section 168(k)(4) and qualifies for the expensing election under section 179. Pursuant to paragraph §1.168(k)-1(g)(3)(ii) and paragraph (k)(2)(i) of this section, AB decided to apply §1.168(i)-6 to the exchange of Automobile X1 for Automobile Y1, the replacement MACRS property. AB also makes the election under section 179 for the excess basis of Automobile Y1. AB depreciates Y1 using a five-year recovery period, the double declining balance method and the half-year convention. For 2003, the relinquished automobile section 280F limit for

Automobile X1 is $1,775 and the replacement automobile section 280F limit for 2003 for Automobile Y1 is $10,710.

(i) The 2003 depreciation deduction for Automobile X1 is $576. The depreciation deduction calculated for X1 is $576 (the adjusted depreciable basis of Automobile X1 at the beginning of 2003 of $2,880 × 40% × ¹/₂ year), which is less than the relinquished automobile section 280F limit and the replacement automobile section 280F limit.

(ii) The additional first year depreciation deduction for the exchanged basis is $1,152. The additional first year depreciation deduction of $1,152 (remaining exchanged basis of $2,304 ($2,880 adjusted basis of Automobile X1 at the beginning of 2003 minus $576) × 0.5)) is less than the replacement automobile section 280F limit minus $576.

(iii) AB's MACRS depreciation deduction allowable in 2003 for the remaining exchanged basis of $1,152 is $47 (the relinquished automobile section 280F limit of $1,775 less the depreciation deduction of $576 taken for Automobile X1 less the additional first year depreciation deduction of $1,152 taken for the exchanged basis) which is less than the depreciation deduction calculated for the depreciable exchanged basis.

(iv) For 2003, AB takes a $1,400 section 179 deduction for the excess basis of Automobile Y1. AB must reduce the excess basis of $14,000 by the section 179 deduction of $1,400 to determine the remaining excess basis of $12,600.

(v) For 2003, AB is allowed a 50-percent additional first year depreciation deduction of $6,300 (the remaining excess basis of $12,600 multiplied by .50).

(vi) For 2003, AB's depreciation deduction for the depreciable excess basis is limited to $1,235. The depreciation deduction computed without regard to the replacement automobile section 280F limit is $1,260 ($6,300 depreciable excess basis × 0.4 × 6/12). However the depreciation deduction for the depreciable excess basis is limited to $1,235 ($10,710 (replacement automobile section 280F limit) − $576 (depreciation deduction for Automobile X1) − $1,152 (additional first year depreciation deduction for the exchanged basis) − $47 (depreciation deduction for exchanged basis) $1,400 (section 179 deduction) − $6,300 (additional first year depreciation deduction for remaining excess basis)).

(4) *Involuntary conversion for which the replacement MACRS property is acquired and placed in service before disposition of relinquished MACRS property.*—If, in an involuntary conversion, a taxpayer acquires and places in service the replacement MACRS property before the date of disposition of the relinquished MACRS property, the taxpayer depreciates the unadjusted depreciable basis of the replacement MACRS property under section 168 beginning in the taxable year when the replacement MACRS property is placed in service by the taxpayer and by using the applicable depreciation method, recovery period, and convention prescribed under section 168 for the replacement MACRS property at the placed-in-service date. However, at the time of disposition of the relinquished MACRS property, the taxpayer determines the exchanged basis and the excess basis of the replacement MACRS property and begins to depreciate the depreciable exchanged basis of the replacement MACRS property in accordance with paragraph (c) of this section. The depreciable excess basis of the replacement MACRS property continues to be depreciated by the taxpayer in accordance with the first sentence of this paragraph (d)(4). Further, in the year of disposition of the relinquished MACRS property, the taxpayer must include in taxable income the excess of the depreciation deductions allowable on the unadjusted depreciable basis of the replacement MACRS property over the depreciation deductions that would have been allowable to the taxpayer on the depreciable excess basis of the replacement MACRS property from the date the replacement MACRS property was placed in service by the taxpayer (taking into account the applicable convention) to the time of disposition of the relinquished MACRS property. However, see § 1.168(k)-1(f)(5)(v) for replacement MACRS property that is qualified property or 50-percent bonus depreciation property and § 1.1400L(b)-1(f)(5) for replacement MACRS property that is qualified New York Liberty Zone property. Further, see § 1.168(k)-2(g)(5)(iv) for replacement MACRS property that is qualified property under section 168(k), as amended by the Tax Cuts and Jobs Act, Public Law 115-97 (131 Stat. 2054 (December 22, 2017)).

(e) *Use of optional depreciation tables.*—(1) *Taxpayer not bound by prior use of table.*—If a taxpayer used an optional depreciation table for the relinquished MACRS property, the taxpayer is not required to use an optional table for the depreciable exchanged basis of the replacement MACRS property. Conversely, if a taxpayer did not use an optional depreciation table for the relinquished MACRS property, the taxpayer may use the appropriate table for the depreciable exchanged basis of the replacement MACRS property. If a taxpayer decides not to use the table for the depreciable exchanged basis of the replacement MACRS property, the depreciation allowance for this property for the year of replacement and subsequent taxable years is determined under paragraph (c) of this section. If a taxpayer decides to use the optional depreciation tables, no depreciation deduction is allowable for MACRS property placed in service by the acquiring taxpayer and subsequently exchanged or involuntarily converted by such taxpayer in the same taxable year, and, if, during the same taxable year, MACRS property is placed in service by the acquiring taxpayer, exchanged or involuntarily converted by such taxpayer, and the replacement MACRS property is disposed of by such taxpayer, no depreciation deduction is allowable for either MACRS property.

(2) *Determination of the depreciation deduction.*—(i) *Relinquished MACRS property.*—In the year of disposition, the depreciation allowance for the relinquished MACRS property is computed by multiplying the unadjusted depreciable basis (less the amount of the additional first year depreciation deduction allowed or allowable, whichever is greater, under section 168(k) or section 1400L(b), as applicable) of the relinquished MACRS property by the annual depreciation rate (expressed as a decimal equivalent) specified in the appropriate table for the recovery year corresponding to the year of disposition. This product is then multiplied by a fraction, the numerator of which is the number of months (including fractions of months) the property is deemed to be placed in service during the year of the exchange or involuntary conversion (taking into account the applicable convention) and the denominator of which is 12. However, if the year of disposition is less than 12 months, the depreciation allowance determined under this paragraph (e)(2)(i) must be adjusted for a short taxable year (for further guidance, for example, see Rev. Proc. 89-15 (1989-1 CB 816) and § 601.601(d)(2)(ii)(b) of this chapter).

(ii) *Replacement MACRS property.*—(A) *Determination of the appropriate optional depreciation table.*—If a taxpayer chooses to use the appropriate optional depreciation table for the depreciable exchanged basis, the depreciation allowances for the depreciable exchanged basis beginning in the year of replacement are determined by choosing the optional depreciation table that corresponds to the recovery period, depreciation method, and convention of the replacement MACRS property determined under paragraph (c) of this section.

(B) *Calculating the depreciation deduction for the replacement MACRS property.*—(1) The depreciation deduction for the taxable year is computed by first determining the appropriate recovery year in the table identified under paragraph (e)(2)(ii)(A) of this section. The appropriate recovery year for the year of replacement is the same as the recovery year for the year of disposition, regardless of the taxable year in which the replacement property is acquired. For example, if the recovery year for the year of disposition would have been year 4 in the table that applied before the disposition of the relinquished MACRS property, then the recovery year for the year of replacement is Year 4 in the table identified under paragraph (e)(2)(ii)(A) of this section.

(2) Next, the annual depreciation rate (expressed as a decimal equivalent) for each recovery year is multiplied by a transaction coefficient. The transaction coefficient is the formula $(1 / (1 − x))$ where x equals the sum of the annual depreciation rates from the table identified under paragraph (e)(2)(ii)(A) of this section (expressed as a decimal equivalent) corresponding to the replacement MACRS property (as determined under paragraph (e)(2)(ii)(A) of this section) for the taxable years beginning with the placed-in-service year of the relinquished MACRS property through the taxable year immediately prior to the year of disposition. The product of the annual depreciation rate and the transaction coefficient is multiplied by the depreciable exchanged basis (taking into account paragraph (e)(2)(i) of this section). In the year of replacement, this product is then multiplied by a fraction, the numerator of which is the number of months (including fractions of months) the property is deemed to be placed in service by the acquiring taxpayer during the year of replacement (taking into account the applicable convention) and the denominator of which is 12. However, if the year of replacement is the year the relinquished MACRS property is placed in service by the acquiring taxpayer, the preceding sentence does not apply. In addition, if the year of replacement is less than 12 months, the depreciation allowance determined under paragraph (e)(2)(ii) of this section must be adjusted for a short taxable year (for further guidance, for example, see Rev. Proc. 89-15 (1989-1 CB 816) and § 601.601(d)(2)(ii)(b) of this chapter).

(iii) *Unrecovered basis.*—If the replacement MACRS property would have unrecovered depreciable basis after the final recovery year (for example, due to a deferred exchange), the unrecovered basis is an allowable depreciation deduction in the taxable year that corresponds to the final recovery year unless the unrecovered basis is subject to a depreciation limitation such as section 280F.

(3) *Excess basis.*—As provided in paragraph (d)(1) of this section, any excess basis in the replacement MACRS property is treated as property that is placed in service by the acquiring taxpayer at the time of replacement. Thus, if the taxpayer chooses to use the appropriate optional depreciation table for the depreciable excess basis in the replacement MACRS property, the depreciation allowances for the depreciable excess basis are determined by multiplying the depreciable excess basis by the annual depreciation rate (expressed as a decimal equivalent) specified in the appropriate table for each taxable year. The appropriate table for the depreciable excess basis is based on the depreciation method, recovery period, and convention applicable to the depreciable excess basis under section 168 at the time of replacement. However, If the year of replacement is less than 12 months, the depreciation allowance determined under this paragraph (e)(3) must be adjusted for a short taxable year (for further guidance, for example, see Rev. Proc. 89-15 (1989-1 CB 816) and § 601.601(d)(2)(ii)(*b*) of this chapter).

(4) *Examples.*—The application of this paragraph (e) is illustrated by the following examples:

Example 1. J, a calendar-year taxpayer, acquired 5-year property for $10,000 and placed it in service in January 2001. J uses the optional tables to depreciate the property. J uses the half-year convention and did not make any elections for the property. In December 2003, J exchanges the 5-year property for used 7-year property in a like-kind exchange. Pursuant to paragraph (k)(2)(i) of this section, J decided to apply § 1.168(i)-6 to the exchange of the 5-year property for the 7-year property, the replacement MACRS property. The depreciable exchanged basis of the 7-year property equals the adjusted depreciable basis of the 5-year property at the time of disposition of the relinquished MACRS property, namely $3,840 ($10,000 less $2,000 depreciation in 2001, $3,200 depreciation in 2002, and $960 depreciation in 2003). J must first determine the appropriate optional depreciation table pursuant to paragraph (c) of this section. Since the replacement MACRS property has a longer recovery period and the same depreciation method as the relinquished MACRS property, J uses the optional depreciation table corresponding to a 7-year recovery period, the 200% declining balance method, and the half-year convention (because the 5-year property was depreciated using a half-year convention). Had the replacement MACRS property been placed in service in the same taxable year as the placed-in-service year of the relinquished MACRS property, the depreciation allowance for the replacement MACRS property for the year of replacement would be determined using recovery year 3 of the optional table. The depreciation allowance equals the depreciable exchanged basis ($3,840) multiplied by the annual depreciation rate for the current taxable year (.1749 for recovery year 3) as modified by the transaction coefficient $[1 / (1 - (.1429 + .2449))]$which equals 1.6335. Thus, J multiplies $3,840, its depreciable exchanged basis in the replacement MACRS property, by the product of .1749 and 1.6335, and then by one-half, to determine the depreciation allowance for 2003, $549. For 2004, J multiples its depreciable exchanged basis in the replacement MACRS property determined at the time of replacement of $3,840 by the product of the modified annual depreciation rate for the current taxable year (.1249 for recovery year 4) and the transaction coefficient (1.6335) to determine its depreciation allowance of $783.

Example 2. K, a calendar-year taxpayer, acquired used Asset V for $100,000 and placed it in service in January 1999. K depreciated Asset V under the general depreciation system of section 168(a) by using a 5-year recovery period, the 200-percent declining balance method of depreciation, and the half-year convention. In December 2003, as part of the involuntary conversion, Asset V is involuntarily converted due to an earthquake. In October 2005, K purchases used Asset W with the insurance proceeds from the destruction of Asset V and places Asset W in service to replace Asset V. Pursuant to paragraph (k)(2)(i) of this section, K decided to apply § 1.168(i)-6 to the involuntary conversion of Asset V with the replacement of Asset W, the replacement MACRS property. If Asset W had been placed in service when Asset V was placed in service, it would have been depreciated using a 7-year recovery period, the 200-percent declining balance method, and the half-year convention. K uses the optional depreciation tables to depreciate Asset V and Asset W. For 2003 (recovery year 5 on the optional table), the depreciation deduction for Asset V is $5,760 ((0.1152)($100,000)(1/2)). Thus, the adjusted depreciable basis of Asset V at the time of replacement is $11,520 ($100,000 less $20,000 depreciation in 1999, $32,000 depreciation in 2000, $19,200 depreciation in 2001, $11,520 depreciation in 2002, and $5,760 depreciation in 2003). Under the table that applied to Asset V, the year of disposition was recovery year 5 and the depreciation deduction was determined under the straight line method. The table that applies for Asset W is the table that applies the straight line depreciation method, the half-year convention, and a 7-year recovery period. The appropriate recovery year under this table is recovery year 5. The depreciation deduction for Asset W for 2005 is $1,646

(($11,520)(0.1429)(1/(1 − 0.5))(1/2)). Thus, the depreciation deduction for Asset W in 2006 (recovery year 6) is $3,290 ($11,520)(0.1428)(1/(1 − 0.5)). The depreciation deduction for 2007 (recovery year 7) is $3,292 (($11,520)(.1429)(1/(1 − .5))). The depreciation deduction for 2008 (recovery year 8) is $3292 ($11,520 less allowable depreciation for Asset W for 2005 through 2007 ($1,646 + $3,290 + $3,292)).

Example 3. L, a calendar-year taxpayer, placed in service used Computer X in January 2002 for $5,000. L depreciated Computer X under the general depreciation system of section 168(a) by using the 200-percent declining balance method of depreciation, a 5-year recovery period, and the half-year convention. Computer X is destroyed in a fire in March 2004. For 2004, the depreciation deduction allowable for Computer X equals $480 ([($5,000)(.1920)] × (1/2)). Thus, the adjusted depreciable basis of Computer X was $1,920 when it was destroyed ($5,000 unadjusted depreciable basis less $1,000 depreciation for 2002, $1,600 depreciation for 2003, and $480 depreciation for 2004). In April 2004, as part of the involuntary conversion, L acquired and placed in service used Computer Y with insurance proceeds received due to the loss of Computer X. Computer Y will be depreciated using the same depreciation method, recovery period, and convention as Computer X. L elected to use the optional depreciation tables to compute the depreciation allowance for Computer X and Computer Y. The depreciation deduction allowable for 2004 for Computer Y equals $384 ([$1,920 × (.1920)(1/(1 − .52)] × (1/2)).

(f) *Mid-quarter convention.*—For purposes of applying the 40-percent test under section 168(d) and the regulations under section 168(d), the following rules apply:

(1) *Exchanged basis.*—If, in a taxable year, MACRS property is placed in service by the acquiring taxpayer (but not as a result of a like-kind exchange or involuntary conversion) and—

(i) In the same taxable year, is disposed of by the acquiring taxpayer in a like-kind exchange or an involuntary conversion and replaced by the acquiring taxpayer with replacement MACRS property, the exchanged basis (determined without any adjustments for depreciation deductions during the taxable year) of the replacement MACRS property is taken into account in the year of replacement in the quarter the relinquished MACRS property was placed in service by the acquiring taxpayer; or

(ii) In the same taxable year, is disposed of by the acquiring taxpayer in a like-kind exchange or an involuntary conversion, and in a subsequent taxable year is replaced by the acquiring taxpayer with replacement MACRS property, the exchanged basis (determined without any adjustments for depreciation deductions during the taxable year) of the replacement MACRS property is taken into account in the year of replacement in the quarter the replacement MACRS property was placed in service by the acquiring taxpayer; or

(iii) In a subsequent taxable year, disposed of by the acquiring taxpayer in a like-kind exchange or involuntary conversion, the exchanged basis of the replacement MACRS property is not taken into account in the year of replacement.

(2) *Excess basis.*—Any excess basis is taken into account in the quarter the replacement MACRS property is placed in service by the acquiring taxpayer.

(3) *Depreciable property acquired for nondepreciable property.*—Both the exchanged basis and excess basis of the replacement MACRS property described in paragraph (d)(2)(ii) of this section (depreciable property acquired for nondepreciable property), are taken into account for determining whether the mid-quarter convention applies in the year of replacement.

(g) *Section 179 election.*—In applying the section 179 election, only the excess basis, if any, in the replacement MACRS property is taken into account. If the replacement MACRS property is described in paragraph (d)(2)(ii) of this section (depreciable property acquired for nondepreciable property), only the excess basis in the replacement MACRS property is taken into account.

(h) *Additional first year depreciation deduction.*—See § 1.168(k)-1(f)(5) (for qualified property or 50-percent bonus depreciation property) and § 1.1400L(b)-1(f)(5) (for qualified New York Liberty Zone property). Further, see § 1.168(k)-2(g)(5) for qualified property under section 168(k), as amended by the Tax Cuts and Jobs Act, Public Law 115-97 (131 Stat. 2054 (December 22, 2017)).

(i) *Elections.*—(1) *Election not to apply this section.*—A taxpayer may elect not to apply this section for any MACRS property involved in a like-kind exchange or involuntary conversion. An election under this paragraph (i)(1) applies only to the taxpayer making the election and the election applies to both the relinquished MACRS property and the replacement MACRS property. If an election is made under this paragraph (i)(1), the depreciation allowances for the replacement MACRS property beginning in the year of replacement and for the relinquished MACRS property in the year of disposition are not determined under this section (except as otherwise provided in this paragraph). Instead, for depreciation purposes only, the sum of the exchanged basis and excess basis, if any, in the replacement MACRS property is treated as property placed in service by the taxpayer at the time of replacement and the adjusted depreciable basis of the relinquished MACRS property is treated as being disposed of by the taxpayer at the time of disposition. While the relinquished MACRS property is treated as being disposed of at the time of disposition for depreciation purposes, the election not to apply this section does not affect the application of sections 1031 and 1033 (for example, if a taxpayer does not make the election under this paragraph (i)(1) and does not recognize gain or loss under section 1031, this result would not change if the taxpayer chose to make the election under this paragraph (i)(1)). In addition, the election not to apply this section does not affect the application of sections 1245 and 1250 to the relinquished MACRS property. Paragraphs (c)(5)(i) (determination of depreciation for relinquished MACRS property in the year of disposition), (c)(5)(iii) (rules for deferred transactions), (g) (section 179 election), and (h) (additional first year depreciation deduction) of this section apply to property to which this paragraph (i)(1) applies. See paragraph (j) of this section for the time and manner of making the election under this paragraph (i)(1).

(2) *Election to treat certain replacement property as MACRS property.*—If the tangible depreciable property acquired by a taxpayer in a like-kind exchange or involuntary conversion (the replacement property) replaces tangible depreciable property for which the taxpayer made a valid election under section 168(f)(1) to exclude it from the application of MACRS (the relinquished property), the taxpayer may elect to treat, for depreciation purposes only, the sum of the exchanged basis and excess basis, if any, of the replacement property as MACRS property that is placed in service by the taxpayer at the time of replacement. An election under this paragraph (i)(2) applies only to the taxpayer making the election and the election applies to both the relinquished property and the replacement property. If an election is made under this paragraph (i)(2), the adjusted depreciable basis of the relinquished property is treated as being disposed of by the taxpayer at the time of disposition. Rules similar to those provided in §§ 1.168(i)-6(b)(3) and (4) apply for purposes of determining the time of disposition and time of replacement under this paragraph (i)(2). While the relinquished property is treated as being disposed of at the time of disposition for depreciation purposes, the election under this paragraph (i)(2) does not affect the application of sections 1031 and 1033, and the application of sections 1245 and 1250 to the relinquished property. If an election is made under this paragraph (i)(2), rules similar to those provided in paragraphs (c)(5)(iii) (rules for deferred transactions), (g) (section 179 election), and (h) (additional first year depreciation deduction) of this section apply to property. Except as provided in paragraph (k)(3)(ii) of this section, a taxpayer makes the election under this paragraph (i)(2) by claiming the depreciation allowance as determined under MACRS for the replacement property on the taxpayer's timely filed (including extensions) original Federal tax return for the placed-in-service year of the replacement property as determined under this paragraph (i)(2).

(j) *Time and manner of making election under paragraph (i)(1) of this section.*—(1) *In general.*—The election provided in paragraph (i)(1) of this section is made separately by each person acquiring replacement MACRS property. The election is made for each member of a consolidated group by the common parent of the group, by the partnership (and not by the partners separately) in the case of a partnership, or by the S corporation (and not by the shareholders separately) in the case of an S corporation. A separate election under paragraph (i)(1) of this section is required for each like-kind exchange or involuntary conversion. The election provided in paragraph (i)(1) of this section must be made within the time and manner provided in paragraph (j)(2) and (3) of this section and may not be made by the taxpayer in any other manner (for example, the election cannot be made through a request under section 446(e) to change the taxpayer's method of accounting), except as provided in paragraph (k)(2) of this section.

(2) *Time for making election.*—The election provided in paragraph (i)(1) of this section must be made by the due date (including extensions) of the taxpayer's Federal tax return for the year of *replacement.*

(3) *Manner of making election.*—The election provided in paragraph (i)(1) of this section is made in the manner provided for on Form 4562, Depreciation and Amortization, and its instructions. If Form 4562 is revised or renumbered, any reference in this section to that form is treated as a reference to the revised or renumbered form.

(4) *Revocation.*—The election provided in paragraph (i)(1) of this section, once made, may be revoked only with the consent of the Commissioner of Internal Revenue. Such consent will be granted only in extraordinary circumstances. Requests for consent are re-

quests for a letter ruling and must be filed with the Commissioner of Internal Revenue, Washington, DC, 20224. Requests for consent may not be made in any other manner (for example, through a request under section 446(e) to change the taxpayer's method of accounting).

(k) *Effective date.*—(1) *In general.*—Except as provided in paragraphs (k)(3) and (4) of this section, this section applies to a like-kind exchange or an involuntary conversion of MACRS property for which the time of disposition and the time of replacement both occur after February 27, 2004.

(2) *Application to pre-effective date like-kind exchanges and involuntary conversions.*—For a like-kind exchange or an involuntary conversion of MACRS property for which the time of disposition, the time of replacement, or both occur on or before February 27, 2004, a taxpayer may—

(i) Apply the provisions of this section. If a taxpayer's applicable Federal tax return has been filed on or before February 27, 2004, and the taxpayer has treated the replacement MACRS property as acquired, and the relinquished MACRS property as disposed of, in a like-kind exchange or an involuntary conversion, the taxpayer changes its method of accounting for depreciation of the replacement MACRS property and relinquished MACRS property in accordance with this paragraph (k)(2)(i) by following the applicable administrative procedures issued under § 1.446-1(e)(3)(ii) for obtaining the Commissioner's automatic consent to a change in method of accounting (for further guidance, see Rev. Proc. 2002-9 (2002-1 CB 327) and § 601.601(d)(2)(ii)(*b*) of this chapter); or

(ii) Rely on prior guidance issued by the Internal Revenue Service for determining the depreciation deductions of replacement MACRS property and relinquished MACRS property (for further guidance, for example, see Notice 2000-4 (2001-1 CB 313) and § 601.601(d)(2)(ii)(*b*) of this chapter). In relying on such guidance, a taxpayer may use any reasonable, consistent method of determining depreciation in the year of disposition and the year of replacement. If a taxpayer's applicable Federal tax return has been filed on or before February 27, 2004, and the taxpayer has treated the replacement MACRS property as acquired, and the relinquished MACRS property as disposed of, in a like-kind exchange or an involuntary conversion, the taxpayer changes its method of accounting for depreciation of the replacement MACRS property and relinquished MACRS property in accordance with this paragraph (k)(2)(ii) by following the applicable administrative procedures issued under § 1.446-1(e)(3)(ii) for obtaining the Commissioner's automatic consent to a change in method of accounting (for further guidance, see Rev. Proc. 2002-9 (2002-1 CB 327) and § 601.601(d)(2)(ii)(*b*) of this chapter).

(3) *Like-kind exchanges and involuntary conversions where the taxpayer made the election under section 168(f)(1) for the relinquished property.*—(i) *In general.*—If the tangible depreciable property acquired by a taxpayer in a like-kind exchange or involuntary conversion (the replacement property) replaces tangible depreciable property for which the taxpayer made a valid election under section 168(f)(1) to exclude it from the application of MACRS (the relinquished property), paragraph (i)(2) of this section applies to such relinquished property and replacement property for which the time of disposition and the time of replacement (both as determined under paragraph (i)(2) of this section) both occur after February 26, 2007.

(ii) *Application of paragraph (i)(2) of this section to pre-February 26, 2007 like-kind exchanges and involuntary conversions.*—If the tangible depreciable property acquired by a taxpayer in a like-kind exchange or involuntary conversion (the replacement property) replaces tangible depreciable property for which the taxpayer made a valid election under section 168(f)(1) to exclude it from the application of MACRS (the relinquished property), the taxpayer may apply paragraph (i)(2) of this section to the relinquished property and the replacement property for which the time of disposition, the time of replacement (both as determined under paragraph (i)(2) of this section), or both occur on or before February 26, 2007. If the taxpayer wants to apply paragraph (i)(2) of this section and the taxpayer's applicable Federal tax return has been filed on or before February 26, 2007, the taxpayer must change its method of accounting for depreciation of the replacement property and relinquished property in accordance with this paragraph (k)(3)(ii) by following the applicable administrative procedures issued under § 1.446-1(e)(3)(ii) for obtaining the Commissioner's automatic consent to a change in method of accounting (for further guidance, see Rev. Proc. 2002-9 (2002-1 CB 327) and § 601.601(d)(2)(ii)(*b*) of this chapter).

(4) *Qualified property under section 168(k) acquired and placed in service after September 27, 2017.*—(i) *In general.*—The language "1.168(k)-2(g)(5)," in paragraphs (d)(3)(ii)(B) and (E) of this section and the final sentence in paragraphs (d)(4) and (h) of this section apply to a like-kind exchange or an involuntary conversion of MACRS property, which is qualified property under section

168(k)(2), for which the time of replacement occurs on or after September 24, 2019.

(ii) *Early application.*—A taxpayer may choose to apply the language "1.168(k)-2(g)(5)," in paragraphs (d)(3)(ii)(B) and (E) of this section and the final sentence in paragraphs (d)(4) and (h) of this section to a like-kind exchange or an involuntary conversion of MACRS property, which is qualified property under section 168(k)(2), for which the time of replacement occurs on or after September 28, 2017.

(iii) *Early application of regulation project REG-104397-18.*—A taxpayer may rely on the language "1.168(k)-2(f)(5)," in paragraphs (d)(3)(ii)(B) and (E) of this section and the final sentence in paragraphs (d)(4) and (h) of this section in regulation project REG-104397-18 (2018-41 I.R.B. 558) (see §601.601(d)(2)(ii)(b) of this chapter) for a like-kind exchange or an involuntary conversion of MACRS property, which is qualified property under section 168(k)(2), for which the time of replacement occurs on or after September 28, 2017, and occurs before September 24, 2019. [Reg. §1.168(i)-6.]

☐ [*T.D. 9314, 2-26-2007 Amended by T.D. 9874, 9-17-2019.*]

[Reg. §1.168(i)-7]

§1.168(i)-7. Accounting for MACRS property.—(a) *In general.*—A taxpayer may account for MACRS property (as defined in §1.168(b)-1(a)(2)) by treating each individual asset as an account (a "single asset account" or an "item account") or by combining two or more assets in a single account (a "multiple asset account" or a "pool"). A taxpayer may establish as many accounts for MACRS property as the taxpayer wants. This section does not apply to assets included in general asset accounts. For rules applicable to general asset accounts, see §1.168(i)-1.

(b) *Required use of single asset accounts.*—A taxpayer must account for an asset in a single asset account if the taxpayer uses the asset both in a trade or business or for the production of income and in a personal activity, or if the taxpayer places in service and disposes of the asset during the same taxable year. Also, if general asset account treatment for an asset terminates under §1.168(i)-1(c)(1)(ii)(A), (e)(3)(iii), (e)(3)(v), (e)(3)(vii), (g), or (h)(1), as applicable, the taxpayer must account for the asset in a single asset account beginning in the taxable year in which the general asset account treatment for the asset terminates. If a taxpayer accounts for an asset in a multiple asset account or a pool and the taxpayer disposes of the asset, the taxpayer must account for the asset in a single asset account beginning in the taxable year in which the disposition occurs. See §1.168(i)-8(h)(2)(i). If a taxpayer disposes of a portion of an asset and §1.168(i)-8(d)(1) applies to that disposition, the taxpayer must account for the disposed portion in a single asset account beginning in the taxable year in which the disposition occurs. See §1.168(i)-8(h)(3)(i).

(c) *Establishment of multiple asset accounts or pools.*—(1) *Assets eligible for multiple asset accounts or pools.*—Except as provided in paragraph (b) of this section, assets that are subject to either the general depreciation system of section 168(a) or the alternative depreciation system of section 168(g) may be accounted for in one or more multiple asset accounts or pools.

(2) *Grouping assets in multiple asset accounts or pools.*—(i) *General rules.*—Assets that are eligible to be grouped into a single multiple asset account or pool may be divided into more than one multiple asset account or pool. Each multiple asset account or pool must include only assets that—

(A) Have the same applicable depreciation method;

(B) Have the same applicable recovery period;

(C) Have the same applicable convention; and

(D) Are placed in service by the taxpayer in the same taxable year.

(ii) *Special rules.*—In addition to the general rules in paragraph (c)(2)(i) of this section, the following rules apply when establishing multiple asset accounts or pools—

(A) Assets subject to the mid-quarter convention may only be grouped into a multiple asset account or pool with assets that are placed in service in the same quarter of the taxable year;

(B) Assets subject to the mid-month convention may only be grouped into a multiple asset account or pool with assets that are placed in service in the same month of the taxable year;

(C) Passenger automobiles for which the depreciation allowance is limited under section 280F(a) must be grouped into a separate multiple asset account or pool;

(D) Assets not eligible for any additional first year depreciation deduction (including assets for which the taxpayer elected not to deduct the additional first year depreciation) provided by, for

example, section 168(k) through (n), 1400L(b), or 1400N(d), must be grouped into a separate multiple asset account or pool;

(E) Assets eligible for the additional first year depreciation deduction may only be grouped into a multiple asset account or pool with assets for which the taxpayer claimed the same percentage of the additional first year depreciation (for example, 30 percent, 50 percent, or 100 percent);

(F) Except for passenger automobiles described in paragraph (c)(2)(ii)(C) of this section, listed property (as defined in section 280F(d)(4)) must be grouped into a separate multiple asset account or pool;

(G) Assets for which the depreciation allowance for the placed-in-service year is not determined by using an optional depreciation table (for further guidance, see section 8 of Rev. Proc. 87-57, 1987-2 CB 687, 693 (see §601.601(d)(2) of this chapter)) must be grouped into a separate multiple asset account or pool; and

(H) Mass assets (as defined in §1.168(i)-8(b)(3)) that are or will be subject to §1.168(i)-8(g)(2)(iii) (disposed of or converted mass asset is identified by a mortality dispersion table) must be grouped into a separate multiple asset account or pool.

(d) *Cross references.*—See §1.167(a)-7(c) for the records to be maintained by a taxpayer for each account. In addition, see §1.168(i)-1(l)(3) for the records to be maintained by a taxpayer for each general asset account.

(e) *Effective/applicability dates.*—(1) *In general.*—This section applies to taxable years beginning on or after January 1, 2014.

(2) *Early application of this section.*—A taxpayer may choose to apply the provisions of this section to taxable years beginning on or after January 1, 2012.

(3) *Early application of regulation project REG-110732-13.*—A taxpayer may rely on the provisions of this section in regulation project REG-110732-13 (2013-43 IRB 404) (see §601.601(d)(2) of this chapter) for taxable years beginning on or after January 1, 2012. However, a taxpayer may not rely on the provisions of this section in regulation project REG-110732-13 for taxable years beginning on or after January 1, 2014.

(4) *Optional application of TD 9564.*—A taxpayer may choose to apply §1.168(i)-7T as contained in 26 CFR part 1 edition revised as of April 1, 2013, to taxable years beginning on or after January 1, 2012. However, a taxpayer may not apply §1.168(i)-7T as contained in 26 CFR part 1 edition revised as of April 1, 2013, to taxable years beginning on or after January 1, 2014.

(5) *Change in method of accounting.*—A change to comply with this section for depreciable assets placed in service in a taxable year ending on or after December 30, 2003, is a change in method of accounting to which the provisions of section 446(e) and the regulations under section 446(e) apply. A taxpayer also may treat a change to comply with this section for depreciable assets placed in service in a taxable year ending before December 30, 2003, as a change in method of accounting to which the provisions of section 446(e) and the regulations under section 446(e) apply. [Reg. §1.168(i)-7.]

☐ [*T.D. 9636, 9-13-2013. Amended by T.D. 9689, 8-14-2014 (corrected 12-30-2014).*]

[Reg. §1.168(i)-8]

§1.168(i)-8. Dispositions of MACRS property.—(a) *Scope.*—This section provides rules applicable to dispositions of MACRS property (as defined in §1.168(b)-1(a)(2)) or to depreciable property (as defined in §1.168(b)-1(a)(1)) that would be MACRS property but for an election made by the taxpayer either to expense all or some of the property's cost under section 179, section 179A, section 179B, section 179C, section 179D, or section 1400I(a)(1), or any similar provision, or to amortize all or some of the property's cost under section 1400I(a)(2) or any similar provision. This section also applies to dispositions described in paragraph (d)(1) of this section of a portion of such property. Except as provided in §1.168(i)-1(e)(3), this section does not apply to dispositions of assets included in a general asset account. For rules applicable to dispositions of assets included in a general asset account, see §1.168(i)-1(e).

(b) *Definitions.*—For purposes of this section—

(1) *Building* has the same meaning as that term is defined in §1.48-1(e)(1).

(2) *Disposition* occurs when ownership of the asset is transferred or when the asset is permanently withdrawn from use either in the taxpayer's trade or business or in the production of income. A disposition includes the sale, exchange, retirement, physical abandonment, or destruction of an asset. A disposition also occurs when an asset is transferred to a supplies, scrap, or similar account, or when a portion of an asset is disposed of as described in paragraph

Itemized Deductions for Individuals and Corps.
See p. 20,601 for regulations not amended to reflect law changes
25,479

(d)(1) of this section. If a structural component, or a portion thereof, of a building is disposed of in a disposition described in paragraph (d)(1) of this section, a disposition also includes the disposition of such structural component or such portion thereof.

(3) *Mass assets* is a mass or group of individual items of depreciable assets—

(i) That are not necessarily homogenous;

(ii) Each of which is minor in value relative to the total value of the mass or group;

(iii) Numerous in quantity;

(iv) Usually accounted for only on a total dollar or quantity basis;

(v) With respect to which separate identification is impracticable; and

(vi) Placed in service in the same taxable year.

(4) *Portion of an asset* is any part of an asset that is less than the entire asset as determined under paragraph (c)(4) of this section.

(5) *Structural component* has the same meaning as that term is defined in § 1.48-1(e)(2).

(6) *Unadjusted depreciable basis of the multiple asset account or pool* is the sum of the unadjusted depreciable bases (as defined in § 1.168(b)-1(a)(3)) of all assets included in the multiple asset account or pool.

(c) *Special rules.*—(1) *Manner of disposition.*—The manner of disposition (for example, normal retirement, abnormal retirement, ordinary retirement, or extraordinary retirement) is not taken into account in determining whether a disposition occurs or gain or loss is recognized.

(2) *Disposition by transfer to a supplies account.*—If a taxpayer made an election under § 1.162-3(d) to treat the cost of any rotable spare part, temporary spare part, or standby emergency spare part (as defined in § 1.162-3(c)) as a capital expenditure subject to the allowance for depreciation, the taxpayer can dispose of the rotable, temporary, or standby emergency spare part by transferring it to a supplies account only if the taxpayer has obtained the consent of the Commissioner to revoke the § 1.162-3(d) election. If a taxpayer made an election under § 1.162-3T(d) to treat the cost of any material and supply (as defined in § 1.162-3T(c)(1)) as a capital expenditure subject to the allowance for depreciation, the taxpayer can dispose of the material and supply by transferring it to a supplies account only if the taxpayer has obtained the consent of the Commissioner to revoke the § 1.162-3T(d) election. See § 1.162-3(d)(3) for the procedures for revoking a § 1.162-3(d) or a § 1.162-3T(d) election.

(3) *Leasehold improvements.*—This section also applies to—

(i) A lessor of leased property that made an improvement to that property for the lessee of the property, has a depreciable basis in the improvement, and disposes of the improvement, or disposes of a portion of the improvement under paragraph (d)(1) of this section, before or upon the termination of the lease with the lessee. See section 168(i)(8)(B); and

(ii) A lessee of leased property that made an improvement to that property, has a depreciable basis in the improvement, and disposes of the improvement, or disposes of a portion of the improvement under paragraph (d)(1) of this section, before or upon the termination of the lease.

(4) *Determination of asset disposed of.*—(i) *General rules.*—For purposes of applying this section, the facts and circumstances of each disposition are considered in determining what is the appropriate asset disposed of. The asset for disposition purposes may not consist of items placed in service by the taxpayer on different dates, without taking into account the applicable convention. For purposes of determining what is the appropriate asset disposed of, the unit of property determination under § 1.263(a)-3(e) or in published guidance in the Internal Revenue Bulletin (see § 601.601(d)(2) of this chapter) under section 263(a) and the distinct asset determination under § 1.1031(a)-3(a)(4) do not apply.

(ii) *Special rules.*—In addition to the general rules in paragraph (c)(4)(i) of this section, the following rules apply for purposes of applying this section:

(A) Each building, including its structural components, is the asset, except as provided in § 1.1250-1a(2)(ii) or in paragraph (c)(4)(ii)(B) or (D) of this section.

(B) If a building has two or more condominium or cooperative units, each condominium or cooperative unit, including its structural components, is the asset, except as provided in § 1.1250-1a(2)(ii) or in paragraph (c)(4)(ii)(D) of this section.

(C) If a taxpayer properly includes an item in one of the asset classes 00.11 through 00.4 of Rev. Proc. 87-56 (1987-2 CB 674) (see § 601.601(d)(2) of this chapter) or properly classifies an item in one of the categories under section 168(e)(3), except for a category that includes buildings or structural components (for example, retail

motor fuels outlet, qualified leasehold improvement property, qualified restaurant property, and qualified retail improvement property), each item is the asset provided paragraph (c)(4)(ii)(D) of this section does not apply to the item. For example, each desk is the asset, each computer is the asset, and each qualified smart electric meter is the asset.

(D) If the taxpayer places in service an improvement or addition to an asset after the taxpayer placed the asset in service, the improvement or addition and, if applicable, its structural components are a separate asset.

(d) *Disposition of a portion of an asset.*—(1) *In general.*—For purposes of applying this section, a disposition includes a disposition of a portion of an asset as a result of a casualty event described in section 165, a disposition of a portion of an asset for which gain, determined without regard to section 1245 or section 1250, is not recognized in whole or in part under section 1031 or section 1033, a transfer of a portion of an asset in a transaction described in section 168(i)(7)(B), or a sale of a portion of an asset, even if the taxpayer does not make the election under paragraph (d)(2)(i) of this section for that disposed portion. For other transactions, a disposition includes a disposition of a portion of an asset only if the taxpayer makes the election under paragraph (d)(2)(i) of this section for that disposed portion.

(2) *Partial disposition election.*—(i) *In general.*—A taxpayer may make an election under this paragraph (d)(2) to apply this section to a disposition of a portion of an asset. If the asset is properly included in one of the asset classes 00.11 through 00.4 of Rev. Proc. 87-56, a taxpayer may make an election under this paragraph (d)(2) to apply this section to a disposition of a portion of such asset only if the taxpayer classifies the replacement portion of the asset under the same asset class as the disposed portion of the asset.

(ii) *Time and manner for making election.*—(A) *Time for making election.*—Except as provided in paragraph (d)(2)(iii) or (iv) of this section, a taxpayer must make the election specified in paragraph (d)(2)(i) of this section by the due date, including extensions, of the original Federal tax return for the taxable year in which the portion of an asset is disposed of by the taxpayer.

(B) *Manner of making election.*—Except as provided in paragraph (d)(2)(iii) or (iv) of this section, a taxpayer must make the election specified in paragraph (d)(2)(i) of this section by applying the provisions of this section for the taxable year in which the portion of an asset is disposed of by the taxpayer, by reporting the gain, loss, or other deduction on the taxpayer's timely filed, including extensions, original Federal tax return for that taxable year, and, if the asset is properly included in one of the asset classes 00.11 through 00.4 of Rev. Proc. 87-56, by classifying the replacement portion of such asset under the same asset class as the disposed portion of the asset in the taxable year in which the replacement portion is placed in service by the taxpayer. Except as provided in paragraph (d)(2)(iii) or (iv)(B) of this section or except as otherwise expressly provided by other guidance published in the Internal Revenue Bulletin (see § 601.601(d)(2) of this chapter), the election specified in paragraph (d)(2)(i) of this section may not be made through the filing of an application for change in accounting method.

(iii) *Special rule for subsequent Internal Revenue Service adjustment.*—This paragraph (d)(2)(iii) applies when a taxpayer deducted the amount paid or incurred for the replacement of a portion of an asset as a repair under § 1.162-4, the taxpayer did not make the election specified in paragraph (d)(2)(i) of this section for the disposed portion of that asset within the time and in the manner under paragraph (d)(2)(ii) or (iv) of this section, and as a result of an examination of the taxpayer's Federal tax return, the Internal Revenue Service disallows the taxpayer's repair deduction for the amount paid or incurred for the replacement of the portion of that asset and instead capitalizes such amount under § 1.263(a)-2 or § 1.263(a)-3. If this paragraph (d)(2)(iii) applies, the taxpayer may make the election specified in paragraph (d)(2)(i) of this section for the disposition of the portion of the asset to which the Internal Revenue Service's adjustment pertains by filing an application for change in accounting method, provided the asset of which the disposed portion was a part is owned by the taxpayer at the beginning of the year of change (as defined for purposes of section 446(e)).

(iv) *Special rules for 2012 or 2013 returns.*—If, under paragraph (j)(2) of this section, a taxpayer chooses to apply the provisions of this section to a taxable year beginning on or after January 1, 2012, and ending on or before September 19, 2013 (applicable taxable year), and the taxpayer did not make the election specified in paragraph (d)(2)(i) of this section on its timely filed original Federal tax return for the applicable taxable year, including extensions, the taxpayer must make the election specified in paragraph (d)(2)(i) of this section for the applicable taxable year by filing either—

(A) An amended Federal tax return for the applicable taxable year on or before 180 days from the due date including extensions of the taxpayer's Federal tax return for the applicable taxable year, notwithstanding that the taxpayer may not have extended the due date; or

(B) An application for change in accounting method with the taxpayer's timely filed original Federal tax return for the first or second taxable year succeeding the applicable taxable year.

(v) *Revocation.*—A taxpayer may revoke the election specified in paragraph (d)(2)(i) of this section only by filing a request for a private letter ruling and obtaining the Commissioner's consent to revoke the election. The Commissioner may grant a request to revoke this election if the taxpayer acted reasonably and in good faith, and the revocation will not prejudice the interests of the Government. See generally § 301.9100-3 of this chapter. The election specified in paragraph (d)(2)(i) of this section may not be revoked through the filing of an application for change in accounting method.

(e) *Gain or loss on dispositions.*—Solely for purposes of this paragraph (e), the term *asset* is an asset within the scope of this section or the portion of such asset that is disposed of in a disposition described in paragraph (d)(1) of this section. Except as provided by section 280B and § 1.280B-1, the following rules apply when an asset is disposed of during a taxable year:

(1) If an asset is disposed of by sale, exchange, or involuntary conversion, gain or loss must be recognized under the applicable provisions of the Internal Revenue Code.

(2) If an asset is disposed of by physical abandonment, loss must be recognized in the amount of the adjusted depreciable basis (as defined in § 1.168(b)-1(a)(4)) of the asset at the time of the abandonment, taking into account the applicable convention. However, if the abandoned asset is subject to nonrecourse indebtedness, paragraph (e)(1) of this section applies to the asset instead of this paragraph (e)(2). For a loss from physical abandonment to qualify for recognition under this paragraph (e)(2), the taxpayer must intend to discard the asset irrevocably so that the taxpayer will neither use the asset again nor retrieve it for sale, exchange, or other disposition.

(3) If an asset is disposed of other than by sale, exchange, involuntary conversion, physical abandonment, or conversion to personal use (as, for example, when the asset is transferred to a supplies or scrap account), gain is not recognized. Loss must be recognized in the amount of the excess of the adjusted depreciable basis of the asset at the time of the disposition, taking into account the applicable convention, over the asset's fair market value at the time of the disposition, taking into account the applicable convention.

(f) *Basis of asset disposed of.*—(1) *In general.*—The adjusted basis of an asset disposed of for computing gain or loss is its adjusted depreciable basis at the time of the asset's disposition, as determined under the applicable convention for the asset.

(2) *Assets disposed of are in multiple accounts.*—(i) If the taxpayer accounts for the asset disposed of in a multiple asset account or pool and it is impracticable from the taxpayer's records to determine the unadjusted depreciable basis (as defined in § 1.168(b)-1(a)(3)) of the asset disposed of, the taxpayer may use any reasonable method that is consistently applied to all assets in the same multiple asset account or pool for purposes of determining the unadjusted depreciable basis of assets disposed of. Examples of a reasonable method include, but are not limited to, the following:

(A) If the replacement asset is a restoration (as defined in § 1.263(a)-3(k)), and is not a betterment (as defined in § 1.263(a)-3(j)) or an adaptation to a new or different use (as defined in § 1.263(a)-3(l)), discounting the cost of the replacement asset to its placed-in-service year cost using the Producer Price Index for Finished Goods or its successor, the Producer Price Index for Final Demand, or any other index designated by guidance in the Internal Revenue Bulletin (see § 601.601(d)(2) of this chapter) for purposes of this paragraph (f)(2);

(B) A pro rata allocation of the unadjusted depreciable basis of the multiple asset account or pool based on the replacement cost of the disposed asset and the replacement cost of all of the assets in the multiple asset account or pool; and

(C) A study allocating the cost of the asset to its individual components.

(ii) To determine the adjusted depreciable basis of an asset disposed of in a multiple asset account or pool, the depreciation allowable for the asset disposed of is computed by using the depreciation method, recovery period, and convention applicable to the multiple asset account or pool in which the asset disposed of was included and by including the additional first year depreciation deduction claimed for the asset disposed of.

(3) *Disposition of a portion of an asset.*—(i) This paragraph (f)(3) applies only when a taxpayer disposes of a portion of an asset and

paragraph (d)(1) of this section applies to that disposition. For computing gain or loss, the adjusted basis of the disposed portion of the asset is the adjusted depreciable basis of that disposed portion at the time of its disposition, as determined under the applicable convention for the asset. If it is impracticable from the taxpayer's records to determine the unadjusted depreciable basis (as defined in § 1.168(b)-1(a)(3)) of the disposed portion of the asset, the taxpayer may use any reasonable method for purposes of determining the unadjusted depreciable basis (as defined in § 1.168(b)-1(a)(3)) of the disposed portion of the asset. If a taxpayer disposes of more than one portion of the same asset and it is impracticable from the taxpayer's records to determine the unadjusted depreciable basis (as defined in § 1.168(b)-1(a)(3)) of the first disposed portion of the asset, the reasonable method used by the taxpayer must be consistently applied to all portions of the same asset for purposes of determining the unadjusted depreciable basis of each disposed portion of the asset. If the asset, a portion of which is disposed of, is in a multiple asset account or pool and it is impracticable from the taxpayer's records to determine the unadjusted depreciable basis (as defined in § 1.168(b)-1(a)(3)) of the disposed portion of the asset, the reasonable method used by the taxpayer must be consistently applied to all assets in the same multiple asset account or pool for purposes of determining the unadjusted depreciable basis of assets disposed of or any disposed portion of the assets. Examples of a reasonable method include, but are not limited to, the following:

(A) If the replacement portion is a restoration (as defined in § 1.263(a)-3(k)), and is not a betterment (as defined in § 1.263(a)-3(j)) or an adaptation to a new or different use (as defined in § 1.263(a)-3(l)), discounting the cost of the replacement portion of the asset to its placed-in-service year cost using the Producer Price Index for Finished Goods or its successor, the Producer Price Index for Final Demand, or any other index designated by guidance in the Internal Revenue Bulletin (see § 601.601(d)(2) of this chapter) for purposes of this paragraph (f)(3);

(B) A pro rata allocation of the unadjusted depreciable basis of the asset based on the replacement cost of the disposed portion of the asset and the replacement cost of the asset; and

(C) A study allocating the cost of the asset to its individual components.

(ii) To determine the adjusted depreciable basis of the disposed portion of the asset, the depreciation allowable for the disposed portion is computed by using the depreciation method, recovery period, and convention applicable to the asset in which the disposed portion was included and by including the portion of the additional first year depreciation deduction claimed for the asset that is attributable to the disposed portion.

(g) *Identification of asset disposed of.*—(1) *In general.*—Except as provided in paragraph (g)(2) or (3) of this section, a taxpayer must use the specific identification method of accounting to identify which asset is disposed of by the taxpayer. Under this method of accounting, the taxpayer can determine the particular taxable year in which the asset disposed of was placed in service by the taxpayer.

(2) *Asset disposed of is in a multiple asset account.*—If a taxpayer accounts for the asset disposed of in a multiple asset account or pool and the total dispositions of assets with the same recovery period during the taxable year are readily determined from the taxpayer's records, but it is impracticable from the taxpayer's records to determine the particular taxable year in which the asset disposed of was placed in service by the taxpayer, the taxpayer must identify the asset disposed of by using—

(i) A first-in, first-out method of accounting if the unadjusted depreciable basis of the asset disposed of cannot be readily determined from the taxpayer's records. Under this method of accounting, the taxpayer identifies the multiple asset account or pool with the earliest placed-in-service year that has the same recovery period as the asset disposed of and that has assets at the beginning of the taxable year of the disposition, and the taxpayer treats the asset disposed of as being from that multiple asset account or pool;

(ii) A modified first-in, first-out method of accounting if the unadjusted depreciable basis of the asset disposed of can be readily determined from the taxpayer's records. Under this method of accounting, the taxpayer identifies the multiple asset account or pool with the earliest placed-in-service year that has the same recovery period as the asset disposed of and that has assets at the beginning of the taxable year of the disposition with the same unadjusted depreciable basis as the asset disposed of, and the taxpayer treats the asset disposed of as being from that multiple asset account or pool;

(iii) A mortality dispersion table if the asset disposed of is a mass asset. The mortality dispersion table must be based upon an acceptable sampling of the taxpayer's actual disposition experience for mass assets or other acceptable statistical or engineering techniques. To use a mortality dispersion table, the taxpayer must adopt

Itemized Deductions for Individuals and Corps.
See p. 20,601 for regulations not amended to reflect law changes
25,481

recordkeeping practices consistent with the taxpayer's prior practices and consonant with good accounting and engineering practices; or

(iv) Any other method as the Secretary may designate by publication in the **Federal Register** or in the Internal Revenue Bulletin (see §601.601(d)(2) of this chapter) on or after September 19, 2013. See paragraph (g)(4) of this section regarding the last-in, first-out method of accounting.

(3) *Disposition of a portion of an asset.*—If a taxpayer disposes of a portion of an asset and paragraph (d)(1) of this section applies to that disposition, but it is impracticable from the taxpayer's records to determine the particular taxable year in which the asset was placed in service, the taxpayer must identify the asset by using any applicable method provided in paragraph (g)(2) of this section, after taking into account paragraph (g)(4) of this section.

(4) *Last-in, first-out method of accounting.*—For purposes of this paragraph (g), a last-in, first-out method of accounting may not be used. Examples of a last-in, first-out method of accounting include the taxpayer identifying the multiple asset account or pool with the most recent placed-in-service year that has the same recovery period as the asset disposed of and that has assets at the beginning of the taxable year of the disposition, and the taxpayer treating the asset disposed of as being from that multiple asset account or pool, or the taxpayer treating the disposed portion of an asset as being from an asset with the most recent placed-in-service year that is the same as the asset of which the disposed portion is a part.

(h) *Accounting for asset disposed of.*—(1) *Depreciation ends.*—Depreciation ends for an asset at the time of the asset's disposition, as determined under the applicable convention for the asset. See §1.167(a)-10(b). If the asset disposed of is in a single asset account initially or as a result of §1.168(i)-8(h)(2)(i), §1.168(i)-8(h)(3)(i), or general asset account treatment for the asset terminated under §1.168(i)-1(c)(1)(ii)(A), (e)(3)(iii), (e)(3)(v), (e)(3)(vii), (g), or (h)(1), as applicable, the single asset account terminates at the time of the asset's disposition, as determined under the applicable convention for the asset. If a taxpayer disposes of a portion of an asset and paragraph (d)(1) of this section applies to that disposition, depreciation ends for that disposed portion of the asset at the time of the disposition of the disposed portion, as determined under the applicable convention for the asset.

(2) *Asset disposed of in a multiple asset account or pool.*—If the taxpayer accounts for the asset disposed of in a multiple asset account or pool, then—

(i) As of the first day of the taxable year in which the disposition occurs, the asset disposed of is removed from the multiple asset account or pool and is placed into a single asset account. See §1.168(i)-7(b);

(ii) The unadjusted depreciable basis of the multiple asset account or pool must be reduced by the unadjusted depreciable basis of the asset disposed of as of the first day of the taxable year in which the disposition occurs. See paragraph (f)(2)(i) of this section for determining the unadjusted depreciable basis of the asset disposed of;

(iii) The depreciation reserve of the multiple asset account or pool must be reduced by the greater of the depreciation allowed or allowable for the asset disposed of as of the end of the taxable year immediately preceding the year of disposition. The allowable depreciation is computed by using the depreciation method, recovery period, and convention applicable to the multiple asset account or pool in which the asset disposed of was included and by including the additional first year depreciation deduction claimed for the asset disposed of; and

(iv) In determining the adjusted depreciable basis of the asset disposed of at the time of disposition, taking into account the applicable convention, the depreciation allowable for the asset disposed of is computed by using the depreciation method, recovery period, and convention applicable to the multiple asset account or pool in which the asset disposed of was included and by including the additional first year depreciation deduction claimed for the asset disposed of.

(3) *Disposition of a portion of an asset.*—This paragraph (h)(3) applies only when a taxpayer disposes of a portion of an asset and paragraph (d)(1) of this section applies to that disposition. In this case—

(i) As of the first day of the taxable year in which the disposition occurs, the disposed portion is placed into a single asset account. See §1.168(i)-7(b);

(ii) The unadjusted depreciable basis of the asset must be reduced by the unadjusted depreciable basis of the disposed portion as of the first day of the taxable year in which the disposition occurs. See paragraph (f)(3)(i) of this section for determining the unadjusted depreciable basis of the disposed portion;

(iii) The depreciation reserve of the asset must be reduced by the greater of the depreciation allowed or allowable for the disposed portion as of the end of the taxable year immediately preceding the year of disposition. The allowable depreciation is computed by using the depreciation method, recovery period, and convention applicable to the asset in which the disposed portion was included and by including the portion of the additional first year depreciation deduction claimed for the asset that is attributable to the disposed portion; and

(iv) In determining the adjusted depreciable basis of the disposed portion at the time of disposition, taking into account the applicable convention, the depreciation allowable for the disposed portion is computed by using the depreciation method, recovery period, and convention applicable to the asset in which the disposed portion was included and by including the portion of the additional first year depreciation deduction claimed for the asset that is attributable to the disposed portion.

(i) *Examples.*—The application of this section is illustrated by the following examples:

Example 1. A owns an office building with four elevators. A replaces one of the elevators. The elevator is a structural component of the office building. In accordance with paragraph (c)(4)(ii)(A) of this section, the office building, including its structural components, is the asset for disposition purposes. A does not make the partial disposition election provided under paragraph (d)(2) of this section for the elevator. Thus, the retirement of the replaced elevator is not a disposition. As a result, depreciation continues for the cost of the building, including the cost of the retired elevator and the building's other structural components, and A does not recognize a loss for this retired elevator. If A must capitalize the amount paid for the replacement elevator pursuant to §1.263(a)-3, the replacement elevator is a separate asset for disposition purposes pursuant to paragraph (c)(4)(ii)(D) of this section and for depreciation purposes pursuant to section 168(i)(6).

Example 2. The facts are the same as in *Example 1*, except A accounts for each structural component of the office building as a separate asset in its fixed asset system. Although A treats each structural component as a separate asset in its records, the office building, including its structural components, is the asset for disposition purposes in accordance with paragraph (c)(4)(ii)(A) of this section. Accordingly, the result is the same as in *Example 1*.

Example 3. The facts are the same as in *Example 1*, except A makes the partial disposition election provided under paragraph (d)(2) of this section for the elevator. Although the office building, including its structural components, is the asset for disposition purposes, the result of A making the partial disposition election for the elevator is that the retirement of the replaced elevator is a disposition. Thus, depreciation for the retired elevator ceases at the time of its retirement, taking into account the applicable convention, and A recognizes a loss upon this retirement. Further, A must capitalize the amount paid for the replacement elevator pursuant to §1.263(a)-3(k)(1)(i), and the replacement elevator is a separate asset for disposition purposes pursuant to paragraph (c)(4)(ii)(D) of this section and for depreciation purposes pursuant to section 168(i)(6).

Example 4. B, a calendar-year commercial airline company, owns several aircraft that are used in the commercial carrying of passengers and described in asset class 45.0 of Rev. Proc. 87-56. B replaces the existing engines on one of the aircraft with new engines. Assume each aircraft is a unit of property as determined under §1.263(a)-3(e)(3) and each engine of an aircraft is a major component or substantial structural part of the aircraft as determined under §1.263(a)-3(k)(6). Assume also that B treats each aircraft as the asset for disposition purposes in accordance with paragraph (c)(4) of this section. B makes the partial disposition election provided under paragraph (d)(2) of this section for the engines in the aircraft. Although the aircraft is the asset for disposition purposes, the result of B making the partial disposition election for the engines is that the retirement of the replaced engines is a disposition. Thus, depreciation for the retired engines ceases at the time of their retirement, taking into account the applicable convention, and B recognizes a loss upon this retirement. Further, B must capitalize the amount paid for the replacement engines pursuant to §1.263(a)-3(k)(1)(i), and the replacement engines are a separate asset for disposition purposes pursuant to paragraph (c)(4)(ii)(D) of this section and for depreciation purposes pursuant to section 168(i)(6).

Example 5. The facts are the same as in *Example 4*, except B does not make the partial disposition election provided under paragraph (d)(2) of this section for the engines. Thus, the retirement of the replaced engines on one of the aircraft is not a disposition. As a result, depreciation continues for the cost of the aircraft, including the cost of the retired engines, and B does not recognize a loss for these retired engines. If B must capitalize the amount paid for the replacement engines pursuant to §1.263(a)-3, the replacement engines are a separate asset for disposition purposes pursuant to paragraph (c)(4)(ii)(D) of this section and for depreciation purposes pursuant to section 168(i)(6).

Example 6. C, a corporation, owns several trucks that are used in its trade or business and described in asset class 00.241 of Rev. Proc. 87-56. C replaces the engine on one of the trucks with a new engine. Assume each truck is a unit of property as determined under § 1.263(a)-3(e)(3) and each engine is a major component or substantial structural part of the truck as determined under § 1.263(a)-3(k)(6). Because the trucks are described in asset class 00.241 of Rev. Proc. 87-56, C must treat each truck as the asset for disposition purposes. C does not make the partial disposition election provided under paragraph (d)(2) of this section for the engine. Thus, the retirement of the replaced engine on the truck is not a disposition. As a result, depreciation continues for the cost of the truck, including the cost of the retired engine, and C does not recognize a loss for this retired engine. If C must capitalize the amount paid for the replacement engine pursuant to § 1.263(a)-3, the replacement engine is a separate asset for disposition purposes pursuant to paragraph (c)(4)(ii)(D) of this section and for depreciation purposes pursuant to section 168(i)(6).

Example 7. D owns a retail building. D replaces 60% of the roof of this building. In accordance with paragraph (c)(4)(ii)(A) of this section, the retail building, including its structural components, is the asset for disposition purposes. Assume D must capitalize the costs incurred for replacing 60% of the roof pursuant to § 1.263(a)-3(k)(1)(vi). D makes the partial disposition election provided under paragraph (d)(2) of this section for the 60% of the replaced roof. Thus, the retirement of 60% of the roof is a disposition. As a result, depreciation for 60% of the roof ceases at the time of its retirement, taking into account the applicable convention, and D recognizes a loss upon this retirement. Further, D must capitalize the amount paid for the 60% of the roof pursuant to § 1.263(a)-3(k)(1)(i) and (vi) and the replacement 60% of the roof is a separate asset for disposition purposes pursuant to paragraph (c)(4)(ii)(D) of this section and for depreciation purposes pursuant to section 168(i)(6).

Example 8. (i) The facts are the same as in *Example 7.* Ten years after replacing 60% of the roof, D replaces 55% of the roof of the building. In accordance with paragraph (c)(4)(ii)(A) and (D) of this section, for disposition purposes, the retail building, including its structural components, except the replacement 60% of the roof, is an asset and the replacement 60% of the roof is a separate asset. Assume D must capitalize the costs incurred for replacing 55% of the roof pursuant to § 1.263(a)-3(k)(1)(vi). D makes the partial disposition election provided under paragraph (d)(2) of this section for the 55% of the replaced roof. Thus, the retirement of 55% of the roof is a disposition.

(ii) However, D cannot determine from its records whether the replaced 55% is part of the 60% of the roof replaced ten years ago or whether the replaced 55% includes part or all of the remaining 40% of the original roof. Pursuant to paragraph (g)(3) of this section, D identifies which asset it disposed of by using the first-in, first-out method of accounting. As a result, D disposed of the remaining 40% of the original roof and 25% of the 60% of the roof replaced ten years ago.

(iii) Thus, depreciation for the remaining 40% of the original roof ceases at the time of its retirement, taking into account the applicable convention, and D recognizes a loss upon this retirement. Further, depreciation for 25% of the 60% of the roof replaced ten years ago ceases at the time of its retirement, taking into account the applicable convention, and D recognizes a loss upon this retirement. Also, D must capitalize the amount paid for the 55% of the roof pursuant to § 1.263(a)-3(k)(1)(i) and (vi), and the replacement 55% of the roof is a separate asset for disposition purposes pursuant to paragraph (c)(4)(ii)(D) of this section and for depreciation purposes pursuant to section 168(i)(6).

Example 9. (i) On July 1, 2011, E, a calendar-year taxpayer, purchased and placed in service an existing multi-story office building that costs $20,000,000. The cost of each structural component of the building was not separately stated. E accounts for the building and its structural components in its tax and financial accounting records as a single asset with a cost of $20,000,000. E depreciates the building as nonresidential real property and uses the optional depreciation table that corresponds with the general depreciation system, the straight-line method, a 39-year recovery period, and the mid-month convention. As of January 1, 2014, the depreciation reserve for the building is $1,261,000.

(ii) On June 30, 2014, E replaces one of the two elevators in the office building. E did not dispose of any other structural components of this building in 2014 and prior years. E makes the partial disposition election provided under paragraph (d)(2) of this section for this elevator. Although the office building, including its structural components, is the asset for disposition purposes, the result of E making the partial disposition election for the elevator is that the retirement of the replaced elevator is a disposition. Assume the replacement elevator is a restoration under § 1.263(a)-3(k), and not a betterment under § 1.263(a)-3(j)) or an adaptation to a new or different use under

§ 1.263(a)-3(l)). Because E cannot identify the cost of the elevator from its records and the replacement elevator is a restoration under § 1.263(a)-3(k), E determines the cost of the disposed elevator by discounting the cost of the replacement elevator to its placed-in-service year cost using the Producer Price Index for Final Demand. Using this reasonable method, E determines the cost of the retired elevator by discounting the cost of the replacement elevator to its cost in 2011 (the placed-in-service year) using the Producer Price Index for Final Demand, resulting in $150,000 of the $20,000,000 purchase price for the building to be the cost of the retired elevator. Using the optional depreciation table that corresponds with the general depreciation system, the straight-line method, a 39-year recovery period, and the mid-month convention, the depreciation allowed or allowable for the retired elevator as of December 31, 2013, is $9,458.

(iii) For E's 2014 Federal tax return, the loss for the retired elevator is determined as follows. The depreciation allowed or allowable for 2014 for the retired elevator is $1,763 ((unadjusted depreciable basis of $150,000 × depreciation rate of 2.564% for 2014) × 5.5/12 months). Thus, the adjusted depreciable basis of the retired elevator is $138,779 (the adjusted depreciable basis of $140,542 removed from the building cost less the depreciation allowed or allowable of $1,763 for 2014). As a result, E recognizes a loss of $138,779 for the retired elevator in 2014.

(iv) For E's 2014 Federal tax return, the depreciation allowance for the building is computed as follows. As of January 1, 2014, the unadjusted depreciable basis of the building is reduced from $20,000,000 to $19,850,000 ($20,000,000 less the unadjusted depreciable basis of $150,000 for the retired elevator), and the depreciation reserve of the building is reduced from $1,261,000 to $1,251,542 ($1,261,000 less the depreciation allowed or allowable of $9,458 for the retired elevator as of December 31, 2013). Consequently, the depreciation allowance for the building for 2014 is $508,954 ($19,850,000 × depreciation rate of 2.564% for 2014).

(v) E also must capitalize the amount paid for the replacement elevator pursuant to § 1.263(a)-3(k)(1). The replacement elevator is a separate asset for disposition purposes pursuant to paragraph (c)(4)(ii)(D) of this section and for depreciation purposes pursuant to section 168(i)(6).

Example 10. (i) Since 2005, F, a calendar year taxpayer, has accounted for items of MACRS property that are mass assets in pools. Each pool includes only the mass assets that have the same depreciation method, recovery period, and convention, and are placed in service by F in the same taxable year. None of the pools are general asset accounts under section 168(i)(4) and the regulations under section 168(i)(4). F identifies any dispositions of these mass assets by specific identification.

(ii) During 2014, F sells 10 items of mass assets with a 5-year recovery period each for $100. Under the specific identification method, F identifies these mass assets as being from the pool established by F in 2012 for mass assets with a 5-year recovery period. Assume F depreciates this pool using the optional depreciation table that corresponds with the general depreciation system, the 200-percent declining balance method, a 5-year recovery period, and the half-year convention. F elected not to deduct the additional first year depreciation provided by section 168(k) for 5-year property placed in service during 2012. As of January 1, 2014, this pool contains 100 similar items of mass assets with a total cost of $25,000 and a total depreciation reserve of $13,000. Because all the items of mass assets in the pool are similar, F allocates the cost and depreciation allowed or allowable for the pool ratably among each item in the pool. This allocation is a reasonable method because all the items of mass assets in the pool are similar. Using this reasonable method, F allocates a cost of $250 ($25,000 × (1/100)) to each disposed of mass asset and depreciation allowed or allowable of $130 ($13,000 × (1/100)) to each disposed of mass asset. The depreciation allowed or allowable in 2014 for each disposed of mass asset is $24 (($250 × 19.2%) / 2). As a result, the adjusted depreciable basis of each disposed of mass asset under section 1011 is $96 ($250 - $130 - $24). Thus, F recognizes a gain of $4 for each disposed of mass asset in 2014, which is subject to section 1245.

(iii) Further, as of January 1, 2014, the unadjusted depreciable basis of the 2012 pool of mass assets with a 5-year recovery period is reduced from $25,000 to $22,500 ($25,000 less the unadjusted depreciable basis of $2,500 for the 10 disposed of items), and the depreciation reserve of this 2012 pool is reduced from $13,000 to $11,700 ($13,000 less the depreciation allowed or allowable of $1,300 for the 10 disposed of items as of December 31, 2013). Consequently, as of January 1, 2014, the 2012 pool of mass assets with a 5-year recovery period has 90 items with a total cost of $22,500 and a depreciation reserve of $11,700. Thus, the depreciation allowance for this pool for 2014 is $4,320 ($22,500 × 19.2%).

Example 11. (i) The facts are the same as in *Example 10.* Because of changes in F's recordkeeping in 2015, it is impracticable for F to continue to identify disposed of mass assets using specific identification and to determine the unadjusted depreciable basis of the disposed of mass assets. As a result, F files a Form 3115, Application for Change in Accounting Method, to change to a first-in, first-out method beginning with the taxable year beginning on January 1, 2015, on a modified cut-off basis. See §1.446-1(e)(2)(ii)(d)(2)(vii). Under the first-in, first-out method, the mass assets disposed of in a taxable year are deemed to be from the pool with the earliest placed-in-service year that has assets as of the beginning of the taxable year of the disposition with the same recovery period as the asset disposed of. The Commissioner of Internal Revenue consents to this change in method of accounting.

(ii) During 2015, F sells 20 items of mass assets with a 5-year recovery period each for $50. As of January 1, 2015, the 2008 pool is the pool with the earliest placed-in-service year for mass assets with a 5-year recovery period, and this pool contains 25 items of mass assets with a total cost of $10,000 and a total depreciation reserve of $10,000. Thus, F allocates a cost of $400 ($10,000 × (1/25)) to each disposed of mass asset and depreciation allowed or allowable of $400 to each disposed of mass asset. As a result, the adjusted depreciable basis of each disposed of mass asset is $0. Thus, F recognizes a gain of $50 for each disposed of mass asset in 2015, which is subject to section 1245.

(iii) Further, as of January 1, 2015, the unadjusted depreciable basis of the 2008 pool of mass assets with a 5-year recovery period is reduced from $10,000 to $2,000 ($10,000 less the unadjusted depreciable basis of $8,000 for the 20 disposed of items ($400 × 20)), and the depreciation reserve of this 2008 pool is reduced from $10,000 to $2,000 ($10,000 less the depreciation allowed or allowable of $8,000 for the 20 disposed of items as of December 31, 2014). Consequently, as of January 1, 2015, the 2008 pool of mass assets with a 5-year recovery period has 5 items with a total cost of $2,000 and a depreciation reserve of $2,000.

(j) *Effective/applicability dates.*—(1) *In general.*—Except as provided in paragraph (j)(5) of this section, this section applies to taxable years beginning on or after January 1, 2014.

(2) *Early application of this section.*—A taxpayer may choose to apply the provisions of this section to taxable years beginning on or after January 1, 2012.

(3) *Early application of regulation project REG-110732-13.*—A taxpayer may rely on the provisions of this section in regulation project REG-110732-13 (2013-43 IRB 404) (see §601.601(d)(2) of this chapter) for taxable years beginning on or after January 1, 2012. However, a taxpayer may not rely on the provisions of this section in regulation project REG-110732-13 for taxable years beginning on or after January 1, 2014.

(4) *Optional application of TD 9564.*—A taxpayer may choose to apply §1.168(i)-8T as contained in 26 CFR part 1 edition revised as of April 1, 2014, to taxable years beginning on or after January 1, 2012. However, a taxpayer may not apply §1.168(i)-8T as contained in 26 CFR part 1 edition revised as of April 1, 2014, to taxable years beginning on or after January 1, 2014.

(5) *Application of paragraph (c)(4)(i).*—The language "and the distinct asset determination under §1.1031(a)-3(a)(4) do not apply." in the last sentence of paragraph (c)(4)(i) of this section applies on or after December 2, 2020. Paragraph (c)(4)(i) of this section as contained in 26 CFR part 1 edition revised as of April 1, 2020, applies before December 2, 2020.

(6) *Change in method of accounting.*—A change to comply with this section for depreciable assets placed in service in a taxable year ending on or after December 30, 2003, is a change in method of accounting to which the provisions of section 446(e) and the regulations under section 446(e) apply. A taxpayer also may treat a change to comply with this section for depreciable assets placed in service in a taxable year ending before December 30, 2003, as a change in method of accounting to which the provisions of section 446(e) and the regulations under section 446(e) apply. This paragraph (j)(5) does not apply to a change to comply with paragraph (d)(2) of this section, except as provided in paragraph (d)(2)(iii) or (iv)(B) of this section or otherwise provided by other guidance published in the Internal Revenue Bulletin (see §601.601(d)(2) of this chapter). [Reg. §1.168(i)-8.]

☐ [*T.D. 9689*, 8-14-2014 (*corrected* 12-30-2014). *Amended by T.D.* 9935, 11-30-2020.]

[Reg. §1.168(j)-1T]

§1.168(j)-1T. Questions and answers concerning tax-exempt entity leasing rules (Temporary).—The following questions and answers concern tax-exempt entity leasing under section 168(j) of the Internal Revenue Code of 1954, as enacted by section 31 of the Tax Reform Act of 1984 ("TRA") (Pub. L. 98-369): *Consequences of tax-exempt use status:*

Q-1. If recovery property is subject to the tax-exempt entity leasing provisions of section 168(j), how must the taxpayer compute the property's recovery deductions?

A-1. The taxpayer must compute the property's recovery deductions in accordance with section 168(j)(1) and (2); that is, the taxpayer must use the straight line method and the specified recovery period. For property other than 18-year real property, the applicable recovery percentages for the specified recovery period are to be determined with reference to the tables contained in Prop. Treas. Reg. §1.168-2(g)(3)(iv)(A). For 18-year real property for which a 40-year recovery period is required, the applicable recovery percentages are to be determined under the following table:

40-Year Straight Line Method (Assuming Mid-Month Convention)

If the recovery year is:	And the month in the first recovery year the property is placed in service is:											
	1	2	3	4	5	6	7	8	9	10	11	12
	The applicable recovery percentage is:											
1	2.4	2.2	2.0	1.8	1.6	1.4	1.1	0.9	0.7	0.5	0.3	0.1
2	2.5	2.5	2.5	2.5	2.5	2.5	2.5	2.5	2.5	2.5	2.5	2.5
3	2.5	2.5	2.5	2.5	2.5	2.5	2.5	2.5	2.5	2.5	2.5	2.5
4	2.5	2.5	2.5	2.5	2.5	2.5	2.5	2.5	2.5	2.5	2.5	2.5
5	2.5	2.5	2.5	2.5	2.5	2.5	2.5	2.5	2.5	2.5	2.5	2.5
6	2.5	2.5	2.5	2.5	2.5	2.5	2.5	2.5	2.5	2.5	2.5	2.5
7	2.5	2.5	2.5	2.5	2.5	2.5	2.5	2.5	2.5	2.5	2.5	2.5
8	2.5	2.5	2.5	2.5	2.5	2.5	2.5	2.5	2.5	2.5	2.5	2.5
9	2.5	2.5	2.5	2.5	2.5	2.5	2.5	2.5	2.5	2.5	2.5	2.5
10	2.5	2.5	2.5	2.5	2.5	2.5	2.5	2.5	2.5	2.5	2.5	2.5
11	2.5	2.5	2.5	2.5	2.5	2.5	2.5	2.5	2.5	2.5	2.5	2.5
12	2.5	2.5	2.5	2.5	2.5	2.5	2.5	2.5	2.5	2.5	2.5	2.5
13	2.5	2.5	2.5	2.5	2.5	2.5	2.5	2.5	2.5	2.5	2.5	2.5
14	2.5	2.5	2.5	2.5	2.5	2.5	2.5	2.5	2.5	2.5	2.5	2.5
15	2.5	2.5	2.5	2.5	2.5	2.5	2.5	2.5	2.5	2.5	2.5	2.5
16	2.5	2.5	2.5	2.5	2.5	2.5	2.5	2.5	2.5	2.5	2.5	2.5
17	2.5	2.5	2.5	2.5	2.5	2.5	2.5	2.5	2.5	2.5	2.5	2.5
18	2.5	2.5	2.5	2.5	2.5	2.5	2.5	2.5	2.5	2.5	2.5	2.5
19	2.5	2.5	2.5	2.5	2.5	2.5	2.5	2.5	2.5	2.5	2.5	2.5
20	2.5	2.5	2.5	2.5	2.5	2.5	2.5	2.5	2.5	2.5	2.5	2.5
21	2.5	2.5	2.5	2.5	2.5	2.5	2.5	2.5	2.5	2.5	2.5	2.5
22	2.5	2.5	2.5	2.5	2.5	2.5	2.5	2.5	2.5	2.5	2.5	2.5
23	2.5	2.5	2.5	2.5	2.5	2.5	2.5	2.5	2.5	2.5	2.5	2.5
24	2.5	2.5	2.5	2.5	2.5	2.5	2.5	2.5	2.5	2.5	2.5	2.5
25	2.5	2.5	2.5	2.5	2.5	2.5	2.5	2.5	2.5	2.5	2.5	2.5
26	2.5	2.5	2.5	2.5	2.5	2.5	2.5	2.5	2.5	2.5	2.5	2.5
27	2.5	2.5	2.5	2.5	2.5	2.5	2.5	2.5	2.5	2.5	2.5	2.5

40-Year Straight Line Method (Assuming Mid-Month Convention)

If the recovery year is:	And the month in the first recovery year the property is placed in service is:											
	1	2	3	4	5	6	7	8	9	10	11	12
	The applicable recovery percentage is:											
28	2.5	2.5	2.5	2.5	2.5	2.5	2.5	2.5	2.5	2.5	2.5	2.5
29	2.5	2.5	2.5	2.5	2.5	2.5	2.5	2.5	2.5	2.5	2.5	2.5
30	2.5	2.5	2.5	2.5	2.5	2.5	2.5	2.5	2.5	2.5	2.5	2.5
31	2.5	2.5	2.5	2.5	2.5	2.5	2.5	2.5	2.5	2.5	2.5	2.5
32	2.5	2.5	2.5	2.5	2.5	2.5	2.5	2.5	2.5	2.5	2.5	2.5
33	2.5	2.5	2.5	2.5	2.5	2.5	2.5	2.5	2.5	2.5	2.5	2.5
34	2.5	2.5	2.5	2.5	2.5	2.5	2.5	2.5	2.5	2.5	2.5	2.5
35	2.5	2.5	2.5	2.5	2.5	2.5	2.5	2.5	2.5	2.5	2.5	2.5
36	2.5	2.5	2.5	2.5	2.5	2.5	2.5	2.5	2.5	2.5	2.5	2.5
37	2.5	2.5	2.5	2.5	2.5	2.5	2.5	2.5	2.5	2.5	2.5	2.5
38	2.5	2.5	2.5	2.5	2.5	2.5	2.5	2.5	2.5	2.5	2.5	2.5
39	2.5	2.5	2.5	2.5	2.5	2.5	2.5	2.5	2.5	2.5	2.5	2.5
40	2.5	2.5	2.5	2.5	2.5	2.5	2.5	2.5	2.5	2.5	2.5	2.5
41	0.1	0.3	0.5	0.7	0.9	1.1	1.4	1.6	1.8	2.0	2.2	2.4

Q-2. If recovery property that was placed in service after December 31, 1980 by a taxable entity subsequently becomes tax-exempt use property, how are such property's cost recovery deductions under section 168 affected?

A-2. A change to tax-exempt use property, as defined in section 168(j)(3), will cause the cost recovery deductions under the accelerated cost recovery system (ACRS) to be recomputed. The allowable recovery deduction for the taxable year in which the change occurs (and for subsequent taxable years) must be determined as if the property had originally been tax-exempt use property. Proper adjustment must be made under the principles of Prop. Treas. Reg. §1.168-2(j)(3)(i)(B) to account for the difference between the deductions allowable with respect to the property prior to the year of change and those which would have been allowable had the taxpayer used the recovery period and method for tax-exempt use property under section 168(j)(1) and (2). However, no adjustment is made pursuant to the provisions of this A-2 if section 168(j)(2)(C) applies, that is, if the taxpayer had selected a longer recovery period in the year the property was placed in service than the recovery period prescribed for such property under section 168(j)(1).

Example (1). On July 1, 1983, X, a calendar year taxpayer, places in service 5-year recovery property with an unadjusted basis of $100. For 1983, X's allowable deduction is $15 (*i.e.*, .15 × $100). In 1984, the property becomes tax-exempt use property. Under section 168(j), assume the prescribed recovery period is 12 years. For 1984 (and subsequent taxable years), X's allowable deduction is determined as if the property had been tax-exempt use property since 1983, that is, the year it was placed in service. Thus, taxable year 1984 is the property's second recovery year of its 12-year recovery period. Additionally, X must account for the excess allowable recovery deduction of $11 (*i.e.*, the difference between the recovery allowance for 1983 ($15) and the allowance for that year had the property been tax-exempt use property ($4)) in accordance with the principles of Prop. Treas. Reg. §1.168-2(j)(3)(i)(B). Thus, the recovery allowances in 1984 and 1985 are $7.97, determined as follows:

Unadjusted basis multiplied by the applicable recovery percentage for second recovery year ($100 × .09)	$9.00
Excess allowable recovery deduction multiplied by the applicable recovery percentage for second recovery year divided by the sum of the remaining unused applicable percentages for tax-exempt use property existing as of the taxable year of change (1984) (($11 × .09)/.96)	− 1.03
Difference—allowable deduction for 1984	$7.97
Unadjusted basis multiplied by the applicable recovery percentage for third recovery year ($100 × .09)	$9.00
Excess allowable recovery deduction multiplied by the applicable recovery percentage for third recovery year divided by the sum of the remaining unused applicable percentages for tax-exempt use property existing as of the taxable year of change (1984) (($11 × .09)/.96)	− 1.03
Difference—allowable deduction for 1985	$7.97

Additionally, X must make a similar adjustment for the taxable years 1986 through 1995, that is, his fourth through thirteenth recovery years.

Example (2). Assume the same facts as in Example (1) except that in 1983, X elected under section 168(b)(3) with respect to the 5-year property to use the optional recovery percentages over a 25-year recovery period. Based on these facts, the provisions of this A-2 do not apply.

Definition of tax-exempt use property

—*Mixed leases of real and personal property:*

Q-3. How is a mixed lease of real property and personal property (*e.g.*, a building with furniture) to be treated for purposes of applying the rules of section 168(j)(3) defining which property constitutes tax-exempt use property?

A-3. The general rule is that 18-year real property and property other than 18-year real property are tested separately to determine whether each constitutes tax-exempt use property. However, if a lease of section 1245 class property is incidental to a lease of 18-year real property, and the 18-year real property is not tax-exempt use property, then the section 1245 class property also does not constitute tax-exempt use property. A lease of section 1245 class property will be considered incidental if the adjusted basis of all section 1245 class property leased in the same transaction is 1 percent or less of the adjusted basis of all 18-year real property leased in such transaction.

—*Buildings which are partially tax-exempt use property:*

Q-4. If part of a building is leased to a tax-exempt entity in a disqualified lease and part of the building is leased other than to a tax-exempt entity in a disqualified lease, to what extent do the tax-exempt entity leasing rules apply to such building?

A-4. The taxpayer must determine the amount of the building's unadjusted basis that is properly allocable to the portion of the building that is tax-exempt use property; the section 168(j) rules apply to the allocated amount. Solely for purposes of determining what percentage of the building's basis is subject to the tax-exempt entity leasing rules, no part of the basis is allocated to common areas.

Example. A constructs a 3-story building in 1984 at a cost of $900,000. Each floor consists of 30,000 square feet. The only common area (10,000 square feet) in the building is on the first floor. A leases the first floor (other than the common areas) to a firm that is not a tax-exempt entity. A leases the top two floors to a tax-exempt entity in a 25-year lease. The top two floors constitute tax-exempt use property. Assume that square footage is the appropriate method for allocating basis in this case. Thus, A must allocate $675,000 of the $900,000 basis to the tax-exempt use portion, determined as follows:

$$\frac{\text{square footage of building which is tax-exempt use property (excluding common areas)}}{\text{total square footage in the building (excluding common areas)}} = \frac{60,000 \text{ sq. feet}}{80,000 \text{ sq. feet}} = \frac{3}{4}$$

$$^3/_4 × \$900,000 = \$675,000$$

A must compute his recovery deductions on this portion of the basis ($675,000) in accordance with the rules of section 168(j)(1) and (2).

—*Requirement of a lease:*

Q-5. Can the use of property by a party other than a tax-exempt entity result in the property being treated as tax-exempt use property within the meaning of section 168(j)(3)?

A-5. Yes, if based on all the facts and circumstances it is more appropriate to characterize the transaction as a lease to a tax-exempt entity. A transaction can be characterized as a lease to a tax-exempt entity under section 168(j)(6)(A), which provides that "the term 'lease' includes any grant of a right to use property"; or under the

Itemized Deductions for Individuals and Corps.
See p. 20,601 for regulations not amended to reflect law changes
25,485

service contract rules of section 7701(e). See Q & A #18 for rules regarding service contracts.

Example. A trust is executed on January 1, 1984, to create a pooled income fund (P) that meets the requirements of section 642(c)(5). A university (U) that is tax-exempt under section 501(c)(3) is the remainderman of the pooled income fund. P's purpose is to construct and operate an athletic center on land adjacent to U's campus. Construction of the athletic center, which has a 50-year useful life, was completed and the center was placed in service on February 1, 1985. The athletic center is managed for a fee by M, an unrelated taxable organization which operates athletic facilities open to the public. Office space at the facility is occupied rent-free by both the U athletic department and M. Scheduling of activities at the center is handled jointly by members of U's athletic department and M. General operating expenses of the athletic center are paid by P. Although the athletic center is open to the public for a membership fee, the majority of members are U's students who pay membership fees as part of their tuition. These fees are remitted by U to P. This arrangement is in substance a grant to U of a right to use the facility, and therefore a lease to U under section 168(j)(6)(A). U, as remainderman, will have obtained title to the entire building when the last pooled income fund donor dies. This arrangement is a disqualified lease because either (1) U has the equivalent of a fixed price purchase option under section 168(j)(3)(B)(ii)(II) (if U receives title as remainderman before the end of the useful life of the building), or (2) the lease has a term in excess of 20 years under section 168(j)(3)(B)(ii)(III) (if U does not receive title as remainderman until 20 years have elapsed), or both. Therefore, the allowable recovery deductions (without regard to salvage value) must be computed in accordance with section 168(j)(1) and (2). In addition, because this arrangement is treated as a lease under section 168(j), the facility is used by U for purposes of section 48(a)(4), and thus no investment tax credit is permitted with respect to any portion of the facility. This arrangement also may be treated as a lease to U for all purposes of chapter 1 of the Internal Revenue Code under section 7701(e).

—*"More than 35 percent of the property" test*:

Q-6. How is the percentage of 18-year real property leased to a tax-exempt entity in a disqualified lease to be determined for purposes of the "more than 35 percent of the property" test of section 168(j)(3)(B)(iii)?

A-6. The phrase "more than 35 percent of the property" means more than 35 percent of the net rentable floor space of the property. The net rentable floor space in a building does not include the common areas of the building, regardless of the terms of the lease. For purposes of the "more than 35 percent of the property" rule, two or more buildings will be treated as separate properties unless they are part of the same project, in which case they will be treated as one property. Two or more buildings will be treated as part of the same project if the buildings are constructed, under a common plan, within a reasonable time of each other on the same site and will be used in an integrated manner.

Q-7. Are disqualified leases to different tax-exempt entities (regardless of whether they are related) aggregated in determining whether 18-year real property is tax-exempt use property?

A-7. Yes.

Example. A tax-exempt entity participates in industrial development bond financing for the acquisition of a new building by a taxable entity. The tax-exempt entity leases 60 percent of the net rentable floor space in the building for 5 years. Sixty percent of the building is tax-exempt use property. If the same tax-exempt entity leased only 19 percent of the net rentable floor space in the building for 5 years, no portion of the building would be tax-exempt use property because not more than 35 percent of the property is leased to a tax-exempt entity pursuant to a disqualified lease. If such tax-exempt entity leased only 19 percent of the net rentable floor space in the building for 5 years and another tax-exempt entity leased 20 percent of the net rentable floor space in the building for a term in excess of 20 years (or a related entity leased 20 percent of the building for 5 years), 39 percent of the building would be tax-exempt use property. See A-4 regarding the determination of the amount of the building unadjusted basis that is properly allocable to the portion of the building that is tax-exempt use property.

—*"Predominantly used" test*:

Q-8. What does the term "predominantly used" mean for purposes of the section 168(j)(3)(D) exception to the tax-exempt use property rules?

A-8. "Predominantly used" means that for more than 50 percent of the time used, as determined for each taxable year, the real or personal property is used in an unrelated trade or business the income of which is subject to tax under section 511 (determined without regard to the debt-financed income rules of section 514). If only a portion of property is predominantly used in an unrelated trade or business, the remainder may nevertheless be tax-exempt use property.

Q-9. How is the "predominantly used" test of section 168(j)(3)(D) to be applied to a building?

A-9. The "predominantly used" test is to be applied to a building in the following manner:

(i) Identify the discrete portions (excluding common areas) of the building which are leased to a tax-exempt entity in a disqualified lease under section 168(j)(3)(B)(ii). A discrete portion of a building is an area physically separated from other areas. An area is physically separated from other areas if separated by permanent walls or by partitions serving as room dividers if such partitions remain in place throughout the taxable year. A discrete portion can be the entire building, floors, wings, offices, rooms, or a combination thereof. For example, a building whose entire internal space consists of a single large room used as a gymnasium has only one discrete portion. On the other hand, if the building has 3 stories with 10 offices on each floor, each of the 30 offices is a discrete portion.

(ii) Determine whether each discrete portion is predominantly used in an unrelated trade or business subject to tax under section 511. See A-8 for the rules regarding how to make this determination.

(iii) Once the discrete portions of the building that constitute tax-exempt use property have been identified, an appropriate allocation of basis must be made to such discrete portions. See A-4 for rules regarding how to make such allocation.

(iv) The application of these rules is illustrated by the following example:

Example. A building, constructed in 1985, is leased in its entirety to a tax-exempt entity (E) pursuant to a 25-year lease. The building has 25,000 square feet of net rentable floor space and consists of an auditorium (15,000 square feet), a retail shop (10,000 square feet), plus common area of 5,000 square feet. E uses the auditorium 80 percent of the time in its exempt activity and 20 percent of the time in an unrelated trade or business subject to tax under section 511. The retail shop is used 90 percent of the time in an unrelated trade or business subject to tax under section 511 and 10 percent of the time in an exempt activity. Thus, the auditorium is tax-exempt use property; the retail shop is not. An appropriate allocation of basis to the auditorium must be made. See A-4

Definition of tax-exempt entity:

Q-10. What elections must be made in order to avoid the "5-year lookback" rule of section 168(j)(4)(E)(i)?

A-10. Only organizations which were exempt from tax under section 501(a) as organizations described in section 501(c)(12) (and which are no longer tax-exempt) may avoid the 5-year lookback rule of section 168(j)(4)(E)(i). In order to avoid the 5-year lookback rule with respect to any property, two elections are required. First, the organization must elect not to be exempt from tax under section 501(a) during the tax-exempt use period (as defined in section 168(j)(4)(E)(ii)(II)) with respect to the property. Second, the organization must elect to be taxed on the exempt arbitrage profits as provided in section 31(g)(16) of the Tax Reform Act of 1984. See Temp. Treas. Reg. § 301.9100-6T(a) for the time and manner of making these elections. These elections, once made, are irrevocable.

Q-11. Does the term "tax-exempt entity" include tax-exempt plans of deferred compensation and similar arrangements?

A-11. Yes. For purposes of section 168(j), the term "tax-exempt entity" includes trusts or other entities that are tax-qualified under section 401(a), individual retirement accounts, simplified employee pensions, and other tax-exempt arrangements described in subchapter D of chapter 1 of the Internal Revenue Code.

Special rules for high technology equipment:

Q-12. What effect do the tax-exempt entity leasing provisions have on "qualified technological equipment"?

A-12. "Qualified technological equipment" which is leased to a tax-exempt entity for a term of 5 years or less shall not constitute tax-exempt use property. If "qualified technological equipment" which is leased to a tax-exempt entity for a term of more than 5 years constitutes tax-exempt use property (as defined in section 168(j)(3)) and is not used predominantly outside the United States, the rules of section 168(j)(1) and (2) apply except that the recovery period to be used for such equipment shall be 5 years regardless of the length of the lease term. For purposes of section 168(j)(5), "qualified technological equipment" means (1) any computer or peripheral equipment, (2) any high technology telephone station equipment installed on the customer's premises, and (3) any high technology medical equipment. For definitions of these terms, see A-13 through A-16.

Q-13. What is a "computer" as that term is used in section 168(j)(5)(C)(i)(I)?

A-13. Computers are electronically activated devices that are programmable by the user and that are capable of accepting information, applying prescribed processes to it, and supplying the results of those processes with or without human intervention. Computers consist of a central processing unit containing extensive storage, logic, arithmetic, and control capabilities. A computer does not include any equipment which is an integral part of property that is not a user-programmable device, any video games or other devices used by the user primarily for amusement or entertainment purposes, or any typewriters, calculators, adding or accounting machines, copiers, duplicating equipment, or similar equipment. A computer does not include any equipment that is not tangible personal property.

Q-14. What is "peripheral equipment" as that term is used in section 168(j)(5)(C)(i)(I)?

A-14. Peripheral equipment means tangible personal property such as auxiliary machines, whether on-line or off-line, that are designed to be placed under the control of the central processing unit of the computer. Some examples of peripheral equipment are: card readers, card punches, magnetic tape feeds, high speed printers, optical character readers, tape cassettes, mass storage units, paper tape equipment, keypunches, data entry devices, teleprinters, terminals, tape drives, disc drives, disc files, disc packs, visual image projector tubes, card sorters, plotters, and collators. Peripheral equipment does not include equipment not included in Asset Depreciation Range (ADR) 00.12 listed in section 3 of Rev. Proc. 83-35, 1983-1 C.B. 745, 746. Peripheral equipment also does not include any equipment that is an integral part of property that is not a user-programmable device, any video games or other devices used by the user primarily for amusement or entertainment purposes, or any typewriters, calculators, adding or accounting machines, copiers, duplicating equipment, or similar equipment.

Q-15. What does "high technology telephone station equipment" mean as that term is used in section 168(j)(5)(C)(i)(II)?

A-15. High technology telephone station equipment includes only tangible personal property described in asset depreciation range (ADR) class 48.13 listed in section 3 of Rev. Proc. 83-35, 1983-1 C.B. 745, 758 that has a high technology content and which, because of such high technology content, can reasonably be expected to become obsolete before the expiration of its physical useful life. For example, telephone booths and telephones which include only a standard dialing feature are not high technology equipment. However, telephones with features such as an abbreviated dialing short program, an automatic callback, or conference call feature may qualify as high technology equipment. High technology telephone station equipment may include terminal equipment including such extra features but not terminal equipment used in conjunction with features offered through central office capacity. There are no current plans to utilize the regulatory authority provided in section 168(j)(5)(C)(iv).

Q-16. What is "high technology medical equipment" as that term is used in section 168(j)(5)(C)(i)(III)?

A-16. High technology medical equipment is any electronic, electromechanical, or computer-based high technology equipment which is tangible personal property used in the screening, monitoring, observation, diagnosis, or treatment of human patients in a laboratory, medical, or hospital environment. High technology medical equipment includes only equipment that has a high technology content and which, because of such high technology content, can reasonably be expected to become obsolete before the expiration of its physical useful life. High technology medical equipment may include computer axial tomography (C.A.T.) scanners, nuclear magnetic resonance equipment, clinical chemistry analyzers, drug monitors, diagnostic ultrasound scanners, nuclear cameras, radiographic and fluoroscopic systems, Holter monitors, and bedside monitors. Incidental use of any such equipment for other purposes, such as research, will not prevent it from qualifying as high technology medical equipment. There are no current plans to utilize the regulatory authority provided in section 168(j)(5)(C)(iv).

Lease term:

Q-17. What is included in determining the length of a lease term?

A-17. (i) The lease term starts when the property is first made available to the lessee under the lease. The lease term includes not only the stated duration, but also any additional period of time which is within the "realistic contemplation of the parties at the time the property is first put into service." *Hokanson v. Commissioner,* 730 F.2d 1245, 1248 (9th Cir. 1984). A subsequent period of time is included in the term of the original lease if the circumstances indicate that the parties, upon entering into the original lease, had informally agreed that there would be an extension of the original lease.

(ii) With respect to personal property, the lease term includes all periods for which the tax-exempt lessee or a related party (as defined under section 168(j)(7)) has a legally enforceable option to renew the lease, or the lessor has a legally enforceable option to compel its renewal by the tax-exempt entity or a related party. This is true regardless of the renewal terms of the lease agreement or whether the lease is in fact renewed.

(iii) With respect to real property, the lease term includes all periods for which the tax-exempt lessee or a related party (as defined under section 168(j)(7)) has a legally enforceable option to renew the lease, or the lessor has a legally enforceable option to compel its renewal by the tax-exempt entity or a related party, unless the option to renew is at fair market value, determined at the time of renewal.

The *Hokanson* facts and circumstances test (see (i) above) may cause the term of a fair market value renewal option to be treated as part of the original lease term.

(iv) Successive leases that are part of the same transaction or a series of related transactions concerning the same or substantially similar property shall be treated as one lease. This rule applies if at substantially the same time or as part of one arrangement the parties enter into multiple leases covering the same or substantially similar property, each having a different term. If so, then the original lease term will be treated as running through the term of the lease that has the last expiration date of the multiple leases. The multiple lease rule will not apply merely because the parties enter into a new lease at fair market rental value at the end of the original lease term.

(v) The application of the above rules is illustrated by the following examples:

Example (1). On December 30, 1984, X, a taxable corporation, and Y, a tax-exempt entity, enter into a requirements contract for a period of 3 years. The requirements contract sets the terms and conditions under which X and Y will do business on those occasions when X actually leases items of personal property to Y. The requirements contract imposes no obligation on either party to actually enter into a lease agreement. Pursuant to this requirements contract, on January 1, 1985, X and Y enter into three separate leases. Under the leases, Y obtained the use of three identical items of personal property, each for a term of six months beginning on January 1, 1985. On March 1, 1985, Y entered into a fourth lease for the use of a fourth item of personal property substantially similar to the other three items for a term of 20 months beginning on that date. The mere fact that all 4 leases were entered into pursuant to the same requirements contract and involved the same or substantially similar property does not require aggregation of the terms of such leases under section 168(j)(6)(B).

Example (2). Assume the same facts as in Example (1) except that, instead of the 4 leases entered into in Example (1), on January 1, 1985, pursuant to the requirements contract, X and Y enter into a lease for an item of personal property for one year. On January 10, 1986, after the end of the one-year lease term, X and Y enter into a second lease with respect to the same or substantially similar equipment. Assuming that the requirements contract itself is not a lease and assuming that the parties did not have any informal or implicit understanding (other than the general expectation of doing some business in the future) to enter into the second lease when the first lease was entered into, these two leases are not aggregated. The mere fact that the parties entered into two leases under the requirements contract does not result in the application of the section 168(j)(6)(B) rules for successsive leases.

Example (3). The facts are the same as in Example (2) except that the parties did have an understanding, informal or otherwise, at the time of the first lease that they would enter into a second lease of the same personal property. The terms of the leases are aggregated.

Example (4). The facts are the same as in Example (2) except that, instead of the leases entered into in Example (2), on January 1, 1985, X and Y enter into two separate leases, each for a term of one year. One lease is for the period beginning on January 1, 1985 and ending on December 31, 1985. The other lease is for the period beginning on January 1, 1986 and ending on December 31, 1986. Both leases involve the same or substantially similar personal property. Under the successive lease rule, the terms of both leases are aggregated for purposes of determining the term of either lease under section 168(j)(6)(B). This result occurs because the two leases were entered into as part of the same transaction, and they relate to the same or substantially similar personal property.

Service contract issues:

Q-18. How is the treatment of service contracts affected by the service contract rules set forth in section 7701(e)?

A-18. If a contract which purports to be a service contract is treated as a lease under section 7701(e), such contract is to be treated as a lease for all purposes of Chapter 1 of the Internal Revenue Code (including, for example, section 168(j) and section 48(a)(4) and (5)).

Q-19. Does a contract to provide heating, maintenance, etc. services in low-income housing come within the low-income housing exception in section 7701(e)(5) to the service contract rules set forth in section 7701(e)?

A-19. No. Although certain low-income housing operated by or for an organization described in paragraphs (3) or (4) of section 501(c) is not subject to the service contract rules in section 7701(e), a contract, for instance, to provide heating services to low-income housing units, such as by installing and operating a furnace, does not constitute "low-income housing" within the meaning of section 7701(e)(5). Thus, the rules of section 7701(e) apply to such contracts in determining whether they are properly treated as leases.

Partnership issues:

Q-20. Do the provisions applicable to property leased to partnerships, set forth in section 168(j)(8), and the provisions applicable to

Itemized Deductions for Individuals and Corps.
See p. 20,601 for regulations not amended to reflect law changes
25,487

property owned by partnerships, set forth in section 168(j)(9), apply to pass-through entities other than partnerships.

A-20. Yes. Rules similar to those provided in paragraphs (8), (9)(A), (9)(B), and (9)(C) of section 168(j) and those provided in Q & A's 21–26 apply to pass-through entities other than partnerships.

Q-21. What rules apply to property owned by a partnership in which one or more partners is a tax-exempt entity?

A-21. If property is owned by a partnership having both taxable and tax-exempt entities as partners, and any allocation to a tax-exempt entity partner is not a "qualified allocation" under section 168(j)(9)(B), then such entity's proportionate share of the property is to be treated as tax-exempt use property for all purposes. However, the property will not be tax-exempt use property if it is predominantly used by the partnership in an activity which, with respect to the tax-exempt entity, is an unrelated trade or business. An activity is an unrelated trade or business with respect to a tax-exempt entity if such entity's distributive share of the partnership's gross income from the activity is includible in computing its unrelated business taxable income under section 512(c) (determined without regard to the debt-financed income rules of section 514). A tax-exempt entity partner's proportionate share of property of a partnership equals such partner's share of that item of the partnership's income or gain (excluding income or gain allocated under section 704(c)) in which the tax-exempt entity has the highest share. If the tax-exempt entity partner's share of any item of income or gain (excluding income or gain allocated under section 704(c)) may vary during the period it is a partner, the previous sentence shall be applied with reference to the highest share of any such item that it may receive at any time during such period. The application of these rules is illustrated by the following example:

Example. A partnership (P) operates a factory, which consists of a building and various items of machinery. P has one tax-exempt entity (E) as a partner, and E's proportionate share is 10 percent (*i.e.*, 10 percent is the largest share of any item of income or gain that E may receive during the time E is a partner). Unless P's allocations to E are qualified under section 168(j)(9)(B), 10 percent of each item of partnership property (including the building) is tax-exempt use property, notwithstanding the 35 percent threshold test of section 168(j)(3)(B)(iii) that is otherwise applicable to 18-year real property. However, the property will not be tax-exempt use property if it is predominantly used by the partnership in an activity which, with respect to E, is an unrelated trade or business (determined without regard to the debt-financed income rules of section 514).

Q-22. What constitutes a "qualified allocation" under section 168(j)(9)(B)?

A-22. (i) A "qualified allocation" means any allocation to a tax-exempt entity which is consistent with such entity's being allocated the same share (*i.e.*, the identical percentage) of each and every item of partnership income, gain, loss, deduction, credit, and basis during the entire period such entity is a partner. Except as provided in A-23, an allocation is not qualified if it does not have substantial economic effect under section 704(b). However, for purposes of the two preceding sentences, items allocated under section 704(c) (relating to contributed property) are not taken into account. An allocation is not a "qualified allocation" under section 168(j)(9)(B) if the partnership agreement provides for, or the partners have otherwise formally or informally agreed to, any change (regardless of whether such change is contingent upon the happening of one or more events) in the tax-exempt entity's distributive share of income, gain, loss, deduction, credit, or basis at any time during the entire period the tax-exempt entity is a partner.

(ii) A change in a tax-exempt entity's distributive share of income, gain, loss, deduction, credit, or basis which occurs as a result of a sale or redemption of a partnership interest (or portion thereof) or a contribution of cash or property to the partnership shall be disregarded in determining whether the partnership allocations are qualified, provided that such transaction is based on fair market value at the time of the transaction and that the allocations are qualified after the change. For this purpose, the consideration determined by the parties dealing at arm's length and with adverse interests normally will be deemed to satisfy the fair market value requirement. In addition, a change in a tax-exempt entity's distributive share which occurs as a result of a partner's default (other than a prearranged *default*) *under the terms of the partnership agreement* will be disregarded, provided that the allocations are qualified after the change, and that the change does not have the effect of avoiding the restrictions of section 168(j)(9). Any of the above-described transactions between existing partners (and parties related to them) will be closely scrutinized.

Example (1). A, a taxable entity, and B, a tax-exempt entity, form a partnership in 1985. A contributes $800,000 to the partnership; B contributes $200,000. The partnership agreement allocates 95 percent of each item of income, gain, loss, deduction, credit, and basis to A; B's share of each of these items is 5 percent. Liquidation proceeds are,

throughout the term of the partnership, to be distributed in accordance with the partner's capital account balances, and any partner with a deficit in his capital account following the distribution of liquidation proceeds is required to restore the amount of such deficit to the partnership. Assuming that these allocations have substantial economic effect within the meaning of section 704(b)(2), they are qualified because B's distributive share of each item of income, gain, loss, deduction, credit, and basis will remain the same during the entire period that B is a partner. The fact that the liquidation proceeds may be distributed in a ratio other than 95 percent/5 percent does not cause the allocations not to be qualified.

Example (2). A, B, and E are members of a partnership formed on July 1, 1984. On that date the partnership places in service a building and section 1245 class property. A and B are taxable entities; E is a tax-exempt entity. The partnership agreement provides that during the first 5 years of the partnership, A and B are each allocated 40 percent of each item of income, gain, loss, deduction, credit, and basis; E is allocated 20 percent. Thereafter, A, B, and E are each allocated 33$^{1}/_{3}$ percent of each item of income, gain, loss, deduction, credit, and basis. Assume that these allocations meet the substantial economic effect test of section 704(b)(2) and E's distributive share of the partnership's income is not unrelated trade or business income subject to tax under section 511. The allocations to E are not qualified allocations under section 168(j)(9)(B) because E's distributive share of partnership items does not remain the same during the entire period that E is a partner in the partnership. Thus, 33$^{1}/_{3}$ percent of the building and 33$^{1}/_{3}$ percent of the section 1245 class property are tax-exempt use property from the time each is placed in service by the partnership and are thus subject to the cost recovery rules of section 168(j)(1) and (2). In addition, no investment tax credit is allowed for 33$^{1}/_{3}$ percent of the section 1245 class property because of section 48(a)(4).

Q-23. In determining whether allocations constitute qualified allocations, what rules are applied to test allocations that are not governed by the substantial economic effect rules?

A-23. A-22 provides the general rules to be used in determining whether an allocation is a qualified allocation, including the rule that the allocation must have substantial economic effect. However, certain allocations are not governed by the substantial economic effect rules (*e.g.*, an allocation of basis of an oil and gas property is generally governed by section 613A(c)(7)(D), rather than section 704(b)), and other allocations cannot satisfy the substantial economic effect rules (*e.g.*, allocations of credits, allocations of deduction and loss attributable to nonrecourse debt, and allocations of percentage depletion in excess of basis). Since allocations in either of these categories cannot be tested under the substantial economic effect test, these allocations, in order to be qualified, must comply with the relevant Code or regulation section that governs the particular allocation (*e.g.*, in the case of an allocation of basis of an oil and gas property, section 613A(c)(7)(D)).

Q-24. Will the Internal Revenue Service issue letter rulings on the issue of whether an allocation is a "qualified allocation" for purposes of section 168(j)(9)?

A-24. The Internal Revenue Service will accept requests for rulings on the question of whether an allocation is a "qualified allocation" for purposes of section 168(j)(9). Such requests should be submitted in accordance with the appropriate revenue procedure. One requirement of a qualified allocation is that such allocation must have substantial economic effect under section 704(b)(2). Currently, the Service will not rule on the question of whether an allocation has substantial economic effect under section 704(b)(2). Therefore, unless and until this policy is changed, a ruling request regarding a qualified allocation must contain a representation that the subject allocation has substantial economic effect (or complies with A-23, if applicable).

Q-25. Do priority cash distributions which constitute guaranteed payments under section 707(c) disqualify an otherwise qualified allocation?

A-25. Priority cash distributions to partners which constitute guaranteed payments will not disqualify an otherwise qualified allocation if the priority cash distributions are reasonable in amount (*e.g.*, equal to the Federal short-term rate described in section 1274(d)) and are made in equal priorities to all partners in proportion to their capital in the partnership. Other guaranteed payments will be closely scrutinized and, in appropriate cases, will disqualify an otherwise qualified allocation.

Example. A and B form Partnership AB to operate a manufacturing business. A is a tax-exempt entity; B is a taxable person. A contributes $500,000 to the partnership; B contributes $100,000. The partnership agreement provides that A and B are each entitled to cash distributions each year, in equal priority, in an amount equal to 8 percent of their capital contribution. Assume that these payments are reasonable in amount and constitute guaranteed payments under section 707(c). Without taking into consideration the guaranteed payments, all allocations constitute qualified allocations under section 168(j)(9)(B) and A-22. These guaranteed payments will not disqualify such allocations.

Q-26. Can property be treated as tax-exempt use property under both the general rule of section 168(j)(3) and the partnership provisions of section 168(j)(9)?

A-26. Yes. For example, a tax-exempt entity may be a partner in a partnership that owns a building 60 percent of which is tax-exempt use property because it is leased to an unrelated tax-exempt entity under a 25-year lease. The status of the remaining 40 percent depends on whether or not allocations under the parntership agreement are qualified under section 168(j)(9). If the allocations are not qualified under section 168(j)(9), the tax-exempt entity's proportionate share (as determined under section 168(j)(9)(C)) of the remaining 40 percent will be tax-exempt use property. For example, if the tax-exempt entity's proportionate share is 30 percent, then 12 percent of the remaining 40 percent (i.e., .30 times .40) is tax-exempt use property and a total of 72 percent of the property (60 percent + 12 percent) is tax-exempt use property.

Effective date questions:

Q-27. Does an amendment to a lease (or sublease) to a tax-exempt entity of property which, pursuant to the effective date provisions of section 31(g) of TRA, is not subject to section 168(j) cause such property to be subject to the provisions of section 168(j)?

A-27. An amendment to such a lease (or sublease) does not cause such property to be subject to the provisions of section 168(j) unless the amendment increases the term of the lease (or sublease). However, if the amendment increases the amount of property subject to the lease, the additional property must be tested independently under the effective date provisions of section 31(g) of TRA. See A-31 for special rules regarding improvements to property.

Example. On May 1, 1983, X, a taxable entity, and E, a tax-exempt entity, enter into a lease whereby X will lease to E the top 4 floors of a ten-story building for a lease term of 25 years. In 1985, the lease is amended to provide that E will lease an additional floor for the balance of the lease term. At that time the annual rent due under the lease is increased. Pursuant to the provisions of section 31(g)(2)(A) of TRA, section 168(j) does not apply to the lease to E of the top 4 floors of the building. Assuming that no other provision of section 31(g) of TRA provides otherwise, the floor added to the lease in 1985 is subject to the provisions of section 168(j).

Q-28. If property which is not subject to section 168(j) by virtue of the effective date provisions of section 31(g) of TRA is sold, subject to the lease to the tax-exempt entity, what are the consequences?

A-28. Property to which section 168(j) does not apply by virtue of the effective date provisions set forth in section 31(g)(2), (3), and (4) of TRA will not become subject to section 168(j) merely because of a transfer of the property subject to the lease by the lessor (or a transfer of the contract to acquire, construct, reconstruct, or rehabilitate the property), so long as the lessee (or party obligated to lease) does not change. For purposes of the preceding sentence, the term "transfer" includes the sale-leaseback by a taxable lessor of its interest in the property, subject to the underlying lease to the tax-exempt entity. However, if property is transferred to a partnership or other pass-through entity after the effective date of section 168(j)(9) (see section 31(g) of TRA), such property is subject to the provisions of section 168(j)(9).

Q-29. Can property which was leased to a tax-exempt entity after May 23, 1983 and acquired by a partnership before October 22, 1983 be tax-exempt use property?

A-29. Yes. Because the property was leased to a tax-exempt entity after May 23, 1983 it may be tax-exempt use property under section 168(j)(3) and section 31(g)(1) of TRA. However, if the partnership included a tax-exempt entity as a partner, section 168(j)(9) would be inapplicable under section 31(g)(3)(B) of TRA because the partnership acquired the property before October 22, 1983.

Q-30. What is a binding contract for purposes of the transitional rules in section 31(g) of TRA?

A-30. (i) A contract is binding only if it is enforceable under State law against the taxpayer or a predecessor and does not limit damages to a specified amount, as for example, by a liquidated damages provision. A contract that limits damages to an amount equal to at least 5 percent of the total contract price will not be treated as limiting damages for this purpose. In determining whether a contract limits damages, the fact that there may be little or no damages because the contract price does not significantly differ from fair market value will not be taken into account. For example, if a taxpayer entered into an irrevocable contract to purchase an asset for $100 and the contract contained no provision for liquidated damages, the contract is considered binding notwithstanding the fact that the property had a fair market value of $99 and under local law the seller would only recover the difference in the event the purchaser failed to perform. If the contract provided for a refund of the purchase price in

lieu of any damages allowable by law in the event of breach or cancellation, the contract is not considered binding.

(ii) A contract is binding even if subject to a condition, so long as the condition is not within the control of either party or a predecessor in interest. A contract will not be treated as ceasing to be binding merely because the parties make insubstantial changes in its terms or because any term is to be determined by a standard beyond the control of either party. A contract which imposes significant obligations on the taxpayer (or a predecessor) will be treated as binding notwithstanding the fact that insubstantial terms remain to be negotiated by the parties to the contract.

(iii) A binding contract to acquire a component part of a larger piece of property will not be treated as a binding contract to acquire the larger piece of property. For example, if a tax-exempt entity entered into a binding contract on May 1, 1983 to acquire a new aircraft engine, there would be a binding contract to acquire only the engine, not the entire aircraft.

Q-31. If an improvement is made to a property that is "grandfathered" (i.e., property that is not subject to section 168(j) because of the effective date provisions of section 31(g) of TRA), to what extent will such improvement be grandfathered?

A-31. Section 31(g)(20)(B) provides that a "substantial improvement" to property is treated as a separate property for purposes of the effective date provisions of section 31(g) of TRA. As a result, a "substantial improvement" will not be grandfathered unless such "substantial improvement" is grandfathered under a provision other than section 31(g)(20)(B). A property that is grandfathered will not become subject to section 168(j) merely because an improvement is made to such property, regardless of whether the improvement is a "substantial improvement". If an improvement other than a "substantial improvement" is made to property (other than land) that is grandfathered, that improvement also will be grandfathered. The determination of whether new construction constitutes an improvement to property or the creation of a new separate property will be based on all facts and circumstances. Furthermore, any improvement to land will be treated as a separate property.

Example. On January 3, 1983, T, a taxable entity, entered into a lease of a parking lot to E, a tax-exempt entity. On January 1, 1985, T begins construction of a building for use by E on the site of the parking lot. The building is completed and placed in service in November 1985. The building is treated as a separate property, and is thus subject to the provisions of section 168(j), unless the building is grandfathered under a provision other than section 31(g)(20)(B) of TRA.

Q-32. What is "significant official governmental action" for purposes of the section 31(g)(4) transitional rule of TRA?

A-32. (i) "Significant official governmental action" involves three separate requirements. First, the action must be an official action. Second, the action must be specific action with respect to a particular project. Third, the action must be taken by a governmental entity having authority to commit the tax-exempt entity to the project, to provide funds for it, or to approve the project under State or local law.

(ii) The first requirement of official action means that the governing body must adopt a resolution or ordinance, or take similar official action, on or before November 1, 1983. The action qualifies only if it conforms with Federal, State, and local law (as applicable) and is a proper exercise of the powers of the governing body. Moreover, the action must not have been withdrawn. There must be satisfactory written evidence of the action that was in existence on or before November 1, 1983. Satisfactory written evidence includes a formal resolution or ordinance, minutes of meetings, and binding contracts with third parties pursuant to which third parties are to render services in furtherance of the project.

(iii) The second requirement of specific action is directed at the substance of the action taken. The action must be a specific action with respect to a particular project in which the governing body indicates an intent to have the project (or the design work for it) proceed. This requires that a specific project have been formulated and that the significant official action be a step toward consummation of the project. If the action does not relate to a specific project or merely directs that a proposal or recommendation be formulated, it will not qualify. The following set of actions with respect to a particular project constitute specific action: the hiring of bond counsel or bond underwriters necessary to assist in the issuance and sale of bonds to finance a particular project or the adoption of an inducement resolution relating to bonds to be issued for such a project; applying for an Urban Development Action Grant on behalf of the project described in the application, receiving such a grant concerning the project, or the recommendation of a city planning authority to proceed with a project; the enactment of a State law authorizing the sale, lease, or construction of the property; the appropriation of funds for the property or authorization of a feasibility study or a development services contract with respect to it; the approval of financing

Itemized Deductions for Individuals and Corps.
See p. 20,601 for regulations not amended to reflect law changes
25,489

arrangements by a regulatory agency; the enactment of a State law designed to provide funding for a project; the certification of a building as a historic structure by a State agency and the Department of the Interior; or the endorsement of the application for a certification of need with respect to a medical facility by a regulatory agency other than the agency empowered to issue such a certificate.

(iv) The third requirement for significant official governmental action is that the action must be taken by a Federal, State, or local governing body having authority to commit the tax-exempt entity to the project, to provide funds for it, or to approve the project under applicable law. If the chief executive or another representative of a governing body has such authority, action by such representative would satisfy the requirement of this (iv). A governing body may have the authority to commit the tax-exempt entity to a project notwithstanding the fact that the project cannot be consummated without other governmental action being taken. For example, a city council will be treated as having authority to commit a city to do a sale-leaseback of its city hall notwithstanding the fact that State law needs to be amended to permit such a transaction. Similarly, if a local project cannot be completed without Federal approval, either legislative or administrative, the obtaining of such approval satisfies the requirements of this (iv).

(v) Routine governmental action at a local level will not qualify as significant official governmental action. Routine governmental action includes the granting of building permits or zoning changes and the issuance of environmental impact statements.

(vi) In order to qualify under the transitional rule of TRA section 31(g)(4), a sale and leaseback pursuant to a building contract entered into before January 1, 1985 must be part of the project as to which there was significant official governmental action. Except as provided in the following sentence, where there has been significant official governmental action on or before November 1, 1983 with respect to the construction, reconstruction or rehabilitation of a property, the sale and leaseback of such property pursuant to a binding contract entered into before January 1, 1985 will be treated as part of the project which was the subject of the significant official governmental action. However, if the construction, reconstruction or rehabilitation was substantially completed prior to January 1, 1983, the sale and leaseback of such property will be treated as a separate project, unless the sale and leaseback was contemplated at the time of the significant official governmental action. Nevertheless, where the sale and leaseback is treated as a separate project, section 31(g)(4) may apply if there was significant official governmental action on or before November 1, 1983, with respect to such sale and leaseback. The application of this provision is illustrated by the following example:

Example. In the summer of 1927, the Board of Aldermen of City C passed a resolution authorizing the design and construction of a new city hall and appropriated the funds necessary for such project. Construction was completed in 1928. At the time of the significant official governmental action, City C had no plan to enter into a sale-leaseback arrangement with respect to the facility. On December 15, 1984, City C entered into a binding sale-leaseback arrangement concerning the city hall. This transaction will not qualify for exclusion from section 168(j) under section 31(g)(4) of TRA since construction of the facility in question was substantially completed before January 1, 1983. If, however, there had been significant official governmental action on or before November 1, 1983 with respect to the sale-leaseback project, then the transitional rule of section 31(g)(4) of TRA would apply. [Temporary Reg. § 1.168(j)-1T.]

□ [*T.D. 8033, 6-28-85. Amended by T.D. 8435, 9-18-92.*]

[Reg. § 1.168(k)-0]

§ 1.168(k)-0. Table of contents.—This section lists the major paragraphs contained in §§ 1.168(k)-1 and 1.168(k)-2.

(iii) Definition.
(iv) Examples.
(3) Section 1245 and 1250 depreciation recapture.
(4) Coordination with section 169.
(5) Like-kind exchanges and involuntary conversions.
  (i) Scope.
  (ii) Definitions.
  (iii) Computation.
    (A) In general.
    (B) Year of disposition and year of replacement.
    (C) Property having a longer production period.
    (D) Alternative minimum tax.
  (iv) Sale-leasebacks.
  (v) Acquired MACRS property or acquired computer software that is acquired and placed in service before disposition of involuntarily converted MACRS property or involuntarily converted computer software.
    (A) Time of replacement.
    (B) Depreciation of acquired MACRS property or acquired computer software.
  (vi) Examples.
(6) Change in use.
  (i) Change in use of depreciable property.
  (ii) Conversion to personal use.
  (iii) Conversion to business or income-producing use.
    (A) During the same taxable year.
    (B) Subsequent to the acquisition year.
  (iv) Depreciable property changes use subsequent to the placed-in-service year.
  (v) Examples.
(7) Earnings and profits.
(8) Limitation of amount of depreciation for certain passenger automobiles.
(9) Section 754 election.
(10) Coordination with section 47.
(11) Coordination with section 514(a)(3).
(g) Effective date.
(1) In general.
(2) Technical termination of a partnership or section 168(i)(7) transactions.
(3) Like-kind exchanges and involuntary conversions.
(4) Change in method of accounting.
  (i) Special rules for 2000 or 2001 returns.
  (ii) Like-kind exchanges and involuntary conversions.
(5) Revisions to paragraphs (b)(3)(ii)(B) and (b)(5)(ii)(B).
(6) Rehabilitation credit.

§1.168(k)-2 *Additional first year depreciation deduction for property acquired and placed in service after September 27, 2017.*
(a) Scope and definitions.
(1) Scope.
(2) Definitions.
(b) Qualified property.
(1) In general.
(2) Description of qualified property.
  (i) In general.
  (ii) Property not eligible for additional first year depreciation deduction.
  (iii) Examples.
(3) Original use or used property acquisition requirements.
  (i) In general.
  (ii) Original use.
    (A) In general.
    (B) Conversion to business or income-producing use.
    (C) Fractional interests in property.
  (iii) Used property acquisition requirements.
    (A) In general.
    (B) Property was not used by the taxpayer at any time prior to acquisition.
    (C) Special rules for a series of related transactions.
  (iv) Application to partnerships.
    (A) Section 704(c) remedial allocations.
    (B) Basis determined under section 732.
    (C) Section 734(b) adjustments.
    (D) Section 743(b) adjustments.
  (v) Application to members of a consolidated group.
  (vi) Syndication transaction.
  (vii) Examples.
(4) Placed-in-service date.
  (i) In general.
  (ii) Specified plant.

  (iii) Qualified film, television, or live theatrical production.
    (A) Qualified film or television production.
    (B) Qualified live theatrical production.
  (iv) Syndication transaction.
  (v) Technical termination of a partnership.
  (vi) Section 168(i)(7) transactions.
(5) Acquisition of property.
  (i) In general.
  (ii) Acquisition date.
    (A) In general.
    (B) Determination of acquisition date for property acquired pursuant to a written binding contract.
  (iii) Definition of binding contract.
    (A) In general.
    (B) Conditions.
    (C) Options.
    (D) Letter of intent.
    (E) Supply agreements.
    (F) Components.
    (G) Acquisition of a trade or business or an entity.
  (iv) Self-constructed property.
    (A) In general.
    (B) When does manufacture, construction, or production begin.
    (C) Components of self-constructed property.
  (v) Determination of acquisition date for property not acquired pursuant to a written binding contract.
  (vi) Qualified film, television, or live theatrical production.
    (A) Qualified film or television production.
    (B) Qualified live theatrical production.
  (vii) Specified plant.
  (viii) Examples.
(c) Election for components of larger self-constructed property for which the manufacture, construction, or production begins before September 28, 2017.
(1) In general.
(2) Eligible larger self-constructed property.
  (i) In general.
  (ii) Residential rental property or nonresidential real property.
  (iii) Beginning of manufacture, construction, or production.
  (iv) Exception.
(3) Eligible components.
  (i) In general.
  (ii) Acquired components.
  (iii) Self-constructed components.
(4) Special rules.
  (i) Installation costs.
  (ii) Property described in section 168(k)(2)(B).
(5) Computation of additional first year depreciation deduction.
  (i) Election is made.
  (ii) Election is not made.
(6) Time and manner for making election.
  (i) Time for making election.
  (ii) Manner of making election.
(7) Revocation of election.
  (i) In general.
  (ii) Automatic 6-month extension.
(8) Additional procedural guidance.
(9) Examples.
(d) Property described in section 168(k)(2)(B) or (C).
(1) In general.
(2) Definition of binding contract.
(3) Self-constructed property.
  (i) In general.
  (ii) When does manufacture, construction, or production begin.
    (A) In general.
    (B) Safe harbor.
  (iii) Components of self-constructed property.
    (A) Acquired components.
    (B) Self-constructed components.
  (iv) Determination of acquisition date for property not acquired pursuant to a written binding contract.
(4) Examples.
(e) Computation of depreciation deduction for qualified property.
(1) Additional first year depreciation deduction.
  (i) Allowable taxable year.
  (ii) Computation.
  (iii) Property described in section 168(k)(2)(B).
  (iv) Alternative minimum tax.

(A) In general.

(B) Special rules.

(2) Otherwise allowable depreciation deduction.

  (i) In general.

  (ii) Alternative minimum tax.

(3) Examples.

(f) Elections under section 168(k).

(1) Election not to deduct additional first year depreciation.

  (i) In general.

  (ii) Definition of class of property.

  (iii) Time and manner for making election.

    (A) Time for making election.

    (B) Manner of making election.

  (iv) Failure to make election.

(2) Election to apply section 168(k)(5) for specified plants.

  (i) In general.

  (ii) Time and manner for making election.

    (A) Time for making election.

    (B) Manner of making election.

  (iii) Failure to make election.

(3) Election for qualified property placed in service during the 2017 taxable year.

  (i) In general.

  (ii) Time and manner for making election.

    (A) Time for making election.

    (B) Manner of making election.

  (iii) Failure to make election.

(4) Alternative minimum tax.

(5) Revocation of election.

  (i) In general.

  (ii) Automatic 6-month extension.

(6) Special rules for 2016 and 2017 returns.

(7) Additional procedural guidance.

(g) Special rules.

(1) Property placed in service and disposed of in the same taxable year.

  (i) In general.

  (ii) Technical termination of a partnership.

  (iii) Section 168(i)(7) transactions.

  (iv) Examples.

(2) Redetermination of basis.

  (i) Increase in basis.

  (ii) Decrease in basis.

  (iii) Definitions.

  (iv) Examples.

(3) Sections 1245 and 1250 depreciation recapture.

(4) Coordination with section 169.

(5) Like-kind exchanges and involuntary conversions.

  (i) Scope.

  (ii) Definitions.

  (iii) Computation.

    (A) In general.

    (B) Year of disposition and year of replacement.

    (C) Property described in section 168(k)(2)(B).

    (D) Effect of § 1.168(i)-6(i)(1) election.

    (E) Alternative minimum tax.

  (iv) Replacement MACRS property or replacement computer software that is acquired and placed in service before disposition of relinquished MACRS property or relinquished computer software.

  (v) Examples.

(6) Change in use.

  (i) Change in use of MACRS property.

  (ii) Conversion to personal use.

  (iii) Conversion to business or income-producing use.

    (A) During the same taxable year.

    (B) Subsequent to the acquisition year.

  (iv) Depreciable property changes use subsequent to the placed-in-service year.

  (v) Examples.

(7) Earnings and profits.

(8) Limitation of amount of depreciation for certain passenger automobiles.

(9) Coordination with section 47.

  (i) In general.

  (ii) Example.

(10) Coordination with section 514(a)(3).

(11) Mid-quarter convention.

(h) Applicability dates.

(1) In general.

(2) Applicability of this section for prior taxable years.

(3) Early application of this section and § 1.1502-68.

  (i) In general.

  (ii) Early application to certain transactions.

  (iii) Bound by early application.

[Reg. § 1.168(k)-0.]

☐ [*T.D.* 9091, 9-5-2003. *Redesignated and amended by T.D.* 9283, 8-28-2006, *T.D.* 9874, 9-17-2019 *and T.D.* 9916, 11-5-2020.]

[Reg. § 1.168(k)-1]

§ 1.168(k)-1. Additional first year depreciation deduction.— (a) *Scope and definitions.*—(1) *Scope.*—This section provides the rules for determining the 30-percent additional first year depreciation deduction allowable under section 168(k)(1) for qualified property and the 50-percent additional first year depreciation deduction allowable under section 168(k)(4) for 50-percent bonus depreciation property.

(2) *Definitions.*—For purposes of section 168(k) and this section, the following definitions apply:

(i) *Depreciable property* is property that is of a character subject to the allowance for depreciation as determined under section 167 and the regulations thereunder.

(ii) *MACRS property* is tangible, depreciable property that is placed in service after December 31, 1986 (or after July 31, 1986, if the taxpayer made an election under section 203(a)(1)(B) of the Tax Reform Act of 1986; 100 Stat. 2143) and subject to section 168, except for property excluded from the application of section 168 as a result of section 168(f) or as a result of a transitional rule.

(iii) *Unadjusted depreciable basis* is the basis of property for purposes of section 1011 without regard to any adjustments described in section 1016(a)(2) and (3). This basis reflects the reduction in basis for the percentage of the taxpayer's use of property for the taxable year other than in the taxpayer's trade or business (or for the production of income), for any portion of the basis the taxpayer properly elects to treat as an expense under section 179 or section 179C, and for any adjustments to basis provided by other provisions of the Internal Revenue Code and the regulations thereunder (other than section 1016(a)(2) and (3)) (for example, a reduction in basis by the amount of the disabled access credit pursuant to section 44(d)(7)). For property subject to a lease, see section 167(c)(2).

(iv) *Adjusted depreciable basis* is the unadjusted depreciable basis of the property, as defined in § 1.168(k)-1(a)(2)(iii), less the adjustments described in section 1016(a)(2) and (3).

(b) *Qualified property or 50-percent bonus depreciation property.*— (1) *In general.*—Qualified property or 50-percent bonus depreciation property is depreciable property that meets all the following requirements in the first taxable year in which the property is subject to depreciation by the taxpayer whether or not depreciation deductions for the property are allowable:

(i) The requirements in § 1.168(k)-1(b)(2) (description of property);

(ii) The requirements in § 1.168(k)-1(b)(3) (original use);

(iii) The requirements in § 1.168(k)-1(b)(4) (acquisition of property); and

(iv) The requirements in § 1.168(k)-1(b)(5) (placed-in-service date).

(2) *Description of qualified property or 50-percent bonus depreciation property.*—(i) *In general.*—Depreciable property will meet the requirements of this paragraph (b)(2) if the property is—

(A) MACRS property (as defined in § 1.168(k)-1(a)(2)(ii)) that has a recovery period of 20 years or less. For purposes of this paragraph (b)(2)(i)(A) and section 168(k)(2)(B)(i)(II) and 168(k)(4)(C), the recovery period is determined in accordance with section 168(c) regardless of any election made by the taxpayer under section 168(g)(7);

(B) Computer software as defined in, and depreciated under, section 167(f)(1) and the regulations thereunder;

(C) Water utility property as defined in section 168(e)(5) and depreciated under section 168; or

(D) Qualified leasehold improvement property as defined in paragraph (c) of this section and depreciated under section 168.

(ii) *Property not eligible for additional first year depreciation deduction.*—(A) *Property that is not qualified.*—For purposes of the 30-percent additional first year depreciation deduction, depreciable property will not meet the requirements of this paragraph (b)(2) if the property is—

(1) Described in section 168(f);

(2) Required to be depreciated under the alternative depreciation system of section 168(g) pursuant to section 168(g)(1)(A) through (D) or other provisions of the Internal Revenue Code (for example, property described in section 263A(e)(2)(A) if the taxpayer (or any related person as defined in section 263A(e)(2)(B)) has made

an election under section 263A(d)(3), or property described in section 280F(b)(1)).

(3) Included in any class of property for which the taxpayer elects not to deduct the 30-percent additional first year depreciation (for further guidance, see paragraph (e) of this section); or

(4) Qualified New York Liberty Zone leasehold improvement property as defined in section 1400L(c)(2).

(B) *Property that is not 50-percent bonus depreciation property.*—For purposes of the 50-percent additional first year depreciation deduction, depreciable property will not meet the requirements of this paragraph (b)(2) if the property is—

(1) Described in paragraph (b)(2)(ii)(A)(1), (2), or (4) of this section; or

(2) Included in any class of property for which the taxpayer elects the 30-percent, instead of the 50-percent, additional first year depreciation deduction or elects not to deduct any additional first year depreciation (for further guidance, see paragraph (e) of this section).

(3) *Original use.*—(i) *In general.*—For purposes of the 30-percent additional first year depreciation deduction, depreciable property will meet the requirements of this paragraph (b)(3) if the original use of the property commences with the taxpayer after September 10, 2001. For purposes of the 50-percent additional first year depreciation deduction, depreciable property will meet the requirements of this paragraph (b)(3) if the original use of the property commences with the taxpayer after May 5, 2003. Except as provided in paragraphs (b)(3)(iii) and (iv) of this section, original use means the first use to which the property is put, whether or not that use corresponds to the use of the property by the taxpayer. Thus, additional capital expenditures incurred by a taxpayer to recondition or rebuild property acquired or owned by the taxpayer satisfies the original use requirement. However, the cost of reconditioned or rebuilt property does not satisfy the original use requirement. The question of whether property is reconditioned or rebuilt property is a question of fact. For purposes of this paragraph (b)(3)(i), property that contains used parts will not be treated as reconditioned or rebuilt if the cost of the used parts is not more than 20 percent of the total cost of the property, whether acquired or self-constructed.

(ii) *Conversion to business or income-producing use.*—(A) *Personal use to business or income-producing use.*—If a taxpayer initially acquires new property for personal use and subsequently uses the property in the taxpayer's trade or business or for the taxpayer's production of income, the taxpayer is considered the original user of the property. If a person initially acquires new property for personal use and a taxpayer subsequently acquires the property from the person for use in the taxpayer's trade or business or for the taxpayer's production of income, the taxpayer is not considered the original user of the property.

(B) *Inventory to business or income-producing use.*—If a taxpayer initially acquires new property and holds the property primarily for sale to customers in the ordinary course of the taxpayer's business and subsequently withdraws the property from inventory and uses the property primarily in the taxpayer's trade or business or primarily for the taxpayer's production of income, the taxpayer is considered the original user of the property. If a person initially acquires new property and holds the property primarily for sale to customers in the ordinary course of the person's business and a taxpayer subsequently acquires the property from the person for use primarily in the taxpayer's trade or business or primarily for the taxpayer's production of income, the taxpayer is considered the original user of the property. For purposes of this paragraph (b)(3)(ii)(B), the original use of the property by the taxpayer commences on the date on which the taxpayer uses the property primarily in the taxpayer's trade or business or primarily for the taxpayer's production of income.

(iii) *Sale-leaseback, syndication, and certain other transactions.*—(A) *Sale-leaseback transaction.*—If new property is originally placed in service by a person after September 10, 2001 (for qualified property), or after May 5, 2003 (for 50-percent bonus depreciation property), and is sold to a taxpayer and leased back to the person by the taxpayer within three months after the date the property was originally placed in service by the person, the taxpayer-lessor is considered the original user of the property.

(B) *Syndication transaction and certain other transactions.*—If new property is originally placed in service by a lessor (including by operation of paragraph (b)(5)(ii)(A) of this section) after September 10, 2001 (for qualified property), or after May 5, 2003 (for 50-percent bonus depreciation property), and is sold by the lessor or any subsequent purchaser within three months after the date the property was originally placed in service by the lessor (or, in the case of multiple units of property subject to the same lease, within three months after

the date the final unit is placed in service, so long as the period between the time the first unit is placed in service and the time the last unit is placed in service does not exceed 12 months), and the user of the property after the last sale during the three-month period remains the same as when the property was originally placed in service by the lessor, the purchaser of the property in the last sale during the three-month period is considered the original user of the property.

(C) *Sale-leaseback transaction followed by a syndication transaction and certain other transactions.*—If a sale-leaseback transaction that satisfies the requirements in paragraph (b)(3)(iii)(A) of this section is followed by a transaction that satisfies the requirements in paragraph (b)(3)(iii)(B) of this section, the original user of the property is determined in accordance with paragraph (b)(3)(iii)(B) of this section.

(iv) *Fractional interests in property.*—If, in the ordinary course of its business, a taxpayer sells fractional interests in property to third parties unrelated to the taxpayer, each first fractional owner of the property is considered as the original user of its proportionate share of the property. Furthermore, if the taxpayer sells the property before all of the fractional interests of the property are sold but the property continues to be held primarily for sale by the taxpayer, the original use of any fractional interest sold to a third party unrelated to the taxpayer subsequent to the taxpayer's use of the property begins with the first purchaser of that fractional interest. For purposes of this paragraph (b)(3)(iv), persons are not related if they do not have a relationship described in section 267(b) or 707(b) and the regulations thereunder.

(v) *Examples.*—The application of this paragraph (b)(3) is illustrated by the following examples:

Example 1. On August 1, 2002, A buys from B for $20,000 a machine that has been previously used by B in B's trade or business. On March 1, 2003, A makes a $5,000 capital expenditure to recondition the machine. The $20,000 purchase price does not qualify for the additional first year depreciation deduction because the original use requirement of this paragraph (b)(3) is not met. However, the $5,000 expenditure satisfies the original use requirement of this paragraph (b)(3) and, assuming all other requirements are met, qualifies for the 30-percent additional first year depreciation deduction, regardless of whether the $5,000 is added to the basis of the machine or is capitalized as a separate asset.

Example 2. C, an automobile dealer, uses some of its automobiles as demonstrators in order to show them to prospective customers. The automobiles that are used as demonstrators by C are held by C primarily for sale to customers in the ordinary course of its business. On September 1, 2002, D buys from C an automobile that was previously used as a demonstrator by C. D will use the automobile solely for business purposes. The use of the automobile by C as a demonstrator does not constitute a "use" for purposes of the original use requirement and, therefore, D will be considered the original user of the automobile for purposes of this paragraph (b)(3). Assuming all other requirements are met, D's purchase price of the automobile qualifies for the 30-percent additional first year depreciation deduction for D, subject to any limitation under section 280F.

Example 3. On April 1, 2000, E acquires a horse to be used in E's thoroughbred racing business. On October 1, 2003, F buys the horse from E and will use the horse in F's horse breeding business. The use of the horse by E in its racing business prevents the original use of the horse from commencing with F. Thus, F's purchase price of the horse does not qualify for the additional first year depreciation deduction.

Example 4. In the ordinary course of its business, G sells fractional interests in its aircraft to unrelated parties. G holds out for sale eight equal fractional interests in an aircraft. On January 1, 2003, G sells five of the eight fractional interests in the aircraft to H, an unrelated party, and H begins to use its proportionate share of the aircraft immediately upon purchase. On June 1, 2003, G sells to I, an unrelated party to G, the remaining unsold $3/8$ fractional interests in the aircraft. H is considered the original user as to its $5/8$ fractional interest in the aircraft and I is considered the original user as to its $3/8$ fractional interest in the aircraft. Thus, assuming all other requirements are met, H's purchase price for its $5/8$ fractional interest in the aircraft qualifies for the 30-percent additional first year depreciation deduction and I's purchase price for its $3/8$ fractional interest in the aircraft qualifies for the 50-percent additional first year depreciation deduction.

Example 5. On September 1, 2001, JJ, an equipment dealer, buys new tractors that are held by JJ primarily for sale to customers in the ordinary course of its business. On October 15, 2001, JJ withdraws the tractors from inventory and begins to use the tractors primarily for producing rental income. The holding of the tractors by JJ as inventory does not constitute a "use" for purposes of the original use requirement and, therefore, the original use of the tractors commences with JJ on October 15, 2001, for purposes of para-

Itemized Deductions for Individuals and Corps.
See p. 20,601 for regulations not amended to reflect law changes
25,493

graph (b)(3) of this section. However, the tractors are not eligible for the additional first year depreciation deduction because JJ acquired the tractors before September 11, 2001.

(4) *Acquisition of property.*—(i) *In general.*—(A) *Qualified property.*—For purposes of the 30-percent additional first year depreciation deduction, depreciable property will meet the requirements of this paragraph (b)(4) if the property is—

(1) Acquired by the taxpayer after September 10, 2001, and before January 1, 2005, but only if no written binding contract for the acquisition of the property was in effect before September 11, 2001; or

(2) Acquired by the taxpayer pursuant to a written binding contract that was entered into after September 10, 2001, and before January 1, 2005.

(B) *50-percent bonus depreciation property.*—For purposes of the 50-percent additional first year depreciation deduction, depreciable property will meet the requirements of this paragraph (b)(4) if the property is—

(1) Acquired by the taxpayer after May 5, 2003, and before January 1, 2005, but only if no written binding contract for the acquisition of the property was in effect before May 6, 2003; or

(2) Acquired by the taxpayer pursuant to a written binding contract that was entered into after May 5, 2003, and before January 1, 2005.

(ii) *Definition of binding contract.*—(A) *In general.*—A contract is binding only if it is enforceable under State law against the taxpayer or a predecessor, and does not limit damages to a specified amount (for example, by use of a liquidated damages provision). For this purpose, a contractual provision that limits damages to an amount equal to at least 5 percent of the total contract price will not be treated as limiting damages to a specified amount. In determining whether a contract limits damages, the fact that there may be little or no damages because the contract price does not significantly differ from fair market value will not be taken into account. For example, if a taxpayer entered into an irrevocable written contract to purchase an asset for $100 and the contract contained no provision for liquidated damages, the contract is considered binding notwithstanding the fact that the asset had a fair market value of $99 and under local law the seller would only recover the difference in the event the purchaser failed to perform. If the contract provided for a full refund of the purchase price in lieu of any damages allowable by law in the event of breach or cancellation, the contract is not considered binding.

(B) *Conditions.*—A contract is binding even if subject to a condition, as long as the condition is not within the control of either party or a predecessor. A contract will continue to be binding if the parties make insubstantial changes in its terms and conditions or because any term is to be determined by a standard beyond the control of either party. A contract that imposes significant obligations on the taxpayer or a predecessor will be treated as binding notwithstanding the fact that certain terms remain to be negotiated by the parties to the contract.

(C) *Options.*—An option to either acquire or sell property is not a binding contract.

(D) *Supply agreements.*—A binding contract does not include a supply or similar agreement if the amount and design specifications of the property to be purchased have not been specified. The contract will not be a binding contract for the property to be purchased until both the amount and the design specifications are specified. For example, if the provisions of a supply or similar agreement state the design specifications of the property to be purchased, a purchase order under the agreement for a specific number of assets is treated as a binding contract.

(E) *Components.*—A binding contract to acquire one or more components of a larger property will not be treated as a binding contract to acquire the larger property. If a binding contract to acquire the component does not satisfy the requirements of this paragraph (b)(4), the component does not qualify for the 30-percent or 50-percent additional first year depreciation deduction, as applicable.

(iii) *Self-constructed property.*—(A) *In general.*—If a taxpayer manufactures, constructs, or produces property for use by the taxpayer in its trade or business (or for its production of income), the acquisition rules in paragraph (b)(4)(i) of this section are treated as met for qualified property if the taxpayer begins manufacturing, constructing, or producing the property after September 10, 2001, and before January 1, 2005, and for 50-percent bonus depreciation property if the taxpayer begins manufacturing, constructing, or producing the property after May 5, 2003, and before January 1, 2005. Property that is manufactured, constructed, or produced for the

taxpayer by another person under a written binding contract (as defined in paragraph (b)(4)(ii) of this section) that is entered into prior to the manufacture, construction, or production of the property for use by the taxpayer in its trade or business (or for its production of income) is considered to be manufactured, constructed, or produced by the taxpayer. If a taxpayer enters into a written binding contract (as defined in paragraph (b)(4)(ii) of this section) after September 10, 2001, and before January 1, 2005, with another person to manufacture, construct, or produce property described in section 168(k)(2)(B) (longer production period property) or section 168(k)(2)(C) (certain aircraft) and the manufacture, construction, or production of this property begins after December 31, 2004, the acquisition rule in paragraph (b)(4)(i)(A)(2) or (b)(4)(i)(B)(2) of this section is met.

(B) *When does manufacture, construction, or production begin.*—(1) *In general.*—For purposes of paragraph (b)(4)(iii) of this section, manufacture, construction, or production of property begins when physical work of a significant nature begins. Physical work does not include preliminary activities such as planning or designing, securing financing, exploring, or researching. The determination of when physical work of a significant nature begins depends on the facts and circumstances. For example, if a retail motor fuels outlet or other facility is to be constructed on-site, construction begins when physical work of a significant nature commences at the site; that is, when work begins on the excavation for footings, pouring the pads for the outlet, or the driving of foundation pilings into the ground. Preliminary work, such as clearing a site, test drilling to determine soil condition, or excavation to change the contour of the land (as distinguished from excavation for footings) does not constitute the beginning of construction. However, if a retail motor fuels outlet or other facility is to be assembled on-site from modular units manufactured off-site and delivered to the site where the outlet will be used, manufacturing begins when physical work of a significant nature commences at the off-site location.

(2) *Safe harbor.*—For purposes of paragraph (b)(4)(iii)(B)(1) of this section, a taxpayer may choose to determine when physical work of a significant nature begins in accordance with this paragraph (b)(4)(iii)(B)(2). Physical work of a significant nature will not be considered to begin before the taxpayer incurs (in the case of an accrual basis taxpayer) or pays (in the case of a cash basis taxpayer) more than 10 percent of the total cost of the property (excluding the cost of any land and preliminary activities such as planning or designing, securing financing, exploring, or researching). When property is manufactured, constructed, or produced for the taxpayer by another person, this safe harbor test must be satisfied by the taxpayer. For example, if a retail motor fuels outlet or other facility is to be constructed for an accrual basis taxpayer by another person for the total cost of $200,000 (excluding the cost of any land and preliminary activities such as planning or designing, securing financing, exploring, or researching), construction is deemed to begin for purposes of this paragraph (b)(4)(iii)(B)(2) when the taxpayer has incurred more than 10 percent (more than $20,000) of the total cost of the property. A taxpayer chooses to apply this paragraph (b)(4)(iii)(B)(2) by filing an income tax return for the placed-in-service year of the property that determines when physical work of a significant nature begins consistent with this paragraph (b)(4)(iii)(B)(2).

(C) *Components of self-constructed property.*—(1) *Acquired components.*—If a binding contract (as defined in paragraph (b)(4)(ii) of this section) to acquire a component does not satisfy the requirements of paragraph (b)(4)(i) of this section, the component does not qualify for the 30-percent or 50-percent additional first year depreciation deduction, as applicable. A binding contract (as defined in paragraph (b)(4)(ii) of this section) to acquire one or more components of a larger self-constructed property will not preclude the larger self-constructed property from satisfying the acquisition rules in paragraph (b)(4)(iii)(A) of this section. Accordingly, the unadjusted depreciable basis of the larger self-constructed property that is eligible for the 30-percent or 50-percent additional first year depreciation deduction, as applicable (assuming all other requirements are met), must not include the unadjusted depreciable basis of any component that does not satisfy the requirements of paragraph (b)(4)(i) of this section. If the manufacture, construction, or production of the larger self-constructed property begins before September 11, 2001, for qualified property, or before May 6, 2003, for 50-percent bonus depreciation property, the larger self-constructed property and any acquired components related to the larger self-constructed property do not qualify for the 30-percent or 50-percent additional first year depreciation deduction, as applicable. If a binding contract to acquire the component is entered into after September 10, 2001, for qualified property, or after May 5, 2003, for 50-percent bonus depreciation property, and before January 1, 2005, but the manufacture, construction, or production of the larger self-constructed property does not begin before January 1, 2005, the component qualifies for the additional first year depreciation deduction (assuming all other requirements are met) but the larger self-constructed property does not.

(2) *Self-constructed components.*—If the manufacture, construction, or production of a component does not satisfy the requirements of paragraph (b)(4)(iii)(A) of this section, the component does not qualify for the 30-percent or 50-percent additional first year depreciation deduction, as applicable. However, if the manufacture, construction, or production of a component does not satisfy the requirements of paragraph (b)(4)(iii)(A) of this section, but the manufacture, construction, or production of the larger self-constructed property satisfies the requirements of paragraph (b)(4)(iii)(A) of this section, the larger self-constructed property qualifies for the 30-percent or 50-percent additional first year depreciation deduction, as applicable (assuming all other requirements are met) even though the component does not qualify for the 30-percent or 50-percent additional first year depreciation deduction. Accordingly, the unadjusted depreciable basis of the larger self-constructed property that is eligible for the 30-percent or 50-percent additional first year depreciation deduction, as applicable (assuming all other requirements are met), must not include the unadjusted depreciable basis of any component that does not qualify for the 30-percent or 50-percent additional first year depreciation deduction. If the manufacture, construction, or production of the larger self-constructed property began before September 11, 2001, for qualified property, or before May 6, 2003, for 50-percent bonus depreciation property, the larger self-constructed property and any self-constructed components related to the larger self-constructed property do not qualify for the 30-percent or 50-percent additional first year depreciation deduction, as applicable. If the manufacture, construction, or production of a component begins after September 10, 2001, for qualified property, or after May 5, 2003, for 50-percent bonus depreciation property, and before January 1, 2005, but the manufacture, construction, or production of the larger self-constructed property does not begin before January 1, 2005, the component qualifies for the additional first year depreciation deduction (assuming all other requirements are met) but the larger self-constructed property does not.

(iv) *Disqualified transactions.*—(A) *In general.*—Property does not satisfy the requirements of this paragraph (b)(4) if the user of the property as of the date on which the property was originally placed in service (including by operation of paragraphs (b)(5)(ii), (iii), and (iv) of this section), or a related party to the user or to the taxpayer, acquired, or had a written binding contract (as defined in paragraph (b)(4)(ii) of this section) in effect for the acquisition of the property at any time before September 11, 2001 (for qualified property), or before May 6, 2003 (for 50-percent bonus depreciation property). In addition, property manufactured, constructed, or produced for the use by the user of the property or by a related party to the user or to the taxpayer does not satisfy the requirements of this paragraph (b)(4) if the manufacture, construction, or production of the property for the user or the related party began at any time before September 11, 2001 (for qualified property), or before May 6, 2003 (for 50-percent bonus depreciation property).

(B) *Related party defined.*—For purposes of this paragraph (b)(4)(iv), persons are related if they have a relationship specified in section 267(b) or 707(b) and the regulations thereunder.

(v) *Examples.*—The application of this paragraph (b)(4) is illustrated by the following examples:

Example 1. On September 1, 2001, *J*, a corporation, entered into a written agreement with *K*, a manufacturer, to purchase 20 new lamps for $100 each within the next two years. Although the agreement specifies the number of lamps to be purchased, the agreement does not specify the design of the lamps to be purchased. Accordingly, the agreement is not a binding contract pursuant to paragraph (b)(4)(ii)(D) of this section.

Example 2. Same facts as *Example 1.* On December 1, 2001, *J* placed a purchase order with *K* to purchase 20 new model XPC5 lamps for $100 each for a total amount of $2,000. Because the agreement specifies the number of lamps to be purchased and the purchase order specifies the design of the lamps to be purchased, the purchase order placed by *J* with *K* on December 1, 2001, is a binding contract pursuant to paragraph (b)(4)(ii)(D) of this section. Accordingly, the cost of the 20 lamps qualifies for the 30-percent additional first year depreciation deduction.

Example 3. Same facts as *Example 1* except that the written agreement between *J* and *K* is to purchase 100 model XPC5 lamps for $100 each within the next two years. Because this agreement specifies *the amount and design of the lamps to be purchased*, the agreement is a binding contract pursuant to paragraph (b)(4)(ii)(D) of this section. Accordingly, because the agreement was entered into before September 11, 2001, any lamp acquired by *J* under this contract does not qualify for the additional first year depreciation deduction.

Example 4. On September 1, 2001, *L* began constructing an electric generation power plant for its own use. On November 1, 2002, *L* ceases construction of the power plant prior to its completion. Between September 1, 2001, and November 1, 2002, *L* incurred $3,000,000 for the construction of the power plant. On May 6, 2003, *L* resumed construction of the power plant and completed its construction on August 31, 2003. Between May 6, 2003, and August 31, 2003, *L* incurred another $1,600,000 to complete the construction of the power plant and, on September 1, 2003, *L* placed the power plant in service. None of *L*'s total expenditures of $4,600,000 qualify for the additional first year depreciation deduction because, pursuant to paragraph (b)(4)(iii)(A) of this section, *L* began constructing the power plant before September 11, 2001.

Example 5. Same facts as *Example 4* except that *L* began constructing the electric generation power plant for its own use on October 1, 2001. *L*'s total expenditures of $4,600,000 qualify for the additional first year depreciation deduction because, pursuant to paragraph (b)(4)(iii)(A) of this section, *L* began constructing the power plant after September 10, 2001, and placed the power plant in service before January 1, 2005. Accordingly, the additional first year depreciation deduction for the power plant will be $1,380,000, computed as $4,600,000 multiplied by 30 percent.

Example 6. On August 1, 2001, *M* entered into a written binding contract to acquire a new turbine. The new turbine is a component part of a new electric generation power plant that is being constructed on *M*'s behalf. The construction of the new electric generation power plant commenced in November 2001, and the new electric generation power plant was completed in November 2002. Because *M* entered into a written binding contract to acquire a component part (the new turbine) prior to September 11, 2001, pursuant to paragraph (b)(4)(iii)(C) of this section, the component part does not qualify for the additional first year depreciation deduction. However, pursuant to paragraphs (b)(4)(iii)(A) and (C) of this section, the new plant constructed for *M* will qualify for the 30-percent additional first year depreciation deduction because construction of the new plant began after September 10, 2001, and before May 6, 2003. Accordingly, the unadjusted depreciable basis of the new plant that is eligible for the 30-percent additional first year depreciation deduction must not include the unadjusted depreciable basis of the new turbine.

Example 7. Same facts as *Example 6* except that *M* entered into the written binding contract to acquire the new turbine on September 30, 2002, and construction of the new plant commenced on August 1, 2001. Because *M* began construction of the new plant prior to September 11, 2001, pursuant to paragraphs (b)(4)(iii)(A) and (C) of this section, neither the new plant constructed for *M* nor the turbine will qualify for the additional first year depreciation deduction because self-construction of the new plant began prior to September 11, 2001.

Example 8. On September 1, 2001, *N* began constructing property for its own use. On October 1, 2001, *N* sold its rights to the property to *O*, a related party under section 267(b). Pursuant to paragraph (b)(4)(iv) of this section, the property is not eligible for the additional first year depreciation deduction because *N* and *O* are related parties and construction of the property by *N* began prior to September 11, 2001.

Example 9. On September 1, 2001, *P* entered into a written binding contract to acquire property. On October 1, 2001, *P* sold its rights to the property to *Q*, a related party under section 267(b). Pursuant to paragraph (b)(4)(iv) of this section, the property is not eligible for the additional first year depreciation deduction because *P* and *Q* are related parties and a written binding contract for the acquisition of the property was in effect prior to September 11, 2001.

Example 10. Prior to September 11, 2001, *R* began constructing an electric generation power plant for its own use. On May 1, 2003, prior to the completion of the power plant, *R* transferred the rights to own and use this power plant to *S*, an unrelated party, for $6,000,000. Between May 6, 2003, and June 30, 2003, *S*, a calendar-year taxpayer, began construction, and incurred another $1,200,000 to complete the construction, of the power plant and, on August 1, 2003, *S* placed the power plant in service. Because *R* and *S* are not related parties, the transaction between *R* and *S* will not be a disqualified transaction pursuant to paragraph (b)(4)(iv) of this section. Accordingly, *S*'s total expenditures of $7,200,000 for the power plant qualify for the additional first year depreciation deduction. *S*'s additional first year depreciation deduction for the power plant will be $2,400,000, computed as $6,000,000 multiplied by 30 percent, plus $1,200,000 multiplied by 50 percent. The $6,000,000 portion of the total $7,200,000 unadjusted depreciable basis qualifies for the 30-percent additional first year depreciation deduction because that portion of the total unadjusted depreciable basis was acquired by *S* after September 10, 2001, and before May 6, 2003. However, because *S* began construction to complete the power plant after May 5, 2003, the $1,200,000 portion of the total $7,200,000 unadjusted depreciable basis qualifies for the 50-percent additional first year depreciation deduction.

Example 11. On September 1, 2001, *T* acquired and placed in service equipment. On October 15, 2001, *T* sells the equipment to *U*, an unrelated party, and leases the property back from *U* in a sale-leaseback transaction. Pursuant to paragraph (b)(4)(iv) of this section, the equipment does not qualify for the additional first year depreciation deduction because *T*, the user of the equipment, acquired the equipment prior to September 11, 2001. In addition, the sale-leaseback rules in paragraphs (b)(3)(iii)(A) and (b)(5)(ii)(A) of this section do not apply because the equipment was originally placed in service by *T* before September 11, 2001.

Example 12. On July 1, 2001, KK began constructing property for its own use. KK placed this property in service on September 15, 2001. On October 15, 2001, KK sells the property to LL, an unrelated party, and leases the property back from LL in a sale-leaseback transaction. Pursuant to paragraph (b)(4)(iv) of this section, the property does not qualify for the additional first year depreciation deduction because the property was constructed for KK, the user of the property, and that construction began prior to September 11, 2001.

Example 13. On June 1, 2004, MM decided to construct property described in section 168(k)(2)(B) for its own use. However, one of the component parts of the property had to be manufactured by another person for MM. On August 15, 2004, MM entered into a written binding contract with NN to acquire this component part of the property for $100,000. The manufacture of the component part commenced on September 1, 2004, and MM received the completed component part on February 1, 2005. The cost of this component part is 9 percent of the total cost of the property to be constructed by MM. MM began constructing the property described in section 168(k)(2)(B) on January 15, 2005, and placed this property (including all component parts) in service on November 1, 2005. Pursuant to paragraph (b)(4)(iii)(C)(2) of this section, the self-constructed component part of $100,000 manufactured by NN for MM is eligible for the additional first year depreciation deduction (assuming all other requirements are met) because the manufacturing of the component part began after September 10, 2001, and before January 1, 2005, and the property described in section 168(k)(2)(B), the larger self-constructed property, was placed in service by MM before January 1, 2006. However, pursuant to paragraph (b)(4)(iii)(A) of this section, the cost of the property described in section 168(k)(2)(B) (excluding the cost of the self-constructed component part of $100,000 manufactured by NN for MM) is not eligible for the additional first year depreciation deduction because construction of the property began after December 31, 2004.

Example 14. On December 1, 2004, OO entered into a written binding contract (as defined in paragraph (b)(4)(ii) of this section) with PP to manufacture an aircraft described in section 168(k)(2)(C) for use in OO's trade or business. PP begins to manufacture the aircraft on February 1, 2005. OO places the aircraft in service on August 1, 2005. Pursuant to paragraph (b)(4)(iii)(A) of this section, the aircraft meets the requirements of paragraph (b)(4)(i)(B)(2) of this section because the aircraft was acquired by OO pursuant to a written binding contract entered into after May 5, 2003, and before January 1, 2005.

(5) *Placed-in-service date.*—(i) *In general.*—Depreciable property will meet the requirements of this paragraph (b)(5) if the property is placed in service by the taxpayer for use in its trade or business or for production of income before January 1, 2005, or, in the case of property described in section 168(k)(2)(B) or (C), is placed in service by the taxpayer for use in its trade or business or for production of income before January 1, 2006 (or placed in service by the taxpayer for use in its trade or business or for production of income before January 1, 2007, in the case of property described in section 168(k)(2)(B) or (C) to which section 105 of the Gulf Opportunity Zone Act of 2005 (Public Law 109-135, 119 Stat. 2577) applies (for further guidance, see Announcement 2006-29 (2006-19 I.R.B. 879) and §601.601(d)(2)(ii)(*b*) of this chapter)).

(ii) *Sale-leaseback, syndication, and certain other transactions.*—(A) *Sale-leaseback transaction.*—If qualified property is originally placed in service after September 10, 2001, or 50-percent bonus depreciation property is originally placed in service after May 5, 2003, by a person and sold to a taxpayer and leased back to the person by the taxpayer within three months after the date the property was originally placed in service by the person, the property is treated as originally placed in service by the taxpayer-lessor not earlier than the date on which the property is used by the lessee under the leaseback.

(B) *Syndication transaction and certain other transactions.*—If qualified property is originally placed in service after September 10, 2001, or 50-percent bonus depreciation property is originally placed in service after May 5, 2003, by a lessor (including by operation of paragraph (b)(5)(ii)(A) of this section) and is sold by the lessor or any subsequent purchaser within three months after the date the property was originally placed in service by the lessor (or, in the case of

multiple units of property subject to the same lease, within three months after the date the final unit is placed in service, so long as the period between the time the first unit is placed in service and the time the last unit is placed in service does not exceed 12 months), and the user of the property after the last sale during this three-month period remains the same as when the property was originally placed in service by the lessor, the property is treated as originally placed in service by the purchaser of the property in the last sale during the three-month period but not earlier than the date of the last sale.

(C) *Sale-leaseback transaction followed by a syndication transaction and certain other transactions.*—If a sale-leaseback transaction that satisfies the requirements in paragraph (b)(5)(ii)(A) of this section is followed by a transaction that satisfies the requirements in paragraph (b)(5)(ii)(B) of this section, the placed-in-service date of the property is determined in accordance with paragraph (b)(5)(ii)(B) of this section.

(iii) *Technical termination of a partnership.*—For purposes of this paragraph (b)(5), in the case of a technical termination of a partnership under section 708(b)(1)(B), qualified property or 50-percent bonus depreciation property placed in service by the terminated partnership during the taxable year of termination is treated as originally placed in service by the new partnership on the date the qualified property or the 50-percent bonus depreciation property is contributed by the terminated partnership to the new partnership.

(iv) *Section 168(i)(7) transactions.*—For purposes of this paragraph (b)(5), if qualified property or 50-percent bonus depreciation property is transferred in a transaction described in section 168(i)(7) in the same taxable year that the qualified property or the 50-percent bonus depreciation property is placed in service by the transferor, the transferred property is treated as originally placed in service on the date the transferor placed in service the qualified property or the 50-percent bonus depreciation property, as applicable. In the case of multiple transfers of qualified property or 50-percent bonus depreciation property in multiple transactions described in section 168(i)(7) in the same taxable year, the placed in service date of the transferred property is deemed to be the date on which the first transferor placed in service the qualified property or the 50-percent bonus depreciation property, as applicable.

(v) *Example.*—The application of this paragraph (b)(5) is illustrated by the following example:

Example. On September 15, 2004, QQ acquired and placed in service new equipment. This equipment is not described in section 168(k)(2)(B) or (C). On December 1, 2004, QQ sells the equipment to RR and leases the equipment back from RR in a sale-leaseback transaction. On February 15, 2005, RR sells the equipment to TT subject to the lease with QQ. As of February 15, 2005, QQ is still the user of the equipment. The sale-leaseback transaction of December 1, 2004, between QQ and RR satisfies the requirements of paragraph (b)(5)(ii)(A) of this section. The sale transaction of February 15, 2005, between RR and TT satisfies the requirements of paragraph (b)(5)(ii)(B) of this section. Consequently, pursuant to paragraph (b)(5)(ii)(C) of this section, the equipment is treated as originally placed in service by TT on February 15, 2005. Further, pursuant to paragraph (b)(3)(iii)(C) of this section, TT is considered the original user of the equipment. Accordingly, the equipment is not eligible for the additional first year depreciation deduction.

(c) *Qualified leasehold improvement property.*—(1) *In general.*—For purposes of section 168(k), qualified leasehold improvement property means any improvement, which is section 1250 property, to an interior portion of a building that is nonresidential real property if—

(i) The improvement is made under or pursuant to a lease by the lessee (or any sublessee) of the interior portion, or by the lessor of that interior portion;

(ii) The interior portion of the building is to be occupied exclusively by the lessee (or any sublessee) of that interior portion; and

(iii) The improvement is placed in service more than 3 years after the date the building was first placed in service by any person.

(2) *Certain improvements not included.*—Qualified leasehold improvement property does not include any improvement for which the expenditure is attributable to:

(i) The enlargement of the building;

(ii) Any elevator or escalator;

(iii) Any structural component benefiting a common area; or

(iv) The internal structural framework of the building.

(3) *Definitions.*—For purposes of this paragraph (c), the following definitions apply:

(i) *Building* has the same meaning as that term is defined in §1.48-1(e)(1).

(ii) *Common area* means any portion of a building that is equally available to all users of the building on the same basis for uses that are incidental to the primary use of the building. For example, stairways, hallways, lobbies, common seating areas, interior and exterior pedestrian walkways and pedestrian bridges, loading docks and areas, and rest rooms generally are treated as common areas if they are used by different lessees of a building.

(iii) *Elevator* and *escalator* have the same meanings as those terms are defined in § 1.48-1(m)(2).

(iv) *Enlargement* has the same meaning as that term is defined in § 1.48-12(c)(10).

(v) *Internal structural framework* has the same meaning as that term is defined in § 1.48-12(b)(3)(i)(D)(iii).

(vi) *Lease* has the same meaning as that term is defined in section 168(h)(7). In addition, a commitment to enter into a lease is treated as a lease, and the parties to the commitment are treated as lessor and lessee. However, a lease between related persons is not considered a lease. For purposes of the preceding sentence, related persons are—

(A) Members of an affiliated group (as defined in section 1504 and the regulations thereunder); and

(B) Persons having a relationship described in section 267(b) and the regulations thereunder. For purposes of applying section 267(b), the language "80 percent or more" is used instead of "more than 50 percent."

(vii) *Nonresidential real property* has the same meaning as that term is defined in section 168(e)(2)(B).

(viii) *Structural component* has the same meaning as that term is defined in § 1.48-1(e)(2).

(d) *Computation of depreciation deduction for qualified property or 50-percent bonus depreciation property.*—(1) *Additional first year depreciation deduction.*—(i) *In general.*—Except as provided in paragraph (f) of this section, the additional first year depreciation deduction is allowable in the first taxable year in which the qualified property or 50-percent bonus depreciation property is placed in service by the taxpayer for use in its trade or business or for the production of income. Except as provided in paragraph (f)(5) of this section, the allowable additional first year depreciation deduction for qualified property is determined by multiplying the unadjusted depreciable basis (as defined in § 1.168(k)-1(a)(2)(iii)) of the qualified property by 30 percent. Except as provided in paragraph (f)(5) of this section, the allowable additional first year depreciation deduction for 50-percent bonus depreciation property is determined by multiplying the unadjusted depreciable basis (as defined in § 1.168(k)-1(a)(2)(iii)) of the 50-percent bonus depreciation property by 50 percent. Except as provided in paragraph (f)(1) of this section, the 30-percent or 50-percent additional first year depreciation deduction is not affected by a taxable year of less than 12 months. See paragraph (f)(1) of this section for qualified property or 50-percent bonus depreciation property placed in service and disposed of in the same taxable year. See paragraph (f)(5) of this section for qualified property or 50-percent bonus depreciation property acquired in a like-kind exchange or as a result of an involuntary conversion.

(ii) *Property having a longer production period.*—For purposes of paragraph (d)(1)(i) of this section, the unadjusted depreciable basis (as defined in § 1.168(k)-1(a)(2)(iii)) of qualified property or 50-percent bonus depreciation property described in section 168(k)(2)(B) is limited to the property's unadjusted depreciable basis attributable to the property's manufacture, construction, or production after September 10, 2001 (for qualified property), or May 5, 2003 (for 50-percent bonus depreciation property), and before January 1, 2005.

(iii) *Alternative minimum tax.*—The 30-percent or 50-percent additional first year depreciation deduction is allowed for alternative minimum tax purposes for the taxable year in which the qualified property or the 50-percent bonus depreciation property is placed in service by the taxpayer. In general, the 30-percent or 50-percent additional first year depreciation deduction for alternative minimum tax purposes is based on the unadjusted depreciable basis of the property for alternative minimum tax purposes. However, see paragraph (f)(5)(iii)(D) of this section for qualified property or 50-percent bonus depreciation property acquired in a like-kind exchange or as a result of an involuntary conversion.

(2) *Otherwise allowable depreciation deduction.*—(i) *In general.*—Before determining the amount otherwise allowable as a depreciation deduction for the qualified property or the 50-percent bonus depreciation property for the placed-in-service year and any subsequent taxable year, the taxpayer must determine the remaining adjusted depreciable basis of the qualified property or the 50-percent bonus depreciation property. This remaining adjusted depreciable basis is equal to the unadjusted depreciable basis of the qualified property or the 50-percent bonus depreciation property reduced by the amount

of the additional first year depreciation allowed or allowable, whichever is greater. The remaining adjusted depreciable basis of the qualified property or the 50-percent bonus depreciation property is then depreciated using the applicable depreciation provisions under the Internal Revenue Code for the qualified property or the 50-percent bonus depreciation property. The remaining adjusted depreciable basis of the qualified property or the 50-percent bonus depreciation property that is MACRS property is also the basis to which the annual depreciation rates in the optional depreciation tables apply (for further guidance, see section 8 of Rev. Proc. 87-57 (1987-2 C.B. 687) and § 601.601(d)(2)(ii)(b) of this chapter). The depreciation deduction allowable for the remaining adjusted depreciable basis of the qualified property or the 50-percent bonus depreciation property is affected by a taxable year of less than 12 months.

(ii) *Alternative minimum tax.*—For alternative minimum tax purposes, the depreciation deduction allowable for the remaining adjusted depreciable basis of the qualified property or the 50-percent bonus depreciation property is based on the remaining adjusted depreciable basis for alternative minimum tax purposes. The remaining adjusted depreciable basis of the qualified property or the 50-percent bonus depreciable property for alternative minimum tax purposes is depreciated using the same depreciation method, recovery period (or useful life in the case of computer software), and convention that apply to the qualified property or the 50-percent bonus depreciation property for regular tax purposes.

(3) *Examples.*—This paragraph (d) is illustrated by the following examples:

Example 1. On March 1, 2003, *V*, a calendar-year taxpayer, purchased and placed in service qualified property that costs $1 million and is 5-year property under section 168(e). *V* depreciates its 5-year property placed in service in 2003 using the optional depreciation table that corresponds with the general depreciation system, the 200-percent declining balance method, a 5-year recovery period, and the half-year convention. For 2003, *V* is allowed a 30-percent additional first year depreciation deduction of $300,000 (the unadjusted depreciable basis of $1 million multiplied by .30). Next, *V* must reduce the unadjusted depreciable basis of $1 million by the additional first year depreciation deduction of $300,000 to determine the remaining adjusted depreciable basis of $700,000. Then, *V*'s depreciation deduction allowable in 2003 for the remaining adjusted depreciable basis of $700,000 is $140,000 (the remaining adjusted depreciable basis of $700,000 multiplied by the annual depreciation rate of .20 for recovery year 1).

Example 2. On June 1, 2003, *W*, a calendar-year taxpayer, purchased and placed in service 50-percent bonus depreciation property that costs $126,000. The property qualifies for the expensing election under section 179 and is 5-year property under section 168(e). *W* did not purchase any other section 179 property in 2003. *W* makes the election under section 179 for the property and depreciates its 5-year property placed in service in 2003 using the optional depreciation table that corresponds with the general depreciation system, the 200-percent declining balance method, a 5-year recovery period, and the half-year convention. For 2003, *W* is first allowed a $100,000 deduction under section 179. Next, *W* must reduce the cost of $126,000 by the section 179 deduction of $100,000 to determine the unadjusted depreciable basis of $26,000. Then, for 2003, *W* is allowed a 50-percent additional first year depreciation deduction of $13,000 (the unadjusted depreciable basis of $26,000 multiplied by .50). Next, *W* must reduce the unadjusted depreciable basis of $26,000 by the additional first year depreciation deduction of $13,000 to determine the remaining adjusted depreciable basis of $13,000. Then, *W*'s depreciation deduction allowable in 2003 for the remaining adjusted depreciable basis of $13,000 is $2,600 (the remaining adjusted depreciable basis of $13,000 multiplied by the annual depreciation rate of .20 for recovery year 1).

(e) *Election not to deduct additional first year depreciation.*—(1) *In general.*—If a taxpayer makes an election under this paragraph (e), the election applies to all qualified property or 50-percent bonus depreciation property, as applicable, that is in the same class of property and placed in service in the same taxable year. The rules of this paragraph (e) apply to the following elections provided under section 168(k):

(i) *Qualified property.*—A taxpayer may make an election not to deduct the 30-percent additional first year depreciation for any class of property that is qualified property placed in service during the taxable year. If this election is made, no additional first year depreciation deduction is allowable for the property placed in service during the taxable year in the class of property.

(ii) *50-percent bonus depreciation property.*—For any class of property that is 50-percent bonus depreciation property placed in service during the taxable year, a taxpayer may make an election—

Itemized Deductions for Individuals and Corps.
See p. 20,601 for regulations not amended to reflect law changes
25,497

(A) To deduct the 30-percent, instead of the 50-percent, additional first year depreciation. If this election is made, the allowable additional first year depreciation deduction is determined as though the class of property is qualified property under section 168(k)(2); or

(B) Not to deduct both the 30-percent and the 50-percent additional first year depreciation. If this election is made, no additional first year depreciation deduction is allowable for the class of property.

(2) *Definition of class of property.*—For purposes of this paragraph (e), the term class of property means:

(i) Except for the property described in paragraphs (e)(2)(ii) and (iv) of this section, each class of property described in section 168(e) (for example, 5-year property);

(ii) Water utility property as defined in section 168(e)(5) and depreciated under section 168;

(iii) Computer software as defined in, and depreciated under, section 167(f)(1) and the regulations thereunder; or

(iv) Qualified leasehold improvement property as defined in paragraph (c) of this section and depreciated under section 168.

(3) *Time and manner for making election.*—(i) *Time for making election.*—Except as provided in paragraph (e)(4) of this section, any election specified in paragraph (e)(1) of this section must be made by the due date (including extensions) of the Federal return for the taxable year in which the qualified property or the 50-percent bonus depreciation property, as applicable, is placed in service by the taxpayer.

(ii) *Manner of making election.*—Except as provided in paragraph (e)(4) of this section, any election specified in paragraph (e)(1) of this section must be made in the manner prescribed on Form 4562, "Depreciation and Amortization," and its instructions. The election is made separately by each person owning qualified property or 50-percent bonus depreciation property (for example, for each member of a consolidated group by the common parent of the group, by the partnership, or by the S corporation). If Form 4562 is revised or renumbered, any reference in this section to that form shall be treated as a reference to the revised or renumbered form.

(4) *Special rules for 2000 or 2001 returns.*—For the election specified in paragraph (e)(1)(i) of this section for qualified property placed in service by the taxpayer during the taxable year that included September 11, 2001, the taxpayer should refer to the guidance provided by the Internal Revenue Service for the time and manner of making this election on the 2000 or 2001 Federal tax return for the taxable year that included September 11, 2001 (for further guidance, see sections 3.03(3) and 4 of Rev. Proc. 2002-33 (2002-1 C.B. 963), Rev. Proc. 2003-50 (2003-29 I.R.B. 119), and §601.601(d)(2)(ii)(b) of this chapter).

(5) *Failure to make election.*—If a taxpayer does not make the applicable election specified in paragraph (e)(1) of this section within the time and in the manner prescribed in paragraph (e)(3) or (4) of this section, the amount of depreciation allowable for that property under section 167(f)(1) or under section 168, as applicable, must be determined for the placed-in-service year and for all subsequent taxable years by taking into account the additional first year depreciation deduction. Thus, any election specified in paragraph (e)(1) of this section shall not be made by the taxpayer in any other manner (for example, the election cannot be made through a request under section 446(e) to change the taxpayer's method of accounting).

(6) *Alternative minimum tax.*—If a taxpayer makes an election specified in paragraph (e)(1) of this section for a class of property, the depreciation adjustments under section 56 and the regulations under section 56 apply to the property to which that election applies for purposes of computing the taxpayer's alternative minimum taxable income.

(7) *Revocation of election.*—(i) *In general.*—Except as provided in paragraph (e)(7)(ii) of this section, an election specified in paragraph (e)(1) of this section, once made, may be revoked only with the written consent of the Commissioner of Internal Revenue. To seek the Commissioner's consent, the taxpayer must submit a request for a letter ruling.

(ii) *Automatic 6-month extension.*—If a taxpayer made an election specified in paragraph (e)(1) of this section for a class of property, an automatic extension of 6 months from the due date of the taxpayer's Federal tax return (excluding extensions) for the placed-in-service year of the class of property is granted to revoke that election, provided the taxpayer timely filed the taxpayer's Federal tax return for the placed-in-service year of the class of property and, within this 6-month extension period, the taxpayer (and all taxpayers whose tax liability would be affected by the election) files an amended Federal tax return for the placed-in-service year of the class of property in a manner that is consistent with the revocation of the election.

(f) *Special rules.*—(1) *Property placed in service and disposed of in the same taxable year.*—(i) *In general.*—Except as provided in paragraphs (f)(1)(ii) and (iii) of this section, the additional first year depreciation deduction is not allowed for qualified property or 50-percent bonus depreciation property placed in service and disposed of during the same taxable year. Also if qualified property or 50-percent bonus depreciation property is placed in service and disposed of during the same taxable year and then reacquired and again placed in service in a subsequent taxable year, the additional first year depreciation deduction is not allowable for the property in the subsequent taxable year.

(ii) *Technical termination of a partnership.*—In the case of a technical termination of a partnership under section 708(b)(1)(B), the additional first year depreciation deduction is allowable for any qualified property or 50-percent bonus depreciation property placed in service by the terminated partnership during the taxable year of termination and contributed by the terminated partnership to the new partnership. The allowable additional first year depreciation deduction for the qualified property or the 50-percent bonus depreciation property shall not be claimed by the terminated partnership but instead shall be claimed by the new partnership for the new partnership's taxable year in which the qualified property or the 50-percent bonus depreciation property was contributed by the terminated partnership to the new partnership. However, if qualified property or 50-percent bonus depreciation property is both placed in service and contributed to a new partnership in a transaction described in section 708(b)(1)(B) by the terminated partnership during the taxable year of termination, and if such property is disposed of by the new partnership in the same taxable year the new partnership received such property from the terminated partnership, then no additional first year depreciation deduction is allowable to either partnership.

(iii) *Section 168(i)(7) transactions.*—If any qualified property or 50-percent bonus depreciation property is transferred in a transaction described in section 168(i)(7) in the same taxable year that the qualified property or the 50-percent bonus depreciation property is placed in service by the transferor, the additional first year depreciation deduction is allowable for the qualified property or the 50-percent bonus depreciation property. The allowable additional first year depreciation deduction for the qualified property or the 50-percent bonus depreciation property for the transferor's taxable year in which the property is placed in service is allocated between the transferor and the transferee on a monthly basis. This allocation shall be made in accordance with the rules in §1.168(d)-1(b)(7)(ii) for allocating the depreciation deduction between the transferor and the transferee. However, if qualified property or 50-percent bonus depreciation property is both placed in service and transferred in a transaction described in section 168(i)(7) by the transferor during the same taxable year, and if such property is disposed of by the transferee (other than by a transaction described in section 168(i)(7)) during the same taxable year the transferee received such property from the transferor, then no additional first year depreciation deduction is allowable to either party.

(iv) *Examples.*—The application of this paragraph (f)(1) is illustrated by the following examples:

Example 1. X and Y are equal partners in *Partnership XY*, a general partnership. On February 1, 2002, *Partnership XY* purchased and placed in service new equipment at a cost of $30,000. On March 1, 2002, X sells its entire 50 percent interest to Z in a transfer that terminates the partnership under section 708(b)(1)(B). As a result, terminated *Partnership XY* is deemed to have contributed the equipment to new *Partnership XY*. Pursuant to paragraph (f)(1)(ii) of this section, new *Partnership XY*, not terminated *Partnership XY*, is eligible to claim the 30-percent additional first year depreciation deduction allowable for the equipment for the taxable year 2002 (assuming all other requirements are met).

Example 2. On January 5, 2002, BB purchased and placed in service new office desks for a total amount of $8,000. On August 20, 2002, BB transferred the office desks to *Partnership BC* in a transaction described in section 721. BB and *Partnership BC* are calendar-year taxpayers. Because the transaction between BB and *Partnership BC* is a transaction described in section 168(i)(7), pursuant to paragraph (f)(1)(iii) of this section the 30-percent additional first year depreciation deduction allowable for the desks is allocated between BB and *Partnership BC* in accordance with the rules in §1.168(d)-1(b)(7)(ii) for allocating the depreciation deduction between the transferor and the transferee. Accordingly, the 30-percent additional first year depreciation deduction allowable for the desks for 2002 of $2,400 (the unadjusted depreciable basis of $8,000 multiplied by .30) is allocated between BB and *Partnership BC* based on the number of months that

Reg. §1.168(k)-1(f)(1)(iv)

BB and *Partnership BC* held the desks in service. Thus, because the desks were held in service by *BB* for 7 of 12 months, which includes the month in which *BB* placed the desks in service but does not include the month in which the desks were transferred, *BB* is allocated $1,400 ($7/12 \times$ $2,400 additional first year depreciation deduction). *Partnership BC* is allocated $1,000, the remaining $5/12$ of the $2,400 additional first year depreciation deduction allowable for the desks.

(2) *Redetermination of basis.*—If the unadjusted depreciable basis (as defined in §1.168(k)-1(a)(2)(iii)) of qualified property or 50-percent bonus depreciation property is redetermined (for example, due to contingent purchase price or discharge of indebtedness) before January 1, 2005, or, in the case of property described in section 168(k)(2)(B) or (C), is redetermined before January 1, 2006 (or redetermined before January 1, 2007, in the case of property described in section 168(k)(2)(B) or (C) to which section 105 of the Gulf Opportunity Zone Act of 2005 (Public Law 109-135, 119 Stat. 2577) applies (for further guidance, see Announcement 2006-29 (2006-19 I.R.B. 879) and §601.601(d)(2)(ii)(*b*) of this chapter)), the additional first year depreciation deduction allowable for the qualified property or the 50-percent bonus depreciation property is redetermined as follows:

(i) *Increase in basis.*—For the taxable year in which an increase in basis of qualified property or 50-percent bonus depreciation property occurs, the taxpayer shall claim an additional first year depreciation deduction for qualified property by multiplying the amount of the increase in basis for this property by 30 percent or, for 50-percent bonus depreciation property, by multiplying the amount of the increase in basis for this property by 50 percent. For purposes of this paragraph (f)(2)(i), the 30-percent additional first year depreciation deduction applies to the increase in basis if the underlying property is qualified property and the 50-percent additional first year depreciation deduction applies to the increase in basis if the underlying property is 50-percent bonus depreciation property. To determine the amount otherwise allowable as a depreciation deduction for the increase in basis of qualified property or 50-percent bonus depreciation property, the amount of the increase in basis of the qualified property or the 50-percent bonus depreciation property must be reduced by the additional first year depreciation deduction allowed or allowable, whichever is greater, for the increase in basis and the remaining increase in basis of—

(A) Qualified property or 50-percent bonus depreciation property (except for computer software described in paragraph (b)(2)(i)(B) of this section) is depreciated over the recovery period of the qualified property or the 50-percent bonus depreciation property, as applicable, remaining as of the beginning of the taxable year in which the increase in basis occurs, and using the same depreciation method and convention applicable to the qualified property or 50-percent bonus depreciation property, as applicable, that applies for the taxable year in which the increase in basis occurs; and

(B) Computer software (as defined in paragraph (b)(2)(i)(B) of this section) that is qualified property or 50-percent bonus depreciation property is depreciated ratably over the remainder of the 36-month period (the useful life under section 167(f)(1)) as of the beginning of the first day of the month in which the increase in basis occurs.

(ii) *Decrease in basis.*—For the taxable year in which a decrease in basis of qualified property or 50-percent bonus depreciation property occurs, the taxpayer shall reduce the total amount otherwise allowable as a depreciation deduction for all of the taxpayer's depreciable property by the excess additional first year depreciation deduction previously claimed for the qualified property or the 50-percent bonus depreciation property. If, for such taxable year, the excess additional first year depreciation deduction exceeds the total amount otherwise allowable as a depreciation deduction for all of the taxpayer's depreciable property, the taxpayer shall take into account a negative depreciation deduction in computing taxable income. The excess additional first year depreciation deduction for qualified property is determined by multiplying the amount of the decrease in basis for this property by 30 percent. The excess additional first year depreciation deduction for 50-percent bonus depreciation property is determined by multiplying the amount of the decrease in basis for this property by 50 percent. For purposes of this paragraph (f)(2)(ii), the 30-percent additional first year depreciation deduction applies to the decrease in basis if the underlying property is qualified property and the 50-percent additional first year depreciation deduction applies to the decrease in basis if the underlying property is 50-percent bonus depreciation property. Also, if the taxpayer establishes by adequate records or other sufficient evidence that the taxpayer claimed less than the additional first year depreciation deduction allowable for the qualified property or the 50-percent bonus depreciation property before the decrease in basis or if the taxpayer claimed more than the additional first year depreciation deduction allowable for the qualified property or the 50-percent bonus depreciation prop-

erty before the decrease in basis, the excess additional first year depreciation deduction is determined by multiplying the amount of the decrease in basis by the additional first year depreciation deduction percentage actually claimed by the taxpayer for the qualified property or the 50-percent bonus depreciation property, as applicable, before the decrease in basis. To determine the amount to reduce the total amount otherwise allowable as a depreciation deduction for all of the taxpayer's depreciable property for the excess depreciation previously claimed (other than the additional first year depreciation deduction) resulting from the decrease in basis of the qualified property or the 50-percent bonus depreciation property, the amount of the decrease in basis of the qualified property or the 50-percent bonus depreciation property must be adjusted by the excess additional first year depreciation deduction that reduced the total amount otherwise allowable as a depreciation deduction (as determined under this paragraph) and the remaining decrease in basis of—

(A) Qualified property or 50-percent bonus depreciation property (except for computer software described in paragraph (b)(2)(i)(B) of this section) reduces the amount otherwise allowable as a depreciation deduction over the recovery period of the qualified property or the 50-percent bonus depreciation property, as applicable, remaining as of the beginning of the taxable year in which the decrease in basis occurs, and using the same depreciation method and convention of the qualified property or 50-percent bonus depreciation property, as applicable, that applies in the taxable year in which the decrease in basis occurs. If, for any taxable year, the reduction to the amount otherwise allowable as a depreciation deduction (as determined under this paragraph (f)(2)(ii)(A)) exceeds the total amount otherwise allowable as a depreciation deduction for all of the taxpayer's depreciable property, the taxpayer shall take into account a negative depreciation deduction in computing taxable income; and

(B) Computer software (as defined in paragraph (b)(2)(i)(B) of this section) that is qualified property or 50-percent bonus depreciation property reduces the amount otherwise allowable as a depreciation deduction over the remainder of the 36-month period (the useful life under section 167(f)(1)) as of the beginning of the first day of the month in which the decrease in basis occurs. If, for any taxable year, the reduction to the amount otherwise allowable as a depreciation deduction (as determined under this paragraph (f)(2)(ii)(B)) exceeds the total amount otherwise allowable as a depreciation deduction for all of the taxpayer's depreciable property, the taxpayer shall take into account a negative depreciation deduction in computing taxable income.

(iii) *Definition.*—Except as otherwise expressly provided by the Internal Revenue Code (for example, section 1017(a)), the regulations under the Internal Revenue Code, or other guidance published in the Internal Revenue Bulletin (see §601.601(d)(2)(ii)(*b*) of this chapter), for purposes of this paragraph (f)(2)—

(A) An increase in basis occurs in the taxable year an amount is taken into account under section 461; and

(B) A decrease in basis occurs in the taxable year an amount would be taken into account under section 451.

(iv) *Examples.*—The application of this paragraph (f)(2) is illustrated by the following examples:

Example 1. (i) On May 15, 2002, *CC*, a cash-basis taxpayer, purchased and placed in service qualified property that is 5-year property at a cost of $200,000. In addition to the $200,000, *CC* agrees to pay the seller 25 percent of the gross profits from the operation of the property in 2002. On May 15, 2003, *CC* paid to the seller an additional $10,000. *CC* depreciates the 5-year property placed in service in 2002 using the optional depreciation table that corresponds with the general depreciation system, the 200-percent declining balance method, a 5-year recovery period, and the half-year convention.

(ii) For 2002, *CC* is allowed a 30-percent additional first year depreciation deduction of $60,000 (the unadjusted depreciable basis of $200,000 multiplied by .30). In addition, *CC*'s depreciation deduction for 2002 for the remaining adjusted depreciable basis of $140,000 (the unadjusted depreciable basis of $200,000 reduced by the additional first year depreciation deduction of $60,000) is $28,000 (the remaining adjusted depreciable basis of $140,000 multiplied by the annual depreciation rate of .20 for recovery year 1).

(iii) For 2003, *CC*'s depreciation deduction for the remaining adjusted depreciable basis of $140,000 is $44,800 (the remaining adjusted depreciable basis of $140,000 multiplied by the annual depreciation rate of .32 for recovery year 2). In addition, pursuant to paragraph (f)(2)(i) of this section, *CC* is allowed an additional first year depreciation deduction for 2003 for the $10,000 increase in basis of the qualified property. Consequently, *CC* is allowed an additional first year depreciation deduction of $3,000 (the increase in basis of $10,000 multiplied by .30). Also, *CC* is allowed a depreciation deduction for 2003 attributable to the remaining increase in basis of $7,000 (the increase in basis of $10,000 reduced by the additional first year

Itemized Deductions for Individuals and Corps.
See p. 20,601 for regulations not amended to reflect law changes
25,499

depreciation deduction of $3,000). The depreciation deduction allowable for 2003 attributable to the remaining increase in basis of $7,000 is $3,111 (the remaining increase in basis of $7,000 multiplied by .4444, which is equal to 1/remaining recovery period of 4.5 years at January 1, 2003, multiplied by 2). Accordingly, for 2003, CC's total depreciation deduction allowable for the qualified property is $50,911.

Example 2. (i) On May 15, 2002, DD, a calendar-year taxpayer, purchased and placed in service qualified property that is 5-year property at a cost of $400,000. To purchase the property, DD borrowed $250,000 from Bank2. On May 15, 2003, Bank2 forgives $50,000 of the indebtedness. DD makes the election provided in section 108(b)(5) to apply any portion of the reduction under section 1017 to the basis of the depreciable property of the taxpayer. DD depreciates the 5-year property placed in service in 2002 using the optional depreciation table that corresponds with the general depreciation system, the 200-percent declining balance method, a 5-year recovery period, and the halfyear convention.

(ii) For 2002, DD is allowed a 30-percent additional first year depreciation deduction of $120,000 (the unadjusted depreciable basis of $400,000 multiplied by .30). In addition, DD's depreciation deduction allowable for 2002 for the remaining adjusted depreciable basis of $280,000 (the unadjusted depreciable basis of $400,000 reduced by the additional first year depreciation deduction of $120,000) is $56,000 (the remaining adjusted depreciable basis of $280,000 multiplied by the annual depreciation rate of .20 for recovery year 1).

(iii) For 2003, DD's deduction for the remaining adjusted depreciable basis of $280,000 is $89,600 (the remaining adjusted depreciable basis of $280,000 multiplied by the annual depreciation rate .32 for recovery year 2). Although Bank2 forgave the indebtedness in 2003, the basis of the property is reduced on January 1, 2004, pursuant to sections 108(b)(5) and 1017(a) under which basis is reduced at the beginning of the taxable year following the taxable year in which the discharge of indebtedness occurs.

(iv) For 2004, DD's deduction for the remaining adjusted depreciable basis of $280,000 is $53,760 (the remaining adjusted depreciable basis of $280,000 multiplied by the annual depreciation rate .192 for recovery year 3). However, pursuant to paragraph (f)(2)(ii) of this section, DD must reduce the amount otherwise allowable as a depreciation deduction for 2004 by the excess depreciation previously claimed for the $50,000 decrease in basis of the qualified property. Consequently, DD must reduce the amount of depreciation otherwise allowable for 2004 by the excess additional first year depreciation of $15,000 (the decrease in basis of $50,000 multiplied by .30). Also, DD must reduce the amount of depreciation otherwise allowable for 2004 by the excess depreciation attributable to the remaining decrease in basis of $35,000 (the decrease in basis of $50,000 reduced by the excess additional first year depreciation of $15,000). The reduction in the amount of depreciation otherwise allowable for 2004 for the remaining decrease in basis of $35,000 is $19,999 (the remaining decrease in basis of $35,000 multiplied by .5714, which is equal to 1/remaining recovery period of 3.5 years at January 1, 2004, multiplied by 2). Accordingly, assuming the qualified property is the only depreciable property owned by DD, for 2004, DD's total depreciation deduction allowable for the qualified property is $18,761 ($53,760 minus $15,000 minus $19,999).

(3) *Section 1245 and 1250 depreciation recapture.*—For purposes of section 1245 and the regulations thereunder, the additional first year depreciation deduction is an amount allowed or allowable for depreciation. Further, for purposes of section 1250(b) and the regulations thereunder, the additional first year depreciation deduction is not a straight line method.

(4) *Coordination with section 169.*—The additional first year depreciation deduction is allowable in the placed-in-service year of a certified pollution control facility (as defined in § 1.169-2(a)) that is qualified property or 50-percent bonus depreciation property, even if the taxpayer makes the election to amortize the certified pollution control facility under section 169 and the regulations thereunder in the certified pollution control facility's placed-in-service year.

(5) *Like-kind exchanges and involuntary conversions.*—(i) *Scope.*—The rules of this paragraph (f)(5) apply to acquired MACRS property or acquired computer software that is qualified property or 50-percent bonus depreciation property at the time of replacement provided the time of replacement is after September 10, 2001, and before January 1, 2005, or, in the case of acquired MACRS property or acquired computer software that is qualified property, or 50-percent bonus depreciation property, described in section 168(k)(2)(B) or (C), the time of replacement is after September 10, 2001, and before January 1, 2006, or (the time of replacement is after September 10, 2001, and before January 1, 2007, in the case of property described in section 168(k)(2)(B) or (C) to which section 105 of the Gulf Opportunity Zone Act of 2005 (Public Law 109-135, 119 Stat. 2577) applies (for

further guidance, see Announcement 2006-29 (2006-19 I.R.B. 879) and § 601.601(d)(2)(ii)(b) of this chapter)).

(ii) *Definitions.*—For purposes of this paragraph (f)(5), the following definitions apply:

(A) *Acquired MACRS property* is MACRS property in the hands of the acquiring taxpayer that is acquired in a transaction described in section 1031(a), (b), or (c) for other MACRS property or that is acquired in connection with an involuntary conversion of other MACRS property in a transaction to which section 1033 applies.

(B) *Exchanged or involuntarily converted MACRS property* is MACRS property that is transferred by the taxpayer in a transaction described in section 1031(a), (b), or (c), or that is converted as a result of an involuntary conversion to which section 1033 applies.

(C) *Acquired computer software* is computer software (as defined in paragraph (b)(2)(i)(B) of this section) in the hands of the acquiring taxpayer that is acquired in a like-kind exchange under section 1031 or as a result of an involuntary conversion under section 1033.

(D) *Exchanged or involuntarily converted computer software* is computer software (as defined in paragraph (b)(2)(i)(B) of this section) that is transferred by the taxpayer in a like-kind exchange under section 1031 or that is converted as a result of an involuntary conversion under section 1033.

(E) *Time of disposition* is when the disposition of the exchanged or involuntarily converted MACRS property or the exchanged or involuntarily converted computer software, as applicable, takes place.

(F) Except as provided in paragraph (f)(5)(v) of this section, the *time of replacement* is the later of—

(1) When the acquired MACRS property or acquired computer software is placed in service; or

(2) The time of disposition of the exchanged or involuntarily converted property.

(G) *Carryover basis* is the lesser of:

(1) the basis in the acquired MACRS property or acquired computer software, as applicable and as determined under section 1031(d) or 1033(b) and the regulations thereunder; or

(2) the adjusted depreciable basis of the exchanged or involuntarily converted MACRS property or the exchanged or involuntarily converted computer software, as applicable.

(H) *Excess basis* is any excess of the basis in the acquired MACRS property or acquired computer software, as applicable and as determined under section 1031(d) or 1033(b) and the regulations thereunder, over the carryover basis as determined under paragraph (f)(5)(ii)(G) of this section.

(I) *Remaining carryover basis* is the carryover basis as determined under paragraph (f)(5)(ii)(G) of this section reduced by—

(1) The percentage of the taxpayer's use of property for the taxable year other than in the taxpayer's trade or business (or for the production of income); and

(2) Any adjustments to basis provided by other provisions of the Code and the regulations thereunder (including section 1016(a)(2) and (3)) for periods prior to the disposition of the exchanged or involuntarily converted property.

(J) *Remaining excess basis* is the excess basis as determined under paragraph (f)(5)(ii)(H) of this section reduced by—

(1) The percentage of the taxpayer's use of property for the taxable year other than in the taxpayer's trade or business (or for the production of income);

(2) Any portion of the basis the taxpayer properly elects to treat as an expense under section 179 or section 179C;

(3) Any adjustments to basis provided by other provisions of the Code and the regulations thereunder.

(K) *Year of disposition* is the taxable year that includes the time of disposition.

(L) *Year of replacement* is the taxable year that includes the time of replacement.

(iii) *Computation.*—(A) *In general.*—Assuming all other requirements of section 168(k) and this section are met, the remaining carryover basis for the year of replacement and the remaining excess basis, if any, for the year of replacement for the acquired MACRS property or the acquired computer software, as applicable, are eligible for the additional first year depreciation deduction. The 30-percent additional first year depreciation deduction applies to the remaining carryover basis and the remaining excess basis, if any, of the acquired MACRS property or the acquired computer software if the time of replacement is after September 10, 2001, and before May 6, 2003, or if the taxpayer made the election provided in paragraph (e)(1)(ii)(A) of this section. The 50-percent additional first year depreciation deduction applies to the remaining carryover basis and the remaining excess basis, if any, of the acquired MACRS property or

Reg. § 1.168(k)-1(f)(5)(iii)(A)

the acquired computer software if the time of replacement is after May 5, 2003, and before January 1, 2005, or, in the case of acquired MACRS property or acquired computer software that is 50-percent bonus depreciation property described in section 168(k)(2)(B) or (C), the time of replacement is after May 5, 2003, and before January 1, 2006 (or the time of replacement is after May 5, 2003, and before January 1, 2007, in the case of 50-percent bonus depreciation property described in section 168(k)(2)(B) or (C) to which section 105 of the Gulf Opportunity Zone Act of 2005 (Public Law 109-135, 119 Stat. 2577) applies (for further guidance, see Announcement 2006-29 (2006-19 I.R.B. 879) and §601.601(d)(2)(ii)(b) of this chapter). The additional first year depreciation deduction is computed separately for the remaining carryover basis and the remaining excess basis.

(B) *Year of disposition and year of replacement.*—The additional first year depreciation deduction is allowable for the acquired MACRS property or acquired computer software in the year of replacement. However, the additional first year depreciation deduction is not allowable for the exchanged or involuntarily converted MACRS property or the exchanged or involuntarily converted computer software if the exchanged or involuntarily converted MACRS property or the exchanged or involuntarily converted computer software, as applicable, is placed in service and disposed of in an exchange or involuntary conversion in the same taxable year.

(C) *Property having a longer production period.*—For purposes of paragraph (f)(5)(iii)(A) of this section, the total of the remaining carryover basis and the remaining excess basis, if any, of the acquired MACRS property that is qualified property or 50-percent bonus depreciation property described in section 168(k)(2)(B) is limited to the total of the property's remaining carryover basis and remaining excess basis, if any, attributable to the property's manufacture, construction, or production after September 10, 2001 (for qualified property), or May 5, 2003 (for 50-percent bonus depreciation property), and before January 1, 2005.

(D) *Alternative minimum tax.*—The 30-percent or 50-percent additional first year depreciation deduction is allowed for alternative minimum tax purposes for the year of replacement of acquired MACRS property or acquired computer software that is qualified property or 50-percent bonus depreciation property. The 30-percent or 50-percent additional first year depreciation deduction for alternative minimum tax purposes is based on the remaining carryover basis and the remaining excess basis, if any, of the acquired MACRS property or the acquired computer software for alternative minimum tax purposes.

(iv) *Sale-leaseback transaction.*—For purposes of this paragraph (f)(5), if MACRS property or computer software is sold to a taxpayer and leased back to a person by the taxpayer within three months after the time of disposition of the MACRS property or computer software, as applicable, the time of replacement for this MACRS property or computer software, as applicable, shall not be earlier than the date on which the MACRS property or computer software, as applicable, is used by the lessee under the leaseback.

(v) *Acquired MACRS property or acquired computer software that is acquired and placed in service before disposition of involuntarily converted MACRS property or involuntarily converted computer software.*—If, in an involuntary conversion, a taxpayer acquires and places in service the acquired MACRS property or the acquired computer software before the time of disposition of the involuntarily converted MACRS property or the involuntarily converted computer software and the time of disposition of the involuntarily converted MACRS property or the involuntarily converted computer software is after December 31, 2004, or, in the case of property described in section 168(k)(2)(B) or (C), after December 31, 2005 (or after December 31, 2006, in the case of property described in section 168(k)(2)(B) or (C) to which section 105 of the Gulf Opportunity Zone Act of 2005 (Public Law 109-135, 119 Stat. 2577) applies (for further guidance, see Announcement 2006-29 (2006-19 I.R.B. 879) and §601.601(d)(2)(ii)(b) of this chapter)), then—

(A) *Time of replacement.*—The time of replacement for purposes of this paragraph (f)(5) is when the acquired MACRS property or acquired computer software is placed in service by the taxpayer, provided the threat or imminence of requisition or condemnation of the involuntarily converted MACRS property or involuntarily converted computer software existed before January 1, 2005, or, in the case of property described in section 168(k)(2)(B) or (C), existed before January 1, 2006 (or existed before January 1, 2007, in the case of property described in section 168(k)(2)(B) or (C) to which section 105 of the Gulf Opportunity Zone Act of 2005 (Public Law 109-135, 119 Stat. 2577) applies (for further guidance, see Announcement 2006-29 (2006-19 I.R.B. 879) and §601.601(d)(2)(ii)(b) of this chapter)); and

(B) *Depreciation of acquired MACRS property or acquired computer software.*—The taxpayer depreciates the acquired MACRS property or acquired computer software in accordance with paragraph (d) of this section. However, at the time of disposition of the involuntarily converted MACRS property, the taxpayer determines the exchanged basis (as defined in §1.168(i)-6(b)(7)) and the excess basis (as defined in §1.168(i)-6(b)(8)) of the acquired MACRS property and begins to depreciate the depreciable exchanged basis (as defined in §1.168(i)-6(b)(9) of the acquired MACRS property in accordance with §1.168(i)-6(c). The depreciable excess basis (as defined in §1.168(i)-6(b)(10)) of the acquired MACRS property continues to be depreciated by the taxpayer in accordance with the first sentence of this paragraph (f)(5)(v)(B). Further, in the year of disposition of the involuntarily converted MACRS property, the taxpayer must include in taxable income the excess of the depreciation deductions allowable, including the additional first year depreciation deduction allowable, on the unadjusted depreciable basis of the acquired MACRS property over the additional first year depreciation deduction that would have been allowable to the taxpayer on the remaining carryover basis of the acquired MACRS property at the time of replacement (as defined in paragraph (f)(5)(v)(A) of this section) plus the depreciation deductions that would have been allowable, including the additional first year depreciation deduction allowable, to the taxpayer on the depreciable excess basis of the acquired MACRS property from the date the acquired MACRS property was placed in service by the taxpayer (taking into account the applicable convention) to the time of disposition of the involuntarily converted MACRS property. Similar rules apply to acquired computer software.

(vi) *Examples.*—The application of this paragraph (f)(5) is illustrated by the following examples:

Example 1. (i) In December 2002, EE, a calendar-year corporation, acquired for $200,000 and placed in service Canopy V1, a gas station canopy. Canopy V1 is qualified property under section 168(k)(1) and is 5-year property under section 168(e). EE depreciated Canopy V1 under the general depreciation system of section 168(a) by using the 200-percent declining balance method of depreciation, a 5-year recovery period, and the half-year convention. EE elected to use the optional depreciation tables to compute the depreciation allowance for Canopy V1. On January 1, 2003, Canopy V1 was destroyed in a fire and was no longer usable in EE's business. On June 1, 2003, in an involuntary conversion, EE acquired and placed in service new Canopy W1 with all of the $160,000 of insurance proceeds EE received due to the loss of Canopy V1. Canopy W1 is 50-percent bonus depreciation property under section 168(k)(4) and is 5-year property under section 168(e). Pursuant to paragraph (g)(3)(ii) of this section and §1.168(i)-6(k)(2)(i), EE decided to apply §1.168(i)-6 to the involuntary conversion of Canopy V1 with the replacement of Canopy W1, the acquired MACRS property.

(ii) For 2002, EE is allowed a 30-percent additional first year depreciation deduction of $60,000 for Canopy V1 (the unadjusted depreciable basis of $200,000 multiplied by .30), and a regular MACRS depreciation deduction of $28,000 for Canopy V1 (the remaining adjusted depreciable basis of $140,000 multiplied by the annual depreciation rate of .20 for recovery year 1).

(iii) For 2003, EE is allowed a regular MACRS depreciation deduction of $22,400 for Canopy V1 (the remaining adjusted depreciable basis of $140,000 multiplied by the annual depreciation rate of .32 for recovery year 2 × $^{1}/_{2}$ year).

(iv) Pursuant to paragraph (f)(5)(iii)(A) of this section, the additional first year depreciation deduction allowable for Canopy W1 equals $44,800 (.50 of Canopy W1's remaining carryover basis at the time of replacement of $89,600 (Canopy V1's remaining adjusted depreciable basis of $140,000 minus 2002 regular MACRS depreciation deduction of $28,000 minus 2003 regular MACRS depreciation deduction of $22,400).

Example 2. (i) Same facts as in *Example 1,* except EE elected not to deduct the additional first year depreciation for 5-year property placed in service in 2002. EE deducted the additional first year depreciation for 5-year property placed in service in 2003.

(ii) For 2002, EE is allowed a regular MACRS depreciation deduction of $40,000 for Canopy V1 (the unadjusted depreciable basis of $200,000 multiplied by the annual depreciation rate of .20 for recovery year 1).

(iii) For 2003, EE is allowed a regular MACRS depreciation deduction of $32,000 for Canopy V1 (the unadjusted depreciable basis of $200,000 multiplied by the annual depreciation rate of .32 for recovery year 2 × $^{1}/_{2}$ year).

(iv) Pursuant to paragraph (f)(5)(iii)(A) of this section, the additional first year depreciation deduction allowable for Canopy W1 equals $64,000 (.50 of Canopy W1's remaining carryover basis at the time of replacement of $128,000 (Canopy V1's unadjusted depreciable basis of $200,000 minus 2002 regular MACRS depreciation deduction of $40,000 minus 2003 regular MACRS depreciation deduction of $32,000)).

Example 3. (i) In December 2001, FF, a calendar-year corporation, acquired for $10,000 and placed in service Computer X2. Computer X2 is qualified property under section 168(k)(1) and is 5-year property under section 168(e). FF depreciated Computer X2 under the general depreciation system of section 168(a) by using the 200-percent declining balance method of depreciation, a 5-year recovery period, and the half-year convention. FF elected to use the optional depreciation tables to compute the depreciation allowance for Computer X2. On January 1, 2002, FF acquired new Computer Y2 by exchanging Computer X2 and $1,000 cash in a like-kind exchange. Computer Y2 is qualified property under section 168(k)(1) and is 5-year property under section 168(e). Pursuant to paragraph (g)(3)(ii) of this section and §1.168(i)-6(k)(2)(i), FF decided to apply §1.168(i)-6 to the exchange of Computer X2 for Computer Y2, the acquired MACRS property.

(ii) For 2001, FF is allowed a 30-percent additional first year depreciation deduction of $3,000 for Computer X2 (unadjusted basis of $10,000 multiplied by .30), and a regular MACRS depreciation deduction of $1,400 for Computer X2 (the remaining adjusted depreciable basis of $7,000 multiplied by the annual depreciation rate of .20 for recovery year 1).

(iii) For 2002, FF is allowed a regular MACRS depreciation deduction of $1,120 for Computer X2 (the remaining adjusted depreciable basis of $7,000 multiplied by the annual depreciation rate of .32 for recovery year 2 × ¹/₂ year).

(iv) Pursuant to paragraph (f)(5)(iii)(A) of this section, the 30-percent additional first year depreciation deduction for Computer Y2 is allowable for the remaining carryover basis at the time of replacement of $4,480 (Computer X2's unadjusted depreciable basis of $10,000 minus additional first year depreciation deduction allowable of $3,000 minus 2001 regular MACRS depreciation deduction of $1,400 minus 2002 regular MACRS depreciation deduction of $1,120) and for the remaining excess basis at the time of replacement of $1,000 (cash paid for Computer Y2). Thus, the 30-percent additional first year depreciation deduction for the remaining carryover basis at the time of replacement equals $1,344 ($4,480 multiplied by .30) and for the remaining excess basis at the time of replacement equals $300 ($1,000 multiplied by .30), which totals $1,644.

Example 4. (i) In September 2002, GG, a June 30 year-end corporation, acquired for $20,000 and placed in service Equipment X3. Equipment X3 is qualified property under section 168(k)(1) and is 5-year property under section 168(e). GG depreciated Equipment X3 under the general depreciation system of section 168(a) by using the 200-percent declining balance method of depreciation, a 5-year recovery period, and the half-year convention. GG elected to use the optional depreciation tables to compute the depreciation allowance for Equipment X3. In December 2002, GG acquired new Equipment Y3 by exchanging Equipment X3 and $5,000 cash in a like-kind exchange. Equipment Y3 is qualified property under section 168(k)(1) and is 5-year property under section 168(e). Pursuant to paragraph (g)(3)(ii) of this section and §1.168(i)-6(k)(2)(i), GG decided to apply §1.168(i)-6 to the exchange of Equipment X3 for Equipment Y3, the acquired MACRS property.

(ii) Pursuant to paragraph (f)(5)(iii)(B) of this section, no additional first year depreciation deduction is allowable for Equipment X3 and, pursuant to §1.168(d)-1T(b)(3)(ii), no regular depreciation deduction is allowable for Equipment X3, for the taxable year ended June 30, 2003.

(iii) Pursuant to paragraph (f)(5)(iii)(A) of this section, the 30-percent additional first year depreciation deduction for Equipment Y3 is allowable for the remaining carryover basis at the time of replacement of $20,000 (Equipment X3's unadjusted depreciable basis of $20,000) and for the remaining excess basis at the time of replacement of $5,000 (cash paid for Equipment Y3). Thus, the 30-percent additional first year depreciation deduction for the remaining carryover basis at the time of replacement equals $6,000 ($20,000 multiplied by .30) and for the remaining excess basis at the time of replacement equals $1,500 ($5,000 multiplied by .30), which totals $7,500.

Example 5. (i) Same facts as in *Example 4*. GG depreciated Equipment Y3 under the general depreciation system of section 168(a) by using the 200-percent declining balance method of depreciation, a 5-year recovery period, and the half-year convention. GG elected to use the optional depreciation tables to compute the depreciation allowance for Equipment Y3. On July 1, 2003, GG acquired new Equipment Z1 by exchanging Equipment Y3 in a like-kind exchange. Equipment Z1 is 50-percent bonus depreciation property under section 168(k)(4) and is 5-year property under section 168(e). Pursuant to paragraph (g)(3)(ii) of this section and §1.168(i)-6(k)(2)(i), GG decided to apply §1.168(i)-6 to the exchange of Equipment Y3 for Equipment Z1, the acquired MACRS property.

(ii) For the taxable year ending June 30, 2003, the regular MACRS depreciation deduction allowable for the remaining carryover basis at the time of replacement (after taking into account the

additional first year depreciation deduction) of Equipment Y3 is $2,800 (the remaining carryover basis at the time of replacement of $20,000 minus the additional first year depreciation deduction of $6,000, multiplied by the annual depreciation rate of .20 for recovery year 1) and for the remaining excess basis at the time of replacement (after taking into account the additional first year depreciation deduction) of Equipment Y3 is $700 (the remaining excess basis at the time of replacement of $5,000 minus the additional first year depreciation deduction of $1,500, multiplied by the annual depreciation rate of .20 for recovery year 1), which totals $3,500.

(iii) For the taxable year ending June 30, 2004, the regular MACRS depreciation deduction allowable for the remaining carryover basis (after taking into account the additional first year depreciation deduction) of Equipment Y3 is $2,240 (the remaining carryover basis at the time of replacement of $20,000 minus the additional first year depreciation deduction of $6,000, multiplied by the annual depreciation rate of .32 for recovery year 2 × ¹/₂ year) and for the remaining excess basis (after taking into account the additional first year depreciation deduction) of Equipment Y3 is $560 (the remaining excess basis at the time of replacement of $5,000 minus the additional first year depreciation deduction of $1,500, multiplied by the annual depreciation rate of .32 for recovery year 2 × ¹/₂ year), which totals $2,800.

(iv) For the taxable year ending June 30, 2004, pursuant to paragraph (f)(5)(iii)(A) of this section, the 50-percent additional first year depreciation deduction for Equipment Z1 is allowable for the remaining carryover basis at the time of replacement of $11,200 (Equipment Y3's unadjusted depreciable basis of $25,000 minus the total additional first year depreciation deduction of $7,500 minus the total 2003 regular MACRS depreciation deduction of $3,500 minus the total 2004 regular depreciation deduction (taking into account the half-year convention) of $2,800). Thus, the 50-percent additional first year depreciation deduction for the remaining carryover basis at the time of replacement equals $5,600 ($11,200 multiplied by .50).

Example 6. (i) In April 2004, SS, a calendar year-end corporation, acquired and placed in service Equipment K89. Equipment K89 is 50-percent bonus depreciation property under section 168(k)(4). In November 2004, SS acquired and placed in service used Equipment N78 by exchanging Equipment K89 in a like-kind exchange.

(ii) Pursuant to paragraph (f(5)(iii)(B) of this section, no additional first year deduction is allowable for Equipment K89 and, pursuant to §1.168(d)-1T(b)(3)(ii), no regular depreciation deduction is allowable for Equipment K89, for the taxable year ended December 31, 2004.

(iii) Equipment N78 is not qualified property under section 168(k)(1) or 50-percent bonus depreciation property under section 168(k)(4) because the original use requirement of paragraph (b)(3) of this section is not met. Accordingly, no additional first year depreciation deduction is allowable for Equipment N78.

(6) *Change in use.*—(i) *Change in use of depreciable property.*—The determination of whether the use of depreciable property changes is made in accordance with section 168(i)(5) and regulations thereunder.

(ii) *Conversion to personal use.*—If qualified property or 50-percent bonus depreciation property is converted from business or income-producing use to personal use in the same taxable year in which the property is placed in service by a taxpayer, the additional first year depreciation deduction is not allowable for the property.

(iii) *Conversion to business or income-producing use.*—(A) *During the same taxable year.*—If, during the same taxable year, property is acquired by a taxpayer for personal use and is converted by the taxpayer from personal use to business or income-producing use, the additional first year depreciation deduction is allowable for the property in the taxable year the property is converted to business or income-producing use (assuming all of the requirements in paragraph (b) of this section are met). See paragraph (b)(3)(ii) of this section relating to the original use rules for a conversion of property to business or income-producing use.

(B) *Subsequent to the acquisition year.*—If property is acquired by a taxpayer for personal use and, during a subsequent taxable year, is converted by the taxpayer from personal use to business or income-producing use, the additional first year depreciation deduction is allowable for the property in the taxable year the property is converted to business or income-producing use (assuming all of the requirements in paragraph (b) of this section are met). For purposes of paragraphs (b)(4) and (5) of this section, the property must be acquired by the taxpayer for personal use after September 10, 2001 (for qualified property), or after May 5, 2003 (for 50-percent bonus depreciation property), and converted by the taxpayer from personal use to business or income-producing use by January 1, 2005. See paragraph (b)(3)(ii) of this section relating to the original use rules for a conversion of property to business or income-producing use.

(iv) *Depreciable property changes use subsequent to the placed-in-service year.*—(A) If the use of qualified property or 50-percent bonus depreciation property changes in the hands of the same taxpayer subsequent to the taxable year the qualified property or the 50-percent bonus depreciation property, as applicable, is placed in service and, as a result of the change in use, the property is no longer qualified property or 50-percent bonus depreciation property, as applicable, the additional first year depreciation deduction allowable for the qualified property or the 50-percent bonus depreciation property, as applicable, is not redetermined.

(B) If depreciable property is not qualified property or 50-percent bonus depreciation property in the taxable year the property is placed in service by the taxpayer, the additional first year depreciation deduction is not allowable for the property even if a change in the use of the property subsequent to the taxable year the property is placed in service results in the property being qualified property or 50-percent bonus depreciation property in the taxable year of the change in use.

(v) *Examples.*—The application of this paragraph (f)(6) is illustrated by the following examples:

Example 1. (i) On January 1, 2002, *HH*, a calendar year corporation, purchased and placed in service several new computers at a total cost of $100,000. *HH* used these computers within the United States for 3 months in 2002 and then moved and used the computers outside the United States for the remainder of 2002. On January 1, 2003, *HH* permanently returns the computers to the United States for use in its business.

(ii) For 2002, the computers are considered as used predominantly outside the United States in 2002 pursuant to §1.48-1(g)(1)(i). As a result, the computers are required to be depreciated under the alternative depreciation system of section 168(g). Pursuant to paragraph (b)(2)(ii)(A)(2) of this section, the computers are not qualified property in 2002, the placed-in-service year. Thus, pursuant to (f)(6)(iv)(B) of this section, no additional first year depreciation deduction is allowed for these computers, regardless of the fact that the computers are permanently returned to the United States in 2003.

Example 2. (i) On February 8, 2002, *II*, a calendar year corporation, purchased and placed in service new equipment at a cost of $1,000,000 for use in its California plant. The equipment is 5-year property under section 168(e) and is qualified property under section 168(k). *II* depreciates its 5-year property placed in service in 2002 using the optional depreciation table that corresponds with the general depreciation system, the 200-percent declining balance method, a 5-year recovery period, and the half-year convention. On June 4, 2003, due to changes in *II*'s business circumstances, *II* permanently moves the equipment to its plant in Mexico.

(ii) For 2002, *II* is allowed a 30-percent additional first year depreciation deduction of $300,000 (the adjusted depreciable basis of $1,000,000 multiplied by .30). In addition, *II*'s depreciation deduction allowable in 2002 for the remaining adjusted depreciable basis of $700,000 (the unadjusted depreciable basis of $1,000,000 reduced by the additional first year depreciation deduction of $300,000) is $140,000 (the remaining adjusted depreciable basis of $700,000 multiplied by the annual depreciation rate of .20 for recovery year 1).

(iii) For 2003, the equipment is considered as used predominantly outside the United States pursuant to §1.48-1(g)(1)(i). As a result of this change in use, the adjusted depreciable basis of $560,000 for the equipment is required to be depreciated under the alternative depreciation system of section 168(g) beginning in 2003. However, the additional first year depreciation deduction of $300,000 allowed for the equipment in 2002 is not redetermined.

(7) *Earnings and profits.*—The additional first year depreciation deduction is not allowable for purposes of computing earnings and profits.

(8) *Limitation of amount of depreciation for certain passenger automobiles.*—For a passenger automobile as defined in section 280F(d)(5), the limitation under section 280F(a)(1)(A)(i) is increased by—

(i) $4,600 for qualified property acquired by a taxpayer after September 10, 2001, and before May 6, 2003; and

(ii) $7,650 for qualified property or 50-percent bonus depreciation property acquired by a taxpayer after May 5, 2003.

(9) *Section 754 election.*—In general, for purposes of section 168(k) any increase in basis of qualified property or 50-percent bonus depreciation property due to a section 754 election is not eligible for the additional first year depreciation deduction. However, if qualified property or 50-percent bonus depreciation property is placed in service by a partnership in the taxable year the partnership terminates under section 708(b)(1)(B), any increase in basis of the qualified property or the 50-percent bonus depreciation property due to a section 754 election is eligible for the additional first year depreciation deduction.

(10) *Coordination with section 47.*—(i) *In general.*—If qualified rehabilitation expenditures (as defined in section 47(c)(2) and §1.48-12(c)) incurred by a taxpayer with respect to a qualified rehabilitated building (as defined in section 47(c)(1) and §1.48-12(b)) are qualified property or 50-percent bonus depreciation property, the taxpayer may claim the rehabilitation credit provided by section 47(a) (provided the requirements of section 47 are met)—

(A) With respect to the portion of the basis of the qualified rehabilitated building that is attributable to the qualified rehabilitation expenditures if the taxpayer makes the applicable election under paragraph (e)(1)(i) or (e)(1)(ii)(B) of this section not to deduct any additional first year depreciation for the class of property that includes the qualified rehabilitation expenditures; or

(B) With respect to the portion of the remaining rehabilitated basis of the qualified rehabilitated building that is attributable to the qualified rehabilitation expenditures if the taxpayer claims the additional first year depreciation deduction on the unadjusted depreciable basis (as defined in paragraph (a)(2)(iii) of this section but before the reduction in basis for the amount of the rehabilitation credit) of the qualified rehabilitation expenditures and the taxpayer depreciates the remaining adjusted depreciable basis (as defined in paragraph (d)(2)(i) of this section) of such expenditures using straight line cost recovery in accordance with section 47(c)(2)(B)(i) and §1.48-12(c)(7)(i). For purposes of this paragraph (f)(10)(i)(B), the remaining rehabilitated basis is equal to the unadjusted depreciable basis (as defined in paragraph (a)(2)(iii) of this section but before the reduction in basis for the amount of the rehabilitation credit) of the qualified rehabilitation expenditures that are qualified property or 50-percent bonus depreciation property reduced by the additional first year depreciation allowed or allowable, whichever is greater.

(ii) *Example.*—The application of this paragraph (f)(10) is illustrated by the following example.

Example. (i) Between February 8, 2004, and June 4, 2004, *UU*, a calendar-year taxpayer, incurred qualified rehabilitation expenditures of $200,000 with respect to a qualified rehabilitated building that is nonresidential real property under section 168(e). These qualified rehabilitation expenditures are 50-percent bonus depreciation property and qualify for the 10-percent rehabilitation credit under section 47(a)(1). *UU*'s basis in the qualified rehabilitated building is zero before incurring the qualified rehabilitation expenditures and *UU* placed the qualified rehabilitated building in service in July 2004. *UU* depreciates its nonresidential real property placed in service in 2004 under the general depreciation system of section 168(a) by using the straight line method of depreciation, a 39-year recovery period, and the mid-month convention. *UU* elected to use the optional depreciation tables to compute the depreciation allowance for its depreciable property placed in service in 2004. Further, for 2004, *UU* did not make any election under paragraph (e) of this section.

(ii) Because *UU* did not make any election under paragraph (e) of this section, *UU* is allowed a 50-percent additional first year depreciation deduction of $100,000 for the qualified rehabilitation expenditures for 2004 (the unadjusted depreciable basis of $200,000 (before reduction in basis for the rehabilitation credit) multiplied by .50). For 2004, *UU* also is allowed to claim a rehabilitation credit of $10,000 for the remaining rehabilitated basis of $100,000 (the unadjusted depreciable basis (before reduction in basis for the rehabilitation credit) of $200,000 less the additional first year depreciation deduction of $100,000). Further, *UU*'s depreciation deduction for 2004 for the remaining adjusted depreciable basis of $90,000 (the unadjusted depreciable basis (before reduction in basis for the rehabilitation credit) of $200,000 less the additional first year depreciation deduction of $100,000 less the rehabilitation credit of $10,000) is $1,059.30 (the remaining adjusted depreciable basis of $90,000 multiplied by the depreciation rate of .01177 for recovery year 1, placed in service in month 7).

(11) *Coordination with section 514(a)(3).*—The additional first year depreciation deduction is not allowable for purposes of section 514(a)(3).

(g) *Effective date.*—(1) *In general.*—Except as provided in paragraphs (g)(2), (3), and (5) of this section, this section applies to qualified property under section 168(k)(2) acquired by a taxpayer after September 10, 2001, and to 50-percent bonus depreciation property under section 168(k)(4) acquired by a taxpayer after May 5, 2003.

(2) *Technical termination of a partnership or section 168(i)(7) transactions.*—If qualified property or 50 percent bonus depreciation property is transferred in a technical termination of a partnership under section 708(b)(1)(B) or in a transaction described in section 168(i)(7) for a taxable year ending on or before September 8, 2003, and the additional first year depreciation deduction allowable for the property was not determined in accordance with paragraph (f)(1)(ii) or (iii) of this section, as applicable, the Internal Revenue Service will allow any reasonable method of determining the additional first year

Itemized Deductions for Individuals and Corps.
See p. 20,601 for regulations not amended to reflect law changes
25,503

depreciation deduction allowable for the property in the year of the transaction that is consistently applied to the property by all parties to the transaction.

(3)(i) *Like-kind exchanges and involuntary conversions.*—If a taxpayer did not claim on a federal tax return for a taxable year ending on or before September 8, 2003, the additional first year depreciation deduction for the remaining carryover basis of qualified property or 50-percent bonus depreciation property acquired in a transaction described in section 1031(a), (b), or (c), or in a transaction to which section 1033 applies and the taxpayer did not make an election not to deduct the additional first year depreciation deduction for the class of property applicable to the remaining carryover basis, the Internal Revenue Service will treat the taxpayer's method of not claiming the additional first year depreciation deduction for the remaining carryover basis as a permissible method of accounting and will treat the amount of the additional first year depreciation deduction allowable for the remaining carryover basis as being equal to zero, provided the taxpayer does not claim the additional first year depreciation deduction for the remaining carryover basis in accordance with paragraph (g)(4)(ii) of this section.

(ii) Paragraphs (f)(5)(ii)(F)(2) and (f)(5)(v) of this section apply to a like-kind exchange or an involuntary conversion of MACRS property and computer software for which the time of disposition and the time of replacement both occur after February 27, 2004. For a like-kind exchange or an involuntary conversion of MACRS property for which the time of disposition, the time of replacement, or both occur on or before February 27, 2004, see § 1.168(i)-6(k)(2)(ii). For a like-kind exchange or involuntary conversion of computer software for which the time of disposition, the time of replacement, or both occur on or before February 27, 2004, a taxpayer may rely on prior guidance issued by the Internal Revenue Service for determining the depreciation deductions of the acquired computer software and the exchanged or involuntarily converted computer software (for further guidance, see § 1.168(k)-1T(f)(5) published in the **Federal Register** on September 8, 2003 (68 FR 53000)). In relying on such guidance, a taxpayer may use any reasonable, consistent method of determining depreciation in the year of disposition and the year of replacement.

(4) *Change in method of accounting.*—(i) *Special rules for 2000 or 2001 returns.*—If a taxpayer did not claim on the Federal tax return for the taxable year that included September 11, 2001, any additional first year depreciation deduction for a class of property that is qualified property and did not make an election not to deduct the additional first year depreciation deduction for that class of property, the taxpayer should refer to the guidance provided by the Internal Revenue Service for the time and manner of claiming the additional first year depreciation deduction for the class of property (for further guidance, see section 4 of Rev. Proc. 2002-33 (2002-1 C.B. 963), Rev. Proc. 2003-50 (2003-29 I.R.B. 119), and § 601.601(d)(2)(ii)(b) of this chapter).

(ii) *Like-kind exchanges and involuntary conversions.*—If a taxpayer did not claim on a federal tax return for any taxable year ending on or before September 8, 2003, the additional first year depreciation deduction allowable for the remaining carryover basis of qualified property or 50-percent bonus depreciation property acquired in a transaction described in section 1031(a), (b), or (c), or in a transaction to which section 1033 applies and the taxpayer did not make an election not to deduct the additional first year depreciation deduction for the class of property applicable to the remaining carryover basis, the taxpayer may claim the additional first year depreciation deduction allowable for the remaining carryover basis in accordance with paragraph (f)(5) of this section either:

(A) by filing an amended return (or a qualified amended return, if applicable (for further guidance, see Rev. Proc. 94-69 (1994-2 C.B. 804) and § 601.601(d)(2)(ii)(b) of this chapter)) on or before December 31, 2003, for the year of replacement and any affected subsequent taxable year; or,

(B) by following the applicable administrative procedures issued under § 1.446-1(e)(3)(ii) for obtaining the Commissioner's automatic consent to a change in method of accounting (for further guidance, see Rev. Proc. 2002-9 (2002-1 C.B. 327) and § 601.601(d)(2)(ii)(b) of this chapter).

(5) *Revision to paragraphs (b)(3)(iii)(B) and (b)(5)(ii)(B) of this section.*—The addition of "(or, in the case of multiple units of property subject to the same lease, within three months after the date the final unit is placed in service, so long as the period between the time the first unit is placed in service and the time the last unit is placed in service does not exceed 12 months)" to paragraphs (b)(3)(iii)(B) and (b)(5)(ii)(B) of this section applies to property sold after June 4, 2004.

(6) *Rehabilitation credit.*—If a taxpayer did not claim on a Federal tax return for any taxable year ending on or before September 1,

2006, the rehabilitation credit provided by section 47(a) with respect to the portion of the basis of a qualified rehabilitated building that is attributable to qualified rehabilitation expenditures and the qualified rehabilitation expenditures are qualified property or 50-percent bonus depreciation property, and the taxpayer did not make the applicable election specified in paragraph (e)(1)(i) or (e)(1)(ii)(B) of this section for the class of property that includes the qualified rehabilitation expenditures, the taxpayer may claim the rehabilitation credit for the remaining rehabilitated basis (as defined in paragraph (f)(10)(i)(B) of this section) of the qualified rehabilitated building that is attributable to the qualified rehabilitation expenditures (assuming all the requirements of section 47 are met) in accordance with paragraph (f)(10)(i)(B) of this section by filing an amended Federal tax return for the taxable year for which the rehabilitation credit is to be claimed. The amended Federal tax return must include the adjustment to the tax liability for the rehabilitation credit and any collateral adjustments to taxable income or to the tax liability (for example, the amount of depreciation allowed or allowable in that taxable year for the qualified rehabilitated building). Such adjustments must also be made on amended Federal tax returns for any affected succeeding taxable years. [Reg. § 1.168(k)-1.]

☐ [*T.D. 9091, 9-5-2003 (corrected 11-7-2003). Amended by T.D. 9115, 2-27-2004 (corrected 4-2-2004). Redesignated and amended by T.D. 9283, 8-28-2006. Amended by T.D. 9314, 2-26-2007.*]

[Reg. § 1.168(k)-2]

§ 1.168(k)-2. Additional first year depreciation deduction for property acquired and placed in service after September 27, 2017.—(a) *Scope and definitions.*—(1) *Scope.*—This section provides rules for determining the additional first year depreciation deduction allowable under section 168(k) for qualified property acquired and placed in service after September 27, 2017, except as provided in paragraph (c) of this section.

(2) *Definitions.*—For purposes of this section—

(i) *Act* is the Tax Cuts and Jobs Act, Public Law 115-97 (131 Stat. 2054 (December 22, 2017));

(ii) *Applicable percentage* is the percentage provided in section 168(k)(6);

(iii) *Initial live staged performance* is the first commercial exhibition of a production to an audience. However, the term *initial live staged performance* does not include limited exhibition prior to commercial exhibition to general audiences if the limited exhibition is primarily for purposes of publicity, determining the need for further production activity, or raising funds for the completion of production. For example, an initial live staged performance does not include a preview of the production if the preview is primarily to determine the need for further production activity; and

(iv) *Predecessor* includes—

(A) A transferor of an asset to a transferee in a transaction to which section 381(a) applies;

(B) A transferor of the asset to a transferee in a transaction in which the transferee's basis in the asset is determined, in whole or in part, by reference to the basis of the asset in the hands of the transferor;

(C) A partnership that is considered as continuing under section 708(b)(2) and § 1.708-1; or

(D) The decedent in the case of an asset acquired by the estate.

(b) *Qualified property.*—(1) *In general.*—Qualified property is depreciable property, as defined in § 1.168(b)-1(a)(1), that meets all the following requirements in the first taxable year in which the property is subject to depreciation by the taxpayer whether or not depreciation deductions for the property are allowable:

(i) The requirements in § 1.168(k)-2(b)(2) (description of qualified property);

(ii) The requirements in § 1.168(k)-2(b)(3) (original use or used property acquisition requirements);

(iii) The requirements in § 1.168(k)-2(b)(4) (placed-in-service date); and

(iv) The requirements in § 1.168(k)-2(b)(5) (acquisition of property).

(2) *Description of qualified property.*—(i) *In general.*—Depreciable property will meet the requirements of this paragraph (b)(2) if the property is—

(A) MACRS property, as defined in § 1.168(b)-1(a)(2), that has a recovery period of 20 years or less. For purposes of this paragraph (b)(2)(i)(A) and section 168(k)(2)(A)(i)(I), the recovery period is determined in accordance with section 168(c) regardless of any election made by the taxpayer under section 168(g)(7). This paragraph (b)(2)(i)(A) includes the following MACRS property that is acquired by the taxpayer after September 27, 2017, and placed in service by the taxpayer after September 27, 2017, and before January 1, 2018:

(1) Qualified leasehold improvement property as defined in section 168(e)(6) as in effect on the day before amendment by section 13204(a)(1) of the Act;

(2) Qualified restaurant property, as defined in section 168(e)(7) as in effect on the day before amendment by section 13204(a)(1) of the Act, that is qualified improvement property as defined in § 1.168(b)-1(a)(5)(i)(C) and (a)(5)(ii); and

(3) Qualified retail improvement property as defined in section 168(e)(8) as in effect on the day before amendment by section 13204(a)(1) of the Act;

(B) Computer software as defined in, and depreciated under, section 167(f)(1) and § 1.167(a)-14;

(C) Water utility property as defined in section 168(e)(5) and depreciated under section 168;

(D) Qualified improvement property as defined in § 1.168(b)-1(a)(5)(i)(C) and (a)(5)(ii) and depreciated under section 168;

(E) A qualified film or television production, as defined in section 181(d) and § 1.181-3, for which a deduction would have been allowable under section 181 and §§ 1.181-1 through 1.181-6 without regard to section 181(a)(2) and (g), § 1.181-1(b)(1)(i) and (ii), and (b)(2)(i), or section 168(k). Only production costs of a qualified film or television production are allowable as a deduction under section 181 and §§ 1.181-1 through 1.181-6 without regard, for purposes of section 168(k), to section 181(a)(2) and (g), § 1.181-1(b)(1)(i) and (ii), and (b)(2)(i). The taxpayer that claims the additional first year depreciation deduction under this section for the production costs of a qualified film or television production must be the owner, as defined in § 1.181-1(a)(2), of the qualified film or television production. See § 1.181-1(a)(3) for the definition of production costs;

(F) A qualified live theatrical production, as defined in section 181(e), for which a deduction would have been allowable under section 181 and §§ 1.181-1 through 1.181-6 without regard to section 181(a)(2) and (g), § 1.181-1(b)(1)(i) and (ii), and (b)(2)(i), or section 168(k). Only production costs of a qualified live theatrical production are allowable as a deduction under section 181 and §§ 1.181-1 through 1.181-6 without regard, for purposes of section 168(k), to section 181(a)(2) and (g), § 1.181-1(b)(1)(i) and (ii), and (b)(2)(i). The taxpayer that claims the additional first year depreciation deduction under this section for the production costs of a qualified live theatrical production must be the owner, as defined in § 1.181-1(a)(2), of the qualified live theatrical production. In applying § 1.181-1(a)(2)(ii) to a person that acquires a finished or partially-finished qualified live theatrical production, such person is treated as an owner of that production, but only if the production is acquired prior to its initial live staged performance. Rules similar to the rules in § 1.181-1(a)(3) for the definition of production costs of a qualified film or television production apply for defining production costs of a qualified live theatrical production; or

(G) A specified plant, as defined in section 168(k)(5)(B), for which the taxpayer has properly made an election to apply section 168(k)(5) for the taxable year in which the specified plant is planted, or grafted to a plant that has already been planted, by the taxpayer in the ordinary course of the taxpayer's farming business, as defined in section 263A(e)(4) (for further guidance, see paragraph (f) of this section).

(ii) *Property not eligible for additional first year depreciation deduction.*—Depreciable property will not meet the requirements of this paragraph (b)(2) if the property is—

(A) Described in section 168(f) (for example, automobiles for which the taxpayer uses the optional business standard mileage rate);

(B) Required to be depreciated under the alternative depreciation system of section 168(g) pursuant to section 168(g)(1)(A), (B), (C), (D), (F), or (G), or other provisions of the Internal Revenue Code (for example, property described in section 263A(e)(2)(A) if the taxpayer or any related person, as defined in section 263A(e)(2)(B), has made an election under section 263A(d)(3), or property described in section 280F(b)(1)). If section 168(h)(6) applies to the property, only the tax-exempt entity's proportionate share of the property, as determined under section 168(h)(6), is treated as tax-exempt use property described in section 168(g)(1)(B) and in this paragraph (b)(2)(ii)(B). This paragraph (b)(2)(ii)(B) does not apply to property for which the adjusted basis is required to be determined using the alternative depreciation system of section 168(g) pursuant to section 250(b)(2)(B) or 951A(d)(3), as applicable, or to property for which the adjusted basis is required to be determined using the alternative depreciation system of section 168(g) for allocating business interest expense between excepted and non-excepted trades or businesses under section 163(j), but only if the property is not required to be depreciated under the alternative depreciation system of section 168(g) pursuant

to section 168(g)(1)(A), (B), (C), (D), (F), or (G), or other provisions of the Code, other than section 163(j), 250(b)(2)(B), or 951A(d)(3), as applicable;

(C) Included in any class of property for which the taxpayer elects not to deduct the additional first year depreciation (for further guidance, see paragraph (f) of this section);

(D) A specified plant that is placed in service by the taxpayer during the taxable year and for which the taxpayer made an election to apply section 168(k)(5) for a prior taxable year;

(E) Included in any class of property for which the taxpayer elects to apply section 168(k)(4). This paragraph (b)(2)(ii)(E) applies to property placed in service by the taxpayer in any taxable year beginning before January 1, 2018;

(F) Primarily used in a trade or business described in section 163(j)(7)(A)(iv) and §§ 1.163(j)-1(b)(15)(i) and 1.163(j)-10(c)(3)(iii)(C)(3), and placed in service by the taxpayer in any taxable year beginning after December 31, 2017. For purposes of section 168(k)(9)(A) and this paragraph (b)(2)(ii)(F), the term *primarily used* has the same meaning as that term is used in § 1.167(a)-11(b)(4)(iii)(*b*) and (e)(3)(iii) for classifying property. This paragraph (b)(2)(ii)(F) does not apply to property that is leased to a lessee's trade or business described in section 163(j)(7)(A)(iv) and §§ 1.163(j)-1(b)(15)(i) and 1.163(j)-10(c)(3)(iii)(C)(3), by a lessor's trade or business that is not described in section 163(j)(7)(A)(iv) and §§ 1.163(j)-1(b)(15)(i) and 1.163(j)-10(c)(3)(iii)(C)(3) for the taxable year; or

(G) Used in a trade or business that has had floor plan financing indebtedness, as defined in section 163(j)(9)(B) and § 1.163(j)-1(b)(18), if the floor plan financing interest expense, as defined in section 163(j)(9)(A) and § 1.163(j)-1(b)(19), related to such indebtedness is taken into account under section 163(j)(1)(C) for the taxable year. Such property also must be placed in service by the taxpayer in any taxable year beginning after December 31, 2017. Solely for purposes of section 168(k)(9)(B) and this paragraph (b)(2)(ii)(G), floor plan financing interest expense is taken into account for the taxable year by a trade or business that has had floor plan financing indebtedness only if the business interest expense, as defined in section 163(j)(5) and § 1.163(j)-1(b)(3), of the trade or business for the taxable year (which includes floor plan financing interest expense) exceeds the sum of the amounts calculated under section 163(j)(1)(A) and (B) for the trade or business for the taxable year. If the trade or business has taken floor plan financing interest expense into account pursuant to this paragraph (b)(2)(ii)(G) for a taxable year, this paragraph (b)(2)(ii)(G) applies to any property placed in service by that trade or business in that taxable year. This paragraph (b)(2)(ii)(G) does not apply to property that is leased to a lessee's trade or business that has had floor plan financing indebtedness, by a lessor's trade or business that has not had floor plan financing indebtedness during the taxable year or that has had floor plan financing indebtedness but did not take into account floor plan financing interest expense for the taxable year pursuant to this paragraph (b)(2)(ii)(G).

(iii) *Examples.*—The application of this paragraph (b)(2) is illustrated by the following examples. Unless the facts specifically indicate otherwise, assume that the parties are not related within the meaning of section 179(d)(2)(A) or (B) and § 1.179-4(c), and are not described in section 163(j)(3):

(A) *Example 1.* On February 8, 2018, *A* finishes the production of a qualified film, as defined in § 1.181-3. On June 4, 2018, *B* acquires this finished production from A. The initial release or broadcast, as defined in § 1.181-1(a)(7), of this qualified film is on July 28, 2018. Because *B* acquired the qualified film before its initial release or broadcast, *B* is treated as the owner of the qualified film for purposes of section 181 and § 1.181-1(a)(2). Assuming all other requirements of this section are met and all requirements of section 181 and §§ 1.181-1 through 1.181-6, other than section 181(a)(2) and (g), and § 1.181-1(b)(1)(i) and (ii), and (b)(2)(i), are met, B's acquisition cost of the qualified film qualifies for the additional first year depreciation deduction under this section.

(B) *Example 2.* The facts are the same as in *Example 1* of paragraph (b)(2)(iii)(A) of this section, except that *B* acquires a limited license or right to release the qualified film in Europe. As a result, *B* is not treated as the owner of the qualified film pursuant to § 1.181-1(a)(2). Accordingly, paragraph (b)(2)(i)(E) of this section is not satisfied, and B's acquisition cost of the license or right does not qualify for the additional first year depreciation deduction.

(C) *Example 3.* *C* owns a film library. All of the films in this film library are completed and have been released or broadcasted. In 2018, *D* buys this film library from C. Because *D* acquired the films after their initial release or broadcast, D's acquisition cost of the film library does not qualify for a deduction under section 181. As a result, paragraph (b)(2)(i)(E) of this section is not satisfied, and D's acquisition cost of the film library does not qualify for the additional first year depreciation deduction.

(D) *Example 4.* During 2019, E Corporation, a domestic corporation, acquired new equipment for use in its manufacturing trade or business in Mexico. To determine its qualified business asset investment for purposes of section 250, E Corporation must determine the adjusted basis of the new equipment using the alternative depreciation system of section 168(g) pursuant to sections 250(b)(2)(B) and 951A(d)(3). E Corporation also is required to depreciate the new equipment under the alternative depreciation system of section 168(g) pursuant to section 168(g)(1)(A). As a result, the new equipment does not qualify for the additional first year depreciation deduction pursuant to paragraph (b)(2)(ii)(B) of this section.

(E) *Example 5.* The facts are the same as in *Example 4* of paragraph (b)(2)(iii)(D) of this section, except E Corporation acquired the new equipment for use in its manufacturing trade or business in California. The new equipment is not described in section 168(g)(1)(A), (B), (C), (D), (F), or (G). No other provision of the Internal Revenue Code, other than section 250(b)(2)(B) or 951A(d)(3), requires the new equipment to be depreciated using the alternative depreciation system of section 168(g). To determine its qualified business asset investment for purposes of section 250, E Corporation must determine the adjusted basis of the new equipment using the alternative depreciation system of section 168(g) pursuant to sections 250(b)(2)(B) and 951A(d)(3). Because E Corporation is not required to depreciate the new equipment under the alternative depreciation system of section 168(g), paragraph (b)(2)(ii)(B) of this section does not apply to this new equipment. Assuming all other requirements are met, the new equipment qualifies for the additional first year depreciation deduction under this section.

(F) *Example 6.* In 2019, a financial institution buys new equipment for $1 million and then leases this equipment to a lessee that primarily uses the equipment in a trade or business described in section 163(j)(7)(A)(iv) and §§ 1.163(j)-1(b)(15)(i) and 1.163(j)-10(c)(3)(iii)(C)(3). The financial institution is not described in section 163(j)(7)(A)(iv) and §§ 1.163(j)-1(b)(15)(i) and 1.163(j)-10(c)(3)(iii)(C)(3). As a result, paragraph (b)(2)(ii)(F) of this section does not apply to this new equipment. Assuming all other requirements are met, the financial institution's purchase price of $1 million for the new equipment qualifies for the additional first year depreciation deduction under this section.

(G) *Example 7.* During its taxable year beginning in 2020, F, a corporation that is an automobile dealer, buys new computers for $50,000 for use in its trade or business of selling automobiles. For purposes of section 163(j), F has the following for 2020: $700 of adjusted taxable income, $40 of business interest income, $400 of business interest expense (which includes $100 of floor plan financing interest expense). The sum of the amounts calculated under section 163(j)(1)(A) and (B) for F for 2020 is $390 ($40 + ($700 x 50 percent)). F's business interest expense, which includes floor plan financing interest expense, for 2020 is $400. As a result, F's floor plan financing interest expense is taken into account by F for 2020 pursuant to paragraph (b)(2)(ii)(G) of this section. Accordingly, F's purchase price of $50,000 for the computers does not qualify for the additional first year depreciation deduction under this section.

(H) *Example 8.* The facts are the same as in *Example 7* in paragraph (b)(2)(iii)(G) of this section, except F buys new computers for $30,000 for use in its trade or business of selling automobiles and, for purposes of section 163(j), F has $1,300 of adjusted taxable income. The sum of the amounts calculated under section 163(j)(1)(A) and (B) for F for 2020 is $690 ($40 + ($1,300 x 50 percent)). F's business interest expense, which includes floor plan financing interest expense, for 2020 is $400. As a result, F's floor plan financing interest expense is not taken into account by F for 2020 pursuant to paragraph (b)(2)(ii)(G) of this section. Assuming all other requirements are met, F's purchase price of $30,000 for the computers qualifies for the additional first year depreciation deduction under this section.

(I) *Example 9.* (1) G, a calendar-year taxpayer, owns an office building for use in its trade or business and G placed in service such building in 2000. In November 2018, G made and placed in service an improvement to the inside of such building at a cost of $100,000. In January 2019, G entered into a written contract with H for H to construct an improvement to the inside of the building. In March 2019, H completed construction of the improvement at a cost of $750,000 and G placed in service such improvement. Both improvements to the building are section 1250 property and are not described in § 1.168(b)-1(a)(5)(ii).

(2) Both the improvement to the office building made by G in November 2018 and the improvement to the office building that was constructed by H for G in 2019 are improvements made by G under § 1.168(b)-1(a)(5)(i)(A). Further, each improvement is made to the inside of the office building, is section 1250 property, and is not described in § 1.168(b)-1(a)(5)(ii). As a result, each improvement meets the definition of qualified improvement property in section 168(e)(6) and § 1.168(b)-1(a)(5)(i)(A) and (a)(5)(ii). Accordingly, each

improvement is 15-year property under section 168(e)(3) and is described in § 1.168(k)-2(b)(2)(i)(A). Assuming all other requirements of this section are met, each improvement made by G qualifies for the additional first year depreciation deduction for G under this section.

(3) *Original use or used property acquisition requirements.*—(i) *In general.*—Depreciable property will meet the requirements of this paragraph (b)(3) if the property meets the original use requirements in paragraph (b)(3)(ii) of this section or if the property meets the used property acquisition requirements in paragraph (b)(3)(iii) of this section.

(ii) *Original use.*—(A) *In general.*—Depreciable property will meet the requirements of this paragraph (b)(3)(ii) if the original use of the property commences with the taxpayer. Except as provided in paragraphs (b)(3)(ii)(B) and (C) of this section, original use means the first use to which the property is put, whether or not that use corresponds to the use of the property by the taxpayer. Additional capital expenditures paid or incurred by a taxpayer to recondition or rebuild property acquired or owned by the taxpayer satisfy the original use requirement. However, the cost of reconditioned or rebuilt property does not satisfy the original use requirement (but may satisfy the used property acquisition requirements in paragraph (b)(3)(iii) of this section). The question of whether property is reconditioned or rebuilt property is a question of fact. For purposes of this paragraph (b)(3)(ii)(A), property that contains used parts will not be treated as reconditioned or rebuilt if the cost of the used parts is not more than 20 percent of the total cost of the property, whether acquired or self-constructed.

(B) *Conversion to business or income-producing use.*—(1) *Personal use to business or income-producing use.*—If a taxpayer initially acquires new property for personal use and subsequently uses the property in the taxpayer's trade or business or for the taxpayer's production of income, the taxpayer is considered the original user of the property. If a person initially acquires new property for personal use and a taxpayer subsequently acquires the property from the person for use in the taxpayer's trade or business or for the taxpayer's production of income, the taxpayer is not considered the original user of the property.

(2) *Inventory to business or income-producing use.*—If a taxpayer initially acquires new property and holds the property primarily for sale to customers in the ordinary course of the taxpayer's business and subsequently withdraws the property from inventory and uses the property primarily in the taxpayer's trade or business or primarily for the taxpayer's production of income, the taxpayer is considered the original user of the property. If a person initially acquires new property and holds the property primarily for sale to customers in the ordinary course of the person's business and a taxpayer subsequently acquires the property from the person for use primarily in the taxpayer's trade or business or primarily for the taxpayer's production of income, the taxpayer is considered the original user of the property. For purposes of this paragraph (b)(3)(ii)(B)(2), the original use of the property by the taxpayer commences on the date on which the taxpayer uses the property primarily in the taxpayer's trade or business or primarily for the taxpayer's production of income.

(C) *Fractional interests in property.*—If, in the ordinary course of its business, a taxpayer sells fractional interests in new property to third parties unrelated to the taxpayer, each first fractional owner of the property is considered as the original user of its proportionate share of the property. Furthermore, if the taxpayer uses the property before all of the fractional interests of the property are sold but the property continues to be held primarily for sale by the taxpayer, the original use of any fractional interest sold to a third party unrelated to the taxpayer subsequent to the taxpayer's use of the property begins with the first purchaser of that fractional interest. For purposes of this paragraph (b)(3)(ii)(C), persons are not related if they do not have a relationship described in section 267(b) and § 1.267(b)-1, or section 707(b) and § 1.707-1.

(iii) *Used property acquisition requirements.*—(A) *In general.*—Depreciable property will meet the requirements of this paragraph (b)(3)(iii) if the acquisition of the used property meets the following requirements:

(1) Such property was not used by the taxpayer or a predecessor at any time prior to such acquisition;

(2) The acquisition of such property meets the requirements of section 179(d)(2)(A), (B), and (C), and § 1.179-4(c)(1)(ii), (iii), and (iv); or § 1.179-4(c)(2) (property is acquired by purchase); and

(3) The acquisition of such property meets the requirements of section 179(d)(3) and § 1.179-4(d) (cost of property) (for further guidance regarding like-kind exchanges and involuntary conversions, see paragraph (g)(5) of this section).

(B) *Property was not used by the taxpayer at any time prior to acquisition.*—(1) In general. Solely for purposes of paragraph (b)(3)(iii)(A)(1) of this section, the property is treated as used by the taxpayer or a predecessor at any time prior to acquisition by the taxpayer or predecessor if the taxpayer or the predecessor had a depreciable interest in the property at any time prior to such acquisition, whether or not the taxpayer or the predecessor claimed depreciation deductions for the property. To determine if the taxpayer or a predecessor had a depreciable interest in the property at any time prior to the acquisition, only the five calendar years immediately prior to the current calendar year in which the property is placed in service by the taxpayer, and the portion of such current calendar year before the placed-in-service date of the property without taking into account the applicable convention, are taken into account (lookback period). If the taxpayer and a predecessor have not been in existence for this entire five-year period, only the number of calendar years the taxpayer and the predecessor have been in existence is taken into account. If either the taxpayer or a predecessor, or both, have not been in existence for the entire lookback period, only the portion of the lookback period during which the taxpayer or a predecessor, or both, as applicable, have been in existence is taken into account to determine if the taxpayer or a predecessor had a depreciable interest in the property at any time prior to the acquisition.

(2) *Taxpayer has a depreciable interest in a portion of the property.*—If a taxpayer initially acquires a depreciable interest in a portion of the property and subsequently acquires a depreciable interest in an additional portion of the same property, such additional depreciable interest is not treated as used by the taxpayer at any time prior to its acquisition by the taxpayer under paragraphs (b)(3)(iii)(A)(1) and (b)(3)(iii)(B)(1) of this section. This paragraph (b)(3)(iii)(B)(2) does not apply if the taxpayer or a predecessor previously had a depreciable interest in the subsequently acquired additional portion. For purposes of this paragraph (b)(3)(iii)(B)(2), a portion of the property is considered to be the percentage interest in the property. If a taxpayer holds a depreciable interest in a portion of the property, sells that portion or a part of that portion, and subsequently acquires a depreciable interest in another portion of the same property, the taxpayer will be treated as previously having a depreciable interest in the property up to the amount of the portion for which the taxpayer held a depreciable interest in the property before the sale.

(3) *Substantial renovation of property.*—If a taxpayer acquires and places in service substantially renovated property and the taxpayer or a predecessor previously had a depreciable interest in the property before it was substantially renovated, the taxpayer's or predecessor's depreciable interest in the property before it was substantially renovated is not taken into account for determining whether the substantially renovated property was used by the taxpayer or a predecessor at any time prior to its acquisition by the taxpayer under paragraphs (b)(3)(iii)(A)(1) and (b)(3)(iii)(B)(1) of this section. For purposes of this paragraph (b)(3)(iii)(B)(3), property is substantially renovated if the cost of the used parts is not more than 20 percent of the total cost of the substantially renovated property, whether acquired or self-constructed.

(4) *De minimis use of property.*—If a taxpayer acquires and places in service property, the taxpayer or a predecessor did not previously have a depreciable interest in the property, the taxpayer disposes of the property to an unrelated party within 90 calendar days after the date the property was originally placed in service by the taxpayer, without taking into account the applicable convention, and the taxpayer reacquires and again places in service the property, then the taxpayer's depreciable interest in the property during that 90-day period is not taken into account for determining whether the property was used by the taxpayer or a predecessor at any time prior to its reacquisition by the taxpayer under paragraphs (b)(3)(iii)(A)(1) and (b)(3)(iii)(B)(1) of this section. If the taxpayer originally acquired the property before September 28, 2017, as determined under §1.168(k)-1(b)(4), and the taxpayer reacquires and again places in service the property during the same taxable year the taxpayer disposed of the property to the unrelated party, then this paragraph (b)(3)(iii)(B)(4) does not apply. For purposes of this paragraph (b)(3)(iii)(B)(4), an *unrelated party* is a person not described in section 179(d)(2)(A) or (B), and §1.179-4(c)(1)(ii) or (iii) or (c)(2).

(C) *Special rules for a series of related transactions.*—(1) In general.—Solely for purposes of paragraph (b)(3)(iii) of this section, each transferee in a series of related transactions tests its relationship under section 179(d)(2)(A) or (B) with the transferor from which the transferee *directly* acquires the depreciable property (immediate transferor) and with the original transferor of the depreciable property in the series. The transferee is treated as related to the immediate transferor or the original transferor if the relationship exists either when the transferee acquires, or immediately before the first transfer

of, the depreciable property in the series. A series of related transactions may include, for example, a transfer of partnership assets followed by a transfer of an interest in the partnership that owned the assets; or a disposition of property and a disposition, directly or indirectly, of the transferor or transferee of the property. For special rules that may apply when the transferor and transferee of the property are members of a consolidated group, as defined in §1.1502-1(h), see §1.1502-68.

(2) *Special rules.*—(i) *Property placed in service and disposed of in same taxable year or property not placed in service.*—Any party in a series of related transactions that is neither the original transferor nor the ultimate transferee is disregarded (disregarded party) for purposes of testing the relationships under paragraph (b)(3)(iii)(C)(1) of this section if the party places in service and disposes of the depreciable property subject to the series, other than in a transaction described in paragraph (g)(1)(iii) of this section, during the party's same taxable year, or if the party does not place in service the depreciable property subject to the series for use in the party's trade or business or production of income. In either case, the party to which the disregarded party disposed of the depreciable property tests its relationship with the party from which the disregarded party acquired the depreciable property and with the original transferor of the depreciable property in the series. If the series has consecutive disregarded parties, the party to which the last disregarded party disposed of the depreciable property tests its relationship with the party from which the first disregarded party acquired the depreciable property and with the original transferor of the depreciable property in the series. The rules for testing the relationships in paragraph (b)(3)(iii)(C)(1) of this section continue to apply for the other transactions in the series.

(ii) *All section 168(i)(7) transactions.*—This paragraph (b)(3)(iii)(C) does not apply if all transactions in a series of related transactions are described in paragraph (g)(1)(iii) of this section (section 168(i)(7) transactions in which property is transferred in the same taxable year that the property is placed in service by the transferor).

(iii) *One or more section 168(i)(7) transactions.*—Any step in a series of related transactions that is neither the original step nor the ultimate step is disregarded (disregarded step) for purposes of testing the relationships under paragraph (b)(3)(iii)(C)(1) of this section if the step is a transaction described in paragraph (g)(1)(iii) of this section. In this case, the relationship is not tested between the transferor and transferee of that transaction. Instead, the relationship is tested between the transferor in the disregarded step and the party to which the transferee in the disregarded step disposed of the depreciable property, the transferee in the disregarded step and the party to which the transferee in the disregarded step disposed of the depreciable property, and the original transferor of the depreciable property in the series and the party to which the transferee in the disregarded step disposed of the depreciable property. If the series has consecutive disregarded steps, the relationship is tested between the transferor in the first disregarded step and the party to which the transferee in the last disregarded step disposed of the depreciable property, the transferee in the last disregarded step and the party to which the transferee in the last disregarded step disposed of the depreciable property, and the original transferor of the depreciable property in the series and the party to which the transferee in the last disregarded step disposed of the depreciable property. The rules for testing the relationships in paragraph (b)(3)(iii)(C)(1) of this section continue to apply for the other transactions in the series.

(iv) *Syndication transaction.*—This paragraph (b)(3)(iii)(C) does not apply to a syndication transaction described in paragraph (b)(3)(vi) of this section.

(v) *Certain relationships disregarded.*—If a party acquires depreciable property in a series of related transactions in which the party acquires stock, meeting the requirements of section 1504(a)(2), of a corporation in a fully taxable transaction followed by a liquidation of the acquired corporation under section 331, any relationship created as part of such series of related transactions is disregarded in determining whether any party is related to such acquired corporation for purposes of testing the relationships under paragraph (b)(3)(iii)(C)(1) of this section.

(vi) *Transferors that cease to exist for Federal tax purposes.*—Any transferor in a series of related transactions that ceases to exist for Federal tax purposes during the series is deemed, for purposes of testing the relationships under paragraph (b)(3)(iii)(C)(1) of this section, to be in existence at the time of any transfer in the series.

(vii) *Newly created party.*—If a transferee in a series of related transactions acquires depreciable property from a transferor that was not in existence immediately prior to the first transfer of

Itemized Deductions for Individuals and Corps.
See p. 20,601 for regulations not amended to reflect law changes
25,507

such property in such series (new transferor), the transferee tests its relationship with the party from which the new transferor acquired such property and with the original transferor of the depreciable property in the series for purposes of paragraph (b)(3)(iii)(C)(1) of this section. If the series has consecutive new transferors, the party to which the last new transferor disposed of the depreciable property tests its relationship with the party from which the first new transferor acquired the depreciable property and with the original transferor of the depreciable property in the series. The rules for testing the relationships in paragraph (b)(3)(iii)(C)(1) of this section continue to apply for the other transactions in the series.

(viii) Application of paragraph (g)(1) of this section.—Paragraph (g)(1) of this section applies to each step in a series of related transactions.

(iv) Application to partnerships.—(A) *Section 704(c) remedial allocations.*—Remedial allocations under section 704(c) do not satisfy the requirements of paragraph (b)(3) of this section. See § 1.704-3(d)(2).

(B) *Basis determined under section 732.*—Any basis of distributed property determined under section 732 does not satisfy the requirements of paragraph (b)(3) of this section.

(C) *Section 734(b) adjustments.*—Any increase in basis of depreciable property under section 734(b) does not satisfy the requirements of paragraph (b)(3) of this section.

(D) *Section 743(b) adjustments.*—(1) *In general.*—For purposes of determining whether the transfer of a partnership interest meets the requirements of paragraph (b)(3)(iii)(A) of this section, each partner is treated as having a depreciable interest in the partner's proportionate share of partnership property. Any increase in basis of depreciable property under section 743(b) satisfies the requirements of paragraph (b)(3)(iii)(A) of this section if—

(i) At any time prior to the transfer of the partnership interest that gave rise to such basis increase, neither the transferee partner nor a predecessor of the transferee partner had any depreciable interest in the portion of the property deemed acquired to which the section 743(b) adjustment is allocated under section 755 and § 1.755-1; and

(ii) The transfer of the partnership interest that gave rise to such basis increase satisfies the requirements of paragraphs (b)(3)(iii)(A)(2) and (3) of this section.

(2) Relatedness tested at partner level.—Solely for purposes of paragraph (b)(3)(iv)(D)(1)(ii) of this section, whether the parties are related or unrelated is determined by comparing the transferor and the transferee of the transferred partnership interest.

(v) Application to members of a consolidated group.—For rules applicable to the acquisition of depreciable property by a member of a consolidated group, see § 1.1502-68.

(vi) Syndication transaction.—If new property is acquired and placed in service by a lessor, or if used property is acquired and placed in service by a lessor and the lessor or a predecessor did not previously have a depreciable interest in the used property, and the property is sold by the lessor or any subsequent purchaser within three months after the date the property was originally placed in service by the lessor (or, in the case of multiple units of property subject to the same lease, within three months after the date the final unit is placed in service, so long as the period between the time the first unit is placed in service and the time the last unit is placed in service does not exceed 12 months), and the user of the property after the last sale during the three-month period remains the same as when the property was originally placed in service by the lessor, the purchaser of the property in the last sale during the three-month period is considered the taxpayer that acquired the property for purposes of applying paragraphs (b)(3)(ii) and (iii) of this section. The purchaser of the property in the last sale during the three-month period is treated, for purposes of applying paragraph (b)(3) of this section, as—

(A) The original user of the property in this transaction if the lessor acquired and placed in service new property; or

(B) The taxpayer having the depreciable interest in the property in this transaction if the lessor acquired and placed in service used property.

(vii) Examples.—The application of this paragraph (b)(3) is illustrated by the following examples. Unless the facts specifically indicate otherwise, assume that the parties are not related within the meaning of section 179(d)(2)(A) or (B) and § 1.179-4(c), no corporation is a member of a consolidated or controlled group, and the parties do not have predecessors:

(A) *Example 1.* (1) On August 1, 2018, *A* buys a new machine for $35,000 from an unrelated party for use in *A*'s trade or business.

On July 1, 2020, *B* buys that machine from *A* for $20,000 for use in *B*'s trade or business. On October 1, 2020, *B* makes a $5,000 capital expenditure to recondition the machine. *B* did not have any depreciable interest in the machine before *B* acquired it on July 1, 2020.

(2) *A*'s purchase price of $35,000 satisfies the original use requirement of paragraph (b)(3)(ii) of this section and, assuming all other requirements are met, qualifies for the additional first year depreciation deduction under this section.

(3) *B*'s purchase price of $20,000 does not satisfy the original use requirement of paragraph (b)(3)(ii) of this section, but it does satisfy the used property acquisition requirements of paragraph (b)(3)(iii) of this section. Assuming all other requirements are met, the $20,000 purchase price qualifies for the additional first year depreciation deduction under this section. Further, *B*'s $5,000 expenditure satisfies the original use requirement of paragraph (b)(3)(ii) of this section and, assuming all other requirements are met, qualifies for the additional first year depreciation deduction under this section, regardless of whether the $5,000 is added to the basis of the machine or is capitalized as a separate asset.

(B) *Example 2. C*, an automobile dealer, uses some of its automobiles as demonstrators in order to show them to prospective customers. The automobiles that are used as demonstrators by *C* are held by *C* primarily for sale to customers in the ordinary course of its business. On November 1, 2017, *D* buys from *C* an automobile that was previously used as a demonstrator by *C*. *D* will use the automobile solely for business purposes. The use of the automobile by *C* as a demonstrator does not constitute a "use" for purposes of the original use requirement and, therefore, *D* will be considered the original user of the automobile for purposes of paragraph (b)(3)(ii) of this section. Assuming all other requirements are met, *D*'s purchase price of the automobile qualifies for the additional first year depreciation deduction for *D* under this section, subject to any limitation under section 280F.

(C) *Example 3.* On April 1, 2015, *E* acquires a horse to be used in *E*'s thoroughbred racing business. On October 1, 2018, *F* buys the horse from *E* and will use the horse in *F*'s horse breeding business. *F* did not have any depreciable interest in the horse before *F* acquired it on October 1, 2018. The use of the horse by *E* in its racing business prevents *F* from satisfying the original use requirement of paragraph (b)(3)(ii) of this section. However, *F*'s acquisition of the horse satisfies the used property acquisition requirements of paragraph (b)(3)(iii) of this section. Assuming all other requirements are met, *F*'s purchase price of the horse qualifies for the additional first year depreciation deduction for *F* under this section.

(D) *Example 4.* In the ordinary course of its business, *G* sells fractional interests in its aircraft to unrelated parties. *G* holds out for sale eight equal fractional interests in an aircraft. On October 1, 2017, *G* sells five of the eight fractional interests in the aircraft to *H* and *H* begins to use its proportionate share of the aircraft immediately upon purchase. On February 1, 2018, *G* sells to *I* the remaining unsold $3/8$ fractional interests in the aircraft. *H* is considered the original user as to its $5/8$ fractional interest in the aircraft and *I* is considered the original user as to its $3/8$ fractional interest in the aircraft. Thus, assuming all other requirements are met, *H*'s purchase price for its $5/8$ fractional interest in the aircraft qualifies for the additional first year depreciation deduction under this section and *I*'s purchase price for its $3/8$ fractional interest in the aircraft qualifies for the additional first year depreciation deduction under this section.

(E) *Example 5.* On September 1, 2017, *J*, an equipment dealer, buys new tractors that are held by *J* primarily for sale to customers in the ordinary course of its business. On October 15, 2017, *J* withdraws the tractors from inventory and begins to use the tractors primarily for producing rental income. The holding of the tractors by *J* as inventory does not constitute a "use" for purposes of the original use requirement and, therefore, the original use of the tractors commences with *J* on October 15, 2017, for purposes of paragraph (b)(3)(ii) of this section. However, the tractors are not eligible for the additional first year depreciation deduction under this section because *J* acquired the tractors before September 28, 2017.

(F) *Example 6. K* is in the trade or business of leasing equipment to others. During 2016, *K* buys a new machine (Machine #1) and then leases it to *L* for use in *L*'s trade or business. The lease between *K* and *L* for Machine #1 is a true lease for Federal income tax purposes. During 2018, *L* enters into a written binding contract with *K* to buy Machine #1 at its fair market value on May 15, 2018. *L* did not have any depreciable interest in Machine #1 before *L* acquired it on May 15, 2018. As a result, *L*'s acquisition of Machine #1 satisfies the used property acquisition requirements of paragraph (b)(3)(iii) of this section. Assuming all other requirements are met, *L*'s purchase price of Machine #1 qualifies for the additional first year depreciation deduction for *L* under this section.

(G) *Example 7.* The facts are the same as in *Example 6* of paragraph (b)(3)(vii)(F) of this section, except that *K* and *L* are related parties within the meaning of section 179(d)(2)(A) or (B) and

§1.179-4(c). As a result, L's acquisition of Machine #1 does not satisfy the used property acquisition requirements of paragraph (b)(3)(iii) of this section. Thus, Machine #1 is not eligible for the additional first year depreciation deduction for L.

(H) *Example 8.* The facts are the same as in *Example 6* of paragraph (b)(3)(vii)(F) of this section, except L incurred capital expenditures of $5,000 to improve Machine #1 on September 5, 2017, and has a depreciable interest in such improvements. L's purchase price of $5,000 for the improvements to Machine #1 satisfies the original use requirement of §1.168(k)-1(b)(3)(i) and, assuming all other requirements are met, qualifies for the 50-percent additional first year depreciation deduction. Because L has a depreciable interest only in the improvements to Machine #1, L's acquisition of Machine #1, excluding L's improvements to such machine, satisfies the used property acquisition requirements of paragraph (b)(3)(iii) of this section. Assuming all other requirements are met, L's unadjusted depreciable basis of Machine #1, excluding the amount of such unadjusted depreciable basis attributable to L's improvements to Machine #1, qualifies for the additional first year depreciation deduction for L under this section.

(I) *Example 9.* During 2016, M and N purchased used equipment for use in their trades or businesses and each own a 50 percent interest in such equipment. Prior to this acquisition, M and N did not have any depreciable interest in the equipment. Assume this ownership arrangement is not a partnership. During 2018, N enters into a written binding contract with M to buy M's interest in the equipment. Pursuant to paragraph (b)(3)(iii)(B)(2) of this section, N is not treated as using M's interest in the equipment prior to N's acquisition of M's interest. As a result, N's acquisition of M's interest in the equipment satisfies the used property acquisition requirements of paragraph (b)(3)(iii) of this section. Assuming all other requirements are met, N's purchase price of M's interest in the equipment qualifies for the additional first year depreciation deduction for N under this section.

(J) *Example 10.* The facts are the same as in *Example 9* of paragraph (b)(3)(vii)(I) of this section, except N had a 100-percent depreciable interest in the equipment during 2011 through 2015, and M purchased from N a 50-percent interest in the equipment during 2016. Pursuant to paragraph (b)(3)(iii)(B)(1) of this section, the lookback period is 2013 through 2017 to determine if N had a depreciable interest in M's 50-percent interest in the equipment N acquired from M in 2018. Because N had a 100-percent depreciable interest in the equipment during 2013 through 2015, N had a depreciable interest in M's 50-percent interest in the equipment during the lookback period. As a result, N's acquisition of M's interest in the equipment during 2018 does not satisfy the used property acquisition requirements of paragraphs (b)(3)(iii)(A)(1) and (b)(3)(iii)(B)(1) of this section. Paragraph (b)(3)(iii)(B)(2) of this section does not apply because N initially acquired a 100-percent depreciable interest in the equipment. Accordingly, N's purchase price of M's interest in the equipment during 2018 does not qualify for the additional first year depreciation deduction for N.

(K) *Example 11.* The facts are the same as in *Example 9* of paragraph (b)(3)(vii)(I) of this section, except N had a 100-percent depreciable interest in the equipment only during 2011, and M purchased from N a 50-percent interest in the equipment during 2012. Pursuant to paragraph (b)(3)(iii)(B)(1) of this section, the lookback period is 2013 through 2017 to determine if N had a depreciable interest in M's 50-percent interest in the equipment N acquired from M in 2018. Because N had a depreciable interest in only its 50-percent interest in the equipment during this lookback period, N's acquisition of M's interest in the equipment during 2018 satisfies the used property acquisition requirements of paragraphs (b)(3)(iii)(A)(1) and (b)(3)(iii)(B)(1) of this section. Assuming all other requirements are met, N's purchase price of M's interest in the equipment during 2018 qualifies for the additional first year depreciation deduction for N under this section.

(L) *Example 12.* The facts are the same as in *Example 9* of paragraph (b)(3)(vii)(I) of this section, except during 2018, M also enters into a written binding contract with N to buy N's interest in the equipment. Pursuant to paragraph (b)(3)(iii)(B)(2) of this section, both M and N are treated as previously having a depreciable interest in a 50-percent portion of the equipment. Accordingly, the acquisition by M of N's 50-percent interest and the acquisition by N of M's 50-percent interest in the equipment during 2018 do not qualify for the additional first year depreciation deduction.

(M) *Example 13.* O and P form an equal partnership, OP, in 2018. O contributes cash to OP, and P contributes equipment to OP. OP's basis in the equipment contributed by P is determined under section 723. Because OP's basis in such equipment is determined in whole or in part by reference to P's adjusted basis in such equipment, OP's acquisition of such equipment does not satisfy section 179(d)(2)(C) and §1.179-4(c)(1)(iv) and, thus, does not satisfy the used property acquisition requirements of paragraph (b)(3)(iii) of this

section. Accordingly, OP's acquisition of such equipment is not eligible for the additional first year depreciation deduction.

(N) *Example 14.* Q, R, and S form an equal partnership, QRS, in 2019. Each partner contributes $100, which QRS uses to purchase a retail motor fuels outlet for $300. Assume this retail motor fuels outlet is QRS' only property and is qualified property under section 168(k)(2)(A)(i). QRS makes an election not to deduct the additional first year depreciation for all qualified property placed in service during 2019. QRS has a section 754 election in effect. QRS claimed depreciation of $15 for the retail motor fuels outlet for 2019. During 2020, when the retail motor fuels outlet's fair market value is $600, Q sells all of its partnership interest to T in a fully taxable transaction for $200. T never previously had a depreciable interest in the retail motor fuels outlet. T takes an outside basis of $200 in the partnership interest previously owned by Q. T's share of the partnership's previously taxed capital is $95. Accordingly, T's section 743(b) adjustment is $105 and is allocated entirely to the retail motor fuels outlet under section 755. Assuming all other requirements are met, T's section 743(b) adjustment qualifies for the additional first year depreciation deduction under this section.

(O) *Example 15.* The facts are the same as in *Example 14* of paragraph (b)(3)(vii)(N) of this section, except that Q sells his partnership interest to U, a related person within the meaning of section 179(d)(2)(A) or (B) and §1.179-4(c). U's section 743(b) adjustment does not qualify for the additional first year depreciation deduction.

(P) *Example 16.* The facts are the same as in *Example 14* of paragraph (b)(3)(vii)(N) of this section, except that Q dies and his partnership interest is transferred to V. V takes a basis in Q's partnership interest under section 1014. As a result, section 179(d)(2)(C)(ii) and §1.179-4(c)(1)(iv) are not satisfied, and V's section 743(b) adjustment does not qualify for the additional first year depreciation deduction.

(Q) *Example 17.* The facts are the same as in *Example 14* of paragraph (b)(3)(vii)(N) of this section, except that QRS purchased the retail motor fuels outlet from T prior to T purchasing Q's partnership interest in QRS. T had a depreciable interest in such retail motor fuels outlet. Because T had a depreciable interest in the retail motor fuels outlet before T acquired its interest in QRS, T's section 743(b) adjustment does not qualify for the additional first year depreciation deduction.

(R) *Example 18.* (1) W, a freight transportation company, acquires and places in service a used aircraft during 2019 (Airplane #1). Prior to this acquisition, W never had a depreciable interest in this aircraft. During September 2020, W enters into a written binding contract with a third party to renovate Airplane #1. The third party begins to renovate Airplane #1 in October 2020 and delivers the renovated aircraft (Airplane #2) to W in February 2021. To renovate Airplane #1, the third party used mostly new parts but also used parts from Airplane #1. The cost of the used parts is not more than 20 percent of the total cost of the renovated airplane, Airplane #2. W uses Airplane #2 in its trade or business.

(2) Although Airplane #2 contains used parts, the cost of the used parts is not more than 20 percent of the total cost of Airplane #2. As a result, Airplane #2 is not treated as reconditioned or rebuilt property, and W is considered the original user of Airplane #2, pursuant to paragraph (b)(3)(ii)(A) of this section. Accordingly, assuming all other requirements are met, the amount paid or incurred by W for Airplane #2 qualifies for the additional first year depreciation deduction for W under this section.

(S) *Example 19.* (1) X, a freight transportation company, acquires and places in service a new aircraft in 2019 (Airplane #1). During 2022, X sells Airplane #1 to AB and AB uses Airplane #1 in its trade or business. Prior to this acquisition, AB never had a depreciable interest in Airplane #1. During January 2023, AB enters into a written binding contract with a third party to renovate Airplane #1. The third party begins to renovate Airplane #1 in February 2023 and delivers the renovated aircraft (Airplane #2) to AB in June 2023. To renovate Airplane #1, the third party used mostly new parts but also used parts from Airplane #1. The cost of the used parts is not more than 20 percent of the total cost of the renovated airplane, Airplane #2. AB uses Airplane #2 in its trade or business. During 2025, AB sells Airplane #2 to X and X uses Airplane #2 in its trade or business.

(2) With respect to X's purchase of Airplane #1 in 2019, X is the original user of this airplane pursuant to paragraph (b)(3)(ii)(A) of this section. Accordingly, assuming all other requirements are met, X's purchase price for Airplane #1 qualifies for the additional first year depreciation deduction for X under this section.

(3) Because AB never had a depreciable interest in Airplane #1 prior to its acquisition in 2022, the requirements of paragraphs (b)(3)(iii)(A)(1) and (b)(3)(ii)(B)(1) of this section are satisfied. Accordingly, assuming all other requirements are met, AB's purchase price for Airplane #1 qualifies for the additional first year depreciation deduction for AB under this section.

(4) Although Airplane #2 contains used parts, the cost of the used parts is not more than 20 percent of the total cost of Airplane #2. As a result, Airplane #2 is not treated as reconditioned or rebuilt property, and *AB* is considered the original user of Airplane #2, pursuant to paragraph (b)(3)(ii)(A) of this section. Accordingly, assuming all other requirements are met, the amount paid or incurred by *AB* for Airplane #2 qualifies for the additional first year depreciation deduction for *AB* under this section.

(5) With respect to *X*'s purchase of Airplane #2 in 2025, Airplane #2 is substantially renovated property pursuant to paragraph (b)(3)(iii)(B)(*3*) of this section. Also, pursuant to paragraph (b)(3)(iii)(B)(*3*) of this section, *X*'s depreciable interest in Airplane #1 is not taken into account for determining if *X* previously had a depreciable interest in Airplane #2 prior to its acquisition during 2025. As a result, Airplane #2 is not treated as used by *X* at any time before its acquisition of Airplane #2 in 2025 pursuant to paragraph (b)(3)(iii)(B)(*3*) of this section. Accordingly, assuming all other requirements are met, *X*'s purchase price of Airplane #2 qualifies for the additional first year depreciation deduction for *X* under this section.

(T) *Example 20.* In November 2017, AA Corporation purchases a used drill press costing $10,000 and is granted a trade-in allowance of $2,000 on its old drill press. The used drill press is qualified property under section 168(k)(2)(A)(i). The old drill press had a basis of $1,200. Under sections 1012 and 1031(d), the basis of the used drill press is $9,200 ($1,200 basis of old drill press plus cash expended of $8,000). Only $8,000 of the basis of the used drill press satisfies the requirements of section 179(d)(3) and §1.179-4(d) and, thus, satisfies the used property acquisition requirement of paragraph (b)(3)(iii) of this section. The remaining $1,200 of the basis of the used drill press does not satisfy the requirements of section 179(d)(3) and §1.179-4(d) because it is determined by reference to the old drill press. Accordingly, assuming all other requirements are met, only $8,000 of the basis of the used drill press is eligible for the additional first year depreciation deduction under this section.

(U) *Example 21.* (1) M Corporation acquires and places in service a used airplane on March 26, 2018. Prior to this acquisition, M Corporation never had a depreciable interest in this airplane. On March 26, 2018, M Corporation also leases the used airplane to N Corporation, an airline company. On May 27, 2018, M Corporation sells to O Corporation the used airplane subject to the lease with N Corporation. M Corporation and O Corporation are related parties within the meaning of section 179(d)(2)(A) or (B) and §1.179-4(c). As of May 27, 2018, N Corporation is still the lessee of the used airplane. Prior to this acquisition, O Corporation never had a depreciable interest in the used airplane. O Corporation is a calendar-year taxpayer.

(2) The sale transaction of May 27, 2018, satisfies the requirements of a syndication transaction described in paragraph (b)(3)(vi) of this section. As a result, O Corporation is considered the taxpayer that acquired the used airplane for purposes of applying the used property acquisition requirements in paragraph (b)(3)(iii) of this section. In applying these rules, the fact that M Corporation and O Corporation are related parties is not taken into account because O Corporation, not M Corporation, is treated as acquiring the used airplane. Also, O Corporation, not M Corporation, is treated as having the depreciable interest in the used airplane. Further, pursuant to paragraph (b)(4)(iv) of this section, the used airplane is treated as originally placed in service by O Corporation on May 27, 2018. Because O Corporation never had a depreciable interest in the used airplane and assuming all other requirements are met, O Corporation's purchase price of the used airplane qualifies for the additional first year depreciation deduction for O Corporation under this section.

(V) *Example 22.* (1) The facts are the same as in *Example 21* of paragraph (b)(3)(vii)(U)(*1*) of this section. Additionally, on September 5, 2018, O Corporation sells to P Corporation the used airplane subject to the lease with N Corporation. Prior to this acquisition, P Corporation never had a depreciable interest in the used airplane.

(2) Because O Corporation, a calendar-year taxpayer, placed in service and disposed of the used airplane during 2018, the used airplane is not eligible for the additional first year depreciation deduction for O Corporation pursuant to paragraph (g)(1)(i) of this section.

(3) Because P Corporation never had a depreciable interest in the used airplane and assuming all other requirements are met, P Corporation's purchase price of the used airplane qualifies for the additional first year depreciation deduction for P Corporation under this section.

(W) *Example 23.* (1) The facts are the same as in *Example 21* of paragraph (b)(3)(vii)(U)(*1*) of this section, except M Corporation and O Corporation are not related parties within the meaning of section 179(d)(2)(A) or (B) and §1.179-4(c). Additionally, on March 26, 2020,

O Corporation sells to M Corporation the used airplane subject to the lease with N Corporation.

(2) The sale transaction of May 27, 2018, satisfies the requirements of a syndication transaction described in paragraph (b)(3)(vi) of this section. As a result, O Corporation is considered the taxpayer that acquired the used airplane for purposes of applying the used property acquisition requirements in paragraph (b)(3)(iii) of this section. Also, O Corporation, not M Corporation, is treated as having the depreciable interest in the used airplane. Further, pursuant to paragraph (b)(4)(iv) of this section, the used airplane is treated as originally placed in service by O Corporation on May 27, 2018. Because O Corporation never had a depreciable interest in the used airplane before its acquisition in 2018 and assuming all other requirements are met, O Corporation's purchase price of the used airplane qualifies for the additional first year depreciation deduction for O Corporation under this section.

(3) Prior to its acquisition of the used airplane on March 26, 2020, M Corporation never had a depreciable interest in the used airplane pursuant to paragraph (b)(3)(vi) of this section. Assuming all other requirements are met, M Corporation's purchase price of the used airplane on March 26, 2020, qualifies for the additional first year depreciation deduction for M Corporation under this section.

(X) *Example 24.* (1) J, K, and L are corporations that are unrelated parties within the meaning of section 179(d)(2)(A) or (B) and §1.179-4(c). None of J, K, or L is a member of a consolidated group. J has a depreciable interest in Equipment #5. During 2018, J sells Equipment #5 to K. During 2020, J merges into L in a transaction described in section 368(a)(1)(A). In 2021, L acquires Equipment #5 from K.

(2) Because J is the predecessor of L, and because J previously had a depreciable interest in Equipment #5, L's acquisition of Equipment #5 does not satisfy paragraphs (b)(3)(iii)(A)(*1*) and (b)(3)(iii)(B)(*1*) of this section. Thus, L's acquisition of Equipment #5 does not satisfy the used property acquisition requirements of paragraph (b)(3)(iii) of this section. Accordingly, L's acquisition of Equipment #5 is not eligible for the additional first year depreciation deduction.

(Y) *Example 25.* (1) JL is a fiscal year taxpayer with a taxable year ending June 30. On April 22, 2020, JL acquires and places in service a new machine for use in its trade or business. On May 1, 2022, JL sells this machine to JM, an unrelated party, for use in JM's trade or business. JM is a fiscal year taxpayer with a taxable year ending March 31. On February 1, 2023, JL buys the machine from JM and places the machine in service. JL uses the machine in its trade or business for the remainder of its taxable year ending June 30, 2023.

(2) JL's acquisition of the machine on April 22, 2020, satisfies the original use requirement in paragraph (b)(3)(ii) of this section. Assuming all other requirements are met, JL's purchase price of the machine qualifies for the additional first year depreciation deduction for JL for the taxable year ending June 30, 2020, under this section.

(3) JM placed in service the machine on May 1, 2022, and disposed of it on February 1, 2023. As a result, JM placed in service and disposed of the machine during the same taxable year (JM's taxable year beginning April 1, 2022, and ending March 31, 2023). Accordingly, JM's acquisition of the machine on May 1, 2022, does not qualify for the additional first year depreciation deduction pursuant to paragraph (g)(1)(i) of this section.

(4) Pursuant to paragraph (b)(3)(iii)(B)(*1*) of this section, the lookback period is calendar years 2018 through 2022 and January 1, 2023, through January 31, 2023, to determine if JL had a depreciable interest in the machine when JL reacquired it on February 1, 2023. As a result, JL's depreciable interest in the machine during the period April 22, 2020, to April 30, 2022, is taken into account for determining whether the machine was used by JL or a predecessor at any time prior to its reacquisition by JL on February 1, 2023. Accordingly, the reacquisition of the machine by JL on February 1, 2023, does not qualify for the additional first year depreciation deduction.

(Z) *Example 26.* (1) EF has owned and had a depreciable interest in Property since 2012. On January 1, 2016, EF contributes assets (not including Property) to existing *Partnership T* in a transaction described in section 721, in exchange for a partnership interest in *Partnership T*, and *Partnership T* placed in service these assets for use in its trade or business. On July 1, 2016, EF sells Property to EG, a party unrelated to either EF or *Partnership T*. On April 1, 2018, *Partnership T* buys Property from EG and places it in service for use in its trade or business.

(2) EF is not *Partnership T*'s predecessor with respect to Property within the meaning of paragraph (a)(2)(iv)(B) of this section. Pursuant to paragraph (3)(iii)(B)(*1*) of this section, the lookback period is 2013-2017, plus January through March 2018, to determine if *Partnership T* had a depreciable interest in Property that *Partnership T* acquired on April 1, 2018. EF need not be examined in the lookback period to see if EF had a depreciable interest in Property, because EF is not *Partnership T*'s predecessor. Because *Partnership T* did not have

Reg. §1.168(k)-2(b)(3)(vii)

a depreciable interest in Property in the lookback period prior to its acquisition of Property on April 1, 2018, *Partnership T*'s acquisition of Property on April 1, 2018, satisfies the used property acquisition requirement of paragraph (b)(3)(iii)(B)(1) of this section. Assuming all other requirements of this section are satisfied, *Partnership T's* purchase price of Property qualifies for the additional first year depreciation deduction under this section.

(AA) *Example 27.* (1) The facts are the same as in *Example 26* of paragraph (b)(3)(vii)(Z)(1) of this section, except that on January 1, 2016, *EF's* contribution of assets to *Partnership T* includes Property. On July 1, 2016, *Partnership T* sells Property to *EG*.

(2) *Partnership T's* acquisition of Property on January 1, 2016, does not satisfy the original use requirement of §1.168(k)-1(b)(3) and is not eligible for the additional first year depreciation deduction under section 168(k) as in effect prior to the enactment of the Act.

(3) With respect to *Partnership T's* acquisition of Property on April 1, 2018, *EF* is *Partnership T's* predecessor with respect to Property within the meaning of paragraph (a)(2)(iv)(B) of this section. Pursuant to paragraph (b)(3)(iii)(B)(1) of this section, the lookback period is 2013-2017, plus January through March 2018, to determine if *EF* or *Partnership T* had a depreciable interest in Property that *Partnership T* acquired on April 1, 2018. Because *EF* had a depreciable interest in Property from 2013 to 2015 and *Partnership T* had a depreciable interest in Property from January through June 2016, *Partnership T's* acquisition of Property on April 1, 2018, does not satisfy the used property acquisition requirement of paragraph (b)(3)(iii)(B)(1) of this section and is not eligible for the additional first year depreciation deduction.

(BB) *Example 28.* (1) X Corporation has owned and had a depreciable interest in Property since 2012. On January 1, 2015, X Corporation sold Property to *Q*, an unrelated party. Y Corporation is formed July 1, 2015. On January 1, 2016, Y Corporation merges into X Corporation in a transaction described in section 368(a)(1)(A). On April 1, 2018, X Corporation buys Property from *Q* and places it in service for use in its trade or business.

(2) Pursuant to paragraph (a)(2)(iv)(A) of this section, Y Corporation is X Corporation's predecessor. Pursuant to paragraph (b)(3)(iii)(B)(1) of this section, the lookback period is 2013-2017, plus January through March 2018, to determine if Y Corporation or X Corporation had a depreciable interest in Property that X Corporation acquired on April 1, 2018. Y Corporation did not have a depreciable interest in Property at any time during the lookback period. Because X Corporation had a depreciable interest in Property from 2013 through 2014, X Corporation's acquisition of Property on April 1, 2018, does not satisfy the used property acquisition requirement of paragraph (b)(3)(iii)(B)(1) of this section and is not eligible for the additional first year depreciation deduction.

(CC) *Example 29.* (1) Y Corporation has owned and had a depreciable interest in Property since 2012. On January 1, 2015, Y Corporation sells Property to *Q*, an unrelated party. X Corporation is formed on July 1, 2015. On January 1, 2016, Y Corporation merges into X Corporation in a transaction described in section 368(a)(1)(A). On April 1, 2018, X Corporation buys Property from *Q* and places it in service for use in its trade or business.

(2) Pursuant to paragraph (a)(2)(iv)(A) of this section, Y Corporation is X Corporation's predecessor. Pursuant to paragraph (b)(3)(iii)(B)(1) of this section, the lookback period is 2013-2017, plus January through March 2018, to determine if X Corporation or Y Corporation had a depreciable interest in Property that X Corporation acquired on April 1, 2018. Because Y Corporation had a depreciable interest in Property from 2013 through 2014, X Corporation's acquisition of Property on April 1, 2018, does not satisfy the used property acquisition requirement of paragraph (b)(3)(iii)(B)(1) of this section and is not eligible for the additional first year depreciation deduction.

(DD) *Example 30.* (1) On September 5, 2017, *Y*, a calendar-year taxpayer, acquires and places in service a new machine (Machine #1), and begins using Machine #1 in its manufacturing trade or business. On November 1, 2017, *Y* sells Machine #1 to *Z*, then *Z* leases Machine #1 back to *Y* for 4 years, and *Y* continues to use Machine #1 in its manufacturing trade or business. The lease agreement contains a purchase option provision allowing *Y* to buy Machine #1 at the end of the lease term. On November 1, 2021, *Y* exercises the purchase option in the lease agreement and buys Machine #1 from *Z*. The lease between *Y* and *Z* for Machine #1 is a true lease for Federal tax purposes.

(2) Because *Y*, a calendar-year taxpayer, placed in service and disposed of Machine #1 during 2017, Machine #1 is not eligible for the additional first year depreciation deduction for *Y* pursuant to §1.168(k)-1(f)(1)(i).

(3) The use of Machine #1 by *Y* prevents *Z* from satisfying the original use requirement of paragraph (b)(3)(ii) of this section. However, *Z*'s acquisition of Machine #1 satisfies the used property acquisition requirements of paragraph (b)(3)(iii) of this section. Assuming

all other requirements are met, *Z*'s purchase price of Machine #1 qualifies for the additional first year depreciation deduction for *Z* under this section.

(4) During 2017, *Y* sold Machine #1 within 90 calendar days of placing Machine #1 in service originally on September 5, 2017. Pursuant to paragraph (b)(3)(iii)(B)(4) of this section, *Y*'s depreciable interest in Machine #1 during that 90-day period is not taken into account for determining whether Machine #1 was used by *Y* or a predecessor at any time prior to its reacquisition by *Y* on November 1, 2021. Accordingly, assuming all other requirements are met, *Y*'s purchase price of Machine #1 on November 1, 2021, qualifies for the additional first year depreciation deduction for *Y* under this section.

(EE) *Example 31.* (1) On October 15, 2019, *FA*, a calendar-year taxpayer, buys and places in service a new machine for use in its trade or business. On January 10, 2020, *FA* sells this machine to *FB* for use in *FB's* trade or business. *FB* is a calendar-year taxpayer and is not related to *FA*. On March 30, 2020, *FA* buys the machine from *FB* and places the machine in service. *FA* uses the machine in its trade or business for the remainder of 2020.

(2) *FA's* acquisition of the machine on October 15, 2019, satisfies the original use requirement in paragraph (b)(3)(ii) of this section. Assuming all other requirements are met, *FA's* purchase price of the machine qualifies for the additional first year depreciation deduction for *FA* for the 2019 taxable year under this section.

(3) Because *FB* placed in service the machine on January 10, 2020, and disposed of it on March 30, 2020, *FB's* acquisition of the machine on January 10, 2020, does not qualify for the additional first year depreciation deduction pursuant to §1.168(k)-2(g)(1)(i).

(4) *FA* sold the machine to *FB* in 2020 and within 90 calendar days of placing the machine in service originally on October 15, 2019. Pursuant to paragraph (b)(3)(iii)(B)(4) of this section, *FA's* depreciable interest in the machine during that 90-day period is not taken into account for determining whether the machine was used by *FA* or a predecessor at any time prior to its reacquisition by *FA* on March 30, 2020. Accordingly, assuming all other requirements are met, *FA's* purchase price of the machine on March 30, 2020, qualifies for the additional first year depreciation deduction for *FA* for the 2020 taxable year under this section.

(FF) *Example 32.* (1) The facts are the same as in *Example 31* of paragraph (b)(3)(vii)(EE)(1) of this section, except that on November 1, 2020, *FB* buys the machine from *FA* and places the machine in service. *FB* uses the machine in its trade or business for the remainder of 2020.

(2) Because *FA* placed in service the machine on March 30, 2020, and disposed of it on November 1, 2020, *FA's* reacquisition of the machine on March 30, 2020, does not qualify for the additional first year depreciation deduction pursuant to paragraph (g)(1)(i) of this section.

(3) During 2020, *FB* sold the machine to *FA* within 90 calendar days of placing the machine in service originally on January 10, 2020. After *FB* reacquired the machine on November 1, 2020, *FB* did not dispose of the property during the remainder of 2020. Pursuant to paragraph (b)(3)(iii)(B)(4) of this section, *FB's* depreciable interest in the machine during that 90-day period is not taken into account for determining whether the machine was used by *FB* or a predecessor at any time prior to its reacquisition by *FB* on November 1, 2020. Accordingly, assuming all other requirements are met, *FB's* purchase price of the machine on November 1, 2020, qualifies for the additional first year depreciation deduction for *FB* under this section.

(GG) *Example 33.* (1) The facts are the same as in *Example 32* of paragraph (b)(3)(vii)(FF)(1) of this section, except *FB* sells the machine to *FC*, an unrelated party, on December 31, 2020.

(2) Because *FB* placed in service the machine on November 1, 2020, and disposed of it on December 31, 2020, *FB's* reacquisition of the machine on November 1, 2020, does not qualify for the additional first year depreciation deduction pursuant to paragraph (g)(1)(i) of this section.

(3) *FC's* acquisition of the machine on December 31, 2020, satisfies the used property acquisition requirement of paragraph (b)(3)(iii)(A)(2) of this section. Accordingly, assuming all other requirements of this section are satisfied, *FC's* purchase price of the machine qualifies for the additional first year depreciation deduction under this section.

(HH) *Example 34.* (1) In August 2017, *FD*, a calendar-year taxpayer, entered into a written binding contract with *X* for *X* to manufacture a machine for *FD* for use in its trade or business. Before September 28, 2017, *FD* incurred more than 10 percent of the total cost of the machine. On February 8, 2020, *X* delivered the machine to *FD* and *FD* placed in service the machine. The machine is property described in section 168(k)(2)(B) as in effect on the day before the date of the enactment of the Act. *FD's* entire unadjusted depreciable basis of the machine is attributable to the machine's manufacture before January 1, 2020. *FD* uses the safe harbor test in §1.168(k)-1(b)(4)(iii)(B)(2) to determine when manufacturing of the machine began. On March 26, 2020, *FD* sells the machine to *FE* for use in *FE's* trade or business. *FE* is a calendar-year taxpayer and is not related to *FD*. On November 7, 2020, *FD* buys the machine from *FE* and places in service the machine. *FD* uses the machine in its trade or business for the remainder of 2020.

(2) Because *FD* incurred more than 10 percent of the cost of the machine before September 28, 2017, and *FD* uses the safe harbor test in § 1.168(k)-1(b)(4)(iii)(B)(*2*) to determine when the manufacturing of the machine began, *FD* acquired the machine before September 28, 2017. If *FD* had not disposed of the machine on March 26, 2020, the cost of the machine would have qualified for the 30-percent additional first year depreciation deduction pursuant to section 168(k)(8), assuming all requirements are met under section 168(k)(2) as in effect on the day before the date of the enactment of the Act. However, because *FD* placed in service the machine on February 8, 2020, and disposed of it on March 26, 2020, FD's acquisition of the machine on February 8, 2020, does not qualify for the additional first year depreciation deduction pursuant to § 1.168(k)-1(f)(1)(i).

(3) Because *FE* placed in service the machine on March 26, 2020, and disposed of it on November 7, 2020, *FE's* acquisition of the machine on March 26, 2020, does not qualify for the additional first year depreciation deduction pursuant to paragraph (g)(1)(i) of this section.

(4) During 2020, *FD* sold the machine to *FE* within 90 calendar days of placing the machine in service originally on February 8, 2020. After *FD* reacquired the machine on November 7, 2020, *FD* did not dispose of the machine during the remainder of 2020. *FD* originally acquired this machine before September 28, 2017. As a result, paragraph (b)(3)(iii)(B)(*4*) of this section does not apply. Pursuant to paragraph (b)(3)(iii)(B)(*1*) of this section, the lookback period is 2015 through 2019 and January 1, 2020, through November 6, 2020, to determine if *FD* had a depreciable interest in the machine when *FD* reacquired it on November 7, 2020. As a result, *FD's* depreciable interest in the machine during the period February 8, 2020, to March 26, 2020, is taken into account for determining whether the machine was used by *FD* or a predecessor at any time prior to its reacquisition by *FD* on November 7, 2020. Accordingly, the reacquisition of the machine by *FD* on November 7, 2020, does not qualify for the additional first year depreciation deduction.

(II) *Example 35.* (*1*) In a series of related transactions, a father sells a machine to an unrelated individual on December 15, 2019, who sells the machine to the father's daughter on January 2, 2020, for use in the daughter's trade or business. Pursuant to paragraph (b)(3)(iii)(C)(*1*) of this section, a transferee tests its relationship with the transferor from which the transferee directly acquires the depreciable property, and with the original transferor of the depreciable property in the series. The relationship is tested when the transferee acquires, and immediately before the first transfer of, the depreciable property in the series. As a result, the following relationships are tested under section 179(d)(2)(A): the unrelated individual tests its relationship to the father as of December 15, 2019; and the daughter tests her relationship to the unrelated individual as of January 2, 2020, and December 15, 2019, and to the father as of January 2, 2020, and December 15, 2019.

(2) Because the individual is not related to the father within the meaning of section 179(d)(2)(A) and § 1.179-4(c)(1)(ii) as of December 15, 2019, the individual's acquisition of the machine satisfies the used property acquisition requirement of paragraph (b)(3)(iii)(A)(*2*) of this section. Accordingly, assuming the unrelated individual placed the machine in service for use in its trade or business in 2019 and all other requirements of this section are satisfied, the unrelated individual's purchase price of the machine qualifies for the additional first year depreciation deduction under this section.

(3) The individual and the daughter are not related parties within the meaning of section 179(d)(2)(A) and § 1.179-4(c)(1)(ii) as of January 2, 2020, or December 15, 2019. However, the father and his daughter are related parties within the meaning of section 179(d)(2)(A) and § 1.179-4(c)(1)(ii) as of January 2, 2020, or December 15, 2019. Accordingly, the daughter's acquisition of the machine does not satisfy the used property acquisition requirements of paragraph (b)(3)(iii) of this section and is not eligible for the additional first year depreciation deduction.

(JJ) *Example 36.* (*1*) The facts are the same as in *Example 35* of paragraph (b)(3)(vii)(II)(*1*) of this section, except that instead of selling to an unrelated individual, the father sells the machine to his son on December 15, 2019, who sells the machine to his sister (the father's daughter) on January 2, 2020. Pursuant to paragraph (b)(3)(iii)(C)(*1*) of this section, a transferee tests its relationship with the transferor from which the transferee directly acquires the depreciable property, and with the original transferor of the depreciable property in the series. The relationship is tested when the transferee acquires, and immediately before the first transfer of, the depreciable property in the series. As a result, the following relationships are tested under section 179(d)(2)(A): the son tests his relationship to the father as of December 15, 2019; and the daughter tests her relationship to her brother as of January 2, 2020, and December 15, 2019, and to the father as of January 2, 2020, and December 15, 2019.

(2) Because the father and his son are related parties within the meaning of section 179(d)(2)(A) and § 1.179-4(c)(1)(ii) as of December 15, 2019, the son's acquisition of the machine does not satisfy the used property acquisition requirements of paragraph (b)(3)(iii) of this section. Accordingly, the son's acquisition of the machine is not eligible for the additional first year depreciation deduction.

(3) The son and his sister are not related parties within the meaning of section 179(d)(2)(A) and § 1.179-4(c)(1)(ii) as of January 2, 2020, or December 15, 2019. However, the father and his daughter are related parties within the meaning of section 179(d)(2)(A) and § 1.179-4(c)(1)(ii) as of January 2, 2020, or December 15, 2019. Accordingly, the daughter's acquisition of the machine does not satisfy the used property acquisition requirements of paragraph (b)(3)(iii) of this section and is not eligible for the additional first year depreciation deduction.

(KK) *Example 37.* (*1*) In June 2018, *BA*, an individual, bought and placed in service a new machine from an unrelated party for use in its trade or business. In a series of related transactions, *BA* sells the machine to *BB* and *BB* places it in service on October 1, 2019, *BB* sells the machine to *BC* and *BC* places it in service on December 1, 2019, and *BC* sells the machine to *BD* and *BD* places it in service on January 2, 2020. *BA* and *BB* are related parties within the meaning of section 179(d)(2)(A) and § 1.179-4(c)(1)(ii). *BB* and *BC* are related parties within the meaning of section 179(d)(2)(B) and § 1.179-4(c)(1)(iii). *BC* and *BD* are not related parties within the meaning of section 179(d)(2)(A) and § 1.179-4(c)(1)(ii), or section 179(d)(2)(B) and § 1.179-4(c)(1)(iii). *BA* is not related to *BC* or to *BD* within the meaning of section 179(c)(2)(A) and § 1.179-4(c)(1)(ii). All parties are calendar-year taxpayers.

(2) *BA's* purchase of the machine in June 2018 satisfies the original use requirement of paragraph (b)(3)(ii) of this section and, assuming all other requirements of this section are met, *BA's* purchase price of the machine qualifies for the additional first year depreciation deduction under this section.

(3) Pursuant to paragraph (b)(3)(iii)(C)(*1*) of this section, a transferee tests its relationship with the transferor from which the transferee directly acquires the depreciable property, and with the original transferor of the depreciable property in the series. The relationship is tested when the transferee acquires, and immediately before the first transfer of, the depreciable property in the series. However, because *BB* placed in service and disposed of the machine in the same taxable year, *BB* is disregarded pursuant to paragraph (b)(3)(iii)(C)(*2*)(*i*) of this section. As a result, the following relationships are tested under section 179(d)(2)(A) and (B): *BC* tests its relationship to *BA* as of December 1, 2019, and October 1, 2019; and *BD* tests its relationship to *BC* as of January 2, 2020, and October 1, 2019, and to *BA* as of January 2, 2020, and October 1, 2020.

(4) Because *BA* is not related to *BC* within the meaning of section 179(d)(2)(A) and § 1.179-4(c)(1)(ii) as of December 1, 2019, or October 1, 2019, *BC's* acquisition of the machine satisfies the used property acquisition requirement of paragraph (b)(3)(iii)(A)(*2*) of this section. Accordingly, assuming all other requirements of this section are satisfied, *BC's* purchase price of the machine qualifies for the additional first year depreciation deduction under this section.

(5) Because *BC* is not related to *BD* and *BA* is not related to *BD* within the meaning of section 179(d)(2)(A) and § 1.179-4(c)(1)(ii), or section 179(d)(2)(B) and § 1.179-4(c)(1)(iii) as of January 2, 2020, or October 1, 2019, *BD's* acquisition of the machine satisfies the used property acquisition requirement of paragraph (b)(3)(iii)(A)(*2*) of this section. Accordingly, assuming all other requirements of this section are satisfied, *BD's* purchase price of the machine qualifies for the additional first year depreciation deduction under this section.

(LL) *Example 38.* (*1*) In June 2018, *CA*, an individual, bought and placed in service a new machine from an unrelated party for use in his trade or business. In a series of related transactions, *CA* sells the machine to *CB* and *CB* places it in service on September 1, 2019, *CB* transfers the machine to *CC* in a transaction described in paragraph (g)(1)(iii) of this section and *CC* places it in service on November 1, 2019, and *CC* sells the machine to *CD* and *CD* places it in service on January 2, 2020. *CA* and *CB* are not related parties within the meaning of section 179(d)(2)(A) and § 1.179-4(c)(1)(ii). *CB* and *CC* are related parties within the meaning of section 179(d)(2)(B) and § 1.179-4(c)(1)(iii). *CB* and *CD* are related parties within the meaning of section 179(d)(2)(A) and § 1.179-4(c)(1)(ii), or section 179(d)(2)(B) and § 1.179-4(c)(1)(iii). *CC* and *CD* are not related parties within the meaning of section 179(d)(2)(A) and § 1.179-4(c)(1)(ii), or section 179(d)(2)(B) and § 1.179-4(c)(1)(iii). *CA* is not related to *CC* or to *CD* within the meaning of section 179(d)(2)(A) and § 1.179-4(c)(1)(ii). All parties are calendar-year taxpayers.

(2) *CA's* purchase of the machine in June 2018 satisfies the original use requirement of paragraph (b)(3)(ii) of this section and, assuming all other requirements of this section are met, *CA's* purchase price of the machine qualifies for the additional first year depreciation deduction under this section.

(3) Pursuant to paragraph (b)(3)(iii)(C)(*1*) of this section, a transferee tests its relationship with the transferor from which the transferee directly acquires the depreciable property, and with the original transferor of the depreciable property in the series. The relationship is tested when the transferee acquires, and immediately before the first transfer of, the depreciable property in the series. However, because *CB* placed in service and transferred the machine in the same taxable year in a transaction described in paragraph (g)(1)(iii) of this section, the section 168(i)(7) transaction between *CB* and *CC* is disregarded pursuant to paragraph (b)(3)(iii)(C)(2)(iii) of this section. As a result, the following relationships are tested under section 179(d)(2)(A) and (B): *CB* tests its relationship to *CA* as of September 1, 2019; and *CD* tests its relationship to *CB*, *CC*, and *CA* as of January 2, 2020, and September 1, 2019.

(4) Because *CA* is not related to *CB* within the meaning of section 179(d)(2)(A) and §1.179-4(c)(1)(ii) as of September 1, 2019, *CB's* acquisition of the machine satisfies the used property acquisition requirement of paragraph (b)(3)(iii)(A)(2) of this section. Accordingly, assuming all other requirements of this section are satisfied, *CB's* purchase price of the machine qualifies for the additional first year depreciation deduction under this section. Pursuant to paragraph (g)(1)(iii) of this section, *CB* is allocated 2/12 of its 100-percent additional first year depreciation deduction for the machine, and *CC* is allocated the remaining portion of *CB's* 100-percent additional first year depreciation deduction for the machine.

(5) *CC* is not related to *CD* and *CA* is not related to *CD* within the meaning of section 179(d)(2)(A) and §1.179-4(c)(1)(ii), or section 179(d)(2)(B) and §1.179-4(c)(1)(iii) as of January 2, 2020, or September 1, 2019. However, *CB* and *CD* are related parties within the meaning of section 179(d)(2)(A) and §1.179-4(c)(1)(ii), or section 179(d)(2)(B) and §1.179-4(c)(1)(iii) as of January 2, 2020, or September 1, 2019. Accordingly, *CD's* acquisition of the machine does not satisfy the used property acquisition requirements of paragraph (b)(3)(iii) of this section and is not eligible for the additional first year depreciation deduction.

(MM) *Example 39.* (*1*) In a series of related transactions, on January 2, 2018, *DA*, a corporation, bought and placed in service a new machine from an unrelated party for use in its trade or business. As part of the same series, *DB* purchases 100 percent of the stock of *DA* on January 2, 2019, and such stock acquisition meets the requirements of section 1504(a)(2). *DB* and *DA* were not related prior to the acquisition within the meaning of section 179(d)(2)(A) and §1.179-4(c)(1)(ii) or section 179(d)(2)(B) and §1.179-4(c)(1)(iii). Immediately after acquiring the *DA* stock, and *DB* liquidates *DA* under section 331. In the liquidating distribution, *DB* receives the machine that was acquired by *DA* on January 2, 2018. As part of the same series, on March 1, 2020, *DB* sells the machine to *DC* and *DC* places it in service. Throughout the series, *DC* is not related to *DB* or *DA* within the meaning of section 179(d)(2)(A) and §1.179-4(c)(1)(ii) or section 179(d)(2)(B) and §1.179-4(c)(1)(iii).

(2) *DA's* purchase of the machine on January 2, 2018, satisfies the original use requirement of paragraph (b)(3)(ii) of this section and, assuming all other requirements of this section are met, *DA's* purchase price of the machine qualifies for the additional first year depreciation deduction under this section.

(3) Pursuant to paragraph (b)(3)(iii)(C)(1) of this section, a transferee tests its relationship with the transferor from which the transferee directly acquires the depreciable property, and with the original transferor of the depreciable property in the series. The relationship is tested when the transferee acquires, and immediately before the first transfer of, the depreciable property in the series. Although *DA* is no longer in existence as of the date *DC* acquires the machine, pursuant to paragraph (b)(3)(iii)(C)(2)(*vi*) of this section, *DA* is deemed to be in existence at the time of each transfer for purposes of testing relationships under paragraph (b)(3)(iii)(C)(*1*). As a result, the following relationships are tested under section 179(d)(2)(A) and (B): *DB* tests its relationship to *DA* as of January 2, 2019, and January 2, 2018; and *DC* tests its relationship to *DB* and *DA* as of March 1, 2020, and January 2, 2018.

(4) Because *DB* acquired the machine in a series of related transactions in which *DB* acquired stock, meeting the requirements of section 1504(a)(2), of *DA* followed by a liquidation of *DA* under section 331, the relationship of *DB* and *DA* created thereof is disregarded for purposes of testing the relationship pursuant to paragraph (b)(3)(iii)(C)(2)(v) of this section. Therefore, *DA* is not related to *DB* within the meaning of section 179(d)(2)(A) and §1.179-4(c)(1)(ii) or section 179(d)(2)(B) and §1.179-4(c)(1)(iii) as of January 2, 2019, or January 2, 2018, and *DB's* acquisition of the machine satisfies the used property acquisition requirement of paragraph (b)(3)(iii)(A)(2)

of this section. Accordingly, assuming all other requirements of this section are satisfied, *DB's* depreciable basis of the machine as a result of the liquidation of *DA* qualifies for the additional first year depreciation deduction under this section.

(5) Because *DC* is not related to *DB* or *DA* within the meaning of section 179(d)(2)(A) and §1.179-4(c)(1)(ii) or section 179(d)(2)(B) and §1.179-4(c)(1)(iii) as of March 1, 2020, or January 2, 2018, *DC's* acquisition of the machine satisfies the used property acquisition requirements of paragraph (b)(3)(iii)(A)(2) of this section. Accordingly, assuming all other requirements of this section are satisfied, *DC's* purchase price of the machine qualifies for the additional first year depreciation deduction.

(NN) *Example 40.* (*1*) Pursuant to a series of related transactions, on January 2, 2018, *EA* bought and placed in service a new machine from an unrelated party for use in its trade or business. As part of the same series, *EA* sells the machine to *EB* and *EB* places it in service on January 2, 2019. As part of the same series, *EB* sells the machine to *EC* and *EC* places it in service on January 2, 2020. Throughout the series, *EA* is not related to *EB* or *EC* within the meaning of section 179(d)(2)(B) and §1.179-4(c)(1)(iii). *EB* and *EC* were related parties within the meaning of section 179(d)(2)(B) and §1.179-4(c)(1)(iii) until July 1, 2019, at which time, they ceased to be related.

(2) *EA's* purchase of the machine on January 2, 2018, satisfies the original use requirement of paragraph (b)(3)(ii) of this section and, assuming all other requirements of this section are met, *EA's* purchase price of the machines qualifies for the additional first year depreciation deduction under this section.

(3) Pursuant to paragraph (b)(3)(iii)(C)(1) of this section, a transferee tests its relationship with the transferor from which the transferee directly acquires the depreciable property, and with the original transferor of the depreciable property in the series. The relationship is tested when the transferee acquires, and immediately before the first transfer of, the depreciable property in the series. As a result, the following relationships are tested under section 179(d)(2)(A) and (B): *EB* tests its relationship to *EA* as of January 2, 2019, and January 2, 2018; and *EC* tests its relationship to *EA* and *EB* as of January 2, 2020, and January 2, 2018.

(4) Because *EA* is not related to *EB* within the meaning of section 179(d)(2)(B) and §1.179-4(c)(1)(iii) as of January 2, 2019, or January 2, 2018, *EB's* acquisition of the machine satisfies the used property acquisition requirement of paragraph (b)(3)(iii)(A)(2) of this section. Accordingly, assuming all other requirements of this section are satisfied, *EB's* purchase price of the machine qualifies for the additional first year depreciation deduction under this section.

(5) *EC* and *EA* are not related parties within the meaning of section 179(d)(2)(B) and §1.179-4(c)(1)(iii) as of January 2, 2020, or January 2, 2018. Within the meaning of section 179(d)(2)(B) and §1.179-4(c)(1)(iii), *EC* is not related to *EB* as of January 2, 2020; however, *EC* is related to *EB* as of January 2, 2018. Accordingly, *EC's* acquisition of the machine does not satisfy the used property acquisition requirement of paragraph (b)(3)(iii) of this section and is not eligible for the additional first year depreciation deduction.

(OO) *Example 41.* (*1*) The facts are the same as in *Example 40* of paragraph (b)(3)(vii)(NN)(1) of this section, except that instead of selling to *EC*, *EB* sells the machine to *EE*, and *EE* places in service on January 2, 2020, and *EE* sells the machine to *EC* and *EC* places in service on January 2, 2021. *EE* was not in existence until July 2019 and is not related to *EA* or *EB*.

(2) *EA's* purchase of the machine on January 2, 2018, satisfies the original use requirement of paragraph (b)(3)(ii) of this section and, assuming all other requirements of this section are met, *EA's* purchase price of the machine qualifies for the additional first year depreciation deduction under this section.

(3) Pursuant to paragraph (b)(3)(iii)(C)(*1*) of this section, a transferee tests its relationship with the transferor from which the transferee directly acquires the depreciable property, and with the original transferor of the depreciable property in the series. The relationship is tested when the transferee acquires, and immediately before the first transfer of, the depreciable property in the series. However, because *EE* was not in existence immediately prior to the first transfer of the depreciable property in the series, *EC* tests its relationship with *EB* and *EA* pursuant to paragraph (b)(3)(iii)(C)(2)(vii) of this section. As a result, the following relationships are tested under section 179(d)(2)(A) and (B): *EB* tests its relationship to *EA* as of January 2, 2019, and January 2, 2018; *EE* tests its relationship to *EA* and *EB* as of January 2, 2020, and January 2, 2018; and *EC* tests its relationship to *EA* and *EB* as of January 2, 2021, and January 2, 2018.

(4) Because *EA* is not related to *EB* within the meaning of section 179(d)(2)(B) and §1.179-4(c)(1)(iii) as of January 2, 2019, or January 2, 2018, *EB's* acquisition of the machine satisfies the used property acquisition requirement of paragraph (b)(3)(iii)(A)(2) of this section. Accordingly, assuming all other requirements of this section

are satisfied, *EB's* purchase price of the machine qualifies for the additional first year depreciation deduction under this section.

(5) Because *EE* is not related to *EA* or *EB* within the meaning of section 179(d)(2)(B) and §1.179-4(c)(1)(iii) as of January 2, 2020, or January 2, 2018, *EE's* acquisition of the machine satisfies the used property acquisition requirement of paragraph (b)(3)(iii)(A)(2) of this section. Accordingly, assuming all other requirements of this section are satisfied, *EE's* purchase price of the machine qualifies for the additional first year depreciation deduction under this section.

(6) Within the meaning of section 179(d)(2)(B) and §1.179-4(c)(1)(iii), *EC* is not related to *EA* as of January 2, 2021, or January 2, 2018; however, *EC* is related to *EB* as of January 2, 2018. Accordingly, *EC's* acquisition of the machine does not satisfy the used property acquisition requirement of paragraph (b)(3)(iii) of this section and is not eligible for the additional first year depreciation deduction.

(4) *Placed-in-service date.*—(i) *In general.*—Depreciable property will meet the requirements of this paragraph (b)(4) if the property is placed in service by the taxpayer for use in its trade or business or for production of income after September 27, 2017; and, except as provided in paragraphs (b)(2)(i)(A) and (D) of this section, before January 1, 2027, or, in the case of property described in section 168(k)(2)(B) or (C), before January 1, 2028.

(ii) *Specified plant.*—If the taxpayer has properly made an election to apply section 168(k)(5) for a specified plant, the requirements of this paragraph (b)(4) are satisfied only if the specified plant is planted before January 1, 2027, or is grafted before January 1, 2027, to a plant that has already been planted, by the taxpayer in the ordinary course of the taxpayer's farming business, as defined in section 263A(e)(4).

(iii) *Qualified film, television, or live theatrical production.*—(A) *Qualified film or television production.*—For purposes of this paragraph (b)(4), a qualified film or television production is treated as placed in service at the time of initial release or broadcast as defined under §1.181-1(a)(7). The taxpayer that places in service a qualified film or television production must be the owner, as defined in §1.181-1(a)(2), of the qualified film or television production.

(B) *Qualified live theatrical production.*—For purposes of this paragraph (b)(4), a qualified live theatrical production is treated as placed in service at the time of the initial live staged performance. The taxpayer that places in service a qualified live theatrical production must be the owner, as defined in paragraph (b)(2)(i)(F) of this section and in §1.181-1(a)(2), of the qualified live theatrical production.

(iv) *Syndication transaction.*—If new property is acquired and placed in service by a lessor, or if used property is acquired and placed in service by a lessor and the lessor and any predecessor did not previously have a depreciable interest in the used property, and the property is sold by the lessor or any subsequent purchaser within three months after the date the property was originally placed in service by the lessor (or, in the case of multiple units of property subject to the same lease, within three months after the date the final unit is placed in service, so long as the period between the time the first unit is placed in service and the time the last unit is placed in service does not exceed 12 months), and the user of the property after the last sale during this three-month period remains the same as when the property was originally placed in service by the lessor, the property is treated as originally placed in service by the purchaser of the property in the last sale during the three-month period but not earlier than the date of the last sale for purposes of sections 167 and 168, and §§1.46-3(d) and 1.167(a)-11(e)(1).

(v) *Technical termination of a partnership.*—For purposes of this paragraph (b)(4), in the case of a technical termination of a partnership under section 708(b)(1)(B) occurring in a taxable year beginning before January 1, 2018, qualified property placed in service by the terminated partnership during the taxable year of termination is treated as originally placed in service by the new partnership on the date the qualified property is contributed by the terminated partnership to the new partnership.

(vi) *Section 168(i)(7) transactions.*—For purposes of this paragraph (b)(4), if qualified property is transferred in a transaction described in section 168(i)(7) in the same taxable year that the qualified property is placed in service by the transferor, the transferred property is treated as originally placed in service on the date the transferor placed in service the qualified property. In the case of multiple transfers of qualified property in multiple transactions described in section 168(i)(7) in the same taxable year, the placed-in-service date of the transferred property is deemed to be the date on which the first transferor placed in service the qualified property.

(5) *Acquisition of property.*—(i) *In general.*—This paragraph (b)(5) provides rules for the acquisition requirements in section 13201(h) of the Act. These rules apply to all property, including self-constructed property or property described in section 168(k)(2)(B) or (C).

(ii) *Acquisition date.*—(A) *In general.*—Except as provided in paragraph (b)(5)(vi) of this section, depreciable property will meet the requirements of this paragraph (b)(5) if the property is acquired by the taxpayer after September 27, 2017, or is acquired by the taxpayer pursuant to a written binding contract entered into by the taxpayer after September 27, 2017. Property that is manufactured, constructed, or produced for the taxpayer by another person under a written binding contract that is entered into prior to the manufacture, construction, or production of the property for use by the taxpayer in its trade or business or for its production of income is not acquired pursuant to a written binding contract but is considered to be self-constructed property under this paragraph (b)(5). For determination of acquisition date, see paragraph (b)(5)(ii)(B) of this section for property acquired pursuant to a written binding contract, paragraph (b)(5)(iv) of this section for self-constructed property, and paragraph (b)(5)(v) of this section for property not acquired pursuant to a written binding contract.

(B) *Determination of acquisition date for property acquired pursuant to a written binding contract.*—Except as provided in paragraphs (b)(5)(vi) and (vii) of this section, the acquisition date of property that the taxpayer acquired pursuant to a written binding contract is the later of—

(1) The date on which the contract was entered into;

(2) The date on which the contract is enforceable under State law;

(3) If the contract has one or more cancellation periods, the date on which all cancellation periods end. For purposes of this paragraph (b)(5)(ii)(B)(3), a cancellation period is the number of days stated in the contract for any party to cancel the contract without penalty; or

(4) If the contract has one or more contingency clauses, the date on which all conditions subject to such clauses are satisfied. For purposes of this paragraph (b)(5)(ii)(B)(4), a contingency clause is one that provides for a condition (or conditions) or action (or actions) that is within the control of any party or a predecessor.

(iii) *Definition of binding contract.*—(A) *In general.*—Except as provided in paragraph (b)(5)(iii)(G) of this section, a contract is binding only if it is enforceable under State law against the taxpayer or a predecessor, and does not limit damages to a specified amount (for example, by use of a liquidated damages provision). For this purpose, any contractual provision that limits damages to an amount equal to at least 5 percent of the total contract price will not be treated as limiting damages to a specified amount. If a contract has multiple provisions that limit damages, only the provision with the highest damages is taken into account in determining whether the contract limits damages. Also, in determining whether a contract limits damages, the fact that there may be little or no damages because the contract price does not significantly differ from fair market value will not be taken into account. For example, if a taxpayer entered into an irrevocable written contract to purchase an asset for $100 and the contract did not contain a provision for liquidated damages, the contract is considered binding notwithstanding the fact that the asset had a fair market value of $99 and under local law the seller would only recover the difference in the event the purchaser failed to perform. If the contract provided for a full refund of the purchase price in lieu of any damages allowable by law in the event of breach or cancellation, the contract is not considered binding.

(B) *Conditions.*—Except as provided in paragraph (b)(5)(iii)(G) of this section, a contract is binding even if subject to a condition, as long as the condition is not within the control of either party or a predecessor. A contract will continue to be binding if the parties make insubstantial changes in its terms and conditions or if any term is to be determined by a standard beyond the control of either party. A contract that imposes significant obligations on the taxpayer or a predecessor will be treated as binding notwithstanding the fact that certain terms remain to be negotiated by the parties to the contract.

(C) *Options.*—An option to either acquire or sell property is not a binding contract.

(D) *Letter of intent.*—A letter of intent for an acquisition is not a binding contract.

(E) *Supply agreements.*—A binding contract does not include a supply or similar agreement if the amount and design specifications of the property to be purchased have not been specified. The contract will not be a binding contract for the property to be purchased until both the amount and the design specifications are specified. For example, if the provisions of a supply or similar agreement state the design specifications of the property to be purchased, a purchase order under the agreement for a specific number of assets is treated as a binding contract.

(F) *Components.*—A binding contract to acquire one or more components of a larger property will not be treated as a binding contract to acquire the larger property. If a binding contract to acquire the component does not satisfy the requirements of this paragraph (b)(5), the component does not qualify for the additional first year depreciation deduction under this section.

(G) *Acquisition of a trade or business or an entity.*—A contract to acquire all or substantially all of the assets of a trade or business or to acquire an entity (for example, a corporation, a partnership, or a limited liability company) is binding if it is enforceable under State law against the parties to the contract. The presence of a condition outside the control of the parties, including, for example, regulatory agency approval, will not prevent the contract from being a binding contract. Further, the fact that insubstantial terms remain to be negotiated by the parties to the contract, or that customary conditions remain to be satisfied, does not prevent the contract from being a binding contract. This paragraph (b)(5)(iii)(G) also applies to a contract for the sale of the stock of a corporation that is treated as an asset sale as a result of an election under section 338 or under section 336(e) made for a disposition described in § 1.336-2(b)(1).

(iv) *Self-constructed property.*—(A) *In general.*—If a taxpayer manufactures, constructs, or produces property for use by the taxpayer in its trade or business or for its production of income, the acquisition rules in paragraph (b)(5)(ii) of this section are treated as met for the property if the taxpayer begins manufacturing, constructing, or producing the property after September 27, 2017. Property that is manufactured, constructed, or produced for the taxpayer by another person under a written binding contract, as defined in paragraph (b)(5)(iii) of this section, that is entered into prior to the manufacture, construction, or production of the property for use by the taxpayer in its trade or business or for its production of income is considered to be manufactured, constructed, or produced by the taxpayer. If a taxpayer enters into a written binding contract, as defined in paragraph (b)(5)(iii) of this section, before September 28, 2017, with another person to manufacture, construct, or produce property and the manufacture, construction, or production of this property begins after September 27, 2017, the acquisition rules in paragraph (b)(5)(ii) of this section are met.

(B) *When does manufacture, construction, or production begin.*—(1) *In general.*—For purposes of paragraph (b)(5)(iv)(A) of this section, manufacture, construction, or production of property begins when physical work of a significant nature begins. Physical work does not include preliminary activities such as planning or designing, securing financing, exploring, or researching. The determination of when physical work of a significant nature begins depends on the facts and circumstances. For example, if a retail motor fuels outlet is to be constructed on-site, construction begins when physical work of a significant nature commences at the site; that is, when work begins on the excavation for footings, pouring the pads for the outlet, or the driving of foundation pilings into the ground. Preliminary work, such as clearing a site, test drilling to determine soil condition, or excavation to change the contour of the land (as distinguished from excavation for footings) does not constitute the beginning of construction. However, if a retail motor fuels outlet is to be assembled on-site from modular units manufactured off-site and delivered to the site where the outlet will be used, manufacturing begins when physical work of a significant nature commences at the off-site location.

(2) *Safe harbor.*—For purposes of paragraph (b)(5)(iv)(B)(1) of this section, a taxpayer may choose to determine when physical work of a significant nature begins in accordance with this paragraph (b)(5)(iv)(B)(2). Physical work of a significant nature will be considered to begin at the time the taxpayer incurs (in the case of an accrual basis taxpayer) or pays (in the case of a cash basis taxpayer) more than 10 percent of the total cost of the property, excluding the cost of any land and preliminary activities such as planning or designing, securing financing, exploring, or researching. When property is manufactured, constructed, or produced for the taxpayer by another person, this safe harbor test must be satisfied by the taxpayer. For example, if a retail motor fuels outlet or other facility is to be constructed for an accrual basis taxpayer by another person for the total cost of $200,000, excluding the cost of any land and preliminary activities such as planning or designing, securing financing, exploring, or researching, construction is deemed to begin for purposes of this paragraph (b)(5)(iv)(B)(2) when the taxpayer has incurred more than 10 percent (more than $20,000) of the total cost of the property. A taxpayer chooses to apply this paragraph

(b)(5)(iv)(B)(2) by filing a Federal income tax return for the placed-in-service year of the property that determines when physical work of a significant nature begins consistent with this paragraph (b)(5)(iv)(B)(2).

(C) *Components of self-constructed property.*—(1) *Acquired components.*—If a binding contract, as defined in paragraph (b)(5)(iii) of this section, to acquire a component does not satisfy the requirements of paragraph (b)(5)(ii) of this section, the component does not qualify for the additional first year depreciation deduction under this section. A binding contract described in the preceding sentence to acquire one or more components of a larger self-constructed property will not preclude the larger self-constructed property from satisfying the acquisition rules in paragraph (b)(5)(iv)(A) of this section. Accordingly, the unadjusted depreciable basis of the larger self-constructed property that is eligible for the additional first year depreciation deduction under this section, assuming all other requirements are met, must not include the unadjusted depreciable basis of any component that does not satisfy the requirements of paragraph (b)(5)(ii) of this section. If the manufacture, construction, or production of the larger self-constructed property begins before September 28, 2017, the larger self-constructed property and any acquired components related to the larger self-constructed property do not qualify for the additional first year depreciation deduction under this section. If a binding contract to acquire the component is entered into after September 27, 2017, but the manufacture, construction, or production of the larger self-constructed property does not begin before January 1, 2027, the component qualifies for the additional first year depreciation deduction under this section, assuming all other requirements are met, but the larger self-constructed property does not, except as provided in paragraph (c) of this section.

(2) *Self-constructed components.*—If the manufacture, construction, or production of a component does not satisfy the requirements of this paragraph (b)(5)(iv), the component does not qualify for the additional first year depreciation deduction under this section. However, if the manufacture, construction, or production of a component does not satisfy the requirements of this paragraph (b)(5)(iv), but the manufacture, construction, or production of the larger self-constructed property satisfies the requirements of this paragraph (b)(5)(iv), the larger self-constructed property qualifies for the additional first year depreciation deduction under this section, assuming all other requirements are met, even though the component does not qualify for the additional first year depreciation deduction under this section. Accordingly, the unadjusted depreciable basis of the larger self-constructed property that is eligible for the additional first year depreciation deduction under this section, assuming all other requirements are met, must not include the unadjusted depreciable basis of any component that does not qualify for the additional first year depreciation deduction under this section. If the manufacture, construction, or production of the larger self-constructed property began before September 28, 2017, the larger self-constructed property and any self-constructed components related to the larger self-constructed property do not qualify for the additional first year depreciation deduction under this section. If the manufacture, construction, or production of a component begins after September 27, 2017, but the manufacture, construction, or production of the larger self-constructed property does not begin before January 1, 2027, the component qualifies for the additional first year depreciation deduction under this section, assuming all other requirements are met, but the larger self-constructed property does not, except as provided in paragraph (c) of this section.

(v) *Determination of acquisition date for property not acquired pursuant to a written binding contract.*—Except as provided in paragraphs (b)(5)(iv), (vi), and (vii) of this section, the acquisition date of property that the taxpayer acquires pursuant to a contract that does not meet the definition of a written binding contract in paragraph (b)(5)(iii) of this section, is the date on which the taxpayer paid, in the case of a cash basis taxpayer, or incurred, in the case of an accrual basis taxpayer, more than 10 percent of the total cost of the property, excluding the cost of any land and preliminary activities such as planning and designing, securing financing, exploring, or researching. The preceding sentence also applies to property that is manufactured, constructed, or produced for the taxpayer by another person under a written contract that does not meet the definition of a binding contract in paragraph (b)(5)(iii) of this section, and that is entered into prior to the manufacture, construction, or production of the property for use by the taxpayer in its trade or business or for its production of income. This paragraph (b)(5)(v) does not apply to an acquisition described in paragraph (b)(5)(iii)(G) of this section.

(vi) *Qualified film, television, or live theatrical production.*—(A) *Qualified film or television production.*—For purposes of section 13201(h)(1)(A) of the Act, a qualified film or television production is treated as acquired on the date principal photography commences.

(B) *Qualified live theatrical production.*—For purposes of section 13201(h)(1)(A) of the Act, a qualified live theatrical production is treated as acquired on the date when all of the necessary elements for producing the live theatrical production are secured. These elements may include a script, financing, actors, set, scenic and costume designs, advertising agents, music, and lighting.

(vii) *Specified plant.*—If the taxpayer has properly made an election to apply section 168(k)(5) for a specified plant, the requirements of this paragraph (b)(5) are satisfied if the specified plant is planted after September 27, 2017, or is grafted after September 27, 2017, to a plant that has already been planted, by the taxpayer in the ordinary course of the taxpayer's farming business, as defined in section 263A(e)(4).

(viii) *Examples.*—The application of this paragraph (b)(5) is illustrated by the following examples. Unless the facts specifically indicate otherwise, assume that the parties are not related within the meaning of section 179(d)(2)(A) or (B) and §1.179-4(c), paragraph (c) of this section does not apply, and the parties do not have predecessors:

(A) *Example 1.* On September 1, 2017, *BB*, a corporation, entered into a written agreement with *CC*, a manufacturer, to purchase 20 new lamps for $100 each within the next two years. Although the agreement specifies the number of lamps to be purchased, the agreement does not specify the design of the lamps to be purchased. Accordingly, the agreement is not a binding contract pursuant to paragraph (b)(5)(iii)(E) of this section.

(B) *Example 2.* The facts are the same as in *Example 1* of paragraph (b)(5)(viii)(A) of this section. On December 1, 2017, *BB* placed a purchase order with *CC* to purchase 20 new model XPC5 lamps for $100 each for a total amount of $2,000. Because the agreement specifies the number of lamps to be purchased and the purchase order specifies the design of the lamps to be purchased, the purchase order placed by *BB* with *CC* on December 1, 2017, is a binding contract pursuant to paragraph (b)(5)(iii)(E) of this section. Accordingly, assuming all other requirements are met, the cost of the 20 lamps qualifies for the 100-percent additional first year depreciation deduction.

(C) *Example 3.* The facts are the same as in *Example 1* of paragraph (b)(5)(viii)(A) of this section, except that the written agreement between *BB* and *CC* is to purchase 100 model XPC5 lamps for $100 each within the next two years. Because this agreement specifies the amount and design of the lamps to be purchased, the agreement is a binding contract pursuant to paragraph (b)(5)(iii)(E) of this section. However, because the agreement was entered into before September 28, 2017, no lamp acquired by *BB* under this contract qualifies for the 100-percent additional first year depreciation deduction.

(D) *Example 4.* On September 1, 2017, *DD* began constructing a retail motor fuels outlet for its own use. On November 1, 2018, *DD* ceases construction of the retail motor fuels outlet prior to its completion. Between September 1, 2017, and November 1, 2018, *DD* incurred $3,000,000 of expenditures for the construction of the retail motor fuels outlet. On May 1, 2019, *DD* resumed construction of the retail motor fuels outlet and completed its construction on August 31, 2019. Between May 1, 2019, and August 31, 2019, *DD* incurred another $1,600,000 of expenditures to complete the construction of the retail motor fuels outlet and, on September 1, 2019, *DD* placed the retail motor fuels outlet in service. None of *DD*'s total expenditures of $4,600,000 qualify for the 100-percent additional first year depreciation deduction because, pursuant to paragraph (b)(5)(iv)(A) of this section, *DD* began constructing the retail motor fuels outlet before September 28, 2017.

(E) *Example 5.* The facts are the same as in *Example 4* of paragraph (b)(5)(viii)(D) of this section except that *DD* began constructing the retail motor fuels outlet for its own use on October 1, 2017, and *DD* incurred the $3,000,000 between October 1, 2017, and November 1, 2018. *DD*'s total expenditures of $4,600,000 qualify for the 100-percent additional first year depreciation deduction because, pursuant to paragraph (b)(5)(iv)(A) of this section, *DD* began constructing the retail motor fuels outlet after September 27, 2017, and *DD* placed the retail motor fuels outlet in service on September 1, 2019. Accordingly, assuming all other requirements are met, the additional first year depreciation deduction for the retail motor fuels outlet will be $4,600,000, computed as $4,600,000 multiplied by 100 percent.

(F) *Example 6.* On August 15, 2017, *EE*, an accrual basis taxpayer, entered into a written binding contract with *FF* to manufacture an aircraft described in section 168(k)(2)(C) for use in *EE*'s trade or business. *FF* begins to manufacture the aircraft on October 1, 2017. The completed aircraft is delivered to *EE* on February 15, 2018, at which time *EE* incurred the total cost of the aircraft. *EE* places the aircraft in service on March 1, 2018. Pursuant to paragraphs (b)(5)(ii)(A) and (b)(5)(iv)(A) of this section, the aircraft is considered to be manufactured by *EE*. Because *EE* began manufacturing the aircraft after September 27, 2017, the aircraft qualifies for the 100-percent additional first year depreciation deduction, assuming all other requirements are met.

(G) *Example 7.* On June 1, 2017, *HH* entered into a written binding contract with GG to acquire a new component part of property that is being constructed by *HH* for its own use in its trade or business. *HH* commenced construction of the property in November 2017, and placed the property in service in November 2018. Because *HH* entered into a written binding contract to acquire a component part prior to September 28, 2017, pursuant to paragraphs (b)(5)(ii) and (b)(5)(iv)(C)(1) of this section, the component part does not qualify for the 100-percent additional first year depreciation deduction. However, pursuant to paragraphs (b)(5)(iv)(A) and (b)(5)(iv)(C)(1) of this section, the property constructed by *HH* will qualify for the 100-percent additional first year depreciation deduction, because construction of the property began after September 27, 2017, assuming all other requirements are met. Accordingly, the unadjusted depreciable basis of the property that is eligible for the 100-percent additional first year depreciation deduction must not include the unadjusted depreciable basis of the component part.

(H) *Example 8.* The facts are the same as in *Example 7* of paragraph (b)(5)(viii)(G) of this section except that *HH* entered into the written binding contract with GG to acquire the new component part on September 30, 2017, and *HH* commenced construction of the property on August 1, 2017. Pursuant to paragraphs (b)(5)(iv)(A) and (C) of this section, neither the property constructed by *HH* nor the component part will qualify for the 100-percent additional first year depreciation deduction, because *HH* began construction of the property prior to September 28, 2017.

(I) *Example 9.* On September 1, 2017, II acquired and placed in service equipment. On January 15, 2018, II sells the equipment to *JJ* and leases the property back from *JJ* in a sale-leaseback transaction. Pursuant to paragraph (b)(5)(ii) of this section, II's cost of the equipment does not qualify for the 100-percent additional first year depreciation deduction because II acquired the equipment prior to September 28, 2017. However, *JJ* acquired used equipment from an unrelated party after September 27, 2017, and, assuming all other requirements are met, *JJ*'s cost of the used equipment qualifies for the 100-percent additional first year depreciation deduction for *JJ*.

(J) *Example 10.* On July 1, 2017, *KK* began constructing property for its own use in its trade or business. *KK* placed this property in service on September 15, 2017. On January 15, 2018, *KK* sells the property to *LL* and leases the property back from *LL* in a sale-leaseback transaction. Pursuant to paragraph (b)(5)(iv) of this section, *KK*'s cost of the property does not qualify for the 100-percent additional first year depreciation deduction because *KK* began construction of the property prior to September 28, 2017. However, *LL* acquired used property from an unrelated party after September 27, 2017, and, assuming all other requirements are met, *LL*'s cost of the used property qualifies for the 100-percent additional first year depreciation deduction for *LL*.

(K) *Example 11.* *MM*, a calendar year taxpayer, is engaged in a trade or business described in section 163(j)(7)(A)(iv). In December 2018, *MM* began constructing a new electric generation power plant for its own use. *MM* placed in service this new power plant, including all component parts, in 2020. Even though *MM* began constructing the power plant after September 27, 2017, none of *MM*'s total expenditures of the power plant qualify for the additional first year depreciation deduction under this section because, pursuant to paragraph (b)(2)(ii)(F) of this section, the power plant is property that is primarily used in a trade or business described in section 163(j)(7)(A)(iv) and the power plant was placed in service in *MM*'s taxable year beginning after 2017.

(c) *Election for components of larger self-constructed property for which the manufacture, construction, or production begins before September 28, 2017.*—(1) *In general.*—A taxpayer may elect to treat any acquired or self-constructed component, as described in paragraph (c)(3) of this section, of the larger self-constructed property, as described in paragraph (c)(2) of this section, as being eligible for the additional first year depreciation deduction under this section, assuming all requirements of section 168(k) and this section are met. The taxpayer may make this election for one or more such components.

(2) *Eligible larger self-constructed property.*—(i) *In general.*—Solely for purposes of this paragraph (c), a larger self-constructed property is property that is manufactured, constructed, or produced by the taxpayer for its own use in its trade or business or production of income. Solely for purposes of this paragraph (c), property that is manufactured, constructed, or produced for the taxpayer by another person under a written binding contract, as defined in paragraph (b)(5)(iii) of this section, or under a written contract that does not meet the definition of a binding contract in paragraph (b)(5)(iii) of this section, that is entered into prior to the manufacture, construc-

tion, or production of the property for use by the taxpayer in its trade or business or production of income is considered to be manufactured, constructed, or produced by the taxpayer. Except as provided in paragraph (c)(2)(iv) of this section, such larger self-constructed property must be property—

(A) That is described in paragraph (b)(2)(i)(A), (B), (C), or (D) of this section. Solely for purposes of the preceding sentence, the requirement that property has to be acquired after September 27, 2017, is disregarded;

(B) That meets the requirements under paragraph (b) of this section, determined without regard to the acquisition date requirement in paragraph (b)(5) of this section; and

(C) For which the taxpayer begins the manufacture, construction, or production before September 28, 2017.

(ii) *Residential rental property or nonresidential real property.*—If the taxpayer constructs, manufactures, or produces residential rental property or nonresidential real property, as defined in section 168(e)(2), or an improvement to such property, for use in its trade or business or production of income, all property that is constructed, manufactured, or produced as part of such residential rental property, nonresidential real property, or improvement, as applicable, and that is described in paragraph (c)(2)(i)(A) of this section is the larger self-constructed property for purposes of applying the rules in this paragraph (c).

(iii) *Beginning of manufacturing, construction, or production.*— Solely for purposes of paragraph (c)(2)(i)(C) of this section, the determination of when manufacture, construction, or production of the larger self-constructed property begins is made in accordance with the rules in paragraph (b)(5)(iv)(B) of this section if the larger self-constructed property is manufactured, constructed, or produced by the taxpayer for its own use in its trade or business or production of income, or is manufactured, constructed, or produced for the taxpayer by another person under a written binding contract, as defined in paragraph (b)(5)(iii) of this section, that is entered into prior to the manufacture, construction, or production of the property for use by the taxpayer in its trade or business or production of income. If the larger self-constructed property is manufactured, constructed, or produced for the taxpayer by another person under a written contract that does not meet the definition of a binding contract in paragraph (b)(5)(iii) of this section, that is entered into prior to the manufacture, construction, or production of the property for use by the taxpayer in its trade or business or production of income, the determination of when manufacture, construction, or production of the larger self-constructed property begins is made in accordance with the rules in paragraph (b)(5)(v) of this section. If the taxpayer enters into a written binding contract, as defined in paragraph (b)(5)(iii) of this section, before September 28, 2017, with another person to manufacture, construct, or produce the larger self-constructed property and the manufacture, construction, or production of this property begins after September 27, 2017, as determined under paragraph (b)(5)(iv)(B) of this section, this paragraph (c) does not apply. If the taxpayer enters into a written contract that does not meet the definition of a binding contract in paragraph (b)(5)(iii) of this section before September 28, 2017, with another person to manufacture, construct, or produce the larger self-constructed property and the manufacture, construction, or production of this property begins after September 27, 2017, as determined under paragraph (b)(5)(v) of this section, this paragraph (c) does not apply.

(iv) *Exception.*—This paragraph (c) does not apply to any larger self-constructed property that is included in a class of property for which the taxpayer made an election under section 168(k)(7) (formerly section 168(k)(2)(D)(iii)) not to deduct the additional first year depreciation deduction.

(3) *Eligible components.*—(i) *In general.*—Solely for purposes of this paragraph (c), a component of the larger self-constructed property, as described in paragraph (c)(2) of this section, must be qualified property under section 168(k)(2) and paragraph (b) of this section. Solely for purposes of the preceding sentence, a component will satisfy the acquisition date requirement in paragraph (b)(5) of this section if it satisfies the requirements in paragraph (c)(3)(ii) or (iii) of this section, as applicable.

(ii) *Acquired components.*—If a component of the larger self-constructed property is acquired pursuant to a written binding contract, as defined in paragraph (b)(5)(iii) of this section, the component must be acquired by the taxpayer after September 27, 2017, as determined under the rules in paragraph (b)(5)(ii)(B) of this section. If a component of the larger self-constructed property is acquired pursuant to a written contract that does not meet the definition of a binding contract in paragraph (b)(5)(iii) of this section, the component must be acquired by the taxpayer after September 27, 2017, as determined under the rules in paragraph (b)(5)(v) of this section.

(iii) *Self-constructed components.*—The manufacture, construction, or production of a component of a larger self-constructed property must begin after September 27, 2017. The determination of when manufacture, construction, or production of the component begins is made in accordance with the rules in—

(A) Paragraph (b)(5)(iv)(B) of this section if the component is manufactured, constructed, or produced by the taxpayer for its own use in its trade or business or for its production of income, or is manufactured, constructed, or produced for the taxpayer by another person under a written binding contract, as defined in paragraph (b)(5)(iii) of this section, that is entered into prior to the manufacture, construction, or production of the component for use by the taxpayer in its trade or business or for its production of income; or

(B) (B) Paragraph (b)(5)(v) of this section if the component is manufactured, constructed, or produced for the taxpayer by another person under a written contract that does not meet the definition of a binding contract in paragraph (b)(5)(iii) of this section, that is entered into prior to the manufacture, construction, or production of the component for use by the taxpayer in its trade or business or for its production of income.

(4) *Special rules.*—(i) *Installation costs.*—If the taxpayer pays, in the case of a cash basis taxpayer, or incurs, in the case of an accrual basis taxpayer, costs, including labor costs, to install a component of the larger self-constructed property, as described in paragraph (c)(2) of this section, such costs are eligible for the additional first year depreciation under this section, assuming all requirements are met, only if the component being installed meets the requirements in paragraph (c)(3) of this section.

(ii) *Property described in section 168(k)(2)(B).*—The rules in paragraph (e)(1)(iii) of this section apply for determining the unadjusted depreciable basis, as defined in § 1.168(b)-1(a)(3), of larger self-constructed property described in paragraph (c)(2) of this section and in section 168(k)(2)(B).

(5) *Computation of additional first year depreciation deduction.*— (i) *Election is made.*—Before determining the allowable additional first year depreciation deduction for the larger self-constructed property, as described in paragraph (c)(2) of this section, for which the taxpayer makes the election specified in this paragraph (c) for one or more components of such property, the taxpayer must determine the portion of the unadjusted depreciable basis, as defined in § 1.168(b)-1(a)(3), of the larger self-constructed property, including all components, attributable to the component that meets the requirements of paragraphs (c)(3) and (c)(4)(i) of this section (component basis). The additional first year depreciation deduction for the component basis is determined by multiplying such component basis by the applicable percentage for the placed-in-service year of the larger self-constructed property. The additional first year depreciation deduction, if any, for the remaining unadjusted depreciable basis of the larger self-constructed property, as described in paragraph (c)(2) of this section, is determined under section 168(k), as in effect on the day before the date of the enactment of the Act, and section 168(k)(8). For purposes of this paragraph (c), the remaining unadjusted depreciable basis of the larger self-constructed property is equal to the unadjusted depreciable basis, as defined in § 1.168(b)-1(a)(3), of the larger self-constructed property, including all components, reduced by the sum of the component basis of the components for which the taxpayer makes the election specified in this paragraph (c).

(ii) *Election is not made.*—If the taxpayer does not make the election specified in this paragraph (c), the additional first year depreciation deduction, if any, for the larger self-constructed property, including all components, is determined under section 168(k), as in effect on the day before the date of the enactment of the Act, and section 168(k)(8).

(6) *Time and manner for making election.*—(i) *Time for making election.*—The election specified in this paragraph (c) must be made by the due date, including extensions, of the Federal tax return for the taxable year in which the taxpayer placed in service the larger self-constructed property.

(ii) *Manner of making election.*—The election specified in this paragraph (c) must be made by attaching a statement to such return indicating that the taxpayer is making the election provided in this paragraph (c) and whether the taxpayer is making the election for all or some of the components described in paragraph (c)(3) of this section. The election is made separately by each person owning qualified property (for example, for each member of a consolidated group by the agent for the group (within the meaning of § 1.1502-77(a) and (c)), by the partnership (including a lower-tier partnership), or by the S corporation).

(7) *Revocation of election.*—(i) *In general.*—Except as provided in paragraph (c)(7)(ii) of this section, the election specified in this para-

graph (c), once made, may be revoked only by filing a request for a private letter ruling and obtaining the Commissioner of Internal Revenue's written consent to revoke the election. The Commissioner may grant a request to revoke the election if the taxpayer acted reasonably and in good faith, and the revocation will not prejudice the interests of the Government. See generally § 301.9100-3 of this chapter. The election specified in this paragraph (c) may not be revoked through a request under section 446(e) to change the taxpayer's method of accounting.

(ii) *Automatic 6-month extension.*—If a taxpayer made the election specified in this paragraph (c), an automatic extension of 6 months from the due date of the taxpayer's Federal tax return, excluding extensions, for the placed-in-service year of the larger self-constructed property is granted to revoke that election, provided the taxpayer timely filed the taxpayer's Federal tax return for that placed-in-service year and, within this 6-month extension period, the taxpayer, and all taxpayers whose tax liability would be affected by the election, file an amended Federal tax return for the placed-in-service year in a manner that is consistent with the revocation of the election.

(8) *Additional procedural guidance.*—The IRS may publish procedural guidance in the Internal Revenue Bulletin (see § 601.601(d)(2)(ii)(b) of this chapter) that provides alternative procedures for complying with paragraph (c)(6) or (c)(7)(i) of this section.

(9) *Examples.*—The application of this paragraph (c) is illustrated by the following examples. Unless the facts specifically indicate otherwise, assume that the larger self-constructed property is described in paragraph (c)(2) of this section, the components that are acquired or self-constructed after September 27, 2017, are described in paragraph (c)(3) of this section, the taxpayer is an accrual basis taxpayer, and none of the costs paid or incurred after September 27, 2017, are for the installation of components that do not meet the requirements of paragraph (c)(3) of this section.

(i) *Example 1.*—(A) BC, a calendar year taxpayer, is engaged in a trade or business described in section 163(j)(7)(A)(iv) and §§ 1.163(j)-1(b)(15)(i) and 1.163(j)-10(c)(3)(iii)(C)(3). In December 2015, BC decided to construct an electric generation power plant for its own use. This plant is property described in section 168(k)(2)(B) as in effect on the day before the date of the enactment of the Act. However, the turbine for the plant had to be manufactured by another person for BC. In January 2016, BC entered into a written binding contract with CD to acquire the turbine. BC received the completed turbine in August 2017 at which time BC incurred the cost of the turbine. The cost of the turbine is 11 percent of the total cost of the electric generation power plant to be constructed by BC. BC began constructing the electric generation power plant in October 2017 and placed in service this new power plant, including all component parts, in 2020.

(B) The larger self-constructed property is the electric generation power plant to be constructed by BC. For determining if the construction of this power plant begins before September 28, 2017, paragraph (b)(5)(iv)(B) of this section provides that manufacture, construction, or production of property begins when physical work of a significant nature begins. BC uses the safe harbor test in paragraph (b)(5)(iv)(B)(2) of this section to determine when physical work of a significant nature begins for the electric generation power plant. Because the turbine that was manufactured by CD for BC is more than 10 percent of the total cost of the electric generation power plant, physical work of a significant nature for this plant began before September 28, 2017.

(C) The power plant is described in section 168(k)(9)(A) and paragraph (b)(2)(ii)(F) of this section and, therefore, is not larger self-constructed property eligible for the election pursuant to paragraph (c)(2)(i)(B) of this section. Accordingly, none of BC's expenditures for components of the power plant that are acquired or self-constructed after September 27, 2017, are eligible for the election specified in this paragraph (c). Assuming all requirements are met under section 168(k)(2) as in effect on the day before the date of the enactment of the Act, the unadjusted depreciable basis of the power plant, including all components, attributable to its construction before January 1, 2020, is eligible for the 30-percent additional first year depreciation deduction pursuant to section 168(k)(8).

(ii) *Example 2.*—(A) In August 2017, BD, a calendar-year taxpayer, entered into a written binding contract with CE for CE to manufacture a locomotive for BD for use in its trade or business. Before September 28, 2017, BD acquired or self-constructed components of the locomotive. These components cost $500,000, which is more than 10 percent of the total cost of the locomotive, and BD incurred such costs before September 28, 2017. After September 27, 2017, BD acquired or self-constructed components of the locomotive and these components cost $4,000,000. In February 2019, CE deliv-

ered the locomotive to BD and BD placed in service the locomotive. The total cost of the locomotive is $4,500,000. The locomotive is property described in section 168(k)(2)(B) as in effect on the day before the date of the enactment of the Act. On its timely filed Federal income tax return for 2019, BD made the election specified in this paragraph (c).

(B) The larger self-constructed property is the locomotive being manufactured by CE for BD. For determining if the manufacturing of this locomotive begins before September 28, 2017, paragraph (b)(5)(iv)(B) of this section provides that manufacture, construction, or production of property begins when physical work of a significant nature begins. BD uses the safe harbor test in paragraph (b)(5)(iv)(B)(2) of this section to determine when physical work of a significant nature begins for the locomotive. Because BD had incurred more than 10 percent of the total cost of the locomotive before September 28, 2017, physical work of a significant nature for this locomotive began before September 28, 2017.

(C) Because BD made the election specified in this paragraph (c), the cost of $4,000,000 for the locomotive's components acquired or self-constructed after September 27, 2017, qualifies for the 100-percent additional first year depreciation deduction under this section, assuming all other requirements are met. The remaining cost of the locomotive is $500,000 and such amount qualifies for the 40-percent additional first year depreciation deduction pursuant to section 168(k)(8), assuming all other requirements in section 168(k) as in effect on the day before the date of the enactment of the Act are met.

(iii) *Example 3.*—(A) In February 2016, BF, a calendar-year taxpayer, entered into a written binding contract with CG for CG to manufacture a vessel for BF for use in its trade or business. Before September 28, 2017, BF acquired or self-constructed components for the vessel. These components cost $30,000,000, which is more than 10 percent of the total cost of the vessel, and BF incurred such costs before September 28, 2017. After September 27, 2017, BF acquired or self-constructed components for the vessel and these components cost $15,000,000. In February 2021, CG delivered the vessel to BF and BF placed in service the vessel. The vessel is property described in section 168(k)(2)(B) as in effect on the day before the date of the enactment of the Act. The total cost of the vessel is $45,000,000. On its timely filed Federal income tax return for 2021, BF made the election specified in this paragraph (c).

(B) The larger self-constructed property is the vessel being manufactured by CG for BF. For determining if the manufacturing of this vessel begins before September 28, 2017, paragraph (b)(5)(iv)(B) of this section provides that manufacture, construction, or production of property begins when physical work of a significant nature begins. BF uses the safe harbor test in paragraph (b)(5)(iv)(B)(2) of this section to determine when physical work of a significant nature begins for the vessel. Because BF had incurred more than 10 percent of the total cost of the vessel before September 28, 2017, physical work of a significant nature for this vessel began before September 28, 2017.

(C) Because BF made the election specified in this paragraph (c), the cost of $15,000,000 for the vessel's components acquired or self-constructed after September 27, 2017, qualifies for the 100-percent additional first year depreciation deduction under this section, assuming all other requirements are met. Pursuant to section 168(k)(8) and because BF placed in service the vessel after 2020, none of the remaining cost of the vessel is eligible for any additional first year depreciation deduction under section 168(k) and this section nor under section 168(k) as in effect on the day before the date of the enactment of the Act.

(iv) *Example 4.*—(A) In March 2017, BG, a calendar year taxpayer, entered into a written contract with CH for CH to construct a building for BG to use in its retail business. This written contract does not meet the definition of a binding contract in paragraph (b)(5)(iii) of this section. In September 2019, the construction of the building was completed and placed in service by BG. The total cost is $10,000,000. Of this amount, $3,000,000 is the total cost for all section 1245 properties constructed as part of the building, and $7,000,000 is for the building. Under section 168(e), section 1245 properties in the total amount of $2,400,000 are 5-year property and in the total amount of $600,000 are 7-year property. The building is nonresidential real property under section 168(e). Before September 28, 2017, BG acquired or self-constructed certain components and the total cost of these components is $500,000 for the section 1245 properties and $3,000,000 for the building. BG incurred these costs before September 28, 2017. After September 27, 2017, BG acquired or self-constructed the remaining components of the section 1245 properties and these components cost $2,500,000. BG incurred these costs of $2,500,000 after September 27, 2017. On its timely filed Federal income tax return for 2019, BG made the election specified in this paragraph (c).

(B) All section 1245 properties are constructed as part of the construction of the building and are described in paragraph (b)(2)(i)(A) of this section. The building is not described in paragraph (b)(2)(i)(A), (B), (C), or (D) of this section. As a result, under paragraph (c)(2)(ii) of this section, the larger self-constructed property is all section 1245 properties with a total cost of $3,000,000. For determining if the construction of these section 1245 properties begins before September 28, 2017, paragraph (b)(5)(v) of this section provides that manufacture, construction, or production of property begins when the taxpayer incurs more than 10 percent of the total cost of the property. Because *BG* incurred more than 10 percent of the total cost of the section 1245 properties before September 28, 2017, construction of the section 1245 properties began before September 28, 2017.

(C) Because *BG* made the election specified in this paragraph (c), the cost of $2,500,000 for the section 1245 components acquired or self-constructed by *BG* after September 27, 2017, qualifies for the 100-percent additional first year depreciation deduction under this section, assuming all other requirements are met. The remaining cost of the section 1245 components is $500,000 and such amount qualifies for the 30-percent additional first year depreciation deduction pursuant to section 168(k)(8), assuming all other requirements in section 168(k), as in effect on the day before the date of the enactment of the Act, are met. Because the building is not qualified property under section 168(k), as in effect on the day before the date of the enactment of the Act, none of the cost of $7,000,000 for the building is eligible for any additional first year depreciation deduction under section 168(k) and this section or under section 168(k), as in effect on the day before the date of the enactment of the Act.

(d) *Property described in section 168(k)(2)(B) or (C)*.—(1) *In general.*—Property described in section 168(k)(2)(B) or (C) will meet the acquisition requirements of section 168(k)(2)(B)(i)(III) or (k)(2)(C)(i) if the property is acquired by the taxpayer before January 1, 2027, or acquired by the taxpayer pursuant to a written binding contract that is entered into before January 1, 2027. Property described in section 168(k)(2)(B) or (C), including its components, also must meet the acquisition requirement in section 13201(h)(1)(A) of the Act (for further guidance, see paragraph (b)(5) of this section).

(2) *Definition of binding contract.*—For purposes of this paragraph (d), the rules in paragraph (b)(5)(iii) of this section for a binding contract apply.

(3) *Self-constructed property.*—(i) *In general.*—If a taxpayer manufactures, constructs, or produces property for use by the taxpayer in its trade or business or for its production of income, the acquisition rules in paragraph (d)(1) of this section are treated as met for the property if the taxpayer begins manufacturing, constructing, or producing the property before January 1, 2027. Property that is manufactured, constructed, or produced for the taxpayer by another person under a written binding contract, as defined in paragraph (b)(5)(iii) of this section, that is entered prior to the manufacture, construction, or production of the property for use by the taxpayer in its trade or business or for its production of income is considered to be manufactured, constructed, or produced by the taxpayer. If a taxpayer enters into a written binding contract, as defined in paragraph (b)(5)(iii) of this section, before January 1, 2027, with another person to manufacture, construct, or produce property described in section 168(k)(2)(B) or (C) and the manufacture, construction, or production of this property begins after December 31, 2026, the acquisition rule in paragraph (d)(1) of this section is met.

(ii) *When does manufacture, construction, or production begin.*—(A) *In general.*—For purposes of this paragraph (d)(3), manufacture, construction, or production of property begins when physical work of a significant nature begins. Physical work does not include preliminary activities such as planning or designing, securing financing, exploring, or researching. The determination of when physical work of a significant nature begins depends on the facts and circumstances. For example, if a retail motor fuels outlet is to be constructed on-site, construction begins when physical work of a significant nature commences at the site; that is, when work begins on the excavation for footings, pouring the pads for the outlet, or the driving of foundation pilings into the ground. Preliminary work, such as clearing a site, test drilling to determine soil condition, or excavation to change the contour of the land (as distinguished from excavation for footings) does not constitute the beginning of construction. However, if a retail motor fuels outlet is to be assembled on-site from modular units manufactured off-site and delivered to the site where the outlet will be used, manufacturing begins when physical work of a significant nature commences at the off-site location.

(B) *Safe harbor.*—For purposes of paragraph (d)(3)(ii)(A) of this section, a taxpayer may choose to determine when physical work of a significant nature begins in accordance with this paragraph (d)(3)(ii)(B). Physical work of a significant nature will be considered to begin at the time the taxpayer incurs (in the case of an accrual basis taxpayer) or pays (in the case of a cash basis taxpayer) more

than 10 percent of the total cost of the property, excluding the cost of any land and preliminary activities such as planning or designing, securing financing, exploring, or researching. When property is manufactured, constructed, or produced for the taxpayer by another person, this safe harbor test must be satisfied by the taxpayer. For example, if a retail motor fuels outlet is to be constructed for an accrual basis taxpayer by another person for the total cost of $200,000, excluding the cost of any land and preliminary activities such as planning or designing, securing financing, exploring, or researching, construction is deemed to begin for purposes of this paragraph (d)(3)(ii)(B) when the taxpayer has incurred more than 10 percent (more than $20,000) of the total cost of the property. A taxpayer chooses to apply this paragraph (d)(3)(ii)(B) by filing a Federal income tax return for the placed-in-service year of the property that determines when physical work of a significant nature begins consistent with this paragraph (d)(3)(ii)(B).

(iii) *Components of self-constructed property.*—(A) *Acquired components.*—If a binding contract, as defined in paragraph (b)(5)(iii) of this section, to acquire a component does not satisfy the requirements of paragraph (d)(1) of this section, the component does not qualify for the additional first year depreciation deduction under this section. A binding contract described in the preceding sentence to acquire one or more components of a larger self-constructed property will not preclude the larger self-constructed property from satisfying the acquisition rules in paragraph (d)(3)(i) of this section. Accordingly, the unadjusted depreciable basis of the larger self-constructed property that is eligible for the additional first year depreciation deduction under this section, assuming all other requirements are met, must not include the unadjusted depreciable basis of any component that does not satisfy the requirements of paragraph (d)(1) of this section. If a binding contract to acquire the component is entered into before January 1, 2027, but the manufacture, construction, or production of the larger self-constructed property does not begin before January 1, 2027, the component qualifies for the additional first year depreciation deduction under this section, assuming all other requirements are met, but the larger self-constructed property does not.

(B) *Self-constructed components.*—If the manufacture, construction, or production of a component by the taxpayer does not satisfy the requirements of paragraph (d)(3)(i) of this section, the component does not qualify for the additional first year depreciation deduction under this section. However, if the manufacture, construction, or production of a component does not satisfy the requirements of paragraph (d)(3)(i) of this section, but the manufacture, construction, or production of the larger self-constructed property satisfies the requirements of paragraph (d)(3)(i) of this section, the larger self-constructed property qualifies for the additional first year depreciation deduction under this section, assuming all other requirements are met, even though the component does not qualify for the additional first year depreciation deduction under this section. Accordingly, the unadjusted depreciable basis of the larger self-constructed property that is eligible for the additional first year depreciation deduction under this section, assuming all other requirements are met, must not include the unadjusted depreciable basis of any component that does not qualify for the additional first year depreciation deduction under this section. If the manufacture, construction, or production of a component begins before January 1, 2027, but the manufacture, construction, or production of the larger self-constructed property does not begin before January 1, 2027, the component qualifies for the additional first year depreciation deduction under this section, assuming all other requirements are met, but the larger self-constructed property does not.

(iv) *Determination of acquisition date for property not acquired pursuant to a written binding contract.*—For purposes of the acquisition rules in paragraph (d)(1) of this section, the following property is acquired by the taxpayer before January 1, 2027, if the taxpayer paid, in the case of a cash basis taxpayer, or incurred, in the case of an accrual basis taxpayer, more than 10 percent of the total cost of the property before January 1, 2027, excluding the cost of any land and preliminary activities such as planning and designing, securing financing, exploring, or researching:

(A) Property that the taxpayer acquires pursuant to a contract that does not meet the definition of a written binding contract in paragraph (b)(5)(iii) of this section; or

(B) Property that is manufactured, constructed, or produced for the taxpayer by another person under a written contract that does not meet the definition of a binding contract in paragraph (b)(5)(iii) of this section, and that is entered into prior to the manufacture, construction, or production of the property for use by the taxpayer in its trade or business or production of income.

(4) *Examples.*—The application of this paragraph (d) is illustrated by the following examples:

(A) *Example 1.* (*1*) On June 1, 2016, *NN* decided to construct property described in section 168(k)(2)(B) for its own use. However, one of the component parts of the property had to be manufactured by another person for *NN*. On August 15, 2016, *NN* entered into a written binding contract with *OO* to acquire this component part of the property for $100,000. *OO* began manufacturing the component part on November 1, 2016, and delivered the completed component part to *NN* on September 1, 2017, at which time *NN* incurred $100,000 for the cost of the component. The cost of this component part is 9 percent of the total cost of the property to be constructed by *NN*. *NN* did not incur any other cost of the property to be constructed before *NN* began construction. *NN* began constructing the property described in section 168(k)(2)(B) on October 15, 2017, and placed in service this property, including all component parts, on November 1, 2020. *NN* uses the safe harbor test in paragraph (d)(3)(ii)(B) of this section to determine when physical work of a significant nature begins for the property described in section 168(k)(2)(B).

(*2*) Because the component part of $100,000 that was manufactured by *OO* for *NN* is not more than 10 percent of the total cost of the property described in section 168(k)(2)(B), physical work of a significant nature for the property described in section 168(k)(2)(B) did not begin before September 28, 2017.

(*3*) Pursuant to paragraphs (b)(5)(iv)(C)(*2*) and (d)(1) of this section, the self-constructed component part of $100,000 manufactured by *OO* for *NN* is not eligible for the 100-percent additional first year depreciation deduction because the manufacturing of such component part began before September 28, 2017. However, pursuant to paragraph (d)(3)(i) of this section, the cost of the property described in section 168(k)(2)(B), excluding the cost of the component part of $100,000 manufactured by *OO* for *NN*, is eligible for the 100-percent additional first year depreciation deduction, assuming all other requirements are met, because construction of the property began after September 27, 2017, and before January 1, 2027, and the property described in section 168(k)(2)(B) was placed in service by *NN* during 2020.

(B) *Example 2.* (*1*) On June 1, 2026, *PP* decided to construct property described in section 168(k)(2)(B) for its own use. However, one of the component parts of the property had to be manufactured by another person for *PP*. On August 15, 2026, *PP* entered into a written binding contract with *XP* to acquire this component part of the property for $100,000. *XP* began manufacturing the component part on September 1, 2026, and delivered the completed component part to *PP* on February 1, 2027, at which time *PP* incurred $100,000 for the cost of the component. The cost of this component part is 9 percent of the total cost of the property to be constructed by *PP*. *PP* did not incur any other cost of the property to be constructed before *PP* began construction. *PP* began constructing the property described in section 168(k)(2)(B) on January 15, 2027, and placed this property, including all component parts, in service on November 1, 2027.

(*2*) Pursuant to paragraph (d)(3)(iii)(B) of this section, the self-constructed component part of $100,000 manufactured by *XP* for *PP* is eligible for the additional first year depreciation deduction under this section, assuming all other requirements are met, because the manufacturing of the component part began before January 1, 2027, and the property described in section 168(k)(2)(B), the larger self-constructed property, was placed in service by *PP* before January 1, 2028. However, pursuant to paragraph (d)(3)(i) of this section, the cost of the property described in section 168(k)(2)(B), excluding the cost of the self-constructed component part of $100,000 manufactured by *XP* for *PP*, is not eligible for the additional first year depreciation deduction under this section because construction of the property began after December 31, 2026.

(C) *Example 3.* On December 1, 2026, *QQ* entered into a written binding contract, as defined in paragraph (b)(5)(iii) of this section, with *RR* to manufacture an aircraft described in section 168(k)(2)(C) for use in *QQ*'s trade or business. *RR* begins to manufacture the aircraft on February 1, 2027. *QQ* places the aircraft in service on August 1, 2027. Pursuant to paragraph (d)(3)(i) of this section, the aircraft meets the requirements of paragraph (d)(1) of this section because the aircraft was acquired by *QQ* pursuant to a written binding contract entered into before January 1, 2027. Further, the aircraft was placed in service by *QQ* before January 1, 2028. Thus, assuming all other requirements are met, *QQ*'s cost of the aircraft is eligible for the additional first year depreciation deduction under this section.

(e) *Computation of depreciation deduction for qualified property.*—(1) *Additional first year depreciation deduction.*—(i) *Allowable taxable year.*—The additional first year depreciation deduction is allowable—

(A) Except as provided in paragraph (e)(1)(i)(B) or (g) of this section, in the taxable year in which the qualified property is placed in service by the taxpayer for use in its trade or business or for the production of income; or

(B) In the taxable year in which the specified plant is planted, or grafted to a plant that has already been planted, by the taxpayer in the ordinary course of the taxpayer's farming business, as defined in section 263A(e)(4), if the taxpayer properly made the election to apply section 168(k)(5) (for further guidance, see paragraph (f) of this section).

(ii) *Computation.*—Except as provided in paragraph (g)(5) of this section, the allowable additional first year depreciation deduction for qualified property is determined by multiplying the unadjusted depreciable basis, as defined in § 1.168(b)-1(a)(3), of the qualified property by the applicable percentage. Except as provided in paragraph (g)(1) of this section, the additional first year depreciation deduction is not affected by a taxable year of less than 12 months. See paragraph (g)(1) of this section for qualified property placed in service or planted or grafted, as applicable, and disposed of during the same taxable year. See paragraph (g)(5) of this section for qualified property acquired in a like-kind exchange or as a result of an involuntary conversion.

(iii) *Property described in section 168(k)(2)(B).*—For purposes of paragraph (e)(1)(ii) of this section, the unadjusted depreciable basis, as defined in § 1.168(b)-1(a)(3), of qualified property described in section 168(k)(2)(B) is limited to the property's unadjusted depreciable basis attributable to the property's manufacture, construction, or production before January 1, 2027. The amounts of unadjusted depreciable basis attributable to the property's manufacture, construction, or production before January 1, 2027, are referred to as "progress expenditures." Rules similar to the rules in section 4.02(1)(b) of Notice 2007-36 (2007-17 I.R.B. 1000) (see § 601.601(d)(2)(ii)(*b*) of this chapter) apply for determining progress expenditures, regardless of whether the property is manufactured, constructed, or produced for the taxpayer by another person under a written binding contract, as defined in paragraph (b)(5)(iii) of this section, or under a written contract that does not meet the definition of a binding contract in paragraph (b)(5)(iii) of this section. The IRS may publish procedural guidance in the Internal Revenue Bulletin (see § 601.601(d)(2)(ii)(*b*) of this chapter) that provides alternative procedures for complying with this paragraph (e)(1)(iii).

(iv) *Alternative minimum tax.*—(A) *In general.*—The additional first year depreciation deduction is allowable for alternative minimum tax purposes—

(*1*) Except as provided in paragraph (e)(1)(iv)(A)(*2*) of this section, in the taxable year in which the qualified property is placed in service by the taxpayer; or

(*2*) In the taxable year in which a specified plant is planted by the taxpayer, or grafted by the taxpayer to a plant that was previously planted, if the taxpayer properly made the election to apply section 168(k)(5) (for further guidance, see paragraph (f) of this section).

(B) *Special rules.*—In general, the additional first year depreciation deduction for alternative minimum tax purposes is based on the unadjusted depreciable basis of the property for alternative minimum tax purposes. However, see paragraph (g)(5)(iii)(E) of this section for qualified property acquired in a like-kind exchange or as a result of an involuntary conversion.

(2) *Otherwise allowable depreciation deduction.*—(i) *In general.*—Before determining the amount otherwise allowable as a depreciation deduction for the qualified property for the placed-in-service year and any subsequent taxable year, the taxpayer must determine the remaining adjusted depreciable basis of the qualified property. This remaining adjusted depreciable basis is equal to the unadjusted depreciable basis, as defined in § 1.168(b)-1(a)(3), of the qualified property reduced by the amount of the additional first year depreciation allowed or allowable, whichever is greater. The remaining adjusted depreciable basis of the qualified property is then depreciated using the applicable depreciation provisions under the Internal Revenue Code for the qualified property. The remaining adjusted depreciable basis of the qualified property that is MACRS property is also the basis to which the annual depreciation rates in the optional depreciation tables apply (for further guidance, see section 8 of Rev. Proc. 87-57 (1987-2 C.B. 687) and § 601.601(d)(2)(ii)(*b*) of this chapter). The depreciation deduction allowable for the remaining adjusted depreciable basis of the qualified property is affected by a taxable year of less than 12 months.

(ii) *Alternative minimum tax.*—For alternative minimum tax purposes, the depreciation deduction allowable for the remaining adjusted depreciable basis of the qualified property is based on the remaining adjusted depreciable basis for alternative minimum tax purposes. The remaining adjusted depreciable basis of the qualified property for alternative minimum tax purposes is depreciated using the same depreciation method, recovery period (or useful life in the case of computer software), and convention that apply to the qualified property for regular tax purposes.

25,520
Itemized Deductions for Individuals and Corps.
See p. 20,601 for regulations not amended to reflect law changes

(3) *Examples.*—This paragraph (e) is illustrated by the following examples:

(i) *Example 1.* On March 1, 2023, *SS*, a calendar-year taxpayer, purchased and placed in service qualified property that costs $1 million and is 5-year property under section 168(e). *SS* depreciates its 5-year property placed in service in 2023 using the optional depreciation table that corresponds with the general depreciation system, the 200-percent declining balance method, a 5-year recovery period, and the half-year convention. For 2023, *SS* is allowed an 80-percent additional first year depreciation deduction of $800,000 (the unadjusted depreciable basis of $1 million multiplied by 0.80). Next, *SS* must reduce the unadjusted depreciable basis of $1 million by the additional first year depreciation deduction of $800,000 to determine the remaining adjusted depreciable basis of $200,000. Then, *SS'* depreciation deduction allowable in 2023 for the remaining adjusted depreciable basis of $200,000 is $40,000 (the remaining adjusted depreciable basis of $200,000 multiplied by the annual depreciation rate of 0.20 for recovery year 1).

(ii) *Example 2.* On June 1, 2023, *TT*, a calendar-year taxpayer, purchased and placed in service qualified property that costs $1,500,000. The property qualifies for the expensing election under section 179 and is 5-year property under section 168(e). *TT* did not purchase any other section 179 property in 2023. *TT* makes the election under section 179 for the property and depreciates its 5-year property placed in service in 2023 using the optional depreciation table that corresponds with the general depreciation system, the 200-percent declining balance method, a 5-year recovery period, and the half-year convention. Assume the maximum section 179 deduction for 2023 is $1,000,000. For 2023, *TT* is first allowed a $1,000,000 deduction under section 179. Next, *TT* must reduce the cost of $1,500,000 by the section 179 deduction of $1,000,000 to determine the unadjusted depreciable basis of $500,000. Then, for 2023, *TT* is allowed an 80-percent additional first year depreciation deduction of $400,000 (the unadjusted depreciable basis of $500,000 multiplied by 0.80). Next, *TT* must reduce the unadjusted depreciable basis of $500,000 by the additional first year depreciation deduction of $400,000 to determine the remaining adjusted depreciable basis of $100,000. Then, *TT*'s depreciation deduction allowable in 2023 for the remaining adjusted depreciable basis of $100,000 is $20,000 (the remaining adjusted depreciable basis of $100,000 multiplied by the annual depreciation rate of 0.20 for recovery year 1).

(f) *Elections under section 168(k).*—(1) *Election not to deduct additional first year depreciation.*—(i) *In general.*—A taxpayer may make an election not to deduct the additional first year depreciation for any class of property that is qualified property placed in service during the taxable year. If this election is made, the election applies to all qualified property that is in the same class of property and placed in service in the same taxable year, and no additional first year depreciation deduction is allowable for the property placed in service during the taxable year in the class of property, except as provided in § 1.743-1(j)(4)(i)(B)(*1*).

(ii) *Definition of class of property.*—For purposes of this paragraph (f)(1), the term *class of property* means:

(A) Except for the property described in paragraphs (f)(1)(ii)(B) and (D), and (f)(2) of this section, each class of property described in section 168(e) (for example, 5-year property);

(B) Water utility property as defined in section 168(e)(5) and depreciated under section 168;

(C) Computer software as defined in, and depreciated under, section 167(f)(1) and § 1.167(a)-14(b);

(D) Qualified improvement property as defined in § 1.168(b)-1(a)(5)(i)(C) and (a)(5)(ii) (acquired by the taxpayer after September 27, 2017, and placed in service by the taxpayer after September 27, 2017, and before January 1, 2018), and depreciated under section 168;

(E) Each separate production, as defined in § 1.181-3(b), of a qualified film or television production;

(F) Each separate production, as defined in section 181(e)(2), of a qualified live theatrical production; or

(G) Each partner's basis adjustment in partnership assets under section 743(b) for each class of property described in paragraphs (f)(1)(ii)(A) through (F), and (f)(2) of this section (for further guidance, see § 1.743-1(j)(4)(i)(B)(*1*)).

(iii) *Time and manner for making election.*—(A) *Time for making election.*—Except as provided in paragraph (f)(6) of this section, any election specified in paragraph (f)(1)(i) of this section must be made by the due date, including extensions, of the Federal tax return for the taxable year in which the qualified property is placed in service by the taxpayer.

(B) *Manner of making election.*—Except as provided in paragraph (f)(6) of this section, any election specified in paragraph (f)(1)(i) of this section must be made in the manner prescribed on Form 4562, "Depreciation and Amortization," and its instructions. The election is made separately by each person owning qualified property (for example, for each member of a consolidated group by the common parent of the group, by the partnership (including a lower-tier partnership; also including basis adjustments in the partnership assets under section 743(b)), or by the S corporation). If Form 4562 is revised or renumbered, any reference in this section to that form shall be treated as a reference to the revised or renumbered form.

(iv) *Failure to make election.*—If a taxpayer does not make the election specified in paragraph (f)(1)(i) of this section within the time and in the manner prescribed in paragraph (f)(1)(iii) of this section, the amount of depreciation allowable for that property under section 167 or 168, as applicable, must be determined for the placed-in-service year and for all subsequent taxable years by taking into account the additional first year depreciation deduction. Thus, any election specified in paragraph (f)(1)(i) of this section shall not be made by the taxpayer in any other manner (for example, the election cannot be made through a request under section 446(e) to change the taxpayer's method of accounting).

(2) *Election to apply section 168(k)(5) for specified plants.*—(i) *In general.*—A taxpayer may make an election to apply section 168(k)(5) to one or more specified plants that are planted, or grafted to a plant that has already been planted, by the taxpayer in the ordinary course of the taxpayer's farming business, as defined in section 263A(e)(4). If this election is made for a specified plant, such plant is not treated as qualified property under section 168(k) and this section in its placed-in-service year.

(ii) *Time and manner for making election.*—(A) *Time for making election.*—Except as provided in paragraph (f)(6) of this section, any election specified in paragraph (f)(2)(i) of this section must be made by the due date, including extensions, of the Federal tax return for the taxable year in which the taxpayer planted or grafted the specified plant to which the election applies.

(B) *Manner of making election.*—Except as provided in paragraph (f)(6) of this section, any election specified in paragraph (f)(2)(i) of this section must be made in the manner prescribed on Form 4562, "Depreciation and Amortization," and its instructions. The election is made separately by each person owning specified plants (for example, for each member of a consolidated group by the common parent of the group, by the partnership (including a lower-tier partnership), or by the S corporation). If Form 4562 is revised or renumbered, any reference in this section to that form shall be treated as a reference to the revised or renumbered form.

(iii) *Failure to make election.*—If a taxpayer does not make the election specified in paragraph (f)(2)(i) of this section for a specified plant within the time and in the manner prescribed in paragraph (f)(2)(ii) of this section, the specified plant is treated as qualified property under section 168(k), assuming all requirements are met, in the taxable year in which such plant is placed in service by the taxpayer. Thus, any election specified in paragraph (f)(2)(i) of this section shall not be made by the taxpayer in any other manner (for example, the election cannot be made through a request under section 446(e) to change the taxpayer's method of accounting).

(3) *Election for qualified property placed in service during the 2017 taxable year.*—(i) *In general.*—A taxpayer may make an election to deduct 50 percent, instead of 100 percent, additional first year depreciation for all qualified property acquired after September 27, 2017, by the taxpayer and placed in service by the taxpayer during its taxable year that includes September 28, 2017. If a taxpayer makes an election to apply section 168(k)(5) for its taxable year that includes September 28, 2017, the taxpayer also may make an election to deduct 50 percent, instead of 100 percent, additional first year depreciation for all specified plants that are planted, or grafted to a plant that has already been planted, after September 27, 2017, by the taxpayer in the ordinary course of the taxpayer's farming business during such taxable year.

(ii) *Time and manner for making election.*—(A) *Time for making election.*—Except as provided in paragraph (f)(6) of this section, any election specified in paragraph (f)(3)(i) of this section must be made by the due date, including extensions, of the Federal tax return for the taxpayer's taxable year that includes September 28, 2017.

(B) *Manner of making election.*—Except as provided in paragraph (f)(6) of this section, any election specified in paragraph (f)(3)(i) of this section must be made in the manner prescribed on the 2017 Form 4562, "Depreciation and Amortization," and its instructions. The election is made separately by each person owning qualified property (for example, for each member of a consolidated group by the common parent of the group, by the partnership (including a lower-tier partnership), or by the S corporation).

(iii) *Failure to make election.*—If a taxpayer does not make the election specified in paragraph (f)(3)(i) of this section within the time and in the manner prescribed in paragraph (f)(3)(ii) of this section, the amount of depreciation allowable for qualified property under section 167 or 168, as applicable, acquired and placed in service, or planted or grafted, as applicable, by the taxpayer after September 27, 2017, must be determined for the taxable year that includes September 28, 2017, and for all subsequent taxable years by taking into account the 100-percent additional first year depreciation deduction, unless the taxpayer makes the election specified in paragraph (f)(1)(i) of this section within the time and in the manner prescribed in paragraph (f)(1)(iii) of this section for the class of property in which the qualified property is included. Thus, any election specified in paragraph (f)(3)(i) of this section shall not be made by the taxpayer in any other manner (for example, the election cannot be made through a request under section 446(e) to change the taxpayer's method of accounting).

(4) *Alternative minimum tax.*—If a taxpayer makes an election specified in paragraph (f)(1) of this section for a class of property or in paragraph (f)(2) of this section for a specified plant, the depreciation adjustments under section 56 and the regulations in this part under section 56 do not apply to the property or specified plant, as applicable, to which that election applies for purposes of computing the taxpayer's alternative minimum taxable income. If a taxpayer makes an election specified in paragraph (f)(3) of this section for all qualified property, see paragraphs (e)(1)(iv) and (e)(2)(ii) of this section.

(5) *Revocation of election.*—(i) *In general.*—Except as provided in paragraphs (f)(5)(ii) and (f)(6) of this section, an election specified in this paragraph (f), once made, may be revoked only by filing a request for a private letter ruling and obtaining the Commissioner of Internal Revenue's written consent to revoke the election. The Commissioner may grant a request to revoke the election if the taxpayer acted reasonably and in good faith, and the revocation will not prejudice the interests of the Government. See generally § 301.9100-3 of this chapter. An election specified in this paragraph (f) may not be revoked through a request under section 446(e) to change the taxpayer's method of accounting.

(ii) *Automatic 6-month extension.*—If a taxpayer made an election specified in this paragraph (f), an automatic extension of 6 months from the due date of the taxpayer's Federal tax return, excluding extensions, for the placed-in-service year or the taxable year in which the specified plant is planted or grafted, as applicable, is granted to revoke that election, provided the taxpayer timely filed the taxpayer's Federal tax return for the placed-in-service year or the taxable year in which the specified plant is planted or grafted, as applicable, and, within this 6-month extension period, the taxpayer, and all taxpayers whose tax liability would be affected by the election, file an amended Federal tax return for the placed-in-service year or the taxable year in which the specified plant is planted or grafted, as applicable, in a manner that is consistent with the revocation of the election.

(6) *Special rules for 2016 and 2017 returns.*—For an election specified in this paragraph (f) for qualified property placed in service, or for a specified plant that is planted, or grafted to a plant that has already been planted, by the taxpayer during its taxable year that included September 28, 2017, the taxpayer should refer to Rev. Proc. 2019-33 (2019-34 I.R.B. 662) (see § 601.601(d)(2)(ii)(b)of this chapter) for the time and manner of making the election on the 2016 or 2017 Federal tax return.

(7) *Additional procedural guidance.*—The IRS may publish procedural guidance in the Internal Revenue Bulletin (see § 601.601(d)(2)(ii)(b) of this chapter) that provides alternative procedures for complying with paragraph (f)(1)(iii), (f)(1)(iv), (f)(2)(ii), (f)(2)(iii), (f)(3)(ii), (f)(3)(iii), or (f)(5)(i) of this section.

(g) *Special rules.*—(1) *Property placed in service and disposed of in the same taxable year.*—(i) *In general.*—Except as provided in paragraphs (g)(1)(ii) and (iii) and by the application of paragraph (b)(3)(iii)(B)(4) of this section, the additional first year depreciation deduction is not allowed for qualified property placed in service or planted or grafted, as applicable, and disposed of during the same taxable year. If a partnership interest is acquired and disposed of during the same taxable year, the additional first year depreciation deduction is not allowed for any section 743(b) adjustment arising from the initial acquisition. Also, if qualified property is placed in service and disposed of during the same taxable year and then reacquired and again placed in service in a subsequent taxable year, the additional first year depreciation deduction is not allowable for the property in the subsequent taxable year, except as otherwise provided by the application of paragraph (b)(3)(iii)(B) of this section.

(ii) *Technical termination of a partnership.*—In the case of a technical termination of a partnership under section 708(b)(1)(B) in a taxable year beginning before January 1, 2018, the additional first year depreciation deduction is allowable for any qualified property placed in service or planted or grafted, as applicable, by the terminated partnership during the taxable year of termination and contributed by the terminated partnership to the new partnership. The allowable additional first year depreciation deduction for the qualified property shall not be claimed by the terminated partnership but instead shall be claimed by the new partnership for the new partnership's taxable year in which the qualified property was contributed by the terminated partnership to the new partnership. However, if qualified property is both placed in service or planted or grafted, as applicable, and contributed to a new partnership in a transaction described in section 708(b)(1)(B) by the terminated partnership during the taxable year of termination, and if such property is disposed of by the new partnership in the same taxable year the new partnership received such property from the terminated partnership, then no additional first year depreciation deduction is allowable to either partnership.

(iii) *Section 168(i)(7) transactions.*—If any qualified property is transferred in a transaction described in section 168(i)(7) in the same taxable year that the qualified property is placed in service or planted or grafted, as applicable, by the transferor, the additional first year depreciation deduction is allowable for the qualified property. If a partnership interest is purchased and transferred in a transaction described in section 168(i)(7) in the same taxable year, the additional first year depreciation deduction is allowable for any section 743(b) adjustment that arises from the initial acquisition with respect to qualified property held by the partnership, provided the requirements of paragraph (b)(3)(iv)(D) of this section and all other requirements of section 168(k) and this section are satisfied. The allowable additional first year depreciation deduction for the qualified property for the transferor's taxable year in which the property is placed in service or planted or grafted, as applicable, is allocated between the transferor and the transferee on a monthly basis. The allowable additional first year depreciation deduction for a section 743(b) adjustment with respect to qualified property held by the partnership is allocated between the transferor and the transferee on a monthly basis notwithstanding that under § 1.743-1(f) a transferee's section 743(b) adjustment is determined without regard to a transferors section 743(b) adjustment. These allocations shall be made in accordance with the rules in § 1.168(d)-1(b)(7)(ii) for allocating the depreciation deduction between the transferor and the transferee. However, solely for purposes of this section, if the qualified property is transferred in a section 721(a) transaction to a partnership that has as a partner a person, other than the transferor, who previously had a depreciable interest in the qualified property, in the same taxable year that the qualified property is acquired or planted or grafted, as applicable, by the transferor, the qualified property is deemed to be placed in service or planted or grafted, as applicable, by the transferor during that taxable year, and the allowable additional first year depreciation deduction is allocated entirely to the transferor and not to the partnership. Additionally, if qualified property is both placed in service or planted or grafted, as applicable, and transferred in a transaction described in section 168(i)(7) by the transferor during the same taxable year, and if such property is disposed of by the transferee, other than by a transaction described in section 168(i)(7), during the same taxable year the transferee received such property from the transferor, then no additional first year depreciation deduction is allowable to either party.

(iv) *Examples.*—The application of this paragraph (g)(1) is illustrated by the following examples:

(A) *Example 1.* UU and VV are equal partners in *Partnership JL*, a general partnership. *Partnership JL* is a calendar-year taxpayer. On October 1, 2017, *Partnership JL* purchased and placed in service qualified property at a cost of $30,000. On November 1, 2017, UU sells its entire 50 percent interest to WW in a transfer that terminates the partnership under section 708(b)(1)(B). As a result, terminated *Partnership JL* is deemed to have contributed the qualified property to new *Partnership JL*. Pursuant to paragraph (g)(1)(ii) of this section, new *Partnership JL*, not terminated *Partnership JL*, is eligible to claim the 100-percent additional first year depreciation deduction allowable for the qualified property for the taxable year 2017, assuming all other requirements are met.

(B) *Example 2.* On January 5, 2018, XX purchased and placed in service qualified property for a total amount of $9,000. On August 20, 2018, XX transferred this qualified property to *Partnership BC* in a transaction described in section 721(a). No other partner of *Partnership BC* has ever had a depreciable interest in the qualified property. XX and *Partnership BC* are calendar-year taxpayers. Because the transaction between XX and *Partnership BC* is a transaction described in section 168(i)(7), pursuant to paragraph (g)(1)(iii) of this section, the 100-percent additional first year depreciation deduction allowable for the qualified property is allocated between XX and *Partnership BC* in accordance with the rules in §1.168(d)-1(b)(7)(ii) for allocating the depreciation deduction between the transferor and the transferee. Accordingly, the 100-percent additional first year depreciation deduction allowable of $9,000 for the qualified property for 2018 is allocated between XX and *Partnership BC* based on the number of months that XX and *Partnership BC* held the qualified property in service during 2018. Thus, because the qualified property was held in service by XX for 7 of 12 months, which includes the month in which XX placed the qualified property in service but does not include the month in which the qualified property was transferred, XX is allocated $5,250 ($7/12 × $9,000 additional first year depreciation deduction). *Partnership BC* is allocated $3,750, the remaining $5/12 of the $9,000 additional first year depreciation deduction allowable for the qualified property.

(2) *Redetermination of basis.*—If the unadjusted depreciable basis, as defined in §1.168(b)-1(a)(3), of qualified property is redetermined (for example, due to contingent purchase price or discharge of indebtedness) before January 1, 2027, or in the case of property described in section 168(k)(2)(B) or (C), is redetermined before January 1, 2028, the additional first year depreciation deduction allowable for the qualified property is redetermined as follows:

(i) *Increase in basis.*—For the taxable year in which an increase in basis of qualified property occurs, the taxpayer shall claim an additional first year depreciation deduction for qualified property by multiplying the amount of the increase in basis for this property by the applicable percentage for the taxable year in which the underlying property was placed in service by the taxpayer. For purposes of this paragraph (g)(2)(i), the additional first year depreciation deduction applies to the increase in basis only if the underlying property is qualified property. To determine the amount otherwise allowable as a depreciation deduction for the increase in basis of qualified property, the amount of the increase in basis of the qualified property must be reduced by the additional first year depreciation deduction allowed or allowable, whichever is greater, for the increase in basis and the remaining increase in basis of—

(A) Qualified property, except for computer software described in paragraph (b)(2)(i)(B) of this section, a qualified film or television production described in paragraph (b)(2)(i)(E) of this section, or a qualified live theatrical production described in paragraph (b)(2)(i)(F) of this section, is depreciated over the recovery period of the qualified property remaining as of the beginning of the taxable year in which the increase in basis occurs, and using the same depreciation method and convention applicable to the qualified property that applies for the taxable year in which the increase in basis occurs; and

(B) Computer software, as defined in paragraph (b)(2)(i)(B) of this section, that is qualified property is depreciated ratably over the remainder of the 36-month period, the useful life under section 167(f)(1), as of the beginning of the first day of the month in which the increase in basis occurs.

(ii) *Decrease in basis.*—For the taxable year in which a decrease in basis of qualified property occurs, the taxpayer shall reduce the total amount otherwise allowable as a depreciation deduction for all of the taxpayer's depreciable property by the excess additional first year depreciation deduction previously claimed for the qualified property. If, for such taxable year, the excess additional first year depreciation deduction exceeds the total amount otherwise allowable as a depreciation deduction for all of the taxpayer's depreciable property, the taxpayer shall take into account a negative depreciation deduction in computing taxable income. The excess additional first year depreciation deduction for qualified property is determined by multiplying the amount of the decrease in basis for this property by the applicable percentage for the taxable year in which the underlying property was placed in service by the taxpayer. For purposes of this paragraph (g)(2)(ii), the additional first year depreciation deduction applies to the decrease in basis only if the underlying property is qualified property. Also, if the taxpayer establishes by adequate records or other sufficient evidence that the taxpayer claimed less than the additional first year depreciation deduction allowable for the qualified property before the decrease in basis, or if the taxpayer claimed more than the additional first year depreciation deduction allowable for the qualified property before the decrease in basis, the excess additional first year depreciation deduction is determined by multiplying the amount of the decrease in basis by the additional first year depreciation deduction percentage actually claimed by the taxpayer for the qualified property before the decrease in basis. To determine the amount to reduce the total amount otherwise allowable as a depreciation deduction for all of the taxpayer's depreciable property for the excess depreciation previously claimed, other than the additional first year depreciation deduction, resulting from the decrease in basis of the qualified property, the amount of the decrease in basis of the qualified property must be adjusted by the excess additional first year depreciation deduction that reduced the total amount otherwise allowable as a depreciation deduction, as determined under this paragraph (g)(2)(ii), and the remaining decrease in basis of—

(A) Qualified property, except for computer software described in paragraph (b)(2)(i)(B) of this section, a qualified film or television production described in paragraph (b)(2)(i)(E) of this section, or a qualified live theatrical production described in paragraph (b)(2)(i)(F) of this section, reduces the amount otherwise allowable as a depreciation deduction over the recovery period of the qualified property remaining as of the beginning of the taxable year in which the decrease in basis occurs, and using the same depreciation method and convention of the qualified property that applies in the taxable year in which the decrease in basis occurs. If, for any taxable year, the reduction to the amount otherwise allowable as a depreciation deduction, as determined under this paragraph (g)(2)(ii)(A), exceeds the total amount otherwise allowable as a depreciation deduction for all of the taxpayer's depreciable property, the taxpayer shall take into account a negative depreciation deduction in computing taxable income; and

(B) Computer software, as defined in paragraph (b)(2)(i)(B) of this section, that is qualified property reduces the amount otherwise allowable as a depreciation deduction over the remainder of the 36-month period, the useful life under section 167(f)(1), as of the beginning of the first day of the month in which the decrease in basis occurs. If, for any taxable year, the reduction to the amount otherwise allowable as a depreciation deduction, as determined under this paragraph (g)(2)(ii)(B), exceeds the total amount otherwise allowable as a depreciation deduction for all of the taxpayer's depreciable property, the taxpayer shall take into account a negative depreciation deduction in computing taxable income.

(iii) *Definitions.*—Except as otherwise expressly provided by the Internal Revenue Code (for example, section 1017(a)), the regulations under the Internal Revenue Code, or other guidance published in the Internal Revenue Bulletin for purposes of this paragraph (g)(2)—

(A) An increase in basis occurs in the taxable year an amount is taken into account under section 461; and

(B) A decrease in basis occurs in the taxable year an amount would be taken into account under section 451.

(iv) *Examples.*—The application of this paragraph (g)(2) is illustrated by the following examples:

(A) *Example 1.* (1) On May 15, 2023, YY, a cash-basis taxpayer, purchased and placed in service qualified property that is 5-year property at a cost of $200,000. In addition to the $200,000, YY agrees to pay the seller 25 percent of the gross profits from the operation of the property in 2023. On May 15, 2024, YY paid to the seller an additional $10,000. YY depreciates the 5-year property placed in service in 2023 using the optional depreciation table that corresponds with the general depreciation system, the 200-percent declining balance method, a 5-year recovery period, and the half-year convention.

(2) For 2023, YY is allowed an 80-percent additional first year depreciation deduction of $160,000 (the unadjusted depreciable basis of $200,000 multiplied by 0.80). In addition, YY's depreciation deduction for 2023 for the remaining adjusted depreciable basis of $40,000 (the unadjusted depreciable basis of $200,000 reduced by the additional first year depreciation deduction of $160,000) is $8,000 (the remaining adjusted depreciable basis of $40,000 multiplied by the annual depreciation rate of 0.20 for recovery year 1).

(3) For 2024, YY's depreciation deduction for the remaining adjusted depreciable basis of $40,000 is $12,800 (the remaining adjusted depreciable basis of $40,000 multiplied by the annual depreciation rate of 0.32 for recovery year 2). In addition, pursuant to paragraph (g)(2)(i) of this section, YY is allowed an additional first year depreciation deduction for 2024 for the $10,000 increase in basis of the qualified property. Consequently, YY is allowed an additional first year depreciation deduction of $8,000 (the increase in basis of $10,000 multiplied by 0.80, the applicable percentage for 2023). Also, YY is allowed a depreciation deduction for 2024 attributable to the remaining increase in basis of $2,000 (the increase in basis of $10,000 reduced by the additional first year depreciation deduction of $8,000). The depreciation deduction allowable for 2024 attributable to the remaining increase in basis of $2,000 is $889 (the remaining increase in basis of $2,000 multiplied by 0.4444, which is equal to 1/remaining recovery period of 4.5 years at January 1, 2024, multiplied by 2). Accordingly, for 2024, YY's total depreciation deduction allowable for the qualified property is $21,689 ($12,800 plus $8,000 plus $889).

(B) *Example 2.* (1) On May 15, 2023, ZZ, a calendar-year taxpayer, purchased and placed in service qualified property that is 5-year property at a cost of $400,000. To purchase the property, ZZ borrowed $250,000 from Bank1. On May 15, 2024, Bank1 forgives

$50,000 of the indebtedness. ZZ makes the election provided in section 108(b)(5) to apply any portion of the reduction under section 1017 to the basis of the depreciable property of the taxpayer. ZZ depreciates the 5-year property placed in service in 2023 using the optional depreciation table that corresponds with the general depreciation system, the 200-percent declining balance method, a 5-year recovery period, and the half-year convention.

(2) For 2023, ZZ is allowed an 80-percent additional first year depreciation deduction of $320,000 (the unadjusted depreciable basis of $400,000 multiplied by 0.80). In addition, ZZ's depreciation deduction allowable for 2023 for the remaining adjusted depreciable basis of $80,000 (the unadjusted depreciable basis of $400,000 reduced by the additional first year depreciation deduction of $320,000) is $16,000 (the remaining adjusted depreciable basis of $80,000 multiplied by the annual depreciation rate of 0.20 for recovery year 1).

(3) For 2024, ZZ's deduction for the remaining adjusted depreciable basis of $80,000 is $25,600 (the remaining adjusted depreciable basis of $80,000 multiplied by the annual depreciation rate 0.32 for recovery year 2). Although Bank1 forgave the indebtedness in 2024, the basis of the property is reduced on January 1, 2025, pursuant to sections 108(b)(5) and 1017(a) under which basis is reduced at the beginning of the taxable year following the taxable year in which the discharge of indebtedness occurs.

(4) For 2025, ZZ's deduction for the remaining adjusted depreciable basis of $80,000 is $15,360 (the remaining adjusted depreciable basis of $80,000 multiplied by the annual depreciation rate 0.192 for recovery year 3). However, pursuant to paragraph (g)(2)(ii) of this section, ZZ must reduce the amount otherwise allowable as a depreciation deduction for 2025 by the excess depreciation previously claimed for the $50,000 decrease in basis of the qualified property. Consequently, ZZ must reduce the amount of depreciation otherwise allowable for 2025 by the excess additional first year depreciation of $40,000 (the decrease in basis of $50,000 multiplied by 0.80, the applicable percentage for 2023). Also, ZZ must reduce the amount of depreciation otherwise allowable for 2025 by the excess depreciation attributable to the remaining decrease in basis of $10,000 (the decrease in basis of $50,000 reduced by the excess additional first year depreciation of $40,000). The reduction in the amount of depreciation otherwise allowable for 2025 for the remaining decrease in basis of $10,000 is $5,714 (the remaining decrease in basis of $10,000 multiplied by 0.5714, which is equal to (1/remaining recovery period of 3.5 years at January 1, 2025, multiplied by 2). Accordingly, assuming the qualified property is the only depreciable property owned by ZZ, for 2025, ZZ has a negative depreciation deduction for the qualified property of $30,354 ($15,360 minus $40,000 minus $5,714).

(3) *Sections 1245 and 1250 depreciation recapture.*—For purposes of section 1245 and §§ 1.1245-1 through -6, the additional first year depreciation deduction is an amount allowed or allowable for depreciation. Further, for purposes of section 1250(b) and § 1.1250-2, the additional first year depreciation deduction is not a straight line method.

(4) *Coordination with section 169.*—The additional first year depreciation deduction is allowable in the placed-in-service year of a certified pollution control facility, as defined in § 1.169-2(a), that is qualified property even if the taxpayer makes the election to amortize the certified pollution control facility under section 169 and §§ 1.169-1 through -4 in the certified pollution control facility's placed-in-service year.

(5) *Like-kind exchanges and involuntary conversions.*—(i) *Scope.*—The rules of this paragraph (g)(5) apply to replacement MACRS property or replacement computer software that is qualified property at the time of replacement provided the time of replacement is after September 27, 2017, and before January 1, 2027; or, in the case of replacement MACRS property or replacement computer software that is qualified property described in section 168(k)(2)(B) or (C), the time of replacement is after September 27, 2017, and before January 1, 2028.

(ii) *Definitions.*—For purposes of this paragraph (g)(5), the following definitions apply:

(A) *Replacement MACRS property* has the same meaning as that term is defined in § 1.168(i)-6(b)(1).

(B) *Relinquished MACRS property* has the same meaning as that term is defined in § 1.168(i)-6(b)(2).

(C) *Replacement computer software* is computer software, as defined in paragraph (b)(2)(i)(B) of this section, in the hands of the acquiring taxpayer that is acquired for other computer software in a like-kind exchange or in an involuntary conversion.

(D) *Relinquished computer software* is computer software that is transferred by the taxpayer in a like-kind exchange or in an involuntary conversion.

(E) *Time of disposition* has the same meaning as that term is defined in § 1.168(i)-6(b)(3) for relinquished MACRS property. For relinquished computer software, *time of disposition* is when the disposition of the relinquished computer software takes place under the convention determined under § 1.167(a)-14(b).

(F) Except as provided in paragraph (g)(5)(iv) of this section, the *time of replacement* has the same meaning as that term is defined in § 1.168(i)-6(b)(4) for replacement MACRS property. For replacement computer software, the *time of replacement* is, except as provided in paragraph (g)(5)(iv) of this section, the later of—

(1) When the replacement computer software is placed in service under the convention determined under § 1.167(a)-14(b); or

(2) The time of disposition of the relinquished property.

(G) *Exchanged basis* has the same meaning as that term is defined in § 1.168(i)-6(b)(7) for MACRS property, as defined in § 1.168(b)-1(a)(2). For computer software, the *exchanged basis* is determined after the amortization deductions for the year of disposition are determined under § 1.167(a)-14(b) and is the lesser of—

(1) The basis in the replacement computer software, as determined under section 1031(d) and § 1.1031(d)-1, 1.1031(d)-2, 1.1031(j)-1, or 1.1031(k)-1; or section 1033(b) and § 1.1033(b)-1; or

(2) The adjusted depreciable basis of the relinquished computer software.

(H) *Excess basis* has the same meaning as that term is defined in § 1.168(i)-6(b)(8) for replacement MACRS property. For replacement computer software, the *excess basis* is any excess of the basis in the replacement computer software, as determined under section 1031(d) and § 1.1031(d)-1, 1.1031(d)-2, 1.1031(j)-1, or 1.1031(k)-1; or section 1033(b) and § 1.1033(b)-1, over the exchanged basis as determined under paragraph (g)(5)(ii)(G) of this section.

(I) *Remaining exchanged basis* is the exchanged basis as determined under paragraph (g)(5)(ii)(G) of this section reduced by—

(1) The percentage of such basis attributable to the taxpayer's use of property for the taxable year other than in the taxpayer's trade or business or for the production of income; and

(2) Any adjustments to basis provided by other provisions of the Code and the regulations under the Code (including section 1016(a)(2) and (3)) for periods prior to the disposition of the relinquished property.

(J) *Remaining excess basis* is the excess basis as determined under paragraph (g)(5)(ii)(H) of this section reduced by—

(1) The percentage of such basis attributable to the taxpayer's use of property for the taxable year other than in the taxpayer's trade or business or for the production of income;

(2) Any portion of the basis the taxpayer properly elects to treat as an expense under section 179 or 179C; and

(3) Any adjustments to basis provided by other provisions of the Code and the regulations under the Code.

(K) *Year of disposition* has the same meaning as that term is defined in § 1.168(i)-6(b)(5).

(L) *Year of replacement* has the same meaning as that term is defined in § 1.168(i)-6(b)(6).

(M) *Like-kind exchange* has the same meaning as that term is defined in § 1.168(i)-6(b)(11).

(N) *Involuntary conversion* has the same meaning as that term is defined in § 1.168(i)-6(b)(12).

(iii) *Computation.*—(A) *In general.*—If the replacement MACRS property or the replacement computer software, as applicable, meets the original use requirement in paragraph (b)(3)(ii) of this section and all other requirements of section 168(k) and this section, the remaining exchanged basis for the year of replacement and the remaining excess basis, if any, for the year of replacement for the replacement MACRS property or the replacement computer software, as applicable, are eligible for the additional first year depreciation deduction under this section. If the replacement MACRS property or the replacement computer software, as applicable, meets the used property acquisition requirements in paragraph (b)(3)(iii) of this section and all other requirements of section 168(k) and this section, only the remaining excess basis for the year of replacement for the replacement MACRS property or the replacement computer software, as applicable, is eligible for the additional first year depreciation deduction under this section. See paragraph (b)(3)(iii)(A)(3) of this section. The additional first year depreciation deduction applies to the remaining exchanged basis and any remaining excess basis, as applicable, of the replacement MACRS property or the replacement computer software, as applicable, if the time of replacement is after September 27, 2017, and before January 1, 2027; or, in the case of replacement MACRS property or replacement computer software, as applicable, described in section 168(k)(2)(B) or (C), the time of replacement is after September 27, 2017, and before January 1, 2028. The additional first year depreciation deduction is computed separately for the remaining exchanged basis and any remaining excess basis, as applicable.

(B) *Year of disposition and year of replacement.*—The additional first year depreciation deduction is allowable for the replacement MACRS property or replacement computer software in the year of replacement. However, the additional first year depreciation deduction is not allowable for the relinquished MACRS property or the relinquished computer software, as applicable, if the relinquished MACRS property or the relinquished computer software, as applicable, is placed in service and disposed of in a like-kind exchange or in an involuntary conversion in the same taxable year.

(C) *Property described in section 168(k)(2)(B).*—For purposes of paragraph (g)(5)(iii)(A) of this section, the total of the remaining exchanged basis and the remaining excess basis, if any, of the replacement MACRS property that is qualified property described in section 168(k)(2)(B) and meets the original use requirement in paragraph (b)(3)(ii) of this section is limited to the total of the property's remaining exchanged basis and remaining excess basis, if any, attributable to the property's manufacture, construction, or production after September 27, 2017, and before January 1, 2027. For purposes of paragraph (g)(5)(iii)(A) of this section, the remaining excess basis, if any, of the replacement MACRS property that is qualified property described in section 168(k)(2)(B) and meets the used property acquisition requirements in paragraph (b)(3)(iii) of this section is limited to the property's remaining excess basis, if any, attributable to the property's manufacture, construction, or production after September 27, 2017, and before January 1, 2027.

(D) *Effect of §1.168(i)-6(i)(1) election.*—If a taxpayer properly makes the election under §1.168(i)-6(i)(1) not to apply §1.168(i)-6 for any MACRS property, as defined in §1.168(b)-1(a)(2), involved in a like-kind exchange or involuntary conversion, then:

(1) If the replacement MACRS property meets the original use requirement in paragraph (b)(3)(ii) of this section and all other requirements of section 168(k) and this section, the total of the exchanged basis, as defined in §1.168(i)-6(b)(7), and the excess basis, as defined in §1.168(i)-6(b)(8), if any, in the replacement MACRS property is eligible for the additional first year depreciation deduction under this section; or

(2) If the replacement MACRS property meets the used property acquisition requirements in paragraph (b)(3)(iii) of this section and all other requirements of section 168(k) and this section, only the excess basis, as defined in §1.168(i)-6(b)(8), if any, in the replacement MACRS property is eligible for the additional first year depreciation deduction under this section.

(E) *Alternative minimum tax.*—The additional first year depreciation deduction is allowed for alternative minimum tax purposes for the year of replacement of replacement MACRS property or replacement computer software, as applicable, that is qualified property. If the replacement MACRS property or the replacement computer software, as applicable, meets the original use requirement in paragraph (b)(3)(ii) of this section and all other requirements of section 168(k) and this section, the additional first year depreciation deduction for alternative minimum tax purposes is based on the remaining exchanged basis and the remaining excess basis, if any, of the replacement MACRS property or the replacement computer software, as applicable, for alternative minimum tax purposes. If the replacement MACRS property or the replacement computer software, as applicable, meets the used property acquisition requirements in paragraph (b)(3)(iii) of this section and all other requirements of section 168(k) and this section, the additional first year depreciation deduction for alternative minimum tax purposes is based on the remaining excess basis, if any, of the replacement MACRS property or the replacement computer software, as applicable, for alternative minimum tax purposes.

(iv) *Replacement MACRS property or replacement computer software that is acquired and placed in service before disposition of relinquished MACRS property or relinquished computer software.*—If, in an involuntary conversion, a taxpayer acquires and places in service the replacement MACRS property or the replacement computer software, as applicable, before the time of disposition of the involuntarily converted MACRS property or the involuntarily converted computer software, as applicable; and the time of disposition of the involuntarily converted MACRS property or the involuntarily converted computer software, as applicable, is after December 31, 2026, or, in the case of property described in service 168(k)(2)(B) or (C), after December 31, 2027, then—

(A) The time of replacement for purposes of this paragraph (g)(5) is when the replacement MACRS property or replacement computer software, as applicable, is placed in service by the taxpayer, provided the threat or imminence of requisition or condemnation of the involuntarily converted MACRS property or involuntarily converted computer software, as applicable, existed before January 1, 2027, or, in the case of property described in section 168(k)(2)(B) or (C), existed before January 1, 2028; and

(B) The taxpayer depreciates the replacement MACRS property or replacement computer software, as applicable, in accordance with paragraph (e) of this section. However, at the time of disposition of the involuntarily converted MACRS property, the taxpayer determines the exchanged basis, as defined in §1.168(i)-6(b)(7), and the excess basis, as defined in §1.168(i)-6(b)(8), of the replacement MACRS property and begins to depreciate the depreciable exchanged basis, as defined in §1.168(i)-6(b)(9), of the replacement MACRS property in accordance with §1.168(i)-6(c). The depreciable excess basis, as defined in §1.168(i)-6(b)(10), of the replacement MACRS property continues to be depreciated by the taxpayer in accordance with the first sentence of this paragraph (g)(5)(iv)(B). Further, in the year of disposition of the involuntarily converted MACRS property, the taxpayer must include in taxable income the excess of the depreciation deductions allowable, including the additional first year depreciation deduction allowable, on the unadjusted depreciable basis of the replacement MACRS property over the additional first year depreciation deduction that would have been allowable to the taxpayer on the remaining exchanged basis of the replacement MACRS property at the time of replacement, as defined in paragraph (g)(5)(iv)(A) of this section, plus the depreciation deductions that would have been allowable, including the additional first year depreciation deduction allowable, to the taxpayer on the depreciable excess basis of the replacement MACRS property from the date the replacement MACRS property was placed in service by the taxpayer, taking into account the applicable convention, to the time of disposition of the involuntarily converted MACRS property. Similar rules apply to replacement computer software.

(v) *Examples.*—The application of this paragraph (g)(5) is illustrated by the following examples:

(A) *Example 1.* (1) In April 2016, *CSK*, a calendar-year corporation, acquired for $200,000 and placed in service Canopy V1, a gas station canopy. Canopy V1 is qualified property under section 168(k)(2), as in effect on the day before amendment by the Act, and is 5-year property under section 168(e). *CSK* depreciated Canopy V1 under the general depreciation system of section 168(a) by using the 200-percent declining balance method of depreciation, a 5-year recovery period, and the half-year convention. *CSK* elected to use the optional depreciation tables to compute the depreciation allowance for Canopy V1. In November 2017, Canopy V1 was destroyed in a fire and was no longer usable in *CSK*'s business. In December 2017, in an involuntary conversion, *CSK* acquired and placed in service Canopy W1 with all of the $160,000 of insurance proceeds *CSK* received due to the loss of Canopy V1. Canopy W1 is qualified property under section 168(k)(2) and this section, and is 5-year property under section 168(e). Canopy W1 also meets the original use requirement in paragraph (b)(3)(ii) of this section. *CSK* did not make the election under §1.168(i)-6(i)(1).

(2) For 2016, *CSK* is allowed a 50-percent additional first year depreciation deduction of $100,000 for Canopy V1 (the unadjusted depreciable basis of $200,000 multiplied by 0.50), and a regular MACRS depreciation deduction of $20,000 for Canopy V1 (the remaining adjusted depreciable basis of $100,000 multiplied by the annual depreciation rate of 0.20 for recovery year 1).

(3) For 2017, *CSK* is allowed a regular MACRS depreciation deduction of $16,000 for Canopy V1 (the remaining adjusted depreciable basis of $100,000 multiplied by the annual depreciation rate of 0.32 for recovery year $2 \times \frac{1}{2}$ year).

(4) Pursuant to paragraph (g)(5)(iii)(A) of this section, the additional first year depreciation deduction allowable for Canopy W1 for 2017 equals $64,000 (100 percent of Canopy W1's remaining exchanged basis at the time of replacement of $64,000 (Canopy V1's remaining adjusted depreciable basis of $100,000 minus 2016 regular MACRS depreciation deduction of $20,000 minus 2017 regular MACRS depreciation deduction of $16,000)).

(B) *Example 2.* (1) The facts are the same as in *Example 1* of paragraph (g)(5)(v)(A)(1) of this section, except *CSK* elected not to deduct the additional first year depreciation for 5-year property placed in service in 2016. *CSK* deducted the additional first year depreciation for 5-year property placed in service in 2017.

(2) For 2016, *CSK* is allowed a regular MACRS depreciation deduction of $40,000 for Canopy V1 (the unadjusted depreciable basis of $200,000 multiplied by the annual depreciation rate of 0.20 for recovery year 1).

(3) For 2017, *CSK* is allowed a regular MACRS depreciation deduction of $32,000 for Canopy V1 (the unadjusted depreciable basis of $200,000 multiplied by the annual depreciation rate of 0.32 for recovery year $2 \times \frac{1}{2}$ year).

(4) Pursuant to paragraph (g)(5)(iii)(A) of this section, the additional first year depreciation deduction allowable for Canopy W1 for 2017 equals $128,000 (100 percent of Canopy W1's remaining exchanged basis at the time of replacement of $128,000 (Canopy V1's unadjusted depreciable basis of $200,000 minus 2016 regular MACRS

depreciation deduction of $40,000 minus 2017 regular MACRS depreciation deduction of $32,000)).

(C) *Example 3.* The facts are the same as in *Example 1* of paragraph (g)(5)(v)(A)(*1*) of this section, except Canopy W1 meets the used property acquisition requirements in paragraph (b)(3)(iii) of this section. Because the remaining excess basis of Canopy W1 is zero, *CSK* is not allowed any additional first year depreciation for Canopy W1 pursuant to paragraph (g)(5)(iii)(A) of this section.

(D) *Example 4.* (*1*) In December 2016, *AB*, a calendar-year corporation, acquired for $10,000 and placed in service Computer X2. Computer X2 is qualified property under section 168(k)(2), as in effect on the day before amendment by the Act, and is 5-year property under section 168(e). *AB* depreciated Computer X2 under the general depreciation system of section 168(a) by using the 200-percent declining balance method of depreciation, a 5-year recovery period, and the half-year convention. *AB* elected to use the optional depreciation tables to compute the depreciation allowance for Computer X2. In November 2017, *AB* acquired Computer Y2 by exchanging Computer X2 and $1,000 cash in a like-kind exchange. Computer Y2 is qualified property under section 168(k)(2) and this section, and is 5-year property under section 168(e). Computer Y2 also meets the original use requirement in paragraph (b)(3)(ii) of this section. *AB* did not make the election under §1.168(i)-6(i)(1).

(*2*) For 2016, *AB* is allowed a 50-percent additional first year depreciation deduction of $5,000 for Computer X2 (unadjusted basis of $10,000 multiplied by 0.50), and a regular MACRS depreciation deduction of $1,000 for Computer X2 (the remaining adjusted depreciable basis of $5,000 multiplied by the annual depreciation rate of 0.20 for recovery year 1).

(*3*) For 2017, *AB* is allowed a regular MACRS depreciation deduction of $800 for Computer X2 (the remaining adjusted depreciable basis of $5,000 multiplied by the annual depreciation rate of 0.32 for recovery year 2 × $^1/_2$ year).

(*4*) Pursuant to paragraph (g)(5)(iii)(A) of this section, the 100-percent additional first year depreciation deduction for Computer Y2 for 2017 is allowable for the remaining exchanged basis at the time of replacement of $3,200 (Computer X2's unadjusted depreciable basis of $10,000 minus additional first year depreciation deduction allowable of $5,000 minus the 2016 regular MACRS depreciation deduction of $1,000 minus the 2017 regular MACRS depreciation deduction of $800) and for the remaining excess basis at the time of replacement of $1,000 (cash paid for Computer Y2). Thus, the 100-percent additional first year depreciation deduction allowable for Computer Y2 totals $4,200 for 2017.

(E) *Example 5.* (*1*) In July 2017, *BC*, a calendar-year corporation, acquired for $20,000 and placed in service Equipment X3. Equipment X3 is qualified property under section 168(k)(2), as in effect on the day before amendment by the Act, and is 5-year property under section 168(e). *BC* depreciated Equipment X3 under the general depreciation system of section 168(a) by using the 200-percent declining balance method of depreciation, a 5-year recovery period, and the half-year convention. *BC* elected to use the optional depreciation tables to compute the depreciation allowance for Equipment X3. In December 2017, *BC* acquired Equipment Y3 by exchanging Equipment X3 and $5,000 cash in a like-kind exchange. Equipment Y3 is qualified property under section 168(k)(2) and this section, and is 5-year property under section 168(e). Equipment Y3 also meets the used property acquisition requirements in paragraph (b)(3)(iii) of this section. *BC* did not make the election under §1.168(i)-6(i)(1).

(*2*) Pursuant to §1.168(k)-1(f)(5)(iii)(B), no additional first year depreciation deduction is allowable for Equipment X3 and, pursuant to §1.168(d)-1(b)(3)(ii), no regular depreciation deduction is allowable for Equipment X3, for 2017.

(*3*) Pursuant to paragraph (g)(5)(iii)(A) of this section, no additional first year depreciation deduction is allowable for Equipment Y3's remaining exchanged basis at the time of replacement of $20,000 (Equipment X3's unadjusted depreciable basis of $20,000). However, pursuant to paragraph (g)(5)(iii)(A) of this section, the 100-percent additional first year depreciation deduction is allowable for Equipment Y3's remaining excess basis at the time of replacement of $5,000 (cash paid for Equipment Y3). Thus, the 100-percent additional first year depreciation deduction allowable for Equipment Y3 is $5,000 for 2017.

(F) *Example 6.* (*1*) The facts are the same as in *Example 5* of paragraph (g)(5)(v)(E)(*1*) of this section, except *BC* properly makes the election under §1.168(i)-6(i)(1) not to apply §1.168(i)-6 to Equipment X3 and Equipment Y3.

(*2*) Pursuant to §1.168(k)-1(f)(5)(iii)(B), no additional first year depreciation deduction is allowable for Equipment X3 and, pursuant to §1.168(d)-1(b)(3)(ii), no regular depreciation deduction is allowable for Equipment X3, for 2017.

(*3*) Pursuant to §1.168(i)-6(i)(1), *BC* is treated as placing Equipment Y3 in service in December 2017 with a basis of $25,000 (the total of the exchanged basis of $20,000 and the excess basis of $5,000).

However, pursuant to paragraph (g)(5)(iii)(D)(*2*) of this section, the 100-percent additional first year depreciation deduction is allowable only for Equipment Y3's excess basis at the time of replacement of $5,000 (cash paid for Equipment Y3). Thus, the 100-percent additional first year depreciation deduction allowable for Equipment Y3 is $5,000 for 2017.

(6) *Change in use.*—(i) *Change in use of MACRS property.*—The determination of whether the use of MACRS property, as defined in §1.168(b)-1(a)(2), changes is made in accordance with section 168(i)(5) and §1.168(i)-4.

(ii) *Conversion to personal use.*—If qualified property is converted from business or income-producing use to personal use in the same taxable year in which the property is placed in service by a taxpayer, the additional first year depreciation deduction is not allowable for the property.

(iii) *Conversion to business or income-producing use.*— (A) *During the same taxable year.*—If, during the same taxable year, property is acquired by a taxpayer for personal use and is converted by the taxpayer from personal use to business or income-producing use, the additional first year depreciation deduction is allowable for the property in the taxable year the property is converted to business or income-producing use, assuming all of the requirements in paragraph (b) of this section are met. See paragraph (b)(3)(ii) of this section relating to the original use rules for a conversion of property to business or income-producing use. See §1.168(i)-4(b)(1) for determining the depreciable basis of the property at the time of conversion to business or income-producing use.

(B) *Subsequent to the acquisition year.*—If property is acquired by a taxpayer for personal use and, during a subsequent taxable year, is converted by the taxpayer from personal use to business or income-producing use, the additional first year depreciation deduction is allowable for the property in the taxable year the property is converted to business or income-producing use, assuming all of the requirements in paragraph (b) of this section are met. For purposes of paragraphs (b)(4) and (5) of this section, the property must be acquired by the taxpayer for personal use after September 27, 2017, and converted by the taxpayer from personal use to business or income-producing use by January 1, 2027. See paragraph (b)(3)(ii) of this section relating to the original use rules for a conversion of property to business or income-producing use. See §1.168(i)-4(b)(1) for determining the depreciable basis of the property at the time of conversion to business or income-producing use.

(iv) *Depreciable property changes use subsequent to the placed-in-service year.*—(A) If the use of qualified property changes in the hands of the same taxpayer subsequent to the taxable year the qualified property is placed in service and, as a result of the change in use, the property is no longer qualified property, the additional first year depreciation deduction allowable for the qualified property is not redetermined.

(B) If depreciable property is not qualified property in the taxable year the property is placed in service by the taxpayer, the additional first year depreciation deduction is not allowable for the property even if a change in the use of the property subsequent to the taxable year the property is placed in service results in the property being qualified property in the taxable year of the change in use.

(v) *Examples.*—The application of this paragraph (g)(6) is illustrated by the following examples:

(A) *Example 1.* (*1*) On January 1, 2019, *FFF*, a calendar year corporation, purchased and placed in service several new computers at a total cost of $100,000. *FFF* used these computers within the United States for 3 months in 2019 and then moved and used the computers outside the United States for the remainder of 2019. On January 1, 2020, *FFF* permanently returns the computers to the United States for use in its business.

(*2*) For 2019, the computers are considered as used predominantly outside the United States in 2019 pursuant to §1.48-1(g)(1)(i). As a result, the computers are required to be depreciated under the alternative depreciation system of section 168(g). Pursuant to paragraph (b)(2)(ii)(B) of this section, the computers are not qualified property in 2019, the placed-in-service year. Thus, pursuant to paragraph (g)(6)(iv)(B) of this section, no additional first year depreciation deduction is allowed for these computers, regardless of the fact that the computers are permanently returned to the United States in 2020.

(B) *Example 2.* (*1*) On February 8, 2023, *GGG*, a calendar year corporation, purchased and placed in service new equipment at a cost of $1,000,000 for use in its California plant. The equipment is 5-year property under section 168(e) and is qualified property under section 168(k). *GGG* depreciates its 5-year property placed in service in 2023 using the optional depreciation table that corresponds with the general depreciation system, the 200-percent declining balance method, a 5-year recovery period, and the half-year convention. On June 4, 2024, due to changes in *GGG*'s business circumstances, *GGG* permanently moves the equipment to its plant in Mexico.

(2) For 2023, *GGG* is allowed an 80-percent additional first year depreciation deduction of $800,000 (the adjusted depreciable basis of $1,000,000 multiplied by 0.80). In addition, *GGG*'s depreciation deduction allowable in 2023 for the remaining adjusted depreciable basis of $200,000 (the unadjusted depreciable basis of $1,000,000 reduced by the additional first year depreciation deduction of $800,000) is $40,000 (the remaining adjusted depreciable basis of $200,000 multiplied by the annual depreciation rate of 0.20 for recovery year 1).

(3) For 2024, the equipment is considered as used predominantly outside the United States pursuant to §1.48-1(g)(1)(i). As a result of this change in use, the adjusted depreciable basis of $160,000 for the equipment is required to be depreciated under the alternative depreciation system of section 168(g) beginning in 2024. However, the additional first year depreciation deduction of $800,000 allowed for the equipment in 2023 is not redetermined.

(7) *Earnings and profits.*—The additional first year depreciation deduction is not allowable for purposes of computing earnings and profits.

(8) *Limitation of amount of depreciation for certain passenger automobiles.*—For a passenger automobile as defined in section 280F(d)(5), the limitation under section 280F(a)(1)(A)(i) is increased by $8,000 for qualified property acquired and placed in service by a taxpayer after September 27, 2017.

(9) *Coordination with section 47.*—(i) *In general.*—If qualified rehabilitation expenditures, as defined in section 47(c)(2) and §1.48-12(c), incurred by a taxpayer with respect to a qualified rehabilitated building, as defined in section 47(c)(1) and §1.48-12(b), are qualified property, the taxpayer may claim the rehabilitation credit provided by section 47(a), provided the requirements of section 47 are met—

(A) With respect to the portion of the basis of the qualified rehabilitated building that is attributable to the qualified rehabilitation expenditures if the taxpayer makes the applicable election under paragraph (f)(1)(i) of this section not to deduct any additional first year depreciation for the class of property that includes the qualified rehabilitation expenditures; or

(B) With respect to the portion of the remaining rehabilitated basis of the qualified rehabilitated building that is attributable to the qualified rehabilitation expenditures if the taxpayer claims the additional first year depreciation deduction on the unadjusted depreciable basis, as defined in §1.168(b)-1(a)(3) but before the reduction in basis for the amount of the rehabilitation credit, of the qualified rehabilitation expenditures; and the taxpayer depreciates the remaining adjusted depreciable basis, as defined in paragraph (e)(2)(i) of this section, of such expenditures using straight line cost recovery in accordance with section 47(c)(2)(B)(i) and §1.48-12(c)(7)(i). For purposes of this paragraph (g)(9)(i)(B), the remaining rehabilitated basis is equal to the unadjusted depreciable basis, as defined in §1.168(b)-1(a)(3) but before the reduction in basis for the amount of the rehabilitation credit, of the qualified rehabilitation expenditures that are qualified property reduced by the additional first year depreciation allowed or allowable, whichever is greater.

(ii) *Example.*—The application of this paragraph (g)(9) is illustrated by the following example:

(A) Between February 8, 2023, and June 4, 2023, *JM*, a calendar-year taxpayer, incurred qualified rehabilitation expenditures of $200,000 with respect to a qualified rehabilitated building that is nonresidential real property under section 168(e). These qualified rehabilitation expenditures are qualified property and qualify for the 20-percent rehabilitation credit under section 47(a)(1). *JM*'s basis in the qualified rehabilitated building is zero before incurring the qualified rehabilitation expenditures and *JM* placed the qualified rehabilitated building in service in July 2023. *JM* depreciates its nonresidential real property placed in service in 2023 under the general depreciation system of section 168(a) by using the straight line method of depreciation, a 39-year recovery period, and the mid-month convention. *JM* elected to use the optional depreciation tables to compute the depreciation allowance for its depreciable property placed in service in 2023. Further, for 2023, *JM* did not make any election under paragraph (f) of this section.

(B) Because *JM* did not make any election under paragraph (f) of this section, *JM* is allowed an 80-percent additional first year depreciation deduction of $160,000 for the qualified rehabilitation expenditures for 2023 (the unadjusted depreciable basis of $200,000 *(before reduction in basis for the rehabilitation credit)* multiplied by 0.80). *JM* also is allowed to claim a rehabilitation credit of $8,000 for the remaining rehabilitated basis of $40,000 (the unadjusted depreciable basis (before reduction in basis for the rehabilitation credit) of

$200,000 less the additional first year depreciation deduction of $160,000, multiplied by 0.20 to calculate the rehabilitation credit). For 2023, the ratable share of the rehabilitation credit of $8,000 is $1,600. Further, *JM*'s depreciation deduction for 2023 for the remaining adjusted depreciable basis of $32,000 (the unadjusted depreciable basis (before reduction in basis for the rehabilitation credit) of $200,000 less the additional first year depreciation deduction of $160,000 less the rehabilitation credit of $8,000) is $376.64 (the remaining adjusted depreciable basis of $32,000 multiplied by the depreciation rate of 0.01177 for recovery year 1, placed in service in month 7).

(10) *Coordination with section 514(a)(3).*—The additional first year depreciation deduction is not allowable for purposes of section 514(a)(3).

(11) *Mid-quarter convention.*—In determining whether the mid-quarter convention applies for a taxable year under section 168(d)(3) and §1.168(d)-1, the depreciable basis, as defined in §1.168(d)-1(b)(4), for the taxable year the qualified property is placed in service by the taxpayer is not reduced by the allowed or allowable additional first year depreciation deduction for that taxable year. See §1.168(d)-1(b)(4).

(h) *Applicability dates.*—(1) *In general.*—Except as provided in paragraphs (h)(2) and (3) of this section, this section applies to—

(i) Depreciable property acquired after September 27, 2017, by the taxpayer and placed in service by the taxpayer during or after the taxpayer's taxable year that begins on or after January 1, 2021;

(ii) A specified plant for which the taxpayer properly made an election to apply section 168(k)(5) and that is planted, or grafted to a plant that was previously planted, by the taxpayer during or after the taxpayer's taxable year that begins on or after January 1, 2021; and

(iii) Components acquired or self-constructed after September 27, 2017, of larger self-constructed property described in paragraph (c)(2) of this section and placed in service by the taxpayer during or after the taxpayer's taxable year that begins on or after January 1, 2021.

(2) *Applicability of this section for prior taxable years.*—For taxable years beginning before January 1, 2021, see §1.168(k)-2 as contained in 26 CFR part 1, revised as of April 1, 2020.

(3) *Early application of this section and §1.1502-68.*—(i) *In general.*—Subject to paragraphs (h)(3)(ii) and (iii) of this section, and provided that all members of a consolidated group consistently apply the same set of rules, a taxpayer may choose to apply both the rules of this section and the rules of §1.1502-68 (to the extent relevant), in their entirety and in a consistent manner, to—

(A) Depreciable property acquired after September 27, 2017, by the taxpayer and placed in service by the taxpayer during a taxable year ending on or after September 28, 2017;

(B) A specified plant for which the taxpayer properly made an election to apply section 168(k)(5) and that is planted, or grafted to a plant that was previously planted, after September 27, 2017, by the taxpayer during a taxable year ending on or after September 28, 2017; and

(C) Components acquired or self-constructed after September 27, 2017, of larger self-constructed property described in paragraph (c)(2) of this section and placed in service by the taxpayer during a taxable year ending on or after September 28, 2017.

(ii) *Early application to certain transactions.*—In the case of property described in §1.1502-68(e)(2)(i) that is acquired in a transaction that satisfies the requirements of §1.1502-68(c)(1)(ii) or (c)(2)(ii), the taxpayer may apply the rules of this section and the rules of §1.1502-68 (to the extent relevant), in their entirety and in a consistent manner, to such property only if those rules are applied, in their entirety and in a consistent manner, by all parties to the transaction, including the transferor member, the transferee member, and the target, as applicable, and the consolidated groups of which they are members, for the taxable year(s) in which the transaction occurs and the taxable year(s) that includes the day after the deconsolidation date, as defined in §1.1502-68(a)(2)(iii).

(iii) *Bound by early application.*—Once a taxpayer applies the rules of this section and the rules of §1.1502-68 (to the extent relevant), in their entirety, for a taxable year, the taxpayer must continue to apply the rules of this section and the rules of §1.1502-68 (to the extent relevant), in their entirety, for the taxpayer's subsequent taxable years. [Reg. §1.168(k)-2.]

☐ [*T.D. 9874, 9-17-2019. Amended by T.D. 9916, 11-5-2020.*]

[Reg. §1.169-1]

§1.169-1. Amortization of pollution control facilities.—
(a) *Allowance of deduction.*—(1) *In general.*—Under section 169(a),

every person, at his election, shall be entitled to a deduction with respect to the amortization of the amortizable basis (as defined in §1.169-3) of any certified pollution control facility (as defined in §1.169-2), based on a period of 60 months. Under section 169(b) and paragraph (a) of §1.169-4, the taxpayer may further elect to begin such 60-month period either with the month following the month in which the facility is completed or acquired or with the first month of the taxable year succeeding the taxable year in which such facility is completed or acquired. Under section 169(c), a taxpayer who has elected under section 169(b) to take the amortization deduction provided by section 169(a) may, at any time after making such election and prior to the expiration of the 60-month amortization period, elect to discontinue the amortization deduction for the remainder of the 60-month period in the manner prescribed in paragraph (b)(1) of §1.169-4. In addition, if on or before May 18, 1971, an election under section 169(a) has been made, consent is hereby given to revoke such election without the consent of the Commissioner in the manner prescribed in paragraph (b)(2) of §1.169-4.

(2) *Amount of deduction.*—With respect to each month of such 60-month period which falls within the taxable year, the amortization deduction shall be an amount equal to the amortizable basis of the certified pollution control facility at the end of such month divided by the number of months (including the month for which the deduction is computed) remaining in such 60-month period. The amortizable basis at the end of any month shall be computed without regard to the amortization deduction for such month. The total amortization deduction with respect to a certified pollution control facility for a taxable year is the sum of the amortization deductions allowable for each month of the 60-month period which falls within such taxable year. If a certified pollution control facility is sold or exchanged or otherwise disposed of during one month, the amortization deduction (if any) allowable to the original holder in respect of such month shall be that portion of the amount to which such person would be entitled for a full month which the number of days in such month during which the facility was held by such person bears to the total number of days in such month.

(3) *Effect on other deductions.*—(i) The amortization deduction provided by section 169 with respect to any month shall be in lieu of the depreciation deduction which would otherwise be allowable under section 167 or a deduction in lieu of depreciation which would otherwise be allowable under paragraph (b) of §1.162-11 for such month.

(ii) If the adjusted basis of such facility as computed under section 1011 for purposes other than the amortization deduction provided by section 169 is in excess of the amortizable basis, as computed under §1.169-3, such excess shall be recovered through depreciation deductions under the rules of section 167. See section 169(g).

(iii) See section 179 and paragraph (e)(1)(ii) of §1.179-1 and paragraph (b)(2) of §1.169-3 for additional first-year depreciation in respect of a certified pollution control facility.

(4) [Deleted.]

(5) *Special rules.*—(i) In the case of a certified pollution control facility held by one person for life with the remainder to another person, the amortization deduction under section 169(a) shall be computed as if the life tenant were the absolute owner of the property and shall be allowable to the life tenant during his life.

(ii) If the assets of a corporation which has elected to take the amortization deduction under section 169(a) are acquired by another corporation in a transaction to which section 381 (relating to carryovers in certain corporate acquisitions) applies, the acquiring corporation is to be treated as if it were the distributor or transferor corporation for purposes of this section.

(iii) For the right of estates and trusts to amortize pollution control facilities see section 642(f) and §1.642(f)-1. For the allowance of the amortization deduction in the case of pollution control facilities of partnerships, see section 703 and §1.703-1.

(6) *Depreciation subsequent to discontinuance or in the case of revocation of amortization.*—A taxpayer which elects in the manner prescribed under paragraph (b)(1) of §1.169-4 to discontinue amortization deductions or under paragraph (b)(2) of §1.169-4 to *revoke an election under section 169(a)* with respect to a certified pollution control facility is entitled, if such facility is of a character subject to the allowance for depreciation provided in section 167, to a deduction for depreciation (to the extent allowable) with respect to such facility. In the case of an election to discontinue an amortization deduction, the deduction for depreciation shall begin with the first month as to which such amortization deduction is not applicable and shall be computed on the adjusted basis of the property as of the beginning of such month (see section 1011 and the regulations thereunder). Such depreciation deduction shall be based upon the remaining portion of the period authorized under section 167 for the facility,

as determined, as of the first day of the first month as of which the amortization deduction is not applicable. If the taxpayer so elects to discontinue the amortization deduction under section 169(a), such taxpayer shall not be entitled to any further amortization deduction under this section and section 169(a) with respect to such pollution control facility. In the case of a revocation of an election under section 169(a), the deduction for depreciation shall begin as of the time such depreciation deduction would have been taken but for the election under section 169(a). See paragraph (b)(2) of §1.169-4 for rules as to filing amended returns for years for which amortization deductions have been taken.

(7) *Definitions.*—Except as otherwise provided in §1.169-2, all terms used in section 169 and the regulations thereunder shall have the meaning provided by this section and §§1.169-2 through 1.169-4.

(b) *Examples.*—This section may be illustrated by the following examples:

Example (1). On September 30, 1970, the X Corporation, which uses the calendar year as its taxable year, completes the installation of a facility all of which qualifies as a certified pollution control facility within the meaning of paragraph (a) of §1.169-2. The cost of the facility is $120,000 and the period referred to in paragraph (a)(6) of §1.169-2 is 10 years. In accordance with the rules set forth in paragraph (a) of §1.169-4, on its income tax return filed for 1970, X elects to take amortization deductions under section 169(a) with respect to the facility and to begin the 60-month amortization period with October 1970, the month following the month in which it was completed. The amortizable basis at the end of October 1970 (determined without regard to the amortization deduction under section 169(a) for that month) is $120,000. The allowable amortization deduction with respect to such facility for the taxable year 1970 is $6,000, computed as follows:

Monthly amortization deductions:

October: $120,000 divided by 60	$2,000
November: $118,000 (that is, $120,000 minus $2,000) divided by 59	2,000
December: $116,000 (that is, $118,000 minus $2,000) divided by 58	2,000
Total amortization deduction for 1970	$6,000

Example (2). Assume the same facts as in example (1). Assume further that on May 20, 1972, X properly files notice of its election to discontinue the amortization deductions with the month of June 1972. The adjusted basis of the facility as of June 1, 1972, is $80,000, computed as follows:

Yearly amortization deductions:

1970 (as computed in example (1))	$6,000
1971 (computed in accordance with example (1)) .	24,000
1972 (for the first five months of 1972 computed in accordance with example (1))	10,000
Total amortization deduction for 20 months . . .	40,000
Adjusted basis at beginning of amortization period . .	120,000
Less: Amortization deductions	40,000
Adjusted basis as of June 1, 1972	$80,000

Beginning as of June 1, 1972, the deduction for depreciation under section 167 is allowable with respect to the property on its adjusted basis of $80,000. [Reg. §1.169-1.]

☐ [T.D. 7116, 5-17-71. Amended by T.D. 7203, 8-24-72.]

[Reg. §1.169-2]

§1.169-2. Definitions.—(a) *Certified pollution control facility.*—(1) *In general.*—Under section 169(d), the term "certified pollution control facility" means a facility which—

(i) The Federal certifying authority certifies, in accordance with the rules prescribed in paragraph (c) of this section, is a "treatment facility" described in subparagraph (2) of this paragraph, and

(ii) Is "a new identifiable facility" (as defined in paragraph (b) of this section).

For profitmaking abatement works limitation, see paragraph (d) of this section.

(2) *Treatment facility.*—For purposes of subparagraph (1)(i) of this paragraph, a "treatment facility" is a facility which (i) is used to abate or control water or atmospheric pollution or contamination by removing, altering, disposing, or storing of pollutants, contaminants, wastes, or heat and (ii) is used in connection with a plant or other property in operation before January 1, 1969. Determinations under subdivision (i) of this subparagraph shall be made solely by the Federal certifying authority. See subparagraph (3) of this paragraph. For meaning of the phrases "plant or other property" and "in operation before January 1, 1969," see subparagraphs (4) and (5), respectively, of this paragraph.

(3) *Facilities performing multiple functions or used in connection with several plants, etc.*—(i) If a facility is designed to perform or does perform a function in addition to abating or controlling water or atmospheric pollution or contamination by removing, altering, disposing or storing pollutants, contaminants, wastes, or heat, such facility shall be a treatment facility only with respect to that part of the cost thereof which is certified by the Federal certifying authority as attributable to abating or controlling water or atmospheric pollution or contamination. For example, if a machine which performs a function in addition to abating water pollution is installed at a cost of $100,000 in, and is used only in connection with, a plant which was in operation before January 1, 1969, and if the Federal certifying authority certifies that $30,000 of the cost of such machine is allocable to its function of abating water pollution, such $30,000 will be deemed to be the adjusted basis for purposes of determining gain for purposes of paragraph (a) of §1.169-3.

(ii) If a facility is used in connection with more than one plant or other property, and at least one such plant or other property was not in operation before January 1, 1969, such facility shall be a treatment facility only to the extent of that part of the cost thereof certified by the Federal certifying authority as attributable to abating or controlling water or atmospheric pollution in connection with plants or other property in operation before January 1, 1969. For example, if a machine is constructed after December 31, 1968, at a cost of $100,000 and is used in connection with a number of plants only some of which were in operation before January 1, 1969, and if the Federal certifying authority certifies that $20,000 of the cost of such machine is allocable to its function of abating or controlling water pollution in connection with the plants or other property in operation before January 1, 1969, such $20,000 will be deemed to be the adjusted basis for purposes of determining gain for purposes of paragraph (a) of §1.169-3. In a case in which the Federal certifying authority certifies the percentage of a facility which is used in connection with plants or other property in operation before January 1, 1969, the adjusted basis for the purposes of determining gain for purposes of paragraph (a) of §1.169-3 of the portion of the facility so used shall be the adjusted basis for determining gain of the entire facility multiplied by such percentage.

(4) *Plant or other property.*—As used in subparagraph (2) of this paragraph, the phrase "plant or other property" means any tangible property whether or not such property is used in the trade or business or held for the production of income. Such term includes, for example, a papermill, a motor vehicle, or a furnace in an apartment house.

(5) *In operation before January 1, 1969.*—(i) For purposes of subparagraph (2) of this paragraph and section 169(d), a plant or other property will be considered to be in operation before January 1, 1969, if prior to that date such plant or other property was actually performing the function for which it was constructed or acquired. For example, a papermill which is completed in July 1968, but which is not actually used to produce paper until 1969 would not be considered to be in operation before January 1, 1969. The fact that such plant or other property was only operating at partial capacity prior to January 1, 1969, or was being used as a standby facility prior to such date, shall not prevent its being considered to be in operation before such date.

(ii)*(a)* A piece of machinery which replaces one which was in operation prior to January 1, 1969, and which was a part of the manufacturing operation carried on by the plant but which does not substantially increase the capacity of the plant will be considered to be in operation prior to January 1, 1969. However, an additional machine that is added to a plant which was in operation before January 1, 1969, and which represents a substantial increase in the plant's capacity will not be considered to have been in operation before such date. There shall be deemed to be a substantial increase in the capacity of a plant or other property as of the time its capacity exceeds by more than 20 percent its capacity on December 31, 1968.

(b) In addition, if the total replacements of equipment in any single taxable year beginning after December 31, 1968, represent the replacement of a substantial portion of a manufacturing plant which had been in operation before such date, such replacement shall be considered to result in a new plant which was not in operation before such date. Thus, if a substantial portion of a plant which was in existence before January 1, 1969, is subsequently destroyed by fire and such substantial portion is replaced in a taxable year beginning after that date, such replacement property shall not be considered to have been in operation before January 1, 1969. The replacement of a substantial portion of a plant or other property shall be deemed to have occurred if, during a single taxable year, the taxpayer replaces manufacturing or production facilities or equipment, which comprises such plant or other property, and which has an adjusted basis (determined without regard to the adjustments provided in section 1016(a)(2) and (3)) in excess of 20 percent of the adjusted basis (so

determined) of such plant or other property determined as of the first day of such taxable year.

(6) *Useful life.*—For purposes of section 169 and the regulations thereunder, the terms "useful life" and "actual useful life" shall mean the shortest period authorized under section 167 and the regulations thereunder if an election were not made under section 169.

(b) *New identifiable facility.*—(1) *In general.*—For purposes of paragraph (a)(1)(ii) of this section, the term "new identifiable facility" includes only tangible property (not including a building and its structural components referred to in subparagraph (2)(i) of this paragraph, other than a building and its structural components which under subparagraph (2)(ii) of this paragraph is exclusively a treatment facility) which—

(i) Is of a character subject to the allowance for depreciation provided in section 167,

(ii)*(a)* Is property the construction, reconstruction, or erection (as defined in subparagraph (2)(iii) of this paragraph) of which is completed by the taxpayer after December 31, 1968, or

(b) Is property acquired by the taxpayer after December 31, 1968, if the original use of the property commences with the taxpayer and commences after such date (see subparagraph (2)(ii) of this paragraph), and

(iii) Is placed in service (as defined in subparagraph (2)(iv) of this paragraph) prior to January 1, 1975.

(2) *Meaning of terms.*—(i) For purposes of subparagraph (1) of this paragraph, the terms "building" and "structural component" shall be construed in a manner consistent with the principles set forth in paragraph (e) of §1-48-1. Thus, for example, the following rules are applicable:

(a) The term "building" generally means any structure or edifice enclosing a space within its walls, and usually covered by a roof, the purpose of which is, for example, to provide shelter or housing, or to provide working, office, parking, display, or sales space. The term includes, for example, structures such as apartment houses, factory and office buildings, warehouses, barns, garages, railway or bus stations, and stores. Such term includes any such structure constructed by, or for, a lessee even if such structure must be removed, or ownership of such structure reverts to the lessor, at the termination of the lease. Such term does not include *(1)* a structure which is essentially an item of machinery or equipment, or *(2)* an enclosure which is so closely combined with the machinery or equipment which it supports, houses, or serves that it must be replaced, retired, or abandoned contemporaneously with such machinery or equipment, and which is depreciated over the life of such machinery or equipment. Thus, the term "building" does not include such structures as oil and gas storage tanks, grain storage bins, silos, fractioning towers, blast furnaces, coke ovens, brick kilns, and coal tipples.

(b) The term "structural components" includes, for example, chimneys, and other components relating to the operating or maintenance of a building. However, the term "structural components" does not include machinery or a device which serves no function other than the abatement or control of water or atmospheric pollution.

(ii) For purposes of subparagraph (1) of this paragraph, a building and its structural components is exclusively a treatment facility if the Federal certifying authority certifies that its only function is the abatement or control of air or water pollution. However, the incidental recovery of profits from wastes or otherwise shall not be deemed to be a function other than the abatement or control of air or water pollution. A building and its structural components which serve no function other than the treatment of wastes will be considered to be exclusively a treatment facility even if its contains areas for employees to operate the treatment facility, rest rooms for such workers, and an office for the management of such treatment facility. However, for example, if a portion of a building is used for the treatment of sewage and another portion of the building is used for the manufacture of machinery, the building is not exclusively a treatment facility. The Federal certifying authority will not certify as to what is a building and its structural components within the meaning of subdivision (i) of this subparagraph.

(iii) For purposes of subparagraph (1)(ii) *(a)* and *(b)* of this paragraph (relating to construction, reconstruction, or erection after December 31, 1968, and original use after December 31, 1968) and paragraph (b)(1) of §1.169-3 (relating to definition of amortizable basis), the principles set forth in paragraph (a)(1) and (2) of §1.167(c)-1 and in paragraphs (b) and (c) of §1.48-2 shall be applied. Thus, for example, the following rules are applicable:

(a) Property is considered as constructed, reconstructed, or erected by the taxpayer if the work is done for him in accordance with his specifications.

(b) The portion of the basis of property attributable to construction, reconstruction, or erection after December 31, 1968, consists of all costs of construction, reconstruction, or erection allocable to the period after December 31, 1968, including the cost or other basis of materials entering into such work (but not including, in the case of reconstruction of property, the adjusted basis of the property as of the time such reconstruction is commenced).

(c) It is not necessary that materials entering into construction, reconstruction or erection be acquired after December 31, 1968, or that they be new in use.

(d) If construction or erection by the taxpayer began after December 31, 1968, the entire cost or other basis of such construction or erection may be taken into account for purposes of determining the amortizable basis under section 169.

(e) Construction, reconstruction, or erection by the taxpayer begins when physical work is started on such construction, reconstruction, or erection.

(f) Property shall be deemed to be acquired when reduced to physical possession or control.

(g) The term "original use" means the first use to which the property is put, whether or not such use corresponds to the use of such property by the taxpayer. For example, a reconditioned or rebuilt machine acquired by the taxpayer after December 31, 1968, for pollution control purposes will not be treated as being put to original use by the taxpayer regardless of whether it was used for purposes other than pollution control by its previous owner. Whether property is reconditioned or rebuilt property is a question of fact. Property will not be treated as reconditioned or rebuilt merely because it contains some used parts.

(iv) For purposes of subparagraph (1)(iii) of this paragraph (relating to property placed in service prior to January 1, 1975), the principles set forth in paragraph (d) of § 1.46-3 are applicable. Thus, property shall be considered placed in service in the earlier of the following taxable years:

(a) The taxable year in which, under the taxpayer's depreciation practice, the period for depreciation with respect to such property begins or would have begun; or

(b) The taxable year in which the property is placed in a condition or state or readiness and availability for the abatement or control of water or atmospheric pollution.

Thus, if property meets the conditions of *(b)* of this subdivision in a taxable year, it shall be considered placed in service in such year notwithstanding that the period for depreciation with respect to such property begins or would have begun in a succeeding taxable year because, for example, under the taxpayer's depreciation practice such property is or would have been accounted for in a multiple asset account and depreciation is or would have been computed under an "averaging convention" (see § 1.167(a)-10), or depreciation with respect to such property would have been computed under the completed contract method, the unit of production method, or the retirement method. In the case of property acquired by a taxpayer for use in his trade or business (or in the production of income), property shall be considered in a condition or state of readiness and availability for the abatement or control of water or atmospheric pollution if, for example, equipment is acquired for the abatement or control of water or atmospheric pollution and is operational but is undergoing testing to eliminate any defects. However, materials and parts acquired to be used in the construction of an item of equipment shall not be considered in a condition or state of readiness and availability for the abatement or control of water or atmospheric pollution.

(c) Certification.—(1) *In general.*—For purposes of paragraph (a)(1) of this section, a facility is certified in accordance with the rules prescribed in this paragraph if—

(i) The State certifying authority (as defined in subparagraph (2) of this paragraph) having jurisdiction with respect to such facility has certified to the Federal certifying authority (as defined in subparagraph (3) of this paragraph) that the facility was constructed, reconstructed, erected, or acquired in conformity with the State program or requirements for the abatement or control of water or atmospheric pollution or contamination applicable at the time of such certification, and

(ii) The Federal certifying authority has certified such facility *to the Secretary* or his delegate as *(a)* being in compliance with the applicable regulations of Federal agencies (such as, for example, the Atomic Energy Commission's regulations pertaining to radiological discharge (10 CFR Part 20)) and *(b)* being in furtherance of the general policy of the United States for cooperation with the States in the prevention and abatement of water pollution under the Federal Water Pollution Control Act, as amended (33 U.S.C. 1151-1175) or in the prevention and abatement of atmospheric pollution and contamination under the Clear Air Act, as amended (42 U.S.C. 1857 et seq.).

(2) State certifying authority.—The term "state certifying authority" means—

(i) In the case of water pollution, the State water pollution control agency as defined in section 23(a) of the Federal Water Pollution Control Act, as amended (33 U.S.C. 1173(a)),

(ii) In the case of air pollution, the air pollution control agency designated pursuant to section 302(b)(1) of the Clean Air Act, as amended (42 U.S.C. 1857h(b)), and

(iii) Any interstate agency authorized to act in place of a certifying authority of a State. See section 23(a) of the Federal Water Pollution Control Act, as amended (33 U.S.C. 1173(b)) and section 302(c) of the Clean Air Act, as amended (42 U.S.C. 1857h(c)).

(3) Federal certifying authority.—The term "Federal certifying authority" means the Administrator of the Environmental Protection Agency (see Reorganization Plan No. 3 of 1970, 35 F.R. 15623).

(d) Profitmaking abatement works, etc.—(1) *In general.*—Section 169(e) provides that the Federal certifying authority shall not certify any property to the extent it appears that by reason of estimated profits to be derived through the recovery of wastes or otherwise in the operation of such property its costs will be recovered over the period referred to in paragraph (a)(6) of this section for such property. The Federal certifying authority need not certify the amount of estimated profits to be derived from such recovery of wastes or otherwise with respect to such facility. Such estimated profits shall be determined pursuant to subparagraph (2) of this paragraph. However, the Federal certifying authority shall certify—

(i) Whether, in connection with any treatment facility so certified, there is potential cost recovery through the recovery of wastes or otherwise, and

(ii) A specific description of the wastes which will be recovered, or the nature of such cost recovery if otherwise than through the recovery of wastes.

For effect on computation of amortizable basis, see paragraph (c) of § 1.169-3.

(2) Estimated profits.—For purpose of this paragraph, the term "estimated profits" means the estimated gross receipts from the sale of recovered wastes reduced by the sum of the (i) estimated average annual maintenance and operating expenses, including utilities and labor, allocable to that portion of the facility which is certified as a treatment facility pursuant to paragraph (a)(1)(i) of this section which produces the recovered waste from which the gross receipts are derived, and (ii) estimated selling expenses. However, in determining expenses to be subtracted neither depreciation nor amortization of the facility is to be taken into account. Estimated profits shall not include any estimated savings to the taxpayer by reason of the taxpayer's reuse or recycling of wastes or other items recovered in connection with the operation of the plant or other property served by the treatment facility.

(3) Special rules.—The estimates of cost recovery required by subparagraph (2) of this paragraph shall be based on the period referred to in paragraph (a)(6) of this section. Such estimates shall be made at the time the election provided for by section 169 is made and shall also be set out in the application for certification made to the Federal certifying authority. There shall be no redetermination of estimated profits due to unanticipated fluctuations in the market price for wastes or other items, to an unanticipated increase or decrease in the costs of extracting them from the gas or liquid released, or to other unanticipated factors or events occurring after certification [Reg. § 1.169-2.]

☐ [T.D. 7116, 5-17-71.]

[Reg. § 1.169-3]

§ 1.169-3. Amortizable basis.—(a) *In general.*—The amortizable basis of a certified pollution control facility for the purpose of computing the amortization deduction under section 169 is the adjusted basis of the facility for purposes of determining gain (see part II (section 1011 and following), subchapter O, chapter 1 of the Internal Revenue Code), in conjunction with paragraphs (b), (c), and (d) of this section. The adjusted basis for purposes of determining gain (computed without regard to paragraphs (b), (c), and (d) of this section) of a facility that performs a function in addition to pollution control, or that is used in connection with more than one plant or other property, or both, is determined under § 1.169-2(a)(3). For rules as to additions and improvements to such a facility, see paragraph (f) of this section. Before computing the amortization deduction allowable under section 169, the adjusted basis for purposes of determining gain for a facility that is placed in service by a taxpayer after September 10, 2001, and that is qualified property under section 168(k)(2) or § 1.168(k)-1, 50-percent bonus depreciation property under section 168(k)(4) or § 1.168(k)-1, or qualified New York Liberty Zone property under section 1400L(b) or § 1.1400L(b)-1 must be reduced by the amount of the additional first year depreciation deduction allowed or allowable, whichever is greater, under section

168(k) or section 1400L(b), as applicable, for the facility. Further, before computing the amortization deduction allowable under section 169, the adjusted basis for purposes of determining gain for a facility that is acquired and placed in service after September 27, 2017, and that is qualified property under section 168(k), as amended by the Tax Cuts and Jobs Act, Public Law 115-97 (131 Stat. 2054 (December 22, 2017)) (the "Act"), or §1.168(k)-2, must be reduced by the amount of the additional first year depreciation deduction allowed or allowable, whichever is greater, under section 168(k), as amended by the Act.

(b) *Limitation on post-1968 construction, reconstruction, or erection.*— (1) If the construction, reconstruction, or erection was begun before January 1, 1969, there shall be included in the amortizable basis only so much of the adjusted basis of such facility for purposes of determining gain (referred to in paragraph (a) of this section) as is properly attributable under the rules set forth in paragraph (b)(2)(iii) of §1.169-2 to construction, reconstruction, or erection after December 31, 1968. See section 169(d)(4). For example, assume a certified pollution control facility for which the shortest period authorized under section 167 is 10 years has a cost of $500,000, of which $450,000 is attributable to construction after December 31, 1968. Further, assume such facility does not perform a function in addition to pollution control and is used only in connection with a plant in operation before January 1, 1969. The facility would have an amortizable basis of $450,000 (computed without regard to paragraphs (c) and (d) of this section). For depreciation of the remaining portion ($50,000) of the cost, see section 169(g) and paragraph (a)(3)(ii) of §1.169-1. For the definition of the term "certified pollution control facility," see paragraph (a) of §1.169-2.

(2) If the taxpayer elects to begin the 60-month amortization period with the first month of the taxable year succeeding the taxable year in which the facility is completed or acquired and a depreciation deduction is allowable under section 167 (including an additional first-year depreciation allowance under former section 179; for a facility that is acquired by the taxpayer after September 10, 2001, and that is qualified property under section 168(k)(2) or §1.168(k)-1 or qualified New York Liberty Zone property under section 1400L(b) or §1.1400L(b)-1, the additional first year depreciation deduction under section 168(k)(1) or 1400L(b), as applicable; and for a facility that is acquired by the taxpayer after May 5, 2003, and that is 50-percent bonus depreciation property under section 168(k)(4) or §1.168(k)-1, the additional first year depreciation deduction under section 168(k)(4)) with respect to the facility for the taxable year in which it is completed or acquired, the amount determined under paragraph (b)(1) of this section shall be reduced by an amount equal to the amount of the depreciation deduction allowed or allowable, whichever is greater, multiplied by a fraction the numerator of which is the amount determined under paragraph (b)(1) of this section, and the denominator of which is the facility's total cost. The additional first-year allowance for depreciation under former section 179 will be allowable only for the taxable year in which the facility is completed or acquired and only if the taxpayer elects to begin the amortization deduction under section 169 with the taxable year succeeding the taxable year in which such facility is completed or acquired. For a facility that is acquired by a taxpayer after September 10, 2001, and that is qualified property under section 168(k)(2) or §1.168(k)-1 or qualified New York Liberty Zone property under section 1400L(b) or §1.1400L(b)-1, see §1.168(k)-1(f)(4) or §1.1400L(b)-1(f)(4), as applicable, with respect to when the additional first year depreciation deduction under section 168(k)(1) or 1400L(b) is allowable. For a facility that is acquired by a taxpayer after May 5, 2003, and that is 50-percent bonus depreciation property under section 168(k)(4) or §1.168(k)-1, see §1.168(k)-1(f)(4) with respect to when the additional first year depreciation deduction under section 168(k)(4) is allowable.

(c) *Modification for profitmaking abatement works, etc.*—If it appears that by reason of estimated profits to be derived through the recovery of wastes or otherwise (as determined by applying the rules prescribed in paragraph (d) of §1.169-2) a portion or all of the total costs of the certified pollution control facility will be recovered over the period referred to in paragraph (a)(6) of §1.169-2, its amortizable basis (computed without regard to this paragraph and paragraph (d) of this section) shall be reduced by an amount equal to (1) its amortizable basis (so computed) multiplied by (2) a fraction the numerator of which is such estimated profits and the denominator of which is its adjusted basis for purposes of determining gain. See section 169(e).

(d) *Cases in which the period referred to in paragraph (a)(6) of §1.169-2 exceeds 15 years.*—If as to a certified pollution control facility the period referred to in paragraph (a)(6) of §1.169-2 exceeds 15 years (determined as of the first day of the first month for which a deduction is allowable under the election made under section 169(b) and paragraph (a) of §1.169-4), the amortizable basis of such facility shall be an amount equal to (1) its amortizable basis (computed

without regard to this paragraph) multiplied by (2) a fraction the numerator of which is 15 years and the denominator of which is the number of years of such period. See section 169(f)(2)(A).

(e) *Examples.*—This section may be illustrated by the following examples:

Example (1). The X Corporation, which uses the calendar year as its taxable year, began the installation of a facility on November 1, 1968, and completed the installation on June 30, 1970, at a cost of $400,000. All of the facility qualifies as a certified pollution control facility within the meaning of paragraph (a) of §1.169-2. $40,000 of such cost is attributable to construction prior to January 1, 1969. The X Corporation elects to take amortization deductions under section 169(a) with respect to the facility and to begin the 60-month amortization period with January 1, 1971. The corporation takes a depreciation deduction under sections 167 and 179 of $10,000 (the amount allowable, of which $2,000 is for additional first year depreciation under section 179) for the last 6 months of 1970. It is estimated that over the period referred to in paragraph (a)(6) of §1.169-2 (20 years) as to such facility, $80,000 in profits will be realized from the sale of wastes recovered in its operation. The amortizable basis of the facility for purposes of computing the amortization deduction as of January 1, 1971, is $210,600, computed as follows:

(1)	Portion of $400,000 cost attributable to post-1968 construction, reconstruction, or erection	$360,000
(2)	Reduction for portion of depreciation deduction taken for the taxable year in which the facility was completed:	
	(a) $10,000 depreciation deduction taken for last 6 months of 1970 including $2,000 for additional first year depreciation under section 179 .... $10,000	
	(b) Multiplied by the amount in line (1) and divided by the total cost of the facility ($360,000/$400,000) 0.9	$9,000
(3)	Subtotal	$351,000
(4)	Modification for profitmaking abatement works: Multiply line (3) by estimated profits through waste recovery ($80,000) and divide by the adjusted basis for determining gain of the facility ($400,000)	
(5)	Reduction	70,200
(6)	Subtotal	$280,800
(7)	Modification for period referred to in paragraph (a)(6) of §1.169-2 exceeding 15 years: Multiply by 15 years and divide by such period (determined in accordance with paragraph (d) of this section) (20 years)	$0.75
(8)	Amortizable basis	$210,600

Example (2). Assume the same facts as in example (1), except that the facility is used in connection with a number of separate plants, some of which were in operation before January 1, 1969, that the Federal certifying authority certifies that 80 percent of the capacity of the facility is allocable to the plants which were in operation before such date, and that all of the waste recovery is allocable to the portion of the facility used in connection with the plants in operation before January 1, 1969. The amortizable basis of such facility, for purposes of computing the amortization deduction as of January 1, 1971, is $157,950 computed as follows:

(1)	Adjusted basis for purposes of determining gain: Multiply percent certified as allocable to plants in operation before January 1, 1969 (80 percent) by cost of entire facility ($400,000) ...	$320,000
(2)	Portion of adjusted basis for determining gain attributable to post-1968 construction, reconstruction, or erection: Multiply line (1) by portion of total cost of facility attributable to post-1968 construction, reconstruction, or erection ($360,000) and divide by the total cost of the facility ($400,000)	$288,000
(3)	Reduction for portion of depreciation deduction taken for the taxable year in which the facility was completed:	
	(a) $10,000 depreciation deduction taken for last 6 months of 1970 including $2,000 for additional first year depreciation under section 170 .... $10,000	

(b) Multiplied by the amount in line (2) and divided by the total cost of the facility ($288,000/$400,000)	0.72	7,200
(4) Subtotal		$280,800
(5) Modification for profit making abatement works; Multiply line (4) by estimated profits through waste recovery ($80,000) and divide by the amount in line (1) ($320,000)		
(6) Reduction		$70,200
(7) Subtotal		$210,600
(8) Modification for period referred to in paragraph (a)(6) of §1.169-2 exceeding 15 years: Multiply by 15 years and divide by such period (determined in accordance with paragraph (d) of this section) (20 years)	0.75	
(9) Amortizable basis		$157,950

(f) *Additions or improvements.*—(1) If after the completion or acquisition of a certified pollution control facility further expenditures are made for additional construction, reconstruction, or improvements, the cost of such additions or improvements made prior to the beginning of the amortization period shall increase the amortizable basis of such facility, but the cost of additions or improvements made after the amortization period has begun shall not increase the amortizable basis. See section 169(f)(2)(B).

(2) If expenditures for such additional construction, reconstruction, or improvements result in a facility which is new and is separately certified as a certified pollution control facility as defined in section 169(d)(1) and paragraph (a) of §1.169-2, and, if proper election is made, such expenditures shall be taken into account in computing under paragraph (a) of this section the amortizable basis of such new and separately certified pollution control facility.

(g) *Effective date for qualified property, 50-percent bonus depreciation property, and qualified New York Liberty Zone property.*—This section applies to a certified pollution control facility. This section also applies to a certified pollution control facility that is qualified property under section 168(k)(2) or qualified New York Liberty Zone property under section 1400L(b) acquired by a taxpayer after September 10, 2001, and to a certified pollution control facility that is 50-percent bonus depreciation property under section 168(k)(4) acquired by a taxpayer after May 5, 2003. The last sentence of paragraph (a) of this section applies to a certified pollution control facility that is qualified property under section 168(k)(2) and placed in service by a taxpayer during or after the taxpayer's taxable year that includes September 24, 2019. However, a taxpayer may choose to apply the last sentence of paragraph (a) of this section to a certified pollution control facility that is qualified property under section 168(k)(2) and acquired and placed in service after September 27, 2017, by the taxpayer during taxable years ending on or after September 28, 2017. A taxpayer may rely on the last sentence in paragraph (a) of this section in regulation project REG-104397-18 (2018-41 IRB 558) (see §601.601(d)(2)(ii)(b) of this chapter) for a certified pollution control facility that is qualified property under section 168(k)(2) and acquired and placed in service after September 27, 2017, by the taxpayer during taxable years ending on or after September 28, 2017, and ending before the taxpayer's taxable year that includes September 24, 2019. [Reg. §1.169-3.]

☐ [T.D. 7116, 5-17-71. Amended by T.D. 9091, 9-5-2003, T.D. 9283, 8-28-2006 and T.D. 9874, 9-17-2019.]

[Reg. §1.169-4]

§1.169-4. Time and manner of making elections.—(a) *Election of amortization.*—(1) *In general.*—Under section 169(b), an election by the taxpayer to take an amortization deduction with respect to a certified pollution control facility and to begin the 60-month amortization period (either with the month following the month in which the facility is completed or acquired, or with the first month of the taxable year succeeding the taxable year in which such facility is completed or acquired) shall be made by a statement to that effect attached to its return for the taxable year in which falls the first month of the 60-month amortization period so elected. Such statement shall include the following information (if not otherwise included in the documents referred to in subdivision (ix) of this subparagraph):

(i) A description clearly identifying each certified pollution control facility for which an amortization deduction is claimed;

(ii) The date on which such facility was completed or acquired (see paragraph (b)(2)(iii) of §1.169-2);

(iii) The period referred to in paragraph (a)(6) of §1.169-2 for the facility as of the date the property is placed in service;

(iv) The date as of which the amortization period is to begin;

(v) The date the plant or other property to which the facility is connected began operating (see paragraph (a)(5) of §1.169-2);

(vi) The total costs and expenditures paid or incurred in the acquisition, construction, and installation of such facility;

(vii) A description of any wastes which the facility will recover during the course of its operation, and a reasonable estimate of the profits which will be realized by the sale of such wastes whether pollutants or otherwise, over the period referred to in paragraph (a)(6) of §1.169-2 as to the facility. Such estimate shall include a schedule setting forth a detailed computation illustrating how the estimate was computed including every element prescribed in the definition of estimated profits in paragraph (d)(2) of §1.169-2;

(viii) A computation showing the amortizable basis (as defined in §1.169-3) of the facility as of the first month for which the amortization deduction provided for by section 169(a) is elected; and

(ix) (a) A statement that the facility has been certified by the Federal certifying authority, together with a copy of such certification, and a copy of the application for certification which was filed with and approved by the Federal certifying authority or (b), if the facility has not been certified by the Federal certifying authority, a statement that application has been made to the proper State certifying authority (see paragraph (c)(2) of §1.169-2) together with a copy of such application and (except in the case of an election to which subparagraph (4) of this paragraph applies) a copy of the application filed or to be filed with the Federal certifying authority.

If subdivision (ix)(b) of this subparagraph applies, within 90 days after receipt by the taxpayer, the certification from the Federal certifying authority shall be filed by the taxpayer with the district director, or with the director of the internal revenue service center, with whom the return referred to in this subparagraph was filed.

(2) *Special rule.*—If the return for the taxable year in which falls the first month of the 60-month amortization period to be elected is filed before November 16, 1971, without making the election for such year, then on or before December 31, 1971 (or if there is no State certifying authority in existence on November 16, 1971, on or before the 90th day after such authority is established), the election may be made by a statement attached to an amended income tax return for the taxable year in which falls the first month of the 60-month amortization period so elected. Amended income tax returns or claims for credit or refund must also be filed at this time for other taxable years which are within the amortization period and which are subsequent to the taxable year for which the election is made. Nothing in this paragraph should be construed as extending the time specified in section 6511 within which a claim for credit or refund may be filed.

(3) *Other requirements and considerations.*—No method of making the election provided for in section 169(a) other than that prescribed in this section shall be permitted on or after May 18, 1971. A taxpayer which does not elect in the manner prescribed in this section to take amortization deductions with respect to a certified pollution control facility shall not be entitled to such deductions. In the case of a taxpayer which elects prior to May 18, 1971, the statement required by subparagraph (1) of this paragraph shall be attached to its income tax return for either its taxable year in which December 31, 1971 occurs or its taxable year preceding such year.

(4) *Elections filed before February 29, 1972.*—If a statement of election required by subparagraph (1) of this paragraph is attached to a return (including an amended return referred to in subparagraph (2) of this paragraph) filed before February 29, 1972, such statement of election need not include a copy of the Federal application to be filed with the Federal certifying authority but a copy of such application must be filed no later than February 29, 1972, by the taxpayer with the district director, or with the director of the internal revenue service center, with whom the return or amended return referred to in this subparagraph was filed.

(b) *Election to discontinue or revoke amortization.*—(1) *Election to discontinue.*—An election to discontinue the amortization deduction provided by section 169(c) and paragraph (a)(1) of §1.169-1 shall be made by a statement in writing filed with the district director, or with the director of the internal revenue service center, with whom the return of the taxpayer is required to be filed for its taxable year in which falls the first month for which the election terminates. Such statement shall specify the month as of the beginning of which the taxpayer elects to discontinue such deductions. Unless the election to discontinue amortization is one to which subparagraph (2) of this paragraph applies, such statement shall be filed before the beginning of the month specified therein. In addition, such statement shall contain a description clearly identifying the certified pollution control facility with respect to which the taxpayer elects to discontinue the amortization deduction, and, if a certification has previously been issued, a copy of the certification by the Federal certifying authority. If at the time of such election a certification has not been issued (or if one has been issued but has not been filed as provided in paragraph (a)(1) of this section), the taxpayer shall file, with respect to any taxable year or years for which a deduction under section 169 has been taken, a copy of such certification within 90 days after receipt thereof. For purposes of this paragraph, notification to the Secretary or his delegate from the Federal certifying authority that the facility no longer meets the requirements under which certification was originally granted by the State or Federal certifying authority shall have the same effect as a notice from the taxpayer electing to terminate amortization as of the month following the month such facility ceased functioning in accordance with such requirements.

(2) *Revocation of elections made prior to May 18, 1971.*—If on or before May 18, 1971, an election under section 169(a) has been made, such election may be revoked (see paragraph (a)(1) of §1.169-1) by filing on or before August 16, 1971, a statement of revocation of an election under section 169(a) in accordance with the requirements in subparagraph (1) of this paragraph for filing a notice to discontinue an election. If such election to revoke is for a period which falls within one or more taxable years for which an income tax return has been filed, amended income tax returns shall be filed for any such taxable years in which deductions were taken under section 169 on or before August 16, 1971. [Reg. §1.169-4.]

☐ [*T.D.* 7116, 5-17-71. *Amended by T.D.* 7135, 7-30-71 *and T.D.* 7153, 12-27-71.]

[Reg. §20.1]

§20.1. Applicability.—The regulations of this part apply to certifications by the Administrator of water or air pollution control facilities for purposes of section 169 of the Internal Revenue Code of 1954, as amended, 26 U.S.C. 169, as to which the amortization period began after December 31, 1975. Certification of air or water pollution control facilities as to which the amortization period began before January 1, 1976, will continue to be governed by Environmental Protection Agency regulations published November 25, 1971, at 36 FR 22382. Applicable regulations of the Department of Treasury are at 26 CFR 1.169 et seq. [Reg. §20.1.]

☐ [*Adopted* 11-25-71. *Amended* 1-9-78.]

[Reg. §20.2]

§20.2. Definitions.—As used in this part, the following terms shall have the meaning indicated below:

(a) "Act" means, when used in connection with water pollution control facilities, the Federal Water Pollution Control Act, as amended (33 U.S.C. 1251 et seq.) or, when used in connection with air pollution control facilities, the Clean Air Act, as amended (42 U.S.C. 1857 et seq.).

(b) "State certifying authority" means:

(1) For water pollution control facilities, the State pollution control agency as defined in section 502 of the Act;

(2) For air pollution control facilities, the air pollution control agency designated pursuant to section 302(b)(1) of the Act; or

(3) For both air and water pollution control facilities, any interstate agency authorized to act in place of the certifying agency of a State.

(c) "Applicant" means any person who files an application with the Administrator for certification that a facility is in compliance with the applicable regulations of Federal agencies and in furtherance of the general policies of the United States for cooperation with the States in the prevention and abatement of water or air pollution under the Act.

(d) "Administrator" means the Administrator, Environmental Protection Agency.

(e) "Regional Administrator" means the Regional designee appointed by the Administrator to certify facilities under this part.

(f) "Facility" means property comprising any new identifiable treatment facility which removes, alters, disposes of, stores, or prevents the creation of pollutants, contaminants, wastes, or heat.

(g) "State" means the States, the District of Columbia, the Commonwealth of Puerto Rico, the Canal Zone, Guam, American Samoa, the Virgin Islands, and the Trust Territory of the Pacific Islands. [Reg. §20.2.]

☐ [*Adopted* 11-25-71. *Amended* 1-9-78.]

[Reg. §20.3]

§20.3. General provisions.—(a) An applicant shall file an application in accordance with this part for each separate facility for which certification is sought: *Provided,* That one application shall suffice in the case of substantially identical facilities which the applicant has installed or plans to install in connection with substantially identical properties: *Provided further,* That an application may incorporate by

reference material contained in an application previously submitted by the applicant under this part and pertaining to substantially identical facilities.

(b) The applicant shall, at the time of application to the State certifying authority, submit an application in the form prescribed by the Administrator to the Regional Administrator for the region in which the facility is located.

(c) Applications will be considered complete and will be processed when the Regional Administrator receives the completed State certification.

(d) Applications may be filed prior or subsequent to the commencement of construction, acquisition, installation, or operation of the facility.

(e) An amendment to an application shall be submitted in the same manner as the original application and shall be considered a part of the original application.

(f) If the facility is certified by the Regional Administrator, notice of certification will be issued to the Secretary of the Treasury or his delegate, and a copy of the notice shall be forwarded to the applicant and to the State certifying authority. If the facility is denied certification, the Regional Administrator will advise the applicant and State certifying authority in writing of the reasons therefor.

(g) No certification will be made by the Regional Administrator for any facility prior to the time it is placed in operation and the application, or amended application, in connection with such facility so states.

(h) An applicant may appeal any decision of the Regional Administrator which:

(1) Denies certification;

(2) Disapproves the applicant's suggested method of allocating costs pursuant to §20.8(e); or

(3) Revokes a certification pursuant to §20.10.

Any such appeal may be taken by filing with the Administrator within 30 days from the date of the decision of the Regional Administrator a written statement of objections to the decision appealed from. Within 60 days after receipt of such appeal the Administrator shall affirm, modify, or revoke the decision of the Regional Administrator, stating in writing his reasons therefor. [Reg. §20.3.]

☐ [*Adopted* 11-25-71. *Amended* 1-9-78.]

[Reg. §20.4]

§20.4. Notice of intent to certify.—(a) On the basis of applications submitted prior to the construction, reconstruction, erection, acquisition, or operation of a facility, the Regional Administrator may notify applicants that such facility will be certified if:

(1) The Regional Administrator determines that such facility, if constructed, reconstructed, erected, acquired, installed, and operated in accordance with such application, will be in compliance with requirements identified in §20.8; and if

(2) The application is accompanied by a statement from the State certifying authority that such facility, if constructed, reconstructed, acquired, erected, installed, and operated in accordance with such application, will be in conformity with the State program or requirements for abatement or control of water or air pollution.

(b) Notice of actions taken under this section will be given to the appropriate State certifying authority. [Reg. §20.4.]

☐ [*Adopted* 11-25-71.]

[Reg. §20.5]

§20.5. Applications.—Applications for certification under this part shall be submitted in such manner as the Administrator may prescribe, shall be signed by the applicant or agent thereof, and shall include the following information:

(a) Name, address, and Internal Revenue Service identifying number of the applicant;

(b) Type and narrative description of the new identifiable facility for which certification is (or will be) sought, including a copy of schematic or engineering drawings, and a description of the function and operation of such facility;

(c) Address (or proposed address) of facility location;

(d) A general description of the operation in connection with which the facility is (or will be) used and a description of the specific process or processes resulting in discharges or emissions which are (or will be) controlled or prevented by the facility;

(e) If the facility is (or will be) used in connection with more than one plant or other property, one or more of which were not in operation before January 1, 1976, a description of the operations of the facility in respect to each plant or other property, including a reasonable allocation of the costs of the facility among the plants being serviced, and a description of the reasoning and accounting method or methods used to arrive at these allocations;

(f) A description of the effect of the facility in terms of type and quantity of pollutants, contaminants, wastes, or heat, removed, altered, stored, disposed of, or prevented by the facility;

(g) If the facility performs a function other than removal, alteration, storage, prevention, or disposal of pollutants, contaminants, wastes, or heat, a description of all functions performed by the facility, including a reasonable identification of the costs of the facility allocable to removal, alteration, storage, prevention, or disposal of pollutants, contaminants, wastes, or heat and a description of the reasoning and accounting method or methods used to arrive at the allocation;

(h) Date when such construction, reconstruction, or erection will be completed or when such facility was (or will be) acquired;

(i) Date when such facility is placed (or is intended to be placed) in operation;

(j) Identification of the applicable State and local water or air pollution control requirements and standards, if any;

(k) Expected useful life of facility;

(l) Cost of construction, acquisition, installation, operation, and maintenance of the facility;

(m) Estimated profits reasonably expected to be derived through the recovery of wastes or otherwise in the operation of the facility over the period referred to in paragraph (a)(6) of 26 CFR 1.169-2;

(n) The percentage (if any, and if the taxpayer claims that the percentage is 5 percent or less) by which the facility (1) increases the output or capacity, (2) extends the useful life, or (3) reduces the total operating costs of the operating unit of the plant or other property most directly associated with the pollution control facility and a description of the reasoning and accounting method or methods used to arrive at this percentage.

(o) Such other information as the Administrator deems necessary for certification. [Reg. § 20.5.]

□ [*Adopted* 11-25-71. *Amended* 1-9-78.]

[Reg. § 20.6]

§ 20.6. State certification.—The State certification shall be by the State certifying authority having jurisdiction with respect to the facility in accordance with 26 U.S.C. 169(d)(1)(A) and (d)(2). The certification shall state that the facility described in the application has been constructed, reconstructed, erected, or acquired in conformity with the State program or requirements for abatement or control of water or air pollution. It shall be executed by an agent or officer authorized to act on behalf of the State certifying authority. [Reg. § 20.6.]

□ [*Adopted* 11-25-71.]

[Reg. § 20.7]

§ 20.7. General policies.—(a) The general policies of the United States for cooperation with the States in the prevention and abatement of water pollution are: To enhance the quality and value of our water resources; to eliminate or reduce the pollution of the nation's waters and tributaries thereof; to improve the sanitary condition of surface and underground waters; and to conserve such waters for public water supplies, propagation of fish and aquatic life and wildlife, recreational purposes, and agricultural, industrial, and other legitimate uses.

(b) The general policy of the United States for cooperation with the States in the prevention and abatement of air pollution is to cooperate with and to assist the States and local governments in protecting and enhancing the quality of the Nation's air resources by the prevention and abatement of conditions which cause or contribute to air pollution which endangers the public health or welfare. [Reg. § 20.7.]

□ [*Adopted* 11-25-71.]

[Reg. § 20.8]

§ 20.8. Requirements for certification.—(a) Subject to § 20.9, the Regional Administrator will certify a facility if he makes the following determinations:

(1) It has been certified by the State certifying authority.

(2) That the facility:

(i) Removes, alters, disposes of, stores, or prevents the creation of pollutants, contaminants, wastes, or heat, which, but for the facility, would be released into the environment;

(ii) Does not by a factor or more than 5 percent: (A) Increase the output or capacity, (B) extend the useful life, or (C) reduce the total operating costs of the operating unit (of the plant or other property) most directly associated with the pollution control facility; and

(iii) Does not significantly alter the nature of the manufacturing or production process or facility.

(3) The applicant is in compliance with all regulations of Federal agencies applicable to use of the facility, including conditions specified in any NPDES permit issued to the applicant under section 402 of the Act.

(4) The facility furthers the general policies of the United States and the States in the prevention and abatement of pollution.

(5) The applicant has complied with all the other requirements of this part and has submitted all requested information.

(b) In determining whether use of a facility furthers the general policies of the United States and the States in the prevention and abatement of water pollution, the Regional Administrator shall consider whether such facility is consistent with the following, insofar as they are applicable to the waters which will be affected by the facility:

(1) All applicable water quality standards, including water quality criteria and plans of implementation and enforcement established pursuant to section 303 of the Act or State laws or regulations;

(2) Decisions issued pursuant to section 310 of the Act;

(3) Water pollution control programs required pursuant to any one or more of the following sections of the Act: Section 306, section 307, section 311, section 318, or section 405; or in order to be consistent with a plan under section 208.

(c) In determining whether use of a facility furthers the general policies of the United States and the States in the prevention and abatement of air pollution, the Regional Administrator shall consider whether such facility is consistent with and meets the following requirements, insofar as they are applicable to the air which will be affected by the facility;

(1) Plans for the implementation, maintenance, and enforcement of ambient air quality standards adopted or promulgated pursuant to section 110 of the Act;

(2) Recommendations issued pursuant to sections 103(e) and 115 of the Act which are applicable to facilities of the same type and located in the area to which the recommendations are directed;

(3) Local government requirements for control of air pollution, including emission standards;

(4) Standards promulgated by the Administrator pursuant to the Act.

(d) A facility that removes elements or compounds from fuels that would be released as pollutants when such fuels are burned is eligible for certification if the facility is—

(1) Used in connection with a plant or other property in operation before January 1, 1976 (whether located and used at a particular plant or as a centralized facility for one or more plants), and

(2) Is otherwise eligible for certification.

(e) Where a facility is used in connection with more than one plant or other property, one or more of which were not in operation before January 1, 1976, or where a facility will perform a function other than the removal, alteration, storage, disposal, or prevention of pollutants, contaminants, wastes, or heat, the Regional Administrator will so indicate on the notice of certification and will approve or disapprove the applicant's suggested method of allocating costs. If the Regional Administrator disapproves the applicant's suggested method, he shall identify the proportion of costs allocable to each such plant, or to the removal, alteration, storage. disposal, or prevention of pollutants, contaminants, wastes, or heat. [Reg. § 20.8.]

□ [*Adopted* 11–25–71. *Amended* 1-9-78.]

[Reg. § 20.9]

§ 20.9. Cost recovery.—Where it appears that, by reason of estimated profits to be derived through the recovery of wastes, through separate charges for use of the facility in question, or otherwise in the operation of such facility, all or a portion of its costs may be recovered over the period referred to in paragraph (a)(6) of 26 CFR 1.169-2, the Regional Administrator shall so signify in the notice of certification. Determinations as to the meaning of the term "estimated profits" and as to the percentage of the cost of a certified facility which will be recovered over such period shall be made by the Secretary of the Treasury, or his delegate: *Provided*, That in no event shall estimated profits be deemed to arise from the use or reuse by the applicant of recovered waste. [Reg. § 20.9.]

□ [*Adopted* 11-25-71.]

[Reg. § 20.10]

§ 20.10. Revocation.—Certification hereunder may be revoked by the Regional Administrator on 30 days written notice to the applicant, served by certified mail, whenever the Regional Administrator shall determine that the facility in question is no longer being operated consistent with the § 20.8(b) and (c) [20.8(b) and (c)] criteria in effect at the time the facility was placed in service. Within such 30-day period, the applicant may submit to the Regional Administrator such evidence, data or other written materials as the applicant may deem appropriate to show why the certification hereunder should not be revoked. Notification of a revocation under this section shall be given to the Secretary of the Treasury or his delegate. See 26 CFR 1.169-4(b)(1). [Reg. § 20.10.]

☐ [*Adopted* 11-25-71.]

[Reg. § 1.170A-1]

§ 1.170A-1. Charitable, etc., contributions and gifts; allowance of deduction.—(a) *Allowance of deduction.*—Any charitable contribution, as defined in section 170(c), actually paid during the taxable year is allowable as a deduction in computing taxable income irrespective of the method of accounting employed or of the date on which the contribution is pledged. However, charitable contributions by corporations may under certain circumstances be deductible even though not paid during the taxable year, as provided in section 170(a)(2) and § 1.170A-11. For rules relating to record keeping and return requirements in support of deductions for charitable contributions (whether by an itemizing or nonitemizing taxpayer), see §§ 1.170A-13 (generally applicable to contributions on or before July 30, 2018), 1.170A-14, 1.170A-15, 1.170A-16, 1.170A-17, and 1.170A-18. The deduction is subject to the limitations of section 170(b) and § 1.170A-8 or § 1.170A-11. Subject to the provisions of section 170(d) and §§ 1.170A-10 and 1.170A-11, certain excess charitable contributions made by individuals and corporations shall be treated as paid in certain succeeding taxable years. For provisions relating to direct charitable deductions under section 63 by nonitemizers, see section 63(b)(1)(C) and (i) and section 170(i). For rules relating to the determination of, and the deduction for, amounts paid to maintain certain students as members of the taxpayer's household and treated under section 170(g) as paid for the use of an organization described in section 170(c)(2), (3), or (4), see § 1.170A-2. For the reduction of any charitable contributions for interest on certain indebtedness, see section 170(f)(5) and § 1.170A-3. For a special rule relating to the computation of the amount of the deduction with respect to a charitable contribution of certain ordinary income or capital gain property, see section 170(e) and § 1.170A-4 and § 1.170A-4A. For rules for postponing the time for deduction of a charitable contribution of a future interest in tangible personal property, see section 170(a)(3) and § 1.170A-5. For rules with respect to transfers in trust and of partial interests in property, see section 170(e), section 170(f)(2) and (3), § 1.170A-4, § 1.170A-6, and § 1.170A-7. For definition of the term "section 170(b)(1)(A) organization," see § 1.170A-9. For valuation of a remainder interest in real property, see section 170(f)(4) and the regulations thereunder. The deduction for charitable contributions is subject to verification by the district director.

(b) *Time of making contribution.*—Ordinarily, a contribution is made at the time delivery is effected. The unconditional delivery or mailing of a check which subsequently clears in due course will constitute an effective contribution on the date of delivery or mailing. If a taxpayer unconditionally delivers or mails a properly endorsed stock certificate to a charitable donee or the donee's agent, the gift is completed on the date of delivery or, if such certificate is received in the ordinary course of the mails, on the date of mailing. If the donor delivers the stock certificate to his bank or broker as the donor's agent, or to the issuing corporation or its agent, for transfer into the name of the donee, the gift is completed on the date the stock is transferred on the books of the corporation. For rules relating to the date of payment of a contribution consisting of a future interest in tangible personal property, see section 170(a)(3) and § 1.170A-5.

(c) *Value of a contribution in property.*—(1) If a charitable contribution is made in property other than money, the amount of the contribution is the fair market value of the property at the time of the contribution reduced as provided in section 170(e)(1) and paragraph (a) of § 1.170A-4, or section 170(e)(3) and paragraph (c) of § 1.170A-4A.

(2) The fair market value is the price at which the property would change hands between a willing buyer and a willing seller, neither being under any compulsion to buy or sell and both having reasonable knowledge of relevant facts. If the contribution is made in property of a type which the taxpayer sells in the course of his business, the fair market value is the price which the taxpayer would have received if he had sold the contributed property in the usual market in which he customarily sells, at the time and place of the contribution and, in the case of a contribution of goods in quantity, in the quantity contributed. The usual market of a manufacturer or other producer consists of the wholesalers or other distributors to or through whom he customarily sells, but if he sells only at retail the usual market consists of his retail customers.

(3) If the donor makes a charitable contribution of property, such as stock in trade, at a time when he could not reasonably have been expected to realize its usual selling price, the value of the gift is not the usual selling price but is the amount for which the quantity of property contributed would have been sold by the donor at the time of the contribution.

(4) Any costs and expenses pertaining to the contributed property which were incurred in taxable years preceding the year of contribution and are properly reflected in the opening inventory for the year of contribution must be removed from inventory and are not a part of the cost of goods sold for purposes of determining gross income for the year of contribution. Any costs and expenses pertaining to the contributed property which are incurred in the year of contribution and would, under the method of accounting used, be properly reflected in the cost of goods sold for such year are to be treated as part of the cost of goods sold for such year. If costs and expenses incurred in producing or acquiring the contributed property are, under the method of accounting used, properly deducted under section 162 or other section of the Code, such costs and expenses will be allowed as deductions for the taxable year in which they are paid or incurred, whether or not such year is the year of the contribution. Any such costs and expenses which are treated as part of the cost of goods sold for the year of contribution, and any such costs and expenses which are properly deducted under section 162 or other section of the Code, are not to be treated under any section of the Code as resulting in any basis for the contributed property. Thus, for example, the contributed property has no basis for purposes of determining under section 170(e)(1)(A) and paragraph (a) of § 1.170A-4 the amount of gain which would have been recognized if such property had been sold by the donor at its fair market value at the time of its contribution. The amount of any charitable contribution for the taxable year is not to be reduced by the amount of any costs or expenses pertaining to the contributed property which was properly deducted under section 162 or other section of the Code for any taxable year preceding the year of the contribution. This subparagraph applies only to property which was held by the taxpayer for sale in the course of a trade or business. The application of this subparagraph may be illustrated by the following examples:

Example (1). In 1970, A, an individual using the calendar year as the taxable year and the accrual method of accounting, contributed to a church property from inventory having a fair market value of $600. The closing inventory at the end of 1969 properly included $400 of costs attributable to the acquisition of such property, and in 1969 A properly deducted under section 162 $50 of administrative and other expenses attributable to such property. Under section 170(e)(1)(A) and paragraph (a) of § 1.170A-4, the amount of the charitable contribution allowed for 1970 is $400 ($600 – [$600 – $400]). Pursuant to this subparagraph, the cost of goods sold to be used in determining gross income for 1970 may not include the $400 which was included in opening inventory for that year.

Example (2). The facts are the same as in example (1) except that the contributed property was acquired in 1970 at a cost of $400. The $400 cost of the property is included in determining the cost of goods sold for 1970, and $50 is allowed as a deduction for that year under section 162. A is not allowed any deduction under section 170 for the contributed property, since under section 170(e)(1)(A) and paragraph (a) of § 1.170A-4 the amount of the charitable contribution is reduced to zero ($600 – [$600 – $0]).

Example (3). In 1970, B, an individual using the calendar year as the taxable year and the accrual method of accounting, contributed to a church property from inventory having a fair market value of $600. Under § 1.471-3(c), the closing inventory at the end of 1969 properly included $450 costs attributable to the production of such property, including $50 of administrative and other indirect expenses which, under his method of accounting, was properly added to inventory rather than deducted as a business expense. Under section 170(e)(1)(A) and paragraph (a) of § 1.170A-4, the amount of the charitable contribution allowed for 1970 is $450 ($600 – [$600 – $450]). Pursuant to this subparagraph, the cost of goods sold to be used in determining gross income for 1970 may not include the $450 which was included in opening inventory for that year.

Example (4). The facts are the same as in example (3) except that the contributed property was produced in 1970 at a cost of $450, including $50 of administrative and other indirect expenses. The $450 cost of the property is included in determining the cost of goods sold for 1970. B is not allowed any deduction under section 170 for the contributed property, since under section 170(e)(1)(A) and paragraph (a) of § 1.170A-4 the amount of the charitable contribution is reduced to zero ($600 – [$600 – $0]).

Example (5). In 1970, C, a farmer using the cash method of accounting and the calendar year as the taxable year, contributed to a church a quantity of grain which he had raised having a fair market value of $600. In 1969, C paid expenses of $450 in raising the property which he properly deducted for such year under section 162. Under section 170(e)(1)(A) and paragraph (a) of § 1.170A-4, the amount of the charitable contribution in 1970 is reduced to zero ($600 – [$600 – $0]). Accordingly, C is not allowed any deduction under section 170 for the contributed property.

Example (6). The facts are the same as in example (5) except that the $450 expenses incurred in raising the contributed property were

Itemized Deductions for Individuals and Corps.
See p. 20,601 for regulations not amended to reflect law changes

25,535

paid in 1970. The result is the same as in example (5), except the amount of $450 is deductible under section 162 for 1970.

(5) For payments or transfers to an entity described in section 170(c) by a taxpayer carrying on a trade or business, see §1.162-15(a).

(d) *Purchase of an annuity.*—(1) In the case of an annuity or portion thereof purchased from an organization described in section 170(c), there shall be allowed as a deduction the excess of the amount paid over the value at the time of purchase of the annuity or portion purchased.

(2) The value of the annuity or portion is the value of the annuity determined in accordance with paragraph (e)(1)(iii)(b)(2) of §1.101-2.

(3) For determining gain on any such transaction constituting a bargain sale, see section 1011(b) and §1.1011-2.

(e) *Transfers subject to a condition or power.*—If as of the date of a gift a transfer for charitable purposes is dependent upon the performance of some act or the happening of a precedent event in order that it might become effective, no deduction is allowable unless the possibility that the charitable transfer will not become effective is so remote as to be negligible. If an interest in property passes to, or is vested in, charity on the date of the gift and the interest would be defeated by the subsequent performance of some act or the happening of some event, the possibility of occurrence of which appears on the date of the gift to be so remote as to be negligible, the deduction is allowable. For example, A transfers land to a city government for as long as the land is used by the city for a public park. If on the date of the gift the city does plan to use the land for a park and the possibility that the city will not use the land for a public park is so remote as to be negligible, A is entitled to a deduction under section 170 for his charitable contribution.

(f) *Special rules applicable to certain contributions.*—(1) See section 14 of the Wild and Scenic Rivers Act (Public Law 90-542, 82 Stat. 918) for provisions relating to the claim and allowance of the value of certain easements as a charitable contribution under section 170.

(2) For treatment of gifts accepted by the Secretary of State or the Secretary of Commerce, for the purpose of organizing and holding an international conference to negotiate a Patent Corporation Treaty, as gifts to or for the use of the United States, see section 3 of Joint Resolution of December 24, 1969 (Public Law 91-160, 83 Stat. 443).

(3) For treatment of gifts accepted by the Secretary of the Department of Housing and Urban Development, for the purpose of aiding or facilitating the work of the Department, as gifts to or for the use of the United States, see section 7(k) of the Department of Housing and Urban Development Act (42 U.S.C. 3535), as added by section 905 of Public Law 91-609 (84 Stat. 1809).

(g) *Contributions of services.*—No deduction is allowable under section 170 for a contribution of services. However, unreimbursed expenditures made incident to the rendition of services to an organization contributions to which are deductible may constitute a deductible contribution. For example, the cost of a uniform without general utility which is required to be worn in performing donated services is deductible. Similarly, out-of-pocket transportation expenses necessarily incurred in performing donated services are deductible. Reasonable expenditures for meals and lodging necessarily incurred while away from home in the course of performing donated services also are deductible. For the purposes of this paragraph, the phrase "while away from home" has the same meaning as that phrase is used for purposes of section 162 and the regulations thereunder.

(h) *Payment in exchange for consideration.*—(1) *Burden on taxpayer to show that all or part of payment is a charitable contribution or gift.* No part of a payment that a taxpayer makes to or for the use of an organization described in section 170(c) that is in consideration for (as defined in paragraph (h)(4)(i) of this section) goods or services (as defined in paragraph (h)(4)(ii) of this section) is a contribution or gift within the meaning of section 170(c) unless the taxpayer—

(i) Intends to make a payment in an amount that exceeds the fair market value of the goods or services; and

(ii) Makes a payment in an amount that exceeds the fair market value of the goods or services.

(2) *Limitation on amount deductible.*—(i) *In general.*—The charitable contribution deduction under section 170(a) for a payment a taxpayer makes partly in consideration for goods or services may not exceed the excess of—

(A) The amount of any cash paid and the fair market value of any property (other than cash) transferred by the taxpayer to an organization described in section 170(c); over

(B) The fair market value of the goods or services received or expected to be received in return.

(ii) *Special rules.*—For special limits on the deduction for charitable contributions of ordinary income and capital gain property, see section 170(e) and §§1.170A-4 and 1.170A-4A.

(3) *Payments resulting in state or local tax benefits.*—(i) *State or local tax credits.*—Except as provided in paragraph (h)(3)(vi) of this section, if a taxpayer makes a payment or transfers property to or for the use of an entity described in section 170(c), the amount of the taxpayer's charitable contribution deduction under section 170(a) is reduced by the amount of any state or local tax credit that the taxpayer receives or expects to receive in consideration for the taxpayer's payment or transfer.

(ii) *State or local tax deductions.*—(A) *In general.*—If a taxpayer makes a payment or transfers property to or for the use of an entity described in section 170(c), and the taxpayer receives or expects to receive state or local tax deductions that do not exceed the amount of the taxpayer's payment or the fair market value of the property transferred by the taxpayer to the entity, the taxpayer is not required to reduce its charitable contribution deduction under section 170(a) on account of the state or local tax deductions.

(B) *Excess state or local tax deductions.*—If the taxpayer receives or expects to receive a state or local tax deduction that exceeds the amount of the taxpayer's payment or the fair market value of the property transferred, the taxpayer's charitable contribution deduction under section 170(a) is reduced.

(iii) *In consideration for.*—For purposes of paragraph (h) of this section, the term *in consideration for* has the meaning set forth in paragraph (h)(4)(i) of this section.

(iv) *Amount of reduction.*—For purposes of paragraph (h)(3)(i) of this section, the amount of any state or local tax credit is the maximum credit allowable that corresponds to the amount of the taxpayer's payment or transfer to the entity described in section 170(c).

(v) *State or local tax.*—For purposes of paragraph (h)(3) of this section, the term *state or local tax* means a tax imposed by a State, a possession of the United States, or by a political subdivision of any of the foregoing, or by the District of Columbia.

(vi) *Exception.*—Paragraph (h)(3)(i) of this section shall not apply to any payment or transfer of property if the total amount of the state and local tax credits received or expected to be received by the taxpayer is 15 percent or less of the taxpayer's payment, or 15 percent or less of the fair market value of the property transferred by the taxpayer.

(vii) *Examples.*—The following examples illustrate the provisions of this paragraph (h)(3). The examples in paragraph (h)(6) of this section are not illustrative for purposes of this paragraph (h)(3).

(A) *Example 1.* A, an individual, makes a payment of $1,000 to X, an entity described in section 170(c). In exchange for the payment, A receives or expects to receive a state tax credit of 70 percent of the amount of A's payment to X. Under paragraph (h)(3)(i) of this section, A's charitable contribution deduction is reduced by $700 (0.70 x $1,000). This reduction occurs regardless of whether A is able to claim the state tax credit in that year. Thus, A's charitable contribution deduction for the $1,000 payment to X may not exceed $300.

(B) *Example 2.* B, an individual, transfers a painting to Y, an entity described in section 170(c). At the time of the transfer, the painting has a fair market value of $100,000. In exchange for the painting, B receives or expects to receive a state tax credit equal to 10 percent of the fair market value of the painting. Under paragraph (h)(3)(vi) of this section, B is not required to apply the general rule of paragraph (h)(3)(i) of this section because the amount of the tax credit received or expected to be received by B does not exceed 15 percent of the fair market value of the property transferred to Y. Accordingly, the amount of B's charitable contribution deduction for the transfer of the painting is not reduced under paragraph (h)(3)(i) of this section.

(C) *Example 3.* C, an individual, makes a payment of $1,000 to Z, an entity described in section 170(c). In exchange for the payment, under state M law, C is entitled to receive a state tax deduction equal to the amount paid by C to Z. Under paragraph (h)(3)(ii)(A) of this section, C's charitable contribution deduction under section 170(a) is not required to be reduced on account of C's state tax deduction for C's payment to Z.

(viii) *Safe harbor for payments by C corporations and specified passthrough entities.*—For payments by a C corporation or by a specified passthrough entity to an entity described in section 170(c), where the C corporation or specified passthrough entity receives or expects to receive a State or local tax credit that reduces the charitable contribution deduction for such payments under paragraph (h)(3) of this section, see § 1.162-15(a)(3) (providing safe harbors under section 162(a) to the extent of that reduction).

(ix) *Safe harbor for individuals.*—Under certain circumstances, an individual who itemizes deductions and makes a payment to an entity described in section 170(c) in consideration for a State or local tax credit may treat the portion of such payment for which a charitable contribution deduction is disallowed under paragraph (h)(3) of this section as a payment of State or local taxes under section 164. See § 1.164-3(j), providing a safe harbor for certain payments by individuals in exchange for State or local tax credits.

(x) *Effective/applicability date.*—This paragraph (h)(3) applies to amounts paid or property transferred by a taxpayer after August 27, 2018.

(4) *Definitions.*—For purposes of this paragraph (h), the following definitions apply:

(i) *In consideration for.*—A taxpayer receives goods or services in consideration for a taxpayer's payment or transfer to an entity described in section 170(c) if, at the time the taxpayer makes the payment to such entity, the taxpayer receives or expects to receive goods or services from that entity or any other party in return.

(ii) *Goods or services.*—Goods or services means cash, property, services, benefits, and privileges.

(iii) *Applicability date.*—The definitions provided in this paragraph (h)(4) are applicable to amounts paid or property transferred on or after December 17, 2019.

(5) *Certain goods or services disregarded.*—For purposes of section 170(a) and paragraphs (h)(1) and (h)(2) of this section, goods or services described in § 1.170A-13(f)(8)(i) or § 1.170A-13(f)(9)(i) are disregarded.

(6) *Donee estimates of the value of goods or services may be treated as fair market value.*—(i) *In general.*—For purposes of section 170(a), a taxpayer may rely on either a contemporaneous written acknowledgment provided under section 170(f)(8) and § 1.170A-13(f) or a written disclosure statement provided under section 6115 for the fair market value of any goods or services provided to the taxpayer by the donee organization.

(ii) *Exception.*—A taxpayer may not treat an estimate of the value of goods or services as their fair market value if the taxpayer knows, or has reason to know, that such treatment is unreasonable. For example, if a taxpayer knows, or has reason to know, that there is an error in an estimate provided by an organization described in section 170(c) pertaining to goods or services that have a readily ascertainable value, it is unreasonable for the taxpayer to treat the estimate as the fair market value of the goods or services. Similarly, if a taxpayer is a dealer in the type of goods or services provided in consideration for the taxpayer's payment and knows, or has reason to know, that the estimate is in error, it is unreasonable for the taxpayer to treat the estimate as the fair market value of the goods or services.

(7) *Examples.*—The following examples illustrate the rules of this paragraph (h).

Example 1. Certain goods or services disregarded. Taxpayer makes a $50 payment to Charity *B*, an organization described in section 170(c), in exchange for a family membership. The family membership entitles Taxpayer and members of Taxpayer's family to certain benefits. These benefits include free admission to weekly poetry readings, discounts on merchandise sold by *B* in its gift shop or by mail order, and invitations to special events for members only, such as lectures or informal receptions. When *B* first offers its membership package for the year, *B* reasonably projects that each special event for members will have a cost to *B*, excluding any allocable overhead, of $5 or less per person attending the event. Because the family membership benefits are disregarded pursuant to § 1.170A-13(f)(8)(i), Taxpayer may treat the $50 payment as a contribution or gift within the meaning of section 170(c), regardless of Taxpayer's intent and whether or not the payment exceeds the fair market value of the goods or services. Furthermore, any charitable contribution deduction available to Taxpayer may be calculated without regard to the membership benefits.

Example 2. Treatment of good faith estimate at auction as the fair market value. Taxpayer attends an auction held by Charity *C*, an organization described in section 170(c). Prior to the auction, *C* publishes a catalog that meets the requirements for a written disclosure statement under section 6115(a) (including *C's* good faith estimate of the value of items that will be available for bidding). A representative of *C* gives a copy of the catalog to each individual (including Taxpayer) who attends the auction. Taxpayer notes that in the catalog *C's* estimate of the value of a vase is $100. Taxpayer has no reason to doubt the accuracy of this estimate. Taxpayer successfully bids and pays $500 for the vase. Because Taxpayer knew, prior to making her payment, that the estimate in the catalog was less than the amount of her payment, Taxpayer satisfies the requirement of paragraph (h)(1)(i) of this section. Because Taxpayer makes a payment in an amount that exceeds that estimate, Taxpayer satisfies the requirements of paragraph (h)(1)(ii) of this section. Taxpayer may treat *C's* estimate of the value of the vase as its fair market value in determining the amount of her charitable contribution deduction.

Example 3. Good faith estimate not in error. Taxpayer makes a $200 payment to Charity *D*, an organization described in section 170(c). In return for Taxpayer's payment, *D* gives Taxpayer a book that Taxpayer could buy at retail prices typically ranging from $18 to $25. *D* provides Taxpayer with a good faith estimate, in a written disclosure statement under section 6115(a), of $20 for the value of the book. Because the estimate is within the range of typical retail prices for the book, the estimate contained in the written disclosure statement is not in error. Although Taxpayer knows that the book is sold for as much as $25, Taxpayer may treat the estimate of $20 as the fair market value of the book in determining the amount of his charitable contribution deduction.

(i) [Reserved]

(j) *Exceptions and other rules.*—(1) The provisions of section 170 do not apply to contributions by an estate; nor do they apply to a trust unless the trust is a private foundation which, pursuant to section 642(c)(6) and § 1.642(c)-4, is allowed a deduction under section 170 subject to the provisions applicable to individuals.

(2) No deduction shall be allowed under section 170 for a charitable contribution to or for the use of an organization or trust described in section 508(d) or 4948(c)(4), subject to the conditions specified in such sections and the regulations thereunder.

(3) For disallowance of deductions for contributions to or for the use of communist controlled organizations, see section 11(a) of the Internal Security Act of 1950, as amended (50 U.S.C. 790).

(4) For denial of deductions for charitable contributions as trade or business expenses and rules with respect to treatment of payments to organizations other than those described in section 170(c), see section 162 and the regulations thereunder.

(5) No deduction shall be allowed under section 170 for amounts paid to an organization:

(i) Which is disqualified for tax exemption under section 501(c)(3) by reason of attempting to influence legislation, or

(ii) Which participates in, or intervenes in (including the publishing or distributing of statements), any political campaign on behalf of or in opposition to any candidate for public office.

For purposes of determining whether an organization is attempting to influence legislation or is engaging in political activities, see sections 501(c)(3), 501(h), 4911 and the regulations thereunder.

(6) No deduction shall be allowed under section 170 for expenditures for lobbying purposes, the promotion or defeat of legislation, etc. See also the regulations under sections 162 and 4945.

(7) No deduction for charitable contributions is allowed in computing the taxable income of a common trust fund or of a partnership. See sections 584(d)(3) and 703(a)(2)(D). However, a partner's distributive share of charitable contributions actually paid by a partnership during its taxable year may be allowed as a deduction in the partner's separate return for his taxable year with or within which the taxable year of the partnership ends, to the extent that the aggregate of his share of the partnership contributions and his own contributions does not exceed the limitations in section 170(b).

(8) For charitable contributions paid by a nonresident alien individual or a foreign corporation, see § 1.170A-4(b)(5) and sections 873, 876, 877, and 882(c), and the regulations thereunder.

(9) Charitable contributions paid by bona fide residents of a section 931 possession as defined in § 1.931-1(c)(1) or Puerto Rico are deductible only to the extent allocable to income that is not excluded under section 931 or 933. For the rules for allocating deductions for charitable contributions, see the regulations under section 861.

(10) For carryover of excess charitable contributions in certain corporate acquisitions, see section 381(c)(19) and the regulations thereunder.

(11) No deduction shall be allowed under section 170 for out-of-pocket expenditures on behalf of an eligible organization (within the meaning of § 1.501(h)-2(b)(1)) if the expenditure is made in connection with influencing legislation (within the meaning of section 501(c)(3) or § 56.4911-2), or in connection with the payment of the organization's tax liability under section 4911. For the treatment of similar expenditures on behalf of other organizations see paragraph (h)(6) of this section.

(k) *Effective/applicability date.*—In general this section applies to contributions made in taxable years beginning after December 31, 1969. Paragraph (j)(11) of this section, however, applies only to out-of-pocket expenditures made in taxable years beginning after December 31, 1976. In addition, paragraph (h) of this section applies only to payments made on or after December 16, 1996. However, taxpayers may rely on the rules of paragraph (h) of this section for payments made on or after January 1, 1994. Paragraph (j)(9) of this section is applicable for taxable years ending after April 9, 2008. The third sentence of paragraph (a) applies as provided in the sections referenced in that sentence. [Reg. § 1.170A-1.]

☐ [*T.D. 7207, 10-3-72. Amended by T.D. 7340, 1-6-75; T.D. 7807, 1-29-82; T.D. 8002, 12-26-84; T.D. 8308, 8-30-90; T.D. 8690, 12-13-96; T.D. 9194, 4-6-2005, T.D. 9391, 4-4-2008, T.D. 9836, 7-27-2018 (corrected 9-10-2018), T.D. 9864, 6-11-2019 and T.D. 9907, 8-7-2020.*]

[Reg. § 1.170A-2]

§1.170A-2. Amounts paid to maintain certain students as members of the taxpayer's household.—(a) *In general.*—(1) The term "charitable contributions" includes amounts paid by the taxpayer during the taxable year to maintain certain students as members of his household which, under the provisions of section 170(h) and this section, are treated as amounts paid for the use of an organization described in section 170(c)(2), (3), or (4), and such amounts, to the extent they do not exceed the limitations under section 170(h)(2) and paragraph (b) of this section, are contributions deductible under section 170. In order for such amounts to be so treated, the student must be an individual who is neither a dependent (as defined in section 152) of the taxpayer nor related to the taxpayer in a manner described in any of the paragraphs (1) through (8) of section 152(a), and such individual must be a member of the taxpayer's household pursuant to a written agreement between the taxpayer and an organization described in section 170(c)(2), (3), or (4) to implement a program of the organization to provide educational opportunities for pupils or students placed in private homes by such organization. Furthermore, such amounts must be paid to maintain such individual during the period in the taxable year he is a member of the taxpayer's household and is a full-time pupil or student in the twelfth or any lower grade at an educational institution, as defined in section 151(e)(4) and §1.151-3, located in the United States. Amounts paid outside of such period, but within the taxable year, for expenses necessary for the maintenance of the student during the period will qualify for the charitable contributions deduction if the other limitation requirements of the section are met.

(2) For purposes of subparagraph (1) of this paragraph, amounts treated as charitable contributions include only those amounts actually paid by the taxpayer during the taxable year which are directly attributable to the maintenance of the student while he is a member of the taxpayer's household and is attending an educational institution on a full-time basis. This would include amounts paid to ensure the well-being of the individual and to carry out the purpose for which the individual was placed in the taxpayer's home. For example, a deduction under section 170 would be allowed for amounts paid for books, tuition, food, clothing, transportation, medical and dental care, and recreation for the individual. Amounts treated as charitable contributions under this section do not include amounts which the taxpayer would have expended had the student not been in the household. They would not include, for example, amounts paid in connection with the taxpayer's home for taxes, insurance, interest on a mortgage, repairs, etc. Moreover, such amounts do not include any depreciation sustained by the taxpayer in maintaining such student or students in his household, nor do they include the value of any services rendered on behalf of such student or students by the taxpayer or any member of the taxpayer's household.

(3) For purposes of section 170(h) and this section, an individual will be considered to be a full-time pupil or student at an educational institution only if he is enrolled for a course of study prescribed for a full-time student at such institution and is attending classes on a full-time basis. Nevertheless, such individual may be absent from school due to special circumstances and still be considered to be in full-time attendance. Periods during the regular school term when the school is closed for holidays, such as Christmas and Easter, and for periods between semesters are treated as periods during which the pupil or student is in full-time attendance at the school. Also, absences during the regular school term due to illness of such individual shall not prevent him from being considered as a full-time pupil or student. Similarly, absences from the taxpayer's household due to special circumstances will not disqualify the student as a member of the household. Summer vacations between regular school terms are not considered periods of school attendance.

(4) When claiming a deduction for amounts described in section 170(h) and this section, the taxpayer must submit with his return a copy of his agreement with the organization sponsoring the individual placed in the taxpayer's household, together with a summary of the various items for which amounts were paid to maintain such individual, and a statement as to the date the individual became a member of the household and the period of his full-time attendance at school and the name and location of such school. Substantiation of amounts claimed must be supported by adequate records of the amounts actually paid. Due to the nature of certain items, such as food, a record of amounts spent for all members of the household, with an equal portion thereof allocated to each member, will be acceptable.

(b) *Limitations.*—Section 170(h) and this section shall apply to amounts paid during the taxable year only to the extent that the amounts paid in maintaining each pupil or student do not exceed $50 multiplied by the number of full calendar months in the taxable year that the pupil or student is maintained in accordance with the provisions of this section. For purposes of such limitation if 15 or more days of a calendar month fall within the period to which the maintenance of such pupil or student relates, such month is considered as a full calendar month. To the extent that such amounts qualify as charitable contributions under section 170(c), the aggregate of such amounts plus other contributions made during the taxable year for the use of an organization described in section 170(c) is deductible under section 170 subject to the limitation provided in section 170(b)(1)(B) and paragraph (c) of § 1.170A-8.

(c) *Compensation or reimbursement.*—Amounts paid during the taxable year to maintain a pupil or student as a member of the taxpayer's household as provided in paragraph (a) of this section, shall not be taken into account under section 170(h) and this section, if the taxpayer receives any money or other property as compensation or reimbursement for any portion of such amounts. The taxpayer will not be denied the benefits of section 170(h) if he prepays an extraordinary or non-recurring expense, such as a hospital bill or vacation trip, at the request of the individual's parents or the sponsoring organization and is reimbursed for such prepayment. The value of services performed by the pupil or student in attending to ordinary chores of the household will generally not be considered to constitute compensation or reimbursement. However, if the pupil or student is taken into the taxpayer's household to replace a former employee of the taxpayer or gratuitously to perform substantial services for the taxpayer, the facts and circumstances may warrant a conclusion that the taxpayer received reimbursement for maintaining the pupil or student.

(d) *No other amount allowed as deduction.*—Except to the extent that amounts described in section 170(h) and this section are treated as charitable contributions under section 170(c) and, therefore, deductible under section 170(a), no deduction is allowed for any amount paid to maintain an individual, as a member of the taxpayer's household, in accordance with the provisions of section 170(h) and this section.

(e) *Illustrations.*—The application of this section may be illustrated by the following examples:

Example (1). The X organization is an organization described in section 170(c)(2) and is engaged in a program under which a number of European children are placed in the homes of U.S. residents in order to further the children's high school education. In accordance with paragraph (a) of this section, the taxpayer, A, who reports his income on the calendar year basis, agreed with X to take two of the children, and they were placed in the taxpayer's home on January 2, 1970, where they remained until January 21, 1971, during which time they were fully maintained by the taxpayer. The children enrolled at the local high school for the full course of study prescribed for 10th grade students and attended the school on a full-time basis for the spring semester starting January 18, 1970, and ending June 3, 1970, and for the fall semester starting September 1, 1970, and ending January 13, 1971. The total cost of food paid by A in 1970 for himself, his wife, and the two children amounted to $1,920, or $40 per month for each member of the household. Since the children were actually full-time students for only 8½ months during 1970, the amount paid for food for each child during that period amounted to $340. Other amounts paid during the 8½ month period for each child for laundry, lights, water, recreation, and school supplies amounted to $160. Thus, the amounts treated under section 170(h) and this section as paid for the use of X would, with respect to each child, total $500 ($340 + $160), or a total for both children of $1,000, subject to the limitations of paragraph (b) of this section. Since, for purposes of such limitations, the children were full-time students for only 8 full calendar months during 1970 (less than 15 days in January 1970), the taxpayer may treat only $800 as a charitable contribution made in 1970, that is, $50 multiplied by the 8 full calendar months, or $400 paid for the maintenance of each child. Neither the excess payments nor amounts paid to maintain the children during the period before school opened and for the period in summer between regular school terms is taken into account by reason of section 170(h). Also, because the children were full-time students for less than 15 days in January 1971 (although maintained in the taxpayer's household for 21 days), amounts paid to maintain the children during 1971 would not qualify as a charitable contribution.

Example (2). A religious organization described in section 170(c)(2) has a program for providing educational opportunities for children it places in private homes. In order to implement the program, the taxpayer, H, who resides with his wife, son, and daughter of high school age in a town in the United States, signs an agreement with the organization to maintain a girl sponsored by the organization as a member of his household while the child attends the local high school for the regular 1970-71 school year. The child is a full-time student at the school during the school year starting September 6, 1970, and ending June 6, 1971, and is a member of the taxpayer's household during that period. Although the taxpayer pays $200 during the school period falling in 1970, and $240 during the school period falling in 1971, to maintain the child, he cannot claim either amount as a charitable contribution because the child's parents, from time to time during the school year, send butter, eggs, meat, and vegetables to H to help defray the expenses of maintaining the child. This is considered property received as reimbursement under paragraph (c) of this section. Had her parents not contributed the food, the fact that the child, in addition to the normal chores she shared with the taxpayer's daughter, such as cleaning their own rooms and helping with the shopping and cooking, was responsible for the family laundry and for the heavy cleaning of the entire house while the taxpayer's daughter had no comparable responsibilities would also preclude a claim for a charitable contributions deduction. These substantial gratuitous services are considered property received as reimbursement under paragraph (c) of this section.

Example (3). A taxpayer resides with his wife in a city in the eastern United States. He agrees, in writing, with a fraternal society described in section 170(c)(4) to accept a child selected by the society for maintenance by him as a member of his household during 1971 in order that the child may attend the local grammar school as a part of the society's program to provide elementary education for certain children selected by it. The taxpayer maintains the child, who has as his principal place of abode the home of the taxpayer, and is a member of the taxpayer's household, during the entire year 1971. The child is a full-time student at the local grammar school for 9 full calendar months during the year. Under the agreement, the society pays the taxpayer $30 per month to help maintain the child. Since the $30 per month is considered as compensation or reimbursement to the taxpayer for some portion of the maintenance paid on behalf of the child, no amounts paid with respect to such maintenance can be treated as amounts paid in accordance with section 170(h). In the absence of the $30 per month payments, if the child qualifies as a dependent of the taxpayer under section 152(a)(9), that fact would also prevent the maintenance payments from being treated as charitable contributions paid for the use of the fraternal society.

(f) *Effective date.*—This section applies only to contributions paid in taxable years beginning after December 31, 1969. [Reg. § 1.170A-2.]

□ [*T.D.* 7207, 10-3-72.]

[Reg. § 1.170A-3]

§1.170A-3. Reduction of charitable contribution for interest on certain indebtedness.—(a) *In general.*—Section 170(f)(5) requires that the amount of a charitable contribution be reduced for certain interest to the extent necessary to avoid the deduction of the same amount both as an interest deduction under section 163 and as a deduction for charitable contributions under section 170. The reduction is to be determined in accordance with paragraphs (b) and (c) of this section.

(b) *Interest attributable to postcontribution period.*—In determining the amount to be taken into account as a charitable contribution for purposes of section 170, the amount determined without regard to section 170(f)(5) or this section shall be reduced by the amount of interest which has been paid, or is to be paid, by the taxpayer, which is attributable to any liability connected with the contribution, and which is attributable to any period of time after the making of the contribution. The deduction otherwise allowable for charitable contributions under section 170 is required to be reduced pursuant to section 170(f)(5) and this section only if, in connection with a charitable contribution, a liability is assumed by the recipient of the contribution or by any other person or if the charitable contribution is of property which is subject to a liability. Thus, if a charitable contribution is made in property and the transfer is conditioned upon the assumption of a liability by the donee or by some other person, the contribution must be reduced by the amount of any interest which has been paid, or will be paid, by the taxpayer, which is attributable to the liability, and which is attributable to any period after the making of the contribution. The adjustment referred to in this paragraph must also be made where the contributed property is subject to a liability and the value of the property reflects the payment by the donor of interest with respect to a period of time after the making of the contribution.

(c) *Interest attributable to precontribution period.*—If, in connection with the charitable contribution of a bond, a liability is assumed by the recipient or by any other person, or if the bond is subject to a liability, then, in determining the amount to be taken into account as a charitable contribution under section 170, the amount determined without regard to section 170(f)(5) and this section shall, without regard to whether any reduction may be required by paragraph (b) of this section, also be reduced for interest which has been paid, or is to be paid, by the taxpayer on indebtedness incurred or continued to purchase or carry such bond, and which is attributable to any period before the making of the contribution. However, the reduction referred to in this paragraph shall be made only to the extent that such reduction does not exceed the interest (including bond discount and other interest equivalent) receivable on the bond, and attributable to any period before the making of the contribution which is not, by reason of the taxpayer's method of accounting, includible in the taxpayer's gross income for any taxable year. For purposes of section 170(f)(5) and this section the term "bond" means any bond, debenture, note, or certificate or other evidence of indebtedness.

(d) *Illustrations.*—The application of this section may be illustrated by the following examples:

Example (1). On January 1, 1970, A, a cash basis taxpayer using the calendar year as the taxable year, contributed to a charitable organization real estate having a fair market value and adjusted basis of $10,000. In connection with the contribution the charitable organization assumed an indebtedness of $8,000 which A had incurred. On December 31, 1969, A prepaid one year's interest on that indebtedness for 1970, amounting to $960, and took an interest deduction of $960 for such amount. The amount of the gift, determined without regard to this section, is $2,960 ($10,000 less $8,000, the outstanding indebtedness, plus $960, the amount of prepaid interest). In determining the amount of the deduction for the charitable contribution, the value of the gift ($2,960) must be reduced by $960 to eliminate from the computation of such deduction that portion thereof for which A has been allowed an interest deduction.

Example (2). (a) On January 1, 1970, B, an individual using the cash receipts and disbursements method of accounting, purchased for $9,950 a 5½ percent $10,000, 20-year M Corporation bond, the interest on which was payable semi-annually on June 30 and December 31. The M Corporation had issued the bond on January 1, 1960, at a discount of $720 from the principal amount. On December 1, 1970, B donated the bond to a charitable organization, and, in connection with the contribution, the charitable organization assumed an indebtedness of $7,000 which B had incurred to purchase and carry the bond.

(b) During the calendar year 1970 B paid accrued interest of $330 on the indebtedness for the period from January 1, 1970, to December 1, 1970, and has taken an interest deduction of $330 for such amount. No portion of the bond discount of $36 a year ($720 divided by 20 years) has been included in B's income, and of the $550 of annual interest receivable on the bond, he included in income only the June 30, 1970, payment of $275.

(c) The market value of the bond on December 1, 1970, was $9,902. Such value includes $229 of interest receivable which had accrued from July 1 to December 1, 1970.

(d) The amount of the charitable contribution determined without regard to this section is $2,902 ($9,902, the value of the property on the date of gift, less $7,000, the amount of the liability assumed by the charitable organization). In determining the amount of the allowable deduction for charitable contributions, the value of the gift ($2,902) must be reduced to eliminate from the deduction that portion thereof for which B has been allowed an interest deduction. Although the amount of such interest deduction was $330, the reduction required by this section is limited to $262, since the reduction is not in excess of the amount of interest income on the bond ($229 of accrued interest plus $33, the amount of bond discount attributable to the 11-month period B held the bond).

(e) *Effective date.*—This section applies only to contributions paid in taxable years beginning after December 31, 1969. [Reg. § 1.170A-3.]

□ [*T.D.* 7207, 10-3-72.]

[Reg. § 1.170A-4]

§1.170A-4. Reduction in amount of charitable contributions of certain appreciated property.—(a) *Amount of reduction.*—Section 170(e)(1) requires that the amount of the charitable contribution which would be taken into account under section 170(a) without regard to section 170(e) shall be reduced before applying the percentage limitations under section 170(b)—

(1) In the case of a contribution by an individual or by a corporation of ordinary income property, as defined in paragraph (b)(1) of this section, by the amount of gain (hereinafter in this section referred to as ordinary income) which would have been recognized as gain which is not long-term capital gain if the property had been sold by

the donor at its fair market value at the time of its contribution to the charitable organization,

(2) In the case of a contribution by an individual of section 170(e) capital gain property, as defined in paragraph (b)(2) of this section, by 50 percent of the amount of gain (hereinafter in this section referred to as long-term capital gain) which would have been recognized as long-term capital gain if the property had been sold by the donor at its fair market value at the time of its contribution to the charitable organization, and

(3) In the case of a contribution by a corporation of section 170(e) capital gain property, as defined in paragraph (b)(2) of this section by 62¹/₂ percent of the amount of gain (hereinafter in this section referred to as long-term capital gain) which would have been recognized as long-term capital gain if the property had been sold by the donor at its fair market value at the time of its contribution to the charitable organization,

Section 170(e)(1) and this paragraph do not apply to reduce the amount of the charitable contribution where, by reason of the transfer of the contributed property, ordinary income or capital gain is recognized by the donor in the same taxable year in which the contribution is made. Thus, where income or gain is recognized under section 453(d) upon the transfer of an installment obligation to a charitable organization, or under section 454(b) upon the transfer of an obligation issued at a discount to such an organization, or upon the assignment of income to such an organization, section 170(e)(1) and this paragraph do not apply if recognition of the income or gain occurs in the same taxable year in which the contribution is made. Section 170(e)(1) and this paragraph apply to a charitable contribution of an interest in ordinary income property or section 170(e) capital gain property which is described in paragraph (b) of §1.170A-6 or paragraph (b) of §1.170A-7. For purposes of applying section 170(e)(1) and this paragraph it is immaterial whether the charitable contribution is made "to" the charitable organization or whether it is made "for the use of" the charitable organization. See §1.170A-8(a)(2).

(b) *Definitions and other rules.*—For purposes of this section—

(1) *Ordinary income property.*—The term "ordinary income property" means property any portion of the gain on which would not have been long-term capital gain if the property had been sold by the donor at its fair market value at the time of its contribution to the charitable organization. Such term includes, for example, property held by the donor primarily for sale to customers in the ordinary course of his trade or business, a work of art created by the donor, a manuscript prepared by the donor, letters and memorandums prepared by or for the donor, a capital asset held by the donor for not more than 1 year (6 months for taxable years beginning before 1977; 9 months for taxable years beginning in 1977), and stock described in section 306(a), 341(a) or 1248(a) to the extent that, after applying such section, gain on its disposition would not have been long-term capital gain. The term does not include an income interest in respect of which a deduction is allowed under section 170(f)(2)(B) and paragraph (c) of §1.170A-6.

(2) *Section 170(e) capital gain property.*—The term "section 170(e) capital gain property" means property any portion of the gain on which would have been treated as long-term capital gain if the property had been sold by the donor at its fair market value at the time of its contribution to the charitable organization and which—

(i) Is contributed to or for the use of a private foundation, as defined in section 509(a) and the regulations thereunder, other than a private foundation described in section 170(b)(1)(E),

(ii) Constitutes tangible personal property contributed to or for the use of a charitable organization, other than a private foundation to which subdivision (i) of this subparagraph applies, which is put to an unrelated use by the charitable organization within the meaning of subparagraph (3) of this paragraph, or

(iii) Constitutes property not described in subdivision (i) or (ii) of this subparagraph which is 30-percent capital gain property to which an election under paragraph (d)(2) of §1.170A-8 applies.

For purposes of this subparagraph a fixture which is intended to be severed from real property shall be treated as tangible personal property.

(3) *Unrelated use.*—(i) *In general.*—The term "unrelated use" means a use which is unrelated to the purpose or function constituting the basis of the charitable organization's exemption under section 501 or, in the case of a contribution of property to a governmental unit, the use of such property by such unit for other than exclusively public purposes. For example, if a painting contributed to an educational institution is used by that organization for educational purposes by being placed in its library for display and study by art students, the use is not an unrelated use; but if the painting is sold and the proceeds used by the organization for educational purposes, the use of the property is an unrelated use. If furnishings contributed

to a charitable organization are used by it in its offices and buildings in the course of carrying out its functions, the use of the property is not an unrelated use. If a set or collection of items of tangible personal property is contributed to a charitable organization or governmental unit, the use of the set or collection is not an unrelated use if the donee sells or otherwise disposes of only an insubstantial portion of the set or collection. The use by a trust of tangible personal property contributed to it for the benefit of a charitable organization is an unrelated use if the use by the trust is one which would have been unrelated if made by the charitable organization.

(ii) *Proof of use.*—For purposes of applying subparagraph (2)(ii) of this paragraph, a taxpayer who makes a charitable contribution of tangible personal property to or for the use of a charitable organization or governmental unit may treat such property as not being put to an unrelated use by the donee if—

(a) He establishes that the property is not in fact put to an unrelated use by the donee, or

(b) At the time of the contribution or at the time the contribution is treated as made, it is reasonable to anticipate that the property will not be put to an unrelated use by the donee. In the case of a contribution of tangible personal property to or for the use of a museum, if the object donated is of a general type normally retained by such museum or other museums for museum purposes, it will be reasonable for the donor to anticipate, unless he has actual knowledge to the contrary, that the object will not be put to an unrelated use by the donee, whether or not the object is later sold or exchanged by the donee.

(4) *Property used in trade or business.*—For purposes of applying subparagraphs (1) and (2) of this paragraph, property which is used in the trade or business, as defined in section 1231(b), shall be treated as a capital asset, except that any gain in respect of such property which would have been recognized if the property had been sold by the donor at its fair market value at the time of its contribution to the charitable organization shall be treated as ordinary income to the extent that such gain would have constituted ordinary income by reason of the application of section 617(d)(1), 1245(a), 1250(a), 1251(c), 1252(a), or 1254(a).

(5) *Nonresident alien individuals and foreign corporations.*—The reduction in the case of a nonresident alien individual or a foreign corporation shall be determined by taking into account the gain which would have been recognized and subject to tax under chapter 1 of the Code if the property had been sold or disposed of within the United States by the donor at its fair market value at the time of its contribution to the charitable organization. However, the amount of such gain which would have been subject to tax under section 871(a) or 881 (relating to gain not effectively connected with the conduct of a trade or business within the United States) if there had been a sale or other disposition within the United States shall be treated as long-term capital gain. Thus, a charitable contribution by a nonresident alien individual or a foreign corporation of property the sale or other disposition of which within the United States would have resulted in gain subject to tax under section 871(a) or 881 will be reduced only as provided in section 170(e)(1)(B) and paragraph (a)(2) or (3) of this section, but only if the property contributed is described in subdivision (i), (ii), or (iii) of subparagraph (2) of this paragraph. A charitable contribution by a nonresident alien individual or a foreign corporation of property the sale or other disposition of which within the United States would have resulted in gain subject to tax under section 871(a) or 881 will in no case be reduced under section 170(e)(1)(A) and paragraph (a)(1) of this section.

(c) *Allocation of basis and gain.*—(1) *In general.*—Except as provided in subparagraph (2) of this paragraph—

(i) If a taxpayer makes a charitable contribution of less than his entire interest in appreciated property, whether or not the transfer is made in trust, as, for example, in the case of a transfer of appreciated property to a pooled income fund described in section 642(c)(5) and §1.642(c)-5, and is allowed a deduction under section 170 for a portion of the fair market value of such property, then for purposes of applying the reduction rules of section 170(e)(1) and this section to the contributed portion of the property the taxpayer's adjusted basis in such property at the time of the contribution shall be allocated under section 170(e)(2) between the contributed portion of the property and the noncontributed portion.

(ii) The adjusted basis of the contributed portion of the property shall be that portion of the adjusted basis of the entire property which bears the same ratio to the total adjusted basis as the fair market value of the contributed portion of the property bears to the fair market value of the entire property.

(iii) The ordinary income and the long-term capital gain which shall be taken into account in applying section 170(e)(1) and paragraph (a) of this section to the contributed portion of the property shall be the amount of gain which would have been recognized as ordinary income and long-term capital gain if such contributed portion had been sold by the donor at its fair market value at the time of its contribution to the charitable organization.

(2) *Bargain sale.*—(i) Section 1011(b) and §1.1011-2 apply to bargain sales of property to charitable organizations. For purposes of applying the reduction rules of section 170(e)(1) and this section to the contributed portion of the property in the case of a bargain sale, there shall be allocated under section 1011(b) to the contributed portion of the property that portion of the adjusted basis of the entire property that bears the same ratio to the total adjusted basis as the fair market value of the contributed portion of the property bears to the fair market value of the entire property. For purposes of applying section 170(e)(1) and paragraph (a) of this section to the contributed portion of the property in such a case, there shall be allocated to the contributed portion the amount of gain that is not recognized on the bargain sale but that would have been recognized if such contributed portion had been sold by the donor at its fair market value at the time of its contribution to the charitable organization.

(ii) The term "bargain sale", as used in this subparagraph, means a transfer of property which is in part a sale or exchange of the property and in part a charitable contribution, as defined in section 170(c), of the property.

(3) *Ratio of ordinary income and capital gain.*—For purposes of applying subparagraphs (1)(iii) and (2)(i) of this paragraph, the amount of ordinary income (or long-term capital gain) which would have been recognized if the contributed portion of the property had been sold by the donor at its fair market value at the time of its

contribution shall be that amount which bears the same ratio to the ordinary income (or long-term capital gain) which would have been recognized if the entire property had been sold by the donor at its fair market value at the time of its contribution as (i) the fair market value of the contributed portion at such time bears to (ii) the fair market value of the entire property at such time. In the case of a bargain sale, the fair market value of the contributed portion for purposes of subdivision (i) is the amount determined by subtracting from the fair market value of the entire property the amount realized on the sale.

(4) *Donee's basis of property acquired.*—The adjusted basis of the contributed portion of the property as determined under subparagraph (1) or (2) of this paragraph, shall be used by the donee in applying to the contributed portion such provisions as section 514(a)(1), relating to adjusted basis of debt-financed property; section 1015(a), relating to basis of property acquired by gift; section 4940(c)(4), relating to capital gains and losses in determination of net investment income; and section 4942(f)(2)(B), relating to net short-term capital gain in determination of tax on failure to distribute income. The fair market value of the contributed portion of the property at the time of the contribution shall not be used by the donee as the basis of such contributed portion.

(d) *Illustrations.*—The application of this section may be illustrated by the following examples:

Example (1). (a) On July 1, 1970, C, an individual, makes the following charitable contributions, all of which are made to a church except in the case of the stock (as indicated):

Property	Fair Market Value	Adjusted Basis	Recognized Gain if Sold
Ordinary income property	$50,000	$35,000	$15,000
Property which, if sold, would produce long-term capital gain:			
(1) Stock held more than 6 months contributed to—			
(i) A church	25,000	21,000	4,000
(ii) A private foundation not described in section 170(b)(1)(E)	15,000	10,000	5,000
(2) Tangible personal property held more than 6 months (put to unrelated use by church)	12,000	6,000	6,000
Total	$102,000	$72,000	$30,000

(b) After making the reductions required by paragraph (a) of this section, the amount of charitable contributions allowed (before application of section 170(b) limitations) is as follows:

Property	Fair Market Value	Reduction	Contribution Allowed
Ordinary income property	$50,000	$15,000	$35,000
Property which, if sold, would produce long-term capital gain:			
(1) Stock contributed to—			
(i) The church	25,000	...	25,000
(ii) The private foundation	15,000	2,500	12,500
(2) Tangible personal property	12,000	3,000	9,000
Total	$102,000	$20,500	$81,500

(c) If C were a corporation, rather than an individual, the amount of charitable contributions allowed (before application of section 170(b) limitation) would be as follows:

Property	Fair Market Value	Reduction	Contribution Allowed
Ordinary income property	$50,000	$15,000	$35,000
Property which, if sold, would produce long-term capital gain:			
(1) Stock contributed to—			
(i) The church	25,000	...	25,000
(ii) The private foundation	15,000	3,125	11,875
(2) Tangible personal property	12,000	3,750	8,250
Total	$102,000	$21,875	$80,125

Example (2). On March 1, 1970, D, an individual, contributes to a church intangible property to which section 1245 applies which has a fair market value of $60,000 and an adjusted basis of $10,000. At the time of the contribution D has used the property in his business for more than 6 months. If the property had been sold by D at its fair market value at the time of its contribution, it is assumed that under section 1245 $20,000 of the gain of $50,000 would have been treated as ordinary income and $30,000 would have been long-term capital gain. Under paragraph (a)(1) of this section, D's contribution of $60,000 is reduced by $20,000.

Example (3). The facts are the same as in example (2) except that the property is contributed to a private foundation not described in section 170(b)(1)(E). Under paragraph (a)(1) and (2) of this section, D's contribution is reduced by $35,000 (100% of the ordinary income of $20,000 and 50% of the long-term capital gain of $30,000).

Example (4). (a) In 1971, E, an individual calendar-year taxpayer, contributes to a church stock held for more than 6 months which has a fair market value of $90,000 and an adjusted basis of $10,000. In 1972, E also contributes to a church stock held for more than 6 months which has a fair market value of $20,000 and an adjusted basis of $10,000. E's contribution base for 1971 is $200,000; and for 1972, is $150,000. E makes no other charitable contributions for these 2 taxable years.

(b) For 1971 the amount of the contribution which may be taken into account under section 170(a) is limited by section 170(b)(1)(D)(i) to $60,000 ($200,000 × 30%), and A is allowed a deduction for $60,000. Under section 170(b)(1)(D)(ii), E has a $30,000 carryover to 1972 of 30-percent capital gain property, as defined in paragraph (d)(3) of §1.170A-8. For 1972 the amount of the charitable contributions deduction is $45,000 (total contributions of $50,000 [$30,000 + $20,000] but not to exceed 30% of $150,000).

(c) Assuming, however, that in 1972 E elects under section 170(b)(1)(D)(iii) and paragraph (d)(2) of §1.170A-8 to have section 170(e)(1)(B) apply to his contributions and carryovers of 30-percent capital gain property, he must apply section 170(d)(1) as if section 170(e)(1)(B) had applied to the contribution for 1971. If section 170(e)(1)(B) had applied in 1971 to his contributions of 30-percent capital gain property, E's contribution would have been reduced from $90,000 to $50,000, the reduction of $40,000 being 50 percent of the gain of $80,000 ($90,000 − $10,000) which would have been recognized as long-term capital gain if the property had been sold by E at its fair market value at the time of its contribution to the church. Accordingly, by taking the election into account, E has no carryover of 30-percent capital gain property to 1972 since the charitable contributions deduction of $60,000 allowed for 1971 in respect of that property exceeds the reduced contribution of $50,000 for 1971 which may be taken into account by reason of the election. The charitable contributions deduction of $60,000 allowed for 1971 is not reduced by reason of the election.

(d) Since by reason of the election E is allowed under paragraph (a)(2) of this section a charitable contributions deduction for 1972 of $15,000 ($20,000 − [($20,000 − $10,000) × 50%]) and since the $30,000 carryover from 1971 is eliminated, it would not be to E's advantage to make the election under section 170(b)(1)(D)(iii) in 1972.

Example (5). In 1970, F, an individual calendar-year taxpayer, sells to a church for $4,000 ordinary income property with a fair market value of $10,000 and an adjusted basis of $4,000. F's contribution base for 1970 is $20,000, and F makes no other charitable contributions in 1970. Thus, F makes a charitable contribution to the church of $6,000 ($10,000 − $4,000 amount realized), which is 60% of the value of the property. The amount realized on the bargain sale is 40% ($4,000/$10,000) of the value of the property. In applying section 1011(b) to the bargain sale, adjusted basis in the amount of $1,600 ($4,000 adjusted basis × 40%) is allocated under §1.1011-2(b) to the noncontributed portion of the property, and F recognizes $2,400 ($4,000 amount realized less $1,600 adjusted basis) of ordinary income. Under paragraphs (a)(1) and (c)(2)(i) of this section, F's contribution of $6,000 is reduced by $3,600 ($6,000 − [$4,000 adjusted basis × 60%]) (*i.e.,* the amount of ordinary income that would have been recognized on the contributed portion had the property been sold). The reduced contribution of $2,400 consists of the portion ($4,000 × 60%) of the adjusted basis not allocated to the noncontributed portion of the property. That is, the reduced contribution consists of the portion of the adjusted basis allocated to the contributed portion. Under sections 1012 and 1015(a) the basis of the property to the church is $6,400 ($4,000 + $2,400).

Example (6). In 1970, G, an individual calendar-year taxpayer, sells to a church for $6,000 ordinary income property with a fair market value of $10,000 and an adjusted basis of $4,000. G's contribution base for 1970 is $20,000, and G makes no other charitable contributions in 1970. Thus, G makes a charitable contribution to the church of $4,000 ($10,000 − $6,000 amount realized), which is 40% of the value of the property. The amount realized on the bargain sale is 60% ($6,000/$10,000) of the value of the property. In applying section 1011(b) to the bargain sale, adjusted basis in the amount of $2,400 ($4,000 adjusted basis × 60%) is allocated under §1.1011-2(b) to the noncontributed portion of the property, and G recognizes $3,600 ($6,000 amount realized less $2,400 adjusted basis) of ordinary income. Under paragraphs (a)(1) and (c)(2)(i) of this section, G's contribution of $4,000 is reduced by $2,400 ($4,000 − [$4,000 adjusted basis × 40%]) (*i.e.,* the amount of ordinary income that would have been recognized on the contributed portion had the property been sold). The reduced contribution of $1,600 consists of the portion ($4,000 × 40%) of the adjusted basis not allocated to the noncontributed portion of the property. That is, the reduced contribution consists of the portion of the adjusted basis allocated to the contributed portion. Under sections 1012 and 1015(a) the basis of the property to the church is $7,600 ($6,000 + $1,600).

Example (7). In 1970, H, an individual calendar-year taxpayer, sells to a church for $2,000 stock held for not more than 6 months which has an adjusted basis of $4,000 and a fair market value of $10,000. H's contribution base for 1970 is $20,000, and H makes no other charitable contributions in 1970. Thus, H makes a charitable contribution to the church of $8,000 ($10,000 − $2,000 amount realized), which is 80%

of the value of the property. The amount realized on the bargain sale is 20% ($2,000/$10,000) of the value of the property. In applying section 1011(b) to the bargain sale, adjusted basis in the amount of $800 ($4,000 adjusted basis × 20%) is allocated under §1.1011-2(b) to the noncontributed portion of the property, and H recognizes $1,200 ($2,000 amount realized less $800 adjusted basis) of ordinary income. Under paragraphs (a)(1) and (c)(2)(i) of this section, H's contribution of $8,000 is reduced by $4,800 ($8,000 − [$4,000 adjusted basis × 80%]) (*i.e.,* the amount of ordinary income that would have been recognized on the contributed portion had the property been sold). The reduced contribution of $3,200 consists of the portion ($4,000 × 80%) of the adjusted basis not allocated to the noncontributed portion of the property. That is, the reduced contribution consists of the portion of the adjusted basis allocated to the contributed portion. Under sections 1012 and 1015(a) the basis of the property to the church is $5,200 ($2,000 + $3,200).

Example (8). In 1970, F, an individual calendar-year taxpayer, sells for $4,000 to a private foundation not described in section 170(b)(1)(E) property to which section 1245 applies which has a fair market value of $10,000 and an adjusted basis of $4,000. F's contribution base for 1970 is $20,000, and F makes no other charitable contributions in 1970. At the time of the bargain sale, F has used the property in his business for more than 6 months. Thus, F makes a charitable contribution of $6,000 ($10,000 − $4,000 amount realized), which is 60% of the value of the property. The amount realized on the bargain sale is 40% ($4,000/$10,000) of the value of the property. If the property had been sold by F at its fair market value at the time of its contribution, it is assumed that under section 1245 $4,000 of the gain of $6,000 ($10,000 − $4,000 adjusted basis) would have been treated as ordinary income and $2,000 would have been long-term capital gain. In applying section 1011(b) to the bargain sale, adjusted basis in the amount of $1,600 ($4,000 adjusted basis × 40%) is allocated under §1.1011-2(b) to the noncontributed portion of the property, and F's recognized gain of $2,400 ($4,000 amount realized less $1,600 adjusted basis) consists of $1,600 ($4,000 × 40%) of ordinary income and $800 ($2,000 × 40%) of long-term capital gain. Under paragraphs (a) and (c)(2)(i) of this section, F's contribution of $6,000 is reduced by $3,000 (the sum of $2,400 ($4,000 × 60%) of ordinary income and $600 ([$2,000 × 60%] × 50%) of long-term capital gain) (*i.e.,* the amount of gain that would have been recognized on the contributed portion had the property been sold). The reduced contribution of $3,000 consists of $2,400 ($4,000 × 60%) of adjusted basis and $600 ([$2,000 × 60%] × 50%) of long-term capital gain not used as a reduction under paragraph (a)(2) of this section. Under sections 1012 and 1015(a) the basis of the property to the private foundation is $6,400 ($4,000 + $2,400).

Example (9). On January 1, 1970, A, an individual, transfers to a charitable remainder annuity trust described in section 664(d)(1) stock which he has held for more than 6 months and which has a fair market value of $250,000 and an adjusted basis of $50,000, an irrevocable remainder interest in the property being contributed to a private foundation not described in section 170(b)(1)(E). The trust provides that an annuity of $12,500 a year is payable to A at the end of each year for 20 years. By reference to §20.2031-7A(c) of this chapter (Estate Tax Regulations) the figure in column (2) opposite 20 years is 11.4699. Therefore, under §1.664-2 the fair market value of the gift of the remainder interest to charity is $106,626.25 ($250,000 − [$12,500 × 11.4699]). Under paragraph (c)(1)(ii) of this section, the adjusted basis allocated to the contributed portion of the property is $21,325.25 ($50,000 × $106,626.25/$250,000). Under paragraphs (a)(2) and (c)(1) of this section, A's contribution is reduced by $42,650.50 (50% × [$106,626.25 − $21,325.25]) to $63,975.75 ($106,626.25 − $42,650.50). If, however, the irrevocable remainder interest in the property had been contributed to a section 170(b)(1)(A) organization, A's contribution of $106,626.25 would not be reduced under paragraph (a) of this section.

Example (10). (a) On July 1, 1970, B, a calendar-year individual taxpayer, sells to a church for $75,000 intangible property to which section 1245 applies which has a fair market value of $250,000 and an adjusted basis of $75,000. Thus, B makes a charitable contribution to the church of $175,000 ($250,000 − $75,000 amount realized), which is 70% ($175,000/$250,000) of the value of the property, the amount realized on the bargain sale is 30% ($75,000/$250,000) of the value of the property. At the time of the bargain sale, B has used the property in his business for more than 6 months. B's contribution base for 1970 is $500,000, and B makes no other charitable contributions in 1970. If the property had been sold by B at its fair market value at the time of its contribution, it is assumed that under section 1245 $105,000 of the gain of $175,000 ($250,000 − $75,000 adjusted basis) would have been treated as ordinary income and $70,000 would have been long-term capital gain. In applying section 1011(b) to the bargain sale, adjusted basis in the amount of $22,500 ($75,000 adjusted basis × 30%) is allocated under §1.1011-2(b) to the noncontributed portion of the property, and B's recognized gain of $52,500 ($75,000 amount realized less $22,500 adjusted basis) consists of $31,500 ($105,000 × 30%)

of ordinary income and $21,000 ($70,000 × 30%) of long-term capital gain.

(b) Under paragraphs (a)(1) and (c)(2)(i) of this section B's contribution of $175,000 is reduced by $73,500 ($105,000 × 70%) (*i.e.*, the amount of ordinary income that would have been recognized on the contributed portion had the property been sold). The reduced contribution of $101,500 consists of $52,500 [$75,000 × 70%] of adjusted basis allocated to the contributed portion of the property and $49,000 [$70,000 × 70%] of long-term capital gain allocated to the contributed portion. Under sections 1012 and 1015(a) the basis of the property to the church is $127,500 ($75,000 + $52,500).

(e) *Effective date.*—This section applies only to contributions paid after December 31, 1969, except that, in the case of a charitable contribution of a letter, memorandum, or property similar to a letter or memorandum, it applies to contributions paid after July 25, 1969. [Reg. § 1.170A-4.]

☐ [*T.D. 7207, 10-3-72. Amended by T.D. 7728, 10-31-80, T.D. 7807, 1-29-82, T.D. 8176, 2-24-88 and T.D. 8540, 6-9-94.*]

[Reg. § 1.170A-4A]

§ 1.170A-4A. Special rule for the deduction of certain charitable contributions of inventory and other property.—(a) *Introduction.*—Section 170(e)(3) provides a special rule for the deduction of certain qualified contributions of inventory and certain other property. To be treated as a "qualified contribution," a contribution must meet the restrictions and requirements of section 170(e)(3)(A) and paragraph (b) of this section. Paragraph (b)(1) of this section describes the corporations whose contributions may be subject to this section, the exempt organizations to which these contributions may be made, and the kinds of property which may be contributed. Under paragraph (b)(2) of this section, the use of the property must be related to the purpose or function constituting the ground for the exemption of the organization to which the contribution is made. Also, the property must be used for the care of the ill, needy, or infants. Under paragraph (b)(3) of this section, the recipient organization may not, except as there provided, require or receive in exchange money, property, or services for the transfer or use of property contributed under section 170(e)(3). Under paragraph (b)(4) of this section, the recipient organization must provide the contributing taxpayer with a written statement representing that the organization intends to comply with the restrictions set forth in paragraph (b)(2) and (3) of this section on the use and transfer of the property. Under paragraph (b)(5) of this section, the contributed property must conform to any applicable provisions of the Federal Food, Drug, and Cosmetic Act (as amended), and the regulations thereunder, at the date of contribution and for the immediately preceding 180 days. Paragraph (c) of this section provides the rules for determining the amount of reduction of the charitable contribution under section 170(e)(3). In general, the amount of the reduction is equal to one-half of the amount of gain (other than gain described in paragraph (d) of this section) which would not have been long-term capital gain if the property had been sold by the donor-taxpayer at fair market value at the date of contribution. If, after this reduction, the amount of the deduction would be more than twice the basis of the contributed property, the amount of the deduction is accordingly further reduced under paragraph (c)(1) of this section. The basis of contributed property which is inventory is determined under paragraph (c)(2) of this section, and the donor's cost of goods sold for the year of contribution must be adjusted under paragraph (c)(3) of this section. Under paragraph (d) of this section, a deduction is not allowed for any amount which, if the property had been sold by the donor-taxpayer, would have been gain to which the recapture provisions of section 617, 1245, 1250, 1251, or 1252 would have applied. For purposes of section 170(e)(3), the rules of § 1.170A-4 apply where not inconsistent with the rules of this section.

(b) *Qualified contributions.*—(1) *In general.*—A contribution of property qualifies under section 170(e)(3) of this section only if it is a charitable contribution—

(i) By a corporation, other than a corporation which is an electing small business corporation within the meaning of section 1371(b);

(ii) To an organization described in section 501(c)(3) and exempt under section 501(a), other than a private foundation, as defined in section 509(a), which is not an operating foundation, as defined in section 4942(j)(e);

(iii) Of property described in section 1221(1) or (2);

(iv) Which contribution meets the restrictions and requirements of paragraph (b)(2) through (5) of this section.

(2) *Restrictions on use of contributed property.*—In order for the contribution to qualify under this section, the contributed property is subject to the following restrictions in use. If the transferred property

is used or transferred by the donee organization (or by any subsequent transferee that furnished to the donee organization the written statement described in paragraph (b)(4)(ii) of this section) in a manner inconsistent with the requirements of subdivision (i) or (ii) of this paragraph (b)(2) or the requirements of paragraph (b)(3) of this section, the donor's deduction is reduced to the amount allowable under section 170 of the regulations thereunder, determined without regard to section 170(e)(3) of this section. If, however, the donor establishes that, at the time of the contribution, the donor reasonably anticipated that the property would be used in a manner consistent with those requirements, then the donor's deduction is not reduced.

(i) *Requirement of use for exempt purpose.*—The use of the property must be related to the purpose or function constituting the ground for exemption under section 501(c)(3) of the organization to which the contribution is made. The property may not be used in connection with any activity which gives rise to unrelated trade or business income, as defined in sections 512 and 513 and the regulations thereunder.

(ii) *Requirement of use for care of the ill, needy, or infants.*—(A) *In general.*—The property must be used for the care of the ill, needy, or infants, as defined in this subdivision (ii). The property itself must ultimately either be transferred to (or for the use of) the ill, needy, or infants for their care or be retained for their care. No other person may use the contributed property except as incidental to primary use in the care of the ill, needy, or infants. The organization may satisfy the requirement of this subdivision by transferring the property to a relative, custodian, parent or guardian of the ill or needy individual or infant, or to any other individual if it makes a reasonable effort to ascertain that the property will ultimately be used primarily for the care of the ill or needy individual, or infant, and not for the primary benefit of any other person. The recipient organization may transfer the property to another exempt organization within the jurisdiction of the United States which meets the description contained in paragraph (b)(1)(ii) of this section, or to an organization not within the jurisdiction of the United States that, but for the fact that it is not within the jurisdiction of the United States, would be described in paragraph (b)(1)(ii) of this section. If an organization transfers the property to another organization, the transferring organization must obtain a written statement from the transferee organization as set forth in paragraph (b)(4) of this section. If the property is ultimately transferred to, or used for the benefit of, ill or needy persons, or infants, not within the jurisdiction of the United States, the organization which so transfers the property outside the jurisdiction of the United States must necessarily be a corporation. See section 170(c)(2) and § 1.170A-11(a). For purposes of this subdivision, if the donee-organization charges for its transfer of contributed property (other than a fee allowed by paragraph (b)(3)(ii) of this section) the requirement of this subdivision is not met. See paragraph (b)(3) of this section.

(B) *Definition of the ill.*—An ill person is a person who requires medical care within the meaning of § 1.213-1(e). Examples of ill persons include a person suffering from physical injury, a person with a significant impairment of a bodily organ, a person with an existing handicap, whether from birth or later injury, a person suffering from malnutrition, a person with a disease, sickness, or infection which significantly impairs physical health, a person partially or totally incapable of self-care (including incapacity due to old age). A person suffering from mental illness is included if the person is hospitalized or institutionalized for the mental disorder, or, although the person is nonhospitalized or noninstitutionalized, if the person's mental illness constitutes a significant health impairment.

(C) *Definition of care of the ill.*—Care of the ill means alleviation or cure of an existing illness and includes care of the physical, mental, or emotional needs of the ill.

(D) *Definition of the needy.*—A needy person is a person who lacks the necessities of life, involving physical, mental, or emotional well-being, as a result of poverty or temporary distress. Examples of needy persons include a person who is financially impoverished as a result of low income and lack of financial resources, a person who temporarily lacks food or shelter (and the means to provide for it), a person who is the victim of a natural disaster (such as fire or flood), a person who is the victim of a civil disaster (such as a civil disturbance), a person who is temporarily not self-sufficient as a result of a sudden and severe personal or family crisis (such as a person who is the victim of a crime of violence or who has been physically abused), a person who is a refugee or immigrant and who is experiencing language, cultural, or financial difficulties, a minor child who is not self-sufficient and who is not cared for by a parent or guardian, and a person who is not self-sufficient as a result of previous institutionalization (such as a former prisoner or a former patient in a mental institution).

(E) *Definition of care of the needy.*—Care of the needy means alleviation or satisfaction of an existing need. Since a person may be needy in some respects and not needy in other respects, care of the needy must relate to the particular need which causes the person to be needy. For example, a person whose temporary need arises from a natural disaster may need temporary shelter and food but not recreational facilities.

(F) *Definition of infant.*—An infant is a minor child (as determined under the laws of the jurisdiction in which the child resides).

(G) *Definition of care of an infant.*—Care of an infant means performance of parental functions and provision for the physical, mental, and emotional needs of the infant.

(3) *Restrictions on transfer of contributed property.*—(i) *In general.*—Except as otherwise provided in subdivision (ii) of this paragraph (b)(3), a contribution will not qualify under this section, if the donee-organization or any transferee of the donee-organization requires or receives any money, property, or services for the transfer or use of property contributed under section 170(e)(3). For example, if an organization provides temporary shelter for a fee, and also provides free meals to ill or needy individuals, or infants using food contributed under this section the contribution of food is subject to this section (if the other requirements of this section are met). However, the fee charged by the organization for the shelter may not be increased merely because meals are served to the ill or needy individuals or infants.

(ii) *Exception.*—A contribution may qualify under this section if the donee-organization charges a fee to another organization in connection with its transfer of the donated property, if—

(A) The fee is small or nominal in relation to the value of the transferred property and is not determined by this value; and

(B) The fee is designed to reimburse the donee-organization for its administrative, warehousing, or other similar costs.
For example, if a charitable organization (such as a food bank) accepts surplus food to distribute to other charities which give the food to needy persons, a small fee may be charged to cover administrative, warehousing, and other similar costs. This fee may be charged on the basis of the total number of pounds of food distributed to the transferee charity but not on the basis of the value of the food distributed. The provisions of this subdivision (ii) do not apply to a transfer of donated property directly from an organization to ill or needy individuals, or infants.

(4) *Requirement of a written statement.*—(i) *Furnished to taxpayer.*—In the case of any contribution made on or after [Date which is 30 days after the issuance of these regulations by Treasury decision], the donee-organization must furnish to the taxpayer a written statement which—

(A) Describes the contributed property, stating the date of its receipt;

(B) Represents that the property will be used in compliance with section 170(e)(3) and paragraphs (b)(2) and (3) of this section;

(C) Represents that the donee-organization meets the requirements of paragraph (b)(1)(ii) of this section; and

(D) Represents that adequate books and records will be maintained, and made available to the Internal Revenue Service upon request.
The written statement must be furnished within a reasonable period after the contribution, but not later than the date (including extensions) by which the donor is required to file a United States corporate income tax return for the year in which the contribution was made. The books and records described in (D) of this subdivision (i) need not trace the receipt and disposition of specific items of donated property if they disclose compliance with the requirements by reference to aggregate quantities of donated property. The books and records are adequate if they reflect total amounts received and distributed (or used), and outline the procedure used for determining that the ultimate recipient of the property is an ill or needy individual, or infant. However, the books and records need not reflect the names of the ultimate individual recipients or the property distributed to (or used by) each one.

(ii) *Furnished to transferring organization.*—If an organization that received a contribution under this section transfers the contributed property to another organization on or after [Date which is 30 days after the issuance of these regulations by Treasury decision], the transferee organization must furnish to the transferring organization a written statement which contains the information required in paragraph (b)(4)(i)(A), (B) and (D) of this section. The statement must also represent that the transferee organization meets the requirements of paragraph (b)(1)(ii) of this section (or, in the case of a transferee organization which is a foreign organization not within the jurisdiction of the United States, that, but for such fact, the organization

would meet the requirements of paragraph (b)(1)(ii) of this section). The written statement must be furnished within a reasonable period after the transfer.

(5) *Requirement of compliance with the Federal Food, Drug, and Cosmetic Act.*—(i) *In general.*—With respect to property contributed under this section which is subject to the Federal Food, Drug, and Cosmetic Act (as amended), and regulations thereunder, the contributed property must comply with the applicable provisions of that Act and regulations thereunder at the date of the contribution and for the immediately preceding 180 days. In the case of specific items of contributed property not in existence for the entire period of 180 days immediately preceding the date of contribution, the requirement of this paragraph (b)(5) is considered met if the contributed property complied with that Act and the regulations thereunder during the period of its existence and at the date of contribution and if, for the 180 day period prior to contribution other property (if any) held by the taxpayer at any time during that period, which property was fungible with the contributed property, complied with that Act and the regulations thereunder during the period held by the taxpayer.

(ii) *Example.*—The rule of this paragraph (b)(5) may be illustrated by the following example.
Example. Corporation X, a grocery store, contributes 12 crates of navel oranges. The oranges were picked and placed in the grocery store's stock two weeks prior to the date of contribution. The contribution satisfies the requirements of this paragraph (b)(5) if X complied with the Act and regulations thereunder for 180 days prior to the date of contribution with respect to all navel oranges in stock during that period.

(c) *Amount of reduction.*—(1) *In general.*—Section 170(e)(3)(B) requires that the amount of the charitable contribution subject to this section which would be taken into account under section 170(a), without regard to section 170(e), must be reduced before applying the percentage limitations under section 170(b). The amount of the first reduction is equal to one-half of the amount of gain which would not have been long-term capital gain if the property had been sold by the donor-taxpayer at its fair market value on the date of its contribution, excluding, however, any amount described in paragraph (d) of this section. If the amount of the charitable contribution which remains after this reduction exceeds twice the basis of the contributed property, then the amount of the charitable contribution is reduced a second time to an amount which is equal to twice the amount of the basis of the property.

(2) *Basis of contributed property which is inventory.*—For the purposes of this section, notwithstanding the rules of §1.170A-1(c)(4), the basis of contributed property which is inventory must be determined under the donor's method of accounting for inventory for purposes of United States income tax. The donor must use as the basis of the contributed item the inventoriable carrying cost assigned to any similar item not included in closing inventory. For example, under the LIFO dollar value method of accounting for inventory, where there has been an invasion of a prior year's layer, the donor may choose to treat the item contributed as having a basis of the unit's cost with reference to the layer(s) of prior year(s) cost or with reference to the current year cost.

(3) *Adjustment to cost of goods sold.*—Notwithstanding the rules of §1.170A-1(c)(4), the donor of the property which is inventory contributed under this section must make a corresponding adjustment to cost of goods sold by decreasing the cost of goods sold by the lesser of the fair market value of the contributed item or the amount of basis determined under paragraph (c)(2) of this section.

(4) *Examples.*—The rules of this paragraph (c) may be illustrated by the following examples:
Example (1). During 1978 corporation X, a calendar year taxpayer, makes a qualified contribution of women's coats which were section 1221(1) property. The fair market value of the property at the date of contribution is $1,000, and the basis of the property is $200. The amount of the charitable contribution which would be taken into account under section 170(a) is the fair market value ($1,000). The amount of gain which would not have been long-term capital gain if the property had been sold is $800 ($1,000 – $200). The amount of the contribution is reduced by one-half the amount which would not have been capital gain if the property had been sold ($800/2 = $400).
After this reduction, the amount of the contribution which may be taken into account is $600 ($1,000 – $400). A second reduction is made in the amount of the charitable contribution because this amount (as first reduced to $600) is more than $400 which is an amount equal to twice the basis of the property. The amount of the further reduction is $200 [$600 – (2 × $200)], and the amount of the contribution as finally reduced is $400 [$1,000 – ($400 + $200)]. X would also have to decrease its cost of goods sold for the year of contribution by $200.

Reg. §1.170A-4A(c)(4)

Example (2). Assume the same facts as set forth in example (1) except that the basis of the property is $600. The amount of the first reduction is $200 (($1,000 – $600)/2).

As reduced, the amount of the contribution which may be taken into account is $800 ($1,000 – $200). There is no second reduction because $800 is less than $1,200 which is twice the basis of the property. However, X would have to decrease its cost of goods sold for the year of contribution by $600.

(d) *Recapture excluded.*—A deduction is not allowed under section 170(e)(3) or this section for any amount which, if the property had been sold by the donor-taxpayer on the date of its contribution for an amount equal to its fair market value, would have been treated as ordinary income under section 617, 1245, 1250, 1251, or 1252. Thus, before making either reduction required by section 170(e)(3)(B) and paragraph (c) of this section, the fair market value of the contributed property must be reduced by the amount of gain that would have been recognized (if the property had been sold) as ordinary income under section 617, 1245, 1250, 1251, or 1252.

(e) *Effective date.*—This section applies to qualified contributions made after October 4, 1976. [Reg. § 1.170A-4A.]

☐ [*T.D. 7807, 1-29-82. Amended by T.D. 7962, 6-28-84.*]

[Reg. § 1.170A-5]

§1.170A-5. Future interests in tangible personal property.— (a) *In general.*—(1) A contribution consisting of a transfer of a future interest in tangible personal property shall be treated as made only when all intervening interests in, and rights to the actual possession or enjoyment of, the property—

　(i) Have expired, or

　(ii) Are held by persons other than the taxpayer or those standing in a relationship to the taxpayer described in section 267(b) and the regulations thereunder, relating to losses, expenses, and interest with respect to transactions between related taxpayers.

(2) Section 170(a)(3) and this section have no application in respect of a transfer of an undivided present interest in property. For example, a contribution of an undivided one-quarter interest in a painting with respect to which the donee is entitled to possession during three months of each year shall be treated as made upon the receipt by the donee of a formally executed and acknowledged deed of gift. However, the period of initial possession by the donee may not be deferred in time for more than one year.

(3) Section 170(a)(3) and this section have no application in respect of a transfer of a future interest in intangible personal property or in real property. However, a fixture which is intended to be severed from real property shall be treated as tangible personal property. For example, a contribution of a future interest in a chandelier which is attached to a building is considered a contribution which consists of a future interest in tangible personal property if the transferor intends that it be detached from the building at or prior to the time when the charitable organization's right to possession or enjoyment of the chandelier is to commence.

(4) For purposes of section 170(a)(3) and this section, the term "future interest" has generally the same meaning as it has when used in section 2503 and § 25.2503-3 of this chapter (Gift Tax Regulations); it includes reversions, remainders, and other interests or estates, whether vested or contingent, and whether or not supported by a particular interest or estate, which are limited to commence in use, possession, or enjoyment at some future date or time. The term "future interest" includes situations in which a donor purports to give tangible personal property to a charitable organization, but has an understanding, arrangement, agreement, etc., whether written or oral, with the charitable organization which has the effect of reserving to, or retaining in, such donor a right to the use, possession, or enjoyment of the property.

(5) In the case of a charitable contribution of a future interest to which section 170(a)(3) and this section apply, the other provisions of section 170 and the regulations thereunder are inapplicable to the contribution until such time as the contribution is treated as made under section 170(a)(3).

(b) *Illustrations.*—The application of this section may be illustrated by the following examples:

Example (1). On December 31, 1970, A, an individual who reports his income on the calendar year basis, conveys by deed of gift to a museum title to a painting, but reserves to himself the right to use, possession, and enjoyment of the painting during his lifetime. It is assumed that there was no intention to avoid the application of section 170(f)(3)(A) by the conveyance. At the time of the gift the value of the painting is $90,000. Since the contribution consists of a future interest in tangible personal property in which the donor has retained an intervening interest, no contribution is considered to have been made in 1970.

Example (2). Assume the same facts as in example (1) except that on December 31, 1971, A relinquishes all of his right to the use, possession, and enjoyment of the painting and delivers the painting to the museum. Assuming that the value of the painting has increased to $95,000, A is treated as having made a charitable contribution of $95,000 in 1971 for which a deduction is allowable without regard to section 170(f)(3)(A).

Example (3). Assume the same facts as in example (1) except A dies without relinquishing his right to the use, possession, and enjoyment of the painting. Since A did not relinquish his right to the use, possession, and enjoyment of the property during his life, A is treated as not having made a charitable contribution of the painting for income tax purposes.

Example (4). Assume the same facts as in example (1) except A, on December 31, 1971, transfers his interest in the painting to his son, B, who reports his income on the calendar year basis. Since the relationship between A and B is one described in section 267(b), no contribution of the remainder interest in the painting is considered to have been made in 1971.

Example (5). Assume the same facts as in example (4). Also assume that on December 31, 1972, B conveys to the museum the interest measured by A's life. B has made a charitable contribution of the present interest in the painting conveyed to the museum. In addition, since all intervening interests in, and rights to the actual possession or enjoyment of the property, have expired, a charitable contribution of the remainder interest is treated as having been made by A in 1972 for which a deduction is allowable without regard to section 170(f)(3)(A). Such remainder interest is valued according to § 20.2031-7A(c) of this chapter (Estate Tax Regulations), determined by subtracting the value of B's interest measured by A's life expectancy in 1972, and B receives a deduction in 1972 for the life interest measured by A's life expectancy and valued according to Table A (1) in such section.

Example (6). On December 31, 1970, C, an individual who reports his income on the calendar year basis, transfers a valuable painting to a pooled income fund described in section 642(c)(5), which is maintained by a university. C retains for himself for life an income interest in the painting, the remainder interest in the painting being contributed to the university. Since the contribution consists of a future interest in tangible personal property in which the donor has retained an intervening interest, no charitable contribution is considered to have been made in 1970.

Example (7). On January 15, 1972, D, an individual who reports his income on the calendar year basis, transfers a capital asset held for more than 6 months consisting of a valuable painting to a pooled income fund described in section 642(c)(5), which is maintained by a university, and creates an income interest in such painting for E for life. E is an individual not standing in a relationship to D described in section 267(b). The remainder interest in the property is contributed by D to the university. The trustee of the pooled income fund puts the painting to an unrelated use within the meaning of paragraph (b)(3) of § 1.170A-4. Accordingly, D is allowed a deduction under section 170 in 1972 for the present value of the remainder interest in the painting, after reducing such amount under section 170(e)(1)(B)(i) and paragraph (a)(2) of § 1.170A-4. This reduction in the amount of the contribution is required since under paragraph (b)(3) of that section the use by the pooled income fund of the painting is a use which would have been an unrelated use if it had been made by the university.

(c) *Effective date.*—This section applies only to contributions paid in taxable years beginning after December 31, 1969. [Reg. § 1.170A-5.]

☐ [*T.D. 7207, 10-3-72. Amended by T.D. 8540, 6-9-94.*]

[Reg. § 1.170A-6]

§1.170A-6. Charitable contributions in trust.—(a) *In general.*— (1) No deduction is allowed under section 170 for the fair market value of a charitable contribution of any interest in property which is less than the donor's entire interest in the property and which is transferred in trust unless the transfer meets the requirements of paragraph (b) or (c) of this section. If the donor's entire interest in the property is transferred in trust and is contributed to a charitable organization described in section 170(c), a deduction is allowed under section 170. Thus, if on July 1, 1972, property is transferred in trust with the requirement that the income of the trust be paid for a term of 20 years to a church and thereafter the remainder be paid to an educational organization described in section 170(b)(1)(A), a deduction is allowed for the value of such property. See section 170(f)(2) and (3)(B), and paragraph (b)(1) of § 1.170A-7.

(2) A deduction is allowed without regard to this section for a contribution of a partial interest in property if such interest is the taxpayer's entire interest in the property, such as an income interest or a remainder interest. If, however, the property in which such partial interest exists was divided in order to create such interest and

thus avoid section 170(f)(2), the deduction will not be allowed. Thus, for example, assume that a taxpayer desires to contribute to a charitable organization the reversionary interest in certain stocks and bonds which he owns. If the taxpayer transfers such property in trust with the requirement that the income of the trust be paid to his son for life and that the reversionary interest be paid to himself and immediately after creating the trust contributes the reversionary interest to a charitable organization, no deduction will be allowed under section 170 for the contribution of the taxpayer's entire interest consisting of the reversionary interest in the trust.

(b) *Charitable contribution of a remainder interest in trust.*—(1) *In general.*—No deduction is allowed under section 170 for the fair market value of a charitable contribution of a remainder interest in property which is less than the donor's entire interest in the property and which the donor transfers in trust unless the trust is—

(i) A pooled income fund described in section 642(c)(5) and §1.642(c)-5,

(ii) A charitable remainder annuity trust described in section 664(d)(1) and §1.664-2, or

(iii) A charitable remainder unitrust described in section 664(d)(2) and §1.664-3.

(2) *Value of a remainder interest.*—The fair market value of a remainder interest in a pooled income fund shall be computed under §1.642(c)-6. The fair market value of a remainder interest in a charitable remainder annuity trust shall be computed under §1.664-2. The fair market value of a remainder interest in a charitable remainder unitrust shall be computed under §1.664-4. However, in some cases a reduction in the amount of a charitable contribution of the remainder interest may be required. See section 170(e) and §1.170A-4.

(c) *Charitable contribution of an income interest in trust.*—(1) *In general.*—No deduction is allowed under section 170 for the fair market value of a charitable contribution of an income interest in property which is less than the donor's entire interest in the property and which the donor transfers in trust unless the income interest is either a guaranteed annuity interest or a unitrust interest, as defined in paragraph (c) (2) of this section, and the grantor is treated as the owner of such interest for purposes of applying section 671, relating to grantors and others treated as substantial owners. See section 4947(a)(2) for the application to such income interests in trust of the provisions relating to private foundations and section 508(e) for rules relating to provisions required in the governing instruments.

(2) *Definitions.*—For purposes of this paragraph—

(i) *Guaranteed annuity interest.*—(A) An income interest is a "guaranteed annuity interest" only if it is an irrevocable right pursuant to the governing instrument of the trust to receive a guaranteed annuity. A guaranteed annuity is an arrangement under which a determinable amount is paid periodically, but not less often than annually, for a specified term of years or for the life or lives of certain individuals, each of whom must be living at the date of transfer and can be ascertained at such date. Only one or more of the following individuals may be used as measuring lives: the donor, the donor's spouse, and an individual who, with respect to all remainder beneficiaries (other than charitable organizations described in section 170, 2055, or 2522), is either a lineal ancestor or the spouse of a lineal ancestor of those beneficiaries. A trust will satisfy the requirement that all noncharitable remainder beneficiaries are lineal descendants of the individual who is the measuring life, or that individual's spouse, if there is less than a 15% probability that individuals who are not lineal descendants will receive any trust corpus. This probability must be computed, based on the current applicable Life Table contained in §20.2031-7, at the time property is transferred to the trust taking into account the interests of all primary and contingent remainder beneficiaries who are living at that time. An interest payable for a specified term of years can qualify as a guaranteed annuity interest even if the governing instrument contains a savings clause intended to ensure compliance with a rule against perpetuities. The savings clause must utilize a period for vesting of 21 years after the deaths of measuring lives who are selected to maximize, rather than limit, the term of the trust. The rule in this paragraph that a charitable interest may be payable for the life or lives of only certain specified individuals does not apply in the case of a charitable guaranteed annuity interest payable under a charitable remainder trust described in section 664. An amount is determinable if the exact amount which must be paid under the conditions specified in the governing instrument of the trust can be ascertained as of the date of transfer. For example, the amount to be paid may be a stated sum for a term of years, or for the life of the donor, at the expiration of which it may be changed by a specified amount, but it may not be redetermined by reference to a fluctuating index such as the cost of living index. In further illustration, the amount to be paid may be expressed

in terms of a fraction or percentage of the cost of living index on the date of transfer.

(B) An income interest is a guaranteed annuity interest only if it is a guaranteed annuity interest in every respect. For example, if the income interest is the right to receive from a trust each year a payment equal to the lesser of a sum certain or a fixed percentage of the net fair market value of the trust assets, determined annually, such interest is not a guaranteed annuity interest.

(C) Where a charitable interest is in the form of a guaranteed annuity interest, the governing instrument of the trust may provide that income of the trust which is in excess of the amount required to pay the guaranteed annuity interest shall be paid to or for the use of a charitable organization Nevertheless, the amount of the deduction under section 170(f)(2)(B) shall be limited to the fair market value of the guaranteed annuity interest as determined under paragraph (c)(3) of this section. For a rule relating to treatment by the grantor of any contribution made by the trust in excess of the amount required to pay the guaranteed annuity interest, see paragraph (d)(2)(ii) of this section.

(D) If the present value on the date of transfer of all the income interests for a charitable purpose exceeds 60 percent of the aggregate fair market value of all amounts in the trust (after the payment of liabilities), the income interest will not be considered a guaranteed annuity interest unless the governing instrument of the trust prohibits both the acquisition and the retention of assets which would give rise to a tax under section 4944 if the trustee had acquired such assets. The requirement in this subdivision (D) for a prohibition in the governing instrument against the retention of assets which would give rise to a tax under section 4944 if the trustee had acquired the assets shall not apply to a transfer in trust made on or before May 21, 1972.

(E) Where a charitable interest in the form of a guaranteed annuity interest is transferred after May 21, 1972, the charitable interest generally is not a guaranteed annuity interest if any amount may be paid by the trust for a private purpose before the expiration of all the charitable annuity interests. There are two exceptions to this general rule. First, the charitable interest is a guaranteed annuity interest if the amount payable for a private purpose is in the form of a guaranteed annuity interest and the trust's governing instrument does not provide for any preference or priority in the payment of the private annuity as opposed to the charitable annuity. Second, the charitable interest is a guaranteed annuity interest if under the trust's governing instrument the amount that may be paid for a private purpose is payable only from a group of assets that are devoted exclusively to private purposes and to which section 4947(a)(2) is inapplicable by reason of section 4947(a)(2)(B). For purposes of this paragraph (c)(2)(i)(E), an amount is not paid for a private purpose if it is paid for an adequate and full consideration in money or money's worth. See §53.4947-1(c) of this chapter for rules relating to the inapplicability of section 4947(a)(2) to segregated amounts in a split-interest trust.

(F) For rules relating to certain governing instrument requirements and to the imposition of certain excise taxes where the guaranteed annuity interest is in trust and for rules governing payment of private income interests by a split-interest trust, see section 4947(a)(2) and (b)(3)(A), and the regulations thereunder.

(ii) *Unitrust interest.*—(A) An income interest is a "unitrust interest" only if it is an irrevocable right pursuant to the governing instrument of the trust to receive payment, not less often than annually, of a fixed percentage of the net fair market value of the trust assets, determined annually. In computing the net fair market value of the trust assets, all assets and liabilities shall be taken into account without regard to whether particular items are taken into account in determining the income of the trust. The net fair market value of the trust assets may be determined on any one date during the year or by taking the average of valuations made on more than one date during the year, provided that the same valuation date or dates and valuation methods are used each year. Where the governing instrument of the trust does not specify the valuation date or dates, the trustee shall select such date or dates and shall indicate his selection on the first return on Form 1041 which the trust is required to file. Payments under a unitrust interest may be paid for a specified term of years or for the life or lives of certain individuals, each of whom must be living at the date of transfer and can be ascertained at such date. Only one or more of the following individuals may be used as measuring lives: the donor, the donor's spouse, and an individual who, with respect to all remainder beneficiaries (other than charitable organizations described in section 170, 2055, or 2522), is either a lineal ancestor or the spouse of a lineal ancestor of those beneficiaries. A trust will satisfy the requirement that all noncharitable remainder beneficiaries are lineal descendants of the individual who is the measuring life, or that individual's spouse, if there is less than a 15% probability that individuals who are not lineal descendants will receive any trust corpus. This probability must be computed, based on the current applicable Life Table contained in §20.2031-7, at the time property is transferred to the trust taking into account the interests of all primary and contingent remainder beneficiaries who are living at that time. An interest payable for a specified term of years can qualify as a unitrust interest even if the governing instrument contains a savings clause intended to ensure compliance with a rule against perpetuities. The savings clause must utilize a period for vesting of 21 years after the deaths of measuring lives who are selected to maximize, rather than limit, the term of the trust. The rule in this paragraph that a charitable interest may be payable for the life or lives of only certain specified individuals does not apply in the case of a charitable unitrust interest payable under a charitable remainder trust described in section 664.

(B) An income interest is a unitrust interest only if it is a unitrust interest in every respect. For example, if the income interest is the right to receive from a trust each year a payment equal to the lesser of a sum certain or a fixed percentage of the net fair market value of the trust assets, determined annually, such interest is not a unitrust interest.

(C) Where a charitable interest is in the form of a unitrust interest, the governing instrument of the trust may provide that income of the trust which is in excess of the amount required to pay the unitrust interest shall be paid to or for the use of a charitable organization. Nevertheless, the amount of the deduction under section 170(f)(2)(B) shall be limited to the fair market value of the unitrust interest as determined under paragraph (c)(3) of this section. For a rule relating to treatment by the grantor of any contribution made by the trust in excess of the amount required to pay the unitrust interest, see paragraph (d)(2)(ii) of this section.

(D) Where a charitable interest is in the form of a unitrust interest, the charitable interest generally is not a unitrust interest if any amount may be paid by the trust for a private purpose before the expiration of all the charitable unitrust interests. There are two exceptions to this general rule. First, the charitable interest is a unitrust interest if the amount payable for a private purpose is in the form of a unitrust interest and the trust's governing instrument does not provide for any preference or priority in the payment of the private unitrust interest as opposed to the charitable unitrust interest. Second, the charitable interest is a unitrust interest if under the trust's governing instrument the amount that may be paid for a private purpose is payable only from a group of assets that are devoted exclusively to private purposes and to which section 4947(a)(2) is inapplicable by reason of section 4947(a)(2)(B). For purposes of this paragraph (c)(2)(ii)(D), an amount is not paid for a private purpose if it is paid for an adequate and full consideration in money or money's worth. See §53.4947-1(c) of this chapter for rules relating to the inapplicability of section 4947(a)(2) to segregated amounts in a split-interest trust.

(E) For rules relating to certain governing instrument requirements and to the imposition of certain excise taxes where the unitrust interest is in trust and for rules governing payment of private income interests by a split-interest trust, see section 4947(a)(2) and (b)(3)(A), and the regulations thereunder.

(3) *Valuation of income interest.*—(i) The deduction allowed by section 170(f)(2)(B) for a charitable contribution of a guaranteed annuity interest is limited to the fair market value of such interest on the date of contribution, as computed under §20.2031-7 or, for certain prior periods, §20.2031-7A of this chapter (Estate Tax Regulations).

(ii) The deduction allowed under section 170(f)(2)(B) for a charitable contribution of a unitrust interest is limited to the fair market value of the unitrust interest on the date of contribution. The fair market value of the unitrust interest shall be determined by subtracting the present value of all interests in the transferred property other than the unitrust interest from the fair market value of the transferred property.

(iii) If by reason of all the conditions and circumstances surrounding a transfer of an income interest in property in trust it appears that the charity may not receive the beneficial enjoyment of the interest, a deduction will be allowed under paragraph (c) (1) of this section only for the minimum amount it is evident the charity will receive. The application of this subdivision may be illustrated by the following examples:

Example (1). In 1972, B transfers $20,000 in trust with the requirement that M Church be paid a guaranteed annuity interest (as defined in subparagraph (2)(i) of this paragraph) of $4,000, payable annually at the end of each year for 9 years, and that the residue revert to himself. Since the fair market value of an annuity of $4,000 a year for a period of 9 years, as determined under §20.2031-7A(c) of this chapter, is $27,206.80 ($4,000 × 6.8017), it appears that M will not *receive the beneficial enjoyment of the income interest.* Accordingly, even though B is treated as the owner of the trust under section 673, he is allowed a deduction under subparagraph (1) of this paragraph for only $20,000, which is the minimum amount it is evident M will receive.

Example (2). In 1975, C transfers $40,000 in trust with the requirement that D, an individual, and X Charity be paid simultaneously guaranteed annuity interests (as defined in subparagraph (2)(i) of this paragraph) of $5,000 a year each, payable annually at the end of each year, for a period of 5 years and that the remainder be paid to C's children. The fair market value of two annuities of $5,000 each a year for a period of 5 years is $42,124 ([$5,000 × 4.2124] × 2), as determined under §20.2031-7A(c) of this chapter. The trust instrument provides that in the event the trust fund is insufficient to pay both annuities in a given year, the trust fund will be evenly divided between the charitable and private annuitants. The deduction under subparagraph (1) of this paragraph with respect to the charitable annuity will be limited to $20,000, which is the minimum amount it is evident X will receive.

Example (3). In 1975, D transfers $65,000 in trust with the requirement that a guaranteed annuity interest (as defined in subparagraph (2)(i) of this paragraph) of $5,000 a year, payable annually at the end of each year, be paid to Y Charity for a period of 10 years and that a guaranteed annuity interest (as defined in subparagraph (2)(i) of this paragraph) of $5,000 a year, payable annually at the end of each year, be paid to W, his wife, aged 62, for 10 years or until her prior death. The annuities are to be paid simultaneously, and the remainder is to be paid to D's children. The fair market value of the private annuity is $33,877 ($5,000 × 6.7754), as determined pursuant to §20.2031-7A(c) of this chapter and by the use of factors involving one life and a term of years as published in Publication 723A (12-70). The fair market value of the charitable annuity is $36,800.50 ($5,000 × 7.3601), as determined under §20.2031-7A(c) of this chapter. It is not evident from the governing instrument of the trust or from local law that the trustee would be required to apportion the trust fund between the wife and charity in the event the fund were insufficient to pay both annuities in a given year. Accordingly, the deduction under subparagraph (1) of this paragraph with respect to the charitable annuity will be limited to $31,123 ($65,000 less $33,877 [the value of the private annuity]), which is the minimum amount it is evident Y will receive.

(iv) See paragraph (b)(1) of §1.170A-4 for rule that the term "ordinary income property" for purposes of section 170(e) does not include an income interest in respect of which a deduction is allowed under section 170(f)(2)(B) and this paragraph.

(4) *Recapture upon termination of treatment as owner.*—If for any reason the donor of an income interest in property ceases at any time before the termination of such interest to be treated as the owner of such interest for purposes of applying section 671, as for example, where he dies before the termination of such interest, he shall for purposes of this chapter be considered as having received, on the date he ceases to be so treated, an amount of income equal to (i) the amount of any deduction he was allowed under section 170 for the contribution of such interest reduced by (ii) the discounted value of all amounts which were required to be, and actually were, paid with respect to such interest under the terms of trust to the charitable organization before the time at which he ceases to be treated as the owner of the interest. The discounted value of the amounts described in subdivision (ii) of this subparagraph shall be computed by treating each such amount as a contribution of a remainder interest after a term of years and valuing such amount as of the date of contribution of the income interest by the donor, such value to be determined under §20.2031-7 of this chapter consistently with the manner in which the fair market value of the income interest was determined pursuant to subparagraph (3)(i) of this paragraph. The application of this subparagraph will not be construed to disallow a deduction to the trust for amounts paid by the trust to the charitable organization after the time at which the donor ceased to be treated as the owner of the trust.

(5) *Illustrations.*—The application of this paragraph may be illustrated by the following examples:

Example (1). On January 1, 1971, A contributes to a church in trust a 9-year irrevocable income interest in property. Both A and the trust report income on a calendar year basis. The fair market value of the property placed in trust is $10,000. The trust instrument provides that the church will receive an annuity of $500, payable annually at the end of each year for 9 years. The income interest is a guaranteed annuity interest as defined in subparagraph (2)(i) of this paragraph; upon termination of such interest the residue of the trust is to revert to A. By reference to §20.2031-7A(c) of this chapter, it is found that the figure in column (2) opposite 9 years is 6.8017. The present value of the annuity is therefore $3,400.85 ($500 × 6.8017). The present value of the income interest and A's charitable contribution for 1971 is $3,400.85.

Example (2). (a) On January 1, B contributes to a church in trust a 9-year irrevocable income interest in property. Both B and the trust report income on a calendar year basis. The fair market value of the property placed in trust is $10,000. The trust instrument provides that

Itemized Deductions for Individuals and Corps.
See p. 20,601 for regulations not amended to reflect law changes
25,547

the trust will pay to the church at the end of each year for 9 years 5 percent of the fair market value of all property in the trust at the beginning of the year. The income interest is a unitrust interest as defined in subparagraph (2)(ii) of this paragraph; upon termination of such interest the residue of the trust is to revert to B.

(b) The section 7520 rate at the time of the transfer was 6.0 percent. By reference to Table F(6.0) in §1.664-4(e)(6), the adjusted payout rate is 4.717% (5% × 0.943396). The present value of the reversion is $6,473.75, computed by reference to Table D in §1.664-4(e)(6), as follows:

Factor at 4.6 percent for 9 years	0.654539
Factor at 4.8 percent for 9 years	.642292
Difference	.012247

Interpolation adjustment:

$$\frac{4.717\% - 4.6\%}{0.2\%} = \frac{x}{0.012247}$$

$$x = 0.007164$$

Factor at 4.6 percent for 9 years	0.654539
Less: Interpolation adjustment	.007164
Interpolated factor	.647375

Annuity payment date	Amount paid
12/31/71	$500
12/31/72	500
12/31/73	500
Total discounted value	

(c) Pursuant to subparagraph (4) of this paragraph, there must be included in C's gross income for 1973 the amount of $2,064.34 ($3,400.85 less $1,336.51).

(d) For deduction by the trust for amounts paid to the church after December 31, 1973, see section 642(c)(1) and the regulations thereunder.

(d) *Denial of deduction for certain contributions by a trust.*—(1) If by reason of section 170(f)(2)(B) and paragraph (c) of this section a charitable contributions deduction is allowed under section 170 for the fair market value of an income interest transferred in trust, neither the grantor of the income interest, the trust, nor any other person shall be allowed a deduction under section 170 or any other section for the amount of any charitable contribution made by the trust with respect to, or in fulfillment of, such income interest.

(2) Section 170(f)(2)(C) and subparagraph (1) of this paragraph shall not be construed, however, to—

(i) Disallow a deduction to the trust, pursuant to section 642(c)(1) and the regulations thereunder, for amounts paid by the trust after the grantor ceases to be treated as the owner of the income interest for purposes of applying section 671 and which are not taken into account in determining the amount of recapture under paragraph (c)(4) of this section, or

(ii) Disallow a deduction to the grantor under section 671 and §1.671-2(c) for a charitable contribution made by the trust in excess of the contribution required to be made by the trust under the terms of the trust instrument with respect to, or in fulfillment of, the income interest.

(3) Although a deduction for the fair market value of an income interest in property which is less than the donor's entire interest in the property and which the donor transfers in trust is disallowed under section 170 because such interest is not a guaranteed annuity interest, or a unitrust interest, as defined in paragraph (c)(2) of this section, the donor may be entitled to a deduction under section 671 and §1.671-2(c) for any charitable contributions made by the trust if he is treated as the owner of such interest for purposes of applying section 671.

(e) *Effective date.*—This section applies only to transfers in trust made after July 31, 1969. In addition, the rule in paragraphs (c)(2)(i)(A) and (ii)(A) of this section that guaranteed annuity interests and unitrust interests, respectively, may be payable for a specified term of years or for the life or lives of only certain individuals applies to transfers made on or after April 4, 2000. If a transfer is made to a trust on or after April 4, 2000 that uses an individual other than one permitted in paragraphs (c)(2)(i)(A) and (ii)(A) of this section, the trust may be reformed to satisfy this rule. As an alternative to reformation, rescission may be available for a transfer made on or before March 6, 2001. See §25.2522(c)-3(e) of this chapter for the requirements concerning reformation or possible rescission of these interests. [Reg. §1.170A-6.]

☐ [*T.D.* 7207, 10-3-72. *Amended by T.D.* 7340, 1-6-75; *T.D.* 7955, 5-10-84; *T.D.* 8540, 6-9-94; *T.D.* 8819, 4-29-99 (*corrected* 6-21-99); *T.D.* 8923, 1-4-2001 *and T.D.* 9068, 7-3-2003.]

Present value of reversion	
($10,000 × 0.647375)	$6,473.75

(c) The present value of the income interest and B's charitable contribution is $3,526.25 ($10,000 – $6,473.75).

Example (3). (a) On January 1, 1971, C contributes to a church in trust a 9-year irrevocable income interest in property. Both C and the trust report income on a calendar year basis. The fair market value of the property placed in trust is $10,000. The trust instrument provides that the church will receive an annuity of $500, payable annually at the end of each year for 9 years. The income interest is a guaranteed annuity interest as defined in subparagraph (2)(i) of this paragraph; upon termination of such interest the residue of the trust is to revert to C. C's charitable contribution for 1971 is $3,400.85, determined as provided in example (1). The trust earns income of $600 in 1971, $400 in 1972, and $500 in 1973, all of which is taxable to C under section 671. The church is paid $500 at the end of 1971, 1972, and 1973, respectively. On December 31, 1973, C dies and ceases to be treated as the owner of the income interest under section 673.

(b) Pursuant to subparagraph (4) of this paragraph, the discounted value as of January 1, 1971, of the amounts paid to the church by the trust is $1,336.51, determined by reference to column (4) of Table B in §20.2031-7A(c) of this chapter, as follows:

Years from 1/1/71 to payment date	Discount factor	Discounted value as of 1/1/71
1	.943396	$471.70
2	.889996	445.00
3	.839619	419.81
		$1,336.51

[Reg. §1.170A-7]

§1.170A-7. Contributions not in trust of partial interests in property.—(a) *In general.*—(1) In the case of a charitable contribution, not made by a transfer in trust, of any interest in property which consists of less than the donor's entire interest in such property, no deduction is allowed under section 170 for the value of such interest unless the interest is an interest described in paragraph (b) of this section. See section 170(f)(3)(A). For purposes of this section, a contribution of the right to use property which the donor owns, for example, a rent-free lease, shall be treated as a contribution of less than the taxpayer's entire interest in property.

(2)(i) A deduction is allowed without regard to this section for a contribution of a partial interest in property if such interest is the taxpayer's entire interest in the property, such as an income interest or a remainder interest. Thus, if securities are given to A for life, with the remainder over to B, and B makes a charitable contribution of his remainder interest to an organization described in section 170(c), a deduction is allowed under section 170 for the present value of B's remainder interest in the securities. If, however, the property in which such partial interest exists was divided in order to create such interest and thus avoid section 170 f)(3)(A), the deduction will not be allowed. Thus, for example, assume that a taxpayer desires to contribute to a charitable organization an income interest in property held by him, which is not of a type described in paragraph (b)(2) of this section. If the taxpayer transfers the remainder interest in such property to his son and immediately thereafter contributes the income interest to a charitable organization, no deduction shall be allowed under section 170 for the contribution of the taxpayer's entire interest consisting of the retained income interest. In further illustration, assume that a taxpayer desires to contribute to a charitable organization the reversionary interest in certain stocks and bonds held by him, which is not of a type described in paragraph (b)(2) of this section. If the taxpayer grants a life estate in such property to his son and immediately thereafter contributes the reversionary interest to a charitable organization, no deduction will be allowed under section 170 for the contribution of the taxpayer's entire interest consisting of the reversionary interest.

(ii) A deduction is allowed without regard to this section for a contribution of a partial interest in property if such contribution constitutes part of a charitable contribution not in trust in which all interests of the taxpayer in the property are given to a charitable organization described in section 170(c). Thus, if on March 1, 1971, an income interest in property is given not in trust to a church and the remainder interest in the property is given not in trust to an educational organization described in section 170(b)(1)(A), a deduction is allowed for the value of such property.

(3) A deduction shall not be disallowed under section 170(f)(3)(A) and this section merely because the interest which passes to, or is vested in, the charity may be defeated by the performance of some act or the happening of some event, if on the date of the gift it appears that the possibility that such act or event will occur is so remote as to be negligible. See paragraph (e) of §1.170A-1.

(b) *Contributions of certain partial interests in property for which a deduction is allowed.*—A deduction is allowed under section 170 for a contribution not in trust of a partial interest which is less than the donor's entire interest in property and which qualifies under one of the following subparagraphs:

(1) *Undivided portion of donor's entire interest.*—(i) A deduction is allowed under section 170 for the value of a charitable contribution not in trust of an undivided portion of a donor's entire interest in property. An undivided portion of a donor's entire interest in property must consist of a fraction or percentage or each and every substantial interest or right owned by the donor in such property and must extend over the entire term of the donor's interest in such property and in other property into which such property is converted. For example, assuming that in 1967 B has been given a life estate in an office building for the life of A and that B has no other interest in the office building, B will be allowed a deduction under section 170 for his contribution in 1972 to charity of a one-half interest in such life estate in a transfer which is not made in trust. Such contribution by B will be considered a contribution of an undivided portion of the donor's entire interest in property. In further illustration, assuming that in 1968 C has been given the remainder interest in a trust created under the will of his father and C has no other interest in the trust, C will be allowed a deduction under section 170 for his contribution in 1972 to charity of a 20-percent interest in such remainder interest in a transfer which is not made in trust. Such contribution by C will be considered a contribution of an undivided portion of the donor's entire interest in property. If a taxpayer owns 100 acres of land and makes a contribution of 50 acres to a charitable organization, the charitable contribution is allowed as a deduction under section 170. A deduction is allowed under section 170 for a contribution of property to a charitable organization whereby such organization is given the right, as a tenant in common with the donor, to possession, dominion, and control of the property for a portion of each year appropriate to its interest in such property. However, for purposes of this subparagraph a charitable contribution in perpetuity of an interest in property not in trust where the donor transfers some specific rights and retains other substantial rights will not be considered a contribution of an undivided portion of the donor's entire interest in property to which section 170(f)(3)(A) does not apply. Thus, for example, a deduction is not allowable for the value of an immediate and perpetual gift not in trust of an interest in original historic motion picture films to a charitable organization where the donor retains the exclusive right to make reproductions of such films and to exploit such reproductions commercially.

(ii) With respect to contributions made on or before December 17, 1980, for purposes of this subparagraph a charitable contribution of an open space easement in gross in perpetuity shall be considered a contribution of an undivided portion of the donor's entire interest in property to which section 170(f)(3)(A) does not apply. For this purpose an easement in gross is a mere personal interest in, or right to use, the land of another; it is not supported by a dominant estate but is attached to, and vested in, the person to whom it is granted. Thus, for example, a deduction is allowed under section 170 for the value of a restrictive easement gratuitously conveyed to the United States in perpetuity whereby the donor agrees to certain restrictions on the use of his property, such as, restrictions on the type and height of buildings that may be erected, the removal of trees, the erection of utility lines, the dumping of trash, and the use of signs. For the deductibility of a qualified conservation contribution, see § 1.170A-14.

(2) *Partial interests in property which would be deductible in trust.*—A deduction is allowed under section 170 for the value of a charitable contribution not in trust of a partial interest in property which is less than the donor's entire interest in the property and which would be deductible under section 170(f)(2) and § 1.170A-6 if such interest had been transferred in trust.

(3) *Contribution of a remainder interest in a personal residence.*—A deduction is allowed under section 170 for the value of a charitable contribution not in trust of an irrevocable remainder interest in a personal residence which is not the donor's entire interest in such property. Thus, for example, if a taxpayer contributes not in trust to an organization described in section 170(c) a remainder interest in a personal residence and retains an estate in such property for life or for a term of years, a deduction is allowed under section 170 for the value of such remainder interest not transferred in trust. For purposes of section 170(f)(3)(B)(i) and this subparagraph, the term "personal residence" means any property used by the taxpayer as his personal residence even though it is not used as his principal residence. For example, the taxpayer's vacation home may be a personal residence for purposes of this subparagraph. The term "personal residence" also includes stock owned by a taxpayer as a tenant-stockholder in a cooperative housing corporation (as those terms are defined in section 216(b)(1) and (2)) if the dwelling which the tax-

payer is entitled to occupy as such stockholder is used by him as his personal residence.

(4) *Contribution of a remainder interest in a farm.*—A deduction is allowed under section 170 for the value of a charitable contribution not in trust of an irrevocable remainder interest in a farm which is not the donor's entire interest in such property. Thus, for example, if a taxpayer contributes not in trust to an organization described in section 170(c) a remainder interest in a farm and retains an estate in such farm for life or for a term of years, a deduction is allowed under section 170 for the value of such remainder interest not transferred in trust. For purposes of section 170(f)(3)(B)(i) and this subparagraph, the term "farm" means any land used by the taxpayer or his tenant for the production of crops, fruits, or other agricultural products or for the sustenance of livestock. The term "livestock" includes cattle, hogs, horses, mules, donkeys, sheep, goats, captive fur-bearing animals, chickens, turkeys, pigeons, and other poultry. A farm includes the improvements thereon.

(5) *Qualified conservation contribution.*—A deduction is allowed under section 170 for the value of a qualified conservation contribution. For the definition of a qualified conservation contribution, see § 1.170A-14.

(c) *Valuation of a partial interest in property.*—Except as provided in § 1.170A-14, the amount of the deduction under section 170 in the case of a charitable contribution of a partial interest in property to which paragraph (b) of this section applies is the fair market value of the partial interest at the time of the contribution. See § 1.170A-1(c). the fair market value of such partial interest must be determined in accordance with § 20.2031-7 of this chapter (Estate Tax Regulations), except that, in the case of a charitable contribution of a remainder interest in real property which is not transferred in trust, the fair market value of such interest must be determined in accordance with section 170(f)(4) and § 1.170A-12. In the case of a charitable contribution of a remainder interest in the form of a remainder interest in a pooled income fund, a charitable remainder annuity trust, or a charitable remainder unitrust, the fair market value of the remainder interest must be determined as provided in paragraph (b)(2) of § 1.170A-6. However, in some cases a reduction in the amount of a charitable contribution of the remainder interest may be required. See section 170(e) and paragraph (a) of § 1.170A-4.

(d) *Illustrations.*—The application of this section may be illustrated by the following examples:

Example (1). A, an individual owning a 10-story office building, donates the rent-free use of the top floor of the building for the year 1971 to a charitable organization. Since A's contribution consists of a partial interest to which section 170(f)(3)(A) applies, he is not entitled to a charitable contributions deduction for the contribution of such partial interest.

Example (2). In 1971, B contributes to a charitable organization an undivided one-half interest in 100 acres of land, whereby as tenants in common they share in the economic benefits from the property. The present value of the contributed property is $50,000. Since B's contribution consists of an undivided portion of his entire interest in the property to which section 170(f)(3)(B) applies, he is allowed a deduction in 1971 for his charitable contribution of $50,000.

Example (3). In 1971, D loans $10,000 in cash to a charitable organization and does not require the organization to pay any interest for the use of the money. Since D's contribution consists of a partial interest to which section 170(f)(3)(A) applies, he is not entitled to a charitable contributions deduction for the contribution of such partial interest.

(e) *Effective date.*—This section applies only to contributions made after July 31, 1969. The deduction allowable under § 1.170A-7(b)(1)(ii) shall be available only for contributions made on or before December 17, 1980. Except as otherwise provided in § 1.170A-14(g)(4)(ii), the deduction allowable under § 1.170A-7(b)(5) shall be available for contributions made on or after December 18, 1980. [Reg. § 1.170A-7.]

□ [*T.D. 7207, 10-3-72. Amended by T.D. 7955, 5-10-84 T.D. 8069, 1-14-86 and T.D. 8540, 6-9-94.*]

[Reg. § 1.170A-8]

§ 1.170A-8. Limitations on charitable deductions by individuals.—(a) *Percentage limitations.*—(1) *In general.*—An individual's charitable contributions deduction is subject to 20, 30, and 50-percent limitations unless the individual qualifies for the unlimited charitable contributions deduction under section 170(b)(1)(C). For a discussion of these limitations and examples of their application, see paragraphs (b) through (f) of this section. If a husband and wife make a joint return, the deduction for contributions is the aggregate of the contributions made by the spouses, and the limitations in section 170(b) and this section are based on the aggregate contribution base of the spouses. A charitable contribution by an individual to an organization described in section 170(c) is deductible even though all, or some portion, of the funds of the organization may be used in foreign countries for charitable or educational purposes.

(2) *"To" or "for the use of" defined.*—For purposes of section 170, a contribution of an income interest in property, whether or not such contributed interest is transferred in trust, for which a deduction is allowed under section 170(f)(2)(B) or (3)(A) shall be considered as made "for the use of" rather than "to" the charitable organization. A contribution of a remainder interest in property, whether or not such contributed interest is transferred in trust, for which a deduction is allowed under section 170(f)(2)(A) or (3)(A), shall be considered as made "to" the charitable organization except that, if such interest is transferred in trust and, pursuant to the terms of the trust instrument, the interest contributed is, upon termination of the predecessor estate, to be held in trust for the benefit of such organization, the contribution shall be considered as made "for the use of" such organization. Thus, for example, assume that A transfers property to a charitable remainder annuity trust described in section 664(d)(1) which is required to pay to B for life an annuity equal to 5 percent of the initial fair market value of the property transferred in trust. The trust instrument provides that after B's death the remainder interest in the trust is to be transferred to M Church or, in the event M Church is not an organization described in section 170(c) when the amount is to be irrevocably transferred to such church, to an organization which is described in section 170(c) at that time. The contribution by A of the remainder interest shall be considered as made "to" M Church. However, if in the trust instrument A had directed that after B's death the remainder interest is to be held in trust for the benefit of M Church, the contribution shall be considered as made "for the use of" M Church. This subparagraph does not apply to the contribution of a partial interest in property, or of an undivided portion of such partial interest, if such partial interest is the donor's entire interest in the property and such entire interest was not created to avoid section 170(f)(2) or (3)(A). See paragraph (a)(2) of § 1.170A-6 and paragraphs (a)(2)(i) and (b)(1) of § 1.170A-7.

(b) *50-percent limitation.*—An individual may deduct charitable contributions made during a taxable year to any one or more section 170(b)(1)(A) organizations, as defined in § 1.170A-9, to the extent that such contributions in the aggregate do not exceed 50-percent of his contribution base, as defined in section 170(b)(1)(F) and paragraph (e) of this section, for the taxable year. However, see paragraph (d) of this section for a limitation on the amount of charitable contributions of 30-percent capital gain property. To qualify for the 50-percent limitation the contributions must be made "to", and not merely "for the use of", one of the specified organizations. A contribution to an organization referred to in section 170(c)(2), other than a section 170(b)(1)(A) organization, will not qualify for the 50-percent limitation even though such organization makes the contribution available to an organization which is a section 170(b)(1)(A) organization. For provisions relating to the carryover of contributions in excess of 50-percent of an individual's contribution base see section 170(d)(1) and paragraph (b) of § 1.170A-10.

(c) *20-percent limitation.*—(1) An individual may deduct charitable contributions made during a taxable year—

(i) To any one or more charitable organizations described in section 170(c) other than section 170(b)(1)(A) organizations, as defined in § 1.170A-9, and,

(ii) For the use of any charitable organization described in section 170(c),

to the extent that such contributions in the aggregate do not exceed the lesser of the limitations under subparagraph (2) of this paragraph.

(2) For purposes of subparagraph (1) of this paragraph the limitations are—

(i) 20 percent of the individual's contribution base, as defined in paragraph (e) of this section, for the taxable year, or

(ii) The excess of 50 percent of the individual's contribution base, as so defined, for the taxable year over the total amount of the charitable contributions allowed under section 170(b)(1)(A) and paragraph (b) of this section, determined by first reducing the amount of *such contributions under section 170(e)(1) and paragraph (a) of* § 1.170A-4 but without applying the 30-percent limitation under section 170(b)(1)(D)(i) and paragraph (d)(1) of this section.

However, see paragraph (d) of this section for a limitation on the amount of charitable contributions of 30-percent capital gain property. If an election under section 170(b)(1)(D)(iii) and paragraph (d)(2) of this section applies to any contributions of 30-percent capital gain property made during the taxable year or carried over to the taxable year, the amount allowed for the taxable year under paragraph (b) of this section with respect to such contributions for purposes of applying subdivision (ii) of this subparagraph shall be the

reduced amount of such contributions determined by applying paragraph (d)(2) of this section.

(d) *30-percent limitation.*—(1) *In general.*—An individual may deduct charitable contributions of 30-percent capital gain property, as defined in subparagraph (3) of this paragraph, made during a taxable year to or for the use of any charitable organization described in section 170(c) to the extent that such contributions in the aggregate do not exceed 30-percent of his contribution base, as defined in paragraph (e) of this section, subject, however, to the 50 and 20-percent limitations prescribed by paragraphs (b) and (c) of this section. For purposes of applying the 50-percent and 20-percent limitations described in paragraphs (b) and (c) of this section, charitable contributions of 30-percent capital gain property paid during the taxable year, and limited as provided by this subparagraph, shall be taken into account after all other charitable contributions paid during the taxable year. For provisions relating to the carryover of certain contributions of 30-percent capital gain property in excess of 30-percent of an individual's contribution base, see section 170(b)(1)(D)(ii) and paragraph (c) of § 1.170A-10.

(2) *Election by an individual to have section 170(e)(1)(B) apply to contributions.*—(i) *In general.*—(a) An individual may elect under section 170(b)(1)(D)(iii) for any taxable year to have the reduction rule of section 170(e)(1)(B) and paragraph (a) of § 1.170A-4 apply to all his charitable contributions of 30-percent capital gain property made during such taxable year or carried over to such taxable year from a taxable year beginning after December 31, 1969. If such election is made such contributions shall be treated as contributions of section 170(e) capital gain property in accordance with paragraph (b)(2)(iii) of § 1.170A-4. The election may be made with respect to contributions of 30-percent capital gain property carried over to the taxable year even though the individual has not made any contribution of 30-percent capital gain property in such year. If such an election is made, section 170(b)(1)(D)(i) and (ii) and subparagraph (1) of this paragraph shall not apply to such contributions made during such year. However, such contributions must be reduced as required under section 170(e)(1)(B) and paragraph (a) of § 1.170A-4.

(b) If there are carryovers to such taxable year of charitable contributions of 30-percent capital gain property made in preceding taxable years beginning after December 31, 1969, the amount of such contributions in each such preceding year shall be reduced as if section 170(e)(1)(B) had applied to them in the preceding year and shall be carried over to the taxable year and succeeding taxable years under section 170(d)(1) and paragraph (b) of § 1.170A-10 as contributions of property other than 30-percent capital gain property. For purposes of applying the immediately preceding sentence, the percentage limitations under section 170(b) for the preceding taxable year and for any taxable years intervening between such year and the year of the election shall not be redetermined and the amount of any deduction allowed for such years under section 170 in respect of the charitable contributions of 30-percent capital gain property in the preceding taxable year shall not be redetermined. However, the amount of the deduction so allowed under section 170 in the preceding taxable year must be subtracted from the reduced amount of the charitable contributions made in such year in order to determine the excess amount which is carried over from such year under section 170(d)(1). If the amount of the deduction so allowed in the preceding taxable year equals or exceeds the reduced amount of the charitable contributions, there shall be no carryover from such year to the year of the election.

(c) An election under this subparagraph may be made for each taxable year in which charitable contributions of 30-percent capital gain property are made or to which they are carried over under section 170(b)(1)(D)(ii). If there are also carryovers under section 170(d)(1) to the year of the election by reason of an election made under this subparagraph for a previous taxable year, such carryovers under section 170(d)(1) shall not be redetermined by reason of the subsequent election.

(ii) *Husband and wife making joint return.*—If a husband and wife make a joint return of income for a contribution year and one of the spouses elects under this subparagraph in a later year when he files a separate return, or if a spouse dies after a contribution year for which a joint return is made, any excess contribution of 30-percent capital gain property which is carried over to the election year from the contribution year shall be allocated between the husband and wife as provided in paragraph (d)(4)(i) and (iii) of § 1.170A-10. If a husband and wife file separate returns in a contribution year, any election under this subparagraph in a later year when a joint return is filed shall be applicable to any excess contributions of 30-percent capital gain property of either taxpayer carried over from the contribution year to the election year. The immediately preceding sentence shall also apply where two single individuals are subsequently married and file a joint return. A remarried individual who filed a joint return with his former spouse for a contribution year and thereafter

Reg. § 1.170A-8(d)(2)(ii)

files a joint return with his present spouse shall treat the carryover to the election year as provided in paragraph (d)(4)(ii) of §1.170A-10.

(iii) *Manner of making election.*—The election under subdivision (i) of this subparagraph shall be made by attaching to the income tax return for the election year a statement indicating that the election under section 170(b)(1)(D)(iii) and this subparagraph is being made. If there is a carryover to the taxable year of any charitable contributions of 30-percent capital gain property from a previous taxable year or years, the statement shall show a recomputation, in accordance with this subparagraph and §1.170A-4, of such carryover, setting forth sufficient information with respect to the previous taxable year or any intervening year to show the basis of the recomputation. The statement shall indicate the district director, or the director of the internal revenue service center, with whom the return for the previous taxable year or years was filed, the name or names in which such return or returns were filed, and whether each such return was a joint or separate return.

(3) *30-percent capital gain property defined.*—If there is a charitable contribution of a capital asset which, if it were sold by the donor at its fair market value at the time of its contribution, would result in the recognition of gain all, or any portion, of which would be long-term capital gain and if the amount of such contribution is not required to be reduced under section 170(e)(1)(B) and §1.170A-4(a)(2), such capital asset shall be treated as "30-percent capital gain property" for purposes of section 170 and the regulations thereunder. For such purposes any property which is property used in the trade or business, as defined in section 1231(b), shall be treated as a capital asset. However, see paragraph (b)(4) of §1.170A-4. For the treatment of such property as section 170(e) capital gain property, see paragraph (b)(2)(iii) of §1.170A-4.

(e) *Contribution base defined.*—For purposes of section 170 the term "contribution base" means adjusted gross income under section 62, computed without regard to any net operating loss carryback to the taxable year under section 172. See section 170(b)(1)(F).

(f) *Illustrations.*—The application of this section may be illustrated by the following examples:

Example (1). B, an individual, reports his income on the calendar-year basis and for 1970 has a contribution base of $100,000. During 1970 he makes charitable contributions of $70,000 in cash, of which $40,000 is given to section 170(b)(1)(A) organizations and $30,000 is given to other organizations described in section 170(c). Accordingly, B is allowed a charitable contributions deduction of $50,000 (50% of $100,000), which consists of the $40,000 contributed to section 170(b)(1)(A) organizations and $10,000 of the $30,000 contributed to the other organizations. Under paragraph (c) of this section, only $10,000 of the $30,000 contributed to the other organizations is allowed as a deduction since such contribution of $30,000 is allowed to the extent of the lesser of $20,000 (20% of $100,000) or $10,000 ([50% of $100,000] – $40,000 (contributions allowed under section 170(b)(1)(A) and paragraph (b) of this section)). Under section 170(b)(1)(D)(ii) and (d)(1) and §1.170A-10, B is not allowed a carryover to 1971 or to any other taxable year for any of the $20,000 ($30,000 – $10,000) not deductible under section 170(b)(1)(B) and paragraph (c) of this section.

Example (2). C, an individual, reports his income on the calendar-year basis and for 1970 has a contribution base of $100,000. During 1970 he makes charitable contributions of $40,000 in 30-percent capital gain property to section 170(b)(1)(A) organizations and of $30,000 in cash to other organizations described in section 170(c). The 20-percent limitation in section 170(b)(1)(B) and paragraph (c) of this section is applied before the 30-percent limitation in section 170(b)(1)(D)(i) and paragraph (d) of this section; accordingly section 170(b)(1)(B)(ii) limits the deduction for the $30,000 cash contribution to $10,000 ([50% of $100,000] – $40,000). The amount of the contribution of 30-percent capital gain property is limited by section 170(b)(1)(D)(i) and paragraph (d) of this section to $30,000 (30% of $100,000). Accordingly, C's charitable contributions deduction for 1970 is limited to $40,000 ($10,000 + $30,000). Under section 170(b)(1)(D)(ii) and paragraph (c) of §1.170A-10, C is allowed a carryover to 1971 of $10,000 ($40,000 – $30,000) in respect of his contributions of 30-percent capital gain property. C is not allowed a carryover to 1971 or to any other taxable year for any of the $20,000 cash ($30,000 – $10,000) not deductible under section 170(b)(1)(B) and paragraph (c) of this section.

Example (3). (a) D, an individual, reports his income on the calendar-year basis and for 1970 has a contribution base of $100,000. During 1970 he makes charitable contributions of $70,000 in cash, of which $40,000 is given to section 170(b)(1)(A) organizations and $30,000 is given to other organizations described in section 170(c). During 1971 D makes charitable contributions to a section 170(b)(1)(A) organization of $12,000, consisting of cash of $1,000 and

$11,000 in 30-percent capital gain property. His contribution base for 1971 is $10,000.

(b) For 1970, D is allowed a charitable contributions deduction of $50,000 (50% of $100,000), which consists of the $40,000 contributed to section 170(b)(1)(A) organizations and $10,000 of the $30,000 contributed to the other organizations. Under paragraph (c) of this section, only $10,000 of the $30,000 contributed to the other organizations is allowed as a deduction since such contribution of $30,000 is allowed to the extent of the lesser of $20,000 (20% of $100,000) or $10,000 ([50% of $100,000] – $40,000 (contributions allowed under section 170(b)(1)(A) and paragraph (d) of this section)). D is not allowed a carryover to 1971 or to any other taxable year for any of the $20,000 ($30,000 – $10,000) not deductible under section 170(b)(1)(B) and paragraph (c) of this section.

(c) For 1971, D is allowed a charitable contributions deduction of $4,000, consisting of $1,000 cash and $3,000 of the 30-percent capital gain property (30% of $10,000). Under section 170(b)(1)(D)(ii) and paragraph (c) of §1.170A-10, D is allowed a carryover to 1972 of $8,000 ($11,000 – $3,000) in respect of his contribution of 30-percent capital gain property in 1971.

Example (4). (a) E, an individual, reports his income on the calendar-year basis and for 1970 has a contribution base of $100,000. During 1970 he makes charitable contributions of $70,000 in cash, of which $40,000 is given to section 170(b)(1)(A) organizations and $30,000 is given to other organizations described in section 170(c). During 1971 E makes charitable contributions to a section 170(b)(1)(A) organization of $14,000 consisting of cash of $3,000 and $11,000 in 30-percent capital gain property. His contribution base for 1971 is $10,000.

(b) For 1970, E is allowed a charitable contributions deduction of $50,000 (50% of $100,000), which consists of the $40,000 contributed to section 170(b)(1)(A) organizations and $10,000 of the $30,000 contributed to the other organizations. Under paragraph (c) of this section, only $10,000 of the $30,000 contributed to the other organizations is allowed as a deduction since such contribution of $30,000 is allowed to the extent of the lesser of $20,000 (20% of $100,000) or $10,000 ([50% of $100,000] – $40,000 (contributions allowed under section 170(b)(1)(A) and paragraph (b) of this section)). E is not allowed a carryover to 1971 or to any other taxable year for any of the $20,000 ($30,000 – $10,000) not deductible under section 170(b)(1)(B) and paragraph (c) of this section.

(c) For 1971, E is allowed a charitable contribution deduction of $5,000 (50% of $10,000), consisting of $3,000 cash and $2,000 of the $3,000 (30% of $10,000) 30-percent capital gain property which is taken into account. This result is reached because, as provided in section 170(b)(1)(D)(i) and paragraph (d)(1) of this section, cash contributions are taken into account before charitable contributions of 30-percent capital gain property. Under section 170(b)(1)(D)(ii) and (d)(1) and paragraphs (b) and (c) of §1.170A-10, E is allowed a carryover of $9,000 ([$11,000 – $3,000] plus [$6,000 – $5,000]) to 1972 in respect of his contribution of 30-percent capital gain property in 1971.

Example (5). In 1970, C, a calendar-year individual taxpayer, contributes to section 170(b)(1)(A) organizations the amount of $8,000, consisting of $3,000 in cash and $5,000 in 30-percent capital gain property. In 1970, C also makes charitable contributions of $8,500 in 30-percent capital gain property to other organizations described in section 170(c). C's contribution base for 1970 is $20,000. The 20-percent limitation in section 170(b)(1)(B) and paragraph (c) of this section is applied before the 30-percent limitation in section 170(b)(1)(D)(i) and paragraph (d) of this section; accordingly, section 170(b)(1)(B)(ii) limits the deduction for the $8,500 of contributions to the other organizations described in section 170(c) to $2,000 ([50% of $20,000] – [$3,000 + $5,000]). However, the total amount of contributions of 30-percent capital gain property which is allowed as a deduction for 1970 is limited by section 170(b)(1)(D)(i) and paragraph (d) of this section to $6,000 (30% of $20,000), consisting of the $5,000 contribution to the section 170(b)(1)(A) organizations and $1,000 of the contributions to the other organizations described in section 170(c). Accordingly, C is allowed a charitable contributions deduction for 1970 of $9,000, which consists of $3,000 cash and $6,000 of the $13,500 of 30-percent capital gain property. C is not allowed to carry over to 1971 or any other year the remaining $7,500 because his contributions of 30-percent capital gain property for 1970 to section 170(b)(1)(A) organizations amount only to $5,000 and do not exceed $6,000 (30% of $20,000). Thus, the requirement of section 170(b)(1)(D)(ii) is not satisfied.

Example (6). During 1971, D, a calendar-year individual taxpayer, makes a charitable contribution to a church of $8,000, consisting of $5,000 in cash and $3,000 in 30-percent capital gain property. For such year, D's contribution base is $10,000. Accordingly, D is allowed a charitable contributions deduction for 1971 of $5,000 (50% of $10,000) of cash. Under section 170(d)(1) and paragraph (b) of §1.170A-10, D is allowed a carryover to 1972 of his $3,000 contribution of 30-percent capital gain property, even though such amount does not exceed 30 percent of his contribution base for 1971.

Example (7). In 1970, E, a calendar-year individual taxpayer, makes a charitable contribution to a section 170(b)(1)(A) organization in the amount of $10,000, consisting of $8,000 in 30-percent capital gain property and of $2,000 (after reduction under section 170(e)) in other property. E's contribution base of 1970 is $20,000. Accordingly, E is allowed a charitable contributions deduction for 1970 of $8,000, consisting of the $2,000 of property the amount of which was reduced under section 170(e) and $6,000 (30% of $20,000) of the 30-percent capital gain property. Under section 170(b)(1)(D)(ii) and paragraph (c) of §1.170A-10, E is allowed to carry over to 1971 $2,000 ($8,000–$6,000) of his contribution of 30-percent capital gain property.

Example (8). (a) In 1972, F, a calendar-year individual taxpayer, makes a charitable contribution to a church of $4,000, consisting of $1,000 in cash and $3,000 in 30-percent capital gain property. In addition, F makes a charitable contribution in 1972 of $2,000 in cash to an organization described in section 170(c)(4). F also has a carryover from 1971 under section 170(d)(1) of $5,000 (none of which consists of contributions of 30-percent capital gain property) and a carryover from 1971 under section 170(b)(1)(D)(ii) of $6,000 of contributions of 30-percent capital gain property. F's contribution base for 1972 is $11,000. Accordingly, F is allowed a charitable contributions deduction for 1972 of $5,500 (50% of $11,000), which consists of $1,000 cash contributed in 1972 to the church, $3,000 of 30-percent capital gain property contributed in 1972 to the church, and $1,500 (carryover of $5,000 but not to exceed [$5,500 – ($1,000 + $3,000)]) of the carryover from 1971 under section 170(d)(1).

(b) No deduction is allowed for 1972 for the contribution in that year of $2,000 cash to the section 170(c)(4) organization since section 170(b)(1)(B)(ii) and paragraph (c) of this section limit the deduction for such contribution to $0 ([50% of $11,000] – [$1,000 + $1,500 + $3,000]). Moreover, F is not allowed a carryover to 1973 or to any other year for any of such $2,000 cash contributed to the section 170(c)(4) organization.

(c) Under section 170(d)(1) and paragraph (b) of §1.170A-10, F is allowed a carryover to 1973 from 1971 of $3,500 ($5,000 – $1,500) of contributions of other than 30-percent capital gain property. Under section 170(b)(1)(D)(ii) and paragraph (c) of §1.170A-10, F is allowed a carryover to 1973 from 1971 of $6,000 ($6,000 – $0 of such carryover treated as paid in 1972) of contributions of 30-percent capital gain property. The portion of such $6,000 carryover from 1971 which is treated as paid in 1972 is $0 ([50% of $11,000]– [$4,000 contributions to the church in 1972 plus $1,500 of section 170(d)(1) carryover treated as paid in 1972]).

Example (9). (a) In 1970, A, a calendar-year individual taxpayer, makes a charitable contribution to a church of 30-percent capital gain property having a fair market value of $60,000 and an adjusted basis of $10,000. A's contribution base for 1970 is $50,000, and he makes no other charitable contributions in that year. A does not elect for 1970 under paragraph (d)(2) of this section to have section 170(e)(1)(B) apply to such contribution. Accordingly, under section 170(b)(1)(D)(i) and paragraph (d) of this section, A is allowed a charitable contributions deduction for 1970 of $15,000 (30% of $50,000). Under section 170(b)(1)(D)(ii) and paragraph (c) of §1.170A-10, A is allowed a carryover to 1971 of $45,000 ($60,000–$15,000) for his contribution of 30-percent capital gain property.

(b) In 1971, A makes a charitable contribution to a church of 30-percent capital gain property having a fair market value of $11,000 and an adjusted basis of $10,000. A's contribution base for 1971 is $60,000, and he makes no other charitable contributions in that year. A elects for 1971 under paragraph (d)(2) of this section to have section 170(e)(1)(B) and §1.170A-4 apply to his contribution of $11,000 in that year and to his carryover of $45,000 from 1970. Accordingly, he is required to recompute his carryover from 1970 as if section 170(e)(1)(B) had applied to his contribution of 30-percent capital gain property in that year.

(c) If section 170(e)(1)(B) had applied in 1970 to his contribution of 30-percent capital gain property, A's contribution would have been reduced from $60,000 to $35,000, the reduction of $25,000 being 50 percent of the gain of $50,000 ($60,000–$10,000) which would have been recognized as long-term capital gain if the property had been *sold by A at its fair market value at the time of the contribution* in 1970. Accordingly, by taking the election under paragraph (d)(2) of this section into account, A has a recomputed carryover to 1971 of $20,000 ($35,000–$15,000) of his contribution of 30-percent capital gain property in 1970. However, A's charitable contributions deduction of $15,000 allowed for 1970 is not recomputed by reason of the election.

(d) Pursuant to the election for 1971, the contribution of 30-percent capital gain property for 1971 is reduced from $11,000 to $10,500, the reduction of $500 being 50 percent of the gain of $1,000 ($11,000–$10,000) which would have been recognized as long-term

capital gain if the property had been sold by A at its fair market value at the time of its contribution in 1971.

(e) Accordingly, A is allowed a charitable contributions deduction for 1971 of $30,000 (total contributions of $30,500 [$20,000+$10,500]but not to exceed 50% of $60,000).

(f) Under section 170(d)(1) and paragraph (b) of §1.170A-10, A is allowed a carryover of $500 ($30,500–$30,000) to 1972 and the 3 succeeding taxable years. The $500 carryover, which by reason of the election is no longer treated as a contribution of 30-percent capital gain property, is treated as carried over under paragraph (b) of §1.170A-10 from 1970 since in 1971 current year contributions are deducted before contributions which are carried over from preceding taxable years.

Example (10). The facts are the same as in example (9) except that A also makes a charitable contribution in 1971 of $2,000 cash to a private foundation not described in section 170(b)(1)(E) and that A's contribution base for that year is $62,000, instead of $60,000. Accordingly, A is allowed a charitable contributions deduction for 1971 of $31,000, determined in the following manner. Under section 170(b)(1)(A) and paragraph (b) of this section, A is allowed a charitable contributions deduction for 197_ of $30,500, consisting of $10,500 of property contributed to the church in 1971 and of $20,000 (carryover of $20,000 but not to exceed [($62,000×50%)–$10,500]) of contributions of property carried over to 1971 under section 170(d)(1) and paragraph (b) of §1.170A-10. Under section 170(b)(1)(B) and paragraph (c) of this section, A is allowed a charitable contributions deduction for 1971 of $500 ([50% of $62,000]–[$10,500+$20,000]) of cash contributed to the private foundation in that year. A is not allowed a carryover to 1972 or to any other taxable year for any of the $1,500 ($2,000–$500) cash not deductible in 1971 under section 170(b)(1)(B) and paragraph (c) of this section.

Example (11). The facts are the same as in example (9) except that A's contribution base for 1970 is $120,000. Thus, before making the election under paragraph (d)(2) of this section for 1971, A is allowed a charitable contributions deduction for 1970 of $36,000 (30% of $120,000) and is allowed a carryover to 1971 of $24,000 ($60,000–$36,000). By making the election for 1971, A is required to recompute the carryover from 1970, which is reduced from $24,000 to zero, since the charitable contributions deduction of $36,000 allowed for 1970 exceeds the reduced $35,000 contribution for 1970 which may be taken into account by reason of the election for 1971. Accordingly, A is allowed a deduction for 1971 of $10,500 and is allowed no carryover to 1972, since the reduced contribution for 1971 ($10,500) does not exceed the limitation of $30,000 (50% of $60,000) for 1971 which applies under section 170(d)(1) and paragraph (b) of §1.170A-10. A's charitable contributions deduction of $36,000 allowed for 1970 is not recomputed by reason of the election. Thus, it is not to A's advantage to make the election under paragraph (d)(2) of this section.

Example (12). (a) B, an individual, reports his income on the calendar year basis and for 1970 has a contribution base of $100,000. During 1970 he makes charitable contributions of $70,000, consisting of $50,000 in 30-percent capital gain property contributed to a church and $20,000 in cash contributed to a private foundation not described in section 170(b)(1)(E). For 1971, B's contribution base is $40,000, and in that year he makes a charitable contribution of $5,000 in cash to such private foundation. During the years involved B makes no other charitable contributions.

(b) The amount of the contribution of 30-percent capital gain property which may be taken into account for 1970 is limited by section 170(b)(1)(D)(i) and paragraph (d) of this section to $30,000 (30% of $100,000). Accordingly, under section 170(b)(1)(A) and paragraph (b) of this section B is allowed a deduction for 1970 of $30,000 of 30-percent capital gain property (contribution of $30,000 but not to exceed $50,000 [50% of $100,000]). No deduction is allowed for 1970 for the contribution in that year of $20,000 of cash to the private foundation since section 170(b)(1)(B)(ii) and paragraph (c) of this section limit the deduction for such contribution to $0 ([50% of $100,000]—$50,000, the amount of the contribution of 30-percent capital gain property).

(c) Under section 170(b)(1)(D)(ii) and paragraph (c) of §1.170A-10, B is allowed a carryover to 1971 of $20,000 ($50,000–[30% of $100,000]) of his contribution in 1970 of 30-percent capital gain property. B is not allowed a carryover to 1971 or to any other taxable year for any of the $20,000 cash contribution in 1970 which is not deductible under section 170(b)(1)(B) and paragraph (c) of this section.

(d) The amount of the contribution of 30-percent capital gain property which may be taken into account for 1971 is limited by section 170(b)(1)(D)(i) and paragraph (d) of this section to $12,000 (30% of $40,000). Accordingly, under section 170(b)(1)(A) and paragraph (b) of this section B is allowed a deduction for 1971 of $12,000 of 30-percent capital gain property (contribution of $12,000 but not to exceed $20,000 [50% of $40,000]). No deduction is allowed for 1971 for the contribution in that year of $5,000 of cash to the private foundation, since section 170(b)(1)(B)(ii) and paragraph (c) of this section limit the deduction for such contribution to $0 ([50% of $40,000] – $20,000 carryover of 30-percent capital gain property from 1970).

(e) Under section 170(b)(1)(D)(ii) and paragraph (c) of §1.170A-10, B is allowed a carryover to 1972 of $8,000 ($20,000–[30% of $40,000]) of his contribution in 1970 of 30-percent capital gain property. B is not allowed a carryover to 1972 or to any other taxable year for any of the $5,000 cash contribution for 1971 which is not deductible under section 170(b)(1)(B) and paragraph (c) of this section.

Example (13). D, an individual, reports his income on the calendar-year basis and for 1970 has a contribution base of $100,000. On March 1, 1970, he contributes to a church intangible property to which section 1245 applies which has a fair market value of $60,000 and an adjusted basis of $10,000. At the time of the contribution D has used the property in his business for more than 6 months. If the property had been sold by D at its fair market value at the time of its contribution, it is assumed that under section 1245 $20,000 of the gain of $50,000 would have been treated as ordinary income and $30,000 would have been long-term capital gain. Since the property contributed is ordinary income property within the meaning of paragraph (b)(1) of §1.170A-4, D's contribution of $60,000 is reduced under paragraph (a)(1) of such section to $40,000 ($60,000 – $20,000 ordinary income). However, since the property contributed is also 30-percent capital gain property within the meaning of paragraph (d)(3) of this section, D's deduction for 1970 is limited by section 170(b)(1)(D)(i) and paragraph (d) of this section to $30,000(30% of $100,000). Under section 170(b)(1)(D)(ii) and paragraph (c) of §1.170A-10, D is allowed to carry over to 1971 $10,000 ($40,000 – $30,000) of his contribution of 30-percent capital gain property.

Example (14). C, an individual, reports his income on the calendar-year basis and for 1970 has a contribution base of $50,000. During 1970 he makes charitable contributions to a church of $57,000, consisting of $2,000 cash and of 30-percent capital gain property with a fair market value of $55,000 and an adjusted basis of $15,000. In addition, C contributes $3,000 cash in 1970 to a private foundation not described in section 170(b)(1)(E). For 1970, C elects under paragraph (d)(2) of this section to have section 170(e)(1)(B) and §1.170A-4(a) apply to his contribution of property to the church. Accordingly, for 1970 C's contribution of property to the church is reduced from $55,000 to $35,000, the reduction of $20,000 being 50 percent of the gain of $40,000 ($55,000 – $15,000) which would have been recognized as long-term capital gain if the property had been sold by C at its fair market value at the time of its contribution to the church. Under section 170(b)(1)(A) and paragraph (b) of this section, C is allowed a charitable contributions deduction for 1970 of $25,000 ([$2,000 + $35,000] but not to exceed [$50,000 × 50%]). Under section 170(d)(1) and paragraph (b) of §1.170A-10, C is allowed a carryover from 1970 to 1971 of $12,000 ($37,000 – $25,000). No deduction is allowed for 1970 for the contribution in that year of $3,000 cash to the private foundation since section 170(b)(1)(B) and paragraph (c) of this section limit the deduction for such contribution to the smaller of $10,000 ($50,000 × 20%) or $0 ([$50,000 × 50%] – $25,000). C is not allowed a carryover from 1970 for any of the $3,000 cash contribution in that year which is not deductible under section 170(b)(1)(B) and paragraph (c) of this section.

Example (15). (a) D, an individual, reports his income on the calendar-year basis and for 1970 has a contribution base of $100,000. During 1970 he makes a charitable contribution to a church of 30-percent capital gain property with a fair market value of $40,000 and an adjusted basis of $21,000. In addition, he contributes $23,000 cash in 1970 to a private foundation not described in section 170(b)(1)(E). For 1970, D elects under paragraph (d)(2) of this section to have section 170(e)(1)(B) and §1.170A-4(a) apply to his contribution of property to the church. Accordingly, for 1970 D's contribution of property to the church is reduced from $40,000 to $30,500, the reduction of $9,500 being 50 percent of the gain of $19,000 ($40,000 – $21,000) which would have been recognized as long-term capital gain if the property had been sold by D at its fair market value at the time of its contribution to the church. Under section 170(b)(1)(A) and paragraph (b) of this section, D is allowed a charitable contributions deduction for 1970 of $30,500 for the property contributed to the church. In addition, under section 170(b)(1)(B) and paragraph (c) of this section, D is allowed a deduction of $19,500 for the cash contributed to the private foundation, since such contribution of $23,000 is allowed to the extent of the lesser of $20,000 (20% of $100,000) or $19,500 ([$100,000 × 50%] – $30,500). D is not allowed a carryover to 1971 or to any other taxable year for any of the $3,500 (23,000 – $19,500) of cash not deductible under section 170(b)(1)(B) and paragraph (c) of this section.

(b) If D had not made the election under paragraph (d)(2) of this section for 1970, his deduction for 1970 under section 170(a) for the $40,000 contribution of property to the church would have been limited by section 170(b)(1)(D)(i) and paragraph (d) of this section to $30,000 (30% of $100,000), and under section 170(b)(1)(D)(ii) and

paragraph (c) of §1.170A-10 he would have been allowed a carryover to 1971 of $10,000 ($40,000 – $30,000) for his contribution of such property. In addition, he would have been allowed under section 170(b)(1)(B)(ii) and paragraph (c) of this section for 1970 a charitable contributions deduction of $10,000 ([$100,000 × 50%] – $40,000) for the cash contributed to the private foundation. In such case, D would not have been allowed a carryover to 1971 or to any other taxable year for any of the $13,000 ($23,000 – $10,000) of cash not deductible under section 170(b)(1)(B) and paragraph (c) of this section.

(g) *Effective date.*—This section applies only to contributions paid in taxable years beginning after December 31, 1969. [Reg. §1.170A-8.]

☐ [T.D. 7207, 10-3-72.]

[Reg. §1.170A-9]

§1.170A-9. Definition of section 170(b)(1)(A) organization.— (a) The term *section 170(b)(1)(A) organization* as used in the regulations under section 170 means any organization described in paragraphs (b) through (j) of this section, effective with respect to taxable years beginning after December 31, 1969, except as otherwise provided. Section 1.170-2(b) shall continue to be applicable with respect to taxable years beginning prior to January 1, 1970. The term *one or more organizations described in section 170(b)(1)(A) (other than clauses (vii) and (viii))* as used in sections 507 and 509 of the Internal Revenue Code (Code) and the regulations means one or more organizations described in paragraphs (b) through (f) of this section, except as modified by the regulations under part II of subchapter F of chapter 1 or under chapter 42.

(b) *Church or a convention or association of churches.*—An organization is described in section 170(b)(1)(A)(i) if it is a church or a convention or association of churches.

(c) *Educational organization and organizations for the benefit of certain State and municipal colleges and universities.*—(1) *Educational organization.*—An educational organization is described in section 170(b)(1)(A)(ii) if its primary function is the presentation of formal instruction and it normally maintains a regular faculty and curriculum and normally has a regularly enrolled body of pupils or students in attendance at the place where its educational activities are regularly carried on. The term includes institutions such as primary, secondary, preparatory, or high schools, and colleges and universities. It includes Federal, State, and other public-supported schools which otherwise come within the definition. It does not include organizations engaged in both educational and noneducational activities unless the latter are merely incidental to the educational activities. A recognized university which incidentally operates a museum or sponsors concerts is an educational organization within the meaning of section 170(b)(1)(A)(ii). However, the operation of a school by a museum does not necessarily qualify the museum as an educational organization within the meaning of this subparagraph.

(2) *Organizations for the benefit of certain State and municipal colleges and universities.*—(i) An organization is described in section 170(b)(1)(A)(iv) if it meets the support requirements of subdivision (ii) of this subparagraph and is organized and operated exclusively to receive, hold, invest, and administer property and to make expenditures to or for the benefit of a college or university which is an organization described in subdivision (iii) of this subparagraph. The phrase "expenditures to or for the benefit of a college or university" includes expenditures made for any one or more of the normal functions of colleges and universities such as the acquisition and maintenance of real property comprising part of the campus area; the erection of, or participation in the erection of, college or university buildings; the acquisition and maintenance of equipment and furnishings used for, or in conjunction with, normal functions of colleges and universities; or expenditures for scholarships, libraries and student loans.

(ii) To qualify under section 170(b)(1)(A)(iv), the organization receiving the contribution must normally receive a substantial part of its support from the United States or any State or political subdivision thereof or from direct or indirect contributions from the general public, or from a combination of two or more of such sources. For such purposes, the term "support" does not include income received in the exercise or performance by the organization of its charitable, educational, or other purpose or function constituting the basis for its exemption under section 501(a). An example of an indirect contribution from the public is the receipt by the organization of its share of the proceeds of an annual collection campaign of a community chest, community fund, or united fund. In determining the amount of support received by such organization with respect to a contribution of property which is subject to reduction under section 170(e), the fair market value of the property shall be taken into account.

(iii) The college or university (including a land grant college or university) to be benefited must be an educational organization referred to in section 170(b)(1)(A)(ii) and subparagraph (1) of this paragraph which is an agency or instrumentality of a State or political subdivision thereof, or which is owned or operated by a State or political subdivision thereof or by an agency or instrumentality of one more States or political subdivisions.

(d) *Hospitals and medical research organizations.*—(1) *Hospitals.*—An organization (other than one described in paragraph (d)(2) of this section) is described in section 170(b)(1)(A)(iii) if—

(i) It is a hospital; and

(ii) Its principal purpose or function is the providing of medical or hospital care or medical education or medical research.

(A) The term *hospital* includes—

(*1*) Federal hospitals; and

(*2*) State, county, and municipal hospitals which are instrumentalities of governmental units referred to in section 170(c)(1) and otherwise come within the definition. A rehabilitation institution, outpatient clinic, or community mental health or drug treatment center may qualify as a "hospital" within the meaning of paragraph (d)(1)(i) of this section if its principal purpose or function is the providing of hospital or medical care. For purposes of this paragraph (d)(1)(ii), the term *medical care* shall include the treatment of any physical or mental disability or condition, whether on an inpatient or outpatient basis, provided the cost of such treatment is deductible under section 213 by the person treated. An organization, all the accommodations of which qualify as being part of a "skilled nursing facility" within the meaning of 42 U.S.C. 1395x(j), may qualify as a "hospital" within the meaning of paragraph (d)(1)(i) of this section if its principal purpose or function is the providing of hospital or medical care. For taxable years ending after June 28, 1968, the term hospital also includes cooperative hospital service organizations which meet the requirements of section 501(e) and § 1.501(e)-1.

(B) The term *hospital* does not, however, include convalescent homes or homes for children or the aged, nor does the term include institutions whose principal purpose or function is to train handicapped individuals to pursue some vocation. An organization whose principal purpose or function is the providing of medical education or medical research will not be considered a "hospital" within the meaning of paragraph (d)(1)(i) of this section, unless it is also actively engaged in providing medical or hospital care to patients on its premises or in its facilities, on an inpatient or outpatient basis, as an integral part of its medical education or medical research functions. See, however, paragraph (d)(2) of this section with respect to certain medical research organizations.

(2) *Certain medical research organizations.*—(i) *Introduction.*—A medical research organization is described in section 170(b)(1)(A)(iii) if the principal purpose or functions of such organization are medical research and if it is directly engaged in the continuous active conduct of medical research in conjunction with a hospital. In addition, for purposes of the 50 percent limitation of section 170(b)(1)(A) with respect to a contribution, during the calendar year in which the contribution is made such organization must be committed to spend such contribution for such research before January 1 of the fifth calendar year which begins after the date such contribution is made. An organization need not receive contributions deductible under section 170 to qualify as a medical research organization and such organization need not be committed to spend amounts to which the limitation of section 170(b)(1)(A) does not apply within the 5-year period referred to in this paragraph (d)(2)(i). However, the requirement of continuous active conduct of medical research indicates that the type of organization contemplated in this paragraph (d)(2) is one which is primarily engaged directly in the continuous active conduct of medical research, as compared to an inactive medical research organization or an organization primarily engaged in funding the programs of other medical research organizations. As in the case of a hospital, since an organization is ordinarily not described in section 170(b)(1)(A)(iii) as a hospital unless it functions primarily as a hospital, similarly a medical research organization is not so described unless it is primarily engaged directly in the continuous active conduct of medical research in conjunction with a hospital. Accordingly, the rules of this paragraph (d)(2) shall only apply with respect to such medical research organizations.

(ii) *General rule.*—An organization (other than a hospital described in paragraph (d)(1) of this section) is described in section 170(b)(1)(A)(iii) only if within the meaning of this paragraph (d)(2):

(A) The principal purpose or functions of such organization are to engage primarily in the conduct of medical research; and

(B) It is primarily engaged directly in the continuous active conduct of medical research in conjunction with a hospital which is—

(*1*) Described in section 501(c)(3);

(*2*) A Federal hospital; or

(*3*) An instrumentality of a governmental unit referred to in section 170(c)(1).

(C) In order for a contribution to such organization to qualify for purposes of the 50 percent limitation of section 170(b)(1)(A), during the calendar year in which such contribution is made or treated as made, such organization must be committed (within the meaning of paragraph (d)(2)(viii) of this section) to spend such contribution for such active conduct of medical research before January 1 of the fifth calendar year beginning after the date such contribution is made. For the meaning of the term "medical research" see paragraph (d)(2)(iii) of this section. For the meaning of the term "principal purpose or functions" see paragraph (d)(2)(iv) of this section. For the meaning of the term "primarily engaged directly in the continuous active conduct of medical research" see paragraph (d)(2)(v) of this section. For the meaning of the term "medical research in conjunction with a hospital" see paragraph (d)(2)(vii) of this section.

(iii) *Definition of medical research.*—*Medical research* means the conduct of investigations, experiments, and studies to discover, develop, or verify knowledge relating to the causes, diagnosis, treatment, prevention, or control of physical or mental diseases and impairments of man. To qualify as a medical research organization, the organization must have or must have continuously available for its regular use the appropriate equipment and professional personnel necessary to carry out its principal function. Medical research encompasses the associated disciplines spanning the biological, social and behavioral sciences. Such disciplines include chemistry (biochemistry, physical chemistry, bioorganic chemistry, etc.), behavioral sciences (psychiatry, physiological psychology, neurophysiology, neurology, neurobiology, and social psychology, etc.), biomedical engineering (applied biophysics, medical physics, and medical electronics, for example, developing pacemakers and other medically related electrical equipment), virology, immunology, biophysics, cell biology, molecular biology, pharmacology, toxicology, genetics, pathology, physiology, microbiology, parasitology, endocrinology, bacteriology, and epidemiology.

(iv) *Principal purpose or functions.*—An organization must be organized for the principal purpose of engaging primarily in the conduct of medical research in order to be an organization meeting the requirements of this paragraph (d)(2). An organization will normally be considered to be so organized if it is expressly organized for the purpose of conducting medical research and is actually engaged primarily in the conduct of medical research. Other facts and circumstances, however, may indicate that an organization does not meet the principal purpose requirement of this paragraph (d)(2)(iv) even where its governing instrument so expressly provides. An organization that otherwise meets all of the requirements of this paragraph (d)(2) (including this paragraph (d)(2)(iv)) to qualify as a medical research organization will not fail to so qualify solely because its governing instrument does not specifically state that its principal purpose is to conduct medical research.

(v) *Primarily engaged directly in the continuous active conduct of medical research.*—(A) In order for an organization to be primarily engaged directly in the continuous active conduct of medical research, the organization must either devote a substantial part of its assets to, or expend a significant percentage of its endowment for, such purposes, or both. Whether an organization devotes a substantial part of its assets to, or makes significant expenditures for, such continuous active conduct depends upon the facts and circumstances existing in each specific case. An organization will be treated as devoting a substantial part of its assets to, or expending a significant percentage of its endowment for, such purposes if it meets the appropriate test contained in paragraph (d)(2)(v)(B) of this section. If an organization fails to satisfy both of such tests, in evaluating the facts and circumstances, the factor given most weight is the margin by which the organization failed to meet such tests. Some of the other facts and circumstances to be considered in making such a determination are—

(*1*) If the organization fails to satisfy the tests because it failed to properly value its assets or endowment, then upon determination of the improper valuation it devotes additional assets to, or makes additional expenditures for, such purposes, so that it satisfies such tests on an aggregate basis for the prior year in addition to such tests for the current year;

(*2*) The organization acquires new assets or has a significant increase in the value of its securities after it had developed a budget in a prior year based on the assets then owned and the then current values;

(*3*) The organization fails to make expenditures in any given year because of the interrelated aspects of its budget and long-term planning requirements, for example, where an organization prematurely terminates an unsuccessful program and because of long-term planning requirements it will not be able to establish a fully operational replacement program immediately; and

(4) The organization has as its objective to spend less than a significant percentage in a particular year but make up the difference in the subsequent few years, or to budget a greater percentage in an earlier year and a lower percentage in a later year.

(B) For purposes of this section, an organization which devotes more than one half of its assets to the continuous active conduct of medical research will be considered to be devoting a substantial part of its assets to such conduct within the meaning of paragraph (d)(2)(v)(A) of this section. An organization which expends funds equaling 3.5 percent or more of the fair market value of its endowment for the continuous active conduct of medical research will be considered to have expended a significant percentage of its endowment for such purposes within the meaning of paragraph (d)(2)(v)(A) of this section.

(C) Engaging directly in the continuous active conduct of medical research does not include the disbursing of funds to other organizations for the conduct of research by them or the extending of grants or scholarships to others. Therefore, if an organization's primary purpose is to disburse funds to other organizations for the conduct of research by them or to extend grants or scholarships to others, it is not primarily engaged directly in the continuous active conduct of medical research.

(vi) *Special rules.*—The following rules shall apply in determining whether a substantial part of an organization's assets are devoted to, or its endowment is expended for, the continuous active conduct of medical research activities:

(A) An organization may satisfy the tests of paragraph (d)(2)(v)(B) of this section by meeting such tests either for a computation period consisting of the immediately preceding taxable year, or for the computation period consisting of the immediately preceding four taxable years. In addition, for taxable years beginning in 1970, 1971, 1972, 1973, and 1974, if an organization meets such tests for the computation period consisting of the first four taxable years beginning after December 31, 1969, an organization will be treated as meeting such tests, not only for the taxable year beginning in 1974, but also for the preceding four taxable years. Thus, for example, if a calendar year organization failed to satisfy such tests for a computation period consisting of 1969, 1970, 1971, and 1972, but on the basis of a computation period consisting of the years 1970 through 1973, it expended funds equaling 3.5 percent or more of the fair market value of its endowment for the continuous active conduct of medical research, such organization will be considered to have expended a significant percentage of its endowment for such purposes for the taxable years 1970 through 1974. In applying such tests for a four-year computation period, although the organization's expenditures for the entire four-year period shall be aggregated, the fair market value of its endowment for each year shall be summed, even though, in the case of an asset held throughout the four-year period, the fair market value of such an asset will be counted four times. Similarly, the fair market value of an organization's assets for each year of a four-year computation period shall be summed.

(B) Any property substantially all the use of which is "substantially related" (within the meaning of section 514(b)(1)(A)) to the exercise or performance of the organization's medical research activities will not be treated as part of its endowment.

(C) The valuation of assets must be made with commonly accepted methods of valuation. A method of valuation made in accordance with the principles stated in the regulations under section 2031 constitutes an acceptable method of valuation. Assets may be valued as of any day in the organization's taxable year to which such valuation applies, provided the organization follows a consistent practice of valuing such asset as of such date in all taxable years. For purposes of paragraph (d)(2)(v) of this section, an asset held by the organization for part of a taxable year shall be taken into account by multiplying the fair market value of such asset by a fraction, the numerator of which is the number of days in such taxable year that the organization held such asset and the denominator of which is the number of days in such taxable year.

(vii) *Medical research in conjunction with a hospital.*—The organization need not be formally affiliated with a hospital to be considered primarily engaged directly in the continuous active conduct of medical research in conjunction with a hospital, but in any event there must be a joint effort on the part of the research organization and the hospital pursuant to an understanding that the two organizations will maintain continuing close cooperation in the active conduct of medical research. For example, the necessary joint effort will normally be found to exist if the activities of the medical research organization are carried on in space located within or adjacent to a hospital, the organization is permitted to utilize the facilities (including equipment, case studies, etc.) of the hospital on a continuing basis directly in the active conduct of medical research, and there is substantial evidence of the close cooperation of the members of the staff of the research organization and members of the staff of the

particular hospital or hospitals. The active participation in medical research by members of the staff of the particular hospital or hospitals will be considered to be evidence of such close cooperation. Because medical research may involve substantial investigation, experimentation and study not immediately connected with hospital or medical care, the requisite joint effort will also normally be found to exist if there is an established relationship between the research organization and the hospital which provides that the cooperation of appropriate personnel and the use of facilities of the particular hospital or hospitals will be required whenever it would aid such research.

(viii) *Commitment to spend contributions.*—The organization's commitment that the contribution will be spent within the prescribed time only for the prescribed purposes must be legally enforceable. A promise in writing to the donor in consideration of his making a contribution that such contribution will be so spent within the prescribed time will constitute a commitment. The expenditure of contributions received for plant, facilities, or equipment, used solely for medical research purposes (within the meaning of paragraph (d)(2)(ii) of this section), shall ordinarily be considered to be an expenditure for medical research. If a contribution is made in other than money, it shall be considered spent for medical research if the funds from the proceeds of a disposition thereof are spent by the organization within the five-year period for medical research; or, if such property is of such a kind that it is used on a continuing basis directly in connection with such research, it shall be considered spent for medical research in the year in which it is first so used. A medical research organization will be presumed to have made the commitment required under this paragraph (d)(2)(viii) with respect to any contribution if its governing instrument or by-laws require that every contribution be spent for medical research before January 1 of the fifth year which begins after the date such contribution is made.

(ix) *Organizational period for new organizations.*—A newly created organization, for its "organizational" period, shall be considered to be primarily engaged directly in the continuous active conduct of medical research in conjunction with a hospital within the meaning of paragraphs (d)(2)(v) and (d)(2)(vii) of this section if during such period the organization establishes to the satisfaction of the Commissioner that it reasonably can be expected to be so engaged by the end of such period. The information to be submitted shall include detailed plans showing the proposed initial medical research program, architectural drawings for the erection of buildings and facilities to be used for medical research in accordance with such plans, plans to assemble a professional staff and detailed projections showing the timetable for the expected accomplishment of the foregoing. The "organizational" period shall be that period which is appropriate to implement the proposed plans, giving effect to the proposed amounts involved and the magnitude and complexity of the projected medical research program, but in no event in excess of three years following organization.

(x) *Examples.*—The application of this paragraph (d)(2) may be illustrated by the following examples:

Example 1. N, an organization referred to in section 170(c)(2), was created to promote human knowledge within the field of medical research and medical education. All of N's assets were contributed to it by A and consist of a diversified portfolio of stocks and bonds. N's endowment earns 3.5 percent annually, which N expends in the conduct of various medical research programs in conjunction with Y hospital. N is located adjacent to Y hospital, makes substantial use of Y's facilities, and there is close cooperation between the staffs of N and Y. N is directly engaged in the continuous active conduct of medical research in conjunction with a hospital, meets the principal purpose test described in paragraph (d)(2)(iv) of this section, and is therefore an organization described in section 170(b)(1)(A)(iii).

Example 2. O, an organization referred to in section 170(c)(2), was created to promote human knowledge within the field of medical research and medical education. All of O's assets consist of a diversified portfolio of stocks and bonds. O's endowment earns 3.5 percent annually, which O expends in the conduct of various medical research programs in conjunction with certain hospitals. However, in 1974, O receives a substantial bequest of additional stocks and bonds. O's budget for 1974 does not take into account the bequest and as a result O expends only 3.1 percent of its endowment in 1974. However, O establishes that it will expend at least 3.5 percent of its endowment for the active conduct of medical research for taxable years 1975 through 1978. O is therefore directly engaged in the continuous active conduct of medical research in conjunction with a hospital for taxable year 1975. Since O also meets the principal purpose test described in paragraph (d)(2)(iv) of this section, it is therefore an organization described in section 170(b)(1)(A)(iii) for taxable year 1975.

Example 3. M, an organization referred to in section 170(c)(2), was created to promote human knowledge within the field of medical research and medical education. M's activities consist of the

Itemized Deductions for Individuals and Corps.
See p. 20,601 for regulations not amended to reflect law changes

25,555

conduct of medical research programs in conjunction with various hospitals. Under such programs, researchers employed by M engage in research at laboratories set aside for M within the various hospitals. Substantially all of M's assets consists of 100 percent of the stock of X corporation, which has a fair market value of approximately 100 million dollars. X pays M approximately 3.3 million dollars in dividends annually, which M expends in the conduct of its medical research programs. Since M expends only 3.3 percent of its endowment, which does not constitute a significant percentage, in the active conduct of medical research, M is not an organization described in section 170(b)(1)(A)(iii) because M is not engaged in the continuous active conduct of medical research.

(xi) *Special rule for organizations with existing ruling.*—This paragraph (d)(2)(xi) shall apply to an organization that prior to January 1, 1970, had received a ruling or determination letter which has not been expressly revoked holding the organization to be a medical research organization described in section 170(b)(1)(A)(iii) and with respect to which the facts and circumstances on which the ruling was based have not substantially changed. An organization to which this paragraph (d)(2)(xi) applies shall be treated as an organization described in section 170(b)(1)(A)(iii) for a period not ending prior to 90 days after February 13, 1976 (or where appropriate, for taxable years beginning before such 90th day). In addition, with respect to a grantor or contributor under sections 170, 507, 545(b)(2), 556(b)(2), 642(c), 4942, 4945, 2055, 2106(a)(2), and 2522, the status of an organization to which this paragraph (d)(2)(xi) applies will not be affected until notice of change of status under section 170(b)(1)(A)(iii) is made to the public (such as by publication in the Internal Revenue Bulletin). The preceding sentence shall not apply if the grantor or contributor had previously acquired knowledge that the Internal Revenue Service had given notice to such organization that it would be deleted from classification as a section 170(b)(1)(A)(iii) organization.

(e) *Governmental unit.*—A governmental unit is described in section 170(b)(1)(A)(v) if it is referred to in section 170(c)(1).

(f) *Definition of section 170(b)(1)(A)(vi) organization.*—(1) *In general.*—An organization is described in section 170(b)(1)(A)(vi) if it—

(i) Is referred to in section 170(c)(2) (other than an organization specifically described in paragraphs (b) through (e) of this section); and

(ii) Normally receives a substantial part of its support from a governmental unit referred to in section 170(c)(1) or from direct or indirect contributions from the general public ("publicly supported"). For purposes of this paragraph (f), an organization is publicly supported if it meets the requirements of either paragraph (f)(2) of this section (33. percent support test) or paragraph (f)(3) of this section (facts and circumstances test). Paragraph (f)(4) of this section defines "normally" for purposes of the 33. percent support test and the facts and circumstances test, and for new organizations in the first five years of the organization's existence as a section 501(c)(3) organization. Paragraph (f)(5) of this section provides for determinations of foundation classification and rules for reliance by donors and contributors. Paragraphs (f)(6), (f)(7), and (f)(8) of this section list the items that are included and excluded from the term support. Paragraph (f)(9) of this section provides examples of the application of this paragraph. Types of organizations that, subject to the provisions of this paragraph (f), generally qualify under section 170(b)(1)(A)(vi) as "publicly supported" are publicly or governmentally supported museums of history, art, or science, libraries, community centers to promote the arts, organizations providing facilities for the support of an opera, symphony orchestra, ballet, or repertory drama or for some other direct service to the general public.

(2) *Determination whether an organization is "publicly supported"; 33⅓ percent support test.*—An organization is publicly supported if the total amount of support (see paragraphs (f)(6), (f)(7), and (f)(8) of this section) that the organization normally (see paragraph (f)(4)(i) of this section) receives from governmental units referred to in section 170(c)(1), from contributions made directly or indirectly by the general public, or from a combination of these sources, equals at least 33. percent of the total support normally received by the organization. See paragraph (f)(9), *Example 1* of this section.

(3) *Determination whether an organization is "publicly supported"; facts and circumstances test.*—Even if an organization fails to meet the 33. percent support test described in paragraph (f)(2) of this section, it is publicly supported if it normally (see paragraph (f)(4)(i) of this section) receives a substantial part of its support from governmental units, from contributions made directly or indirectly by the general public, or from a combination of these sources, and meets the other requirements of this paragraph (f)(3). In order to satisfy the facts and circumstances test, an organization must meet the requirements of paragraphs (f)(3)(i) and (f)(3)(ii) of this section. In addition, the organization must be in the nature of an organization that is publicly

supported, taking into account all pertinent facts and circumstances, including the factors listed in paragraphs (f)(3)(iii)(A) through (f)(3)(iii)(E) of this section.

(i) *Ten-percent support limitation.*—The percentage of support (see paragraphs (f)(6), (f)(7) and (f)(8) of this section) normally received by an organization from governmental units, from contributions made directly or indirectly by the general public, or from a combination of these sources, must be substantial. For purposes of this paragraph (f)(3), an organization will not be treated as normally receiving a substantial amount of governmental or public support unless the total amount of governmental and public support normally received equals at least 10 percent of the total support normally received by such organization.

(ii) *Attraction of public support.*—An organization must be so organized and operated as to attract new and additional public or governmental support on a continuous basis. An organization will be considered to meet this requirement if it maintains a continuous and bona fide program for solicitation of funds from the general public, community, or membership group involved, or if it carries on activities designed to attract support from governmental units or other organizations described in section 170(b)(1)(A)(i) through (b)(1)(A)(vi). In determining whether an organization maintains a continuous and bona fide program for solicitation of funds from the general public or community, consideration will be given to whether the scope of its fundraising activities is reasonable in light of its charitable activities. Consideration will also be given to the fact that an organization, in its early years of existence, may limit the scope of its solicitation to persons deemed most likely to provide seed money in an amount sufficient to enable it to commence its charitable activities and expand its solicitation program.

(iii) In addition to the requirements set forth in paragraphs (f)(3)(i) and (f)(3)(ii) of this section that must be satisfied, all pertinent facts and circumstances, including the following factors, will be taken into consideration in determining whether an organization is "publicly supported" within the meaning of paragraph (f)(1) of this section. However, an organization is not generally required to satisfy all of the factors in paragraphs (f)(3)(iii)(A) through (f)(3)(iii)(E) of this section. The factors relevant to each case and the weight accorded to any one of them may differ depending upon the nature and purpose of the organization and the length of time it has been in existence.

(A) *Percentage of financial support.*—The percentage of support received by an organization from public or governmental sources will be taken into consideration in determining whether an organization is "publicly supported." The higher the percentage of support above the 10 percent requirement of paragraph (f)(3)(i) of this section from public or governmental sources, the lesser will be the burden of establishing the publicly supported nature of the organization through other factors, including those described in this paragraph (f)(3), while the lower the percentage, the greater will be the burden. If the percentage of the organization's support from public or governmental sources is low because it receives a high percentage of its total support from investment income on its endowment funds, such fact will be treated as evidence of an organization being "publicly supported" if such endowment funds were originally contributed by a governmental unit or by the general public. However, if such endowment funds were originally contributed by a few individuals or members of their families, such fact will increase the burden on the organization of establishing that it is "publicly supported" taking into account all pertinent facts and circumstances, including the other factors described in paragraph (f)(3)(iii) of this section.

(B) *Sources of support.*—The fact that an organization meets the requirement of paragraph (f)(3)(i) of this section through support from governmental units or directly or indirectly from a representative number of persons, rather than receiving almost all of its support from the members of a single family, will be considered evidence of an organization being "publicly supported." In determining what is a "representative number of persons," consideration will be given to the type of organization involved, the length of time it has been in existence, and whether it limits its activities to a particular community or region or to a special field which can be expected to appeal to a limited number of persons.

(C) *Representative governing body.*—The fact that an organization has a governing body which represents the broad interests of the public, rather than the personal or private interests of a limited number of donors (or persons standing in a relationship to such donors which is described in section 4946(a)(1)(C) through (a)(1)(G)), will be considered evidence of an organization being "publicly supported." An organization will be treated as having a representative governing body if it has a governing body (whether designated in the organization's governing instrument or bylaws as a Board of Directors, Board of Trustees, or similar governing body) which is comprised of public officials acting in their capacities as such; of individuals selected by public officials acting in their capacities as such; of persons having special knowledge or expertise in the particular field or discipline in which the organization is operating; of community leaders, such as elected or appointed officials, clergymen, educators, civic leaders, or other such persons representing a broad cross-section of the views and interests of the community; or, in the case of a membership organization, of individuals elected pursuant to the organization's governing instrument or bylaws by a broadly based membership.

(D) *Availability of public facilities or services; public participation in programs or policies.*—(1) The fact that an organization generally provides facilities or services directly for the benefit of the general public on a continuing basis (such as a museum or library which holds open its building or facilities to the public, a symphony orchestra which gives public performances, a conservation organization which provides educational services to the public through the distribution of educational materials, or an old age home which provides domiciliary or nursing services for members of the general public) will be considered evidence that such organization is "publicly supported."

(2) The fact that an organization is an educational or research institution which regularly publishes scholarly studies that are widely used by colleges and universities or by members of the general public will also be considered evidence that such organization is "publicly supported."

(3) The following factors will also be considered evidence that an organization is "publicly supported":

(i) The participation in, or sponsorship of, the programs of the organization by members of the public having special knowledge or expertise, public officials, or civic or community leaders.

(ii) The maintenance of a definitive program by an organization to accomplish its charitable work in the community, such as combating community deterioration in an economically depressed area that has suffered a major loss of population and jobs.

(iii) The receipt of a significant part of its funds from a public charity or governmental agency to which it is in some way held accountable as a condition of the grant, contract, or contribution.

(E) *Additional factors pertinent to membership organizations.*— The following are additional factors to be considered in determining whether a membership organization is "publicly supported":

(1) Whether the solicitation for dues-paying members is designed to enroll a substantial number of persons in the community or area, or in a particular profession or field of special interest (taking into account the size of the area and the nature of the organization's activities).

(2) Whether membership dues for individual (rather than institutional), members have been fixed at rates designed to make membership available to a broad cross section of the interested public, rather than to restrict membership to a limited number of persons.

(3) Whether the activities of the organization will be likely to appeal to persons having some broad common interest or purpose, such as educational activities in the case of alumni associations, musical activities in the case of symphony societies, or civic affairs in the case of parent-teacher associations. See *Example 2* through *Example 5* contained in paragraph (f)(9) of this section for illustrations of this paragraph (f)(3).

(4) *Definition of normally; general rule.*—(i) *Normally; 33⅓ percent support test.*—An organization "normally" receives the requisite amount of public support and meets the 33⅓ percent support test for a taxable year and the taxable year immediately succeeding that year, if, for the taxable year being tested and the four taxable years immediately preceding that taxable year, the organization meets the 33⅓ percent support test on an aggregate basis.

(ii) *Normally; facts and circumstances test.*—An organization "normally" receives the requisite amount of public support and meets the facts and circumstances test of paragraph (f)(3) for a taxable year and the taxable year immediately succeeding that year, if, for the taxable year being tested and the four taxable years immediately preceding that taxable year, the organization meets the facts and circumstances test on an aggregate basis. In the case of paragraphs (f)(3)(iii)(A) and (f)(3)(iii)(B) of this section, facts pertinent to years preceding the five-year period may also be taken into consideration. The combination of factors set forth in paragraphs (f)(3)(iii)(A) through (f)(3)(iii)(E) of this section that an organization normally must meet does not have to be the same for each five-year period so long as there exists a sufficient combination of factors to show compliance with the facts and circumstances test.

(iii) *Special rule.*—The fact that an organization has normally met the requirements of the 33⅓ percent support test for a current taxable year, but is unable normally to meet such requirements for a succeeding taxable year, will not in itself prevent such organization from meeting the facts and circumstances test for such succeeding taxable year.

(iv) *Example.*—The application of paragraphs (f)(4)(i), (f)(4)(ii), and (f)(4)(iii) of this section may be illustrated by the following example:

Example. (i) X is recognized as an organization described in section 501(c)(3). On the basis of support received during taxable years 2008, 2009, 2010, 2011, and 2012, in the aggregate, X receives at least 33⅓ percent of its support from governmental units referred to in section 170(c)(1), from contributions made directly or indirectly by the general public, or from a combination of these sources. Consequently, X meets the 33⅓ percent support test for taxable year 2012 (the current taxable year). X also meets the 33⅓ support test for 2013, as the immediately succeeding taxable year.

(ii) In taxable years 2009, 2010, 2011, 2012, and 2013, in the aggregate, X does not receive at least 33⅓ percent of its support from governmental units referred to in section 170(c)(1), from contributions made directly or indirectly by the general public, or from a combination of these sources. However, X still meets the 33⅓ percent support test for taxable year 2013 based on the aggregate support received for taxable years 2008 through 2012.

(iii) In taxable years 2010, 2011, 2012, 2013, and 2014, in the aggregate, X does not receive at least 33⅓ percent of its support from governmental units referred to in section 170(c)(1), from contributions made directly or indirectly by the general public, or from a combination of these sources. X does not meet the 33⅓ percent support test for taxable year 2014.

(iv) X meets the facts and circumstances test for taxable year 2013 and for taxable year 2014 (the immediately succeeding taxable year) based on the aggregate support X receives, X's fundraising program, and consideration of other factors, including those listed in paragraphs (f)(3)(iii)(A) through (f)(3)(iii)(E) of this section, during taxable years 2009, 2010, 2011, 2012, and 2013. Therefore, even though X does not meet the 33⅓ percent support test for taxable year 2014, X is still an organization described in section 170(b)(1)(A)(vi) for that year.

(v) *Normally; first five years of an organization's existence.*— (A) An organization "normally" receives the requisite amount of public support and meets the 33⅓ percent public support test or the facts and circumstances test during its first five taxable years as a section 501(c)(3) organization if the organization can reasonably be expected to meet the requirements of the 33⅓ percent support test or the facts and circumstances test during that period. With respect to such organization's sixth taxable year, the general definition of normally set forth in paragraphs (f)(4)(i), (f)(4)(ii), and (f)(4)(iii) of this section apply. Alternatively, the organization shall be treated as "normally" meeting the 33⅓ percent support test or the facts and circumstances test for its sixth taxable year (but not its seventh taxable year) if it meets the 33⅓ percent support test or the facts and circumstances test under the definition of normally set forth in paragraphs (f)(4)(i), (f)(4)(ii), and (f)(4)(iii) of this section for its fifth taxable year (based on support received in its first through fifth taxable years).

(B) *Basic consideration.*—In determining whether an organization can reasonably be expected (within the meaning of paragraph (f)(4)(v)(A) of this section) to meet the requirements of the 33⅓ percent support test or the facts and circumstances test during its first five taxable years, the basic consideration is whether its organizational structure, current or proposed programs or activities, and actual or intended method of operation are such as can reasonably be expected to attract the type of broadly based support from the general public, public charities, and governmental units that is necessary to meet such tests. The factors that are relevant to this determination, and the weight accorded to each of them, may differ from case to case, depending on the nature and functions of the organization. The information to be considered for this purpose shall consist of all pertinent facts and circumstances, including the factors set forth in paragraph (f)(3) of this section.

(vi) *Example.*—The application of paragraph (f)(4)(v) of this section may be illustrated by the following example:

Example. (i) Organization Y was formed in January 2008, and uses a taxable year ending December 31. After September 9, 2008, and before December 31, 2008, Organization Y filed Form 1023 requesting recognition of exemption as an organization described in section 501(c)(3) and in sections 170(b)(1)(A)(vi) and 509(a)(1). In its application, Organization Y established that it can reasonably be expected to operate as a publicly supported organization under paragraph (f)(2) or (f)(3) and paragraph (f)(4)(v) of this section.

Itemized Deductions for Individuals and Corps.
See p. 20,601 for regulations not amended to reflect law changes
25,557

Subsequently, Organization Y received a ruling or determination letter that it is an organization described in section 501(c)(3) and sections 170(b)(1)(A)(vi) and 509(a)(1) effective as of the date of its formation.

(ii) Organization Y is described in sections 170(b)(1)(A)(vi) and 509(a)(1) for its first five taxable years (the taxable years ending December 31, 2008, through December 31, 2012).

(iii) Organization Y can qualify as a publicly supported organization for the taxable year ending December 31, 2013, if Organization Y can meet the requirements of either paragraph (f)(2) or paragraph (f)(3) of this section or §1.509(a)-3(a) and §1.509(a)-(3)(b) for the taxable years ending December 31, 2009, through December 31, 2013, or for the taxable years ending December 31, 2008, through December 31, 2012.

(vii) *Organizations reclassified as private foundations.*—(A) *New publicly supported organizations.*—If a new publicly supported organization described under section 170(b)(1)(A)(vi) cannot meet the requirements of the 33 1/3 percent test of paragraph (f)(2) or the facts and circumstances test of paragraph (f)(3) for its sixth taxable year under the general definition of normally set forth in paragraphs (f)(4)(i), (f)(4)(ii), and (f)(4)(iii) of this section or under the alternate rule set forth in paragraph (f)(4)(v) of this section (effectively failing to meet a public support test for both its fifth and sixth taxable years), it will be treated as a private foundation as of the first day of its sixth taxable year only for purposes of sections 507, 4940, and 6033. Such an organization must file a Form 990-PF, "Return of Private Foundation or Section 4947(a)(1) Nonexempt Charitable Trust Treated as a Private Foundation," and will be liable for the net investment tax imposed by section 4940 and, if applicable, the private foundation termination tax imposed by section 507(c), for its sixth taxable year. For succeeding taxable years, the organization will be treated as a private foundation for all purposes.

(B) *Other publicly supported organizations.*—A publicly supported organization described in section 170(b)(1)(A)(vi) (other than a new publicly supported organization described in paragraph (f)(4)(vii)(A) of this section) that has failed to meet both the 33^1/$_3$ percent support test and the facts and circumstances test for any two consecutive taxable years will be treated as a private foundation as of the first day of the second consecutive taxable year only for purposes of sections 507, 4940, and 6033. Such an organization must file a Form 990-PF, "Return of Private Foundation or Section 4947(a)(1) Nonexempt Charitable Trust Treated as a Private Foundation," and will be liable for the net investment tax imposed by section 4940 and, if applicable, the private foundation termination tax imposed by section 507(c), for the second consecutive failed taxable year. For succeeding taxable years, the organization will be treated as a private foundation for all purposes.

(5) *Determinations of foundation classification and reliance.*—(i) A ruling or determination letter that an organization is described in section 170(b)(1)(A)(vi) may be issued to an organization. Such determination may be made in conjunction with the recognition of the organization's tax-exempt status or at such other time as the organization believes it is described in section 170(b)(1)(A)(vi). The ruling or determination letter that the organization is described in section 170(b)(1)(A)(vi) may be revoked if, upon examination, the organization has not met the requirements of paragraph (f) of this section. The ruling or determination letter that the organization is described in section 170(b)(1)(A)(vi) also may be revoked if the organization's application for a ruling or determination contained one or more material misstatements or omissions of fact or if such application was part of a scheme or plan to avoid or evade any provision of the Internal Revenue Code. The revocation of the determination that an organization is described in section 170(b)(1)(A)(vi) does not preclude revocation of the determination that the organization is described in section 501(c)(3).

(ii) *Status of grantors or contributors.*—For purposes of sections 170, 507, 545(b)(2), 642(c), 4942, 4945, 4966, 2055, 2106(a)(2), and 2522, grantors or contributors may rely upon a determination letter or ruling that an organization is described in section 170(b)(1)(A)(vi) until the IRS publishes notice of a change of status (for example, in the Internal Revenue Bulletin or Publication 78, "Cumulative List of Organizations described in Section 170(c) of the Internal Revenue Code of 1986," which can be searched at www.irs.gov). For this purpose, grantors or contributors also may rely on an advance ruling that expires on or after June 9, 2008. However, a grantor or contributor may not rely on such an advance ruling or any determination letter or ruling if the grantor or contributor was responsible for, or aware of, the act or failure to act that resulted in the organization's loss of classification under section 170(b)(1)(A)(vi) or acquired knowledge that the IRS had given notice to such organization that it would be deleted from such classification.

(iii) *Reliance by grantors or contributors.*—A grantor or contributor, other than one of the organization's founders, creators, or foundation managers (within the meaning of section 4946(b)), will not be considered to be responsible for, or aware of, the act or failure to act that resulted in the loss of the organization's "publicly supported" classification under section 170(b)(1)(A)(vi), if such grantor or contributor has made such grant or contribution in reliance upon a written statement by the grantee organization that such grant or contribution will not result in the loss of such organization's classification as a publicly supported organization as described in section 170(b)(1)(A)(vi). Such statement must be signed by a responsible officer of the grantee organization and must set forth sufficient information, including a summary of the pertinent financial data for the five taxable years immediately preceding the current taxable year, to assure a reasonably prudent person that his grant or contribution will not result in the loss of the grantee organization's classification as a publicly supported organization as described in section 170(b)(1)(A)(vi). If a reasonable doubt exists as to the effect of such grant or contribution, or if the grantor or contributor is one of the organization's founders, creators, or foundation managers, the procedure set forth in paragraph (f)(6)(iv) of this section for requesting a determination from the IRS may be followed by the grantee organization for the protection of the grantor or contributor.

(6) *Definition of support; meaning of general public.*—(i) *In general.*—In determining whether the 33^1/$_2$ [33^1/$_3$] percent support test or the 10 percent support limitation described in paragraph (f)(3)(i) of this section is met, contributions by an individual, trust, or corporation shall be taken into account as support from direct or indirect contributions from the general public only to the extent that the total amount of the contributions by any such individual, trust, or corporation during the period described in paragraph (f)(4)(i) or paragraph (f)(4)(ii) of this section does not exceed two percent of the organization's total support for such period, except as provided in paragraph (f)(6)(ii) of this section. Therefore, for example, any contribution by one individual will be included in full in the denominator of the fraction determining the 33^1/$_2$ [33^1/$_3$] percent support or the 10 percent support limitation, but will be includible in the numerator of such fraction only to the extent that such amount does not exceed two percent of the denominator. In applying the two percent limitation, all contributions made by a donor and by any person or persons standing in a relationship to the donor that is described in section 4946(a)(1)(C) through (a)(1)(G) and the related regulations shall be treated as made by one person. The two percent limitation shall not apply to support received from governmental units referred to in section 170(c)(1) or to contributions from organizations described in section 170(b)(1)(A)(vi), except as provided in paragraph (f)(6)(v) of this section. For purposes of paragraphs (f)(2), (f)(3)(i), and (f)(7)(iii)(A)(2) of this section, the term *indirect contributions from the general public* includes contributions received by the organization from organizations (such as section 170(b)(1)(A)(vi) organizations) that normally receive a substantial part of their support from direct contributions from the general public, except as provided in paragraph (f)(6)(v) of this section. See the examples in paragraph (f)(9) of this section for the application of this paragraph (f)(6)(i). For purposes of this paragraph (f), the term *contributions* includes qualified sponsorship payments (as defined in §1.513-4) in the form of money or property (but not services).

(ii) *Exclusion of unusual grants.*—(A) For purposes of applying the two percent limitation described in paragraph (f)(6)(i) of this section to determine whether the 33 percent support test or the 10 percent support limitation in paragraph (f)(3)(i) of this section is satisfied, one or more contributions may be excluded from both the numerator and the denominator of the applicable support fraction if such contributions meet the requirements of paragraph (f)(6)(iii) of this section. The exclusion provided by this paragraph (f)(6)(ii) is generally intended to apply to substantial contributions or bequests from disinterested parties, which contributions or bequests—

(1) Are attracted by reason of the publicly supported nature of the organization;

(2) Are unusual or unexpected with respect to the amount thereof; and

(3) Would, by reason of their size, adversely affect the status of the organization as normally being publicly supported for the applicable period described in paragraph (f)(4) of this section.

(B) In the case of a grant (as defined in §1.509(a)-3(g)) that meets the requirements of this paragraph (f)(6)(ii), if the terms of the granting instrument require that the funds be paid to the recipient organization over a period of years, the grant amounts received by the organization may be excluded for such year or years in which they would otherwise be includible in computing support under the method of accounting on the basis of which the organization regularly computes its income in keeping its books under section 446. However, no item of gross investment income may be excluded under this paragraph (f)(6). The provisions of this paragraph (f)(6) shall apply to exclude unusual grants made during any of the applicable periods described in paragraph (f)(4) or paragraph (f)(6) of this section. See paragraph (f)(6)(iv) of this section as to reliance by a grantee organization upon an unusual grant ruling under this paragraph (f)(6).

(iii) *Determining factors.*—In determining whether a particular contribution may be excluded under paragraph (f)(6)(ii) of this section, all pertinent facts and circumstances will be taken into consideration. No single factor will necessarily be determinative. For some of the factors similar to the factors to be considered, see § 1.509(a)-3(c)(4).

(iv) *Grantors and contributors.*—Prior to the making of any grant or contribution that will allegedly meet the requirements for exclusion under paragraph (f)(6)(ii) of this section, a potential grantee organization may request a determination whether such grant or contribution may be so excluded. Requests for such determination may be filed by the grantee organization in the time and manner specified by revenue procedure or other guidance published in the Internal Revenue Bulletin. The issuance of such determination will be at the sole discretion of the Commissioner. The organization must submit all information necessary to make a determination on the factors referred to in paragraph (f)(6)(iii) of this section. If a favorable determination is issued, such determination may be relied upon by the grantor or contributor of the particular contribution in question for purposes of sections 170, 507, 545(b)(2), 642(c), 4942, 4945, 4966, 2055, 2106(a)(2), and 2522 and by the grantee organization for purposes of paragraph (f)(6)(ii) of this section.

(v) *Grants from public charities.*—Pursuant to paragraph (f)(6)(i) of this section, contributions received from a governmental unit or from a section 170(b)(1)(A)(vi) organization are not subject to the two percent limitation described in paragraph (f)(6)(i) of this section unless such contributions represent amounts which have been expressly or impliedly earmarked by a donor to such governmental unit or section 170(b)(1)(A)(vi) organization as being for, or for the benefit of, the particular organization claiming section 170(b)(1)(A)(vi) status. See § 1.509(a)-3(j)(3) for examples illustrating the rules of this paragraph (f)(6)(v).

(7) *Definition of support; special rules and meaning of terms.*— (i) *Definition of support.*—For purposes of this paragraph (f), the term "support" shall be as defined in section 509(d) (without regard to section 509(d)(2)). The term "support" does not include—

(A) Any amounts received from the exercise or performance by an organization of its charitable, educational, or other purpose or function constituting the basis for its exemption under section 501(a). In general, such amounts include amounts received from any activity the conduct of which is substantially related to the furtherance of such purpose or function (other than through the production of income); or

(B) Contributions of services for which a deduction is not allowable.

(ii) For purposes of the 33. percent support test and the 10 percent support limitation in paragraph (f)(3)(i) of this section, all amounts received that are described in paragraph (f)(7)(i)(A) or paragraph (f)(7)(i)(B) of this section are to be excluded from both the numerator and the denominator of the fractions determining compliance with such tests, except as provided in paragraph (f)(7)(iii) of this section.

(iii) *Organizations dependent primarily on gross receipts from related activities.*—(A) Notwithstanding the provisions of paragraph (f)(7)(i) of this section, an organization will not be treated as satisfying the 33. percent support test or the 10 percent support limitation in paragraph (f)(3)(i) of this section if it receives—

(1) Almost all of its support (as defined in section 509(d)) from gross receipts from related activities; and

(2) An insignificant amount of its support from governmental units (without regard to amounts referred to in paragraph (f)(7)(i)(A) of this section) and contributions made directly or indirectly by the general public.

(B) *Example.*—The application of this paragraph (f)(7)(iii) may be illustrated by the following example:

Example. Z, an organization described in section 501(c)(3), is controlled by A, its president. Z received $500,000 during the period consisting of the current taxable year and the four immediately preceding taxable years under a contract with the Department of Transportation, pursuant to which Z has engaged in research to improve a particular vehicle used primarily by the Federal govern-

ment. During this same period, the only other support received by Z consisted of $5,000 in small contributions primarily from Z's employees and business associates. The $500,000 amount constitutes support under sections 509(d)(2) and 509(a)(2)(A). Under these circumstances, Z meets the conditions of paragraphs (f)(7)(iii)(A)(1) and (f)(7)(iii)(A)(2) of this section and will not be treated as meeting the requirements of either the 33⅓ percent support test or the facts and circumstances test. As to the rules applicable to organizations that fail to qualify under section 170(b)(1)(A)(vi) because of the provisions of this paragraph (f)(7)(iii), see section 509(a)(2) and the related regulations. For the distinction between gross receipts (as referred to in section 509(d)(2)) and gross investment income (as referred to in section 509(d)(4)), see § 1.509(a)-3(m).

(iv) *Membership fees.*—For purposes of this paragraph (f)(7), the term *support* shall include "membership fees" within the meaning of § 1.509(a)-3(h) (that is, if the basic purpose for making a payment is to provide support for the organization rather than to purchase admissions, merchandise, services, or the use of facilities).

(v) *Unrelated business activities.*—The term *net income from unrelated business activities* in section 509(d)(3) includes (but is not limited to) an organization's unrelated business taxable income (UBTI) within the meaning of section 512. However, when calculating UBTI for purposes of determining support (within the meaning of this paragraph (f)(7)), section 512(a)(6) does not apply. Accordingly, in the case of an organization that derives gross income from the regular conduct of two or more unrelated business activities, support includes the aggregate of gross income from all such unrelated business activities less the aggregate of the deductions allowed with respect to all such unrelated business activities. Nonetheless, when determining support, such organization can use either its UBTI calculated under section 512(a)(6) or its UBTI calculated in the aggregate.

(8) *Support from a governmental unit.*—(i) For purposes of the 33⅓ percent support test and the 10 percent support limitation described in paragraph (f)(3)(i) of this section, the term *support from a governmental unit* includes any amounts received from a governmental unit, including donations or contributions and amounts received in connection with a contract entered into with a governmental unit for the performance of services or in connection with a government research grant. However, such amounts will not constitute support from a governmental unit for such purposes if they constitute amounts received from the exercise or performance of the organization's exempt functions as provided in paragraph (f)(7)(i)(A) of this section.

(ii) For purposes of paragraph (f)(8)(i) of this section, any amount paid by a governmental unit to an organization is not to be treated as received from the exercise or performance of its charitable, educational, or other purpose or function constituting the basis for its exemption under section 501(a) (within the meaning of paragraph (f)(7)(i)(A) of this section) if the purpose of the payment is primarily to enable the organization to provide a service to, or maintain a facility for, the direct benefit of the public (regardless of whether part of the expense of providing such service or facility is paid for by the public), rather than to serve the direct and immediate needs of the payor. For example—

(A) Amounts paid for the maintenance of library facilities which are open to the public;

(B) Amounts paid under government programs to nursing homes or homes for the aged in order to provide health care or domiciliary services to residents of such facilities; and

(C) Amounts paid to child placement or child guidance organizations under government programs for services rendered to children in the community, are considered payments the purpose of which is primarily to enable the recipient organization to provide a service or maintain a facility for the direct benefit of the public, rather than to serve the direct and immediate needs of the payor. Furthermore, any amount received from a governmental unit under circumstances such that the amount would be treated as a "grant" within the meaning of § 1.509(a)-3(g) will generally constitute "support from a governmental unit" described in this paragraph (f)(8), rather than an amount described in paragraph (f)(7)(i)(A) of this section.

(9) *Examples.*—The application of paragraphs (f)(1) through (f)(8) of this section may be illustrated by the following examples:

Example 1. (i) M is recognized as an organization described in section 501(c)(3). For the years 2008 through 2012 (the applicable period with respect to the taxable year 2012 under paragraph (f)(4) of this section), M received support (as defined in paragraphs (f)(6) through (8) of this section) of $600,000 from the following sources:

Investment income	$ 300,000
City R (a governmental unit described in section 170(c)(1))	40,000
United Fund (an organization described in section 170(b)(1)(A)(vi))	40,000
Contributions (including six contributions in excess of the two-percent limit, totaling $170,000)	220,000
Total support	$ 600,000

(ii) With respect to the taxable year 2012, M's public support is computed as follows:

Support from a governmental unit described in section 170(c)(1)	40,000
Indirect contributions from the general public (United Fund)	40,000
Contributions by various donors that were not in excess of $12,000, or two percent of total support	50,000
Six contributions that were each in excess of $12,000, or two percent of total support, up to the two-percent limitation, 6 × $12,000	72,000
	202,000

(iii) M's support from governmental units referred to in section 170(c)(1) and from direct and indirect contributions from the general public (as defined in paragraph (f)(6) of this section) with respect to the taxable year 2012 normally exceeds 33⅓ percent of M's total support ($202,000/$600,000 = 33.67 percent) for the applicable period (2008 through 2012). M meets the 33⅓ percent support test with respect to 2012 and is therefore publicly supported for the taxable years 2012 and 2013.

Example 2. (i) N is recognized as an organization described in section 501(c)(3). It was created to maintain public gardens containing botanical specimens and displaying statuary and other art objects. The facilities, works of art, and a large endowment were all contributed by a single contributor. The members of the governing body of the organization are unrelated to its creator. The gardens are open to the public without charge and attract a substantial number of visitors each year. For the current taxable year and the four taxable years immediately preceding the current taxable year, 95 percent of the organization's total support was received from investment income from its original endowment. N also maintains a membership society that is supported by members of the general public who wish to contribute to the upkeep of the gardens by paying a small annual membership fee. Over the five-year period in question, these fees from the general public constituted the remaining five percent of the organization's total support for such period.

(ii) Under these circumstances, N does not meet the 33⅓ percent support test for its current taxable year. Furthermore, because only five percent of its total support is, with respect to the current taxable year, normally received from the general public, N does not satisfy the 10 percent support limitation described in paragraph (f)(3)(i) of this section and therefore does not qualify as publicly supported under the facts and circumstances test. Because N has failed to satisfy the 10 percent support limitation under paragraph (f)(3)(i) of this section, none of the other requirements or factors set forth in paragraphs (f)(3)(iii)(A) through (f)(3)(iii)(E) of this section can be considered in determining whether N qualifies as a publicly supported organization. For its current taxable year, therefore, N is not an organization described in section 170(b)(1)(A)(vi).

Example 3. (i) O, an art museum, is recognized as an organization described in section 501(c)(3). In 1930, O was founded in S City by the members of a single family to collect, preserve, interpret, and display to the public important works of art. O is governed by a Board of Trustees that originally consisted almost entirely of members of the founding family. However, since 1945, members of the founding family or persons standing in a relationship to the members of such family described in section 4946(a)(1)(C) through (G) have annually constituted less than one-fifth of the Board of Trustees. The remaining board members are citizens of S City from a variety of professions and occupations who represent the interests and views of the people of S City in the activities carried on by the organization rather than the personal or private interests of the founding family. O solicits contributions from the general public and, for the current taxable year and each of the four taxable years immediately preceding the current taxable year, O has received total contributions (in small sums of less than $100, none of which exceeds two percent of

O's total support for such period) in excess of $10,000. These contributions from the general public (as defined in paragraph (f)(6) of this section) represent 25 percent of the organization's total support for such five-year period. For this same period, investment income from several large endowment funds has constituted 75 percent of O's total support. O expends substantially all of its annual income for its exempt purposes and thus depends upon the funds it annually solicits from the public as well as its investment income in order to carry out its activities on a normal and continuing basis and to acquire new works of art. O has, for the entire period of its existence, been open to the public and more than 300,000 people (from S City and elsewhere) have visited the museum in each of the current taxable year and the four immediately preceding taxable years.

(ii) Under these circumstances, O does not meet the 33⅓ percent support test for its current year because it has received only 25 percent of its total support for the applicable five-year period from the general public. However, under the facts set forth above, O meets the 10 percent support limitation under paragraph (f)(3)(i) of this section, as well as the requirements of paragraph (f)(3)(ii) of this section. Under all of the facts set forth in this example, O is considered as meeting the requirements of the facts and circumstances test on the basis of satisfying paragraphs (f)(3)(i) and (f)(3)(ii) of this section and the factors set forth in paragraphs (f)(3)(iii)(A) through (f)(3)(iii)(D) of this section. O is therefore publicly supported for its current taxable year and the immediately succeeding taxable year.

Example 4. (i) In 1960, the P Philharmonic Orchestra was organized in T City through the combined efforts of a local music society and a local women's club to present to the public a wide variety of musical programs intended to foster music appreciation in the community. P is recognized as an organization described in section 501(c)(3). The orchestra is composed of professional musicians who are paid by the association. Twelve performances open to the public are scheduled each year. A small admission fee is charged for each of these performances. In addition, several performances are staged annually without charge. During the current taxable year and the four taxable years immediately preceding the current taxable year, P has received separate contributions of $200,000 each from A and B (not members of a single family) and support of $120,000 from the T Community Chest, a public federated fundraising organization operating in T City. P depends on these funds in order to carry out its activities and will continue to depend on contributions of this type to be made in the future. P has also begun a fundraising campaign in an attempt to expand its activities for the coming years. P is governed by a Board of Directors comprised of five individuals. A faculty member of a local college, the president of a local music society, the head of a local banking institution, a prominent doctor, and a member of the governing body of the local chamber of commerce currently serve on P's Board and represent the interests and views of the community in the activities carried on by P.

(ii) With respect to P's current taxable year, P's sources of support are computed on the basis of the current taxable year and the four taxable years immediately preceding the current taxable year, as follows:

Contributions	$520,000
Receipts from performances	100,000
Total support	$ 620,000
Less:	
Receipts from performances (excluded under paragraph (f)(7)(i)(A) of this section)	100,000
Total support for purposes of paragraphs (f)(2) and (f)(3)(i) of this section	$ 520,000

(iii) For purposes of paragraphs (f)(2) and (f)(3)(i) of this section, P's public support is computed as follows:

T Community Chest (indirect support from the general public)	$ 120,000
Two contributions from A & B (each in excess of $10,400—2 percent of total support) 2 × $10,400	20,800
Total	$ 140,800

(iv) Under these circumstances, P does not meet the 33⅓ percent support test for its current year because it has received only 27 percent of its total support ($140,800/$520,000) for the applicable five-year period from the general public. However, under the facts

set forth above, P meets the 10 percent support limitation under paragraph (f)(3)(i) of this section, as well as the requirements of paragraph (f)(3)(ii) of this section. Under all of the facts set forth in this example, P is considered as meeting the requirements of the facts and circumstances test on the basis of satisfying paragraphs (f)(3)(i) and (f)(3)(ii) of this section and the factors set forth in paragraphs (f)(3)(iii)(A) through (f)(3)(iii)(D) of this section. P is therefore publicly supported for its current taxable year and the immediately succeeding taxable year.

Example 5. (i) Q is recognized as an organization described in section 501(c)(3). It is a philanthropic organization founded in 1965 by C for the purpose of making annual contributions to worthy charities. C created Q as a charitable trust by the transfer of appreciated securities worth $500,000 to Q. Pursuant to the trust agreement, C and two other members of his family are the sole trustees of Q and are vested with the right to appoint successor trustees. In each of the current taxable year and the four taxable years immediately preced-

Investment income	$ 60,000
Contributions	40,000
Total support	$ 100,000

(iii) For purposes of paragraphs (f)(2) and (f)(3)(i) of this section, Q's public support is computed as follows:

Contributions from the general public	$ 15,000
C's contribution (in excess of $ 2,000 — 2 percent of total support) 1 X $2,000	2,000
Total	$ 17,000

(iv) Under these circumstances, Q does not meet the 33⅓ percent support test for its current year because it has received only 17 percent of its total support ($17,000/$100,000) for the applicable five-year period from the general public. Thus, Q's classification as a "publicly supported" organization depends on whether it meets the requirements of the facts and circumstances test. Even though it satisfies the 10 percent support limitation under paragraph (f)(3)(i) of this section, its method of solicitation makes it questionable whether Q satisfies the requirements of paragraph (f)(3)(ii) of this section. Because of its method of operating, Q also has a greater burden of establishing its publicly supported nature under paragraph (f)(3)(iii)(A) of this section. Based upon the foregoing facts and circumstances, including Q's failure to receive favorable consideration under the factors set forth in paragraphs (f)(3)(iii)(B), (f)(3)(iii)(C), and (f)(3)(iii)(D) of this section, Q does not satisfy the facts and circumstances test.

(10) *Community trust; introduction.*—Community trusts have often been established to attract large contributions of a capital or endowment nature for the benefit of a particular community or area, and often such contributions have come initially from a small number of donors. While the community trust generally has a governing body comprised of representatives of the particular community or area, its contributions are often received and maintained in the form of separate trusts or funds, which are subject to varying degrees of control by the governing body. To qualify as a "publicly supported" organization, a community trust must meet the 33⅓ percent support test, or, if it cannot meet that test, be organized and operated so as to attract new and additional public or governmental support on a continuous basis sufficient to meet the facts and circumstances test. Such facts and circumstances test includes a requirement of attraction of public support in paragraph (f)(3)(ii) of this section which, as applied to community trusts, generally will be satisfied if they seek gifts and bequests from a wide range of potential donors in the community or area served, through banks or trust companies, through attorneys or other professional persons, or in other appropriate ways that call attention to the community trust as a potential recipient of gifts and bequests made for the benefit of the community or area served. A community trust is not required to engage in periodic, community-wide, fundraising campaigns directed toward attracting a large number of small contributions in a manner similar to campaigns conducted by a community chest or united fund. Paragraph (f)(11) of this section provides rules for determining the extent to which separate trusts or funds may be treated as component parts of a community trust, fund, or foundation (herein collectively referred to as a "community trust," and sometimes referred to as an "organization") for purposes of meeting the requirements of this paragraph for classification as a publicly supported organization. Paragraph (f)(12) of this section contains rules for trusts or funds that are prevented from qualifying as component parts of a community trust by paragraph (f)(11) of this section.

(11) *Community trusts; requirements for treatment as a single entity.*—(i) *General rule.*—For purposes of sections 170, 501, 507, 508, 509, and Chapter 42, any organization that meets the requirements contained in paragraphs (f)(11)(iii) through (f)(11)(vi) of this section will be treated as a single entity, rather than as an aggregation of separate funds, and except as otherwise provided, all funds associated with such organization (whether a trust, not-for-profit corporation, unincorporated association, or a combination thereof) which meet the requirements of paragraph (f)(11)(ii) of this section will be treated as component parts of such organization.

ing the current taxable year, Q received $12,000 in investment income from its original endowment. Each year Q makes a solicitation for funds by operating a charity ball at C's residence. Guests are invited and requested to make contributions of $100 per couple. During the five-year period at issue, $15,000 was received from the proceeds of these events. C and his family have also made contributions to Q of $25,000 over the five-year period at issue. Q makes disbursements each year of substantially all of its net income to the public charities chosen by the trustees.

(ii) Q's sources of support for the current taxable year and the four taxable years immediately preceding the current taxable year as follows:

(ii) *Component part of a community trust.*—In order to be treated as a component part of a community trust referred to in this paragraph (f)(11) (rather than as a separate trust or not-for-profit corporation or association), a trust or fund—

(A) Must be created by a gift, bequest, legacy, devise, or other transfer to a community trust which is treated as a single entity under this paragraph (f)(11); and

(B) May not be directly or indirectly subjected by the transferor to any material restriction or condition (within the meaning of § 1.507-2(a)(7)) with respect to the transferred assets. For purposes of this paragraph (f)(11)(ii)(B), if the transferor is not a private foundation, the provisions of § 1.507-2(a)(7) shall be applied to the trust or fund as if the transferor were a private foundation established and funded by the person establishing the trust or fund and such foundation transferred all its assets to the trust or fund. Any transfer made to a fund or trust which is treated as a component part of a community trust under this paragraph (f)(11)(ii) will be treated as a transfer made "to" a "publicly supported" community trust for purposes of sections 170(b)(1)(A) and 507(b)(1)(A) if such community trust meets the requirements of section 170(b)(1)(A)(vi) as a "publicly supported" organization at the time of the transfer, except as provided in paragraph (f)(5)(ii) of this section or §§ 1.508-1(b)(4) and 1.508-1(b)(6) (relating, generally, to reliance by grantors and contributors). See also paragraphs (f)(12)(ii) and (f)(12)(iii) of this section for special provisions relating to split-interest trusts and certain private foundations described in section 170(b)(1)(F)(iii).

(iii) *Name.*—The organization must be commonly known as a community trust, fund, foundation, or other similar name conveying the concept of a capital or endowment fund to support charitable activities (within the meaning of section 170(c)(1) or section 170(c)(2)(B)) in the community or area it serves.

(iv) *Common instrument.*—All funds of the organization must be subject to a common governing instrument or a master trust or agency agreement (herein referred to as the "governing instrument"), which may be embodied in a single document or several documents containing common language. Language in an instrument of transfer to the community trust making a fund subject to the community trust's governing instrument or master trust or agency agreement will satisfy the requirements of this paragraph (f)(11)(iv). In addition, if a community trust adopts a new governing instrument (or creates a corporation) to put into effect new provisions (applying to future transfers to the community trust), the adoption of such new governing instrument (or creation of a corporation with a governing instrument) which contains common language with the existing governing instrument shall not preclude the community trust from meeting the requirements of this paragraph (f)(11)(iv).

(v) *Common governing body.*—(A) The organization must have a common governing body or distribution committee (herein referred to as the "governing body") which either directs or, in the case of a fund designated for specified beneficiaries, monitors the distribution of all of the funds exclusively for charitable purposes (within the meaning of section 170(c)(1) or section 170(c)(2)(B)). For purposes of this paragraph (f)(11)(v), a fund is designated for specified beneficiaries only if no person is left with the discretion to direct the distribution of the fund.

(B) *Powers of modification and removal.*—The fact that the exercise of any power described in this paragraph (f)(11)(v)(B) is reviewable by an appropriate State authority will not preclude the community trust from meeting the requirements of this paragraph (f)(11)(v)(B). Except as provided in paragraph (f)(11)(v)(C) of this section, the governing body must have the power in the governing instrument, the instrument of transfer, the resolutions or by-laws of the governing body, a written agreement, or otherwise

(1) To modify any restriction or condition on the distribution of funds for any specified charitable purposes or to specified organizations if in the sole judgment of the governing body (without the necessity of the approval of any participating trustee, custodian, or agent), such restriction or condition becomes, in effect, unnecessary, incapable of fulfillment, or inconsistent with the charitable needs of the community or area served;

(2) To replace any participating trustee, custodian, or agent for breach of fiduciary duty under State law; and

(3) To replace any participating trustee, custodian, or agent for failure to produce a reasonable (as determined by the governing body) return of net income (within the meaning of paragraph (f)(11)(v)(F) of this section) over a reasonable period of time (as determined by the governing body).

(C) *Transitional rule.*—(1) Notwithstanding paragraph (f)(11)(v)(B) of this section, if a community trust meets the requirements of paragraph (f)(11)(v)(C)(3) of this section, then in the case of any instrument of transfer which is executed before July 19, 1977, and is not revoked or amended thereafter (with respect to any dispositive provision affecting the transfer to the community trust), and in the case of any instrument of transfer which is irrevocable on January 19, 1982, the governing body must have the power to cause proceedings to be instituted (by request to the appropriate State authority)

(i) To modify any restriction or condition on the distribution of funds for any specified charitable purposes or to specified organizations if in the judgment of the governing body such restriction or condition becomes, in effect, unnecessary, incapable of fulfillment, or inconsistent with the charitable needs of the community or area served; and

(ii) To remove any participating trustee, custodian, or agent for breach of fiduciary duty under State law.

(2) The necessity for the governing body to obtain the approval of a participating trustee to exercise the powers described in paragraph (f)(11)(v)(C)(1) of this section shall be treated as not preventing the governing body from having such power, unless (and until) such approval has been (or is) requested by the governing body and has been (or is) denied.

(3) Paragraph (f)(11)(v)(C)(1) of this section shall not apply unless the community trust meets the requirements of paragraph (f)(11)(v)(B) of this section, with respect to funds other than those under instruments of transfer described in the first sentence of such paragraph (f)(11)(v)(C)(1) of this section, by January 19, 1978, or such later date as the Commissioner may provide for such community trust, and unless the community trust does not, once it so complies, thereafter solicit for funds that will not qualify under the requirements of paragraph (f)(11)(v)(B) of this section.

(D) *Inconsistent State law.*—(1) For purposes of paragraphs (f)(11)(v)(B)(1), (f)(11)(v)(B)(2), (f)(11)(v)(B)(3), (f)(11)(v)(C)(1)(i), (f)(11)(v)(C)(1)(ii), and (f)(11)(v)(E) of this section, if a power described in such a provision is inconsistent with State law even if such power were expressly granted to the governing body by the governing instrument and were accepted without limitation under an instrument of transfer, then the community trust will be treated as meeting the requirements of such a provision if it meets such requirements to the fullest extent possible consistent with State law (if such power is or had been so expressly granted).

(2) For example, if, under the conditions of paragraph (f)(11)(v)(D)(1) of this section, the power to modify is inconsistent with State law, but the power to institute proceedings to modify, if so expressly granted, would be consistent with State law, the community trust will be treated as meeting such requirements to the fullest extent possible if the governing body has the power (in the governing instrument or otherwise) to institute proceedings to modify a condition or restriction. On the other hand, if in such a case the community trust has only the power to cause proceedings to be instituted to modify a condition or restriction, it will not be treated as meeting such requirements to the fullest extent possible.

(3) In addition, if, for example, under the conditions of paragraph (f)(11)(v)(D)(1) of this section, the power to modify and the power to institute proceedings to modify a condition or restriction is inconsistent with State law, but the power to cause such proceedings to be instituted would be consistent with State law, if it were expressly granted in the governing instrument and if the approval of the State Attorney General were obtained, then the community trust will be treated as meeting such requirements to the fullest extent possible if it has the power (in the governing instrument or otherwise) to cause such proceedings to be instituted, even if such

proceedings can be instituted only with the approval of the State Attorney General.

(E) *Exercise of powers.*—The governing body shall (by resolution or otherwise) commit itself to exercise the powers described in paragraphs (f)(11)(v)(B), (f)(11)(v)(C), and (f)(11)(v)(D) of this section in the best interests of the community trust. The governing body will be considered not to be so committed where it has grounds to exercise such a power and fails to exercise it by taking appropriate action. Such appropriate action may include, for example, consulting with the appropriate State authority prior to taking action to replace a participating trustee.

(F) *Reasonable return.*—In addition to the requirements of paragraphs (f)(11)(v)(B), (f)(11)(v)(C), (f)(11)(v)(D), or (f)(11)(v)(E) of this section, the governing body shall (by resolution or otherwise) commit itself to obtain information and take other appropriate steps with the view to seeing that each participating trustee, custodian, or agent, with respect to each restricted trust or fund that is, and with respect to the aggregate of the unrestricted trusts or funds that are, a component part of the community trust, administers such trust or fund in accordance with the terms of its governing instrument and accepted standards of fiduciary conduct to produce a reasonable return of net income (or appreciation where not inconsistent with the community trust's need for current income), with due regard to safety of principal, in furtherance of the exempt purposes of the community trust (except for assets held for the active conduct of the community trust's exempt activities). In the case of a low return of net income (and, where appropriate, appreciation), the IRS will examine carefully whether the governing body has, in fact, committed itself to take the appropriate steps. For purposes of this paragraph (f)(11)(v)(F), any income that has been designated by the donor of the gift or bequest to which such income is attributable as being available only for the use or benefit of a broad charitable purpose, such as the encouragement of higher education or the promotion of better health care in the community, will be treated as unrestricted. However, any income that has been designated for the use or benefit of a named charitable organization or agency or for the use or benefit of a particular class of charitable organizations or agencies, the members of which are readily ascertainable and are less than five in number, will be treated as restricted.

(vi) *Common reports.*—The organization must prepare periodic financial reports treating all of the funds which are held by the community trust, either directly or in component parts, as funds of the organization.

(12) *Community trusts; treatment of trusts and not-for-profit corporations and associations not included as components.*—(i) For purposes of sections 170, 501, 507, 508, 509, and Chapter 42, any trust or not-for-profit corporation or association that is alleged to be a component part of a community trust, but that fails to meet the requirements of paragraph (f)(11)(ii) of this section, shall not be treated as a component part of a community trust and, if a trust, shall be treated as a separate trust and be subject to the provisions of section 501, section 4947(a)(1), or section 4947(a)(2), as the case may be. If such organization is a not-for-profit corporation or association, it will be treated as a separate entity, and, if it is described in section 501(c)(3), it will be treated as a private foundation unless it is described in section 509(a)(1), section 509(a)(2), section 509(a)(3), or section 509(a)(4). In the case of a fund that is ultimately treated as not being a component part of a community trust pursuant to this paragraph (f)(12), if the Forms 990 filed annually by the community trust included financial information with respect to such fund and treated such fund in the same manner as other component parts thereof, such returns filed by the community trust prior to the taxable year in which the Commissioner notifies such fund that it will not be treated as a component part will be treated as its separate return for purpose of Subchapter A of Chapter 61 of Subtitle F, and the first such return filed by the community trust will be treated as the notification required of the separate entity for purposes of section 508(a).

(ii) If a transfer is made in trust to a community trust to make income or other payments for a period of a life or lives in being or a term of years to any individual or for any noncharitable purpose, followed by payments to or for the use of the community trust (such as in the case of a charitable remainder annuity trust or a charitable remainder unitrust described in section 664 or a pooled income fund described in section 642(c)(5)), such trust will be treated as a component part of the community trust upon the termination of all intervening noncharitable interests and rights to the actual possession or enjoyment of the property if such trust satisfies the requirements of paragraph (f)(11) of this section at such time. Until such time, the trust will be treated as a separate trust. If a transfer is made in trust to a community trust to make income or other payments to or for the use of the community trust, followed by payments to any individual or for any noncharitable purpose, such trust will be treated as a separate trust rather than as a component part of the community trust. See section 4947(a)(2) and the related regulations for the treatment of such split-interest trusts. The provisions of this paragraph (f)(12)(ii) provide rules only for determining when a charitable remainder trust or pooled income fund may be treated as a component part of a community trust and are not intended to preclude a community trust from maintaining a charitable remainder trust or pooled income fund. For purposes of grantors and contributors, a pooled income fund of a publicly supported community trust shall be treated no differently than a pooled income fund of any other publicly supported organization.

(iii) An organization described in section 170(b)(1)(F)(iii) will not ordinarily satisfy the requirements of paragraph (f)(11)(ii) of this section because of the unqualified right of the donor to designate the recipients of the income and principal of the trust. Such organization will therefore ordinarily be treated as other than a component part of a community trust under paragraph (f)(12)(i) of this section. However, see section 170(b)(1)(F)(iii) and the related regulations with respect to the treatment of contributions to such organizations.

(13) *Method of accounting.*—For purposes of section 170(b)(1)(A)(vi), an organization's support will be determined under the method of accounting on the basis of which the organization regularly computes its income in keeping its books under section 446. For example, if a grantor makes a grant to an organization payable over a term of years, such grant will be includible in the support fraction of the grantee organization under the method of accounting on the basis of which the grantee organization regularly computes its income in keeping its books under section 446.

(14) *Transition rules.*—(i) An organization that received an advance ruling, that expires on or after June 9, 2008, that it will be treated as an organization described in sections 170(b)(1)(A)(vi) and 509(a)(1) will be treated as meeting the requirements of paragraph (f)(2) or paragraph (f)(3) of this section for the first five taxable years of its existence as a section 501(c)(3) organization unless the IRS issued to the organization a proposed determination prior to September 9, 2008, that the organization is not described in sections 170(b)(1)(A)(vi) and 509(a)(1) or in section 509(a)(2).

(ii) Paragraph (f)(4)(v) of this section shall not apply with respect to an organization that received an advance ruling that expired prior to June 9, 2008, and that did not timely file with the Internal Revenue Service the required information to establish that it is an organization described in sections 170(b)(1)(A)(vi) and 509(a)(1) or in section 509(a)(2).

(iii) An organization that fails to meet a public support test for its first taxable year beginning on or after January 1, 2008, under the regulations in this section may use the prior tests set forth in § 1.170A-9(e)(2) or § 1.170A-9(e)(3), or in § § 1.509(a)-3(a)(2) and 1.509(a)-3(a)(3), as in effect before September 9, 2008 (as contained in 26 CFR part 1 revised April 1, 2008), to determine whether the organization was publicly supported for its 2008 taxable year based on its satisfaction of a public support test for taxable year 2007, computed over the period 2003 through 2006.

(iv) *Examples.*—The application of this paragraph (f)(14) may be illustrated by the following examples:

Example 1. (i) Organization X was formed in January 2004 and uses a taxable year ending June 30. Organization X received an advance ruling letter that it is recognized as an organization described in section 501(c)(3) effective as of the date of its formation and that it is treated as a publicly supported organization under sections 170(b)(1)(A)(vi) and 509(a)(1) during the five-year advance ruling period that will end on June 30, 2008. This date is on or after June 9, 2008.

(ii) Under the transition rule, Organization X is a publicly supported organization described in sections 170(b)(1)(A)(vi) and 509(a)(1) for the taxable years ending June 30, 2004, through June 30, 2008. Organization X does not need to establish within 90 days after June 30, 2008, that it met a public support test under § 1.170A-9(e) or § 1.509(a)-3, as in effect prior to September 9, 2008, (as contained in 26 CFR part 1 revised April 1, 2008), for its advance ruling period.

(iii) Organization X can qualify as a publicly supported organization for the taxable year ending June 30, 2009, if Organization X can meet the requirements of paragraph (f)(2) or (f)(3) of this section or § § 1.509(a)-3(a)(2) and 1.509(a)-3(a)(3) for the taxable years ending June 30, 2005, through June 30, 2009, or for the taxable years ending June 30, 2004, through June 30, 2008. In addition, for its taxable year ending June 30, 2009, Organization X may qualify as a publicly supported organization by availing itself of the transition rule contained in paragraph (f)(14)(iii) of this section, which looks to support received by X in the taxable years ending June 30, 2004, through June 30, 2007.

Example 2. (i) Organization Y was formed in January 2000, and uses a taxable year ending December 31. Organization Y received a

final determination that it was recognized as tax-exempt under section 501(c)(3) and as a publicly supported organization prior to September 9, 2008.

(ii) For taxable year 2008, Organization Y will qualify as publicly supported if it meets the requirements under either paragraph (f)(2) or (f)(3) of this section or § § 1.509(a)-3(a)(2) or 1.509(a)-3(a)(3) for the five-year period January 1, 2004, through December 31, 2008. Organization Y will also qualify as publicly supported for taxable year 2008 if it meets the requirements under § 1.170A-9(e)(2) or § 1.170A-9(e)(3), or under § § 1.509(a)-3(a)(2) and 1.509(a)-3(a)(3), as in effect prior to September 9, 2008, (as contained in 26 CFR part 1 revised April 1, 2008) for taxable year 2007, using the four-year period from January 1, 2003, through December 31, 2006.

(g) *Private operating foundation.*—An organization is described in section 170(b)(1)(A)(vii) and (E)(i) if it is a private "operating foundation" as defined in section 4942(j)(3) and the regulations thereunder.

(h) *Private nonoperating foundation distributing amount equal to all contributions received.*—(1) *In general.*—(i) An organization is described in section 170(b)(1)(A)(vii) and (E)(ii) if it is a private foundation which, not later than the 15th day of the third month after the close of its taxable year in which any contributions are received, distributes an amount equal in value to 100 percent of all contributions received in such year. Such distributions must be qualifying distributions (as defined in section 4942(g) without regard to paragraph (3) thereof) which are treated, after the application of section 4942(g)(3), as distributions out of corpus in accordance with section 4942(h). Qualifying distributions, as defined in section 4942(g) without regard to paragraph (3) thereof, cannot be made to (i) an organization controlled directly or indirectly by the foundation or by one or more disqualified persons (as defined in section 4946) with respect to the foundation or (ii) a private foundation which is not an operating foundation (as defined in section 4942(j)(3)). The phrase "after the application of section 4942(g)(3)" means that every contribution described in section 4942(g)(3) received by a private foundation described in this subparagraph in a particular taxable year must be distributed (within the meaning of section 4942(g)(3)(A)) by such foundation not later than the 15th day of the third month after the close of such taxable year in order for any other distribution by such foundation to be counted toward the 100-percent requirement described in this subparagraph.

(ii) In order for an organization to meet the distribution requirements of subdivision (i) of this subparagraph, it must, not later than the 15th day of the third month after the close of its taxable year in which any contributions are received, distribute (within the meaning of subdivision (i) of this subparagraph) an amount equal in value to 100 percent of all contributions received in such year and have no remaining undistributed income for such year.

(iii) The provisions of this subparagraph may be illustrated by the following examples:

Example (1). X is a private foundation on a calendar year basis. As of January 1, 1971, X had no undistributed income for 1970. X's distributable amount for 1971 was $600,000. In July 1971, A, an individual, contributed $500,000 (fair market value determined at the time of the contribution) of appreciated property to X (which, if sold, would give rise to long-term capital gain). X did not receive any other contribution in either 1970 or 1971. During 1971, X made qualifying distributions of $700,000 which were treated as made out of the undistributed income for 1971 and $100,000 out of corpus. X will meet the requirements of section 170(b)(1)(E)(ii) for 1971 if it makes additional qualifying distributions of $400,000 out of corpus by March 15, 1972.

Example (2). Assume the facts as stated in Example (1), except that as of January 1, 1971, X had $100,000 of undistributed income for 1970. Under these circumstances, the $700,000 distributed by X in 1971 would be treated as made out of the undistributed income for 1970 and 1971. X would therefore have to make additional qualifying distributions of $500,000 out of corpus between January 1, 1972, and March 15, 1972, in order to meet the requirements of section 170(b)(1)(E)(ii) for 1971.

(2) *Special rules.*—In applying subparagraph (1) of this paragraph—

(i) For purposes of section 170(b)(1)(A)(vii), an organization described in section 170(b)(1)(E)(ii) must distribute all contributions received in any year, whether of cash or property. However, solely for purposes of section 170(e)(1)(B)(ii), an organization described in section 170(b)(1)(E)(ii) is required to distribute all contributions of property only received in any year. Contributions for purposes of this paragraph do not include bequests, legacies, devises, or transfers within the meaning of section 2055 or 2106(a)(2) with respect to which a deduction was not allowed under section 170.

(ii) Any distributions made by a private foundation pursuant to subparagraph (1) of this paragraph with respect to a particular taxable year shall be treated as made first out of contributions of property and then out of contributions of cash received by such foundation in such year.

(iii) A private foundation is not required to trace specific contributions of property, or amounts into which such contributions are converted, to specific distributions.

(iv) For purposes of satisfying the requirements of section 170(b)(1)(D)(ii), except as provided to the contrary in this subdivision (iv), the fair market value of contributed property, determined on the date of contribution, is required to be used for purposes of determining whether an amount equal in value to 100 percent of the contributions received has been distributed. However, reasonable selling expenses, if any, incurred by the foundation in the sale of the contributed property may be deducted from the fair market value of the contributed property on the date of contribution, and distribution of the balance of the fair market value will satisfy the 100 percent distribution requirement. If a private foundation receives a contribution of property and, within 30 days thereafter, either sells the property or makes an in kind distribution of the property to a public charity, then at the choice of the private foundation the gross amount received on the sale (less reasonable selling expenses incurred) or the fair market value of the contributed property at the date of its distribution to the public charity, and not the fair market value of the contributed property on the date of contribution (less reasonable selling expenses, if any), is considered to be the amount of the fair market value of the contributed property for purposes of the requirements of section 170(b)(1)(D)(ii).

(v) A private foundation may satisfy the requirements of subparagraph (1) of this paragraph for a particular taxable year by electing (pursuant to section 4942(h)(2) and the regulations thereunder) to treat a portion or all of one or more distributions, made not later than the 15th day of the third month after the close of such year, as made out of corpus.

(3) *Transitional rules.*—(i) *Taxable years beginning before January 1, 1970, and ending after December 31, 1969.*—In order for an organization to meet the distribution requirements of subparagraph (1)(i) of this paragraph for a taxable year which begins before January 1, 1970 and ends after December 31, 1969, it must, not later than the 15th day of the third month after the close of such taxable year, distribute (within the meaning of subparagraph (1)(i) of this paragraph) an amount equal in value to 100 percent of all contributions (other than contributions described in section 4942(g)(3)) which were received between January 1, 1970 and the last day of such taxable year. Because the organization is not subject to the provisions of section 4942 for such year, the organization need not satisfy subparagraph (1)(ii) of this paragraph or the phrase "after the application of section 4942(g)(3)" for such year.

(ii) *Extension of period.*—For purposes of section 170(b)(1)(A)(vii) and (e)(1)(B)(ii), in the case of a taxable year ending in either 1970, 1971 or 1972, the period referred to in section 170(b)(1)(E)(ii) for making distributions shall not expire before April 2, 1973.

(4) *Adequate records required.*—A taxpayer claiming a deduction under section 170 for a charitable contribution to a foundation described in subparagraph (1) of this paragraph must obtain adequate records or other sufficient evidence from such foundation showing that the foundation made the required qualifying distributions within the time prescribed. Such records or other evidence must be attached to the taxpayer's return for the taxable year for which the charitable contribution deduction is claimed. If necessary, an amended income tax return or claim for refund may be filed in accordance with § 301.6402-2 and § 301.6402-3 of this chapter (Procedure and Administration Regulations).

(i) *Private foundation maintaining a common fund.*—(1) *Designation by substantial contributors.*—An organization is described in section 170(b)(1)(A)(vii) and (E)(iii) if it is a private foundation all of the contributions to which are pooled in a common fund and which would be described in section 509(a)(3) but for the right of any donor who is a substantial contributor or his spouse to designate annually the recipients, from among private charities, of the income attributable to the donor's contribution to the fund and to direct (by deed or by will) the payment, to public charities, of the corpus in the common fund attributable to the donor's contribution. For purposes of this paragraph the private foundation is to be treated as meeting the requirements of section 509(a)(3)(A) and (B) even though donors to the foundation, or their spouses, retain the right to, and in fact do, designate public charities to receive income or corpus from the fund.

(2) *Distribution requirements.*—To qualify under subparagraph (1) of this paragraph, the private foundation described therein must be

required by its governing instrument to distribute, and it must in fact distribute (including administrative expenses)—

(i) All of the adjusted net income (as defined in section 4942(f)) of the common fund to one or more public charities not later than the 15th day of the third month after the close of the taxable year in which such income is realized by the fund, and

(ii) All the corpus attributable to any donor's contribution to the fund to one or more public charities not later than one year after the donor's death or after the death of the donor's surviving spouse if such surviving spouse has the right to designate the recipients of such corpus.

(3) *Failure to designate.*—A private foundation will not fail to qualify under this paragraph merely because a substantial contributor or his spouse fails to exercise his right to designate the recipients of income or corpus of the fund provided that the income and corpus attributable to his contribution are distributed as required by subparagraph (2) of this paragraph.

(4) *Definitions.*—For purposes of this paragraph—

(i) The term "substantial contributor" is as defined in section 507(d)(2) and the regulations thereunder.

(ii) The term "public charity" means an organization described in section 170(b)(1)(A)(i) through (vi). If an organization is described in section 170(b)(1)(A)(i) through (vi), and is also described in section 170(b)(1)(A)(viii), it shall be treated as a public charity for purposes of this paragraph.

(iii) The term "income attributable to" means the income earned by the fund which is properly allocable to the contributed amount by any reasonable and consistently applied method. See, for example, § 1.642(c)-5(c).

(iv) The term "corpus attributable to" means the portion of the corpus of the fund attributable to the contributed amount. Such portion may be determined by any reasonable and consistently applied method.

(v) The term "donor" means any individual who makes a contribution (whether of cash or property) to the private foundation, whether or not such individual is a substantial contributor.

(j) *Section 509(a)(2) or (3) organization.*—An organization is described in section 170(b)(1)(A)(viii) if it is described in section 509(a)(2) or (3) and the regulations thereunder.

(k) *Effective/applicability date.*—(1) *In general.*—These regulations shall apply to taxable years beginning after December 31, 1969.

(2) *Applicability date.*—The regulations in paragraph (f) of this section shall apply to taxable years beginning on or after January 1, 2008. For tax years beginning after December 31, 1969, and beginning before January 1, 2008, see § 1.170A-9(e) (as contained in 26 CFR part 1 revised April 1, 2008).

(3) *Applicability date.*—Paragraph (f)(7)(v) of this section applies to taxable years beginning on or after December 2, 2020. Taxpayers may choose to apply this section to taxable years beginning on or after January 1, 2018, and before December 2, 2020. [Reg. § 1.170A-9].

☐ [*T.D. 7242, 12-29-72. Amended by T.D. 7406, 2-13-76; T.D. 7440, 11-11-76; T.D. 7465, 1-19-77; T.D. 7579, 2-28-80; T.D. 8100, 9-3-86; T.D. 8991, 4-24-2002; T.D. 9423, 9-8-2008, T.D. 9549, 9-7-2011 and T.D. 9933, 11-30-2020.*]

[Reg. § 1.170A-10]

§ 1.170A-10. Charitable contributions carryovers of individuals.—(a) *In general.*—(1) Section 170(d)(1), relating to carryover of charitable contributions in excess of 50 percent of contribution base, and section 170(b)(1)(D)(ii), relating to carryover of charitable contributions in excess of 30 percent of contribution base, provide for excess charitable contributions carryovers by individuals of charitable contributions to section 170(b)(1)(A) organizations described in § 1.170A-9. These carryovers shall be determined as provided in paragraphs (b) and (c) of this section. No excess charitable contributions carryover shall be allowed with respect to contributions "for the use of", rather than "to", section 170(b)(1)(A) organizations or with respect to contributions "to" or "for the use of" organizations which are not section 170(b)(1)(A) organizations. See § 1.170A-8(a)(2) for definitions of "to" or "for the use of" a charitable organization.

(2) The carryover provisions apply with respect to contributions made during a taxable year in excess of the applicable percentage limitation even though the taxpayer elects under section 144 to take the standard deduction in that year instead of itemizing the deduction allowable in computing taxable income for that year.

(3) For provisions requiring a reduction of the excess charitable contribution computed under paragraph (b)(1) or (c)(1) of this section when there is a net operating loss carryover to the taxable year, see paragraph (d)(1) of this section.

(4) The provisions of section 170(b)(1)(D)(ii) and (d)(1) and this section do not apply to contributions by an estate; nor do they apply to a trust unless the trust is a private foundation which, pursuant to §1.642(c)-4, is allowed a deduction under section 170 subject to the provisions applicable to individuals.

(b) *50-percent charitable contributions carryover of individuals.*— (1) *Computation of excess of charitable contributions made in a contribution year.*—Under section 170(d)(1), subject to certain conditions and limitations, the excess of—

(i) The amount of the charitable contributions made by an individual in a taxable year (hereinafter in this paragraph referred to as the "contribution year") to section 170(b)(1)(A) organizations described in §1.170A-9, over

(ii) 50 percent of his contribution base, as defined in section 170(b)(1)(F), for such contribution year,

shall be treated as a charitable contribution paid by him to a section 170(b)(1)(A) organization in each of the 5 taxable years immediately succeeding the contribution year in order of time. However, such excess to the extent it consists of contributions of 30-percent capital gain property, as defined in §1.170-A-8(d)(3), shall be subject to the rules of section 170(b)(1)(D)(ii) and paragraph (c) of this section in the years to which it is carried over. A charitable contribution made in a taxable year beginning before January 1, 1970, to a section 170(b)(1)(A) organization and carried over to a taxable year beginning after December 31, 1969, under section 170(b)(5) (before its amendment by the Tax Reform Act of 1969) shall be treated in such taxable year beginning after December 31, 1969, as a charitable contribution of cash subject to the limitations of this paragraph, whether or not such carryover consists of contributions of 30-percent capital gain property or of ordinary income property described in §1.170A-4(b)(1). For purposes of applying this paragraph and paragraph (c) of this section, such a carryover from a taxable year beginning before January 1, 1970, which is so treated as paid to a section 170(b)(1)(A) organization in a taxable year beginning after December 31, 1969, shall be treated as paid to such an organization under section 170(d)(1) of this section. The provisions of this subparagraph may be illustrated by the following examples:

Example (1). Assume that H and W (husband and wife) have a contribution base for 1970 of $50,000 and for 1971 of $40,000 and file a joint return for each year. Assume further that in 1970 they make a charitable contribution in cash of $26,500 to a church and $1,000 to X (not a section 170(b)(1)(A) organization) and in 1971 they make a charitable contribution in cash of $19,000 to a church and $600 to X. They may claim a charitable contributions deduction of $25,000 in 1970, and the excess of $26,500 (contribution to the church) over $25,000 (50 percent of contribution base), or $1,500, constitutes a charitable contributions carryover which shall be treated as a charitable contribution paid by them to a section 170(b)(1)(A) organization in each of the 5 succeeding taxable years in order of time. No carryover is allowed with respect to the $1,000 contribution made to X in 1970. Since 50 percent of their contribution base for 1971 ($20,000) exceeds the charitable contributions of $19,000 made by them in 1971 to section 170(b)(1)(A) organizations (computed without regard to section 170(b)(1)(D)(ii) and (d)(1) and this section), the portion of the 1970 carryover equal to such excess of $1,000 ($20,000 minus $19,000) is treated, pursuant to the provisions of subparagraph (2) of this paragraph, as paid to a section 170(b)(1)(A) organization in 1971; the remaining $500 constitutes an unused charitable contributions carryover. No deduction for 1971, and no carryover, are allowed with respect to the $600 contribution made to X in 1971.

Example (2). Assume the same facts as in example (1) except that H and W have a contribution base for 1971 of $42,000. Since 50 percent of their contribution base for 1971 ($21,000) exceeds by $2,000 the charitable contribution of $19,000 made by them in 1971 to the section 170(b)(1)(A) organization (computed without regard to section 170(b)(1)(D)(ii) and (d)(1) and this section), the full amount of the 1970 carryover of $1,500 is treated, pursuant to the provisions of subparagraph (2) of this paragraph, as paid to a section 170(b)(1)(A) organization in 1971. They may also claim a charitable contribution of $500 ($21,000 – $20,500 [$19,000 + $1,500]) with respect to the gift to X in 1971. No carryover is allowed with respect to the $100 ($600 – $500) of the contribution to X which is not deductible in 1971.

(2) *Determination of amount treated as paid in taxable years succeeding contribution year.*—In applying the provisions of subparagraph (1) of this paragraph, the amount of the excess computed in accordance with the provisions of such subparagraph and paragraph (d)(1) of this section which is to be treated as paid in any one of the 5 taxable years immediately succeeding the contribution year to a section 170(b)(1)(A) organization shall not exceed the lesser of the amounts computed under subdivision (i) to (iii), inclusive, of this subparagraph:

(i) The amount by which 50 percent of the taxpayer's contribution base for such succeeding taxable year exceeds the sum of—

(a) The charitable contributions actually made (computed without regard to the provisions of section 170(b)(1)(D)(ii) and (d)(1) and this section) by the taxpayer in such succeeding taxable year to section 170(b)(1)(A) organizations, and

(b) The charitable contributions, other than contributions of 30 percent capital gain property, made to section 170(b)(1)(A) organizations in taxable years preceding the contribution year which, pursuant to the provisions of section 170(d)(1) and this section, are treated as having been paid to a section 170(b)(1)(A) organization in such succeeding taxable year.

(ii) In the case of the first taxable year succeeding the contribution year, the amount of the excess charitable contribution in the contribution year, computed under subparagraph (1) of this paragraph and paragraph (d)(1) of this section.

(iii) In the case of the second, third, fourth, and fifth taxable years succeeding the contribution year, the portion of the excess charitable contribution in the contribution year, computed under subparagraph (1) of this paragraph and paragraph (d)(1) of this section, which has not been treated as paid to a section 170(b)(1)(A) organization in a year intervening between the contribution year and such succeeding taxable year.

For purposes of applying subdivision (i)(a) of this subparagraph, the amount of charitable contributions of 30-percent capital gain property actually made in a taxable year succeeding the contribution year shall be determined by first applying the 30-percent limitation of section 170(b)(1)(D)(i) and paragraph (d) of §1.170A-8. If a taxpayer, in any one of the 4 taxable years succeeding a contribution year, elects under section 144 to take the standard deduction instead of itemizing the deductions allowable in computing taxable income, there shall be treated as paid (but not allowable as a deduction) in such standard deduction year the lesser of the amounts determined under subdivisions (i) to (iii), inclusive, of this subparagraph. The provisions of this subparagraph may be illustrated by the following examples:

Example (1). Assume that B has a contribution base for 1970 of $20,000 and for 1971 of $30,000. Assume further than in 1970 B contributed $12,000 in cash to a church and in 1971 he contributed $13,500 in cash to the church. B may claim a charitable contributions deduction of $10,000 in 1970, and the excess of $12,000 (contribution to the church) over $10,000 (50 percent of B's contribution base), or $2,000, constitutes a charitable contributions carryover which shall be treated as a charitable contribution paid by B to a section 170(b)(1)(A) organization in the 5 taxable years succeeding 1970 in order of time. B may claim a charitable contributions deduction of $15,000 in 1971. Such $15,000 consists of the $13,500 contribution to the church in 1971 and $1,500 carried over from 1970 and treated as a charitable contribution paid to a section 170(b)(1)(A) organization in 1971. The $1,500 contribution treated as paid in 1971 is computed as follows:

1970 excess contributions		$2,000
50 percent of B's contribution base for 1971		15,000
Less:		
Contributions actually made in 1971 to section 170(b)(1)(A) organizations	$13,500	
Contributions made to section 170(b)(1)(A) organizations in taxable years prior to 1970 treated as having been paid in 1971	0	$13,500
Balance		1,500

Amount of 1970 excess treated as paid in 1971—the lesser of $2,000 (1970 excess contributions) or $1,500 (excess of 50 percent of contribution base for 1971 ($15,000) over the sum of the section 170(b)(1)(A) contributions actually made in 1971 ($13,500) and the section 170(b)(1)(A) contributions made in years prior to 1970 treated as having been paid in 1971 ($0)) 1,500

If the excess contributions made by B in 1971 had been $1,000 instead of $2,000, then, for purposes of this example, the amount of the 1970 excess treated as paid in 1971 would be $1,000 rather than $1,500.

Example (2). Assume the same facts as in example (1), and, in addition, that B has a contribution base for 1972 of $10,000 and for 1973 of $20,000. Assume further with respect to 1972 that B elects

Itemized Deductions for Individuals and Corps.
See p. 20,601 for regulations not amended to reflect law changes
25,565

under section 144 to take the standard deduction in computing taxable income and that his actual contributions to section 170(b)(1)(A) organizations in that year are $300 in cash. Assume further that with respect to 1973 that B itemizes his deductions, which include a $5,000 cash contribution to a church. B's deductions for 1972 are not increased by reason of the $500 available as a charitable contributions carryover from 1970 (excess contributions made in 1970 ($2,000) less the amount of such excess treated as paid in 1971 ($1,500)), since B elected to take the standard deduction in 1972. However, for purposes of determining the amount of the excess charitable contributions made in 1970 which is available as a carryover to 1973, B is required to treat such $500 as -a charitable contribu-

tion paid in 1972—the lesser of $500 or $4,700 (50 percent of contribution base ($5,000) over contributions actually made in 1972 to section 170(b)(1)(A) organizations (S300)). Therefore, even though the $5,000 contribution made by B in 1973 to a church does not amount to 50 percent of B's contribution base for 1973 (50 percent of $20,000), B may claim a charitable contributions deduction of only the $5,000 actually paid in 1973 since the entire excess charitable contribution made in 1970 ($2,000) has been treated as paid in 1971 ($1,500) and 1972 ($500).

Example (3). Assume the following factual situation for C who itemizes his deductions in computing taxable income for each of the years set forth in the example:

	1970	1971	1972	1973	1974
Contribution base	$10,000	$7,000	$15,000	$10,000	$9,000
Contributions of cash to section 170(b)(1)(A) organizations (no other contributions)	$6,000	$4,400	$8,000	$3,000	$1,500
Allowable charitable contributions deductions computed without regard to carryover of contribution	5,000	3,500	7,500	3,000	1,500
Excess contributions for taxable year to be treated as paid in 5 succeeding taxable years	1,000	900	500	0	0

Since C's contributions in 1973 and 1974 to section 170(b)(1)(A) organizations are less than 50 percent of his contribution base for such years, the excess contributions for 1970, 1971, and 1972 are treated as having been paid to section 170(b)(1)(A) organizations in 1973 and 1974 as follows:

1970	$1,000	0	$1,000
1971	900	0	900
1972	500	0	500
Total			2,400

50 percent of B's contribution base for 1973	5,000
Less: Charitable contributions made in 1973 to section 170(b)(1)(A) organizations	3,000
	2,000

Amount of excess contributions treated as paid in 1973—lesser of $2,400 (available carryovers to 1973) or $2,000 (excess of 50 percent of contribution base ($5,000) over contributions actually made in 1973 to section 170(b)(1)(A) organizations ($3,000)) **$2,000**

1970	$1,000	$1,000	0
1971	900	900	0
1972	500	100	$400
1973	0	0	0
Total			400

50 percent of B's contribution base for 1974	$4,500
Less: Charitable contributions made in 1974 to section 170(b)(1)(A) organizations	1,500
	3,000

Amount of excess contributions treated as paid in 1974—the lesser of $400 (available carryovers to 1974) or $3,000 (excess of 50 percent of contribution base ($4,500) over contributions actually made in 1974 to section 170(b)(1)(A) organizations ($1,500)) **$400**

(c) *30-percent charitable contributions carryover of individuals.*— (1) *Computation of excess of charitable contributions made in a contribution year.*—Under section 170(b)(1)(D)(ii), subject to certain conditions and limitations, the excess of—

(i) The amount of the charitable contributions of 30-percent capital gain property, as defined in §1.170A-8(d)(3), made by an individual in a taxable year (hereinafter in this paragraph referred to as the "contribution year") to section 170(b)(1)(A) organizations described in §1.170A-9, over

(ii) 30 percent of his contribution base for such contribution year, shall, subject to section 170(b)(1)(A) and paragraph (b) of §1.170A-8, be treated as a charitable contribution of 30-percent capital gain property paid by him to a section 170(b)(1)(A) organization in each of the 5 taxable years immediately succeeding the contribution year in order of time. In addition, any charitable contribution of 30-percent capital gain property which is carried over to such years under section 170(d)(1) and paragraph (b) of this section shall also be treated as though it were a carryover of 30-percent capital gain property under section 170(b)(1)(D)(ii) and this paragraph. The provisions of this subparagraph may be illustrated by the following examples:

Example (1). Assume that H and W (husband and wife) have a contribution base for 1970 of $50,000 and for 1971 of $40,000 and file a joint return for each year. Assume further that in 1970 they contribute $20,000 cash and $13,000 of 30-percent capital gain property to a church, and that in 1971 they contribute $5,000 cash and $10,000 of 30-percent capital gain property to a church. They may claim a charitable contributions deduction of $25,000 in 1970 and the excess of $33,000 (contributed to the church) over $25,000 (50 percent of contribution base), or $8,000, constitutes a charitable contributions

carryover which shall be treated as a charitable contribution of 30-percent capital gain property paid by them to a section 170(b)(1)(A) organization in each of the 5 succeeding taxable years in order of time. Since 30 percent cf their contribution base for 1971 ($12,000) exceeds the charitable contributions of 30-percent capital gain property ($10,000) made by them in 1971 to section 170(b)(1)(A) organizations (computed without regard to section 170(b)(1)(D)(ii) and (d)(1) and this section), the portion of the 1970 carryover equal to such excess of $2,000 ($12,000 – $10,000) is treated, pursuant to the provisions of subparagraph (2) of this paragraph, as paid to a section 170(b)(1)(A) organization in 1971; the remaining $6,000 constitutes an unused charitable contributions carryover in respect of 30-percent capital gain property from 1970.

Example (2). Assume the same facts as in example (1) except the $33,000 of charitable contributions in 1970 are all 30-percent capital gain property. Since their charitable contributions in 1970 exceed 30 percent of their contribution base ($15,000) by $18,000 ($33,000 – $15,000), they may claim a charitable contributions deduction of $15,000 in 1970, and the excess of $33,000 over $15,000, or $18,000, constitutes a charitable contributions carryover which shall be treated as a charitable contribution of 30-percent capital gain property paid by them to a section 170(b)(1)(A) organization in each of the 5 succeeding taxable years in order of time. Since they are allowed to treat only $2,000 of their 1970 contribution as paid in 1971, they have a remaining unused charitable contributions carryover of $16,000 in respect to 30-percent capital gain property from 1970.

(2) *Determination of amount treated as paid in taxable years succeeding contribution year.*—In applying the provisions of subparagraph (1) of this paragraph, the amount of the excess computed in

accordance with the provisions of such subparagraph and paragraph (d)(1) of this section which is to be treated as paid in any one of the 5 taxable years immediately succeeding the contribution year to a section 170(b)(1)(A) organization shall not exceed the least of the amounts computed under subdivisions (i) to (iv), inclusive, of this subparagraph:

(i) The amount by which 30 percent of the taxpayer's contribution base for such succeeding taxable year exceeds the sum of—

(a) The charitable contributions of 30-percent capital gain property actually made (computed without regard to the provisions of section 170(b)(1)(D)(ii) and (d)(1) and this section) by the taxpayer in such succeeding taxable year to section 170(b)(1)(A) organizations, and

(b) The charitable contributions of 30-percent capital gain property made to section 170(b)(1)(A) organizations in taxable years preceding the contribution year, which, pursuant to the provisions of section 170(b)(1)(D)(ii) and (d)(1) and this section, are treated as having been paid to a section 170(b)(1)(A) organization in such succeeding year.

(ii) The amount by which 50 percent of the taxpayer's contribution base for such succeeding taxable year exceeds the sum of—

(a) The charitable contributions actually made (computed without regard to the provisions of section 170(b)(1)(D)(ii) and (d)(1) and this section) by the taxpayer in such succeeding taxable year to section 170(b)(1)(A) organizations,

(b) The charitable contributions of 30-percent capital gain property made to section 170(b)(1)(A) organizations in taxable years preceding the contribution year which, pursuant to the provisions of section 170(b)(1)(D)(ii) and (d)(1) and this section, are treated as having been paid to a section 170(b)(1)(A) organization in such succeeding year, and

(c) The charitable contributions, other than contributions of 30-percent capital gain property, made to section 170(b)(1)(A) organi-

zations which, pursuant to the provisions of section 170(d)(1) and paragraph (b) of this section, are treated as having been paid to a section 170(b)(1)(A) organization in such succeeding year.

(iii) In the case of the first taxable year succeeding the contribution year, the amount of the excess charitable contribution of 30-percent capital gain property in the contribution year, computed under subparagraph (1) of this paragraph and paragraph (d)(1) of this section.

(iv) In the case of the second, third, fourth, and fifth succeeding taxable years succeeding the contribution year, the portion of the excess charitable contribution of 30-percent capital gain property in the contribution year (computed under subparagraph (1) of this paragraph and paragraph (d)(1) of this section) which has not been treated as paid to a section 170(b)(1)(A) organization in a year intervening between the contribution year and such succeeding taxable year.

For purposes of applying subdivisions (i) and (ii) of this subparagraph, the amount of charitable contributions of 30-percent capital gain property actually made in a taxable year succeeding the contribution year shall be determined by first applying the 30-percent limitation of section 170(b)(1)(D)(i) and paragraph (d) of §1.170A-8. If a taxpayer, in any one of the four taxable years succeeding a contribution year, elects under section 144 to take the standard deduction instead of itemizing the deductions allowable in computing taxable income, there shall be treated as paid (but not allowable as a deduction) in the standard deduction year the least of the amounts determined under subdivisions (1) to (iv), inclusive, of this subparagraph. The provisions of this subparagraph may be illustrated by the following example:

Example. Assume the following factual situation for C who itemizes his deductions in computing taxable income for each of the years set forth in the example:

	1970	1971	1972	1973	1974
Contribution base	$10,000	$15,000	$20,000	$15,000	$33,000
Contributions of cash to section 170(b)(1)(A) organizations	2,000	8,500	0	14,000	700
Contributions of 30-percent capital gain property to section 170(b)(1)(A) organizations	5,000	0	7,800	0	6,400
Allowable charitable contributions deductions (computed without regard to carryover of contributions) subject to limitations of:					
50 percent	2,000	7,500	0	7,500	700
30 percent	3,000	0	6,000	0	6,400
Total	5,000	7,500	6,000	7,500	7,100
Excess of contributions for taxable year to be treated as paid in 5 succeeding taxable years:					
Carryover of contributions of property other than 30-percent capital gain property	0	$1,000	0	$6,500	0
Carryover of contributions of 30-percent capital gain property	$2,000	0	$1,800	0	0

C's excess contributions for 1970, 1971, 1972, and 1973 which are treated as having been paid to section 170(b)(1)(A) organizations in 1972, 1973 and 1974 are indicated below. The portion of the excess

charitable contribution for 1972 of 30-percent capital gain property which is not treated as paid in 1974 ($1,800–$900) is available as a carryover to 1975.

1971

Contribution year	50%	Total excess 30%	Less: Amount treated as paid in years prior to 1971 50%	Available charitable contributions carryovers 30%
1970	0	$2,000	0	$2,000

	50%	30%
50 percent of C's contribution base for 1971	$7,500	
30 percent of C's contribution base for 1971		4,500
Less: Charitable contributions actually made in 1971 to section 170(b)(1)(A) organizations ($8,500, but not to exceed 50% of contribution base)	7,500	0
Excess	0	4,500

The amount of excess contributions for 1970 of 30-percent capital gain property which is treated as paid in 1971 is the least of—

(i)	Available carryover from 1970 to 1971 of contributions of 30-percent capital gain property	2,000
(ii)	Excess of 50 percent of contribution base for 1971 ($7,500) over sum of contributions actually made in 1971 to section 170(b)(1)(A) organizations ($7,500)	0
(iii)	Excess of 30 percent of contribution base for 1971 ($4,500) over contributions of 30-percent capital gain property actually made in 1971 to section 170(b)(1)(A) organizations ($0)	$4,500
	Amount treated as paid	0

1972

Contribution year	Total excess 50%	Total excess 30%	Less: Amount treated as paid in years prior to 1972	Available charitable contributions carryovers 50%	Available charitable contributions carryovers 30%
1970	0	$2,000	0	0	$2,000
1971	$1,000	0	0	$1,000	0
				1,000	2,000

50 percent of C's contribution base for 1972 10,000

30 percent of C's contribution base for 1972 6,000

Less: Charitable contributions actually made in 1972 to section 170(b)(1)(A) organizations ($7,800, but not to exceed 30% of contribution base) . . . . 0 / 6,000

Excess . . . . 10,000 / 0

(1) The amount of excess contributions for 1971 of property other than 30-percent capital gain property which is treated as paid in 1972 is the lesser of—

  (i) Available carryover from 1971 to 1972 of contributions of property other than 30-percent capital gain property $1,000

  (ii) Excess of 50 percent of contribution base for 1972 ($10,000) over contributions actually made in 1972 to section 170(b)(1)(A) organizations ($6,000) 4,000

      Amount treated as paid $1,000

(2) The amount of excess contributions for 1970 of 30-percent capital gain property which is treated as paid in 1972 is the least of—

  (i) Available carryover from 1970 to 1972 of contributions of 30-percent capital gain property $2,000

  (ii) Excess of 50 percent of contribution base for 1972 ($10,000) over sum of contributions actually made in 1972 to section 170(b)(1)(A) organizations ($6,000) and excess contributions for 1971 treated under item (1) above as paid in 1972 ($1,000) 3,000

  (iii) Excess of 30 percent of contribution base for 1972 ($6,000) over contributions of 30-percent capital gain property actually made in 1972 to section 170(b)(1)(A) organizations ($6,000) 0

      Amount treated as paid 0

1973

Contribution year	Total excess 50%	Total excess 30%	Less: Amount treated as paid in years prior to 1973	Available charitable contributions carryovers 50%	Available charitable contributions carryovers 30%
1970	0	$2,000	0	0	$2,000
1971	$1,000	0	$1,000	0	0
1972	0	1,800	0	0	1,800
				0	3,800

50 percent of C's contribution base for 1973 . . . . $7,500

30 percent of C's contribution base for 1973 4,500

Less: Charitable contributions actually made in 1973 to section 170(b)(1)(A) organizations ($14,000, but not to exceed 50% of contribution base) . . . . 7,500 / 0

Excess . . . . 0 / 4,500

(1) The amount of excess contributions for 1970 of 30-percent capital gain property which is treated as paid in 1973 is the least of

  (i) Available carryover from 1970 to 1973 of contributions of 30-percent capital gain property . . $2,000

  (ii) Excess of 50 percent of contribution base for 1973 ($7,500) over contributions actually made in 1973 to section 170(b)(1)(A) organizations ($7,500) 0

  (iii) Excess of 30 percent of contribution base for 1973 ($4,500) over contributions of 30-percent capital gain property actually made in 1973 to section 170(b)(1)(A) organizations ($0) 4,500

      Amount treated as paid 0

(2) The amount of excess contributions for 1972 of 30-percent capital gain property which is treated as paid in 1973 is the least of—

  (i) Available carryover from 1972 to 1973 of contributions of 30-percent capital gain property . . $1,800

  (ii) Excess of 50 percent of contribution base for 1973 ($7,500) over contributions actually made in 1973 to section 170(b)(1)(A) organizations ($7,500) 0

  (iii) Excess of 30 percent of contribution base for 1973 ($4,500) over sum of contributions of 30-percent capital gain property actually made in 1973 to section 170(b)(1)(A) organizations ($0) and excess contributions for 1970 treated under item (1) above as paid in 1973 ($0) $4,500

      Amount treated as paid 0

1974

Contribution year	Total excess 50%	Total excess 30%	Less: Amount treated as paid in years prior to 1974	Available charitable contributions carryovers 50%	Available charitable contributions carryovers 30%
1970	0	$2,000		0	$2,000
1971	$1,000	0	$1,000	0	0
1972	0	1,800	0	0	1,800
1973	6,500	0	0	$6,500	0
				$6,500	$3,800

50 percent of C's contribution base of 1974 . . . . $16,500

30 percent of C's contribution base for 1974 . . . . $9,900

Less: Charitable contributions actually made in 1974 to section 170(b)(1)(A) organizations . . . . 700 / 6,400

Excess		15,800	3,500

(1) The amount of excess contributions for 1973 of property other than 30-percent capital gain property which is treated as paid in 1974 is the lesser of

	(i)	Available carryover from 1973 to 1974 of contributions of property other than 30-percent capital gain property	6,500	
	(ii)	Excess of 50 percent of contribution base for 1974 ($16,500) over contributions actually made in 1974 to section 170(b)(1)(A) organizations ($7,100)	9,400	
		Amount treated as paid		6,500

(2) The amount of excess contributions for 1970 of 30-percent capital gain property which is treated as paid in 1974 is the least of—

	(i)	Available carryover from 1970 to 1974 of contributions of 30-percent capital gain property . . .	$2,000	
	(ii)	Excess of 50 percent of contribution base for 1974 ($16,500) over sum of contributions actually made in 1974 to section 170(b)(1)(A) organizations ($7,100) and excess contributions for 1973 of property other than 30-percent capital gain property treated under item (1) above as paid in 1974 ($6,500)	2,900	
	(iii)	Excess of 30 percent of contribution base for 1974 ($9,900) over contributions of 30-percent capital gain property actually made in 1974 to section 170(b)(1)(A) organizations ($6,400) . .	3,500	
		Amount treated as paid		2,000

(3) The amount of excess contributions for 1972 of 30-percent capital gain property which is treated as paid in 1974 is the least of—

	(i)	Available carryover from 1972 to 1974 of contributions of 30-percent capital gain property . . .	1,800	
	(ii)	Excess of 50 percent of contribution base for 1974 ($16,500) over sum of contributions actually made in 1974 to section 170(b)(1)(A) organizations ($7,100) and excess contributions for 1973 and 1970 treated under items (1) and (2) above as paid in 1974 ($8,500)	$900	
	(iii)	Excess of 30 percent of contribution base for 1974 ($9,900) over sum of contributions of 30-percent capital gain property actually made in 1974 to section 170(b)(1)(A) organizations ($6,400) and excess contributions for 1970 of 30-percent capital gain property treated under item (2) above as paid in 1974 ($2,000)	1,500	
		Amount treated as paid		$900

(d) *Adjustments.*—(1) *Effect of net operating loss carryovers on carryover of excess contributions.*—An individual having a net operating loss carryover from a prior taxable year which is available as a deduction in a contribution year must apply the special rule of section 170(d)(1)(B) and this subparagraph in computing the excess described in paragraph (b)(1) or (c)(1) of this section for such contribution year. In determining the amount of excess charitable contributions that shall be treated as paid in each of the 5 taxable years succeeding the contribution year, the excess charitable contributions described in paragraph (b)(1) or (c)(1) of this section must be reduced by the amount by which such excess reduces taxable income (for purposes of determining the portion of a net operating loss which shall be carried to taxable years succeeding the contribution year under the second sentence of section 172(b)(2)) and increases the net operating loss which is carried to a succeeding taxable year. In reducing taxable income under the second sentence of section 172(b)(2), an individual who has made charitable contributions in the contribution year to both section 170(b)(1)(A) organizations, as defined in §1.170A-9, and to organizations which are not section 170(b)(1)(A) organizations must first deduct contributions made to the section 170(b)(1)(A) organizations from his adjusted gross income computed without regard to his net operating loss deduction before any of the contributions made to organizations which are not section 170(b)(1)(A) organizations may be deducted from such adjusted gross income. Thus, if the excess of the contributions made in the contribution year to section 170(b)(1)(A) organizations over the amount deductible in such contribution year is utilized to reduce taxable income (under the provisions of section 172(b)(2)) for such year, thereby serving to increase the amount of the net operating loss carryover to a succeeding year or years, no part of the excess charitable contributions made in such contribution year shall be treated as paid in any of the 5 immediately succeeding taxable years. If only a portion of the excess charitable contributions is so used, the excess charitable contributions shall be reduced only to that extent. The provisions of this subparagraph may be illustrated by the following examples:

Example (1). B, an individual, reports his income on the calendar year basis and for the year 1970 has adjusted gross income (computed without regard to any net operating loss deduction) of $50,000. During 1970 he made charitable contributions of cash in the amount of $30,000 all of which were to section 170(b)(1)(A) organizations. B has a net operating loss carryover from 1969 of $50,000. In the absence of the net operating loss deduction B would have been allowed a deduction for charitable contributions of $25,000. After the application of the net operating loss deduction, B is allowed no deduction for charitable contributions, and there is (before applying the special rule of section 170(d)(1)(B) and this subparagraph) a tentative excess charitable contribution of $30,000. For purposes of determining the net operating loss which remains to be carried over to 1971, B computes his taxable income for 1970 under section 172(b)(2) by deducting the $25,000 charitable contribution. After the $50,000 net operating loss carryover is applied against the $25,000 of taxable income for 1970 (computed in accordance with section

172(b)(2), assuming no deductions other than the charitable contributions deduction are applicable in making such computation) there remains a $25,000 net operating loss carryover to 1971. Since the application of the net operating loss carryover of $50,000 from 1969 reduces the 1970 adjusted gross income (for purposes of determining 1970 tax liability) to zero, no part of the $25,000 of charitable contributions in that year is deductible under section 170(b)(1). However, in determining the amount of the excess charitable contributions which shall be treated as paid in taxable years 1971, 1972, 1973, 1974, and 1975, the $30,000 must be reduced to $5,000 by the portion of the excess charitable contributions ($25,000) which was used to reduce taxable income for 1970 (as computed for purposes of the second sentence of section 172(b)(2)) and which thereby served to increase the net operating loss carryover to 1971 from zero to $25,000.

Example (2). Assume the same facts as in example (1), except that B's total charitable contributions of $30,000 in cash made during 1970 consisted of $25,000 to section 170(b)(1)(A) organizations and $5,000 to organizations other than section 170(b)(1)(A) organizations. Under these facts there is a tentative excess charitable contribution of $25,000, rather than $30,000 as in example (1). For purposes of determining the net operating loss which remains to be carried over to 1971, B computes his taxable income for 1970 under section 172(b)(2) by deducting the $25,000 of charitable contributions made to section 170(b)(1)(A) organizations. Since the excess charitable contribution of $25,000 determined in accordance with paragraph (b)(1) of this section was used to reduce taxable income for 1970 (as computed for purposes of the second sentence of section 172(b)(2)) and thereby served to increase the net operating loss carryover to 1971 from zero to $25,000, no part of such excess charitable contributions made in the contribution year shall be treated as paid in any of the five immediately succeeding taxable years. No carryover is allowed with respect to the $5,000 of charitable contributions made in 1970 to organizations other than section 170(b)(1)(A) organizations.

Example (3). Assume the same facts as in example (1), except that B's total contributions of $30,000 made during 1970 were of 30-percent capital gain property. Under these facts there is a tentative excess charitable contribution of $30,000. For purposes of determining the net operating loss which remains to be carried over to 1971, B computes his taxable income for 1970 under section 172(b)(2)(B) by deducting the $15,000 (30 percent of $50,000) contribution of 30-percent capital gain property which would have been deductible in 1970 absent the net operating loss deduction. Since $15,000 of the excess charitable contribution of $30,000 determined in accordance with paragraph (c)(1) of this section was used to reduce taxable income for 1970 (as computed for purposes of the second sentence of section 172(b)(2)) and thereby served to increase the net operating loss carryover to 1971 from zero to $15,000, only $15,000 ($30,000 – $15,000) of such excess shall be treated as paid in taxable years 1971, 1972, 1973, 1974, and 1975.

(2) *Effect of net operating loss carryback to contribution year.*—The amount of the excess contribution for a contribution year computed as provided in paragraph (b)(1) or (c)(1) of this section and subpara-

Reg. §1.170A-10(d)(1)

graph (1) of this paragraph shall not be increased because a net operating loss carryback is available as a deduction in the contribution year. Thus, for example, assuming that in 1970 there is an excess contribution of $50,000 (determined as provided in paragraph (b)(1) of this section) which is to be carried to the 5 succeeding taxable years and that in 1973 the taxpayer has a net operating loss which may be carried back to 1970, the excess contribution of $50,000 for 1970 is not increased by reason of the fact that the adjusted gross income for 1970 (on which such excess contribution was based) is subsequently decreased by the carryback of the net operating loss from 1973. In addition, in determining under the provisions of section 172(b)(2) the amount of the net operating loss for any year subsequent to the contribution year which is a carryback or carryover to taxable years succeeding the contribution year, the amount of contributions made to section 170(b)(1)(A) organizations shall be limited to the amount of such contributions which did not exceed 50 percent or, in the case of 30-percent capital gain property, 30 percent of the donor's contribution base, computed without regard to any of the modifications referred to in section 172(d), for the contribution year. Thus, for example, assume that the taxpayer has a net operating loss in 1973 which is carried back to 1970 and in turn to 1971 and that he has made charitable contributions in 1970 to section 170(b)(1)(A) organizations. In determining the maximum amount of such charitable contributions which may be deducted in 1970 for purposes of determining the taxable income for 1970 which is deducted under section 172(b)(2) from the 1973 loss in order to ascertain the amount of such loss which is carried back to 1971, the 50-percent limitation of section 170(b)(1)(A) is based upon the adjusted gross income for 1970 computed without taking into account the net operating loss carryback from 1973 and without making any of the modifications specified in section 172(d).

(3) *Effect of net operating loss carryback to taxable years succeeding the contribution year.*—The amount of the charitable contribution from a preceding taxable year which is treated as paid, as provided in paragraph (b)(2) or (c)(2) of this section, in a current taxable year (hereinafter referred to in this subparagraph as the "deduction year") shall not be reduced because a net operating loss carryback is available as a deduction in the deduction year. In addition, in determining under the provisions of section 172(b)(2) the amount of the net operating loss for any taxable year subsequent to the deduction year which is a carryback or carryover to taxable years succeeding the deduction year, the amount of contributions made to section 170(b)(1)(A) organizations in the deduction year shall be limited to the amount of such contributions, which were actually made in such year and those which were treated as paid in such year, which did not exceed 50 percent or, in the case of 30-percent capital gain property, 30 percent of the donor's contribution based, computed without regard to any of the modifications referred to in section 172(d), for the deduction year.

(4) *Husband and wife filing joint returns.*—(i) *Change from joint return to separate returns.*—If a husband and wife—

(a) Make a joint return for a contribution year and compute an excess charitable contribution for such year in accordance with the provisions of paragraph (b)(1) or (c)(1) of this section and subparagraph (1) of this paragraph, and

(b) Make separate returns for one or more of the 5 taxable years immediately succeeding such contribution year,

any excess charitable contribution for the contribution year which is unused at the beginning of the first such taxable year for which separate returns are filed shall be allocated between the husband and wife. For purposes of the allocation, a computation shall be made of the amount of any excess charitable contribution which each spouse would have computed in accordance with paragraph (b)(1) or (c)(1) of this section and subparagraph (1) of this paragraph if separate returns (rather than a joint return) had been filed for the contribution year. The portion of the total unused excess charitable contribution for the contribution year allocated to each spouse shall be an amount which bears the same ratio to such unused excess charitable contribution as such spouse's excess contribution, based on the separate return computation, bears to the total excess contributions of both spouses, based on the separate return computation. To the extent that a portion of the amount allocated to either spouse in accordance with the foregoing provisions of this subdivision is not treated in accordance with the provisions of paragraph (b)(2) or (c)(2) of this section as a charitable contribution paid to a section 170(b)(1)(A) organization in the taxable year in which a separate return or separate returns are filed, each spouse shall for purposes of paragraph (b)(2) or (c)(2) of this section treat his respective unused portion as the available charitable contributions carryover to the next succeeding taxable year in which the joint excess charitable contribution may be treated as paid in accordance with paragraph (b)(1) or (c)(1) of this section. If such husband and wife make a joint return in one of the five taxable years immediately succeeding the contribution year with respect to which a joint excess charitable contribution is computed and following such first taxable year for which such husband and wife filed a separate return, the amounts allocated to each spouse in accordance with this subdivision for such first year reduced by the portion of such amounts treated as paid to a section 170(b)(1)(A) organization in such first year and in any taxable year intervening between such first year and the succeeding taxable year in which the joint return is filed shall be aggregated for purposes of determining the amount of the available charitable contributions carryover to such succeeding taxable year. The provisions of this subdivision may be illustrated by the following example:

Example. (a) H and W file joint returns for 1970, 1971, and 1972, and in 1973 they file separate returns. In each such year H and W itemize their deductions in computing taxable income. Assume the following factual situation with respect to H and W for 1970:

1970

	H	W	Joint return
Contribution base	$50,000	$40,000	$90,000
Contributions of cash to section 170(b)(1)(A) organizations (no other contributions)	37,000	28,000	65,000
Allowable charitable contributions deductions	$25,000	$20,000	$45,000
Excess contributions for taxable year to be treated as paid in 5 succeeding taxable years	$12,000	$8,000	$20,000

(b) The joint excess charitable contribution of $20,000 is to be treated as having been paid to a section 170(b)(1)(A) organization in the five succeeding taxable years. Assume that in 1971 the portion of such excess treated as paid by H and W is $3,000, and that in 1972 the portion of such excess treated as paid is $7,000. Thus, the unused portion of the excess charitable contribution made in the contribution year is $10,000 ($20,000 less $3,000 [amount treated as paid in 1971] and $7,000 [amount treated as paid in 1972]). Since H and W file separate returns in 1973, $6,000 of such $10,000 is allocable to H, and $4,000 is allocable to W. Such allocation is computed as follows:

$$\frac{\$12,000 \text{ (excess charitable contributions made by H (based on separate return computation) in 1970)}}{\$20,000 \text{ (total excess charitable contributions made by H and W (based on separate return computation) in 1970)}} \times \$10,000 = \$6,000$$

$$\frac{\$8,000 \text{ (excess charitable contributions made by W (based on separate return computation) in 1970)}}{\$20,000 \text{ (Total excess charitable contributions made by H and W (based on separate return computation) in 1970)}} \times \$10,000 = \$4,000$$

(c) In 1973 H has a contribution base of $70,000, and he contributes $14,000 in cash to a section 170(b)(1)(A) organization. In 1973 W has a contribution base of $50,000, and she contributes $10,000 in cash to a section 170(b)(1)(A) organization. Accordingly, H may claim a charitable contributions deduction of $20,000 in 1973, and W may claim a charitable contributions deduction of $14,000 in 1973. H's $20,000 deduction consists of the $14,000 contribution made to the section 170(b)(1)(A) organization in 1973 and the $6,000 carried over from 1970 and treated as a charitable contribution paid by him to a section 170(b)(1)(A) organization in 1973. W's $14,000 deduction consists of the $10,000 contribution made to a section 170(b)(1)(A) organization in 1973 and the $4,000 carried over from 1970 and treated as a charitable contribution paid by her to a section 170(b)(1)(A) organization in 1973.

(d) The $6,000 contribution treated as paid in 1973 by H, and the $4,000 contribution treated as paid in 1973, by W, are computed as follows:

	H	W
Available charitable contribution carryover (see computations in (b))	$6,000	$4,000
50-percent of contribution base	35,000	25,000
Contributions of cash made in 1973 to section 170(b)(1)(A) organizations (no other contributions)	14,000	10,000
	21,000	15,000

Amount of excess contributions treated as paid in 1973:

The lesser of $6,000 (available carryover of H to 1973) or $21,000 (excess of 50 percent of contribution base ($35,000) over contributions actually made in 1973 to section 170(b)(1)(A) organizations ($14,000)) $6,000

The lesser of $4,000 (available carryover of W to 1973) or $15,000 (excess of 50 percent of contribution base ($25,000) over contributions actually made in 1973 to section 170(b)(1)(A) organizations ($10,000)) $4,000

(e) It is assumed that H and W made no contributions of 30-percent capital gain property during these years. If they had made such contributions, there would have been similar adjustments based on 30 percent of the contribution base.

(ii) *Change from separate returns to joint return.*—If in the case of a husband and wife—

(a) Either or both of the spouses make a separate return for a contribution year and compute an excess charitable contribution for such year in accordance with the provisions of paragraph (b)(1) or (c)(1) of this section and subparagraph (1) of this paragraph, and

(b) Such husband and wife make a joint return for one or more of the taxable years succeeding such contribution year, the excess charitable contribution of the husband and wife for the contribution year which is unused at the beginning of the first taxable year for which a joint return is filed shall be aggregated for purposes of determining the portion of such unused charitable contribution which shall be treated in accordance with paragraph (b)(2) or (c)(2) of this section as a charitable contribution paid to a section 170(b)(1)(A) organization. The provisions of this subdivision also apply in the case of two single individuals who are subsequently married and file a joint return. A remarried taxpayer who filed a joint return with a former spouse in a contribution year with respect to which an excess charitable contribution was computed and who in any one of the five taxable years succeeding such contribution year files a joint return with his or her present spouse shall treat the unused portion of such excess charitable contribution allocated to him or her in accordance with subdivision (i) of this subparagraph in the same manner as the unused portion of an excess charitable contribution computed in a contribution year in which he filed a separate return, for purposes of determining the amount which in accordance with paragraph (b)(2) or (c)(2) of this section shall be treated as paid to an organization specified in section 170(b)(1)(A) in such succeeding year.

(iii) *Unused excess charitable contribution of deceased spouse.*—In case of the death of one spouse, any unused portion of an excess charitable contribution which is allocable in accordance with subdivision (i) of this subparagraph to such spouse shall not be treated as paid in the taxable year in which such death occurs or in any subsequent taxable year except on a separate return made for the deceased spouse by a fiduciary for the taxable year which ends with the date of death or on a joint return for the taxable year in which such death occurs. The application of this subdivision may be illustrated by the following example:

Example. Assume the same facts as in the example in subdivision (i) of this subparagraph except that H dies in 1972 and W files a separate return for 1973. W made a joint return for herself and H for 1972. In that example, the unused excess charitable contribution as of January 1, 1973, was $10,000, of which $6,000 was allocable to H and $4,000 to W. No portion of the $6,000 allocable to H may be treated as paid by W or any other person in 1973 or any subsequent year.

(e) *Information required in support of a deduction of an amount carried over and treated as paid.*—If, in a taxable year, a deduction is claimed in respect of an excess charitable contribution which, in accordance with the provisions of paragraph (b)(2) or (c)(2) of this section, is treated (in whole or in part) as paid in such taxable year, the taxpayer shall attach to his return a statement showing:

(1) The contribution year (or years) in which the excess charitable contributions were made,

(2) The excess charitable contributions made in each contribution year, and the amount of such excess charitable contributions consisting of 30-percent capital gain property,

(3) The portion of such excess, or of each such excess, treated as paid in accordance with paragraph (b)(2) or (c)(2) of this section in any taxable year intervening between the contribution year and the

taxable year for which the return is made, and the portion of such excess which consists of 30-percent capital gain property,

(4) Whether or not an election under section 170(b)(1)(D)(iii) has been made which affects any of such excess contributions of 30-percent capital gain property, and

(5) Such other information as the return or the instructions relating thereto may require.

(f) *Effective date.*—This section applies only to contributions paid in taxable years beginning after December 31, 1969. For purposes of applying section 170(d)(1) with respect to contributions paid in a taxable year beginning before January 1, 1970, subsection (b)(1)(D), subsection (e), and paragraphs (1), (2), (3), and (4) of subsection (f) of section 170 shall not apply. See section 201(g)(1)(D) of the Tax Reform Act of 1969 (83 Stat. 564). [Reg. §1.170A-10.]

☐ [*T.D. 7207, 10-3-72. Amended by T.D. 7340, 1-6-75.*]

[Reg. §1.170-3]

§1.170-3. Contributions or gifts by corporations (before amendment by Tax Reform Act of 1969).—[The text of Reg. §1.170-3, pertaining to taxable years beginning before January 1, 1970, is no longer reproduced by CCH.]

[Reg. §1.170A-11]

§1.170A-11. Limitation on, and carryover of, contributions by corporations.—(a). *In general.*—The deduction by a corporation in any taxable year for charitable contributions, as defined in section 170(c), is limited to 5 percent of its taxable income for the year, computed without regard to—

(1) The deduction under section 170 for charitable contributions,

(2) The special deductions for corporations allowed under part VIII (except section 248), subchapter B, chapter 1 of the Code,

(3) Any net operating loss carryback to the taxable year under section 172, and

(4) Any capital loss carryback to the taxable year under section 1212(a)(1).

A charitable contribution by a corporation to a trust, chest, fund, or foundation described in section 170(c)(2) is deductible under section 170 only if the contribution is to be used in the United States or its possessions exclusively for religious, charitable, scientific, literary, or educational purposes or for the prevention of cruelty to children or animals. For the purposes of section 170, amounts excluded from the gross income of a corporation under section 114, relating to sports programs conducted for the American National Red Cross, are not to be considered contributions or gifts.

(b) *Election by corporations on an accrual method.*—(1) A corporation reporting its taxable income on an accrual method may elect to have a charitable contribution treated as paid during the taxable year, if payment is actually made on or before the 15th day of the third month following the close of such year and if, during such year, its board of directors authorizes the charitable contribution. If by reason of such an election a charitable contribution (other than a contribution of a letter, memorandum, or property similar to a letter or memorandum) paid in a taxable year beginning after December 31, 1969, is treated as paid during a taxable year beginning before January 1, 1970, the provisions of §1.170A-4 shall not be applied to reduce the amount of such contribution. However, see section 170(e) before its amendment by the Tax Reform Act of 1969.

(2) The election must be made at the time the return for the taxable year is filed, by reporting the contribution on the return. There shall be attached to the return when filed a written declaration stating that the resolution authorizing the contribution was adopted by the board of directors during the taxable year. For taxable years beginning before January 1, 2003, the declaration shall be verified by a statement signed by an officer authorized to sign the return that it

is made under penalties of perjury, and there shall also be attached to the return when filed a copy of the resolution of the board of directors authorizing the contribution. For taxable years beginning after December 31, 2002, the declaration must also include the date of the resolution, the declaration shall be verified by signing the return, and a copy of the resolution of the board of directors authorizing the contribution is a record that the taxpayer must retain and keep available for inspection in the manner required by § 1.6001-1(e).

(c) *Charitable contributions carryover of corporations.*—(1) *In general.*—Subject to the reduction provided in subparagraph (2) of this paragraph, any charitable contributions made by a corporation in a taxable year (hereinafter in this paragraph referred to as the "contribution year") in excess of the amount deductible in such contribution year under the 5-percent limitation of section 170(b)(2) are deductible in each of the five succeeding taxable years in order of time, but only to the extent of the lesser of the following amounts:

(i) The excess of the maximum amount deductible for such succeeding taxable year under the 5-percent limitation of section 170(b)(2) over the sum of the charitable contributions made in that year plus the aggregate of the excess contributions which were made in taxable years before the contribution year and which are deductible under this paragraph in such succeeding taxable year; or

(ii) In the case of the first taxable year succeeding the contribution year, the amount of the excess charitable contributions, and in the case of the second, third, fourth, and fifth taxable years succeeding the contribution year, the portion of the excess charitable contributions not deductible under this subparagraph for any taxable year intervening between the contribution year and such succeeding taxable year.

This paragraph applies to excess charitable contributions by a corporation, whether or not such contributions are made to, or for the use of, the donee organization and whether or not such organization is a section 170(b)(1)(A) organization, as defined in §1.170A-9. For purposes of applying this paragraph, a charitable contribution made in a taxable year beginning before January 1, 1970, which is carried over to a taxable year beginning after December 31, 1969, under section 170(b)(2) (before its amendment by the Tax Reform Act of 1969) and is deductible in such taxable year beginning after December 31, 1969, shall be treated as deductible under section 170(d)(1) and this paragraph. The application of this subparagraph may be illustrated by the following example:

Example. A corporation which reports its income on the calendar year basis makes a charitable contribution of $20,000 in 1970. Its taxable income (determined without regard to any deduction for charitable contributions) for 1970 is $100,000. Accordingly, the charitable contributions deduction for that year is limited to $5,000 (5 percent of $100,000). The excess charitable contribution not deductible in 1970 ($15,000) is a carryover to 1971. The corporation has taxable income (determined without regard to any deduction for charitable contributions) of $150,000 in 1971 and makes a charitable contribution of $5,000 in that year. For 1971 the corporation may deduct as a charitable contribution the amount of $7,500 (5 percent of $150,000). This amount consists of the $5,000 contribution made in 1971 and of the $2,500 carried over from 1970. The remaining $12,500 carried over from 1970 and not allowable as a deduction for 1971 because of the 5-percent limitation may be carried over to 1972. The corporation has taxable income (determined without regard to any deduction for charitable contributions) of $200,000 in 1972 and makes a charitable contribution of $5,000 in that year. For 1972 the corporation may deduct the amount of $10,000 (5 percent of $200,000). This amount consists of the $5,000 contributed in 1972, and $5,000 of the $12,500 carried over from 1970 to 1972. The remaining $7,500 of the carryover from 1970 is available for purposes of computing the charitable contributions carryover from 1970 to 1973, 1974, and 1975.

(2) *Effect of net operating loss carryovers on carryover of excess contributions.*—A corporation having a net operating loss carryover from any taxable year must apply the special rule of section 170(d)(2)(B) and this subparagraph before computing under subparagraph (1) of this paragraph the excess charitable contributions carryover from any taxable year. In determining the amount of excess charitable contributions that may be deducted in accordance with subparagraph (1) of this paragraph in taxable years succeeding the contribution year, the excess of the charitable contributions made by a corporation in the contributions year over the amount deductible in such year must be reduced by the amount by which such excess reduces taxable income for purposes of determining the net operating loss carryover under the second sentence of section 172(b)(2) and increases a net operating loss carryover to a succeeding taxable year. Thus, if the excess of the contributions made in a taxable year over the amount deductible in the taxable year is utilized to reduce taxable income (under the provisions of section 172(b)(2)) for such year, thereby serving to increase the amount of the net operating loss carryover to a succeeding taxable year or years, no charitable contri-

butions carryover will be allowed. If only a portion of the excess charitable contributions is so used, the charitable contributions carryover will be reduced only to that extent. The application of this subparagraph may be illustrated by the following example:

Example. A corporation, which reports its income on the calendar year basis, makes a charitable contribution of $10,000 during 1971. Its taxable income for 1971 is $80,000 (computed without regard to any net operating loss deduction and computed in accordance with section 170(b)(2) without regard to any deduction for charitable contributions). The corporation has a net operating loss carryover from 1970 of $80,000. In the absence of the net operating loss deduction the corporation would have been allowed a deduction for charitable contributions of $4,000 (5 percent of $80,000). After the application of the net operating loss deduction the corporation is allowed no deduction for charitable contributions, and there is a tentative charitable contribution carryover from 1971 of $10,000. For purposes of determining the net operating loss carryover to 1972 the corporation computes its taxable income for 1971 under section 172 (b)(2) by deducting the $4,000 charitable contribution. Thus, after the $80,000 net operating loss carryover is applied against the $76,000 of taxable income for 1971 (computed in accordance with section 172(b)(2)), there remains a $4,000 net operating loss carryover to 1972. Since the application of the net operating loss carryover of $80,000 from 1970 reduces the taxable income for 1971 to zero, no part of the $10,000 of charitable contributions in that year is deductible under section 170(b)(2). However, in determining the amount of the allowable charitable contributions carryover from 1971 to 1972, 1973, 1974, 1975, and 1976, the $10,000 must be reduced by the portion thereof ($4,000) which was used to reduce taxable income for 1971 (as computed for purposes of the second sentence of section 172(b)(2)) and which thereby served to increase the net operating loss carryover from 1970 to 1972 from zero to $4,000.

(3) *Effect of net operating loss carryback to contribution year.*—The amount of the excess contribution for a contribution year computed as provided in subparagraph (1) of this paragraph shall not be increased because a net operating loss carryback is available as a deduction in the contribution year. In addition, in determining under the provisions of section 172(b)(2) the amount of the net operating loss for any year subsequent to the contribution year which is a carryback or carryover to taxable years succeeding the contribution year, the amount of any charitable contributions shall be limited to the amount of such contributions which did not exceed 5 percent of the donor's taxable income, computed as provided in paragraph (a) of this section and without regard to any of the modifications referred to in section 172(d), for the contribution year. For illustrations see paragraph (d)(2) of §1.170A-1C.

(4) *Effect of net operating loss carryback to taxable year succeeding the contribution year.*—The amount of the charitable contribution from a preceding taxable year which is deductible (as provided in this paragraph) in a current taxable year (hereinafter referred to in this subparagraph as the "deduction year") shall not be reduced because a net operating loss carryback is available as a deduction in the deduction year. In addition, in determining under the provisions of section 172(b)(2) the amount of the net operating loss for any taxable year subsequent to the deduction year which is a carryback or a carryover to taxable years succeeding the deduction year, the amount of contributions made in the deduction year shall be limited to the amount of such contributions, which were actually made in such year and those which were deductible in such year under section 170(d)(2), which did not exceed 5 percent of the donor's taxable income, computed as provided in paragraph (a) of this section and without regard to any of the modifications referred to in section 172(d), for the deduction year.

(5) *Year contribution is made.*—For purposes of this paragraph, contributions made by a corporation in a contribution year include contributions which, in accordance with the provisions of section 170(a)(2) and paragraph (b) of this section, are considered as paid during such contribution year.

(d) *Effective date.*—This section applies only to contributions paid in taxable years beginning after December 31, 1969. For purposes of applying section 170(d)(2) with respect to contributions paid, or treated under section 170(a)(2) as paid, in a taxable year beginning before January 1, 1970, subsection (e), and paragraphs (1), (2), (3), and (4) of subsection (f) of section 170 shall not apply. See section 201(g)(1)(D) of the Tax Reform Act of 1969 (83 Stat. 564). [Reg. § 1.170A-11.]

☐ [*T.D. 7207*, 10-3-72. *Amended by T.D. 7807*, 1-29-82; *T.D. 9100*, 12-18-2003 *and T.D. 9300*, 12-7-2006.]

[Reg. § 1.170A-12]

§1.170A-12. Valuation of a remainder interest in real property for contributions made after July 31, 1969.—(a) *In general.*—(1) Section 170(f)(4) provides that, in determining the value of a remainder interest in real property for purposes of section 170, depreciation and depletion of such property shall be taken into account. Depreciation shall be computed by the straight line method and depletion shall be computed by the cost depletion method. Section 170(f)(4) and this section apply only in the case of a contribution, not made in trust, of a remainder interest in real property made after July 31, 1969, for which a deduction is otherwise allowable under section 170.

(2) In the case of the contribution of a remainder interest in real property consisting of a combination of both depreciable and nondepreciable property, or of both depletable and nondepletable property, and allocation of the fair market value of the property at the time of the contribution shall be made between the depreciable and nondepreciable property, or the depletable and nondepletable property, and depreciation or depletion shall be taken into account only with respect to the depreciable or depletable property. The expected value at the end of its "estimated useful life" (as defined in paragraph (d) of this section) of that part of the remainder interest consisting of depreciable property shall be considered to be nondepreciable property for purposes of the required allocation. In the case of the contribution of a remainder interest in stock in a cooperative housing corporation (as defined in section 216(b)(1)), an allocation of the fair market value of the stock at the time of the contribution shall be made to reflect the respective values of the depreciable and nondepreciable property underlying such stock, and depreciation on the depreciable part shall be taken into account for purposes of valuing the remainder interest in such stock.

(3) If the remainder interest that has been contributed follows only one life, the value of the remainder interest shall be computed under the rules contained in paragraph (b) of this section. If the remainder interest that has been contributed follows a term for years, the value of the remainder interest shall be computed under the rules contained in paragraph (c) of this section. If the remainder interest that has been contributed is dependent upon the continuation or the termination of more than one life or upon a term certain concurrent with one or more lives, the provisions of paragraph (e) of this section shall apply. In every case where it is provided in this section that the rules contained in §25.2512-5 (or, for certain prior periods, §25.2512-5A) of this chapter (Gift Tax Regulations) apply, such rules shall apply notwithstanding the general effective date for such rules contained in paragraph (a) of such sections. Except as provided in §1.7520-3(b) of this chapter, for transfers of remainder interests after April 30, 1989, the present value of the remainder interest is determined under §25.2512-5 of this chapter by use of the interest rate component on the date the interest is transferred unless an election is made under section 7520 and §1.7520-2 of this chapter to compute the present value of the interest transferred by use of the interest rate component for either of the 2 months preceding the month in which the interest is transferred. In some cases, a reduction in the amount of a charitable contribution of a remainder interest, after the computa-

tion of its value under section 170(f)(4) and this section, may be required. See section 170(e) and §1.170A-4.

(b) *Valuation of a remainder interest following only one life.*—(1) *General rule.*—The value of a remainder interest in real property following only one life is determined under the rules provided in §20.2031-7 (or for certain prior periods, §20.2031-7A) of this chapter (Estate Tax Regulations), using the interest rate and life contingencies prescribed for the date of the gift. See, however, §1.7520-3(b) (relating to exceptions to the use of prescribed tables under certain circumstances). However, if any part of the real property is subject to exhaustion, wear and tear, or obsolescence, the special factor determined under paragraph (b)(2) of this section shall be used in valuing the remainder interest in that part. Further, if any part of the property is subject to depletion of its natural resources, such depletion is taken into account in determining the value of the remainder interest.

(2) *Computation of depreciation factor.*—If the valuation of the remainder interest in depreciable property is dependent upon the continuation of one life, a special factor must be used. The factor determined under this paragraph (b)(2) is carried to the fifth decimal place. The special factor is to be computed on the basis of the interest rate and life contingencies prescribed in §20.2031-7 of this chapter (or for periods before May 1, 2009, §20.2031-7A) and on the assumption that the property depreciates on a straight-line basis over its estimated useful life. For transfers for which the valuation date is on or after May 1, 2009, special factors for determining the present value of a remainder interest following one life and an example describing the computation are contained in Internal Revenue Service Publication 1459, "Actuarial Valuations Version 3C" (2009). This publication is available, at no charge, electronically via the IRS Internet site at *www.irs.gov*. For transfers for which the valuation date is after April 30, 1999, and before May 1, 2009, special factors for determining the present value of a remainder interest following one life and an example describing the computation are contained in Internal Revenue Service Publication 1459, "Actuarial Values, Book Gimel," (7-99). For transfers for which the valuation date is after April 30, 1989, and before May 1, 1999, special factors for determining the present value of a remainder interest following one life and an example describing the computation are contained in Internal Revenue Service Publication 1459, "Actuarial Values, Gamma Volume," (8-89). These publications are no longer available for purchase from the Superintendent of Documents, United States Government Printing Office. However, they may be obtained by requesting a copy from: CC:PA:LPD:PR (IRS Publication 1459), room 5205, Internal Revenue Service, P.O.Box 7604, Ben Franklin Station, Washington, DC 20044. See, however, §1.7520-3(b) (relating to exceptions to the use of prescribed tables under certain circumstances). Otherwise, in the case of the valuation of a remainder interest following one life, the special factor may be obtained through use of the following formula:

$$\left(1+\frac{i}{2}\right)\sum_{t=0}^{n-1} v^{t+1}\left[\left(1-\frac{l_{x+t+1}}{l_x}\right)-\left(1-\frac{l_{x+t}}{l_x}\right)\right]\left(1-\frac{1}{2n}-\frac{t}{n}\right)$$

Where:

n = the estimated number of years of useful life,

i = the applicable interest rate under section 7520 of the Internal Revenue Code,

v = 1 divided by the sum of 1 plus the applicable interest rate under section 7520 of the Internal Revenue Code,

x = the age of the life tenant, and

lx = number of persons living at age x as set forth in Table 2000CM of §20.2031-7 of this chapter (or, for periods before May 1, 2009, the tables set forth under §20.2031-7A).

(3) The following example illustrates the provisions of this paragraph (b):

Example. A, who is 62, donates to Y University a remainder interest in a personal residence, consisting of a house and land, subject to a reserved life estate in A. At the time of the gift, the land has a value of $30,000 and the house has a value of $100,000 with an estimated useful life of 45 years, at the end of which period the value of the house is expected to be $20,000. The portion of the property *considered to be depreciable is $80,000 (the value of the house ($100,000) less its expected value at the end of 45 years ($20,000)). The portion of the property considered to be nondepreciable is $50,000 (the value of the land at the time of the gift ($30,000) plus the expected value of the house at the end of 45 years ($20,000)). At the

time of the gift, the interest rate prescribed under section 7520 is 8.4 percent. Based on an interest rate of 8.4 percent, the remainder factor for $1.00 prescribed in §20.2031-7(d) for a person age 62 is 0.26534. The value of the nondepreciable remainder interest is $13,267.00 (0.26534 times $50,000). The value of the depreciable remainder interest is $15,053.60 (0.18817, computed under the formula described in paragraph (b)(2) of this section, times $80,000). Therefore, the value of the remainder interest is $28,320.60.

(c) *Valuation of a remainder interest following a term for years.*—The value of a remainder interest in real property following a term for years shall be determined under the rules provided in §25.2512-5 (or, for certain prior periods, §25.2512-5A) of this chapter (Gift Tax Regulations) using Table B provided in §20.2031-7(d)(6) of this chapter. However, if any part of the real property is subject to exhaustion, wear and tear, or obsolescence, in valuing the remainder interest in that part the value of such part is adjusted by subtracting from the value of such part the amount determined by multiplying such value by a fraction, the numerator of which is the number of years in the term or, if less, the estimated useful life of the property, and the denominator of which is the estimated useful life of the property. The resultant figure is the value of the property to be used in §25.2512-5 (or, for certain prior periods, §25.2512-5A) of this chapter (Gift Tax Regulations). Further, if any part of the property is subject to depletion of its natural resources, such depletion shall be taken into account in determining the value of the remainder interest. The provisions of this paragraph as it relates to depreciation are illustrated by the following example:

Example. In 1972, B donates to Z University a remainder interest in his personal residence, consisting of a house and land, subject to a 20 year term interest provided for his sister. At such time the house has a value of $60,000, and an expected useful life of 45 years, at the end of which time it is expected to have a value of 10,000, and the land has a value of $8,000. The value of the portion of the property considered to be depreciable is $50,000 (the value of the house ($60,000) less its expected value at the end of 45 years ($10,000)), and this is multiplied by the fraction 20/45. The product, $22,222.22, is subtracted from $68,000, the value of the entire property, and the balance, $45,777.78, is multiplied by the factor .311805 (see §25.2512-5A(c)). The result, $14,273.74, is the value of the remainder interest in the property.

(d) *Definition of estimated useful life.*—For the purposes of this section, the determination of the estimated useful life of depreciable property shall take account of the expected use of such property during the period of the life estate or term for years. The term "estimated useful life" means the estimated period (beginning with the date of the contribution) over which such property may reasonably be expected to be useful for such expected use. This period shall be determined by reference to the experience based on any prior use of the property for such purposes if such prior experience is adequate. If such prior experience is inadequate or if the property has not been previously used for such purposes, the estimated useful life shall be determined by reference to the general experience of persons normally holding similar property for such expected use, taking into account present conditions and probable future developments. The estimated useful life of such depreciable property is not limited to the period of the life estate or term for years preceding the remainder interest. In determining the expected use and the estimated useful life of the property, consideration is to be given to the provisions of the governing instrument creating the life estate or term for years or applicable local law, if any, relating to use, preservation, and mainte-

nance of the property during the life estate or term for years. In arriving at the estimated useful life of the property, estimates, if available, of engineers or other persons skilled in estimating the useful life of similar property may be taken into account. At the option of the taxpayer, the estimated useful life of property contributed after December 31, 1970, for purposes of this section, shall be an asset depreciation period selected by the taxpayer that is within the permissible asset depreciation range for the relevant asset guideline class established pursuant to §1.167(a)-11(b)(4)(ii). For purposes of the preceding sentence, such period, range, and class shall be those which are in effect at the time that the contribution of the remainder interest was made. At the option of the taxpayer, in the case of property contributed before January 1, 1971, the estimated useful life, for purposes of this section, shall be the guideline life provided in Revenue Procedure 62-21 for the relevant asset guideline class.

(e) *Valuation of a remainder interest following more than one life or a term certain concurrent with one or more lives.*—(1)(i) If the valuation of the remainder interest in the real property is dependent upon the continuation or the termination of more than one life or upon a term certain concurrent with one or more lives, a special factor must be used.

(ii) The special factor is to be computed on the basis of—

(A) Interest at the rate prescribed under §25.2512-5 (or, for certain prior periods, §25.2512-5A) of this chapter, compounded annually;

(B) Life contingencies determined from the values that are set forth in the mortality table in §20.2031-7 (or, for certain prior periods, §20.2031-7A) of this chapter; and

(C) If depreciation is involved, the assumption that the property depreciates on a straight-line basis over its estimated useful life.

(iii) If any part of the property is subject to depletion of its natural resources, such depletion must be taken into account in determining the value of the remainder interest.

(2) In the case of the valuation of a remainder interest following two lives, the special factor may be obtained through use of the following formula:

$$\left(1 + \frac{i}{2}\right) \sum_{t=0}^{n-1} v^{(t+1)} \left[\left(1 - \frac{l_{x+t+1}}{l_x}\right)\left(1 - \frac{l_{y+t+1}}{l_y}\right) - \left(1 - \frac{l_{x+t}}{l_x}\right)\left(1 - \frac{l_{y+t}}{l_y}\right)\right]\left(1 - \frac{1}{2n} - \frac{t}{n}\right)$$

Where:

n = the estimated number of years of useful life,

i = the applicable interest rate under section 7520 of the Internal Revenue Code,

v = 1 divided by the sum of 1 plus the applicable interest rate under section 7520 of the Internal Revenue Code,

x and y = the ages of the life tenants, and

lx and ly = the number of persons living at ages x and y as set forth in Table 2000CM in §20.2031-7 (or, for prior periods, in §20.2031-7A) of this chapter.

(3) Notwithstanding that the taxpayer may be able to compute the special factor in certain cases under paragraph (2), if a special factor is required in the case of an actual contribution, the Commissioner will furnish the factor to the donor upon request. The request must be accompanied by a statement of the sex and date of birth of each person the duration of whose life may affect the value of the remainder interest, copies of the relevant instruments, and, if depreciation is involved, a statement of the estimated useful life of the depreciable property. However, since remainder interests in that part of any property which is depletable cannot be valued on a purely actuarial basis, special factors will not be furnished with respect to such part. Requests should be forwarded to the Commissioner of Internal Revenue, Attention: OP:E:EP:A:1, Washington, D.C. 20224.

(f) *Effective/applicability date.*—This section applies to contributions made after July 31, 1969, except that paragraphs (b)(2) and (b)(3) apply to all contributions made on or after May 1, 2009. [Reg. §1.170A-12.]

☐ *[T.D. 7370, 7-14-75. Amended by T.D. 7955, 5-10-84; T.D. 8540, 6-9-94; T.D. 8819, 4-29-99; T.D. 8886, 6-9-2000; T.D. 9448, 5-1-2009 (corrected 6-5-2009) and T.D. 9540, 8-9-2011.]*

[Reg. §1.170A-13]

§1.170A-13. Recordkeeping and return requirements for deductions for charitable contributions.—(a) *Charitable contributions of money made in taxable years beginning after December 31, 1982.*—(1) *In general.*—If a taxpayer makes a charitable contribution of money in a taxable year beginning after December 31, 1982, the taxpayer shall maintain for each contribution one of the following:

(i) A cancelled check.

(ii) A receipt from the donee charitable organization showing the name of the donee, the date of the contribution, and the amount of the contribution. A letter or other communication from the donee charitable organization acknowledging receipt of a contribution and showing the date and amount of the contribution constitutes a receipt for purposes of this paragraph (a).

(iii) In the absence of a canceled check or receipt from the donee charitable organization, other reliable written records showing the name of the donee, the date of the contribution, and the amount of the contribution.

(2) *Special rules.*—(i) *Reliability of records.*—The reliability of the written records described in paragraph (a)(1)(iii) of this section is to be determined on the basis of all of the facts and circumstances of a particular case. In all events, however, the burden shall be on the taxpayer to establish reliability. Factors indicating that the written records are reliable include, but are not limited to:

(A) The contemporaneous nature of the writing evidencing the contribution.

(B) The regularity of the taxpayer's recordkeeping procedures. For example, a contemporaneous diary entry stating the amount and date of the donation and the name of the donee charitable organization made by a taxpayer who regularly makes such diary entries would generally be considered reliable.

(C) In the case of a contribution of a small amount, the existence of any written or other evidence from the donee charitable organization evidencing receipt of a donation that would not otherwise constitute a receipt under paragraph (a)(1)(ii) of this section (including an emblem, button, or other token traditionally associated with a charitable organization and regularly given by the organization to persons making cash donations).

(ii) *Information stated in income tax return.*—The information required by paragraph (a)(1)(iii) of this section shall be stated in the taxpayer's income tax return if required by the return form or its instructions.

(3) *Taxpayer option to apply paragraph (d)(1) to pre-1985 contributions.*—See paragraph (d)(1) of this section with regard to contributions of money made on or before December 31, 1984.

(b) *Charitable contributions of property other than money made in taxable years beginning after December 31, 1982.*—(1) *In general.*—Except in the case of certain charitable contributions of property made after December 31, 1984, to which paragraph (c) of this section applies, any taxpayer who makes a charitable contribution of property other than money in a taxable year beginning after December 31, 1982, shall maintain for each contribution a receipt from the donee showing the following information:

(i) The name of the donee.

(ii) The date and location of the contribution.

(iii) A description of the property in detail reasonably sufficient under the circumstances. Although the fair market value of the property is one of the circumstances to be taken into account in determining the amount of detail to be included on the receipt, such value need not be stated on the receipt.

A letter or other written communication from the donee acknowledging receipt of the contribution, showing the date of the contribution, and containing the required description of the property contributed constitutes a receipt for purposes of this paragraph. A receipt is not required if the contribution is made in circumstances where it is impractical to obtain a receipt (*e.g.*, by depositing property at a charity's unattended drop site). In such cases, however, the taxpayer shall maintain reliable written records with respect to each item of donated property that include the information required by paragraph (b)(2)(ii) of this section.

(2) *Special rules.*—(i) *Reliability of records.*—The rules described in paragraph (a)(2)(i) of this section also apply to this paragraph (b) for determining the reliability of the written records described in paragraph (b)(1) of this section.

(ii) *Content of records.*—The written records described in paragraph (b)(1) of this section shall include the following information and such information shall be stated in the taxpayer's income tax return if required by the return form or its instructions:

(A) The name and address of the donee organization to which the contribution was made.

(B) The date and location of the contribution.

(C) A description of the property in detail reasonable under the circumstances (including the value of the property), and, in the case of securities, the name of the issuer, the type of security, and whether or not such security is regularly traded on a stock exchange or in an over-the-counter market.

(D) The fair market value of the property at the time the contribution was made, the method utilized in determining the fair market value, and, if the valuation was determined by appraisal, a copy of the signed report of the appraiser.

(E) In the case of property to which section 170(e) applies, the cost or other basis, adjusted as provided by section 1016, the reduction by reason of section 170(e)(1) in the amount of the charitable contribution otherwise taken into account, and the manner in which such reduction was determined. A taxpayer who elects under paragraph (d)(2) of §1.170A-8 to apply section 170(e)(1) to contributions and carryovers of 30 percent capital gain property shall maintain a written record indicating the years for which the election was made and showing the contributions in the current year and carryovers from preceding years to which it applies. For the definition of the term "30-percent capital gain property," see paragraph (d)(3) of §1.170A-8.

(F) If less than the entire interest in the property is contributed during the taxable year, the total amount claimed as a deduction for the taxable year due to the contribution of the property, and the amount claimed as a deduction in any prior year or years for contributions of other interests in such property, the name and address of each organization to which any such contribution was made, the place where any such property which is tangible property is located or kept, and the name of any person, other than the organization to which the property giving rise to the deduction was contributed, having actual possession of the property.

(G) The terms of any agreement or understanding entered into by or on behalf of the taxpayer which relates to the use, sale, or other disposition of the property contributed, including for example, the terms of any agreement or understanding which—

(1) Restricts temporarily or permanently the donee's right to use or dispose of the donated property,

(2) Reserves to, or confers upon, anyone (other than the donee organization or an organization participating with the donee organization in cooperative fund-raising) any right to the income from donated property or to the possession of the property, including the right to vote donated securities, to acquire the property by purchase or otherwise, or to designate the person having such income, possession, or right to acquire, or

(3) Earmarks donated property for a particular use.

(3) *Deductions in excess of $500 claimed for a charitable contribution of property other than money.*—(i) *In general.*—In addition to the information required under paragraph (b)(2)(ii) of this section, if a taxpayer makes a charitable contribution of property other than money in a taxable year beginning after December 31, 1982, and claims a deduction in excess of $500 in respect of the contribution of such item, the taxpayer shall maintain written records that include the following information with respect to such item of donated property, and shall state such information in his or her income tax return if required by the return form or its instructions:

(A) The manner of acquisition, as, for example by purchase, gift, bequest, inheritance, or exchange, and the approximate date of acquisition of the property by the taxpayer or, if the property was created, produced, or manufactured by or for the taxpayer, the approximate date the property was substantially completed.

(B) The cost or other basis, adjusted as provided by section 1016, of property, other than publicly traded securities, held by the taxpayer for a period of less than 12 months (6 months for property contributed in taxable years beginning after December 31, 1982, and on or before June 6, 1988) immediately preceding the date on which the contribution was made and, when the information is available, of property, other than publicly traded securities, held for a period of 12 months or more (6 months or more for property contributed in taxable years beginning after December 31, 1982, and on or before June 6, 1988) preceding the date on which the contribution was made.

(ii) *Information on acquisition date or cost basis not available.*—If the return form or its instructions require the taxpayer to provide information on either the acquisition date of the property or the cost basis as described in paragraph (b)(3)(i)(A) and (B), respectively, of this section, and the taxpayer has reasonable cause for not being able to provide such information, the taxpayer shall attach an explanatory statement to the return. If a taxpayer has reasonable cause for not being able to provide such information, the taxpayer shall not be disallowed a charitable contribution deduction under section 170 for failure to comply with paragraph (b)(3)(i)(A) and (B) of the section.

(4) *Taxpayer option to apply paragraph (d)(1) and (2) to pre-1985 contributions.*—See paragraph (d)(1) and (2) of this section with regard to contributions of property made on or before December 31, 1984.

(c) *Deductions in excess of $5,000 for certain charitable contributions of property made after December 31, 1984.*—(1) *General Rule.*—(i) *In general.*—This paragraph applies to any charitable contribution made after December 31, 1984, by an individual, closely held corporation, personal service corporation, partnership, or S corporation of an item of property (other than money and publicly traded securities to which §1.170A-13(c)(7)(xi)(B) does not apply) if the amount claimed or reported as a deduction under section 170 with respect to such item exceeds $5,000. This paragraph also applies to charitable contributions by C corporations (as defined in section 1361(a)(2) of the Code) to the extent described in paragraph (c)(2)(ii) of this section. No deduction under section 170 shall be allowed with respect to a charitable contribution to which this paragraph applies unless the substantiation requirements described in paragraph (c)(2) of this section are met. For purposes of this paragraph (c), the amount claimed or reported as a deduction for an item of property is the aggregate amount claimed or reported as a deduction for a charitable contribution under section 170 for such items of property and all similar items of property (as defined in paragraph (c)(7)(iii) of this section) by the same donor for the same taxable year (whether or not donated to the same donee).

(ii) *Special rule for property to which section 170(e)(3) or (4) applies.*—For purposes of this paragraph (c), in computing the amount claimed or reported as a deduction for donated property to which section 170(e)(3) or (4) applies (pertaining to certain contributions of inventory and scientific equipment) there shall be taken into account only the amount claimed or reported as a deduction in excess of the amount which would have been taken into account for tax purposes by the donor as costs of goods sold if the donor had sold the contributed property to the donee. For example, assume that a donor makes a contribution from inventory of clothing for the care of the needy to which section 170(e)(3) applies. The cost of the property to the donor was $5,000, and, pursuant to section 170(e)(3)(B), the donor claims a charitable contribution deduction of $8,000 with respect to the property. Therefore, $3,000 ($8,000 – $5,000) is the amount taken into account for purposes of determining whether the $5,000 threshold of this paragraph (c)(1) is met.

(2) *Substantiation requirements.*—(i) *In general.*—Except as provided in paragraph (c)(2)(ii) of this section, a donor who claims or reports a deduction with respect to a charitable contribution to which

this paragraph (c) applies must comply with the following three requirements:

(A) Obtain a qualified appraisal (as defined in paragraph (c)(3) of this section) for such property contributed. If the contributed property is a partial interest, the appraisal shall be of the partial interest.

(B) Attach a fully completed appraisal summary (as defined in paragraph (c)(4) of this section) to the tax return (or, in the case of a donor that is a partnership or S corporation, the information return) on which the deduction for the contribution is first claimed (or reported) by the donor.

(C) Maintain records containing the information required by paragraph (b)(2)(ii) of this section.

(ii) *Special rules for certain nonpublicly traded stock, certain publicly traded securities, and contributions by certain C corporations.*—(A) In cases described in paragraph (c)(2)(ii)(B) of this section, a qualified appraisal is not required, and only a partially completed appraisal summary form (as described in paragraph (c)(4)(iv)(A) of this section) is required to be attached to the tax or information return specified in paragraph (c)(2)(i)(B) of this section. However, in all cases donors must maintain records containing the information required by paragraph (b)(2)(ii) of this section.

(B) This paragraph (c)(2)(ii) applies in each of the following cases:

(1) The contribution of nonpublicly traded stock, if the amount claimed or reported as a deduction for the charitable contribution of such stock is greater than $5,000 but does not exceed $10,000;

(2) The contribution of a security to which paragraph (c)(7)(xi)(B) of this section applies; and

(3) The contribution of an item of property or of similar items of property described in paragraph (c)(1) of this section made after June 6, 1988, by a C corporation (as defined in section 1361(a)(2) of the Code), other than a closely held corporation or a personal service corporation.

(3) *Qualified appraisal.*—(i) *In general.*—For purposes of this paragraph (c), the term "qualified appraisal" means an appraisal document that—

(A) Relates to an appraisal that is made not earlier than 60 days prior to the date of contribution of the appraised property nor later than the date specified in paragraph (c)(3)(iv)(B) of this section;

(B) Is prepared, signed, and dated by a qualified appraiser (within the meaning of paragraph (c)(5) of this section);

(C) Includes the information required by paragraph (c)(3)(ii) of this section; and

(D) Does not involve an appraisal fee prohibited by paragraph (c)(6) of this section.

(ii) *Information included in qualified appraisal.*—A qualified appraisal shall include the following information:

(A) A description of the property in sufficient detail for a person who is not generally familiar with the type of property to ascertain that the property that was appraised is the property that was (or will be) contributed;

(B) In the case of tangible property, the physical condition of the property;

(C) The date (or expected date) of contribution to the donee;

(D) The terms of any agreement or understanding entered into (or expected to be entered into) by or on behalf of the donor or donee that relates to the use, sale, or other disposition of the property contributed, including, for example, the terms of any agreement or understanding that—

(1) Restricts temporarily or permanently a donee's right to use or dispose of the donated property,

(2) Reserves to, or confers upon, anyone (other than a donee organization or an organization participating with a donee organization in cooperative fund-raising) any right to the income from the contributed property or to the possession of the property, including the right to vote donated securities, to acquire the property by purchase or otherwise, or to designate the person having such income, possession, or right to acquire, or

(3) Earmarks donated property for a particular use;

(E) The name, address, and (if a taxpayer identification number is otherwise required by section 6109 and the regulations thereunder) the identifying number of the qualified appraiser; and, if the qualified appraiser is acting in his or her capacity as a partner in a partnership, an employee of any person (whether an individual, corporation, or partnerships), or an independent contractor engaged by a person other than the donor, the name, address, and taxpayer identification number (if a number is otherwise required by section 6109 and the regulations thereunder) of the partnership or the person who employs or engages the qualified appraiser;

(F) The qualifications of the qualified appraiser who signs the appraisal, including the appraiser's background, experience, education, and membership, if any, in professional appraisal associations;

(G) A statement that the appraisal was prepared for income tax purposes;

(H) The date (or dates) on which the property was appraised;

(I) The appraised fair market value (within the meaning of §1.170A-1(c)(2)) of the property on the date (or expected date) of contribution;

(J) The method of valuation used to determine the fair market value, such as the income approach, the market-data approach, and the replacement-cost-less-depreciation approach; and

(K) The specific basis for the valuation, such as specific comparable sales transactions or statistical sampling, including a justification for using sampling and an explanation of the sampling procedure employed.

(iii) *Effect of signature of the qualified appraiser.*—Any appraiser who falsely or fraudulently overstates the value of the contributed property referred to in a qualified appraisal or appraisal summary (as defined in paragraph (c)(3) and (4), respectively, of this section) that the appraiser has signed may be subject to a civil penalty under section 6701 for aiding and abetting an understatement of tax liability and, moreover, may have appraisals disregarded pursuant to 31 U.S.C. §330(c).

(iv) *Special rules.*—(A) *Number of qualified appraisals.*—For purposes of paragraph (c)(2)(i)(A) of this section, a separate qualified appraisal is required for each item of property that is not included in a group of similar items of property. See paragraph (c)(7)(iii) of this section for the definition of similar items of property. Only one qualified appraisal is required for a group of similar items of property contributed in the same taxable year of the donor, although a donor may obtain separate qualified appraisals for each item of property. A qualified appraisal prepared with respect to a group of similar items of property shall provide all the information required by paragraph (c)(3)(ii) of this section for each item of similar property, except that the appraiser may select any items whose aggregate value is appraised at $100 or less and provide a group description of such items.

(B) *Time of receipt of qualified appraisal.*—The qualified appraisal must be received by the donor before the due date (including extensions) of the return on which a deduction is first claimed (or reported in the case of a donor that is a partnership or S corporation) under section 170 with respect to the donated property, or, in the case of a deduction first claimed (or reported) on an amended return, the date on which the return is filed.

(C) *Retention of qualified appraisal.*—The donor must retain the qualified appraisal in the donor's records for so long as it may be relevant in the administration of any internal revenue law.

(D) *Appraisal disregarded pursuant to 31 U.S.C. §330(c).*—If an appraisal is disregarded pursuant to 31 U.S.C. §330(c) it shall have no probative effect as to the value of the appraised property. Such appraisal will, however, otherwise constitute a "qualified appraisal" for purposes of this paragraph (c) if the appraisal summary includes the declaration described in paragraph (c)(4)(ii)(L)(2) and the taxpayer had no knowledge that such declaration was false as of the time described in paragraph (c)(4)(i)(B) of this section.

(4) *Appraisal summary.*—(i) *In general.*—For purposes of this paragraph (c), except as provided in paragraph (c)(4)(iv)(A) of this section, the term "appraisal summary" means a summary of a qualified appraisal that—

(A) Is made on the form prescribed by the Internal Revenue Service;

(B) Is signed and dated (as described in paragraph (c)(4)(iii) of this section) by the donee (or presented to the donee for signature in cases described in paragraph (c)(4)(iv)(C)(2) of this section);

(C) Is signed and dated by the qualified appraiser (within the meaning of paragraph (c)(5) of this section) who prepared the qualified appraisal (within the meaning of paragraph (c)(3) of this section); and

(D) Includes the information required by paragraph (c)(4)(ii) of this section.

(ii) *Information included in an appraisal summary.*—An appraisal summary shall include the following information:

(A) The name and taxpayer identification number of the donor (social security number if the donor is an individual or employer identification number if the donor is a partnership or corporation);

(B) A description of the property in sufficient detail for a person who is not generally familiar with the type of property to ascertain that the property that was appraised is the property that was contributed;

(C) In the case of tangible property, a brief summary of the overall physical condition of the property at the time of the contribution;

(D) The manner of acquisition (*e.g.*, purchase, exchange, gift, or bequest) and the date of acquisition of the property by the donor, or, if the property was created, produced, or manufactured by or for the donor, a statement to that effect and the approximate date the property was substantially completed;

(E) The cost or other basis of the property adjusted as provided by section 1016;

(F) The name, address, and taxpayer identification number of the donee;

(G) The date the donee received the property;

(H) For charitable contributions made after June 6, 1988, a statement explaining whether or not the charitable contribution was made by means of a bargain sale and the amount of any consideration received from the donee for the contribution;

(I) The name, address, and (if a taxpayer identification number is otherwise required by section 6109 and the regulations thereunder) the identifying number of the qualified appraiser who signs the appraisal summary and of other persons as required by paragraph (c)(3)(ii)(E) of this section;

(J) The appraised fair market value of the property on the date of contribution;

(K) The declaration by the appraiser described in paragraph (c)(5)(i) of this section;

(L) A declaration by the appraiser stating that—

(1) The fee charged for the appraisal is not of a type prohibited by paragraph (c)(6) of this section; and

(2) Appraisals prepared by the appraiser are not being disregarded pursuant to 31 U.S.C. §330(c) on the date the appraisal summary is signed by the appraiser; and

(M) Such other information as may be specified by the form.

(iii) *Signature of the original donee.*—The person who signs the appraisal summary for the donee shall be an official authorized to sign the tax or information returns of the donee, or a person specifically authorized to sign appraisal summaries by an official authorized to sign the tax or information returns of such donee. In the case of a donee that is a governmental unit, the person who signs the appraisal summary for such donee shall be the official authorized by such donee to sign appraisal summaries. The signature of the donee on the appraisal summary does not represent concurrence in the appraised value of the contributed property. Rather, it represents acknowledgment of receipt of the property described in the appraisal summary on the date specified in the appraisal summary and that the donee understands the information reporting requirements imposed by section 6050L and §1.6050L-1. In general, §1.6050L-1 requires the donee to file an information return with the Internal Revenue Service in the event the donee sells, exchanges, consumes, or otherwise disposes of the property (or any portion thereof) described in the appraisal summary within 2 years after the date of the donor's contribution of such property.

(iv) *Special rules.*—(A) *Content of appraisal summary required in certain cases.*—With respect to contributions of nonpublicly traded stock described in paragraph (c)(2)(ii)(B)(1) of this section, contributions of securities described in paragraph (c)(7)(xi)(B) of this section, and contributions by C corporations described in paragraph (c)(2)(ii)(B)(3) of this section, the term "appraisal summary" means a document that—

(1) Complies with the requirements of paragraph (c)(4)(i)(A) and (B) of this section,

(2) Includes the information required by paragraph (c)(4)(ii)(A) through (H) of this section,

(3) Includes the amount claimed or reported as a charitable contribution deduction, and

(4) In the case of securities described in paragraph (c)(7)(xi)(B) of this section, also includes the pertinent average trading price (as described in paragraph (c)(7)(xi)(B)(2)(iii) of this section).

(B) *Number of appraisal summaries.*—A separate appraisal summary for each item of property described in paragraph (c)(1) of this section must be attached to the donor's return. If, during the donor's taxable year, the donor contributes similar items of property described in paragraph (c)(1) of this section to more than one donee, the donor shall attach to the donor's return a separate appraisal summary for each donee. See paragraph (c)(7)(iii) of this section for

the definition of similar items of property. If, however, during the donor's taxable year, a donor contributes similar items of property described in paragraph (c)(1) of this section to the same donee, the donor may attach to the donor's return a single appraisal summary with respect to all similar items of property contributed to the same donee. Such an appraisal summary shall provide all the information required by paragraph (c)(4)(ii) of this section for each item of property, except that the appraiser may select any items whose aggregate value is appraised at $100 or less and provide a group description for such items.

(C) *Manner of acquisition, cost basis and donee's signature.*— (1) If a taxpayer has reasonable cause for being unable to provide the information required by paragraph (c)(4)(ii)(D) and (E) of this section (relating to the manner of acquisition and basis of the contributed property), an appropriate explanation should be attached to the appraisal summary. The taxpayer's deduction will not be disallowed simply because of the inability (for reasonable cause) to provide these items of information.

(2) In rare and unusual circumstances in which it is impossible for the taxpayer to obtain the signature of the donee on the appraisal summary as required by paragraph (c)(4)(i)(B) of this section, the taxpayer's deduction will not be disallowed for that reason provided that the taxpayer attaches a statement to the appraisal summary explaining, in detail, why it was not possible to obtain the donee's signature. For example, if the donee ceases to exist as an entity subsequent to the date of the contribution and prior to the date when the appraisal summary must be signed, and the donor acted reasonably in not obtaining the donee's signature at the time of the contribution, relief under this paragraph (c)(4)(iv)(C)(2) would generally be appropriate.

(D) *Information excluded from certain appraisal summaries.*— The information required by paragraph (c)(4)(i)(C), paragraph (c)(4)(ii)(D), (E), (H) through (M), and paragraph (c)(4)(iv)(A)(3), and the average trading price referred to in paragraph (c)(4)(iv)(A)(4) of this section do not have to be included on the appraisal summary at the time it is signed by the donee or a copy is provided to the donee pursuant to paragraph (c)(4)(iv)(E) of this section.

(E) *Statement to be furnished by donors to donees.*—Every donor who presents an appraisal summary to a donee for signature after June 6, 1988, in order to comply with paragraph (c)(4)(i)(B) of this section shall furnish a copy of the appraisal summary to such donee.

(F) *Appraisal summary required to be provided to partners and S corporation shareholders.*—If the donor is a partnership or S corporation, the donor shall provide a copy of the appraisal summary to every partner or shareholder, respectively, who receives an allocation of a charitable contribution deduction under section 170 with respect to the property described in the appraisal summary.

(G) *Partners and S corporation shareholders.*—A partner of a partnership or shareholder of an S corporation who receives an allocation of a deduction under section 170 for a charitable contribution of property to which this paragraph (c) applies must attach a copy of the partnership's or S corporation's appraisal summary to the tax return on which the deduction for the contribution is first claimed. If such appraisal summary is not attached, the partner's or shareholder's deduction shall not be allowed except as provided for in paragraph (c)(4)(iv)(H) of this section.

(H) *Failure to attach appraisal summary.*—In the event that a donor fails to attach to the donor's return an appraisal summary as required by paragraph (c)(2)(i)(B) of this section, the Internal Revenue Service may request that the donor submit the appraisal summary within 90 days of the request. If such a request is made and the donor complies with the request within the 90-day period, the deduction under section 170 shall not be disallowed for failure to attach the appraisal summary, provided that the donor's failure to attach the appraisal summary was a good faith omission and the requirements of paragraph (c)(3) and (4) of this section are met (including the completion of the qualified appraisal prior to the date specified in paragraph (c)(3)(iv)(B) of this section).

(5) *Qualified appraiser.*—(i) *In general.*—The term "qualified appraiser" means an individual (other than a person described in paragraph (c)(5)(iv) of this section) who includes on the appraisal summary (described in paragraph (c)(4) of this section), a declaration that—

(A) The individual either holds himself or herself out to the public as an appraiser or performs appraisals on a regular basis;

(B) Because of the appraiser's qualifications as described in the appraisal (pursuant to paragraph (c)(3)(ii)(F) of this section), the appraiser is qualified to make appraisals of the type of property being valued;

(C) The appraiser is not one of the persons described in paragraph (c)(5)(iv) of this section; and

(D) The appraiser understands that an intentionally false or fraudulent overstatement of the value of the property described in the qualified appraisal or appraisal summary may subject the appraiser to a civil penalty under section 6701 for aiding and abetting an understatement of tax liability, and, moreover, the appraiser may have appraisals disregarded pursuant to 31 U.S.C. § 330(c) (see paragraph (c)(3)(iii) of this section).

(ii) *Exception.*—An individual is not a qualified appraiser with respect to a particular donation, even if the declaration specified in paragraph (c)(5)(i) of this section is provided in the appraisal summary, if the donor had knowledge of facts that would cause a reasonable person to expect the appraiser falsely to overstate the value of the donated property (*e.g.,* the donor and the appraiser make an agreement concerning the amount at which the property will be valued and the donor knows that such amount exceeds the fair market value of the property).

(iii) *Numbers of appraisers.*—More than one appraiser may appraise the donated property. If more than one appraiser appraises the property, the donor does not have to use each appraiser's appraisal for purposes of substantiating the charitable contribution deduction pursuant to this paragraph (c). If the donor uses the appraisal of more than one appraiser, or if two or more appraisers contribute to a single appraisal, each appraiser shall comply with the requirements of this paragraph (c), including signing the qualified appraisal and appraisal summary as required by paragraphs (c)(3)(i)(B) and (c)(4)(i)(C) of this section, respectively.

(iv) *Qualified appraiser exclusions.*—The following persons cannot be qualified appraisers with respect to particular property:

(A) The donor or the taxpayer who claims or reports a deduction under section 170 for the contribution of the property that is being appraised.

(B) A party to the transaction in which the donor acquired the property being appraised (*i.e.,* the person who sold, exchanged, or gave the property to the donor, or any person who acted as an agent for the transferor or for the donor with respect to such sale, exchange, or gift), unless the property is donated within 2 months of the date of acquisition and its appraised value does not exceed its acquisition price.

(C) The donee of the property.

(D) Any person employed by any of the foregoing persons (*e.g.,* if the donor acquired a painting from an art dealer, neither the art dealer nor persons employed by the dealer can be qualified appraisers with respect to that painting).

(E) Any person related to any of the foregoing persons under section 267(b), or with respect to appraisals made after June 6, 1988, married to a person who is in a relationship described in section 267(b) with any of the foregoing persons.

(F) An appraiser who is regularly used by any person described in paragraph (c)(5)(iv)(A), (B), or (C) of this section and who does not perform a majority of his or her appraisals made during his or her taxable year for other persons.

(6) *Appraisal fees.*—(i) *In general.*—Except as otherwise provided in paragraph (c)(6)(ii) of this section, no part of the fee arrangement for a qualified appraisal can be based, in effect, on a percentage (or set of percentages) of the appraised value of the property. If a fee arrangement for an appraisal is based in whole or in part on the amount of the appraised value of the property, if any, that is allowed as a deduction under section 170, after Internal Revenue Service examination or otherwise, it shall be treated as a fee based on a percentage of the appraised value of the property. For example, an appraiser's fee that is subject to reduction by the same percentage as the appraised value may be reduced by the Internal Revenue Service would be treated as a fee that violates this paragraph (c)(6).

(ii) *Exception.*—Paragraph (c)(6)(i) of this section does not apply to a fee paid to a generally recognized association that regulates appraisers provided all of the following requirements are met:

(A) The association is not organized for profit and no part of the net earnings of the association inures to the benefit of any private shareholder or individual (these terms have the same meaning as in section 501(c)),

(B) The appraiser does not receive any compensation from the association or any other persons for making the appraisal, and

(C) The fee arrangement is not based in whole or in part on the amount of the appraised value of the donated property, if any, that is allowed as a deduction under section 170 after Internal Revenue Service examination or otherwise.

(7) *Meaning of terms.*—For purposes of this paragraph (c)—

(i) *Closely held corporation.*—The term "closely held corporation" means any corporation (other than an S corporation) with respect to which the stock ownership requirement of paragraph (2) of section 542(a) of the Code is met.

(ii) *Personal service corporation.*—The term "personal service corporation" means any corporation (other than an S corporation) which is a service organization (within the meaning of section 414(m)(3) of the Code).

(iii) *Similar items of property.*—The phrase "similar items of property" means property of the same generic category or type, such as stamp collections (including philatelic supplies and books on stamp collecting), coin collections (including numismatic supplies and books on coin collecting), lithographs, paintings, photographs, books, nonpublicly traded stock, nonpublicly traded securities other than nonpublicly traded stock, land, buildings, clothing, jewelry, furniture, electronic equipment, household appliances, toys, everyday kitchenware, china, crystal, or silver. For example, if a donor claims on her return for the year deductions of $2,000 for books given by her to College A, $2,500 for books given by her to College B, and $900 for books given by her to College C, the $5,000 threshold of paragraph (c)(1) of this section is exceeded. Therefore, the donor must obtain a qualified appraisal for the books and attach to her return three appraisal summaries for the books donated to A, B, and C. For rules regarding the number of qualified appraisals and appraisal summaries required when similar items of property are contributed, see paragraphs (c)(3)(iv)(A) and (c)(4)(iv)(B), respectively, of this section.

(iv) *Donor.*—The term "donor" means a person or entity (other than an organization described in section 170(c) to which the donated property was previously contributed) that makes a charitable contribution of property.

(v) *Donee.*—The term "donee" means—

(A) Except as provided in paragraph (c)(7)(v)(B) and (C) of this section, an organization described in section 170(c) to which property is contributed,

(B) Except as provided in paragraph (c)(7)(v)(C) of this section, in the case of a charitable contribution of property placed in trust for the benefit of an organization described in section 170(c), the trust, or

(C) In the case of a charitable contribution of property placed in trust for the benefit of an organization described in section 170(c) made on or before June 6, 1988, the beneficiary that is an organization described in section 170(c), or if the trust has assumed the duties of a donee by signing the appraisal summary pursuant to paragraph (c)(4)(i)(B) of this section, the trust.

In general, the term refers only to the original donee. However, with respect to paragraph (c)(3)(ii)(D), the last sentence of paragraph (c)(4)(iii), and paragraph (c)(5)(iv)(C) of this section, the term "donee" means the original donee and all successor donees in cases where the original donee transfers the contributed property to a successor donee after June 6, 1988.

(vi) *Original donee.*—The term "original donee" means the donee to or for which property is initially donated by a donor.

(vii) *Successor donee.*—The term "successor donee" means any donee of property other than its original donee (*i.e.,* a transferee of property for less than fair market value from an original donee or another successor donee).

(viii) *Fair market value.*—For the meaning of the term "fair market value," see section 1.170A-1(c)(2).

(ix) *Nonpublicly traded securities.*—The term "nonpublicly traded securities" means securities (within the meaning of section 165(g)(2) of the Code) which are not publicly traded securities as defined in paragraph (c)(7)(xi) of this section.

(x) *Nonpublicly traded stock.*—The term "nonpublicly traded stock" means any stock of a corporation (evidence by a stock certificate) which is not a publicly traded security. The term stock does not include a debenture or any other evidence of indebtedness.

(xi) *Publicly traded securities.*—(A) *In general.*—Except as provided in paragraph (c)(7)(xi)(C) of this section, the term "publicly traded securities" means securities (within the meaning of section 165(g)(2) of the Code) for which (as of the date of the contribution) market quotations are readily available on an established securities market. For purposes of this section, market quotations are readily available on an established securities market with respect to a security if:

(1) The security is listed on the New York Stock Exchange, the American Stock Exchange, or any copy or regional exchange in which quotations are published on a daily basis, including

foreign securities listed on a recognized foreign, national, or regional exchange in which quotations are published daily basis;

(2) The security is regularly traded in the national or regional over-the-counter market, for which published quotations are available; or

(3) The security is a share of an open-end investment company (commonly known as a mutual fund) registered under the Investment Company Act of 1940, as amended (15 U.S.C. 80a-1 to 80b-2), for which quotations are published on a daily basis in a newspaper of general circulation throughout the United States.
(If the market value of an issue of a security is reflected only on an interdealer quotation system, the issue shall not be considered to be publicly traded unless the special rule described in paragraph (c)(7)(xi)(B) of this section is satisfied.)

(B) *Special rule.*—(1) *In General.*—An issue of a security that does not satisfy the requirements of paragraph (c)(7)(xi)(A)(1), (2), or (3) of this section shall nonetheless be considered to have market quotations readily available on an established securities market for purposes of paragraph (c)(7)(xi)(A) of this section if all of the following five requirements are met:

(i) The issue is regularly traded during the computational period (as defined in paragraph (c)(7)(xi)(B)(2)(iv) of this section) in a market that is reflected by the existence of an interdealer quotation system for the issue,

(ii) The issuer or an agent of the issuer computes the average trading price (as defined in paragraph (c)(7)(xi)(B)(2)(iii) of this section) for the issue for the computational period,

(iii) The average trading price and total volume of the issue during the computational period are published in a newspaper of general circulation throughout the United States not later than the last day of the month following the end of the calendar quarter in which the computational period ends,

(iv) The issuer or its agent keeps books and records that list for each transaction during the computational period involving each issue covered by this procedure the date of the settlement of the transaction, the name and address of the broker or dealer making the market in which the transaction occurred, and the trading price and volume, and

(v) The issuer or its agent permits the Internal Revenue Service to review the books and records described in paragraph (c)(7)(xi)(B)(1)(iv) of this section with respect to transactions during the computational period upon giving reasonable notice to the issuer or agent.

(2) *Definitions.*—For purposes of this paragraph (c)(7)(xi)(B)—

(i) *Issue of a security.*—The term "issue of a security" means a class of debt securities with the same obligor and identical terms except as to their relative denominations (amounts) or a class of stock having identical rights.

(ii) *Interdealer quotation system.*—The term "interdealer quotation system" means any system of general circulation to brokers and dealers that regularly disseminates quotations of obligations by two or more identified brokers or dealers, who are not related to either the issuer of the security or to the issuer's agent, who compute the average trading price of the security. A quotation sheet prepared and distributed by a broker or dealer in the regular course of its business and containing only quotations of such broker or dealer is not an interdealer quotation system.

(iii) *Average trading price.*—The term "average trading price" means the mean price of all transactions (weighted by volume), other than original issue or redemption transactions, conducted through a United States office of a broker or dealer who maintains a market in the issue of the security during the computational period. For this purpose, bid and asked quotations are not taken into account.

(iv) *Computational period.*—For calendar quarters beginning on or after June 6, 1988, the term "computational period" means weekly during October through December (beginning with the first Monday in October and ending with the first Sunday following the last Monday in December) and monthly during January through September (beginning January 1). For calendar quarters beginning before June 6, 1988, the term "computational period" means weekly during October through December and monthly during January through September.

(C) *Exception.*—Securities described in paragraph (c)(7)(xi)(A) or (B) of this section shall not be considered publicly traded securities if—

(1) The securities are subject to any restrictions that materially affect the value of the securities to the donor or prevent the securities from being freely traded, or

(2) If the amount claimed or reported as a deduction with respect to the contribution of the securities is different than the amount listed in the market quotations that are readily available on an established securities market pursuant to paragraph (c)(7)(xi)(A) or (B) of this section.

(D) *Market quotations and fair market value.*—The fair market value of a publicly traded security, as defined in this paragraph (c)(7)(xi), is not necessarily equal to its market quotation, its average trading price (as defined in paragraph (c)(7)(xi)(B)(2)(iii) of this section), or its face value, if any. See section 1.170A-1(c)(2) for the definition of "fair market value."

(d) *Charitable contributions; information required in support of deductions for taxable years beginning before January 1, 1983.*—(1) *In general.*—This paragraph (d)(1) shall apply to deductions for charitable contributions made in taxable years beginning before January 1, 1983. At the option of the taxpayer the requirements of this paragraph (d)(1) shall also apply to all charitable contributions made on or before December 31, 1984 (in lieu of the requirements of paragraphs (a) and (b) of this section). In connection with claims for deductions for charitable contributions, taxpayers shall state in their income tax returns the name of each organization to which a contribution was made and the amount and date of the actual payment of each contribution. If a contribution is made in property other than money, the taxpayer shall state the kind of property contributed, for example, used clothing, paintings, or securities, the method utilized in determining the fair market value of the property at the time the contribution was made, and whether or not the amount of the contribution was reduced under section 170(e). If a taxpayer makes more than one cash contribution to an organization during the taxable year, then in lieu of listing each cash contribution and the date of payment the taxpayer may state the total cash payments made to such organization during the taxable year. A taxpayer who elects under paragraph (d)(2) of § 1.170A-8 to apply section 170(e)(1) to his contributions and carryovers of 30-percent capital gain property must file a statement with his return indicating that he has made the election and showing the contributions in the current year and carryovers from preceding years to which it applies. For the definition of the term "30-percent capital gain property", see paragraph (d)(3) of § 1.170A-8.

(2) *Contribution by individual of property other than money.*—This paragraph (d)(2) shall apply to deductions for charitable contributions made in taxable years beginning before January 1, 1983. At the option of the taxpayer, the requirements of this paragraph (d)(2) shall also apply to contributions of property made on or before December 31, 1984 (in lieu of the requirements of paragraph (b) of this section).

(i) The name and address of the organization to which the contribution was made.

(ii) The date of the actual contribution.

(iii) A description of the property in sufficient detail to identify the particular property contributed, including in the case of tangible property the physical condition of the property at the time of contribution, and, in the case of securities, the name of the issuer, the type of security, and whether or not such security is regularly traded on a stock exchange or in an over-the-counter market.

(iv) The manner of acquisition, as, for example, by purchase, gift, bequest, inheritance, or exchange, and the approximate date of acquisition of the property by the taxpayer or, if the property was created, produced, or manufactured by or for the taxpayer, the approximate date the property was substantially completed.

(v) The fair market value of the property at the time the contribution was made, the method utilized in determining the fair market value, and, if the valuation was determined by appraisal, a copy of the signed report of the appraiser.

(vi) The cost or other basis, adjusted as provided by section 1016, of property, other than securities, held by the taxpayer for a period of less than five years immediately preceding the date on which the contribution was made and, when the information is available, of property, other than securities, held for a period of five years or more preceding the date on which the contribution was made.

(vii) In the case of property to which section 170(e) applies, the cost or other basis, adjusted as provided in section 1016, the reduction by reason of section 170(e)(1) in the amount of the charitable contribution otherwise taken into account, and the manner in which such reduction was determined.

(viii) The terms of any agreement or understanding entered into by or on behalf of the taxpayer which relates to the use, sale, or disposition of the property contributed, as, for example, the terms of any agreement or understanding which—

(A) Restricts temporarily or permanently the donee's right to dispose of the donated property.

(B) Reserves to, or confers upon, anyone other than the donee organization or other than an organization participating with such organization in cooperative fund raising, any right to the income from such property, to the possession of the property, including the right to vote securities, to acquire such property by purchase or otherwise, or to designate the person to have such income, possession, or right to acquire, or

(C) Earmarks contributed property for a particular charitable use, such as the use of donated furniture in the reading room of the donee organization's library.

(ix) The total amount claimed as a deduction for the taxable year due to the contribution of the property and, if less than the entire interest in the property is contributed during the taxable year, the amount claimed as a deduction in any prior year or years for contributions of other interests in such property, the name and address of each organization to which any such contribution was made, the place where any such property which is tangible property is located or kept, and the name of any person, other than the organization to which the property giving rise to the deduction was contributed, having actual possession of the property.

(e) [Reserved]

(f) *Substantiation of charitable contributions of $250 or more.*—(1) *In general.*—No deduction is allowed under section 170(a) for all or part of any contribution of $250 or more unless the taxpayer substantiates the contribution with a contemporaneous written acknowledgment from the donee organization. A taxpayer who makes more than one contribution of $250 or more to a donee organization in a taxable year may substantiate the contributions with one or more contemporaneous written acknowledgments. Section 170(f)(8) does not apply to a payment of $250 or more if the amount contributed (as determined under §1.170A-1(h)) is less than $250. Separate contributions of less than $250 are not subject to the requirements of section 170(f)(8), regardless of whether the sum of the contributions made by a taxpayer to a donee organization during a taxable year equals $250 or more.

(2) *Written acknowledgment.*—Except as otherwise provided in paragraphs (f)(8) through (f)(11) and (f)(13) of this section, a written acknowledgment from a donee organization must provide the following information—

(i) The amount of any cash the taxpayer paid and a description (but not necessarily the value) of any property other than cash the taxpayer transferred to the donee organization;

(ii) A statement of whether or not the donee organization provides any goods or services in consideration, in whole or in part, for any of the cash or other property transferred to the donee organization;

(iii) If the donee organization provides any goods or services other than intangible religious benefits (as described in section 170(f)(8)), a description and good faith estimate of the value of those goods or services; and

(iv) If the donee organization provides any intangible religious benefits, a statement to that effect.

(3) *Contemporaneous.*—A written acknowledgment is contemporaneous if it is obtained by the taxpayer on or before the earlier of—

(i) The date the taxpayer files the original return for the taxable year in which the contribution was made; or

(ii) The due date (including extensions) for filing the taxpayer's original return for that year.

(4) *Donee organization.*—For purposes of this paragraph (f), a donee organization is an organization described in section 170(c).

(5) *Goods or services.*—Goods or services means cash, property, services, benefits, and privileges.

(6) *In consideration for.*—A donee organization provides goods or services in consideration for a taxpayer's payment if, at the time the taxpayer makes the payment to the donee organization, the taxpayer receives or expects to receive goods or services in exchange for that payment. Goods or services a donee organization provides in consideration for a payment by a taxpayer include goods or services provided in a year other than the year in which the taxpayer makes the payment to the donee organization.

(7) *Good faith estimate.*—For purposes of this section, good faith estimate means a donee organization's estimate of the fair market value of any goods or services, without regard to the manner in which the organization in fact made that estimate. See §1.170A-1(h)(6) for rules regarding when a taxpayer may treat a donee organization's estimate of the value of goods or services as the fair market value.

(8) *Certain goods or services disregarded.*—(i) *In general.*—For purposes of section 170(f)(8), the following goods or services are disregarded—

(A) Goods or services that have insubstantial value under the guidelines provided in Revenue Procedures 90-12, 1990-1 C.B. 471, 92-49, 1992-1 C.B. 987, and any successor documents. (See §601.601(d)(2)(ii) of the Statement of Procedural Rules, 26 CFR part 601.); and

(B) Annual membership benefits offered to a taxpayer in exchange for a payment of $75 or less per year that consist of—

(1) Any rights or privileges, other than those described in section 170(l), that the taxpayer can exercise frequently during the membership period. Examples of such rights and privileges may include, but are not limited to, free or discounted admission to the organization's facilities or events, free or discounted parking, preferred access to goods or services, and discounts on the purchase of goods or services; and

(2) Admission to events during the membership period that are open only to members of a donee organization and for which the donee organization reasonably projects that the cost per person (excluding any allocable overhead) attending each such event is within the limits established for "low cost articles" under section 513(h)(2). The projected cost to the donee organization is determined at the time the organization first offers its membership package for the year (using section 3.07 of Revenue Procedure 90-12, or any successor documents, to determine the cost of any items or services that are donated).

(ii) *Examples.*—The following examples illustrate the rules of this paragraph (f)(8).

Example 1. Membership benefits disregarded. Performing Arts Center E is an organization described in section 170(c). In return for a payment of $75, E offers a package of basic membership benefits that includes the right to purchase tickets to performances one week before they go on sale to the general public, free parking in E's garage during evening and weekend performances, and a 10% discount on merchandise sold in E's gift shop. In return for a payment of $150, E offers a package of preferred membership benefits that includes all of the benefits in the $75 package as well as a poster that is sold in E's gift shop for $20. The basic membership and the preferred membership are each valid for twelve months, and there are approximately 50 performances of various productions at E during a twelve-month period. E's gift shop is open for several hours each week and at performance times. F, a patron of the arts, is solicited by E to make a contribution. E offers F the preferred membership benefits in return for a payment of $150 or more. F makes a payment of $300 to E. F can satisfy the substantiation requirement of section 170(f)(8) by obtaining a contemporaneous written acknowledgment from E that includes a description of the poster and a good faith estimate of its fair market value ($20) and disregards the remaining membership benefits.

Example 2. Contemporaneous written acknowledgment need not mention rights or privileges that can be disregarded. The facts are the same as in Example 1, except that F made a payment of $300 and received only a basic membership. F can satisfy the section 170(f)(8) substantiation requirement with a contemporaneous written acknowledgment stating that no goods or services were provided.

Example 3. Rights or privileges that cannot be exercised frequently. Community Theater Group G is an organization described in section 170(c). Every summer, G performs four different plays. Each play is performed two times. In return for a membership fee of $60, G offers its members free admission to any of its performances. Non-members may purchase tickets on a performance by performance basis for $15 a ticket. H, an individual who is a sponsor of the theater, is solicited by G to make a contribution. G tells H that the membership benefit will be provided in return for any payment of $60 or more. H chooses to make a payment of $350 to G and receives in return the membership benefit. G's membership benefit of free admission is not described in paragraph (f)(8)(i)(B) of this section because it is not a privilege that can be exercised frequently (due to the limited number of performances offered by G). Therefore, to meet the requirements of section 170(f)(8), a contemporaneous written acknowledgment of H's $350 payment must include a description of the free admission benefit and a good faith estimate of its value.

Example 4. Multiple memberships. In December of each year, K, an individual, gives each of her six grandchildren a junior membership in Dinosaur Museum, an organization described in section 170(c). Each junior membership costs $50, and K makes a single payment of $300 for all six memberships. A junior member is entitled to free admission to the museum and to weekly films, slide shows, and lectures about dinosaurs. In addition, each junior member receives a bi-monthly, non-commercial quality newsletter with information about dinosaurs and upcoming events. K's contemporaneous written acknowledgment from Dinosaur Museum may state that no goods or services were provided in exchange for K's payment.

(9) *Goods or services provided to employees or partners of donors.*—(i) *Certain goods or services disregarded.*—For purposes of section 170(f)(8), goods or services provided by a donee organization to employees of a donor, or to partners of a partnership that is a donor, in return for a payment to the organization may be disregarded to the extent that the goods or services provided to each employee or partner are the same as those described in paragraph (f)(8)(i) of this section.

(ii) *No good faith estimate required for other goods or services.*—If a taxpayer makes a contribution of $250 or more to a donee organization and, in return, the donee organization offers the taxpayer's employees or partners goods or services other than those described in paragraph (f)(9)(i) of this section, the contemporaneous written acknowledgment of the taxpayer's contribution is not required to include a good faith estimate of the value of such goods or services but must include a description of those goods or services.

(iii) *Example.*—The following example illustrates the rules of this paragraph (f)(9).

Example. Museum *J* is an organization described in section 170(c). For a payment of $40, *J* offers a package of basic membership benefits that includes free admission and a 10% discount on merchandise sold in *J*'s gift shop. *J*'s other membership categories are for supporters who contribute $100 or more. Corporation *K* makes a payment of $50,000 to *J* and, in return, *J* offers *K*'s employees free admission for one year, a tee-shirt with *J*'s logo that costs *J* $4.50, and a gift shop discount of 25% for one year. The free admission for *K*'s employees is the same as the benefit made available to holders of the $40 membership and is otherwise described in paragraph (f)(8)(i)(B) of this section. The tee-shirt given to each of *K*'s employees is described in paragraph (f)(8)(i)(A) of this section. Therefore, the contemporaneous written acknowledgment of *K*'s payment is not required to include a description or good faith estimate of the value of the free admission or the tee-shirts. However, because the gift shop discount offered to *K*'s employees is different than that offered to those who purchase the $40 membership, the discount is not described in paragraph (f)(8)(i) of this section. Therefore, the contemporaneous written acknowledgment of *K*'s payment is required to include a description of the 25% discount offered to *K*'s employees.

(10) *Substantiation of out-of-pocket expenses.*—A taxpayer who incurs unreimbursed expenditures incident to the rendition of services, within the meaning of §1.170A-1(g), is treated as having obtained a contemporaneous written acknowledgment of those expenditures if the taxpayer—

(i) Has adequate records under paragraph (a) of this section to substantiate the amount of the expenditures; and

(ii) Obtains by the date prescribed in paragraph (f)(3) of this section a statement prepared by the donee organization containing—

(A) A description of the services provided by the taxpayer;

(B) A statement of whether or not the donee organization provides any goods or services in consideration, in whole or in part, for the unreimbursed expenditures; and

(C) The information required by paragraphs (f)(2)(iii) and (iv) of this section.

(11) *Contributions made by payroll deduction.*—(i) *Form of substantiation.*—A contribution made by means of withholding from a taxpayer's wages and payment by the taxpayer's employer to a donee organization may be substantiated, for purposes of section 170(f)(8), by both—

(A) A pay stub, Form W-2, or other document furnished by the employer that sets forth the amount withheld by the employer for the purpose of payment to a donee organization; and

(B) A pledge card or other document prepared by or at the direction of the donee organization that includes a statement to the effect that the organization does not provide goods or services in whole or partial consideration for any contributions made to the organization by payroll deduction.

(ii) *Application of $250 threshold.*—For the purpose of applying the $250 threshold provided in section 170(f)(8)(A) to contributions made by the means described in paragraph (f)(11)(i) of this section, the amount withheld from each payment of wages to a taxpayer is treated as a separate contribution.

(12) *Distributing organizations as donees.*—An organization described in section 170(c), or an organization described in 5 CFR 950.105 (a Principal Combined Fund Organization for purposes of the Combined Federal Campaign) and acting in that capacity, that *receives a payment made as a contribution is treated as a donee* organization solely for purposes of section 170(f)(8), even if the organization (pursuant to the donor's instructions or otherwise) distributes the amount received to one or more organizations described in section 170(c). This paragraph (f)(12) does not apply, however, to a

case in which the distributee organization provides goods or services as part of a transaction structured with a view to avoid taking the goods or services into account in determining the amount of the deduction to which the donor is entitled under section 170.

(13) *Transfers to certain trusts.*—Section 170(f)(8) does not apply to a transfer of property to a trust described in section 170(f)(2)(B), a charitable remainder annuity trust (as defined in section 664(d)(1)), or a charitable remainder unitrust (as defined in section 664(d)(2) or (d)(3) or §1.664-3(a)(1)(i)(*b*)). Section 170(f)(8) does apply, however, to a transfer to a pooled income fund (as defined in section 642(c)(5)); for such a transfer, the contemporaneous written acknowledgment must state that the contribution was transferred to the donee organization's pooled income fund and indicate whether any goods or services (in addition to an income interest in the fund) were provided in exchange for the transfer. The contemporaneous written acknowledgment is not required to include a good faith estimate of the income interest.

(14) *Substantiation of payments to a college or university for the right to purchase tickets to athletic events.*—For purposes of paragraph (f)(2)(iii) of this section, the right to purchase tickets for seating at an athletic event in exchange for a payment described in section 170(l) is treated as having a value equal to twenty percent of such payment. For example, when a taxpayer makes a payment of $312.50 for the right to purchase tickets for seating at an athletic event, the right to purchase tickets is treated as having a value of $62.50. The remaining $250 is treated as a charitable contribution, which the taxpayer must substantiate in accordance with the requirements of this section.

(15) *Substantiation of charitable contributions made by a partnership or an S corporation.*—If a partnership or an S corporation makes a charitable contribution of $250 or more, the partnership or S corporation will be treated as the taxpayer for purposes of section 170(f)(8). Therefore, the partnership or S corporation must substantiate the contribution with a contemporaneous written acknowledgment from the donee organization before reporting the contribution on its income tax return for the year in which the contribution was made and must maintain the contemporaneous written acknowledgment in its records. A partner of a partnership or a shareholder of an S corporation is not required to obtain any additional substantiation for his or her share of the partnership's or S corporation's charitable contribution.

(16) *Purchase of an annuity.*—If a taxpayer purchases an annuity from a charitable organization and claims a charitable contribution deduction of $250 or more for the excess of the amount paid over the value of the annuity, the contemporaneous written acknowledgment must state whether any goods or services in addition to the annuity were provided to the taxpayer. The contemporaneous written acknowledgment is not required to include a good faith estimate of the value of the annuity. See §1.170A-1(d)(2) for guidance in determining the value of the annuity.

(17) *Substantiation of matched payments.*—(i) *In general.*—For purposes of section 170, if a taxpayer's payment to a donee organization is matched, in whole or in part, by another payor, and the taxpayer receives goods or services in consideration for its payment and some or all of the matching payment, those goods or services will be treated as provided in consideration for the taxpayer's payment and not in consideration for the matching payment.

(ii) *Example.*—The following example illustrates the rules of this paragraph (f)(17).

Example. Taxpayer makes a $400 payment to Charity *L*, a donee organization. Pursuant to a matching payment plan, Taxpayer's employer matches Taxpayer's $400 payment with an additional payment of $400. In consideration for the combined payments of $800, *L* gives Taxpayer an item that it estimates has a fair market value of $100. *L* does not give the employer any goods or services in consideration for its contribution. The contemporaneous written acknowledgment provided to the employer must include a statement that no goods or services were provided in consideration for the employer's $400 payment. The contemporaneous written acknowledgment provided to Taxpayer must include a statement of the amount of Taxpayer's payment, a description of the item received by Taxpayer, and a statement that *L*'s good faith estimate of the value of the item received by Taxpayer is $100.

(18) *Effective date.*—This paragraph (f) applies to contributions made on or after December 16, 1996. However, taxpayers may rely on the rules of this paragraph (f) for contributions made on or after January 1, 1994. [Reg. §1.170A-13.]

☐ [*T.D. 8002, 12-26-84. Amended by T.D. 8003, 12-26-84; T.D. 8199, 5-4-88; T.D. 8623, 10-11-95, T.D. 8690, 12-13-96, T.D. 9836, 7-27-2018, T.D. 9864, 6-11-2019 and T.D. 9907, 8-7-2020.*]

[Reg. §1.170A-14]

§1.170A-14. Qualified conservation contributions.—(a) *Qualified conservation contributions.*—A deduction under section 170 is generally not allowed for a charitable contribution of any interest in property that consists of less than the donor's entire interest in the property other than certain transfers in trust (see §1.170A-6 relating to charitable contributions in trust and §1.170A-7 relating to contributions not in trust of partial interests in property). However, a deduction may be allowed under section 170(f)(3)(B)(iii) for the value of a qualified conservation contribution if the requirements of this section are met. A qualified conservation contribution is the contribution of a qualified real property interest to a qualified organization exclusively for conservation purposes. To be eligible for a deduction under this section, the conservation purpose must be protected in perpetuity.

(b) *Qualified real property interest.*—(1) *Entire interest of donor other than qualified mineral interest.*—(i) The entire interest of the donor other than a qualified mineral interest is a qualified real property interest. A qualified mineral interest is the donor's interest in subsurface oil, gas, or other minerals and the right of access to such minerals.

(ii) A real property interest shall not be treated as an entire interest other than a qualified mineral interest by reason of section 170(h)(2)(A) and this paragraph (b)(1) if the property in which the donor's interest exists was divided prior to the contribution in order to enable the donor to retain control of more than a qualified mineral interest or to reduce the real property interest donated. See Treasury regulations §1.170A-7(a)(2)(i). An entire interest in real property may consist of an undivided interest in the property. But see section 170(h)(5)(A) and the regulations thereunder (relating to the requirement that the conservation purpose which is the subject of the donation must be protected in perpetuity).

Minor interests, such as rights-of-way, that will not interfere with the conservation purposes of the donation, may be transferred prior to the conservation contribution without affecting the treatment of a property interest as a qualified real property interest under this paragraph (b)(1).

(2) *Perpetual conservation restriction.*—A perpetual conservation restriction is a qualified real property interest. A "perpetual conservation restriction" is a restriction granted in perpetuity on the use which may be made of real property—including, an easement or other interest in real property that under state law has attributes similar to an easement (e.g., a restrictive covenant or equitable servitude). For purposes of this section, the terms "easement", "conservation restriction", and "perpetual conservation restriction" have the same meaning. The definition of "perpetual conservation restriction" under this paragraph (b)(3) is not intended to preclude the deductibility of a donation of affirmative rights to use a land or water area under §1.170A-13(d)(2). Any rights reserved by the donor in the donation of a perpetual conservation restriction must conform to the requirements of this section. See *e.g.,* paragraphs (d)(4)(ii), (d)(5)(i), (e)(3), and (g)(4) of this section.

(c) *Qualified organization.*—(1) *Eligible donee.*—To be considered an eligible donee under this section, an organization must be a qualified organization, have a commitment to protect the conservation purposes of the donation, and have the resources to enforce the restrictions. A conservation group organized or operated primarily or substantially for one of the conservation purposes specified in section 170(b)(4)(A) will be considered to have the commitment required by the preceding sentence. A qualified organization need not set aside funds to enforce the restrictions that are the subject of the contribution. For purposes of this section, the term "qualified organization" means:

(i) A governmental unit described in section 170(b)(1)(A)(v);

(ii) An organization described in section 170(b)(1)(A)(vi);

(iii) A charitable organization described in section 501(c)(3) that meets the public support test of section 509(a)(2);

(iv) A charitable organization described in section 501(c)(3) that meets the requirements of section 509(a)(3) and is controlled by an organization described in paragraphs (c)(1)(i), (ii), or (iii) of this *section.*

(2) *Transfers by donee.*—A deduction shall be allowed for a contribution under this section only if in the instrument of conveyance the donor prohibits the donee from subsequently transferring the easement (or, in the case of a remainder interest or the reservation of a qualified mineral interest, the property), whether or not for consideration, unless the donee organization, as a condition of the subsequent transfer, requires that the conservation purposes which the contribution was originally intended to advance continue to be carried out. Moreover, subsequent transfers must be restricted to organizations qualifying, at the time of the subsequent transfer, as an

eligible donee under paragraph (c)(1) of this section. When a later unexpected change in the conditions surrounding the property that is the subject of a donation under paragraphs (b)(1), (2), or (3) of this section makes impossible or impractical the continued use of the property for conservation purposes, the requirements of this paragraph will be met if the property is sold or exchanged and any proceeds are used by the donee organization in a manner consistent with the conservation purposes of the original contribution. In the case of a donation under paragraph (b)(3) of this section to which the preceding sentence applies, see also paragraph (g)(5)(ii) of this section.

(d) *Conservation purposes.*—(1) *In general.*—For purposes of section 170(h) and this section, the term "conservation purposes" means—

(i) The preservation of land areas for outdoor recreation by, or the education of, the general public, within the meaning of paragraph (d)(2) of this section,

(ii) The protection of a relatively natural habitat of fish, wildlife, or plants, or similar ecosystem, within the meaning of paragraph (d)(3) of this section,

(iii) The preservation of certain open space (including farmland and forest land) within the meaning of paragraph (d)(4) of this section, or

(iv) The preservation of an historically important land area or a certified historic structure, within the meaning of paragraph (d)(5) of this section.

(2) *Recreation or education.*—(i) *In general.*—The donation of a qualified real property interest to preserve land areas for the outdoor recreation of the general public or for the education of the general public will meet the conservation purposes test of this section. Thus, conservation purposes would include, for example, the preservation of a water area for the use of the public for boating or fishing, or a nature or hiking trail for the use of the public.

(ii) *Access.*—The preservation of land areas for recreation or education will not meet the test of this section unless the recreation or education is for the substantial and regular use of the general public.

(3) *Protection of environmental system.*—(i) *In general.*—The donation of a qualified real property interest to protect a significant relatively natural habitat in which a fish, wildlife, or plant community, or similar ecosystem, normally lives will meet the conservation purposes test of this section. The fact that the habitat or environment has been altered to some extent by human activity will not result in a deduction being denied under this section if the fish, wildlife, or plants continue to exist there in a relatively natural state. For example, the preservation of a lake formed by a man-made dam or a salt pond formed by a man-made dike would meet the conservation purposes test if the lake or pond were a natural feeding area for a wildlife community that included rare, endangered, or threatened native species.

(ii) *Significant habitat or ecosystem.*—Significant habitats and ecosystems include, but are not limited to, habitats for rare, endangered, or threatened species of animals, fish, or plants; natural areas that represent high quality examples of a terrestrial community or aquatic community, such as islands that are undeveloped or not intensely developed where the coastal ecosystem is relatively intact; and natural areas which are included in, or which contribute to, the ecological viability of a local, state, or national park, nature preserve, wildlife refuge, wilderness area, or other similar conservation area.

(iii) Limitations on public access to property that is the subject of a donation under this paragraph (d)(3) shall not render the donation nondeductible. For example, a restriction on all public access to the habitat of a threatened native animal species protected by a donation under this paragraph (d)(3) would not cause the donation to be nondeductible.

(4) *Preservation of open space.*—(i) *In general.*—The donation of a qualified real property interest to preserve open space (including farmland and forest land) will meet the conservation purposes test of this section if such a preservation is—

(A) Pursuant to a clearly delineated federal, state, or local governmental conservation policy and will yield a significant public benefit, or

(B) For the scenic enjoyment of the general public and will yield a significant public benefit.

An open space easement donated on or after December 18, 1980, must meet the requirements of section 170(h) in order to be deductible.

(ii) *Scenic enjoyment.*—(A) *Factors.*—A contribution made for the preservation of open space may be for the scenic enjoyment of the general public. Preservation of land may be for the scenic enjoyment of the general public if development of the property would impair

Reg. §1.170A-14(d)(4)(ii)(A)

the scenic character of the local rural or urban landscape or would interfere with a scenic panorama that can be enjoyed from a park, nature preserve, road, waterbody, trail, or historic structure or land area, and such area or transportation way is open to, or utilized by, the public. "Scenic enjoyment" will be evaluated by considering all pertinent facts and circumstances germane to the contribution. Regional variations in topography, geology, biology, and cultural and economic conditions require flexibility in the application of this test, but do not lessen the burden on the taxpayer to demonstrate the scenic characteristics of a donation under this paragraph. The application of a particular objective factor to help define a view as "scenic" in one setting may in fact be entirely inappropriate in another setting. Among the factors to be considered are:

(1) The compatibility of the land use with other land in the vicinity;

(2) The degree of contrast and variety provided by the visual scene;

(3) The openness of the land (which would be a more significant factor in an urban or densely populated setting or in a heavily wooded area);

(4) Relief from urban closeness;

(5) The harmonious variety of shapes and textures;

(6) The degree to which the land use maintains the scale and character of the urban landscape to preserve open space, visual enjoyment, and sunlight for the surrounding area;

(7) The consistency of the proposed scenic view with a methodical state scenic identification program, such as a state landscape inventory; and

(8) The consistency of the proposed scenic view with a regional or local landscape inventory made pursuant to a sufficiently rigorous review process, especially if the donation is endorsed by an appropriate state or local governmental agency.

(B) *Access.*—To satisfy the requirement of scenic enjoyment by the general public, visual (rather than physical) access to or across the property by the general public is sufficient. Under the terms of an open space easement on scenic property, the entire property need not be visible to the public for a donation to qualify under this section, although the public benefit from the donation may be insufficient to qualify for a deduction if only a small portion of the property is visible to the public.

(iii) *Governmental conservation policy.*—(A) *In general.*—The requirement that the preservation of open space be pursuant to a clearly delineated Federal, state, or local governmental policy is intended to protect the types of property identified by representatives of the general public as worthy of preservation or conservation. A general declaration of conservation goals by a single official or legislative body is not sufficient. However, a governmental conservation policy need not be a certification program that identifies particular lots or small parcels of individually owned property. This requirement will be met by donations that further a specific, identified conservation project, such as the preservation of land within a state or local landmark district that is locally recognized as being significant to that district; the preservation of a wild or scenic river; the preservation of farmland pursuant to a state program for flood prevention and control; or the protection of the scenic, ecological, or historic character of land that is contiguous to, or an integral part of, the surroundings of existing recreation or conservation sites. For example, the donation of a perpetual conservation restriction to a qualified organization pursuant to a formal resolution or certification by a local governmental agency established under state law specifically identifying the subject property as worthy of protection for conservation purposes will meet the requirement of this paragraph. A program need not be funded to satisfy this requirement, but the program must involve a significant commitment by the government with respect to the conservation project. For example, a governmental program according preferential tax assessment or preferential zoning for certain property deemed worthy of protection for conservation purposes would constitute a significant commitment by the government.

(B) *Effect of acceptance by governmental agency.*—Acceptance of an easement by an agency of the Federal Government or by an agency of a state or local government (or by a commission, authority, or similar body duly constituted by the state or local government and acting on behalf of the state or local government) tends to establish the requisite clearly delineated governmental policy, although such acceptance, without more, is not sufficient. The more rigorous the review process by the governmental agency, the more the acceptance of the easement tends to establish the requisite clearly delineated governmental policy. For example, in a state where the legislature has established an Environmental Trust to accept gifts to the state which meet certain conservation purposes and to submit the gifts to a review that requires the approval of the state's highest officials,

acceptance of a gift by the Trust tends to establish the requisite clearly delineated governmental policy. However, if the Trust merely accepts such gifts without a review process, the requisite clearly delineated governmental policy is not established.

(C) *Access.*—A limitation on public access to property subject to a donation under this paragraph (d)(4)(iii) shall not render the deduction nondeductible unless the conservation purpose of the donation would be undermined or frustrated without public access. For example, a donation pursuant to a governmental policy to protect the scenic character of land near a river requires visual access to the same extent as would a donation under paragraph (d)(4)(ii) of this section.

(iv) *Significant public benefit.*—(A) *Factors.*—All contributions made for the preservation of open space must yield a significant public benefit. Public benefit will be evaluated by considering all pertinent facts and circumstances germane to the contribution. Factors germane to the evaluation of public benefit from one contribution may be irrelevant in determining public benefit from another contribution. No single factor will necessarily be determinative. Among the factors to be considered are:

(1) The uniqueness of the property to the area;

(2) The intensity of land development in the vicinity of the property (both existing development and foreseeable trends of development);

(3) The consistency of the proposed open space use with public programs (whether Federal, state or local) for conservation in the region, including programs for outdoor recreation, irrigation or water supply protection, water quality maintenance or enhancement, flood prevention and control, erosion control, shoreline protection, and protection of land areas included in, or related to, a government approved master plan or land management area;

(4) The consistency of the proposed open space use with existing private conservation programs in the area, as evidenced by other land, protected by easement or fee ownership by organizations referred to in §1.170A-14(c)(1), in close proximity to the property;

(5) The likelihood that development of the property would lead to or contribute to degradation of the scenic, natural, or historic character of the area;

(6) The opportunity for the general public to use the property or to appreciate its scenic values;

(7) The importance of the property in preserving a local or regional landscape or resource that attracts tourism or commerce to the area;

(8) The likelihood that the donee will acquire equally desirable and valuable substitute property or property rights;

(9) The cost to the donee of enforcing the terms of the conservation restriction;

(10) The population density in the area of the property; and

(11) The consistency of the proposed open space use with a legislatively mandated program identifying particular parcels of land for future protection.

(B) *Illustrations.*—The preservation of an ordinary tract of land would not in and of itself yield a significant public benefit, but the preservation of ordinary land areas in conjunction with other factors that demonstrate significant public benefit or the preservation of a unique land area for public enjoyment would yield a significant public benefit. For example, the preservation of a vacant downtown lot would not by itself yield a significant public benefit, but the preservation of the downtown lot as a public garden would, absent countervailing factors, yield a significant public benefit. The following are other examples of contributions which would, absent countervailing factors, yield a significant public benefit: the preservation of farmland pursuant to a state program for flood prevention and control; the preservation of a unique natural land formation for the enjoyment of the general public; the preservation of woodland along a public highway pursuant to a government program to preserve the appearance of the area so as to maintain the scenic view from the highway; and the preservation of a stretch of undeveloped property located between a public highway and the ocean in order to maintain the scenic ocean view from the highway.

(v) *Limitation.*—A deduction will not be allowed for the preservation of open space under section 170(h)(4)(A)(iii), if the terms of the easement permit a degree of intrusion or future development that would interfere with the essential scenic quality of the land or with the governmental conservation policy that is being furthered by the donation. See §1.170A-14(e)(2) for rules relating to inconsistent use.

(vi) *Relationship of requirements.*—(A) *Clearly delineated governmental policy and significant public benefit.*—Although the requirements of "clearly delineated governmental policy" and "significant public benefit" must be met independently, for purposes of this section the two requirements may also be related. The more specific the governmental policy with respect to the particular site to be protected, the more likely the governmental decision, by itself, will tend to establish the significant public benefit associated with the donation. For example, while a statute in State X permitting preferential assessment for farmland is, by definition, governmental policy, it is distinguishable from a state statute, accompanied by appropriations, naming the X River as a valuable resource and articulating the legislative policy that the X River and the relatively natural quality of its surroundings be protected. On these facts, an open space easement on farmland in State X would have to demonstrate additional factors to establish "significant public benefit." The specificity of the legislative mandate to protect the X River, however, would by itself tend to establish the significant public benefit associated with an open space easement on land fronting the X River.

(B) *Scenic enjoyment and significant public benefit.*—With respect to the relationship between the requirements of "scenic enjoyment" and "significant public benefit," since the degrees of scenic enjoyment offered by a variety of open space easements are subjective and not as easily delineated as are increasingly specific levels of governmental policy, the significant public benefit of preserving a scenic view must be independently established in all cases.

(C) *Donations may satisfy more than one test.*—In some cases, open space easements may be both for scenic enjoyment and pursuant to a clearly delineated governmental policy. For example, the preservation of a particular scenic view identified as part of a scenic landscape inventory by a rigorous governmental review process will meet the tests of both paragraphs (d)(4)(i)(A) and (d)(4)(i)(B) of this section.

(5) *Historic preservation.*—(i) *In general.*—The donation of a qualified real property interest to preserve an historically important land area or a certified historic structure will meet the conservation purposes test of this section. When restrictions to preserve a building or land area within a registered historic district permit future development on the site, a deduction will be allowed under this section only if the terms of the restrictions require that such development conform with appropriate local, state, or Federal standards for construction or rehabilitation within the district. See also, § 1.170A-14(h)(3)(ii).

(ii) *Historically important land area.*—The term "historically important land area" includes:

(A) An independently significant land area including any related historic resources (for example, an archaeological site or a Civil War battlefield with related monuments, bridges, cannons, or houses) that meets the National Register Criteria for Evaluation in 36 CFR 60.4 (Pub. L. 89-665, 80 Stat. 915);

(B) Any land area within a registered historic district including any buildings on the land area that can reasonably be considered as contributing to the significance of the district; and

(C) Any land area (including related historic resources) adjacent to a property listed individually in the National Register of Historic Places (but not within a registered historic district) in a case where the physical or environmental features of the land area contribute to the historic or cultural integrity of the property.

(iii) *Certified historic structure.*—(A) *Definition.*—The term "certified historic structure," for purposes of this section, means any building, structure or land area which is—

(A) Listed in the National Register, or

(B) Located in a registered historic district (as defined in section 48(g)(3)(B)) and is certified by the Secretary of the Interior (pursuant to 36 CFR 67.4) to the Secretary of the Treasury as being of historic significance to the district.

A "structure" for purposes of this section means any structure, whether or not it is depreciable. Accordingly, easements on private residences may qualify under this section. In addition, a structure would be considered to be a certified historic structure if it were certified either at the time the transfer was made or at the due date (including extensions) for filing the donor's return for the taxable year in which the contribution was made.

(iv) *Access.*—(A) In order for a conservation contribution described in section 170(h)(4)(A)(iv) and this paragraph (d)(5) to be deductible, some visual public access to the donated property is required. In the case of an historically important land area, the entire property need not be visible to the public for a donation to qualify under this section. However, the public benefit from the donation may be insufficient to qualify for a deduction if only a small portion of the property is so visible. Where the historic land area or certified historic structure which is the subject of the donation is not visible from a public way (*e.g.*, the structure is hidden from view by a wall or shrubbery, the structure is too far from the public way, or interior characteristics and features of the structure are the subject of the easement), the terms of the easement must be such that the general public is given the opportunity on a regular basis to view the characteristics and features of the property which are preserved by the easement to the extent consistent with the nature and condition of the property.

(B) Factors to be considered in determining the type and amount of public access required under paragraph (d)(5)(iv)(A) of this section include the historical significance of the donated property, the nature of the features that are the subject of the easement, the remoteness or accessibility of the site of the donated property, the possibility of physical hazards to the public visiting the property (for example, an unoccupied structure in a dilapidated condition), the extent to which public access would be an unreasonable intrusion on any privacy interests of individuals living on the property, the degree to which public access would impair the preservation interests which are the subject of the donation, and the availability of opportunities for the public to view the property by means other than visits to the site.

(C) The amount of access afforded the public by the donation of an easement shall be determined with reference to the amount of access permitted by the terms of the easement which are established by the donor, rather than the amount of access actually provided by the donee organization. However, if the donor is aware of any facts indicating that the amount of access that the donee organization will provide is significantly less than the amount of access permitted under the terms of the easement, then the amount of access afforded the public shall be determined with reference to this lesser amount.

(v) *Examples.*—The provisions of paragraph (d)(5)(iv) of this section may be illustrated by the following examples:

Example (1). A and his family live in a house in a certified historic district in the State of X. The entire house, including its interior, has architectural features representing classic Victorian period architecture. A donates an exterior and interior easement on the property to a qualified organization but continues to live in the house with his family. A's house is surrounded by a high stone wall which obscures the public's view of it from the street. Pursuant to the terms of the easement, the house may be opened to the public from 10:00 a.m. to 4:00 p.m. on one Sunday in May and one Sunday in November each year for house and garden tours. These tours are to be under the supervision of the donee and open to members of the general public upon payment of a small fee. In addition, under the terms of the easement, the donee organization is given the right to photograph the interior and exterior of the house and distribute such photographs to magazines, newsletters, or other publicly available publications. The terms of the easement also permit persons affiliated with educational organizations, professional architectural associations, and historical societies to make an appointment through the donee organization to study the property. The donor is not aware of any facts indicating that the public access to be provided by the donee organization will be significantly less than that permitted by the terms of the easement. The 2 opportunities for public visits per year, when combined with the ability of the general public to view the architectural characteristics and features that are the subject of the easement through photographs, the opportunity for scholarly study of the property, and the fact that the house is used as an occupied residence, will enable the donation to satisfy the requirement of public access.

Example (2). B owns an unoccupied farmhouse built in the 1840's and located on a property that is adjacent to a Civil War battlefield. During the Civil War the farmhouse was used as quarters for Union troops. The battlefield is visited year round by the general public. The condition of the farmhouse is such that the safety of visitors will not be jeopardized and opening it to the public will not result in significant deterioration. The farmhouse is not visible from the battlefield or any public way. It is accessible only by way of a private road owned by B. B donates a conservation easement on the farmhouse to a qualified organization. The terms of the easement provide that the donee organization may open the property (via B's road) to the general public on four weekends each year from 8:30 a.m. to 4:00 p.m. The donation does not meet the public access requirement because the farmhouse is safe, unoccupied, and easily accessible to the general public who have come to the site to visit Civil War historic land areas (and related resources), but will only be open to the public on four weekends each year. However, the donation would meet the public access requirement if the terms of the easement permitted the donee organization to open the property to the public every other weekend during the year and the donor is not aware of any facts indicating that the donee organization will provide significantly less access than that permitted.

(e) *Exclusively for conservation purposes.*—(1) *In general.*—To meet the requirements of this section, a donation must be exclusively for conservation purposes. See paragraphs (c)(1) and (g)(1) through (g)(6)(ii) of this section. A deduction will not be denied under this

Reg. § 1.170A-14(e)(1)

section when incidental benefit inures to the donor merely as a result of conservation restrictions limiting the uses to which the donor's property may be put.

(2) *Inconsistent use.*—Except as provided in paragraph (e)(4) of this section, a deduction will not be allowed if the contribution would accomplish one of the enumerated conservation purposes but would permit destruction of other significant conservation interests. For example, the preservation of farmland pursuant to a state program for flood prevention and control would not qualify under paragraph (d)(4) of this section if under the terms of the contribution a significant naturally occurring ecosystem could be injured or destroyed by the use of pesticides in the operation of the farm. However, this requirement is not intended to prohibit uses of the property, such as selective timber harvesting or selective farming if, under the circumstances, those uses do not impair significant conservation interests.

(3) *Inconsistent use permitted.*—A use that is destructive of conservation interests will be permitted only if such use is necessary for the protection of the conservation interests that are the subject of the contribution. For example, a deduction for the donation of an easement to preserve an archaeological site that is listed on the National Register of Historic Places will not be disallowed if site excavation consistent with sound archaeological practices may impair a scenic view of which the land is a part. A donor may continue a pre-existing use of the property that does not conflict with the conservation purposes of the gift.

(f) *Examples.*—The provisions of this section relating to conservation purposes may be illustrated by the following examples.

Example (1). State S contains many large tract forests that are desirable recreation and scenic areas for the general public. The forests' scenic values attract millions of people to the State. However, due to the increasing intensity of land development in State S, the continued existence of forestland parcels greater than 45 acres is threatened. J grants a perpetual easement on a 100-acre parcel of forestland that is part of one of the State's scenic areas to a qualifying organization. The easement imposes restrictions on the use of the parcel for the purpose of maintaining its scenic values. The restrictions include a requirement that the parcel be maintained forever as open space devoted exclusively to conservation purposes and wildlife protection, and that there be no commercial, industrial, residential, or other development use of such parcel. The law of State S recognizes a limited public right to enter private land, particularly for recreational pursuits, unless such land is posted or the landowner objects. The easement specifically restricts the landowner from posting the parcel, or from objecting, thereby maintaining public access to the parcel according to the custom of the State. J's parcel provides the opportunity for the public to enjoy the use of the property and appreciate its scenic values. Accordingly, J's donation qualifies for a deduction under this section.

Example (2). A qualified conservation organization owns Greenacre in fee as a nature preserve. Greenacre contains a high quality example of a tall grass prairie ecosystem. Farmacre, an operating farm, adjoins Greenacre and is a compatible buffer to the nature preserve. Conversion of Farmacre to a more intense use, such as a housing development, would adversely affect the continued use of Greenacre as a nature preserve because of human traffic generated by the development. The owner of Farmacre donates an easement preventing any future development on Farmacre to the qualified conservation organization for conservation purposes. Normal agricultural uses will be allowed on Farmacre. Accordingly, the donation qualifies for a deduction under this section.

Example (3). H owns Greenacre, a 900-acre parcel of woodland, rolling pasture, and orchards on the crest of a mountain. All of Greenacre is clearly visible from a nearby national park. Because of the strict enforcement of an applicable zoning plan, the highest and best use of Greenacre is as a subdivision of 40-acre tracts. H wishes to donate a scenic easement on Greenacre to a qualifying conservation organization, but H would like to reserve the right to subdivide Greenacre into 90-acre parcels with no more than one single-family home allowable on each parcel. Random building on the property, even as little as one home for each 90 acres, would destroy the scenic character of the view. Accordingly, no deduction would be allowable under this section.

Example (4). Assume the same facts as in *example (3)*, except that not all of Greenacre is visible from the park and the deed of easement allows for limited cluster development of no more than five nine-acre clusters (with four houses on each cluster) located in areas generally not visible from the national park and subject to site and building plan approval by the donee organization in order to preserve the scenic view from the park. The donor and the donee have already identified sites where limited cluster development would not be visible from the park or would not impair the view. Owners of

homes in the clusters will not have any rights with respect to the surrounding Greenacre property that are not also available to the general public. Accordingly, the donation qualifies for a deduction under this section.

Example (5). In order to protect State S's declining open space that is suited for agricultural use from increasing development pressure that has led to a marked decline in such open space, the Legislature of State S passed a statute authorizing the purchase of "agricultural land development rights" on open acreage. Agricultural land development rights allow the State to place agricultural preservation restrictions on land designated as worthy of protection in order to preserve open space and farm resources. Agricultural preservation restrictions prohibit or limit construction or placement of buildings except those used for agricultural purposes or dwellings used for family living by the farmer and his family and employees; removal of mineral substances in any manner that adversely affects the land's agricultural potential; or other uses detrimental to retention of the land for agricultural use. Money has been appropriated for this program and some landowners have in fact sold their "agricultural land development rights" to State S. K owns and operates a small dairy farm in State S located in an area designated by the Legislature as worthy of protection. K desires to preserve his farm for agricultural purposes in perpetuity. Rather than selling the development rights to State S, K grants to a qualified organization an agricultural preservation restriction on his property in the form of a conservation easement. K reserves to himself, his heirs and assigns the right to manage the farm consistent with sound agricultural and management practices. The preservation of K's land is pursuant to a clearly delineated governmental policy of preserving open space available for agricultural use, and will yield a significant public benefit by preserving open space against increasing development pressures. Accordingly, a deduction is allowed under this section.

(g) *Enforceable in perpetuity.*—(1) *In general.*—In the case of any donation under this section, any interest in the property retained by the donor (and the donor's successors in interest) must be subject to legally enforceable restrictions (for example, by recordation in the land records of the jurisdiction in which the property is located) that will prevent uses of the retained interest inconsistent with the conservation purposes of the donation. In the case of a contribution of a remainder interest, the contribution will not qualify if the tenants, whether they are tenants for life or a term of years, can use the property in a manner that diminishes the conservation values which are intended to be protected by the contributions.

(2) *Protection of a conservation purpose in case of donation of property subject to a mortgage.*—In the case of conservation contributions made after February 13, 1986, no deduction will be permitted under this section for an interest in property which is subject to a mortgage unless the mortgagee subordinates its rights in the property to the right of the qualified organization to enforce the conservation purposes of the gift in perpetuity. For conservation contributions made prior to February 14, 1986, the requirement of section 170(h)(5)(A) is satisfied in the case of mortgaged property (with respect to which the mortgagee has not subordinated its rights) only if the donor can demonstrate that the conservation purpose is protected in perpetuity without subordination of the mortgagee's rights.

(3) *Remote future event.*—A deduction shall not be disallowed under section 170(f)(3)(B)(iii) and this section merely because the interest which passes to, or is vested in, the donee organization may be defeated by the performance of some act or the happening of some event, if on the date of the gift it appears that the possibility that such act or event will occur is so remote as to be negligible. See paragraph (e) of § 1.170A-1. For example, a state's statutory requirement that use restrictions must be rerecorded every 30 years to remain enforceable shall not, by itself, render an easement nonperpetual.

(4) *Retention of qualified mineral interest.*—(i) *In general.*—Except as otherwise provided in paragraph (g)(4)(ii) of this section, the requirements of this section are not met and no deduction shall be allowed in the case of a contribution of any interest when there is a retention by any person of a qualified mineral interest (as defined in paragraph (b)(1)(i) of this section) if at any time there may be extractions or removal of minerals by any surface mining method. Moreover, in the case of a qualified mineral interest gift, the requirement that the conservation purposes be protected in perpetuity is not satisfied if any method of mining that is inconsistent with the particular conservation purposes of a contribution is permitted at any time. See also § 1.170A-14(e)(2). However, a deduction under this section will not be denied in the case of certain methods of mining that may have limited, localized impact on the real property but that are not irremediably destructive of significant conservation interests. For example, a deduction will not be denied in a case where production facilities are concealed or compatible with existing topography and

Itemized Deductions for Individuals and Corps.
See p. 20,601 for regulations not amended to reflect law changes
25,585

landscape and when surface alteration is to be restored to its original state.

(ii) *Exception for qualified conservation contributions after July 1984.*—(A) A contribution made after July 18, 1984, of a qualified real property interest described in section 170(h)(2)(A) shall not be disqualified under the first sentence of paragraph (g)(4)(i) of this section if the following requirements are satisfied.

(1) The ownership of the surface estate and mineral interest were separated before June 13, 1976, and remain so separated up to and including the time of the contribution.

(2) The present owner of the mineral interest is not a person whose relationship to the owner of the surface estate is described at the time of the contribution in section 267(b) or section 707(b), and

(3) The probability of extraction or removal of minerals by any surface mining method is so remote as to be negligible.

Whether the probability of extraction or removal of minerals by surface mining is so remote as to be negligible is a question of fact and is to be made on a case by case basis. Relevant factors to be considered in determining if the probability of extraction or removal of minerals by surface mining is so remote as to be negligible include: geological, geophysical or economic data showing the absence of mineral reserves on the property, or the lack of commercial feasibility at the time of the contribution of surface mining the mineral interest.

(B) If the ownership of the surface estate and mineral interest first became separated after June 12, 1976, no deduction is permitted for a contribution under this section unless surface mining on the property is completely prohibited.

(iii) *Examples.*—The provisions of paragraph (g)(4)(i) and (ii) of this section may be illustrated by the following examples.

Example (1). K owns 5,000 acres of bottomland hardwood property along a major watershed system in the southern part of the United States. Agencies within the Department of the Interior have determined that southern bottomland hardwoods are a rapidly diminishing resource and a critical ecosystem in the south because of the intense pressure to cut the trees and convert the land to agricultural use. These agencies have further determined (and have indicated in correspondence with K) that bottomland hardwoods provide a superb habitat for numerous species and play an important role in controlling floods and in purifying rivers. K donates to a qualified organization his entire interest in this property other than his interest in the gas and oil deposits that have been identified under K's property. K covenants and can ensure that, although drilling for gas and oil on the property may have some temporary localized impact on the real property, the drilling will not interfere with the overall conservation purpose of the gift, which is to protect the unique bottomland hardwood ecosystem. Accordingly, the donation qualifies for a deduction under this section.

Example (2). Assume the same facts as in example (1), except that in 1979, K sells the mineral interest to A, an unrelated person, in an arm's-length transaction, subject to a recorded prohibition on the removal of any minerals by any surface mining method and a recorded prohibition against any mining technique that will harm the bottomland hardwood ecosystem. After the sale to A, K donates a qualified real property interest to a qualified organization to protect the bottomland hardwood ecosystem. Since at the time of the transfer, surface mining and any mining technique that will harm the bottomland hardwood ecosystem are completely prohibited, the donation qualifies for a deduction under this section.

(5) *Protection of conservation purpose where taxpayer reserves certain rights.*—(i) *Documentation.*—In the case of a donation made after February 13, 1986, of any qualified real property interest where the donor reserves rights the exercise of which may impair the conservation interests associated with the property, for a deduction to be allowable under this section the donor must make available to the donee, prior to the time the donation is made, documentation sufficient to establish the condition of the property at the time of the gift. Such documentation is designed to protect the conservation interests associated with the property, which although protected in perpetuity by the easement, could be adversely affected by the exercise of the reserved rights. Such documentation may include:

(A) The appropriate survey maps from the United States Geological Survey, showing the property line and other contiguous or nearby protected areas;

(B) A map of the area drawn to scale showing all existing man-made improvements or incursions (such as roads, buildings, fences, or gravel pits), vegetation and identification of flora and fauna (including, for example, rare species locations, animal breeding and roosting areas, and migration routes), land use history (including present uses and recent past disturbances), and distinct natural features (such as large trees and aquatic areas);

(C) An aerial photograph of the property at an appropriate scale taken as close as possible to the date the donation is made; and

(D) On-site photographs taken at appropriate locations on the property.

If the terms of the donation contain restrictions with regard to a particular natural resource to be protected, such as water quality or air quality, the condition of the resource at or near the time of the gift must be established. The documentation, including the maps and photographs, must be accompanied by a statement signed by the donor and a representative of the donee clearly referencing the documentation and in substance saying "This natural resources inventory is an accurate representation of [the protected property]at the time of the transfer."

(ii) *Donee's right to inspection and legal remedies.*—In the case of any donation referred to in paragraph (g)(5)(i) of this section, the donor must agree to notify the donee, in writing, before exercising any reserved right, *e.g.,* the right to extract certain minerals which may have an adverse impact on the conservation interests associated with the qualified real property interest. The terms of the donation must provide a right of the donee to enter the property at reasonable times for the purpose of inspecting the property to determine if there is compliance with the terms of the donation. Additionally, the terms of the donation must provide a right of the donee to enforce the conservation restrictions by appropriate legal proceedings including, but not limited to, the right to require the restoration of the property to its condition at the time of the donation.

(6) *Extinguishment.*—(i) *In general.*—If a subsequent unexpected change in the conditions surrounding the property that is the subject of a donation under this paragraph can make impossible or impractical the continued use of the property for conservation purposes, the conservation purpose can nonetheless be treated as protected in perpetuity if the restrictions are extinguished by judicial proceeding and all of the donee's proceeds (determined under paragraph (g)(6)(ii) of this section) from a subsequent sale or exchange of the property are used by the donee organization in a manner consistent with the conservation purposes of the original contribution.

(ii) *Proceeds.*—In the case of a donation made after February 13, 1986, for a deduction to be allowed under this section, at the time of the gift the donor must agree that the donation of the perpetual conservation restriction gives rise to a property right, immediately vested in the donee organization, with a fair market value that is at least equal to the proportionate value that the perpetual conservation restriction at the time of the gift bears to the value of the property as a whole at that time. See §1.170A-14(h)(3)(iii) relating to the allocation of basis. For purposes of this paragraph (g)(6)(ii), that proportionate value of the donee's property rights shall remain constant. Accordingly, when a change in conditions gives rise to the extinguishment of a perpetual conservation restriction under paragraph (g)(6)(i) of this section, the donee organization, on a subsequent sale, exchange,or involuntary conversion of the subject property, must be entitled to a portion of the proceeds at least equal to that proportionate value of the perpetual conservation restriction, unless state law provides that the donor is entitled to the full proceeds from the conversion without regard to the terms of the prior perpetual conservation restriction.

(h) *Valuation.*—(1) *Entire interest of donor other than qualified mineral interest.*—The value of the contribution under section 170 in the case of a contribution of a taxpayer's entire interest in property other than a qualified mineral interest is the fair market value of the surface rights in the property contributed. The value of the contribution shall be computed without regard to the mineral rights. See paragraph (h)(4), *example (1),* of this section.

(2) *Remainder interest in real property.*—In the case of a contribution of any remainder interest in real property, section 170(f)(4) provides that in determining the value of such interest for purposes of section 170, depreciation and depletion of such property shall be taken into account. See §170A-12. In the case of the contribution of a remainder interest for conservation purposes, the current fair market value of the property (against which the limitations of §1.170A-12 are applied) must take into account any pre-existing or contemporaneously recorded rights limiting, for conservation purposes, the uses to which the subject property may be put.

(3) *Perpetual conservation restriction.*—(i) *In general.*—The value of the contribution under section 170 in the case of a charitable contribution of a perpetual conservation restriction is the fair market value of the perpetual conservation restriction at the time of the contribution. See §1.170A-7(c). If there is a substantial record of sales of easements comparable to the donated easement (such as purchases pursuant to a governmental program), the fair market value of the donated easement is based on the sales prices of such comparable easements. If no substantial record of market-place sales is available

to use as a meaningful or valid comparison, as a general rule (but not necessarily in all cases) the fair market value of a perpetual conservation restriction is equal to the difference between the fair market value of the property it encumbers before the granting of the restriction and the fair market value of the encumbered property after the granting of the restriction. The amount of the deduction in the case of a charitable contribution of a perpetual conservation restriction covering a portion of the contiguous property owned by a donor and the donor's family as defined in section 267(c)(4) is the difference between the fair market value of the entire contiguous parcel of property before and after the granting of the restriction. If the granting of a perpetual conservation restriction after January 14, 1986, has the effect of increasing the value of any other property owned by the donor or a related person, the amount of the deduction for the conservation contribution shall be reduced by the amount of the increase in the value of the other property, whether or not such property is contiguous. If, as a result of the donation of a perpetual conservation restriction, the donor or a related person receives, or can reasonably expect to receive, financial or economic benefits that are greater than those that will inure to the general public from the transfer, no deduction is allowable under this section. However, if the donor or a related person receives, or can reasonably expect to receive, a financial or economic benefit that is substantial, but it is clearly shown that the benefit is less than the amount of the transfer, then a deduction under this section is allowable for the excess of the amount transferred over the amount of the financial or economic benefit received or reasonably expected to be received by the donor or the related person. For purposes of this paragraph (h)(3)(i), related person shall have the same meaning as in either section 267(b) or section 707(b). (See *example (10)* of paragraph (h)(4) of this section.)

(ii) *Fair market value of property before and after restriction.*—If before and after valuation is used, the fair market value of the property before contribution of the conservation restriction must take into account not only the current use of the property but also an objective assessment of how immediate or remote the likelihood is that the property, absent the restriction, would in fact be developed, as well as any effect from zoning, conservation, or historic preservation laws that already restrict the property's potential highest and best use. Further, there may be instances where the grant of a conservation restriction may have no material effect on the value of the property or may in fact serve to enhance, rather than reduce, the value of property. In such instances, no deduction would be allowable. In the case of a conservation restriction that allows for any development, however limited, on the property to be protected, the fair market value of the property after contribution of the restriction must take into account the effect of the development. In the case of a conservation easement such as an easement on a certified historic structure, the fair market value of the property after contribution of the restriction must take into account the amount of access permitted by the terms of the easement. Additionally, if before and after valuation is used, an appraisal of the property after contribution of the restriction must take into account the effect of restrictions that will result in a reduction of the potential fair market value represented by highest and best use but will, nevertheless, permit uses of the property that will increase its fair market value above that represented by the property's current use. The value of a perpetual conservation restriction shall not be reduced by reason of the existence of restrictions on transfer designed solely to ensure that the conservation restriction will be dedicated to conservation purposes. See § 1.170A-14(c)(3).

(iii) *Allocation of basis.*—In the case of the donation of a qualified real property interest for conservation purposes, the basis of the property retained by the donor must be adjusted by the elimination of that part of the total basis of the property that is properly allocable to the qualified real property interest granted. The amount of the basis that is allocable to the qualified real property interest shall bear the same ratio to the total basis of the property as the fair market value of the qualified real property interest bears to the fair market value of the property before the granting of the qualified real property interest. When a taxpayer donates to a qualifying conservation organization an easement on a structure with respect to which deductions are taken for depreciation, the reduction required by this paragraph (h)(3)(ii) in the basis of the property retained by the taxpayer must be allocated between the structure and the underlying land.

(4) *Examples.*—The provisions of this section may be illustrated by the following examples. In examples illustrating the value or *deductibility of donations,* the applicable restrictions and limitations of § 1.170A-4, with respect to reduction in amount of charitable contributions of certain appreciated property, and § 1.170A-8, with respect to limitations on charitable deductions by individuals, must also be taken into account.

Example (1). A owns Goldacre, a property adjacent to a state park. A wants to donate Goldacre to the state to be used as part of the park, but A wants to reserve a qualified mineral interest in the property, to exploit currently and to devise at death. The fair market value of the surface rights in Goldacre is $200,000 and the fair market value of the mineral rights is $100,000. In order to ensure that the quality of the park will not be degraded, restrictions must be imposed on the right to extract the minerals that reduce the fair market value of the mineral rights to $80,000. Under this section, the value of the contribution is $200,000 (the value of the surface rights).

Example (2). In 1984, B, who is 62, donates a remainder interest in Greenacre to a qualifying organization for conservation purposes. Greenacre is a tract of 200 acres of undeveloped woodland that is valued at $200,000 at its highest and best use. Under § 1.170A-12(b), the value of a remainder interest in real property following one life is determined under § 25.2512-5 of this chapter (Gift Tax Regulations). (See § 25.2512-5A of this chapter with respect to the valuation of annuities, interests for life or term of years, and remainder or reversionary interests transferred before May 1, 2009). Accordingly, the value of the remainder interest, and thus the amount eligible for an income tax deduction under section 170(f), is $55,996 ($200,000 × .27998).

Example (3). Assume the same facts as in *example (2),* except that Greenacre is B's 200-acre estate with a home built during the colonial period. Some of the acreage around the home is cleared; the balance of Greenacre, except for access roads, is wooded and undeveloped. See section 170(f)(3)(B)(i). However, B would like Greenacre to be maintained in its current state after his death, so he donates a remainder interest in Greenacre to a qualifying organization for conservation purposes pursuant to sections 170(f)(3)(B)(iii) and (h)(2)(B). At the time of the gift the land has a value of $200,000 and the house has a value of $100,000. The value of the remainder interest, and thus the amount eligible for an income tax deduction under section 170(f), is computed pursuant to § 1.170A-12. See § 1.170A-12(b)(3).

Example (4). Assume the same facts as in *example (2),* except that at age 62 instead of donating a remainder interest B donates an easement in Greenacre to a qualifying organization for conservation purposes. The fair market value of Greenacre after the donation is reduced to $110,000. Accordingly, the value of the easement, and thus the amount eligible for a deduction under section 170(f), is $90,000 ($200,000 less $110,000).

Example (5). Assume the same facts as in *example (4),* and assume that three years later, at age 65, B decides to donate a remainder interest in Greenacre to a qualifying organization for conservation purposes. Increasing real estate values in the area have raised the fair market value of Greenacre (subject to the easement) to $130,000. Accordingly, the value of the remainder interest, and thus the amount eligible for a deduction under section 170(f), is $41,639 ($130,000 × .32030).

Example (6). Assume the same facts as in *example (2),* except that at the time of the donation of a remainder interest in Greenacre, B also donates an easement to a different qualifying organization for conservation purposes. Based on all the facts and circumstances, the value of the easement is determined to be $100,000. Therefore, the value of the property after the easement is $100,000 and the value of the remainder interest, and thus the amount eligible for deduction under section 170(f), is $27,998 ($100,000 × .27998).

Example (7). C owns Greenacre, a 200-acre estate containing a house built during the colonial period. At its highest and best use, for home development, the fair market value of Greenacre is $300,000. C donates an easement (to maintain the house and Greenacre in their current state) to a qualifying organization for conservation purposes. The fair market value of Greenacre after the donation is reduced to $125,000. Accordingly, the value of the easement and the amount eligible for a deduction under section 170(f) is $175,000 ($300,000 less $125,000).

Example (8). Assume the same facts as in *example (7),* and assume that three years later, C decides to donate a remainder interest in Greenacre to a qualifying organization for conservation purposes. Increasing real estate values in the area have raised the fair market value of Greenacre to $180,000. Assume that because of the perpetual easement prohibiting any development of the land, the value of the house is $120,000 and the value of the land is $60,000. The value of the remainder interest, and thus the amount eligible for an income tax deduction under section 170(f), is computed pursuant to § 1.170A-12. See § 1.170A-12(b)(3).

Example (9). D owns property with a basis of $20,000 and a fair market value of $80,000. D donates to a qualifying organization an easement for conservation purposes that is determined under this section to have a fair market value of $60,000. The amount of basis allocable to the easement is $15,000 ($60,000/$80,000 = $15,000/$20,000). Accordingly, the basis of the property is reduced to $5,000 ($20,000 minus $15,000).

Example (10). E owns 10 one-acre lots that are currently woods and parkland. The fair market value of each of E's lots is $15,000 and the basis of each lot is $3,000. E grants to the county a perpetual easement for conservation purposes to use and maintain eight of the acres as a public park and to restrict any future development on those eight acres. As a result of the restrictions, the value of the eight acres is reduced to $1,000 an acre. However, by perpetually restricting development on this portion of the land, E has ensured that the two remaining acres will always be bordered by parkland, thus increasing their fair market value to $22,500 each. If the eight acres represented all of E's land, the fair market value of the easement would be $112,000, an amount equal to the fair market value of the land before the granting of the easement (8 × $15,000 = $120,000) minus the fair market value of the encumbered land after the granting of the easement (8 × $1,000 = $8,000). However, because the easement only covered a portion of the taxpayer's contiguous land, the amount of the deduction under section 170 is reduced to $97,000 ($150,000 − $53,000), that is, the difference between the fair market value of the entire tract of land before ($150,000) and after ((8 × $1,000) + (2 × $22,500)) the granting of the easement.

Example (11). Assume the same facts as in *example (10).* Since the easement covers a portion of E's land, only the basis of that portion is adjusted. Therefore, the amount of basis allocable to the easement is $22,400 ((8 × $3,000) × ($112,000/$120,000)). Accordingly, the basis of the eight acres encumbered by the easement is reduced to $1,600 ($24,000 − $22,400), or $200 for each acre. The basis of the two remaining acres is not affected by the donation.

Example (12). F owns and uses as professional offices a two-story building that lies within a registered historic district. F's building is an outstanding example of period architecture with a fair market value of $125,000. Restricted to its current use, which is the highest and best use of the property without making changes to the facade, the building and lot would have a fair market value of $100,000, of which $80,000 would be allocable to the building and $20,000 would be allocable to the lot. F's basis in the property is $50,000, of which $40,000 is allocable to the building and $10,000 is allocable to the lot. F's neighborhood is a mix of residential and commercial uses, and it is possible that F (or another owner) could enlarge the building for more extensive commercial use, which is its highest and best use. However, this would require changes to the facade. F would like to donate to a qualifying preservation organization an easement restricting any changes to the facade and promising to maintain the facade in perpetuity. The donation would qualify for a deduction under this section. The fair market value of the easement is $25,000 (the fair market value of the property before the easement, $125,000, minus the fair market value of the property after the easement, $100,000). Pursuant to § 1.170A-14(h)(3)(iii), the basis allocable to the easement is $10,000 and the basis of the underlying property (building and lot) is reduced to $40,000.

(i) *Substantiation requirement.*—If a taxpayer makes a qualified conservation contribution and claims a deduction, the taxpayer must maintain written records of the fair market value of the underlying property before and after the donation and the conservation purpose furthered by the donation, and such information shall be stated in the taxpayer's income tax return if required by the return or its instructions. See also § 1.170A-13(c) (relating to substantiation requirements for deductions in excess of $5,000 for charitable contributions made on or before July 30, 2018); § 1.170A-16(d) (relating to substantiation of charitable contributions of more than $5,000 made after July 30, 2018); § 1.170A-17 (relating to the definitions of qualified appraisal and qualified appraiser for substantiation of contributions made on or after January 1, 2019); and section 6662 (relating to the imposition of an accuracy-related penalty on underpayments). Taxpayers may rely on the rules in § 1.170A-16(d) for contributions made after June 3, 2004, or appraisals prepared for returns or submissions filed after August 17, 2006. Taxpayers may rely on the rules in § 1.170A-17 for appraisals prepared for returns or submissions filed after August 17, 2006.

(j) *Effective/applicability dates.*—Except as otherwise provided in § 1.170A-14(g)(4)(ii) and § 1.170A-14(i), this section applies only to contributions made on or after December 18, 1980. [Reg. § 1.170A-14.]

☐ [*T.D. 8069, 1-13-86. Amended by T.D. 8199, 5-4-88; T.D. 8540, 6-9-94; T.D. 8819, 4-29-99, T.D. 9448, 5-1-2009 and T.D. 9836, 7-27-2018.*]

[Reg. § 1.170A-15]

§ 1.170A-15. Substantiation requirements for charitable contribution of a cash, check, or other monetary gift.—(a) *In general.*—(1) *Bank record or written communication required.*—No deduction is allowed under sections 170(a) and 170(f)(17) for a charitable contribution in the form of a cash, check, or other monetary gift, as described in paragraph (b)(1) of this section, unless the donor substantiates the deduction with a bank record, as described in paragraph (b)(2) of this section, or a written communication, as described in paragraph (b)(3) of this section, from the donee showing the name of the donee, the date of the contribution, and the amount of the contribution.

(2) *Additional substantiation required for contributions of $250 or more.*—No deduction is allowed under section 170(a) for any contribution of $250 or more unless the donor substantiates the contribution with a contemporaneous written acknowledgment, as described in section 170(f)(8) and § 1.170A-13(f), from the donee.

(3) *Single document may be used.*—The requirements of paragraphs (a)(1) and (2) of this section may be met by a single document that contains all the information required by paragraphs (a)(1) and (2) of this section, if the document is obtained by the donor no later than the date prescribed by paragraph (c) of this section.

(b) *Terms.*—(1) *Monetary gift* includes a transfer of a gift card redeemable for cash, and a payment made by credit card, electronic fund transfer (as described in section 5061(e)(2)), an online payment service, or payroll deduction.

(2) *Bank record* includes a statement from a financial institution, an electronic fund transfer receipt, a canceled check, a scanned image of both sides of a canceled check obtained from a bank website, or a credit card statement.

(3) *Written communication* includes email.

(c) *Deadline for receipt of substantiation.*—The substantiation described in paragraph (a) of this section must be received by the donor on or before the earlier of—

(1) The date the donor files the original return for the taxable year in which the contribution was made; or

(2) The due date, including any extension, for filing the donor's original return for that year.

(d) *Special rules.*—(1) *Contributions made by payroll deduction.*—In the case of a charitable contribution made by payroll deduction, a donor is treated as meeting the requirements of section 170(f)(17) and paragraph (a) of this section if, no later than the date described in paragraph (c) of this section, the donor obtains—

(i) A pay stub, Form W-2, "Wage and Tax Statement," or other employer-furnished document that sets forth the amount withheld during the taxable year for payment to a donee; and

(ii) A pledge card or other document prepared by or at the direction of the donee that shows the name of the donee.

(2) *Distributing organizations as donees.*—The following organizations are treated as donees for purposes of section 170(f)(17) and paragraph (a) of this section, even if the organization (pursuant to the donor's instructions or otherwise) distributes the amount received to one or more organizations described in section 170(c):

(i) An organization described in section 170(c).

(ii) An organization described in 5 CFR 950.105 (a Principal Combined Fund Organization (PCFO) for purposes of the Combined Federal Campaign (CFC) and acting in that capacity. For purposes of the requirement for a written communication under section 170(f)(17), if the donee is a PCFO, the name of the local CFC campaign may be treated as the name of the donee organization.

(e) *Substantiation of out-of-pocket expenses.*—Paragraph (a)(1) of this section does not apply to a donor who incurs unreimbursed expenses of less than $250 incident to the rendition of services, within the meaning of § 1.170A-1(g). For substantiation of unreimbursed out-of-pocket expenses of $250 or more, see § 1.170A-13(f)(10).

(f) Charitable contributions made by partnership or S corporation.—If a partnership or an S corporation makes a charitable contribution, the partnership or S corporation is treated as the donor for purposes of section 170(f)(17) and paragraph (a) of this section.

(g) *Transfers to certain trusts.*—The requirements of section 170(f)(17) and paragraphs (a)(1) and (3) of this section do not apply to a transfer of a cash, check, or other monetary gift to a trust described in section 170(f)(2)(B); a charitable remainder annuity trust, as described in section 664(d)(1) and the corresponding regulations; or a charitable remainder unitrust, as described in section 664(d)(2) or (d)(3) and the corresponding regulations. The requirements of section 170(f)(17) and paragraphs (a)(1) and (2) of this section do apply, however, to a transfer to a pooled income fund, as defined in section 642(c)(5).

(h) *Effective/applicability date.*—This section applies to contributions made after July 30, 2018. Taxpayers may rely on the rules of this section for contributions made in taxable years beginning after August 17, 2006. [Reg. § 1.170A-15.]

☐ [*T.D. 9836, 7-27-2018.*]

[Reg. §1.170A-16]

§1.170A-16. Substantiation and reporting requirements for non-cash charitable contributions.—(a) *Substantiation of charitable contributions of less than $250.—*(1) *Individuals, partnerships, and certain corporations required to obtain receipt.—*Except as provided in paragraph (a)(2) of this section, no deduction is allowed under section 170(a) for a noncash charitable contribution of less than $250 by an individual, partnership, S corporation, or C corporation that is a personal service corporation or closely held corporation unless the donor maintains for each contribution a receipt from the donee showing the following information:

(i) The name and address of the donee;

(ii) The date of the contribution;

(iii) A description of the property in sufficient detail under the circumstances (taking into account the value of the property) for a person who is not generally familiar with the type of property to ascertain that the described property is the contributed property; and

(iv) In the case of securities, the name of the issuer, the type of security, and whether the securities are publicly traded securities within the meaning of § 1.170A-13(c)(7)(xi).

(2) *Substitution of reliable written records.—*(i) *In general.—*If it is impracticable to obtain a receipt (for example, where a donor deposits property at a donee's unattended drop site), the donor may satisfy the recordkeeping rules of this paragraph (a) by maintaining reliable written records, as described in paragraphs (a)(2)(ii) and (iii) of this section, for the contributed property.

(ii) *Reliable written records.—*The reliability of written records is to be determined on the basis of all of the facts and circumstances of a particular case, including the proximity in time of the written record to the contribution.

(iii) *Contents of reliable written records.—*Reliable written records must include—

(A) The information required by paragraph (a)(1) of this section;

(B) The fair market value of the property on the date the contribution was made;

(C) The method used in determining the fair market value; and

(D) In the case of a contribution of clothing or a household item as defined in § 1.170A-18(c), the condition of the item.

(3) *Additional substantiation rules may apply.—*For additional substantiation rules, see paragraph (f) of this section.

(b) *Substantiation of charitable contributions of $250 or more but not more than $500.—*No deduction is allowed under section 170(a) for a noncash charitable contribution of $250 or more but not more than $500 unless the donor substantiates the contribution with a contemporaneous written acknowledgment, as described in section 170(f)(8) and § 1.170A-13(f).

(c) *Substantiation of charitable contributions of more than $500 but not more than $5,000.—*(1) *In general.—*No deduction is allowed under section 170(a) for a noncash charitable contribution of more than $500 but not more than $5,000 unless the donor substantiates the contribution with a contemporaneous written acknowledgment, as described in section 170(f)(8) and § 1.170A-13(f), and meets the applicable requirements of this section.

(2) *Individuals, partnerships, and certain corporations also required to file Form 8283 (Section A).—*No deduction is allowed under section 170(a) for a noncash charitable contribution of more than $500 but not more than $5,000 by an individual, partnership, S corporation, or C corporation that is a personal service corporation or closely held corporation unless the donor completes Form 8283 (Section A), "Noncash Charitable Contributions," as provided in paragraph (c)(3) of this section, or a successor form, and files it with the return on which the deduction is claimed.

(3) *Completion of Form 8283 (Section A).—*A completed Form 8283 (Section A) includes—

(i) The donor's name and taxpayer identification number (for example, a social security number or employer identification number);

(ii) The name and address of the donee;

(iii) The date of the contribution;

(iv) The following information about the contributed property:

(A) A description of the property in sufficient detail under the circumstances, taking into account the value of the property, for a person who is not generally familiar with the type of property to ascertain that the described property is the contributed property;

(B) In the case of real or tangible personal property, the condition of the property;

(C) In the case of securities, the name of the issuer, the type of security, and whether the securities are publicly traded securities within the meaning of § 1.170A-13(c)(7)(xi);

(D) The fair market value of the property on the date the contribution was made and the method used in determining the fair market value;

(E) The manner of acquisition (for example, by purchase, gift, bequest, inheritance, or exchange), and the approximate date of acquisition of the property by the donor (except that in the case of a contribution of publicly traded securities as defined in § 1.170A-13(c)(7)(xi), a representation that the donor held the securities for more than one year is sufficient) or, if the property was created, produced, or manufactured by or for the donor, the approximate date the property was substantially completed;

(F) The cost or other basis, adjusted as provided by section 1016, of the property (except that the cost or basis is not required for contributions of publicly traded securities (as defined in § 1.170A-13(c)(7)(xi)) that would have resulted in long-term capital gain if sold on the contribution date, unless the donor has elected to limit the deduction to basis under section 170(b)(1)(C)(iii));

(G) In the case of tangible personal property, whether the donee has certified it for a use related to the purpose or function constituting the donee's basis for exemption under section 501, or in the case of a governmental unit, an exclusively public purpose; and

(v) Any other information required by Form 8283 (Section A) or the instructions to Form 8283 (Section A).

(4) *Additional requirement for certain vehicle contributions.—*In the case of a contribution of a qualified vehicle described in section 170(f)(12)(E) for which an acknowledgment by the donee organization is required under section 170(f)(12)(D), the donor must attach a copy of the acknowledgment to the Form 8283 (Section A) for the return on which the deduction is claimed.

(5) *Additional substantiation rules may apply.—*For additional substantiation rules, see paragraph (f) of this section.

(d) *Substantiation of charitable contributions of more than $5,000.—*(1) *In general.—*Except as provided in paragraph (d)(2) of this section, no deduction is allowed under section 170(a) for a noncash charitable contribution of more than $5,000 unless the donor—

(i) Substantiates the contribution with a contemporaneous written acknowledgment, as described in section 170(f)(8) and § 1.170A-13(f);

(ii) Obtains a qualified appraisal, as defined in § 1.170A-17(a)(1), prepared by a qualified appraiser, as defined in § 1.170A-17(b)(1); and

(iii) Completes Form 8283 (Section B), as provided in paragraph (d)(3) of this section, or a successor form, and files it with the return on which the deduction is claimed.

(2) *Exception for certain noncash contributions.—*A qualified appraisal is not required, and a completed Form 8283 (Section A) containing the information required in paragraph (c)(3) of this section meets the requirements of paragraph (d)(1)(iii) of this section for contributions of—

(i) Publicly traded securities as defined in § 1.170A-13(c)(7)(xi);

(ii) Property described in section 170(e)(1)(B)(iii) (certain intellectual property);

(iii) A qualified vehicle described in section 170(f)(12)(A)(ii) for which an acknowledgment under section 170(f)(12)(B)(iii) is provided; and

(iv) Property described in section 1221(a)(1) (inventory and property held by the donor primarily for sale to customers in the ordinary course of the donor's trade or business).

(3) *Completed Form 8283 (Section B).—*A completed Form 8283 (Section B) includes—

(i) The donor's name and taxpayer identification number (for example, a social security number or employer identification number);

(ii) The donee's name, address, taxpayer identification number, signature, the date signed by the donee, and the date the donee received the property;

(iii) The appraiser's name, address, taxpayer identification number, appraiser declaration, as described in paragraph (d)(4) of this section, signature, and the date signed by the appraiser;

(iv) The following information about the contributed property:

(A) The fair market value on the valuation effective date, as defined in § 1.170A-17(a)(5)(i).

(B) A description in sufficient detail under the circumstances, taking into account the value of the property, for a person who is not generally familiar with the type of property to ascertain that the described property is the contributed property.

(C) In the case of real property or tangible personal property, the condition of the property;

(v) The manner of acquisition (for example, by purchase, gift, bequest, inheritance, or exchange), and the approximate date of acquisition of the property by the donor, or, if the property was created, produced, or manufactured by or for the donor, the approximate date the property was substantially completed;

(vi) The cost or other basis of the property, adjusted as provided by section 1016;

(vii) A statement explaining whether the charitable contribution was made by means of a bargain sale and, if so, the amount of any consideration received for the contribution; and

(viii) Any other information required by Form 8283 (Section B) or the instructions to Form 8283 (Section B).

(4) *Appraiser declaration.*—The appraiser declaration referred to in paragraph (d)(3)(iii) of this section must include the following statement: "I understand that my appraisal will be used in connection with a return or claim for refund. I also understand that, if there is a substantial or gross valuation misstatement of the value of the property claimed on the return or claim for refund that is based on my appraisal, I may be subject to a penalty under section 6695A of the Internal Revenue Code, as well as other applicable penalties. I affirm that I have not been at any time in the three-year period ending on the date of the appraisal barred from presenting evidence or testimony before the Department of the Treasury or the Internal Revenue Service pursuant to 31 U.S.C. section 330(c)."

(5) *Donee signature.*—(i) *Person authorized to sign.*—The person who signs Form 8283 (Section B) for the donee must be either an official authorized to sign the tax or information returns of the donee, or a person specifically authorized to sign Forms 8283 (Section B) by that official. In the case of a donee that is a governmental unit, the person who signs Form 8283 (Section B) for the donee must be an official of the governmental unit.

(ii) *Effect of donee signature.*—The signature of the donee on Form 8283 (Section B) does not represent concurrence in the appraised value of the contributed property. Rather, it represents acknowledgment of receipt of the property described in Form 8283 (Section B) on the date specified in Form 8283 (Section B) and that the donee understands the information reporting requirements imposed by section 6050L and § 1.6050L-1.

(iii) *Certain information not required on Form 8283 (Section B) before donee signs.*—Before Form 8283 (Section B) is signed by the donee, Form 8283 (Section B) must be completed (as described in paragraph (d)(3) of this section), except that it is not required to contain the following:

(A) The appraiser declaration or information about the qualified appraiser.

(B) The manner or date of acquisition.

(C) The cost or other basis of the property.

(D) The appraised fair market value of the contributed property.

(E) The amount claimed as a charitable contribution.

(6) *Additional substantiation rules may apply.*—For additional substantiation rules, see paragraph (f) of this section.

(7) *More than one appraiser.*—More than one appraiser may appraise the donated property. If more than one appraiser appraises the property, the donor does not have to use each appraiser's appraisal for purposes of substantiating the charitable contribution deduction under this paragraph (d). If the donor uses the appraisal of more than one appraiser, or if two or more appraisers contribute to a single appraisal, each appraiser shall comply with the requirements of this paragraph (d) and the requirements in § 1.170A-17, including signing the qualified appraisal and appraisal summary.

(e) *Substantiation of noncash charitable contributions of more than $500,000.*—(1) *In general.*—Except as provided in paragraph (e)(2) of this section, no deduction is allowed under section 170(a) for a noncash charitable contribution of more than $500,000 unless the donor—

(i) Substantiates the contribution with a contemporaneous written acknowledgment, as described in section 170(f)(8) and § 1.170A-13(f);

(ii) Obtains a qualified appraisal, as defined in § 1.170A-17(a)(1), prepared by a qualified appraiser, as defined in § 1.170A-17(b)(1);

(iii) Completes, as described in paragraph (d)(3) of this section, Form 8283 (Section B) and files it with the return on which the deduction is claimed; and

(iv) Attaches the qualified appraisal of the property to the return on which the deduction is claimed.

(2) *Exception for certain noncash contributions.*—For contributions of property described in paragraph (d)(2) of this section, a qualified appraisal is not required, and a completed Form 8283 (Section A), containing the information required in paragraph (c)(3) of this section, meets the requirements of paragraph (e)(1)(iii) of this section.

(3) *Additional substantiation rules may apply.*—For additional substantiation rules, see paragraph (f) of this section.

(f) *Additional substantiation rules.*—(1) *Form 8283 (Section B) furnished by donor to donee.*—A donor who presents a Form 8283 (Section B) to a donee for signature must furnish to the donee a copy of the Form 8283 (Section B).

(2) *Number of Forms 8283 (Section A or Section B).*—(i) *In general.*—For each item of contributed property for which a Form 8283 (Section A or Section B) is required under paragraphs (c), (d), or (e) of this section, a donor must attach a separate Form 8283 (Section A or Section B) to the return on which the deduction for the item is claimed.

(ii) *Exception for similar items.*—The donor may attach a single Form 8283 (Section A or Section B) for all similar items of property, as defined in § 1.170A-13(c)(7)(iii), contributed to the same donee during the donor's taxable year, if the donor includes on Form 8283 (Section A or Section B) the information required by paragraph (c)(3) or (d)(3) of this section for each item of property.

(3) *Substantiation requirements for carryovers of noncash contribution deductions.*—The rules in paragraphs (c), (d), and (e) of this section (regarding substantiation that must be submitted with a return) also apply to the return for any carryover year under section 170(d).

(4) *Partners and S corporation shareholders.*—(i) *Form 8283 (Section A or Section B) must be provided to partners and S corporation shareholders.*—If the donor is a partnership or S corporation, the donor must provide a copy of the completed Form 8283 (Section A or Section B) to every partner or shareholder who receives an allocation of a charitable contribution deduction under section 170 for the property described in Form 8283 (Section A or Section B). Similarly, a recipient partner or shareholder that is a partnership or S corporation must provide a copy of the completed Form 8283 (Section A or Section B) to each of its partners or shareholders who receives an allocation of a charitable contribution deduction under section 170 for the property described in Form 8283 (Section A or Section B).

(ii) *Partners and S corporation shareholders must attach Form 8283 (Section A or Section B) to return.*—A partner of a partnership or shareholder of an S corporation who receives an allocation of a charitable contribution deduction under section 170 for property to which paragraph (c), (d), or (e) of this section applies must attach a copy of the partnership's or S corporation's completed Form 8283 (Section A or Section B) to the return on which the deduction is claimed.

(5) *Determination of deduction amount for purposes of substantiation rules.*—(i) *In general.*—In determining whether the amount of a donor's deduction exceeds the amounts set forth in section 170(f)(11)(B) (noncash contributions exceeding $500), 170(f)(11)(C) (noncash contributions exceeding $5,000), or 170(f)(11)(D) (noncash contributions exceeding $500,000), the rules of paragraphs (f)(5)(ii) and (iii) of this section apply.

(ii) *Similar items of property must be aggregated.*—Under section 170(f)(11)(F), the donor must aggregate the amount claimed as a deduction for all similar items of property, as defined in § 1.170A-13(c)(7)(iii), contributed during the taxable year. For rules regarding the number of qualified appraisals and Forms 8283 (Section A or Section B) required if similar items of property are contributed, see § 1.170A-13(c)(3)(iv)(A) and (4)(iv)(B).

(iii) *For contributions of certain inventory and scientific property, excess of amount claimed over cost of goods sold taken into account.*—(A) *In general.*—In determining the amount of a donor's contribution of property to which section 170(e)(3) (relating to contributions of inventory and other property) or (e)(4) (relating to contributions of scientific property used for research) applies, the donor must take into account only the excess of the amount claimed as a deduction over the amount that would have been treated as the cost of goods sold if the donor had sold the contributed property to the donee.

Reg. §1.170A-16(f)(5)(iii)(A)

(B) *Example.*—The following example illustrates the rule of this paragraph (f)(5)(iii):

Example. X Corporation makes a contribution of inventory described in section 1221(a)(2). The contribution, described in section 170(e)(3), is for the care of the needy. The cost of the property to X Corporation is $5,000 and the fair market value of the property at the time of the contribution is $11,000. Pursuant to section 170(e)(3)(B), X Corporation claims a charitable contribution deduction of $8,000 ($5,000 + 1/2 × ($11,000 − 5,000) = $8,000). The amount taken into account for purposes of determining the $5,000 threshold of paragraph (d) of this section is $3,000 ($8,000-$5,000).

(g) *Effective/applicability date.*—This section applies to contributions made after July 30, 2018. Taxpayers may rely on the rules of this section for contributions made after June 3, 2004, or appraisals prepared for returns or submissions filed after August 17, 2006. [Reg. §1.170A-16.]

☐ [T.D. 9836, 7-27-2018.]

[Reg. §1.170A-17]

§1.170A-17. Qualified appraisal and qualified appraiser.—
(a) *Qualified appraisal.*—(1) *Definition.*—For purposes of section 170(f)(11) and §1.170A-16(d)(1)(ii) and (e)(1)(ii), the term *qualified appraisal* means an appraisal document that is prepared by a qualified appraiser (as defined in paragraph (b)(1) of this section) in accordance with generally accepted appraisal standards (as defined in paragraph (a)(2) of this section) and otherwise complies with the requirements of this paragraph (a).

(2) *Generally accepted appraisal standards defined.*—For purposes of paragraph (a)(1) of this section, *generally accepted appraisal standards* means the substance and principles of the Uniform Standards of Professional Appraisal Practice, as developed by the Appraisal Standards Board of the Appraisal Foundation.

(3) *Contents of qualified appraisal.*—A qualified appraisal must include—

(i) The following information about the contributed property:

(A) A description in sufficient detail under the circumstances, taking into account the value of the property, for a person who is not generally familiar with the type of property to ascertain that the appraised property is the contributed property.

(B) In the case of real property or tangible personal property, the condition of the property.

(C) The valuation effective date, as defined in paragraph (a)(5)(i) of this section.

(D) The fair market value, within the meaning of §1.170A-1(c)(2), of the contributed property on the valuation effective date;

(ii) The terms of any agreement or understanding by or on behalf of the donor and donee that relates to the use, sale, or other disposition of the contributed property, including, for example, the terms of any agreement or understanding that—

(A) Restricts temporarily or permanently a donee's right to use or dispose of the contributed property;

(B) Reserves to, or confers upon, anyone, other than a donee or an organization participating with a donee in cooperative fundraising, any right to the income from the contributed property or to the possession of the property, including the right to vote contributed securities, to acquire the property by purchase or otherwise, or to designate the person having income, possession, or right to acquire; or

(C) Earmarks contributed property for a particular use;

(iii) The date, or expected date, of the contribution to the donee;

(iv) The following information about the appraiser:

(A) Name, address, and taxpayer identification number.

(B) Qualifications to value the type of property being valued, including the appraiser's education and experience.

(C) If the appraiser is acting in his or her capacity as a partner in a partnership, an employee of any person, whether an individual, corporation, or partnership, or an independent contractor engaged by a person other than the donor, the name, address, and taxpayer identification number of the partnership or the person who employs or engages the qualified appraiser;

(v) The signature of the appraiser and the date signed by the appraiser (appraisal report date);

(vi) The following declaration by the appraiser: "I understand that my appraisal will be used in connection with a return or claim for refund. *I also understand that, if there is a substantial or gross valuation misstatement of the value of the property claimed on the return or claim for refund that is based on my appraisal, I may be subject to a penalty under section 6695A of the Internal Revenue Code, as well as other applicable penalties. I affirm that I have not*

been at any time in the three-year period ending on the date of the appraisal barred from presenting evidence or testimony before the Department of the Treasury or the Internal Revenue Service pursuant to 31 U.S.C. section 330(c)";

(vii) A statement that the appraisal was prepared for income tax purposes;

(viii) The method of valuation used to determine the fair market value, such as the income approach, the market-data approach, or the replacement-cost-less-depreciation approach; and

(ix) The specific basis for the valuation, such as specific comparable sales transactions or statistical sampling, including a justification for using sampling and an explanation of the sampling procedure employed.

(4) *Timely appraisal report.*—A qualified appraisal must be signed and dated by the qualified appraiser no earlier than 60 days before the date of the contribution and no later than—

(i) The due date, including extensions, of the return on which the deduction for the contribution is first claimed;

(ii) In the case of a donor that is a partnership or S corporation, the due date, including extensions, of the return on which the deduction for the contribution is first reported; or

(iii) In the case of a deduction first claimed on an amended return, the date on which the amended return is filed.

(5) *Valuation effective date.*—(i) *Definition.*—The *valuation effective date* is the date to which the value opinion applies.

(ii) *Timely valuation effective date.*—For an appraisal report dated before the date of the contribution, as described in §1.170A-1(b), the valuation effective date must be no earlier than 60 days before the date of the contribution and no later than the date of the contribution. For an appraisal report dated on or after the date of the contribution, the valuation effective date must be the date of the contribution.

(6) *Exclusion for donor knowledge of falsity.*—An appraisal is not a qualified appraisal for a particular contribution, even if the requirements of this paragraph (a) are met, if the donor either failed to disclose or misrepresented facts, and a reasonable person would expect that this failure or misrepresentation would cause the appraiser to misstate the value of the contributed property.

(7) *Number of appraisals required.*—A donor must obtain a separate qualified appraisal for each item of property for which an appraisal is required under section 170(f)(11)(C) and (D) and paragraph (d) or (e) of §1.170A-16 and that is not included in a group of similar items of property, as defined in §1.170A-13(c)(7)(iii). For rules regarding the number of appraisals required if similar items of property are contributed, see section 170(f)(11)(F) and §1.170A-13(c)(3)(iv)(A).

(8) *Time of receipt of qualified appraisal.*—The qualified appraisal must be received by the donor before the due date, including extensions, of the return on which a deduction is first claimed, or reported in the case of a donor that is a partnership or S corporation, under section 170 with respect to the donated property, or, in the case of a deduction first claimed, or reported, on an amended return, the date on which the return is filed.

(9) *Prohibited appraisal fees.*—The fee for a qualified appraisal cannot be based to any extent on the appraised value of the property. For example, a fee for an appraisal will be treated as based on the appraised value of the property if any part of the fee depends on the amount of the appraised value that is allowed by the Internal Revenue Service after an examination.

(10) *Retention of qualified appraisal.*—The donor must retain the qualified appraisal for so long as it may be relevant in the administration of any internal revenue law.

(11) *Effect of appraisal disregarded pursuant to 31 U.S.C. section 330(c).*—If an appraiser has been prohibited from practicing before the Internal Revenue Service by the Secretary under 31 U.S.C. section 330(c) at any time during the three-year period ending on the date the appraisal is signed by the appraiser, any appraisal prepared by the appraiser will be disregarded as to value, but could constitute a qualified appraisal if the requirements of this section are otherwise satisfied, and the donor had no knowledge that the signature, date, or declaration was false when the appraisal and Form 8283 (Section B) were signed by the appraiser.

(12) *Partial interest.*—If the contributed property is a partial interest, the appraisal must be of the partial interest.

(b) *Qualified appraiser.*—(1) *Definition.*—For purposes of section 170(f)(11) and §1.170A-16(d)(1)(ii) and (e)(1)(ii), the term *qualified appraiser* means an individual with verifiable education and experience in valuing the type of property for which the appraisal is performed, as described in paragraphs (b)(2) through (4) of this section.

(2) *Education and experience in valuing the type of property.*—(i) *In general.*—An individual is treated as having education and experience in valuing the type of property within the meaning of paragraph (b)(1) of this section if, as of the date the individual signs the appraisal, the individual has—

(A) Successfully completed (for example, received a passing grade on a final examination) professional or college-level coursework, as described in paragraph (b)(2)(ii) of this section, in valuing the type of property, as described in paragraph (b)(3) of this section, and has two or more years of experience in valuing the type of property, as described in paragraph (b)(3) of this section; or

(B) Earned a recognized appraiser designation, as described in paragraph (b)(2)(iii) of this section, for the type of property, as described in paragraph (b)(3) of this section.

(ii) *Coursework must be obtained from an educational organization, generally recognized professional trade or appraiser organization, or employer educational program.*—For purposes of paragraph (b)(2)(i)(A) of this section, the coursework must be obtained from—

(A) A professional or college-level educational organization described in section 170(b)(1)(A)(ii);

(B) A generally recognized professional trade or appraiser organization that regularly offers educational programs in valuing the type of property; or

(C) An employer as part of an employee apprenticeship or educational program substantially similar to the educational programs described in paragraphs (b)(2)(ii)(A) and (B) of this section.

(iii) *Recognized appraiser designation defined.*—A *recognized appraiser designation* means a designation awarded by a generally recognized professional appraiser organization on the basis of demonstrated competency.

(3) *Type of property defined.*—(i) *In general.*—The type of property means the category of property customary in the appraisal field for an appraiser to value.

(ii) *Examples.*—The following examples illustrate the rule of paragraphs (b)(2)(i) and (b)(3)(i) of this section:

Example (1). Coursework in valuing type of property. There are very few professional-level courses offered in widget appraising, and it is customary in the appraisal field for personal property appraisers to appraise widgets. Appraiser *A* has successfully completed professional-level coursework in valuing personal property generally but has completed no coursework in valuing widgets. The coursework completed by Appraiser *A* is for the type of property under paragraphs (b)(2)(i) and (b)(3)(i) of this section.

Example (2). Experience in valuing type of property. It is customary for professional antique appraisers to appraise antique widgets. Appraiser *B* has 2 years of experience in valuing antiques generally and is asked to appraise an antique widget. Appraiser *B* has obtained experience in valuing the type of property under paragraphs (b)(2)(i) and (b)(3)(i) of this section.

Example (3). No experience in valuing type of property. It is not customary for professional antique appraisers to appraise new widgets. Appraiser *C* has experience in appraising antiques generally but no experience in appraising new widgets. Appraiser *C* is asked to appraise a new widget. Appraiser *C* does not have experience in valuing the type of property under paragraphs (b)(2)(i) and (b)(3)(i) of this section.

(4) *Verifiable.*—For purposes of paragraph (b)(1) of this section, education and experience in valuing the type of property are verifiable if the appraiser specifies in the appraisal the appraiser's education and experience in valuing the type of property, as described in paragraphs (b)(2) and (3) of this section, and the appraiser makes a declaration in the appraisal that, because of the appraiser's education and experience, the appraiser is qualified to make appraisals of the type of property being valued.

(5) *Individuals who are not qualified appraisers.*—The following individuals are not qualified appraisers for the appraised property:

(i) An individual who receives a fee prohibited by paragraph (a)(9) of this section for the appraisal of the appraised property.

(ii) The donor of the property.

(iii) A party to the transaction in which the donor acquired the property (for example, the individual who sold, exchanged, or gave the property to the donor, or any individual who acted as an agent for the transferor or for the donor for the sale, exchange, or gift), unless the property is contributed within 2 months of the date of acquisition and its appraised value does not exceed its acquisition price.

(iv) The donee of the property.

(v) Any individual who is either—

(A) Related, within the meaning of section 267(b), to, or an employee of, an individual described in paragraph (b)(5)(ii), (iii), or (iv) of this section;

(B) Married to an individual described in paragraph (b)(5)(v)(A) of this section; or

(C) An independent contractor who is regularly used as an appraiser by any of the individuals described in paragraph (b)(5)(ii), (iii), or (iv) of this section, and who does not perform a majority of his or her appraisals for others during the taxable year.

(vi) An individual who is prohibited from practicing before the Internal Revenue Service by the Secretary under 31 U.S.C. section 330(c) at any time during the three-year period ending on the date the appraisal is signed by the individual.

(c) *Effective/applicability date.*—This section applies to contributions made on or after January 1, 2019. Taxpayers may rely on the rules of this section for appraisals prepared for returns or submissions filed after August 17, 2006. [Reg. § 1.170A-17.]

☐ [*T.D.* 9836, 7-27-2018.]

[Reg. § 1.170A-18]

§ 1.170A-18. Contributions of clothing and household items.—(a) *In general.*—Except as provided in paragraph (b) of this section, no deduction is allowed under section 170(a) for a contribution of clothing or a household item (as described in paragraph (c) of this section) unless—

(1) The item is in good used condition or better at the time of the contribution; and

(2) The donor meets the substantiation requirements of § 1.170A-16.

(b) *Certain contributions of clothing or household items with claimed value of more than $500.*—The rule described in paragraph (a)(1) of this section does not apply to a contribution of a single item of clothing or a household item for which a deduction of more than $500 is claimed, if the donor submits with the return on which the deduction is claimed a qualified appraisal, as defined in § 1.170A-17(a)(1), of the property prepared by a qualified appraiser, as defined in § 1.170A-17(b)(1), and a completed Form 8283 (Section B), "Noncash Charitable Contributions," as described in § 1.170A-16(d)(3).

(c) *Definition of household items.*—For purposes of section 170(f)(16) and this section, the term *household items* includes furniture, furnishings, electronics, appliances, linens, and other similar items. Food, paintings, antiques, and other objects of art, jewelry, gems, and collections are not household items.

(d) *Effective/applicability date.*—This section applies to contributions made after July 30, 2018. Taxpayers may rely on the rules of this section for contributions made after August 17, 2006. [Reg. § 1.170A-18.]

☐ [*T.D.* 9836, 7-27-2018.]

[Reg. § 1.171-1]

§ 1.171-1. Bond premium.—(a) *Overview.*—(1) *In general.*—This section and § § 1.171-2 through 1.171-5 provide rules for the determination and amortization of bond premium by a holder. In general, a holder amortizes bond premium by offsetting the interest allocable to an accrual period with the premium allocable to that period. Bond premium is allocable to an accrual period based on a constant yield. The use of a constant yield to amortize bond premium is intended to generally conform the treatment of bond premium to the treatment of original issue discount under sections 1271 through 1275. Unless otherwise provided, the terms used in this section and § § 1.171-2 through 1.171-5 have the same meaning as those terms in sections 1271 through 1275 and the corresponding regulations. Moreover, unless otherwise provided, the provisions of this section and § § 1.171-2 through 1.171-5 apply in a manner consistent with those of sections 1271 through 1275 and the corresponding regulations. In addition, the anti-abuse rule in § 1.1275-2(g) applies for purposes of this section and § § 1.171-2 through 1.171-5.

(2) *Cross-references.*—For rules dealing with the adjustments to a holder's basis to reflect the amortization of bond premium, see § 1.1016-5(b). For rules dealing with the treatment of bond issuance premium by an issuer, see § 1.163-13.

(b) *Scope.*—(1) *In general.*—Except as provided in paragraph (b)(2) of this section and § 1.171-5, this section and § § 1.171-2 through 1.171-4 apply to any bond that, upon its acquisition by the holder, is held with bond premium. For purposes of this section and § § 1.171-2 through 1.171-5, the term *bond* has the same meaning as the term *debt instrument* in §1.1275-1(d).

(2) *Exceptions.*—This section and §§1.171-2 through 1.171-5 do not apply to—

(i) A bond described in section 1272(a)(6)(C) (regular interests in a REMIC, qualified mortgages held by a REMIC, and certain other debt instruments, or pools of debt instruments, with payments subject to acceleration);

(ii) A bond to which §1.1275-4 applies (relating to certain debt instruments that provide for contingent payments);

(iii) A bond held by a holder that has made a §1.1272-3 election with respect to the bond;

(iv) A bond that is stock in trade of the holder, a bond of a kind that would properly be included in the inventory of the holder if on hand at the close of the taxable year, or a bond held primarily for sale to customers in the ordinary course of the holder's trade or business; or

(v) A bond issued before September 28, 1985, unless the bond bears interest and was issued by a corporation or by a government or political subdivision thereof.

(c) *General rule.*—(1) *Tax-exempt obligations.*—A holder must amortize bond premium on a bond that is a tax-exempt obligation. See §1.171-2(c) *Example 4.*

(2) *Taxable bonds.*—A holder may elect to amortize bond premium on a taxable bond. Except as provided in paragraph (c)(3) of this section, a taxable bond is any bond other than a tax-exempt obligation. See §1.171-4 for rules relating to the election to amortize bond premium on a taxable bond.

(3) *Bonds the interest on which is partially excludable.*—For purposes of this section and §§1.171-2 through 1.171-5, a bond the interest on which is partially excludable from gross income is treated as two instruments, a tax-exempt obligation and a taxable bond. The holder's basis in the bond and each payment on the bond are allocated between the two instruments based on a reasonable method.

(d) *Determination of bond premium.*—(1) *In general.*—A holder acquires a bond at a premium if the holder's basis in the bond immediately after its acquisition by the holder exceeds the sum of all amounts payable on the bond after the acquisition date (other than payments of qualified stated interest). This excess is bond premium, which is amortizable under §1.171-2.

(2) *Additional rules for amounts payable on certain bonds.*—Additional rules apply to determine the amounts payable on a variable rate debt instrument, an inflation-indexed debt instrument, a bond that provides for certain alternative payment schedules, and a bond that provides for remote or incidental contingencies. See §1.171-3.

(e) *Basis.*—A holder determines its basis in a bond under this paragraph (e). This determination of basis applies only for purposes of this section and §§1.171-2 through 1.171-5. Because of the application of this paragraph (e), the holder's basis in the bond for purposes of these sections may differ from the holder's basis for determining gain or loss on the sale or exchange of the bond.

(1) *Determination of basis.*—(i) *In general.*—In general, the holder's basis in the bond is the holder's basis for determining loss on the sale or exchange of the bond.

(ii) *Bonds acquired in certain exchanges.*—If the holder acquired the bond in exchange for other property (other than in a reorganization defined in section 368) and the holder's basis in the bond is determined in whole or in part by reference to the holder's basis in the other property, the holder's basis in the bond may not exceed its fair market value immediately after the exchange. See paragraph (f) *Example 1* of this section. If the bond is acquired in a reorganization, see section 171(b)(4)(B).

(iii) *Convertible bonds.*—(A) *General rule.*—If the bond is a convertible bond, the holder's basis in the bond is reduced by an amount equal to the value of the conversion option. The value of the conversion option may be determined under any reasonable method. For example, the holder may determine the value of the conversion option by comparing the market price of the convertible bond to the market prices of similar bonds that do not have conversion options. See paragraph (f) *Example 2* of this section.

(B) *Convertible bonds acquired in certain exchanges.*—If the bond is a convertible bond acquired in a transaction described in paragraph (e)(1)(ii) of this section, the holder's basis in the bond may not exceed its fair market value immediately after the exchange reduced by the value of the conversion option.

(C) *Definition of convertible bond.*—A convertible bond is a bond that provides the holder with an option to convert the bond

into stock of the issuer, stock or debt of a related party (within the meaning of section 267(b) or 707(b)(1)), or into cash or other property in an amount equal to the approximate value of such stock or debt. For bonds issued on or after February 5, 2013, the term *stock* in the preceding sentence means an equity interest in any entity that is classified, for Federal tax purposes, as either a partnership or a corporation.

(2) *Basis in bonds held by certain transferees.*—Notwithstanding paragraph (e)(1) of this section, if the bond is transferred basis property (as defined in section 7701(a)(43)) and the transferor had acquired the bond at a premium, the holder's basis in the bond is—

(i) The holder's basis for determining loss on the sale or exchange of the bond; reduced by

(ii) Any amounts that the transferor could not have amortized under this paragraph (e) or under §1.171-4(c), except to the extent that the holder's basis already reflects a reduction attributable to such nonamortizable amounts.

(f) *Examples.*—The following examples illustrate the rules of this section:

Example 1. Bond received in liquidation of a partnership interest—(i) *Facts.* PR is a partner in partnership PRS. PRS does not have any unrealized receivables or inventory items as defined in section 751. On January 1, 1998, PRS distributes to PR a taxable bond, issued by an unrelated corporation, in liquidation of PR's partnership interest. At that time, the fair market value of PR's partnership interest is $40,000 and the basis is $100,000. The fair market value of the bond is $40,000.

(ii) *Determination of basis.* Under section 732(b), PR's basis in the bond is equal to PR's basis in the partnership interest. Therefore, PR's basis for determining loss on the sale or exchange of the bond is $100,000. However, because the distribution is treated as an exchange for purposes of section 171(b)(4), PR's basis in the bond is $40,000 for purposes of this section and §§1.171-2 through 1.171-5. See paragraph (e)(1)(ii) of this section.

Example 2. Convertible bond—(i) *Facts.* On January 1, A purchases for $1,100 B corporation's bond maturing in three years from the purchase date, with a stated principal amount of $1,000, payable at maturity. The bond provides for unconditional payments of interest of $30 on January 1 and July 1 of each year. In addition, the bond is convertible into 15 shares of B corporation stock at the option of the holder. On the purchase date, B corporation's nonconvertible, publicly-traded, three-year debt of comparable credit quality trades at a price that reflects a yield of 6.75 percent, compounded semiannually.

(ii) *Determination of basis.* A's basis for determining loss on the sale or exchange of the bond is $1,100. As of the purchase date, discounting the remaining payments on the bond at the yield at which B's similar nonconvertible bonds trade (6.75 percent, compounded semiannually) results in a present value of $980. Thus, the value of the conversion option is $120. Under paragraph (e)(1)(iii)(A) of this section, A's basis is $980 ($1,100 - $120) for purposes of this section and §§1.171-2 through 1.171-5. The sum of all amounts payable on the bond other than qualified stated interest is $1,000. Because A's basis (as determined under paragraph (e)(1)(iii)(A) of this section) does not exceed $1,000, A does not acquire the bond at a premium.

(iii) *Applicability date.* Notwithstanding §1.171-5(a)(1), this *Example 2* applies to bonds acquired on or after July 6, 2011.

[Reg. §1.171-1.]

☐ [T.D. 6278, 12-10-57. *Amended by* T.D. 8746, 12-30-97; T.D. 9533, 7-1-2011; T.D. 9612, 2-4-2013 *and* T.D. 9637, 9-5-2013.]

[Reg. §1.171-2]

§1.171-2. Amortization of bond premium.—(a) *Offsetting qualified stated interest with premium.*—(1) *In general.*—A holder amortizes bond premium by offsetting the qualified stated interest allocable to an accrual period with the bond premium allocable to the accrual period. This offset occurs when the holder takes the qualified stated interest into account under the holder's regular method of accounting.

(2) *Qualified stated interest allocable to an accrual period.*—See §1.446-2(b) to determine the accrual period to which qualified stated interest is allocable and to determine the accrual of qualified stated interest within an accrual period.

(3) *Bond premium allocable to an accrual period.*—The bond premium allocable to an accrual period is determined under this paragraph (a)(3). Within an accrual period, the bond premium allocable to the period accrues ratably.

(i) *Step one: Determine the holder's yield.*—The holder's yield is the discount rate that, when used in computing the present value of all remaining payments to be made on the bond (including payments of qualified stated interest), produces an amount equal to the holder's basis in the bond as determined under §1.171-1(e). For this purpose, the remaining payments include only payments to be made after the date the holder acquires the bond. The yield is calculated as of the date the holder acquires the bond, must be constant over the term of the bond, and must be calculated to at least two decimal places when expressed as a percentage.

(ii) *Step two: Determine the accrual periods.*—A holder determines the accrual periods for the bond under the rules of §1.1272-1(b)(1)(ii).

(iii) *Step three: Determine the bond premium allocable to the accrual period.*—The bond premium allocable to an accrual period is the excess of the qualified stated interest allocable to the accrual period over the product of the holder's adjusted acquisition price (as defined in paragraph (b) of this section) at the beginning of the accrual period and the holder's yield. In performing this calculation, the yield must be stated appropriately taking into account the length of the particular accrual period. Principles similar to those in §1.1272-1(b)(4) apply in determining the bond premium allocable to an accrual period.

(4) *Bond premium in excess of qualified stated interest.*—(i) *Taxable bonds.*—(A) *Bond premium deduction.*—In the case of a taxable bond, if the bond premium allocable to an accrual period exceeds the qualified stated interest allocable to the accrual period, the excess is treated by the holder as a bond premium deduction under section 171(a)(1) for the accrual period. However, the amount treated as a bond premium deduction is limited to the amount by which the holder's total interest inclusions on the bond in prior accrual periods exceed the total amount treated by the holder as a bond premium deduction on the bond in prior accrual periods. A deduction determined under this paragraph (a)(4)(i)(A) is not subject to section 67 (the 2-percent floor on miscellaneous itemized deductions). See *Example 1* of §1.171-3(e).

(B) *Carryforward.*—If the bond premium allocable to an accrual period exceeds the sum of the qualified stated interest allocable to the accrual period and the amount treated as a deduction for the accrual period under paragraph (a)(4)(i)(A) of this section, the excess is carried forward to the next accrual period and is treated as bond premium allocable to that period.

(C) *Carryforward in holder's final accrual period.*—(1) *Bond premium deduction.*—If there is a bond premium carryforward determined under paragraph (a)(4)(i)(B) of this section as of the end of the holder's accrual period in which the bond is sold, retired, or otherwise disposed of, the holder treats the amount of the carryforward as a bond premium deduction under section 171(a)(1) for the holder's taxable year in which the sale, retirement, or other disposition occurs. For purposes of §1.1016-5(b), the holder's basis in the bond is reduced by the amount of bond premium allowed as a deduction under this paragraph (a)(4)(i)(C)(1).

(2) *Effective/applicability date.*—Notwithstanding §1.171-5(a)(1), paragraph (a)(4)(i)(C)(1) of this section applies to a bond acquired on or after January 4, 2013. A taxpayer, however, may rely on paragraph (a)(4)(i)(C)(1) of this section for a bond acquired before that date.

(ii) *Tax-exempt obligations.*—In the case of a tax-exempt obligation, if the bond premium allocable to an accrual period exceeds the qualified stated interest allocable to the accrual period, the excess is a nondeductible loss. If a regulated investment company (RIC) within the meaning of section 851 has excess bond premium for an accrual period that would be a nondeductible loss under the prior sentence, the RIC must use this excess bond premium to reduce its tax-exempt interest income on other tax-exempt obligations held during the accrual period.

(5) *Additional rules for certain bonds.*—Additional rules apply to determine the amortization of bond premium on a variable rate debt instrument, an inflation-indexed debt instrument, a bond that provides for certain alternative payment schedules, and a bond that provides for remote or incidental contingencies. See §1.171-3.

(b) *Adjusted acquisition price.*—The adjusted acquisition price of a bond at the beginning of the first accrual period is the holder's basis as determined under §1.171-1(e). Thereafter, the adjusted acquisition price is the holder's basis in the bond decreased by—

(1) The amount of bond premium previously allocable under paragraph (a)(3) of this section; and

(2) The amount of any payment previously made on the bond other than a payment of qualified stated interest.

(c) *Examples.*—The following examples illustrate the rules of this section. Each example assumes the holder uses the calendar year as its taxable year and has elected to amortize bond premium, effective for all relevant taxable years. In addition, each example assumes a 30-day month and 360-day year. Although, for purposes of simplicity, the yield as stated is rounded to two decimal places, the computations do not reflect this rounding convention. The examples are as follows:

Example 1. Taxable bond—(i) *Facts.* On February 1, 1999, A purchases for $110,000 a taxable bond maturing on February 1, 2006, with a stated principal amount of $100,000, payable at maturity. The bond provides for unconditional payments of interest of $10,000, payable on February 1 of each year. A uses the cash receipts and disbursements method of accounting, and A decides to use annual accrual periods ending on February 1 of each year.

(ii) *Amount of bond premium.* The interest payments on the bond are qualified stated interest. Therefore, the sum of all amounts payable on the bond (other than the interest payments) is $100,000. Under §1.171-1, the amount of bond premium is $10,000 ($110,000 – $100,000).

(iii) *Bond premium allocable to the first accrual period.* Based on the remaining payment schedule of the bond and A's basis in the bond, A's yield is 8.07 percent, compounded annually. The bond premium allocable to the accrual period ending on February 1, 2000, is the excess of the qualified stated interest allocable to the period ($10,000) over the product of the adjusted acquisition price at the beginning of the period ($110,000) and A's yield (8.07 percent, compounded annually). Therefore, the bond premium allocable to the accrual period is $1,118.17 ($10,000 – $8,881.83).

(iv) *Premium used to offset interest.* Although A receives an interest payment of $10,000 on February 1, 2000, A only includes in income $8,881.83, the qualified stated interest allocable to the period ($10,000) offset with bond premium allocable to the period ($1,118.17). Under §1.1016-5(b), A's basis in the bond is reduced by $1,118.17 on February 1, 2000.

Example 2. Alternative accrual periods—(i) *Facts.* The facts are the same as in *Example 1* of this paragraph (c) except that A decides to use semiannual accrual periods ending on February 1 and August 1 of each year.

(ii) *Bond premium allocable to the first accrual period.* Based on the remaining payment schedule of the bond and A's basis in the bond, A's yield is 7.92 percent, compounded semiannually. The bond premium allocable to the accrual period ending on August 1, 1999, is the excess of the qualified stated interest allocable to the period ($5,000) over the product of the adjusted acquisition price at the beginning of the period ($110,000) and A's yield, stated appropriately taking into account the length of the accrual period (7.92 percent/2). Therefore, the bond premium allocable to the accrual period is $645.29 ($5,000 – $4,354.71). Although the accrual period ends on August 1, 1999, the qualified stated interest of $5,000 is not taken into income until February 1, 2000, the date it is received. Likewise, the bond premium of $645.29 is not taken into account until February 1, 2000. The adjusted acquisition price of the bond on August 1, 1999, is $109,354.71 (the adjusted acquisition price at the beginning of the period ($110,000) less the bond premium allocable to the period ($645.29)).

(iii) *Bond premium allocable to the second accrual period.* Because the interval between payments of qualified stated interest contains more than one accrual period, the adjusted acquisition price at the beginning of the second accrual period must be adjusted for the accrued but unpaid qualified stated interest. See paragraph (a)(3)(iii) of this section and §1.1272-1(b)(4)(i)(B). Therefore, the adjusted acquisition price on August 1, 1999, is $114,354.71 ($109,354.71 + $5,000). The bond premium allocable to the accrual period ending on February 1, 2000, is the excess of the qualified stated interest allocable to the period ($5,000) over the product of the adjusted acquisition price at the beginning of the period ($114,354.71) and A's yield, stated appropriately taking into account the length of the accrual period (7.92 percent/2). Therefore, the bond premium allocable to the accrual period is $472.88 ($5,000 – $4,527.12).

(iv) *Premium used to offset interest.* Although A receives an interest payment of $10,000 on February 1, 2000, A only includes in income $8,881.83, the qualified stated interest of $10,000 ($5,000 allocable to the accrual period ending on August 1, 1999, and $5,000 allocable to the accrual period ending on February 1, 2000) offset with bond premium of $1,118.17 ($645.29 allocable to the accrual period ending on August 1, 1999, and $472.88 allocable to the accrual period ending on February 1, 2000). As indicated in *Example 1* of this paragraph (c), this same amount would be taken into income at the same time had A used annual accrual periods.

Example 3. Holder uses accrual method of accounting—(i) *Facts.* The facts are the same as in *Example 1* of this paragraph (c) except that A uses an accrual method of accounting. Thus, for the accrual period ending on February 1, 2000, the qualified stated interest allocable to the period is $10,000, and the bond premium allocable to the period is $1,118.17. Because the accrual period extends beyond the end of A's taxable year, A must allocate these amounts between the two taxable years.

(ii) *Amounts allocable to the first taxable year.* The qualified stated interest allocable to the first taxable year is $9,166.67 ($10,000 × 11/12). The bond premium allocable to the first taxable year is $1,024.99 ($1,118.17 × 11/12).

(iii) *Premium used to offset interest.* For 1999, A includes in income $8,141.68, the qualified stated interest allocable to the period ($9,166.67) offset with bond premium allocable to the period ($1,024.99). Under § 1.1016-5(b), A's basis in the bond is reduced by $1,024.99 in 1999.

(iv) *Amounts allocable to the next taxable year.* The remaining amounts of qualified stated interest and bond premium allocable to the accrual period ending on February 1, 2000, are taken into account for the taxable year ending on December 31, 2000.

Example 4. Tax-exempt obligation—(i) *Facts.* On January 15, 1999, C purchases for $120,000 a tax-exempt obligation maturing on January 15, 2006, with a stated principal amount of $100,000, payable at maturity. The obligation provides for unconditional payments of interest of $9,000, payable on January 15 of each year. C uses the cash receipts and disbursements method of accounting, and C decides to use annual accrual periods ending on January 15 of each year.

(ii) *Amount of bond premium.* The interest payments on the obligation are qualified stated interest. Therefore, the sum of all amounts payable on the obligation (other than the interest payments) is $100,000. Under § 1.171-1, the amount of bond premium is $20,000 ($120,000 – $100,000).

(iii) *Bond premium allocable to the first accrual period.* Based on the remaining payment schedule of the obligation and C's basis in the obligation, C's yield is 5.48 percent, compounded annually. The bond premium allocable to the accrual period ending on January 15, 2000, is the excess of the qualified stated interest allocable to the period ($9,000) over the product of the adjusted acquisition price at the beginning of the period ($120,000) and C's yield (5.48 percent, compounded annually). Therefore, the bond premium allocable to the accrual period is $2,420.55 ($9,000 – $6,579.45).

(iv) *Premium used to offset interest.* Although C receives an interest payment of $9,000 on January 15, 2000, C only receives tax-exempt interest income of $6,579.45, the qualified stated interest allocable to the period ($9,000) offset with bond premium allocable to the period ($2,420.55). Under § 1.1016-5(b), C's basis in the obligation is reduced by $2,420.55 on January 15, 2000.
[Reg. § 1.171-2.]

☐ [*T.D. 6278*, 12-10-57. *Amended by T.D. 6647*, 4-10-63; *T.D. 6984*, 12-23-68; *T.D. 8746*, 12-30-97 *and T.D. 9653*, 1-14-2014.]

[Reg. § 1.171-3]

§ 1.171-3. Special rules for certain bonds.—(a) *Variable rate debt instruments.*—A holder determines bond premium on a variable rate debt instrument by reference to the stated redemption price at maturity of the equivalent fixed rate debt instrument constructed for the variable rate debt instrument. The holder also allocates any bond premium among the accrual periods by reference to the equivalent fixed rate debt instrument. The holder constructs the equivalent fixed rate debt instrument, as of the date the holder acquires the variable rate debt instrument, by using the principles of § 1.1275-5(e). See paragraph (e) *Example 1* of this section.

(b) *Inflation-indexed debt instruments.*—A holder determines bond premium on an inflation-indexed debt instrument by assuming that there will be no inflation or deflation over the remaining term of the instrument. The holder also allocates any bond premium among the accrual periods by assuming that there will be no inflation or deflation over the remaining term of the instrument. The bond premium allocable to an accrual period offsets qualified stated interest allocable to the period. Notwithstanding § 1.171-2(a)(4), if the bond premium allocable to an accrual period exceeds the qualified stated interest allocable to the period, the excess is treated as a deflation adjustment under § 1.1275-7(f)(1)(i). However, the rules in § 1.171-2(a)(4)(i)(C) apply to any remaining deflation adjustment attributable to bond premium as of the end of the holder's accrual period in which the bond is sold, retired, or otherwise disposed of. See § 1.1275-7 for other rules relating to inflation-indexed debt instruments.

(c) *Yield and remaining payment schedule of certain bonds subject to contingencies.*—(1) *Applicability.*—This paragraph (c) provides rules that apply in determining the yield and remaining payment schedule of certain bonds that provide for an alternative payment schedule (or schedules) applicable upon the occurrence of a contingency (or contingencies). This paragraph (c) applies, however, only if the timing and amounts of the payments that comprise each payment schedule are known as of the date the holder acquires the bond (the acquisition date) and the bond is subject to paragraph (c)(2), (3), or (4) of this section. A bond does not provide for an alternative payment schedule merely because there is a possibility of impairment of a payment (or payments) by insolvency, default, or similar circumstances. See

§ 1.1275-4 for the treatment of a bond that provides for a contingency that is not described in this paragraph (c).

(2) *Remaining payment schedule that is significantly more likely than not to occur.*—If, based on all the facts and circumstances as of the acquisition date, a single remaining payment schedule for a bond is significantly more likely than not to occur, this remaining payment schedule is used to determine and amortize bond premium under §§ 1.171-1 and 1.171-2.

(3) *Mandatory sinking fund provision.*—Notwithstanding paragraph (c)(2) of this section, if a bond is subject to a mandatory sinking fund provision described in § 1.1272-1(c)(3), the provision is ignored for purposes of determining and amortizing bond premium under §§ 1.171-1 and 1.171-2.

(4) *Treatment of certain options.*—(i) *Applicability.*—Notwithstanding paragraphs (c)(2) and (3) of this section, the rules of this paragraph (c)(4) determine the remaining payment schedule of a bond that provides the holder or issuer with an unconditional option or options, exercisable on one or more dates during the remaining term of the bond, to alter the bond's remaining payment schedule.

(ii) *Operating rules.*—A holder determines the remaining payment schedule of a bond by assuming that each option will (or will not) be exercised under the following rules:

(A) *Issuer options.*—In general, the issuer is deemed to exercise or not exercise an option or combination of options in the manner that minimizes the holder's yield on the obligation. However, the issuer of a taxable bond is deemed to exercise or not exercise a call option or combination of call options in the manner that maximizes the holder's yield on the bond.

(B) *Holder options.*—A holder is deemed to exercise or not exercise an option or combination of options in the manner that maximizes the holder's yield on the bond.

(C) *Multiple options.*—If both the issuer and the holder have options, the rules of paragraphs (c)(4)(ii)(A) and (B) of this section are applied to the options in the order that they may be exercised. Thus, the deemed exercise of one option may eliminate other options that are later in time.

(5) *Subsequent adjustments.*—(i) *In general.*—Except as provided in paragraph (c)(5)(ii) of this section, if a contingency described in this paragraph (c) (including the exercise of an option described in paragraph (c)(4) of this section) actually occurs or does not occur, contrary to the assumption made pursuant to paragraph (c) of this section (a change in circumstances), then solely for purposes of section 171, the bond is treated as retired and reacquired by the holder on the date of the change in circumstances for an amount equal to the adjusted acquisition price of the bond as of that date. If, however, the change in circumstances results in a substantially contemporaneous pro-rata prepayment as defined in § 1.1275-2(f)(2), the pro-rata prepayment is treated as a payment in retirement of a portion of the bond. See paragraph (e) *Example 2* of this section.

(ii) *Bond premium deduction on the issuer's call of a taxable bond.*—If a change in circumstances results from an issuer's call of a taxable bond or a partial call that is a pro-rata prepayment, the holder may deduct as bond premium an amount equal to the excess, if any, of the holder's adjusted acquisition price of the bond over the greater of—

(A) The amount received on redemption; and

(B) The amounts that would have been payable under the bond (other than payments of qualified stated interest) if no change in circumstances had occurred.

(d) *Remote and incidental contingencies.*—For purposes of determining and amortizing bond premium, if a bond provides for a contingency that is remote or incidental (within the meaning of § 1.1275-2(h)), the holder takes the contingency into account under the rules for remote and incidental contingencies in § 1.1275-2(h).

(e) *Examples.*—The following examples illustrate the rules of this section. Each example assumes the holder uses the calendar year as its taxable year and has elected to amortize bond premium, effective for all relevant taxable years. In addition, each example assumes a 30-day month and 360-day year. Although, for purposes of simplicity, the yield as stated is rounded to two decimal places, the computations do not reflect this rounding convention. The examples are as follows:

Example 1. Variable rate debt instrument—(i) *Facts.* On March 1, 1999, E purchases for $110,000 a taxable bond maturing on March 1, 2007, with a stated principal amount of $100,000, payable at maturity. The bond provides for unconditional payments of interest on March 1 of each year based on the percentage appreciation of a nationally-known commodity index. On March 1, 1999, it is reasonably expected that the bond will yield 12 percent, compounded annually. E uses the cash receipts and disbursements method of accounting, and E decides to use annual accrual periods ending on March 1 of each year. Assume that the bond is a variable rate debt instrument under § 1.1275-5.

(ii) *Amount of bond premium.* Because the bond is a variable rate debt instrument, E determines and amortizes its bond premium by reference to the equivalent fixed rate debt instrument constructed for the bond as of March 1, 1999. Because the bond provides for interest at a single objective rate that is reasonably expected to yield 12 percent, compounded annually, the equivalent fixed rate debt instrument for the bond is an eight-year bond with a principal amount of $100,000, payable at maturity. It provides for annual payments of interest of $12,000. E's basis in the equivalent fixed rate debt instrument is $110,000. The sum of all amounts payable on the equivalent fixed rate debt instrument (other than payments of qualified stated

Accrual period ending	
3/1/00	
3/1/01	
3/1/02	
3/1/03	
3/1/04	
3/1/05	
3/1/06	
3/1/07	

(iv) *Qualified stated interest for each accrual period.* Assume the bond actually pays the following amounts of qualified stated interest:

Accrual period ending	Qualified stated interest
3/1/00	$2,000.00
3/1/01	0.00
3/1/02	0.00
3/1/03	10,000.00
3/1/04	8,000.00
3/1/05	12,000.00
3/1/06	15,000.00
3/1/07	8,500.00

(v) *Premium used to offset interest.* E's interest income for each accrual period is determined by offsetting the qualified stated interest allocable to the period with the bond premium allocable to the period. For the accrual period ending on March 1, 2000, E includes in income $1,129.29, the qualified stated interest allocable to the period ($2,000) offset with the bond premium allocable to the period

Accrual period ending	Qualified stated interest	Premium allocable to accrual period
3/1/00	$2,000.00	$870.71
3/1/01	0.00	958.81
3/1/02	0.00	1,055.82
3/1/03	10,000.00	1,162.64
3/1/04	8,000.00	1,280.27
3/1/05	12,000.00	1,409.80
3/1/06	15,000.00	1,552.44
3/1/07	8,500.00	1,709.51
		$10,000.00

Example 2. Partial call that results in a pro-rata prepayment—(i) *Facts.* On April 1, 1999, M purchases for $110,000 N's taxable bond maturing on April 1, 2006, with a stated principal amount of $100,000, payable at maturity. The bond provides for unconditional payments of interest of $10,000, payable on April 1 of each year. N has the option to call all or part of the bond on April 1, 2001, at a 5 percent premium over the principal amount. M uses the cash receipts and disbursements method of accounting.

(ii) *Determination of yield and the remaining payment schedule.* M's yield determined without regard to the call option is 8.07 percent, compounded annually. M's yield determined by assuming N exercises its call option is 6.89 percent, compounded annually. Under paragraph (c)(4)(ii)(A) of this section, it is assumed N will not exercise the call option because exercising the option would minimize M's yield. Thus, for purposes of determining and amortizing bond premium, the bond is assumed to be a seven-year bond with a single principal payment at maturity of $100,000.

(iii) *Amount of bond premium.* The interest payments on the bond are qualified stated interest. Therefore, the sum of all amounts payable on the bond (other than the interest payments) is $100,000. Under

interest) is $100,000. Under § 1.171-1, the amount of bond premium is $10,000 ($110,000 – $100,000).

(iii) *Bond premium allocable to each accrual period.* E allocates bond premium to the remaining accrual periods by reference to the payment schedule on the equivalent fixed rate debt instrument. Based on the payment schedule of the equivalent fixed rate debt instrument and E's basis in the bond, E's yield is 10.12 percent, compounded annually. The bond premium allocable to the accrual period ending on March 1, 2000, is the excess of the qualified stated interest allocable to the period for the equivalent fixed rate debt instrument ($12,000) over the product of the adjusted acquisition price at the beginning of the period ($110,000) and E's yield (10.12 percent, compounded annually). Therefore, the bond premium allocable to the accrual period is $870.71 ($12,000 – $11,129.29). The bond premium allocable to all the accrual periods is listed in the following schedule:

Adjusted acquisition price at beginning of accrual period	Premium allocable to accrual period
$110,000.00	$870.71
109,129.29	958.81
108,170.48	1,055.82
107,114.66	1,162.64
105,952.02	1,280.27
104,671.75	1,409.80
103,261.95	1,552.44
101,709.51	1,709.51
	$10,000.00

($870.71). For the accrual period ending on March 1, 2001, the bond premium allocable to the accrual period ($958.81) exceeds the qualified stated interest allocable to the period ($0) and, therefore, E does not have interest income for this accrual period. However, under § 1.171-2(a)(4)(i)(A), E may deduct as bond premium $958.81, the excess of the bond premium allocable to the accrual period ($958.81) over the qualified stated interest allocable to the accrual period ($0). For the accrual period ending on March 1, 2002, the bond premium allocable to the accrual period ($1,055.82) exceeds the qualified stated interest allocable to the accrual period ($0) and, therefore, E does not have interest income for the accrual period. Under § 1.171-2(a)(4)(i)(A), E's deduction for bond premium for the accrual period is limited to $170.48, the excess of E's total interest inclusions on the bond in prior accrual periods ($1,129.29) over the total amount treated by E as a bond premium deduction in prior accrual periods ($958.81). Under § 1.171-2(a)(4)(i)(B), E must carry forward the remaining $885.34 of bond premium allocable to the period ending March 1, 2002, and treat it as bond premium allocable to the period ending March 1, 2003. The amount E includes in income for each accrual period is shown in the following schedule:

Interest income	Premium deduction	Premium carryforward
$1,129.29	$958.81	
0.00		
0.00		$885.34
7,951.93	170.48	
6,719.73		
10,590.20		
13,447.56		
6,790.49		

§ 1.171-1, the amount of bond premium is $10,000 ($110,000 – $100,000).

(iv) *Bond premium allocable to the first two accrual periods.* For the accrual period ending on April 1, 2000, M includes in income $8,881.83, the qualified stated interest allocable to the period ($10,000) offset with bond premium allocable to the period ($1,118.17). The adjusted acquisition price on April 1, 2000, is $108,881.83 ($110,000 – $1,118.17). For the accrual period ending on April 1, 2001, M includes in income $8,791.54, the qualified stated interest allocable to the period ($10,000) offset with bond premium allocable to the period ($1,208.46). The adjusted acquisition price on April 1, 2001, is $107,673.37 ($108,881.83 – $1,208.46).

(v) *Partial call.* Assume N calls one-half of M's bond for $52,500 on April 1, 2001. Because it was assumed the call would not be exercised, the call is a change in circumstances. However, the partial call is also a pro-rata prepayment within the meaning of § 1.1275-2(f)(2). As a result, the call is treated as a retirement of one-half of the bond. Under paragraph (c)(5)(ii) of this section, M may deduct $1,336.68, the excess of its adjusted acquisition price in the retired portion of the bond ($107,673.37/2, or $53,836.68) over the amount received on redemption ($52,500). M's adjusted basis in the portion of the bond that remains outstanding is $53,836.68 ($107,673.37 – $53,836.68). [Reg. § 1.171-3.]

☐ [*T.D. 6278, 12-10-57. Amended by T.D. 8746, 12-30-97; T.D. 8838, 9-3-99; T.D. 9609, 1-3-2013 and T.D. 9653, 1-14-2014.*]

[Reg. § 1.171-4]

§ 1.171-4. Election to amortize bond premium on taxable bonds.—(a) *Time and manner of making the election.*—(1) *In general.*— A holder makes the election to amortize bond premium by offsetting interest income with bond premium in the holder's timely filed federal income tax return for the first taxable year to which the holder desires the election to apply. The holder should attach to the return a statement that the holder is making the election under this section.

(2) *Coordination with OID election.*—If a holder makes an election under § 1.1272-3 for a bond with bond premium, the holder is deemed to have made the election under this section.

(b) *Scope of election.*—The election under this section applies to all taxable bonds held during or after the taxable year for which the election is made.

(c) *Election to amortize made in a subsequent taxable year.*—(1) *In general.*—If a holder elects to amortize bond premium and holds a taxable bond acquired before the taxable year for which the election is made, the holder may not amortize amounts that would have been amortized in prior taxable years had an election been in effect for those prior years.

(2) *Example.*—The following example illustrates the rule of this paragraph (c):

Example—(i) *Facts.* On May 1, 1999, C purchases for $130,000 a taxable bond maturing on May 1, 2006, with a stated principal amount of $100,000, payable at maturity. The bond provides for unconditional payments of interest of $15,000, payable on May 1 of each year. C uses the cash receipts and disbursements method of accounting and the calendar year as its taxable year. C has not previously elected to amortize bond premium, but does so for 2002.

(ii) *Amount to amortize.* C's basis for determining loss on the sale or exchange of the bond is $130,000. Thus, under § 1.171-1, the amount of bond premium is $30,000. Under § 1.171-2, if a bond premium election were in effect for the prior taxable years, C would have amortized $3,257.44 of bond premium on May 1, 2000, and $3,551.68 of bond premium on May 1, 2001, based on annual accrual periods ending on May 1. Thus, for 2002 and future years to which the election applies, C may amortize only $23,190.88 ($30,000 – $3,257.44 – $3,551.68).

(d) *Revocation of election.*—The election under this section may not be revoked unless approved by the Commissioner. Because a revocation of the election is a change in accounting method, a taxpayer must follow the rules under § 1.446-1(e)(3)(i) to request the Commissioner's consent to revoke the election. A revocation of the election applies to all taxable bonds held during or after the taxable year for which the revocation is effective. The holder may not amortize any remaining bond premium on bonds held at the beginning of the taxable year for which the revocation is effective. Therefore, no adjustment under section 481 is allowed upon the revocation of the election because no items of income or deduction are omitted or duplicated. [Reg. § 1.171-4.]

☐ [*T.D. 6278, 12-10-57. Amended by T.D. 8746, 12-30-97.*]

[Reg. § 1.171-5]

§ 1.171-5. Effective date and transition rules.—(a) *Effective date.*— (1) *In general.*—Sections 1.171-1 through 1.171-4 apply to bonds acquired on or after March 2, 1998. However, if a holder makes the election under § 1.171-4 for the taxable year containing March 2, 1998, or any subsequent taxable year, §§ 1.171-1 through 1.171-4 apply to bonds held on or after the first day of the taxable year in which the election is made.

(2) *Transition rule for use of constant yield.*—Notwithstanding paragraph (a)(1) of this section, § 1.171-2(a)(3) (providing that the bond premium allocable to an accrual period is determined with reference to a constant yield) does not apply to a bond issued before September 28, 1985.

(b) *Coordination with existing election.*—A holder is deemed to have made the election under § 1.171-4 for the taxable year containing March 2, 1998, if the holder elected to amortize bond premium under section 171 and that election is effective on March 2, 1998. If the holder is deemed to have made the election under § 1.171-4 for the taxable year containing March 2, 1998, §§ 1.171-1 through 1.171-4

apply to bonds acquired on or after the first day of that taxable year. See § 1.171-4(d) for rules relating to a revocation of an election under section 171.

(c) *Accounting method changes.*—(1) *Consent to change.*—A holder required to change its method of accounting for bond premium to comply with §§ 1.171-1 through 1.171-3 must secure the consent of the Commissioner in accordance with the requirements of § 1.446-1(e). Paragraph (c)(2) of this section provides the Commissioner's automatic consent for certain changes. A holder making the election under § 1.171-4 does not need the Commissioner's consent to make the election.

(2) *Automatic consent.*—The Commissioner grants consent for a holder to change its method of accounting for bond premium with respect to taxable bonds to which §§ 1.171-1 through 1.171-3 apply. Because this change is made on a cut-off basis, no items of income or deduction are omitted or duplicated and, therefore, no adjustment under section 481 is allowed. The consent granted by this paragraph (c)(2) applies provided—

(i) The holder elected to amortize bond premium under section 171 for a taxable year prior to the taxable year containing March 2, 1998, and that election has not been revoked;

(ii) The change is made for the first taxable year for which the holder must account for a bond under §§ 1.171-1 through 1.171-3; and

(iii) The holder attaches to its return for the taxable year containing the change a statement that it has changed its method of accounting under this section. [Reg. § 1.171-5.]

☐ [*T.D. 8746, 12-30-97.*]

[Reg. § 1.172-1]

§ 1.172-1. Net operating loss deduction.—(a) *Allowance of deduction.*—Section 172(a) allows as a deduction in computing taxable income for any taxable year subject to the Code the aggregate of the net operating loss carryovers and net operating loss carrybacks to such taxable year. This deduction is referred to as the net operating loss deduction. The net operating loss is the basis for the computation of the net operating loss carryovers and net operating loss carrybacks and ultimately for the net operating loss deduction itself. The net operating loss deduction shall not be disallowed for any taxable year merely because the taxpayer has no income from a trade or business for the taxable year.

(b) *Steps in computation of net operating loss deduction.*—The three steps to be taken in the ascertainment of the net operating loss deduction for any taxable year subject to the Code are as follows:

(1) Compute the net operating loss for any preceding or succeeding taxable year from which a net operating loss may be carried over or carried back to such taxable year.

(2) Compute the net operating loss carryovers to such taxable year from such preceding taxable years and the net operating loss carrybacks to such taxable year from such succeeding taxable years.

(3) Add such net operating loss carryovers and carrybacks in order to determine the net operating loss deduction for such taxable year.

(c) *Statement with tax return.*—Every taxpayer claiming a net operating loss deduction for any taxable year shall file with his return for such year a concise statement setting forth the amount of the net operating loss deduction claimed and all material and pertinent facts relative thereto, including a detailed schedule showing the computation of the net operating loss deduction.

(d) *Ascertainment of deduction dependent upon net operating loss carryback.*—If the taxpayer is entitled in computing his net operating loss deduction to a carryback which he is not able to ascertain at the time his return is due, he shall compute the net operating loss deduction on his return without regard to such net operating loss carryback. When the taxpayer ascertains the net operating loss carryback, he may within the applicable period of limitations file a claim for credit or refund of the overpayment, if any, resulting from the failure to compute the net operating loss deduction for the taxable year with the inclusion of such carryback; or he may file an application under the provisions of section 6411 for a tentative carryback adjustment.

(e) *Law applicable to computations.*—(1) In determining the amount of any net operating loss carryback or carryover to any taxable year, the necessary computations involving any other taxable year shall be made under the law applicable to such other taxable year.

(2) The net operating loss for any taxable year shall be determined under the law applicable to that year without regard to the year to which it is to be carried and in which, in effect, it is to be deducted as part of the net operating loss deduction.

(3) The amount of the net operating loss deduction which shall be allowed for any taxable year shall be determined under the law applicable to that year.

(f) *Electing small business corporations.*—In determining the amount of the net operating loss deduction of any corporation, there shall be disregarded the net operating loss of such corporation for any taxable year for which such corporation was an electing small business corporation under subchapter S (section 1371 and following), chapter 1 of the Code. In applying section 172(b)(1) and (2) to a net operating loss sustained in a taxable year in which the corporation was not an electing small business corporation, a taxable year in which the corporation was an electing small business corporation is counted as a taxable year to which such net operating loss is carried back or over. However, the taxable income for such year as determined under section 172(b)(2) is treated as if it were zero for purposes of computing the balance of the loss available to the corporation as a carryback or carryover to other taxable years in which the corporation is not an electing small business corporation. See section 1374 and the regulations thereunder for allowance of a deduction to shareholders for a net operating loss sustained by an electing small business corporation.

(g) *Husband and wife.*—The net operating loss deduction of a husband and wife shall be determined in accordance with this section, but subject also to the provisions of §1.172-7. [Reg. §1.172-1.]

☐ [T.D. 6192, 7-23-56. *Amended by T.D. 6486, 8-12-60 and T.D. 8107,* 12-1-86.]

[Reg. §1.172-2]

§1.172-2. Net operating loss in case of a corporation.—(a) *Modification of deductions.*—A net operating loss is sustained by a corporation in any taxable year if and to the extent that, for such year, there is an excess of deductions allowed by chapter 1 of the Code over gross income computed thereunder. In determining the excess of deductions over gross income for such purpose—

(1) *Items not deductible.*—No deduction shall be allowed under—
(i) Section 172 for the net operating loss deduction, and
(ii) Section 922 in respect of Western Hemisphere trade corporations;

(2) *Dividends received.*—The 85-percent limitation provided by section 246(b) shall not apply to the deductions otherwise allowed under—
(i) Section 243(a) in respect of dividends received from domestic corporations,
(ii) Section 244 in respect of dividends received on preferred stock of public utilities, and
(iii) Section 245 in respect of dividends received from foreign corporations; and

(3) *Dividends paid.*—The deduction granted by section 247 in respect of dividends paid on the preferred stock of public utilities shall be computed without regard to subsection (a)(1)(B) of section 247.

(b) *Example.*—The following example illustrates the application of paragraph (a):

Example. For the calendar year 1981, the X corporation has gross income of $400,000 and total deductions allowed by chapter 1 of the Code of $375,000, exclusive of any net operating loss deduction and exclusive of any deduction for dividends received or paid. Corporation X in 1981 received $100,000 of dividends entitled to the benefits of section 243(a). These dividends are included in Corporation X's $400,000 gross income. Corporation X has no other deductions to which section 172(d) applies.

On the basis of these facts, Corporation X has a net operating loss for the year 1981 of $60,000, computed as follows:

Deductions for 1981	$375,000
Plus: Deduction for dividends received, computed without regard to the limitation provided in section 246(b) (85% of $100,000)	85,000
Total	460,000
Less: Gross income for 1981 (including $100,000 dividends)	400,000
Net operating loss for 1981	$60,000

(c) *Qualified real estate investment trusts.*—For taxable years ending after October 4, 1976, the net operating loss of a qualified real estate investment trust (as defined in §1.172-10(b)) is computed by taking into account the adjustments described in section 857(b)(2) (other than the deduction for dividends paid, as defined in section 561), as well as the modifications required by paragraph (a)(1) of this section. Thus, for example, the special deductions for dividends received,

etc., provided in part VIII of subchapter B (other than section 248), as well as the net operating loss deduction under section 172, are not allowed in computing the net operating loss of a qualified real estate investment trust. [Reg. §1.172-2.]

☐ [T.D. 6192, 7-23-56. *Amended by T.D. 6486, 8-12-60, T.D. 7767,* 2-3-81 *and T.D. 8107, 12-1-86.]*

[Reg. §1.172-3]

§1.172-3. Net operating loss in case of a taxpayer other than a corporation.—(a) *Modification of deductions.*—A net operating loss is sustained by a taxpayer other than a corporation in any taxable year if and to the extent that, for such year, there is an excess of deductions allowed by chapter 1 of the Internal Revenue Code over gross income computed thereunder. In determining the excess of deductions over gross income for such purpose—

(1) *Items not deductible.*—No deduction shall be allowed under—
(i) Section 151 for the personal exemptions or under any other section which grants a deduction in lieu of the deductions allowed by section 151,
(ii) Section 172 for the net operating loss deduction, and
(iii) Section 1202 in respect of net long-term capital gain.

(2) *Capital losses.*—(i) The amount deductible on account of business capital losses shall not exceed the sum of the amount includible on account of business capital gains and that portion of nonbusiness capital gains which is computed in accordance with paragraph (c) of this section.

(ii) The amount deductible on account of nonbusiness capital losses shall not exceed the amount includible on account of nonbusiness capital gains.

(3) *Nonbusiness deductions.*—(i) *Ordinary deductions.*—Ordinary nonbusiness deductions shall be taken into account without regard to the amount of business deductions and shall be allowed in full to the extent, but not in excess, of that amount which is the sum of the ordinary nonbusiness gross income and the excess of nonbusiness capital gains over nonbusiness capital losses. See paragraph (c) of this section. For purposes of section 172, nonbusiness deductions and income are those deductions and that income which are not attributable to, or derived from, a taxpayer's trade or business. Wages and salary constitute income attributable to the taxpayer's trade or business for such purposes.

(ii) *Sale of business property.*—Any gain or loss on the sale or other disposition of property which is used in the taxpayer's trade or business and which is of a character that is subject to the allowance for depreciation provided in section 167, or of real property used in the taxpayer's trade or business, shall be considered, for purposes of section 172(d)(4), as attributable to, or derived from, the taxpayer's trade or business. Such gains and losses are to be taken into account fully in computing a net operating loss without regard to the limitation on nonbusiness deductions. Thus, a farmer who sells at a loss land used in the business of farming may, in computing a net operating loss, include in full the deduction otherwise allowable with respect to such loss, without regard to the amount of his nonbusiness income and without regard to whether he is engaged in the trade or business of selling farms. Similarly, an individual who sells at a loss machinery which is used in his trade or business and which is of a character that is subject to the allowance for depreciation may, in computing the net operating loss, include in full the deduction otherwise allowable with respect to such loss.

(iii) *Casualty losses.*—Any deduction allowable under section 165(c)(3) for losses of property not connected with a trade or business shall not be considered, for purposes of section 172(d)(4), to be a nonbusiness deduction but shall be treated as a deduction attributable to the taxpayer's trade or business.

(iv) *Self-employed retirement plans.*—Any deduction allowed under section 404, relating to contributions of an employer to an employees' trust or annuity plan, or under section 405(c), relating to contributions to a bond purchase plan, to the extent attributable to contributions made on behalf of an individual while he is an employee within the meaning of section 401(c)(1), shall not be treated, for purposes of section 172(d)(4), as attributable to, or derived from, the taxpayer's trade or business, but shall be treated as a nonbusiness deduction.

(v) *Limitation.*—The provisions of this subparagraph shall not be construed to permit the deduction of items disallowed by subparagraph (1) of this paragraph.

(b) *Treatment of capital loss carryovers.*—Because of the distinction between business and nonbusiness capital gains and losses, a taxpayer who has a capital loss carryover from a preceding taxable year, includible by virtue of section 1212 among the capital losses for the taxable year in issue, is required to determine how much of such capital loss carryover is a business capital loss and how much is a nonbusiness capital loss. In order to make this determination, the taxpayer shall first ascertain what proportion of the net capital loss for such preceding taxable year was attributable to an excess of business capital losses over business capital gains for such year, and what proportion was attributable to an excess of nonbusiness capital losses over nonbusiness capital gains. The same proportion of the capital loss carryover from such preceding taxable year shall be treated as a business capital loss and a nonbusiness capital loss, respectively. In order to determine the composition (business—nonbusiness) of a net capital loss for a taxable year, for purposes of this paragraph, if such net capital loss is computed under paragraph (b) of §1.1212-1 and takes into account a capital loss carryover from a preceding taxable year, the composition (business—nonbusiness) of the net capital loss for such preceding taxable year must also be determined. For purposes of this paragraph, the term "capital loss carryover" means the sum of the short-term and long-term capital loss carryovers from such year This paragaraph may be illustrated by the following examples:

Example (1). (i) A, an individual, has $5,000 ordinary taxable income (computed without regard to the deductions for personal exemptions) for the calendar year 1954 and also has the following capital gains and losses for such year: Business capital gains of $2,000; business capital losses of $3,200; nonbusiness capital gains of $1,000; and nonbusiness capital losses of $1,200.

(ii) A's net capital loss for the taxable year 1954 is $400, computed as follows:

Capital losses	$4,400
Capital gains	3,000
Excess of capital losses over capital gains	$1,400
Less: $1,000 of such ordinary taxable income	1,000
Net capital loss for 1954	$400

(iii) A's capital losses for 1954 exceeded his capital gains for such year by $1,400. Since A's business capital losses for 1954 exceeded his business capital gains for such year by $1,200, 6/7ths ($1,200/$1,400) of A's net capital loss for 1954 is attributable to an excess of his business capital losses over his business capital gains for such year. Similarly, 1/7th of the net capital loss is attributable to the excess of nonbusiness capital losses over nonbusiness capital gains. Since the capital loss carryover for 1954 to 1955 is $400, 6/7ths of $400, or $342.86, shall be treated as a business capital loss in 1955; and 1/7th of $400, or $57.14, as a nonbusiness capital loss.

Example (2). (i) A, an individual who is computing a net operating loss for the calendar year 1966, has a capital loss carryover from 1965 of $8,000. In order to apply the provisions of this paragraph, A must determine what portion of the $8,000 carryover is attributable to the excess of business capital losses over business capital gains and what portion thereof is attributable to the excess of nonbusiness capital losses over nonbusiness capital gains. For 1965, A had $10,000 ordinary taxable income (computed without regard to the deductions for personal exemptions), and a short-term capital loss carryover of $6,000 from 1964. In order to determine the composition (business—nonbusiness) of the $8,000 carryover from 1965, A first determines that of the $6,000 carryover from 1964, $5,000 is a business capital loss and $1,000 is a nonbusiness capital loss. This must be done since, under paragraph (b) of §1.1212-1, the net capital loss for 1965 is computed by taking into account the capital loss carryover from 1964. A's capital gains and losses for 1965 are as follows:

	1965	Carried over from 1964
Business capital gains	$2,000	
Business capital losses	3,000	$5,000
Nonbusiness capital gains	4,000	
Nonbusiness capital losses	6,000	1,000

(ii) A's net capital loss for the taxable year 1965 is $8,000, computed as follows:

Capital losses (including carryovers)	$15,000
Capital gains	6,000
Excess of capital losses over capital gains	$9,000
Less: $1,000 of such ordinary taxable income	1,000
Net capital loss for 1965	$8,000

(iii) A's capital losses, including carryovers, for 1965 exceeded his capital gains for such year by $9,000. Since A's business capital losses for 1965 exceeded his business capital gains for such year by $6,000, 2/3rds ($6,000/$9,000) of A's net capital loss for 1965 is attributable to an excess of his business capital losses over his business capital gains for such year. Similarly, 1/3rd of the net capital loss is attributable to the excess of nonbusiness capital losses over nonbusiness

capital gains. Since the total capital loss carryover from 1965 to 1966 is $8,000, 2/3rds of $8,000, or $5,333.33, shall be treated as a business capital loss in 1966; and 1/3rd of $8,000, or $2,666.67, as a nonbusiness capital loss.

(c) *Determination of portion of nonbusiness capital gains available for the deduction of business capital losses.*—In the computation of a net operating loss a taxpayer other than a corporation must use his nonbusiness capital gains for the deduction of his nonbusiness capital losses. Any amount not necessary for this purpose shall then be used for the deduction of any excess of ordinary nonbusiness deductions over ordinary nonbusiness gross income. The remainder, computed by applying the excess ordinary nonbusiness deductions against the excess nonbusiness capital gains, shall be treated as nonbusiness capital gains and used for the purpose of determining the deductibility of business capital losses under paragraph (a)(2)(i) of this section. This principle may be illustrated by the following example:

Example. (1) A, an individual, has a total nonbusiness gross income of $20,500, computed as follows:

Ordinary gross income	$7,500
Capital gains	13,000
Total gross income	20,500

(2) A also has total nonbusiness deductions of $16,000, computed as follows:

Ordinary deductions	$9,000
Capital loss	7,000
Total deductions	16,000

(3) The portion of nonbusiness capital gains to be used for the purpose of determining the deductibility of business capital losses is $4,500, computed as follows:

Nonbusiness capital gains		$13,000
Less: Nonbusiness capital loss		7,000
Excess to be taken into account for purposes of paragraph (a)(3)(i) of this section		6,000
Ordinary nonbusiness deductions	$9,000	
Less: Ordinary nonbusiness gross income	7,500	1,500
Portion of nonbusiness capital gains to be used for purposes of paragraph (a)(2)(i) of this section		4,500

(d) *Joint net operating loss of husband and wife.*—In the case of a husband and wife, the joint net operating loss for any taxable year for which a joint return is filed is to be computed on the basis of the combined income and deductions of both spouses, and the modifications prescribed in paragraph (a) of this section are to be computed as if the combined income and deductions of both spouses were the income and deductions of one individual.

(e) *Illustration of computation of net operating loss of a taxpayer other than a corporation.*—(1) *Facts.*—For the calendar year 1954, A, an individual, has gross income of $483,000 and allowable deductions of $540,000. The latter amount does not include the net operating loss deduction or any deduction on account of the sale or exchange of capital assets. Included in gross income are business capital gains of $50,000 and ordinary nonbusiness income of $10,000. Included among the deductions are ordinary nonbusiness deductions of $12,000 and a deduction of $600 for his personal exemption. A has a business capital loss of $60,000 in 1954. A has no other items of income or deductions to which section 172(d) applies.

(2) *Computation.*—On the basis of these facts, A has a net operating loss for 1954 of $104,400, computed as follows:

Deductions for 1954 (as specified in first sentence of subparagraph (1))		$540,000
Plus: Amount of business capital loss ($60,000) to extent such amount does not exceed business capital gains ($50,000)		50,000
Total		590,000
Less: Excess of ordinary nonbusiness deductions over ordinary nonbusiness gross income ($12,000 minus $10,000)	$2,000	
Deduction for personal exemption	600	2,600
Deductions for 1954 adjusted as required by section 172(d)		587,400
Gross income for 1954		483,000
Net operating loss for 1954		104,400

[Reg. §1.172-3.]

□ [T.D. 6192, 7-23-56. *Amended by* T.D. 6828, 6-16-65, T.D. 6862, 11-17-65 *and* T.D. 8107, 12-1-86.]

Itemized Deductions for Individuals and Corps.
See p. 20,601 for regulations not amended to reflect law changes
25,599

[Reg. §1.172-4]

§1.172-4. Net operating loss carrybacks and net operating loss carryovers.—(a) *General provisions.*—(1) *Years to which loss may be carried.*—(i) *In general.*—In order to compute the net operating loss deduction the taxpayer must first determine the part of any net operating losses for any preceding or succeeding taxable years which are carrybacks or carryovers to the taxable year in issue.

(ii) *General rule for carrybacks and carryovers.*—Except as provided in section 172(b)(1)(C), (D), (E), (F), (G), (H), (I), and (J), paragraphs (a)(1)(iii), (iv), (v), and (vi) of this section, and §1.172-10(a), a net operating loss shall be carried back to the 3 preceding taxable years and carried over to the 15 succeeding taxable years (5 succeeding taxable years for a loss sustained in a taxable year ending before January 1, 1976).

(iii) *Loss of a regulated transportation corporation.*—Except as provided in subdivision (iv) of this subparagraph and §1.172-10(a), a net operating loss sustained by a taxpayer which is a regulated transportation corporation (as defined in section 172(g)(1)) in a taxable year ending before January 1, 1976, shall, subject to the provisions of section 172(g) and §1.172-8, be carried back to the taxable years specified in paragraph (a)(1)(ii) of this section and shall be carried over to the 7 succeeding taxable years.

(iv) *Loss attributable to foreign expropriation.*—If the provisions of section 172(b)(3)(A) and §1.172-8 are satisfied, the portion of a net operating loss attributable to a foreign expropriation loss (as defined in section 172(h)) shall not be a net operating loss carryback to any taxable year preceding the taxable year of such loss and shall be a net operating loss carryover to each of the 10 taxable years following the taxable year of such loss.

(v) *Loss of a financial institution.*—A net operating loss sustained in a taxable year beginning after December 31, 1975, by a taxpayer to which section 585, 586, or 593 applies shall be carried back (except as provided in §1.172-10(a)) to the 10 preceding taxable years and shall be carried over to the 5 succeeding taxable years.

(vi) *Loss of a Bank for Cooperatives.*—A net operating loss sustained by a taxpayer which is a Bank for Cooperatives (organized and chartered pursuant to section 2 of the Farm Credit Act of 1933 (12 U.S.C. 1134)) shall be carried back (except as provided in §1.172-10(a)) to the 10 preceding taxable years and shall be carried over to the 5 succeeding taxable years.

(2) *Periods of less than 12 months.*—A fractional part of a year which is a taxable year under sections 441(b) and 7701(a)(23) is a preceding or a succeeding taxable year for the purpose of determining under section 172 the first, second, etc., preceding or succeeding taxable year.

(3) *Amount of loss to be carried.*—The amount which is carried back or carried over to any taxable year is the net operating loss to the extent it was not absorbed in the computation of the taxable (or net) income for other taxable years, preceding such taxable year, to which it may be carried back or carried over. For the purpose of determining the taxable (or net) income for any such preceding taxable year, the various net operating loss carryovers and carrybacks to such taxable year are considered to be applied in reduction of the taxable (or net) income in the order of the taxable years from which such losses are carried over or carried back, beginning with the loss for the earliest taxable year.

(4) *Husband and wife.*—The net operating loss carryovers and carrybacks of a husband and wife shall be determined in accordance with this section, but subject also to the provisions of §1.172-7.

(5) *Corporate acquisitions.*—For the computation of the net operating loss carryovers in the case of certain acquisitions of the assets of a corporation by another corporation, see section 381 and the regulations thereunder.

(6) *Special limitations.*—For special limitations on the net operating loss carryovers in certain cases of change in both the ownership and the trade or business of a corporation and in certain cases of corporate reorganization lacking specified continuity of ownership, see section 382 and the regulations thereunder.

(7) *Electing small business corporations.*—For special rule applicable to corporations which were electing small business corporations under subchapter S (section 1361 and following), chapter 1 of the Code, during one or more of the taxable years described in section 172(b)(1), see paragraph (f) of §1.172-1.

(b) *Portion of net operating loss which is a carryback or a carryover to the taxable year in issue.*—(1) A net operating loss shall first be carried to the earliest of the several taxable years for which such loss is allowable as a carryback or a carryover, and shall then be carried to the next earliest of such several taxable years, etc. Except as provided in §1.172-9, the entire net operating loss shall be carried back to such earliest year.

(2) The portion of the loss which shall be carried to any of such several taxable years subsequent to the earliest taxable year is the excess of such net operating loss over the sum of the taxable incomes (computed as provided in §1.172-3) for all of such several taxable years preceding such subsequent taxable year.

(3) If a portion of the net operating loss for a taxable year is attributable to a foreign expropriation loss (as defined in section 172(h)) and if an election under paragraph (c) of §1.172-9 is made with respect to such portion of the net operating loss, then see §1.172-9 for the separate treatment of such portion of the net operating loss.

(c) *Illustration.*—The principles of this section are illustrated in §1.172-6. [Reg. §1.172-4.]

☐ [T.D. 6192, 7-23-56. *Amended by T.D. 6486, 8-12-60, T.D. 6862, 11-17-65, T.D. 7444, 12-6-76, T.D. 7767, 2-3-81, T.D. 8096, 8-27-86 and T.D. 8107, 12-1-86.*]

[Reg. §1.172-5]

§1.172-5. Taxable income which is subtracted from net operating loss to determine carryback or carryover.—(a) *Taxable year subject to Internal Revenue Code of 1954.*—The taxable income for any taxable year subject to the Internal Revenue Code of 1954 which is subtracted from the net operating loss for any other taxable year to determine the portion of such net operating loss which is a carryback or a carryover to a particular taxable year is computed with the modifications prescribed in this paragraph. These modifications shall be made independently of, and without reference to, the modifications required by §§1.172-2(a) and 1.172-3(a) for purposes of computing the net operating loss itself.

(1) *Modifications applicable to unincorporated taxpayers only.*—In the case of a taxpayer other than a corporation, in computing taxable income and adjusted gross income—

(i) No deduction shall be allowed under section 151 for the personal exemptions (or under any other section which grants a deduction in lieu of the deductions allowed by section 151) and under section 1202 in respect of net long-term capital gain.

(ii) The amount deductible on account of losses from sales or exchanges of capital assets shall not exceed the amount includible on account of gains from sales or exchanges of capital assets.

(2) *Modifications applicable to all taxpayers.*—In the case either of a corporation or of a taxpayer other than a corporation—

(i) *Net operating loss deduction.*—The net operating loss deduction for such taxable year shall be computed by taking into account only such net operating losses otherwise allowable as carrybacks or carryovers to such taxable year as were sustained in taxable years preceding the taxable year in which the taxpayer sustained the net operating loss from which the taxable income is to be deducted. Thus, for such purposes, the net operating loss for the loss year or any taxable year thereafter shall not be taken into account.

Example. The taxpayer's income tax returns are made on the basis of the calendar year. In computing the net operating loss deduction for 1954, the taxpayer has a carryover from 1952 of $9,000, a carryover from 1953 of $6,000, a carryback from 1955 of $18,000, and a carryback from 1956 of $10,000, or an aggregate of $43,000 in carryovers and carrybacks. Thus, the net operating loss deduction for 1954, for purposes of determining the tax liability for 1954, is $43,000. However, in computing the taxable income for 1954 which is subtracted from the net operating loss for 1955 for the purpose of determining the portion of such loss which may be carried over to subsequent taxable years, the net operating loss deduction for 1954 is $15,000, that is, the aggregate of the $9,000 carryover from 1952 and the $6,000 carryover from 1953. In computing the net operating loss deduction for such purpose, the $18,000 carryback from 1955 and the $10,000 carryback from 1956 are disregarded. In computing the taxable income for 1954, however, which is subtracted from the net operating loss for 1956 for the purpose of determining the portion of such loss which may be carried over to subsequent taxable years, the net operating loss deduction for 1954 is $33,000, that is, the aggregate of the $9,000 carryover from 1952, the $6,000 carryover from 1953, and the $18,000 carryback from 1955. In computing the net operating loss deduction for such purpose, the $10,000 carryback from 1956 is disregarded.

(ii) *Recomputation of percentage limitations.*—Unless otherwise specifically provided in this subchapter, any deduction which is limited in amount to a percentage of the taxpayer's taxable income or adjusted gross income shall be recomputed upon the basis of the taxable income or adjusted gross income, as the case may be, determined with the modifications prescribed in this paragraph. Thus, in the case of an individual the deduction for medical expenses would be recomputed after making all the modifications prescribed in this paragraph, whereas the deduction for charitable contributions would be determined without regard to any net operating loss carryback but with regard to any other modifications so prescribed. See, however, the regulations under paragraph (g) of §1.170-2 (relating to charitable contributions carryover of individuals) and paragraph (c) of §1.170-3 (relating to charitable contributions carryover of corporations) for special rules regarding charitable contributions in excess of the percentage limitations which may be treated as paid in succeeding taxable years.

Example (1). For the calendar year 1954 the taxpayer, an individual, files a return showing taxable income of $4,800, computed as follows:

Salary		$5,000
Net long-term capital gain		4,000
Total gross income		9,000
Less: Deduction allowed by section 1202 in respect of net long-term capital gain	$2,000	
Adjusted gross income		7,000
Less:		
Deduction for personal exemption	$600	
Deduction for medical expense ($410 actually paid but allowable only to extent in excess of 3 percent of adjusted gross income)	200	
Deduction for charitable contributions ($2,000 actually paid but allowable only to extent not in excess of 20 percent of adjusted gross income)	1,400	2,200
Taxable income		4,800

In 1955 the taxpayer undertakes the operation of a trade or business and sustains therein a net operating loss of $3,000. Under section 172(b)(2), it is determined that the entire $3,000 is a carryback to 1954. In 1956 he sustains a net operating loss of $10,000 in the operation of the business. In determining the amount of the carryover of the 1956 loss to 1957, the taxable income for 1954 as computed under this paragraph is $3,970, determined as follows:

Salary		$5,000
Net long-term capital gain		4,000
Total gross income		9,000
Less: Deduction for carryback of 1955 net operating loss		3,000
Less:		
Deduction for medical expense ($410 actually paid but allowable only to extent in excess of 3 percent of adjusted gross income as modified under this paragraph)	$230	
Deduction for charitable contributions ($2,000 actually paid but allowable only to extent not in excess of 20 percent of adjusted gross income determined with all the modifications prescribed in this paragraph other than the net operating loss carryback)	$1,800	$2,030
Taxable income		3,970

Example (2). For the calendar year 1959 the taxpayer, an individual, files a return showing taxable income of $5,700, computed as follows:

Salary		$5,000
Net long-term capital gain		4,000
Total gross income		9,000
Less: Deduction allowed by section 1202 in respect of net long-term capital gain		2,000
Adjusted gross income		7,000
Less:		
Deduction for personal exemption	$600	
Standard deduction allowed by section 141	700	1,300
Taxable income		5,700

In 1960 the taxpayer undertakes the operation of a trade or business and sustains therein a net operating loss of $4,700. In 1961 he sustains a net operating loss of $10,000 in the operation of the business. Under section 172(b)(2), it is determined that the entire amount of each loss, $4,700 and $10,000, is a carryback to 1959. In determining the amount of the carryover of the 1961 less to 1962, the taxable income for 1959 as computed under this paragraph is $3,870, determined as follows:

Salary		$5,000
Net long-term capital gain		4,000
Total gross income		9,000
Less: Deduction for carryback of 1960 net operating loss		4,700
Adjusted gross income		4,300
Less: Standard deduction		430
Taxable income		3,870

(iii) *Minimum limitation.*—The taxable income, as modified under this paragraph, shall in no case be considered less than zero.

(3) *Electing small business corporations.*—For special rule applicable to corporations which were electing small business corporations under subchapter S (section 1361 and following), chapter 1 of the Code, during one or more of the taxable years described in section 172(b)(1), see paragraph (f) of §1.172-1.

(4) *Qualified real estate investment trust.*—Where a net operating loss is carried over to a qualified taxable year (as defined in §1.172-10(b)) ending after October 4, 1976, the real estate investment trust taxable income (as defined in section 857(b)(2)) shall be used as the "taxable income" for that taxable year to determine, under section 172(b)(2), the balance of the net operating loss available as a carryover to a subsequent taxable year. The real estate investment trust taxable income, however, is computed by applying the rules applicable to corporations in paragraph (a)(2) of this section. Thus, in computing real estate investment trust taxable income for purposes of section 172(b)(2), the net operating loss deduction for the taxable year shall be computed in accordance with paragraph (a)(2)(i) of this section. The principles of this subparagraph may be illustrated by the following examples:

Example (1). Corporation X, a calendar year taxpayer, is formed on January 1, 1977. X incurs a net operating loss of $100,000 for its taxable year 1977, which, under section 172(b)(2), is a carryover to 1978. For 1978 X is a qualified real estate investment trust (as defined in §1.172-10(b)) and has real estate investment trust taxable income (determined without regard to the deduction for dividends paid or the net operating loss deduction) of $150,000, all of which consists of ordinary income. X pays dividends in 1978 totaling $120,000 that qualify for the deduction for dividends paid under section 857(b)(2)(B). The portion of the 1977 net operating loss available as a carryover to 1979 and subsequent years is $70,000 (*i.e.*, the excess of the amount of the net operating loss ($100,000) over the amount of the real estate investment trust taxable income for 1978 ($30,000), determined by taking into account the deduction for dividends paid allowable under section 857(b)(2)(B) and without taking into account the net operating loss for 1977).

Example (2). (i) Assume the same facts as in example (1), except that the $150,000 of real estate investment trust taxable income (determined without the net operating loss deduction or the dividends paid deduction) consists of $80,000 of ordinary income and $70,000 of net capital gain. The amount of capital gain dividends which may be paid for 1978 is limited to $50,000, that is, the amount of the real estate investment trust taxable income for 1978, determined by taking into account the net operating loss deduction for the taxable year, but not the deduction for dividends paid ($150,000 minus $100,000). See §1.857-6(e)(1)(ii).

(ii) X designated $50,000 of the $120,000 of dividends paid as capital gains dividends (as defined in section 857(b)(3)(C) and §1.857-6(e)). Thus, $70,000 is an ordinary dividend. Since both ordinary dividends and capital gains dividends are taken into account in computing the deduction for dividends paid under section 857(b)(2)(B), the result will be the same as in example (1); that is, the portion of the 1977 net operating loss available as a carryover to 1979 and subsequent years is $70,000.

(b) Reserved.

[Reg. §1.172-5]

☐ [T.D. 6192, 7-23-56. *Amended by* T.D. 6486, 8-12-60, T.D. 6862, 11-17-65, T.D. 6900, 11-16-66, T.D. 7767, 2-3-81 *and* T.D. 8107, 12-1-86.]

[Reg. §1.172-6]

§1.172-6. Illustration of net operating loss carrybacks and carryovers.—The application of §1.172-4 may be illustrated by the following example:

(a) *Facts.*—The books of the taxpayer, whose return is made on the basis of the calendar year, reveal the following facts:

Taxable year	Taxable income	Net operating loss
1954	$15,000	....
1955	30,000	....
1956	....	($75,000)
1957	20,000	....

Itemized Deductions for Individuals and Corps.
See p. 20,601 for regulations not amended to reflect law changes

25,601

Taxable year	Taxable income	Net operating loss
1958	. . . .	(150,000)
1959	30,000	. . . .
1960	35,000	. . . .
1961	75,000	. . . .
1962	17,000	. . . .
1963	53,000	. . . .

The taxable income thus shown is computed without any net operating loss deduction. The assumption is also made that none of the other modifications prescribed in §1.172-5 apply. There are no net operating losses for 1950, 1951, 1952, 1953, 1964, or 1966.

(b) *Loss sustained in 1956.*—The portions of the $75,000 net operating loss for 1956 which shall be used as carrybacks to 1954 and 1955 and as carryovers to 1957, 1958, 1959, 1960, and 1961 are computed as follows:

(1) *Carryback to 1954.*—The carryback to this year is $75,000, that is, the amount of the net operating loss.

(2) *Carryback to 1955.*—The carryback to this year is $60,000, computed as follows:

Net operating loss		$75,000
Less:		
Taxable income for 1954 (computed without the deduction of the carryback from 1956)		15,000
Carryback		60,000

(3) *Carryover to 1957.*—The carryover to this year is $30,000, computed as follows:

Net operating loss		$75,000
Less:		
Taxable income for 1954 (computed without the deduction of the carryback from 1956)	$15,000	
Taxable income for 1955 (computed without the deduction of the carryback from 1956 or the carryback from 1958)	30,000	45,000
Carryover		30,000

(4) *Carryover to 1958.*—The carryover to this year is $10,000, computed as follows:

Net operating loss		$75,000
Less:		
Taxable income for 1954 (computed without the deduction of the carryback from 1956)	$15,000	
Taxable income for 1955 (computed without the deduction of the carryback from 1956 or the carryback from 1958)	30,000	
Taxable income for 1957 (computed without the deduction of the carryover from 1956 or the carryback from 1958)	20,000	
		65,000
Carryover		10,000

(5) *Carryover to 1959.*—The carryover to this year is $10,000, computed as follows:

Net operating loss		$75,000
Less:		
Taxable income for 1954 (computed without the deduction of the carryback from 1956)	$15,000	
Taxable income for 1955 (computed without the deduction of the carryback from 1956 or the carryback from 1958)	30,000	
Taxable income for 1957 (computed without the deduction of the carryover from 1956 or the carryback from 1958)	20,000	
Taxable income for 1958 (a year in which a net operating loss was sustained)	0	
		65,000
		10,000

(6) *Carryover to 1960.*—The carryover to this year is $0, computed as follows:

Net operating loss		$75,000
Less:		

Taxable income for 1954 (computed without the deduction of the carryback from 1956) $15,000

Taxable income for 1955 (computed without the deduction of the carryback from 1956 or the carryback from 1958) $30,000

Taxable income for 1957 (computed without the deduction of the carryover from 1956 or the carryback from 1958) 20,000

Taxable income for 1958 (a year in which a net operating loss was sustained) 0

Taxable income for 1959 (computed without the deduction of the carryover from 1956 or the carryover from 1958) 30,000

		$95,000
Carryover		0

(7) *Carryover to 1961.*—The carryover to this year is $0, computed as follows:

Net operating loss $75,000
Less:

Taxable income for 1954 (computed without the deduction of the carryback from 1956) $15,000

Taxable income for 1955 (computed without the deduction of the carryback from 1956 or the carryback from 1958) 30,000

Taxable income for 1957 (computed without the deduction of the carryover from 1956 or the carryback from 1958) 20,000

Taxable income for 1958 (a year in which a net operating loss was sustained) 0

Taxable income for 1959 (computed without the deduction of the carryover

Taxable income for 1960 (computed without the deduction of the carryover from 1956 or the carryover from 1958) 35,000

		$130,000
Carryover		0

(c) *Loss sustained in 1958.*—The portions of the $150,000 net operating loss for 1958 which shall be used as carrybacks to 1955, 1956, and 1957 and as carryovers to 1959, 1960, 1961, 1962, and 1963 are computed as follows:

(1) *Carryback to 1955.*—The carryback to this year is $150,000, that is, the amount of the net operating loss.

(2) *Carryback to 1956.*—The carryback to this year is $150,000, computed as follows:

Net operating loss		$150,000
Less:		
Taxable income for 1955 (the $30,000 taxable income for such year reduced by the carryback to such year of $60,000 from 1956, the carryback from 1958 to 1955 not being taken into account)		0
Carryback		150,000

(3) *Carryback to 1957.*—The carryback to this year is $150,000, computed as follows:

Net operating loss		$150,000
Less:		
Taxable income for 1955 (the $30,000 taxable income for such year reduced by the carryback to such year of $60,000 from 1956, the carryback from 1958 to 1955 not being taken into account)	$0	
Taxable income for 1956 (a year in which a net operating loss was sustained)	0	
		0
Carryback		150,000

(4) *Carryover to 1959.*—The carryover to this year is $150,000, computed as follows:

Net operating loss $150,000
Less:

Taxable income for 1955 (the $30,000 taxable income for such year reduced by the carryback to such year of $60,000 from 1956, the carryback from 1958 to 1955 not being taken into account) $0

Taxable income for 1956 (a year in which a net operating loss was sustained) 0

Taxable income for 1957 (the $20,000 taxable income for such year reduced by the carryover to such year of $30,000 from 1956, the carryback from 1958 to 1957 not being taken into account) 0

                                                        0
                                                  _____
        Carryover   150,000

(5) *Carryover to 1960.*—The carryover to this year is $130,000, computed as follows:

Net operating loss $150,000
Less:

Taxable income for 1955 (the $30,000 taxable income for such year reduced by the carryback to such year of $60,000 from 1956, the carryback from 1958 to 1955 not being taken into account) $0

Taxable income for 1956 (a year in which a net operating loss was sustained) 0

Taxable income for 1957 (the $20,000 taxable income for such year reduced by the carryover to such year of $30,000 from 1956, the carryback from 1958 to 1957 not being taken into account) 0

Taxable income for 1959 (the $30,000 taxable income for such year reduced by the carryover to such year of $10,000 from 1956, the carryover from 1958 to 1959 not being taken into account) $20,000
                                                  _____
                                                        $20,000
                                                          130,000
        Carryover   130,000

(6) *Carryover to 1961.*—The carryover to this year is $95,000, computed as follows:

Net operating loss $150,000
Less:

Taxable income for 1955 (the $30,000 taxable income for such year reduced by the carryback to such year of $60,000 from 1956, the carryback from 1958 to 1955 not being taken into account) $0

Taxable income for 1956 (a year in which a net operating loss was sustained) 0

Taxable income for 1957 (the $20,000 taxable income for such year reduced by the carryover to such year of $30,000 from 1956, the carryback from 1958 to 1957 not being taken into account) 0

Taxable income for 1959 (the $30,000 taxable income for such year reduced by the carryover to such year of $10,000 from 1956, the carryover from 1958 to 1959 not being taken into account) 20,000

Taxable income for 1960 (the $35,000 taxable income for such year reduced by the carryover to such year of $0 from 1956, the carryover from 1958 to 1960 not being taken into account) . 35,000
                                                  _____
                                                        55,000
        Carryover   95,000

(7) *Carryover to 1962.*—The carryover to this year is $20,000, computed as follows:

Net operating loss $150,000
Less:

Taxable income for 1955 (the $30,000 taxable income for such year reduced by the carryback to such year of $60,000 from 1956, the carryback from 1958 to 1955 not being taken into account) $0

Taxable income for 1956 (a year in which a net operating loss was sustained) $0

Taxable income for 1957 (the $20,000 taxable income for such year reduced by the carryover to such year of $30,000 from 1956, the carryback from 1958 to 1957 not being taken into account) 0

Taxable income for 1959 (the $30,000 taxable income for such year reduced by the carryover to such year of $10,000 from 1956, the carryover from 1958 to 1959 not being taken into account) 20,000

Taxable income for 1960 (the $35,000 taxable income for such year reduced by the carryover to such year of $0 from 1956, the carryover from 1958 to 1960 not being taken into account) . 35,000

Taxable income for 1961 (the $75,000 taxable income for such year reduced by the carryover to such year of $0 from 1956, the carryover from 1958 to 1961 not being taken into account) . 75,000
                                                  _____
                                                        $130,000
        Carryover   20,000

(8) *Carryover to 1963.*—The carryover to this year is $3,000, computed as follows:

Net operating loss $150,000
Less:

Taxable income for 1955 (the $30,000 taxable income for such year reduced by the carryback to such year of $60,000 from 1956, the carryback from 1958 to 1955 not being taken into account) $0

Taxable income for 1956 (a year in which a net operating loss was sustained) 0

Taxable income for 1957 (the $20,000 taxable income for such year reduced by the carryover to such year of $30,000 from 1956, the carryback from 1958 to 1957 not being taken into account) 0

Taxable income for 1959 (the $30,000 taxable income for such year reduced by the carryover to such year of $10,000 from 1956, the carryover from 1958 to 1959 not being taken into account) 20,000

Taxable income for 1960 (the $35,000 taxable income for such year reduced by the carryover to such year of $0 from 1956, the carryover from 1958 to 1960 not being taken into account) . 35,000

Taxable income for 1961 (the $75,000 taxable income for such year reduced by the carryover to such year of $0 from 1956, the carryover from 1958 to 1961 not being taken into account) . 75,000

Taxable income for 1962 (computed without the deduction of the carryover from 1958) 17,000
                                                  _____
                                                        147,000
        Carryover   3,000

(d) *Determination of net operating loss deduction for each year.*—The carryovers and carrybacks computed under paragraphs (b) and (c) of this section are used as a basis for the computation of the net operating loss deduction in the following manner:

Reg. §1.172-6(c)(5)

	Carryover			Carryback		
Taxable year	From 1956	From 1958		From 1956	From 1958	Net operating loss deduction
1954	...	...		$75,000	...	$75,000
1955	...	...		60,000	$150,000	210,000
1957	$30,000	...		...	150,000	180,000
1959	10,000	$150,000		...	...	160,000
1960	...	130,000		...	...	130,000
1961	...	95,000		...	...	95,000
1962	...	20,000		...	...	20,000
1963	...	3,000		...	...	3,000

[Reg. § 1.172-6.]

☐ [*T.D. 6192, 7-23-56. Amended by T.D. 6486, 8-12-60.*]

[Reg. § 1.172-7]

§ 1.172-7. Joint return by husband and wife.—(a) *In general.*—This section prescribes additional rules for computing the net operating loss carrybacks and carryovers of a husband and wife making a joint return for one or more of the taxable years involved in the computation of the net operating loss deduction.

(b) *From separate to joint return.*—If a husband and wife, making a joint return for any taxable year, did not make a joint return for any of the taxable years involved in the computation of a net operating loss carryover or a net operating loss carryback to the taxable year for which the joint return is made, such separate net operating loss carryover or separate net operating loss carryback is a joint net operating loss carryover or joint net operating loss carryback to such taxable year.

(c) *Continuous use of joint return.*—If a husband and wife making a joint return for a taxable year made a joint return for each of the taxable years involved in the computation of a net operating loss carryover or net operating loss carryback to such taxable year, the joint net operating loss carryover or joint net operating loss carryback to such taxable year is computed in the same manner as the net operating loss carryover or net operating loss carryback of an individual under § 1.172-4 but upon the basis of the joint net operating losses and the combined taxable income of both spouses.

(d) *From joint to separate return.*—If a husband and wife making separate returns for a taxable year made a joint return for any, or all, of the taxable years involved in the computation of a net operating loss carryover or net operating loss carryback to such taxable year, the separate net operating loss carryover or separate net operating loss carryback of each spouse to the taxable year is computed in the manner set forth in § 1.172-4 but with the following modifications:

(1) *Net operating loss.*—The net operating loss of each spouse for a taxable year for which a joint return was made shall be deemed to be that portion of the joint net operating loss (computed in accordance with paragraph (d) of § 1.172-3) which is attributable to the gross income and deductions of such spouse, gross income and deductions being taken into account to the same extent that they are taken into account in computing the joint net operating loss.

(2) *Taxable income to be subtracted.*—(i) *Net operating loss of other spouse.*—The taxable income of a particular spouse for any taxable year which is subtracted from the net operating loss of such spouse for another taxable year in order to determine the amount of such loss which may be carried back or carried over to still another taxable year is deemed to be, in a case in which such taxable income was reported in a joint return, the sum of the following:

(a) That portion of the combined taxable income of both spouses for such year for which the joint return was made which is attributable to the gross income and deductions of the particular spouse, gross income and deductions being taken into account to the same extent that they are taken into account in computing such combined taxable income, and

(b) That portion of such combined taxable income which is attributable to the other spouse; but, if such other spouse sustained a net operating loss in a taxable year beginning on the same date as the taxable year in which the particular spouse sustained the net operating loss from which the taxable income is subtracted, then such portion shall first be reduced by such net operating loss of such other spouse.

(ii) *Modifications.*—For purposes of this subparagraph, the combined taxable income shall be computed as though the combined income and deductions of both spouses were those of one individual. The provisions of § 1.172-5 shall apply in computing the combined taxable income for such purposes except that the net operating loss deduction shall be determined without taking into account any separate net operating loss of either spouse, or any joint net operating loss of both spouses, which was sustained in a taxable year beginning on

or after the date of the beginning of the taxable year in which the particular spouse sustained the net operating loss from which the taxable income is subtracted.

(e) *Recurrent use of joint return.*—If a husband and wife making a joint return for any taxable year made a joint return for one or more, but not all, of the taxable years involved in the computation of a net operating loss carryover or net operating loss carryback to such taxable year, such net operating loss carryover or net operating loss carryback to the taxable year is computed in the manner set forth in paragraph (d) of this section. Such net operating loss carryover or net operating loss carryback is considered a joint net operating loss carryover or joint net operating loss carryback to such taxable year.

(f) *Joint carryovers and carrybacks.*—The joint net operating loss carryovers and the joint net operating loss carrybacks to any taxable year for which a joint return is made are all the net operating loss carryovers and net operating loss carrybacks of both spouses to such taxable year. For example, a husband and wife file a joint return for the calendar year 1956, having a joint taxable income for such year. The wife filed a separate return for the calendar years 1954 and 1955, in which years she sustained net operating losses. The husband filed separate returns for his fiscal year ending June 30, 1955, and, having received permission to change his accounting period to a calendar year basis, for the 6-month period ending December 31, 1955. The husband sustained net operating losses in both such taxable years. Since the husband and wife did not file a joint return for any taxable year involved in the computation of the net operating loss carryovers to 1956 from 1954 and 1955, the joint net operating loss carryovers to 1956 are the separate net operating loss carryovers of the wife from the calendar years 1954 and 1955 and the separate net operating loss carryovers of the husband from the fiscal year ending June 30, 1955, and from the short taxable year ending December 31, 1955. If the husband and wife also file joint returns for the calendar years 1957, 1958, and 1959, having a joint taxable income in 1957 and 1958 and a joint net operating loss in 1959, the joint net operating loss carrybacks to 1956, 1957, and 1958 from 1959 are computed on the basis of the joint net operating loss for 1959, since separate returns were not made for any taxable year involved in the computation of such carrybacks.

(g) *Illustration of principles.*—In the following examples, which illustrate the application of this section, it is assumed that there are no items of adjustment under section 172(b)(2)(A) and that the taxable income or loss in each case is the taxable income or loss determined without any net operating loss deduction. The taxpayers in each example, H, a husband, and W, his wife, report their income on the calendar-year basis.

Example (1). H and W filed joint returns for 1954 and 1955. They sustained a joint net operating loss of $1,000 for 1954 and a joint net operating loss of $2,000 for 1955. For 1954 the deductions of H exceeded his gross income by $700, and the deductions of W exceeded her gross income by $300, the total of such amounts being $1,000. Therefore, $700 of the $1,000 joint net operating loss for 1954 is considered the net operating loss of H for 1954, and $300 of such joint net operating loss is considered the net operating loss of W for 1954. For 1955 the gross income of H exceeded his deductions, so that his separate taxable income would be $1,500, and the deductions of W exceeded her gross income by $3,500. Therefore, all of the $2,000 joint net operating loss for 1955 is considered the separate net operating loss of W for 1955.

Example (2). (i) H and W filed joint returns for 1954 and 1956, and separate returns for 1955 and 1957. For the years 1954, 1955, 1956, and 1957 they had taxable incomes and net operating losses as follows, losses being indicated in parentheses:

	1954	1955	1956	1957
H	($5,000)	($2,500)	$6,500	($4,000)
W	(3,000)	2,000	3,000	(1,500)
Total	(8,000)	...	9,500	...

(ii) The net operating loss carryover of H from 1957 to 1958 is $4,000, that is, his $4,000 net operating loss for 1957 which is not reduced by any part of the taxable income for 1956, since none of such taxable income is attributable to H and the portion attributable

Reg. § 1.172-7(g)

to W is entirely offset by her separate net operating loss for her taxable year 1957, which taxable year begins on the same date as H's taxable year 1957. H's $4,000 net operating loss for 1957 likewise is not reduced by reference to 1955 since H sustained a loss in 1955. The $0 taxable income for 1956 which reduces H's net operating loss for 1957 is computed as follows:

(iii) The combined taxable income of $9,500 for 1956 is reduced to $1,000 by the net operating loss deduction for such year of $8,500. This net operating loss deduction is computed without taking into account any net operating loss of either H or W sustained in a taxable year beginning on or after January 1,1957, the date of the beginning of the taxable year in which H sustained the net operating loss from which the taxable income is subtracted. This $8,500 is composed of H's carryovers of $5,000 from 1954 and $2,500 from 1955, and of W's carryover of $1,000 from 1954 (the excess of W's $3,000 loss for 1954 over her $2,000 income for 1955). None of the $1,000 combined taxable income for 1956 (computed with the net operating loss deduction described above) is attributable to H since it is caused by W's income (computed after deducting her separate carryover) offsetting H's loss (computed by deducting from his income his separate carryovers). No part of the $1,000 combined taxable income for 1956 which is attributable to W is used to reduce H's net operating loss for 1957 since such taxable income attributable to W must first be reduced by W's $1,500 net operating loss for 1957, her taxable year beginning on the same date as the taxable year of H in which he sustained the net operating loss from which the taxable income is subtracted.

(iv) The net operating loss carryover of W from 1957 to 1958 is $500, her $1,500 loss reduced by the sum of her $0 taxable income for 1955 (computed by taking into account her $3,000 carryover from 1954) and her $1,000 taxable income for 1956, that is, the portion of the combined taxable income for 1956 which is attributable to her.

Example (3). (i) Assume the same facts as in example (2) except that for 1957 the net operating loss of W is $200 instead of $1,500.

(ii) The net operating loss carryover of H from 1957 to 1958 is $3,200, that is, his $4,000 net operating loss for 1957 reduced by the sum of his $0 taxable income for 1955 (a year in which he sustained a loss) and his $800 taxable income for 1956. Such $800 is computed as follows:

(iii) The combined taxable income for 1956, computed with the net operating loss deduction in the manner described in example (2), remains $1,000, no part of which is attributable to H. To the $0 taxable income attributable to H for 1956 there is added $800, the excess of the $1,000 taxable income for such year attributable to W over her $200 net operating loss sustained in 1957, a taxable year beginning on the same date as the taxable year of H in which he sustained the $4,000 net operating loss from which the taxable income is subtracted.

(iv) W has no net operating loss carryover from 1957 to 1958 since her net operating loss of $200 for 1957 does not exceed the $1,000 taxable income for 1956 attributable to her.

Example (4). (i) Assume the same facts as in example (2), except that W changes her accounting period in 1957 to a fiscal year ending on January 31, and has neither income nor losses for the taxable year January 1, 1957, to January 31, 1957, or for the fiscal year February 1, 1957, to January 31, 1958, but has a net operating loss of $200 for the fiscal year February 1, 1958, to January 31, 1959.

(ii) The net operating loss carryover of H from 1957 to 1958 is $3,000, that is, his net operating loss of $4,000 for 1957 reduced by the sum of his $0 taxable income for 1955 (a year in which he sustained a loss) and his $1,000 taxable income for 1956. Such $1,000 is computed as follows:

(iii) The combined taxable income for 1956, computed with the net operating loss deduction in the manner described in example (2), remains $1,000, no part of which is attributable to H. To the $0 taxable income attributable to H for 1956 there is added the $1,000 taxable income attributable to W for such year. The taxable income attributable to W is not reduced by any amount since she does not have a net operating loss for her taxable year beginning on January 1, 1957, the date of the beginning of the taxable year of H in which he sustained the $4,000 net operating loss from which his taxable income is subtracted.

(iv) The net operating loss carryover of W from the fiscal year beginning February 1, 1958, to her next fiscal year is $200, that is, her net operating loss of $200 for the fiscal year beginning February 1, 1958, reduced by the sum of her $0 taxable income for 1956, her $0 taxable income for the taxable year January 1, 1957, to January 31, 1957 (a year in which she had neither income nor loss), and her $0 taxable income for the fiscal year February 1, 1957, to January 31, 1958 (also a year in which she had neither income nor loss). The $0 taxable income for 1956 is computed as follows:

(v) The combined taxable income of $9,500 for 1956 is reduced to $0 amount by the net operating loss deduction for such year of $12,500. This net operating loss deduction is computed by taking into account the net operating loss of H for 1957 since it was sustained in

a taxable year beginning before February 1, 1958, the date of the beginning of the taxable year of W in which she sustained the $200 net operating loss from which her taxable income is subtracted. This $12,500 is composed of H's carryovers of $5,000 from 1954 and $2,500 from 1955 and of his carryback of $4,000 from 1957, plus W's carryover of $1,000 from 1954 (the excess of W's $3,000 loss for 1954 over her $2,000 income for 1955). Since there is no combined taxable income for 1956, there is no taxable income attributable to W for such year. [Reg. §1.172-7.]

☐ [*T.D. 6192, 7-23-56. Amended by T.D. 6486, 8-12-60, and T.D. 8170, 12-1-86.*]

[Reg. §1.172-8]

§1.172-8. Net operating loss carryovers for regulated transportation corporations.—(a) *In general.*—A net operating loss sustained in a taxable year ending before January 1, 1976, shall be a carryover to the 7 succeeding taxable years if the taxpayer is a regulated transportation corporation (as defined in paragraph (b) of this section) for the loss year and for the 6th and 7th succeeding taxable years. If, however, the taxpayer is a regulated transportation corporation for the loss year and for the 6th succeeding taxable year, but not for the 7th succeeding taxable year, then the loss shall be a carryover to the 6 succeeding taxable years. If the taxpayer is not a regulated transportation corporation for the 6th succeeding taxable year then this section shall not apply. A net operating loss sustained in a taxable year ending after December 31, 1975, shall be a carryover to the 15 succeeding taxable years.

(b) *Regulated transportation corporations.*—A corporation is a "regulated transportation corporation" for a taxable year if it is included within one or more of the following categories:

(1) Eighty percent or more of the corporation's gross income (computed without regard to dividends and capital gains and losses) for such taxable year is income from transportation sources described in paragraph (c) of this section.

(2) The corporation is a railroad corporation, subject to Part I of the Interstate Commerce Act, which is either a lessor railroad corporation described in section 7701(a)(33)(G) or a common parent railroad corporation described in section 7701(a)(33)(H).

(3) The corporation is a member of a regulated transportation system for the taxable year. For purposes of this section, a member of a regulated transportation system for a taxable year means a member of an affiliated group of corporations making a consolidated return for such year, if 80 percent or more of the sum of the gross incomes of the members of the affiliated group for such year (computed without regard to dividends, capital gains and losses, or eliminations for intercompany transactions) is derived from transportation sources described in paragraph (c) of this section. For purposes of this subparagraph, income derived by a corporation described in subparagraph (2) of this paragraph from leases described in section 7701(a)(33)(G) shall be considered as income from transportation sources described in paragraph (c) of this section.

(c) *Transportation sources.*—For purposes of this section, income from "transportation sources" means income received directly in consideration for transportation services, and income from the furnishing or sale of essential facilities, products, and other services which are directly necessary and incidental to the furnishing of transportation services. For purposes of the preceding sentence, the term "transportation services" means—

(1) Transportation by railroad as a common carrier subject to the jurisdiction of the Interstate Commerce Commission;

(2)(i) Transportation, which is not included in subparagraph (1) of this paragraph—

(*a*) On an intrastate, suburban, municipal, or interurban electric railroad,

(*b*) On an intrastate, municipal, or suburban trackless trolley system,

(*c*) On a municipal or suburban bus system, or

(*d*) By motor vehicle not otherwise included in this subparagraph,

if the rates for the furnishing or sale of such transportation are established or approved by a regulatory body described in section 7701(a)(33)(A);

(ii) In the case of a corporation which establishes to the satisfaction of the district director that—

(*a*) Its revenue from regulated rates from transportation services described in subdivision (i) of this subparagraph and its revenue derived from unregulated rates are derived from its operation of a single interconnected and coordinated system or from the operation of more than one such system, and

(*b*) The unregulated rates have been and are substantially as favorable to users and consumers as are the regulated rates,

transportation, which is not included in subparagraph (1) of this paragraph, from which such revenue from unregulated rates is derived.

(3) Transportation by air as a common carrier subject to the jurisdiction of the Civil Aeronautics Board; and

(4) Transportation by water by common carrier subject to the jurisdiction of either the Interstate Commerce Commission under Part III of the Interstate Commerce Act (54 Stat. 929), or the Federal Maritime Board under the Intercoastal Shipping Act, 1933 (52 Stat. 965).

(d) *Corporate acquisitions.*—This section shall apply to a carryover of a net operating loss sustained by a regulated transportation corporation (as defined in paragraph (b) of this section) to which an acquiring corporation succeeds under section 381(a) only if the acquiring corporation is a regulated transportation corporation (as defined in paragraph (b) of this section)—

(1) For the sixth succeeding taxable year in the case of a carryover to the sixth succeeding taxable year, and

(2) For the sixth and seventh succeeding taxable years in the case of a carryover to the seventh succeeding taxable year. [Reg. § 1.172-8.]

. ☐ [*T.D. 6862, 11-17-65. Amended by T.D. 8107, 12-1-86.*]

[Reg. § 1.172-9]

§ 1.172-9. Election with respect to portion of net operating loss attributable to foreign expropriation loss.—(a) *In general.*—If a taxpayer has a net operating loss for a taxable year ending after December 31, 1958, and if the foreign expropriation loss for such year (as defined in paragraph (b)(1) of this section) equals or exceeds 50 percent of the net operating loss for such year, then the taxpayer may elect (at the time and in the manner provided in paragraph (c)(1) or (2) of this section, whichever is applicable) to have the provisions of this section apply. If the taxpayer so elects, the portion of the net operating loss for such taxable year attributable (under paragraph (b)(2) of this section) to such foreign expropriation loss shall not be a net operating loss carryback to any taxable year preceding the taxable year of such loss and shall be a net operating loss carryover to each of the ten taxable years following the taxable year of such loss. In such case, the portion, if any, of the net operating loss not attributable to a foreign expropriation loss shall be carried back or carried over as provided in paragraph (a)(1)(ii) of § 1.172-4.

(b) *Determination of "foreign expropriation loss".*—(1) *Definition of "foreign expropriation loss".*—The term "foreign expropriation loss" means, for any taxable year, the sum of the losses allowable as deductions under section 165 (other than losses from, or which under section 165(g) or 1231(a) are treated or considered as losses from, sales or exchanges of capital assets and other than losses described in section 165(i)(1)) sustained by reason of the expropriation, intervention, seizure, or similar taking of property by the government of any foreign country, any political subdivision thereof, or any agency or instrumentality of the foregoing. For purposes of the preceding sentence, a debt which becomes worthless in whole or in part, shall, to the extent of any deduction allowed under section 166(a), be treated as a loss allowable as a deduction under section 165.

(2) *Portion of the net operating loss attributable to a foreign expropriation loss.*—(i) Except as provided in subdivision (ii) of this subparagraph, the portion of the net operating loss for any taxable year attributable to a foreign expropriation loss is the amount of the foreign expropriation loss for such taxable year (determined under subparagraph (1) of this paragraph).

(ii) The portion of the net operating loss for a taxable year attributable to a foreign expropriation loss shall not exceed the amount of the net operating loss, computed under section 172(c), for such year.

(3) *Examples.*—The application of this paragraph may be illustrated by the following examples:

Example (1). M Corporation, a domestic calendar year corporation manufacturing cigars in the United States, owns, in country X, a tobacco plantation having an adjusted basis of $400,000 and farm equipment having an adjusted basis of $300,000. On January 15, 1961, country X expropriates the plantation and equipment without any allowance for compensation. For the taxable year 1961, M Corporation sustains a loss from the operation of its business (not including losses from the seizure of its plantation and equipment in country X) of $200,000, which loss would not have been sustained in the absence of the seizure. Accordingly, M has a net operating loss of $900,000 (the sum of $400,000, $300,000, and $200,000). For purposes of section 172(k)(1), M Corporation has a foreign expropriation loss for 1961 of $700,000 (the sum of $400,000 and $300,000, the losses directly sustained by reason of the seizure of its property by country X). Since the foreign expropriation loss for 1961, $700,000, equals or exceeds 50

percent of the net operating loss for such year, or $450,000 (i.e., 50 percent of $900,000) M Corporation may make the election under paragraph (c)(2) of this section with respect to $700,000, the portion of the net operating loss attributable to the foreign expropriation loss.

Example (2). Assume the same facts as in example (1) except that for 1961, M Corporation has operating profits of $300,000 (not including losses from the seizure of its plantation and equipment in country X) so that its net operating loss (as defined in section 172(c)) is only $400,000. Under the provisions of section 172(k)(2) and paragraph (b)(2) of this section, the portion of the net operating loss for 1961 attributable to a foreign expropriation loss is limited to $400,000, the amount of the net operating loss.

(c) *Time and manner of making election.*—(1) *Taxable years ending after December 31, 1963.*—In the case of a taxpayer who has a foreign expropriation loss for a taxable year ending after December 31, 1963, the election referred to in paragraph (a) of this section shall be made by attaching to the taxpayer's income tax return (filed within the time prescribed by law, including extensions of time) for the taxable year of such foreign expropriation loss a statement containing the information required by subparagraph (3) of this paragraph. Such election shall be irrevocable after the due date (including extensions of time) of such return.

(2) *Information required.*—The statement referred to in subparagraph (1) of this paragraph shall contain the following information:

(i) The name, address, and taxpayer account number of the taxpayer;

(ii) A statement that the taxpayer elects under section 172(b)(3)(A)(ii) or (iii), whichever is applicable, to have section 172(b)(1)(D) of the Code apply;

(iii) The amount of the net operating loss for the taxable year; and

(iv) The amount of the foreign expropriation loss for the taxable year, including a schedule showing the computation of such foreign expropriation loss.

(d) *Amount of foreign expropriation loss which is a carryover to the taxable year in issue.*—(1) *General.*—If a portion of a net operating loss for the taxable year is attributable to a foreign expropriation loss and if an election under paragraph (a) of this section has been made with respect to such portion of the net operating loss, then such portion shall be considered to be a separate net operating loss for such year, and, for the purpose of determining the amount of such separate loss which may be carried over to other taxable years, such portion shall be applied after the other portion (if any) of such net operating loss. Such separate loss shall be carried to the earliest of the several taxable years to which such separate loss is allowable as a carryover under the provisions of paragraph (a)(1)(iv) of § 1.172-4, and the amount of such separate loss which shall be carried over to any taxable year subsequent to such earliest year is an amount (not exceeding such separate loss) equal to the excess of—

(i) The sum of (a) such separate loss and (b) the other portion (if any) of the net operating loss (i.e., that portion not attributable to a foreign expropriation loss) to the extent such other portion is a carryover to such earliest taxable year, over

(ii) The sum of the aggregate of the taxable incomes (computed as provided in § 1.172-5) for all of such several taxable years preceding such subsequent taxable year.

(2) *Cross reference.*—The portion of a net operating loss which is not attributable to a foreign expropriation loss shall be carried back or carried over, in accordance with the rules provided in paragraph (b)(1) of § 1.172-4, as if such portion were the only net operating loss for such year.

(3) *Examples.*—The application of this paragraph may be illustrated by the following examples:

Example (1). Corporation A, organized in 1960 and whose return is made on the basis of the calendar year, incurs for 1960 a net operating loss of $10,000, of which $7,500 is attributable to a foreign expropriation loss. With respect to such $7,500, A makes the election described in paragraph (a) of this section. In each of the years 1961, 1962, 1963, 1964, and 1965, A has taxable income in the amount of $600 (computed without any net operating loss deduction). The assumption is made that none of the other modifications prescribed in § 1.172-5 apply. The portion of the net operating loss attributable to the foreign expropriation loss which is a carryover to the year 1966 is $7,000, which is the sum of $7,500 (the portion of the net operating loss attributable to the foreign expropriation loss) and $2,500 (the other portion of the net operating loss available as a carryover to 1961), minus $3,000 (the aggregate of the taxable incomes for taxable years 1961 through 1965).

Example (2). Assume the same facts as in example (1) except that taxable income for each of the years 1961 through 1965 is $400 (computed without any net operating loss deduction). The carryover to the year 1966 is $7,500, that is, the sum of $7,500 (the portion of the net operating loss attributable to the foreign expropriation loss) and $2,500 (the other portion of the net operating loss available as a carryover to 1961), minus $2,000 (the aggregate of the taxable incomes for taxable years 1961 through 1965), but limited to $7,500 (the portion of the net operating loss attributable to the foreign expropriation loss).

(e) *Taxable income which is subtracted from net operating loss to determine carryback or carryover.*—In computing taxable income for a taxable year (hereinafter called a "prior taxable year") for the purpose of determining the portion of a net operating loss for another taxable year which shall be carried to each of the several taxable years subsequent to the earliest taxable year to which such loss may be carried, the net operating loss deduction for any such prior taxable year shall be determined without regard to that portion, if any, of a net operating loss for a taxable year attributable to a foreign expropriation loss, if such portion may not, under the provisions of section 172(b)(1)(D) and paragraph (a)(1)(iv) of §1.172-4, be carried back to such prior taxable year. Thus, if the taxpayer has a foreign expropriation loss for 1962 and elects the 10-year carryover with respect to the portion of his net operating loss for 1962 attributable to the foreign expropriation loss, then in computing taxable income for the year 1960 for the purpose of determining the portion of a net operating loss for 1963 which is carried to years subsequent to 1960, the net operating loss deduction for 1960 is determined without regard to the portion of the net operating loss for 1962 attributable to the foreign expropriation loss, since under the provisions of section 172(b)(1)(D) and paragraph (a)(1)(iv) of §1.172-4 such portion of the net operating loss for 1962 may not be carried back to 1960. [Reg. §1.172-9.]

☐ [*T.D. 6862, 11-17-65. Amended by T.D. 8107, 12-1-86.*]

[Reg. §1.172-10]

§1.172-10. Net operating losses of real estate investment trusts.—
(a) *Taxable years to which a loss may be carried.*—(1) A net operating loss sustained by a qualified real estate investment trust (as defined in paragraph (b)(1) of this section) in a qualified taxable year (as defined in paragraph (b)(2) of this section) ending after October 4, 1976, shall not be carried back to a preceding taxable year.

(2) A net operating loss sustained by a qualified real estate investment trust in a qualified taxable year ending before October 5, 1976, shall be carried back to the 3 preceding taxable years. However, see §1.857-2(a)(5), which does not allow the net operating loss deduction in computing real estate investment trust taxable income for taxable years ending before October 5, 1976.

(3) A net operating loss sustained by a qualified real estate investment trust in a qualified taxable year ending after December 31, 1972, shall be carried over to the 15 succeeding taxable years. However, see §1.857-2(a)(5).

(4) A net operating loss sustained by a qualified real estate investment trust in a qualified taxable year ending before January 1, 1973, shall be carried over to the 8 succeeding taxable years. However, see §1.857-2(a)(5).

(5) A net operating loss sustained in a taxable year for which the taxpayer is not a qualified real estate investment trust generally may be carried back to the 3 preceding taxable years; however, a net operating loss sustained in a taxable year ending after December 31, 1975, shall not be carried back to any qualified taxable year. However, see §1.857-2(a)(5) with respect to a net operating loss sustained in a taxable year ending before January 1, 1976.

(6) A net operating loss sustained in a taxable year ending after December 31, 1975, for which the taxpayer is not a qualified real estate investment trust generally may be carried over to the 15 succeeding taxable years.

(7)(i) A net operating loss sustained in a taxable year ending before January 1, 1976, for which the taxpayer is not a qualified real estate investment trust generally may be a net operating loss carryover to each of the 5 succeeding taxable years. However, where the loss was a net operating loss carryback to one or more qualified taxable years, the net operating loss, in accordance with paragraph (a)(7)(ii) of this section, shall be—

(A) Carried over to the 15 succeeding taxable years if the loss could be a net operating loss carryover to a taxable year ending in 1981, or

(B) Carried over to the 5, 6, 7, or 8 succeeding taxable years if paragraph (a)(7)(i)(A) of this section does not apply.

(ii) For purposes of determining whether a net operating loss could be a carryover to a taxable year ending in 1981 under paragraph (a)(7)(i)(A) of this section or, where paragraph (a)(7)(i)(A) of this section does not apply, to determine the actual carryover period under paragraph (a)(7)(i)(B) of this section, the net operating loss shall have a carryover period of 5 years, and such period shall be increased (to a number not greater than 8) by the number of qualified taxable years to which such loss was a net operating loss carryback;

however, where the taxpayer acted so as to cause itself to cease to be a qualified real estate investment trust and the principal purpose for such action was to secure the benefit of the allowance of a net operating loss carryover under section 172(b)(1)(B), the net operating loss carryover period shall be limited to 5 years. However, see §1.857-2(a)(5).

(8) A qualified taxable year is a taxable year preceding or following the taxable year of the net operating loss, for purposes of section 172(b)(1), even though the loss may not be carried to, or allowed as a deduction in, such qualified taxable year. Thus, a qualified taxable year ending before October 5, 1976 (for which no net operating loss deduction is allowable) is nevertheless a preceding or following taxable year for purposes of section 172(b)(1). Moreover, a qualified taxable year ending after October 4, 1976 (to which a net operating loss cannot be carried back because of section 172(b)(1)(E)) is nevertheless a preceding taxable year for purposes of section 172(b)(1). For purposes of determining, under section 172(b)(2), the balance of the loss available as a carryback or carryover to other taxable years, however, the net operating loss is not reduced on account of such qualified taxable year being a preceding or following taxable year.

(b) *Definitions.*—For purposes of this section and §§1.172-2 and 1.172-5—

(1) The term "qualified real estate investment trust" means, with respect to any taxable year, a real estate investment trust within the meaning of part II of subchapter M which is taxable for such year under that part as a real estate investment trust, and

(2) The term "qualified taxable year" means a taxable year for which the taxpayer is a qualified real estate investment trust.

(c) *Examples.*—The provisions of this section may be illustrated by the following examples:

Example (1)-(i) *Facts.* X was a qualified real estate investment trust for the taxable years ending on December 31, 1972, and December 31, 1973. X was not a qualified real estate investment trust for the taxable years ending on December 31, 1971, and December 31, 1974. X sustained a net operating loss for the taxable year ending on December 31, 1974.

(ii) *Applicable carryback and carryover periods.* The net operating loss must be carried back to the 3 preceding taxable years. Under §1.857-2(a)(5) the net operating loss deduction shall not be allowed in computing real estate investment trust taxable income for the years ending December 31, 1972, and December 31, 1973. Where a net operating loss is sustained in a taxable year ending before January 1, 1976, for which the taxpayer is not a qualified real estate investment trust and the loss is a net operating loss carryback to one or more qualified taxable years, the carryover period is determined under §1.172-10(a)(7); the carryover period is determined by first applying the rule provided in paragraph (a)(7)(ii) of this section to obtain the carryover period for purposes of determining whether the net operating loss could have been a net operating loss carryover to a taxable year ending in 1981. Under these facts, paragraph (a)(7)(ii) of this section provides for a 7-year carryover period (5 years increased by the 2 qualified taxable years to which the loss was a net operating loss carryback); therefore, since the carryover period provided for by paragraph (a)(7)(ii) of this section would allow the net operating loss to be a net operating loss carryover to a taxable year ending in 1981, under paragraph (a)(7)(ii)(A) of this section the applicable carryover period is 15 years (provided that X did not act so as to cause itself to cease to qualify as a real estate investment trust for the principal purpose of securing the benefit of a net operating loss carryover under section 172(b)(1)(B)).

Example (2)-(i) *Facts.* The facts are the same as in *example* (1) except that the taxable year ending December 31, 1973, was not a qualified taxable year for X.

(ii) *Applicable carryback and carryover periods.* The net operating loss must be carried back to the 3 preceding taxable years. Section 1.857-2(a)(5) provides that the net operating loss deduction shall not be allowed in computing real estate investment trust taxable income for the year ending December 31, 1972. Under these facts the carryover period is determined under §1.172-10(a)(7). Paragraph (a)(7)(ii) of this section provides for a 6 year carryover period (5 years increased by the 1 qualified taxable year to which the loss was a net operating loss carryback); therefore, since a 6 year carryover period would not allow the net operating loss to be a net operating loss carryover to a taxable year ending in 1981, under paragraph (a)(7)(ii)(A) of this section the applicable carryover period is 15 years (provided that X did not act so as to cause itself to cease to qualify as a real estate investment trust for the principal purpose of securing the benefit of a net operating loss carryover under section 172(b)(1)(B)).

(d) *Cross references.*—See §§1.172-2(e) and 1.172-5(a)(5) for the computation of the net operating loss of a qualified real estate investment trust for a taxable year ending after October 4, 1976, and the amount of a net operating loss which is absorbed when carried over to a qualified taxable year ending after October 4, 1976. See §1.857-2(a)(5), which provides that for a taxable year ending before October 5, 1976, the net operating loss deduction is not allowed in computing the real estate investment trust taxable income of a qualified real estate investment trust. [Reg. §1.172-10.]

☐ [*T.D. 7767, 2-3-81. Amended by T.D. 8107, 12-1-86.*]

[Reg. §1.172-13]

§1.172-13. Product liability losses.—(a) *Entitlement to 10-year carryback.*—(1) *In general.*—Unless an election is made pursuant to paragraph (c) of this section, in the case of a taxpayer which has a product liability loss (as defined in section 172(j) and paragraph (b)(1) of this section) for a taxable year beginning after September 30, 1979 (hereinafter "loss year"), the product liability loss shall be a net operating loss carryback to each of the 10 taxable years preceding the loss year.

(2) *Years to which loss may be carried.*—A product liability loss shall first be carried to the earliest of the taxable years to which such loss is allowable as a carryback and shall then be carried to the next earliest of such taxable years, etc.

(3) *Example.*—The application of this paragraph may be illustrated as follows:

Example. Taxpayer A incurs a net operating loss for taxable year 1980 of $80,000, of which $60,000 is a product liability loss. A's taxable income for each of the 10 years immediately preceding taxable year 1980 was $5,000. The product liability loss of $60,000 is first carried back to the 10th through the 4th preceding taxable years ($5,000 per year), thus offsetting $35,000 of the loss. The remaining $25,000 of product liability loss is added to the remaining portion of the total net operating loss for taxable year 1980 which was not a product liability loss ($20,000), and the total is then carried back to the 3rd through 1st years preceding taxable year 1980, which offsets $15,000 of this loss. The remaining loss ($30,000) is carried forward pursuant to section 172(b)(1) and the regulations thereunder without regard to whether all or any portion thereof originated as a product liability loss.

(b) *Definitions.*—(1) *Product liability loss.*—The term "product liability loss" means, for any taxable year, the lesser of—

(i) The net operating loss for the current taxable year (not including the portion of such net operating loss attributable to foreign expropriation losses, as defined in §1.172-11), or

(ii) The total of the amounts allowable as deductions under sections 162 and 165 directly attributable to—

(A) Product liability (as defined in paragraph (b)(2) of this section), and

(B) Expenses (including settlement payments) incurred in connection with the investigation or settlement of or opposition to claims against the taxpayer on account of alleged product liability.

Indirect corporate expense, or overhead, is not to be allocated to product liability claims so as to become a product liability loss.

(2) *Product liability.*—(i) The term "product liability" means the liability of a taxpayer for damages resulting from physical injury or emotional harm to individuals, or damage to or loss of the use of property, on account of any defect in any product which is manufactured, leased, or sold by the taxpayer. The preceding sentence applies only to the extent that the injury, harm, or damage occurs after the taxpayer has completed or terminated operations with respect to the product, including, but not limited to the manufacture, installation, delivery, or testing of the product, and has relinquished possession of such product.

(ii) The term "product liability" does not include liabilities arising under warranty theories relating to repair or replacement of the property that are essentially contract liabilities. For example, the costs incurred by a taxpayer in repairing or replacing defective products under the terms of a warranty, express or implied, are not product liability losses. On the other hand, the taxpayer's liability for damage done to other property or for harm done to persons that is attributable to a defective product may be product liability losses *regardless of whether the claim sounds in tort or contract.* Further, liability incurred as a result of services performed by a taxpayer is not product liability. For purposes of the preceding sentence, where both a product and services are integral parts of a transaction, product liability does not arise until all operations with respect to the product are completed and the taxpayer has relinquished possession of it. On the other hand, any liability that arises after completion of the initial delivery, installation, servicing, testing, etc., is considered "product liability" even if such liability arises during the subsequent servicing of the product pursuant to a service agreement or otherwise.

(iii) Liability for injury, harm, or damage due to a defective product as described in this subparagraph shall be "product liability" notwithstanding that the liability is not considered product liability under the law of the State in which such liability arose.

(iv) Amounts paid for insurance against product liability risks are not paid on account of product liability.

(v) Notwithstanding subparagraph (iv), an amount is paid on account of product liability (even if such amount is paid to an insurance company) if the amount satisfies the provisions of paragraph (b)(2)(i) through (iii) of this section and the amount—

(A) Is paid on account of specific claims against the taxpayer (or on account of expenses incurred in connection with the investigation or settlement of or opposition to such claims), subsequent to the events giving rise to the claims and pursuant to a contract entered into before those events,

(B) Is not refundable, and

(C) Is not applicable to other claims, other expenses or to subsequent coverage.

(3) *Examples.*—Paragraph (b)(2) of this section is illustrated by the following examples:

Example (1). X, a manufacturer of heating equipment, sells a boiler to A, a homeowner. Subsequent to the sale and installation of the boiler, the boiler explodes due to a defect causing physical injury to A. A sues X for damages for the injuries sustained in the explosion and is awarded $250,000, which X pays. The payment was made on account of product liability.

Example (2). Assume the same facts as in example (1) and that A also sues under the contract with X to recover for the cost of the boiler and recovers $1,000, the boiler's replacement cost. The $1,000 payment is not a payment on account of product liability. Similarly, if X agrees to repair the destroyed boiler, any amount expended by X for such repair is not payment made on account of product liability.

Example (3). Y, a professional medical association, is sued by B, a patient, in an action based on the malpractice of one of its doctors. B recovers $25,000. Because the suit was based on the service of B, the payment is not made on account of product liability.

Example (4). R, a retailer of communications equipment, sells a telecommunication device to C. R also contracts with C to service the equipment for 3 years. While R is installing the equipment, the unit catches on fire due to faulty wiring within the unit and destroys C's office. Because R had not relinquished possession of this equipment when the fire started, any amount paid to C by R for the damage to C's property on account of the defective product is not payment on account of product liability.

Example (5). Assume the same facts as in example (4) except that the fire and resulting property damages occurred after R had installed the equipment and relinquished possession of it. Any amount paid for the property damages sustained on account of the defective product is payment on account of product liability.

Example (6). Assume the same facts as in example (4) except that the equipment catches on fire during the subsequent servicing of the unit. Because C is in possession of the unit during the servicing, any amount paid for the property damage sustained on account of the defective product would be payment on account of product liability.

Example (7). X, a manufacturer of computers, sells a computer to A. X also has its employees periodically service the computer for A from time to time after it is placed in service. After the initial delivery, installation, servicing, and testing of the computer is completed, the computer catches on fire while X's employee is servicing the equipment. This fire causes property damage to A's office and physical injury to A. Any amount paid for the property or physical damage sustained on account of the defective product is payment on account of product liability.

(c) *Election.*—(1) *In general.*—The 10-year carryback provision of this section applies, except as provided in this paragraph, to any taxpayer who, for a taxable year beginning after September 30, 1979, incurs a product liability loss. Any taxpayer entitled to a 10-year carryback under paragraph (a) of this section in any loss year may elect (at the time and in the manner provided in paragraph (c)(2) of this section) to have the carryback period with respect to the product liability loss determined without regard to the carryback rules provided by paragraph (a) of this section. If the taxpayer so elects, the product liability loss shall not be carried back to the 10th through the 4th taxable years preceding the loss year. In such case, the product liability loss shall be carried back or carried over as provided by section 172(b) (except subparagraph (1)(I) thereof) and the regulations thereunder.

(2) *Time and manner of making election.*—An election by any taxpayer entitled to the 10-year carryback for the product liability loss to have the carryback with respect to such loss determined without regard to the 10-year carryback provision of paragraph (a) of this section must be made by attaching to the taxpayer's tax return (filed

within the time prescribed by law, including extensions of time) for the taxable year in which such product liability loss is sustained, a statement containing the information required by paragraph (c)(3) of this section. Such election, once made for any taxable year, shall be irrevocable after the due date (including extensions of time) of the taxpayer's tax return for that taxable year.

(3) *Information required.*—In the case of a statement filed after April 25, 1983, the statement referred to in paragraph (c)(2) of this section shall contain the following information:

　(i) The name, address, and taxpayer identifying number of the taxpayer; and

　(ii) A statement that the taxpayer elects under section 172(j)(3) not to have section 172(b)(1)(I) apply.

(4) *Relationship with section 172(b)(3)(C) election.*—If a taxpayer sustains during the taxable year both a net operating loss not attributable to product liability and a product liability loss (as defined in section 172(j)(1) and paragraph (b)(1) of this section), an election pursuant to section 172(b)(3)(C) (relating to election to relinquish the entire carryback period) does not preclude the product liability loss from being carried back 10 years under section 172(b)(1)(I) and paragraph (a)(1) of this section. [Reg. § 1.172-13.]

☐ [T.D. 8096, 8-26-86.]

[Reg. § 1.173-1]

§1.173-1. Circulation expenditures.—(a) *Allowance of deduction.*—Section 173 provides for the deduction from gross income of all expenditures to establish, maintain, or increase the circulation of a newspaper, magazine, or other periodical, subject to the following limitations:

(1) No deduction shall be allowed for expenditures for the purchase of land or depreciable property or for the acquisition of circulation through the purchase of any part of the business of another publisher of a newspaper, magazine, or other periodical;

(2) The deduction shall be allowed only to the publisher making the circulation expenditures; and

(3) The deduction shall be allowed only for the taxable year in which such expenditures are paid or incurred.

Subject to the provisions of paragraph (c) of this section, the deduction permitted under section 173 and this paragraph shall be allowed without regard to the method of accounting used by the taxpayer and notwithstanding the provisions of section 263 and the regulations thereunder, relating to capital expenditures.

(b) *Deferred expenditures.*—Notwithstanding the provisions of paragraph (a)(3) of this section, expenditures paid or incurred in a taxable year subject to the Internal Revenue Code of 1939 which are deferrable pursuant to I.T. 3369 (C.B. 1940-1, 46), as modified by Rev. Rul. 57-87 (C.B. 1957-1, 507), may be deducted in the taxable year subject to the Internal Revenue Code of 1954 to which so deferred.

(c) *Election to capitalize.*—(1) A taxpayer entitled to the deduction for circulation expenditures provided in section 173 and paragraph (a) of this section may, in lieu of taking such deduction, elect to capitalize the portion of such circulation expenditures which is properly chargeable to capital account. As a general rule, expenditures normally made from year to year in an effort to maintain circulation are not properly chargeable to capital account; conversely, expenditures made in an effort to establish or to increase circulation are properly chargeable to capital account. For example, if a newspaper normally employs five persons to obtain renewals of subscriptions by telephone, the expenditures in connection therewith would not be properly chargeable to capital account. However, if such newspaper, in a special effort to increase its circulation, hires for a limited period 20 additional employees to obtain new subscriptions by means of telephone calls to the general public, the expenditures in connection therewith would be properly chargeable to capital account. If an election is made by a taxpayer to treat any portion of his circulation expenditures as chargeable to capital account, the election must apply to all such expenditures which are properly so chargeable. In such case, no deduction shall be allowed under section 173 for any such expenditures. In particular cases, the extent to which any deductions attributable to the amortization of capital expenditures are allowed may be determined under sections 162, 263, and 461.

(2) A taxpayer may make the election referred to in subparagraph (1) of this paragraph by attaching a statement to his return for the first taxable year to which the election is applicable. Once an election is made, the taxpayer must continue in subsequent taxable years to charge to capital account all circulation expenditures properly so chargeable, unless the Commissioner, on application made to him in writing by the taxpayer, permits a revocation of such election for any subsequent taxable year or years. Permission to revoke such election may be granted subject to such conditions as the Commissioner deems necessary.

(3) Elections filed under section 23(bb) of the Internal Revenue Code of 1939 shall be given the same effect as if they were filed under section 173. (See section 7807(b)(2).) [Reg. § 1.173-1.]

☐ [T.D. 6254, 9-27-57.]

[Reg. § 1.174-1]

§1.174-1. Research and experimental expenditures; in general.—Section 174 provides two methods for treating research or experimental expenditures paid or incurred by the taxpayer in connection with his trade or business. These expenditures may be treated as expenses not chargeable to capital account and deducted in the year in which they are paid or incurred (see § 1.174-3), or they may be deferred and amortized (see § 1.174-4). Research or experimental expenditures which are neither treated as expenses nor deferred and amortized under section 174 must be charged to capital account. The expenditures to which section 174 applies may relate either to a general research program or to a particular project. See § 1.174-2 for the definition of research and experimental expenditures. The term "paid or incurred", as used in section 174 and in §§ 1.174-1 to 1.174-4, inclusive, is to be construed according to the method of accounting used by the taxpayer in computing taxable income. See section 7701(a)(25). [Reg. § 1.174-1.]

☐ [T.D. 6255, 10-3-57.]

[Reg. § 1.174-2]

§1.174-2. Definition of research and experimental expenditures.—(a) *In general.*—(1) *Research or experimental expenditures defined.*—The term *research or experimental expenditures*, as used in section 174, means expenditures incurred in connection with the taxpayer's trade or business which represent research and development costs in the experimental or laboratory sense. The term generally includes all such costs incident to the development or improvement of a product. The term includes the costs of obtaining a patent, such as attorneys' fees expended in making and perfecting a patent application. Expenditures represent research and development costs in the experimental or laboratory sense if they are for activities intended to discover information that would eliminate uncertainty concerning the development or improvement of a product. Uncertainty exists if the information available to the taxpayer does not establish the capability or method for developing or improving the product or the appropriate design of the product. Whether expenditures qualify as research or experimental expenditures depends on the nature of the activity to which the expenditures relate, not the nature of the product or improvement being developed or the level of technological advancement the product or improvement represents. The ultimate success, failure, sale, or use of the product is not relevant to a determination of eligibility under section 174. Costs may be eligible under section 174 if paid or incurred after production begins but before uncertainty concerning the development or improvement of the product is eliminated.

(2) *Production costs.*—Except as provided in paragraph (a)(5) of this section (the rule concerning the application of section 174 to components of a product), costs paid or incurred in the production of a product after the elimination of uncertainty concerning the development or improvement of the product are not eligible under section 174.

(3) *Product defined.*—For purposes of this section, the term *product* includes any pilot model, process, formula, invention, technique, patent, or similar property, and includes products to be used by the taxpayer in its trade or business as well as products to be held for sale, lease, or license.

(4) *Pilot model defined.*—For purposes of this section, the term *pilot model* means any representation or model of a product that is produced to evaluate and resolve uncertainty concerning the product during the development or improvement of the product. The term includes a fully-functional representation or model of the product or, to the extent paragraph (a)(5) of this section applies, a component of the product.

(5) *Application of section 174 to components of a product.*—If the requirements of paragraph (a)(1) of this section are not met at the level of a product (as defined in paragraph (a)(3) of this section), then whether expenditures represent research and development costs is determined at the level of the component or subcomponent of the product. The presence of uncertainty concerning the development or improvement of certain components of a product does not necessarily indicate the presence of uncertainty concerning the development or improvement of other components of the product or the product as a whole. The rule in this paragraph (a)(5) is not itself applied as a reason to exclude research or experimental expenditures from section 174 eligibility.

(6) *Research or experimental expenditures—exclusions.*—The term *research or experimental expenditures* does not include expenditures for—

    (i) The ordinary testing or inspection of materials or products for quality control (quality control testing);

    (ii) Efficiency surveys;

    (iii) Management studies;

    (iv) Consumer surveys;

    (v) Advertising or promotions;

    (vi) The acquisition of another's patent, model, production or process; or

    (vii) Research in connection with literary, historical, or similar projects.

(7) *Quality control testing.*—For purposes of paragraph (a)(6)(i) of this section, testing or inspection to determine whether particular units of materials or products conform to specified parameters is quality control testing. However, quality control testing does not include testing to determine if the design of the product is appropriate.

(8) *Expenditures for literary, historical, or similar research—cross reference.*—See section 263A and the regulations thereunder for cost capitalization rules which apply to expenditures paid or incurred for research in connection with literary, historical, or similar projects involving the production of property, including the production of films, sound recordings, video tapes, books, or similar properties.

(9) *Research or experimental expenditures limited to reasonable amounts.*—Section 174 applies to a research or experimental expenditure only to the extent that the amount of the expenditure is reasonable under the circumstances. In general, the amount of an expenditure for research or experimental activities is reasonable if the amount would ordinarily be paid for like activities by like enterprises under like circumstances. Amounts supposedly paid for research that are not reasonable under the circumstances may be characterized as disguised dividends, gifts, loans, or similar payments. The reasonableness requirement of this paragraph (a)(9) does not apply to the reasonableness of the type or nature of the activities themselves.

(10) *Amounts paid to others for research or experimentation.*—The provisions of this section apply not only to costs paid or incurred by the taxpayer for research or experimentation undertaken directly by him but also to expenditures paid or incurred for research or experimentation carried on in his behalf by another person or organization (such as a research institute, foundation, engineering company, or similar contractor). However, any expenditures for research or experimentation carried on in the taxpayer's behalf by another person are not expenditures to which section 174 relates, to the extent that they represent expenditures for the acquisition or improvement of land or depreciable property, used in connection with the research or experimentation, to which the taxpayer acquires rights of ownership.

(11) *Examples.*—The following examples illustrate the application of this paragraph (a).

Example 1. Amounts paid to others for research or experimentation allowed as a deduction A engages B to undertake research and experimental work in order to create a particular product. B will be paid annually a fixed sum plus an amount equivalent to his actual expenditures. In 1957, A pays to B in respect of the project the sum of $150,000 of which $25,000 represents an addition to B's laboratory and the balance represents charges for research and experimentation on the project. It is agreed between the parties that A will absorb the entire cost of this addition to B's laboratory which will be retained by B. A may treat the entire $150,000 as expenditures under section 174.

Example 2. Amounts paid to others not allowable as a deduction. S Corporation, a manufacturer of explosives, contracts with the T research organization to attempt through research and experimentation the creation of a new process for making certain explosives. Because of the danger involved in such an undertaking, T is compelled to acquire an isolated tract of land on which to conduct the research and experimentation. It is agreed that upon completion of the project T will transfer this tract, including any improvements thereon, to S. Section 174 does not apply to the amount paid to T representing the costs of the tract of land and improvements.

Example 3. Pilot model. U is engaged in the manufacture and sale of custom machines. U contracts to design and produce a machine to meet a customer's specifications. Because U has never designed a machine with these specifications, U is uncertain regarding the appropriate design of the machine, and particularly whether features desired by the customer can be designed and integrated into a functional machine. U incurs a total of $31,000 on the project. Of the $31,000, U incurs $10,000 of costs on materials and labor to produce a model that is used to evaluate and resolve the uncertainty concerning the appropriate design. U also incurs $1,000 of costs using the model to test whether certain features can be integrated into the design of the machine. This $11,000 of costs represents research and development costs in the experimental or laboratory sense. After uncertainty is eliminated, U incurs $20,000 to produce the machine for sale to the customer based on the appropriate design. The model produced and used to evaluate and resolve uncertainty is a pilot model within the meaning of paragraph (a)(4) of this section. Therefore, the $10,000 incurred to produce the model and the $1,000 incurred on design testing activities qualifies as research or experimental expenditures under section 174. However, section 174 does not apply to the $20,000 that U incurred to produce the machine for sale to the customer based on the appropriate design. See paragraph (a)(2) of this section (relating to production costs).

Example 4. Product component redesign. Assume the same facts as *Example 3*, except that during a quality control test of the machine, a component of the machine fails to function due to the component's inappropriate design. U incurs an additional $8,000 (including design retesting) to reconfigure the component's design. The $8,000 of costs represents research and development costs in the experimental or laboratory sense. After the elimination of uncertainty regarding the appropriate design of the component, U incurs an additional $2,000 on its production. The reconfigured component produced and used to evaluate and resolve uncertainty with respect to the component is a pilot model within the meaning of paragraph (a)(4) of this section. Therefore, in addition to the $11,000 of research and experimental expenditures previously incurred, the $8,000 incurred on design activities to establish the appropriate design of the component qualifies as research or experimental expenditures under section 174. However, section 174 does not apply to the additional $2,000 that U incurred for the production after the elimination of uncertainty of the re-designed component based on the appropriate design or to the $20,000 previously incurred to produce the machine. See paragraph (a)(2) of this section (relating to production costs).

Example 5. Multiple pilot models. V is a manufacturer that designs a new product. V incurs $5,000 to produce a number of models of the product that are to be used in testing the appropriate design before the product is mass-produced for sale. The $5,000 of costs represents research and development costs in the experimental or laboratory sense. Multiple models are necessary to test the design in a variety of different environments (exposure to extreme heat, exposure to extreme cold, submersion, and vibration). In some cases, V uses more than one model to test in a particular environment. Upon completion of several years of testing, V enters into a contract to sell one of the models to a customer and uses another model in its trade or business. The remaining models were rendered inoperable as a result of the testing process. Because V produced the models to resolve uncertainty regarding the appropriate design of the product, the models are pilot models under paragraph (a)(4) of this section. Therefore, the $5,000 that V incurred in producing the models qualifies as research or experimental expenditures under section 174. See also paragraph (a)(1) of this section (ultimate use is not relevant).

Example 6. Development of a new component; pilot model. W wants to improve a machine for use in its trade or business and incurs $20,000 to develop a new component for the machine. The $20,000 is incurred for engineering labor and materials to produce a model of the new component that is used to eliminate uncertainty regarding the development of the new component for the machine. The $20,000 of costs represents research and experimental costs in the experimental or laboratory sense. After W completes its research and experimentation on the new component, W incurs $10,000 for materials and labor to produce the component and incorporate it into the machine. The model produced and used to evaluate and resolve uncertainty with respect to the new component is a pilot model within the meaning of paragraph (a)(4) of this section. Therefore, the $20,000 incurred to produce the model and eliminate uncertainty regarding the development of the new component qualifies as research or experimental expenditures under section 174. However, section 174 does not apply to the $10,000 of production costs of the component because those costs were not incurred for research or experimentation. See paragraph (a)(2) of this section (relating to production costs).

Example 7. Disposition of a pilot model. X is a manufacturer of aircraft. X is researching and developing a new, experimental aircraft that can take off and land vertically. To evaluate and resolve uncertainty during the development or improvement of the product and test the appropriate design of the experimental aircraft, X produces a working aircraft at a cost of $5,000,000. The $5,000,000 of costs represents research and development costs in the experimental or laboratory sense. In a later year, X sells the aircraft. Because X produced the aircraft to resolve uncertainty regarding the appropriate design of the product during the development of the experimental aircraft, the aircraft is a pilot model under paragraph (a)(4) of this section. Therefore, the $5,000,000 of costs that X incurred in producing the aircraft qualifies as research or experimental expenditures under section 174. Further, it would not matter if X sold the pilot model or incorporated it in its own business as a demonstration model. See paragraph (a)(1) of this section (ultimate use is not relevant).

Example 8. Development of new component; pilot model. Y is a manufacturer of aircraft engines. Y is researching and developing a new type of compressor blade, a component of an aircraft engine, to improve the performance of an existing aircraft engine design that Y already manufactures and sells. To test the appropriate design of the new compressor blade and evaluate the impact of fatigue on the compressor blade design, Y produces and installs the compressor blade on an aircraft engine held by Y in its inventory. The costs of producing and installing the compressor blade component that Y incurred represent research and development costs in the experimental or laboratory sense. Because Y produced the compressor blade component to resolve uncertainty regarding the appropriate design of the component, the component is a pilot model under paragraph (a)(4) of this section. Therefore, the costs that Y incurred to produce and install the component qualify as research or experimental expenditures under section 174. See paragraph (a)(5) of this section (regarding the application of section 174 to components of a product). However, section 174 does not apply to Y's costs of producing the aircraft engine on which the component was installed. See paragraph (a)(2) of this section (relating to production costs).

Example 9. Variant product. T is a fuselage manufacturer for commercial and military aircraft. T is modifying one of its existing fuselage products, Class 20XX-1, to enable it to carry a larger passenger and cargo load. T modifies the Class 20XX-1 design by extending its length by 40 feet. T incurs $1,000,000 to develop and evaluate different designs to resolve uncertainty with respect to the appropriate design of the new fuselage class, Class 20XX-2. The $1,000,000 of costs represents research and development costs in the experimental or laboratory sense. Although Class 20XX-2, is a variant of Class 20XX-1, Class 20XX-2 is a new product because the information available to T as a result of T's development of Class 20XX-1 does not resolve uncertainty with respect to T's development of Class 20XX-2. Therefore, the $1,000,000 of costs that T incurred to develop and evaluate the Class 20XX-2 qualifies as research or experimental expenditures under section 174. Paragraph (a)(5) of this section does not apply, as the requirements of paragraph (a)(1) of this section are met with respect to the entire product.

Example 10. New process development. Z is a wine producer. Z is researching and developing a new wine production process that involves the use of a different method of crushing the wine grapes. In order to test the effectiveness of the new method of crushing wine grapes, Z incurs $2,000 in labor and materials to conduct the test on this part of the new manufacturing process. The $2,000 of costs represents research and development costs in the experimental or laboratory sense. Therefore, the $2,000 incurred qualifies as research or experimental expenditures under section 174 because it is a cost incident to the development or improvement of a component of a process.

(b) *Certain expenditures with respect to land and other property.*— (1) *Land and other property.*—Expenditures by the taxpayer for the acquisition or improvement of land, or for the acquisition or improvement of property which is subject to an allowance for depreciation under section 167 or depletion under section 611, are not deductible under section 174, irrespective of the fact that the property or improvements may be used by the taxpayer in connection with research or experimentation. However, allowances for depreciation or depletion of property are considered as research or experimental expenditures, for purposes of section 174, to the extent that the property to which the allowances relate is used in connection with research or experimentation. If any part of the cost of acquisition or improvement of depreciable property is attributable to research or experimentation (whether made by the taxpayer or another), see subparagraphs (2), (3), and (4) of this paragraph.

(2) *Expenditure resulting in depreciable property.*—Expenditures for research or experimentation which result, as an end product of the research or experimentation, in depreciable property to be used in the taxpayer's trade or business may, subject to the limitations of subparagraph (4) of this paragraph, be allowable as a current expense deduction under section 174(a). Such expenditures cannot be amortized under section 174(b) except to the extent provided in paragraph (a)(4) of § 1.174-4.

(3) *Amounts paid to others for research or experimentation resulting in depreciable property.*—If expenditures for research or experimentation are incurred in connection with the construction or manufacture of depreciable property by another, they are deductible under section 174(a) only if made upon the taxpayer's order and at his risk. No deduction will be allowed (i) if the taxpayer purchases another's product under a performance guarantee (whether express, implied, or imposed by local law) unless the guarantee is limited, to engineering specifications or otherwise, in such a way that economic utility is not taken into account; or (ii) for any part of the purchase price of a

product in regular production. For example, if a taxpayer orders a specially-built automatic milling machine under a guarantee that the machine will be capable of producing a given number of units per hour, no portion of the expenditure is deductible since none of it is made at the taxpayer's risk. Similarly, no deductible expense is incurred if a taxpayer enters into a contract for the construction of a new type of chemical processing plant under a turn-key contract guaranteeing a given annual production and a given consumption of raw material and fuel per unit. On the other hand, if the contract contained no guarantee of quality of production and of quantity of units in relation to consumption of raw material and fuel, and if real doubt existed as to the capabilities of the process, expenses for research or experimentation under the contract are at the taxpayer's risk and are deductible under section 174(a). However, see subparagraph (4) of this paragraph.

(4) *Deductions limited to amounts expended for research or experimentation.*—The deductions referred to in paragraphs (b)(2) and (3) of this section for expenditures in connection with the acquisition or production of depreciable property to be used in the taxpayer's trade or business are limited to amounts expended for research or experimentation within the meaning of section 174 and paragraph (a) of this section.

(5) *Examples.*—The following examples illustrate the application of paragraph (b) of this section.

Example 1. Amounts paid to others for research or experimentation resulting in depreciable property. X is a tool manufacturer. X has developed a new tool design, and orders a specially-built machine from Y to produce X's new tool. The machine is built upon X's order and at X's risk, and Y does not provide a guarantee of economic utility. There is uncertainty regarding the appropriate design of the machine. Under X's contract with Y, X pays $15,000 for Y's engineering and design labor, $5,000 for materials and supplies used to develop the appropriate design of the machine, and $10,000 for Y's machine production materials and labor. The $15,000 of engineering and design labor costs and the $5,000 of materials and supplies costs represent research and development costs in the experimental or laboratory sense. Therefore, the $15,000 X pays Y for Y's engineering and design labor and the $5,000 for materials and supplies used to develop the appropriate design of the machine are for research or experimentation under section 174. However, section 174 does not apply to the $10,000 of production costs of the machine because those costs were not incurred for research or experimentation. See paragraph (a)(2) of this section (relating to production costs) and paragraph (b)(4) of this section (limiting deduction to amounts expended for research or experimentation).

Example 2. Expenditures with respect to other property. Z is an aircraft manufacturer. Z incurs $5,000,000 to construct a new test bed that will be used in the development and improvement of Z's aircraft. No portion of Z's $5,000,000 of costs to construct the new test bed represent research and development costs in the experimental or laboratory sense to develop or improve the test bed. Because no portion of the costs to construct the new test bed were incurred for research or experimentation, the $5,000,000 will be considered an amount paid or incurred in the production of depreciable property to be used in the taxpayer's trade or business that are not allowable under section 174. However, the allowances for depreciation of the test bed are considered research and experimental expenditures of other products, for purposes of section 174, to the extent the test bed is used in connection with research or experimentation of other products. See paragraph (b)(1) of this section (depreciation allowances may be considered research or experimental expenditures).

Example 3. Expenditure resulting in depreciable property. Assume the same facts as *Example 2*, except that $50,000 of the costs of the test bed relates to costs to resolve uncertainties regarding the new test bed design. The $50,000 of costs represents research and development costs in the experimental or laboratory sense. Because $50,000 of Z's costs to construct the new test bed was incurred for research and experimentation, the costs qualify as research and experimental expenditures under section 174. Paragraph (b)(2) of this section applies to $50,000 of Z's costs for the test bed because they are expenditures for research or experimentation that result in depreciable property to be used in the taxpayer's trade or business. Z's remaining $4,950,000 of costs is not allowable under section 174 because these costs were not incurred for research or experimentation.

(c) *Exploration expenditures.*—The provisions of section 174 are not applicable to any expenditures paid or incurred for the purpose of ascertaining the existence, location, extent, or quality of any deposit of ore, oil, gas or other mineral. See sections 617 and 263.

(d) *Effective/applicability date.*—The eighth and ninth sentences of § 1.174-2(a)(1); § 1.174-2(a)(2); § 1.174-2(a)(4); § 1.174-2(a)(5); § 1.174-2(a)(11) *Example 3* through *Example 10*; § 1.174-2(b)(4); and § 1.174-2(b)(5) apply to taxable years ending on or after July 21, 2014.

Taxpayers may apply the provisions enumerated in the preceding sentence to taxable years for which the limitations for assessment of tax has not expired. [Reg. § 1.174-2.]

☐ [*T.D. 6255, 10-3-57. Amended by T.D. 8131, 3-24-87; T.D. 8562, 9-30-94 and T.D. 9680. 7-18-2014.*]

[Reg. § 1.174-3]

§ 1.174-3. Treatment as expenses.—(a) *In general.*—Research or experimental expenditures paid or incurred by a taxpayer during the taxable year in connection with his trade or business are deductible as expenses, and are not chargeable to capital account, if the taxpayer adopts the method provided in section 174(a). See paragraph (b) of this section. If adopted, the method shall apply to all research and experimental expenditures paid or incurred in the taxable year of adoption and all subsequent taxable years, unless a different method is authorized by the Commissioner under section 174(a)(3) with respect to part or all of the expenditures. See paragraph (b)(3) of this section. Thus, if a change to the deferred expense method under section 174(b) is authorized by the Commissioner with respect to research or experimental expenditures attributable to a particular project or projects, the taxpayer, for the taxable year of the change and for subsequent taxable years, must apply the deferred expense method to all such expenditures paid or incurred during any of those taxable years in connection with the particular project or projects, even though all other research and experimental expenditures are required to be deducted as current expenses under this section. In no event will the taxpayer be permitted to adopt the method described in this section as to part of the expenditures relative to a particular project and adopt for the same taxable year a different method of treating the balance of the expenditures relating to the same project.

(b) *Adoption and change of method.*—(1) *Adoption without consent.*—The method described in this section may be adopted for any taxable year beginning after December 31, 1953, and ending after August 16, 1954. The consent of the Commissioner is not required if the taxpayer adopts the method for the first such taxable year in which he pays or incurs research or experimental expenditures. The taxpayer may do so by claiming in his income tax return for such year a deduction for his research or experimental expenditures. If the taxpayer fails to adopt the method for the first taxable year in which he incurs such expenditures, he cannot do so in subsequent taxable years unless he obtains the consent of the Commissioner under section 174(a)(2)(B) and subparagraph (2) of this paragraph. See, however, subparagraph (4) of this paragraph, relating to extensions of time.

(2) *Adoption with consent.*—A taxpayer may, with the consent of the Commissioner, adopt at any time the method provided in section 174(a). The method adopted in this manner shall be applicable only to expenditures paid or incurred during the taxable year for which the request is made and in subsequent taxable years. A request to adopt this method shall be in writing and shall be addressed to the Commissioner of Internal Revenue, Attention: T:R, Washington 25, D.C. The request shall set forth the name and address of the taxpayer, the first taxable year for which the adoption of the method is requested, and a description of the project or projects with respect to which research or experimental expenditures are to be, or have already been, paid or incurred. The request shall be signed by the taxpayer (or his duly authorized representative) and shall be filed not later than the last day of the first taxable year for which the adoption of the method is requested. See, however, subparagraph (4) of this paragraph, relating to extensions of time.

(3) *Change of method.*—An application for permission to change to a different method of treating research or experimental expenditures shall be in writing and shall be addressed to the Commissioner of Internal Revenue, Attention: T:R, Washington 25, D.C. The application shall include the name and address of the taxpayer, shall be signed by the taxpayer (or his duly authorized representative), and shall be filed not later than the last day of the first taxable year for which the change in method is to apply. See, however, subparagraph (4) of this paragraph, relating to extensions of time. The application shall—

(i) State the first year to which the requested change is to be *applicable;*

(ii) State whether the change is to apply to all research or experimental expenditures paid or incurred by the taxpayer, or only to expenditures attributable to a particular project or projects;

(iii) Include such information as will identify the project or projects to which the change is applicable;

(iv) Indicate the number of months (not less than 60) selected for amortization of the expenditures, if any, which are to be treated as deferred expenses under section 174(b);

(v) State that, upon approval of the application, the taxpayer will make an accounting segregation on his books and records of the research or experimental expenditures to which the change in method is to apply; and

(vi) State the reasons for the change.

If permission is granted to make the change, the taxpayer shall attach a copy of the letter granting permission to his income tax return for the first taxable year in which the different method is effective.

(4) *Special rules.*—If the last day prescribed by law for filing a return for any taxable year (including extensions thereof) to which section 174(a) is applicable falls before January 2, 1958, consent is hereby given for the taxpayer to adopt the expense method or to change from the expense method to a different method. In the case of a change from the expense method to a different method, the taxpayer, on or before January 2, 1958, must submit to the district director for the internal revenue district in which the return was filed the information required by subparagraph (3) of this paragraph. For any taxable year for which the expense method or a different method is adopted pursuant to this subparagraph, an amended return reflecting such method shall be filed on or before January 2, 1958, if such return is necessary. [Reg. § 1.174-3.]

☐ [*T.D. 6255, 10-3-57.*]

[Reg. § 1.174-4]

§ 1.174-4. Treatment as deferred expenses.—(a) *In general.*—(1) If a taxpayer has not adopted the method provided in section 174(a) of treating research or experimental expenditures paid or incurred by him in connection with his trade or business as currently deductible expenses, he may, for any taxable year beginning December 31, 1953, elect to treat such expenditures as deferred expenses under section 174(b), subject to the limitations of subparagraph (2) of this paragraph. If a taxpayer has adopted the method of treating such expenditures as expenses under section 174(a), he may not elect to defer and amortize any such expenditures unless permission to do so is granted under section 174(a)(3). See paragraph (b) of this section.

(2) The election to treat research or experimental expenditures as deferred expenses under section 174(b) applies only to those expenditures which are chargeable to capital account but which are not chargeable to property of a character subject to an allowance for depreciation or depletion under section 167 or 611, respectively. Thus, the election under section 174(b) applies only if the property resulting from the research or experimental expenditures has no determinable useful life. If the property resulting from the expenditures has a determinable useful life, section 174(b) is not applicable, and the capitalized expenditures must be amortized or depreciated over the determinable useful life. Amounts treated as deferred expenses are properly chargeable to capital account for purposes of section 1016(a)(1), relating to adjustments to basis of property. See section 1016(a)(14). See section 174(c) and paragraph (b)(1) of § 1.174-2 for treatment of expenditures for the acquisition or improvement of land or of depreciable or depletable property to be used in connection with the research or experimentation.

(3) Expenditures which are treated as deferred expenses under section 174(b) are allowable as a deduction ratably over a period of not less than 60 consecutive months beginning with the month in which the taxpayer first realizes benefits from the expenditures. The length of the period shall be selected by the taxpayer at the time he makes the election to defer the expenditures. If a taxpayer has two or more separate projects, he may select a different amortization period for each project. In the absence of a showing to the contrary, the taxpayer will be deemed to have begun to realize benefits from the deferred expenditures in the month in which the taxpayer first puts the process, formula, invention, or similar property to which the expenditures relate to an income-producing use. See section 1016(a)(14) for adjustments to basis of property for amounts allowed as deductions under section 174(b) and this section. See section 165 and the regulations thereunder for rules relating to the treatment of losses resulting from abandonment.

(4) If expenditures which the taxpayer has elected to defer and deduct ratably over a period of time in accordance with section 174(b) result in the development of depreciable property, deductions for the unrecovered expenditures, beginning with the time the asset becomes depreciable in character, shall be determined under section 167 (relating to depreciation) and the regulations thereunder. For example, for the taxable year 1954, A, who reports his income on the basis of a calendar year, elects to defer and deduct ratably over a period of 60 months research and experimental expenditures made in connection with a particular project. In 1956, the total of the deferred expenditures amounts to $60,000. At that time, A has developed a process which he seeks to patent. On July 1, 1956, A first realized benefits from the marketing of products resulting from this process. Therefore, the expenditures deferred are deductible ratably over the 60-month period beginning with July 1, 1956 (when A first realized benefits from the project). In his return for the year 1956, A deducted $6,000; in 1957, A deducted $12,000 ($1,000 per month). On July 1,

1958, a patent protecting his process is obtained by A. In his return for 1958, A is entitled to a deduction of $6,000, representing the amortizable portion of the deferred expenses attributable to the period prior to July 1, 1958. The balance of the unrecovered expenditures ($60,000 minus $24,000, or $36,000) is to be recovered as a depreciation deduction over the life of the patent commencing with July 1, 1958. Thus, one-half of the annual depreciation deduction based upon the useful life of the patent is also deductible for 1958 (from July 1 to December 31).

(5) The election shall be applicable to all research and experimental expenditures paid or incurred by the taxpayer or, if so limited by the taxpayer's election, to all such expenditures with respect to the particular project, subject to the limitations of subparagraph (2) of this paragraph. The election shall apply for the taxable year for which the election is made and for all subsequent taxable years, unless a change to a different treatment is authorized by the Commissioner under section 174(b)(2). See paragraph (b)(2) of this section. Likewise, the taxpayer shall adhere to the amortization period selected at the time of the election unless a different period of amortization with respect to a part or all of the expenditures is similarly authorized. However, no change in method will be permitted with respect to expenditures paid or incurred before the taxable year to which the change is to apply. In no event will the taxpayer be permitted to treat part of the expenditures with respect to a particular project as deferred expenses under section 174(b) and to adopt a different method of treating the balance of the expenditures relating to the same project for the same taxable year. The election under this section shall not apply to any expenditures paid or incurred before the taxable year for which the taxpayer makes the election.

(b) *Election and change of method.*—(1) *Election.*—The election under section 174(b) shall be made not later than the time (including extensions) prescribed by law for filing the return for the taxable year for which the method is to be adopted. The election shall be made by attaching a statement to the taxpayer's return for the first taxable year to which the election is applicable. The statement shall be signed by the taxpayer (or his duly authorized representative), and shall—

(i) Set forth the name and address of the taxpayer;

(ii) Designate the first taxable year to which the election is to apply;

(iii) State whether the election is intended to apply to all expenditures within the permissible scope of the election, or only to a particular project or projects, and, if the latter, include such information as will identify the project or projects as to which the election is to apply;

(iv) Set forth the amount of all research or experimental expenditures paid or incurred during the taxable year for which the election is made;

(v) Indicate the number of months (not less than 60) selected for amortization of the deferred expenses for each project; and

(vi) State that the taxpayer will make an accounting segregation in his books and records of the expenditures to which the election relates.

(2) *Change to a different method or period.*—Application for permission to change to a different method of treating research or experimental expenditures or to a different period of amortization for deferred expenses shall be in writing and shall be addressed to the Commissioner of Internal Revenue, Attention: T:R, Washington 25, D.C. The application shall include the name and address of the taxpayer, shall be signed by the taxpayer (or his duly authorized representative), and shall be filed not later than the end of the first taxable year in which the different method or different amortization period is to be used (unless subparagraph (3) of this paragraph, relating to extensions of time, is applicable). The application shall set forth the following information with regard to the research or experimental expenditures which are being treated under section 174(b) as deferred expenses:

(i) Total amount of research or experimental expenditures attributable to each project;

(ii) Amortization period applicable to each project; and

(iii) Unamortized expenditures attributable to each project at the beginning of the taxable year in which the application is filed.
In addition, the application shall set forth the length of the new period or periods proposed, or the new method of treatment proposed, the reasons for the proposed change, and such information as will identify the project or projects to which the expenditures affected by the change relate. If permission is granted to make the change, the taxpayer shall attach a copy of the letter granting the permission to his income tax return for the first taxable year in which the different method or period is to be effective.

(3) *Special rules.*—If the last day prescribed by law for filing a return for any taxable year for which the deferred method provided in section 174(b) has been adopted falls before January 2, 1958,

consent is hereby given for the taxpayer to change from such method and adopt a different method of treating research or experimental expenditures, provided that on or before January 2, 1958, he submits to the district director for the district in which the return was filed the information required by subparagraph (2) of this paragraph, relating to a change to a different method or period. For any taxable year for which the different method is adopted pursuant to this subparagraph, an amended return reflecting such method shall be filed on or before January 2, 1958.

(c) *Example.*—The application of this section is illustrated by the following example:

Example. N Corporation is engaged in the business of manufacturing chemical products. On January 1, 1955, work is begun on a special research project. N Corporation elects, pursuant to section 174(b), to defer the expenditures relating to the special project and to amortize the expenditures over a period of 72 months beginning with the month in which benefits from the expenditures are first realized. On January 1, 1955, N Corporation also purchased for $57,600 a building having a remaining useful life of 12 years as of the date of purchase and no salvage value at the end of the period. Fifty per cent of the building's facilities are to be used in connection with the special research project. During 1955, N Corporation pays or incurs the following expenditures relating to the special research project:

Salaries	$15,000
Heat, light and power	700
Drawings	2,000
Models	6,500
Laboratory materials	8,000
Attorneys' fees	1,400
Depreciation on building attributable to project (50 percent of $4,800 allowable depreciation)	2,400
Total research and development expenditures	$36,000

The above expenditures result in a process which is marketable but not patentable and which has no determinable useful life. N Corporation first realizes benefits from the process in January 1956. N Corporation is entitled to deduct the amount of $6,000

$$\left(\frac{\$36,000 \times 12 \text{ months}}{72 \text{ months}} \right)$$

as deferred expenses under section 174(b) in computing taxable income for 1956. [Reg. §1.174-4.]

☐ [*T.D. 6255, 10-3-57.*]

[Reg. §1.175-1]

§1.175-1. Soil and water conservation expenditures; in general.—Under section 175, a farmer may deduct his soil or water conservation expenditures which do not give rise to a deduction for depreciation and which are not otherwise deductible. The amount of the deduction is limited annually to 25 percent of the taxpayer's gross income from farming. Any excess may be carried over and deducted in succeeding taxable years. As a general rule, once a farmer has adopted this method of treating soil and water conservation expenditures, he must deduct all such expenditures (subject to the 25-percent limitation) for the current and subsequent taxable years. If a farmer does not adopt this method, such expenditures increase the basis of the property to which they relate. For rules relating to the allocation of expenditures that benefit both land used in farming and other land of the taxpayer, see §1.175-7. [Reg. §1.175-1.]

☐ [*T.D. 6235, 5-31-57. Amended by T.D. 7740, 12-21-80.*]

[Reg. §1.175-2]

§1.175-2. Definition of soil and water conservation expenditures.—(a) *Expenditures treated as a deduction.*—(1) The method described in section 175 applies to expenditures paid or incurred for the purpose of soil or water conservation in respect of land used in farming, or for the prevention or erosion of land used in farming, but only if such expenditures are made in the furtherance of the business of farming. More specifically, a farmer may deduct expenditures made for these purposes which are for (i) the treatment or moving of earth, (ii) the construction, control, and protection of diversion channels, drainage ditches, irrigation ditches, earthen dams, watercourses, outlets, and ponds, (iii) the eradication of brush, and (iv) the planting of windbreaks. Expenditures for the treatment or moving of earth include but are not limited to expenditures for leveling, conditioning, grading, terracing, contour furrowing, and restoration of soil fertility.

(2) The following are examples of soil and water conservation: (i) constructing terraces, or the like, to detain or control the flow of water, to check soil erosion on sloping land, to intercept run-off, and to divert excess water to protected outlets; (ii) constructing water detention or sediment retention dams to prevent or fill gullies, to retard or reduce run-off of water, or to collect stock water; and (iii)

Itemized Deductions for Individuals and Corps.
See p. 20,601 for regulations not amended to reflect law changes
25,613

constructing earthen floodways, levees, or dikes, to prevent flood damage to farmland.

(b) *Expenditures not subject to section 175 treatment.*—(1) The method described in section 175 applies only to expenditures for nondepreciable items. Accordingly, a taxpayer may not deduct expenditures for the purchase, construction, installation, or improvement of structures, appliances, or facilities subject to the allowance for depreciation. Thus, the method does not apply to depreciable nonearthen items such as those made of masonry or concrete (see section 167). For example, expenditures in respect of depreciable property include those for materials, supplies, wages, fuel, hauling, and dirt moving for making structures such as tanks, reservoirs, pipes, conduits, canals, dams, wells, or pumps composed of masonry, concrete, tile, metal, or wood. However, the method applies to expenditures for earthen items which are not subject to a depreciation allowance. For example, expenditures for earthen terraces and dams which are nondepreciable are deductible under section 175. For taxable years beginning after December 31, 1959, in the case of expenditures paid or incurred by farmers for fertilizer, lime, etc., for purposes other than soil or water conservation, see section 180 and the regulations thereunder.

(2) The method does not apply to expenses deductible apart from section 175. Adoption of the method is not necessary in order to deduct such expenses in full without limitation. Thus, the method does not apply to interest (deductible under section 163), nor to taxes (deductible under section 164). It does not apply to expenses for the repair of completed soil or water conservation structures, such as costs of annual removal of sediment from a drainage ditch. It does not apply to expenditures paid or incurred primarily to produce an agricultural crop even though they incidentally conserve soil. Thus, the cost of fertilizing (the effectiveness of which does not last beyond one year) used to produce hay is deductible without adoption of the method prescribed in section 175. For taxable years beginning after December 31, 1959, in the case of expenditures paid or incurred by farmers for fertilizer, lime, etc., for purposes other than soil or water conservation. See section 180 and the regulations thereunder. However, the method would apply to expenses incurred to produce vegetation primarily to conserve soil or water or to prevent erosion. Thus, for example, the method would apply to such expenditures as the cost of dirt moving, lime, fertilizer, seed and planting stock used in gulley stabilization, or in stabilizing severely eroded areas, in order to obtain a soil binding stand of vegetation on raw or infertile land.

(c) *Assessments.*—The method applies also to that part of assessments levied by a soil or water conservation or drainage district to reimburse it for its expenditures which, if actually paid or incurred during the taxable year by the taxpayer directly, would be deductible under section 175. Depending upon the farmer's method of accounting, the time when the farmer pays or incurs the assessment, and not the time when the expenditures are paid or incurred by the district, controls the time the deduction must be taken. The provisions of this paragraph may be illustrated by the following example:

Example. In 1955 a soil and water conservation district levies an assessment of $700 upon a farmer on the cash method of accounting. The assessment is to reimburse the district for its expenditures in 1954. The farmer's share of such expenditures is as follows: $400 for digging drainage ditches for soil conservation and $300 for assets subject to the allowance for depreciation. If the farmer pays the assessment in 1955 and has adopted the method of treating expenditures for soil or water conservation as current expenses under section 175, he may deduct in 1955 the $400 attributable to the digging of drainage ditches as a soil conservation expenditure subject to the 25-percent limitation. [Reg. § 1.175-2.]

☐ [*T.D. 6235, 5-31-57. Amended by T.D. 6548, 2-21-61.*]

[Reg. § 1.175-3]

§ 1.175-3. Definition of "the business of farming".—The method described in section 175 is available only to a taxpayer engaged in "the business of farming". A taxpayer is engaged in the business of farming if he cultivates, operates, or manages a farm for gain or profit, either as owner or tenant. For the purpose of section 175, a taxpayer who receives a rental (either in cash or in kind) which is based upon farm production is engaged in the business of farming. However, a taxpayer who receives a fixed rental (without reference to production) is engaged in the business of farming only if he participates to a material extent in the operation or management of the farm. A taxpayer engaged in forestry or the growing of timber is not thereby engaged in the business of farming. A person cultivating or operating a farm for recreation on pleasure rather than a profit is not engaged in the business of farming. For the purpose of this section, the term "farm" is used in its ordinary, accepted sense and includes stock, dairy, poultry, fish, fruit, and truck farms, and also plantations, ranches, ranges, and orchards. A fish farm is an area

where fish are grown or raised, as opposed to merely caught or harvested; that is, an area where they are artificially fed, protected, cared for, etc. A taxpayer is engaged in "the business of farming" if he is a member of a partnership engaged in the business of farming. See paragraphs (a)(8)(i) and (c)(1)(iv) of § 1.702-1. [Reg. § 1.175-3.]

☐ [*T.D. 6235, 5-31-57. Amended by T.D. 6649, 4-17-63.*]

[Reg. § 1.175-4]

§ 1.175-4. Definition of "land used in farming".—(a) *Requirements.*—For purposes of section 175, the term "land used in farming" means land which is used in the business of farming and which meets both of the following requirements:

(1) The land must be used for the production of crops, fruits, or other agricultural products, including fish, or for the sustenance of livestock. The term "livestock" includes cattle, hogs, horses, mules, donkeys, sheep, goats, captive fur-bearing animals, chickens, turkeys, pigeons, and other poultry. Land used for the sustenance of livestock includes land used for grazing such livestock.

(2) The land must be or have been so used either by the taxpayer or his tenant at some time before, or at the same time as, the taxpayer makes the expenditure for soil or water conservation or for the prevention of the erosion of land. The taxpayer will be considered to have used the land in farming before making such expenditure if he or his tenant has employed the land in a farming use in the past. If the expenditures are made by the taxpayer in respect to land newly acquired from one who immediately prior to the acquisition was using it in farming, the taxpayer will be considered to be using the land in farming at the time that such expenditures are made, if the use which is made by the taxpayer of the land from the time of its acquisition by him is substantially a continuation of its use in farming, whether for the same farming use as that of the taxpayer's predecessor or for one of the other uses specified in paragraph (a)(1) of this section.

(b) *Example.*—The provisions of paragraph (a) of this section may be illustrated by the following examples:

Example (1). A purchases an operating farm from B in the autumn after B has harvested his crops. Prior to spring plowing and planting when the land is idle because of the season, A makes certain soil and water conservation expenditures on this farm. At the time such expenditures are made the land is considered to be used by A in farming, and A may deduct such expenditures under section 175, subject to the other requisite conditions of such section.

Example (2). C acquires uncultivated land, not previously used in farming, which he intends to develop for farming. Prior to putting this land into production it is necessary for C to clear brush, construct earthern terraces and ponds, and make other soil and water conservation expenditures. The land is not used in farming at the same time that such expenditures are made. Therefore, C may not deduct such expenditures under section 175.

Example (3). D acquires several tracts of land from persons who had used such land immediately prior to D's acquisition for grazing cattle. D intends to use the land for growing grapes. In order to make the land suitable for this use, D constructs earthern terraces, builds drainage ditches and irrigation ditches, extensively treats the soil, and makes other soil and water conservation expenditures. The land is considered to be used in farming by D at the time he makes such expenditures, even though it is being prepared for a different type of farming activity than that engaged in by D's predecessors. Therefore, D may deduct such expenditures under section 175, subject to the other requisite conditions of such section.

(c) *Cross reference.*—For rules relating to the allocation of expenditures that benefit both land used in farming and other land of the taxpayer, see § 1.175-7. [Reg. § 1.175-4.]

☐ [*T.D. 6235, 5-31-57. Amended by T.D. 6649, 4-17-63 and T.D. 7740, 11-21-80.*]

[Reg. § 1.175-5]

§ 1.175-5. Percentage limitation and carryover.—(a) *The limitation.*—(1) *General rule.*—The amount of soil and water conservation expenditures which the taxpayer may deduct under section 175 in any one taxable year is limited to 25 percent of his "gross income from farming".

(2) *Definition of "gross income from farming".*—For the purpose of section 175, the term "gross income from farming" means the gross income of the taxpayer, derived in "the business of farming" as defined in § 1.175-3, from the production of crops, fruits, or other agricultural products, including fish, or from livestock (including livestock held for draft, breeding, or dairy purposes). It includes such income from land used in farming other than that upon which expenditures are made for soil or water conservation or for the prevention or erosion of land. It does not include gains from sales of

assets such as farm machinery or gains from the disposition of land. A taxpayer shall compute his "gross income from farming" in accordance with his accounting method used in determining gross income. (See the regulations under section 61 relating to accounting methods used by farmers in determining gross income.) The provisions of this subparagraph may be illustrated by the following example:

Example. A, who uses the cash receipts and disbursements method of accounting, includes in his "gross income from farming" for purposes of determining the 25-percent limitation the following items:

Proceeds from sale of his 1955 yield of corn	$10,000
Gain from disposition of old breeding cows replaced by younger cows	500
Total gross income from farming	10,500

A must exclude from "gross income from farming" the following items which are included in his gross income:

Gain from sale of tractor	$100
Gain from sale of 40 acres of taxpayer's farm	8,000
Interest on loan to neighboring farmer	100

(3) *Deduction qualifies for net operating loss deduction.*—Any amount allowed as a deduction under section 175, either for the year in which the expenditure is paid or incurred or for the year to which it is carried, is taken into account in computing a net operating loss for such taxable year. If a deduction for soil or water conservation expenditures has been taken into account in computing a net operating loss carryback or carryover, it shall not be considered a soil or water conservation expenditure for the year to which the loss is carried, and therefore, is not subject to the 25-percent limitation for

that year. The provisions of this subparagraph may be illustrated by the following example:

Example. Assume that in 1956 A has gross income from farming of $4,000, soil and water conservation expenditures of $1,600, and deductible farm expenses of $3,500. Of the soil and water conservation expenditures, $1,000 is deductible in 1956. The $600 in excess of 25 percent of A's gross income from farming is carried over into 1957. Assuming that A has no other income, his deductions of $4,500 ($1,000 plus $3,500) exceed his gross income of $4,000 by $500. This $500 will constitute a net operating loss which he must carry back two years and carry forward five years, until it has offset $500 of taxable income. No part of this $500 net operating loss carryback or carryover will be taken into account in determining the amount of soil and water conservation expenditures in the years to which it is carried.

(b) *Carryover of expenditures in excess of deduction.*—The deduction for soil and water conservation expenditures in any one taxable year is limited to 25 percent of the taxpayer's gross income from farming. The taxpayer may carry over the excess of such expenditures over 25 percent of his gross income from farming into his next taxable year, and, if not deductible in that year, into the next year, and so on without limit as to time. In determining the deductible amount of such expenditures for any taxable year, the actual expenditures of that year shall be added to any such expenditures carried over from prior years, before applying the 25-percent limitation. Any such expenditures in excess of the deductible amount may be carried over during the taxpayer's entire existence. For this purpose in a farm partnership, since the 25-percent limitation is applied to each partner, not the partnership, the carryover may be carried forward during the life of the partner. The provisions of this paragraph may be illustrated by the following example:

Example. Assume the expenditures and income shown in the following table:

	Deductible soil and water conservation expenditures				
Year	Paid or incurred during taxable year	Carried forward from prior year	Total	25 percent of gross income from farming	Excess to be carried forward
1954	$900	None	$900	$800	$100
1955	1,000	$100	1,100	900	200
1956	None	200	200	1,000	None

The deduction for 1954 is limited to $800. The remainder, $100 ($900 minus $800), not being deductible for 1954, is a carryover to 1955. For 1955, accordingly, the total of the expenditures to be taken into account is $1,100 (the $100 carryover and the $1,000 actually paid in that year). The deduction for 1955 is limited to $900, and the remainder of the $1,100 total, or $200, is a carryover to 1956. The deduction for 1956 consists solely of this carryover of $200. Since the total expenditures, actual and carried-over, for 1956 are less than 25 percent of gross income from farming, there is no carryover into 1957. [Reg. §1.175-5.]

☐ [*T.D. 6235, 5-31-57. Amended by T.D. 6649, 4-17-63.*]

[Reg. §1.175-6]

§1.175-6. Adoption or change of method.—(a) *Adoption without consent.*—A taxpayer may, without consent, adopt the method of treating expenditures for soil or water conservation as expenses for the first taxable year:

(1) Which begins after December 31, 1953, and ends after August 16, 1954, and

(2) For which soil or water conservation expenditures described in section 175(a) are paid or incurred.

Such adoption shall be made by claiming the deduction on his income tax return. For a taxable year ending prior to May 31, 1957, the adoption of the method described in section 175 shall be made by claiming the deduction on such return for that year, or by claiming the deduction on an amended return filed for that year on or before August 30, 1957.

(b) *Adoption with consent.*—A taxpayer may adopt the method of treating soil and water conservation expenditures as provided by section 175 for any taxable year to which the section is applicable if consent is obtained from the district director for the internal revenue district in which the taxpayer's return is required to be filed.

(c) *Change of method.*—A taxpayer who has adopted the method of treating expenditures for soil or water conservation, as provided by section 175, may change from this method and capitalize such expenditures made after the effective date of the change, if he obtains

the consent of the district director for the internal revenue district in which his return is required to be filed.

(d) *Request for consent to adopt or change method.*—Where the consent of the district director is required under paragraph (b) or (c) of this section, the request for his consent shall be in writing, signed by the taxpayer or his authorized representative, and shall be filed not later than the date prescribed by law for filing the income tax return for the first taxable year to which the adoption of, or change of, method is to apply, or not later than August 20, 1957, following their adoption, whichever is later. The request shall:

(1) Set forth the name and address of the taxpayer;

(2) Designate the first taxable year to which the method or change of method is to apply;

(3) State whether the method or change of method is intended to apply to all expenditures within the permissible scope of section 175, or only to a particular project or farm and, if the latter, include such information as will identify the project or farm as to which the method or change of method is to apply;

(4) Set forth the amount of all soil and water conservation expenditures paid or incurred during the first taxable year for which the method or change of method is to apply; and

(5) State that the taxpayer will make an accounting segregation in his books and records of the expenditures to which the election relates.

(e) *Scope of method.*—Except with the consent of the district director as provided in paragraph (b) or (c) of this section, the taxpayer's method of treating soil and water conservation expenditures described in section 175 shall apply to all such expenditures for the taxable year of adoption and all subsequent taxable years. Although a taxpayer may have elected to deduct soil and water conservation expenditures, he may request an authorization to capitalize his soil and water conservation expenditures attributable to a special project or single farm. Similarly, a taxpayer who has not elected to deduct such expenditures may request an authorization to deduct his soil and water conservation expenditures attributable to a special project or single farm. The authorization with respect to the special project or single farm will not affect the method adopted with respect to the

Itemized Deductions for Individuals and Corps.
See p. 20,601 for regulations not amended to reflect law changes
25,615

taxpayer's regularly incurred soil and water conservation expenditures. No adoption of, or change of, the method under section 175 will be permitted as to expenditures actually paid or incurred before the taxable year to which the method or change of method is to apply. Thus, if a taxpayer adopts such method for 1956, he cannot deduct any part of such expenditures which he capitalized, or should have capitalized, in 1955. Likewise, if a taxpayer who has adopted such method has an unused carryover of such expenditures in excess of the 25-percent limitation, and is granted consent to capitalize soil and water conservation expenditures beginning in 1956, he cannot capitalize any part of the unused carryover. The excess expenditures carried over continue to be deductible to the extent of 25 percent of the taxpayer's gross income from farming. No adjustment to the basis of land shall be made under section 1016 for expenditures to which the method under section 175 applies. For example, A has an unused carryover of soil and water conservation expenditures amounting to $5,000 as of December 31, 1956. On January 1, 1957, A sells his farm and goes out of the business of farming. The unused carryover of $5,000 cannot be added to the basis of the farm for purposes of determining gain or loss on its sale. In 1959, A purchases another farm and resumes the business of farming. In such year, A may deduct the amount of the unused carryover to the extent of 25 percent of his gross income from farming and may carry over any excess to subsequent years. [Reg. §1.175-6.]

□ [T.D. 6235, 5-31-57.]

[Reg. §1.175-7]

§1.175-7. Allocation of expenditures in certain circumstances.—(a) *General rule.*—If at the time the taxpayer paid or incurred expenditures for the purpose of soil or water conservation, or for the prevention of erosion of land, it was reasonable to believe that such expenditures would directly and substantially benefit land of the taxpayer which does not qualify as "land used in farming", as defined in §1.175-4, as well as land of the taxpayer which does so qualify, then, for purposes of section 175, only a part of the taxpayer's total expenditures is in respect of "land used in farming".

(b) *Method of allocation.*—The part of expenditures allocable to "land used in farming" generally equals the amount which bears the same proportion to the total amount of such expenditures as the area of land of the taxpayer used in farming which it was reasonable to believe would be directly and substantially benefited as a result of the expenditures bears to the total area of land of the taxpayer which it was reasonable to believe would be so benefited. If it is established by clear and convincing evidence that, in the light of all the facts and circumstances, another method of allocation is more reasonable than the method provided in the preceding sentence, the taxpayer may allocate the expenditures under that other method. For purposes of this section, the term "land of the taxpayer" means land with respect to which the taxpayer has title, leasehold, or some other substantial interest.

(c) *Examples.*—The provisions of this section may be illustrated by the following examples:

Example (1). A owns a 200-acre tract of land, 80 acres of which qualify as "land used in farming". A makes expenditures for the purpose of soil and water conservation which can reasonably be expected to directly and substantially benefit the entire 200-acre tract. In the absence of clear and convincing evidence that a different allocation is more reasonable, A may deduct 40 percent (80/200) of such expenditures under section 175. The same result would obtain if A had made the expenditures after newly acquiring the tract from a person who had used 80 of the 200 acres in farming immediately prior to A's acquisition.

Example (2). Assume the same facts as in example (1), except that A's expenditures for the purpose of soil and water conservation can reasonably be expected to directly and substantially benefit only the 80 acres which qualify as land used in farming; any benefit to the other 120 acres would be minor and incidental. A may deduct all of such expenditures under section 175.

Example (3). Assume the same facts as in example (1), except that A's expenditures for the purpose of soil and water conservation can reasonably be expected to directly and substantially benefit only the 120 acres which do not qualify as land used in farming. A may not deduct any of such expenditures under section 175. The same result would obtain even if A had leased the 200-acre tract to B in the expectation that B would farm the entire tract. [Reg. §1.175-7.]

□ [T.D. 7740, 11-21-80.]

[Reg. §1.178-1]

§1.178-1. Depreciation or amortization of improvements on leased property and cost of acquiring a lease.—(a) *In general.*—Section 178 provides rules for determining the amount of the deduction allowable for any taxable year to a lessee for depreciation or amortization of improvements made on leased property and as amortization of the cost of acquiring a lease. For purposes of section 178 the term "depreciation" means the deduction allowable for exhaustion, wear and tear, or obsolescence under provisions of the Code such as section 167 or 611 and the regulations thereunder and the term "amortization" means the deduction allowable for amortization of buildings or other improvements made on leased property or for amortization of the cost of acquiring a lease under provisions of the Code such as section 162 or 212 and the regulations thereunder. The provisions of section 178 are applicable with respect to costs of acquiring a lease incurred, and improvements begun, after July 28, 1958, other than improvements which, on July 28, 1958, and at all times thereafter, the lessee was under a binding legal obligation to make.

(b) *Determination of amount of deduction.*—(1) In determining the amount of the deduction allowable to a lessee (other than a lessee who is related to the lessor within the meaning of §1.178-2) for any taxable year for depreciation or amortization of improvements made on leased property, or for amortization in respect of the cost of acquiring a lease, the term of the lease shall, except as provided in subparagraph (2) of this paragraph, be treated as including all periods for which the lease may be renewed, extended, or continued pursuant to an option or options exercisable by the lessee (whether or not specifically provided for in the lease) if—

(i) In the case of any building erected, or other improvements made, by the lessee on the leased property, the portion of the term of the lease (excluding all periods for which the lease may subsequently be renewed, extended, or continued pursuant to an option or options exercisable by the lessee) remaining upon the completion of such building or other improvements is less than 60 percent of the estimated useful life of such building or other improvements; or

(ii) In the case of any cost of acquiring the lease, less than 75 percent of such cost is attributable to the portion of the term of the lease (excluding all periods for which the lease may be renewed, extended, or continued pursuant to an option or options exercisable by the lessee) remaining on the date of its acquisition.

(2) The rules provided in subparagraph (1) of this paragraph shall not apply if the lessee establishes that, as of the close of the taxable year, it is more probable that the lease will not be renewed, extended, or continued than that the lease will be renewed, extended, or continued. In such case, the cost of improvements made on leased property or the cost of acquiring a lease shall be amortized over the remaining term of the lease without regard to any options exercisable by the lessee to renew, extend, or continue the lease. The probability test referred to in the first sentence of this subparagraph shall be applicable to each option period to which the lease may be renewed, extended, or continued. The establishment by a lessee as of the close of the taxable year that it is more probable that the lease will not be renewed, extended, or continued will ordinarily be effective as of the close of such taxable year and any subsequent taxable year, and the deduction for amortization will be based on the term of the lease without regard to any periods for which the lease may be renewed, extended, or continued pursuant to an option or options exercisable by the lessee. However, in appropriate cases, if the facts as of the close of any subsequent taxable year indicate that it is more probable that the lease will be renewed, extended, or continued, the deduction for amortization (or depreciation) shall, beginning with the first day of such subsequent taxable year, be determined by including in the remaining term of the lease all periods for which it is more probable that the lease will be renewed, extended, or continued.

(3) If at any time the remaining term of the lease determined in accordance with section 178 and this section is equal to or of longer duration than the then estimated useful life of the improvements made on the leased property by the lessee, the cost of such improvements shall be depreciated over the estimated useful life of such improvements under the provisions of section 167 and the regulations thereunder.

(4) For purposes of section 178(a)(1) and this section, the date on which the building erected or other improvements made are completed is the date on which the building or improvements are usable, whether or not used.

(5)(i) For purposes of section 178(a)(2) and this section, the portion of the cost of acquiring a lease which is attributable to the term of the lease remaining on the date of its acquisition without regard to options exercisable by the lessee to renew, extend, or continue the lease shall be determined on the basis of the facts and circumstances of each case. In some cases, it may be appropriate to determine such portion of the cost of acquiring a lease by applying the principles used to measure the present value of an annuity. Where that method is used, such portion shall be determined by multiplying the cost of the lease by a fraction, the numerator comprised of a factor representing the present value of an annually recurring savings of $1 per year for the period of the remaining term of the lease (without regard to options to renew, extend, or continue the lease) at an appropriate rate of interest (determined on the basis of all the facts and circumstances in each case), and the denominator comprised of a factor representing the present value of $1 per year for the period of the remaining term of the lease including the options to renew, extend, or continue the lease at an appropriate rate of interest.

(ii) The provisions of this subparagraph may be illustrated by the following example:

Example. Lessee A acquires a lease with respect to unimproved property at a cost of $100,000 at which time there are 21 years remaining in the original term of the lease with two renewal options

is 67.21% or $67,210 determined as follows:

(6) The provisions of this paragraph may be illustrated by the following examples:

Example (1). Lessee A constructs a building on land leased from lessor B. The construction is commenced on August 1, 1958, and is completed and placed in service on December 31, 1958, at which time A has 15 years remaining on his lease with an option to renew for an additional 20 years. Lessee A computes his taxable income on a calendar year basis. Lessee A was not, on July 28, 1958, under a binding legal obligation to erect the building. The building has an estimated useful life of 30 years. A is not related to B. Since the portion of the term of the lease (without regard to any renewals) remaining upon completion of the building (15 years) is less than 60 percent of the estimated useful life of the building (60 percent of 30 years, or 18 years), the term of the lease shall be treated as including the remaining portion of the original lease period and the renewal period, or 35 years. Since the estimated useful life of the building (30 years) is less than 35 years, the cost of the building shall, in accord with paragraph (b)(3) of this section, be depreciated under the provisions of section 167, over its estimated useful life. If, however, lessee A establishes, as of the close of the taxable year 1958, it is more probable that the lease will not be renewed than that it will be renewed, then in such case the remaining term of the lease shall be treated as including only the 15-year period remaining in the original lease. Since this is less than the estimated useful life of the building, the remaining cost of the building would be amortized over such 15-year period under the provisions of section 162 and the regulations thereunder.

Example (2). Assume the same facts as in example (1), except that A has 21 years remaining on his lease with an option to renew for an additional 10 years. Section 178(a) and paragraph (b)(1) of this section do not apply since the term of the lease remaining on the date of completion of the building (21 years) is not less than 60 percent of the estimated useful life of the building (60 percent of 30 years, or 18 years).

Example (3). Assume the same facts as in example (1), except that A has no renewal option until July 1, 1961, when lessor B grants A an option to renew the lease for a 10-year period. Because there is no option to renew the lease, the term of the lease is, for the taxable years 1959 and 1960 and for the first six months of the taxable year 1961, determined without regard to section 178(a). However, as of July 1, 1961, the date the renewal option is granted, section 178(a) and paragraph (b)(1) of this section become applicable since the portion of the term of the lease remaining upon completion of the building (15 years) was less than 60 percent of the estimated useful life of the building (60 percent of 30 years, or 18 years). As of July 1, 1961, the term of the lease shall be treated as including the remaining portion of the original lease period (12¹/₂ years) and the 10-year renewal period, of 22¹/₂ years, unless lessee A can establish that, as of the close of 1961, it is more probable that the lease will not be renewed than that it will be.

Example (4). On January 1, 1959, lessee A pays $10,000 to acquire a lease for 20 years with two options exercisable by him to renew for periods of 5 years each. Of the total $10,000 cost to acquire the lease, $7,000 was paid for the original 20-year lease period and the balance of $3,000 was paid for the renewal options. Since the $7,000 cost of acquiring the initial lease is less than 75 percent of the $10,000 cost of the lease ($7,500), the term of the lease shall be treated as including the original lease period and the 2 renewal periods, or 30 years. However, if lessee A establishes that, as of the close of the taxable year 1959, it is more probable that the lease will not be renewed than that it will be renewed, the term of the lease shall be treated as including only the original lease period, or 20 years.

Example (5). Assume the same facts as in example (4), except that the portion of the total cost ($10,000) paid for the 20-year original lease period is $8,000. Since the $8,000 cost of acquiring the original lease is not less than 75 percent of the $10,000 cost of the lease ($7,500), section 178(a) and paragraph (b)(1) of this section do not apply.

of 21 years each. The lease provides for a uniform annual rental for the remaining term of the lease and the renewal periods. It has been determined that this is an appropriate case for the application of the principles used to measure the present value of an annuity. Assume that in this case appropriate rate of interest is 5 percent. By applying the tables (Inwood) used to measure the present value of an annuity of $1 per year, the factor representing the present value of $1 per annum for 21 years at 5% is ascertained to be 12.821, and the factor representing the present value of $1 per annum for 63 years at 5% is 19.075. The portion of the cost of the lease ($100,000) attributable to the remaining term of the original lease (21 years)

$$\frac{12.821}{19.075} \text{ or } 67.21\%.$$

(c) *Application of section 178(a) where lessee gives notice to lessor of intention to exercise option.*—(1) If the lessee has given notice to the lessor of his intention to renew, extend, or continue a lease, the lessee shall, for purposes of applying the provisions of section 178(a) and paragraph (b)(1) of this section, take into account such renewal or extension in determining the portion of the term of the lease remaining upon the completion of the improvements or on the date of the acquisition of the lease.

(2) The application of the provisions of this paragraph may be illustrated by the following examples:

Example (1). Lessee A constructs a building on land leased from lessor B. The construction was commenced on September 1, 1958, and was completed and placed in service on December 31, 1958. Lessee A was not, on July 28, 1958, under a binding legal obligation to erect the building. A and B are not related. At the time the building was completed (December 31, 1958), lessee A had 3 years remaining on his lease with 2 options to renew for periods of 20 years each. The estimated useful life of the building is 50 years. Prior to completion of the building, lessee A gives notice to lessor B of his intention to exercise the first 20-year option. Therefore, the portion of the term of the lease remaining on January 1, 1959, shall be the 3 years remaining in the original lease period plus the 20-year renewal period, or 23 years. Since the term of the lease remaining upon completion of the building (23 years) is less than 60 percent of the estimated useful life of the building (60 percent of 50 years, or 30 years), the provisions of section 178(a) and paragraph (b)(1) of this section are applicable. Accordingly, the term of the lease shall be treated as including the aggregate of the remaining term of the original lease (23 years) and the second 20-year renewal period or 43 years, unless lessee A establishes that it is more probable that the lease will not be renewed, extended, or continued under the second 20-year option than that it will be so renewed, extended, or continued under such option. If this is established by lessee A, then the term of the lease shall be treated as including only the remaining portion of the original lease period and the first 20-year renewal period, or 23 years.

Example (2). Assume the same facts as in example (1), except that the estimated useful life of the building is 30 years. Since the term of the lease remaining upon completion of the building (23 years) is not less than 60 percent of the estimated life of the building (60 percent of 30 years, or 18 years), the provisions of section 178(a) and paragraph (b)(1) of this section do not apply.

Example (3). If in examples (1) and (2), the lessee failed to give notice of his intention to exercise the renewal option, the renewal period would not be taken into account in computing the percentage requirements under section 178(a) and paragraph (b)(1) of this section. Thus, unless lessee A establishes the required probability, the provisions of section 178(a) and paragraph (b)(1) of this section would apply in both examples since the term of the lease remaining upon completion of the building (3 years) is less than 60 percent of the estimated useful life of the building in either example (60 percent of 50 years, or 30 years; 60 percent of 30 years, or 18 years).

(d) *Application of section 178 where lessee is related to lessor.*—(1)(i) If the lessee and lessor are related persons within the meaning of section 178(b)(2) and §1.178-2 at any time during the taxable year, the lease shall be treated as including a period of not less duration than the remaining estimated useful life of improvements made by the lessee on leased property for purposes of determining the amount of deduction allowable to the lessee for such taxable year for depreciation or amortization in respect of any building erected or other improvements made on leased property. If the lessee and lessor cease to be related persons during any taxable year, then for the immediately following and subsequent taxable years during which they continue to be unrelated, the amount allowable to the lessee as a deduction shall be determined without reference to section 178(b) and in accordance with section 178(a) or section 178(c), whichever is applicable.

(ii) Although the related lessee and lessor rule of section 178(b) and §1.178-2 does not apply in determining the period over which the cost of acquiring a lease may be amortized, the relation-

Itemized Deductions for Individuals and Corps.
See p. 20,601 for regulations not amended to reflect law changes
25,617

ship between a lessee and lessor will be a significant factor in applying section 178(a) and (c) in cases in which the lease may be renewed, extended, or continued pursuant to an option or options exercisable by the lessee.

(2) The application of the provisions of this paragraph may be illustrated by the following examples:

Example (1). Lessee A constructs a building on land leased from lessor B. The construction was commenced on August 1, 1958, and was completed and put in service on December 31, 1958. Lessee A was not on July 28, 1958, under a binding legal obligation to erect the building. On the completion date of the building, lessee A had 20 years remaining in his original lease period with an option to renew for an additional 20 years. The building has an estimated useful life of 50 years. During the taxable years 1959 and 1960, A and B are related persons within the meaning of section 178(b)(2) and §1.178-2, but they are not related persons at any time during the taxable year 1961 or during any subsequent taxable year. Since A and B are related persons during the taxable years 1959 and 1960, the term of the lease shall, for each of those years, be treated as 50 years. Section 178(a) and paragraph (b)(1) of this section become applicable in the taxable year 1961 since A and B are not related persons at any time during that year and because the portion of the original lease period remaining at the time the building was completed (20 years) is less than 60 percent of the estimated useful life of the building (60 percent of 50 years, or 30 years). Thus, the term of the lease shall, beginning on January 1, 1961, be treated as including the remaining portion of the original lease period (18 years) and the renewal period (20 years), or 38 years, unless lessee A can establish that, as of the close of the taxable year 1961 or any subsequent taxable year, it is more probable that the lease will not be renewed than that it will be renewed.

Example (2). Assume the same facts as in example (1), except that the estimated useful life of the building is 30 years. During the taxable years 1959 and 1960, the term of the lease shall be treated as 30 years. For the taxable year 1961, however, neither section 178(a) nor section 178(b) apply since the percentage requirement of section 178(a) and paragraph (b) of this section are not satisfied and A and B are not related persons within the meaning of section 178(b)(2) and §1.178-2. [Reg. §1.178-1.]

□ [T.D. 6520, 12-23-60.]

[Reg. §1.179-0]

§1.179-0. Table of contents.—This section lists captioned paragraphs contained in §§1.179-1 through 1.179-6.

(d) Election or revocation must not be made in any other manner.

§ 1.179-6. *Effective dates.*

(a) *In general.*

(b) Section 179 property placed in service by the taxpayer in a taxable year beginning after 2002 and before 2008.

(c) Application of § 1.179–5(d).

[Reg. § 1.179–0.]

☐ [*T.D.* 8455, 12-23-92. *Amended by T.D.* 9146, 8-3-2004 *and T.D.* 9209, 7-12-2005.]

[Reg. § 1.179-1]

§ 1.179-1. Election to expense certain depreciable assets.—(a) *In general.*—Section 179(a) allows a taxpayer to elect to expense the cost (as defined in § 1.179-4(d)), or a portion of the cost, of section 179 property (as defined in § 1.179-4(a)) for the taxable year in which the property is placed in service (as defined in § 1.179-4(e)). The election is not available for trusts, estates, and certain noncorporate lessors. See paragraph (i)(2) of this section for rules concerning noncorporate lessors. However, section 179(b) provides certain limitations on the amount that a taxpayer may elect to expense in any one taxable year. See §§ 1.179-2 and 1.179-3 for rules relating to the dollar and taxable income limitations and the carryover of disallowed deduction rules. For rules describing the time and manner of making an election under section 179, see § 1.179-5. For the effective date, see § 1.179-6.

(b) *Cost subject to expense.*—The expense deduction under section 179 is allowed for the entire cost or a portion of the cost of one or more items of section 179 property. This expense deduction is subject to the limitations of section 179(b) and § 1.179-2. The taxpayer may select the properties that are subject to the election as well as the portion of each property's cost to expense.

(c) *Proration not required.*—(1) *In general.*—The expense deduction under section 179 is determined without any proration based on—

(i) The period of time the section 179 property has been in service during the taxable year; or

(ii) The length of the taxable year in which the property is placed in service.

(2) *Example.*—The following example illustrates the provisions of paragraph (c)(1) of this section.

Example. On December 1, 1991, X, a calendar-year corporation, purchases and places in service section 179 property costing $20,000. For the taxable year ending December 31, 1991, X may elect to claim a section 179 expense deduction on the property (subject to the limitations imposed under section 179(b)) without proration of its cost for the number of days in 1991 during which the property was in service.

(d) *Partial business use.*—(1) *In general.*—If a taxpayer uses section 179 property for trade or business as well as other purposes, the portion of the cost of the property attributable to the trade or business use is eligible for expensing under section 179 provided that more than 50 percent of the property's use in the taxable year is for trade or business purposes. The limitations of section 179(b) and § 1.179-2 are applied to the portion of the cost attributable to the trade or business use.

(2) *Example.*—The following example illustrates the provisions of paragraph (d)(1) of this section.

Example. A purchases section 179 property costing $10,000 in 1991 for which 80 percent of its use will be in A's trade or business. The cost of the property adjusted to reflect the business use of the property is $8,000 (80 percent × $10,000). Thus, A may elect to expense up to $8,000 of the cost of the property (subject to the limitations imposed under section 179(b) and § 1.179-2).

(3) *Additional rules that may apply.*—If a section 179 election is made for "listed property" within the meaning of section 280F(d)(4) and there is personal use of the property, section 280F(d)(1), which provides rules that coordinate section 179 with the section 280F limitation on the amount of depreciation, may apply. If section 179 property is no longer predominantly used in the taxpayer's trade or business, paragraphs (e)(1) through (4) of this section, relating to recapture of the section 179 deduction, may apply.

(e) *Change in use; recapture.*—(1) *In general.*—If a taxpayer's section 179 property is not used predominantly in a trade or business of the taxpayer at any time before the end of the property's recovery period, the taxpayer must recapture in the taxable year in which the section 179 property is not used predominantly in a trade or business any benefit derived from expensing such property. The benefit derived from expensing the property is equal to the excess of the amount expensed under this section over the total amount that would have been allowable for prior taxable years and the taxable year of recap-

ture as a deduction under section 168 (had section 179 not been elected) for the portion of the cost of the property to which the expensing relates (regardless of whether such excess reduced the taxpayer's tax liability). For purposes of the preceding sentence, (i) the "amount expensed under this section" shall not include any amount that was not allowed as a deduction to a taxpayer because the taxpayer's aggregate amount of allowable section 179 expenses exceeded the section 179(b) dollar limitation, and (ii) in the case of an individual who does not elect to itemize deductions under section 63(g) in the taxable year of recapture, the amount allowable as a deduction under section 168 in the taxable year of recapture shall be determined by treating property used in the production of income other than rents or royalties as being property used for personal purposes. The amount to be recaptured shall be treated as ordinary income for the taxable year in which the property is no longer used predominantly in a trade or business of the taxpayer. For taxable years following the year of recapture, the taxpayer's deductions under section 168(a) shall be determined as if no section 179 election with respect to the property had been made. However, see section 280F(d)(1) relating to the coordination of section 179 with the limitation on the amount of depreciation for luxury automobiles and where certain property is used for personal purposes. If the recapture rules of both section 280F(b)(2) and this paragraph (e)(1) apply to an item of section 179 property, the amount of recapture for such property shall be determined only under the rules of section 280F(b)(2).

(2) *Predominant use.*—Property will be treated as not used predominantly in a trade or business of the taxpayer if 50 percent or more of the use of such property during any taxable year within the recapture period is for a use other than in a trade or business of the taxpayer. If during any taxable year of the recapture period the taxpayer disposes of the property (other than in a disposition to which section 1245(a) applies) or ceases to use the property in a trade or business in a manner that had the taxpayer claimed a credit under section 38 for such property such disposition or cessation in use would cause recapture under section 47, the property will be treated as not used in a trade or business of the taxpayer. However, for purposes of applying the recapture rules of section 47 pursuant to the preceding sentence, converting the use of the property from use in a trade or business to use in the production of income will be treated as a conversion to personal use.

(3) *Basis; application with section 1245.*—The basis of property with respect to which there is recapture under paragraph (e)(1) of this section shall be increased immediately before the event resulting in such recapture by the amount recaptured. If section 1245(a) applies to a disposition of property, there is no recapture under paragraph (e)(1) of this section.

(4) *Carryover of disallowed deduction.*—See § 1.179-3 for rules on applying the recapture provisions of this paragraph (e) when a taxpayer has a carryover of disallowed deduction.

(5) *Example.*—The following example illustrates the provisions of paragraphs (e)(1) through (e)(4) of this section.

Example. A, a calendar-year taxpayer, purchases and places in service on January 1, 1991, section 179 property costing $15,000. The property is 5-year property for section 168 purposes and is the only item of depreciable property placed in service by A during 1991. A properly elects to expense $10,000 of the cost and elects under section 168(b)(5) to depreciate the remaining cost under the straight-line method. On January 1, 1992, A converts the property from use in A's business to use for the production of income, and A uses the property in the latter capacity for the entire year. A elects to itemize deductions for 1992. Because the property was not predominantly used in A's trade or business in 1992, A must recapture any benefit derived from expensing the property under section 179. Had A not elected to expense the $10,000 in 1991, A would have been entitled to deduct, under section 168, 10 percent of the $10,000 in 1991, and 20 percent of the $10,000 in 1992. Therefore, A must include $7,000 in ordinary income for the 1992 taxable year, the excess of $10,000 (the section 179 expense amount) over $3,000 (30 percent of $10,000).

(f) *Basis.*—(1) *In general.*—A taxpayer who elects to expense under section 179 must reduce the depreciable basis of the section 179 property by the amount of the section 179 expense deduction.

(2) *Special rules for partnerships and S Corporations.*—Generally the basis of a partnership or S corporation's section 179 property must be reduced to reflect the amount of section 179 expense elected by the partnership or S corporation. This reduction must be made in the basis of partnership or S corporation property even if the limitations of section 179(b) and § 1.179-2 prevent a partner in a partnership or a shareholder in an S corporation from deducting all or a portion of the amount of the section 179 expense allocated by the partnership or S corporation. See § 1.179-3 for rules on applying the basis provisions

of this paragraph (f) when a person has a carryover of disallowed deduction.

(3) *Special rules with respect to trusts and estates which are partners or S corporation shareholders.*—Since the section 179 election is not available for trusts or estates, a partner or S corporation shareholder that is a trust or estate, may not deduct its allocable share of the section 179 expense elected by the partnership or S corporation. The partnership or S corporation's basis in section 179 property shall not be reduced to reflect any portion of the section 179 expense that is allocable to the trust or estate. Accordingly, the partnership or S corporation may claim a depreciation deduction under section 168 or a section 38 credit (if available) with respect to any depreciable basis resulting from the trust or estate's inability to claim its allocable portion of the section 179 expense.

(g) *Disallowance of the section 38 credit.*—If a taxpayer elects to expense under section 179, no section 38 credit is allowable for the portion of the cost expensed. In addition, no section 38 credit shall be allowed under section 48(d) to a lessee of property for the portion of the cost of the property that the lessor expensed under section 179.

(h) *Partnerships and S corporations.*—(1) *In general.*—In the case of property purchased and placed in service by a partnership or an S corporation, the determination of whether the property is section 179 property is made at the partnership or S corporation level. The election to expense the cost of section 179 property is made by the partnership or the S corporation. See sections 703(b), 1363(c), 6221, 6231(a)(3), 6241, and 6245.

(2) *Example.*—The following example illustrates the provisions of paragraph (h)(1) of this section.

Example. A owns certain residential rental property as an investment. A and others form ABC partnership whose function is to rent and manage such property. A and ABC partnership file their income tax returns on a calendar-year basis. In 1991, ABC partnership purchases and places in service office furniture costing $20,000 to be used in the active conduct of ABC's business. Although the office furniture is used with respect to an investment activity of A, the furniture is being used in the active conduct of ABC's trade or business. Therefore, because the determination of whether property is section 179 property is made at the partnership level, the office furniture is section 179 property and ABC may elect to expense a portion of its cost under section 179.

(i) *Leasing of section 179 property.*—(1) *In general.*—A lessor of section 179 property who is treated as the owner of the property for Federal tax purposes will be entitled to the section 179 expense deduction if the requirements of section 179 and the regulations thereunder are met. These requirements will not be met if the lessor merely holds the property for the production of income. For certain leases entered prior to January 1, 1984, the safe harbor provisions of section 168(f)(8) apply in determining whether an agreement is treated as a lease for Federal tax purposes.

(2) *Noncorporate lessor.*—In determining the class of taxpayers (other than an estate or trust) for which section 179 is applicable, section 179(d)(5) provides that if a taxpayer is a noncorporate lessor (*i.e.*, a person who is not a corporation and is a lessor), the taxpayer shall not be entitled to claim a section 179 expense for section 179 property purchased and leased by the taxpayer unless the taxpayer has satisfied all of the requirements of section 179(d)(5)(A) or (B).

(j) *Application of sections 263 and 263A.*—Under section 263(a)(1)(G), expenditures for which a deduction is allowed under section 179 and this section are excluded from capitalization under section 263(a). Under this paragraph (j), amounts allowed as a deduction under section 179 and this section are excluded from the application of the uniform capitalization rules of section 263A.

(k) *Cross references.*—See section 453(i) and the regulations thereunder with respect to installment sales of section 179 property. See section 1033(g)(3) and the regulations thereunder relating to the condemnation of outdoor advertising displays. See section 1245(a) and the regulations thereunder with respect to recapture rules for section 179 property. [Reg. § 1.179-1.]

☐ [*T.D. 8121, 1-5-87. Amended by T.D. 8455, 12-23-92.*]

[Reg. § 1.179-2]

§1.179-2. Limitations on amount subject to section 179 election.—(a) *In general.*—Sections 179(b)(1) and (2) limit the aggregate cost of section 179 property that a taxpayer may elect to expense under section 179 for any one taxable year (dollar limitation). See paragraph (b) of this section. Section 179(b)(3)(A) limits the aggregate cost of section 179 property that a taxpayer may deduct in any taxable year (taxable income limitation). See paragraph (c) of this section. Any cost that is elected to be expensed but that is not

currently deductible because of the taxable income limitation may be carried forward to the next taxable year (carryover of disallowed deduction). See § 1.179-3 for rules relating to carryovers of disallowed deductions. See also sections 280F(a), (b), and (d)(1) relating to the coordination of section 179 with the limitations on the amount of depreciation for luxury automobiles and other listed property. The dollar and taxable income limitations apply to each taxpayer and not to each trade or business in which the taxpayer has an interest.

(b) *Dollar limitation.*—(1) *In general.*—The aggregate cost of section 179 property that a taxpayer may elect to expense under section 179 for any taxable year beginning in 2003 and thereafter is $25,000 ($100,000 in the case of taxable years beginning after 2002 and before 2008 under section 179(b)(1), indexed annually for inflation under section 179(b)(5) for taxable years beginning after 2003 and before 2008), reduced (but not below zero) by the amount of any excess section 179 property (described in paragraph (b)(2) of this section) placed in service during the taxable year.

(2) *Excess section 179 property.*—The amount of any excess section 179 property for a taxable year equals the excess (if any) of—

(i) The cost of section 179 property placed in service by the taxpayer in the taxable year; over

(ii) $200,000 ($400,000 in the case of taxable years beginning after 2002 and before 2008 under section 179(b)(2), indexed annually for inflation under section 179(b)(5) for taxable years beginning after 2003 and before 2008).

(3) *Application to partnerships.*—(i) *In general.*—The dollar limitation of this paragraph (b) applies to the partnership as well as to each partner. In applying the dollar limitation to a taxpayer that is a partner in one or more partnerships, the partner's share of section 179 expenses allocated to the partner from each partnership is aggregated with any nonpartnership section 179 expenses of the taxpayer for the taxable year. However, in determining the excess section 179 property placed in service by a partner in a taxable year, the cost of section 179 property placed in service by the partnership is not attributed to any partner.

(ii) *Example.*—The following example illustrates the provisions of paragraph (b)(3)(i) of this section.

Example. During 1991, CD, a calendar-year partnership, purchases and places in service section 179 property costing $150,000 and elects under section 179(c) and § 1.179-5 to expense $10,000 of the cost of that property. CD properly allocates to C, a calendar-year taxpayer and a partner in CD, $5,000 of section 179 expenses (C's distributive share of CD's section 179 expenses for 1991). In applying the dollar limitation to C for 1991, C must include the $5,000 of section 179 expenses allocated from CD. However, in determining the amount of any excess section 179 property C placed in service during 1991, C does not include any of the cost of section 179 property placed in service by CD, including the $5,000 of cost represented by the $5,000 of section 179 expenses allocated to C by the partnership.

(iii) *Partner's share of section 179 expenses.*—Section 704 and the regulations thereunder govern the determination of a partner's share of a partnership's section 179 expenses for any taxable year. However, no allocation among partners of the section 179 expenses may be modified after the due date of the partnership return (without regard to extensions of time) for the taxable year for which the election under section 179 is made.

(iv) *Taxable year.*—If the taxable years of a partner and the partnership do not coincide, then for purposes of section 179, the amount of the partnership's section 179 expenses attributable to a partner for a taxable year is determined under section 706 and the regulations thereunder (generally the partner's distributive share of partnership section 179 expenses for the partnership year that ends with or within the partner's taxable year).

(v) *Example.*—The following example illustrates the provisions of paragraph (b)(3)(iv) of this section.

Example. AB partnership has a taxable year ending January 31. A, a partner of AB, has a taxable year ending December 31. AB purchases and places in service section 179 property on March 10, 1991, and elects to expense a portion of the cost of that property under section 179. Under section 706 and § 1.706-1(a)(1), A will be unable to claim A's distributive share of any of AB's section 179 expenses attributable to the property placed in service on March 10, 1991, until A's taxable year ending December 31, 1992.

(4) *S Corporations.*—Rules similar to those contained in paragraph (b)(3) of this section apply in the case of S corporations (as defined in section 1361(a)) and their shareholders. Each shareholder's share of the section 179 expenses of an S corporation is determined under section 1366.

(5) *Joint returns.*—(i) *In general.*—A husband and wife who file a joint income tax return under section 6013(a) are treated as one taxpayer in determining the amount of the dollar limitation under paragraph (b)(1) of this section, regardless of which spouse purchased the property or placed it in service.

(ii) *Joint returns filed after separate returns.*—In the case of a husband and wife who elect under section 6013(b) to file a joint income tax return for a taxable year after the time prescribed by law for filing the return for such taxable year has expired, the dollar limitation under paragraph (b)(1) of this section is the lesser of—

(A) The dollar limitation (as determined under paragraph (b)(5)(i) of this section); or

(B) The aggregate cost of section 179 property elected to be expensed by the husband and wife on their separate returns.

(iii) *Example.*—The following example illustrates the provisions of paragraph (b)(5)(ii) of this section.

Example. During 1991, Mr. and Mrs. B, both calendar-year taxpayers, purchase and place in service section 179 property costing $100,000. On their separate returns for 1991, Mr. B elects to expense $3,000 of section 179 property as an expense and Mrs. B elects to expense $4,000. After the due date of the return they elect under section 6013(b) to file a joint income tax return for 1991. The dollar limitation for their joint income tax return is $7,000, the lesser of the dollar limitation ($10,000) or the aggregate cost elected to be expensed under section 179 on their separate returns ($3,000 elected by Mr. B plus $4,000 elected by Mrs. B, or $7,000).

(6) *Married individuals filing separately.*—(i) *In general.*—In the case of an individual who is married but files a separate income tax return for a taxable year, the dollar limitation of this paragraph (b) for such taxable year is the amount that would be determined under paragraph (b)(5)(i) of this section if the individual filed a joint income tax return under section 6013(a) multiplied by either the percentage elected by the individual under this paragraph (b)(6) or 50 percent. The election in the preceding sentence is made in accordance with the requirements of section 179(c) and §1.179-5. However, the amount determined under paragraph (b)(5)(i) of this section must be multiplied by 50 percent if either the individual or the individual's spouse does not elect a percentage under this paragraph (b)(6) or the sum of the percentages elected by the individual and the individual's spouse does not equal 100 percent. For purposes of this paragraph (b)(6), marital status is determined under section 7703 and the regulations thereunder.

(ii) *Example.*—The following example illustrates the provisions of paragraph (b)(6)(i) of this section.

Example. Mr. and Mrs. D, both calendar-year taxpayers, file separate income tax returns for 1991. During 1991, Mr. D places $195,000 of section 179 property in service and Mrs. D places $9,000 of section 179 property in service. Neither of them elects a percentage under paragraph (b)(6)(i) of this section. The 1991 dollar limitation for both Mr. D and Mrs. D is determined by multiplying by 50 percent the dollar limitation that would apply had they filed a joint income tax return. Had Mr. and Mrs. D filed a joint return for 1991, the dollar limitation would have been $6,000, $10,000 reduced by the excess section 179 property placed in service during 1991 ($195,000 placed in service by Mr. D plus $9,000 placed in service by Mrs. D less $200,000, or $4,000). Thus, the 1991 dollar limitation for Mr. and Mrs. D is $3,000 each ($6,000 multiplied by 50 percent).

(7) *Component members of a controlled group.*—(i) *In general.*—Component members of a controlled group (as defined in §1.179-4(f)) on a December 31 are treated as one taxpayer in applying the dollar limitation of sections 179(b)(1) and (2) and this paragraph (b). The expense deduction may be taken by any one component member or allocated (for the taxable year of each member that includes that December 31) among the several members in any manner. Any allocation of the expense deduction must be pursuant to an allocation by the common parent corporation if a consolidated return is filed for all component members of the group, or in accordance with an agreement entered into by the members of the group if separate returns are filed. If a consolidated return is filed by some component members of the group and separate returns are filed by other component members, the common parent of the group filing the consolidated return must enter into an agreement with those members that do not join in filing the consolidated return allocating the amount between the group filing the consolidated return and the other component members of the controlled group that do not join in filing the consolidated return. The amount of the expense allocated to any component member, however, may not exceed the cost of section 179 property actually purchased and placed in service by the member in the taxable year. If the component members have different taxable years, the term "taxable year" in sections 179(b)(1) and (2) means the

taxable year of the member whose taxable year begins on the earliest date.

(ii) *Statement to be filed.*—If a consolidated return is filed, the common parent corporation must file a separate statement attached to the income tax return on which the election is made to claim an expense deduction under section 179. See §1.179-5. If separate returns are filed by some or all component members of the group, each component member not included in a consolidated return must file a separate statement attached to the income tax return on which an election is made to claim a deduction under section 179. The statement must include the name, address, employer identification number, and the taxable year of each component member of the controlled group, a copy of the allocation agreement signed by persons duly authorized to act on behalf of the component members, and a description of the manner in which the deduction under section 179 has been divided among the component members.

(iii) *Revocation.*—If a consolidated return is filed for all component members of the group, an allocation among such members of the expense deduction under section 179 may not be revoked after the due date of the return (including extensions of time) of the common parent corporation for the taxable year for which an election to take an expense deduction is made. If some or all of the component members of the controlled group file separate returns for taxable years including a particular December 31 for which an election to take the expense deduction is made, the allocation as to all members of the group may not be revoked after the due date of the return (including extensions of time) of the component member of the controlled group whose taxable year that includes such December 31 ends on the latest date.

(c) *Taxable income limitation.*—(1) *In general.*—The aggregate cost of section 179 property elected to be expensed under section 179 that may be deducted for any taxable year may not exceed the aggregate amount of taxable income of the taxpayer for such taxable year that is derived from the active conduct by the taxpayer of any trade or business during the taxable year. For purposes of section 179(b)(3) and this paragraph (c), the aggregate amount of taxable income derived from the active conduct by an individual, a partnership, or an S corporation of any trade or business is computed by aggregating the net income (or loss) from all of the trades or businesses actively conducted by the individual, partnership, or S corporation during the taxable year. Items of income that are derived from the active conduct of a trade or business include section 1231 gains (or losses) from the trade or business and interest from working capital of the trade or business. Taxable income derived from the active conduct of a trade or business is computed without regard to the deduction allowable under section 179, any section 164(f) deduction, any net operating loss carryback or carryforward, and deductions suspended under any section of the Code. See paragraph (c)(6) of this section for rules on determining whether a taxpayer is engaged in the active conduct of a trade or business for this purpose.

(2) *Application to partnerships and partners.*—(i) *In general.*—The taxable income limitation of this paragraph (c) applies to the partnership as well as to each partner. Thus, the partnership may not allocate to its partners as a section 179 expense deduction for any taxable year more than the partnership's taxable income limitation for that taxable year, and a partner may not deduct as a section 179 expense deduction for any taxable year more than the partner's taxable income limitation for that taxable year.

(ii) *Taxable year.*—If the taxable year of a partner and the partnership do not coincide, then for purposes of section 179, the amount of the partnership's taxable income attributable to a partner for a taxable year is determined under section 706 and the regulations thereunder (generally the partner's distributive share of partnership taxable income for the partnership year that ends with or within the partner's taxable year).

(iii) *Example.*—The following example illustrates the provisions of paragraph (c)(2)(ii) of this section.

Example. AB partnership has a taxable year ending January 31. A, a partner of AB, has a taxable year ending December 31. For AB's taxable year ending January 31, 1992, AB has taxable income from the active conduct of its trade or business of $100,000, $90,000 of which was earned during 1991. Under section 706 and §1.706-1(a)(1), A includes A's entire share of partnership taxable income in computing A's taxable income limitation for A's taxable year ending December 31, 1992.

(iv) *Taxable income of a partnership.*—The taxable income (or loss) derived from the active conduct by a partnership of any trade or business is computed by aggregating the net income (or loss) from all of the trades or businesses actively conducted by the partnership during the taxable year. The net income (or loss) from a trade or business actively conducted by the partnership is determined by taking into account the aggregate amount of the partnership's items described in section 702(a) (other than credits, tax-exempt income, and guaranteed payments under section 707(c)) derived from that trade or business. For purposes of determining the aggregate amount of partnership items, deductions and losses are treated as negative income. Any limitation on the amount of a partnership item described in section 702(a) which may be taken into account for purposes of computing the taxable income of a partner shall be disregarded in computing the taxable income of the partnership.

(v) *Partner's share of partnership taxable income.*—A taxpayer who is a partner in a partnership and is engaged in the active conduct of at least one of the partnership's trades or businesses includes as taxable income derived from the active conduct of a trade or business the amount of the taxpayer's allocable share of taxable income derived from the active conduct by the partnership of any trade or business (as determined under paragraph (c)(2)(iv) of this section).

(3) *S corporations and S corporation shareholders.*—(i) *In general.*—Rules similar to those contained in paragraphs (c)(2)(i) and (ii) of this section apply in the case of S corporations (as defined in section 1361(a)) and their shareholders. Each shareholder's share of the taxable income of an S corporation is determined under section 1366.

(ii) *Taxable income of an S corporation.*—The taxable income (or loss) derived from the active conduct by an S corporation of any trade or business is computed by aggregating the net income (or loss) from all of the trades or businesses actively conducted by the S corporation during the taxable year. The net income (or loss) from a trade or business actively conducted by an S corporation is determined by taking into account the aggregate amount of the S corporation's items described in section 1366(a) (other than credits, tax-exempt income, and deductions for compensation paid to an S corporation's shareholder-employees) derived from that trade or business. For purposes of determining the aggregate amount of S corporation items, deductions and losses are treated as negative income. Any limitation on the amount of an S corporation item described in section 1366(a) which may be taken into account for purposes of computing the taxable income of a shareholder shall be disregarded in computing the taxable income of the S corporation.

(iii) *Shareholder's share of S corporation taxable income.*—Rules similar to those contained in paragraph (c)(2)(v) and (c)(6)(ii) of this section apply to a taxpayer who is a shareholder in an S corporation and is engaged in the active conduct of the S corporation's trades or businesses.

(4) *Taxable income of a corporation other than an S corporation.*—The aggregate amount of taxable income derived from the active conduct by a corporation other than an S corporation of any trade or business is the amount of the corporation's taxable income before deducting its net operating loss deduction and special deductions (as reported on the corporation's income tax return), adjusted to reflect those items of income or deduction included in that amount that were not derived by the corporation from a trade or business actively conducted by the corporation during the taxable year.

(5) *Ordering rule for certain circular problems.*—(i) *In general.*—A taxpayer who elects to expense the cost of section 179 property (the deduction of which is subject to the taxable income limitation) also may have to apply another Internal Revenue Code section that has a limitation based on the taxpayer's taxable income. Except as provided in paragraph (c)(1) of this section, this section provides rules for applying the taxable income limitation under section 179 in such a case. First, taxable income is computed for the other section of the Internal Revenue Code. In computing the taxable income of the taxpayer for the other section of the Internal Revenue Code, the taxpayer's section 179 deduction is computed by assuming that the taxpayer's taxable income is determined without regard to the deduction under the other Internal Revenue Code section. Next, after reducing taxable income by the amount of the section 179 deduction so computed, a hypothetical amount of deduction is determined for the other section of the Internal Revenue Code. The taxable income limitation of the taxpayer under section 179(b)(3) and this paragraph (c) then is computed by including that hypothetical amount in determining taxable income.

(ii) *Example.*—The following example illustrates the ordering rule described in paragraph (c)(5)(i) of this section.
Example. X, a calendar-year corporation, elects to expense $10,000 of the cost of section 179 property purchased and placed in service during 1991. Assume X's dollar limitation is $10,000. X also gives a charitable contribution of $5,000 during the taxable year. X's taxable income for purposes of both sections 179 and 170(b)(2), but without regard to any deduction allowable under either section 179

or section 170, is $11,000. In determining X's taxable income limitation under section 179(b)(3) and this paragraph (c), X must first compute its section 170 deduction. However, section 170(b)(2) limits X's charitable contribution to 10 percent of its taxable income determined by taking into account its section 179 deduction. Paragraph (c)(5)(i) of this section provides that in determining X's section 179 deduction for 1991, X first computes a hypothetical section 170 deduction by assuming that its section 179 deduction is not affected by the section 170 deduction. Thus, in computing X's hypothetical section 170 deduction, X's taxable income limitation under section 179 is $11,000 and its section 179 deduction is $10,000. X's hypothetical section 170 deduction is $100 (10 percent of $1,000 ($11,000 less $10,000 section 179 deduction)). X's taxable income limitation for section 179 purposes is then computed by deducting the hypothetical charitable contribution of $100 for 1991. Thus, X's section 179 taxable income limitation is $10,900 ($11,000 less hypothetical $100 section 170 deduction), and its section 179 deduction for 1991 is $10,000. X's section 179 deduction so calculated applies for all purposes of the Code, including the computation of its actual section 170 deduction.

(6) *Active conduct by the taxpayer of a trade or business.*—(i) *Trade or business.*—For purposes of this section and §1.179-4(a), the term "trade or business" has the same meaning as in section 162 and the regulations thereunder. Thus, property held merely for the production of income or used in an activity not engaged in for profit (as described in section 183) does not qualify as section 179 property and taxable income derived from property held for the production of income or from an activity not engaged in for profit is not taken into account in determining the taxable income limitation.

(ii) *Active conduct.*—For purposes of this section, the determination of whether a trade or business is actively conducted by the taxpayer is to be made from all the facts and circumstances and is to be applied in light of the purpose of the active conduct requirement of section 179(b)(3)(A). In the context of section 179, the purpose of the active conduct requirement is to prevent a passive investor in a trade or business from deducting section 179 expenses against taxable income derived from that trade or business. Consistent with this purpose, a taxpayer generally is considered to actively conduct a trade or business if the taxpayer meaningfully participates in the management or operations of the trade or business. Generally, a partner is considered to actively conduct a trade or business of the partnership if the partner meaningfully participates in the management or operations of the trade or business. A mere passive investor in a trade or business does not actively conduct the trade or business.

(iii) *Example.*—The following example illustrates the provisions of paragraph (c)(6)(ii) of this section.
Example. A owns a salon as a sole proprietorship and employs B to operate it. A periodically meets with B to review developments relating to the business. A also approves the salon's annual budget that is prepared by B. B performs all the necessary operating functions, including hiring beauticians, acquiring the necessary beauty supplies, and writing the checks to pay all bills and the beauticians' salaries. In 1991, B purchased, as provided for in the salon's annual budget, equipment costing $9,500 for use in the active conduct of the salon. There were no other purchases of section 179 property during 1991. A's net income from the salon, before any section 179 deduction, totaled $8,000. A also is a partner in PRS, a calendar-year partnership, which owns a grocery store. C, a partner in PRS, runs the grocery store for the partnership, making all the management and operating decisions. PRS did not purchase any section 179 property during 1991. A's allocable share of partnership net income was $6,000. Based on the facts and circumstances, A meaningfully participates in the management of the salon. However, A does not meaningfully participate in the management or operations of the trade or business of PRS. Under section 179(b)(3)(A) and this paragraph (c), A's aggregate taxable income derived from the active conduct by A of any trade or business is $8,000, the net income from the salon.

(iv) *Employees.*—For purposes of this section, employees are considered to be engaged in the active conduct of the trade or business of their employment. Thus, wages, salaries, tips, and other compensation (not reduced by unreimbursed employee business expenses) derived by a taxpayer as an employee are included in the aggregate amount of taxable income of the taxpayer under paragraph (c)(1) of this section.

(7) *Joint returns.*—(i) *In general.*—The taxable income limitation of this paragraph (c) is applied to a husband and wife who file a joint income tax return under section 6013(a) by aggregating the taxable income of each spouse (as determined under paragraph (c)(1) of this section).

(ii) *Joint returns filed after separate returns.*—In the case of a husband and wife who elect under section 6013(b) to file a joint income tax return for a taxable year after the time prescribed by law for filing the return for such taxable year, the taxable income limitation of this paragraph (c) for the taxable year for which the joint return is filed is determined under paragraph (c)(7)(i) of this section.

(8) *Married individuals filing separately.*—In the case of an individual who is married but files a separate tax return for a taxable year, the taxable income limitation for that individual is determined under paragraph (c)(1) of this section by treating the husband and wife as separate taxpayers.

(d) *Examples.*—The following examples illustrate the provisions of paragraphs (b) and (c) of this section.

Example 1. (i) During 1991, PRS, a calendar-year partnership, purchases and places in service $50,000 of section 179 property. The taxable income of PRS derived from the active conduct of all its trades or businesses (as determined under paragraph (c)(1) of this section) is $8,000.

(ii) Under the dollar limitation of paragraph (b) of this section, PRS may elect to expense $10,000 of the cost of section 179 property purchased in 1991. Assume PRS elects under section 179(c) and §1.179-5 to expense $10,000 of the cost of section 179 property purchased in 1991.

(iii) Under the taxable income limitation of paragraph (c) of this section, PRS may allocate to its partners as a deduction only $8,000 of the cost of section 179 property in 1991. Under section 179(b)(3)(B) and §1.179-3(a), PRS may carry forward the remaining $2,000 it elected to expense, which would have been deductible under section 179(a) for 1991 absent the taxable income limitation.

Example 2. (i) The facts are the same as in *Example 1*, except that on December 31, 1991, PRS allocates to A, a calendar-year taxpayer and a partner in PRS, $7,000 of section 179 expenses and $2,000 of taxable income. A was engaged in the active conduct of a trade or business of PRS during 1991.

(ii) In addition to being a partner in PRS, A conducts a business as a sole proprietor. During 1991, A purchases and places in service $201,000 of section 179 property in connection with the sole proprietorship. A's 1991 taxable income derived from the active conduct of this business is $6,000.

(iii) Under the dollar limitation, A may elect to expense only $9,000 of the cost of section 179 property purchased in 1991, the $10,000 limit reduced by $1,000 (the amount by which the cost of section 179 property placed in service during 1991 ($201,000) exceeds $200,000). Under paragraph (b)(3)(i) of this section, the $7,000 of section 179 expenses allocated from PRS is subject to the $9,000 limit. Assume that A elects to expense $2,000 of the cost of section 179 property purchased by A's sole proprietorship in 1991. Thus, A has elected to expense under section 179 an amount equal to the dollar limitation for 1991 ($2,000 elected to be expensed by A's sole proprietorship plus $7,000, the amount of PRS's section 179 expenses allocated to A in 1991).

(iv) Under the taxable income limitation, A may only deduct $8,000 of the cost of section 179 property elected to be expensed in 1991, the aggregate taxable income derived from the active conduct of A's trades or businesses in 1991 ($2,000 from PRS and $6,000 from A's sole proprietorship). The entire $2,000 of taxable income allocated from PRS is included by A as taxable income derived from the active conduct by A of a trade or business because it was derived from the active conduct of a trade or business by PRS and A was engaged in the active conduct of a trade or business of PRS during 1991. Under section 179(b)(3)(B) and §1.179-3(a), A may carry forward the remaining $1,000 A elected to expense, which would have been deductible under section 179(a) for 1991 absent the taxable income limitation. [Reg. §1.179-2.]

□ [T.D. 8121, 1-5-87. *Amended by T.D.* 8455, 12-23-92; *T.D.* 9146, 8-3-2004 *and T.D. 9209, 7-12-2005.*]

[Reg. §1.179-3]

§1.179-3. Carryover of disallowed deduction.—(a) *In general.*—Under section 179(b)(3)(B), a taxpayer may carry forward for an unlimited number of years the amount of any cost of section 179 property elected to be expensed in a taxable year but disallowed as a deduction in that taxable year because of the taxable income limitation of section 179(b)(3)(A) and §1.179-2(c) ("carryover of disallowed deduction"). This carryover of disallowed deduction may be deducted under section 179(a) and §1.179-1(a) in a future taxable year as provided in paragraph (b) of this section.

(b) *Deduction of carryover of disallowed deduction.*—(1) *In general.*—The amount allowable as a deduction under section 179(a) and §1.179-1(a) for any taxable year is increased by the lesser of—

(i) The aggregate amount disallowed under section 179(b)(3)(A) and §1.179-2(c) for all prior taxable years (to the extent not previously allowed as a deduction by reason of this section); or

(ii) The amount of any unused section 179 expense allowance for the taxable year (as described in paragraph (c) of this section).

(2) *Cross references.*—See paragraph (f) of this section for rules that apply when a taxpayer disposes of or otherwise transfers section 179 property for which a carryover of disallowed deduction is outstanding. See paragraph (g) of this section for special rules that apply to partnerships and S corporations and paragraph (h) of this section for special rules that apply to partners and S corporation shareholders.

(c) *Unused section 179 expense allowance.*—The amount of any unused section 179 expense allowance for a taxable year equals the excess (if any) of—

(1) The maximum cost of section 179 property that the taxpayer may deduct under section 179 and §1.179-1 for the taxable year after applying the limitations of section 179(b) and §1.179-2; over

(2) The amount of section 179 property that the taxpayer actually elected to expense under section 179 and §1.179-1(a) for the taxable year.

(d) *Example.*—The following example illustrates the provisions of paragraphs (b) and (c) of this section.

Example. A, a calendar-year taxpayer, has a $3,000 carryover of disallowed deduction for an item of section 179 property purchased and placed in service in 1991. In 1992, A purchases and places in service an item of section 179 property costing $25,000. A's 1992 taxable income from the active conduct of all A's trades or businesses is $100,000. A elects, under section 179(c) and §1.179-5, to expense $8,000 of the cost of the item of section 179 property purchased in 1992. Under paragraph (b) of this section, A may deduct $2,000 of A's carryover of disallowed deduction from 1991 (the lesser of A's total outstanding carryover of disallowed deductions ($3,000), or the amount of any unused section 179 expense allowance for 1992 ($10,000 limit less $8,000 elected to be expensed, or $2,000)). For 1993, A has a $1,000 carryover of disallowed deduction for the item of section 179 property purchased and placed in service in 1991.

(e) *Recordkeeping requirement and ordering rule.*—The properties and the apportionment of cost that will be subject to a carryover of disallowed deduction are selected by the taxpayer in the year the properties are placed in service. This selection must be evidenced on the taxpayer's books and records and be applied consistently in subsequent years. If no selection is made, the total carryover of disallowed deduction is apportioned equally over the items of section 179 property elected to be expensed for the taxable year. For this purpose, the taxpayer treats any section 179 expense amount allocated from a partnership (or an S corporation) for a taxable year as one item of section 179 property. If the taxpayer is allowed to deduct a portion of the total carryover of disallowed deduction under paragraph (b) of this section, the taxpayer must deduct the cost of section 179 property carried forward from the earliest taxable year.

(f) *Dispositions and other transfers of section 179 property.*—(1) *In general.*—Upon a sale or other disposition of section 179 property, or a transfer of section 179 property in a transaction in which gain or loss is not recognized in whole or in part (including transfers at death), immediately before the transfer the adjusted basis of the section 179 property is increased by the amount of any outstanding carryover of disallowed deduction with respect to the property. This carryover of disallowed deduction is not available as a deduction to the transferor or the transferee of the section 179 property.

(2) *Recapture under section 179(d)(10).*—Under §1.179-1(e), if a taxpayer's section 179 property is subject to recapture under section 179(d)(10), the taxpayer must recapture the benefit derived from expensing the property. Upon recapture, any outstanding carryover of disallowed deduction with respect to the property is no longer available for expensing. In determining the amount subject to recapture under section 179(d)(10) and §1.179-1(e), any outstanding carryover of disallowed deduction with respect to that property is not treated as an amount expensed under section 179.

(g) *Special rules for partnerships and S corporations.*—(1) *In general.*—Under section 179(d)(8) and §1.179-2(c), the taxable income limitation applies at the partnership level as well as at the partner level. Therefore, a partnership may have a carryover of disallowed deduction with respect to the cost of its section 179 property. Similar rules apply to S corporations. This paragraph (g) provides special rules that apply when a partnership or an S corporation has a carryover of disallowed deduction.

(2) *Basis adjustment.*—Under §1.179-1(f)(2), the basis of a partnership's section 179 property must be reduced to reflect the amount of section 179 expense elected by the partnership. This reduction must be made for the taxable year for which the election is made even if the section 179 expense amount, or a portion thereof, must be carried forward by the partnership. Similar rules apply to S corporations.

(3) *Dispositions and other transfers of section 179 property by a partnership or an S corporation.*—The provisions of paragraph (f) of this section apply in determining the treatment of any outstanding carryover of disallowed deduction with respect to section 179 property disposed of, or transferred in a nonrecognition transaction, by a partnership or an S corporation.

(4) *Example.*—The following example illustrates the provisions of this paragraph (g).

Example. ABC, a calendar-year partnership, owns and operates a restaurant business. During 1992, ABC purchases and places in service two items of section 179 property—a cash register costing $4,000 and office furniture costing $6,000. ABC elects to expense under section 179(c) the full cost of the cash register and the office furniture. For 1992, ABC has $6,000 of taxable income derived from the active conduct of its restaurant business. Therefore, ABC may deduct only $6,000 of section 179 expenses and must carry forward the remaining $4,000 of section 179 expenses at the partnership level. ABC must reduce the adjusted basis of the section 179 property by the full amount elected to be expensed. However, ABC may not allocate to its partners any portion of the carryover of disallowed deduction until ABC is able to deduct it under paragraph (b) of this section.

(h) *Special rules for partners and S corporation shareholders.*—(1) *In general.*—Under section 179(d)(8) and §1.179-2(c), a partner may have a carryover of disallowed deduction with respect to the cost of section 179 property elected to be expensed by the partnership and allocated to the partner. A partner who is allocated section 179 expenses from a partnership must reduce the basis of his or her partnership interest by the full amount allocated regardless of whether the partner may deduct for the taxable year the allocated section 179 expenses or is required to carry forward all or a portion of the expenses. Similar rules apply to S corporation shareholders.

(2) *Dispositions and other transfers of a partner's interest in a partnership or a shareholder's interest in an S corporation.*—A partner who disposes of a partnership interest, or transfers a partnership interest in a transaction in which gain or loss is not recognized in whole or in part (including transfers of a partnership interest at death), may have an outstanding carryover of disallowed deduction of section 179 expenses allocated from the partnership. In such a case, immediately before the transfer the partner's basis in the partnership interest is increased by the amount of the partner's outstanding carryover of disallowed deduction with respect to the partnership interest. This carryover of disallowed deduction is not available as a deduction to the transferor or transferee partner of the section 179 property. Similar rules apply to S corporation shareholders.

(3) *Examples.*—The following examples illustrate the provisions of this paragraph (h).

Example 1. (i) G is a general partner in GD, a calendar-year partnership, and is engaged in the active conduct of GD's business. During 1991, GD purchases and places section 179 property in service and elects to expense a portion of the cost of the property under section 179. GD allocates $2,500 of section 179 expenses and $15,000 of taxable income (determined without regard to the section 179 deduction) to G. The income was derived from the active conduct by GD of a trade or business.

(ii) In addition to being a partner in GD, G conducts a business as a sole proprietor. During 1991, G purchases and places in service office equipment costing $25,000 and a computer costing $10,000 in connection with the sole proprietorship. G elects under section 179(c) and §1.179-5 to expense $7,500 of the cost of the office equipment. G has a taxable loss (determined without regard to the section 179 deduction) derived from the active conduct of this business of $12,500.

(iii) G has no other taxable income (or loss) derived from the active conduct of a trade or business during 1991. G's taxable income limitation for 1991 is $2,500 ($15,000 taxable income allocated from GD less $12,500 taxable loss from the sole proprietorship). Therefore, G may deduct during 1991 only $2,500 of the $10,000 of section 179 expenses. G notes on the appropriate books and records that G expenses the $2,500 of section 179 expenses allocated from GD and carries forward the $7,500 of section 179 expenses with respect to the *office equipment purchased by G's sole proprietorship.*

(iv) On January 1, 1992, G sells the office equipment G's sole proprietorship purchased and placed in service in 1991. Under paragraph (f) of this section, immediately before the sale G increases the adjusted basis of the office equipment by $7,500, the amount of the outstanding carryover of disallowed deduction with respect to the office equipment.

Example 2. (i) Assume the same facts as in *Example 1*, except that G notes on the appropriate books and records that G expenses $2,500 of section 179 expenses relating to G's sole proprietorship and carries forward the remaining $5,000 of section 179 expenses relating to G's

sole proprietorship and $2,500 of section 179 expenses allocated from GD.

(ii) On January 1, 1992, G sells G's partnership interest to A. Under paragraph (h)(2) of this section, immediately before the sale G increases the adjusted basis of G's partnership interest by $2,500, the amount of the outstanding carryover of disallowed deduction with respect to the partnership interest. [Reg. §1.179-3.]

☐ [T.D. 8455, 12-23-92.]

[Reg. §1.179-4]

§1.179-4. Definitions.—The following definitions apply for purposes of section 179 and §§1.179-1 through 1.179-6:

(a) *Section 179 property.*—The term *section 179 property* means any tangible property described in section 179(d)(1) that is acquired by purchase for use in the active conduct of the taxpayer's trade or business (as described in §1.179-2(c)(6)). For taxable years beginning after 2002 and before 2008, the term *section 179 property* includes computer software described in section 179(d)(1) that is placed in service by the taxpayer in a taxable year beginning after 2002 and before 2008 and is acquired by purchase for use in the active conduct of the taxpayer's trade or business (as described in §1.179-2(c)(6)). For purposes of this paragraph (a), the term *trade or business* has the same meaning as in section 162 and the regulations under section 162.

(b) *Section 38 property.*—The term "section 38 property" shall have the same meaning assigned to it in section 48(a) and the regulations thereunder.

(c) *Purchase.*—(1)(i) Except as otherwise provided in paragraph (c)(2) of this section, the term "purchase" means any acquisition of the property, but only if all the requirements of paragraphs (c)(1)(ii), (iii), and (iv) of this section are satisfied.

(ii) Property is not acquired by purchase if it is acquired from a person whose relationship to the person acquiring it would result in the disallowance of losses under section 267 or 707(b). The property is considered not acquired by purchase only to the extent that losses would be disallowed under section 267 or 707(b). Thus, for example, if property is purchased by a husband and wife jointly from the husband's father, the property will be treated as not acquired by purchase only to the extent of the husband's interest in the property. However, in applying the rules of section 267(b) and (c) for this purpose, section 267(c)(4) shall be treated as providing that the family of an individual will include only his spouse, ancestors, and lineal descendants. For example, a purchase of property from a corporation by a taxpayer who owns, directly or indirectly, more than 50 percent in value of the outstanding stock of such corporation does not qualify as a purchase under section 179(d)(2); nor does the purchase of property by a husband from his wife. However, the purchase of section 179 property by a taxpayer from his brother or sister does qualify as a purchase for purposes of section 179(d)(2).

(iii) The property is not acquired by purchase if acquired from a component member of a controlled group of corporations (as defined in paragraph (g) of this section) by another component member of the same group.

(iv) The property is not acquired by purchase if the basis of the property in the hands of the person acquiring it is determined in whole or in part by reference to the adjusted basis of such property in the hands of the person from whom acquired, is determined under section 1014(a), relating to property acquired from a decedent, or is determined under section 1022, relating to property acquired from certain decedents who died in 2010. For example, property acquired by gift or bequest does not qualify as property acquired by purchase for purposes of section 179(d)(2); nor does property received in a corporate distribution the basis of which is determined under section 301(d)(2)(B), property acquired by a corporation in a transaction to which section 351 applies, property acquired by a partnership through contribution (section 723), or property received in a partnership distribution which has a carryover basis under section 732(a)(1).

(2) Property deemed to have been acquired by a new target corporation as a result of a section 338 election (relating to certain stock purchases treated as asset acquisitions) or a section 336(e) election (relating to certain stock dispositions treated as asset transfers) made for a disposition described in §1.336-2(b)(1) will be considered acquired by purchase.

(d) *Cost.*—The cost of section 179 property does not include so much of the basis of such property as is determined by reference to the basis of other property held at any time by the taxpayer. For example, X Corporation purchases a new drill press costing $10,000 in November 1984 which qualifies as section 179 property, and is granted a trade-in allowance of $2,000 on its old drill press. The old drill press had a basis of $1,200. Under the provisions of sections 1012 and 1031(d), the basis of the new drill press is $9,200 ($1,200 basis of old drill press plus cash expended of $8,000). However, only $8,000 of the basis of the new drill press qualifies as cost for purposes of the section 179 expense deduction; the remaining $1,200 is not part of the cost because it is determined by reference to the basis of the old drill press.

(e) *Placed in service.*—The term "placed in service" means the time that property is first placed by the taxpayer in a condition or state of readiness and availability for a specifically assigned function, whether for use in a trade or business, for the production of income, in a tax-exempt activity, or in a personal activity. See § 1.46-3(d)(2) for examples regarding when property shall be considered in a condition or state of readiness and availability for a specifically assigned function.

(f) *Controlled group of corporations and component member of controlled group.*—The terms "controlled group of corporations" and "component member" of a controlled group of corporations shall have the same meaning assigned to those terms in section 1563(a) and (b), except that the phrase "more than 50 percent" shall be substituted for the phrase "at least 80 percent" each place it appears in section 1563(a)(1). [Reg. § 1.179-4.]

☐ [*T.D. 8121, 1-5-87. Amended by T.D. 8455, 12-23-92; T.D. 9146, 8-3-2004, T.D. 9209, 7-12-2005, T.D. 9811, 1-18-2017 and T.D. 9874, 9-17-2019.*]

[Reg. § 1.179-5]

§ 1.179-5. Time and manner of making election.—(a) *Election.*—A separate election must be made for each taxable year in which a section 179 expense deduction is claimed with respect to section 179 property. The election under section 179 and § 1.179-1 to claim a section 179 expense deduction for section 179 property shall be made on the taxpayer's first income tax return for the taxable year to which the election applies (whether or not the return is timely) or on an amended return filed within the time prescribed by law (including extensions) for filing the return for such taxable year. The election shall be made by showing as a separate item on the taxpayer's income tax return the following items:

(1) The total section 179 expense deduction claimed with respect to all section 179 property selected; and

(2) The portion of that deduction allocable to each specific item. The person shall maintain records which permit specific identification of each piece of section 179 property and reflect how and from whom such property was acquired and when such property was placed in service. However, for this purpose a partner (or an S corporation shareholder) treats partnership (or S corporation) section 179 property for which section 179 expenses are allocated from a partnership (or an S corporation) as one item of section 179 property. The election to claim a section 179 expense deduction under this section, with respect to any property, is irrevocable and will be binding on the taxpayer with respect to such property for the taxable year for which the election is made and for all subsequent taxable years, unless the Commissioner consents to the revocation of the election. Similarly, the selection of section 179 property by the taxpayer to be subject to the expense deduction and apportionment scheme must be adhered to in computing the taxpayer's taxable income for the taxable year for which the election is made and for all subsequent taxable years, unless consent to change is given by the Commissioner.

(b) *Revocation.*—Any election made under section 179, and any specification contained in such election, may not be revoked except with the consent of the Commissioner. Such consent will be granted only in extraordinary circumstances. Requests for consent must be filed with the Commissioner of Internal Revenue, Washington, D.C., 20224. The request must include the name, address, and taxpayer identification number of the taxpayer and must be signed by the taxpayer or his duly authorized representative. It must be accompanied by a statement showing the year and property involved, and must set forth in detail the reasons for the request.

(c) *Section 179 property placed in service by the taxpayer in a taxable year beginning after 2002 and before 2008.*—(1) *In general.*—For any taxable year beginning after 2002 and before 2008, a taxpayer is permitted to make or revoke an election under section 179 without the consent of the Commissioner on an amended Federal tax return for that taxable year. This amended return must be filed within the time prescribed by law for filing an amended return for such taxable year.

(2) *Election.*—(i) *In general.*—For any taxable year beginning after 2002 and before 2008, a taxpayer is permitted to make an election under section 179 on an amended Federal tax return for that taxable year without the consent of the Commissioner. Thus, the election under section 179 and § 1.179-1 to claim a section 179 expense deduction for section 179 property may be made on an amended Federal

tax return for the taxable year to which the election applies. The amended Federal tax return must include the adjustment to taxable income for the section 179 election and any collateral adjustments to taxable income or to the tax liability (for example, the amount of depreciation allowed or allowable in that taxable year for the item of section 179 property to which the election pertains). Such adjustments must also be made on amended Federal tax returns for any affected succeeding taxable years.

(ii) *Specifications of elections.*—Any election under section 179 must specify the items of section 179 property and the portion of the cost of each such item to be taken into account under section 179(a). Any election under section 179 must comply with the specification requirements of section 179(c)(1)(A), § 1.179-1(b), and § 1.179-5(a). If a taxpayer elects to expense only a portion of the cost basis of an item of section 179 property for a taxable year beginning after 2002 and before 2008 (or did not elect to expense any portion of the cost basis of the item of section 179 property), the taxpayer is permitted to file an amended Federal tax return for that particular taxable year and increase the portion of the cost of the item of section 179 property to be taken into account under section 179(a) (or elect to expense any portion of the cost basis of the item of section 179 property if no prior election was made) without the consent of the Commissioner. Any such increase in the amount expensed under section 179 is not deemed to be a revocation of the prior election for that particular taxable year.

(3) *Revocation.*—(i) *In general.*—Section 179(c)(2) permits the revocation of an entire election or specification, or a portion of the selected dollar amount of a specification. The term *specification* in section 179(c)(2) refers to both the selected specific item of section 179 property subject to a section 179 election and the selected dollar amount allocable to the specific item of section 179 property. Any portion of the cost basis of an item of section 179 property subject to an election under section 179 for a taxable year beginning after 2002 and before 2008 may be revoked by the taxpayer without the consent of the Commissioner by filing an amended Federal tax return for that particular taxable year. The amended Federal tax return must include the adjustment to taxable income for the section 179 revocation and any collateral adjustments to taxable income or to the tax liability (for example, allowable depreciation in that taxable year for the item of section 179 property to which the revocation pertains). Such adjustments must also be made on amended Federal tax returns for any affected succeeding taxable years. Reducing or eliminating a specified dollar amount for any item of section 179 property with respect to any taxable year beginning after 2002 and before 2008 results in a revocation of that specified dollar amount.

(ii) *Effect of revocation.*—Such revocation, once made, shall be irrevocable. If the selected dollar amount reflects the entire cost of the item of section 179 property subject to the section 179 election, a revocation of the entire selected dollar amount is treated as a revocation of the section 179 election for that item of section 179 property and the taxpayer is unable to make a new section 179 election with respect to that item of property. If the selected dollar amount is a portion of the cost of the item of section 179 property, revocation of a selected dollar amount shall be treated as a revocation of only that selected dollar amount. The revoked dollars cannot be the subject of a new section 179 election for the same item of property.

(4) *Examples.*—The following examples illustrate the rules of this paragraph (c):

Example 1. Taxpayer, a sole proprietor, owns and operates a jewelry store. During 2003, Taxpayer purchased and placed in service two items of section 179 property — a cash register costing $4,000 (5-year MACRS property) and office furniture costing $10,000 (7-year MACRS property). On his 2003 Federal tax return filed on April 15, 2004, Taxpayer elected to expense under section 179 the full cost of the cash register and, with respect to the office furniture, claimed the depreciation allowable. In November 2004, Taxpayer determines it would have been more advantageous to have made an election under section 179 to expense the full cost of the office furniture rather than the cash register. Pursuant to paragraph (c)(1) of this section, Taxpayer is permitted to file an amended Federal tax return for 2003 revoking the section 179 election for the cash register, claiming the depreciation allowable in 2003 for the cash register, and making an election to expense under section 179 the cost of the office furniture. The amended return must include an adjustment for the depreciation previously claimed in 2003 for the office furniture, an adjustment for the depreciation allowable in 2003 for the cash register, and any other collateral adjustments to taxable income or to the tax liability. In addition, once Taxpayer revokes the section 179 election for the entire cost basis of the cash register, Taxpayer can no longer expense under section 179 any portion of the cost of the cash register.

Example 2. Taxpayer, a sole proprietor, owns and operates a machine shop that does specialized repair work on industrial equip-

Itemized Deductions for Individuals and Corps.
See p. 20,601 for regulations not amended to reflect law changes
25,625

ment. During 2003, Taxpayer purchased and placed in service one item of section 179 property — a milling machine costing $135,000. On Taxpayer's 2003 Federal tax return filed on April 15, 2004, Taxpayer elected to expense under section 179 $5,000 of the cost of the milling machine and claimed allowable depreciation on the remaining cost. Subsequently, Taxpayer determines it would have been to Taxpayer's advantage to have elected to expense $100,000 of the cost of the milling machine on Taxpayer's 2003 Federal tax return. In November 2004, Taxpayer files an amended Federal tax return for 2003, increasing the amount of the cost of the milling machine that is to be taken into account under section 179(a) to $100,000, decreasing the depreciation allowable in 2003 for the milling machine, and making any other collateral adjustments to taxable income or to the tax liability. Pursuant to paragraph (c)(2)(ii) of this section, increasing the amount of the cost of the milling machine to be taken into account under section 179(a) supplements the portion of the cost of the milling machine that was already taken into account by the original section 179 election made on the 2003 Federal tax return and no revocation of any specification with respect to the milling machine has occurred.

Example 3. Taxpayer, a sole proprietor, owns and operates a real estate brokerage business located in a rented storefront office. During 2003, Taxpayer purchases and places in service two items of section 179 property — a laptop computer costing $2,500 and a desktop computer costing $1,500. On Taxpayer's 2003 Federal tax return filed on April 15, 2004, Taxpayer elected to expense under section 179 the full cost of the laptop computer and the full cost of the desktop computer. Subsequently, Taxpayer determines it would have been to Taxpayer's advantage to have originally elected to expense under section 179 only $1,500 of the cost of the laptop computer on Taxpayer's 2003 Federal tax return. In November 2004, Taxpayer files an amended Federal tax return for 2003 reducing the amount of the cost of the laptop computer that was taken into account under section 179(a) to $1,500, claiming the depreciation allowable in 2003 on the remaining cost of $1,000 for that item, and making any other collateral adjustments to taxable income or to the tax liability. Pursuant to paragraph (c)(3)(ii) of this section, the $1,000 reduction represents a revocation of a portion of the selected dollar amount and no portion of those revoked dollars may be the subject of a new section 179 election for the laptop computer.

Example 4. Taxpayer, a sole proprietor, owns and operates a furniture making business. During 2003, Taxpayer purchases and places in service one item of section 179 property — an industrial-grade cabinet table saw costing $5,000. On Taxpayer's 2003 Federal tax return filed on April 15, 2004, Taxpayer elected to expense under section 179 $3,000 of the cost of the saw and, with respect to the remaining $2,000 of the cost of the saw, claimed the depreciation allowable. In November 2004, Taxpayer files an amended Federal tax return for 2003 revoking the selected $3,000 amount for the saw, claiming the depreciation allowable in 2003 on the $3,000 cost of the saw, and making any other collateral adjustments to taxable income or to the tax liability. Subsequently, in December 2004, Taxpayer files a second amended Federal tax return for 2003 selecting a new dollar amount of $2,000 for the saw, including an adjustment for the depreciation previously claimed in 2003 on the $2,000, and making any other collateral adjustments to taxable income or to the tax liability. Pursuant to paragraph (c)(2)(ii) of this section, Taxpayer is permitted to select a new selected dollar amount to expense under section 179 encompassing all or a part of the initially non-elected portion of the cost of the elected item of section 179 property. However, no portion of the revoked $3,000 may be the subject of a new section 179 dollar amount selection for the saw. In December 2005, Taxpayer files a third amended Federal tax return for 2003 revoking the entire selected $2,000 amount with respect to the saw, claiming the depreciation allowable in 2003 for the $2,000, and making any other collateral adjustments to taxable income or to the tax liability. Because Taxpayer elected to expense, and subsequently revoke, the entire cost basis of the saw, the section 179 election for the saw has been revoked and Taxpayer is unable to make a new section 179 election with respect to the saw.

(d) *Election or revocation must not be made in any other manner.*—Any election or revocation specified in this section must be made in the manner prescribed in paragraphs (a), (b), and (c) of this section. Thus, this election or revocation must not be made by the taxpayer in any other manner (for example, an election or a revocation of an election cannot be made through a request under section 446(e) to change the taxpayer's method of accounting), except as otherwise expressly provided by the Internal Revenue Code, the regulations under the Code, or other guidance published in the Internal Revenue Bulletin. [Reg. §1.179-5.]

☐ [*T.D.* 8121, 1-5-87. *Amended by T.D.* 8455, 12-23-92; *T.D.* 9146, 8-3-2004 *and T.D.* 9209, 7-12-2005.]

[Reg. §1.179-6]

§1.179-6. Effective/applicability dates.—(a) *In general.*—Except as provided in paragraphs (b), (c), (d), and (e) of this section, the provisions of §§1.179-1 through 1.179-5 apply for property placed in service by the taxpayer in taxable years ending after January 25, 1993. However, a taxpayer may apply the provisions of §§1.179-1 through 1.179-5 to property placed in service by the taxpayer after December 31, 1986, in taxable years ending on or before January 25, 1993. Otherwise, for property placed in service by the taxpayer after December 31, 1986, in taxable years ending on or before January 25, 1993, the final regulations under section 179 as in effect for the year the property was placed in service apply, except to the extent modified by the changes made to section 179 by the Tax Reform Act of 1986 (100 Stat. 2085), the Technical and Miscellaneous Revenue Act of 1988 (102 Stat. 3342) and the Revenue Reconciliation Act of 1990 (104 Stat. 1388-400). For that property, a taxpayer may apply any reasonable method that clearly reflects income in applying the changes to section 179, provided the taxpayer consistently applies the method to the property.

(b) *Section 179 property placed in service by the taxpayer in a taxable year beginning after 2002 and before 2008.*—The provisions of §1.179-2(b)(1) and (b)(2)(ii), the second sentence of §1.179-4(a), and the provisions of §1.179-5(c), reflecting changes made to section 179 by the Jobs and Growth Tax Relief Reconciliation Act of 2003 (117 Stat. 752) and the American Jobs Creation Act of 2004 (118 Stat. 1418), apply for property placed in service in taxable years beginning after 2002 and before 2008.

(c) *Application of §1.179-5(d).*—Section 1.179-5(d) applies on or after July 12, 2005.

(d) *Application of §1.179-4(c)(1)(iv).*—The provisions of §1.179-4(c)(1)(iv) relating to section 1022 are effective on and after January 19, 2017.

(e) *Application of §1.179-4(c)(2).*—(1) *In general.*—Except as provided in paragraphs (e)(2) and (3) of this section, the provisions of §1.179-4(c)(2) relating to section 336(e) are applicable on or after September 24, 2019.

(2) *Early application of §1.179-4(c)(2).*—A taxpayer may choose to apply the provisions of §1.179-4(c)(2) relating to section 336(e) for the taxpayer's taxable years ending on or after September 28, 2017.

(3) *Early application of regulation project REG-104397-18.*—A taxpayer may rely on the provisions of §1.179-4(c)(2) relating to section 336(e) in regulation project REG-104397-18 (2018-41 I.R.B. 558) (see §601.601(d)(2)(ii)(*b*) of this chapter) for the taxpayer's taxable years ending on or after September 28, 2017, and ending before September 24, 2019. [Reg. §1.179-6.]

☐ [*T.D.* 9146, 8-3-2004. *Redesignated and amended by T.D.* 9209, 7-12-2005, *T.D.* 9811, 1-18-2017 *and T.D.* 9874, 9-17-2019.]

[Reg. §1.179A-1]

§1.179A-1. [Reserved].

☐ [*T.D.* 8606, 8-2-95. *Removed and reserved by T.D.* 9849, 3-11-2019.]

[Reg. §1.179B-1T]

§1.179B-1T. Deduction for capital costs incurred in complying with Environmental Protection Agency sulfur regulations (temporary).—(a) *Scope and definitions.*—(1) *Scope.*—This section provides the rules for determining the amount of the deduction allowable under section 179B(a) for qualified capital costs paid or incurred by a small business refiner to comply with the highway diesel fuel sulfur control requirements of the Environmental Protection Agency (EPA). This section also provides rules for making elections under section 179B.

(2) *Definitions.*—For purposes of section 179B and this section, the following definitions apply:

(i) The *applicable EPA regulations* are the EPA regulations establishing the highway diesel fuel sulfur control program (40 CFR part 80, subpart I).

(ii) The *average daily domestic refinery run* for a refinery is the lesser of—

(A) The total amount of crude oil input (in barrels) to the refinery's domestic processing units during the 1-year period ending on December 31, 2002, divided by 365; or

(B) The total amount of refined petroleum product (in barrels) produced by the refinery's domestic processing units during such 1-year period divided by 365.

(iii) The *aggregate average domestic daily refinery run* for a refiner is the sum of the average daily domestic refinery runs for all refineries that were owned by the refiner or a related person on April 1, 2003.

(iv) *Cooperative owner* is a person that—

(A) Directly holds an ownership interest in a cooperative small business refiner, as defined in paragraph (a)(2)(v) of this section; and

(B) Is a cooperative to which part 1 of subchapter T of the Internal Revenue Code (Code) applies.

(v) *Cooperative small business refiner* is a small business refiner that is a cooperative to which part 1 of subchapter T of the Code applies.

(vi) *Low sulfur diesel fuel* has the meaning prescribed in section 45H(c)(5).

(vii) *Qualified capital costs* are qualified costs as defined in section 45H(c)(2) that are properly chargeable to capital account.

(viii) *Related person* has the meaning prescribed in section 613A(d)(3) and the regulations under section 613A(d)(3).

(ix) *Small business refiner* has the meaning prescribed in section 45H(c)(1).

(b) *Section 179B deduction.*—(1) *In general.*—Section 179B(a) allows a deduction with respect to the qualified capital costs paid or incurred by a small business refiner (the section 179B deduction). The deduction is allowable with respect to the qualified capital costs paid or incurred during a taxable year only if the small business refiner makes an election under paragraph (d) of this section for the taxable year. The certification requirement in section 45H(e) (relating to the certification required to support a credit under section 45H) does not apply for purposes of the section 179B deduction. Accordingly, the section 179B deduction is allowable with respect to the qualified capital costs of an electing small business refiner even if the refiner never obtains a certification under section 45H(e) with respect to those costs.

(2) *Computation of section 179B deduction.*—(i) *In general.*—Except as provided in paragraphs (b)(2)(ii) and (c)(3) of this section, a small business refiner that makes an election under paragraph (d) of this section for a taxable year is allowed a section 179B deduction in an amount equal to 75 percent of qualified capital costs that are paid or incurred by the small business refiner during the taxable year.

(ii) *Reduced percentage.*—A small business refiner's section 179B deduction is reduced if the refiner's aggregate average daily domestic refinery run is in excess of 155,000 barrels. In that case, the number of percentage points used in computing the deduction under paragraph (b)(2)(i) of this section (75) is reduced (not below zero) by the product of 75 and the ratio of the excess barrels to 50,000 barrels.

(3) *Example.*—The application of this paragraph (b) is illustrated by the following example:

Example. (i) A, an accrual method taxpayer, is a small business refiner with a taxable year ending December 31. On April 1, 2003, A owns a refinery with an average daily domestic refinery run (that is, an average daily run during calendar year 2002) of 100,000 barrels and a person related to A owns a refinery with an average daily domestic refinery run of 85,000 barrels. These are the only domestic refineries owned by A and persons related to A. A's aggregate average daily domestic refinery run for the two refineries is 185,000 barrels. A incurs qualified capital costs of $10 million in the taxable year ended December 31, 2007. The costs are incurred with respect to property that is placed in service in year 2008. A makes the election under paragraph (d) of this section for the 2007 taxable year.

(ii) Because A's aggregate average daily domestic refinery run is 185,000 barrels, the percentage of the qualified capital costs that is deductible under section 179B(a) is reduced from 75 percent to 30 percent (75 percent reduced by 75 percent multiplied by 0.6 ((185,000 barrels minus 155,000 barrels)/50,000 barrels)). Thus, for 2007, A's deduction under section 179B(a) is $3,000,000 ($10,000,000 qualified capital costs multiplied by .30).

(c) *Effect on basis.*—(1) *In general.*—If qualified capital costs are included in the basis of property, the basis of the property is reduced by the amount of the section 179B deduction allowed with respect to such costs.

(2) *Treatment as depreciation.*—If qualified capital costs are included in the basis of depreciable property, the amount of the section 179B deduction allowed with respect to such costs is treated as a depreciation deduction for purposes of section 1245.

(d) *Election to deduct qualified capital costs.*—(1) *In general.*—(i) *Section 179B election.*—This paragraph (d) prescribes rules for the election to deduct the qualified capital costs paid or incurred by a small business refiner during a taxable year (the section 179B election). A small business refiner making the section 179B election for a taxable year consents to, and agrees to apply, all of the provisions of section 179B and this section to qualified capital costs paid or in-

curred by the refiner during the taxable year. The section 179B election for a taxable year applies with respect to all qualified capital costs paid or incurred by the small business refiner during that taxable year.

(ii) *Year-by-year election.*—A separate section 179B election must be made for each taxable year in which the taxpayer seeks to deduct qualified capital costs under section 179B. A small business refiner may make the section 179B election for some taxable years and not for other taxable years.

(iii) *Elections for cooperative small business refiners.*—See paragraph (e) of this section for the rules applicable to the election provided under section 179B(e), relating to the election to allocate the section 179B deduction to cooperative owners of a cooperative small business refiner (the section 179B(e) election).

(2) *Time and manner for making section 179B election.*—(i) *Time for making election.*—Except as provided in paragraph (d)(2)(iii) of this section, a taxpayer's section 179B election for a taxable year must be made by the due date (including extensions) for filing the taxpayer's Federal income tax return for the taxable year.

(ii) *Manner of making election.*—(A) *In general.*—Except as provided in paragraph (d)(2)(iii) of this section, the section 179B election for a taxable year is made by claiming a section 179B deduction on the taxpayer's original Federal income tax return for the taxable year and attaching the statement described in paragraph (d)(2)(ii)(B) of this section to the return. The section 179B election with respect to qualified capital costs paid or incurred by a partnership is made by the partnership and the section 179B election with respect to qualified capital costs paid or incurred by an S corporation is made by the S corporation. In the case of qualified capital costs paid or incurred by the members of a consolidated group (within the meaning of § 1.1502-1(h)), the section 179B election with respect to such costs is made for each member by the common parent of the group.

(B) *Information required in election statement.*—The election statement attached to the taxpayer's return must contain the following information:

(1) The name and identification number of the small business refiner.

(2) The amount of the qualified capital costs paid or incurred during the taxable year for which the election is made.

(3) The aggregate average daily domestic refinery run (as determined under paragraph (a)(2)(iii) of this section).

(4) The date by which the small business refiner must comply with the applicable EPA regulations. If this date is not June 1, 2006, the statement also must explain why compliance is not required by June 1, 2006.

(5) The calculation of the section 179B deduction for the taxable year.

(6) For each property that will have its basis reduced on account of the section 179B deduction for the taxable year, a description of the property, the amount included in the basis of the property on account of qualified capital costs paid or incurred during the taxable year, and the amount of the basis reduction to that property on account of the section 179B deduction for the taxable year.

(iii) Except as otherwise expressly provided by the Code, the regulations under the Code, or other guidance published in the Internal Revenue Bulletin, a section 179B election is valid only if made at the time and in the manner prescribed in this paragraph (d)(2). For example, except as otherwise expressly provided, the 179B election cannot be made for a taxable year to which this section applies through a request under section 446(e) to change the taxpayer's method of accounting.

(3) *Revocation of election.*—An election made under this paragraph (d) may not be revoked without the prior written consent of the Commissioner of Internal Revenue. To seek the Commissioner's consent, the taxpayer must submit a request for a private letter ruling (for further guidance, see, for example, Rev. Proc. 2008-1 (2008-1 IRB 1) and § 601.601(d)(2)(ii)(*b*) of this chapter).

(4) *Failure to make election.*—If a small business refiner does not make the section 179B election for a taxable year at the time and in the manner prescribed in paragraph (d)(2) of this section, no deduction is allowed for the qualified capital costs that the refiner paid or incurred during the year. Instead these qualified capital costs are chargeable to a capital account in that taxable year, the basis of the property to which these costs are capitalized is not reduced on account of section 179B, and the amount of depreciation allowable for the property attributable to these costs is determined by reference to these costs unreduced by section 179B.

(5) *Elections for taxable years ending before June 26, 2008.*—This section does not apply to section 179B elections for taxable years

ending before June 26, 2008. The rules for making the section 179B election for a taxable year ending before June 26, 2008 are provided in Notice 2006-47 (2006-20 IRB 892). See §601.601(d)(2)(ii)(b) of this chapter.

(e) *Election under section 179B(e) to allocate section 179B deduction to cooperative owners.*—(1) *In general.*—A cooperative small business refiner may elect to allocate part or all of its cooperative owners' ratable shares of the section 179B deduction for a taxable year to the cooperative owners (the section 179B(e) election). The section 179B deduction allocated to a cooperative owner is equal to the cooperative owner's ratable share of the total section 179B deduction allocated. A cooperative owner's ratable share is determined for this purpose on the basis of the cooperative owner's ownership interest in the cooperative small business refiner during the cooperative small business refiner's taxable year. If the cooperative owners' interests vary during the year, the cooperative small business refiner shall determine the owners' ratable shares under a consistently applied method that reasonably takes into account the owners' varying interests during the taxable year.

(2) *Cooperative small business refiner denied section 1382 deduction for allocated portion.*—In computing taxable income under section 1382, a cooperative small business refiner must reduce its section 179B deduction for the taxable year by an amount equal to the section 179B deduction allocated under this paragraph (e) to the refiner's cooperative owners for the taxable year.

(3) *Time and manner for making election.*—(i) *Time for making election.*—The section 179B(e) election for a taxable year must be made by the due date (including extensions) for filing the cooperative small business refiner's Federal income tax return for the taxable year.

(ii) *Manner of making election.*—The section 179B(e) election for a taxable year is made by attaching a statement to the cooperative small business refiner's Federal income tax return for the taxable year. The election statement must contain the following information:

(A) The name and identification number of the cooperative small business refiner.

(B) The amount of the section 179B deduction allowable to the cooperative small business refiner for the taxable year (determined before the application of section 179B(e) and this paragraph (e)).

(C) The name and identification number of each cooperative owner to which the cooperative small business refiner is allocating all or some of the section 179B deduction.

(D) The amount of the section 179B deduction that is allocated to each cooperative owner listed in response to paragraph (e)(3)(ii)(C) of this section.

(4) *Irrevocable election.*—A section 179B(e) election for a taxable year, once made, is irrevocable for that taxable year.

(5) *Written notice to owners.*—A cooperative small business refiner that makes a section 179B(e) election for a taxable year must notify each cooperative owner of the amount of the section 179B deduction that is allocated to that cooperative owner. This notification must be provided in a written notice that is mailed by the cooperative small business refiner to its cooperative owner before the due date (including extensions) of the cooperative small business refiner's Federal income tax return for the election year. In addition, the cooperative small business refiner must report the amount of the cooperative owner's section 179B deduction on Form 1099-PATR, "Taxable Distributions Received From Cooperatives," issued to the cooperative owner. If Form 1099-PATR is revised or renumbered, the amount of the cooperative owner's section 179B deduction must be reported on the revised or renumbered form.

(f) *Effective/applicability date.*—(1) *In general.*—This section applies to taxable years ending on or after June 26, 2008.

(2) *Application to taxable years ending before June 26, 2008.*—A small business refiner may apply this section to a taxable year ending before June 26, 2008, provided that the small business refiner applies all provisions in this section, with the modifications described in paragraph (f)(3) of this section, to the taxable year.

(3) *Modifications applicable to taxable years ending before June 26, 2008.*—The following modifications to the rules of this section apply to a small business refiner that applies those rules to a taxable year ending before June 26, 2008:

(i) *Rules relating to section 179B election.*—The section 179B election for a taxable year ending before June 26, 2008 may be made under the rules provided in Notice 2006-47, rather than under the rules set forth in paragraph (d) of this section.

(ii) *Rules relating to section 179B(e) election.*—A section 179B(e) election for a taxable year ending before June 26, 2008 will be treated as satisfying the requirements of paragraph (f) if the cooperative small business refiner has allocated its tax liability in a manner consistent with the election and has used any reasonable method consistent with the principles of section 179B(e) to inform the Internal Revenue Service that an election has been made under section 179B(e) and to inform cooperative owners of the amount of the section 179B deduction they have been allocated.

(4) *Expiration date.*—The applicability of §179B-1T expires on June 24, 2011. [Temporary Reg. §1.179B-1T.]

☐ [T.D. 9404, 6-26-2008.]

[Reg. §1.179C-1]

§1.179C-1. Election to expense certain refineries.—(a) *Scope and definitions.*—(1) *Scope.*—This section provides the rules for determining the deduction allowable under section 179C(a) for the cost of any qualified refinery property. The provisions of this section apply only to a taxpayer that elects to apply section 179C in the manner prescribed under paragraph (d) of this section.

(2) *Definitions.*—For purposes of section 179C and this section, the following definitions apply:

(i) *Applicable environmental laws* are any applicable federal, state, or local environmental laws.

(ii) *Qualified fuels* has the meaning set forth in section 45K(c).

(iii) *Cost* is the unadjusted depreciable basis (as defined in §1.168(b)-1(a)(3), but without regard to the reduction in basis for any portion of the basis the taxpayer properly elects to treat as an expense under section 179C and this section) of the property.

(iv) *Throughput* is a volumetric rate measuring the flow of crude oil, qualified fuels, or, in the case of property placed in service after October 3, 2008, and before January 1, 2014, shale or tar sands, processed over a given period of time, typically referenced on the basis of barrels per calendar day.

(v) *Barrels per calendar day* is the amount of fuels that a facility can process under usual operating conditions, expressed in terms of capacity during a 24-hour period and reduced to account for down time and other limitations.

(vi) *United States* has the same meaning as that term is defined in section 7701(a)(9).

(b) *Qualified refinery property.*—(1) *In general.*—Qualified refinery property is any property that meets the requirements set forth in paragraphs (b)(2) through (b)(7) of this section.

(2) *Description of qualified refinery property.*—(i) *In general.*—Property that comprises any portion of a qualified refinery may be qualified refinery property. For purposes of section 179C and this section, a qualified refinery is any refinery located in the United States that —

(A) In the case of property placed in service after August 8, 2005, and on or before October 3, 2008, is designed to serve the primary purpose of processing liquid fuel from crude oil or qualified fuels; or

(B) In the case of property placed in service after October 3, 2008, and before January 1, 2014, is designed to serve the primary purpose of processing liquid fuel from crude oil, qualified fuels, or directly from shale or tar sands.

(ii) *Nonqualified refinery property.*—Refinery property is not qualified refinery property for purposes of this paragraph (b)(2) if—

(A) The primary purpose of the refinery property is for use as a topping plant, asphalt plant, lube oil facility, crude or product terminal, or blending facility; or

(B) The refinery property is built solely to comply with consent decrees or projects mandated by Federal, State, or local governments.

(3) *Original use.*—(i) *In general.*—For purposes of the deduction allowable under section 179C(a), refinery property will meet the requirements of this paragraph (b)(3) if the original use of the property commences with the taxpayer. Except as provided in paragraph (b)(3)(ii) of this section, original use means the first use to which the property is put, whether or not that use corresponds to the use of the property by the taxpayer. Thus, if a taxpayer incurs capital expenditures to recondition or rebuild property acquired or owned by the taxpayer, only the capital expenditures incurred by the taxpayer to recondition or rebuild the property acquired or owned by the taxpayer satisfy the original use requirement. However, the cost of reconditioned or rebuilt property acquired by a taxpayer does not satisfy the original use requirement. Whether property is reconditioned or rebuilt property is a question of fact. For purposes of this paragraph (b)(3)(i), acquired or self-constructed property that contains used parts will be treated as reconditioned or rebuilt only if the

cost of the used parts is more than 20 percent of the total cost of the property.

(ii) *Sale-leaseback.*—If any new portion of a qualified refinery is originally placed in service by a person after August 8, 2005, and is sold to a taxpayer and leased back to the person by the taxpayer within three months after the date the property was originally placed in service by the person, the taxpayer-lessor is considered the original user of the property.

(4) *Placed-in-service date.*—(i) *In general.*—Refinery property will meet the requirements of this paragraph (b)(4) if the property is placed in service by the taxpayer after August 8, 2005, and before January 1, 2014.

(ii) *Sale-leaseback.*—If a new portion of refinery property is originally placed in service by a person after August 8, 2005, and is sold to a taxpayer and leased back to the person by the taxpayer within three months after the date the property was originally placed in service by the person, the property is treated as originally placed in service by the taxpayer-lessor not earlier than the date on which the property is used by the lessee under the leaseback.

(5) *Production capacity.*—(i) *In general.*—Refinery property is considered qualified refinery property if—

(A) It enables the existing qualified refinery to increase the total volume output, determined without regard to asphalt or lube oil, by at least 5 percent on an average daily basis;

(B) In the case of property placed in service after August 8, 2005, and on or before October 3, 2008, it enables the existing qualified refinery to increase the percentage of total throughput attributable to processing qualified fuels to a rate that is at least 25 percent of total throughput on an average daily basis; or

(C) In the case of property placed in service after October 3, 2008, and before January 1, 2014, it enables the existing qualified refinery to increase the percentage of total throughput attributable to processing qualified fuels, shale, or tar sands to a rate that is at least 25 percent of total throughput on an average daily basis.

(ii) *When production capacity is tested.*—The production capacity requirement of this paragraph (b)(5) is determined as of the date the property is placed in service by the taxpayer. Any reasonable method may be used to determine the appropriate baseline for measuring capacity increases and to demonstrate and substantiate that the capacity of the existing qualified refinery has been sufficiently increased.

(iii) *Multi-stage projects.*—In the case of multi-stage projects, a taxpayer must satisfy the reporting requirements of paragraph (f)(2) of this section, sufficient to establish that the production capacity requirements of this paragraph (b)(5) will be met as a result of the taxpayer's overall plan.

(6) *Applicable environmental laws.*—(i) *In general.*—The environmental compliance requirement applies only with respect to refinery property, or any portion of refinery property, that is placed in service after August 8, 2005. A refinery's failure to meet applicable environmental laws with respect to a portion of the refinery that was in service prior to August 8, 2005 will not disqualify a taxpayer from making the election under section 179C(a) with respect to otherwise qualifying refinery property.

(ii) *Waiver under the Clean Air Act.*—Refinery property must comply with the Clean Air Act, notwithstanding any waiver received by the taxpayer under that Act.

(7) *Construction of property.*—(i) *In general.*—Qualified property will meet the requirements of this paragraph (b)(7) if no written binding contract for the construction of the property was in effect before June 14, 2005, and if—

(A) The construction of the property is subject to a written binding contract entered into before January 1, 2010;

(B) The property is placed in service before January 1, 2010; or

(C) In the case of self-constructed property, the construction of the property began after June 14, 2005, and before January 1, 2010.

(ii) *Definition of binding contract.*—(A) *In general.*—A contract is binding only if it is enforceable under state law against the taxpayer or a predecessor, and does not limit damages to a specified amount (for example, by use of a liquidated damages provision). For this purpose, a contractual provision that limits damages to an amount equal to at least 5 percent of the total contract price will not be treated as limiting damages to a specified amount. In determining whether a contract limits damages, the fact that there may be little or no damages because the contract price does not significantly differ from fair market value will not be taken into account.

(B) *Conditions.*—A contract is binding even if subject to a condition, as long as the condition is not within the control of either party or the predecessor of either party. A contract will continue to be binding if the parties make insubstantial changes in its terms and conditions, or if any term is to be determined by a standard beyond the control of either party. A contract that imposes significant obligations on the taxpayer or a predecessor will be treated as binding, notwithstanding the fact that insubstantial terms remain to be negotiated by the parties to the contract.

(C) *Options.*—An option to either acquire or sell property is not a binding contract.

(D) *Supply agreements.*—A binding contract does not include a supply or similar agreement if the payment amount and design specification of the property to be purchased have not been specified.

(E) *Components.*—A binding contract to acquire one or more components of a larger property will not be treated as a binding contract to acquire the larger property. If a binding contract to acquire a component does not satisfy the requirements of this paragraph (b)(7), the component is not qualified refinery property.

(iii) *Self-constructed property.*—(A) *In general.*—Except as provided in paragraph (b)(7)(iii)(B) of this section, if a taxpayer manufactures, constructs, or produces property for use by the taxpayer in its trade or business (or for the production of income by the taxpayer), the construction of property rules in this paragraph (b)(7) are treated as met for qualified refinery property if the taxpayer begins manufacturing, constructing, or producing the property after June 14, 2005, and before January 1, 2010. Property that is manufactured, constructed, or produced for the taxpayer by another person under a written binding contract (as defined in paragraph (b)(7)(ii) of this section) that is entered into prior to the manufacture, construction, or production of the property for use by the taxpayer in its trade or business (or for the production of income) is considered to be manufactured, constructed, or produced by the taxpayer.

(B) *When construction begins.*—For purposes of this paragraph (b)(7)(iii), construction of property generally begins when physical work of a significant nature begins. Physical work does not include preliminary activities such as planning or designing, securing financing, exploring, or researching. The determination of when physical work of a significant nature begins depends on the facts and circumstances.

(C) *Components of self-constructed property.*—(1) *Acquired components.*—If a binding contract (as defined in paragraph (b)(7)(ii) of this section) to acquire a component of self-constructed property is in effect on or before June 14, 2005, the component does not satisfy the requirements of paragraph (b)(7)(i) of this section, and is not qualified refinery property. However, if construction of the self-constructed property begins after June 14, 2005, the self-constructed property may be qualified refinery property if it meets all other requirements of section 179C and this section (including paragraph (b)(7)(i) of this section), even though the component is not qualified refinery property. If the construction of self-constructed property begins before June 14, 2005, neither the self-constructed property nor any component related to the self-constructed property is qualified refinery property. If the component is acquired before January 1, 2010, but the construction of the self-constructed property begins after December 31, 2009, the component may qualify as qualified refinery property even if the self-constructed property is not qualified refinery property.

(2) *Self-constructed components.*—If the manufacture, construction, or production of a component fails to meet any of the requirements of paragraph (b)(7)(iii) of this section, the component is not qualified refinery property. However, if the manufacture, construction, or production of a component fails to meet any of the requirements provided in paragraph (b)(7)(iii) of this section, but the construction of the self-constructed property begins after June 14, 2005, the self constructed property may qualify as qualified refinery property if it meets all other requirements of section 179C and this section (including paragraph (b)(7)(i) of this section). If the construction of the self-constructed property begins before June 14, 2005, neither the self-constructed property nor any components related to the self-constructed property are qualified refinery property. If the component was self-constructed before January 1, 2010, but the construction of the self-constructed property begins after December 31, 2009, the component may qualify as qualified refinery property, although the self-constructed property is not qualified refinery property.

(c) *Computation of expense deduction for qualified refinery property.*—In general, the allowable deduction under paragraph (d) of this section for qualified refinery property is determined by multiplying by 50 percent the cost of the qualified refinery property paid or incurred by the taxpayer.

(d) *Election.*—(1) *In general.*—A taxpayer may make an election to deduct as an expense 50 percent of the cost of any qualified refinery property. A taxpayer making this election takes the 50 percent deduction for the taxable year in which the qualified refinery property is placed in service.

(2) *Time and manner for making election.*—(i) *Time for making election.*—An election specified in this paragraph (d) generally must be made not later than the due date (including extensions) for filing the original Federal income tax return for the taxable year in which the qualified refinery property is placed in service by the taxpayer.

(ii) *Manner of making election.*—The taxpayer makes an election under section 179C(a) and this paragraph (d) by entering the amount of the deduction at the appropriate place on the taxpayer's timely filed original Federal income tax return for the taxable year in which the qualified refinery property is placed in service, and attaching a report as specified in paragraph (f) of this section to the taxpayer's timely filed original federal income tax return for the taxable year in which the qualified refinery property is placed in service.

(3) *Revocation of election.*—(i) *In general.*—An election made under section 179C(a) and this paragraph (d), and any specification contained in such election, may not be revoked except with the consent of the Commissioner of Internal Revenue.

(ii) *Revocation prior to the revocation deadline.*—A taxpayer is deemed to have requested, and to have been granted, the consent of the Commissioner to revoke an election under section 179C(a) and this paragraph (d) if the taxpayer revokes the election before the revocation deadline. The revocation deadline is 24 months after the due date (including extensions) for filing the taxpayer's Federal income tax return for the taxable year for which the election applies. An election under section 179C(a) and this paragraph (d) is revoked by attaching a statement to an amended return for the taxable year for which the election applies. The statement must specify the name and address of the refinery for which the election applies and the amount deducted on the taxpayer's original Federal income tax return for the taxable year for which the election applies.

(iii) *Revocation after the revocation deadline.*—An election under section 179C(a) and this paragraph (d) may not be revoked after the revocation deadline. The revocation deadline may not be extended under §301.9100-1.

(iv) *Revocation by cooperative taxpayer.*—A taxpayer that has made an election to allocate the section 179C deduction to cooperative owners under section 179C(g) and paragraph (e) of this section may not revoke its election under section 179C(a).

(e) *Election to allocate section 179C deduction to cooperative owners.*—(1) *In general.*—If a cooperative taxpayer makes an election under section 179C(g) and this paragraph (e), the cooperative taxpayer may elect to allocate all, some, or none of the deduction allowable under section 179C(a) for that taxable year to the cooperative owner(s). This allocation is equal to the cooperative owner(s)' ratable share of the total amount allocated, determined on the basis of each cooperative owner's ownership interest in the cooperative taxpayer. For purposes of this section, a cooperative taxpayer is an organization to which part I of subchapter T applies, and in which another organization to which part I of subchapter T applies (cooperative owner) directly holds an ownership interest. No deduction shall be allowed under section 1382 for any amount allocated under this paragraph (e).

(2) *Time and manner for making election.*—(i) *Time for making election.*—A cooperative taxpayer must make the election under section 179C(g) and this paragraph (e) by the due date (including extensions) for filing the cooperative taxpayer's original Federal income tax return for the taxable year to which the cooperative taxpayer's election under section 179C(a) and paragraph (d) of this section applies.

(ii) *Manner of making election.*—An election under this paragraph (e) is made by attaching to the cooperative taxpayer's timely filed Federal income tax return for the taxable year (including extensions) to which the cooperative taxpayer's election under section 179C(a) and paragraph (d) of this section applies a statement providing the following information:

(A) The name and taxpayer identification number of the cooperative taxpayer.

(B) The amount of the deduction allowable to the cooperative taxpayer for the taxable year to which the election under section 179C(a) and paragraph (d) of this section applies.

(C) The name and taxpayer identification number of each cooperative owner to which the cooperative taxpayer is allocating all or some of the deduction allowable.

(D) The amount of the allowable deduction that is allocated to each cooperative owner listed in paragraph (e)(2)(ii)(C) of this section.

(3) *Written notice to owners.*—If any portion of the deduction allowable under section 179C(a) is allocated to a cooperative owner, the cooperative taxpayer must notify the cooperative owner of the amount of the deduction allocated to the cooperative owner in a written notice, and on Form 1099-PATR, "Taxable Distributions Received from Cooperatives." This notice must be provided on or before the due date (including extensions) of the cooperative taxpayer's original federal income tax return for the taxable year for which the cooperative taxpayer's election under section 179C(a) and paragraph (d) of this section applies.

(4) *Irrevocable election.*—A section 179C(g) election, once made, is irrevocable.

(f) *Reporting requirement.*—(1) *In general.*—A taxpayer may not claim a deduction under section 179C(a) for any taxable year unless the taxpayer files a report with the Secretary containing information with respect to the operation of the taxpayer's refineries.

(2) *Information to be included in the report.*—The taxpayer must specify—

(i) The name and address of the refinery;

(ii) Under which production capacity requirement under section 179C(e) and paragraph (b)(5)(i)(A), (B), and (C) of this section the taxpayer's qualified refinery qualifies;

(iii) Whether the refinery is qualified refinery property under section 179C(d) and paragraph (b)(2) of this section, sufficient to establish that the primary purpose of the refinery is to process liquid fuel from crude oil, qualified fuels, or directly from shale or tar sands.

(iv) The total cost basis of the qualified refinery property at issue for the taxpayer's current taxable year; and

(v) The depreciation treatment of the capitalized portion of the qualified refinery property.

(3) *Time and manner for submitting report.*—(i) *Time for submitting report.*—The taxpayer is required to submit the report specified in this paragraph (f) not later than the due date (including extensions) of the taxpayer's Federal income tax return for the taxable year in which the qualified refinery property is placed in service.

(ii) *Manner of submitting report.*—The taxpayer must attach the report specified in this paragraph (f) to the taxpayer's timely filed original Federal income tax return for the taxable year in which the qualified refinery property is placed in service.

(g) *Effective/applicability date.*—This section is applicable for taxable years ending on or after August 22, 2011. For taxable years ending before August 22, 2011, taxpayers may apply the proposed regulations published on July 9, 2008 [Temporary Reg. §1.179C-1T, as it appeared in the April 1, 2011 CFR], or, in the alternative, may apply these final regulations. [Reg. §1.179C-1.]

☐ [*T.D. 9547, 8-22-2011.*]

[Reg. §1.180-1]

§1.180-1. Expenditures by farmers for fertilizer, etc.—(a) *In general.*—A taxpayer engaged in the business of farming may elect, for any taxable year beginning after December 31, 1959, to treat as deductible expenses those expenditures otherwise chargeable to capital account which are paid or incurred by him during the taxable year for the purchase or acquisition of fertilizer, lime, ground limestone, marl, or other materials to enrich, neutralize, or condition land used in farming, and those expenditures otherwise chargeable to capital account paid or incurred for the application of such items and materials to such land. No election is required to be made for those expenditures which are not capital in nature. Section 180, §1.180-2, and this section are not applicable to those expenses which are deductible under section 162 and the regulations thereunder or which are subject to the method described in section 175 and the regulations thereunder.

(b) *Land used in farming.*—For purposes of section 180(a) and of paragraph (a) of this section, the term "land used in farming" means land used (before or simultaneously with the expenditures described in such section and such paragraph) by the taxpayer or his tenant for the production of crops, fruits, or other agricultural products or for the sustenance of livestock. See section 180(b). Expenditures for the initial preparation of land never previously used for farming purposes by the taxpayer or his tenant (although chargeable to capital account) are not subject to the election. The principles stated in §§1.175-3 and 1.175-4 are equally applicable under this section in determining whether the taxpayer is engaged in the business of farming and whether the land is used in farming. [Reg. §1.180-1.]

☐ [*T.D. 6548, 2-21-61.*]

[Reg. §1.180-2]

§1.180-2. Time and manner of making election and revocation.—
(a) *Election.*—The claiming of a deduction on the taxpayer's return for an amount to which section 180 applies for amounts (otherwise chargeable to capital account) expended for fertilizer, lime, etc., shall constitute an election under section 180 and paragraph (a) of §1.180-1. Such election shall be effective only for the taxable year for which the deduction is claimed.

(b) *Revocation.*—Once the election is made for any taxable year such election may not be revoked without the consent of the district director for the district in which the taxpayer's return is required to be filed. Such requests for consent shall be in writing and signed by the taxpayer or his authorized representative and shall set forth—

(1) The name and address of the taxpayer;

(2) The taxable year to which the revocation of the election is to apply;

(3) The amount of expenditures paid or incurred during the taxable year, or portions thereof (where applicable), previously taken as a deduction on the return in respect of which the revocation of the election is to be applicable; and

(4) The reasons for the request to revoke the election. [Reg. §1.180-2.]

☐ [T.D. 6548, 2-21-61.]

[Reg. §1.181-0]

§1.181-0. Table of contents.—This section lists the table of contents for §§1.181-1 through 1.181-6.

☐ [T.D. 9551, 9-29-2011. *Amended by* T.D. 9603, 12-6-2012.]

[Reg. §1.181-1]

§1.181-1. Deduction for qualified film and television production costs.—(a) *Deduction.*—(1) *In general.*—(i) An owner (as defined in paragraph (a)(2) of this section) of any film or television production (production, as defined in §1.181-3(b)) that the owner reasonably expects will be, upon completion, a qualified film or television production (as defined in §1.181-3(a)) may elect to treat production costs paid or incurred by that owner (subject to the limits imposed under paragraph (b) of this section) as an expense that is deductible for the taxable year in which the costs are paid (for an owner who uses the cash receipts and disbursements method of accounting) or incurred (for an owner who uses an accrual method of accounting). The deduction under section 181 is subject to recapture if the owner's expectations are later determined to be inaccurate.

(ii) This section provides rules for determining the owner of a production, the production costs (as defined in paragraph (a)(3) of this section), the maximum amount of aggregate production costs (as defined in paragraph (a)(4) of this section) that may be paid or incurred for a pre-amendment production (as defined in paragraph (a)(5) of this section) for which the owner makes an election under section 181, and the maximum amount of aggregate production costs that may be claimed as a deduction for a post-amendment production (as defined in paragraph (a)(6) of this section) for which the owner makes an election under section 181. Section 1.181-2 provides rules for making the election under section 181. Section 1.181-3 provides definitions and rules concerning qualified film and television productions. Section 1.181-4 provides special rules, including rules for recapture of the deduction. Section 1.181-5 provides examples of the application of §§1.181-1 through 1.181-4, while §1.181-6 provides the effective date of §§1.181-1 through 1.181-5.

(2) *Owner.*—(i) For purposes of this section and §§1.181-2 through 1.181-6, an owner of a production is any person that is required under section 263A to capitalize the costs of producing the production into the cost basis of the production, or that would be required to do so if section 263A applied to that person.

(ii) Further, a person that acquires a finished or partially-finished production is treated as an owner of that production for purposes of this section and §§1.181-2 through 1.181-6, but only if the production is acquired prior to its initial release or broadcast (as defined in paragraph (a)(7) of this section). Moreover, a person that acquires only a limited license or right to exploit a production, or receives an interest or profit participation in a production, as compensation for services, is not an owner of the production for purposes of this section and §§1.181-2 through 1.181-6.

(3) *Production costs.*—(i) For purposes of this section and §§1.181-2 through 1.181-6, the term *production costs* means all costs that are paid or incurred by an owner in producing a production that are required, absent the provisions of section 181, to be capitalized under section 263A, or that would be required to be capitalized if section 263A applied to the owner, and, if applicable, all costs that are paid or incurred by an owner in acquiring a production prior to its initial release or broadcast. Production costs include, but are not limited to, participations and residuals paid or incurred, compensation paid or incurred for services, compensation paid or incurred for property rights, non-compensation costs, and costs paid or incurred in connection with obtaining financing for the production (for example, premiums paid or incurred to obtain a completion bond for the production).

(ii) Production costs do not include costs paid or incurred to distribute or exploit a production (including advertising and print costs).

(iii) Production costs do not include the costs to prepare a new release or new broadcast of an existing production after the initial release or broadcast of the production (for example, the preparation of a DVD release of a theatrically-released film, or the preparation of an edited version of a theatrically-released film for television broadcast). Costs paid or incurred to prepare a new release or a new broadcast of a production after its initial release or broadcast, therefore, are not taken into account for purposes of paragraph (b)(1) of this section, and may not be deducted under this paragraph (a).

(iv) If a pre-amendment production is acquired from any person prior to its initial release or broadcast, the acquiring person must use as its initial aggregate costs the greater of —

(A) The cost of acquisition; or

(B) The seller's aggregate production costs.

(v) Production costs do not include costs that the owner has deducted or begun to amortize prior to the taxable year the owner makes an election under §1.181-2 for the production (for example, costs described in §1.181-2(a)(2)). These costs, however, are included in aggregate production costs to the extent they would have been treated as production costs by the owner notwithstanding this paragraph (a)(3)(v).

(4) *Aggregate production costs.*—The term *aggregate production costs* means all production costs described in paragraph (a)(3) of this section paid or incurred by any person, whether paid or incurred directly by an owner or indirectly on behalf of an owner.

(5) *Pre-amendment production.*—The term *pre-amendment production* means a qualified film or television production commencing after October 22, 2004, and before January 1, 2008.

(6) *Post-amendment production.*—The term *post-amendment production* means a qualified film or television production commencing on or after January 1, 2008.

(7) *Initial release or broadcast.*—Solely for purposes of this section and §§1.181-2 through 1.181-6, the term *initial release or broadcast* means the first commercial exhibition or broadcast of a production to an audience. However, the term "initial release or broadcast" does not include limited exhibition prior to commercial exhibition to general audiences if the limited exhibition is primarily for purposes of publicity, marketing to potential purchasers or distributors, determining the need for further production activity, or raising funds for the completion of production. For example, the term initial release or broadcast does not include exhibition to a test audience to determine the need for further production activity, or exhibition at a film festival for promotional purposes, if the exhibition precedes commercial exhibition to general audiences.

(8) *Special rule.*—The provisions of this paragraph (a) apply notwithstanding the treatment of participations and residuals permitted under the income forecast method in section 167(g)(7)(D).

(b) *Limit on amount of aggregate production costs and amount of deduction.*—(1) *In general.*—(i) *Pre-amendment production.*—Except as provided under paragraph (b)(2) of this section, no deduction is allowed under section 181 for any pre-amendment production, the aggregate production costs of which exceed $15,000,000. See also paragraph (a)(3)(iv) of this section. For a pre-amendment production for which the aggregate production costs do not exceed $15,000,000 (or, if applicable under paragraph (b)(2) of this section, $20,000,000), an owner may deduct under section 181 all of the production costs paid or incurred by that owner.

(ii) *Post-amendment production.*—Section 181 permits a deduction for the first $15,000,000 (or, if applicable under paragraph (b)(2) of this section, $20,000,000) of the aggregate production costs of any post-amendment production.

(iii) *Special rules.*—The owner's deduction under section 181 is limited to the owner's acquisition costs of the production plus any further production costs paid or incurred by the owner. The deduction under section 181 is not available for any portion of the acquisition costs, and any subsequent production costs, of a production with an initial release or broadcast that is prior to the date of acquisition.

(2) *Higher limit for productions in certain areas.*—(i) *In general.*—This section is applied by substituting $20,000,000 for $15,000,000 in paragraph (b)(1) of this section for any production the aggregate production costs of which are significantly paid or incurred in an area eligible for designation as—

(A) A low income community under section 45D; or

(B) A distressed county or isolated area of distress by the Delta Regional Authority established under 7 U.S.C section 2009aa-1.

(ii) *Significantly paid or incurred for live action productions.*—The aggregate production costs of a live action production are significantly paid or incurred within one or more areas specified in paragraph (b)(2)(i) of this section if—

(A) At least 20 percent of the aggregate production costs paid or incurred in connection with first-unit principal photography for the production are paid or incurred in connection with first-unit principal photography that takes place in such areas; or

(B) At least 50 percent of the total number of days of first-unit principal photography for the production consists of days during which first-unit principal photography takes place in such areas.

(iii) *Significantly paid or incurred for animated productions.*—For purposes of an animated production, the aggregate production costs of the production are significantly paid or incurred within one or more areas specified in paragraph (b)(2)(i) of this section if—

(A) At least 20 percent of the aggregate production costs paid or incurred in connection with keyframe animation, in-between animation, animation photography, and the recording of voice acting performances for the production are paid or incurred in connection with such activities that take place in such areas; or

(B) At least 50 percent of the total number of days of keyframe animation, inbetween animation, animation photography, and the recording of voice acting performances for the production consists of days during which such activities take place in such areas.

(iv) *Significantly paid or incurred for productions incorporating both live action and animation.*—For purposes of a production incorporating both live action and animation, the aggregate production costs of the production are significantly paid or incurred within one or more areas specified in paragraph (b)(2)(i) of this section if—

(A) At least 20 percent of the aggregate production costs paid or incurred in connection with first-unit principal photography, keyframe animation, in-between animation, animation photography, and the recording of voice acting performances for the production are paid or incurred in connection with such activities that take place in such areas; or

(B) At least 50 percent of the total number of days of first-unit principal photography, keyframe animation, in-between animation, animation photography, and the recording of voice acting performances for the production consists of days during which such activities take place in such areas.

(v) *Establishing qualification.*—An owner intending to utilize the higher aggregate production costs limit under this paragraph (b)(2) must establish qualification under this paragraph (b)(2).

(vi) *Allocation.*—Solely for purposes of determining whether a production qualifies for the higher production cost limit (for pre-amendment productions) or deduction limit (for post-amendment productions) provided under this paragraph (b)(2), compensation to actors (as defined in §1.181-3(f)(1)), directors, producers, and other relevant production personnel (as defined in §1.181-3 (f)(2)) is allocated entirely to first-unit principal photography.

(c) *Effect on depreciation or amortization of a qualified film or television production.*—(1) *Pre-amendment production.*—Except as provided in §§1.181-1(a)(3)(v) and 1.181-2(a)(2), an owner that elects to deduct production costs under section 181 for a preamendment production may not deduct production costs for that production under any provision of the Internal Revenue Code other than section 181 unless the recapture requirements of §1.181-4(a) apply to the production.

(2) *Post-amendment production.*—Amounts not allowable as a deduction under section 181 for a post-amendment production may be deducted under any other applicable provision of the Code. [Reg. §1.181-1.]

☐ [T.D. 9551, 9-29-2011. *Amended by T.D.* 9552, 10-18-2011 *and T.D.* 9603, 12-6-2012.]

[Reg. §1.181-2]

§1.181-2. Election to deduct production costs.—(a) *Election.*—(1) *In general.*—Except as provided in paragraph (a)(2) of this section, an owner may make an election under section 181 to deduct production costs of a production only if that owner has not deducted in a previous taxable year any production costs for that production under any provision of the Internal Revenue Code (Code) other than section 181.

(2) *Exception.*—An owner may make an election under section 181 despite prior deductions under any other provision of the Code for amortization of the costs of acquiring or developing screenplays, scripts, story outlines, motion picture production rights to books and plays, and other similar properties for purposes of potential future development or production of a production, if such costs were paid or incurred before the first taxable year for which an election may be

made under §1.181-2(b) and are included in aggregate production costs.

(b) *Time of making election.*—(1) *In general.*—The election to deduct production costs for a production under section 181 must be made by the due date (including any extension) for filing the owner's Federal income tax return for the first taxable year in which:

(i) Any aggregate production costs have been paid or incurred;

(ii) The owner reasonably expects (based on all of the facts and circumstances) that the production will be set for production and will, upon completion, be a qualified film or television production; and

(iii) For any pre-amendment production, the owner reasonably expects (based on all of the facts and circumstances) that the aggregate production costs paid or incurred for the pre-amendment production will, at no time, exceed the applicable aggregate production costs limit set forth under §1.181-1(b)(1)(i) or (b)(2).

(2) *Special rule.*—If paragraph (b)(1) of this section is not satisfied until a taxable year subsequent to the taxable year in which any aggregate production costs were first paid or incurred, the owner must make the election for the taxable year in which paragraph (b)(1) of this section is first satisfied, and any production costs paid or incurred prior to the taxable year in which the owner makes the election and not deducted in a prior taxable year are treated as production costs (except costs described in §1.181-2(a)(2)) that are deductible under §1.181-1(a)(1)(i) for the taxable year paragraph (b)(1) of this section is first satisfied and the election is made.

(3) *Six-month extension.*—See §301.9100-2 for a six-month extension of time to make the election in certain circumstances.

(c) *Manner of making election.*—(1) *In general.*—An owner must make the election under section 181 separately for each production. For a production owned by an entity, the election must be made by the entity. For example, if the production is owned by a partnership or S corporation, the partnership or S corporation must make the election.

(2) *Information required.*—(i) *Initial election.*—For each production to which the election applies, the owner must attach a statement to the owner's Federal income tax return for the taxable year of the election stating that the owner is making an election under section 181 and providing—

(A) The name (or other unique identifying designation) of the production;

(B) The date aggregate production costs were first paid or incurred for the production;

(C) The amount of aggregate production costs paid or incurred for the production during the taxable year (including costs described in §§1.181-1(a)(3)(v) and 1.181-2(b)(2));

(D) The amount of qualified compensation (as defined in §1.181-3(d)) paid or incurred for the production during the taxable year (including costs described in §1.181-2(b)(2));

(E) The amount of compensation (as defined in §1.181-3(c)) paid or incurred for the production during the taxable year (including costs described in §1.181-2(b)(2));

(F) If the owner expects that the aggregate production costs of the production will be significantly paid or incurred in (or, if applicable, if a significant portion of the total number of days of first-unit principal photography will occur in) one or more of the areas specified in §1.181-1(b)(2)(i), the identity of the area or areas, the amount of aggregate production costs paid or incurred (or the number of days of first-unit principal photography engaged in) for the applicable activities described in §1.181-1(b)(2)(ii), (b)(2)(iii), or (b)(2)(iv), as applicable, that took place within such areas (including costs described in §§ 1.181-1(a)(3)(v) and 1.181-2(b)(2)), and the aggregate production costs paid or incurred (or the total number of days of first-unit principal photography engaged in) for such activities (whether or not they took place in such areas), for the taxable year (including costs described in §§1.181-1(a)(3)(v) and 1.181-2(b)(2));

(G) A declaration that the owner reasonably expects (based on all of the facts and circumstances at the time the election is made) both that the production will be set for production (or has been set for production) and will be a qualified film or television production; and

(H) For any pre-amendment production, a declaration that *the owner reasonably expects (based on all of the facts and circum-* stances at the time the election is made) that the aggregate production costs paid or incurred for the pre-amendment production will not, at any time, exceed the applicable aggregate production costs limit set forth under §1.181-1(b)(1)(i) or (b)(2).

(ii) *Subsequent taxable years.*—If the owner pays or incurs additional production costs in any taxable year subsequent to the taxable year for which production costs are first deducted under section 181, the owner must attach a statement to its Federal income tax return for that subsequent taxable year providing—

(A) The name (or other unique identifying designation) of the production that was used in the initial election, and any revised name (or unique identifying designation) subsequently used for the production;

(B) The date the aggregate production costs were first paid or incurred for the production;

(C) The amount of aggregate production costs paid or incurred for the production during the current taxable year;

(D) The amount of qualified compensation paid or incurred for the production during the current taxable year;

(E) The amount of compensation paid or incurred for the production during the current taxable year, and the aggregate amount of compensation paid or incurred for the production in all prior taxable years;

(F) If the owner expects that the aggregate production costs of the production will be significantly paid or incurred in (or, if applicable, if a significant portion of the total number of days of first-unit principal photography will occur in) one or more of the areas specified in §1.181-1(b)(2)(i), the identity of the area or areas, the amount of aggregate production costs paid or incurred (or the number of days of first-unit principal photography engaged in) for the applicable activities described in §1.181-1(b)(2)(ii), (b)(2)(iii), or (b)(2)(iv), as applicable, that took place within such areas, and the aggregate production costs paid or incurred (or the number of days of first-unit principal photography engaged in) for such activities (whether or not they took place in such areas), for the current taxable year;

(G) A declaration that the owner continues to reasonably expect (based on all of the facts and circumstances at the end of the current taxable year) both that the production will be set for production (or has been set for production) and will be a qualified film or television production; and

(H) For any pre-amendment production, a declaration that the owner continues to reasonably expect (based on all of the facts and circumstances at the end of the current taxable year) that the aggregate production costs paid or incurred for the preamendment production will not, at any time, exceed the applicable aggregate production costs limit set forth under §1.181-1(b)(1)(i) or (b)(2).

(3) *Deductions by more than one person.*—If more than one person will claim deductions under section 181 with respect to the production for the taxable year, each person claiming the deduction (but not the members of an entity who are issued a Schedule K-1 by the entity with respect to their interest in the production) must provide a list of the names and taxpayer identification numbers of all such persons, the dollar amount that each such person will deduct under section 181, and the information required by paragraph (c)(2) of this section for all such persons. Notwithstanding the preceding sentence, whether or not multiple persons form a partnership with respect to the production will be determined in accordance with §301.7701-3 of this chapter.

(d) *Revocation of election.*—(1) *In general.*—An owner may revoke an election made under this section only with the consent of the Commissioner. Except as provided in paragraph (d)(2) of this section, an owner seeking consent to revoke an election made under this section must submit a letter ruling request, other than a Form 3115, "Application for Change in Accounting Method," under the appropriate revenue procedure. See, for example, Rev. Proc. 2011-1, 2011-1 CB 1 (updated annually) (see §601.601(d)(2)(ii)(b) of this chapter).

(2) *Consent granted.*—The Commissioner grants consent to an owner to revoke an election under this section for a particular production if the owner—

(i) Complies with the recapture provisions of §1.181-4(a)(3) on a timely filed (including any extension) original Federal income tax return for the taxable year of the revocation; and

(ii) Attaches a statement to that Federal income tax return that includes the name of the production that was in the owner's original election statement, and any revised name (or other unique identifying designation) of the production, and a statement that the owner revokes the election under section 181 for that production, pursuant to §1.181-2(d)(2). [Reg. §1.181-2.]

☐ [*T.D.* 9551, 9-29-2011.]

[Reg. §1.181-3]

§1.181-3. Qualified film or television production.—(a) *In general.*—The term *qualified film or television production* means any production (as defined in paragraph (b) of this section) for which not less than 75 percent of the aggregate amount of compensation (as defined in paragraph (c) of this section) paid or incurred for the production is qualified compensation (as defined in paragraph (d) of this section).

(b) *Production.*—(1) *In general.*—Except as provided in paragraph (b)(3) of this section, for purposes of this section and §§ 1.181-1, 1.181-2, 1.181-4, 1.181-5, and 1.181-6, the term *production* means any motion picture film or video tape (including digital video) production the production costs of which are subject to capitalization under section 263A, or that would be subject to capitalization if section 263A applied to the owner of the production. If, prior to its initial release or broadcast, a person acquires a completed motion picture film or video tape (including digital video) that the seller was entitled to treat as a production under this paragraph (b)(1), then the new owner may treat the acquired asset as a production within the meaning of this paragraph (b)(1).

(2) *Special rules for television productions.*—Each episode of a television series is a separate production to which the rules, limits, and election requirements of this section and §§ 1.181-1, 1.181-2, 1.181-4, 1.181-5, and 1.181-6 apply. An owner may elect to deduct production costs under section 181 only for the first 44 episodes of a television series (including pilot episodes). A television series may include more than one season of programming.

(3) *Exception for certain sexually explicit productions.*—A production does not include property for which records are required to be maintained under 18 U.S.C. 2257.

(c) *Compensation.*—The term *compensation* means, for purposes of this section and § 1.181-2(c)(2), all amounts paid or incurred either directly by the owner or indirectly on the owner's behalf for services performed by actors (as defined in paragraph (f)(1) of this section), directors, producers, and other production personnel (as defined in paragraph (f)(2) of this section) for the production. Examples of indirect payments paid or incurred on the owner's behalf are payments by a partner on behalf of an owner that is a partnership, payments by a shareholder on behalf of an owner that is a corporation, and payments by a contract producer on behalf of the owner. Payments for services are all elements of compensation as provided for in §§ 1.263A-1(e)(2)(i)(B) and (e)(3)(ii)(D). Compensation is not limited to wages reported on Form W-2, "Wage and Tax Statement," and includes compensation paid or incurred to independent contractors. However, solely for purposes of paragraph (a) of this section, the term "compensation" does not include participations and residuals (as defined in section 167(g)(7)(B)). See § 1.181-1(a)(3) for additional rules concerning participations and residuals.

(d) *Qualified compensation.*—The term *qualified compensation* means, for purposes of this section and § 1.181-2(c)(2), all compensation (as defined in paragraph (c) of this section) paid or incurred for services performed in the United States (as defined in paragraph (f)(3) of this section) by actors, directors, producers, and other production personnel for the production. A service is performed in the United States for purposes of this paragraph (d) if the principal photography to which the compensated service relates occurs within the United States and the person performing the service is physically present in the United States. For purposes of an animated film or animated television production, the location where production activities such as keyframe animation, in-between animation, animation photography, and the recording of voice acting performances are performed is considered in lieu of the location of principal photography. For purposes of a production incorporating both live action and animation, the location where production activities such as keyframe animation, inbetween animation, animation photography, and the recording of voice acting performances for the production is considered in addition to the location of principal photography.

(e) *Special rule for acquired productions.*—A person who acquires a production from a prior owner must take into account all compensation paid or incurred by or on behalf of the seller and any previous owners in determining if the production is a qualified film or television production as defined in paragraph (a) of this section. Any owner that elects to deduct as production costs the costs of acquiring a production and any subsequent production costs must obtain from the seller detailed records concerning the compensation paid or incurred for the production and, for a pre-amendment production, concerning aggregate production costs, in order to demonstrate the eligibility of the production under section 181.

(f) *Other definitions.*—The following definitions apply for purposes of this section and §§ 1.181-1, 1.181-2, 1.181-4, 1.181-5, and 1.181-6:

(1) *Actors.*—The term *actors* means players, newscasters, or any other persons who are compensated for their performance or appearance in a production.

(2) *Production personnel.*—The term *production personnel* means persons who are compensated for providing services directly related to the production, such as writers, choreographers, composers, casting agents, camera operators, set designers, lighting technicians, and make-up artists.

(3) *United States.*—The term *United States* means the 50 states, the District of Columbia, the territorial waters of the continental United States, the airspace or space over the continental United States and its territorial waters, and the seabed and subsoil of those submarine areas that are adjacent to the territorial waters of the continental United States and over which the United States has exclusive rights, in accordance with international law, for the exploration and exploitation of natural resources. The term "United States" does not include possessions and territories of the United States (or the airspace or space over these areas). [Reg. § 1.181-3.]

□ [T.D. 9551, 9-29-2011.]

[Reg. § 1.181-4]

§ 1.181-4. Special rules.—(a) *Recapture.*—(1) *Applicability.*—(i) *In general.*—The requirements of this paragraph (a) apply notwithstanding whether an owner has satisfied the revocation requirements of § 1.181-2(d). An owner that claimed a deduction under section 181 for a production in any taxable year in an amount in excess of the amount that would be allowable as a deduction for that year in the absence of section 181 must recapture the excess amount as provided for in paragraph (a)(3) of this section for the production in the first taxable year for which—

(A) For any pre-amendment production, the aggregate production costs of the production exceed the applicable aggregate production costs limit under § 1.181-1(b)(1)(i) or (b)(2);

(B) For any pre-amendment production, the owner no longer reasonably expects (based on all of the facts and circumstances at the end of the current taxable year) that the aggregate production costs of the production will not, at any time, exceed the applicable aggregate production costs limit set forth under § 1.181-1(b)(1)(i) or (b)(2);

(C) The owner no longer reasonably expects (based on all of the facts and circumstances at the end of the current taxable year) either that the production will be set for production or that the production will be a qualified film or television production; or

(D) The owner revokes the election pursuant to § 1.181-2(d).

(ii) *Special rule.*—An owner that claimed a deduction under section 181 and disposes of the production prior to its initial release or broadcast must recapture the entire amount specified under paragraph (a)(3) of this section in the year the owner disposes of the production before computing gain or loss from the disposition.

(2) *Principal photography not commencing prior to the date of expiration of section 181.*—If an owner claims a deduction under section 181 for a production for which principal photography does not commence prior to the date of expiration of section 181, the owner must recapture deductions as provided for in paragraph (a)(3) of this section in the owner's taxable year that includes the date of expiration of section 181.

(3) *Amount of recapture.*—An owner subject to the recapture requirements under this section must, for the taxable year in which recapture is required, include in the owner's gross income as ordinary income and add to the owner's adjusted basis in the property—

(i) For a production that is placed in service in a taxable year prior to the taxable year for which recapture is required, the difference between the aggregate amount the owner claimed as a deduction under section 181 for the production for all such prior taxable years and the aggregate depreciation deductions that would have been allowable for the production for such prior taxable years (or that the owner could have elected to deduct in the taxable year that the production was placed in service) for the production under the owner's method of accounting; or

(ii) For a production that has not been placed in service, the aggregate amount claimed as a deduction under section 181 for the production for all such prior taxable years.

(b) *Recapture under section 1245.*—For purposes of recapture under section 1245, any deduction allowed under section 181 is treated as a deduction allowable for amortization. [Reg. § 1.181-4.]

□ [T.D. 9551, 9-29-2011.]

[Reg. § 1.181-5]

§ 1.181-5. Examples.—The following examples illustrate the application of §§ 1.181-1 through 1.181-4:

Example 1. X, a corporation that uses an accrual method of accounting and files Federal income tax returns on a calendar-year basis, is a producer of films. X is the owner (within the meaning of

§ 1.181-1(a)(2)) of film ABC. X incurs production costs in year 1, but does not commence principal photography for film ABC until year 2. In year 1, X reasonably expects, based on all of the facts and circumstances, that film ABC will be set for production and will be a qualified film or television production. Provided that X satisfies all other requirements of § § 1.181-1 through 1.181-4 and § 1.181-6, X may deduct in year 1 the production costs for film ABC that X incurred in year 1.

Example 2. The facts are the same as in *Example 1.* In year 2, X begins, but does not complete, principal photography for film ABC. Most of the scenes that X films in year 2 are shot outside the United States and, as of December 31, year 2, less than 75 percent of the total compensation paid for film ABC is qualified compensation. Nevertheless, X still reasonably expects, based on all of the facts and circumstances, that film ABC will be a qualified film or television production. Provided that X satisfies all other requirements of § § 1.181-1 through 1.181-4 and § 1.181-6, X may deduct in year 2 the production costs for film ABC that X incurred in year 2.

Example 3. The facts are the same as in *Example 2.* In year 3, X continues, but does not complete, production of film ABC. Due to changes in the expected production costs of film ABC, X no longer expects film ABC to qualify under section 181. X files a statement with its return for year 3 identifying the film and stating that X revokes its election under section 181. X includes in income in year 3 the deductions claimed in year 1 and in year 2 as provided for in § 1.181-4(a)(3). X has successfully revoked its election pursuant to § 1.181-2(d). [Reg. § 1.181-5.]

☐ [*T.D. 9551, 9-29-2011.*]

[Reg. § 1.181-6]

§ 1.181-6. Effective/applicability date.—(a) *In general.*—Except as otherwise provided in this section, § § 1.181-1 through 1.181-5 apply to productions the first day of principal photography for which occurs on or after September 29, 2011. Paragraphs 1.181-1(a)(1)(ii), (a)(6), (b)(1)(ii), (b)(2)(vi), and (c)(2) of § 1.181-1 apply to productions to which section 181 is applicable and for which the first day of principal photography or in-between animation occurs on or after December 7, 2012.

(b) *Pre-effective date productions.*—For any taxable year for which the period of limitation on refund or credit under section 6511 has not expired, the owner may apply § § 1.181-1 through 1.181-5 to any production to which section 181 applies and for which the first day of principal photography (or in-between animation) occurred before December 7, 2012, provided the owner applies all relevant provisions of § § 1.181-1 through 1.181-5 to the production. [Reg. § 1.181-6.]

☐ [*T.D. 9551, 9-29-2011. Amended by T.D. 9603, 12-6-2012.*]

[Reg. § 1.182-1]

§ 1.182-1. Expenditures by farmers for clearing land; in general.—Under section 182, a taxpayer engaged in the business of farming may elect, in the manner provided in § 1.182-6, to deduct certain expenditures paid or incurred by him in any taxable year beginning after December 31, 1962, in the clearing of land. The expenditures to which the election applies are all expenditures paid or incurred during the taxable year in clearing land for the purpose of making the "land suitable for use in farming" (as defined in § 1.182-4) which are not otherwise deductible (exclusive of expenditures for or in connection with depreciable items referred to in paragraph (b)(1) of § 1.182-3), but only if such expenditures are made in furtherance of the taxpayer's business of farming. The term "expenditures" to which the election applies also includes a reasonable allowance for depreciation (not otherwise allowable) on equipment used in the clearing of land provided such equipment, if used in the carrying on of a trade or business, would be subject to the allowance for depreciation under section 167. (See paragraph (c) of § 1.182-3.) (See section 175 and the regulations thereunder for deductibility of certain expenditures for treatment or moving of earth by a farmer where the land already qualifies as land used in farming as defined in § 1.175.4.) The amount deductible for any taxable year is limited to the lesser of $5,000 or 25 percent of the taxable income derived from farming (as defined in paragraph (a)(2) of § 1.182-5) during the taxable year. Expenditures paid or incurred in a taxable year in excess of the amount deductible under section 182 for such taxable year shall be treated as capital expenditures and shall constitute an adjustment to the basis of the land under section 1016(a). [Reg. § 1.182-1.]

☐ [*T.D. 6794, 1-25-65.*]

[Reg. § 1.182-2]

§ 1.182-2. Definition of "the business of farming".—Under section 182, the election to deduct expenditures incurred in the clearing of land is applicable only to a taxpayer who is engaged in "the

business of farming" during the taxable year. A taxpayer is engaged in the business of farming if he cultivates, operates, or manages a farm for gain or profit, either as owner or tenant. For purposes of section 182, a taxpayer who receives a rental (either in cash or in kind) which is based upon farm production is engaged in the business of farming. However, a taxpayer who receives a fixed rental (without reference to production) is engaged in the business of farming only if he participates to a material extent in the operation or management of the farm. A taxpayer engaged in forestry or the growing of timber is not thereby engaged in the business of farming. A person cultivating or operating a farm for recreation or pleasure rather than for profit is not engaged in the business of farming. For purposes of section 182 and this section, the term "farm" is used in its ordinary, accepted sense and includes stock, dairy, poultry, fish, fruit, and truck farms, and also plantations, ranches, ranges, and orchards. A fish farm is an area where fish are grown or raised, as opposed to merely caught or harvested; that is, an area where they are artificially fed, protected, cared for, etc. A taxpayer is engaged in "the business of farming" if he is a member of a partnership engaged in the business of farming. See § 1.702-1. [Reg. § 1.182-2.]

☐ [*T.D. 6794, 1-25-65.*]

[Reg. § 1.182-3]

§ 1.182-3. Definition, exceptions, etc., relating to deductible expenditures.—(a) *"Clearing of land".*—(1) For purposes of section 182, the term "clearing of land" includes (but is not limited to)—

(i) The removal of rocks, stones, trees, stumps, brush or other natural impediments to the use of the land in farming through blasting, cutting, burning, bulldozing, plowing, or in any other way;

(ii) The treatment or moving of earth, including the construction, repair or removal of nondepreciable earthen structures, such as dikes or levies, if the purpose of such treatment or moving of earth is to protect, level, contour, terrace, or condition the land so as to permit its use as farming land; and

(iii) The diversion of streams and watercourses, including the construction of nondepreciable drainage facilities, provided that the purpose is to remove or divert water from the land so as to make it available for use in farming.

(2) The following are examples of land clearing activities:

(i) The cutting of trees, the blasting of the resulting stumps, and the burning of the residual undergrowth;

(ii) The leveling of land so as to permit irrigation or planting;

(iii) The removal of salt or other minerals which might inhibit cultivation of the soil;

(iv) The draining and filling in of a swamp or marsh; and

(v) The diversion of a stream from one watercourse to another.

(b) *Expenditures not allowed as a deduction under section 182.*—(1) Section 182 applies only to expenditures for nondepreciable items. Accordingly, a taxpayer may not deduct expenditures for the purchase, construction, installation, or improvement of structures, appliances, or facilities which are of a character which is subject to the allowance for depreciation under section 167 and the regulations thereunder. Expenditures in respect of such depreciable property include those for materials, supplies, wages, fuel, freight, and the moving of earth, paid or incurred with respect to tanks, reservoirs, pipes, conduits, canals, dams, wells, or pumps constructed of masonry, concrete, tile, metal, wood, or other nonearthen material.

(2) Expenditures which are deductible without regard to section 182 are not deductible under section 182. Thus, such expenditures are deductible without being subject to the limitations imposed by section 182(b) and § 1.182-5. For example, section 182 does not apply to the ordinary and necessary expenses incurred in the business of farming which are deductible under section 162 even though they might otherwise be considered to be clearing of land expenditures. Section 182 also does not apply to interest (deductible under section 163) nor to taxes (deductible under section 164). Similarly, section 182 does not apply to any expenditures (whether or not currently deductible) paid or incurred for the purpose of soil or water conservation in respect of land used in farming, or for the prevention of erosion of land used in farming, within the meaning of section 175 and the regulations thereunder, nor to expenditures deductible under section 180 and the regulations thereunder relating to expenditures for fertilizer, etc.

(c) *Depreciation.*—In addition to expenditures for the activities described in paragraph (a) of this section, there also shall be treated as an expenditure to which section 182 applies a reasonable allowance for depreciation not otherwise deductible on property of the taxpayer which is used in the clearing of land for the purpose of making such land suitable for use in farming, provided the property is property which, if used in a trade or business, would be subject to the allowance for depreciation under section 167. Depreciation allowable as a deduction under section 182 is limited to the portion of depreciation which is attributable to the use of the property in the clearing of land. The depreciation shall be computed in accordance with section 167 and the regulations thereunder. To the extent an amount representing a reasonable allowance for depreciation with respect to property used in clearing land is treated as an expenditure to which section 182 applies, such depreciation shall, for purposes of chapter 1 of the Code, be treated as an amount allowed under section 167 for depreciation. Thus, if a deduction is allowed for depreciation under section 182 in respect of property used in clearing land, proper adjustment to the basis of the property so used shall be made under section 1016(a). [Reg. § 1.182-3.]

☐ [T.D. 6794, 1-25-65.]

[Reg. § 1.182-4]

§ 1.182-4. Definition of "land suitable for use in farming", etc.— For purposes of section 182, the term "land suitable for use in farming" means land which, as a result of the land clearing activities described in paragraph (a) of § 1.182-3, could be used by the taxpayer or his tenant for the production of crops, fruits, or other agricultural products, including fish, or for the sustenance of livestock. The term "livestock" includes cattle, hogs, horses, mules, donkeys, sheep, goats, captive fur-bearing animals, chickens, turkeys, pigeons, and other poultry. Land used for the sustenance of livestock includes land used for grazing such livestock. Expenditures are considered to be for the purpose of making land suitable for use in farming by the taxpayer or his tenant only if made to prepare the land which is cleared for use by the taxpayer or his tenant in farming. Thus, if the taxpayer pays or incurs expenditures to clear land for the purpose of sale (whether or not for use in farming by the purchaser) or to be held by the taxpayer or his tenant other than for use in farming, section 182 does not apply to such expenditures. Whether the land is cleared for the purpose of making it suitable for use in farming by the taxpayer or his tenant, is a question of fact which must be resolved on the basis of all the relevant facts and circumstances. For purposes of section 182, it is not necessary that the land cleared actually be used in farming following the clearing activities. However, the fact that following the clearing operation, the land is used by the taxpayer or his tenant in the business of farming will, in most cases, constitute evidence that the purpose of the clearing was to make land suitable for use in farming by the taxpayer or his tenant. On the other hand, if the land cleared is sold or converted to nonfarming use soon after the taxpayer has completed his clearing activities, there will be a presumption that the expenditures were not made for the purpose of making the land suitable for use in farming by the taxpayer or his tenant. Other factors which will be considered in determining the taxpayer's purpose for clearing the land are, for example, the acreage, location, and character of the land cleared, the

nature of the taxpayer's farming operation, and the use to which adjoining or nearby land is put. [Reg. § 1.182-4.]

☐ [T.D. 6794, 1-25-65.]

[Reg. § 1.182-5]

§ 1.182-5. Limitation.—(a) *Limitation.—*(1) *General rule.—*The amount of land clearing expenditures which the taxpayer may deduct under section 182 in any one taxable year is limited to the lesser of $5,000 or 25 percent of his "taxable income derived from farming". Expenditures in excess of the applicable limitation are to be charged to the capital account and constitute additions to the taxpayer's basis in the land.

(2) *Definition of "taxable income derived from farming".—*For purposes of section 182, the term "taxable income derived from farming" means the gross income derived from the business of farming reduced by the deductions attributable to such gross income. Gross income derived from the business of farming is the gross income of the taxpayer derived from the production of crops, fruits, or other agricultural products, including fish, or from livestock (including livestock held for draft, breeding or dairy purposes). It does not include gains from sales of assets such as farm machinery or gains from the disposition of land. The deductions attributable to the business of farming are all the deductions allowed by chapter 1 of the Code (other than the deduction allowed by section 182) for expenditures or charges (including depreciation and amortization) paid or incurred in connection with the production or raising of crops, fruits, or other agricultural products, including fish, or livestock. However, the deduction under section 1202 (relating to the capital gains deduction) attributable to gain on the sale or other disposition of assets (other than draft, breeding, or dairy stock), and the net operating loss deduction (computed under section 172) shall not be taken into account in computing "taxable income derived from farming." Similarly, deductible losses on the sale, disposition, destruction, condemnation, or abandonment of assets (other than draft, breeding, or dairy stock) shall not be considered as deductions attributable to the business of farming. A taxpayer shall compute his gross income from farming in accordance with his accounting method used in determining gross income. (See the regulations under section 61 relating to accounting methods used by farmers in determining gross income.)

(b) *Examples.—*The provisions of paragraph (a) of this section may be illustrated by the following examples:

Example 1. For the taxable year 1963, A, who uses the cash receipts and disbursements method of accounting, incurs expenditures to which section 182 applies in the amount of $2,000 and makes the election under section 182. A has the following items of income and deductions (without regard to section 182 expenditures).

Income:

Proceeds from sale of his 1963 yield of corn	$10,000
Proceeds from sale of milk	8,000
Gain from disposition of old breeding cows	500
Gain from sale of tractor	100
Gain from sale of farmland	5,000
Interest on loan to brother	100
	$23,700

Deductions:

Cost of labor	$4,000	
Cost of feed	3,000	
Depreciation on farm equipment and buildings	2,500	
Cost of maintenance, fuel, etc	2,000	
Interest paid, mortgage on farm buildings	1,000	
Interest paid, personal loan	500	
Loss on destruction of barn	2,000	
Loss on sale of truck	300	
Section 1202 deduction—gain on sale of cows ($500 × ¹/₂)	250	
Section 1202 deduction—net gain on disposition of section 1231 property, other than cows [$2,800 ($5,100 − $2,300) × ¹/₂]	1,400	$16,950
Net income before section 182 deduction		$6,750

For purposes of computing taxable income derived from farming under section 182, the following items of income and deductions are not taken into account:

Income:		
Gain from the sale of tractor	$100	
Gain from the sale of farmland	5,000	
Interest on loan to brother	100	$5,200
Deductions:		
Interest paid, personal loan	$500	
Loss on destruction of barn	2,000	
Loss on sale of truck	300	
Section 1202 deduction—Net gain from disposition of section 1231 assets other than cows	1,400	$4,200

A's "taxable income derived from farming" for purposes of section 182 is $5,750; income of $18,500 ($23,700 – $5,200), less deductions of $12,750 ($16,950 – $4,200). A may deduct $1,437.50 (25% of $5,750) under section 182. The excess expenditures in the amount of $562.50 are to be charged to capital account and serve to increase the taxpayer's basis of the land.

Example 2. Assume the same facts as in example (1) and in addition, assume that A is allowed a deduction for a net operating loss carryback from the taxable year 1966 in the amount of $3,000. The net operating loss deduction will not be taken into account in computing A's "taxable income derived from farming" for 1963. Accordingly, A will not be required to recompute such taxable income for purposes of applying the limitation on the deduction provided in section 182 and the deduction of $1,437.50 will not be reduced. [Reg. § 1.182-5.]

☐ [T.D. 6794, 1-25-66.]

[Reg. § 1.182-6]

§ 1.182-6. Election to deduct land clearing expenditures.—
(a) *Manner of making election.*—The election to deduct expenditures for land clearing provided by section 182(a) shall be made by means of a statement attached to the taxpayer's income tax return for the taxable year for which such election is to apply. The statement shall include the name and address of the taxpayer, shall be signed by the taxpayer (or his duly authorized representative), and shall be filed not later than the time prescribed by law for filing the income tax return (including extensions thereof) for the taxable year for which the election is to apply. The statement shall also set forth the amount and description of the expenditures for land clearing claimed as a deduction under section 182, and shall include a computation of "taxable income derived from farming", if the amount of such income is not the same as the net income from farming shown on Schedule F of Form 1040, increased by the amount of the deduction claimed under section 182.

(b) *Scope of election.*—An election under section 182(a) shall apply only to the taxable year for which made. However, once made, an election applies to all expenditures described in § 1.182-3 paid or incurred during the taxable year, and is binding for such taxable year unless the district director consents to a revocation of such election. Requests for consent to revoke an election under section 182 shall be made by means of a letter to the district director for the district in which the taxpayer is required to file his return, setting forth the taxpayer's name, address and identification number, the year for which it is desired to revoke the election, and the reasons therefor. However, consent will not be granted where the only reason therefor is a change in tax consequences. [Reg. § 1.182-6.]

☐ [T.D. 6794, 1-25-65.]

[Reg. § 1.183-1]

§ 1.183-1. Activities not engaged in for profit.—(a) *In general.*— Section 183 provides rules relating to the allowance of deductions in the case of activities (whether active or passive in character) not engaged in for profit by individuals and electing small business corporations, creates a presumption that an activity is engaged in for profit if certain requirements are met, and permits the taxpayer to elect to postpone determination of whether such presumption applies until he has engaged in the activity for at least five taxable years, or, in certain cases, seven taxable years. Whether an activity is engaged in for profit is determined under section 162 and section 212(1) and (2) except insofar as section 183(d) creates a presumption that the activity is engaged in for profit. If deductions are not allowable under sections 162 and 212(1) and (2), the deduction allowance rules of section 183(b) and this section apply. Pursuant to section 641(b), the taxable income of an estate or trust is computed in the same manner as in the case of an individual, with certain exceptions not here relevant. Accordingly, where an estate or trust engages in an activity or activities which are not for profit, the rules of section 183 and this section apply in computing the allowable deductions of such trust or estate. No inference is to be drawn from the provisions of section 183 and the regulations thereunder that any activity of a corporation (other than an electing small business corporation) is or is not a business or engaged in for profit. For rules relating to the deductions that may be taken into account by taxable membership organizations which are operated primarily to furnish services, facilities, or goods to members, see section 277 and the regulations thereunder. For the definition of an activity not engaged in for profit, see § 1.183-2. For rules relating to the election contained in section 183(e), *see* § 1.183-3.

(b) *Deductions allowable.*—(1) *Manner and extent.*—If an activity is not engaged in for profit, deductions are allowable under section 183(b) in the following order and only to the following extent:

(i) Amounts allowable as deductions during the taxable year under chapter 1 of the Code without regard to whether the activity giving rise to such amounts was engaged in for profit are allowable to the full extent allowed by the relevant sections of the Code, determined after taking into account any limitations or exceptions with respect to the allowability of such amounts. For example, the allowability-of-interest expenses incurred with respect to activities not engaged in for profit is limited by the rules contained in section 163(d).

(ii) Amounts otherwise allowable as deductions during the taxable year under chapter 1 of the Code, but only if such allowance does not result in an adjustment to the basis of property, determined as if the activity giving rise to such amounts was engaged in for profit, are allowed only to the extent the gross income attributable to such activity exceeds the deductions allowed or allowable under subdivision (i) of this subparagraph.

(iii) Amounts otherwise allowable as deductions for the taxable year under chapter 1 of the Code which result in (or if otherwise allowed would have resulted in) an adjustment to the basis of property, determined as if the activity giving rise to such amounts was engaged in for profit, are allowed only to the extent the gross income attributable to such activity exceeds the deductions allowed or allowable under subdivisions (i) and (ii) of this subparagraph. Deductions falling within this subdivision include such items as depreciation, partial losses with respect to property, partially worthless debts, amortization, and amortizable bond premium.

(2) *Rule for deductions involving basis adjustments.*—(i) *In general.*—If deductions are allowed under subparagraph, (1)(iii) of this paragraph, and such deductions are allowed with respect to more than one asset, the deduction allowed with respect to each asset shall be determined separately in accordance with the computation set forth in subdivision (ii) of this paragraph.

(ii) *Basis adjustment fraction.*—The deduction allowed under subparagraph (1)(iii) of this paragraph is computed by multiplying the amount which would have been allowed, had the activity been engaged in for profit, as a deduction with respect to each particular asset which involves a basis adjustment, by the basis adjustment fraction—

(a) The numerator of which is the total of deductions allowable under subparagraph (1)(iii) of this paragraph, and

(b) The denominator of which is the total of deductions which involve basis adjustments which would have been allowed with respect to the activity had the activity been engaged in for profit.

The amount resulting from this computation is the deduction allowed under subparagraph (1)(iii) of this paragraph with respect to the particular asset. The basis of such asset is adjusted only to the extent of such deduction.

(3) *Examples.*—The provisions of subparagraphs (1) and (2) of this paragraph may be illustrated by the following examples:

Example (1). A, an individual, maintains a herd of dairy cattle, which is an "activity not engaged in for profit" within the meaning of section 183(c). A sold milk for $1,000 during the year. During the year A paid $300 State taxes on gasoline used to transport the cows, milk, etc., and paid $1,200 for feed for the cows. For the year A also had a casualty loss attributable to this activity of $500. A determines the amount of his allowable deductions under section 183 as follows:

(i) First, A computes his deductions allowable under subparagraph (1)(i) of this paragraph as follows:

State gasoline taxes specifically allowed under section 164(a)(5) without regard to whether the activity is engaged in for profit	$300
Casualty loss specifically allowed under section 165(c)(3) without regard to whether the activity is engaged in for profit ($500 less $100 limitation)	400
Deductions allowable under subparagraph (1)(i) of this paragraph	$700

(ii) Second, A computes his deductions allowable under subparagraph (1)(ii) of this paragraph (deductions which would be allowed under chapter 1 of the Code if the activity were engaged in for profit and which do not involve basis adjustments) as follows:

Maximum amount of deductions allowable under subparagraph (1)(ii) of this paragraph:	
Income from milk sales	$1,000
Gross income from activity	$1,000
Less: deductions allowable under subparagraph (1)(i) of this paragraph	700

Maximum amount of deductions allowable under subparagraph (1)(ii) of this paragraph	$300
Feed for cows	$1,200
Deduction allowed under subparagraph (1)(ii) of this paragraph	$300

$900 of the feed expense is not allowed as a deduction under section 183 because the total feed expense ($1,200) exceeds the maximum amount of deductions allowable under subparagraph (1)(ii) of this paragraph ($300). In view of these circumstances, it is not necessary to determine deductions allowable under subparagraph (1)(iii) of this paragraph which would be allowable under chapter 1 of the Code if the activity were engaged in for profit and which involve basis adjustment (the $100 of casualty loss not allowable under subparagraph (1)(i) of this paragraph because of the limitation in section 165(c)(3)) because none of such amount will be allowed as a deduction under section 183.

Example (2). Assume the same facts as in example (1), except that A also had income from sales of hay grown on the farm of $1,200 and that depreciation of $750 with respect to a barn, and $650 with respect to a tractor would have been allowed with respect to the activity had it been engaged in for profit. A determines the amount of his allowable deductions under section 183 as follows:

(i) First, A computes his deductions allowable under subparagraph (1)(i) of this paragraph as follows:

State gasoline taxes specifically allowed under section 164(a)(5) without regard to whether the activity is engaged in for profit	$300
Casualty loss specifically allowed under section 165(c)(3) without regard to whether the activity is engaged in for profit ($500 less $100 limitation)	400
Deductions allowable under subparagraph (1)(i) of this paragraph	$700

(ii) Second, A computes his deductions allowable under subparagraph (1)(ii) of this paragraph (deductions which would be allowable under chapter 1 of the Code if the activity were engaged in for profit and which do not involve basis adjustments) as follows:

Maximum amount of deductions allowable under subparagraph (1)(ii) of this paragraph:	
Income from milk sales	$1,000
Income from hay sales	1,200
Gross income from activity	$2,200
Less: deductions allowable under subparagraph (1)(i) of this paragraph	700
Maximum amount of deductions allowable under subparagraph (1)(ii) of this paragraph	$1,500
Feed for cows	$1,200

The entire $1,200 of expenses relating to feed for cows is allowable as a deduction under subparagraph (1)(ii) of this paragraph, since it does not exceed the maximum amount of deductions allowable under such subparagraph.

(iii) Last, A computes the deductions allowable under subparagraph (1)(iii) of this paragraph (deductions which would be allowable under chapter 1 of the Code if the activity were engaged in for profit and which involve basis adjustments) as follows:

Maximum amount of deductions allowable under subparagraph (1)(iii) of this paragraph:		
Gross income from farming		$2,200
Less: Deductions allowed under subparagraph (1)(i) of this paragraph . . .	$700	
Deductions allowed under subparagraph (1)(ii) of this paragraph	1,200	1,900
Maximum amount of deductions allowable under subparagraph (1)(iii) of this paragraph		$300

(iv) Since the total of A's deductions under chapter 1 of the Code (determined as if the activity was engaged in for profit) which involve basis adjustments ($750 with respect to barn, $650 with respect to tractor, and $100 with respect to limitation on casualty loss) exceeds the maximum amount of the deductions allowable under subparagraph (1)(iii) of this paragraph ($300), A computes his allowable deductions with respect to such assets as follows:

A first computes his basis adjustment fraction under subparagraph (2)(ii) of this paragraph as follows:

The numerator of the fraction is the maximum of deductions allowable under subparagraph (1)(iii) of this paragraph which involve basis adjustments	$300

The denominator of the fraction is the total of deductions that involve basis adjustments which would have been allowed with respect to the activity had the activity been engaged in for profit $1,500

The basis adjustment fraction is then applied to the amount of each deduction which would have been allowable if the activity were engaged in for profit and which involves a basis adjustment as follows:

Depreciation allowed with respect to barn (300/1,500 × $750)	$150
Depreciation allowed with respect to tractor (300/1,500 × $650)	$130
Deduction allowed with respect to limitation on casualty loss (300/1,500 × $100)	$20

The basis of the barn and of the tractor are adjusted only by the amount of depreciation actually allowed under section 183 with respect to each (as determined by the above computation). The basis of the asset with regard to which the casualty loss was suffered is adjusted only to the extent of the amount of the casualty loss actually allowed as a deduction under subparagraph (1)(i) and (iii) of this paragraph.

(4) *Rule for capital gains and losses.*—(i) *In general.*—For purposes of section 183 and the regulations thereunder, the gross income from any activity not engaged in for profit includes the total of all capital gains attributable to such activity determined without regard to the section 1202 deduction. Amounts attributable to an activity not engaged in for profit which would be allowable as a deduction under section 1202, without regard to section 183, shall be allowable as a deduction under section 183(b)(1) in accordance with the rules stated in this subparagraph.

(ii) *Cases where deduction not allowed under section 183.*—No deduction is allowable under section 183(b)(1) with respect to capital gains attributable to an activity not engaged in for profit if—

(a) Without regard to section 183 and the regulations thereunder, there is no excess of net long-term capital gain over net short-term capital loss for the year, or

(b) There is no excess of net long-term capital gain attributable to the activity over net short-term capital loss attributable to the activity.

(iii) *Allocation of deduction.*—If there is—

(a) An excess of net long-term capital gain over net short-term capital loss attributable to an activity not engaged in for profit, and

(b) Such an excess attributable to all activities, determined without regard to section 183 and the regulations thereunder,

the deduction allowable under section 183(b)(1) attributable to capital gains with respect to each activity not engaged in for profit (with respect to which there is an excess of net long-term capital gain over net short-term capital loss for the year) shall be an amount equal to the deduction allowable under section 1202 for the taxable year (determined without regard to section 183) multiplied by a fraction the numerator of which is the excess of the net long-term capital gain attributable to the activity over the net short-term capital loss attributable to the activity and the denominator of which is an amount equal to the total excess of net long-term capital gain over net short-term capital loss for all activities with respect to which there is such excess. The amount of the total section 1202 deduction allowable for the year shall be reduced by the amount determined to be allocable to activities not engaged in for profit and accordingly allowed as a deduction under section 183(b)(1).

(iv) *Example.*—The provisions of this subparagraph may be illustrated by the following example:

Example. A, an individual who uses the cash receipts and disbursement method of accounting and the calendar year as the taxable year, has three activities not engaged in for profit. For his taxable year ending on December 31, 1973, A has a $200 net long-term capital gain from activity No. 1, a $100 net short-term capital loss from activity No. 2, and a $300 net long-term capital gain from activity No. 3. In addition, A has a $500 net long-term capital gain from another activity which he engages in for profit. A computes his deductions for capital gains for calendar year 1973 as follows:

Section 1202 deduction without regard to section 183 is determined as follows:

Net long-term capital gain from activity No. 1	$200
Net long-term capital gain from activity No. 3	300
Net long-term capital gain from activity engaged in for profit	500

Total net long-term capital gain from all activities	$1,000
Less: Net short-term capital loss attributable to activity No. 2	$100
Aggregate net long-term capital gain over net short-term capital loss from all activities	$900
Section 1202 deduction determined without regard to section 183 (one-half of $900)	$450

Allocation of the total section 1202 deduction among A's various activities:

Portion allocable to activity No. 1 which is deductible under section 183(b)(1) (Excess net long-term capital gain attributable to activity No. 1 ($200) over total excess net long-term capital gain attributable to all of A's activities with respect to which there is such an excess ($1,000) times amount of section 1202 deduction ($450))	$90
Portion allocable to activity No. 3 which is deductible under section 183(b)(1) (Excess net long-term capital gain attributable to activity No. 3 ($300) over total excess net long-term capital gain attributable to all of A's activities with respect to which there is such an excess ($1,000) times amount of section 1202 deduction ($450))	135
Portion allocable to all activities engaged in for profit (total section 1202 deduction ($450) less section 1202 deduction allowable to activities No. 1 and 3 ($225)	225
Total section 1202 deduction deductible under sections 1202 and 183(b)(1)	$450

(c) *Presumption that activity is engaged in for profit.*—(1) *In general.*—If for—

(i) Any two of seven consecutive taxable years, in the case of an activity which consists in major part of the breeding, training, showing, or racing of horses, or

(ii) Any two of five consecutive taxable years, in the case of any other activity, the gross income derived from an activity exceeds the deductions attributable to such activity which would be allowed or allowable if the activity were engaged in for profit, such activity is presumed, unless the Commissioner establishes to the contrary, to be engaged in for profit. For purposes of this determination the deduction permitted by section 1202 shall not be taken into account. Such presumption applies with respect to the second profit year and all years subsequent to the second profit year within the five- or seven-year period beginning with the first profit year. This presumption arises only if the activity is substantially the same activity for each of the relevant taxable years, including the taxable year in question. If the taxpayer does not meet the requirements of section 183(d) and this paragraph, no inference that the activity is not engaged in for profit shall arise by reason of the provisions of section 183. For purposes of this paragraph, a net operating loss deduction is not taken into account as a deduction. For purposes of this subparagraph a short taxable year constitutes a taxable year.

(2) *Examples.*—The provisions of subparagraph (1) of this paragraph may be illustrated by the following examples, in each of which it is assumed that the taxpayer has not elected, in accordance with section 183(e), to postpone determination of whether the presumption described in section 183(d) and this paragraph is applicable.

Example (1). For taxable years 1970-74, A, an individual who uses the cash receipts and disbursement method of accounting and the calendar year as the taxable year, is engaged in the activity of farming. In taxable years 1971, 1973, and 1974, A's deductible expenditures with respect to such activity exceed his gross income from the activity. In taxable years 1970 and 1972 A has income from the sale of farm produce of $30,000 for each year. In each of such years A had expenses for feed for his livestock of $10,000, depreciation of equipment of $10,000, and fertilizer cost of $5,000 which he elects to take as a deduction. A also has a net operating loss carryover to taxable year 1970 of $6,000. A is presumed, for taxable years 1972, 1973, and 1974, to have engaged in the activity of farming for profit, since for 2 years of a 5-consecutive-year period the gross income from the activity ($30,000 for each year) exceeded the deductions (computed without regard to the net operating loss) which are allowable in the case of the activity ($25,000 for each year).

Example (2). For the taxable years 1970 and 1971, B, an individual who uses the cash receipts and disbursement method of accounting and the calendar year as the taxable year, engaged in raising pure-bred Charolais cattle for breeding purposes. The operation showed a loss during 1970. At the end of 1971, B sold a substantial portion of his herd and the cattle operation showed a profit for that year. For all subsequent relevant taxable years B continued to keep a few Charolais bulls at stud. In 1972, B started to raise Tennessee Walking Horses for breeding and show purposes, utilizing substantially the same

pasture land, barns, and (with structural modifications) the same stalls. The Walking Horse operations showed a small profit in 1973 and losses in 1972 and 1974 through 1976.

(i) Assuming that under paragraph (d)(1) of this section the raising of cattle and raising of horses are determined to be separate activities, no presumption that the Walking Horse operation was carried on for profit arises under section 183(d) and this paragraph since this activity was not the same activity that generated the profit in 1971 and there are not, therefore, 2 profit years attributable to the horse activity.

(ii) Assuming the same facts as in (i) above, if there were no stud fees received in 1972 with respect to Charolais bulls, but for 1973 stud fees with respect to such bulls exceed deductions attributable to maintenance of the bulls in that year, the presumption will arise under section 183(d) and this paragraph with respect to the activity of raising and maintaining Charolais cattle for 1973 and for all subsequent years within the five-year period beginning with taxable year 1971, since the activity of raising and maintaining Charolais cattle is the same activity in 1971 and in 1973, although carried on by B on a much reduced basis and in a different manner. Since it has been assumed that the horse and cattle operations are separate activities, no presumption will arise with respect to the Walking Horse operation because there are not 2 profit years attributable to such horse operation during the period in question.

(iii) Assuming, alternatively, that the raising of cattle and raising of horses would be considered a single activity under paragraph (d)(1) of this section, B would receive the benefit of the presumption beginning in 1973 with respect to both the cattle and horses since there were profits in 1971 and 1973. The presumption would be effective through 1977 (and longer if there is an excess of income over deductions in this activity in 1974, 1975, 1976, or 1977 which would extend the presumption) if, under section 183(d) and subparagraph (3) of this paragraph, it was determined that the activity consists in major part of the breeding, training, showing, or racing of horses. Otherwise, the presumption would be effective only through 1975 (assuming no excess of income over deductions in this activity in 1974 or 1975 which would extend the presumption).

(3) *Activity which consists in major part of the breeding, training, showing, or racing of horses.*—For purposes of this paragraph an activity consists in major part of the breeding, training, showing, or racing of horses for the taxable year if the average of the portion of expenditures attributable to breeding, training, showing, and racing of horses for the 3 taxable years preceding the taxable year (or, in the case of an activity which has not been conducted by the taxpayer for 3 years, for so long as it has been carried on by him) was at least 50 percent of the total expenditures attributable to the activity for such prior taxable years.

(4) *Transitional rule.*—In applying the presumption described in section 183(d) and this paragraph, only taxable years beginning after December 31, 1969, shall be taken into account. Accordingly, in the case of an activity referred to in subparagraph (1)(i) or (ii) of this paragraph, section 183(d) does not apply prior to the second profitable taxable year beginning after December 31, 1969, since taxable years prior to such date are not taken into account.

(5) *Cross reference.*—For rules relating to section 183(e) which permits a taxpayer to elect to postpone determination of whether any activity shall be presumed to be "an activity engaged in for profit" by operation of the presumption described in section 183(d) and this paragraph until after the close of the fourth taxable year (sixth taxable year, in the case of activity which consists in major part of breeding, training, showing, or racing of horses) following the taxable year in which the taxpayer first engages in the activity, see § 1.183-3.

(d) *Activity defined.*—(1) *Ascertainment of activity.*—In order to determine whether, and to what extent, section 183 and the regulations thereunder apply, the activity or activities of the taxpayer must be ascertained. For instance, where the taxpayer is engaged in several undertakings, each of these may be a separate activity, or several undertakings may constitute one activity. In ascertaining the activity or activities of the taxpayer, all the facts and circumstances of the case must be taken into account. Generally, the most significant facts and circumstances in making this determination are the degree of organizational and economic interrelationship of various undertakings, the business purpose which is (or might be) served by carrying on the various undertakings separately or together in a trade or business or in an investment setting, and the similarity of various undertakings. Generally, the Commissioner will accept the characterization by the taxpayer of several undertakings either as a single activity or as separate activities. The taxpayer's characterization will not be accepted, however, when it appears that his characterization is artificial and cannot be reasonably supported under the facts and circumstances of the case. If the taxpayer engages in two or more

Reg. §1.183-1(c)(1)

Itemized Deductions for Individuals and Corps.
See p. 20,601 for regulations not amended to reflect law changes
25,639

separate activities, deductions and income from each separate activity are not aggregated either in determining whether a particular activity is engaged in for profit or in applying section 183. Where land is purchased or held primarily with the intent to profit from increase in its value, and the taxpayer also engages in farming on such land, the farming and the holding of the land will ordinarily be considered a single activity only if the farming activity reduces the net cost of carrying the land for its appreciation in value. Thus, the farming and holding of the land will be considered a single activity only if the income derived from farming exceeds the deductions attributable to the farming activity which are not directly attributable to the holding of the land (that is, deductions other than those directly attributable to the holding of the land such as interest on a mortgage secured by the land, annual property taxes attributable to the land and improvements, and depreciation of improvements to the land).

(2) *Rules for allocation of expenses.*—If the taxpayer is engaged in more than one activity, an item of deduction or income may be allocated between two or more of these activities. Where property is used in several activities, and one or more of such activities is determined not to be engaged in for profit, deductions relating to such property must be allocated between the various activities on a reasonable and consistently applied basis.

(3) *Example.*—The provisions of this paragraph may be illustrated by the following example:

Example. (i) A, an individual, owns a small house located near the beach in a resort community. Visitors come to the area for

Maintenance expense $600 . . . .
Utilities expense $300 . . . .
Depreciation $1,200 . . . .

    Total . . . .

The $700 of expenses and depreciation allocated to the personal use of the beach house are disallowed as a deduction under section 262. In addition, the allowability of each of the expenses and the depreciation allocated to section 183(b)(2) is determined under paragraph (b)(1)(ii) and (iii) of this section. Thus, the maximum amount allowable as a deduction under section 183(b)(2) is $200 ($2,000 gross income from activity, less $1,800 deductions under section 183(b)(1)). Since the amounts described in section 183(b)(2) ($1,400) exceed the maximum amount allowable ($200), and since the amounts described in paragraph (b)(1)(ii) of this section ($600) exceed such maximum amount allowable ($200), none of the depreciation (an amount described in paragraph (b)(1)(iii) of this section) is allowable as a deduction.

(e) *Gross income from activity not engaged in for profit defined.*—For purposes of section 183 and the regulations thereunder, gross income derived from an activity not engaged in for profit includes the total of all gains from the sale, exchange, or other disposition of property, and all other gross receipts derived from such activity. Such gross income shall include, for instance, capital gains, and rents received for the use of property which is held in connection with the activity. The taxpayer may determine gross income from any activity by subtracting the cost of goods sold from the gross receipts so long as he consistently does so and follows generally accepted methods of accounting in determining such gross income.

(f) *Rule for electing small business corporations.*—Section 183 and this section shall be applied at the corporate level in determining the allowable deductions of an electing small business corporation. [Reg. § 1.183-1.]

☐ *[T.D. 7198, 7-12-72.]*

[Reg. § 1.183-2]

§ 1.183-2. Activity not engaged in for profit defined.—(a) *In general.*—For purposes of section 183 and the regulations thereunder, the term "activity not engaged in for profit" means any activity other than one with respect to which deductions are allowable for the taxable year under section 162 or under paragraph (1) or (2) of section 212. Deductions are allowable under section 162 for expenses of carrying on activities which constitute a trade or business of the taxpayer and under section 212 for expenses incurred in connection with activities engaged in for the production or collection of income or for the management, conservation, or maintenance of property held for the production of income. Except as provided in section 183 and § 1.183-1, no deductions are allowable for expenses incurred in connection with activities which are not engaged in for profit. Thus, for example, deductions are not allowable under section 162 or 212

recreational purposes during only three months of the year. During the remaining 9 months of the year houses such as A's are not rented. Customarily, A arranges that the house will be leased for 2 months of 3-month recreational season to vacationers and reserves the house for his own vacation during the remaining month of the recreational season. In 1971, A leases the house for 2 months for $1,000 per month and actually uses the house for his own vacation during the other month of the recreational season. For 1971, the expenses attributable to the house are $1,200 interest, $600 real estate taxes, $600 maintenance, $300 utilities, and $1,200 which would have been allowed as depreciation had the activity been engaged in for profit. Under these facts and circumstances, A is engaged in a single activity, holding the beach house primarily for personal purposes, which is an "activity not engaged in for profit" within the meaning of section 183(c). See paragraph (b)(9) of § 1.183-2.

(ii) Since the $1,200 of interest and the $600 of real estate taxes are specifically allowable as deductions under sections 163 and 164(a) without regard to whether the beach house activity is engaged in for profit, no allocation of these expenses between the uses of the beach house is necessary. However, since section 262 specifically disallows personal, living, and family expenses as deductions, the maintenance and utilities expenses and the depreciation from the activity must be allocated between the rental use and the personal use of the beach house. Under the particular facts and circumstances, 2/3 (2 months of rental use over 3 months of total use) of each of these expenses are allocated to the rental use, and 1/3 (1 month of personal use over 3 months of total use) of each of these expenses are allocated to the personal use as follows:

Rental use 2/3— expenses allocable to section 183(b)(2)	Personal use 1/3— expenses allocable to section 262
$400	$200
200	100
800	400
$1,400	$700

for activities which are carried on primarily as a sport, hobby, or for recreation. The determination whether an activity is engaged in for profit is to be made by reference to objective standards, taking into account all of the facts and circumstances of each case. Although a reasonable expectation of profit is not required, the facts and circumstances must indicate that the taxpayer entered into the activity, or continued the activity, with the objective of making a profit. In determining whether such an objective exists, it may be sufficient that there is a small chance of making a large profit. Thus it may be found that an investor in a wildcat oil well who incurs very substantial expenditures is in the venture for profit even though the expectation of a profit might be considered unreasonable. In determining whether an activity is engaged in for profit, greater weight is given to objective facts than to the taxpayer's mere statement of his intent.

(b) *Relevant factors.*—In determining whether an activity is engaged in for profit, all facts and circumstances with respect to the activity are to be taken into account. No one factor is determinative in making this determination. In addition, it is not intended that only the factors described in this paragraph are to be taken into account in making the determination, or that a determination is to be made on the basis that the number of factors (whether or not listed in this paragraph) indicating a lack of profit objective exceeds the number of factors indicating a profit objective, or vice versa. Among the factors which should normally be taken into account are the following:

(1) *Manner in which the taxpayer carries on the activity.*—The fact that the taxpayer carries on the activity in a businesslike manner and maintains complete and accurate books and records may indicate that the activity is engaged in for profit. Similarly, where an activity is carried on in a manner substantially similar to other activities of the same nature which are profitable, a profit motive may be indicated. A change of operating methods, adoption of new techniques or abandonment of unprofitable methods in a manner consistent with an intent to improve profitability may also indicate a profit motive.

(2) *The expertise of the taxpayer or his advisors.*—Preparation for the activity by extensive study of its accepted business, economic, and scientific practices, or consultation with those who are expert therein, may indicate that the taxpayer has a profit motive where the taxpayer carries on the activity in accordance with such practices. Where a taxpayer has such preparation or procures such expert advice, but does not carry on the activity in accordance with such practices, a lack of intent to derive profit may be indicated unless it appears that the taxpayer is attempting to develop new or superior techniques which may result in profits from the activity.

(3) *The time and effort expended by the taxpayer in carrying on the activity.*—The fact that the taxpayer devotes much of his personal time and effort to carrying on an activity, particularly if the activity does not have substantial personal or recreational aspects, may indicate an intention to derive a profit. A taxpayer's withdrawal from another occupation to devote most of his energies to the activity may also be evidence that the activity is engaged in for profit. The fact that the taxpayer devotes a limited amount of time to an activity does not necessarily indicate a lack of profit motive where the taxpayer employs competent and qualified persons to carry on such activity.

(4) *Expectation that assets used in activity may appreciate in value.*—The term "profit" encompasses appreciation in the value of assets, such as land, used in the activity. Thus, the taxpayer may intend to derive a profit from the operation of the activity, and may also intend that, even if no profit from current operations is derived, an overall profit will result when appreciation in the value of land used in the activity is realized since income from the activity together with the appreciation of land will exceed expenses of operation. See, however, paragraph (d) of § 1.183-1 for definition of an activity in this connection.

(5) *The success of the taxpayer in carrying on other similar or dissimilar activities.*—The fact that the taxpayer has engaged in similar activities in the past and converted them from unprofitable to profitable enterprises may indicate that he is engaged in the present activity for profit, even though the activity is presently unprofitable.

(6) *The taxpayer's history of income or losses with respect to the activity.*—A series of losses during the initial or start-up stage of an activity may not necessarily be an indication that the activity is not engaged in for profit. However, where losses continue to be sustained beyond the period which customarily is necessary to bring the operation to profitable status, if not explainable, as due to customary business risks or reverses, may be indicative that the activity is not being engaged in for profit. If losses are sustained because of unforeseen or fortuitous circumstances which are beyond the control of the taxpayer, such as drought, disease, fire, theft, weather damages, other involuntary conversions, or depressed market conditions, such losses would not be an indication that the activity is not engaged in for profit. A series of years in which net income was realized would of course be strong evidence that the activity is engaged in for profit.

(7) *The amount of occasional profits, if any, which are earned.*—The amount of profits in relation to the amount of losses incurred, and in relation to the amount of the taxpayer's investment and the value of the assets used in the activity, may provide useful criteria in determining the taxpayer's intent. An occasional small profit from an activity generating large losses, or from an activity in which the taxpayer has made a large investment, would not generally be determinative that the activity is engaged in for profit. However, substantial profit, though only occasional, would generally be indicative that an activity is engaged in for profit, where the investment or losses are comparatively small. Moreover, an opportunity to earn a substantial ultimate profit in a highly speculative venture is ordinarily sufficient to indicate that the activity is engaged in for profit even though losses or only occasional small profits are actually generated.

(8) *The financial status of the taxpayer.*—The fact that the taxpayer does not have substantial income or capital from sources other than the activity may indicate that an activity is engaged in for profit. Substantial income from sources other than the activity (particularly if the losses from the activity generate substantial tax benefits) may indicate that the activity is not engaged in for profit especially if there are personal or recreational elements involved.

(9) *Elements of personal pleasure or recreation.*—The presence of personal motives in carrying on of an activity may indicate that the activity is not engaged in for profit, especially where there are recreational or personal elements involved. On the other hand, a profit motivation may be indicated where an activity lacks any appeal other than profit. It is not, however, necessary that an activity be engaged in with the exclusive intention of deriving a profit or with the intention of maximizing profits. For example, the availability of other investments which would yield a higher return, or which would be more likely to be profitable, is not evidence that an activity is not engaged in for profit. An activity will not be treated as not engaged in for profit merely because the taxpayer has purposes or motivations other than solely to make a profit. Also, the fact that the taxpayer derives personal pleasure from engaging in the activity is *not sufficient to cause the activity to be classified as not engaged in for profit if the activity is in fact engaged in for profit* as evidenced by other factors whether or not listed in this paragraph.

(c) *Examples.*—The provisions of this section may be illustrated by the following examples:

Example (1). The taxpayer inherited a farm from her husband in an area which was becoming largely residential, and is now nearly all so. The farm had never made a profit before the taxpayer inherited it, and the farm has since had substantial losses in each year. The decedent from whom the taxpayer inherited the farm was a stockbroker, and he also left the taxpayer substantial stock holdings which yield large income from dividends. The taxpayer lives on an area of the farm which is set aside exclusively for living purposes. A farm manager is employed to operate the farm, but modern methods are not used in operating the farm. The taxpayer was born and raised on a farm, and expresses a strong preference for living on a farm. The taxpayer's activity of farming, based on all the facts and circumstances, could be found not to be engaged in for profit.

Example (2). The taxpayer is a wealthy individual who is greatly interested in philosophy. During the past thirty years he has written and published at his own expense several pamphlets, and he has engaged in extensive lecturing activity, advocating and disseminating his ideas. He has made a profit from these activities in only occasional years, and the profits in those years were small in relation to the amounts of the losses in all other years. The taxpayer has very sizable income from securities (dividends and capital gains) which constitutes the principal source of his livelihood. The activity of lecturing, publishing pamphlets, and disseminating his ideas is not an activity engaged in by the taxpayer for profit.

Example (3). The taxpayer, very successful in the business of retailing soft drinks, raises dogs and horses. He began raising a particular breed of dogs many years ago in the belief that the breed was in danger of declining, and he has raised and sold the dogs in each year since. The taxpayer recently began raising and racing thoroughbred horses. The losses from the taxpayer's dog and horse activities have increased in magnitude over the years, and he has not made a profit on these operations during any of the last 15 years. The taxpayer generally sells the dogs only to friends, does not advertise the dogs for sale, and shows the dogs only infrequently. The taxpayer races his horses only at the "prestige" tracks at which he combines his racing activities with social and recreational activities. The horse and dog operations are conducted at a large residential property on which the taxpayer also lives, which includes substantial living quarters and attractive recreational facilities for the taxpayer and his family. Since (i) the activity of raising dogs and horses and racing the horses is of a sporting and recreational nature, (ii) the taxpayer has substantial income from his business activities of retailing soft drinks, (iii) the horse and dog operations are not conducted in a businesslike manner, and (iv) such operations have a continuous record of losses, it could be determined that the horse and dog activities of the taxpayer are not engaged in for profit.

Example (4). The taxpayer inherited a farm of 65 acres from his parents when they died 6 years ago. The taxpayer moved to the farm from his house in a small nearby town, and he operates it in the same manner as his parents operated the farm before they died. The taxpayer is employed as a skilled machine operator in a nearby factory, for which he is paid approximately $8,500 per year. The farm has not been profitable for the past 15 years because of rising costs of operating farms in general, and because of the decline in the price of the produce of this farm in particular. The taxpayer consults the local agent of the State agricultural service from time-to-time, and the suggestions of the agent have generally been followed. The manner in which the farm is operated by the taxpayer is substantially similar to the manner in which farms of similar size, and which grow similar crops in the area are operated. Many of these other farms do not make profits. The taxpayer does much of the required labor around the farm himself, such as fixing fences, planting crops, etc. The activity of farming could be found, based on all the facts and circumstances, to be engaged in by the taxpayer for profit.

Example (5). A, an independent oil and gas operator, frequently engages in the activity of searching for oil on undeveloped and unexplored land which is not near proven fields. He does so in a manner substantially similar to that of others who engage in the same activity. The chances, based on the experience of A and others who engaged in this activity, are strong that A will not find a commercially profitable oil deposit when he drills on land not established geologically to be proven oil bearing land. However, on the rare occasions that these activities do result in discovering a well, the operator generally realizes a very large return from such activity. Thus, there is a small chance that A will make a large profit from his oil exploration activity. Under these circumstances, A is engaged in the activity of oil drilling for profit.

Example (6). C, a chemist, is employed by a large chemical company and is engaged in a wide variety of basic research projects for his employer. Although he does no work for his employer with respect to the development of new plastics, he has always been interested in such development and has outfitted a workshop in his home at his own expense which he uses to experiment in the field. He has patented several developments at his own expense but as yet has realized no income from his inventions or from such patents. C conducts his research on a regular, systematic basis, incurs fees to secure consultation on his projects from time to time, and makes extensive efforts to "market" his developments. C has devoted substantial time and expense in an effort to develop a plastic sufficiently hard, durable, and malleable that it could be used in lieu of sheet steel in many major applications, such as automobile bodies. Although there may be only a small chance that C will invent new plastics, the return from any such development would be so large that it induces C to incur the costs of his experimental work. C is sufficiently qualified by his background that there is some reasonable basis for his experimental activities. C's experimental work does not involve substantial personal or recreational aspects and is conducted in an effort to find practical applications for his work. Under these circumstances, C may be found to be engaged in the experimental activities for profit. [Reg. § 1.183-2.]

☐ [T.D. 7198, 7-12-72.]

[Reg. § 1.183-3]

§ 1.183-3. Election to postpone determination with respect to the presumption described in section 183(d).—[Reserved]

[Reg. § 12.9]

§ 12.9. Election to postpone determination with respect to the presumption described in section 183(d).—(a) *In general.*—An individual, electing small business corporation, trust or estate may elect in accordance with the rules set forth in this section to postpone a determination whether the presumption described in section 183(d) applies with respect to any activity in which the taxpayer engages until after the close of the fourth taxable year (sixth taxable year, in the case of an activity described in § 1.183-1(c)(3)) following the taxable year in which the taxpayer first engages in such activity. The election must be made in accordance with the applicable requirements of paragraphs (b), (c) and (d) of this section. Except as otherwise provided in paragraphs (c) and (e) of this section, an election made pursuant to this section shall be binding for the first taxable year in which the taxpayer first engages in the activity and for all subsequent taxable years in the five (or seven) year period referred to in the first sentence of this paragraph. For purposes of this section, a taxpayer shall be treated as not having engaged in an activity during any taxable year beginning before January 1, 1970.

(b) *Period to which an election applies.*—An individual, trust, estate, or small business corporation may make the election. The five year presumption period (seven year presumption period in the case of an activity described in § 1.183-1(c)(3)) to which the election shall apply shall be the five (or seven) consecutive taxable years of such taxpayer beginning with the taxable year in which such taxpayer first engages in the activity. For purposes of this section, a taxpayer who engages in an activity as a partner, engages in it in each of his taxable years with or within which ends a partnership year during which the activity was carried on by the partnership.

(c) *Time for making an election.*—A taxpayer who is an individual, trust, estate or small business corporation may make the election provided in section 183(e) by filing the statement and consents required by paragraph (d) of this section within—

(1) 3 years after the due date of such taxpayer's return (determined without extensions) for the taxable year in which such taxpayer first engages in the activity, but not later than

(2) 60 days after such taxpayer receives a written notice (if any) from a district director that the district director proposes to disallow deductions attributable to an activity not engaged in for profit under section 183. The provisions of paragraph (c)(2) of this section shall in no event be construed to extend the period described in (c)(1) of this section for making such election. Notwithstanding the time periods prescribed in paragraph (c)(1) and (2) of this section, if no election has been made before a suit or proceeding described in section 7422(a) is maintained or a petition is filed in the Tax Court for a redetermination of a deficiency for any taxable year within the presumption period to which the election would apply, no election may be made except with the consent of the Commissioner which will not be given unless no appreciable delay in the suit or proceeding will be caused.

(d) *Manner of making election.*—(1) The election shall be made by the *individual, trust, estate, or electing small business corporation, as* the case may be, engaged in the activity, by filing a statement which sets forth the following information—

(i) The name, address, and taxpayer identification number of such taxpayer, and, if applicable, of the partnership in which he engages in the activity,

(ii) A declaration stating that the taxpayer elects to postpone a determination as to whether the presumption described in section 183(d) applies until after the close of the taxpayer's fourth taxable year (sixth taxable year, in the case of an activity described in § 1.183-1(c)(3)) following the taxable year in which the taxpayer first

engaged in such activity and identifying that first such taxable year, and,

(iii) A description of each activity (as defined in § 1.183-1(d)(1)) with respect to which the election is being made.

(2) For an election to be effective, there must be attached to the statement properly executed consents, in the form prescribed by the Commissioner, extending the period prescribed by section 6501 for the assessment of any tax to a date which is not earlier than 18 months after the due date of the return (determined without extensions) for the final year in the presumption period to which the election applies, as follows:

(i) Consents for each of the taxpayer's taxable years in the presumption period to which the election applies,

(ii) If the election is made by an electing small business corporation, a consent of each person who is a shareholder during any taxable year to which the election applies, for each of such shareholder's taxable years with or within which end each of the corporation's taxable years in the presumption period,

(iii) If a taxpayer referred to in paragraph (d)(2)(i) of this section or shareholder referred to in paragraph (d)(2)(ii) of this section is married at the time of the election, in the case of his present spouse, a consent for each of such spouse's taxable years which correspond to the taxable years (other than prior years of the shareholder during no part of which he was a shareholder) for which consents are required by paragraph (d)(2)(i) or (ii) of this section as the case may be. Such consents shall not be construed to shorten the period described in section 6501 for any taxable year within the presumption period to which the election applies.

(3) The statement, with the required consents attached, shall be filed—

(i) With the service center at which the taxpayer making the election is required to file his return, or

(ii) If the taxpayer is notified by a district director that, pursuant to section 183, he is proposing to disallow deductions with respect to an activity not engaged in for profit, with such district director.

(e) *Subsequent invalidations.*—If, after a timely election has been made, but still within the presumption period, a suit or proceeding (as described in section 7422(a)) is maintained by the electing taxpayer, a shareholder referred to in paragraph (d)(2)(ii) of this section, or spouse referred to in paragraph (d)(2)(iii) of this section for any taxable year for which a consent is required by this section and the taxpayer, shareholder, or spouse has not been issued a notice of deficiency (as described in section 6212(a)) with respect to such taxable year, such election shall not be effective to postpone the determination whether the presumption applies, for such taxable year, but the consents extending the statute of limitations filed with the election shall not thereby be invalidated. The immediately preceding sentence shall not apply to a suit or proceeding maintained by the spouse of an electing taxpayer for a taxable year for which such spouse has filed a separate return, or a suit or proceeding maintained by a shareholder for a taxable year in which he was not such a shareholder. An election by an individual taxpayer or electing small business corporation, shall be subsequently invalidated for all years in the presumption period to which it had applied if—

(1) The electing taxpayer or shareholder taxpayer files a joint return for one of the first three (five, in the case of an activity described in § 1.183-1(c)(3)) taxable years in such presumption period, and

(2) The spouse with whom he files such joint return has not previously executed a consent described in paragraph (d)(2)(iii) of this section, and

(3) Within one year after the filing of such joint return (or, if later, 90 days after March 14, 1974), such spouse has not filed a consent described in paragraph (d)(2) of this section.

An election by an electing small business corporation shall be invalidated for all years in the presumption period to which it applies if a person who was not a shareholder on the date of election becomes a shareholder during the first three (or five) years of the presumption period to which the election applies and does not, within 90 days after the date on which he becomes a shareholder (or, if later, 90 days after March 14, 1974), file a consent required by paragraph (d)(2) of this section. Invalidation of the election by operation of this paragraph will in no case affect the validity of the consents filed with such election.

(f) *Extension of time for filing election in hardship cases.*—The Commissioner may, upon application by a taxpayer, consent to an extension of time prescribed in this section for making an election if he finds that such an extension would be justified by hardship incurred by reason of the time at which this section is published. The burden will be on the taxpayer to establish that under the relevant facts the Commissioner should so consent. [Temporary Reg. § 12.9.]

☐ [T.D. 7308, 3-14-74.]

[Reg. §1.183-4]

§1.183-4. Taxable years affected.—The provisions of section 183 and the regulations thereunder shall apply only with respect to taxable years beginning after December 31, 1969. For provisions applicable to prior taxable years, see section 270 and §1.270-1. [Reg. §1.183-4.]

☐ [T.D. 7198, 7-12-72.]

[Reg. §1.186-1]

§1.186-1. Recoveries of damages for antitrust violations, etc.—(a) *Allowance of deduction.*—Under section 186, when a compensatory amount which is included in gross income is received or accrued during a taxable year for a compensable injury, a deduction is allowed in an amount equal to the lesser of (1) such compensatory amount, or (2) the unrecovered losses sustained as a result of such compensable injury.

(b) *Compensable injury.*—(1) *In general.*—For purposes of this section, the term "compensable injury" means any of the injuries described in subparagraph (2), (3), or (4) of this paragraph.

(2) *Patent infringement.*—An injury sustained as a result of an infringement of a patent issued by the United States (whether or not issued to the taxpayer or another person or persons) constitutes a compensable injury. The term "patent issued by the United States" means any patent issued or granted by the United States under the authority of the Commissioner of Patents pursuant to 35 U.S.C. 153.

(3) *Breach of contract or of fiduciary duty or relationship.*—An injury sustained as a result of a breach of contract (including an injury sustained by a third party beneficiary) or a breach of fiduciary duty or relationship constitutes a compensable injury.

(4) *Injury suffered under certain antitrust law violations.*—An injury sustained in business, or to property, by reason of any conduct forbidden in the antitrust laws for which a civil action may be brought under section 4 of the Act of October 15, 1914 (15 U.S.C. 15), commonly known as the Clayton Act, constitutes a compensable injury.

(c) *Compensatory amount.*—(1) *In general.*—For purposes of this section, the term "compensatory amount" means any amount received or accrued during the taxable year as damages as a result of an award in, or in settlement of, a civil action for recovery for a compensable injury, reduced by any amounts paid or incurred in the taxable year in securing such award or settlement. The term "compensatory amount" includes only amounts compensating for actual economic injury. Thus, additional amounts representing punitive, exemplary, or treble damages are not included within the term. Where, for example, a taxpayer recovers treble damages under section 4 of the Clayton Act, only one-third of the recovery representing economic injury constitutes a compensatory amount. In the absence of any indication to the contrary, amounts received in settlement of an action shall be deemed to be a recovery for an actual economic injury except to the extent such settlement amounts exceed actual damages claimed by the taxpayer in such action.

(2) *Interest on a compensatory amount.*—Interest attributable to a compensatory amount shall not be included within the term "compensatory amount."

(3) *Settlement of a civil action for damages.*—(i) *Necessity for an action.*—The term "compensatory amount" does not include an amount received or accrued in settlement of a claim for a compensable injury if the amount is received or accrued prior to institution of an action. An action shall be considered as instituted upon completion of service of process, in accordance with the laws and rules of the court in which the action has been commenced or to which the action has been removed, upon all defendants who pay or incur an obligation to pay a compensatory amount.

(ii) *Specifications of the parties.*—If an action for a compensable injury is settled, the specifications of the parties will generally determine compensatory amounts unless such specifications are not reasonably supported by the facts and circumstances of the case. For example, the parties may provide that the sum of $1,000 represents actual damages sustained as the result of antitrust violations and that the total amount of the settlement after the trebling of damages is $3,000. In such case, only the sum of $1,000 would be a compensatory amount. In the absence of specifications of the parties, the complaint filed by the taxpayer may be considered in determining what portion of the amount of the settlement is a compensatory amount.

(4) *Amounts paid or incurred in securing the award or settlement.*—For purposes of this section, the term "amounts paid or incurred in the taxable year in securing such award or settlement" shall include

legal expenses such as attorney's fees, witness fees, accountant fees, and court costs. Expenses incurred in securing a recovery of both a compensatory amount and other amounts from the same action shall be allocated among such amounts in the ratio each of such amounts bears to the total recovery. For instance, where a taxpayer incurs attorney's fees and other expenses of $3,000 in recovering $10,000 as a compensatory amount, $5,000 as a return of capital, and $25,000 as punitive damages from the same action, the taxpayer shall allocate $750 of the expenses to the compensatory amount (10,000/40,000 × 3,000), $375 to the return of capital (5,000/40,000 × 3,000), and $1,875 to the punitive damages (25,000/40,000 × 3,000).

(d) *Unrecovered losses.*—(1) *In general.*—For purposes of this section, the term "unrecovered losses sustained as a result of such compensable injury" means the sum of the amounts of the net operating losses for each taxable year in whole or in part within the injury period, to the extent that such net operating losses are attributable to such compensable injury, reduced by (i) the sum of any amounts of such net operating losses which were allowed as a net operating loss carryback or carryover for any prior taxable year under the provisions of section 172, and (ii) the sum of any amounts allowed as deductions under section 186(a) and this section for all prior taxable years with respect to the same compensable injury. Accordingly, a deduction is permitted under section 186(a) and this section with respect to net operating losses whether or not the period for carryover under section 172 has expired.

(2) *Injury period.*—For purposes of this section, the term "injury period" means (i) with respect to an infringement of a patent, the period during which the infringement of the patent continued, (ii) with respect to a breach of contract or breach of fiduciary duty or relationship, the period during which amounts would have been received or accrued but for such breach of contract or breach of fiduciary duty or relationship, or (iii) with respect to injuries sustained by reason of a violation of section 4 of the Clayton Act, the period during which such injuries were sustained. The injury period will be determined on the basis of the facts and circumstances of the taxpayer's situation. The injury period may include periods before and after the period covered by the civil action instituted.

(3) *Net operating losses attributable to compensable injuries.*—A net operating loss for any taxable year shall be treated as attributable (whether actually attributable or not) to a compensable injury to the extent the compensable injury is sustained during the taxable year. For purposes of determining the extent of the compensable injury sustained during a taxable year, a judgment for a compensable injury apportioning the amount of the recovery (not reduced by any amounts paid or incurred in securing such recovery) to specific taxable years within the injury period will be conclusive. If a judgment for a compensable injury does not apportion the amount of the recovery to specific taxable years within the injury period, the amount of the recovery will be prorated among the years within the injury period in the proportion that the net operating loss sustained in each of such years bears to the total net operating losses sustained for all such years. If an action is settled, the specifications of the parties will generally determine the apportionment of the amount of the recovery unless such specifications are not reasonably supported by the facts and circumstances of the case. In the absence of specifications of the parties, the amount of the recovery will be prorated among the years within the injury period in the proportion that the net operating loss sustained in each of such years bears to the total net operating losses sustained for all such years.

(4) *Application of losses attributable to a compensable injury.*—If only a portion of a net operating loss for any taxable year is attributable to a compensable injury, such portion shall (in applying section 172 for purposes of this section) be considered to be a separate net operating loss for such year to be applied after the other portion of such net operating loss. If, for example, in the year of the compensable injury the net operating loss was $1,000 and the amount of the compensable injury was $600, the amount of $400 not attributable to the compensable injury would be used first to offset profits in the carryover or carryback periods as prescribed by section 172. After the amount not attributable to the compensable injury is used to offset profits in other years, then the amount attributable to the compensable injury will be applied against profits in the carryover or carryback periods.

(e) *Effect on net operating loss carryovers.*—(1) *In general.*—Under section 186(e) if for the taxable year in which a compensatory amount is received or accrued any portion of the net operating loss carryovers to such year are attributable to the compensable injury for which such amount is received or accrued, such portion of the net operating loss carryovers must be reduced by the excess, if any, of (i) the amount computed under section 186(e)(1) with respect to such compensatory amount, over (ii) the amount computed under section 186(e)(2) with respect to such compensable injury.

(2) *Amount computed under section 186(e)(1).*—The amount computed under section 186(e)(1) is equal to the deduction allowed under section 186(a) with respect to the compensatory amount received or accrued for the taxable year.

(3) *Amount computed under section 186(e)(2).*—The amount computed under section 186(e)(2) is equal to that portion of the unrecovered losses sustained as a result of the compensable injury with respect to which, as of the beginning of the taxable year, the period for carryover under section 172 has expired without benefit to the taxpayer, but only to the extent that such portion of the unrecovered losses did not reduce an amount computed under section 186(e)(1) for any prior taxable year.

(4) *Increase in income under section 172(b)(2).*—If there is a reduction for any taxable year under subparagraph (1) of this paragraph in the portion of the net operating loss carryovers to such year attributable to a compensable injury, then, solely for purposes of determining the amount of such portion which may be carried to subsequent taxable years, the income of such taxable year, as computed under section 172(b)(2), shall be increased by the amount of the reduction computed under subparagraph (1) of this paragraph, for such year.

(f) *Illustration.*—The provisions of section 186 and this section may be illustrated by the following example:

Example. (i) As of the beginning of this taxable year 1969, taxpayer A has a net operating loss carryover from his taxable year 1966 of $550 of which $250 is attributable to a compensable injury. In addition, he has a net operating loss attributable to the compensable injury of $150 with respect to which the period for carryover under section 172 has expired without benefit to the taxpayer. In 1969, he receives a $100 compensatory amount with respect to that injury and he has $75 in other income. Thus, A has gross income of $175 and he is entitled to a $100 deduction (the compensatory amount received) under section 186(a) and this section since this amount is less than the unrecovered losses sustained as a result of the compensable injury ($250 + $150 = $400). No portion of the net operating loss carryover to the current taxable year attributable to the compensable injury is reduced under section 186(e) since the amount determined under section 186(e)(1) ($100) does not exceed the amount determined under section 186(e)(2) ($150). Therefore, A applies a net operating loss carryover of $550 against his remaining income of $75 and retains a net operating loss carryover of $475 to following years of which amount $250 remains attributable to the compensable injury. In addition, he retains $50 of net operating losses attributable to the compensable injury with respect to which the period for carryover under section 172 has expired without benefit to the taxpayer.

(ii) In 1970, A receives a $200 compensatory amount with respect to the same compensable injury and has $75 of other income. Thus, A has gross income of $275 and he is entitled to a $200 deduction (the compensatory amount received) under section 186(a) and this section since this amount is less than the remaining unrecovered loss sustained as a result of the compensable injury ($250 + $50 = $300). The net operating loss carryover to the current taxable year of $250 attributable to the compensable injury is reduced under section 186(e) by $150, which is the excess of the amount determined under section 186(e)(1) ($200) over the amount determined under section 186(e)(2) ($50). Therefore, A applies net operating loss carryovers of $325 ($225 not attributable to the compensable injury, + $100 attributable to such injury) against his remaining income of $75. A retains net operating loss carryovers of $250 for following years, of which amount $100 is attributable to the compensable injury. A has used all of his net operating losses attributable to the compensable injury with respect to which the period for carryover under section 172 has expired without benefit to the taxpayer.

(iii) In 1971, A receives a $200 compensatory amount with respect to the same compensable injury and has $75 of other income. Thus, A has gross income of $275 and he is entitled to a $100 deduction (the amount of unrecovered losses) under section 186(a) and this section since this amount is less than the compensatory amount received ($200). The net operating loss carryover to the current taxable year of $100 attributable to the compensable injury is reduced under section 186(e) by $100, which is the excess of the amount determined under section 186(e)(1) ($100) over the amount determined under section 186(e)(2) ($0). Therefore, A applies net operating loss carryovers of $150 against his remaining income of $175 ($100 compensatory amount plus $75 other income) which leaves $25 taxable income. No net operating loss carryover remains for following years.

(g) *Effective date.*—The provisions of this section are applicable as to compensatory amounts received or accrued in taxable years beginning after December 31, 1968, even though the compensable injury

was sustained in taxable years beginning before such date. [Reg. §1.186-1.]

☐ [T.D. 7220, 11-20-72.]

[Reg. §1.190-1]

§1.190-1. Expenditures to remove architectural and transportation barriers to the handicapped and elderly.—(a) *In general.*—Under section 190 of the Internal Revenue Code of 1954, a taxpayer may elect, in the manner provided in §1.190-3 of this chapter, to deduct certain amounts paid or incurred by him in any taxable year beginning after December 31, 1976. and before January 1, 1980, for qualified architectural and transportation barrier removal expenses (as defined in §1.190-2(b) of this chapter). In the case of a partnership, the election shall be made by the partnership. The election applies to expenditures paid or incurred during the taxable year which (but for the election) are chargeable to capital account.

(b) *Limitation.*—The maximum deduction for a taxpayer (including an affiliated group of corporations filing a consolidated return) for any taxable year is $25,000. The $25,000 limitation applies to a partnership and to each partner. Expenditures paid or incurred in a taxable year in excess of the amount deductible under section 190 for such taxable year are capital expenditures and are adjustments to basis under section 1016(a). A partner must combine his distributive share of the partnership's deductible expenditures (after application of the $25,000 limitation at the partnership level) with that partner's distributive share of deductible expenditures from any other partnership plus that partner's own section 190 expenditures, if any (if he makes the election with respect to his own expenditures), and apply the partner's $25,000 limitation to the combined total to determine the aggregate amount deductible by that partner. In so doing, the partner may allocate the partner's $25,000 limitation among the partner's own section 190 expenditures and the partner's distributive share of partnership deductible expenditures in any manner. If such allocation results in all or a portion of the partner's distributive share of a partnership's deductible expenditures not being an allowable deduction by the partner, the partnership may capitalize such unallowable portion by an appropriate adjustment to the basis of the relevant partnership property under section 1016. For purposes of adjustments to the basis of properties held by a partnership, however, it shall be presumed that each partner's distributive share of partnership deductible expenditures (after application of the $25,000 limitation at the partnership level) was allowable in full to the partner. This presumption can be rebutted only by clear and convincing evidence that all or any portion of a partner's distributive share of the partnership section 190 deduction was not allowable as a deduction to the partner because it exceeded that partner's $25,000 limitation as allocated by him. For example, suppose for 1978 A's distributive share of the ABC partnership's deductible section 190 expenditures (after application of the $25,000 limitation at the partnership level) is $15,000. A also made section 190 expenditures of $20,000 in 1978 which he elects to deduct. A allocates $10,000 of his $25,000 limitation to his distributive share of the ABC expenditures and $15,000 to his own expenditures. A may capitalize the excess $5,000 of his own expenditures. In addition, if ABC obtains from A evidence which meets the requisite burden of proof, it may capitalize the $5,000 of A's distributive share which is not allowable as a deduction to A. [Reg. §1.190-1.]

☐ [T.D. 7634, 7-19-79.]

[Reg. §1.190-2]

§1.190-2. Definitions.—For purposes of section 190 and the regulations thereunder—

(a) *Architectural and transportation barrier removal expenses.*—The term "architectural and transportation barrier removal expenses" means expenditures for the purpose of making any facility, or public transportation vehicle, owned or leased by the taxpayer for use in connection with his trade or business more accessible to, or usable by, handicapped individuals or elderly individuals. For purposes of this section—

(1) The term "facility" means all or any portion of buildings, structures, equipment, roads, walks, parking lots, or similar real or personal property.

(2) The term "public transportation vehicle" means a vehicle, such as a bus, a railroad car, or other conveyance, which provides to the public general or special transportation service (including such service rendered to the customers of a taxpayer who is not in the trade or business of rendering transportation services).

(3) The term "handicapped individual" means any individual who has—

(i) A physical or mental disability (including, but not limited to, blindness or deafness) which for such individual constitutes or results in a functional limitation to employment, or

(ii) A physical or mental impairment (including, but not limited to, a sight or hearing impairment) which substantially limits one or more of such individual's major life activities, such as performing manual tasks, walking, speaking, breathing, learning, or working.

(4) The term "elderly individual" means an individual age 65 or over.

(b) *Qualified architectural and transportation barrier removal expense.*—(1) *In general.*—The term "qualified architectural and transportation barrier removal expense" means an architectural or transportation barrier removal expenses (as defined in paragraph (a) of this section) with respect to which the taxpayer establishes, to the satisfaction of the Commissioner or his delegate, that the resulting removal of any such barrier conforms a facility or public transportation vehicle to all the requirements set forth in one or more of paragraphs (b)(2) through (22) of this section or in one or more of the subdivisions of paragraph (b)(20) or (21). Such term includes only expenses specifically attributable to the removal of an existing architectural or transportation barrier. It does not include any part of any expense paid or incurred in connection with the construction or comprehensive renovation of a facility or public transportation vehicle or the normal replacement of depreciable property. Such term may include expenses of construction, as, for example, the construction of a ramp to remove the barrier posed for wheelchair users by steps. Major portions of the standards set forth in this paragraph were adapted from "American National Standard Specifications for Making Buildings and Facilities Accessible to, and Usable by, the Physically Handicapped" (1971), the copyright for which is held by the American National Standards Institute, 1430 Broadway, New York, New York 10018.

(2) *Grading.*—The grading of ground, even contrary to existing topography, shall attain a level with a normal entrance to make a facility accessible to individuals with physical disabilities.

(3) *Walks.*—(i) A public walk shall be at least 48 inches wide and shall have a gradient not greater than 5 percent. A walk of maximum or near maximum grade and of considerable length shall have level areas at regular intervals. A walk or driveway shall have a nonslip surface.

(ii) A walk shall be of a continuing common surface and shall not be interrupted by steps or abrupt changes in level.

(iii) Where a walk crosses a walk, a driveway, or a parking lot, they shall blend to a common level. However, the preceding sentence does not require the elimination of those curbs which are a safety feature for the handicapped, particularly the blind.

(iv) An inclined walk shall have a level platform at the top and at the bottom. If a door swings out onto the platform toward the walk, such platform shall be at least 5 feet deep and 5 feet wide. If a door does not swing onto the platform or toward the walk, such platform shall be at least 3 feet deep and 5 feet wide. A platform shall extend at least 1 foot beyond the strike jamb side of any doorway.

(4) *Parking lots.*—(i) At least one parking space that is accessible and approximate to a facility shall be set aside and identified for use by the handicapped.

(ii) A parking space shall be open on one side to allow room for individuals in wheelchairs and individuals on braces or crutches to get in and out of an automobile onto a level surface which is suitable for wheeling and walking.

(iii) A parking space for the handicapped, when placed between two conventional diagonal or head-on parking spaces, shall be at least 12 feet wide.

(iv) A parking space shall be positioned so that individuals in wheelchairs and individuals on braces or crutches need not wheel or walk behind parked cars.

(5) *Ramps.*—(i) A ramp shall not have a slope greater than 1 inch rise in 12 inches.

(ii) A ramp shall have at least one handrail that is 32 inches in height, measured from the surface of the ramp, that is smooth, and that extends 1 foot beyond the top and bottom of the ramp. However, the preceding sentence does not require a handrail extension which is itself a hazard.

(iii) A ramp shall have a nonslip surface.

(iv) A ramp shall have a level platform at the top and at the bottom. If a door swings out onto the platform or toward the ramp, such platform shall be at least 5 feet deep and 5 feet wide. If a door does not swing onto the platform or toward the ramp, such platform shall be at least 3 feet deep and 5 feet wide. A platform shall extend *at least 1 foot beyond the strike jamb side of any doorway.*

(v) A ramp shall have level platforms at not more than 30-foot intervals and at any turn.

(vi) A curb ramp shall be provided at an intersection. The curb ramp shall not be less than 4 feet wide; it shall not have a slope

greater than 1 inch rise in 12 inches. The transition between the two surfaces shall be smooth. A curb ramp shall have a nonslip surface.

(6) *Entrances.*—A building shall have at least one primary entrance which is usable by individuals in wheelchairs and which is on a level accessible to an elevator.

(7) *Doors and doorways.*—(i) A door shall have a clear opening of no less than 32 inches and shall be operable by a single effort.

(ii) The floor on the inside and outside of a doorway shall be level for a distance of at least 5 feet from the door in the direction the door swings and shall extend at least 1 foot beyond the strike jamb side of the doorway.

(iii) There shall be no sharp inclines or abrupt changes in level at a doorway. The threshold shall be flush with the floor. The door closer shall be selected, placed, and set so as not to impair the use of the door by the handicapped.

(8) *Stairs.*—(i) Stairsteps shall have round nosing of between 1 and 1¹/₂ inch radius.

(ii) Stairs shall have a handrail 32 inches high as measured from the tread at the face of the riser.

(iii) Stairs shall have at least one handrail that extends at least 18 inches beyond the top step and beyond the bottom step. The preceding sentence does not require a handrail extension which is itself a hazard.

(iv) Steps shall have risers which do not exceed 7 inches.

(9) *Floors.*—(i) Floors shall have a nonslip surface.

(ii) Floors on a given story of a building shall be of a common level or shall be connected by a ramp in accordance with subparagraph (5) of this paragraph.

(10) *Toilet rooms.*—(i) A toilet room shall have sufficient space to allow traffic of individuals in wheelchairs.

(ii) A toilet room shall have at least one toilet stall that—

(A) Is at least 36 inches wide;

(B) Is at least 56 inches deep;

(C) Has a door, if any, that is at least 32 inches wide and swings out;

(D) Has handrails on each side, 33 inches high and parallel to the floor, 1¹/₂ inches in outside diameter, 1¹/₂ inches clearance between rail and wall, and fastened securely at ends and center; and

(E) Has a water closet with a seat 19 to 20 inches from the finished floor.

(iii) A toilet room shall have, in addition to or in lieu of a toilet stall described in (ii), at least one toilet stall that—

(A) Is at least 66 inches wide;

(B) Is at least 60 inches deep;

(C) Has a door, if any, that is at least 32 inches wide and swings out;

(D) Has a handrail on one side, 33 inches high and parallel to the floor, 1¹/₂ inches in outside diameter, 1¹/₂ inches clearance between rail and wall, and fastened securely at ends and center; and

(E) Has a water closet with a seat 19 to 20 inches from the finished floor, centerline located 18 inches from the side wall on which the handrail is located.

(iv) A toilet room shall have lavatories with narrow aprons. Drain pipes and hot water pipes under a lavatory shall be covered or insulated.

(v) A mirror and a shelf above a lavatory shall be no higher than 40 inches above the floor, measured from the top of the shelf and the bottom of the mirror.

(vi) A toilet room for men shall have wall-mounted urinals with the opening of the basin 15 to 19 inches from the finished floor or shall have floor-mounted urinals that are level with the main floor of the toilet room.

(vii) Towel racks, towel dispensers, and other dispensers and disposal units shall be mounted no higher than 40 inches from the floor.

(11) *Water fountains.*—(i) A water fountain and a cooler shall have upfront spouts and controls.

(ii) A water fountain and a cooler shall be hand-operated or hand-and-foot-operated.

(iii) A water fountain mounted on the side of a floor-mounted cooler shall not be more than 30 inches above the floor.

(iv) A wall-mounted, hand-operated water cooler shall be mounted with the basin 36 inches from the floor.

(v) A water fountain shall not be fully recessed and shall not be set into an alcove unless the alcove is at least 36 inches wide.

(12) *Public telephones.*—(i) A public telephone shall be placed so that the dial and the headset can be reached by individuals in wheelchairs.

(ii) A public telephone shall be equipped for those with hearing disabilities and so identified with instructions for use.

(iii) Coin slots of public telephones shall be not more than 48 inches from the floor.

(13) *Elevators.*—(i) An elevator shall be accessible to, and usable by, the handicapped or the elderly on the levels they use to enter the building and all levels and areas normally used.

(ii) Cab size shall allow for the turning of a wheelchair. It shall measure at least 54 by 68 inches.

(iii) Door clear opening width shall be at least 32 inches.

(iv) All essential controls shall be within 48 to 54 inches from cab floor. Such controls shall be usable by the blind and shall be tactilely identifiable.

(14) *Controls.*—Switches and controls for light, heat, ventilation, windows, draperies, fire alarms, and all similar controls of frequent or essential use, shall be placed within the reach of individuals in wheelchairs. Such switches and controls shall be no higher than 48 inches from the floor.

(15) *Identification.*—(i) Raised letters or numbers shall be used to identify a room or an office. Such identification shall be placed on the wall to the right or left of the door at a height of 54 inches to 66 inches, measured from the finished floor.

(ii) A door that might prove dangerous if a blind person were to exit or enter by it (such as a door leading to a loading platform, boiler room, stage, or fire escape) shall be tactilely identifiable.

(16) *Warning signals.*—(i) An audible warning signal shall be accompanied by a simultaneous visual signal for the benefit of those with hearing disabilities.

(ii) A visual warning signal shall be accompanied by a simultaneous audible signal for the benefit of the blind.

(17) *Hazards.*—Hanging signs, ceiling lights, and similar objects and fixtures shall be placed at a minimum height of 7 feet, measured from the floor.

(18) *International accessibility symbol.*—The international accessibility symbol (see illustration) shall be displayed on routes to and at wheelchair-accessible entrances to facilities and public transportation vehicles.

(19) *Additional standards for rail facilities.*—(i) A rail facility shall contain a fare control area with at least one entrance with a clear opening at least 36 inches wide.

(ii) A boarding platform edge bordering a drop-off or other dangerous condition shall be marked with a warning device consisting of a strip of floor material differing in color and texture from the remaining floor surface. The gap between boarding platform and vehicle doorway shall be minimized.

(20) *Standards for buses.*—(i) A bus shall have a level change mechanism (*e.g.*, lift or ramp) to enter the bus and sufficient clearance to permit a wheelchair user to reach a secure location.

(ii) A bus shall have a wheelchair securement device. However, the preceding sentence does not require a wheelchair securement device which is itself a barrier or hazard.

(iii) The vertical distance from a curb or from street level to the first front door step shall not exceed 8 inches; the riser height for each front doorstep after the first step up from the curb or street level shall also not exceed 8 inches; and the tread depth of steps at front and rear doors shall be no less than 12 inches.

(iv) A bus shall contain clearly legible signs that indicate that seats in the front of the bus are priority seats for handicapped or

elderly persons, and that encourage other passengers to make such seats available to handicapped and elderly persons who wish to use them.

(v) Handrails and stanchions shall be provided in the entranceway to the bus in a configuration that allows handicapped and elderly persons to grasp such assists from outside the bus while starting to board and to continue to use such assists throughout the boarding and fare collection processes. The configuration of the passenger assist system shall include a rail across the front of the interior of the bus located to allow passengers to lean against it while paying fares. Overhead handrails shall be continuous except for a gap at the rear doorway.

(vi) Floors and steps shall have nonslip surfaces. Step edges shall have a band of bright contrasting color running the full width of the step.

(vii) A stepwell immediately adjacent to the driver shall have, when the door is open, at least 2 foot-candles of illumination measured on the step tread. Other stepwells shall have, at all times, at least 2 foot-candles of illumination measured on the step tread.

(viii) The doorways of the bus shall have outside lighting that provides at least 1 foot-candle of illumination on the street surface for a distance of 3 feet from all points on the bottom step tread edge. Such lighting shall be located below window level and shall be shielded to protect the eyes of entering and exiting passengers.

(ix) The fare box shall be located as far forward as practicable and shall not obstruct traffic in the vestibule.

(21) *Standards for rapid and light rail vehicles.*—(i) Passenger doorways on the vehicle sides shall have clear openings at least 32 inches wide.

(ii) Audible or visual warning signals shall be provided to alert handicapped and elderly persons of closing doors.

(iii) Handrails and stanchions shall be sufficient to permit safe boarding, onboard circulation, seating and standing assistance, and unboarding by handicapped and elderly persons. On a level entry vehicle, handrails, stanchions, and seats shall be located so as to allow a wheelchair user to enter the vehicle and position the wheelchair in a location which does not obstruct the movement of other passengers. On a vehicle that requires the use of steps in the boarding process, handrails and stanchions shall be provided in the entranceway to the vehicle in a configuration that allows handicapped and elderly persons to grasp such assists from outside the vehicle while starting to board, and to continue using such assists throughout the boarding process.

(iv) Floors shall have nonslip surfaces. Step edges on a light rail vehicle shall have a band of bright contrasting color running the full width of the step.

(v) A stepwell immediately adjacent to the driver shall have, when the door is open, at least 2 foot-candles of illumination measured on the step tread. Other stepwells shall have, at all times, at least 2 foot-candles of illumination measured on the step tread.

(vi) Doorways on a light rail vehicle shall have outside lighting that provides at least 1 foot-candle of illumination on the street surface for a distance of 3 feet from all points on the bottom step tread edge. Such lighting shall be located below window level and shall be shielded to protect the eyes of entering and exiting passengers.

(22) *Other barrier removals.*—The provisions of this subparagraph apply to any barrier which would not be removed by compliance with paragraphs (b)(2) through (21) of this section. The requirements of this subparagraph are:

(i) A substantial barrier to the access to or use of a facility or public transportation vehicle by handicapped or elderly individuals is removed;

(ii) The barrier which is removed had been a barrier for one or more major classes of such individuals (such as the blind, deaf, or wheelchair users); and

(iii) The removal of that barrier is accomplished without creating any new barrier that significantly impairs access to or use of the facility or vehicle by such class or classes. [Reg. §1.190-2.]

☐ [*T.D. 7634, 7-19-79.*]

[Reg. §1.190-3]

§1.190-3. Election to deduct architectural and transportation barrier removal expenses.—(a) *Manner of making election.*—The election to deduct expenditures for removal of architectural and transportation barriers provided by section 190(a) shall be made by claiming the deduction as a separate item identified as such on the taxpayer's income tax return for the taxable year for which such election is to apply (or, in the case of a partnership, to the return of partnership income for such year). For the election to be valid, the return must be filed not later than the time prescribed by law for filing the return (including extensions thereof) for the taxable year for which the election is to apply.

(b) *Scope of election.*—An election under section 190(a) shall apply to all expenditures described in § 1.190-2 (or, in the case of a taxpayer whose architectural and transportation barrier removal expenses exceed $25,000 for the taxable year, to the $25,000 of such expenses with respect to which the deduction is claimed) paid or incurred during the taxable year for which made and shall be irrevocable after the date by which any such election must have been made.

(c) *Records to be kept.*—In any case in which an election is made under section 190(a), the taxpayer shall have available, for the period prescribed by paragraph (e) of § 1.6001-1 of this chapter (Income Tax Regulations), records and documentation, including architectural plans and blueprints, contracts, and any building permits, of all the facts necessary to determine the amount of any deduction to which he is entitled by reason of the election, as well as the amount of any adjustment to basis made for expenditures in excess of the amount deductible under section 190. [Reg. § 1.190-3.]

□ [T.D. 7634, 7-19-79.]

[Reg. §1.193-1]

§1.193-1. Deduction for tertiary injectant expenses.—(a) *In general.*—Subject to the limitations and restrictions of paragraphs (c) and (d) of this section, there shall be allowed as a deduction from gross income an amount equal to the qualified tertiary injectant expenses of the taxpayer. This deduction is allowed for the later of—

(1) The taxable year in which the injectant is injected, or

(2) The taxable year in which the expenses are paid or incurred.

(b) *Definitions.*—(1) *Qualified tertiary injectant expenses.*—Except as otherwise provided in this section, the term "qualified tertiary injectant expense" means any cost paid or incurred for any tertiary injectant which is used as part of a tertiary recovery method.

(2) *Tertiary recovery method.*—"Tertiary recovery method" means—

(i) Any method which is described in subparagraphs (1) through (9) of section 212.78(c) of the June 1979 energy regulations (as defined by section 4996(b)(8)(C)),

(ii) Any method for which the taxpayer has obtained the approval of the Associate Chief Counsel (Technical), under section 4993(d)(1)(B) for purposes of Chapter 45 of the Internal Revenue Code,

(iii) Any method which is approved in the regulations under section 4993(d)(1)(B), or

(iv) Any other method to provide tertiary enhanced recovery for which the taxpayer obtains the approval of the Associate Chief Counsel (Technical) for purposes of section 193.

(c) *Special rules for hydrocarbons.*—(1) *In general.*—If an injectant contains more than an insignificant amount of recoverable hydrocarbons, the amount deductible under section 193 and paragraph (a) of this section shall be limited to the cost of the injectant reduced by the lesser of—

(i) The fair market value of the hydrocarbon component in the form in which it is recovered, or

(ii) The cost to the taxpayer of the hydrocarbon component of the injectant. Price levels at the time of injection are to be used in determining the fair market value of the recoverable hydrocarbons.

(2) *Presumption of recoverability.*—Except to the extent that the taxpayer can demonstrate otherwise, all hydrocarbons shall be presumed recoverable and shall be presumed to have the same value on recovery that they would have if separated from the other components of the injectant before injection. Estimates based on generally accepted engineering practices may provide evidence of limitations on the amount or value of recoverable hydrocarbons.

(3) *Significant amount.*—For purposes of section 193 and this section, an injectant contains more than an insignificant amount of recoverable hydrocarbons if the fair market value of the recoverable hydrocarbon component of the injectant, in the form in which it is recovered, equals or exceeds 25 percent of the cost of the injectant.

(4) *Hydrocarbon defined.*—For purposes of section 193 and this section, the term hydrocarbon means all forms of natural gas and crude oil (which includes oil recovered from sources such as oil shale and condensate).

(5) *Injectant defined.*—For purposes of applying this paragraph (c), an injectant is the substance or mixture of substances injected at a particular time. Substances injected at different times are not treated as components of a single injectant even if the injections are part of a single tertiary recovery process.

(d) *Application with other deductions.*—No deduction shall be allowed under section 193 and this section for any expenditure—

(1) With respect to which the taxpayer has made an election under section 263(c) or

(2) With respect to which a deduction is allowed or allowable under any other provision of chapter 1 of the Code.

(e) *Examples.*—The application of this section may be illustrated by the following examples:

Example (1). B, a calendar year taxpayer who uses the cash receipts and disbursements method of accounting, uses an approved tertiary recovery method for the enhanced recovery of crude oil from one of B's oil properties. During 1980, B pays $100x for a tertiary injectant which contains 1,000y units of hydrocarbon; if separated from the other components of the injectant before injection, the hydrocarbons would have a fair market value of $80x. B uses this injectant during the recovery effort during 1981. B has not made any election under section 263(c) with respect to the expenditures for the injectant, and no section of chapter 1 of the Code other than section 193 allows a deduction for the expenditure. B is unable to demonstrate that the value of the injected hydrocarbons recovered during production will be less than $80x. B's deduction under section 193 is limited to the excess of the cost for the injectant over the fair market value of the hydrocarbon component expected to be recovered ($100x – $80x=$20x). B may claim the deduction only for 1981, the year of the injection.

Example (2). Assume the same facts as in example (1) except that through engineering studies B has shown that 700y units or 70 percent of the hydrocarbon injected is nonrecoverable. The recoverable hydrocarbons have a fair market value of $24x (30 percent of $80x). The recoverable hydrocarbon portion of the injectant is 24 percent of the cost of the injectant ($24x divided by $100x). The injectant does not contain a significant amount of recoverable hydrocarbons. B may claim a deduction for $100x, the entire cost of the injectant.

Example (3). Assume the same facts as in example (1) except that through laboratory studies B has shown that because of chemical changes in the course of production the injected hydrocarbons that are recovered will have a fair market value of only $40x. B may claim a deduction for $60x, the excess of the cost of the injectant ($100x) over the fair market value of the recoverable hydrocarbons ($40x).

Example (4). B prepares an injectant from crude oil and certain nonhydrocarbon materials purchased by B. The total cost of the injectant to B is $100x, of which $24x is attributable to the crude oil. The fair market value of the crude oil used in the injectant is $27x. B is unable to demonstrate that the value of the crude oil from the injectant that will be recovered is less than $27x. The injectant contains more than an insignificant amount of recoverable hydrocarbons because the value of the recoverable crude oil ($27x) exceeds $25x (25 percent of $100x, the cost of the injectant). Because the cost to B of the hydrocarbon component of the injectant ($24x) is less than the fair market value of the hydrocarbon component in the form in which it is recovered ($27x), the cost rather than the value is taken into account in the adjustment required under paragraph (c)(1) of this section. B's deduction under section 193 is limited to the excess of the cost of the injectant over the cost of the hydrocarbon component ($100x – $24x = $76x). [Reg. § 1.193-1]

□ [T.D. 7980, 10-2-84.]

[Reg. §1.194-1]

§1.194-1. Amortization of reforestation expenditures.—(a) *In general.*—Section 194 allows a taxpayer to elect to amortize over an 84-month period, up to $10,000 of reforestation expenditures (as defined in §1.194-3(c)) incurred by the taxpayer in a taxable year in connection with qualified timber property (as defined in §1.194-3(a)). The election is not available to trusts. Only those reforestation expenditures which result in additions to capital accounts after December 31, 1979 are eligible for this special amortization.

(b) *Determination of amortization period.*—The amortization period must begin on the first day of the first month of the last half of the taxable year during which the taxpayer incurs the reforestation expenditures. For example, the 84-month amortization period begins on July 1 of a taxable year for a calendar year taxpayer, regardless of whether the reforestation expenditures are incurred in January or December of that taxable year. Therefore, a taxpayer will be allowed to claim amortization deductions for only six months of each of the first and eighth taxable years of the period over which the reforestation expenditures will be amortized.

(c) *Recapture.*—If a taxpayer disposes of qualified timber property within ten years of the year in which the amortizable basis was created and the taxpayer has claimed amortization deductions under section 194, part or all of any gain on the disposition may be recaptured as ordinary income. See section 1245. [Reg. § 1.194-1.]

□ [T.D. 7927, 12-15-83.]

[Reg. §1.194-2]

§1.194-2. Amount of deduction allowable.—(a) *General rule.*—The allowable monthly deduction with respect to reforestation expenditures made in a taxable year is determined by dividing the amount of reforestation expenditures made in such taxable year (after applying the limitations of paragraph (b) of this section) by 84. In order to determine the total allowable amortization deduction for a given month, a taxpayer should add the monthly amortization deductions computed under the preceding sentence for qualifying expenditures made by the taxpayer in the taxable year and the preceding seven taxable years.

(b) *Dollar limitation.*—(1) *Maximum amount subject to election.*—A taxpayer may elect to amortize up to $10,000 of qualifying reforestation expenditures each year under section 194. However, the maximum amortizable amount is $5,000 in the case of a married individual (as defined in section 143) filing a separate return. No carryover or carryback of expenditures in excess of $10,000 is permitted. The maximum annual amortization deduction for expenditures incurred in any taxable year is $1,428.57 ($10,000/7). The maximum deduction in the first and eighth taxable years of the amortization period is one-half that amount, or $714.29, because of the half-year convention provided in §1.194-1(b). Total deductions for any one year under this section will reach $10,000 only if a taxpayer incurs and elects to amortize the maximum $10,000 of expenditures each year over an 8-year period.

(2) *Allocation of amortizable basis among taxpayer's timber properties.*—The limit of $10,000 on amortizable reforestation expenditures applies to expenditures paid or incurred during a taxable year on all of the taxpayer's timber properties. A taxpayer who incurs more than $10,000 in qualifying expenditures in connection with more than one qualified timber property during a taxable year may select the properties for which section 194 amortization will be elected as well as the manner in which the $10,000 limitation on amortizable basis is allocated among such properties. For example, A incurred $10,000 of qualifying reforestation expenditures on each of four properties in 1981. A may elect under section 194 to amortize $2,500 of the amount spent on each property, $5,000 of the amount spent on any two properties, the entire $10,000 spent on any one property, or A may allocate the $10,000 maximum amortizable basis among some or all of the properties in any other manner.

(3) *Basis.*—(i) *In general.*—Except as provided in paragraph (b)(3)(ii) of this section, the basis of a taxpayer's interest in qualified timber property for which an election is made under section 194 shall be adjusted to reflect the amount of the section 194 amortization deduction allowable to the taxpayer.

(ii) *Special rule for trusts.*—Although a trust may be a partner of a partnership, income beneficiary of an estate, or (for taxable years beginning after December 31, 1982) shareholder of an S corporation, it may not deduct its allocable share of a section 194 amortization deduction allowable to such partnership, estate, or S corporation. In addition, the basis of the interest held by the partnership, estate, or S corporation in the qualified timber property shall not be adjusted to reflect the portion of the section 194 amortization deduction that is allocable to the trust.

(4) *Allocation of amortizable basis among component members of a controlled group.*—Component members of a controlled group (as defined in §1.194-3(d)) on a December 31 shall be treated as one taxpayer in applying the $10,000 limitation of paragraph (b)(1) of this section. The amortizable basis may be allocated to any one such member or allocated (for the taxable year of each such member which includes such December 31) among the several members in any manner, provided that the amount of amortizable basis allocated to any member does not exceed the amount of amortizable basis actually acquired by the member in the taxable year. The allocation is to be made (1) by the common parent corporation if a consolidated return is filed for all component members of the group, or (2) in accordance with an agreement entered into by the members of the group if separate returns are filed. If a consolidated return is filed by some component members of the group and separate returns are filed by other component members, then the common parent of the group filing the consolidated return shall enter into an agreement with those members who do not join in filing the consolidated return allocating the amount between the group filing the return and the other component members of the controlled group who do not join in filing the consolidated return. If a consolidated return is filed, the common parent corporation shall file a separate statement attached to the income tax return on which an election is made to amortize reforestation costs under section 194. See §1.194-4. If separate returns are filed by some or all component members of the group, each component member to which is allocated any part of the deduction

under section 194 shall file a separate statement attached to the income tax return in which an election is made to amortize reforestation expenditures. See §1.194-4. Such statement shall include the name, address, employer identification number, and the taxable year of each component member of the controlled group, a copy of the allocation agreement signed by persons duly authorized to act on behalf of those members who file separate returns, and a description of the manner in which the deduction under section 194 has been divided among them.

(5) *Partnerships.*—(i) *Election to be made by partnership.*—A partnership makes the election to amortize qualified reforestation expenditures of the partnership. See section 703(b).

(ii) *Dollar limitations applicable to partnerships.*—The dollar limitations of section 194 apply to the partnership as well as to each partner. Thus, a partnership may not elect to amortize more than $10,000 of reforestation expenditures under section 194 in any taxable year.

(iii) *Partner's share of amortizable basis.*—Section 704 and the regulations thereunder shall govern the determination of a partner's share of a partnership's amortizable reforestation expenditures for any taxable year.

(iv) *Dollar limitation applicable to partners.*—A partner shall in no event be entitled in any taxable year to claim a deduction for amortization based on more than $10,000 ($5,000 in the case of a married taxpayer who files a separate return) of amortizable basis acquired in such taxable year regardless of the source of the amortizable basis. In the case of a partner who is a member of two or more partnerships that elect under section 194, the partner's aggregate share of partnership amortizable basis may not exceed $10,000 or $5,000, whichever is applicable. In the case of a member of a partnership that elects under section 194 who also has separately acquired qualified timber property, the aggregate of the member's partnership and nonpartnership amortizable basis may not exceed $10,000 or $5,000, whichever is applicable.

(6) *S corporations.*—For taxable years beginning after December 31, 1982, rules similar to those contained in paragraph (b)(5)(ii) and (iv) of this section shall apply in the case of S corporations (as defined in section 1361(a)) and their shareholders.

(7) *Estates.*—Estates may elect to amortize in each taxable year up to a maximum of $10,000 of qualifying reforestation expenditures under section 194. Any amortizable basis acquired by an estate shall be apportioned between the estate and the income beneficiary on the basis of the income of the estate allocable to each. The amount of amortizable basis apportioned from an estate to a beneficiary shall be taken into account in determining the $10,000 (or $5,000) amount of amortizable basis allowable to such beneficiary under this section.

(c) *Life tenant and remainderman.*—If property is held by one person for life with remainder to another person, the life tenant is entitled to the full benefit of any amortization allowable under section 194 on qualifying expenditures he or she makes. Any remainder interest in the property is ignored for this purpose. [Reg. §1.194-2.]

☐ [*T.D. 7927, 12-15-83.*]

[Reg. §1.194-3]

§1.194-3. Definitions.—(a) *Qualified timber property.*—The term "qualified timber property" means property located in the United States which will contain trees in significant commercial quantities. The property may be a woodlot or other site but must consist of at least one acre which is planted with tree seedlings in the manner normally used in forestation or reforestation. The property must be held by the taxpayer for the growing and cutting of timber which will either be sold for use in, or used by the taxpayer in, the commercial production of timber products. A taxpayer does not have to own the property in order to be eligible to elect to amortize costs attributable to it under section 194. Thus, a taxpayer may elect to amortize qualifying reforestation expenditures incurred by such taxpayer on leased qualified timber property. Qualified timber property does not include property on which the taxpayer has planted shelter belts (for which current deductions are allowed under section 175) or ornamental trees, such as Christmas trees.

(b) *Amortizable basis.*—The term "amortizable basis" means that portion of the basis of qualified timber property which is attributable to reforestation expenditures.

(c) *Reforestation expenditures.*—(1) *In general.*—The term "reforestation expenditures" means direct costs incurred to plant or seed for forestation or reforestation purposes. Qualifying expenditures include amounts spent for site preparation, seed or seedlings, and labor and tool costs, including depreciation on equipment used in planting or seeding. Only those costs which must be capitalized and are included in the adjusted basis of the property qualify as reforestation expenditures. Costs which are currently deductible do not qualify.

(2) *Cost-sharing programs.*—Any expenditures for which the taxpayer has been reimbursed under any governmental reforestation cost-sharing program do not qualify as reforestation expenditures unless the amounts reimbursed have been included in the gross income of the taxpayer.

(d) *Definitions of controlled group of corporations and component member of controlled group.*—For purposes of section 194, the terms "controlled group of corporations" and "component member" of a controlled group of corporations shall have the same meaning assigned to those terms in section 1563(a) and (b), except that the phrase "more than 50 percent" shall be substituted for the phrase "at least 80 percent" each place it appears in section 1563(a)(1). [Reg. § 1.194-3.]

☐ [T.D. 7927, 12-15-83.]

[Reg. § 1.194-4]

§ 1.194-4. Time and manner of making election.—(a) *In general.*— Except as provided in paragraph (b) of this section, an election to amortize reforestation expenditures under section 194 shall be made by entering the amortization deduction claimed at the appropriate place on the taxpayer's income tax return for the year in which the expenditures were incurred, and by attaching a statement to such return. The statement should state the amounts of the expenditures, describe the nature of the expenditures, and give the date on which each was incurred. The statement should also state the type of timber being grown and the purpose for which it is being grown. A separate statement must be included for each property for which reforestation expenditures are being amortized under section 194. The election

may only be made on a timely return (taking into account extensions of the time for filing) for the taxable year in which the amortizable expenditures were made.

(b) *Special rule.*—With respect to any return filed before March 15, 1984 on which a taxpayer was eligible to, but did not make an election under section 194, the election to amortize reforestation expenditures under section 194 may be made by a statement on, or attached to, the income tax return (or an amended return) for the taxable year, indicating that an election is being made under section 194 and setting forth the information required under paragraph (a) of this section. An election made under the provisions of this paragraph (b) must be made not later than,

(1) The time prescribed by law (including extension thereof) for filing the income tax return for the year in which the reforestation expenditures were made, or

(2) March 15, 1984, whichever is later. Nothing in this paragraph shall be construed as extending the time specified in section 6511 within which a claim for credit or refund may be filed.

(c) *Revocation.*—An application for consent to revoke an election under section 194 shall be in writing and shall be addressed to the Commissioner of Internal Revenue, Washington, D.C. 20224. The application shall set forth the name and address of the taxpayer, state the taxable years for which the election was in effect, and state the reason for revoking the election. The application shall be signed by the taxpayer or a duly authorized representative of the taxpayer and shall be filed at least 90 days prior to the time prescribed by law (without regard to extensions thereof) for filing the income tax return for the first taxable year for which the election is to terminate. Ordinarily, the request for consent to revoke the election will not be granted if it appears from all the facts and circumstances that the only reason for the desired change is to obtain a tax advantage. [Reg. § 1.194-4.]

☐ [T.D. 7927, 12-15-83.]

≫→ *Caution: Reg. §1.195-1, below, prior to amendment by T.D. 9411 and T.D. 9542, applies to start-up expenditures paid or incurred on or before September 8, 2008. Certain taxpayers may apply the provisions of Reg. §1.195-1, as amended by T.D. 9542, to start-up expenditures paid or incurred after October 22, 2004.*

[Reg. § 1.195-1]

§ 1.195-1. Election to amortize start-up expenditures.—(a) *In general.*—Under section 195(b), a taxpayer may elect to amortize start-up expenditures (as defined in section 195(c)(1)). A taxpayer who elects to amortize start-up expenditures must, at the time of the election, select an amortization period of not less than 60 months, beginning with the month in which the active trade or business begins. The election applies to all of the taxpayer's start-up expenditures with respect to the trade or business. The election to amortize startup expenditures is irrevocable, and the amortization period selected by the taxpayer in making the election may not subsequently be changed.

(b) *Time and manner of making election.*—The election to amortize start-up expenditures under section 195 shall be made by attaching a statement containing the information described in paragraph (c) of this section to the taxpayer's return. The statement must be filed no later than the date prescribed by law for filing the return (including any extensions of time) for the taxable year in which the active trade or business begins. The statement may be filed with a return for any taxable year prior to the year in which the taxpayer's active trade or business begins, but no later than the date prescribed in the preceding sentence. Accordingly, an election under section 195 filed for any taxable year prior to the year in which the taxpayer's active trade or

business begins (and pursuant to which the taxpayer commenced amortizing start-up expenditures in that prior year) will become effective in the month of the year in which the taxpayer's active trade or business begins.

(c) *Information required.*—The statement shall set forth a description of the trade or business to which it relates with sufficient detail so that expenses relating to the trade or business can be identified properly for the taxable year in which the statement is filed and for all future taxable years to which it relates. The statement also shall include the number of months (not less than 60) over which the expenditures are to be amortized, and to the extent known at the time the statement is filed, a description of each start-up expenditure incurred (whether or not paid) and the month in which the active trade or business began (or was acquired). A revised statement may be filed to include any start-up expenditures not included in the taxpayer's original election statement, but the revised statement may not include any expenditures for which the taxpayer had previously taken a position on a return inconsistent with their treatment as start-up expenditures. The revised statement may be filed with a return filed after the return that contained the election.

(d) *Effective date.*—This section applies to elections filed on or after December 17, 1998. [Reg. § 1.195-1.]

☐ [T.D. 8797, 12-16-98.]

≫→ *Caution: Reg. §1.195-1, below, as amended by T.D. 9411 and T.D. 9542, generally applies to start-up expenditures paid or incurred after August 16, 2011. For other applicability provisions, see Reg. §1.195-1(d).*

[Reg. § 1.195-1]

§ 1.195-1. Election to amortize start-up expenditures.—(a) *In general.*—Under section 195(b), a taxpayer may elect to amortize start-up expenditures as defined in section 195(c)(1). In the taxable year in which a taxpayer begins an active trade or business, an electing taxpayer may deduct an amount equal to the lesser of the amount of the start-up expenditures that relate to the active trade or business, or $5,000 (reduced (but not below zero) by the amount by which the start-up expenditures exceed $50,000). The remainder of the start-up expenditures is deductible ratably over the 180-month period beginning with the month in which the active trade or business begins. All start-up expenditures that relate to the active trade or business are considered in determining whether the start-up expenditures exceed $50,000, including expenditures incurred on or before October 22, 2004.

(b) *Time and manner of making election.*—A taxpayer is deemed to have made an election under section 195(b) to amortize start-up expenditures as defined in section 195(c)(1) for the taxable year in

which the active trade or business to which the expenditures relate begins. A taxpayer may choose to forgo the deemed election by affirmatively electing to capitalize its start-up expenditures on a timely filed Federal income tax return (including extensions) for the taxable year in which the active trade or business to which the expenditures relate begins. The election either to amortize startup expenditures under section 195(b) or to capitalize start-up expenditures is irrevocable and applies to all start-up expenditures that are related to the active trade or business. A change in the characterization of an item as a start-up expenditure is a change in method of accounting to which sections 446 and 481(a) apply if the taxpayer treated the item consistently for two or more taxable years. A change in the determination of the taxable year in which the active trade or business begins also is treated as a change in method of accounting if the taxpayer amortized start-up expenditures for two or more taxable years.

(c) *Examples.*—The following examples illustrate the application of this section:

⮞⮞→ *Caution: Reg. §1.195-1, below, as amended by T.D. 9411 and T.D. 9542, generally applies to start-up expenditures paid or incurred after August 16, 2011. For other applicability provisions, see Reg. §1.195-1(d).*

Example 1. Expenditures of $5,000 or less. Corporation X, a calendar year taxpayer, incurs $3,000 of start-up expenditures after October 22, 2004, that relate to an active trade or business that begins on July 1, 2011. Under paragraph (b) of this section, Corporation X is deemed to have elected to amortize start-up expenditures under section 195(b) in 2011. Therefore, Corporation X may deduct the entire amount of the start-up expenditures in 2011, the taxable year in which the active trade or business begins.

Example 2. Expenditures of more than $5,000 but less than or equal to $50,000. The facts are the same as in *Example 1* except that Corporation X incurs start-up expenditures of $41,000. Under paragraph (b) of this section, Corporation X is deemed to have elected to amortize start-up expenditures under section 195(b) in 2011. Therefore, Corporation X may deduct $5,000 and the portion of the remaining $36,000 that is allocable to July through December of 2011 ($36,000/180 × 6 = $1,200) in 2011, the taxable year in which the active trade or business begins. Corporation X may amortize the remaining $34,800 ($36,000 - $1,200 = $34,800) ratably over the remaining 174 months.

Example 3. Subsequent change in the characterization of an item. The facts are the same as in *Example 2* except that Corporation X determines in 2013 that Corporation X incurred $10,000 for an additional start-up expenditure erroneously deducted in 2011 under section 162 as a business expense. Under paragraph (b) of this section, Corporation X is deemed to have elected to amortize start-up expenditures under section 195(b) in 2011, including the additional $10,000 of start-up expenditures. Corporation X is using an impermissible method of accounting for the additional $10,000 of start-up expenditures and must change its method under §1.446-1(e) and the applicable general administrative procedures in effect in 2013.

Example 4. Subsequent redetermination of year in which business begins. The facts are the same as in *Example 2* except that, in 2012, Corporation X deducted the start-up expenditures allocable to January through December of 2012 ($36,000/180 x 12 = $2,400). In addition, in 2013 it is determined that Corporation X actually began business in 2012. Under paragraph (b) of this section, Corporation X is deemed to have elected to amortize start-up expenditures under section 195(b) in 2012. Corporation X impermissibly deducted start-up expenditures in 2011, and incorrectly determined the amount of start-up expenditures deducted in 2012. Therefore, Corporation X is using an impermissible method of accounting for the start-up expenditures and must change its method under §1.446-1(e) and the applicable general administrative procedures in effect in 2013.

Example 5. Expenditures of more than $50,000 but less than or equal to $55,000. The facts are the same as in *Example 1* except that Corporation X incurs start-up expenditures of $54,500. Under paragraph (b) of this section, Corporation X is deemed to have elected to amortize start-up expenditures under section 195(b) in 2011. Therefore, Corporation X may deduct $500 ($5,000 - $4,500) and the portion of the remaining $54,000 that is allocable to July through December of 2011 ($54,000/180 × 6 = $1,800) in 2011, the taxable year in which the active trade or business begins. Corporation X may amortize the remaining $52,200 ($54,000 - $1,800 = $52,200) ratably over the remaining 174 months.

Example 6. Expenditures of more than $55,000. The facts are the same as in *Example 1* except that Corporation X incurs start-up expenditures of $450,000. Under paragraph (b) of this section, Corporation X is deemed to have elected to amortize startup expenditures under section 195(b) in 2011. Therefore, Corporation X may deduct the amounts allocable to July through December of 2011 ($450,000/180 × 6 = $15,000) in 2011, the taxable year in which the active trade or business begins. Corporation X may amortize the remaining $435,000 ($450,000 - $15,000 = $435,000) ratably over the remaining 174 months.

(d) *Effective/applicability date.*—This section applies to start-up expenditures paid or incurred after August 16, 2011. However, taxpayers may apply all the provisions of this section to start-up expenditures paid or incurred after October 22, 2004, provided that the period of limitations on assessment of tax for the year the election under paragraph (b) of this section is deemed made has not expired. For start-up expenditures paid or incurred on or before September 8, 2008, taxpayers may instead apply §1.195-1, as in effect prior to that date (§1.195-1 as contained in 26 CFR part 1 edition revised as of April 1, 2008). [Reg. §1.195-1.]

☐ [*T.D. 8797, 12-16-98. Amended by T.D. 9411, 7-7-2008 and T.D. 9542, 8-16-2011.*]

[Reg. §1.195-2]

§1.195-2. Technical termination of a partnership.—(a) *In general.*—If a partnership that has elected to amortize start-up expenditures under section 195(b) and §1.195-1 terminates in a transaction (or a series of transactions) described in section 708(b)(1)(B) or

§1.708-1(b)(2), the termination shall not be treated as resulting in a disposition of the partnership's trade or business for purposes of section 195(b)(2). See §1.708-1(b)(6) for rules concerning the treatment of these start-up expenditures by the new partnership.

(b) *Effective/applicability date.*—This section applies to a technical termination of a partnership under section 708(b)(1)(B) that occurs on or after December 9, 2013. [Reg. §1.195-2.]

☐ [*T.D. 9681, 7-22-2014.*]

[Reg. §1.197-0]

§1.197-0. Table of contents.—This section lists the headings that appear in §1.197-2.

(1) In general.
(2) Treatment of contingent amounts.
  (i) Amounts added to basis during 15-year period.
  (ii) Amounts becoming fixed after expiration of 15-year period.
  (iii) Rules for including amounts in basis.
(3) Basis determinations for certain assets.
  (i) Covenants not to compete.
  (ii) Contracts for the use of section 197 intangibles; acquired as part of a trade or business.
    (A) In general.
    (B) Know-how and certain information base.
  (iii) Contracts for the use of section 197 intangibles; not acquired as part of a trade or business.
  (iv) Applicable rules.
    (A) Franchises, trademarks, and trade names.
    (B) Certain amounts treated as payable under a debt instrument.
      (1) In general.
      (2) Rights granted by governmental units.
      (3) Treatment of other parties to transaction.
      (4) Basis determinations in certain transactions.
        (i) Certain renewal transactions.
        (ii) Transactions subject to section 338 or 1060.
        (iii) Certain reinsurance transactions.
(g) Special rules.
  (1) Treatment of certain dispositions.
    (i) Loss disallowance rules.
      (A) In general.
      (B) Abandonment or worthlessness.
      (C) Certain nonrecognition transfers.
    (ii) Separately acquired property.
    (iii) Disposition of a covenant not to compete.
    (iv) Taxpayers under common control.
      (A) In general.
      (B) Treatment of disallowed loss.
  (2) Treatment of certain nonrecognition and exchange transactions.
    (i) Relationship to anti-churning rules.
    (ii) Treatment of nonrecognition and exchange transactions generally.
      (A) Transfer disregarded.
      (B) Application of general rule.
      (C) Transactions covered.
    (iii) Certain exchanged-basis property.
    (iv) Transfers under section 708(b)(1).
      (A) In general.
      (B) Termination by sale or exchange of interest.
      (C) Other terminations.
  (3) Increase in the basis of partnership property under section 732(b), 734(b), 743(b), or 732(d).
  (4) Section 704(c) allocations.
    (i) Allocations where the intangible is amortizable by the contributor.
    (ii) Allocations where the intangible is not amortizable by the contributor.
  (5) Treatment of certain insurance contracts acquired in an assumption reinsurance transaction.
    (i) In general.
    (ii) Determination of adjusted basis of amortizable section 197 intangible resulting from an assumption reinsurance transaction.
      (A) In general.
      (B) Amount paid or incurred by acquirer (reinsurer) under the assumption reinsurance transaction.
      (C) Amount required to be capitalized under section 848 in connection with the transaction.
        (1) In general.
        (2) Required capitalization amount.
        (3) General deductions allocable to the assumption reinsurance transaction.
        (4) Treatment of a capitalization shortfall allocable to the reinsurance agreement.
          (i) In general.
          (ii) Treatment of additional capitalized amounts as the result of an election under §1.848-2(g)(8).
      (5) Cross references and special rules.
      (D) Examples.
      (E) Effective/applicability date.

    (iii) Application of loss disallowance rule upon a disposition of an insurance contract acquired in an assumption reinsurance transaction.
      (A) Disposition.
        (1) In general.
        (2) Treatment of indemnity reinsurance transactions.
      (B) Loss.
      (C) Examples.
    (iv) Effective dates.
      (A) In general.
      (B) Application to pre-effective date acquisitions and dispositions.
      (C) Change in method of accounting.
        (1) In general.
        (2) Acquisitions and dispositions on or after effective date.
        (3) Acquisitions and dispositions before the effective date.
  (6) Amounts paid or incurred for a franchise, trademark, or trade name.
  (7) Amounts properly taken into account in determining the cost of property that is not a section 197 intangible.
  (8) Treatment of amortizable section 197 intangibles as depreciable property.
(h) Anti-churning rules.
  (1) Scope and purpose.
    (i) Scope.
    (ii) Purpose.
  (2) Treatment of section 197(f)(9) intangibles.
  (3) Amounts deductible under section 1253(d) or §1.162-11.
  (4) Transition period.
  (5) Exceptions.
  (6) Related person.
    (i) In general.
    (ii) Time for testing relationships.
    (iii) Certain relationships disregarded.
    (iv) De minimis rule.
      (A) In general.
      (B) Determination of beneficial ownership interest.
  (7) Special rules for entities that owned or used property at any time during the transition period and that are no longer in existence.
  (8) Special rules for section 338 deemed acquisitions.
  (9) Gain-recognition exception.
    (i) Applicability.
    (ii) Effect of exception.
    (iii) Time and manner of election.
    (iv) Special rules for certain entities.
    (v) Effect of nonconforming elections.
    (vi) Notification requirements.
    (vii) Revocation.
    (viii) Election Statement.
    (ix) Determination of highest marginal rate of tax and amount of other Federal income tax on gain.
      (A) Marginal rate.
        (1) Noncorporate taxpayers.
        (2) Corporations and tax-exempt entities.
      (B) Other Federal income tax on gain.
    (x) Coordination with other provisions.
      (A) In general.
      (B) Section 1374.
      (C) Procedural and administrative provisions.
      (D) Installment method.
    (xi) Special rules for persons not otherwise subject to Federal income tax.
  (10) Transactions subject to both anti-churning and nonrecognition rules.
  (11) Avoidance purpose.
  (12) Additional partnership anti-churning rules
    (i) In general.
    (ii) Section 732(b) adjustments. [Reserved]
    (iii) Section 732(d) adjustments.
    (iv) Section 734(b) adjustments. [Reserved]
    (v) Section 743(b) adjustments.
    (vi) Partner is or becomes a user of partnership intangible.
      (A) General rule.
      (B) Anti-churning partner.
      (C) Effect of retroactive elections.
    (vii) Section 704(c) elections.

(A) Allocations where the intangible is amortizable by the contributor.

(B) Allocations where the intangible is not amortizable by the contributor.

(viii) Operating rule for transfers upon death.

(i) Reserved

(j) General anti-abuse rule.

(k) Examples.

(l) Effective dates.

  (1) In general.

  (2) Application to pre-effective date acquisitions.

  (3) Application of regulation project REG-209709-94 to pre-effective date acquisitions.

  (4) Change in method of accounting.

    (i) In general.

    (ii) Application to pre-effective date transactions.

    (iii) Automatic change procedures.

[Reg. §1.197-0.]

☐ [*T.D. 8865, 1-20-2000. Amended by T.D. 9257, 4-7-2006 and T.D. 9377, 1-22-2008.*]

[Reg. §1.197-1T]

§1.197-1T. Certain elections for intangible property (temporary).—(a) *In general.*—This section provides rules for making the two elections under section 13261 of the Omnibus Budget Reconciliation Act of 1993 (OBRA '93). Paragraph (c) of this section provides rules for making the section 13261(g)(2) election (the retroactive election) to apply the intangibles provisions of OBRA '93 to property acquired after July 25, 1991, and on or before August 10, 1993 (the date of enactment of OBRA '93). Paragraph (d) of this section provides rules for making the section 13261(g)(3) election (binding contract election) to apply prior law to property acquired pursuant to a written binding contract in effect on August 10, 1993, and at all times thereafter before the date of acquisition. The provisions of this section apply only to property for which an election is made under paragraph (c) or (d) of this section.

(b) *Definitions and special rules—.*—(1) *Intangibles provisions of OBRA '93.*—The intangibles provisions of OBRA '93 are sections 167(f) and 197 of the Internal Revenue Code (Code) and all other pertinent provisions of section 13261 of OBRA '93 (e.g., the amendment of section 1253 in the case of a franchise, trademark, or trade name).

(2) *Transition period property.*—The transition period property of a taxpayer is any property that was acquired by the taxpayer after July 25, 1991, and on or before August 10, 1993.

(3) *Eligible section 197 intangibles.*—The eligible section 197 intangibles of a taxpayer are any section 197 intangibles that—

  (i) Are transition period property; and

  (ii) Qualify as amortizable section 197 intangibles (within the meaning of section 197(c)) if an election under section 13261(g)(2) of OBRA '93 applies.

(4) *Election date.*—The election date is the date (determined after application of section 7502(a)) on which the taxpayer files the original or amended return to which the election statement described in paragraph (e) of this section is attached.

(5) *Election year.*—The election year is the taxable year of the taxpayer that includes August 10, 1993.

(6) *Common control.*—A taxpayer is under common control with the electing taxpayer if, at any time after August 2, 1993, and on or before the election date (as defined in paragraph (b)(4) of this section), the two taxpayers would be treated as a single taxpayer under section 41(f)(1)(A) or (B).

(7) *Applicable convention for sections 197 and 167(f) intangibles.*—For purposes of computing the depreciation or amortization deduction allowable with respect to transition period property described in section 167(f)(1) or (3) or with respect to eligible section 197 intangibles—

  (i) *Property acquired at any time during the month is treated as acquired as of the first day of the month and is eligible for depreciation or amortization during the month;* and

  (ii) *Property is not eligible for depreciation or amortization in the month of disposition.*

(8) *Application to adjustment to basis of partnership property under section 734(b) or 743(b).*—Any increase in the basis of partnership property under section 734(b) (relating to the optional adjustment to basis of undistributed partnership property) or section 743(b) (relating to the optional adjustment to the basis of partnership property) will be taken into account under this section by a partner if the increased portion of the basis were attributable to the partner's acquisition of the underlying partnership property on the date the distribution or transfer occurs. For example, if a section 754 election is in effect and, as a result of its acquisition of a partnership interest, a taxpayer obtains an increased basis in an intangible held through the partnership, the increased portion of the basis in the intangible will be treated as an intangible asset newly acquired by that taxpayer on the date of the transaction.

(9) *Former member.*—A former member of a consolidated group is a corporation that was a member of the consolidated group at any time after July 25, 1991, and on or before August 2, 1993, but that is not under common control with the common parent of the group for purposes of paragraph (c)(1)(ii) of this section.

(c) *Retroactive election—.*—(1) *Effect of election.*—(i) *On taxpayer.*—Except as provided in paragraph (c)(1)(v) of this section, if a taxpayer makes the retroactive election, the intangibles provisions of OBRA '93 will apply to all the taxpayer's transition period property. Thus, for example, section 197 will apply to all the taxpayer's eligible section 197 intangibles.

  (ii) *On taxpayers under common control.*—If a taxpayer makes the retroactive election, the election applies to each taxpayer that is under common control with the electing taxpayer. If the retroactive election applies to a taxpayer under common control, the intangibles provisions of OBRA '93 apply to that taxpayer's transition period property in the same manner as if that taxpayer had itself made the retroactive election. However, a retroactive election that applies to a non-electing taxpayer under common control is not treated as an election by that taxpayer for purposes of re-applying the rule of this paragraph (c)(1)(ii) to any other taxpayer.

  (iii) *On former members of consolidated group.*—A retroactive election by the common parent of a consolidated group applies to transition period property acquired by a former member while it was a member of the consolidated group and continues to apply to that property in each subsequent consolidated or separate return year of the former member.

  (iv) *On transferred assets.*—(A) *In general.*—If property is transferred in a transaction described in paragraph (c)(1)(iv)(C) of this section and the intangibles provisions of OBRA '93 applied to such property in the hands of the transferor, the property remains subject to the intangibles provisions of OBRA '93 with respect to so much of its adjusted basis in the hands of the transferee as does not exceed its adjusted basis in the hands of the transferor. The transferee is not required to apply the intangibles provisions of OBRA '93 to any other transition period property that it owns, however, unless such provisions are otherwise applicable under the rules of this paragraph (c)(1).

  (B) *Transferee election.*—If property is transferred in a transaction described in paragraph (c)(1)(iv)(C)(1) of this section and the transferee makes the retroactive election, the transferor is not required to apply the intangibles provisions of OBRA '93 to any of its transition period property (including the property transferred to the transferee in the transaction described in paragraph (c)(1)(iv)(C)(1) of this section), unless such provisions are otherwise applicable under the rules of this paragraph (c)(1).

  (C) *Transactions covered.*—This paragraph (c)(1)(iv) applies to—

    (1) Any transaction described in section 332, 351, 361, 721, 731, 1031, or 1033; and

    (2) Any transaction between corporations that are members of the same consolidated group immediately after the transaction.

  (D) *Exchanged basis property.*—In the case of a transaction involving exchanged basis property (e.g., a transaction subject to section 1031 or 1033)—

    (1) Paragraph (c)(1)(iv)(A) of this section shall not apply; and

    (2) If the intangibles provisions of OBRA '93 applied to the property by reference to which the exchanged basis is determined (the predecessor property), the exchanged basis property becomes subject to the intangibles provisions of OBRA '93 with respect to so much of its basis as does not exceed the predecessor property's basis.

  (E) *Acquisition date.*—For purposes of paragraph (b)(2) of this section (definition of transition period property), property (other than exchanged basis property) acquired in a transaction described in paragraph (c)(1)(iv)(C)(1) of this section generally is treated as acquired when the transferor acquired (or was treated as acquiring) the property (or predecessor property). However, if the adjusted basis of the property in the hands of the transferee exceeds the adjusted basis of the property in the hands of the transferor, the property, with

25,652
Itemized Deductions for Individuals and Corps.
See p. 20,601 for regulations not amended to reflect law changes

respect to that excess basis, is treated as acquired at the time of the transfer. The time at which exchanged basis property is considered acquired is determined by applying similar principles to the transferee's acquisition of predecessor property.

(v) *Special rule for property of former member of consolidated group.*—(A) *Intangibles provisions inapplicable for certain periods.*—If a former member of a consolidated group makes a retroactive election pursuant to paragraph (c)(1)(i) of this section or if an election applies to the former member under the common control rule of paragraph (c)(1)(ii) of this section, the intangibles provisions of OBRA '93 generally apply to all transition period property of the former member. The intangibles provisions of OBRA '93 do not apply, however, to the transition period property of a former member (including a former member that makes or is bound by a retroactive election) during the period beginning immediately after July 25, 1991, and ending immediately before the earlier of—

(1) The first day after July 25, 1991, that the former member was not a member of a consolidated group; or

(2) The first day after July 25, 1991, that the former member was a member of a consolidated group that is otherwise required to apply the intangibles provisions of OBRA '93 to its transition period property (e.g., because the common control election under paragraph (c)(1)(ii) of this section applies to the group).

(B) *Subsequent adjustments.*—See paragraph (c)(5) of this section for adjustments when the intangibles provisions of OBRA '93 first apply to the transition period property of the former member after the property is acquired.

(2) *Making the election.*—(i) *Partnerships, S corporations, estates, and trusts.*—Except as provided in paragraph (c)(2)(ii) of this section, in the case of transition period property of a partnership, S corporation, estate, or trust, only the entity may make the retroactive election for purposes of paragraph (c)(1)(i) of this section.

(ii) *Partnerships for which a section 754 election is in effect.*—In the case of increased basis that is treated as transition period property of a partner under paragraph (b)(8) of this section, only that partner may make the retroactive election for purposes of paragraph (c)(1)(i) of this section.

(iii) *Consolidated groups.*—An election by the common parent of a consolidated group applies to members and former members as described in paragraphs (c)(1)(ii) and (iii) of this section. Further, for purposes of paragraph (c)(1)(ii) of this section, an election by the common parent is not treated as an election by any subsidiary member. A retroactive election cannot be made by a corporation that is a subsidiary member of a consolidated group on August 10, 1993, but an election can be made on behalf of the subsidiary member under paragraph (c)(1)(ii) of this section (e.g., by the common parent of the group). See paragraph (c)(1)(iii) of this section for rules concerning the effect of the common parent's election on transition period property of a former member.

(3) *Time and manner of election.*—(i) *Time.*—In general, the retroactive election must be made by the due date (including extensions of time) of the electing taxpayer's Federal income tax return for the election year. If, however, the taxpayer's original Federal income tax return for the election year is filed before April 14, 1994, the election may be made by amending that return no later than September 12, 1994.

(ii) *Manner.*—The retroactive election is made by attaching the election statement described in paragraph (e) of this section to the taxpayer's original or amended income tax return for the election year. In addition, the taxpayer must—

(A) Amend any previously filed return when required to do so under paragraph (c)(4) of this section; and

(B) Satisfy the notification requirements of paragraph (c)(6) of this section.

(iii) *Effect of nonconforming elections.*—An attempted election that does not satisfy the requirements of this paragraph (c)(3) (including an attempted election made on a return for a taxable year prior to the election year) is not valid.

(4) *Amended return requirements.*—(i) *Requirements.*—A taxpayer subject to this paragraph (c)(4) must amend all previously filed income tax returns as necessary to conform the taxpayer's treatment of transition period property to the treatment required under the intangibles provisions of OBRA '93. See paragraph (c)(5) of this section for certain adjustments that may be required on the amended returns required under this paragraph (c)(4) in the case of certain consolidated group member dispositions and tax-free transactions.

(ii) *Applicability.*—This paragraph (c)(4) applies to a taxpayer if—

(A) The taxpayer makes the retroactive election; or

(B) Another person's retroactive election applies to the taxpayer or to any property acquired by the taxpayer.

(5) *Adjustment required with respect to certain consolidated group member dispositions and tax-free transactions.*—(i) *Application.*—This paragraph (c)(5) applies to transition period property if the intangibles provisions of OBRA '93 first apply to the property while it is held by the taxpayer but do not apply to the property for some period (the "interim period") after the property is acquired (or considered acquired) by the taxpayer. For example, this paragraph (c)(5) may apply to transition period property held by a former member of a consolidated group if a retroactive election is made by or on behalf of the former member but is not made by the consolidated group. See paragraph (c)(1)(v) of this section.

(ii) *Required adjustment to income.*—If this paragraph (c)(5) applies, an adjustment must be taken into account in computing taxable income of the taxpayer for the taxable year in which the intangibles provisions of OBRA '93 first apply to the property. The amount of the adjustment is equal to the difference for the transition period property between—

(A) The sum of the depreciation, amortization, or other cost recovery deductions that the taxpayer (and its predecessors) would have been permitted if the intangibles provisions of OBRA '93 applied to the property during the interim period; and

(B) The sum of the depreciation, amortization, or other cost recovery deductions that the taxpayer (and its predecessors) claimed during that interim period.

(iii) *Required adjustment to basis.*—The taxpayer also must make a corresponding adjustment to the basis of its transition period property to reflect any adjustment to taxable income with respect to the property under this paragraph (c)(5).

(6) *Notification requirements.*—(i) *Notification of commonly controlled taxpayers.*—A taxpayer that makes the retroactive election must provide written notification of the retroactive election (on or before the election date) to each taxpayer that is under common control with the electing taxpayer.

(ii) *Notification of certain former members, former consolidated groups, and transferees.*—This paragraph (c)(6)(ii) applies to a common parent of a consolidated group that makes or is notified of a retroactive election that applies to transition period property of a former member, a corporation that makes or is notified of a retroactive election that affects any consolidated group of which the corporation is a former member, or a taxpayer that makes or is notified of a retroactive election that applies to transition period property the taxpayer transfers in a transaction described in paragraph (c)(1)(iv)(C) of this section. Such common parent, former member, or transferor must provide written notification of the retroactive election to any affected former member, consolidated group, or transferee. The written notification must be provided on or before the election date in the case of an election by the common parent, former member, or transferor, and within 30 days of the election date in the case of an election by a person other than the common parent, former member, or transferor.

(7) *Revocation.*—Once made, the retroactive election may be revoked only with the consent of the Commissioner.

(8) *Examples.*—The following examples illustrate the application of this paragraph (c).

Example 1. (i) X is a partnership with 5 equal partners, A through E. X acquires in 1989, as its sole asset, intangible asset M. X has a section 754 election in effect for all relevant years. F, an unrelated individual, purchases A's entire interest in the X partnership in January 1993 for $700. At the time of F's purchase, X's inside basis for M is $2,000, and its fair market value is $3,500.

(ii) Under section 743(b), X makes an adjustment to increase F's basis in asset M by $300, the difference between the allocated purchase price and M's inside basis ($700 − $400 = $300). Under paragraphs (b)(8) and (c)(2)(ii) of this section, if F makes the retroactive election, the section 743(b) basis increase of $300 in M is an amortizable section 197 intangible even though asset M is not an amortizable section 197 intangible in the hands of X. F's increase in the basis of asset M is amortizable over 15 years beginning with the month of F's acquisition of the partnership interest. With respect to the remaining $400 of basis, F is treated as stepping into A's shoes and continues A's amortization (if any) in asset M. F's retroactive election applies to all other intangibles acquired by F or a taxpayer under common control with F.

Example 2. A, a calendar year taxpayer, is under common control with B, a June 30 fiscal year taxpayer. A files its original election year Federal income tax return on March 15, 1994, and does not make either the retroactive election or the binding contract election. B files its election year tax return on September 15, 1994, and makes the retroactive election. B is required by paragraph (c)(6)(i) of this section to notify A of its election. Even though A had already filed its election year return, A is bound by B's retroactive election under the common control rules. Additionally, if A had made a binding contract election, it would have been negated by B's retroactive election. Because of B's retroactive election, A must comply with the requirements of this paragraph (c), and file amended returns for the election year and any affected prior years as necessary to conform the treatment of transition period property to the treatment required under the intangibles provisions of OBRA '93.

Example 3. (i) P and Y, calendar year taxpayers, are the common parents of unrelated calendar year consolidated groups. On August 15, 1991, S, a subsidiary member of the P group, acquires a section 197 intangible with an unadjusted basis of \$180. Under prior law, no amortization or depreciation was allowed with respect to the acquired intangible. On November 1, 1992, a member of the Y group acquires the S stock in a taxable transaction. On the P group's 1993 consolidated return, P makes the retroactive election. The P group also files amended returns for its affected prior years. Y does not make the retroactive election for the Y group.

(ii) Under paragraph (c)(1)(iii) of this section, a retroactive election by the common parent of a consolidated group applies to all transition period property acquired by a former member while it was a member of the group. The section 197 intangible acquired by S is transition period property that S, a former member of the P group, acquired while a member of the P group. Thus, P's election applies to the acquired asset. P must notify S of the election pursuant to paragraph (c)(6)(ii) of this section.

(iii) S amortizes the unadjusted basis of its eligible section 197 intangible (\$180) over the 15-year amortization period using the applicable convention beginning as of the first day of the month of acquisition (August 1, 1991). Thus, the P group amends its 1991 consolidated tax return to take into account \$5 of amortization (\$180/15 years × $^5/_{12}$ year = \$5) for S.

(iv) For 1992, S is entitled to \$12 of amortization (\$180/15). Assume that under §1.1502-76, \$10 of S's amortization for 1992 is allocated to the P group's consolidated return and \$2 is allocated to the Y group's return. The P group amends its 1992 consolidated tax return to reflect the \$10 deduction for S. The Y group must amend its 1992 return to reflect the \$2 deduction for S.

Example 4. (i) The facts are the same as in *Example 3*, except that the retroactive election is made for the Y group, not for the P group.

(ii) The Y group amends its 1992 consolidated return to claim a section 197 deduction of \$2 (\$180/15 years × $^2/_{12}$ year = \$2) for S.

(iii) Under paragraph (c)(1)(ii) of this section, the retroactive election by Y applies to all transition period property acquired by S. However, under paragraph (c)(1)(v)(A) of this section, the intangibles provisions of OBRA '93 do not apply to S's transition period property during the period when it held such property as a member of P group. Instead, these provisions become applicable to S's transition period property beginning on November 1, 1992, when S becomes a member of Y group.

(iv) Because the P group did not make the retroactive election, there is an interim period during which the intangibles provisions of OBRA '93 do not apply to the asset acquired by S. Thus, under paragraph (c)(5) of this section, the Y group must take into account in computing taxable income in 1992 an adjustment equal to the difference between the section 197 deduction that would have been permitted if the intangibles provisions of OBRA '93 applied to the property for the interim period (i.e., the period for which S was included in the P group's 1991 and 1992 consolidated returns) and any amortization or depreciation deductions claimed by S for the transferred intangible for that period. The retroactive election does not affect the P group, and the P group is not required to amend its returns.

Example 5. The facts are the same as in *Example 3*, except that both P and Y make the retroactive election. P must notify S of its election pursuant to paragraph (c)(6)(ii) of this section. Further, both the P and Y groups must file amended returns for affected prior years. Because there is no period of time during which the intangibles provisions of OBRA '93 do not apply to the asset acquired by S, the Y group is permitted no adjustment under paragraph (c)(5) of this section for the asset.

(d) *Binding contract election.*—(1) *General rule.*—(i) *Effect of election.*—If a taxpayer acquires property pursuant to a written binding contract in effect on August 10, 1993, and at all times thereafter before the acquisition (an eligible acquisition) and makes the binding contract election with respect to the contract, the law in effect prior to the enactment of OBRA '93 will apply to all property acquired pursuant to the contract. A separate binding contract election must be made with respect to each eligible acquisition to which the law in effect prior to the enactment of OBRA '93 is to apply.

(ii) *Taxpayers subject to retroactive election.*—A taxpayer may not make the binding contract election if the taxpayer or a person under common control with the taxpayer makes the retroactive election under paragraph (c) of this section.

(iii) *Revocation.*—A binding contract election, once made, may be revoked only with the consent of the Commissioner.

(2) *Time and manner of election*—(i) *Time.*—In general, the binding contract election must be made by the due date (including extensions of time) of the electing taxpayer's Federal income tax return for the election year. If, however, the taxpayer's original Federal income tax return for the election year is filed before April 14, 1994, the election may be made by amending that return no later than September 12, 1994.

(ii) *Manner.*—The binding contract election is made by attaching the election statement described in paragraph (e) of this section to the taxpayer's original or amended income tax return for the election year.

(iii) *Effect of nonconforming election.*—An attempted election that does not satisfy the requirements of this paragraph (d)(2) is not valid.

(e) *Election statement.*—(1) *Filing requirements.*—For an election under paragraph (c) or (d) of this section to be valid, the electing taxpayer must:

(i) File (with its Federal income tax return for the election year and with any affected amended returns required under paragraph (c)(4) of this section) a written election statement, as an attachment to Form 4562 (Depreciation and Amortization), that satisfies the requirements of paragraph (e)(2) of this section; and

(ii) Forward a copy of the election statement to the Statistics Branch (QAM:S:6111), IRS Ogden Service Center, ATTN: Chief, Statistics Branch, P.O. Box 9941, Ogden, UT 84409.

(2) *Content of the election statement.*—The written election statement must include the information in paragraphs (e)(2)(i) through (vi) and (ix) of this section in the case of a retroactive election, and the information in paragraphs (e)(2)(i) and (vii) through (ix) of this section in the case of a binding contract election. The required information should be arranged and identified in accordance with the following order and numbering system—

(i) The name, address and taxpayer identification number (TIN) of the electing taxpayer (and the common parent if a consolidated return is filed).

(ii) A statement that the taxpayer is making the retroactive election.

(iii) Identification of the transition period property affected by the retroactive election, the name and TIN of the person from which the property was acquired, the manner and date of acquisition, the basis at which the property was acquired, and the amount of depreciation, amortization, or other cost recovery under section 167 or any other provision of the Code claimed with respect to the property.

(iv) Identification of each taxpayer under common control (as defined in paragraph (b)(6) of this section) with the electing taxpayer by name, TIN, and Internal Revenue Service Center where the taxpayer's income tax return is filed.

(v) If any persons are required to be notified of the retroactive election under paragraph (c)(6) of this section, identification of such persons and certification that written notification of the election has been provided to such persons.

(vi) A statement that the transition period property being amortized under section 197 is not subject to the anti-churning rules of section 197(f)(9).

(vii) A statement that the taxpayer is making the binding contract election.

(viii) Identification of the property affected by the binding contract election, the name and TIN of the person from which the property was acquired, the manner and date of acquisition, the basis at which the property was acquired, and whether any of the property is subject to depreciation under section 167 or to amortization or other cost recovery under any other provision of the Code.

(ix) The signature of the taxpayer or an individual authorized to sign the taxpayer's Federal income tax return.

(f) *Effective date.*—These regulations are effective March 15, 1994. [Temporary Reg. §1.197-1T.]

☐ [T.D. 8528, 3-10-94.]

[Reg. §1.197-2]

§1.197-2. Amortization of goodwill and certain other intangibles.—(a) *Overview.*—(1) *In general.*—Section 197 allows an amortization deduction for the capitalized costs of an amortizable section 197 intangible and prohibits any other depreciation or amortization with respect to that property. Paragraphs (b), (c), and (e) of this section provide rules and definitions for determining whether property is a section 197 intangible, and paragraphs (d) and (e) of this section provide rules and definitions for determining whether a section 197 intangible is an amortizable section 197 intangible. The amortization deduction under section 197 is determined by amortizing basis ratably over a 15-year period under the rules of paragraph (f) of this section. Section 197 also includes various special rules pertaining to the disposition of amortizable section 197 intangibles, nonrecognition transactions, anti-churning rules, and anti-abuse rules. Rules relating to these provisions are contained in paragraphs (g), (h), and (j) of this section. Examples demonstrating the application of these provisions are contained in paragraph (k) of this section. The effective date of the rules in this section is contained in paragraph (l) of this section.

(2) *Section 167(f) property.*—Section 167(f) prescribes rules for computing the depreciation deduction for certain property to which section 197 does not apply. See §1.167(a)-14 for rules under section 167(f) and paragraphs (c)(4), (6), (7), (11), and (13) of this section for a description of the property subject to section 167(f).

(3) *Amounts otherwise deductible.*—Section 197 does not apply to amounts that are not chargeable to capital account under paragraph (f)(3) (relating to basis determinations for covenants not to compete and certain contracts for the use of section 197 intangibles) of this section and are otherwise currently deductible. For this purpose, an amount described in §1.162-11 is not currently deductible if, without regard to §1.162-11, such amount is properly chargeable to capital account.

(b) *Section 197 intangibles; in general.*—Except as otherwise provided in paragraph (c) of this section, the term *section 197 intangible* means any property described in section 197(d)(1). The following rules and definitions provide guidance concerning property that is a section 197 intangible unless an exception applies:

(1) *Goodwill.*—Section 197 intangibles include goodwill. Goodwill is the value of a trade or business attributable to the expectancy of continued customer patronage. This expectancy may be due to the name or reputation of a trade or business or any other factor.

(2) *Going concern value.*—Section 197 intangibles include going concern value. Going concern value is the additional value that attaches to property by reason of its existence as an integral part of an ongoing business activity. Going concern value includes the value attributable to the ability of a trade or business (or a part of a trade or business) to continue functioning or generating income without interruption notwithstanding a change in ownership, but does not include any of the intangibles described in any other provision of this paragraph (b). It also includes the value that is attributable to the immediate use or availability of an acquired trade or business, such as, for example, the use of the revenues or net earnings that otherwise would not be received during any period if the acquired trade or business were not available or operational.

(3) *Workforce in place.*—Section 197 intangibles include workforce in place. Workforce in place (sometimes referred to as agency force or assembled workforce) includes the composition of a workforce (for example, the experience, education, or training of a workforce), the terms and conditions of employment whether contractual or otherwise, and any other value placed on employees or any of their attributes. Thus, the amount paid or incurred for workforce in place includes, for example, any portion of the purchase price of an acquired trade or business attributable to the existence of a highly-skilled workforce, an existing employment contract (or contracts), or a relationship with employees or consultants (including, but not limited to, any key employee contract or relationship). Workforce in place does not include any covenant not to compete or other similar arrangement described in paragraph (b)(9) of this section.

(4) *Information base.*—Section 197 intangibles include any information base, including a customer-related information base. For this purpose, an information base includes business books and records, operating systems, and any other information base (regardless of the method of recording the information) and a customer-related information base is any information base that includes lists or other information with respect to current or prospective customers. Thus, the amount paid or incurred for information base includes, for example, any portion of the purchase price of an acquired trade or business attributable to the intangible value of technical manuals, *training manuals or programs, data files,* and accounting or inventory control systems. Other examples include the cost of acquiring customer lists, subscription lists, insurance expirations, patient or client files, or lists of newspaper, magazine, radio, or television advertisers.

(5) *Know-how, etc.*—Section 197 intangibles include any patent, copyright, formula, process, design, pattern, know-how, format, package design, computer software (as defined in paragraph (c)(4)(iv) of this section), or interest in a film, sound recording, video tape, book, or other similar property. (See, however, the exceptions in paragraph (c) of this section.)

(6) *Customer-based intangibles.*—Section 197 intangibles include any customer-based intangible. A customer-based intangible is any composition of market, market share, or other value resulting from the future provision of goods or services pursuant to contractual or other relationships in the ordinary course of business with customers. Thus, the amount paid or incurred for customer-based intangibles includes, for example, any portion of the purchase price of an acquired trade or business attributable to the existence of a customer base, a circulation base, an undeveloped market or market growth, insurance in force, the existence of a qualification to supply goods or services to a particular customer, a mortgage servicing contract (as defined in paragraph (c)(11) of this section), an investment management contract, or other relationship with customers involving the future provision of goods or services. (See, however, the exceptions in paragraph (c) of this section.) In addition, customer-based intangibles include the deposit base and any similar asset of a financial institution. Thus, the amount paid or incurred for customer-based intangibles also includes any portion of the purchase price of an acquired financial institution attributable to the value represented by existing checking accounts, savings accounts, escrow accounts, and other similar items of the financial institution. However, any portion of the purchase price of an acquired trade or business attributable to accounts receivable or other similar rights to income for goods or services provided to customers prior to the acquisition of a trade or business is not an amount paid or incurred for a customer-based intangible.

(7) *Supplier-based intangibles.*—(i) *In general.*—Section 197 intangibles include any supplier-based intangible. A *supplier-based intangible* is the value resulting from the future acquisition, pursuant to contractual or other relationships with suppliers in the ordinary course of business, of goods or services that will be sold or used by the taxpayer. Thus, the amount paid or incurred for supplier-based intangibles includes, for example, any portion of the purchase price of an acquired trade or business attributable to the existence of a favorable relationship with persons providing distribution services (such as favorable shelf or display space at a retail outlet), or the existence of favorable supply contracts. The amount paid or incurred for supplier-based intangibles does not include any amount required to be paid for the goods or services themselves pursuant to the terms of the agreement or other relationship. In addition, see the exceptions in paragraph 2(c) of this section, including the exception in paragraph 2(c)(6) of this section for certain rights to receive tangible property or services from another person.

(ii) *Applicability date.*—This section applies to supplier-based intangibles acquired after July 6, 2011.

(8) *Licenses, permits, and other rights granted by governmental units.*—Section 197 intangibles include any license, permit, or other right granted by a governmental unit (including, for purposes of section 197, an agency or instrumentality thereof) even if the right is granted for an indefinite period or is reasonably expected to be renewed for an indefinite period. These rights include, for example, a liquor license, a taxi-cab medallion (or license), an airport landing or takeoff right (sometimes referred to as a slot), a regulated airline route, or a television or radio broadcasting license. The issuance or renewal of a license, permit, or other right granted by a governmental unit is considered an acquisition of the license, permit, or other right. (See, however, the exceptions in paragraph (c) of this section, including the exceptions in paragraph (c)(3) of this section for an interest in land, paragraph (c)(6) of this section for certain rights to receive tangible property or services, paragraph (c)(8) of this section for an interest under a lease of tangible property, and paragraph (c)(13) of this section for certain rights granted by a governmental unit. See paragraph (b)(10) of this section for the treatment of franchises.)

(9) *Covenants not to compete and other similar arrangements.*—Section 197 intangibles include any covenant not to compete, or agreement having substantially the same effect, entered into in connection with the direct or indirect acquisition of an interest in a trade or business or a substantial portion thereof. For purposes of this paragraph (b)(9), an acquisition may be made in the form of an asset acquisition (including a qualified stock purchase that is treated as a purchase of assets under section 338), a stock acquisition or redemption, and the acquisition or redemption of a partnership interest. An agreement requiring the performance of services for the acquiring taxpayer or the provision of property or its use to the acquiring taxpayer does not have substantially the same effect as a covenant

not to compete to the extent that the amount paid under the agreement represents reasonable compensation for the services actually rendered or for the property or use of the property actually provided.

(10) *Franchises, trademarks, and trade names.*—(i) Section 197 intangibles include any franchise, trademark, or trade name. The term *franchise* has the meaning given in section 1253(b)(1) and includes any agreement that provides one of the parties to the agreement with the right to distribute, sell, or provide goods, services, or facilities, within a specified area. The term *trademark* includes any word, name, symbol, or device, or any combination thereof, adopted and used to identify goods or services and distinguish them from those provided by others. The term *trade name* includes any name used to identify or designate a particular trade or business or the name or title used by a person or organization engaged in a trade or business. A license, permit, or other right granted by a governmental unit is a franchise if it otherwise meets the definition of a franchise. A trademark or trade name includes any trademark or trade name arising under statute or applicable common law, and any similar right granted by contract. The renewal of a franchise, trademark, or trade name is treated as an acquisition of the franchise, trademark, or trade name.

(ii) Notwithstanding the definitions provided in paragraph (b)(10)(i) of this section, any amount that is paid or incurred on account of a transfer, sale, or other disposition of a franchise, trademark, or trade name and that is subject to section 1253(d)(1) is not included in the basis of a section 197 intangible. (See paragraph (g)(6) of this section.)

(11) *Contracts for the use of, and term interests in, section 197 intangibles.*—Section 197 intangibles include any right under a license, contract, or other arrangement providing for the use of property that would be a section 197 intangible under any provision of this paragraph (b) (including this paragraph (b)(11)) after giving effect to all of the exceptions provided in paragraph (c) of this section. Section 197 intangibles also include any term interest (whether outright or in trust) in such property.

(12) *Other similar items.*—Section 197 intangibles include any other intangible property that is similar in all material respects to the property specifically described in section 197(d)(1)(C)(i) through (v) and paragraphs (b)(3) through (7) of this section. (See paragraph (g)(5) of this section for special rules regarding certain reinsurance transactions.)

(c) *Section 197 intangibles; exceptions.*—The term *section 197 intangible* does not include property described in section 197(e). The following rules and definitions provide guidance concerning property to which the exceptions apply:

(1) *Interests in a corporation, partnership, trust, or estate.*—Section 197 intangibles do not include an interest in a corporation, partnership, trust, or estate. Thus, for example, amortization under section 197 is not available for the cost of acquiring stock, partnership interests, or interests in a trust or estate, whether or not the interests are regularly traded on an established market. (See paragraph (g)(3) of this section for special rules applicable to property of a partnership when a section 754 election is in effect for the partnership.)

(2) *Interests under certain financial contracts.*—Section 197 intangibles do not include an interest under an existing futures contract, foreign currency contract, notional principal contract, interest rate swap, or other similar financial contract, whether or not the interest is regularly traded on an established market. However, this exception does not apply to an interest under a mortgage servicing contract, credit card servicing contract, or other contract to service another person's indebtedness, or an interest under an assumption reinsurance contract. (See paragraph (g)(5) of this section for the treatment of assumption reinsurance contracts. See paragraph (c)(11) of this section and §1.167(a)-14(d) for the treatment of mortgage servicing rights.)

(3) *Interests in land.*—Section 197 intangibles do not include any interest in land. For this purpose, an interest in land includes a fee interest, life estate, remainder, easement, mineral right, timber right, grazing right, riparian right, air right, zoning variance, and any other similar right, such as a farm allotment, quota for farm commodities, or crop acreage base. An interest in land does not include an airport landing or takeoff right, a regulated airline route, or a franchise to provide cable television service. The cost of acquiring a license, permit, or other land improvement right, such as a building construction or use permit, is taken into account in the same manner as the underlying improvement.

(4) *Certain computer software.*—(i) *Publicly available.*—Section 197 intangibles do not include any interest in computer software that is (or has been) readily available to the general public on similar terms, is subject to a nonexclusive license, and has not been substantially modified. Computer software will be treated as readily available to

the general public if the software may be obtained on substantially the same terms by a significant number of persons that would reasonably be expected to use the software. This requirement can be met even though the software is not available through a system of retail distribution. Computer software will not be considered to have been substantially modified if the cost of all modifications to the version of the software that is readily available to the general public does not exceed the greater of 25 percent of the price at which the unmodified version of the software is readily available to the general public or $2,000. For the purpose of determining whether computer software has been substantially modified—

(A) Integrated programs acquired in a package from a single source are treated as a single computer program; and

(B) Any cost incurred to install the computer software on a system is not treated as a cost of the software. However, the costs for customization, such as tailoring to a user's specifications (other than embedded programming options) are costs of modifying the software.

(ii) *Not acquired as part of trade or business.*—Section 197 intangibles do not include an interest in computer software that is not acquired as part of a purchase of a trade or business.

(iii) *Other exceptions.*—For other exceptions applicable to computer software, see paragraph (a)(3) of this section (relating to otherwise deductible amounts) and paragraph (g)(7) of this section (relating to amounts properly taken into account in determining the cost of property that is not a section 197 intangible).

(iv) *Computer software defined.*—For purposes of this section, computer software is any program or routine (that is, any sequence of machine-readable code) that is designed to cause a computer to perform a desired function or set of functions, and the documentation required to describe and maintain that program or routine. It includes all forms and media in which the software is contained, whether written, magnetic, or otherwise. Computer programs of all classes, for example, operating systems, executive systems, monitors, compilers and translators, assembly routines, and utility programs as well as application programs, are included. Computer software also includes any incidental and ancillary rights that are necessary to effect the acquisition of the title to, the ownership of, or the right to use the computer software, and that are used only in connection with that specific computer software. Such incidental and ancillary rights are not included in the definition of trademark or trade name under paragraph (b)(10)(i) of this section. For example, a trademark or trade name that is ancillary to the ownership or use of a specific computer software program in the taxpayer's trade or business and is not acquired for the purpose of marketing the computer software is included in the definition of computer software and is not included in the definition of trademark or trade name. Computer software does not include any data or information base described in paragraph (b)(4) of this section unless the data base or item is in the public domain and is incidental to a computer program. For this purpose, a copyrighted or proprietary data or information base is treated as in the public domain if its availability through the computer program does not contribute significantly to the cost of the program. For example, if a word-processing program includes a dictionary feature used to spell-check a document or any portion thereof, the entire program (including the dictionary feature) is computer software regardless of the form in which the feature is maintained or stored.

(5) *Certain interests in films, sound recordings, video tapes, books, or other similar property.*—Section 197 intangibles do not include any interest (including an interest as a licensee) in a film, sound recording, video tape, book, or other similar property (such as the right to broadcast or transmit a live event) if the interest is not acquired as part of a purchase of a trade or business. A film, sound recording, video tape, book, or other similar property includes any incidental and ancillary rights (such as a trademark or trade name) that are necessary to effect the acquisition of title to, the ownership of, or the right to use the property and are used only in connection with that property. Such incidental and ancillary rights are not included in the definition of trademark or trade name under paragraph (b)(10)(i) of this section. For purposes of this paragraph (c)(5), computer software (as defined in paragraph (c)(4)(iv) of this section) is not treated as other property similar to a film, sound recording, video tape, or book. (See section 167 for amortization of excluded intangible property or interests.)

(6) *Certain rights to receive tangible property or services.*—Section 197 intangibles do not include any right to receive tangible property or services under a contract or from a governmental unit if the right is not acquired as part of a purchase of a trade or business. Any right that is described in the preceding sentence is not treated as a section 197 intangible even though the right is also described in section

197(d)(1)(D) and paragraph (b)(8) of this section (relating to certain governmental licenses, permits, and other rights) and even though the right fails to meet one or more of the requirements of paragraph (c)(13) of this section (relating to certain rights of fixed duration or amount. (See § 1.167(a)-14(c)(1) and (3) for applicable rules.)

(7) *Certain interests in patents or copyrights.*—Section 197 intangibles do not include any interest (including an interest as a licensee) in a patent, patent application, or copyright that is not acquired as part of a purchase of a trade or business. A patent or copyright includes any incidental and ancillary rights (such as a trademark or trade name) that are necessary to effect the acquisition of title to, the ownership of, or the right to use the property and are used only in connection with that property. Such incidental and ancillary rights are not included in the definition of trademark or trade name under paragraph (b)(10)(i) of this section. (See § 1.167(a)-14(c)(4) for applicable rules.)

(8) *Interests under leases of tangible property.*—(i) *Interest as a lessor.*—Section 197 intangibles do not include any interest as a lessor under an existing lease or sublease of tangible real or personal property. In addition, the cost of acquiring an interest as a lessor in connection with the acquisition of tangible property is taken into account as part of the cost of the tangible property. For example, if a taxpayer acquires a shopping center that is leased to tenants operating retail stores, any portion of the purchase price attributable to favorable lease terms is taken into account as part of the basis of the shopping center and in determining the depreciation deduction allowed with respect to the shopping center. (See section 167(c)(2).)

(ii) *Interest as a lessee.*—Section 197 intangibles do not include any interest as a lessee under an existing lease of tangible real or personal property. For this purpose, an airline lease of an airport passenger or cargo gate is a lease of tangible property. The cost of acquiring such an interest is taken into account under section 178 and § 1.162-11(a). If an interest as a lessee under a lease of tangible property is acquired in a transaction with any other intangible property, a portion of the total purchase price may be allocable to the interest as a lessee based on all of the relevant facts and circumstances.

(9) *Interests under indebtedness.*—(i) *In general.*—Section 197 intangibles do not include any interest (whether as a creditor or debtor) under an indebtedness in existence when the interest was acquired. Thus, for example, the value attributable to the assumption of an indebtedness with a below-market interest rate is not amortizable under section 197. In addition, the premium paid for acquiring a debt instrument with an above-market interest rate is not amortizable under section 197. See section 171 for rules concerning the treatment of amortizable bond premium.

(ii) *Exceptions.*—For purposes of this paragraph (c)(9), an interest under an existing indebtedness does not include the deposit base (and other similar items) of a financial institution. An interest under an existing indebtedness includes mortgage servicing rights, however, to the extent the rights are stripped coupons under section 1286.

(10) *Professional sports franchises.*—Section 197 intangibles do not include any franchise to engage in professional baseball, basketball, football, or any other professional sport, and any item (even though otherwise qualifying as a section 197 intangible) acquired in connection with such a franchise.

(11) *Mortgage servicing rights.*—Section 197 intangibles do not include any right described in section 197(e)(7) (concerning rights to service indebtedness secured by residential real property that are not acquired as part of a purchase of a trade or business). (See § 1.167(a)-14(d) for applicable rules.)

(12) *Certain transaction costs.*—Section 197 intangibles do not include any fees for professional services and any transaction costs incurred by parties to a transaction in which all or any portion of the gain or loss is not recognized under part III of subchapter C of the Internal Revenue Code.

(13) *Rights of fixed duration or amount.*—(i) Section 197 intangibles do not include any right under a contract or any license, permit, or other right granted by a governmental unit if the right—

(A) Is acquired in the ordinary course of a trade or business (or an activity described in section 212) and not as part of a purchase of a trade or business;

(B) Is not described in section 197(d)(1)(A), (B), (E), or (F);

(C) Is not a customer-based intangible, a customer-related information base, or any other similar item; and

(D) Either—

(1) Has a fixed duration of less than 15 years; or

(2) Is fixed as to amount and the adjusted basis thereof is properly recoverable (without regard to this section) under a method similar to the unit-of-production method.

(ii) See § 1.167(a)-14(c)(2) and (3) for applicable rules.

(d) *Amortizable section 197 intangibles.*—(1) *Definition.*—Except as otherwise provided in this paragraph (d), the term *amortizable section 197 intangible* means any section 197 intangible acquired after August 10, 1993 (or after July 25, 1991, if a valid retroactive election under § 1.197-1T has been made), and held in connection with the conduct of a trade or business or an activity described in section 212.

(2) *Exception for self-created intangibles.*—(i) *In general.*—Except as provided in paragraph (d)(2)(iii) of this section, amortizable section 197 intangibles do not include any section 197 intangible created by the taxpayer (a self-created intangible).

(ii) *Created by the taxpayer.*—(A) *Defined.*—A section 197 intangible is created by the taxpayer to the extent the taxpayer makes payments or otherwise incurs costs for its creation, production, development, or improvement, whether the actual work is performed by the taxpayer or by another person under a contract with the taxpayer entered into before the contracted creation, production, development, or improvement occurs. For example, a technological process developed specifically for a taxpayer under an arrangement with another person pursuant to which the taxpayer retains all rights to the process is created by the taxpayer.

(B) *Contracts for the use of intangibles.*—A section 197 intangible is not a self-created intangible to the extent that it results from the entry into (or renewal of) a contract for the use of an existing section 197 intangible. Thus, for example, the exception for self-created intangibles does not apply to capitalized costs, such as legal and other professional fees, incurred by a licensee in connection with the entry into (or renewal of) a contract for the use of know-how or similar property.

(C) *Improvements and modifications.*—If an existing section 197 intangible is improved or otherwise modified by the taxpayer or by another person under a contract with the taxpayer, the existing intangible and the capitalized costs (if any) of the improvements or other modifications are each treated as a separate section 197 intangible for purposes of this paragraph (d).

(iii) *Exceptions.*—(A) The exception for self-created intangibles does not apply to any section 197 intangible described in section 197(d)(1)(D) (relating to licenses, permits or other rights granted by a governmental unit), 197(d)(1)(E) (relating to covenants not to compete), or 197(d)(1)(F) (relating to franchises, trademarks, and trade names). Thus, for example, capitalized costs incurred in the development, registration, or defense of a trademark or trade name do not qualify for the exception and are amortized over 15 years under section 197.

(B) The exception for self-created intangibles does not apply to any section 197 intangible created in connection with the purchase of a trade or business (as defined in paragraph (e) of this section).

(C) If a taxpayer disposes of a self-created intangible and subsequently reacquires the intangible in an acquisition described in paragraph (h)(5)(ii) of this section, the exception for self-created intangibles does not apply to the reacquired intangible.

(3) *Exception for property subject to anti-churning rules.*—Amortizable section 197 intangibles do not include any property to which the anti-churning rules of section 197(f)(9) and paragraph (h) of this section apply.

(e) *Purchase of a trade or business.*—Several of the exceptions in section 197 apply only to property that is not acquired in (or created in connection with) a transaction or series of related transactions involving the acquisition of assets constituting a trade or business or a substantial portion thereof. Property acquired in (or created in connection with) such a transaction or series of related transactions is referred to in this section as property acquired as part of (or created in connection with) a purchase of a trade or business. For purposes of section 197 and this section, the applicability of the limitation is determined under the following rules:

(1) *Goodwill or going concern value.*—An asset or group of assets constitutes a trade or business or a substantial portion thereof if their use would constitute a trade or business under section 1060 (that is, if goodwill or going concern value could under any circumstances attach to the assets). See § 1.1060-1(b)(2). For this purpose, all the facts and circumstances, including any employee relationships that continue (or covenants not to compete that are entered into) as part of the transfer of the assets, are taken into account in determining whether goodwill or going concern value could attach to the assets.

(2) *Franchise, trademark, or trade name.*—(i) *In general.*—The acquisition of a franchise, trademark, or trade name constitutes the acquisition of a trade or business or a substantial portion thereof.

(ii) *Exceptions.*—For purposes of this paragraph (e)(2)—

(A) A trademark or trade name is disregarded if it is included in computer software under paragraph (c)(4) of this section or in an interest in a film, sound recording, video tape, book, or other similar property under paragraph (c)(5) of this section;

(B) A franchise, trademark, or trade name is disregarded if its value is nominal or the taxpayer irrevocably disposes of it immediately after its acquisition; and

(C) The acquisition of a right or interest in a trademark or trade name is disregarded if the grant of the right or interest is not, under the principles of section 1253, a transfer of all substantial rights to such property or of an undivided interest in all substantial rights to such property.

(3) *Acquisitions to be included.*—The assets acquired in a transaction (or series of related transactions) include only assets (including a beneficial or other indirect interest in assets where the interest is of a type described in paragraph (c)(1) of this section) acquired by the taxpayer and persons related to the taxpayer from another person and persons related to that other person. For purposes of this paragraph (e)(3), persons are related only if their relationship is described in section 267(b) or 707(b) or they are engaged in trades or businesses under common control within the meaning of section 41(f)(1).

(4) *Substantial portion.*—The determination of whether acquired assets constitute a substantial portion of a trade or business is to be based on all of the facts and circumstances, including the nature and the amount of the assets acquired as well as the nature and amount of the assets retained by the transferor. The value of the assets acquired relative to the value of the assets retained by the transferor is not determinative of whether the acquired assets constitute a substantial portion of a trade or business.

(5) *Deemed asset purchases under section 338.*—A qualified stock purchase that is treated as a purchase of assets under section 338 is treated as a transaction involving the acquisition of assets constituting a trade or business only if the direct acquisition of the assets of the corporation would have been treated as the acquisition of assets constituting a trade or business or a substantial portion thereof.

(6) *Mortgage servicing rights.*—Mortgage servicing rights acquired in a transaction or series of related transactions are disregarded in determining for purposes of paragraph (c)(11) of this section whether the assets acquired in the transaction or transactions constitute a trade or business or substantial portion thereof.

(7) *Computer software acquired for internal use.*—Computer software acquired in a transaction or series of related transactions solely for internal use in an existing trade or business is disregarded in determining for purposes of paragraph (c)(4) of this section whether the assets acquired in the transaction or series of related transactions constitute a trade or business or substantial portion thereof.

(f) *Computation of amortization deduction.*—(1) *In general.*—Except as provided in paragraph (f)(2) of this section, the amortization deduction allowable under section 197(a) is computed as follows:

(i) The basis of an amortizable section 197 intangible is amortized ratably over the 15-year period beginning on the later of—

(A) The first day of the month in which the property is acquired; or

(B) In the case of property held in connection with the conduct of a trade or business or in an activity described in section 212, the first day of the month in which the conduct of the trade or business or the activity begins.

(ii) Except as otherwise provided in this section, basis is determined under section 1011 and salvage value is disregarded.

(iii) Property is not eligible for amortization in the month of disposition.

(iv) The amortization deduction for a short taxable year is based on the number of months in the short taxable year.

(2) *Treatment of contingent amounts.*—(i) *Amounts added to basis during 15-year period.*—Any amount that is properly included in the basis of an amortizable section 197 intangible after the first month of the 15-year period described in paragraph (f)(1)(i) of this section and before the expiration of that period is amortized ratably over the remainder of the 15-year period. For this purpose, the remainder of the 15-year period begins on the first day of the month in which the basis increase occurs.

(ii) *Amounts becoming fixed after expiration of 15-year period.*—Any amount that is not properly included in the basis of an amortiza-

ble section 197 intangible until after the expiration of the 15-year period described in paragraph (f)(1)(i) of this section is amortized in full immediately upon the inclusion of the amount in the basis of the intangible.

(iii) *Rules for including amounts in basis.*—See §§ 1.1275-4(c)(4) and 1.483-4(a) for rules governing the extent to which contingent amounts payable under a debt instrument given in consideration for the sale or exchange of an amortizable section 197 intangible are treated as payments of principal and the time at which the amount treated as principal is included in basis. See § 1.461-1(a)(1) and (2) for rules governing the time at which other contingent amounts are taken into account in determining the basis of an amortizable section 197 intangible.

(3) *Basis determinations for certain assets.*—(i) *Covenants not to compete.*—In the case of a covenant not to compete or other similar arrangement described in paragraph (b)(9) of this section (a covenant), the amount chargeable to capital account includes, except as provided in this paragraph (f)(3), all amounts that are required to be paid pursuant to the covenant, whether or not any such amount would be deductible under section 162 if the covenant were not a section 197 intangible.

(ii) *Contracts for the use of section 197 intangibles; acquired as part of a trade or business.*—(A) *In general.*—Except as provided in this paragraph (f)(3), any amount paid or incurred by the transferee on account of the transfer of a right or term interest described in paragraph (b)(11) of this section (relating to contracts for the use of, and term interests in, section 197 intangibles) by the owner of the property to which such right or interest relates and as part of a purchase of a trade or business is chargeable to capital account, whether or not such amount would be deductible under section 162 if the property were not a section 197 intangible.

(B) *Know-how and certain information base.*—The amount chargeable to capital account with respect to a right or term interest described in paragraph (b)(11) of this section is determined without regard to the rule in paragraph (f)(3)(ii)(A) of this section if the right or interest relates to property (other than a customer-related information base) described in paragraph (b)(4) or (5) of this section and the acquiring taxpayer establishes that—

(1) The transfer of the right or interest is not, under the principles of section 1235, a transfer of all substantial rights to such property or of an individed interest in all substantial rights to such property; and

(2) The right or interest was transferred for an arm's-length consideration.

(iii) *Contracts for the use of section 197 intangibles; not acquired as part of a trade or business.*—The transfer of a right or term interest described in paragraph (b)(11) of this section by the owner of the property to which such right or interest relates but not as part of a purchase of a trade or business will be closely scrutinized under the principles of section 1235 for purposes of determining whether the transfer is a sale or exchange and, accordingly, whether amounts paid on account of the transfer are chargeable to capital account. If under the principles of section 1235 the transaction is not a sale or exchange, amounts paid on account of the transfer are not chargeable to capital account under this paragraph (f)(3).

(iv) *Applicable rules.*—(A) *Franchises, trademarks, and trade names.*—For purposes of this paragraph (f)(3), section 197 intangibles described in paragraph (b)(11) of this section do not include any property that is also described in paragraph (b)(10) of this section (relating to franchises, trademarks, and trade names).

(B) *Certain amounts treated as payable under a debt instrument.*—(1) *In general.*—For purposes of applying any provision of the Internal Revenue Code to a person making payments of amounts that are otherwise chargeable to capital account under this paragraph (f)(3) and are payable after the acquisition of the section 197 intangible to which they relate, such amounts are treated as payable under a debt instrument given in consideration for the sale or exchange of the section 197 intangible.

(2) *Rights granted by governmental units.*—For purposes of applying any provision of the Internal Revenue Code to any amounts that are otherwise chargeable to capital account with respect to a license, permit, or other right described in paragraph (b)(8) of this section (relating to rights granted by a governmental unit or agency or instrumentality thereof) and are payable after the acquisition of the section 197 intangible to which they relate, such amounts are treated, except as provided in paragraph (f)(4)(i) of this section (relating to renewal transactions), as payable under a debt instrument given in consideration for the sale or exchange of the section 197 intangible.

(3) Treatment of other parties to transaction.—No person shall be treated as having sold, exchanged, or otherwise disposed of property in a transaction for purposes of any provision of the Internal Revenue Code solely by reason of the application of this paragraph (f)(3) to any other party to the transaction.

(4) Basis determinations in certain transactions.—*(i) Certain renewal transactions.*—The costs paid or incurred for the renewal of a franchise, trademark, or trade name or any license, permit, or other right granted by a governmental unit or an agency or instrumentality thereof are amortized over the 15-year period that begins with the month of renewal. Any costs paid or incurred for the issuance, or earlier renewal, continue to be taken into account over the remaining portion of the amortization period that began at the time of the issuance, or earlier renewal. Any amount paid or incurred for the protection, expansion, or defense of a trademark or trade name and chargeable to capital account is treated as an amount paid or incurred for a renewal.

(ii) Transactions subject to section 338 or 1060.—In the case of a section 197 intangible deemed to have been acquired as the result of a qualified stock purchase within the meaning of section 338(d)(3), the basis shall be determined pursuant to section 338(b)(5) and the regulations thereunder. In the case of a section 197 intangible acquired in an applicable asset acquisition within the meaning of section 1060(c), the basis shall be determined pursuant to section 1060(a) and the regulations thereunder.

(iii) Certain reinsurance transactions.—See paragraph (g)(5)(ii) of this section for special rules regarding the adjusted basis of an insurance contract acquired through an assumption reinsurance transaction.

(g) Special rules.—*(1) Treatment of certain dispositions.*—*(i) Loss disallowance rules.*—*(A) In general.*—No loss is recognized on the disposition of an amortizable section 197 intangible if the taxpayer has any retained intangibles. The retained intangibles with respect to the disposition of any amortizable section 197 intangible (the transferred intangible) are all amortizable section 197 intangibles, or rights to use or interests (including beneficial or other indirect interests) in amortizable section 197 intangibles (including the transferred intangible) that were acquired in the same transaction or series of related transactions as the transferred intangible and are retained after its disposition. Except as otherwise provided in paragraph (g)(1)(iv)(B) of this section, the adjusted basis of each of the retained intangibles is increased by the product of—

(1) The loss that is not recognized solely by reason of this rule; and

(2) A fraction, the numerator of which is the adjusted basis of the retained intangible on the date of the disposition and the denominator of which is the total adjusted bases of all the retained intangibles on that date.

(B) Abandonment or worthlessness.—The abandonment of an amortizable section 197 intangible, or any other event rendering an amortizable section 197 intangible worthless, is treated as a disposition of the intangible for purposes of this paragraph (g)(1), and the abandoned or worthless intangible is disregarded (that is, it is not treated as a retained intangible) for purposes of applying this paragraph (g)(1) to the subsequent disposition of any other amortizable section 197 intangible.

(C) Certain nonrecognition transfers.—The loss disallowance rule in paragraph (g)(1)(i)(A) of this section also applies when a taxpayer transfers an amortizable section 197 intangible from an acquired trade or business in a transaction in which the intangible is transferred basis property and, after the transfer, retains other amortizable section 197 intangibles from the trade or business. Thus, for example, the transfer of an amortizable section 197 intangible to a corporation in exchange for stock in the corporation in a transaction described in section 351, or to a partnership in exchange for an interest in the partnership in a transaction described in section 721, when other amortizable section 197 intangibles acquired in the same transaction are retained, followed by a sale of the stock or partnership interest received, will not avoid the application of the loss disallowance provision to the extent the adjusted basis of the transferred intangible at the time of the sale exceeds its fair market value at that time.

(ii) Separately acquired property.—Paragraph (g)(1)(i) of this section does not apply to an amortizable section 197 intangible that is not acquired in a transaction or series of related transactions in which the taxpayer acquires other amortizable section 197 intangibles (a separately acquired intangible). Consequently, a loss may be recognized upon the disposition of a separately acquired amortizable section 197 intangible. However, the termination or worthlessness of only a portion of an amortizable section 197 intangible is not the disposition of a separately acquired intangible. For example, neither the loss of several customers from an acquired customer list nor the worthlessness of only some information from an acquired data base constitutes the disposition of a separately acquired intangible.

(iii) Disposition of a covenant not to compete.—If a covenant not to compete or any other arrangement having substantially the same effect is entered into in connection with the direct or indirect acquisition of an interest in one or more trades or businesses, the disposition or worthlessness of the covenant or other arrangement will not be considered to occur until the disposition or worthlessness of all interests in those trades or businesses. For example, a covenant not to compete entered into in connection with the purchase of stock continues to be amortized ratably over the 15-year recovery period (even after the covenant expires or becomes worthless) unless all the trades or businesses in which an interest was acquired through the stock purchase (or all the purchaser's interests in those trades or businesses) also are disposed of or become worthless.

(iv) Taxpayers under common control.—*(A) In general.*—Except as provided in paragraph (g)(1)(iv)(B) of this section, all persons that would be treated as a single taxpayer under section 41(f)(1) are treated as a single taxpayer under this paragraph (g)(1). Thus, for example, a loss is not recognized on the disposition of an amortizable section 197 intangible by a member of a controlled group of corporations (as defined in section 41(f)(5)) if, after the disposition, another member retains other amortizable section 197 intangibles acquired in the same transaction as the amortizable section 197 intangible that has been disposed of.

(B) Treatment of disallowed loss.—If retained intangibles are held by a person other than the person incurring the disallowed loss, only the adjusted basis of intangibles retained by the person incurring the disallowed loss is increased, and only the adjusted basis of those intangibles is included in the denominator of the fraction described in paragraph (g)(1)(i)(A) of this section. If none of the retained intangibles are held by the person incurring the disallowed loss, the loss is allowed ratably, as a deduction under section 197, over the remainder of the period during which the intangible giving rise to the loss would have been amortized, except that any remaining disallowed loss is allowed in full on the first date on which all other retained intangibles have been disposed of or become worthless.

(2) Treatment of certain nonrecognition and exchange transactions.—*(i) Relationship to anti-churning rules.*—This paragraph (g)(2) provides rules relating to the treatment of section 197 intangibles acquired in certain transactions. If these rules apply to a section 197(f)(9) intangible (within the meaning of paragraph (h)(1)(i) of this section), the intangible is, notwithstanding its treatment under this paragraph (g)(2), treated as an amortizable section 197 intangible only to the extent permitted under paragraph (h) of this section.

(ii) Treatment of nonrecognition and exchange transactions generally.—*(A) Transfer disregarded.*—If a section 197 intangible is transferred in a transaction described in paragraph (g)(2)(ii)(C) of this section, the transfer is disregarded in determining—

(1) Whether, with respect to so much of the intangible's basis in the hands of the transferee as does not exceed its basis in the hands of the transferor, the intangible is an amortizable section 197 intangible; and

(2) The amount of the deduction under section 197 with respect to such basis.

(B) Application of general rule.—If the intangible described in paragraph (g)(2)(ii)(A) of this section was an amortizable section 197 intangible in the hands of the transferor, the transferee will continue to amortize its adjusted basis, to the extent it does not exceed the transferor's adjusted basis, ratably over the remainder of the transferor's 15-year amortization period. If the intangible was not an amortizable section 197 intangible in the hands of the transferor, the transferee's adjusted basis, to the extent it does not exceed the transferor's adjusted basis, cannot be amortized under section 197. In either event, the intangible is treated, with respect to so much of its adjusted basis in the hands of the transferee as exceeds its adjusted basis in the hands of the transferor, in the same manner for purposes of section 197 as an intangible acquired from the transferor in a transaction that is not described in paragraph (g)(2)(ii)(C) of this section. The rules of this paragraph (g)(2)(ii) also apply to any subsequent transfers of the intangible in a transaction described in paragraph (g)(2)(ii)(C) of this section.

(C) Transactions covered.—The transactions described in this paragraph (g)(2)(ii)(C) are—

(1) Any transaction described in section 332, 351, 361, 721, or 731; and

(2) Any transaction between corporations that are members of the same consolidated group immediately after the transaction.

(iii) *Certain exchanged-basis property.*—This paragraph (g)(2)(iii) applies to property that is acquired in a transaction subject to section 1031 or 1033 and is permitted to be acquired without recognition of gain (replacement property). Replacement property is treated as if it were the property by reference to which its basis is determined (the predecessor property) in determining whether, with respect to so much of its basis as does not exceed the basis of the predecessor property, the replacement property is an amortizable section 197 intangible and the amortization period under section 197 with respect to such basis. Thus, if the predecessor property was an amortizable section 197 intangible, the taxpayer will amortize the adjusted basis of the replacement property, to the extent it does not exceed the adjusted basis of the predecessor property, ratably over the remainder of the 15-year amortization period for the predecessor property. If the predecessor property was not an amortizable section 197 intangible, the adjusted basis of the replacement property, to the extent it does not exceed the adjusted basis of the predecessor property, may not be amortized under section 197. In either event, the replacement property is treated, with respect to so much of its adjusted basis as exceeds the adjusted basis of the predecessor property, in the same manner for purposes of section 197 as property acquired from the transferor in a transaction that is not subject to section 1031 or 1033.

(iv) *Transfers under section 708(b)(1).*—(A) *In general.*—Paragraph (g)(2)(ii) of this section applies to transfers of section 197 intangibles that occur or are deemed to occur by reason of the termination of a partnership under section 708(b)(1).

(B) *Termination by sale or exchange of interest.*—In applying paragraph (g)(2)(ii) of this section to a partnership that is terminated pursuant to section 708(b)(1)(B) (relating to deemed terminations from the sale or exchange of an interest), the terminated partnership is treated as the transferor and the new partnership is treated as the transferee with respect to any section 197 intangible held by the terminated partnership immediately preceding the termination. (See paragraph (g)(3) of this section for the treatment of increases in the bases of property of the terminated partnership under section 743(b).)

(C) *Other terminations.*—In applying paragraph (g)(2)(ii) of this section to a partnership that is terminated pursuant to section 708(b)(1)(A) (relating to cessation of activities by a partnership), the terminated partnership is treated as the transferor and the distributee partner is treated as the transferee with respect to any section 197 intangible held by the terminated partnership immediately preceding the termination.

(3) *Increase in the basis of partnership property under section 732(b), 734(b), 743(b), or 732(d).*—Any increase in the adjusted basis of a section 197 intangible under sections 732(b) or 732(d) (relating to a partner's basis in property distributed by a partnership), section 734(b) (relating to the optional adjustment to the basis of undistributed partnership property after a distribution of property to a partner), or section 743(b) (relating to the optional adjustment to the basis of partnership property after transfer of a partnership interest) is treated as a separate section 197 intangible. For purposes of determining the amortization period under section 197 with respect to the basis increase, the intangible is treated as having been acquired at the time of the transaction that causes the basis increase, except as provided in §1.743-1(j)(4)(i)(B)(2). The provisions of paragraph (f)(2) of this section apply to the extent that the amount of the basis increase is determined by reference to contingent payments. For purposes of the effective date and anti-churning provisions (paragraphs (l)(1) and (h) of this section) for a basis increase under section 732(d), the intangible is treated as having been acquired by the transferee partner at the time of the transfer of the partnership interest described in section 732(d).

(4) *Section 704(c) allocations.*—(i) *Allocations where the intangible is amortizable by the contributor.*—To the extent that the intangible was an amortizable section 197 intangible in the hands of the contributing partner, a partnership may make allocations of amortization deductions with respect to the intangible to all of its partners under any of the permissible methods described in the regulations under section 704(c). See §1.704-3.

(ii) *Allocations where the intangible is not amortizable by the contributor.*—To the extent that the intangible was not an amortizable section 197 intangible in the hands of the contributing partner, the intangible is not amortizable under section 197 by the partnership. However, if a partner contributes a section 197 intangible to a partnership and the partnership adopts the remedial allocation method for making section 704(c) allocations of amortization deductions, the partnership generally may make remedial allocations of amortization deductions with respect to the contributed section 197 intangible in accordance with §1.704-3(d). See paragraph (h)(12) of this section to determine the application of the anti-churning rules in the context of remedial allocations.

(5) *Treatment of certain insurance contracts acquired in an assumption reinsurance transaction.*—(i) *In general.*—Section 197 generally applies to insurance and annuity contracts acquired from another person through an assumption reinsurance transaction. See §1.809-5(a)(7)(ii) for the definition of assumption reinsurance. The transfer of insurance or annuity contracts and the assumption of related liabilities deemed to occur by reason of a section 338 election for a target insurance company is treated as an assumption reinsurance transaction. The transfer of a reinsurance contract by a reinsurer (transferor) to another reinsurer (acquirer) is treated as an assumption reinsurance transaction if the transferor's obligations are extinguished as a result of the transaction.

(ii) *Determination of adjusted basis of amortizable section 197 intangible resulting from an assumption reinsurance transaction.*—(A) *In general.*—Section 197(f)(5) determines the basis of an amortizable section 197 intangible for insurance or annuity contracts acquired in an assumption reinsurance transaction. The basis of such intangible is the excess, if any, of—

(1) The amount paid or incurred by the acquirer (reinsurer) under the assumption reinsurance transaction; over

(2) The amount, if any, required to be capitalized under section 848 in connection with such transaction.

(B) *Amount paid or incurred by acquirer (reinsurer) under the assumption reinsurance transaction.*—The amount paid or incurred by the acquirer (reinsurer) under the assumption reinsurance transaction is—

(1) In a deemed asset sale resulting from an election under section 338, the amount of the adjusted grossed-up basis (AGUB) allocable thereto (see §§1.338-6 and 1.338-11(b)(2);

(2) In an applicable asset acquisition within the meaning of section 1060, the amount of the consideration allocable thereto (see §§1.338-6, 1.338-11(b)(2), and 1.1060-1(c)(5)); and

(3) In any other transaction, the excess of the increase in the reinsurer's tax reserves resulting from the transaction (computed in accordance with sections 807, 832(b)(4)(B), and 846) over the value of the net assets received from the ceding company in the transaction.

(C) *Amount required to be capitalized under section 848 in connection with the transaction.*—(1) *In general.*—The amount required to be capitalized under section 848 for specified insurance contracts (as defined in section 848(e)) acquired in an assumption reinsurance transaction is the lesser of—

(i) The reinsurer's required capitalization amount for the assumption reinsurance transaction; or

(ii) The reinsurer's general deductions (as defined in section 848(c)(2)) allocable to the transaction.

(2) *Required capitalization amount.*—The reinsurer determines the required capitalization amount for an assumption reinsurance transaction by multiplying the net positive or net negative consideration for the transaction by the applicable percentage set forth in section 848(c)(1) for the category of specified insurance contracts acquired in the transaction. See §1.848-2(g)(5). If more than one category of specified insurance contracts is acquired in an assumption reinsurance transaction, the required capitalization amount for each category is determined as if the transfer of the contracts in that category were made under a separate assumption reinsurance transaction. See §1.848-2(f)(7).

(3) *General deductions allocable to the assumption reinsurance transaction.*—The reinsurer determines the general deductions allocable to the assumption reinsurance transaction in accordance with the procedure set forth in §1.848-2(g)(6). Accordingly, the reinsurer must allocate its general deductions to the amount required under section 848(c)(1) on specified insurance contracts that the reinsurer has issued directly before determining the general deductions allocable to the assumption reinsurance transaction. For purposes of allocating its general deductions under §1.848-2(g)(6), the reinsurer includes premiums received on the acquired specified insurance contracts after the assumption reinsurance transaction in determining the amount required under section 848(c)(1) on specified insurance contracts that the reinsurer has issued directly. If the reinsurer has entered into multiple reinsurance agreements during the taxable year, the reinsurer determines the general deductions allocable to each reinsurance agreement (including the assumption reinsurance transaction) by allocating the general deductions allocable to reinsurance agreements under §1.848-2(g)(6) to each reinsurance agreement with a positive required capitalization amount.

(4) Treatment of a capitalization shortfall allocable to the reinsurance agreement.—(i) In general.—The reinsurer determines any capitalization shortfall allocable to the assumption reinsurance transaction in the manner provided in §§ 1.848-2(g)(4) and 1.848-2(g)(7). If the reinsurer has a capitalization shortfall allocable to the assumption reinsurance transaction, the ceding company must reduce the net negative consideration (as determined under §1.848-2(f)(2)) for the transaction by the amount described in §1.848-2(g)(3) unless the parties make the election provided in §1.848-2(g)(8) to determine the amounts capitalized under section 848 in connection with the transaction without regard to the general deductions limitation of section 848(c)(2).

(ii) Treatment of additional capitalized amounts as the result of an election under §1.848-2(g)(8).—The additional amounts capitalized by the reinsurer as the result of the election under §1.848-2(g)(8) reduce the adjusted basis of any amortizable section 197 intangible with respect to specified insurance contracts acquired in the assumption reinsurance transaction. If the additional capitalized amounts exceed the adjusted basis of the amortizable section 197 intangible, the reinsurer must reduce its deductions under section 805 or section 832 by the amount of such excess. The additional capitalized amounts are treated as specified policy acquisition expenses attributable to the premiums and other consideration on the assumption reinsurance transaction and are deducted ratably over a 120-month period as provided under section 848(a)(2).

(5) Cross references and special rules.—In general, for rules applicable to the determination of specified policy acquisition expenses, net premiums, and net consideration, see section 848(c) and (d), and §1.848-2(a) and (f). However, the following special rules apply for purposes of this paragraph (g)(5)(ii)(C)—

(i) The amount required to be capitalized under section 848 in connection with the assumption reinsurance transaction cannot be less than zero;

(ii) For purposes of determining the company's general deductions under section 848(c)(2) for the taxable year of the assumption reinsurance transaction, the reinsurer takes into account a tentative amortization deduction under section 197(a) as if the entire amount paid or incurred by the reinsurer for the specified insurance contracts were allocated to an amortizable section 197 intangible with respect to insurance contracts acquired in an assumption reinsurance transaction; and

(iii) Any reduction of specified policy acquisition expenses pursuant to an election under §1.848-2(i)(4) (relating to an assumption reinsurance transaction with an insolvent insurance company) is disregarded.

(D) Examples.—The following examples illustrate the principles of this paragraph (g)(5)(ii):

Example 1. (i) *Facts.* On January 15, 2006, P acquires all of the stock of T, an insurance company, in a qualified stock purchase and makes a section 338 election for T. T issues individual life insurance contracts which are specified insurance contracts as defined in section 848(e)(1). P and new T are calendar year taxpayers. Under §§ 1.338-6 and 1.338-11(b)(2), the amount of AGUB allocated to old T's individual life insurance contracts is $300,000. On the acquisition date, the tax reserves for old T's individual life insurance contracts are $2,000,000. After the acquisition date, new T receives $1,000,000 of net premiums with respect to new and renewal individual life insurance contracts and incurs $100,000 of general deductions under section 848(c)(2) through December 31, 2006. New T engages in no other reinsurance transactions other than the assumption reinsurance transaction treated as occurring by reason of the section 338 election.

(ii) *Analysis.* The transfer of insurance contracts and the assumption of related liabilities deemed to occur by reason of the election under section 338 is treated as an assumption reinsurance transaction. New T determines the adjusted basis under section 197(f)(5) for the life insurance contracts acquired in the assumption reinsurance transaction as follows. The amount paid or incurred for the individual life insurance contracts is $300,000. To determine the amount required to be capitalized under section 848 in connection with the assumption reinsurance transaction, new T compares the required capitalization amount for the assumption reinsurance transaction with the general deductions allocable to the transaction. The required capitalization amount for the assumption reinsurance transaction is $130,900, which is determined by multiplying the $1,700,000 net positive consideration for the transaction ($2,000,000 reinsurance premium less $300,000 ceding commission) by the applicable percentage under section 848(c)(1) for the acquired individual life insurance contracts (7.7 percent). To determine its general deductions, new T takes into account a tentative amortization deduction under section 197(a) as if the entire amount paid or incurred for old T's individual life insurance contracts ($300,000) were allocable to a amortizable section 197 intangible with respect to insurance contracts acquired in the assumption reinsurance transaction. Accordingly, for the year of

the assumption reinsurance transaction, new T is treated as having general deductions under section 848(c)(2) of $120,000 ($100,000 + $300,000/15). Under §1.848-2(g)(6), these general deductions are first allocated to the $77,000 capitalization requirement for new T's directly written business ($1,000,000 × .077). Thus, $43,000 ($120,000 − $77,000) of the general deductions are allocable to the assumption reinsurance transaction. Because the general deductions allocable to the assumption reinsurance transaction ($43,000) are less than the required capitalization amount for the transaction ($130,900), new T has a capitalization shortfall of $87,900 ($130,900 − $43,000) with regard to the transaction. Under §1.848-2(g), this capitalization shortfall would cause old T to reduce the net negative consideration taken into account with respect to the assumption reinsurance transaction by $1,141,558 ($87,900 ÷ .077) unless the parties make the election under §1.848-2(g)(8) to capitalize specified policy acquisition expenses in connection with the assumption reinsurance transaction without regard to the general deductions limitation. If the parties make the election, the amount capitalized by new T under section 848 in connection with the assumption reinsurance transaction would be $130,900. The $130,900 capitalized by new T under section 848 would reduce new T's adjusted basis of the amortizable section 197 intangible with respect to the specified insurance contracts acquired in the assumption reinsurance transaction. Accordingly, new T would have an adjusted basis under section 197(f)(5) with respect to the individual life insurance contracts acquired from old T of $169,100 ($300,000 − $130,900). New T's actual amortization deduction under section 197(a) with respect to the amortizable section 197 intangible for insurance contracts acquired in the assumption reinsurance transaction would be $11,273 ($169,100 ÷15).

Example 2. (i) *Facts.* The facts are the same as *Example 1*, except that T only issues accident and health insurance contracts that are qualified long-term care contracts under section 7702B. Under section 7702B(a)(5), T's qualified long-term care insurance contracts are treated as guaranteed renewable accident and health insurance contracts, and, therefore, are considered specified insurance contracts under section 848(e)(1). Under §§ 1.338-6 and 1.338-11(b)(2), the amount of AGUB allocable to T's qualified long-term care insurance contracts is $250,000. The amount of T's tax reserves for the qualified long-term care contracts on the acquisition date is $7,750,000. Following the acquisition, new T receives net premiums of $500,000 with respect to qualified long-term care contracts and incurs general deductions of $75,000 through December 31, 2006.

(ii) *Analysis.* The transfer of insurance contracts and the assumption of related liabilities deemed to occur by reason of the election under section 338 is treated as an assumption reinsurance transaction. New T determines the adjusted basis under section 197(f)(5) for the insurance contracts acquired in the assumption reinsurance transaction as follows. The amount paid or incurred for the insurance contracts is $250,000. To determine the amount required to be capitalized under section 848 in connection with the assumption reinsurance transaction, new T compares the required capitalization amount for the assumption reinsurance transaction with the general deductions allocable to the transaction. The required capitalization amount for the assumption reinsurance transaction is $577,500, which is determined by multiplying the $7,500,000 net positive consideration for the transaction ($7,750,000 reinsurance premium less $250,000 ceding commission) by the applicable percentage under section 848(c)(1) for the acquired insurance contracts (7.7 percent). To determine its general deductions, new T takes into account a tentative amortization deduction under section 197(a) as if the entire amount paid or incurred for old T's insurance contracts ($250,000) were allocable to an amortizable section 197 intangible with respect to insurance contracts acquired in the assumption reinsurance transaction. Accordingly, for the year of the assumption reinsurance transaction, new T is treated as having general deductions under section 848(c)(2) of $91,667 ($75,000 + $250,000/15). Under §1.848-2(g)(6), these general deductions are first allocated to the $38,500 capitalization requirement for new T's directly written business ($500,000 × .077). Thus, $53,167 ($91,667 − $38,500) of general deductions are allocable to the assumption reinsurance transaction. Because the general deductions allocable to the assumption reinsurance transaction ($53,167) are less than the required capitalization amount for the transaction ($577,500), new T has a capitalization shortfall of $524,333 ($577,500 - $53,167) with regard to the transaction. Under §1.848-2(g), this capitalization shortfall would cause old T to reduce the net negative consideration taken into account with respect to the assumption reinsurance transaction by $6,809,519 ($524,333 ÷ .077) unless the parties make the election under §1.848-2(g)(8) to capitalize specified policy acquisition expenses in connection with the assumption reinsurance transaction without regard to the general deductions limitation. If the parties make the election, the amount capitalized by new T under section 848 in connection with the assumption reinsurance transaction would increase from $53,167 to $577,500. Pursuant to paragraph (g)(5)(ii)(C)(4) of this section, the additional $524,333 ($577,500 - $53,167) capitalized by new T under section 848 would reduce new T's adjusted basis of the amortizable section 197 intangible with respect to the insurance contracts acquired in the assumption reinsurance transaction. Accordingly, new T's adjusted basis of the section 197 intangible with regard to the insurance contracts is reduced from $196,833 ($250,000 - $53,167) to $0. Because the additional $524,333 capitalized pursuant to the § 1.848-2(g)(8) election exceeds the $196,833 adjusted basis of the section 197 intangible before the reduction, new T is required to reduce its deductions under section 805 by the $327,500 ($524,333 - $196,833).

(E) *Effective/applicability date.*—This section applies to acquisitions and dispositions of insurance contracts on or after April 10, 2006.

(iii) *Application of loss disallowance rule upon a disposition of an insurance contract acquired in an assumption reinsurance transaction.*—The following rules apply for purposes of applying the loss disallowance rules of section 197(f)(1)(A) to the disposition of a section 197(f)(5) intangible. For this purpose, a section 197(f)(5) intangible is an amortizable section 197 intangible the basis of which is determined under section 197(f)(5).

(A) *Disposition.*—(1) *In general.*—A disposition of a section 197 intangible is any event as a result of which, absent section 197, recovery of basis is otherwise allowed for Federal income tax purposes.

(2) *Treatment of indemnity reinsurance transactions.*—The transfer through indemnity reinsurance of the right to the future income from the insurance contracts to which a section 197(f)(5) intangible relates does not preclude the recovery of basis by the ceding company, provided that sufficient economic rights relating to the reinsured contracts are transferred to the reinsurer. However, the ceding company is not permitted to recover basis in an indemnity reinsurance transaction if it has a right to experience refunds reflecting a significant portion of the future profits on the reinsured contracts, or if it retains an option to reacquire a significant portion of the future profits on the reinsured contracts through the exercise of a recapture provision. In addition, the ceding company is not permitted to recover basis in an indemnity reinsurance transaction if the reinsurer assumes only a limited portion of the ceding company's risk relating to the reinsured contracts (excess loss reinsurance).

(B) *Loss.*—The loss, if any, recognized by a taxpayer on the disposition of a section 197(f)(5) intangible equals the amount by which the taxpayer's adjusted basis in the section 197(f)(5) intangible immediately before the disposition exceeds the amount, if any, that the taxpayer receives from another person for the future income right from the insurance contracts to which the section 197(f)(5) intangible relates. In determining the amount of the taxpayer's loss on the disposition of a section 197(f)(5) intangible through a reinsurance transaction, any effect of the transaction on the amounts capitalized by the taxpayer as specified policy acquisition expenses under section 848 is disregarded.

(C) *Examples.*—The following examples illustrate the principles of this paragraph (g)(5)(iii):

Example 1. (i) *Facts.* In a prior taxable year, as a result of a section 338 election with respect to T, new T was treated as purchasing all of old T's insurance contracts that were in force on the acquisition date in an assumption reinsurance transaction. Under §§ 1.338-6 and 1.338-11(b)(2), the amount of AGUB allocable to the future income right from the purchased insurance contracts was $15, net of the amounts required to be capitalized under section 848 as a result of the assumption reinsurance transaction. At the beginning of the current taxable year, as a result of amortization deductions allowed by section 197(a), new T's adjusted basis in the section 197(f)(5) intangible resulting from the assumption reinsurance transaction is $12. During the current taxable year, new T enters into an indemnity reinsurance agreement with R, another insurance company, in which R assumes 100 percent of the risk relating to the insurance contracts to which the section 197(f)(5) intangible relates. In the indemnity reinsurance agreement, R agrees to pay new T a ceding commission of $10 in exchange for the future profits on the underlying reinsured policies. Under the indemnity reinsurance agreement, new T continues to administer the reinsured policies, but transfers investment assets equal to the required reserves for the reinsured policies together with all future premiums to R. The indemnity reinsurance agreement does not contain an experience refund provision or a provision allowing new T to terminate the reinsurance agreement at its sole option. New T retains the insurance licenses and other amortizable section 197 intangibles acquired in the deemed asset sale and continues to underwrite and issue new insurance contracts.

(ii) *Analysis.* The indemnity reinsurance agreement constitutes a disposition of the section 197(f)(5) intangible because it involves the transfer of sufficient economic rights attributable to the insurance contracts to which the section 197(f)(5) intangible relates such that recovery of basis is allowed. For purposes of applying the loss disallowance rules of section 197(f)(1) and paragraph (g) of this section, new T's loss is $2 (new T's adjusted basis in the section 197(f)(5) intangible immediately before the disposition ($12) less the ceding commission ($10)). Therefore, new T applies $10 of the adjusted basis in the section 197(f)(5) intangible against the amount received from R for the future income right on the reinsured policies and increases its basis in the amortizable section 197 intangibles that it acquired and retained from the deemed asset sale by $2, the amount of the disallowed loss. The amount of new T's disallowed loss under section 197(f)(1)(A) is determined without regard to the effect of the indemnity reinsurance transaction on the amounts capitalized by new T as specified policy acquisition expenses under section 848.

Example 2. (i) *Facts.* Assume the same facts as in *Example 1,* except that under the indemnity reinsurance agreement R agrees to pay new T a ceding commission of $5 with respect to the underlying reinsured contracts. In addition, under the indemnity reinsurance agreement, new T is entitled to an experience refund equal to any future profits on the reinsured contracts in excess of the ceding commission plus an annual risk charge. New T also has a right to recapture the business at any time after R has recovered an amount equal to the ceding commission.

(ii) *Analysis.* The indemnity reinsurance agreement between new T and R does not represent a disposition because it does not involve the transfer of sufficient economic rights with respect to the future income on the reinsured contracts. Therefore, new T may not recover its basis in the section 197(f)(5) intangible to which the contracts relate and must continue to amortize ratably the adjusted basis of the section 197(f)(5) intangible over the remainder of the 15-year recovery period and cannot apply any portion of this adjusted basis to offset the ceding commission received from R in the indemnity reinsurance transaction.

(iv) *Effective dates.*—(A) *In general.*—This paragraph (g)(5) applies to acquisitions and dispositions on or after April 10, 2006. For rules applicable to acquisitions and dispositions before that date, see § 1.197-2 in effect before that date (see 26 CFR part 1, revised April 1, 2001).

(B) *Application to pre-effective date acquisitions and dispositions.*—A taxpayer may choose, on a transaction-by-transaction basis, to apply the provisions of this paragraph (g)(5) to property acquired and disposed of before April 10, 2006.

(C) *Change in method of accounting.*—(1) *In general.*—A change in a taxpayer's treatment of all property acquired and disposed under paragraph (g)(5) is a change in method of accounting to which the provisions of sections 446 and 481 and the regulations thereunder apply.

(2) *Acquisitions and dispositions on or after effective date.*—A Taxpayer is granted the consent of the Commissioner under section 446(e) to change its method of accounting to comply with this paragraph (g)(5) for acquisitions and dispositions on or after April 10, 2006. The change must be made on a cut-off basis with no section 481(a) adjustment. Notwithstanding § 1.446-1(e)(3), a taxpayer should not file a Form 3115, "Application for Change in Accounting Method," to obtain the consent of the Commissioner to change its method of accounting under this paragraph (g)(5)(iv)(C)(2). Instead, a taxpayer must make the change by using the new method on its federal income tax returns.

(3) *Acquisitions and dispositions before the effective date.*—For the first taxable year ending after April 10, 2006, a taxpayer is granted consent of the Commissioner to change its method of accounting for all property acquired in transactions described in paragraph (g)(5)(iv)(B) to comply with this paragraph (g)(5) unless the proper treatment of any such property is an issue under consideration in an examination, before an Appeals office, or before a Federal Court. (For the definition of when an issue is under consideration, see, Rev. Proc. 97-27 (1997-1 C.B. 680); and, § 601.601(d)(2) of this chapter). A taxpayer changing its method of accounting in accordance with this paragraph (g)(5)(iv)(C)(3) must follow the applicable administrative procedures for obtaining the Commissioner's automatic consent to a change in method of accounting (for further guidance, see, for example, Rev. Proc. 2002-9 (2002-1 C.B. 327) as modified and clarified by Announcement 2002-17 (2002-1 C.B. 561), modified and amplified by Rev. Proc. 2002-19 (2002-1 C.B. 696), and amplified, clarified and modified by Rev. Proc. 2002-54 (2002-2 C.B. 432); and, § 601.601(d)(2) of this chapter), except, for purposes of this paragraph (g)(5)(iv)(C)(3), any limitations in such administrative procedures for obtaining the automatic consent of the Commissioner shall not apply. However, if the taxpayer is under examination, before an appeals office, or before a Federal court, the taxpayer must

provide a copy of the application to the examining agent(s), appeals officer, or counsel for the government, as appropriate, at the same time that it files the copy of the application with the National Office. The application must contain the name(s) and telephone number(s) of the examining agent(s), appeals officer, or counsel for the government, as appropriate. For purposes of From 3115, "Application for Change in Accounting Method," the designated number for the automatic accounting method change authorized by this paragraph (g)(5)(iv)(C)(3) is "98". A change in method of accounting in accordance with this paragraph (g)(5)(iv)(C)(3) requires an adjustment under section 481(a).

(6) *Amounts paid or incurred for a franchise, trademark, or trade name.*—If an amount to which section 1253(d) (relating to the transfer, sale, or other disposition of a franchise, trademark, or trade name) applies is described in section 1253(d)(1)(B) (relating to contingent serial payments deductible under section 162), the amount is not included in the adjusted basis of the intangible for purposes of section 197. Any other amount, whether fixed or contingent, to which section 1253(d) applies is chargeable to capital account under section 1253(d)(2) and is amortizable only under section 197.

(7) *Amounts properly taken into account in determining the cost of property that is not a section 197 intangible.*—Section 197 does not apply to an amount that is properly taken into account in determining the cost of property that is not a section 197 intangible. The entire cost of acquiring the other property is included in its basis and recovered under other applicable Internal Revenue Code provisions. Thus, for example, section 197 does not apply to the cost of an interest in computer software to the extent such cost is included, without being separately stated, in the cost of the hardware or other tangible property and is consistently treated as part of the cost of the hardware or other tangible property.

(8) *Treatment of amortizable section 197 intangibles as depreciable property.*—An amortizable section 197 intangible is treated as property of a character subject to the allowance for depreciation under section 167. Thus, for example, an amortizable section 197 intangible is not a capital asset for purposes of section 1221, but if used in a trade or business and held for more than one year, gain or loss on its disposition generally qualifies as section 1231 gain or loss. Also, an amortizable section 197 intangible is section 1245 property and section 1239 applies to any gain recognized upon its sale or exchange between related persons (as defined in section 1239(b)).

(h) *Anti-churning rules.*—(1) *Scope and purpose.*—(i) *Scope.*—This paragraph (h) applies to section 197(f)(9) intangibles. For this purpose, section 197(f)(9) intangibles are goodwill and going concern value that was held or used at any time during the transition period and any other section 197 intangible that was held or used at any time during the transition period and was not depreciable or amortizable under prior law.

(ii) *Purpose.*—To qualify as an amortizable section 197 intangible, a section 197 intangible must be acquired after the applicable date (July 25, 1991, if the acquiring taxpayer has made a valid retroactive election pursuant to §1.197-1T; August 10, 1993, in all other cases). The purpose of the anti-churning rules of section 197(f)(9) and this paragraph (h) is to prevent the amortization of section 197(f)(9) intangibles unless they are transferred after the applicable effective date in a transaction giving rise to a significant change in ownership or use. (Special rules apply for purposes of determining whether transactions involving partnerships give rise to a significant change in ownership or use. See paragraph (h)(12) of this section.) The anti-churning rules are to be applied in a manner that carries out their purpose.

(2) *Treatment of section 197(f)(9) intangibles.*—Except as otherwise provided in this paragraph (h), a section 197(f)(9) intangible acquired by a taxpayer after the applicable effective date does not qualify for amortization under section 197 if—

(i) The taxpayer or a related person held or used the intangible or an interest therein at any time during the transition period;

(ii) The taxpayer acquired the intangible from a person that held the intangible at any time during the transition period and, as part of the transaction, the user of the intangible does not change; or

(iii) The taxpayer grants the right to use the intangible to a person that held or used the intangible at any time during the transition period (or to a person related to that person), but only if the transaction in which the taxpayer grants the right and the transaction in which the taxpayer acquired the intangible are part of a series of related transactions.

(3) *Amounts deductible under section 1253(d) or §1.162-11.*—For purposes of this paragraph (h), deductions allowable under section 1253(d)(2) or pursuant to an election under section 1253(d)(3) (in either case as in effect prior to the enactment of section 197) and

deductions allowable under §1.162-11 are treated as deductions allowable for amortization under prior law.

(4) *Transition period.*—For purposes of this paragraph (h), the transition period is July 25, 1991, if the acquiring taxpayer has made a valid retroactive election pursuant to §1.197-1T and the period beginning on July 25, 1991, and ending on August 10, 1993, in all other cases.

(5) *Exceptions.*—The anti-churning rules of this paragraph (h) do not apply to—

(i) The acquisition of a section 197(f)(9) intangible if the acquiring taxpayer's basis in the intangible is determined under section 1014(a) or 1022; or

(ii) The acquisition of a section 197(f)(9) intangible that was an amortizable section 197 intangible in the hands of the seller (or transferor), but only if the acquisition transaction and the transaction in which the seller (or transferor) acquired the intangible or interest therein are not part of a series of related transactions.

(6) *Related person.*—(i) *In general.*—Except as otherwise provided in paragraph (h)(6)(ii) of this section, a person is related to another person for purposes of this paragraph (h) if—

(A) The person bears a relationship to that person that would be specified in section 267(b) (determined without regard to section 267(e)) and, by substitution, section 267(f)(1), if those sections were amended by substituting 20 percent for 50 percent; or

(B) The person bears a relationship to that person that would be specified in section 707(b)(1) if that section were amended by substituting 20 percent for 50 percent; or

(C) The persons are engaged in trades or businesses under common control (within the meaning of section 41(f)(1)(A) and (B)).

(ii) *Time for testing relationships.*—Except as provided in paragraph (h)(6)(iii) of this section, a person is treated as related to another person for purposes of this paragraph (h) if the relationship exists—

(A) In the case of a single transaction, immediately before or immediately after the transaction in which the intangible is acquired; and

(B) In the case of a series of related transactions (or a series of transactions that together comprise a qualified stock purchase within the meaning of section 338(d)(3)), immediately before the earliest such transaction or immediately after the last such transaction.

(iii) *Certain relationships disregarded.*—In applying the rules in paragraph (h)(7) of this section, if a person acquires an intangible in a series of related transactions in which the person acquires stock (meeting the requirements of section 1504(a)(2)) of a corporation in a fully taxable transaction followed by a liquidation of the acquired corporation under section 331, any relationship created as part of such series of transactions is disregarded in determining whether any person is related to such acquired corporation immediately after the last transaction.

(iv) *De minimis rule.*—(A) *In general.*—Two corporations are not treated as related persons for purposes of this paragraph (h) if—

(1) The corporations would (but for the application of this paragraph (h)(6)(iv)) be treated as related persons solely by reason of substituting "more than 20 percent" for "more than 50 percent" in section 267(f)(1)(A); and

(2) The beneficial ownership interest of each corporation in the stock of the other corporation represents less than 10 percent of the total combined voting power of all classes of stock entitled to vote and less than 10 percent of the total value of the shares of all classes of stock outstanding.

(B) *Determination of beneficial ownership interest.*—For purposes of this paragraph (h)(6)(iv), the beneficial ownership interest of one corporation in the stock of another corporation is determined under the principles of section 318(a), except that—

(1) In applying section 318(a)(2)(C), the 50-percent limitation contained therein is not applied; and

(2) Section 318(a)(3)(C) is applied by substituting "20 percent" for "50 percent".

(7) *Special rules for entities that owned or used property at any time during the transition period and that are no longer in existence.*—A corporation, partnership, or trust that owned or used a section 197 intangible at any time during the transition period and that is no longer in existence is deemed, for purposes of determining whether a taxpayer acquiring the intangible is related to such entity, to be in existence at the time of the acquisition.

(8) *Special rules for section 338 deemed acquisitions.*—In the case of a qualified stock purchase that is treated as a deemed sale and

purchase of assets pursuant to section 338, the corporation treated as purchasing assets as a result of an election thereunder (new target) is not considered the person that held or used the assets during any period in which the assets were held or used by the corporation treated as selling the assets (old target). Thus, for example, if a corporation (the purchasing corporation) makes a qualified stock purchase of the stock of another corporation after the transition period, new target will not be treated as the owner during the transition period of assets owned by old target during that period even if old target and new target are treated as the same corporation for certain other purposes of the Internal Revenue Code or old target and new target are the same corporation under the laws of the State or other jurisdiction of its organization. However, the anti-churning rules of this paragraph (h) may nevertheless apply to a deemed asset purchase resulting from a section 338 election if new target is related (within the meaning of paragraph (h)(6) of this section) to old target.

(9) *Gain-recognition exception.*—(i) *Applicability.*—A section 197(f)(9) intangible qualifies for the gain-recognition exception if—

(A) The taxpayer acquires the intangible from a person that would not be related to the taxpayer but for the substitution of 20 percent for 50 percent under paragraph (h)(6)(i)(A) of this section; and

(B) That person (whether or not otherwise subject to Federal income tax) elects to recognize gain on the disposition of the intangible and agrees, notwithstanding any other provision of law or treaty, to pay for the taxable year in which the disposition occurs an amount of tax on the gain that, when added to any other Federal income tax on such gain, equals the gain on the disposition multiplied by the highest marginal rate of tax for that taxable year.

(ii) *Effect of exception.*—The anti-churning rules of this paragraph (h) apply to a section 197(f)(9) intangible that qualifies for the gain-recognition exception only to the extent the acquiring taxpayer's basis in the intangible exceeds the gain recognized by the transferor.

(iii) *Time and manner of election.*—The election described in this paragraph (h)(9) must be made by the due date (including extensions of time) of the electing taxpayer's Federal income tax return for the taxable year in which the disposition occurs. The election is made by attaching an election statement satisfying the requirements of paragraph (h)(9)(viii) of this section to the electing taxpayer's original or amended income tax return for that taxable year (or by filing the statement as a return for the taxable year under paragraph (h)(9)(xi) of this section). In addition, the taxpayer must satisfy the notification requirements of paragraph (h)(9)(vi) of this section. The election is binding on the taxpayer and all parties whose Federal tax liability is affected by the election.

(iv) *Special rules for certain entities.*—In the case of a partnership, S corporation, estate or trust, the election under this paragraph (h)(9) is made by the entity rather than by its owners or beneficiaries. If a partnership or S corporation makes an election under this paragraph (h)(9) with respect to the disposition of a section 197(f)(9) intangible, each of its partners or shareholders is required to pay a tax determined in the manner described in paragraph (h)(9)(i)(B) of this section on the amount of gain that is properly allocable to such partner or shareholder with respect to the disposition.

(v) *Effect of nonconforming elections.*—An attempted election that does not substantially comply with each of the requirements of this paragraph (h)(9) is disregarded in determining whether a section 197(f)(9) intangible qualifies for the gain-recognition exception.

(vi) *Notification requirements.*—A taxpayer making an election under this paragraph (h)(9) with respect to the disposition of a section 197(f)(9) intangible must provide written notification of the election on or before the due date of the return on which the election is made to the person acquiring the section 197 intangible. In addition, a partnership or S corporation making an election under this paragraph (h)(9) must attach to the Schedule K-1 furnished to each partner or shareholder a written statement containing all information necessary to determine the recipient's additional tax liability under this paragraph (h)(9).

(vii) *Revocation.*—An election under this paragraph (h)(9) may be revoked only with the consent of the Commissioner.

(viii) *Election Statement.*—An election statement satisfies the requirements of this paragraph (h)(9)(viii) if it is in writing and contains the information listed below. The required information should be arranged and identified in accordance with the following order and numbering system:

(A) The name and address of the electing taxpayer.

(B) Except in the case of a taxpayer that is not otherwise subject to Federal income tax, the taxpayer identification number (TIN) of the electing taxpayer.

(C) A statement that the taxpayer is making the election under section 197(f)(9)(B).

(D) Identification of the transaction and each person that is a party to the transaction or whose tax return is affected by the election (including, except in the case of persons not otherwise subject to Federal income tax, the TIN of each such person).

(E) The calculation of the gain realized, the applicable rate of tax, and the amount of the taxpayer's additional tax liability under this paragraph (h)(9).

(F) The signature of the taxpayer or an individual authorized to sign the taxpayer's Federal income tax return.

(ix) *Determination of highest marginal rate of tax and amount of other Federal income tax on gain.*—(A) *Marginal rate.*—The following rules apply for purposes of determining the highest marginal rate of tax applicable to an electing taxpayer:

(1) *Noncorporate taxpayers.*—In the case of an individual, estate, or trust, the highest marginal rate of tax is the highest marginal rate of tax in effect under section 1, determined without regard to section 1(h).

(2) *Corporations and tax-exempt entities.*—In the case of a corporation or an entity that is exempt from tax under section 501(a), the highest marginal rate of tax is the highest marginal rate of tax in effect under section 11, determined without regard to any rate that is added to the otherwise applicable rate in order to offset the effect of the graduated rate schedule.

(B) *Other Federal income tax on gain.*—The amount of Federal income tax (other than the tax determined under this paragraph (h)(9)) imposed on any gain is the lesser of—

(1) The amount by which the taxpayer's Federal income tax liability (determined without regard to this paragraph (h)(9)) would be reduced if the amount of such gain were not taken into account; or

(2) The amount of the gain multiplied by the highest marginal rate of tax for the taxable year.

(x) *Coordination with other provisions.*—(A) *In general.*—The amount of gain subject to the tax determined under this paragraph (h)(9) is not reduced by any net operating loss deduction under section 172(a), any capital loss under section 1212, or any other similar loss or deduction. In addition, the amount of tax determined under this paragraph (h)(9) is not reduced by any credit of the taxpayer. In computing the amount of any net operating loss, capital loss, or other similar loss or deduction, or any credit that may be carried to any taxable year, any gain subject to the tax determined under this paragraph (h)(9) and any tax paid under this paragraph (h)(9) is not taken into account.

(B) *Section 1374.*—No provision of paragraph (h)(9)(iv) of this section precludes the application of section 1374 (relating to a tax on certain built-in gains of S corporations) to any gain with respect to which an election under this paragraph (h)(9) is made. In addition, neither paragraph (h)(9)(iv) nor paragraph (h)(9)(x)(A) of this section precludes a taxpayer from applying the provisions of section 1366(f)(2) (relating to treatment of the tax imposed by section 1374 as a loss sustained by the S corporation) in determining the amount of tax payable under paragraph (h)(9) of this section.

(C) *Procedural and administrative provisions.*—For purposes of subtitle F, the amount determined under this paragraph (h)(9) is treated as a tax imposed by section 1 or 11, as appropriate.

(D) *Installment method.*—The gain subject to the tax determined under paragraph (h)(9)(i) of this section may not be reported under the method described in section 453(a). Any such gain that would, but for the application of this paragraph (h)(9)(x)(D), be taken into account under section 453(a) shall be taken into account in the same manner as if an election under section 453(d) (relating to the election not to apply section 453(a)) had been made.

(xi) *Special rules for persons not otherwise subject to Federal income tax.*—If the person making the election under this paragraph (h)(9) with respect to a disposition is not otherwise subject to Federal income tax, the election statement satisfying the requirements of paragraph (h)(9)(viii) of this section must be filed with the Philadelphia Service Center. For purposes of this paragraph (h)(9) and subtitle F, the statement is treated as an income tax return for the calendar year in which the disposition occurs and as a return due on or before March 15 of the following year.

(10) *Transactions subject to both anti-churning and nonrecognition rules.*—If a person acquires a section 197(f)(9) intangible in a transaction described in paragraph (g)(2) of this section from a person in whose hands the intangible was an amortizable section 197 intangible, and immediately after the transaction (or series of transactions

described in paragraph (h)(6)(ii)(B) of this section) in which such intangible is acquired, the person acquiring the section 197(f)(9) intangible is related to any person described in paragraph (h)(2) of this section, the intangible is, notwithstanding its treatment under paragraph (g)(2) of this section, treated as an amortizable section 197 intangible only to the extent permitted under this paragraph (h). (See, for example, paragraph (h)(5)(ii) of this section.)

(11) *Avoidance purpose.*—A section 197(f)(9) intangible acquired by a taxpayer after the applicable effective date does not qualify for amortization under section 197 if one of the principal purposes of the transaction in which it is acquired is to avoid the operation of the anti-churning rules of section 197(f)(9) and this paragraph (h). A transaction will be presumed to have a principal purpose of avoidance if it does not effect a significant change in the ownership or use of the intangible. Thus, for example, if section 197(f)(9) intangibles are acquired in a transaction (or series of related transactions) in which an option to acquire stock is issued to a party to the transaction, but the option is not treated as having been exercised for purposes of paragraph (h)(6) of this section, this paragraph (h)(11) may apply to the transaction.

(12) *Additional partnership anti-churning rules.*—(i) *In general.*—In determining whether the anti-churning rules of this paragraph (h) apply to any increase in the basis of a section 197(f)(9) intangible under section 732(b), 732(d), 734(b), or 743(b), the determinations are made at the partner level and each partner is treated as having owned and used the partner's proportionate share of partnership property. In determining whether the anti-churning rules of this paragraph (h) apply to any transaction under another section of the Internal Revenue Code, the determinations are made at the partnership level, unless under §1.701-2(e) the Commissioner determines that the partner level is more appropriate.

(ii) *Section 732(b) adjustments.*—(A) *In general.*—The anti-churning rules of this paragraph (h) apply to any increase in the adjusted basis of a section 197(f)(9) intangible under section 732(b) to the extent that the basis increase exceeds the total unrealized appreciation from the intangible allocable to—

(1) Partners other than the distributee partner or persons related to the distributee partner;

(2) The distributee partner and persons related to the distributee partner if the distributed intangible is a section 197(f)(9) intangible acquired by the partnership on or before August 10, 1993, to the extent that—

(i) The distributee partner and related persons acquired an interest or interests in the partnership after August 10, 1993;

(ii) Such interest or interests were held after August 10, 1993, by a person or persons other than either the distributee partner or persons who were related to the distributee partner; and

(iii) The acquisition of such interest or interests by such person or persons was not part of a transaction or series of related transactions in which the distributee partner (or persons related to the distributee partner) subsequently acquired such interest or interests; and

(3) The distributee partner and persons related to the distributee partner if the distributed intangible is a section 197(f)(9) intangible acquired by the partnership after August 10, 1993, that is not amortizable with respect to the partnership, to the extent that—

(i) The distributee partner and persons related to the distributee partner acquired an interest or interests in the partnership after the partnership acquired the distributed intangible;

(ii) Such interest or interests were held after the partnership acquired the distributed intangible, by a person or persons other than either the distributee partner or persons who were related to the distributee partner; and

(iii) The acquisition of such interest or interests by such person or persons was not part of a transaction or series of related transactions in which the distributee partner (or persons related to the distributee partner) subsequently acquired such interest or interests.

(B) *Effect of retroactive elections.*—For purposes of paragraph (h)(12)(ii)(A) of this section, references to August 10, 1993, are treated as references to July 25, 1991, if the relevant party made a valid retroactive election under §1.197-1T.

(C) *Intangible still subject to anti-churning rules.*—Notwithstanding paragraph (h)(12)(ii) of this section, in applying the provisions of this paragraph (h) with respect to subsequent transfers, the distributed intangible remains subject to the provisions of this paragraph (h) in proportion to a fraction (determined at the time of the distribution), as follows—

(1) The numerator of which is equal to the sum of—

(i) The amount of the distributed intangible's basis that is nonamortizable under paragraph (g)(2)(ii)(B) of this section; and

(ii) The total unrealized appreciation inherent in the intangible reduced by the amount of the increase in the adjusted basis of the distributed intangible under section 732(b) to which the anti-churning rules do not apply; and

(2) The denominator of which is the fair market value of such intangible.

(D) *Partner's allocable share of unrealized appreciation from the intangible.*—The amount of unrealized appreciation from an intangible that is allocable to a partner is the amount of taxable gain that would have been allocated to that partner if the partnership had sold the intangible immediately before the distribution for its fair market value in a fully taxable transaction.

(E) *Acquisition of partnership interest by contribution.*—Solely for purposes of paragraphs (h)(12)(ii)(A)(2) and (3) of this section, a partner who acquires an interest in a partnership in exchange for a contribution of property to the partnership is deemed to acquire a pro rata portion of that interest in the partnership from each person who is a partner in the partnership at the time of the contribution based on each partner's respective proportionate interest in the partnership.

(iii) *Section 732(d) adjustments.*—The anti-churning rules of this paragraph (h) do not apply to an increase in the basis of a section 197(f)(9) intangible under section 732(d) if, had an election been in effect under section 754 at the time of the transfer of the partnership interest, the distributee partner would have been able to amortize the basis adjustment made pursuant to section 743(b).

(iv) *Section 734(b) adjustments.*—(A) *In general.*—The anti-churning rules of this paragraph (h) do not apply to a continuing partner's share of an increase in the basis of a section 197(f)(9) intangible held by a partnership under section 734(b) to the extent that the continuing partner is an eligible partner.

(B) *Eligible partner.*—For purposes of this paragraph (h)(12)(iv), eligible partner means—

(1) A continuing partner that is not the distributee partner or a person related to the distributee partner;

(2) A continuing partner that is the distributee partner or a person related to the distributee partner, with respect to any section 197(f)(9) intangible acquired by the partnership on or before August 10, 1993, to the extent that—

(i) The distributee partner's interest in the partnership was acquired after August 10, 1993;

(ii) Such interest was held after August 10, 1993 by a person or persons who were not related to the distributee partner; and

(iii) The acquisition of such interest by such person or persons was not part of a transaction or series of related transactions in which the distributee partner or persons related to the distributee partner subsequently acquired such interest; or

(3) A continuing partner that is the distributee partner or a person related to the distributee partner, with respect to any section 197(f)(9) intangible acquired by the partnership after August 10, 1993, that is not amortizable with respect to the partnership, to the extent that—

(i) The distributee partner's interest in the partnership was acquired after the partnership acquired the relevant intangible;

(ii) Such interest was held after the partnership acquired the relevant intangible by a person or persons who were not related to the distributee partner; and

(iii) The acquisition of such interest by such person or persons was not part of a transaction or series of related transactions in which the distributee partner or persons related to the distributee partner subsequently acquired such interest.

(C) *Effect of retroactive elections.*—For purposes of paragraph (h)(12)(iv)(A) of this section, references to August 10, 1993, are treated as references to July 25, 1991, if the distributee partner made a valid retroactive election under §1.197-1T.

(D) *Partner's share of basis increase.*—(1) *In general.*—Except as provided in paragraph (h)(12)(iv)(D)(2) of this section, for purposes of this paragraph (h)(12)(iv), a continuing partner's share of a basis increase under section 734(b) is equal to—

(i) The total basis increase allocable to the intangible; multiplied by

(ii) A fraction the numerator of which is the amount of the continuing partner's post-distribution capital account (determined immediately after the distribution in accordance with the capital accounting rules of §1.704-1(b)(2)(iv)), and the denominator of which is the total amount of the post-distribution capital accounts (determined immediately after the distribution in accordance with

Itemized Deductions for Individuals and Corps.
See p. 20,601 for regulations not amended to reflect law changes
25,665

the capital accounting rules of §1.704-1(b)(2)(iv)) of all continuing partners.

(2) Exception where partnership does not maintain capital accounts.—If a partnership does not maintain capital accounts in accordance with §1.704-1(b)(2)(iv), then for purposes of this paragraph (h)(12)(iv), a continuing partner's share of a basis increase is equal to—

(i) The total basis increase allocable to the intangible; multiplied by

(ii) The partner's overall interest in the partnership as determined under §1.704-1(b)(3) immediately after the distribution.

(E) Interests acquired by contribution.—*(1) Application of paragraphs (h)(12)(iv)(B)(2) and (3) of this section.*—Solely for purposes of paragraphs (h)(12)(iv)(B)(2) and (3) of this section, a partner who acquires an interest in a partnership in exchange for a contribution of property to the partnership is deemed to acquire a pro rata portion of that interest in the partnership from each person who is a partner in the partnership at the time of the contribution based on each such partner's proportionate interest in the partnership.

(2) Special rule with respect to paragraph (h)(12)(iv)(B)(1) of this section.—Solely for purposes of paragraph (h)(12)(iv)(B)(1) of this section, if a distribution that gives rise to an increase in the basis under section 734(b) of a section 197(f)(9) intangible held by the partnership is undertaken as part of a series of related transactions that include a contribution of the intangible to the partnership by a continuing partner, the continuing partner is treated as related to the distributee partner in analyzing the basis adjustment with respect to the contributed section 197(f)(9) intangible.

(F) Effect of section 734(b) adjustments on partners' capital accounts.—If one or more partners are subject to the anti-churning rules under this paragraph (h) with respect to a section 734(b) adjustment allocable to an intangible asset, taxpayers may use any reasonable method to determine amortization of the asset for book purposes, provided that the method used does not contravene the purposes of the anti-churning rules under section 197 and this paragraph (h). A method will be considered to contravene the purposes of the anti-churning rules if the effect of the book adjustments resulting from the method is such that any portion of the tax deduction for amortization attributable to the section 734 adjustment is allocated, directly or indirectly, to a partner who is subject to the anti-churning rules with respect to such adjustment.

(v) Section 743(b) adjustments.—*(A) General rule.*—The anti-churning rules of this paragraph (h) do not apply to an increase in the basis of a section 197 intangible under section 743(b) if the person acquiring the partnership interest is not related to the person transferring the partnership interest. In addition, the anti-churning rules of this paragraph (h) do not apply to an increase in the basis of a section 197 intangible under section 743(b) to the extent that—

(1) The partnership interest being transferred was acquired after August 10, 1993, provided—

(i) The section 197(f)(9) intangible was acquired by the partnership on or before August 10, 1993;

(ii) The partnership interest being transferred was held after August 10, 1993, by a person or persons (the post-1993 person or persons) other than the person transferring the partnership interest or persons who were related to the person transferring the partnership interest; and

(iii) The acquisition of such interest by the post-1993 person or persons was not part of a transaction or series of related transactions in which the person transferring the partnership interest or persons related to the person transferring the partnership interest acquired such interest; or

(2) The partnership interest being transferred was acquired after the partnership acquired the section 197(f)(9) intangible, provided—

(i) The section 197(f)(9) intangible was acquired by the partnership after August 10, 1993, and is not amortizable with respect to the partnership;

(ii) The partnership interest being transferred was held *after the partnership* acquired the section 197(f)(9) intangible by a person or persons (the post-contribution person or persons) other than the person transferring the partnership interest or persons who were related to the person transferring the partnership interest; and

(iii) The acquisition of such interest by the post-contribution person or persons was not part of a transaction or series of related transactions in which the person transferring the partnership interest or persons related to the person transferring the partnership interest acquired such interest.

(B) Acquisition of partnership interest by contribution.—Solely for purposes of paragraph (h)(12)(v)(A)(1) and (2) of this section, a partner who acquires an interest in a partnership in exchange for a contribution of property to the partnership is deemed to acquire a pro rata portion of that interest in the partnership from each person who is a partner in the partnership at the time of the contribution based on each such partner's proportionate interest in the partnership.

(C) Effect of retroactive elections.—For purposes of paragraph (h)(12)(v)(A) of this section, references to August 10, 1993, are treated as references to July 25, 1991, if the transferee partner made a valid retroactive election under §1.197-1T.

(vi) Partner is or becomes a user of partnership intangible.—*(A) General rule.*—If, as part of a series of related transactions that includes a transaction described in paragraph (h)(12)(ii), (iii), (iv), or (v) of this section, an anti-churning partner or related person (other than the partnership) becomes (or remains) a direct user of an intangible that is treated as transferred in the transaction (as a result of the partners being treated as having owned their proportionate share of partnership assets), the anti-churning rules of this paragraph (h) apply to the proportionate share of such intangible that is treated as transferred by such anti-churning partner, notwithstanding the application of paragraph (h)(12)(ii), (iii), (iv), or (v) of this section.

(B) Anti-churning partner.—For purposes of this paragraph (h)(12)(vi), anti-churning partner means—

(1) With respect to all intangibles held by a partnership on or before August 10, 1993, any partner, but only to the extent that

(i) The partner's interest in the partnership was acquired on or before August 10, 1993, or

(ii) The interest was acquired from a person related to the partner on or after August 10, 1993, and such interest was not held by any person other than persons related to such partner at any time after August 10, 1993 (disregarding, for this purpose, a person's holding of an interest if the acquisition of such interest was part of a transaction or series of related transactions in which the partner or persons related to the partner subsequently acquired such interest),

(2) With respect to any section 197(f)(9) intangible acquired by a partnership after August 10, 1993, that is not amortizable with respect to the partnership, any partner, but only to the extent that

(i) The partner's interest in the partnership was acquired on or before the date the partnership acquired the section 197(f)(9) intangible, or

(ii) The interest was acquired from a person related to the partner on or after the date the partnership acquired the section 197(f)(9) intangible, and such interest was not held by any person other than persons related to such partner at any time after the date the partnership acquired the section 197(f)(9) intangible (disregarding, for this purpose, a person's holding of an interest if the acquisition of such interest was part of a transaction or series of related transactions in which the partner or persons related to the partner subsequently acquired such interest).

(C) Effect of retroactive elections.—For purposes of paragraph (h)(12)(vi)(B) of this section, references to August 10, 1993, are treated as references to July 25, 1991, if the relevant party made a valid retroactive election under §1.197-1T.

(vii) Section 704(c) allocations.—*(A) Allocations where the intangible is amortizable by the contributor.*—The anti-churning rules of this paragraph (h) do not apply to the curative or remedial allocations of amortization with respect to a section 197(f)(9) intangible if the intangible was an amortizable section 197 intangible in the hands of the contributing partner (unless paragraph (h)(10) of this section applies so as to cause the intangible to cease to be an amortizable section 197 intangible in the hands of the partnership).

(B) Allocations where the intangible is not amortizable by the contributor.—If a section 197(f)(9) intangible was not an amortizable section 197 intangible in the hands of the contributing partner, a noncontributing partner generally may receive remedial allocations of amortization under section 704(c) that are deductible for Federal income tax purposes. However, such a partner may not receive remedial allocations of amortization under section 704(c) if that partner is related to the partner that contributed the intangible or if, as part of a series of related transactions that includes the contribution of the section 197(f)(9) intangible to the partnership, the contributing partner or related person (other than the partnership) becomes (or remains) a direct user of the contributed intangible. Taxpayers may use any reasonable method to determine amortization of the asset for book purposes, provided that the method used does not contravene the purposes of the anti-churning rules under section 197 and this paragraph (h). A method will be considered to contravene the purposes of the anti-churning rules if the effect of the book adjustments resulting from the method is such that any portion of the tax deduction for amortization attributable to section 704(c) is allocated, di-

rectly or indirectly, to a partner who is subject to the anti-churning rules with respect to such adjustment.

(C) *Rules for section 721(c) partnerships.*—See §1.704-3(d)(5)(iii) if there is a contribution of a section 197(f)(9) intangible to a section 721(c) partnership (as defined in §1.721(c)-1(b)(14)).

(viii) *Operating rule for transfers upon death.*—For purposes of this paragraph (h) (12), if the basis of a partner's interest in a partnership is determined under section 1014(a) or 1022, such partner is treated as acquiring such interest from a person who is not related to such partner, and such interest is treated as having previously been held by a person who is not related to such partner.

(i) [Reserved]

(j) *General anti-abuse rule.*—The Commissioner will interpret and apply the rules in this section as necessary and appropriate to prevent avoidance of the purposes of section 197. If one of the principal purposes of a transaction is to achieve a tax result that is inconsistent with the purposes of section 197, the Commissioner will recast the transaction for Federal tax purposes as appropriate to achieve tax results that are consistent with the purposes of section 197, in light of the applicable statutory and regulatory provisions and the pertinent facts and circumstances.

(k) *Examples.*—The following examples illustrate the application of this section:

Example 1. Advertising costs. (i) Q manufactures and sells consumer products through a series of wholesalers and distributors. In order to increase sales of its products by encouraging consumer loyalty to its products and to enhance the value of the goodwill, trademarks, and trade names of the business, Q advertises its products to the consuming public. It regularly incurs costs to develop radio, television, and print advertisements. These costs generally consist of employee costs and amounts paid to independent advertising agencies. Q also incurs costs to run these advertisements in the various media for which they were developed.

(ii) The advertising costs are not chargeable to capital account under paragraph (f)(3) of this section (relating to costs incurred for covenants not to compete, rights granted by governmental units, and contracts for the use of section 197 intangibles) and are currently deductible as ordinary and necessary expenses under section 162. Accordingly, under paragraph (a)(3) of this section, section 197 does not apply to these costs.

Example 2. Computer software. (i) X purchases all of the assets of an existing trade or business from Y. One of the assets acquired is all of Y's rights in certain computer software previously used by Y under the terms of a nonexclusive license from the software developer. The software was developed for use by manufacturers to maintain a comprehensive accounting system, including general and subsidiary ledgers, payroll, accounts receivable and payable, cash receipts and disbursements, fixed asset accounting, and inventory cost accounting and controls. The developer modified the software for use by Y at a cost of $1,000 and Y made additional modifications at a cost of $500. The developer does not maintain wholesale or retail outlets but markets the software directly to ultimate users. Y's license of the software is limited to an entity that is actively engaged in business as a manufacturer.

(ii) Notwithstanding these limitations, the software is considered to be readily available to the general public for purposes of paragraph (c)(4)(i) of this section. In addition, the software is not substantially modified because the cost of the modifications by the developer and Y to the version of the software that is readily available to the general public does not exceed $2,000. Accordingly, the software is not a section 197 intangible.

Example 3. Acquisition of software for internal use. (i) B, the owner and operator of a worldwide package-delivery service, purchases from S all rights to software developed by S. The software will be used by B for the sole purpose of improving its package-tracking operations. B does not purchase any other assets in the transaction or any related transaction.

(ii) Because B acquired the software solely for internal use, it is disregarded in determining for purposes of paragraph (c)(4)(ii) of this section whether the assets acquired in the transaction or series of related transactions constitute a trade or business or substantial portion thereof. Since no other assets were acquired, the software is not acquired as part of a purchase of a trade or business and under paragraph (c)(4)(ii) of this section is not a section 197 intangible.

Example 4. Governmental rights of fixed duration. (i) City M operates a municipal water system. In order to induce X to locate a new manufacturing business in the city, M grants X the right to purchase water for 16 years at a specified price.

(ii) The right granted by M is a right to receive tangible property or services described in section 197(e)(4)(B) and paragraph (c)(6) of this section and, thus, is not a section 197 intangible. This exclusion applies even though the right does not qualify for exclusion as a right of fixed duration or amount under section 197(e)(4)(D) and paragraph (c)(13) of this section because the duration exceeds 15 years and the right is not fixed as to amount. It is also immaterial that the right would not qualify for exclusion as a self-created intangible under section 197(c)(2) and paragraph (d)(2) of this section because it is granted by a governmental unit.

Example 5. Separate acquisition of franchise. (i) S is a franchiser of retail outlets for specialty coffees. G enters into a franchise agreement (within the meaning of section 1253(b)(1)) with S pursuant to which G is permitted to acquire and operate a store using the S trademark and trade name at the location specified in the agreement. G agrees to pay S $100,000 upon execution of the agreement and also agrees to pay, throughout the term of the franchise, additional amounts that are deductible under section 1253(d)(1). The agreement contains detailed specifications for the construction and operation of the business, but G is not required to purchase from S any of the materials necessary to construct the improvements at the location specified in the franchise agreement.

(ii) The franchise is a section 197 intangible within the meaning of paragraph (b)(10) of this section. The franchise does not qualify for the exclusion relating to self-created intangibles described in section 197(c)(2) and paragraph (d)(2) of this section because the franchise is described in section 197(d)(1)(F). In addition, because the acquisition of the franchise constitutes the acquisition of an interest in a trade or business or a substantial portion thereof, the franchise may not be excluded under section 197(e)(4). Thus, the franchise is an amortizable section 197 intangible, the basis of which must be recovered over a 15-year period. However, the amounts that are deductible under section 1253(d)(1)are not subject to the provisions of section 197 by reason of section 197(f)(4)(C) and paragraph (b)(10)(ii) of this section.

Example 6. Acquisition and amortization of covenant not to compete. (i) As part of the acquisition of a trade or business from C, B and C enter into an agreement containing a covenant not to compete. Under this agreement, C agrees that it will not compete with the business acquired by B within a prescribed geographical territory for a period of three years after the date on which the business is sold to B. In exchange for this agreement, B agrees to pay C $90,000 per year for each year in the term of the agreement. The agreement further provides that, in the event of a breach by C of his obligations under the agreement, B may terminate the agreement, cease making any of the payments due thereafter, and pursue any other legal or equitable remedies available under applicable law. The amounts payable to C under the agreement are not contingent payments for purposes of §1.1275-4. The present fair market value of B's rights under the agreement is $225,000. The aggregate consideration paid excluding any amount treated as interest or original issue discount under applicable provisions of the Internal Revenue Code, for all assets acquired in the transaction (including the covenant not to compete) exceeds the sum of the amount of Class I assets and the aggregate fair market value of all Class II, Class III, Class IV, Class V, and Class VI assets by $50,000. See §1.338-6(b) for rules for determining the assets in each class.

(ii) Because the covenant is acquired in an applicable asset acquisition (within the meaning of section 1060(c)), paragraph (f)(4)(ii) of this section applies and the basis of B in the covenant is determined pursuant to section 1060(a) and the regulations thereunder. Under §§1.1060-1(c)(2) and 1.338-6(c)(1), B's basis in the covenant cannot exceed its fair market value. Thus, B's basis in the covenant immediately after the acquisition is $225,000. This basis is amortized ratably over the 15-year period beginning on the first day of the month in which the agreement is entered into. All of the remaining consideration after allocation to the covenant and other Class VI assets, ($50,000) is allocated to Class VII assets (goodwill and going concern value). See §§1.1060-1(c)(2) and 1.338-6(b).

Example 7. Stand-alone license of technology. (i) X is a manufacturer of consumer goods that does business throughout the world through subsidiary corporations organized under the laws of each country in which business is conducted. X licenses to Y, its subsidiary organized and conducting business in Country K, all of the patents, formulas, designs, and know-how necessary for Y to manufacture the same products that X manufactures in the United States. Assume that the license is not considered a sale or exchange under the principles of section 1235. The license is for a term of 18 years, and there are no facts to indicate that the license does not have a fixed duration. Y agrees to pay X a royalty equal to a specified, fixed percentage of the revenues obtained from selling products manufactured using the licensed technology. Assume that the royalty is reasonable and is not subject to adjustment under section 482. The license is not entered into in connection with any other transaction. Y incurs capitalized costs in connection with entering into the license.

(ii) The license is a contract for the use of a section 197 intangible within the meaning of paragraph (b)(11) of this section. It does not qualify for the exception in section 197(e)(4)(D) and paragraph (c)(13) of this section (relating to rights of fixed duration or amount) because it does not have a term of less than 15 years, and the other exceptions in section 197(e) and paragraph (c) of this section are also inapplicable. Accordingly, the license is a section 197 intangible.

(iii) The license is not acquired as part of a purchase of a trade or business. Thus, under paragraph (f)(3)(iii) of this section, the license will be closely scrutinized under the principles of section 1235 for purposes of determining whether the transfer is a sale or exchange and, accordingly, whether the payments under the license are chargeable to capital account. Because the license is not a sale or exchange under the principles of section 1235, the royalty payments are not chargeable to capital account for purposes section 197. The capitalized costs of entering into the license are not within the exception under paragraph (d)(2) of this section for self-created intangibles, and thus are amortized under section 197.

Example 8. License of technology and trademarks. (i) The facts are the same as in *Example 7*, except that the license also includes the use of the trademarks and trade names that X uses to manufacture and distribute its products in the United States. Assume that under the principles of section 1253 the transfer is not a sale or exchange of the trademarks and trade names or an undivided interest therein and that the royalty payments are described in section 1253(d)(1)(B).

(ii) As in *Example 7*, the license is a section 197 intangible. Although the license conveys an interest in X's trademarks and trade names to Y, the transfer of the interest is disregarded for purposes of paragraph (e)(2) of this section unless the transfer is considered a sale or exchange of the trademarks and trade names or an undivided interest therein. Accordingly, the licensing of the technology and the trademarks and trade names is not treated as part of a purchase of a trade or business under paragraph (e)(2) of this section.

(iii) Because the technology license is not part of the purchase of a trade or business, it is treated in the manner described in *Example 7*. The royalty payments for the use of the trademarks and trade names are deductible under section 1253(d)(1) and, under section 197(f)(4)(C) and paragraph (b)(10)(ii) of this section, are not chargeable to capital account for purposes of section 197. The capitalized costs of entering into the license are treated in the same manner as in example 7.

Example 9. Disguised sale. (i) The facts are the same as in *Example 7*, except that Y agrees to pay X, in addition to the contingent royalty, a fixed minimum royalty immediately upon entering into the agreement and there are sufficient facts present to characterize the transaction, for federal tax purposes, as a transfer of ownership of the intellectual property from X to Y.

(ii) The purported license of technology is, in fact, an acquisition of an intangible described in section 197(d)(1)(C)(iii) and paragraph (b)(5) of this section (relating to know-how, etc.). As in *Example 7*, the exceptions in section 197(e) and paragraph (c) of this section do not apply to the transfer. Accordingly, the transferred property is a section 197 intangible. Y's basis in the transferred intangible includes the capitalized costs of entering into the agreement and the fixed minimum royalty payment payable at the time of the transfer. In addition, except to the extent that a portion of any payment will be treated as interest or original issue discount under applicable provisions of the Internal Revenue Code, all of the contingent payments under the purported license are properly chargeable to capital account for purposes of section 197 and this section. The extent to which such payments are treated as payments of principal and the time at which any amount treated as a payment of principal is taken into account in determining basis are determined under the rules of §1.1275-4(c)(4) or 1.483-4(a), whichever is applicable. Any contingent amount that is included in basis after the month in which the acquisition occurs is amortized under the rules of paragraph (f)(2)(i) or (ii) of this section.

Example 10. License of technology and customer list as part of sale of a trade or business. (i) X is a computer manufacturer that produces, in separate operating divisions, personal computers, servers, and peripheral equipment. In a transaction that is the purchase of a trade or business for purposes of section 197, Y (who is unrelated to X) purchases from X all assets of the operating division producing personal computers, except for certain patents that are also used in the division manufacturing servers and customer lists that are also used in the division manufacturing peripheral equipment. As part of the transaction, X transfers to Y the right to use the retained patents and customer lists solely in connection with the manufacture and sale of personal computers. The transfer agreement requires annual royalty payments contingent on the use of the patents and also requires a payment for each use of the customer list. In addition, Y incurs capitalized costs in connection with entering into the licenses.

(ii) The rights to use the retained patents and customer lists are contracts for the use of section 197 intangibles within the meaning of paragraph (b)(11) of this section. The rights do not qualify for the exception in 197(e)(4)(D) and paragraph (c)(13) of this section (relating to rights of fixed duration or amount) because they are trans-

ferred as part of a purchase of a trade or business and the other exceptions in section 197(e) and paragraph (c) of this section are also inapplicable. Accordingly, the licenses are section 197 intangibles.

(iii) Because the right to use the retained patents is described in paragraph (b)(11) of this section and the right is transferred as part of a purchase of a trade or business, the treatment of the royalty payments is determined under paragraph (f)(3)(ii) of this section. In addition, however, the retained patents are described in paragraph (b)(5) of this section. Thus, the annual royalty payments are chargeable to capital account under the general rule of paragraph (f)(3)(ii)(A) of this section unless Y establishes that the license is not a sale or exchange under the principles of section 1235 and the royalty payments are an arm's length consideration for the rights transferred. If these facts are established, the exception in paragraph (f)(3)(ii)(B) of this section applies and the royalty payments are not chargeable to capital account for purposes of section 197. The capitalized costs of entering into the license are treated in the same manner as in Example 7.

(iv) The right to use the retained customer list is also described in paragraph (b)(11) of this section and is transferred as part of a purchase of a trade or business. Thus, the treatment of the payments for use of the customer list is also determined under paragraph (f)(3)(ii) of this section. The customer list, although described in paragraph (b)(6) of this section, is a customer-related information base. Thus, the exception in paragraph (f)(3)(ii)(B) of this section does not apply. Accordingly, payments for use of the list are chargeable to capital account under the general rule of paragraph (f)(3)(ii)(A) of this section and are amortized under section 197. In addition, the capitalized costs of entering into the contract for use of the customer list are treated in the same manner as in *Example 7*.

Example 11. Loss disallowance rules involving related persons. (i) Assume that X and Y are treated as a single taxpayer for purposes of paragraph (g)(1) of this section. In a single transaction, X and Y acquired from Z all of the assets used by Z in a trade or business. Z had operated this business at two locations, and X and Y each acquired the assets used by Z at one of the locations. Three years after the acquisition, X sold all of the assets it acquired, including amortizable section 197 intangibles, to an unrelated purchaser. The amortizable section intangibles are sold at a loss of $120,000.

(ii) Because X and Y are treated as a single taxpayer for purposes of the loss disallowance rules of section 197(f)(1) and paragraph (g)(1) of this section, X's loss on the sale of the amortizable section 197 intangibles is not recognized. Under paragraph (g)(1)(iv)(B) of this section, X's disallowed loss is allowed ratably, as a deduction under section 197, over the remainder of the 15-year period during which the intangibles would have been amortized, and Y may not increase the basis of the amortizable section 197 intangibles that it acquired from Z by the amount of X's disallowed loss.

Example 12. Disposition of retained intangibles by related person. (i) The facts are the same as in *Example 11*, except that 10 years after the acquisition of the assets by X and Y and 7 years after the sale of the assets by X, Y sells all of the assets acquired from Z, including amortizable section 197 intangibles, to an unrelated purchaser.

(ii) Under paragraph (g)(1)(iv)(B) of this section, X may recognize, on the date of the sale by Y, any loss that has not been allowed as a deduction under section 197. Accordingly, X recognizes a loss of $50,000, the amount obtained by reducing the loss on the sale of the assets at the end of the third year ($120,000) by the amount allowed as a deduction under paragraph (g)(1)(iv)(B) of this section during the 7 years following the sale by X ($70,000).

Example 13. Acquisition of an interest in partnership with no section 754 election. (i) A, B, and C each contribute $1,500 for equal shares in general partnership P. On January 1, 1998, P acquires as its sole asset an amortizable section 197 intangible for $4,500. P still holds the intangible on January 1, 2003, at which time the intangible has an adjusted basis to P of $3,000, and A, B, and C have an adjusted basis of $1,000 in their partnership interests. D (who is not related to A) acquires A's interest in P for $1,600. No section 754 election is in effect for 2003.

(ii) Because there is no change in the basis of the intangible under section 743(b), D merely steps into the shoes of A with respect to the intangible. D's proportionate share of P's adjusted basis in the intangible is $1,000, which continues to be amortized over the 10 years remaining in the original 15-year amortization period for the intangible.

Example 14. Acquisition of an interest in partnership with a section 754 election. (i) The facts are the same as in *Example 13*, except that a section 754 election is in effect for 2003.

(ii) Pursuant to paragraph (g)(3) of this section, for purposes of section 197, D is treated as if P owns two assets. D's proportionate share of P's adjusted basis in one asset is $1,000, which continues to be amortized over the 10 years remaining in the original 15-year amortization period. For the other asset, D's proportionate share of P's adjusted basis is $600 (the amount of the basis increase under section 743 as a result of the section 754 election), which is amortized over a new 15-year period beginning January 2003. With respect to B and C, P's remaining $2,000 adjusted basis in the intangible continues to be amortized over the 10 years remaining in the original 15-year amortization period.

Example 15. Payment to a retiring partner by partnership with a section 754 election. (i) The facts are the same as in *Example 13*, except that a section 754 election is in effect for 2003 and, instead of D acquiring A's interest in P, A retires from P. A, B, and C are not related to each other within the meaning of paragraph (h)(6) of this section. P borrows $1,600, and A receives a payment under section 736 from P of such amount, all of which is in exchange for A's interest in the intangible asset owned by P. (Assume, for purposes of this example, that the borrowing by P and payment of such funds to A does not give rise to a disguised sale of A's partnership interest under section 707(a)(2)(B).) P makes a positive basis adjustment of $600 with respect to the section 197 intangible under section 734(b).

(ii) Pursuant to paragraph (g)(3) of this section, because of the section 734 adjustment, P is treated as having two amortizable section 197 intangibles, one with a basis of $3,000 and a remaining amortization period of 10 years and the other with a basis of $600 and a new amortization period of 15 years.

Example 16. Termination of partnership under section 708(b)(1)(B). (i) A and B are partners with equal shares in the capital and profits of general partnership P. P's only asset is an amortizable section 197 intangible, which P had acquired on January 1, 1995. On January 1, 2000, the asset had a fair market value of $100 and a basis to P of $50. On that date, A sells his entire partnership interest in P to C, who is unrelated to A, for $50. At the time of the sale, the basis of each of A and B in their respective partnership interests is $25.

(ii) The sale causes a termination of P under section 708(b)(1)(B). Under section 708, the transaction is treated as if P transfers its sole asset to a new partnership in exchange for the assumption of its liabilities and the receipt of all of the interests in the new partnership. Immediately thereafter, P is treated as if it is liquidated, with B and C each receiving their proportionate share of the interests in the new partnership. The contribution by P of its asset to the new partnership is governed by section 721, and the liquidating distributions by P of the interests in the new partnership are governed by section 731. C does not realize a basis adjustment under section 743 with respect to the amortizable section 197 intangible unless P had a section 754 election in effect for its taxable year in which the transfer of the partnership interest to C occurred or the taxable year in which the deemed liquidation of P occurred.

(iii) Under section 197, if P had a section 754 election in effect, C is treated as if the new partnership had acquired two assets from P immediately preceding its termination. Even though the adjusted basis of the new partnership in the two assets is determined solely under section 723, because the transfer of assets is a transaction described in section 721, the application of sections 743(b) and 754 to P immediately before its termination causes P to be treated as if it held two assets for purposes of section 197. See paragraph (g)(3) of this section. B's and C's proportionate share of the new partnership's adjusted basis is $25 each in one asset, which continues to be amortized over the 10 years remaining in the original 15-year amortization period. For the other asset, C's proportionate share of the new partnership's adjusted basis is $25 (the amount of the basis increase resulting from the application of section 743 to the sale or exchange by A of the interest in P), which is amortized over a new 15-year period beginning in January 2000.

(iv) If P did not have a section 754 election in effect for its taxable year in which the sale of the partnership interest by A to C occurred or the taxable year in which the deemed liquidation of P occurred, the adjusted basis of the new partnership in the amortizable section 197 intangible is determined solely under section 723, because the transfer is a transaction described in section 721, and P does not have a basis increase in the intangible. Under section 197(f)(2) and paragraph (g)(2)(ii) of this section, the new partnership continues to amortize the intangible over the 10 years remaining in the original 15-year amortization period. No additional amortization is allowable with respect to this asset.

Example 17. Disguised sale to partnership. (i) E and F are individuals who are unrelated to each other within the meaning of paragraph (h)(6) of this section. E has been engaged in the active conduct of a trade or business as a sole proprietor since 1990. E and F form EF Partnership. E transfers all of the assets of the business, having a fair market value of $100, to EF, and F transfers $40 of cash to EF. E receives a 60 percent interest in EF and the $40 of cash contributed by F, and F receives a 40 percent interest in EF, under circumstances in which the transfer by E is partially treated as a sale of property to EF under § 1.707-3(b).

(ii) Under § 1.707-3(a)(1), the transaction is treated as if E had sold to EF a 40 percent interest in each asset for $40 and contributed the remaining 60 percent interest in each asset to EF in exchange solely for an interest in EF. Because E and EF are related persons within the meaning of paragraph (h)(6) of this section, no portion of any transferred section 197(f)(9) intangible that E held during the transition period (as defined in paragraph (h)(4) of this section) is an amortizable section 197 intangible pursuant to paragraph (h)(2) of this section. Section 197(f)(9)(E) and paragraph (g)(3) of this section do not apply to any portion of the section 197 intangible in the hands of EF because the basis of EF in these assets was not increased under any of sections 732, 734, or 743.

Example 18. Acquisition by related person in nonrecognition transaction. (i) A owns a nonamortizable intangible that A acquired in 1990. In 2000, A sells a one-half interest in the intangible to B for cash. Immediately after the sale, A and B, who are unrelated to each other, form partnership P as equal partners. A and B each contribute their one-half interest in the intangible to P.

(ii) P has a transferred basis in the intangible from A and B under section 723. The nonrecognition transfer rule under paragraph (g)(2)(ii) of this section applies to A's transfer of its one-half interest in the intangible to P, and consequently P steps into A's shoes with respect to A's nonamortizable transferred basis. The anti-churning rules of paragraph (h) of this section apply to B's transfer of its one-half interest in the intangible to P, because A, who is related to P under paragraph (h)(6) of this section immediately after the series of transactions in which the intangible was acquired by P, held B's one-half interest in the intangible during the transition period. Pursuant to paragraph (h)(10) of this section, these rules apply to B's transfer of its one-half interest to P even though the nonrecognition transfer rule under paragraph (g)(2)(ii) of this section would have permitted P to step into B's shoes with respect to B's otherwise amortizable basis. Therefore, P's entire basis in the intangible is nonamortizable. However, if A (not B) elects to recognize gain under paragraph (h)(9) of this section on the transfer of each of the one-half interests in the intangible to B and P, then the intangible would be amortizable by P to the extent provided in section 197(f)(9)(B) and paragraph (h)(9) of this section.

Example 19. Acquisition of partnership interest following formation of partnership. (i) The facts are the same as in *Example 18* except that, in 2000, A formed P with an affiliate, S, and contributed the intangible to the partnership and except that in a subsequent year, in a transaction that is properly characterized as a sale of a partnership interest for Federal tax purposes, B purchases a 50 percent interest in P from A. P has a section 754 election in effect and holds no assets other than the intangible and cash.

(ii) For the reasons set forth in *Example 16*(iii), B is treated as if P owns two assets. B's proportionate share of P's adjusted basis in one asset is the same as A's proportionate share of P's adjusted basis in that asset, which is not amortizable under section 197. For the other asset, B's proportionate share of the remaining adjusted basis of P is amortized over a new 15-year period.

Example 20. Acquisition by related corporation in nonrecognition transaction. (i) The facts are the same as in *Example 18*, except that A and B form corporation P as equal owners.

(ii) P has a transferred basis in the intangible from A and B under section 362. Pursuant to paragraph (h)(10) of this section, the application of the nonrecognition transfer rule under paragraph (g)(2)(ii) of this section and the anti-churning rules of paragraph (h) of this section to the facts of this *Example 18* is the same as in *Example 16*. Thus, P's entire basis in the intangible is nonamortizable.

Example 21. Acquisition from corporation related to purchaser through remote indirect interest. (i) X, Y, and Z are each corporations that have only one class of issued and outstanding stock. X owns 25 percent of the stock of Y and Y owns 25 percent of the outstanding stock of Z. No other shareholder of any of these corporations is related to any other shareholder or to any of the corporations. On June 30, 2000, X purchases from Z section 197(f)(9) intangibles that Z owned during the transition period (as defined in paragraph (h)(4) of this section).

(ii) Pursuant to paragraph (h)(6)(iv)(B) of this section, the beneficial ownership interest of X in Z is 6.25 percent, determined by treating X as if it owned a proportionate (25 percent) interest in the stock of Z that is actually owned by Y. Thus, even though X is related to Y and Y is related to Z, X and Z are not considered to be related for purposes of the anti-churning rules of section 197.

Example 22. Gain recognition election. (i) B owns 25 percent of the stock of S, a corporation that uses the calendar year as its taxable year. No other shareholder of B or S is related to each other. S is not a member of a controlled group of corporations within the meaning of section 1563(a). S has section 197(f)(9) intangibles that it owned during the transition period. S has a basis of $25,000 in the intangibles. In 2001, S sells these intangibles to B for $75,000. S recognizes a gain of $50,000 on the sale and has no other items of income, deduction, gain, or loss for the year, except that S also has a net operating loss of $20,000 from prior years that it would otherwise be entitled to use in 2001 pursuant to section 172(b). S makes a valid gain recognition election pursuant to section 197(f)(9)(B) and paragraph (h)(9) of this section. In 2001, the highest marginal tax rate applicable to S is 35 percent. But for the election, all of S's taxable income would be taxed at a rate of 15 percent.

(ii) If the gain recognition election had not been made, S would have taxable income of $30,000 for 2001 and a tax liability of $4,500. If the gain were not taken into account, S would have no tax liability for the taxable year. Thus, the amount of tax (other than the tax imposed under paragraph (h)(9) of this section) imposed on the gain is also $4,500. The gain on the disposition multiplied by the highest marginal tax rate is $17,500 ($50,000 × .35). Accordingly, S's tax liability for the year is $4,500 plus an additional tax under paragraph (h)(9) of this section of $13,000 ($17,500 – $4,500).

(iii) Pursuant to paragraph (h)(9)(x)(A) of this section, S determines the amount of its net operating loss deduction in subsequent years without regard to the gain recognized on the sale of the section 197 intangible to B. Accordingly, the entire $20,000 net operating loss deduction that would have been available in 2001 but for the gain recognition election may be used in 2002, subject to the limitations of section 172.

(iv) B has a basis of $75,000 in the section 197(f)(9) intangibles acquired from S. As the result of the gain recognition election by S, B may amortize $50,000 of its basis under section 197. Under paragraph (h)(9)(ii) of this section, the remaining basis does not qualify for the gain-recognition exception and may not be amortized by B.

Example 23. Section 338 election. (i) Corporation P makes a qualified stock purchase of the stock of T corporation from two shareholders in July 2000, and a section 338 election is made by P. No shareholder of either T or P owns stock in both of these corporations, and no other shareholder is related to any other shareholder of either corporation.

(ii) Pursuant to paragraph (h)(8) of this section, in the case of a qualified stock purchase that is treated as a deemed sale and purchase of assets pursuant to section 338, the corporation treated as purchasing assets as a result of an election thereunder (new target) is not considered the person that held or used the assets during any period in which the assets were held or used by the corporation treated as selling the assets (old target). Because there are no relationships described in paragraph (h)(6) of this section among the parties to the transaction, any nonamortizable section 197(f)(9) intangible held by old target is an amortizable section 197 intangible in the hands of new target.

(iii) Assume the same facts as set forth in paragraph (i) of this *Example 23*, except that one of the selling shareholders is an individual who owns 25 percent of the total value of the stock of each of the T and P corporation.

(iv) Old target and new target (as these terms are defined in §1.338-2(c)(17)) are members of a controlled group of corporations under section 267(b)(3), as modified by section 197(f)(9)(C)(i), and any nonamortizable section 197(f)(9) intangible held by old target is not an amortizable section 197 intangible in the hands of new target. However, a gain recognition election under paragraph (h)(9) of this section may be made with respect to this transaction.

Example 24. Relationship created as part of public offering. (i) On January 1, 2001, Corporation X engages in a series of related transactions to discontinue its involvement in one line of business. X forms a new corporation, Y, with a nominal amount of cash. Shortly thereafter, X transfers all the stock of its subsidiary conducting the unwanted business (Target) to Y in exchange for 100 shares of Y common stock and a Y promissory note. Target owns a nonamortizable section 197(f)(9) intangible. Prior to January 1, 2001, X and an underwriter (U) had entered into a binding agreement pursuant to which U would purchase 85 shares of Y common stock from X and then sell those shares in a public offering. On January 6, 2001, the public offering closes. X and Y make a section 338(h)(10) election for Target.

(ii) Pursuant to paragraph (h)(8) of this section, in the case of a qualified stock purchase that is treated as a deemed sale and purchase of assets pursuant to section 338, the corporation treated as purchasing assets as a result of an election thereunder (new target) is not considered the person that held or used the assets during any period in which the assets were held or used by the corporation treated as selling the assets (old target). Further, for purposes of determining whether the nonamortizable section 197(f)(9) intangible is acquired by new target from a related person, because the transactions are a series of related transactions, the relationship between old target and new target must be tested immediately before the first transaction in the series (the formation of Y) and immediately after the last transaction in the series (the sale to U and the public offering). See paragraph (h)(6)(ii)(B) of this section. Because there was no relationship between old target and new target immediately before the formation of Y (because the section 338 election had not been made) and only a 15% relationship between old target and new target immediately after, old target is not related to new target for purposes of applying the anti-churning rules of paragraph (h) of this section. Accordingly, Target may amortize the section 197 intangible.

Example 25. Other transfers to controlled corporations. (i) In 2001, Corporation A transfers a section 197(f)(9) intangible that it held during the transition period to X, a newly formed corporation, in exchange for 15% of X's stock. As part of the same transaction, B transfers property to X in exchange for the remaining 85% of X stock.

(ii) Because the acquisition of the intangible by X is part of a qualifying section 351 exchange, under section 197(f)(2) and paragraph (g)(2)(ii) of this section, X is treated in the same manner as the transferor of the asset. Accordingly, X may not amortize the intangible. If, however, at the time of the exchange, B has a binding commitment to sell 25 percent of the X stock to C, an unrelated third party, the exchange, including A's transfer of the section 197(f)(9) intangible, would fail to qualify as a section 351 exchange. Because the formation of X, the transfers of property to X, and the sale of X stock by B are part of a series of related transactions, the relationship between A and X must be tested immediately before the first transaction in the series (the transfer of property to X) and immediately after the last transaction in the series (the sale of X stock to C). See paragraph (h)(6)(ii)(B) of this section. Because there was no relationship between A and X immediately before and only a 15% relationship immediately after, A is not related to X for purposes of applying the anti-churning rules of paragraph (h) of this section. Accordingly, X may amortize the section 197 intangible.

Example 26. Relationship created as part of stock acquisition followed by liquidation. (i) In 2001, Partnership P purchases 100 percent of the stock of Corporation X. P and X were not related prior to the acquisition. Immediately after acquiring the X stock, and as part of a series of related transactions, P liquidates X under section 331. In the liquidating distribution, P receives a section 197(f)(9) intangible that was held by X during the transition period.

(ii) Because the relationship between P and X was created pursuant to a series of related transactions where P acquires stock (meeting the requirements of section 1504(a)(2)) in a fully taxable transaction followed by a liquidation under section 331, the relationship immediately after the last transaction in the series (the liquidation) is disregarded. See paragraph (h)(6)(iii) of this section. Accordingly, P is entitled to amortize the section 197(f)(9) intangible.

Example 27. Section 743(b) adjustment with no change in user. (i) On January 1, 2001, A forms a partnership (PRS) with B in which A owns a 40-percent, and B owns a 60-percent, interest in profits and capital. A contributes a nonamortizable section 197(f)(9) intangible with a value of $80 and an adjusted basis of $0 to PRS in exchange for its PRS interest and B contributes $120 cash. At the time of the contribution, PRS licenses the section 197(f)(9) intangible to A. On February 1, 2001, A sells its entire interest in PRS to C, an unrelated person, for $80. PRS has a section 754 election in effect.

(ii) The section 197(f)(9) intangible contributed to PRS by A is not amortizable in the hands of PRS. Pursuant to section (g)(2)(ii) of this section, PRS steps into the shoes of A with respect to A's nonamortizable transferred basis in the intangible.

(iii) When A sells the PRS interest to C, C will have a basis adjustment in the PRS assets under section 743(b) equal to $80. The entire basis adjustment will be allocated to the intangible because the only other asset held by PRS is cash. Ordinarily, under paragraph (h)(12)(v) of this section, the anti-churning rules will not apply to an increase in the basis of partnership property under section 743(b) if the person acquiring the partnership interest is not related to the person transferring the partnership interest. However, A is an anti-churning partner under paragraph (h)(12)(vi)(B)(2)(i) of this section. As a result of the license agreement, A remains a direct user of the section 197(f)(9) intangible after the transfer to C. Accordingly, paragraph (h)(12)(vi)(A) of this section will cause the anti-churning rules to apply to the entire basis adjustment under section 743(b).

Example 28. Distribution of section 197(f)(9) intangible to partner who acquired partnership interest prior to the effective date. (i) In 1990, A, B, and C each contribute $150 cash to form general partnership ABC for the purpose of engaging in a consulting business and a software manufacturing business. The partners agree to share partnership profits and losses equally. In 2000, the partnership distributes the consulting business to A in liquidation of A's entire interest in ABC. The only asset of the consulting business is a nonamortizable intangible, which has a fair market value of $180 and a basis of $0. At the time of the distribution, the adjusted basis of A's interest in ABC is $150. A is not related to B or C. ABC does not have a section 754 election in effect.

(ii) Under section 732(b), A's adjusted basis in the intangible distributed by ABC is $150, a $150 increase over the basis of the intangible in ABC's hands. In determining whether the anti-churning rules apply to any portion of the basis increase, A is treated as having owned and used A's proportionate share of partnership property. Thus, A is treated as holding an interest in the intangible during the transition period. Because the intangible was not amortizable prior to the enactment of section 197, the section 732(b) increase in the basis of the intangible may be subject to the anti-churning provisions.

Reg. §1.197-2(k)

Paragraph (h)(12)(ii) of this section provides that the anti-churning provisions apply to the extent that the section 732(b) adjustment exceeds the total unrealized appreciation from the intangible allocable to partners other than A or persons related to A, as well as certain other partners whose purchase of their interests meet certain criteria. Because B and C are not related to A, and A's acquisition of its partnership interest does not satisfy the necessary criteria, the section 732(b) basis increase is subject to the anti-churning provisions to the extent that it exceeds B and C's proportionate share of the unrealized appreciation from the intangible. B and C's proportionate share of the unrealized appreciation from the intangible is $120 (2/3 of $180). This is the amount of gain that would be allocated to B and C if the partnership sold the intangible immediately before the distribution for its fair market value of $180. Therefore, $120 of the section 732(b) basis increase is not subject to the anti-churning rules. The remaining $30 of the section 732(b) basis increase is subject to the anti-churning rules. Accordingly, A is treated as having two intangibles, an amortizable section 197 intangible with an adjusted basis of $120 and a new amortization period of 15 years and a nonamortizable intangible with an adjusted basis of $30.

(iii) In applying the anti-churning rules to future transfers of the distributed intangible, under paragraph (h)(12)(ii)(C) of this section, one-third of the intangible will continue to be subject to the anti-churning rules, determined as follows: The sum of the amount of the distributed intangible's basis that is nonamortizable under paragraph (g)(2)(ii)(B) of this section ($0) and the total unrealized appreciation inherent in the intangible reduced by the amount of the increase in the adjusted basis of the distributed intangible under section 732(b) to which the anti-churning rules do not apply ($180–$120=$60), over the fair market value of the distributed intangible ($180).

Example 29. Distribution of section 197(f)(9) intangible to partner who acquired partnership interest after the effective date. (i) The facts are the same as in *Example 28*, except that B and C form ABC in 1990. A does not acquire an interest in ABC until 1995. In 1995, A contributes $150 to ABC in exchange for a one-third interest in ABC. At the time of the distribution, the adjusted basis of A's interest in ABC is $150.

(ii) As in *Example 28*, the anti-churning rules do not apply to the increase in the basis of the intangible distributed to A under section 732(b) to the extent that it does not exceed the unrealized appreciation from the intangible allocable to B and C. Under paragraph (h)(12)(ii) of this section, the anti-churning provisions also do not apply to the section 732(b) basis increase to the extent of A's allocable share of the unrealized appreciation from the intangible because A acquired the ABC interest from an unrelated person after August 10, 1993, and the intangible was acquired by the partnership before A acquired the ABC interest. Under paragraph (h)(12)(ii)(E) of this section, A is deemed to acquire the ABC partnership interest from an unrelated person because A acquired the ABC partnership interest in exchange for a contribution to the partnership of property other than the distributed intangible and, at the time of the contribution, no partner in the partnership was related to A. Consequently, the increase in the basis of the intangible under section 732(b) is not subject to the anti-churning rules to the extent of the total unrealized appreciation from the intangible allocable to A, B, and C. The total unrealized appreciation from the intangible allocable to A, B, and C is $180 (the gain the partnership would have recognized if it had sold the intangible for its fair market value immediately before the distribution). Because this amount exceeds the section 732(b) basis increase of $150, the entire section 732(b) basis increase is amortizable.

(iii) In applying the anti-churning rules to future transfers of the distributed intangible, under paragraph (h)(12)(ii)(C) of this section, one-sixth of the intangible will continue to be subject to the anti-churning rules, determined as follows: The sum of the amount of the distributed intangible's basis that is nonamortizable under paragraph (g)(2)(ii)(B) of this section ($0) and the total unrealized appreciation inherent in the intangible reduced by the amount of the increase in the adjusted basis of the distributed intangible under section 732(b) to which the anti-churning rules do not apply ($180–$150=$30), over the fair market value of the distributed intangible ($180).

Example 30. Distribution of section 197(f)(9) intangible contributed to the partnership by a partner. (i) The facts are the same as in *Example 29*, except that C purchased the intangible used in the consulting business in 1988 for $60 and contributed the intangible to ABC in 1990. At that time, the intangible had a fair market value of $150 and an adjusted tax basis of $60. When ABC distributes the intangible to A in 2000, the intangible has a fair market value of $180 and a basis of $60.

(ii) As in *Examples 28* and *29*, the adjusted basis of the intangible in A's hands is $150 under section 732(b). However, the increase in the adjusted basis of the intangible under section 732(b) is only $90 ($150 adjusted basis after the distribution compared to $60 basis before the distribution). Pursuant to paragraph (g)(2)(ii)(B) of this section, A steps into the shoes of ABC with respect to the $60 of A's adjusted basis in the intangible that corresponds to ABC's basis in the intangible and this portion of the basis is nonamortizable. B and C are not

related to A, A acquired the ABC interest from an unrelated person after August 10, 1993, and the intangible was acquired by ABC before A acquired the ABC interest. Therefore, under paragraph (h)(12)(ii) of this section, the section 732(b) basis increase is amortizable to the extent of A, B, and C's allocable share of the unrealized appreciation from the intangible. The total unrealized appreciation from the intangible that is allocable to A, B, and C is $120. If ABC had sold the intangible immediately before the distribution to A for its fair market value of $180, it would have recognized gain of $120, which would have been allocated $10 to A, $10 to B, and $100 to C under section 704(c). Because A, B, and C's allocable share of the unrealized appreciation from the intangible exceeds the section 732(b) basis increase in the intangible, the entire $90 of basis increase is amortizable by A. Accordingly, after the distribution, A will be treated as having two intangibles, an amortizable section 197 intangible with an adjusted basis of $90 and a new amortization period of 15 years and a nonamortizable intangible with an adjusted basis of $60.

(iii) In applying the anti-churning rules to future transfers of the distributed intangible, under paragraph (h)(12)(ii)(C) of this section, one-half of the intangible will continue to be subject to the anti-churning rules, determined as follows: The sum of the amount of the distributed intangible's basis that is nonamortizable under paragraph (g)(2)(ii)(B) of this section ($60) and the total unrealized appreciation inherent in the intangible reduced by the amount of the increase in the adjusted basis of the distributed intangible under section 732(b) to which the anti-churning rules do not apply ($120–$90=$30), over the fair market value of the distributed intangible ($180).

Example 31. Partnership distribution causing section 734(b) basis adjustment to section 197(f)(9) intangible. (i) On January 1, 2001, A, B, and C form a partnership (ABC) in which each partner shares equally in capital and income, gain, loss, and deductions. On that date, A contributes a section 197(f)(9) intangible with a zero basis and a value of $150, and B and C each contribute $150 cash. A and B are related, but neither A nor B is related to C. ABC does not adopt the remedial allocation method for making section 704(c) allocations of amortization expenses with respect to the intangible. On December 1, 2004, when the value of the intangible has increased to $600, ABC distributes $300 to B in complete redemption of B's interest in the partnership. ABC has an election under section 754 in effect for the taxable year that includes December 1, 2004. (Assume that, at the time of the distribution, the basis of A's partnership interest remains zero, and the basis of each of B's and C's partnership interest remains $150.)

(ii) Immediately prior to the distribution, the assets of the partnership are revalued pursuant to § 1.704-1(b)(2)(iv)(f), so that the section 197(f)(9) intangible is reflected on the books of the partnership at a value of $600. B recognizes $150 of gain under section 731(a)(1) upon the distribution of $300 in redemption of B's partnership interest. As a result, the adjusted basis of the intangible held by ABC increases by $150 under section 734(b). A does not satisfy any of the tests set forth under paragraph (h)(12)(iv)(B) and thus is not an eligible partner. C is not related to B and thus is an eligible partner under paragraph (h)(12)(iv)(B)(1) of this section. The capital accounts of A and C are equal immediately after the distribution, so, pursuant to paragraph (h)(12)(iv)(D)(1) of this section, each partner's share of the basis increase is equal to $75. Because A is not an eligible partner, the anti-churning rules apply to A's share of the basis increase. The anti-churning rules do not apply to C's share of the basis increase.

(iii) For book purposes, ABC determines the amortization of the asset as follows: First, the intangible that is subject to adjustment under section 734(b) will be divided into three assets: the first, with a basis and value of $75 will be amortizable for both book and tax purposes; the second, with a basis and value of $75 will be amortizable for book, but not tax purposes; and a third asset with a basis of zero and a value of $450 will not be amortizable for book or tax purposes. Any subsequent revaluation of the intangible pursuant to § 1.704-1(b)(2)(iv)(f) will be made solely with respect to the third asset (which is not amortizable for book purposes). The book and tax attributes from the first asset (i.e., book and tax amortization) will be specially allocated to C. The book and tax attributes from the second asset (i.e., book amortization and non-amortizable tax basis) will be specially allocated to A. Upon disposition of the intangible, each partner's share of gain or loss will be determined first by allocating among the partners an amount realized equal to the book value of the intangible attributable to such partner, with any remaining amount realized being allocated in accordance with the partnership agreement. Each partner then will compare its share of the amount realized with its remaining basis in the intangible to arrive at the gain or loss to be allocated to such partner. This is a reasonable method for amortizing the intangible for book purposes, and the results in allocating the income, gain, loss, and deductions attributable to the intangible do not contravene the purposes of the anti-churning rules under section 197 or paragraph (h) of this section.

(l) *Effective dates.*—(1) *In general.*—This section applies to property acquired after January 25, 2000, except that paragraph (c)(13) of this section (exception from section 197 for separately acquired rights of fixed duration or amount) applies to property acquired after August 10, 1993 (or July 25, 1991, if a valid retroactive election has been made under § 1.197-IT), and paragraphs (h)(12)(ii), (iii), (iv), (v), (vi)(A), and (vii)(B) of this section (anti-churning rules applicable to partnerships) apply to partnership transactions occurring on or after November 20, 2000.

(2) *Application to pre-effective date acquisitions.*—A taxpayer may choose, on a transaction-by-transaction basis, to apply the provisions of this section and § 1.167(a)-14 to property acquired (or partnership transactions occurring) after August 10, 1993 (or July 25, 1991, if a valid retroactive election has been made under § 1.197-IT) and—

(i) On or before January 25, 2000; or

(ii) With respect to paragraphs (h)(12)(ii), (iii), (iv), (v), (vi) (A), and (vii) (B) of this section, before November 20, 2000.

(3) *Application of regulation project REG-209709-94 to pre-effective date acquisitions.*—A taxpayer may rely on the provisions of regulation project REG-209709-94 (1997-1 C.B. 731) for property acquired after August 10, 1993 (or July 25, 1991, if a valid retroactive election has been made under § 1.197-1T) and on or before January 25, 2000.

(4) *Change in method of accounting.*—(i) *In general.*—For the first taxable year ending after January 25, 2000, a taxpayer that has acquired property to which the exception in § 1.197-2(c)(13) applies is granted consent of the Commissioner to change its method of accounting for such property to comply with the provisions of this section and § 1.167(a)-14 unless the proper treatment of such property is an issue under consideration (within the meaning of Rev. Proc. 97-27 (1997-21 IRB 10)(see § 601.601(d)(2) of this chapter)) in an examination, before an Appeals office, or before a Federal court.

(ii) *Application to pre-effective date acquisitions.*—For the first taxable year ending after January 25, 2000, a taxpayer is granted consent of the Commissioner to change its method of accounting for all property acquired in transactions described in paragraph (l)(2) of this section to comply with the provisions of this section and § 1.167(a)-14 unless the proper treatment of any such property is an issue under consideration (within the meaning of Rev. Proc. 97-27 (1997-21 IRB 10)(see § 601.601(d)(2) of this chapter)) in an examination, before an Appeals office, or before a Federal court.

(iii) *Automatic change procedures.*—A taxpayer changing its method of accounting in accordance with this paragraph (l)(4) must follow the automatic change in accounting method provisions of Rev. Proc. 99-49 (1999-52 IRB 725) (see § 601.601(d)(2) of this chapter) except, for purposes of this paragraph (l)(4), the scope limitations in section 4.02 of Rev. Proc. 99-49 (1999-52 IRB 725) are not applicable. However, if the taxpayer is under examination, before an appeals office, or before a Federal court, the taxpayer must provide a copy of the application to the examining agent(s), appeals officer, or counsel for the government, as appropriate, at the same time that it files the copy of the application with the National Office. The application must contain the name(s) and telephone number(s) of the examining agent(s), appeals officer, or counsel for the government, as appropriate.

(5) *Applicability dates for section 721(c) partnerships.*—(i) *In general.*—Except as provided in paragraph (l)(5)(ii) of this section, paragraph (h)(12)(vii)(C) of this section applies with respect to contributions occurring on or after January 18, 2017, and with respect to contributions that occurred before January 18, 2017 resulting from an entity classification election made under § 301.7701-3 of this chapter that was effective on or before January 18, 2017 but was filed on or after January 18, 2017.

(ii) *Application of the provisions described in paragraph (l)(5)(i)(A) of this section retroactively.*—Paragraph (h)(12)(vii)(C) of this section may be applied with respect to a contribution occurring on or after August 6, 2015, and to a contribution that occurred before August 6, 2015 resulting from an entity classification election made under § 301.7701-3 of this chapter that was effective on or before August 6, 2015 but was filed on or after August 6, 2015. A taxpayer applying paragraph (h)(12)(vii)(C) of this section retroactively must apply paragraph (h)(12)(vii)(C) of this section on a timely filed original *return (including extensions) or an amended return filed no later than July 18, 2017.* [Reg. § 1.197-2.]

☐ [*T.D.* 8865, 1-20-2000 (*corrected* 3-27-2000 *and* 10-11-2000). *Amended by T.D.* 8907, 11-17-2000; *T.D.* 8940, 2-12-2001; *T.D.* 9257, 4-7-2006; *T.D.* 9377, 1-22-2008; *T.D.* 9533, 7-1-2011, *T.D.* 9637, 9-5-2013, *T.D.* 9811, 1-18-2017, *T.D.* 9814, 1-18-2017 *and T.D.* 9891, 1-17-2020.]

[Reg. § 1.199A-0]

§ 1.199A-0. Table of Contents.—This section lists the section headings that appear in § § 1.199A-1 through 1.199A-6.

(iii) Requirement that wages must be reported on return filed with the Social Security Administration.

    (A) In general.

    (B) Corrected return filed to correct a return that was filed within 60 days of the due date.

    (C) Corrected return filed to correct a return that was filed later than 60 days after the due date.

    (iv) Methods for calculating W-2 wages.

        (A) In general.

        (B) Acquisition or disposition of a trade or business.

            (1) In general.

            (2) Acquisition or disposition.

        (C) Application in the case of a person with a short taxable year.

            (1) In general.

            (2) Short taxable year that does not include December 31.

        (D) Remuneration paid for services performed in the Commonwealth of Puerto Rico.

    (3) Allocation of wages to trades or businesses.

    (4) Allocation of wages to QBI.

    (5) Non-duplication rule.

  (c) UBIA of qualified property.

    (1) Qualified property.

      (i) In general.

      (ii) Improvements to qualified property.

      (iii) Adjustments under sections 734(b) and 743(b).

      (iv) Property acquired at end of year.

    (2) Depreciable period.

      (i) In general.

      (ii) Additional first-year depreciation under section 168.

      (iii) Qualified property acquired in transactions subject to section 1031 or section 1033.

        (A) Replacement property received in a section 1031 or 1033 transaction.

        (B) Other property received in a section 1031 or 1033 transaction.

      (iv) Qualified property acquired in transactions subject to section 168(i)(7)(B).

      (v) Excess section 743(b) basis adjustment.

    (3) Unadjusted basis immediately after acquisition.

      (i) In general.

      (ii) Qualified property acquired in a like-kind exchange.

        (A) In general.

        (B) Excess boot.

      (iii) Qualified property acquired pursuant to an involuntary conversion.

        (A) In general.

        (B) Excess boot.

      (iv) Qualified property acquired in transactions described in section 168(i)(7)(B).

      (v) Qualified property acquired from a decedent.

      (vi) Property acquired in a nonrecognition transaction with principal purpose of increasing UBIA.

    (4) Examples.

  (d) Applicability date.

    (1) General rule.

    (2) Exceptions.

      (i) Anti-abuse rules.

      (ii) Non-calendar year RPE.

§ 1.199A-3 Qualified business income, qualified REIT dividends, and qualified PTP income.

  (a) In general.

  (b) Definition of qualified business income.

    (1) In general.

      (i) Section 751 gain.

      (ii) Guaranteed payments for the use of capital.

      (iii) Section 481 adjustments.

      (iv) Previously disallowed losses

        (A) In general.

        (B) Partial allowance.

        (C) Attributes of disallowed loss determined in year loss is incurred.

            (1) In general.

            (2) Specified service trades or businesses.

        (D) Examples.

      (v) Net operating losses.

      (vi) Other deductions.

    (2) Qualified items of income, gain, deduction, and loss.

      (i) In general.

      (ii) Items not taken into account.

    (3) Commonwealth of Puerto Rico.

    (4) Wages.

    (5) Allocation of items among directly-conducted trades or businesses.

  (c) Qualified REIT dividends and qualified PTP income.

    (1) In general.

    (2) Qualified REIT dividend.

    (3) Qualified PTP income.

      (i) In general.

      (ii) Special rules.

  (d) Section 199A dividends paid by a regulated investment company.

    (1) In general.

    (2) Definition of section 199A dividend.

      (i) In general.

      (ii) Reduction in the case of excess reported amounts.

      (iii) Allocation of excess reported amount.

        (A) In general.

        (B) Special rule for noncalendar-year RICs.

    (3) Definitions.

      (i) Reported section 199A dividend amount.

      (ii) Excess reported amount.

      (iii) Aggregate reported amount.

      (iv) Post-December reported amount.

      (v) Qualified REIT dividend income.

    (4) Treatment of section 199A dividends by shareholders.

      (i) In general.

      (ii) Holding period.

    (5) Example.

  (e) Applicability date.

    (1) General rule.

    (2) Exceptions.

      (i) Anti-abuse rules.

      (ii) Non-calendar year RPE.

      (iii) Previously disallowed losses.

      (iv) Section 199A dividends.

§ 1.199A-4 Aggregation.

  (a) Scope and purpose.

  (b) Aggregation rules.

    (1) General rule.

    (2) Operating rules.

      (i) Individuals.

      (ii) RPEs.

  (c) Reporting and consistency.

    (1) For individual.

    (2) Individual disclosure.

      (i) Required annual disclosure.

      (ii) Failure to disclose.

    (3) For RPEs.

      (i) Required annual disclosure.

      (ii) Failure to disclose.

  (d) Examples.

  (e) Applicability date.

    (1) General rule.

    (2) Exception for non-calendar year RPE.

§ 1.199A-5 Specified service trades or businesses and the trade or business of performing services as an employee.

  (a) Scope and effect.

    (1) Scope.

    (2) Effect of being an SSTB.

    (3) Trade or business of performing services as an employee.

  (b) Definition of specified service trade or business.

    (1) Listed SSTBs.

    (2) Additional rules for applying section 199A(d)(2) and paragraph (b) of this section.

      (i) In general.

        (A) No effect on other tax rules.

        (B) Hedging transactions.

      (ii) Meaning of services performed in the field of health.

      (iii) Meaning of services performed in the field of law.

      (iv) Meaning of services performed in the field of accounting.

      (v) Meaning of services performed in the field of actuarial science.

      (vi) Meaning of services performed in the field of performing arts.

      (vii) Meaning of services performed in the field of consulting.

      (viii) Meaning of services performed in the field of athletics.

      (ix) Meaning of services performed in the field of financial services.

(x) Meaning of services performed in the field of brokerage services.

(xi) Meaning of the provision of services in investing and investment management.

(xii) Meaning of the provision of services in trading.

(xiii) Meaning of the provision of services in dealing.

(A) Dealing in securities.

(B) Dealing in commodities.

(1) Qualified active sale.

(2) Active conduct of a commodities business.

(3) Directly holds commodities as inventory or similar property.

(4) Directly incurs substantial expenses in the ordinary course.

(5) Significant activities for purposes of paragraph (b)(2)(xiii)(B)(*4*)(*iii*) of this section.

(C) Dealing in partnership interests.

(xiv) Meaning of trade or business where the principal asset of such trade or business is the reputation or skill of one or more of its employees or owners.

(3) Examples.

(c) Special rules.

(1) De minimis rule.

(i) Gross receipts of $25 million or less.

(ii) Gross receipts of greater than $25 million.

(2) Services or property provided to an SSTB.

(i) In general.

(ii) 50 percent or more common ownership.

(iii) Examples.

(d) Trade or business of performing services as an employee.

(1) In general.

(2) Employer's Federal employment tax classification of employee immaterial.

(3) Presumption that former employees are still employees.

(i) Presumption.

(ii) Rebuttal of presumption.

(iii) Examples.

(e) Applicability date.

(1) General rule.

(2) Exceptions.

(i) Anti-abuse rules.

(ii) Non-calendar year RPE.

§1.199A-6 Relevant passthrough entities (RPEs), publicly traded partnerships (PTPs), trusts, and estates.

(a) Overview.

(b) Computational and reporting rules for RPEs.

(1) In general.

(2) Computational rules.

(3) Reporting rules for RPEs.

(i) Trade or business directly engaged in.

(ii) Other items.

(iii) Failure to report information.

(c) Computational and reporting rules for PTPs.

(1) Computational rules.

(2) Reporting rules.

(d) Application to trusts, estates, and beneficiaries.

(1) In general.

(2) Grantor trusts.

(3) Non-grantor trusts and estates.

(i) Calculation at entity level.

(ii) Allocation among trust or estate and beneficiaries.

(iii) Separate shares.

(iv) Threshold amount.

(v) Charitable remainder trusts.

(vi) Electing small business trusts.

(vii) Anti-abuse rule for creation of a trust to avoid exceeding the threshold amount.

(viii) Example.

(e) Applicability date.

(1) General rule.

(2) Exceptions.

(i) Anti-abuse rules.

(ii) Non-calendar year RPE.

(iii) Separate shares.

(iv) Charitable remainder trusts.

[Reg. §1.199A-0.]

☐ [T.D. 9847, 2-4-2019 (corrected 4-17-2019). *Amended by* T.D. 9899, 6-24-2020.]

[Reg. §1.199A-1]

§1.199A-1. Operational rules.—(a) *Overview.*—(1) *In general.*—This section provides operational rules for calculating the section 199A(a) qualified business income deduction (section 199A deduction) under section 199A of the Internal Revenue Code (Code). This section refers to the rules in §§1.199A-2 through 1.199A-6. This paragraph (a) provides an overview of this section. Paragraph (b) of this section provides definitions that apply for purposes of section 199A and §§1.199A-1 through 1.199A-6. Paragraph (c) of this section provides computational rules and examples for individuals whose taxable income does not exceed the threshold amount. Paragraph (d) of this section provides computational rules and examples for individuals whose taxable income exceeds the threshold amount. Paragraph (e) of this section provides special rules for purposes of section 199A and §§1.199A-1 through 1.199A-6. This section and §§1.199A-2 through 1.199A-6 do not apply for purposes of calculating the deduction in section 199A(g) for specified agricultural and horticultural cooperatives.

(2) *Usage of term individual.*—For purposes of applying the rules of §§1.199A-1 through 1.199A-6, a reference to an individual includes a reference to a trust (other than a grantor trust) or an estate to the extent that the section 199A deduction is determined by the trust or estate under the rules of §1.199A-6.

(b) *Definitions.*—For purposes of section 199A and §§1.199A-1 through 1.199A-6, the following definitions apply:

(1) *Aggregated trade or business* means two or more trades or businesses that have been aggregated pursuant to §1.199A-4.

(2) *Applicable percentage* means, with respect to any taxable year, 100 percent reduced (not below zero) by the percentage equal to the ratio that the taxable income of the individual for the taxable year in excess of the threshold amount, bears to $50,000 (or $100,000 in the case of a joint return).

(3) *Net capital gain* means *net capital gain* as defined in section 1222(11) plus any *qualified dividend income* (as defined in section 1(h)(11)(B)) for the taxable year.

(4) *Phase-in range* means a range of taxable income between the threshold amount and the threshold amount plus $50,000 (or $100,000 in the case of a joint return).

(5) *Qualified business income (QBI)* means the net amount of qualified items of income, gain, deduction, and loss with respect to any trade or business (or aggregated trade or business) as determined under the rules of §1.199A-3(b).

(6) *QBI component* means the amount determined under paragraph (d)(2) of this section.

(7) *Qualified PTP income* is defined in §1.199A-3(c)(3).

(8) *Qualified REIT dividends* are defined in §1.199A-3(c)(2).

(9) *Reduction amount* means, with respect to any taxable year, the excess amount multiplied by the ratio that the taxable income of the individual for the taxable year in excess of the threshold amount, bears to $50,000 (or $100,000 in the case of a joint return). For purposes of this paragraph (b)(9), the *excess amount* is the amount by which 20 percent of QBI exceeds the greater of 50 percent of W-2 wages or the sum of 25 percent of W-2 wages plus 2.5 percent of the UBIA of qualified property.

(10) *Relevant passthrough entity (RPE)* means a partnership (other than a PTP) or an S corporation that is owned, directly or indirectly, by at least one individual, estate, or trust. Other passthrough entities including common trust funds as described in §1.6032-1T and religious or apostolic organizations described in section 501(d) are also treated as RPEs if the entity files a Form 1065, *U.S. Return of Partnership Income,* and is owned, directly or indirectly, by at least one individual, estate, or trust. A trust or estate is treated as an RPE to the extent it passes through QBI, W-2 wages, UBIA of qualified property, qualified REIT dividends, or qualified PTP income.

(11) *Specified service trade or business (SSTB)* means a specified service trade or business as defined in §1.199A-5(b).

(12) *Threshold amount* means, for any taxable year beginning before 2019, $157,500 (or $315,000 in the case of a taxpayer filing a joint return). In the case of any taxable year beginning after 2018, the threshold amount is the dollar amount in the preceding sentence increased by an amount equal to such dollar amount, multiplied by the cost-of-living adjustment determined under section 1(f)(3) of the Code for the calendar year in which the taxable year begins, determined by substituting "calendar year 2017" for "calendar year 2016" in section 1(f)(3)(A)(ii). The amount of any increase under the preceding sentence is rounded as provided in section 1(f)(7) of the Code.

(13) *Total QBI amount* means the net total QBI from all trades or businesses (including the individual's share of QBI from trades or business conducted by RPEs).

(14) *Trade or business* means a trade or business that is a trade or business under section 162 (a section 162 trade or business) other than the trade or business of performing services as an employee. In

addition, rental or licensing of tangible or intangible property (rental activity) that does not rise to the level of a section 162 trade or business is nevertheless treated as a trade or business for purposes of section 199A, if the property is rented or licensed to a trade or business conducted by the individual or an RPE which is commonly controlled under § 1.199A-4(b)(1)(i) (regardless of whether the rental activity and the trade or business are otherwise eligible to be aggregated under § 1.199A-4(b)(1)).

(15) *Unadjusted basis immediately after acquisition of qualified property (UBIA of qualified property)* is defined in § 1.199A-2(c).

(16) *W-2 wages* means W-2 wages of a trade or business (or aggregated trade or business) properly allocable to QBI as determined under § 1.199A-2(b).

(c) *Computation of the section 199A deduction for individuals with taxable income not exceeding threshold amount.*—(1) *In general.*—The section 199A deduction is determined for individuals with taxable income for the taxable year that does not exceed the threshold amount by adding 20 percent of the total QBI amount (including the individual's share of QBI from an RPE and QBI attributable to an SSTB) and 20 percent of the combined amount of qualified REIT dividends and qualified PTP income (including the individual's share of qualified REIT dividends and qualified PTP income from RPEs and qualified PTP income attributable to an SSTB). That sum is then compared to 20 percent of the amount by which the individual's taxable income exceeds net capital gain. The lesser of these two amounts is the individual's section 199A deduction.

(2) *Carryover rules.*—(i) *Negative total QBI amount.*—If the total QBI amount is less than zero, the portion of the individual's section 199A deduction related to QBI is zero for the taxable year. The negative total QBI amount is treated as negative QBI from a separate trade or business in the succeeding taxable years of the individual for purposes of section 199A and this section. This carryover rule does not affect the deductibility of the loss for purposes of other provisions of the Code.

(ii) *Negative combined qualified REIT dividends/qualified PTP income.*—If the combined amount of REIT dividends and qualified PTP income is less than zero, the portion of the individual's section 199A deduction related to qualified REIT dividends and qualified PTP income is zero for the taxable year. The negative combined amount must be carried forward and used to offset the combined amount of REIT dividends and qualified PTP income in the succeeding taxable years of the individual for purposes of section 199A and this section. This carryover rule does not affect the deductibility of the loss for purposes of other provisions of the Code.

(3) *Examples.*—The following examples illustrate the provisions of this paragraph (c). For purposes of these examples, unless indicated otherwise, assume that all of the trades or businesses are trades or businesses as defined in paragraph (b)(14) of this section and all of the tax items are effectively connected to a trade or business within the United States within the meaning of section 864(c). Total taxable income does not include the section 199A deduction.

(i) *Example 1.* A, an unmarried individual, owns and operates a computer repair shop as a sole proprietorship. The business generates $100,000 in net taxable income from operations in 2018. A has no capital gains or losses. After allowable deductions not relating to the business, A's total taxable income for 2018 is $81,000. The business's QBI is $100,000, the net amount of its qualified items of income, gain, deduction, and loss. A's section 199A deduction for 2018 is equal to $16,200, the lesser of 20% of A's QBI from the business ($100,000 x 20% = $20,000) and 20% of A's total taxable income for the taxable year ($81,000 x 20% = $16,200).

(ii) *Example 2.* Assume the same facts as in *Example 1* of paragraph (c)(3)(i) of this section, except that A also has $7,000 in net capital gain for 2018 and that, after allowable deductions not relating to the business, A's taxable income for 2018 is $74,000. A's taxable income minus net capital gain is $67,000 ($74,000 - $7,000). A's section 199A deduction is equal to $13,400, the lesser of 20% of A's QBI from the business ($100,000 x 20% = $20,000) and 20% of A's total taxable income minus net capital gain for the taxable year ($67,000 x 20% = $13,400).

(iii) *Example 3.* B and C are married and file a joint individual income tax return. B earns $50,000 in wages as an employee of an unrelated company in 2018. C owns 100% of the shares of X, an S corporation that provides landscaping services. X generates $100,000 in net income from operations in 2018. X pays C $150,000 in wages in 2018. B and C have no capital gains or losses. After allowable deductions not related to X, B and C's total taxable income for 2018 is $270,000. B's and C's wages are not considered to be income from a trade or business for purposes of the section 199A deduction. Because X is an S corporation, its QBI is determined at the S corporation level. X's QBI is $100,000, the net amount of its qualified items of income, gain, deduction, and loss. The wages paid by X to C are

considered to be a qualified item of deduction for purposes of determining X's QBI. The section 199A deduction with respect to X's QBI is then determined by C, X's sole shareholder, and is claimed on the joint return filed by B and C. B and C's section 199A deduction is equal to $20,000, the lesser of 20% of C's QBI from the business ($100,000 x 20% = $20,000) and 20% of B and C's total taxable income for the taxable year ($270,000 x 20% = $54,000).

(iv) *Example 4.* Assume the same facts as in *Example 3* of paragraph (c)(3)(iii) of this section except that B also earns $1,000 in qualified REIT dividends and $500 in qualified PTP income in 2018, increasing taxable income to $271,500. B and C's section 199A deduction is equal to $20,300, the lesser of:

(A) 20% of C's QBI from the business ($100,000 x 20% = $20,000) plus 20% of B's combined qualified REIT dividends and qualified PTP income ($1500 x 20% = $300); and

(B) 20% of B and C's total taxable for the taxable year ($271,500 x 20% = $54,300).

(d) *Computation of the section 199A deduction for individuals with taxable income above threshold amount.*—(1) *In general.*—The section 199A deduction is determined for individuals with taxable income for the taxable year that exceeds the threshold amount by adding the QBI component described in paragraph (d)(2) of this section and the qualified REIT dividends/qualified PTP income component described in paragraph (d)(3) of this section (including the individual's share of qualified REIT dividends and qualified PTP income from RPEs). That sum is then compared to 20 percent of the amount by which the individual's taxable income exceeds net capital gain. The lesser of these two amounts is the individual's section 199A deduction.

(2) *QBI component.*—An individual with taxable income for the taxable year that exceeds the threshold amount determines the QBI component using the following computational rules, which are to be applied in the order they appear.

(i) *SSTB exclusion.*—If the individual's taxable income is within the phase-in range, then only the applicable percentage of QBI, W-2 wages, and UBIA of qualified property for each SSTB is taken into account for all purposes of determining the individual's section 199A deduction, including the application of the netting and carryover rules described in paragraph (d)(2)(iii) of this section. If the individual's taxable income exceeds the phase-in range, then none of the individual's share of QBI, W-2 wages, or UBIA of qualified property attributable to an SSTB may be taken into account for purposes of determining the individual's section 199A deduction.

(ii) *Aggregated trade or business.*—If an individual chooses to aggregate trades or businesses under the rules of § 1.199A-4, the individual must combine the QBI, W-2 wages, and UBIA of qualified property of each trade or business within an aggregated trade or business prior to applying the netting and carryover rules described in paragraph (d)(2)(iii) of this section and the W-2 wage and UBIA of qualified property limitations described in paragraph (d)(2)(iv) of this section.

(iii) *Netting and carryover.*—(A) *Netting.*—If an individual's QBI from at least one trade or business (including an aggregated trade or business) is less than zero, the individual must offset the QBI attributable to each trade or business (or aggregated trade or business) that produced net positive QBI with the QBI from each trade or business (or aggregated trade or business) that produced net negative QBI in proportion to the relative amounts of net QBI in the trades or businesses (or aggregated trades or businesses) with positive QBI. The adjusted QBI is then used in paragraph (d)(2)(iv) of this section. The W-2 wages and UBIA of qualified property from the trades or businesses (including aggregated trades or businesses) that produced net negative QBI are not taken into account for purposes of this paragraph (d) and are not carried over to the subsequent year.

(B) *Carryover of negative total QBI amount.*—If an individual's QBI from all trades or businesses (including aggregated trades or businesses) combined is less than zero, the QBI component is zero for the taxable year. This negative amount is treated as negative QBI from a separate trade or business in the succeeding taxable years of the individual for purposes of section 199A and this section. This carryover rule does not affect the deductibility of the loss for purposes of other provisions of the Code. The W-2 wages and UBIA of qualified property from the trades or businesses (including aggregated trades or businesses) that produced net negative QBI are not taken into account for purposes of this paragraph (d) and are not carried over to the subsequent year.

(iv) *QBI component calculation.*—(A) *General rule.*—Except as provided in paragraph (d)(2)(iv)(B) of this section, the QBI component is the sum of the amounts determined under this paragraph (d)(2)(iv)(A) for each trade or business (or aggregated trade or busi-

Itemized Deductions for Individuals and Corps.
See p. 20,601 for regulations not amended to reflect law changes
25,675

ness). For each trade or business (or aggregated trade or business) (including trades or businesses operated through RPEs) the individual must determine the lesser of—

    (1) 20 percent of the QBI for that trade or business (or aggregated trade or business); or

    (2) The greater of—

        (i) 50 percent of W-2 wages with respect to that trade or business (or aggregated trade or business); or

        (ii) The sum of 25 percent of W-2 wages with respect to that trade or business (or aggregated trade or business) plus 2.5 percent of the UBIA of qualified property with respect to that trade or business (or aggregated trade or business).

    (B) *Taxpayers with taxable income within phase-in range.*—If the individual's taxable income is within the phase-in range and the amount determined under paragraph (d)(2)(iv)(A)(2) of this section for a trade or business (or aggregated trade or business) is less than the amount determined under paragraph (d)(2)(iv)(A)(1) of this section for that trade or business (or aggregated trade or business), the amount determined under paragraph (d)(2)(iv)(A) of this section for such trade or business (or aggregated trade or business) is modified. Instead of the amount determined under paragraph (d)(2)(iv)(A)(2) of this section, the QBI component for the trade or business (or aggregated trade or business) is the amount determined under paragraph (d)(2)(iv)(A)(1) of this section reduced by the reduction amount as defined in paragraph (b)(9) of this section. This reduction amount does not apply if the amount determined in paragraph (d)(2)(iv)(A)(2) of this section is greater than the amount determined under paragraph (d)(2)(iv)(A)(1) of this section (in which circumstance the QBI component for the trade or business (or aggregated trade or business) will be the unreduced amount determined in paragraph (d)(2)(iv)(A)(1) of this section).

    (3) *Qualified REIT dividends/qualified PTP income component.*— (i) *In general.*—The qualified REIT dividend/qualified PTP income component is 20 percent of the combined amount of qualified REIT dividends and qualified PTP income received by the individual (including the individual's share of qualified REIT dividends and qualified PTP income from RPEs).

    (ii) *SSTB exclusion.*—If the individual's taxable income is within the phase-in range, then only the applicable percentage of qualified PTP income generated by an SSTB is taken into account for purposes of determining the individual's section 199A deduction, including the determination of the combined amount of qualified REIT dividends and qualified PTP income described in paragraph (d)(1) of this section. If the individual's taxable income exceeds the phase-in range, then none of the individual's share of qualified PTP income generated by an SSTB may be taken into account for purposes of determining the individual's section 199A deduction.

    (iii) *Negative combined qualified REIT dividends/qualified PTP income.*—If the combined amount of REIT dividends and qualified PTP income is less than zero, the portion of the individual's section 199A deduction related to qualified REIT dividends and qualified PTP income is zero for the taxable year. The negative combined amount must be carried forward and used to offset the combined amount of REIT dividends/qualified PTP income in the succeeding taxable years of the individual for purposes of section 199A and this section. This carryover rule does not affect the deductibility of the loss for purposes of other provisions of the Code.

    (4) *Examples.*—The following examples illustrate the provisions of this paragraph (d). For purposes of these examples, unless indicated otherwise, assume that all of the trades or businesses are trades or businesses as defined in paragraph (b)(14) of this section, none of the trades or businesses are SSTBs as defined in paragraph (b)(11) of this section and § 1.199A-5(b); and all of the tax items associated with the trades or businesses are effectively connected to a trade or business within the United States within the meaning of section 864(c). Also assume that the taxpayers report no capital gains or losses or other tax items not specified in the examples. Total taxable income does not include the section 199A deduction.

    (i) *Example 1.*—D, an unmarried individual, operates a business as a sole proprietorship. The business generates $1,000,000 of QBI in 2018. Solely for purposes of this example, assume that the business paid no wages and holds no qualified property for use in the business. After allowable deductions unrelated to the business, D's total taxable income for 2018 is $980,000. Because D's taxable income exceeds the applicable threshold amount, D's section 199A deduction is subject to the W-2 wage and UBIA of qualified property limitations. D's section 199A deduction is limited to zero because the business paid no wages and held no qualified property.

    (ii) *Example 2.*—Assume the same facts as in *Example 1* of paragraph (d)(4)(i) of this section, except that D holds qualified property with a UBIA of $10,000,000 for use in the trade or business. D reports $4,000,000 of QBI for 2020. After allowable deductions unrelated to the business, D's total taxable income for 2020 is $3,980,000. Because D's taxable income is above the threshold amount, the QBI component of D's section 199A deduction is subject to the W-2 wage and UBIA of qualified property limitations. Because the business has no W-2 wages, the QBI component of D's section 199A deduction is limited to the lesser of 20% of the business's QBI or 2.5% of its UBIA of qualified property. Twenty percent of the $4,000,000 of QBI is $800,000. Two and one-half percent of the $10,000,000 UBIA of qualified property is $250,000. The QBI component of D's section 199A deduction is thus limited to $250,000. D's section 199A deduction is equal to the lesser of:

    (A) 20% of the QBI from the business as limited ($250,000); or

    (B) 20% of D's taxable income ($3,980,000 x 20% = $796,000). Therefore, D's section 199A deduction for 2020 is $250,000.

    (iii) *Example 3.*—E, an unmarried individual, is a 30% owner of LLC, which is classified as a partnership for Federal income tax purposes. In 2018, the LLC has a single trade or business and reports QBI of $3,000,000. The LLC pays total W-2 wages of $1,000,000, and its total UBIA of qualified property is $100,000. E is allocated 30% of all items of the partnership. For the 2018 taxable year, E reports $900,000 of QBI from the LLC. After allowable deductions unrelated to LLC, E's taxable income is $880,000. Because E's taxable income is above the threshold amount, the QBI component of E's section 199A deduction will be limited to the lesser of 20% of E's share of LLC's QBI or the greater of the W-2 wage or UBIA of qualified property limitations. Twenty percent of E's share of QBI of $900,000 is $180,000. The W-2 wage limitation equals 50% of E's share of the LLC's wages ($300,000) or $150,000. The UBIA of qualified property limitation equals $75,750, the sum of 25% of E's share of LLC's wages ($300,000) or $75,000 plus 2.5% of E's share of UBIA of qualified property ($30,000) or $750. The greater of the limitation amounts ($150,000 and $75,750) is $150,000. The QBI component of E's section 199A deduction is thus limited to $150,000, the lesser of 20% of QBI ($180,000) and the greater of the limitations amounts ($150,000). E's section 199A deduction is equal to the lesser of 20% of the QBI from the business as limited ($150,000) or 20% of E's taxable income ($880,000 x 20% = $176,000). Therefore, E's section 199A deduction is $150,000 for 2018.

    (iv) *Example 4.*—F, an unmarried individual, owns a 50% interest in Z, an S corporation for Federal income tax purposes that conducts a single trade or business. In 2018, Z reports QBI of $6,000,000. Z pays total W-2 wages of $2,000,000, and its total UBIA of qualified property is $200,000. For the 2018 taxable year, F reports $3,000,000 of QBI from Z. F is not an employee of Z and receives no wages or reasonable compensation from Z. After allowable deductions unrelated to Z and a deductible qualified net loss from a PTP of ($10,000), F's taxable income is $1,880,000. Because F's taxable income is above the threshold amount, the QBI component of F's section 199A deduction will be limited to the lesser of 20% of F's share of Z's QBI or the greater of the W-2 wage and UBIA of qualified property limitations. Twenty percent of F's share of Z's QBI ($3,000,000) is $600,000. The W-2 wage limitation equals 50% of F's share of Z's W-2 wages ($1,000,000) or $500,000. The UBIA of qualified property limitation equals $252,500, the sum of 25% of F's share of Z's W-2 wages ($1,000,000) or $250,000 plus 2.5% of E's share of UBIA of qualified property ($100,000) or $2,500. The greater of the limitation amounts ($500,000 and $252,500) is $500,000. The QBI component of F's section 199A deduction is thus limited to $500,000, the lesser of 20% of QBI ($600,000) and the greater of the limitations amounts ($500,000). F reports a qualified loss from a PTP and has no qualified REIT dividend. F does not net the ($10,000) loss from the PTP against QBI. Instead, the portion of F's section 199A deduction related to qualified REIT dividends and qualified PTP income is zero for 2018. F's section is 199A deduction is equal to the lesser of 20% of the QBI from the business as limited ($500,000) or 20% of F's taxable income over net capital gain ($1,880,000 x 20% = $376,000). Therefore, F's section 199A deduction is $376,000 for 2018. F must also carry forward the ($10,000) qualified loss from a PTP to be netted against F's qualified REIT dividends and qualified PTP income in the succeeding taxable year.

    (v) *Example 5.*—*Phase-in range.* (A) B and C are married and file a joint individual income tax return. B is a shareholder in M, an entity taxed as an S corporation for Federal income tax purposes that conducts a single trade or business. M holds no qualified property. B's share of the M's QBI is $300,000 in 2018. B's share of the W-2 wages from M in 2018 is $40,000. C earns wage income from employment by an unrelated company. After allowable deductions unrelated to M, B and C's taxable income for 2018 is $375,000. B and C are within the phase-in range because their taxable income exceeds the applicable threshold amount, $315,000, but does not exceed the threshold amount plus $100,000, or $415,000. Consequently, the QBI component of B and C's section 199A deduction may be limited by the W-2 wage and UBIA of qualified property limitations but the limitations will be phased in.

(B) Because M does not hold qualified property, only the W-2 wage limitation must be calculated. In order to apply the W-2 wage limitation, B and C must first determine 20% of B's share of M's QBI. Twenty percent of B's share of M's QBI of $300,000 is $60,000. Next, B and C must determine 50% of B's share of M's W-2 wages. Fifty percent of B's share of M's W-2 wages of $40,000 is $20,000. Because 50% of B's share of M's W-2 wages ($20,000) is less than 20% of B's share of M's QBI ($60,000), B and C must determine the QBI component of their section 199A deduction by reducing 20% of B's share of M's QBI by the reduction amount.

(C) B and C are 60% through the phase-in range (that is, their taxable income exceeds the threshold amount by $60,000 and their phase-in range is $100,000). B and C must determine the excess amount, which is the excess of 20% of B's share of M's QBI, or $60,000, over 50% of B's share of M's W-2 wages, or $20,000. Thus, the excess amount is $40,000. The reduction amount is equal to 60% of the excess amount, or $24,000. Thus, the QBI component of B and C's section 199A deduction is equal to $36,000, 20% of B's $300,000 share M's QBI (that is, $60,000), reduced by $24,000. B and C's section 199A deduction is equal to the lesser of 20% of the QBI from the business as limited ($36,000) or 20% of B and C's taxable income ($375,000 x 20% = $75,000). Therefore, B and C's section 199A deduction is $36,000 for 2018.

(vi) *Example 6.*— (A) Assume the same facts as in *Example 5* of paragraph (d)(4)(v) of this section, except that M is engaged in an SSTB. Because B and C are within the phase-in range, B must reduce the QBI and W-2 wages allocable to B from M to the applicable percentage of those items. B and C's applicable percentage is 100% reduced by the percentage equal to the ratio that their taxable income for the taxable year ($375,000) exceeds their threshold amount ($315,000), or $60,000, bears to $100,000. Their applicable percentage is 40%. The applicable percentage of B's QBI is ($300,000 x 40% =) $120,000, and the applicable percentage of B's share of W-2 wages is ($40,000 x 40% =) $16,000. These reduced numbers must then be used to determine how B's section 199A deduction is limited.

(B) B and C must apply the W-2 wage limitation by first determining 20% of B's share of M's QBI as limited by paragraph (d)(4)(vi)(A) of this section. Twenty percent of B's share of M's QBI of $120,000 is $24,000. Next, B and C must determine 50% of B's share of M's W-2 wages. Fifty percent of B's share of M's W-2 wages of $16,000 is $8,000. Because 50% of B's share of M's W-2 wages ($8,000) is less than 20% of B's share of M's QBI ($24,000), B and C's must determine the QBI component of their section 199A deduction by reducing 20% of B's share of M's QBI by the reduction amount.

(C) B and C are 60% through the phase-in range (that is, their taxable income exceeds the threshold amount by $60,000 and their phase-in range is $100,000). B and C must determine the excess amount, which is the excess of 20% of B's share of M's QBI, as adjusted in paragraph (d)(4)(vi)(A) of this section or $24,000, over 50% of B's share of M's W-2 wages, as adjusted in paragraph (d)(4)(vi)(A) of this section, or $8,000. Thus, the excess amount is $16,000. The reduction amount is equal to 60% of the excess amount or $9,600. Thus, the QBI component of B and C's section 199A deduction is equal to $14,400, 20% of B's share M's QBI of $24,000, reduced by $9,600. B and C's section 199A deduction is equal to the lesser of 20% of the QBI from the business as limited ($14,400) or 20% of B's and C's taxable income ($375,000 x 20% = $75,000). Therefore, B and C's section 199A deduction is $14,400 for 2018.

(vii) *Example 7.*—(A) F, an unmarried individual, owns as a sole proprietor 100 percent of three trades or businesses, Business X, Business Y, and Business Z. None of the businesses hold qualified property. F does not aggregate the trades or businesses under §1.199A-4. For taxable year 2018, Business X generates $1 million of QBI and pays $500,000 of W-2 wages with respect to the business. Business Y also generates $1 million of QBI but pays no wages. Business Z generates $2,000 of QBI and pays $500,000 of W-2 wages with respect to the business. F also has $750,000 of wage income from employment with an unrelated company. After allowable deductions unrelated to the businesses, F's taxable income is $2,722,000.

(B) Because F's taxable income is above the threshold amount, the QBI component of F's section 199A deduction is subject to the W-2 wage and UBIA of qualified property limitations. These limitations must be applied on a business-by-business basis. None of the businesses hold qualified property, therefore only the 50% of W-2 wage limitation must be calculated. Because QBI from each business is positive, F applies the limitation by determining the lesser of 20% of QBI and 50% of W-2 wages for each business. For Business X, the lesser of 20% of QBI ($1,000,000 x 20 percent = $200,000) and 50% of Business X's W-2 wages ($500,000 x 50% = $250,000) is $200,000. Business Y pays no W-2 wages. The lesser of 20% of Business Y's QBI

($1,000,000 x 20% = $200,000) and 50% of its W-2 wages (zero) is zero. For Business Z, the lesser of 20% of QBI ($2,000 x 20% = $400) and 50% of W-2 wages ($500,000 x 50% = $250,000) is $400.

(C) Next, F must then combine the amounts determined in paragraph (d)(4)(vii)(B) of this section and compare that sum to 20% of F's taxable income. The lesser of these two amounts equals F's section 199A deduction. The total of the combined amounts in paragraph (d)(4)(vii)(B) of this section is $200,400 ($200,000 + zero + 400). Twenty percent of F's taxable income is $544,400 ($2,722,000 x 20%). Thus, F's section 199A deduction for 2018 is $200,400.

(viii) *Example 8.*—(A) Assume the same facts as in *Example 7* of paragraph (d)(4)(vii) of this section, except that F aggregates Business X, Business Y, and Business Z under the rules of §1.199A-4.

(B) Because F's taxable income is above the threshold amount, the QBI component of F's section 199A deduction is subject to the W-2 wage and UBIA of qualified property limitations. Because the businesses are aggregated, these limitations are applied on an aggregated basis. None of the businesses holds qualified property, therefore only the W-2 wage limitation must be calculated. F applies the limitation by determining the lesser of 20% of the QBI from the aggregated businesses, which is $400,400 ($2,002,000 x 20%) and 50% of W-2 wages from the aggregated businesses, which is $500,000 ($1,000,000 x 50%). F's section 199A deduction is equal to the lesser of $400,400 and 20% of F's taxable income ($2,722,000 x 20% = $544,400). Thus, F's section 199A deduction for 2018 is $400,400.

(ix) *Example 9.*—(A) Assume the same facts as in *Example 7* of paragraph (d)(4)(vii) of this section, except that for taxable year 2018, Business Z generates a loss that results in ($600,000) of negative QBI and pays $500,000 of W-2 wages. After allowable deductions unrelated to the businesses, F's taxable income is $2,120,000. Because Business Z had negative QBI, F must offset the positive QBI from Business X and Business Y with the negative QBI from Business Z in proportion to the relative amounts of positive QBI from Business X and Business Y. Because Business X and Business Y produced the same amount of positive QBI, the negative QBI from Business Z is apportioned equally among Business X and Business Y. Therefore, the adjusted QBI for each of Business X and Business Y is $700,000 ($1 million plus 50% of the negative QBI of $600,000). The adjusted QBI in Business Z is $0, because its negative QBI has been fully apportioned to Business X and Business Y.

(B) Because F's taxable income is above the threshold amount, the QBI component of F's section 199A deduction is subject to the W-2 wage and UBIA of qualified property limitations. These limitations must be applied on a business-by-business basis. None of the businesses hold qualified property, therefore only the 50% of W-2 wage limitation must be calculated. For Business X, the lesser of 20% of QBI ($700,000 x 20% = $140,000) and 50% of W-2 wages ($500,000 x 50% = $250,000) is $140,000. Business Y pays no W-2 wages. The lesser of 20% of Business Y's QBI ($700,000 x 20% = $140,000) and 50% of its W-2 wages (zero) is zero.

(C) F must combine the amounts determined in paragraph (d)(4)(ix)(B) of this section and compare the sum to 20% of taxable income. F's section 199A deduction equals the lesser of these two amounts. The combined amount from paragraph (d)(4)(ix)(B) of this section is $140,000 ($140,000 + zero) and 20% of F's taxable income is $424,000 ($2,120,000 x 20%). Thus, F's section 199A deduction for 2018 is $140,000. There is no carryover of any loss into the following taxable year for purposes of section 199A.

(x) *Example 10.*—(A) Assume the same facts as in *Example 9* of paragraph (d)(4)(ix) of this section, except that F aggregates Business X, Business Y, and Business Z under the rules of §1.199A-4.

(B) Because F's taxable income is above the threshold amount, the QBI component of F's section 199A deduction is subject to the W-2 wage and UBIA of qualified property limitations. Because the businesses are aggregated, these limitations are applied on an aggregated basis. None of the businesses holds qualified property, therefore only the W-2 wage limitation must be calculated. F applies the limitation by determining the lesser of 20% of the QBI from the aggregated businesses ($1,400,000 x 20% = $280,000) and 50% of W-2 wages from the aggregated businesses ($1,000,000 x 50% = $500,000), or $280,000. F's section 199A deduction is equal to the lesser of $280,000 and 20% of F's taxable income ($2,120,000 x 20% = $424,000). Thus, F's section 199A deduction for 2018 is $280,000. There is no carryover of any loss into the following taxable year for purposes of section 199A.

(xi) *Example 11.*—(A) Assume the same facts as in *Example 7* of paragraph (d)(4)(vii) of this section, except that Business Z generates a loss that results in ($2,150,000) of negative QBI and pays $500,000 of W-2 wages with respect to the business in 2018. Thus, F has a negative combined QBI of ($150,000) when the QBI from all of the businesses are added together ($1 million plus $1 million minus the loss of ($2,150,000)). Because F has a negative combined QBI for 2018,

F has no section 199A deduction with respect to any trade or business for 2018. Instead, the negative combined QBI of ($150,000) carries forward and will be treated as negative QBI from a separate trade or business for purposes of computing the section 199A deduction in the next taxable year. None of the W-2 wages carry forward. However, for income tax purposes, the $150,000 loss may offset F's $750,000 of wage income (assuming the loss is otherwise allowable under the Code).

(B) In taxable year 2019, Business X generates $200,000 of net QBI and pays $100,000 of W-2 wages with respect to the business. Business Y generates $150,000 of net QBI but pays no wages. Business Z generates a loss that results in ($120,000) of negative QBI and pays $500 of W-2 wages with respect to the business. F also has $750,000 of wage income from employment with an unrelated company. After allowable deductions unrelated to the businesses, F's taxable income is $960,000. Pursuant to paragraph (d)(2)(iii)(B) of this section, the ($150,000) of negative QBI from 2018 is treated as arising in 2019 from a separate trade or business. Thus, F has overall net QBI of $80,000 when all trades or businesses are taken together ($200,000) plus $150,000 minus $120,000 minus the carryover loss of ($150,000). Because Business Z had negative QBI and F also has a negative QBI carryover amount, F must offset the positive QBI from Business X and Business Y with the negative QBI from Business Z and the carryover amount in proportion to the relative amounts of positive QBI from Business X and Business Y. Because Business X produced 57.14% of the total QBI from Business X and Business Y, 57.14% of the negative QBI from Business Z and the negative QBI carryforward must be apportioned to Business X, and the remaining 42.86% allocated to Business Y. Therefore, the adjusted QBI in Business X is $45,722 ($200,000 minus 57.14% of the loss from Business Z ($68,568), minus 57.14% of the carryover loss ($85,710). The adjusted QBI in Business Y is $34,278 ($150,000, minus 42.86% of the loss from Business Z ($51,432) minus 42.86% of the carryover loss ($64,290)). The adjusted QBI in Business Z is $0, because its negative QBI has been apportioned to Business X and Business Y.

(C) Because F's taxable income is above the threshold amount, the QBI component of F's section 199A deduction is subject to the W-2 wage and UBIA of qualified property limitations. These limitations must be applied on a business-by-business basis. None of the businesses hold qualified property, therefore only the 50% of W-2 wage limitation must be calculated. For Business X, 20% of QBI is $9,144 ($45,722 x 20%) and 50% of W-2 wages is $50,000 ($100,000 x 50%), so the lesser amount is $9,144. Business Y pays no W-2 wages. Twenty percent of Business Y's QBI is $6,856 ($34,278 x 20%) and 50% of its W-2 wages (zero) is zero, so the lesser amount is zero.

(D) F must then compare the combined amounts determined in paragraph (d)(4)(xi)(C) of this section to 20% of F's taxable income. The section 199A deduction equals the lesser of these amounts. F's combined amount from paragraph (d)(4)(xi)(C) of this section is $9,144 ($9,144 plus zero) and 20% of F's taxable income is $192,000 ($960,000 x 20%) Thus, F's section 199A deduction for 2019 is $9,144. There is no carryover of any negative QBI into the following taxable year for purposes of section 199A.

(xii) *Example 12.*—(A) Assume the same facts as in *Example 11* of paragraph (d)(4)(xi) of this section, except that F aggregates Business X, Business Y, and Business Z under the rules of § 1.199A-4. For 2018, F's QBI from the aggregated trade or business is ($150,000). Because F has a combined negative QBI for 2018, F has no section 199A deduction with respect to any trade or business for 2018. Instead, the negative combined QBI of ($150,000) carries forward and will be treated as negative QBI from a separate trade or business for purposes of computing the section 199A deduction in the next taxable year. However, for income tax purposes, the $150,000 loss may offset taxpayer's $750,000 of wage income (assuming the loss is otherwise allowable under the Code).

(B) In taxable year 2019, F will have QBI of $230,000 and W-2 wages of $100,500 from the aggregated trade or business. F also has $750,000 of wage income from employment with an unrelated company. After allowable deductions unrelated to the businesses, F's taxable income is $960,000. F must treat the negative QBI carryover loss ($150,000) from 2018 as a loss from a separate trade or business for purposes of section 199A. This loss will offset the positive QBI from the aggregated trade or business, resulting in an adjusted QBI of $80,000 ($230,000 - $150,000).

(C) Because F's taxable income is above the threshold amount, the QBI component of F's section 199A deduction is subject to the W-2 wage and UBIA of qualified property limitations. These limitations must be applied on a business-by-business basis. None of the businesses hold qualified property, therefore only the 50% of W-2 wage limitation must be calculated. For the aggregated trade or business, the lesser of 20% of QBI ($80,000 x 20% = $16,000) and 50% of W-2 wages ($100,500 x 50% = $50,250) is $16,000. F's section 199A deduction equals the lesser of that amount ($16,000) and 20% of F's taxable income ($960,000 x 20% = $192,000). Thus, F's section 199A

deduction for 2019 is $16,000. There is no carryover of any negative QBI into the following taxable year for purposes of section 199A.

(e) *Special rules.*—(1) *Effect of deduction.*—In the case of a partnership or S corporation, section 199A is applied at the partner or shareholder level. The rules of subchapter K and subchapter S of the Code apply in their entirety for purposes of determining each partner's or shareholder's share of QBI, W-2 wages, UBIA of qualified property, qualified REIT dividends, and qualified PTP income or loss. The section 199A deduction has no effect on the adjusted basis of a partner's interest in the partnership, the adjusted basis of a shareholder's stock in an S corporation, or an S corporation's accumulated adjustments account.

(2) *Disregarded entities.*—An entity with a single owner that is treated as disregarded as an entity separate from its owner under any provision of the Code is disregarded for purposes of section 199A and §§ 1.199A-1 through 1.199A-6.

(3) *Self-employment tax and net investment income tax.*—The deduction allowed under section 199A does not reduce net earnings from self-employment under section 1402 or net investment income under section 1411.

(4) *Commonwealth of Puerto Rico.*—If all of an individual's QBI from sources within the Commonwealth of Puerto Rico is taxable under section 1 of the Code for a taxable year, then for purposes of determining the QBI of such individual for such taxable year, the term "United States" includes the Commonwealth of Puerto Rico.

(5) *Coordination with alternative minimum tax.*—For purposes of determining alternative minimum taxable income under section 55, the deduction allowed under section 199A(a) for a taxable year is equal in amount to the deduction allowed under section 199A(a) in determining taxable income for that taxable year (that is, without regard to any adjustments under sections 56 through 59).

(6) *Imposition of accuracy-related penalty on underpayments.*—For rules related to the imposition of the accuracy-related penalty on underpayments for taxpayers who claim the deduction allowed under section 199A, see section 6662(d)(1)(C).

(7) *Reduction for income received from cooperatives.*—In the case of any trade or business of a patron of a *specified agricultural or horticultural cooperative*, as defined in section 199A(g)(4), the amount of section 199A deduction determined under paragraph (c) or (d) of this section with respect to such trade or business must be reduced by the lesser of:

(i) Nine percent of the QBI with respect to such trade or business as is properly allocable to qualified payments received from such cooperative; or

(ii) 50 percent of the W-2 wages with respect to such trade or business as are so allocable as determined under § 1.199A-2.

(f) *Applicability date.*—(1) *General rule.*—Except as provided in paragraph (f)(2) of this section, the provisions of this section apply to taxable years ending after February 8, 2019.

(2) *Exception for non-calendar year RPE.*—For purposes of determining QBI, W-2 wages, UBIA of qualified property, and the aggregate amount of qualified REIT dividends and qualified PTP income, if an individual receives any of these items from an RPE with a taxable year that begins before January 1, 2018, and ends after December 31, 2017, such items are treated as having been incurred by the individual during the individual's taxable year in which or with which such RPE taxable year ends. [Reg. § 1.199A-1.]

☐ [T.D. 9847, 2-4-2019 (corrected 4-17-2019).]

[Reg. § 1.199A-2]

§ 1.199A-2. Determination of W-2 wages and unadjusted basis immediately after acquisition of qualified property.—(a) *Scope.*—(1) *In general.*—This section provides guidance on calculating a trade or business's W-2 wages properly allocable to QBI (W-2 wages) and the trade or business's unadjusted basis immediately after acquisition of all qualified property (UBIA of qualified property). The provisions of this section apply solely for purposes of section 199A of the Internal Revenue Code (Code).

(2) *W-2 wages.*—Paragraph (b) of this section provides guidance on the determination of W-2 wages. The determination of W-2 wages must be made for each trade or business by the individual or RPE that directly conducts the trade or business (or aggregated trade or business). In the case of W-2 wages paid by an RPE, the RPE must determine and report W-2 wages for each trade or business (or aggregated trade or business) conducted by the RPE. W-2 wages are presumed to be zero if not determined and reported for each trade or business (or aggregated trade or business).

(3) *UBIA of qualified property.*—(i) *In general.*—Paragraph (c) of this section provides guidance on the determination of the UBIA of qualified property. The determination of the UBIA of qualified property must be made for each trade or business (or aggregated trade or business) by the individual or RPE that directly conducts the trade or business (or aggregated trade or business). The UBIA of qualified property is presumed to be zero if not determined and reported for each trade or business (or aggregated trade or business).

(ii) *UBIA of qualified property held by a partnership.*—In the case of qualified property held by a partnership, each partner's share of the UBIA of qualified property is determined in accordance with how the partnership would allocate depreciation under § 1.704-1(b)(2)(iv)(*g*) on the last day of the taxable year.

(iii) *UBIA of qualified property held by an S corporation.*—In the case of qualified property held by an S corporation, each shareholder's share of the UBIA of qualified property is the share of the unadjusted basis proportionate to the ratio of shares in the S corporation held by the shareholder on the last day of the taxable year over the total issued and outstanding shares of the S corporation.

(iv) *UBIA and section 743(b) basis adjustments.*—(A) *In general.*—A partner will be allowed to take into account UBIA with respect to an item of qualified property in addition to the amount of UBIA with respect to such qualified property determined under paragraphs (a)(3)(i) and (c) of this section and allocated to such partner under paragraph (a)(3)(ii) of this section to the extent of the partner's excess section 743(b) basis adjustment with respect to such item of qualified property.

(B) *Excess section 743(b) basis adjustments.*—A partner's *excess section 743(b) basis adjustment* is an amount that is determined with respect to each item of qualified property and is equal to an amount that would represent the partner's section 743(b) basis adjustment with respect to the same item of qualified property, as determined under § § 1.743-1(b) and 1.755-1, but calculated as if the adjusted basis of all of the partnership's property was equal to the UBIA of such property. The absolute value of the excess section 743(b) basis adjustment cannot exceed the absolute value of the total section 743(b) basis adjustment with respect to qualified property.

(C) *Computation of partner's share of UBIA with excess section 743(b) basis adjustments.*—The partnership first computes its UBIA with respect to qualified property under paragraphs (a)(3)(i) and (c) of this section and allocates such UBIA under paragraph (a)(3)(ii) of this section. If the sum of the excess section 743(b) basis adjustment for all of the items of qualified property is a negative number, that amount will be subtracted from the partner's UBIA of qualified property determined under paragraphs (a)(3)(i) and (c) of this section and allocated under paragraph (a)(3)(ii) of this section. A partner's UBIA of qualified property may not be below $0. Excess section 743(b) basis adjustments are computed with respect to all section 743(b) adjustments, including adjustments made as a result of a substantial built-in loss under section 743(d).

(D) *Examples.*—The provisions of this paragraph (a)(3)(iv) are illustrated by the following examples:

(1) *Example 1*—(i) *Facts.* A, B, and C are equal partners in partnership, PRS. PRS has a single trade or business that generates QBI. PRS has no liabilities and only one asset, a single item of qualified property with a UBIA equal to $900,000. Each partner's share of the UBIA is $300,000. A sells its one-third interest in PRS to T for $350,000 when a section 754 election is in effect. At the time of the sale, the tax basis of the qualified property held by PRS is $750,000. The amount of gain that would be allocated to T from a hypothetical transaction under § 1.743-1(d)(2) is $100,000. Thus, T's interest in PRS's previously taxed capital is equal to $250,000 ($350,000, the amount of cash T would receive if PRS liquidated immediately after the hypothetical transaction, decreased by $100,000, T's share of gain from the hypothetical transaction). The amount of T's section 743(b) basis adjustment to PRS's qualified property is $100,000 (the excess of $350,000, T's cost basis for its interest, over $250,000, T's share of the adjusted basis to PRS of the partnership's property).

(iii) *Analysis.* In order for T to determine its UBIA, T must calculate its excess section 743(b) basis adjustment. T's excess section 743(b) basis adjustment is equal to an amount that would represent T's section 743(b) basis adjustment with respect to the same item of qualified property, as determined under § § 1.743-1(b) and 1.755-1, but calculated as if the adjusted basis of all of PRS's property was equal to the UBIA of such property. T's section 743(b) basis adjustment calculated as if adjusted basis of the qualified property were equal to its UBIA is $50,000 (the excess of $350,000, T's cost basis for its interest, over $300,000, T's share of the adjusted basis to PRS of the partnership's property). Thus, T's excess section 743(b) basis adjustment is equal to $50,000. For purposes of applying the UBIA limitation to T's share of QBI from PRS's trade or business, T's UBIA is

equal to $350,000 ($300,000, T's one-third share of the qualified property's UBIA, plus $50,000, T's excess section 743(b) basis adjustment).

(2) *Example 2*—(i) *Facts.* Assume the same facts as in *Example 1* of paragraph (a)(3)(iv)(D)(*1*) of this section, except that A sells its one-third interest in PRS to T for $200,000 when a section 754 election is in effect. At the time of the sale, the tax basis of the qualified property held by PRS is $750,000, and the amount of loss that would be allocated to T from a hypothetical transaction under § 1.743-1(d)(2) is $50,000. Thus, T's interest in PRS's previously taxed capital is equal to $250,000 ($200,000, the amount of cash T would receive if PRS liquidated immediately after the hypothetical transaction, increased by $50,000, T's share of loss from the hypothetical transaction). The amount of T's section 743(b) basis adjustment to PRS's qualified property is negative $50,000 (the excess of $250,000, T's share of the adjusted basis to PRS of the partnership's property, over $200,000, T's cost basis for its interest).

(ii) *Analysis.* In order for T to determine its UBIA, T must calculate its excess section 743(b) basis adjustment. T's excess section 743(b) basis adjustment is equal to an amount that would represent T's section 743(b) basis adjustment with respect to the same item of qualified property, as determined under § § 1.743-1(b) and 1.755-1, but calculated as if the adjusted basis of all of PRS's property was equal to the UBIA of such property. T's section 743(b) basis adjustment calculated as if adjusted basis of the qualified property were equal to its UBIA is negative $100,000 (the excess of $300,000, T's share of the adjusted basis to PRS of the partnership's property, over $200,000, T's cost basis for its interest). T's excess section 743(b) basis adjustment to the qualified property is limited to the amount of T's section 743(b) basis adjustment of negative $50,000. Thus, T's excess section 743(b) basis adjustment is equal to negative $50,000. For purposes of applying the UBIA limitation to T's share of QBI from PRS's trade or business, T's UBIA is equal to $250,000 ($300,000, T's one-third share of the qualified property's UBIA, reduced by T's negative $50,000 excess section 743(b) basis adjustment).

(b) *W-2 wages.*—(1) *In general.*—Section 199A(b)(2)(B) provides limitations on the section 199A deduction based on the W-2 wages paid with respect to each trade or business (or aggregated trade or business). Section 199A(b)(4)(B) provides that W-2 wages do not include any amount which is not properly allocable to QBI for purposes of section 199A(c)(1). This section provides a three step process for determining the W-2 wages paid with respect to a trade or business that are properly allocable to QBI. First, each individual or RPE must determine its total W-2 wages paid for the taxable year under the rules in paragraph (b)(2) of this section. Second, each individual or RPE must allocate its W-2 wages between or among one or more trades or businesses under the rules in paragraph (b)(3) of this section. Third, each individual or RPE must determine the amount of such wages with respect to each trade or business, which are allocable to the QBI of the trade or business (or aggregated trade or business) under the rules in paragraph (b)(4) of this section.

(2) *Definition of W-2 wages.*—(i) *In general.*—Section 199A(b)(4)(A) provides that the term W-2 wages means with respect to any person for any taxable year of such person, the amounts described in section 6051(a)(3) and (8) paid by such person with respect to employment of employees by such person during the calendar year ending during such taxable year. Thus, the term W-2 wages includes the total amount of wages as defined in section 3401(a) plus the total amount of elective deferrals (within the meaning of section 402(g)(3)), the compensation deferred under section 457, and the amount of designated Roth contributions (as defined in section 402A). For this purpose, except as provided in paragraphs (b)(2)(iv)(C)(*2*) and (b)(2)(iv)(D) of this section, the Forms W-2, "Wage and Tax Statement," or any subsequent form or document used in determining the amount of W-2 wages, are those issued for the calendar year ending during the individual's or RPE's taxable year for wages paid to employees (or former employees) of the individual or RPE for employment by the individual or RPE. For purposes of this section, employees of the individual or RPE are limited to employees of the individual or RPE as defined in section 3121(d)(1) and (2). (For purposes of section 199A, this includes officers of an S corporation and employees of an individual or RPE under common law.)

(ii) *Wages paid by a person other than a common law employer.*—In determining W-2 wages, an individual or RPE may take into account any W-2 wages paid by another person and reported by the other person on Forms W-2 with the other person as the employer listed in Box c of the Forms W-2, provided that the W-2 wages were paid to common law employees or officers of the individual or RPE for employment by the individual or RPE. In such cases, the person paying the W-2 wages and reporting the W-2 wages on Forms W-2 is precluded from taking into account such wages for purposes of determining W-2 wages with respect to that person. For purposes of this paragraph (b)(2)(ii), persons that pay and report W-2 wages on behalf of or with respect to others can include, but are not limited to, certified professional employer organizations under section 7705, statutory employers under section 3401(d)(1), and agents under section 3504.

(iii) *Requirement that wages must be reported on return filed with the Social Security Administration (SSA).*—(A) *In general.*—Pursuant to section 199A(b)(4)(C), the term W-2 wages does not include any amount that is not properly included in a return filed with SSA on or before the 60th day after the due date (including extensions) for such return. Under § 31.6051-2 of this chapter, each Form W-2 and the transmittal Form W-3, "Transmittal of Wage and Tax Statements," together constitute an information return to be filed with SSA. Similarly, each Form W-2c, "Corrected Wage and Tax Statement," and the transmittal Form W-3 or W-3c, "Transmittal of Corrected Wage and Tax Statements," together constitute an information return to be filed with SSA. In determining whether any amount has been properly included in a return filed with SSA on or before the 60th day after the due date (including extensions) for such return, each Form W-2 together with its accompanying Form W-3 will be considered a separate information return and each Form W-2c together with its accompanying Form W-3 or Form W-3c will be considered a separate information return. Section 6071(c) provides that Forms W-2 and W-3 must be filed on or before January 31 of the year following the calendar year to which such returns relate (but see the special rule in § 31.6071(a)-1T(a)(3)(i) of this chapter for monthly returns filed under § 31.6011(a)-5(a) of this chapter). Corrected Forms W-2 are required to be filed with SSA on or before January 31 of the year following the year in which the correction is made.

(B) *Corrected return filed to correct a return that was filed within 60 days of the due date.*—If a corrected information return (Return B) is filed with SSA on or before the 60th day after the due date (including extensions) of Return B to correct an information return (Return A) that was filed with SSA on or before the 60th day after the due date (including extensions) of the information return (Return A) and paragraph (b)(2)(iii)(C) of this section does not apply, then the wage information on Return B must be included in determining W-2 wages. If a corrected information return (Return D) is filed with SSA later than the 60th day after the due date (including extensions) of Return D to correct an information return (Return C) that was filed with SSA on or before the 60th day after the due date (including extensions) of the information return (Return C), and if Return D reports an increase (or increases) in wages included in determining W-2 wages from the wage amounts reported on Return C, then such increase (or increases) on Return D will be disregarded in determining W-2 wages (and only the wage amounts on Return C may be included in determining W-2 wages). If Return D reports a decrease (or decreases) in wages included in determining W-2 wages from the amounts reported on Return C, then, in determining W-2 wages, the wages reported on Return C must be reduced by the decrease (or decreases) reflected on Return D.

(C) *Corrected return filed to correct a return that was filed later than 60 days after the due date.*—If an information return (Return F) is filed to correct an information return (Return E) that was not filed with SSA on or before the 60th day after the due date (including extensions) of Return E, then Return F (and any subsequent information returns filed with respect to Return E) will not be considered filed on or before the 60th day after the due date (including extensions) of Return F (or the subsequent corrected information return). Thus, if a Form W-2c is filed to correct a Form W-2 that was not filed with SSA on or before the 60th day after the due date (including extensions) of the Form W-2 (or to correct a Form W-2c relating to Form W-2 that had not been filed with SSA on or before the 60th day after the due date (including extensions) of the Form W-2), then this Form W-2c will not be considered to have been filed with SSA on or before the 60th day after the due date (including extensions) for this Form W-2c (or corrected Form W-2), regardless of when the Form W-2c is filed.

(iv) *Methods for calculating W-2 wages.*—(A) *In general.*—The Secretary may provide for methods to be used in calculating W-2 wages, including W-2 wages for short taxable years by publication in the Internal Revenue Bulletin (see § 601.601(d)(2)(ii)(b) of this chapter).

(B) *Acquisition or disposition of a trade or business.*—(1) *In general.*—In the case of an acquisition or disposition of a trade or business, the major portion of a trade or business, or the major portion of a separate unit of a trade or business that causes more than one individual or entity to be an employer of the employees of the acquired or disposed of trade or business during the calendar year, the W-2 wages of the individual or entity for the calendar year of the acquisition or disposition are allocated between each individual or entity based on the period during which the employees of the ac-

quired or disposed of trade or business were employed by the individual or entity, regardless of which permissible method is used for reporting predecessor and successor wages on Form W-2, "Wage and Tax Statement." For this purpose, the period of employment is determined consistently with the principles for determining whether an individual is an employee described in paragraph (b) of this section.

(2) *Acquisition or disposition.*—For purposes of this paragraph (b)(2)(iv)(B), the term *acquisition or disposition* includes an incorporation, a formation, a liquidation, a reorganization, or a purchase or sale of assets.

(C) *Application in the case of a person with a short taxable year.*—(1) *In general.*—In the case of an individual or RPE with a short taxable year, subject to the rules of paragraph (b)(2) of this section, the W-2 wages of the individual or RPE for the short taxable year include only those wages paid during the short taxable year to employees of the individuals or RPE, only those elective deferrals (within the meaning of section 402(g)(3)) made during the short taxable year by employees of the individual or RPE and only compensation actually deferred under section 457 during the short taxable year with respect to employees of the individual or RPE.

(2) *Short taxable year that does not include December 31.*—If an individual or RPE has a short taxable year that does not contain a calendar year ending during such short taxable year, wages paid to employees for employment by such individual or RPE during the short taxable year are treated as W-2 wages for such short taxable year for purposes of paragraph (b) of this section (if the wages would otherwise meet the requirements to be W-2 wages under this section but for the requirement that a calendar year must end during the short taxable year).

(D) *Remuneration paid for services performed in the Commonwealth of Puerto Rico.*—In the case of an individual or RPE that conducts a trade or business in the Commonwealth of Puerto Rico, the determination of W-2 wages of such individual or RPE will be made without regard to any exclusion under section 3401(a)(8) for remuneration paid for services performed in the Commonwealth of Puerto Rico. The individual or RPE must maintain sufficient documentation (for example, Forms 499R-2/W-2PR) to substantiate the amount of remuneration paid for services performed in the Commonwealth of Puerto Rico that is used in determining the W-2 wages of such individual or RPE with respect to any trade or business conducted in the Commonwealth of Puerto Rico.

(3) *Allocation of wages to trades or businesses.*—After calculating total W-2 wages for a taxable year, each individual or RPE that directly conducts more than one trade or business must allocate those wages among its various trades or businesses. W-2 wages must be allocated to the trade or business that generated those wages. In the case of W-2 wages that are allocable to more than one trade or business, the portion of the W-2 wages allocable to each trade or business is determined in the same manner as the expenses associated with those wages are allocated among the trades or businesses under § 1.199A-3(b)(5).

(4) *Allocation of wages to QBI.*—Once W-2 wages for each trade or business have been determined, each individual or RPE must identify the amount of W-2 wages properly allocable to QBI for each trade or business (or aggregated trade or business). W-2 wages are properly allocable to QBI if the associated wage expense is taken into account in computing QBI under § 1.199A-3. In the case of an RPE, the wage expense must be allocated and reported to the partners or shareholders of the RPE as required by the Code, including subchapters K and S of chapter 1 of subtitle A of the Code. The RPE must also identify and report the associated W-2 wages to its partners or shareholders.

(5) *Non-duplication rule.*—Amounts that are treated as W-2 wages for a taxable year under any method cannot be treated as W-2 wages of any other taxable year. Also, an amount cannot be treated as W-2 wages by more than one trade or business (or aggregated trade or business).

(c) *UBIA of qualified property.*—(1) *Qualified property.*—(i) *In general.*—The term *qualified property* means, with respect to any trade or business (or aggregated trade or business) of an individual or RPE for a taxable year, tangible property of a character subject to the allowance for depreciation under section 167(a)—

(A) Which is held by, and available for use in, the trade or business (or aggregated trade or business) at the close of the taxable year;

(B) Which is used at any point during the taxable year in the trade or business's (or aggregated trade or business's) production of QBI; and

(C) The depreciable period for which has not ended before the close of the individual's or RPE's taxable year.

(ii) *Improvements to qualified property.*—In the case of any addition to, or improvement of, qualified property that has already been placed in service by the individual or RPE, such addition or improvement is treated as separate qualified property first placed in service on the date such addition or improvement is placed in service for purposes of paragraph (c)(2) of this section.

(iii) *Adjustments under sections 734(b) and 743(b).*—Excess section 743(b) basis adjustments as defined in paragraph (a)(3)(iv)(B) of this section are treated as qualified property. Otherwise, basis adjustments under sections 734(b) and 743(b) are not treated as qualified property.

(iv) *Property acquired at end of year.*—Property is not qualified property if the property is acquired within 60 days of the end of the taxable year and disposed of within 120 days of acquisition without having been used in a trade or business for at least 45 days prior to disposition, unless the taxpayer demonstrates that the principal purpose of the acquisition and disposition was a purpose other than increasing the section 199A deduction.

(2) *Depreciable period.*—(i) *In general.*—The term *depreciable period* means, with respect to qualified property of a trade or business, the period beginning on the date the property was first placed in service by the individual or RPE and ending on the later of—

(A) The date that is 10 years after such date; or

(B) The last day of the last full year in the applicable recovery period that would apply to the property under section 168(c), regardless of any application of section 168(g).

(ii) *Additional first-year depreciation under section 168.*—The additional first-year depreciation deduction allowable under section 168 (for example, under section 168(k) or (m)) does not affect the applicable recovery period under this paragraph for the qualified property.

(iii) *Qualified property acquired in transactions subject to section 1031 or section 1033.*—Solely for purposes of paragraph (c)(2)(i) of this section, the following rules apply to qualified property acquired in a like-kind exchange or in an involuntary conversion (replacement property).

(A) *Replacement property received in a section 1031 or 1033 transaction.*—The date on which replacement property that is of like-kind to relinquished property or is similar or related in service or use to involuntarily converted property was first placed in service by the individual or RPE is determined as follows—

(1) For the portion of the individual's or RPE's UBIA, as defined in paragraph (c)(3) of this section, in such replacement property that does not exceed the individual's or RPE's UBIA in the relinquished property or involuntarily converted property, the date such portion in the replacement property was first placed in service by the individual or RPE is the date on which the relinquished property or involuntarily converted property was first placed in service by the individual or RPE; and

(2) For the portion of the individual's or RPE's UBIA, as defined in paragraph (c)(3) of this section, in such replacement property that exceeds the individual's or RPE's UBIA in the relinquished property or involuntarily converted property, such portion in the replacement property is treated as separate qualified property that the individual or RPE first placed in service on the date on which the replacement property was first placed in service by the individual or RPE.

(B) *Other property received in a section 1031 or 1033 transaction.*—Other property, as defined in paragraph (c)(3)(ii) or (iii) of this section, that is qualified property is treated as separate qualified property that the individual or RPE first placed in service on the date on which such other property was first placed in service by the individual or RPE.

(iv) *Qualified property acquired in transactions described in section 168(i)(7)(B).*—If an individual or RPE acquires qualified property in a transaction described in section 168(i)(7)(B) (pertaining to treatment of transferees in certain nonrecognition transactions), the individual or RPE must determine the date on which the qualified property was first placed in service solely for purposes of paragraph (c)(2)(i) of this section as follows—

(A) For the portion of the transferee's UBIA in the qualified property that does not exceed the transferor's UBIA in such property, the date such portion was first placed in service by the transferee is the date on which the transferor first placed the qualified property in service; and

(B) For the portion of the transferee's UBIA in the qualified property that exceeds the transferor's UBIA in such property, such portion is treated as separate qualified property that the transferee first placed in service on the date of the transfer.

(v) *Excess section 743(b) basis adjustment.*—Solely for purposes of paragraph (c)(2)(i) of this section, an excess section 743(b) basis adjustment with respect to an item of partnership property that is qualified property is treated as being placed in service when the transfer of the partnership interest occurs, and the recovery period for such property is determined under §1.743-1(j)(4)(i)(B) with respect to positive basis adjustments and §1.743-1(j)(4)(ii)(B) with respect to negative basis adjustments.

(3) *Unadjusted basis immediately after acquisition.*—(i) *In general.*—Except as provided in paragraphs (c)(3)(ii) through (v) of this section, the term *unadjusted basis immediately after acquisition* (UBIA) means the basis on the placed in service date of the property as determined under section 1012 or other applicable sections of chapter 1 of the Code, including the provisions of subchapters O (relating to gain or loss on dispositions of property), C (relating to corporate distributions and adjustments), K (relating to partners and partnerships), and P (relating to capital gains and losses). UBIA is determined without regard to any adjustments described in section 1016(a)(2) or (3), to any adjustments for tax credits claimed by the individual or RPE (for example, under section 50(c)), or to any adjustments for any portion of the basis which the individual or RPE has elected to treat as an expense (for example, under sections 179, 179B, or 179C). However, UBIA does reflect the reduction in basis for the percentage of the individual's or RPE's use of property for the taxable year other than in the trade or business.

(ii) *Qualified property acquired in a like-kind exchange.*—(A) *In general.*—Solely for purposes of this section, if property that is qualified property (replacement property) is acquired in a like-kind exchange that qualifies for deferral of gain or loss under section 1031, then the UBIA of such property is the same as the UBIA of the qualified property exchanged (relinquished property), decreased by excess boot or increased by the amount of money paid or the fair market value of property not of a like kind to the relinquished property (other property) transferred by the taxpayer to acquire the replacement property. If the taxpayer acquires more than one piece of qualified property as replacement property that is of a like kind to the relinquished property in an exchange described in section 1031, UBIA is apportioned between or among the qualified replacement properties in proportion to their relative fair market values. Other property received by the taxpayer in a section 1031 transaction that is qualified property has a UBIA equal to the fair market value of such other property.

(B) *Excess boot.*—For purposes of paragraph (c)(3)(ii)(A) of this section, *excess boot* is the amount of any money or the fair market value of other property received by the taxpayer in the exchange over the amount of appreciation in the relinquished property. Appreciation for this purpose is the excess of the fair market value of the relinquished property on the date of the exchange over the fair market value of the relinquished property on the date of the acquisition by the taxpayer.

(iii) *Qualified property acquired pursuant to an involuntary conversion.*—(A) *In general.*—Solely for purposes of this section, if qualified property is compulsorily or involuntarily converted (converted property) within the meaning of section 1033 and qualified replacement property is acquired in a transaction that qualifies for deferral of gain under section 1033, then the UBIA of the replacement property is the same as the UBIA of the converted property, decreased by excess boot or increased by the amount of money paid or the fair market value of property not similar or related in service or use to the converted property (other property) transferred by the taxpayer to acquire the replacement property. If the taxpayer acquires more than one piece of qualified replacement property that meets the similar or related in service or use requirements in section 1033, UBIA is apportioned between the qualified replacement properties in proportion to their relative fair market values. Other property acquired by the taxpayer with the proceeds of an involuntary conversion that is qualified property has a UBIA equal to the fair market value of such other property.

(B) *Excess boot.*—For purposes of paragraph (c)(3)(iii)(A) of this section, *excess boot* is the amount of any money or the fair market value of other property received by the taxpayer in the conversion over the amount of appreciation in the converted property. Appreciation for this purpose is the excess of the fair market value of the converted property on the date of the conversion over the fair market value of the converted property on the date of the acquisition by the taxpayer.

(iv) *Qualified property acquired in transactions described in section 168(i)(7)(B).*—Solely for purposes of this section, if qualified property is acquired in a transaction described in section 168(i)(7)(B) (pertaining to treatment of transferees in certain nonrecognition transactions), the transferee's UBIA in the qualified property shall be the same as the transferor's UBIA in the property, decreased by the amount of money received by the transferor in the transaction or increased by the amount of money paid by the transferee to acquire the property in the transaction.

(v) *Qualified property acquired from a decedent.*—In the case of qualified property acquired from a decedent and immediately placed in service, the UBIA of the property will generally be the fair market value at the date of the decedent's death under section 1014. See section 1014 and the regulations thereunder. Solely for purposes of paragraph (c)(2)(i) of this section, a new depreciable period for the property commences as of the date of the decedent's death.

(vi) *Property acquired in a nonrecognition transaction with principal purpose of increasing UBIA.*—If qualified property is acquired in a transaction described in section 1031, 1033, or 168(i)(7) with the principal purpose of increasing the UBIA of the qualified property, the UBIA of the acquired qualified property is its basis as determined under relevant Code sections and not under the rules described in paragraphs (c)(3)(i) through (iv) of this section. For example, in a section 1031 transaction undertaken with the principal purpose of increasing the UBIA of the replacement property, the UBIA of the replacement property is its basis as determined under section 1031(d).

(4) *Examples.*—The provisions of this paragraph (c) are illustrated by the following examples:

(i) *Example 1.* (A) On January 5, 2012, A purchases Real Property X for $1 million and places it in service in A's trade or business. A's trade or business is not an SSTB. A's basis in Real Property X under section 1012 is $1 million. Real Property X is qualified property within the meaning of section 199A(b)(6). As of December 31, 2018, A's basis in Real Property X, as adjusted under section 1016(a)(2) for depreciation deductions under section 168(a), is $821,550.

(B) For purposes of section 199A(b)(2)(B)(ii) and this section, A's UBIA of Real Property X is its $1 million cost basis under section 1012, regardless of any later depreciation deductions under section 168(a) and resulting basis adjustments under section 1016(a)(2).

(ii) *Example 2.* (A) The facts are the same as in *Example 1* of paragraph (c)(4)(i) of this section, except that on January 15, 2019, A enters into a like-kind exchange under section 1031 in which A exchanges Real Property X for Real Property Y. Real Property Y has a value of $1 million. No cash or other property is involved in the exchange. As of January 15, 2019, A's basis in Real Property X, as adjusted under section 1016(a)(2) for depreciation deductions under section 168(a), is $820,482.

(B) A's UBIA in Real Property Y is $1 million as determined under paragraph (c)(3)(ii) of this section. Pursuant to paragraph (c)(2)(iii)(A) of this section, Real Property Y is first placed in service by A on January 5, 2012, which is the date on which Real Property X was first placed in service by A.

(iii) *Example 3.* (A) The facts are the same as in *Example 1* of paragraph (c)(4)(i) of this section, except that on January 15, 2019, A enters into a like-kind exchange under section 1031, in which A exchanges Real Property X for Real Property Y. Real Property X has appreciated in value to $1.3 million, and Real Property Y also has a value of $1.3 million. No cash or other property is involved in the exchange. As of January 15, 2019, A's basis in Real Property X, as adjusted under section 1016(a)(2), is $820,482.

(B) A's UBIA in Real Property Y is $1 million as determined under paragraph (c)(3)(ii) of this section. Pursuant to paragraph (c)(2)(iii)(A) of this section, Real Property Y is first placed in service by A on January 5, 2012, which is the date on which Real Property X was first placed in service by A.

(iv) *Example 4.* (A) The facts are the same as in *Example 1* of paragraph (c)(4)(i) of this section, except that on January 15, 2019, A enters into a like-kind exchange under section 1031, in which A exchanges Real Property X for Real Property Y. Real Property X has appreciated in value to $1.3 million, but Real Property Y has a value of $1.5 million. A therefore adds $200,000 in cash to the exchange of Real Property X for Real Property Y. On January 15, 2019, A places Real Property Y in service. As of January 15, 2019, A's basis in Real Property X, as adjusted under section 1016(a)(2), is $820,482.

(B) A's UBIA in Real Property Y is $1.2 million as determined under paragraph (c)(3)(ii) of this section ($1 million in UBIA from Real Property X plus $200,000 cash paid by A to acquire Real Property Y). Because the UBIA of Real Property Y exceeds the UBIA of Real Property X, Real Property Y is treated as being two separate qualified properties for purposes of applying paragraph (c)(2)(iii)(A) of this section. One property has a UBIA of $1 million (the portion of A's UBIA of $1.2 million in Real Property Y that does not exceed A's UBIA of $1 million in Real Property X) and it is first placed in service

by A on January 5, 2012, which is the date on which Real Property X was first placed in service by A. The other property has a UBIA of $200,000 (the portion of A's UBIA of $1.2 million in Real Property Y that exceeds A's UBIA of $1 million in Real Property X) and it is first placed in service by A on January 15, 2019, which is the date on which Real Property Y was first placed in service by A.

(v) *Example 5.* (A) The facts are the same as in *Example 1* of paragraph (c)(4)(i) of this section, except that on January 15, 2019, A enters into a like-kind exchange under section 1031, in which A exchanges Real Property X for Real Property Y. Real Property X has appreciated in value to $1.3 million. Real Property Y has a fair market value of $1 million. As of January 15, 2019, A's basis in Real Property X, as adjusted under section 1016(a)(2), is $820,482. Pursuant to the exchange, A receives Real Property Y and $300,000 in cash.

(B) A's UBIA in Real Property Y is $1 million as determined under paragraph (c)(3)(ii) of this section ($1 million in UBIA from Real Property X, less $0 excess boot ($300,000 cash received in the exchange over $300,000 in appreciation in Property X, which is equal to the excess of the $1.3 million fair market value of Property X on the date of the exchange over $1 million fair market value of Property X on the date of acquisition by the taxpayer)). Pursuant to paragraph (c)(2)(iii)(A) of this section, Real Property Y is first placed in service by A on January 5, 2012, which is the date on which Real Property X was first placed in service by A.

(vi) *Example 6.* (A) The facts are the same as in *Example 1* of paragraph (c)(4)(i) of this section, except that on January 15, 2019, A enters into a like-kind exchange under section 1031, in which A exchanges Real Property X for Real Property Y. Real Property X has appreciated in value to $1.3 million. Real Property Y has a fair market value of $900,000. Pursuant to the exchange, A receives Real Property Y and $400,000 in cash. As of January 15, 2019, A's basis in Real Property X, as adjusted under section 1016(a)(2), is $820,482.

(B) A's UBIA in Real Property Y is $900,000 as determined under paragraph (c)(3)(ii) of this section ($1 million in UBIA from Real Property X less $100,000 excess boot ($400,000 in cash received in the exchange over $300,000 in appreciation in Property X, which is equal to the excess of the $1.3 million fair market value of Property X on the date of the exchange over the $1 million fair market value of Property X on the date of acquisition by the taxpayer)). Pursuant to paragraph (c)(2)(iii)(A) of this section, Real Property Y is first placed in service by A on January 5, 2012, which is the date on which Real Property X was first placed in service by A.

(vii) *Example 7.* (A) The facts are the same as in *Example 1* of paragraph (c)(4)(i) of this section, except that on January 15, 2019, A enters into a like-kind exchange under section 1031, in which A exchanges Real Property X for Real Property Y. Real Property X has declined in value to $900,000, and Real Property Y also has a value of $900,000. No cash or other property is involved in the exchange. As of January 15, 2019, A's basis in Real Property X, as adjusted under section 1016(a)(2), is $820,482.

(B) Even though Real Property Y is worth only $900,000, A's UBIA in Real Property Y is $1 million as determined under paragraph (c)(3)(ii) of this section because no cash or other property was involved in the exchange. Pursuant to paragraph (c)(2)(iii)(A) of this section, Real Property Y is first placed in service by A on January 5, 2012, which is the date on which Real Property X was first placed in service by A.

(viii) *Example 8.* (A) C operates a trade or business that is not an SSTB as a sole proprietorship. On January 5, 2011, C purchases Machinery Y for $10,000 and places it in service in C's trade or business. C's basis in Machinery Y under section 1012 is $10,000. Machinery Y is qualified property within the meaning of section 199A(b)(6). Assume that Machinery Y's recovery period under section 168(c) is 10 years, and C depreciates Machinery Y under the general depreciation system by using the straight-line depreciation method, a 10-year recovery period, and the half-year convention. As of December 31, 2018, C's basis in Machinery Y, as adjusted under section 1016(a)(2) for depreciation deductions under section 168(a), is $2,500. On January 1, 2019, C incorporates the sole proprietorship and elects to treat the newly formed entity as an S corporation for Federal income tax purposes. C contributes Machinery Y and all other assets of the trade or business to the S corporation in a nonrecognition transaction under section 351. The S corporation immediately places all the assets in service.

(B) For purposes of section 199A(b)(2)(B)(ii) and this section, C's UBIA of Machinery Y from 2011 through 2018 is its $10,000 cost basis under section 1012, regardless of any later depreciation deductions under section 168(a) and resulting basis adjustments under section 1016(a)(2). The S corporation's basis of Machinery Y is $2,500, the basis of the property under section 362 at the time the S corporation places the property in service. Pursuant to paragraph (c)(3)(iv) of this section, S corporation's UBIA of Machinery Y is $10,000, which is C's UBIA of Machinery Y. Pursuant to paragraph (c)(2)(iv)(A) of this section, for purposes of determining the depreciable period of Machinery Y, the S corporation's placed in service date of Machinery Y will be January 5, 2011, which is the date C originally placed the property in service in 2011. Therefore, Machinery Y may be qualified property of the S corporation (assuming it continues to be used in the business) for 2019 and 2020 and will not be qualified property of the S corporation after 2020, because its depreciable period will have expired.

(ix) *Example 9.* (A) LLC, a partnership, operates a trade or business that is not an SSTB. On January 5, 2011, LLC purchases Machinery Z for $30,000 and places it in service in LLC's trade or business. LLC's basis in Machinery Z under section 1012 is $30,000. Machinery Z is qualified property within the meaning of section 199A(b)(6). Assume that Machinery Z's recovery period under section 168(c) is 10 years, and LLC depreciates Machinery Z under the general depreciation system by using the straight-line depreciation method, a 10-year recovery period, and the half-year convention. As of December 31, 2018, LLC's basis in Machinery Z, as adjusted under section 1016(a)(2) for depreciation deductions under section 168(a), is $7,500. On January 1, 2019, LLC distributes Machinery Z to Partner A in full liquidation of Partner A's interest in LLC. Partner A's outside basis in LLC is $35,000.

(B) For purposes of section 199A(b)(2)(B)(ii) and this section, LLC's UBIA of Machinery Z from 2011 through 2018 is its $30,000 cost basis under section 1012, regardless of any later depreciation deductions under section 168(a) and resulting basis adjustments under section 1016(a)(2). Prior to the distribution to Partner A, LLC's basis of Machinery Z is $7,500. Under section 732(b), Partner A's basis in Machinery Z is $35,000. Pursuant to paragraph (c)(3)(iv) of this section, upon distribution of Machinery Z, Partner A's UBIA of Machinery Z is $30,000, which was LLC's UBIA of Machinery Z.

(d) *Applicability date.*—(1) *General rule.*—Except as provided in paragraph (d)(2) of this section, the provisions of this section apply to taxable years ending after February 8, 2019.

(2) *Exceptions.*—(i) *Anti-abuse rules.*—The provisions of paragraph (c)(1)(iv) of this section apply to taxable years ending after December 22, 2017.

(ii) *Non-calendar year RPE.*—For purposes of determining QBI, W-2 wages, UBIA of qualified property, and the aggregate amount of qualified REIT dividends and qualified PTP income if an individual receives any of these items from an RPE with a taxable year that begins before January 1, 2018, and ends after December 31, 2017, such items are treated as having been incurred by the individual during the individual's taxable year in which or with which such RPE taxable year ends. [Reg. § 1.199A-2.]

☐ [T.D. 9847, 2-4-2019 (corrected 4-17-2019).]

[Reg. § 1.199A-3]

§ 1.199A-3. Qualified business income, qualified REIT dividends, and qualified PTP income.—(a) *In general.*—This section provides rules on the determination of a trade or business's qualified business income (QBI), as well as the determination of qualified real estate investment trust (REIT) dividends and qualified publicly traded partnership (PTP) income. The provisions of this section apply solely for purposes of section 199A of the Internal Revenue Code (Code). Paragraph (b) of this section provides rules for the determination of QBI. Paragraph (c) of this section provides rules for the determination of qualified REIT dividends and qualified PTP income. QBI must be determined and reported for each trade or business by the individual or relevant passthrough entity (RPE) that directly conducts the trade or business before applying the aggregation rules of § 1.199A-4.

(b) *Definition of qualified business income.*—(1) *In general.*—For purposes of this section, the term *qualified business income* or *QBI* means, for any taxable year, the net amount of qualified items of income, gain, deduction, and loss with respect to any trade or business of the taxpayer as described in paragraph (b)(2) of this section, provided the other requirements of this section and section 199A are satisfied (including, for example, the exclusion of income not effectively connected with a United States trade or business).

(i) *Section 751 gain.*—With respect to a partnership, if section 751(a) or (b) applies, then gain or loss attributable to assets of the partnership giving rise to ordinary income under section 751(a) or (b) is considered attributable to the trades or businesses conducted by the partnership, and is taken into account for purposes of computing QBI.

(ii) *Guaranteed payments for the use of capital.*—Income attributable to a guaranteed payment for the use of capital is not considered to be attributable to a trade or business, and thus is not taken into account for purposes of computing QBI except to the extent properly allocable to a trade or business of the recipient. The partnership's

deduction associated with the guaranteed payment will be taken into account for purposes of computing QBI if such deduction is properly allocable to the trade or business and is otherwise deductible for Federal income tax purposes.

(iii) *Section 481 adjustments.*—Section 481 adjustments (whether positive or negative) are taken into account for purposes of computing QBI to the extent that the requirements of this section and section 199A are otherwise satisfied, but only if the adjustment arises in taxable years ending after December 31, 2017.

(iv) *Previously disallowed losses.*—(A) *In general.*—Previously disallowed losses or deductions allowed in the taxable year generally are taken into account for purposes of computing QBI to the extent the disallowed loss or deduction is otherwise allowed by section 199A. These previously disallowed losses include, but are not limited to losses disallowed under sections 461(l), 465, 469, 704(d) and 1366(d). These losses are used for purposes of section 199A and this section in order from the oldest to the most recent on a first-in, first-out (FIFO) basis and are treated as losses from a separate trade or business. To the extent such losses relate to a PTP, they must be treated as a loss from a separate PTP in the taxable year the losses are taken into account. However, losses or deductions that were disallowed, suspended, limited, or carried over from taxable years ending before January 1, 2018 (including under sections 465, 469, 704(d) and 1366(d)), are not taken into account in a subsequent taxable year for purposes of computing QBI.

(B) *Partial allowance.*—If a loss or deduction attributable to a trade or business is only partially allowed during the taxable year in which incurred, only the portion of the allowed loss or deduction that is attributable to QBI will be considered in determining QBI from the trade or business in the year the loss or deduction is incurred. The portion of the allowed loss or deduction attributable to QBI is determined by multiplying the total amount of the allowed loss by a fraction, the numerator of which is the portion of the total loss incurred during the taxable year that is attributable to QBI and the denominator of which is the amount of the total loss incurred during the taxable year.

(C) *Attributes of disallowed loss or deduction determined in year loss is incurred.*—(1) *In general.*—Whether a disallowed loss or deduction is attributable to a trade or business, and otherwise meets the requirements of this section, is determined in the year the loss is incurred.

(2) *Specified service trades or businesses.*—If a disallowed loss or deduction is attributable to a specified service trade or business (SSTB), whether an individual has taxable income at or below the threshold amount as defined in § 1.199A-1(b)(12), within the phase-in range as defined in § 1.199A-1(b)(4), or in excess of the phase-in range is determined in the year the loss or deduction is incurred. If the individual's taxable income is at or below the threshold amount in the year the loss or deduction is incurred, the entire disallowed loss or deduction must be taken into account when applying paragraph (b)(1)(iv)(A) of this section. If the individual's taxable income is within the phase-in range, then only the applicable percentage, as defined in § 1.199A-1(b)(2), of the disallowed loss or deduction is taken into account when applying paragraph (b)(1)(iv)(A) of this section. If the individual's taxable income exceeds the phase-in range, none of the disallowed loss or deduction will be taken into account in applying paragraph (b)(1)(iv)(A) of this section.

(D) *Examples.*—The following examples illustrate the provisions of this paragraph (b)(1)(iv).

(1) *Example 1.*—A is an unmarried individual and a 50% owner of LLC, an entity classified as a partnership for Federal income tax purposes. In 2018, A's allocable share of loss from LLC is $100,000 of which $80,000 is negative QBI. Under section 465, $60,000 of the allocable loss is allowed in determining A's taxable income. A has no other previously disallowed losses under section 465 or any other provision of the Code for 2018 or prior years. Because 80% of A's allocable loss is attributable to QBI ($80,000/$100,000), A will reduce the amount A takes into account in determining QBI proportionately. Thus, A will include $48,000 of the allowed loss in negative QBI (80% of $60,000) in determining A's section 199A deduction in 2018. The remaining $32,000 of negative QBI is treated as negative QBI from a separate trade or business for purposes of computing the section 199A deduction in the year the loss is taken into account in determining taxable income as described in § 1.199A-1(d)(2)(iii).

(2) *Example 2.*—B is an unmarried individual and a 50% owner of LLC, an entity classified as a partnership for Federal income tax purposes. After allowable deductions other than the section 199A deduction, B's taxable income for 2018 is $177,500. In 2018, LLC has a single trade or business that is an SSTB. B's allocable share of loss is $100,000, all of which is suspended under section 465.

B's allocable share of negative QBI is also $100,000. B has no other previously disallowed losses under section 465 or any other provision of the Code for 2018 or prior years. Because the entire loss is suspended, none of the negative QBI is taken into account in determining B's section 199A deduction for 2018. Further, because the negative QBI is from an SSTB and B's taxable income before the section 199A deduction is within the phase-in range, B must determine the applicable percentage of the negative QBI that must be taken into account in the year that the loss is taken into account in determining taxable income. B's applicable percentage is 100% reduced by 40% (the percentage equal to the amount that B's taxable income for the taxable year exceeds B's threshold amount ($20,000=$177,500-$157,500) over $50,000). Thus, B's applicable percentage is 60%. Therefore, B will have $60,000 (60% of $100,000) of negative QBI from a separate trade or business to be applied proportionately to QBI in the year(s) the loss is taken into account in determining taxable income, regardless of the amount of taxable income and how rules under §1.199A-5 apply in the year the loss is taken into account in determining taxable income.

(v) *Net operating losses.*—Generally, a net operating loss deduction under section 172 is not considered with respect to a trade or business and therefore, is not taken into account in computing QBI. However, an excess business loss under section 461(l) is treated as a net operating loss carryover to the following taxable year and is taken into account for purposes of computing QBI in the subsequent taxable year in which it is deducted.

(vi) *Other deductions.*—Generally, deductions attributable to a trade or business are taken into account for purposes of computing QBI to the extent that the requirements of section 199A and this section are otherwise satisfied. For purposes of section 199A only, deductions such as the deductible portion of the tax on self-employment income under section 164(f), the self-employed health insurance deduction under section 162(l), and the deduction for contributions to qualified retirement plans under section 404 are considered attributable to a trade or business to the extent that the individual's gross income from the trade or business is taken into account in calculating the allowable deduction, on a proportionate basis to the gross income received from the trade or business.

(2) *Qualified items of income, gain, deduction, and loss.*—(i) *In general.*—The term *qualified items of income, gain, deduction, and loss* means items of gross income, gain, deduction, and loss to the extent such items are—

(A) Effectively connected with the conduct of a trade or business within the United States (within the meaning of section 864(c), determined by substituting "trade or business (within the meaning of section 199A)" for "nonresident alien individual or a foreign corporation" or for "a foreign corporation" each place it appears); and

(B) Included or allowed in determining taxable income for the taxable year.

(ii) *Items not taken into account.*—Notwithstanding paragraph (b)(2)(i) of this section and in accordance with section 199A(c)(3)(B) and (c)(4), the following items are not taken into account as qualified items of income, gain, deduction, or loss and thus are not included in determining QBI:

(A) Any item of short-term capital gain, short-term capital loss, long-term capital gain, or long-term capital loss, including any item treated as one of such items under any other provision of the Code. This provision does not apply to the extent an item is treated as anything other than short-term capital gain, short-term capital loss, long-term capital gain, or long-term capital loss.

(B) Any dividend, income equivalent to a dividend, or payment in lieu of dividends described in section 954(c)(1)(G). Any amount described in section 1385(a)(1) is not treated as described in this clause.

(C) Any interest income other than interest income which is properly allocable to a trade or business. For purposes of section 199A and this section, interest income attributable to an investment of working capital, reserves, or similar accounts is not properly allocable to a trade or business.

(D) Any item of gain or loss described in section 954(c)(1)(C) (transactions in commodities) or section 954(c)(1)(D) (excess foreign currency gains) applied in each case by substituting "trade or business (within the meaning of section 199A)" for "controlled foreign corporation."

(E) Any item of income, gain, deduction, or loss described in section 954(c)(1)(F) (income from notional principal contracts) determined without regard to section 954(c)(1)(F)(ii) and other than items attributable to notional principal contracts entered into in transactions qualifying under section 1221(a)(7).

(F) Any amount received from an annuity which is not received in connection with the trade or business.

(G) Any qualified REIT dividends as defined in paragraph (c)(2) of this section or qualified PTP income as defined in paragraph (c)(3) of this section.

(H) Reasonable compensation received by a shareholder from an S corporation. However, the S corporation's deduction for such reasonable compensation will reduce QBI if such deduction is properly allocable to the trade or business and is otherwise deductible for Federal income tax purposes.

(I) Any guaranteed payment described in section 707(c) received by a partner for services rendered with respect to the trade or business, regardless of whether the partner is an individual or an RPE. However, the partnership's deduction for such guaranteed payment will reduce QBI if such deduction is properly allocable to the trade or business and is otherwise deductible for Federal income tax purposes.

(J) Any payment described in section 707(a) received by a partner for services rendered with respect to the trade or business, regardless of whether the partner is an individual or an RPE. However, the partnership's deduction for such payment will reduce QBI if such deduction is properly allocable to the trade or business and is otherwise deductible for Federal income tax purposes.

(3) *Commonwealth of Puerto Rico.*—For the purposes of determining QBI, the term *United States* includes the Commonwealth of Puerto Rico in the case of any taxpayer with QBI for any taxable year from sources within the Commonwealth of Puerto Rico, if all of such receipts are taxable under section 1 for such taxable year. This paragraph (b)(3) only applies as provided in section 199A(f)(1)(C).

(4) *Wages.*—Expenses for all wages paid (or incurred in the case of an accrual method taxpayer) must be taken into account in computing QBI (if the requirements of this section and section 199A are satisfied) regardless of the application of the W-2 wage limitation described in §1.199A-1(d)(2)(iv).

(5) *Allocation of items among directly-conducted trades or businesses.*—If an individual or an RPE directly conducts multiple trades or businesses, and has items of QBI that are properly attributable to more than one trade or business, the individual or RPE must allocate those items among the several trades or businesses to which they are attributable using a reasonable method based on all the facts and circumstances. The individual or RPE may use a different reasonable method with respect to different items of income, gain, deduction, and loss. The chosen reasonable method for each item must be consistently applied from one taxable year to another and must clearly reflect the income and expenses of each trade or business. The overall combination of methods must also be reasonable based on all facts and circumstances. The books and records maintained for a trade or business must be consistent with any allocations under this paragraph (b)(5).

(c) *Qualified REIT Dividends and Qualified PTP Income.*—(1) *In general.*—Qualified REIT dividends and qualified PTP income are the sum of qualified REIT dividends as defined in paragraph (c)(2) of this section earned directly or through an RPE and the net amount of qualified PTP income as defined in paragraph (c)(3) of this section earned directly or through an RPE.

(2) *Qualified REIT dividend.*—(i) The term *qualified REIT dividend* means any dividend from a REIT received during the taxable year which—

(A) Is not a capital gain dividend, as defined in section 857(b)(3); and

(B) Is not qualified dividend income, as defined in section 1(h)(11).

(ii) The term qualified REIT dividend does not include any REIT dividend received with respect to any share of REIT stock—

(A) That is held by the shareholder for 45 days or less (taking into account the principles of section 246(c)(3) and (4)) during the 91-day period beginning on the date which is 45 days before the date on which such share becomes ex-dividend with respect to such dividend; or

(B) To the extent that the shareholder is under an obligation (whether pursuant to a short sale or otherwise) to make related payments with respect to positions in substantially similar or related property.

(3) *Qualified PTP income.*—(i) *In general.*—The term *qualified PTP income* means the sum of—

(A) The net amount of such taxpayer's allocable share of income, gain, deduction, and loss from a PTP as defined in section 7704(b) that is not taxed as a corporation under section 7704(a); plus

(B) Any gain or loss attributable to assets of the PTP giving rise to ordinary income under section 751(a) or (b) that is considered attributable to the trades or businesses conducted by the partnership.

(ii) *Special rules.*—The rules applicable to the determination of QBI described in paragraph (b) of this section also apply to the determination of a taxpayer's allocable share of income, gain, deduction, and loss from a PTP. An individual's allocable share of income from a PTP, and any section 751 gain or loss is qualified PTP income only to the extent the items meet the qualifications of section 199A and this section, including the requirement that the item is included or allowed in determining taxable income for the taxable year, and the requirement that the item be effectively connected with the conduct of a trade or business within the United States. For example, if an individual owns an interest in a PTP, and for the taxable year is allocated a distributive share of net loss which is disallowed under the passive activity rules of section 469, such loss is not taken into account for purposes of section 199A. The specified service trade or business limitations described in §§1.199A-1(d)(3) and 1.199A-5 also apply to income earned from a PTP. Furthermore, each PTP is required to determine its qualified PTP income for each trade or business and report that information to its owners as described in §1.199A-6(b)(3).

(d) *Section 199A dividends paid by a regulated investment company.*—(1) *In general.*—If section 852(b) applies to a regulated investment company (RIC) for a taxable year, the RIC may pay section 199A dividends, as defined in this paragraph (d).

(2) *Definition of section 199A dividend.*—(i) *In general.*—Except as provided in paragraph (d)(2)(ii) of this section, a section 199A dividend is any dividend or part of such a dividend that a RIC pays to its shareholders and reports as a section 199A dividend in written statements furnished to its shareholders.

(ii) *Reduction in the case of excess reported amounts.*—If the aggregate reported amount with respect to the RIC for any taxable year exceeds the RIC's qualified REIT dividend income for the taxable year, then a section 199A dividend is equal to—

(A) The reported section 199A dividend amount; reduced by

(B) The excess reported amount that is allocable to that reported section 199A dividend amount.

(iii) *Allocation of excess reported amount.*—(A) *In general.*—Except as provided in paragraph (d)(2)(iii)(B) of this section, the excess reported amount (if any) that is allocable to the reported section 199A dividend amount is that portion of the excess reported amount that bears the same ratio to the excess reported amount as the reported section 199A dividend amount bears to the aggregate reported amount.

(B) *Special rule for noncalendar-year RICs.*—In the case of any taxable year that does not begin and end in the same calendar year, if the post-December reported amount equals or exceeds the excess reported amount for that taxable year, paragraph (d)(2)(iii)(A) of this section is applied by substituting "post-December reported amount" for "aggregate reported amount," and no excess reported amount is allocated to any dividend paid on or before December 31 of that taxable year.

(3) *Definitions.*—For purposes of paragraph (d) of this section—

(i) *Reported section 199A dividend amount.*—The term *reported section 199A dividend amount* means the amount of a dividend distribution reported to the RIC's shareholders under paragraph (d)(2)(i) of this section as a section 199A dividend.

(ii) *Excess reported amount.*—The term *excess reported amount* means the excess of the aggregate reported amount over the RIC's qualified REIT dividend income for the taxable year.

(iii) *Aggregate reported amount.*—The term *aggregate reported amount* means the aggregate amount of dividends reported by the RIC under paragraph (d)(2)(i) of this section as section 199A dividends for the taxable year (including section 199A dividends paid after the close of the taxable year and described in section 855).

(iv) *Post-December reported amount.*—The term *post-December reported amount* means the aggregate reported amount determined by taking into account only dividends paid after December 31 of the taxable year.

(v) *Qualified REIT dividend income.*—The term *qualified REIT dividend income* means, with respect to a taxable year of a RIC, the excess of the amount of qualified REIT dividends, as defined in paragraph (c)(2) of this section, includible in the RIC's taxable income for the taxable year over the amount of the RIC's deductions that are properly allocable to such income.

(4) *Treatment of section 199A dividends by shareholders.*—(i) *In general.*—For purposes of section 199A, and §§1.199A-1 through 1.199A-6, a section 199A dividend is treated by a taxpayer that receives the section 199A dividend as a qualified REIT dividend.

(ii) *Holding period.*—Paragraph (d)(4)(i) of this section does not apply to any dividend received with respect to a share of RIC stock—

(A) That is held by the shareholder for 45 days or less (taking into account the principles of section 246(c)(3) and (4)) during the 91-day period beginning on the date which is 45 days before the date on which the share becomes ex-dividend with respect to such dividend; or

(B) To the extent that the shareholder is under an obligation (whether pursuant to a short sale or otherwise) to make related payments with respect to positions in substantially similar or related property.

(5) *Example.*—The following example illustrates the provisions of this paragraph (d).

(i) X is a corporation that has elected to be a RIC. For its taxable year ending March 31, 2021, X has $25,000x of net long-term capital gain, $60,000x of qualified dividend income, $25,000x of taxable interest income, $15,000x of net short-term capital gain, and $25,000x of qualified REIT dividends. X has $15,000x of deductible expenses, of which $3,000x is allocable to the qualified REIT dividends. On December 31, 2020, X pays a single dividend of $100,000x, and reports $20,000x of the dividend as a section 199A dividend in written statements to its shareholders. On March 31, 2021, X pays a dividend of $35,000x, and reports $5,000x of the dividend as a section 199A dividend in written statements to its shareholders.

(ii) X's qualified REIT dividend income under paragraph (d)(3)(v) of this section is $22,000x, which is the excess of X's $25,000x of qualified REIT dividends over $3,000x in allocable expenses. The reported section 199A dividend amounts for the December 31, 2020, and March 31, 2021, distributions are $20,000x and $5,000x, respectively. For the taxable year ending March 31, 2021, the aggregate reported amount of section 199A dividends is $25,000x, and the excess reported amount under paragraph (d)(3)(ii) of this section is $3,000x. Because X is a noncalendar-year RIC and the post-December reported amount of $5,000x exceeds the excess reported amount of $3,000x, the entire excess reported amount is allocated under paragraphs (d)(2)(iii)(A) and (B) of this section to the reported section 199A dividend amount for the March 31, 2021, distribution. No portion of the excess reported amount is allocated to the reported section 199A dividend amount for the December 31, 2020, distribution. Thus, the section 199A dividend on March 31, 2021, is $2,000x, which is the reported section 199A dividend amount of $5,000x reduced by the $3,000x of allocable excess reported amount. The section 199A dividend on December 31, 2020, is the $20,000x that X reports as a section 199A dividend.

(iii) Shareholder A, a United States person, receives a dividend from X of $100x on December 31, 2020, of which $20x is reported as a section 199A dividend. If A meets the holding period requirements in paragraph (d)(4)(ii) of this section with respect to the stock of X, A treats $20x of the dividend from X as a qualified REIT dividend for purposes of section 199A for A's 2020 taxable year.

(iv) A receives a dividend from X of $35x on March 31, 2021, of which $5x is reported as a section 199A dividend. Only $2x of the dividend is a section 199A dividend. If A meets the holding period requirements in paragraph (d)(4)(ii) of this section with respect to the stock of X, A may treat the $2x section 199A dividend as a qualified REIT dividend for A's 2021 taxable year.

(e) *Applicability date.*—(1) *General rule.*—Except as provided in paragraph (e)(2) of this section, the provisions of this section apply to taxable years ending after February 8, 2019.

(2) *Exceptions.*—(i) *Anti-abuse rules.*—The provisions of paragraph (c)(2)(ii) of this section apply to taxable years ending after December 22, 2017.

(ii) *Non-calendar year RPE.*—For purposes of determining QBI, W-2 wages, UBIA of qualified property, and the aggregate amount of qualified REIT dividends and qualified PTP income if an individual receives any of these items from an RPE with a taxable year that begins before January 1, 2018, and ends after December 31, 2017, such items are treated as having been incurred by the individual during the individual's taxable year in which or with which such RPE taxable year ends.

(iii) *Previously disallowed losses.*—The provisions of paragraph (b)(1)(iv) of this section apply to taxable years beginning after August 24, 2020. Taxpayers may choose to apply the rules in paragraph (b)(1)(iv) of this section for taxable years beginning on or before August 24, 2020, so long as the taxpayers consistently apply the rules in paragraph (b)(1)(iv) of this section for each such year.

(iv) *Section 199A dividends.*—The provisions of paragraph (d) of this section apply to taxable years beginning after August 24, 2020.

Taxpayers may choose to apply the rules in paragraph (d) of this section for taxable years beginning on or before August 24, 2020, so long as the taxpayers consistently apply the rules in paragraph (d) of this section for each such year. [Reg. § 1.199A-3.]

☐ [T.D. 9847, 2-4-2019. *Amended by T.D. 9899, 6-24-2020.*]

[Reg. § 1.199A-4]

§ 1.199A-4. Aggregation.—(a) *Scope and purpose.*—An individual or RPE may be engaged in more than one trade or business. Except as provided in this section, each trade or business is a separate trade or business for purposes of applying the limitations described in § 1.199A-1(d)(2)(iv). This section sets forth rules to allow individuals and RPEs to aggregate trades or businesses, treating the aggregate as a single trade or business for purposes of applying the limitations described in § 1.199A-1(d)(2)(iv). Trades or businesses may be aggregated only to the extent provided in this section, but aggregation by taxpayers is not required.

(b) *Aggregation rules.*—**(1)** *General rule.*—Trades or businesses may be aggregated only if an individual or RPE can demonstrate that—

(i) The same person or group of persons, directly or by attribution under sections 267(b) or 707(b), owns 50 percent or more of each trade or business to be aggregated, meaning in the case of such trades or businesses owned by an S corporation, 50 percent or more of the issued and outstanding shares of the corporation, or, in the case of such trades or businesses owned by a partnership, 50 percent or more of the capital or profits in the partnership;

(ii) The ownership described in paragraph (b)(1)(i) of this section exists for a majority of the taxable year, including the last day of the taxable year, in which the items attributable to each trade or business to be aggregated are included in income;

(iii) All of the items attributable to each trade or business to be aggregated are reported on returns with the same taxable year, not taking into account short taxable years;

(iv) None of the trades or businesses to be aggregated is a *specified service trade or business* (SSTB) as defined in § 1.199A-5; and

(v) The trades or businesses to be aggregated satisfy at least two of the following factors (based on all of the facts and circumstances):

(A) The trades or businesses provide products, property, or services that are the same or customarily offered together.

(B) The trades or businesses share facilities or share significant centralized business elements, such as personnel, accounting, legal, manufacturing, purchasing, human resources, or information technology resources.

(C) The trades or businesses are operated in coordination with, or reliance upon, one or more of the businesses in the aggregated group (for example, supply chain interdependencies).

(2) *Operating rules.*—**(i)** *Individuals.*—An individual may aggregate trades or businesses operated directly or through an RPE to the extent an aggregation is not inconsistent with the aggregation of an RPE. If an individual aggregates multiple trades or businesses under paragraph (b)(1) of this section, QBI, W-2 wages, and UBIA of qualified property must be combined for the aggregated trades or businesses for purposes of applying the W-2 wage and UBIA of qualified property limitations described in § 1.199A-1(d)(2)(iv). An individual may not subtract from the trades or businesses aggregated by an RPE but may aggregate additional trades or businesses with the RPE's aggregation if the rules of this section are otherwise satisfied.

(ii) *RPEs.*—An RPE may aggregate trades or businesses operated directly or through a lower-tier RPE to the extent an aggregation is not inconsistent with the aggregation of a lower-tier RPE. If an RPE itself does not aggregate, multiple owners of an RPE need not aggregate in the same manner. If an RPE aggregates multiple trades or businesses under paragraph (b)(1) of this section, the RPE must compute and report QBI, W-2 wages, and UBIA of qualified property for the aggregated trade or business under the rules described in § 1.199A-6(b). An RPE may not subtract from the trades or businesses aggregated by a lower-tier RPE but may aggregate additional trades or businesses with a lower-tier RPE's aggregation if the rules of this section are otherwise satisfied.

(c) *Reporting and consistency requirements.*—**(1)** *Individuals.*—Once an individual chooses to aggregate two or more trades or businesses, the individual must consistently report the aggregated trades or businesses in all subsequent taxable years. A failure to aggregate will not be considered to be an aggregation for purposes of this rule. An individual that fails to aggregate may not aggregate trades or businesses on an amended return (other than an amended return for the 2018 taxable year). However, an individual may add a newly created or newly acquired (including through nonrecognition transfers) trade or business to an existing aggregated trade or business (including the

aggregated trade or business of an RPE) if the requirements of paragraph (b)(1) of this section are satisfied. In a subsequent year, if there is a significant change in facts and circumstances such that an individual's prior aggregation of trades or businesses no longer qualifies for aggregation under the rules of this section, then the trades or businesses will no longer be aggregated within the meaning of this section, and the individual must reapply the rules in paragraph (b)(1) of this section to determine a new permissible aggregation (if any). An individual also must report aggregated trades or businesses of an RPE in which the individual holds a direct or indirect interest.

(2) *Individual disclosure.*—**(i)** *Required annual disclosure.*—For each taxable year, individuals must attach a statement to their returns identifying each trade or business aggregated under paragraph (b)(1) of this section. The statement must contain —

(A) A description of each trade or business;

(B) The name and EIN of each entity in which a trade or business is operated;

(C) Information identifying any trade or business that was formed, ceased operations, was acquired, or was disposed of during the taxable year;

(D) Information identifying any aggregated trade or business of an RPE in which the individual holds an ownership interest; and

(E) Such other information as the Commissioner may require in forms, instructions, or other published guidance.

(ii) *Failure to disclose.*—If an individual fails to attach the statement required in paragraph (c)(2)(i) of this section, the Commissioner may disaggregate the individual's trades or businesses. The individual may not aggregate trades or businesses that are disaggregated by the Commissioner for the subsequent three taxable years.

(3) *RPEs.*—Once an RPE chooses to aggregate two or more trades or businesses, the RPE must consistently report the aggregated trades or businesses in all subsequent taxable years. A failure to aggregate will not be considered to be an aggregation for purposes of this rule. An RPE that fails to aggregate may not aggregate trades or businesses on an amended return (other than an amended return for the 2018 taxable year). However, an RPE may add a newly created or newly acquired (including through non-recognition transfers) trade or business to an existing aggregated trade or business (including the aggregated trade or business of a lower-tier RPE) if the requirements of paragraph (b)(1) of this section are satisfied. In a subsequent year, if there is a significant change in facts and circumstances such that an RPE's prior aggregation of trades or businesses no longer qualifies for aggregation under the rules of this section, then the trades or businesses will no longer be aggregated within the meaning of this section, and the RPE must reapply the rules in paragraph (b)(1) of this section to determine a new permissible aggregation (if any). An RPE also must report aggregated trades or businesses of a lower-tier RPE in which the RPE holds a direct or indirect interest.

(4) *RPE disclosure.*—**(i)** *Required annual disclosure.*—For each taxable year, RPEs (including each RPE in a tiered structure) must attach a statement to each owner's Schedule K-1 identifying each trade or business aggregated under paragraph (b)(1) of this section. The statement must contain —

(A) A description of each trade or business;

(B) The name and EIN of each entity in which a trade or business is operated;

(C) Information identifying any trade or business that was formed, ceased operations, was acquired, or was disposed of during the taxable year;

(D) Information identifying any aggregated trade or business of an RPE in which the RPE holds an ownership interest; and

(E) Such other information as the Commissioner may require in forms, instructions, or other published guidance.

(ii) *Failure to disclose.*—If an RPE fails to attach the statement required in paragraph (c)(4)(i) of this section, the Commissioner may disaggregate the RPE's trades or businesses. The RPE may not aggregate trades or businesses that are disaggregated by the Commissioner for the subsequent three taxable years.

(d) *Examples.*—The following examples illustrate the principles of this section. For purposes of these examples, assume the taxpayer is a United States citizen, all individuals and RPEs use a calendar taxable year, there are no ownership changes during the taxable year, all trades or businesses satisfy the requirements under section 162, all tax items are effectively connected to a trade or business within the United States within the meaning of section 864(c), and none of the trades or businesses is an SSTB within the meaning of § 1.199A-5. Except as otherwise specified, a single capital letter denotes an individual taxpayer.

(1) *Example 1*—(i) *Facts.* A wholly owns and operates a catering business and a restaurant through separate disregarded entities. The catering business and the restaurant share centralized purchasing to obtain volume discounts and a centralized accounting office that performs all of the bookkeeping, tracks and issues statements on all of the receivables, and prepares the payroll for each business. A maintains a website and print advertising materials that reference both the catering business and the restaurant. A uses the restaurant kitchen to prepare food for the catering business. The catering business employs its own staff and owns equipment and trucks that are not used or associated with the restaurant.

(ii) *Analysis.* Because the restaurant and catering business are held in disregarded entities, A will be treated as operating each of these businesses directly and thereby satisfies paragraph (b)(1)(i) of this section. Under paragraph (b)(1)(v) of this section, A satisfies the following factors: paragraph (b)(1)(v)(A) of this section is met as both businesses offer prepared food to customers; and paragraph (b)(1)(v)(B) of this section is met because the two businesses share the same kitchen facilities in addition to centralized purchasing, marketing, and accounting. Having satisfied paragraphs (b)(1)(i) through (v) of this section, A may treat the catering business and the restaurant as a single trade or business for purposes of applying § 1.199A-1(d).

(2) *Example 2*—(i) *Facts.* Assume the same facts as in *Example 1* of paragraph (d)(1) of this section, but the catering and restaurant businesses are owned in separate partnerships and A, B, C, and D each own a 25% interest in each of the two partnerships. A, B, C, and D are unrelated.

(ii) *Analysis.* Because under paragraph (b)(1)(i) of this section A, B, C, and D together own more than 50% of each of the two partnerships, they may each treat the catering business and the restaurant as a single trade or business for purposes of applying § 1.199A-1(d).

(3) *Example 3*—(i) *Facts.* W owns a 75% interest in S1, an S corporation, and a 75% interest in PRS, a partnership. S1 manufactures clothing and PRS is a retail pet food store. W manages S1 and PRS.

(ii) *Analysis.* W owns more than 50% of the stock of S1 and more than 50% of PRS thereby satisfying paragraph (b)(1)(i) of this section. Although W manages both S1 and PRS, W is not able to satisfy the requirements of paragraph (b)(1)(v) of this section as the two businesses do not provide goods or services that are the same or customarily offered together; there are no significant centralized business elements; and no facts indicate that the businesses are operated in coordination with, or reliance upon, one another. W must treat S1 and PRS as separate trades or businesses for purposes of applying § 1.199A-1(d).

(4) *Example 4*—(i) *Facts.* E owns a 60% interest in each of four partnerships (PRS1, PRS2, PRS3, and PRS4). Each partnership operates a hardware store. A team of executives oversees the operations of all four of the businesses and controls the policy decisions involving the business as a whole. Human resources and accounting are centralized for the four businesses. E reports PRS1, PRS3, and PRS4 as an aggregated trade or business under paragraph (b)(1) of this section and reports PRS2 as a separate trade or business. Only PRS2 generates a net taxable loss.

(ii) *Analysis.* E owns more than 50% of each partnership thereby satisfying paragraph (b)(1)(i) of this section. Under paragraph (b)(1)(v) of this section, the following factors are satisfied: paragraph (b)(1)(v)(A) of this section because each partnership operates a hardware store; and paragraph (b)(1)(v)(B) of this section because the businesses share accounting and human resource functions. E's decision to aggregate only PRS1, PRS3, and PRS4 into a single trade or business for purposes of applying § 1.199A-1(d) is permissible. The loss from PRS2 will be netted against the aggregate profits of PRS1, PRS3, and PRS4 pursuant to § 1.199A-1(d)(2)(iii).

(5) *Example 5*—(i) *Facts.* Assume the same facts as *Example 4* of paragraph (d)(4) of this section, and that F owns a 10% interest in PRS1, PRS2, PRS3, and PRS4.

(ii) *Analysis.* Because under paragraph (b)(1)(i) of this section E owns more than 50% of the four partnerships, F may aggregate PRS 1, PRS2, PRS3, and PRS4 as a single trade or business for purposes of applying § 1.199A-1(d), provided that F can demonstrate that the ownership test is met by E.

(6) *Example 6*—(i) *Facts.* D owns 75% of the stock of S1, S2, and S3, each of which is an S corporation. Each S corporation operates a grocery store in a separate state. S1 and S2 share centralized purchasing functions to obtain volume discounts and a centralized accounting office that performs all of the bookkeeping, tracks and issues statements on all of the receivables, and prepares the payroll for each business. S3 is operated independently from the other businesses.

(ii) *Analysis.* D owns more than 50% of the stock of each S corporation thereby satisfying paragraph (b)(1)(i) of this section. Under paragraph (b)(1)(v) of this section, the grocery stores satisfy paragraph (b)(1)(v)(A) of this section because they are in the same trade or business. Only S1 and S2 satisfy paragraph (b)(1)(v)(B) of this section because of their centralized purchasing and accounting of-

fices. D is only able to show that the requirements of paragraph (b)(1)(v)(B) of this section are satisfied for S1 and S2; therefore, D only may aggregate S1 and S2 into a single trade or business for purposes of § 1.199A-1(d). D must report S3 as a separate trade or business for purposes of applying § 1.199A-1(d).

(7) *Example 7*—(i) *Facts.* Assume the same facts as *Example 6* of paragraph (d)(6) of this section except each store is independently operated and S1 and S2 do not have centralized purchasing or accounting functions.

(ii) *Analysis.* Although the stores provide the same products and services within the meaning of paragraph (b)(1)(v)(A) of this section, D cannot show that another factor under paragraph (b)(1)(v) of this section is present. Therefore, D must report S1, S2, and S3 as separate trades or businesses for purposes of applying § 1.199A-1(d).

(8) *Example 8*—(i) *Facts.* G owns 80% of the stock in S1, an S corporation and 80% of LLC1 and LLC2, each of which is a partnership for Federal tax purposes. LLC1 manufactures and supplies all of the widgets sold by LLC2. LLC2 operates a retail store that sells LLC1's widgets. S1 owns the real property leased to LLC1 and LLC2 for use by the factory and retail store. The entities share common advertising and management.

(ii) *Analysis.* G owns more than 50% of the stock of S1 and more than 50% of LLC1 and LLC2 thus satisfying paragraph (b)(1)(i) of this section. LLC1, LLC2, and S1 share significant centralized business elements and are operated in coordination with, or in reliance upon, one or more of the businesses in the aggregated group. G can treat the business operations of LLC1 and LLC2 as a single trade or business for purposes of applying § 1.199A-1(d). S1 is eligible to be included in the aggregated group because it leases property to a trade or business within the aggregated trade or business as described in § 1.199A-1(b)(14) and meets the requirements of paragraph (b)(1) of this section.

(9) *Example 9*—(i) *Facts.* Same facts as *Example 8* of paragraph (d)(8) of this section, except G owns 80% of the stock in S1 and 20% of each of LLC1 and LLC2. B, G's son, owns a majority interest in LLC2, and M, G's mother, owns a majority interest in LLC1. B does not own an interest in S1 or LLC1, and M does not own an interest in S1 or LLC2.

(ii) *Analysis.* Under the rules in paragraph (b)(1) of this section, B and M's interest in LLC2 and LLC1, respectively, are attributable to G and G is treated as owning a majority interest in LLC2 and LLC1; G thus satisfies paragraph (b)(1)(i) of this section. G may aggregate his interests in LLC1, LLC2, and S1 as a single trade or business for purposes of applying § 1.199A-1(d). Under paragraph (b)(1) of this section, S1 is eligible to be included in the aggregated group because it leases property to a trade or business within the aggregated trade or business as described in § 1.199A-1(b)(14) and meets the requirements of paragraph (b)(1) of this section.

(10) *Example 10*—(i) *Facts.* F owns a 75% interest and G owns a 5% interest in five partnerships (PRS1-PRS5). H owns a 10% interest in PRS1 and PRS2. Each partnership operates a restaurant and each restaurant separately constitutes a trade or business for purposes of section 162. G is the executive chef of all of the restaurants and as such he creates the menus and orders the food supplies.

(ii) *Analysis.* F owns more than 50% of the partnerships thereby satisfying paragraph (b)(1)(i) of this section. Under paragraph (b)(1)(v) of this section, the restaurants satisfy paragraph (b)(1)(v)(A) of this section because they are in the same trade or business, and paragraph (b)(1)(v)(B) of this section is satisfied as G is the executive chef of all of the restaurants and the businesses share a centralized function for ordering food and supplies. F can show the requirements under paragraph (b)(1) of this section are satisfied as to all of the restaurants. Because F owns a majority interest in each of the partnerships, G can demonstrate that paragraph (b)(1)(i) of this section is satisfied. G can also aggregate all five restaurants into a single trade or business for purposes of applying § 1.199A-1(d). H, however, only owns an interest in PRS1 and PRS2. Like G, H satisfies paragraph (b)(1)(i) of this section because F owns a majority interest. H can, therefore, aggregate PRS1 and PRS2 into a single trade or business for purposes of applying § 1.199A-1(d).

(11) *Example 11*—(i) *Facts.* H, J, K, and L own interests in PRS1 and PRS2, each a partnership, and S1 and S2, each an S corporation. H, J, K, and L also own interests in C, an entity taxable as a C corporation. H owns 30%, J owns 20%, K owns 5%, and L owns 45% of each of the five entities. All of the entities satisfy 2 of the 3 factors under paragraph (b)(1)(v) of this section. For purposes of section 199A the taxpayers report the following aggregated trades or businesses: H aggregates PRS1 and S1 together and aggregates PRS2 and S2 together; J aggregates PRS1, S1 and S2 together and reports PRS2 separately; K aggregates PRS1 and PRS2 together and aggregates S1 and S2 together; and L aggregates S1, S2, and PRS2 together and reports PRS1 separately. C cannot be aggregated.

(ii) *Analysis.* Under paragraph (b)(1)(i) of this section, because H, J, and K together own a majority interest in PRS1, PRS2, S1, and S2, H, J, K, and L are permitted to aggregate under paragraph (b)(1) of this section. Further, the aggregations reported by the taxpayers are permitted, but not required for each of H, J, K, and L. C's income is not eligible for the section 199A deduction and it cannot be aggregated for purposes of applying §1.199A-1(d).

(12) *Example 12*—(i) *Facts.* L owns 60% of PRS1, a partnership, a business that sells non-food items to grocery stores. L also owns 55% of PRS2, a partnership, which owns and operates a distribution trucking business. The predominant portion of PRS2's business is transporting goods for PRS1.

(ii) *Analysis.* L is able to meet paragraph (b)(1)(i) of this section as the majority owner of PRS1 and PRS2. Under paragraph (b)(1)(v) of this section, L is only able to show the operations of PRS1 and PRS2 are operated in reliance of one another under paragraph (b)(1)(v)(C) of this section. For purposes of applying §1.199A-1(d), L must treat PRS1 and PRS2 as separate trades or businesses.

(13) *Example 13*—(i) *Facts.* C owns a majority interest in a sailboat racing team and also owns an interest in PRS1 which operates a marina. PRS1 is a trade or business under section 162, but the sailboat racing team is not a trade or business within the meaning of section 162.

(ii) *Analysis.* C has only one trade or business for purposes of section 199A and, therefore, cannot aggregate the interest in the racing team with PRS1 under paragraph (b)(1) of this section.

(14) *Example 14*—(i) *Facts.* Trust wholly owns LLC1, LLC2, and LLC3. LLC1 operates a trucking company that delivers lumber and other supplies sold by LLC2. LLC2 operates a lumber yard and supplies LLC3 with building materials. LLC3 operates a construction business. LLC1, LLC2, and LLC3 have a centralized human resources department, payroll, and accounting department.

(ii) *Analysis.* Because Trust owns 100% of the interests in LLC1, LLC2, and LLC3, Trust satisfies paragraph (b)(1)(i) of this section. Trust can also show that it satisfies paragraph (b)(1)(v)(B) of this section as the trades or businesses have a centralized human resources department, payroll, and accounting department. Trust also can show is meets paragraph (b)(1)(v)(C) of this section as the trades or businesses are operated in coordination, or reliance upon, one or more in the aggregated group. Trust can aggregate LLC1, LLC2, and LLC3 for purposes of applying §1.199A-1(d).

(15) *Example 15*—(i) *Facts.* PRS1, a partnership, directly operates a food service trade or business and owns 60% of PRS2, which directly operates a movie theater trade or business and a food service trade or business. PRS2's movie theater and food service businesses operate in coordination with, or reliance upon, one another and share a centralized human resources department, payroll, and accounting department. PRS1's and PRS2's food service businesses provide products and services that are the same and share centralized purchasing and shipping to obtain volume discounts.

(ii) *Analysis.* PRS2 may aggregate its movie theater and food service businesses. Paragraph (b)(1)(v) of this section is satisfied because the businesses operate in coordination with one another and share centralized business elements. If PRS2 does aggregate the two businesses, PRS1 may not aggregate its food service business with PRS2's aggregated trades or businesses. Because PRS1 owns more than 50% of PRS2, thereby satisfying paragraph (b)(1)(i) of this section, PRS1 may aggregate its food service businesses with PRS2's food service business if PRS2 has not aggregated its movie theater and food service businesses. Paragraph (b)(1)(v) of this section is satisfied because the businesses provide the same products and services and share centralized business elements. Under either alternative, PRS1's food service business and PRS2's movie theater cannot be aggregated because there are no factors in paragraph (b)(1)(v) of this section present between the businesses.

(16) *Example 16*—(i) *Facts.* PRS1, a partnership, owns 60% of a commercial rental office building in state A, and 80% of a commercial rental office building in state B. Both commercial rental office building operations share centralized accounting, legal, and human resource functions. PRS1 treats the two commercial rental office buildings as an aggregated trade or business under paragraph (b)(1) of this section.

(ii) *Analysis.* PRS1 owns more than 50% of each trade or business thereby satisfying paragraph (b)(1)(i) of this section. Under paragraph (b)(1)(v) of this section, PRS1 may aggregate its commercial rental office buildings because the businesses provide the same type of property and share accounting, legal, and human resource functions.

(17) *Example 17*—(i) *Facts.* S, an S corporation owns 100% of the interests in a residential condominium building and 100% of the interests in a commercial rental office building. Both building operations share centralized accounting, legal, and human resource functions.

(ii) *Analysis.* S owns more than 50% of each trade or business thereby satisfying paragraph (b)(1)(i) of this section. Although both businesses share significant centralized business elements, S cannot show that another factor under paragraph (b)(1)(v) of this section is present because the two building operations are not of the same type of property. S must treat the residential condominium building and the commercial rental office building as separate trades or businesses for purposes of applying §1.199A-1(d).

(18) *Example 18*—(i) *Facts.* M owns 75% of a residential apartment building. M also owns 80% of PRS2. PRS2 owns 80% of the interests in a residential condominium building and 80% of the interests in a residential apartment building. PRS2's residential condominium building and residential apartment building operations share centralized back office functions and management. M's residential apartment building and PRS2's residential condominium and apartment building operate in coordination with each other in renting apartments to tenants.

(ii) *Analysis.* PRS2 may aggregate its residential condominium and residential apartment building operations. PRS2 owns more than 50% of each trade or business thereby satisfying paragraph (b)(1)(i) of this section. Paragraph (b)(1)(v) of this section is satisfied because the businesses are of the same type of property and share centralized back office functions and management. M may also add its residential apartment building operations to PRS2's aggregated residential condominium and apartment building operations. M owns more than 50% of each trade or business thereby satisfying paragraph (b)(1)(i) of this section. Paragraph (b)(1)(v) of this section is also satisfied because the businesses operate in coordination with each other.

(e) *Applicability date.*—(1) *General rule.*—Except as provided in paragraph (e)(2) of this section, the provisions of this section apply to taxable years ending after February 8, 2019.

(2) *Exception for non-calendar year RPE.*—For purposes of determining QBI, W-2 wages, and UBIA of qualified property, and the aggregate amount of qualified REIT dividends and qualified PTP income, if an individual receives any of these items from an RPE with a taxable year that begins before January 1, 2018, and ends after December 31, 2017, such items are treated as having been incurred by the individual during the individual's taxable year in which or with which such RPE taxable year ends. [Reg. §1.199A-4.]

☐ [T.D. 9847, 2-4-2019 (corrected 4-17-2019).]

[Reg. §1.199A-5]

§1.199A-5. Specified service trades or businesses and the trade or business of performing services as an employee.—(a) *Scope and effect.*—(1) *Scope.*—This section provides guidance on specified service trades or businesses (SSTBs) and the trade or business of performing services as an employee. This paragraph (a) describes the effect of a trade or business being an SSTB and the trade or business of performing services as an employee. Paragraph (b) of this section provides definitional guidance on SSTBs. Paragraph (c) of this section provides special rules related to SSTBs. Paragraph (d) of this section provides guidance on the trade or business of performing services as an employee. The provisions of this section apply solely for purposes of section 199A of the Internal Revenue Code (Code).

(2) *Effect of being an SSTB.*—If a trade or business is an SSTB, no qualified business income (QBI), W-2 wages, or unadjusted basis immediately after acquisition (UBIA) of qualified property from the SSTB may be taken into account by any individual whose taxable income exceeds the phase-in range as defined in §1.199A-1(b)(4), even if the item is derived from an activity that is not itself a specified service activity. The SSTB limitation also applies to income earned from a publicly traded partnership (PTP). If a trade or business conducted by a relevant passthrough entity (RPE) or PTP is an SSTB, this limitation applies to any direct or indirect individual owners of the business, regardless of whether the owner is passive or participated in any specified service activity. However, the SSTB limitation does not apply to individuals with taxable income below the threshold amount as defined in §1.199A-1(b)(12). A phase-in rule, provided in §1.199A-1(d)(2), applies to individuals with taxable income within the phase-in range, allowing them to take into account a certain "applicable percentage" of QBI, W-2 wages, and UBIA of qualified property from an SSTB. The phase-in rule also applies to income earned from a PTP. A direct or indirect owner of a trade or business engaged in the performance of a specified service is engaged in the performance of the specified service for purposes of section 199A and this section, regardless of whether the owner is passive or participated in the specified service activity.

(3) *Trade or business of performing services as an employee.*—The trade or business of performing services as an employee is not a trade or business for purposes of section 199A and the regulations thereunder. Therefore, no items of income, gain, deduction, or loss from the trade or business of performing services as an employee constitute QBI within the meaning of section 199A and §1.199A-3. No taxpayer may claim a section 199A deduction for wage income, regardless of the amount of taxable income.

(b) *Definition of specified service trade or business.*—Except as provided in paragraph (c)(1) of this section, the term *specified service trade or business (SSTB)* means any of the following:

(1) *Listed SSTBs.*—Any trade or business involving the performance of services in one or more of the following fields:

(i) *Health* as described in paragraph (b)(2)(ii) of this section;

(ii) *Law* as described in paragraph (b)(2)(iii) of this section;

(iii) *Accounting* as described in paragraph (b)(2)(iv) of this section;

(iv) *Actuarial science* as described in paragraph (b)(2)(v) of this section;

(v) *Performing arts* as described in paragraph (b)(2)(vi) of this section;

(vi) *Consulting* as described in paragraph (b)(2)(vii) of this section;

(vii) *Athletics* as described in paragraph (b)(2)(viii) of this section;

(viii) *Financial services* as described in paragraph (b)(2)(ix) of this section;

(ix) *Brokerage services* as described in paragraph (b)(2)(x) of this section;

(x) *Investing and investment management* as described in paragraph (b)(2)(xi) of this section;

(xi) *Trading* as described in paragraph (b)(2)(xii) of this section;

(xii) *Dealing in securities (as defined in section 475(c)(2)), partnership interests, or commodities (as defined in section 475(e)(2))* as described in paragraph (b)(2)(xiii) of this section; or

(xiii) *Any trade or business where the principal asset of such trade or business is the reputation or skill of one or more of its employees or owners* as defined in paragraph (b)(2)(xiv) of this section.

(2) *Additional rules for applying section 199A(d)(2) and paragraph (b) of this section.*—(i) *In general.*—(A) *No effect on other tax rules.*—This paragraph (b)(2) provides additional rules for determining whether a business is an SSTB within the meaning of section 199A(d)(2) and paragraph (b) of this section only. The rules of this paragraph (b)(2) apply solely for purposes of section 199A and therefore may not be taken into account for purposes of applying any provision of law or regulation other than section 199A and the regulations thereunder, except to the extent such provision expressly refers to section 199A(d) or this section.

(B) *Hedging transactions.*—Income, deduction, gain or loss from a *hedging transaction* (as defined in §1.1221-2(b)) entered into by an individual or RPE in the normal course of the individual's or RPE's trade or business is treated as income, deduction, gain, or loss from that trade or business for purposes of this paragraph (b)(2). See also §1.446-4.

(ii) *Meaning of services performed in the field of health.*—For purposes of section 199A(d)(2) and paragraph (b)(1)(i) of this section only, the *performance of services in the field of health* means the provision of medical services by individuals such as physicians, pharmacists, nurses, dentists, veterinarians, physical therapists, psychologists, and other similar healthcare professionals performing services in their capacity as such. The performance of services in the field of health does not include the provision of services not directly related to a medical services field, even though the services provided may purportedly relate to the health of the service recipient. For example, the performance of services in the field of health does not include the operation of health clubs or health spas that provide physical exercise or conditioning to their customers, payment processing, or the research, testing, and manufacture and/or sales of pharmaceuticals or medical devices.

(iii) *Meaning of services performed in the field of law.*—For purposes of section 199A(d)(2) and paragraph (b)(1)(ii) of this section only, the *performance of services in the field of law* means the performance of legal services by individuals such as lawyers, paralegals, legal arbitrators, mediators, and similar professionals performing services in their capacity as such. The performance of services in the field of law does not include the provision of services that do not require skills unique to the field of law; for example, the provision of services in the field of law does not include the provision of services by printers, delivery services, or stenography services.

(iv) *Meaning of services performed in the field of accounting.*—For purposes of section 199A(d)(2) and paragraph (b)(1)(iii) of this section only, the *performance of services in the field of accounting* means the provision of services by individuals such as accountants, enrolled agents, return preparers, financial auditors, and similar professionals performing services in their capacity as such.

(v) *Meaning of services performed in the field of actuarial science.*—For purposes of section 199A(d)(2) and paragraph (b)(1)(iv) of this section only, the *performance of services in the field of actuarial science* means the provision of services by individuals such as actuaries and similar professionals performing services in their capacity as such.

(vi) *Meaning of services performed in the field of performing arts.*—For purposes of section 199A(d)(2) and paragraph (b)(1)(v) of this section only, the *performance of services in the field of the performing arts* means the performance of services by individuals who participate in the creation of performing arts, such as actors, singers, musicians, entertainers, directors, and similar professionals performing services in their capacity as such. The performance of services in the field of performing arts does not include the provision of services that do not require skills unique to the creation of performing arts, such as the maintenance and operation of equipment or facilities for use in the performing arts. Similarly, the performance of services in the field of the performing arts does not include the provision of services by persons who broadcast or otherwise disseminate video or audio of performing arts to the public.

(vii) *Meaning of services performed in the field of consulting.*—For purposes of section 199A(d)(2) and paragraph (b)(1)(vi) of this section only, the *performance of services in the field of consulting* means the provision of professional advice and counsel to clients to assist the client in achieving goals and solving problems. Consulting includes providing advice and counsel regarding advocacy with the intention of influencing decisions made by a government or governmental agency and all attempts to influence legislators and other government officials on behalf of a client by lobbyists and other similar professionals performing services in their capacity as such. The performance of services in the field of consulting does not include the performance of services other than advice and counsel, such as sales (or economically similar services) or the provision of training and educational courses. For purposes of the preceding sentence, the determination of whether a person's services are sales or economically similar services will be based on all the facts and circumstances of that person's business. Such facts and circumstances include, for example, the manner in which the taxpayer is compensated for the services provided. Performance of services in the field of consulting does not include the performance of consulting services embedded in, or ancillary to, the sale of goods or performance of services on behalf of a trade or business that is otherwise not an SSTB (such as typical services provided by a building contractor) if there is no separate payment for the consulting services. Services within the fields of architecture and engineering are not treated as consulting services.

(viii) *Meaning of services performed in the field of athletics.*—For purposes of section 199A(d)(2) and paragraph (b)(1)(vii) of this section only, the *performance of services in the field of athletics* means the performance of services by individuals who participate in athletic competition such as athletes, coaches, and team managers in sports such as baseball, basketball, football, soccer, hockey, martial arts, boxing, bowling, tennis, golf, skiing, snowboarding, track and field, billiards, and racing. The performance of services in the field of athletics does not include the provision of services that do not require skills unique to athletic competition, such as the maintenance and operation of equipment or facilities for use in athletic events. Similarly, the performance of services in the field of athletics does not include the provision of services by persons who broadcast or otherwise disseminate video or audio of athletic events to the public.

(ix) *Meaning of services performed in the field of financial services.*—For purposes of section 199A(d)(2) and paragraph (b)(1)(viii) of this section only, the *performance of services in the field of financial services* means the provision of financial services to clients including managing wealth, advising clients with respect to finances, developing retirement plans, developing wealth transition plans, the provision of advisory and other similar services regarding valuations, mergers, acquisitions, dispositions, restructurings (including in title 11 of the Code or similar cases), and raising financial capital by underwriting, or acting as a client's agent in the issuance of securities and similar services. This includes services provided by financial advisors, investment bankers, wealth planners, retirement advisors, and other similar professionals performing services in their capacity as such. Solely for purposes of section 199A, the performance of services in the field of financial services does not include taking deposits or making loans, but does include arranging lending transactions between a lender and borrower.

(x) *Meaning of services performed in the field of brokerage services.*—For purposes of section 199A(d)(2) and paragraph (b)(1)(ix) of this section only, the *performance of services in the field of brokerage services* includes services in which a person arranges transactions between a buyer and a seller with respect to securities (as defined in section 475(c)(2)) for a commission or fee. This includes services provided by stock brokers and other similar professionals, but does not include services provided by real estate agents and brokers, or insurance agents and brokers.

(xi) *Meaning of the provision of services in investing and investment management.*—For purposes of section 199A(d)(2) and paragraph (b)(1)(x) of this section only, the *performance of services that consist of investing and investment management* refers to a trade or business involving the receipt of fees for providing investing, asset management, or investment management services, including providing advice with respect to buying and selling investments. The performance of services of investing and investment management does not include directly managing real property.

(xii) *Meaning of the provision of services in trading.*—For purposes of section 199A(d)(2) and paragraph (b)(1)(xi) of this section only, the *performance of services that consist of trading* means a trade or business of trading in securities (as defined in section 475(c)(2)), commodities (as defined in section 475(e)(2)), or partnership interests. Whether a person is a trader in securities, commodities, or partnership interests is determined by taking into account all relevant facts and circumstances, including the source and type of profit that is associated with engaging in the activity regardless of whether that person trades for the person's own account, for the account of others, or any combination thereof.

(xiii) *Meaning of the provision of services in dealing.*—(A) *Dealing in securities.*—For purposes of section 199A(d)(2) and paragraph (b)(1)(xii) of this section only, the *performance of services that consist of dealing in securities (as defined in section 475(c)(2))* means regularly purchasing securities from and selling securities to customers in the ordinary course of a trade or business or regularly offering to enter into, assume, offset, assign, or otherwise terminate positions in securities with customers in the ordinary course of a trade or business. Solely for purposes of the preceding sentence, the performance of services to originate a loan is not treated as the purchase of a security from the borrower in determining whether the lender is dealing in securities.

(B) *Dealing in commodities.*—For purposes of section 199A(d)(2) and paragraph (b)(1)(xii) of this section only, the *performance of services that consist of dealing in commodities (as defined in section 475(e)(2))* means regularly purchasing commodities from and selling commodities to customers in the ordinary course of a trade or business or regularly offering to enter into, assume, offset, assign, or otherwise terminate positions in commodities with customers in the ordinary course of a trade or business. Solely for purposes of the preceding sentence, gains and losses from qualified active sales as defined in paragraph (b)(2)(xiii)(B)(1) of this section are not taken into account in determining whether a person is engaged in the trade or business of dealing in commodities.

(1) *Qualified active sale.*—The term *qualified active sale* means the sale of commodities in the active conduct of a commodities business as a producer, processor, merchant, or handler of commodities if the trade or business is as an active producer, processor, merchant or handler of commodities. A hedging transaction described in paragraph (b)(2)(i)(B) of this section is treated as a qualified active sale. The sale of commodities held by a trade or business other than in its capacity as an active producer, processor, merchant, or handler of commodities is not a qualified active sale. For example, the sale by a trade or business of commodities that were held for investment or speculation would not be a qualified active sale.

(2) *Active conduct of a commodities business.*—For purposes of paragraph (b)(2)(xiii)(B)(1) of this section, a trade or business is engaged in the active conduct of a commodities business as a producer, processor, merchant, or handler of commodities only with respect to commodities for which each of the conditions described in paragraphs (b)(2)(xiii)(B)(3) through (5) of this section are satisfied.

(3) *Directly holds commodities as inventory or similar property.*—The commodities trade or business holds the commodities directly, and not through an agent or independent contractor, as inventory or similar property. The term inventory or similar property means property that is stock in trade of the trade or business or other property of a kind that would properly be included in the inventory of the trade or business if on hand at the close of the taxable year, or property held by the trade or business primarily for sale to customers in the ordinary course of its trade or business.

(4) *Directly incurs substantial expenses in the ordinary course.*—The commodities trade or business incurs substantial expenses in the ordinary course of the commodities trade or business from engaging in one or more of the following activities directly, and not through an agent or independent contractor—

(i) Substantial activities in the production of the commodities, including planting, tending or harvesting crops, raising or slaughtering livestock, or extracting minerals;

(ii) Substantial processing activities prior to the sale of the commodities, including the blending and drying of agricultural commodities, or the concentrating, refining, mixing, crushing, aerating or milling of commodities; or

(iii) Significant activities as described in paragraph (b)(2)(xiii)(B)(5) of this section.

(5) *Significant activities for purposes of paragraph (b)(2)(xiii)(B)(4)(iii) of this section.*—The commodities trade or business performs significant activities with respect to the commodities that consists of—

(i) The physical movement, handling and storage of the commodities, including preparation of contracts and invoices, arranging transportation, insurance and credit, arranging for receipt, transfer or negotiation of shipping documents, arranging storage or warehousing, and dealing with quality claims;

(ii) Owning and operating facilities for storage or warehousing; or

(iii) Owning, chartering, or leasing vessels or vehicles for the transportation of the commodities.

(C) *Dealing in partnership interests.*—For purposes of section 199A(d)(2) and paragraph (b)(1)(xii) of this section only, the *performance of services that consist of dealing in partnership interests* means regularly purchasing partnership interests from and selling partnership interests to customers in the ordinary course of a trade or business or regularly offering to enter into, assume, offset, assign, or otherwise terminate positions in partnership interests with customers in the ordinary course of a trade or business.

(xiv) *Meaning of trade or business where the principal asset of such trade or business is the reputation or skill of one or more employees or owners.*—For purposes of section 199A(d)(2) and paragraph (b)(1)(xiii) of this section only, the term *any trade or business where the principal asset of such trade or business is the reputation or skill of one or more of its employees or owners* means any trade or business that consists of any of the following (or any combination thereof):

(A) A trade or business in which a person receives fees, compensation, or other income for endorsing products or services;

(B) A trade or business in which a person licenses or receives fees, compensation, or other income for the use of an individual's image, likeness, name, signature, voice, trademark, or any other symbols associated with the individual's identity; or

(C) Receiving fees, compensation, or other income for appearing at an event or on radio, television, or another media format.

(D) For purposes of paragraphs (b)(2)(xiv)(A) through (C) of this section, the term *fees, compensation, or other income* includes the receipt of a partnership interest and the corresponding distributive share of income, deduction, gain, or loss from the partnership, or the receipt of stock of an S corporation and the corresponding income, deduction, gain, or loss from the S corporation stock.

(3) *Examples.*—The following examples illustrate the rules in paragraphs (a) and (b) of this section. The examples do not address all types of services that may or may not qualify as specified services. Unless otherwise provided, the individual in each example has taxable income in excess of the threshold amount.

(i) *Example 1.* B is a board-certified pharmacist who contracts as an independent contractor with X, a small medical facility in a rural area. X employs one full time pharmacist, but contracts with B when X's needs exceed the capacity of its full-time staff. When engaged by X, B is responsible for receiving and reviewing orders from physicians providing medical care at the facility; making recommendations on dosing and alternatives to the ordering physician; performing inoculations, checking for drug interactions, and filling pharmaceutical orders for patients receiving care at X. B is engaged in the performance of services in the field of health within the meaning of section 199A(d)(2) and paragraphs (b)(1)(i) and (b)(2)(ii) of this section.

(ii) *Example 2.* X is the operator of a residential facility that provides a variety of services to senior citizens who reside on campus. For residents, X offers standard domestic services including housing management and maintenance, meals, laundry, entertainment, and other similar services. In addition, X contracts with local professional healthcare organizations to offer residents a range of medical and health services provided at the facility, including skilled nursing care, physical and occupational therapy, speech-language pathology services, medical social services, medications, medical supplies and equipment used in the facility, ambulance transportation to the nearest supplier of needed services, and dietary counseling. X receives all of its income from residents for the costs associated with residing at the facility. Any health and medical services are billed directly by the healthcare providers to the senior citizens for those professional healthcare services even though those services are provided at the facility. X does not perform services in the field of health within the meaning of section 199A(d)(2) and paragraphs (b)(1)(i) and (b)(2)(ii) of this section.

(iii) *Example 3.* Y operates specialty surgical centers that provide outpatient medical procedures that do not require the patient to remain overnight for recovery or observation following the procedure. Y is a private organization that owns a number of facilities throughout the country. For each facility, Y ensures compliance with state and Federal laws for medical facilities and manages the facility's operations and performs all administrative functions. Y does not employ physicians, nurses, and medical assistants, but enters into agreements with other professional medical organizations or directly with the medical professionals to perform the procedures and provide all medical care. Patients are billed by Y for the facility costs relating to their procedure and by the healthcare professional or their affiliated organization for the actual costs of the procedure conducted by the physician and medical support team. Y does not perform services in the field of health within the meaning of section 199A(d)(2) and paragraphs (b)(1)(i) and (b)(2)(ii) of this section.

(iv) *Example 4.* Z is the developer and the only provider of a patented test used to detect a particular medical condition. Z accepts test orders only from health care professionals (Z's clients), does not have contact with patients, and Z's employees do not diagnose, treat, or manage any aspect of patient care. A, who manages Z's testing operations, is the only employee with an advanced medical degree. All other employees are technical support staff and not healthcare professionals. Z's workers are highly educated, but the skills the workers bring to the job are not often useful for Z's testing methods. In order to perform the duties required by Z, employees receive more than a year of specialized training for working with Z's test, which is of no use to other employers. Upon completion of an ordered test, Z analyses the results and provides its clients a report summarizing the findings. Z does not discuss the report's results, or the patient's diagnosis or treatment with any health care provider or the patient. Z is not informed by the healthcare provider as to the healthcare provider's diagnosis or treatment. Z is not providing services in the field of health within the meaning of section 199A(d)(2) and paragraphs (b)(1)(i) and (b)(2)(ii) of this section or where the principal asset of the trade or business is the reputation or skill of one or more of its employees within the meaning of paragraphs (b)(1)(xiii) and (b)(2)(xiv) of this section.

(v) *Example 5.* A, a singer and songwriter, writes and records a song. A is paid a mechanical royalty when the song is licensed or streamed. A is also paid a performance royalty when the recorded song is played publicly. A is engaged in the performance of services in an SSTB in the field of performing arts within the meaning of section 199A(d)(2) or paragraphs (b)(1)(v) and (b)(2)(vi) of this section. The royalties that A receives for the song are not eligible for a deduction under section 199A.

(vi) *Example 6.* B is a partner in Movie LLC, a partnership. Movie LLC is a film production company. Movie LLC plans and coordinates film production. Movie LLC shares in the profits of the films that it produces. Therefore, Movie LLC is engaged in the performance of services in an SSTB in the field of performing arts within the meaning of section 199A(d)(2) or paragraphs (b)(1)(v) and (b)(2)(vi) of this section. B is a passive owner in Movie LLC and does not provide any services with respect to Movie LLC. However, because Movie LLC is engaged in an SSTB in the field of performing arts, B's distributive share of the income, gain, deduction, and loss with respect to Movie LLC is not eligible for a deduction under section 199A.

(vii) *Example 7.* C is a partner in Partnership, which solely owns and operates a professional sports team. Partnership employs athletes and sells tickets and broadcast rights for games in which the sports team competes. Partnership sells the broadcast rights to Broadcast LLC, a separate trade or business. Broadcast LLC solely broadcasts the games. Partnership is engaged in the performance of services in an SSTB in the field of athletics within the meaning of section 199A(d)(2) or paragraphs (b)(1)(vii) and (b)(2)(viii) of this section. The tickets sales and the sale of the broadcast rights are both the performance of services in the field of athletics. C is a passive owner in Partnership and C does not provide any services with respect to Partnership or the sports team. However, because Partnership is engaged in an SSTB in the field of athletics, C's distributive share of the income, gain, deduction, and loss with respect to Partnership is not eligible for a deduction under section 199A. Broadcast LLC is not engaged in the performance of services in an SSTB in the field of athletics.

(viii) *Example 8.* D is in the business of providing services that *assist unrelated entities in making their personnel structures more* efficient. D studies its client's organization and structure and compares it to peers in its industry. D then makes recommendations and provides advice to its client regarding possible changes in the client's personnel structure, including the use of temporary workers. D does

not provide any temporary workers to its clients and D's compensation and fees are not affected by whether D's clients used temporary workers. D is engaged in the performance of services in an SSTB in the field of consulting within the meaning of section 199A(d)(2) or paragraphs (b)(1)(vi) and (b)(2)(vii) of this section.

(ix) *Example 9.* E is an individual who owns and operates a temporary worker staffing firm primarily focused on the software consulting industry. Business clients hire E to provide temporary workers that have the necessary technical skills and experience with a variety of business software to provide consulting and advice regarding the proper selection and operation of software most appropriate for the business they are advising. E does not have a technical software engineering background and does not provide software consulting advice herself. E reviews resumes and refers candidates to the client when the client indicates a need for temporary workers. E does not evaluate her clients' needs about whether the client needs workers and does not evaluate the clients' consulting contracts to determine the type of expertise needed. Rather, the client provides E with a job description indicating the required skills for the upcoming consulting project. E is paid a fixed fee for each temporary worker actually hired by the client and receives a bonus if that worker is hired permanently within a year of referral. E's fee is not contingent on the profits of its clients. E is not considered to be engaged in the performance of services in the field of consulting within the meaning of section 199A(d)(2) or (b)(1)(vi) and (b)(2)(vii) of this section.

(x) *Example 10.* F is in the business of licensing software to customers. F discusses and evaluates the customer's software needs with the customer. The taxpayer advises the customer on the particular software products it licenses. F is paid a flat price for the software license. After the customer licenses the software, F helps to implement the software. F is engaged in the trade or business of licensing software and not engaged in an SSTB in the field of consulting within the meaning of section 199A(d)(2) or paragraphs (b)(1)(vi) and (b)(2)(vii) of this section.

(xi) *Example 11.* G is in the business of providing services to assist clients with their finances. G will study a particular client's financial situation, including, the client's present income, savings, and investments, and anticipated future economic and financial needs. Based on this study, G will then assist the client in making decisions and plans regarding the client's financial activities. Such financial planning includes the design of a personal budget to assist the client in monitoring the client's financial situation, the adoption of investment strategies tailored to the client's needs, and other similar services. G is engaged in the performance of services in an SSTB in the field of financial services within the meaning of section 199A(d)(2) or paragraphs (b)(1)(viii) and (b)(2)(ix) of this section.

(xii) *Example 12.* H is in the business of franchising a brand of personal financial planning offices, which generally provide personal wealth management, retirement planning, and other financial advice services to customers for a fee. H does not provide financial planning services itself. H licenses the right to use the business tradename, other branding intellectual property, and a marketing plan to third-party financial planner franchisees that operate the franchised locations and provide all services to customers. In exchange, the franchisees compensate H based on a fee structure, which includes a one-time fee to acquire the franchise. H is not engaged in the performance of services in the field of financial services within the meaning of section 199A(d)(2) or paragraphs (b)(1)(viii) and (b)(2)(ix) of this section.

(xiii) *Example 13.* J is in the business of executing transactions for customers involving various types of securities or commodities generally traded through organized exchanges or other similar networks. Customers place orders with J to trade securities or commodities based on the taxpayer's recommendations. J's compensation for its services typically is based on completion of the trade orders. J is engaged in an SSTB in the field of brokerage services within the meaning of section 199A(d)(2) or paragraphs (b)(1)(ix) and (b)(2)(x) of this section.

(xiv) *Example 14.* K owns 100% of Corp, an S corporation, which operates a bicycle sales and repair business. Corp has 8 employees, including K. Half of Corp's net income is generated from sales of new and used bicycles and related goods, such as helmets, and bicycle-related equipment. The other half of Corp's net income is generated from bicycle repair services performed by K and Corp's other employees. Corp's assets consist of inventory, fixtures, bicycle repair equipment, and a leasehold on its retail location. Several of the employees and K have worked in the bicycle business for many years, and have acquired substantial skill and reputation in the field. Customers often consult with the employees on the best bicycle for purchase. K is in the business of sales and repairs of bicycles and is not engaged in an SSTB within the meaning of section 199A(d)(2) or paragraphs (b)(1)(xiii) and (b)(2)(xiv) of this section.

(xv) *Example 15.* L is a well-known chef and the sole owner of multiple restaurants each of which is owned in a disregarded entity.

Itemized Deductions for Individuals and Corps.
See p. 20,601 for regulations not amended to reflect law changes
25,691

Due to L's skill and reputation as a chef, L receives an endorsement fee of $500,000 for the use of L's name on a line of cooking utensils and cookware. L is in the trade or business of being a chef and owning restaurants and such trade or business is not an SSTB. However, L is also in the trade or business of receiving endorsement income. L's trade or business consisting of the receipt of the endorsement fee for L's skill and/or reputation is an SSTB within the meaning of section 199A(d)(2) or paragraphs (b)(1)(xiii) and (b)(2)(xiv) of this section.

(xvi) *Example 16.* M is a well-known actor. M entered into a partnership with Shoe Company, in which M contributed her likeness and the use of her name to the partnership in exchange for a 50% interest in the partnership and a guaranteed payment. M's trade or business consisting of the receipt of the partnership interest and the corresponding distributive share with respect to the partnership interest for M's likeness and the use of her name is an SSTB within the meaning of section 199A(d)(2) or paragraphs (b)(1)(xiii) and (b)(2)(xiv) of this section.

(c) *Special rules.*—(1) *De minimis rule.*—(i) *Gross receipts of $25 million or less.*—For a trade or business with gross receipts of $25 million or less for the taxable year, a trade or business is not an SSTB if less than 10 percent of the gross receipts of the trade or business are attributable to the performance of services in a field described in paragraph (b) of this section. For purposes of determining whether this 10 percent test is satisfied, the performance of any activity incident to the actual performance of services in the field is considered the performance of services in that field.

(ii) *Gross receipts of greater than $25 million.*—For a trade or business with gross receipts of greater than $25 million for the taxable year, the rules of paragraph (c)(1)(i) of this section are applied by substituting "5 percent" for "10 percent" each place it appears.

(iii) *Examples.*—The following examples illustrate the provisions of paragraph (c)(1) of this section.

(A) *Example 1.* Landscape LLC sells lawn care and landscaping equipment and also provides advice and counsel on landscape design for large office parks and residential buildings. The landscape design services include advice on the selection and placement of trees, shrubs, and flowers and are considered to be the performance of services in the field of consulting under paragraphs (b)(1)(vi) and (b)(2)(vii) of this section. Landscape LLC separately invoices for its landscape design services and does not sell the trees, shrubs, or flowers it recommends for use in the landscape design. Landscape LLC maintains one set of books and records and treats the equipment sales and design services as a single trade or business for purposes of sections 162 and 199A. Landscape LLC has gross receipts of $2 million. $250,000 of the gross receipts is attributable to the landscape design services, an SSTB. Because the gross receipts from the consulting services exceed 10 percent of Landscape LLC's total gross receipts, the entirety of Landscape LLC's trade or business is considered an SSTB.

(B) *Example 2.* Animal Care LLC provides veterinarian services performed by licensed staff and also develops and sells its own line of organic dog food at its veterinarian clinic and online. The veterinarian services are considered to be the performance of services in the field of health under paragraphs (b)(1)(i) and (b)(2)(ii) of this section. Animal Care LLC separately invoices for its veterinarian services and the sale of its organic dog food. Animal Care LLC maintains separate books and records for its veterinarian clinic and its development and sale of its dog food. Animal Care LLC also has separate employees who are unaffiliated with the veterinary clinic and who only work on the formulation, marketing, sales, and distribution of the organic dog food products. Animal Care LLC treats its veterinary practice and the dog food development and sales as separate trades or businesses for purposes of section 162 and 199A. Animal Care LLC has gross receipts of $3,000,000. $1,000,000 of the gross receipts is attributable to the veterinary services, an SSTB. Although the gross receipts from the services in the field of health exceed 10 percent of Animal Care LLC's total gross receipts, the dog food development and sales business is not considered an SSTB due to the fact that the veterinary practice and the dog food development and sales are separate trades or businesses under section 162.

(2) *Services or property provided to an SSTB.*—(i) *In general.*—If a trade or business provides property or services to an SSTB within the meaning of this section and there is 50 percent or more common ownership of the trades or businesses, that portion of the trade or business of providing property or services to the 50 percent or more commonly-owned SSTB will be treated as a separate SSTB with respect to the related parties.

(ii) *50 percent or more common ownership.*—For purposes of paragraph (c)(2)(i) and (ii) of this section, 50 percent or more common ownership includes direct or indirect ownership by related parties within the meaning of sections 267(b) or 707(b).

(iii) *Examples.*—The following examples illustrate the provisions of paragraph (c)(2) of this section.

(A) *Example 1.* Law Firm is a partnership that provides legal services to clients, owns its own office building and employs its own administrative staff. Law Firm divides into three partnerships. Partnership 1 performs legal services to clients. Partnership 2 owns the office building and rents the entire building to Partnership 1. Partnership 3 employs the administrative staff and through a contract with Partnership 1 provides administrative services to Partnership 1 in exchange for fees. All three of the partnerships are owned by the same people (the original owners of Law Firm). Because Partnership 2 provides all of its property to Partnership 1, and Partnership 3 provides all of its services to Partnership 1, Partnerships 2 and 3 will each be treated as an SSTB under paragraph (c)(2) of this section.

(B) *Example 2.* Assume the same facts as in Example 1 of this paragraph (c)(2), except that Partnership 2, which owns the office building, rents 50 percent of the building to Partnership 1, which provides legal services, and the other 50 percent to various unrelated third party tenants. Because Partnership 2 is owned by the same people as Partnership 1, the portion of Partnership 2's leasing activity related to the lease of the building to Partnership 1 will be treated as a separate SSTB. The remaining 50 percent of Partnership 2's leasing activity will not be treated as an SSTB.

(d) *Trade or business of performing services as an employee.*—(1) *In general.*—The trade or business of performing services as an employee is not a trade or business for purposes of section 199A and the regulations thereunder. Therefore, no items of income, gain, deduction, and loss from the trade or business of performing services as an employee constitute QBI within the meaning of section 199A and §1.199A-3. Except as provided in paragraph (d)(3) of this section, income from the trade or business of performing services as an employee refers to all wages (within the meaning of section 3401(a)) and other income earned in a capacity as an employee, including payments described in §1.6041-2(a)(1) (other than payments to individuals described in section 3121(d)(3)) and §1.6041-2(b)(1).

(2) *Employer's Federal employment tax classification of employee immaterial.*—For purposes of determining whether wages are earned in a capacity as an employee as provided in paragraph (d)(1) of this section, the treatment of an employee by an employer as anything other than an employee for Federal employment tax purposes is immaterial. Thus, if a worker should be properly classified as an employee, it is of no consequence that the employee is treated as a non-employee by the employer for Federal employment tax purposes.

(3) *Presumption that former employees are still employees.*—(i) *Presumption.*—Solely for purposes of section 199A(d)(1)(B) and paragraph (d)(1) of this section, an individual that was properly treated as an employee for Federal employment tax purposes by the person to which he or she provided services and who is subsequently treated as other than an employee by such person with regard to the provision of substantially the same services directly or indirectly to the person (or a related person), is presumed, for three years after ceasing to be treated as an employee for Federal employment tax purposes, to be in the trade or business of performing services as an employee with regard to such services. As provided in paragraph (d)(3)(ii) of this section, this presumption may be rebutted upon a showing by the individual that, under Federal tax law, regulations, and principles (including common-law employee classification rules), the individual is performing services in a capacity other than as an employee. This presumption applies regardless of whether the individual provides services directly or indirectly through an entity or entities.

(ii) *Rebuttal of presumption.*—Upon notice from the IRS, an individual rebuts the presumption in paragraph (d)(3)(i) of this section by providing records, such as contracts or partnership agreements, that provide sufficient evidence to corroborate the individual's status as a non-employee.

(iii) *Examples.*—The following examples illustrate the provision of paragraph (d)(3) of this section. Unless otherwise provided, the individual in each example has taxable income in excess of the threshold amount.

(A) *Example 1.* A is employed by PRS, a partnership for Federal tax purposes, as a fulltime employee and is treated as such for Federal employment tax purposes. A quits his job for PRS and enters into a contract with PRS under which A provides substantially the same services that A previously provided to PRS in A's capacity as an employee. Because A was treated as an employee for services he provided to PRS, and now is no longer treated as an employee with regard to such services, A is presumed (solely for purposes of section

199A(d)(1)(B) and paragraphs (a)(3) and (d) of this section) to be in the trade or business of performing services as an employee with regard to his services performed for PRS. Unless the presumption is rebutted with a showing that, under Federal tax law, regulations, and principles (including the common-law employee classification rules), A is not an employee, any amounts paid by PRS to A with respect to such services will not be QBI for purposes of section 199A. The presumption would apply even if, instead of contracting directly with PRS, A formed a disregarded entity, or a passthrough entity, and the entity entered into the contract with PRS.

(B) *Example 2.* C is an attorney employed as an associate in a law firm (Law Firm 1) and was treated as such for Federal employment tax purposes. C and the other associates in Law Firm 1 have taxable income below the threshold amount. Law Firm 1 terminates its employment relationship with C and its other associates. C and the other former associates form a new partnership, Law Firm 2, which contracts to perform legal services for Law Firm 1. Therefore, in form, C is now a partner in Law Firm 2 which earns income from providing legal services to Law Firm 1. C continues to provide substantially the same legal services to Law Firm 1 and its clients. Because C was previously treated as an employee for services she provided to Law Firm 1, and now is no longer treated as an employee with regard to such services, C is presumed (solely for purposes of section 199A(d)(1)(B) and paragraphs (a)(3) and (d) of this section) to be in the trade or business of performing services as an employee with respect to the services C provides to Law Firm 1 indirectly through Law Firm 2. Unless the presumption is rebutted with a showing that, under Federal tax law, regulations, and principles (including common-law employee classification rules), C is not an employee, C's distributive share of Law Firm 2 income (including any guaranteed payments) will not be QBI for purposes of section 199A. The results in this example would not change if, instead of contracting with Law Firm 1, Law Firm 2 was instead admitted as a partner in Law Firm 1.

(C) *Example 3.* E is an engineer employed as a senior project engineer in an engineering firm, Engineering Firm. Engineering Firm is a partnership for Federal tax purposes and structured such that after 10 years, senior project engineers are considered for partner if certain career milestones are met. After 10 years, E meets those career milestones and is admitted as a partner in Engineering Firm. As a partner in Engineering Firm, E shares in the net profits of Engineering Firm, and also otherwise satisfies the requirements under Federal tax law, regulations, and principles (including common-law employee classification rules) to be respected as a partner. E is presumed (solely for purposes of section 199A(d)(1)(B) and paragraphs (a)(3) and (d) of this section) to be in the trade or business of performing services as an employee with respect to the services E provides to Engineering Firm. However, E is able to rebut the presumption by showing that E became a partner in Engineering Firm as a career milestone, shares in the overall net profits in Engineering Firm, and otherwise satisfies the requirements under Federal tax law, regulations, and principles (including common-law employee classification rules) to be respected as a partner.

(D) *Example 4.* F is a financial advisor employed by a financial advisory firm, Advisory Firm, a partnership for Federal tax purposes, as a fulltime employee and is treated as such for Federal employment tax purposes. F has taxable income below the threshold amount. Advisory Firm is a partnership and offers F the opportunity to be admitted as a partner. F elects to be admitted as a partner to Advisory Firm and is admitted as a partner to Advisory Firm. As a partner in Advisory Firm, F shares in the net profits of Advisory Firm, is obligated to Advisory Firm in ways that F was not previously obligated as an employee, is no longer entitled to certain benefits available only to employees of Advisory Firm, and has materially modified his relationship with Advisory Firm. F's share of net profits is not subject to a floor or capped at a dollar amount. F is presumed (solely for purposes of section 199A(d)(1)(B) and paragraphs (a)(3) and (d) of this section) to be in the trade or business of performing services as an employee with respect to the services F provides to Advisory Firm. However, F is able to rebut the presumption by showing that F became a partner in Advisory Firm by sharing in the profits of Advisory Firm, materially modifying F's relationship with Advisory Firm, and otherwise satisfying the requirements under Federal tax law, regulations, and principles (including common-law employee classification rules) to be respected as a partner.

(e) *Applicability date.*—(1) *General rule.*—Except as provided in paragraph (e)(2) of this section, the provisions of this section apply to taxable years ending after February 8, 2019.

(2) *Exceptions.*—(i) *Anti-abuse rules.*—The provisions of paragraphs (c)(2) and (d)(3) of this section apply to taxable years ending after December 22, 2017.

(ii) *Non-calendar year RPE.*—For purposes of determining QBI, W-2 wages, UBIA of qualified property, and the aggregate amount of

qualified REIT dividends and qualified PTP income, if an individual receives any of these items from an RPE with a taxable year that begins before January 1, 2018, and ends after December 31, 2017, such items are treated as having been incurred by the individual during the individual's taxable year in which or with which such RPE taxable year ends. [Reg. § 1.199A-5.]

☐ [T.D. 9847, 2-4-2019 (corrected 4-17-2019).]

[Reg. § 1.199A-6]

§ 1.199A-6. Relevant passthrough entities (RPEs), publicly traded partnerships (PTPs), trusts, and estates.—(a) *Overview.*—This section provides special rules for RPEs, PTPs, trusts, and estates necessary for the computation of the section 199A deduction of their owners or beneficiaries. Paragraph (b) of this section provides computational and reporting rules for RPEs necessary for individuals who own interests in RPEs to calculate their section 199A deduction. Paragraph (c) of this section provides computational and reporting rules for PTPs necessary for individuals who own interests in PTPs to calculate their section 199A deduction. Paragraph (d) of this section provides computational and reporting rules for trusts (other than grantor trusts) and estates necessary for their beneficiaries to calculate their section 199A deduction.

(b) *Computational and reporting rules for RPEs.*—(1) *In general.*—An RPE must determine and report information attributable to any trades or businesses it is engaged in necessary for its owners to determine their section 199A deduction.

(2) *Computational rules.*—Using the following four rules, an RPE must determine the items necessary for individuals who own interests in the RPE to calculate their section 199A deduction under § 1.199A-1(c) or (d). An RPE that chooses to aggregate trades or businesses under the rules of § 1.199A-4 may determine these items for the aggregated trade or business.

(i) First, the RPE must determine if it is engaged in one or more trades or businesses. The RPE must also determine whether any of its trades or businesses is an SSTB under the rules of § 1.199A-5.

(ii) Second, the RPE must apply the rules in § 1.199A-3 to determine the QBI for each trade or business engaged in directly.

(iii) Third, the RPE must apply the rules in § 1.199A-2 to determine the W-2 wages and UBIA of qualified property for each trade or business engaged in directly.

(iv) Fourth, the RPE must determine whether it has any qualified REIT dividends as defined in § 1.199A-3(c)(1) earned directly or through another RPE. The RPE must also determine the amount of qualified PTP income as defined in § 1.199A-3(c)(2) earned directly or indirectly through investments in PTPs.

(3) *Reporting rules for RPEs.*—(i) *Trade or business directly engaged in.*—An RPE must separately identify and report on the Schedule K-1 issued to its owners for any trade or business (including an aggregated trade or business) engaged in directly by the RPE—

(A) Each owner's allocable share of QBI, W-2 wages, and UBIA of qualified property attributable to each such trade or business; and

(B) Whether any of the trades or businesses described in paragraph (b)(3)(i) of this section is an SSTB.

(ii) *Other items.*—An RPE must also report on an attachment to the Schedule K-1, any QBI, W-2 wages, UBIA of qualified property, or SSTB determinations, reported to it by any RPE in which the RPE owns a direct or indirect interest. The RPE must also report each owner's allocated share of any qualified REIT dividends received by the RPE (including through another RPE) as well as any qualified PTP income or loss received by the RPE for each PTP in which the RPE holds an interest (including through another RPE). Such information can be reported on an amended or late filed return to the extent that the period of limitations remains open.

(iii) *Failure to report information.*—If an RPE fails to separately identify or report on the Schedule K-1 (or any attachments thereto) issued to an owner an item described in paragraph (b)(3)(i) of this section, the owner's share (and the share of any upper-tier indirect owner) of each unreported item of positive QBI, W-2 wages, or UBIA of qualified property attributable to trades or businesses engaged in by that RPE will be presumed to be zero.

(c) *Computational and reporting rules for PTPs.*—(1) *Computational rules.*—Each PTP must determine its QBI under the rules of § 1.199A-3 for each trade or business in which the PTP is engaged in directly. The PTP must also determine whether any of the trades or businesses it is engaged in directly is an SSTB.

(2) *Reporting rules.*—Each PTP is required to separately identify and report the information described in paragraph (c)(1) of this

Itemized Deductions for Individuals and Corps.
See p. 20,601 for regulations not amended to reflect law changes
25,693

section on Schedules K-1 issued to its partners. Each PTP must also determine and report any qualified REIT dividends or qualified PTP income or loss received by the PTP including through an RPE, a REIT, or another PTP. A PTP is not required to determine or report W-2 wages or the UBIA of qualified property attributable to trades or businesses it is engaged in directly.

(d) *Application to trusts, estates, and beneficiaries.*—(1) *In general.*—A trust or estate computes its section 199A deduction based on the QBI, W-2 wages, UBIA of qualified property, qualified REIT dividends, and qualified PTP income that are allocated to the trust or estate. An individual beneficiary of a trust or estate takes into account any QBI, W-2 wages, UBIA of qualified property, qualified REIT dividends, and qualified PTP income allocated from a trust or estate in calculating the beneficiary's section 199A deduction, in the same manner as though the items had been allocated from an RPE. For purposes of this section and §§ 1.199A-1 through 1.199A-5, a trust or estate is treated as an RPE to the extent it allocates QBI and other items to its beneficiaries, and is treated as an individual to the extent it retains the QBI and other items.

(2) *Grantor trusts.*—To the extent that the grantor or another person is treated as owning all or part of a trust under sections 671 through 679, such person computes its section 199A deduction as if that person directly conducted the activities of the trust with respect to the portion of the trust treated as owned by the grantor or other person.

(3) *Non-grantor trusts and estates.*—(i) *Calculation at entity level.*—A trust or estate must calculate its QBI, W-2 wages, UBIA of qualified property, qualified REIT dividends, and qualified PTP income. The QBI of a trust or estate must be computed by allocating qualified items of deduction described in section 199A(c)(3) in accordance with the classification of those deductions under § 1.652(b)-3(a), and deductions not directly attributable within the meaning of § 1.652(b)-3(b) (other deductions) are allocated in a manner consistent with the rules in § 1.652(b)-3(b). Any depletion and depreciation deductions described in section 642(e) and any amortization deductions described in section 642(f) that otherwise are properly included in the computation of QBI are included in the computation of QBI of the trust or estate, regardless of how those deductions may otherwise be allocated between the trust or estate and its beneficiaries for other purposes of the Code.

(ii) *Allocation among trust or estate and beneficiaries.*—The QBI (including any amounts that may be less than zero as calculated at the trust or estate level), W-2 wages, UBIA of qualified property, qualified REIT dividends, and qualified PTP income of a trust or estate are allocated to each beneficiary and to the trust or estate based on the relative proportion of the trust's or estate's *distributable net income (DNI)*, as defined by section 643(a), for the taxable year that is distributed or required to be distributed to the beneficiary or is retained by the trust or estate. For this purpose, the trust's or estate's DNI is determined with regard to the separate share rule of section 663(c), but without regard to section 199A. If the trust or estate has no DNI for the taxable year, any QBI, W-2 wages, UBIA of qualified property, qualified REIT dividends, and qualified PTP income are allocated entirely to the trust or estate.

(iii) *Separate shares.*—In the case of a trust or estate described in section 663(c) with substantially separate and independent shares for multiple beneficiaries, such trust or estate will be treated as a single trust or estate for purposes of determining whether the taxable income of the trust or estate exceeds the threshold amount; determining taxable income, net capital gain, net QBI, W-2 wages, UBIA of qualified property, qualified REIT dividends, and qualified PTP income for each trade or business of the trust and estate; and computing the W-2 wage and UBIA of qualified property limitations. The allocation of these items to the separate shares of a trust or estate will be governed by the rules under §§ 1.663(c)-1 through 1.663(c)-5, as they may be adjusted or clarified by publication in the Internal Revenue Bulletin (see § 601.601(d)(2)(ii)(*b*) of this chapter).

(iv) *Threshold amount.*—The threshold amount applicable to a trust or estate is $157,500 for any taxable year beginning before 2019. For taxable years beginning after 2018, the threshold amount shall be $157,500 increased by the cost-of-living adjustment as outlined in § 1.199A-1(b)(12). For purposes of determining whether a trust or estate has taxable income in excess of the threshold amount, the taxable income of the trust or estate is determined after taking into account any distribution deduction under sections 651 or 661.

(v) *Charitable remainder trusts.*—A charitable remainder trust described in section 664 is not entitled to and does not calculate a section 199A deduction, and the threshold amount described in section 199A(e)(2) does not apply to the trust. However, any taxable recipient of a unitrust or annuity amount from the trust must deter-

mine and apply the recipient's own threshold amount for purposes of section 199A taking into account any annuity or unitrust amounts received from the trust. A recipient of a unitrust or annuity amount from a trust may take into account QBI, qualified REIT dividends, or qualified PTP income for purposes of determining the recipient's section 199A deduction for the taxable year to the extent that the unitrust or annuity amount distributed to such recipient consists of such section 199A items under § 1.664-1(d). For example, if a charitable remainder trust has investment income of $500, qualified dividend income of $200, and qualified REIT dividends of $1,000, and distributes $1,000 to the recipient, the trust would be treated as having income in two classes within the category of income, described in § 1.664-1(d)(1)(i)(*a*)(1), for purposes of § 1.664-1(d)(1)(ii)(*b*). Because the annuity amount first carries out income in the class subject to the highest income tax rate, the entire annuity payment comes from the class with the investment income and qualified REIT dividends. Thus, the charitable remainder trust would be treated as distributing a proportionate amount of the investment income ($500/(1,000+500)*1,000 = $333) and qualified REIT dividends ($1000/(1,000+500)*1000 = $667) because the investment income and qualified REIT dividends are taxed at the same rate and within the same class, which is higher than the rate of tax for the qualified dividend income in a separate class. The charitable remainder trust in this example would not be treated as distributing any of the qualified dividend income until it distributed all the investment income and qualified REIT dividends (more than $1,500 in total) to the recipient. To the extent that a trust is treated as distributing QBI, qualified REIT dividends, or qualified PTP income to more than one unitrust or annuity recipient in the taxable year, the distribution of such income will be treated as made to the recipients proportionately, based on their respective shares of total QBI, qualified REIT dividends, or qualified PTP income distributed for that year. The trust allocates and reports any W-2 wages or UBIA of qualified property to the taxable recipient of the annuity or unitrust interest based on each recipient's share of the trust's total QBI (whether or not distributed) for that taxable year. Accordingly, if 10 percent of the QBI of a charitable remainder trust is distributed to the recipient and 90 percent of the QBI is retained by the trust, 10 percent of the W-2 wages and UBIA of qualified property is allocated and reported to the recipient and 90 percent of the W-2 wages and UBIA of qualified property is treated as retained by the trust. However, any W-2 wages retained by the trust cannot be used to compute W-2 wages in a subsequent taxable year for section 199A purposes. Any QBI, qualified REIT dividends, or qualified PTP income of the trust that is unrelated business taxable income is subject to excise tax and that tax must be allocated to the corpus of the trust under § 1.664-1(c).

(vi) *Electing small business trusts.*—An electing small business trust (ESBT) is entitled to the deduction under section 199A. Any section 199A deduction attributable to the assets in the S portion of the ESBT is to be taken into account by the S portion. The S portion of the ESBT must take into account the QBI and other items from any S corporation owned by the ESBT, the grantor portion of the ESBT must take into account the QBI and other items from any assets treated as owned by a grantor or another person (owned portion) of a trust under sections 671 through 679, and the non-S portion of the ESBT must take into account any QBI and other items from any other entities or assets owned by the ESBT. For purposes of determining whether the taxable income of an ESBT exceeds the threshold amount, the S portion and the non-S portion of an ESBT are treated as a single trust. See § 1.641(c)-1.

(vii) *Anti-abuse rule for creation of a trust to avoid exceeding the threshold amount.*—A trust formed or funded with a principal purpose of avoiding, or of using more than one, threshold amount for purposes of calculating the deduction under section 199A will not be respected as a separate trust entity for purposes of determining the threshold amount for purposes of section 199A. See also § 1.643(f)-1 of the regulations.

(viii) *Example.*—The following example illustrates the application of paragraph (d) of this section.

(A) *Example*—(1) *Computation of DNI and inclusion and deduction amounts*—(i) *Trust's distributive share of partnership items.* Trust, an irrevocable testamentary complex trust, is a 25% partner in PRS, a family partnership that operates a restaurant that generates QBI and W-2 wages. A and B, Trust's beneficiaries, own the remaining 75% of PRS directly. In 2018, PRS properly allocates gross income from the restaurant of $55,000, and expenses directly allocable to the restaurant of $45,000 (including W-2 wages of $25,000, and miscellaneous expenses of $20,000) to Trust. These items are properly included in Trust's DNI. PRS distributes $10,000 of cash to Trust in 2018.

(ii) *Trust's activities.* In addition to its interest in PRS, Trust also operates a family bakery conducted through an LLC wholly-owned by the Trust that is treated as a disregarded entity. In 2018, the bakery produces $100,000 of gross income and $155,000 of expenses directly allocable to operation of the bakery (including W-2 wages of $50,000, rental expense of $75,000, miscellaneous expenses of $25,000, and depreciation deductions of $5,000). (The net loss from the bakery operations is not subject to any loss disallowance provisions outside of section 199A.) Trust maintains a reserve of $5,000 for depreciation. Trust also has $125,000 of UBIA of qualified property in the bakery. For purposes of computing its section 199A deduction, Trust and its beneficiaries have properly chosen to aggregate the family restaurant conducted through PRS with the bakery conducted directly by Trust under §1.199A-4. Trust also owns various investment assets that produce portfolio-type income consisting of dividends ($25,000), interest ($15,000), and tax-exempt interest ($15,000). Accordingly, Trust has the following items which are properly included in Trust's DNI:

Table 1 to Paragraph (d)(3)(viii)(A)(1)(ii)

Interest Income	15,000
Dividends	25,000
Tax-exempt interest	15,000
Net business loss from PRS and bakery	(45,000)
Trustee commissions	3,000
State and local taxes	5,000

(iii) *Allocation of deductions under §1.652(b)-3 (Directly attributable expenses).* In computing Trust's DNI for the taxable year, the distributive share of expenses of PRS are directly attributable under §1.652(b)-3(a) to the distributive share of income of PRS. Accordingly, Trust has gross business income of $155,000 ($55,000 from PRS and $100,000 from the bakery) and direct business expenses of $200,000 ($45,000 from PRS and $155,000 from the bakery). In addition, $1,000 of the trustee commissions and $1,000 of state and local taxes are directly attributable under §1.652(b)-3(a) to Trust's business income. Accordingly, Trust has excess business deductions of $47,000. Pursuant to its authority recognized under §1.652(b)-3(d), Trust allocates the $47,000 excess business deductions as follows: $15,000 to the interest income, resulting in $0 interest income, $25,000 to the dividends, resulting in $0 dividend income, and $7,000 to the tax exempt interest.

(iv) *Allocation of deductions under §1.652(b)-3 (Non-directly attributable expenses).* The trustee must allocate the sum of the balance of the trustee commissions ($2,000) and state and local taxes ($4,000) to Trust's remaining tax-exempt interest income, resulting in $2,000 of tax exempt interest.

(v) *Amounts included in taxable income.* For 2018, Trust has DNI of $2,000. Pursuant to Trust's governing instrument, Trustee distributes 50%, or $1,000, of that DNI to A, an individual who is a discretionary beneficiary of Trust. In addition, Trustee is required to distribute 25%, or $500, of that DNI to B, a current income beneficiary of Trust. Trust retains the remaining 25% of DNI. Consequently, with respect to the $1,000 distribution A receives from Trust, A properly excludes $1,000 of tax-exempt interest income under section 662(b). With respect to the $500 distribution B receives from Trust, B properly excludes $500 of tax exempt interest income under section 662(b). Because the DNI consists entirely of tax-exempt income, Trust deducts $0 under section 661 with respect to the distributions to A and B.

(2) *Section 199A deduction*—(i) *Trust's W-2 wages and QBI.* For the 2018 taxable year, prior to allocating the beneficiaries' shares of the section 199A items, Trust has $75,000 ($25,000 from PRS + $50,000 of Trust) of W-2 wages. Trust also has $125,000 of UBIA of qualified property. Trust has negative QBI of ($47,000) ($155,000 gross income from aggregated businesses less the sum of $200,000 direct expenses from aggregated businesses and $2,000 directly attributable business expenses from Trust under the rules of §1.652(b)-3(a)).

(ii) *A's Section 199A deduction computation.* Because the $1,000 Trust distribution to A equals one-half of Trust's DNI, A has W-2 wages from Trust of $37,500. A also has W-2 wages of $2,500 from a trade or business outside of Trust (computed without regard to A's interest in Trust), which A has properly aggregated under §1.199A-4 with the Trust's trade or businesses (the family's restaurant and bakery), for a total of $40,000 of W-2 wages from the aggregate trade or businesses. A also has $62,500 of UBIA from Trust and $25,000 of UBIA of qualified property from the trade or business outside of Trust for $87,500 of total UBIA of qualified property. A has $100,000 of QBI from the non-Trust trade or businesses in which A owns an interest. Because the $1,000 Trust distribution to A equals one-half of Trust's DNI, A has (negative) QBI from Trust of ($23,500). A's total QBI is determined by combining the $100,000 QBI from non-Trust sources with the ($23,500) QBI from Trust for a total of $76,500 of QBI. Assume that A's taxable income is $357,500, which exceeds A's applicable threshold amount for 2018 by $200,000. A's tentative deductible amount is $15,300 (20% x $76,500 of QBI), limited to the greater of (i) $20,000 (50% x $40,000 of W-2 wages), or (ii) $12,187.50 ($10,000, 25% x $40,000 of W-2 wages, plus $2,187.50, 2.5% x $87,500 of UBIA of qualified property). A's section 199A deduction is equal to the lesser of $15,300, or $71,500 (20% x $357,500 of taxable income). Accordingly, A's section 199A deduction for 2018 is $15,300.

(iii) *B's Section 199A deduction computation.* For 2018, B's taxable income is below the threshold amount so B is not subject to the W-2 wage limitation. Because the $500 Trust distribution to B equals one-quarter of Trust's DNI, B has a total of ($11,750) of QBI. B also has no QBI from non-Trust trades or businesses, so B has a total of ($11,750) of QBI. Accordingly, B's section 199A deduction for 2018 is zero. The ($11,750) of QBI is carried over to 2019 as a loss from a qualified business in the hands of B pursuant to section 199A(c)(2).

(iv) *Trust's Section 199A deduction computation.* For 2018, Trust's taxable income is below the threshold amount so it is not subject to the W-2 wage limitation. Because Trust retained 25% of Trust's DNI, Trust is allocated 25% of its QBI, which is ($11,750). Trust's section 199A deduction for 2018 is zero. The ($11,750) of QBI is carried over to 2019 as a loss from a qualified business in the hands of Trust pursuant to section 199A(c)(2).

(B) [Reserved]

(e) *Applicability date.*—(1) *General rule.*—Except as provided in paragraph (e)(2) of this section, the provisions of this section apply to taxable years ending after February 8, 2019.

(2) *Exceptions.*—(i) *Anti-abuse rules.*—The provisions of paragraph (d)(3)(vii) of this section apply to taxable years ending after December 22, 2017.

(ii) *Non-calendar year RPE.*—For purposes of determining QBI, W-2 wages, UBIA of qualified property, and the aggregate amount of qualified REIT dividends and qualified PTP income, if an individual receives any of these items from an RPE with a taxable year that begins before January 1, 2018, and ends after December 31, 2017, such items are treated as having been incurred by the individual during the individual's taxable year in which or with which such RPE taxable year ends.

(iii) *Separate shares.*—The provisions of paragraph (d)(3)(iii) of this section apply to taxable years beginning after August 24, 2018. Taxpayers may choose to apply the rules in paragraph (d)(3)(iii) of this section for taxable years beginning on or before August 24, 2020, so long as the taxpayers consistently apply the rules in paragraph (d)(3)(iii) of this section for each such year.

(iv) *Charitable remainder trusts.*—The provisions of paragraph (d)(3)(v) of this section apply to taxable years beginning after August 24, 2020. Taxpayers may choose to apply the rules in paragraph (d) of this section for taxable years beginning on or before August 24, 2020, so long as the taxpayers consistently apply the rules in paragraph (d)(3)(v) of this section for each such year. [Reg. §1.199A-6.]

☐ [T.D. 9847, 2-4-2019. Amended by T.D. 9899, 6-24-2020.]

[Reg. §1.199A-7]

§1.199A-7. Section 199A(a) Rules for Cooperatives and their Patrons.—(a) *Overview.*—(1) *In general.*—This section provides guidance and special rules on the application of the rules of §§1.199A-1 through 1.199A-6 regarding the deduction for qualified business income (QBI) under section 199A(a) (section 199A(a) deduction) of the Internal Revenue Code (Code) by patrons (patrons) of cooperatives to which Part I of subchapter T of chapter 1 of the Code (subchapter T) applies (Cooperatives). Unless otherwise provided in this section, all the rules in §§1.199A-1 through 1.199A-6 relating to calculating the section 199A(a) deduction apply to patrons and Cooperatives. Paragraph (b) of this section provides special rules for patrons relating to trades or businesses. Paragraph (c) of this section provides special rules for patrons and Cooperatives relating to the definition of QBI. Paragraph (d) of this section provides special rules for patrons and Cooperatives relating to specified service trades or businesses (SSTBs). Paragraph (e) of this section provides special rules for patrons relating to the statutory limitations based on W-2 wages and unadjusted basis immediately after acquisition (UBIA) of qualified property. Paragraph (f) of this section provides special rules for specified agricultural or horticultural cooperatives (Specified Co-operatives) and paragraph (g) of this section provides examples for Specified Cooperatives and their patrons. Paragraph (h) of this section sets forth the applicability date of this section and a special transition rule relating to Specified Cooperatives and their patrons.

(2) *At patron level.*—The section 199A(a) deduction is applied at the patron level, and patrons who are individuals (as defined in §1.199A-1(a)(2)) may take the section 199A(a) deduction.

(3) *Definitions.*—For purposes of section 199A and §1.199A-7, the following definitions apply—

(i) *Individual* is defined in §1.199A-1(a)(2).

(ii) *Patron* is defined in §1.1388-1(e).

(iii) *Patronage and nonpatronage* is defined in §1.1388-1(f).

(iv) *Relevant Passthrough Entity (RPE)* is defined in §1.199A-1(a)(9).

(v) *Qualified payment* is defined in §1.199A-8(d)(2)(ii).

(vi) *Specified Cooperative* is defined in §1.199A-8(a)(2) and is a subset of Cooperatives defined in §1.199A-7(a)(1).

(b) *Trade or business.*—A patron (whether the patron is an RPE or an individual), and not a Cooperative, must determine whether it has one or more trades or businesses that it directly conducts as defined in §1.199A-1(b)(14). To the extent a patron operating a trade or business has income directly from that business, the patron must follow the rules of §§1.199A-1 through 1.199A-6 to calculate the section 199A(a) deduction. Patronage dividends or similar payments are considered to be generated from the trade or business the Cooperative conducts on behalf of or with the patron. A Cooperative that distributes patronage dividends or similar payments, as described in paragraph (c)(1) of this section, must determine and report information to its patrons relating to qualified items of income, gain, deduction, and loss in accordance with paragraphs (c)(3) and (d)(3) of this section. A patron that receives patronage dividends or similar payments, as described in paragraph (c)(1) of this section, from a Cooperative must follow the rules of paragraphs (c) through (e) of this section to calculate the section 199A(a) deduction.

(c) *Qualified Business Income.*—(1) *In general.*—QBI means the net amount of qualified items of income, gain, deduction, and loss with respect to any trade or business as determined under the rules of section 199A(c)(3) and §1.199A-3(b). A qualified item of income includes distributions under section 1382(b) and (c)(2) (including patronage dividends or similar payments, such as money, property, qualified written notices of allocations, and qualified per-unit retain certificates, as well as money or property paid in redemption of a nonqualified written notice of allocation (collectively patronage dividends or similar payments)), provided such distribution is otherwise a qualified item of income, gain, deduction, or loss. *See* special rule in paragraph (d)(3) of this section relating to SSTBs that may affect QBI.

(2) *QBI determinations made by patron.*—A patron must determine QBI for each trade or business it directly conducts. In situations where the patron receives distributions described in paragraph (c)(1) of this section, the Cooperative must determine whether those distributions include qualified items of income, gain, deduction, and loss as determined under rules of section 199A(c)(3) and §1.199A-3(b). These distributions may be included in the QBI of the patron's trade or business to the extent that:

(i) The distributions are related to the patron's trade or business as defined in §1.199A-1(b)(14);

(ii) The distributions are qualified items of income, gain, deduction, and loss as determined under rules of section 199A(c)(3) and §1.199A-3(b) at the Cooperative's trade or business level;

(iii) The distributions are not items from an SSTB as defined in section 199A(d)(2) at the Cooperative's trade or business level (except as permitted by the threshold rules in section 199A(d)(3) and §1.199A-5(a)(2)); and

(iv) Certain information is reported by the Cooperative about these payments as provided in paragraphs (c)(3) and (d)(3) of this section.

(3) *Qualified items of income, gain, deduction, and loss determinations made and reported by Cooperatives.*—In the case of a Cooperative that makes distributions described in paragraph (c)(1) of this section to a patron, the Cooperative must determine the amount of qualified items of income, gain, deduction, and loss as determined under the rules of section 199A(c)(3) and §1.199A-3(b) in those distributions. A patron must determine whether these qualified items relate to one or more trades or businesses that it directly conducts as defined in §1.199A-1(b)(14). Pursuant to this paragraph (c)(3), the Cooperative must report the net amount of qualified items with respect to non-SSTBs of the Cooperative in the distributions made to the patron on an attachment to or on the Form 1099-PATR, Taxable Distributions

Received From Cooperatives, (or any successor form) issued by the Cooperative to the patron, unless otherwise provided by the instructions to the Form. If the Cooperative does not report on or before the due date of the Form 1099-PATR the amount of such qualified items of income, gain, deduction, and loss in the distributions to the patron, the amount of distributions from the Cooperative that may be included in the patron's QBI is presumed to be zero. *See* special rule in paragraph (d)(3) of this section relating to reporting of qualified items of income, gain, deduction, and loss with respect to SSTBs of the Cooperative.

(d) *Specified Service Trades or Businesses.*—(1) *In general.*—This section provides guidance on the determination of SSTBs as defined in section 199A(d)(2) and §1.199A-5. Unless otherwise provided in this section, all of the rules in §1.199A-5 relating to SSTBs apply to patrons of Cooperatives.

(2) *SSTB determinations made by patron.*—A patron (whether an RPE or an individual) must determine whether each trade or business it directly conducts is an SSTB.

(3) *SSTB determinations made and reported by Cooperatives.*—(i) *In general.*—In the case of a Cooperative that makes distributions described in paragraph (c)(1) of this section to a patron, the Cooperative must determine the amount of qualified items of income, gain, deduction, and loss as determined under the rules of section 199A(c)(3) and §1.199A-3(b) with respect to SSTBs directly conducted by the Cooperative. A patron must determine whether these qualified items relate to one or more trades or businesses that it directly conducts as defined in §1.199A-1(b)(14). The Cooperative must report the net amount of qualified items with respect to the SSTBs of the Cooperative in the distributions made to the patron on an attachment to or on the Form 1099-PATR, Taxable Distributions Received from Cooperatives, (or any successor form) issued by the Cooperative to the patron, unless otherwise provided by the instructions to the Form. If the Cooperative does not report the amount on or before the due date of the Form 1099-PATR, then only the amount that a Cooperative reports as qualified items of income, gain, deduction, and loss under §1.199A-7(c)(3) may be included in the patron's QBI, and the remaining amount of distributions from the Cooperative that may be included in the patron's QBI is presumed to be zero.

(ii) *Patron allocation of expenses paid to Cooperative for SSTB items of income reported by Cooperative.*—(A) *In general.*—When a Cooperative reports SSTB items to a patron, a patron may allocate a deductible expense that was paid to the Cooperative in connection with the patron's qualified trade or business between a patron's qualified trade or business income and the SSTB income reported to it by the Cooperative only if the SSTB income directly relates to the deductible expense. A patron can allocate the deductible expense paid by the patron to the Cooperative only up to the amount of SSTB income reported by the Cooperative.

(B) *Example Patron allocating expenses between qualified trade or business and SSTB income from a Cooperative.*—(1) Cooperative provides to its patrons a service that is an SSTB under section 199A(d)(2). P, a patron, runs a qualified trade or business under section 199A(d)(1) and incurs expenses for the service from the Cooperative in P's qualified trade or business. P pays the Cooperative $1,000 for the service. Cooperative later pays P a patronage dividend of $50 related to the service.

(2) Cooperative reports the $50 as SSTB income on the Form 1099-PATR issued to P.

(3) Since P's deductible expense for services from the Cooperative was in connection with a qualified trade or business and the SSTB income directly relates to that expense, P may allocate the expense under paragraph (d)(3)(ii) of this section. Accordingly, $50 of the $1,000 expense is allocated to P's SSTB income, and $950 of the expense is allocated to P's qualified trade or business and is included in P's QBI calculation.

(e) *W-2 wages and unadjusted basis immediately after acquisition of qualified property.*—(1) *In general.*—This section provides guidance on calculating a trade or business's W-2 wages and the UBIA of qualified property properly allocable to QBI.

(2) *Determinations made by patron.*—The determination of W-2 wages and UBIA of qualified property must be made for each trade or business by the patron (whether an RPE or individual) that directly conducts the trade or business before applying the aggregation rules of §1.199A-4. Unlike RPEs, Cooperatives do not compute and allocate their W-2 wages and UBIA of qualified property to patrons.

(f) *Special rules for patrons of Specified Cooperatives.*—(1) *Section 199A(b)(7) reduction.*—A patron of a Specified Cooperative that receives a qualified payment must reduce its section 199A(a) deduction as provided in §1.199A-1(e)(7). This reduction applies whether the Specified Cooperative passes through all, some, or none of the Specified Cooperative's section 199A(g) deduction to the patron in that taxable year. The rules relating to the section 199A(g) deduction can be found in §§1.199A-8 through 1.199A-12.

(2) *Reduction calculation.*—(i) *Allocation method.*—If in any taxable year, a patron receives income or gain related to qualified payments and income or gain that is not related to qualified payments in a trade or business, the patron must allocate the income or gain and related deductions, losses and W-2 wages using a reasonable method based on all the facts and circumstances for purposes of calculating the reduction in §1.199A-1(e)(7). Different reasonable methods may be used for different items and related deductions of income, gain, deduction, and loss. The chosen reasonable method for each item must be consistently applied from one taxable year of the patron to another, and must clearly reflect the income and expenses of each trade or business. The overall combination of methods must also be reasonable based on all the facts and circumstances. The books and records maintained for a trade or business must be consistent with any allocations under this paragraph (f)(2)(i).

(ii) *Safe harbor.*—A patron with taxable income under the threshold amount set forth in section 199A(e)(2) is eligible to use the safe harbor set forth in this paragraph (f)(2)(ii) to apportion its deductions, losses and W-2 wages instead of the allocation method set forth in paragraph (f)(2)(i) of this section for any taxable year in which the patron receives income or gain related to qualified payments and income or gain not related to qualified payments in a trade or business. Under the safe harbor the patron may apportion its deductions, losses and W-2 wages ratably between income or gain related to qualified payments and income or gain that is not related to qualified payments for purposes of calculating the reduction in paragraph (f)(1) of this section. Accordingly, the amount of deductions and losses apportioned to determine QBI allocable to qualified payments is equal to the proportion of the total deductions and losses that the amount of income or gain related to qualified payments bears to total income or gain used to determine QBI. The same proportion applies to determine the amount of W-2 wages allocable to the portion of the trade or business that received qualified payments.

(3) *Qualified payments notice requirement.*—A Specified Cooperative must report the amount of the qualified payments made to the eligible taxpayer, as defined in section 199A(g)(2)(D), on an attachment to or on the Form 1099-PATR (or any successor form) issued by the Cooperative to the patron, unless otherwise provided by the instructions to the Form.

(g) *Examples.*—The following examples illustrate the provisions of paragraph (f) of this section. For purposes of these examples, assume that the Specified Cooperative has satisfied the applicable written notice requirements in paragraphs (c)(3), (d)(3) and (f)(3) of this section.

(1) *Example 1. Patron of Specified Cooperative with W-2 wages.*—(i) P, a grain farmer and patron of nonexempt Specified Cooperative C, delivered to C during 2020 2% of all grain marketed through C during such year. During 2021, P receives $20,000 in patronage dividends and $1,000 of allocated section 199A(g) deduction from C related to the grain delivered to C during 2020.

(ii) P has taxable income of $75,000 for 2021 (determined without regard to section 199A) and has a filing status of married filing jointly. P's QBI related to its grain trade or business for 2021 is $50,000, which consists of gross receipts of $150,000 from sales to an independent grain elevator, per-unit retain allocations received from C during 2021 of $80,000, patronage dividends received from C during 2021 related to C's 2020 net earnings of $20,000, and expenses of $200,000 (including $50,000 of W-2 wages).

(iii) The portion of QBI from P's grain trade or business related to qualified payments received from C during 2021 is $10,000, which consists of per-unit retain allocations received from C during 2021 of $80,000, patronage dividends received from C during 2021 related to C's 2020 net earnings of $20,000, and properly allocable expenses of $90,000 (including $25,000 of W-2 wages).

(iv) P's deductible amount related to the grain trade or business is 20% of QBI ($10,000) reduced by the lesser of 9% of QBI related to qualified payments received from C ($900) or 50% of W-2 wages related to qualified payments received from C ($12,500), or $9,100. As P does not have any other trades or businesses, the combined QBI amount is also $9,100.

(v) P's deduction under section 199A for 2021 is $10,100, which consists of the combined QBI amount of $9,100, plus P's deduction passed through from C of $1,000.

(2) *Example 2. Patron of Specified Cooperative without W-2 wages.*—(i) C and P have the same facts for 2020 and 2021 as *Example 1*, except

that P has expenses of $200,000 that include zero W-2 wages during 2021.

(ii) P's deductible amount related to the grain trade or business is 20% of QBI ($10,000) reduced by the lesser of 9% of QBI related to qualified payments received from C ($900) or 50% of W-2 wages related to qualified payments received from C ($0), or $10,000.

(iii) P's deduction under section 199A for 2021 is $11,000, which consists of the combined QBI amount of $10,000, plus P's deduction passed through from C of $1,000.

(3) *Example 3. Patron of Specified Cooperative – Qualified Payments do not equal QBI and no section 199A(g) passthrough.*—(i) P, a grain farmer and a patron of a nonexempt Specified Cooperative C, during 2020, receives $60,000 in patronage dividends, $100,000 in per-unit retain allocations, and $0 of allocated section 199A(g) deduction from C related to the grain delivered to C. C notifies P that only $150,000 of the patronage dividends and per-unit retain allocations are qualified payments because $10,000 of the payments are not attributable to C's QPAI.

(ii) P has taxable income of $90,000 (determined without regard to section 199A) and has a filing status of married filing jointly. P's QBI related to its grain trade or business is $45,000, which consists of gross receipts of $95,000 from sales to an independent grain elevator, plus $160,000 from C (all payments from C qualify as qualified items of income, gain, deduction, and loss), less expenses of $210,000 (including $30,000 of W-2 wages).

(iii) The portion of QBI from P's grain trade or business related to qualified payments received from C is $25,000, which consists of the qualified payments received from C of $150,000, less the properly allocable expenses of $125,000 (including $18,000 of W-2 wages), which were determined using a reasonable method under paragraph (f)(2)(ii) of this section.

(iv) P's patron reduction is $2,250, which is the lesser of 9% of QBI related to qualified payments received from C, $2,250 (9% x $25,000), or 50% of W-2 wages related to qualified payments received from C, $9,000 (50% x $18,000). As P does not have any other trades or businesses, the combined QBI amount is $6,750 (20% of P's total QBI, $9,000 (20% x $45,000), reduced by the patron reduction of $2,250).

(v) P's deduction under section 199A is $6,750, which consists of the combined QBI amount of $6,750.

(4) *Example 4. Patron of Specified Cooperative – Reasonable Method under paragraph (f)(2)(i) of this section.*—P is a grain farmer that has $45,000 of QBI related to P's grain trade or business in 2020. P's QBI consists of $105,000 of sales to an independent grain elevator, $100,000 of per-unit retain allocations, and $50,000 of patronage dividends from a nonexempt Specified Cooperative C, for which C reports $150,000 of qualified payments to P as required by paragraph (f)(3) of this section. P's grain trade or business has $210,000 of expenses (including $30,000 of W-2 wages). P delivered 65x bushels of grain to C and sold 35x bushels of comparable grain to the independent grain elevator. To allocate the expenses between qualified payments ($150,000) and other income ($105,000), P compares the bushels of grain delivered to C (65x) to the total bushels of grain delivered to C and sold to the independent grain elevator (100x). P determines $136,500 (65% x $210,000) of expenses (including $19,500 of W-2 wages) are properly allocable to the qualified payments. The portion of QBI from P's grain trade or business related to qualified payments received from C is $13,500, which consists of qualified payments of $150,000 less the properly allocable expenses of $136,500 (including $19,500 of W-2 wages). P's method of allocating expenses is a reasonable method under paragraph (f)(2)(i) of this section.

(5) *Example 5. Patron of Specified Cooperative using safe harbor to allocate.*—(i) P is a grain farmer with taxable income of $100,000 for 2021 (determined without regard to section 199A) and has a filing status of married filing jointly. P's QBI related to P's grain trade or business for 2021 is $50,000, which consists of gross receipts of $180,000 from sales to an independent grain elevator, per-unit retain allocations received from a Specified Cooperative C during 2021 of $15,000, patronage dividends received from C during 2021 related to C's 2020 net earnings of $5,000, and expenses of $150,000 (including $50,000 of W-2 wages). C also passed through $1,800 of the section 199A(g) deduction to P, which related to the grain delivered by P to the Specified Cooperative during 2020. P uses the safe harbor in paragraph (f)(2)(ii) of this section to determine the expenses (including W-2 wages) allocable to the qualified payments.

(ii) Using the safe harbor to allocate P's $150,000 of expenses, P allocates $15,000 of the expenses to the qualified payments ($150,000 of expenses multiplied by the ratio (0.10) of qualified payments ($20,000) to total gross receipts ($200,000)). Using the same ratio, P also determines there are $5,000 of W-2 wages allocable ($50,000 multiplied by 0.10) to the qualified payments.

(iii) The portion of QBI from P's grain trade or business related to qualified payments received from C during 2021 is $5,000, which consists of per-unit retain allocations received from C during 2021 of $15,000, patronage dividends of $5,000, and properly allocable expenses of $15,000 (including $5,000 of W-2 wages).

(iv) P's QBI related to the grain trade or business is 20% of QBI ($10,000) reduced by the lesser of 9% of QBI related to qualified payments received from C ($450) or 50% of W-2 wages related to qualified payments received from C ($2,500), or $9,550. As P does not have any other trades or businesses, the combined QBI amount is also $9,550.

(v) P's deduction under section 199A for 2021 is $11,350, which consists of the combined QBI amount of $9,550, plus P's deduction passed through from C of $1,800.

(h) *Applicability date.*—(1) *General rule.*—Except as provided in paragraph (h)(2) of this section, the provisions of this section apply to taxable years beginning after January 19, 2021. Taxpayers, however, may choose to apply the rules of §§ 1.199A-7 through 1.199A-12 for taxable years beginning on or before that date, provided taxpayers apply the rules in their entirety and in a consistent manner.

(2) *Transition rule for qualified payments of patrons of Cooperatives.*—See the transition rule for qualified payments of patrons of Cooperatives for a taxable year of a Cooperative beginning before January 1, 2018 in the Consolidated Appropriations Act, 2018 (Public Law 115-141, 132 Stat. 348) Division T, section 101(c).

(3) *Notice from the Cooperative.*—If a patron of a Cooperative cannot claim a deduction under section 199A for any qualified payments described in the transition rule set forth in paragraph (h)(2) of this section, the Cooperative must use a reasonable method to identify the qualified payments to its patrons. A reasonable method includes reporting this information on an attachment to or on the Form 1099-PATR (or any successor form) issued by the Cooperative to the patron, unless otherwise provided by the instructions to the Form. [Reg. § 1.199A-7.]

☐ [*T.D.* 9947, 1-14-2021 (corrected 11-16-2022).]

[Reg. § 1.199A-8]

§ 1.199A-8. Deduction for income attributable to domestic production activities of specified agricultural or horticultural cooperatives.—(a) *Overview.*—(1) *In general.*—This section provides rules relating to the deduction for income attributable to domestic production activities of a specified agricultural or horticultural cooperative (Specified Cooperative). This paragraph (a) provides an overview and definitions of certain terms. Paragraph (b) of this section provides rules explaining the steps a nonexempt Specified Cooperative performs to calculate its section 199A(g) deduction and includes definitions of relevant terms. Paragraph (c) of this section provides rules explaining the steps an exempt Specified Cooperative performs to calculate its section 199A(g) deduction. Paragraph (d) of this section provides rules for Specified Cooperatives passing through the section 199A(g) deduction to patrons. Paragraph (e) of this section provides examples that illustrate the provisions of paragraphs (b), (c), and (d) of this section. Paragraph (f) of this section provides guidance for Specified Cooperatives that are partners in a partnership. Paragraph (g) of this section provides guidance on the recapture of a claimed section 199A(g) deduction. Paragraph (h) of this section provides effective dates. For additional rules addressing an expanded affiliated group (EAG), to which the principles of this section apply, *see* § 1.199A-12. The provisions of this section apply solely for purposes of section 199A of the Internal Revenue Code (Code).

(2) *Specified Cooperative.*—(i) *In general.*—Specified Cooperative means a cooperative to which Part I of subchapter T of chapter 1 of the Code applies and which—

(A) Manufactures, produces, grows, or extracts (MPGE) in whole or significant part within the United States any agricultural or horticultural product, or

(B) Is engaged in the marketing of agricultural or horticultural products that have been MPGE in whole or significant part within the United States by the patrons of the cooperative.

(C) See § 1.199A-9 for rules to determine if a Specified Cooperative has MPGE an agricultural or horticultural product in whole or significant part within the United States.

(ii) *Types of Specified Cooperatives.*—A Specified Cooperative that is qualified as a farmer's cooperative organization under section 521 is an *exempt Specified Cooperative*, while a Specified Cooperative not so qualified is a *nonexempt Specified Cooperative*.

(3) *Patron* is defined in § 1.1388-1(e).

(4) *Agricultural or horticultural products* are agricultural, horticultural, viticultural, and dairy products, livestock and the products thereof, the products of poultry and bee raising, the edible products

of forestry, and any and all products raised or produced on farms and processed or manufactured products thereof within the meaning of the Cooperative Marketing Act of 1926, 44 Stat. 802 (1926). Agricultural or horticultural products also include aquatic products that are farmed. Some examples of agricultural or horticultural products include, but are not limited to, fruits, grains, oilseeds, rice, vegetables, legumes, grasses (including hay), plants of all kinds, flowers (including hops), seeds, tobacco, cotton, sugar cane and sugar beets. Some examples of livestock products include, but are not limited to, wool, fur, hides, eggs, down, honey, and silk. Some examples of edible forestry products include, but are not limited to, fruits, nuts, berries and mushrooms. Some examples of aquatic products include, but are not limited to, fish, crustaceans, shellfish and seaweed. In addition, agricultural or horticultural products include fertilizer, diesel fuel, and other supplies (for example, seed, feed, herbicides, and pesticides) used in agricultural or horticultural production that are MPGE by a Specified Cooperative. Agricultural or horticultural products, however, do not include intangible property other than when incorporated into a tangible agricultural or horticultural product (other than as provided in the exception in § 1.199A-9(b)(2)). Intangible property for this purpose includes, for example, the rights to MPGE and sell an agricultural or horticultural product with certain characteristics protected by a patent, or the rights to a trademark or tradename. This exclusion of intangible property does not apply to intangible characteristics of any particular agricultural or horticultural product. For example, gross receipts from the sale of different varieties of oranges would be considered from the disposition of agricultural or horticultural products. However, gross receipts from the license of the right to produce and sell a certain variety of an orange would be considered separate from the orange and not from an agricultural or horticultural product.

(b) *Steps for a nonexempt Specified Cooperative in calculating deduction.*—(1) *In general.*—Except as provided in paragraph (c)(3) of this section, this paragraph (b) applies only to nonexempt Specified Cooperatives.

(2) *Step 1 - Gross receipts and related deductions.*—(i) *Identify.*—To determine the section 199A(g) deduction, a Specified Cooperative first identifies its patronage and nonpatronage gross receipts and related cost of goods sold (COGS), deductible expenses, W-2 wages, etc. (deductions) and allocates them between patronage and nonpatronage. A single definition for the term *patronage and nonpatronage* is found in § 1.1388-1(f).

(ii) *Applicable gross receipts and deductions.*—Except as described in this paragraph (b)(ii), for all purposes of the section 199A(g) deduction, a Specified Cooperative can use only patronage gross receipts and related deductions to calculate qualified production activities income (QPAI) as defined in paragraph (b)(4)(ii) of this section, oil-related QPAI as defined in paragraph (b)(7)(ii) of this section, the W-2 wage limitation in paragraph (b)(5)(ii)(B) of this section, or taxable income as defined in paragraph (b)(5)(ii)(C) of this section. A Specified Cooperative cannot use its nonpatronage gross receipts and related deductions to calculate its section 199A(g) deduction, other than treating all of its nonpatronage gross receipts as patronage non-DPGR for purposes of applying the de minimis rules in § 1.199A-9(c)(3). If a Specified Cooperative treats all nonpatronage gross receipts as DPGR under § 1.199A-9(c)(3)(i), then a Specified Cooperative shall also treat its deductions related to the nonpatronage gross receipts as patronage in calculating QPAI, oil-related QPAI, the W-2 wage limitation, or taxable income for purposes of the section 199A(g) deduction.

(iii) *Gross receipts* are the Specified Cooperative's receipts for the taxable year that are recognized under the Specified Cooperative's methods of accounting used for Federal income tax purposes for the taxable year. See § 1.199A-12 if the gross receipts are recognized in an intercompany transaction within the meaning of § 1.1502-13. Gross receipts include total sales (net of returns and allowances) and all amounts received for services. In addition, gross receipts include any income from investments and from incidental or outside sources. For example, gross receipts include interest (except interest under section 103 but including original issue discount), dividends, rents, royalties, and annuities, regardless of whether the amounts are derived in the ordinary course of the Specified Cooperative's trade or business. Gross receipts are not reduced by COGS or by the cost of property sold if such property is described in section 1221(a)(1), (2), (3), (4), or (5). Finally, gross receipts do not include amounts received by the Specified Cooperative with respect to sales tax or other similar state or local taxes if, under the applicable state or local law, the tax is legally imposed on the purchaser of the good or service and the Specified Cooperative merely collects and remits the tax to the taxing authority. If, in contrast, the tax is imposed on the Specified Cooperative under the applicable law, then gross receipts include the amounts received that are allocable to the payment of such tax.

(3) *Step 2 – Determine gross receipts that are DPGR.*—(i) *In general.*—A Specified Cooperative examines its patronage gross receipts to determine which of these are DPGR. A Specified Cooperative does not use nonpatronage gross receipts to determine DPGR.

(ii) *DPGR* are the gross receipts of the Specified Cooperative that are derived from any lease, rental, license, sale, exchange, or other disposition of an agricultural or horticultural product that is MPGE by the Specified Cooperative or its patrons in whole or significant part within the United States. DPGR does not include gross receipts derived from services or the lease, rental, license, sale, exchange, or other disposition of land unless a de minimis or other exception applies. See § 1.199A-9 for additional rules on determining if gross receipts are DPGR.

(4) *Step 3 – Determine QPAI.*—(i) *In general.*—A Specified Cooperative determines QPAI from patronage DPGR and patronage deductions identified in paragraphs (b)(3)(ii) and (b)(2)(i) of this section, respectively. A Specified Cooperative does not use nonpatronage gross receipts or deductions to determine QPAI.

(ii) *QPAI* for the taxable year means an amount equal to the excess (if any) of—

(A) DPGR for the taxable year, over

(B) The sum of—

(1) COGS that are allocable to DPGR, and

(2) Other expenses, losses, or deductions (other than the section 199A(g) deduction that are properly allocable to DPGR.

(C) *QPAI computational rules.*—QPAI is computed without taking into account the section 199A(g) deduction or any deduction allowed under section 1382(b). *See* § 1.199A-10 for additional rules on calculating QPAI.

(5) *Step 4 – Calculate deduction.*—(i) *In general.*—From QPAI and taxable income, a Specified Cooperative calculates its section 199A(g) deduction as provided in paragraph (b)(5)(ii) of this section.

(ii) *Deduction.*—(A) *In general.*—A Specified Cooperative is allowed a deduction equal to 9 percent of the lesser of—

(1) QPAI of the Specified Cooperative for the taxable year, or

(2) Taxable income of the Specified Cooperative for the taxable year.

(B) *W-2 wage limitation.*—The deduction allowed under paragraph (b)(5)(ii)(A) of this section for any taxable year cannot exceed 50 percent of the patronage W-2 wages attributable to DPGR for the taxable year. *See* § 1.199A-11 for additional rules on calculating the patronage W-2 wage limitation.

(C) *Taxable income.*—Taxable income is defined in section 63, and adjusted under section 1382 and § 1.1382-1 and § 1.1382-2. For purposes of determining the amount of the deduction allowed under paragraph (b)(5)(ii) of this section, taxable income is limited to taxable income and related deductions from patronage sources, other than as allowed under paragraph (b)(2)(ii) of this section. Taxable income is computed without taking into account the section 199A(g) deduction or any deduction allowable under section 1382(b). Patronage net operating losses (NOLs) reduce taxable income in the amount that the Specified Cooperative would use to reduce taxable income (no lower than zero) before using the section 199A(g) deduction, but do not reduce taxable income that is the result of not taking into account any deduction allowable under section 1382(b).

(6) *Use of patronage section 199A(g) deduction.*—Except as provided in § 1.199A-12(c)(2) related to the rules for EAGs, the patronage section 199A(g) deduction cannot create or increase a patronage or nonpatronage NOL or the amount of a patronage or nonpatronage NOL carryover or carryback, if applicable, in accordance with section 172. A patronage section 199A(g) deduction can be applied only against patronage income and deductions. A patronage section 199A(g) deduction that is not used in the appropriate taxable year is lost. To the extent that a Specified Cooperative passes through the section 199A(g) deduction to patrons and appropriately adjusts the section 1382 deduction under § 1.199A-8(d), the amount passed through is not considered to create or increase a patronage or nonpatronage NOL or the amount of a patronage or nonpatronage NOL carryover or carryback, if applicable, in accordance with section 172.

(7) *Special rules for nonexempt Specified Cooperatives that have oil-related QPAI.*—(i) *Reduction of section 199A(g) deduction.*—If a Specified Cooperative has oil-related QPAI for any taxable year, the amount otherwise allowable as a deduction under paragraph (b)(5)(ii) of this section must be reduced by 3 percent of the least of—

(A) Oil-related QPAI of the Specified Cooperative for the taxable year,

(B) QPAI of the Specified Cooperative for the taxable year, or

(C) Taxable income of the Specified Cooperative for the taxable year.

(ii) *Oil-related QPAI.*—means, for any taxable year, the patronage QPAI that is attributable to the production, refining, processing, transportation, or distribution of oil, gas, or any primary product thereof (within the meaning of section 927(a)(2)(C), as in effect before its repeal) during such taxable year. Oil-related QPAI for any taxable year is an amount equal to the excess (if any) of patronage DPGR derived from the production, refining or processing of oil, gas, or any primary product thereof (oil-related DPGR) over the sum of—

(A) COGS of the Specified Cooperative that is allocable to such receipts; and

(B) Other expenses, losses, or deductions (other than section 199A(g) deduction) that are properly allocable to such receipts.

(iii) *Special rule for patronage oil-related DPGR.*—Oil-related DPGR does not include gross receipts derived from the transportation or distribution of oil, gas, or any primary product thereof. However, to the extent that the nonexempt Specified Cooperative treats gross receipts derived from transportation or distribution of oil, gas, or any primary product thereof as part of DPGR under § 1.199A-9(c)(3)(i), or under § 1.199A-9(j)(3)(i)(B), then the Specified Cooperative must treat those patronage gross receipts as oil-related DGPR.

(iv) *Oil* includes oil recovered from both conventional and non-conventional recovery methods, including crude oil, shale oil, and oil recovered from tar/oil sands. The *primary product from oil* includes all products derived from the destructive distillation of oil, including volatile products, light oils such as motor fuel and kerosene, distillates such as naphtha, lubricating oils, greases and waxes, and residues such as fuel oil. The *primary product from gas* means all gas and associated hydrocarbon components from gas wells or oil wells, whether recovered at the lease or upon further processing, including natural gas, condensates, liquefied petroleum gases such as ethane, propane, and butane, and liquid products such as natural gasoline. The primary products from oil and gas provided in this paragraph (b)(7)(iv) are not intended to represent either the only primary products from oil or gas, or the only processes from which primary products may be derived under existing and future technologies. Examples of non-primary products include, but are not limited to, petrochemicals, medicinal products, insecticides, and alcohols.

(c) *Exempt Specified Cooperatives.*—(1) *In general.*—This paragraph (c) applies only to exempt Specified Cooperatives.

(2) *Two section 199A(g) deductions.*—The Specified Cooperative must calculate two separate section 199A(g) deductions, one patronage sourced and the other nonpatronage sourced, unless a Specified Cooperative treats all of its nonpatronage gross receipts and related deductions as patronage as described in paragraph (b)(2)(ii) of this section. Patronage and nonpatronage gross receipts, related COGS that are allocable to DPGR, and other expenses, losses, or deductions (other than the section 199A(g) deduction) that are properly allocable to DPGR (deductions), DPGR, QPAI, NOLs, W-2 wages, etc. are not netted to calculate these two separate section 199A(g) deductions.

(3) *Exempt Specified Cooperative patronage section 199A(g) deduction.*—The Specified Cooperative calculates its patronage section 199A(g) deduction following steps 1 through 4 in paragraphs (b)(2) through (5) of this section as if it were a nonexempt Specified Cooperative.

(4) *Exempt Specified Cooperative nonpatronage section 199A(g) deduction.*—(i) *In general.*—The Specified Cooperative calculates its nonpatronage section 199A(g) deduction following steps 2 through 4 in paragraphs (b)(2) through (5) of this section using only nonpatronage gross receipts and related nonpatronage deductions, unless a Specified Cooperative treats all of its nonpatronage gross receipts and related deductions as patronage as described in paragraph (b)(2)(ii) of this section. For purposes of determining the amount of the nonpatronage section 199A(g) deduction allowed under paragraph (b)(5)(ii) of this section, taxable income is limited to taxable income and related deductions from nonpatronage sources. Nonpatronage NOLs reduce taxable income. Taxable income is computed without taking into account the section 199A(g) deduction or any deduction allowable under section 1382(c).

(ii) *Use of nonpatronage section 199A(g) deduction.*—Except as provided in § 1.199A-12(c)(2) related to the rules for EAGs, the nonpatronage section 199A(g) deduction cannot create or increase a nonpatronage NOL or the amount of nonpatronage NOL carryover or carryback, if applicable, in accordance with section 172. A Specified Cooperative cannot pass through its nonpatronage section 199A(g) deduction under paragraph (d) of this section and can apply

Itemized Deductions for Individuals and Corps.
See p. 20,601 for regulations not amended to reflect law changes
25,699

the nonpatronage section 199A(g) deduction only against its nonpatronage income and deductions. As is the case for the patronage section 199A(g) deduction, the nonpatronage section 199A(g) deduction that a Specified Cooperative does not use in the appropriate taxable year is lost.

(d) *Discretion to pass through deduction.*—(1) *Permitted amount.*—(i) *In general.*—A Specified Cooperative may, at its discretion, pass through all, some, or none of its patronage section 199A(g) deduction to all patrons. Only eligible taxpayers as defined in section 199A(g)(2)(D) may claim the section 199A(g) deduction that is passed through. A Specified Cooperative member of a federated cooperative may pass through the patronage section 199A(g) deduction it receives from the federated cooperative to its member patrons.

(ii) *Specified Cooperative identifies eligibility of patron.*—If a Specified Cooperative determines that a patron is not an eligible taxpayer, then the Specified Cooperative may, at its discretion, retain any of the patronage section 199A(g) deduction attributable to the patron that would otherwise be passed through and lost under the general rule in paragraph (d)(1)(i) of this section.

(2) *Amount of deduction being passed through.*—(i) *In general.*—A Specified Cooperative is permitted to pass through an amount equal to the portion of the Specified Cooperative's section 199A(g) deduction that is allowed with respect to the portion of the cooperative's QPAI that is attributable to the qualified payments the Specified Cooperative distributed to the patron during the taxable year and identified on the notice required in § 1.199A-7(f)(3) on an attachment to or on the Form 1099–PATR, Taxable Distributions Received From Cooperatives (Form 1099–PATR), (or any successor form) issued by the Specified Cooperative to the patron, unless otherwise provided by the instructions to the Form 1099–PATR. The notice requirement to pass through the section 199A(g) deduction is in paragraph (d)(3) of this section.

(ii) *Qualified payment* means any amount of a patronage dividend or per-unit retain allocation, as described in section 1385(a)(1) or (3) received by a patron from a Specified Cooperative that is attributable to the portion of the Specified Cooperative's QPAI, for which the cooperative is allowed a section 199A(g) deduction. For this purpose, patronage dividends include any advances on patronage and per-unit retain allocations include per-unit retains paid in money during the taxable year.

(3) *Notice requirement to pass through deduction.*—A Specified Cooperative must identify in a written notice the amount of the section 199A(g) deduction being passed through to its patrons. This written notice must be mailed by the Specified Cooperative to the patron no later than the 15th day of the ninth month following the close of the taxable year of the Specified Cooperative. The Specified Cooperative may use the same written notice, if any, that it uses to notify the patron of the patron's respective allocations of patronage distributions, or may use a separate timely written notice(s) to comply with this section. The Specified Cooperative must report the amount of section 199A(g) deduction passed through to the patron on an attachment to or on the Form 1099–PATR (or any successor form) issued by the Specified Cooperative to the patron, unless otherwise provided by the instructions to the Form 1099–PATR.

(4) *Section 199A(g) deduction allocated to eligible taxpayer.*—An eligible taxpayer may deduct the lesser of the section 199A(g) deduction identified on the notice described in paragraph (d)(3) of this section or the eligible taxpayer's taxable income in the taxable year in which the eligible taxpayer receives the timely written notice described in paragraph (d)(3) of this section. For this purpose, the eligible taxpayer's taxable income is determined without taking into account the section 199A(g) deduction being passed through to the eligible taxpayer and after taking into account any section 199A(a) deduction allowed to the eligible taxpayer. Any section 199A(g) deduction the eligible taxpayer does not use in the taxable year in which the eligible taxpayer receives the notice (received on or before the due date of the Form 1099-PATR) is lost and cannot be carried forward or back to other taxable years. The taxable income limitation for the section 199A(a) deduction set forth in section 199A(b)(3) and § 1.199A-1(a) and (b) does not apply to limit the deductibility of the section 199A(g) deduction passed through to the eligible taxpayer.

(5) *Special rules for eligible taxpayers that are Specified Cooperatives.*—Any Specified Cooperative that receives a section 199A(g) deduction as an eligible taxpayer can take the deduction against patronage gross income and related deductions to the extent it relates to its patronage gross income and related deductions. Only a patron that is an exempt Specified Cooperative may take a section 199A(g) deduction passed through from another Specified Cooperative if the deduction relates to the patron Specified Cooperative's nonpatronage gross income and related deductions.

(6) *W-2 wage limitation.*—The W-2 wage limitation described in paragraph (b)(5)(ii)(B) of this section is applied at the cooperative level whether or not the Specified Cooperative chooses to pass through some or all of the section 199A(g) deduction. Any section 199A(g) deduction that has been passed through by a Specified Cooperative to an eligible taxpayer is not subject to the W-2 wage limitation a second time at the eligible taxpayer's level.

(7) *Specified Cooperative denied section 1382 deduction for portion of qualified payments.*—A Specified Cooperative must reduce its section 1382 deduction by an amount equal to the portion of any qualified payment that is attributable to the Specified Cooperative's section 199A(g) deduction passed through. This means the Specified Cooperative must reduce its section 1382 deduction in an amount equal to the section 199A(g) deduction passed through.

(8) *No double counting.*—A qualified payment received by a Specified Cooperative that is a patron of a Specified Cooperative is not taken into account by the patron for purposes of section 199A(g).

(e) *Examples.*—The following examples illustrate the application of paragraphs (a), (b), (c), and (d) of this section. The examples of this section apply solely for purposes of section 199A of the Code. Assume for each example that the Specified Cooperative sent all required notices to patrons on or before the due date of the Form 1099-PATR.

(1) *Example 1. Nonexempt Specified Cooperative calculating section 199A(g) deduction.*—(i) C is a grain marketing nonexempt Specified Cooperative, with $5,250,000 in gross receipts during 2020 from the sale of grain grown by its patrons. C paid $4,000,000 to its patrons at the time the grain was delivered in the form of per-unit retain allocations and another $1,000,000 in patronage dividends after the close of the 2020 taxable year. C has other expenses of $250,000 during 2020, including $100,000 of W-2 wages.

(ii) C has DPGR of $5,250,000 and QPAI as defined in § 1.199A-8(b)(4)(ii) of $5,000,000 for 2020. C's section 199A(g) deduction is equal to the least of 9% of QPAI ($450,000), 9% of taxable income ($450,000), or 50% of W-2 wages ($50,000). C passes through the entire section 199A(g) deduction to its patrons. Accordingly, C reduces its $5,000,000 deduction allowable under section 1382(b) (relating to the $1,000,000 patronage dividends and $4,000,000 per-unit retain allocations) by $50,000.

(2) *Example 2. Nonexempt Specified Cooperative determines amounts included in QPAI and taxable income.*—(i) C, a nonexempt Specified Cooperative, offers harvesting services and markets the grain of patrons and nonpatrons. C had gross receipts from harvesting services and grain sales, and expenses related to both. All of C's harvesting services were performed for their patrons, and 75% of the grain sales were for patrons.

(ii) C identifies 75% of the gross receipts and related expenses from grain sales and 100% of the gross receipts and related expenses from the harvesting services as patronage sourced. C identifies 25% of the gross receipts and related expenses from grain sales as nonpatronage sourced.

(iii) C does not include any nonpatronage gross receipts or related expenses from grain sales in either QPAI or taxable income when calculating the section 199A(g) deduction. C's QPAI includes the patronage DPGR, less related expenses (allocable COGS, wages and other expenses). C's taxable income includes the patronage gross receipts, whether such gross receipts are DPGR or non-DPGR.

(iv) C allocates and reports patronage dividends to its harvesting patrons and grain marketing patrons. C also notifies its grain marketing patrons (in accordance with the requirements of § 1.199A-7(f)(3)) that their patronage dividends are qualified payments used in C's section 199A(g) computation. The patrons must use this information for purposes of computing their section 199A(b)(7) reduction to their section 199A(a) deduction (*see* § 1.199A-7(f)).

(3) *Example 3. Nonexempt Specified Cooperative with patronage and nonpatronage gross receipts and related deductions.*—(i) C, a nonexempt Specified Cooperative, markets corn grown by its patrons in the United States. For the calendar year ending December 31, 2020, C derives gross receipts from the marketing activity of $1,800. Such gross receipts qualify as DPGR. Assume C has $800 of expenses (including COGS, other expenses, and $400 of W-2 wages) properly allocable to DPGR, and a $1,000 deduction allowed under section 1382(b). C also derives gross receipts from nonpatronage sources in the amount of $500, and has nonpatronage deductions in the amount of $400 (including COGS, other expenses, and $100 of W-2 wages).

(ii) C does not include any gross receipts or deductions from nonpatronage sources when calculating the deduction under paragraph (b)(5)(ii) of this section. C's QPAI and taxable income both equal $1,000 ($1,800–$800). C's deduction under paragraph (b)(5)(ii) of this section for the taxable year is equal to $90 (9% of $1,000), which does not exceed $200 (50% of C's W-2 wages properly allocable to DPGR). C passes through $90 of the deduction to patrons and C reduces its section 1382(b) deduction by $90.

(4) *Example 4. Exempt Specified Cooperative with patronage and nonpatronage income and deductions.*—(i) C, an exempt Specified Cooperative, markets corn MPGE by its patrons in the United States. For the calendar year ending December 31, 2020, C derives gross receipts from the marketing activity of $1,800. For this activity assume C has $800 of expenses (including COGS, other expenses, and $400 of W-2 wages) properly allocable to DPGR, and a $1,000 deduction under section 1382(b). C also derives gross receipts from nonpatronage sources in the amount of $500. Assume the gross receipts qualify as DPGR. For this activity assume C has $400 of expenses (including COGS, other expenses, and $20 of W-2 wages) properly allocable to DPGR and no deduction under section 1382(c).

(ii) C calculates two separate section 199A(g) deduction amounts. C's section 199A(g) deduction attributable to patronage sources is the same as the deduction calculated by the nonexempt Specified Cooperative in *Example* 3 in paragraph (e)(3) of this section.

(iii) C's nonpatronage QPAI and taxable income is equal to $100 ($500 − $400). C's deduction under paragraph (c)(4) of this section that directs C to use paragraph (b)(5)(ii) of this section attributable to nonpatronage sources is equal to $9 (9% of $100), which does not exceed $10 (50% of C's W-2 wages properly allocable to DPGR). C cannot pass through any of the nonpatronage section 199A(g) deduction amount to its patrons.

(5) *Example 5. NOL.*—(i) In 2021, E, a nonexempt Specified Cooperative that is not part of an EAG, generates QPAI and taxable income of $100 (without taking into account any section 1382(b) deductions, NOLs, or the section 199A(g) deduction). E pays out patronage dividends of $91 that are deductible under section 1382(b). E has an NOL carryover of $500 attributable to losses incurred prior to 2018. While taxable income and QPAI do not take into account the section 1382(b) deduction, taxable income does take into account NOLs. When calculating its section 199A(g) deduction, E must take into account the NOL carryover when calculating taxable income, unless the taxable income is the result of not taking into account any deduction allowable under section 1382(b). In this case $91 of taxable income is the result of not taking into account the deduction allowed under section 1382(b) and the remaining $9 should be reduced by the NOL carryover so that taxable income equals $91. E calculates a section 199A(g) deduction of $8.19 (.09 x $91 (which is the lesser of $100 QPAI or $91 taxable income)).

(ii) E may pass through the entire $8.19 of section 199A(g) deduction to patrons (which will reduce its section 1382(b) deduction from $91 to $82.81). However, if E does not pass the deduction through, paragraph (b)(6) of this section prohibits E from claiming any of the section 199A(g) deduction in 2021.

(iii) If E passes through the deduction to patrons, E's taxable income under section 172(b)(2) for NOL absorption purposes is $9 ($100 - $82.81 - $9 NOL - $8.19 section 199A(g) deduction). If E does not pass through the deduction, then E's taxable income under section 172(b)(2) for NOL absorption purposes is $9 ($100 - $91 - $9 NOL).

(iv) Assuming E passes through the deduction to patrons, E would use $9 of the NOL carryover and have a $491 NOL carryover remaining. To the extent E does not pass through the deduction, E would still use $9 of the NOL carryover and have a $491 NOL carryover remaining.

(6) *Example 6. Nonexempt Specified Cooperative not passing through the section 199A(g) deduction to patrons.*—(i) D, a nonexempt Specified Cooperative, markets corn grown by its patrons within the United States. For its calendar year ended December 31, 2020, D has gross receipts of $1,500,000, all derived from the sale of corn grown by its patrons within the United States. D pays $300,000 for its patrons' corn at the time the grain was delivered in the form of per-unit retain allocations and its W–2 wages (as defined in §1.199A-11) for 2020 total $300,000. D has no other costs. Patron A is a patron of D. Patron A is a cash basis taxpayer and files Federal income tax returns on a calendar year basis. All corn grown by Patron A in 2020 is sold through D and Patron A is eligible to share in patronage dividends paid by D for that year.

(ii) All of D's gross receipts from the sale of its patrons' corn qualify as DPGR (as defined paragraph (8)(b)(3)(ii) of this section). D's QPAI and taxable income is $1,200,000. D's section 199A(g) deduction for its taxable year 2020 is $108,000 (.09 × $1,200,000). Because this amount is less than 50% of D's W–2 wages, the entire amount is allowed as a section 199A(g) deduction. D decides not to pass any of its section 199A(g) deduction to its patrons. The section 199A(g) deduction of $108,000 is applied to, and reduces, D's taxable income.

(7) *Example 7. Nonexempt Specified Cooperative passing through the section 199A(g) deduction to patrons paid a patronage dividend.*—(i) The

facts are the same as in Example 6 except that D decides to pass its entire section 199A(g) deduction through to its patrons. D declares a patronage dividend for its 2020 taxable year of $900,000, which it pays on March 15, 2021. Pursuant to paragraph (d)(3) of this section, D notifies patrons in written notices that accompany the patronage dividend notification that D is allocating to them the section 199A(g) deduction D is entitled to claim in the calendar year 2020. On March 15, 2021, Patron A receives a $9,000 patronage dividend that is a qualified payment under paragraph (d)(2)(ii) of this section from D. In the notice that accompanies the patronage dividend, Patron A is designated a $1,080 section 199A(g) deduction. Under paragraph (a) of this section, Patron A may claim a $1,080 section 199A(g) deduction for the taxable year ending December 31, 2021, subject to the limitations set forth under paragraph (d)(4) of this section. D must report the allowable amount of Patron A's section 199A(g) deduction on Form 1099-PATR, "Taxable Distributions Received From Cooperatives," issued to Patron A for the calendar year 2021.

(ii) Under paragraph (d)(7) of this section, D is required to reduce its section 1382 deduction of $1,200,000 by the $108,000 section 199A(g) deduction passed through to patrons (whether D pays patronage dividends on book or Federal income tax net earnings). As a consequence, D is entitled to a section 1382 deduction for the taxable year ending December 31, 2020, in the amount of $1,092,000 ($1,200,000 − $108,000) and to a section 199A(g) deduction in the amount of $108,000 ($1,200,000 × .09). Its taxable income for 2020 is $0.

(8) *Example 8. Nonexempt Specified Cooperative passing through the section 199A(g) deduction to patrons paid a patronage dividend and advances on expected patronage net earnings.*—(i) The facts are the same as in Example 6 except that D paid out $500,000 to its patrons as advances on expected patronage net earnings. In 2020, D pays its patrons a $400,000 ($900,000 − $500,000 already paid) patronage dividend in cash or a combination of cash and qualified written notices of allocation. Under paragraph (d)(7) of this section and section 1382, D is allowed a deduction of $1,092,000 ($1,200,000 − $108,000 section 199A(g) deduction), whether patronage net earnings are distributed on book or Federal income tax net earnings.

(ii) The patrons will have received a gross amount of $1,200,000 in qualified payments under paragraph (d)(2)(ii) of this section from Cooperative D ($300,000 paid as per-unit retain allocations, $500,000 paid during the taxable year as advances, and the additional $400,000 paid as patronage dividends). If D passes through its entire section 199A(g) deduction to its patrons by providing the notice required by paragraph (d)(3) of this section, then the patrons will be allowed a $108,000 section 199A(g) deduction, resulting in a net $1,092,000 taxable distribution from D. Pursuant to paragraph (d)(8) of this section, any of the $1,200,000 received by patrons that are Specified Cooperatives from D is not taken into account for purposes of calculating the patrons' section 199A(g) deduction. Patrons that are not Specified Cooperatives must include those payments in the section 199A(b)(7) reduction when calculating a section 199A(a) deduction as applicable.

(9) *Example 9. Intangible property transaction as part of disposition of agricultural or horticultural products.*—F, a Specified Cooperative, markets patrons' oranges by processing the oranges into orange juice, and then bottling and selling the orange juice to customers. F markets the orange juice under its own brand name, but F also licenses from G, an unrelated third party, the rights to use G's brand name on the bottled orange juice. F's gross receipts from the sale of both brands of orange juice qualify as DPGR, assuming all other requirements of this section are met.

(10) *Example 10. Intangible property transaction that is not a disposition of an agricultural or horticultural product.*—H, a Specified Cooperative, licenses H's brand name to J, an unrelated third party. J purchases oranges, produces orange juice, and then bottles and sells the orange juice to customers. Gross receipts that H derives from the license of the brand name to J are not DPGR from the disposition of an agricultural or horticultural product.

(11) *Example 11. Allocation rules when Specified Cooperative retains the section 199A(g) deduction attributable to non-eligible taxpayers.*—K, a Specified Cooperative, for the taxable year has $200 of taxable income and QPAI ($100 is attributable to business done for patrons that are C corporation patrons and $100 is attributable to business done for patrons that are eligible taxpayers). K calculates an $18 section 199A(g) deduction. K passes through $9 to its patrons that are eligible taxpayers, distributes $191 to patrons in distributions that are deductible under section 1382(b)(including patronage dividends that were paid out in the same amounts to C corporation patrons and eligible taxpayer patrons because the value of their business,$100 each, was the same), and adjusts its deduction under section 1382 by $9 (the amount of the section 199A(g) deduction passed through). K's

taxable income after the section 199A deduction and distributions is $0.

(f) *Special rule for Specified Cooperative partners.*—In the case described in section 199A(g)(5)(B), where a Specified Cooperative is a partner in a partnership, the partnership must separately identify and report on the Schedule K–1 of the Form 1065, U.S. Return of Partnership Income (or any successor form) issued to the Specified Cooperative partner the cooperative's share of gross receipts and related deductions, W–2 wages, and COGS, unless otherwise provided by the instructions to the Form. The Specified Cooperative partner determines what gross receipts reported by the partnership qualify as DPGR and includes these gross receipts and related deductions, W-2 wages, and COGS to calculate one section 199A(g) deduction (in the case of a nonexempt Specified Cooperative) or two section 199A(g) deductions (in the case of an exempt Specified Cooperative) using the steps set forth in paragraphs (b) and (c) of this section. For purposes of determining whether gross receipts are DPGR, the MPGE activities of the Specified Cooperative partner may be attributed to the partnership, and the partnership's MPGE activities may be attributed to the Specified Cooperative partner.

(g) *Recapture of section 199A(g) deduction.*—If the amount of the section 199A(g) deduction that was passed through to eligible taxpayers exceeds the amount allowable as a section 199A(g) deduction as determined on examination or reported on an amended return, then recapture of the excess will occur at the Specified Cooperative level in the taxable year the Specified Cooperative took the excess section 199A(g) deduction.

(h) *Applicability date.*—Except as provided in paragraph (h)(2) of §1.199A-7, the provisions of this section apply to taxable years beginning after January 19, 2021. Taxpayers, however, may choose to apply the rules of §§1.199A-7 through 1.199A-12 for taxable years beginning on or before that date, provided the taxpayers apply the rules in their entirety and in a consistent manner. [Reg. §1.199A-8.]

□ [T.D. 9947, 1-14-2021 (corrected 11-16-2022).]

[Reg. §1.199A-9]

§1.199A-9. Domestic production gross receipts.—(a) *Domestic production gross receipts.*—(1) *In general.*—The provisions of this section apply solely for purposes of section 199A(g) of the Internal Revenue Code (Code). The provisions of this section provide guidance to determine what gross receipts (defined in §1.199A-8(b)(2)(iii)) are domestic production gross receipts (DPGR) (defined in §1.199A-8(b)(3)(ii)). DPGR does not include gross receipts derived from services or the lease, rental, license, sale, exchange, or other disposition of land unless a de minimis or other exception applies. Partners, including partners in an EAG partnership described in §1.199A-12(i)(1), may not treat guaranteed payments under section 707(c) as DPGR.

(2) *Application to marketing cooperatives.*—For purposes of determining DPGR, a Specified Cooperative (defined in §1.199A-8(a)(2)) will be treated as having manufactured, produced, grown, or extracted (MPGE) (defined in paragraph (f) of this section) in whole or significant part (defined in paragraph (h) of this section) any agricultural or horticultural product (defined in §1.199A-8(a)(4)) within the United States (defined in paragraph (i) of this section) marketed by the Specified Cooperative which its patrons (defined in §1.1388-1(e)) have so MPGE.

(b) *Related persons.*—(1) *In general.*—Pursuant to section 199A(g)(3)(D)(ii), DPGR does not include any gross receipts derived from agricultural or horticultural products leased, licensed, or rented by the Specified Cooperative for use by any related person. A person is treated as related to another person if both persons are treated as a single employer under either section 52(a) or (b) (without regard to section 1563(b)), or section 414(m) or (o). Any other person is an unrelated person for purposes of the section 199A(g) deduction.

(2) *Exceptions.*—Notwithstanding paragraph (b)(1) of this section, gross receipts derived from any agricultural or horticultural product leased or rented by the Specified Cooperative to a related person may qualify as DPGR if the agricultural or horticultural product is held for sublease or rent, or is subleased or rented, by the related person to an unrelated person for the ultimate use of the unrelated person. Similarly, notwithstanding paragraph (b)(1) of this section, gross receipts derived from a license of the right to reproduce an agricultural or horticultural product to a related person for reproduction and sale, exchange, lease, or rental to an unrelated person for the ultimate use of the unrelated person are treated as gross receipts from a disposition of an agricultural or horticultural product and may qualify as DPGR.

(c) *Allocating gross receipts.*—(1) *In general.*—A Specified Cooperative must determine the portion of its gross receipts for the taxable

year that is DPGR and the portion of its gross receipts that is non-DPGR using a reasonable method based on all the facts and circumstances. Applicable Federal income tax principles apply to determine whether a transaction is, in substance, a lease, rental, license, sale, exchange, or other disposition the gross receipts of which may constitute DPGR, whether it is a service the gross receipts of which may constitute non-DPGR, or some combination thereof. For example, if a Specified Cooperative sells an agricultural or horticultural product and, in connection with that sale, also provides services, the Specified Cooperative must allocate its gross receipts from the transaction using a reasonable method based on all the facts and circumstances that accurately identifies the gross receipts that constitute DPGR and non-DPGR in accordance with the requirements of §1.199A-8(b) and/or (c). The chosen reasonable method must be consistently applied from one taxable year to another and must clearly reflect the portion of gross receipts for the taxable year that is DPGR and the portion of gross receipts that is non-DPGR. The books and records maintained for gross receipts must be consistent with any allocations under this paragraph (c)(1).

(2) *Reasonable method of allocation.*—If a Specified Cooperative has the information readily available and can, without undue burden or expense, specifically identify whether the gross receipts are derived from an item (and thus, are DPGR), then the Specified Cooperative must use that specific identification to determine DPGR. If the Specified Cooperative does not have information readily available to specifically identify whether gross receipts are derived from an item or cannot, without undue burden or expense, specifically identify whether gross receipts are derived from an item, then the Specified Cooperative is not required to use a method that specifically identifies whether the gross receipts are derived from an item but can use a reasonable allocation method. Factors taken into consideration in determining whether the Specified Cooperative's method of allocating gross receipts between DPGR and non-DPGR is reasonable include whether the Specified Cooperative uses the most accurate information available; the relationship between the gross receipts and the method used; the accuracy of the method chosen as compared with other possible methods; whether the method is used by the Specified Cooperative for internal management or other business purposes; whether the method is used for other Federal or state income tax purposes; the time, burden, and cost of using alternative methods; and whether the Specified Cooperative applies the method consistently from year to year.

(3) *De minimis rules.*—(i) *DPGR.*—A Specified Cooperative's applicable gross receipts as provided in §1.199A-8(b) and/or (c) may be treated as DPGR if less than 10 percent of the Specified Cooperative's total gross receipts are non-DPGR (after application of the exceptions provided in §1.199A-9(j)(3)). If the amount of the Specified Cooperative's gross receipts that are non-DPGR equals or exceeds 10 percent of the Specified Cooperative's total gross receipts, then, except as provided in paragraph (c)(3)(ii) of this section, the Specified Cooperative is required to allocate all gross receipts between DPGR and non-DPGR in accordance with paragraph (c)(1) of this section. If a Specified Cooperative is a member of an expanded affiliated group (EAG) (defined in §1.199A-12), but is not a member of a consolidated group, then the determination of whether less than 10 percent of the Specified Cooperative's total gross receipts are non-DPGR is made at the Specified Cooperative level. If a Specified Cooperative is a member of a consolidated group, then the determination of whether less than 10 percent of the Specified Cooperative's total gross receipts are non-DPGR is made at the consolidated group level. *See* §1.199A-12(d).

(ii) *Non-DPGR.*—A Specified Cooperative's applicable gross receipts as provided in §1.199A-8(b) and/or (c) may be treated as non-DPGR if less than 10 percent of the Specified Cooperative's total gross receipts are DPGR. If a Specified Cooperative is a member of an EAG, but is not a member of a consolidated group, then the determination of whether less than 10 percent of the Specified Cooperative's total gross receipts are DPGR is made at the Specified Cooperative level. If a Specified Cooperative is a member of a consolidated group, then the determination of whether less than 10 percent of the Specified Cooperative's total gross receipts are DPGR is made at the consolidated group level.

(d) *Use of historical data for multiple-year transactions.*—If a Specified Cooperative recognizes and reports gross receipts from upfront payments or other similar payments on a Federal income tax return for a taxable year, then the Specified Cooperative's use of historical data in making an allocation of gross receipts from the transaction between DPGR and non-DPGR may constitute a reasonable method. If a Specified Cooperative makes allocations using historical data, and subsequently updates the data, then the Specified Cooperative must use the more recent or updated data, starting in the taxable year in which the update is made.

(e) *Determining DPGR item-by-item.*—(1) *In general.*—For purposes of the section 199A(g) deduction, a Specified Cooperative determines, using a reasonable method based on all the facts and circumstances, whether gross receipts qualify as DPGR on an item-by-item basis (and not, for example, on a division-by-division, product line-by-product line, or transaction-by-transaction basis). The chosen reasonable method must be consistently applied from one taxable year to another and must clearly reflect the portion of gross receipts that is DPGR. The books and records maintained for gross receipts must be consistent with any allocations under this paragraph (e)(1).

(i) The term *item* means the agricultural or horticultural product offered by the Specified Cooperative in the normal course of its trade or business for lease, rental, license, sale, exchange, or other disposition (for purposes of this paragraph (e), collectively referred to as disposition) to customers, if the gross receipts from the disposition of such product qualify as DPGR; or

(ii) If paragraph (e)(1)(i) of this section does not apply to the product, then any component of the product described in paragraph (e)(1)(i) of this section is treated as the item, provided that the gross receipts from the disposition of the product described in paragraph (e)(1)(i) of this section that are attributable to such component qualify as DPGR. Each component that meets the requirements under this paragraph (e)(1)(ii) must be treated as a separate item and a component that meets the requirements under this paragraph (e)(1)(ii) may not be combined with a component that does not meet these requirements.

(2) *Special rules.*—(i) For purposes of paragraph (e)(1)(i) of this section, in no event may a single item consist of two or more products unless those products are offered for disposition, in the normal course of the Specified Cooperative's trade or business, as a single item (regardless of how the products are packaged).

(ii) In the case of agricultural or horticultural products customarily sold by weight or by volume, the item is determined using the most common custom of the industry (for example, barrels of oil).

(3) *Exception.*—If the Specified Cooperative MPGE agricultural or horticultural products within the United States that it disposes of, and the Specified Cooperative leases, rents, licenses, purchases, or otherwise acquires property that contains or may contain the agricultural or horticultural products (or a portion thereof), and the Specified Cooperative cannot reasonably determine, without undue burden and expense, whether the acquired property contains any of the original agricultural or horticultural products MPGE by the Specified Cooperative, then the Specified Cooperative is not required to determine whether any portion of the acquired property qualifies as an item for purposes of paragraph (e)(1) of this section. Therefore, the gross receipts derived from the disposition of the acquired property may be treated as non-DPGR. Similarly, the preceding sentences apply if the Specified Cooperative can reasonably determine that the acquired property contains agricultural or horticultural products (or a portion thereof) MPGE by the Specified Cooperative, but cannot reasonably determine, without undue burden or expense, how much, or what type, grade, etc., of the agricultural or horticultural MPGE by the Specified Cooperative the acquired property contains.

(f) *Definition of manufactured, produced, grown, or extracted (MPGE).*—(1) *In general.*—Except as provided in paragraphs (f)(2) and (3) of this section, the term *MPGE* includes manufacturing, producing, growing, extracting, installing, developing, improving, and creating agricultural or horticultural products; making agricultural or horticultural products out of material by processing, manipulating, refining, or changing the form of an article, or by combining or assembling two or more articles; cultivating soil, raising livestock, and farming aquatic products. The term MPGE also includes storage, handling, or other processing activities (other than transportation activities) within the United States related to the sale, exchange, or other disposition of agricultural or horticultural products only if the products are consumed in connection with or incorporated into the MPGE of agricultural or horticultural products, whether or not by the Specified Cooperative. The Specified Cooperative (or the patron if §1.199A-9(a)(2) applies) must have the benefits and burdens of ownership of the agricultural or horticultural products under Federal income tax principles during the period the MPGE activity occurs for the gross receipts derived from the MPGE of the agricultural or horticultural products to qualify as DPGR.

(2) *Packaging, repackaging, or labeling.*—If the Specified Cooperative packages, repackages, or labels agricultural or horticultural products and engages in no other MPGE activity with respect to those agricultural or horticultural products, the packaging, repackaging, or labeling does not qualify as MPGE with respect to those agricultural or horticultural products.

(3) *Installing.*—If a Specified Cooperative installs agricultural or horticultural products and engages in no other MPGE activity with respect to the agricultural or horticultural products, the Specified Cooperative's installing activity does not qualify as an MPGE activity. Notwithstanding paragraph (j)(3)(i)(A) of this section, if the Specified Cooperative installs agricultural or horticultural products MPGE by the Specified Cooperative and the Specified Cooperative has the benefits and burdens of ownership of the agricultural or horticultural products under Federal income tax principles during the period the installing activity occurs, then the portion of the installing activity that relates to the agricultural or horticultural products is an MPGE activity.

(4) *Consistency with section 263A.*—A Specified Cooperative that has MPGE agricultural or horticultural products for the taxable year must treat itself as a producer under section 263A with respect to the agricultural or horticultural products unless the Specified Cooperative is not subject to section 263A. A Specified Cooperative that currently is not properly accounting for its production activities under section 263A, and wishes to change its method of accounting to comply with the producer requirements of section 263A, must follow the applicable administrative procedures issued under §1.446-1(e)(3)(ii) for obtaining the Commissioner's consent to a change in accounting method (for further guidance, for example, *see* Rev. Proc. 2015-13, 2015-5 IRB 419, or any applicable subsequent guidance (*see* §601.601(d)(2) of this chapter)).

(5) *Examples.*—The following examples illustrate the application of paragraphs (f)(1), (2), and (3) of this section.

(i) *Example 1. MPGE activities conducted within United States.*—A, B, and C are unrelated persons. A is a Specified Cooperative, B is an individual patron of A, and C is a C corporation. B grows agricultural products outside of the United States and A markets those agricultural products for B. A stores the agricultural products in agricultural storage bins in the United States and has the benefits and burdens of ownership under Federal income tax principles of the agricultural products while they are being stored. A sells the agricultural products to C, who processes them into refined agricultural products in the United States. The gross receipts from A's activities are DPGR from the MPGE of agricultural products.

(ii) *Example 2. MPGE activities conducted within and outside United States.*—The facts are the same as in Example 1 except that B grows the agricultural products outside the United States and C processes them into refined agricultural products outside the United States. Pursuant to paragraph (f)(1) of this section, the gross receipts derived by A from its sale of the agricultural products to C are DPGR from the MPGE of agricultural products within the United States.

(g) *By the taxpayer.*—With respect to the exception of the rules applicable to an EAG and EAG partnerships under §1.199A-12, only one Specified Cooperative may claim the section 199A(g) deduction with respect to any qualifying activity under paragraph (f) of this section performed in connection with the same agricultural or horticultural product. If an unrelated party performs a qualifying activity under paragraph (f) of this section pursuant to a contract with a Specified Cooperative (or its patron as relevant under paragraph (a)(2) of this section), then only if the Specified Cooperative (or its patron) has the benefits and burdens of ownership of the agricultural or horticultural product under Federal income tax principles during the period in which the qualifying activity occurs is the Specified Cooperative (or its patron) treated as engaging in the qualifying activity.

(h) *In whole or significant part defined.*—(1) *In general.*—Agricultural or horticultural products must be MPGE in whole or significant part by the Specified Cooperative (or its patrons in the case described in paragraph (a)(2) of this section) and in whole or significant part within the United States to qualify under section 199A(g)(3)(D)(i). If a Specified Cooperative enters into a contract with an unrelated person for the unrelated person to MPGE agricultural or horticultural products for the Specified Cooperative and the Specified Cooperative has the benefits and burdens of ownership of the agricultural or horticultural products under applicable Federal income tax principles during the period the MPGE activity occurs, then, pursuant to paragraph (g) of this section, the Specified Cooperative is considered to MPGE the agricultural or horticultural products under this section. The unrelated person must perform the MPGE activity on behalf of the Specified Cooperative in whole or significant part within the United States in order for the Specified Cooperative to satisfy the requirements of this paragraph (h)(1).

(2) *Substantial in nature.*—Agricultural or horticultural products will be treated as MPGE in whole or in significant part by the Specified Cooperative (or its patrons in the case described in paragraph (a)(2) of this section) within the United States for purposes of paragraph (h)(1) of this section. However, MPGE of the agricultural or horticultural products by the Specified Cooperative within the

United States must be substantial in nature taking into account all the facts and circumstances, including the relative value added by, and relative cost of, the Specified Cooperative's MPGE within the United States, the nature of the agricultural or horticultural products, and the nature of the MPGE activity that the Specified Cooperative performs within the United States. The MPGE of a key component of an agricultural or horticultural product does not, in itself, meet the substantial-in-nature requirement with respect to an agricultural or horticultural product under this paragraph (h)(2). In the case of an agricultural or horticultural product, research and experimental activities under section 174 and the creation of intangible assets are not taken into account in determining whether the MPGE of the agricultural or horticultural product is substantial in nature.

(3) *Safe harbor.*—(i) *In general.*—A Specified Cooperative (or its patrons in the case described in paragraph (a)(2) of this section) will be treated as having MPGE an agricultural or horticultural product in whole or in significant part within the United States for purposes of paragraph (h)(1) of this section if the direct labor and overhead of such Specified Cooperative to MPGE the agricultural or horticultural product within the United States account for 20 percent or more of the Specified Cooperative's COGS of the agricultural or horticultural product, or in a transaction without COGS (for example, a lease, rental, or license), account for 20 percent or more of the Specified Cooperative's unadjusted depreciable basis (as defined in paragraph (h)(3)(ii) of this section) in property included in the definition of agricultural or horticultural products. For Specified Cooperatives subject to section 263A, overhead is all costs required to be capitalized under section 263A except direct materials and direct labor. For Specified Cooperatives not subject to section 263A, overhead may be computed using a reasonable method based on all the facts and circumstances, but may not include any cost, or amount of any cost, that would not be required to be capitalized under section 263A if the Specified Cooperative were subject to section 263A. Research and experimental expenditures under section 174 and the costs of creating intangible assets are not taken into account in determining direct labor or overhead for any agricultural or horticultural product. In the case of agricultural or horticultural products, research and experimental expenditures under section 174 and any other costs incurred in the creation of intangible assets may be excluded from COGS or unadjusted depreciable basis for purposes of determining whether the Specified Cooperative meets the safe harbor under this paragraph (h)(3). For Specified Cooperatives not subject to section 263A, the chosen reasonable method to compute overhead must be consistently applied from one taxable year to another and must clearly reflect the Specified Cooperative's portion of overhead not subject to section 263A. The method must also be reasonable based on all the facts and circumstances. The books and records maintained for overhead must be consistent with any allocations under this paragraph (h)(3)(i).

(ii) *Unadjusted depreciable basis.*—The term unadjusted depreciable basis means the basis of property for purposes of section 1011 without regard to any adjustments described in section 1016(a)(2) and (3). This basis does not reflect the reduction in basis for—

(A) Any portion of the basis the Specified Cooperative properly elects to treat as an expense under sections 179 or 179C; or

(B) Any adjustments to basis provided by other provisions of the Code and the regulations under the Code (for example, a reduction in basis by the amount of the disabled access credit pursuant to section 44(d)(7)).

(4) *Special rules.*—(i) *Contract with an unrelated person.*—If a Specified Cooperative enters into a contract with an unrelated person for the unrelated person to MPGE an agricultural or horticultural product within the United States for the Specified Cooperative, and the Specified Cooperative is considered to MPGE the agricultural or horticultural product pursuant to paragraph (f)(1) of this section, then, for purposes of the substantial-in-nature requirement under paragraph (h)(2) of this section and the safe harbor under paragraph (h)(3)(i) of this section, the Specified Cooperative's MPGE activities or direct labor and overhead must include both the Specified Cooperative's MPGE activities or direct labor and overhead to MPGE the agricultural or horticultural product within the United States as well as the MPGE activities or direct labor and overhead of the unrelated *person to MPGE the agricultural or horticultural product within the* United States under the contract.

(ii) *Aggregation.*—In determining whether the substantial-in-nature requirement under paragraph (h)(2) of this section or the safe harbor under paragraph (h)(3)(i) of this section is met at the time the Specified Cooperative disposes of an agricultural or horticultural product—

(A) An EAG member must take into account all the previous MPGE activities or direct labor and overhead of the other members of the EAG;

(B) An EAG partnership as defined in §1.199A-12(i)(1) must take into account all of the previous MPGE activities or direct labor and overhead of all members of the EAG in which the partners of the EAG partnership are members (as well as the previous MPGE activities of any other EAG partnerships owned by members of the same EAG); and

(C) A member of an EAG in which the partners of an EAG partnership are members must take into account all of the previous MPGE activities or direct labor and overhead of the EAG partnership (as well as those of any other members of the EAG and any previous MPGE activities of any other EAG partnerships owned by members of the same EAG).

(i) *United States defined.*—For purposes of section 199A(g), the term *United States* includes the 50 states, the District of Columbia, the territorial waters of the United States, and the seabed and subsoil of those submarine areas that are adjacent to the territorial waters of the United States and over which the United States has exclusive rights, in accordance with international law, with respect to the exploration and exploitation of natural resources. Consistent with its definition in section 7701(a)(9), the term *United States* does not include possessions and territories of the United States or the airspace or space over the United States and these areas.

(j) *Derived from the lease, rental, license, sale, exchange, or other disposition.*—(1) *In general.*—(i) *Definition.*—The term *derived from the lease, rental, license, sale, exchange, or other disposition* is defined as, and limited to, the gross receipts directly derived from the lease, rental, license, sale, exchange, or other disposition of agricultural or horticultural products even if the Specified Cooperative has already recognized receipts from a previous lease, rental, license, sale, exchange, or other disposition of the same agricultural or horticultural products. Applicable Federal income tax principles apply to determine whether a transaction is, in substance, a lease, rental, license, sale, exchange, or other disposition, whether it is a service, or whether it is some combination thereof.

(ii) *Lease income.*—The financing and interest components of a lease of agricultural or horticultural products are considered to be derived from the lease of such agricultural or horticultural products. However, any portion of the lease income that is attributable to services or non-qualified property as defined in paragraph (j)(3) of this section is not derived from the lease of agricultural or horticultural products.

(iii) *Income substitutes.*—The proceeds from business interruption insurance, governmental subsidies, and governmental payments not to produce are treated as gross receipts derived from the lease, rental, license, sale, exchange, or other disposition to the extent they are substitutes for gross receipts that would qualify as DPGR.

(iv) *Exchange of property.*—(A) *Taxable exchanges.*—The value of property received by the Specified Cooperative in a taxable exchange of agricultural or horticultural products MPGE in whole or in significant part by the Specified Cooperative within the United States is DPGR for the Specified Cooperative (assuming all the other requirements of this section are met). However, unless the Specified Cooperative meets all of the requirements under this section with respect to any additional MPGE by the Specified Cooperative of the agricultural or horticultural products received in the taxable exchange, any gross receipts derived from the sale by the Specified Cooperative of the property received in the taxable exchange are non-DPGR, because the Specified Cooperative did not MPGE such property, even if the property was an agricultural or horticultural product in the hands of the other party to the transaction.

(B) *Safe harbor.*—For purposes of paragraph (j)(1)(iv)(A) of this section, the gross receipts derived by the Specified Cooperative from the sale of eligible property (as defined in paragraph (j)(1)(iv)(C) of this section) received in a taxable exchange, net of any adjustments between the parties involved in the taxable exchange to account for differences in the eligible property exchanged (for example, location differentials and product differentials), may be treated as the value of the eligible property received by the Specified Cooperative in the taxable exchange. For purposes of the preceding sentence, the taxable exchange is deemed to occur on the date of the sale of the eligible property received in the taxable exchange by the Specified Cooperative, to the extent the sale occurs no later than the last day of the month following the month in which the exchanged eligible property is received by the Specified Cooperative. In addition, if the Specified Cooperative engages in any further MPGE activity with respect to the eligible property received in the taxable exchange, then, unless the Specified Cooperative meets the in-whole-or-in-significant-part requirement under paragraph (h)(1) of this section with respect to the property sold, for purposes of this paragraph (j)(1)(iv)(B), the Specified Cooperative must also value the property sold without taking into account the gross receipts attributable to the further MPGE activity.

(C) *Eligible property.*—For purposes of paragraph (j)(1)(iv)(B) of this section, eligible property is—

(1) Oil, natural gas, or petrochemicals, or products derived from oil, natural gas, or petrochemicals; or

(2) Any other property or product designated by publication in the Internal Revenue Bulletin (*see* §601.601(d)(2)(ii)(b) of this chapter).

(3) For this purpose, the term *natural gas* includes only natural gas extracted from a natural deposit and does not include, for example, methane gas extracted from a landfill. In the case of natural gas, production activities include all activities involved in extracting natural gas from the ground and processing the gas into pipeline quality gas.

(2) *Hedging transactions.*—(i) *In general.*—For purposes of this section, if a transaction is a hedging transaction within the meaning of section 1221(b)(2)(A) and §1.1221-2(b), is properly identified as a hedging transaction in accordance with §1.1221-2(f), and the risk being hedged relates to property described in section 1221(a)(1) that gives rise to DPGR or to property described in section 1221(a)(8) that is consumed in an activity that gives rise to DPGR, then—

(A) In the case of a hedge of purchases of property described in section 1221(a)(1), income, deduction, gain, or loss on the hedging transaction must be taken into account in determining COGS;

(B) In the case of a hedge of sales of property described in section 1221(a)(1), income, deduction, gain, or loss on the hedging transaction must be taken into account in determining DPGR; and

(C) In the case of a hedge of purchases of property described in section 1221(a)(8), income, deduction, gain, or loss on the hedging transaction must be taken into account in determining DPGR.

(ii) *Allocation.*—The income, deduction, gain and loss from hedging transactions described in paragraph (j)(2) of this section must be allocated between the patronage and nonpatronage (defined in §1.1388-1(f)) sourced income and related deductions of the Specified Cooperatives consistent with the cooperative's method for determining patronage and nonpatronage income and deductions.

(iii) *Effect of identification and nonidentification.*—The principles of §1.1221-2(g) apply to a Specified Cooperative that identifies or fails to identify a transaction as a hedging transaction, except that the consequence of identifying as a hedging transaction a transaction that is not in fact a hedging transaction described in paragraph (j)(2) of this section, or of failing to identify a transaction that the Specified Cooperative has no reasonable grounds for treating as other than a hedging transaction described in paragraph (j)(2) of this section, is that deduction or loss (but not income or gain) from the transaction is taken into account under paragraph (j)(2) of this section.

(iv) *Other rules.*—See §1.1221-2(e) for rules applicable to hedging by members of a consolidated group and §1.446-4 for rules regarding the timing of income, deductions, gains or losses with respect to hedging transactions.

(3) *Allocation of gross receipts to embedded services and non-qualified property.*—(i) *Embedded services and non-qualified property.*—(A) *In general.*—Except as otherwise provided in paragraph (j)(3)(i)(B) of this section, gross receipts derived from the performance of services do not qualify as DPGR. In the case of an embedded service, that is, a service the price of which, in the normal course of the business, is not separately stated from the amount charged for the lease, rental, license, sale, exchange, or other disposition of agricultural or horticultural products, DPGR includes only the gross receipts derived from the lease, rental, license, sale, exchange, or other disposition of agricultural or horticultural products (assuming all the other requirements of this section are met) and not any receipts attributable to the embedded service. In addition, DPGR does not include gross receipts derived from the lease, rental, license, sale, exchange, or other disposition of property that does not meet all of the requirements under this section (non-qualified property). The allocation of the gross receipts attributable to the embedded services or non-qualified property will be deemed to be reasonable if the allocation reflects the fair market value of the embedded services or non-qualified property.

(B) *Exceptions.*—There are five exceptions to the rules under paragraph (j)(3)(i)(A) of this section regarding embedded services and non-qualified property. A Specified Cooperative may include in DPGR, if all the other requirements of this section are met with respect to the underlying item of agricultural or horticultural products to which the embedded services or non-qualified property relate, the gross receipts derived from—

(1) A qualified warranty, that is, a warranty that is provided in connection with the lease, rental, license, sale, exchange, or other disposition of agricultural or horticultural products if, in the normal course of the Specified Cooperative's business—

(i) The price for the warranty is not separately stated from the amount charged for the lease, rental, license, sale, exchange, or other disposition of the agricultural or horticultural products; and

(ii) The warranty is neither separately offered by the Specified Cooperative nor separately bargained for with customers (that is, a customer cannot purchase the agricultural or horticultural products without the warranty).

(2) A qualified delivery, that is, a delivery or distribution service that is provided in connection with the lease, rental, license, sale, exchange, or other disposition of agricultural or horticultural products if, in the normal course of the Specified Cooperative's business—

(i) The price for the delivery or distribution service is not separately stated from the amount charged for the lease, rental, license, sale, exchange, or other disposition of the agricultural or horticultural products; and

(ii) The delivery or distribution service is neither separately offered by the Specified Cooperative nor separately bargained for with customers (that is, a customer cannot purchase the agricultural or horticultural products without the delivery or distribution service).

(3) A qualified operating manual, that is, a manual of instructions that is provided in connection with the lease, rental, license, sale, exchange, or other disposition of the agricultural or horticultural products if, in the normal course of the Specified Cooperative's business—

(i) The price for the manual is not separately stated from the amount charged for the lease, rental, license, sale, exchange, or other disposition of the agricultural or horticultural products;

(ii) The manual is neither separately offered by the Specified Cooperative nor separately bargained for with customers (that is, a customer cannot purchase the agricultural or horticultural products without the manual); and

(iii) The manual is not provided in connection with a training course for customers.

(4) A qualified installation, that is, an installation service for agricultural or horticultural products that is provided in connection with the lease, rental, license, sale, exchange, or other disposition of the agricultural or horticultural products if, in the normal course of the Specified Cooperative's business—

(i) The price for the installation service is not separately stated from the amount charged for the lease, rental, license, sale, exchange, or other disposition of the agricultural or horticultural products; and

(ii) The installation is neither separately offered by the Specified Cooperative nor separately bargained for with customers (that is, a customer cannot purchase the agricultural or horticultural products without the installation service).

(5) A de minimis amount of gross receipts from embedded services and non-qualified property for each item of agricultural or horticultural products may qualify. For purposes of this exception, a de minimis amount of gross receipts from embedded services and non-qualified property is less than 5 percent of the total gross receipts derived from the lease, rental, license, sale, exchange, or other disposition of each item of agricultural or horticultural products. In the case of gross receipts derived from the lease, rental, license, sale, exchange, or other disposition of agricultural or horticultural products that are received over a period of time (for example, a multi-year lease or installment sale), this de minimis exception is applied by taking into account the total gross receipts for the entire period derived (and to be derived) from the lease, rental, license, sale, exchange, or other disposition of the item of agricultural or horticultural products. For purposes of the preceding sentence, if a Specified Cooperative treats gross receipts as DPGR under this de minimis exception, then the Specified Cooperative must treat the gross receipts recognized in each taxable year consistently as DPGR. The gross receipts that the Specified Cooperative treats as DPGR under paragraphs (j)(3)(i)(B)(1) through (4) of this section are treated as DPGR for purposes of applying this de minimis exception. This de minimis exception does not apply if the price of a service or non-qualified property is separately stated by the Specified Cooperative, or if the service or non-qualified property is separately offered or separately bargained for with the customer (that is, the customer can purchase the agricultural or horticultural products without the service or non-qualified property).

(ii) *Non-DPGR.*—Applicable gross receipts as provided in §§1.199A-8(b) and/or (c) derived from the lease, rental, license, sale, exchange or other disposition of an item of agricultural or horticultural products may be treated as non-DPGR if less than 5 percent of the Specified Cooperative's total gross receipts derived from the lease, rental, license, sale, exchange or other disposition of that item are DPGR (taking into account embedded services and non-qualified property included in such disposition, but not part of the item). In the case of gross receipts derived from the lease, rental, license, sale, exchange, or other disposition of agricultural or horticultural products that are received over a period of time (for example, a multi-year lease or installment sale), this paragraph (j)(5)(ii) is applied by taking into account the total gross receipts for the entire period derived (and to be derived) from the lease, rental, license, sale, exchange, or other disposition of the item of agricultural or horticultural products. For purposes of the preceding sentence, if the Specified Cooperative treats gross receipts as non-DPGR under this de minimis exception, then the Specified Cooperative must treat the gross receipts recognized in each taxable year consistently as non-DPGR.

(k) *Applicability date.*—The provisions of this section apply to taxable years beginning after January 19, 2021. Taxpayers, however, may choose to apply the rules of §§ 1.199A-7 through 1.199A-12 for taxable years beginning on or before that date, provided the taxpayers apply the rules in their entirety and in a consistent manner. [Reg. § 1.199A-9.]

☐ [T.D. 9947, 1-14-2021 (corrected 11-16-2022).]

[Reg. § 1.199A-10]

§1.199A-10. Allocation of cost of goods sold (COGS) and other deductions to domestic production gross receipts (DPGR), and other rules.—(a) *In general.*—The provisions of this section apply solely for purposes of section 199A(g) of the Internal Revenue Code (Code). The provisions of this section provide additional guidance on determining qualified production activities income (QPAI) as described and defined in § 1.199A-8(b)(4)(ii).

(b) *COGS allocable to DPGR.*—(1) *In general.*—When determining its QPAI, the Specified Cooperative (defined in § 1.199A-8(a)(2)) must subtract from its DPGR (defined in § 1.199A-8(b)(3)(ii)) the COGS allocable to its DPGR. The Specified Cooperative determines its COGS allocable to DPGR in accordance with this paragraph (b)(1) or, if applicable, paragraph (f) of this section. In the case of a sale, exchange, or other disposition of inventory, COGS is equal to beginning inventory of the Specified Cooperative plus purchases and production costs incurred during the taxable year and included in inventory costs by the Specified Cooperative, less ending inventory of the Specified Cooperative. In determining its QPAI, the Specified Cooperative does not include in COGS any payment made, whether during the taxable year, or included in beginning inventory, for which a deduction is allowed under section 1382(b) and/or (c), as applicable. *See* § 1.199A-8(b)(4)(ii)(C). COGS is determined under the methods of accounting that the Specified Cooperative uses to compute taxable income. *See* sections 263A, 471, and 472. If section 263A requires the Specified Cooperative to include additional section 263A costs (as defined in § 1.263A-1(d)(3)) in inventory, additional section 263A costs must be included in determining COGS. COGS also include the Specified Cooperative's inventory valuation adjustments such as writedowns under the lower of cost or market method. In the case of a sale, exchange, or other disposition (including, for example, theft, casualty, or abandonment) by the Specified Cooperative of non-inventory property, COGS for purposes of this section includes the adjusted basis of the property.

(2) *Allocating COGS.*—(i) *In general.*—A Specified Cooperative must use a reasonable method based on all the facts and circumstances to allocate COGS between DPGR and non-DPGR. Whether an allocation method is reasonable is based on all the facts and circumstances, including whether the Specified Cooperative uses the most accurate information available; the relationship between COGS and the method used; the accuracy of the method chosen as compared with other possible methods; whether the method is used by the Specified Cooperative for internal management or other business purposes; whether the method is used for other Federal or state income tax purposes; the availability of costing information; the time, burden, and cost of using alternative methods; and whether the Specified Cooperative applies the method consistently from year to year. Depending on the facts and circumstances, reasonable methods may include methods based on gross receipts (defined in § 1.199A-8(b)(2)(iii)), number of units sold, number of units produced, or total production costs. Ordinarily, if a Specified Cooperative uses a method to allocate gross receipts between DPGR and non-DPGR, then the use of a different method to allocate COGS that is not demonstrably more accurate than the method used to allocate gross receipts will not be considered reasonable. However, if a Specified Cooperative has information readily available to specifically identify COGS allocable to DPGR and can specifically identify that amount without undue burden or expense, COGS allocable to DPGR is that amount irrespective of whether the Specified Cooperative uses an-

other allocation method to allocate gross receipts between DPGR and non-DPGR. A Specified Cooperative that does not have information readily available to specifically identify COGS allocable to DPGR and that cannot, without undue burden or expense, specifically identify that amount is not required to use a method that specifically identifies COGS allocable to DPGR. The chosen reasonable method must be consistently applied from one taxable year to another and must clearly reflect the portion of COGS between DPGR and non-DPGR. The method must also be reasonable based on all the facts and circumstances. The books and records maintained for COGS must be consistent with any allocations under this paragraph (b)(2).

(ii) *Gross receipts recognized in an earlier taxable year.*—If the Specified Cooperative (other than a Specified Cooperative that uses the small business simplified overall method of paragraph (f) of this section) recognizes and reports gross receipts on a Federal income tax return for a taxable year, and incurs COGS related to such gross receipts in a subsequent taxable year, then regardless of whether the gross receipts ultimately qualify as DPGR, the Specified Cooperative must allocate the COGS to—

(A) DPGR if the Specified Cooperative identified the related gross receipts as DPGR in the prior taxable year; or

(B) Non-DPGR if the Specified Cooperative identified the related gross receipts as non-DPGR in the prior taxable year or if the Specified Cooperative recognized under the Specified Cooperative's methods of accounting those gross receipts in a taxable year to which section 199A(g) does not apply.

(iii) *COGS associated with activities undertaken in an earlier taxable year.*—(A) *In general.*—A Specified Cooperative must allocate its COGS between DPGR and non-DPGR under the rules provided in paragraphs (b)(2)(i) and (iii) of this section, regardless of whether certain costs included in its COGS can be associated with activities undertaken in an earlier taxable year (including a year prior to the effective date of section 199A(g)). A Specified Cooperative may not segregate its COGS into component costs and allocate those component costs between DPGR and non-DPGR.

(B) *Example.*—The following example illustrates an application of paragraph (b)(2)(iii)(A) of this section.

(1) *Example 1.* During the 2020 taxable year, nonexempt Specified Cooperative X grew and sold Horticultural Product A. All of the patronage gross receipts from sales recognized by X in 2020 were from the sale of Horticultural Product A and qualified as DPGR. Employee 1 of X was involved in X's production process until he retired in 2013. In 2020, X paid $30 directly from its general assets for Employee 1's medical expenses pursuant to an unfunded, self-insured plan for retired X employees. For purposes of computing X's 2020 taxable income, X capitalized those medical costs to inventory under section 263A. In 2020, the COGS for a unit of Horticultural Product A was $100 (including the applicable portion of the $30 paid for Employee 1's medical costs that was allocated to COGS under X's allocation method for additional section 263A costs). X has information readily available to specifically identify COGS allocable to DPGR and can identify that amount without undue burden and expense because all of X's gross receipts from sales in 2020 are attributable to the sale of Horticultural Product A and qualify as DPGR. The inventory cost of each unit of Horticultural Product A sold in 2020, including the applicable portion of retiree medical costs, is related to X's gross receipts from the sale of Horticultural Product A in 2020. X may not segregate the 2020 COGS by separately allocating the retiree medical costs, which are components of COGS, to DPGR and non-DPGR. Thus, even though the retiree medical costs can be associated with activities undertaken in prior years, $100 of inventory cost of each unit of Horticultural Product A sold in 2020, including the applicable portion of the retiree medical expense cost component, is allocable to DPGR in 2020.

(3) *Special allocation rules.*—Section 199A(g)(3)(C) provides the following two special rules—

(i) For purposes of determining the COGS that are allocable to DPGR, any item or service brought into the United States (defined in § 1.199A-9(i)) is treated as acquired by purchase, and its cost is treated as not less than its value immediately after it entered the United States. A similar rule applies in determining the adjusted basis of leased or rented property where the lease or rental gives rise to DPGR.

(ii) In the case of any property described in paragraph (b)(3)(i) of this section that has been exported by the Specified Cooperative for further manufacture, the increase in cost or adjusted basis under paragraph (b)(3)(i) of this section cannot exceed the difference between the value of the property when exported and the value of the property when brought back into the United States after the further manufacture. For the purposes of this paragraph (b)(3), the value of property is its customs value as defined in section 1059A(b)(1).

(4) *Rules for inventories valued at market or bona fide selling prices.*— If part of COGS is attributable to the Specified Cooperative's inventory valuation adjustments, then COGS allocable to DPGR includes inventory adjustments to agricultural or horticultural products that are MPGE in whole or significant part within the United States. Accordingly, a Specified Cooperative that values its inventory under §1.471-4 (inventories at cost or market, whichever is lower) or §1.471-2(c) (subnormal goods at bona fide selling prices) must allocate a proper share of such adjustments (for example, write-downs) to DPGR based on a reasonable method based on all the facts and circumstances. Factors taken into account in determining whether the method is reasonable include whether the Specified Cooperative uses the most accurate information available; the relationship between the adjustment and the allocation base chosen; the accuracy of the method chosen as compared with other possible methods; whether the method is used by the Specified Cooperative for internal management or other business purposes; whether the method is used for other Federal or state income tax purposes; the time, burden, and cost of using alternative methods; and whether the Specified Cooperative applies the method consistently from year to year. If the Specified Cooperative has information readily available to specifically identify the proper amount of inventory valuation adjustments allocable to DPGR, then the Specified Cooperative must allocate that amount to DPGR. The Specified Cooperative that does not have information readily available to specifically identify the proper amount of its inventory valuation adjustments allocable to DPGR and that cannot, without undue burden or expense, specifically identify the proper amount of its inventory valuation adjustments allocable to DPGR, is not required to use a method that specifically identifies inventory valuation adjustments to DPGR. The chosen reasonable method must be consistently applied from one taxable year to another and must clearly reflect inventory adjustments. The method must also be reasonable based on all the facts and circumstances. The books and records maintained for inventory adjustments must be consistent with any allocations under this paragraph (b)(4).

(5) *Rules applicable to inventories accounted for under the last-in, first-out inventory method.*—(i) *In general.*—This paragraph (b)(5) applies to inventories accounted for using the specific goods last-in, first-out (LIFO) method or the dollar-value LIFO method. Whenever a specific goods grouping or a dollar-value LIFO pool contains agricultural or horticultural products that produce DPGR and goods that do not, the Specified Cooperative must allocate COGS attributable to that grouping or pool between DPGR and non-DPGR using a reasonable method based on all the facts and circumstances. Whether a method of allocating COGS between DPGR and non-DPGR is reasonable must be determined in accordance with paragraph (b)(2) of this section. In addition, this paragraph (b)(5) provides methods that a Specified Cooperative may use to allocate COGS for a Specified Cooperative's inventories accounted for using the LIFO method. If the Specified Cooperative uses the LIFO/FIFO ratio method provided in paragraph (b)(5)(ii) of this section or the change in relative base-year cost method provided in paragraph (b)(5)(iii) of this section, then the Specified Cooperative must use that method for all of the Specified Cooperative's inventory accounted for under the LIFO method. The chosen reasonable method must be consistently applied from one taxable year to another and must clearly reflect the inventory method. The method must also be reasonable based on all the facts and circumstances. The books and records maintained for the inventory method must be consistent with any allocations under this paragraph (b)(5).

(ii) *LIFO/FIFO ratio method.*—The LIFO/FIFO ratio method is applied with respect to the LIFO inventory on a grouping-by-grouping or pool-by-pool basis. Under the LIFO/FIFO ratio method, a Specified Cooperative computes the COGS of a grouping or pool allocable to DPGR by multiplying the COGS of agricultural or horticultural products (defined in §1.199A-8(a)(4)) in the grouping or pool that produced DPGR computed using the FIFO method by the LIFO/FIFO ratio of the grouping or pool. The LIFO/FIFO ratio of a grouping or pool is equal to the total COGS of the grouping or pool computed using the LIFO method over the total COGS of the grouping or pool computed using the FIFO method.

(iii) *Change in relative base-year cost method.*—A Specified Cooperative using the dollar-value LIFO method may use the change in relative base-year cost method. The change in relative base-year cost method for a Specified Cooperative using the dollar-value LIFO method is applied to all LIFO inventory on a pool-by-pool basis. The change in relative base-year cost method determines the COGS allocable to DPGR by increasing or decreasing the total production costs (*section 471 costs and additional section 263A costs*) of agricultural or horticultural products that generate DPGR by a portion of any increment or liquidation of the dollar-value pool. The portion of an increment or liquidation allocable to DPGR is determined by multiplying the LIFO value of the increment or liquidation (expressed as a

positive number) by the ratio of the change in total base-year cost (expressed as a positive number) of agricultural or horticultural products that will generate DPGR in ending inventory to the change in total base-year cost (expressed as a positive number) of all goods in ending inventory. The portion of an increment or liquidation allocable to DPGR may be zero but cannot exceed the amount of the increment or liquidation. Thus, a ratio in excess of 1.0 must be treated as 1.0.

(6) *Specified Cooperative using a simplified method for additional section 263A costs to ending inventory.*—A Specified Cooperative that uses a simplified method specifically described in the section 263A regulations to allocate additional section 263A costs to ending inventory must follow the rules in paragraph (b)(2) of this section to determine the amount of additional section 263A costs allocable to DPGR. Allocable additional section 263A costs include additional section 263A costs included in the Specified Cooperative's beginning inventory as well as additional section 263A costs incurred during the taxable year by the Specified Cooperative. Ordinarily, if the Specified Cooperative uses a simplified method specifically described in the section 263A regulations to allocate its additional section 263A costs to its ending inventory, the additional section 263A costs must be allocated in the same proportion as section 471 costs are allocated.

(c) *Other deductions properly allocable to DPGR or gross income attributable to DPGR.*—(1) *In general.*—In determining its QPAI, the Specified Cooperative must subtract from its DPGR (in addition to the COGS), the deductions that are properly allocable and apportioned to DPGR. A Specified Cooperative generally must allocate and apportion these deductions using the rules of the section 861 method provided in paragraph (d) of this section. In lieu of the section 861 method, an eligible Specified Cooperative may apportion these deductions using the simplified deduction method provided in paragraph (e) of this section. Paragraph (f) of this section provides a small business simplified overall method that may be used by a qualifying small Specified Cooperative. A Specified Cooperative using the simplified deduction method or the small business simplified overall method must use that method for all deductions. A Specified Cooperative eligible to use the small business simplified overall method may choose at any time for any taxable year to use the small business simplified overall method or the simplified deduction method for a taxable year.

(2) *Treatment of net operating losses.*—A deduction under section 172 for a net operating loss (NOL) is not allocated or apportioned to DPGR or gross income attributable to DPGR.

(3) *W-2 wages.*—Although only W-2 wages as described in §1.199A-11 are taken into account in computing the W-2 wage limitation, all wages paid (or incurred in the case of an accrual method taxpayer) in the taxable year are taken into account in computing QPAI for that taxable year.

(d) *Section 861 method.*—Under the section 861 method, the Specified Cooperative must allocate and apportion its deductions using the allocation and apportionment rules provided under the section 861 regulations under which section 199A(g) is treated as an operative section described in §1.861-8(f). Accordingly, the Specified Cooperative applies the rules of the section 861 regulations to allocate and apportion deductions (including, if applicable, its distributive share of deductions from passthrough entities) to gross income attributable to DPGR. If the Specified Cooperative applies the allocation and apportionment rules of the section 861 regulations for section 199A(g) and another operative section, then the Specified Cooperative must use the same method of allocation and the same principles of apportionment for purposes of all operative sections. Research and experimental expenditures must be allocated and apportioned in accordance with §1.861-17 without taking into account the exclusive apportionment rule of §1.861-17(b). Deductions for charitable contributions (as allowed under section 170 and section 873(b)(2) or 882(c)(1)(B)) must be ratably apportioned between gross income attributable to DPGR and gross income attributable to non-DPGR based on the relative amounts of gross income.

(e) *Simplified deduction method.*—(1) *In general.*—An eligible Specified Cooperative (defined in paragraph (e)(2) of this section) may use the simplified deduction method to apportion business deductions between DPGR and non-DPGR. The simplified deduction method does not apply to COGS. Under the simplified deduction method, the business deductions (except the NOL deduction) are ratably apportioned between DPGR and non-DPGR based on relative gross receipts. Accordingly, the amount of deductions for the current taxable year apportioned to DPGR is equal to the proportion of the total business deductions for the current taxable year that the amount of DPGR bears to total gross receipts.

(2) *Eligible Specified Cooperative.*—For purposes of this paragraph (e), an eligible Specified Cooperative is—

(i) A Specified Cooperative that has average annual total gross receipts (as defined in paragraph (g) of this section) of $100,000,000 or less; or

(ii) A Specified Cooperative that has total assets (as defined in paragraph (e)(3) of this section) of $10,000,000 or less.

(3) *Total assets.*—(i) *In general.*—For purposes of the simplified deduction method, total assets mean the total assets the Specified Cooperative has at the end of the taxable year.

(ii) *Members of an expanded affiliated group.*—To compute the total assets of an expanded affiliated group (EAG) at the end of the taxable year, the total assets at the end of the taxable year of each member of the EAG at the end of the taxable year that ends with or within the taxable year of the computing member (as described in §1.199A-12(g)) are aggregated.

(4) *Members of an expanded affiliated group.*—(i) *In general.*— Whether the members of an EAG may use the simplified deduction method is determined by reference to all the members of the EAG. If the average annual gross receipts of the EAG are less than or equal to $100,000,000 or the total assets of the EAG are less than or equal to $10,000,000, then each member of the EAG may individually determine whether to use the simplified deduction method, regardless of the cost allocation method used by the other members.

(ii) *Exception.*—Notwithstanding paragraph (e)(4)(i) of this section, all members of the same consolidated group must use the same cost allocation method.

(f) *Small business simplified overall method.*—(1) *In general.*—A qualifying small Specified Cooperative may use the small business simplified overall method to apportion COGS and deductions between DPGR and non-DPGR. Under the small business simplified overall method, a Specified Cooperative's total costs for the current taxable year (as defined in paragraph (f)(3) of this section) are apportioned between DPGR and non-DPGR based on relative gross receipts. Accordingly, the amount of total costs for the current taxable year apportioned to DPGR is equal to the proportion of total costs for the current taxable year that the amount of DPGR bears to total gross receipts.

(2) *Qualifying small Specified Cooperative.*—For purposes of this paragraph (f), a qualifying small Specified Cooperative is a Specified Cooperative that has average annual total gross receipts (as defined in paragraph (g) of this section) of $25,000,000 or less.

(3) *Total costs for the current taxable year.*—For purposes of the small business simplified overall method, total costs for the current taxable year means the total COGS and deductions for the current taxable year. Total costs for the current taxable year are determined under the methods of accounting that the Specified Cooperative uses to compute taxable income.

(4) *Members of an expanded affiliated group.*—(i) *In general.*— Whether the members of an EAG may use the small business simplified overall method is determined by reference to all the members of the EAG. If the average annual gross receipts of the EAG are less than or equal to $25,000,000 then each member of the EAG may individually determine whether to use the small business simplified overall method, regardless of the cost allocation method used by the other members.

(ii) *Exception.*—Notwithstanding paragraph (f)(4)(i) of this section, all members of the same consolidated group must use the same cost allocation method.

(g) *Average annual gross receipts.*—(1) *In general.*—For purposes of the simplified deduction method and the small business simplified overall method, average annual gross receipts means the average annual gross receipts of the Specified Cooperative for the 3 taxable years (or, if fewer, the taxable years during which the taxpayer was in existence) preceding the current taxable year, even if one or more of such taxable years began before the effective date of section 199A(g). In the case of any taxable year of less than 12 months (a short taxable year), the gross receipts of the Specified Cooperative are annualized by multiplying the gross receipts for the short period by 12 and dividing the result by the number of months in the short period.

(2) *Members of an expanded affiliated group.*—(i) *In general.*—To compute the average annual gross receipts of an EAG, the gross receipts for the entire taxable year of each member that is a member of the EAG at the end of its taxable year that ends with or within the taxable year are aggregated. For purposes of this paragraph (g)(2), a consolidated group is treated as one member of an EAG.

(ii) *Exception.*—Notwithstanding paragraph (g)(1)(i) of this section, all members of the same consolidated group must use the same cost allocation method.

(h) *Cost allocation methods for determining oil-related QPAI.*—(1) *Section 861 method.*—A Specified Cooperative that uses the section 861 method to determine deductions that are allocated and apportioned to gross income attributable to DPGR must use the section 861 method to determine deductions that are allocated and apportioned to gross income attributable to oil-related DPGR.

(2) *Simplified deduction method.*—A Specified Cooperative that uses the simplified deduction method to apportion deductions between DPGR and non-DPGR must determine the portion of deductions allocable to oil-related DPGR by multiplying the deductions allocable to DPGR by the ratio of oil-related DPGR to DPGR from all activities.

(3) *Small business simplified overall method.*—A Specified Cooperative that uses the small business simplified overall method to apportion total costs (COGS and deductions) between DPGR and non-DPGR must determine the portion of total costs allocable to oil-related DPGR by multiplying the total costs allocable to DPGR by the ratio of oil-related DPGR to DPGR from all activities.

(i) *Applicability date.*—The provisions of this section apply to taxable years beginning after January 19, 2021. Taxpayers, however, may choose to apply the rules of §§1.199A-7 through 1.199A-12 for taxable years beginning on or before that date, provided the taxpayers apply the rules in their entirety and in a consistent manner. [Reg. §1.199A-10.]

☐ [T.D. 9947, 1-14-2021.]

[Reg. §1.199A-11]

§1.199A-11. Wage limitation for the section 199A(g) deduction.— (a) *Rules of application.*—(1) *In general.*—The provisions of this section apply solely for purposes of section 199A(g) of the Internal Revenue Code (Code). The provisions of this section provide guidance on determining the W-2 wage limitation as defined in §1.199A-8(b)(5)(ii)(B). Except as provided in paragraph (d)(2) of this section, the Form W-2, Wage and Tax Statement, or any subsequent form or document used in determining the amount of W-2 wages, are those issued for the calendar year ending during the taxable year of the Specified Cooperative (defined in §1.199A-8(a)(2)) for wages paid to employees (or former employees) of the Specified Cooperative for employment by the Specified Cooperative. Employees are limited to employees defined in section 3121(d)(1) and (2) (that is, officers of a corporate taxpayer and employees of the taxpayer under the common law rules). See paragraph (a)(5) of this section for the requirement that W-2 wages must have been included in a return filed with the Social Security Administration (SSA) within 60 days after the due date (including extensions) of the return. *See also* section 199A(a)(4)(C).

(2) *Wage limitation for section 199A(g) deduction.*—The amount of the deduction allowable under section 199A(g) to the Specified Cooperative for any taxable year cannot exceed 50 percent of the W-2 wages (as defined in section 199A(g)(1)(B)(ii) and paragraph (b) of this section) for the taxable year that are attributable to domestic production gross receipts (DPGR), defined in §1.199A-8(b)(3)(ii), of agricultural or horticultural products defined in §1.199A-8(a)(4).

(3) *Wages paid by entity other than common law employer.*—In determining W-2 wages, the Specified Cooperative may take into account any W-2 wages paid by another entity and reported by the other entity on Forms W-2 with the other entity as the employer listed in Box c of the Forms W-2, provided that the W-2 wages were paid to common law employees or officers of the Specified Cooperative for employment by the Specified Cooperative. In such cases, the entity paying the W-2 wages and reporting the W-2 wages on Forms W-2 is precluded from taking into account such wages for purposes of determining W-2 wages with respect to that entity. For purposes of this paragraph (a)(4), entities that pay and report W-2 wages on behalf of or with respect to other taxpayers can include, but are not limited to, certified professional employer organizations under section 7705, statutory employers under section 3401(d)(1), and agents under section 3504.

(4) *Requirement that wages must be reported on return filed with the Social Security Administration.*—(i) *In general.*—Pursuant to section 199A(g)(1)(B)(ii) and section 199A(b)(4)(C), the term W-2 wages does not include any amount that is not properly included in a return filed with SSA on or before the 60th day after the due date (including extensions) for such return. Under §31.6051-2 of this chapter, each Form W-2 and the transmittal Form W-3, Transmittal of Wage and Tax Statements, together constitute an information return to be filed with SSA. Similarly, each Form W-2c, Corrected Wage and Tax State-

ment, and the transmittal Form W-3 or W-3c, Transmittal of Corrected Wage and Tax Statements, together constitute an information return to be filed with SSA. In determining whether any amount has been properly included in a return filed with SSA on or before the 60th day after the due date (including extensions) for such return, each Form W-2 together with its accompanying Form W-3 is considered a separate information return and each Form W-2c together with its accompanying Form W-3 or Form W-3c is considered a separate information return. Section 6071(c) provides that Forms W-2 and W-3 must be filed on or before January 31 of the year following the calendar year to which such returns relate (but see the special rule in § 31.6071(a)-1T(a)(3)(1) of this chapter for monthly returns filed under § 31.6011(a)-5(a) of this chapter). Corrected Forms W-2 are required to be filed with SSA on or before January 31 of the year following the year in which the correction is made.

(ii) *Corrected return filed to correct a return that was filed within 60 days of the due date.*—If a corrected information return (Return B) is filed with SSA on or before the 60th day after the due date (including extensions) of Return B to correct an information return (Return A) that was filed with SSA on or before the 60th day after the due date (including extensions) of the information return (Return A) and paragraph (a)(5)(iii) of this section does not apply, then the wage information on Return B must be included in determining W-2 wages. If a corrected information return (Return D) is filed with SSA later than the 60th day after the due date (including extensions) of Return D to correct an information return (Return C) that was filed with SSA on or before the 60th day after the due date (including extensions) of the information return (Return C), then if Return D reports an increase (or increases) in wages included in determining W-2 wages from the wage amounts reported on Return C, such increase (or increases) on Return D is disregarded in determining W-2 wages (and only the wage amounts on Return C may be included in determining W-2 wages). If Return D reports a decrease (or decreases) in wages included in determining W-2 wages from the amounts reported on Return C, then, in determining W-2 wages, the wages reported on Return C must be reduced by the decrease (or decreases) reflected on Return D.

(iii) *Corrected return filed to correct a return that was filed later than 60 days after the due date.*—If an information return (Return F) is filed to correct an information return (Return E) that was not filed with SSA on or before the 60th day after the due date (including extensions) of Return E, then Return F (and any subsequent information returns filed with respect to Return E) will not be considered filed on or before the 60th day after the due date (including extensions) of Return F (or the subsequent corrected information return). Thus, if a Form W-2c is filed to correct a Form W-2 that was not filed with SSA on or before the 60th day after the due date (including extensions) of the Form W-2 (or to correct a Form W-2c relating to a Form W-2 that had not been filed with SSA on or before the 60th day after the due date (including extensions) of the Form W-2), then this Form W-2c is not to be considered to have been filed with SSA on or before the 60th day after the due date (including extensions) for this Form W-2c, regardless of when the Form W-2c is filed.

(b) *Definition of W-2 wages.*—(1) *In general.*—Section 199A(g)(1)(B)(ii) provides that the W-2 wages of the Specified Cooperative must be determined in the same manner as under section 199A(b)(4) (without regard to section 199A(b)(4)(B) and after application of section 199A(b)(5)). Section 199A(b)(4)(A) provides that the term W-2 wages means with respect to any person for any taxable year of such person, the amounts described in paragraphs (3) and (8) of section 6051(a) paid by such person with respect to employment of employees by such person during the calendar year ending during such taxable year. Thus, the term W-2 wages includes the total amount of wages as defined in section 3401(a); the total amount of elective deferrals (within the meaning of section 402(g)(3)); the compensation deferred under section 457; and the amount of designated Roth contributions (as defined in section 402A).

(2) *Section 199A(g) deduction.*—Pursuant to section 199A(g)(3)(A), W-2 wages do not include any amount which is not properly allocable to DPGR for purposes of calculating qualified production activities income (QPAI) as defined in § 1.199A-8(b)(4)(ii). The Specified Cooperative may determine the amount of wages that is properly allocable to DPGR using a reasonable method based on all the facts and circumstances. The chosen reasonable method must be consistently applied from one taxable year to another and must clearly reflect the wages allocable to DPGR for purposes of QPAI. The books and records maintained for wages allocable to DPGR for purposes of QPAI must be consistent with any allocations under this paragraph (b)(2).

(c) *Methods for calculating W-2 wages.*—The Secretary may provide for methods that may be used in calculating W-2 wages, including

W-2 wages for short taxable years by publication in the Internal Revenue Bulletin (*see* § 601.601(d)(2)(ii)(b) of this chapter).

(d) *Wage limitation — acquisitions, dispositions, and short taxable years.*—(1) *In general.*—For purposes of computing the deduction under section 199A(g) of the Specified Cooperative, in the case of an acquisition or disposition (as defined in section 199A(b)(5) and paragraph (d)(3) of this section) that causes more than one Specified Cooperative to be an employer of the employees of the acquired or disposed of Specified Cooperative during the calendar year, the W-2 wages of the Specified Cooperative for the calendar year of the acquisition or disposition are allocated between or among each Specified Cooperative based on the period during which the employees of the acquired or disposed of Specified Cooperatives were employed by the Specified Cooperative, regardless of which permissible method is used for reporting predecessor and successor wages on Form W-2, Wage and Tax Statement.

(2) *Short taxable year that does not include December 31.*—If the Specified Cooperative has a short taxable year that does not contain a calendar year ending during such short taxable year, wages paid to employees for employment by the Specified Cooperative during the short taxable year are treated as W-2 wages for such short taxable year for purposes of paragraph (a) of this section (if the wages would otherwise meet the requirements to be W-2 wages under this section but for the requirement that a calendar year must end during the short taxable year).

(3) *Acquisition or disposition.*—For purposes of paragraph (d)(1) and (2) of this section, the terms *acquisition* and *disposition* include an incorporation, a liquidation, a reorganization, or a purchase or sale of assets.

(e) *Application in the case of a Specified Cooperative with a short taxable year.*—In the case of a Specified Cooperative with a short taxable year, subject to the rules of paragraph (a) of this section, the W-2 wages of the Specified Cooperative for the short taxable year can include only those wages paid during the short taxable year to employees of the Specified Cooperative, only those elective deferrals (within the meaning of section 402(g)(3)) made during the short taxable year by employees of the Specified Cooperative, and only compensation actually deferred under section 457 during the short taxable year with respect to employees of the Specified Cooperative.

(f) *Non-duplication rule.*—Amounts that are treated as W-2 wages for a taxable year under any method cannot be treated as W-2 wages of any other taxable year. Also, an amount cannot be treated as W-2 wages by more than one taxpayer. Finally, an amount cannot be treated as W-2 wages by the Specified Cooperative both in determining patronage and nonpatronage W-2 wages.

(g) *Wage expense safe harbor.*—(1) *In general.*—A Specified Cooperative using either the section 861 method of cost allocation under § 1.199A-10(d) or the simplified deduction method under § 1.199A-10(e) may determine the amount of W-2 wages that are properly allocable to DPGR for a taxable year by multiplying the amount of W-2 wages determined under paragraph (b)(1) of this section for the taxable year by the ratio of the Specified Cooperative's wage expense included in calculating QPAI for the taxable year to the Specified Cooperative's total wage expense used in calculating the Specified Cooperative's taxable income for the taxable year, without regard to any wage expense disallowed by section 465, 469, 704(d), or 1366(d). A Specified Cooperative that uses either the section 861 method of cost allocation or the simplified deduction method to determine QPAI must use the same expense allocation and apportionment methods that it uses to determine QPAI to allocate and apportion wage expense for purposes of this safe harbor. For purposes of this paragraph (g)(1), the term wage expense means wages (that is, compensation paid by the employer in the active conduct of a trade or business to its employees) that are properly taken into account under the Specified Cooperative's method of accounting.

(2) *Wage expense included in cost of goods sold.*—For purposes of paragraph (g)(1) of this section, a Specified Cooperative may determine its wage expense included in cost of goods sold (COGS) using a reasonable method based on all the facts and circumstances, such as using the amount of direct labor included in COGS or using section 263A labor costs (as defined in § 1.263A-1(h)(4)(ii)) included in COGS. The chosen reasonable method must be consistently applied from one taxable year to another and must clearly reflect the portion of wage expense included in COGS. The method must also be reasonable based on all the facts and circumstances. The books and records maintained for wage expense included in COGS must be consistent with any allocations under this paragraph (g)(2).

(3) *Small business simplified overall method safe harbor.*—The Specified Cooperative that uses the small business simplified overall method under § 1.199A-10(f) may use the small business simplified

overall method safe harbor for determining the amount of W-2 wages determined under paragraph (b)(1) of this section that is properly allocable to DPGR. Under this safe harbor, the amount of W-2 wages determined under paragraph (b)(1) of this section that is properly allocable to DPGR is equal to the same proportion of W-2 wages determined under paragraph (b)(1) of this section that the amount of DPGR bears to the Specified Cooperative's total gross receipts.

(h) *Applicability date.*—The provisions of this section apply to taxable years beginning after January 19, 2021. Taxpayers, however, may choose to apply the rules of §§ 1.199A-7 through 1.199A-12 for taxable years beginning on or before that date, provided the taxpayers apply the rules in their entirety and in a consistent manner. [Reg. § 1.199A-11.]

☐ [*T.D. 9947*, 1-14-2021.]

[Reg. § 1.199A-12]

§ 1.199A-12. Expanded affiliated groups.—(a) *In general.*—The provisions of this section apply solely for purposes of section 199A(g) of the Internal Revenue Code (Code). Except as otherwise provided in the Code or regulations issued under the relevant section of the Code (for example, sections 199A(g)(3)(D)(ii) and 267, § 1.199A-8(c), paragraph (a)(3) of this section, and the consolidated return regulations under section 1502), each nonexempt Specified Cooperative (defined in § 1.199A-8(a)(2)(ii)) that is a member of an expanded affiliated group (EAG) (defined in paragraph (a)(1) of this section) computes its own taxable income or loss, qualified production activities income (QPAI) (defined in § 1.199A-8(b)(4)(ii)), and W-2 wages (defined in § 1.199A-11(b)). For purposes of this section unless otherwise specified, the term *Specified Cooperative* means a nonexempt Specified Cooperative. If a Specified Cooperative is also a member of a consolidated group, see paragraph (d) of this section.

(1) *Definition of an expanded affiliated group.*—An EAG is an affiliated group as defined in section 1504(a), determined by substituting "more than 50 percent" for "at least 80 percent" in each place it appears and without regard to section 1504(b)(2) and (4).

(2) *Identification of members of an expanded affiliated group.*—(i) *In general.*—Each Specified Cooperative must determine if it is a member of an EAG on a daily basis.

(ii) *Becoming or ceasing to be a member of an expanded affiliated group.*—If a Specified Cooperative becomes or ceases to be a member of an EAG, the Specified Cooperative is treated as becoming or ceasing to be a member of the EAG at the end of the day on which its status as a member changes.

(3) *Attribution of activities.*—(i) *In general.*—Except as provided in paragraph (a)(3)(iv) of this section, if a Specified Cooperative that is a member of an EAG (disposing member) derives gross receipts (defined in § 1.199A-8(b)(2)(iii)) from the lease, rental, license, sale, exchange, or other disposition (defined in § 1.199A-9(j)) of agricultural or horticultural products (defined in § 1.199A-8(a)(4)) that were manufactured, produced, grown or extracted (MPGE) (defined in § 1.199A-9(f)), in whole or significant part (defined in § 1.199A-9(h)), in the United States (defined in § 1.199A-9(i)) by another Specified Cooperative, then the disposing member is treated as conducting the previous activities conducted by such other Specified Cooperative with respect to the agricultural or horticultural products in determining whether its gross receipts are domestic production gross receipts (DPGR) (defined in § 1.199A-8(b)(3)(ii)) if—

(A) Such property was MPGE by such other Specified Cooperative, and

(B) The disposing member is a member of the same EAG as such other Specified Cooperative at the time that the disposing member disposes of the agricultural or horticultural products.

(ii) *Date of disposition for leases, rentals, or licenses.*—Except as provided in paragraph (a)(3)(iv) of this section, with respect to a lease, rental, or license, the disposing member described in paragraph (a)(3)(i) of this section is treated as having disposed of the agricultural or horticultural products on the date or dates on which it takes into account the gross receipts derived from the lease, rental, or license under its methods of accounting.

(iii) *Date of disposition for sales, exchanges, or other dispositions.*—Except as provided in paragraph (a)(3)(iv) of this section, with respect to a sale, exchange, or other disposition, the disposing member is treated as having disposed of the agricultural or horticultural products on the date on which it ceases to own the agricultural or horticultural products for Federal income tax purposes, even if no gain or loss is taken into account.

(iv) *Exception.*—A Specified Cooperative is not attributed non-patronage activities conducted by another Specified Cooperative. *See* § 1.199A-8(b)(2)(ii).

(4) *Marketing Specified Cooperatives.*—A Specified Cooperative is treated as having MPGE in whole or significant part any agricultural or horticultural product within the United States marketed by the Specified Cooperative which its patrons have so MPGE. Patrons are defined in § 1.1388-1(e).

(5) *Anti-avoidance rule.*—If a transaction between members of an EAG is engaged in or structured with a principal purpose of qualifying for, or increasing the amount of, the section 199A(g) deduction of the EAG or the portion of the section 199A(g) deduction allocated to one or more members of the EAG, the Secretary may make adjustments to eliminate the effect of the transaction on the computation of the section 199A(g) deduction.

(b) *Computation of EAG's section 199A(g) deduction.*—(1) *In general.*—The section 199A(g) deduction for an EAG is determined by separately computing the section 199A(g) deduction from the patronage sources of Specified Cooperatives that are members of the EAG. The section 199A(g) deduction from patronage sources of Specified Cooperatives is determined by aggregating the income or loss, QPAI, and W-2 wages, if any, of each patronage source of a Specified Cooperative that is a member of the EAG. For purposes of this determination, a member's QPAI may be positive or negative. A Specified Cooperative's taxable income or loss and QPAI is determined by reference to the Specified Cooperative's method of accounting. For purposes of determining the section 199A(g) deduction for an EAG, taxable income or loss, QPAI, and W-2 wages of a Specified Cooperative from nonpatronage sources are considered to be zero, other than as allowed under § 1.199A-8(b)(2)(ii).

(2) *Example.*—The following example illustrates the application of paragraph (b)(1) of this section.

(i) *Facts.* Nonexempt Specified Cooperatives X, Y, and Z, calendar year taxpayers, are the only members of an EAG and are not members of a consolidated group. X has patronage source taxable income of $50,000, QPAI of $15,000, and W-2 wages of $0. Y has patronage source taxable income of ($20,000), QPAI of ($1,000), and W-2 wages of $750. Z has patronage source taxable income of $0, QPAI of $0, and W-2 wages of $3,000.

(ii) *Analysis.* In determining the EAG's section 199A(g) deduction, the EAG aggregates each member's patronage source taxable income or loss, QPAI, and W-2 wages. Thus, the EAG has patronage source taxable income of $30,000, the sum of X's patronage source taxable income of $50,000, Y's patronage source taxable income of ($20,000), and Z's patronage source taxable income of $0. The EAG has QPAI of $14,000, the sum of X's QPAI of $15,000, Y's QPAI of ($1,000), and Z's QPAI of $0. The EAG has W-2 wages of $3,750, the sum of X's W-2 wages of $0, Y's W-2 wages of $750, and Z's W-2 wages of $3,000. Accordingly, the EAG's section 199A(g) deduction equals $1,260, 9% of $14,000, the lesser of the QPAI and patronage source taxable income, but not greater than $1,875, 50% of its W-2 wages of $3,750. This result would be the same if X had a nonpatronage source income or loss, because nonpatronage source income of a nonexempt Specified Cooperative is not taken into account in determining the section 199A(g) deduction.

(3) *Net operating loss carryovers/carrybacks.*—In determining the taxable income of an EAG, if a Specified Cooperative has a net operating loss (NOL) from its patronage sources that may be carried over or carried back (in accordance with section 172) to the taxable year, then for purposes of determining the taxable income of the Specified Cooperative, the amount of the NOL used to offset taxable income cannot exceed the taxable income of the patronage source of that Specified Cooperative.

(4) *Losses used to reduce taxable income of an expanded affiliated group.*—The amount of an NOL sustained by a Specified Cooperative member of an EAG that is used in the year sustained in determining an EAG's taxable income limitation under § 1.199A-8(b)(5)(ii)(C) is not treated as an NOL carryover to any taxable year in determining the taxable income limitation under § 1.199A-8(b)(5)(ii)(C). For purposes of this paragraph (b)(4), an NOL is considered to be used if it reduces an EAG's aggregate taxable income from patronage sources or nonpatronage sources, as the case may be, regardless of whether the use of the NOL actually reduces the amount of the section 199A(g) deduction that the EAG would otherwise derive. An NOL is not considered to be used to the extent that it reduces an EAG's aggregate taxable income from patronage sources to an amount less than zero. If more than one Specified Cooperative has an NOL used in the same taxable year to reduce the EAG's taxable income from patronage sources, the respective NOLs are deemed used in proportion to the amount of each Specified Cooperative's NOL.

(5) *Example.*—The following example illustrates the application of paragraph (b)(4) of this section.

(i) *Facts.* Nonexempt Specified Cooperatives A and B are the only two members of an EAG. A and B are both calendar year taxpayers and they do not join in the filing of a consolidated Federal income tax return. Neither A nor B had taxable income or loss prior to 2020. In 2020, A has patronage QPAI and patronage taxable income of $1,000 and B has patronage QPAI of $1,000 and a patronage NOL of $1,500. A also has nonpatronage income of $3,000. B has no activities other than from its patronage activities. In 2021, A has patronage QPAI of $2,000 and patronage taxable income of $1,000 and B has patronage QPAI of $2,000 and patronage taxable income prior to the NOL deduction allowed under section 172 of $2,000. Neither A nor B has nonpatronage activities in 2021. A's and B's patronage activities have aggregate W-2 wages in excess of the section 199A(g)(1)(B) wage limitation in both 2020 and 2021.

(ii) *Section 199A(g) deduction for 2020.* In determining the EAG's section 199A(g) deduction for 2020, A's $1,000 of QPAI and B's $1,000 of QPAI are aggregated, as are A's $1,000 of taxable income from its patronage activities and B's $1,500 NOL from its patronage activities. A's nonpatronage income is not included. Thus, for 2020, the EAG has patronage QPAI of $2,000 and patronage taxable income of ($500). The EAG's section 199A(g) deduction for 2020 is 9% of the lesser of its patronage QPAI or its patronage taxable income. Because the EAG has a taxable loss from patronage sources in 2020, the EAG's section 199A(g) deduction is $0.

(iii) *Section 199A(a) deduction for 2021.* In determining the EAG's section 199A deduction for 2021, A's patronage QPAI of $2,000 and B's patronage QPAI of $2,000 are aggregated, resulting in the EAG having patronage QPAI of $4,000. Also, $1,000 of B's patronage NOL from 2020 was used in 2020 to reduce the EAG's taxable income from patronage sources to $0. The remaining $500 of B's patronage NOL from 2020 is not considered to have been used in 2020 because it reduced the EAG's patronage taxable income to less than $0. Accordingly, for purposes of determining the EAG's taxable income limitation under § 1.199A-8(b)(5) in 2021, B is deemed to have only a $500 NOL carryover from its patronage sources from 2020 to offset a portion of its 2021 taxable income from its patronage sources. Thus, B's taxable income from its patronage sources in 2021 is $1,500, which is aggregated with A's $1,000 of taxable income from its patronage sources. The EAG's taxable income limitation in 2021 is $2,500. The EAG's section 199A(g) deduction is 9% of the lesser of its patronage sourced QPAI of $4,000 and its taxable income from patronage sources of $2,500. Thus, the EAG's section 199A(g) deduction in 2021 is 9% of $2,500, or $225. The results for 2021 would be the same if neither A nor B had patronage sourced QPAI in 2020.

(c) *Allocation of an expanded affiliated group's section 199A(g) deduction among members of the expanded affiliated group.*—(1) *In general.*—An EAG's section 199A(g) deduction from its patronage sources, as determined in paragraph (b) of this section, is allocated among the Specified Cooperatives that are members of the EAG in proportion to each Specified Cooperative's patronage QPAI, regardless of whether the Specified Cooperative has patronage taxable income or W-2 wages for the taxable year. For these purposes, if a Specified Cooperative has negative patronage QPAI, such QPAI is treated as zero. Pursuant to § 1.199A-8(b)(6), a patronage section 199A(g) deduction can be applied only against patronage income and deductions.

(2) *Use of section 199A(g) deduction to create or increase a net operating loss.*—If a Specified Cooperative that is a member of an EAG has some or all of the EAG's section 199A(g) deduction allocated to it under paragraph (c)(1) of this section and the amount allocated exceeds patronage taxable income, determined as described in this section and prior to allocation of the section 199A(g) deduction, the section 199A(g) deduction will create an NOL for the patronage source. Similarly, if a Specified Cooperative that is a member of an EAG, prior to the allocation of some or all of the EAG's section 199A(g) deduction to the member, has a patronage NOL for the taxable year, the portion of the EAG's section 199A(g) deduction allocated to the member will increase such NOL.

(d) *Special rules for members of the same consolidated group.*—(1) *Intercompany transactions.*—In the case of an intercompany transaction between consolidated group members S and B (as the terms intercompany transaction, S, and B are defined in § 1.1502-13(b)(1)), S takes the intercompany transaction into account in computing the section 199A(g) deduction at the same time and in the same proportion as S takes into account the income, gain, deduction, or loss from the intercompany transaction under § 1.1502-13.

(2) *Application of the simplified deduction method and the small business simplified overall method.*—For purposes of applying the simplified deduction method under § 1.199A-10(e) and the small business simplified overall method under § 1.199A-10(f), a Specified

Cooperative that is part of a consolidated group determines its QPAI using its members' DPGR, non-DPGR, cost of goods sold (COGS), and all other deductions, expenses, or losses (hereinafter deductions), determined after the application of § 1.1502-13.

(3) *Determining the section 199A(g) deduction.*—(i) *Expanded affiliated group consists of consolidated group and non-consolidated group members.*—In determining the section 199A(g) deduction, if an EAG includes Specified Cooperatives that are members of the same consolidated group and Specified Cooperatives that are not members of the same consolidated group, the consolidated taxable income or loss, QPAI, and W-2 wages, from patronage sources, if any, of the consolidated group (and not the separate taxable income or loss, QPAI, and W-2 wages from patronage sources of the members of the consolidated group), are aggregated with the taxable income or loss, QPAI, and W-2 wages, from patronage sources, if any, of the non-consolidated group members. For example, if A, B, C, S1, and S2 are Specified Cooperatives that are members of the same EAG, and A, S1, and S2 are members of the same consolidated group (the A consolidated group), then the A consolidated group is treated as one member of the EAG. Accordingly, the EAG is considered to have three members—the A consolidated group, B, and C. The consolidated taxable income or loss, QPAI, and W-2 wages from patronage sources, if any, of the A consolidated group are aggregated with the taxable income or loss from patronage sources, QPAI, and W-2 wages, if any, of B and C in determining the EAG's section 199A(g) deduction from patronage sources. Pursuant to § 1.199A-8(b)(6), a patronage section 199A(g) deduction can be applied only against patronage income and deductions.

(ii) *Expanded affiliated group consists only of members of a single consolidated group.*—If all of the Specified Cooperatives that are members of an EAG are also members of the same consolidated group, the consolidated group's section 199A(g) deduction is determined using the consolidated group's consolidated taxable income or loss, QPAI, and W-2 wages, from patronage sources rather than the separate taxable income or loss, QPAI, and W-2 wages from patronage sources of its members.

(4) *Allocation of the section 199A(g) deduction of a consolidated group among its members.*—The section 199A(g) deduction from patronage sources of a consolidated group (or the section 199A(g) deduction allocated to a consolidated group that is a member of an EAG) is allocated among the patronage sources of Specified Cooperatives in proportion to each Specified Cooperative's patronage QPAI, regardless of whether the Specified Cooperative has patronage separate taxable income or W-2 wages for the taxable year. In allocating the section 199A(g) deduction of a patronage source of a Specified Cooperative that is part of a consolidated group among patronage sources of other members of the same group, any redetermination of a member's patronage receipts, COGS, or other deductions from an intercompany transaction under § 1.1502-13(c)(1)(i) or (c)(4) is not taken into account for purposes of section 199A(g). Also, for purposes of this allocation, if a patronage source of a Specified Cooperative that is a member of a consolidated group has negative QPAI, the QPAI of the patronage source is treated as zero.

(e) *Examples.*—The following examples illustrate the application of paragraphs (a) through (d) of this section.

(1) *Example 1.*—Specified Cooperatives X, Y, and Z are members of the same EAG but are not members of a consolidated group. X, Y, and Z each files Federal income tax returns on a calendar year basis. None of X, Y, or Z have activities other than from its patronage sources. Prior to 2020, X had no taxable income or loss. In 2020, X has taxable income of $0, QPAI of $2,000, and W-2 wages of $0, Y has taxable income of $4,000, QPAI of $3,000, and W-2 wages of $500, and Z has taxable income of $4,000, QPAI of $5,000, and W-2 wages of $2,500. Accordingly, the EAG's patronage source taxable income is $8,000, the sum of X's taxable income of $0, Y's taxable income of $4,000, and Z's taxable income of $4,000. The EAG has QPAI of $10,000, the sum of X's QPAI of $2,000, Y's QPAI of $3,000, and Z's QPAI of $5,000. The EAG's W-2 wages are $3,000, the sum of X's W-2 wages of $0, Y's W-2 wages of $500, and Z's W-2 wages of $2,500. Thus, the EAG's section 199A(g) deduction for 2020 is $720 (9% of the lesser of the EAG's patronage source taxable income of $8,000 and the EAG's QPAI of $10,000, but no greater than 50% of its W-2 wages of $3,000, that is $1,500). Pursuant to paragraph (c)(1) of this section, the $720 section 199A(g) deduction is allocated to X, Y, and Z in proportion to their respective amounts of QPAI, that is $144 to X ($720 × $2,000/$10,000), $216 to Y ($720 × $3,000/$10,000), and $360 to Z ($720 × $5,000/$10,000). Although X's patronage source taxable income for 2020 determined prior to allocation of a portion of the EAG's section 199A(g) deduction to it was $0, pursuant to paragraph (c)(2) of this section, X will have an NOL from its patronage source for 2020 equal to $144, which will be a carryover to 2021.

Itemized Deductions for Individuals and Corps.
See p. 20,601 for regulations not amended to reflect law changes
25,711

(2) *Example 2.*—(i) *Facts.*—Corporation X is the common parent of a consolidated group, consisting of X and Y, which has filed a consolidated Federal income tax return for many years. Corporation P is the common parent of a consolidated group, consisting of P and S, which has filed a consolidated Federal income tax return for many years. The X and P consolidated groups each file their consolidated Federal income tax returns on a calendar year basis. X, Y, P, and S are each Specified Cooperatives, and none of X, Y, P, or S has ever had activities other than from its patronage sources. The X consolidated group and the P consolidated group are members of the same EAG in 2021. In 2020, the X consolidated group incurred a consolidated net operating loss (CNOL) of $25,000. Neither P nor S (nor the P consolidated group) has ever incurred an NOL. In 2021, the X consolidated group has (prior to the deduction under section 172) taxable income of $8,000 and the P consolidated group has taxable income of $20,000. X's QPAI is $8,000, Y's QPAI is ($13,000), P's QPAI is $16,000 and S's QPAI is $4,000. There are sufficient W-2 wages to exceed the section 199A(g)(1)(B) limitation.

(ii) *Analysis.*—The X consolidated group uses $8,000 of its CNOL from 2020 to offset the X consolidated group's taxable income in 2021. None of the X consolidated group's remaining CNOL may be used to offset taxable income of the P consolidated group under paragraph (b)(3) of this section. Accordingly, for purposes of determining the EAG's section 199A(g) deduction for 2021, the EAG has taxable income of $20,000 (the X consolidated group's taxable income, after the deduction under section 172, of $0 plus the P consolidated group's taxable income of $20,000). The EAG has QPAI of $15,000 (the X consolidated group's QPAI of ($5,000) (X's $8,000 + Y's ($13,000)), and the P consolidated group's QPAI of $20,000 (P's $16,000 + S's $4,000)). The EAG's section 199A(g) deduction equals $1,350, 9% of the lesser of its taxable income of $20,000 and its QPAI of $15,000. The section 199A(g) deduction is allocated between the X and P consolidated groups in proportion to their respective QPAI. Because the X consolidated group has negative QPAI, all of the section 199A(g) deduction of $1,350 is allocated to the P consolidated group. This $1,350 is allocated between P and S, the members of the P consolidated group, in proportion to their QPAI. Accordingly, P is allocated $1,080 ($1,350 × $16,000/$20,000) and S is allocated $270 ($1,350 × $4,000/ $20,000).

(f) *Allocation of patronage income and loss by a Specified Cooperative that is a member of the expanded affiliated group for only a portion of the year.*—(1) *In general.*—A Specified Cooperative that becomes or ceases to be a member of an EAG during its taxable year must allocate its taxable income or loss, QPAI, and W-2 wages between the portion of the taxable year that the Specified Cooperative is a member of the EAG and the portion of the taxable year that the Specified Cooperative is not a member of the EAG. This allocation of items is made by using the pro rata allocation method described in this paragraph (f)(1). Under the pro rata allocation method, an equal portion of patronage taxable income or loss, QPAI, and W-2 wages is assigned to each day of the Specified Cooperative's taxable year. Those items assigned to those days that the Specified Cooperative was a member of the EAG are then aggregated.

(2) *Coordination with rules relating to the allocation of income under §1.1502-76(b).*—If §1.1502-76(b) (relating to items included in a consolidated return) applies to a Specified Cooperative that is a member of an EAG, then any allocation of items required under this paragraph (f) is made only after the allocation of the items pursuant to §1.1502-76(b).

(g) *Total section 199A(g) deduction for a Specified Cooperative that is a member of an expanded affiliated group for some or all of its taxable year.*—(1) *Member of the same EAG for the entire taxable year.*—If a Specified Cooperative is a member of the same EAG for its entire taxable year, the Specified Cooperative's section 199A(g) deduction for the taxable year is the amount of the section 199A(g) deduction allocated to it by the EAG under paragraph (c)(1) of this section.

(2) *Member of the expanded affiliated group for a portion of the taxable year.*—If a Specified Cooperative is a member of an EAG for only a portion of its taxable year and is either not a member of any EAG or is a member of another EAG, or both, for another portion of the taxable year, the Specified Cooperative's section 199A(g) deduction for the taxable year is the sum of its section 199A(g) deductions for each portion of the taxable year.

(3) *Example.*—The following example illustrates the application of paragraphs (f) and (g) of this section.

(i) *Facts.* Specified Cooperatives X and Y, calendar year taxpayers, are members of the same EAG for the entire 2020 taxable year. Specified Cooperative Z, also a calendar year taxpayer, is a member of the EAG of which X and Y are members for the first half of 2020 and not a member of any EAG for the second half of 2020. None of X, Y, or Z have activities other than from its patronage sources. Assume

that X, Y, and Z each has W-2 wages in excess of the section 199A(g)(1)(B) wage limitation for all relevant periods. In 2020, X has taxable income of $2,000 and QPAI of $600, Y has taxable loss of $400 and QPAI of ($200), and Z has taxable income of $1,400 and QPAI of $2,400.

(ii) *Analysis.* Pursuant to the pro rata allocation method, $700 of Z's 2020 taxable income and $1,200 of its QPAI are allocated to the first half of the 2020 taxable year (the period in which Z is a member of the EAG) and $700 of Z's 2020 taxable income and $1,200 of its QPAI are allocated to the second half of the 2020 taxable year (the period in which Z is not a member of any EAG). Accordingly, in 2020, the EAG has taxable income from patronage sources of $2,300 ($2,000 + ($400) + $700) and QPAI of $1,600 ($600 + ($200) + $1,200). The EAG's section 199A(g) deduction for 2020 is $144 (9% of the lesser of the EAG's taxable income of $2,300 or QPAI of $1,600). Pursuant to §1.199A-12(c)(1), this $144 deduction is allocated to X, Y, and Z in proportion to their respective QPAI. Accordingly, X is allocated $48 of the EAG's section 199A(g) deduction ($144 x ($600/($600 + $0 + $1,200))), Y is allocated $0 of the EAG's section 199A(g) deduction ($144 x ($0 / ($600 + $0 + $1,200))), and Z is allocated $96 of the EAG's section 199A(g) deduction ($144 x ($1,200 / ($600 + $0 + $1,200))). For the second half of 2020, Z has taxable income of $700 and QPAI of $1,200. Therefore, for the second half of 2020, Z has a section 199A(g) deduction of $63 (9% of the lesser of its taxable income of $700 or its QPAI of $1,200). Accordingly, X's 2020 section 199A(g) deduction is $48 and Y's 2020 section 199A(g) deduction is $0. Z's 2020 section 199A(g) deduction is $159, the sum of $96, the portion of the EAG's section 199A(g) deduction allocated to Z for the first half of 2020 and Z's $63 section 199A(g) deduction for the second half of 2020.

(h) *Computation of section 199A(g) deduction for members of an expanded affiliated group with different taxable years.*—(1) *In general.*—If Specified Cooperatives that are members of an EAG have different taxable years, in determining the section 199A(g) deduction of a member (the computing member), the computing member is required to take into account the taxable income or loss, determined without regard to the section 199A(g) deduction, QPAI, and W-2 wages of each other group member that are both—

(i) Attributable to the period that each other member of the EAG and the computing member are members of the EAG; and

(ii) Taken into account in a taxable year that begins after the effective date of section 199A(g) and ends with or within the taxable year of the computing member with respect to which the section 199A(g) deduction is computed.

(2) *Example.*—The following example illustrates the application of this paragraph (h).

(i) *Facts.* Specified Cooperatives X, Y, and Z are members of the same EAG. Neither X, Y, nor Z is a member of a consolidated group. X and Y are calendar year taxpayers and Z is a June 30 fiscal year taxpayer. Z came into existence on July 1, 2020. None of X, Y, or Z have activities other than from its patronage sources. Each Specified Cooperative has taxable income that exceeds its QPAI and W-2 wages in excess of the section 199A(g)(1)(B) wage limitation. For the taxable year ending December 31, 2020, X's QPAI is $8,000 and Y's QPAI is ($6,000). For its taxable year ending June 30, 2021, Z's QPAI is $2,000.

(ii) *2020 Computation.* In computing X's and Y's respective section 199A(g) deductions for their taxable years ending December 31, 2020, X's taxable income or loss, QPAI and W-2 wages and Y's taxable income or loss, QPAI, and W-2 wages from their respective taxable years ending December 31, 2020, are aggregated. The EAG's QPAI for this purpose is $2,000 (X's QPAI of $8,000 + Y's QPAI of ($6,000)). Accordingly, the EAG's section 199A(g) deduction is $180 (9% × $2,000). The $180 deduction is allocated to each of X and Y in proportion to their respective QPAI as a percentage of the QPAI of each member of the EAG that was taken into account in computing the EAG's section 199A(g) deduction. Pursuant to paragraph (c)(1) of this section, in allocating the section 199A(g) deduction between X and Y, because Y's QPAI is negative, Y's QPAI is treated as being $0. Accordingly, X's section 199A(g) deduction for its taxable year ending December 31, 2020, is $180 ($180 × $8,000/($8,000 + $0)). Y's section 199A(g) deduction for its taxable year ending December 31, 2020, is $0 ($180 × $0/($8,000 + $0)).

(iii) *2021 Computation.* In computing Z's section 199A(g) deduction for its taxable year ending June 30, 2021, X's and Y's items from their respective taxable years ending December 31, 2020, are taken into account. Therefore, X's taxable income or loss and Y's taxable income or loss, determined without regard to the section 199A(g) deduction, QPAI, and W-2 wages from their taxable years ending December 31, 2020, are aggregated with Z's taxable income or loss, QPAI, and W-2 wages from its taxable year ending June 30, 2021. The EAG's QPAI is $4,000 (X's QPAI of $8,000 + Y's QPAI of ($6,000) + Z's QPAI of $2,000). The EAG's section 199A(g) deduction is $360 (9% ×

$4,000). A portion of the $360 deduction is allocated to Z in proportion to its QPAI as a percentage of the QPAI of each member of the EAG that was taken into account in computing the EAG's section 199A(g) deduction. Pursuant to paragraph (c)(1) of this section, in allocating a portion of the $360 deduction to Z, Y's QPAI is treated as being $0 because Y's QPAI is negative. Z's section 199A(g) deduction for its taxable year ending June 30, 2021, is $72 ($360 × ($2,000/($8,000 + $0 + $2,000))).

(i) *Partnership owned by expanded affiliated group.*—(1) *In general.*—For purposes of section 199A(g)(3)(D) relating to DPGR, if all of the interests in the capital and profits of a partnership are owned by members of a single EAG at all times during the taxable year of such partnership (EAG partnership), then the EAG partnership and all members of that EAG are treated as a single taxpayer during such period.

(2) *Attribution of activities.*—(i) *In general.*—If a Specified Cooperative which is a member of an EAG (disposing member) derives gross receipts from the lease, rental, license, sale, exchange, or other disposition of property that was MPGE by an EAG partnership, all the partners of which are members of the same EAG to which the disposing member belongs at the time that the disposing member disposes of such property, then the disposing member is treated as conducting the MPGE activities previously conducted by the EAG partnership with respect to that property. The previous sentence applies only for those taxable years in which the disposing member is a member of the EAG of which all the partners of the EAG partnership are members for the entire taxable year of the EAG partnership. With respect to a lease, rental, or license, the disposing member is treated as having disposed of the property on the date or dates on which it takes into account its gross receipts from the lease, rental, or license under its method of accounting. With respect to a sale, exchange, or other disposition, the disposing member is treated as having disposed of the property on the date it ceases to own the property for Federal income tax purposes, even if no gain or loss is taken into account. Likewise, if an EAG partnership derives gross receipts from the lease, rental, license, sale, exchange, or other disposition of property that was MPGE by a member (or members) of the same EAG (the producing member) to which all the partners of the EAG partnership belong at the time that the EAG partnership disposes of such property, then the EAG partnership is treated as conducting the MPGE activities previously conducted by the producing member with respect to that property. The previous sentence applies only for those taxable years in which the producing member is a member of the EAG of which all the partners of the EAG partnership are members for the entire taxable year of the EAG partnership. With respect to a lease, rental, or license, the EAG partnership is treated as having disposed of the property on the date or dates on which it takes into account its gross receipts derived from the lease, rental, or license under its method of accounting. With respect to a sale, exchange, or other disposition, the EAG partnership is treated as having disposed of the property on the date it ceases to own the property for Federal income tax purposes, even if no gain or loss is taken into account.

(ii) *Attribution between expanded affiliated group partnerships.*—If an EAG partnership (disposing partnership) derives gross receipts from the lease, rental, license, sale, exchange, or other disposition of property that was MPGE by another EAG partnership (producing partnership), then the disposing partnership is treated as conducting the MPGE activities previously conducted by the producing partnership with respect to that property, provided that each of these partnerships (the producing partnership and the disposing partnership) is owned for its entire taxable year in which the disposing partnership disposes of such property by members of the same EAG. With respect to a lease, rental, or license, the disposing partnership is treated as having disposed of the property on the date or dates on which it takes into account its gross receipts from the lease, rental, or license under its method of accounting. With respect to a sale, exchange, or other disposition, the disposing partnership is treated as having disposed of the property on the date it ceases to own the property for Federal income tax purposes, even if no gain or loss is taken into account.

(j) *Applicability date.*—The provisions of this section apply to taxable years beginning after January 19, 2021. Taxpayers, however, may choose to apply the rules of §§ 1.199A-7 through 1.199A-12 for taxable years beginning on or before that date, provided the taxpayers apply the rules in their entirety and in a consistent manner. [Reg. § 1.199A-12.]

☐ [*T.D.* 9947, 1-14-2021 (corrected 11-16-2022).]

Additional Itemized Deductions for Individuals

[Reg. § 1.211-1]

§1.211-1. Allowance of deductions.—In computing taxable income under section 63(a), the deductions provided by sections 212, 213, 214, 215, 216 and 217 shall be allowed subject to the exceptions provided in part IX, subchapter B, chapter 1 of the Code (section 261 and following, relating to items not deductible). [Reg. § 1.211-1.]

☐ [*T.D.* 6279, 12-13-57. *Amended by T.D.* 6796, 1-29-65.]

[Reg. § 1.212-1]

§1.212-1. Nontrade or nonbusiness expenses.—(a) An expense may be deducted under section 212 only if—

(1) It has been paid or incurred by the taxpayer during the taxable year (i) for the production or collection of income which, if and when realized, will be required to be included in income for Federal income tax purposes, or (ii) for the management, conservation, or maintenance of property held for the production of such income, or (iii) in connection with the determination, collection, or refund of any tax; and

(2) It is an ordinary and necessary expense for any of the purposes stated in subparagraph (1) of this paragraph.

(b) The term "income" for the purpose of section 212 includes not merely income of the taxable year but also income which the taxpayer has realized in a prior taxable year or may realize in subsequent taxable years; and is not confined to recurring income but applies as well to gains from the disposition of property. For example, if defaulted bonds, the interest from which if received would be includible in income, are purchased with the expectation of realizing capital gain on their resale, even though no current yield thereon is anticipated, ordinary and necessary expenses thereafter paid or incurred in connection with such bonds are deductible. Similarly, ordinary and necessary expenses paid or incurred in the management, conservation, or maintenance of a building devoted to rental purposes are deductible notwithstanding that there is actually no income therefrom in the taxable year, and regardless of the manner in which or the purpose for which the property in question was acquired. Expenses paid or incurred in managing, conserving, or maintaining property held for investment may be deductible under section 212 even though the property is not currently productive and there is no likelihood that the property will be sold at a profit or will otherwise be productive of income and even though the property is held merely to minimize a loss with respect thereto.

(c) In the case of taxable years beginning before January 1, 1970, expenses of carrying on transactions which do not constitute a trade or business of the taxpayer and are not carried on for the production or collection of income or for the management, conservation, or maintenance of property held for the production of income, but which are carried on primarily as a sport, hobby, or recreation are not allowable as nontrade or nonbusiness expenses. The question whether or not a transaction is carried on primarily for the production of income or for the management, conservation, or maintenance of property held for the production or collection of income, rather than primarily as a sport, hobby, or recreation, is not to be determined solely from the intention of the taxpayer but rather from all the circumstances of the case. For example, consideration will be given to the record of prior gain or loss of the taxpayer in the activity, the relation between the type of activity and the principal occupation of the taxpayer, and the uses to which the property or what it produces is put by the taxpayer. For provisions relating to activities not engaged in for profit applicable to taxable years beginning after December 31, 1969, see section 183 and the regulations thereunder.

(d) Expenses, to be deductible under section 212, must be "ordinary and necessary". Thus, such expenses must be reasonable in amount and must bear a reasonable and proximate relation to the production or collection of taxable income or to the management, conservation, or maintenance of property held for the production of income.

(e) A deduction under section 212 is subject to the restrictions and limitations in part IX (section 261 and following), subchapter B, chapter 1 of the Code, relating to items not deductible. Thus, no deduction is allowable under section 212 for any amount allocable to the production or collection of one or more classes of income which are not includible in gross income, or for any amount allocable to the management, conservation, or maintenance of property held for the production of income which is not included in gross income. See section 265. Nor does section 212 allow the deduction of any expenses which are disallowed by any of the provisions of subtitle A of the Code, even though such expenses may be paid or incurred for one of the purposes specified in section 212.

(f) Among expenditures not allowable as deductions under section 212 are the following: Commuter's expenses; expenses of taking special courses or training; expenses for improving personal appearance; the cost of rental of a safe-deposit box for storing jewelry and other personal effects; expenses such as those paid or incurred in seeking employment or in placing oneself in a position to begin rendering personal services for compensation, campaign expenses of a candidate for public office, bar examination fees and other expenses paid or incurred in securing admission to the bar, and corresponding fees and expenses paid or incurred by physicians, dentists, accountants, and other taxpayers for securing the right to practice their respective professions. See, however, section 162 and the regulations thereunder.

(g) Fees for services of investment counsel, custodial fees, clerical help, office rent, and similar expenses paid or incurred by a taxpayer in connection with investments held by him are deductible under section 212 only if (1) they are paid or incurred by the taxpayer for the production or collection of income or for the management, conservation, or maintenance of investments held by him for the production of income; and (2) they are ordinary and necessary under all the circumstances, having regard to the type of investment and to the relation of the taxpayer to such investment.

(h) Ordinary and necessary expenses paid or incurred in connection with the management, conservation, or maintenance of property held for use as a residence by the taxpayer are not deductible. However, ordinary and necessary expenses paid or incurred in connection with the management, conservation, or maintenance of property held by the taxpayer as rental property are deductible even though such property was formerly held by the taxpayer for use as a home.

(i) Reasonable amounts paid or incurred by the fiduciary of an estate or trust on account of administration expenses, including fiduciaries' fees and expenses of litigation, which are ordinary and necessary in connection with the performance of the duties of administration are deductible under section 212 notwithstanding that the estate or trust is not engaged in a trade or business, except to the extent that such expenses are allocable to the production or collection of tax-exempt income. But see section 642(g) and the regulations thereunder for disallowance of such deductions to an estate where such items are allowed as a deduction under section 2053 or 2054 in computing the net estate subject to the estate tax.

(j) Reasonable amounts paid or incurred for the services of a guardian or committee for a ward or minor, and other expenses of guardians and committees which are ordinary and necessary, in connection with the production or collection of income inuring to the ward or minor, or in connection with the management, conservation, or maintenance of property, held for the production of income, belonging to the ward or minor, are deductible.

(k) Expenses paid or incurred in defending or perfecting title to property, in recovering property (other than investment property and amounts of income which, if and when recovered, must be included in gross income), or in developing or improving property, constitute a part of the cost of the property and are not deductible expenses. Attorneys' fees paid in a suit to quiet title to lands are not deductible; but if the suit is also to collect accrued rents thereon, that portion of such fees is deductible which is properly allocable to the services rendered in collecting such rents. Expenses paid or incurred in protecting or asserting one's rights to property of a decedent as heir or legatee, or as beneficiary under a testamentary trust, are not deductible.

(l) Expenses paid or incurred by an individual in connection with the determination, collection, or refund of any tax, whether the taxing authority be Federal, State, or municipal, and whether the tax be income, estate, gift, property, or any other tax, are deductible. Thus, expenses paid or incurred by a taxpayer for tax counsel or expenses paid or incurred in connection with the preparation of his tax returns or in connection with any proceedings involved in determining the extent of tax liability or in contesting his tax liability are deductible.

(m) An expense (not otherwise deductible) paid or incurred by an individual in determining or contesting a liability asserted against him does not become deductible by reason of the fact that property held by him for the production of income may be required to be used or sold for the purpose of satisfying such liability.

(n) Capital expenditures are not allowable as nontrade or nonbusiness expenses. The deduction of an item otherwise allowable under section 212 will not be disallowed simply because the taxpayer was entitled under subtitle A of the Code to treat such item as a capital expenditure, rather than to deduct it as an expense. For example, see section 266. Where, however, the item may properly be treated only as a capital expenditure or where it was properly so treated under an option granted in subtitle A, no deduction is allowable under section 212; and this is true regardless of whether any basis adjustment is allowed under any other provision of the Code.

(o) The provisions of section 212 are not intended in any way to disallow expenses which would otherwise be allowable under section 162 and the regulations thereunder. Double deductions are not permitted. Amounts deducted under one provision of the Internal Revenue Code of 1954 cannot again be deducted under any other provision thereof.

(p) *Frustration of public policy.*—The deduction of a payment will be disallowed under section 212 if the payment is of a type for which a deduction would be disallowed under section 162(c), (f), or (g) and the regulations thereunder in the case of a business expense. [Reg. § 1.212-1.]

☐ [*T.D. 6279, 12-13-57. Amended by T.D. 7198, 7-12-72 and T.D. 7345, 2-19-75.*]

[Reg. § 1.213-1]

§ 1.213-1. **Medical, dental, etc., expenses.**—(a) *Allowance of deduction.*—(1) Section 213 permits a deduction of payments for certain medical expenses (including expenses for medicine and drugs). Except as provided in paragraph (d) of this section (relating to special rule for decedents) a deduction is allowable only to individuals and only with respect to medical expenses actually paid during the taxable year, regardless of when the incident or event which occasioned the expenses occurred and regardless of the method of accounting employed by the taxpayer in making his income tax return. Thus, if the medical expenses are incurred but not paid during the taxable year, no deduction for such expenses shall be allowed for such year.

(2) Except as provided in subparagraphs (4)(i) and (5)(i) of this paragraph, only such medical expenses (including the allowable expenses for medicine and drugs) are deductible as exceed 3 percent of the adjusted gross income for the taxable year. For taxable years beginning after December 31, 1966, the amounts paid during the taxable year for insurance that constitute expenses paid for medical care shall, for purposes of computing total medical expenses, be reduced by the amount determined under subparagraph (5)(i) of this paragraph. For the amounts paid during the taxable year for medicine and drugs which may be taken into account in computing total medical expenses, see paragraph (b) of this section. For the maximum deduction allowable under section 213 in the case of certain taxable years, see paragraph (c) of this section. As to what constitutes "adjusted gross income", see section 62 and the regulations thereunder.

(3)(i) For medical expenses paid (including expenses paid for medicine and drugs) to be deductible, they must be for medical care of the taxpayer, his spouse, or a dependent of the taxpayer and not be compensated for by insurance or otherwise. Expenses paid for the medical care of a dependent, as defined in section 152 and the regulations thereunder, are deductible under this section even though the dependent has gross income equal to or in excess of the amount determined pursuant to § 1.151-2 applicable to the calendar year in which the taxable year of the taxpayer begins. Where such expenses are paid by two or more persons and the conditions of section 152(c) and the regulations thereunder are met, the medical expenses are deductible only by the person designated in the multiple support agreement filed by such persons and such deduction is limited to the amount of medical expenses paid by such person.

(ii) An amount excluded from gross income under section 105(c) or (d) (relating to amounts received under accident and health plans) and the regulations thereunder shall not constitute compensation for expenses paid for medical care. Exclusion of such amounts from gross income will not affect the treatment of expenses paid for medical care.

(iii) The application of the rule allowing a deduction for medical expenses to the extent not compensated for by insurance or otherwise may be illustrated by the following example in which it is assumed that neither the taxpayer nor his wife has attained the age of 65:

Example. Taxpayer H, married to W and having one dependent child, had adjusted gross income for 1956 of $3,000. During 1956 he paid $300 for medical care, of which $100 was for treatment of his dependent child and $200 for an operation on W which was performed in September 1955. In 1956, he received a payment of $50 for health insurance to cover a portion of the cost of W's operation performed during 1955. The deduction allowable under section 213 for the calendar year 1956, provided the taxpayer itemizes his deductions and does not compute his tax under section 3 by use of the tax table, is $160, computed as follows:

Payments in 1956 for medical care	$300
Less: Amount of insurance received in 1956	50
Payments in 1956 for medical care not compensated for during 1956	$250
Less: 3 percent of $3,000 (adjusted gross income)	90

Reg. § 1.213-1(a)(3)(iii)

Excess, allowable as a deduction for 1956 . . . . $160

(4)(i) For taxable years beginning before January 1, 1967, where either the taxpayer or his spouse has attained the age of 65 before the close of the taxable year, the 3-percent limitation on the deduction for medical expenses does not apply with respect to expenses for medical care of the taxpayer or his spouse. Moreover, for taxable years beginning after December 31, 1959, and before January 1, 1967, the 3-percent limitation on the deduction for medical expenses does not apply to amounts paid for the medical care of a dependent (as defined in sec. 152) who is the mother or father of the taxpayer or his spouse and who has attained the age of 65 before the close of the taxpayer's taxable year. For taxable years beginning before January 1, 1964, and for taxable years beginning after December 31, 1966, all amounts paid by the taxpayer for medicine and drugs are subject to the 1-percent limitation provided by section 213(b). For taxable years beginning after December 31, 1963, and before January 1, 1967, the 1-percent limitation provided by section 213(b) does not apply, under certain circumstances, to amounts paid by the taxpayer for medicine and drugs for the taxpayer and his spouse or for a dependent (as defined in sec. 152) who is the mother or father of the taxpayer or of his spouse. (For additional provisions relating to the 1-percent limitation with respect to medicine and drugs, see paragraph (b) of this section.) For taxable years beginning before January 1, 1967, whether or not the 3-percent or 1-percent limitation applies, the total medical expenses deductible under section 213 are subject to the limitations described in section 213(c) and paragraph (c) of this section and, where applicable, to the limitations described in section 213(g) and §1.213-2.

(ii) The age of a taxpayer shall be determined as of the last day of his taxable year. In the event of the taxpayer's death, his taxable year shall end as of the date of his death. The age of a taxpayer's spouse shall be determined as of the last day of the taxpayer's taxable year, except that, if the spouse dies within such taxable year, her age shall be determined as of the date of her death. Likewise, the age of the taxpayer's dependent who is the mother or father of the taxpayer or of his spouse shall be determined as of the last day of the taxpayer's taxable year but not later than the date of death of such dependent.

(iii) The application of subdivision (i) of this subparagraph may be illustrated by the following examples:

Example (1). Taxpayer A, who attained the age of 65 on February 22, 1956, makes his return on the basis of the calendar year. During the year 1956, A had adjusted gross income of $8,000, and paid the following medical bills: (*a*) $560 (7 percent of adjusted gross income) for the medical care of himself and his spouse, and (*b*) $160 (2 percent of adjusted gross income) for the medical care of his dependent son. No part of these payments was for medicine and drugs nor compensated for by insurance or otherwise. The allowable deduction under section 213 for 1956 is $560, the full amount of the medical expenses for the taxpayer and his spouse. No deduction is allowable for the amount of $160 paid for medical care of the dependent son since the amount of such payment (determined without regard to the payments for the care of the taxpayer and his spouse) does not exceed 3 percent of adjusted gross income.

Example (2). H and W, who have a dependent child, made a joint return for the calendar year 1956. H became 65 years of age on August 15, 1956. The adjusted gross income of H and W in 1956 was $40,000 and they paid in such year the following amounts for medical care: (*a*) $3,000 for the medical care of H; (*b*) $2,000 for the medical care of W; and (*c*) $3,000 for the medical care of the dependent child. No part of these payments was for medicine and drugs nor compensated for by insurance or otherwise. The allowable deduction under section 213 for medical expenses paid in 1956 is $6,800 computed as follows:

Payments for medical care of H and W in 1956		$5,000
Payments for medical care of the dependent in 1956	$3,000	
Less: 3 percent of $40,000 (adjusted gross income)	1,200	1,800
Allowable deduction for 1956		$6,800

Example (3). D and his wife, E, made a joint income tax return for the calendar year 1962, and reported adjusted gross income of $30,000. On December 13, 1962, D attained the age of 65. During the year 1962, D's father, F, who was 87 years of age, received over half of his support from, and was a dependent (as defined in section 152) of, D. However, D could not claim an exemption under section 151 for F because F had gross income from rents in 1962 of $800. D paid the following medical expenses in 1962, none of which were compensated for by insurance or otherwise: hospital and doctor bills for D and E, $6,500; hospital and doctor bills for F, $4,850; medicine and drugs for D and E, $225, and for F, $225. Since none of the medical expenses are subject to the 3-percent limitation, the amount of medi-

cal expenses to be taken into account (before computing the maximum deduction) is $11,500, computed as follows:

Hospital and doctor bills—for D and E		$6,500
Hospital and doctor bills—for F		4,850
Medicine and drugs—for D and E	$225	
Medicine and drugs—for F	225	
Total medicine and drugs	$450	
Less: 1 percent of adjusted gross income ($30,000)	300	
Allowable expenses for medicine and drugs	$150	
Total medical expenses taken into account		$11,500

Since an exemption cannot be claimed for F on the 1962 return of D and E, their deduction for medical expenses (assuming that section 213(g) does not apply) is limited to $10,000 for that year ($5,000 multiplied by the two exemptions allowed for D and E under section 151(b)). If these identical facts had occurred in a taxable year beginning before January 1, 1962, the medical expense deduction for D and E would, for such taxable year, be limited to $5,000 ($2,500 multiplied by the two exemptions allowed for D and E under section 151(b)). See paragraph (c) of this section.

Example (4). Assume the same facts in Example (3), except that D furnished the entire support of his father's twin sister, G, who had no gross income during 1962 and for whom D was entitled to a dependency exemption. In addition, D paid $4,800 to doctors and hospitals during 1962 for the medical care of G. No part of the $4,800 was for medicine and drugs, and no amount was compensated for by insurance or otherwise. For purposes of the maximum limitation under section 213(c), the maximum deduction for medical expenses on the 1962 return of D and E is limited to $15,000 ($5,000 multiplied by 3, the number of exemptions allowed under section 151, exclusive of the exemptions for old age or blindness). If these identical facts had occurred in a taxable year beginning before January 1, 1962, the medical expense deduction for D and E would, for such taxable year, be limited to $7,500 ($2,500 multiplied by the three exemptions allowed under section 151, exclusive of the exemptions for old age or blindness). The medical expenses to be taken into account by D and E for 1962 and the maximum deductions allowable for such expenses are $15,400 and $15,000, respectively, computed as follows:

Medical expenses per example (3)		$11,500
Add: Expenses paid for G	$4,800	
Less: 3 percent of adjusted gross income ($30,000)	900	3,900
Total medical expenses taken into account		$15,400
Maximum deduction for 1962 ($5,000 multiplied by 3 exemptions)		15,000
Medical expenses not deductible		$400

Example (5). Assume that the facts set forth in Example (3) had occurred in respect of the calendar year 1964 rather than the calendar year 1962. Since both D and his father, F, had attained the age of 65 before the close of the taxable year, the 1-percent limitation does not apply to the amounts paid for medicine and drugs for D, E, and F. Accordingly, the total medical expenses taken into account by D and E for 1964 would be $11,800 (rather than $11,500 as in Example (3)) computed as follows:

Hospital and doctor bills—for D and E		$6,500
Hospital and doctor bills—for F		4,850
Medicine and drugs—for D and E		225
Medicine and drugs—for F		225
Total medical expenses taken into account		$11,800

(5)(i) For taxable years beginning after December 31, 1966, there may be deducted without regard to the 3-percent limitation the lessor of—(*a*) One-half of the amounts paid during the taxable year for insurance which constitute expenses for medical care for the taxpayer, his spouse, and dependents; or (*b*) $150.

(ii) The application of subdivision (i) of this subparagraph may be illustrated by the following example:

Example. H and W made a joint return for the calendar year 1967. The adjusted gross income of H and W for 1967 was $10,000 and they paid in such year $370 for medical care of which amount $350 was paid for insurance which constitutes medical care for H and W. No part of the payment was for medicine and drugs or was compensated for by insurance or otherwise. The allowable deduction under section 213 for medical expenses paid in 1967 is $150, computed as follows:

(1)	Lesser of $175 (one-half of amounts paid for insurance) or	$150	$150
(2)	Payments for medical care .	$370	
(3)	Less line 1	150	

(4) Medical expenses to be taken into account under 3-percent limitation (line 2 minus line 3) $220

(5) Less: 3 percent of $10,000 (adjusted gross income) $300

(6) Excess allowable as a deduction for 1967 (excess of line 4 over line 5) $0

(7) Allowable medical expense deduction for 1967 (line 1 plus line 6) $150

(b) *Limitation with respect to medicine and drugs.*—(1) *Taxable years beginning before January 1, 1964.*—(i) Amounts paid during taxable years beginning before January 1, 1964, for medicine and drugs are to be taken into account in computing the allowable deduction for medical expenses paid during the taxable year only to the extent that the aggregate of such amounts exceeds 1 percent of the adjusted gross income for the taxable year. Thus, if the aggregate of the amounts paid for medicine and drugs exceeds 1 percent of adjusted gross income, the excess is added to other medical expenses for the purpose of computing the medical expense deduction. The application of this subdivision may be illustrated by the following example:

Example. The taxpayer, a single individual with no dependents, had an adjusted gross income of $6,000 for the calendar year 1956. During 1956, he paid a doctor $300 for medical services, a hospital $100 for hospital care, and also spent $100 for medicine and drugs. These payments were not compensated for by insurance or otherwise. The deduction allowable under section 213 for the calendar year 1956 is $260, computed as follows:

Payments for medical care in 1956:

Doctor $300
Hospital 100
Medicine and drugs $100
Less: 1 percent of $6,000 (adjusted gross income) 60   40

Total medical expenses taken into account $440
Less: 3 percent of $6,000 (adjusted gross income) . . . 180

Allowable deduction for 1956 . . . . $260

(ii) For taxable years beginning before January 1, 1964, the 1-percent limitation is applicable to all amounts paid by a taxpayer during the taxable year for medicine and drugs. Moreover, this limitation applies regardless of the fact that the amounts paid are for medicine and drugs for the taxpayer, his spouse, or dependent parent (the mother or father of the taxpayer or of his spouse) who has attained the age of 65 before the close of the taxable year. In a case where either a taxpayer or his spouse has attained the age of 65 and the taxpayer pays an amount in excess of 1 percent of adjusted gross income for medicine and drugs for himself, his spouse, and his dependents, it is necessary to apportion the 1 percent of adjusted gross income (the portion which is not taken into account as expenses paid for medical care) between the taxpayer and his spouse on the one hand and his dependents on the other. The part of the 1 percent allocable to the taxpayer and his spouse is an amount which bears the same ratio to 1 percent of his adjusted gross income which the amount paid for medicine and drugs for the taxpayer and his spouse bears to the total amount paid for medicine and drugs for the taxpayer, his spouse, and his dependents. The balance of the 1 percent shall be allocated to his dependents. The amount paid for medicine and drugs in excess of the allocated part of the 1 percent shall be taken into account as payments for medical care for the taxpayer and his spouse on the one hand and his dependents on the other, respectively. A similar apportionment must be made in the case of a dependent parent (65 years of age or over) of the taxpayer or his spouse. The application of this subdivision (ii) may be illustrated by the following example:

Example. H and W, who have a dependent child, made a joint return for the calendar year 1956. H became 65 years of age on September 15, 1956. The adjusted gross income of H and W for 1956 is $10,000. During the year, H and W paid the following amounts for medical care: (i) $1,000 for doctors and hospital expenses and $180 for medicine and drugs for themselves; and (ii) $500 for doctors and hospital expenses and $140 for medicine and drugs for the dependent child. These payments were not compensated for by insurance or otherwise. The deduction allowable under section 213(a)(2) for medical expenses paid in 1956 is $1,420, computed as follows:

H and W:
Payments for doctors and hospital $1,000.00
Payments for medicine and drugs . . . $180.00
Less: Limitation for medicine and drugs (see computation below) 56.25
    123.75

Medical expenses for H and W to be taken into account $1,123.75

Dependent:
Payments for doctors and hospital . . . $500.00
Payments for medicine and drugs $140.00
Less: Limitation for medicine and drugs (see computation below) . . . 43.75
    96.25

Total medical expenses $596.25
Less: 3 percent of $10,000 (adjusted gross income) 300.00

Medical expenses for the dependent to be taken into account 296.25

Allowable deduction for 1956 . . . . $1,420.00

Payments for medicine and drugs:
H and W $180.00
Dependent 140.00

Total payments $320.00
Less: 1 percent of $10,000 (adjusted gross income) . 100.00

Payments to be taken into account $220.00

Allocation of 1-percent exclusion:

H and W $\dfrac{180}{320} \times \$100 =$ $56.25

Dependent $\dfrac{140}{320} \times \$100 =$ 43.75

Total $100.00

(2) *Taxable years beginning after December 31, 1963.*—(i) Except as otherwise provided in subdivision (ii) of this subparagraph, amounts paid during taxable years beginning after December 31, 1963, for medicine and drugs are to be taken into account in computing the allowable deduction for medical expenses paid during the taxable year only to the extent that the aggregate of such amounts exceeds 1 percent of the adjusted gross income for the taxable year. Thus, if the aggregate of the amounts paid for medicine and drugs which are subject to the 1-percent limitation exceeds 1 percent of adjusted gross income, the excess is added to other medical expenses for the purpose of computing the medical expense deduction.

(ii) The 1-percent limitation provided by section 213 does not apply to amounts paid by a taxpayer during a taxable year beginning after December 31, 1963, and before January 1, 1967, for medicine and drugs for the medical care of the taxpayer and his spouse if either has attained the age of 65 before the close of the taxable year. Moreover, for taxable years beginning after December 31, 1963, and before January 1, 1967, the 1-percent limitation with respect to medicine and drugs does not apply to amounts paid for the medical care of a dependent (as defined in sec. 152) who is the mother or father of the taxpayer or of his spouse and who has attained the age of 65 before the close of the taxpayer's taxable year. Amounts paid for medicine and drugs which are not subject to the limitation on medicine and drugs are added to other medical expenses of a taxpayer and his spouse or the dependent (as the case may be) for the purpose of computing the medical expense deduction.

(iii) The application of this subparagraph may be illustrated by the following examples:

Example (1). H and W, who have a dependent child, C, were both under 65 years of age at the close of the calendar year 1964 and made a joint return for that calendar year. During the year 1964, H's mother, M, attained the age of 65, and was a dependent (as defined in section 152) of H. The adjusted gross income of H and W in 1964 was $12,000. During 1964 H and W paid the following amounts for medical care: (i) $600 for doctors and hospital expenses and $120 for medicine and drugs for themselves; (ii) $350 for doctors and hospital expenses and $60 for medicine and drugs for C; and (iii) $400 for doctors and hospital expenses and $100 for medicine and drugs for M. These payments were not compensated for by insurance or otherwise. The deduction allowable under section 213(a)(1) for medical expenses paid in 1964 is $1,150, computed as follows:

H, W and C:
Payments for doctors and hospital $950
Payments for medicine and drugs $180
Less: 1 percent of $12,000 (adjusted gross income) 120   60

Total medical expenses . . . $1,010

Reg. §1.213-1(b)(2)(iii)

Less: 3 percent of $12,000
(adjusted gross income)   360

    Medical expenses of H, W
    and C to be taken into
    account $650

M:

Payments for doctors and
hospitals $400
Payments for medicine and
drugs   100

    Medical expenses of M to be
    taken into account $500

Allowable deduction for 1964 $1,150

Example (2). H and W, who have a dependent child, C, made a joint return for the calendar year 1964, and reported adjusted gross income of $12,000. H became 65 years of age on January 23, 1964. F, the 87 year old father of W, was a dependent of H. During 1964, H and W paid the following amounts for medical care: (i) $400 for doctors and hospital expenses and $75 for medicine and drugs for H; (ii) $200 for doctors and hospital expenses and $100 for medicine and drugs for W; (iii) $200 for doctors and hospital expenses and $175 for medicine and drugs for C; and (iv) $700 for doctors and hospital expenses and $150 for medicine and drugs for F. These payments were not compensated for by insurance or otherwise. The deduction allowable under section 213(a)(2) for medical expenses paid in 1964 is $1,625, computed as follows:

H and W:

Payments for doctors and
hospital $600
Payments for medicine and
drugs   175

    Medical expenses for H and
    W to be taken into account $775

F:

Payments for doctors and
hospital   700
Payments for medicine and
drugs   150

    Medical expenses for F to be
    taken into account $850

C:

Payments for doctors and
hospital $200
Payments for medicine and
drugs $175
Less: 1 percent of $12,000
(adjusted gross income)   120   55

    Total medical expenses . . . $255
Less: 3 percent of $12,000
(adjusted gross income)   360

    Medical expenses for C to be
    taken into account $0

      Allowable deduction for
      1964 . . . . $1,625

Example (3). Assume the same facts as example (2) except that the calendar year of the return is 1967 and the amounts paid for medical care were paid during 1967. The deduction allowable under section 213(a) for medical expenses paid in 1967 is $1,520, computed as follows:

Payments for doctors
and hospitals:
H $400
W   200
C   200
F   700

                $1,500

Payments for
medicine and drugs:
H $75
W   100
C   175
F   150

           $500
Less: 1 percent of $12,000
(adjusted gross income) . .   120 $380

Medical expenses to be taken into account $1,880
Less: 3 percent of $12,000 (adjusted gross income) . .   360

Allowable medical expense deduction for 1967 . . . $1,520

Reg. §1.213-1(b)(3)

---

(3) *Definition of medicine and drugs.*—For definition of medicine and drugs, see paragraph (e)(2) of this section.

(c) *Maximum limitations.*—(1) For taxable years beginning after December 31, 1966, there shall be no maximum limitation on the amount of the deduction allowable for payment of medical expenses.

(2) Except as provided in section 213(g) and § 1.213-2 (relating to maximum limitations with respect to certain aged and disabled individuals for taxable years beginning before January 1, 1967), for taxable years beginning after December 31, 1961, and before January 1, 1967, the maximum deduction allowable for medical expenses paid in any one taxable year is the lesser of:

(i) $5,000 multiplied by the number of exemptions allowed under section 151 (exclusive of exemptions allowed under section 151(c) for a taxpayer or spouse attaining the age of 65, or section 151(d) for a taxpayer who is blind or a spouse who is blind);

(ii) $10,000, if the taxpayer is single, not the head of a household (as defined in section 1(b)(2)) and not a surviving spouse (as defined in section 2(b)), or is married and files a separate return; or

(iii) $20,000, if the taxpayer is married and files a joint return with his spouse under section 6013, or is the head of a household (as defined in section 1(b)(2)), or a surviving spouse (as defined in section 2(b)).

(3) The application of subparagraph (2) of this paragraph may be illustrated by the following example:

Example. H and W made a joint return for the calendar year 1962 and were allowed five exemptions (exclusive of exemptions under section 151(c) and (d)), one for each taxpayer and three for their dependents. The adjusted gross income of H and W in 1962 was $80,000. They paid during such year $26,000 for medical care, no part of which is compensated for by insurance or otherwise. The deduction allowable under section 213 for the calendar year 1962 is $20,000, computed as follows:

Payments for medical care in 1962 . . . . $26,000
Less: 3 percent of $80,000 (adjusted gross income)   2,400

    Excess of medical expenses in 1962 over 3 percent of
    adjusted gross income $23,600
Allowable deduction for 1962 ($5,000 multiplied by five
exemptions allowed under sec. 151(b) and (e) but not in
excess of $20,000) $20,000

(4) Except as provided in section 213(g) and § 1.213-2 (relating to certain aged and disabled individuals), for taxable years beginning before January 1, 1962, the maximum deduction allowable for medical expenses paid in any one taxable year is the lesser of:

(i) $2,500 multiplied by the number of exemptions allowed under section 151 (exclusive of exemptions allowed under section 151(c) for a taxpayer or spouse attaining the age of 65, or section 151(d) for a taxpayer who is blind or a spouse who is blind);

(ii) $5,000, if the taxpayer is single, not the head of a household (as defined in section 1(b)(2)) and not a surviving spouse (as defined in section 2(b)), or is married and files a separate return; or

(iii) $10,000, if the taxpayer is married and files a joint return with his spouse under section 6013, or is head of a household (as defined in section 1(b)(2)), or a surviving spouse (as defined in section 2(b)).

(5) For the maximum deduction allowable for taxable years beginning before January 1, 1967, if the taxpayer or his spouse is age 65 or over and is disabled, see § 1.213-2.

(d) *Special rule for decedents.*—(1) For the purpose of section 213(a), expenses for medical care of the taxpayer which are paid out of his estate during the 1-year period beginning with the day after the date of his death shall be treated as paid by the taxpayer at the time the medical services were rendered. However, no credit or refund of tax shall be allowed for any taxable year for which the statutory period for filing a claim has expired. See section 6511 and the regulations thereunder.

(2) The rule prescribed in subparagraph (1) of this paragraph shall not apply where the amount so paid is allowable under section 2053 as a deduction in computing the taxable estate of the decedent unless there is filed in duplicate (i) a statement that such amount has not been allowed as a deduction under section 2053 in computing the taxable estate of the decedent and (ii) a waiver of the right to have such amount allowed at any time as a deduction under section 2053. The statement and waiver shall be filed with or for association with the return, amended return, or claim for credit or refund for the decedent for any taxable year for which such an amount is claimed as a deduction.

(e) *Definitions.*—(1) *General.*—(i) The term "medical care" includes the diagnosis, cure, mitigation, treatment, or prevention of disease. Expenses paid for "medical care" shall include those paid for the purpose of affecting any structure or function of the body or for transportation primarily for and essential to medical care. See subparagraph (4) of this paragraph for provisions relating to medical insurance.

(ii) Amounts paid for operations or treatments affecting any portion of the body, including obstetrical expenses and expenses of therapy or X-ray treatments, are deemed to be for the purpose of affecting any structure or function of the body and are therefore paid for medical care. Amounts expended for illegal operations or treatments are not deductible. Deductions for expenditures for medical care allowable under section 213 will be confined strictly to expenses incurred primarily for the prevention or alleviation of a physical or mental defect or illness. Thus, payments for the following are payments for medical care: Hospital services, nursing services (including nurses' board where paid by the taxpayer), medical, laboratory, surgical, dental and other diagnostic and healing services, X-rays, medicine and drugs (as defined in subparagraph (2) of this paragraph, subject to the 1 percent limitation in paragraph (b) of this section), artificial teeth or limbs, and ambulance hire. However, an expenditure which is merely beneficial to the general health of an individual, such as an expenditure for a vacation, is not an expenditure for medical care.

(iii) Capital expenditures are generally not deductible for Federal income tax purposes. See section 263 and the regulations thereunder. However, an expenditure which otherwise qualifies as a medical expense under section 213 shall not be disqualified merely because it is a capital expenditure. For purposes of section 213 and this paragraph, a capital expenditure made by the taxpayer may qualify as a medical expense, if it has as its primary purpose the medical care (as defined in subdivisions (i) and (ii) of this subparagraph) of the taxpayer, his spouse, or his dependent. Thus, a capital expenditure which is related only to the sick person and is not related to permanent improvement or betterment of property, if it otherwise qualifies as an expenditure for medical care, shall be deductible; for example, an expenditure for eye glasses, a seeing eye dog, artificial teeth and limbs, a wheel chair, crutches, an inclinator or an air conditioner which is detachable from the property and purchased only for the use of a sick person, etc. Moreover, a capital expenditure for permanent improvement or betterment of property which would not ordinarily be for the purpose of medical care (within the meaning of this paragraph) may, nevertheless, qualify as a medical expense to the extent that the expenditure exceeds the increase in the value of the related property, if the particular expenditure is related directly to medical care. Such a situation could arise, for example, where a taxpayer is advised by a physician to install an elevator in his residence so that the taxpayer's wife who is afflicted with heart disease will not be required to climb stairs. If the cost of installing the elevator is $1,000 and the increase in the value of the residence is determined to be only $700, the difference of $300, which is the amount in excess of the value enhancement, is deductible as a medical expense. If, however, by reason of this expenditure, it is determined that the value of the residence has not been increased, the entire cost of installing the elevator would qualify as a medical expense. Expenditures made for the operation or maintenance of a capital asset are likewise deductible medical expenses if they have as their primary purpose the medical care (as defined in subdivisions (i) and (ii) of this subparagraph) of the taxpayer, his spouse, or his dependent. Normally, if a capital expenditure qualifies as a medical expense, expenditures for the operation or maintenance of the capital asset would also qualify provided that the medical reason for the capital expenditure still exists. The entire amount of such operation and maintenance expenditures qualifies, even if none or only a portion of the original cost of the capital asset itself qualified.

(iv) Expenses paid for transportation primarily for and essential to the rendition of the medical care are expenses paid for medical care. However, an amount allowable as a deduction for "transportation primarily for and essential to medical care" shall not include the cost of any meals and lodging while away from home receiving medical treatment. For example, if a doctor prescribes that a taxpayer go to a warm climate in order to alleviate a specific chronic ailment, the cost of meals and lodging while there would not be deductible. On the other hand, if the travel is undertaken merely for the general improvement of a taxpayer's health, neither the cost of transportation nor the cost of meals and lodging would be deductible. If a doctor prescribes an operation or other medical care, and the taxpayer chooses for purely personal considerations to travel to another locality (such as a resort area) for the operation or the other medical care, neither the cost of transportation nor the cost of meals and lodging (except where paid as part of a hospital bill) is deductible.

(v) The cost of in-patient hospital care (including the cost of meals and lodging therein) is an expenditure for medical care. The extent to which expenses for care in an institution other than a hospital shall constitute medical care is primarily a question of fact which depends upon the condition of the individual and the nature of the services he receives (rather than the nature of the institution). A private establishment which is regularly engaged in providing the types of care or services outlined in this subdivision shall be considered an institution for purposes of the rules provided herein. In general, the following rules will be applied:

(a) Where an individual is in an institution because his condition is such that the availability of medical care (as defined in subdivisions (i) and (ii) of this subparagraph) in such institution is a principal reason for his presence there, and meals and lodging are furnished as a necessary incident to such care, the entire cost of medical care and meals and lodging at the institution, which are furnished while the individual requires continual medical care, shall constitute an expense for medical care. For example, medical care includes the entire cost of institutional care for a person who is mentally ill and unsafe when left alone. While ordinary education is not medical care, the cost of medical care includes the cost of attending a special school for a mentally or physically handicapped individual, if his condition is such that the resources of the institution for alleviating such mental or physical handicap are a principal reason for his presence there. In such a case, the cost of attending such a special school will include the cost of meals and lodging, if supplied, and the cost of ordinary education furnished which is incidental to the special services furnished by the school. Thus, the cost of medical care includes the cost of attending a special school designed to compensate for or overcome a physical handicap, in order to qualify the individual for future normal education or for normal living, such as a school for the teaching of braille or lip reading. Similarly, the cost of care and supervision, or of treatment and training, of a mentally retarded or physically handicapped individual at an institution is within the meaning of the term "medical care."

(b) Where an individual is in an institution, and his condition is such that the availability of medical care in such institution is not a principal reason for his presence there, only that part of the cost of care in the institution as is attributable to medical care (as defined in subdivisions (i) and (ii) of this subparagraph) shall be considered as a cost of medical care; meals and lodging at the institution in such a case are not considered a cost of medical care for purposes of this section. For example, an individual is in a home for the aged for personal or family considerations and not because he requires medical or nursing attention. In such case, medical care consists only of that part of the cost for care in the home which is attributable to medical care or nursing attention furnished to him; his meals and lodging at the home are not considered a cost of medical care.

(c) It is immaterial for purposes of this subdivision whether the medical care is furnished in a Federal or State institution or in a private institution.

(vi) See section 262 and the regulations thereunder for disallowance of deduction for personal, living, and family expenses not falling within the definition of medical care.

(2) *Medicine and drugs.*—The term "medicine and drugs" shall include only items which are legally procured and which are generally accepted as falling within the category of medicine and drugs (whether or not requiring a prescription). Such term shall not include toiletries or similar preparations (such as toothpaste, shaving lotion, shaving cream, etc.) nor shall it include cosmetics (such as face creams, deodorants, hand lotions, etc., or any similar preparation used for ordinary cosmetic purposes) or sundry items. Amounts expended for items which, under this subparagraph, are excluded from the term "medicine and drugs" shall not constitute amounts expended for "medical care."

(3) *Status as spouse or dependent.*—In the case of medical expenses for the care of a person who is the taxpayer's spouse or dependent, the deduction under section 213 is allowable if the status of such person as "spouse" or "dependent" of the taxpayer exists either at the time the medical services were rendered or at the time the expenses were paid. In determining whether such status as "spouse" exists, a taxpayer who is legally separated from his spouse under a decree of separate maintenance is not considered as married. Thus, payments made in June 1956 by A, for medical services rendered in 1955 to B, his wife, may be deducted by A for 1956 even though, before the payments were made, B may have died or in 1956 secured a divorce. Payments made in July 1956 by C, for medical services rendered to D in 1955 may be deducted by C for 1956 even though C and D were not married until June 1956.

(4) *Medical insurance.*—(i)(a) For taxable years beginning after December 31, 1966, expenditures for insurance shall constitute expenses paid for medical care only to the extent that such amounts are paid for insurance covering expenses of medical care referred to in subparagraph (1) of this paragraph. In the case of an insurance contract under which amounts are payable for other than medical care (as, for example, a policy providing an indemnity for loss of income or for loss of life, limb, or sight)—

(1) No amount shall be treated as paid for insurance covering expenses of medical care referred to in subparagraph (1) of this paragraph unless the charge for such insurance is either sepa-

rately stated in the contract or furnished to the policyholder by the insurer in a separate statement,

(2) The amount taken into account as the amount paid for such medical insurance shall not exceed such charge, and

(3) No amount shall be treated as paid for such medical insurance if the amount specified in the contract (or furnished to the policyholder by the insurer in a separate statement) as the charge for such insurance is unreasonably large in relation to the total charges under the contract.

For purposes of the preceding sentence, amounts will be considered payable for other than medical care under the contract if the contract provides for the waiver of premiums upon the occurrence of an event. In determining whether a separately stated charge for insurance covering expenses of medical care is unreasonably large in relation to the total premium, the relationship of the coverages under the contract together with all of the facts and circumstances shall be considered. In determining whether a contract constitutes an "insurance" contract it is irrelevant whether the benefits are payable in cash or in services. For example, amounts paid for hospitalization insurance, for membership in an association furnishing cooperative or so-called free-choice medical service, or for group hospitalization and clinical care are expenses paid for medical care. Premiums paid under Part B, Title XVIII of the Social Security Act (42 U.S.C. 1395j–1395w), relating to supplementary medical insurance benefits for the aged, are amounts paid for insurance covering expenses of medical care. Taxes imposed by any governmental unit do not, however, constitute amounts paid for such medical insurance.

(b) For taxable years beginning after December 31, 1966, subject to the rules of (a) of this subdivision, premiums paid during a taxable year by a taxpayer under the age of 65 for insurance covering expenses of medical care for the taxpayer, his spouse, or a dependent after the taxpayer attains the age of 65 are to be treated as expenses paid during the taxable year for insurance covering expenses of medical care if the premiums for such insurance are payable (on a level payment basis) under the contract—

(1) For a period of 10 years or more, or

(2) Until the year in which the taxpayer attains the age of 65 (but in no case for a period of less than 5 years).

For purposes of this subdivision (b), premiums will be considered payable on a level payment basis if the total premium under the contract is payable in equal annual or more frequent installments. Thus, a total premium of $10,000 payable over a period of 10 years at $1,000 a year shall be considered payable on a level payment basis.

(ii) For taxable years beginning before January 1, 1967, expenses paid for medical care shall include amounts paid for accident or health insurance. In determining whether a contract constitutes an "insurance" contract it is irrelevant whether the benefits are payable in cash or in services. For example, amounts paid for hospitalization insurance, for membership in an association furnishing cooperative or so-called free-choice medical service, or for group hospitalization and clinical care are expenses paid for medical care.

(f) *Exclusion of amounts allowed for care of certain dependents.*— Amounts allowable under section 44A in computing a credit for the care of certain dependents shall not be treated as expenses paid for medical care.

(g) *Reimbursement for expenses paid in prior years.*—(1) Where reimbursement, from insurance or otherwise, for medical expenses is received in a taxable year subsequent to a year in which a deduction was claimed on account of such expenses, the reimbursement must be included in gross income in such subsequent year to the extent attributable to (and not in excess of) deductions allowed under section 213 for any prior taxable year. See section 104, relating to compensation for injuries or sickness, and section 105(b), relating to amounts expended for medical care, and the regulations thereunder, with regard to amounts in excess of or not attributable to deductions allowed.

(2) If no medical expense deduction was taken in an earlier year, for example, if the standard deduction under section 141 was taken for the earlier year, the reimbursement received in the taxable year for the medical expense of the earlier year is not includible in gross income.

(3) In order to allow the same aggregate medical expense deductions as if the reimbursement received in a subsequent year or years had been received in the year in which the payments for medical care were made, the following rules shall be followed:

(i) If the amount of the reimbursement is equal to or less than the amount which was deducted in a prior year, the entire amount of the reimbursement shall be considered attributable to the deduction taken in such prior year (and hence includible in gross income); or

(ii) *If the amount of the reimbursement received in such subsequent year or years is greater than the amount which was deducted for the prior year, that portion of the reimbursement received which is equal in amount to the deduction taken in the prior year shall be*

considered as attributable to such deduction (and hence includible in gross income); but

(iii) If the deduction for the prior year would have been greater but for the limitations on the maximum amount of such deduction provided by section 213(c), then the amount of the reimbursement attributable to such deduction (and hence includible in gross income) shall be the amount of the reimbursement received in a subsequent year or years reduced by the amount disallowed as a deduction because of the maximum limitation, but not in excess of the deduction allowed for the previous year.

(4) The application of subparagraphs (1), (2), and (3) of this paragraph may be illustrated by the following examples. Examples (1) and (2) reflect the maximum limitation on the medical expense deduction applicable to taxable years beginning after December 31, 1961. Examples (3) and (4) reflect the maximum limitation on the medical expense deduction applicable to taxable years beginning prior to January 1, 1962. For explanation of such maximum medical expense limitations, see paragraph (c) of this section.

Example (1). Taxpayer A, a single individual (not the head of a household and not a surviving spouse) with one dependent, is entitled to two exemptions under the provisions of section 151. He had an adjusted gross income of $35,000 for the calendar year 1962. During 1962 he paid $16,000 for medical care. A received no reimbursement for such medical expenses in 1962, but in 1963 he received $6,000 upon an insurance policy covering the medical expenses which he paid in 1962. A was allowed a deduction of $10,000 (the maximum) from his adjusted gross income for 1962. The amount which A must include in his gross income for 1963 is $1,050, and the amount to be excluded from gross income for 1963 is $4,950, computed as follows:

Payments for medical care in 1962 (not reimbursed in 1962)	$16,000
Less: 3 percent of $35,000 (adjusted gross income)	1,050
Excess of medical expenses not reimbursed in 1962 over 3 percent of adjusted gross income	14,950
Allowable deduction for 1962	$10,000
Amount by which the medical deduction for 1962 would have been greater than $10,000 but for the limitations on the maximum amount provided by section 213	4,950
Reimbursement received in 1963 . . $6,000	
Less: Amount by which the medical deduction for 1962 would have been greater than $10,000 but for the limitations on the maximum amount provided by section 213 4,950	
Reimbursement received in 1963 reduced by the amount by which the medical deduction for 1962 would have been greater than $10,000 but for the limitations on the maximum amount provided by section 213	1,050
Amount attributed to medical deduction taken for 1962	1,050
Amount to be included in gross income for 1963	1,050
Amount to be excluded from gross income for 1963 ($6,000 less $1,050)	4,950

Example (2). Assuming that A, in example (1), received $15,000 in 1963 as reimbursement for the medical expenses which he paid in 1962, the amount which A must include in his gross income for 1963 is $10,000, and the amount to be excluded from gross income for 1963 is $5,000, computed as follows:

Reimbursement received in 1963	$15,000
Less: Amount by which the medical deduction for 1962 would have been greater than $10,000 but for the limitations on the maximum amount provided by section 213	4,950
Reimbursement received in 1963 reduced by the amount by which the medical deduction for 1962 would have been greater than $10,000 but for the limitations on the maximum amount provided by section 213	$10,500
Deduction allowable for 1962	10,000
Amount of reimbursement received in 1963 to be included in gross income for 1963 as attributable to deduction allowable for 1962	10,000
Amount to be excluded from gross income for 1963 ($15,000 less $10,000)	5,000

Example (3). Taxpayer A, a single individual (not the head of a household and not a surviving spouse) with one dependent, is entitled to two exemptions under the provisions of section 151. He had an adjusted gross income of $35,000 for the calendar year 1956. During 1956 he paid $9,000 for medical care. A received no reimbursement for such medical expenses in 1956, but in 1957 he received

$6,000 upon an insurance policy covering the medical expenses which he paid in 1956. A was allowed a deduction of $5,000 (the maximum) from his adjusted gross income for 1956. The amount which A must include in his gross income for 1957 is $3,050 and the amount to be excluded from gross income for 1957 is $2,950, computed as follows:

Payments for medical care in 1956 (not reimbursed in 1956)	$9,000
Less: 3 percent of $35,000 (adjusted gross income)	1,050
Excess of medical expenses not reimbursed in 1956 over 3 percent of adjusted gross income	$7,950
Allowable deduction for 1956	5,000
Amount by which the medical deductions for 1956 would have been greater than $5,000 but for the limitations on the maximum amount provided by section 213	2,950
Reimbursement received in 1957	$6,000
Less: Amount by which the medical deduction for 1956 would have been greater than $5,000 but for the limitations on the maximum amount provided by section 213	2,950
Reimbursement received in 1957 reduced by the amount by which the medical deduction for 1956 would have been greater than $5,000 but for the limitations on the maximum amount provided by section 213	3,050
Amount attributed to medical deduction taken for 1956	3,050
Amount to be included in gross income for 1957	3,050
Amount to be excluded from gross income for 1957 ($6,000 less $3,050)	2,950

Example (4). Assuming that A, in example (3), received $8,000 in 1957 as reimbursement for the medical expenses which he paid in 1956, the amount which A must include in his gross income for 1957 is $5,000 and the amount to be excluded from gross income for 1957 is $3,000 computed as follows:

Reimbursement received in 1957	$8,000
Less: Amount by which the medical deduction for 1956 would have been greater than $5,000 but for the limitations on the maximum amount provided by section 213	2,950
Reimbursement received in 1957 reduced by the amount by which the medical deduction for 1956 would have been greater than $5,000 but for the limitations on the maximum amount provided by section 213	$5,050
Deduction allowable for 1956	5,000
Amount of reimbursement received in 1957 to be included in gross income for 1957 as attributable to deduction allowable for 1956	5,000
Amount to be excluded from gross income for 1957 ($8,000 less $5,000)	3,000

(h) *Substantiation of deductions.*—In connection with claims for deductions under section 213, the taxpayer shall furnish the name and address of each person to whom payment for medical expenses was made and the amount and date of the payment thereof in each case. If payment was made in kind, such fact shall be so reflected. Claims for deductions must be substantiated, when requested by the district director, by a statement or itemized invoice from the individual or entity to which payment for medical expenses was made showing the nature of the service rendered, and to or for whom rendered; the nature of any other item of expense and for whom incurred and for what specific purpose, the amount paid therefor and the date of the payment thereof; and by such other information as the district director may deem necessary. [Reg. § 1.213-1.]

☐ [T.D. 6279, 12-13-57. *Amended by T.D. 6451, 2-3-60; T.D. 6604, 7-23-62; T.D. 6661, 6-26-63; T.D. 6761, 9-28-64; T.D. 6946, 2-12-68; T.D. 6985, 12-26-68; T.D. 7114, 5-17-71; T.D. 7317, 6-27-74 and T.D. 7643, 8-27-79.]*

[Reg. § 1.215-1]

§ 1.215-1. Periodic alimony, etc., payments.—(a) A deduction is allowable under section 215 with respect to periodic payments in the nature of, or in lieu of, alimony or an allowance for support actually paid by the taxpayer during his taxable year and required to be included in the income of the payee wife or former wife, as the case may be, under section 71. As to the amounts required to be included in the income of such wife or former wife, see section 71 and the regulations thereunder. For definition of "husband" and "wife" see section 7701(a)(17).

(b) The deduction under section 215 is allowed only to the obligor spouse. It is not allowed to an estate, trust, corporation, or any other person who may pay the alimony obligation of such obligor spouse. The obligor spouse, however, is not allowed a deduction for any periodic payment includible under section 71 in the income of the wife or former wife, which payment is attributable to property transferred in discharge of his obligation and which, under section 71(d) or section 682, is not includible in his gross income.

(c) The following examples, in which both H and W file their income tax returns on the basis of a calendar year, illustrate cases in which a deduction is or is not allowed under section 215:

Example (1). Pursuant to the terms of a decree of divorce, H, in 1956, transferred securities valued at $100,000 in trust for the benefit of W, which fully discharged all his obligations to W. The periodic payments made by the trust to W are required to be included in W's income under section 71. Such payments are stated in section 71(d) not to be includible in H's income and, therefore, under section 215 are not deductible from his income.

Example (2). A decree of divorce obtained by W from H incorporated a previous agreement of H to establish a trust, the trustees of which were instructed to pay W $5,000 a year for the remainder of her life. The court retained jurisdiction to order H to provide further payments if necessary for the support of W. In 1956 the trustee paid to W $4,000 from the income of the trust and $1,000 from the corpus of the trust. Under the provisions of sections 71 and 682(b), W would include $5,000 in her income for 1956. H would not include any part of the $5,000 in his income nor take a deduction therefor. If H had paid the $1,000 to W pursuant to court order rather than allowing the trustees to pay it out of corpus, he would have been entitled to a deduction of $1,000 under the provisions of section 215.

(d) For other examples, see sections 71 and 682 and the regulations thereunder. [Reg. § 1.215-1.]

☐ [T.D. 6279, 12-13-57.]

[Reg. § 1.215-1T]

§ 1.215-1T. Alimony, etc., payments (temporary).—
Q-1. What information is required by the Internal Revenue Service when an alimony or separate maintenance payment is claimed as a deduction by a payor?

A-1. The payor spouse must include on his/her first filed return of tax (Form 1040) for the taxable year in which the payment is made the payee's social security number, which the payee is required to furnish to the payor. For penalties applicable to a payor spouse who fails to include such information on his/her return of tax or to a payee spouse who fails to furnish his/her social security number to the payor spouse, see section 6676. [Temporary Reg. § 1.215-1T.]

☐ [T.D. 7973, 8-30-84.]

[Reg. § 1.216-1]

§ 1.216-1. Amounts representing taxes and interest paid to cooperative housing corporation.—(a) *General rule.*—A tenant-stockholder of a cooperative housing corporation may deduct from his gross income amounts paid or accrued within his taxable year to a cooperative housing corporation representing his proportionate share of:

(1) The real estate taxes allowable as a deduction to the corporation under section 164 which are paid or incurred by the corporation before the close of the taxable year of the tenant-stockholder on the houses (or apartment building) and the land on which the houses (or apartment building) are situated, or

(2) The interest allowable as a deduction to the corporation under section 163 which is paid or incurred by the corporation before the close of the taxable year of the tenant-stockholder on its indebtedness contracted in the acquisition, construction, alteration, rehabilitation, or maintenance of the houses (or apartment building), or in the acquisition of the land on which the houses (or apartment building) are situated.

(b) *Limitation.*—The deduction allowable under section 216 shall not exceed the amount of the tenant-stockholder's proportionate share of the taxes and interest described therein. If a tenant-stockholder pays or incurs only a part of his proportionate share of such taxes and interest to the corporation, only the amount so paid or incurred which represents taxes and interest is allowable as a deduction under section 216. If a tenant-stockholder pays an amount, or incurs an obligation for an amount, to the corporation on account of such taxes and interest and other items, such as maintenance, overhead expenses, and reduction of mortgage indebtedness, the amount representing such taxes and interest is an amount which bears the same ratio to the total amount of the tenant-stockholder's payment or liability, as the case may be, as the total amount of the tenant-stockholder's proportionate share of such taxes and interest bears to the total amount of the tenant-stockholder's proportionate share of the taxes, interest, and other items on account of which such payment is made or liability incurred. No deduction is allowable under section 216 for that part of amounts representing the taxes or interest described in that section which are deductible by a tenant-stockholder under any other provision of the Code.

(c) *Disallowance of deduction for certain payments to the corporation.*— For taxable years beginning after December 31, 1986, no deduction shall be allowed to a stockholder during any taxable year for any amount paid or accrued to a cooperative housing corporation (in excess of the stockholder's proportionate share of the items described in paragraph (a)(1) and (2) of this section) which is allocable to amounts that are paid or incurred at any time by the cooperative housing corporation and which is chargeable to the corporation's capital account. Examples of expenditures chargeable to the corporation's capital account include the cost of paving a community parking lot, the purchase of a new boiler or roof, and the payment of the principal of the corporation's building mortgage. The adjusted basis of the stockholder's stock in such corporation shall be increased by the amount of such disallowance. This paragraph may be illustrated by the following example:

Example. The X corporation is a cooperative housing corporation within the meaning of section 216. In 1988 X uses $275,000 that it received from its shareholders in such year to purchase and place in service a new boiler. The $275,000 will be chargeable to the corporation's capital account. A owns 10% of the shares of X and uses in a trade or business the dwelling unit appurtenant to A's shares and was responsible for paying 10% of the cost of the boiler. A is thus responsible for $27,500 of the cost of the boiler, which amount A will not be able to deduct currently. A will, however, add the $27,500 to A's basis for A's shares in X.

(d) *Tenant-stockholder's proportionate share.*—(1) *General rule.*—The tenant-stockholder's proportionate share is that proportion which the stock of the cooperative housing corporation owned by the tenant-stockholder is of the total outstanding stock of the corporation, including any stock held by the corporation. For taxable years beginning after December 31, 1969, if the cooperative housing corporation has issued stock to a governmental unit, as defined in paragraph (g) of this section, then in determining the total outstanding stock of the corporation, the governmental unit shall be deemed to hold the number of shares that it would have held, with respect to the apartments or houses it is entitled to occupy, if it had been a tenant-stockholder. That is, the number of shares the governmental unit is deemed to hold is determined in the same manner as if stock had been issued to it as a tenant-stockholder. For example, if a cooperative housing corporation requires each tenant-stockholder to buy one share of stock for each one thousand dollars of value of the apartment he is entitled to occupy, a governmental unit shall be deemed to hold one share of stock for each one thousand dollars of value of the apartments it is entitled to occupy, regardless of the number of shares formally issued to it.

(2) *Special rule.*—(i) *In general.*—For taxable years beginning after December 31, 1986, if a cooperative housing corporation allocates to each tenant-stockholder a portion of the real estate taxes or interest (or both) that reasonably reflects the cost to the corporation of the taxes or interest attributable to each tenant-stockholder's dwelling unit (and the unit's share of the common areas), the cooperative housing corporation may elect to treat the amounts so allocated as the tenant-stockholders' proportionate shares.

(ii) *Time and manner of making election.*—The election referred to in paragraph (d)(2)(i) of this section is effective only if, by January 31 of the year following the first calendar year that includes any period to which the election applies, the cooperative housing corporation furnishes to each person that is a tenant-stockholder during that period a written statement showing the amount of real estate taxes or interest (or both) allocated to the tenant-stockholder with respect to the tenant-stockholder's dwelling unit or units and share of common areas for that period. The election must be made by attaching a statement to the corporation's timely filed tax return (taking extensions into account) for the first taxable year for which the election is to be effective. The statement must contain the name, address, and taxpayer identification number of the cooperative housing corporation, identify the election as an election under section 216(b)(3)(B)(ii) of the Code, indicate whether the election is being made with respect to the allocation of real estate taxes or interest (or both), and include a description of the method of allocation being elected. The election applies for the taxable year and succeeding taxable years. It is revocable only with the consent of the Commissioner and will be binding on all tenant-stockholders.

(iii) *Reasonable allocation.*—It is reasonable to allocate to each tenant-stockholder a portion of the real estate taxes or interest (or both) that bears the same ratio to the cooperative housing corporation's total interest or real estate taxes as the fair market value of each

dwelling unit (including the unit's share of the common areas) bears to the fair market value of all the dwelling units with respect to which stock is outstanding (including stock held by the corporation) at the time of allocation. If real estate taxes are separately assessed on each dwelling unit by the relevant taxing authority, an allocation of real estate taxes to tenant-stockholders based on separate assessments is a reasonable allocation. If one or more of the tenant-stockholders prepays any portion of the principal of the indebtedness that gives rise to interest, an allocation of interest to those tenant-stockholders will be a reasonable allocation of interest if the allocation is reduced to reflect the reduction in the debt service attributable to the prepayment. In addition, similar kinds of allocations may also be reasonable, depending on the facts and circumstances.

(3) *Examples.*—The provisions of this paragraph may be illustrated by the following examples.

Example (1). The X Corporation is a cooperative housing corporation within the meaning of section 216. In 1970, it acquires a building containing 40 category A apartments and 25 category B apartments for $750,000. The value of each category A apartment is $12,500, and of each category B apartment is $10,000. X values each share of stock issued with respect to category A apartments at $125, and sells 4,000 shares of its stock, along with the right to occupy the 40 category A apartments, to 40 tenant-stockholders for $500,000. X also sells 1,000 shares of nonvoting stock to G, a State housing authority qualifying as a governmental unit under paragraph (f) of this section for $250,000. The purchase of this stock gives G the right to occupy all the category B apartments. G is deemed to hold the number of shares that it would have held if it had been a tenant-stockholder. G is therefore deemed to own 2,000 shares of stock in X. All stockholders are required to pay a specified part of the corporation's expenses. F, one of the tenant-stockholders, purchased 100 shares of the category A stock for $12,500 in order to obtain a right to occupy a category A apartment. Since there are 6,000 total shares deemed outstanding, F's proportionate share is 1/60 (100/6,000).

Example (2). The X Corporation is a cooperative housing corporation within the meaning of section 216. In 1960 it acquired a housing development containing 100 detached houses, each house having the same value. X issued one share of stock to each of 100 tenant-stockholders, each share carrying the right to occupy one of the houses. In 1971 X redeemed 40 of its 100 shares. It then sold to G, a municipal housing authority qualifying as a governmental unit under paragraph (f) of this section, 1,000 shares preferred stock and the right to occupy the 40 houses with respect to which the stock had been redeemed. X sold the preferred stock to G for an amount equal to the cost of redeeming the 40 shares. G also agreed to pay 40 percent of X's expenses. For purposes of determining the total stock which X has outstanding, G is deemed to hold 40 shares of X.

Example (3). The X Corporation is a cooperative housing corporation within the meaning of section 216. In 1987, it acquires for $1,000,000 a building containing 10 category A apartments, 10 category B apartments, and 10 category C apartments. The value of each category A apartment is $20,000, of each category B apartment is $30,000 and of each category C apartment is $50,000. X issues 1 share of stock to each of the 30 tenant-stockholders, each share carrying the right to occupy one of the apartments. X allocates the real estate taxes and interest to the tenant-stockholders on the basis of the fair market value of their respective apartments. Since the total fair market value of all of the apartments is $1,000,000, the allocation of taxes and interest to each tenant-stockholder that has the right to occupy a category A apartment is 2/100 ($20,000/$1,000,000). Similarly, the allocation of taxes and interest to each tenant-stockholder who has a right to occupy a category B apartment is 3/100 ($30,000/$1,000,000) and of a category C apartment is 5/100 ($50,000/$1,000,000). X may elect in accordance with the rules described in paragraph (d)(2) of this section to treat the amounts so allocated as each tenant-stockholder's proportionate share of real estate taxes and interest.

Example (4). The Y Corporation is a cooperative housing corporation within the meaning of section 216. In 1987, it acquires a housing development containing 5 detached houses for $1,500,000, incurring an indebtedness of $1,000,000 for the purchase of the property. Each house is valued at $300,000, although the shares appurtenant to those houses have been sold to tenant-stockholders for $100,000. Y issues one share of stock to each of the five tenant-stockholders, each share carrying the right to occupy one of the houses. A, a tenant-stockholder, prepays all of the corporation's indebtedness allocable to A's house. The periodic charges payable to Y by A are reduced commensurately with the reduction in Y's debt service. Because no part of the indebtedness remains outstanding with respect to A's house, A's share of the interest expense is $0. The other four tenant-stockholders do not prepay their share of the indebtedness. Accordingly, 1/4 of the interest is allocated to each of the tenant-stockholders other than A. Y may elect in accordance with the rules described in paragraph (d)(2) of this section to treat the amounts so allocated as each tenant-stockholder's proportionate share of interest.

Example (5). The Z Corporation is a cooperative housing corporation within the meaning of section 216. In 1987, it acquires a building containing 10 apartments. One of the apartments is occupied by a senior citizen. Under local law, a senior citizen who owns and occupies a residential apartment is entitled to a $500 reduction in local property taxes assessed upon the apartment. As a result, Z corporation is eligible under local law for a reduction in local property taxes assessed upon the building. Z's real estate tax assessment for the year would have been $10,000, however, with the senior citizen reduction, the assessment is $9,500. The proprietary lease provides for a reduced maintenance fee to the senior citizen tenant-stockholder in accordance with the real estate tax reduction. Accordingly, each apartment owner is assessed $1,000 for local real estate taxes, except the senior citizen tenant-stockholder, who is assessed $500. Z may elect in accordance with the rules described in paragraph (d)(2) of this section to treat the amounts so allocated as each tenant-stockholder's proportionate share of taxes.

(e) *Cooperative housing corporation.*—In order to qualify as a "cooperative housing corporation" under section 216, the requirements of subparagraphs (1) through (4) of this paragraph must be met.

(1) *One class of stock.*—The corporation shall have one and only one class of stock outstanding. However, a special classification of preferred stock, in a nominal amount not exceeding $100, issued to a Federal housing agency or other governmental agency solely for the purpose of creating a security device on the mortgage indebtedness of the corporation, shall be disregarded for purposes of determining whether the corporation has one class of stock outstanding and such agency will not be considered a stockholder for purposes of section 216 and this section. Furthermore, for taxable years beginning after December 31, 1969, a special class of stock issued to a governmental unit, as defined in paragraph (g) of this section, shall also be disregarded for purposes of this paragraph in determining whether the corporation has one class of stock outstanding.

(2) *Right of occupancy.*—Each stockholder of the corporation, whether or not the stockholder qualifies as a tenant-stockholder under section 216(b)(2) and paragraph (f) of this section, must be entitled to occupy for dwelling purposes an apartment in a building or a unit in a housing development owned or leased by such corporation. The stockholder is not required to occupy the premises. The right as against the corporation to occupy the premises is sufficient. Such right must be conferred on each stockholder solely by reasons of his or her ownership of stock in the corporation. That is, the stock must entitle the owner thereof either to occupy the premises or to a lease of the premises. The fact that the right to continue to occupy the premises is dependent upon the payment of charges to the corporation in the nature of rentals or assessments is immaterial. For taxable years beginning after December 31, 1986, the fact that, by agreement with the cooperative housing corporation, a person or his nominee may not occupy the house or apartment without the prior approval of such corporation will not be taken into account for purposes of this paragraph in the following cases:

(i) In any case where a person acquires stock of the cooperative housing corporation by operation of law, by inheritance, or by foreclosure (or by instrument in lieu of foreclosure),

(ii) In any case where a person other than an individual acquires stock in the cooperative housing corporation, and

(iii) In any case where the person from whom the corporation has acquired the apartments or houses (or leaseholds therein) acquires any stock of the cooperative housing corporation from the corporation not later than one year after the date on which the apartments or houses (or leaseholds therein) are transferred to the corporation by such person. For purposes of the preceding sentence, paragraph (e)(2)(i) and (ii) of this section will not apply to acquisitions of stock by foreclosure by the person from whom the corporation has acquired the apartments or houses (or leaseholds therein).

(3) *Distributions.*—None of the stockholders of the corporation may be entitled, either conditionally or unconditionally, except upon a complete or partial liquidation of the corporation, to receive any distribution other than out of earnings and profits of the corporation.

(4) *Gross income.*—Eighty percent or more of the gross income of the corporation for the taxable year of the corporation in which the taxes and interest are paid or incurred must be derived from the tenant-stockholders. For purposes of the 80-percent test, in taxable years beginning after December 31, 1969, gross income attributable to any house or apartment which a governmental unit is entitled to occupy, pursuant to a lease or stock ownership, shall be disregarded.

(f) *Tenant-stockholder.*—The term "tenant-stockholder" means a person that is a stockholder in a cooperative housing corporation, as defined in section 216(b)(1) and paragraph (e) of this section, and whose stock is fully paid up in an amount at least equal to an amount shown to the satisfaction of the district director as bearing a reasona-

ble relationship to the portion of the fair market value, as of the date of the original issuance of the stock, of the corporation's equity in the building and the land on which it is situated that is attributable to the apartment or housing unit which such person is entitled to occupy (within the meaning of paragraph (e)(2) of this section). Notwithstanding the preceding sentence, for taxable years beginning before January 1, 1987, tenant-stockholders include only individuals, certain lending institutions, and certain persons from whom the cooperative housing corporation has acquired the apartments or houses (or leaseholds thereon).

(g) *Governmental unit.*—For purposes of section 216(b) and this section, the term "governmental unit" means the United States or any of its possessions, a State or any political subdivision thereof, or any agency or instrumentality of the foregoing empowered to acquire shares in a cooperative housing corporation for the purpose of providing housing facilities.

(h) *Examples.*—The application of section 216(a) and (b) and this section may be illustrated by the following examples, which refer to apartments but which are equally applicable to housing units:

Example (1). The X Corporation is a cooperative housing corporation within the meaning of section 216. In 1970, at a total cost of $200,000, it purchased a site and constructed thereon a building with 15 apartments. The fair market value of the land and building was $200,000 at the time of completion of the building. The building contains five category A apartment units, each of equal value, and 10 category B apartment units. The total value of all of the category A apartment units is $100,000. The total value of all of the category B apartments is also $100,000. Upon completion of the building, the X Corporation mortgaged the land and building for $100,000, and sold its total authorized capital for $100,000. The stock attributable to the category A apartments was purchased by five individuals, each of whom paid $10,000 for 100 shares, or $100 a share. Each certificate for 100 shares of such stock provides that the holder thereof is entitled to a lease of a particular apartment in the building for a specified term of years. The stock attributable to the category B apartments was purchased by a governmental unit for $50,000. Since the shares sold to the tenant-stockholders are valued at $100 per share, the governmental unit is deemed to hold a total of 500 shares. The certificate of such stock provides that the governmental unit is entitled to a lease of all of the category B apartments. All leases provide that the lessee shall pay his proportionate part of the corporation's expenses. In 1970 the original owner of 100 shares of stock attributable to the Category A apartments and to the lease to apartment No. 1 made a gift of the stock and lease to A, an individual. The taxable year of A and of the X Corporation is the calendar year. The corporation computes its taxable income on an accrual method, while A computes his taxable income on the cash receipts and disbursements method. In 1971, the X Corporation incurred expenses aggregating $13,800, including $4,000 for the real estate taxes on the land and building, and $5,000 for the interest on the mortgage. In 1972, A pays the X Corporation $1,380, representing his proportionate part of the expenses incurred by the corporation. The entire gross income of the X Corporation for 1971 was derived from the five tenant-stockholders and from the governmental unit. A is entitled under section 216 to a deduction of $900 in computing his taxable income for 1972. The deduction is computed as follows:

Shares of X Corporation owned by A		$100
Shares of X Corporation owned by four other tenant-stockholders		400
Shares of stock of X Corporation deemed owned by governmental unit		500
Total shares of stock of X Corporation outstanding		1,000
A's proportionate share of stock of X Corporation (100/1,000)		1/10
Expenses incurred by X Corporation:		
Real estate taxes	$4,000	
Interest	5,000	
Other	4,800	
Total		$13,800
Amount paid by A		$1,380
A's proportionate share of real estate taxes and interest based on his stock ownership (1/10 of $9,000)		$900
A's proportionate share of total corporate expenses based on his stock ownership (1/10 of $13,800)		$1,380
Amount of A's payment representing real estate taxes and interest (900/1,380 of $1,380)		$900
A's allowable deduction		$900

Since the stock which A acquired by gift was fully paid up by his donor in an amount equal to the portion of the fair market value, as of the date of the original issuance of the stock, of the corporation's equity in the land and building which is attributable to apartment No. 1, the requirement of section 216 in this regard is satisfied. The fair market value at the time of the gift of the corporation's equity attributable to the apartment is immaterial.

Example (2). The facts are the same as in example (1) except that the building constructed by the X Corporation contained, in addition to the 15 apartments, business space on the ground floor, which the corporation rented at $2,400 for the calendar year 1971. The corporation deducted the $2,400 from its expenses in determining the amount of the expenses to be prorated among its tenant-stockholders. The amount paid by A to the corporation in 1972 is $1,140 instead of $1,380. More than 80 percent of the gross income of the corporation for 1971 was derived from tenant-stockholders. A is entitled under section 216 to a deduction of $743.48 in computing his taxable income for 1972. The deduction is computed as follows:

Expenses incurred by X Corporation	$13,800.00
Less: Rent from business space	2,400.00
Expenses to be prorated among tenant-stockholders	$11,400.00
Amount paid by A	1,140.00
A's proportionate share of real estate taxes and interest based on his stock ownership (1/10 of $9,000)	900.00
A's proportionate share of total corporate expenses based on his stock ownership (1/10 of $13,800)	1,380.00
Amount of A's payment representing real estate taxes and interest (900/1380 of $1,140)	743.48
A's allowable deduction	743.48

Since the portion of A's payment allocable to real estate taxes and interest is only $743.48, that amount instead of $900 is allowable as a deduction in computing A's taxable income for 1972.

Example (3). The facts are the same as in example (1) except that the amount paid by A to the X Corporation in 1972 is $1,000 instead of $1,380. A is entitled under section 216 to a deduction of $652.17 in computing his taxable income for 1972. The deduction is computed as follows:

Amount paid by A	$1,000.00
A's proportionate share of real estate taxes and interest based on his stock ownership (1/10 of $9,000)	$900.00
A's proportionate share of total corporate expenses based on his stock ownership (1/10 of $13,800)	$1,380.00
Amount of A's payment representing real estate taxes and interest (900/1380 of $1,000)	$652.17
A's allowable deduction	$652.17

Since the portion of A's payment allocable to real estate taxes and interest is only $652.17, that amount instead of $900 is allowable as a deduction in computing A's taxable income for 1972.

Example (4). The facts are the same as in example (1) except that X Corporation leases recreational facilities from Y Corporation for use by the tenant-stockholders of X. Under the terms of the lease, X is obligated to pay an annual rental of $5,000 plus all real estate taxes assessed against the facilities. In 1971 X paid, in addition to the $13,800 of expenses enumerated in example (1), $5,000 rent and $1,000 real estate taxes. In 1972 A pays the X Corporation $2,000, no part of which is refunded to him in 1972. A is entitled under section 216 to a deduction of $900 in computing his taxable income for 1972. The deduction is computed as follows:

Expenses to be prorated among tenant-stockholders	$19,800
Total amount paid by A	$2,000
A's proportionate share of real estate taxes and interest based on stock ownership (1/10 of $9,000)	$900
A's proportionate share of total corporate expenses based on his stock ownership (1/10 of $19,800)	$1,980
Amount of A's payment representing real estate taxes and interest (900/1,980 of $1,980)	$900
A's allowable deduction	$900

The $1,000 of real estate taxes assessed against the recreational facilities constitutes additional rent and hence is not deductible by A as taxes under section 216. A's allowable deduction is limited to his proportionate share of real estate taxes and interest based on stock ownership and cannot be increased by the payment of an amount in excess of his proportionate share. [Reg. §1.216-1.]

☐ [*T.D. 6277, 12-19-57. Amended by T.D. 7092, 3-9-71 and T.D. 8316, 10-16-90.*]

[Reg. §1.216-2]

§1.216-2. Treatment as property subject to depreciation.— (a) *General rule.*—For taxable years beginning after December 31, 1961, stock in a cooperative housing corporation (as defined by section 216(b)(1) and paragraph (c) of §1.216-1) owned by a tenant-stockholder (as defined by section 216(b)(2) and paragraph (d) of §1.216-1) who uses the proprietary lease or right of tenancy, which

was conferred on him solely by reason of his ownership of such stock, in a trade or business or for the production of income shall be treated as property subject to the allowance for depreciation under section 167(a) in the manner and to the extent prescribed in this section.

(b) *Determination of allowance for depreciation.*—(1) *In general.*—Subject to the special rules provided in subparagraphs (2) and (3) of this paragraph and the limitation provided in paragraph (c) of this section, the allowance for depreciation for the taxable year with respect to stock of a tenant-stockholder, subject to the extent provided in this section to an allowance for depreciation, shall be determined—

(i) By computing the amount of depreciation (amortization in the case of a leasehold) which would be allowable under one of the methods of depreciation prescribed in section 167(b) and the regulations thereunder (in paragraph (a) of §1.162-11 and §1.167(a)-4 in the case of a leasehold) in respect of the depreciable (amortizable) real property owned by the cooperative housing corporation in which such tenant-stockholder has a proprietary lease or right of tenancy,

(ii) By reducing the amount of depreciation (amortization) so computed in the same ratio as the the rentable space in such property which is not subject to a proprietary lease or right of tenancy by reason of stock ownership but which is held for rental purposes bears to the total rentable space in such property, and

(iii) By computing such tenant-stockholder's proportionate share of such annual depreciation (amortization), so reduced. As used in this section, the terms "depreciation" and "depreciable real property" include amortization and amortizable leasehold of real property. As used in this section, the tenant-stockholder's proportionate share is that proportion which stock of the cooperative housing corporation owned by the tenant-stockholder is of the total outstanding stock of the corporation, including any stock held by the corporation. In order to determine whether a tenant-stockholder may use one of the methods of depreciation prescribed in section 167(b)(2), (3), or (4) for purposes of subdivision (i) of this subparagraph, the limitations provided in section 167(c) on the use of such methods of depreciation shall be applied with respect to the depreciable real property owned by the cooperative housing corporation in which the tenant-stockholder has a proprietary lease or right of tenancy, rather than with respect to the stock in the cooperative housing corporation owned by the tenant-stockholder or with respect to the proprietary lease or right of tenancy conferred on the tenant-stockholder by reason of his ownership of such stock. The allowance for depreciation determined under this subparagraph shall be properly adjusted where only a portion of the property occupied under a proprietary lease or right of tenancy is used in a trade or business or for the production of income.

(2) *Stock acquired subsequent to first offering.*—Except as provided in subparagraph (3) of this paragraph, in the case of a tenant-stockholder who purchases stock other than as part of the first offering of stock by the corporation, the basis of the depreciable real property for purposes of the computation required by subparagraph (1)(i) of this paragraph shall be the amount obtained by—

(i) Multiplying the taxpayer's cost per share by the total number of outstanding shares of stock of the corporation, including any shares held by the corporation,

(ii) Adding thereto the mortgage indebtedness to which such depreciable real property is subject on the date of purchase of such stock, and

(iii) Subtracting from the sum so obtained the portion thereof not properly allocable as of the date such stock was purchased to the depreciable real property owned by the cooperative housing corporation in which such tenant-stockholder has a proprietary lease or right of tenancy.

In order to prevent an overstatement or understatement of the basis of the depreciable real property for purposes of the computation required by subparagraph (1)(i) of this paragraph, appropriate adjustment for purposes of the computations described in subdivisions (i) and (ii) of this subparagraph shall be made in respect of prepayments and delinquencies on account of the corporation's mortgage indebtedness. Thus, for purposes of subdivision (i) of this subparagraph, the taxpayer's cost per share shall be reduced by an amount determined by dividing the total mortgage indebtedness prepayments in respect of the shares purchased by the taxpayer by the number of such shares. For purposes of subdivision (ii) of this subparagraph, the mortgage indebtedness shall be increased by the sum of all prepayments applied in reduction of the mortgage indebtedness and shall be decreased by any amount due under the terms of the mortgage and unpaid.

(3) *Conversion subsequent to date of acquisition.*—In the case of a tenant-stockholder whose proprietary lease or right of tenancy is converted, in whole or in part, to use in a trade or business or for the production of income on a date subsequent to the date on which he

acquired the stock conferring on him such lease or right of tenancy, the basis of the depreciable real property for purposes of the computation required by subparagraph (1)(i) of this paragraph shall be the fair market value of such depreciable real property on the date of the conversion if the fair market value is less than the adjusted basis of such property in the hands of the cooperative housing corporation provided in section 1011 without taking into account any adjustment for depreciation required by section 1016(a)(2). Such fair market value shall be deemed to be equal to the adjusted basis of such property, taking into account adjustments required by section 1016(a)(2) computed as if the corporation had used the straight line method of depreciation, in the absence of evidence establishing that the fair market value so attributed to the property is unrealistic. In the case of a tenant-stockholder who purchases stock other than as part of the first offering of stock of the corporation, and at a later date converts his proprietary lease to use for business or production of income—

(i) The adjusted basis of the cooperative housing corporation's depreciable real property without taking into account any adjustment for depreciation shall be the amount determined in accordance with subdivisions (i), (ii), and (iii) of subparagraph (2) of this paragraph, and

(ii) The fair market value shall be deemed to be equal to such adjusted basis reduced by the amount of depreciation, computed under the straight line method, which would have been allowable in respect of depreciable real property having a cost or other basis equal to the amount representing such adjusted basis in the absence of evidence establishing that the fair market value so attributed to the property is unrealistic.

(c) *Limitation.*—If the allowance for depreciation for the taxable year determined in accordance with the provisions of paragraph (b) of this section exceeds the adjusted basis (provided in section 1011) of the stock described in paragraph (a) of this section allocable to the tenant-stockholder's proprietary lease or right of tenancy used in a trade or business or for the production of income, such excess is not allowable as a deduction. For taxable years beginning after December 31, 1986, such excess, subject to the provisions of this paragraph (c), is allowable as a deduction for depreciation in the succeeding taxable year. To determine the portion of the adjusted basis of such stock which is allocable to such proprietary lease or right of tenancy, the adjusted basis is reduced by taking into account the same factors as are taken into account under paragraph (b)(1) of this section in determining the allowance for depreciation.

(d) *Examples.*—The provisions of section 216(c) and this section may be illustrated by the following examples:

Example (1). The Y corporation, a cooperative housing corporation within the meaning of section 216, in 1961 purchased a site and constructed thereon a building with 10 apartments at a total cost of $250,000 ($200,000 being allocable to the building and $50,000 being allocable to the land). Such building was completed on January 1, 1962, and at that time had an estimated useful life of 50 years, with an estimated salvage value of $20,000. Each apartment is of equal value. Upon completion of the building, Y corporation mortgaged the land and building for $150,000 and sold its total authorized capital stock, consisting of 1000 shares of common stock, for $100,000. The stock was purchased by 10 individuals each of whom paid $10,000 for 100 shares. Each certificate for 100 shares provides that the holder thereof is entitled to a proprietary lease of a particular apartment in the building. Each lease provides that the lessee shall pay his proportionate share of the corporation's expenses including an amount on account of the curtailment of Y's mortgage indebtedness. B, a calendar year taxpayer, is the original owner of 100 shares of stock in Y corporation. On January 1, 1962, B subleases his apartment for a term of 5 years. B's stock in Y corporation is treated as property subject to the allowance for depreciation under section 167(a), and B, who uses the straight line method of depreciation for purposes of the computation prescribed by paragraph (b)(1)(i) of this section, computes the allowance for depreciation for the taxable year 1962 with respect to such stock as follows:

Y's basis in the building	$200,000
Less: Estimated salvage value	20,000
Y's basis for depreciation	180,000
Annual straight line depreciation on Y's building (1/50 of $180,000)	$3,600
Proportion of outstanding shares of stock of Y corporation (1,000) owned by B (100)	1/10
B's proportionate share of annual depreciation (1/10 of $3,600)	$360
Depreciation allowance for 1962 with respect to B's stock (if the limitation in paragraph (c) of this section is not applicable)	360

Example (2). The facts are the same as in example (1) except that the building constructed by Y corporation contained, in addition to the 10 apartments, space on the ground floor for 2 stores which were rented to persons who do not have a proprietary lease of such space by reason of stock ownership. Y corporation's building has a total area of 16,000 square feet, the 10 apartments in such building have an area of 10,000 square feet, and the 2 stores on the ground floor have an area of 2,000 square feet. Thus, the total rentable space in Y corporation's building is 12,000 square feet. B, who uses the straight line method of depreciation for purposes of the computation prescribed by paragraph (b)(1)(i) of this section, computes the allowance for depreciation for the taxable year 1962 with respect to his stock in Y corporation as follows:

Y's basis in the building	$200,000
Less: Estimated salvage value	20,000
Y's basis for depreciation	180,000
Annual straight line depreciation on Y's building (1/50 of $180,000)	3,600
Less: Amount representing rentable space not subject to proprietary lease but held for rental purposes over total rentable space 2,000 ÷ 12,000 (of $3,600)	$600
Annual depreciation, as reduced	3,000
B's proportionate share of annual depreciation (1/10 of $3,000)	$300
Depreciation allowance for 1962 with respect to B's stock (if the limitation in paragraph (c) of this section is not applicable)	300

Example (3). The facts are the same as in example (1) except that B occupies his apartment from January 1, 1962, until December 31, 1966, and that on January 1, 1967, B sells his stock to C, an individual, for $15,000. C thereby obtains a proprietary lease from Y corporation with the same rights and obligations as B's lease provided. Y corporation's records disclose that its outstanding mortgage indebtedness is $135,000 on January 1, 1967. C, a physician, uses the entire apartment solely as an office. C's stock in Y corporation is treated as property subject to the allowance for depreciation under section 167(a), and C, who uses the straight line method of depreciation for purposes of the computation prescribed by paragraph (b)(1)(i) of this section, computes the allowance for depreciation for the taxable year 1967 with respect to such stock as follows:

Price paid for each share of stock in Y corporation purchased by C on 1/1/67 ($15,000 ÷ 100)	$150
Per share price paid by C multiplied by total shares of stock in Y corporation outstanding on 1/1/67 ($150 × 1,000)	150,000
Y's mortgage indebtedness outstanding on 1/1/67	135,000
	285,000
Less: Amount attributable to land (assumed to be 1/5 of $285,000)	57,000
	228,000
Less: Estimated salvage value	20,000
Basis of Y's building for purposes of computing C's depreciation	208,000
Annual straight line depreciation (1/45 of $208,000)	$4,622.22
C's proportionate share of annual depreciation (1/10 of $4,622.22)	462.22
Depreciation allowance for 1967 with respect to C's stock (if the limitation in paragraph (c) of this section is not applicable	462.22

[Reg. § 1.216-2.]

☐ [*T.D. 6725, 4-28-64. Amended by T.D. 8316, 10-16-90.*]

[Reg. §1.217-2]

1.217-2. Deduction for moving expenses paid or incurred in taxable years beginning after December 31, 1969.—(a) *Allowance of deduction.*—(1) *In general.*—Section 217(a) allows a deduction from gross income for moving expenses paid or incurred by the taxpayer during the taxable year in connection with his commencement of work as an employee or as a self-employed individual at a new principal place of work. For purposes of this section, amounts are considered as being paid or incurred by an individual whether goods or services are furnished to the taxpayer directly (by an employer, a client, a customer, or similar person) or indirectly (paid to a third party on behalf of the taxpayer by an employer, a client, a customer, or similar person). A cash basis taxpayer will treat moving expenses as being paid for purposes of section 217 and this section in the year in which the taxpayer is considered to have received such payment under section 82 and §1.82-1. No deduction is allowable under section 162 for any expenses incurred by the taxpayer in connection with moving from one residence to another residence unless such expenses are deductible under section 162 without regard to such change in residence. To qualify for the deduction under section 217 the expenses must meet the definition of the term "moving expenses" provided in section 217(b) and the taxpayer must meet the conditions set forth in section 217(c). The term "employee" as used in this section has the same meaning as in § 31.3401(c)-1 of this chapter (Employment Tax Regulations). The term "self-employed individual" as used in this section is defined in paragraph (f)(1) of this section.

(2) *Expenses paid in a taxable year other than the taxable year in which reimbursement representing such expenses is received.*—In general, moving expenses are deductible in the year paid or incurred. If a taxpayer who uses the cash receipts and disbursements method of accounting receives reimbursement for a moving expense in a taxable year other than the taxable year the taxpayer pays such expense, he may elect to deduct such expense in the taxable year that he receives such reimbursement, rather than the taxable year when he paid such expense in any case where—

(i) The expense is paid in a taxable year prior to the taxable year in which the reimbursement is received, or

(ii) The expense is paid in the taxable year immediately following the taxable year in which the reimbursement is received, provided that such expense is paid on or before the due date prescribed for filing the return (determined with regard to any extension of time for such filing) for the taxable year in which the reimbursement is received.

An election to deduct moving expenses in the taxable year that the reimbursement is received shall be made by claiming the deduction on the return, amended return, or claim for refund for the taxable year in which the reimbursement is received.

(3) *Commencement of work.*—(i) To be deductible, the moving expenses must be paid or incurred by the taxpayer in connection with his commencement of work at a new principal place of work (see paragraph (c)(3) of this section for a discussion of the term "principal place of work"). Except for those expenses described in section 217(b)(1)(C) and (D) it is not necessary for the taxpayer to have made arrangements to work prior to his moving to a new location; however, a deduction is not allowable unless employment or self-employment actually does occur. The term "commencement" includes (a) the beginning of work by a taxpayer as an employee or as a self-employed individual for the first time or after a substantial period of unemployment or part-time employment, (b) the beginning of work by a taxpayer for a different employer or in the case of a self-employed individual in a new trade or business, or (c) the beginning of work by a taxpayer for the same employer or in the case of a self-employed individual in the same trade or business at a new location. To qualify as being in connection with the commencement of work, the move must bear a reasonable proximity both in time and place to such commencement at the new principal place of work. In general, moving expenses incurred within one year of the date of the commencement of work are considered to be reasonably proximate in time to such commencement. Moving expenses incurred after the 1-year period may be considered reasonably proximate in time if it can be shown that circumstances existed which prevented the taxpayer from incurring the expenses of moving within the 1-year period allowed. Whether circumstances existed which prevented the taxpayer from incurring the expenses of moving within the period allowed is dependent upon the facts and circumstances of each case. The length of the delay and the fact that the taxpayer may have incurred part of the expenses of the move within the 1-year period allowed shall be taken into account in determining whether expenses incurred after such period are allowable. In general, a move is not considered to be reasonably proximate in place to the commencement of work at the new principal place of work where the distance between the taxpayer's new residence and his new principal place of work exceeds the distance between his former residence and his new principal place of work. A move to a new residence which does not satisfy this test may, however, be considered reasonably proximate in place to the commencement of work if the taxpayer can demonstrate, for example, that he is required to live at such residence as a condition of employment or that living at such residence will result in an actual decrease in commuting time or expense. For example, assume that in 1977 A is transferred by his employer to a new principal place of work and the distance between his former residence and his new principal place of work is 35 miles greater than was the distance between his former residence and his former principal place of work. However, the distance between his new residence and his new principal place of work is 10 miles greater than was the distance between his former residence and his new principal place of work. Although the minimum distance requirement of section 217(c)(1) is met the expenses of moving to the new residence are not considered as incurred in connection with A's commencement of work at his

new principal place of work since the new residence is not proximate in place to the new place of work. If, however, A can demonstrate, for example, that he is required to live at such new residence as a condition of employment or if living at such new residence will result in an actual decrease in commuting time or expense, the expenses of the move may be considered as incurred in connection with A's commencement of work at his new principal place of work.

(ii) The provisions of subdivision (i) of this subparagraph may be illustrated by the following examples:

Example (1). Assume that A is transferred by his employer from Boston, Massachusetts, to Washington, D.C. A moves to a new residence in Washington, D.C., and commences to work on February 1, 1971. A's wife and his two children remain in Boston until June 1972 in order to allow A's children to complete their grade school education in Boston. On June 1, 1972, A sells his home in Boston and his wife and children move to the new residence in Washington, D.C. The expenses incurred on June 1, 1972, in selling the old residence and in moving A's family, their household goods, and personal effects to the new residence in Washington are allowable as a deduction although they were incurred 16 months after the date of the commencement of work by A since A has moved to and established a new residence in Washington, D.C., and thus incurred part of the total expenses of the move prior to the expiration of the 1-year period.

Example (2). Assume that A is transferred by his employer from Washington, D.C., to Baltimore, Maryland. A commences work on January 1, 1971 in Baltimore. A commutes from his residence in Washington to his new principal place of work in Baltimore for a period of 18 months. On July 1, 1972, A decides to move to and establish a new residence in Baltimore. None of the moving expenses otherwise allowable under section 217 may be deducted since A neither incurred the expenses within 1 year nor has shown circumstances under which he was prevented from moving within such period.

(b) *Definition of moving expenses.*—(1) *In general.*—Section 217(b) defines the term "moving expenses" to mean only the reasonable expenses (i) of moving household goods and personal effects from the taxpayer's former residence to his new residence, (ii) of traveling (including meals and lodging) from the taxpayer's former residence to his new place of residence, (iii) of traveling (including meals and lodging), after obtaining employment, from the taxpayer's former residence to the general location of his new principal place of work and return, for the principal purpose of searching for a new residence, (iv) of meals and lodging while occupying temporary quarters in the general location of the new principal place of work during any period of 30 consecutive days after obtaining employment, or (v) of a nature constituting qualified residence sale, purchase, or lease expenses. Thus, the test of deductibility is whether the expenses are reasonable and are incurred for the items set forth in subdivisions (i) through (v) of this subparagraph.

(2) *Reasonable expenses.*—(i) The term "moving expenses" includes only those expenses which are reasonable under the circumstances of the particular move. Expenses paid or incurred in excess of a reasonable amount are not deductible. Generally, expenses paid or incurred for movement of household goods and personal effects or for travel (including meals and lodging) are reasonable only to the extent that they are paid or incurred for such movement or travel by the shortest and most direct route available from the former residence to the new residence by the conventional mode or modes of transportation actually used and in the shortest period of time commonly required to travel the distance involved by such mode. Thus, if moving or travel arrangements are made to provide a circuitous route for scenic, stopover, or other similar reasons, additional expenses resulting therefrom are not deductible since they are not reasonable nor related to the commencement of work at the new principal place of work. In addition, expenses paid or incurred for meals and lodging while traveling from the former residence to the new place of residence or to the general location of the new principal place of work and return or occupying temporary quarters in the general location of the new principal place of work are reasonable only if under the facts and circumstances involved such expenses are not lavish or extravagant.

(ii) The application of this subparagraph may be illustrated by the following example:

Example. A, an employee of the M Company works and maintains his residence in Boston, Massachusetts. Upon receiving orders from his employer that he is to be transferred to M's Los Angeles, California office, A motors to Los Angeles with his family with stopovers at various cities between Boston and Los Angeles to visit friends and relatives. In addition, A detours into Mexico for sightseeing. Because of the stopovers and tour into Mexico, A's travel time and distance are increased over what they would have been had he proceeded directly to Los Angeles. To the extent that A's route of travel between Boston and Los Angeles is in a generally southwesterly direction it may be said that he is traveling by the shortest and most direct route available by motor vehicle. Since A's excursion into Mexico is away from the usual Boston-Los Angeles route, the portion of the expenses paid or incurred attributable to such excursion is not deductible. Likewise, that portion of the expenses attributable to A's delay en route in visiting personal friends and sightseeing are not deductible.

(3) *Expenses of moving household goods and personal effects.*—Expenses of moving household goods and personal effects include expenses of transporting such goods and effects from the taxpayer's former residence to his new residence, and expenses of packing, crating, and in-transit storage and insurance for such goods and effects. Such expenses also include any costs of connecting or disconnecting utilities required because of the moving of household goods, appliances, or personal effects. Expenses of storing and insuring household goods and personal effects constitute in-transit expenses if incurred within any consecutive 30-day period after the day such goods and effects are moved from the taxpayer's former residence and prior to delivery at the taxpayer's new residence. Expenses paid or incurred in moving household goods and personal effects to the taxpayer's new residence from a place other than his former residence are allowable, but only to the extent that such expenses do not exceed the amount which would be allowable had such goods and effects been moved from the taxpayer's former residence. Expenses of moving household goods and personal effects do not include, for example, storage charges (other than in-transit), costs incurred in the acquisition of property, costs incurred and losses sustained in the disposition of property, penalties for breaking leases, mortgage penalties, expenses of refitting rugs or draperies, losses sustained on the disposal of memberships in clubs, tuition fees, and similar items. The above expenses may, however, be described in other provisions of section 217(b) and if so a deduction may be allowed for them subject to the allowable dollar limitations.

(4) *Expenses of traveling from the former residence to the new place of residence.*—Expenses of traveling from the former residence to the new place of residence include the cost of transportation and of meals and lodging en route (including the date of arrival) from the taxpayer's former residence to his new place of residence and lodging incurred in the general location of the former residence within 1 day after the former residence is no longer suitable for occupancy because of the removal of household goods and personal effects shall be considered as expenses of traveling for purposes of this subparagraph. The date of arrival is the day the taxpayer secures lodging at the new place of residence, even if on a temporary basis. Expenses of traveling from the taxpayer's former residence to his new place of residence do not include, for example, living or other expenses following the date of arrival at the new place of residence and while waiting to enter the new residence or waiting for household goods to arrive, expenses in connection with house or apartment hunting, living expenses preceding date of departure for the new place of residence (other than expenses of meals and lodging incurred within 1 day after the former residence is no longer suitable for occupancy), expenses of trips for purposes of selling property, expenses of trips to the former residence by the taxpayer pending the move by his family to the new place of residence, or any allowance for depreciation. The above expenses may, however, be described in other provisions of section 217(b) and if so a deduction may be allowed for them subject to the allowable dollar limitations. The deduction for traveling expenses from the former residence to the new place of residence is allowable for only one trip made by the taxpayer and members of his household; however, it is not necessary that the taxpayer and all members of his household travel together or at the same time.

(5) *Expenses of traveling for the principal purpose of looking for a new residence.*—Expenses of traveling, after obtaining employment, from the former residence to the general location of the new principal place of work and return, for the principal purpose of searching for a new residence include the cost of transportation and meals and lodging during such travel and while at the general location of the new place of work for the principal purpose of searching for a new residence. However, such expenses do not include, for example, expenses of meals and lodging of the taxpayer and members of his household before departing for the new principal place of work, expenses for trips for purposes of selling property, expenses of trips to the former residence by the taxpayer pending the move by his family to the place of residence, or any allowance for depreciation. The above expenses may, however, be described in other provisions of section 217(b) and if so a deduction may be allowed for them. The deduction for expenses of traveling for the principal purpose of looking for a new residence is not limited to any number of trips by the taxpayer and by members of his household. In addition, the taxpayer and all members of his household need not travel together or at the same time. Moreover, a trip need not result in acquisition of

a lease of property or purchase of property. An employee is considered to have obtained employment in the general location of the new principal place of work after he has obtained a contract or agreement of employment. A self-employed individual is considered to have obtained employment when he has made substantial arrangements to commence work at the new principal place of work (see paragraph (f)(2) of this section for a discussion of the term "made substantial arrangements to commence to work").

(6) *Expenses of occupying temporary quarters.*—Expenses of occupying temporary quarters include only the cost of meals and lodging while occupying temporary quarters in the general location of the new principal place of work during any period of 30 consecutive days after the taxpayer has obtained employment in such general location. Thus, expenses of occupying temporary quarters do not include, for example, the cost of entertainment, laundry, transportation, or other personal, living, family expenses, or expenses of occupying temporary quarters in the general location of the former place of work. The 30 consecutive day period is any one period of 30 consecutive days which can begin, at the option of the taxpayer, on any day after the day the taxpayer obtains employment in the general location of the new principal place of work.

(7) *Qualified residence sale, purchase, or lease expenses.*—Qualified residence sale, purchase, or lease expenses (hereinafter "qualified real estate expenses") are only reasonable amounts paid or incurred for any of the following purposes:

(i) Expenses incident to the sale or exchange by the taxpayer or his spouse of the taxpayer's former residence which, but for section 217(b) and (e), would be taken into account in determining the amount realized on the sale or exchange of the residence. These expenses include real estate commissions, attorneys' fees, title fees, escrow fees, so called "points" or loan placement charges which the seller is required to pay, State transfer taxes and similar expenses paid or incurred in connection with the sale or exchange. No deduction, however, is permitted under section 217 and this section for the cost of physical improvements intended to enhance salability by improving the condition or appearance of the residence.

(ii) Expenses incident to the purchase by the taxpayer or his spouse of a new residence in the general location of the new principal place of work which, but for section 217(b) and (e), would be taken into account in determining either the adjusted basis of the new residence or the cost of a loan. These expenses include attorneys' fees, escrow fees, appraisal fees, title costs, so-called "points" or loan placement charges not representing payments or prepayments of interest, and similar expenses paid or incurred in connection with the purchase of the new residence. No deduction, however, is permitted under section 217 and this section for any portion of real estate taxes or insurance, so-called "points" or loan placement charges which are, in essence, prepayments of interest, or the purchase price of the residence.

(iii) Expenses incident to the settlement of an unexpired lease held by the taxpayer or his spouse on property used by the taxpayer as his former residence. These expenses include consideration paid to a lessor to obtain a release from a lease, attorneys' fees, real estate commissions, or similar expenses incident to obtaining a release from a lease or to obtaining an assignee or a sublessee such as the difference between rent paid under a primary lease and rent received under a sublease. No deduction, however, is permitted under section 217 and this section for the cost of physical improvements intended to enhance marketability of the leasehold by improving the condition or appearance of the residence.

(iv) Expenses incident to the acquisition of a lease by the taxpayer or his spouse. These expenses include the cost of fees or commissions for obtaining a lease, a sublease, or an assignment of an interest in property used by the taxpayer as his new residence in the general location of the new principal place of work. No deduction, however, is permitted under section 217 and this section for payments or prepayments of rent or payments representing the cost of a security or other similar deposit.

Qualified real estate expenses do not include losses sustained on the disposition of property or mortgage penalties, to the extent that such penalties are otherwise deductible as interest.

(8) *Residence.*—The term "former residence" refers to the taxpayer's principal residence before his departure for his new principal place of work. The term "new residence" refers to the taxpayer's principal residence within the general location of his new principal place of work. Thus, neither term includes other residences owned or maintained by the taxpayer or members of his family or seasonal residences such as a summer beach cottage. Whether or not property is used by the taxpayer as his principal residence depends upon all the facts and circumstances in each case. Property used by the taxpayer as his principal residence may include a houseboat, a house-trailer, or similar dwelling. The term "new place of residence"

generally includes the area within which the taxpayer might reasonably be expected to commute to his new principal place of work.

(9) *Dollar limitations.*—(i) Expenses described in subparagraphs (A) and (B) of section 217(b)(1) are not subject to an overall dollar limitation. Thus, assuming all other requirements of section 217 are satisfied, a taxpayer who, in connection with his commencement of work at a new principal place of work, pays or incurs reasonable expenses of moving household goods and personal effects from his former residence to his new place of residence and reasonable expenses of traveling, including meals and lodging, from his former residence to his new place of residence is permitted to deduct the entire amount of these expenses.

(ii) Expenses described in subparagraphs (C), (D), and (E) of section 217(b)(1) are subject to an overall dollar limitation for each commencement of work of $3,000 ($2,500 in the case of a commencement of work in a taxable year beginning before January 1, 1977) of which the expenses described in subparagraphs (C) and (D) of section 217(b)(1) cannot cannot exceed $1,500 ($1,000 in the case of a commencement of work in a taxable year beginning before January 1, 1977). The dollar limitation applies to the amount of expenses paid or incurred in connection with each commencement of work and not to the amount of expenses paid or incurred in each taxable year. Thus, for example, a taxpayer who paid or incurred $2,000 of expenses described in subparagraphs (C), (D), and (E) of section 217(b)(1) in taxable year 1977 in connection with his commencement of work at a principal place of work and paid or incurred an additional $2,000 of such expenses in taxable year 1978 in connection with the same commencement of work is permitted to deduct the $2,000 of such expenses paid or incurred in taxable year 1977 and only $1,000 of such expenses paid or incurred in taxable year 1978.

(iii) A taxpayer who pays or incurs expenses described in subparagraphs (C), (D), and (E) of section 217(b)(1) in connection with the same commencement of work may choose to deduct any combination of such expenses within the dollar amounts specified in subdivision (ii) of this subparagraph. For example, a taxpayer who pays or incurs such expenses in connection with the same commencement of work may either choose to deduct: (*a*) expenses described in subparagraphs (C) and (D) of section 217(b)(1) to the extent of $1,500 ($1,000 in the case of a commencement of work in a taxable year beginning before January 1, 1977) before deducting any of the expenses described in subparagraph (E) of such section, or (*b*) expenses described in subparagraph (E) of section 217(b)(1) to the extent of $3,000 ($2,500 in the case of a commencement of work in a taxable year beginning before January 1, 1977) before deducting any of the expenses described in subparagraphs (C) and (D) of such section.

(iv) For the purpose of computing the dollar limitation contained in subparagraph (A) of section 217(b)(3) a commencement of work by a taxpayer at a new principal place of work and a commencement of work by his spouse at a new principal place of work which are in the same general location constitute a single commencement of work. Two principal places of work are treated as being in the same general location where the taxpayer and his spouse reside together and commute to their principal places of work. Two principal places of work are not treated as being in the same general location where, as of the close of the taxable year, the taxpayer and his spouse have not shared the same new residence nor made specific plans to share the same new residence within a determinable time. Under such circumstances, the separate commencements of work by a taxpayer and his spouse will be considered separately in assigning the dollar limitations and expenses to the appropriate return in the manner described in subdivisions (v) and (vi) of this subparagraph.

(v) Moving expenses (described in subparagraphs (C), (D), and (E) of section 217(b)(1)), paid or incurred with respect to the commencement of work by both a husband and wife which is considered a single commencement of work under subdivision (iv) of this subparagraph are subject to an overall dollar limitation of $3,000 ($2,500 in the case of a commencement of work in a taxable year beginning before January 1, 1977) per move of which the expenses described in subparagraphs (C) and (D) of section 217(b)(1) cannot exceed $1,500 ($1,000 in the case of a commencement of work in a taxable year beginning before January 1, 1977). If separate returns are filed with respect to the commencement of work by both a husband and wife which is considered a single commencement of work under subdivision (iv) of this subparagraph, moving expenses (described in subparagraphs (C), (D), and (E) of section 217(b)(1) are subject to an overall dollar limitation of $1,500 ($1,250 in the case of a commencement of work in a taxable year beginning before January 1, 1977) per move of which the expenses described in subparagraphs (C) and (D) of section 217(b)(1) cannot exceed $750 ($500 in the case of a commencement of work in a taxable year beginning before January 1, 1977) with respect to each return. Where moving expenses are paid or incurred in more than one taxable year with respect to a single commencement of work by a husband and wife they shall, for

purposes of applying the dollar limitations to such move, be subject to a $3,000 and $1,500 limitation ($2,500 and $1,000, respectively, in the case of a commencement of work in a taxable year beginning before January 1, 1977) for all such years that they file a joint return and shall be subject to a separate $1,500 and $750 limitation ($1,250 and $500, respectively, in the case of a commencement of work in a taxable year beginning before January 1, 1977) for all such years that they file separate returns. If a joint return is filed for the first taxable year moving expenses are paid or incurred with respect to a move but separate returns are filed in a subsequent year, the unused portion of the amount which may be deducted shall be allocated equally between the husband and wife in the later year. If separate returns are filed for the first taxable year such moving expenses are paid or incurred but a joint return is filed in a subsequent year, the deductions claimed on their separate returns shall be aggregated for purposes of determining the unused portion of the amount which may be deducted in the later year.

(vi) The application of subdivisions (iv) and (v) of this subparagraph may be illustrated by the following examples:

Example (1). A, who was transferred by his employer, effective January 15, 1977, moved from Boston, Massachusetts, to Washington, D.C. A's wife was transferred by her employer, effective January 15, 1977, from Boston, Massachusetts, to Baltimore, Maryland. A and his wife reside together at the same residence. A and his wife are cash basis taxpayers and file a joint return for taxable year 1977. Because A and his wife reside together at the new residence, the commencement of work by both is considered a single commencement of work under subdivision (iv) of this subparagraph. They are permitted to deduct with respect to their commencement of work in Washington and Baltimore up to $3,000 of the expenses described in subparagraphs (C), (D), and (E) of section 217(b)(1) of which the expenses described in subparagraphs (C) and (D) of such section cannot exceed $1,500.

Example (2). Assume the same facts as in example (1) except that for taxable year 1977, A and his wife file separate returns. Because A and his wife reside together, the commencement of work by both is considered a single commencement of work under subdivision (iv) of this subparagraph. A is permitted to deduct with respect to his commencement of work in Washington up to $1,500 of the expenses described in subparagraphs (C), (D), and (E) of section 217(b)(1) of which the expenses described in subparagraphs (C) and (D) cannot exceed $750. A is not permitted to deduct any of the expenses described in subparagraphs (C), (D), and (E) of section 217(b)(1) paid by his wife in connection with her commencement of work at a new principal place of work. A's wife is permitted to deduct with respect to her commencement of work in Baltimore up to $1,500 of the expenses described in subparagraphs (C), (D), and (E) of section 217(b)(1) that are paid by her of which the expenses described in subparagraphs (C) and (D) cannot exceed $750. A's wife is not permitted to deduct any of the expenses described in subparagraphs (C), (D), and (E) of the section 217(b)(1) paid by A in connection with his commencement of work in Washington, D.C.

Example (3). Assume the same facts as in example (1) except that A and his wife take up separate residences in Washington and Baltimore, do not reside together during the entire taxable year, and have no specific plans to reside together. The commencement of work by A in Washington, D.C., and by his wife in Baltimore are considered separate commencements of work since their principal places of work are not treated as being in the same general location. If A and his wife file a joint return for taxable year 1977, the moving expenses described in subparagraphs (C), (D), and (E) of section 217(b)(1) paid in connection with the commencement of work by A in Washington, D.C., and his wife in Baltimore, Maryland, are subject to an overall limitation of $6,000 of which the expenses described in subparagraphs (C) and (D) cannot exceed $3,000. If A and his wife file separate returns for taxable year 1977, A may deduct up to $3,000 of the expenses described in subparagraphs (C), (D), and (E) of which the expenses described in subparagraphs (C) and (D) cannot exceed $1,500. A's wife may deduct up to $3,000 of the expenses described in subparagraphs (C), (D), and (E) of which the expenses described in subparagraphs (C) and (D) cannot exceed $1,500.

(10) *Individuals other than taxpayer.*—(i) In addition to the expenses set forth in subparagraphs (A) through (D) of section 217(b)(1) attributable to the taxpayer alone, the same type of expenses attributable to certain individuals other than the taxpayer, if paid or incurred by the taxpayer, are deductible. These other individuals must be members of the taxpayer's household, and have both the taxpayer's former residence and his new residence as their principal place of abode. A member of the taxpayer's household includes any individual residing at the taxpayer's residence who is neither a tenant nor an employee of the taxpayer. Thus, for example, a member of the taxpayer's household may not be an individual such as a servant, governess, chauffeur, nurse, valet, or personal attendant. However, for purposes of this paragraph, a tenant or employee will be considered a member of the taxpayer's household where the

tenant or employee is a dependent of the taxpayer as defined in section 152.

(ii) In addition to the expenses set forth in section 217(b)(2) paid or incurred by the taxpayer attributable to property sold, purchased, or leased by the taxpayer alone, the same type of expenses paid or incurred by the taxpayer attributable to property sold, purchased, or leased by the taxpayer's spouse or by the taxpayer and his spouse are deductible providing such property is used by the taxpayer as his principal place of residence.

(c) *Conditions for allowance.*—(1) *In general.*—Section 217(c) provides two conditions which must be satisfied in order for a deduction of moving expenses to be allowed under section 217(a). The first is a minimum distance condition prescribed by section 217(c)(1), and the second is a minimum period of employment condition prescribed by section 217(c)(2).

(2) *Minimum distance.*—For purposes of applying the minimum distance condition of section 217(c)(1) all taxpayers are divided into one or the other of the following categories: Taxpayers having a former principal place of work, and taxpayers not having a former principal place of work. Included in this latter category are individuals who are seeking fulltime employment for the first time either as an employee or on a self-employed basis (for example, recent high school or college graduates), or individuals who are reentering the labor force after a substantial period of unemployment or part-time employment.

(i) In the case of a taxpayer having a former principal place of work, section 217(c)(1)(A) provides that no deduction is allowable unless the distance between the former residence and the new principal place of work exceeds by at least 35 miles (50 miles in the case of expenses paid or incurred in taxable years beginning before January 1, 1977) the distance between the former residence and the former principal place of work.

(ii) In the case of a taxpayer not having a former principal place of work, section 217(c)(1)(B) provides that no deduction is allowable unless the distance between the former residence and the new principal place of work is at least 35 miles (50 miles in the case of expenses paid or incurred in taxable years beginning before January 1, 1977).

(iii) For purposes of measuring distances under section 217(c)(1) the distance between two geographic points is measured by the shortest of the more commonly traveled routes between such points. The shortest of the more commonly traveled routes refers to the line of travel and the mode or modes of transportation commonly used to go between two geographic points comprising the shortest distance between such points irrespective of the route used by the taxpayer.

(3) *Principal place of work.*—(i) A taxpayer's "principal place of work" usually is the place where he spends most of his working time. The principal place of work of a taxpayer who performs services as an employee is his employer's plant, office, shop, store, or other property. The principal place of work of a taxpayer who is self-employed is the plant, office, shop, store, or other property which serves as the center of his business activities. However, a taxpayer may have a principal place of work even if there is no one place where he spends a substantial portion of his working time. In such case, the taxpayer's principal place of work is the place where his business activities are centered—for example, because he reports there for work, or is required either by his employer or the nature of his employment to "base" his employment there. Thus, while a member of a railroad crew may spend most of his working time aboard a train, his principal place of work is his home terminal, station, or other such central point where he reports in, checks out, or receives instructions. The principal place of work of a taxpayer who is employed by a number of employers on a relatively short-term basis and secures employment by means of a union hall system (such as a construction or building trades worker) would be the union hall.

(ii) Where a taxpayer has more than one employment (i.e., the taxpayer is employed by more than one employer, or is self-employed in more than one trade or business, or is an employee and is self-employed at any particular time) his principal place of work is determined with reference to his principal employment. The location of a taxpayer's principal place of work is a question of fact determined on the basis of the particular circumstances in each case. The more important factors to be considered in making this determination are (a) the total time ordinarily spent by the taxpayer at each place, (b) the degree of the taxpayer's business activity at each place, and (c) the relative significance of the financial return to the taxpayer from each place.

(iii) Where a taxpayer maintains inconsistent positions by claiming a deduction for expenses of meals and lodging while away from home (incurred in the general location of the new principal place of work) under section 162 (relating to trade or business expenses) and by claiming a deduction under this section for moving expenses incurred in connection with the commencement of work at such place of work, it will be a question of facts and circumstances as to whether such new place of work will be considered a principal place of work, and accordingly which category of deductions he will be allowed.

(4) *Minimum period of employment.*—(i) Under section 217(c)(2) no deduction is allowed unless—

(a) Where a taxpayer is an employee, during the 12-month period immediately following his arrival in the general location of the new principal place of work, he is a full-time employee, in such general location, during at least 39 weeks, or

(b) Where a taxpayer is a self-employed individual (including a taxpayer who is also an employee, but is unable to satisfy the requirements of the 39-week test of (a) of this subdivision (i)), during the 24-month period immediately following his arrival in the general location of the new principal place of work, he is a full-time employee or performs services as a self-employed individual on a full-time basis, in such general location, during at least 78 weeks, of which not less than 39 weeks are during the 12-month period referred to above.

Where a taxpayer works as an employee and at the same time performs services as a self-employed individual his principal employment (determined according to subdivision (i) of subparagraph (3) of this paragraph) governs whether the 39-week or 78-week test is applicable.

(ii) The 12-month period and the 39-week period set forth in subparagraph (A) of section 217(c)(2) and the 12- and 24-month periods as well as 39- and 78-week periods set forth in subparagraph (B) of such section are measured from the date of the taxpayer's arrival in the general location of the new principal place of work. Generally, date of arrival is the date of the termination of the last trip preceding the taxpayer's commencement of work on a regular basis and is not the date the taxpayer's family or household goods and effects arrive.

(iii) The taxpayer need not remain in the employ of the same employer or remain self-employed in the same trade or business for the required number of weeks. However, he must be employed in the same general location of the new principal place of work during such period. The "general location" of the new principal place of work refers to a general commutation area and is usually the same area as the "new place of residence"; see paragraph (b)(8) of this section.

(iv) Only those weeks during which the taxpayer is a full-time employee or during which he performs services as a self-employed individual on a full-time basis qualify as a week of work for purposes of the minimum period of employment condition of section 217(c)(2).

(a) Whether an employee is a full-time employee during any particular week depends upon the customary practices of the occupation in the geographic area in which the taxpayer works. Where employment is on a seasonal basis, weeks occurring in the off-season when no work is required or available may be counted as weeks of full-time employment only if the employee's contract or agreement of employment covers the off-season period and such period is less than 6 months. Thus, for example, a school teacher whose employment contract covers a 12-month period and who teaches on a full-time basis for more than 6 months is considered a full-time employee during the entire 12-month period. A taxpayer will be treated as a full-time employee during any week of involuntary temporary absence from work because of illness, strikes, shutouts, layoffs, natural disasters, etc. A taxpayer will, also, be treated as a full-time employee during any week in which he voluntarily absents himself from work for leave or vacation provided for in his contract or agreement of employment.

(b) Whether a taxpayer performs services as a self-employed individual on a full-time basis during any particular week depends on the practices of the trade or business in the geographic area in which the taxpayer works. For example, a self-employed dentist maintaining office hours 4 days a week is considered to perform services as a self-employed individual on a full-time basis providing it is not unusual for other self-employed dentists in the geographic area in which the taxpayer works to maintain office hours only 4 days a week. Where a trade or business is seasonal, weeks occurring during the off-season when no work is required or available may be counted as weeks of performance of services on a full-time basis only if the off-season is less than 6 months and the taxpayer performs services on a full-time basis both before and after the off-season. For example, a taxpayer who owns and operates a motel at a beach resort is considered to perform services as a self-employed individual on a full-time basis if the motel is closed for a period not exceeding 6 months during the off-season and if he performs services on a full-time basis as the operator of a motel both before and after the off-season. A taxpayer will be treated as performing services as a self-employed individual on a full-time basis during any week of involuntary temporary absence from work because of illness, strikes, natural disasters, etc.

(v) Where taxpayers file a joint return, either spouse may satisfy the minimum period of employment condition. However, weeks worked by one spouse may not be added to weeks worked by the other spouse in order to satisfy such condition. The taxpayer seeking to satisfy the minimum period of employment condition must satisfy the condition applicable to him. Thus, if a taxpayer is subject to the 39-week condition and his spouse is subject to the 78-week condition and the taxpayer satisfies the 39-week condition, his spouse need not satisfy the 78-week condition. On the other hand, if the taxpayer does not satisfy the 39-week condition, his spouse in such case must satisfy the 78-week condition.

(vi) The application of this subparagraph may be illustrated by the following examples:

Example (1). A is an electrician residing in New York City. He moves himself, his family, and his household goods and personal effects, at his own expense, to Denver where he commences employment with the M Aircraft Corporation. After working full-time for 30 weeks he voluntarily leaves his job, and he subsequently moves to and commences employment in Los Angeles, California, which employment lasts for more than 39 weeks. Since A was not employed in the general location of his new principal place of employment in Denver for at least 39 weeks, no deduction is allowable for moving expenses paid or incurred between New York City and Denver. A will be allowed to deduct only those moving expenses attributable to his move from Denver to Los Angeles, assuming all other conditions of section 217 are met.

Example (2). Assume the same facts as in example (1), except that A's wife commences employment in Denver at the same time as A, and that she continues to work in Denver for at least 9 weeks after A's departure for Los Angeles. Since she has met the 39-week requirement in Denver, and assuming all other requirements of section 217 are met, the moving expenses paid by A attributable to the move from New York City to Denver will be allowed as a deduction, provided A and his wife file a joint return. If A and his wife file separate returns moving expenses paid by A's wife attributable to the move from New York City to Denver will be allowed as a deduction on A's wife's return.

Example (3). Assume the same facts as in example (1), except that A's wife commences employment in Denver on the same day that A departs for Los Angeles, and continues to work in Denver for 9 weeks thereafter. Since neither A (who has worked 30 weeks) nor his wife (who has worked 9 weeks) has independently satisfied the 39-week requirement, no deduction for moving expenses attributable to the move from New York City to Denver is allowable.

(d) *Rules for application of section 217(c)(2).*—(1) *Inapplicability of minimum period of employment condition in certain cases.*—Section 217(d)(1) provides that the minimum period of employment condition of section 217(c)(2) does not apply in the case of a taxpayer who is unable to meet such condition by reason of—

(i) Death or disability, or

(ii) Involuntary separation (other than for willful misconduct) from the service of an employer or separation by reason of transfer for the benefit of an employer after obtaining full-time employment in which the taxpayer could reasonably have been expected to satisfy such condition.

For purposes of subdivision (i) of this subparagraph disability shall be determined according to the rules in section 72(m)(7) and § 1.72-17(f). Subdivision (ii) of this subparagraph applies only where the taxpayer has obtained full-time employment in which he could reasonably have been expected to satisfy the minimum period of employment condition. A taxpayer could reasonably have been expected to satisfy the minimum period of employment condition if at the time he commences work at the new principal place of work he could have been expected, based upon the facts known to him at such time, to satisfy such condition. Thus, for example, if the taxpayer at the time of transfer was not advised by his employer that he planned to transfer him within 6 months to another principal place of work, the taxpayer could, in the absence of other factors, reasonably have been expected to satisfy the minimum employment period condition at the time of the first transfer. On the other hand, a taxpayer could not reasonably have been expected to satisfy the minimum employment condition if at the time of the commencement of the move he knew that his employer's retirement age policy would prevent his satisfying the minimum employment period condition.

(2) *Election of deduction before minimum period of employment condition is satisfied.*—(i) Paragraph (2) of section 217(d) provides a rule which applies where a taxpayer paid or incurred, in a taxable year, moving expenses which would be deductible in that taxable year except that the minimum period of employment condition of section 217(c)(2) has not been satisfied before the time prescribed by law for filing the return for such taxable year. The rule provides that where a taxpayer has paid or incurred moving expenses and as of the date prescribed by section 6072 for filing his return for such taxable year

(determined with regard to extensions of time for filing) there remains unexpired a sufficient portion of the 12-month or the 24-month period so that it is still possible for the taxpayer to satisfy the applicable period of employment condition, the taxpayer may elect to claim a deduction for such moving expenses on the return for such taxable year. The election is exercised by taking the deduction on the return.

(ii) Where a taxpayer does not elect to claim a deduction for moving expenses on the return for the taxable year in which such expenses were paid or incurred in accordance with subdivision (i) of this subparagraph and the applicable minimum period of employment condition of section 217(c)(2) (as well as all other requirements of section 217) is subsequently satisfied, the taxpayer may file an amended return or a claim for refund for the taxable year such moving expenses were paid or incurred on which he may claim a deduction under section 217.

(iii) The application of this subparagraph may be illustrated by the following examples:

Example (1). A is transferred by his employer from Boston, Massachusetts, to Cleveland, Ohio. He begins working there on November 1, 1970. Moving expenses are paid by A in 1970 in connection with this move. On April 15, 1971, when he files his income tax return for the year 1970, A has been a full-time employee in Cleveland for approximately 24 weeks. Although he has not satisfied the 39-week employment condition at this time, A may elect to claim his 1970 moving expenses on his 1970 income tax return as there is still sufficient time remaining before November 1, 1971, to satisfy such condition.

Example (2). Assume the same facts as in example (1), except that on April 15, 1971, A has voluntarily left his employer and is looking for other employment in Cleveland. A may not be sure he will be able to meet the 39-week employment condition by November 1, 1971. Thus, he may if he wishes wait until such condition is met and file an amended return claiming as a deduction the expenses paid in 1970. Instead of filing an amended return A may file a claim for refund based on a deduction for such expenses. If A fails to meet the 39-week employment condition on or before November 1, 1971, no deduction is allowable for such expenses.

Example (3). B is a self-employed accountant. He moves from Rochester, N.Y., to New York, N.Y., and begins to work there on December 1, 1970. Moving expenses are paid by B in 1970 and 1971 in connection with this move. On April 15, 1971, when he files his income tax return for the year 1970, B has been performing services as a self-employed individual on a full-time basis in New York City for approximately 20 weeks. Although he has not satisfied the 78-week employment condition at this time, A may elect to claim his 1970 moving expenses on his 1970 income tax return as there is still sufficient time remaining before December 1, 1972, to satisfy such condition. On April 15, 1972, when he files his income tax return for the year 1971, B has been performing services as a self-employed individual on a full-time basis in New York City for approximately 72 weeks. Although he has not met the 78-week employment condition at this time, B may elect to claim his 1971 moving expenses on his 1971 income tax return as there is still sufficient time remaining before December 1, 1972, to satisfy such requirement.

(3) *Recapture of deduction.*—Paragraph (3) of section 217(d) provides a rule which applies where a taxpayer has deducted moving expenses under the election provided in section 217(d)(2) prior to satisfying the applicable minimum period of employment condition and such condition cannot be satisfied at the close of a subsequent taxable year. In such cases an amount equal to the expenses deducted must be included in the taxpayer's gross income for the taxable year in which the taxpayer is no longer able to satisfy such minimum period of employment condition. Where the taxpayer has deducted moving expenses under the election provided in section 217(d)(2) for the taxable year and subsequently files an amended return for such year on which he does not claim the deduction, such expenses are not treated as having been deducted for purposes of the recapture rule of the preceding sentence.

(e) *Denial of double benefit.*—(1) *In general.*—Section 217(e) provides a rule for computing the amount realized and the basis where qualified real estate expenses are allowed as a deduction under section 217(a).

(2) *Sale or exchange of residence.*—Section 217(e) provides that the amount realized on the sale or exchange of a residence owned by the taxpayer, by the taxpayer's spouse, or by the taxpayer and his spouse and used by the taxpayer as his principal place of residence is not decreased by the amount of any expenses described in subparagraph (A) of section 217(b)(2) and deducted under section 217(a). For the purposes of section 217(e) and of this paragraph the term "amount realized" has the same meaning as under section 1001(b) and the regulations thereunder. Thus, for example, if the taxpayer sells a residence used as his principal place of residence and real estate

commissions or similar expenses described in subparagraph (A) of section 217(b)(2) are deducted by him pursuant to section 217(a), the amount realized on the sale of the residence is not reduced by the amount of such real estate commissions or such similar expenses described in subparagraph (A) of section 217(b)(2).

(3) *Purchase of a residence.*—Section 217(e) provides that the basis of a residence purchased or received in exchange for other property by the taxpayer, by the taxpayer's spouse, or by the taxpayer and his spouse and used by the taxpayer as his principal place of residence is not increased by the amount of any expenses described in subparagraph (B) of section 217(b)(2) and deducted under section 217(a). For the purposes of section 217(e) and of this paragraph the term "basis" has the same meaning as under section 1011 and the regulations thereunder. Thus, for example, if a taxpayer purchases a residence to be used as his principal place of residence and attorneys' fees or similar expenses described in subparagraph (B) of section 217(b)(2) are deducted pursuant to section 217(a), the basis of such residence is not increased by the amount of such attorneys' fees or such similar expenses described in subparagraph (B) of section 217(b)(2).

(4) *Inapplicability of section 217(e).*—(i) Section 217(e) and paragraphs (1) through (3) of this paragraph do not apply to any expenses with respect to which an amount is included in gross income under section 217(d)(3). Thus, the amount of any expenses described in subparagraph (A) of section 217(b)(2) deducted in the year paid or incurred pursuant to the election under section 217(d)(2) and subsequently recaptured pursuant to section 217(d)(3) may be taken into account in computing the amount realized on the sale or exchange of the residence described in such subparagraph. Also, the amount of expenses described in subparagraph (B) of section 217(b)(2) deducted in the year paid or incurred pursuant to such election under section 217(d)(2) and subsequently recaptured pursuant to section 217(d)(3) may be taken into account as an adjustment to the basis of the residence described in such subparagraph.

(ii) The application of subdivision (i) of this subparagraph may be illustrated by the following examples:

Example (1). A was notified of his transfer effective December 15, 1972, from Seattle, Wash., to Philadelphia, Pa. In connection with the transfer A sold his house in Seattle on November 10, 1972. Expenses incident to the sale of the house of $2,500 were paid by A prior to or at the time of the closing of the contract of sale on December 10, 1972. The amount realized on the sale of the house was $47,500 and the adjusted basis of the house was $30,000. Pursuant to the election provided in section 217(d)(2), A deducted the expenses of moving from Seattle to Philadelphia including the expenses incident to the sale of his former residence in taxable year 1972. Dissatisfied with his position with his employer in Philadelphia, A took a position with an employer in Chicago, Ill., on July 15, 1973. Since A was no longer able to satisfy the minimum period employment condition at the close of taxable year 1973 he included an amount equal to the amount deducted as moving expenses including the expenses incident to the sale of his former residence in gross income for taxable year 1973. A is permitted to decrease the amount realized on the sale of the house by the amount of the expenses incident to the sale of the house deducted from gross income and subsequently included in gross income. Thus, the amount realized on the sale of the house is decreased from $47,500 to $45,000 and thus, the gain on the sale of the house is reduced from $17,500 to $15,000. A is allowed to file an amended return or a claim for refund in order to reflect the recomputation of the amount realized.

Example (2). B, who is self-employed, decided to move from Washington, D.C., to Los Angeles, Calif. In connection with the commencement of work in Los Angeles on March 1, 1973, B purchased a house in a suburb of Los Angeles for $65,000. Expenses incident to the purchase of the house in the amount of $1,500 were paid by B prior to or at the time of the closing of the contract of sale on September 15, 1973. Pursuant to the election provided in section 217(d)(2), B deducted the expenses of moving from Washington to Los Angeles including the expenses incident to the purchase of his new residence in taxable year 1973. Dissatisfied with his prospects in Los Angeles, B moved back to Washington on July 1, 1974. Since B was no longer able to satisfy the minimum period of employment condition at the close of taxable year 1974 he included an amount equal to the amount deducted as moving expenses incident to the purchase of the former residence in gross income for taxable year 1974. B is permitted to increase the basis of the house by the amount of the expenses incident to the purchase of the house deducted from gross income and subsequently included in gross income. Thus, the basis of the house is increased to $66,500.

(f) *Rules for self-employed individuals.*—(1) *Definition.*—Section 217(f)(1) defines the term "self-employed individual" for purposes of section 217 to mean an individual who performs personal services either as the owner of the entire interest in an unincorporated trade or business or as a partner in a partnership carrying on a trade or business. The term "self-employed individual" does not include the semiretired, part-time students, or other similarly situated taxpayers who work only a few hours each week. The application of this subparagraph may be illustrated by the following example:

Example. A is the owner of the entire interest in an unincorporated construction business. A hires a manager who performs all of the daily functions of the business including the negotiation of contracts with customers, the hiring and firing of employees, the purchasing of materials used on the projects, and other similar services. A and his manager discuss the operations of the business about once a week over the telephone. Otherwise A does not perform any managerial services for the business. For the purposes of section 217, A is not considered to be a self-employed individual.

(2) *Rule for application of subsection (b)(1)(C) and (D).*—Section 217(f)(2) provides that for purposes of subparagraphs (C) and (D) of section 217(b)(1) an individual who commences work at a new principal place of work as a self-employed individual is treated as having obtained employment when he has made substantial arrangements to commence such work. Whether the taxpayer has made substantial arrangements to commerce work at a new principal place of work is determined on the basis of all the facts and circumstances in each case. The factors to be considered in this determination depend upon the nature of the taxpayer's trade or business and include such considerations as whether the taxpayer has: (i) leased or purchased a plant, office, shop, store, equipment, or other property to be used in the trade or business, (ii) made arrangements to purchase inventory or supplies to be used in connection with the operation of the trade or business, (iii) entered into commitments with individuals to be employed in the trade or business, and (iv) made arrangements to contact customers or clients in order to advertise the business in the general location of the new principal place of work. The application of this subparagraph may be illustrated by the following examples:

Example (1). A, a partner in a growing chain of drug stores, decided to move from Houston, Tex., to Dallas, Tex., in order to open a drug store in Dallas. A made several trips to Dallas for the purpose of looking for a site for the drug store. After the signing of a lease on a building in a shopping plaza, suppliers were contacted, equipment was purchased, and employees were hired. Shortly before the opening of the store A and his wife moved from Houston to Dallas and took up temporary quarters in a motel until the time their apartment was available. By the time he and his wife took up temporary quarters in the motel A was considered to have made substantial arrangements to commence work at the new principal place of work.

Example (2). B, who is a partner in a securities brokerage firm in New York, N.Y., decided to move to Rochester, N.Y., to become the resident partner in the firm's new Rochester office. After a lease was signed on an office in downtown Rochester B moved to Rochester and took up temporary quarters in a motel until his apartment became available. Before the opening of the office B supervised the decoration of the office, the purchase of equipment and supplies necessary for the operation of the office, the hiring of personnel for the office, as well as other similar activities. By the time B took up temporary quarters in the motel he was considered to have made substantial arrangements to commence to work at the new principal place of work.

Example (3). C, who is about to complete his residency in ophthalmology at a hospital in Pittsburgh, Pa., decided to fly to Philadelphia, Pa., for the purpose of looking into opportunities for practicing in that city. Following his arrival in Philadelphia C decided to establish his practice in that city. He leased an office and an apartment. At the time he departed Pittsburgh for Philadelphia C was not considered to have made substantial arrangements to commence work at the new principal place of work, and, therefore, is not allowed to deduct expenses described in subparagraph (C) of section 217(b)(1) (relating to expenses of traveling (including meals and lodging), after obtaining employment, from the former residence to the general location of the new principal place of work and return, for the principal purpose of searching for a new residence).

(g) *Rules for members of the Armed Forces of the United States.*—(1) *In general.*—The rules in paragraphs (a)(1) and (2), (b), and (e) of this section apply to moving expenses paid or incurred by members of the Armed Forces of the United States on active duty who move pursuant to a military order and incident to a permanent change of station, except as provided in this paragraph (g). However, if the moving expenses are not paid or incurred incident to a permanent change of station, this paragraph (g) does not apply, but all other paragraphs of this section do apply. The provisions of this paragraph apply to taxable years beginning after December 31, 1975.

(2) *Treatment of services or reimbursement provided by Government.*—(i) *Services in kind.*—The value of any moving or storage services furnished by the United States Government to members of the Armed Forces, their spouses, or their dependents in connection

with a permanent change of station is not includible in gross income. The Secretary of Defense and (in cases involving members of the peace-time Coast Guard) the Secretary of Transportation are not required to report or withhold taxes with respect to those services. Services furnished by the Government include services rendered directly by the Government or rendered by a third party who is compensated directly by the Government for the services.

(ii) *Reimbursements.*—The following rules apply to reimbursements or allowances by the Government to members of the Armed Forces, their spouses, or their dependents for moving or storage expenses paid or incurred by them in connection with a permanent change of station. If the reimbursement or allowance exceeds the actual expenses paid or incurred, the excess is includible in the gross income of the member, and the Secretary of Defense or Secretary of Transportation must report the excess as payment of wages and withhold income taxes under section 3402 and the employee taxes under section 3102 with respect to that excess. If the reimbursement or allowance does not exceed the actual expenses, the reimbursement or allowance is not includible in gross income, and no reporting or withholding by the Secretary of Defense or Secretary of Transportation is required. If the actual expenses, as limited by paragraph (b)(9) of this section, exceed the reimbursement or allowance, the member may deduct the excess if the other requirements of this section, as modified by this paragraph, are met. The determination of the limitation on actual expenses under paragraph (b)(9) of this section is made without regard to any services in kind furnished by the Government.

(3) *Permanent change of station.*—For purposes of this section, the term "permanent change of station" includes the following situations:

(i) A move from home to the first post of duty when appointed, reappointed, reinstated, called to active duty, enlisted, or inducted.

(ii) A move from the last post of duty to home or a nearer point in the United States in connection with retirement, discharge, resignation, separation under honorable conditions, transfer, relief from active duty, temporary disability retirement, or transfer to a Fleet Reserve, if such move occurs within 1 year of such termination of active duty or within the period prescribed by the Joint Travel Regulations promulgated under the authority contained in sections 404 throuth 411 of title 37 of the United States Code.

(iii) A move from one permanent post of duty to another permanent post of duty at a different duty station, even if the member separates from the Armed Forces immediately or shortly after the move.

The terms "permanent", "post of duty", "duty station", and "honorable" have the meanings given them in appropriate Department of Defense or Department of Transportation rules and regulations.

(4) *Storage expenses.*—This paragraph applies to storage expenses as well as to moving expenses described in paragraph (b)(1) of this section. The term "storage expenses" means the cost of storing personal effects of members of the Armed Forces, their spouses, and their dependents.

(5) *Moves of spouses and dependents.*—(i) The following special rule applies for purposes of paragraphs (b)(9) and (10) of this section, if the spouse or dependents of a member of the Armed Forces move to or from a different location than does the member. In this case, the spouse is considered to have commenced work as an employee at a new principal place of work that is within the same general location as the location to which the member moves.

(ii) The following special rule applies for purposes of this paragraph to moves by spouses or dependents of members of the Armed Forces who die, are imprisoned, or desert while on active duty. In these cases, a move to a member's place of enlistment or induction or the member's, spouse's, or dependents' home of record or nearer point in the United States is considered incident to a permanent change of station.

(6) *Disallowance of deduction.*—No deduction is allowed under this section for any moving or storage expense reimbursed by an allowance that is excluded from gross income.

(h) *Special rules for foreign moves.*—(1) *Increase in limitations.*—In the case of a foreign move (as defined in paragraph (h)(3) of this section), paragraph (b)(6) of this section shall be applied by substituting "90 consecutive" for "30 consecutive" each time it appears. Paragraph (b)(9)(ii), (iii) and (v) of this section shall be applied by substituting "$6,000" for "$3,000" each time it appears and by substituting "$4,500" for "$1,500" each time it appears. Paragraph (b)(9)(ii) of this section shall be applied by substituting "$5,000" for "$2,000" each time it appears and by substituting "1979" for "1977" and "1980" for "1978" each time they appear in the last sentence. Paragraph (b)(9)(v) of this section shall be applied by substituting "$2,250" for "$750"

each time it appears. Paragraph (b)(9)(vi) of this section does not apply.

(2) *Allowance of certain storage fees.*—In the case of a foreign move, for purposes of this section, the moving expenses described in paragraph (b)(3) of this section shall include the reasonable expenses of moving household goods and personal effects to and from storage, and of storing such goods and effects for part or all of the period during which the new place of work continues to be the taxpayer's principal place of work.

(3) *Foreign move.*—For purposes of this paragraph, the term "foreign move" means a move in connection with the commencement of work by the taxpayer at a new principal place of work located outside the United States. Thus, a move from the United States to a foreign country or from one foreign country to another foreign country qualifies as a foreign move. A move within a foreign country also qualifies as a foreign move. A move from a foreign country to the United States does not qualify as a foreign move.

(4) *United States.*—For purposes of this paragraph, the term "United States" includes the possessions of the United States.

(5) *Effective date.*—The provisions of this paragraph apply to expenses paid or incurred in taxable years beginning after December 31, 1978. The paragraph also applies to the expenses paid or incurred in the taxable year beginning during 1978 of taxpayers who do not make an election pursuant to section 209(c) of the Foreign Earned Income Act of 1978 (Pub. Law 95-615, 92 Stat. 3109) to have section 911 under prior law apply to that taxable year.

(i) *Allowance of deductions in case of retirees or decedents who were working abroad.*—(1) *In general.*—In the case of any qualified retiree moving expenses or qualified survivor moving expenses, this section (other than paragraph (h)) shall be applied to such expenses as if they were incurred in connection with the commencement of work by the taxpayer as an employee at a new principal place of work located within the United States and the limitations of paragraph (c)(4) of this section (relating to the minimum period of employment) shall not apply.

(2) *Qualified retiree moving expenses.*—For purposes of this paragraph, the term "qualified retiree moving expenses" means any moving expenses which are incurred by an individual whose former principal place of work and former residence were outside the United States and which are incurred for a move to a new residence in the United States in connection with the bona fide retirement of the individual. "Bona fide retirement" means the permanent withdrawal from gainful full-time employment and self-employment. An individual who at the time of withdrawal from gainful full-time employment or self-employment intends the withdrawal to be permanent shall be considered to be a "bona fide retiree" even though the individual ultimately resumes gainful full-time employment or self-employment. An individual's intention may be evidenced by relevant facts and circumstances which include the age and health of the individual, the customary retirement age of employees engaged in similar work, whether the individual is receiving a retirement allowance under a pension annuity, retirement or similar fund or system, and the length of time before resuming full-time employment or self-employment.

(3) *Qualified survivor moving expenses.*—(i) For purposes of this paragraph, the term "qualified survivor moving expenses" means any moving expenses—

(A) Which are paid or incurred by the spouse or any dependent (as defined in section 152) of any decedent who (as of the time of his death) had a principal place of work outside the United States, and

(B) Which are incurred for a move which begins within 6 months after the death of the decedent and which is to a residence in the United States from a former residence outside the United States which (as of the time of the decedent's death) was the residence of such decedent and the individual paying or incurring the expense.

(ii) For purposes of subdivision (i)(B), a move begins when—

(A) The taxpayer contracts for the moving of his or her household goods and personal effects to a residence in the United States but only if the move is completed within a reasonable time thereafter;

(B) The taxpayer's household goods and personal effects are packed and in transit to a residence in the United States; or

(C) The taxpayer leaves the former residence to travel to a new place of residence in the United States.

(4) *United States.*—For purposes of this paragraph, the term "United States" includes the possessions of the United States.

(5) *Effective date.*—The provisions of this paragraph apply to expenses paid or incurred in taxable years beginning after December

31, 1978. The paragraph also applies to the expenses paid or incurred in the taxable year beginning during 1978 of taxpayers who do not make an election pursuant to section 209(c) of the Foreign Earned Income Act of 1978 (Pub. Law 95-615, 92 Stat. 3109) to have section 911 under prior law apply to that taxable year.

(j) *Effective date.*—(1) *In general.*—This section, except as provided in subparagraphs (2) and (3) of this paragraph, is applicable to items paid or incurred in taxable years beginning after December 31, 1969.

(2) *Reimbursement not included in gross income.*—This section does not apply to items to the extent that the taxpayer received or accrued in a taxable year beginning before January 1, 1970, a reimbursement or other expense allowance for such items which was not included in his gross income.

(3) *Election in cases of expenses paid or incurred before January 1, 1971, in connection with certain moves.*—(i) *In general.*—A taxpayer who was notified by his employer on or before December 19, 1969, of a transfer to a new principal place of work and who pays or incurs moving expenses after December 31, 1969, but before January 1, 1971, in connection with such transfer may elect to have the rules governing moving expenses in effect prior to the effective date of section 231 of the Tax Reform Act of 1969 (83 Stat. 577) govern such expenses. If such election is made, this section and section 82 and the regulations thereunder do not apply to such expenses. A taxpayer is considered to have been notified on or before December 19, 1969, by his employer of a transfer, for example, if before such date the employer has sent a notice to all employees or a reasonably defined group of employees, which includes such taxpayer, of a relocation of the operations of such employer from one plant or facility to another plant or facility. An employee who is transferred to a new principal place of work for the benefit of his employer and who makes an election under this paragraph is permitted to exclude amounts received or accrued, directly or indirectly, as payment for or reimbursement of expenses of moving household goods and personal effects from the former residence to the new residence and of traveling (including meals and lodging) from the former residence to the new place of residence. Such exclusion is limited to amounts received or accrued, directly or indirectly, as a payment for or reimbursement of the expenses described above. Amounts in excess of actual expenses paid or incurred must be included in gross income. No deduction is allowable under section 217 for expenses representing amounts excluded from gross income. Also, an employee who is transferred to a new principal place of work which is less than 50 miles but at least 20 miles farther from his former residence than was his former principal place of work and who is not reimbursed, either directly or indirectly, for the expenses described above is permitted to deduct such expenses providing all of the requirements of section 217 and the regulations thereunder prior to the effective date of section 231 of the Tax Reform Act of 1969 (83 Stat. 577) are satisfied.

(ii) *Election made before the date of publication of this notice as a Treasury decision.*—An election under this subparagraph made before the date of publication of this notice as a Treasury decision shall be made pursuant to the procedure prescribed in temporary income tax regulations relating to treatment of payments of expenses of moving from one residence to another residence (Part 13 of this chapter) T.D. 7032 (35 F.R. 4330, approved March 11, 1970).

(iii) *Election made on or after the date of publication of this notice as a Treasury decision.*—An election made under this subparagraph on or after the date of publication of this notice as a Treasury decision shall be made not later than the time, including extensions thereof, prescribed by law for filing the income tax return for the year in which the expenses were paid or incurred or 30 days after the date of publication of this notice as a Treasury decision, whichever occurs last. The election shall be made by a statement attached to the return (or the amended return) for the taxable year, setting forth the following information:

(a) The items to which the election relates;

(b) The amount of each item;

(c) The date each item was paid or incurred; and

(d) The date the taxpayer was informed by his employer of his transfer to the new principal place of work.

(iv) *Revocation of election.*—An election made in accordance with this subparagraph is revocable upon the filing by the taxpayer of an amended return or a claim for refund with the district director, or the director of the Internal Revenue Service center with whom the election was filed not later than the time prescribed by law, including extensions thereof, for the filing of a claim for refund with respect to the items to which the election relates. [Reg. § 1.217-2.]

☐ [T.D. 7195, 7-10-72. *Amended by* T.D. 7578, 12-19-78; T.D. 7605, 3-29-79; T.D. 7689, 3-28-80; T.D. 7810, 2-5-82 *and* T.D. 8607, 8-4-95.]

[Reg. § 1.219-1]

§ 1.219-1. Deduction for retirement savings.—(a) *In general.*—Subject to the limitations and restrictions of paragraph (b) and the special rules of paragraph (c)(3) of this section, there shall be allowed a deduction under section 62 from gross income of amounts paid for the taxable year of an individual on behalf of such individual to an individual retirement account described in section 408(a), for an individual retirement annuity described in section 408(b), or for a retirement bond described in section 409. The deduction described in the preceding sentence shall be allowed only to the individual on whose behalf such individual retirement account, individual retirement annuity, or retirement bond is maintained. The first sentence of this paragraph shall apply only in the case of a contribution of cash. A contribution of property other than cash is not allowable as a deduction under this section. In the case of a retirement bond, a deduction will not be allowed if the bond is redeemed within 12 months of its issue date.

(b) *Limitations and restrictions.*—(1) *Maximum deduction.*—The amount allowable as a deduction under section 219(a) to an individual for any taxable year cannot exceed an amount equal to 15 percent of the compensation includible in the gross income of the individual for such taxable year, or $1,500, whichever is less.

(2) *Restrictions.*—(i) *Individuals covered by certain other plans.*—No deduction is allowable under section 219(a) to an individual for the taxable year if for any part of such year—

(A) He was an active participant in—

(1) A plan described in section 401(a) which includes a trust exempt from tax under section 501(a),

(2) An annuity plan described in section 403(a),

(3) A qualified bond purchase plan described in section 405(a), or

(4) A retirement plan established for its employees by the United States, by a State or political subdivision thereof, or by an agency or instrumentality of any of the foregoing, or

(B) Amounts were contributed by his employer for an annuity contract described in section 403(b) (whether or not the individual's rights in such contract are nonforfeitable).

(ii) *Contributions after age 70½.*—No deduction is allowable under section 219(a) to an individual for the taxable year of the individual, if he has attained the age of 70½ before the close of such taxable year.

(iii) *Rollover contributions.*—No deduction is allowable under section 219 for any taxable year of an individual with respect to a rollover contribution described in section 402(a)(5), 402(a)(7), 403(a)(4), 403(b)(8), 408(d)(3), or 409(b)(3)(C).

(3) *Amounts contributed under endowment contracts.*—(i) For any taxable year, no deduction is allowable under section 219(a) for amounts paid under an endowment contract described in § 1.408-3(e) which is allocable under subdivision (ii) of this subparagraph to the cost of life insurance.

(ii) For any taxable year, the cost of current life insurance protection under an endowment contract described in paragraph (b)(3)(i) of this section is the product of the net premium cost, as determined by the Commissioner, and the excess, if any, of the death benefit payable under the contract during the policy year beginning in the taxable year over the cash value of the contract at the end of such policy year.

(iii) The provisions of this subparagraph may be illustrated by the following examples:

Example (1). A, an individual who is otherwise entitled to the maximum deduction allowed under section 219, purchases, at age 20, an endowment contract described in § 1.408-3(e) which provides for the payment of an annuity of $100 per month, at age 65, with a minimum death benefit of $10,000, and an annual premium of $220. The cash value at the end of the first policy year is 0. The net premium cost, as determined by the Commissioner, for A's age is $1.61 per thousand dollars of life insurance protection. The cost of current life insurance protection is $16.10 ($1.61 × 10). A's maximum deduction under section 219 with respect to amounts paid under the endowment contract for the taxable year in which the first policy year begins is $203.90 ($220 – $16.10).

Example (2). Assume the same facts as in example (1), except that the cash value at the end of the second policy year is $200 and the net premium cost is $1.67 per thousand for A's age. The cost of current life insurance protection is $16.37 ($1.67 × 9.8). A's maximum deduction under section 219 with respect to amounts paid under the endowment contract for the taxable year in which the second policy year begins is $203.63 ($220–$16.37).

(c) *Definitions and special rules.*—(1) *Compensation.*—For purposes of this section, the term "compensation" means wages, salaries, professional fees, or other amounts derived from or received for personal service actually rendered (including, but not limited to, commissions paid salesmen, compensation for services on the basis of a percentage of profits, commissions on insurance premiums, tips, and bonuses) and includes earned income, as defined in section 401(c)(2), but does not include amounts derived from or received as earnings or profits from property (including, but not limited to, interest and dividends) or amounts not includible in gross income.

(2) *Active participant.*—For the definition of active participant, see §1.219-2.

(3) *Special rules.*—(i) The maximum deduction allowable under section 219(b)(1) is computed separately for each individual. Thus, if a husband and wife each has compensation of $10,000 for the taxable year and they are each otherwise eligible to contribute to an individual retirement account and they file a joint return, then the maximum amount allowable as a deduction under section 219 is $3,000, the sum of the individual maximums of $1,500. However, if, for example, the husband has compensation of $20,000, the wife has no compensation, each is otherwise eligible to contribute to a individual retirement account for the taxable year, and they file a joint return, the maximum amount allowable as a deduction under section 219 is $1,500.

(ii) Section 219 is to be applied without regard to any community property laws. Thus, if, for example, a husband and wife, who are otherwise eligible to contribute to an individual retirement account, live in a community property jurisdiction and the husband alone has compensation of $20,000 for the taxable year, then the maximum amount allowable as a deduction under section 219 is $1,500.

(4) *Employer contributions.*—For purposes of this chapter, any amount paid by an employer to an individual retirement account or for an individual retirement annuity or retirement bond constitutes the payment of compensation to the employee (other than a self-employed individual who is an employee within the meaning of section 401(c)(1)) includible in his gross income, whether or not a deduction for such payment is allowable under section 219 to such employee after the application of section 219(b). Thus, an employer will be entitled to a deduction for compensation paid to an employee for amounts the employer contributes on the employee's behalf to an individual retirement account, for an individual retirement annuity, or for a retirement bond if such deduction is otherwise allowable under section 162. [Reg. §1.219-1.]

☐ [T.D. 7714, 8-7-80.]

[Reg. §1.219-2]

§1.219-2. Definition of active participant.—(a) *In general.*—This section defines the term "active participant" for individuals who participate in retirement plans described in section 219(b)(2). Any individual who is an active participant in such a plan is not allowed a deduction under section 219(a) for contributions to an individual retirement account.

(b) *Defined benefit plans.*—(1) *In general.*—Except as provided in subparagraphs (2), (3) and (4) of this paragraph, an individual is an active participant in a defined benefit plan if for any portion of the plan year ending with or within such individual's taxable year he is not excluded under the eligibility provisions of the plan. An individual is not an active participant in a particular taxable year merely because the individual meets the plan's eligibility requirements during a plan year beginning in that particular taxable year but ending in a later taxable year of the individual. However, for purposes of this section, an individual is deemed not to satisfy the eligibility provisions for a particular plan year if his compensation is less than the minimum amount of compensation needed under the plan to accrue a benefit. For example, assume a plan is integrated with Social Security and only those individuals whose compensation exceeds a certain amount accrue benefits under the plan. An individual whose compensation for the plan year ending with or within his taxable year is less than the amount necessary under the plan to accrue a benefit is not an active participant in such plan.

(2) *Rules for plans maintained by more than one employer.*—In the case of a defined benefit plan described in section 413(a) and funded at least in part by service-related contributions, *e.g.*, so many cents-per-hour, an individual is an active participant if an employer is contributing or is required to contribute to the plan an amount based on that individual's service taken into account for the plan year ending with or within the individual's taxable year. The general rule in par agraph (b)(1) of this section applies in the case of plans described in section 413(a) and funded only on some non-service-related unit, *e.g.*, so many cents-per-ton of coal.

(3) *Plans in which accruals for all participants have ceased.*—In the case of a defined benefit plan in which accruals for all participants

have ceased, an individual in such a plan is not an active participant. However, any benefit that may vary with future compensation of an individual provides additional accruals. For example, a plan in which future benefit accruals have ceased, but the actual benefit depends upon final average compensation will not be considered as one in which accruals have ceased.

(4) *No accruals after specified age.*—An individual in a defined benefit plan who accrues no additional benefits in a plan year ending with or within such individual's taxable year by reason of attaining a specified age is not an active participant by reason of his participation in that plan.

(c) *Money purchase plan.*—An individual is an active participant in a money purchase plan if under the terms of the plan employer contributions must be allocated to the individual's account with respect to the plan year ending with or within the individual's taxable year. This rule applies even if an individual is not employed at any time during the individual's taxable year.

(d) *Profit-sharing and stock-bonus plans.*—(1) *In general.*—This paragraph applies to profit-sharing and stock bonus plans. An individual is an active participant in such plans in a taxable year if a forfeiture is allocated to his account as of a date in such taxable year. An individual is also an active participant in a taxable year in such plans if an employer contribution is added to the participant's account in such taxable year. A contribution is added to a participant's account as of the later of the following two dates: the date the contribution is made or the date as of which it is allocated. Thus, if a contribution is made in an individual's taxable year 2 and allocated as of a date in individual's taxable year 1, the later of the relevant dates is the date the contribution is made. Consequently, the individual is an active participant in year 2 but not in year 1 as a result of that contribution.

(2) *Special rule.*—An individual is not an active participant for a particular taxable year by reason of a contribution made in such year allocated to a previous year if such individual was an active participant in such previous year by reason of a prior contribution that was allocated as of a date in such previous year.

(e) *Employee contributions.*—If an employee makes a voluntary or mandatory contribution to a plan described in paragraphs (b), (c), or (d) of this section, such employee is an active participant in the plan for the taxable year in which such contribution is made.

(f) *Certain individuals not active participants.*—For purposes of this section, an individual is not an active participant under a plan for any taxable year of such individual for which such individual elects, pursuant to the plan, not to participate in such plan.

(g) *Retirement savings for married individuals.*—The provisions of this section apply in determining whether an individual or his spouse is an active participant in a plan for purposes of section 220 (relating to retirement savings for certain married individuals).

(h) *Examples.*—The provisions of this section may be illustrated by the following examples:

Example (1). The X Corporation maintains a defined benefit plan which has the following rules on participation and accrual of benefits. Each employee who has attained the age of 25 or has completed one year of service is a participant in the plan. The plan further provides that each participant shall receive upon retirement $12 per month for each year of service in which the employee completes 1,000 hours of service. The plan year is the calendar year. B, a calendar-year taxpayer, enters the plan on January 2, 1980, when he is 27 years of age. Since B has attained the age of 25, he is a participant in the plan. However, B completes less than 1,000 hours of service in 1980 and 1981. Although B is not accruing any benefits under the plan in 1980 and 1981, he is an active participant under section 219(b)(2) because he is a participant in the plan. Thus, B cannot make deductible contributions to an individual retirement arrangement for his taxable years of 1980 and 1981.

Example (2). The Y Corporation maintains a profit-sharing plan for its employees. The plan year of the plan is the calendar year. C is a calendar-year taxpayer and a participant in the plan. On June 30, 1980, the employer makes a contribution for 1980 which is allocated on July 31, 1980. In 1981 the employer makes a second contribution for 1980, allocated as of December 31, 1980. Under the general rule stated in §1.219-2(d)(1), C is an active participant in 1980. Under the special rule stated in §1.219-2(d)(2), however, C is not an active participant in 1981 by reason of that contribution made in 1981.

(i) *Effective date.*—The provisions set forth in this section are effective for taxable years beginning after December 31, 1978. [Reg. §1.219-2.]

☐ [T.D. 7714, 8-7-80.]

[Reg. §1.221-1]

§1.221-1. Deduction for interest paid on qualified education loans after December 31, 2001.—(a) *In general.*—(1) *Applicability.*— Under section 221, an individual taxpayer may deduct from gross income certain interest paid by the taxpayer during the taxable year on a qualified education loan. See paragraph (b)(4) of this section for rules on payments of interest by third parties. The rules of this section are applicable to periods governed by section 221 as amended in 2001, which relates to deductions for interest paid on qualified education loans after December 31, 2001, in taxable years ending after December 31, 2001, and on or before December 31, 2010. For rules applicable to interest due and paid on qualified education loans after January 21, 1999, if paid before January 1, 2002, see §1.221-2. Taxpayers also may apply §1.221-2 to interest due and paid on qualified education loans after December 31, 1997, but before January 21, 1999. To the extent that the effective date limitation (sunset) of the 2001 amendment remains in force unchanged, section 221 before amendment in 2001, to which §1.221-2 relates, also applies to interest due and paid on qualified education loans in taxable years beginning after December 31, 2010.

(2) *Example.*—The following example illustrates the rules of this paragraph (a). In the example, assume that the institution the student attends is an eligible educational institution, the loan is a qualified education loan, the student is legally obligated to make interest payments under the terms of the loan, and any other applicable requirements, if not otherwise specified, are fulfilled. The example is as follows:

Example. Effective dates. Student A begins to make monthly interest payments on her loan beginning January 1, 1997. Student A continues to make interest payments in a timely fashion. However, under the effective date provisions of section 221, no deduction is allowed for interest Student A pays prior to January 1, 1998. Student A may deduct interest due and paid on the loan after December 31, 1997. Student A may apply the rules of §1.221-2 to interest due and paid during the period beginning January 1, 1998, and ending January 20, 1999. Interest due and paid during the period January 21, 1999, and ending December 31, 2001, is deductible under the rules of §1.221-2, and interest paid after December 31, 2001, is deductible under the rules of this section.

(b) *Eligibility.*—(1) *Taxpayer must have a legal obligation to make interest payments.*—A taxpayer is entitled to a deduction under section 221 only if the taxpayer has a legal obligation to make interest payments under the terms of the qualified education loan.

(2) *Claimed dependents not eligible.*—(i) *In general.*—An individual is not entitled to a deduction under section 221 for a taxable year if the individual is a dependent (as defined in section 152) for whom another taxpayer is allowed a deduction under section 151 on a Federal income tax return for the same taxable year (or, in the case of a fiscal year taxpayer, the taxable year beginning in the same calendar year as the individual's taxable year).

(ii) *Examples.*—The following examples illustrate the rules of this paragraph (b)(2):

Example 1. Student not claimed as dependent. Student B pays $750 of interest on qualified education loans during 2003. Student B's parents are not allowed a deduction for her as a dependent for 2003. Assuming fulfillment of all other relevant requirements, Student B may deduct under section 221 the $750 of interest paid in 2003.

Example 2. Student claimed as dependent. Student C pays $750 of interest on qualified education loans during 2003. Only Student C has the legal obligation to make the payments. Student C's parent claims him as a dependent and is allowed a deduction under section 151 with respect to Student C in computing the parent's 2003 Federal income tax. Student C is not entitled to a deduction under section 221 for the $750 of interest paid in 2003. Because Student C's parent was not legally obligated to make the payments, Student C's parent also is not entitled to a deduction for the interest.

(3) *Married taxpayers.*—If a taxpayer is married as of the close of a taxable year, he or she is entitled to a deduction under this section only if the taxpayer and the taxpayer's spouse file a joint return for that taxable year.

(4) *Payments of interest by a third party.*—(i) *In general.*—If a third party who is not legally obligated to make a payment of interest on a qualified education loan makes a payment of interest on behalf of a taxpayer who is legally obligated to make the payment, then the taxpayer is treated as receiving the payment from the third party and, in turn, paying the interest.

(ii) *Examples.*—The following examples illustrate the rules of this paragraph (b)(4):

Example 1. Payment by employer. Student D obtains a qualified education loan to attend college. Upon Student D's graduation from college, Student D works as an intern for a non-profit organization during which time Student D's loan is in deferment and Student D makes no interest payments. As part of the internship program, the non-profit organization makes an interest payment on behalf of Student D after the deferment period. This payment is not excluded from Student D's income under section 108(f) and is treated as additional compensation includible in Student D's gross income. Assuming fulfillment of all other requirements of section 221, Student D may deduct this payment of interest for Federal income tax purposes.

Example 2. Payment by parent. Student E obtains a qualified education loan to attend college. Upon graduation from college, Student E makes legally required monthly payments of principal and interest. Student E's mother makes a required monthly payment of interest as a gift to Student E. A deduction for Student E as a dependent is not allowed on another taxpayer's tax return for that taxable year. Assuming fulfillment of all other requirements of section 221, Student E may deduct this payment of interest for Federal income tax purposes.

(c) *Maximum deduction.*—The amount allowed as a deduction under section 221 for any taxable year may not exceed $2,500.

(d) *Limitation based on modified adjusted gross income.*—(1) *In general.*—The deduction allowed under section 221 is phased out ratably for taxpayers with modified adjusted gross income between $50,000 and $65,000 ($100,000 and $130,000 for married individuals who file a joint return). Section 221 does not allow a deduction for taxpayers with modified adjusted gross income of $65,000 or above ($130,000 or above for married individuals who file a joint return). See paragraph (d)(3) of this section for inflation adjustment of amounts in this paragraph (d)(1).

(2) *Modified adjusted gross income defined.*—The term *modified adjusted gross income* means the adjusted gross income (as defined in section 62) of the taxpayer for the taxable year increased by any amount excluded from gross income under section 911, 931, or 933 (relating to income earned abroad or from certain United States possessions or Puerto Rico). Modified adjusted gross income must be determined under this section after taking into account the inclusions, exclusions, deductions, and limitations provided by sections 86 (social security and tier 1 railroad retirement benefits), 135 (redemption of qualified United States savings bonds), 137 (adoption assistance programs), 219 (deductible qualified retirement contributions), and 469 (limitation on passive activity losses and credits), but before taking into account the deductions provided by sections 221 and 222 (qualified tuition and related expenses).

(3) *Inflation adjustment.*—For taxable years beginning after 2002, the amounts in paragraph (d)(1) of this section will be increased for inflation occurring after 2001 in accordance with section 221(f)(1). If any amount adjusted under section 221(f)(1) is not a multiple of $5,000, the amount will be rounded to the next lowest multiple of $5,000.

(e) *Definitions.*—(1) *Eligible educational institution.*—In general, an *eligible educational institution* means any college, university, vocational school, or other postsecondary educational institution described in section 481 of the Higher Education Act of 1965 (20 U.S.C. 1088), as in effect on August 5, 1997, and certified by the U.S. Department of Education as eligible to participate in student aid programs administered by the Department, as described in section 25A(f)(2) and §1.25A-2(b). For purposes of this section, an eligible educational institution also includes an institution that conducts an internship or residency program leading to a degree or certificate awarded by an institution, a hospital, or a health care facility that offers postgraduate training.

(2) *Qualified higher education expenses.*—(i) *In general.*—Qualified *higher education expenses* means the cost of attendance (as defined in section 472 of the Higher Education Act of 1965, 20 U.S.C. 1087ll, as in effect on August 4, 1997), at an eligible educational institution, reduced by the amounts described in paragraph (e)(2)(ii) of this section. Consistent with section 472 of the Higher Education Act of 1965, a student's cost of attendance is determined by the eligible educational institution and includes tuition and fees normally assessed a student carrying the same academic workload as the student, an allowance for room and board, and an allowance for books, supplies, transportation, and miscellaneous expenses of the student.

(ii) *Reductions.*—Qualified higher education expenses are reduced by any amount that is paid to or on behalf of a student with respect to such expenses and that is—

(A) A qualified scholarship that is excludable from income under section 117;

(B) An educational assistance allowance for a veteran or member of the armed forces under chapter 30, 31, 32, 34 or 35 of title 38, United States Code, or under chapter 1606 of title 10, United States Code;

(C) Employer-provided educational assistance that is excludable from income under section 127;

(D) Any other amount that is described in section 25A(g)(2)(C) (relating to amounts excludable from gross income as educational assistance);

(E) Any otherwise includible amount excluded from gross income under section 135 (relating to the redemption of United States savings bonds);

(F) Any otherwise includible amount distributed from a Coverdell education savings account and excluded from gross income under section 530(d)(2); or

(G) Any otherwise includible amount distributed from a qualified tuition program and excluded from gross income under section 529(c)(3)(B).

(3) *Qualified education loan.*—(i) *In general.*—A *qualified education loan* means indebtedness incurred by a taxpayer solely to pay qualified higher education expenses that are—

(A) Incurred on behalf of a student who is the taxpayer, the taxpayer's spouse, or a dependent (as defined in section 152) of the taxpayer at the time the taxpayer incurs the indebtedness;

(B) Attributable to education provided during an academic period, as described in section 25A and the regulations thereunder, when the student is an eligible student as defined in section 25A(b)(3) (requiring that the student be a degree candidate carrying at least half the normal full-time workload); and

(C) Paid or incurred within a reasonable period of time before or after the taxpayer incurs the indebtedness.

(ii) *Reasonable period.*—Except as otherwise provided in this paragraph (e)(3)(ii), what constitutes a reasonable period of time for purposes of paragraph (e)(3)(i)(C) of this section generally is determined based on all the relevant facts and circumstances. However, qualified higher education expenses are treated as paid or incurred within a reasonable period of time before or after the taxpayer incurs the indebtedness if—

(A) The expenses are paid with the proceeds of education loans that are part of a Federal postsecondary education loan program; or

(B) The expenses relate to a particular academic period and the loan proceeds used to pay the expenses are disbursed within a period that begins 90 days prior to the start of that academic period and ends 90 days after the end of that academic period.

(iii) *Related party.*—A qualified education loan does not include any indebtedness owed to a person who is related to the taxpayer, within the meaning of section 267(b) or 707(b)(1). For example, a parent or grandparent of the taxpayer is a related person. In addition, a qualified education loan does not include a loan made under any qualified employer plan as defined in section 72(p)(4) or under any contract referred to in section 72(p)(5).

(iv) *Federal issuance or guarantee not required.*—A loan does not have to be issued or guaranteed under a Federal postsecondary education loan program to be a qualified education loan.

(v) *Refinanced and consolidated indebtedness.*—(A) *In general.*—A qualified education loan includes indebtedness incurred solely to refinance a qualified education loan. A qualified education loan includes a single, consolidated indebtedness incurred solely to refinance two or more qualified education loans of a borrower.

(B) *Treatment of refinanced and consolidated indebtedness.*—[Reserved.]

(4) *Examples.*—The following examples illustrate the rules of this paragraph (e):

Example 1. Eligible educational institution. University F is a postsecondary educational institution described in section 481 of the Higher Education Act of 1965. The U.S. Department of Education has certified that University F is eligible to participate in federal financial aid programs administered by that Department, although University F chooses not to participate. University F is an eligible educational institution.

Example 2. Qualified higher education expenses. Student G receives a $3,000 qualified scholarship for the 2003 fall semester that is excludable from Student G's gross income under section 117. Student G receives no other forms of financial assistance with respect to the 2003 fall semester. Student G's cost of attendance for the 2003 fall semester, as determined by Student G's eligible educational institution for purposes of calculating a student's financial need in accordance with section 472 of the Higher Education Act, is $16,000. For

the 2003 fall semester, Student G has qualified higher education expenses of $13,000 (the cost of attendance as determined by the institution ($16,000) reduced by the qualified scholarship proceeds excludable from gross income ($3,000)).

Example 3. Qualified education loan. Student H borrows money from a commercial bank to pay qualified higher education expenses related to his enrollment on a half-time basis in a graduate program at an eligible educational institution. Student H uses all the loan proceeds to pay qualified higher education expenses incurred within a reasonable period of time after incurring the indebtedness. The loan is not federally guaranteed. The commercial bank is not related to Student H within the meaning of section 267(b) or 707(b)(1). Student H's loan is a qualified education loan within the meaning of section 221.

Example 4. Qualified education loan. Student I signs a promissory note for a loan on August 15, 2003, to pay for qualified higher education expenses for the 2003 fall and 2004 spring semesters. On August 20, 2003, the lender disburses loan proceeds to Student I's college. The college credits them to Student I's account to pay qualified higher education expenses for the 2003 fall semester, which begins on August 25, 2003. On January 26, 2004, the lender disburses additional loan proceeds to Student I's college. The college credits them to Student I's account to pay qualified higher education expenses for the 2004 spring semester, which began on January 12, 2004. Student I's qualified higher education expenses for the two semesters are paid within a reasonable period of time, as the first loan disbursement occurred within the 90 days prior to the start of the fall 2003 semester and the second loan disbursement occurred during the spring 2004 semester.

Example 5. Qualified education loan. The facts are the same as in *Example 4* except that in 2005 the college is not an eligible educational institution because it loses its eligibility to participate in certain federal financial aid programs administered by the U.S. Department of Education. The qualification of Student I's loan, which was used to pay for qualified higher education expenses for the 2003 fall and 2004 spring semesters, as a qualified education loan is not affected by the college's subsequent loss of eligibility.

Example 6. Mixed-use loans. Student J signs a promissory note for a loan secured by Student J's personal residence. Student J will use part of the loan proceeds to pay for certain improvements to Student J's residence and part of the loan proceeds to pay qualified higher education expenses of Student J's spouse. Because Student J obtains the loan not solely to pay qualified higher education expenses, the loan is not a qualified education loan.

(f) *Interest.*—(1) *In general.*—Amounts paid on a qualified education loan are deductible under section 221 if the amounts are interest for Federal income tax purposes. For example, interest includes—

(i) Qualified stated interest (as defined in § 1.1273-1(c)); and

(ii) Original issue discount, which generally includes capitalized interest. For purposes of section 221, capitalized interest means any accrued and unpaid interest on a qualified education loan that, in accordance with the terms of the loan, is added by the lender to the outstanding principal balance of the loan.

(2) *Operative rules for original issue discount.*—(i) *In general.*—The rules to determine the amount of original issue discount on a loan and the accruals of the discount are in sections 163(e), 1271 through 1275, and the regulations thereunder. In general, original issue discount is the excess of a loan's stated redemption price at maturity (all payments due under the loan other than qualified stated interest payments) over its issue price (the amount loaned). Although original issue discount generally is deductible as it accrues under section 163(e) and § 1.163-7, original issue discount on a qualified education loan is not deductible until paid. See paragraph (f)(3) of this section to determine when original issue discount is paid.

(ii) *Treatment of loan origination fees by the borrower.*—If a loan origination fee is paid by the borrower other than for property or services provided by the lender, the fee reduces the issue price of the loan, which creates original issue discount (or additional original issue discount) on the loan in an amount equal to the fee. See § 1.1273-2(g). For an example of how a loan origination fee is taken into account, see *Example 2* of paragraph (f)(4) of this section.

(3) *Allocation of payments.*—See § § 1.446-2(e) and 1.1275-2(a) for rules on allocating payments between interest and principal. In general, these rules treat a payment first as a payment of interest to the extent of the interest that has accrued and remains unpaid as of the date the payment is due, and second as a payment of principal. The characterization of a payment as either interest or principal under these rules applies regardless of how the parties label the payment (either as interest or principal). Accordingly, the taxpayer may deduct the portion of a payment labeled as principal that these rules treat as a payment of interest on the loan, including any portion attributable to capitalized interest or loan origination fees.

(4) *Examples.*—The following examples illustrate the rules of this paragraph (f). In the examples, assume that the institution the student attends is an eligible educational institution, the loan is a qualified education loan, the student is legally obligated to make interest payments under the terms of the loan, and any other applicable requirements, if not otherwise specified, are fulfilled. The examples are as follows:

Example 1. Capitalized interest. Interest on Student K's loan accrues while Student K is in school, but Student K is not required to make any payments on the loan until six months after he graduates or otherwise leaves school. At that time, the lender capitalizes all accrued but unpaid interest and adds it to the outstanding principal amount of the loan. Thereafter, Student K is required to make monthly payments of interest and principal on the loan. The interest payable on the loan, including the capitalized interest, is original issue discount. See section 1273 and the regulations thereunder. Therefore, in determining the total amount of interest paid on the loan each taxable year, Student K may deduct any payments that §1.1275-2(a) treats as payments of interest, including any principal payments that are treated as payments of capitalized interest. See paragraph (f)(3) of this section.

Example 2. Allocation of payments. The facts are the same as in *Example 1*, except that, in addition, the lender charges Student K a loan origination fee, which is not for any property or services provided by the lender. Under §1.1273-2(g), the loan origination fee reduces the issue price of the loan, which reduction increases the amount of original issue discount on the loan by the amount of the fee. The amount of original issue discount (which includes the capitalized interest and loan origination fee) that accrues each year is determined under section 1272 and §1.1272-1. In effect, the loan origination fee accrues over the entire term of the loan. Because the loan has original issue discount, the payment ordering rules in §1.1275-2(a) must be used to determine how much of each payment is interest for federal tax purposes. See paragraph (f)(3) of this section. Under §1.1275-2(a), each payment (regardless of its designation by the parties as either interest or principal) generally is treated first as a payment of original issue discount, to the extent of the original issue discount that has accrued as of the date the payment is due and has not been allocated to prior payments, and second as a payment of principal. Therefore, in determining the total amount of interest paid on the qualified education loan for a taxable year, Student K may deduct any payments that the parties label as principal but that are treated as payments of original issue discount under §1.1275-2(a).

(g) *Additional rules.*—(1) *Payment of interest made during period when interest payment not required.*—Payments of interest on a qualified education loan to which this section is applicable are deductible even if the payments are made during a period when interest payments are not required because, for example, the loan has not yet entered repayment status or is in a period of deferment or forbearance.

(2) *Denial of double benefit.*—No deduction is allowed under this section for any amount for which a deduction is allowable under another provision of Chapter 1 of the Internal Revenue Code. No deduction is allowed under this section for any amount for which an exclusion is allowable under section 108(f) (relating to cancellation of indebtedness).

(3) *Examples.*—The following examples illustrate the rules of this paragraph (g). In the examples, assume that the institution the student attends is an eligible educational institution, the loan is a qualified education loan, and the student is legally obligated to make interest payments under the terms of the loan:

Example 1. Voluntary payment of interest before loan has entered repayment status. Student L obtains a loan to attend college. The terms of the loan provide that interest accrues on the loan while Student L earns his undergraduate degree but that Student L is not required to begin making payments of interest until six full calendar months after he graduates or otherwise leaves school. Nevertheless, Student L voluntarily pays interest on the loan during 2003, while enrolled in college. Assuming all other relevant requirements are met, Student L is allowed a deduction for interest paid while attending college even though the payments were made before interest payments were required.

Example 2. Voluntary payment during period of deferment or forbearance. The facts are the same as in *Example 2*, except that Student L makes no payments on the loan while enrolled in college. Student L graduates in June 2003 and begins making monthly payments of principal and interest on the loan in January 2004, as required by the terms of the loan. In August 2004, Student L enrolls in graduate school on a fulltime basis. Under the terms of the loan, Student L may apply for deferment of the loan payments while Student L is enrolled in graduate school. Student L applies for and receives a deferment on the outstanding loan. However, Student L continues to make some monthly payments of interest during graduate school.

Student L may deduct interest paid on the loan during the period beginning in January 2004, including interest paid while Student L is enrolled in graduate school.

(h) *Effective date.*—This section is applicable to periods governed by section 221 as amended in 2001, which relates to interest paid on a qualified education loan after December 31, 2001, in taxable years ending after December 31, 2001, and on or before December 31, 2010. [Reg. §1.221-1.]

☐ [T.D. 9125, 5-6-2004.]

[Reg. §1.221-2]

§1.221-2. Deduction for interest due and paid on qualified education loans before January 1, 2002.—(a) *In general.*—Under section 221, an individual taxpayer may deduct from gross income certain interest due and paid by the taxpayer during the taxable year on a qualified education loan. The deduction is allowed only with respect to interest due and paid on a qualified education loan during the first 60 months that interest payments are required under the terms of the loan. See paragraph (e) of this section for rules relating to the 60-month rule. See paragraph (b)(4) of this section for rules on payments of interest by third parties. The rules of this section are applicable to interest due and paid on qualified education loans after January 21, 1999, if paid before January 1, 2002. Taxpayers also may apply the rules of this section to interest due and paid on qualified education loans after December 31, 1997, but before January 21, 1999. To the extent that the effective date limitation ("sunset") of the 2001 amendment remains in force unchanged, section 221 before amendment in 2001, to which this section relates, also applies to interest due and paid on qualified education loans in taxable years beginning after December 31, 2010. For rules applicable to periods governed by section 221 as amended in 2001, which relates to deductions for interest paid on qualified education loans after December 31, 2001, in taxable years ending after December 31, 2001, and before January 1, 2011, see §1.221-1.

(b) *Eligibility.*—(1) *Taxpayer must have a legal obligation to make interest payments.*—A taxpayer is entitled to a deduction under section 221 only if the taxpayer has a legal obligation to make interest payments under the terms of the qualified education loan.

(2) *Claimed dependents not eligible.*—(i) *In general.*—An individual is not entitled to a deduction under section 221 for a taxable year if the individual is a dependent (as defined in section 152) for whom another taxpayer is allowed a deduction under section 151 on a Federal income tax return for the same taxable year (or, in the case of a fiscal year taxpayer, the taxable year beginning in the same calendar year as the individual's taxable year).

(ii) *Examples.*—The following examples illustrate the rules of this paragraph (b)(2):

Example 1. Student not claimed as dependent. Student A pays $750 of interest on qualified education loans during 1998. Student A's parents are not allowed a deduction for her as a dependent for 1998. Assuming fulfillment of all other relevant requirements, Student A may deduct the $750 of interest paid in 1998 under section 221.

Example 2. Student claimed as dependent. Student B pays $750 of interest on qualified education loans during 1998. Only Student B has the legal obligation to make the payments. Student B's parent claims him as a dependent and is allowed a deduction under section 151 with respect to Student B in computing the parent's 1998 Federal income tax. Student B may not deduct the $750 of interest paid in 1998 under section 221. Because Student B's parent was not legally obligated to make the payments, Student B's parent also may not deduct the interest.

(3) *Married taxpayers.*—If a taxpayer is married as of the close of a taxable year, he or she is entitled to a deduction under this section only if the taxpayer and the taxpayer's spouse file a joint return for that taxable year.

(4) *Payments of interest by a third party.*—(i) *In general.*—If a third party who is not legally obligated to make a payment of interest on a qualified education loan makes a payment of interest on behalf of a taxpayer who is legally obligated to make the payment, then the taxpayer is treated as receiving the payment from the third party and, in turn, paying the interest.

(ii) *Examples.*—The following examples illustrate the rules of this paragraph (b)(4):

Example 1. Payment by employer. Student C obtains a qualified education loan to attend college. Upon Student C's graduation from college, Student C works as an intern for a non-profit organization during which time Student C's loan is in deferment and Student C makes no interest payments. As part of the internship program, the non-profit organization makes an interest payment on behalf of Student C after the deferment period. This payment is not excluded from Student C's income under section 108(f) and is treated as additional compensation includible in Student C's gross income. Assuming fulfillment of all other requirements of section 221, Student C may deduct this payment of interest for Federal income tax purposes.

Example 2. Payment by parent. Student D obtains a qualified education loan to attend college. Upon graduation from college, Student D makes legally required monthly payments of principal and interest. Student D's mother makes a required monthly payment of interest as a gift to Student D. A deduction for Student D as a dependent is not allowed on another taxpayer's tax return for that taxable year. Assuming fulfillment of all other requirements of section 221, Student D may deduct this payment of interest for Federal income tax purposes.

(c) Maximum deduction.—In any taxable year beginning before January 1, 2002, the amount allowed as a deduction under section 221 may not exceed the amount determined in accordance with the following table:

Taxable Year Beginning in	Maximum Deduction
1998	$1,000
1999	$1,500
2000	$2,000
2001	$2,500

(d) Limitation based on modified adjusted gross income.—(1) In general.—The deduction allowed under section 221 is phased out ratably for taxpayers with modified adjusted gross income between $40,000 and $55,000 ($60,000 and $75,000 for married individuals who file a joint return). Section 221 does not allow a deduction for taxpayers with modified adjusted gross income of $55,000 or above ($75,000 or above for married individuals who file a joint return).

(2) Modified adjusted gross income defined.—The term modified adjusted gross income means the adjusted gross income (as defined in section 62) of the taxpayer for the taxable year increased by any amount excluded from gross income under section 911, 931, or 933 (relating to income earned abroad or from certain United States possessions or Puerto Rico). Modified adjusted gross income must be determined under this section after taking into account the inclusions, exclusions, deductions, and limitations provided by sections 86 (social security and tier 1 railroad retirement benefits), 135 (redemption of qualified United States savings bonds), 137 (adoption assistance programs), 219 (deductible qualified retirement contributions), and 469 (limitation on passive activity losses and credits), but before taking into account the deduction provided by section 221.

(e) 60-month rule.—(1) In general.—A deduction for interest paid on a qualified education loan is allowed only for payments made during the first 60 months that interest payments are required on the loan. The 60-month period begins on the first day of the month that includes the date on which interest payments are first required and ends 60 months later, unless the 60-month period is suspended for periods of deferment or forbearance within the meaning of paragraph (e)(3) of this section. The 60-month period continues to run regardless of whether the required interest payments are actually made. The date on which the first interest payment is required is determined under the terms of the loan agreement or, in the case of a loan issued or guaranteed under a federal postsecondary education loan program (such as loan programs under Title IV of the Higher Education Act of 1965 (20 U.S.C. 1070) and Titles VII and VIII of the Public Health Service Act (42 U.S.C. 292., and 42 U.S.C. 296)) under applicable Federal regulations. For a discussion of interest, see paragraph (h) of this section. For special rules relating to loan refinancings, consolidated loans, and collapsed loans, see paragraph (i) of this section.

(2) Loans that entered repayment status prior to January 1, 1998.—In the case of any qualified education loan that entered repayment status prior to January 1, 1998, section 221 allows no deduction for interest paid during the portion of the 60-month period described in paragraph (e)(1) of this section that occurred prior to January 1, 1998. Section 221 allows a deduction only for interest due and paid during that portion, if any, of the 60-month period remaining after December 31, 1997.

(3) Periods of deferment or forbearance.—The 60-month period described in paragraph (e)(1) of this section generally is suspended for any period when interest payments are not required on a qualified education loan because the lender has granted the taxpayer a period of deferment or forbearance (including postponement in anticipation of cancellation). However, in the case of a qualified education loan that is not issued or guaranteed under a Federal postsecondary education loan program, the 60-month period will be suspended under this paragraph (e)(3) only if the promissory note contains conditions substantially similar to the conditions for deferment or

forbearance established by the U.S. Department of Education for Federal student loan programs under Title IV of the Higher Education Act of 1965, such as half-time study at a postsecondary educational institution, study in an approved graduate fellowship program or in an approved rehabilitation program for the disabled, inability to find full-time employment, economic hardship, or the performance of services in certain occupations or federal programs, and the borrower satisfies one of those conditions. For any qualified education loan, the 60-month period is not suspended if under the terms of the loan interest continues to accrue while the loan is in deferment or forbearance and either—

(i) In the case of deferment, the taxpayer agrees to pay interest currently during the deferment period; or

(ii) In the case of forbearance, the taxpayer agrees to make reduced payments, or payments of interest only, during the forbearance period.

(4) Late payments.—A deduction is allowed for a payment of interest required in one month but actually made in a subsequent month prior to the expiration of the 60-month period. A deduction is not allowed for a payment of interest required in one month but actually made in a subsequent month after the expiration of the 60-month period. A late payment made during a period of deferment or forbearance is treated, solely for purposes of determining whether it is made during the 60-month period, as made on the date it is due.

(5) Examples.—The following examples illustrate the rules of this paragraph (e). In the examples, assume that the institution the student attends is an eligible educational institution, the loan is a qualified education loan and is issued or guaranteed under a federal postsecondary education loan program, the student is legally obligated to make interest payments under the terms of the loan, the interest payments occur after December 31, 1997, but before January 1, 2002, and with respect to any period after December 31, 1997, but before January 21, 1999, the taxpayer elects to apply the rules of this section. The examples are as follows:

Example 1. Payment prior to 60-month period. Student E obtains a loan to attend college. The terms of the loan provide that interest accrues on the loan while Student E earns his undergraduate degree but that Student E is not required to begin making payments of interest until six full calendar months after he graduates. Nevertheless, Student E voluntarily pays interest on the loan while attending college. Student E is not allowed a deduction for interest paid during that period, because those payments were made prior to the start of the 60-month period. Similarly, Student E would not be allowed a deduction for any interest paid during the six month grace period after graduation when interest payments are not required.

Example 2. Deferment option not exercised. The facts are the same as in Example 1 except that Student E makes no payments on the loan while enrolled in college. Student E graduates in June 1999, and is required to begin making monthly payments of principal and interest on the loan in January 2000. The 60-month period described in paragraph (e)(1) of this section begins in January 2000. In August 2000, Student E enrolls in graduate school on a full-time basis. Under the terms of the loan, Student E may apply for deferment of the loan payments while enrolled in graduate school. However, Student E elects not to apply for deferment and continues to make required monthly payments on the loan during graduate school. Assuming fulfillment of all other relevant requirements, Student E may deduct interest paid on the loan during the 60-month period beginning in January 2000, including interest paid while enrolled in graduate school.

Example 3. Late payment, within 60-month period. The facts are the same as in Example 2 except that, after the loan enters repayment status in January 2000, Student E makes no interest payments until March 2000. In March 2000, Student E pays interest required for the months of January, February, and March 2000. Assuming fulfillment of all other relevant requirements, Student E may deduct the interest paid in March for the months of January, February, and March because the interest payments are required under the terms of the loan and are paid within the 60-month period, even though the January and February interest payments may be late.

Example 4. Late payment during deferment but within 60-month period. The terms of Student F's loan require her to begin making monthly payments of interest on the loan in January 2000. The 60-month period described in paragraph (e)(1) of this section begins in January 2000. Student F fails to make the required interest payments for the months of November and December 2000. In January 2001, Student F enrolls in graduate school on a half-time basis. Under the terms of the loan, Student F obtains a deferment of the loan payments due while enrolled in graduate school. The deferment becomes effective January 1, 2001. In March 2001, while the loan is in deferment, Student F pays the interest due for the months of November and December 2000. Assuming fulfillment of all other relevant requirements, Student F may deduct interest paid in March 2001, for the months of November and December 2000, because the late interest payments are treated, solely for purposes of determining whether they were made during the 60-month period, as made in November and December 2000.

Example 5. 60-month period. The terms of Student G's loan require him to begin making monthly payments of interest on the loan in November 1999. The 60-month period described in paragraph (e)(1) of this section begins in November 1999. In January 2000, Student G enrolls in graduate school on a half-time basis. As permitted under the terms of the loan, Student G applies for deferment of the loan payments due while enrolled in graduate school. While awaiting formal approval from the lender of his request for deferment, Student G pays interest due for the month of January 2000. In February 2000, the lender approves Student G's request for deferment, effective as of January 1, 2000. Assuming fulfillment of all other relevant requirements, Student G may deduct interest paid in January 2000, prior to his receipt of the lender's approval, even though the deferment was retroactive to January 1, 2000. As of February 2000, there are 57 months remaining in the 60-month period for that loan. Because Student G is not required to make interest payments during the period of deferment, the 60-month period is suspended. After January 2000, Student G may not deduct any voluntary payments of interest made during the period of deferment.

Example 6. 60-month period. The terms of Student H's loan require her to begin making monthly payments of interest on the loan in November 1999. The 60-month period described in paragraph (e)(1) of this section begins in November 1999. In January 2000, Student H enrolls in graduate school on a half-time basis. As permitted under the terms of the loan, Student H applies to make reduced payments of principal and interest while enrolled in graduate school. After the lender approves her application, Student H pays principal and interest due for the month of January 2000 at the reduced rate. Assuming fulfillment of all other relevant requirements, Student H may deduct interest paid in January 2000. As of February 2000, there are 57 months remaining in the 60-month period for that loan.

Example 7. Reduction of 60-month period for months prior to January 1, 1998. The first payment of interest on a loan is due in January 1997. Thereafter, interest payments are required on a monthly basis. The 60-month period described in paragraph (e)(1) of this section for this loan begins on January 1, 1997, the first day of the month that includes the date on which the first interest payment is required. However, the borrower may not deduct interest paid prior to January 1, 1998, under the effective date provisions of section 221. Assuming fulfillment of all other relevant requirements, the borrower may deduct interest due and paid on the loan during the 48 months beginning on January 1, 1998 (unless such period is extended for periods of deferment or forbearance under paragraph (e)(3) of this section).

(f) *Definitions.*—(1) *Eligible educational institution.*—In general, an *eligible educational institution* means any college, university, vocational school, or other post-secondary educational institution described in section 481 of the Higher Education Act of 1965, 20 U.S.C. 1088, as in effect on August 5, 1997, and certified by the U.S. Department of Education as eligible to participate in student aid programs administered by the Department, as described in section 25A(f)(2) and § 1.25A-2(b). For purposes of this section, an eligible educational institution also includes an institution that conducts an internship or residency program leading to a degree or certificate awarded by an institution, a hospital, or a health care facility that offers postgraduate training.

(2) *Qualified higher education expenses.*—(i) *In general.*—*Qualified higher education expenses* means the cost of attendance (as defined in section 472 of the Higher Education Act of 1965, 20 U.S.C. 1087ll, as in effect on August 4, 1997), at an eligible educational institution, reduced by the amounts described in paragraph (f)(2)(ii) of this section. Consistent with section 472 of the Higher Education Act of 1965, a student's cost of attendance is determined by the eligible educational institution and includes tuition and fees normally assessed a student carrying the same academic workload as the student, an allowance for room and board, and an allowance for books, supplies, transportation, and miscellaneous expenses of the student.

(ii) *Reductions.*—Qualified higher education expenses are reduced by any amount that is paid to or on behalf of a student with respect to such expenses and that is—

(A) A qualified scholarship that is excludable from income under section 117;

(B) An educational assistance allowance for a veteran or member of the armed forces under chapter 30, 31, 32, 34 or 35 of title 38, United States Code, or under chapter 1606 of title 10, United States Code;

(C) Employer-provided educational assistance that is excludable from income under section 127;

(D) Any other amount that is described in section 25A(g)(2)(C) (relating to amounts excludable from gross income as educational assistance);

(E) Any otherwise includible amount excluded from gross income under section 135 (relating to the redemption of United States savings bonds); or

(F) Any otherwise includible amount distributed from a Coverdell education savings account and excluded from gross income under section 530(d)(2).

(3) *Qualified education loan.*—(i) *In general.*—A *qualified education loan* means indebtedness incurred by a taxpayer solely to pay qualified higher education expenses that are—

(A) Incurred on behalf of a student who is the taxpayer, the taxpayer's spouse, or a dependent (as defined in section 152) of the taxpayer at the time the taxpayer incurs the indebtedness;

(B) Attributable to education provided during an academic period, as described in section 25A and the regulations thereunder, when the student is an eligible student as defined in section 25A(b)(3) (requiring that the student be a degree candidate carrying at least half the normal full-time workload); and

(C) Paid or incurred within a reasonable period of time before or after the taxpayer incurs the indebtedness.

(ii) *Reasonable period.*—Except as otherwise provided in this paragraph (f)(3)(ii), what constitutes a reasonable period of time for purposes of paragraph (f)(3)(i)(C) of this section generally is determined based on all the relevant facts and circumstances. However, qualified higher education expenses are treated as paid or incurred within a reasonable period of time before or after the taxpayer incurs the indebtedness if—

(A) The expenses are paid with the proceeds of education loans that are part of a federal postsecondary education loan program; or

(B) The expenses relate to a particular academic period and the loan proceeds used to pay the expenses are disbursed within a period that begins 90 days prior to the start of that academic period and ends 90 days after the end of that academic period.

(iii) *Related party.*—A qualified education loan does not include any indebtedness owed to a person who is related to the taxpayer, within the meaning of section 267(b) or 707(b)(1). For example, a parent or grandparent of the taxpayer is a related person. In addition, a qualified education loan does not include a loan made under any qualified employer plan as defined in section 72(p)(4) or under any contract referred to in section 72(p)(5).

(iv) *Federal issuance or guarantee not required.*—A loan does not have to be issued or guaranteed under a federal postsecondary education loan program to be a qualified education loan.

(v) *Refinanced and consolidated indebtedness.*—(A) *In general.*—A qualified education loan includes indebtedness incurred solely to refinance a qualified education loan. A qualified education loan includes a single, consolidated indebtedness incurred solely to refinance two or more qualified education loans of a borrower.

(B) *Treatment of refinanced and consolidated indebtedness.*—[Reserved.]

(4) *Examples.*—The following examples illustrate the rules of this paragraph (f):

Example 1. Eligible educational institution. University J is a postsecondary educational institution described in section 481 of the Higher Education Act of 1965. The U.S. Department of Education has certified that University J is eligible to participate in federal financial aid programs administered by that Department, although University J chooses not to participate. University J is an eligible educational institution.

Example 2. Qualified higher education expenses. Student K receives a $3,000 qualified scholarship for the 1999 fall semester that is excludable from Student K's gross income under section 117. Student K receives no other forms of financial assistance with respect to the 1999 fall semester. Student K's cost of attendance for the 1999 fall semester, as determined by Student K's eligible educational institution for purposes of calculating a student's financial need in accordance with section 472 of the Higher Education Act, is $16,000. For the 1999 fall semester, Student K has qualified higher education expenses of $13,000 (the cost of attendance as determined by the institution ($16,000) reduced by the qualified scholarship proceeds excludable from gross income ($3,000)).

Example 3. Qualified education loan. Student L borrows money from a commercial bank to pay qualified higher education expenses related to his enrollment on a half-time basis in a graduate program at an eligible educational institution. Student L uses all the loan proceeds to pay qualified higher education expenses incurred within a reasonable period of time after incurring the indebtedness. The loan is not federally guaranteed. The commercial bank is not related to Student L within the meaning of section 267(b) or 707(b)(1). Student L's loan is a qualified education loan within the meaning of section 221.

Example 4. Qualified education loan. Student M signs a promissory note for a loan on August 15, 1999, to pay for qualified higher education expenses for the 1999 fall and 2000 spring semesters. On August 20, 1999, the lender disburses loan proceeds to Student M's college. The college credits them to Student M's account to pay qualified higher education expenses for the 1999 fall semester, which begins on August 23, 1999. On January 25, 2000, the lender disburses additional loan proceeds to Student M's college. The college credits them to Student M's account to pay qualified higher education expenses for the 2000 spring semester, which began on January 10, 2000. Student M's qualified higher education expenses for the two semesters are paid within a reasonable period of time, as the first loan disbursement occurred within the 90 days prior to the start of the fall 1999 semester, and the second loan disbursement occurred during the spring 2000 semester.

Example 5. Qualified education loan. The facts are the same as in *Example 4,* except that in 2001 the college is not an eligible educational institution because it loses its eligibility to participate in certain federal financial aid programs administered by the U.S. Department of Education. The qualification of Student M's loan, which was used to pay for qualified higher education expenses for the 1999 fall and 2000 spring semesters, as a qualified education loan is not affected by the college's subsequent loss of eligibility.

Example 6. Mixed-use loans. Student N signs a promissory note for a loan that is secured by Student N's personal residence. Student N will use part of the loan proceeds to pay for certain improvements to Student N's residence and part of the loan proceeds to pay qualified higher education expenses of Student N's spouse. Because Student N obtains the loan not solely to pay qualified higher education expenses, the loan is not a qualified education loan.

(g) *Denial of double benefit.*—No deduction is allowed under this section for any amount for which a deduction is allowable under another provision of Chapter 1 of the Internal Revenue Code. No deduction is allowed under this section for any amount for which an exclusion is allowable under section 108(f) (relating to cancellation of indebtedness).

(h) *Interest.*—(1) *In general.*—Amounts paid on a qualified education loan are deductible under section 221 if the amounts are interest for Federal income tax purposes. For example, interest includes—

(i) Qualified stated interest (as defined in § 1.1273-1(c)); and

(ii) Original issue discount, which generally includes capitalized interest. For purposes of section 221, capitalized interest means any accrued and unpaid interest on a qualified education loan that, in accordance with the terms of the loan, is added by the lender to the outstanding principal balance of the loan.

(2) *Operative rules for original issue discount.*—(i) *In general.*—The rules to determine the amount of original issue discount on a loan and the accruals of the discount are in sections 163(e), 1271 through 1275, and the regulations thereunder. In general, original issue discount is the excess of a loan's stated redemption price at maturity (all payments due under the loan other than qualified stated interest payments) over its issue price (the amount loaned). Although original issue discount generally is deductible as it accrues under section 163(e) and § 1.163-7, original issue discount on a qualified education loan is not deductible until paid. See paragraph (h)(3) of this section to determine when original issue discount is paid.

(ii) *Treatment of loan origination fees by the borrower.*—If a loan origination fee is paid by the borrower other than for property or services provided by the lender, the fee reduces the issue price of the loan, which creates original issue discount (or additional original issue discount) on the loan in an amount equal to the fee. See § 1.1273-2(g). For an example of how a loan origination fee is taken into account, see *Example 2* of paragraph (h)(4) of this section.

(3) *Allocation of payments.*—See § § 1.446-2(e) and 1.1275-2(a) for rules on allocating payments between interest and principal. In general, these rules treat a payment first as a payment of interest to the extent of the interest that has accrued and remains unpaid as of the date the payment is due, and second as a payment of principal. The characterization of a payment as either interest or principal under these rules applies regardless of how the parties label the payment (either as interest or principal). Accordingly, the taxpayer may deduct the portion of a payment labeled as principal that these rules treat as a payment of interest on the loan, including any portion *attributable to capitalized interest or loan origination fees.*

(4) *Examples.*—The following examples illustrate the rules of this paragraph (h). In the examples, assume that the institution the student attends is an eligible educational institution, the loan is a

qualified education loan, the student is legally obligated to make interest payments under the terms of the loan, and any other applicable requirements, if not otherwise specified, are fulfilled. The examples are as follows:

Example 1. Capitalized interest. Interest on Student O's qualified education loan accrues while Student O is in school, but Student O is not required to make any payments on the loan until six months after he graduates or otherwise leaves school. At that time, the lender capitalizes all accrued but unpaid interest and adds it to the outstanding principal amount of the loan. Thereafter, Student O is required to make monthly payments of interest and principal on the loan. The interest payable on the loan, including the capitalized interest, is original issue discount. Therefore, in determining the total amount of interest paid on the qualified education loan during the 60-month period described in paragraph (e)(1) of this section, Student O may deduct any payments that § 1.1275-2(a) treats as payments of interest, including any principal payments that are treated as payments of capitalized interest. See paragraph (h)(3) of this section.

Example 2. Allocation of payments. The facts are the same as in *Example 1* of this paragraph (h)(4), except that, in addition, the lender charges Student O a loan origination fee, which is not for any property or services provided by the lender. Under § 1.1273-2(g), the loan origination fee reduces the issue price of the loan, which reduction increases the amount of original issue discount on the loan by the amount of the fee. The amount of original issue discount (which includes the capitalized interest and loan origination fee) that accrues each year is determined under section 1272 and § 1.1272-1. In effect, the loan origination fee accrues over the entire term of the loan. Because the loan has original issue discount, the payment ordering rules in § 1.1275-2(a) must be used to determine how much of each payment is interest for federal tax purposes. See paragraph (h)(3) of this section. Under § 1.1275-2(a), each payment (regardless of its designation by the parties as either interest or principal) generally is treated first as a payment of original issue discount, to the extent of the original issue discount that has accrued as of the date the payment is due and has not been allocated to prior payments, and second as a payment of principal. Therefore, in determining the total amount of interest paid on the qualified education loan during the 60-month period described in paragraph (e)(1) of this section, Student O may deduct any payments that the parties label as principal but that are treated as payments of original issue discount under § 1.1275-2(a). The 60-month period does not begin in the month in which the lender charges Student O the loan origination fee.

(i) *Special rules regarding 60-month limitation.*—(1) *Refinancing.*—A qualified education loan and all indebtedness incurred solely to refinance that loan constitute a single loan for purposes of calculating the 60-month period described in paragraph (e)(1) of this section.

(2) *Consolidated loans.*—A consolidated loan is a single loan that refinances more than one qualified education loan of a borrower. For consolidated loans, the 60-month period described in paragraph (e)(1) of this section begins on the latest date on which any of the underlying loans entered repayment status and includes any subsequent month in which the consolidated loan is in repayment status.

(3) *Collapsed loans.*—A collapsed loan is two or more qualified education loans of a single taxpayer that constitute a single qualified education loan for loan servicing purposes and for which the lender or servicer does not separately account. For a collapsed loan, the 60-month period described in paragraph (e)(1) of this section begins on the latest date on which any of the underlying loans entered repayment status and includes any subsequent month in which any of the underlying loans is in repayment status.

(4) *Examples.*—The following examples illustrate the rules of this paragraph (i):

Example 1. Refinancing. Student P obtains a qualified education loan to pay for an undergraduate degree at an eligible educational institution. After graduation, Student P is required to make monthly interest payments on the loan beginning in January 2000. Student P makes the required interest payments for 15 months. In April 2001, Student P borrows money from another lender exclusively to repay the first qualified education loan. The new loan requires interest payments to start immediately. At the time Student P must begin interest payments on the new loan, which is a qualified education loan, there are 45 months remaining of the original 60-month period referred to in paragraph (e)(1) of this section.

Example 2. Collapsed loans. To finance his education, Student Q obtains four separate qualified education loans from Lender R. The loans enter repayment status, and their respective 60-month periods described in paragraph (e)(1) of this section begin, in July, August, September, and December of 1999. After all of Student Q's loans have entered repayment status, Lender R informs Student Q that Lender R will transfer all four loans to Lender S. Following the transfer, Lender

S treats the loans as a single loan for loan servicing purposes. Lender S sends Student Q a single statement that shows the total principal and interest, and does not keep separate records with respect to each loan. With respect to the single collapsed loan, the 60-month period described in paragraph (e)(1) of this section begins in December 1999.

(j) *Effective date.*—This section is applicable to interest due and paid on qualified education loans after January 21, 1999, if paid before January 1, 2002. Taxpayers also may apply this section to interest due and paid on qualified education loans after December 31, 1997, but before January 21, 1999. This section also applies to interest due and paid on qualified education loans in a taxable year beginning after December 31, 2010. [Reg. §1.221-2.]

☐ [*T.D.* 9125, 5-6-2004.]

Special Deductions for Corporations

[Reg. §1.241-1]

§1.241-1. Allowance of special deductions.—A corporation, in computing its taxable income, is allowed as deductions the items specified in part VIII (section 242 and following), subchapter B, chapter 1 of the Code, in addition to the deductions provided in Part VI (section 161 and following) subchapter B, chapter 1 of the Code. [Reg. §1.241-1.]

☐ [*T.D.* 6183, 6-13-56.]

[Reg. §1.243-1]

§1.243-1. Deduction for dividends received by corporations.—(a)(1) A corporation is allowed a deduction under section 243 for dividends received from a domestic corporation which is subject to taxation under chapter 1 of the Internal Revenue Code of 1954.

(2) Except as provided in section 243(c) and in section 246, the deduction is:

(i) For the taxable year, an amount equal to 85 percent of the dividends received from such domestic corporations during the taxable year (other than dividends to which subdivision (ii) or (iii) of this subparagraph applies).

(ii) For a taxable year beginning after September 2, 1958, an amount equal to 100 percent of the dividends received from such domestic corporations if at the time of receipt of such dividends the recipient corporation is a Federal licensee under the Small Business Investment Act of 1958 (15 U.S.C. ch. 14B). However, to claim the deduction provided by section 243(a)(2) the company must file with its return a statement that it was a Federal licensee under the Small Business Investment Act of 1958 at the time of the receipt of the dividends.

(iii) For a taxable year ending after December 31, 1963, an amount equal to 100 percent of the dividends received which are "qualifying dividends," as defined in section 243(b) and §1.243-4.

(3) To determine the amount of the distribution to a recipient corporation and the amount of the dividend, see §§1.301-1 and 1.316-1.

(b) For limitation on the dividends received deduction, see section 246 and the regulations thereunder. [Reg. §1.243-1.]

☐ [*T.D.* 6183, 6-13-56. *Amended by T.D.* 6449, 1-27-60 *and T.D.* 6992, 1-17-69.]

[Reg. §1.243-2]

§1.243-2. Special rules for certain distributions.—(a) *Dividends paid by mutual savings banks, etc.*—In determining the deduction provided in section 243(a), any amount allowed as a deduction under section 591 (relating to deduction for dividends paid by mutual savings banks, cooperative banks, and domestic building and loan associations) shall not be considered as a dividend.

(b) *Dividends received from regulated investment companies.*—In determining the deduction provided in section 243(a), dividends received from a regulated investment company shall be subject to the limitations provided in section 854.

(c) *Dividends received from real estate investment trusts.*—See section 857(c) and paragraph (d) of §1.857-6 for special rules which deny a deduction under section 243 in the case of dividends received from a real estate investment trust with respect to a taxable year for which such trust is taxable under part II, subchapter M, chapter 1 of the Code.

(d) *Dividends received on preferred stock of a public utility.*—The deduction allowed by section 243(a) shall be determined without regard to any dividends described in section 244 (relating to dividends on the preferred stock of a public utility). That is, such deduction shall be determined without regard to any dividends received on the preferred stock of a public utility which is subject to taxation under chapter 1 of the Code and with respect to which a deduction is allowed by section 247 (relating to dividends paid on certain preferred stock of public utilities). For a deduction with respect to such dividends received on the preferred stock of a public utility, see section 244. If a deduction for dividends paid is not allowable to the distributing corporation under section 247 with respect to the dividends on its preferred stock, such dividends received from a domestic public utility corporation subject to taxation under chapter 1 of the Code are includible in determining the deduction allowed by section 243(a). [Reg. §1.243-2.]

☐ [*T.D.* 6183, 6-13-56. *Amended by T.D.* 6449, 1-27-60, *T.D.* 6598, 4-25-62, *T.D.* 6992, 1-17-69, *and T.D.* 7767, 2-3-81.]

[Reg. §1.243-3]

§1.243-3. Certain dividends from foreign corporations.—(a) *In general.*—(1) In determining the deduction provided in section 243(a), section 243(d) provides that a dividend received from a foreign corporation after December 31, 1959, shall be treated as a dividend from a domestic corporation which is subject to taxation under chapter 1 of the Code, but only to the extent that such dividend is out of earnings and profits accumulated by a domestic corporation during a period with respect to which such domestic corporation was subject to taxation under chapter 1 of the Code (or corresponding provisions of prior law). Thus, for example, if a domestic corporation accumulates earnings and profits during a period or periods with respect to which it is subject to taxation under chapter 1 of the Code (or corresponding provisions of prior law) and subsequently such domestic corporation reincorporates in a foreign country, any dividends paid out of such earnings and profits after such reincorporation are eligible for the deduction provided in section 243(a)(1) and (2).

(2) Section 243(d) and this section do not apply to dividends paid out of earnings and profits accumulated (i) by a corporation organized under the China Trade Act, 1922, (ii) by a domestic corporation during any period with respect to which such corporation was exempt from taxation under section 501 (relating to certain charitable, etc. organizations) or 521 (relating to farmers' cooperative associations), or (iii) by a domestic corporation during any period to which section 931 (relating to income from sources within possessions of the United States), as in effect for taxable years beginning before January 1, 1976, applied.

(b) *Establishing separate earnings and profits accounts.*—A foreign corporation shall, for purposes of section 243(d), maintain a separate account for earnings and profits to which it succeeds which were accumulated by a domestic corporation, and such foreign corporation shall treat such earnings and profits as having been accumulated during the accounting periods in which earned by such domestic corporation. Such foreign corporation shall also maintain such a separate account for the earnings and profits, or deficit in earnings and profits, accumulated by it or accumulated by any other corporations to the earnings and profits of which it succeeds.

(c) *Effect of dividends on earnings and profits accounts.*—Dividends paid out of the accumulated earnings and profits (see section 316(a)(1)) of such foreign corporation shall be treated as having been paid out of the most recently accumulated earnings and profits of such corporation. A deficit in an earnings and profits account for any accounting period shall reduce the most recently accumulated earnings and profits for a prior accounting period in such account. If there are no accumulated earnings and profits in an earnings and profits account because of a deficit incurred in a prior accounting period, such deficit must be restored before earnings and profits can be accumulated in a subsequent accounting period. If a dividend is paid out of earnings and profits of a foreign corporation which maintains two or more accounts (established under the provisions of paragraph (b) of this section) with respect to two or more accounting periods ending on the same day, then the portion of such dividend considered as paid out of each account shall be the same proportion of the total dividend as the amount of earnings and profits in that account bears to the sum of the earnings and profits in all such accounts.

(d) *Illustration.*—The application of the principles of this section in the determination of the amount of the dividends received deduction may be illustrated by the following example:

Example. On December 31, 1960, corporation X, a calendar-year corporation organized in the United States on January 1, 1958, consolidated with corporation Y, a foreign corporation organized on

January 1, 1958, which used an annual accounting period based on the calendar year, to form corporation Z, a foreign corporation not engaged in trade or business within the United States. Corporation Z is a wholly-owned subsidiary of corporation M, a domestic corporation. On January 1, 1961, corporation Z's accumulated ubsidiary of corporation M, a domestic corporation. On January 1, 1961, corporation Z's accumulated earnings and profits of $31,000 are, under the provisions of paragraph (b) of this section, maintained in separate earnings and profits accounts containing the following amounts:

Earnings and profits accumulated for—	Domestic corporation X	Foreign corporation Y
1958	($ 1,000)	$11,000
1959	10,000	9,000
1960	5,000	(3,000)

Corporation Z had earnings and profits of $10,000 in each of the years 1961, 1962, and 1963 and makes distributions with respect to its stock to corporation M for such years in the following amounts:

1961 . . . . :	$14,000
1962	23,000
1963	16,000

(1) For 1961, a deduction of $3,400 is allowable to M with respect to the $14,000 distribution from Z, computed as follows:

(i) Dividend from current year earnings and profits (1961) $10,000

(ii) Dividend from earnings and profits of corporation X accumulated for 1960 4,000

(iii) Deduction: 85 percent of $4,000 (the amount distributed from the accumulated earnings and profits of corporation X) 3,400

(2) For 1962, a deduction of $6,970 is allowable to corporation M with respect to the $23,000 distribution from corporation Z, computed as follows:

(i) Dividend from current year earnings and profits (1962) $10,000

(ii) Dividend from earnings and profits of corporation X accumulated for:
1960 . . . . $1,000
1959: $9,000 (i.e., $10,000 – $1,000) divided by $15,000 (i.e., $9,000 + $9,000 – $3,000) multiplied by $12,000 (i.e., $23,000– $11,000) . .   7,200

Total $8,200

(iii) Dividend from earnings and profits of corporation Y accumulated for:
1959: $6,000/$15,000 × $12,000 . . . . $4,800

(iv) Deduction: 85 percent of $8,200 (the amount distributed from the accumulated earnings and profits of corporation X) 6,970

(3) For 1963, a deduction of $1,530 is allowable to M with respect to the $16,000 distribution from Z, computed as follows:

(i) Dividend from current year earnings and profits (1963) $10,000

(ii) Dividend from earnings and profits of corporation X accumulated for 1959:
Earnings and profits remaining after 1962 distribution (i.e., $9,000 – $7,200) 1,800

(iii) Dividend from earnings and profits of corporation Y accumulated for 1959:
Earnings and profits remaining after 1962 distribution (i.e., $6,000 – $4,800) 1,200
1958 3,000

(iv) Deduction: 85 percent of $1,800 (the amount distributed from the accumulated earnings and profits of corporation X) 1,530

[Reg. §1.243-3.]

☐ [T.D. 6830, 6-22-65. Amended by T.D. 9194, 4-6-2005.]

[Reg. §1.243-4]

§1.243-4. Qualifying dividends.—(a) *Definition of qualifying dividends.*—(1) *General.*—For purposes of section 243(a)(3), the term "qualifying dividends" means dividends received by a corporation if—

(i) At the close of the day the dividends are received, such corporation is a member of the same affiliated group of corporations (*as defined in paragraph (b) of this section*) as the corporation distributing the dividends,

(ii) An election by such affiliated group under section 243(b)(2) and paragraph (c) of this section is effective for the taxable years of its members which include such day, and

(iii) The dividends are distributed out of earnings and profits specified in subparagraph (2) of this paragraph.

(2) *Earnings and profits.*—The earnings and profits specified in this subparagraph are earnings and profits of a taxable year of the distributing corporation (or a predecessor corporation) which satisfies each of the following conditions:

(i) Such year must end after December 31, 1963;

(ii) On each day of such year the distributing corporation (or the predecessor corporation) and the corporation receiving the dividends must have been members of the affiliated group of which the distributing corporation and the corporation receiving the dividends are members on the day the dividends are received; and

(iii) An election under section 1562 (relating to the election of multiple surtax exemptions) was never effective (or is no longer effective pursuant to section 1562(c)) for such year.

(3) *Special rule for insurance companies.*—Notwithstanding the provisions of subparagraph (2) of this paragraph, if an insurance company subject to taxation under section 802 or 821 distributes a dividend out of earnings and profits of a taxable year with respect to which the company would have been a component member of a controlled group of corporations within the meaning of section 1563 were it not for the application of section 1563(b)(2)(D), such dividend shall not be treated as a qualifying dividend unless an election under section 243(b)(2) is effective for such taxable year.

(4) *Predecessor corporations.*—For purposes of this paragraph, a corporation shall be considered to be a predecessor corporation with respect to a distributing corporation if the distributing corporation succeeds to the earnings and profits of such corporation, for example, as the result of a transaction to which section 381(a) applies. A distributing corporation shall, for purposes of this section, maintain, in respect of each predecessor corporation, a separate account for earnings and profits to which it succeeds, and such earnings and profits shall be considered to be earnings and profits of the predecessor's taxable year in which the earnings and profits were accumulated.

(5) *Mere change in form.*—(i) For purposes of subparagraph (2)(ii) of this paragraph, the affiliated group in existence during the taxable year out of the earnings and profits of which the dividend is distributed shall not be considered as a different group from that in existence on the day on which the dividend is received merely because—

(a) The common parent corporation has undergone a mere change in identity, form, or place of organization (within the meaning of section 368(a)(1)((F)), or

(b) A newly organized corporation (the "acquiring corporation") has acquired substantially all of the outstanding stock of the common parent corporation (the "acquired corporation") solely in exchange for stock of such acquiring corporation, and the stockholders (immediately before the acquisition) of the acquired corporation, as a result of owning stock of the acquired corporation, own (immediately after the acquisition) all of the outstanding stock of the acquiring corporation.

If a transaction described in the preceding sentence has occurred, the acquiring corporation shall be treated as having been a member of the affiliated group for the entire period during which the acquired corporation was a member of such group.

(ii) For purposes of subdivision (i)(b) of this subparagraph, if immediately before the acquisition—

(a) The stockholders of the acquired corporation also owned all of the outstanding stock of another corporation (the "second corporation"), and

(b) Stock of the acquired corporation and of the second corporation could be acquired or transferred only as a unit (hereinafter referred to as the "limitation on transferability"),

then the second corporation shall be treated as an acquired corporation and such second corporation shall be treated as having been a member of the affiliated group for the entire period (while such group was in existence) during which the limitation on transferability was in existence, and if the second corporation is itself the common parent corporation of an affiliated group (the "second group") any other member of the second group shall be treated as having been a member of the affiliated group for the entire period during which it was a member of the second group while the limitation on transferability existed. For purposes of (a) of this subdivision and subdivision (i)(b) of this subparagraph, if the limitation on transferability of stock of the acquired corporation and the second corporation is achieved by using a voting trust, then the stock owned by the trust shall be considered as owned by the holders of the beneficial interests in the trust.

(6) *Source of distributions.*—In determining from what year's earnings and profits a dividend is treated as having been distributed

for purposes of this section, the principles of paragraph (a) of §1.316-2 shall apply. A dividend shall be considered to be distributed, first, out of the earnings and profits of the taxable year which includes the date the dividend is distributed, second, out of the earnings and profits accumulated for the immediately preceding taxable year, third, out of the earnings and profits accumulated for the second preceding taxable year, etc. A deficit in an earnings and profits account for any taxable year shall reduce the most recently accumulated earnings and profits for a prior year in such account. If there are no accumulated earnings and profits in an earnings and profits account because of a deficit incurred in a prior year, such deficit must be restored before earnings and profits can be accumulated in a subsequent year. If a dividend is distributed out of separate earnings and profits accounts (established under the provisions of subparagraph (4) of this paragraph) for two or more taxable years ending on the same day, then the portion of such dividend considered as distributed out of each account shall be the same proportion of the total dividend as the amount of earnings and profits in that account bears to the sum of the earnings and profits in all such accounts.

(7) *Examples.*—The provisions of this paragraph may be illustrated by the following examples:

Example (1). On March 1, 1965, corporation P, a publicly owned corporation, acquires all of the stock of corporation S and continues to hold the stock throughout the remainder of 1965 and all of 1966. P and S are domestic corporations which file separate returns on the basis of a calendar year. The affiliated group consisting of P and S makes an election under section 243(b)(2) which is effective for the 1966 taxable years of P and S. A multiple surtax exemption election under section 1562 is not effective for their 1965 taxable years. On February 1, 1966, S distributes $50,000 with respect to its stock which is received by P on the same date. S had earnings and profits of $40,000 for 1966 (computed without regard to distributions during 1966). S also had earnings and profits accumulated for 1965 of $70,000. Since $40,000 was distributed out of earnings and profits for 1966 and since each one of the conditions prescribed in subparagraphs (1) and (2) of this paragraph is satisfied, P is entitled to a 100-percent dividends received deduction with respect to $40,000 of the $50,000 distribution. However, since $10,000 was distributed out of earnings and profits accumulated for 1965, and since on each day of 1965 S and P were not members of the affiliated group of which S and P were members on February 1, 1966, $10,000 of the $50,000 distribution does not satisfy the condition specified in subparagraph (2)(ii) of this paragraph and thus does not qualify for the 100-percent dividends received deduction.

Example (2). Assume the same facts as in example (1), except that corporation P acquires all the stock of corporation S on January 1, 1965, and sells such stock on November 1, 1966. Since $10,000 is distributed out of earnings and profits for 1965, and since each of the conditions prescribed in subparagraphs (1) and (2) of this paragraph is satisfied, P is entitled to a 100-percent dividends received deduction with respect to $10,000 of the $50,000 distribution. However, since $40,000 of the $50,000 distribution was made out of earnings and profits of S for its 1966 taxable year, and on each day of such year S and P were not members of the affiliated group of which S and P were members on February 1, 1966, $40,000 of the distribution does not satisfy the condition specified in subparagraph (2)(ii) of this paragraph and thus does not qualify for the 100-percent dividends received deduction.

Example (3). Assume the same facts as in example (1), except that corporation P acquires all the stock of corporation S on January 1, 1965, and that a multiple surtax exemption election under section 1562 is effective for P's and S's 1965 taxable years. Further assume that the section 1562 election is terminated effective with respect to their 1966 taxable years, and that an election under section 243(b)(2) is effective for such taxable years. Since $10,000 of the February 1, 1966, distribution was made out of earnings and profits of S for its 1965 taxable year and since a multiple surtax exemption election is effective for such year, $10,000 of the distribution does not satisfy the condition specified in subparagraph (2)(iii) of this paragraph and thus does not qualify for the 100-percent dividends received deduction. However, the portion of the distribution which was distributed out of earnings and profits of S's 1966 year ($40,000) qualifies for the 100-percent dividends received deduction.

Example (4). Assume the same facts as in example (1), except that corporation P acquires all the stock of corporation S on January 1, 1965, and that S is a life insurance company subject to taxation under section 802. Accordingly, S would have been a member of a controlled group of corporations except for the application of section 1563(b)(2)(D). Since $10,000 of the distribution was made out of earnings and profits of S for its 1965 taxable year, and since with respect to such year an election under section 243(b)(2) was not effective, $10,000 of the distribution is not a qualifying dividend by reason of subparagraph (3) of this paragraph. On the other hand, the portion of the distribution which was distributed out of earnings and profits for S's 1966 year ($40,000) does qualify for the 100-percent dividends received deduction because the distribution was out of earnings and profits of a year for which an election under section 243(b)(2) is effective, and because the other conditions specified in subparagraphs (1) and (2) of this paragraph are satisfied. However, if P were also a life insurance company subject to taxation under section 802, then subparagraph (3) of this paragraph would not result in the disqualification of the portion of the distribution made out of S's 1965 earnings and profits because S would be a component member of an insurance group of corporations (as defined in section 1563(a)(4)), consisting of P and S, with respect to its 1965 year.

Example (5). Corporation X owns all the stock of corporation Y from January 1, 1965, through December 31, 1969. X and Y are domestic corporations which file separate returns on the basis of a calendar year. On June 30, 1965, Y acquired all the stock of domestic corporation Z, a calendar year taxpayer, and on December 31, 1967, Y acquired the assets of Z in a transaction to which section 381(a) applied. A multiple surtax exemption election under section 1562 was not effective for any taxable year of X, Y, or Z, and an election under section 243(b)(2) is effective for the 1968 and 1969 taxable years of X and Y. On January 1, 1968, Y's accumulated earnings and profits are, under the provisions of subparagraph (4) of this paragraph, maintained in separate earnings and profits accounts containing the following amounts:

Earnings and profits accumulated for:	Corporation Y	Corporation Z
1964	$60,000	$40,000
1965	30,000	15,000
1966	(5,000)	2,000
1967	12,000	6,000

Corporation Y had earnings and profits of $10,000 in each of the years 1968 and 1969, and made distributions during such years in the following amounts:

1968	$29,000
1969	31,000

(i) The source of the 1968 distribution, determined in accordance with the rules of subparagraph (6) of this paragraph, is as follows:

(a)	Dividend from Y's current year's earnings and profits (1968)	$10,000
(b)	Dividend from earnings and profits of Y accumulated for 1967	12,000
(c)	Dividend from earnings and profits of Z accumulated for:	
	1967	6,000
	1966	1,000
		$29,000

Since the 1968 dividend is considered paid out of earnings and profits of Y's 1968 and 1967 years, and Z's 1967 and 1966 years, and since each of these years satisfies each of the conditions specified in subparagraph (2) of this paragraph. X is entitled to a 100-percent dividends received deduction with respect to the entire 1968 distribution of $29,000 from Y.

(ii) The source of the 1969 distribution of $31,000, determined in accordance with the rules of subparagraph (6) of this paragraph, is as follows:

(a)	Dividend from Y's current year's earnings and profits (1969)	$10,000
(b)	Dividend from earnings and profits of Z accumulated for 1966 (1966 earnings and profits remaining after 1968 distribution, i.e., $2,000 − $1,000)	1,000
(c)	Dividend from earnings and profits of Y and Z accumulated for 1965:	
	Corporation Y: $25,000 (i.e., $30,000 − $5,000 deficit) divided by $40,000 (i.e., the sum of the 1965 earnings and profits of Y and Z) multiplied by $20,000 (the portion of the distribution from the 1965 earnings and profits of Y and Z)	12,500
	Corporation Z: $15,000 divided by $40,000 multiplied by $20,000	7,500
		$31,000

The sum of the dividends from Y's 1969 year ($10,000), Z's 1966 year ($1,000), and Y's 1965 year ($12,500), or $23,500, qualifies for the 100-percent dividends received deduction. However, the dividends paid out of Z's 1965 year ($7,500) do not qualify because on each day of 1965 Z and X were not members of the affiliated group of which Y (the distributing corporation) and X (the corporation receiving the dividends) were members on the day in 1969 when the dividends were received by X.

(b) *Definition of affiliated group.*—For purposes of this section and §1.243-5, the term "affiliated group" shall have the meaning assigned to it by section 1504(a), except that insurance companies subject to taxation under section 802 or 821 shall be treated as includible corporations (notwithstanding section 1504(b)(2)), and the provisions of section 1504(c) shall not apply.

(c) *Election.*—(1) *Manner and time of making election.*—(i) *General.*— The election provided by section 243(b)(2) shall be made for an affiliated group by the common parent corporation and shall be made for a particular taxable year of the common parent corporation. Such election may not be made for any taxable year of the common parent corporation for which a multiple surtax exemption election under section 1562 is effective. The election shall be made by means of a statement, signed by any person who is duly authorized to act on behalf of the common parent corporation, stating that the affiliated group elects under section 243(b)(2) for such taxable year. The statement shall be filed with the district director for the internal revenue district in which is located the principal place of business or principal office or agency of the common parent. The statement shall set forth the name, address, taxpayer account number, and taxable year of each corporation (including wholly-owned subsidiaries) that is a member of the affiliated group at the time the election is filed. The statement may be filed at any time, provided that, with respect to each corporation the tax liability of which for its matching taxable year of election (or for any subsequent taxable year) would be increased because of the election, at the time of filing there is at least 1 year remaining in the statutory period (including any extensions thereof) for the assessment of a deficiency against such corporation for such year. (If there is less than 1 year remaining with respect to any taxable year, the district director for the internal revenue district in which is located the principal place of business or principal office or agency of the corporation will ordinarily, upon request, enter into an agreement to extend such statutory period for assessment and collection of deficiencies.)

(ii) *Information statement by common parent.*—If a corporation becomes a member of the affiliated group after the date on which the election is filed and during its matching taxable year of election, then the common parent shall file, within 60 days after such corporation becomes a member of the affiliated group, an additional statement containing the name, address, taxpayer account number, and taxable year of such corporation. Such additional statement shall be filed with the internal revenue officer with whom the election was filed.

(iii) *Definition of matching taxable year of election.*—For purposes of this paragraph and paragraphs (d) and (e) of this section, the term "matching taxable year of election" shall mean the taxable year of each member (including the common parent corporation) of the electing affiliated group which includes the last day of the taxable year of the common parent corporation for which an election by the affiliated group is made under section 243(b)(2).

(2) *Consents by subsidiary corporations.*—(i) *General.*—Each corporation (other than the common parent corporation) which is a member of the electing affiliated group (including any member which joins in the filing of a consolidated return) at any time during its matching taxable year of election must consent to such election in the manner and time provided in subdivision (ii) or (iii) of this subparagraph, whichever is applicable.

(ii) *Wholly owned subsidiary.*—If all of the stock of a corporation is owned by a member or members of the affiliated group on each day of such corporation's matching taxable year of election, then such corporation (referred to in this paragraph as a "wholly owned subsidiary") shall be deemed to consent to such election.

(iii) *Other members.*—The consent of each member of the affiliated group (other than a wholly-owned subsidiary) shall be made by means of a statement, signed by any person who is duly authorized to act on behalf of the consenting member, stating that such member consents to the election under section 243(b)(2). The statement shall set forth the name, address, taxpayer account number, and taxable year of the consenting member and of the common parent corporation, and in the case of a statement filed after December 31, 1968, the identity of the internal revenue district in which is located the principal place of business or principal office or agency of the common parent corporation. The consent of more than one such member may be incorporated in a single statement. The statement (or statements) shall be attached to the election filed by the common parent corporation. The consent of a corporation that, after the date the election was filed and during its matching taxable year of election, either (a) becomes a member, or (b) ceases to be a wholly-owned subsidiary but continues to be a member, shall be filed with the internal revenue officer with whom the election was filed and shall be filed on or before the date prescribed by law (including extensions of time) for

the filing of the consenting member's income tax return for such taxable year, or on or before June 10, 1964, whichever is later.

(iv) *Statement attached to return.*—Each corporation that consents to an election by means of a statement described in subdivision (iii) of this subparagraph should attach a copy of the statement to its income tax return for its matching taxable year of election, or, if such return has already been filed, to its first income tax return filed on or after the date on which the statement is filed. However, if such return is filed on or before June 10, 1964, a copy of such statement should be filed on or before June 10, 1964, with the district director with whom such return is filed. Each wholly-owned subsidiary should attach a statement to its income tax return for its matching taxable year of election, or, if such return has already been filed, to its first income tax return filed on or after the date on which the statement is filed stating that it is subject to an election under section 243(b)(2) and the taxable year to which the election applies, and setting forth the name, address, taxpayer account number, and taxable year of the common parent corporation, and in the case of a statement filed after December 31, 1968, the identity of the internal revenue district in which is located the principal place of business or principal office or agency of the common parent corporation. However, if the due date for such return (including extensions of time) is before June 10, 1964, such statement should be filed on or before June 10, 1964, with the district director with whom such return is filed.

(3) *Information statement by member.*—If a corporation becomes a member of the affiliated group during a taxable year that begins after the last day of the common parent corporation's matching taxable year of election, then (unless such election has been terminated) such corporation should attach a statement to its income tax return for such taxable year stating that it is subject to an election under section 243(b)(2) for such taxable year and setting forth the name, address, taxpayer account number, and taxable year of the common parent corporation, and the identity of the internal revenue district in which is located the principal place of business or principal office or agency of the common parent corporation. In the case of an affiliated group that made an election under the rules provided in Treasury Decision 6721, approved April 8, 1964 (29 F.R. 4997, C.B. 1964-1 (Part 1), 625), such statement shall be filed, on or before March 15, 1969, with the district director for the internal revenue district in which is located such member's principal place of business or principal office or agency.

(4) *Years for which election effective.*—(i) *General rule.*—An election under section 243(b)(2) by an affiliated group shall be effective—

(a) In the case of each corporation which is a member of such group at any time during its matching taxable year of election, for such taxable year, and

(b) In the case of each corporation which is a member of such group at any time during a taxable year ending after the last day of the common parent's taxable year of election but which does not include such last day, for such taxable year, unless the election is terminated under section 243(b)(4) and paragraph (e) of this section. Thus, the election has a continuing effect and need not be renewed annually.

(ii) *Special rule for certain taxable years ending in 1964.*—In the case of a taxable year of a member (other than the common parent corporation) of the affiliated group (a) which begins in 1963 and ends in 1964, and (b) for which an election is not effective under subdivision (i)(a) of this subparagraph, if an election under section 243(b)(2) is effective for the taxable year of the common parent corporation which includes the last day of such taxable year of such member, then such election shall be effective for such taxable year of such member if such member files a separate consent with respect to such taxable year. However, in order for a dividend distributed by such member during such taxable year to meet the requirements of section 243(b)(1), an election under section 243(b)(2) must be effective for the taxable year of each member of the affiliated group which includes the date such dividend is received. See section 243(b)(1)(A) and paragraph (a)(1) of this section. Accordingly, if the dividend is to qualify for the 100-percent dividends received deduction under section 243(a)(3), a consent must be filed under this subdivision by each member of the affiliated group with respect to its taxable year which includes the day the dividend is received (unless an election is effective for such taxable year under subdivision (i)(a) of this subparagraph). For purposes of this subdivision, a consent shall be made by means of a statement meeting the requirements of subparagraph (2)(iii) of this paragraph, and shall be attached to the election made by the common parent corporation for its taxable year which includes the last day of the taxable year of the member with respect to which the consent is made. A copy of the statement should be filed, within 60 days after such election is filed by the common parent corporation, with the district director with whom the consenting member filed its income tax return for such taxable year.

(iii) *Examples.*—The provisions of subdivision (ii) of this subparagraph, relating to the special rule for certain taxable years ending in 1964, may be illustrated by the following examples:

Example (1). P Corporation owns all the stock of S-1 Corporation on each day of 1963, 1964, and 1965. P uses the calendar year as its taxable year and S-1 uses a fiscal year ending June 30 as its taxable year. P makes an election under section 243(b)(2) for 1964. Since S-1 is a wholly owned subsidiary for its taxable year ending June 30, 1965, it is deemed to consent to the election. However, in order for the election to be effective with respect to S-1's taxable year ending June 30, 1964, a statement specifying that S-1 consents to the election with respect to such taxable year and containing the information required in a statement of consent under subparagraph (2)(iii) of this paragraph must be attached to the election.

Example (2). Assume the same facts as in example (1), except that P also owns all the stock of S-2 Corporation on each day of 1963, 1964, and 1965. S-2 uses a fiscal year ending May 31 as its taxable year. If S-1 distributes a dividend to P on January 15, 1964, the dividend may qualify under section 243(a)(3) only if S-1 and S-2 both consent to the election made by P for 1964 with respect to their taxable years ending in 1964.

Example (3). Assume the same facts as in example (1), except that P uses a fiscal year ending on January 31 as its taxable year and makes an election under subparagraph (1) of this paragraph for its taxable year ending January 31, 1964. Since S-1's taxable year beginning in 1963 and ending in 1964 includes January 31, 1964, the last day of P's taxable year for which the election was made, the election is effective under subdivision (i)(a) of this subparagraph, for S-1's taxable year ending June 30, 1964. Accordingly, the special rule of subdivision (ii) of this subparagraph has no application.

(d) *Effect of election.*—For restrictions and limitations applicable to corporations which are members of an electing affiliated group on each day of their taxable years, see § 1.243-5.

(e) *Termination of election.*—(1) *In general.*—An election under section 243(b)(2) by an affiliated group may be terminated with respect to any taxable year of the common parent corporation after the matching taxable year of election of the common parent corporation. The election is terminated as a result of one of the occurrences described in subparagraph (2) or (3) of this paragraph. For years affected by termination, see subparagraph (4) of this paragraph.

(2) *Consent of members.*—(i) *General.*—An election may be terminated for an affiliated group by its common parent corporation with respect to a taxable year of the common parent corporation provided each corporation (other than the common parent) that was a member of the affiliated group at any time during its taxable year that includes the last day of such year of the common parent (the "matching taxable year of termination") consents to such termination. The statement of termination may be filed by the common parent corporation at any time, provided that, with respect to each corporation the tax liability of which its matching taxable year of termination (or for any subsequent taxable year) would be increased because of the termination, at the time of filing there is at least 1 year remaining in the statutory period (including any extensions thereof) for the assessment of a deficiency against such corporation for such year. (If there is less than 1 year remaining with respect to any taxable year, the district director for the internal revenue district in which is located the principal place of business or principal office or agency of the corporation will ordinarily, upon request, enter into an agreement to extend such statutory period for assessment and collection of deficiencies.)

(ii) *Statements filed after December 31, 1968.*—With respect to statements of termination filed after December 31, 1968—

(a) The statement shall be filed with the district director for the internal revenue district in which is located the principal place of business or principal office or agency of the common parent corporation;

(b) The statement shall be signed by any person who is duly authorized to act on behalf of the common parent corporation and shall state that the affiliated group terminates the election under section 243(b)(2) for such taxable year;

(c) The statement shall set forth the name, address, taxpayer account number, and taxable year of each corporation (including wholly-owned subsidiaries) which is a member of the affiliated group at the time the termination is filed; and

(d) The consents to the termination shall be given in accordance with the rules prescribed in paragraph (c)(2) of this section, relating to manner and time for giving consents to an election under section 243(b)(2).

(3) *Refusal by new member to consent.*—(i) *Manner of giving refusal.*—If any corporation which is a new member of an affiliated group with respect to a taxable year of the common parent corpora-

tion (other than the matching taxable year of election of the common parent corporation) files a statement that it does not consent to an election under section 243(b)(2) with respect to such taxable year, then such election shall terminate with respect to such taxable year. Such statement shall be signed by any person who is duly authorized to act on behalf of the new member, and shall be filed with the timely filed income tax return of such new member for its taxable year within which falls the last day of such taxable year of the common parent corporation. In the event of a termination under this subparagraph, each corporation (other than such new member) that is a member of the affiliated group at any time during its taxable year which includes such last day should, within 30 days after such new member files the statement of refusal to consent, notify the district director of such termination. Such notification should be filed with the district director for the internal revenue district in which is located the principal place of business or principal office or agency of the corporation.

(ii) *Corporation considered as new member.*—For purposes of subdivision (i) of this subparagraph, a corporation shall be considered to be a new member of an affiliated group of corporations with respect to a taxable year of the common parent corporation if such corporation—

(a) Is a member of the affiliated group at any time during such taxable year of the common parent corporation, and

(b) Was not a member of the affiliated group at any time during the common parent corporation's immediately preceding taxable year.

(4) *Effect of termination.*—A termination under subparagraph (2) or (3) of this paragraph is effective with respect to (i) the common parent corporation's taxable year referred to in the particular subparagraph under which the termination occurs, and (ii) the taxable years of the other members of the affiliated group which include the last day of such taxable year of the common parent. An election, once terminated, is no longer effective. Accordingly, the termination is also effective with respect to the succeeding taxable years of the members of the group. However, the affiliated group may make a new election in accordance with the provisions of section 243(b)(2) and paragraph (c) of this section. [Reg. § 1.243-4.]

□ [T.D. 6992, 1-17-69.]

[Reg. § 1.243-5]

§ 1.243-5. Effect of election.—(a) *General.*—(1) *Corporations subject to restrictions and limitations.*—If an election by an affiliated group under section 243(b)(2) is effective with respect to a taxable year of the common parent corporation, then each corporation (including the common parent corporation) which is a member of such group on each day of its matching taxable year shall be subject to the restrictions and limitations prescribed by paragraphs (b), (c), and (d) of this section for such taxable year. For purposes of this section, the term "matching taxable year" shall mean the taxable year of each member (including the common parent corporation) of an affiliated group which includes the last day of a particular taxable year of the common parent corporation for which an election by the affiliated group under section 243(b)(2) is effective. If a corporation is a member of an affiliated group on each day of a short taxable year which does not include the last day of a taxable year of the common parent corporation, and if an election under section 243(b)(2) is effective for such short year, see paragraph (g) of this section. In the case of taxable years beginning in 1963 and ending in 1964 for which an election under section 243(b)(2) is effective under paragraph (c)(4)(ii) of § 1.243-4, see paragraph (f)(9) of this section.

(2) *Members filing consolidated returns.*—The restrictions and limitations prescribed by this section shall apply notwithstanding the fact that some of the corporations which are members of the electing affiliated group (within the meaning of section 243(b)(5)) join in the filing of a consolidated return. Thus, for example, if an electing affiliated group includes one or more corporations taxable under section 11 of the Code and two or more insurance companies taxable under section 802 of the Code, and if the insurance companies join in the filing of a consolidated return, the amount of such companies' exemptions from estimated tax (for purposes of sections 6016 and 6655) shall be the amounts determined under paragraph (d)(5) of this section and not the amounts determined pursuant to the regulations under section 1502.

(b) *Multiple surtax exemption election.*—(1) *General rule.*—If an election by an affiliated group under section 243(b)(2) is effective with respect to a taxable year of the common parent corporation, then no corporation which is a member of such affiliated group on each day of its matching taxable year may consent (or shall be deemed to consent) to an election under section 1562(a)(1), relating to election of multiple surtax exemptions, which would be effective for such matching taxable year. Thus, each corporation which is a component member of the controlled group of corporations with respect to its matching taxable year (determined by applying section 1563(b) without regard to paragraph (2)(D) thereof) shall determine its surtax exemption for such taxable year in accordance with section 1561 and the regulations thereunder.

(2) *Special rule for certain insurance companies.*—Under section 243(b)(6)(A), if the provisions of subparagraph (1) of this paragraph apply with respect to the taxable year of an insurance company subject to taxation under section 802 or 821, then the surtax exemption of such insurance company for such taxable year shall be determined by applying part II (section 1561 and following), subchapter B, chapter 6 of the Code, with respect to such insurance company and the other corporations which are component members of the controlled group of corporations (as determined under section 1563 without regard to subsections (a)(4) and (b)(2)(D) thereof) of which such insurance company is a member, without regard to section 1563(a)(4) (relating to certain insurance companies treated as a separate controlled group) and section 1563(b)(2)(D) (relating to certain insurance companies treated as excluded members).

(3) *Example.*—The provisions of this paragraph may be illustrated by the following example:

Example. Throughout 1965 corporation M owns all the stock of corporations L-1, L-2, S-1, and S-2. M is a domestic mutual insurance company subject to tax under section 821 of the Code, L-1 and L-2 are domestic life insurance companies subject to tax under section 802 of the Code, and S-1 and S-2 are domestic corporations subject to tax under section 11 of the Code. Each corporation uses the calendar year as its taxable year. M makes a valid election under section 243(b)(2) for the affiliated group consisting of M, L-1, L-2, S-1, and S-2. If part II, subchapter B, chapter 6 of the Code were applied with respect to the 1965 taxable years of the corporations without regard to section 243(b)(6)(A), the following would result: S-1 and S-2 would be treated as component members of a controlled group of corporations on such date; L-1 and L-2 would be treated as component members of a separate controlled group on such date; and M would be treated as an excluded member. However, since section 243(b)(6)(A) requires that part II of subchapter B be applied without regard to section 1563(a)(4) and (b)(2)(D), for purposes of determining the surtax exemptions of M, L-1, L-2, S-1, and S-2 for their 1965 taxable years, such corporations are treated for purposes of such part II as component members of a single controlled group of corporations on December 31, 1965. Moreover, by reason of having made the election under section 243(b)(2), M, L-1, L-2, S-1, and S-2 cannot consent to multiple surtax exemption elections under section 1562 which would be effective for their 1965 taxable years. Thus, such corporations are limited to a single $25,000 surtax exemption for such taxable years (to be apportioned among such corporations in accordance with section 1561 and the regulations thereunder).

(c) *Foreign tax credit.*—(1) *General.*—If an election by an affiliated group under section 243(b)(2) is effective with respect to a taxable year of the common parent corporation, then—

(i) The credit under section 901 for taxes paid or accrued to any foreign country or possession of the United States shall be allowed to a corporation which is a member of such affiliated group for each day of its matching taxable year only if such other corporation which pays or accrues such foreign taxes to any foreign country or possession, and which is a member of such group on each day of its matching taxable year, does not deduct such taxes in computing its tax liability for its matching taxable year, and

(ii) A corporation which is a member of such affiliated group on each day of its matching taxable year may use the overall limitation provided in section 904(a)(2) for such matching taxable year only if each other corporation which pays or accrues foreign taxes to any foreign country or possession, and which is a member of such group on each day of its matching taxable year, uses such limitation for its matching taxable year.

(2) *Consent of the Commissioner.*—In the absence of unusual circumstances, a request by a corporation for the consent of the Commissioner to the revocation of an election of the overall limitation, or to a new election of the overall limitation, for the purpose of satisfying the requirements of subparagraph (1)(ii) of this paragraph will be given favorable consideration, notwithstanding the fact that there has been no change in the basic nature of the corporation's business or changes in conditions in a foreign country which substantially affect the corporation's business. See paragraph (d)(3) of § 1.904-1.

(d) *Other restrictions and limitations.*—(1) *General rule.*—If an election by an affiliated group under section 243(b)(2) is effective with respect to a taxable year of the common parent corporation, then, except to the extent that an apportionment plan adopted under paragraph (f) of this section for such taxable year provides otherwise with respect to a restriction or limitation described in this paragraph, the rules provided in subparagraphs (2), (3), (4), and (5) of this paragraph shall apply to each corporation which is a member of such affiliated group on each day of its matching taxable year for the purpose of computing the amount of such restriction or limitation for its matching taxable year. For purposes of this paragraph, each corporation which is a member of an electing affiliated group (including any member which joins in filing a consolidated return) shall be treated as a separate corporation for purposes of determining the amount of such restrictions and limitations.

(2) *Accumulated earnings credit.*—(i) *General.*—Except as provided in subdivision (ii) of this subparagraph, in determining the minimum accumulated earnings credit under section 535(c)(2) (or the accumulated earnings credit of a mere holding or investment company under section 535(c)(3)) for each corporation which is a member of the affiliated group on each day of its matching taxable year, in lieu of the $150,000 amount ($100,000 amount in the case of taxable years beginning before January 1, 1975) mentioned in such sections there shall be substituted an amount equal to (a) $150,000 ($100,000 in the case of taxable years ending before January 1, 1975), divided by (b) the number of such members.

(ii) *Allocation of excess.*—If, with respect to one or more members, the amount determined under subdivision (i) of this subparagraph exceeds the sum of (a) such member's accumulated earnings and profits as of the close of the preceding taxable year, plus (b) such member's earnings and profits for the taxable year which are retained (within the meaning of section 535(c)(1)), then any such excess shall be subtracted from the amount determined under subdivision (i) of this subparagraph and shall be divided equally among those remaining members of the affiliated group that do not have such an excess (until no such excess remains to be divided among those remaining members that have not had such an excess). The excess so divided among such remaining members shall be added to the amount determined under subdivision (i) with respect to such members.

(iii) *Apportionment plan not allowed.*—An affiliated group may not adopt an apportionment plan, as provided in paragraph (f) of this section, with respect to the amounts computed under the provisions of this subparagraph.

(iv) *Example.*—The provisions of this subparagraph may be illustrated by the following example:

Example. An affiliated group is composed of four member corporations, W, X, Y, and Z. The sum of the accumulated earnings and profits (as of the close of the preceding taxable year ending December 31, 1975) plus the earnings and profits for the taxable year ending December 31, 1976 which are retained is $15,000, $75,000, $37,500, and $300,000 in the case of W, X, Y and Z, respectively. The amounts determined under this subparagraph for W, X, Y, and Z are $15,000, $48,750, $37,500, and $48,750, respectively, computed as follows:

	Component members			
	W	X	Y	Z
Earnings and profits	$15,000	$75,000	$37,500	$300,000
Amount computed under subpar. (1)	37,500	37,500	37,500	37,500
Excess	22,500	0	0	0
Allocation of excess	...	7,500	7,500	7,500
New excess	...	...	7,500	...
Reallocation of new excess	...	3,750	...	3,750
Amount to be used for purposes of sec. 535(c)(2) and (3)	15,000	48,750	37,500	48,750

(3) *Mine exploration expenditures.*—(i) *Limitation under section 615 (a).*—If the aggregate of the expenditures to which section 615(a) applies, which are paid or incurred by corporations which are members of the affiliated group on each day of their matching taxable years (duing such taxable years) exceeds $100,000, then the deduc-

tion (or amount deferrable) under section 615 for any such member for its matching taxable year shall be limited to an amount equal to the amount which bears the same ratio to $100,000 as the amount deductible or deferrable by such member under section 615 (computed without regard to this subdivision) bears to the aggregate of the amounts deductible or deferrable under section 615 (as so computed) by all such members.

(ii) *Limitation under section 615(c).*—If the aggregate of the expenditures to which section 615(a) applies which are paid or incurred by the corporations which are members of such affiliated group on each day of their matching taxable years (during such taxable years) would, when added to the aggregate of the amounts deducted or deferred in prior taxable years which are taken into account by such corporations in applying the limitation of section 615(c), exceed $400,000, then section 615 shall not apply to any such expenditure so paid or incurred by any such member to the extent such expenditure would exceed the amount which bears the same ratio to (a) the amount, if any, by which $400,000 exceeds the amounts so deducted or deferred in prior years, as (b) such member's deduction (or amount deferrable) under section 615 (computed without regard to this subdivision) for such expenditures paid or incurred by such member during its matching taxable year, bears to (c) the aggregate of the amounts deductible or deferable under section 615 (as so computed) by all such members during their matching taxable years.

(iii) *Treatment of corporations filing consolidated returns.*—For purposes of making the computations under subdivisions (i) and (ii) of this subparagraph, a corporation which joins in the filing of a consolidated return shall be treated as if it filed a separate return.

(iv) *Estimate of exploration expenditures.*—If, on the date a corporation (which is a member of an affiliated group on each day of its matching taxable year) files its income tax return for such taxable year, it cannot be determined whether or not the $100,000 limitation prescribed by subdivision (i) of this subparagraph, or the $400,000 limitation prescribed by subdivision (ii) of this subparagraph, will apply with respect to such taxable year, then such member shall, for purposes of such return, apply the provisions of such subdivisions (i) and (ii) with respect to such taxable year on the basis of an estimate of the aggregate of the exploration expenditures by all such members of the affiliated group for their matching taxable years. Such estimate shall be made on the basis of the facts and circumstances known at the time of such estimate. If an estimate is used by any such member of the affiliated group pursuant to this subdivision, and if the actual expenditures by all such members differ from the estimate, then each such member shall file as soon as possible an original or amended return reflecting an amended apportionment (either pursuant to an apportionment plan adopted under paragraph (f) of this section or pursuant to the application of the rule provided by subdivision (i) or (ii) of this subparagraph) based upon such actual expenditures.

(v) *Amount apportioned under apportionment plan.*—If an electing affiliated group adopts an apportionment plan as provided in paragraph (f) of this section with respect to the limitation under section 615(a) or 615(e), then the amount apportioned under such plan to any corporation which is a member of such group may not exceed the amount which such member could have deducted (or deferred) under section 615 had such affiliated group not filed an election under section 243(b)(2).

(4) *Small business deductions of life insurance companies.*—In the case of a life insurance company taxable under section 802 which is a member of such affiliated group on each day of its matching taxable year, the small business deduction under sections 804(a)(4) and 809(d)(10) shall not exceed an amount equal to $25,000 divided by the number of life insurance companies taxable under section 802 which are members of such group on each day of their matching taxable years.

(5) *Estimated tax.*—(i) *Exemption from estimated tax.*—Except as otherwise provided in subdivision (ii) of this subparagraph, the exemption from estimated tax (for purposes of estimated tax filing requirements under section 6016 and the addition to tax under section 6655 for failure to pay estimated tax) of each corporation which is a member of such affiliated group on each day of its matching taxable year shall be (in lieu of the $100,000 amount specified in section 6016(a) and (b)(2)(A) and in section 6655(d)(1) and (e)(2)(A)) an amount equal to $100,000 divided by the number of such members.

(ii) *Nonapplication to certain taxable years beginning in 1963 and ending in 1964.*—For purposes of this section, if a corporation has a taxable year beginning in 1963 and ending in 1964 the last day of the 8th month of which falls on or before April 10, 1964, then (notwithstanding the fact that an election under section 243(b)(2) is effective for such taxable year) subdivision (i) of this subparagraph shall not apply to such corporation for such taxable year. Thus, such corporation shall be entitled to a $100,000 exemption from estimated tax for such taxable year. Also, with respect to a taxable year described in

the first sentence of this subdivision, any such corporation shall not be considered to be a member of the affiliated group for purposes of determining the number of members referred to in subdivision (i) of this subparagraph.

(iii) *Examples.*—The provisions of subdivision (i) of this subparagraph may be illustrated by the following examples:

Example (1). Corporation P owns all the stock of corporation S-1 on each day of 1965. On March 1, 1965, P acquires all the stock of corporation S-2. Corporations P, S-1, and S-2 file separate returns on a calendar year basis. On March 31, 1965, the affiliated group consisting of P, S-1, and S-2 anticipates making an election under section 243(b)(2) for P's 1965 taxable year. If the affiliated group does make a valid election under section 243(b)(2) for P's 1965 year, under subdivision (i) of this subparagraph the exemption from estimated tax of P for 1965, and the exemption from estimated tax of S-1 for 1965, will be (assuming an apportionment plan is not filed pursuant to paragraph (f) of this section) an amount equal to $50,000 ($100,000 ÷ 2). (Since S-2 is not a member of the affiliated group on each day of 1965, S-2's exemption from estimated tax will be determined for the year 1965 without regard to subdivision (i) of this subparagraph, whether or not the affiliated group makes the election under section 243(b)(2).) P and S-1 file declarations of estimated tax on April 15, 1965, on such basis and make payments with respect to such declarations on such basis. Thus, if the affiliated group does make a valid election under section 243(b)(2) for P's 1965 year, P and S-1 will not incur (as a result of the application of subdivision (i) of this subparagraph to their 1965 years) additions to tax under section 6655 for failure to pay estimated tax.

Example (2). Assume the same facts as in example (1), except that, on March 31, 1965, S-1 anticipates that it will incur a loss for its 1965 year. Accordingly, in anticipation of making an election under section 243(b)(2) for P's 1965 year and adopting an apportionment plan under paragraph (f) of this section, P computes its estimated tax liability for 1965 on the basis of a $100,000 exemption, and S-1 computes its estimated tax liability for 1965 on the basis of a zero exemption. Assume S-1 incurs a loss for 1965 as anticipated. Thus, if P does make the election for 1965, and an apportionment plan is adopted apportioning $100,000 to P and zero to S-1 (for their 1965 years), P and S-1 will not incur (as a result of the application of subdivision (i) of this subparagraph to their 1965 years) additions to tax under section 6655 for failure to pay estimated tax.

Example (3). Assume the same facts as in example (1), except that P and S-1 file declarations of estimated tax on April 15, 1965, on the basis of separate $100,000 exemptions from estimated tax for their 1965 years, and make payments with respect to such declarations on such basis. Assume that the affiliated group makes an election under section 243(b)(2) for P's 1965 year. Under subdivision (i) of this subparagraph, P and S-1 are limited in the aggregate to a single $100,000 exemption from estimated tax for their 1965 years. The provisions of section 6655 will be applied to the 1965 year of P and the 1965 year of S-1 on the basis of a $50,000 exemption from estimated tax for each corporation, unless a different apportionment of the $100,000 amount is adopted under paragraph (f) of this section. Since the election was made under section 243(b)(2), regardless of whether or not the affiliated group anticipated making the election, P or S-1 (or both) may incur additions to tax under section 6655 for failure to pay estimated tax.

(e) *Effect of election for certain taxable years beginning in 1963 and ending in 1964.*—If an election under section 243(b)(2) by an affiliated group is effective for a taxable year of a corporation under paragraph (c)(4)(ii) of §1.243-4 (relating to election for certain taxable years beginning in 1963 and ending in 1964), and if such corporation is a member of such group on each day of such taxable year, then the restrictions and limitations prescribed by paragraphs (b), (c), and (d) of this section shall apply to all such members having such taxable years (for such taxable years). For purposes of this paragraph, such paragraphs shall be applied with respect to such taxable years as if such taxable years included the last day of a taxable year of the common parent corporation for which an election was effective under section 243(b)(2), i.e., as if such taxable years were matching taxable years. For apportionment plans with respect to such taxable years, see paragraph (f)(9) of this section.

(f) *Apportionment plans.*—(1) *In general.*—In the case of corporations which are members of an affiliated group of corporations on each day of their matching taxable years—

(i) The $100,000 amount referred to in paragraph (d)(3)(i) of this section (relating to limitation under section 615(a)),

(ii) The amount determined under paragraph (d)(3)(ii)(a) of this section (relating to limitation under section 615(c)),

(iii) The $25,000 amount referred to in paragraph (d)(4) of this section (relating to small business deduction of life insurance companies), and

(iv) The $100,000 amount referred to in paragraph (d)(5)(i) of this section (relating to exemption from estimated tax),

may be apportioned among such members (for such taxable years) if the common parent corporation files an apportionment plan with respect to such taxable years in the manner provided in subparagraph (4) of this paragraph, and if all other members consent to the plan, in the manner provided in subparagraph (5) or (6) of this paragraph (whichever is applicable). The plan may provide for the apportionment to one or more of such members, in fixed dollar amounts, of one or more of the amounts referred to in subdivisions (i), (ii), (iii), and (iv) of this subparagraph, but in no event shall the sum of the amounts so apportioned in respect to any such subdivision exceed the amount referred to in such subdivision. See also paragraph (d)(3)(v) of this section, relating to the maximum amount that may be apportioned to a corporation under this subparagraph with respect to exploration expenditures to which section 615 applies.

(2) *Time for adopting plan.*—An affiliated group may adopt an apportionment plan with respect to the matching taxable years of its members only if, at the time such plan is sought to be adopted, there is at least 1 year remaining in the statutory period (including any extensions thereof) for the assessment of a deficiency against any corporation the tax liability of which for any taxable year would be increased by the adoption of such plan. (If there is less than 1 year remaining with respect to any taxable year, the district director for the internal revenue district in which is located the principal place of business or principal office or agency of the corporation will ordinarily, upon request, enter into an agreement to extend such statutory period for assessment and collection of deficiencies.)

(3) *Years for which effective.*—A valid apportionment plan with respect to matching taxable years of members of an affiliated group shall be effective for such matching taxable years, and for all succeeding matching taxable years of such members, unless the plan is amended in accordance with subparagraph (8) of this paragraph or is terminated. Thus, the apportionment plan (including any amendments thereof) has a continuing effect and need not be renewed annually. An apportionment plan with respect to a particular taxable year of the common parent shall terminate with respect to the taxable years of the members of the affiliated group which include the last day of a succeeding taxable year of the common parent if—

(i) Any corporation which was a member of the affiliated group on each day of its matching taxable year which included the last day of the particular taxable year of the common parent is not a member of such group on each day of its taxable year which includes the last day of such succeeding taxable year of the common parent, or

(ii) Any corporation which was not a member of such group on each day of its taxable year which included the last day of the particular taxable year of the common parent is a member of such group on each day of its taxable year which includes the last day of such succeeding taxable year of the common parent.

An apportionment plan, once terminated, is no longer effective. Accordingly, unless a new apportionment plan is filed and consented to (or the section 243(b)(2) election is terminated) the amounts referred to in subparagraph (1) of this paragraph will be apportioned among the corporations which are members of the affiliated group on each day of their matching taxable years in accordance with the rules provided in paragraphs (d)(3)(i), (d)(3)(ii), (d)(4), and (d)(5)(i) of this section.

(4) *Filing of plan.*—The apportionment plan shall be in the form of a statement filed by the common parent corporation with the district director for the internal revenue district in which is located the principal place of business or principal office or agency of such common parent. The statement shall be signed by any person who is duly authorized to act on behalf of the common parent corporation and shall set forth the name, address, internal revenue district, taxpayer account number, and taxable year of each member to whom the common parent could apportion an amount under subparagraph (1) of this paragraph (or, in the case of an apportionment plan referred to in subparagraph (9) of this paragraph, each member to whom the common parent could apportion an amount under such subparagraph) and the amount (or amounts) apportioned to each such member under the plan.

(5) *Consent of wholly owned subsidiaries.*—If all the stock of a corporation which is a member of the affiliated group on each day of its matching taxable year is owned on each such day by another corporation (or corporations) which is a member of such group on each day of its matching taxable year, such corporation (hereinafter in this paragraph referred to as a "wholly owned subsidiary") shall be deemed to consent to the apportionment plan. Each wholly owned subsidiary should attach a copy of the plan filed by the common parent corporation to an income tax return, amended return, or claim for refund for its matching taxable year.

(6) *Consent of other members.*—The consent of each member (other than the common parent corporation and wholly owned subsidiaries) to an apportionment plan shall be in the form of a statement, signed by any person who is duly authorized to act on behalf of the member consenting to the plan, stating that such member consents to the plan. The consent of more than one such member may be incorporated in a single statement. The statement (or statements) shall be attached to the apportionment plan filed by the common parent corporation. The consent of any such member which, after the date the apportionment plan was filed and during its matching taxable year referred to in subparagraph (1) of this paragraph, ceases to be a wholly owned subsidiary but continues to be a member, shall be filed with the district director with whom the apportionment plan is filed (as soon as possible after it ceases to be a wholly owned subsidiary) Each consenting member should attach a copy of the apportionment plan filed by the common parent to an income tax return, amended return, or claim for refund for its matching taxable year which includes the last day of the taxable year of the common parent corporation for which the apportionment plan was filed.

(7) *Members of group filing consolidated return.*—(i) *General rule.*—Except as provided in subdivision (ii) of this subparagraph, if the members of an affiliated group of corporations include one or more corporations taxable under section 11 of the Code and one or more insurance companies taxable under section 802 or 821 of the Code and if the affiliated group includes corporations which join in the filing of a consolidated return, then, for purposes of determining the amount to be apportioned to a corporation under an apportionment plan adopted under this paragraph, the corporations filing the consolidated return shall be treated as a single member.

(ii) *Consenting to an apportionment plan.*—For purposes of consenting to an apportionment plan under subparagraphs (5) and (6) of this paragraph, if the members of an affiliated group of corporations include corporations which join in the filing of a consolidated return, each corporation which joins in filing the consolidated return shall be treated as a separate member.

(8) *Amendment of plan.*—An apportionment plan, which is effective for the matching taxable years of members of an affiliated group, may be amended if an amended plan is filed (and consented to) within the time and in accordance with the rules prescribed in this paragraph for the adoption of an original plan with respect to such taxable years.

(9) *Certain taxable years beginning in 1963 and ending in 1964.*—In the case of corporations which are members of an affiliated group of corporations on each day of their taxable years referred to in paragraph (e) of this section—

(i) The $100,000 amount referred to in paragraph (d)(3)(i) of this section (relating to limitation under section 615(a)),

(ii) The amount determined under paragraph (d)(3)(ii)(*a*) of this section (relating to limitation under section 615(c)),

(iii) The $25,000 amount referred to in paragraph (d)(4) of this section (relating to small business deduction of life insurance companies), and

(iv) The $100,000 amount referred to in paragraph (d)(5)(i) of this section (relating to exemption from estimated tax),

may be apportioned among such members (for such taxable years) if an apportionment plan is filed (and consented to) with respect to such taxable years in accordance with the rules provided in subparagraphs (2), (4), (5), (6), (7), and (8) of this paragraph. For purposes of this subparagraph, such subparagraphs shall be applied as if such taxable years included the last day of a taxable year of the common parent corporation, i.e., as if such taxable years were matching taxable years. An apportionment plan adopted under this subparagraph shall be effective only with respect to taxable years referred to in paragraph (e) of this section. The plan may provide for the apportionment to one or more of such members, in fixed dollar amounts, of one or more of the amounts referred to in subdivisions (i), (ii), (iii), and (iv) of this subparagraph, but in no event shall the sum of the amounts so apportioned in respect of any such subdivision exceed the amount referred to in such subdivision. See also paragraph (d) (3) (v) of this section, relating to the maximum amount that may be apportioned to a corporation under an apportionment plan described in this subparagraph with respect to exploration expenditures to which section 615 applies.

(g) *Short taxable years.*—(1) *General.*—If—

(i) The return of a corporation is for a short period (ending after December 31, 1963) on each day of which such corporation is a member of an affiliated group,

(ii) The last day of the common parent's taxable year does not end with or within such short period, and

(iii) An election under section 243(b)(2) by such group is effective under paragraph (c)(4)(i) of §1.243-4 for the taxable year of the common parent within which falls such short period,

then the restrictions and limitations prescribed by section 243(b)(3) shall be applied in the manner provided in subparagraph (2) of this paragraph.

(2) *Manner of applying restrictions.*—In the case of a corporation described in subparagraph (1) of this paragraph having a short period described in such subparagraph—

(i) Such corporation may not consent to an election under section 1562, relating to election of multiple surtax exemptions, which would be effective for such short period;

(ii) The credit under section 901 shall be allowed to such corporation for such short period if, and only if, each corporation, which pays or accrues foreign taxes and which is a member of the affiliated group on each day of its taxable year which includes the last day of the common parent's taxable year within which falls such short period, does not deduct such taxes in computing its tax liability for its taxable year which includes such last day;

(iii) The overall limitation provided in section 904(a)(2) shall be allowed to such corporation for such short period if, and only if, each corporation, which pays or accrues foreign taxes and which is a member of the affiliated group on each day of its taxable year which includes the last day of the common parent's taxable year within which falls such short period, uses such limitation for its taxable year which includes such last day;

(iv) The minimum accumulated earnings credit provided by section 535(c)(2) (or in the case of a mere holding or investment company, the accumulated earnings credit provided by section 535(c)(3)) allowable for such short period shall be the amount computed by dividing (*a*) the amount (if any) by which $100,000 exceeds the aggregate of the accumulated earnings and profits of the corporations, which are members of the affiliated group on the last day of such short period, as of the close of their taxable years preceding the taxable year which includes the last day of such short period, by (*b*) the number of such members on the last day of such short period;

(v) The deduction allowable under section 615(a) for such short period shall be limited to an amount equal to $100,000 divided by the number of corporations which are members of the affiliated group on the last day of such short period;

(vi) If the expenditures to which section 615(a) applies which are paid or incurred by such corporation during such short period would, when added to the aggregate of the amounts deducted or deferred (in taxable years ending before the last day of such short period) which are taken into account in applying the limitation of section 615(c) by corporations which are members of the affiliated group on the last day of such short period exceed $400,000, then section 615 shall not apply to any such expenditure so paid or incurred by such corporation to the extent such expenditure would exceed an amount equal to (*a*) the amount (if any) by which $400,000 exceeds the aggregate of the amounts so deducted or deferred in such taxable years (computed as if each member filed a separate return), divided by (*b*) the number of corporations in the group which have taxable years ending on such last day;

(vii) If such corporation is a life insurance company taxable under section 802, the small business deduction under sections 804(a)(4) and 809(d)(10) shall not exceed an amount equal to (*a*) $25,000, divided by (*b*) the number of life insurance companies taxable under section 802 which are members of the affiliated group on the last day of such short period; and

(viii) The exemption from estimated tax (for purposes of estimated tax filing requirements under section 6016 and the addition to tax under section 6655 for failure to pay estimated tax) for such short period shall be an amount equal to $100,000 divided by the number of corporations which are members of the affiliated group on the last day of such short period. [Reg. §1.243-5.]

☐ [T.D. 6992, 1-17-69. *Amended by T.D. 7376, 9-15-75.*]

[Reg. §1.245-1]

§1.245-1. Dividends received from certain foreign corporations.—(a) *General rule.*—(1) A corporation is allowed a deduction *under section 245(a)* for dividends received from a foreign corporation (other than a *foreign personal holding company as defined in* section 552) which is subject to taxation under chapter 1 of the Code if, for an uninterrupted period of not less than 36 months ending with the close of the foreign corporation's taxable year in which the dividends are paid, (i) the foreign corporation is engaged in trade or business in the United States, and (ii) 50 percent or more of the foreign corporation's entire gross income is effectively connected with the conduct of a trade or business in the United States by that corporation. If the foreign corporation has been in existence less than 36 months as of the close of the taxable year in which the dividends are paid, then the applicable uninterrupted period to be taken into

consideration in lieu of the uninterrupted period of 36 or more months is the entire period such corporation has been in existence as of the close of such taxable year. An uninterrupted period which satisfied the twofold requirement with respect to business activity and gross income may start at a date later than the date on which the foreign corporation first commenced an uninterrupted period of engaging in trade or business within the United States, but the applicable uninterrupted period is in any event the longest uninterrupted period which satisfies such twofold requirement. The deduction under section 245(a) is allowable to any corporation, whether foreign or domestic, receiving dividends from a distributing corporation which meets the requirements of that section.

(2) Any taxable year of a foreign corporation which falls within the uninterrupted period described in section 245(a)(2) shall not be taken into account in applying section 245(a)(2) and this paragraph if the 100 percent dividends received deduction would be allowable under paragraph (b) of this section, whether or not in fact allowed, with respect to any dividends payable, whether or not in fact paid, out of the earnings and profits of such foreign corporation for that taxable year. Thus, in such case the foreign corporation shall be treated as having no earnings and profits for that taxable year for purposes of determining the dividends received deduction allowance under section 245(a) and this paragraph. However, that taxable year may be taken into account for purposes of determining whether the foreign corporation meets the requirements of section 245(a) that, for the uninterrupted period specified therein, the foreign corporation is engaged in trade or business in the United States and meets the 50 percent gross income requirement.

(b) *Dividends from wholly owned foreign subsidiaries.*—(1) A domestic corporation is allowed a deduction under section 245(b) for any taxable year beginning after December 31, 1966, for dividends received from a foreign corporation (other than a foreign personal holding company as defined in section 552) which is subject to taxation under chapter 1 of the Code if—

(i) The domestic corporation owns either directly or indirectly all of the outstanding stock of the foreign corporation during the entire taxable year of the domestic corporation in which the dividends are received, and

(ii) The dividends are paid out of earnings and profits of a taxable year of the foreign corporation during which (*a*) the domestic corporation receiving the dividends owns directly or indirectly throughout such year all of the outstanding stock of the foreign corporation, and (*b*) all of the gross income of the foreign corporation from all sources is effectively connected for that year with the conduct of a trade or business in the United States by that corporation.

(2) The deduction allowed by section 245(b) does not apply if an election under section 1562, relating to the privilege of a controlled group of corporations to elect multiple surtax exemptions, is effective for either the taxable year of the domestic corporation in which the dividends are received or the taxable year of the foreign corporation out of the earnings and profits of which the dividends are paid.

(c) *Rules of application.*—(1) Except as provided in section 246, the deduction provided by section 245 for any taxable year is the sum of the amounts computed under paragraphs (1) and (2) of section 245(a) plus, in the case of a domestic corporation for any taxable year beginning after December 31, 1966, the sum of the amounts computed under section 245(b)(2).

(2) To the extent that a dividend received from a foreign corporation is treated as a dividend from a domestic corporation in accordance with section 243(d) and §1.243-3, it shall not be treated as a dividend received from a foreign corporation for purposes of this section.

(3) For purposes of section 245(a) and (b), the amount of a distribution shall be determined under subparagraph (B) (without reference to subparagraph (C)) of section 301(b)(1).

(4) In determining from what year's earnings and profits a dividend is treated as having been distributed for purposes of this section, the principles of paragraph (a) of §1.316-2 shall apply. A dividend shall be considered to be distributed, first, out of the earnings and profits of the taxable year which includes the date the dividend is distributed, second, out of the earnings and profits accumulated for the immediately preceding taxable year, third, out of the earnings and profits accumulated for the second preceding taxable year, etc. A deficit in an earnings and profits account for any taxable year shall reduce the most recently accumulated earnings and profits for a prior year in such account. If there are no accumulated earnings and profits in an earnings and profits account because of a deficit incurred in a prior year, such deficit must be restored before earnings and profits can be accumulated in a subsequent accounting year. See also paragraph (c) of §1.243-3 and paragraph (a)(6) of §1.243-4.

(5) For purposes of this section the gross income of a foreign corporation for any period before its first taxable year beginning after

December 31, 1966, which is from sources within the United States shall be treated as gross income which is effectively connected for that period with the conduct of a trade or business in the United States by that corporation.

(6) For the determination of the source of income and the income which is effectively connected with the conduct of a trade or business in the United States, see sections 861 through 864, and the regulations thereunder.

(d) *Illustrations.*—The application of this section may be illustrated by the following examples:

Example (1). Corporation A (a foreign corporation filing its income tax returns on a calendar year basis) whose stock is 100 percent owned by Corporation B (a domestic corporation filing its income tax returns on a calendar year basis) for the first time engaged in trade or business within the United States on January 1, 1943, and qualifies under section 245 for the entire period beginning on that date and ending on December 31, 1954. Corporation A had accumulated earnings and profits of $50,000 immediately prior to January 1, 1943, and had earnings and profits of $10,000 for each taxable year during the uninterrupted period from January 1, 1943, through December 31, 1954. It derived for the period from January 1, 1943, through December 31, 1953, 90 percent of its gross income from sources within the United States and in 1954 derived 95 percent of its gross income from sources within the United States. During the calendar years 1943, 1944, 1945, 1946, and 1947 Corporation A distributed in each year $15,000; during the calendar years 1948, 1949, 1950, 1951, 1952, and 1953 it distributed in each year $5,000; and during the year 1954, $50,000. An analysis of the accumulated earnings and profits under the above statement of facts discloses that at December 31, 1953, the accumulation amounted to $55,000, of which $25,000 was accumulated prior to the "uninterrupted period" and $30,000 was accumulated during the uninterrupted period. (See section 316(a) and paragraph (c) of this section.) For 1954 a deduction under section 245 of $31,025 ($8,075 on 1954 earnings of the foreign corporation, plus $22,950 from the $30,000 accumulation at December 31, 1953) for dividends received from a foreign corporation is allowable to Corporation B with respect to the $50,000 received from Corporation A, computed as follows:

(i) $8,075, which is $8,500 (85 percent—the percent specified in section 243 for the calendar year 1954—of the $10,000 of earnings and profits of the taxable year) multiplied by 95 percent (the portion of the gross income of Corporation A derived during the taxable year 1954 from sources within the United States), plus

(ii) $22,950, which is $25,500 (85 percent—the percent specified in section 243 for the calendar year 1954—of $30,000, the part of the earnings and profits accumulated after the beginning of the uninterrupted period) multiplied by 90 percent (the portion of the gross income of Corporation A derived from sources within the United States during that portion of the uninterrupted period ending at the beginning of the taxable year 1954).

Example (2). If in example (1) Corporation A for the taxable year 1954 had incurred a deficit of $10,000 (shown to have been incurred before December 31) the amount of the earnings and profits accumulated after the beginning of the uninterrupted period would be $20,000. If Corporation A had distributed $50,000 on December 31, 1954, the deduction under section 245 for dividends received from a foreign corporation allowable to Corporation B for 1954 would be $15,300, computed by multiplying $17,000 (85 percent—the percent specified in section 243 for the calendar year 1954—of $20,000 earnings and profits accumulated after the beginning of the uninterrupted period) by 90 percent (the portion of the gross income of Corporation A derived from United States sources during that portion of the uninterrupted period ending at the beginning of the taxable year 1954).

Example (3). Corporation A (a foreign corporation filing its income tax returns on a calendar year basis) whose stock is 100 percent owned by corporation B (a domestic corporation filing its income tax returns on a calendar year basis) for the first time engaged in trade or business within the United States on January 1, 1960, and qualifies under section 245 for the entire period beginning on that date and ending on December 31, 1963. In 1963, A derived 75 percent of its gross income from sources within the United States. A's earnings and profits for 1963 (computed as of the close of the taxable year without diminution by reason of any distributions made during the taxable year) are $200,000. On December 31, 1963, corporation A distributes to corporation B 100 shares of corporation C stock which have an adjusted basis in A's hands of $40,000 and a fair market value of $100,000. For purposes of computing the deduction under section 245 for dividends received from a foreign corporation, the amount of the *distribution is $40,000.* B is allowed a deduction under section 245 of $25,500, i.e., $34,000 ($40,000 multiplied by 85 percent, the percent specified in section 243 for 1963), multiplied by 75 percent (the portion of the gross income of corporation A derived during 1963 from sources within the United States). [Reg. § 1.245-1.]

☐ [*T.D.* 6183, 6-13-56. *Amended by T.D.* 6752, 9-8-64, *T.D.* 6830, 6-22-65 *and T.D.* 7293, 11-27-73.]

[Reg. § 1.245A-1]

§1.245A-1. [Reserved].
☐ [*T.D.* 9909, 8-21-2020.]

[Reg. § 1.245A-2]

§1.245A-2. [Reserved].
☐ [*T.D.* 9909, 8-21-2020.]

[Reg. § 1.245A-3]

§1.245A-3. [Reserved].
☐ [*T.D.* 9909, 8-21-2020.]

[Reg. § 1.245A-4]

§1.245A-4. [Reserved].
☐ [*T.D.* 9909, 8-21-2020.]

[Reg. § 1.245A-5]

§1.245A-5. Limitation of section 245A deduction and section 954(c)(6) exception.—(a) *Overview.*—This section provides rules that limit a deduction under section 245A(a) to the portion of a dividend that exceeds the ineligible amount of such dividend or the applicability of section 954(c)(6) when a portion of a dividend is paid out of an extraordinary disposition account or when an extraordinary reduction occurs. Paragraph (b) of this section provides rules regarding ineligible amounts. Paragraph (c) of this section provides rules for determining ineligible amounts attributable to an extraordinary disposition. Paragraph (d) of this section provides rules that limit the application of section 954(c)(6) when one or more section 245A shareholders of a lower-tier CFC have an extraordinary disposition account. Paragraph (e) of this section provides rules for determining ineligible amounts attributable to an extraordinary reduction. Paragraph (f) of this section provides rules that limit the application of section 954(c)(6) when a lower-tier CFC has an extraordinary reduction amount. Paragraph (g) of this section provides special rules for purposes of applying this section. Paragraph (h) of this section provides an anti-abuse rule. Paragraph (i) of this section provides definitions. Paragraph (j) of this section provides examples illustrating the application of this section. Paragraph (k) of this section provides the applicability date of this section.

(b) *Limitation of deduction under section 245A.*—(1) *In general.*—A section 245A shareholder is allowed a section 245A deduction for any dividend received from an SFC (provided all other applicable requirements are satisfied) only to the extent that the dividend exceeds the ineligible amount of the dividend. See paragraphs (j)(2), (4), and (5) of this section for examples illustrating the application of this paragraph (b)(1).

(2) *Definition of ineligible amount.*—The term *ineligible amount* means, with respect to a dividend received by a section 245A shareholder from an SFC, an amount equal to the sum of—

(i) 50 percent of the extraordinary disposition amount (as determined under paragraph (c) of this section); and

(ii) The extraordinary reduction amount (as determined under paragraph (e) of this section).

(c) *Rules for determining extraordinary disposition amount.*—(1) *Definition of extraordinary disposition amount.*—The term *extraordinary disposition amount* means the portion of a dividend received by a section 245A shareholder from an SFC that is paid out of the extraordinary disposition account with respect to the section 245A shareholder. See paragraph (j)(2) of this section for an example illustrating the application of this paragraph (c).

(2) *Determination of portion of dividend paid out of extraordinary disposition account.*—(i) *In general.*—For purposes of determining the portion of a dividend received by a section 245A shareholder from an SFC that is paid out of the extraordinary disposition account with respect to the section 245A shareholder, the following rules apply—

(A) The dividend is first considered paid out of non-extraordinary disposition E&P with respect to the section 245A shareholder; and

(B) The dividend is next considered paid out of the extraordinary disposition account to the extent of the section 245A shareholder's extraordinary disposition account balance.

(ii) *Definition of non-extraordinary disposition E&P.*—The term *non-extraordinary disposition E&P* means, with respect to a section 245A shareholder and an SFC, an amount of earnings and profits of the SFC equal to the excess, if any, of—

(A) The product of—

(1) The amount of the SFC's earnings and profits described in section 959(c)(3), determined as of the end of the SFC's taxable year (for purposes of paragraph (c)(2)(ii) of this section, without regard to distributions during the taxable year other than as provided in this paragraph (c)(2)(ii)(A)(1)), but, if during the taxable year the SFC pays more than one dividend, reduced (but not below zero) by the amounts of any dividends paid by the SFC earlier in the taxable year; and

(2) The percentage of the stock (by value) of the SFC that the section 245A shareholder owns directly or indirectly immediately before the distribution; over

(B) The balance of the section 245A shareholder's extraordinary disposition account with respect to the SFC, determined immediately before the distribution.

(3) Definitions with respect to extraordinary disposition accounts.—*(i) Extraordinary disposition account.*—*(A) In general.*—The term *extraordinary disposition account* means, with respect to a section 245A shareholder of an SFC, an account, the balance of which is equal to the product of the extraordinary disposition ownership percentage and the extraordinary disposition E&P, reduced (but not below zero) by the prior extraordinary disposition amount and as provided in §1.245A-7 or §1.245A-8, and adjusted under paragraph (c)(4) of this section, as applicable. An extraordinary disposition account is maintained in the same functional currency as the extraordinary disposition E&P.

(B) Extraordinary disposition ownership percentage.—The term *extraordinary disposition ownership percentage* means the percentage of stock (by value) of an SFC that a section 245A shareholder owns directly or indirectly at the beginning of the disqualified period or, if later, on the first day during the disqualified period on which the SFC is a CFC, regardless of whether the section 245A shareholder owns directly or indirectly such stock of the SFC on the date of an extraordinary disposition giving rise to extraordinary disposition E&P; if not, see paragraph (c)(4) of this section.

(C) Extraordinary disposition E&P.—The term *extraordinary disposition E&P* means an amount of earnings and profits of an SFC equal to the sum of the net gain recognized by the SFC with respect to specified property in each extraordinary disposition. In the case of an extraordinary disposition with respect to the SFC arising as a result of a disposition of specified property by a specified entity (other than a foreign corporation), an interest of which is owned directly or indirectly (through one or more other specified entities that are not foreign corporations) by the SFC, the net gain taken into account for purposes of the preceding sentence is the SFC's distributive share of the net gain recognized by the specified entity with respect to the specified property.

(D) Prior extraordinary disposition amount.—*(1) General rule.*—The term *prior extraordinary disposition amount* means, with respect to an SFC and a section 245A shareholder, the sum of the extraordinary disposition amount of each prior dividend received by the section 245A shareholder from the SFC by reason of paragraph (c)(1) of this section and 200 percent of the sum of the amounts included in the section 245A shareholder's gross income under section 951(a) by reason of paragraph (d) of this section (in the case in which the SFC is, or has been, a lower-tier CFC). A section 245A shareholder's prior extraordinary disposition amount also includes—

(i) A prior dividend received by the section 245A shareholder from the SFC to the extent not an extraordinary reduction amount and to the extent the dividend would have been an extraordinary disposition amount but for the failure of the dividend to qualify for the section 245A deduction by reason of one or more of the following: application of section 245A(e); the recipient domestic corporation does not satisfy the holding period requirement of section 246; or the recipient domestic corporation is not a United States shareholder with respect to the foreign corporation from whose earnings and profits the dividend is sourced;

(ii) The portion of a prior dividend (to the extent not a tiered extraordinary disposition amount by reason of paragraph (d) of this section) received by an upper-tier CFC from the SFC that by reason of section 245A(e) or being properly allocable to subpart F income of the SFC for the taxable year of the dividend pursuant to section 954(c)(6)(A) was included in the upper-tier CFC's foreign personal holding company income and was included in gross income by the section 245A shareholder under section 951(a) but would have been a tiered extraordinary disposition amount by reason of paragraph (d) of this section had paragraph (d) applied to the dividend;

(iii) If a prior dividend received by an upper-tier CFC from a lower-tier CFC gives rise to a tiered extraordinary disposition amount with respect to the section 245A shareholder by reason of paragraph (d) of this section, the qualified portion; and

(iv) 200 percent of an amount included in the gross income of a domestic corporation under section 951(a)(1)(B) with respect to a CFC for the taxable year of the domestic corporation in which or with which the CFC's taxable year ends, to the extent so included by reason of the application of this section to the hypothetical distribution described in §1.956-1(a)(2), or to the extent the amount would have been so included by reason of the application of this section to the hypothetical distribution but for the application of section 245A(e) or the holding period requirement in section 246 to the hypothetical distribution.

(2) Definition of qualified portion.—*(i) In general.*—The term *qualified portion* means, with respect to a tiered extraordinary disposition amount of a section 245A shareholder and a lower-tier CFC, 200 percent of the portion of the disqualified amount with respect to the tiered extraordinary disposition amount equal to the sum of the amounts included in gross income by each U.S. tax resident under section 951(a) in the taxable year in which the tiered extraordinary disposition amount arose with respect to the lower-tier CFC by reason of paragraph (d) of this section. For purposes of the preceding sentence, the reference to a U.S. tax resident does not include any section 245A shareholder with a tiered extraordinary disposition amount with respect to the lower-tier CFC.

(ii) Determining a qualified portion if multiple section 245A shareholders have tiered extraordinary disposition amounts. For the purposes of applying paragraph (c)(3)(i)(D)(2)(i) of this section, if more than one section 245A shareholder has a tiered extraordinary disposition amount with respect to a dividend received by an upper-tier CFC from a lower-tier CFC, then the qualified portion with respect to each section 245A shareholder is equal to the amount described in paragraph (c)(3)(i)(D)(2)(i) of this section, without regard to this paragraph (c)(3)(i)(D)(2)(ii), multiplied by a fraction, the numerator of which is the section 245A shareholder's tiered extraordinary disposition amount with respect to the lower-tier CFC and the denominator of which is the sum of the tiered extraordinary disposition amounts with respect to each section 245A shareholder and the lower-tier CFC.

(ii) Extraordinary disposition.—*(A) In general.*—Except as provided in paragraph (c)(3)(ii)(E) of this section, the term *extraordinary disposition* means, with respect to an SFC, any disposition of specified property by the SFC on a date on which it was a CFC and during the SFC's disqualified period to a related party if the disposition occurs outside of the ordinary course of the SFC's activities. An extraordinary disposition also includes a disposition during the disqualified period on a date on which the SFC is not a CFC if there is a plan, agreement, or understanding involving a section 245A shareholder to cause the SFC to recognize gain that would give rise to an extraordinary disposition if the SFC were a CFC.

(B) Facts and circumstances.—A determination as to whether a disposition is undertaken outside of the ordinary course of an SFC's activities is made on the basis of facts and circumstances, taking into account whether the transaction is consistent with the SFC's past activities, including with respect to quantity and frequency. In addition, a disposition of specified property by an SFC to a related party may be considered outside of the ordinary course of the SFC's activities notwithstanding that the SFC regularly disposes of property of the same type of, or similar to, the specified property to persons that are not related parties.

(C) Per se rules.—*(1) In general.*—Even if a disposition would otherwise be considered to be undertaken in the ordinary course of an SFC's activities under the requirements of paragraph (c)(3)(ii)(B) of this section, that disposition is treated as occurring outside of the ordinary course of an SFC's activities if the disposition is undertaken with a principal purpose of generating earnings and profits during the disqualified period or, except as provided in paragraph (c)(3)(ii)(C)(2) of this section, if the disposition is of intangible property, as defined in section 367(d)(4).

(2) Exception to the per se rule for certain property.—*(i) Exception.*—Paragraph (c)(3)(ii)(C)(1) of this section does not apply to a disposition of intangible property that is not described in section 367(d)(4)(C) or (F), provided that the property is transferred to a related person during the disqualified period with a reasonable expectation that the related person will resell the property to an unrelated customer within one year. Subject to paragraph (c)(3)(ii)(C)(2)(ii) of this section, a disposition of intangible property that satisfies the requirements of this paragraph (c)(3)(ii)(C)(2)(i) is determined to be within or without the ordinary course of an SFC's activities based on the test described in paragraph (c)(3)(ii)(B) of this section.

(ii) Facts and circumstances presumption for property described in section 367(d)(4)(A).—Notwithstanding paragraph (c)(3)(ii)(B) of this section, any disposition described in paragraph (c)(3)(ii)(C)(2)(i) of this section of a copyright right within the meaning of §1.861-18 or of intangible property described in section

367(d)(4)(A) is presumed to take place outside of the ordinary course of an SFC's activities for purposes of paragraph (c)(3)(ii)(A) of this section. The presumption in the preceding sentence may be rebutted only if the taxpayer can show that the facts and circumstances clearly establish that the disposition took place in the ordinary course of the SFC's activities.

(D) *Treatment of dispositions by certain specified entities.*—For purposes of paragraph (c)(3)(ii)(A) of this section, an extraordinary disposition with respect to an SFC includes a disposition by a specified entity other than a foreign corporation, provided that immediately before or immediately after the disposition the specified entity is a related party with respect to the SFC, the SFC directly or indirectly (through one or more other specified entities other than foreign corporations) owns an interest in the specified entity, and the disposition would have otherwise qualified as an extraordinary disposition had the specified entity been a foreign corporation.

(E) *De minimis exception to extraordinary disposition.*—If the sum of the net gain recognized by an SFC with respect to specified property in all dispositions otherwise described in paragraph (c)(3)(ii)(A) of this section does not exceed the lesser of $50 million or 5 percent of the gross value of all of the SFC's property held immediately before the beginning of its disqualified period, then no disposition of specified property by the SFC is an extraordinary disposition.

(iii) *Disqualified period.*—The term *disqualified period* means, with respect to an SFC that is a CFC on any day during the taxable year that includes January 1, 2018, the period beginning on January 1, 2018, and ending as of the close of the taxable year of the SFC, if any, that begins before January 1, 2018, and ends after December 31, 2017.

(iv) *Specified property.*—The term *specified property* means any property if gain recognized with respect to such property during the disqualified period is not described in section 951A(c)(2)(A)(i)(I) through (V). If only a portion of the gain recognized with respect to property during the disqualified period is gain that is not described in section 951A(c)(2)(A)(i)(I) through (V), then a portion of the property is treated as specified property in an amount that bears the same ratio to the value of the property as the amount of gain not described in section 951A(c)(2)(A)(i)(I) through (V) bears to the total amount of gain recognized with respect to such property during the disqualified period. Specified property is also property with respect to which a loss was recognized during the disqualified period if the loss is properly allocable to income not described in section 951A(c)(2)(A)(i)(I) through (V) under the principles of section 954(b)(5) (specified loss). If only a portion of the loss recognized with respect to property during the disqualified period is specified loss, then a portion of the property is treated as specified property in an amount that bears the same ratio to the value of the property as the amount of specified loss bears to the total amount of loss recognized with respect to such property during the disqualified period.

(4) *Successor rules for extraordinary disposition accounts.*—This paragraph (c)(4) applies with respect to an extraordinary disposition account upon certain direct or indirect transfers of stock of an SFC by a section 245A shareholder.

(i) *Another section 245A shareholder succeeds to all or portion of account.*—Except as provided in paragraph (c)(4)(vi) of this section, paragraphs (c)(4)(i)(A) through (D) of this section apply when a section 245A shareholder of an SFC (the *transferor*) transfers directly or indirectly a share of stock (or a portion of a share of stock) of the SFC that it owns directly or indirectly (the share or portion thereof, a *transferred share*).

(A) If immediately after the transfer (taking into account all transactions related to the transfer) another person is a section 245A shareholder of the SFC, then such other person's extraordinary disposition account with respect to the SFC is increased by the person's proportionate share of the amount allocated to the transferred share.

(B) For purposes of paragraph (c)(4)(i)(A) of this section, the amount allocated to a transferred share is equal to the product of—

(1) The balance of the transferor's extraordinary disposition account with respect to the SFC, determined after any reduction pursuant to paragraph (c)(3) of this section by reason of dividends and before the application of this paragraph (c)(4)(i)(B); and

(2) A fraction, the numerator of which is the value of the transferred share and the denominator of which is the value of all of the stock of the SFC that the transferor owns directly or indirectly immediately before the transfer.

(C) For purposes of paragraph (c)(4)(i)(A) of this section, a person's proportionate share of the amount allocated to a transferred share under paragraph (c)(4)(i)(B) of this section is equal to the product of—

(1) The amount allocated to the share; and

(2) The percentage of the share (by value) that the person owns directly or indirectly immediately after the transfer (taking into account all transactions related to the transfer).

(D) The transferor's extraordinary disposition account with respect to the SFC is decreased by the amount by which another person's extraordinary disposition account with respect to the SFC is increased pursuant to paragraph (c)(4)(i)(A) of this section.

(ii) *Certain section 381 transactions.*—(A) *In general.*—If assets of an SFC (the *acquired corporation*) are acquired by another SFC (the *acquiring corporation*) pursuant to a transaction described in section 381(a) in which the acquired corporation is the transferor corporation for purposes of section 381, then a section 245A shareholder's extraordinary disposition account with respect to the acquiring corporation is increased by the balance of its extraordinary disposition account with respect to the acquired corporation, determined after any reduction pursuant to paragraph (c)(3) of this section by reason of dividends and before the application of this paragraph (c)(4)(ii)(A).

(B) *Certain triangular asset reorganizations.*—If, in a transaction described in paragraph (c)(4)(ii)(A) of this section, the section 245A shareholder receives stock of a domestic corporation that controls (within the meaning of section 368(c)) the acquiring corporation, the domestic corporation's extraordinary disposition account with respect to the acquiring corporation is increased by the balance of the section 245A shareholder's extraordinary disposition account with respect to the acquired corporation, determined after any reduction pursuant to paragraph (c)(3) of this section by reason of dividends and before the application of this paragraph (c)(4)(ii)(B).

(iii) *Certain distributions involving section 355 or 356.*—In the case of a transaction involving a distribution under section 355 (or so much of section 356 as it relates to section 355) by an SFC (the *distributing corporation*) of stock of another SFC (the *controlled corporation*), a section 245A shareholder's extraordinary disposition account with respect to the distributing corporation is attributed to (and treated as) an extraordinary disposition account with respect to the controlled corporation in a manner similar to how earnings and profits of the distributing corporation and the controlled corporation are adjusted under §1.312-10. To the extent that a section 245A shareholder's extraordinary disposition account with respect to the distributing CFC is not so attributed to (and treated as) an extraordinary disposition account with respect to the controlled corporation, the extraordinary disposition account remains as an extraordinary disposition account with respect to the distributing corporation.

(iv) *Transfer of all of the stock of the SFC owned by a section 245A shareholder.*—(A) *In general.*—If, in a transaction described in paragraph (c) of this section, a section 245A shareholder of an SFC transfers directly or indirectly all of the stock of the SFC that it owns directly or indirectly, then, except as provided in paragraph (c)(4)(iv)(B) of this section, any remaining balance of the section 245A shareholder's extraordinary disposition account that is not allocated or attributed under paragraph (c) of this section is eliminated and therefore not taken into account by any person.

(B) *Related party retains the extraordinary distribution account.*—If any related party with respect to the section 245A shareholder described in paragraph (c)(4)(iv)(A) of this section is a section 245A shareholder with respect to the SFC immediately after the transfer (taking into account all transactions related to the transfer), then the remaining balance of the section 245A shareholder's extraordinary disposition account with respect to the SFC is added to the related party's extraordinary disposition account. If multiple related parties are section 245A shareholders of the SFC, then the remaining balance of the extraordinary disposition account is allocated between the related parties in proportion to the value of the stock of the SFC that they own directly or indirectly immediately after the transfer (taking into account all transactions related to the transfer).

(v) *Effect of section 338(g) election.*—(A) *In general.*—Except as provided in paragraph (c)(4)(v)(B) of this section, if an election under section 338(g) is made with respect to a qualified stock purchase (as defined in section 338(d)(3)) of stock of an SFC, then a section 245A shareholder's extraordinary disposition account with respect to the old target (as defined in §1.338-2(c)(17)) is not treated as (or attributed to) an extraordinary disposition account with respect to the new target (as defined in §1.338-2(c)(17)). Accordingly, the remaining balance of the old target's extraordinary disposition account is eliminated and is not thereafter taken into account by any person.

(B) *Special rules regarding carryover foreign target stock.*—If an election under section 338(g) is made with respect to a qualified stock purchase (as described in section 338(d)(3)) of stock of an SFC and there are one or more shares of carryover foreign target stock ("FT stock") (as described in §1.338-9(b)(3)(i)), then the following rules apply as to a section 245A shareholder of the new target that after the qualified stock purchase directly or indirectly owns carryover FT stock (such shareholder, the *carryover FT stock shareholder*):

(1) In a case in which before the qualified stock purchase the carryover FT stock shareholder directly or indirectly owned carryover FT stock, the carryover FT stock shareholder's extraordinary disposition account with respect to the old target, determined after any reduction pursuant to paragraph (c)(3) of this section by reason of dividends, is treated as its extraordinary disposition account with respect to the new target.

(2) In a case in which before the qualified stock purchase the carryover FT stock shareholder did not directly or indirectly own carryover FT stock, but the stock retains its character as carryover FT stock (taking into account §1.338-9(b)(3)(vi)), a ratable portion of each section 245A shareholder's extraordinary disposition account with respect to the old target, determined after any reduction pursuant to paragraph (c)(3) of this section by reason of dividends, is treated as the carryover FT stock shareholder's extraordinary disposition account with respect to the new target, based on the value of the carryover FT stock that the carryover FT stock shareholder owns directly or indirectly after the qualified stock purchase relative to the value of all of the stock of the new target.

(vi) *Certain transfers described in §1.1248-8(a)(1).*—(A) *In general.*—If a person transfers stock of an SFC with respect to which a section 245A shareholder has an extraordinary disposition account to a foreign acquiring corporation in a transaction described §1.1248-8(a)(1) (other than a transfer that is also described in §1.1248(f)-1(b)(2) or (3)) in which stock of a foreign corporation is received by the transferor, then, except in the case in which the transfer is also described in paragraph (c)(4)(ii) or (iii) of this section, the section 245A shareholder's extraordinary disposition account is not adjusted under this paragraph (c)(4).

(B) *Certain transfers described in §1.1248(f)-1(b).*—In the case of a transfer directly or indirectly of stock of an SFC by a section 245A shareholder described in §1.1248(f)-1(b)(2) or (3), but which does not result in an income inclusion, in whole or in part, by reason of §1.1248-2, the section 245A shareholder's extraordinary disposition account with respect to the SFC, determined after any reduction pursuant to paragraph (c)(3) of this section by reason of dividends and before the application of this paragraph (c)(4)(vi)(B), is allocated and adjusted in the same manner as under paragraph (c)(4)(i) of this section, except that, for purposes of applying paragraphs (c)(4)(i)(B) and (C) of this section, stock of the SFC that is owned directly or indirectly by persons who are not section 1248 shareholders (as defined in §1.1248(f)-1(c)(12)) is disregarded.

(vii) *Anti-abuse rule.*—Pursuant to paragraph (h) of this section, if a principal purpose of a transaction or series of transactions is to shift to another person, or to avoid, an amount of a section 245A shareholder's extraordinary disposition account with respect to an SFC or otherwise avoid the purposes of this section, then appropriate adjustments are made for purposes of this section, including disregarding the transaction or series of transactions. A principal purpose described in the preceding sentence is deemed to exist if stock of an SFC is directly or indirectly acquired by one of more section 245A shareholders within one year of a transaction or transactions to which paragraph (c)(4)(iv)(A) of this section would otherwise apply.

(d) *Limitation of amount eligible for section 954(c)(6) when there is an extraordinary disposition account with respect to a lower-tier CFC.*—(1) *In general.*—If an upper-tier CFC receives a dividend from a lower-tier CFC, then the dividend is eligible for the exception to foreign personal holding company income under section 954(c)(6) (provided all other applicable requirements are satisfied) with respect to the portion of the dividend that exceeds the disqualified amount. With respect to the portion of the dividend that does not exceed the disqualified amount, the exception to foreign personal holding company income under section 954(c)(6) is allowed (provided all applicable requirements are satisfied) only for the amount equal to 50 percent of the portion of the dividend that does not exceed the disqualified amount. The disqualified amount is the quotient of the amounts described in paragraphs (d)(1)(i) and (ii) of this section.

(i) The sum of each section 245A shareholder's tiered extraordinary disposition amount with respect to the lower-tier CFC.

(ii) The percentage of stock of the upper-tier CFC (by value) owned, in the aggregate, by U.S. tax residents that include in gross income their pro rata share of the upper-tier CFC's subpart F income under section 951(a) on the last day of the upper-tier CFC's taxable year. If a U.S. tax resident is a direct or indirect partner in a domestic partnership that is a United States shareholder of the upper-tier CFC, the amount of stock owned by the U.S. tax resident for purposes of the preceding sentence is determined under the principles of paragraph (g)(3) of this section.

(2) *Definition of tiered extraordinary disposition amount.*—(i) *In general.*—The term *tiered extraordinary disposition amount* means, with respect to a dividend received by an upper-tier CFC from a lower-tier CFC and a section 245A shareholder, the portion of the dividend that would be an extraordinary disposition amount if the section 245A shareholder received as a dividend its pro rata share of the dividend from the lower-tier CFC. The preceding sentence does not apply to an amount treated as a dividend received by an upper-tier CFC from a lower-tier CFC by reason of section 964(e)(4) (in such case, see paragraphs (b)(1) and (g)(2) of this section).

(ii) *Section 245A shareholder's pro rata share of a dividend received by an upper-tier CFC.*—For the purposes of paragraph (d)(2)(i) of this section, a section 245A shareholder's pro rata share of the amount of a dividend received by an upper-tier CFC from a lower-tier CFC equals the amount by which the dividend would increase the section 245A shareholder's pro rata share of the upper-tier CFC's subpart F income under section 951(a)(2) and §1.951-1(b) and (e) if the dividend were included in the upper-tier CFC's foreign personal holding company income under section 951(a)(1), determined without regard to section 952(c) and as if the upper-tier CFC had no deductions properly allocable to the dividend under section 954(b)(5).

(e) *Extraordinary reduction amount.*—(1) *In general.*—Except as provided in paragraph (e)(3) of this section, the term *extraordinary reduction amount* means, with respect to a dividend received by a controlling section 245A shareholder from a CFC during a taxable year of the CFC ending after December 31, 2017, in which an extraordinary reduction occurs with respect to the controlling section 245A shareholder's ownership of the CFC, the lesser of the amounts described in paragraph (e)(1)(i) or (ii) of this section. *See* paragraphs (j)(4) through (6) of this section for examples illustrating the application of this paragraph (e).

(i) The amount of the dividend.

(ii) The amount equal to the sum of the controlling section 245A shareholder's pre-reduction pro rata share of the CFC's subpart F income (as defined in section 952(a)) and tested income (as defined in section 951A(c)(2)(A)) for the taxable year, reduced, but not below zero, by the prior extraordinary reduction amount.

(2) *Rules regarding extraordinary reduction amounts.*—(i) *Extraordinary reduction.*—(A) *In general.*—Except as provided in paragraph (e)(2)(i)(C) of this section, an *extraordinary reduction* occurs, with respect to a controlling section 245A shareholder's ownership of a CFC during a taxable year of the CFC, if either of the conditions described in paragraph (e)(2)(i)(A)(1) or (2) of this section is satisfied. See paragraphs (j)(4) and (5) of this section for examples illustrating an extraordinary reduction.

(1) The condition of this paragraph (e)(2)(i)(A)(1) requires that during the taxable year, the controlling section 245A shareholder transfers directly or indirectly (other than by reason of a transfer occurring pursuant to an exchange described in section 368(a)(1)(E) or (F)), in the aggregate, more than 10 percent (by value) of the stock of the CFC that the section 245A shareholder owns directly or indirectly as of the beginning of the taxable year of the CFC, provided the stock transferred, in the aggregate, represents at least 5 percent (by value) of the outstanding stock of the CFC as of the beginning of the taxable year of the CFC; or

(2) The condition of this paragraph (e)(2)(i)(A)(2) requires that, as a result of one or more transactions occurring during the taxable year, the percentage of stock (by value) of the CFC that the controlling section 245A shareholder owns directly or indirectly as of the close of the last day of the taxable year of the CFC is less than 90 percent of the percentage of stock (by value) that the controlling section 245A shareholder owns directly or indirectly on either of the dates described in paragraphs (e)(2)(i)(B)(1) and (2) of this section (such percentage, the *initial percentage*), provided the difference between the initial percentage and percentage at the end of the year is at least five percentage points.

(B) *Dates for purposes of the initial percentage.*—For purposes of paragraph (e)(2)(i)(A)(2) of this section, the dates described in paragraphs (e)(2)(i)(B)(1) and (2) of this section are—

(1) The day of the taxable year on which the controlling section 245A shareholder owns directly or indirectly its highest percentage of stock (by value) of the CFC; and

(2) The day immediately before the first day on which stock was transferred directly or indirectly in the preceding taxable year in a transaction (or a series of transactions) occurring pursuant to a plan to reduce the percentage of stock (by value) of the CFC that the controlling section 245A shareholder owns directly or indirectly.

(C) *Transactions pursuant to which CFC's taxable year ends.*—A controlling section 245A shareholder's direct or indirect transfer of stock of a CFC that but for this paragraph (e)(2)(i)(C) would give rise to an extraordinary reduction under paragraph (e)(2)(i)(A) of this section does not give rise to an extraordinary reduction if the taxable year of the CFC ends immediately after the transfer, provided that the controlling section 245A shareholder directly or indirectly owns the stock on the last day of such year. Thus, for example, if a controlling section 245A shareholder exchanges all the stock of a CFC pursuant to a complete liquidation of the CFC, the exchange does not give rise to an extraordinary reduction.

(ii) *Rules for determining pre-reduction pro rata share.*—(A) *In general.*—Except as provided in paragraph (e)(2)(ii)(B) of this section, the term *pre-reduction pro rata share* means, with respect to a controlling section 245A shareholder and the subpart F income or tested income of a CFC, the controlling section 245A shareholder's pro rata share of the CFC's subpart F income or tested income under section 951(a)(2) and §1.951-1(b) and (e) or section 951A(e)(1) and §1.951A-1(d)(1), respectively, determined based on the controlling section 245A shareholder's direct or indirect ownership of stock of the CFC immediately before the extraordinary reduction (or, if the extraordinary reduction occurs by reason of multiple transactions, immediately before the first transaction) and without regard to section 951(a)(2)(B) and §1.951-1(b)(1)(ii), but only to the extent that such subpart F income or tested income is not included in the controlling section 245A shareholder's pro rata share of the CFC's subpart F income or tested income under section 951(a)(2) and §1.951-1(b) and (e) or section 951A(e)(1) and §1.951A-1(d)(1), respectively.

(B) *Decrease in section 245A shareholder's pre-reduction pro rata share for amounts taken into account by U.S. tax resident.*—A controlling section 245A shareholder's pre-reduction pro rata share of subpart F income or tested income of a CFC for a taxable year is reduced by an amount equal to the sum of the amounts by which each U.S. tax resident's pro rata share of the subpart F income or tested income is increased as a result of a transfer directly or indirectly of stock of the CFC by the controlling section 245A shareholder or an issuance of stock by the CFC (such an amount with respect to a U.S. tax resident, a *specified amount*), in either case, during the taxable year in which the extraordinary reduction occurs. For purposes of this paragraph (e)(2)(ii)(B), if there are extraordinary reductions with respect to more than one controlling section 245A shareholder during the CFC's taxable year, then a U.S. tax resident's specified amount attributable to an acquisition of stock from the CFC is prorated with respect to each controlling section 245A shareholder based on its relative decrease in ownership of the CFC. See paragraph (j)(5) of this section for an example illustrating a decrease in a section 245A shareholder's pre-reduction pro rata share for amounts taken into account by a U.S. tax resident.

(C) *Prior extraordinary reduction amount.*—The term *prior extraordinary reduction amount* means, with respect to a CFC and section 245A shareholder and a taxable year of the CFC in which an extraordinary reduction occurs, the sum of the extraordinary reduction amount of each prior dividend received by the section 245A shareholder from the CFC during the taxable year. A section 245A shareholder's prior extraordinary reduction amount also includes—

(1) A prior dividend received by the section 245A shareholder from the CFC during the taxable year to the extent the dividend was not eligible for the section 245A deduction by reason of section 245A(e) or the holding period requirement of section 246 not being satisfied but would have been an extraordinary reduction amount had this paragraph (e) applied to the dividend;

(2) If the CFC is a lower-tier CFC for a portion of the taxable year during which the lower-tier CFC pays any dividend to an upper tier-CFC, the portion of a prior dividend received by an upper-tier CFC from the lower-tier CFC during the taxable year of the lower-tier CFC that, by reason of section 245A(e), was included in the upper-tier CFC's foreign personal holding company income and that by reason of section 951(a) was included in income of the section 245A shareholder, and that would have given rise to a tiered extraordinary reduction amount by reason of paragraph (f) of this section had paragraph (f) applied to the dividend of which the section 245A shareholder would have included a pro rata share of the tiered extraordinary reduction amount in income by reason of section 951(a); and

(3) If the CFC is a lower-tier CFC for a portion of the taxable year during which the lower-tier CFC pays any dividend to an upper-tier CFC, the sum of the portion of the tiered extraordinary reduction amount of each prior dividend received by an upper-tier CFC from the lower-tier CFC during the taxable year that is included in income of the section 245A shareholder by reason of section 951(a).

(3) *Exceptions.*—(i) *Elective exception to close CFC's taxable year.*— (A) *In general.*—For a taxable year of a CFC in which an extraordinary reduction occurs with respect to a controlling section 245A shareholder and for which, absent this paragraph (e)(3)(i), there would be an extraordinary reduction amount or tiered extraordinary

reduction amount greater than zero, no amount is considered an extraordinary reduction amount or tiered extraordinary reduction amount with respect to the controlling section 245A shareholder if each controlling section 245A shareholder elects, and each U.S. tax resident described in paragraph (e)(3)(i)(C)(2) of this section agrees, pursuant to this paragraph (e)(3)(i), to close the CFC's taxable year for all purposes of the Internal Revenue Code (and, therefore, as to all shareholders of the CFC) as of the end of the date on which the extraordinary reduction occurs, or, if the extraordinary reduction occurs by reason of multiple transactions, as of the end of each date on which a transaction forming a part of the extraordinary reduction occurs. Because the determination as to whether there would be an extraordinary reduction amount or tiered extraordinary reduction amount greater than zero is made without regard to this paragraph (e)(3)(i), this determination is made without taking into account any elections that may be available, or other events that may occur, solely by reason of an election described in this paragraph (e)(3)(i), such as the application of section 954(b)(4) to a short taxable year created as a result of the election. If an election is made pursuant to this paragraph (e)(3)(i), all shareholders of the CFC that are a controlling section 245A shareholder or a U.S. tax resident described in paragraph (e)(3)(i)(C)(2) of this section must file their respective U.S. income tax and information returns consistently with the election. If each controlling section 245A shareholder elects to close the CFC's taxable year, that closing will be treated as a change in accounting period for purposes of the notice requirement in §1.964-1(c)(3)(iii), treating any controlling section 245A shareholders as controlling domestic shareholders for this purpose. However, the notice described in §1.964-1(c)(3)(iii) does not need to be provided to persons that are U.S. tax residents described in paragraph (e)(3)(i)(C) of this section. For purposes of applying this paragraph (e)(3)(i), a controlling section 245A shareholder that has an extraordinary reduction (or a transaction forming a part thereof) with respect to a CFC is treated as owning the same amount of stock it owned in the CFC immediately before the extraordinary reduction (or a transaction forming a part thereof) on the end of the date on which the extraordinary reduction occurs (or such transaction forming a part thereof occurs). To the extent that shares of a CFC are treated as owned by a controlling section 245A shareholder as of the close of the CFC's taxable year pursuant to the preceding sentence, such shares are treated as not being owned by any other person as of the close of the CFC's taxable year.

(B) *Allocation of foreign taxes.*—If an election is made pursuant to this paragraph (e)(3) to close a CFC's taxable year and the CFC's taxable year under foreign law (if any) does not close at the end of the date on which the CFC's taxable year closes as a result of the election, foreign taxes paid or accrued with respect to such foreign taxable year are allocated between the period of the foreign taxable year that ends with, and the period of the foreign taxable year that begins after, the date on which the CFC's taxable year closes as a result of the election. If there is more than one date on which the CFC's taxable year closes as a result of the election, foreign taxes paid or accrued with respect to the foreign taxable year are allocated to all such periods. The allocation is made based on the respective portions of the taxable income of the CFC (as determined under foreign law) for the foreign taxable year that are attributable under the principles of §1.1502-76(b) to the periods during the foreign taxable year. Foreign taxes allocated to a period under this paragraph (e)(3)(i)(B) are treated as paid or accrued by the CFC as of the close of that period.

(C) *Time and manner of making election.*—(1) *Election by controlling section 245A shareholder.*—An election pursuant to this paragraph (e)(3) is made and effective if the statement described in paragraph (e)(3)(i)(D) of this section is timely filed (including extensions) by each controlling section 245A shareholder making the election with its original U.S. tax return for the taxable year in which the extraordinary reduction occurs. If a controlling section 245A shareholder is a member of a consolidated group (within the meaning of §1.1502-1(h)) and participates in the extraordinary reduction, the agent for such group (within the meaning of §1.1502-77(c)(1)) must file the election described in this paragraph (e)(3) on behalf of such member.

(2) *Binding agreement.*—Before the filing of the statement described in paragraph (e)(3)(i)(D) of this section, each controlling section 245A shareholder must enter into a written, binding agreement with each U.S. tax resident that on the end of the date on which the extraordinary reduction occurs (or, if the extraordinary reduction occurs by reason of multiple transactions, each U.S. tax resident that on the end of each date on which a transaction forming a part of the extraordinary reduction occurs) owns directly or indirectly, without regard to the final two sentences of paragraph (e)(3)(i)(A) of this section, stock of the CFC and is a United States shareholder with respect to the CFC. In the case of a U.S. tax resident that owns stock

of the CFC indirectly through one or more partnerships, the partnership that directly owns the stock of the CFC may enter into the binding agreement on behalf of the U.S. tax resident partner provided that, before the due date of the partner's original Federal income tax return, including extensions, the partner delegated the authority to the partnership to enter into the binding agreement pursuant to a written partnership agreement (within the meaning of § 1.704-1(b)(2)(ii)(h)). The written, binding agreement must provide that each controlling section 245A shareholder will elect to close the taxable year of the CFC.

(3) *Transition rule.*—In the case of an extraordinary reduction occurring before August 27, 2020, the statement described in paragraph (e)(3)(i)(D) of this section is considered timely filed if it is attached by each controlling section 245A shareholder to an original or amended return for the taxable year in which the extraordinary reduction occurs. In the case of an amended return, the statement is considered timely filed only if it is filed with an amended return no later than February 23, 2021.

(D) *Form and content of statement.*—The statement required by paragraph (e)(3)(i)(C) of this section is to be titled "Elective Section 245A Year-Closing Statement." The statement must—

(1) Identify (by name and tax identification number, if any) each controlling section 245A shareholder, each U.S tax resident described in paragraph (e)(3)(i)(C) of this section, and the CFC;

(2) State the date of the extraordinary reduction (or, if the extraordinary reduction includes transactions on more than one date, the dates of all such transactions) to which the election applies;

(3) State the filing controlling section 245A shareholder's pro rata share of the subpart F income, tested income, and foreign taxes described in section 960 with respect to the stock of the CFC subject to the extraordinary reduction, and, if applicable, the amount of earnings and profits attributable to such stock within the meaning of section 1248, as of the date of the extraordinary reduction;

(4) State that each controlling section 245A shareholder and each U.S tax resident described in paragraph (e)(3)(i)(C) of this section have entered into a written, binding agreement to elect to close the CFC's taxable year in accordance with paragraph (e)(3)(i)(C) of this section; and

(5) Be filed in the manner, if any, prescribed by forms, publications, or other guidance published in the Internal Revenue Bulletin.

(E) *Consistency requirements.*—If multiple extraordinary reductions occur with respect to one or more controlling section 245A shareholders' ownership in a single CFC during one or more taxable years of the CFC, then to the extent those extraordinary reductions occur pursuant to a plan or series of related transactions, the election described in this paragraph (e)(3) section may be made only if it is made for all such extraordinary reductions with respect to the CFC for which there was an extraordinary reduction amount. Furthermore, if an extraordinary reduction occurs with respect to a controlling section 245A shareholders' ownership in one or more CFCs, then, to the extent those extraordinary reductions occur pursuant to a plan or series of related transactions, the election described in this paragraph (e)(3) may be made only if it is made for each extraordinary reduction for which there was an extraordinary reduction amount with respect to all of the CFCs that have the same or related (within the meaning of section 267(b) or 707(b)) controlling section 245A shareholders.

(ii) *De minimis subpart F income and tested income.*—For a taxable year of a CFC in which an extraordinary reduction occurs, no amount is considered an extraordinary reduction amount (or, with respect to a lower-tier CFC, a tiered extraordinary reduction amount under paragraph (f) of this section) with respect to a controlling section 245A shareholder of the CFC if the sum of the CFC's subpart F income and tested income (as defined in section 951A(c)(2)(A)) for the taxable year does not exceed the lesser of $50 million or 5 percent of the CFC's total income for the taxable year.

(f) *Limitation of amount eligible for section 954(c)(6) where extraordinary reduction occurs with respect to lower-tier CFCs.*—(1) *In general.*—If an extraordinary reduction occurs with respect to a lower-tier CFC and an upper-tier CFC receives a dividend from the lower-tier CFC in the taxable year in which the extraordinary reduction occurs, then the dividend is eligible for the exception to foreign personal holding company income under section 954(c)(6) (provided all other applicable requirements are satisfied) only with respect to the portion of the dividend that exceeds the tiered extraordinary reduction amount. The preceding sentence does not apply to an amount treated as a dividend received by an upper-tier CFC by reason of section 964(e)(4) (in this case, see paragraphs (b)(1) and (g)(2) of this section). See paragraph (j)(7) of this section for an example illustrating the application of this paragraph (f)(1).

(2) *Definition of tiered extraordinary reduction amount.*—The term *tiered extraordinary reduction amount* means, with respect to the portion of a dividend received by an upper-tier CFC from a lower-tier CFC during a taxable year of the lower-tier CFC, the amount of such dividend equal to the excess, if any, of—

(i) The product of—

(A) The sum of the amount of the subpart F income and tested income of the lower-tier CFC for the taxable year; and

(B) The percentage (by value) of stock of the lower-tier CFC owned (within the meaning of section 958(a)(2)) by the upper-tier CFC immediately before the extraordinary reduction (or the first transaction forming a part thereof); over

(ii) The following amounts—

(A) The sum of each U.S. tax resident's pro rata share of the lower-tier CFC's subpart F income and tested income under section 951(a) or 951A(a), respectively, that is attributable to shares of the lower-tier CFC owned (within the meaning of section 958(a)(2)) by the upper-tier CFC immediately prior to the extraordinary reduction (or the first transaction forming a part thereof), computed without the application of this paragraph (f);

(B) The sum of each prior tiered extraordinary reduction amount and sum of each amount included in an upper-tier CFC's subpart F income by reason of section 245A(e) with respect to prior dividends from the lower-tier CFC during the taxable year;

(C) The sum of each U.S. tax resident's pro rata share of an upper-tier CFC's subpart F income under section 951(a) and § 1.951-1(e) that is attributable to dividends received from the lower-tier CFC in the taxable year of the extraordinary reduction that do not qualify for the exception to foreign personal holding company income under section 954(c)(6) because the dividends, or portions thereof, are properly allocable to subpart F income of the lower-tier CFC for the taxable year of the extraordinary reduction pursuant to section 954(c)(6)(A);

(D) The sum of the prior extraordinary reduction amounts (but, for this purpose, computed without regard to amounts described in paragraphs (e)(2)(ii)(C)(2) and (3) of this section) of each controlling section 245A shareholder with respect to shares of the lower-tier CFC that were owned by such controlling section 245A shareholder (including indirectly through a specified entity other than a foreign corporation) for a portion of the taxable year but are owned by an upper-tier CFC (including indirectly through a specified entity other than a foreign corporation) at the time of the distribution of the dividend; and

(E) The product of the amount described in paragraph (f)(2)(i)(B) of this section and the sum of the amounts of each U.S. tax resident's pro rata share of subpart F income and tested income for the taxable year under section 951(a) or 951A(a), respectively, attributable to shares of the lower-tier CFC directly or indirectly acquired by the U.S. tax resident from the lower-tier CFC during the taxable year.

(3) *Transition rule for computing tiered extraordinary reduction amount.*—Solely for purposes of applying this paragraph (f) in taxable years of a lower-tier CFC beginning on or after January 1, 2018, and ending before June 14, 2019, a tiered extraordinary reduction amount is determined by treating the lower-tier CFC's subpart F income for the taxable year as if it were neither subpart F income nor tested income.

(g) *Special rules.*—The rules in this paragraph (g) apply for purposes of this section.

(1) *Source of dividends.*—A dividend received by any person is considered received directly by such person from the foreign corporation whose earnings and profits give rise to the dividend. Therefore, for example, if a section 245A shareholder sells or exchanges stock of an upper-tier CFC and the gain recognized on the sale or exchange is included in the gross income of the section 245A shareholder as a dividend under section 1248(a), then, to the extent the dividend is attributable under section 1248(c)(2) to the earnings and profits of a lower-tier CFC owned, within the meaning of section 958(a)(2), by the section 245A shareholder through the upper-tier CFC, the dividend is considered received directly by the section 245A shareholder from the lower-tier CFC.

(2) *Certain section 964(e) inclusions treated as dividends.*—An amount included in the gross income of a section 245A shareholder under section 951(a)(1)(A) by reason of section 964(e)(4) is considered a dividend received by the section 245A shareholder directly from the foreign corporation whose earnings and profits give rise to the amount described in section 964(e)(1). Therefore, for example, if an upper-tier CFC sells or exchanges stock of a lower-tier CFC, and, as a result of the sale or exchange, a section 245A shareholder with respect to the upper-tier CFC includes an amount in gross income under section 951(a)(1)(A) by reason of section 964(e)(4), then the inclusion is treated as a dividend received directly by the section 245A shareholder from the lower-tier CFC whose earnings and prof-

its give rise to the dividend, and the section 245A shareholder is not allowed a section 245A deduction for the dividend to the extent of the ineligible amount of such dividend.

(3) *Rules regarding stock ownership and stock transfers.*— (i) *Determining indirect ownership of stock of an SFC or a CFC.*—For purposes of this section, if a person owns an interest in, or stock of, a specified entity, including through a chain of ownership of one or more other specified entities, then the person is considered to own indirectly a pro rata share of stock of an SFC or a CFC owned by the specified entity. To determine a person's pro rata share of stock owned by a specified entity, the principles of section 958(a) apply without regard to whether the specified entity is foreign or domestic.

(ii) *Determining indirect transfers for stock owned indirectly.*—If, under paragraph (g)(3)(i) of this section, a person is considered to own indirectly stock of an SFC or CFC that is owned by a specified entity, then the following rules apply in determining if the person transfers stock of the SFC or CFC—

(A) To the extent the specified entity transfers stock that is considered owned indirectly by the person immediately before the transfer, the person is considered to transfer indirectly such stock;

(B) If the person transfers an interest in, or stock of, the specified entity, then the person is considered to transfer indirectly the stock of the SFC or CFC attributable to the interest in, or the stock of, the specified entity that is transferred; and

(C) In the case in which the person owns the specified entity through a chain of ownership of one or more other specified entities, if there is a transfer of an interest in, or stock of, another specified entity in the chain of ownership, then the person is considered to transfer indirectly the stock of the SFC or CFC attributable to the interest in, or the stock of, the other specified entity transferred.

(iii) *Definition of specified entity.*—The term *specified entity* means any partnership, trust (other than a trust treated as a corporation for U.S. income tax purposes), or estate (in each case, domestic or foreign), or any foreign corporation.

(4) *Coordination rules.*—(i) *General rule.*—A dividend is first subject to section 245A(e). To the extent the dividend is not a hybrid dividend or tiered hybrid dividend under section 245A(e), the dividend is subject to paragraph (e) or (f) of this section, as applicable, and then, to the extent the dividend is not subject to paragraph (e) or (f) of this section, it is subject to paragraph (c) or (d) of this section, as applicable.

(ii) *Coordination rule for paragraphs (c) and (d) and (e) and (f) of this section, respectively.*—If an SFC or CFC pays a dividend (or simultaneous dividends), a portion of which may be subject to paragraph (c) or (e) of this section and a portion of which may be subject to paragraph (d) or (f) of this section, the rules of this section apply by treating the portion of the dividend or dividends that may be subject to paragraph (c) or (e) of this section as if it occurred immediately before the portion of the dividend or dividends that may be subject to paragraph (d) or (f) of this section. For example, if a dividend arising under section 964(e)(4) occurs at the same time as a dividend that would be eligible for the exception to foreign personal holding company income under section 954(c)(6) but for the potential application of paragraph (d) this section, then the tiered extraordinary disposition amount with respect to the other dividend is determined as if the dividend arising under section 964(e)(4) occurs immediately before the other dividend.

(5) *Ordering rule for multiple dividends made by an SFC or a CFC during a taxable year.*—If an SFC or a CFC pays dividends on more than one date during its taxable year or at different times on the same date, this section applies based on the order in which the dividends are paid.

(6) *Partner's distributive share of a domestic partnership's pro rata share of subpart F income or tested income.*—If a section 245A shareholder or a U.S. tax resident is a direct or indirect partner in a domestic partnership that is a United States shareholder with respect to a CFC and includes in gross income its distributive share of the domestic partnership's inclusion under section 951(a) or 951A(a) with respect to the CFC then, solely for purposes of this section, a reference to the section 245A shareholder's or U.S. tax resident's pro rata share of the CFC's subpart F income or tested income included in gross income under section 951(a) or 951A(a), respectively, includes such person's distributive share of the domestic partnership's pro rata share of the CFC's subpart F income or tested income. A person is an indirect partner with respect to a domestic partnership if the person indirectly owns the domestic partnership through one or more specified entities (other than a foreign corporation).

(7) *Related domestic corporations treated as a single domestic corporation for certain purposes.*—For purposes of determining the extent that

a dividend is an extraordinary disposition amount or a tiered extraordinary disposition amount, as well as for purposes of determining the extent to which an extraordinary disposition account is reduced by a prior extraordinary disposition amount, domestic corporations that are related parties are treated as a single domestic corporation. Thus, for example, if two domestic corporations are related parties and either or both of them are section 245A shareholders with respect to an SFC, then the extent to which a dividend received by either domestic corporation from the SFC is an extraordinary disposition amount is based on the sum of each domestic corporation's extraordinary disposition account with respect to the SFC. When, by reason of this paragraph (g)(7), the extent to which a dividend is an extraordinary disposition amount or tiered extraordinary disposition amount is determined based on the sum of two or more extraordinary disposition accounts, a pro rata amount in each extraordinary disposition account is considered to give rise to the extraordinary disposition amount or tiered extraordinary disposition amount, if any.

(h) *Anti-abuse rule.*—Appropriate adjustments are made pursuant to this section, including adjustments that would disregard a transaction or arrangement in whole or in part, to any amounts determined under (or subject to the application of) this section if a transaction or arrangement is engaged in with a principal purpose of avoiding the purposes of this section. For examples illustrating the application of this paragraph (h), see paragraphs (j)(8) through (10) of this section.

(i) *Definitions.*—The following definitions apply for purposes of this section.

(1) *Controlled foreign corporation.*—The term *controlled foreign corporation* (or *CFC*) has the meaning provided in section 957.

(2) *Controlling section 245A shareholder.*—The term *controlling section 245A shareholder* means, with respect to a CFC, any section 245A shareholder that owns directly or indirectly more than 50 percent (by vote or value) of the stock of the CFC. For purposes of determining whether a section 245A shareholder is a controlling section 245A shareholder with respect to a CFC, all stock of the CFC owned by a related party with respect to the section 245A shareholder or by other persons acting in concert with the section 245A shareholder to undertake an extraordinary reduction is considered owned by the section 245A shareholder. If section 964(e)(4) applies to a sale or exchange of a lower-tier CFC with respect to a controlling section 245A shareholder, all United States shareholders of the CFC are considered to act in concert with regard to the sale or exchange. In addition, if all persons selling stock in a CFC, held directly, sell such stock to the same buyer or buyers (or a related party with respect to the buyer or buyers) as part of the same plan, all sellers will be considered to act in concert with regard to the sale or exchange.

(3) *Disqualified amount.*—The term *disqualified amount* has the meaning set forth in paragraph (d)(1) of this section.

(4) *Disqualified period.*—The term *disqualified period* has the meaning set forth in paragraph (c)(3)(iii) of this section.

(5) *Extraordinary disposition.*—The term *extraordinary disposition* has the meaning set forth in paragraph (c)(3)(ii) of this section.

(6) *Extraordinary disposition account.*—The term *extraordinary disposition amount* has the meaning set forth in paragraph (c)(3)(i) of this section.

(7) *Extraordinary disposition amount.*—The term *extraordinary disposition amount* has the meaning set forth in paragraph (c)(1) of this section.

(8) *Extraordinary disposition E&P.*—The term *extraordinary disposition E&P* has the meaning set forth in paragraph (c)(3)(i)(C) of this section.

(9) *Extraordinary disposition ownership percentage.*—The term *extraordinary disposition ownership percentage* has the meaning set forth in paragraph (c)(3)(i)(B) of this section.

(10) *Extraordinary reduction.*—The term *extraordinary reduction* has the meaning set forth in paragraph (e)(2)(i)(A) of this section.

(11) *Extraordinary reduction amount.*—The term *extraordinary reduction amount* has the meaning set forth in paragraph (e)(1) of this section.

(12) *Ineligible amount.*—The term *ineligible amount* has the meaning set forth in paragraph (b)(2) of this section.

(13) *Lower-tier CFC.*—The term *lower-tier CFC* means a CFC whose stock is owned (within the meaning of section 958(a)(2)), in whole or in part, by another CFC.

(14) *Non-extraordinary disposition E&P.*—The term *non-extraordinary disposition E&P* has the meaning set forth in paragraph (c)(2)(ii) of this section.

(15) *Pre-reduction pro rata share.*—The term *pre-reduction pro rata share* has the meaning set forth in paragraph (e)(2)(ii) of this section.

(16) *Prior extraordinary disposition amount.*—The term *prior extraordinary disposition amount* has the meaning set forth in paragraph (c)(3)(i)(D) of this section.

(17) *Prior extraordinary reduction amount.*—The term *prior extraordinary reduction amount* has the meaning set forth in paragraph (e)(2)(ii)(C) of this section.

(18) *Qualified portion.*—The term *qualified portion* has the meaning set forth in paragraph (c)(3)(i)(D)(2)(i) of this section.

(19) *Related party.*—The term *related party* means, with respect to a person, another person bearing a relationship described in section 267(b) or 707(b) to the person, in which case such persons are *related*.

(20) *Section 245A deduction.*—The term *section 245A deduction* means, with respect to a dividend received by a section 245A shareholder from an SFC, the amount of the deduction allowed to the section 245A shareholder by reason of the dividend.

(21) *Section 245A shareholder.*—The term *section 245A shareholder* means a domestic corporation that is a United States shareholder with respect to an SFC and that owns directly or indirectly stock of the SFC.

(22) *Specified 10-percent owned foreign corporation (SFC).*—The term *specified 10-percent owned foreign corporation* (or *SFC*) has the meaning provided in section 245A(b)(1).

(23) *Specified entity.*—The term *specified entity* has the meaning set forth in paragraph (g)(3)(iii) of this section.

(24) *Specified property.*—The term *specified property* has the meaning set forth in paragraph (c)(3)(iv) of this section.

(25) *Tiered extraordinary disposition amount.*—The term *tiered extraordinary disposition amount* has the meaning set forth in paragraph (d)(2)(i) of this section.

(26) *Tiered extraordinary reduction amount.*—The term *tiered extraordinary reduction amount* has the meaning set forth in paragraph (f)(2) of this section.

(27) *United States shareholder.*—The term *United States shareholder* has the meaning provided in section 951(b).

(28) *Upper-tier CFC.*—The term *upper-tier CFC* means a CFC that owns (within the meaning of section 958(a)(2)) stock in another CFC.

(29) *U.S. tax resident.*—The term *U.S. tax resident* means a United States person described in section 7701(a)(30)(A) or (C).

(j) *Examples.*—The application of this section is illustrated by the examples in this paragraph (j).

(1) *Facts.*—Except as otherwise stated, the facts described in this paragraph (j)(1) are assumed for purposes of the examples.

(i) US1 and US2 are domestic corporations, each with a calendar taxable year, and are not related parties with respect to each other.

(ii) CFC1, CFC2, and CFC3 are foreign corporations that are SFCs and CFCs.

(iii) Each entity uses the U.S. dollar as its functional currency.

(iv) Year 2 begins on or after January 1, 2018 and has 365 days.

(v) Absent application of this section, dividends received by US1 and US2 from a CFC meet the requirements to qualify for the section 245A deduction, and dividends received by one CFC from another CFC qualify for the exception to foreign personal holding company income under section 954(c)(6).

(vi) The de minimis rules in paragraphs (c)(3)(ii)(E) and (e)(3)(ii) of this section do not apply.

(vii) Section 1059 is not relevant to the tax results described in the examples in this paragraph (j).

(2) *Example 1. Extraordinary disposition.*—(i) *Facts.* US1 and US2 own 60% and 40%, respectively, of the single class of stock of CFC1. CFC1 owns all of the single class of stock of CFC2. CFC1 and CFC2 use the taxable year ending November 30 as their taxable year. On November 1, 2018, CFC1 sells specified property to CFC2 in exchange for $200x of cash (the "Property Transfer"). The Property Transfer is outside of CFC1's ordinary course of activities. The transferred property has a basis of $100x in the hands of CFC1. CFC1 recognizes $100x of gain as a result of the Property Transfer ($200x −

$100x). On December 1, 2018, CFC1 distributes $80x pro rata to US1 ($48x) and US2 ($32x), all of which is a dividend within the meaning of section 316 and treated as a distribution out of earnings described in section 959(c)(3). No other distributions are made by CFC1 to either US1 or US2 in CFC1's taxable year ending November 30, 2019. For its taxable year ending on November 30, 2019, CFC1 has $110x of earnings and profits described in section 959(c)(3), without regard to any distributions during the taxable year.

(ii) *Analysis*—(A) *Identification of extraordinary disposition.* Because CFC1 is a CFC and uses the taxable year ending on November 30, under paragraph (c)(3)(iii) of this section, it has a disqualified period beginning on January 1, 2018, and ending on November 30, 2018. In addition, under paragraph (c)(3)(ii) of this section, the Property Transfer is an extraordinary disposition because it: is a disposition of specified property by CFC1 on a date on which it was a CFC and during CFC1's disqualified period; is to CFC2, a related party with respect to CFC1; occurs outside of the ordinary course of CFC1's activities; and, is not subject to the de minimis rule in paragraph (c)(3)(ii)(E) of this section.

(B) *Determination of section 245A shareholders and their extraordinary disposition accounts.* Because CFC1 undertook an extraordinary disposition, under paragraph (c)(3)(i) of this section, a portion of CFC1's earnings and profits are extraordinary disposition E&P and, therefore, give rise to an extraordinary disposition account with respect to each of CFC1's section 245A shareholders. Under paragraph (i)(21) of this section, US1 and US2 are both section 245A shareholders with respect to CFC1. The amount of the extraordinary disposition account with respect to US1 is $60x, which is equal to the product of the extraordinary disposition E&P (the amount of the net gain recognized by CFC1 as a result of the Property Transfer ($100x)) and the extraordinary disposition ownership percentage (the percentage of the stock of CFC1 owned directly or indirectly by US1 on January 1, 2018 (60%)), reduced by the prior extraordinary disposition amount ($0). *See* paragraph (c)(3)(i) of this section. Similarly, the amount of the extraordinary disposition account with respect to US2 is $40x, which is equal to the product of the extraordinary disposition E&P (the net gain recognized by CFC1 as a result of the Property Transfer ($100x)) and extraordinary disposition ownership percentage (the percentage of the stock of CFC1 owned directly or indirectly by US2 on January 1, 2018 (40%)), reduced by the prior extraordinary disposition amount ($0).

(C) *Determination of extraordinary disposition amount with respect to US1.* The dividend of $48x paid to US1 on December 1, 2018, is an extraordinary disposition amount to the extent the dividend is paid out of the extraordinary disposition account with respect to US1. *See* paragraph (c)(1) of this section. Under paragraph (c)(2)(i) of this section, the dividend is first considered paid out of non-extraordinary disposition E&P with respect to US1, to the extent thereof. With respect to US1, $6x of CFC1's earnings and profits is non-extraordinary disposition E&P, calculated as the excess of $66x (the product of $110x of earnings and profits described in section 959(c)(3), without regard to the $80x distribution, and 60%) over $60x (the balance of US1's extraordinary disposition account with respect to CFC1, immediately before the distribution). *See* paragraph (c)(2)(ii) of this section. Thus, $6x of the dividend is considered paid out of non-extraordinary disposition E&P with respect to US1. Under paragraph (c)(2)(i)(B) of this section, the remaining $42x of the dividend is next considered paid out of US1's extraordinary disposition account with respect to CFC1, to the extent thereof. Accordingly, $42x of the dividend is considered paid out of the extraordinary disposition account with respect to CFC1 and gives rise to $42x of an extraordinary disposition amount. As a result, US1's prior extraordinary disposition amount is increased by $42x under paragraph (c)(3)(i)(D) of this section, and US1's extraordinary disposition account is reduced to $18x ($60x − $42x) under paragraph (c)(3)(i)(A) of this section.

(D) *Determination of extraordinary disposition amount with respect to US2.* The dividend of $32x paid to US2, on December 1, 2018, is an extraordinary disposition amount to the extent the dividend is paid out of extraordinary disposition E&P with respect to US2. *See* paragraph (c)(1) of this section. Under paragraph (c)(2)(i) of this section, the dividend is first considered paid out of non-extraordinary disposition E&P with respect to US2, to the extent thereof. With respect to US2, $4x of CFC1's earnings and profits is non-extraordinary disposition E&P, calculated as the excess of $44x (the product of $110x of earnings and profits described in section 959(c)(3), without regard to the $80x distribution, and 40%) over $40x (the balance of US2's extraordinary disposition account with respect to CFC1, immediately before the distribution). *See* paragraph (c)(2)(ii) of this section. Thus, $4x of the dividend is considered paid out of non-extraordinary disposition E&P with respect to US2. Under paragraph (c)(2)(i)(B) of this section, the remaining $28x of the dividend is next considered paid out of US2's extraordinary disposition account with respect to CFC1, to the extent thereof. Accordingly, $28x of the dividend is considered paid out of the extraordinary disposition account with respect to US2 and gives rise to $28x of an extraordinary disposition amount. As a result, US2's prior extraordinary disposition amount is increased by $28x under paragraph (c)(3)(i)(D) of this section, and US2's extraordinary disposition account is reduced to $12x ($40x - $28x) under paragraph (c)(3)(i)(A) of this section.

(E) *Determination of ineligible amount with respect to US1 and US2.* Under paragraph (b)(2) of this section, with respect to US1 and the dividend of $48x, the ineligible amount is $21x, the sum of 50 percent of the extraordinary disposition amount ($42x) and extraordinary reduction amount ($0). Therefore, with respect to the dividend received by US1 of $48x, $27x is eligible for a section 245A deduction. With respect to US2 and the dividend of $32x, the ineligible amount is $14x, the sum of 50% of the extraordinary disposition amount ($28x) and extraordinary reduction amount ($0). Therefore, with respect to the dividend received by US2 of $32x, $18x is eligible for a section 245A deduction.

(3) *Example 2. Application of section 954(c)(6) exception with extraordinary disposition account.—*(i) *Facts.* The facts are the same as in paragraph (j)(2)(i) of this section (the facts in *Example 1*) except that the Property Transfer is a sale by CFC2 to CFC1 instead of a sale by CFC1 to CFC2, the $80x distribution is by CFC2 to CFC1 in a separate transaction that is unrelated to the Property Transfer, and the description of the earnings and profits of CFC1 is applied to CFC2. Additionally, absent the application of this section, section 954(c)(6) would apply to the distribution by CFC2 to CFC1. Under section 951(a)(2) and §1.951-1(b) and (e), US1's pro rata share of any subpart F income of CFC1 is 60% and US2's pro rata share of any subpart F income of CFC2 is 40%.

(ii) *Analysis—*(A) *Identification of extraordinary disposition.* The Property Transfer is an extraordinary disposition under the same analysis as provided in paragraph (j)(2)(ii)(A) of this section (the analysis in *Example 1*).

(B) *Determination of section 245A shareholders and their extraordinary disposition accounts.* Both US1 and US2 are section 245A shareholders with respect to CFC2, US1 has an extraordinary disposition account of $60x with respect to CFC2, and US2 has an extraordinary disposition account of $40x with respect to CFC2 under the same analysis as provided in paragraph (j)(2)(ii)(B) of this section (the analysis in *Example 1*).

(C) *Determination of tiered extraordinary disposition amount—*(1) *In general.* US1 and US2 each have a tiered extraordinary disposition amount with respect to the $80x dividend paid by CFC2 to CFC1 to the extent that US1 and US2 would have an extraordinary disposition amount if each had received as a dividend its pro rata share of the dividend from CFC2. *See* paragraph (d)(2)(i) of this section. Under paragraph (d)(2)(ii) of this section, US1's pro rata share of the dividend is $48x (60% x $80x), that is, the increase to US1's pro rata share of the subpart F income if the dividend were included in CFC1's foreign personal holding company income, without regard to section 952(c) and the allocation of expenses. Similarly, US2's pro rata share of the dividend is $32x (40% x $80x).

(2) *Determination of tiered extraordinary disposition amount with respect to US1.* The extraordinary disposition amount with respect to US1 is $42x, under the same analysis provided in paragraph (j)(2)(ii)(C) of this section (the analysis in *Example 1*). Accordingly, the tiered extraordinary disposition amount with respect to US1 is $42x.

(3) *Determination of extraordinary disposition amount with respect to US2.* The extraordinary disposition amount with respect to US2 is $28x, under the same analysis provided in paragraph (j)(2)(ii)(D) of this section (the analysis in *Example 1*). Accordingly, the tiered extraordinary disposition amount with respect to US2 is $28x.

(D) *Limitation of section 954(c)(6) exception.* The sum of US1 and US2's tiered extraordinary disposition amounts is $70x ($42x + $28x). The portion of the stock of CFC1 (by value) owned (within the meaning of section 958(a)) by U.S. tax residents on the last day of CFC1's taxable year is 100%. Under paragraph (d)(1) of this section, the disqualified amount with respect to the dividend is $70x ($70x/100%). Accordingly, the portion of the $80x dividend from CFC2 to CFC1 that is eligible for the exception to foreign personal holding company income under section 954(c)(6) is $45x, equal to the sum of $10x (the portion of the $80x dividend that exceeds the $70x disqualified amount) and $35x (50 percent of $70x, the portion of the dividend that does not exceed the disqualified amount). Under section 951(a)(2) and §1.951-1(b) and (e), US1 includes $21x (60% x $35x) and US2 includes $14x (40% x $35x) in income under section 951(a).

(E) *Changes in extraordinary disposition account of US1.* Under paragraph (c)(3)(i)(D)(1) of this section, US1's prior extraordinary disposition amount with respect to CFC2 is increased by $42x, or 200% of $21x, the amount US1 included in income under section 951(a) with respect to CFC1. Under paragraph (c)(3)(i)(D)(1)(iii) of this section, US1 has no qualified portion because all of the owners of CFC2 are section 245A shareholders with a tiered extraordinary disposition amount with respect to CFC2. As a result, US1's extraordinary disposition account is reduced to $18x ($60x - $42x) under paragraph (c)(3)(i)(A) of this section.

(F) *Changes in extraordinary disposition account of US2.* Under paragraph (c)(3)(i)(D)(1) of this section, US2's prior extraordinary disposition amount with respect to CFC2 is increased by $28x, or 200% of $14x, the amount US2 included in income under section 951(a) with respect to CFC1. Under paragraph (c)(3)(i)(D)(1)(iii) of this section, US2 has no qualified portion because all of the owners of CFC2 are section 245A shareholders with a tiered extraordinary disposition amount with respect to CFC2. As a result, US2's extraordinary disposition account is reduced to $12x ($40x - $28x) under paragraph (c)(3)(i)(A) of this section.

(4) *Example 3. Extraordinary reduction.—*(i) *Facts.* At the beginning of CFC1's taxable year ending on December 31, Year 2, US1 owns all of the single class of stock of CFC1, and no person transferred any CFC1 stock directly or indirectly in Year 1 pursuant to a plan to reduce the percentage of stock (by value) of CFC1 owned by US1. Also as of the beginning of Year 2, CFC1 has no earnings and profits described in section 959(c)(1) or (2), and US1 does not have an extraordinary disposition account with respect to CFC1. As of the end of Year 2, CFC1 has $160x of tested income and no other income. CFC1 has $160x of earnings and profits for Year 2. On October 19, Year 2, US1 sells all of its CFC1 stock to US2 for $100x in a transaction (the "Stock Sale") in which US1 recognizes $90x of gain. Under section 1248(a), the entire $90x of gain is included in US1's gross income as a dividend and, pursuant to section 1248(j), the $90x is treated as a dividend for purposes of applying section 245A. At the end of Year 2, under section 951A, US2 takes into account $70x of tested income, calculated as $160x (100% of the $160x of tested income) less $90x, the amount described in section 951(a)(2)(B). The amount described in section 951(a)(2)(B) is the lesser of $90x, the amount of dividends received by US1 with respect to the transferred stock, and $128x, the amount of tested income attributable to the transferred stock ($160x) multiplied by 292/365 (the ratio of the number of days in Year 2 that US2 did not own the transferred stock to the total number of days in Year 2). US1 does not make an election pursuant to paragraph (e)(3)(i) of this section.

(ii) *Analysis—*(A) *Determination of controlling section 245A shareholder and extraordinary reduction of ownership.* Under paragraph (i)(2) of this section, US1 is a controlling section 245A shareholder with respect to CFC1. In addition, the Stock Sale results in an extraordinary reduction with respect to US1's ownership of CFC1. *See* paragraph (e)(2)(i) of this section. The extraordinary reduction occurs because during Year 2, US1 transferred 100% of the CFC1 stock it owned at the beginning of the year and such amount is more than 5% of the total value of the stock of CFC1 at the beginning of Year 2; it also occurs because on the last day of the year the percentage of stock (by value) of CFC1 that US1 owns directly or indirectly (0%) (the end of year percentage) is less than 90% of the stock (by value) of CFC1 that US1 owns directly or indirectly on the day of the taxable year when it owned the highest percentage of CFC1 stock by value (100%) (the initial percentage), no transactions occurred in the preceding year pursuant to a plan to reduce the percentage of CFC1 stock owned by US1, and the difference between the initial percentage and the end of year percentage (100 percentage points) is at least 5 percentage points.

(B) *Determination of extraordinary reduction amount.* Under paragraph (e)(1) of this section, the entire $90x dividend to US1 is an extraordinary reduction amount with respect to US1 because the dividend is at least equal to US1's pre-reduction pro rata share of CFC1's Year 2 tested income described in paragraph (e)(2)(ii)(A) of this section ($160x), reduced by the amount of tested income taken into account by US2, a U.S. tax resident, under paragraph (e)(2)(ii)(B) of this section ($70x).

(C) *Determination of ineligible amount.* Under paragraph (b)(2) of this section, with respect to US1 and the dividend of $90x, the ineligible amount is $90x, the sum of 50% of the extraordinary disposition amount ($0) and extraordinary reduction amount ($90x). Therefore, with respect to the dividend received of $90x, no portion is eligible for the dividends received deduction allowed under section 245A(a).

(iii) *Alternative facts – election to close CFC's taxable year.* The facts are the same as in paragraph (j)(4)(i) of this section (the facts of this *Example 3*), except that, pursuant to paragraph (e)(3)(i) of this section, US1 elects to close CFC1's Year 2 taxable year for all purposes of the Code as of the end of October 19, Year 2, the date on which the Stock Sale occurs; in addition, US1 and US2 enter into a written, binding agreement that US1 will elect to close CFC1's Year 2 taxable year. Accordingly, under section 951A(a), US1 takes into account 100% of CFC1's tested income for the taxable year beginning January 1, Year 2, and ending October 19, Year 2, and US2 takes into account 100% of CFC1's tested income for the taxable year beginning October 20, Year 2, and ending December 31, Year 2. Under paragraph (e)(3)(i)(A) of this section, no amount is considered an extraordinary reduction amount with respect to US1.

(5) *Example 4. Extraordinary reduction; decrease in section 245A shareholder's pre-reduction pro rata share for amounts taken into account by U.S. tax residents.*—(i) *Facts.* At the beginning of CFC1's taxable year ending December 31, Year 2, US1 owns all of the single class of stock of CFC1, and no person transferred any CFC1 stock directly or indirectly in Year 1 pursuant to a plan to reduce the percentage of stock (by value) of CFC1 owned by US1. CFC1 generates $120x of subpart F income during its taxable year ending on December 31, Year 2. On October 1, Year 2, CFC1 distributes a $120x dividend to US1. On October 19, Year 2, US1 sells 100% of its stock of CFC1 to PRS, a domestic partnership, in a transaction in which no gain or loss is realized (the "Stock Sale"). A, an individual who is a citizen of the United States, and B, a foreign individual who is not a U.S. tax resident, each own 50% of the capital and profits interests of PRS. On December 1, Year 2, US2 and FP, a foreign corporation, contribute property to CFC1; in exchange, each of US2 and FP receives 25% of the stock of CFC1. PRS owns the remaining 50% of the stock of CFC1. US1 does not make an election pursuant to paragraph (e)(3)(i) of this section.

(ii) *Analysis*—(A) *Determination of controlling section 245A shareholder and extraordinary reduction.* Under paragraph (i)(2) of this section, US1 is a controlling section 245A shareholder with respect to CFC1. In addition, the Stock Sale results in an extraordinary reduction with respect to US1's ownership of CFC1. *See* paragraph (e)(2)(i) of this section. The extraordinary reduction occurs because during Year 2, US1 transferred 100% of the CFC1 stock it owns on the first day of Year 2, and that amount is more than 5% of the total value of the stock of CFC1 at the beginning of Year 2; it also occurs because on the last day of Year 2 the percentage of stock (by value) of CFC1 that US1 owns directly or indirectly (0%) (the end of year percentage) is less than 90% of the highest percentage of stock (by value) of CFC1 that US1 owns directly or indirectly on the day of the taxable year when it owned the highest percentage of CFC1 stock by value (100%) (the initial percentage), no transactions occurred in the preceding year pursuant to a plan to reduce the percentage of CFC1 stock owned by US1, and the difference between the initial percentage and the end of year percentage (100 percentage points) is at least 5 percentage points.

(B) *Determination of pre-reduction pro rata share.* Before the extraordinary reduction, US1 owned 100% of the stock of CFC1. Thus, under paragraph (e)(2)(ii)(A) of this section, the tentative amount of US1's pre-reduction pro rata share of CFC1's subpart F income is $120x. A and US2 are U.S. tax residents pursuant to paragraph (i)(29) of this section because they are United States persons described in section 7701(a)(30)(A) or (C). Thus, US1's pre-reduction pro rata share amount is subject to the reduction described in paragraph (e)(2)(ii)(B) of this section because U.S. tax residents directly or indirectly acquire stock of CFC1 from US1 or CFC1 during the taxable year in which the extraordinary reduction occurs. With respect to US1's pre-reduction pro rata share of CFC1's subpart F income, the reduction equals the amount of subpart F income of CFC1 taken into account under section 951(a) by these U.S. tax residents.

(C) *Determination of decrease in pre-reduction pro rata share for amounts taken into account by U.S. tax resident.* On December 31, Year 2, both PRS and US2 will be United States shareholders with respect to CFC1 and will include in gross income their pro rata share of CFC1's subpart F income under section 951(a). With respect to US2, this amount will be $30x, which is equal to 25% of CFC1's subpart F income for the taxable year. With respect to PRS, its pro rata share of $60x under section 951(a)(2)(A) (50% of $120x) will be reduced under section 951(a)(2)(B) by $48x. The section 951(a)(2)(B) reduction is equal to the lesser of the $120x dividend paid with respect to those shares to US1 or $48x (50% x $120x x 292/365, the period during the taxable year that PRS did not own CFC1 stock). Thus, PRS includes $12x in gross income pursuant to section 951(a). Of this amount, $6x is allocated to A (as a 50% partner of PRS) and, therefore, treated as taken into account by A under paragraphs (e)(2)(ii)(B) and (g)(6) of this section. Thus, A and US2 take into account a total of $36x of CFC1's subpart F income under section 951(a). This amount reduces US1's pre-reduction pro rata share of CFC1's subpart F income to $84x ($120x - $36x) under paragraph (e)(2)(ii)(B) of this section. CFC1 did not generate tested income during the taxable year and, therefore, no amount is taken into account under section 951A with respect to CFC1, and US1 has no pre-reduction pro rata share with respect to tested income of CFC1.

(D) *Determination of extraordinary reduction amount.* Under paragraph (e)(1) of this section, the extraordinary reduction amount equals $84x, which is the lesser of the amount of the dividend received by US1 from CFC1 during Year 2 ($120x) and the sum of US1's pre-reduction pro rata share of CFC1's subpart F income ($84x) and tested income ($0).

(E) *Determination of ineligible amount.* Under paragraph (b)(2) of this section, with respect to US1 and the dividend of $120x, the ineligible amount is $84x, the sum of 50% of the extraordinary

disposition amount ($0) and extraordinary reduction amount ($84x). Therefore, with respect to the dividend received by US1 from CFC1, $36x ($120x - $84x) is eligible for a section 245A deduction.

(6) *Example 5. Controlling section 245A shareholder.*—(i) *Facts.* US1 and US2 own 30% and 25% of the stock of CFC1, respectively. FP, a foreign corporation that is not a CFC, owns all of the stock of US1 and US2. FP owns the remaining 45% of the stock of CFC1. On September 30, Year 2, US1 sells all of its stock of CFC1 to US3, a domestic corporation that is not a related party with respect to FP, US1, or US2. No person transferred any stock of CFC1 directly or indirectly in Year 1 pursuant to a plan to reduce the percentage of stock (by value) of CFC1 owned by US1.

(ii) *Analysis.* Under paragraph (i)(21) of this section, US1 is a section 245A shareholder with respect to CFC1, an SFC. Because US1 owns, together with US2 and FP (related persons with respect to US1), more than 50% of the stock of CFC1, US1 is a controlling section 245A shareholder of CFC1. The sale of US1's CFC1 stock results in an extraordinary reduction occurring with respect to US1's ownership of CFC1. The extraordinary reduction occurs because during Year 2, US1 transferred 100% of the stock of CFC1 that it owned at the beginning of the year and that amount is more than 5% of the total value of the stock of CFC1 at the beginning of Year 2. The extraordinary disposition also occurs because on the last day of the year the percentage of stock (by value) of CFC1 that US1 directly or indirectly owns (0%) (the end of year percentage) is less than 90% of the stock (by value) of CFC1 that US1 directly or indirectly owned on the day of the taxable year when it owned the highest percentage of CFC1 stock by value (30%) (the initial percentage), no transactions occurred in the preceding year pursuant to a plan to reduce the percentage of CFC1 stock owned by US1, and the difference between the initial percentage and end of year percentage (30 percentage points) is at least 5 percentage points.

(7) *Example 6. Limitation of section 954(c)(6) exception with respect to an extraordinary reduction.*—(i) *Facts.* At the beginning of CFC1 and CFC2's taxable year ending on December 31, Year 2, US1 and A, an individual who is a citizen of the United States, own 80% and 20% of the single class of stock of CFC1, respectively. CFC1 owns 100% of the stock of CFC2. Both US1 and A are United States shareholders with respect to CFC1 and CFC2, and US1 and A are not related parties with respect to each other. No person transferred CFC2 stock directly or indirectly in Year 2 pursuant to a plan to reduce the percentage of stock (by value) of CFC2 owned by US1, and US1 does not have an extraordinary disposition account with respect to CFC2. At the end of Year 2, and without regard to any distributions during Year 2, CFC2 had $150x of tested income and no other income, and CFC1 had no income or expenses. On June 30, Year 2, CFC2 distributed $150x as a dividend to CFC1, which would qualify for the exception from foreign personal holding company income under section 954(c)(6) but for the application of this section. On August 7, Year 2, CFC1 sells all of its CFC2 stock to US2 for $100x in a transaction (the "Stock Sale") in which CFC1 realizes no gain or loss. At the end of Year 2, under section 951A, US2 takes into account $60x of tested income, calculated as $150x (100% of the $150x of tested income) less $90x, the amount described in section 951(a)(2)(B). The amount described in section 951(a)(2)(B) is the lesser of $150x, the amount of dividends received by CFC1 during Year 2 with respect to the transferred stock, and $90x, the amount of tested income attributable to the transferred stock ($150x) multiplied by 219/365 (the ratio of the number of days in Year 2 that US2 did not own the transferred stock to the total number of days in Year 2). US1 does not make an election pursuant to paragraph (e)(3)(i) of this section.

(ii) *Analysis*—(A) *Determination of controlling section 245A shareholder and extraordinary reduction of ownership.* Under paragraph (i)(2) of this section, US1 is a controlling section 245A shareholder with respect to CFC2, but A is not. In addition, the Stock Sale results in an extraordinary reduction with respect to US1's ownership of CFC2. *See* paragraph (e)(2)(i) of this section. The extraordinary reduction occurs because during Year 2, US1 transferred indirectly 100% of the CFC2 stock it owned at the beginning of the year and such amount is more than 5% of the total value of the stock of CFC2 at the beginning of Year 2. The extraordinary disposition also occurs because on the last day of the year the percentage of stock (by value) of CFC2 that US1 owns directly or indirectly (0%) (the end of year percentage) is less than 90% of the stock (by value) of CFC2 that US1 owns directly or indirectly on the day of the taxable year when it owned the highest percentage of CFC2 stock by value (80%) (the initial percentage), no transactions occurred in the preceding year pursuant to a plan to reduce the percentage of CFC2 stock owned by US1, and the difference between the initial percentage and the end of year percentage (80 percentage points) is at least 5 percentage points. Because there is an extraordinary reduction with respect to CFC2 in Year 2 and CFC1 received a dividend from CFC2 in Year 2, under paragraph (f)(1) of this section, it is necessary to determine the limitation on the amount of the dividend eligible for the exception under section 954(c)(6).

(B) *Determination of tiered extraordinary reduction amount.* The limitation on the amount of the dividend eligible for the exception under section 954(c)(6) is based on the tiered extraordinary reduction amount. The sum of the amount of subpart F income and tested income of CFC2 for Year 2 is $150x, and immediately before the extraordinary reduction, CFC1 held 100% of the stock of CFC2. Additionally, US2 is a U.S. tax resident as defined in paragraph (i)(29) of this section because it is a United States person described in section 7701(a)(30)(A) or (C), and US2 has a pro rata share of $60x of tested income under section 951A with respect to CFC2. Accordingly, under paragraph (f)(2) of this section, the tiered extraordinary reduction amount is $90x ((($150x x 100%) - $60x).

(C) *Limitation of section 954(c)(6) exception.* Under paragraph (f)(1) of this section, the portion of the $150x dividend from CFC2 to CFC1 that is eligible for the exception to foreign personal holding company income under section 954(c)(6) is $60x ($150x - $90x). To the extent that the $90x that does not qualify for the exception gives rise to additional subpart F income to CFC1, both US1 and A will take into account their pro rata share of that subpart F income under section 951(a)(2) and § 1.951-1(b) and (e).

(8) *Example 7. Application of anti-abuse rule to a prepayment of a royalty.*—(i) *Facts.* US1 owns 100% of the single class of stock of CFC1 and CFC2. CFC1 has a November 30 taxable year, and CFC2 has a calendar year taxable year. There is a license agreement between CFC1 and CFC2 pursuant to which CFC2 is obligated to pay annual royalties to CFC1 for the use of intangible property. As of November 1, 2018, the remaining term of the agreement is 10 years. On November 1, 2018, CFC1 receives from CFC2, and accrues into income, $100x of pre-paid royalties that are for the use of the intangible property for the subsequent 10 years. The form of the arrangement as a license, including the prepayment of the royalty, is respected for U.S. tax purposes; therefore CFC1's receipt of the $100x royalty prepayment does not constitute a disposition of the intangible property and is excluded from CFC1's subpart F income pursuant to section 954(c)(6). A principal purpose of CFC2 prepaying the royalty is for CFC1 to generate earnings and profits during the disqualified period that would not be subject to current U.S. tax yet may be eligible for the section 245A deduction and could, for example, be used to reduce the amount of gain recognized on a disposition of the stock of CFC1 that would be subject to U.S. tax by increasing the portion of such gain treated as a dividend.

(ii) *Analysis.* Because the royalty prepayment was carried out with a principal purpose of avoiding the purposes of this section, appropriate adjustments are required to be made under the anti-abuse rule in paragraph (h) of this section. CFC1 is a CFC that has a November 30 taxable year, so under paragraph (c)(3)(iii) of this section, CFC1 has a disqualified period beginning on January 1, 2018, and ending on November 30, 2018. In addition, even though the intangible property licensed by CFC1 to CFC2 is specified property, CFC2's prepayment of the royalty would not be treated as a disposition of the specified property by CFC1 and, therefore, would not constitute an extraordinary disposition (and thus would not give rise to extraordinary disposition E&P), absent the application of the anti-abuse rule of paragraph (h) of this section. Pursuant to paragraph (h) of this section, the earnings and profits of CFC1 generated as a result of the $100x of prepaid royalty are treated as extraordinary disposition E&P for purposes of this section and, therefore, US1 has an extraordinary disposition account with respect to CFC1 of $100x. In addition, the prepaid royalty gives rise to a disqualified payment (as defined in § 1.951A-2(c)(6)(ii)(A)) of $100x. As a result, § 1.245A-7(b) or § 1.245A-8(b), as applicable, applies to reduce the disqualified payment in the same manner as if the disqualified payment were disqualified basis, and § 1.245A-7(c) or § 1.245A-8(c), as applicable, applies to reduce the extraordinary disposition account in the same manner as if the deductions directly or indirectly related to the disqualified payment were deductions attributable to disqualified basis of an item of specified property that corresponds to the extraordinary disposition account.

(9) *Example 8. Application of anti-abuse rule to restructuring transaction.*—(i) *Facts.* FP, a foreign corporation with no United States shareholders, owns 100% of the single class of stock of US1. US1 owns 100% of the single class of stock of CFC1 that, in turn, owns 100% of the single class of stock of CFC2. CFC2 has $100x of extraordinary disposition E&P, and US1 has a $100x extraordinary disposition account with respect to CFC2. In Year 1, FP transfers property to CFC1 in exchange for newly issued stock of CFC1. After the transfer, *FP and US1 own, respectively, 90% and 10%* of the single class of stock of CFC1. In Year 3, CFC2 pays a $100x dividend to CFC1, and the dividend gives rise to a tiered extraordinary disposition amount with respect to US1 of $10x. US1 includes $10x in gross income under section 951(a) with respect to the tiered extraordinary disposition

amount. The $10x tiered extraordinary disposition amount reduces US1's extraordinary disposition account from $100x to $90x. In Year 5, CFC1 redeems all of the stock of CFC1 held by US1 in exchange for $100x of cash. Under sections 302(d) and 301(c)(1), the redemption results in a $100x dividend to US1. Under section 959(a), $10x of the $100x dividend is not included in US1's gross income and, but for the application of paragraph (h) of this section, US1 would claim a section 245A deduction of $90x with respect to $90x of the dividend. The transfer of property from FP to CFC1 in exchange for stock of CFC1, the $100x dividend from CFC2 to CFC1, and CFC1's redemption of all of its stock held by US1 (together, the "Transaction") were undertaken with the principal purpose of avoiding the application of this section to distributions from CFC2. As a result of the redemption, CFC2 is wholly owned by FP through CFC1, and CFC2's earnings and profits can be distributed without incurring U.S. tax irrespective of the availability of the section 245A deduction or the exception under section 954(c)(6).

(ii) *Analysis.* Because the Transaction was carried out with a principal purpose of avoiding the purposes of this section, appropriate adjustments are required to be made under the anti-abuse rule in paragraph (h) of this section. Pursuant to paragraph (h) of this section, all $90x of the dividend included in US1's income in Year 5 is treated as an extraordinary disposition amount. Therefore, $45x of the dividend is treated as an ineligible amount for which US1 cannot claim a section 245A deduction pursuant to paragraph (b)(2)(i) of this section (that is, 50% of the extraordinary disposition amount) and, accordingly, US1 is only allowed a section 245A deduction of $45x ($90x dividend received, less the $45x ineligible amount) with respect to the $90x dividend from CFC1 that it included in income. In addition, US1's extraordinary disposition account with respect to CFC2 is reduced from $90x to zero pursuant to paragraph (c)(3)(i)(A) and (D) of this section.

(10) *Example 9. Application of anti-abuse rule to a related-party loan.*—(i) *Facts.* US1 owns 100% of the single class of stock of CFC1 and CFC2. US1 does not own stock of any other foreign corporation. US1 intends to repatriate $100x cash from CFC1 at the end of taxable year Y1. At the end of taxable year Y1, CFC1 has $100x of earnings and profits described in section 959(c)(3) (all of which is extraordinary disposition E&P) and $100x of cash, and US1 has an extraordinary disposition account balance with respect to CFC1 equal to $100x. In addition, at the end of taxable year Y1, CFC2 has $100x of earnings and profits described in section 959(c)(3). US1 does not have an extraordinary disposition account with respect to CFC2. Anticipating the application of this section to a distribution from CFC1, US1 instead causes CFC1 to loan $100x of cash to CFC2 during taxable year Y1 in exchange for a $100x note. The form of the transaction is respected as a loan for U.S. tax purposes. At the end of taxable Y1, CFC2 distributes $100x of cash to US1. The loan and distribution are part of a plan a principal purpose of which is to repatriate CFC1's $100x cash without triggering the application of this section.

(ii) *Analysis.* Because the loan from CFC1 to CFC2 and the subsequent distribution of cash were carried out with a principal purpose of avoiding the purposes of this section, appropriate adjustments are required to be made under the anti-abuse rule in paragraph (h) of this section. Pursuant to that rule, the distribution of $100x of cash is treated as a distribution out of US1's extraordinary disposition account with respect to CFC1. Accordingly, the $100x distribution is taxed as a dividend, and only $50x of the dividend received by US1 is eligible for the section 245A deduction pursuant to paragraph (b)(1) of this section. As a result of the distribution, the balance of US1's extraordinary disposition account with respect to CFC1 is reduced by $100x to zero pursuant to paragraph (c)(3)(i)(A) of this section.

(k) *Applicability date.*—(1) *In general.*—This section applies to taxable periods of a foreign corporation ending on or after June 14, 2019, and to taxable periods of section 245A shareholders in which or with which such taxable periods end. For taxable periods described in the previous sentence, this section (and not § 1.245A-5T) applies regardless of whether, but for this paragraph (k)(1), § 1.245A-5T would apply. See § 1.245A-5T as contained in 26 CFR part 1 edition revised as of April 1, 2020 for distributions occurring after December 31, 2017, as to which this section does not apply.

(2) *Early application of this section.*—Notwithstanding paragraph (k)(1) of this section, a taxpayer may choose to apply this section to taxable periods of a foreign corporation ending before June 14, 2019, and to taxable periods of section 245A shareholders in which or with which such taxable periods end, provided that the taxpayer and all persons bearing a relationship to the taxpayer described in section 267(b) or 707(b) apply this section in its entirety for all such taxable periods. [Reg. § 1.245A-5.]

☐ [T.D. 9909, 8-21-2020 (corrected 11-12-2020). Amended by T.D. 9934, 11-25-2020]

[Reg. §1.245A-6]

§1.245A-6. Coordination of extraordinary disposition and disqualified basis rules.—(a) *Scope.*—This section and §§1.245A-7 through 1.245A-11 coordinate the application of the extraordinary disposition rules of §1.245A-5(c) and (d) and the disqualified basis rule of §1.951A-2(c)(5). Section 1.245A-7 provides coordination rules for simple cases, and §1.245A-8 provides coordination rules for complex cases. Section 1.245A-9 provides definitions and other rules, including rules of general applicability for purposes of this section and §§1.245A-7 through 1.245A-11. Section 1.245A-10 provides examples illustrating the application of this section and §§1.245A-7 through 1.245A-9. Section 1.245A-11 provides applicability dates.

(b) *Conditions to apply coordination rules for simple cases.*—For a taxable year of a section 245A shareholder for which the conditions described in paragraphs (b)(1) and (2) of this section are satisfied, the section 245A shareholder may apply the coordination rules of §1.245A-7 (rules for simple cases) to an extraordinary disposition account of the section 245A shareholder with respect to an SFC and disqualified basis of an item of specified property that corresponds to the extraordinary disposition account (as determined pursuant to §1.245A-9(b)(1)). If the conditions are not satisfied, then the coordination rules of §1.245A-8 (rules for complex cases) apply beginning with the first day of the first taxable year of the section 245A shareholder for which the conditions are not satisfied and all taxable years thereafter. If the conditions are satisfied for a taxable year of the section 245A shareholder but the section 245A shareholder chooses not to apply the coordination rules of §1.245A-7 for that taxable year, then the coordination rules of §1.245A-8 apply to that taxable year (though, for a subsequent taxable year, the section 245A shareholder may apply the coordination rules of §1.245A-7, provided that the conditions described in paragraphs (b)(1) and (2) of this section are satisfied for such subsequent taxable year and have been satisfied for all earlier taxable years). For purposes of applying paragraphs (b)(1) and (2) of this section, a reference to a section 245A shareholder, an SFC, or a CFC does not include a successor of the section 245A shareholder, the SFC, or the CFC, respectively.

(1) *Requirements related to the SFC.*—The condition of this paragraph (b)(1) is satisfied for a taxable year of the section 245A shareholder if the following requirements are satisfied:

(i) On January 1, 2018, the section 245A shareholder owns (within the meaning of section 958(a)) all of the stock (by vote and value) of the SFC.

(ii) On each day of the taxable year of the section 245A shareholder, the section 245A shareholder owns (within the meaning of section 958(a)) all of the stock (by vote and value) of the SFC.

(iii) On no day during the taxable year of the section 245A shareholder was the SFC a distributing or controlled corporation in a transaction described in a section 355, or did the SFC acquire the assets of a corporation as to which there is an extraordinary disposition account pursuant to a transaction described in section 381 (that is, taking into account the requirements of this paragraph (b)(1) and paragraph (b)(2) of this section, the section 245A shareholder's extraordinary disposition account with respect to the SFC has not been not been adjusted pursuant to the rules of §1.245A-5(c)(4)).

(2) *Requirements related to an item of specified property that corresponds to an extraordinary disposition account and a CFC holding the item.*—The condition of this paragraph (b)(2) is satisfied for a taxable year of a section 245A shareholder if the following requirements are satisfied:

(i) For each item of specified property with disqualified basis that corresponds to the extraordinary disposition account, the item of specified property is held by a CFC immediately after the extraordinary disposition of the item of specified property.

(ii) For each CFC described in paragraph (b)(2)(i) of this section—

(A) All of the stock (by vote and value) of the CFC is owned (within the meaning of section 958(a)) by the section 245A shareholder and any domestic affiliates of the section 245A shareholder immediately after the extraordinary disposition described in paragraph (b)(2)(i) of this section;

(B) For each taxable year of the CFC that ends with or within the taxable year of the section 245A shareholder, there is no extraordinary disposition account with respect to the CFC, and the sum of the balance of the hybrid deduction accounts (as described in §1.245A(e)-1(d)(1) with respect to shares of stock of the CFC is zero (determined as of the end of the taxable year of the CFC and taking into account any adjustments to the accounts for the taxable year); and

(C) On each day of each taxable year of the CFC that ends with or within the taxable year of the section 245A shareholder, and on each day of each taxable year of the CFC that begins with or within the taxable year of the section 245A shareholder—

(1) The CFC holds the item of specified property described in paragraph (b)(1)(i) of this section;

(2) The section 245A shareholder and any domestic affiliates own (within the meaning of section 958(a)) all of the stock (by vote and value) of the CFC;

(3) The CFC does not hold any item of specified property with disqualified basis other than an item of specified property that corresponds to the extraordinary disposition account;

(4) The CFC does not own an interest in a partnership, trust, or estate (directly or indirectly through one or more other partnerships, trusts, or estates) that holds an item of specified property with disqualified basis; and

(5) The CFC is not engaged in the conduct of a trade or business in the United States and therefore does not have ECTI, and the CFC does not have any deficit in earnings and profits subject to §1.381(c)(2)-1(a)(5). [Reg. §1.245A-6.]

☐ [T.D. 9934, 11-25-2020.]

[Reg. §1.245A-7]

§1.245A-7. Coordination rules for simple cases.—(a) *Scope.*—This section applies for a taxable year of a section 245A shareholder for which the conditions of §1.245A-6(b)(1) and (2) are satisfied and for which the section 245A shareholder chooses to apply this section (in lieu of §1.245A-8).

(b) *Reduction of disqualified basis by reason of an extraordinary disposition amount or tiered extraordinary disposition amount.*—(1) *In general.*—If, for a taxable year of a section 245A shareholder, an extraordinary disposition account of the section 245A shareholder gives rise to one or more extraordinary disposition amounts or tiered extraordinary disposition amounts, then, with respect to an item of specified property that corresponds to the extraordinary disposition account, the disqualified basis of the item of specified property is, solely for purposes of §1.951A-2(c)(5), reduced (but not below zero) by an amount (determined in the functional currency in which the extraordinary disposition account is maintained) equal to the product of—

(i) The sum of the extraordinary disposition amounts and the tiered extraordinary disposition amounts; and

(ii) A fraction, the numerator of which is the disqualified basis of the item of specified property, and the denominator of which is the sum of the disqualified basis of each item of specified property that corresponds to the extraordinary disposition account.

(2) *Timing rules regarding disqualified basis.*—See §1.245A-9(b)(2) for timing rules regarding the determination of, and reduction to, disqualified basis of an item of specified property.

(3) *Special rule regarding prior extraordinary disposition amounts.*—For purposes of paragraph (b)(1) of this section, to the extent that an extraordinary disposition account of a section 245A shareholder is reduced under §1.245A-5(c)(3)(i)(A) by reason of a prior extraordinary disposition amount described in §1.245A-5(c)(3)(i)(D)(1)(i) through (iv), the extraordinary disposition account is considered to give rise to an extraordinary disposition amount or tiered extraordinary disposition amount (and the amount by which the account is reduced is treated as an extraordinary disposition amount or tiered extraordinary disposition amount).

(c) *Reduction of extraordinary disposition account by reason of the allocation and apportionment of deductions or losses attributable to disqualified basis.*—(1) *In general.*—If, for a taxable year of a CFC, the CFC holds one or more items of specified property that correspond to an extraordinary disposition account of a section 245A shareholder with respect to an SFC, then the extraordinary disposition account is reduced (but not below zero) by the lesser of the amounts described in paragraphs (c)(1)(i) and (ii) of this section (each determined in the functional currency of the CFC).

(i) The excess (if any) of the adjusted earnings of the CFC for the taxable year of the CFC, over the sum of the previously taxed earnings and profits accounts with respect to the CFC for purposes of section 959 (determined as of the end of the taxable year of the CFC and taking into account any adjustments to the accounts for the taxable year).

(ii) The balance of the section 245A shareholder's RGI account with respect to the CFC (determined as of the end of the taxable year of the CFC, but without regard to the application of paragraph (c)(4)(ii) of this section for the taxable year).

(2) *Timing of reduction to extraordinary disposition account.*—See §1.245A-9(b)(3) for timing rules regarding the reduction to an extraordinary disposition account.

(3) *Adjusted earnings.*—The term *adjusted earnings* means, with respect to a CFC and a taxable year of the CFC, the earnings and profits of the CFC, determined as of the end of the CFC's taxable year

(taking into account all distributions during the taxable year), and with the adjustments described in paragraphs (c)(3)(i) through (iii) of this section.

(i) The earnings and profits are increased by the amount of any deduction or loss that is or was allocated and apportioned to residual CFC gross income of the CFC solely by reason of §1.951A-2(c)(5)(i).

(ii) The earnings and profits are decreased by the amount by which an RGI account with respect to the CFC has been decreased pursuant to paragraph (c)(4)(ii) of this section for a prior taxable year of the CFC.

(iii) The earnings and profits are determined without regard to income described in section 245(a)(5)(A) or dividends described in section 245(a)(5)(B) (determined without regard to section 245(a)(12)).

(4) *RGI account.*—For a taxable year of a CFC, the following rules apply to determine the balance of a section 245A shareholder's RGI account with respect to the CFC:

(i) The balance of the RGI account is increased by the sum of the amounts of deductions and losses of the CFC that, but for §1.951A-2(c)(5)(i), would have decreased one or more categories of the CFC's positive subpart F income or the CFC's tested income, or increased or given rise to a tested loss or one or more qualified deficits of the CFC.

(ii) The balance of the RGI account is decreased to the extent that, by reason of the application of paragraph (c)(1) of this section with respect to the taxable year of the CFC, there is a reduction to the extraordinary disposition account of the section 245A shareholder. [Reg. §1.245A-7.]

☐ [*T.D. 9934, 11-25-2020.*]

[Reg. §1.245A-8]

§1.245A-8. Coordination rules for complex cases.—(a) *Scope.*—This section applies beginning with the first day of the first taxable year of a section 245A shareholder for which §1.245A-7 does not apply and for all taxable years thereafter, or for a taxable year of a section 245A shareholder for which the section 245A shareholder chooses not to apply §1.245A-7.

(b) *Reduction of disqualified basis by reason of an extraordinary disposition amount or tiered extraordinary disposition amount.*—(1) *In general.*—If, for a taxable year of a section 245A shareholder, an extraordinary disposition account of the section 245A shareholder gives rise to one or more extraordinary disposition amounts or tiered extraordinary disposition amounts, then, with respect to an item of specified property that corresponds to the extraordinary disposition account and for which the ownership requirement of paragraph (b)(3)(i) of this section is satisfied for the taxable year of the section 245A shareholder, solely for purposes of §1.951A-2(c)(5), the disqualified basis of the item of specified property is reduced (but not below zero) by an amount (determined in the functional currency in which the extraordinary disposition account is maintained) equal to the product of—

(i) The excess (if any) of—

(A) The sum of the extraordinary disposition amounts and the tiered extraordinary disposition amounts; over

(B) The basis benefit account with respect to the extraordinary disposition account (determined as of the end of the taxable year of the section 245A shareholder, and without regard to the application of paragraph (b)(4)(i)(B) of this section for the taxable year); and

(ii) A fraction, the numerator of which is the disqualified basis of the item of specified property, and the denominator of which is the sum of the disqualified basis of each item of specified property that corresponds to the extraordinary disposition account and for which the ownership requirement of paragraph (b)(3)(i) of this section is satisfied for the taxable year of the section 245A shareholder.

(2) *Timing rules regarding disqualified basis.*—See §1.245A-9(b)(2) for timing rules regarding the determination of, and reduction to, disqualified basis of an item of specified property.

(3) *Ownership requirement with respect to an item of specified property.*—(i) *In general.*—For a taxable year of a section 245A shareholder, the ownership requirement of this paragraph (b)(3)(i) is satisfied with respect to an item of specified property if, on at least one day that falls within the taxable year, the item of specified property is held by—

(A) The section 245A shareholder;

(B) A person (other than the section 245A shareholder) that, on at least one day that falls within the section 245A shareholder's taxable year, is a related party with respect to the section 245A shareholder (such a person, a *qualified related party* with respect to the section 245A shareholder for the taxable year of the section 245A shareholder); or

(C) A specified entity at least 10 percent of the interests of which are, on at least one day that falls within the section 245A shareholder's taxable year, owned directly or indirectly through one or more other specified entities by the section 245A shareholder or a qualified related party.

(ii) *Rules for determining an interest in a specified entity.*—For purposes of paragraph (b)(3)(i)(C) of this section, the phrase *at least 10 percent of the interests* means—

(A) If the specified entity is a foreign corporation, at least 10 percent of the stock (by vote or value) of the foreign corporation;

(B) If the specified entity is a partnership, at least 10 percent of the interests in the capital or profits of the partnership; or

(C) If the specified entity is not a foreign corporation or a partnership, at least 10 percent of the value of the interests in the specified entity.

(4) *Basis benefit account.*—(i) *General rules.*—The term *basis benefit account* means, with respect to an extraordinary disposition account of a section 245A shareholder, an account of the section 245A shareholder (the initial balance of which is zero), adjusted pursuant to the rules of paragraphs (b)(4)(i)(A) and (B) of this section on the last day of each taxable year of the section 245A shareholder. The basis benefit account must be maintained in the same functional currency as the extraordinary disposition account.

(A) The balance of the basis benefit account is increased to the extent that a basis benefit amount with respect to an item of specified property that corresponds to the section 245A shareholder's extraordinary disposition account is assigned to the taxable year of the section 245A shareholder. However, if the extraordinary disposition ownership percentage applicable to the section 245A shareholder's extraordinary disposition account is less than 100 percent, then, the basis benefit account is instead increased by the amount equal to the basis benefit amount multiplied by the extraordinary disposition ownership percentage.

(B) The balance of the basis benefit account is decreased to the extent that, for a taxable year that includes the date on which the section 245A shareholder's taxable year ends, disqualified basis of an item of specified property would have been reduced pursuant to paragraph (b)(1) of this section but for an amount in the basis benefit account.

(ii) *Rules for determining a basis benefit amount.*—(A) *In general.*—The term *basis benefit amount* means, with respect to an item of specified property that has disqualified basis, the portion of disqualified basis that, for a taxable year, is directly (or indirectly through one or more specified entities that are not corporations) taken into account for U.S. tax purposes by a U.S. tax resident, a CFC described in §1.267A-5(a)(17), or a specified foreign person and—

(1) Reduces the amount of the U.S. tax resident's taxable income, one or more categories of the CFC's positive subpart F income, the CFC's tested income, or the specified foreign person's ECTI, as applicable; or

(2) Prevents a decrease or offset of the amount of the CFC's tested loss or qualified deficits.

(B) *Rules for determining whether disqualified basis of an item of specified property is taken into account.*—For purposes of paragraph (b)(4)(ii)(A) of this section, disqualified basis of an item of specified property is taken into account for U.S. tax purposes without regard to whether the disqualified basis is reduced or eliminated under §1.951A-3(h)(2)(ii)(B)(1).

(C) *Timing rules when disqualified basis gives rise to a deferred or disallowed loss.*—To the extent disqualified basis of an item of specified property gives rise to a deduction or loss during a taxable year that is deferred, then the determination of whether the item of deduction or loss gives rise to a basis benefit amount under paragraph (b)(4)(ii)(A) of this section is made when the item of deduction or loss is no longer deferred. In addition, to the extent disqualified basis of an item of specified property gives rise to a deduction or loss during a taxable year that is disallowed under section 267(a)(1), then a basis benefit amount is treated as occurring in the taxable year when and to the extent that gain is reduced pursuant to section 267(d), and provided that the gain is described in paragraph (b)(4)(ii)(A) of this section.

(iii) *Rules for assigning a basis benefit amount to a taxable year of a section 245A shareholder.*—(A) *In general.*—For purposes of applying paragraph (b)(4)(i)(A) of this section with respect to a section 245A shareholder, a basis benefit amount with respect to an item of specified property is assigned to a taxable year of the section 245A shareholder if—

(1) With respect to the item of specified property, the ownership requirement of paragraph (b)(3)(i) of this section is satisfied for the taxable year of the section 245A shareholder; and

(2) The basis benefit amount occurs during the taxable year of the section 245A shareholder, or a taxable year of a U.S. tax resident (other than the section 245A shareholder), a CFC described in §1.267A-5(a)(17), or a specified foreign person, as applicable, that—

(i) Ends with or within the taxable year of the section 245A shareholder; or

(ii) Begins with or within the taxable year of the section 245A shareholder, but only in a case in which but for this paragraph (b)(4)(iii)(A)(2)(ii) the basis benefit amount would not be assigned to a taxable year of the section 245A shareholder.

(B) *Anti-duplication rule.*—For purposes of paragraph (b)(4)(i)(A) of this section, to the extent that disqualified basis of an item of specified property gives rise to a basis benefit amount that is assigned to a taxable year of a section 245A shareholder under paragraph (b)(4)(iii)(A) of this section, and thereafter such disqualified basis gives rise to an additional basis benefit amount, the additional basis benefit amount cannot be assigned to another taxable year of any section 245A shareholder. Thus, for example, if the entire amount of disqualified basis of an item of specified property gives rise to a basis benefit amount for a particular taxable year of a CFC and is assigned to a taxable year of a section 245A shareholder but, pursuant to §1.951A-3(h)(2)(ii)(B)(1)(ii), the disqualified basis is not reduced or eliminated in such taxable year of the CFC (because, for example, the buyer is a CFC that is a related party) and, as a result, the disqualified basis thereafter gives rise to an additional basis benefit amount, then no portion of the additional basis benefit amount is assigned to a taxable year of any section 245A shareholder.

(iv) *Successor rules for basis benefit accounts.*—To the extent that an extraordinary disposition account of a section 245A shareholder is adjusted pursuant to §1.245A-5(c)(4), a basis benefit account with respect to the extraordinary disposition account is adjusted in a similar manner.

(5) *Special rules regarding duplicate DQB of an item of exchanged basis property.*—(i) *Adjustments to certain rules in applying paragraph (b)(1) of this section.*—For purposes of paragraph (b)(1) of this section for a taxable year of a section 245A shareholder, the following rules apply with respect to duplicate DQB of an item of exchanged basis property:

(A) Duplicate DQB of the item of exchanged basis property with respect to an item of specified property to which the item of exchanged property relates is not taken into account for purposes of paragraph (b)(1) of this section if the disqualified basis of the item of specified property is taken into account for purposes of paragraph (b)(1) of this section. Thus, for example, if for a taxable year of a section 245A shareholder the ownership requirement of paragraph (b)(3) of this section is satisfied with respect to an item of specified property and an item of exchanged basis property that relates to the item of specified property, all of the disqualified basis of which is duplicate DQB with respect to the item of specified property, then only the disqualified basis of the item of specified property is taken into account for purposes of, and is subject to reduction under, paragraph (b)(1) of this section.

(B) If, pursuant to paragraph (b)(5)(i)(A) of this section, duplicate DQB of an item of exchanged basis property with respect to an item of specified property is not taken into account for purposes of paragraph (b)(1) of this section, then, solely for purposes of §1.951A-2(c)(5), the duplicate DQB of the item of exchanged basis property is reduced (in the same manner as it would be if the disqualified basis were taken into account for purposes of paragraph (b)(1) of this section) by the product of the amounts described in paragraphs (b)(5)(i)(B)(1) and (2) of this section.

(1) The reduction, under paragraph (b)(1) of this section for the taxable year of the section 245A shareholder, to the disqualified basis of the item of specified property to which the item of exchanged basis property relates.

(2) A fraction, the numerator of which is the duplicate DQB of the item of exchanged basis property with respect to the item of specified property, and the denominator of which is the sum of the amounts of duplicate DQB with respect to the item of specified property of each item of exchanged basis property that relates to the item of specified property and for which the ownership requirement of paragraph (b)(3)(i) of this section is satisfied for the taxable year of the section 245A shareholder. For purposes of determining this fraction, duplicate DQB of an item of exchanged basis property is determined pursuant to the rules of paragraph (b)(2)(i) of this section (by replacing the term "paragraph (b)(1)" in that paragraph with the term "paragraph (b)(5)(i)(B)"). In addition, duplicate DQB of an item of exchanged basis property is excluded from the denominator of the fraction to the extent the duplicate DQB is attributable to duplicate DQB of another item of exchanged basis property that is included in the denominator of the fraction.

(ii) *Adjustments to certain rules in applying paragraph (b)(4) of this section.*—For purposes of paragraph (b)(4)(i)(A) of this section, to the extent that disqualified basis of an item of specified property gives rise to a basis benefit amount that is assigned to a taxable year of a section 245A shareholder under paragraph (b)(4)(iii)(A) of this section, and thereafter duplicate DQB attributable to such disqualified basis of the item of specified property gives rise to an additional basis benefit amount, the additional basis benefit amount cannot be assigned to another taxable year of any section 245A shareholder. Similarly, for purposes of paragraph (b)(4)(i)(A) of this section, to the extent that duplicate DQB attributable to disqualified basis of an item of specified property gives rise to a basis benefit amount that is assigned to a taxable year of a section 245A shareholder under paragraph (b)(4)(iii)(A) of this section, and thereafter such disqualified basis of the item of specified property (or duplicate DQB attributable to such disqualified basis of the item of specified property) gives rise to an additional basis benefit amount, the additional basis benefit amount cannot be assigned to another taxable year of any section 245A shareholder.

(6) *Special rule regarding prior extraordinary disposition amounts.*—For purposes of paragraph (b)(1) of this section, to the extent that an extraordinary disposition account of a section 245A shareholder is reduced under §1.245A-5(c)(3)(i)(A) by reason of a prior extraordinary disposition amount described in §1.245A-5(c)(3)(i)(D)(1)(i) through (iv), the extraordinary disposition account is considered to give rise to an extraordinary disposition amount or tiered extraordinary disposition amount (and the amount by which the account is reduced is treated as an extraordinary disposition amount or tiered extraordinary disposition amount).

(c) *Reduction of extraordinary disposition account by reason of the allocation and apportionment of deductions or losses attributable to disqualified basis.*—(1) *In general.*—For a taxable year of a CFC, if there is an RGI account with respect to the CFC that relates to an extraordinary disposition account of a section 245A shareholder with respect to an SFC, and the section 245A shareholder satisfies the ownership requirement of paragraph (c)(5) of this section for the taxable year of the CFC, then, subject to the limitations in paragraphs (c)(6) and (7) of this section, the extraordinary disposition account is reduced (but not below zero) by the lesser of the following amounts (each determined in the functional currency of the CFC)—

(i) The excess (if any) of—

(A) The product of—

(1) The adjusted earnings of the CFC for the taxable year of the CFC; and

(2) The percentage of stock of the CFC (by value) that, in aggregate, is owned directly or indirectly through one or more specified entities by the section 245A shareholder and any domestic affiliates on the last day of the taxable year of the CFC; over

(B) The sum of—

(1) The sum of the balance of the section 245A shareholder's and any domestic affiliates' previously taxed earnings and profits accounts with respect to the CFC for purposes of section 959 (determined as of the end of the taxable year of the CFC and taking into account any adjustments to the accounts for the taxable year);

(2) The sum of the balance of the hybrid deduction accounts (as described in §1.245A(e)-1(d)(1)) with respect to shares of stock of the CFC that the section 245A shareholder and any domestic affiliates own (within the meaning of section 958(a), and determined by treating a domestic partnership as foreign) as of the end of the taxable year of the CFC and taking into account any adjustments to the accounts for the taxable year; and

(3) The sum of the balance of the section 245A shareholder's and any domestic affiliates' extraordinary disposition accounts with respect to the CFC (determined as of the end of the taxable year of the CFC and taking into account any adjustments to the accounts for the taxable year). However, if the section 245A shareholder or a domestic affiliate has an RGI account with respect to the CFC that relates to an extraordinary disposition account with respect to the CFC, then only the excess, if any, of the balance of the extraordinary disposition account over the balance of the RGI account that relates to the extraordinary disposition account (determined as of the end of the taxable year of the CFC, but without regard to the application of paragraph (c)(4)(i)(B) of this section for the taxable year) is taken into account for purposes of this paragraph (c)(1)(i)(B)(3). In addition, for purposes of this paragraph (c)(1)(i)(B)(3), an extraordinary disposition account that but for paragraph (e)(1) of this section would be with respect to the CFC for purposes of this section is treated as an extraordinary disposition account with respect to the CFC and thus is taken into account for purposes of this paragraph (c)(1)(i)(B)(3).

(ii) The balance of the RGI account with respect to the CFC that relates to the section 245A shareholder's extraordinary disposition account with respect to the SFC (determined as of the end of the taxable year of the CFC, but without regard to the application of paragraph (c)(4)(i)(B) of this section for the taxable year).

(2) *Timing of reduction to extraordinary disposition account.*—See §1.245A-9(b)(3) for timing rules regarding the reduction to an extraordinary disposition account.

(3) *Adjusted earnings.*—The term *adjusted earnings* means, with respect to a CFC and a taxable year of the CFC, the earnings and profits of the CFC, determined as of the end of the CFC's taxable year (taking into account all distributions during the taxable year, and not taking into account any deficit in earnings and profits subject to §1.381(c)(2)-1(a)(5)) and with the adjustments described in paragraphs (c)(3)(i) through (iv) of this section.

(i) The earnings and profits are increased by the amount of any deduction or loss that—

(A) Is or was attributable to disqualified basis of an item of specified property, but only to the extent that gain recognized on the extraordinary disposition of the item of specified property was included in the initial balance of an extraordinary disposition account;

(B) Is or was allocated and apportioned to residual CFC gross income of the CFC (or a predecessor) solely by reason of §1.951A-2(c)(5)(i); and

(C) Does not or has not given rise to or increased a deficit in earnings and profits subject to §1.381(c)(2)-1(a)(5), determined as of the end of the taxable year of the CFC.

(ii) The earnings and profits are decreased by the amount by which any RGI account with respect to the CFC has been decreased pursuant to paragraph (c)(4)(i)(B) of this section for a prior taxable year of the CFC.

(iii) The earnings and profits are determined without regard to earnings attributable to income described in section 245(a)(5)(A) or dividends described in section 245(a)(5)(B) (determined without regard to section 245(a)(12)).

(iv) The earnings and profits are decreased by the amount of any deduction or loss that, but for paragraph (c)(3)(i)(C) of this section, would be described in paragraph (c)(3)(i) of this section.

(4) *RGI account.*—(i) *In general.*—For a taxable year of a CFC, the following rules apply to determine the balance of a section 245A shareholder's RGI account that is with respect to the CFC and that relates to an extraordinary disposition account of the section 245A shareholder with respect to an SFC:

(A) The balance of the RGI account is increased by the product of the amounts described in paragraphs (c)(4)(i)(A)(*1*) and (*2*) of this section for a taxable year of the CFC.

(*1*) The sum of the amounts of deductions and losses of the CFC that—

(*i*) Are attributable to disqualified basis of one or more items of specified property that correspond to the extraordinary disposition account; and

(*ii*) But for §1.951A-2(c)(5)(i), would have decreased one or more categories of the CFC's positive subpart F income, the CFC's tested income, or the CFC's ECTI, or increased or given rise to a tested loss or one or more qualified deficits of the CFC.

(*2*) The lesser of—

(*i*) A fraction (expressed as a percentage), the numerator of which is the sum of the portions of the CFC's subpart F income and tested income or tested loss (expressed as a positive number) taken into account under sections 951(a)(1)(A) and 951A(a) (as determined under the rules of §§1.951-1(b) and (e) and 1.951A-1(d)) by the section 245A shareholder and any domestic affiliates of the section 245A shareholder and the section 245A shareholder's and any domestic affiliates' pro rata shares of the CFC's qualified deficits (expressed as a positive number), and the denominator of which is the sum of the CFC's subpart F income, tested income or tested loss (expressed as a positive number), and qualified deficits (expressed as a positive number), but for purposes of this paragraph (c)(4)(i)(A)(*2*)(*i*) treating ECTI (expressed as a positive number) as if it were subpart F income; and

(*ii*) The extraordinary disposition ownership percentage applicable as to the section 245A shareholder's extraordinary disposition account.

(B) The balance of the RGI account is decreased to the extent that, by reason of the application of paragraph (c)(1) of this section with respect to the taxable year of the CFC, there is a reduction to the extraordinary disposition account of the section 245A shareholder.

(ii) *Successor rules for RGI accounts.*—To the extent that an extraordinary disposition account of a section 245A shareholder is adjusted pursuant to §1.245A-5(c)(4), an RGI account of a CFC with respect to the extraordinary disposition account is adjusted in a similar manner.

(5) *Ownership requirement with respect to a CFC.*—For a taxable year of a CFC, a section 245A shareholder satisfies the ownership requirement of this paragraph (c)(5) if, on the last day of the CFC's taxable year, the section 245A shareholder or a domestic affiliate is a United States shareholder with respect to the CFC.

(6) *Allocation of reductions among multiple extraordinary disposition accounts.*—This paragraph (c)(6) applies if, by reason of the application of paragraph (c)(1) of this section with respect to a taxable year of a CFC (and but for the application of this paragraph (c)(6) and paragraph (c)(7) of this section), the sum of the reductions under paragraph (c)(1) of this section to two or more extraordinary disposition accounts of a section 245A shareholder or a domestic affiliate of the section 245A shareholder would exceed the amount described in paragraph (c)(1)(i)(A) of this section (the amount of such excess, the *excess amount*). When this paragraph (c)(6) applies, the reduction to each extraordinary disposition account described in the previous sentence is equal to the reduction that would occur but for this paragraph (c)(6) and paragraph (c)(7) of this section, less the product of the excess amount and a fraction, the numerator of which is the balance of the extraordinary disposition account, and the denominator of which is the sum of the balances of all of the extraordinary dispositions accounts described in the previous sentence. For purposes of determining this fraction, the balance of an extraordinary disposition account is determined as of the end of the taxable year of the section 245A shareholder or the domestic affiliate, as applicable, that includes the date on which the CFC's taxable year ends (and after the determination of any extraordinary disposition amounts or tiered extraordinary disposition amounts for the taxable year of the section 245A shareholder or the domestic affiliate, as applicable, and adjustments to the extraordinary disposition account for prior extraordinary disposition amounts).

(7) *Extraordinary disposition account not reduced below balance of basis benefit account.*—An extraordinary disposition account of a section 245A shareholder cannot be reduced pursuant to paragraph (c)(1) of this section below the balance of the basis benefit account with respect to the extraordinary disposition account (determined when a reduction to the extraordinary disposition account would occur under paragraph (c)(1) of this section).

(d) *Special rules for determining when specified property corresponds to an extraordinary disposition account.*—(1) *Substituted property.*—(i) *Treatment as specified property that corresponds to an extraordinary disposition account.*—For purposes of this section, an item of substituted property is treated as an item of specified property that corresponds to an extraordinary disposition account to which the related item of specified property (that is, the item of specified property to which the item of substituted property relates, as described in paragraph (d)(1)(ii) of this section) corresponds. In addition, in a case in which an item of substituted property relates to an item of specified property that corresponds to a particular extraordinary disposition account and an item of specified property that corresponds to another extraordinary disposition account (such that, pursuant to this paragraph (d)(1)(i), the item of substituted property is treated as corresponding to multiple extraordinary disposition accounts), only the disqualified basis of the item of substituted property attributable to the first item of specified property is taken into account for purposes of applying this section as to the first extraordinary disposition account, and, similarly, only the disqualified basis of the item of substituted property attributable to the second item of specified property is taken into account for purposes of applying this section as to the second extraordinary disposition account.

(ii) *Definition of substituted property.*—The term *substituted property* means an item of property the disqualified basis of which is, pursuant to §1.951A-3(h)(2)(ii)(B)(2)(*i*) or (*iii*), increased by reason of a reduction under §1.951A-3(h)(2)(ii)(B)(1) in disqualified basis of an item of specified property. An item of substituted property relates to an item of specified property if the disqualified basis of the item of substituted property was increased by reason of a reduction in disqualified basis of the item of specified property.

(2) *Exchanged basis property.*—(i) *Treatment as specified property that corresponds to an extraordinary disposition account for certain purposes.*—For purposes of this section, an item of exchanged basis property is treated as an item of specified property that corresponds to an extraordinary disposition account to which the related item of specified property (that is, the item of specified property to which the item of exchanged basis property relates) corresponds.

(ii) *Definition of exchanged basis property.*—The term *exchanged basis property* means an item of property the disqualified basis of which, pursuant to §1.951A-3(h)(2)(ii)(B)(2)(*ii*), includes disqualified basis of an item of specified property. An item of exchanged basis property relates to an item of specified property if the disqualified basis of the item of exchanged basis property includes disqualified basis of the item of specified property.

(iii) *Definition of duplicate DQB.*—(A) *In general.*—The term *duplicate DQB* means, with respect to an item of exchanged basis property and the item of specified property to which the exchanged basis property relates, the disqualified basis of the item of exchanged basis property that includes or is attributable to disqualified basis of the item of specified property.

(B) *Certain nonrecognition transfers involving stock or a partnership interest.*—To the extent that an item of exchanged basis property that is stock or an interest in a partnership *(lower-tier item)* includes disqualified basis of an item of specified property to which the lower-tier item relates *(contributed item)*, and another item of exchanged basis property that is stock or a partnership interest *(upper-tier item)* includes disqualified basis of the lower-tier item that is attributable to disqualified basis of the contributed item, the disqualified basis of the upper-tier item is attributable to disqualified basis of the contributed item and the upper-tier item is an item of exchanged basis property that relates to the contributed item. The principles of the preceding sentence apply each time disqualified basis of an item of exchanged basis property that is stock or an interest in a partnership is included in disqualified basis of another item of exchanged basis property that is stock or an interest in a partnership.

(C) *Multiple nonrecognition transfers of an item of specified property.*—To the extent that multiple items of exchanged basis property that are stock or interests in a partnership include disqualified basis of the same item of specified property *(contributed item)* to which the items of exchanged basis property relate, and the issuer of one of the items of exchanged basis property *(upper-tier successor item)* receives the other item of exchanged basis property *(lower-tier successor item)* in exchange for the contributed property, the disqualified basis of the upper-tier successor item is attributable to disqualified basis of the lower-tier successor item and the upper-tier successor item is an item of exchanged basis property that relates to the lower-tier successor item. The principles of the preceding sentence apply each time disqualified basis of an item of specified property to which an item of exchanged basis property that is stock or an interest in partnership relates is included in disqualified basis of another item of exchanged basis property that is stock or an interest in a partnership.

(e) *Special rules when extraordinary disposition accounts are adjusted pursuant to §1.245A-5(c)(4).*—(1) *Extraordinary disposition account with respect to multiple SFCs.*—This paragraph (e)(1) applies if, pursuant to §1.245A-5(c)(4)(ii) or (iii) (the transaction or transactions by reason of which §1.245A-5(c)(4)(ii) or (iii) applies, the *adjustment transaction*), an extraordinary disposition account of a section 245A shareholder with respect to an SFC (such extraordinary disposition account, the *transferor ED account;* and such SFC, the *transferor SFC)* gives rise to an increase in the balance of an extraordinary disposition account with respect to another SFC (such extraordinary disposition account, the *transferee ED account;* such SFC, the *transferee SFC;* and such increase, the *adjustment amount).* When this paragraph (e)(1) applies, the following rules apply for purposes of this section:

(i) A ratable portion of the transferee ED account is treated as retaining its status as an extraordinary disposition account with respect to the transferor SFC and is not treated as an extraordinary disposition account with respect to the transferee SFC (the transferee ED account to such extent, the *deemed transferor ED account),* based on the adjustment amount relative to the balance of the transferee ED account (without regard to this paragraph (e)(1)) immediately after the adjustment transaction. Thus, for example, whether or not the transferor SFC is in existence immediately after the transaction, the items of specified property that correspond to the deemed transferor ED account are the same as the items of specified property that correspond to the transferor ED account. As an additional example, whether or not the transferor SFC is in existence immediately after the transaction the extraordinary disposition ownership percentage with respect to the deemed transferor ED account is the same as the extraordinary disposition ownership percentage with respect to the transferor ED account (except to the extent the extraordinary disposition ownership percentage is adjusted pursuant to the rules of paragraph (e)(2) of this section).

(ii) In the case of an amount (such as an extraordinary disposition amount or tiered extraordinary disposition amount) determined by reference to the transferee ED account (without regard to this paragraph (e)(1)), the portion of the amount that is considered attributable to the deemed transferor ED account (and not the transferee ED account) is equal to the product of such amount and a fraction, the numerator of which is the balance of the deemed transferor ED account, and the denominator of which is the balance of the transferee ED account (determined without regard to this paragraph (e)(1)). Thus, for example, if after an adjustment transaction the

transferee ED account (without regard to this paragraph (e)(1)) gives rise to an extraordinary disposition amount, and if the fraction (expressed as a percentage) is 40, then, for purposes of this section, 40 percent of the extraordinary disposition amount is treated as attributable to the deemed transferor ED account and the remaining 60 percent of the extraordinary disposition amount is attributable to the transferee ED account, and the balance of each of the deemed transferor ED account and the transferee ED account is correspondingly reduced.

(2) *Extraordinary disposition accounts with respect to a single SFC.*—If an extraordinary disposition account of a section 245A shareholder with respect to an SFC is reduced by reason of §1.245A-5(c)(4), then, except as provided in paragraph (e)(1) of this section, for purposes of this section, the extraordinary disposition ownership percentage as to the extraordinary disposition account (as well as the extraordinary disposition ownership percentage as to any extraordinary disposition account with respect to the SFC that is increased by reason of the reduction) is adjusted in a similar manner. [Reg. §1.245A-8.]

☐ [*T.D.* 9934, 11-25-2020.]

[Reg. §1.245A-9]

§1.245A-9. Other rules and definitions.—(a) *In general.*—This section provides rules of general applicability for purposes of §§1.245A-6 through 1.245A-10, a transition rule to revoke an election to eliminate disqualified basis, and definitions.

(b) *Rules of general applicability.*—(1) *Correspondence.*—An item of specified property corresponds to a section 245A shareholder's extraordinary disposition account if gain was recognized on the extraordinary disposition of the item and the gain was taken into account in determining the initial balance of the account. See §1.245A-8(d) for additional rules regarding when an item of property is treated as corresponding to an extraordinary disposition account in certain complex cases.

(2) *Timing rules related to disqualified basis for purposes of applying §§1.245A-7(b) and 1.245A-8(b).*—(i) *Determination of disqualified basis.*—For purposes of determining the fraction described in §1.245A-7(b)(1)(ii) or §1.245A-8(b)(1)(ii) when applying §1.245A-7(b)(1) or §1.245A-8(b)(1)(ii), respectively, for a taxable year of a section 245A shareholder, disqualified basis of an item of specified property is determined as of the beginning of the taxable year of the CFC that holds the item of specified property (in a case in which §1.245A-7(b) applies) or the specified property owner (in a case in which §1.245A-8(b) applies), in either case, that includes the date on which the section 245A shareholder's taxable year ends (and without regard to any reductions to the disqualified basis of the item of specified property pursuant to §1.245A-7(b)(1) or §1.245A-8(b)(1) for such taxable year of the CFC or the specified property owner, as applicable). However, if disqualified basis of the item of specified property arose as a result of an extraordinary disposition that occurred after the beginning of the taxable year of the CFC or the specified property owner described in the preceding sentence, then the disqualified basis of the item of specified property is determined as of the date on which the extraordinary disposition occurred (and without regard to any reductions to the disqualified basis of the item of specified property pursuant to paragraph (b)(1) of this section for such taxable year of the CFC or the specified property owner).

(ii) *Reduction to disqualified basis of an item of specified property.*—The reduction to disqualified basis of an item of specified property pursuant to §1.245A-7(b)(1) or §1.245A-8(b)(1) occurs on the date described in paragraph (b)(2)(i) of this section.

(iii) *Definition of specified property owner.*—For purposes of applying §1.245A-8(b)(1) and paragraphs (b)(2)(i) and (ii) of this section for a taxable year of a section 245A shareholder, the term *specified property owner* means, with respect to an item of specified property, the person that, on at least one day of the taxable year of the person that includes the date on which the section 245A shareholder's taxable year ends, held the item of specified property. However, if, but for this sentence, there would be more than one specified property owner with respect to the item of specified property, then the specified property owner is the person that held the item of specified property on the earliest date that falls within the section 245A shareholder's taxable year.

(3) *Timing rules for reducing an extraordinary disposition account under §§1.245A-7(c) and 1.245A-8(c).*—For purposes of §1.245A-7(c)(1) or §1.245A-8(c)(1), as applicable, with respect to a taxable year of a CFC, the reduction to an extraordinary disposition account pursuant to §1.245A-7(c)(1) or §1.245A-8(c)(1) occurs as of the end of the taxable year of the section 245A shareholder that includes the date on which the CFC's taxable year ends (and after the determination of any extraordinary disposition amounts or tiered

extraordinary amounts, adjustments to the extraordinary disposition account for prior extraordinary disposition amounts, and the application of §1.245A-7(b) or §1.245A-8(b), as applicable, each for the taxable year of the section 245A shareholder.

(4) *Currency translation.*—For purposes of applying §§1.245A-7(b) and 1.245A-8(b), the disqualified basis of (and, if applicable, a basis benefit amount with respect to) an item of specified property that corresponds to an extraordinary disposition account are translated (if necessary) into the functional currency in which the extraordinary disposition account is maintained, using the spot rate on the date the extraordinary disposition occurred. A reduction in disqualified basis of an item of specified property determined under §1.245A-7(b)(1) or §1.245A-8(b)(1) is translated (if necessary) into the functional currency in which the disqualified basis of the item of specified property is maintained, and a reduction in an extraordinary disposition account determined under §1.245A-7(c) or §1.245A-8(c) section is translated (if necessary) into the functional currency in which the extraordinary disposition account is maintained, in each case using the spot rate described in the preceding sentence.

(5) *Anti-avoidance rule.*—Appropriate adjustments are made pursuant to this paragraph (b)(5), including adjustments that would disregard a transaction or arrangement in whole or in part, to any amounts determined under (or subject to application of) this section if a transaction or arrangement is engaged in with a principal purpose of avoiding the purposes of §§1.245A-6 through 1.245A-10.

(c) *Transition rule to revoke election to eliminate disqualified basis.*—(1) *In general.*—This paragraph (c)(1) applies to an election that is filed, pursuant to §1.951A-3(h)(2)(ii)(B)(3), to eliminate the disqualified basis of an item of specified property. An election to which this paragraph (c)(1) applies may be revoked if, on or before March 1, 2021—

(i) All controlling domestic shareholders (as defined in §1.964-1(c)(5)) of the CFC (or, in the case of an election made by a partnership, the partnership) each attach a revocation statement (in the manner described in paragraph (c)(2) of this section) to an amended return, for the taxable year to which the election applies, that revokes the election (or, in the case of a partnership subject to subchapter C of chapter 63 of the Internal Revenue Code, requests administrative adjustment under section 6227); and

(ii) The controlling domestic shareholders (or the partnership) each file an amended tax return, for any other taxable years reflecting the election to eliminate the disqualified basis, that reflects the election having been revoked (or, in the case of a partnership subject to subchapter C of chapter 63, requests administrative adjustment under section 6227).

(2) *Revocation statement.*—Except as otherwise provided in publications, forms, instructions, or other guidance, a revocation statement attached by a person to an amended tax return must include the person's name, taxpayer identification number, and a statement that the revocation statement is filed pursuant to paragraph (c)(1) of this section to revoke an election pursuant to §1.951A-3(h)(2)(ii)(B)(3). In addition, the revocation statement must be filed in the manner prescribed in publications, forms, instructions, or other guidance.

(d) *Definitions.*—In addition to the definitions in §1.245A-5, the following definitions apply for purposes of §§1.245A-6 through 1.245A-11.

(1) The term *adjusted earnings* has the meaning provided in §1.245A-7(c)(3) or §1.245A-8(c)(3), as applicable.

(2) The term *basis benefit account* has the meaning provided in §1.245A-8(b)(4)(i).

(3) The term *basis benefit amount* has the meaning provided in §1.245A-8(b)(4)(ii).

(4) The term *disqualified basis* has the meaning provided in §1.951A-3(h)(2)(ii).

(5) The term *domestic affiliate* means, with respect to a section 245A shareholder, a domestic corporation that is a related party with respect to the section 245A shareholder. *See also* §1.245A-5(i)(19) (defining related party).

(6) The term *duplicate DQB* has the meaning provided in §1.245A-8(d)(2)(iii).

(7) The term *ECTI* means, with respect to a taxable year of a specified foreign person, the taxable income (or loss) of the specified foreign person determined by taking into account only items of income and gain that are, or are treated as, effectively connected with the conduct of a trade or business in the United States (as described in §1.882-4(a)(1)) and are not exempt from U.S. tax pursuant to a treaty obligation of the United States, and items of deduction and loss that are allocated and apportioned to such items of income and gain.

(8) The term *exchanged basis property* has the meaning provided in §1.245A-8(d)(2)(ii).

(9) The term *qualified deficit* has the meaning provided in section 952(c)(1)(B)(ii).

(10) The term *qualified related party* has the meaning provided in §1.245A-8(b)(3)(ii).

(11) The term *RGI account* means, with respect to a CFC and an extraordinary disposition account of a section 245A shareholder with respect to an SFC, an account of the section 245A shareholder with respect to an SFC (the initial balance of which is zero), adjusted at the end of each taxable year of the CFC pursuant to the rules of §1.245A-7(c)(4) or §1.245A-8(c)(4), as applicable. The RGI account must be maintained in the functional currency of the CFC.

(12) The term *specified foreign person* means a nonresident alien individual (as defined in section 7701(b) and the regulations under section 7701(b)) or a foreign corporation (including a CFC) that conducts, or is treated as conducting, a trade or business in the United States (as described in §1.882-4(a)(1)).

(13) The term *specified property owner* has the meaning provided in §1.245A-8(b)(2)(iii).

(14) The term *subpart F income* has the meaning provided in section 952(a).

(15) The term *substituted property* has the meaning provided in §1.245A-8(d)(1)(ii).

(16) The term *tested income* has the meaning provided in section 951A(c)(2)(A).

(17) The term *tested loss* has the meaning provided in section 951A(c)(2)(B). [Reg. §1.245A-9.]

☐ [T.D. 9934, 11-25-2020.]

[Reg. §1.245A-10]

§1.245A-10. Examples.—(a) *Scope.*—This section provides examples illustrating the application of §§1.245A-6 through 1.245A-9.

(b) *Presumed facts.*—For purposes of the examples in the section, except as otherwise stated, the following facts are presumed:

(1) US1 and US2 are both domestic corporations that have calendar taxable years.

(2) CFC1, CFC2, CFC3, and CFC4 are all SFCs and CFCs that have taxable years ending November 30.

(3) Each entity uses the U.S. dollar as its functional currency.

(4) There are no items of deduction or loss attributable to an item of specified property.

(5) Absent the application of §1.245A-5, any dividends received by US1 from CFC1 would meet the requirements to qualify for the section 245A deduction.

(6) All dispositions of items of specified property by an SFC during a disqualified period of the SFC to a related party give rise to an extraordinary disposition.

(7) None of the CFCs have a deficit subject to §1.381(c)(2)-1(a)(5), and none of the CFCs are engaged in the conduct of a trade or business in the United States (and therefore none of the CFCs have ECTI).

(8) There is no previously taxed earnings and profits account with respect to any CFC for purposes of section 959. In addition, each hybrid deduction account with respect to a share of stock of a CFC has a zero balance at all times. Further, there is no extraordinary disposition account with respect to any CFC.

(9) Under §1.245A-11(b), taxpayers choose to apply §§1.245A-6 through 1.245A-11 to the relevant taxable years.

(c) *Examples.*—(1) *Example 1. Reduction of disqualified basis under rule for simple cases by reason of dividend paid out of extraordinary disposition account.*—(i) *Facts.* US1 owns 100% of the single class of stock of CFC1 and CFC2. On November 30, 2018, in a transaction that is an extraordinary disposition, CFC1 sells two items of specified property, Item 1 and Item 2, to CFC2 in exchange for $150x of cash (the "Disqualified Transfer"). Item 1 is sold for $90x and Item 2 is sold for $60x. Item 1 and Item 2 each has a basis of $0 in the hands of CFC1 immediately before the Disqualified Transfer, and therefore CFC1 recognizes $150x of gain as a result of the Disqualified Transfer ($150x - $0). After the Disqualified Transfer, CFC2's only assets are Item 1 and Item 2. On November 30, 2018, and thus during US1's taxable year ending December 31, 2018, CFC1 distributes $150x of cash to US1, and all of the distribution is characterized as a dividend under section 301(c)(1) and treated as a distribution out of earnings and profits described in section 959(c)(3). For CFC1's taxable year ending on November 30, 2018, CFC1 has $160x of earnings and profits described in section 959(c)(3), without regard to any distributions during the taxable year. CFC2 continues to hold Item 1 and Item 2. Lastly, because the conditions of §1.245A-6(b)(1) and (2) are satisfied for US1's 2018 taxable year, US1 chooses to apply §1.245A-7 (rules for simple cases) in lieu of §1.245A-8 (rules for complex cases) for that taxable year.

(ii) *Analysis*—(A) *Application of §§ 1.245A-5 and 1.951A-2 as a result of the Disqualified Transfer.* As a result of the Disqualified Transfer, under § 1.951A-2(c)(5), Item 1 has disqualified basis of $90x, and Item 2 has disqualified basis of $60x. In addition, as a result of the Disqualified Transfer, under § 1.245A-5(c)(3)(i)(A), US1 has an extraordinary disposition account with respect to CFC1 with an initial balance of $150x. Under § 1.245A-5(c)(2)(i), $10x of the dividend is considered paid out of non-extraordinary disposition E&P of CFC1 with respect to US1, and $140x of the dividend is considered paid out of US1's extraordinary disposition account with respect to CFC1 to the extent of the balance of the extraordinary disposition account ($150x). Thus, the dividend of $150x is an extraordinary disposition amount, within the meaning of § 1.245A-5(c)(1), to the extent of $140x. As a result, the balance of the extraordinary disposition account is reduced to $10x ($150x - $140x).

(B) *Correspondence requirement.* Under § 1.245A-9(b)(1), each of Item 1 and Item 2 corresponds to US1's extraordinary disposition account with respect to CFC1, because as a result of the Disqualified Transfer CFC1 recognized gain with respect to Item 1 and Item 2, and the gain was taken into account in determining the initial balance of US1's extraordinary disposition account with respect to CFC1.

(C) *Reduction of disqualified basis of Item 1.* Because Item 1 corresponds to US1's extraordinary disposition account, the disqualified basis of Item 1 is reduced pursuant to § 1.245A-7(b)(1) by reason of US1's $140x extraordinary disposition amount for US1's 2018 taxable year. Paragraphs (c)(2)(ii)(C)(*1*) through (*3*) of this section describe the determinations pursuant to § 1.245A-7(b)(1).

(*1*) To determine the reduction to the disqualified basis of Item 1, the disqualified basis of Item 1, as well as the disqualified basis of Item 2, must be determined as of the date described in § 1.245A-9(b)(2)(i) (and before the application of § 1.245A-7(b)(1)). *See* § 1.245A-7(b)(1)(ii). For each of Item 1 and Item 2, that date is December 1, 2018. December 1, 2018, is the first day of the taxable year of CFC2 (the CFC that holds Item 1 and Item 2) beginning on December 1, 2018, which is the taxable year of CFC2 that includes December 31, 2018, the date on which US1's 2018 taxable year ends. *See* § 1.245A-9(b)(2)(i).

(*2*) Pursuant to § 1.245A-7(b)(1), the disqualified basis of Item 1 is reduced by $84x, computed as the product of—

(*i*) $140x, the extraordinary disposition amount; and

(*ii*) A fraction, the numerator of which is $90x (the disqualified basis of Item 1 on December 1, 2018, and before the application of § 1.245A-7(b)(1)), and the denominator of which is $150x (the disqualified basis of Item 1, $90x, plus the disqualified basis of Item 2, $60x, in each case determined on December 1, 2018, and before the application of § 1.245A-7(b)(1)). *See* § 1.245A-7(b)(1).

(*3*) The $84x reduction to the disqualified basis of Item 1 occurs on December 1, 2018, the date on which the disqualified basis of Item 1 is determined for purposes of determining the reduction pursuant to § 1.245A-7(b)(1). *See* § 1.245A-9(b)(2)(ii).

(D) *Reduction of disqualified basis of Item 2.* For reasons similar to those described in paragraph (c)(2)(ii)(C) of this section, on December 1, 2018, the disqualified basis of Item 2 is reduced by $56x, the amount equal to the product of $140x, the extraordinary disposition amount, and a fraction, the numerator of which is $60x (the disqualified basis of Item 2 on December 1, 2018, and before the application of § 1.245A-7(b)(1)), and the denominator of which is $150x (the disqualified basis of Item 1, $90x, plus the disqualified basis of Item 2, $60x, in each case determined on December 1, 2018, and before the application of § 1.245A-7(b)(1)).

(2) *Example 2. Basis benefit amount and impact on reduction to disqualified basis under rule for complex cases*—(i) *Facts.* The facts are the same as in paragraph (c)(1)(i) of this section (*Example 1*) (and the results are the same as in paragraph (c)(1)(ii)(A) of this section), except that, on December 1, 2018, CFC2 sells Item 1 for $90x of cash to an individual that is not a related party with respect to US1 or CFC2 (such transaction, the "Sale," and such individual, "Individual A"). At the time of the Sale, CFC2's basis in Item 1 is $90x (all of which is disqualified basis, as described in § 1.951A-3(h)(2)(ii)(A)). CFC2 takes into the account the disqualified basis of Item 1 for purposes of determining the amount of gain recognized on the Sale, which is $0 ($90x - $90x); but for the disqualified basis, CFC2 would have had $90x of gain that would have been taken into account in computing its tested income. As a result of the Sale, the condition of § 1.245A-6(b)(2) is not satisfied, because on at least one day of CFC2's taxable year beginning on December 1, 2018 (which begins within US1's 2018 taxable year) CFC2 does not hold Item 1. *See* § 1.245A-6(b)(2)(ii)(C)(*1*). US1 therefore applies § 1.245A-8 (rules for complex cases) for its 2018 taxable year. *See* § 1.245A-6(b).

(ii) *Analysis*—(A) *Ownership requirement.* With respect to each of Item 1 and Item 2, the ownership requirement of § 1.245A-8(b)(3)(i) is satisfied for US1's 2018 taxable year. This is because on at least one day that falls within US1's 2018 taxable year, each of Item 1 and Item 2 is held by CFC2, and US1 directly owns all of the stock of CFC2

throughout such taxable year (and thus, for purposes of applying § 1.245A-8(b)(3)(i), US1 owns at least 10% of the interests of CFC2 on at least one day that falls within such taxable year). *See* § 1.245A-8(b)(3).

(B) *Basis benefit amount with respect to Item 1 as a result of the Sale.* Under § 1.245A-8(b)(4)(i), US1 has a basis benefit account with respect to its extraordinary disposition account with respect to CFC1. As described in paragraphs (c)(2)(ii)(B)(*1*) through (*3*) of this section, the balance of the basis benefit account (which is initially zero) is, on December 31, 2018, increased by $90x, the basis benefit amount with respect to Item 1 and assigned to US1's 2018 taxable year.

(*1*) By reason of the Sale, for CFC2's taxable year beginning December 1, 2018, and ending November 30, 2019, the entire $90x of disqualified basis of Item 1 is taken into account for U.S. tax purposes by CFC2 and, as a result, reduces CFC2's tested income or increases CFC2's tested loss. Accordingly, for such taxable year, there is a $90x basis benefit amount with respect to Item 1. *See* § 1.245A-8(b)(4)(ii)(A). The result would be the same if the Sale were to a related person and thus, pursuant to § 1.951A-3(h)(2)(ii)(B)(*1*)(*ii*), no portion of the $90x of disqualified basis were eliminated or reduced by reason of the Sale. *See* § 1.245A-8(b)(4)(ii)(B).

(*2*) The $90x basis benefit amount with respect to Item 1 is assigned to US1's 2018 taxable year. This is because the ownership requirement of § 1.245A-8(b)(3)(i) is satisfied with respect to Item 1 for US1's 2018 taxable year, and the basis benefit amount occurs in CFC2's taxable year beginning December 1, 2018, a taxable year of CFC2 that begins within US1's 2018 taxable year (and, but for § 1.245A-8(b)(4)(iii)(A)(*2*)(*ii*), the basis benefit amount would not be assigned to a taxable year of US1, such as the taxable year of US1 beginning January 1, 2019, given that, as result of the Sale, the ownership requirement of § 1.245A-8(b)(3)(i) would not be satisfied with respect to Item 1 for such taxable year). *See* § 1.245A-8(b)(4)(iii)(A).

(*3*) On December 31, 2018 (the last day of US1's 2018 taxable year), US1's basis benefit account with respect to its extraordinary disposition account with respect to CFC1 is increased by $90x, the $90x basis benefit amount with respect to Item 1 and assigned to US1's 2018 taxable year. The basis benefit account is increased by such amount because Item 1 corresponds to US1's extraordinary disposition account with respect to CFC1, and the extraordinary disposition ownership percentage applicable to such extraordinary disposition account is 100. *See* § 1.245A-8(b)(4)(i)(A).

(C) *Basis benefit amount limitation on reduction to disqualified basis.* By reason of US1's $140x extraordinary disposition amount for US1's 2018 taxable year, the disqualified basis of Item 1 is reduced by $30x, and the disqualified basis of Item 2 is reduced by $20x, pursuant to § 1.245A-8(b)(1). *See* § 1.245A-8(b). Paragraphs (c)(2)(ii)(C)(*1*) through (*4*) of this section describe the determinations pursuant to § 1.245A-8(b)(1).

(*1*) For purposes of determining the reduction to the disqualified bases of Item 1 and Item 2, the disqualified bases of the Items are determined on December 1, 2018 (and before the application of § 1.245A-8(b)(1)). *See* § 1.245A-8(b)(1)(ii). The disqualified bases of the Items are determined on December 1, 2018, because that date is the first day of the taxable year of CFC2 beginning on December 1, 2018, which is the taxable year of CFC2 (the specified property owner of each of Item 1 and Item 2) that includes December 31, 2018, the date on which US1's 2018 taxable year ends. *See* § 1.245A-8(b)(2)(i). For purposes of applying § § 1.245A-8(b)(1) and § 1.245A-9(b)(2) for US1's 2018 taxable year, CFC2 is the specified property owner of each of Item 1 and Item 2 because, on at least one day of CFC2's taxable year that includes the date on which US1's 2018 taxable year ends (that is, on at least one day of CFC2's taxable year beginning December 1, 2018), CFC2 held the Item. *See* § 1.245A-9(b)(2)(iii). CFC2 is the specified property owner of Item 1 even though Individual A also held Item 1 during Individual A's taxable year that includes the date on which US1's 2018 taxable year ends because CFC2 held Item 1 on an earlier date than Individual A. *See* § 1.245A-9(b)(2)(iii).

(*2*) Pursuant to § 1.245A-8(b)(1), the disqualified basis of Item 1 is reduced by $30x, computed as the product of—

(*i*) $50x, the excess of the extraordinary disposition amount ($140x) over the balance of the basis benefit account with respect to US1's extraordinary disposition with respect to CFC1 ($90x); and

(*ii*) A fraction, the numerator of which is $90x (the disqualified basis of Item 1 on December 1, 2018, and before the application of § 1.245A-8(b)(1)), and the denominator of which is $150x (the disqualified basis of Item 1, $90x, plus the disqualified basis of Item 2, $60x, in each case determined on December 1, 2018, and before the application of § 1.245A-8(b)(1)). *See* paragraph 1.245A-8(b)(1).

(*3*) Pursuant to § 1.245A-8(b)(1), the disqualified basis of Item 2 is reduced by $20x, computed as the product of—

(*i*) $50x, the excess of the extraordinary disposition amount ($140x) over the balance of the basis benefit account with respect to US1's extraordinary disposition with respect to CFC1 ($90x); and (*ii*) A fraction, the numerator of which is $60x (the disqualified basis of Item 2 on December 1, 2018, and before the application of paragraph (b)(1) of this section), and the denominator of which is $150x (the disqualified basis of Item 1, $90x, plus the disqualified basis of Item 2, $60x, in each case determined on December 1, 2018, and before the application of §1.245A-8(b)(1)). *See* §1.245A-8(b)(1).

(4) The $30x and $20x reductions to the disqualified bases of Item 1 and Item 2, respectively, occur on December 1, 2018, the date on which the disqualified bases of the Items are determined for purposes of determining the reductions pursuant to §1.245A-8(b)(1). *See* §1.245A-9(b)(2)(ii).

(D) *Reduction of basis benefit account.* The balance of the basis benefit account with respect to US1's extraordinary disposition account with respect to CFC1 is decreased by $90x, the amount by which, for CFC2's taxable year beginning December 1, 2018, the disqualified bases of Item 1 and Item 2 would have been reduced pursuant to §1.245A-8(b)(1) but for the $90x balance of the basis benefit account. *See* §1.245A-8(b)(4)(i)(B). The reduction to the balance of the basis benefit account occurs on December 31, 2018, and after the completion of all other computations pursuant to §1.245A-8(b). *See* §1.245A-8(b)(4)(i)(B).

(3) *Example 3. Reduction in balance of extraordinary disposition account under rules for simple cases by reason of allocation and apportionment of deductions to residual CFC gross income.*—(i) *Facts.* The facts are the same as in paragraph (c)(1)(i) of this section (*Example 1*) (and the results are the same as in paragraph (c)(1)(ii)(A) of this section), except that CFC1 does not make a distribution to US1. In addition, during CFC2's taxable year beginning December 1, 2018, and ending November 30, 2019, the disqualified basis of Item 1 gives rise to a $6x amortization deduction, and the disqualified basis of Item 2 gives rise to a $4x amortization deduction, and each of the amortization deductions is allocated and apportioned to residual CFC gross income of CFC2 solely by reason of §1.951A-2(c)(5) (though, but for §1.951A-2(c)(5), would have been allocated and apportioned to gross tested income of CFC2). Further, as of the end of CFC2's taxable year ending November 30, 2019, CFC2 has $15x of earnings and profits. Lastly, because the conditions of §1.245A-6(b)(1) and (2) are satisfied for US1's 2018 taxable year, US1 chooses to apply §1.245A-7 (rules for simple cases) in lieu of §1.245A-8 (rules for complex cases) for that taxable year.

(ii) *Analysis.* Pursuant to §1.245A-7(c)(1), US1's extraordinary disposition account with respect to CFC1 is reduced by the lesser of the amount described in §1.245A-7(c)(1)(i) with respect to US1, and the RGI account of US1 with respect to CFC2 that relates to its extraordinary disposition account with respect to CFC1. *See* §1.245A-7(c)(1). Paragraphs (c)(3)(ii)(A) through (D) of this section describe the determinations pursuant to §1.245A-8(c)(1).

(A) *Computation of adjusted earnings of CFC2, and amount described in §1.245A-7(c)(1)(i) with respect to US1.* To determine the amount described in §1.245A-7(c)(1)(i) with respect to US1, the adjusted earnings of CFC2 must be computed for CFC2's taxable year ending November 30, 2019. *See* §1.245A-7(c)(1)(i). Paragraphs (c)(3)(ii)(A)(*1*) and (2) of this section describe these determinations.

(*1*) The adjusted earnings of CFC2 for its taxable year ending November 30, 2019, is $25x, computed as $15x (CFC2's earnings and profits as of November 30, 2019, the last day of that taxable year), plus $10x (the sum of the $6x and $4x amortization deductions of CFC2 for that taxable year, which is the amount of all deductions or losses of CFC2 that is or was attributable to disqualified basis of items of specified property and allocated and apportioned to residual CFC gross income of CFC2 solely by reason of §1.951A-2(c)(5)(i)). *See* §1.245A-7(c)(3).

(*2*) For CFC2's taxable year ending November 30, 2019, the amount described in §1.245A-7(c)(1)(i) with respect to US1 is $25x, computed as the excess of $25x (the adjusted earnings) over $0 (the sum of the balance of the previously taxed earnings and profits accounts with respect to CFC2).

(B) *Increase to balance of RGI account.* Under §1.245A-9(d)(11), US1 has an RGI account with respect to CFC2 that relates to its extraordinary disposition account with respect to CFC1. On November 30, 2019 (the last day of CFC2's taxable year), the balance of the RGI account (which is initially zero) is increased by $10x, the sum of the $6x and $4x amortization deductions of CFC2 for its taxable year ending November 30, 2019. *See* §1.245A-7(c)(4)(i). Each of the amortization deductions is taken into account for this purpose because, but for §1.951A-2(c)(5)(i), the deduction would have decreased CFC2's tested income or increased or given rise to a tested loss of CFC2. *See* §1.245A-7(c)(4)(i).

(C) *Reduction in balance of extraordinary disposition account.* Pursuant to §1.245A-7(c)(1), US1's extraordinary disposition account with respect to CFC1 is reduced by $10x, the lesser of the amount described in §1.245A-7(c)(1)(i) with respect to US1 for CFC2's taxable year ending November 30, 2019 ($25x), and the balance of US1's RGI account with respect to CFC2 that relates to its extraordinary disposi-

tion account with respect to CFC1 ($10x, determined as of November 30, 2019, but without regard to the application of §1.245A-7(c)(4)(ii) for the taxable year of CFC2 ending on that date). *See* §1.245A-7(c)(1). The $10x reduction in the balance of US1's extraordinary disposition account occurs on December 31, 2019, the last day of US1's taxable year that includes November 30, 2019 (the last day of CFC2's taxable year). *See* §1.245A-9(c)(3).

(D) *Reduction in balance of RGI account.* On November 30, 2019 (the last day of CFC2's taxable year), the balance of US1's RGI account with respect to CFC2 that relates to its extraordinary disposition account with respect to CFC1 is decreased by $10x, the amount of the reduction, pursuant to §1.245A-7(c)(1) section and by reason of the RGI account, to US1's extraordinary disposition account with respect to CFC1. *See* §1.245A-7(c)(4)(ii). Therefore, following that reduction, the balance of the RGI account is zero ($10x - $10x).

(iii) *Alternative facts in which the reduction is limited by earnings and profits.* The facts are the same as in paragraph (c)(3)(i) of this section (*Example 3*), except that CFC2 has a $5x deficit in its earnings and profits as of the end of its taxable year ending November 30, 2019. In this case—

(A) The adjusted earnings of CFC2 for its taxable year ending November 30, 2019, is $5x, computed as -$5x (CFC2's deficit in earnings and profits as of November 30, 2019) plus $10x (the sum of the $6x and $4x amortization deductions of CFC2), *see* §1.245A-7(c)(3);

(B) The amount described in §1.245A-7(c)(1)(i) with respect to US1 for CFC's taxable year ending November 30, 2019, is $5x, computed as the excess of $5x (the adjusted earnings) over $0 (the sum of the balance of the previously taxed earnings and profits accounts with respect to CFC2), *see* §1.245A-7(c)(1)(i);

(C) On December 31, 2019, US1's extraordinary disposition account with respect to CFC1 is reduced by $5x, the lesser of the amount described in §1.245A-7(c)(1)(i) with respect to US1 for CFC2's taxable year ending November 30, 2019 ($5x), and the balance of US1's RGI account with respect to CFC2 that relates to its extraordinary disposition account with respect to CFC1 ($10x, determined as of November 30, 2019, but without regard to the application of §1.245A-8(c)(4)(i)(B) for the taxable year of CFC2 ending on that date), *see* §§1.245A-7(c)(1) and 1.245A-9(c)(3); and

(D) On November 30, 2019 (the last day of CFC2's taxable year), the balance of US1's RGI account with respect to CFC2 is decreased by $5x (the amount of the reduction, pursuant to §1.245A-7(c)(1) and by reason of the RGI account, to US1's extraordinary disposition account with respect to CFC1) and, therefore, following such reduction, the balance of the RGI account is $5x ($10x - $5x), *see* §1.245A-7(c)(4)(ii).

(4) *Example 4. Reduction to extraordinary disposition accounts limited by §1.245A-8(c)(6).*—(i) *Facts.* The facts are the same as in paragraph (c)(3)(iii) of this section (*Example 3*, alternative facts in which the reduction is limited by earnings and profits) (and the results are the same as in paragraph (c)(1)(ii)(A) of this section), except that US1 also owns 100% of the stock of US2, which owns 100% of the stock of CFC3, and on November 30, 2018, in a transaction that was an extraordinary disposition, CFC3 sold an item of specified property ("Item 3") to CFC2 in exchange for $200x of cash. Item 3 had a basis of $0 in the hands of CFC3 immediately before the sale and, therefore, CFC3 recognized $200x of gain as a result of the sale ($200x - $0), Item 3 has $200x of disqualified basis under §1.951A-2(c)(5), and US2 has an extraordinary disposition account with respect to CFC3 with an initial balance of $200x under §1.245A-5(c)(3)(i)(A). Moreover, during CFC2's taxable year beginning December 1, 2018, and ending November 30, 2019, the disqualified basis of Item 3 gives rise to a $20x amortization deduction, which is allocated and apportioned to residual CFC gross income of CFC2 solely by reason of §1.951A-2(c)(5) (though, but for §1.951A-2(c)(5), would have been allocated and apportioned to gross tested income of CFC2). Further, as of the end of US1's 2018 taxable year, the balance of US1's basis benefit account with respect to its extraordinary disposition account with respect to CFC1 is $0; similarly, as of the end of US2's 2018 taxable year, the balance of US2's basis benefit account with respect to its extraordinary disposition account with respect to CFC2 is $0. Because CFC2 holds items of specified property that correspond to more than one extraordinary disposition account (that is, Item 1 and Item 2 correspond to US1's extraordinary disposition account with respect to CFC2, and Item 3 corresponds to US2's extraordinary disposition account with respect to CFC2), the condition of §1.245A-6(b)(2) is not satisfied. *See* §1.245A-6(b)(2)(ii)(C)(3). US1 and US2 therefore apply §1.245A-8 (rules for complex cases) for their 2018 taxable years.

(ii) *Analysis.* Pursuant to §1.245A-8(c)(1), US1's extraordinary disposition account with respect to CFC1 is, subject to the limitation in §1.245A-8(c)(6), reduced by the lesser of the amount described in §1.245A-8(c)(1)(i) with respect to US1, and the RGI account of US1 with respect to CFC2 that relates to its extraordinary disposition account with respect to CFC1. *See* §1.245A-8(c)(1). Similarly, US2's extraordinary disposition account with respect to CFC3 is, subject to the limitation in §1.245A-8(c)(6), reduced by the lesser of the amount described in §1.245A-8(c)(1)(i) with respect to US2, and the RGI account of US2 with respect to CFC2 that relates to its extraordinary disposition account with respect to CFC3. *See* §1.245A-8(c)(1). Paragraphs (c)(4)(ii)(A) through (F) of this section describe the determinations pursuant to §1.245A-8(c)(1).

(A) *Ownership requirement.* Each of US1 and US2 satisfy the ownership requirement of §1.245A-8(c)(5) for CFC2's taxable year ending November 30, 2019, because on the last day of that taxable year each is a United States shareholder with respect to CFC2. *See* §1.245A-8(c)(5).

(B) *Computation of adjusted earnings of CFC2, and amount described in §1.245A-8(c)(1)(i) with respect to US1 and US2.* The adjusted earnings of CFC2 for its taxable year ending November 30, 2019, is $25x, computed as -$5x (CFC2's deficit in earnings and profits as of November 30, 2019), plus $30x (the sum of the $6x, $4x, and $20x amortization deductions of CFC2). *See* §1.245A-8(c)(3). For CFC2's taxable year ending November 30, 2019, the amount described in §1.245A-8(c)(1)(i) with respect to US1 is $25x, computed as the excess of the product of $25x (the adjusted earnings) and 100% (the percentage of the stock of CFC2 that US1 and its domestic affiliate, US2, own), over $0 (the sum of the balance of certain previously taxed earnings and profits accounts and hybrid deduction accounts). *See* §1.245A-8(c)(1)(i). Similarly, for CFC2's taxable year ending November 30, 2019, the amount described in §1.245A-8(c)(1)(i) with respect to US2 is $25x, computed as the excess of the product of $25x (the adjusted earnings) and 100% (the percentage of the stock of CFC2 that US2 and its domestic affiliate, US1, own), over $0 (the sum of the balance of certain previously taxed earnings and profits accounts and hybrid deduction accounts). *See* §1.245A-8(c)(1)(i).

(C) *Increase to balance of RGI account.* As described in paragraph (c)(3)(ii)(B) of this section, US1 has an RGI account with respect to CFC2 that relates to its extraordinary disposition account with respect to CFC1, and the balance of the RGI account is $10x on November 30, 2019 (the last day of CFC2's taxable year). Similarly, US2 has an RGI account with respect to CFC2 that relates to its extraordinary disposition account with respect to CFC3, and the balance of the RGI account is $20x on November 30, 2019 (reflecting a $20x increase to the balance of the account for the $20x amortization deduction of CFC2 for its taxable year ending November 30, 2019). *See* §1.245A-8(c)(4)(i).

(D) *Reduction in balance of extraordinary disposition accounts but for §1.245A-8(c)(6).* But for the application of §1.245A-8(c)(6), US1's extraordinary disposition account with respect to CFC2 would be reduced by $10x, which is the lesser of $25x, the amount described in §1.245A-8(c)(1)(i) with respect to US1 for CFC2's taxable year ending November 30, 2019, and $10x, the balance of the RGI account of US1 with respect to CFC2 that relates to its extraordinary disposition account with respect to CFC1 (determined as of November 30, 2019, but without regard to the application of §1.245A-8(c)(4)(i)(B) for the taxable year of CFC2 ending on that date). *See* §1.245A-8(c)(1)(i) and (ii). Similarly, but for the application of §1.245A-8(c)(6), US2's extraordinary disposition account with respect to CFC3 would be reduced by $20x, which is the lesser of $25x, the amount described in §1.245A-8(c)(1)(i) with respect to US2 for CFC2's taxable year ending November 30, 2019, and $20x, the balance of the RGI account of US2 with respect to CFC2 that relates to its extraordinary disposition account with respect to CFC3 (determined as of November 30, 2019, but without regard to the application of §1.245A-8(c)(4)(i)(B) for the taxable year of CFC2 ending on that date). *See* §1.245A-8(c)(1)(i) and (ii).

(E) *Application of limitation of §1.245A-8(c)(6).* As described in paragraph (c)(4)(ii)(D) of this section, but for the application of §1.245A-8(c)(6), there would be a total of $30x of reductions to US1's extraordinary disposition account with respect to CFC1, and US2's extraordinary disposition account with respect to CFC3, by reason of the application of §1.245A-8(c)(1) with respect to CFC2's taxable year ending November 30, 2019. Because that $30x exceeds the amount described in §1.245A-8(c)(1)(i) with respect to US1 and US2 ($25x)—

(1) US1's extraordinary disposition account with respect to CFC1 is reduced by $7.86x, computed as $10x (the reduction that would occur but for §1.245A-8(c)(6)) less the product of $5x (the excess amount, computed as $30x, the total reductions that would occur but for the application of §1.245A-8(c)(6), less $25x, the amount described in §1.245A-8(c)(1)(i)) and a fraction, the numerator of which is $150x (the balance of US1's extraordinary disposition account with respect to CFC1) and the denominator of which is $350x ($150x, the balance of US1's extraordinary disposition account with respect to CFC1, plus $200x, the balance of US2's extraordinary disposition account with respect to CFC3), *see* §1.245A-8(c)(6); and

(2) US2's extraordinary disposition account with respect to CFC3 is reduced by $17.14x, computed as $20x (the reduction that would occur but for §1.245A-8(c)(6)) less the product of $5x (the excess amount, computed as $30x, the total reductions that would occur but for the application of §1.245A-8(c)(6), less $25x, the amount described in §1.245A-8(c)(1)(i)) and a fraction, the numerator of which is $200x (the balance of US2's extraordinary disposition account with respect to CFC3) and the denominator of which is $350x ($150x, the balance of US1's extraordinary disposition account with respect to CFC1, plus $200x, the balance of US2's extraordinary disposition account with respect to CFC3), *see* §1.245A-8(c)(6) of this section.

(F) *Reduction in balance of RGI accounts.* On November 30, 2019 (the last day of CFC2's taxable year)—

(1) The balance of US1's RGI account with respect to CFC2 that relates to its extraordinary disposition account with respect to CFC1 is decreased by $7.86x (the amount of the reduction, pursuant to §1.245A-8(c)(1) and by reason of the RGI account, to US1's extraordinary disposition account with respect to CFC1) and, thus, following that reduction, the balance of the RGI account is $2.14x ($10x - $7.86x), *see* §1.245A-8(c)(4)(i)(B); and

(2) The balance of US2's RGI account with respect to CFC2 that relates to its extraordinary disposition account with respect to CFC3 is decreased by $17.14x (the amount of the reduction, pursuant to §1.245A-8(c)(1) and by reason of the RGI account, to US2's extraordinary disposition account with respect to CFC3) and, thus, following that reduction, the balance of the RGI account is $2.86x ($20x - $17.14x), *see* §1.245A-8(c)(4)(i)(B).

(5) *Example 5. Computation of duplicate DQB.*—(i) *Facts.* The facts are the same as in paragraph (c)(1)(i) of this section (*Example 1*) (and the results are the same as in paragraph (c)(1)(ii)(A) of this section), except that CFC1 does not make any distribution to US1, and on November 30, 2018, immediately after the Disqualified Transfer, CFC2 transfers Item 1 to newly-formed CFC3 solely in exchange for the sole share of stock of CFC3 (the contribution, "Contribution 1," and the share of stock of CFC3, the "CFC3 Share") and, immediately after Contribution 1, CFC3 transfers Item 1 to newly-formed CFC4 solely in exchange for the sole share of stock of CFC4 (the contribution, "Contribution 2," and the share of stock of CFC4, the "CFC4 Share"). Pursuant to section 358(a)(1), CFC2's basis in its share of stock of CFC3 is $90x, and CFC3's basis in its share of stock of CFC4 is $90x basis. As a result of Contribution 1, the condition of §1.245A-6(b)(2) is not satisfied, because on at least one day of CFC2's taxable year ending on November 30, 2018 (which ends within US1's 2018 taxable year), CFC2 does not hold Item 1. *See* §1.245A-6(b)(2)(ii)(C)(*1*). US1 therefore applies §1.245A-8 (rules for complex cases) for its 2018 taxable year. *See* §1.245A-6(b).

(ii) *Analysis*—(A) *Application of exchanged basis rule under section 951A to Contribution 1 and Contribution 2.* As a result of Contribution 1, pursuant to §1.951A-3(h)(2)(ii)(B)(2)(*ii*), the disqualified basis of CFC3 Share includes the disqualified basis of Item 1 ($90x), and therefore the disqualified basis of CFC3 Share is $90x. Similarly, as a result of Contribution 2, pursuant to §1.951A-3(h)(2)(ii)(B)(2)(*ii*), the disqualified basis of CFC4 Share also includes the disqualified basis of Item 1 ($90x), and therefore the disqualified basis of CFC4 Share is $90x.

(B) *Determination of duplicate DQB of CFC3 Share as a result of Contribution 1.* Because the disqualified basis of CFC3 Share includes the disqualified basis of Item 1, CFC3 Share is an item of exchanged basis property that relates to Item 1. *See* §1.245A-8(d)(2)(ii). In addition, because CFC3 Share is an item of exchanged basis property that relates to Item 1 (which corresponds to US1's extraordinary disposition account with respect to CFC1), CFC3 Share is, for purposes of §1.245A-8, treated as an item of specified property that corresponds to US1's extraordinary disposition account with respect to CFC1. *See* §1.245A-8(d)(2)(i). Further, the duplicate DQB of CFC3 Share as to Item 1 is $90x, the portion of the disqualified basis of CFC3 Share that includes Item 1's disqualified basis of $90x. *See* §1.245A-8(d)(2)(iii)(A).

(C) *Determination of duplicate DQB of CFC4 Share as a result of Contribution 2.* For reasons similar to those described in paragraph (c)(5)(ii)(B) of this section, CFC4 Share is an item of exchanged basis property that relates to Item 1, CFC4 is treated for purposes of §1.245A-8 as an item of specified property that corresponds to US1's extraordinary disposition account with respect to CFC1, and the duplicate DQB of CFC4 Share as to Item 1 is $90x.

(D) *Determination of duplicate DQB of CFC3 Share as a result of Contribution 2.* Because the disqualified basis of CFC3 Share and the disqualified basis of CFC4 Share each includes $90x of the disqualified basis of Item 1 and CFC3 receives the CFC4 Share in Contribution 2, the $90x of disqualified basis of CFC3 Share is attributable to the $90x of disqualified basis of CFC4 Share, and CFC3 Share is an item of exchanged basis property that relates to CFC4 Share. *See* §1.245A-8(d)(2)(i) and (d)(2)(iii)(C). In addition, the duplicate DQB of CFC3 Share as to CFC4 Share is $90x. *See* §1.245A-8(d)(2)(iii)(A).

(E) *Application of duplicate basis rules in §1.245A-8(b)(5).* For purposes of computing the fraction described in §1.245A-8(b)(1)(ii), if

US1's extraordinary disposition account with respect to CFC1 were to give rise to an extraordinary disposition amount or a tiered extraordinary disposition amount during US1's 2018 taxable year, then the duplicate DQB of CFC3 Share and the duplicate DQB of CFC4 Share would not be taken into account, because the disqualified basis of Item 1 (an item of specified property that corresponds to US1's extraordinary disposition account and as to which each of CFC3 Share and CFC4 share relates) would be taken into account. *See* § 1.245A-8(b)(1)(ii) and (b)(5)(i)(A). Accordingly, in such a case, for US1's 2018 taxable year, the numerator of the fraction described in § 1.245A-8(b)(1)(ii) would reflect only the disqualified basis of Item 1 or Item 2, as applicable, and the denominator would reflect only the sum of the disqualified basis of each of Item 1 and Item 2. *See* § 1.245A-8(b)(1)(ii) and (b)(5)(i)(A). Furthermore, to the extent there were to be a reduction under § 1.245A-8(b)(1) to the disqualified basis of Item 1, then the duplicate DQB of CFC4 Share would be reduced (but not below zero) by the product of the reduction to the disqualified basis of Item 1 and a fraction, the numerator of which would be $90x (the duplicate DQB of CFC4 Share), and the denominator of which would also be $90x (the duplicate DQB of CFC4 Share). *See* § 1.245A-8(b)(5)(i)(B). The $90x of duplicate DQB of CFC3 Share would be excluded from the denominator of the fraction described in the previous sentence because it is attributable to the $90x of duplicate DQB of CFC4 Share. *See* § 1.245A-8(b)(5)(i)(B)(2) (last sentence). For reasons similar to those described in this paragraph (c)(4)(ii)(E) with respect to the application of § 1.245A-8(b)(5)(i)(B) to CFC4 Share, the duplicate DQB of CFC3 Share would be reduced (but not below zero) by the product of the reduction to the disqualified basis of Item 1 and a fraction, the numerator of which would be $90x, and the denominator of which would also be $90x. [Reg. § 1.245A-10.]

☐ [*T.D.* 9934, 11-25-2020.]

[Reg. § 1.245A-11]

§ 1.245A-11. Applicability dates.—(a) *In general.*—Sections 1.245A-6 through 1.245A-11 apply to taxable years of a foreign corporation beginning on or after December 1, 2020 and to taxable years of section 245A shareholders in which or with which such taxable years end.

(b) *Exception.*—Notwithstanding paragraph (a) of this section, a taxpayer may choose to apply §§ 1.245A-6 through 1.245A-11 for a taxable year of a foreign corporation beginning before December 1, 2020 and to a taxable year of a section 245A shareholder in which or with which such taxable year ends, provided that the taxpayer and all persons bearing a relationship to the taxpayer described in section 267(b) or 707(b) apply §§ 1.245A-6 through 1.245A-11, in their entirety, and § 1.6038-2(f)(18) for all such taxable years and any subsequent taxable years beginning before December 1, 2020. [Reg. § 1.245A-11.]

☐ [*T.D.* 9934, 11-25-2020.]

[Reg. § 1.245A(d)-1]

§ 1.245A(d)-1. Disallowance of foreign tax credit or deduction.—(a) *No foreign tax credit or deduction allowed under section 245A(d).*—(1) *Foreign income taxes paid or accrued by domestic corporations or successors.*—No credit under section 901 or deduction is allowed in any taxable year for:

(i) Foreign income taxes paid or accrued by a domestic corporation that are attributable to section 245A(d) income of the domestic corporation;

(ii) Foreign income taxes paid or accrued by a successor to a domestic corporation that are attributable to section 245A(d) income of the successor; and

(iii) Foreign income taxes paid or accrued by a domestic corporation that is a United States shareholder of a foreign corporation, other than a foreign corporation that is a passive foreign investment company (as defined in section 1297) with respect to the domestic corporation and that is not a controlled foreign corporation, that are attributable to non-inclusion income of the foreign corporation and are not otherwise disallowed under paragraph (a)(1)(i) or (ii) of this section.

(2) *Foreign income taxes paid or accrued by foreign corporations.*—No credit under section 901 or deduction is allowed in any taxable year for foreign income taxes paid or accrued by a foreign corporation that are attributable to section 245A(d) income, and such taxes are not eligible to be deemed paid under section 960 in any taxable year.

(3) *Effect of disallowance on earnings and profits.*—The disallowance of a credit or deduction for foreign income taxes under this paragraph (a) does not affect whether the foreign income taxes reduce earnings and profits of a corporation.

(b) *Attribution of foreign income taxes.*—(1) *Section 245A(d) income.*—Foreign income taxes are attributable to section 245A(d) income to the extent that the foreign income taxes are allocated and apportioned under § 1.861-20 to the section 245A(d) income group. For purposes of this paragraph (b)(1), § 1.861-20 is applied by treating the section 245A(d) income group in each section 904 category of a domestic corporation, successor, or foreign corporation as a statutory grouping and treating all other income, including the receipt of a distribution of previously taxed earnings and profits other than section 245A(d) PTEP, as income in the residual grouping. See § 1.861-20(d)(2) through (3) for rules regarding the allocation and apportionment of foreign income taxes to the statutory and residual groupings if the taxpayer does not realize, recognize, or take into account a corresponding U.S. item in the U.S. taxable year in which the foreign income taxes are paid or accrued. In the case of a foreign law distribution or foreign law disposition, a corresponding U.S. item is assigned to the statutory and residual groupings under § 1.861-20(d)(2)(ii)(B) and (C) without regard to the application of section 246(c), the holding periods described in sections 964(e)(4)(A) and 1248(j), and § 1.245A-5.

(2) *Non-inclusion income of a foreign corporation.*—(i) *Scope.*—This paragraph (b)(2) provides rules for attributing foreign income taxes paid or accrued by a domestic corporation that is a United States shareholder of a foreign corporation to non-inclusion income of the foreign corporation. It applies only in cases in which the foreign income taxes are allocated and apportioned under § 1.861-20 by reference to the characterization of the tax book value of stock, whether the stock is held directly or indirectly through a partnership or other passthrough entity, for purposes of allocating and apportioning the domestic corporation's interest expense, or by reference to the income of a foreign corporation that is a reverse hybrid or foreign law CFC.

(ii) *Foreign income taxes on a remittance, U.S. return of capital amount, or U.S. return of partnership basis amount.*—This paragraph (b)(2)(ii) applies to foreign income taxes paid or accrued by a domestic corporation that is a United States shareholder of a foreign corporation with respect to foreign taxable income that the domestic corporation includes by reason of a remittance, a distribution (including a foreign law distribution) that is a U.S. return of capital amount or U.S. return of partnership basis amount, or a disposition (including a foreign law disposition) that gives rise to a U.S. return of capital amount or a U.S. return of partnership basis amount. These foreign income taxes are attributable to non-inclusion income of the foreign corporation to the extent that they are allocated and apportioned to the domestic corporation's section 245A subgroup of general category stock, section 245A subgroup of passive category stock, or section 245A subgroup of U.S. source category stock in applying § 1.861-20 for purposes of section 904 as the operative section. For purposes of this paragraph (b)(2)(ii), § 1.861-20 is applied by treating the domestic corporation's section 245A subgroup of general category stock, section 245A subgroup of passive category stock, and section 245A subgroup of U.S. source category stock as the statutory groupings and treating the tax book value of the non-section 245A subgroup of stock for each separate category as tax book value in the residual grouping.

(iii) *Foreign income taxes on income of a reverse hybrid or a foreign law CFC.*—This paragraph (b)(2)(iii) applies to foreign income taxes paid or accrued by a domestic corporation, other than a regulated investment company (as defined in section 851), real estate investment trust (as defined in section 856), or S corporation (as defined in section 1361), that is a United States shareholder of a foreign corporation that is a reverse hybrid or foreign law CFC with respect to the foreign law pass-through income or foreign law inclusion regime income of the reverse hybrid or foreign law CFC, respectively. These taxes are attributable to the non-inclusion income of a reverse hybrid or foreign law CFC to the extent that they are allocated and apportioned to the non-inclusion income group under § 1.861-20. For purposes of this paragraph (b)(2)(iii), § 1.861-20 is applied by treating the non-inclusion income group in each section 904 category of the domestic corporation and the foreign corporation as a statutory grouping and treating all other income as income in the residual grouping.

(3) *Anti-avoidance rule.*—Foreign income taxes are treated as attributable to section 245A(d) income of a domestic corporation or foreign corporation, or non-inclusion income of a foreign corporation, if a transaction, series of related transactions, or arrangement is undertaken with a principal purpose of avoiding the purposes of section 245A(d) and this section with respect to such foreign income taxes, including, for example, by separating foreign income taxes from the income, or earnings and profits, to which such foreign income taxes relate or by making distributions (or causing inclusions) under foreign law in multiple years that give rise to foreign income taxes that are allocated and apportioned with reference to the same

previously taxed earnings and profits. See paragraph (d)(4) of this section (*Example 3*).

(c) *Definitions.*—The following definitions apply for purposes of this section.

(1) *Corresponding U.S. item.*—The term *corresponding U.S. item* has the meaning set forth in § 1.861-20(b).

(2) *Foreign income tax.*—The term *foreign income tax* has the meaning set forth in § 1.901-2(a).

(3) *Foreign law CFC.*—The term *foreign law CFC* has the meaning set forth in § 1.861-20(b).

(4) *Foreign law disposition.*—The term *foreign law disposition* has the meaning set forth in § 1.861-20(b).

(5) *Foreign law distribution.*—The term *foreign law distribution* has the meaning set forth in § 1.861-20(b).

(6) *Foreign law inclusion regime.*—The term *foreign law inclusion regime* has the meaning set forth in § 1.861-20(b).

(7) *Foreign law inclusion regime income.*—The term *foreign law inclusion regime income* has the meaning set forth in § 1.861-20(b).

(8) *Foreign law pass-through income.*—The term *foreign law pass-through income* has the meaning set forth in § 1.861-20(b).

(9) *Foreign taxable income.*—The term *foreign taxable income* has the meaning set forth in § 1.861-20(b).

(10) *Gross included tested income.*—The term *gross included tested income* means, with respect to a foreign corporation that is described in paragraph (b)(2)(iii) of this section, an item of gross tested income multiplied by the inclusion percentage of a domestic corporation that is described in paragraph (b)(2)(iii) of this section for the domestic corporation's U.S. taxable year with or within which the foreign corporation's taxable year described in § 1.861-20(d)(3)(i)(C) or § 1.861-20(d)(3)(iii) ends.

(11) *Hybrid dividend.*—The term *hybrid dividend* has the meaning set forth in § 1.245A(e)-1(b)(2).

(12) *Inclusion percentage.*—The term *inclusion percentage* has the meaning set forth in § 1.960-1(b).

(13) *Non-inclusion income.*—The term *non-inclusion income* means the items of gross income of a foreign corporation other than items that are described in § 1.960-1(d)(2)(ii)(B)(2) (items of income assigned to the subpart F income groups) and section 245(a)(5) (without regard to section 245(a)(12)), and other than gross included tested income.

(14) *Non-inclusion income group.*—The term *non-inclusion income group* means the income group within a section 904 category that consists of non-inclusion income.

(15) *Non-section 245A subgroup.*—The term *non-section 245A subgroup* means each non-section 245A subgroup determined under § 1.861-13(a)(5), applied as if the foreign corporation whose stock is being characterized were a controlled foreign corporation.

(16) *Pass-through entity.*—The term *pass-through entity* has the meaning set forth in § 1.904-5(a)(4).

(17) *Remittance.*—The term *remittance* has the meaning set forth in § 1.861-20(d)(3)(v)(E).

(18) *Reverse hybrid.*—The term *reverse hybrid* has the meaning set forth in § 1.861-20(b).

(19) *Section 245A subgroup.*—The term *section 245A subgroup* means each section 245A subgroup determined under § 1.861-13(a)(5), applied as if the foreign corporation whose stock is being characterized were a controlled foreign corporation.

(20) *Section 245A(d) income.*—With respect to a domestic corporation, the term *section 245A(d) income* means a dividend (including a *section 1248 dividend* and a dividend received indirectly through a pass-through entity) or an inclusion under section 951(a)(1)(A) for which a deduction under section 245A(a) is allowed, a distribution of section 245A(d) PTEP, a hybrid dividend, or an inclusion under section 245A(e)(2) and § 1.245A(e)-1(c)(1) by reason of a tiered hybrid dividend. With respect to a successor of a domestic corporation, the term *section 245A(d) income* means the receipt of a distribution of section 245A(d) PTEP. With respect to a foreign corporation, the term *section 245A(d) income* means an item of subpart F income that gave rise to a deduction under section 245A(a), a tiered hybrid dividend or a distribution of section 245A(d) PTEP. An item described in this paragraph (c)(20) that qualifies for the deduction under section

245A(a) is considered section 245A(d) income regardless of whether the domestic corporation claims the deduction on its return with respect to the item.

(21) *Section 245A(d) income group.*—The term *section 245A(d) income group* means an income group within a section 904 category that consists of section 245A(d) income.

(22) *Section 245A(d) PTEP.*—The term *section 245A(d) PTEP* means previously taxed earnings and profits described in § 1.960-3(c)(2)(v) or (ix) if such previously taxed earnings and profits arose either as a result of a dividend that gave rise to a deduction under section 245A(a), or as a result of a tiered hybrid dividend that, by reason of section 245A(e)(2) and § 1.245A(e)-1(c)(1), gave rise to an inclusion in the gross income of a United States shareholder. For purposes of this paragraph (c)(22), a dividend that qualifies for the deduction under section 245A(a) is considered to have given rise to a deduction under section 245A(a) regardless of whether the domestic corporation claims the deduction on its return with respect to the dividend.

(23) *Section 904 category.*—The term *section 904 category* has the meaning set forth in § 1.960-1(b).

(24) *Section 1248 dividend.*—The term *section 1248 dividend* means an amount of gain that is treated as a dividend under section 1248.

(25) *Successor.*—The term *successor* means a person, including an individual who is a citizen or resident of the United States, that acquires from any person any portion of the interest of a United States shareholder in a foreign corporation for purposes of section 959(a).

(26) *Tested income.*—The term *tested income* has the meaning set forth in § 1.960-1(b).

(27) *Tiered hybrid dividend.*—The term *tiered hybrid dividend* has the meaning set forth in § 1.245A(e)-1(c)(2).

(28) *U.S. capital gain amount.*—The term *U.S. capital gain amount* has the meaning set forth in § 1.861-20(b).

(29) *U.S. return of capital amount.*—The term *U.S. return of capital amount* has the meaning set forth in § 1.861-20(b).

(30) *U.S. return of partnership basis amount.*—The term *U.S. return of partnership basis amount* means, with respect to a partnership in which a domestic corporation is a partner, the portion of a distribution by the partnership to the domestic corporation, or the portion of the proceeds of a disposition of the domestic corporation's interest in the partnership, that exceeds the U.S. capital gain amount.

(d) *Examples.*—The following examples illustrate the application of this section.

(1) *Presumed facts.*—Except as otherwise provided, the following facts are presumed for purposes of the examples:

   (i) USP is a domestic corporation;

   (ii) CFC is a controlled foreign corporation organized in Country A, and is not a reverse hybrid or a foreign law CFC;

   (iii) USP owns all of the outstanding stock of CFC;

   (iv) USP would be allowed a deduction under section 245A(a) for dividends received from CFC.

   (v) All parties have a U.S. dollar functional currency and a U.S. taxable year and foreign taxable year that correspond to the calendar year; and

   (vi) References to income are to gross items of income, and no party has deductions for Country A tax purposes or deductions for Federal income tax purposes (other than foreign income tax expense).

(2) *Example 1: Distribution for foreign and Federal income tax purposes.*—(i) *Facts.* As of December 31, Year 1, CFC has $800x of section 951A PTEP (as defined in § 1.960-3(c)(2)(viii)) in a single annual PTEP account (as defined in § 1.960-3(c)(1)), and $500x of earnings and profits described in section 959(c)(3). On December 31, Year 1, CFC distributes $1,000x of cash to USP. For Country A tax purposes, the entire $1,000x distribution is a dividend and is therefore a foreign dividend amount (as defined in § 1.861-20(b)). Country A imposes a withholding tax on USP of $150x with respect to the $1,000x of foreign gross dividend income under Country A law. For Federal income tax purposes, USP includes in gross income $200x of the distribution as a dividend for which a deduction is allowable under section 245A(a). The remaining $800x of the distribution is a distribution of PTEP that is excluded from USP's gross income and not treated as a dividend under section 959(a) and (d), respectively. The entire $1,000x dividend is a U.S. dividend amount (as defined in § 1.861-20(b)).

   (ii) *Analysis*—(A) *In general.* The rules of this section are applied by first determining the portion of the $150x Country A withholding tax that is attributable under paragraph (b)(1) of this section to the section 245A(d) income of USP, and then by determining the portion of the $150x Country A withholding tax that is described in paragraph (b)(2)(i) of this section and that is attributable under either paragraph (b)(2)(ii) or (b)(2)(iii) of this section to the non-inclusion income of CFC. No credit or deduction is allowed in any taxable year under paragraph (a)(1)(i) of this section for any portion of the $150x Country A withholding tax that is attributable to the section 245A(d) income of USP, or, under paragraph (a)(1)(iii) of this section, for any portion of that tax that is attributable to the non-inclusion income of CFC, to the extent the tax is not disallowed under paragraph (a)(1)(i) of this section.

(B) *Attribution of foreign income taxes to section 245A(d) income.* Under paragraph (b)(1) of this section, the $150x Country A withholding tax is attributable to the section 245A(d) income of USP to the extent that it is allocated and apportioned to the section 245A(d) income group (the statutory grouping) under §1.861-20. Section 1.861-20(c) allocates and apportions foreign income tax to the statutory and residual groupings to which the items of foreign gross income that were included in the foreign tax base are assigned under §1.861-20(d). Section 1.861-20(d)(3)(i) assigns foreign gross income that is a foreign dividend amount, to the extent of the U.S. dividend amount, to the statutory and residual groupings to which the U.S. dividend amount is assigned. The $1,000x foreign dividend amount is therefore assigned to the statutory and residual groupings to which the $1,000x U.S. dividend amount is assigned under Federal income tax law. The $1,000x U.S. dividend amount comprises a $200x dividend for which a deduction under section 245A(a) is allowed, which is an item of section 245A(d) income, and $800x of section 951A PTEP, the receipt of which is income in the residual grouping. Accordingly, $200x of the $1,000x of foreign gross dividend income is assigned to the section 245A(d) income group, and $800x is assigned to the residual grouping. Under §1.861-20(f), $30x ($150x × $200x/ $1,000x) of the $150x Country A withholding tax is apportioned to the section 245A(d) income group and is attributable to the section 245A(d) income of USP. The remaining $120x ($150x × $800x/ $1,000x) of the tax is apportioned to the residual grouping.

(C) *Attribution of foreign income taxes to non-inclusion income.* Under paragraph (b)(2) of this section, the $150x Country A withholding tax may be attributed to non-inclusion income of CFC if the tax is allocated and apportioned under §1.861-20 by reference to either the characterization of the tax book value of stock under §1.861-9 or the income of a foreign corporation that is a reverse hybrid or foreign law CFC. CFC is neither a reverse hybrid nor a foreign law CFC. In addition, no portion of the $150x Country A withholding tax is allocated and apportioned under §1.861-20 by reference to the characterization of the tax book value of CFC's stock. See §1.861-20(d)(3)(i). Therefore, none of the tax is attributable to non-inclusion income of CFC.

(D) *Disallowance.* Under paragraph (a)(1)(i) of this section, no credit under section 901 or deduction is allowed in any taxable year to USP for the $30x portion of the Country A withholding tax that is attributable to section 245A(d) income of USP.

(3) *Example 2: Distribution for foreign law purposes.*—(i) *Facts.* As of December 31, Year 1, CFC has $800x of section 951A PTEP (as defined in §1.960-3(c)(2)(viii)) in a single annual PTEP account (as defined in §1.960-3(c)(1)), and $500x of earnings and profits described in section 959(c)(3). On December 31, Year 1, CFC distributes $1,000x of its stock to USP. For Country A tax purposes, the entire $1,000x stock distribution is treated as a dividend to USP and is therefore a foreign dividend amount (as defined in §1.861-20(b)). Country A imposes a withholding tax on USP of $150x with respect to the $1,000x of foreign gross dividend income that USP includes under Country A law. For Federal income tax purposes, USP does not recognize gross income as a result of the stock distribution under section 305(a). The $1,000x stock distribution is therefore a foreign law distribution.

(ii) *Analysis*—(A) *In general.* The rules of this section are applied by first determining the portion of the $150x Country A withholding tax that is attributable under paragraph (b)(1) of this section to the section 245A(d) income of USP, and then by determining the portion of the $150x Country A withholding tax that is described in paragraph (b)(2)(i) of this section and that is attributable under either paragraph (b)(2)(ii) or (b)(2)(iii) of this section to the non-inclusion income of CFC. No credit or deduction is allowed in any taxable year under paragraph (a)(1)(i) of this section for any portion of the $150x Country A withholding tax that is attributable to the section 245A(d) income of USP or, under paragraph (a)(1)(iii) of this section, for any portion of that tax that is attributable to the non-inclusion income of CFC, to the extent the tax is not disallowed under paragraph (a)(1)(i) of this section.

(B) *Attribution of foreign income taxes to section 245A(d) income.* Under paragraph (b)(1) of this section, the $150x Country A withholding tax is attributable to the section 245A(d) income of USP to

the extent that it is allocated and apportioned to the section 245A(d) income group (the statutory grouping) under §1.861-20. Section 1.861-20(c) allocates and apportions foreign income tax to the statutory and residual groupings to which the items of foreign gross income that were included in the foreign tax base are assigned under §1.861-20(d). In general, §1.861-20(d) assigns foreign gross income to the statutory and residual groupings to which the corresponding U.S. item is assigned. If a taxpayer does not recognize a corresponding U.S. item in the year in which it pays or accrues foreign income tax with respect to foreign gross income that it includes by reason of a foreign law dividend, §1.861-20(d)(2)(ii)(B) assigns the foreign dividend amount to the same statutory or residual groupings to which the foreign dividend amount would be assigned if a distribution were made for Federal income tax purposes in the amount of, and on the date of, the foreign law distribution. Further, §1.861-20(d)(2)(ii)(B) computes the U.S. dividend amount (as defined in §1.861-20(b)) as if the distribution occurred on the date the distribution occurs for foreign law purposes. Therefore, the foreign dividend amount is assigned to the same statutory and residual groupings to which it would be assigned if a $1,000x distribution occurred on December 31, Year 1 for Federal income tax purposes. If such a distribution occurred, it would result in a $200x dividend to USP for which a deduction would be allowed under section 245A(a). The remaining $800x of the distribution would be excluded from USP's gross income and not treated as a dividend under section 959(a) and (d), respectively. Under paragraphs (c)(20) and (b)(1) of this section, the $1,000x U.S. dividend amount comprises a $200x dividend for which a deduction under section 245A(a) would be allowed, which is an item of section 245A(d) income, and $800x of section 951A PTEP, which is income in the residual grouping. Accordingly, $200x of the $1,000x foreign gross dividend income is assigned to the section 245A(d) income group, and $800x is assigned to the residual grouping. Under §1.861-20(f), $30x ($150x × $200x/ $1,000x) of the Country A foreign income tax is apportioned to the section 245A(d) income group and is attributable to the section 245A(d) income of USP. The remaining $120x ($150x × $800x/ $1,000x) of the tax is apportioned to the residual grouping.

(C) *Attribution of foreign income taxes to non-inclusion income.* Under paragraph (b)(2) of this section, the $150x Country A withholding tax may be attributed to non-inclusion income of CFC if the tax is allocated and apportioned under §1.861-20 by reference to either the characterization of the tax book value of stock under §1.861-9 or the income of a foreign corporation that is a reverse hybrid or foreign law CFC. CFC is neither a reverse hybrid nor a foreign law CFC. In addition, no portion of the $150x Country A withholding tax is allocated and apportioned under §1.861-20 by reference to the characterization of the tax book value of CFC's stock. See §1.861-20(d)(3)(i). Therefore, none of the tax is attributable to non-inclusion income of CFC.

(D) *Disallowance.* Under paragraph (a)(1)(i) of this section, no credit under section 901 or deduction is allowed in any taxable year to USP for the $30x portion of the Country A withholding tax that is attributable to section 245A(d) income of USP.

(4) *Example 3: Successive foreign law distributions subject to anti-avoidance rule.*—(i) *Facts.* For Year 1, CFC earns $500x of subpart F income that gives rise to a $500x gross income inclusion to USP under section 951(a), and income that creates $500x of earnings and profits described in section 959(c)(3). CFC earns no income in Years 2 through 4. As of January 1, Year 2, and through December 31, Year 4, CFC has $500x of earnings and profits described in section 959(c)(3) and $500x of section 951(a)(1)(A) PTEP (as defined in §1.960-3(c)(2)(x)) in a single annual PTEP account (as defined in §1.960-3(c)(1)). In each of Years 2 and 3, USP makes a consent dividend election under Country A law that, for Country A tax purposes, deems CFC to distribute to USP, and USP immediately to contribute to CFC, $500x on December 31 of each year. For Country A tax purposes, each deemed distribution is a dividend of $500x to USP, and each deemed contribution is a non-taxable contribution of $500x to the capital of CFC. Each $500x deemed distribution is therefore a foreign dividend amount (as defined in §1.861-20(b)). Country A imposes $150x of withholding tax on USP in each of Years 2 and 3 with respect to the $500x of foreign gross dividend income that USP includes in income under Country A law. For Federal income tax purposes, the Country A deemed distributions in Years 2 and 3 are disregarded such that USP recognizes no income, and the deemed distributions are therefore foreign law distributions. On December 31, Year 4, CFC distributes $1,000x to USP, which for Country A tax purposes is treated as a return of contributed capital on which no withholding tax is imposed. For Federal income tax purposes, $500x of the $1,000x distribution is a dividend to USP for which a deduction under section 245A(a) is allowed; the remaining $500x of the distribution is a distribution of section 951(a)(1)(A) PTEP that is excluded from USP's gross income and not treated as a dividend under section 959(a) and (d), respectively. The entire

$1,000x dividend is a U.S. dividend amount (as defined in §1.861-20(b)). The Country A consent dividend elections in Years 2 and 3 are made with a principal purpose of avoiding the purposes of section 245A(d) and this section to disallow a credit or deduction for Country A withholding tax incurred with respect to USP's section 245A(d) income.

(ii) *Analysis*—(A) *In general.* The rules of this section are applied by first determining the portion of the $150x Country A withholding tax paid by USP in each of Years 2 and 3 that is attributable under paragraph (b)(1) of this section to the section 245A(d) income of USP, and then by determining the portion of the $150x Country A withholding tax paid by USP in each of Years 2 and 3 that is described in paragraph (b)(2)(i) of this section and that is attributable under either paragraph (b)(2)(ii) or (b)(2)(iii) of this section to the non-inclusion income of CFC. Finally, the anti-avoidance rule under paragraph (b)(3) of this section applies to treat any portion of the $150x Country A withholding tax paid by USP in each of Years 2 and 3 as attributable to section 245A(d) income of USP or non-inclusion income of CFC, if a transaction, series of related transactions, or arrangement is undertaken with a principal purpose of avoiding the purposes of section 245A(d) and this section. No credit or deduction is allowed in any taxable year under paragraph (a)(1)(i) of this section for any portion of the $150x Country A withholding tax paid by USP in each of Years 2 and 3 that is attributable to the section 245A(d) income of USP or, under paragraph (a)(1)(iii) of this section, for any portion of that tax that is attributable to the non-inclusion income of CFC, to the extent the tax is not disallowed under paragraph (a)(1)(i) of this section.

(B) *Attribution of foreign income taxes to section 245A(d) income.* Under paragraph (b)(1) of this section, the $150x Country A withholding tax paid by USP in each of Years 2 and 3 is attributable to the section 245A(d) income of USP to the extent that it is allocated and apportioned to the section 245A(d) income group (the statutory grouping) under §1.861-20. Section 1.861-20(c) allocates and apportions foreign income tax to the statutory and residual groupings to which the items of foreign gross income that were included in the foreign tax base are assigned under §1.861-20(d). In general, §1.861-20(d) assigns foreign gross income to the statutory and residual groupings to which the corresponding U.S. item is assigned. If a taxpayer does not recognize a corresponding U.S. item in the year in which it pays or accrues foreign income tax with respect to foreign gross income that it includes by reason of a foreign law dividend, §1.861-20(d)(2)(ii)(B) assigns the foreign dividend amount to the same statutory or residual groupings to which the foreign dividend amount would be assigned if a distribution were made for Federal income tax purposes in the amount of, and on the date of, the foreign law distribution. Therefore, the $500x foreign dividend amount in each of Years 2 and 3 is assigned to the same statutory and residual groupings to which it would be assigned if a $500x distribution occurred on December 31 of each of those years for Federal income tax purposes.

(1) Year 2 $500x deemed distribution. CFC made no distributions in Year 1 and earned no income and made no distributions in Year 2 for Federal income tax purposes. As of December 31, Year 2, CFC has $500x of earnings and profits described in section 959(c)(3) and $500x of section 951(a)(1)(A) PTEP. If CFC distributed $500x on that date, the distribution would be a distribution of section 951(a)(1)(A) PTEP. A distribution of previously taxed earnings and profits is a U.S. dividend amount. Section 1.861-20(d)(3)(i) assigns the foreign dividend amount, to the extent of the U.S. dividend amount, to the statutory and residual groupings to which the U.S. dividend amount is assigned. The receipt of a distribution of previously taxed earnings and profits is assigned to the residual grouping under paragraph (b)(1) of this section. Therefore, all $500x foreign dividend amount would be assigned to the residual grouping, and none of the $150x withholding tax paid or accrued by USP in Year 2 would be treated as attributable to section 245A(d) income of USP.

(2) Year 3 $500x deemed distribution. CFC made no distributions in Year 1 and earned no income and made no distributions in Year 2 or Year 3 for Federal income tax purposes. Consequently, as of December 31, Year 3, CFC has $500x of earnings and profits described in section 959(c)(3) and $500x of section 951(a)(1)(A) PTEP. If CFC distributed $500x on that date, the distribution would be a distribution of section 951(a)(1)(A) PTEP. For the reasons described in paragraph (d)(4)(ii)(B)(1) of this section, all $500x of the foreign dividend amount would be assigned to the residual grouping, and none of the $150x withholding tax paid or accrued by USP in Year 3 would be treated as attributable to section 245A(d) income of USP.

(3) Year 4 $1,000x distribution. The Year 4 $1,000x distribution is, for Country A purposes, a return of capital distribution that is not subject to withholding tax. For Federal income tax purposes, it comprises a $500x dividend for which a deduction under section 245A(a) is allowed, which is an item of section 245A(d) income of USP, and a $500x distribution of section 951(a)(1)(A) PTEP, the receipt of which is income in the residual grouping.

(C) *Attribution of foreign income taxes to non-inclusion income.* Under paragraph (b)(2) of this section, the $150x Country A withholding tax paid by USP in each of Years 2 and 3 may be attributed to non-inclusion income of CFC if the tax is allocated and apportioned under §1.861-20 by reference to either the characterization of the tax book value of stock under §1.861-9 or the income of a foreign corporation that is a reverse hybrid or foreign law CFC. CFC is neither a reverse hybrid nor a foreign law CFC. In addition, no portion of the Country A withholding tax is allocated and apportioned under §1.861-20 by reference to the characterization of the tax book value of CFC's stock. See §1.861-20(d)(3)(i). Therefore, none of the tax is attributable to non-inclusion income of CFC.

(D) *Attribution of foreign income taxes pursuant to anti-avoidance rule.* USP made two successive foreign law distributions in Years 2 and 3 that were subject to Country A withholding tax and that did not individually exceed, but together exceeded, the section 951(a)(1)(A) PTEP of CFC. The Country A withholding tax on each consent dividend is allocated to the residual grouping rather than to the statutory grouping of section 245A(d) income under §§1.861-20(d)(2)(ii) and 1.861-20(d)(3)(i). USP paid no Country A withholding tax on the Year 4 distribution as a result of the Country A consent dividends in Years 2 and 3. If CFC had distributed its earnings and profits in Year 4 without the prior consent dividends, the distribution would have been subject to withholding tax, a portion of which would have been attributable to the section 245A(d) income arising from the distribution. But for the application of the anti-avoidance rule in paragraph (b)(3) of this section, USP would avoid the disallowance under section 245A(d) with respect to this portion of the withholding tax. Because USP made foreign law distributions that caused withholding tax from multiple foreign law distributions to be associated with the same previously taxed earnings and profits with a principal purpose of avoiding the purposes of section 245A(d) and this section, the $150x Country A withholding tax paid by USP in each of Years 2 and 3 is treated as being attributable to section 245A(d) income of USP.

(E) *Disallowance.* Under paragraph (a)(1)(i) of this section, no credit under section 901 or deduction is allowed in any taxable year to USP for the $150x Country A withholding tax paid by USP in each of Years 2 and 3 that is attributable to section 245A(d) income of USP.

(5) Example 4: Distribution that is in part a dividend and in part a return of capital.—(i) *Facts.* CFC uses the modified gross income method to allocate and apportion its interest expense, and its stock has a tax book value of $10,000x. For Year 1, CFC earns $500x of income that is specified foreign source general category gross income as that term is defined in §1.861-13(a)(1)(i)(A)(9) and is therefore neither tested income nor subpart F income of CFC. As of December 31, Year 1, CFC has $500x of earnings and profits described in section 959(c)(3). On that date, CFC distributes $1,000x of cash to USP. For Country A tax purposes, the entire $1,000x distribution is a dividend to USP and is therefore a foreign dividend amount (as defined in §1.861-20(b)). Country A imposes a withholding tax on USP of $150x with respect to the $1,000x of foreign gross dividend income that USP includes under the law of Country A. For Federal income tax purposes, USP includes $500x of the distribution in its gross income as a dividend for which a $500x deduction is allowed to USP under section 245A(a); the remaining $500x of the distribution is applied against and reduces USP's basis in its CFC stock under section 301(c)(2). The portion of the distribution that is a $500x dividend is a U.S. dividend amount (as defined in §1.861-20(b)). The remaining $500x of the distribution is a U.S. return of capital amount.

(ii) *Analysis*—(A) *In general.* The rules of this section are applied by first determining the portion of the $150x Country A withholding tax that is attributable under paragraph (b)(1) of this section to the section 245A(d) income of USP, and then by determining the portion of the $150x Country A withholding tax that is described in paragraph (b)(2)(i) of this section and that is attributable under either paragraph (b)(2)(ii) or (b)(2)(iii) of this section to the non-inclusion income of CFC. No credit or deduction is allowed under paragraph (a)(1)(i) of this section for any portion of the $150x Country A withholding tax that is attributable to the section 245A(d) income of USP or, under paragraph (a)(1)(iii) of this section, for any portion of that tax that is attributable to the non-inclusion income of CFC, to the extent the tax is not disallowed under paragraph (a)(1)(i) of this section.

(B) *Attribution of foreign income taxes to section 245A(d) income.* Under paragraph (b)(1) of this section, the $150x Country A withholding tax is attributable to the section 245A(d) income of USP to the extent that it is allocated and apportioned to the section 245A(d) income group (the statutory grouping) under §1.861-20. Section 1.861-20(c) allocates and apportions foreign income tax to the statutory and residual groupings to which the items of foreign gross income that were included in the foreign tax base are assigned under §1.861-20(d). Section 1.861-20(d)(3)(i) assigns foreign gross income that is a foreign dividend amount, to the extent of the U.S. dividend amount, to the statutory and residual groupings to which the U.S. dividend amount is assigned. Of the $1,000x foreign dividend amount, $500x is therefore assigned to the statutory and residual groupings to which the $500x U.S. dividend amount is assigned under Federal income tax law. The entire $500x U.S. dividend amount is a dividend for which a section 245A(a) deduction is allowed and is therefore section 245A(d) income that is assigned to the section 245A(d) income group. Accordingly, $500x of the foreign dividend amount is assigned to the section 245A(d) income group. Under § 1.861-20(f), $75x ($150x × $500x/$1,000x) of the Country A withholding tax is allocated to the section 245A(d) income group and so under paragraph (b)(1) of this section is attributable to the section 245A(d) income of USP.

(C) *Attribution of foreign income taxes to non-inclusion income.* The remaining $75x of the Country A withholding tax is described in paragraph (b)(2)(i) of this section because the $500x of foreign dividend amount that corresponds to the $500x U.S. return of capital amount is assigned, and the remaining withholding tax imposed on that foreign dividend amount is allocated and apportioned, by reference to the characterization of the tax book value of the stock of CFC. Under paragraph (b)(2)(ii) of this section, the remaining $75x Country A withholding tax is attributable to non-inclusion income of CFC to the extent that the tax is allocated and apportioned under § 1.861-20 to USP's section 245A subgroup of general category stock, section 245A subgroup of passive category stock, and section 245A subgroup of U.S. source category stock (the statutory groupings) for purposes of section 904 as the operative section. Under § 1.861-20(d)(3)(i), the $500x portion of the foreign dividend amount that corresponds to the $500x U.S. return of capital amount is assigned to the statutory and residual groupings to which $500x of earnings of CFC would be assigned if CFC recognized them in Year 1. Those earnings are deemed to arise in the statutory and residual groupings in the same proportions as the proportions of the tax book value of CFC's stock in the groupings for Year 1 for purposes of applying the asset method of expense allocation and apportionment under § 1.861-9. Under § 1.861-9, § 1.861-9T(f), and § 1.861-13, for purposes of section 904 as the operative section, all of the tax book value of the stock of CFC is assigned to USP's section 245A subgroup of general category stock because CFC uses the modified gross income method to allocate and apportion its interest expense and earns only specified foreign source general category gross income for Year 1. Under § 1.861-20(d)(3)(i), if CFC recognized $500x of earnings in Year 1 these earnings would be deemed to arise in the section 245A subgroup of general category stock. Accordingly, the remaining $500x of foreign dividend amount is assigned to USP's section 245A subgroup of general category stock. Under § 1.861-20(f), the remaining $75x of withholding tax is allocated to the section 245A subgroup and, under paragraph (b)(2)(ii) of this section, is attributable to the non-inclusion income of CFC.

(D) *Disallowance.* Under paragraph (a)(1)(i) of this section, no credit under section 901 or deduction is allowed in any taxable year to USP for the $75x portion of the Country A withholding tax that is attributable to section 245A(d) income of USP. Under paragraph (a)(1)(iii) of this section, no credit under section 901 or deduction is allowed in any taxable year to USP for the $75x portion of the Country A withholding tax that is attributable to non-inclusion income of CFC.

(6) *Example 5: Income of a reverse hybrid.*—(i) *Facts.* CFC is a reverse hybrid. In Year 1, CFC earns a $500x item of gain described in section 907(c)(1)(B) that is non-inclusion income. CFC also earns for Federal income tax purposes and Country A tax purposes a $1,000x item of royalty income, of which $500x is gross included tested income and $500x is non-inclusion income. USP includes the $500x item of foreign gain and the $1,000x item of foreign gross royalty income in its Country A taxable income, and the items are foreign law pass-through income. If CFC included these items under Country A tax law, its $1,000x of royalty income for Federal income tax purposes would be the corresponding U.S. item for the foreign gross royalty income, and its $500x of gain for Federal income tax purposes would be the corresponding U.S. item for the foreign gain. Country A imposes a $150x foreign income tax on USP with respect to $1,500x of foreign gross income.

(ii) *Analysis*—(A) *In general.* The rules of this section are applied by first determining the portion of the $150x Country A tax that is attributable under paragraph (b)(1) of this section to the section 245A(d) income of USP, and then by determining the portion of the $150x Country A tax that is described in paragraph (b)(2)(i) of this section and that is attributable under either paragraph (b)(2)(ii) or (iii) of this section to the non-inclusion income of CFC. No credit or deduction is allowed under paragraph (a)(1)(i) of this section for any portion of the $150x Country A tax that is attributable to the section 245A(d) income of USP or, under paragraph (a)(1)(iii) of this section, for any portion of that tax that is attributable to the non-inclusion

income of CFC, to the extent the tax is not disallowed under paragraph (a)(1)(i) of this section.

(B) *Attribution of foreign income taxes to section 245A(d) income.* Under paragraph (b)(1) of this section, the $150x Country A tax is attributable to section 245A(d) income to the extent the tax is allocated and apportioned to the section 245A(d) income group (the statutory grouping) under § 1.861-20. Section 1.861-20(c) allocates and apportions foreign income tax to the statutory and residual groupings to which the items of foreign gross income that were included in the foreign tax base are assigned under § 1.861-20(d). In general, § 1.861-20(d) assigns foreign gross income to the statutory and residual groupings to which the corresponding U.S. item is assigned. Section 1.861-20(d)(3)(i)(C) assigns the foreign law pass-through income that USP includes by reason of its ownership of CFC to the statutory and residual groupings by treating USP's foreign law pass-through income as foreign gross income of CFC, and by treating CFC as paying the $150x of Country A tax in CFC's U.S. taxable year within which its foreign taxable year ends (Year 1). CFC is therefore treated as including a $1,000x foreign gross royalty item and a $500x foreign gross income item of gain and paying $150x of Country A tax in Year 1. These foreign gross income items are assigned to the statutory and residual groupings to which the corresponding U.S. items are assigned under Federal income tax law. No foreign gross income is assigned to the section 245A(d) income group because neither the corresponding U.S. item of royalty income nor the corresponding U.S. item of gain is assigned to the section 245A(d) income group. Therefore, none of USP's Country A tax is allocated to the section 245A(d) income group.

(C) *Attribution of foreign income taxes to non-inclusion income.* The $150x Country A tax is described in paragraph (b)(2) of this section because USP is a United States shareholder of CFC, CFC is a reverse hybrid, and § 1.861-20(d)(3)(i)(C) allocates and apportions the tax by reference to the income of CFC. Under paragraph (b)(2)(iii) of this section, the $150x Country A tax is attributable to the non-inclusion income of CFC to the extent that the foreign income taxes are allocated and apportioned to the non-inclusion income group under § 1.861-20. For the reasons described in paragraph (d)(6)(ii)(B) of this section, under § 1.861-20(d)(3)(i)(C) CFC is treated as including a $1,000x foreign gross royalty item and a $500x foreign gross income item of gain and paying $150x of Country A tax in Year 1. These foreign gross income items are assigned to the statutory and residual groupings to which the corresponding U.S. items are assigned under Federal income tax law. For Federal income tax purposes, the $500x item of gain and $500x of the $1,000x item of royalty income are items of non-inclusion income that are therefore assigned to the non-inclusion income group. The remaining $500x of the foreign gross royalty income item is assigned to the residual grouping. Under § 1.861-20(f), $100x ($150x × $1,000x/$1,500x) of the Country A tax is apportioned to the non-inclusion income group, and $50x ($150x × $500x/$1,500x) is apportioned to the residual grouping. Under paragraph (b)(2)(iii) of this section, the $100x of Country A tax that is apportioned to the non-inclusion income group under § 1.861-20(d)(3)(i)(C) is attributable to non-inclusion income of CFC.

(D) *Disallowance.* Under paragraph (a)(1)(iii) of this section, no credit under section 901 or deduction is allowed in any taxable year to USP for the $100x of Country A foreign income tax that is attributable to non-inclusion income of CFC.

(e) *Applicability date.*—This section applies to taxable years of a foreign corporation that begin after December 31, 2019, and end on or after November 2, 2020, and with respect to a United States person, taxable years in which or with which such taxable years of the foreign corporation end. [Reg. § 1.245A(d)-1.]

☐ [T.D. 9959, 12-28-2021 (*corrected* 7-26-2022).]

[Reg. § 1.245A(e)-1]

§ 1.245A(e)-1. Special rules for hybrid dividends.— (a) *Overview.*—This section provides rules for hybrid dividends. Paragraph (b) of this section disallows the deduction under section 245A(a) for a hybrid dividend received by a United States shareholder from a CFC. Paragraph (c) of this section provides a rule for hybrid dividends of tiered corporations. Paragraph (d) of this section sets forth rules regarding a hybrid deduction account. Paragraph (e) of this section provides an anti-avoidance rule. Paragraph (f) of this section provides definitions. Paragraph (g) of this section illustrates the application of the rules of this section through examples. Paragraph (h) of this section provides the applicability date.

(b) *Hybrid dividends received by United States shareholders.*—(1) *In general.*—If a United States shareholder receives a hybrid dividend, then—

(i) The United States shareholder is not allowed a deduction under section 245A(a) for the hybrid dividend; and

(ii) The rules of section 245A(d) and § 1.245A(d)-1 (disallowance of foreign tax credits and deductions) apply to the hybrid dividend. See paragraph (g)(1) of this section for an example illustrating the application of paragraph (b) of this section.

(2) *Definition of hybrid dividend.*—The term *hybrid dividend* means an amount received by a United States shareholder from a CFC for which, without regard to section 245A(e) and this section as well as § 1.245A-5, the United States shareholder would be allowed a deduction under section 245A(a), to the extent of the sum of the United States shareholder's hybrid deduction accounts (as described in paragraph (d) of this section) with respect to each share of stock of the CFC, determined at the close of the CFC's taxable year (or in accordance with paragraph (d)(5) of this section, as applicable). No other amount received by a United States shareholder from a CFC is a hybrid dividend for purposes of section 245A.

(3) *Special rule for certain dividends attributable to earnings of lower-tier foreign corporations.*—This paragraph (b)(3) applies if a domestic corporation directly or indirectly (as determined under the principles of § 1.245A-5(g)(3)(ii)) sells or exchanges stock of a foreign corporation and, pursuant to section 1248, the gain recognized on the sale or exchange is included in gross income as a dividend. In such a case, for purposes of this section—

(i) To the extent that earnings and profits of a lower-tier CFC gave rise to the dividend under section 1248(c)(2), those earnings and profits are treated as distributed as a dividend by the lower-tier CFC directly to the domestic corporation under the principles of § 1.1248-1(d); and

(ii) To the extent the domestic corporation indirectly owns (within the meaning of section 958(a)(2), and determined by treating a domestic partnership as foreign) shares of stock of the lower-tier CFC, the hybrid deduction accounts with respect to those shares are treated as the domestic corporation's hybrid deduction accounts with respect to stock of the lower-tier CFC. Thus, for example, if a domestic corporation sells or exchanges all the stock of an upper-tier CFC and under this paragraph (b)(3) there is considered to be a dividend paid directly by the lower-tier CFC to the domestic corporation, then the dividend is generally a hybrid dividend to the extent of the sum of the upper-tier CFC's hybrid deduction accounts with respect to stock of the lower-tier CFC.

(4) *Ordering rule.*—Amounts received by a United States shareholder from a CFC are subject to the rules of section 245A(e) and this section based on the order in which they are received. Thus, for example, if on different days during a CFC's taxable year a United States shareholder receives dividends from the CFC, then the rules of section 245A(e) and this section apply first to the dividend received on the earliest date (based on the sum of the United States shareholder's hybrid deduction accounts with respect to each share of stock of the CFC), and then to the dividend received on the next earliest date (based on the remaining sum).

(c) *Hybrid dividends of tiered corporations.*—(1) *In general.*—If a CFC (the *receiving CFC*) receives a tiered hybrid dividend from another CFC, and a domestic corporation is a United States shareholder with respect to both CFCs, then, notwithstanding any other provision of the Code—

(i) For purposes of section 951(a) as to the United States shareholder, the tiered hybrid dividend is treated for purposes of section 951(a)(1)(A) as subpart F income of the receiving CFC for the taxable year of the CFC in which the tiered hybrid dividend is received;

(ii) The United States shareholder includes in gross income an amount equal to its pro rata share (determined in the same manner as under section 951(a)(2)) of the subpart F income described in paragraph (c)(1)(i) of this section; and

(iii) The rules of section 245A(d) and § 1.245A(d)-1 (disallowance of foreign tax credit, including for taxes that would have been deemed paid under section 960(a) or (b), and deductions) apply to the amount included under paragraph (c)(1)(ii) of this section in the United States shareholder's gross income. See paragraph (g)(2) of this section for an example illustrating the application of paragraph (c) of this section.

(2) *Definition of tiered hybrid dividend.*—The term *tiered hybrid dividend* means an amount received by a receiving CFC from another CFC to the extent that the amount would be a hybrid dividend under paragraph (b)(2) of this section if, for purposes of section 245A and the regulations in this part under section 245A (except for section 245A(e)(2) and this paragraph (c)), the receiving CFC were a domestic corporation. A tiered hybrid dividend does not include an amount described in section 959(b). No other amount received by a receiving CFC from another CFC is a tiered hybrid dividend for purposes of section 245A.

(3) *Special rule for certain dividends attributable to earnings of lower-tier foreign corporations.*—This paragraph (c)(3) applies if a CFC directly or indirectly (as determined under the principles of

§ 1.245A-5(g)(3)(ii)) sells or exchanges stock of a foreign corporation and pursuant to section 964(e)(1) the gain recognized on the sale or exchange is included in gross income as a dividend. In such a case, the rules of paragraph (b)(3) of this section apply, by treating the CFC as the domestic corporation described in paragraph (b)(3) of this section and substituting the phrase "sections 964(e)(1) and 1248(c)(2)" for the phrase "section 1248(c)(2)" in paragraph (b)(3)(i) of this section.

(4) *Interaction with rules under section 964(e).*—To the extent a dividend described in section 964(e)(1) (gain on certain stock sales by CFCs treated as dividends) is a tiered hybrid dividend, the rules of section 964(e)(4) do not apply as to a domestic corporation that is a United States shareholder of both of the CFCs described in paragraph (c)(1) of this section and, therefore, such United States shareholder is not allowed a deduction under section 245A(a) for the amount included in gross income under paragraph (c)(1)(ii) of this section.

(d) *Hybrid deduction accounts.*—(1) *In general.*—A specified owner of a share of CFC stock must maintain a hybrid deduction account with respect to the share. The hybrid deduction account with respect to the share must reflect the amount of hybrid deductions of the CFC allocated to the share (as determined under paragraphs (d)(2) and (3) of this section), and must be maintained in accordance with the rules of paragraphs (d)(4) through (6) of this section.

(2) *Hybrid deductions.*—(i) *In general.*—The term *hybrid deduction* of a CFC means a deduction or other tax benefit (such as an exemption, exclusion, or credit, to the extent equivalent to a deduction) for which the requirements of paragraphs (d)(2)(i)(A) and (B) of this section are both satisfied.

(A) The deduction or other tax benefit is allowed to the CFC (or a person related to the CFC) under a relevant foreign tax law, regardless of whether the deduction or other tax benefit is used, or otherwise reduces tax, currently under the relevant foreign tax law.

(B) The deduction or other tax benefit relates to or results from an amount paid, accrued, or distributed with respect to an instrument issued by the CFC and treated as stock for U.S. tax purposes, or is a deduction allowed to the CFC with respect to equity. Examples of such a deduction or other tax benefit include an interest deduction, a dividends paid deduction, and a notional interest deduction (or similar deduction determined with respect to the CFC's equity). However, a deduction or other tax benefit relating to or resulting from a distribution by the CFC that is a dividend for purposes of the relevant foreign tax law is considered a hybrid deduction only to the extent it has the effect of causing the earnings that funded the distribution to not be included in income (determined under the principles of § 1.267A-3(a)) or otherwise subject to tax under such tax law. Thus, for example, upon a distribution by a CFC that is treated as a dividend for purposes of the CFC's tax law to a shareholder of the CFC, a dividends paid deduction allowed to the CFC under its tax law (or a refund to the shareholder, including through a credit, of tax paid by the CFC on the earnings that funded the distribution) pursuant to an integration or imputation system is not a hybrid deduction of the CFC to the extent that the shareholder, if a tax resident of the CFC's country, includes the distribution in income under the CFC's tax law or, if not a tax resident of the CFC's country, is subject to withholding tax (as defined in section 901(k)(1)(B)) on the distribution under the CFC's tax law. As an additional example, upon a distribution by a CFC to a shareholder of the CFC that is a tax resident of the CFC's country, a dividends received deduction allowed to the shareholder under the tax law of such foreign country pursuant to a regime intended to relieve double-taxation within the group is not a hybrid deduction of the CFC (though if the CFC were also allowed a deduction or other tax benefit for the distribution under such tax, such deduction or other tax benefit would be a hybrid deduction of the CFC). See paragraphs (g)(1) and (2) of this section for examples illustrating the application of paragraph (d) of this section.

(ii) *Coordination with foreign disallowance rules.*—The following special rules apply for purposes of determining whether a deduction or other tax benefit is allowed to a CFC (or a person related to the CFC) under a relevant foreign tax law:

(A) Whether the deduction or other tax benefit is allowed is determined without regard to a rule under the relevant foreign tax law that disallows or suspends deductions if a certain ratio or percentage is exceeded (for example, a thin capitalization rule that disallows interest deductions if debt to equity exceeds a certain ratio, or a rule similar to section 163(j) that disallows or suspends interest deductions if interest exceeds a certain percentage of income).

(B) Except as provided in this paragraph (d)(2)(ii)(B), whether the deduction or other tax benefit is allowed is determined without regard to hybrid mismatch rules, if any, under the relevant foreign tax law that may disallow such deduction or other tax benefit. However, whether the deduction or other tax benefit is allowed is determined with regard to hybrid mismatch rules under the relevant foreign tax law if the amount giving rise to the deduction or other tax benefit neither gives rise to a dividend for U.S. tax purposes nor, based on all the facts and circumstances, is reasonably expected to give rise to a dividend for U.S. tax purposes that will be paid within 12 months from the end of the taxable period for which the deduction or other tax benefit would be allowed but for the hybrid mismatch rules. For purposes of this paragraph (d)(2)(ii)(B), the term hybrid mismatch rules has the meaning provided in §1.267A-5(b)(10).

(iii) *Anti-duplication rule.*—A deduction or other tax benefit allowed to a CFC (or a person related to the CFC) under a relevant foreign tax law for an amount paid, accrued, or distributed with respect to an instrument issued by the CFC is not a hybrid deduction to the extent that treating it as a hybrid deduction would have the effect of duplicating a hybrid deduction that is a deduction or other tax benefit allowed under such tax law for an amount paid, accrued, or distributed with respect to an instrument that is issued by a CFC at a higher tier and that has terms substantially similar to the terms of the first instrument. For example, if an upper tier CFC issues to a corporate United States shareholder a hybrid instrument (the "upper tier instrument"), a lower tier CFC issues to the upper tier CFC a hybrid instrument that has terms substantially similar to the terms of the upper tier instrument (the "mirror instrument"), the CFCs are tax residents of the same foreign country, and the upper tier CFC includes in income under its tax law (as determined under the principles of §1.267A-3(a)) amounts accrued with respect to the mirror instrument, then a deduction allowed to the lower tier CFC under such foreign tax law for an amount accrued pursuant to the mirror instrument is not a hybrid deduction (but a deduction allowed to the upper tier CFC under the foreign tax law for an amount accrued with respect to the upper tier instrument is a hybrid deduction).

(iv) *Application limited to items allowed in taxable years ending on or after December 20, 2018; special rule for deductions with respect to equity.*—A deduction or other tax benefit, other than a deduction with respect to equity, allowed to a CFC (or a person related to the CFC) under a relevant foreign tax law is taken into account for purposes of this section only if it was allowed with respect to a taxable year under the relevant foreign tax law ending on or after December 20, 2018. A deduction with respect to equity allowed to a CFC under a relevant foreign tax law is taken into account for purposes of this section only if it was allowed with respect to a taxable year under the relevant foreign tax law beginning on or after December 20, 2018.

(3) *Allocating hybrid deductions to shares.*—A hybrid deduction is allocated to a share of stock of a CFC to the extent that the hybrid deduction (or amount equivalent to a deduction) relates to an amount paid, accrued, or distributed by the CFC with respect to the share. However, in the case of a hybrid deduction that is a deduction with respect to equity (such as a notional interest deduction), the deduction is allocated to a share of stock of a CFC based on the product of—

(i) The amount of the deduction allowed for all of the equity of the CFC; and

(ii) A fraction, the numerator of which is the value of the share and the denominator of which is the value of all of the stock of the CFC.

(4) *Maintenance of hybrid deduction accounts.*—(i) *In general.*—A specified owner's hybrid deduction account with respect to a share of stock of a CFC is, as of the close of the taxable year of the CFC, adjusted pursuant to the following rules.

(A) First, the account is increased by the amount of hybrid deductions of the CFC allocated to the share for the taxable year.

(B) Second, the account is decreased (but not below zero) pursuant to the rules of paragraphs (d)(4)(i)(B)(1) through (3) of this section, in the order set forth in this paragraph (d)(4)(i)(B).

(1) *Adjusted subpart F inclusions.*—(i) *In general.*—Subject to the limitation in paragraph (d)(4)(i)(B)(1)(ii) of this section, the account is reduced by an adjusted subpart F inclusion with respect to the share for the taxable year, as determined pursuant to the rules of paragraph (d)(4)(ii) of this section.

(ii) *Limitation.*—The reduction pursuant to paragraph (d)(4)(i)(B)(1)(i) of this section cannot exceed the hybrid deductions of the CFC allocated to the share for the taxable year multiplied by a fraction, the numerator of which is the sum of the items of gross income of the CFC that give rise to subpart F income (determined without regard to an amount treated as subpart F income by reason of section 964(e)(4)(A)(i), to the extent that a deduction under section 245A(a) is allowed for a portion of the amount included under section 964(e)(4)(A)(ii) in the gross income of a domestic corporation)

of the CFC for the taxable year and the denominator of which is the sum of all the items of gross income of the CFC for the taxable year.

(iii) *Special rule allocating otherwise unused adjusted subpart F inclusions across accounts in certain cases.*—This paragraph (d)(4)(i)(B)(1)(iii) applies after each of the specified owner's hybrid deduction accounts with respect to its shares of stock of the CFC are adjusted pursuant to paragraph (d)(4)(i)(B)(1)(i) of this section but before the accounts are adjusted pursuant to paragraph (d)(4)(i)(B)(2) of this section, to the extent that one or more of the hybrid deduction accounts would have been reduced by an amount pursuant to paragraph (d)(4)(i)(B)(1)(i) of this section but for the limitation in paragraph (d)(4)(i)(B)(1)(ii) of this section (the aggregate of the amounts that would have been reduced but for the limitation, the *unused reduction amount*, and the accounts that would have been reduced by the unused reduction amount, the *unused reduction amount accounts*). When this paragraph (d)(4)(i)(B)(1)(iii) applies, the specified owner's hybrid deduction accounts other than the unused reduction amount accounts (if any) are ratably reduced by the lesser of the unused reduction amount and the difference of the following two amounts: the hybrid deductions of the CFC allocated to the specified owner's shares of stock of the CFC for the taxable year multiplied by the fraction described in paragraph (d)(4)(i)(B)(1)(ii) of this section; and the reductions pursuant to paragraph (d)(4)(i)(B)(1)(i) of this section with respect to the specified owner's shares of stock of the CFC.

(2) *Adjusted GILTI inclusions.*—(i) *In general.*—Subject to the limitation in paragraph (d)(4)(i)(B)(2)(ii) of this section, the account is reduced by an adjusted GILTI inclusion with respect to the share for the taxable year, as determined pursuant to the rules of paragraph (d)(4)(ii) of this section.

(ii) *Limitation.*—The reduction pursuant to paragraph (d)(4)(i)(B)(2)(i) of this section cannot exceed the hybrid deductions of the CFC allocated to the share for the taxable year multiplied by a fraction, the numerator of which is the sum of the items of gross tested income of the CFC for the taxable year and the denominator of which is the sum of all the items of gross income of the CFC for the taxable year.

(iii) *Special rule allocating otherwise unused adjusted GILTI inclusions across accounts in certain cases.*—This paragraph (d)(4)(i)(B)(2)(iii) applies after each of the specified owner's hybrid deduction accounts with respect to its shares of stock of the CFC are adjusted pursuant to paragraph (d)(4)(i)(B)(2)(i) of this section but before the accounts are adjusted pursuant to paragraph (d)(4)(i)(B)(3) of this section, to the extent that one or more of the hybrid deduction accounts would have been reduced by an amount pursuant to paragraph (d)(4)(i)(B)(2)(i) of this section but for the limitation in paragraph (d)(4)(i)(B)(2)(ii) of this section (the aggregate of the amounts that would have been reduced but for the limitation, the *unused reduction amount*, and the accounts that would have been reduced by the unused reduction amount, the *unused reduction amount accounts*). When this paragraph (d)(4)(i)(B)(2)(iii) applies, the specified owner's hybrid deduction accounts other than the unused reduction amount accounts (if any) are ratably reduced by the lesser of the unused reduction amount and the difference of the following two amounts: the hybrid deductions of the CFC allocated to the specified owner's shares of stock of the CFC for the taxable year multiplied by the fraction described in paragraph (d)(4)(i)(B)(2)(ii) of this section; and the reductions pursuant to paragraph (d)(4)(i)(B)(2)(i) of this section with respect to the specified owner's shares of stock of the CFC. *See* paragraph (g)(1)(v)(C) of this section for an illustration of the application of this paragraph (d)(4)(i)(B)(2)(iii).

(3) *Certain section 956 inclusions.*—The account is reduced by an amount included in the gross income of a domestic corporation under sections 951(a)(1)(B) and 956 with respect to the share for the taxable year of the domestic corporation in which or with which the CFC's taxable year ends, to the extent so included by reason of the application of section 245A(e) and this section to the hypothetical distribution described in §1.956-1(a)(2).

(C) Third, the account is decreased by the amount of hybrid deductions in the account that gave rise to a hybrid dividend or tiered hybrid dividend during the taxable year. If the specified owner has more than one hybrid deduction account with respect to its stock of the CFC, then a pro rata amount in each hybrid deduction account is considered to have given rise to the hybrid dividend or tiered hybrid dividend, based on the amounts in the accounts before applying this paragraph (d)(4)(i)(C).

(ii) *Rules regarding adjusted subpart F and GILTI inclusions.*—(A) The term *adjusted subpart F inclusion* means, with respect to a share of stock of a CFC for a taxable year of the CFC, a domestic corporation's pro rata share of the CFC's subpart F income included in gross income under section 951(a)(1)(A) (determined without regard to an amount included in gross income by the domestic corporation by reason of section 964(e)(4)(A)(ii), to the extent a deduction under section 245A(a) is allowed for the amount) for the taxable year of the domestic corporation in which or with which the CFC's taxable year ends, to the extent attributable to the share (as determined under the principles of section 951(a)(2) and §1.951-1(b) and (e)), adjusted (but not below zero) by—

(1) Adding to the amount the associated foreign income taxes with respect to the amount; and

(2) Subtracting from such sum the quotient of the associated foreign income taxes divided by the percentage described in section 11(b).

(B) The term *adjusted GILTI inclusion* means, with respect to a share of stock of a CFC for a taxable year of the CFC, a domestic corporation's GILTI inclusion amount (within the meaning of §1.951A-1(c)(1)) for the U.S. shareholder inclusion year (within the meaning of §1.951A-1(f)(7)), to the extent attributable to the share (as determined under paragraph (d)(4)(ii)(C) of this section), adjusted (but not below zero) by—

(1) Adding to the amount the associated foreign income taxes with respect to the amount;

(2) Multiplying such sum by the difference of 100 percent and the section 250(a)(1)(B)(i) deduction percentage; and

(3) Subtracting from such product the quotient of 80 percent of the associated foreign income taxes divided by the percentage described in section 11(b).

(C) A domestic corporation's GILTI inclusion amount for a U.S. shareholder inclusion year is attributable to a share of stock of the CFC based on a fraction—

(1) The numerator of which is the domestic corporation's pro rata share of the tested income of the CFC for the U.S. shareholder inclusion year, to the extent attributable to the share (as determined under the principles of §1.951A-1(d)(2)); and

(2) The denominator of which is the aggregate of the domestic corporation's pro rata share of the tested income of each tested income CFC (as defined in §1.951A-2(b)(1)) for the U.S. shareholder inclusion year.

(D) The term *associated foreign income taxes* means—

(1) With respect to a domestic corporation's pro rata share of the subpart F income of the CFC included in gross income under section 951(a)(1)(A) and attributable to a share of stock of a CFC for a taxable year of the CFC, current year tax (as described in §1.960-1(b)(4)) allocated and apportioned under §1.960-1(d)(3)(ii) to the subpart F income groups (as described in §1.960-1(b)(30)) of the CFC for the taxable year, to the extent allocated to the share under paragraph (d)(4)(ii)(E) of this section; and

(2) With respect to a domestic corporation's GILTI inclusion amount under section 951A attributable to a share of stock of a CFC for a taxable year of the CFC, the product of—

(i) Current year tax (as described in §1.960-1(b)(4)) allocated and apportioned under §1.960-1(d)(3)(ii) to the tested income groups (as described in §1.960-1(b)(33)) of the CFC for the taxable year, to the extent allocated to the share under paragraph (d)(4)(ii)(F) of this section;

(ii) The domestic corporation's inclusion percentage (as described in §1.960-2(c)(2)); and

(iii) The section 904 limitation fraction with respect to the domestic corporation for the U.S. shareholder inclusion year.

(E) Current year tax allocated and apportioned to a subpart F income group of a CFC for a taxable year is allocated to a share of stock of the CFC by multiplying the foreign income tax by a fraction—

(1) The numerator of which is the domestic corporation's pro rata share of the subpart F income of the CFC for the taxable year, to the extent attributable to the share (as determined under the principles of section 951(a)(2) and §1.951-1(b) and (e)); and

(2) The denominator of which is the subpart F income of the CFC for the taxable year.

(F) Current year tax allocated and apportioned to a tested income group of a CFC for a taxable year is allocated to a share of stock of the CFC by multiplying the foreign income tax by a fraction—

(1) The numerator of which is the domestic corporation's pro rata share of tested income of the CFC for the taxable year, to the extent attributable to the share (as determined under the principles §1.951A-1(d)(2)); and

(2) The denominator of which is the tested income of the CFC for the taxable year.

(G) The term *section 904 limitation fraction* means, with respect to a domestic corporation for a U.S. shareholder inclusion year, a fraction—

(1) The numerator of which is the amount of foreign tax credits for the U.S. shareholder inclusion year that, by reason of sections 901 and 960(d) and taking into account section 904, the

domestic corporation is allowed for the separate category set forth in section 904(d)(1)(A) (amounts includible in gross income under section 951A); and

(2) The denominator of which is the amount of foreign tax credits for the U.S. shareholder inclusion year that, by reason of sections 901 and 960(d) and without regard to section 904, the domestic corporation would be allowed for the separate category set forth in section 904(d)(1)(A) (amounts includible in gross income under section 951A).

(H) The term *section 250(a)(1)(B)(i) deduction percentage* means, with respect to a domestic corporation for a U.S. shareholder inclusion year, a fraction—

(1) The numerator of which is the amount of the deduction under section 250 allowed to the domestic corporation for the U.S. shareholder inclusion year by reason of section 250(a)(1)(B)(i) (taking into account section 250(a)(2)(B)); and

(2) The denominator of which is the domestic corporation's GILTI inclusion amount for the U.S. shareholder inclusion year.

(iii) *Acquisition of account and certain other adjustments.*—(A) *In general.*—The following rules apply when a person (the *acquirer*) directly or indirectly through a partnership, trust, or estate acquires a share of stock of a CFC from another person (the *transferor*).

(1) In the case of an acquirer that is a specified owner of the share immediately after the acquisition, the transferor's hybrid deduction account, if any, with respect to the share becomes the hybrid deduction account of the acquirer.

(2) In the case of an acquirer that is not a specified owner of the share immediately after the acquisition, the transferor's hybrid deduction account, if any, is eliminated and accordingly is not thereafter taken into account by any person.

(B) *Additional rules.*—The following rules apply in addition to the rules of paragraph (d)(4)(iii)(A) of this section.

(1) *Certain section 354 or 356 exchanges.*—The following rules apply when a shareholder of a CFC (the CFC, the *target CFC*; the shareholder, the *exchanging shareholder*) exchanges stock of the target CFC for stock of another CFC (the *acquiring CFC*) pursuant to an exchange described in section 354 or 356 that occurs in connection with a transaction described in section 381(a)(2) in which the target CFC is the transferor corporation.

(i) In the case of an exchanging shareholder that is a specified owner of one or more shares of stock of the acquiring CFC immediately after the exchange, the exchanging shareholder's hybrid deduction accounts with respect to the shares of stock of the target CFC that it exchanges are attributed to the shares of stock of the acquiring CFC that it receives in the exchange.

(ii) In the case of an exchanging shareholder that is not a specified owner of one or more shares of stock of the acquiring CFC immediately after the exchange, the exchanging shareholder's hybrid deduction accounts with respect to its shares of stock of the target CFC are eliminated and accordingly are not thereafter taken into account by any person.

(2) *Section 332 liquidations.*—If a CFC is a distributor corporation in a transaction described in section 381(a)(1) (the *distributor CFC*) in which a controlled foreign corporation is the acquiring corporation (the *distributee CFC*), then each hybrid deduction account with respect to a share of stock of the distributee CFC is increased pro rata by the sum of the hybrid deduction accounts with respect to shares of stock of the distributor CFC.

(3) *Recapitalizations.*—If a shareholder of a CFC exchanges stock of the CFC pursuant to a reorganization described in section 368(a)(1)(E) or a transaction to which section 1036 applies, then the shareholder's hybrid deduction accounts with respect to the stock of the CFC that it exchanges are attributed to the shares of stock of the CFC that it receives in the exchange.

(4) *Certain distributions involving section 355 or 356.*—In the case of a transaction involving a distribution under section 355 (or so much of section 356 as it relates to section 355) by a CFC (the *distributing CFC*) of stock of another CFC (the *controlled CFC*), the balance of the hybrid deduction accounts with respect to stock of the distributing CFC is attributed to stock of the controlled CFC in a manner similar to how earnings and profits of the distributing CFC and controlled CFC are adjusted. To the extent the balance of the hybrid deduction accounts with respect to stock of the distributing CFC is not so attributed to stock of the controlled CFC, such balance remains as the balance of the hybrid deduction accounts with respect to stock of the distributing CFC.

(5) *Effect of section 338(g) election.*—(i) *In general.*—If an election under section 338(g) is made with respect to a qualified stock purchase (as described in section 338(d)(3)) of stock of a CFC, then a hybrid deduction account with respect to a share of stock of the old

target is not treated as (or attributed to) a hybrid deduction account with respect to a share of stock of the new target. Accordingly, immediately after the deemed asset sale described in §1.338-1, the balance of a hybrid deduction account with respect to a share of stock of the new target is zero; the account must then be maintained in accordance with the rules of paragraph (d) of this section.

(ii) *Special rule regarding carryover FT stock.*—Paragraph (d)(4)(iii)(B)(5)(*i*) of this section does not apply as to a hybrid deduction account with respect to a share of carryover FT stock (as described in §1.338-9(b)(3)(i)). A hybrid deduction account with respect to a share of carryover FT stock is attributed to the corresponding share of stock of the new target.

(5) *Determinations and adjustments made during year of transfer in certain cases.*—This paragraph (d)(5) applies if on a date other than the date that is the last day of the CFC's taxable year a United States shareholder of the CFC or an upper-tier CFC with respect to the CFC directly or indirectly (as determined under the principles of §1.245A-5(g)(3)(ii)) transfers a share of stock of the CFC, and, during the taxable year, but on or before the transfer date, the United States shareholder or upper-tier CFC receives an amount from the CFC that is subject to the rules of section 245A(e) and this section. In such a case, the following rules apply:

(i) As to the United States shareholder or upper-tier CFC and the United States shareholder's or upper-tier CFC's hybrid deduction accounts with respect to each share of stock of the CFC (regardless of whether such share is transferred), the determinations and adjustments under this section that would otherwise be made at the close of the CFC's taxable year are made at the close of the date of the transfer. When making these determinations and adjustments at the close of the date of the transfer, each hybrid deduction account described in the previous sentence is pursuant to paragraph (d)(4)(ii)(A) of this section increased by a ratable portion (based on the number of days in the taxable year within the pre-transfer period to the total number of days in the taxable year) of the hybrid deductions of the CFC allocated to the share for the taxable year, and pursuant to paragraph (d)(4)(ii)(C) of this section decreased by the amount of hybrid deductions in the account that gave rise to a hybrid dividend or tiered hybrid dividend during the portion of the taxable year up to and including the transfer date. Thus, for example, if a United States shareholder of a CFC exchanges stock of the CFC in an exchange described in §1.367(b)-4(b)(1)(i) and is required to include in income as a deemed dividend the section 1248 amount attributable to the stock exchanged, then: as of the close of the date of the exchange, each of the United States shareholder's hybrid deductions accounts with respect to a share of stock of the CFC is increased by a ratable portion of the hybrid deductions of the CFC allocated to the share for the taxable year (based on the number of days in the taxable year within the pre-transfer period to the total number of days in the taxable year); the deemed dividend is a hybrid dividend to the extent of the sum of the United States shareholder's hybrid deduction accounts with respect to each share of stock of the CFC; and, as the close of the date of the exchange, each of the accounts is decreased by the amount of hybrid deductions in the account that gave rise to a hybrid dividend during the portion of the taxable year up to and including the date of the exchange.

(ii) As to a hybrid deduction account described in paragraph (d)(5)(i) of this section, the adjustments to the account as of the close of the taxable year of the CFC must take into account the adjustments, if any, occurring with respect to the account pursuant to paragraph (d)(5)(i) of this section. Thus, for example, if an acquisition of a share of stock of a CFC occurs on a date other than the date that is the last day of the CFC's taxable year and pursuant to paragraph (d)(4)(iii)(A)(*1*) of this section the acquirer succeeds to the transferor's hybrid deduction account with respect to the share, then, as of the close of the taxable year of the CFC, the account is increased by a ratable portion of the hybrid deductions of the CFC allocated to the share for the taxable year (based on the number of days in the taxable year within the post-transfer period to the total number of days in the taxable year), and, decreased by the amount of hybrid deductions in the account that gave rise to a hybrid dividend or tiered hybrid dividend during the portion of the taxable year following the transfer date.

(6) *Effects of CFC functional currency.*—(i) *Maintenance of the hybrid deduction account.*—A hybrid deduction account with respect to a share of CFC stock must be maintained in the functional currency (within the meaning of section 985) of the CFC. Thus, for example, the amount of a hybrid deduction and the adjustments described in paragraphs (d)(4)(i)(A) and (B) of this section are determined based on the functional currency of the CFC. In addition, for purposes of this section, the amount of a deduction or other tax benefit allowed to a CFC (or a person related to the CFC) is determined taking into account foreign currency gain or loss recognized with respect to such deduction or other tax benefit under a provision of foreign tax law

comparable to section 988 (treatment of certain foreign currency transactions).

(ii) *Determination of amount of hybrid dividend.*—This paragraph (d)(6)(ii) applies if a CFC's functional currency is other than the functional currency of a United States shareholder or upper-tier CFC that receives an amount from the CFC that is subject to the rules of section 245A(e) and this section. In such a case, the sum of the United States shareholder's or upper-tier CFC's hybrid deduction accounts with respect to each share of stock of the CFC is, for purposes of determining the extent that a dividend is a hybrid dividend or tiered hybrid dividend, translated into the functional currency of the United States shareholder or upper-tier CFC based on the spot rate (within the meaning of §1.988-1(d)) as of the date of the dividend.

(e) *Anti-avoidance rule.*—Appropriate adjustments are made pursuant to this section, including adjustments that would disregard the transaction or arrangement, if a transaction or arrangement is undertaken with a principal purpose of avoiding the purposes of section 245A(e) and this section. For example, if a specified owner of a share of CFC stock transfers the share to another person, and a principal purpose of the transfer is to shift the hybrid deduction account with respect to the share to the other person or to cause the hybrid deduction account to be eliminated, then for purposes of this section the shifting or elimination of the hybrid deduction account is disregarded as to the transferor. As another example, if a transaction or arrangement is undertaken to affirmatively fail to satisfy the holding period requirement under section 246(c)(5) with a principal purpose of avoiding the tiered hybrid dividend rules described in paragraph (c) of this section, the transaction or arrangement is disregarded for purposes of this section. This paragraph (e) will not apply, however, to disregard (or make other adjustments with respect to) a transaction pursuant to which an instrument or arrangement that gives rise to hybrid deductions is eliminated or otherwise converted into another instrument or arrangement that does not give rise to hybrid deductions.

(f) *Definitions.*—The following definitions apply for purposes of this section.

(1) The term *controlled foreign corporation* (or *CFC*) has the meaning provided in section 957.

(2) The term *domestic corporation* means an entity classified as a domestic corporation under section 7701(a)(3) and (4) or otherwise treated as a domestic corporation by the Internal Revenue Code. However, for purposes of this section, a domestic corporation does not include a regulated investment company (as described in section 851), a real estate investment trust (as described in section 856), or an S corporation (as described in section 1361).

(3) The term *person* has the meaning provided in section 7701(a)(1).

(4) The term *related* has the meaning provided in this paragraph (f)(4). A person is related to a CFC if the person is a related person within the meaning of section 954(d)(3). *See also* §1.954-1(f)(2)(iv)(B)(*1*) (neither section 318(a)(3), nor §1.958-2(d) or the principles thereof, applies to attribute stock or other interests).

(5) The term *relevant foreign tax law* means, with respect to a CFC, any regime of any foreign country or possession of the United States that imposes an income, war profits, or excess profits tax with respect to income of the CFC, other than a foreign anti-deferral regime under which a person that owns an interest in the CFC is liable to tax. If a foreign country has an income tax treaty with the United States that applies to taxes imposed by a political subdivision or other local authority of that country, then the tax law of the political subdivision or other local authority is deemed to be a tax law of a foreign country. Thus, the term includes any regime of a foreign country or possession of the United States that imposes income, war profits, or excess profits tax under which—

(i) The CFC is liable to tax as a resident;

(ii) The CFC has a branch that gives rise to a taxable presence in the foreign country or possession of the United States; or

(iii) A person related to the CFC is liable to tax as a resident, provided that under such person's tax law the person is allowed a deduction for amounts paid or accrued by the CFC (because the CFC is fiscally transparent under the person's tax law).

(6) The term *specified owner* means, with respect to a share of stock of a CFC, a person for which the requirements of paragraphs (f)(6)(i) and (ii) of this section are satisfied.

(i) The person is a domestic corporation that is a United States shareholder of the CFC, or is an upper-tier CFC that would be a United States shareholder of the CFC were the upper-tier CFC a domestic corporation (provided that, for purposes of sections 951 and 951A, a domestic corporation that is a United States shareholder of the upper-tier CFC owns (within the meaning of section 958(a), and determined by treating a domestic partnership as foreign) one or more shares of stock of the upper-tier CFC).

(ii) The person owns the share directly or indirectly through a partnership, trust, or estate. Thus, for example, if a domestic corporation directly owns all the shares of stock of an upper-tier CFC and the upper-tier CFC directly owns all the shares of stock of another CFC, the domestic corporation is the specified owner with respect to each share of stock of the upper-tier CFC and the upper-tier CFC is the specified owner with respect to each share of stock of the other CFC.

(7) The term *United States shareholder* has the meaning provided in section 951(b).

(g) *Examples.*—This paragraph (g) provides examples that illustrate the application of this section. For purposes of the examples in this paragraph (g), unless otherwise indicated, the following facts are presumed. US1 is a domestic corporation. FX and FZ are CFCs formed at the beginning of year 1, and the functional currency (within the meaning of section 985) of each of FX and FZ is the dollar. FX is a tax resident of Country X and FZ is a tax resident of Country Z. US1 is a United States shareholder with respect to FX and FZ. No distributed amounts are attributable to amounts which are, or have been, included in the gross income of a United States shareholder under section 951(a). All instruments are treated as stock for U.S. tax purposes. Only the tax law of the United States contains hybrid mismatch rules. No amounts are included in the gross income of US1 under section 951(a)(1)(A), 951A(a), or 951(a)(1)(B) and section 956.

(1) *Example 1. Hybrid dividend resulting from hybrid instrument.*—(i) *Facts.* US1 holds both shares of stock of FX, which have an equal value. One share is treated as indebtedness for Country X tax purposes ("Share A"), and the other is treated as equity for Country X tax purposes ("Share B"). During year 1, under Country X tax law, FX accrues $80x of interest to US1 with respect to Share A and is allowed a deduction for the amount (the "Hybrid Instrument Deduction"). During year 2, FX distributes $30x to US1 with respect to each of Share A and Share B. For U.S. tax purposes, each of the $30x distributions is treated as a dividend for which, without regard to section 245A(e) and this section as well as § 1.245A-5, US1 would be allowed a deduction under section 245A(a). For Country X tax purposes, the $30x distribution with respect to Share A represents a payment of interest for which a deduction was already allowed (and thus FX is not allowed an additional deduction for the amount), and the $30x distribution with respect to Share B is treated as a dividend (for which no deduction is allowed).

(ii) *Analysis.* The entire $30x of each dividend received by US1 from FX during year 2 is a hybrid dividend, because the sum of US1's hybrid deduction accounts with respect to each of its shares of FX stock at the end of year 2 ($80x) is at least equal to the amount of the dividends ($60x). *See* paragraph (b)(2) of this section. This is the case for the $30x dividend with respect to Share B even though there are no hybrid deductions allocated to Share B. *See* paragraph (b)(2) of this section. As a result, US1 is not allowed a deduction under section 245A(a) for the entire $60x of hybrid dividends and the rules of section 245A(d) and § 1.245A(d)-1 (disallowance of foreign tax credits and deductions) apply. *See* paragraph (b)(1) of this section. Paragraphs (g)(1)(ii)(A) through (D) of this section describe the determinations under this section.

(A) At the end of year 1, US1's hybrid deduction accounts with respect to Share A and Share B are $80x and $0, respectively, calculated as follows.

(1) The $80x Hybrid Instrument Deduction allowed to FX under Country X tax law (a relevant foreign tax law) is a hybrid deduction of FX, because the deduction is allowed to FX and relates to or results from an amount accrued with respect to an instrument issued by FX and treated as stock for U.S. tax purposes. *See* paragraph (d)(2)(i) of this section. Thus, FX's hybrid deductions for year 1 are $80x.

(2) The entire $80x Hybrid Instrument Deduction is allocated to Share A, because the deduction was accrued with respect to Share A. *See* paragraph (d)(3) of this section. As there are no additional hybrid deductions of FX for year 1, there are no additional hybrid deductions to allocate to either Share A or Share B. Thus, there are no hybrid deductions allocated to Share B.

(3) At the end of year 1, US1's hybrid deduction account with respect to Share A is increased by $80x (the amount of hybrid deductions allocated to Share A). *See* paragraph (d)(4)(i)(A) of this section. Because FX did not pay any dividends with respect to either Share A or Share B during year 1 (and therefore did not pay any hybrid dividends or tiered hybrid dividends), no further adjustments are made. *See* paragraph (d)(4)(i)(C) of this section. Therefore, at the end of year 1, US1's hybrid deduction accounts with respect to Share A and Share B are $80x and $0, respectively.

(B) At the end of year 2, and before the adjustments described in paragraph (d)(4)(i)(C) of this section, US1's hybrid deduction accounts with respect to Share A and Share B remain $80x and $0, respectively. This is because there are no hybrid deductions of FX for year 2. *See* paragraph (d)(4)(i)(A) of this section.

(C) Because at the end of year 2 (and before the adjustments described in paragraph (d)(4)(i)(C) of this section) the sum of US1's hybrid deduction accounts with respect to Share A and Share B ($80x, calculated as $80x plus $0) is at least equal to the aggregate $60x of year 2 dividends, the entire $60x dividend is a hybrid dividend. *See* paragraph (b)(2) of this section.

(D) At the end of year 2, US1's hybrid deduction account with respect to Share A is decreased by $60x, the amount of the hybrid deductions in the account that gave rise to a hybrid dividend or tiered hybrid dividend during year 2. *See* paragraph (d)(4)(i)(C) of this section. Because there are no hybrid deductions in the hybrid deduction account with respect to Share B, no adjustments with respect to that account are made under paragraph (d)(4)(i)(C) of this section. Therefore, at the end of year 2 and taking into account the adjustments under paragraph (d)(4)(i)(C) of this section, US1's hybrid deduction account with respect to Share A is $20x ($80x less $60x) and with respect to Share E is $0.

(iii) *Alternative facts – notional interest deductions.* The facts are the same as in paragraph (g)(1)(i) of this section, except that for each of year 1 and year 2 FX is allowed $10x of notional interest deductions with respect to its equity, Share B, under Country X tax law (the "NIDs"). In addition, during year 2, FX distributes $47.5x (rather than $30x) to US1 with respect to each of Share A and Share B. For U.S. tax purposes, each of the $47.5x distributions is treated as a dividend for which, without regard to section 245A(e) and this section as well as § 1.245A-5, US1 would be allowed a deduction under section 245A(a). For Country X tax purposes, the $47.5x distribution with respect to Share A represents a payment of interest for which a deduction was already allowed (and thus FX is not allowed an additional deduction for the amount), and the $47.5x distribution with respect to Share B is treated as a dividend (for which no deduction is allowed). The entire $47.5x of each dividend received by US1 from FX during year 2 is a hybrid dividend, because the sum of US1's hybrid deduction accounts with respect to each of its shares of FX stock at the end of year 2 ($80x plus $20x, or $100x) is at least equal to the amount of the dividends ($95x). *See* paragraph (b)(2) of this section. As a result, US1 is not allowed a deduction under section 245A(a) for the $95x hybrid dividend and the rules of section 245A(d) and § 1.245A(d)-1 (disallowance of foreign tax credits and deductions) apply. *See* paragraph (b)(1) of this section. Paragraphs (g)(1)(iii)(A) through (D) of this section describe the determinations under this section.

(A) The $10x of NIDs allowed to FX under Country X tax law in year 1 are hybrid deductions of FX for year 1. *See* paragraph (d)(2)(i) of this section. The $10x of NIDs is allocated equally to each of Share A and Share B, because the hybrid deduction is with respect to equity and the shares have an equal value. *See* paragraph (d)(3) of this section. Thus, $5x of the NIDs is allocated to each of Share A and Share B for year 1. For the reasons described in paragraph (g)(1)(ii)(A)(2) of this section, the entire $80x Hybrid Instrument Deduction is allocated to Share A. Therefore, at the end of year 1, US1's hybrid deduction accounts with respect to Share A and Share B are $85x and $5x, respectively.

(B) Similarly, the $10x of NIDs allowed to FX under Country X tax law in year 2 are hybrid deductions of FX for year 2, and $5x of the NIDs is allocated to each of Share A and Share B for year 2. *See* paragraphs (d)(2)(i) and (d)(3) of this section. Thus, at the end of year 2 (and before the adjustments described in paragraph (d)(4)(i)(C) of this section), US1's hybrid deduction account with respect to Share A is $90x ($85x plus $5x) and with respect to Share B is $10x ($5x plus $5x). *See* paragraph (d)(4)(i) of this section.

(C) Because at the end of year 2 (and before the adjustments described in paragraph (d)(4)(i)(C) of this section) the sum of US1's hybrid deduction accounts with respect to Share A and Share B ($100x, calculated as $90x plus $10x) is at least equal to the aggregate $95x of year 2 dividends, the entire $95x of dividends are hybrid dividends. *See* paragraph (b)(2) of this section.

(D) At the end of year 2, US1's hybrid deduction accounts with respect to Share A and Share B are decreased by the amount of hybrid deductions in the accounts that gave rise to a hybrid dividend or tiered hybrid dividend during year 2. *See* paragraph (d)(4)(i)(C) of this section. A total of $95x of hybrid deductions in the accounts gave rise to a hybrid dividend during year 2. For the hybrid deduction account with respect to Share A, $85.5x in the account is considered to have given rise to a hybrid deduction (calculated as $95x multiplied by $90x/$100x). *See* paragraph (d)(4)(i)(C) of this section. For the hybrid deduction account with respect to Share B, $9.5x in the account is considered to have given rise to a hybrid deduction (calculated as $95x multiplied by $10x/$100x). *See* paragraph (d)(4)(i)(C) of this section. Thus, following these adjustments, at the end of year 2, US1's hybrid deduction account with respect to Share A is $4.5x ($90x less $85.5x) and with respect to Share B is $0.5x ($10x less $9.5x).

(iv) *Alternative facts – deduction in branch country*—(A) *Facts.* The facts are the same as in paragraph (g)(1)(i) of this section, except that for Country X tax purposes Share A is treated as equity (and thus the Hybrid Instrument Deduction does not exist, and under Country X tax law FX is not allowed a deduction for the $30x distributed in year 2 with respect to Share A). However, FX has a branch in Country Z that gives rise to a taxable presence under Country Z tax law, and for Country Z tax purposes Share A is treated as indebtedness and Share B is treated as equity. Also, during year 1, for Country Z tax purposes, FX accrues $80x of interest to US1 with respect to Share A and is allowed an $80x interest deduction with respect to its Country Z branch income. Moreover, for Country Z tax purposes, the $30x distribution with respect to Share A in year 2 represents a payment of interest for which a deduction was already allowed (and thus FX is not allowed an additional deduction for the amount), and the $30x distribution with respect to Share B in year 2 is treated as a dividend (for which no deduction is allowed).

(B) *Analysis.* The $80x interest deduction allowed to FX under Country Z tax law (a relevant foreign tax law) with respect to its Country Z branch income is a hybrid deduction of FX for year 1. *See* paragraphs (d)(2)(i) and (f)(5) of this section. For reasons similar to those discussed in paragraph (g)(1)(ii) of this section, at the end of year 2 (and before the adjustments described in paragraph (d)(4)(i)(C) of this section), US1's hybrid deduction accounts with respect to Share A and Share B are $80x and $0, respectively, and the sum of the accounts is $80x. Accordingly, the entire $60x of the year 2 dividend is a hybrid dividend. *See* paragraph (b)(2) of this section. Further, for the reasons described in paragraph (g)(1)(ii)(D) of this section, at the end of year 2 and taking into account the adjustments under paragraph (d)(4)(i)(C) of this section, US1's hybrid deduction account with respect to Share A is $20x ($80x less $60x) and with respect to Share B is $0.

(v) *Alternative facts — account reduced by adjusted GILTI inclusion*—The facts are the same as in paragraph (g)(1)(i) of this section, except that for taxable year 1 FX has $130x of gross tested income and $10.5x of current year tax (as described in § 1.960-1(b)(4)) that is allocated and apportioned under § 1.960-1(d)(3)(ii) to the tested income groups of FX. US1's ability to credit the $10.5x of current year tax is not limited under section 904(a). In addition, FX has $119.5x of tested income ($130x of gross tested income, less the $10.5x of current year tax deductions properly allocable to the gross tested income). Further, of US1's pro rata share of the tested income ($119.5x), $80x is attributable to Share A and $39.5x is attributable to Share B (as determined under the principles of § 1.951A-1(d)(2)). Moreover, US1's net deemed tangible income return (as defined in § 1.951A-1(c)(3)) for taxable year 1 is $71.7x, and US1 does not own any stock of a CFC other than its stock of FX. Thus, US1's GILTI inclusion amount (within the meaning of § 1.951A-1(c)(1)) for taxable year 1, the U.S. shareholder inclusion year, is $47.8x (net CFC tested income of $119.5x, less net deemed tangible income return of $71.7x) and US1's inclusion percentage (as described in § 1.960-2(c)(2)) is 40 ($47.8x/$119.5x). The deduction allowed to US1 under section 250 by reason of section 250(a)(1)(B)(i) is not limited as a result of section 250(a)(2)(B). At the end of year 1, US1's hybrid deduction account with respect to Share A is: first, increased by $80x (the amount of hybrid deductions allocated to Share A); and second, decreased by $10x (the sum of the adjusted GILTI inclusion with respect to Share A, and the adjusted GILTI inclusion with respect to Share B that is allocated to the hybrid deduction account with respect to Share A) to $70x. *See* paragraphs (d)(4)(i)(A) and (B) of this section. In year 2, the entire $30x of each dividend received by US1 from FX during year 2 is a hybrid dividend, because the sum of US1's hybrid deduction accounts with respect to each of its shares of FX stock at the end of year 2 ($70x) is at least equal to the amount of the dividends ($60x). *See* paragraph (b)(2) of this section. At the end of year 2, US1's hybrid deduction account with respect to Share A is decreased by $60x (the amount of the hybrid deductions in the account that give rise to a hybrid dividend or tiered hybrid dividend during year 2) to $10x. *See* paragraph (d)(4)(i)(C) of this section. Paragraphs (g)(1)(v)(A) through (C) of this section describe the computations pursuant to paragraph (d)(4)(i)(B)(2) of this section.

(A) To determine the adjusted GILTI inclusion with respect to Share A for taxable year 1, it must be determined to what extent US1's $47.8x GILTI inclusion amount is attributable to Share A. *See* paragraph (d)(4)(ii)(B) of this section. Here, $32x of the inclusion is attributable to Share A, calculated as $47.8x multiplied by a fraction, the numerator of which is $80x (US1's pro rata share of the tested income of FX attributable to Share A) and denominator of which is $119.5x (US1's pro rata share of the tested income of FX, its only CFC). *See* paragraph (d)(4)(ii)(C) of this section. Next, the associated foreign income taxes with respect to the $32x GILTI inclusion amount attributable to Share A must be determined. *See* paragraphs (d)(4)(ii)(B) and (D) of this section. Such associated foreign income taxes are $2.8x, calculated as $10.5x (the current year tax allocated and apportioned to the tested income groups of FX) multiplied by a

fraction, the numerator of which is $80x (US1's pro rata share of the tested income of FX attributable to Share A) and the denominator of which is $119.5x (the tested income of FX), multiplied by 40% (US1's inclusion percentage), multiplied by 1 (the section 904 limitation fraction with respect to US1's GILTI inclusion amount). *See* paragraphs (d)(4)(ii)(D), (F), and (G) of this section. Thus, pursuant to paragraph (d)(4)(ii)(B) of this section, the adjusted GILTI inclusion with respect to Share A is $6.7x, computed by—

(1) Adding $2.8x (the associated foreign income taxes with respect to the $32x GILTI inclusion attributable to Share A) to $32x, which is $34.8x;

(2) Multiplying $34.8x (the sum of the amounts in paragraph (g)(1)(v)(A)(1) of this section) by 50% (the difference of 100 percent and the section 250(a)(1)(B)(i) deduction percentage), which is $17.4x; and

(3) Subtracting $10.7x (calculated as $2.24x (80% of the $2.8x of associated foreign income taxes) divided by .21 (the percentage described in section 11(b)) from $17.4x (the product of the amounts in paragraph (g)(1)(v)(A)(2) of this section), which is $6.7x.

(B) Pursuant to computations similar to those discussed in paragraph (g)(1)(v)(A) of this section, the adjusted GILTI inclusion with respect to Share B is $3.3x. However, the hybrid deduction account with respect to Share B is not reduced by such $3.3x, because of the limitation in paragraph (d)(4)(i)(B)(2)(ii) of this section, which, with respect to Share B, limits the reduction pursuant to paragraph (d)(4)(i)(B)(2)(i) of this section to $0 (calculated as $0, the hybrid deductions allocated to the share for the taxable year, multiplied by 1, the fraction described in paragraph (d)(4)(i)(B)(2)(ii) of this section (computed as $130x, the sole item of gross tested income, divided by $130x, the sole item of gross income)). *See* paragraphs (d)(4)(i)(B)(2)(i) and (ii) of this section.

(C) US1's hybrid deduction account with respect to Share A is reduced by the entire $6.7x adjusted GILTI inclusion with respect to the share, as such $6.7x does not exceed the limit in paragraph (d)(4)(i)(B)(2)(ii) of this section ($80x, calculated as $80x, the hybrid deductions allocated to the share for the taxable year, multiplied by 1, the fraction described in paragraph (d)(4)(i)(B)(2)(ii) of this section). *See* paragraphs (d)(4)(i)(B)(2)(i) and (ii) of this section. In addition, the hybrid deduction account is reduced by another $3.3x, the amount of the adjusted GILTI inclusion with respect to Share B that is allocated to the hybrid deduction account with respect to Share A. *See* paragraph (d)(4)(i)(B)(2)(iii) of this section. As a result, pursuant to paragraph (d)(4)(i)(B)(2) of this section, US1's hybrid deduction account with respect to Share A is reduced by $10x ($6.7x plus $3.3x).

(2) *Example 2. Tiered hybrid dividend rule; tax benefit equivalent to a deduction.*—(i) *Facts.* US1 holds all the stock of FX, and FX holds all 100 shares of stock of FZ (the "FZ shares"), which have an equal value. The FZ shares are treated as equity for Country Z tax purposes. At the end of year 1, the sum of FX's hybrid deduction accounts with respect to each of its shares of FZ stock is $0. During year 2, FZ distributes $10x to FX with respect to each of the FZ shares, for a total of $1,000x. The $1,000x is treated as a dividend for U.S. and Country Z tax purposes, and is not deductible for Country Z tax purposes. If FX were a domestic corporation, then, without regard to section 245A(e) and this section as well as § 1.245A-5, FX would be allowed a deduction under section 245A(a) for the $1,000x. Under Country Z tax law, 75% of the corporate income tax paid by a Country Z corporation with respect to a dividend distribution is refunded to the corporation's shareholders (regardless of where such shareholders are tax residents) upon a dividend distribution by the corporation. The corporate tax rate in Country Z is 20%. With respect to FZ's distributions, FX is allowed a refundable tax credit of $187.5x. The $187.5x refundable tax credit is calculated as $1,250x (the amount of pre-tax earnings that funded the distribution, determined as $1,000x (the amount of the distribution) divided by 0.8 (the percentage of pre-tax earnings that a Country Z corporation retains after paying Country Z corporate tax)) multiplied by 0.2 (the Country Z corporate tax rate) multiplied by 0.75 (the percentage of the Country Z tax credit). Under Country Z tax law, FX is not subject to Country Z withholding tax (or any other tax) with respect to the $1,000x dividend distribution.

(ii) *Analysis.* As described in paragraphs (g)(2)(ii)(A) and (B) of this section, the sum of FX's hybrid deduction accounts with respect to each of its shares of FZ stock at the end of year 2 is $937.5x and, as a result, $937.5x of the $1,000x of dividends received by FX from FZ during year 2 is a tiered hybrid dividend. *See* paragraphs (b)(2) and (c)(2) of this section. The $937.5x tiered hybrid dividend is treated for purposes of section 951(a)(1)(A) as subpart F income of FX and US1 must include in gross income its pro rata share of such subpart F income, which is $937.5x. *See* paragraph (c)(1) of this section. This is the case notwithstanding any other provision of the Code, including section 952(c) or section 954(c)(3) or (6). In addition, the rules of section 245A(d) and § 1.245A(d)-1 (disallowance of foreign tax credits and deductions) apply with respect to US1's inclusion. *See* paragraph (c)(1) of this section. Paragraphs (g)(2)(ii)(A) through (C) of this section describe the determinations under this section. The characterization of the FZ stock for Country X tax purposes (or for purposes of any other foreign tax law) does not affect this analysis.

(A) The $187.5x refundable tax credit allowed to FX under Country Z tax law (a relevant foreign tax law) is equivalent to a $937.5x deduction, calculated as $187.5x (the amount of the credit) divided by 0.2 (the Country Z corporate tax rate). The $937.5x is a hybrid deduction of FZ because it is allowed to FX (a person related to FZ), it relates to or results from amounts distributed with respect to instruments issued by FZ and treated as stock for U.S. tax purposes, and it has the effect of causing the earnings that funded the distributions to not be included in income under Country Z tax law. *See* paragraph (d)(2)(i) of this section. $9.375x of the hybrid deduction is allocated to each of the FZ shares, calculated as $937.5x (the amount of the hybrid deduction) multiplied by 1/100 (the value of each FZ share relative to the value of all the FZ shares). *See* paragraph (d)(3) of this section. The result would be the same if FX were instead a tax resident of Country Z (and not Country X), FX were allowed the $187.5x refundable tax credit under Country Z tax law, and under Country Z tax law FX were to not include the $1,000x in income (because, for example, Country Z tax law provides Country Z resident corporations a 100% exclusion or dividends received deduction with respect to dividends received from a resident corporation). *See* paragraph (d)(2)(i) of this section.

(B) At the end of year 2, and before the adjustments described in paragraph (d)(4)(i)(C) of this section, the sum of FX's hybrid deduction accounts with respect to each of its shares of FZ stock is $937.5x, calculated as $9.375x (the amount in each account) multiplied by 100 (the number of accounts). *See* paragraph (d)(4)(i) of this section. Accordingly, $937.5x of the $1,000x dividend received by FX from FZ during year 2 is a tiered hybrid dividend. *See* paragraphs (b)(2) and (c)(2) of this section.

(C) At the end of year 2, each of FX's hybrid deduction accounts with respect to its shares of FZ is decreased by the $9.375x in the account that gave rise to a hybrid dividend or tiered hybrid dividend during year 2. *See* paragraph (d)(4)(i)(C) of this section. Thus, following these adjustments, at the end of year 2, each of FX's hybrid deduction accounts with respect to its shares of FZ stock is $0, calculated as $9.375x (the amount in the account before the adjustments described in paragraph (d)(4)(i)(C) of this section) less $9.375x (the adjustment described in paragraph (d)(4)(i)(C) of this section with respect to the account).

(iii) *Alternative facts – imputation system that taxes shareholders.* The facts are the same as in paragraph (g)(2)(i) of this section, except that under Country Z tax law the $1,000x dividend to FX is subject to a 30% gross basis withholding tax, or $300x, and the $187.5x refundable tax credit is applied against and reduces the withholding tax to $112.5x. The $187.5x refundable tax credit provided to FX is not a hybrid deduction because FX was subject to Country Z withholding tax of $300x on the $1,000x dividend (such withholding tax being greater than the $187.5x credit). *See* paragraph (d)(2)(i) of this section. If instead FZ were allowed a $1,000x dividends paid deduction for the $1,000x dividend (and FX were not allowed the refundable tax credit) and the dividend were subject to 5% gross basis withholding tax (or $50x), then $750x of the dividends paid deduction would be a hybrid deduction, calculated as the excess of $1,000x (the dividends paid deduction) over $250x (the amount of income that under Country Z tax law would produce an amount of tax equal to the $50x of withholding tax, calculated as $50x, the amount of withholding tax, divided by 0.2, the Country Z corporate tax rate). *See* paragraph (d)(2)(i) of this section.

(h) *Applicability dates.*—(1) *In general.*—Except as provided in paragraph (h)(2) of this section, this section applies to distributions made after December 31, 2017, provided that such distributions occur during taxable years ending on or after December 20, 2018. However, taxpayers may apply this section in its entirety to distributions made after December 31, 2017 and occurring during taxable years ending before December 20, 2018. In lieu of applying the regulations in this section, taxpayers may apply the provisions matching this section from the Internal Revenue Bulletin (IRB) 2019-03 (https://www.irs.gov/pub/irs-irbs/irb19-03.pdf) in their entirety for all taxable years ending on or before April 8, 2020.

(2) *Special rules.*—Paragraphs (d)(4)(i)(B) and (d)(4)(ii) of this section (decrease of hybrid deduction accounts; rules regarding adjusted subpart F and GILTI inclusions) apply to taxable years ending on or after November 12, 2020. However, a taxpayer may choose to apply paragraphs (d)(4)(i)(B) and (d)(4)(ii) of this section to a taxable year ending before November 12, 2020, so long as the taxpayer consistently applies paragraphs (d)(4)(i)(B) and (d)(4)(ii) of this section to that taxable year and any subsequent taxable year ending before November 12, 2020. [Reg. § 1.245A(e)-1.]

□ [*T.D. 9896, 4-7-2020. Amended by T.D. 9909, 8-21-2020, T.D. 9922, 11-2-2020 and T.D. 9959, 12-28-2021.*]

[Reg. § 1.246-1]

§ 1.246-1. Deductions not allowed for dividends from certain corporations.—The deductions provided in sections 243 (relating to dividends received by corporations), 244 (relating to dividends received on certain preferred stock), and 245 (relating to dividends received from certain foreign corporations), are not allowable with respect to any dividend received from:

(a) A corporation organized under the China Trade Act, 1922 (15 U.S.C. ch. 4) (see section 941); or

(b) A corporation which is exempt from tax under section 501 (relating to certain charitable, etc., organizations) or section 521 (relating to farmers' cooperative associations) for the taxable year of the corporation in which the distribution is made or for its next preceding taxable year; or

(c) A corporation to which section 931 (relating to income from sources within possessions of the United States) applies for the taxable year of the corporation in which the distribution is made or for its next preceding taxable year; or

(d) A real estate investment trust which, for its taxable year in which the distribution is made, is taxable under part II, subchapter M, chapter 1 of the Code. See section 243(c)(3), paragraph (c) of § 1.243-2, section 857(c), and paragraph (d) of § 1.857-6. [Reg. § 1.246-1.]

□ [*T.D. 6183, 6-13-56. Amended by T.D. 6598, 4-25-62 and T.D. 7767, 2-3-81.*]

[Reg. § 1.246-2]

§ 1.246-2. Limitation on aggregate amount of deductions.—(a) *General rule.*—The sum of the deductions allowed by sections 243(a)(1) (relating to dividends received by corporations), 244(a) (relating to dividends received on certain preferred stock), and 245 (relating to dividends received from certain foreign corporations), except as provided in section 246(b)(2) and in paragraph (b) of this section, is limited to 85 percent of the taxable income of the corporation. The taxable income of the corporation for this purpose is computed without regard to the net operating loss deduction allowed by section 172, the deduction for dividends paid on certain preferred stock of public utilities allowed by section 247, any capital loss carryback under section 1212(a)(1), and the deductions provided in sections 243(a)(1), 244(a), and 245. For definition of the term "taxable income," see section 63.

(b) *Effect of net operating loss.*—If the shareholder corporation has a net operating loss (as determined under section 172) for a taxable year, the limitation provided in section 246(b)(1) and in paragraph (a) of this section is not applicable for such taxable year. In that event, the deductions provided in sections 243(a)(1), 244(a), and 245 shall be allowable for all tax purposes to the shareholder corporation for such taxable year without regard to such limitation. If the shareholder corporation does not have a net operating loss for the taxable year, however, the limitation will be applicable for all tax purposes for such taxable year. In determining whether the shareholder corporation has a net operating loss for a taxable year under section 172, the deductions allowed by sections 243(a)(1), 244(a), and 245 are to be computed without regard to the limitation provided in section 246(b)(1) and in paragraph (a) of this section. [Reg. § 1.246-2.]

□ [*T.D. 6183, 6-13-56. Amended by T.D. 6449, 1-27-60, T.D. 6992, 1-17-69 and T.D. 7301, 1-3-74.*]

[Reg. § 1.246-3]

§ 1.246-3. Exclusion of certain dividends.—(a) *In general.*—Corporate taxpayers are denied, in certain cases, the dividends-received deduction provided by section 243 (dividends received by corporations), section 244 (dividends received on certain preferred stock), and section 245 (dividends received from certain foreign corporations). The above-mentioned dividends-received deductions are denied, under section 246(c)(1), to corporate shareholders:

(1) If the dividend is in respect of any share of stock which is sold or otherwise disposed of in any case where the taxpayer has held such share for 15 days or less; or

(2) If and to the extent that the taxpayer is under an obligation to make corresponding payments with respect to substantially identical stock or securities. It is immaterial whether the obligation has arisen pursuant to a short sale or otherwise.

(b) *Ninety-day rule for certain preference dividends.*—In the case of any stock having a preference in dividends, a special rules is provided by section 246(c)(2) in lieu of the 15-day rule described in section 246(c)(1) and paragraph (a)(1) of this section. If the taxpayer receives dividends on such stock which are attributable to a period or periods aggregating in excess of 366 days, the holding period specified in section 246(c)(1)(A) shall be 90 days (in lieu of 15 days).

(c) *Definitions.*—(1) *"Otherwise disposed of".*—As used in this section the term "otherwise disposed of" includes disposal by gift.

(2) *"Substantially identical stock or securities".*—The term "substantially identical stock or securities" is to be applied according to the facts and circumstances in each case. In general, the term has the same meaning as the corresponding terms in sections 1091 and 1233 and the regulations thereunder. See paragraph (d)(1) of § 1.1233-1.

(3) *Obligation to make corresponding payments.*—(i) Section 246 (c)(1)(B) of the Code denies the dividends-received deduction to a corporate taxpayer to the extent that such taxpayer is under an obligation, with respect to substantially identical stock or securities, to make payments corresponding to the dividend received. Thus, for example, where a corporate taxpayer is in both a "long" and "short" position with respect to the same stock on the date that such stock goes ex-dividend, the dividend received on the stock owned by the taxpayer will not be eligible for the dividends-received deduction to the extent that the taxpayer is obligated to make payments to cover the dividends with respect to its offsetting short position in the same stock. The dividends-received deduction is denied in such a case without regard to the length of time the taxpayer has held the stock on which such dividends are received.

(ii) The provisions of subdivision (i) of this subparagraph may be illustrated by the following example:

Example. Y Corporation owns 100 shares of the Z Corporation's common stock on January 1, 1959. Z Corporation on January 15, 1959, declares a dividend of $1.00 per share payable to shareholders of record on January 30, 1959. On January 21, 1959, Y Corporation sells short 25 shares of the Z Corporation's common stock and remains in the short position on January 31, 1959, the day that Z Corporation's common stock goes ex-dividend. Y Corporation is therefore obligated to make a payment to the lender of the 25 shares of Z Corporation's common stock which were sold short, corresponding to the $1.00 a share dividend that the lender would have received on those 25 shares, or $25.00. Therefore, $25.00 of the $100.00 that the Y Corporation receives as dividends from the Z Corporation with respect to the 100 shares of common stock in which it has a long position is not eligible for the dividends-received deduction.

(d) *Determination of holding period.*—(1) *In general.*—Special rules are provided by paragraph (3) of section 246(c) for determining the period for which the taxpayer has held any share of stock for purposes of the restriction provided by such section. In computing the holding period, the day of disposition but not the day of acquisition shall be taken into account. Also, there shall not be taken into account any day which is more than 15 days after the date on which the share of stock becomes ex-dividend. Thus, the holding period is automatically terminated at the end of such 15-day period without regard to how long the stock may be held after that date. In the case of stock qualifying under paragraph (2) of section 246(c) (as having preference in dividends) a 90-day period is substituted for the 15-day period prescribed in this subparagraph. Finally, section 1223(4), relating to holding periods in the case of wash sales, shall not apply. Therefore, tacking of the holding period of the stock disposed of to the holding period of the stock acquired where a wash sale occurs is not permitted for purposes of determining the holding period described in section 246(c).

(2) *Special rules.*—Section 246(c) requires that the holding periods determined thereunder shall be appropriately reduced for any period that the taxpayer's stock holding is offset by a corresponding short position resulting from an option to sell, a contractual obligation to sell, or a short sale of, substantially identical stock or securities. The holding periods of stock held for a period of 15 days or less on the date such short position is created shall accordingly be reduced to the extent of such short position. Where the amount of stock acquired within such period exceeds the amount as to which the taxpayer establishes a short position, the stock the holding period of which must be reduced because of such short position shall be that most recently acquired within such period. If, on the date the short position is created, the amount of stock subject to the short position exceeds the amount, if any, of stock held by the taxpayer for 15 days or less, the excess shares of stock sold short shall, to the extent thereof, postpone until the termination of the short position the commencement of the holding periods of subsequently acquired stock. Stock having a preference in dividends is also subject to these rules prescribed in this subparagraph, except that the 90-day period provided by paragraph (b) of this section shall apply in lieu of the 15-day period otherwise applicable. These rules may be illustrated by the following examples:

Example (1). L Company purchased 100 shares of Z Corporation's common stock during January 1959. On November 26, 1959, L Company purchased an additional 100 shares of the same stock. On December 1, 1959, Z Corporation declared a dividend payable on its common stock to shareholders of record on December 20, 1959. Also on December 1, L Company sold short 150 shares of Z Corporations' common stock. On December 16, 1959 (before the stock went ex-dividend), L Company closed its short sale with 150 shares purchased on that date. In determining, for purposes of section 246(c), whether L Company has held the 100 shares of stock acquired on November 26 for a period in excess of 15 days, the period of the short position (from December 2 through December 16) shall be excluded. Thus, if on or before December 26, 1959, L Company sold the 100 shares of Z Corporation stock which it purchased on November 26, 1959, it would not be entitled to a dividends-received deduction for the dividends received on such shares because it would have held such shares for 15 days or less on the date of the sale. Since L Company had held the 100 shares acquired during January 1959 for more than 15 days on December 2, 1959, and since it was under no obligation to make payments corresponding to the dividends received thereon, section 246(c) is inapplicable to the dividends received with respect to those shares.

Example (2). Assume the same facts as in example (1) above except that the additional 100 shares of Z Corporation common stock were purchased by L Company on December 10, 1959, rather than November 26, 1959. In determining, for purposes of section 246(c), whether L Company has held such shares for a period in excess of 15 days, the period from December 11, 1959, until December 16, 1959 (the date the short sale made on December 1 was closed), shall be excluded.

(e) *Effective date.*—The provisions of this section shall apply to stock acquired after December 31, 1957, or with respect to stock acquired before that date where the taxpayer has made a short sale of substantially identical stock or securities after that date. [Reg. § 1.246-3.]

☐ [T.D. 6440, 1-4-60.]

[Reg. § 1.246-4]

§ 1.246-4. Dividends from a DISC or former DISC.—The deduction provided in section 243 (relating to dividends received by corporations) is not allowable with respect to any dividend (whether in the form of a deemed or actual distribution or an amount treated as a dividend pursuant to section 995(c)) from a corporation which is a DISC or former DISC (as defined in section 992(a)(1) or (3) as the case may be) to the extent such dividend is from the corporation's accumulated DISC income (as defined in section 996(f)(1)) or previously taxed income (as defined in section 996(f)(2)) or is a deemed distribution pursuant to section 995(b)(1) in a taxable year for which the corporation qualifies (or is treated) as a DISC. To the extent that a dividend is paid out of earnings and profits which are not made up of accumulated DISC income or previously taxed income, the corporate recipient is entitled to the deduction provided in section 243 in the same manner and to the same extent as a dividend from a domestic corporation which is not a DISC or former DISC. [Reg. § 1.246-4.]

☐ [T.D. 7283, 8-2-73.]

[Reg. § 1.246-5]

§ 1.246-5. Reduction of holding periods in certain situations.—(a) *In general.*—Under section 246(c)(4)(C), the holding period of stock for purposes of the dividends received deduction is appropriately reduced for any period in which a taxpayer has diminished its risk of loss by holding one or more other positions with respect to substantially similar or related property. This section provides rules for applying section 246(c)(4)(C).

(b) *Definitions.*—(1) *Substantially similar or related property.*—The term substantially similar or related property is applied according to the facts and circumstances in each case. In general, property is substantially similar or related to stock when—

(i) The fair market values of the stock and the property primarily reflect the performance of—

(A) A single firm or enterprise;

(B) The same industry or industries; or

(C) The same economic factor or factors such as (but not limited to) interest rates, commodity prices, or foreign-currency exchange rates; and

(ii) Changes in the fair market value of the stock are reasonably expected to approximate, directly or inversely, changes in the fair market value of the property, a fraction of the fair market value of the property, or a multiple of the fair market value of the property.

(2) *Diminished risk of loss.*—A taxpayer has diminished its risk of loss on its stock by holding positions with respect to substantially

similar or related property if changes in the fair market values of the stock and the positions are reasonably expected to vary inversely.

(3) *Position.*—For purposes of this section, a position with respect to property is an interest (including a futures or forward contract or an option) in property or any contractual right to a payment, whether or not severable from stock or other property. A position does not include traditional equity rights to demand payment from the issuer, such as the rights traditionally provided by mandatorily redeemable preferred stock.

(4) *Reasonable expectations.*—For purposes of paragraphs (b)(1)(i), (b)(2), or (c)(1)(vi) of this section, reasonable expectations are the expectations of a reasonable person, based on all the facts and circumstances at the later of the time the stock is acquired or the positions are entered into. Reasonable expectations include all explicit or implicit representations made with respect to the marketing or sale of the position.

(c) *Special rules.*—(1) *Positions in more than one stock.*—(i) *In general.*—This paragraph (c)(1) provides rules for the treatment of positions that reflect the value of more than one stock. In general, positions that reflect the value of a portfolio of stocks are treated under the rules of paragraphs (c)(1)(ii) through (iv) of this section, and positions that reflect the value of more than one stock but less than a portfolio are treated under the rules of paragraph (c)(1)(v) of this section. A portfolio for this purpose is any group of stocks of 20 or more unrelated issuers. Paragraph (c)(1)(vi) of this section provides an anti-abuse rule.

(ii) *Portfolios.*—Notwithstanding paragraph (b)(1) of this section, a position reflecting the value of a portfolio of stocks is substantially similar or related to the stocks held by the taxpayer only if the position and the taxpayer's holdings substantially overlap as of the most recent testing date. A position may be substantially similar or related to a taxpayer's entire stock holdings or a portion of a taxpayer's stock holdings.

(iii) *Determining substantial overlap.*—This paragraph (c)(1)(iii) provides rules for determining whether a position and a taxpayer's stock holdings or a portion of a taxpayer's stock holdings substantially overlap. Paragraphs (c)(1)(iii)(A) through (C) of this section determine whether there is substantial overlap as of any testing date.

(A) *Step One.*—Construct a subportfolio (the Subportfolio) that consists of stock in an amount equal to the lesser of the fair market value of each stock represented in the position and the fair market value of the stock in the taxpayer's stock holdings. (The Subportfolio may contain fewer than 20 stocks.)

(B) *Step Two.*—If the fair market value of the Subportfolio is equal to or greater than 70 percent of the fair market value of the stocks represented in the position, the position and the Subportfolio substantially overlap.

(C) *Step Three.*—If the position does not substantially overlap with the Subportfolio, repeat Steps One and Two (paragraphs (c)(1)(iii)(A) and (B) of this section) reducing the size of the position. The largest percentage of the position that results in a substantial overlap is substantially similar or related to the Subportfolio determined with respect to that percentage of the position.

(iv) *Testing date.*—A testing date is any day on which the taxpayer purchases or sells any stock if the fair market value of the stock or the fair market value of substantially similar or related property is reflected in the position, any day on which the taxpayer changes the position, or any day on which the composition of the position changes.

(v) *Nonportfolio positions.*—A position that reflects the fair market value of more than one stock but not of a portfolio of stocks is treated as a separate position with respect to each of the stocks the value of which the position reflects.

(vi) *Anti-abuse rule.*—Notwithstanding paragraphs (c)(1)(i) through (v) of this section, a position that reflects the value of more than one stock is a position in substantially similar or related property to the appropriate portion of the taxpayer's stock holdings if—

(A) Changes in the value of the position or the stocks reflected in the position are reasonably expected to virtually track (directly or inversely) changes in the value of the taxpayer's stock holdings, or any portion of the taxpayer's stock holdings and other positions of the taxpayer; and

(B) The position is acquired or held as part of a plan a principal purpose of which is to obtain tax savings (including by deferring tax) the value of which is significantly in excess of the expected pre-tax economic profits from the plan.

(2) *Options.*—(i) *Options that are significantly out of the money.*—For purposes of paragraph (b)(2) of this section, an option to sell that is significantly out of the money does not diminish the taxpayer's risk of loss on its stock unless the option is held as part of a strategy to substantially offset changes in the fair market value of the stock.

(ii) *Conversion rights.*—Notwithstanding paragraphs (b)(1) and (2) of this section, a taxpayer is treated as diminishing its risk of loss by holding substantially similar or related property if it engages in the following transactions or their substantial equivalents—

(A) A short sale of common stock while holding convertible preferred stock of the same issuer and the price changes of the convertible preferred stock and the common stock are related;

(B) A short sale of a convertible debenture while holding convertible preferred stock into which the debenture is convertible or common stock; or

(C) A short sale of convertible preferred stock while holding common stock.

(3) *Stacking rule.*—If a taxpayer diminishes its risk of loss by holding a position in substantially similar or related property with respect to only a portion of the shares that the taxpayer holds in a particular stock, the holding period of those shares having the shortest holding period is reduced.

(4) *Guarantees, surety agreements, or similar arrangements.*—A taxpayer has diminished its risk of loss on stock by holding a position in substantially similar or related property if the taxpayer is the beneficiary of a guarantee, surety agreement, or similar arrangement and the guarantee, surety agreement, or similar arrangement provides for payments that will substantially offset decreases in the fair market value of the stock.

(5) *Hedges counted only once.*—A position established as a hedge of one outstanding position, transaction, or obligation of the taxpayer (other than stock) is not treated as diminishing the risk of loss with respect to any other position held by the taxpayer. In determining whether a position is established to hedge an outstanding position, transaction, or obligation of the taxpayer, substantial deference will be given to the relationships that are established in its books and records at the time the position is entered into.

(6) *Use of related persons or pass-through entities.*—Positions held by a party related to the taxpayer within the meaning of sections 267(b) or 707(b)(1) are treated as positions held by the taxpayer if the positions are held with a view to avoiding the application of this section or §1.1092(d)-2. In addition, a taxpayer is treated as diminishing its risk of loss by holding substantially similar or related property if the taxpayer holds an interest in, or is the beneficiary of, a pass-through entity, intermediary, or other arrangement with a view to avoiding the application of this section or §1.1092(d)-2.

(7) *Notional principal contracts.*—For purposes of this section, rights and obligations under notional principal contracts are considered separately even though payments with regard to those rights and obligations are generally netted for other purposes. Therefore, if a taxpayer is treated under the preceding sentence as receiving payments under a notional principal contract when the fair market value of the taxpayer's stock declines, the taxpayer has diminished its risk of loss by holding a position in substantially similar or related property regardless of the netting of the payments under the contract for any other purposes.

(d) *Examples.*—The following examples illustrate the provisions of this section:

Example 1. General application to common stock. Corporation A and Corporation B are both automobile manufacturers. The fair market values of Corporation A and Corporation B common stock primarily reflect the value of the same industry. Because Corporation A and Corporation B common stock are affected not only by the general level of growth in the industry but also by individual corporate management decisions and corporate capital structures, changes in the fair market value of Corporation A common stock are not reasonably expected to approximate changes in the fair market value of the Corporation B common stock. Under paragraph (b)(1) of this section, Corporation A common stock is not substantially similar or related to Corporation B common stock.

Example 2. Common stock value primarily reflects commodity price. Corporation C and Corporation D both hold gold as their primary asset, and historically changes in the fair market value of Corporation C common stock approximated changes in the fair market value of Corporation D common stock. Corporation M purchased Corporation C common stock and sold short Corporation D common stock. Corporation C common stock is substantially similar or related to Corporation D common stock because their fair market values primarily reflect the performance of the same economic factor, the price of gold, and changes in the fair market value of Corporation C common stock are reasonably expected to approximate changes in the fair market value of Corporation D common stock. It was reasonably expected that changes in the fair market values of the Corporation C common stock and the short position in Corporation D common stock would vary inversely. Thus, Corporation M has diminished its risk of loss on its Corporation C common stock for purposes of section 246(c)(4)(C) and this section by holding a position in substantially similar or related property.

Stock	Z's Holdings
A	$300
B	300
C	-0-
D	400
E	300
F	300
G	500
H	300
I	-0-
J	400
K	200
L	200
M	200
N	100
O	-0-
P	200
Q	100
R	200
S	100
T	100
Totals	$4,200

(ii) The position is substantially similar or related to Z's stock holdings only if they substantially overlap. To determine whether they substantially overlap, Corporation Z must construct a Subportfolio of stocks with the lesser of the value of the stock as reflected in the RFC and its holdings. The Subportfolio is given in the rightmost column above. The value of the Subportfolio is 60.74 percent of the value of the stocks represented in the position ($4100 + $6750), so the position and the Subportfolio do not substantially overlap.

Stock	Z's Holdings
A	$300
B	300
C	-0-
D	400
E	300
F	300
G	500
H	300
I	-0-
J	400
K	200
L	200
M	200
N	100
O	-0-
P	200
Q	100
R	200
S	100
T	100
Totals	$4,200

(iv) Because $3,780 is 70 percent of $5,400, the Subportfolio substantially overlaps with 80 percent of the position. Under paragraph (c)(3) of this section, Z's stocks having the shortest holding period are treated as included in the Subportfolio. A larger portion of Z's stocks may be treated as substantially similar or related property under the anti-abuse rule of paragraph (c)(1)(vi) of this section.

Example 4. Hedges counted only once. On January 1, 1996, Corporation X owns a $100 million portfolio of stocks all of which would substantially overlap with a $100 million regulated futures contract (RFC) on a commonly used index (the Index). On January 15, Corporation X enters into a $100 million short position in an RFC on the Index with a March delivery date and enters into a $75 million long position in an RFC on the Index for June delivery. Also on January 15, 1996, Corporation X indicates in its books and records that the long and short RFC positions are intended to offset one another. Under paragraph (c)(5) of this section, $75 million of the short position in the RFC is not treated as diminishing the risk of loss on the stock portfolio and instead is treated as a straddle or a hedging transaction, as appropriate, with respect to the $75 million long

Example 3. Portfolios of stocks—(i) Corporation Z holds a portfolio of stocks and acquires a short position on a publicly traded index through a regulated futures contract (RFC) that reflects the value of a portfolio of stocks as defined in paragraph (c)(1)(i) of this section. The index reflects the fair market value of stocks A through T. The values of stocks reflected in the index and the values of the same stocks in Corporation Z's holdings are as follows:

RFC	Subportfolio
$300	$300
300	300
300	-0-
500	400
500	300
500	300
600	500
300	300
300	-0-
450	400
500	200
400	200
500	200
200	100
200	-0-
200	200
300	100
100	100
100	100
200	100
$6,750	$4,100

(iii) To determine whether any portion of the position substantially overlaps with any portion of the Z's stock holdings, the values of the stocks in the RFC are reduced for purposes of the above steps. Eighty percent of the position and the corresponding subportfolio (consisting of stocks with a value of the lesser of the stocks represented in Z's holdings and in 80 percent of the RFC) substantially overlap, computed as follows:

80% of RFC	Subportfolio
$240	$240
240	240
240	-0-
400	400
400	300
400	300
480	480
240	240
240	-0-
360	360
400	200
320	200
400	200
160	100
160	-0-
160	160
240	100
80	80
80	80
160	100
$5,400	$3,780

position in the RFC, under section 1092. The remaining $25 million short position is treated as diminishing the risk of loss on the portfolio by holding a position in substantially similar or related property. The rules of paragraph (c)(1) determine how much of the portfolio is subject to this rule and the rules of paragraph (c)(3) determine which shares have their holding periods tolled.

(e) *Effective date.*—(1) *In general.*—The provisions of this section apply to dividends received on or after March 17, 1995, on stock acquired after July 18, 1984.

(2) *Special rule for dividends received on certain stock.*—Notwithstanding paragraph (e)(1) of this section, this section applies to any dividends received by a taxpayer on stock acquired after July 18, 1984, if the taxpayer has diminished its risk of loss by holding substantially similar or related property involving the following types of transactions—

(i) The short sale of common stock when holding convertible preferred stock of the same issuer and the price changes of the two stocks are related, or the short sale of a convertible debenture while holding convertible preferred stock into which the debenture is convertible (or common stock), or a short sale of convertible preferred stock while holding common stock; or

(ii) The acquisition of a short position in a regulated futures contract on a stock index, or the acquisition of an option to sell the regulated futures contract or the stock index itself, or the grant of a deep-in-the-money option to buy the regulated futures contract or the stock index while holding the stock of an investment company whose principal holdings mimic the performance of the stocks included in the stock index; or alternatively, while holding a portfolio composed of stocks that mimic the performance of the stocks included in the stock index. [Reg. § 1.246-5.]

☐ [T.D. 8590, 3-17-95.]

[Reg. § 1.247-1]

§ 1.247-1. Deduction for dividends paid on preferred stock of public utilities.—(a) *Amount of deduction.*—(1) A deduction is provided in section 247 for dividends paid during the taxable year by certain public utility corporations (see paragraph (b) of this section) on certain preferred stock (see paragraph (c) of this section). This deduction is an amount equal to the product of a specified fraction times the lesser of (i) the amount of the dividends paid during the taxable year by a public utility on its preferred stock (as defined in paragraph (c) of this section), or (ii) the taxable income of the public utility for such taxable year (computed without regard to the deduction allowed by section 247). The specified fraction for any taxable year is the fraction the numerator of which is 14 and the denominator of which is the sum of the corporation normal tax rate and the surtax rate for such taxable year specified in section 11. Since section 11 provides that for the calendar year 1954 the corporation normal tax rate is 30 percent and the surtax rate is 22 percent, the sum of the two tax rates is 52 percent and the specified fraction for the calendar year 1954 is 14/52. If, for example, section 11 should specify that the corporation's normal tax rate is 25 percent and the surtax rate is 22 percent for the calendar year, the sum of two tax rates will be 47 percent and the specified fraction for the calendar year will be 14/47. If Corporation A, a public utility which files its income tax return on the calendar year basis, pays $100,000 dividends on its preferred stock in the calendar year 1954 and if its taxable income for such year is greater than $100,000 the deduction allowable to Corporation A under section 247 for 1954 is $100,000 times 14/52, or $26,923.08. If in 1954 Corporation A's taxable income, computed without regard to the deduction provided in section 247, had been $90,000 (that is, less than the amount of the dividends which it paid on its preferred stock in that year), the deduction allowable under section 247 for 1954 would have been $90,000 times 14/52, or $24,230.77.

(2) For the purpose of determining the amount of the deduction provided in section 247(a) and in subparagraph (1) of this paragraph, the amount of dividends paid in a given taxable year shall not include any amount distributed in such year with respect to dividends unpaid and accumulated in any taxable year ending before October 1, 1942. If any distribution is made in the current taxable year with respect to dividends unpaid and accumulated for a prior taxable year, such distribution will be deemed to have been made with respect to the earliest year or years for which there are dividends unpaid and accumulated. Thus, if a public utility makes a distribution with respect to a prior taxable year, it shall be considered that such distribution was made with respect to the earliest year or years for which there are dividends unpaid and accumulated, whether or not the public utility states that the distribution was made with respect to such year or years and even though the public utility states that the distribution was made with respect to a later year. Even though it has dividends unpaid and accumulated with respect to a taxable year ending before October 1, 1942, a public utility may, however, include the dividends paid with respect to the current taxable year in computing the deduction under section 247. If there are no dividends unpaid and accumulated with respect to a taxable year ending before October 1, 1942, a public utility may include the dividends paid with respect to a prior taxable year which ended after October 1, 1942, in computing the deduction under section 247; such public utility in addition may include the dividends paid with respect to the current taxable year in computing the deduction under section 247. However, if local law or its own charter requires a public utility to pay all unpaid and accumulated dividends before any dividends can be paid with respect to the current taxable year, such public utility may not include any distribution in the current year in computing the deduction under section 247 to the extent that there are dividends unpaid and accumulated with respect to taxable years ending before October 1, 1942.

(3) If a corporation which is engaged in one or more of the four types of business activities (called utility activities in this section) enumerated in section 247(b)(1) (the furnishing of telephone service or the sale of electrical energy, gas, or water) is also engaged in some other business that does not fall within any of the enumerated

categories, the deduction under section 247 is allowable only for such portion of the amount computed under section 247(a) as is allocable to the income from utility activities. For this purpose, the allocation may be made on the basis of the ratio which the total income from the utility activities bears to total income from all sources (total income being considered either gross income or gross receipts, whichever method results in the higher deduction). However, if such an allocation reaches an inequitable result and the books of the corporation are so kept that the taxable income attributable to the utility activities can be readily determined, particularly where the books of the corporation are required by governmental bodies to be so kept for rate making or other purposes, the allocation may be made upon the basis of taxable income. No such apportionment will be required if the income from sources other than utility activities is less than 20 percent of the total income of the corporation, irrespective of the method used in determining such total income.

(b) *Public utility.*—As used in section 247 and this section, public utility means a corporation engaged in the furnishing of telephone service, or in the sale of electric energy, gas, or water if the rates charged by such corporation for such furnishing or sale, as the case may be, have been established or approved by a State or political subdivision thereof or by an agency or instrumentality of the United States or by a public utility or public service commission or other similar body of the District of Columbia or of any State or political subdivision thereof. If a schedule of rates has been filed with any of the above bodies having the power to disapprove such rates, then such rates shall be considered as established or approved rates even though such body has taken no action on the filed schedule. Rates fixed by contract between the corporation and the purchaser, except where the purchaser is the United States, a State, the District of Columbia or an agency or political subdivision of the United States, a State, or the District of Columbia, shall not be considered as established or approved rates in those cases where they are not subject to direct control, or where no maximum rate for such contract rates has been established by the United States, a State, the District of Columbia, or by an agency or political subdivision thereof. The deduction provided in section 247 will not be denied solely because part of the gross income of the corporation consists of revenue derived from such furnishing or sale at rates which are not so regulated, provided the corporation establishes to the satisfaction of the Commissioner (1) that the revenue from regulated rates and the revenue from unregulated rates are derived from the operation of a single interconnected and coordinated system within a single area or region in one or more States, or from the operation of more than one such system and (2) that the regulation to which it is subject in part of its operating territory in one such system is effective to control rates within the unregulated territory of the same system so that the rates within the unregulated territory have been and are substantially as favorable to users and consumers as are the rates within the regulated territory.

(c) *Preferred stock.*—(1) For the purposes of section 247 and this section, preferred stock means stock (i) which was issued before October 1, 1942, (ii) the dividends in respect of which (during the whole of the taxable year, or the part of the taxable year after the actual date of the issue of such stock) were cumulative, nonparticipating as to current distributions, and payable in preference to the payment of dividends on other stock, and (iii) the rate of return on which is fixed and cannot be changed by a vote of the board of directors or by some similar method. However, if there are several classes of preferred stock, all of which meet the above requirements, the deduction provided in section 247 shall not be denied in the case of a given class of preferred stock merely because there is another class of preferred stock whose dividends are to be paid before those of the given class of stock. Likewise, it is immaterial for the purposes of section 247 and this section whether the stock be voting or nonvoting stock.

(2) Preferred stock issued on or after October 1, 1942, under certain circumstances will be considered as having been issued before October 1, 1942, for purposes of the deduction provided in section 247. If the new stock is issued on or after October 1, 1942, to refund or replace bonds or debentures which were issued before October 1, 1942, or to refund or replace other stock which was preferred stock within the meaning of section 247(b)(2) (or the corresponding provision of the Internal Revenue Code of 1939), such new stock shall be considered as having been issued before October 1, 1942. If preferred stock is issued to refund or replace stock which was preferred stock within the meaning of section 247(b)(2) (or the corresponding provision of the Internal Revenue Code of 1939), it shall be immaterial whether the preferred stock so refunded or replaced was issued before, on, or after October 1, 1942. If stock issued on or after October 1, 1942, to refund or replace stock which was issued before October 1, 1942, and which was preferred stock within the meaning of section 247(b)(2) (or the corresponding provision of the Internal Revenue Code of 1939), is not itself preferred stock within the meaning of section 247(b)(2) (or the corresponding provision of the Inter-

nal Revenue Code of 1939), no stock issued to refund or replace such stock can be considered preferred stock for purposes of the deduction provided in section 247.

(3) In the case of any preferred stock issued on or after October 1, 1942, to refund or replace bonds or debentures issued before October 1, 1942, or to refund or replace other stock which was preferred stock within the meaning of section 247(b)(2) (or the corresponding provision of the Internal Revenue Code of 1939), only that portion of the stock issued on or after October 1, 1942, will be considered as having been issued before October 1, 1942, the par or stated value of which does not exceed the par, stated, or face value of such bonds, debentures, or other preferred stock which the new stock was issued to refund or replace. In such case no shares of the new stock issued on or after October 1, 1942, shall be earmarked in determining the deduction allowable under section 247, but the appropriate allocable portion of the total amount of dividends paid on such stock will be considered as having been paid on stock which was issued before October 1, 1942.

(4) The provisions of section 247(b)(2) may be illustrated by the following example:

Example. A public utility has outstanding 1,000 bonds which were issued before October 1, 1942, and each of which has a face value of $100. On or after October 1, 1942, each of such bonds is retired in exchange for 1 1/10 shares of preferred stock issued on or after October 1, 1942, and having a par value of $100 per share. Only 10/11 of the dividends paid on the preferred stock thus issued in exchange for the bonds will be considered as having been paid on stock which was issued before October 1, 1942. Likewise, if preferred stock which is issued on or after October 1, 1942, has no par value but a stated value of $50 per share and such stock is issued in a ratio of three shares to one share to refund or replace preferred stock having a par value of $100 per share, only two-thirds of the dividends paid on the new shares of stock will be considered as having been paid on stock which was issued before October 1, 1942.

(5) Whether or not preferred stock issued on or after October 1, 1942, was issued to refund or replace bonds or debentures issued before October 1, 1942, or to refund or replace other preferred stock, is in each case a question of fact. Among the factors to be considered is whether such stock is new in an economic sense to the corporation or whether it was issued merely to take the place, directly or indirectly, of bonds, debentures, or other preferred stock of such corporation. It is not necessary that the new preferred stock be issued in exchange for such bonds, debentures, or other preferred stock. The mere fact that the bonds, debentures, or other preferred stock remain in existence for a short period of time after the issuance of the new stock (or were retired before the issuance of the new stock) does not necessarily mean that such new stock was not issued to refund or replace such bonds, debentures, or other preferred stock. It is necessary to consider the entire transaction, including the issuance of the new preferred stock, the date of such issuance, the retirement of the old bonds, debentures, or preferred stock, and the date of such retirement, in order to determine whether such new stock really was issued to take the place of bonds, debentures, or other preferred stock of the corporation or whether it represents something essentially new in an economic sense in the corporation's financial structure. If, for example, a public utility, which has outstanding bonds issued before October 1, 1942, issues new preferred stock on October 1, 1954, in order to secure funds with which to retire such bonds and with the money paid in for such stock retires the bonds on November 1, 1954, such stock may be considered as having been issued to refund or replace bonds issued before October 1, 1942. Whether the money used to retire the bonds can be traced back and identified as the money paid in for the stock will have evidentiary value, but will not be conclusive, in determining whether the stock was issued to refund or replace the bonds. Similarly, whether the amount of money used to retire the bonds was smaller than, equal to, or greater than that paid in for the stock, or whether the entire issue of bonds is retired, will be important, but not decisive, in making such determination.

(6) Preferred stock issued on or after October 1, 1942, by a corporation to refund or replace bonds or debentures of a second corporation which were issued before October 1, 1942, or to refund or replace other preferred stock of such second corporation, may be considered as having been issued before October 1, 1942, if such new stock was issued (i) in a transaction which is a reorganization within the meaning of section 368(a) or the corresponding provisions of the Internal Revenue Code of 1939; or (ii) in a transaction to which section 371 (relating to insolvency reorganizations), or the corresponding provisions of the Internal Revenue Code of 1939, is applicable; or (iii) in a transaction which is subject to the provisions of part VI of subchapter O, chapter 1 of the Code, (relating to exchanges and distributions in obedience to orders of the Securities and Exchange Commission) or to the corresponding provisions of the Internal Revenue Code of 1939. Whether the stock actually was issued to refund or replace bonds or debentures of the second corporation issued before October 1, 1942, or to refund or replace preferred stock of such

second corporation, shall be determined under the same principles as if only one corporation were involved. A corporation may issue stock to refund or replace its own bonds, debentures, or other preferred stock in a transaction which is a reorganization within the meaning of section 368(a) or the corresponding provisions of the Internal Revenue Code of 1939, in a transaction to which section 371 or the corresponding provisions of the Internal Revenue Code of 1939 is applicable, or in a transaction which is subject to the provisions of part VI of subchapter O, chapter 1 of the Code or to the corresponding provisions of the Internal Revenue Code of 1939. The provisions of this paragraph, in addition, are applicable in case a corporation issues stock on or after October 1, 1942, to refund or replace its own bonds, debentures, or other preferred stock even though the issuance of such stock may not fall within one of the categories enumerated above.

(7) Even though stock issued on or after October 1, 1942, is considered as having been issued before October 1, 1942, by reason of having been issued to refund or replace bonds or debentures issued before October 1, 1942, or to refund or replace other preferred stock, such stock will not be deemed to be preferred stock within the meaning of section 247(b)(2), and no deduction will be allowable in respect to dividends paid on such stock, unless the stock fulfills all the other requirements of a preferred stock set forth in section 247(b)(2) and in this paragraph. [Reg. §1.247-1.]

☐ [*T.D.* 6183, 6-13-56.]

[Reg. §1.248-1]

§1.248-1. Election to amortize organizational expenditures.—
(a) *In general.*—Under section 248(a), a corporation may elect to amortize organizational expenditures as defined in section 248(b) and §1.248-1(b). In the taxable year in which a corporation begins business, an electing corporation may deduct an amount equal to the lesser of the amount of the organizational expenditures of the corporation, or $5,000 (reduced (but not below zero) by the amount by which the organizational expenditures exceed $50,000). The remainder of the organizational expenditures is deducted ratably over the 180-month period beginning with the month in which the corporation begins business. All organizational expenditures of the corporation are considered in determining whether the organizational expenditures exceed $50,000, including expenditures incurred on or before October 22, 2004.

(b) *Organizational expenditures defined.*—(1) Section 248(b) defines the term "organization expenditures." Such expenditures for purposes of section 248 and this section, are those expenditures which are directly incident to the creation of the corporation. An expenditure, in order to qualify as an organizational expenditure, must be (i) incident to the creation of the corporation, (ii) chargeable to the capital account of the corporation, and (iii) of a character which, if expended incident to the creation of a corporation having a limited life, would be amortizable over such life. An expenditure which fails to meet each of these three tests may not be considered an organizational expenditure for purposes of section 248 and this section.

(2) The following are examples of organizational expenditures within the meaning of section 248 and this section: legal services incident to the organization of the corporation, such as drafting the corporate charter, by-laws, minutes of organizational meetings, terms of original stock certificates, and the like; necessary accounting services; expenses of temporary directors and of organizational meetings of directors or stockholders; and fees paid to State of incorporation.

(3) The following expenditures are not organizational expenditures within the meaning of section 248 and this section:

(i) Expenditures connected with issuing or selling shares of stock or other securities, such as commissions, professional fees, and printing costs. This is so even where the particular issue of stock to which the expenditures relate is for a fixed term of years;

(ii) Expenditures connected with the transfer of assets to a corporation.

(4) Expenditures connected with the reorganization of a corporation, unless directly incident to the creation of a corporation, are not organizational expenditures within the meaning of section 248 and this section.

(c) *Time and manner of making election.*—A corporation is deemed to have made an election under section 248(a) to amortize organizational expenditures as defined in section 248(b) and §1.248-1(b) for the taxable year in which the corporation begins business. A corporation may choose to forgo the deemed election by affirmatively electing to capitalize its organizational expenditures on a timely filed Federal income tax return (including extensions) for the taxable year in which the corporation begins business. The election either to amortize organizational expenditures under section 248(a) or to capitalize organizational expenditures is irrevocable and applies to all organizational expenditures of the corporation. A change in the characterization of an item as an organizational expenditure is a change in method of accounting to which sections 446 and 481(a) apply if the corporation treated the item consistently for two or more taxable years. A change in the determination of the taxable year in which the corporation begins business also is treated as a change in method of accounting if the corporation amortized organizational expenditures for two or more taxable years.

(d) *Determination of when corporation begins business.*—The deduction allowed under section 248 must be spread over a period beginning with the month in which the corporation begins business. The determination of the date the corporation begins business presents a question of fact which must be determined in each case in light of all the circumstances of the particular case. The words "begins business," however, do not have the same meaning as "in existence." Ordinarily, a corporation begins business when it starts the business operations for which it was organized; a corporation comes into existence on the date of its incorporation. Mere organizational activities, such as the obtaining of the corporate charter, are not alone sufficient to show the beginning of business. If the activities of the corporation have advanced to the extent necessary to establish the nature of its business operations, however, it will be deemed to have begun business. For example, the acquisition of operating assets which are necessary to the type of business contemplated may constitute the beginning of business.

(e) *Examples.*—The following examples illustrate the application of this section:

Example 1. Expenditures of $5,000 or less. Corporation X, a calendar year taxpayer, incurs $3,000 of organizational expenditures after October 22, 2004, and begins business on July 1, 2011. Under paragraph (c) of this section, Corporation X is deemed to have elected to amortize organizational expenditures under section 248(a) in 2011. Therefore, Corporation X may deduct the entire amount of the organizational expenditures in 2011, the taxable year in which Corporation X begins business.

Example 2. Expenditures of more than $5,000 but less than or equal to $50,000. The facts are the same as in *Example 1* except that Corporation X incurs organizational expenditures of $41,000. Under paragraph (c) of this section, Corporation X is deemed to have elected to amortize organizational expenditures under section 248(a) in 2011. Therefore, Corporation X may deduct $5,000 and the portion of the remaining $36,000 that is allocable to July through December of 2011 ($36,000/180 × 6 = $1,200) in 2011, the taxable year in which Corporation X begins business. Corporation X may amortize the remaining $34,800 ($36,000 - $1,200 = $34,800) ratably over the remaining 174 months.

Example 3. Subsequent change in the characterization of an item. The facts are the same as in *Example 2* except that Corporation X determines in 2013 that Corporation X incurred $10,000 for an additional organizational expenditure erroneously deducted in 2011 under section 162 as a business expense. Under paragraph (c) of this section, Corporation X is deemed to have elected to amortize organizational expenditures under section 248(a) in 2011, including the additional $10,000 of organizational expenditures. Corporation X is using an impermissible method of accounting for the additional $10,000 of organizational expenditures and must change its method under §1.446-1(e) and the applicable general administrative procedures in effect in 2013.

Example 4. Subsequent redetermination of year in which business begins. The facts are the same as in *Example 2* except that, in 2012, Corporation X deducted the organizational expenditures allocable to January through December of 2012 ($36,000/180 × 12 = $2,400). In addition, in 2013 it is determined that Corporation X actually began business in 2012. Under paragraph (c) of this section, Corporation X is deemed to have elected to amortize organizational expenditures under section 248(a) in 2012. Corporation X impermissibly deducted organizational expenditures in 2011, and incorrectly determined the amount of organizational expenditures deducted in 2012. Therefore, Corporation X is using an impermissible method of accounting for the organizational expenditures and must change its method under §1.446-1(e) and the applicable general administrative procedures in effect in 2013.

Example 5. Expenditures of more than $50,000 but less than or equal to $55,000. The facts are the same as in *Example 1* except that Corporation X incurs organizational expenditures of $54,500. Under paragraph (c) of this section, Corporation X is deemed to have elected to amortize organizational expenditures under section 248(a) in 2011. Therefore, Corporation X may deduct $500 ($5,000 - $4,500) and the portion of the remaining $54,000 that is allocable to July through December of 2011 ($54,000/180 × 6 = $1,800) in 2011, the taxable year in which Corporation X begins business. Corporation X may amortize the remaining $52,200 ($54,000 - $1,800 = $52,200) ratably over the remaining 174 months.

Example 6. Expenditures of more than $55,000. The facts are the same as in *Example 1* except that Corporation X incurs organizational expenditures of $450,000. Under paragraph (c) of this section, Corpo-

ration X is deemed to have elected to amortize organizational expenditures under section 248(a) in 2011. Therefore, Corporation X may deduct the amounts allocable to July through December of 2011 ($450,000/180 × 6 = $15,000) in 2011, the taxable year in which Corporation X begins business. Corporation X may amortize the remaining $435,000 ($450,000 - $15,000 = $435,000) ratably over the remaining 174 months.

(f) *Effective/applicability date.*—This section applies to organizational expenditures paid or incurred after August 16, 2011. However, taxpayers may apply all the provisions of this section to organizational expenditures paid or incurred after October 22, 2004, provided that the period of limitations on assessment of tax for the year the election under paragraph (c) of this section is deemed made has not expired. For organizational expenditures paid or incurred on or before September 8, 2008, taxpayers may instead apply §1.248-1, as in effect prior to that date (§1.248-1 as contained in 26 CFR part 1 edition revised as of April 1, 2008). [Reg. §1.248-1.]

☐ [T.D. 6183, 6-13-56. Amended by T.D. 9411, 7-7-2008 and T.D. 9542, 8-16-2011.]

[Reg. §1.249-1]

§1.249-1. Limitation on deduction of bond premium on repurchase.—(a) *Limitation.*—(1) *General rule.*—No deduction is allowed to the issuing corporation for any "repurchase premium" paid or incurred to repurchase a convertible obligation to the extent the repurchase premium exceeds a "normal call premium."

(2) *Exception.*—Under paragraph (e) of this section, the preceding sentence shall not apply to the extent the corporation demonstrates that such excess is attributable to the cost of borrowing and not to the conversion feature.

(b) *Obligations.*—(1) *Definition.*—For purposes of this section, the term "obligation" means any bond, debenture, note, or certificate or other evidence of indebtedness.

(2) *Convertible obligation.*—Section 249 applies to an obligation which is convertible into the stock of the issuing corporation or a corporation which, at the time the obligation is issued or repurchased, is in control of or controlled by the issuing corporation. For purposes of this subparagraph, the term "control" has the meaning assigned to such term by section 368(c).

(3) *Comparable nonconvertible obligation.*—A nonconvertible obligation is comparable to a convertible obligation if both obligations are of the same grade and classification, with the same issue and maturity dates, and bearing the same rate of interest. The term "comparable nonconvertible obligation" does not include any obligation which is convertible into property.

(c) *Repurchase premium.*—For purposes of this section, the term *repurchase premium* means the excess of the repurchase price paid or incurred to repurchase the obligation over its adjusted issue price (within the meaning of §1.1275-1(b)) as of the repurchase date. For the general rules applicable to the deductibility of repurchase premium, see §1.163-7(c). This paragraph (c) applies to convertible obligations repurchased on or after March 2, 1998.

(d) *Normal call premium.*—(1) *In general.*—Except as provided in subparagraph (2) of this paragraph, for purposes of this section, a "normal call premium" on a convertible obligation is an amount equal to a normal call premium on a nonconvertible obligation which is comparable to the convertible obligation. A normal call premium on a comparable nonconvertible obligation is a call premium specified in dollars under the terms of such obligation. Thus, if such a specified call premium is constant over the entire term of the obligation, the normal call premium is the amount specified. If, however, the specified call premium varies during the period the comparable nonconvertible obligation is callable or if such obligation is not callable over its entire term, the normal call premium is the amount specified for the period during the term of such comparable nonconvertible obligation which corresponds to the period during which the convertible obligation was repurchased.

(2) *One-year's interest rule.*—For a convertible obligation repurchased on or after March 2, 1998, a call premium specified in dollars under the terms of the obligation is considered to be a normal call premium on a nonconvertible obligation if the call premium applicable when the obligation is repurchased does not exceed an amount equal to the interest (including original issue discount) that otherwise would be deductible for the taxable year of repurchase (determined as if the obligation were not repurchased). The provisions of this subparagraph shall not apply if the amount of interest payable for the corporation's taxable year is subject under the terms of the obligation to any contingency other than repurchase prior to the close of such taxable year.

(e) *Exception.*—(1) *In general.*—If a repurchase premium exceeds a normal call premium, the general rule of paragraph (a)(1) of this section does not apply to the extent that the corporation demonstrates to the satisfaction of the Commissioner or his delegate that such repurchase premium is attributable to the cost of borrowing and is not attributable to the conversion feature. For purposes of this paragraph, if a normal call premium cannot be established under paragraph (d) of this section, the amount thereof shall be considered to be zero.

(2) *Determination of the portion of a repurchase premium attributable to the cost of borrowing and not attributable to the conversion feature.*— (i) For purposes of subparagraph (1) of this paragraph, the portion of a repurchase premium which is attributable to the cost of borrowing and which is not attributable to the conversion feature is the amount by which the selling price of the convertible obligation increased between the dates it was issued and repurchased by reason of a decline in yields on comparable nonconvertible obligations traded on an established securities market or, if such comparable traded obligations do not exist, by reason of a decline in yields generally on nonconvertible obligations which are as nearly comparable as possible.

(ii) In determining the amount under paragraph (e)(2)(i) of this section, appropriate consideration shall be given to all factors affecting the selling price or yields of comparable nonconvertible obligations. Such factors include general changes in prevailing yields of comparable obligations between the dates the convertible obligation was issued and repurchased and the amount (if any) by which the selling price of the nonconvertible obligation was affected by reason of any change in the issuing corporation's credit quality or the credit quality of the obligation during such period (determined on the basis of widely published financial information or on the basis of other relevant facts and circumstances which reflect the relative credit quality of the corporation or the comparable obligation).

(iii) The relationship between selling price and yields in subdivision (i) of this subparagraph shall ordinarily be determined by means of standard bond tables.

(f) *Effective/applicability dates.*—(1) *In general.*—Under section 414(c) of the Tax Reform Act of 1969, the provisions of section 249 and this section shall apply to any repurchase of a convertible obligation occurring after April 22, 1969, other than a convertible obligation repurchased pursuant to a binding obligation incurred on or before April 22, 1969, to repurchase such convertible obligation at a specified call premium. A binding obligation on or before such date may arise if, for example, the issuer irrevocably obligates itself, on or before such date, to repurchase the convertible obligation at a specified price after such date, or if, for example, the issuer, without regard to the terms of the convertible obligation, negotiates a contract which, on or before such date, irrevocably obligates the issuer to repurchase the convertible obligation at a specified price after such date. A binding obligation on or before such date does not include a privilege in the convertible obligation permitting the issuer to call such convertible obligation after such date, which privilege was not exercised on or before such date.

(2) *Effect on transactions not subject to this section.*—No inferences shall be drawn from the provisions of section 249 and this section as to the proper treatment of transactions not subject to such provisions because of the effective date limitations thereof. For provisions relating to repurchases of convertible bonds or other evidences of indebtedness to which section 249 and this section do not apply, see §§ 1.163-3(c) and 1.163-4(c).

(3) *Portion of repurchase premium attributable to cost of borrowing.* Paragraph (e)(2)(ii) of this section applies to any repurchase of a convertible obligation occurring on or after July 6, 2011.

(g) *Example.*—The provisions of this section may be illustrated by the following example:

Example. On May 15, 1968, Corporation A issues a callable 20-year convertible bond at face for $1,000 bearing interest at 10 percent per annum. The bond is convertible at any time into 2 shares of the common stock of Corporation A. Under the terms of the bond, the applicable call price prior to May 15, 1975, is $1,100. On June 1, 1974, Corporation A calls the bond for $1,100. Since the repurchase premium, $100 (*i.e.,* $1,100 minus $1,000), was specified in dollars in the obligation and does not exceed one year's interest at the rate fixed in the obligation, the $100 is considered under paragraph (d)(2) of this section to be a normal call premium on a comparable nonconvertible obligation. Accordingly, A may deduct the $100 under § 1.163-3(c). [Reg. § 1.249-1.]

□ [T.D. 7259, 2-9-73. *Amended by* T.D. 8746, 12-30-97; T.D. 9533, 7-1-2011 *and* T.D. 9637, 9-5-2013.]

(1) In general.
(2) Determination of business operations that benefit from the service.
(i) In general.
(ii) Advertising services.
(iii) Electronically supplied services.
(3) Identification of business recipient's operations.
(i) In general.
(ii) Advertising services and electronically supplied services.
(iii) No office or fixed place of business.
(4) Substantiation of the location of a business recipient's operations outside the United States.
(5) Examples.
(f) Proximate services.
(g) Property services.
(1) In general.
(2) Exception for service provided with respect to property temporarily in the United States.
(h) Transportation services.
§1.250(b)-6 Related party transactions.
(a) Scope.
(b) Definitions.
(1) Related party sale.
(2) Related party service.
(3) Unrelated party transaction.
(c) Related party sales.
(1) In general.
(i) Sale of property in an unrelated party transaction.
(ii) Use of property in an unrelated party transaction.
(2) Treatment of foreign related party as seller or renderer.
(3) Transactions between related parties.
(4) Example.
(d) Related party services.
(1) In general.
(2) Substantially similar services.
(3) Special rules.
(i) Rules for determining the location of and price paid by recipients of a service provided by a related party.
(ii) Rules for allocating the benefits provided by and price paid to the renderer of a related party service.
(4) Examples.
[Reg. §1.250-0.]
☐ [*T.D.* 9901, 7-9-2020. (*corrected* 9-28-2020).]

[Reg. §1.250-1]

§1.250-1. Introduction.—(a) *Overview.*—Sections 1.250(a)-1 and 1.250(b)-1 through 1.250(b)-6 provide rules to determine a domestic corporation's section 250 deduction. Section 1.250(a)-1 provides rules to determine the amount of a domestic corporation's deduction for foreign-derived intangible income and global intangible low-taxed income. Section 1.250(b)-1 provides general rules and definitions regarding the computation of foreign-derived intangible income. Section 1.250(b)-2 provides rules for determining a domestic corporation's qualified business asset investment. Section 1.250(b)-3 provides general rules and definitions regarding the determination of gross foreign-derived deduction eligible income. Section 1.250(b)-4 provides rules regarding the determination of gross foreign-derived deduction eligible income from the sale of property. Section 1.250(b)-5 provides rules regarding the determination of gross foreign-derived deduction eligible income from the provision of a service. Section 1.250(b)-6 provides rules regarding the sale of property or provision of a service to a related party.

(b) *Applicability dates.*—Except as otherwise provided in this paragraph (b), §§1.250(a)-1 and §§1.250(b)-1 through 1.250(b)-6 apply to taxable years beginning on or after January 1, 2021. Section 1.250(b)-2(h) applies to taxable years ending on or after March 4, 2019. However, taxpayers may choose to apply §§1.250(a)-1 and 1.250(b)-1 through 1.250(b)-6 for taxable years beginning on or after January 1, 2018, and before January 1, 2021, provided they apply the regulations in their entirety (other than §1.250(b)-3(f) and the applicable provisions in §1.250(b)-4(d)(3) or §1.250(b)-5(e)(4)), but once applied, taxpayers must apply the final regulations for all subsequent taxable years beginning before January 1, 2021. The last sentence in §1.250(b)-2(e)(2) applies to taxable years beginning after December 31, 2017. [Reg. §1.250-1.]

☐ [*T.D.* 9901, 7-9-2020 (*corrected* 10-27-2020). *Amended by T.D.* 9956, 9-21-2021.]

[Reg. §1.250(a)-1]

§1.250(a)-1. Deduction for foreign-derived intangible income (FDII) and global intangible low-taxed income (GILTI).—

(a) *Scope.*—This section provides rules for determining the amount of a domestic corporation's deduction for foreign-derived intangible income (FDII) and global intangible low-taxed income (GILTI). Paragraph (b) of this section provides general rules for determining the amount of the deduction. Paragraph (c) of this section provides definitions relevant for determining the amount of the deduction. Paragraph (d) of this section provides reporting requirements for a domestic corporation claiming the deduction. Paragraph (e) of this section provides a rule for determining the amount of the deduction of a member of a consolidated group. Paragraph (f) of this section provides examples illustrating the application of this section.

(b) *Allowance of deduction.*—(1) *In general.*—A domestic corporation is allowed a deduction for any taxable year equal to the sum of—
(i) 37.5 percent of its foreign-derived intangible income for the year; and
(ii) 50 percent of—
(A) Its global intangible low-taxed income for the year; and
(B) The amount treated as a dividend received by the corporation under section 78 which is attributable to its GILTI for the year.

(2) *Taxable income limitation.*—In the case of a domestic corporation with a section 250(a)(2) amount for a taxable year, for purposes of applying paragraph (b)(1) of this section for the year—
(i) The corporation's FDII for the year (if any) is reduced (but not below zero) by an amount that bears the same ratio to the corporation's section 250(a)(2) amount that the corporation's FDII for the year bears to the sum of the corporation's FDII and GILTI for the year; and
(ii) The corporation's GILTI for the year (if any) is reduced (but not below zero) by the excess of the corporation's section 250(a)(2) amount over the amount of the reduction described in paragraph (b)(2)(i) of this section.

(3) *Reduction in deduction for taxable years after 2025.*—For any taxable year of a domestic corporation beginning after December 31, 2025, paragraph (b)(1) of this section applies by substituting—
(i) 21.875 percent for 37.5 percent in paragraph (b)(1)(i) of this section; and
(ii) 37.5 percent for 50 percent in paragraph (b)(1)(ii) of this section.

(4) *Treatment under section 4940.*—For purposes of section 4940(c)(3)(A), a deduction under section 250(a) is not treated as an ordinary and necessary expense paid or incurred for the production or collection of gross investment income.

(c) *Definitions.*—The following definitions apply for purposes of this section.

(1) *Domestic corporation.*—The term *domestic corporation* has the meaning set forth in section 7701(a), but does not include a regulated investment company (as defined in section 851), a real estate investment trust (as defined in section 856), or an S corporation (as defined in section 1361).

(2) *Foreign-derived intangible income (FDII).*—The term *foreign-derived intangible income* or *FDII* has the meaning set forth in §1.250(b)-1(b).

(3) *Global intangible low-taxed income (GILTI).*—The term *global intangible low-taxed income* or *GILTI* means, with respect to a domestic corporation for a taxable year, the corporation's GILTI inclusion amount under §1.951A-1(c) for the taxable year.

(4) *Section 250(a)(2) amount.*—The term *section 250(a)(2) amount* means, with respect to a domestic corporation for a taxable year, the excess (if any) of the sum of the corporation's FDII and GILTI (determined without regard to section 250(a)(2) and paragraph (b)(2) of this section), over the corporation's taxable income. For a corporation that is subject to the unrelated business income tax under section 511, taxable income is determined only by reference to that corporation's unrelated business taxable income defined under section 512.

(5) *Taxable income.*—(i) *In general.*—The term *taxable income* has the meaning set forth in section 63(a) determined without regard to the deduction allowed under section 250 and this section.
(ii) [Reserved]

(d) *Reporting requirement.*—Each domestic corporation (or individual making an election under section 962) that claims a deduction under section 250 for a taxable year must make an annual return on Form 8993, "Section 250 Deduction for Foreign-Derived Intangible Income (FDII) and Global Intangible Low-Taxed Income (GILTI)" (or any successor form) for such year, setting forth the information, in such form and manner, as Form 8993 (or any successor form) or its instructions prescribe. Returns on Form 8993 (or any successor form) for a taxable year must be filed with the domestic corporation's (or in the case of a section 962 election, the individual's) income tax return on or before the due date (taking into account extensions) for filing the corporation's (or in the case of a section 962 election, the individual's) income tax return.

(e) *Determination of deduction for consolidated groups.*—A member of a consolidated group (as defined in §1.1502-1(h)) determines its deduction under section 250(a) and this section under the rules provided in §1.1502-50(b).

(f) *Example: Application of the taxable income limitation.*—The following example illustrates the application of this section. For purposes of the example, it is assumed that DC is a domestic corporation that is not a member of a consolidated group and the taxable year of DC begins after 2017 and before 2026.

(1) *Facts.* For the taxable year, without regard to section 250(a)(2) and paragraph (b)(2) of this section, DC has FDII of $100x and GILTI of $300x. DC's taxable income (without regard to section 250(a) and this section) is $300x.

(2) *Analysis.* DC has a section 250(a)(2) amount of $100x, which is equal to the excess of the sum of DC's FDII and GILTI of $400x ($100x + $300x) over its taxable income of $300x. As a result, DC's FDII and GILTI are reduced, in the aggregate, by $100x under section 250(a)(2) and paragraph (b)(2) of this section for purposes of calculating DC's deduction allowed under section 250(a)(1) and paragraph (b)(1) of this section. DC's FDII is reduced by $25x, the amount that bears the same ratio to the section 250(a)(2) amount ($100x) as DC's FDII ($100x) bears to the sum of DC's FDII and GILTI ($400x). DC's GILTI is reduced by $75x, which is the remainder of the section 250(a)(2) amount ($100x - $25x). Therefore, for purposes of calculating its deduction under section 250(a)(1) and paragraph (b)(1) of this section, DC's FDII is $75x ($100x - $25x) and its GILTI is $225x ($300x - $75x). Accordingly, DC is allowed a deduction for the taxable year under section 250(a)(1) and paragraph (b)(1) of this section of $140.63x ($75x × 0.375 + $225x × 0.50). [Reg. §1.250(a)-1.]

☐ [T.D. 9901, 7-9-2020.]

[Reg. §1.250(b)-1]

§1.250(b)-1. Computation of foreign-derived intangible income (FDII).—(a) *Scope.*—This section provides rules for computing FDII. Paragraph (b) of this section defines FDII. Paragraph (c) of this section provides definitions that are relevant for computing FDII. Paragraph (d) of this section provides rules for computing gross income and allocating and apportioning deductions for purposes of computing deduction eligible income (DEI) and foreign-derived deduction eligible income (FDDEI). Paragraph (e) of this section provides rules for computing the DEI and FDDEI of a domestic corporate partner. Paragraph (f) of this section provides a rule for computing the FDII of a member of a consolidated group. Paragraph (g) of this section provides a rule for computing the FDII of a tax-exempt corporation.

(b) *Definition of FDII.*—Subject to the provisions of this section, the term *FDII* means, with respect to a domestic corporation for a taxable year, the corporation's deemed intangible income for the year multiplied by the corporation's foreign-derived ratio for the year.

(c) *Definitions.*—This paragraph (c) provides definitions that apply for purposes of this section and §§1.250(b)-2 through 1.250(b)-6.

(1) *Controlled foreign corporation.*—The term *controlled foreign corporation* has the meaning set forth in section 957(a) and §1.957-1(a).

(2) *Deduction eligible income.*—The term *deduction eligible income* or *DEI* means, with respect to a domestic corporation for a taxable year, the excess (if any) of the corporation's gross DEI for the year over the deductions properly allocable to gross DEI for the year, as determined under paragraph (d)(2) of this section.

(3) *Deemed intangible income.*—The term *deemed intangible income* means, with respect to a domestic corporation for a taxable year, the excess (if any) of the corporation's DEI for the year over the corporation's deemed tangible income return for the year.

(4) *Deemed tangible income return.*—The term *deemed tangible income return* means, with respect to a domestic corporation and a taxable year, 10 percent of the corporation's qualified business asset investment for the year.

(5) *Dividend.*—The term *dividend* has the meaning set forth in section 316, and includes any amount treated as a dividend under any other provision of subtitle A of the Internal Revenue Code or the regulations in this part (for example, under section 78, 356(a)(2), 367(b), or 1248).

(6) *Domestic corporation.*—The term *domestic corporation* has the meaning set forth in §1.250(a)-1(c)(1).

(7) *Domestic oil and gas extraction income.*—The term *domestic oil and gas extraction income* means income described in section 907(c)(1), substituting "within the United States" for "without the United States." A taxpayer must use a consistent method to determine the amount of its domestic oil and gas extraction income ("DOGEI") and its foreign oil and gas extraction income ("FOGEI") from the sale of oil or gas that has been transported or processed. For example, a taxpayer must use a consistent method to determine the amount of FOGEI from the sale of gasoline from foreign crude oil sources in computing the exclusion from gross tested income under §1.951A-2(c)(1)(v) and the amount of DOGEI from the sale of gasoline from domestic crude oil sources in computing its section 250 deduction.

(8) *FDDEI sale.*—The term *FDDEI sale* has the meaning set forth in §1.250(b)-4(b).

(9) *FDDEI service.*—The term *FDDEI service* has the meaning set forth in §1.250(b)-5(b).

(10) *FDDEI transaction.*—The term *FDDEI transaction* means a FDDEI sale or a FDDEI service.

(11) *Foreign branch income.*—The term *foreign branch income* has the meaning set forth in section 904(d)(2)(J) and §1.904-4(f)(2).

(12) *Foreign-derived deduction eligible income.*—The term *foreign-derived deduction eligible income* or *FDDEI* means, with respect to a domestic corporation for a taxable year, the excess (if any) of the corporation's gross FDDEI for the year, over the deductions properly allocable to gross FDDEI for the year, as determined under paragraph (d)(2) of this section.

(13) *Foreign-derived ratio.*—The term *foreign-derived ratio* means, with respect to a domestic corporation for a taxable year, the ratio (not to exceed one) of the corporation's FDDEI for the year to the corporation's DEI for the year. If a domestic corporation has no FDDEI for a taxable year, the corporation's foreign-derived ratio is zero for the taxable year.

(14) *Gross RDEI.*—The term *gross RDEI* means, with respect to a domestic corporation or a partnership for a taxable year, the portion of the corporation or partnership's gross DEI for the year that is not included in gross FDDEI.

(15) *Gross DEI.*—The term *gross DEI* means, with respect to a domestic corporation or a partnership for a taxable year, the gross income of the corporation or partnership for the year determined without regard to the following items of gross income—

(i) Amounts included in gross income under section 951(a)(1);

(ii) GILTI (as defined in §1.250(a)-1(c)(3));

(iii) Financial services income (as defined in section 904(d)(2)(D) and §1.904-4(e)(1)(iii));

(iv) Dividends received from a controlled foreign corporation with respect to which the corporation or partnership is a United States shareholder;

(v) Domestic oil and gas extraction income; and

(vi) Foreign branch income.

(16) *Gross FDDEI.*—The term *gross FDDEI* means, with respect to a domestic corporation or a partnership for a taxable year, the portion of the gross DEI of the corporation or partnership for the year which is derived from all of its FDDEI transactions.

(17) *Modified affiliated group*—(i) *In general.*—The term *modified affiliated group* means an affiliated group as defined in section 1504(a) determined by substituting "more than 50 percent" for "at least 80 percent" each place it appears, and without regard to section 1504(b)(2) and (3).

(ii) *Special rule for noncorporate entities.*—Any person (other than a corporation) that is controlled by one or more members of a modified affiliated group (including one or more persons treated as a member or members of a modified affiliated group by reason of this paragraph (c)(17)(ii)) or that controls any such member is treated as a member of the modified affiliated group.

(iii) *Definition of control.*—For purposes of paragraph (c)(17)(ii) of this section, the term *control* has the meaning set forth in section 954(d)(3).

(18) *Qualified business asset investment.*—The term *qualified business asset investment* or *QBAI* has the meaning set forth in §1.250(b)-2(b).

(19) *Related party.*—The term *related party* means, with respect to any person, any member of a modified affiliated group that includes such person.

(20) *United States shareholder.*—The term *United States shareholder* has the meaning set forth in section 951(b) and §1.951-1(g).

(d) *Treatment of cost of goods sold and allocation and apportionment of deductions.*—(1) *Cost of goods sold for determining gross DEI and gross FDDEI.*—For purposes of determining the gross income included in gross DEI and gross FDDEI of a domestic corporation or a partnership, the cost of goods sold of the corporation or partnership is attributed to gross receipts with respect to gross DEI or gross FDDEI under any reasonable method that is applied consistently. Cost of goods sold must be attributed to gross receipts with respect to gross DEI or gross FDDEI regardless of whether certain costs included in cost of goods sold can be associated with activities undertaken in an earlier taxable year (including a year before the effective date of section 250). A domestic corporation or partnership may not segregate cost of goods sold with respect to a particular product into component costs and attribute those component costs disproportionately to gross receipts with respect to amounts excluded from gross DEI or gross FDDEI, as applicable.

(2) *Deductions properly allocable to gross DEI and gross FDDEI.*—(i) *In general.*—For purposes of determining a domestic corporation's deductions that are properly allocable to gross DEI and gross FDDEI, the corporation's deductions are allocated and apportioned to gross DEI and gross FDDEI under the rules of §§1.861-8 through 1.861-14T and 1.861-17 by treating section 250(b) as an operative section described in §1.861-8(f). In allocating and apportioning deductions under §§1.861-8 through 1.861-14T and 1.861-17, gross FDDEI and gross RDEI are treated as separate statutory groupings. The deductions allocated and apportioned to gross DEI equal the sum of the deductions allocated and apportioned to gross FDDEI and gross RDEI. All items of gross income described in paragraphs (c)(15)(i) through (vi) of this section are in the residual grouping.

(ii) *Determination of deductions to allocate.*—For purposes of determining the deductions of a domestic corporation for a taxable year properly allocable to gross DEI and gross FDDEI, the deductions of the corporation for the taxable year are determined without regard to sections 163(j), 170(b)(2), 172, 246(b), and 250.

(3) *Examples.*—The following examples illustrate the application of this paragraph (d).

(i) *Assumed facts.*—The following facts are assumed for purposes of the examples—

(A) DC is a domestic corporation that is not a member of a consolidated group.

(B) All sales and services are provided to persons that are not related parties.

(C) All sales and services to foreign persons qualify as FDDEI transactions.

(ii) *Examples*—

(A) *Example 1: Allocation of deductions.*—(1) *Facts.* For a taxable year, DC manufactures products A and B in the United States. DC sells products A and B and provides services associated with products A and B to United States and foreign persons. DC's QBAI for the taxable year is $1,000x. DC has $300x of deductible interest expense allowed under section 163. DC has assets with a tax book value of $2,500x. The tax book value of DC's assets used to produce products A and B and services is split evenly between assets that produce gross FDDEI and assets that produce gross RDEI. DC has $840x of supportive deductions, as defined in §1.861-8(b)(3), attributable to general and administrative expenses incurred for the purpose of generating the class of gross income that consists of gross DEI. DC apportions the $840x of deductions on the basis of gross income in accordance with §1.861-8T(c)(1). For purposes of determining gross FDDEI and gross DEI under paragraph (d)(1) of this section, DC attributes $200x of cost of goods sold to Product A and $400x of cost of goods sold to Product B, and then attributes the cost of goods sold for each product ratably between the gross receipts of such product sold to foreign persons and the gross receipts of such product sold to United States persons. The manner in which DC attributes the cost of goods sold is a reasonable method. DC has no other items of income, loss, or deduction. For the taxable year, DC has the following income tax items relevant to the determination of its FDII:

Table 1 to paragraph (d)(3)(ii)(A)(1)			
	Product A	Product B	Services	Total
Gross receipts from U.S. persons	$200x	$800x	$100x	$1,100x
Gross receipts from foreign persons	$200x	$800x	$100x	$1,100x
Total gross receipts	$400x	$1,600x	$200x	$2,200x
Cost of goods sold for gross receipts from U.S. persons	$100x	$200x	$0	$300x
Cost of goods sold for gross receipts from foreign persons	$100x	$200x	$0	$300x
Total cost of goods sold	$200x	$400x	$0	$600x
Gross income	$200x	$1,200x	$200x	$1,600x
Tax book value of assets used to produce products/services	$500x	$500x	$1,500x	$2,500x

(2) *Analysis*—(i) *Determination of gross FDDEI and gross RDEI.* Because DC does not have any income described in section 250(b)(3)(A)(i)(I) through (VI) and paragraphs (c)(15)(i) through (vi) of this section, none of its gross income is excluded from gross DEI. DC's gross DEI is $1,600x ($2,200x total gross receipts less $600x total cost of goods sold). DC's gross FDDEI is $800x ($1,100x of gross receipts from foreign persons minus attributable cost of goods sold of $300x).

(ii) *Determination of foreign-derived deduction eligible income.* To calculate its FDDEI, DC must determine the amount of its deductions that are allocated and apportioned to gross FDDEI and then subtract those amounts from gross FDDEI. DC's interest deduction of $300x is allocated and apportioned to gross FDDEI on the basis of the average total value of DC's assets in each grouping. DC has assets with a tax book value of $2,500x split evenly between assets that produce gross FDDEI and assets that produce gross RDEI. Accordingly, an interest expense deduction of $150x is apportioned to DC's gross FDDEI. With respect to DC's supportive deductions of $840x that are related to DC's gross DEI, DC apportions such deductions between gross FDDEI and gross RDEI on the basis of gross income. Accordingly, supportive deductions of $420x are apportioned to DC's gross FDDEI. Thus, DC's FDDEI is $230x, which is equal to its gross FDDEI of $800x less $150x of interest expense deduction and $420x of supportive deductions.

(iii) *Determination of deemed intangible income.* DC's deemed tangible income return is $100x, which is equal to 10 percent of its QBAI of $1,000x. DC's DEI is $460x, which is equal to its gross DEI of $1,600x less $300x of interest expense deductions and $840x of supportive deductions. Therefore, DC's deemed intangible income is $360x, which is equal to the excess of its DEI of $460x over its deemed tangible income return of $100x.

(iv) *Determination of foreign-derived intangible income.* DC's foreign-derived ratio is 50 percent, which is the ratio of DC's FDDEI of $230x to DC's DEI of $460x. Therefore, DC's FDII is $180x, which is equal to DC's deemed intangible income of $360x multiplied by its foreign-derived ratio of 50 percent.

(B) *Example 2: Allocation of deductions with respect to a partnership.*—(1) *Facts*—(i) *DC's operations.* DC is engaged in the production and sale of products consisting of two separate product groups in three-digit Standard Industrial Classification (SIC) Industry Groups, hereafter referred to as Group AAA and Group BBB. All of the gross income of DC is included in gross DEI. DC incurs $250x of research and experimental (R&E) expenditures in the United States that are deductible under section 174. None of the R&E is included in cost of goods sold. For purposes of determining gross FDDEI and gross DEI under paragraph (d)(1) of this section, DC attributes $210x of cost of goods sold to Group AAA products and $900x of cost of goods sold to Group BBB products, and then attributes the cost of goods sold with respect to each such product group ratably between the gross receipts with respect to such product group sold to foreign persons and the gross receipts with respect to such product group not sold to foreign persons. The manner in which DC attributes the cost of goods sold is a reasonable method. For the taxable year, DC has the following income tax items relevant to the determination of its FDII:

	Group AAA Products	Group BBB Products	Total
Table 2 to (d)(3)(ii)(B)(1)(i)			
Gross receipts from U.S. persons	$200x	$800x	$1,000x
Gross receipts from foreign persons	$100x	$400x	$500x
Total gross receipts	$300x	$1,200x	$1,500x
Cost of goods sold for gross receipts from U.S. persons	$140x	$600x	$740x
Cost of goods sold for gross receipts from foreign persons	$70x	$300x	$370x
Total cost of goods sold	$210x	$900x	$1,110x
Gross income	$90x	$300x	$390x
R&E deductions	$40x	$210x	$250x

(ii) *PRS's operations.* In addition to its own operations, DC is a partner in PRS, a partnership that also produces products described in SIC Group AAA. DC is allocated 50 percent of all income, gain, loss, and deductions of PRS. During the taxable year, PRS sells Group AAA products solely to foreign persons, and all of its gross income is included in gross DEI. PRS has $400 of gross receipts from sales of Group AAA products for the taxable year and incurs $100x of research and experimental (R&E) expenditures in the United States that are deductible under section 174. None of the R&E is included in cost of goods sold. For purposes of determining gross FDDEI and gross DEI under paragraph (d)(1) of this section, PRS attributes $200x of cost of goods sold to Group AAA products, and then attributes the cost of goods sold with respect to such product group ratably between the gross receipts with respect to such product group sold to foreign persons and the gross receipts with respect to such product group not sold to foreign persons. The manner in which PRS attributes the cost of goods sold is a reasonable method. DC's distributive share of PRS taxable items is $100x of gross income and $50x of R&E deductions, and DC's share of PRS's gross receipts from sales of Group AAA products for the taxable year is $200x under §1.861-17(f)(3).

(iii) *Application of the sales method to allocate and apportion R&E.* DC applies the sales method to apportion its R&E deductions under §1.861-17. Neither DC nor PRS licenses or sells its intangible property to controlled or uncontrolled corporations in a manner that necessitates including the sales by such corporations for purposes of apportioning DC's R&E deductions.

(2) *Analysis*—(i) *Determination of gross DEI and gross FDDEI.* Under paragraph (e)(1) of this section, DC's gross DEI, gross FDDEI, and deductions allocable to those include its distributive share of gross DEI, gross FDDEI, and deductions of PRS. Thus, DC's gross DEI for the year is $490x ($390x attributable to DC and $100x attributable to DC's interest in PRS). DC's gross income from sales of Group AAA products to foreign persons is $30x ($100x of gross receipts minus attributable cost of goods sold of $70x). DC's gross income from sales of Group BBB products to foreign persons is $100x ($400x of gross receipts minus attributable cost of goods sold of $300x). DC's gross FDDEI for the year is $230x ($30x from DC's sale of Group AAA products plus $100x from DC's sale of Group BBB products plus DC's distributive share of PRS's gross FDDEI of $100x).

(ii) *Allocation and apportionment of R&E deductions.* To determine FDDEI, DC must allocate and apportion its R&E expense of $300x ($250x incurred directly by DC and $50x incurred indirectly through DC's interest in PRS). In accordance with §1.861-17, R&E expenses are first allocated to a class of gross income related to a three-digit SIC group code. DC's R&E expenses related to products in Group AAA are $90x ($40x incurred directly by DC and $50x incurred indirectly through DC's interest in PRS) and its expenses related to Group BBB are $210x. See paragraph (d)(2)(i) of this section. Accordingly, all R&E expense attributable to a particular SIC group code is apportioned on the basis of the amounts of sales within that SIC group code. Total sales within Group AAA were $500x ($300x directly by DC and $200x attributable to DC's interest in PRS), $300x of which were made to foreign persons ($100x directly by DC and $200x attributable to DC's interest in PRS). Therefore, the $90x of R&E expense related to Group AAA is apportioned $54x to gross FDDEI ($90x x $300x/$500x) and $36x to gross RDEI ($90x x $200x/$500x). Total sales within Group BBB were $1,200x, $400x of which were made to foreign persons. Therefore, the $210x of R&E expense related to products in Group BBB is apportioned $70x to gross FDDEI ($210x x $400x/$1,200x) and $140x to gross RDEI ($210x x $800x/$1,200x). Accordingly, DC's FDDEI for the tax year is $106x ($230x gross FDDEI minus $124x of R&E ($54x + $70x) allocated and apportioned to gross FDDEI).

(e) *Domestic corporate partners.*—(1) *In general.*—A domestic corporation's DEI and FDDEI for a taxable year are determined by taking into account the corporation's share of gross DEI, gross FDDEI, and deductions of any partnership (whether domestic or foreign) in which the corporation is a direct or indirect partner. For purposes of the preceding sentence, a domestic corporation's share of each such item of a partnership is determined in accordance with the corporation's distributive share of the underlying items of income, gain, deduction, and loss of the partnership that comprise such amounts. See §1.250(b)-2(g) for rules on calculating the increase to a domestic corporation's QBAI by the corporation's share of partnership QBAI.

(2) *Reporting requirement for partnership with domestic corporate partners.*—A partnership that has one or more direct partners that are domestic corporations and that is required to file a return under section 6031 must furnish to each such partner on or with such partner's Schedule K-1 (Form 1065 or any successor form) by the due date (including extensions) for furnishing Schedule K-1 the partner's share of the partnership's gross DEI, gross FDDEI, deductions that are properly allocable to the partnership's gross DEI and gross FDDEI, and partnership QBAI (as determined under §1.250(b)-2(g)) for each taxable year in which the partnership has gross DEI, gross FDDEI, deductions that are properly allocable to the partnership's gross DEI or gross FDDEI, or partnership specified tangible property (as defined in §1.250(b)-2(g)(5)). In the case of tiered partnerships where one or more partners of an upper-tier partnership are domestic corporations, a lower-tier partnership must report the amount specified in this paragraph (e)(2) to the upper-tier partnership to allow reporting of such information to any partner that is a domestic corporation. To the extent that a partnership cannot determine the information described in the first sentence of this paragraph (e)(2), the partnership must instead furnish to each partner its share of the partnership's attributes that a partner needs to determine the partner's gross DEI, gross FDDEI, deductions that are properly allocable to the partner's gross DEI and gross FDDEI, and the partner's adjusted bases in partnership specified tangible property.

(3) *Examples.*—The following examples illustrate the application of this paragraph (e).

(i) *Assumed facts.*—The following facts are assumed for purposes of the examples—

(A) DC, a domestic corporation, is a partner in PRS, a partnership.

(B) FP and FP2 are foreign persons.

(C) FC is a foreign corporation.

(D) The allocations under PRS's partnership agreement satisfy the requirements of section 704.

(E) No partner of PRS is a related party of DC.

(F) DC, PRS, and FC all use the calendar year as their taxable year.

(G) PRS has no items of income, loss, or deduction for its taxable year, except the items of income described.

(ii) *Examples*—

(A) *Example 1: Sale by partnership to foreign person.*—(1) *Facts.* Under the terms of the partnership agreement, DC is allocated 50 percent of all income, gain, loss, and deductions of PRS. For the taxable year, PRS recognizes $20x of gross income on the sale of general property (as defined in §1.250(b)-3(b)(10)) to FP, a foreign person (as determined under §1.250(b)-4(c)), for a foreign use (as determined under §1.250(b)-4(d)). The gross income recognized on the sale of property is not described in section 250(b)(3)(A)(I) through (VI) or paragraphs (c)(15)(i) through (vi) of this section.

(2) *Analysis.* PRS's sale of property to FP is a FDDEI sale as described in §1.250(b)-4(b). Therefore, the gross income derived from the sale ($20x) is included in PRS's gross DEI and gross FDDEI, and DC's share of PRS's gross DEI and gross FDDEI ($10x) is included in DC's gross DEI and gross FDDEI for the taxable year.

(B) *Example 2: Sale by partnership to foreign person attributable to foreign branch.*—(1) *Facts.* The facts are the same as in paragraph (e)(3)(ii)(A)(1) of this section (the facts in *Example 1*), except the income from the sale of property to FP is attributable to a foreign branch of PRS.

(2) *Analysis.* PRS's sale of property to FP is excluded from PRS's gross DEI under section 250(b)(3)(A)(VI) and paragraph (c)(15)(vi) of this section. Accordingly, DC's share of PRS's gross income of $10x from the sale is not included in DC's gross DEI or gross FDDEI for the taxable year.

(C) *Example 3: Partnership with a loss in gross FDDEI.*—(1) *Facts.* The facts are the same as in paragraph (e)(3)(ii)(A)(1) of this section (the facts in *Example 1*), except that in the same taxable year, PRS also sells property to FP2, a foreign person (as determined under § 1.250(b)-4(c)), for a foreign use (as determined under § 1.250(b)-4(d)). After taking into account both sales, PRS has a gross loss of $30x.

(2) *Analysis.* Both the sale of property to FP and the sale of property to FP2 are FDDEI sales because each sale is described in § 1.250(b)-4(b). DC's share of PRS's gross loss ($15x) from the sales is included in DC's gross DEI and gross FDDEI.

(D) *Example 4: Sale by partnership to foreign related party of the partnership.*—(1) *Facts.* Under the terms of the partnership agreement, DC has 25 percent of the capital and profits interest in the partnership and is allocated 25 percent of all income, gain, loss, and deductions of PRS. PRS owns 100 percent of the single class of stock of FC. In the taxable year, PRS has $20x of gain on the sale of general property (as defined in § 1.250(b)-3(b)(10)) to FC, and FC makes a physical and material change to the property within the meaning of § 1.250(b)-4(d)(1)(iii)(B) outside the United States before selling the property to customers in the United States.

(2) *Analysis.* The sale of property by PRS to FC is described in § 1.250(b)-4(b) without regard to the application of § 1.250(b)-6, since the sale is to a foreign person (as determined under § 1.250(b)-4(c)) for a foreign use (as determined under § 1.250(b)-4(d)). However, FC is a foreign related party of PRS within the meaning of section 250(b)(5)(D) and § 1.250(b)-3(b)(6), because FC and PRS are members of a modified affiliated group within the meaning of paragraph (c)(17) of this section. Therefore, the sale by PRS to FC is a related party sale within the meaning of § 1.250(b)-6(b)(1). Under section 250(b)(5)(C)(i) and § 1.250(b)-6(c), because FC did not sell the property, or use the property in connection with other property sold or the provision of a service, to a foreign unrelated party before the property was subject to a domestic use, the sale by PRS to FC is not a FDDEI sale. See § 1.250(b)-6(c)(1). Accordingly, the gain from the sale ($20x) is included in PRS's gross DEI but not its gross FDDEI, and DC's share of PRS's gain ($5x) is included in DC's gross DEI but not gross FDDEI. This is the result notwithstanding that FC is not a related party of DC because FC and DC are not members of a modified affiliated group within the meaning of paragraph (c)(17) of this section.

(f) *Determination of FDII for consolidated groups.*—A member of a consolidated group (as defined in § 1.1502-1(h)) determines its FDII under the rules provided in § 1.1502-50.

(g) *Determination of FDII for tax-exempt corporations.*—The FDII of a corporation that is subject to the unrelated business income tax under section 511 is determined only by reference to that corporation's items of income, gain, deduction, or loss, and adjusted bases in property, that are taken into account in computing the corporation's unrelated business taxable income (as defined in section 512). For example, if a corporation that is subject to the unrelated business income tax under section 511 has tangible property used in the production of both unrelated business income and gross income that is not unrelated business income, only the portion of the basis of such property taken into account in computing the corporation's unrelated business taxable income is taken into account in determining the corporation's QBAI. Similarly, if a corporation that is subject to the unrelated business income tax under section 511 has tangible property that is used in both the production of gross DEI and the production of gross income that is not gross DEI, only the corporation's unrelated business income is taken into account in determining the corporation's dual use ratio with respect to such property under § 1.250(b)-2(d)(3). [Reg. § 1.250(b)-1.]

☐ [T.D. 9901, 7-9-2020. Amended by T.D. 9959, 12-28-2021.]

[Reg. § 1.250(b)-2]

§ 1.250(b)-2. Qualified business asset investment (QBAI).—(a) *Scope.*—This section provides general rules for determining the qualified business asset investment of a domestic corporation for purposes of determining its deemed tangible income return under § 1.250(b)-1(c)(4). Paragraph (b) of this section defines qualified business asset investment (QBAI). Paragraph (c) of this section defines

tangible property and specified tangible property. Paragraph (d) of this section provides rules for determining the portion of property that is specified tangible property when the property is used in the production of both gross DEI and gross income that is not gross DEI. Paragraph (e) of this section provides rules for determining the adjusted basis of specified tangible property. Paragraph (f) of this section provides rules for determining QBAI of a domestic corporation with a short taxable year. Paragraph (g) of this section provides rules for increasing the QBAI of a domestic corporation by reason of property owned through a partnership. Paragraph (h) of this section provides an anti-avoidance rule that disregards certain transfers when determining the QBAI of a domestic corporation.

(b) *Definition of qualified business asset investment.*—The term *qualified business asset investment (QBAI)* means the average of a domestic corporation's aggregate adjusted bases as of the close of each quarter of the domestic corporation's taxable year in specified tangible property that is used in a trade or business of the domestic corporation and is of a type with respect to which a deduction is allowable under section 167. In the case of partially depreciable property, only the depreciable portion of the property is of a type with respect to which a deduction is allowable under section 167.

(c) *Specified tangible property.*—(1) *In general.*—The term *specified tangible property* means, with respect to a domestic corporation for a taxable year, tangible property of the domestic corporation used in the production of gross DEI for the taxable year. For purposes of the preceding sentence, tangible property of a domestic corporation is used in the production of gross DEI for a taxable year if some or all of the depreciation or cost recovery allowance with respect to the tangible property is either allocated and apportioned to the gross DEI of the domestic corporation for the taxable year under § 1.250(b)-1(d)(2) or capitalized to inventory or other property held for sale, some or all of the gross income or loss from the sale of which is taken into account in determining DEI of the domestic corporation for the taxable year.

(2) *Tangible property.*—The term *tangible property* means property for which the depreciation deduction provided by section 167(a) is eligible to be determined under section 168 without regard to section 168(f)(1), (2), or (5), section 168(k)(2)(A)(i)(II), (IV), or (V), and the date placed in service.

(d) *Dual use property.*—(1) *In general.*—The amount of the adjusted basis in dual use property of a domestic corporation for a taxable year that is treated as adjusted basis in specified tangible property for the taxable year is the average of the domestic corporation's adjusted basis in the property multiplied by the dual use ratio with respect to the property for the taxable year.

(2) *Definition of dual use property.*—The term *dual use property* means, with respect to a domestic corporation and a taxable year, specified tangible property of the domestic corporation that is used in both the production of gross DEI and the production of gross income that is not gross DEI for the taxable year. For purposes of the preceding sentence, specified tangible property of a domestic corporation is used in the production of gross DEI and the production of gross income that is not gross DEI for a taxable year if less than all of the depreciation or cost recovery allowance with respect to the property is either allocated and apportioned to the gross DEI of the domestic corporation for the taxable year under § 1.250(b)-1(d)(2) or capitalized to inventory or other property held for sale, the gross income or loss from the sale of which is taken into account in determining the DEI of the domestic corporation for the taxable year.

(3) *Dual use ratio.*—The term *dual use ratio* means, with respect to dual use property, a domestic corporation, and a taxable year, a ratio (expressed as a percentage) calculated as—

(i) The sum of-

(A) The depreciation deduction or cost recovery allowance with respect to the property that is allocated and apportioned to the gross DEI of the domestic corporation for the taxable year under § 1.250(b)-1(d)(2); and

(B) The depreciation or cost recovery allowance with respect to the property that is capitalized to inventory or other property held for sale, the gross income or loss from the sale of which is taken into account in determining the DEI of the domestic corporation for the taxable year; divided by

(ii) The sum of—

(A) The total amount of the domestic corporation's depreciation deduction or cost recovery allowance with respect to the property for the taxable year; and

(B) The total amount of the domestic corporation's depreciation or cost recovery allowance with respect to the property capitalized to inventory or other property held for sale, the gross income or loss from the sale of which is taken into account in determining the income or loss of the domestic corporation for the taxable year.

(4) *Example.*—The following example illustrates the application of this paragraph (d).

(i) *Facts.* DC, a domestic corporation, owns a machine that produces both gross DEI and income that is not gross DEI. The average adjusted basis of the machine for the taxable year in the hands of DC is $4,000x. The depreciation with respect to the machine for the taxable year is $400x, $320x of which is capitalized to inventory of Product A, gross income or loss from the sale of which is taken into account in determining DC's gross DEI for the taxable year, and $80x of which is capitalized to inventory of Product B, gross income or loss from the sale of which is not taken into account in determining DC's gross DEI for the taxable year. DC also owns an office building for its administrative functions with an average adjusted basis for the taxable year of $10,000x. DC does not capitalize depreciation with respect to the office building to inventory or other property held for sale. DC's depreciation deduction with respect to the office building is $1,000x for the taxable year, $750x of which is allocated and apportioned to gross DEI under § 1.250(b)-1(d)(2), and $250x of which is allocated and apportioned to income other than gross DEI under § 1.250(b)-1(d)(2).

(ii) *Analysis*—(A) *Dual use property.* The machine and office building are property for which the depreciation deduction provided by section 167(a) is eligible to be determined under section 168 (without regard to section 168(f)(1), (2), or (5), section 168(k)(2)(A)(i)(II), (IV), or (V), and the date placed in service). Therefore, under paragraph (c)(2) of this section, the machine and office building are tangible property. Furthermore, because the machine and office building are used in the production of gross DEI for the taxable year within the meaning of paragraph (c)(1) of this section, the machine and office building are specified tangible property. Finally, because the machine and office building are used in both the production of gross DEI and the production of gross income that is not gross DEI for the taxable year within the meaning of paragraph (d)(2) of this section, the machine and office building are dual use property. Therefore, under paragraph (d)(1) of this section, the amount of DC's adjusted basis in the machine and office building that is treated as adjusted basis in specified tangible property for the taxable year is determined by multiplying DC's adjusted basis in the machine and office building by DC's dual use ratio with respect to the machine and office building determined under paragraph (d)(3) of this section.

(B) *Depreciation not capitalized to inventory.* Because none of the depreciation with respect to the office building is capitalized to inventory or other property held for sale, DC's dual use ratio with respect to the office building is determined entirely by reference to the depreciation deduction with respect to the office building. Therefore, under paragraph (d)(3) of this section, DC's dual use ratio with respect to the office building for Year 1 is 75 percent, which is DC's depreciation deduction with respect to the office building that is allocated and apportioned to gross DEI under § 1.250(b)-1(d)(2) for Year 1 ($750x), divided by the total amount of DC's depreciation deduction with respect to the office building for Year 1 ($1000x). Accordingly, under paragraph (d)(1) of this section, $7,500x ($10,000x x 0.75) of DC's average adjusted bases in the office building is taken into account under paragraph (b) of this section in determining DC's QBAI for the taxable year.

(C) *Depreciation capitalized to inventory.* Because all of the depreciation with respect to the machine is capitalized to inventory, DC's dual use ratio with respect to the machine is determined entirely by reference to the depreciation with respect to the machine that is capitalized to inventory and included in cost of goods sold. Therefore, under paragraph (d)(3) of this section, DC's dual use ratio with respect to the machine for the taxable year is 80 percent, which is DC's depreciation with respect to the machine that is capitalized to inventory of Product A, the gross income or loss from the sale of which is taken into account in determining DC's DEI for the taxable year ($320x), divided by DC's depreciation with respect to the machine that is capitalized to inventory, the gross income or loss from the sale of which is taken into account in determining DC's income for Year 1 ($400x). Accordingly, under paragraph (d)(1) of this section, $3,200x ($4,000x x 0.8) of DC's average adjusted basis in the machine is taken into account under paragraph (b) of this section in *determining DC's QBAI for the taxable year.*

(e) *Determination of adjusted basis of specified tangible property.*—(1) *In general.*—The adjusted basis in specified tangible property for purposes of this section is determined by using the cost capitalization methods of accounting used by the domestic corporation for purposes of determining the gross income and deductions of the domestic corporation and the alternative depreciation system under section 168(g), and by allocating the depreciation deduction with respect to such property for the domestic corporation's taxable year ratably to each day during the period in the taxable year to which such depreciation relates. For purposes of the preceding sentence, the period in the taxable year to which such depreciation relates is determined without regard to the applicable convention under section 168(d).

(2) *Effect of change in law.*—The adjusted basis in specified tangible property is determined without regard to any provision of law enacted after December 22, 2017, unless such later enacted law specifically and directly amends the definition of QBAI under section 250 or section 951A. For purposes of applying section 250(b)(2)(B) and this paragraph (e), the technical amendment to section 168(g) (to provide a recovery period of 20 years for qualified improvement property for purposes of the alternative depreciation system) enacted in section 2307(a) of the Coronavirus Aid, Relief, and Economic Security Act, Pub. L. 116-136 (2020) is treated as enacted on December 22, 2017.

(3) *Specified tangible property placed in service before enactment of section 250.*—The adjusted basis in specified tangible property placed in service before December 22, 2017, is determined using the alternative depreciation system under section 168(g), as if this system had applied from the date that the property was placed in service.

(f) *Special rules for short taxable years.*—(1) *In general.*—In the case of a domestic corporation that has a taxable year that is less than twelve months (a *short taxable year*), the rules for determining the QBAI of the domestic corporation under this section are modified as provided in paragraphs (f)(2) and (3) of this section with respect to the taxable year.

(2) *Determination of when the quarter closes.*—For purposes of determining when the quarter closes, in determining the QBAI of a domestic corporation for a short taxable year, the quarters of the domestic corporation for purposes of this section are the full quarters beginning and ending within the short taxable year (if any), determining quarter length as if the domestic corporation did not have a short taxable year, plus one or more short quarters (if any).

(3) *Reduction of qualified business asset investment.*—The QBAI of a domestic corporation for a short taxable year is the sum of—

(i) The sum of the domestic corporation's aggregate adjusted bases in specified tangible property as of the close of each full quarter (if any) in the domestic corporation's taxable year divided by four; plus

(ii) The domestic corporation's aggregate adjusted bases in specified tangible property as of the close of each short quarter (if any) in the domestic corporation's taxable year multiplied by the sum of the number of days in each short quarter divided by 365.

(4) *Example.*—The following example illustrates the application of this paragraph (f).

(i) *Facts.* A, an individual, owns all of the stock of DC, a domestic corporation. A owns DC from the beginning of the taxable year. On July 15 of the taxable year, A sells DC to USP, a domestic corporation that is unrelated to A. DC becomes a member of the consolidated group of which USP is the common parent and as a result, under § 1.1502-76(b)(2)(ii), DC's taxable year is treated as ending on July 15. USP and DC both use the calendar year as their taxable year. DC's aggregate adjusted bases in specified tangible property for the taxable year are $250x as of March 31, $300x as of June 30, $275x as of July 15, $500x as of September 30, and $450x as of December 31.

(ii) *Analysis*—(A) *Determination of short taxable years and quarters.* DC has two short taxable years during the year. The first short taxable year is from January 1 to July 15, with two full quarters (January 1 through March 31 and April 1 through June 30) and one short quarter (July 1 through July 15). The second taxable year is from July 16 to December 31, with one short quarter (July 16 through September 30) and one full quarter (October 1 through December 31).

(B) *Calculation of qualified business asset investment for the first short taxable year.* Under paragraph (f)(2) of this section, for the first short taxable year, DC has three quarter closes (March 31, June 30, and July 15). Under paragraph (f)(3) of this section, the QBAI of DC for the first short taxable year is $148.80x, the sum of $137.50x (($250x + $300x)/4) attributable to the two full quarters and $11.30x ($275x x 15/365) attributable to the short quarter.

(C) *Calculation of qualified business asset investment for the second short taxable year.* Under paragraph (f)(2) of this section, for the second short taxable year, DC has two quarter closes (September 30 and December 31). Under paragraph (f)(3) of this section, the QBAI of DC for the second short taxable year is $217.98x, the sum of $112.50x ($450x/4) attributable to the one full quarter and $105.48x ($500x x 77/365) attributable to the short quarter.

(g) *Partnership property.*—(1) *In general.*—If a domestic corporation holds an interest in one or more partnerships during a taxable year (including indirectly through one or more partnerships that are partners in a lower-tier partnership), the QBAI of the domestic corporation for the taxable year (determined without regard to this paragraph (g)(1)) is increased by the sum of the domestic corporation's partnership QBAI with respect to each partnership for the taxable year.

(2) *Determination of partnership QBAI.*—For purposes of paragraph (g)(1) of this section, the term *partnership QBAI* means, with respect to a partnership, a domestic corporation, and a taxable year, the sum of the domestic corporation's partner adjusted basis in each partnership specified tangible property of the partnership for each partnership taxable year that ends with or within the taxable year. If a partnership taxable year is less than twelve months, the principles of paragraph (f) of this section apply in determining a domestic corporation's partnership QBAI with respect to the partnership.

(3) *Determination of partner adjusted basis.*—(i) *In general.*—For purposes of paragraph (g)(2) of this section, the term *partner adjusted basis* means the amount described in paragraph (g)(3)(ii) of this section with respect to sole use partnership property or paragraph (g)(3)(iii) of this section with respect to dual use partnership property. The principles of section 706(d) apply to this determination.

(ii) *Sole use partnership property.*—(A) *In general.*—The amount described in this paragraph (g)(3)(ii), with respect to sole use partnership property, a partnership taxable year, and a domestic corporation, is the sum of the domestic corporation's proportionate share of the partnership adjusted basis in the sole use partnership property for the partnership taxable year and the domestic corporation's partner-specific QBAI basis in the sole use partnership property for the partnership taxable year.

(B) *Definition of sole use partnership property.*—The term *sole use partnership property* means, with respect to a partnership, a partnership taxable year, and a domestic corporation, partnership specified tangible property of the partnership that is used in the production of only gross DEI of the domestic corporation for the taxable year in which or with which the partnership taxable year ends. For purposes of the preceding sentence, partnership specified tangible property of a partnership is used in the production of only gross DEI for a taxable year if all the domestic corporation's distributive share of the partnership's depreciation deduction or cost recovery allowance with respect to the property (if any) for the partnership taxable year that ends with or within the taxable year is allocated and apportioned to the domestic corporation's gross DEI for the taxable year under §1.250(b)-1(d)(2) and, if any of the partnership's depreciation or cost recovery allowance with respect to the property is capitalized to inventory or other property held for sale, all the domestic corporation's distributive share of the partnership's gross income or loss from the sale of such inventory or other property for the partnership taxable year that ends with or within the taxable year is taken into account in determining the DEI of the domestic corporation for the taxable year.

(iii) *Dual use partnership property.*—(A) *In general.*—The amount described in this paragraph (g)(3)(iii), with respect to dual use partnership property, a partnership taxable year, and a domestic corporation, is the sum of the domestic corporation's proportionate share of the partnership adjusted basis in the property for the partnership taxable year and the domestic corporation's partner-specific QBAI basis in the property for the partnership taxable year, multiplied by the domestic corporation's dual use ratio with respect to the property for the partnership taxable year determined under the principles of paragraph (d)(3) of this section, except that the ratio described in paragraph (d)(3) of this section is determined by reference to the domestic corporation's distributive share of the amounts described in paragraph (d)(3) of this section.

(B) *Definition of dual use partnership property.*—The term *dual use partnership property* means partnership specified tangible property other than sole use partnership property.

(4) *Determination of proportionate share of the partnership's adjusted basis in partnership specified tangible property.*—(i) *In general.*—For purposes of paragraph (g)(3) of this section, the domestic corporation's proportionate share of the partnership adjusted basis in partnership specified tangible property for a partnership taxable year is the partnership adjusted basis in the property multiplied by the domestic corporation's proportionate share ratio with respect to the property for the partnership taxable year. Solely for purposes of determining the proportionate share ratio under paragraph (g)(4)(ii) of this section, the partnership's calculation of, and a partner's distributive share of, any income, loss, depreciation, or cost recovery allowance is determined under section 704(b).

(ii) *Proportionate share ratio.*—The term *proportionate share ratio* means, with respect to a partnership, a partnership taxable year, and a domestic corporation, the ratio (expressed as a percentage) calculated as —

(A) The sum of—

(1) The domestic corporation's distributive share of the partnership's depreciation deduction or cost recovery allowance with respect to the property for the partnership taxable year; and

(2) The amount of the partnership's depreciation or cost recovery allowance with respect to the property that is capitalized to inventory or other property held for sale, the gross income or loss from the sale of which is taken into account in determining the domestic corporation's distributive share of the partnership's income or loss for the partnership taxable year; divided by

(B) The sum of—

(1) The total amount of the partnership's depreciation deduction or cost recovery allowance with respect to the property for the partnership taxable year; and

(2) The total amount of the partnership's depreciation or cost recovery allowance with respect to the property capitalized to inventory or other property held for sale, the gross income or loss from the sale of which is taken into account in determining the partnership's income or loss for the partnership taxable year.

(5) *Definition of partnership specified tangible property.*—The term *partnership specified tangible property* means, with respect to a domestic corporation, tangible property (as defined in paragraph (c)(2) of this section) of a partnership that is—

(i) Used in the trade or business of the partnership;

(ii) Of a type with respect to which a deduction is allowable under section 167; and

(iii) Used in the production of gross income included in the domestic corporation's gross DEI.

(6) *Determination of partnership adjusted basis.*—For purposes of this paragraph (g), the term *partnership adjusted basis* means, with respect to a partnership, partnership specified tangible property, and a partnership taxable year, the amount equal to the average of the partnership's adjusted basis in the partnership specified tangible property as of the close of each quarter in the partnership taxable year determined without regard to any adjustments under section 734(b) except for adjustments under section 734(b)(1)(B) or section 734(b)(2)(B) that are attributable to distributions of tangible property (as defined in paragraph (c)(2) of this section) and for adjustments under section 734(b)(1)(A) or 734(b)(2)(A). The principles of paragraphs (e) and (h) of this section apply for purposes of determining a partnership's adjusted basis in partnership specified tangible property and the proportionate share of the partnership's adjusted basis in partnership specified tangible property.

(7) *Determination of partner-specific QBAI basis.*—For purposes of this paragraph (g), the term *partner-specific QBAI basis* means, with respect to a domestic corporation, a partnership, and partnership specified tangible property, the amount that is equal to the average of the basis adjustment under section 743(b) that is allocated to the partnership specified tangible property of the partnership with respect to the domestic corporation as of the close of each quarter in the partnership taxable year. For this purpose, a negative basis adjustment under section 743(b) is expressed as a negative number. The principles of paragraphs (e) and (h) of this section apply for purposes of determining the partner-specific QBAI basis with respect to partnership specified tangible property.

(8) *Examples.*—The following examples illustrate the rules of this paragraph (g).

(i) *Assumed facts.*—Except as otherwise stated, the following facts are assumed for purposes of the examples:

(A) DC, DC1, DC2, and DC3 are domestic corporations.

(B) PRS is a partnership and its allocations satisfy the requirements of section 704.

(C) All properties are partnership specified tangible property.

(D) All persons use the calendar year as their taxable year.

(E) There is no partner-specific QBAI basis with respect to any property.

(ii) *Example 1: Sole use partnership property.*—(A) *Facts.* DC is a partner in PRS. PRS owns two properties, Asset A and Asset B. The average of PRS's adjusted basis as of the close of each quarter of PRS's taxable year in Asset A is $100x and in Asset B is $500x. In Year 1, PRS's section 704(b) depreciation deduction is $10x with respect to Asset A and $5x with respect to Asset B, and DC's section 704(b) distributive share of the depreciation deduction is $8x with respect to Asset A and $1x with respect to Asset B. None of the depreciation with respect to Asset A or Asset B is capitalized to inventory or other property held for sale. DC's entire distributive share of the depreciation deduction with respect to Asset A and Asset B is allocated and apportioned to DC's gross DEI for Year 1 under §1.250(b)-1(d)(2).

(B) *Analysis*—(1) *Sole use partnership property.* Because all of DC's distributive share of the depreciation deduction with respect to

Asset A and B is allocated and apportioned to gross DEI for Year 1, Asset A and Asset B are sole use partnership property within the meaning of paragraph (g)(3)(ii)(B) of this section. Therefore, under paragraph (g)(3)(ii)(A) of this section, DC's partner adjusted basis in Asset A and Asset B is equal to the sum of DC's proportionate share of PRS's partnership adjusted basis in Asset A and Asset B for Year 1 and DC's partner-specific QBAI basis in Asset A and Asset B for Year 1, respectively.

(2) *Proportionate share.* Under paragraph (g)(4)(i) of this section, DC's proportionate share of PRS's partnership adjusted basis in Asset A and Asset B is PRS's partnership adjusted basis in Asset A and Asset B for Year 1, multiplied by DC's proportionate share ratio with respect to Asset A and Asset B for Year 1, respectively. Because none of the depreciation with respect to Asset A or Asset B is capitalized to inventory or other property held for sale, DC's proportionate share ratio with respect to Asset A and Asset B is determined entirely by reference to the depreciation deduction with respect to Asset A and Asset B. Therefore, DC's proportionate share ratio with respect to Asset A for Year 1 is 80 percent, which is the ratio of DC's section 704(b) distributive share of PRS's section 704(b) depreciation deduction with respect to Asset A for Year 1 ($8x), divided by the total amount of PRS's section 704(b) depreciation deduction with respect to Asset A for Year 1 ($10x). DC's proportionate share ratio with respect to Asset B for Year 1 is 20 percent, which is the ratio of DC's section 704(b) distributive share of PRS's section 704(b) depreciation deduction with respect to Asset B for Year 1 ($1x), divided by the total amount of PRS's section 704(b) depreciation deduction with respect to Asset B for Year 1 ($5x). Accordingly, under paragraph (g)(4)(i) of this section, DC's proportionate share of PRS's partnership adjusted basis in Asset A is $80x ($100x x 0.8), and DC's proportionate share of PRS's partnership adjusted basis in Asset B is $100x ($500x x 0.2).

(3) *Partner adjusted basis.* Because DC has no partner-specific QBAI basis with respect to Asset A and Asset B, DC's partner adjusted basis in Asset A and Asset B is determined entirely by reference to its proportionate share of PRS's partnership adjusted basis in Asset A and Asset B. Therefore, under paragraph (g)(3)(ii)(A) of this section, DC's partner adjusted basis in Asset A is $80x, DC's proportionate share of PRS's partnership adjusted basis in Asset A, and DC's partner adjusted basis in Asset B is $100x, DC's proportionate share of PRS's partnership adjusted basis in Asset B.

(4) *Partnership QBAI.* Under paragraph (g)(2) of this section, DC's partnership QBAI with respect to PRS is $180x, the sum of DC's partner adjusted basis in Asset A ($80x) and DC's partner adjusted basis in Asset B ($100x). Accordingly, under paragraph (g)(1) of this section, DC increases its QBAI for Year 1 by $180x.

(iii) *Example 2: Dual use partnership property.*—(A) *Facts.* DC owns a 50 percent interest in PRS. All section 704(b) and tax items are identical and are allocated equally between DC and its other partner. PRS owns three properties, Asset C, Asset D, and Asset E. PRS sells two products, Product A and Product B. All of DC's distributive share of the gross income or loss from the sale of Product A is taken into account in determining DC's DEI, and none of DC's distributive share of the gross income or loss from the sale of Product B is taken into account in determining DC's DEI.

(1) *Asset C.* The average of PRS's adjusted basis as of the close of each quarter of PRS's taxable year in Asset C is $100x. In Year 1, PRS's depreciation is $10x with respect to Asset C, none of which is capitalized to inventory or other property held for sale. DC's distributive share of the depreciation deduction with respect to Asset C is $5x ($10x x 0.5), $3x of which is allocated and apportioned to DC's gross DEI under § 1.250(b)-1(d)(2).

(2) *Asset D.* The average of PRS's adjusted basis as of the close of each quarter of PRS's taxable year in Asset D is $500x. In Year 1, PRS's depreciation is $50x with respect to Asset D, $10x of which is capitalized to inventory of Product A and $40x is capitalized to inventory of Product B. None of the $10x depreciation with respect to Asset D capitalized to inventory of Product A is capitalized to ending inventory. However, of the $40x capitalized to inventory of Product B, $10x is capitalized to ending inventory. Therefore, the amount of depreciation with respect to Asset D capitalized to inventory of Product A that is taken into account in determining DC's distributive share of the income or loss of PRS for Year 1 is $5x ($10x x 0.5), and the amount of depreciation with respect to Asset D capitalized to inventory of Product B that is taken into account in determining DC's distributive share of the income or loss of PRS for Year 1 is $15x ($30x x 0.5).

(3) *Asset E.* The average of PRS's adjusted basis as of the close of each quarter of PRS's taxable year in Asset E is $600x. In Year 1, PRS's depreciation is $60x with respect to Asset E. Of the $60x depreciation with respect to Asset E, $20x is allowed as a deduction, $24x is capitalized to inventory of Product A, and $16x is capitalized to inventory of Product B. DC's distributive share of the depreciation deduction with respect to Asset E is $10x ($20x x 0.5), $8x of which is

allocated and apportioned to DC's gross DEI under § 1.250(b)-1(d)(2). None of the $24x depreciation with respect to Asset E capitalized to inventory of Product A is capitalized to ending inventory. However, of the $16x depreciation with respect to Asset E capitalized to inventory of Product B, $10x is capitalized to ending inventory. Therefore, the amount of depreciation with respect to Asset E capitalized to inventory of Product A that is taken into account in determining DC's distributive share of the income or loss of PRS for Year 1 is $12x ($24x x 0.5), and the amount of depreciation with respect to Asset E capitalized to inventory of Product B that is taken into account in determining DC's distributive share of the income or loss of PRS for Year 1 is $3x ($6x x 0.5).

(B) *Analysis.* Because Asset C, Asset D, and Asset E are not used in the production of only gross DEI in Year 1 within the meaning of paragraph (g)(3)(ii)(B) of this section, Asset C, Asset D, and Asset E are dual use partnership property within the meaning of paragraph (g)(3)(iii)(B) of this section. Therefore, under paragraph (g)(3)(iii)(A) of this section, DC's partner adjusted basis in Asset C, Asset D, and Asset E is the sum of DC's proportionate share of PRS's partnership adjusted basis in Asset C, Asset D, and Asset E, respectively, for Year 1, and DC's partner-specific QBAI basis in Asset C, Asset D, and Asset E, respectively, for Year 1, multiplied by DC's dual use ratio with respect to Asset C, Asset D, and Asset E, respectively, for Year 1, determined under the principles of paragraph (d)(3) of this section, except that the ratio described in paragraph (d)(3) of this section is determined by reference to DC's distributive share of the amounts described in paragraph (d)(3) of this section.

(1) *Asset C*—(i) *Proportionate share.* Under paragraph (g)(4)(i) of this section, DC's proportionate share of PRS's partnership adjusted basis in Asset C is PRS's partnership adjusted basis in Asset C for Year 1, multiplied by DC's proportionate share ratio with respect to Asset C for Year 1. Because none of the depreciation with respect to Asset C is capitalized to inventory or other property held for sale, DC's proportionate share ratio with respect to Asset C is determined entirely by reference to the depreciation deduction with respect to Asset C. Therefore, DC's proportionate share ratio with respect to Asset C is 50 percent, which is the ratio calculated as the amount of DC's section 704(b) distributive share of PRS's section 704(b) depreciation deduction with respect to Asset C for Year 1 ($5x), divided by the total amount of PRS's section 704(b) depreciation deduction with respect to Asset C for Year 1 ($10x). Accordingly, under paragraph (g)(4)(i) of this section, DC's proportionate share of PRS's partnership adjusted basis in Asset C is $50x ($100x x 0.5).

(ii) *Dual use ratio.* Because none of the depreciation with respect to Asset C is capitalized to inventory or other property held for sale, DC's dual use ratio with respect to Asset C is determined entirely by reference to the depreciation deduction with respect to Asset C. Therefore, DC's dual use ratio with respect to Asset C is 60 percent, which is the ratio calculated as the amount of DC's distributive share of PRS's depreciation deduction with respect to Asset C that is allocated and apportioned to DC's gross DEI under § 1.250(b)-1(d)(2) for Year 1 ($3x), divided by the total amount of DC's distributive share of PRS's depreciation deduction with respect to Asset C for Year 1 ($5x).

(iii) *Partner adjusted basis.* Because DC has no partner-specific QBAI basis with respect to Asset C, DC's partner adjusted basis in Asset C is determined entirely by reference to DC's proportionate share of PRS's partnership adjusted basis in Asset C, multiplied by DC's dual use ratio with respect to Asset C. Under paragraph (g)(3)(iii)(A) of this section, DC's partner adjusted basis in Asset C is $30x, DC's proportionate share of PRS's partnership adjusted basis in Asset C for Year 1 ($50x), multiplied by DC's dual use ratio with respect to Asset C for Year 1 (60 percent).

(2) *Asset D*—(i) *Proportionate share.* Under paragraph (g)(4)(i) of this section, DC's proportionate share of PRS's partnership adjusted basis in Asset D is PRS's partnership adjusted basis in Asset D for Year 1, multiplied by DC's proportionate share ratio with respect to Asset D for Year 1. Because all of the depreciation with respect to Asset D is capitalized to inventory, DC's proportionate share ratio with respect to Asset D is determined entirely by reference to the depreciation with respect to Asset D that is capitalized to inventory and included in cost of goods sold. Therefore, DC's proportionate share ratio with respect to Asset D is 50 percent, which is the ratio calculated as the amount of PRS's section 704(b) depreciation with respect to Asset D capitalized to Product A and Product B that is taken into account in determining DC's section 704(b) distributive share of PRS's income or loss for Year 1 ($20x), divided by the total amount of PRS's section 704(b) depreciation with respect to Asset D capitalized to Product A and Product B that is taken into account in determining PRS's section 704(b) income or loss for Year 1 ($40x). Accordingly, under paragraph (g)(4)(i) of this section, DC's proportionate share of PRS's partnership adjusted basis in Asset D is $250x ($500x x 0.5).

(ii) *Dual use ratio.* Because all of the depreciation with respect to Asset D is capitalized to inventory, DC's dual use ratio with respect to Asset D is determined entirely by reference to the depreciation with respect to Asset D that is capitalized to inventory and included in cost of goods sold. Therefore, DC's dual use ratio with respect to Asset D is 25 percent, which is the ratio calculated as the amount of depreciation with respect to Asset D capitalized to inventory of Product A and Product B that is taken into account in determining DC's DEI for Year 1 ($5x), divided by the total amount of depreciation with respect to Asset D capitalized to inventory of Product A and Product B that is taken into account in determining DC's income or loss for Year 1 ($20x).

(iii) *Partner adjusted basis.* Because DC has no partner-specific QBAI basis with respect to Asset D, DC's partner adjusted basis in Asset D is determined entirely by reference to DC's proportionate share of PRS's partnership adjusted basis in Asset D, multiplied by DC's dual use ratio with respect to Asset D. Under paragraph (g)(3)(iii)(A) of this section, DC's partner adjusted basis in Asset D is $62.50x, DC's proportionate share of PRS's partnership adjusted basis in Asset D for Year 1 ($250x), multiplied by DC's dual use ratio with respect to Asset D for Year 1 (25 percent).

(3) *Asset E—(i) Proportionate share.* Under paragraph (g)(4)(i) of this section, DC's proportionate share of PRS's partnership adjusted basis in Asset E is PRS's partnership adjusted basis in Asset E for Year 1, multiplied by DC's proportionate share ratio with respect to Asset E for Year 1. Because the depreciation with respect to Asset E is partly deducted and partly capitalized to inventory, DC's proportionate share ratio with respect to Asset E is determined by reference to both the depreciation that is deducted and the depreciation that is capitalized to inventory and included in cost of goods sold. Therefore, DC's proportionate share ratio with respect to Asset E is 50 percent, which is the ratio calculated as the sum ($25x) of the amount of DC's section 704(b) distributive share of PRS's section 704(b) depreciation deduction with respect to Asset E for Year 1 ($10x) and the amount of PRS's section 704(b) depreciation with respect to Asset E capitalized to inventory of Product A and Product B that is taken into account in determining DC's section 704(b) distributive share of PRS's income or loss for Year 1 ($15x), divided by the sum ($50x) of the total amount of PRS's section 704(b) depreciation deduction with respect to Asset E for Year 1 ($20x) and the total amount of PRS's section 704(b) depreciation with respect to Asset E capitalized to inventory of Product A and Product B that is taken into account in determining PRS's section 704(b) income or loss for Year 1 ($30x). Accordingly, under paragraph (g)(4)(i) of this section, DC's proportionate share of PRS's partnership adjusted basis in Asset E is $300x ($600x x 0.5).

(ii) *Dual use ratio.* Because the depreciation with respect to Asset E is partly deducted and partly capitalized to inventory, DC's dual use ratio with respect to Asset E is determined by reference to the depreciation that is deducted and the depreciation that is capitalized to inventory and included in cost of goods sold. Therefore, DC's dual use ratio with respect to Asset E is 80 percent, which is the ratio calculated as the sum ($20x) of the amount of DC's distributive share of PRS's depreciation deduction with respect to Asset E that is allocated and apportioned to DC's gross DEI under § 1.250(b)-1(d)(2) for Year 1 ($8x) and the amount of depreciation with respect to Asset E capitalized to inventory of Product A and Product B that is taken into account in determining DC's DEI for Year 1 ($12x), divided by the sum ($25x) of the total amount of DC's distributive share of PRS's depreciation deduction with respect to Asset E for Year 1 ($10x) and the total amount of depreciation with respect to Asset E capitalized to inventory of Product A and Product B that is taken into account in determining DC's income or loss for Year 1 ($15x).

(iii) *Partner adjusted basis.* Because DC has no partner-specific QBAI basis with respect to Asset E, DC's partner adjusted basis in Asset E is determined entirely by reference to DC's proportionate share of PRS's partnership adjusted basis in Asset E, multiplied by DC's dual use ratio with respect to Asset E. Under paragraph (g)(3)(iii)(A) of this section, DC's partner adjusted basis in Asset E is $240x, DC's proportionate share of PRS's partnership adjusted basis in Asset E for Year 1 ($300x), multiplied by DC's dual use ratio with respect to Asset E for Year 1 (80 percent).

(4) *Partnership QBAI.* Under paragraph (g)(2) of this section, DC's partnership QBAI with respect to PRS is $332.50x, the sum of DC's partner adjusted basis in Asset C ($30x), DC's partner adjusted basis in Asset D ($62.50x), and DC's partner adjusted basis in Asset E ($240x). Accordingly, under paragraph (g)(1) of this section, DC increases its QBAI for Year 1 by $332.50x.

(iv) *Example 3: Sole use partnership specified tangible property; section 743(b) adjustments.*—(A) *Facts.* The facts are the same as in paragraph (g)(8)(ii)(A) of this section (the facts in *Example 1*), except that there is an average of $40x positive adjustment to the adjusted basis in Asset A as of the close of each quarter of PRS's taxable year with respect to DC under section 743(b) and an average of $20x negative adjustment to the adjusted basis in Asset B as of the close of

each quarter of PRS's taxable year with respect to DC under section 743(b).

(B) *Analysis.* Under paragraph (g)(3)(ii)(A) of this section, DC's partner adjusted basis in Asset A is $120x, which is the sum of $80x (DC's proportionate share of PRS's partnership adjusted basis in Asset A as illustrated in paragraph (g)(8)(ii)(B)(2) of this section (the analysis in *Example 1*)) and $40x (DC's partner-specific QBAI basis in Asset A). Under paragraph (g)(3)(ii)(A) of this section, DC's partner adjusted basis in Asset B is $80x, the sum of $100x (DC's proportionate share of the partnership adjusted basis in the property as illustrated in paragraph (g)(8)(ii)(B)(2) of this section (the analysis in *Example 1*)) and (-$20x) (DC's partner-specific QBAI basis in Asset B). Therefore, under paragraph (g)(2) of this section, DC's partnership QBAI with respect to PRS is $200x ($120x + $80x). Accordingly, under paragraph (g)(1) of this section, DC increases its QBAI for Year 1 by $200x.

(v) *Example 4: Sale of partnership interest before close of taxable year.*—(A) *Facts.* DC1 owns a 50 percent interest in PRS on January 1 of Year 1. PRS does not have an election under section 754 in effect. On July 1 of Year 1, DC1 sells its entire interest in PRS to DC2. PRS owns Asset G. The average of PRS's adjusted basis as of the close of each quarter of PRS's taxable year in Asset G is $100x. DC1's section 704(b) distributive share of the depreciation deduction with respect to Asset G is 25 percent with respect to PRS's entire year. DC2's section 704(b) distributive share of the depreciation deduction with respect to Asset G is also 25 percent with respect to PRS's entire year. Both DC1's and DC2's entire distributive shares of the depreciation deduction with respect to Asset G are allocated and apportioned under § 1.250(b)-1(d)(2) to DC1's and DC2's gross DEI, respectively, for Year 1. PRS's allocations satisfy section 706(d).

(B) *Analysis—(1) DC1.* Because DC1 owns an interest in PRS during DC1's taxable year and receives a distributive share of partnership items of the partnership under section 706(d), DC1 has partnership QBAI with respect to PRS in the amount determined under paragraph (g)(2) of this section. Under paragraph (g)(3)(i) of this section, DC1's partner adjusted basis in Asset G is $25x, the product of $100x (the partnership's adjusted basis in the property) and 25 percent (DC1's section 704(b) distributive share of depreciation deduction with respect to Asset G). Therefore, DC1's partnership QBAI with respect to PRS is $25x. Accordingly, under paragraph (g)(1) of this section, DC1 increases its QBAI by $25x for Year 1.

(2) *DC2.* DC2's partner adjusted basis in Asset G is also $25x, the product of $100x (the partnership's adjusted basis in the property) and 25 percent (DC2's section 704(b) distributive share of depreciation deduction with respect to Asset G). Therefore, DC2's partnership QBAI with respect to PRS is $25x. Accordingly, under paragraph (g)(1) of this section, DC2 increases its QBAI by $25x for Year 1.

(vi) *Example 5: Partnership adjusted basis; distribution of property in liquidation of partnership interest.*—(A) *Facts.* DC1, DC2, and DC3 are equal partners in PRS, a partnership. DC1 and DC2 each has an adjusted basis of $100x in its partnership interest. DC3 has an adjusted basis of $50x in its partnership interest. PRS has a section 754 election in effect. PRS owns Asset H with a fair market value of $50x and an adjusted basis of $0, Asset I with a fair market value of $100x and an adjusted basis of $100x, and Asset J with a fair market value of $150x and an adjusted basis of $150x. Asset H and Asset J are tangible property, but Asset I is not tangible property. PRS distributes Asset I to DC3 in liquidation of DC3's interest in PRS. None of DC1, DC2, DC3, or PRS recognizes gain on the distribution. Under section 732(b), DC3's adjusted basis in Asset I is $50x. PRS's adjusted basis in Asset H is increased by $50x to $50x under section 734(b)(1)(B), which is the amount by which PRS's adjusted basis in Asset I immediately before the distribution exceeds DC3's adjusted basis in Asset I.

(B) *Analysis.* Under paragraph (g)(6) of this section, PRS's adjusted basis in Asset H is determined without regard to any adjustments under section 734(b) except for adjustments under section 734(b)(1)(B) or section 734(b)(2)(B) that are attributable to distributions of tangible property and for adjustments under section 734(b)(1)(A) or 734(b)(2)(A). The adjustment to the adjusted basis in Asset H is under section 734(b)(1)(B) and is attributable to the distribution of Asset I, which is not tangible property. Accordingly, for purposes of applying paragraph (g)(1) of this section, PRS's adjusted basis in Asset H is $0.

(h) *Anti-avoidance rule for certain transfers of property.*—(1) *In general.*—If, with a principal purpose of decreasing the amount of its deemed tangible income return, a domestic corporation transfers specified tangible property (*transferred property*) to a specified related party of the domestic corporation and, within the disqualified period, the domestic corporation or an FDII-eligible related party of the domestic corporation leases the same or substantially similar property from any specified related party, then, solely for purposes of determining the QBAI of the domestic corporation under paragraph (b) of this section, the domestic corporation is treated as owning the transferred property from the later of the beginning of the term of the lease or date of the transfer of the property until the earlier of the end of the term of the lease or the end of the recovery period of the property.

(2) *Rule for structured arrangements.*—For purposes of paragraph (h)(1) of this section, a transfer of specified tangible property to a person that is not a related party or lease of property from a person that is not a related party is treated as a transfer to or lease from a specified related party if the transfer or lease is pursuant to a structured arrangement. A structured arrangement exists only if either paragraph (h)(2)(i) or (ii) of this section is satisfied.

(i) The reduction in the domestic corporation's deemed tangible income return is priced into the terms of the arrangement with the transferee.

(ii) Based on all the facts and circumstances, the reduction in the domestic corporation's deemed tangible income return is a principal purpose of the arrangement. Facts and circumstances that indicate the reduction in the domestic corporation's deemed tangible income return is a principal purpose of the arrangement include—

(A) Marketing the arrangement as tax-advantaged where some or all of the tax advantage derives from the reduction in the domestic corporation's deemed tangible income return;

(B) Primarily marketing the arrangement to domestic corporations which earn FDDEI;

(C) Features that alter the terms of the arrangement, including the return, in the event the reduction in the domestic corporation's deemed tangible income return is no longer relevant; or

(D) A below-market return absent the tax effects or benefits resulting from the reduction in the domestic corporation's deemed tangible income return.

(3) *Per se rules for certain transactions.*—For purposes of paragraph (h)(1) of this section, a transfer of property by a domestic corporation to a specified related party (including a party deemed to be a specified related party under paragraph (h)(2) of this section) followed by a lease of the same or substantially similar property by the domestic corporation or an FDII-eligible related party from a specified related party (including a party deemed to be a specified related party under paragraph (h)(2) of this section) is treated per se as occurring pursuant to a principal purpose of decreasing the amount of the domestic corporation's deemed tangible income return if both the transfer and the lease occur within a six-month period.

(4) *Definitions related to anti-avoidance rule.*—The following definitions apply for purpose of this paragraph (h).

(i) *Disqualified period.*—The term *disqualified period* means, with respect to a transfer, the period beginning one year before the date of the transfer and ending the earlier of the end of the remaining recovery period (under the system described in section 951A(d)(3)(A)) of the property or one year after the date of the transfer.

(ii) *FDII-eligible related party.*—The term *FDII-eligible related party* means, with respect to a domestic corporation, a member of the same consolidated group as the domestic corporation or a partnership with respect to which at least 80 percent of the interests in partnership capital and profits are owned, directly or indirectly, by the domestic corporation or one or more members of the consolidated group that includes the domestic corporation.

(iii) *Specified related party.*—The term *specified related party* means, with respect to a domestic corporation, a related party other than an FDII-eligible related party.

(iv) *Transfer.*—The term *transfer* means any disposition, exchange, contribution, or distribution of property, and includes an indirect transfer. For example, a transfer of an interest in a partnership is treated as a transfer of the assets of the partnership. In addition, if paragraph (h)(1) of this section applies to treat a domestic corporation as owning specified tangible property by reason of a lease of property, the termination or lapse of the lease of the property is treated as a transfer of the specified tangible property by the domestic corporation to the lessor.

(5) *Transactions occurring before March 4, 2019.*—Paragraph (h)(1) of this section does not apply to a transfer of property that occurs before March 4, 2019.

(6) *Examples.*—The following examples illustrate the application of this paragraph (h).

(i) *Example 1: Sale-leaseback with a related party.*—(A) *Facts.* DC, a domestic corporation, owns Asset A, which is specified tangible property. DC also owns all the single class of stock of DS, a domestic

corporation, and FS1 and FS2, each a controlled foreign corporation. DC and DS are members of the same consolidated group. On January 1, Year 1, DC sells Asset A to FS1. At the time of the sale, Asset A had a remaining recovery period of 10 years under the alternative depreciation system. On February 1, Year 1, FS2 leases Asset B, which is substantially similar to Asset A, to DS for a five-year term ending on January 31, Year 6.

(B) *Analysis.* Because DC transfers specified tangible property (Asset A), to a specified related party of DC (FS1), and, within a six month period (January 1, Year 1 to February 1, Year 1), an FDII-eligible related party of DC (DS) leases a substantially similar property (Asset B) from a specified related party (FS2), DC's transfer of Asset A and lease of Asset B are treated as per se occurring pursuant to a principal purpose of decreasing the amount of its deemed tangible income return. Accordingly, for purposes of determining DC's QBAI, DC is treated as owning Asset A from February 1, Year 1, the later of the date of the transfer of Asset A (January 1, Year 1) and the beginning of the term of the lease of Asset B (February 1, Year 1), until January 31, Year 6, the earlier of the end of the term of the lease of Asset B (January 31, Year 6) or the remaining recovery period of Asset A (December 31, Year 10).

(ii) *Example 2: Sale-leaseback with a related party; lapse of initial lease.*—(A) *Facts.* The facts are the same as in paragraph (h)(6)(i)(A) of this section (the facts in *Example 1*). In addition, DS allows the lease of Asset B to expire on February 1, Year 6. On June 1, Year 6, DS and FS2 renew the lease for a five-year term ending on May 31, Year 11.

(B) *Analysis.* Because DC is treated as owning Asset A under paragraph (h)(1) of this section, the lapse of the lease of Asset B is treated as a transfer of Asset A to FS2 on February 1, Year 6, under paragraph (h)(4)(iv) of this section. Further, because DC is deemed to transfer specified tangible property (Asset A) to a specified related party (FS2) upon the lapse of the lease, and within a six month period (February 1, Year 6 to June 1, Year 6), an FDII-eligible related party of DC (DS) leases a substantially similar property (Asset B), DC's deemed transfer of Asset A under paragraph (h)(4)(iv) of this section and lease of Asset B are treated as per se occurring pursuant to a principal purpose of decreasing the amount of its deemed tangible income return. Accordingly, for purposes of determining DC's QBAI, DC is treated as owning Asset A from June 1, Year 6, the later of the date of the deemed transfer of Asset A (February 1, Year 6) and the beginning of the term of the lease of Asset B (June 1, Year 6), until December 31, Year 10, the earlier of the end of the term of the lease of Asset B (May 31, Year 11) or the remaining recovery period of Asset A (December 31, Year 10). [Reg. § .250(b)-2.]

□ [*T.D.* 9901, 7-9-2020. (*corrected* 9-28-2020). *Amended by T.D.* 9956, 9-21-2021.]

[Reg. § 1.250(b)-3]

§1.250(b)-3. Foreign-derived deduction eligible income (FDDEI) transactions.—(a) *Scope.*—This section provides rules related to the determination of whether a sale of property or provision of a service is a FDDEI transaction. Paragraph (b) of this section provides definitions related to the determination of whether a sale of property or provision of a service is a FDDEI transaction. Paragraph (c) of this section provides rules regarding a sale of property or provision of a service to a foreign government or an agency or instrumentality thereof. Paragraph (d) of this section provides a rule for characterizing a transaction with both sales and services elements. Paragraph (e) of this section provides a rule for determining whether a sale of property or provision of a service to a partnership is a FDDEI transaction. Paragraph (f) of this section provides rules for substantiating certain FDDEI transactions.

(b) *Definitions.*—This paragraph (b) provides definitions that apply for purposes of this section and §§ 1.250(b)-4 through 1.250(b)-6.

(1) *Digital content.*—The term *digital content* means a computer program or any other content in digital format. For example, digital content includes books in digital format, movies in digital format, and music in digital format. For purposes of this section, a computer program is a set of statements or instructions to be used directly or indirectly in a computer or other electronic device in order to bring about a certain result, and includes any media, user manuals, documentation, data base, or similar item if the media, user manuals, documentation, data base, or other similar item is incidental to the operation of the computer program.

(2) *End user.*—Except as modified by §1.250(b)-4(d)(2)(ii), the term *end user* means the person that ultimately uses or consumes property or a person that acquires property in a foreign retail sale. A person that acquires property for resale or otherwise as an intermediary is not an end user.

(3) *FDII filing date.*—The term *FDII filing date* means, with respect to a sale of property by a seller or provision of a service by a

renderer, the date, including extensions, by which the seller or renderer is required to file an income tax return (or in the case of a seller or renderer that is a partnership, a return of partnership income) for the taxable year in which the gross income from the sale of property or provision of a service is included in the gross income of the seller or renderer.

(4) *Finished goods.*—The term *finished goods* means general property that is acquired by an end user.

(5) *Foreign person.*—The term *foreign person* means a person (as defined in section 7701(a)(1)) that is not a United States person and includes a foreign government or an international organization.

(6) *Foreign related party.*—The term *foreign related party* means, with respect to a seller or renderer, any foreign person that is a related party of the seller or renderer.

(7) *Foreign retail sale.*—The term *foreign retail sale* means a sale of general property to a recipient that acquires the general property at a physical retail location (such as a store or warehouse) outside the United States.

(8) *Foreign unrelated party.*—The term *foreign unrelated party* means, with respect to a seller, a foreign person that is not a related party of the seller.

(9) *Fungible mass of general property.*—The term *fungible mass of general property* means multiple units of property for sale with similar or identical characteristics for which the seller does not know the specific identity of the recipient or the end user for a particular unit.

(10) *General property.*—The term *general property* means any property other than: intangible property (as defined in paragraph (b)(11) of this section); a security (as defined in section 475(c)(2)); an interest in a partnership, trust, or estate; a commodity described in section 475(e)(2)(A) that is not a physical commodity; or a commodity described in section 475(e)(2)(B) through (D). A physical commodity described in section 475(e)(2)(A) is treated as general property, including if it is sold pursuant to a forward or option contract (including a contract described in section 475(e)(2)(C), but not a section 1256 contract as defined in section 1256(b) or other similar contract that is traded on a U.S. or non-U.S. regulated exchange and cleared by a central clearing organization in a manner similar to a section 1256 contract) that is physically settled by delivery of the commodity (provided that the taxpayer physically settled the contract pursuant to a consistent practice adopted for business purposes of determining whether to cash or physically settle such contracts under similar circumstances).

(11) *Intangible property.*—The term *intangible property* has the meaning set forth in section 367(d)(4). For purposes of section 250, intangible property does not include a copyrighted article as defined in §1.861-18(c)(3).

(12) *International transportation property.*—The term *international transportation property* means aircraft, railroad rolling stock, vessel, motor vehicle, or similar property that provides a mode of transportation and is capable of traveling internationally.

(13) *IP address.*—The term *IP address* means a device's Internet Protocol address.

(14) *Recipient.*—The term *recipient* means a person that purchases property or services from a seller or renderer.

(15) *Renderer.*—The term *renderer* means a person that provides a service to a recipient.

(16) *Sale.*—The term *sale* means any sale, lease, license, sublicense, exchange, or other disposition of property, and includes any transfer of property in which gain or income is recognized under section 367. In addition, the term *sell* (and any form of the word sell) means any transfer by sale.

(17) *Seller.*—The term *seller* means a person that sells property to a recipient.

(18) *United States.*—The term *United States* has the meaning set forth in section 7701(a)(9), as expanded by section 638(1) with respect to mines, oil and gas wells, and other natural deposits.

(19) *United States person.*—The term *United States person* has the meaning set forth in section 7701(a)(30), except that the term does not include an individual that is a bona fide resident of a United States territory within the meaning of section 937(a).

(20) *United States territory.*—The term *United States territory* means American Samoa, Guam, the Northern Mariana Islands, Puerto Rico, or the U.S. Virgin Islands.

(c) *Foreign military sales and services.*—If a sale of property or a provision of a service is made to the United States or an instrumentality thereof pursuant to 22 U.S.C. 2751 et seq. under which the United States or an instrumentality thereof purchases the property or service for resale or on-service to a foreign government or agency or instrumentality thereof, then the sale of property or provision of a service is treated as a FDDEI sale or FDDEI service without regard to §1.250(b)-4 or §1.250(b)-5.

(d) *Transactions with multiple elements.*—A transaction is classified according to its overall predominant character for purposes of determining whether the transaction is a FDDEI sale under §1.250(b)-4 or a FDDEI service under §1.250(b)-5. For example, whether a transaction that includes both a sales component and a service component is subject to §1.250(b)-4 or §1.250(b)-5 is determined based on whether the overall predominant character, taking into account all relevant facts and circumstances, is a sale or service. In addition, whether a transaction that includes both a sale of general property and a sale of intangible property is subject to §1.250(b)-4(d)(1) or §1.250(b)-4(d)(2) is determined based on whether the overall predominant character, taking into account all relevant facts and circumstances, is a sale of general property or a sale of intangible property.

(e) *Treatment of partnerships.*—(1) *In general.*—For purposes of determining whether a sale of property to or by a partnership or a provision of a service to or by a partnership is a FDDEI transaction, a partnership is treated as a person. Accordingly, for example, a partnership may be a seller, renderer, recipient, or related party, including a foreign related party (as defined in paragraph (b)(6) of this section).

(2) *Examples.*—The following examples illustrate the application of this paragraph (e).

(i) *Example 1: Domestic partner sale to foreign partnership with a foreign branch.*—(A) *Facts.* DC, a domestic corporation, is a partner in PRS, a foreign partnership. DC and PRS are not related parties. PRS has a foreign branch within the meaning of §1.904-4(f)(3)(iii). DC and PRS both use the calendar year as their taxable year. For the taxable year, DC recognizes $20x of gain on the sale of general property to PRS for a foreign use (as determined under §1.250(b)-4(d)). During the same taxable year, PRS recognizes $20x of gain on the sale of other general property to a foreign person for a foreign use (as determined under §1.250(b)-4(d)). PRS's income on the sale of the property is attributable to its foreign branch.

(B) *Analysis.* DC's sale of property to PRS, a foreign partnership, is a FDDEI sale because it is a sale to a foreign person for a foreign use. Therefore, DC's gain of $20x on the sale to PRS is included in DC's gross DEI and gross FDDEI. However, PRS's gain of $20x is not included in the gross DEI or gross FDDEI of PRS because the gain is foreign branch income within the meaning of §1.250(b)-1(c)(11). Accordingly, none of PRS's gain on the sale of property is included in DC's gross DEI or gross FDDEI under §1.250(b)-1(e)(1).

(ii) *Example 2: Domestic partner sale to domestic partnership without a foreign branch.*—(A) *Facts.* The facts are the same as in paragraph (e)(2)(i)(A) of this section (the facts in *Example 1*), except PRS is a domestic partnership that does not have a foreign branch within the meaning of §1.904-4(f)(3)(iii).

(B) *Analysis.* DC's sale of property to PRS, a domestic partnership, is not a FDDEI sale because the sale is to a United States person. Therefore, the gross income from DC's sale to PRS is included in DC's gross DEI but is not included in its gross FDDEI. However, PRS's sale of other general property is a FDDEI sale, and therefore the gain of $20x is included in the gross DEI and gross FDDEI of PRS. Accordingly, DC includes its distributive share of PRS's gain from the sale in determining DC's gross DEI and gross FDDEI for the taxable year under §1.250(b)-1(e)(1).

(f) *Substantiation for certain FDDEI transactions.*—(1) *In general.*—Except as provided in paragraph (f)(2) of this section, for purposes of §1.250(b)-4(d)(1)(ii)(C) (foreign use for sale of general property for resale), §1.250(b)-4(d)(1)(iii) (foreign use for sale of general property subject to manufacturing, assembly, or processing outside the United States), §1.250(b)-4(d)(2) (foreign use for sale of intangible property), and §1.250(b)-5(e) (general services provided to business recipients located outside the United States), a transaction is a FDDEI transaction only if the taxpayer substantiates its determination of foreign use (in the case of sales of property) or location outside the United States (in the case of general services provided to a business recipient) as described in the applicable paragraph of §1.250(b)-4(d)(3) or §1.250(b)-5(e)(4). The substantiating documents must be in existence as of the FDII filing date with respect to the FDDEI transaction, and a taxpayer must provide the required substantiating documents within 30 days of a request by the Commissioner or another period as agreed between the Commissioner and the taxpayer.

(2) *Exception for small businesses.*—Paragraph (f)(1) of this section, and the specific substantiation requirements described in the applicable paragraph of §1.250(b)-4(d)(3) or §1.250(b)-5(e)(4), do not apply to a taxpayer if the taxpayer and all related parties of the taxpayer, in the aggregate, receive less than $25,000,000 in gross receipts during the taxable year prior to the FDDEI transaction. If the taxpayer's prior taxable year was less than 12 months (a short period), gross receipts are annualized by multiplying the gross receipts for the short period by 365 and dividing the result by the number of days in the short period.

(3) *Treatment of certain loss transactions.*—(i) *In general.*—If a domestic corporation fails to satisfy the substantiation requirements described in the applicable paragraph of §1.250(b)-4(d)(3) or §1.250(b)-5(e)(4) with respect to a transaction (including in connection with a related party transaction described in §1.250(b)-6), the gross income from the transaction will be treated as gross FDDEI if—

(A) In the case of a sale of property, the seller knows or has reason to know that property is sold to a foreign person for a foreign use (within the meaning of §1.250(b)-4(d)(1) or (2));

(B) In the case of the provision of a general service to a business recipient, the renderer knows or has reason to know that a service is provided to a business recipient located outside the United States; and

(C) Not treating the transaction as a FDDEI transaction would increase the amount of the corporation's FDDEI for the taxable year relative to its FDDEI that would be determined if the transaction were treated as a FDDEI transaction.

(ii) *Reason to know.*—(A) *Sales to a foreign person for a foreign use.*—For purposes of paragraph (f)(3)(i)(A) of this section, a seller has reason to know that a sale is to a foreign person for a foreign use if the information received as part of the sales process contains information that indicates that the recipient is a foreign person or that the sale is for a foreign use, and the seller fails to obtain evidence establishing that the recipient is not in fact a foreign person or that the sale is not in fact for a foreign use. Information that indicates that a recipient is a foreign person or that the sale is for a foreign use includes, but is not limited to, a foreign phone number, billing address, shipping address, or place of residence; and, with respect to an entity, evidence that the entity is incorporated, formed, or managed outside the United States.

(B) *General services provided to a business recipient located outside the United States.*—For purposes of paragraph (f)(3)(i)(B) of

this section, a renderer has reason to know that the provision of a general service is to a business recipient located outside the United States if the information received as part of the sales process contains information that indicates that the recipient is a business recipient located outside the United States and the seller fails to obtain evidence establishing that the recipient is not in fact a business recipient located outside the United States. Information that indicates that a recipient is a business recipient includes, but is not limited to, indicia of a business status (such as "LLC" or "Company," or similar indicia under applicable domestic or foreign law, in the name) or statements by the recipient indicating that it is a business. Information that indicates that a business recipient is located outside the United States includes, but is not limited to, a foreign phone number, billing address, and evidence that the entity or business is incorporated, formed, or managed outside the United States.

(iii) *Multiple transactions.*—If a seller or renderer engages in more than one transaction described in paragraph (f)(3)(i) of this section in a taxable year, paragraph (f)(3)(i) of this section applies by comparing the corporation's FDDEI if each such transaction were not treated as a FDDEI transaction to its FDDEI if each such transaction were treated as a FDDEI transaction.

(iv) *Example.*—The following example illustrates the application of this paragraph (f)(3).

(A) *Facts.* During a taxable year, DC, a domestic corporation, manufactures products A and B in the United States. DC sells product A and product B to Y, a foreign person that is a distributor, for $200x and $800x, respectively. DC knows or has reason to know that all of its sales of product A and product B will ultimately be sold to end users located outside the United States. Y provides DC with a statement that satisfies the substantiation requirement of paragraph (f)(1) of this section and §1.250(b)-4(d)(3)(ii) that establishes that its sales of product B are for a foreign use but does not obtain substantiation establishing that any sales of product A are for a foreign use. DC's cost of goods sold is $450x. For purposes of determining gross FDDEI, under §1.250(b)-1(d)(1) DC attributes $250x of cost of goods sold to product A and $200x of cost of goods sold to product B, and then attributes the cost of goods sold for each product ratably between the gross receipts of such product sold to foreign persons and the gross receipts of such product not sold to foreign persons. The manner in which DC attributes the cost of goods sold is a reasonable method. DC has no other items of income, loss, or deduction.

Table 1 to paragraph (f)(3)(iv)(A)			
	Product A	Product B	Total
Gross receipts	$200x	$800x	$1,000x
Cost of Goods Sold	$250x	$200x	$450x
Gross Income (Loss)	($50x)	$600x	$550x

(B) *Analysis.* By not treating the sales of product A as FDDEI sales, the amount of DC's FDDEI would increase by $50x relative to its FDDEI if the sales of product A were treated as FDDEI sales. Accordingly, because DC knows or has reason to know that its sales of product A are to foreign persons for a foreign use, the sales of product A constitute FDDEI sales under paragraph (f)(3) of this section, and thus the $50x loss from the sale of product A is included in DC's gross FDDEI. [Reg. §1.250(b)-3.]

☐ [T.D. 9901, 7-9-2020.]

[Reg. §1.250(b)-4]

§1.250(b)-4. Foreign-derived deduction eligible income (FDDEI) sales.—(a) *Scope.*—This section provides rules for determining whether a sale of property is a FDDEI sale. Paragraph (b) of this section defines a FDDEI sale. Paragraph (c) of this section provides rules for determining whether a recipient is a foreign person. Paragraph (d) of this section provides rules for determining whether property is sold for a foreign use. Paragraph (e) of this section provides a special rule for the sale of interests in a disregarded entity. Paragraph (f) of this section provides a rule regarding certain hedging transactions with respect to FDDEI sales.

(b) *Definition of FDDEI sale.*—Except as provided in §1.250(b)-6(c), the term *FDDEI sale* means a sale of general property or intangible property to a recipient that is a foreign person (see paragraph (c) of this section for presumption rules relating to determining foreign person status) and that is for a foreign use (as determined under paragraph (d) of this section). A sale of any property other than general property or intangible property is not a FDDEI sale.

(c) *Presumption of foreign person status.*—(1) *In general.*—The sale of property is presumed to be to a recipient that is a foreign person for

purposes of paragraph (b) of this section if the sale is described in paragraph (c)(2) of this section. However, this presumption does not apply if the seller knows or has reason to know that the sale is not to a foreign person. A seller has reason to know that a sale is not to a foreign person if the information received as part of the sales process contains information that indicates that the recipient is not a foreign person and the seller fails to obtain evidence establishing that the recipient is in fact a foreign person. Information that indicates that a recipient is not a foreign person include, but are not limited to, a United States phone number, billing address, shipping address, or place of residence; and, with respect to an entity, evidence that the entity is incorporated, formed, or managed in the United States.

(2) *Sales of property.*—A sale of a property is described in this paragraph (c)(2) if:

(i) The sale is a foreign retail sale;

(ii) In the case of a sale of general property that is not a foreign retail sale and the general property is delivered (such as through a commercial carrier) to the recipient or an end user, the shipping address of the recipient or end user is outside the United States;

(iii) In the case of a sale of general property that is not described in either paragraph (c)(2)(i) or (ii) of this section, the billing address of the recipient is outside the United States; or

(iv) In the case of a sale of intangible property, the billing address of the recipient is outside the United States.

(d) *Foreign use.*—(1) *Foreign use for general property.*—(i) *In general.*—The sale of general property is for a foreign use for purposes of paragraph (b) of this section if the seller determines that the sale is for a foreign use under the rules of paragraph (d)(1)(ii) or (iii) of this section and the exception in paragraph (d)(1)(iv) of this section does not apply.

(ii) *Rules for determining foreign use.*—(A) *Sales that are delivered to an end user by a carrier or freight forwarder.*—Except as otherwise provided in this paragraph (d)(1)(ii)(A), a sale of general property (other than a sale of general property described in paragraphs (d)(1)(ii)(D) through (F) of this section) that is delivered through a carrier or freight forwarder to a recipient that is an end user is for a foreign use if the end user receives delivery of the general property outside the United States. However, a sale described in the preceding sentence is not treated as a sale to an end user for a foreign use if the sale is made with a principal purpose of having the property transported from its location outside the United States to a location within the United States for ultimate use or consumption.

(B) *Sales to an end user without the use of a carrier or freight forwarder.*—With respect to sales that are not delivered through the use of a carrier or freight forwarder, a sale of general property (other than a sale of general property described in paragraphs (d)(1)(ii)(D) through (F) of this section) to a recipient that is an end user is for a foreign use if the property is located outside the United States at the time of the sale (including as part of foreign retail sales).

(C) *Sales for resale.*—A sale of general property (other than a sale of general property described in paragraphs (d)(1)(ii)(D) through (F) of this section) to a recipient (such as a distributor or retailer) that will resell the general property is for a foreign use if the general property will ultimately be sold to end users outside the United States (including in foreign retail sales) and such sales to end users outside the United States are substantiated under paragraph (d)(3)(ii) of this section. In the case of sales of a fungible mass of general property, the taxpayer may presume that the proportion of its sales that are ultimately sold to end users outside the United States is the same as the proportion of the recipient's resales of that fungible mass to end users outside the United States.

(D) *Sales of digital content.*—A sale of general property that primarily contains digital content that is transferred electronically rather than in a physical medium is for a foreign use if the end user downloads, installs, receives, or accesses the purchased digital content on the end user's device outside the United States (see § 1.250(b)-5(d)(2) and (e)(2)(iii) for rules that apply in the case of digital content that is not purchased in a sale but is electronically supplied as a service). If information about where the digital content is downloaded, installed, received, or accessed (such as the device's IP address) is unavailable, and the gross receipts from all sales with respect to the end user (which may be a business) are in the aggregate less than $50,000 for the seller's taxable year, a sale of general property described in the preceding sentence is for a foreign use if it is to an end user that has a billing address located outside the United States.

(E) *Sales of international transportation property used for compensation or hire.*—A sale of international transportation property used for compensation or hire is for a foreign use if the end user registers the property with a foreign jurisdiction.

(F) *Sales of international transportation property not used for compensation or hire.*—A sale of international transportation property not used for compensation or hire is for a foreign use if the end user registers the property in a foreign jurisdiction and hangars or stores the property primarily outside the United States.

(iii) *Sales for manufacturing, assembly, or other processing.*—(A) *In general.*—A sale of general property is for a foreign use if the sale is to a foreign unrelated party that subjects the property to manufacture, assembly, or other processing outside the United States and such manufacturing, assembly, or other processing outside the United States is substantiated under paragraph (d)(3)(iii) of this section. Property is subject to manufacture, assembly, or other processing only if the property is physically and materially changed (as described in paragraph (d)(1)(iii)(B) of this section) or the property is incorporated as a component into another product (as described in paragraph (d)(1)(iii)(C) of this section).

(B) *Property subject to a physical and material change.*—The determination of whether general property is subject to a physical and material change is made based on all the relevant facts and circumstances. General property is subject to a physical and material change if it is substantially transformed and is distinguishable from and cannot be readily returned to its original state.

(C) *Property incorporated into a product as a component.*—General property is a component incorporated into another product if the incorporation of the general property into another product involves activities that are substantial in nature and generally consid-

ered to constitute the manufacture, assembly, or processing of property based on all the relevant facts and circumstances. However, general property is not considered a component incorporated into another product if it is subject only to packaging, repackaging, labeling, or minor assembly operations. In addition, general property is treated as a component if the seller expects, using reliable estimates, that the fair market value of the property when it is delivered to the recipient will constitute no more than 20 percent of the fair market value of the finished good into which the general property is directly or indirectly incorporated when the finished good is sold to end users (the "20-percent rule"). If the property could be incorporated into a number of different finished goods, a reliable estimate of the fair market value of the finished good may include the average fair market value of a representative range of such goods. For purposes of the 20-percent rule, all general property that is sold by the seller and incorporated into the finished good is treated as a single item of property if the seller sells the property to the recipient and the seller knows or has reason to know that the components will be incorporated into a single item of property (for example, where multiple components are sold as a kit). A seller knows or has reason to know that the components will be incorporated into a single item of property if the information received as part of the sales process indicates that the components will be included in the same second product or the nature of the components compels inclusion into the second product and the seller fails to obtain evidence to the contrary.

(iv) *Sales of property subject to manufacturing, assembly, or other processing in the United States.*—If the seller sells general property to a recipient (other than a related party) for manufacturing, assembly, or other processing within the United States, such property is not sold for a foreign use even if the requirements of paragraph (d)(1)(ii) or (iii) of this section are subsequently satisfied. See § 1.250(b)-6(c) for rules governing sales of general property to a foreign person that is a related party. Property is subject to manufacture, assembly, or other processing only if the property is physically and materially changed (as described in paragraph (d)(1)(iii)(B) of this section) or the property is incorporated as a component into another product (as described in paragraph (d)(1)(iii)(C) of this section).

(v) *Examples.*—The following examples illustrate the application of this paragraph (d)(1).

(A) *Assumed facts.*—The following facts are assumed for purposes of the examples—

(1) DC is a domestic corporation.

(2) FP is a foreign person that is a foreign unrelated party with respect to DC.

(3) To the extent a sale is for a foreign use, any applicable substantiation requirements described in paragraph (d)(3)(ii) or (iii) of this section are satisfied.

(B) *Examples*—

(1) *Example 1: Manufacturing outside the United States.*—(i) *Facts.* DC sells batteries for $18x to FP. DC expects that FP will insert the batteries into tablets as part of the process of assembling tablets outside the United States. While the tablets are manufactured in a way that end users would not easily be able to remove the batteries, the batteries could be removed from the tablets and would resemble their original state following the removal. The finished tablets will be sold to end users within and outside the United States. DC's batteries are used in two types of tablets, Tablet A and Tablet B. Based on an economic analysis, DC determines that the fair market value of Tablet A is $90x and the fair market value of Tablet B is $110x. FP informs DC that the number of sales of Tablet A is approximately equal to the number of sales of Tablet B.

(ii) *Analysis.* Because the batteries could be removed from the tablets and be returned to their original state, the insertion of the batteries into tablets does not constitute a physical and material change described in paragraph (d)(1)(iii)(B) of this section. However, the average fair market value of a representative range of tablets that incorporate the batteries is $100x (the average of $90x for Tablet A and $110x for Tablet B because their sales are approximately equal), and $18x is less than 20 percent of $100x. Therefore, the batteries are considered components of the tablets and treated as subject to manufacture, assembly, or other processing outside the United States. See paragraphs (d)(1)(iii)(A) and (C) of this section. As a result, notwithstanding that some tablets incorporating the batteries may be sold to an end user in the United States, DC's sale of batteries is considered for a foreign use. Accordingly, DC's sale of batteries to FP is for a foreign use under paragraph (d)(1)(iii)(A) and (C) of this section, and the sale is a FDDEI sale.

(2) *Example 2: Manufacturing outside the United States.*—(i) *Facts.* The facts are the same as in paragraph (d)(1)(v)(B)(1) of this section (the facts in *Example 1*), except FP purchases the batteries from DC for $25x. In addition, FP purchased other components of

tablets from other parties. FP has a substantial investment in machinery and tools that are used to assemble tablets.

(ii) *Analysis.* Even though the fair market value of the batteries that FP purchases from DC and incorporates into the tablets exceeds 20 percent of the fair market value of the tablets, because the batteries are used by FP in activities that are substantial in nature and generally considered to constitute the manufacture, assembly or other processing of property, the batteries are components of the tablets. As a result, DC's sale of property to FP is still for a foreign use under paragraph (d)(1)(iii)(A) and (C) of this section, and the sale is a FDDEI sale.

(3) *Example 3: Sale of products to distributor outside the United States.*—(i) *Facts.* DC sells smartphones to FP, a distributor of electronics located within Country A. The sales contract between DC and FP provides that FP may sell the smartphones it purchases from DC only to specified retailers located within Country A. The specified retailers only sell electronics, including smartphones, in foreign retail sales.

(ii) *Analysis.* Although FP does not sell the smartphones it purchases from DC to end users, FP sells to retailers that sell the smartphones in foreign retail sales. All of the sales of smartphones from DC to FP are sales of general property for a foreign use under paragraph (d)(1)(ii)(C) of this section because FP is only allowed to sell the smartphones to retailers who sell such property in foreign retail sales. As a result, DC's sales of smartphones to FP are FDDEI sales.

(4) *Example 4: Sale of a fungible mass of products.*—(i) *Facts.* DC and persons other than DC sell multiple units of printer paper that is considered fungible general property to FP during the taxable year. FP is a distributor that sells paper to retail stores within and outside the United States. FP informs DC that approximately 25 percent of FP's sales of the paper are to retail stores located outside of the United States for foreign retail sales.

(ii) *Analysis.* The sale of paper to FP is for a foreign use to the extent that the paper will be sold to end users located outside the United States under paragraph (d)(1)(ii)(C) of this section. Because a portion of DC's sales to FP are not for a foreign use, DC must determine the amount of paper that is sold for a foreign use. Based on the information provided by FP about its own sales, DC determines under paragraph (d)(1)(ii)(C) of this section that 25 percent of the total units of paper that is fungible general property that FP purchased from all persons in the taxable year will ultimately be sold to end users located outside the United States. Accordingly, DC satisfies the test for a foreign use under paragraph (d)(1)(ii)(C) of this section with respect to 25 percent of its sales of the paper to FP.

(5) *Example 5: Limited use license of copyrighted computer software.*—(i) *Facts.* DC provides FP with a limited use license to copyrighted computer software in exchange for an annual fee of $100x. The limited use license restricts FP's use of the computer software to 100 of FP's employees, who download the software onto their computers. The limited use license prohibits FP from using the computer software in any way other than as an end user, which includes prohibiting sublicensing, selling, reverse engineering, or modifying the computer software. All of FP's employees download the software onto computers that are physically located outside the United States.

(ii) *Analysis.* The software licensed to FP is digital content as defined in §1.250(b)-3(b)(1), and is downloaded by an end user as defined in §1.250(b)-3(b)(2). Accordingly, because the software is downloaded solely onto computers outside the United States, DC's license to FP is for a foreign use and therefore a FDDEI sale under paragraph (d)(1)(ii)(D) of this section. The entire $100x of the license fee is included in DC's gross FDDEI for the taxable year.

(6) *Example 6: Limited use license of copyrighted computer software used within and outside the United States.*—(i) *Facts.* The facts are the same as in paragraph (d)(1)(v)(B)(5) of this section (the facts in *Example 5*), except that FP has offices both within and outside the United States, and DC's internal records indicates that 50 percent of the downloads of the software are onto computers located outside the United States.

(ii) *Analysis.* Because 50 percent of the downloads of the software are onto computers located outside the United States, a portion of DC's license to FP is for a foreign use and therefore such portion is a FDDEI sale. The $50x of license fee derived with respect to such portion is included in DC's gross FDDEI for the taxable year.

(7) *Example 7: Sale of a copyrighted article.*—(i) *Facts.* DC sells copyrighted music available for download on its website. Once downloaded, the recipient listens to the music on electronic devices that do not need to be connected to the internet. DC has data that an individual accesses the website to purchase a song for download on a device located outside the United States. The terms of the sale permit the recipient to use the song for personal use, but convey no other rights to the copyrighted music to the recipient.

(ii) *Analysis.* The music acquired through download is digital content as defined in §1.250(b)-3(b)(1). Because the recipient acquires no ownership in copyright rights to the music, the sale is considered a sale of a copyrighted article, and thus is a sale of general property. See §1.250(b)-3(b)(10) and (11). As a result, the sale is considered for a foreign use under paragraph (d)(1)(ii)(D) of this section because the digital content was installed, received, or accessed on the end user's device outside the United States. The income derived with respect to the sale of the music is included in DC's gross FDDEI for the taxable year. See §1.250(b)-5(d)(3) for an example of digital content provided to consumers as a service rather than as a sale.

(2) *Foreign use for intangible property.*—(i) *In general.*—A sale of rights to exploit intangible property solely outside the United States is for a foreign use. A sale of rights to exploit intangible property solely within the United States is not for a foreign use. A sale of rights to exploit intangible property worldwide is partially for a foreign use and partially not for a foreign use. Whether intangible property is exploited within versus outside the United States is determined based on revenue earned from end users located within versus outside the United States. Therefore, a sale of rights to exploit intangible property both within and outside the United States is for a foreign use in proportion to the revenue earned from end users located outside the United States over the total revenue earned from the exploitation of the intangible property. A sale of intangible property will be treated as a FDDEI sale only if the substantiation requirements of paragraph (d)(3)(iv) of this section are satisfied. For rules specific to determining end users and revenue earned from end users for intangible property used in sales of general property, provision of services, research and development, or consisting of a manufacturing method or process, see paragraph (d)(2)(ii) of this section.

(ii) *Determination of end users and revenue earned from end users.*—(A) *Intangible property embedded in general property or used in connection with the sale of general property.*—If intangible property is embedded in general property that is sold, or used in connection with a sale of general property, then the end user of the intangible property is the end user of the general property. Revenue is earned from the end user of the general property outside the United States to the extent the sale of the general property is for a foreign use under paragraph (d)(1)(ii) or (iii) of this section.

(B) *Intangible property used in providing a service.*—If intangible property is used to provide a service, then the end user of that intangible property is the recipient, consumer, or business recipient of the service or, in the case of a property service or a transportation service that involves the transportation of property, the end user is the owner of the property on which such service is being performed. Such end users are treated as located outside the United States only to the extent the service qualifies as a FDDEI service under §1.250(b)-5. Therefore, in the case of a recipient of a sale of intangible property that uses such intangible property to provide a property service that qualifies as a FDDEI service to another person, that person is the end user and is treated as located outside the United States.

(C) *Intangible property consisting of a manufacturing method or process.*—(1) *In general.*—Except as provided in paragraph (d)(2)(ii)(C)(2) of this section, if intangible property consists of a manufacturing method or process (as defined in paragraph (d)(2)(ii)(C)(3) of this section) and is sold to a foreign unrelated party (including in a sale by a foreign related party), then the foreign unrelated party is treated as an end user located outside the United States, unless the seller knows or has reason to know that the manufacturing method or process will be used in the United States, in which case the foreign unrelated party is treated as an end user located within the United States. A seller has reason to know that the manufacturing method or process will be used in the United States if the information received from the recipient as part of the sales process contains information that indicates that the recipient intends to use the manufacturing method or process in the United States and the seller fails to obtain evidence establishing that the recipient does not intend to use the manufacturing method or process in the United States.

(2) *Exception for certain manufacturing arrangements.*—A sale of intangible property consisting of a manufacturing method or process (including a sale by a foreign related party) to a foreign unrelated party for use in manufacturing products for or on behalf of the seller or any person related to the seller does not qualify as a sale to a foreign unrelated party for purposes of determining the end user under paragraph (d)(2)(ii)(C)(1) of this section.

(3) Manufacturing method or process.—For purposes of this section, a manufacturing method or process consists of a sequence of actions or steps that comprise an overall method or process that is used to manufacture a product or produce a particular manufacturing result, which may be in the form of a patent or know-how. Intangible property consisting of the right to make and sell an item of property is not a manufacturing method or process, whereas intangible property consisting of the right to apply a series of actions or steps to be performed to achieve a particular manufacturing result is a manufacturing method or process. For example, a utility or design patent on an article of manufacture, machine, composition of matter, design, or providing the right to sell equipment to perform a process is not a manufacturing method or process, whereas a utility patent covering a method or process of manufacturing is a manufacturing method or process for purposes of this section.

(D) Intangible property used in research and development.—If intangible property (primary IP) is used to develop new or modify other intangible property (secondary IP), then the end user of the primary IP is the end user (applying paragraph (d)(2)(ii)(A), (B), or (C) of this section) of the secondary IP.

(iii) Determination of revenue for periodic payments versus lump sums.—(A) *Sales in exchange for periodic payments.*—In the case of a sale of intangible property, other than intangible property consisting of a manufacturing method or process that is sold to a foreign unrelated party, to a recipient in exchange for periodic payments, the extent to which the sale is for a foreign use is determined annually based on the actual revenue earned by the recipient from any use of the intangible property for the taxable year in which a periodic payment is received. If actual revenue earned by the recipient cannot be obtained after reasonable efforts, then estimated revenue earned by a recipient that is not a related party of the seller from the use of the intangible property may be used based on the principles of paragraph (d)(2)(iii)(B) of this section.

(B) Sales in exchange for a lump sum.—In the case of a sale of intangible property, other than intangible property consisting of a manufacturing method or process that is sold to a foreign unrelated party, for a lump sum, the extent to which the sale is for a foreign use is determined based on the ratio of the total net present value of revenue the seller would have expected to earn from the exploitation of the intangible property outside the United States to the total net present value of revenue the seller would have expected to earn from the exploitation of the intangible property. In the case of a recipient that is a foreign unrelated party, net present values of revenue that the recipient expected to earn from the exploitation of the intangible property within and outside the United States may also be used if the seller obtained such revenue data from the recipient near the time of the sale and such revenue data was used to negotiate the lump sum price paid for the intangible property. Net present values must be determined using reliable inputs including, but not limited to, reliable revenue, expenses, and discount rates. The extent to which the inputs are used by the parties to determine the sales price agreed to between the seller and a foreign unrelated party purchasing the intangible property will be a factor in determining whether such inputs are reliable. If the intangible property is sold to a foreign related party, the reliability of the inputs used to determine net present values and the net present values are determined under section 482.

(C) Sales to a foreign unrelated party of intangible property consisting of a manufacturing method or process.—In the case of a sale to an unrelated foreign party of intangible property consisting of a manufacturing method or process, the revenue earned from the end user is equal to the amount received from the recipient in exchange for the manufacturing method or process. In the case of a bundled sale of intangible property consisting of a manufacturing method or process and intangible property not consisting of a manufacturing method or process, the revenue earned from the intangible property consisting of the manufacturing method or process equals the total amount paid for the bundled sale multiplied by the proportion that the value of the manufacturing method or process bears to the total value of the intangible property. The value of the manufacturing method or process to the total value of the intangible property must be determined using the principles of section 482.

(iv) Examples.—The following examples illustrate the application of this paragraph (d)(2).

(A) Assumed facts.—The following facts are assumed for purposes of the examples—

(1) DC is a domestic corporation.

(2) Except as otherwise provided, FP and FP2 are foreign persons that are foreign unrelated parties with respect to DC.

(3) All of DC's income is DEI.

(4) Except as otherwise provided, the substantiation requirements described in paragraph (d)(3)(iv) of this section are satisfied.

(5) Except as otherwise provided, inputs used to determine the net present values of the revenue are reliable.

(B) Examples—

(1) Example 1: License of worldwide rights with actual revenue data from recipient.—(i) *Facts.* DC licenses to FP worldwide rights to the copyright to composition A in exchange for annual royalties of 60 percent of revenue from FP's sales of composition A. FP sells composition A to customers through digital downloads from servers. In the taxable year, FP earns $100x in revenue from sales of copies of composition A to customers, of which $60x is from customers located in the United States and the remaining $40x is from customers located outside the United States. FP provides DC with reliable records showing the amount of revenue earned in the taxable year from sales of composition A to establish the royalties owed to DC. These records also provide DC with the amount of revenue earned from sales of composition A to customers located within the United States.

(ii) Analysis. FP is not the end user of the copyright to composition A under paragraph (d)(2)(ii)(A) of this section because the copyright is used in the sale of general property (the sale of copyrighted articles to customers). The customers that purchase a copy of composition A from FP are the end users (as defined in § 1.250(b)-3(b)(2) and paragraph (d)(2)(ii)(A) of this section) because those customers are the recipients of composition A when sold as general property. Based on the actual revenue earned by FP from sales of composition A, 40 percent ($40x/$100x) of the revenue generated by the copyright during the taxable year is earned outside the United States. Accordingly, a portion of DC's license to FP is for a foreign use under paragraph (d)(2) of this section and therefore such portion is a FDDEI sale. The $24x of royalty (0.40 x $60x of total royalties owed to DC during the taxable year) derived with respect to such portion is included in DC's gross FDDEI for the taxable year.

(2) Example 2: Fixed annual payments for worldwide rights without actual revenue data from recipient.—(i) *Facts.* The facts are the same as in paragraph (d)(2)(iv)(B)(*1*)(*i*) of this section (the facts in *Example 1*), except FP pays DC a fixed annual payment of $60x each year for the worldwide rights to the copyright to composition A and does not provide DC with data showing how much revenue FP earned from sales of composition A, even after DC requests that FP provide it with such information. DC also is unable to determine how much revenue FP earned from sales of composition A to customers within the United States from the data it has with respect to FP and publicly available data with respect to FP. However, DC's economic analysis of the revenue DC expected it could earn annually from use of composition A as part of determining the annual payments DC would receive from FP from the license of composition A supports a determination that 40 percent of sales of composition A during the tax year would be to customers located outside the United States. During an examination of DC's return for the taxable year, DC provides the IRS with data explaining the economic analysis, inputs, and results from its valuation of composition A used in determining the amount of annual payments agreed to by DC and FP.

(ii) Analysis. For the same reasons provided in paragraph (d)(2)(iv)(B)(*1*)(*ii*) of this section (the analysis in *Example 1*), the customers that purchase copies of composition A from FP are the end users. DC is allowed to use reliable economic analysis to estimate revenue earned by FP from the use of the copyright to composition A under paragraph (d)(2)(iii)(A) of this section because DC was unable to obtain actual revenue earned by FP from use of the copyright to composition A during the taxable year after reasonable efforts to obtain the actual revenue data. Based on DC's economic analysis, a portion of DC's license to FP is for a foreign use under paragraph (d)(2) of this section and therefore such portion is a FDDEI sale. $24x of the $60x fixed payment to DC (0.40 x $60x) is included in DC's gross FDDEI for the taxable year.

(3) Example 3: Sale of patent rights protected in the United States and other countries; use of financial projections in sale to foreign unrelated party.—(i) *Facts.* DC owns a patent for an active pharmaceutical ingredient ("API") approved for treatment of disease A ("indication A") in the United States and in Countries A, B, and C. The patent is registered in the United States and in Countries A, B, and C. DC sells to FP all of its patent rights to the API for indication A for a lump sum payment of $1,000x. DC has no basis in the patent rights. To determine the sales price for the patent rights, DC projected that the net present value of the revenue it would earn from selling a pharmaceutical product incorporating the API for indication A was $5,000x, with 15 percent of the net present value of revenue earned from sales within the United States and 85 percent of the net present value of revenue earned from sales outside the United States. DC did not obtain revenue projections from the recipient.

(ii) Analysis. FP is not the end user of the patent under paragraph (d)(2)(ii)(A) of this section because the patent is used in the sale of general property (the sale of pharmaceutical products to customers) and FP is not the recipient of that general property. The unrelated party customers that purchase the finished pharmaceutical product from FP are the end users (as defined in §1.250(b)-3(b)(2) and paragraph (d)(2)(ii)(A) of this section) because those customers are the unrelated party recipients of the pharmaceutical product when sold as general property. Based on the financial projections DC used to determine the sales price of the patent that FP purchased, a portion of DC's sale to FP is for a foreign use under paragraph (d)(2) of this section and such portion is a FDDEI sale. The $850x (85 percent x $1,000x) of gain derived with respect to such portion is included in DC's gross FDDEI for the taxable year.

(4) Example 4: Sale of patent rights protected in the United States and other countries; use of financial projections in sale to foreign related party.—(i) Facts. The facts are the same as in paragraph (d)(2)(iv)(B)(3)(i) of this section (the facts in *Example 3*), except that FP is a foreign related party with respect to DC, and DC projected that the net present value of the revenue it would earn from selling a pharmaceutical product incorporating the API for indication A would result in 1 percent of the revenue earned from sales within the United States and 99 percent of the revenue earned from sales outside the United States. During the examination of DC's return for the taxable year, the IRS determines that DC's substantiation allocating the projected revenue from sales within the United States and outside the United States does not reflect reliable inputs to determine the net present values of revenues under section 482, but determines that the total lump sum price FP paid for DC's patent rights is an arm's length price. The IRS determines that the most reliable net present values of revenue DC would have earned from sales within the United States and outside the United States is $750x and $4250x, respectively.

(ii) Analysis. For the same reasons provided in paragraph (d)(2)(iv)(B)(3)(ii) of this section (the analysis in *Example 3*), the customers that purchase the finished pharmaceutical product from FP are the end users. Under paragraph (d)(2)(iii)(B) of this section, the reliability of the inputs DC used to determine the net present values and the net present values are determined under section 482. Based on the sales price of the patent that FP purchased and the IRS-determined net present values of revenue DC would have earned from sales within the United States and outside the United States, a portion of DC's sale to FP is for a foreign use under paragraph (d)(2) of this section and such portion is a FDDEI sale. DC is allowed to include $850x (($4250x divided by $5000x) x $1,000x) of gain in DC's gross FDDEI for the taxable year.

(5) Example 5: Sale of patent of manufacturing method or process protected in the United States and other countries; foreign unrelated party.—(i) Facts. DC owns the worldwide rights to a patent covering a process for refining crude oil. DC sells to FP the right to DC's patented process for refining crude oil for a lump sum payment of $100x. DC has no basis in the patent rights. DC does not know or have reason to know that FP will use the patented process to refine crude oil within the United States or will sell or license the rights to the patent to a person to refine crude oil within the United States.

(ii) Analysis. DC's patent covering a process for refining crude oil is a manufacturing method or process as defined in paragraph (d)(2)(ii)(C)(3) of this section. Under paragraph (d)(2)(ii)(C)(1) of this section, FP is treated as the end user of the patent, and is treated as located outside the United States because FP is a foreign unrelated party and DC does not know or have reason to know that the patented process will be used in the United States. As a result, all of the sale to FP is for a foreign use under paragraph (d)(2) of this section and therefore is a FDDEI sale. The entire $100x lump sum payment is included in DC's gross FDDEI for the taxable year.

(6) Example 6: License of intangible property that includes a patented manufacturing method or process protected in the United States and other countries; foreign unrelated party.—(i) Facts. DC owns worldwide rights to patents, know-how, and a trademark and tradename for product Z. The patents consist of: a patent covering the right to make, use, and sell product Z (article of manufacture), a patent covering the rights to make, use, and sell a composition of substances used in certain components of product Z (composition of matter), and a patent covering the right to use a manufacturing process consisting of a series of manufacturing steps to manufacture product Z (manufacturing method or process as defined in paragraph (d)(2)(ii)(C)(3) of this section) and to sell the product Z that FP manufactures using the manufacturing method or process. The know-how consists entirely of manufacturing know-how used to implement the manufacturing steps that comprise the manufacturing method or process. DC licenses the worldwide rights to the patents, know-how, and the trademark and tradename for product Z to FP in exchange for annual royalties of 60 percent of revenue from sales of

product Z. FP manufactures product Z in country X and sells product Z to DC2, a domestic corporation and unrelated party to DC and FP, for resale to customers located within the United States. FP also sells product Z to FP2, a foreign unrelated party with respect to DC and FP, for resale to customers located outside the United States. During the taxable year, FP sells to DC2 $140x of product Z. Also, during the taxable year, FP sells to FP2 $60x of product Z. DC determines under the principles of section 482 that the licensed know-how and the patented manufacturing method or process comprise 10 percent of the arm's length price of the intangible property DC licenses to FP.

(ii) Analysis—(A) End users. Under paragraph (d)(2)(ii)(C)(1) of this section, FP is treated as the end user of the patent covering the right to use the manufacturing process and the manufacturing know-how used to implement the manufacturing method or process, and is treated as located outside the United States because FP is a foreign unrelated party and DC does not know or have reason to know that the patented process and know-how will be used in the United States. DC2, FP, and FP2 are not the end users of the remaining intangible property under paragraph (d)(2)(ii)(A) of this section because that intangible property is used in the sale of general property (the sale of product Z) and DC2, FP, and FP2 are not the end users of that general property. The unrelated party customers that purchase product Z from DC2 and FP2 are the end users (as defined in §1.250(b)-3(b)(2) and paragraph (d)(2)(ii)(A) of this section) because those customers are the unrelated party recipients of product Z.

(B) Foreign use. Under paragraph (d)(2)(ii)(A) of this section, revenue from royalties paid for the intangible property other than the manufacturing method or process is earned from end users outside the United States to the extent the sale of the general property is for a foreign use under paragraph (d)(1) of this section. FP2 is a reseller of product Z to end users outside the United States, so all sales of product Z to FP2 are for a foreign use under paragraph (d)(1)(ii)(C) of this section. Because DC has determined that 10 percent of the value of the intangible property consists of a manufacturing method or process (as defined in paragraph (d)(2)(ii)(C)(3) of this section) used to manufacture product Z, $12x of the $120x royalty FP pays to DC during the taxable year is for foreign use ($120x total royalty x 0.10) based on the location of FP's manufacturing utilizing the know-how or all of the sequence of actions that comprise the manufacturing method or process under paragraph (d)(2)(ii)(C)(3) of this section. Based on the sales of product Z within and outside the United States, $32.4x of the royalties FP pays DC for rights to the licensed intangible property during the taxable year (($60x of revenue from sales to FP2 for resale to customers located outside the United States divided by $200x total worldwide sales revenue FP receives from DC2 and FP2) x ($120x total royalties less $12 of those royalties attributable to the manufacturing method or process)) qualifies as income earned from the sale of intangible property for a foreign use under paragraph (d)(2) of this section and therefore such portion is a FDDEI sale. As a result, $44.40x of royalties ($12x + $32.40x) is included in DC's gross FDDEI for the taxable year.

(7) Example 7: License of intangible property that includes a patented manufacturing method or process protected in the United States and other countries; foreign related party with third-party manufacturer.—(i) Facts. The facts are the same as in paragraph (d)(2)(iv)(B)(6)(i) of this section (the facts in *Example 6*), except that FP is a foreign related party with respect to DC and FP engages FP2, a foreign unrelated party, to manufacture product Z. FP sublicenses to FP2 the rights to the intangible property FP licenses from DC solely to manufacture product Z and sell product Z to FP. FP2 manufactures product Z in country Y and sells all of product Z it manufactures to FP. During the taxable year, FP sold $80x of product Z to DC2, which DC2 resold to customers located within the United States. Also, during the taxable year, FP sold $120x of product Z to customers located outside the United States.

(ii) Analysis—(A) End users. Under paragraph (d)(2)(ii)(C)(1) of this section, FP is not treated as the end user of the patent covering the right to use the manufacturing process and the manufacturing know-how used to implement the manufacturing method or process because FP is a foreign related party with respect to DC. Under paragraph (d)(2)(ii)(C)(2) of this section, FP2 is also not treated as the end user of the patent covering the right to use the manufacturing process and the manufacturing know-how used to implement the manufacturing method or process because FP2 is using that intangible property to manufacture product Z for FP. DC2 is also not treated as the end user of the patent covering the right to use the manufacturing process and the manufacturing know-how used to implement the manufacturing method or process because DC2 does not use the patent or know-how in manufacturing. DC2, FP, and FP2 are not the end users of the remaining intangible property under paragraph (d)(2)(ii)(A) of this section because that intangible property is used in the sale of general property (the sale of product Z) and DC2, FP, and FP2 are not the end users of that

general property. The unrelated party customers that purchase the Product Z from DC2 and FP are the end users (as defined in §1.250(b)-3(b)(2) and paragraph (d)(2)(ii)(A) of this section) of the intangible property because those customers are the persons that ultimately use or consume product Z.

(B) *Foreign use.* Based on the sales of product Z to customers located within and outside the United States, $72x of the royalties FP pays DC for rights to the licensed intangible property during the taxable year (($120x of revenue from sales to customers located outside the United States divided by $200x total worldwide sales revenue) x $120x total royalties) qualifies as income earned from the sale of intangible property for a foreign use under paragraph (d)(2) of this section and therefore such portion is a FDDEI sale. As a result, $72x of royalties is included in DC's gross FDDEI for the taxable year.

(8) *Example 8: Deemed sale in exchange for contingent payments under section 367(d).*—(i) *Facts.* DC owns 100 percent of the stock of FP, a foreign related party with respect to DC. FP manufactures and sells product A. For the taxable year, DC contributes to FP exclusive worldwide rights to patents, trademarks, know-how, customer lists, and goodwill and going concern value (collectively, intangible property) related to product A in an exchange described in section 351. DC is required to report an annual income inclusion on its Federal income tax return based on the productivity, use, or disposition of the contributed intangible property under section 367(d). DC includes a percentage of FP's revenue in its gross income under section 367(d) each year. In the current taxable year, FP earns $1,000x of revenue from sales of product A. Based on reliable sales records kept by FP for the taxable year, $300x of FP's revenue is earned from sales of product A to customers within the United States, and $700x of its revenue is earned from sales of product A to customers outside the United States.

(ii) *Analysis.* DC's deemed sale of the intangible property to FP in exchange for payments contingent upon the productivity, use, or disposition of the intangible property related to product A under section 367(d) is a sale for purposes of section 250 and this section. See §1.250(b)-3(b)(16). Based on FP's sales records for the taxable year, 70 percent of DC's deemed sale to FP is for a foreign use, and 70 percent of DC's income inclusion under section 367(d) derived with respect to such portion is included in DC's gross FDDEI for the taxable year.

(9) *Example 9: License of intangible property followed by a sale of general property in which the intangible property is embedded; unrelated parties.*—(i) *Facts.* DC owns the worldwide rights to a patent on a silicon chip used in computers, tablets, and smartphones. The patent does not qualify as a manufacturing method or process (as defined in paragraph (d)(2)(ii)(C)(3) of this section). DC licenses the worldwide rights to the patent to FP in exchange for annual royalties of 30 percent of revenue from sales of the silicon chips. During the taxable year, FP manufactures silicon chips protected by the patent and sells all of those chips to FP2 for $1,000x. FP2 also purchases similar silicon chips from other suppliers. FP2 uses the silicon chips in computers, tablets, smartphones, and motherboards that FP2 manufactures in country X and sells to its customers located within the United States and foreign countries. For purposes of this example, FP2's manufacturing qualifies as subjecting the silicon chips to manufacture, assembly, or other processing outside the United States as provided in paragraph (d)(1)(iii) of this section.

(ii) *Analysis.* FP is not the end user or treated as an end user (as defined in §1.250(b)-3(b)(2) and paragraph (d)(2)(ii)(A) of this section) because FP is not the unrelated party recipient of the general property in which the patent is embedded, and the patent does not qualify as a manufacturing method or process. Under paragraph (d)(2)(ii)(A) of this section, revenue from royalties paid for the patent is earned from end users outside the United States to the extent the sale of the general property is for a foreign use under paragraph (d)(1) of this section. Because FP2 is subjecting the silicon chips to manufacture, assembly, or other processing outside the United States, the revenue from royalties FP pays to DC qualifies for foreign use based on the location of FP2's manufacturing and qualifies as a FDDEI sale. As a result, the entire $300x of annual royalties paid by FP to DC during the taxable year is included in DC's gross FDDEI for the taxable year.

(10) *Example 10: License of intangible property followed by a sale of general property in which the intangible property is embedded; related parties.*—(i) *Facts.* The facts are the same as in paragraph (d)(2)(iv)(B)(9)(i) of this section (the facts in *Example 9*), except that FP and FP2 are foreign related parties with respect to DC. FP2 sells and ships computers, tablets, and smartphones it manufactures with the silicon chips it purchases from FP to unrelated party wholesalers located within and outside the United States. The wholesalers within the United States only sell to retailers located within the United States and the wholesalers outside the United States only sell to retailers located outside the United States. The retailers within the

United States only sell to customers located within the United States and the retailers located outside the United States only sell to customers located outside the United States. FP2 earns $15,000x of revenue from sales to unrelated party wholesalers located outside the United States and $10,000x of revenue from sales to unrelated party wholesalers located within the United States. FP2 also sells and ships motherboards with the silicon chips it purchases from FP to unrelated party manufacturers located outside the United States. FP2 does not sell motherboards with the silicon chips it purchases from FP to unrelated party manufacturers located within the United States. FP2 earns $5,000x of revenue from the sales of these motherboards to manufacturers located outside the United States. For purposes of this example, these manufacturers subject the motherboards to manufacture, assembly, or other processing outside the United States as provided in paragraph (d)(1)(iii) of this section.

(ii) *Analysis.* FP is not the end user or treated as an end user (as defined in §1.250(b)-3(b)(2) and paragraph (d)(2)(ii)(A) of this section) of the intangible property because FP is not the end user of the general property in which the patent is embedded (the silicon chips). FP2 is also not the end user (as defined in §1.250(b)-3(b)(2) and paragraph (d)(2)(ii)(A) of this section) of the intangible property because FP2 is not the end user of the silicon chips. Under paragraph (d)(2)(ii)(A) of this section, the customers of the retailers that purchase from the unrelated party wholesalers are the end users. Because the wholesalers located outside the United States only sell to retailers located outside the United States that sell to end users located outside the United States, the location of the wholesalers is a reliable basis for determining the location of the end users. Revenue from royalties paid for the patent is earned from end users outside the United States to the extent the sale of the general property is for a foreign use under paragraph (d)(1) of this section. A portion of the sales to the unrelated party wholesalers qualify as foreign use under paragraph (d)(1) of this section and the sales to the unrelated party manufacturers qualify as foreign use under paragraph (d)(1)(iii) of this section. Accordingly, revenue from royalties FP pays to DC is from a FDDEI sale to the extent of such sales to the unrelated party manufacturers and such portion of sales to unrelated party wholesalers that qualify for foreign use. As a result, $200x of annual royalties paid by FP to DC during the taxable year ((($15,000x of sales to wholesalers located outside the United States plus $5,000x of sales to manufacturers located outside the United States) divided by $30,000x total sales) x $300x) is included in DC's gross FDDEI for the taxable year.

(11) *Example 11: License of intangible property followed by a sale of general property that incorporates the intangible property; unrelated parties with manufacturing within the United States.*—(i) *Facts.* The facts are the same as in paragraph (d)(2)(iv)(B)(9)(i) of this section (the facts in *Example 9*), except that FP2 manufactures its computers, tablets, smartphones, and motherboards in the United States.

(ii) *Analysis.* FP is not the end user or treated as an end user (as defined in §1.250(b)-3(b)(2) and paragraph (d)(2)(ii)(A) of this section) because FP is not the unrelated party recipient of the general property in which the patent is embedded (the silicon chips) and the patent does not qualify as a manufacturing method or process. Under paragraph (d)(2)(ii)(A) of this section, revenue from royalties paid for the patent is earned from end users outside the United States to the extent the sale of the general property is for a foreign use under paragraph (d)(1) of this section. Because FP2 is subjecting the silicon chips to manufacture, assembly, or other processing within the United States, the revenue from royalties FP pays to DC does not qualify as foreign use based on the location of FP2's manufacturing and therefore does not qualify as a FDDEI sale. As a result, none of the $300x of annual royalties paid by FP to DC during the taxable year is included in DC's gross FDDEI for the taxable year.

(12) *Example 12: License of intangible property used to provide a service.*—(i) *Facts.* DC licenses to FP worldwide rights to the copyrights on movies in exchange for an annual royalty of $100x. FP also licenses copyrights on movies from persons other than DC. FP provides a streaming service that meets the definition of an electronically supplied service in §1.250(b)-5(c)(5) to its customers within the United States and foreign countries. FP's streaming service provides its customers a catalog of movies to choose to stream. These movies include the copyrighted movies FP licenses from DC. FP does not provide DC with data showing how much revenue FP earned from streaming services during the taxable year, even after DC requests that FP provide it with such information. DC also is unable to determine how much revenue FP earned from streaming services to customers within the United States from the data it has with respect to FP and publicly available data with respect to FP. However, DC's economic analysis of the revenue DC expected it could earn annually from use of the copyrights as part of determining the annual payments DC would receive from FP from the license of the copyrights

supports a determination that $10,000x of revenue would be earned during the taxable year from customers worldwide, and that 40 percent of that revenue would be earned from customers located outside the United States. During an examination of DC's return for the taxable year, DC provides the IRS with data explaining the economic analysis, inputs, and results from its valuation of the copyrights used in determining the amount of annual payments agreed to by DC and FP.

(ii) *Analysis.* Under paragraph (d)(2)(ii)(B) of this section, FP's customers are the end users of the copyrights FP licenses from DC because FP uses those copyrights to provide the general service to FP's customers. Under paragraph (d)(2)(ii)(B) of this section, revenue from royalties paid for the copyrights is earned from end users outside the United States to the extent the service qualifies as a FDDEI service under §1.250(b)-5. DC is allowed to use reliable economic analysis to estimate revenue earned by FP from streaming the licensed movies under paragraph (d)(2)(iii)(A) of this section because DC was unable to obtain actual revenue earned by FP from use of the copyrights during the taxable year after reasonable efforts to obtain the actual revenue data. Based on DC's reliable economic analysis, $40x of the annual royalty payment to DC (0.40 x $100x total annual royalty payment) is included in DC's gross FDDEI for the taxable year.

(13) *Example 13: License of intangible property used in research and development of other intangible property.*—(i) *Facts.* DC owns a patent ("patent A") for an active pharmaceutical ingredient ("API") approved for treatment of disease A in the United States and in foreign countries. DC licenses to FP worldwide rights to patent A for an annual royalty of $100x. FP uses patent A in research and development of a new API for treatment of disease B. Patent A does not consist of a manufacturing method or process (as defined in paragraph (d)(2)(ii)(C)(3) of this section). FP's research and development is successful, resulting in FP obtaining both a patent for the new API for treatment of disease B and approval for use in the United States and foreign countries. FP does not earn any revenue from sales of finished pharmaceutical products containing the API during years 1 through 4 of the license of patent A. In year 5 of the license of patent A, FP earns $800x of revenue from sales of finished pharmaceutical products containing the API to customers located within the United States and $200x of revenue from sales to customers located in foreign countries.

(ii) *Analysis.* FP is not the end user (as defined in §1.250(b)-3(b)(2) and paragraph (d)(2)(ii)(D) of this section) of patent A because FP is not the end user described in paragraph (d)(2)(ii)(A) of this section of the product in which the API that was developed from patent A is embedded. The unrelated party customers that purchase the finished pharmaceutical product from FP are the end users (as defined in §1.250(b)-3(b)(2) and paragraph (d)(2)(ii)(D) of this section) because those customers are the end users described in paragraph (d)(2)(ii)(A) of this section of the pharmaceutical product in which the newly developed patent is embedded. During the taxable years that include years 1 through 4 of the license of patent A, FP earns no revenue from sales of the API to a foreign person for a foreign use. Under paragraph (d)(2)(ii)(D) of this section, none of the $100x annual royalty payments to DC for each of the tax years that include years 1 through 4 of the license of patent A is included in DC's gross FDDEI. Based on FP's sales of the API during the tax year that includes year 5 of the license of patent A, $20x of the annual royalty payment to DC ($200x of revenue from sales of API to customers located outside the United States divided by $1,000x total worldwide revenue earned from sales of the API) x $100x annual royalty) is included in DC's gross FDDEI for the taxable year.

(3) *Foreign use substantiation for certain sales of property.*—(i) *In general.*—Except as provided in §1.250(b)-3(f)(3) (relating to certain loss transactions), a sale of property described in paragraphs (d)(1)(ii)(C) of this section (foreign use for sale of general property for resale), (d)(1)(iii) of this section (foreign use for sale of general property subject to manufacturing, assembly, or processing outside the United States), or (d)(2) of this section (foreign use for sale of intangible property) is a FDDEI transaction only if the taxpayer satisfies the substantiation requirements described in paragraphs (d)(3)(ii), (iii), or (iv) of this section, as applicable.

(ii) *Substantiation of foreign use for resale.*—A seller satisfies the substantiation requirements with respect to a sale of property described in paragraph (d)(1)(ii)(C) of this section (sales of general property for resale) only if the seller maintains one or more of the following items—

(A) A binding contract that specifically limits subsequent sales to sales outside the United States;

(B) Proof that property is specifically designed, labeled, or adapted for a foreign market;

(C) Proof that the cost of shipping the property back to the United States relative to the value of the property makes it impractical that the property will be resold in the United States;

(D) Credible evidence obtained or created in the ordinary course of business from the recipient evidencing that property will be sold to an end user outside the United States (or, in the case of sales of fungible mass property, stating what portion of the property will be sold to end users outside the United States); or

(E) A written statement prepared by the seller containing the information described in paragraphs (d)(3)(ii)(E)(1) through (7) of this section corroborated by evidence that is credible and sufficient to support the information provided.

(1) The name and address of the recipient;

(2) The date or dates the property was shipped or delivered to the recipient;

(3) The amount of gross income from the sale;

(4) A full description of the property subject to resale;

(5) A description of the method of sales to the end users, such as direct sales by the recipient or sales by the recipient to retail stores;

(6) If known, a description of the end users; and

(7) A description of how the seller determined that property will be ultimately sold to an end user outside the United States (or, in the case of sales of fungible mass property, of how the taxpayer determined what portion of the property that will ultimately be sold to end users outside the United States).

(iii) *Substantiation of foreign use for manufacturing, assembly, or other processing outside the United States.*—A seller satisfies the substantiation requirements with respect to a sale of property described in paragraph (d)(1)(iii) of this section (sales of general property subject to manufacturing, assembly, or other processing outside the United States) if the seller maintains one or more of the following items—

(A) Credible evidence that the property has been sold to a foreign unrelated party that is a manufacturer and such property generally cannot be sold to end users without being subject to a physical and material change (for example, the sale of raw materials that cannot be used except in a manufacturing process);

(B) Credible evidence obtained or created in the ordinary course of business from the recipient to support that the product purchased will be subject to manufacture, assembly, or other processing outside the United States within the meaning of paragraph (d)(1)(iii) of this section; or

(C) A written statement prepared by the seller containing the information described in paragraphs (d)(3)(iii)(C)(1) through (7) of this section corroborated by evidence that is credible and sufficient to support the information provided.

(1) The name and address of the manufacturer of the property;

(2) The date or dates the property was shipped or delivered to the recipient;

(3) The amount of gross income from the sale;

(4) A full description of the general property sold and the type or types of finished goods that will incorporate the general property the taxpayer sold;

(5) A description of the manufacturing, assembly, or other processing operations, including the location or locations of manufacture, assembly, or other processing; how the general property will be used in the finished good; and the nature of the finished good's manufacturing, assembly, or other processing operations as compared to the process used to make the general property used to make the finished good;

(6) A description of how the seller determined the general property was substantially transformed or the activities were substantial in nature within the meaning of paragraph (d)(1)(iii)(B) or (C) of this section, whichever the case may be; and,

(7) If the seller is relying on the rule described in paragraph (d)(1)(iii)(C) of this section (that the fair market value of the general property be no more than twenty percent of the fair market value when incorporated into the finished goods sold to end users), an explanation of how the seller satisfies the requirements in that paragraph.

(iv) *Substantiation of foreign use of intangible property.*—A taxpayer satisfies the substantiation requirements with respect to a sale of property described in paragraph (d)(2) of this section (foreign use for intangible property) if the seller maintains one or more of the following items—

(A) A binding contract that specifically provides that the intangible property can be exploited solely outside the United States;

(B) Credible evidence obtained or created in the ordinary course of business from the recipient establishing the portion of its revenue for a taxable year that was derived from exploiting the intangible property outside the United States; or

(C) A written statement prepared by the seller containing the information described in paragraphs (d)(3)(iv)(C)(1) through (9) of this section corroborated by evidence that is credible and sufficient to support the information provided.

(1) The name and address of the recipient;

(2) The date of the sale;

(3) The amount of gross income from the sale;

(4) A description of the intangible property;

(5) An explanation of how the intangible property will be used by the recipient (embedded in general property, used to provide a service, used as a manufacturing method or process, or used in research and development);

(6) An explanation of how the seller determined what portion of the sale is a FDDEI sale;

(7) If the intangible property consists of a manufacturing method or process, an explanation of how the elements of paragraph (d)(2)(ii)(C) of this section are satisfied;

(8) If the sale is for periodic payments, an explanation of how the seller determined the extent of foreign use based on the actual revenue earned by the recipient from the use of the intangible property for the taxable year in which a periodic payment is received as required by paragraph (d)(2)(iii)(A) of this section, or, if actual revenue cannot be obtained after reasonable efforts, an explanation of why actual revenue is unavailable and how the seller determined the extent of foreign use based on estimated revenue; and

(9) If the sale is for a lump sum, an explanation of how the seller determined the total net present value of revenue it expected to earn from the exploitation of the intangible property outside the United States and the total net present value of revenue it expected to earn from the exploitation of the intangible property as required by paragraph (d)(2)(iii)(B) of this section.

(v) *Examples.*—The following examples illustrate the application of this paragraph (d)(3).

(A) *Assumed facts.*—The following facts are assumed for purposes of the examples—

(1) DC is a domestic corporation.

(2) FP is a foreign person located within Country A that is a foreign unrelated party with respect to DC.

(3) All of DC's income is DEI.

(4) Except as otherwise provided, the substantive rule for foreign use as described in paragraphs (d)(1) and (2) of this section are satisfied.

(B) *Examples*—

(1) *Example 1: Substantiation by seller of sale of products to distributor outside the United States with taxpayer statement and corroborating evidence.*—(i) *Facts.* DC sells smartphones to FP, a distributor of electronics that sells property to end users. As part of their regular business process and pursuant to DC's terms and conditions of sales, DC issues commercial invoices to FP that contain a condition that any subsequent sales must be to end users outside the United States. At or near the time of the FDII filing date, DC prepares a statement containing the information required in paragraph (d)(3)(ii)(E) of this section. During an examination of DC's return for the taxable year, the IRS requests substantiation information of foreign use. DC submits the commercial invoices issued to FP as supporting information that FP's customers are end users outside the United States and all other corroborating evidence to the IRS.

(ii) *Analysis.* DC's sale to FP is a sale of general property for resale subject to the substantiation requirements of paragraph (d)(3)(ii) of this section. DC satisfies the substantiation requirement by providing the statement that satisfies the requirements of paragraph (d)(3)(ii)(E) of this section. The commercial invoices issued pursuant to the terms and conditions of sales sufficiently corroborate DC's statement that the smartphones will ultimately be sold to end users outside of the United States.

(2) *Example 2: Substantiation of sale of products to distributor outside the United States with recipient provided information.*—(i) *Facts.* DC sells cameras to FP, a distributor of electronics that sells property to end users outside the United States. FP issues sales invoices to its end users. The invoices contain detailed information about the nature of the subsequent sales of the cameras and the location of the end users for value added tax (VAT) purposes. DC is able to obtain copies of FP's VAT invoices with respect to the camera sales that were maintained and submitted pursuant to Country A law. Rather than prepare a statement described in paragraph (d)(3)(ii)(E) of this section, DC submits FP's invoices to the IRS as substantiation of foreign use.

(ii) *Analysis.* DC's sale to FP is a sale of general property for resale subject to the substantiation requirements of paragraph

(d)(3)(ii) of this section. DC satisfies the substantiation requirements by providing the invoices that satisfy the requirements of paragraph (d)(3)(ii)(D) of this section. The VAT invoices issued by FP pursuant to Country A law constitute credible evidence from FP that ultimate sales are to end users located outside the United States.

(e) *Sales of interests in a disregarded entity.*—Under Federal income tax principles, the sale of any interest in an entity that is disregarded for Federal income tax purposes is considered the sale of the assets of that entity, and this section applies to the sale of each such asset that is general property or intangible property for purposes of determining whether such sale qualifies as a FDDEI sale.

(f) *FDDEI sales hedging transactions.*—(1) *In general.*—The amount of a corporation's or partnership's gross FDDEI from FDDEI sales of general property in a taxable year is increased by any gain, or decreased by any loss, taken into account in that taxable year with respect to any FDDEI sales hedging transactions (determined by taking into account the applicable Federal income tax accounting rules, including § 1.446-4).

(2) *FDDEI sales hedging transaction.*—The term *FDDEI sales hedging transaction* means a transaction that meets the requirements of § 1.1221-2(a) through (e) and that is identified in accordance with the requirements of § 1.1221-2(f), except that the transaction must manage risk of price changes or currency fluctuations with respect to ordinary property, as provided in § 1.1221-2(b)(1), and the ordinary property whose price risk is being hedged must be general property that is sold in a FDDEI sale. [Reg. § 1.250(b)-4.]

☐ [*T.D. 9901, 7-9-2020 (corrected 9-28-2020 and 10-27-2020).*]

[Reg. § 1.250(b)-5]

§ 1.250(b)-5. Foreign-derived deduction eligible income (FDDEI) services.—(a) *Scope.*—This section provides rules for determining whether a provision of a service is a FDDEI service. Paragraph (b) of this section defines a FDDEI service. Paragraph (c) of this section provides definitions relevant for determining whether a provision of a service is a FDDEI service. Paragraph (d) of this section provides rules for determining whether a general service is provided to a consumer located outside the United States. Paragraph (e) of this section provides rules for determining whether a general service is provided to a business recipient located outside the United States. Paragraph (f) of this section provides rules for determining whether a proximate service is provided to a recipient located outside the United States. Paragraph (g) of this section provides rules for determining whether a service is provided with respect to property located outside the United States. Paragraph (h) of this section provides rules for determining whether a transportation service is provided to a recipient, or with respect to property, located outside the United States.

(b) *Definition of FDDEI service.*—Except as provided in § 1.250(b)-6(d), the term *FDDEI service* means a provision of a service described in any one of paragraphs (b)(1) through (5) of this section. If only a portion of a service is treated as provided to a person, or with respect to property, outside the United States, the provision of the service is a FDDEI service only to the extent of the gross income derived with respect to such portion.

(1) The provision of a general service to a consumer located outside the United States (as determined under paragraph (d) of this section).

(2) The provision of a general service to a business recipient located outside the United States (as determined under paragraph (e) of this section).

(3) The provision of a proximate service to a recipient located outside the United States (as determined under paragraph (f) of this section).

(4) The provision of a property service with respect to tangible property located outside the United States (as determined under paragraph (g) of this section).

(5) The provision of a transportation service to a recipient, or with respect to property, located outside the United States (as determined under paragraph (h) of this section).

(c) *Definitions.*—This paragraph (c) provides definitions that apply for purposes of this section and § 1.250(b)-6.

(1) *Advertising service.*—The term *advertising service* means a general service that consists primarily of transmitting or displaying content (including via the internet) with a purpose to generate revenue based on the promotion of a product or service.

(2) *Benefit.*—The term *benefit* has the meaning set forth in § 1.482-9(l)(3).

(3) *Business recipient.*—The term *business recipient* means a recipient other than a consumer and includes all related parties of the

recipient. However, if the recipient is a related party of the taxpayer, the term does not include the taxpayer.

(4) *Consumer.*—The term *consumer* means a recipient that is an individual that purchases a general service for personal use.

(5) *Electronically supplied service.*—The term *electronically supplied service* means, with respect to a general service other than an advertising service, a service that is delivered primarily over the internet or an electronic network and for which value of the service to the end user is derived primarily from automation or electronic delivery. Electronically supplied services include the provision of access to digital content (as defined in §1.250(b)-3), such as streaming content; on-demand network access to computing resources, such as networks, servers, storage, and software; the provision or support of a business or personal presence on a network, such as a website or a web page; online intermediation platform services; services automatically generated from a computer via the internet or other network in response to data input by the recipient; and similar services. Electronically supplied services do not include services that primarily involve the application of human effort by the renderer (not considering the human effort involved in the development or maintenance of the technology enabling the electronically supplied services). Accordingly, electronically supplied services do not include certain services (such as legal, accounting, medical, or teaching services) involving primarily human effort that are provided electronically.

(6) *General service.*—The term *general service* means any service other than a property service, proximate service, or transportation service. The term *general service* includes advertising services and electronically supplied services.

(7) *Property service.*—The term *property service* means a service, other than a transportation service, provided with respect to tangible property, but only if substantially all of the service is performed at the location of the property and results in physical manipulation of the property such as through manufacturing, assembly, maintenance, or repair. Substantially all of a service is performed at the location of property only if the renderer spends more than 80 percent of the time providing the service at or near the location of the property.

(8) *Proximate service.*—The term *proximate service* means a service, other than a property service or a transportation service, provided to a consumer or business recipient, but only if substantially all of the service is performed in the physical presence of the consumer or, in the case of a business recipient, substantially all of the service is performed in the physical presence of persons working for the business recipient such as employees, contractors, or agents. Substantially all of a service is performed in the physical presence of a consumer or persons working for a business recipient only if the renderer spends more than 80 percent of the time providing the service in the physical presence of such persons.

(9) *Transportation service.*—The term *transportation service* means a service to transport a person or property using aircraft, railroad rolling stock, vessel, motor vehicle, or any other mode of transportation. Transportation services include freight forwarding and similar services.

(d) *General services provided to consumers.*—(1) *In general.*—A general service is provided to a consumer located outside the United States if the consumer of a general service resides outside of the United States when the service is provided. Except as provided in paragraph (d)(2) of this section, if the renderer does not have or cannot after reasonable efforts obtain the consumer's location of residence when the service is provided, the consumer of a general service is treated as residing at the location of the consumer's billing address. However, the rule in the preceding sentence allowing for the use of a consumer's billing address does not apply if the renderer knows or has reason to know that the consumer does not reside outside the United States. A renderer has reason to know that the consumer does not reside outside the United States if the information received as part of the provision of the service indicates that the consumer resides in the United States and the renderer fails to obtain evidence establishing that the consumer resides outside the United States.

(2) *Electronically supplied services.*—The consumer of an electronically supplied service is deemed to reside at the location of the device used to receive the service. Such location may be determined based on the location of the IP address when the electronically supplied service is provided. However, if the renderer does not have or cannot after reasonable efforts obtain the consumer's device location, then the location of the device is treated as being outside the United States if the renderer's billing address for the consumer is outside of the United States, subject to the knowledge and reason to know standards described in paragraph (d)(1) of this section.

(3) *Example.*—The following example illustrates the application of paragraph (d) of this section.

(i) *Facts.* DC, a domestic corporation, provides a streaming movie service on its website. The terms of the service allow consumers to watch movies over the internet. The terms of the service permit the consumer to view the movies for personal use, but convey no ownership of movies to the consumers.

(ii) *Analysis.* The streaming service is a FDDEI service under paragraph (d)(1) of this section to the extent that the service is provided to consumers that reside outside the United States. The service that DC provides is a general service, provided to consumers that is an electronically supplied service under paragraph (c)(5) of this section. Therefore, the consumers are deemed to reside at the location of the devices used to receive the service under paragraph (d)(2) of this section. However, if the renderer cannot reasonably obtain the consumers' device location (such as IP addresses), the device location is treated as being outside the United States if their billing addresses are outside the United States. See §1.250(b)-4(d)(1)(v)(B)(7) for an example of digital content provided to consumers as a sale rather than a service.

(e) *General services provided to business recipients.*—(1) *In general.*—A general service is provided to a business recipient located outside the United States to the extent that the service confers a benefit on the business recipient's operations outside the United States under the rules in paragraph (e)(2) of this section. The location of residence, incorporation, or formation of a business recipient is not relevant to determining the location of the business recipient's operations that benefit from a general service.

(2) *Determination of business operations that benefit from the service.*—(i) *In general.*—Except as otherwise provided in paragraph (e)(2)(ii) and (iii) of this section, the determination of which operations of the business recipient located outside the United States benefit from a general service, and the extent to which such operations benefit, is made under the principles of §1.482-9 by treating the taxpayer as one controlled taxpayer, the portions of the business recipient's operations within the United States (if any) that may benefit from the general service as one or more controlled taxpayers, and the portions of the business recipient's operations outside the United States (if any) that may benefit from the general service, each as one or more controlled taxpayers. The extent to which a business recipient's operations within or outside of the United States are treated as one or more separate controlled taxpayers is determined under any reasonable method (for example, separate controlled taxpayers may be determined on a per entity or per country basis, or by aggregating all of the business recipient's operations outside the United States as one controlled taxpayer). The determination of the amount of the benefit conferred on the business recipient's operations that are treated as controlled taxpayers is determined under a reasonable method consistent with the principles of §1.482-9(k), treating the renderer's gross income from the services provided to the business recipient as if it were a "cost" as that term is used in §1.482-9(k). Reasonable methods may include, for example, allocations based on time spent or costs incurred by the renderer or sales, profits, or assets of the business recipient.

The determination is made when the service is provided based on information obtained from the business recipient or on the renderer's own records (such as time spent working with the business recipient's offices located outside the United States).

(ii) *Advertising services.*—With respect to advertising services, the operations of the business recipient that benefit from the advertising service provided by the renderer are deemed to be located where the advertisements are viewed by individuals. If advertising services are displayed via the internet, the advertising services are located at the location of the device on which the advertisements are viewed. For this purpose, the IP address may be used to establish the location of a device on which an advertisement is viewed.

(iii) *Electronically supplied services.*—With respect to an electronically supplied service, the operations of the business recipient that benefit from that service provided by the renderer are deemed to be located where the business recipient (including employees, contractors, or agents) accesses or otherwise uses the service. If it cannot be determined whether the location is within or outside the United States (such as where the location of access cannot be reliably determined using the location of the IP address of the device used to receive the service), and the gross receipts from all services with respect to the business recipient are in the aggregate less than $50,000 for the renderer's taxable year, the operations of the business recipient that benefit from the service provided by the renderer are deemed to be located at the recipient's billing address; otherwise, the operations of the business recipient that benefit are deemed to be located in the United States. If the renderer provides a service that is partially an electronically supplied service and partially a general service that is not an electronically supplied service (such as a service that is performed partially online and partially by mail or in person), the location of the business recipient is determined using the rule for electronically supplied services in this paragraph (e)(2)(iii) if the primary purpose of the service is to provide electronically supplied services; otherwise, the rule for general services described in paragraph (e)(2)(i) of this section applies.

(3) *Identification of business recipient's operations.*—(i) *In general.*—For purposes of this paragraph (e), except with respect to advertising services and electronically supplied services, a business recipient is treated as having operations where it maintains an office or other fixed place of business. In general, an office or other fixed place of business is a fixed facility, that is, a place, site, structure, or other similar facility, through which the business recipient engages in a trade or business. For purposes of making the determination in this paragraph (e)(3)(i), the renderer may make reliable assumptions based on the information available to it.

(ii) *Advertising services and electronically supplied services.*—The location of a business recipient that receives advertising services or electronically supplied services will be determined under the rules of paragraph (e)(2)(ii) and (iii) of this section, respectively, even if the business recipient does not maintain an office or other fixed place of business in the locations where the advertisements are viewed (in the case of advertising services) or where the general service is accessed (in the case of electronically supplied services).

(iii) *No office or fixed place of business.*—In the case of general services other than advertising services and other than electronically supplied services, if the business recipient does not have an identifiable office or fixed place of business (including the office of a principal manager or managing owner), the business recipient is deemed to be located at its primary billing address.

(4) *Substantiation of the location of a business recipient's operations outside the United States.*—Except as provided in §1.250(b)-3(f)(3) (relating to certain loss transactions), a general service provided to a business recipient is treated as a FDDEI service only if the renderer substantiates its determination of the extent to which the service benefits a business recipient's operations outside the United States. A renderer satisfies the preceding sentence if the renderer maintains one or more of the following items—

(i) Credible evidence obtained or created in the ordinary course of business from the business recipient establishing the extent to which operations of the business recipient outside the United States benefit from the service; or

(ii) A written statement prepared by the renderer containing the information described in paragraphs (e)(4)(ii)(A) through (F) of this section corroborated by evidence that is credible and sufficient to support the information provided.

(A) The name of the business recipient;

(B) The date or dates of the service;

(C) The amount of gross income from the service;

(D) A full description of the service;

(E) A description of how the service will benefit the business recipient; and

(F) An explanation of how the renderer determined what portion of the service will benefit the business recipient's operations located outside the United States.

(5) *Examples.*—The following examples illustrate the application of this paragraph (e).

(i) *Assumed facts.*—The following facts are assumed for purposes of the examples—

(A) DC is a domestic corporation.

(B) A and R are not related parties of DC.

(C) Except as otherwise provided, the substantiation requirements described in paragraph (e)(4) of this section are satisfied.

(ii) *Examples*—

(A) *Example 1: Determination of business operations that benefit from the service.*—(1) *Facts.* For the taxable year, DC provides a consulting service to R, a company that operates restaurants within and outside of the United States, in exchange for $150x. Fifty percent of the sales earned by R and its related parties are from customers located outside of the United States. However, the consulting service that DC provides relates specifically to a single chain of fast food restaurants that R operates. Sales information that R provides to DC indicates that 70 percent of the sales of the fast food restaurant chain are from locations within the United States and 30 percent of the sales are from Country X. DC determines that the use of sales is a reasonable method under the principles of §1.482-9(k) to allocate the benefit of the consulting service among R's fast food operations.

(2) *Analysis.* Under paragraph (e)(1) of this section, DC's service is provided to a person located outside the United States to the extent that DC's service confers a benefit to R's operations outside the United States. Under paragraph (e)(2)(i) of this section, DC, R's fast food operations within the United States, and R's fast food operations in Country X, are treated as if they were controlled taxpayers because only these operations may benefit from DC's service. The principles of §1.482-9(k) apply to determine the amount of DC's service that benefits R's operations outside the United States. DC's gross income is allocated based on the sales of the fast food chain of restaurants that benefits from DC's service because using sales is a reasonable method. Therefore, 30 percent of the provision of the consulting service is treated as the provision of a service to a person located outside the United States and a FDDEI service under paragraph (b)(2) of this section. Accordingly, $45x ($150x x 0.30) of DC's gross income from the provision of the consulting service is included in DC's gross FDDEI for the taxable year.

(B) *Example 2: Determination of business operations that benefit from the service; alternative facts.*—(1) *Facts.* The facts are the same as in paragraph (e)(5)(ii)(A)(1) of this section (the facts in *Example 1*), except that DC provides an information technology service to R that benefits R's entire business. DC determines that the use of sales is a reasonable method under the principles of §1.482-9(k) to allocate the benefit of the information technology service among R's entire business.

(2) *Analysis.* DC, R's operations within the United States, and R's operations in Country X, are treated as if they were controlled taxpayers because the service that DC provides relates to R's entire business. DC's gross income is allocated based on sales of the entire business because using sales is a reasonable method to determine the amount of DC's service that benefits R's operations outside the United States under the principles of §1.482-9(k). Therefore, 50 percent of the provision of the information technology service is treated as a service to a person located outside the United States and a FDDEI service under paragraph (b)(2) of this section. Accordingly, $75x ($150x x 0.50) of DC's gross income from the provision of the information technology service is included in DC's gross FDDEI for the taxable year.

(C) *Example 3: Advertising services.*—(1) *Facts.* The facts are the same as in paragraph (e)(5)(ii)(A)(1) of this section (the facts in *Example 1*), except that DC provides an advertising service to R. DC displays advertisements for R's restaurant chain on its social media website and smartphone application. Based on the IP addresses of the devices on which the advertisements are viewed, 20 percent of the views of the advertisements were from devices located outside the United States.

(2) *Analysis.* Because the service that DC provides is an advertising service, under paragraph (e)(2)(i) of this section, as modified by paragraph (e)(2)(ii) of this section, R's operations that benefit from DC's advertising service are deemed to be where the advertisements are viewed. Therefore, 20 percent of the provision of the advertising service is treated as a service to a person located outside the United States and a FDDEI service under paragraph (b)(2) of this section. Accordingly, $30x ($150x x 0.20) of DC's gross income from the provision of the advertising service is included in DC's gross FDDEI for the taxable year.

(D) *Example 4: No reliable information about which operations benefit from the service or publicly available information.*—(1) *Facts.* For the taxable year, DC provides a consulting service to R, a business-facing company that does not advertise its business. All of DC's interaction with R is through R's employees that report to an office in the United States. Statements made by R's employees indicate that the service will benefit R's business operations located within and outside the United States, but do not provide information that would allow DC to reliably determine the extent to which its service will confer a benefit on R's business operations located outside the United States.

(2) *Analysis.* DC is unable to determine the extent to which its service will confer a benefit on R's business operations located outside the United States under paragraph (e)(2)(i) of this section. Accordingly, DC cannot substantiate a determination of the extent to which the service benefits a business recipient's operations outside the United States under paragraph (e)(4) of this section. Therefore, no portion of DC's service is a FDDEI service.

(E) *Example 5: Electronically supplied services that are accessed by the business recipient's employees.*—(1) *Facts.* DC provides payroll services for R. As part of this service, DC maintains a website through which R can enter payroll information for its employees and through which R's employees can enter and change their personal information. DC also causes R's employees' paychecks to be directly deposited into their bank accounts and pays R's employment taxes on R's behalf. The primary purpose of the service is to pay R's employees. R has 100 user accounts that access DC's website. Sixty of the user accounts that access DC's website access the website from devices that are located outside the United States and forty of the user accounts access the website from devices that are located inside the United States.

(2) *Analysis.* Under paragraph (e)(1) of this section, DC's service is provided to a person located outside the United States to the extent that DC's service confers a benefit to R's operations outside the United States. The service that DC provides to R is an electronically supplied service under paragraph (c)(5) of this section. Accordingly, under paragraph (e)(2)(i) of this section, as modified by paragraph (e)(2)(iii) of this section, R's operations that benefit from DC's services are deemed to be located where R accesses the service, which is where R's employees access the website. See paragraph (e)(2)(iii) of this section. Accordingly, the portion of the payroll service that is treated as a service to a person located outside the United States and a FDDEI service under paragraph (b)(2) of this section is determined based on the extent to which the locations where R accesses the website are located outside the United States. Because 60 percent (60/100) of user accounts access DC's website from locations outside the United States, 60 percent of the provision of the payroll service is treated as a service to a person located outside the United States and a FDDEI service under paragraph (b)(2) of this section.

(F) *Example 6: Electronically supplied services that are accessed by the business recipient's.*—(1) *Facts.* DC maintains an inventory management website for R, a company that sells consumer goods online. R's offices and all of its employees, who use the website, are located in the United States, but R sells its products to customers both within and outside the United States.

(2) *Analysis.* Under paragraph (e)(1) of this section, DC's service is provided to a person located outside the United States to the extent that DC's service confers a benefit to R's operations outside the United States. The service that DC provides to R is an electronically supplied service under paragraph (c)(5) of this section. Accordingly, under paragraph (e)(2)(i) of this section, as modified by paragraph (e)(2)(iii) of this section, R's operations that benefit from DC's services are deemed to be located where the service is accessed by employees. Therefore, none of the provision of the inventory management website is treated as a service to a person located outside the United States and none is a FDDEI service under paragraph (b)(2) of this section.

(G) *Example 7: Service provided to a domestic person.*—(1) *Facts.* A, a domestic corporation that operates solely in the United States, enters into a services agreement with R, a company that operates solely outside the United States. Under the agreement, A agrees to perform a consulting service for R. A hires DC to provide a service to A that A will use in the provision of a consulting service to R.

(2) *Analysis.* Because DC provides a service to A, a person located within the United States, DC's provision of the service to A is not a FDDEI service under paragraph (b)(2) of this section, even though the service is used by A in providing a service to R, a person located outside the United States. See also section 250(b)(5)(B)(ii). However, A's provision of the consulting service to R may be a FDDEI service, in which case A's gross income from the provision of such service would be included in A's gross FDDEI.

(f) *Proximate services.*—A proximate service is provided to a recipient located outside the United States if the proximate service is performed outside the United States. In the case of a proximate service performed partly within the United States and partly outside of the United States, a proportionate amount of the service is treated as provided to a recipient located outside the United States corresponding to the portion of time the renderer spends providing the service outside of the United States.

(g) *Property services.*—(1) *In general.*—Except as provided in paragraph (g)(2) of this section, a property service is provided with respect to tangible property located outside the United States only if the property is located outside the United States for the duration of the period the service is performed.

(2) *Exception for services provided with respect to property temporarily in the United States.*—A property service is deemed to be provided with respect to tangible property located outside the United States if the following conditions are satisfied—

(i) The property is temporarily in the United States for the purpose of receiving the property service;

(ii) After the completion of the service, the property will be primarily hangared, stored, or used outside the United States;

(iii) The property is not used to generate revenue in the United States at any point during the duration of the service; and

(iv) The property is owned by a foreign person that resides or primarily operates outside the United States.

(h) *Transportation services.*—Except as provided in this paragraph (h), a transportation service is provided to a recipient, or with respect to property, located outside the United States only if both the origin and the destination of the service are outside of the United States. However, in the case of a transportation service provided to a recipient, or with respect to property where either the origin or the destination of the service is outside of the United States, but not both, then 50 percent of the gross income from the transportation service is considered derived from services provided to a recipient, or with respect to property, located outside the United States. [Reg. §1.250(b)-5.]

☐ [T.D. 9901, 7-9-2020 (*corrected* 9-28-2020 *and* 10-27-2020). *Amended by* T.D. 9959, 12-28-2021.]

[Reg. §1.250(b)-6]

§1.250(b)-6. Related party transactions.—(a) *Scope.*—This section provides rules for determining whether a sale of property or a provision of a service to a related party is a FDDEI transaction. Paragraph (b) of this section provides definitions relevant for determining whether a sale of property or a provision of a service to a related party is a FDDEI transaction. Paragraph (c) of this section provides rules for determining whether a sale of general property to a foreign related party is a FDDEI sale. Paragraph (d) of this section provides rules for determining whether the provision of a general service to a business recipient that is a related party is a FDDEI service.

(b) *Definitions.*—This paragraph (b) provides definitions that apply for purposes of this section.

(1) *Related party sale.*—The term *related party sale* means a sale of general property to a foreign related party. See §1.250(b)-1(e)(3)(ii)(D) (*Example 4*) for an illustration of a related party sale in the case of a seller that is a partnership.

(2) *Related party service.*—The term *related party service* means a provision of a general service to a business recipient that is a related party of the renderer and that is described in §1.250(b)-5(b)(2) without regard to paragraph (d) of this section.

(3) *Unrelated party transaction.*—The term *unrelated party transaction* means, with respect to property purchased by a foreign related party (the "purchased property") in a related party sale from a seller—

(i) A sale of the purchased property by the foreign related party in the ordinary course of its business to a foreign unrelated party with respect to the seller;

(ii) A sale of property by the foreign related party to a foreign unrelated party with respect to the seller, if the purchased property is a constituent part of the property sold to the foreign unrelated party;

(iii) A sale of property by the foreign related party to a foreign unrelated party with respect to the seller, if the purchased property is not a constituent part of the product sold to the foreign unrelated party but rather is used in connection with producing the property sold to the foreign unrelated party; or

(iv) A provision of a service by the foreign related party to a foreign unrelated party with respect to the seller, if the purchased property was used in connection with the provision of the service.

(c) *Related party sales.*—(1) *In general.*—A related party sale of general property is a FDDEI sale only if the requirements described in either paragraph (c)(1)(i) or (ii) of this section are satisfied with respect to the related party sale. This paragraph (c) does not apply in determining whether a sale of intangible property to a foreign related party is a FDDEI sale.

(i) *Sale of property in an unrelated party transaction.*—A related party sale is a FDDEI sale if an unrelated party transaction described in paragraph (b)(3)(i) or (ii) of this section occurs with respect to the property purchased in the related party sale and such unrelated party transaction is described in §1.250(b)-4(b) (definition of FDDEI sale). The seller in the related party sale may establish that an unrelated party transaction will occur with respect to the property, or what portion of the property will be sold in an unrelated party transaction in the case of sale of a fungible mass of general property, based on contractual terms (including, for example, that the related party is contractually bound to only sell the product to foreign unrelated parties), past practices of the foreign related party (such as practices to only sell products to foreign unrelated parties), a showing that the product sold is designed specifically for a foreign market, or books and records otherwise evidencing that sales will be made to foreign unrelated parties.

(ii) Use of property in an unrelated party transaction.—A related party sale is a FDDEI sale if one or more unrelated party transactions described in paragraph (b)(3)(iii) or (iv) of this section occurs with respect to the property purchased in the related party sale and such unrelated party transaction or transactions would be described in §1.250(b)-4(b) or §1.250(b)-5(b) (definition of FDDEI service). If the property purchased in the related party sale will be used in unrelated party transactions described in the preceding sentence and other transactions, the amount of gross income from the related party sale that is attributable to a FDDEI sale is equal to the gross income from the related party sale multiplied by a fraction, the numerator of which is the revenue that the related party reasonably expects (as of the FDII filing date) to earn from all unrelated party transactions with respect to the property purchased in the related party sale that would be described in §1.250(b)-4(b) or §1.250(b)-5(b) and the denominator of which is the total revenue that the related party reasonably expects (as of the FDII filing date) to earn from all transactions with respect to the property purchased in the related party sale.

(2) Treatment of foreign related party as seller or renderer.—For purposes of determining whether a sale of property or provision of a service by a foreign related party is, or would be, described in §1.250(b)-4(b) or §1.250(b)-5(b), the foreign related party that sells the property or provides the service is treated as a seller or renderer, as applicable, and the foreign unrelated party is treated as the recipient.

(3) Transactions between related parties.—For purposes of determining whether an unrelated party sale has occurred and satisfies the requirements of paragraphs (c)(1) or (2) of this section with respect to a sale to a foreign related party (and not for purposes of determining whether a sale is to a foreign person as required by §1.250(b)-4(b)), the seller and all related parties of the seller are treated as if they are part of a single foreign related party. For purposes of the preceding sentence, in determining whether a United States person is a member of the seller's modified affiliated group, and therefore a related party of the seller, the definition of the term *modified affiliated group* in §1.250(b)-1(c)(17) applies without the substitution of "more than 50 percent" for "at least 80 percent" each place it appears. Accordingly, if a foreign related party sells or uses property purchased in a related party sale in a transaction with a second related party of the seller, transactions between the second related party and an unrelated party may be treated as an unrelated party transaction for purposes of applying paragraph (c)(1) of this section to a related party sale.

(4) Example.—The following example illustrates the application of this paragraph (c).

(i) *Facts.* DC, a domestic corporation, sells a machine to FC, a foreign related party of DC in a transaction described in §1.250(b)-4(b) (without regard to this paragraph (c)). FC uses the machine solely to manufacture product A. As of the FDII filing date for the taxable year, 75 percent of future revenue from sales by FC to unrelated parties of product A will be from sales that would be described in §1.250(b)-4(b).

(ii) *Analysis.* The sale by DC to FC is a related party sale. Because FC uses the machine to make product A, but the machine is not a constituent part of product A because FC does not undertake further manufacturing with respect to the machine itself, FC's sale of product A is an unrelated party transaction described in paragraph (b)(3)(iii) of this section. Therefore, DC's sale of the machine is only a FDDEI sale if the requirements of paragraph (c)(1)(ii) of this section are satisfied. Because 75 percent of the revenue from future sales of product A will be from unrelated party transactions that would be described in §1.250(b)-4(b), 75 percent of the revenues from DC's sale of the machine to FC constitute FDDEI sales.

(d) Related party services.—*(1) In general.*—Except as provided in this paragraph (d)(1), a related party service is a FDDEI service only if the related party service is not substantially similar to a service that has been provided or will be provided by the related party to a person located within the United States. However, if a related party service is substantially similar to a service provided (in whole or in part) by the related party to a person located in the United States solely by reason of paragraph (d)(2)(ii) of this section, the amount of gross income from the related party service attributable to a FDDEI service is equal to the difference between the gross income from the related party service and the amount of the price paid by persons located within the United States that is attributable to the related party service. Section 250(b)(5)(C)(ii) and this paragraph (d)(1) apply only to a general service provided to a related party that is a business recipient and are not applicable with respect to any other service *provided to a related party.*

(2) Substantially similar services.—A related party service is substantially similar to a service provided by the related party to a person located within the United States only if the related party

service is used by the related party in whole or part to provide a service to a person located within the United States and either—

(i) 60 percent or more of the benefits conferred by the related party service are directly used by the related party to confer benefits on consumers or business recipients located within the United States; or

(ii) 60 percent or more of the price paid by consumers or business recipients located within the United States for the service provided by the related party is attributable to the related party service.

(3) Special rules.—For purposes of paragraph (d) of this section, the rules in paragraphs (d)(3)(i) and (ii) of this section apply.

(i) *Rules for determining the location of and price paid by recipients of a service provided by a related party.*—The location of a consumer or business recipient with respect to services provided by the related party is determined under §1.250(b)-5(d) and (e)(2), respectively, but treating the related party as the renderer. Accordingly, if the related party provides a service to a business recipient, the related party is treated as conferring benefits on a person located within the United States to the extent that the service confers a benefit on the business recipient's operations located within the United States. Similarly, for purposes of applying paragraph (d)(2)(ii) of this section with respect to business recipients, the price paid by a business recipient to the related party for services is allocated proportionally based on the locations of the business recipient that benefit from the services provided by the related party.

(ii) *Rules for allocating the benefits provided by and price paid to the renderer of a related party service.*—For purposes of applying paragraph (d)(2)(i) of this section with respect to benefits that are directly used by the related party to confer benefits on its recipients, the benefits provided by the renderer to the related party are allocated to the related party's consumers or business recipients within the United States based on the proportion of benefits conferred by the related party on consumers or business recipients located within the United States. For purposes of determining the amount of the price paid by persons located within the United States that is attributable to the related party service in applying paragraph (d)(2)(ii) of this section, if the related party provides services that confer benefits on persons located within the United States and outside the United States, the price paid for the related party service by the related party to the renderer is allocated proportionally based on the benefits conferred on each location by the related party to its recipients.

(4) Examples.—The following examples illustrate the application of this paragraph (d).

(i) *Assumed facts.*—The following facts are assumed for purposes of the examples—

(A) DC is a domestic corporation.

(B) FC is a foreign corporation and a foreign related party of DC that operates solely outside the United States.

(C) The service DC provides to FC is a general service provided to a business recipient located outside the United States as described in §1.250(b)-5(b)(2) without regard to the application of paragraph (d) of this section.

(D) The benefits conferred by DC's service to FC's customers are not indirect or remote within the meaning of §1.482-9(l)(3)(ii).

(ii) *Examples*—

(A) *Example 1: Services that are substantially similar services under paragraph (d)(2)(i) of this section.*—*(1) Facts.* FC enters into a services agreement with R, a company that operates restaurant chains within and outside the United States. Under the agreement, FC agrees to furnish a design for the renovation of a chain of restaurants that R owns; the design will include architectural plans. FC hires DC to provide an architectural service to FC that FC will use in the provision of its design service to R. The architectural service that DC provides to FC will serve no other purpose than to enable FC to provide its service to R. The service that FC provides will benefit only R's operations within the United States. FC pays an arm's length price of $50x to DC for the architectural service and DC recognizes $50x of gross income from the service. FC incurs additional costs to add additional design elements to the plans and charges R a total of $100x for its service.

(2) Analysis. All of the service that DC provides to FC is directly used in the provision of a service to R because FC uses DC's architectural service to provide its design service to R, and the architectural service that DC provides to FC will serve no purpose other than to enable FC to provide its service to R. In addition, FC is treated as conferring benefits only to persons located within the United States under paragraph (d)(3)(i) of this section because only R's operations within the United States benefit from the service provided by FC that used the service provided by DC. Therefore, the

service provided by DC to FC is substantially similar to the service provided by FC to R under paragraph (d)(2)(i) of this section. Accordingly, DC's provision of the architectural service to FC is not a FDDEI service under paragraph (d)(1) of this section, and DC's gross income from the architectural service ($50x) is not included in its gross FDDEI.

(B) *Example 2: Services that are not substantially similar services under paragraph (d)(2)(i) of this section.*—(1) *Facts.* The facts are the same as paragraph (d)(4)(ii)(A)(1) of this section (the facts in *Example 1*), except that 90 percent of R's operations that will benefit from FC's service are located outside the United States.

(2) *Analysis*—(i) *Analysis under paragraph (d)(2)(i) of this section.* All of the service that DC provides to FC is directly used in the provision of a service to R. However, because 90 percent of R's operations that will benefit from FC's service are located outside the United States under paragraph (d)(3)(i) of this section, only 10 percent of the benefits of FC's service are conferred on persons located within the United States. Further, because FC's service confers a benefit on R's operations located within and outside the United States, the benefit provided by DC to FC is allocated proportionately based on the locations of R that benefit from the services provided by FC under paragraph (d)(3)(ii) of this section. Therefore, only 10 percent of DC's architectural service are directly used by FC to confer benefits on persons located within the United States under paragraph (d)(3)(ii) of this section. Therefore, the architectural service provided by DC to FC is not substantially similar to the design service provided by FC to persons located within the United States under paragraph (d)(2)(i) of this section.

(C) *Example 3: Services that are substantially similar services under paragraph (d)(2)(ii) of this section.*—(1) *Facts.* The facts are the same as paragraph (d)(4)(ii)(B)(1) of this section (the facts in *Example 2*), except that FC pays an arm's length price of $75x to DC for the architectural service and DC recognizes $75x of gross income from the service. As in paragraph (d)(4)(ii)(A)(1) and (d)(4)(ii)(B)(1) of this section (the facts in *Example 1* and *Example 2*), FC charges R a total of $100x for its service.

(2) *Analysis*—(i) *Price paid by persons located within the United States.* Under paragraph (d)(3)(i) of this section, FC is treated as conferring benefits on a person located within the United States to the extent that R's operations that will benefit from FC's service are located within the United States. Further, because FC's service con-

fers a benefit on R's operations located within and outside the United States, the price paid by R to FC ($100x) is allocated proportionately based on the locations of R that benefit from the services provided by FC under paragraph (d)(3)(i) of this section. Accordingly, because 10 percent of R's operations that will benefit from FC's services are located within the United States, persons located within the United States are treated as paying $10x ($100x x 0.10) for FC's services for purposes of applying the test in paragraph (d)(2)(ii) of this section

(ii) *Amount attributable to the related party service.* The service that FC provides to R is attributable in part to DC's service because FC uses the architectural plans that DC provides to provide a service to R. Under paragraph (d)(3)(ii) of this section, because the benefits of the service provided by FC are conferred on persons located within the United States and outside the United States, a proportionate amount (10 percent) of the price paid to DC for the related party service ($75x), or $7.5x, is treated as attributable to the services provided to persons located within the United States.

(iii) *Application of test in paragraph (d)(2)(ii) of this section.* For purposes of applying the test described in paragraph (d)(2)(ii) of this section, the price paid by persons located within the United States for the service provided by the related party (FC) is $10x, as determined in paragraph (d)(4)(ii)(C)(2)(i) of this section (the analysis of this *Example 3*). The amount of the price that is attributable to DC's service is $7.5x, as determined in paragraph (d)(4)(ii)(C)(2)(ii) of this section (the analysis of this *Example 3*). Accordingly, of the price treated as paid to FC by persons located within the United States, 75 percent ($7.5x/$10x) is attributable to the related party service. Because more than 60 percent of the price treated as paid by persons within the United States for FC's service is attributable to DC's service, the service provided by DC to FC is substantially similar to the design service provided by FC to persons located within the United States under paragraph (d)(2)(ii) of this section.

(iv) *Conclusion.* Under paragraph (d)(1) of this section, because the related party service provided by DC is substantially similar to the service provided by FC to a person located in the United States solely by reason of paragraph (d)(2)(ii) of this section, the difference between DC's gross income from the related party service and the amount of the price paid by persons located within the United States that is attributable to the related party service is treated as a FDDEI service. Accordingly, $67.5x ($75x - $7.5x) of DC's gross income from the provision of the service to FC is treated as a FDDEI service. [Reg. § 1.250(b)-6.]

☐ [*T.D. 9901*, 7-9-2020 (*corrected 9-28-2020 and 10-27-2020*).]

Items Not Deductible

[Reg. § 1.261-1]

§ 1.261-1. General rule for disallowance of deductions.—In computing taxable income, no deduction shall be allowed, except as otherwise expressly provided in chapter 1 of the Code, in respect of any of the items specified in part IX (section 262 and following), subchapter B, chapter 1 of the Code and the Regulations thereunder. [Reg. § 1.261-1.]

☐ [*T.D. 6313*, 9-16-58.]

[Reg. § 1.262-1]

§ 1.262-1. Personal, living, and family expenses.—(a) *In general.*—In computing taxable income, no deduction shall be allowed, except as otherwise expressly provided in chapter 1 of the Code, for personal, living, and family expenses.

(b) *Examples of personal, living, and family expenses.*—Personal, living, and family expenses are illustrated in the following examples:

(1) Premiums paid for life insurance by the insured are not deductible. See also section 264 and the regulations thereunder.

(2) The cost of insuring a dwelling owned and occupied by the taxpayer as a personal residence is not deductible.

(3) Expenses of maintaining a household, including amounts paid for rent, water, utilities, domestic service, and the like, are not deductible. A taxpayer who rents a property for residential purposes, but incidentally conducts business there (his place of business being elsewhere) shall not deduct any part of the rent. If, however, he uses part of the house as his place of business, such portion of the rent and other similar expenses as is properly attributable to such place of business is deductible as a business expense. [But see Code Sec. 280A.]

(4) Losses sustained by the taxpayer upon the sale or other disposition of property held for personal, living, and family purposes are not deductible. But see section 165 and the regulations thereunder for deduction of losses sustained to such property by reason of casualty, etc.

(5) Expenses incurred in traveling away from home (which include transportation expenses, meals, and lodging) and any other transportation expenses are not deductible unless they qualify as expenses deductible under section 162 (relating to trade or business expenses), section 170 (relating to charitable contributions), section 212 (relating to expenses for production of income), section 213 (relating to medical expenses), or section 217 (relating to moving expenses), and the regulations under those sections. The taxpayer's costs of commuting to his place of business or employment are personal expenses and do not qualify as deductible expenses. For expenses paid or incurred before October 1, 2014, a taxpayer's expenses for lodging when not traveling away from home (local lodging) are nondeductible personal expenses. However, taxpayers may deduct local lodging expenses that qualify under section 162 and are paid or incurred in taxable years for which the period of limitation on credit or refund under section 6511 has not expired. For expenses paid or incurred on or after October 1, 2014, a taxpayer's local lodging expenses are personal expenses and are not deductible unless they qualify as deductible expenses under section 162. Except as permitted under section 162 or 212, the costs of a taxpayer's meals not incurred in traveling away from home are nondeductible personal expenses.

(6) Amounts paid as damages for breach of promise to marry, and attorney's fees and other costs of suit to recover such damages, are not deductible.

(7) Generally, attorney's fees and other costs paid in connection with a divorce, separation, or decree for support are not deductible by either the husband or the wife. However, the part of an attorney's fee and the part of the other costs paid in connection with a divorce, legal separation, written separation agreement, or a decree for support, which are properly attributable to the production or collection of amounts includible in gross income under section 71 are deductible by the wife under section 212.

(8) The cost of equipment of a member of the armed services is deductible only to the extent that it exceeds nontaxable allowances received for such equipment and to the extent that such equipment is especially required by his profession and does not merely take the

place of articles required in civilian life. For example, the cost of a sword is an allowable deduction in computing taxable income, but the cost of a uniform is not. However, amounts expended by a reservist for the purchase and maintenance of uniforms which may be worn only when on active duty for training for temporary periods, when attending service school courses, or when attending training assemblies are deductible except to the extent that nontaxable allowances are received for such amounts.

(9) Expenditures made by a taxpayer in obtaining an education or in furthering his education are not deductible unless they qualify under section 162 and §1.162-5 (relating to trade or business expenses).

(c) *Cross references.*—Certain items of a personal, living, or family nature are deductible to the extent expressly provided under the following sections, and the regulations under those sections:

(1) Section 163 (interest).

(2) Section 164 (taxes).

(3) Section 165 (losses).

(4) Section 166 (bad debts).

(5) Section 170 (charitable, etc., contributions and gifts).

(6) Section 213 (medical, dental, etc., expenses).

(7) Section 214 (expenses for care of certain dependents). [Now a credit under Code §44A.]

(8) Section 215 (alimony, etc., payments).

(9) Section 216 (amounts representing taxes and interest paid to cooperative housing corporation).

(10) Section 217 (moving expenses). [Reg. §1.262-1.]

☐ [*T.D. 6313, 9-16-58. Amended by T.D. 6796, 1-29-65; T.D. 6918, 5-1-67; T.D. 7207, 10-3-72 and T.D. 9696, 9-30-2014.*]

[Reg. §1.263(a)-0]

§1.263(a)-0. Table of contents.—This section lists the paragraphs in §§1.263(a)-1 through 1.263(a)-3 and §1.263(a)-6.

(B) Unit of property for network assets.
(iv) Leased property other than buildings.
(4) Improvements to property.
(5) Additional rules.
(i) Year placed in service.
(ii) Change in subsequent taxable year.
(6) Examples.
(f) Improvements to leased property.
(1) In general.
(2) Lessee improvements.
(i) Requirement to capitalize.
(ii) Unit of property for lessee improvements.
(3) Lessor improvements.
(i) Requirement to capitalize.
(ii) Unit of property for lessor improvements.
(4) Examples.
(g) Special rules for determining improvement costs.
(1) Certain costs incurred during an improvement.
(i) In general.
(ii) Exception for individuals' residences.
(2) Removal costs.
(i) In general.
(ii) Examples.
(3) Related amounts.
(4) Compliance with regulatory requirements.
(h) Safe harbor for small taxpayers.
(1) In general.
(2) Application with other safe harbor provisions.
(3) Qualifying taxpayer.
(i) In general.
(ii) Application to new taxpayers.
(iii) Treatment of short taxable year.
(iv) Definition of gross receipts.
(4) Eligible building property.
(5) Unadjusted basis.
(i) Eligible building property owned by the taxpayer.
(ii) Eligible building property leased to the taxpayer.
(6) Time and manner of election.
(7) Treatment of safe harbor amounts.
(8) Safe harbor exceeded.
(9) Modification of safe harbor amounts.
(10) Examples.
(i) Safe harbor for routine maintenance.
(1) In general.
(i) Routine maintenance for buildings.
(ii) Routine maintenance for property other than buildings.
(2) Rotable and temporary spare parts.
(3) Exceptions.
(4) Class life.
(5) Coordination with section 263A.
(6) Examples.
(j) Capitalization of betterments.
(1) In general.
(2) Application of betterment rules.
(i) In general.
(ii) Application of betterment rules to buildings.
(iii) Unavailability of replacement parts.
(iv) Appropriate comparison.
(A) In general.
(B) Normal wear and tear.
(C) Damage to property.
(4) Examples.
(k) Capitalization of restorations.
(1) In general.
(2) Application of restorations to buildings.
(3) Exception for losses based on salvage value.
(4) Restoration of damage from casualty.
(i) Limitation.
(ii) Amounts in excess of limitation.
(5) Rebuild to like-new condition.
(6) Replacement of a major component or substantial structural part.
(i) In general.
(A) Major component.
(B) Substantial structural part.
(ii) Major components and substantial structural parts of buildings.
(7) Examples.

(l) Capitalization of amounts to adapt property to a new or different use.
(1) In general.
(2) Application of adaptation rule to buildings.
(3) Examples.
(m) Optional regulatory accounting method.
(1) In general.
(2) Eligibility for regulatory accounting method.
(3) Description of regulatory accounting method.
(4) Examples.
(n) Election to capitalize repair and maintenance costs.
(1) In general.
(2) Time and manner of election.
(3) Exception.
(4) Examples.
(o) Treatment of capital expenditures.
(p) Recovery of capitalized amounts.
(q) Accounting method changes.
(r) Effective/applicability date.
(1) In general.
(2) Early application of this section.
(i) In general.
(ii) Transition rule for elections on 2012 and 2013 returns.
(3) Optional application of TD 9564.

§ 1.263(a)-4 Amounts paid to acquire or create intangibles.
(a) Overview.
(b) Capitalization with respect to intangibles.
(1) In general.
(2) Published guidance.
(3) Separate and distinct intangible asset.
(i) Definition.
(ii) Creation or termination of contract rights.
(iii) Amounts paid in performing services.
(iv) Creation of computer software.
(v) Creation of package design.
(4) Coordination with other provisions of the Internal Revenue Code.
(i) In general.
(ii) Example.
(c) Acquired intangibles.
(1) In general.
(2) Readily available software.
(3) Intangibles acquired from an employee.
(4) Examples.
(d) Created intangibles.
(1) In general.
(2) Financial interests.
(i) In general.
(ii) Amounts paid to create, originate, enter into, renew or renegotiate.
(iii) Renegotiate.
(iv) Coordination with other provisions of this paragraph (d).
(v) Coordination with § 1.263(a)-5.
(vi) Examples.
(3) Prepaid expenses.
(i) In general.
(ii) Examples.
(4) Certain memberships and privileges.
(i) In general.
(ii) Examples.
(5) Certain rights obtained from a government agency.
(i) In general.
(ii) Examples.
(6) Certain contract rights.
(i) In general.
(ii) Amounts paid to create, originate, enter into, renew or renegotiate.
(iii) Renegotiate.
(iv) Right.
(v) De minimis amounts.
(vi) Exception for lessee construction allowances.
(vii) Examples.
(7) Certain contract terminations.
(i) In general.
(ii) Certain break-up fees.
(iii) Examples.
(8) Certain benefits arising from the provision, production, or improvement of real property.

Reg. § 1.263(a)-0

[Reg. § 1.263(a)-0.]

☐ [T.D. 9107, 12-31-2003. *Amended by T.D. 9564, 12-23-2011 and T.D. 9636, 9-13-2013 (corrected 7-18-2014).*]

[Reg. § 1.263(a)-1]

§ 1.263(a)-1. Capital expenditures; in general.—(a) *General rule for capital expenditures.*—Except as provided in chapter 1 of the Internal Revenue Code, no deduction is allowed for—

(1) Any amount paid for new buildings or for permanent improvements or betterments made to increase the value of any property or estate; or

(2) Any amount paid in restoring property or in making good the exhaustion thereof for which an allowance is or has been made.

(b) *Coordination with other provisions of the Internal Revenue Code.*—Nothing in this section changes the treatment of any amount that is specifically provided for under any provision of the Internal Revenue Code or the Treasury Regulations other than section 162(a) or section 212 and the regulations under those sections. For example, see section 263A, which requires taxpayers to capitalize the direct and allocable indirect costs to property produced by the taxpayer and property acquired for resale. See also section 195 requiring taxpayers to capitalize certain costs as start-up expenditures.

(c) *Definitions.*—For purposes of this section, the following definitions apply:

(1) *Amount paid.*—In the case of a taxpayer using an accrual method of accounting, the terms *amount paid* and *payment* mean a liability incurred (within the meaning of § 1.446-1(c)(1)(ii)). A liability may not be taken into account under this section prior to the taxable year during which the liability is incurred.

(2) *Produce* means construct, build, install, manufacture, develop, create, raise, or grow. This definition is intended to have the same meaning as the definition used for purposes of section 263A(g)(1) and § 1.263A-2(a)(1)(i), except that improvements are excluded from the definition in this paragraph (c)(2) and are separately defined and addressed in § 1.263(a)-3.

(d) *Examples of capital expenditures.*—The following amounts paid are examples of capital expenditures:

(1) An amount paid to acquire or produce a unit of real or personal tangible property. See § 1.263(a)-2.

(2) An amount paid to improve a unit of real or personal tangible property. See § 1.263(a)-3.

(3) An amount paid to acquire or create intangibles. See § 1.263(a)-4.

(4) An amount paid or incurred to facilitate an acquisition of a trade or business, a change in capital structure of a business entity, and certain other transactions. See § 1.263(a)-5.

(5) An amount paid to acquire or create interests in land, such as easements, life estates, mineral interests, timber rights, zoning variances, or other interests in land.

(6) An amount assessed and paid under an agreement between bondholders or shareholders of a corporation to be used in a reorganization of the corporation or voluntary contributions by shareholders to the capital of the corporation for any corporate purpose. See section 118 and § 1.118-1.

(7) An amount paid by a holding company to carry out a guaranty of dividends at a specified rate on the stock of a subsidiary corporation for the purpose of securing new capital for the subsidiary and increasing the value of its stockholdings in the subsidiary. This amount must be added to the cost of the stock in the subsidiary.

(e) *Amounts paid to sell property.*—(1) *In general.*—Commissions and other transaction costs paid to facilitate the sale of property are not currently deductible under section 162 or 212. Instead, the amounts are capitalized costs that reduce the amount realized in the taxable year in which the sale occurs or are taken into account in the taxable year in which the sale is abandoned if a deduction is permissible. These amounts are not added to the basis of the property sold or treated as an intangible asset under § 1.263(a)-4. See § 1.263(a)-5(g) for the treatment of amounts paid to facilitate the disposition of assets that constitute a trade or business.

(2) *Dealer in property.*—In the case of a dealer in property, amounts paid to facilitate the sale of such property are treated as ordinary and necessary business expenses.

(3) *Examples.*—The following examples, which assume the sale is not an installment sale under section 453, illustrate the rules of this paragraph (e):

Example 1. Sales costs of real property. A owns a parcel of real estate. A sells the real estate and pays legal fees, recording fees, and sales commissions to facilitate the sale. A must capitalize the fees and commissions and, in the taxable year of the sale, must reduce the amount realized from the sale of the real estate by the fees and commissions.

Example 2. Sales costs of dealers. Assume the same facts as in *Example 1*, except that A is a dealer in real estate. The commissions and fees paid to facilitate the sale of the real estate may be deducted as ordinary and necessary business expenses under section 162.

Example 3. Sales costs of personal property used in a trade or business. B owns a truck for use in B's trade or business. B decides to sell the truck on November 15, Year 1. B pays for an appraisal to determine a reasonable asking price. On February 15, Year 2, B sells the truck to C. In Year 1, B must capitalize the amount paid to appraise the truck, and in Year 2, must reduce the amount realized from the sale of the truck by the amount paid for the appraisal.

Example 4. Costs of abandoned sale of personal property used in a trade or business. Assume the same facts as in *Example 3*, except that, instead of selling the truck on February 15, Year 2, B decides on that date not to sell the truck and takes the truck off the market. In Year 1, B must capitalize the amount paid to appraise the truck. However, B may recognize the amount paid to appraise the truck as a loss under section 165 in Year 2, the taxable year when the sale is abandoned.

Example 5. Sales costs of personal property not used in a trade or business. Assume the same facts as in *Example 3*, except that B does not use the truck in B's trade or business but instead uses it for personal purposes. In Year 1, B must capitalize the amount paid to appraise the truck, and in Year 2, must reduce the amount realized from the sale of the truck by the amount paid for the appraisal.

Example 6. Costs of abandoned sale of personal property not used in a trade or business. Assume the same facts as in *Example 5*, except that, instead of selling the truck on February 15, Year 2, B decides on that date not to sell the truck and takes the truck off the market. In Year 1, B must capitalize the amount paid to appraise the truck. Although B abandons the sale in Year 2, B may not treat the amount paid to appraise the truck as a loss under section 165 because the truck was not used in B's trade or business or in a transaction entered into for profit.

(f) *De minimis safe harbor election.*—(1) *In general.*—Except as otherwise provided in paragraph (f)(2) of this section, a taxpayer electing to apply the de minimis safe harbor under this paragraph (f) may not capitalize under § 1.263(a)-2(d)(1) or § 1.263(a)-3(d) any amount paid

in the taxable year for the acquisition or production of a unit of tangible property nor treat as a material or supply under § 1.162-3(a) any amount paid in the taxable year for tangible property if the amount specified under this paragraph (f)(1) meets the requirements of paragraph (f)(1)(i) or (f)(1)(ii) of this section. However, section 263A and the regulations under section 263A require taxpayers to capitalize the direct and allocable indirect costs of property produced by the taxpayer (for example, property improved by the taxpayer) and property acquired for resale.

(i) *Taxpayer with applicable financial statement.*—A taxpayer electing to apply the de minimis safe harbor may not capitalize under § 1.263(a)-2(d)(1) or § 1.263(a)-3(d) nor treat as a material or supply under § 1.162-3(a) any amount paid in the taxable year for property described in paragraph (f)(1) of this section if—

(A) The taxpayer has an applicable financial statement (as defined in paragraph (f)(4) of this section);

(B) The taxpayer has at the beginning of the taxable year written accounting procedures treating as an expense for non-tax purposes—

(1) Amounts paid for property costing less than a specified dollar amount; or

(2) Amounts paid for property with an economic useful life (as defined in § 1.162-3(c)(4)) of 12 months or less;

(C) The taxpayer treats the amount paid for the property as an expense on its applicable financial statement in accordance with its written accounting procedures; and

(D) The amount paid for the property does not exceed $5,000 per invoice (or per item as substantiated by the invoice) or other amount as identified in published guidance in the **Federal Register** or in the Internal Revenue Bulletin (see § 601.601(d)(2)(ii)(*b*) of this chapter).

(ii) *Taxpayer without applicable financial statement.*—A taxpayer electing to apply the de minimis safe harbor may not capitalize under § 1.263(a)-2(d)(1) or § 1.263(a)-3(c) nor treat as a material or supply under § 1.162-3(a) any amount paid in the taxable year for property described in paragraph (f)(1) of this section if—

(A) The taxpayer does not have an applicable financial statement (as defined in paragraph (f)(4) of this section);

(B) The taxpayer has at the beginning of the taxable year accounting procedures treating as an expense for non-tax purposes—

(1) Amounts paid for property costing less than a specified dollar amount; or

(2) Amounts paid for property with an economic useful life (as defined in § 1.162-3(c)(4)) of 12 months or less;

(C) The taxpayer treats the amount paid for the property as an expense on its books and records in accordance with these accounting procedures; and

(D) The amount paid for the property does not exceed $500 per invoice (or per item as substantiated by the invoice) or other amount as identified in published guidance in the **Federal Register** or in the Internal Revenue Bulletin (see § 601.601(d)(2)(ii)(*b*) of this chapter).

(iii) *Taxpayer with both an applicable financial statement and a non-qualifying financial statement.*—For purposes of this paragraph (f)(1), if a taxpayer has an applicable financial statement defined in paragraph (f)(4) of this section in addition to a financial statement that does not meet requirements of paragraph (f)(4) of this section, the taxpayer must meet the requirements of paragraph (f)(1)(i) of this section to qualify to elect the de minimis safe harbor under this paragraph (f).

(2) *Exceptions to de minimis safe harbor.*—The de minimis safe harbor in paragraph (f)(1) of this section does not apply to the following:

(i) Amounts paid for property that is or is intended to be included in inventory property;

(ii) Amounts paid for land;

(iii) Amounts paid for rotable, temporary, and standby emergency spare parts that the taxpayer elects to capitalize and depreciate under § 1.162-3(d); and

(iv) Amounts paid for rotable and temporary spare parts that the taxpayer accounts for under the optional method of accounting for rotable parts pursuant to § 1.162-3(e).

(3) *Additional rules.*—(i) *Transaction and other additional costs.*—A taxpayer electing to apply the de minimis safe harbor under paragraph (f)(1) of this section is not required to include in the cost of the tangible property the additional costs of acquiring or producing such property if these costs are not included in the same invoice as the tangible property. However, the taxpayer electing to apply the de minimis safe harbor under paragraph (f)(1) of this section must include in the cost of such property all additional costs (for example,

delivery fees, installation services, or similar costs) if these additional costs are included on the same invoice with the tangible property. For purposes of this paragraph, if the invoice includes amounts paid for multiple tangible properties and such invoice includes additional invoice costs related to these multiple properties, then the taxpayer must allocate the additional invoice costs to each property using a reasonable method, and each property, including allocable labor and overhead, must meet the requirements of paragraph (f)(1)(i) or paragraph (f)(1)(ii) of this section, whichever is applicable. Reasonable allocation methods include, but are not limited to specific identification, a pro rata allocation, or a weighted average method based on the property's relative cost. For purposes of this paragraph (f)(3)(i), additional costs consist of the costs of facilitating the acquisition or production of such tangible property under §1.263(a)-2(f) and the costs for work performed prior to the date that the tangible property is placed in service under §1.263(a)-2(d).

(ii) *Materials and supplies.*—If a taxpayer elects to apply the de minimis safe harbor provided under this paragraph (f), then the taxpayer must also apply the de minimis safe harbor to amounts paid for all materials and supplies (as defined under §1.162-3) that meet the requirements of §1.263(a)-1(f). See paragraph (f)(3)(iv) of this section for treatment of materials and supplies under the de minimis safe harbor.

(iii) *Sale or disposition.*—Property to which a taxpayer applies the de minimis safe harbor contained in this paragraph (f) is not treated upon sale or other disposition as a capital asset under section 1221 or as property used in the trade or business under section 1231.

(iv) *Treatment of de minimis amounts.*—An amount paid for property to which a taxpayer properly applies the de minimis safe harbor contained in this paragraph (f) is not treated as a capital expenditure under §1.263(a)-2(d)(1) or §1.263(a)-3(d) or as a material and supply under §1.162-3, and may be deducted under §1.162-1 in the taxable year the amount is paid provided the amount otherwise constitutes an ordinary and necessary expense incurred in carrying on a trade or business.

(v) *Coordination with section 263A.*—Amounts paid for tangible property described in paragraph (f)(1) of this section may be subject to capitalization under section 263A if the amounts paid for tangible property comprise the direct or allocable indirect costs of other property produced by the taxpayer or property acquired for resale. See, for example, §1.263A-1(e)(3)(ii)(R) requiring taxpayers to capitalize the cost of tools and equipment allocable to property produced or property acquired for resale.

(vi) *Written accounting procedures for groups of entities.*—If the taxpayer's financial results are reported on the applicable financial statement (as defined in paragraph (f)(4) of this section) for a group of entities then, for purposes of paragraph (f)(1)(i)(A) of this section, the group's applicable financial statement may be treated as the applicable financial statement of the taxpayer, and for purposes of paragraphs (f)(1)(i)(B) and (f)(1)(i)(C) of this section, the written accounting procedures provided for the group and utilized for the group's applicable financial statement may be treated as the written accounting procedures of the taxpayer.

(vii) *Combined expensing accounting procedures.*—For purposes of paragraphs (f)(1)(i) and (f)(1)(ii) of this section, if the taxpayer has, at the beginning of the taxable year, accounting procedures treating as an expense for non-tax purposes amounts paid for property costing less than a specified dollar amount and amounts paid for property with an economic useful life (as defined in §1.162-3(c)(4)) of 12 months or less, then a taxpayer electing to apply the de minimis safe harbor under this paragraph (f) must apply the provisions of this paragraph (f) to amounts qualifying under either accounting procedure.

(4) *Definition of applicable financial statement.*—For purposes of this paragraph (f), the taxpayer's applicable financial statement (AFS) is the taxpayer's financial statement listed in paragraphs (f)(4)(i) through (iii) of this section that has the highest priority (including within paragraph (f)(4)(ii) of this section). The financial statements are, in descending priority—

(i) A financial statement required to be filed with the Securities and Exchange Commission (SEC) (the 10-K or the Annual Statement to Shareholders);

(ii) A certified audited financial statement that is accompanied by the report of an independent certified public accountant (or in the case of a foreign entity, by the report of a similarly qualified independent professional) that is used for—

(A) Credit purposes;

(B) Reporting to shareholders, partners, or similar persons; or

(C) Any other substantial non-tax purpose; or

(iii) A financial statement (other than a tax return) required to be provided to the federal or a state government or any federal or state agency (other than the SEC or the Internal Revenue Service).

(5) *Time and manner of election.*—A taxpayer that makes the election under this paragraph (f) must make the election for all amounts paid during the taxable year for property described in paragraph (f)(1) of this section and meeting the requirements of paragraph (f)(1)(i) or paragraph (f)(1)(ii) of this section, as applicable. A taxpayer makes the election by attaching a statement to the taxpayer's timely filed original Federal tax return (including extensions) for the taxable year in which these amounts are paid. Sections 301.9100-1 through 301.9100-3 of this chapter provide the rules governing extensions of the time to make regulatory elections. The statement must be titled "Section 1.263(a)-1(f) de minimis safe harbor election" and include the taxpayer's name, address, taxpayer identification number, and a statement that the taxpayer is making the de minimis safe harbor election under §1.263(a)-1(f). In the case of a consolidated group filing a consolidated income tax return, the election is made for each member of the consolidated group by the common parent, and the statement must also include the names and taxpayer identification numbers of each member for which the election is made. In the case of an S corporation or a partnership, the election is made by the S corporation or the partnership and not by the shareholders or partners. An election may not be made through the filing of an application for change in accounting method or, before obtaining the Commissioner's consent to make a late election, by filing an amended Federal tax return. A taxpayer may not revoke an election made under this paragraph (f). The manner of electing the de minimis safe harbor under this paragraph (f) may be modified through guidance of general applicability (see §§601.601(d)(2) and 601.602 of this chapter).

(6) *Anti-abuse rule.*—If a taxpayer acts to manipulate transactions with the intent to achieve a tax benefit or to avoid the application of the limitations provided under paragraphs (f)(1)(i)(B)(*1*), (f)(1)(i)(D), (f)(1)(ii)(B)(*1*), and (f)(1)(ii)(D) of this section, appropriate adjustments will be made to carry out the purposes of this section. For example, a taxpayer is deemed to act to manipulate transactions with an intent to avoid the purposes and requirements of this section if—

(i) The taxpayer applies the de minimis safe harbor to amounts substantiated with invoices created to componentize property that is generally acquired or produced by the taxpayer (or other taxpayers in the same or similar trade or business) as a single unit of tangible property; and

(ii) This property, if treated as a single unit, would exceed any of the limitations provided under paragraphs (f)(1)(i)(B)(*1*), (f)(1)(i)(D), (f)(1)(ii)(B)(*1*), and (f)(1)(ii)(D) of this section, as applicable.

(7) *Examples.*—The following examples illustrate the application of this paragraph (f). Unless otherwise provided, assume that section 263A does not apply to the amounts described.

Example 1. De minimis safe harbor; taxpayer without AFS. In Year 1, A purchases 10 printers at $250 each for a total cost of $2,500 as indicated by the invoice. Assume that each printer is a unit of property under §1.263(a)-3(e). A does not have an AFS. A has accounting procedures in place at the beginning of Year 1 to expense amounts paid for property costing less than $500, and A treats the amounts paid for the printers as an expense on its books and records. The amounts paid for the printers meet the requirements for the de minimis safe harbor under paragraph (f)(1)(ii) of this section. If A elects to apply the de minimis safe harbor under this paragraph (f) in Year 1, A may not capitalize the amounts paid for the 10 printers or any other amounts meeting the criteria for the de minimis safe harbor under paragraph (f)(1). Instead, in accordance with paragraph (f)(3)(iv) of this section, A may deduct these amounts under §1.162-1 in the taxable year the amounts are paid provided the amounts otherwise constitute deductible ordinary and necessary expenses incurred in carrying on a trade or business.

Example 2. De minimis safe harbor; taxpayer without AFS. In Year 1, B purchases 10 computers at $600 each for a total cost of $6,000 as indicated by the invoice. Assume that each computer is a unit of property under §1.263(a)-3(e). B does not have an AFS. B has accounting procedures in place at the beginning of Year 1 to expense amounts paid for property costing less than $1,000, and B treats the amounts paid for the computers as an expense on its books and records. The amounts paid for the printers do not meet the requirements for the de minimis safe harbor under paragraph (f)(1)(ii) of this section because the amount paid for the property exceeds $500 per invoice (or per item as substantiated by the invoice). B may not apply the de minimis safe harbor election to the amounts paid for the 10 computers under paragraph (f)(1) of this section.

Example 3. De minimis safe harbor; taxpayer with AFS. C is a member of a consolidated group for Federal income tax purposes. C's financial results are reported on the consolidated applicable financial statements for the affiliated group. C's affiliated group has a written accounting policy at the beginning of Year 1, which is followed by C, to expense amounts paid for property costing $5,000 or less. In Year 1, C pays $6,250,000 to purchase 1,250 computers at $5,000 each. C receives an invoice from its supplier indicating the total amount due ($6,250,000) and the price per item ($5,000). Assume that each computer is a unit of property under §1.263(a)-3(e). The amounts paid for the computers meet the requirements for the de minimis safe harbor under paragraph (f)(1)(i) of this section. If C elects to apply the de minimis safe harbor under this paragraph (f) for Year 1, C may not capitalize the amounts paid for the 1,250 computers or any other amounts meeting the criteria for the de minimis safe harbor under paragraph (f)(1) of this section. Instead, in accordance with paragraph (f)(3)(iv) of this section, C may deduct these amounts under §1.162-1 in the taxable year the amounts are paid provided the amounts otherwise constitute deductible ordinary and necessary expenses incurred in carrying on a trade or business.

Example 4. De minimis safe harbor; taxpayer with AFS. D is a member of a consolidated group for Federal income tax purposes. D's financial results are reported on the consolidated applicable financial statements for the affiliated group. D's affiliated group has a written accounting policy at the beginning of Year 1, which is followed by D, to expense amounts paid for property costing less than $15,000. In Year 1, D pays $4,800,000 to purchase 800 elliptical machines at $6,000 each. D receives an invoice from its supplier indicating the total amount due ($4,800,000) and the price per item ($6,000). Assume that each elliptical machine is a unit of property under §1.263(a)-3(e). D may not apply the de minimis safe harbor election to the amounts paid for the 800 elliptical machines under paragraph (f)(1) of this section because the amount paid for the property exceeds $5,000 per invoice (or per item as substantiated by the invoice).

Example 5. De minimis safe harbor; additional invoice costs. E is a member of a consolidated group for Federal income tax purposes. E's financial results are reported on the consolidated applicable financial statements for the affiliated group. E's affiliated group has a written accounting policy at the beginning of Year 1, which is followed by E, to expense amounts paid for property costing less than $5,000. In Year 1, E pays $45,000 for the purchase and installation of wireless routers in each of its 10 office locations. Assume that each wireless router is a unit of property under §1.263(a)-3(e). E receives an invoice from its supplier indicating the total amount due ($45,000), including the material price per item ($2,500), and total delivery and installation ($20,000). E allocates the additional invoice costs to the materials on a pro rata basis, bringing the cost of each router to $4,500 ($2,500 materials + $2,000 labor and overhead). The amounts paid for each router, including the allocable additional invoice costs, meet the requirements for the de minimis safe harbor under paragraph (f)(1)(i) of this section. If E elects to apply the de minimis safe harbor under this paragraph (f) for Year 1, E may not capitalize the amounts paid for the 10 routers (including the additional invoice costs) or any other amounts meeting the criteria for the de minimis safe harbor under paragraph (f)(1) of this section. Instead, in accordance with paragraph (f)(3)(iv) of this section, E may deduct these amounts under §1.162-1 in the taxable year the amounts are paid provided the amounts otherwise constitute deductible ordinary and necessary expenses incurred in carrying on a trade or business.

Example 6. De minimis safe harbor; non-invoice additional costs. F is a corporation that provides consulting services to its customer. F does not have an AFS, but F has accounting procedures in place at the beginning of Year 1 to expense amounts paid for property costing less than $500. In Year 1, F pays $600 to an interior designer to shop for, evaluate, and make recommendations regarding purchasing new furniture for F's conference room. As a result of the interior designer's recommendations, F acquires a conference table for $500 and 10 chairs for $300 each. In Year 1, F receives an invoice from the interior designer for $600 for his services, and F receives a separate invoice from the furniture supplier indicating a total amount due of $500 for the table and $300 for each chair. For Year 1, F treats the amount paid for the table and each chair as an expense on its books and records, and F elects to use the de minimis safe harbor for amounts paid for tangible property that qualify under the safe harbor. The amount paid to the interior designer is a cost of facilitating the acquisition of the table and chairs under §1.263(a)-2(f). Under paragraph (f)(3)(i) of this section, F is not required to include in the cost of tangible property the additional costs of acquiring such property if these costs are not included in the same invoice as the tangible property. Thus, F is not required to include a pro rata allocation of the amount paid to the interior designer to determine the application of the de minimis safe harbor to the table and the chairs. Accordingly, the amounts paid by F for the table and each chair meet the requirements for the de minimis safe harbor under paragraph (f)(1)(ii) of this section, and F may not capitalize the amounts paid for the table or each chair under paragraph (f)(1) of this section. In addition, F is not required to capitalize the amounts paid to the interior designer as a cost that facilitates the acquisition of tangible

property under §1.263(a)-2(f)(3)(i). Instead, F may deduct the amounts paid for the table, chairs, and interior designer under §1.162-1 in the taxable year the amounts are paid provided the amounts otherwise constitute deductible ordinary and necessary expenses incurred in carrying on a trade or business.

Example 7. De minimis safe harbor; 12-month economic useful life. G operates a restaurant. In Year 1, G purchases 10 hand-held point-of-service devices at $300 each for a total cost of $3,000 as indicated by invoice. G also purchases 3 tablet computers at $500 each for a total cost of $1,500 as indicated by invoice. Assume each point-of-service device and each tablet computer has an economic useful life of 12 months or less, beginning when they are used in G's business. Assume that each device and each tablet is a unit of property under §1.263(a)-3(e). G does not have an AFS, but G has accounting procedures in place at the beginning of Year 1 to expense amounts paid for property costing $300 or less and to expense amounts paid for property with an economic useful life of 12 months or less. Thus, G expenses the amounts paid for the hand-held devices on its books and records because each device costs $300. G also expenses the amounts paid for the tablet computers on its books and records because the computers have an economic useful life of 12 months of less, beginning when they are used. The amounts paid for the hand-held devices and the tablet computers meet the requirements for the de minimis safe harbor under paragraph (f)(1)(ii) of this section. If G elects to apply the de minimis safe harbor under this paragraph (f) in Year 1, G may not capitalize the amounts paid for the hand-held devices, the tablet computers, or any other amounts meeting the criteria for the de minimis safe harbor under paragraph (f)(1) of this section. Instead, in accordance with paragraph (f)(3)(iv) of this section, G may deduct the amounts paid for the hand-held devices and tablet computers under §1.162-1 in the taxable year the amounts are paid provided the amounts otherwise constitute deductible ordinary and necessary business expenses incurred in carrying on a trade or business.

Example 8. De minimis safe harbor; limitation. Assume the facts as in *Example 7*, except G purchases the 3 tablet computers at $600 each for a total cost of $1,800. The amounts paid for the tablet computers do not meet the de minimis rule safe harbor under paragraphs (f)(1)(ii) and (f)(3)(vii) of this section because the cost of each computer exceeds $500. Therefore, the amounts paid for the tablet computers may not be deducted under the safe harbor.

Example 9. De minimis safe harbor; materials and supplies. H is a corporation that provides consulting services to its customers. H has an AFS and a written accounting policy at the beginning of the taxable year to expense amounts paid for property costing $5,000 or less. In Year 1, H purchases 1,000 computers at $500 each for a total cost of $500,000. Assume that each computer is a unit of property under §1.263(a)-3(e) and is not a material or supply under §1.162-3. In addition, H purchases 200 office chairs at $100 each for a total cost of $20,000 and 250 customized briefcases at $80 each for a total cost of $20,000. Assume that each office chair and each briefcase is a material or supply under §1.162-3(c)(1). H treats the amounts paid for the computers, office chairs, and briefcases as expenses on its AFS. The amounts paid for computers, office chairs, and briefcases meet the requirements for the de minimis safe harbor under paragraph (f)(1)(i) of this section. If H elects to apply the de minimis safe harbor under this paragraph (f) in Year 1, H may not capitalize the amounts paid for the 1,000 computers, the 200 office chairs, and the 250 briefcases under paragraph (f)(1) of this section. H may deduct the amounts paid for the computers, the office chairs, and the briefcases under §1.162-1 in the taxable year the amounts are paid provided the amounts otherwise constitute deductible ordinary and necessary expenses incurred in carrying on a trade or business.

Example 10. De minimis safe harbor; coordination with section 263A. J is a member of a consolidated group for Federal income tax purposes. J's financial results are reported on the consolidated AFS for the affiliated group. J's affiliated group has a written accounting policy at the beginning of Year 1, which is followed by J, to expense amounts paid for property costing less than $1,000 or that has an economic useful life of 12 months or less. In Year 1, J acquires jigs, dies, molds, and patterns for use in the manufacture of J's products. Assume each jig, die, mold, and pattern is a unit of property under §1.263(a)-3(e) and costs less than $1,000. In Year 1, J begins using the jigs, dies, molds and patterns to manufacture its products. Assume these items are materials and supplies under §1.162-3(c)(1)(iii), and J elects to apply the de minimis safe harbor under paragraph (f)(1)(i) of this section to amounts qualifying under the safe harbor in Year 1. Under paragraph (f)(3)(v) of this section, the amounts paid for the jigs, dies, molds, and patterns may be subject to capitalization under section 263A if the amounts paid for these tangible properties comprise the direct or allocable indirect costs of other property produced by the taxpayer or property acquired for resale.

Example 11. De minimis safe harbor; anti-abuse rule. K is a corporation that provides hauling services to its customers. In Year 1, K decides to purchase a truck to use in its business. K does not have an

AFS. K has accounting procedures in place at the beginning of Year 1 to expense amounts paid for property costing less than $500. K arranges to purchase a used truck for a total of $1,500. Prior to the acquisition, K requests the seller to provide multiple invoices for different parts of the truck. Accordingly, the seller provides K with four invoices during Year 1—one invoice of $500 for the cab, one invoice of $500 for the engine, one invoice of $300 for the trailer, and a fourth invoice of $200 for the tires. K treats the amounts paid under each invoice as an expense on its books and records. K elects to apply the de minimis safe harbor under paragraph (f) of this section in Year 1 and does not capitalize the amounts paid for each invoice pursuant to the safe harbor. Under paragraph (f)(6) of this section, K has applied the de minimis rule to amounts substantiated with invoices created to componentize property that is generally acquired as a single unit of tangible property in the taxpayer's type of business, and this property, if treated as single unit, would exceed the limitations provided under the de minimis rule. Accordingly, K is deemed to manipulate the transaction to acquire the truck with the intent to avoid the purposes of this paragraph (f). As a result, K may not apply the de minimis rule to these amounts and is subject to appropriate adjustments.

(g) *Accounting method changes.*—Except for paragraph (f) of this section (the de minimis safe harbor election), a change to comply with this section is a change in method of accounting to which the provisions of sections 446 and 481 and the accompanying regulations apply. A taxpayer seeking to change to a method of accounting permitted in this section must secure the consent of the Commissioner in accordance with § 1.446-1(e) and follow the administrative procedures issued under § 1.446-1(e)(3)(ii) for obtaining the Commissioner's consent to change its accounting method.

(h) *Effective/applicability date.*—(1) *In general.*—Except for paragraph (f) of this section, this section generally applies to taxable years beginning on or after January 1, 2014. Paragraph (f) of this section applies to amounts paid in taxable years beginning on or after January 1, 2014. Except as provided in paragraph (h)(1) and paragraph (h)(2) of this section, § 1.263(a)-1 as contained in 26 CFR part 1 edition revised as of April 1, 2011, applies to taxable years beginning before January 1, 2014.

(2) *Early application of this section.*—(i) *In general.*—Except for paragraph (f) of this section, a taxpayer may choose to apply this section to taxable years beginning on or after January 1, 2012. A taxpayer may choose to apply paragraph (f) of this section to amounts paid in taxable years beginning on or after January 1, 2012.

(ii) *Transition rule for de minimis safe harbor election on 2012 or 2013 returns.*—If under paragraph (h)(2)(i) of this section, a taxpayer chooses to make the election to apply the de minimis safe harbor under paragraph (f) of this section for amounts paid in its taxable year beginning on or after January 1, 2012, and ending on or before September 19, 2013 (applicable taxable year), and the taxpayer did not make the election specified in paragraph (f)(5) of this section on its timely filed original Federal tax return for the applicable taxable year, the taxpayer must make the election specified in paragraph (f)(5) of this section for the applicable taxable year by filing an amended Federal tax return for the applicable taxable year on or before 180 days from the due date including extensions of the taxpayer's Federal tax return for the applicable taxable year, notwithstanding that the taxpayer may not have extended the due date.

(3) *Optional application of TD 9564.*—A taxpayer may choose to apply § 1.263(a)-1T as contained in TD 9564 (76 FR 81060) December 27, 2011, to taxable years beginning on or after January 1, 2012, and before January 1, 2014. [Reg. § 1.263(a)-1.]

☐ [T.D. 6313, 9-16-58. Amended by T.D. 6548, 2-21-61; T.D. 6794, 1-25-65; T.D. 8121, 1-5-87; T.D. 8131, 3-24-87; T.D. 8408, 4-9-92; T.D. 8482, 8-6-93; T.D. 9564, 12-23-2011 and T.D. 9636, 9-13-2013 (corrected 7-18-2014).]

[Reg. § 1.263(a)-2]

§1.263(a)-2. Amounts paid to acquire or produce tangible property.—(a) *Overview.*—This section provides rules for applying section 263(a) to amounts paid to acquire or produce a unit of real or personal property. Paragraph (b) of this section contains definitions. Paragraph (c) of this section contains the rules for coordinating this section with other provisions of the Internal Revenue Code (Code). Paragraph (d) of this section provides the general requirement to capitalize amounts paid to acquire or produce a unit of real or personal property. Paragraph (e) of this section provides the requirement to capitalize amounts paid to defend or perfect title to real or personal property. Paragraph (f) of this section provides the rules for determining the extent to which taxpayers must capitalize transaction costs related to the acquisition of tangible property. Paragraphs (g) and (h) of this section address the treatment and recovery of

capital expenditures. Paragraph (i) of this section provides for changes in methods of accounting to comply with this section, and paragraph (j) of this section provides the effective and applicability dates for the rules under this section.

(b) *Definitions.*—For purposes of this section, the following definitions apply:

(1) *Amount paid.*—In the case of a taxpayer using an accrual method of accounting, the terms *amount paid* and *payment* mean a liability incurred (within the meaning of § 1.446-1(c)(1)(ii)). A liability may not be taken into account under this section prior to the taxable year during which the liability is incurred.

(2) *Personal property* means tangible personal property as defined in § 1.48-1(c).

(3) *Real property* means land and improvements thereto, such as buildings or other inherently permanent structures (including items that are structural components of the buildings or structures) that are not personal property as defined in paragraph (b)(2) of this section. Any property that constitutes other tangible property under § 1.48-1(d) is treated as real property for purposes of this section. Local law is not controlling in determining whether property is real property for purposes of this section.

(4) *Produce* means construct, build, install, manufacture, develop, create, raise, or grow. This definition is intended to have the same meaning as the definition used for purposes of section 263A(g)(1) and § 1.263A-2(a)(1)(i), except that improvements are excluded from the definition in this paragraph (b)(4) and are separately defined and addressed in § 1.263(a)-3.

(c) *Coordination with other provisions of the Code.*—(1) *In general.*—Nothing in this section changes the treatment of any amount that is specifically provided for under any provision of the Code or the Treasury Regulations other than section 162(a) or section 212 and the regulations under those sections. For example, see section 263A requiring taxpayers to capitalize the direct and allocable indirect costs of property produced by the taxpayer and property acquired for resale. See also section 195 requiring taxpayers to capitalize certain costs as start-up expenditures.

(2) *Materials and supplies.*—Nothing in this section changes the treatment of amounts paid to acquire or produce property that is properly treated as materials and supplies under § 1.162-3.

(d) *Acquired or produced tangible property.*—(1) *Requirement to capitalize.*—Except as provided in § 1.162-3 (relating to materials and supplies) and in § 1.263(a)-1(f) (providing a de minimis safe harbor election), a taxpayer must capitalize amounts paid to acquire or produce a unit of real or personal property (as determined under § 1.263(a)-3(e)), including leasehold improvements, land and land improvements, buildings, machinery and equipment, and furniture and fixtures. Section 1.263(a)-3(f) provides the rules for determining whether amounts are for leasehold improvements. Amounts paid to acquire or produce a unit of real or personal property include the invoice price, transaction costs as determined under paragraph (f) of this section, and costs for work performed prior to the date that the unit of property is placed in service by the taxpayer (without regard to any applicable convention under section 168(d)). A taxpayer also must capitalize amounts paid to acquire real or personal property for resale.

(2) *Examples.*—The following examples illustrate the rules of this paragraph (d). Unless otherwise provided, assume that the taxpayer does not elect the de minimis safe harbor under § 1.263(a)-1(f) and that the property is not acquired for resale under section 263A.

Example 1. Acquisition of personal property. A purchases new cash registers for use in its retail store located in leased space in a shopping mall. Assume each cash register is a unit of property as determined under § 1.263(a)-3(e) and is not a material or supply under § 1.162-3. A must capitalize under paragraph (d)(1) of this section the amount paid to acquire each cash register.

Example 2. Acquisition of personal property that is a material or supply; coordination with § 1.162-3. B operates a fleet of aircraft. In Year 1, B acquires a stock of component parts, which it intends to use to maintain and repair its aircraft. Assume that each component part is a material or supply under § 1.162-3(c)(1) and B does not make elections under § 1.162-3(d) to treat the materials and supplies as capital expenditures. In Year 2, B uses the component parts in the repair and maintenance of its aircraft. Because the parts are materials and supplies under § 1.162-3, B is not required to capitalize the amounts paid for the parts under paragraph (d)(1) of this section. Rather, to determine the treatment of these amounts, B must apply the rules under § 1.162-3, governing the treatment of materials and supplies.

Example 3. Acquisition of unit of personal property; coordination with § 1.162-3. C operates a rental business that rents out a variety of small individual items to customers (rental items). C maintains a supply of rental items on hand to replace worn or damaged items. C purchases a large quantity of rental items to be used in its business. Assume that each of these rental items is a unit of property under §1.263(a)-3(e). Also assume that a portion of the rental items are materials and supplies under §1.162-3(c)(1). Under paragraph (d)(1) of this section, C must capitalize the amounts paid for the rental items that are not materials and supplies under §1.162-3(c)(1). However, C must apply the rules in §1.162-3 to determine the treatment of the rental items that are materials and supplies under §1.162-3(c)(1).

Example 4. Acquisition or production cost. D purchases and produces jigs, dies, molds, and patterns for use in the manufacture of D's products. Assume that each of these items is a unit of property as determined under §1.263(a)-3(e) and is not a material and supply under §1.162-3(c)(1). D is required to capitalize under paragraph (d)(1) of this section the amounts paid to acquire and produce the jigs, dies, molds, and patterns.

Example 5. Acquisition of land. F purchases a parcel of undeveloped real estate. F must capitalize under paragraph (d)(1) of this section the amount paid to acquire the real estate. See paragraph (f) of this section for the treatment of amounts paid to facilitate the acquisition of real property.

Example 6. Acquisition of building. G purchases a building. G must capitalize under paragraph (d)(1) of this section the amount paid to acquire the building. See paragraph (f) of this section for the treatment of amounts paid to facilitate the acquisition of real property.

Example 7. Acquisition of property for resale and production of property for sale; coordination with section 263A. H purchases goods for resale and produces other goods for sale. H must capitalize under paragraph (d)(1) of this section the amounts paid to acquire and produce the goods. See section 263A for the amounts required to be capitalized to the property produced or to the property acquired for resale.

Example 8. Production of building; coordination with section 263A. J constructs a building. J must capitalize under paragraph (d)(1) of this section the amount paid to construct the building. See section 263A for the costs required to be capitalized to the real property produced by J.

Example 9. Acquisition of assets constituting a trade or business. K owns tangible and intangible assets that constitute a trade or business. L purchases all the assets of K in a taxable transaction. L must capitalize under paragraph (d)(1) of this section the amount paid for the tangible assets of K. See §1.263(a)-4 for the treatment of amounts paid to acquire or create intangibles and §1.263(a)-5 for the treatment of amounts paid to facilitate the acquisition of assets that constitute a trade or business. See section 1060 for special allocation rules for certain asset acquisitions.

Example 10. Work performed prior to placing the property in service. In Year 1, M purchases a building for use as a business office. Prior to placing the building in service, M pays amounts to repair cement steps, refinish wood floors, patch holes in walls, and paint the interiors and exteriors of the building. In Year 2, M places the building in service and begins using the building as its business office. Assume that the work that M performs does not constitute an improvement to the building or its structural components under §1.263(a)-3. Under §1.263(a)-3(e)(2)(i), the building and its structural components is a single unit of property. Under paragraph (d)(1) of this section, the amounts paid must be capitalized as amounts to acquire the building unit of property because they were for work performed prior to M's placing the building in service.

Example 11. Work performed prior to placing the property in service. In January Year 1, N purchases a new machine for use in an existing production line of its manufacturing business. Assume that the machine is a unit of property under §1.263(a)-3(e) and is not a material or supply under §1.162-3. N pays amounts to install the machine, and after the machine is installed, N pays amounts to perform a critical test on the machine to ensure that it will operate in accordance with quality standards. On November 1, Year 1, the critical test is complete, and N places the machine in service on the production line. N pays amounts to perform periodic quality control testing after the machine is placed in service. Under paragraph (d)(1) of this section, the amounts paid for the installation and the critical test performed before the machine is placed in service must be capitalized by N as amounts to acquire the machine. However, amounts paid for periodic quality control testing after N placed the machine in service are not required to be capitalized as amounts paid to acquire the machine.

(e) *Defense or perfection of title to property.*—(1) *In general.*—Amounts paid to defend or perfect title to real or personal property are amounts paid to acquire or produce property within the meaning of this section and must be capitalized.

(2) *Examples.*—The following examples illustrate the rule of this paragraph (e):

Example 1. Amounts paid to contest condemnation. X owns real property located in County. County files an eminent domain complaint condemning a portion of X's property to use as a roadway. X hires an attorney to contest the condemnation. The amounts that X paid to the attorney must be capitalized because they were to defend X's title to the property.

Example 2. Amounts paid to invalidate ordinance. Y is in the business of quarrying and supplying for sale sand and stone in a certain municipality. Several years after Y establishes its business, the municipality in which it is located passes an ordinance that prohibits the operation of Y's business. Y incurs attorney's fees in a successful prosecution of a suit to invalidate the municipal ordinance. Y prosecutes the suit to preserve its business activities and not to defend Y's title in the property. Therefore, the attorney's fees that Y paid are not required to be capitalized under paragraph (e)(1) of this section.

Example 3. Amounts paid to challenge building line. The board of public works of a municipality establishes a building line across Z's business property, adversely affecting the value of the property. Z incurs legal fees in unsuccessfully litigating the establishment of the building line. The amounts Z paid to the attorney must be capitalized because they were to defend Z's title to the property.

(f) *Transaction costs.*—(1) *In general.*—Except as provided in §1.263(a)-1(f)(3)(i) (for purposes of the de minimis safe harbor), a taxpayer must capitalize amounts paid to facilitate the acquisition of real or personal property. See §1.263(a)-5 for the treatment of amounts paid to facilitate the acquisition of assets that constitute a trade or business. See §1.167(a)-5 for allocations of facilitative costs between depreciable and non-depreciable property.

(2) *Scope of facilitate.*—(i) *In general.*—Except as otherwise provided in this section, an amount is paid to facilitate the acquisition of real or personal property if the amount is paid in the process of investigating or otherwise pursuing the acquisition. Whether an amount is paid in the process of investigating or otherwise pursuing the acquisition is determined based on all of the facts and circumstances. In determining whether an amount is paid to facilitate an acquisition, the fact that the amount would (or would not) have been paid but for the acquisition is relevant but is not determinative. Amounts paid to facilitate an acquisition include, but are not limited to, inherently facilitative amounts specified in paragraph (f)(2)(ii) of this section.

(ii) *Inherently facilitative amounts.*—An amount is paid in the process of investigating or otherwise pursuing the acquisition of real or personal property if the amount is inherently facilitative. An amount is inherently facilitative if the amount is paid for—

(A) Transporting the property (for example, shipping fees and moving costs);

(B) Securing an appraisal or determining the value or price of property;

(C) Negotiating the terms or structure of the acquisition and obtaining tax advice on the acquisition;

(D) Application fees, bidding costs, or similar expenses;

(E) Preparing and reviewing the documents that effectuate the acquisition of the property (for example, preparing the bid, offer, sales contract, or purchase agreement);

(F) Examining and evaluating the title of property;

(G) Obtaining regulatory approval of the acquisition or securing permits related to the acquisition, including application fees;

(H) Conveying property between the parties, including sales and transfer taxes, and title registration costs;

(I) Finders' fees or brokers' commissions, including contingency fees (defined in paragraph (f)(3)(iii) of this section);

(J) Architectural, geological, survey, engineering, environmental, or inspection services pertaining to particular properties; or

(K) Services provided by a qualified intermediary or other facilitator of an exchange under section 1031.

(iii) *Special rule for acquisitions of real property.*—(A) *In general.*—Except as provided in paragraph (f)(2)(ii) of this section (relating to inherently facilitative amounts), an amount paid by the taxpayer in the process of investigating or otherwise pursuing the acquisition of real property does not facilitate the acquisition if it relates to activities performed in the process of determining whether to acquire real property and which real property to acquire.

(B) *Acquisitions of real and personal property in a single transaction.*—An amount paid by the taxpayer in the process of investigating or otherwise pursuing the acquisition of personal property facilitates the acquisition of such personal property, even if such property is acquired in a single transaction that also includes the acquisition of real property subject to the special rule set out in paragraph (f)(2)(iii)(A) of this section. A taxpayer may use a reasonable allocation method to determine which costs facilitate the acquisition of personal property and which costs relate to the acquisition of real property and are subject to the special rule of paragraph (f)(2)(iii)(A) of this section.

(iv) *Employee compensation and overhead costs.*—(A) *In general.*—For purposes of paragraph (f) of this section, amounts paid for employee compensation (within the meaning of § 1.263(a)-4(e)(4)(ii)) and overhead are treated as amounts that do not facilitate the acquisition of real or personal property. However, section 263A provides rules for employee compensation and overhead costs required to be capitalized to property produced by the taxpayer or to property acquired for resale..

(B) *Election to capitalize.*—A taxpayer may elect to treat amounts paid for employee compensation or overhead as amounts that facilitate the acquisition of property. The election is made separately for each acquisition and applies to employee compensation or overhead, or both. For example, a taxpayer may elect to treat overhead, but not employee compensation, as amounts that facilitate the acquisition of property. A taxpayer makes the election by treating the amounts to which the election applies as amounts that facilitate the acquisition in the taxpayer's timely filed original Federal tax return (including extensions) for the taxable year during which the amounts are paid. Sections 301.9100-1 through 301.9100-3 of this chapter provide the rules governing extensions of the time to make regulatory elections. In the case of an S corporation or a partnership, the election is made by the S corporation or by the partnership, and not by the shareholders or partners. A taxpayer may revoke an election made under this paragraph (f)(2)(iv)(B) with respect to each acquisition only by filing a request for a private letter ruling and obtaining the Commissioner's consent to revoke the election. The Commissioner may grant a request to revoke this election if the taxpayer acted reasonably and in good faith and the revocation will not prejudice the interests of Government. See generally § 301.9100-3 of this chapter. The manner of electing and revoking the election to capitalize under this paragraph (f)(2)(iv)(B) may be modified through guidance of general applicability (see § § 606.601(d)(2) and 601.602 of this section). An election may not be made or revoked through the filing of an application for change in accounting method or, before obtaining the Commissioner's consent to make the late election or to revoke the election, by filing an amended Federal tax return.

(3) *Treatment of transaction costs.*—(i) *In general.*—Except as provided under § 1.263(a)-1(f)(3)(i) (for purposes of the de minimis safe harbor), all amounts paid to facilitate the acquisition of real or personal property are capital expenditures. Facilitative amounts allocable to real or personal property must be included in the basis of the property acquired.

(ii) *Treatment of inherently facilitative amounts allocable to property not acquired.*—Inherently facilitative amounts allocable to real or personal property are capital expenditures related to such property, even if the property is not eventually acquired. Except for contingency fees as defined in paragraph (f)(3)(iii) of this section, inherently facilitative amounts allocable to real or personal property not acquired may be allocated to those properties and recovered as appropriate in accordance with the applicable provisions of the Code and the Treasury Regulations (for example, sections 165, 167, or 168). See paragraph (h) of this section for the recovery of capitalized amounts.

(iii) *Contingency Fees.*—For purposes of this section, a contingency fee is an amount paid that is contingent on the successful closing of the acquisition of real or personal property. Contingency fees must be included in the basis of the property acquired and may not be allocated to the property not acquired.

(4) *Examples.*—The following examples illustrate the rules of paragraph (f) of this section. For purposes of these examples, assume that the taxpayer does not elect the de minimis safe harbor under § 1.263(a)-1(f):

Example 1. Broker's fees to facilitate an acquisition. A decides to purchase a building in which to relocate its offices and hires a real estate broker to find a suitable building. A pays fees to the broker to find property for A to acquire. Under paragraph (f)(2)(ii)(I) of this section, A must capitalize the amounts paid to the broker because these costs are inherently facilitative of the acquisition of real property.

Example 2. Inspection and survey costs to facilitate an acquisition. B decides to purchase Building X and pays amounts to third-party contractors for a termite inspection and an environmental survey of Building X. Under paragraph (f)(2)(ii)(J) of this section, B must capitalize the amounts paid for the inspection and the survey of the building because these costs are inherently facilitative of the acquisition of real property.

Example 3. Moving costs to facilitate an acquisition. C purchases all the assets of D and, in connection with the purchase, hires a transportation company to move storage tanks from D's plant to C's plant. Under paragraph (f)(2)(ii)(A) of this section, C must capitalize the

amount paid to move the storage tanks from D's plant to C's plant because this cost is inherently facilitative to the acquisition of personal property.

Example 4. Geological and geophysical costs; coordination with other provisions. E is in the business of exploring, purchasing, and developing properties in the United States for the production of oil and gas. E considers acquiring a particular property but first incurs costs for the services of an engineering firm to perform geological and geophysical studies to determine if the property is suitable for oil or gas production. Assume that the amounts that E paid to the engineering firm constitute geological and geophysical expenditures under section 167(h). Although the amounts that E paid for the geological and geophysical services are inherently facilitative to the acquisition of real property under paragraph (f)(2)(ii)(J) of this section, E is not required to include those amounts in the basis of the real property acquired. Rather, under paragraph (c) of this section, E must capitalize these costs separately and amortize such costs as required under section 167(h) (addressing the amortization of geological and geophysical expenditures).

Example 5. Scope of facilitate. F is in the business of providing legal services to clients. F is interested in acquiring a new conference table for its office. F hires and incurs fees for an interior designer to shop for, evaluate, and make recommendations to F regarding which new table to acquire. Under paragraphs (f)(1) and (2) of this section, F must capitalize the amounts paid to the interior designer to provide these services because they are paid in the process of investigating or otherwise pursuing the acquisition of personal property.

Example 6. Transaction costs allocable to multiple properties. G, a retailer, wants to acquire land for the purpose of building a new distribution facility for its products. G considers various properties on Highway X in State Y. G incurs fees for the services of an architect to advise and evaluate the suitability of the sites for the type of facility that G intends to construct on the selected site. G must capitalize the architect fees as amounts paid to acquire land because these amounts are inherently facilitative to the acquisition of land under paragraph (f)(2)(ii)(J) of this section.

Example 7. Transaction costs; coordination with section 263A. H, a retailer, wants to acquire land for the purpose of building a new distribution facility for its products. H considers various properties on Highway X in State Y. H incurs fees for the services of an architect to prepare preliminary floor plans for a building that H could construct at any of the sites. Under these facts, the architect's fees are not facilitative to the acquisition of land under paragraph (f) of this section. Therefore, H is not required to capitalize the architect fees as amounts paid to acquire land. However, the amounts paid for the architect's fees may be subject to capitalization under section 263A if these amounts comprise the direct or allocable indirect cost of property produced by H, such as the building.

Example 8. Special rule for acquisitions of real property. J owns several retail stores. J decides to examine the feasibility of opening a new store in City X. In October, Year 1, J hires and incurs costs for a development consulting firm to study City X and perform market surveys, evaluate zoning and environmental requirements, and make preliminary reports and recommendations as to areas that J should consider for purposes of locating a new store. In December, Year 1, J continues to consider whether to purchase real property in City X and which property to acquire. J hires, and incurs fees for, an appraiser to perform appraisals on two different sites to determine a fair offering price for each site. In March, Year 2, J decides to acquire one of these two sites for the location of its new store. At the same time, J determines not to acquire the other site. Under paragraph (f)(2)(iii) of this section, J is not required to capitalize amounts paid to the development consultant in Year 1 because the amounts relate to activities performed in the process of determining whether to acquire real property and which real property to acquire, and the amounts are not inherently facilitative costs under paragraph (f)(2)(ii) of this section. However, J must capitalize amounts paid to the appraiser in Year 1 because the appraisal costs are inherently facilitative costs under paragraph (f)(2)(ii)(B) of this section. In Year 2, J must include the appraisal costs allocable to property acquired in the basis of the property acquired. In addition, J may recover the appraisal costs allocable to the property not acquired in accordance with paragraphs (f)(3)(ii) and (h) of this section. See, for example, § 1.165-2 for losses on the permanent withdrawal of non-depreciable property.

Example 9. Contingency fee. K owns several restaurant properties. K decides to open a new restaurant in City X. In October, Year 1, K hires a real estate consultant to identify potential property upon which K may locate its restaurant, and is obligated to compensate the consultant upon the acquisition of property. The real estate consultant identifies three properties, and K decides to acquire one of those properties. Upon closing of the acquisition of that property, K pays the consultant its fee. The amount paid to the consultant constitutes a contingency fee under paragraph (f)(3)(iii) of this section because the payment is contingent on the successful closing of the acquisition of property. Accordingly, under paragraph (f)(3)(iii) of this section, K must include the amount paid to the consultant in the basis of the property acquired. K is not permitted to allocate the amount paid between the properties acquired and not acquired.

Example 10. Employee compensation and overhead. L, a freight carrier, maintains an acquisition department whose sole function is to arrange for the purchase of vehicles and aircraft from manufacturers or other parties to be used in its freight carrying business. As provided in paragraph (f)(2)(iv)(A) of this section, L is not required to capitalize any portion of the compensation paid to employees in its acquisition department or any portion of its overhead allocable to its acquisition department. However, under paragraph (f)(2)(iv)(B) of this section, L may elect to capitalize the compensation and/or overhead costs allocable to the acquisition of a vehicle or aircraft by treating these amounts as costs that facilitate the acquisition of that property in its timely filed original Federal tax return for the year the amounts are paid.

(g) *Treatment of capital expenditures.*—Amounts required to be capitalized under this section are capital expenditures and must be taken into account through a charge to capital account or basis, or in the case of property that is inventory in the hands of a taxpayer, through inclusion in inventory costs.

(h) *Recovery of capitalized amounts.*—(1) *In general.*—Amounts that are capitalized under this section are recovered through depreciation, cost of goods sold, or by an adjustment to basis at the time the property is placed in service, sold, used, or otherwise disposed of by the taxpayer. Cost recovery is determined by the applicable provisions of the Code and regulations relating to the use, sale, or disposition of property.

(2) *Examples.*—The following examples illustrate the rule of paragraph (h)(1) of this section. For purposes of these examples, assume that the taxpayer does not elect the de minimis safe harbor under § 1.263(a)-1(f).

Example 1. Recovery when property placed in service. X owns a 10-unit apartment building. The refrigerator in one of the apartments stops functioning, and X purchases a new refrigerator to replace the old one. X pays for the acquisition, delivery, and installation of the new refrigerator. Assume that the refrigerator is the unit of property, as determined under § 1.263(a)-3(e), and is not a material or supply under § 1.162-3. Under paragraph (d)(1) of this section, X is required to capitalize the amounts paid for the acquisition, delivery, and installation of the refrigerator. Under this paragraph (h), the capitalized amounts are recovered through depreciation, which begins when the refrigerator is placed in service by X.

Example 2. Recovery when property used in the production of property. Y operates a plant where it manufactures widgets. Y purchases a tractor loader to move raw materials into and around the plant for use in the manufacturing process. Assume that the tractor loader is a unit of property, as determined under § 1.263(a)-3(e), and is not a material or supply under § 1.162-3. Under paragraph (d)(1) of this section, Y is required to capitalize the amounts paid to acquire the tractor loader. Under this paragraph (h), the capitalized amounts are recovered through depreciation, which begins when Y places the tractor loader in service. However, because the tractor loader is used in the production of property, under section 263A the cost recovery (that is, the depreciation) may also be capitalized to Y's property produced, and, consequently, recovered through cost of goods sold. See § 1.263A-1(e)(3)(ii)(I).

(i) *Accounting method changes.*—Unless otherwise provided under this section, a change to comply with this section is a change in method of accounting to which the provisions of sections 446 and 481 and the accompanying regulations apply. A taxpayer seeking to change to a method of accounting permitted in this section must secure the consent of the Commissioner in accordance with § 1.446-1(e) and follow the administrative procedures issued under § 1.446-1(e)(3)(ii) for obtaining the Commissioner's consent to change its accounting method.

(j) *Effective/applicability date.*—(1) *In general.*—Except for paragraphs (f)(2)(iii), (f)(2)(iv), and (f)(3)(ii) of this section, this section generally applies to taxable years beginning on or after January 1, 2014. Paragraphs (f)(2)(iii), (f)(2)(iv), and (f)(3)(ii) of this section apply to amounts paid in taxable years beginning on or after January 1, 2014. Except as provided in paragraphs (j)(1) and (j)(2) of this section, § 1.263(a)-2 as contained in 26 CFR part 1 edition revised as of April 1, 2011, applies to taxable years beginning before January 1, 2014.

(2) *Early application of this section-.*—(i) *In general.*—Except for paragraphs (f)(2)(iii), (f)(2)(iv), and (f)(3)(ii) of this section of this section, a taxpayer may choose to apply this section to taxable years beginning on or after January 1, 2012. A taxpayer may choose to apply paragraphs (f)(2)(iii), (f)(2)(iv), and (f)(3)(ii) of this section to amounts paid in taxable years beginning on or after January 1, 2012.

(ii) *Transition rule for election to capitalize employee compensation and overhead costs on 2012 or 2013 returns.*—If under paragraph (j)(2)(i) of this section, a taxpayer chooses to make the election to capitalize employee compensation and overhead costs under paragraph (f)(2)(iv)(B) of this section for amounts paid in its taxable year beginning on or after January 1, 2012, and ending on or before September 19, 2013 (applicable taxable year), and the taxpayer did not make the election specified in paragraph (f)(2)(iv)(B) of this section on its timely filed original Federal tax return for the applicable taxable year, the taxpayer must make the election specified in paragraph (f)(2)(iv)(B) of this section for the applicable taxable year by filing an amended Federal tax return for the applicable taxable year on or before 180 days from the due date including extensions of the taxpayer's Federal tax return for the applicable taxable year, notwithstanding that the taxpayer may not have extended the due date.

(3) *Optional application of TD 9564.*—Except for § 1.263(a)-2T(f)(2)(iii), (f)(2)(iv), (f)(3)(ii), and (g), a taxpayer may choose to apply § 1.263(a)-2T as contained in TD 9564 (76 FR 81060) December 27, 2011, to taxable years beginning on or after January 1, 2012, and before January 1, 2014. A taxpayer may choose to apply § 1.263(a)-2T(f)(2)(iii), (f)(2)(iv), (f)(3)(ii) and (g) as contained in TD 9564 (76 FR 81060) December 27, 2011, to amounts paid in taxable years beginning on or after January 1, 2012, and before January 1, 2014. [Reg. § 1.263(a)-2.]

☐ [T.D. 6313, 9-16-58. *Amended by* T.D. 8131, 3-24-87; T.D. 9564, 12-23-2011 *and* T.D. 9636, 9-13-2013 *(corrected 7-18-2014).*]

[Reg. § 1.263(a)-3]

§ 1.263(a)-3. Amounts paid to improve tangible property.—(a) *Overview.*—This section provides rules for applying section 263(a) to amounts paid to improve tangible property. Paragraph (b) of this section provides definitions. Paragraph (c) of this section provides rules for coordinating this section with other provisions of the Internal Revenue Code (Code). Paragraph (d) of this section provides the requirement to capitalize amounts paid to improve tangible property and provides the general rules for determining whether a unit of property is improved. Paragraph (e) of this section provides the rules for determining the appropriate unit of property. Paragraph (f) of this section provides rules for leasehold improvements. Paragraph (g) of this section provides special rules for determining improvement costs in particular contexts. including indirect costs incurred during an improvement, removal costs, aggregation of related costs, and regulatory compliance costs. Paragraph (h) of this section provides a safe harbor for small taxpayers. Paragraph (i) provides a safe harbor for routine maintenance costs. Paragraph (j) of this section provides rules for determining whether amounts are paid for betterments to the unit of property. Paragraph (k) of this section provides rules for determining whether amounts are paid to restore the unit of property. Paragraph (l) of this section provides rules for amounts paid to adapt the unit of property to a new or different use. Paragraph (m) of this section provides an optional regulatory accounting method. Paragraph (n) of this section provides an election to capitalize repair and maintenance costs consistent with books and records. Paragraphs (o) and (p) of this section provide for the treatment and recovery of amounts capitalized under this section. Paragraphs (q) and (r) of this section provide for accounting method changes and state the effective/applicability date for the rules in this section.

(b) *Definitions.*—For purposes of this section, the following definitions apply:

(1) *Amount paid.*—In the case of a taxpayer using an accrual method of accounting, the terms *amounts paid* and *payment* mean a liability incurred (within the meaning of § 1.446-1(c)(1)(ii)). A liability may not be taken into account under this section prior to the taxable year during which the liability is incurred.

(2) *Personal property* means tangible personal property as defined in § 1.48-1(c).

(3) *Real property* means land and improvements thereto, such as buildings or other inherently permanent structures (including items that are structural components of the buildings or structures) that are not personal property as defined in paragraph (b)(2) of this section. Any property that constitutes other tangible property under § 1.48-1(d) is also treated as real property for purposes of this section. Local law is not controlling in determining whether property is real property for purposes of this section.

(4) *Owner* means the taxpayer that has the benefits and burdens of ownership of the unit of property for Federal income tax purposes.

(c) *Coordination with other provisions of the Code.*—(1) *In general.*—Nothing in this section changes the treatment of any amount that is specifically provided for under any provision of the Code or the regulations other than section 162(a) or section 212 and the regulations under those sections. For example, see section 263A requiring taxpayers to capitalize the direct and allocable indirect costs of property produced and property acquired for resale.

(2) *Materials and supplies.*—A material or supply as defined in §1.162-3(c)(1) that is acquired and used to improve a unit of tangible property is subject to this section and is not treated as a material or supply under §1.162-3.

(3) *Example.*—The following example illustrates the rules of this paragraph (c):

Example. Railroad rolling stock. X is a railroad that properly treats amounts paid for the rehabilitation of railroad rolling stock as deductible expenses under section 263(d). X is not required to capitalize the amounts paid because nothing in this section changes the treatment of amounts specifically provided for under section 263(d).

(d) *Requirement to capitalize amounts paid for improvements.*—Except as provided in paragraph (h) or paragraph (n) of this section or under §1.263(a)-1(f), a taxpayer generally must capitalize the related amounts (as defined in paragraph (g)(3) of this section) paid to improve a unit of property owned by the taxpayer. However, paragraph (f) of this section applies to the treatment of amounts paid to improve leased property. Section 263A provides the requirement to capitalize the direct and allocable indirect costs of property produced by the taxpayer and property acquired for resale. Section 1016 provides for the addition of capitalized amounts to the basis of the property, and section 168 governs the treatment of additions or improvements for depreciation purposes. For purposes of this section, a unit of property is improved if the amounts paid for activities performed after the property is placed in service by the taxpayer—

(1) Are for a betterment to the unit of property (see paragraph (j) of this section);

(2) Restore the unit of property (see paragraph (k) of this section); or

(3) Adapt the unit of property to a new or different use (see paragraph (l) of this section).

(e) *Determining the unit of property.*—(1) *In general.*—The unit of property rules in this paragraph (e) apply only for purposes of section 263(a) and §§1.263(a)-1, 1.263(a)-2, 1.263(a)-3, and 1.162-3. Unless otherwise specified, the unit of property determination is based upon the functional interdependence standard provided in paragraph (e)(3)(i) of this section. However, special rules are provided for buildings (see paragraph (e)(2) of this section), plant property (see paragraph (e)(3)(ii) of this section), network assets (see paragraph (e)(3)(iii) of this section), leased property (see paragraph (e)(2)(v) of this section for leased buildings and paragraph (e)(3)(iv) of this section for leased property other than buildings), and improvements to property (see paragraph (e)(4) of this section). Additional rules are provided if a taxpayer has assigned different MACRS classes or depreciation methods to components of property or subsequently changes the class or depreciation method of a component or other item of property (see paragraph (e)(5) of this section). Property that is aggregated or subject to a general asset account election or accounted for in a multiple asset account (that is, pooled) may not be treated as a single unit of property.

(2) *Building.*—(i) *In general.*—Except as otherwise provided in paragraphs (e)(4), and (e)(5)(ii) of this section, in the case of a building (as defined in §1.48-1(e)(1)), each building and its structural components (as defined in §1.48-1(e)(2)) is a single unit of property ("building"). Paragraph (e)(2)(iii) of this section provides the unit of property for condominiums, paragraph (e)(2)(iv) of this section provides the unit of property for cooperatives, and paragraph (e)(2)(v) of this section provides the unit of property for leased buildings.

(ii) *Application of improvement rules to a building.*—An amount is paid to improve a building under paragraph (d) of this section if the amount is paid for an improvement under paragraphs (j), (k), or paragraph (l) of this section to any of the following:

(A) *Building structure.*—A building structure consists of the building (as defined in §1.48-1(e)(1)), and its structural components (as defined in §1.48-1(e)(2)), other than the structural components designated as buildings systems in paragraph (e)(2)(ii)(B) of this section.

(B) *Building system.*—Each of the following structural components (as defined in §1.48-1(e)(2)), including the components thereof, constitutes a building system that is separate from the building structure, and to which the improvement rules must be applied—

(1) Heating, ventilation, and air conditioning ("HVAC") systems (including motors, compressors, boilers, furnace, chillers, pipes, ducts, radiators);

(2) Plumbing systems (including pipes, drains, valves, sinks, bathtubs, toilets, water and sanitary sewer collection equipment, and site utility equipment used to distribute water and waste

to and from the property line and between buildings and other permanent structures);

(3) Electrical systems (including wiring, outlets, junction boxes, lighting fixtures and associated connectors, and site utility equipment used to distribute electricity from the property line to and between buildings and other permanent structures);

(4) All escalators;

(5) All elevators;

(6) Fire-protection and alarm systems (including sensing devices, computer controls, sprinkler heads, sprinkler mains, associated piping or plumbing, pumps, visual and audible alarms, alarm control panels, heat and smoke detection devices, fire escapes, fire doors, emergency exit lighting and signage, and fire fighting equipment, such as extinguishers, and hoses);

(7) Security systems for the protection of the building and its occupants (including window and door locks, security cameras, recorders, monitors, motion detectors, security lighting, alarm systems, entry and access systems, related junction boxes, associated wiring and conduit);

(8) Gas distribution system (including associated pipes and equipment used to distribute gas to and from the property line and between buildings or permanent structures); and

(9) Other structural components identified in published guidance in the **Federal Register** or in the Internal Revenue Bulletin (see §601.601(d)(2)(ii)(b) of this chapter) that are excepted from the building structure under paragraph (e)(2)(ii)(A) of this section and are specifically designated as building systems under this section.

(iii) *Condominium.*—(A) *In general.*—In the case of a taxpayer that is the owner of an individual unit in a building with multiple units (such as a condominium), the unit of property ("condominium") is the individual unit owned by the taxpayer and the structural components (as defined in §1.48-1(e)(2)) that are part of the unit.

(B) *Application of improvement rules to a condominium.*—An amount is paid to improve a condominium under paragraph (d) of this section if the amount is paid for an improvement under paragraphs (j), (k), or paragraph (l) of this section to the building structure (as defined in paragraph (e)(2)(ii)(A) of this section) that is part of the condominium or to the portion of any building system (as defined in paragraph (e)(2)(ii)(B) of this section) that is part of the condominium. In the case of the condominium management association, the association must apply the improvement rules to the building structure or to any building system described under paragraphs (e)(2)(ii)(A) and (e)(2)(ii)(B) of this section.

(iv) *Cooperative.*—(A) *In general.*—In the case of a taxpayer that has an ownership interest in a cooperative housing corporation, the unit of property ("cooperative") is the portion of the building in which the taxpayer has possessory rights and the structural components (as defined in §1.48-1(e)(2)) that are part of the portion of the building subject to the taxpayer's possessory rights (cooperative).

(B) *Application of improvement rules to a cooperative.*—An amount is paid to improve a cooperative under paragraph (d) of this section if the amount is paid for an improvement under paragraphs (j), (k), or (l) of this section to the portion of the building structure (as defined in paragraph (e)(2)(ii)(A) of this section) in which the taxpayer has possessory rights or to the portion of any building system (as defined in paragraph (e)(2)(ii)(B) of this section) that is part of the portion of the building structure subject to the taxpayer's possessory rights. In the case of a cooperative housing corporation, the corporation must apply the improvement rules to the building structure or to any building system as described under paragraphs (e)(2)(ii)(A) and (e)(2)(ii)(B) of this section.

(v) *Leased building.*—(A) *In general.*—In the case of a taxpayer that is a lessee of all or a portion of a building (such as an office, floor, or certain square footage), the unit of property ("leased building property") is each building and its structural components or the portion of each building subject to the lease and the structural components associated with the leased portion.

(B) *Application of improvement rules to a leased building.*—An amount is paid to improve a leased building property under paragraphs (d) and (f)(2) of this section if the amount is paid for an improvement, under paragraphs (j), (k), or (l) of this section, to any of the following:

(1) *Entire building.*—In the case of a taxpayer that is a lessee of an entire building, the building structure (as defined under paragraph (e)(2)(ii)(A) of this section) or any building system (as defined under paragraph (e)(2)(ii)(B) of this section) that is part of the leased building.

(2) *Portion of a building.*—In the case of a taxpayer that is a lessee of a portion of a building (such as an office, floor, or certain

square footage), the portion of the building structure (as defined under paragraph (e)(2)(ii)(A) of this section) subject to the lease or the portion of any building system (as defined under paragraph (e)(2)(ii)(B) of this section) subject to the lease.

(3) *Property other than building.*—(i) *In general.*—Except as otherwise provided in paragraphs (e)(3), (e)(4), (e)(5), and (f)(1) of this section, in the case of real or personal property other than property described in paragraph (e)(2) of this section, all the components that are functionally interdependent comprise a single unit of property. Components of property are functionally interdependent if the placing in service of one component by the taxpayer is dependent on the placing in service of the other component by the taxpayer.

(ii) *Plant property.*—(A) *Definition.*—For purposes of this paragraph (e), the term *plant property* means functionally interdependent machinery or equipment, other than network assets, used to perform an industrial process, such as manufacturing, generation, warehousing, distribution, automated materials handling in service industries, or other similar activities.

(B) *Unit of property for plant property.*—In the case of plant property, the unit of property determined under the general rule of paragraph (e)(3)(i) of this section is further divided into smaller units comprised of each component (or group of components) that performs a discrete and major function or operation within the functionally interdependent machinery or equipment.

(iii) *Network assets.*—(A) *Definition.*—For purposes of this paragraph (e), the term *network assets* means railroad track, oil and gas pipelines, water and sewage pipelines, power transmission and distribution lines, and telephone and cable lines that are owned or leased by taxpayers in each of those respective industries. The term includes, for example, trunk and feeder lines, pole lines, and buried conduit. It does not include property that would be included as building structure or building systems under paragraphs (e)(2)(ii)(A) and (e)(2)(ii)(B) of this section, nor does it include separate property that is adjacent to, but not part of a network asset, such as bridges, culverts, or tunnels.

(B) *Unit of property for network assets.*—In the case of network assets, the unit of property is determined by the taxpayer's particular facts and circumstances except as otherwise provided in published guidance in the **Federal Register** or in the Internal Revenue Bulletin (see § 601.601(d)(2)(ii)(*b*) of this chapter). For these purposes, the functional interdependence standard provided in paragraph (e)(3)(i) of this section is not determinative.

(iv) *Leased property other than buildings.*—In the case of a taxpayer that is a lessee of real or personal property other than property described in paragraph (e)(2) of this section, the unit of property for the leased property is determined under paragraphs (e)(3)(i),(ii), (iii), and (e)(5) of this section except that, after applying the applicable rules under those paragraphs, the unit of property may not be larger than the property subject to the lease.

(4) *Improvements to property.*—An improvement to a unit of property generally is not a unit of property separate from the unit of property improved. For the unit of property for lessee improvements, see also paragraph (f)(2)(ii)) of this section. If a taxpayer elects to treat as a capital expenditure under § 1.162-3(d) the amount paid for a rotable spare part, temporary spare part, or standby emergency spare part, and such part is used in an improvement to a unit of property, then for purposes of applying paragraph (d) of this section to the unit of property improved, the part is not a unit of property separate from the unit of property improved.

(5) *Additional rules.*—(i) *Year placed in service.*—Notwithstanding the unit of property determination under paragraph (e)(3) of this section, a component (or a group of components) of a unit property must be treated as a separate unit of property if, at the time the unit of property is initially placed in service by the taxpayer, the taxpayer has properly treated the component as being within a different class of property under section 168(e) (MACRS classes) than the class of the unit of property of which the component is a part, or the taxpayer has properly depreciated the component using a different depreciation method than the depreciation method of the unit of property of which the component is a part.

(ii) *Change in subsequent taxable year.*—Notwithstanding the unit of property determination under paragraphs (e)(2), (3), (4), or (5)(i) of this section, in any taxable year after the unit of property is initially placed in service by the taxpayer, if the taxpayer or the Internal Revenue Service changes the treatment of that property (or any portion thereof) to a proper MACRS class or a proper depreciation method (for example, as a result of a cost segregation study or a change in the use of the property), then the taxpayer must change the unit of property determination for that property (or the portion

thereof) under this section to be consistent with the change in treatment for depreciation purposes. Thus, for example, if a portion of a unit of property is properly reclassified to a MACRS class different from the MACRS class of the unit of property of which it was previously treated as a part, then the reclassified portion of the property should be treated as a separate unit of property for purposes of this section.

(6) *Examples.*—The following examples illustrate the application of this paragraph (e) and assume that the taxpayer has not made a general asset account election with regard to property or accounted for property in a multiple asset account. In addition, unless the facts specifically indicate otherwise, assume that the additional rules in paragraph (e)(5) of this section do not apply:

Example 1. Building systems. A owns an office building that contains a HVAC system. The HVAC system incorporates ten roof-mounted units that service different parts of the building. The roof-mounted units are not connected and have separate controls and duct work that distribute the heated or cooled air to different spaces in the building's interior. A pays an amount for labor and materials for work performed on the roof-mounted units. Under paragraph (e)(2)(i) of this section, A must treat the building and its structural components as a single unit of property. As provided under paragraph (e)(2)(ii) of this section, an amount is paid to improve a building if it is for an improvement to the building structure or any designated building system. Under paragraph (e)(2)(ii)(B)(*1*) of this section, the entire HVAC system, including all of the roof-mounted units and their components, comprise a building system. Therefore, under paragraph (e)(2)(ii) of this section, if an amount paid by A for work on the roof-mounted units is an improvement (for example, a betterment) to the HVAC system, A must treat this amount as an improvement to the building.

Example 2. Building systems. B owns a building that it uses in its retail business. The building contains two elevator banks in different locations in its building. Each elevator bank contains three elevators. B pays an amount for labor and materials for work performed on the elevators. Under paragraph (e)(2)(i) of this section, B must treat the building and its structural components as a single unit of property. As provided under paragraph (e)(2)(ii) of this section, an amount is paid to improve a building if it is for an improvement to the building structure or any designated building system. Under paragraph (e)(2)(ii)(B)(*5*) of this section, all six elevators, including all their components, comprise a building system. Therefore, under paragraph (e)(2)(ii) of this section, if an amount paid by B for work on the elevators is an improvement (for example, a betterment) to the elevator system, B must treat this amount as an improvement to the building.

Example 3. Building structure and systems; condominium. C owns a condominium unit in a condominium office building. C uses the condominium unit in its business of providing medical services. The condominium unit contains two restrooms, each of which contains a sink, a toilet, water and drainage pipes and other bathroom fixtures. C pays an amount for labor and materials to perform work on the pipes, sinks, toilets, and plumbing fixtures that are part of the condominium. Under paragraph (e)(2)(iii) of this section, C must treat the individual unit that it owns, including the structural components that are part of that unit, as a single unit of property. As provided under paragraph (e)(2)(iii)(B) of this section, an amount is paid to improve the condominium if it is for an improvement to the building structure that is part of the condominium or to a portion of any designated building system that is part of the condominium. Under paragraph (e)(2)(ii)(B)(*2*) of this section, the pipes, sinks, toilets, and plumbing fixtures that are part of C's condominium comprise the plumbing system for the condominium. Therefore, under paragraph (e)(2)(iii) of this section, if an amount paid by C for work on pipes, sinks, toilets, and plumbing fixtures is an improvement (for example, a betterment) to the portion of the plumbing system that is part of C's condominium, C must treat this amount as an improvement to the condominium.

Example 4. Building structure and systems; property other than buildings. D, a manufacturer, owns a building adjacent to its manufacturing facility that contains office space and related facilities for D's employees that manage and administer D's manufacturing operations. The office building contains equipment, such as desks, chairs, computers, telephones, and bookshelves that are not building structure or building systems. D pays an amount to add an extension to the office building. Under paragraph (e)(2)(i) of this section, D must treat the building and its structural components as a single unit of property. As provided under paragraph (e)(2)(ii) of this section, an amount is paid to improve a building if it is for an improvement to the building structure or any designated building system. Therefore, under paragraph (e)(2)(ii) of this section, if an amount paid by D for the addition of an extension to the office building is an improvement (for example, a betterment) to the building structure or any of the building systems, D must treat this amount as an improvement to the building. In addition, because the equipment contained within the office building constitutes property other than the building, the units of property for the office equipment are initially determined under paragraph (e)(3)(i) of this section and are comprised of all the components that are functionally interdependent (for example, each desk, each chair, and each book shelf).

Example 5. Plant property; discrete and major function. E is an electric utility company that operates a power plant to generate electricity. The power plant includes a structure that is not a building under § 1.48-1(e)(1), and, among other things, one pulverizer that grinds coal, a single boiler that produces steam, one turbine that converts the steam into mechanical energy, and one generator that converts mechanical energy into electrical energy. In addition, the turbine contains a series of blades that cause the turbine to rotate when affected by the steam. Because the plant is composed of real and personal tangible property other than a building, the unit of property for the generating equipment is initially determined under the general rule in paragraph (e)(3)(i) of this section and is comprised of all the components that are functionally interdependent. Under this rule, the initial unit of property is the entire plant because the components of the plant are functionally interdependent. However, because the power plant is plant property under paragraph (e)(3)(ii) of this section, the initial unit of property is further divided into smaller units of property by determining the components (or groups of components) that perform discrete and major functions within the plant. Under this paragraph, E must treat the structure, the boiler, the turbine, the generator, and the pulverizer each as a separate unit of property because each of these components performs a discrete and major function within the power plant. E may not treat components, such as the turbine blades, as separate units of property because each of these components does not perform a discrete and major function within the plant.

Example 6. Plant property; discrete and major function. F is engaged in a uniform and linen rental business. F owns and operates a plant that utilizes many different machines and equipment in an assembly line-like process to treat, launder, and prepare rental items for its customers. F utilizes two laundering lines in its plant, each of which can operate independently. One line is used for uniforms and another line is used for linens. Both lines incorporate a sorter, boiler, washer, dryer, ironer, folder, and waste water treatment system. Because the laundering equipment contained within the plant is property other than a building, the unit of property for the laundering equipment is initially determined under the general rule in paragraph (e)(3)(i) of this section and is comprised of all the components that are functionally interdependent. Under this rule, the initial units of property are each laundering line because each line is functionally independent and is comprised of components that are functionally interdependent. However, because each line is comprised of plant property under paragraph (e)(3)(ii) of this section, F must further divide these initial units of property into smaller units of property by determining the components (or groups of components) that perform discrete and major functions within the line. Under paragraph (e)(3)(ii) of this section, F must treat each sorter, boiler, washer, dryer, ironer, folder, and waste water treatment system in each line as a separate unit of property because each of these components performs a discrete and major function within the line.

Example 7. Plant property; industrial process. G operates a restaurant that prepares and serves food to retail customers. Within its restaurant, G has a large piece of equipment that uses an assembly line-like process to prepare and cook tortillas that G serves only to its restaurant customers. Because the tortilla-making equipment is property other than a building, the unit of property for the equipment is initially determined under the general rule in paragraph (e)(3)(i) of this section and is comprised of all the components that are functionally interdependent. Under this rule, the initial unit of property is the entire tortilla-making equipment because the various components of the equipment are functionally interdependent. The equipment is not plant property under paragraph (e)(3)(ii) of this section because the equipment is not used in an industrial process, as it performs a small-scale function in G's restaurant operations. Thus, G is not required to further divide the equipment into separate units of property based on the components that perform discrete and major functions.

Example 8. Personal property. H owns locomotives that it uses in its railroad business. Each locomotive consists of various components, such as an engine, generators, batteries, and trucks. H acquired a locomotive with all its components. Because H's locomotive is property other than a building, the initial unit of property is determined under the general rule in paragraph (e)(3)(i) of this section and is comprised of the components that are functionally interdependent. Under paragraph (e)(3)(i) of this section, the locomotive is a single unit of property because it consists entirely of components that are functionally interdependent.

Example 9. Personal property. J provides legal services to its clients. J purchased a laptop computer and a printer for its employees to use in providing legal services. Because the computer and printer

are property other than a building, the initial units of property are determined under the general rule in paragraph (e)(3)(i) of this section and are comprised of the components that are functionally interdependent. Under paragraph (e)(3)(i) of this section, the computer and the printer are separate units of property because the computer and the printer are not components that are functionally interdependent (that is, the placing in service of the computer is not dependent on the placing in service of the printer).

Example 10. Building structure and systems; leased building. K is a retailer of consumer products. K conducts its retail sales in a building that it leases from L. The leased building consists of the building structure (including the floor, walls, and roof) and various building systems, including a plumbing system, an electrical system, an HVAC system, a security system, and a fire protection and prevention system. K pays an amount for labor and materials to perform work on the HVAC system of the leased building. Under paragraph (e)(2)(v)(A) of this section, because K leases the entire building, K must treat the leased building and its structural components as a single unit of property. As provided under paragraph (e)(2)(v)(B) of this section, an amount is paid to improve a leased building property if it is for an improvement (for example, a betterment) to the leased building structure or to any building system within the leased building. Therefore, under paragraphs (e)(2)(v)(B)(*1*) and (e)(2)(ii)(B)(*1*) of this section, if an amount paid by K for work on the HVAC system is for an improvement to the HVAC system in the leased building, K must treat this amount as an improvement to the entire leased building property.

Example 11. Production of real property related to leased property. Assume the same facts as in *Example 10*, except that K receives a construction allowance from L, and K uses the construction allowance to build a driveway adjacent to the leased building. Assume that under the terms of the lease, K, the lessee, is treated as the owner of any property that it constructs on or nearby the leased building. Also assume that section 110 does not apply to the construction allowance. Finally, assume that the driveway is not plant property or a network asset. Because the construction of the driveway consists of the production of real property other than a building, all the components of the driveway are functionally interdependent and are a single unit of property under paragraphs (e)(3)(i) and (e)(3)(iv) of this section.

Example 12. Leasehold improvements; construction allowance used for lessor-owned improvements. Assume the same facts as *Example 11*, except that, under the terms of the lease, L, the lessor, is treated as the owner of any property constructed on the leased premises. Because L, the lessor, is the owner of the driveway and the driveway is real property other than a building, all the components of the driveway are functionally interdependent and are a single unit of property under paragraph (e)(3)(i) of this section.

Example 13. Buildings and structural components; leased office space. M provides consulting services to its clients. M conducts its consulting services business in two office spaces in the same building, each of which it leases from N under separate lease agreements. Each office space contains a separate HVAC system, which is part of the leased property. Both lease agreements provide that M is responsible for maintaining, repairing, and replacing the HVAC system that is part of the leased property. M pays amounts to perform work on the HVAC system in each office space. Because M leases two separate office spaces subject to two leases, M must treat the portion of the building structure and the structural components subject to each lease as a separate unit of property under paragraph (e)(2)(v)(A) of this section. As provided under paragraph (e)(2)(v)(B) of this section, an amount is paid to improve a leased building property, if it is for an improvement to the leased portion of the building structure or the portion of any designated building system subject to each lease. Under paragraphs (e)(2)(v)(B)(*1*) and (e)(2)(ii)(B)(*1*) of this section, M must treat the HVAC system associated with each leased office space as a building system of that leased building property. Thus, M must treat the HVAC system associated with the first leased office space as a building system of the first leased office space and the HVAC system associated with the second leased office space as a building system of the second leased office space. Under paragraph (e)(2)(v)(B) of this section, if the amount paid by M for work on the HVAC system in one leased office space is for an improvement (for example, a betterment) to the HVAC system that is part of that leased space, then M must treat the amount as an improvement to that individual leased property.

Example 14. Leased property; personal property. N is engaged in the business of transporting passengers on private jet aircraft. To conduct its business, N leases several aircraft from O. Under paragraph (e)(3)(iv) of this section (referencing paragraph (e)(3)(i) of this section), N must treat all of the components of each leased aircraft that are functionally interdependent as a single unit of property. Thus, N must treat each leased aircraft as a single unit of property.

Example 15. Improvement property. (i) P is a retailer of consumer products. In Year 1, P purchases a building from Q, which P intends to use as a retail sales facility. Under paragraph (e)(2)(i) of this section, P must treat the building and its structural components as a single unit of property. As provided under paragraph (e)(2)(ii) of this section, an amount is paid to improve a building if it is for an improvement to the building structure or any designated building system.

(ii) In Year 2, P pays an amount to construct an extension to the building to be used for additional warehouse space. Assume that the extension involves the addition of walls, floors, roof, and doors, but does not include the addition or extension of any building systems described in paragraph (e)(2)(ii)(B) of this section. Also assume that the amount paid to build the extension is a betterment to the building structure under paragraph (j) of this section, and is therefore treated as an amount paid for an improvement to the entire building under paragraph (e)(2)(ii) of this section. Accordingly, P capitalizes the amount paid as an improvement to the building under paragraph (d) of this section. Under paragraph (e)(4) of this section, the extension is not a unit of property separate from the building, the unit of property improved. Thus, to determine whether any future expenditure constitutes an improvement to the building under paragraph (e)(2)(ii) of this section, P must determine whether the expenditure constitutes an improvement to the building structure, including the building extension, or to any of the designated building systems.

Example 16. Additional rules; year placed in service. R is engaged in the business of transporting freight throughout the United States. To conduct its business, R owns a fleet of truck tractors and trailers. Each tractor and trailer is comprised of various components, including tires. R purchased a truck tractor with all of its components, including tires. The tractor tires have an average useful life to R of more than one year. At the time R placed the tractor in service, it treated the tractor tires as a separate asset for depreciation purposes under section 168. R properly treated the tractor (excluding the cost of the tires) as 3-year property and the tractor tires as 5-year property under section 168(e). Because R's tractor is property other than a building, the initial units of property for the tractor are determined under the general rule in paragraph (e)(3)(i) of this section and are comprised of all the components that are functionally interdependent. Under this rule, R must treat the tractor, including its tires, as a single unit of property because the tractor and the tires are functionally interdependent (that is, the placing in service of the tires is dependent upon the placing in service of the tractor). However, under paragraph (e)(5)(i) of this section, R must treat the tractor and tires as separate units of property because R properly treated the tires as being within a different class of property under section 168(e).

Example 17. Additional rules; change in subsequent year. S is engaged in the business of leasing nonresidential real property to retailers. In Year 1, S acquired and placed in service a building for use in its retail leasing operation. In Year 5, to accommodate the needs of a new lessee, S incurred costs to improve the building structure. S capitalized the costs of the improvement under paragraph (d) of this section and depreciated the improvement in accordance with section 168(i)(6) as nonresidential real property under section 168(e). In Year 7, S determined that the structural improvement made in Year 5 qualified under section 168(e)(8) as qualified retail improvement property and, therefore, was 15-year property under section 168(e). In Year 7, S changed its method of accounting to use a 15-year recovery period for the improvement. Under paragraph (e)(5)(ii) of this section, in Year 7, S must treat the improvement as a unit of property separate from the building.

Example 18. Additional rules; change in subsequent year. In Year 1, T acquired and placed in service a building and parking lot for use in its retail operations. Under §1.263(a)-2 of the regulations, T capitalized the cost of the building and the parking lot and began depreciating the building and the parking lot as nonresidential real property under section 168(e). In Year 3, T completed a cost segregation study under which it properly determined that the parking lot qualified as 15-year property under section 168(e). In Year 3, T changed its method of accounting for the parking lot to use a 15-year recovery period and the 150-percent declining balance method of depreciation. Under paragraph (e)(5)(ii) of this section, beginning in Year 3, T must treat the parking lot as a unit of property separate from the building.

Example 19. Additional rules; change in subsequent year. In Year 1, U acquired and placed in service a building for use in its manufacturing business. U capitalized the costs allocable to the building's wiring *separately from the building and depreciated the wiring as 7-year property under section 168(e).* U capitalized the cost of the building and all other structural components of the building and began depreciating them as nonresidential real property under section 168(e). In Year 3, U completed a cost segregation study under which it properly determined that the wiring is a structural component of the building and, therefore, should have been depreciated as nonresidential real property. In Year 3, U changed its method of accounting to treat the wiring as nonresidential real property. Under paragraph (e)(5)(ii) of this section, U must change the unit of property for the wiring in a manner that is consistent with the change in treatment for deprecia-

tion purposes. Therefore, U must change the unit of property for the wiring to treat it as a structural component of the building, and as part of the building unit of property, in accordance with paragraph (e)(2)(i) of this section.

(f) *Improvements to leased property.*—(1) *In general.*—Except as provided in paragraph (h) of this section (safe harbor for small taxpayers) and under §1.263(a)-1(f) (de minimis safe harbor), this paragraph (f) provides the exclusive rules for determining whether amounts paid by a taxpayer are for an improvement to a leased property and must be capitalized. In the case of a leased building or a leased portion of a building, an amount is paid to improve a leased property if the amount is paid for an improvement to any of the properties specified in paragraph (e)(2)(ii) of this section (for lessor improvements) or in paragraph (e)(2)(v)(B) of this section (for lessee improvements, except as provided in paragraph (f)(2)(ii) of this section). Section 1.263(a)-4 does not apply to amounts paid for improvements to leased property or to amounts paid for the acquisition or production of leasehold improvement property.

(2) *Lessee improvements.*—(i) *Requirement to capitalize.*—A taxpayer lessee must capitalize the related amounts, as determined under paragraph (g)(3) of this section, that it pays to improve, as defined under paragraph (d) of this section, a leased property except to the extent that section 110 applies to a construction allowance received by the lessee for the purpose of such improvement or when the improvement constitutes a substitute for rent. See §1.61-8(c) for the treatment of lessee expenditures that constitute a substitute for rent. A taxpayer lessee must also capitalize the related amounts that a lessor pays to improve, as defined under paragraph (d) of this section, a leased property if the lessee is the owner of the improvement, except to the extent that section 110 applies to a construction allowance received by the lessee for the purpose of such improvement. An amount paid for a lessee improvement under this paragraph (f)(2)(i) is treated as an amount paid to acquire or produce a unit of real or personal property under §1.263(a)-2(d)(1) of the regulations.

(ii) *Unit of property for lessee improvements.*—For purposes of determining whether an amount paid by a lessee constitutes a lessee improvement to a leased property under paragraph (f)(2)(i) of this section, the unit of property and the improvement rules are applied to the leased property in accordance with paragraph (e)(2)(v) (leased buildings) or paragraph (e)(3)(iv) (leased property other than buildings) of this section and include previous lessee improvements. However, if a lessee improvement is comprised of an entire building erected on leased property, then the unit of property for the building and the application of the improvement rules to the building are determined under paragraphs (e)(2)(i) and (e)(2)(ii) of this section.

(3) *Lessor improvements.*—(i) *Requirement to capitalize.*—A taxpayer lessor must capitalize the related amounts, as determined under paragraph (g)(3) of this section, that it pays directly, or indirectly through a construction allowance to the lessee, to improve, as defined in paragraph (d) of this section, a leased property when the lessor is the owner of the improvement or to the extent that section 110 applies to the construction allowance. A lessor must also capitalize the related amounts that the lessee pays to improve a leased property, as defined in paragraph (e) of this section, when the lessee's improvement constitutes a substitute for rent. See §1.61-8(c) for treatment of expenditures by lessees that constitute a substitute for rent. Amounts capitalized by the lessor under this paragraph (f)(3)(i) may not be capitalized by the lessee. If a lessor improvement is comprised of an entire building erected on leased property, then the amount paid for the building is treated as an amount paid by the lessor to acquire or produce a unit of property under §1.263(a)-2(d)(1). See paragraph (e)(2) of this section for the unit of property for a building and paragraph (e)(3) of this section for the unit of property for real or personal property other than a building.

(ii) *Unit of property for lessor improvements.*—In general, an amount capitalized as a lessor improvement under paragraph (f)(3)(i) of this section is not a unit of property separate from the unit of property improved. See paragraph (e)(4) of this section. However, if a lessor improvement is comprised of an entire building erected on leased property, then the unit of property for the building and the application of the improvement rules to the building are determined under paragraphs (e)(2)(i) and (e)(2)(ii) of this section.

(4) *Examples.*—The following examples illustrate the application of this paragraph (f) and do not address whether capitalization is required under another provision of the Code (for example, section 263A). For purposes of the following examples, assume that section 110 does not apply to the lessee and the amounts paid by the lessee are not a substitute for rent.

Example 1. Lessee improvements; additions to building. (i) T is a retailer of consumer products. In Year 1, T leases a building from L, which T intends to use as a retail sales facility. The leased building consists of the building structure under paragraph (e)(2)(ii)(A) of this section and various building systems under paragraph (e)(2)(ii)(B) of this section, including a plumbing system, an electrical system, and an HVAC system. Under the terms of the lease, T is permitted to improve the building at its own expense. Under paragraph (e)(2)(v)(A) of this section, because T leases the entire building, T must treat the leased building and its structural components as a single unit of property. As provided under paragraph (e)(2)(v)(B)(*1*) of this section, an amount is paid to improve a leased building property if the amount is paid for an improvement to the leased building structure or to any building system within the leased building. Therefore, under paragraphs (e)(2)(v)(B)(*1*) and (e)(2)(ii) of this section, if T pays an amount that improves the building structure, the plumbing system, the electrical system, or the HVAC system, then T must treat this amount as an improvement to the entire leased building property.

(ii) In Year 2, T pays an amount to construct an extension to the building to be used for additional warehouse space. Assume that this amount is for a betterment (as defined under paragraph (j) of this section) to T's leased building structure and does not affect any building systems. Accordingly, the amount that T pays for the building extension is for a betterment to the leased building structure, and thus, under paragraph (e)(2)(v)(B)(*1*) of this section, is treated as an improvement to the entire leased building under paragraph (d) of this section. Because T, the lessee, paid an amount to improve a leased building property, T is required to capitalize the amount paid for the building extension as a leasehold improvement under paragraph (f)(2)(i) of this section. In addition, paragraph (f)(2)(i) of this section requires T to treat the amount paid for the improvement as the acquisition or production of a unit of property (leasehold improvement property) under § 1.263(a)-2(d)(1).

(iii) In Year 5, T pays an amount to add a large overhead door to the building extension that it constructed in Year 2 to accommodate the loading of larger products into the warehouse space. Under paragraph (f)(2)(ii) of this section, to determine whether the amount paid by T is for a leasehold improvement, the unit of property and the improvement rules are applied in accordance with paragraph (e)(2)(v) of this section and include T's previous improvements to the leased property. Therefore, under paragraph (e)(2)(v)(A) of this section, the unit of property is the entire leased building, including the extension built in Year 2. In addition, under paragraph (e)(2)(v)(B) of this section, the leased building property is improved if the amount is paid for an improvement to the building structure or any building system. Assume that the amount paid to add the overhead door is for a betterment, under paragraph (j) of this section, to the building structure, which includes the extension. Accordingly, T must capitalize the amounts paid to add the overhead door as a leasehold improvement to the leased building property. In addition, paragraph (f)(2)(i) of this section requires T to treat the amount paid for the improvement as the acquisition or production of a unit of property (leasehold improvement property) under § 1.263(a)-2(d)(1). However, to determine whether a future amount paid by T is for a leasehold improvement to the leased building, the unit of property and the improvement rules are again applied in accordance with paragraph (e)(2)(v) of this section and include the new overhead door.

Example 2. Lessee improvements; additions to certain structural components of buildings. (i) Assume the same facts as *Example 1* except that in Year 2, T also pays an amount to construct an extension of the HVAC system into the building extension. Assume that the extension is a betterment, under paragraph (j) of this section, to the leased HVAC system (a building system under paragraph (e)(2)(ii)(B)(*1*) of this section). Accordingly, the amount that T pays for the extension of the HVAC system is for a betterment to the leased building system, the HVAC system, and thus, under paragraph (e)(2)(v)(B)(*1*) of this section, is treated as an improvement to the entire leased building property under paragraph (d) of this section. Because T, the lessee, pays an amount to improve a leased building property, T is required to capitalize the amount paid as a leasehold improvement under paragraph (f)(2)(i) of this section. Under paragraph (f)(2)(i) of this section, T must treat the amount paid for the HVAC extension as the acquisition and production of a unit of property (leasehold improvement property) under § 1.263(a)-2(d)(1).

(ii) In Year 5, T pays an amount to add an additional chiller to the portion of the HVAC system that it constructed in Year 2 to accommodate the climate control requirements for new product offerings. Under paragraph (f)(2)(ii) of this section, to determine whether the amount paid by T is for a leasehold improvement, the unit of property and the improvement rules are applied in accordance with paragraph (e)(2)(v) of this section and include T's previous improvements to the leased building property. Therefore, under paragraph (e)(2)(v)(B) of this section, the leased building property is improved if the amount is paid for an improvement to the building structure or any building system. Assume that the amount paid to add the chiller is for a betterment, under paragraph (j) of this section,

to the HVAC system, which includes the extension of the system in Year 2. Accordingly, T must capitalize the amounts paid to add the chiller as a leasehold improvement to the leased building property. In addition, paragraph (f)(2)(i) of this section requires T to treat the amount paid for the chiller as the acquisition or production of a unit of property (leasehold improvement property) under § 1.263(a)-2(d)(1). However, to determine whether a future amount paid by T is for a leasehold improvement to the leased building, the unit of property and the improvement rules are again applied in accordance with paragraph (e)(2)(v) of this section and include the new chiller.

Example 3. Lessor Improvements; additions to building. (i) T is a retailer of consumer products. In Year 1, T leases a building from L, which T intends to use as a retail sales facility. Pursuant to the lease, L provides a construction allowance to T, which T intends to use to construct an extension to the retail sales facility for additional warehouse space. Assume that the amount paid for any improvement to the building does not exceed the construction allowance and that L is treated as the owner of any improvement to the building. Under paragraph (e)(2)(i) of this section, L must treat the building and its structural components as a single unit of property. As provided under paragraph (e)(2)(ii) of this section, an amount is paid to improve a building if it is paid for an improvement to the building structure or to any building system.

(ii) In Year 2, T uses L's construction allowance to construct an extension to the leased building to provide additional warehouse space in the building. Assume that the extension is a betterment (as defined under paragraph (j) of this section) to the building structure, and therefore, the amount paid for the extension results in an improvement to the building under paragraph (d) of this section. Under paragraph (f)(3)(i) of this section, L, the lessor and owner of the improvement, must capitalize the amounts paid to T to construct the extension to the retail sales facility. T is not permitted to capitalize the amounts paid for the lessor-owned improvement. Finally, under paragraph (f)(3)(ii) of this section, the extension to L's building is not a unit of property separate from the building and its structural components.

Example 4. Lessee property; personal property added to leased building. T is a retailer of consumer products. T leases a building from L, which T intends to use as a retail sales facility. Pursuant to the lease, L provides a construction allowance to T, which T uses to acquire and construct partitions for fitting rooms, counters, and shelving. Assume that each partition, counter, and shelving unit is a unit of property under paragraph (e)(3) of this section. Assume that for Federal income tax purposes T is treated as the owner of the partitions, counters, and shelving. T's expenditures for the partitions, counters, and shelving are not improvements to the leased property under paragraph (d) of this section, but rather constitute amounts paid to acquire or produce separate units of personal property under § 1.263(a)-2(d)(1).

Example 5. Lessor property; buildings on leased property. L is the owner of a parcel of unimproved real property that L leases to T. Pursuant to the lease, L provides a construction allowance to T of $500,000, which T agrees to use to construct a building costing not more than $500,000 on the leased real property and to lease the building from L after it is constructed. Assume that for Federal income tax purposes, L is treated as the owner of the building that T will construct. T uses the $500,000 to construct the building as required under the lease. The building consists of the building structure and the following building systems: (1) a plumbing system; (2) an electrical system; and (3) an HVAC system. Because L provides a construction allowance to T to construct a building and L is treated as the owner of the building, L must capitalize the amounts that it pays indirectly to T to construct the building as a lessor improvement under paragraph (f)(3)(i) of this section. In addition, the amounts paid by L for the construction allowance are treated as amounts paid by L to acquire and produce the building under § 1.263(a)-2(d)(1). Further, under paragraph (e)(2)(i) of this section, L must treat the building and its structural components as a single unit of property. Under paragraph (f)(3)(i) of this section, T, the lessee, may not capitalize the amounts paid (with the construction allowance received from L) for construction of the building.

Example 6. Lessee contribution to construction costs. Assume the same facts as in *Example 5*, except T spends $600,000 to construct the building. T uses the $500,000 construction allowance provided by L plus $100,000 of its own funds to construct the building that L will own pursuant to the lease. Also assume that the additional $100,000 that T pays is not a substitute for rent. For the reasons discussed in *Example 5*, L must capitalize the $500,000 it paid T to construct the building under § 1.263(a)-2(d)(1). In addition, because T spends its own funds to complete the building, T has a depreciable interest of $100,000 in the building and must capitalize the $100,000 it paid to construct the building as a leasehold improvement under § 1.263(a)-2(d)(1) of the regulations. Under paragraph (e)(2)(i) of this section, L must treat the building as a single unit of property to the extent of its depreciable interest of $500,000 In addition, under paragraphs (f)(2)(ii) and (e)(2)(i) of this section, T must also treat the building as a single unit of property to the extent of its depreciable interest of $100,000.

(g) *Special rules for determining improvement costs.*—(1) *Certain costs incurred during an improvement.*—(i) *In general.*—A taxpayer must capitalize all the direct costs of an improvement and all the indirect costs (including, for example, otherwise deductible repair costs) that directly benefit or are incurred by reason of an improvement. Indirect costs arising from activities that do not directly benefit and are not incurred by reason of an improvement are not required to be capitalized under section 263(a), regardless of whether the activities are performed at the same time as an improvement.

(ii) *Exception for individuals' residences.*—A taxpayer who is an individual may capitalize amounts paid for repairs and maintenance that are made at the same time as capital improvements to units of property not used in the taxpayer's trade or business or for the production of income if the amounts are paid as part of an improvement (for example, a remodeling) of the taxpayer's residence.

(2) *Removal Costs.*—(i) *In general.*—If a taxpayer disposes of a depreciable asset, including a partial disposition under § 1.168(i)-1(e)(1)(ii), or § 1.168(i)-8(d), for Federal income tax purposes and has taken into account the adjusted basis of the asset or component of the asset in realizing gain or loss, then the costs of removing the asset or component are not required to be capitalized under this section. If a depreciable asset is included in a general asset account under section 168(i)(4), and neither the regulations under section 168(i)(4) and § 1.168(i)-1(e)(3), apply to a disposition of such asset, or a portion of such asset under § 1.168(i)-1(e)(1)(ii), a loss is treated as being realized in the amount of zero upon the disposition of the asset solely for purposes of this paragraph (g)(2)(i). If a taxpayer disposes of a component of a unit of property, but the disposal of the component is not a disposition for Federal tax purposes, then the taxpayer must deduct or capitalize the costs of removing the component based on whether the removal costs directly benefit or are incurred by reason of a repair to the unit of property or an improvement to the unit of property. But see § 1.280B-1 for the rules applicable to demolition of structures.

(ii) *Examples.*—The following examples illustrate the application of paragraph (g)(2)(i) of this section and, unless otherwise stated, do not address whether capitalization is required under another provision of this section or another provision of the Code (for example, section 263A). For purposes of the following examples, assume that § 1.168(i)-1(e) or § 1.168(i)-8, applies and that § 1.280B-1 does not apply.

Example 1. Component removed during improvement; no disposition. X owns a factory building with a storage area on the second floor. X pays an amount to remove the original columns and girders supporting the second floor and replace them with new columns and girders to permit storage of supplies with a gross weight 50 percent greater than the previous load-carrying capacity of the storage area. Assume that the replacement of the columns and girders constitutes a betterment to the building structure and is therefore an improvement to the building unit of property under paragraphs (d)(1) and (j) of this section. Assume that X disposes of the original columns and girders and the disposal of these structural components is not a disposition under § 1.168(i)-1(e) or § 1.168(i)-8. Under paragraphs (g)(2)(i) and (j) of this section, the amount paid to remove the columns and girders must be capitalized as a cost of the improvement, because it directly benefits and is incurred by reason of the improvement to the building.

Example 2. Component removed during improvement; disposition. Assume the same facts as *Example 1*, except X disposes of the original columns and girders and elects to treat the disposal of these structural components as a partial disposition of the factory building under § 1.168(i)-8(d), taking into account the adjusted basis of the components in realizing loss on the disposition. Under paragraph (g)(2)(i) of this section, the amount paid to remove the columns and girders is not required to be capitalized as part of the cost of the improvement regardless of their relation to the improvement. However, all the remaining costs of replacing the columns and girders *must be capitalized as improvements to the building unit of property under paragraphs (d)(1), (j), and (g)(1) of this section.*

Example 3. Component removed during repair or maintenance; no disposition. Y owns a building in which it conducts its retail business. The roof over Y's building is covered with shingles. Over time, the shingles begin to wear and Y begins to experience leaks into its retail premises. However, the building still functions in Y's business. To eliminate the problems, a contractor recommends that Y remove the original shingles and replace them with new shingles. Accordingly, Y pays the contractor to replace the old shingles with new but comparable shingles. The new shingles are comparable to original shingles

but correct the leakage problems. Assume that replacement of old shingles with new shingles to correct the leakage is not a betterment or a restoration of the building structure or systems under paragraph (j) or (k) of this section and does not adapt the building structure or systems to a new or different use under paragraph (l) of this section. Thus, the amounts paid by Y to replace the shingles are not improvements to the building unit of property under paragraph (d) of this section. Under paragraph (g)(2)(i) of this section, the amounts paid to remove the shingles are not required to be capitalized because they directly benefit and are incurred by reason of repair or maintenance to the building structure.

Example 4. Component removed with disposition and restoration. Assume the same facts as *Example 3* except Y disposes of the original shingles, and Y elects to treat the disposal of these components as a partial disposition of the building under § 1.168(i)-8(d), and deducts the adjusted basis of the components as a loss on the disposition. Under paragraph (k)(1)(i) of this section, amounts paid for replacement of the shingles constitute a restoration of the building structure because the amounts are paid for the replacement of a component of the structure and the taxpayer has properly deducted a loss for that component. Thus, under paragraphs (d)(2) and (k) of this section, Y is required to capitalize the amounts paid for the replacement of the shingles as an improvement to the building unit of property. However, under paragraph (g)(2)(i) of this section, the amounts paid by Y to remove the original shingles are not required to be capitalized as part of the costs of the improvement, regardless of their relation to the improvement.

(3) *Related amounts.*—For purposes of paragraph (d) of this section, amounts paid to improve a unit of property include amounts paid over a period of more than one taxable year. Whether amounts are related to the same improvement depends on the facts and circumstances of the activities being performed.

(4) *Compliance with regulatory requirements.*—For purposes of this section, a Federal, state, or local regulator's requirement that a taxpayer perform certain repairs or maintenance on a unit of property to continue operating the property is not relevant in determining whether the amount paid improves the unit of property.

(h) *Safe harbor for small taxpayers.*—(1) *In general.*—A qualifying taxpayer (as defined in paragraph (h)(3) of this section) may elect to not apply paragraph (d) or paragraph (f) of this section to an eligible building property (as defined in paragraph (h)(4) of this section) if the total amount paid during the taxable year for repairs, maintenance, improvements, and similar activities performed on the eligible building property does not exceed the lesser of—

(i) 2 percent of the unadjusted basis (as defined under paragraph (h)(5) of this section) of the eligible building property; or

(ii) $10,000.

(2) *Application with other safe harbor provisions.*—For purposes of paragraph (h)(1) of this section, amounts paid for repairs, maintenance, improvements, and similar activities performed on eligible building property include those amounts not capitalized under the de minimis safe harbor election under § 1.263(a)-1(f) and those amounts deemed not to improve property under the safe harbor for routine maintenance under paragraph (i) of this section.

(3) *Qualifying taxpayer.*—(i) *In general.*—For purposes of this paragraph (h), the term *qualifying taxpayer* means a taxpayer whose average annual gross receipts as determined under this paragraph (h)(3) for the three preceding taxable years is less than or equal to $10,000,000.

(ii) *Application to new taxpayers.*—If a taxpayer has been in existence for less than three taxable years, the taxpayer determines its average annual gross receipts for the number of taxable years (including short taxable years) that the taxpayer (or its predecessor) has been in existence.

(iii) *Treatment of short taxable year.*—In the case of any taxable year of less than 12 months (a short taxable year), the gross receipts shall be annualized by—

(A) Multiplying the gross receipts for the short period by 12; and

(B) Dividing the product determined in paragraph (h)(3)(iii)(A) of this section by the number of months in the short period.

(iv) *Definition of gross receipts.*—For purposes of applying paragraph (h)(3)(i) of this section, the term *gross receipts* means the taxpayer's receipts for the taxable year that are properly recognized under the taxpayer's methods of accounting used for Federal income tax purposes for the taxable year. For this purpose, gross receipts include total sales (net of returns and allowances) and all amounts received for services. In addition, gross receipts include any income from investments and from incidental or outside sources. For example, gross receipts include interest (including original issue discount and tax-exempt interest within the meaning of section 103), dividends, rents, royalties, and annuities, regardless of whether such amounts are derived in the ordinary course of the taxpayer's trade of business. Gross receipts are not reduced by cost of goods sold or by the cost of property sold if such property is described in section 1221(a)(1), (3), (4), or (5). With respect to sales of capital assets as defined in section 1221, or sales of property described in section 1221(a)(2) (relating to property used in a trade or business), gross receipts shall be reduced by the taxpayer's adjusted basis in such property. Gross receipts do not include the repayment of a loan or similar instrument (for example, a repayment of the principal amount of a loan held by a commercial lender) and, except to the extent of gain recognized, do not include gross receipts derived from a non-recognition transaction, such as a section 1031 exchange. Finally, gross receipts do not include amounts received by the taxpayer with respect to sales tax or other similar state and local taxes if, under the applicable state or local law, the tax is legally imposed on the purchaser of the good or service, and the taxpayer merely collects and remits the tax to the taxing authority. If, in contrast, the tax is imposed on the taxpayer under the applicable law, then gross receipts include the amounts received that are allocable to the payment of such tax.

(4) *Eligible building property.*—For purposes of this section, the term *eligible building property* refers to each unit of property defined in paragraph (e)(2)(i) (building), paragraph (e)(2)(iii)(A) (condominium), paragraph (e)(2)(iv)(A) (cooperative), or paragraph (e)(2)(v)(A) (leased building or portion of building) of this section, as applicable, that has an unadjusted basis of $1,000,000 or less.

(5) *Unadjusted basis.*—(i) *Eligible building property owned by taxpayer.*—For purposes of this section, the unadjusted basis of eligible building property owned by the taxpayer means the basis as determined under section 1012, or other applicable sections of Chapter 1, including subchapters O (relating to gain or loss on dispositions of property), C (relating to corporate distributions and adjustments), K (relating to partners and partnerships), and P (relating to capital gains and losses). Unadjusted basis is determined without regard to any adjustments described in section 1016(a)(2) or (3) or to amounts for which the taxpayer has elected to treat as an expense (for example, under sections 179, 179B, or 179C).

(ii) *Eligible building property leased to the taxpayer.*—For purposes of this section, the unadjusted basis of eligible building property leased to the taxpayer is the total amount of (undiscounted) rent paid or expected to be paid by the lessee under the lease for the entire term of the lease, including renewal periods if all the facts and circumstances in existence during the taxable year in which the lease is entered indicate a reasonable expectancy of renewal. Section 1.263(a)-4(f)(5)(ii) provides the factors that are significant in determining whether there exists a reasonable expectancy of renewal for purposes of this paragraph.

(6) *Time and manner of election.*—A taxpayer makes the election described in paragraph (h)(1) of this section by attaching a statement to the taxpayer's timely filed original Federal tax return (including extensions) for the taxable year in which amounts are paid for repairs, maintenance, improvements, and similar activities performed on the eligible building property providing that such amounts qualify under the safe harbor provided in paragraph (h)(1) of this section. Sections 301.9100-1 through Reg. § 301.9100-3 of this chapter provide the rules governing extensions of the time to make regulatory elections. The statement must be titled, "Section 1.263(a)-3(h) Safe Harbor Election for Small Taxpayers" and include the taxpayer's name, address, taxpayer identification number, and a description of each eligible building property to which the taxpayer is applying the election. In the case of an S corporation or a partnership, the election is made by the S corporation or by the partnership, and not by the shareholders or partners. An election may not be made through the filing of an application for change in accounting method or, before obtaining the Commissioner's consent to make a late election, by filing an amended Federal tax return. A taxpayer may not revoke an election made under this paragraph (h). The time and manner of making the election under this paragraph (h) may be modified through guidance of general applicability (see §§ 601.601(d)(2) and 601.602 of this chapter).

(7) *Treatment of safe harbor amounts.*—Amounts paid by the taxpayer for repairs, maintenance, improvements, and similar activities to which the taxpayer properly applies the safe harbor under paragraph (h)(1) of this section and for which the taxpayer properly makes the election under paragraph (h)(6) of this section are not treated as improvements under paragraph (d) or (f) of this section and may be deducted under § 1.162-1 or § 1.212-1, as applicable, in

the taxable year these amounts are paid, provided the amounts otherwise qualify for a deduction under these sections.

(8) *Safe harbor exceeded.*—If total amounts paid by a qualifying taxpayer during the taxable year for repairs, maintenance, improvements, and similar activities performed on an eligible building property exceed the safe harbor limitations specified in paragraph (h)(1) of this section, then the safe harbor election is not available for that eligible building property and the taxpayer must apply the general improvement rules under this section to determine whether amounts are for improvements to the unit of property, including the safe harbor for routine maintenance under paragraph (i) of this section. The taxpayer may also elect to apply the de minimis safe harbor under § 1.263(a)-1(f) to amounts qualifying under that safe harbor irrespective of the application of this paragraph (h).

(9) *Modification of safe harbor amounts.*—The amount limitations provided in paragraphs (h)(1)(i), (h)(1)(ii), and (h)(3) of this section may be modified through published guidance in the **Federal Register** or in the Internal Revenue Bulletin (see § 601.601(d)(2)(ii)(*b*) of this chapter).

(10) *Examples.*—The following examples illustrate the rules of this paragraph (h). Assume that § 1.212-1 does not apply to the amounts paid.

Example 1. Safe harbor for small taxpayers applicable. A is a qualifying taxpayer under paragraph (h)(3) of this section. A owns an office building in which A provides consulting services. In Year 1, A's building has an unadjusted basis of $750,000 as determined under paragraph (h)(5)(i) of this section. In Year 1, A pays $5,500 for repairs, maintenance, improvements and similar activities to the office building. Because A's building unit of property has an unadjusted basis of $1,000,000 or less, A's building constitutes eligible building property under paragraph (h)(4) of this section. The aggregate amount paid by A during Year 1 for repairs, maintenance, improvements and similar activities on this eligible building property does not exceed the lesser of $15,000 (2 percent of the building's unadjusted basis of $750,000) or $10,000. Therefore, under paragraph (h)(1) of this section, A may elect to not apply the capitalization rule of paragraph (d) of this section to the amounts paid for repair, maintenance, improvements, or similar activities on the office building in Year 1. If A properly makes the election under paragraph (h)(6) of this section for the office building and the amounts otherwise constitute deductible ordinary and necessary expenses incurred in carrying on a trade or business, A may deduct these amounts under § 1.162-1 in Year 1.

Example 2. Safe harbor for small taxpayers inapplicable. Assume the same facts as in *Example 1*, except that A pays $10,500 for repairs, maintenance, improvements, and similar activities performed on its office building in Year 1. Because this amount exceeds $10,000, the lesser of the two limitations provided in paragraph (h)(1) of this section, A may not apply the safe harbor for small taxpayers under paragraph (h)(1) of this section to the total amounts paid for repairs, maintenance, improvements, and similar activities performed on the building. Therefore, A must apply the general improvement rules under this section to determine which of the aggregate amounts paid are for improvements and must be capitalized under paragraph (d) of this section and which of the amounts are for repair and maintenance under § 1.162-4.

Example 3. Safe harbor applied building-by-building. (i) B is a qualifying taxpayer under paragraph (h)(3) of this section. B owns two rental properties, Building M and Building N. Building M and Building N are both multi-family residential buildings. In Year 1, each property has an unadjusted basis of $300,000 under paragraph (h)(5) of this section. Because Building M and Building N each have an unadjusted basis of $1,000,000 or less, Building M and Building N each constitute eligible building property in Year 1 under paragraph (h)(4) of this section. In Year 1, B pays $5,000 for repairs, maintenance, improvements, and similar activities performed on Building M. In Year 1, B also pays $7,000 for repairs, maintenance, improvements, and similar activities performed on Building N.

(ii) The total amount paid by B during Year 1 for repairs, maintenance, improvements and similar activities on Building M ($5,000) does not exceed the lesser of $6,000 (2 percent of the building's unadjusted basis of $300,000) or $10,000. Therefore, under paragraph (h)(1) of this section, for Year 1, B may elect to not apply the capitalization rule under paragraph (d) of this section to the amounts it paid for repairs, maintenance, improvements, and similar activities on Building M. If B properly makes the election under paragraph (h)(6) of this section for Building M and the amounts otherwise constitute deductible ordinary and necessary expenses incurred in carrying on B's trade or business, B may deduct these amounts under § 1.162-1.

(iii) The total amount paid by B during Year 1 for repairs, maintenance, improvements and similar activities on Building N ($7,000) exceeds $6,000 (2 percent of the building's unadjusted basis of $300,000), the lesser of the two limitations provided under paragraph (h)(1) of this section. Therefore, B may not apply the safe harbor under paragraph (h)(1) of this section to the total amounts paid for repairs, maintenance, improvements, and similar activities performed on Building N. Instead, B must apply the general improvement rules under this section to determine which of the total amounts paid for work performed on Building N are for improvements and must be capitalized under paragraph (d) of this section and which amounts are for repair and maintenance under § 1.162-4.

Example 4. Safe harbor applied to leased building property. C is a qualifying taxpayer under paragraph (h)(3) of this section. C is the lessee of a building in which C operates a retail store. The lease is a triple-net lease, and the lease term is 20 years, including reasonably expected renewals. C pays $4,000 per month in rent. In Year 1, C pays $7,000 for repairs, maintenance, improvements, and similar activities performed on the building. Under paragraph (h)(5)(ii) of this section, the unadjusted basis of C's leased unit of property is $960,000 ($4,000 monthly rent x 12 months × 20 years). Because C's leased building has an unadjusted basis of $1,000,000 or less, the building is eligible building property for Year 1 under paragraph (h)(4) of this section. The total amount paid by C during Year 1 for repairs, maintenance, improvements, and similar activities on the leased building ($7,000) does not exceed the lesser of $19,200 (2 percent of the building's unadjusted basis of $960,000) or $10,000. Therefore, under paragraph (h)(1) of this section, for Year 1, C may elect to not apply the capitalization rule under paragraph (d) of this section to the amounts it paid for repairs, maintenance, improvements, and similar activities on the leased building. If C properly makes the election under paragraph (h)(6) of this section for the leased building and the amounts otherwise constitute deductible ordinary and necessary expenses incurred in carrying on C's trade or business, C may deduct these amounts under § 1.162-1.

(i) *Safe harbor for routine maintenance on property.*—(1) *In general.*— An amount paid for routine maintenance (as defined in paragraph (i)(1)(i) or (i)(1)(ii) of this section, as applicable) on a unit of tangible property, or in the case of a building, on any of the properties designated in paragraphs (e)(2)(ii), (e)(2)(iii)(B), (e)(2)(iv)(B), or paragraph (e)(2)(v)(B) of this section, is deemed not to improve that unit of property.

(i) *Routine maintenance for buildings.*—Routine maintenance for a building unit of property is the recurring activities that a taxpayer expects to perform as a result of the taxpayer's use of any of the properties designated in paragraphs (e)(2)(ii), (e)(2)(iii)(B), (e)(2)(iv)(B), or (e)(2)(v)(B) of this section to keep the building structure or each building system in its ordinarily efficient operating condition. Routine maintenance activities include, for example, the inspection, cleaning, and testing of the building structure or each building system, and the replacement of damaged or worn parts with comparable and commercially available replacement parts. Routine maintenance may be performed any time during the useful life of the building structure or building systems. However, the activities are routine only if the taxpayer reasonably expects to perform the activities more than once during the 10-year period beginning at the time the building structure or the building system upon which the routine maintenance is performed is placed in service by the taxpayer. A taxpayer's expectation will not be deemed unreasonable merely because the taxpayer does not actually perform the maintenance a second time during the 10-year period, provided that the taxpayer can otherwise substantiate that its expectation was reasonable at the time the property was placed in service. Factors to be considered in determining whether maintenance is routine and whether a taxpayer's expectation is reasonable include the recurring nature of the activity, industry practice, manufacturers' recommendations, and the taxpayer's experience with similar or identical property. With respect to a taxpayer that is a lessor of a building or a part of the building, the taxpayer's use of the building unit of property includes the lessee's use of its unit of property.

(ii) *Routine maintenance for property other than buildings.*—Routine maintenance for property other than buildings is the recurring activities that a taxpayer expects to perform as a result of the taxpayer's use of the unit of property to keep the unit of property in its ordinarily efficient operating condition. Routine maintenance activities include, for example, the inspection, cleaning, and testing of the unit of property, and the replacement of damaged or worn parts of the unit of property with comparable and commercially available replacement parts. Routine maintenance may be performed any time during the useful life of the unit of property. However, the activities are routine only if, at the time the unit of property is placed in service by the taxpayer, the taxpayer reasonably expects to perform the activities more than once during the class life (as defined in paragraph (i)(4) of this section) of the unit of property. A taxpayer's expectation will not be deemed unreasonable merely because the taxpayer does not actually perform the maintenance a second time during the class life of the unit of property, provided that the

taxpayer can otherwise substantiate that its expectation was reasonable at the time the property was placed in service. Factors to be considered in determining whether maintenance is routine and whether the taxpayer's expectation is reasonable include the recurring nature of the activity, industry practice, manufacturers' recommendations, and the taxpayer's experience with similar or identical property. With respect to a taxpayer that is a lessor of a unit of property, the taxpayer's use of the unit of property includes the lessee's use of the unit of property.

(2) *Rotable and temporary spare parts.*—Except as provided in paragraph (i)(3) of this section, for purposes of paragraph (i)(1)(ii) of this section, amounts paid for routine maintenance include routine maintenance performed on (and with regard to) rotable and temporary spare parts.

(3) *Exceptions.*—Routine maintenance does not include the following:

(i) Amounts paid for a betterment to a unit of property under paragraph (j) of this section;

(ii) Amounts paid for the replacement of a component of a unit of property for which the taxpayer has properly deducted a loss for that component (other than a casualty loss under § 1.165-7) (see paragraph (k)(1)(i) of this section);

(iii) Amounts paid for the replacement of a component of a unit of property for which the taxpayer has properly taken into account the adjusted basis of the component in realizing gain or loss resulting from the sale or exchange of the component (see paragraph (k)(1)(ii) of this section);

(iv) Amounts paid for the restoration of damage to a unit of property for which the taxpayer is required to take a basis adjustment as a result of a casualty loss under section 165, or relating to a casualty event described in section 165, subject to the limitation in paragraph (k)(4) of this section (see paragraph (k)(1)(iii) of this section);

(v) Amounts paid to return a unit of property to its ordinarily efficient operating condition, if the property has deteriorated to a state of disrepair and is no longer functional for its intended use (see paragraph (k)(1)(iv) of this section);

(vi) Amounts paid to adapt a unit of property to a new or different use under paragraph (l) of this section;

(vii) Amounts paid for repairs, maintenance, or improvement of network assets (as defined in paragraph (e)(3)(iii)(A) of this section); or

(viii) Amounts paid for repairs, maintenance, or improvement of rotable and temporary spare parts to which the taxpayer applies the optional method of accounting for rotable and temporary spare parts under § 1.162-3(e).

(4) *Class life.*—The class life of a unit of property is the recovery period prescribed for the property under sections 168(g)(2) and (3) for purposes of the alternative depreciation system, regardless of whether the property is depreciated under section 168(g). For purposes of determining class life under this section, section 168(g)(3)(A) (relating to tax-exempt use property subject to lease) does not apply. If the unit of property is comprised of components with different class lives, then the class life of the unit of property is deemed to be the same as the component with the longest class life.

(5) *Coordination with section 263A.*—Amounts paid for routine maintenance under this paragraph (i) may be subject to capitalization under section 263A if these amounts comprise the direct or allocable indirect costs of other property produced by the taxpayer or property acquired for resale. See, for example, § 1.263A-1(e)(3)(ii)(O) requiring taxpayers to capitalize the cost of repairing equipment or facilities allocable to property produced or property acquired for resale.

(6) *Examples.*—The following examples illustrate the application of this paragraph (i) and, unless otherwise stated, do not address the treatment under other provisions of the Code (for example, section 263A). In addition, unless otherwise stated, assume that the taxpayer has not applied the optional method of accounting for rotable and temporary spare parts under § 1.162-3(e).

Example 1. Routine maintenance on component. (i) A is a commercial airline engaged in the business of transporting passengers and freight throughout the United States and abroad. To conduct its business, A owns or leases various types of aircraft. As a condition of maintaining its airworthiness certification for these aircraft, A is required by the Federal Aviation Administration (FAA) to establish and adhere to a continuous maintenance program for each aircraft within its fleet. These programs, which are designed by A and the aircraft's manufacturer and approved by the FAA, are incorporated into each aircraft's maintenance manual. The maintenance manuals require a variety of periodic maintenance visits at various intervals. One type of maintenance visit is an engine shop visit (ESV), which A expects to perform on its aircraft engines approximately every 4 years to keep its aircraft in its ordinarily efficient operating condition. In Year 1, A purchased a new aircraft, which included four new engines attached to the airframe. The four aircraft engines acquired with the aircraft are not materials or supplies under § 1.162-3(c)(1)(i) because they are acquired as part of a single unit of property, the aircraft. In Year 5, A performs its first ESV on the aircraft engines. The ESV includes disassembly, cleaning, inspection, repair, replacement, reassembly, and testing of the engine and its component parts. During the ESV, the engine is removed from the aircraft and shipped to an outside vendor who performs the ESV. If inspection or testing discloses a discrepancy in a part's conformity to the specifications in A's maintenance program, the part is repaired, or if necessary, replaced with a comparable and commercially available replacement part. After the ESVs, the engines are returned to A to be reinstalled on another aircraft or stored for later installation. Assume that the class life for A's aircraft, including the engines, is 12 years. Assume that none of the exceptions set out in paragraph (i)(3) of this section apply to the costs of performing the ESVs.

(ii) Because the ESVs involve the recurring activities that A expects to perform as a result of its use of the aircraft to keep the aircraft in ordinarily efficient operating condition and consist of maintenance activities that A expects to perform more than once during the 12 year class life of the aircraft, A's ESVs are within the routine maintenance safe harbor under paragraph (i)(1)(ii) of this section. Accordingly, the amounts paid for the ESVs are deemed not to improve the aircraft and are not required to be capitalized under paragraph (d) of this section.

Example 2. Routine maintenance after class life. Assume the same facts as in *Example 1*, except that in year 15 A pays amounts to perform an ESV on one of the original aircraft engines after the end of the class life of the aircraft. Because this ESV involves the same routine maintenance activities that were performed on aircraft engines in *Example 1*, this ESV also is within the routine maintenance safe harbor under paragraph (i)(1)(ii) of this section. Accordingly, the amounts paid for this ESV, even though performed after the class life of the aircraft, are deemed not to improve the aircraft and are not required to be capitalized under paragraph (d) of this section.

Example 3. Routine maintenance on rotable spare parts. (i) Assume the same facts as in *Example 1*, except that in addition to the four engines purchased as part of the aircraft, A separately purchases four additional new engines that A intends to use in its aircraft fleet to avoid operational downtime when ESVs are required to be performed on the engines previously installed on an aircraft. Later in Year 1, A installs these four engines on an aircraft in its fleet. In Year 5, A performs the first ESVs on these four engines. Assume that these ESVs involve the same routine maintenance activities that were performed on the engines in *Example 1*, and that none of the exceptions set out in paragraph (i)(3) of this section apply to these ESVs. After the ESVs were performed, these engines were reinstalled on other aircraft or stored for later installation.

(ii) The additional aircraft engines are rotable spare parts under § 1.162-3(c)(2) because they were acquired separately from the aircraft, are removable from the aircraft, and are repaired and reinstalled on other aircraft or stored for later installation. Assume the class life of an engine is the same as the airframe, 12 years. Because the ESVs involve the recurring activities that A expects to perform as a result of its use of the engines to keep the engines in ordinarily efficient operating condition, and consist of maintenance activities that A expects to perform more than once during the 12 year class life of the engine, the ESVs fall within the routine maintenance safe harbor under paragraph (i)(1)(ii) of this section. Accordingly, the amounts paid for the ESVs for the four additional engines are deemed not to improve these engines and are not required to be capitalized under paragraph (d) of this section. For the treatment of amounts paid to acquire the engines, see § 1.162-3(a).

Example 4. Routine maintenance resulting from prior owner's use. (i) In January, Year 1, B purchases a used machine for use in its manufacturing operations. Assume that the machine is the unit of property and has a class life of 10 years. B places the machine in service in January, Year 1, and at that time, B expects to perform manufacturer recommended scheduled maintenance on the machine approximately every three years. The scheduled maintenance includes the cleaning and oiling of the machine, the inspection of parts for defects, and the replacement of minor items such as springs, bearings, and seals with comparable and commercially available replacement parts. At the time B purchased the machine, the machine was approaching the end of a three-year scheduled maintenance period. As a result, in February, Year 1, B pays amounts to perform the manufacturer recommended scheduled maintenance. Assume that none of the exceptions set out in paragraph (i)(3) of this section apply to the amounts paid for the scheduled maintenance.

(ii) The majority of B's costs do not qualify under the routine maintenance safe harbor in paragraph (i)(1)(ii) of this section because the costs were incurred primarily as a result of the prior owner's use of the property and not B's use. B acquired the machine just before it

had received its three-year scheduled maintenance. Accordingly, the amounts paid for the scheduled maintenance resulted from the prior owner's, and not B's, use of the property and must be capitalized if those amounts result in a betterment under paragraph (i) of this section, including the amelioration of a material condition or defect, or otherwise result in an improvement under paragraph (d) of this section.

Example 5. Routine maintenance resulting from new owner's use. Assume the same facts as in *Example 4*, except that after B pays amounts for the maintenance in Year 1, B continues to operate the machine in its manufacturing business. In Year 4, B pays amounts to perform the next scheduled manufacturer recommended maintenance on the machine. Assume that the scheduled maintenance activities performed are the same as those performed in *Example 4* and that none of the exceptions set out in paragraph (i)(3) of this section apply to the amounts paid for the scheduled maintenance. Because the scheduled maintenance performed in Year 4 involves the recurring activities that B performs as a result of its use of the machine, keeps the machine in an ordinarily efficient operating condition, and consists of maintenance activities that B expects to perform more than once during the 10-year class life of the machine, B's scheduled maintenance costs are within the routine maintenance safe harbor under paragraph (i)(1)(ii) of this section. Accordingly, the amounts paid for the scheduled maintenance in Year 4 are deemed not to improve the machine and are not required to be capitalized under paragraph (d) of this section.

Example 6. Routine maintenance; replacement of substantial structural part; coordination with section 263A. C is in the business of producing commercial products for sale. As part of the production process, C places raw materials into lined containers in which a chemical reaction is used to convert raw materials into the finished product. The lining, which comprises 60 percent of the total physical structure of the container, is a substantial structural part of the container. Assume that each container, including its lining, is the unit of property and that a container has a class life of 12 years. At the time that C placed the container into service, C was aware that approximately every three years, the container lining would need to be replaced with comparable and commercially available replacement materials. At the end of three years, the container will continue to function, but will become less efficient and the replacement of the lining will be necessary to keep the container in an ordinarily efficient operating condition. In Year 1, C acquired 10 new containers and placed them into service. In Year 4, Year 7, Year 9, and Year 12, C pays amounts to replace the containers' linings with comparable and commercially available replacement parts. Assume that none of the exceptions set out in paragraph (i)(3) of this section apply to the amounts paid for the replacement linings. Because the replacement of the linings involves recurring activities that C expects to perform as a result of its use of the containers to keep the containers in their ordinarily efficient operating condition and consists of maintenance activities that C expects to perform more than once during the 12-year class life of the containers, C's lining replacement costs are within the routine maintenance safe harbor under paragraph (i)(1)(ii) of this section. Accordingly, the amounts that C paid for the replacement of the container linings are deemed not to improve the containers and are not required to be capitalized under paragraph (d) of this section. However, the amounts paid to replace the lining may be subject to capitalization under section 263A if the amounts paid for this maintenance comprise the direct or allocable indirect costs of the property produced by C. See § 1.263A-1(e)(3)(ii)(O).

Example 7. Routine maintenance once during class life. D is a Class I railroad that owns a fleet of freight cars. Assume that a freight car, including all its components, is a unit of property and has a class life of 14 years. At the time that D places a freight car into service, D expects to perform cyclical reconditioning to the car every 8 to 10 years to keep the freight car in ordinarily efficient operating condition. During this reconditioning, D pays amounts to disassemble, inspect, and recondition or replace components of the freight car with comparable and commercially available replacement parts. Ten years after D places the freight car in service, D pays amounts to perform a cyclical reconditioning on the car. Because D expects to perform the reconditioning only once during the 14 year class life of the freight car, the amounts D pays for the reconditioning do not qualify for the routine maintenance safe harbor under paragraph (i)(1)(ii) of this section. Accordingly, D must capitalize the amounts paid for the reconditioning of the freight car if these amounts result in an improvement under paragraph (d) of this section.

Example 8. Routine maintenance; reasonable expectation. Assume the same facts as *Example 7*, except in Year 1, D acquires and places in service several refrigerated freight cars, which also have a class life of 14 years. Because of the special requirements of these cars, at the time they are placed in service, D expects to perform a reconditioning of the refrigeration components of the freight car every 6 years to keep the freight car in an ordinarily efficient operating condition. During the reconditioning, D pays amounts to disassemble, inspect, and recondition or replace the refrigeration components of the freight car with comparable and commercially available replacement parts. Assume that none of the exceptions set out in paragraph (i)(3) of this section apply to the amounts paid for the reconditioning of these freight cars. In Year 6, D pays amounts to perform a reconditioning on the refrigeration components on one of the freight cars. However, because of changes in the frequency that D utilizes this freight car, D does not perform the second reconditioning on the same freight car until Year 15, after the end of the 14-year class life of the car. Under paragraph (i)(1)(ii) of this section, D's reasonable expectation that it would perform the reconditioning every 6 years will not be deemed unreasonable merely because D did not actually perform the reconditioning a second time during the 14-year class life, provided that D can substantiate that its expectation was reasonable at the time the property was placed in service. If D can demonstrate that its expectation was reasonable in Year 1 using the factors provided in paragraph (i)(1)(ii) of this section, then the amounts paid by D to recondition the refrigerated freight car components in Year 6 and in Year 15 are within the routine maintenance safe harbor under paragraph (i)(1)(ii) of this section.

Example 9. Routine maintenance on non-rotable part. E is a towboat operator that owns and leases a fleet of towboats. Each towboat is equipped with two diesel-powered engines. Assume that each towboat, including its engines, is the unit of property and that a towboat has a class life of 18 years. At the time that E places its towboats into service, E is aware that approximately every three to four years E will need to perform scheduled maintenance on the two towboat engines to keep the engines in their ordinarily efficient operating condition. This maintenance is completed while the engines are attached to the towboat and involves the cleaning and inspecting of the engines to determine which parts are within acceptable operating tolerances and can continue to be used, which parts must be reconditioned to be brought back to acceptable tolerances, and which parts must be replaced. Engine parts replaced during these procedures are replaced with comparable and commercially available replacement parts. Assume the towboat engines are not rotable spare parts under § 1.162-3(c)(2). In Year 1, E acquired a new towboat, including its two engines, and placed the towboat into service. In Year 5, E pays amounts to perform scheduled maintenance on both engines in the towboat. Assume that none of the exceptions set out in paragraph (i)(3) of this section apply to the scheduled maintenance costs. Because the scheduled maintenance involves recurring activities that E expects to perform more than once during the 18-year class life of the towboat, the maintenance results from E's use of the towboat, and the maintenance is performed to keep the towboat in an ordinarily efficient operating condition, the scheduled maintenance on E's towboat is within the routine maintenance safe harbor under paragraph (i)(1)(ii) of this section. Accordingly, the amounts paid for the scheduled maintenance to its towboat engines in Year 5 are deemed not to improve the towboat and are not required to be capitalized under paragraph (d) of this section.

Example 10. Routine maintenance with related betterments. Assume the same facts as *Example 9*, except that in Year 9 E's towboat engines are due for another scheduled maintenance visit. At this time, E decides to upgrade the engines to increase their horsepower and propulsion, which would permit the towboats to tow heavier loads. Accordingly, in Year 9, E pays amounts to perform many of the same activities that it would perform during the typical scheduled maintenance activities such as cleaning, inspecting, reconditioning, and replacing minor parts, but at the same time, E incurs costs to upgrade certain engine parts to increase the towing capacity of the boats in excess of the capacity of the boats when E placed them in service. In combination with the replacement of parts with new and upgraded parts, the scheduled maintenance must be completed to perform the horsepower and propulsion upgrade. Thus, the work done on the engines encompasses more than the recurring activities that E expected to perform as a result of its use of the towboats and did more than keep the towboat in its ordinarily efficient operating condition. Rather under paragraph (j) of this section, the amounts paid to increase the horsepower and propulsion of the engines are for a betterment to the towboat, and such amounts are excepted from the routine maintenance safe harbor under paragraph (i)(3)(i) of this section. In addition, under paragraph (g)(1)(i) of this section, the scheduled maintenance procedures directly benefit the upgrades. *Therefore, the amounts that E paid in Year 9 for the maintenance and* upgrade of the engines do not qualify for the routine maintenance safe harbor described under paragraph (i)(1)(ii) of this section. Rather, E must capitalize the amounts paid for maintenance and upgrades of the engines as an improvement to the towboats under paragraph (d) of this section.

Example 11. Routine maintenance with unrelated improvements. Assume the same facts as *Example 9*, except in Year 5, in addition to paying amounts to perform the scheduled engine maintenance on both engines, E also incurs costs to upgrade the communications and navigation systems in the pilot house of the towboat with new state-

of-the-art systems. Assume the amounts paid to upgrade the communications and navigation systems are for betterments under paragraph (j) of this section, and therefore result in an improvement to the towboat under paragraph (d) of this section. In contrast with *Example 9*, the amounts paid for the scheduled maintenance on E's towboat engines are not otherwise related to the upgrades to the navigation systems. Because the scheduled maintenance on the towboat engines does not directly benefit and is not incurred by reason of the upgrades to the communication and navigation systems, the amounts paid for the scheduled engine maintenance are not a direct or indirect cost of the improvement under paragraph (g)(1)(i) of this section. Accordingly, the amounts paid for the scheduled maintenance to its towboat engines in Year 5 are routine maintenance deemed not to improve the towboat and are not required to be capitalized under paragraph (d) of this section.

Example 12. Exceptions to routine maintenance. F owns and operates a farming and cattle ranch with an irrigation system that provides water for crops. Assume that each canal in the irrigation system is a single unit of property and has a class life of 20 years. At the time F placed the canals into service, F expected to have to perform major maintenance on the canals every three years to keep the canals in their ordinarily efficient operating condition. This maintenance includes draining the canals, and then cleaning, inspecting, repairing, and reconditioning or replacing parts of the canal with comparable and commercially available replacement parts. F placed the canals into service in Year 1 and did not perform any maintenance on the canals until Year 6. At that time, the canals had fallen into a state of disrepair and no longer functioned for irrigation. In Year 6, F pays amounts to drain the canals and do extensive cleaning, repairing, reconditioning, and replacing parts of the canals with comparable and commercially available replacement parts. Although the work performed on F's canals was similar to the activities that F expected to perform, but did not perform, every three years, the costs of these activities do not fall within the routine maintenance safe harbor. Specifically, under paragraph (i)(3)(v) of this section, routine maintenance does not include activities that return a unit of property to its former ordinarily efficient operating condition if the property has deteriorated to a state of disrepair and is no longer functional for its intended use. Accordingly, amounts that F pays for work performed on the canals in Year 6 must be capitalized if they result in improvements under paragraph (d) of this section (for example, restorations under paragraph (k) of this section).

Example 13. Routine maintenance on a building; escalator system. In Year 1, G acquires a large retail mall in which it leases space to retailers. The mall contains an escalator system with 40 escalators, which includes landing platforms, trusses, tracks, steps, handrails, and safety brushes. In Year 1, when G placed its building in service, G reasonably expected that it would need to replace the handrails on the escalators approximately every four years to keep the escalator system in its ordinarily efficient operating condition. After a routine inspection and test of the escalator system in Year 4, G determines that the handrails need to be replaced and pays an amount to replace the handrails with comparable and commercially available handrails. The escalator system, including the handrails, is a building system under paragraph (e)(2)(ii)(B)(4) of this section. Assume that none of the exceptions in paragraph (i)(3) of this section apply to the scheduled maintenance costs. Because the replacement of the handrails involves recurring activities that G expects to perform as a result of its use of the escalator system to keep the escalator system in an ordinarily efficient operating condition, and G reasonably expects to perform these activities more than once during the 10-year period beginning at the time building system was placed in service, the amounts paid by G for the handrail replacements are within the routine maintenance safe harbor under paragraph (i)(1)(i) of this section. Accordingly, the amounts paid for the replacement of the handrails in Year 4 are deemed not to improve the building unit of property and are not required to be capitalized under paragraph (d) of this section.

Example 14. Not routine maintenance; escalator system. Assume the same facts as in *Example 13*, except that in Year 9, G pays amounts to replace the steps of the escalators. In Year 1, when G placed its building into service, G reasonably expected that approximately every 18 to 20 years G would need to replace the steps to keep the escalator system in its ordinarily efficient operating condition. Because the replacement does not involve recurring activities that G expects to perform more than once during the 10-year period beginning at the time the building structure or the building system was placed in service, the costs of these activities do not fall within the routine maintenance safe harbor. Accordingly, amounts that G pays to replace the steps in Year 9 must be capitalized if they result in improvements under paragraph (d) of this section (for example, restorations under paragraph (k) of this section).

Example 15. Routine maintenance on building; reasonable expectation. In Year 1, H acquires a new office building, which it uses to provide services. The building contains an HVAC system, which is a building system under paragraph (e)(2)(ii)(B)(*1*) of this section. In Year 1, when H placed its building into service, H reasonably expected that every four years H would need to pay an outside contractor to perform detailed testing, monitoring, and preventative maintenance on its HVAC system to keep the HVAC system in its ordinarily efficient operating condition. This scheduled maintenance includes disassembly, cleaning, inspection, repair, replacement, reassembly, and testing of the HVAC system and many of its component parts. If inspection or testing discloses a problem with any component, the part is repaired, or if necessary, replaced with a comparable and commercially available replacement part. The scheduled maintenance at these intervals is recommended by the manufacturer of the HVAC system and is routinely performed on similar systems in similar buildings. Assume that none of the exceptions in paragraph (i)(3) of this section apply to the amounts paid for the maintenance on the HVAC system. In Year 4, H pays amounts to a contractor to perform the scheduled maintenance. However, H does not perform this scheduled maintenance on its building again until Year 11. Under paragraph (i)(1)(i) of this section, H's reasonable expectation that it would perform the maintenance every 4 years will not be deemed unreasonable merely because H did not actually perform the maintenance a second time during the 10-year period, provided that H can substantiate that its expectation was reasonable at the time the property was placed in service. If H can demonstrate that its expectation was reasonable in Year 1 using the other factors considered in paragraph (i)(1)(i), then the amounts H paid for the maintenance of the HVAC system in Year 4 and in Year 11 are within the routine maintenance safe harbor under paragraph (i)(1)(i) of this section.

(j) *Capitalization of betterments.*—(1) *In general.*—A taxpayer must capitalize as an improvement an amount paid for a betterment to a unit of property. An amount is paid for a betterment to a unit of property only if it—

(i) Ameliorates a material condition or defect that either existed prior to the taxpayer's acquisition of the unit of property or arose during the production of the unit of property, whether or not the taxpayer was aware of the condition or defect at the time of acquisition or production;

(ii) Is for a material addition, including a physical enlargement, expansion, extension, or addition of a major component (as defined in paragraph (k)(6) of this section) to the unit of property or a material increase in the capacity, including additional cubic or linear space, of the unit of property; or

(iii) Is reasonably expected to materially increase the productivity, efficiency, strength, quality, or output of the unit of property.

(2) *Application of betterment rules.*—(i) *In general.*—The applicability of each quantitative and qualitative factor provided in paragraphs (j)(1)(ii) and (j)(1)(iii) of this section to a particular unit of property depends on the nature of the unit of property. For example, if an addition or an increase in a particular factor cannot be measured in the context of a specific type of property, this factor is not relevant in the determination of whether an amount has been paid for a betterment to the unit of property.

(ii) *Application of betterment rules to buildings.*—An amount is paid to improve a building if it is paid for a betterment, as defined under paragraph (j)(1) of this section, to a property specified under paragraph (e)(2)(ii) (building), paragraph (e)(2)(iii)(B) (condominium), paragraph (e)(2)(iv)(B) (cooperative), or paragraph (e)(2)(v)(B) (leased building or leased portion of building) of this section. For example, an amount is paid to improve a building if it is paid for an increase in the efficiency of the building structure or any one of its building systems (for example, the HVAC system).

(iii) *Unavailability of replacement parts.*—If a taxpayer replaces a part of a unit of property that cannot reasonably be replaced with the same type of part (for example, because of technological advancements or product enhancements), the replacement of the part with an improved, but comparable, part does not, by itself, result in a betterment to the unit of property.

(iv) *Appropriate comparison.*—(A) *In general.*—In cases in which an expenditure is necessitated by normal wear and tear or damage to the unit of property that occurred during the taxpayer's use of the unit of property, the determination of whether an expenditure is for the betterment of the unit of property is made by comparing the condition of the property immediately after the expenditure with the condition of the property immediately prior to the circumstances necessitating the expenditure.

(B) *Normal wear and tear.*—If the expenditure is made to correct the effects of normal wear and tear to the unit of property that occurred during the taxpayer's use of the unit of property, the condition of the property immediately prior to the circumstances necessitating the expenditure is the condition of the property after the last time the taxpayer corrected the effects of normal wear and

tear (whether the amounts paid were for maintenance or improvements) or, if the taxpayer has not previously corrected the effects of normal wear and tear, the condition of the property when placed in service by the taxpayer.

(C) *Damage to property.*—If the expenditure is made to correct damage to a unit of property that occurred during the taxpayer's use of the unit of property, the condition of the property immediately prior to the circumstances necessitating the expenditure is the condition of the property immediately prior to damage.

(3) *Examples.*—The following examples illustrate the application of this paragraph (j) only and do not address whether capitalization is required under another provision of this section or another provision of the Internal Revenue Code (for example, section 263A). Unless otherwise provided, assume that the appropriate comparison in paragraph (j)(2)(iv) of this section is not applicable under the facts.

Example 1. Amelioration of pre-existing material condition or defect. In Year 1, A purchases a store located on a parcel of land that contains underground gasoline storage tanks left by prior occupants. Assume that the parcel of land is the unit of property. The tanks had leaked prior to A's purchase, causing soil contamination. A is not aware of the contamination at the time of purchase. In Year 2, A discovers the contamination and incurs costs to remediate the soil. The remediation costs are for a betterment to the land under paragraph (j)(1)(i) of this section because A incurred the costs to ameliorate a material condition or defect that existed prior to A's acquisition of the land.

Example 2. Not amelioration of pre-existing condition or defect. B owns an office building that was constructed with insulation that contained asbestos. The health dangers of asbestos were not widely known when the building was constructed. Several years after B places the building into service, B determines that certain areas of asbestos-containing insulation have begun to deteriorate and could eventually pose a health risk to employees. Therefore, B pays an amount to remove the asbestos-containing insulation from the building structure and replace it with new insulation that is safer to employees, but no more efficient or effective than the asbestos insulation. Under paragraphs (e)(2)(ii) and (j)(2)(ii) of this section, an amount is paid to improve a building unit of property if the amount is paid for a betterment to the building structure or any building system. Although the asbestos is determined to be unsafe under certain circumstances, the presence of asbestos insulation in a building, by itself, is not a preexisting material condition or defect of the building structure under paragraph (j)(1)(i) of this section. In addition, the removal and replacement of the asbestos is not for a material addition to the building structure or a material increase in the capacity of the building structure under paragraphs (j)(1)(ii) and (j)(2)(iv) of this section as compared to the condition of the property prior to the deterioration of the insulation. Similarly, the removal and replacement of asbestos is not reasonably expected to materially increase the productivity, efficiency, strength, quality, or output of the building structure under paragraphs (j)(1)(iii) and (j)(2)(iv) of this section as compared to the condition of the property prior to the deterioration of the insulation. Therefore, the amount paid to remove and replace the asbestos insulation is not for a betterment to the building structure or an improvement to the building under paragraph (j) of this section.

Example 3. Not amelioration of pre-existing material condition or defect. (i) In January, Year 1, C purchased a used machine for use in its manufacturing operations. Assume that the machine is a unit of property and has a class life of 10 years. C placed the machine in service in January, Year 1 and at that time expected to perform manufacturer recommended scheduled maintenance on the machine every three years. The scheduled maintenance includes cleaning and oiling the machine, inspecting parts for defects, and replacing minor items, such as springs, bearings, and seals, with comparable and commercially available replacement parts. The scheduled maintenance does not include any material additions or materially increase the capacity, productivity, efficiency, strength, quality, or output of the machine. At the time C purchased the machine, it was approaching the end of a three-year scheduled maintenance period. As a result, in February, Year 1, C pays an amount to perform the manufacturer recommended scheduled maintenance to keep the machine in its ordinarily efficient operating condition.

(ii) The amount that C pays does not qualify under the routine maintenance safe harbor in paragraph (i) of this section, because the cost primarily results from the prior owner's use of the property and not the taxpayer's use. C acquired the machine just before it had received its three-year scheduled maintenance. Accordingly, the amount that C pays for the scheduled maintenance results from the prior owner's use of the property and ameliorates conditions or defects that existed prior to C's ownership of the machine. Nevertheless, considering the purpose and minor nature of the work performed, this amount does not ameliorate a material condition or defect in the machine under paragraph (j)(1)(i) of this section, is not for a material addition to or increase in capacity of the machine under paragraph (j)(1)(ii) of this section, and is not reasonably expected to materially increase the productivity, efficiency, strength, quality, or output of the machine under paragraph (j)(1)(iii) of this section. Therefore, C is not required to capitalize the amount paid for the scheduled maintenance as a betterment to the unit of property under this paragraph (j).

Example 4. Not amelioration of pre-existing material condition or defect. D purchases a used ice resurfacing machine for use in the operation of its ice skating rink. To comply with local regulations, D is required to routinely monitor the air quality in the ice skating rink. One week after D places the machine into service, during a routine air quality check, D discovers that the operation of the machine is adversely affecting the air quality in the skating rink. As a result, D pays an amount to inspect and retune the machine, which includes replacing minor components of the engine that had worn out prior to D's acquisition of the machine. Assume the resurfacing machine, including the engine, is the unit of property. The routine maintenance safe harbor in paragraph (i) of this section does not apply to the amounts paid, because the activities performed do not relate solely to the taxpayer's use of the machine. The amount that D pays to inspect, retune, and replace minor components of the ice resurfacing machine ameliorates a condition or defect that existed prior to D's acquisition of the equipment. Nevertheless, considering the purpose and minor nature of the work performed, this amount does not ameliorate a material condition or defect in the machine under paragraph (j)(1)(i) of this section. In addition, the amount is not paid for a material addition to the machine or a material increase in the capacity of the machine under paragraph (j)(1)(ii) of this section. Also, the activities are not reasonably expected to materially increase the productivity, efficiency, strength, quality, or output of the machine under paragraph (j)(1)(iii) of this section. Therefore, D is not required to capitalize the amount paid to inspect, retune, and replace minor components of the machine as a betterment under this paragraph (j).

Example 5. Amelioration of material condition or defect. (i) E acquires a building for use in its business of providing assisted living services. Before and after the purchase, the building functions as an assisted living facility. However, at the time of the purchase, E is aware that the building is in a condition that is below the standards that E requires for facilities used in its business. Immediately after the acquisition and during the following two years, while E continues to use the building as an assisted living facility, E pays amounts for extensive repairs and maintenance, and the acquisition of new property to bring the facility into the high-quality condition for which E's facilities are known. The work on E's building includes repairing damaged drywall, repainting, re-wallpapering, replacing windows, repairing and replacing doors, replacing and regrouting tile, repairing millwork, and repairing and replacing roofing materials. The work also involves the replacement of section 1245 property, including window treatments, furniture, and cabinets. The work that E performs affects only the building structure under paragraph (e)(2)(ii)(A) of this section and does not affect any of the building systems described in paragraph (e)(2)(ii)(B) of this section. Assume that each section 1245 property is a separate unit of property.

(ii) Under paragraphs (e)(2)(ii) and (j)(2)(ii) of this section, an amount is paid to improve a building unit of property if the amount is paid for a betterment to the building structure or any building system. Considering the purpose of the expenditure and the effect of the expenditures on the building structure, the amounts that E paid for repairs and maintenance to the building structure comprise a betterment to the building structure under paragraph (j)(1)(i) of this section because the amounts ameliorate material conditions that existed prior to E's acquisition of the building. Therefore, E must treat the amounts paid for the betterment to the building structure as an improvement to the building and must capitalize the amounts under paragraphs (j) and (d)(1) of this section. Moreover, E is required to capitalize the amounts paid to acquire and install each section 1245 property, including each window treatment, each item of furniture, and each cabinet, in accordance with § 1.263(a)-2(d)(1).

Example 6. Not a betterment; building refresh. (i) F owns a nationwide chain of retail stores that sell a wide variety of items. To maintain the appearance and functionality of its store buildings after several years of wear, F periodically pays amounts to refresh the look and layout of its stores. The work that F performs during a refresh consists of cosmetic and layout changes to the store's interiors and general repairs and maintenance to the store building to modernize the store buildings and reorganize the merchandise displays. The work to each store consists of replacing and reconfiguring display tables and racks to provide better exposure of the merchandise, making corresponding lighting relocations and flooring repairs, moving one wall to accommodate the reconfiguration of tables and racks, patching holes in walls, repainting the interior structure with a new color scheme to coordinate with new signage, replacing damaged

ceiling tiles, cleaning and repairing wood flooring throughout the store building, and power washing building exteriors. The display tables and the racks all constitute section 1245 property. F pays amounts to refresh 50 stores during the taxable year. Assume that each section 1245 property within each store is a separate unit of property. Finally, assume that the work does not ameliorate any material conditions or defects that existed when F acquired the store buildings or result in any material additions to the store buildings.

(ii) Under paragraphs (e)(2)(ii) and (j)(2)(ii) of this section, an amount is paid to improve a building unit of property if the amount is paid for a betterment to the building structure or any building system. Considering the facts and circumstances including the purpose of the expenditure, the physical nature of the work performed, and the effect of the expenditure on the buildings' structure and systems, the amounts paid for the refresh of each building are not for any material additions to, or material increases in the capacity of, the buildings' structure or systems as compared with the condition of the structure or systems after the previous refresh. Moreover, the amounts paid are not reasonably expected to materially increase the productivity, efficiency, strength, quality, or output of any building structure or system under as compared to the condition of the structures or systems after the previous refresh. Rather, the work performed keeps F's store buildings' structures and buildings' systems in their ordinarily efficient operating condition. Therefore, F is not required to treat the amounts paid for the refresh of its store buildings' structures and buildings' systems as betterments under paragraphs (j)(1)(ii), (j)(1)(iii), and (j)(2)(iv) of this section. However, F is required to capitalize the amounts paid to acquire and install each section 1245 property in accordance with § 1.263(a)-2(d)(1).

Example 7. Building refresh; limited improvement. (i) Assume the same facts as *Example 6* except, in the course of the refresh to one of its store buildings, F also pays amounts to increase the building's storage space, add a second loading dock, and add a second overhead door. Specifically, at the same time F pays amounts to perform the refresh, F pays additional amounts to construct an addition to the back of the store building, including adding a new overhead door and loading dock to the building. The work also involves upgrades to the electrical system of the building, including the addition of a second service box with increased amperage and new wiring from the service box to provide lighting and power throughout the new space. Although it is performed at the same time, the construction of the additions does not affect, and is not otherwise related to, the refresh of the retail space.

(ii) Under paragraphs (e)(2)(ii) and (j)(2)(ii) of this section, an amount is paid to improve a building unit of property if the amount is paid for a betterment to the building structure or any building system. Under paragraph (j)(1)(ii) of this section, the amounts paid by F to add the storage space, loading dock, overhead door, and expand the electrical system are for betterments to F's building structure and to the electrical system because they are for material additions to, and a material increase in capacity of, the structure and the electrical system of F's store building. Accordingly, F must treat the amounts paid for these betterments as improvements to the building unit of property and capitalize these amounts under paragraphs (d)(1) and (j) of this section. However, for the reasons discussed in *Example 6*, F is not required to treat the amounts paid for the refresh of its store building structure and systems as a betterments under paragraph (j)(1) of this section. In addition, F is not required under paragraph (g)(1) of this section to capitalize the refresh costs described in *Example 6* because these costs do not directly benefit and are not incurred by reason of the additions to the building structure and electrical system. As in *Example 6*, F is required to capitalize the amounts paid to acquire and install each section 1245 property in accordance with § 1.263(a)-2(d)(1).

Example 8. Betterment; building remodel. (i) G owns a large chain of retail stores that sell a variety of items. G determines that due to changes in the retail market, it can no longer compete in its current store class and decides to upgrade its stores to offer higher end products to a different type of customer. To offer these products and attract different types of customers, G must substantially remodel its stores. Thus, G pays amounts to remodel its stores by performing work on the buildings' structures and systems as defined under paragraphs (e)(2)(ii)(A) and (e)(2)(ii)(B) of this section. This work includes replacing large parts of the exterior walls with windows, replacing the escalators with a monumental staircase, adding a new glass enclosed elevator, rebuilding the interior and exterior facades, replacing vinyl floors with ceramic flooring, replacing ceiling tiles with acoustical tiles, and removing and rebuilding walls to move changing rooms and create specialty departments. The work also includes upgrades to increase the capacity of the buildings' electrical system to accommodate the structural changes and the addition of new section 1245 property, such as new product information kiosks and point of sale systems. The work to the electrical system also involves the installation of new more efficient and mood enhancing lighting fixtures. In addition, the work includes remodeling all bathrooms by replacing contractor-grade plumbing fixtures with designer-grade fixtures that conserve water and energy. Finally, G also pays amounts to clean debris resulting from construction during the remodel, patch holes in walls that were made to upgrade the electrical system, repaint existing walls with a new color scheme to match the new interior construction, and to power wash building exteriors to enhance the new exterior facade.

(ii) Under paragraphs (e)(2)(ii) and (j)(2)(ii) of this section, an amount is paid to improve a building unit of property if the amount is paid for a betterment to the building structure or any building system. Considering the facts and circumstances, including the purpose of the expenditure, the physical nature of the work performed, and the effect of the work on the buildings' structures and buildings' systems, the amounts that G pays for the remodeling of its stores result in betterments to the buildings' structures and several of its systems under paragraph (j) of this section. Specifically, the amounts paid to replace large parts of the exterior walls with windows, replace the escalators with a monumental staircase, add a new elevator, rebuild the interior and exterior facades, replace vinyl floors with ceramic flooring, replace the ceiling tiles with acoustical tiles, and to remove and rebuild walls are for material additions, that is the addition of major components, to the building structure under paragraph (j)(1)(ii) of this section and are reasonably expected to increase the quality of the building structure under paragraph (j)(1)(iii) of this section. Similarly, the amounts paid to upgrade the electrical system are to materially increase the capacity of the electrical system under paragraph (j)(1)(ii) of this section and are reasonably expected to increase the quality of this system under paragraph (j)(1)(iii) of this section. In addition, the amounts paid to remodel the bathrooms with higher grade and more resource-efficient materials are reasonably expected to increase the efficiency and quality of the plumbing system under paragraph (j)(1)(iii) of this section. Finally, the amounts paid to clean debris, patch and repaint existing walls with a new color scheme, and to power wash building exteriors, while not betterments by themselves, directly benefited and were incurred by reason of the improvements to G's store buildings' structures and electrical systems under paragraph (g)(1) of this section. Therefore, G must treat the amounts paid for betterments to the store buildings' structures and systems, including the costs of cleaning, patching, repairing, and power washing the building, as improvements to G's buildings and must capitalize these amounts under paragraphs (d)(1) and (j) of this section. Moreover, G is required to capitalize the amounts paid to acquire and install each section 1245 property in accordance with § 1.263(a)-2(d)(1). For the treatment of amounts paid to remove components of property, see paragraph (g)(2) of this section.

Example 9. Not betterment; relocation and reinstallation of personal property. In Year 1, H purchases new cash registers for use in its retail store located in leased space in a shopping mall. Assume that each cash register is a unit of property as determined under paragraph (e)(3) of this section. In Year 1, H capitalizes the costs of acquiring and installing the new cash registers under § 1.263(a)-2(d)(1). In Year 3, H's lease expires, and H decides to relocate its retail store to a different building. In addition to various other costs, H pays $5,000 to move the cash registers and $1,000 to reinstall them in the new store. The cash registers are used for the same purpose and in the same manner that they were used in the former location. The amounts that H pays to move and reinstall the cash registers into its new store do not result in a betterment to the cash registers under paragraph (j) of this section.

Example 10. Betterment; relocation and reinstallation of equipment. J operates a manufacturing facility in Building A, which contains various machines that J uses in its manufacturing business. J decides to expand part of its operations by relocating a machine to Building B to reconfigure the machine with additional components. Assume that the machine is a single unit of property under paragraph (e)(3) of this section. J pays amounts to disassemble the machine, to move the machine to the new location, and to reinstall the machine in a new configuration with additional components. Assume that the reinstallation, including the reconfiguration and the addition of components, is for an increase in capacity of the machine, and therefore is for a betterment to the machine under paragraph (j)(1)(ii) of this section. Accordingly, J must capitalize the costs of reinstalling the machine as an improvement to the machine under paragraphs (j) and (d)(1) of this section. J is also required to capitalize the costs of disassembling and moving the machine to Building B because these costs directly benefit and are incurred by reason of the improvement to the machine under paragraph (g)(1) of this section.

Example 11. Betterment; regulatory requirement. K owns a building that it uses in its business. In Year 1, City C passes an ordinance setting higher safety standards for buildings because of the hazardous conditions caused by earthquakes. To comply with the ordinance, K pays an amount to add expansion bolts to its building structure. These bolts anchor the wooden framing of K's building to its cement foundation, providing additional structural support and

resistance to seismic forces, making the building more resistant to damage from lateral movement. Under paragraphs (e)(2)(ii) and (j)(2)(ii) of this section, an amount is paid to improve a building unit of property if the amount is paid for a betterment to the building structure or any building system. The framing and foundation are part of the building structure as defined in paragraph (e)(2)(ii)(A) of this section. Prior to the ordinance, the old building was in good condition but did not meet City C's new requirements for earthquake resistance. The amount paid by K for the addition of the expansion bolts met City C's new requirement, but also materially increased the strength of the building structure under paragraph (j)(1)(iii) of this section. Therefore, K must treat the amount paid to add the expansion bolts as a betterment to the building structure and must capitalize this amount as an improvement to building under paragraphs (d)(1) and (j) of this section. Under paragraph (g)(4) of this section, City C's new requirement that K's building meet certain safety standards to continue to operate is not relevant in determining whether the amount paid improved the building.

Example 12. Not a betterment; regulatory requirement. L owns a meat processing plant. After operating the plant for many years, L discovers that oil is seeping through the concrete walls of the plant. Federal inspectors advise L that it must correct the seepage problem or shut down its plant. To correct the problem, L pays an amount to add a concrete lining to the walls from the floor to a height of about four feet and also to add concrete to the floor of the plant. Under paragraphs (e)(2)(ii) and (j)(2)(ii) of this section, an amount is paid to improve a building unit of property if the amount is paid for a betterment to the building structure or any building system. The walls are part of the building structure as defined in paragraph (e)(2)(ii)(A) of this section. The condition necessitating the expenditure was the seepage of the oil into the plant. Prior to the seepage, the walls did not leak and were functioning for their intended use. L is not required to treat the amount paid as a betterment under paragraphs (j)(1)(ii) and (j)(2)(iv) of this section because it is not paid for a material addition to, or a material increase in the capacity of, the building's structure as compared to the condition of the structure prior to the seepage of oil. Moreover, the amount paid is not reasonably expected to materially increase the productivity, efficiency, strength, quality, or output of the building structure under paragraphs (j)(1)(iii) and (j)(2)(iv) as compared to the condition of the structure prior to the seepage of the oil. Therefore, L is not required to treat the amount paid to correct the seepage as a betterment to the building under paragraph (d)(1) or (j) of this section. The federal inspectors' requirement that L correct the seepage to continue operating the plant is not relevant in determining whether the amount paid improves the plant.

Example 13. Not a betterment; new roof membrane. M owns a building that it uses for its retail business. Over time, the waterproof membrane (top layer) on the roof of M's building begins to wear, and M began to experience water seepage and leaks throughout its retail premises. To eliminate the problems, a contractor recommends that M put a new rubber membrane on the worn membrane. Accordingly, M pays the contractor to add the new membrane. The new membrane is comparable to the worn membrane when it was originally placed in service by the taxpayer. Under paragraphs (e)(2)(ii) and (j)(2)(ii) of this section, an amount is paid to improve a building unit of property if the amount is paid for a betterment to the building structure or any building system. The roof is part of the building structure under paragraph (e)(2)(ii)(A) of this section. The condition necessitating the expenditure was the normal wear of M's roof. Under paragraph (j)(2)(iv) of this section, to determine whether the amounts are for a betterment, the condition of the building structure after the expenditure must be compared to the condition of the structure when M placed the building into service because M has not previously corrected the effects of normal wear and tear. Under these facts, the amount paid to add the new membrane to the roof is not for a material addition or a material increase in the capacity of the building structure under paragraph (j)(1)(ii) of this section as compared to the condition of the structure when it was placed in service. Moreover, the new membrane is not reasonably expected to materially increase the productivity, efficiency, strength, quality, or output of the building structure under paragraph (j)(1)(iii) of this section as compared to the condition of the building structure when it was placed in service. Therefore, M is not required to treat the amount paid to add the new membrane as a betterment to the building under paragraph (d)(1) or (j) of this section.

Example 14. Material increase in capacity; building. N owns a factory building with a storage area on the second floor. N pays an amount to reinforce the columns and girders supporting the second floor to permit storage of supplies with a gross weight 50 percent greater than the previous load-carrying capacity of the storage area. Under paragraphs (e)(2)(ii) and (j)(2)(ii) of this section, an amount is paid to improve a building unit of property if the amount is paid for a betterment to the building structure or any building system. The columns and girders are part of the building structure defined under paragraph (e)(2)(ii)(A) of this section. N must treat the amount paid to reinforce the columns and girders as a betterment under paragraphs (j)(1)(ii) and (j)(1)(iii) of this section because it materially increases the load-carrying capacity and the strength of the building structure. Therefore, N must capitalize this amount as an improvement to the building under paragraphs (d)(1) and (j) of this section.

Example 15. Material increase in capacity; channel. O owns harbor facilities consisting of a slip for the loading and unloading of barges and a channel leading from the slip to the river. At the time of purchase, the channel was 150 feet wide, 1,000 feet long, and 10 feet deep. Several years after purchasing the harbor facilities, to allow for ingress and egress and for the unloading of larger barges, O decides to deepen the channel to a depth of 20 feet. O pays a contractor to dredge the channel to 20 feet. Assume the channel is the unit of property. O must capitalize the amounts paid for the dredging as an improvement to the channel because they are for a material increase in the capacity of the unit of property under paragraph (j)(1)(ii) of this section.

Example 16. Not a material increase in capacity; channel. Assume the same facts as in *Example 15*, except that the channel was susceptible to siltation and, after dredging to 20 feet, the channel depth had been reduced to 18 feet. O pays a contractor to redredge the channel to a depth of 20 feet. The expenditure was necessitated by the siltation of the channel. Both prior to the siltation and after the redredging, the depth of the channel was 20 feet. Applying the comparison rule under paragraph (j)(2)(iv) of this section, the amounts paid by O to redredge the channel are not for a betterment under paragraph (j)(1)(ii) of this section because they are not for a material addition to, or a material increase in the capacity of, the unit of property as compared to the condition of the property prior to the siltation. Similarly, these amounts are not for a betterment under paragraph (j)(1)(iii) of this section because the amounts are not reasonably expected to increase the productivity, efficiency, strength, quality, or output of the unit of property as compared to the condition of property before the siltation. Therefore, O is not required to capitalize these amounts as improvement under paragraphs (d)(1) and (j) of this section.

Example 17. Material increase in capacity; channel. Assume the same facts as in *Example 16* except that after the redredging, there is more siltation, and the channel depth is reduced back to 18 feet. In addition, to allow for additional ingress and egress and for the unloading of even larger barges, O decides to deepen the channel to a depth of 25 feet. O pays a contractor to redredge the channel to 25 feet. O must capitalize the amounts paid for the dredging as an improvement to the channel because the amounts are for a material increase in the capacity of the unit of property under paragraph (j)(1)(ii) of this section as compared to condition of the unit of property before the siltation. As part of this improvement, O is also required to capitalize the portion of the redredge costs allocable to restoring the depth lost to the siltation because, under paragraph (g)(1)(i) of this section, these amounts directly benefit and are incurred by reason of the improvement to the unit of property.

Example 18. Not a material increase in capacity; building. P owns a building used in its trade or business. The first floor has a drop-ceiling. To fully expose windows on the first floor, P pays an amount to remove the drop-ceiling and repaint the original ceiling. Under paragraphs (e)(2)(ii) and (j)(2)(ii) of this section, an amount is paid to improve a building unit of property if the amount is paid for a betterment to the building structure or any building system. The ceiling is part of the building structure as defined under paragraph (e)(2)(ii)(A) of this section. P is not required to treat the amount paid to remove the drop-ceiling as a betterment to the building because it was not for a material addition or material increase in the capacity of the building structure under paragraph (j)(1)(ii) of this section and it was not reasonably expected to materially increase to the efficiency, strength, or quality of the building structure under paragraph (j)(1)(iii) of this section. In addition, under paragraph (j)(2)(i) of this section, because the effect on productivity and output of the building structure cannot be measured in this context, these factors are not relevant in determining whether there is a betterment to the building structure.

Example 19. Material increase in capacity; building. Q owns a building that it uses in its retail business. The building contains one floor of retail space with very high ceilings. Q pays an amount to add a stairway and a mezzanine for the purposes of adding additional selling space within its building. Under paragraphs (e)(2)(ii) and (j)(2)(ii) of this section, an amount is paid to improve a building unit of property if the amount is paid for a betterment to the building structure or any building system. The stairway and the mezzanine are part of the building structure as defined under paragraph (e)(2)(ii)(A) of this section. Q is required to treat the amount paid to add the stairway and mezzanine as a betterment because it is for a material addition to, and an increase in the capacity of, the building structure under paragraph (j)(1)(ii) of this section. Therefore, Q must

capitalize this amount as an improvement to the building unit of property under paragraphs (d)(1) and (j) of this section.

Example 20. Not material increase in efficiency; HVAC system. R owns an office building that it uses to provide services to customers. The building contains an HVAC system that incorporates 10 roof-mounted units that provide heating and air conditioning for different parts of the building. The HVAC system also consists of controls for the entire system and duct work that distributes the heated or cooled air to the various spaces in the building's interior. After many years of use of the HVAC system, R begins to experience climate control problems in various offices throughout the office building and consults with a contractor to determine the cause. The contractor recommends that R replace two of the roof-mounted units. R pays an amount to replace the two specified units. The two new units are expected to eliminate the climate control problems and to be 10 percent more energy efficient than the replaced units in their original condition. No work is performed on the other roof-mounted heating/cooling units, the duct work, or the controls. Under paragraphs (e)(2)(ii) and (j)(2)(ii) of this section, an amount is paid to improve a building unit of property if the amount is paid for a betterment to the building structure or any building system. The HVAC system, including the two-roof mounted units, is a building system under paragraph (e)(2)(ii)(B)(*1*) of this section. The replacement of the two roof-mounted units is not a material addition to or a material increase in the capacity of the HVAC system under paragraphs (j)(1)(ii) and (j)(3)(ii) of this section as compared to the condition of the system prior to the climate control problems. In addition, given the 10 percent efficiency increase in two units of the entire HVAC system, the replacement is not expected to materially increase the productivity, efficiency, strength, quality, or output of the HVAC system under paragraphs (j)(1)(iii) and (j)(2)(iv) of this section as compared to the condition of the system prior to the climate control problems. Therefore, R is not required to capitalize the amounts paid for these replacements as betterments to the building unit of property under paragraphs (d)(1) and (j) of this section.

Example 21. Material increase in efficiency; building. S owns a building that it uses in its service business. S conducts an energy assessment and determines that it could significantly reduce its energy costs by adding insulation to its building. S pays an insulation contractor to apply a combination of loose-fill, spray foam, and blanket insulation throughout S's building structure, including within the attic, walls, and crawl spaces. S reasonably expects the new insulation to make the building more energy efficient because the contractor indicated that the new insulation would reduce its annual energy and power costs by approximately 50 percent of its annual costs during the last five years. Under paragraphs (e)(2)(ii) and (j)(2)(ii) of this section, an amount is paid to improve a building if the amount is paid for a betterment to the building structure or any building system. Therefore, under paragraphs (d)(1) and (j) of this section, S must capitalize as a betterment the amount paid to add the insulation because the insulation is reasonably expected to materially increase the efficiency of the building structure under paragraph (j)(1)(iii) of this section.

Example 22. Material addition; building. T owns and operates a restaurant, which provides a variety of prepared foods to its customers. To better accommodate its customers and increase customer traffic, T decides to add a drive-through service area. As a result, T pays amounts to partition an area within its restaurant for a drive-through service counter, to construct a service window with necessary security features, to build an overhang for vehicles, and to construct a drive-up menu board. Assume that the drive-up menu board is section 1245 property that is a separate unit of property under paragraph (e)(3) of this section. Under paragraphs (e)(2)(ii) and (j)(2)(ii) of this section, an amount is paid to improve a building unit of property if the amount is paid for a betterment to the building structure or any building system. The amounts paid for the partition, service window and overhang are betterments to the building structure because they comprise a material addition (that is, a physical expansion, extension, and addition of a major component) to the building structure under paragraph (j)(1)(ii) of this section. Accordingly, T must capitalize as an improvement the amounts paid to add the partition, drive-through window, and overhang under paragraphs (d)(1) and (j) of this section. T is also required to capitalize the amounts paid to acquire and install each section 1245 property in accordance with § 1.263(a)-2(d)(1).

Example 23. Costs incurred during betterment. U owns a building that it uses in its service business. To accommodate new employees and equipment, U pays amounts to increase the load capacity of its electrical system by adding a second electrical panel with additional circuits and adding wiring and outlets throughout the electrical system of its building. To complete the upgrades to the electrical system, the contractor makes several holes in walls. As a result, U also incurs costs to patch the holes and repaint several walls. Under paragraphs (e)(2)(ii) and (j)(2)(ii) of this section, an amount is paid to improve a building unit of property if the amount is paid for a betterment to the building structure or any building system. The amounts paid to upgrade the panel and wiring are for betterments to U's electrical system because they increase the capacity of the electrical system under paragraph (j)(1)(ii) of this section and increase the strength and output of the electrical system under paragraph (j)(1)(iii) of this section. Accordingly, U is required to capitalize the costs of the upgrade to the electrical system as an improvement to the building unit of property under paragraphs (d)(1) and (j) of this section. Moreover, under paragraph (g)(1) of this section, U is required to capitalize the amounts paid to patch holes and repaint several walls in its building because these costs directly benefit and are incurred by reason of the improvement to U's building unit of property.

(k) *Capitalization of restorations.*—(1) *In general.*—A taxpayer must capitalize as an improvement an amount paid to restore a unit of property, including an amount paid to make good the exhaustion for which an allowance is or has been made. An amount restores a unit of property only if it—

(i) Is for the replacement of a component of a unit of property for which the taxpayer has properly deducted a loss for that component, other than a casualty loss under § 1.165-7;

(ii) Is for the replacement of a component of a unit of property for which the taxpayer has properly taken into account the adjusted basis of the component in realizing gain or loss resulting from the sale or exchange of the component;

(iii) Is for the restoration of damage to a unit of property for which the taxpayer is required to take a basis adjustment as a result of a casualty loss under section 165, or relating to a casualty event described in section 165, subject to the limitation in paragraph (k)(4) of this section;

(iv) Returns the unit of property to its ordinarily efficient operating condition if the property has deteriorated to a state of disrepair and is no longer functional for its intended use;

(v) Results in the rebuilding of the unit of property to a like-new condition as determined under paragraph (k)(5) of this section after the end of its class life as defined in paragraph (i)(4) of this section; or

(vi) Is for the replacement of a part or combination of parts that comprise a major component or a substantial structural part of a unit of property as determined under paragraph (k)(6) of this section.

(2) *Application of restorations to buildings.*—An amount is paid to improve a building if it is paid to restore, as defined under paragraph (k)(1) of this section, a property specified under paragraph (e)(2)(ii) (building), paragraph (e)(2)(iii)(B) (condominium), paragraph (e)(2)(iv)(B) (cooperative), or paragraph (e)(2)(v)(B) (leased building or portion of building) of this section. For example, an amount is paid to improve a building if it is paid for the replacement of a part or combination of parts that comprise a major component or substantial structural part of the building structure or any one of its building systems (for example, the HVAC system). See paragraph (k)(6) of this section.

(3) *Exception for losses based on salvage value.*—A taxpayer is not required to treat as a restoration amounts paid under paragraph (k)(1)(i) or paragraph (k)(1)(ii) of this section if the unit of property has been fully depreciated and the loss is attributable only to remaining salvage value as computed for federal income tax purposes.

(4) *Restoration of damage from casualty.*—(i) *Limitation.*—For purposes of paragraph (k)(1)(iii) of this section, the amount paid for restoration of damage to the unit of property that must be capitalized under this paragraph (k) is limited to the excess (if any) of—

(A) The amount prescribed by § 1.1011-1 as the adjusted basis of the single, identifiable property (under § 1.167-7(b)(2)(i)) for determining the loss allowable on account of the casualty, over

(B) The amount paid for restoration of damage to the unit of property under paragraph (k)(1)(iii) of this section that also constitutes an improvement under any other provision of paragraph (k)(1) of this section.

(ii) *Amounts in excess of limitation.*—The amounts paid for restoration of damage to a unit of property as described in paragraph (k)(1)(iii) of this section, but that exceed the limitation provided in paragraph (k)(4)(i) of this section, must be treated in accordance with the provisions of the Internal Revenue Code and regulations that are otherwise applicable. See, for example, § 1.162-4 (repairs and maintenance); § 1.263(a)-2 (costs to acquire and produce units of property); and § 1.263(a)-3 (costs to improve units of property).

(5) *Rebuild to like-new condition.*—For purposes of paragraph (k)(1)(v) of this section, a unit of property is rebuilt to a like-new condition if it is brought to the status of new, rebuilt, remanufactured, or a similar status under the terms of any federal regulatory guideline or the manufacturer's original specifications. Generally, a comprehensive maintenance program, even though substantial, does not return a unit of property to a like-new condition.

(6) *Replacement of a major component or a substantial structural part.*—(i) *In general.*—To determine whether an amount is for the replacement of a part or a combination of parts that comprise a major component or a substantial structural part of the unit of property under paragraph (k)(1)(vi) of this section, it is appropriate to consider all the facts and circumstances. These facts and circumstances include the quantitative and qualitative significance of the part or combination of parts in relation to the unit of property.

(A) *Major component.*—A major component is a part or combination of parts that performs a discrete and critical function in the operation of the unit of property. An incidental component of the unit of property, even though such component performs a discrete and critical function in the operation of the unit of property, generally will not, by itself, constitute a major component.

(B) *Substantial structural part.*—A substantial structural part is a part or combination of parts that comprises a large portion of the physical structure of the unit of property.

(ii) *Major components and substantial structural parts of buildings.*—In the case of a building, an amount is for the replacement of a major component or a substantial structural part of the building unit of property if—

(A) The replacement includes a part or combination of parts that comprise a major component (as defined in paragraph (k)(6)(i)(A) of this section), or a significant portion of a major component, of any of the properties designated in paragraph (e)(2)(ii) (building), paragraph (e)(2)(iii)(B) (condominium), paragraph (e)(2)(iv)(B) (cooperative), or paragraph (e)(2)(v)(B) (leased building or leased portion of a building) of this section; or

(B) The replacement includes a part or combination of parts that comprises a large portion of the physical structure of any of the properties designated in paragraph (e)(2)(ii) (building), paragraph (e)(2)(iii)(B) (condominium), paragraph (e)(2)(iv)(B) (cooperative), or paragraph (e)(2)(v)(B) (leased building or portion of building) of this section.

(7) *Examples.*—The following examples illustrate the application of this paragraph (k) only and do not address whether capitalization is required under another provision of this section or another provision of the Code (for example, section 263A). Unless otherwise stated, assume that the taxpayer has not properly deducted a loss for, nor taken into account the adjusted basis on a sale or exchange of, any unit of property, asset, or component of a unit of property that is replaced.

Example 1. Replacement of loss component. A owns a manufacturing building containing various types of manufacturing equipment. A does a cost segregation study of the manufacturing building and properly determines that a walk-in freezer in the manufacturing building is section 1245 property as defined in section 1245(a)(3). The freezer is not part of the building structure or the HVAC system under paragraph (e)(2)(i) or (e)(2)(ii)(B)(1) of this section. Several components of the walk-in freezer cease to function, and A decides to replace them. A abandons the old freezer components and properly recognizes a loss from the abandonment of the components. A replaces the abandoned freezer components with new components and incurs costs to acquire and install the new components. Under paragraph (k)(1)(i) of this section, A must capitalize the amounts paid to acquire and install the new freezer components because A replaced components for which it had properly deducted a loss.

Example 2. Replacement of sold component. Assume the same facts as in *Example 1,* except that A did not abandon the components but instead sold them to another party and properly recognized a loss on the sale. Under paragraph (k)(1)(ii) of this section, A must capitalize the amounts paid to acquire and install the new freezer components because A replaced components for which it had properly taken into account the adjusted basis of the components in realizing a loss from the sale of the components.

Example 3. Restoration after casualty loss. B owns an office building that it uses in its trade or business. A storm damages the office building at a time when the building has an adjusted basis of $500,000. B deducts under section 165 a casualty loss in the amount of $50,000, and properly reduces its basis in the office building to $450,000. B hires a contractor to repair the damage to the building, including the repair of the building roof and the removal of debris from the building premises. B pays the contractor $50,000 for the work. Under paragraph (k)(1)(iii) of this section, B must treat the $50,000 amount paid to the contractor as a restoration of the building structure because B properly adjusted its basis in that amount as a result of a casualty loss under section 165, and the amount does not exceed the limit in paragraph (k)(4) of this section. Therefore, B must treat the amount paid as an improvement to the building unit of property and, under paragraph (d)(2) of this section, must capitalize the amount paid.

Example 4. Restoration after casualty event. Assume the same facts as in *Example 3*, except that B receives insurance proceeds of $50,000 after the casualty to compensate for its loss. B cannot deduct a casualty loss under section 165 because its loss was compensated by insurance. However, B properly reduces its basis in the property by the amount of the insurance proceeds. Under paragraph (k)(1)(iii) of this section, B must treat the $50,000 amount paid to the contractor as a restoration of the building structure because B has properly taken a basis adjustment relating to a casualty event described in section 165, and the amount does not exceed the limit in paragraph (k)(4) of this section. Therefore, B must treat the amount paid as an improvement to the building unit of property and, under paragraph (d)(2) of this section, must capitalize the amount paid.

Example 5. Restoration after casualty loss; limitation. (i) C owns a building that it uses in its trade or business. A storm damages the building at a time when the building has an adjusted basis of $500,000. C determines that the cost of restoring its property is $750,000, deducts a casualty loss under section 165 in the amount of $500,000, and properly reduces its basis in the building to $0. C hires a contractor to repair the damage to the building and pays the contractor $750,000 for the work. The work involves replacing the entire roof structure of the building at a cost of $350,000 and pumping water from the building, cleaning debris from the interior and exterior, and replacing areas of damaged dry wall and flooring at a cost of $400,000. Although resulting from the casualty event, the pumping, cleaning, and replacing damaged drywall and flooring, does not directly benefit and is not incurred by reason of the roof replacement.

(ii) Under paragraph (k)(1)(vi) of this section, C must capitalize as an improvement the $350,000 amount paid to the contractor to replace the roof structure because the roof structure constitutes a major component and a substantial structural part of the building unit of property. In addition, under paragraphs (k)(1)(iii) and (k)(4)(i), C must treat as a restoration the remaining costs, limited to the excess of the adjusted basis of the building over the amounts paid for the improvement under paragraph (k)(1)(vi). Accordingly, C must treat as a restoration $150,000 ($500,000 - $350,000) of the $400,000 paid for the portion of the costs related to repairing and cleaning the building structure under paragraph (k)(1)(iii) of this section. Thus, in addition to the $350,000 to replace the roof structure, C must also capitalize the $150,000 as an improvement to the building unit of property under paragraph (d)(2) of this section. C is not required to capitalize the remaining $250,000 repair and cleaning costs under paragraph (k)(1)(iii) of this section.

Example 6. Restoration of property in a state of disrepair. D owns and operates a farm with several barns and outbuildings. D did not use or maintain one of the outbuildings on a regular basis, and the outbuilding fell into a state of disrepair. The outbuilding previously was used for storage but can no longer be used for that purpose because the building is not structurally sound. D decides to restore the outbuilding and pays an amount to shore up the walls and replace the siding. Under paragraphs (e)(2)(ii) and (k)(2) of this section, an amount is paid to improve a building if the amount is paid to restore the building structure or any building system. The walls and siding are part of the building structure under paragraph (e)(2)(ii)(A) of this section. Under paragraph (k)(1)(iv) of this section, D must treat the amount paid to shore up the walls and replace the siding as a restoration of the building structure because the amounts return the building structure to its ordinarily efficient operating condition after it had deteriorated to a state of disrepair and was no longer functional for its intended use. Therefore, D must treat the amount paid to shore up the walls and replace the siding as an improvement to the building unit of property and, under paragraph (d)(2) of this section, must capitalize the amount paid.

Example 7. Rebuild of property to like-new condition before end of class life. E is a Class I railroad that owns a fleet of freight cars. Assume the freight cars have a recovery period of 7 years under section 168(c) and a class life of 14 years. Every 8 to 10 years, E rebuilds its freight cars. Ten years after E places the freight car in service, E performs a rebuild to the manufacturer's original specification, which includes a complete disassembly, inspection, and reconditioning or replacement of components of the suspension and draft systems, trailer hitches, and other special equipment. E also modifies the car to upgrade various components to the latest engineering standards. The freight car is stripped to the frame, with all of its substantial components either reconditioned or replaced. The frame itself is the longest-lasting part of the car and is reconditioned. The walls of the freight car are replaced or are sandblasted and repainted. New wheels are installed on the car. All the remaining components of the car are restored before they are reassembled. At the end of the rebuild, the freight car has been restored to like-new condition under the manufacturer's specifications. Assume the freight car is the unit of property. E is not required to treat as an improvement and capitalize the

amounts paid to rebuild the freight car under paragraph (k)(1)(v) of this section because, although the amounts paid restore the freight car to like-new condition, the amounts were not paid after the end of the class life of the freight car. However, paragraphs (k)(1)(vi) and (k)(6) of this section are applicable for determining whether any amounts must be capitalized because they are paid for the replacement of a major component or a substantial structural part of the unit of property.

Example 8. Rebuild of property to like-new condition after end of class life. Assume the same facts as in *Example 7*, except that E rebuilds the freight car 15 years after E places it in service. Under paragraph (k)(1)(v) of this section, E must treat as an improvement and capitalize the amounts paid to rebuild the freight car because the amounts paid restore the freight car to like-new condition after the end of the class life of the freight car.

Example 9. Not a rebuild to a like-new condition. F is a commercial airline engaged in the business of transporting freight and passengers. To conduct its business, F owns several aircraft. As a condition of maintaining its airworthiness certificates, F is required by the FAA to establish and adhere to a continuous maintenance program for each aircraft in its fleet. F performs heavy maintenance on its airframes every 8 to 10 years. In Year 1, F purchased an aircraft for $15 million. In Year 16, F paid $2 million for the labor and materials necessary to perform the second heavy maintenance visit on the airframe of an aircraft. To perform the heavy maintenance visit, F extensively disassembles the airframe, removing items such as engines, landing gear, cabin and passenger compartment seats, side and ceiling panels, baggage stowage bins, galleys, lavatories, floor boards, cargo loading systems, and flight control surfaces. As specified by F's maintenance manual for the aircraft, F then performs certain tasks on the disassembled airframe for the purpose of preventing deterioration of the inherent safety and reliability levels of the airframe. These tasks include lubrication and service, operational and visual checks, inspection and functional checks, reconditioning of minor parts and components, and removal, discard, and replacement of certain life-limited single cell parts, such as cartridges, canisters, cylinders, and disks. Reconditioning of parts includes burnishing corrosion, repairing cracks, dents, gouges, punctures, tightening or replacing loose or missing fasteners, replacing damaged seals, gaskets, or valves, and similar activities. In addition to the tasks described above, to comply with certain FAA airworthiness directives, F inspects specific skin locations, applies doublers over small areas where cracks were found, adds structural reinforcements, and replaces skin panels on a small section of the fuselage. However, the heavy maintenance does not include the replacement of any major components or substantial structural parts of the aircraft with new components. In addition, the heavy maintenance visit does not bring the aircraft to the status of new, rebuilt, remanufactured, or a similar status under FAA guidelines or the manufacturer's original specifications. After the heavy maintenance, the aircraft was reassembled. Assume the aircraft, including the engines, is a unit of property and has a class life of 12 years under section 168(c). Although the heavy maintenance is performed after the end of the class life of the aircraft, F is not required to treat the heavy maintenance as a restoration and improvement of the unit of property under paragraph (k)(1)(v) of this section because, although extensive, the amounts paid do not restore the aircraft to like-new condition. See also paragraph (i)(1)(iii) of this section for the application of the safe harbor for routine maintenance.

Example 10. Replacement of major component or substantial structural part; personal property. G is a common carrier that owns a fleet of petroleum hauling trucks. G pays amounts to replace the existing engine, cab, and petroleum tank with a new engine, cab, and tank. Assume the tractor of the truck (which includes the cab and the engine) is a single unit of property and that the trailer (which contains the petroleum tank) is a separate unit of property. The new engine and the cab each constitute a part or combination of parts that comprise a major component of G's tractor, because they perform a discrete and critical function in the operation of the tractor. In addition, the cab constitutes a part or combination of parts that comprise a substantial structural part of G's tractor. Therefore, the amounts paid for the replacement of the engine and the cab must be capitalized under paragraph (k)(1)(vi) of this section. Moreover, the new petroleum tank constitutes a part or combination of parts that comprise a major component and a substantial structural part of the trailer. Accordingly, the amounts paid for the replacement of the tank also must be capitalized under paragraph (k)(1)(vi) of this section.

Example 11. Repair performed during restoration. Assume the same facts as in *Example 10*, except that, at the same time the engine and cab of the tractor are replaced, G pays amounts to paint the cab of the tractor with its company logo and to fix a broken taillight on the tractor. The repair of the broken taillight and the painting of the cab generally are deductible expenses under §1.162-4. However, under paragraph (g)(1)(i) of this section, a taxpayer must capitalize all the direct costs of an improvement and all the indirect costs that directly benefit or are incurred by reason of an improvement. Repairs and maintenance that do not directly benefit or are not incurred by reason of an improvement are not required to be capitalized under section 263(a), regardless of whether they are made at the same time as an improvement. For the amounts paid to paint the logo on the cab, G's need to paint the logo arose from the replacement of the cab with a new cab. Therefore, under paragraph (g)(1)(i) of this section, G must capitalize the amounts paid to paint the cab as part of the improvement to the tractor because these amounts directly benefit and are incurred by reason of the restoration of the tractor. The amounts paid to repair the broken taillight are not for the replacement of a major component, do not directly benefit, and are not incurred by reason of the replacement of the cab or the engine under paragraph (g)(1)(i) of this section, even though the repair was performed at the same time as these replacements. Thus, G is not required to capitalize the amounts paid to repair the broken taillight.

Example 12. Related amounts to replace major component or substantial structural part; personal property. (i) H owns a retail gasoline station, consisting of a paved area used for automobile access to the pumps and parking areas, a building used to market gasoline, and a canopy covering the gasoline pumps. The premises also consist of underground storage tanks (USTs) that are connected by piping to the pumps and are part of the gasoline pumping system used in the immediate retail sale of gas. The USTs are components of the gasoline pumping system. To comply with regulations issued by the Environmental Protection Agency, H is required to remove and replace leaking USTs. In Year 1, H hires a contractor to perform the removal and replacement, which consists of removing the old tanks and installing new tanks with leak detection systems. The removal of the old tanks includes removing the paving material covering the tanks, excavating a hole large enough to gain access to the old tanks, disconnecting any strapping and pipe connections to the old tanks, and lifting the old tanks out of the hole. Installation of the new tanks includes placement of a liner in the excavated hole, placement of the new tanks, installation of a leak detection system, installation of an overfill system, connection of the tanks to the pipes leading to the pumps, backfilling of the hole, and replacement of the paving. H also is required to pay a permit fee to the county to undertake the installation of the new tanks.

(ii) H pays the permit fee to the county on October 15, Year 1. On December 15, Year 1, the contractor completes the removal of the old USTs and bills H for the costs of removal. On January 15, Year 2, the contractor completes the installation of the new USTs and bills H for the remainder of the work. Assume that H computes its taxes on a calendar year basis and H's gasoline pumping system is the unit of property. Under paragraph (k)(1)(vi) of this section, H must capitalize the amounts paid to replace the USTs as a restoration to the gasoline pumping system because the USTs are parts or combinations of parts that comprise a major component and substantial structural part of the gasoline pumping system. Moreover, under paragraph (g)(2) of this section, H must capitalize the costs of removing the old USTs because H has not taken a loss on the disposition of the USTs, and the amounts to remove the USTs directly benefit and are incurred by reason of the restoration of, and improvement to, the gasoline pumping system. In addition, under paragraph (g)(1) of this section, H must capitalize the permit fees because they directly benefit and are incurred by reason of the improvement to the gasoline pumping system. Finally, under paragraph (g)(3) of this section, H must capitalize the related amounts paid to improve the gasoline pumping system, including the permit fees, the amount paid to remove the old USTs, and the amount paid to install the new USTs, even though the amounts were separately invoiced, paid to different parties, and incurred in different tax years.

Example 13. Not replacement of major component; incidental. J owns a machine shop in which it makes dies used by manufacturers. In Year 1, J purchased a drill press for use in its production process. In Year 3, J discovers that the power switch assembly, which controls the supply of electric power to the drill press, has become damaged and cannot operate. To correct this problem, J pays amounts to replace the power switch assembly with comparable and commercially available replacement parts. Assume that the drill press is a unit of property under paragraph (e) of this section and the power switch assembly is a small component of the drill press that may be removed and installed with relative ease. The power switch assembly is not a major component of the unit of property under paragraph (k)(6)(i)(A) of this section because, although the power assembly may affect the function of J's drill press by controlling the supply of electric power, the power assembly is an incidental component of the drill press. In addition, the power assembly is not a substantial structural part of J's drill press under paragraph (k)(6)(i)(B) of this section. Therefore, J is not required to capitalize the costs to replace the power switch assembly under paragraph (k)(1)(vi) of this section.

Example 14. Replacement of major component or substantial structural part; roof. K owns a manufacturing building. K discovers several leaks in the roof of the building and hires a contractor to inspect and fix the roof. The contractor discovers that a major portion of the decking has rotted and recommends the replacement of the entire roof. K pays the contractor to replace the entire roof, including the decking, insulation, asphalt, and various coatings. Under paragraphs (e)(2)(ii) and (k)(2) of this section, an amount is paid to improve a building if the amount is paid to restore the building structure or any building system. The roof is part of the building structure as defined under paragraph (e)(2)(ii)(A) of this section. Because the entire roof performs a discrete and critical function in the building structure, the roof comprises a major component of the building structure under paragraph (k)(6)(ii)(A) of this section. In addition, because the roof comprises a large portion of the physical structure of the building structure, the roof comprises a substantial structural part of the building structure under paragraph (k)(6)(ii)(B) of this section. Therefore, under either analysis, K must treat the amount paid to replace the roof as a restoration of the building under paragraphs (k)(1)(vi) and (k)(2) of this section and must capitalize the amount paid as an improvement under paragraph (d)(2) of this section.

Example 15. Not replacement of major component or substantial structural part; roof membrane. L owns a building in which it conducts its retail business. The roof decking over L's building is covered with a waterproof rubber membrane. Over time, the rubber membrane begins to wear, and L begins to experience leaks into its retail premises. However, the building is still functioning in L's business. To eliminate the problems, a contractor recommends that L replace the membrane on the roof with a new rubber membrane. Accordingly, L pays the contractor to strip the original membrane and replace it with a new rubber membrane. The new membrane is comparable to the original membrane but corrects the leakage problems. Under paragraphs (e)(2)(ii) and (k)(2) of this section, an amount is paid to improve a building if the amount is paid to restore the building structure or any building system. The roof, including the membrane, is part of the building structure as defined under paragraph (e)(2)(ii)(A) of this section. Because the entire roof performs a discrete and critical function in the building structure, the roof comprises a major component of the building structure under paragraph (k)(6)(ii)(A) of this section. Although the replacement membrane may aid in the function of the building structure, it does not, by itself, comprise a significant portion of the roof major component under paragraph (k)(6)(ii)(A) of this section. In addition, the replacement membrane does not comprise a substantial structural part of L's building structure under paragraph (k)(6)(ii)(B) of this section. Therefore, L is not required to capitalize the amount paid to replace the membrane as a restoration of the building under paragraph (k)(1)(vi) of this section.

Example 16. Not a replacement of major component or substantial structural part; HVAC system. M owns a building in which it operates an office that provides medical services. The building contains one HVAC system, which is comprised of three furnaces, three air conditioning units, and duct work that runs throughout the building to distribute the hot or cold air throughout the building. One furnace in M's building breaks down, and M pays an amount to replace it with a new furnace. Under paragraphs (e)(2)(ii) and (k)(2) of this section, an amount is paid to improve a building if the amount is paid to restore the building structure or any building system. The HVAC system, including the furnaces, is a building system under paragraph (e)(2)(ii)(B)(1) of this section. As the parts that provide the heating function in the system, the three furnaces, together, perform a discrete and critical function in the operation of the HVAC system and are therefore a major component of the HVAC system under paragraph (k)(6)(i)(A) of this section. However, the single furnace is not a significant portion of this major component of the HVAC system under paragraph (k)(6)(ii)(A) of this section, or a substantial structural part of the HVAC system under paragraph (k)(6)(ii)(B) of this section. Therefore, M is not required to treat the amount paid to replace the furnace as a restoration of the building under paragraph (k)(1)(vi) of this section.

Example 17. Replacement of major component or substantial structural part; HVAC system. N owns a large office building in which it provides consulting services. The building contains one HVAC system, which is comprised of one chiller unit, one boiler, pumps, duct work, diffusers, air handlers, outside air intake, and a cooling tower. The chiller unit includes the compressor, evaporator, condenser, and expansion valve, and it functions to cool the water used to generate air conditioning throughout the building. N pays an amount to replace the chiller with a comparable unit. Under paragraphs (e)(2)(ii) and (k)(2) of this section, an amount is paid to improve a building if the amount is paid to restore the building structure or any building system. The HVAC system, including the chiller unit, is a building system under paragraph (e)(2)(ii)(B)(1) of this section. The chiller unit performs a discrete and critical function in the operation of the HVAC system because it provides the cooling mechanism for the entire system. Therefore, the chiller unit is a major component of the HVAC system under paragraph (k)(6)(ii)(A) of this section. Because the chiller unit comprises a major component of a building system, N must treat the amount paid to replace the chiller unit as a restoration to the building under paragraphs (k)(1)(vi) and (k)(2) of this section and must capitalize the amount paid as an improvement to the building under paragraph (d)(2) of this section.

Example 18. Not replacement of major component or substantial structural part; HVAC system. O owns an office building that it uses to provide services to customers. The building contains a HVAC system that incorporates ten roof-mounted units that provide heating and air conditioning for the building. The HVAC system also consists of controls for the entire system and duct work that distributes the heated or cooled air to the various spaces in the building's interior. O begins to experience climate control problems in various offices throughout the office building and consults with a contractor to determine the cause. The contractor recommends that O replace three of the roof-mounted heating and cooling units. O pays an amount to replace the three specified units. No work is performed on the other roof-mounted heating and cooling units, the duct work, or the controls. Under paragraphs (e)(2)(ii) and (k)(2) of this section, an amount is paid to improve a building if the amount restores the building structure or any building system. The HVAC system, including the 10 roof-mounted heating and cooling units, is a building system under paragraph (e)(2)(ii)(B)(1) of this section. As the components that generate the heat and the air conditioning in the HVAC system, the 10 roof-mounted units, together, perform a discrete and critical function in the operation of the HVAC system and, therefore, are a major component of the HVAC system under paragraph (k)(6)(ii)(A) of this section. The three roof-mounted heating and cooling units are not a significant portion of a major component of the HVAC system under (k)(6)(ii)(A) of this section, or a substantial structural part of the HVAC system, under paragraph (k)(6)(ii)(B) of this section. Accordingly, O is not required to treat the amount paid to replace the three roof-mounted heating and cooling units as a restoration of the building under paragraph (k)(1)(iv) of this section.

Example 19. Replacement of major component or substantial structural part; fire protection system. P owns a building that it uses to operate its business. P pays an amount to replace the sprinkler system in the building with a new sprinkler system. Under paragraphs (e)(2)(ii) and (k)(2) of this section, an amount is paid to improve a building if the amount restores the building structure or any building system. The fire protection and alarm system, including the sprinkler system, is a building system under paragraph (e)(2)(ii)(B)(6) of this section. As the component that provides the fire suppression mechanism in the system, the sprinkler system performs a discrete and critical function in the operation of the fire protection and alarm system and is therefore a major component of the system under paragraph (k)(6)(ii)(A) of this section. Because the sprinkler system comprises a major component of a building system, P must treat the amount paid to replace the sprinkler system as restoration to the building unit of property under paragraphs (k)(1)(vi) and (k)(2) of this section and must capitalize the amount paid as an improvement to the building under paragraph (d)(2) of this section.

Example 20. Replacement of major component or substantial structural part; electrical system. Q owns a building that it uses to operate its business. Q pays an amount to replace the wiring throughout the building with new wiring that meets building code requirements. Under paragraphs (e)(2)(ii) and (k)(2) of this section, an amount is paid to improve a building if the amount restores the building structure or any building system. The electrical system, including the wiring, is a building system under paragraph (e)(2)(ii)(B)(3) of this section. As the component that distributes the electricity throughout the system, the wiring performs a discrete and critical function in the operation of the electrical system under paragraph (k)(6)(ii)(A) of this section. The wiring also comprises a large portion of the physical structure of the electrical system under paragraph (k)(6)(ii)(B) of this section. Because the wiring comprises a major component and a substantial structural part of a building system, Q must treat the amount paid to replace the wiring as a restoration to the building under paragraphs (k)(1)(vi) and (k)(2) of this section and must capitalize the amount paid as an improvement to the building under paragraph (d)(2) of this section.

Example 21. Not a replacement of major component or substantial structural part; electrical system. R owns a building that it uses to operate its business. R pays an amount to replace 30 percent of the wiring throughout the building with new wiring that meets building code requirements. Under paragraphs (e)(2)(ii) and (k)(2) of this section, an amount is paid to improve a building if the amount restores the building structure or any building system. The electrical system, including the wiring, is a building system under paragraph (e)(2)(ii)(B)(3) of this section. All the wiring in the building comprises a major component because it performs a discrete and critical function in the operation of the electrical system. However, the portion of the wiring that was replaced is not a significant portion of the wiring major component under paragraph (k)(6)(ii)(A) of this section, nor does it comprise a substantial structural part of the electrical system under paragraph (k)(6)(ii)(B) of this section. Therefore, under para-

graph (k)(6) of this section, the replacement of 30 percent of the wiring is not the replacement of a major component or substantial structural part of the building, and R is not required to treat the amount paid to replace 30 percent of the wiring as a restoration to the building under paragraph (k)(1)(iv) of this section.

Example 22. Replacement of major component or substantial structural part; plumbing system. S owns a building in which it conducts a retail business. The retail building has three floors. The retail building has men's and women's restrooms on two of the three floors. S decides to update the restrooms by paying an amount to replace the plumbing fixtures in all of the restrooms, including all the toilets and sinks, with modern style plumbing fixtures of similar quality and function. S does not replace the pipes connecting the fixtures to the building's plumbing system. Under paragraphs (e)(2)(ii) and (k)(2) of this section, an amount is paid to improve a building if the amount restores the building structure or any building system. The plumbing system, including the plumbing fixtures, is a building system under paragraph (e)(2)(ii)(B)(2) of this section. All the toilets together perform a discrete and critical function in the operation of the plumbing system, and all the sinks, together, also perform a discrete and critical function in the operation of the plumbing system. Therefore, under paragraph (k)(6)(ii)(A) of this section, all the toilets comprise a major component of the plumbing system, and all the sinks comprise a major component of the plumbing system. Accordingly, S must treat the amount paid to replace all of the toilets and all of the sinks as a restoration of the building under paragraphs (k)(1)(vi) and (k)(2) of this section and must capitalize the amount paid as an improvement to the building under paragraph (d)(2) of this section.

Example 23. Not replacement of major component or substantial structural part; plumbing system. Assume the same facts as *Example 22* except that S does not update all the bathroom fixtures. Instead, S only pays an amount to replace 8 of the total of 20 sinks located in the various restrooms. The 8 replaced sinks, by themselves, do not comprise a significant portion of a major component (the 20 sinks) of the plumbing system under paragraph (k)(6)(ii)(A) of this section nor do they comprise a large portion of the physical structure of the plumbing system under paragraph (k)(6)(ii)(B) of this section. Therefore, under paragraph (k)(6) of this section, the replacement of the eight sinks does not constitute the replacement of a major component or substantial structural part of the building, and S is not required to treat the amount paid to replace the eight sinks as a restoration of a building under paragraph (k)(1)(iv) of this section.

Example 24. Replacement of major component or substantial structural part; plumbing system. (i) T owns and operates a hotel building. T decides that, to attract customers and to remain competitive, it needs to update the guest rooms in its facility. Accordingly, T pays amounts to replace the bathtubs, toilets, and sinks, and to repair, repaint, and retile the bathroom walls and floors, which is necessitated by the installation of the new plumbing components. The replacement bathtubs, toilets, sinks, and tile are new and in a different style, but are similar in function and quality to the replaced items. T also pays amounts to replace certain section 1245 property, such as the guest room furniture, carpeting, drapes, table lamps, and partition walls separating the bathroom area. T completes this work on two floors at a time, closing those floors and leaving the rest of the hotel open for business. In Year 1, T pays amounts to perform the updates for 4 of the 20 hotel room floors and expects to complete the renovation of the remaining rooms over the next two years.

(ii) Under paragraphs (e)(2)(ii) and (k)(2) of this section, an amount is paid to improve a building if the amount restores the building structure or any building system. The plumbing system, including the bathtubs, toilets, and sinks, is a building system under paragraph (e)(2)(ii)(B)(2) of this section. All the bathtubs, together, all the toilets, together, and all the sinks together in the hotel building perform discrete and critical functions in the operation of the plumbing system under paragraph (k)(6)(ii)(A) of this section and comprise a large portion of the physical structure of the plumbing system under paragraph (k)(6)(ii)(B) of this section. Therefore, under paragraph (k)(6)(ii) of this section, these plumbing components comprise major components and substantial structural parts of the plumbing system, and T must treat the amount paid to replace these plumbing components as a restoration of, and improvement to, the building under paragraphs (k)(1)(vi) and (k)(2) of this section. In addition, under paragraph (g)(1)(i) of this section, T must treat the costs of repairing, repainting, and retiling the bathroom walls and floors as improvement costs because these costs directly benefit and are incurred by reason of the improvement to the building. Further, under paragraph (g)(3) of this section, T must treat the costs incurred in Years 1, 2, and 3 for the bathroom remodeling as improvement costs, even though they are incurred over a period of several taxable years, because they are related amounts paid to improve the building unit of property. Accordingly, under paragraph (d)(2) of this section, T must treat all the amounts it incurs to update its hotel restrooms as an improvement to the hotel building and capitalize these amounts.

In addition, under §1.263(a)-2 of the regulations, T must capitalize the amounts paid to acquire and install each section 1245 property.

Example 25. Not replacement of major component or substantial structural part; windows. U owns a large office building that it uses to provide office space for employees that manage U's operations. The building has 300 exterior windows that represent 25 percent of the total surface area of the building. In Year 1, U pays an amount to replace 100 of the exterior windows that had become damaged. At the time of these replacements, U has no plans to replace any other windows in the near future. Under paragraphs (e)(2)(ii) and (k)(2) of this section, an amount is paid to improve a building if the amount restores the building structure or any building system. The exterior windows are part of the building structure as defined under paragraph (e)(2)(ii)(A) of this section. The 300 exterior windows perform a discrete and critical function in the operation of the building structure and are, therefore, a major component of the building structure under paragraph (k)(6)(i)(A) of this section. However, the 100 windows do not comprise a significant portion of this major component of the building structure under paragraph (k)(6)(ii)(A) of this section or a substantial structural part of the building structure under paragraph (k)(6)(ii)(B) of this section. Therefore, under paragraph (k)(6) of this section, the replacement of the 100 windows does not constitute the replacement of a major component or substantial structural part of the building, and U is not required to treat the amount paid to replace the 100 windows as restoration of the building under paragraph (k)(1)(iv) of this section.

Example 26. Replacement of major component; windows. Assume the same facts as *Example 25*, except that that U replaces 200 of the 300 windows on the building. The 300 exterior windows perform a discrete and critical function in the operation of the building structure and are, therefore, a major component of the building structure under paragraph (k)(6)(i)(A) of this section. The 200 windows comprise a significant portion of this major component of the building structure under paragraph (k)(6)(ii)(A) of this section. Therefore, under paragraph (k)(6) of this section, the replacement of the 200 windows comprise the replacement of a major component of the building structure. Accordingly, U must treat the amount paid to replace the 200 windows as a restoration of the building under paragraphs (k)(1)(vi) and (k)(2) of this section and must capitalize the amount paid as an improvement to the building under paragraph (d)(2) of this section.

Example 27. Replacement of substantial structural part; windows. Assume the same facts as *Example 25*, except that the building is a modern design and the 300 windows represent 90 percent of the total surface area of the building. U replaces 100 of the 300 windows on the building. The 300 exterior windows perform a discrete and critical function in the operation of the building structure and are, therefore, a major component of the building structure under paragraph (k)(6)(i)(A) of this section. The 100 windows do not comprise a significant portion of this major component of the building structure under paragraph (k)(6)(ii)(A) of this section, however, they do comprise a substantial structural part of the building structure under paragraph (k)(6)(ii)(B) of this section. Therefore, under paragraph (k)(6) of this section, the replacement of the 100 windows comprise the replacement of a substantial structural part of the building structure. Accordingly, U must treat the amount paid to replace the 100 windows as a restoration of the building unit of property under paragraphs (k)(1)(vi) and (k)(2) of this section and must capitalize the amount paid as an improvement to the building under paragraph (d)(2) of this section.

Example 28. Not replacement of major component or substantial structural part; floors. V owns and operates a hotel building. V decides to refresh the appearance of the hotel lobby by replacing the floors in the lobby. The hotel lobby comprises less than 10 percent of the square footage of the entire hotel building. V pays an amount to replace the wood flooring in the lobby with new wood flooring of a similar quality. V did not replace any other flooring in the building. Assume that the wood flooring constitutes section 1250 property. Under paragraphs (e)(2)(ii) and (k)(2) of this section, an amount is paid to improve a building if the amount restores the building structure or any building system. The wood flooring is part of the building structure under paragraph (e)(2)(ii)(A) of this section. All the floors in the hotel building comprise a major component of the building structure because they perform a discrete and critical function in the operation of the building structure. However, the lobby floors are not a significant portion of a major component (that is, all the floors) under paragraph (k)(6)(ii)(A) of this section, nor do the lobby floors comprise a substantial structural part of the building structure under paragraph (k)(6)(ii)(B) of this section. Therefore, under paragraph (k)(6) of this section, the replacement of the lobby floors is not the replacement of a major component or substantial structural part of the building unit of property, and V is not required to treat the amount paid for the replacement of the lobby floors as a restoration to the building under paragraph (k)(1)(iv) of this section.

Example 29. Replacement of major component or substantial structural part; floors. Assume the same facts as *Example 28*, except that V decides to refresh the appearance of all the public areas of the hotel building by replacing all the floors in the public areas. To that end, V pays an amount to replace all the wood floors in all the public areas of the hotel building with new wood floors. The public areas include the lobby, the hallways, the meeting rooms, the ballrooms, and other public rooms throughout the hotel interiors. The public areas comprise approximately 40 percent of the square footage of the entire hotel building. All the floors in the hotel building comprise a major component of the building structure because they perform a discrete and critical function in the operation of the building structure. The floors in all the public areas of the hotel comprise a significant portion of a major component (that is, all the building floors) of the building structure. Therefore, under paragraph (k)(6)(ii)(A) of this section, the replacement of all the public area floors constitutes the replacement of a major component of the building structure. Accordingly, V must treat the amount paid to replace the public area floors as a restoration of the building unit of property under paragraphs (k)(1)(vi) and (k)(2) of this section and must capitalize the amounts as an improvement to the building under paragraph (d)(2) of this section.

Example 30. Replacement with no disposition. (i) X owns an office building with four elevators serving all floors in the building. X replaces one of the elevators. The elevator is a structural component of the office building. X chooses to apply §1.168(i)-8 to taxable years beginning on or after January 1, 2012, and before the applicability date of the final regulations. In accordance with §1.168(i)-8(c)(4)(ii)(A), the office building (including its structural components) is the asset for tax disposition purposes. X also does not make the partial disposition election provided under §1.168(i)-8(d)(2), for the elevator. Thus, the retirement of the replaced elevator is not a disposition under section 168, and no loss is taken into account for purposes of paragraph (k)(1)(i) of this section.

(ii) Under paragraphs (e)(2)(ii) and (k)(2) of this section, an amount is paid to improve a building if the amount restores the building structure or any building system. The elevator system, including all four elevators, is a building system under paragraph (e)(2)(ii)(B)(5) of this section. The replacement elevator does not perform a discrete and critical function in the operation of elevator system under paragraph (k)(6)(ii)(A) of this section nor does it comprise a large portion of the physical structure of the elevator system under paragraph (k)(6)(ii)(B) of this section. Therefore, under paragraph (k)(6) of this section, the replacement elevator does not constitute the replacement of a major component or substantial structural part of the elevator system. Accordingly, X is not required to treat the amount paid to replace the elevator as a restoration to the building under either paragraph (k)(1)(i) or paragraph (k)(1)(vi) of this section.

Example 31. Replacement with disposition. The facts are the same as in *Example 30*, except X makes the partial disposition election provided under paragraph §1.168(i)-8(d)(2), for the elevator. Although the office building (including its structural components) is the asset for disposition purposes, the result of X making the partial disposition election for the elevator is that the retirement of the replaced elevator is a disposition. Thus, depreciation for the retired elevator ceases at the time of its retirement (taking into account the applicable convention); and X recognizes a loss upon this retirement. Accordingly, X must treat the amount paid to replace the elevator as a restoration of the building under paragraphs (k)(1)(i) and (k)(2) of this section and must capitalize the amount paid as an improvement to the building under paragraph (d)(2) of this section. In addition, the replacement elevator is treated as a separate asset for tax disposition purposes pursuant to §1.168(i)-8(c)(4)(ii)(D), and for depreciation purposes pursuant to section 168(i)(6).

(l) *Capitalization of amounts to adapt property to a new or different use.*—(1) *In general.*—A taxpayer must capitalize as an improvement an amount paid to adapt a unit of property to a new or different use. In general, an amount is paid to adapt a unit of property to a new or different use if the adaptation is not consistent with the taxpayer's ordinary use of the unit of property at the time originally placed in service by the taxpayer.

(2) *Application of adaption rule to buildings.*—In the case of a building, an amount is paid to improve a building if it is paid to adapt to a new or different use a property specified under paragraph (e)(2)(ii) (building), paragraph (e)(2)(iii)(B) (condominium), paragraph (e)(2)(iv)(B) (cooperative), or paragraph (e)(2)(v)(B) (leased building or leased portion of building) of this section. For example, an amount is paid to improve a building if it is paid to adapt the building structure or any one of its buildings systems to a new or different use.

(3) *Examples.*—The following examples illustrate the application of this paragraph (l) only and do not address whether capitalization

is required under another provision of this section or under another provision of the Code (for example, section 263A). Unless otherwise stated, assume that the taxpayer has not properly deducted a loss for any unit of property, asset, or component of a unit of property that is removed and replaced.

Example 1. New or different use; change in building use. A is a manufacturer and owns a manufacturing building that it has used for manufacturing since Year 1, when A placed it in service. In Year 30, A pays an amount to convert its manufacturing building into a show-room for its business. To convert the facility, A removes and replaces various structural components to provide a better layout for the showroom and its offices. A also repaints the building interiors as part of the conversion. When building materials are removed and replaced, A uses comparable and commercially available replacement materials. Under paragraphs (l)(2) and (e)(2)(ii) of this section, an amount is paid to improve A's manufacturing building if the amount adapts the building structure or any designated building system to a new or different use. Under paragraph (l)(1) of this section, the amount paid to convert the manufacturing building into a showroom adapts the building structure to a new or different use because the conversion to a showroom is not consistent with A's ordinary use of the building structure at the time it was placed in service. Therefore, A must capitalize the amount paid to convert the building into a showroom as an improvement to the building under paragraphs (d)(3) and (l) of this section.

Example 2. Not a new or different use; leased building. B owns and leases out space in a building consisting of twenty retail spaces. The space was designed to be reconfigured; that is, adjoining spaces could be combined into one space. One of the tenants expands its occupancy by leasing two adjoining retail spaces. To facilitate the new lease, B pays an amount to remove the walls between the three retail spaces. Assume that the walls between spaces are part of the building and its structural components. Under paragraphs (l)(2) and (e)(2)(ii) of this section, an amount is paid to improve B's building if it adapts the building structure or any of the building systems to a new or different use. Under paragraph (l)(1) of this section, the amount paid to convert three retail spaces into one larger space for an existing tenant does not adapt B's building structure to a new or different use because the combination of retail spaces is consistent with B's intended, ordinary use of the building structure. Therefore, the amount paid by B to remove the walls does not improve the building under paragraph (l) of this section and is not required to be capitalized under paragraph (d)(3) of this section.

Example 3. Not a new or different use; preparing building for sale. C owns a building consisting of twenty retail spaces. C decides to sell the building. In anticipation of selling the building, C pays an amount to repaint the interior walls and to refinish the hardwood floors. Under paragraphs (l)(2) and (e)(2)(ii) of this section, an amount is paid to improve C's building to a new or different use if it adapts the building structure or any of the building systems to a new or different use. Preparing the building for sale does not constitute a new or different use for the building structure under paragraph (l)(1) of this section. Therefore, the amount paid by C to prepare the building structure for sale does not improve the building under paragraph (l) of this section and is not required to be capitalized under paragraph (d)(3) of this section.

Example 4. New or different use; land. D owns a parcel of land on which it previously operated a manufacturing facility. Assume that the land is the unit of property. During the course of D's operation of the manufacturing facility, the land became contaminated with wastes from its manufacturing processes. D discontinues manufacturing operations at the site and decides to develop the property for residential housing. In anticipation of building residential property, D pays an amount to remediate the contamination caused by D's manufacturing process. In addition, D pays an amount to regrade the land so that it can be used for residential purposes. Amounts that D pays to clean up wastes do not adapt the land to a new or different use, regardless of the extent to which the land was cleaned, because this cleanup merely returns the land to the condition it was in before the land was contaminated in D's operations. Therefore, D is not required to capitalize the amount paid for the cleanup under paragraph (l)(1) of this section. However, the amount paid to regrade the land so that it can be used for residential purposes adapts the land to a new or different use that is inconsistent with D's intended ordinary use of the property at the time it was placed in service. Accordingly, the amounts paid to regrade the land must be capitalized as improvements to the land under paragraphs (d)(3) and (l) of this section.

Example 5. New or different use; part of building. (i) E owns a building in which it operates a retail drug store. The store consists of a pharmacy for filling medication prescriptions and various departments where customers can purchase food, toiletries, home goods, school supplies, cards, over-the-counter medications, and other similar items. E decides to create a walk-in medical clinic where nurse practitioners and physicians' assistants diagnose, treat, and write

prescriptions for common illnesses and injuries, administer common vaccinations, conduct physicals and wellness screenings, and provide routine lab tests and services for common chronic conditions. To create the clinic, E pays amounts to reconfigure the pharmacy building. E incurs costs to build new walls creating an examination room, lab room, reception area, and waiting area. E installs additional plumbing, electrical wiring, and outlets to support the lab. E also acquires section 1245 property, such as computers, furniture, and equipment necessary for the new clinic. E treats the amounts paid for those units of property as costs of acquiring new units of property under § 1.263(a)-2.

(ii) Under paragraphs (l)(2) and (e)(2)(ii) of this section, an amount is paid to improve E's building if it adapts the building structure or any of the building systems to a new or different use. Under paragraph (l)(1) of this section, the amount paid to convert part of the retail drug store building structure into a medical clinic adapts the building structure to a new and different use, because the use of the building structure to provide clinical medical services is not consistent with E's intended ordinary use of the building structure at the time it was placed in service. Similarly, the amounts paid to add to the plumbing system and the electrical systems to support the new medical services is not consistent with E's intended ordinary use of these systems when the systems were placed in service. Therefore, E must treat the amount paid for the conversion of the building structure, plumbing system, and electrical system as an improvement to the building and capitalize the amount under paragraphs (d)(3) and (l) of this section.

Example 6. Not a new or different use; part of building. (i) F owns a building in which it operates a grocery store. The grocery store includes various departments for fresh produce, frozen foods, fresh meats, dairy products, toiletries, and over-the-counter medicines. The grocery store also includes separate counters for deli meats, prepared foods, and baked goods, often made to order. To better accommodate its customers' shopping needs, F decides to add a sushi bar where customers can order freshly prepared sushi from the counter for take-home or to eat at the counter. To create the sushi bar, F pays amounts to add a sushi counter and chairs, add additional wiring and outlets to support the counter, and install additional pipes and a sink, to provide for the safe handling of the food. F also pays amounts to replace flooring and wall coverings in the sushi bar area with decorative coverings to reflect more appropriate décor. Assume the sushi counter and chairs are section 1245 property, and F treats the amounts paid for those units of property as costs of acquiring new units of property under § 1.263(a)-2.

(ii) Under paragraphs (l)(2) and (e)(2)(ii) of this section, an amount is paid to improve F's building if it adapts the building structure or any of the building systems to a new or different use. Under paragraph (l)(1) of this section, the amount paid to convert a part of F's retail grocery into a sushi bar area does not adapt F's building structure, plumbing system, or electrical system to a new or different use, because the sale of sushi is consistent with F's intended, ordinary use of the building structure and these systems in its grocery sales business, which includes selling food to its customers at various specialized counters. Accordingly, the amount paid by F to replace the wall and floor finishes, add wiring, and add plumbing to create the sushi bar space does not improve the building unit of property under paragraph (l) of this section and is not required to be capitalized under paragraph (d)(3) of this section.

Example 7. Not a new or different use; part of building. (i) G owns a hospital with various departments dedicated to the provision of clinical medical care. To better accommodate its patients' needs, G decides to modify the emergency room space to provide both emergency care and outpatient surgery. To modify the space, G pays amounts to move interior walls, add additional wiring and outlets, replace floor tiles and doors, and repaint the walls. To complete the outpatient surgery center, G also pays amounts to install miscellaneous medical equipment necessary for the provision of surgical services. Assume the medical equipment is section 1245 property, and G treats the amounts paid for those units of property as costs of acquiring new units of property under § 1.263(a)-2.

(ii) Under paragraphs (l)(2) and (e)(2)(ii) of this section, an amount is paid to improve G's building if it adapts the building structure or any of the building systems to a new or different use. Under paragraph (l)(1) of this section, the amount paid to convert part of G's emergency room into an outpatient surgery center does not adapt G's building structure or electrical system to a new or different use, because the provision of outpatient surgery is consistent with G's intended, ordinary use of the building structure and these systems in its clinical medical care business. Accordingly, the amounts paid by G to relocate interior walls, add additional wiring and outlets, replace floor tiles and doors, and repaint the walls to create outpatient surgery space do not improve the building under paragraph (l) of this section and are not required to be capitalized under paragraph (d)(3) of this section.

(m) *Optional regulatory accounting method.*—(1) *In general.*—This paragraph (m) provides an optional simplified method (the regulatory accounting method) for regulated taxpayers to determine whether amounts paid to repair, maintain, or improve tangible property are to be treated as deductible expenses or capital expenditures. A taxpayer that uses the regulatory accounting method described in paragraph (m)(3) of this section must use that method for property subject to regulatory accounting instead of determining whether amounts paid to repair, maintain, or improve property are capital expenditures or deductible expenses under the general principles of sections 162(a), 212, and 263(a). Thus, the capitalization rules in paragraph (d) (and the routine maintenance safe harbor described in paragraph (i)) of this section do not apply to amounts paid to repair, maintain, or improve property subject to regulatory accounting by taxpayers that use the regulatory accounting method under this paragraph (m).

(2) *Eligibility for regulatory accounting method.*—A taxpayer that is engaged in a trade or business in a regulated industry is a regulated taxpayer and may use the regulatory accounting method under this paragraph (m). For purposes of this paragraph (m), a taxpayer is in a regulated industry only if the taxpayer is subject to the regulatory accounting rules of the Federal Energy Regulatory Commission (FERC), the Federal Communications Commission (FCC), or the Surface Transportation Board (STB).

(3) *Description of regulatory accounting method.*—Under the regulatory accounting method, a taxpayer must follow the method of accounting for regulatory accounting purposes that it is required to follow for FERC, FCC, or STB (whichever is applicable) in determining whether an amount paid repairs, maintains, or improves property under this section. Therefore, a taxpayer must capitalize for Federal income tax purposes an amount paid that is capitalized as an improvement for regulatory accounting purposes. A taxpayer may not capitalize for Federal income tax purposes under this section an amount paid that is not capitalized as an improvement for regulatory accounting purposes. A taxpayer that uses the regulatory accounting method must use that method for all of its tangible property that is subject to regulatory accounting rules. The method does not apply to tangible property that is not subject to regulatory accounting rules. The method also does not apply to property for the taxable years in which the taxpayer elected to apply the repair allowance under § 1.167(a)-11(d)(2). The regulatory accounting method is a method of accounting under section 446(a).

(4) *Examples.*—The following examples illustrate the application of this paragraph (m):

Example 1. Taxpayer subject to regulatory accounting rules of FERC. W is an electric utility company that operates a power plant that generates electricity and that owns and operates network assets to transmit and distribute the electricity to its customers. W is subject to the regulatory accounting rules of FERC, and W uses the regulatory accounting method under paragraph (m) of this section. W does not capitalize on its books and records for regulatory accounting purposes the cost of repairs and maintenance performed on its turbines or its network assets. Under the regulatory accounting method, W may not capitalize for Federal income tax purposes amounts paid for repairs performed on its turbines or its network assets.

Example 2. Taxpayer not subject to regulatory accounting rules of FERC. X is an electric utility company that operates a power plant to generate electricity. X previously was subject to the regulatory accounting rules of FERC, but currently X is not required to use FERC's regulatory accounting rules. X cannot use the regulatory accounting method provided in this paragraph (m).

Example 3. Taxpayer subject to regulatory accounting rules of FCC. Y is a telecommunications company that is subject to the regulatory accounting rules of the FCC. Y uses the regulatory accounting method under this paragraph (m). Y's assets include a telephone central office switching center, which contains numerous switches and various switching equipment. Y capitalizes on its books and records for regulatory accounting purposes the cost of replacing each switch. Under the regulatory accounting method, Y is required to capitalize for Federal income tax purposes amounts paid to replace each switch.

Example 4. Taxpayer subject to regulatory accounting rules of STB. Z is a Class I railroad that is subject to the regulatory accounting rules of the STB. Z uses the regulatory accounting method under this paragraph (m). Z capitalizes on its books and records for regulatory accounting purposes the cost of locomotive rebuilds. Under the regulatory accounting method, Z is required to capitalize for Federal income tax purposes amounts paid to rebuild its locomotives.

(n) *Election to capitalize repair and maintenance costs.*—(1) *In general.*—A taxpayer may elect to treat amounts paid during the taxable year for repair and maintenance (as defined under § 1.162-4) to tangible property as amounts paid to improve that property under this section and as an asset subject to the allowance for depreciation if the taxpayer incurs these amounts in carrying on the taxpayer's trade or business and if the taxpayer treats these amounts as capital expenditures on its books and records regularly used in computing income ("books and records"). A taxpayer that elects to apply this paragraph (n) in a taxable year must apply this paragraph to all amounts paid for repair and maintenance to tangible property that it treats as capital expenditures on its books and records in that taxable year. Any amounts for which this election is made shall not be treated as amounts paid for repair or maintenance under § 1.162-4.

(2) *Time and manner of election.*—A taxpayer makes this election under this paragraph (n) by attaching a statement to the taxpayer's timely filed original Federal tax return (including extensions) for the taxable year in which the taxpayer pays amounts described under paragraph (n)(1) of this paragraph. Sections 301.9100-1 through 301.9100-3 of this chapter provide the rules governing extensions of the time to make regulatory elections. The statement must be titled "Section 1.263(a)-3(n) Election" and include the taxpayer's name, address, taxpayer identification number, and a statement that the taxpayer is making the election to capitalize repair and maintenance costs under § 1.263(a)-3(n). In the case of a consolidated group filing a consolidated income tax return, the election is made for each member of the consolidated group by the common parent, and the statement must also include the names and taxpayer identification numbers of each member for which the election is made. In the case of an S corporation or a partnership, the election is made by the S corporation or partnership and not by the shareholders or partners. A taxpayer making this election for a taxable year must treat any amounts paid for repairs and maintenance during the taxable year that are capitalized on the taxpayer's books and records as improvements to tangible property. The taxpayer must begin to depreciate the cost of such improvements amounts when they are placed in service by the taxpayer under the applicable provisions of the Code and regulations. An election may not be made through the filing of an application for change in accounting method or, before obtaining the Commissioner's consent to make a late election, by filing an amended Federal tax return. The time and manner of electing to capitalize repair and maintenance costs under this paragraph (n) may be modified through guidance of general applicability (see § § 601.601(d)(2) and 601.602 of this chapter).

(3) *Exception.*—This paragraph (n) does not apply to amounts paid for repairs or maintenance of rotable or temporary spare parts to which the taxpayer applies the optional method of accounting for rotable and temporary spare parts under § 1.162-3(e).

(4) *Examples.*—The following examples illustrate the application of this paragraph (n):

Example 1. Election to capitalize routine maintenance on non-rotable part. (i) Q is a towboat operator that owns a fleet of towboats that it uses in its trade or business. Each towboat is equipped with two diesel-powered engines. Assume that each towboat, including its engines, is the unit of property and that a towboat has a class life of 18 years. Assume the towboat engines are not rotable spare parts under § 1.162-3(c)(2). In Year 1, Q acquired a new towboat, including its two engines, and placed the towboat into service. In Year 4, Q pays amounts to perform scheduled maintenance on both engines in the towboat. Assume that none of the exceptions set out in paragraph (i)(3) of this section apply to the scheduled maintenance costs and that the scheduled maintenance on Q's towboat is within the routine maintenance safe harbor under paragraph (i)(1)(ii) of this section. Accordingly, the amounts paid for the scheduled maintenance to its towboat engines in Year 4 are deemed not to improve the towboat and are not required to be capitalized under paragraph (d) of this section.

(ii) On its books and records, Q treats amounts paid for scheduled maintenance on its towboat engines as capital expenditures. For administrative convenience, Q decides to account for these costs in the same way for Federal income tax purposes. Under paragraph (n) of this section, in Year 4, Q may elect to capitalize the amounts paid for the scheduled maintenance on its towboat engines. If Q elects to capitalize such amounts, Q must capitalize all amounts paid for repair and maintenance to tangible property that Q treats as capital expenditures on its books and records in Year 4.

Example 2. No election to capitalize routine maintenance. Assume the same facts as *Example 1*, except in Year 8, Q pays amounts to perform scheduled maintenance for a second time on the towboat engines. On its books and records, Q treats the amounts paid for this scheduled maintenance as capital expenditures. However, in Year 8, Q decides not to make the election to capitalize the amounts paid for scheduled maintenance under paragraph (n) of this section. Because Q does not make the election under paragraph (n) for Year 8, Q may apply the routine maintenance safe harbor under paragraph (i)(1)(ii) of this section to the amounts paid in Year 8, and not treat these amounts as capital expenditures. Because the election is made for each taxable year, there is no effect on the scheduled maintenance costs capitalized by Q on its Federal tax return for Year 4.

Example 3. Election to capitalize replacement of building component. (i) R owns an office building that it uses to provide services to customers. The building contains a HVAC system that incorporates ten roof-mounted units that provide heating and air conditioning for different parts of the building. In Year 1, R pays an amount to replace 2 of the 10 units to address climate control problems in various offices throughout the office building. Assume that the replacement of the two units does not constitute an improvement to the HVAC system, and, accordingly, to the building unit of property under paragraph (d) of this section, and that R may deduct these amounts as repairs and maintenance under §1.162-4.

(ii) On its books and records, R treats amounts paid for the two HVAC components as capital expenditures. R determines that it would prefer to account for these amounts in the same way for Federal income tax purposes. Under this paragraph (n), in Year 1, R may elect to capitalize the amounts paid for the new HVAC components. If R elects to capitalize such amounts, R must capitalize all amounts paid for repair and maintenance to tangible property that R treats as capital expenditures on its books and records in Year 1.

(o) *Treatment of capital expenditures.*—Amounts required to be capitalized under this section are capital expenditures and must be taken into account through a charge to capital account or basis, or in the case of property that is inventory in the hands of a taxpayer, through inclusion in inventory costs.

(p) *Recovery of capitalized amounts.*—Amounts that are capitalized under this section are recovered through depreciation, cost of goods sold, or by an adjustment to basis at the time the property is placed in service, sold, used, or otherwise disposed of by the taxpayer. Cost recovery is determined by the applicable Code and regulation provisions relating to the use, sale, or disposition of property.

(q) *Accounting method changes.*—Except as otherwise provided in this section, a change to comply with this section is a change in method of accounting to which the provisions of sections 446 and 481 and the accompanying regulations apply. A taxpayer seeking to change to a method of accounting permitted in this section must secure the consent of the Commissioner in accordance with §1.446-1(e) and follow the administrative procedures issued under §1.446-1(e)(3)(ii) for obtaining the Commissioner's consent to change its accounting method.

(r) *Effective/applicability date.*—(1) *In general.*—Except for paragraphs (h), (m), and (n) of this section, this section applies to taxable years beginning on or after January 1, 2014. Paragraphs (h), (m), and (n) of this section apply to amounts paid in taxable years beginning on or after January 1, 2014. Except as provided in paragraphs (r)(2) and (r)(3) of this section, §1.263(a)-3 as contained in 26 CFR part 1 edition revised as of April 1, 2011, applies to taxable years beginning before January 1, 2014.

(2) *Early application of this section.*—(i) *In general.*—Except for paragraphs (h), (m), and (n) of this section, a taxpayer may choose to apply this section to taxable years beginning on or after January 1, 2012. A taxpayer may choose to apply paragraphs (h), (m), and (n) of this section to amounts paid in taxable years beginning on or after January 1, 2012.

(ii) *Transition rule for certain elections on 2012 or 2013 returns.*— If under paragraph (r)(2)(i) of this section, a taxpayer chooses to make the election to apply the safe harbor for small taxpayers under paragraph (h) of this section or the election to capitalize repair and maintenance costs under paragraph (n) of this section for amounts paid in its taxable year beginning on or after January 1, 2012, and ending on or before September 19, 2013 (applicable taxable year), and the taxpayer did not make the election specified in paragraph (h)(6) or paragraph (n)(2) of this section on its timely filed original Federal tax return for the applicable taxable year, the taxpayer must make the election specified in paragraph (h)(6) or paragraph (n)(2) of this section for the applicable taxable year by filing an amended Federal tax return (including the required statements) for the applicable taxable year on or before 180 days from the due date including extensions of the taxpayer's Federal tax return for the applicable taxable year, notwithstanding that the taxpayer may not have extended the due date.

(3) *Optional application of TD 9564.*—A taxpayer may choose to apply §1.263(a)-3T as contained in TD 9564 (76 FR 81060) December 27, 2011, to taxable years beginning on or after January 1, 2012, and before January 1, 2014. [Reg. §1.263(a)-3.]

☐ [*T.D. 6313, 9-16-58. Amended by T.D. 6548, 2-21-61; T.D. 6794, 1-25-65; T.D. 8121, 1-15-87; T.D. 9564, 12-23-2011; T.D. 9636, 9-13-2013 (corrected 7-18-2014) and T.D. 9689, 8-14-2014.]*

[Reg. §1.263(a)-4]

§1.263(a)-4. Amounts paid to acquire or create intangibles.—

(a) *Overview.*—This section provides rules for applying section 263(a) to amounts paid to acquire or create intangibles. Except to the extent provided in paragraph (d)(8) of this section, the rules provided by this section do not apply to amounts paid to acquire or create tangible assets. Paragraph (b) of this section provides a general principle of capitalization. Paragraphs (c) and (d) of this section identify intangibles for which capitalization is specifically required under the general principle. Paragraph (e) of this section provides rules for determining the extent to which taxpayers must capitalize transaction costs. Paragraph (f) of this section provides a 12-month rule intended to simplify the application of the general principle to certain payments that create benefits of a brief duration. Additional rules and examples relating to these provisions are provided in paragraphs (g) through (n) of this section. The applicability date of the rules in this section is provided in paragraph (o) of this section. Paragraph (p) of this section provides rules applicable to changes in methods of accounting made to comply with this section.

(b) *Capitalization with respect to intangibles.*—(1) *In general.*—Except as otherwise provided in this section, a taxpayer must capitalize—

(i) An amount paid to acquire an intangible (see paragraph (c) of this section);

(ii) An amount paid to create an intangible described in paragraph (d) of this section;

(iii) An amount paid to create or enhance a separate and distinct intangible asset within the meaning of paragraph (b)(3) of this section;

(iv) An amount paid to create or enhance a future benefit identified in published guidance in the Federal Register or in the Internal Revenue Bulletin (see §601.601(d)(2)(ii) of this chapter) as an intangible for which capitalization is required under this section; and

(v) An amount paid to facilitate (within the meaning of paragraph (e)(1) of this section) an acquisition or creation of an intangible described in paragraph (b)(1)(i), (ii), (iii) or (iv) of this section.

(2) *Published guidance.*—Any published guidance identifying a future benefit as an intangible for which capitalization is required under paragraph (b)(1)(iv) of this section applies only to amounts paid on or after the date of publication of the guidance.

(3) *Separate and distinct intangible asset.*—(i) *Definition.*—The term *separate and distinct intangible asset* means a property interest of ascertainable and measurable value in money's worth that is subject to protection under applicable state, federal or foreign law and the possession and control of which is intrinsically capable of being sold, transferred or pledged (ignoring any restrictions imposed on assignability) separate and apart from a trade or business. In addition, for purposes of this section, a fund (or similar account) is treated as a separate and distinct intangible asset of the taxpayer if amounts in the fund (or account) may revert to the taxpayer. The determination of whether a payment creates a separate and distinct intangible asset is made based on all of the facts and circumstances existing during the taxable year in which the payment is made.

(ii) *Creation or termination of contract rights.*—Amounts paid to another party to create, originate, enter into, renew or renegotiate an agreement with that party that produces rights or benefits for the taxpayer (and amounts paid to facilitate the creation, origination, enhancement, renewal or renegotiation of such an agreement) are treated as amounts that do not create (or facilitate the creation of) a separate and distinct intangible asset within the meaning of this paragraph (b)(3). Further, amounts paid to another party to terminate (or facilitate the termination of) an agreement with that party are treated as amounts that do not create a separate and distinct intangible asset within the meaning of this paragraph (b)(3). See paragraphs (d)(2), (d)(6), and (d)(7) of this section for rules that specifically require capitalization of amounts paid to create or terminate certain agreements.

(iii) *Amounts paid in performing services.*—Amounts paid in performing services under an agreement are treated as amounts that do not create a separate and distinct intangible asset within the meaning of this paragraph (b)(3), regardless of whether the amounts result in the creation of an income stream under the agreement.

(iv) *Creation of computer software.*—Except as otherwise provided in the Internal Revenue Code, the regulations thereunder, or other published guidance in the Federal Register or in the Internal Revenue Bulletin (see §601.601(d)(2)(ii) of this chapter), amounts paid to develop computer software are treated as amounts that do not create a separate and distinct intangible asset within the meaning of this paragraph (b)(3).

(v) *Creation of package design.*—Amounts paid to develop a package design are treated as amounts that do not create a separate and distinct intangible asset within the meaning of this paragraph (b)(3). For purposes of this section, the term *package design* means the specific graphic arrangement or design of shapes, colors, words, pictures, lettering, and other elements on a given product package, or the design of a container with respect to its shape or function.

(4) *Coordination with other provisions of the Internal Revenue Code.*—(i) *In general.*—Nothing in this section changes the treatment of an amount that is specifically provided for under any other provision of the Internal Revenue Code (other than section 162(a) or 212) or the regulations thereunder.

(ii) *Example.*—The following example illustrates the rule of this paragraph (b)(4):

Example. On January 1, 2004, G enters into an interest rate swap agreement with unrelated counterparty H under which, for a term of five years, G is obligated to make annual payments at 11% and H is obligated to make annual payments at LIBOR on a notional principal amount of $100 million. At the time G and H enter into this swap agreement, the rate for similar on-market swaps is LIBOR to 10%. To compensate for this difference, on January 1, 2004, H pays G a yield adjustment fee of $3,790,786. This yield adjustment fee constitutes an amount paid to create an intangible and would be capitalized under paragraph (d)(2) of this section. However, because the yield adjustment fee is a nonperiodic payment on a notional principal contract as defined in §1.446-3(c), the treatment of this fee is governed by §1.446-3 and not this section.

(c) *Acquired intangibles.*—(1) *In general.*—A taxpayer must capitalize amounts paid to another party to acquire any intangible from that party in a purchase or similar transaction. Examples of intangibles within the scope of this paragraph (c) include, but are not limited to, the following (if acquired from another party in a purchase or similar transaction):

(i) An ownership interest in a corporation, partnership, trust, estate, limited liability company, or other entity.

(ii) A debt instrument, deposit, stripped bond, stripped coupon (including a servicing right treated for federal income tax purposes as a stripped coupon), regular interest in a REMIC or FASIT, or any other intangible treated as debt for federal income tax purposes.

(iii) A financial instrument, such as—

(A) A notional principal contract;

(B) A foreign currency contract;

(C) A futures contract;

(D) A forward contract (including an agreement under which the taxpayer has the right and obligation to provide or to acquire property (or to be compensated for such property, regardless of whether the taxpayer provides or acquires the property));

(E) An option (including an agreement under which the taxpayer has the right to provide or to acquire property (or to be compensated for such property, regardless of whether the taxpayer provides or acquires the property)); and

(F) Any other financial derivative.

(iv) An endowment contract, annuity contract, or insurance contract.

(v) Non-functional currency.

(vi) A lease.

(vii) A patent or copyright.

(viii) A franchise, trademark or tradename (as defined in §1.197-2(b)(10)).

(ix) An assembled workforce (as defined in §1.197-2(b)(3)).

(x) Goodwill (as defined in §1.197-2(b)(1)) or going concern value (as defined in §1.197-2(b)(2)).

(xi) A customer list.

(xii) A servicing right (for example, a mortgage servicing right that is not treated for federal income tax purposes as a stripped coupon).

(xiii) A customer-based intangible (as defined in §1.197-2(b)(6)) or supplier-based intangible (as defined in §1.197-2(b)(7)).

(xiv) Computer software.

(xv) An agreement providing either party the right to use, possess or sell an intangible described in paragraphs (c)(1)(i) through (v) of this section.

(2) *Readily available software.*—An amount paid to obtain a nonexclusive license for software that is (or has been) readily available to the general public on similar terms and has not been substantially modified (within the meaning of §1.197-2(c)(4)) is treated for purposes of this paragraph (c) as an amount paid to another party to acquire an intangible from that party in a purchase or similar transaction.

(3) *Intangibles acquired from an employee.*—Amounts paid to an employee to acquire an intangible from that employee are not required to be capitalized under this section if the amounts are includible in the employee's income in connection with the performance of services under section 61 or 83. For purposes of this section, whether an individual is an employee is determined in accordance with the rules contained in section 3401(c) and the regulations thereunder.

(4) *Examples.*—The following examples illustrate the rules of this paragraph (c):

Example 1. Debt instrument. X corporation, a commercial bank, purchases a portfolio of existing loans from Y corporation, another financial institution. X pays Y $2,000,000 in exchange for the portfolio. The $2,000,000 paid to Y constitutes an amount paid to acquire an intangible from Y and must be capitalized.

Example 2. Option. W corporation owns all of the outstanding stock of X corporation. Y corporation holds a call option entitling it to purchase from W all of the outstanding stock of X at a certain price per share. Z corporation acquires the call option from Y in exchange for $5,000,000. The $5,000,000 paid to Y constitutes an amount paid to acquire an intangible from Y and must be capitalized.

Example 3. Ownership interest in a corporation. Same as *Example 2*, but assume Z exercises its option and purchases from W all of the outstanding stock of X in exchange for $100,000,000. The $100,000,000 paid to W constitutes an amount paid to acquire an intangible from W and must be capitalized.

Example 4. Customer list. N corporation, a retailer, sells its products through its catalog and mail order system. N purchases a customer list from R corporation. N pays R $100,000 in exchange for the customer list. The $100,000 paid to R constitutes an amount paid to acquire an intangible from R and must be capitalized.

Example 5. Goodwill. Z corporation pays W corporation $10,000,000 to purchase all of the assets of W in a transaction that constitutes an applicable asset acquisition under section 1060(c). Of the $10,000,000 consideration paid in the transaction, $9,000,000 is allocable to tangible assets purchased from W and $1,000,000 is allocable to goodwill. The $1,000,000 allocable to goodwill constitutes an amount paid to W to acquire an intangible from W and must be capitalized.

(d) *Created intangibles.*—(1) *In general.*—Except as provided in paragraph (f) of this section (relating to the 12-month rule), a taxpayer must capitalize amounts paid to create an intangible described in this paragraph (d). The determination of whether an amount is paid to create an intangible described in this paragraph (d) is to be made based on all of the facts and circumstances, disregarding distinctions between the labels used in this paragraph (d) to describe the intangible and the labels used by the taxpayer and other parties to the transaction.

(2) *Financial interests.*—(i) *In general.*—A taxpayer must capitalize amounts paid to another party to create, originate, enter into, renew or renegotiate with that party any of the following financial interests, whether or not the interest is regularly traded on an established market:

(A) An ownership interest in a corporation, partnership, trust, estate, limited liability company, or other entity.

(B) A debt instrument, deposit, stripped bond, stripped coupon (including a servicing right treated for federal income tax purposes as a stripped coupon), regular interest in a REMIC or FASIT, or any other intangible treated as debt for federal income tax purposes.

(C) A financial instrument, such as—

(1) A letter of credit;

(2) A credit card agreement;

(3) A notional principal contract;

(4) A foreign currency contract;

(5) A futures contract;

(6) A forward contract (including an agreement under which the taxpayer has the right and obligation to provide or to acquire property (or to be compensated for such property, regardless of whether the taxpayer provides or acquires the property));

(7) An option (including an agreement under which the taxpayer has the right to provide or to acquire property (or to be compensated for such property, regardless of whether the taxpayer provides or acquires the property)); and

(8) Any other financial derivative.

(D) An endowment contract, annuity contract, or insurance contract that has or may have cash value.

(E) Non-functional currency.

(F) An agreement providing either party the right to use, possess or sell a financial interest described in this paragraph (d)(2).

(ii) *Amounts paid to create, originate, enter into, renew or renegotiate.*—An amount paid to another party is not paid to create, originate, enter into, renew or renegotiate a financial interest with that party if the payment is made with the mere hope or expectation of developing or maintaining a business relationship with that party and is not contingent on the origination, renewal or renegotiation of a financial interest with that party.

(iii) *Renegotiate.*—A taxpayer is treated as renegotiating a financial interest if the terms of the financial interest are modified. A taxpayer also is treated as renegotiating a financial interest if the taxpayer enters into a new financial interest with the same party (or substantially the same parties) to a terminated financial interest, the taxpayer could not cancel the terminated financial interest without the consent of the other party (or parties), and the other party (or parties) would not have consented to the cancellation unless the taxpayer entered into the new financial interest. A taxpayer is treated as unable to cancel a financial interest without the consent of the other party (or parties) if, under the terms of the financial interest, the taxpayer is subject to a termination penalty and the other party (or parties) to the financial interest modifies the terms of the penalty.

(iv) *Coordination with other provisions of this paragraph (d).*—An amount described in this paragraph (d)(2) that is also described elsewhere in paragraph (d) of this section is treated as described only in this paragraph (d)(2).

(v) *Coordination with §1.263(a)-5.*—See §1.263(a)-5 for the treatment of borrowing costs and the treatment of amounts paid by an option writer.

(vi) *Examples.*—The following examples illustrate the rules of this paragraph (d)(2):

Example 1. Loan. X corporation, a commercial bank, makes a loan to A in the principal amount of $250,000. The $250,000 principal amount of the loan paid to A constitutes an amount paid to another party to create a debt instrument with that party under paragraph (d)(2)(i)(B) of this section and must be capitalized.

Example 2. Option. W corporation owns all of the outstanding stock of X corporation. Y corporation pays W $1,000,000 in exchange for W's grant of a 3-year call option to Y permitting Y to purchase all of the outstanding stock of X at a certain price per share. Y's payment of $1,000,000 to W constitutes an amount paid to another party to create an option with that party under paragraph (d)(2)(i)(C)(7) of this section and must be capitalized.

Example 3. Partnership interest. Z corporation pays $10,000 to P, a partnership, in exchange for an ownership interest in P. Z's payment of $10,000 to P constitutes an amount paid to another party to create an ownership interest in a partnership with that party under paragraph (d)(2)(i)(A) of this section and must be capitalized.

Example 4. Take or pay contract. Q corporation, a producer of natural gas, pays $1,000,000 to R during 2005 to induce R corporation to enter into a 5-year "take or pay" gas purchase contract. Under the contract, R is liable to pay for a specified minimum amount of gas, whether or not R takes such gas. Q's payment of $1,000,000 is an amount paid to another party to induce that party to enter into an agreement providing Q the right and obligation to provide property or be compensated for such property (regardless of whether the property is provided) under paragraph (d)(2)(i)(C)(6) of this section and must be capitalized.

Example 5. Agreement to provide property. P corporation pays R corporation $1,000,000 in exchange for R's agreement to purchase 1,000 units of P's product at any time within the three succeeding calendar years. The agreement describes P's $1,000,000 as a sales discount. P's $1,000,000 payment is an amount paid to induce R to enter into an agreement providing P the right and obligation to provide property under paragraph (d)(2)(i)(C)(6) of this section and must be capitalized.

Example 6. Customer incentive payment. S corporation, a computer manufacturer, seeks to develop a business relationship with V corporation, a computer retailer. As an incentive to encourage V to purchase computers from S, S enters into an agreement with V under which S agrees that, if V purchases $20,000,000 of computers from S within 3 years from the date of the agreement, S will pay V $2,000,000 on the date that V reaches the $20,000,000 threshold. V reaches the $20,000,000 threshold during the third year of the agreement, and S pays V $2,000,000. S is not required to capitalize its payment to V under this paragraph (d)(2) because the payment does not provide S the right or obligation to provide property and does not create a separate and distinct intangible asset for S within the meaning of paragraph (b)(3)(i) of this section.

(3) *Prepaid expenses.*—(i) *In general.*—A taxpayer must capitalize prepaid expenses.

(ii) *Examples.*—The following examples illustrate the rules of this paragraph (d)(3):

Example 1. Prepaid insurance. N corporation, an accrual method taxpayer, pays $10,000 to an insurer to obtain three years of coverage under a property and casualty insurance policy. The $10,000 is a prepaid expense and must be capitalized under this paragraph (d)(3). Paragraph (d)(2) of this section does not apply to the payment because the policy has no cash value.

Example 2. Prepaid rent. X corporation, a cash method taxpayer, enters into a 24-month lease of office space. At the time of the lease signing, X prepays $240,000. No other amounts are due under the lease. The $240,000 is a prepaid expense and must be capitalized under this paragraph (d)(3).

(4) *Certain memberships and privileges.*—(i) *In general.*—A taxpayer must capitalize amounts paid to an organization to obtain, renew, renegotiate, or upgrade a membership or privilege from that organization. A taxpayer is not required to capitalize under this paragraph (d)(4) an amount paid to obtain, renew, renegotiate or upgrade certification of the taxpayer's products, services, or business processes.

(ii) *Examples.*—The following examples illustrate the rules of this paragraph (d)(4):

Example 1. Hospital privilege. B, a physician, pays $10,000 to Y corporation to obtain lifetime staff privileges at a hospital operated by Y. B must capitalize the $10,000 payment under this paragraph (d)(4).

Example 2. Initiation fee. X corporation pays a $50,000 initiation fee to obtain membership in a trade association. X must capitalize the $50,000 payment under this paragraph (d)(4).

Example 3. Product rating. V corporation, an automobile manufacturer, pays W corporation, a national quality ratings association, $100,000 to conduct a study and provide a rating of the quality and safety of a line of V's automobiles. V's payment is an amount paid to obtain a certification of V's product and is not required to be capitalized under this paragraph (d)(4).

Example 4. Business process certification. Z corporation, a manufacturer, seeks to obtain a certification that its quality control standards meet a series of international standards known as ISO 9000. Z pays $50,000 to an independent registrar to obtain a certification from the registrar that Z's quality management system conforms to the ISO 9000 standard. Z's payment is an amount paid to obtain a certification of Z's business processes and is not required to be capitalized under this paragraph (d)(4).

(5) *Certain rights obtained from a governmental agency.*—(i) *In general.*—A taxpayer must capitalize amounts paid to a governmental agency to obtain, renew, renegotiate, or upgrade its rights under a trademark, trade name, copyright, license, permit, franchise, or other similar right granted by that governmental agency.

(ii) *Examples.*—The following examples illustrate the rules of this paragraph (d)(5):

Example 1. Business license. X corporation pays $15,000 to state Y to obtain a business license that is valid indefinitely. Under this paragraph (d)(5), the amount paid to state Y is an amount paid to a government agency for a right granted by that agency. Accordingly, X must capitalize the $15,000 payment.

Example 2. Bar admission. A, an individual, pays $1,000 to an agency of state Z to obtain a license to practice law in state Z that is valid indefinitely, provided A adheres to the requirements governing the practice of law in state Z. Under this paragraph (d)(5), the amount paid to state Z is an amount paid to a government agency for a right granted by that agency. Accordingly, A must capitalize the $1,000 payment.

(6) *Certain contract rights.*—(i) *In general.*—Except as otherwise provided in this paragraph (d)(6), a taxpayer must capitalize amounts paid to another party to create, originate, enter into, renew or renegotiate with that party—

(A) An agreement providing the taxpayer the right to use tangible or intangible property or the right to be compensated for the use of tangible or intangible property;

(B) An agreement providing the taxpayer the right to provide or to receive services (or the right to be compensated for services regardless of whether the taxpayer provides such services);

(C) A covenant not to compete or an agreement having substantially the same effect as a covenant not to compete (except, in the case of an agreement that requires the performance of services, to the extent that the amount represents reasonable compensation for services actually rendered);

(D) An agreement not to acquire additional ownership interests in the taxpayer; or

(E) An agreement providing the taxpayer (as the covered party) with an annuity, an endowment, or insurance coverage.

(ii) *Amounts paid to create, originate, enter into, renew or renegotiate.*—An amount paid to another party is not paid to create, originate, enter into, renew or renegotiate an agreement with that party if the payment is made with the mere hope or expectation of developing or maintaining a business relationship with that party and is not contingent on the origination, renewal or renegotiation of an agreement with that party.

(iii) *Renegotiate.*—A taxpayer is treated as renegotiating an agreement if the terms of the agreement are modified. A taxpayer also is treated as renegotiating an agreement if the taxpayer enters into a new agreement with the same party (or substantially the same parties) to a terminated agreement, the taxpayer could not cancel the terminated agreement without the consent of the other party (or parties), and the other party (or parties) would not have consented to the cancellation unless the taxpayer entered into the new agreement. A taxpayer is treated as unable to cancel an agreement without the consent of the other party (or parties) if, under the terms of the agreement, the taxpayer is subject to a termination penalty and the other party (or parties) to the agreement modifies the terms of the penalty.

(iv) *Right.*—An agreement does not provide the taxpayer a right to use property or to provide or receive services if the agreement may be terminated at will by the other party (or parties) to the agreement before the end of the period prescribed by paragraph (f)(1) of this section. An agreement is not terminable at will if the other party (or parties) to the agreement is economically compelled not to terminate the agreement until the end of the period prescribed by paragraph (f)(1) of this section. All of the facts and circumstances will be considered in determining whether the other party (or parties) to an agreement is economically compelled not to terminate the agreement. An agreement also does not provide the taxpayer the right to provide services if the agreement merely provides that the taxpayer will stand ready to provide services if requested, but places no obligation on another person to request or pay for the taxpayer's services.

(v) *De minimis amounts.*—A taxpayer is not required to capitalize amounts paid to another party (or parties) to create, originate, enter into, renew or renegotiate with that party (or those parties) an agreement described in paragraph (d)(6)(i) of this section if the aggregate of all amounts paid to that party (or those parties) with respect to the agreement does not exceed $5,000. If the aggregate of all amounts paid to the other party (or parties) with respect to that agreement exceeds $5,000, then all amounts must be capitalized. For purposes of this paragraph (d)(6), an amount paid in the form of property is valued at its fair market value at the time of the payment. In general, a taxpayer must determine whether the rules of this paragraph (d)(6)(v) apply by accounting for the specific amounts paid with respect to each agreement. However, a taxpayer that reasonably expects to create, originate, enter into, renew or renegotiate at least 25 similar agreements during the taxable year may establish a pool of agreements for purposes of determining the amounts paid with respect to the agreements in the pool. Under this pooling method, the amount paid with respect to each agreement included in the pool is equal to the average amount paid with respect to all agreements included in the pool. A taxpayer computes the average amount paid with respect to all agreements included in the pool by dividing the sum of all amounts paid with respect to all agreements included in the pool by the number of agreements included in the pool. See paragraph (h) of this section for additional rules relating to pooling.

(vi) *Exception for lessee construction allowances.*—Paragraph (d)(6)(i) of this section does not apply to amounts paid by a lessor to a lessee as a construction allowance to the extent the lessee expends the amount for the tangible property that is owned by the lessor for federal income tax purposes (see, for example, section 110).

(vii) *Examples.*—The following examples illustrate the rules of this paragraph (d)(6):

Example 1. New lease agreement. V seeks to lease commercial property in a prominent downtown location of city R. V pays Z, the owner of the commercial property, $50,000 in exchange for Z entering into a 10-year lease with V. V's payment is an amount paid to another party to enter into an agreement providing V the right to use tangible property. Because the $50,000 payment exceeds $5,000, no portion of the amount paid to Z is de minimis for purposes of paragraph (d)(6)(v) of this section. Under paragraph (d)(6)(i)(A) of this section, V must capitalize the entire $50,000 payment.

Example 2. Modification of lease agreement. Partnership Y leases a piece of equipment for use in its business from Z corporation. When the lease has a remaining term of 3 years, Y requests that Z modify the existing lease by extending the remaining term by 5 years. Y pays $50,000 to Z in exchange for Z's agreement to modify the existing

lease. Y's payment of $50,000 is an amount paid to another party to renegotiate an agreement providing Y the right to use property. Because the $50,000 payment exceeds $5,000, no portion of the amount paid to Z is de minimis for purposes of paragraph (d)(6)(v) of this section. Under paragraph (d)(6)(i)(A) of this section, Y must capitalize the entire $50,000 payment.

Example 3. Modification of lease agreement. In 2004, R enters into a 5-year, non-cancelable lease of a mainframe computer for use in its business. R subsequently determines that the mainframe computer that R is leasing is no longer adequate for its needs. In 2006, R and P corporation (the lessor) agree to terminate the 2004 lease and to enter into a new 5-year lease for a different and more powerful mainframe computer. R pays P a $75,000 early termination fee. P would not have agreed to terminate the 2004 lease unless R agreed to enter into the 2006 lease. R's payment of $75,000 is an amount paid to another party to renegotiate an agreement providing R the right to use property. Because the $75,000 payment exceeds $5,000, no portion of the amount paid to P is de minimis for purposes of paragraph (d)(6)(v) of this section. Under paragraph (d)(6)(i)(A) of this section, R must capitalize the entire $75,000 payment.

Example 4. Modification of lease agreement. Same as *Example 3*, except the 2004 lease agreement allows R to terminate the lease at any time subject to a $75,000 early termination fee. Because R can terminate the lease without P's approval, R's payment of $75,000 is not an amount paid to another party to renegotiate an agreement. Accordingly, R is not required to capitalize the $75,000 payment under this paragraph (d)(6).

Example 5. Modification of lease agreement. Same as *Example 4*, except P agreed to reduce the early termination fee to $60,000. Because R did not pay an amount to renegotiate the early termination fee, R's payment of $60,000 is not an amount paid to another party to renegotiate an agreement. Accordingly, R is not required to capitalize the $60,000 payment under this paragraph (d)(6).

Example 6. Covenant not to compete. R corporation enters into an agreement with A, an individual, that prohibits A from competing with R for a period of three years. To encourage A to enter into the agreement, R agrees to pay A $100,000 upon the signing of the agreement. R's payment is an amount paid to another party to enter into a covenant not to compete. Because the $100,000 payment exceeds $5,000, no portion of the amount paid to A is de minimis for purposes of paragraph (d)(6)(v) of this section. Under paragraph (d)(6)(i)(C) of this section, R must capitalize the entire $100,000 payment.

Example 7. Standstill agreement. During 2004 through 2005, X corporation acquires a large minority interest in the stock of Z corporation. To ensure that X does not take control of Z, Z pays X $5,000,000 for a standstill agreement under which X agrees not to acquire any more stock in Z for a period of 10 years. Z's payment is an amount paid to another party to enter into an agreement not to acquire additional ownership interests in Z. Because the $5,000,000 payment exceeds $5,000, no portion of the amount paid to X is de minimis for purposes of paragraph (d)(6)(v) of this section. Under paragraph (d)(6)(i)(D) of this section, Z must capitalize the entire $5,000,000 payment.

Example 8. Signing bonus. Employer B pays a $25,000 signing bonus to employee C to induce C to come to work for B. C can leave B's employment at any time to work for a competitor of B and is not required to repay the $25,000 bonus to B. Because C is not economically compelled to continue his employment with B, B's payment does not provide B the right to receive services from C. Accordingly, B is not required to capitalize the $25,000 payment.

Example 9. Renewal. In 2000, M corporation and N corporation enter into a 5-year agreement that gives M the right to manage N's investment portfolio. In 2005, N has the option of renewing the agreement for another three years. During 2004, M pays $10,000 to send several employees of N to an investment seminar. M pays the $10,000 to help develop and maintain its business relationship with N with the expectation that N will renew its agreement with M in 2005. Because M's payment is not contingent on N agreeing to renew the agreement, M's payment is not an amount paid to renew an agreement under paragraph (d)(6)(ii) of this section and is not required to be capitalized.

Example 10. De minimis payments. X corporation is engaged in the business of providing wireless telecommunications services to customers. To induce customer B to enter into a 3-year non-cancelable telecommunications contract, X provides B with a free wireless telephone. The fair market value of the wireless telephone is $300 at the time it is provided to B. X's provision of a wireless telephone to B is an amount paid to B to induce B to enter into an agreement providing X the right to provide services, as described in paragraph (d)(6)(i)(B) of this section. Because the amount of the inducement is $300, the amount of the inducement is de minimis under paragraph (d)(6)(v) of this section. Accordingly, X is not required to capitalize the amount of the inducement provided to B.

(7) *Certain contract terminations.*—(i) *In general.*—A taxpayer must capitalize amounts paid to another party to terminate—

(A) A lease of real or tangible personal property between the taxpayer (as lessor) and that party (as lessee);

(B) An agreement that grants that party the exclusive right to acquire or use the taxpayer's property or services or to conduct the taxpayer's business (other than an intangible described in paragraph (c)(1)(i) through (iv) of this section or a financial interest described in paragraph (d)(2) of this section); or

(C) An agreement that prohibits the taxpayer from competing with that party or from acquiring property or services from a competitor of that party.

(ii) *Certain break-up fees.*—Paragraph (d)(7)(i) of this section does not apply to the termination of a transaction described in §1.263(a)-5(a) (relating to an acquisition of a trade or business, a change in the capital structure of a business entity, and certain other transactions). See §1.263(a)-5(c)(8) for rules governing the treatment of amounts paid to terminate a transaction to which that section applies.

(iii) *Examples.*—The following examples illustrate the rules of this paragraph (d)(7):

Example 1. Termination of exclusive license agreement. On July 1, 2005, N enters into a license agreement with R corporation under which N grants R the exclusive right to manufacture and distribute goods using N's design and trademarks for a period of 10 years. On June 30, 2007, N pays R $5,000,000 in exchange for R's agreement to terminate the exclusive license agreement. N's payment to terminate its license agreement with R constitutes a payment to terminate an exclusive license to use the taxpayer's property, as described in paragraph (d)(7)(i)(B) of this section. Accordingly, N must capitalize its $5,000,000 payment to R.

Example 2. Termination of exclusive distribution agreement. On March 1, 2005, L, a manufacturer, enters into an agreement with M granting M the right to be the sole distributor of L's products in state X for 10 years. On July 1, 2008, L pays M $50,000 in exchange for M's agreement to terminate the distribution agreement. L's payment to terminate its agreement with M constitutes a payment to terminate an exclusive right to acquire L's property, as described in paragraph (d)(7)(i)(B) of this section. Accordingly, L must capitalize its $50,000 payment to M.

Example 3. Termination of covenant not to compete. On February 1, 2005, Y corporation enters into a covenant not to compete with Z corporation that prohibits Y from competing with Z in city V for a period of 5 years. On January 31, 2007, Y pays Z $1,000,000 in exchange for Z's agreement to terminate the covenant not to compete. Y's payment to terminate the covenant not to compete with Z constitutes a payment to terminate an agreement that prohibits Y from competing with Z, as described in paragraph (d)(7)(i)(C) of this section. Accordingly, Y must capitalize its $1,000,000 payment to Z.

Example 4. Termination of merger agreement. N corporation and U corporation enter into an agreement under which N agrees to merge into U. Subsequently, N pays U $10,000,000 to terminate the merger agreement. As provided in paragraph (d)(7)(ii) of this section, N's $10,000,000 payment to terminate the merger agreement with U is not required to be capitalized under this paragraph (d)(7). In addition, N's $10,000,000 does not create a separate and distinct intangible asset for N within the meaning of paragraph (b)(3)(i) of this section. (See §1.263(a)-5 for additional rules regarding termination of merger agreements.)

(8) *Certain benefits arising from the provision, production, or improvement of real property.*—(i) *In general.*—A taxpayer must capitalize amounts paid for real property if the taxpayer transfers ownership of the real property to another person (except to the extent the real property is sold for fair market value) and if the real property can reasonably be expected to produce significant economic benefits to the taxpayer after the transfer. A taxpayer also must capitalize amounts paid to produce or improve real property owned by another (except to the extent the taxpayer is selling services at fair market value to produce or improve the real property) if the real property can reasonably be expected to produce significant economic benefits for the taxpayer.

(ii) *Exclusions.*—A taxpayer is not required to capitalize an amount under paragraph (d)(8)(i) of this section if the taxpayer transfers real property or pays an amount to produce or improve real property owned by another in exchange for services, the purchase or use of property, or the creation of an intangible described in paragraph (d) of this section (other than in this paragraph (d)(8)). The preceding sentence does not apply to the extent the taxpayer does not receive fair market value consideration for the real property that is relinquished or for the amounts that are paid by the taxpayer to produce or improve real property owned by another.

(iii) *Real property.*—For purposes of this paragraph (d)(8), real property includes property that is affixed to real property and that will ordinarily remain affixed for an indefinite period of time, such as roads, bridges, tunnels, pavements, wharves and docks, breakwaters and sea walls, elevators, power generation and transmission facilities, and pollution control facilities.

(iv) *Impact fees and dedicated improvements.*—Paragraph (d)(8)(i) of this section does not apply to amounts paid to satisfy one-time charges imposed by a state or local government against new development (or expansion of existing development) to finance specific offsite capital improvements for general public use that are necessitated by the new or expanded development. In addition, paragraph (d)(8)(i) of this section does not apply to amounts paid for real property or improvements to real property constructed by the taxpayer where the real property or improvements benefit new development or expansion of existing development, are immediately transferred to a state or local government for dedication to the general public use, and are maintained by the state or local government. See section 263A and the regulations thereunder for capitalization rules that apply to amounts referred to in this paragraph (d)(8)(iv).

(v) *Examples.*—The following examples illustrate the rules of this paragraph (d)(8):

Example 1. Amount paid to produce real property owned by another. W corporation operates a quarry on the east side of a river in city Z and a crusher on the west side of the river. City Z's existing bridges are of insufficient capacity to be traveled by trucks in transferring stone from W's quarry to its crusher. As a result, the efficiency of W's operations is greatly reduced. W contributes $1,000,000 to City Z to defray in part the cost of constructing a publicly owned bridge capable of accommodating W's trucks. W's payment to city Z is an amount paid to produce or improve real property (within the meaning of paragraph (d)(8)(iii) of this section) that can reasonably be expected to produce significant economic benefits for W. Under paragraph (d)(8)(i) of this section, W must capitalize the $1,000,000 paid to city Z.

Example 2. Transfer of real property to another. K corporation, a shipping company, uses smaller vessels to unload its ocean-going vessels at port X. There is no natural harbor at port X, and during stormy weather the transfer of freight between K's ocean vessels and port X is extremely difficult and sometimes impossible, which can be very costly to K. Consequently, K constructs a short breakwater at a cost of $50,000. The short breakwater, however, is inadequate, so K persuades the port authority to build a larger breakwater that will allow K to unload its vessels at any time of the year and during all kinds of weather. K contributes the short breakwater and pays $200,000 to the port authority for use in building the larger breakwater. Because the transfer of the small breakwater and $200,000 is reasonably expected to produce significant economic benefits for K, K must capitalize both the adjusted basis of the small breakwater (determined at the time the small breakwater is contributed) and the $200,000 payment under this paragraph (d)(8).

Example 3. Dedicated improvements. X corporation is engaged in the development and sale of residential real estate. In connection with a residential real estate project under construction by X in city Z, X is required by city Z to construct ingress and egress roads to and from its project and immediately transfer the roads to city Z for dedication to general public use. The roads will be maintained by city Z. X pays its subcontractor $100,000 to construct the ingress and egress roads. X's payment is a dedicated improvement within the meaning of paragraph (d)(8)(iv) of this section. Accordingly, X is not required to capitalize the $100,000 payment under this paragraph (d)(8). See section 263A and the regulations thereunder for capitalization rules that apply to amounts referred to in paragraph (d)(8)(iv) of this section.

(9) *Defense or perfection of title to intangible property.*—(i) *In general.*—A taxpayer must capitalize amounts paid to another party to defend or perfect title to intangible property if that other party challenges the taxpayer's title to the intangible property.

(ii) *Certain break-up fees.*—Paragraph (d)(9)(i) of this section does not apply to the termination of a transaction described in §1.263(a)-5(a) (relating to an acquisition of a trade or business, a change in the capital structure of a business entity, and certain other transactions). See §1.263(a)-5 for rules governing the treatment of amounts paid to terminate a transaction to which that section applies. Paragraph (d)(9)(i) of this section also does not apply to an amount paid to another party to terminate an agreement that grants that party the right to purchase the taxpayer's intangible property.

(iii) *Example.*—The following example illustrates the rules of this paragraph (d)(9):

Example. Defense of title. R corporation claims to own an exclusive patent on a particular technology. U corporation brings a lawsuit against R, claiming that U is the true owner of the patent and that R stole the technology from U. The sole issue in the suit involves the validity of R's patent. R chooses to settle the suit by paying U $100,000 in exchange for U's release of all future claim to the patent. R's payment to U is an amount paid to defend or perfect title to intangible property under paragraph (d)(9) of this section and must be capitalized.

(e) *Transaction costs.*—(1) *Scope of facilitate.*—(i) *In general.*—Except as otherwise provided in this section, an amount is paid to facilitate the acquisition or creation of an intangible (the transaction) if the amount is paid in the process of investigating or otherwise pursuing the transaction. Whether an amount is paid in the process of investigating or otherwise pursuing the transaction is determined based on all of the facts and circumstances. In determining whether an amount is paid to facilitate a transaction, the fact that the amount would (or would not) have been paid but for the transaction is relevant, but is not determinative. An amount paid to determine the value or price of an intangible is an amount paid in the process of investigating or otherwise pursuing the transaction.

(ii) *Treatment of termination payments.*—An amount paid to terminate (or facilitate the termination of) an existing agreement does not facilitate the acquisition or creation of another agreement under this section. See paragraph (d)(6)(iii) of this section for the treatment of termination fees paid to the other party (or parties) of a renegotiated agreement.

(iii) *Special rule for contracts.*—An amount is treated as not paid in the process of investigating or otherwise pursuing the creation of an agreement described in paragraph (d)(2) or (d)(6) of this section if the amount relates to activities performed before the earlier of the date the taxpayer begins preparing its bid for the agreement or the date the taxpayer begins discussing or negotiating the agreement with another party to the agreement.

(iv) *Borrowing costs.*—An amount paid to facilitate a borrowing does not facilitate an acquisition or creation of an intangible described in paragraphs (b)(1)(i) through (iv) of this section. See §§1.263(a)-5 and 1.446-5 for the treatment of an amount paid to facilitate a borrowing.

(v) *Special rule for stock redemption costs of open-end regulated investment companies.*—An amount paid by an open-end regulated investment company (within the meaning of section 851) to facilitate a redemption of its stock is treated as an amount that does not facilitate the acquisition of an intangible under this section.

(2) *Coordination with paragraph (d) of this section.*—In the case of an amount paid to facilitate the creation of an intangible described in paragraph (d) of this section, the provisions of this paragraph (e) apply regardless of whether a payment described in paragraph (d) is made. *[handwritten: This means taxpayer do can be the one receiving a pymt for ... taxable]*

(3) *Transaction.*—For purposes of this section, the term *transaction* means all of the factual elements comprising an acquisition or creation of an intangible and includes a series of steps carried out as part of a single plan. Thus, a transaction can involve more than one invoice and more than one intangible. For example, a purchase of intangibles under one purchase agreement constitutes a single transaction, notwithstanding the fact that the acquisition involves multiple intangibles and the amounts paid to facilitate the acquisition are capable of being allocated among the various intangibles acquired.

(4) *Simplifying conventions.*—(i) *In general.*—For purposes of this section, employee compensation (within the meaning of paragraph (e)(4)(ii) of this section), overhead, and de minimis costs (within the meaning of paragraph (e)(4)(iii) of this section) are treated as amounts that do not facilitate the acquisition or creation of an intangible.

(ii) *Employee compensation.*—(A) *In general.*—The term *employee compensation* means compensation (including salary, bonuses and commissions) paid to an employee of the taxpayer. For purposes of this section, whether an individual is an employee is determined in accordance with the rules contained in section 3401(c) and the regulations thereunder.

(B) *Certain amounts treated as employee compensation.*—For purposes of this section, a guaranteed payment to a partner in a partnership is treated as employee compensation. For purposes of this section, annual compensation paid to a director of a corporation is treated as employee compensation. For example, an amount paid to a director of a corporation for attendance at a regular meeting of the board of directors (or committee thereof) is treated as employee compensation for purposes of this section. However, an amount paid

to a director for attendance at a special meeting of the board of directors (or committee thereof) is not treated as employee compensation. An amount paid to a person that is not an employee of the taxpayer (including the employer of the individual who performs the services) is treated as employee compensation for purposes of this section only if the amount is paid for secretarial, clerical, or similar administrative support services. In the case of an affiliated group of corporations filing a consolidated federal income tax return, a payment by one member of the group to a second member of the group for services performed by an employee of the second member is treated as employee compensation if the services provided by the employee are provided at a time during which both members are affiliated.

(iii) *De minimis costs.*—(A) *In general.*—Except as provided in paragraph (e)(4)(iii)(B) of this section, the term *de minimis costs* means amounts (other than employee compensation and overhead) paid in the process of investigating or otherwise pursuing a transaction if, in the aggregate, the amounts do not exceed $5,000 (or such greater amount as may be set forth in published guidance). If the amounts exceed $5,000 (or such greater amount as may be set forth in published guidance), none of the amounts are de minimis costs within the meaning of this paragraph (e)(4)(iii)(A). For purposes of this paragraph (e)(4)(iii), an amount paid in the form of property is valued at its fair market value at the time of the payment. In determining the amount of transaction costs paid in the process of investigating or otherwise pursuing a transaction, a taxpayer generally must account for the specific costs paid with respect to each transaction. However, a taxpayer that reasonably expects to enter into at least 25 similar transactions during the taxable year may establish a pool of similar transactions for purposes of determining the amount of transaction costs paid in the process of investigating or otherwise pursuing the transactions in the pool. Under this pooling method, the amount of transaction costs paid in the process of investigating or otherwise pursuing each transaction included in the pool is equal to the average transaction costs paid in the process of investigating or otherwise pursuing all transactions included in the pool. A taxpayer computes the average transaction costs paid in the process of investigating or otherwise pursuing all transactions included in the pool by dividing the sum of all transaction costs paid in the process of investigating or otherwise pursuing all transactions included in the pool by the number of transactions included in the pool. See paragraph (h) of this section for additional rules relating to pooling.

(B) *Treatment of commissions.*—The term *de minimis costs* does not include commissions paid to facilitate the acquisition of an intangible described in paragraphs (c)(1)(i) through (v) of this section or to facilitate the creation, origination, entrance into, renewal or renegotiation of an intangible in paragraph (d)(2)(i) of this section.

(iv) *Election to capitalize.*—A taxpayer may elect to treat employee compensation, overhead, or de minimis costs paid in the process of investigating or otherwise pursuing a transaction as amounts that facilitate the transaction. The election is made separately for each transaction and applies to employee compensation, overhead, or de minimis costs, or to any combination thereof. For example, a taxpayer may elect to treat overhead and de minimis costs, but not employee compensation, as amounts that facilitate the transaction. A taxpayer makes the election by treating the amounts to which the election applies as amounts that facilitate the transaction in the taxpayer's timely filed original federal income tax return (including extensions) for the taxable year during which the amounts are paid. In the case of an affiliated group of corporations filing a consolidated return, the election is made separately with respect to each member of the group, and not with respect to the group as a whole. In the case of an S corporation or partnership, the election is made by the S corporation or by the partnership, and not by the shareholders or partners. An election made under this paragraph (e)(4)(iv) is revocable with respect to each taxable year for which made only with the consent of the Commissioner.

(5) *Examples.*—The following examples illustrate the rules of this paragraph (e):

Example 1. Costs to facilitate. In December 2005, R corporation, a calendar year taxpayer, enters into negotiations with X corporation to lease commercial property from X for a period of 25 years. R pays A, its outside legal counsel, $4,000 in December 2005 for services rendered by A during December in assisting with negotiations with X. In January 2006, R and X finalize the terms of the lease and execute the lease agreement. R pays B, another of its outside legal counsel, $2,000 in January 2006 for services rendered by B during January in drafting the lease agreement. The agreement between R and X is an agreement providing R the right to use property, as described in paragraph (d)(6)(i)(A) of this section. R's payments to its outside counsel are amounts paid to facilitate the creation of the agreement. As provided in paragraph (e)(4)(iii)(A) of this section, R must aggregate its transaction costs for purposes of determining whether the transaction costs are de minimis. Because R's aggregate transaction costs exceed $5,000, R's transaction costs are not de minimis costs within the meaning of paragraph (e)(4)(iii)(A) of this section. Accordingly, R must capitalize the $4,000 paid to A and the $2,000 paid to B under paragraph (b)(1)(v) of this section.

Example 2. Costs to facilitate. Partnership X leases its manufacturing equipment from Y corporation under a 10-year lease. During 2005, when the lease has a remaining term of 4 years, X enters into a written agreement with Z corporation, a competitor of Y, under which X agrees to lease its manufacturing equipment from Z, subject to the condition that X first successfully terminates its lease with Y. X pays Y $50,000 in exchange for Y's agreement to terminate the equipment lease. Under paragraph (e)(1)(ii), X's $50,000 payment does not facilitate the creation of the new lease with Z. In addition, X's $50,000 payment does not terminate an agreement described in paragraph (d)(7) of this section. Accordingly, X is not required to capitalize the $50,000 termination payment under this section.

Example 3. Costs to facilitate. W corporation enters into a lease agreement with X corporation under which W agrees to lease property to X for a period of 5 years. W pays its outside counsel $7,000 for legal services rendered in drafting the lease agreement and negotiating with X. The agreement between W and X is an agreement providing W the right to be compensated for the use of property, as described in paragraph (d)(6)(i)(A) of this section. Under paragraph (e)(1)(i) of this section, W's payment to its outside counsel is an amount paid to facilitate the creation of that agreement. As provided by paragraph (e)(2) of this section, W must capitalize its $7,000 payment to outside counsel notwithstanding the fact that W made no payment described in paragraph (d)(6)(i) of this section.

Example 4. Costs to facilitate. U corporation, which owns a majority of the common stock of T corporation, votes its controlling interest in favor of a perpetual extension of T's charter. M, a minority shareholder in T, votes against the extension. Under applicable state law, U is required to purchase the stock of T held by M. When U and M are unable to agree on the value of M's shares, U brings an action in state court to appraise the value of M's stock interest. U pays attorney, accountant and appraisal fees of $25,000 for services rendered in connection with the negotiation and litigation with M. Because U's attorney, accountant and appraisal costs help establish the purchase price of M's stock, U's $25,000 payment facilitates the acquisition of stock. Accordingly, U must capitalize the $25,000 payment under paragraph (b)(1)(v) of this section.

Example 5. Costs to facilitate. For several years, H corporation has provided services to J corporation whenever requested by J. H wants to enter into a multiple-year contract with J that would give H the right to provide services to J. On June 10, 2004, H starts to prepare a bid to provide services to J and pays a consultant $15,000 to research potential competitors. On August 10, 2004, H raises the possibility of a multi-year contract with J. On October 10, 2004, H and J enter into a contract giving H the right to provide services to J for five years. During 2004, H pays $7,000 to travel to the city in which J's offices are located to continue providing services to J under their prior arrangement and pays $6,000 for travel to the city in which J's offices are located to further develop H's business relationship with J (for example, to introduce new employees, update J on current developments and take J's executives to dinner). H also pays $8,000 for travel costs to meet with J to discuss and negotiate the contract. Because the contract gives H the right to provide services to J, H must capitalize amounts paid to facilitate the creation of the contract. The $7,000 of travel expenses paid to provide services to J under their prior arrangement does not facilitate the creation of the contract and is not required to be capitalized, regardless of when the travel occurs. The $6,000 of travel expenses paid to further develop H's business relationship with J is paid in the process of pursuing the contract (and therefore must be capitalized) only to the extent the expenses relate to travel on or after June 10, 2004 (the date H begins to prepare a bid) and before October 11, 2004 (the date after H and J enter into the contract). The $8,000 of travel expenses paid to meet with J to discuss and negotiate the contract is paid in the process of pursuing the contact and must be capitalized. The $15,000 of consultant fees is paid to investigate the contract and also must be capitalized.

Example 6. Costs that do not facilitate. X corporation brings a legal action against Y corporation to recover lost profits resulting from Y's alleged infringement of X's copyright. Y does not challenge X's copyright, but argues that it did not infringe upon X's copyright. X pays its outside counsel $25,000 for legal services rendered in pursuing the suit against Y. Because X's title to its copyright is not in question, X's action against Y does not involve X's defense or perfection of title to intangible property. Thus, the amount paid to outside counsel does not facilitate the creation of an intangible described in paragraph (d)(9) of this section. Accordingly, X is not required to capitalize its $25,000 payment under this section.

Example 7. De minimis rule. W corporation, a commercial bank, acquires a portfolio containing 100 loans from Y corporation. As part of the acquisition, W pays an independent appraiser a fee of $10,000 to appraise the portfolio. The fee is an amount paid to facilitate W's acquisition of an intangible. The acquisition of the loan portfolio is a single transaction within the meaning of paragraph (e)(3) of this section. Because the amount paid to facilitate the transaction exceeds $5,000, the amount is not de minimis as defined in paragraph (e)(4)(iii)(A) of this section. Accordingly, W must capitalize the $10,000 fee under paragraph (b)(1)(v) of this section.

Example 8. Compensation and overhead. P corporation, a commercial bank, maintains a loan acquisition department whose sole function is to acquire loans from other financial institutions. As provided in paragraph (e)(4)(i) of this section, P is not required to capitalize any portion of the compensation paid to the employees in its loan acquisition department or any portion of its overhead allocable to the loan acquisition department.

(f) *12-month rule.*—(1) *In general.*—Except as otherwise provided in this paragraph (f), a taxpayer is not required to capitalize under this section amounts paid to create (or to facilitate the creation of) any right or benefit for the taxpayer that does not extend beyond the earlier of—

(i) 12 months after the first date on which the taxpayer realizes the right or benefit; or

(ii) The end of the taxable year following the taxable year in which the payment is made.

(2) *Duration of benefit for contract terminations.*—For purposes of this paragraph (f), amounts paid to terminate a contract or other agreement described in paragraph (d)(7)(i) of this section prior to its expiration date (or amounts paid to facilitate such termination) create a benefit for the taxpayer that lasts for the unexpired term of the agreement immediately before the date of the termination. If the terms of a contract or other agreement described in paragraph (d)(7)(i) of this section permit the taxpayer to terminate the contract or agreement after a notice period, amounts paid by the taxpayer to terminate the contract or agreement before the end of the notice period create a benefit for the taxpayer that lasts for the amount of time by which the notice period is shortened.

(3) *Inapplicability to created financial interests and self-created amortizable section 197 intangibles.*—Paragraph (f)(1) of this section does not apply to amounts paid to create (or facilitate the creation of) an intangible described in paragraph (d)(2) of this section (relating to amounts paid to create financial interests) or to amounts paid to create (or facilitate the creation of) an intangible that constitutes an amortizable section 197 intangible within the meaning of section 197(c).

(4) *Inapplicability to rights of indefinite duration.*—Paragraph (f)(1) of this section does not apply to amounts paid to create (or facilitate the creation of) an intangible of indefinite duration. A right has an indefinite duration if it has no period of duration fixed by agreement or by law, or if it is not based on a period of time, such as a right attributable to an agreement to provide or receive a fixed amount of goods or services. For example, a license granted by a governmental agency that permits the taxpayer to operate a business conveys a right of indefinite duration if the license may be revoked only upon the taxpayer's violation of the terms of the license.

(5) *Rights subject to renewal.*—(i) *In general.*—For purposes of paragraph (f)(1) of this section, the duration of a right includes any renewal period if all of the facts and circumstances in existence during the taxable year in which the right is created indicate a reasonable expectancy of renewal.

(ii) *Reasonable expectancy of renewal.*—The following factors are significant in determining whether there exists a reasonable expectancy of renewal:

(A) *Renewal history.*—The fact that similar rights are historically renewed is evidence of a reasonable expectancy of renewal. On the other hand, the fact that similar rights are rarely renewed is evidence of a lack of a reasonable expectancy of renewal. Where the taxpayer has no experience with similar rights, or where the taxpayer holds similar rights only occasionally, this factor is less indicative of a reasonable expectancy of renewal.

(B) *Economics of the transaction.*—The fact that renewal is necessary for the taxpayer to earn back its investment in the right is evidence of a reasonable expectancy of renewal. For example, if a taxpayer pays $14,000 to enter into a renewable contract with an initial 9-month term that is expected to general income to the taxpayer of $1,000 per month, the fact that renewal is necessary for the taxpayer to earn back its $14,000 payment is evidence of a reasonable expectancy of renewal.

Reg. §1.263(a)-4(f)(5)(ii)(B)

(C) *Likelihood of renewal by other party.*—Evidence that indicates a likelihood of renewal by the other party to a right, such as a bargain renewal option or similar arrangement, is evidence of a reasonable expectancy of renewal. However, the mere fact that the other party will have the opportunity to renew on the same terms as are available to others is not evidence of a reasonable expectancy of renewal.

(D) *Terms of renewal.*—The fact that material terms of the right are subject to renegotiation at the end of the initial term is evidence of a lack of a reasonable expectancy of renewal. For example, if the parties to an agreement must renegotiate price or amount, the renegotiation requirement is evidence of a lack of a reasonable expectancy of renewal.

(E) *Terminations.*—The fact that similar rights are typically terminated prior to renewal is evidence of a lack of a reasonably expectancy of renewal.

(iii) *Safe harbor pooling method.*—In lieu of applying the reasonable expectancy of renewal test described in paragraph (f)(5)(ii) of this section to each separate right created during a taxable year, a taxpayer that reasonably expects to enter into at least 25 similar rights during the taxable year may establish a pool of similar rights for which the initial term does not extend beyond the period prescribed in paragraph (f)(1) of this section and may elect to apply the reasonable expectancy of renewal test to that pool. See paragraph (h) of this section for additional rules relating to pooling. The application of paragraph (f)(1) of this section to each pool is determined in the following manner:

(A) All amounts (except de minimis costs described in paragraph (d)(6)(v) of this section) paid to create the rights included in the pool and all amounts paid to facilitate the creation of the rights included in the pool are aggregated.

(B) If less than 20 percent of the rights in the pool are reasonably expected to be renewed beyond the period prescribed in paragraph (f)(1) of this section, all rights in the pool are treated as having a duration that does not extend beyond the period prescribed in paragraph (f)(1) of this section, and the taxpayer is not required to capitalize under this section any portion of the aggregate amount described in paragraph (f)(5)(iii)(A) of this section.

(C) If more than 80 percent of the rights in the pool are reasonably expected to be renewed beyond the period prescribed in paragraph (f)(1) of this section, all rights in the pool are treated as having a duration that extends beyond the period prescribed in paragraph (f)(1) of this section, and the taxpayer is required to capitalize under this section the aggregate amount described in paragraph (f)(5)(iii)(A) of this section.

(D) If 20 percent or more, but 80 percent or less, of the rights in the pool are reasonably expected to be renewed beyond the period prescribed in paragraph (f)(1) of this section, the aggregate amount described in paragraph (f)(5)(iii)(A) of this section is multiplied by the percentage of the rights in the pool that are reasonably expected to be renewed beyond the period prescribed in paragraph (f)(1) of this section and the taxpayer must capitalize the resulting amount under this section by treating such amount as creating a separate intangible. The amount determined by multiplying the aggregate amount described in paragraph (f)(5)(iii)(A) of this section by the percentage of rights in the pool that are not reasonably expected to be renewed beyond the period prescribed in paragraph (f)(1) of this section is not required to be capitalized under this section.

(6) *Coordination with section 461.*—In the case of a taxpayer using an accrual method of accounting, the rules of this paragraph (f) do not affect the determination of whether a liability is incurred during the taxable year, including the determination of whether economic performance has occurred with respect to the liability. See § 1.461-4 for rules relating to economic performance.

(7) *Election to capitalize.*—A taxpayer may elect not to apply the rule contained in paragraph (f)(1) of this section. An election made under this paragraph (f)(7) applies to all similar transactions during the taxable year to which paragraph (f)(1) of this section would apply (but for the election under this paragraph (f)(7)). For example, a taxpayer may elect under this paragraph (f)(7) to capitalize its costs of prepaying insurance contracts for 12 months, but may continue to apply the rule in paragraph (f)(1) to its costs of entering into non-renewable, 12-month service contracts. A taxpayer makes the election by treating the amounts as capital expenditures in its timely filed original federal income tax return (including extensions) for the taxable year during which the amounts are paid. In the case of an affiliated group of corporations filing a consolidated return, the election is made separately with respect to each member of the group, and not with respect to the group as a whole. In the case of an S corporation or partnership, the election is made by the S corporation or by the partnership, and not by the shareholders or partners.

An election made under this paragraph (f)(7) is revocable with respect to each taxable year for which made only with the consent of the Commissioner.

(8) *Examples.*—The rules of this paragraph (f) are illustrated by the following examples, in which it is assumed (unless otherwise stated) that the taxpayer is a calendar year, accrual method taxpayer that does not have a short taxable year in any taxable year and has not made an election under paragraph (f)(7) of this section:

Example 1. Prepaid expenses. On December 1, 2005, N corporation pays a $10,000 insurance premium to obtain a property insurance policy (with no cash value) with a 1-year term that begins on February 1, 2006. The amount paid by N is a prepaid expense described in paragraph (d)(3) of this section and not paragraph (d)(2) of this section. Because the right or benefit attributable to the $10,000 payment extends beyond the end of the taxable year following the taxable year in which the payment is made, the 12-month rule provided by this paragraph (f) does not apply. N must capitalize the $10,000 payment.

Example 2. Prepaid expenses. (i) Assume the same facts as in *Example 1*, except that the policy has a term beginning on December 15, 2005. The 12-month rule of this paragraph (f) applies to the $10,000 payment because the right or benefit attributable to the payment neither extends more than 12 months beyond December 15, 2005 (the first date the benefit is realized by the taxpayer) nor beyond the end of the taxable year following the taxable year in which the payment is made. Accordingly, N is not required to capitalize the $10,000 payment.

(ii) Alternatively, assume N capitalizes prepaid expenses for financial accounting and reporting purposes and elects under paragraph (f)(7) of this section not to apply the 12-month rule contained in paragraph (f)(1) of this section. N must capitalize the $10,000 payment for federal income tax purposes.

Example 3. Financial interests. On October 1, 2005, X corporation makes a 9-month loan to B in the principal amount of $250,000. The principal amount of the loan to B constitutes an amount paid to create or originate a financial interest under paragraph (d)(2)(i)(B) of this section. The 9-month term of the loan does not extend beyond the period prescribed by paragraph (f)(1) of this section. However, as provided by paragraph (f)(3) of this section, the rules of this paragraph (f) do not apply to intangibles described in paragraph (d)(2) of this section. Accordingly, X must capitalize the $250,000 loan amount.

Example 4. Financial interests. X corporation owns all of the outstanding stock of Z corporation. On December 1, 2005, Y corporation pays X $1,000,000 in exchange for X's grant of a 9-month call option to Y permitting Y to purchase all of the outstanding stock of Z. Y's payment to X constitutes an amount paid to create or originate an option with X under paragraph (d)(2)(i)(C)(7) of this section. The 9-month term of the option does not extend beyond the period prescribed by paragraph (f)(1) of this section. However, as provided by paragraph (f)(3) of this section, the rules of this paragraph (f) do not apply to intangibles described in paragraph (d)(2) of this section. Accordingly, Y must capitalize the $1,000,000 payment.

Example 5. License. (i) On July 1, 2005, R corporation pays $10,000 to state X to obtain a license to operate a business in state X for a period of 5 years. The terms of the license require R to pay state X an annual fee of $500 due on July 1, 2005, and each of the succeeding four years. R pays the $500 fee on July 1 as required by the license.

(ii) R's payment of $10,000 is an amount paid to a governmental agency for a license granted by that agency to which paragraph (d)(5) of this section applies. Because R's payment creates rights or benefits for R that extend beyond 12 months after the first date on which R realizes the rights or benefits attributable to the payment and beyond the end of 2006 (the taxable year following the taxable year in which the payment is made), the rules of this paragraph (f) do not apply to R's payment. Accordingly, R must capitalize the $10,000 payment.

(iii) R's payment of each $500 annual fee is a prepaid expense described in paragraph (d)(3) of this section. R is not required to capitalize the $500 fee in each taxable year. The rules of this paragraph (f) apply to each such payment because each payment provides a right or benefit to R that does not extend beyond 12 months after the first date on which R realizes the rights or benefits attributable to the payment and does not extend beyond the end of the taxable year following the taxable year in which the payment is made.

Example 6. Lease. On December 1, 2005, W corporation enters into a lease agreement with X corporation under which W agrees to lease property to X for a period of 9 months, beginning on December 1, 2005. W pays its outside counsel $7,000 for legal services rendered in drafting the lease agreement and negotiating with X. The agreement between W and X is an agreement providing W the right to be compensated for the use of property, as described in paragraph (d)(6)(i)(A) of this section. W's $7,000 payment to its outside counsel is an amount paid to facilitate W's creation of the lease as described in paragraph (e)(1)(i) of this section. The 12-month rule of this paragraph (f) applies to the $7,000 payment because the right or benefit that the $7,000 payment facilitates the creation of neither extends more than 12 months beyond December 1, 2005 (the first date the benefit is realized by the taxpayer) nor beyond the end of the taxable year following the taxable year in which the payment is made. Accordingly, W is not required to capitalize its payment to its outside counsel.

Example 7. Certain contract terminations. V corporation owns real property that it has leased to A for a period of 15 years. When the lease has a remaining unexpired term of 5 years, V and A agree to terminate the lease, enabling V to use the property in its trade or business. V pays A $100,000 in exchange for A's agreement to terminate the lease. V's payment to A to terminate the lease is described in paragraph (d)(7)(i)(A) of this section. Under paragraph (f)(2) of this section, V's payment creates a benefit for V with a duration of 5 years, the remaining unexpired term of the lease as of the date of the termination. Because the benefit attributable to the expenditure extends beyond 12 months after the first date on which V realizes the rights or benefits attributable to the payment and beyond the end of the taxable year following the taxable year in which the payment is made, the rules of this paragraph (f) do not apply to the payment. V must capitalize the $100,000 payment.

Example 8. Certain contract terminations. Assume the same facts as in *Example 7*, except that the lease is terminated when it has a remaining unexpired term of 10 months. Under paragraph (f)(2) of this section, V's payment creates a benefit for V with a duration of 10 months. The 12-month rule of this paragraph (f) applies to the payment because the benefit attributable to the payment neither extends more than 12 months beyond the date of termination (the first date the benefit is realized by V) nor beyond the end of the taxable year following the taxable year in which the payment is made. Accordingly, V is not required to capitalize the $100,000 payment.

Example 9. Certain contract terminations. Assume the same facts as in *Example 7*, except that either party can terminate the lease upon 12 months notice. When the lease has a remaining unexpired term of 5 years, V wants to terminate the lease, however, V does not want to wait another 12 months. V pays A $50,000 for the ability to terminate the lease with one month's notice. V's payment to A to terminate the lease is described in paragraph (d)(7)(i)(A) of this section. Under paragraph (f)(2) of this section, V's payment creates a benefit for V with a duration of 11 months, the time by which the notice period is shortened. The 12-month rule of this paragraph (f) applies to V's $50,000 payment because the benefit attributable to the payment neither extends more than 12 months beyond the date of termination (the first date the benefit is realized by V) nor beyond the end of the taxable year following the taxable year in which the payment is made. Accordingly, V is not required to capitalize the $50,000 payment.

Example 10. Coordination with section 461. (i) U corporation leases office space from W corporation at a monthly rental rate of $2,000. On August 1, 2005, U prepays its office rent expense for the first six months of 2006 in the amount of $12,000. For purposes of this example, it is assumed that the recurring item exception provided by §1.461-5 does not apply and that the lease between W and U is not a section 467 rental agreement as defined in section 467(d).

(ii) Under §1.461-4(d)(3), U's prepayment of rent is a payment for the use of property by U for which economic performance occurs ratably over the period of time U is entitled to use the property. Accordingly, because economic performance with respect to U's prepayment of rent does not occur until 2006, U's prepaid rent is not incurred in 2005 and therefore is not properly taken into account through capitalization, deduction, or otherwise in 2005. Thus, the rules of this paragraph (f) do not apply to U's prepayment of its rent.

(iii) Alternatively, assume that U uses the cash method of accounting and the economic performance rules in §1.461-4 therefore do not apply to U. The 12-month rule of this paragraph (f) applies to the $12,000 payment because the rights or benefits attributable to U's prepayment of its rent do not extend beyond December 31, 2006. Accordingly, U is not required to capitalize its prepaid rent.

Example 11. Coordination with section 461. N corporation pays R corporation, an advertising and marketing firm, $40,000 on August 1, 2005, for advertising and marketing services to be provided to N throughout calendar year 2006. For purposes of this example, it is assumed that the recurring item exception provided by §1.461-5 does not apply. Under §1.461-4(d)(2), N's payment arises out of the provision of services to N by R for which economic performance occurs as the services are provided. Accordingly, because economic performance with respect to N's prepaid advertising expense does not occur until 2006, N's prepaid advertising expense is not incurred in 2005 and therefore is not properly taken into account through capitalization, deduction, or otherwise in 2005. Thus, the rules of this paragraph (f) do not apply to N's payment.

(g) *Treatment of capitalized costs.*—(1) *In general.*—An amount required to be capitalized by this section is not currently deductible under section 162. Instead, the amount generally is added to the basis of the intangible acquired or created. See section 1012.

(2) *Financial instruments.*—In the case of a financial instrument described in paragraph (c)(1)(iii) or (d)(2)(i)(C) of this section, notwithstanding paragraph (g)(1) of this section, if under other provisions of law the amount required to be capitalized is not required to be added to the basis of the intangible acquired or created, then the other provisions of law will govern the tax treatment of the amount.

(h) *Special rules applicable to pooling.*—(1) *In general.*—Except as otherwise provided, the rules of this paragraph (h) apply to the pooling methods described in paragraph (d)(6)(v) of this section (relating to de minimis rules applicable to certain contract rights), paragraph (e)(4)(iii)(A) of this section (relating to de minimis rules applicable to transaction costs), and paragraph (f)(5)(iii) of this section (relating to the application of the 12-month rule to renewable rights).

(2) *Method of accounting.*—A pooling method authorized by this section constitutes a method of accounting for purposes of section 446. A taxpayer that adopts or changes to a pooling method authorized by this section must use the method for the year of adoption and for all subsequent taxable years during which the taxpayer qualifies to use the pooling method unless a change to another method is required by the Commissioner in order to clearly reflect income, or unless permission to change to another method is granted by the Commissioner as provided in §1 446-1(e).

(3) *Adopting or changing to a pooling method.*—A taxpayer adopts (or changes to) a pooling method authorized by this section for any taxable year by establishing one or more pools for the taxable year in accordance with the rules governing the particular pooling method and the rules prescribed by this paragraph (h), and by using the pooling method to compute its taxable income for the year of adoption (or change).

(4) *Definition of pool.*—A taxpayer may use any reasonable method of defining a pool of similar transactions, agreements or rights, including a method based on the type of customer or the type of product or service provided under a contract. However, a taxpayer that pools similar transactions, agreements or rights must include in the pool all similar transactions, agreements or rights created during the taxable year. For purposes of the pooling methods described in paragraph (d)(6)(v) of this section (relating to de minimis rules applicable to certain contract rights) and paragraph (e)(4)(iii)(A) of this section (relating to de minimis rules applicable to transaction costs), an agreement (or a transaction) is treated as not similar to other agreements (or transactions) included in the pool if the amount at issue with respect to that agreement (or transaction) is reasonably expected to differ significantly from the average amount at issue with respect to the other agreements (or transactions) properly included in the pool.

(5) *Consistency requirement.*—A taxpayer that uses the pooling method described in paragraph (f)(5)(iii) of this section for purposes of applying the 12-month rule to a right or benefit—

(i) Must use the pooling methods described in paragraph (d)(6)(v) of this section (relating to de minimis rules applicable to certain contract rights) and paragraph (e)(4)(iii)(A) of this section (relating to de minimis rules applicable to transaction costs) for purposes of determining the amount paid to create, or facilitate the creation of, the right or benefit; and

(ii) Must use the same pool for purposes of paragraph (d)(6)(v) of this section and paragraph (e)(4)(iii)(A) of this section as is used for purposes of paragraph (f)(5)(iii) of this section.

(6) *Additional guidance pertaining to pooling.*—The Internal Revenue Service may publish guidance in the Internal Revenue Bulletin (see §601.601(d)(2) of this chapter) prescribing additional rules for applying the pooling methods authorized by this section to specific industries or to specific types of transactions.

(7) *Example.*—The following example illustrates the rules of this paragraph (h):

Example. Pooling. (i) In the course of its business, W corporation enters into 3-year non-cancelable contracts that provide W the right to provide services to its customers. W generally pays certain amounts in the process of pursuing an agreement with a customer, including amounts paid to credit reporting agencies to verify the credit history of the potential customer and commissions paid to the independent sales agent who secures the agreement with the customer. In the case of agreements that W enters into with customers who are individuals, the agreements contain substantially similar terms and conditions and W typically pays between $100 and $200 in the process of pursuing each transaction. During 2005, W enters into agreements with 300 individuals. Also during 2005, W enters into an agreement with X corporation containing terms and conditions that are substantially similar to those contained in the agreements W enters into with its customers who are individuals. W pays certain amounts in the process of pursuing the agreement with X that W would not typically incur in the process of pursuing an agreement with its customers who are individuals. For example, W pays amounts to prepare and submit a bid for the agreement with X and amounts to travel to X's headquarters to make a sales presentation to X's management. In the aggregate, W pays $11,000 in the process of obtaining the agreement with X.

(ii) The agreements between W and its customers are agreements providing W the right to provide services, as described in paragraph (d)(6)(i)(B) of this section. Under paragraph (b)(1)(v) of this section, W must capitalize transaction costs paid to facilitate the creation of these agreements. Because W enters into at least 25 similar transactions during 2005, W may pool its transactions for purposes of determining whether its transaction costs are de minimis within the meaning of paragraph (e)(4)(iii)(A) of this section. W adopts a pooling method by establishing one or more pools of similar transactions and by using the pooling method to compute its taxable income beginning in its 2005 taxable year. If W adopts a pooling method, W must include all similar transactions in the pool. Under paragraph (h)(4) of this section, the transaction with X is not similar to the transactions W enters into with its customers who are individuals. While the agreement with X contains terms and conditions that are substantially similar to those contained in the agreements W enters into with its customers who are individuals, the transaction costs paid in the process of pursuing the agreement with X are reasonably expected to differ significantly from the average transaction costs attributable to transactions with its customers who are individuals. Accordingly, W may not include the transaction with X in the pool of transactions with customers who are individuals.

(i) [Reserved].

(j) *Application to accrual method taxpayers.*—For purposes of this section, the terms *amount paid* and *payment* mean, in the case of a taxpayer using an accrual method of accounting, a liability incurred (within the meaning of § 1.446-1(c)(1)(ii)). A liability may not be taken into account under this section prior to the taxable year during which the liability is incurred.

(k) *Treatment of related parties and indirect payments.*—For purposes of this section, references to a party other than the taxpayer include persons related to that party and persons acting for or on behalf of that party (including persons to whom the taxpayer becomes obligated as a result of assuming a liability of that party). For this purpose, persons are related only if their relationship is described in section 267(b) or 707(b) or they are engaged in trades or businesses under common control within the meaning of section 41(f)(1). References to an amount paid to or by a party include an amount paid on behalf of that party.

(l) *Examples.*—The rules of this section are illustrated by the following examples in which it is assumed that the Internal Revenue Service has not published guidance that requires capitalization under paragraph (b)(1)(iv) of this section (relating to amounts paid to create or enhance a future benefit that is identified in published guidance as an intangible for which capitalization is required):

Example 1. License granted by a governmental unit. (i) X corporation pays $25,000 to state R to obtain a license to sell alcoholic beverages in its restaurant. The license is valid indefinitely, provided X complies with all applicable laws regarding the sale of alcoholic beverages in state R. pays its outside counsel $4,000 for legal services rendered in preparing the license application and otherwise representing X during the licensing process. In addition, X determines that $2,000 of salaries paid to its employees is allocable to services rendered by the employees in obtaining the license.

(ii) X's payment of $25,000 is an amount paid to a governmental unit to obtain a license granted by that agency, as described in paragraph (d)(5)(i) of this section. The right has an indefinite duration and constitutes an amortizable section 197 intangible. Accordingly, as provided in paragraph (f)(3) of this section, the provisions of paragraph (f) of this section (relating to the 12-month rule) do not apply to X's payment. X must capitalize its $25,000 payment to obtain the license from state R.

(iii) As provided in paragraph (e)(4) of this section, X is not required to capitalize employee compensation because such amounts are treated as amounts that do not facilitate the acquisition or creation of an intangible. Thus, X is not required to capitalize the $2,000 *of employee compensation allocable to the transaction.*

(iv) X's payment of $4,000 to its outside counsel is an amount paid to facilitate the creation of an intangible, as described in paragraph (e)(1)(i) of this section. Because X's transaction costs do not exceed $5,000, X's transaction costs are de minimis within the meaning of

paragraph (e)(4)(iii)(A) of this section. Accordingly, X is not required to capitalize the $4,000 payment to its outside counsel under this section.

Example 2. Franchise agreement. (i) R corporation is a franchisor of income tax return preparation outlets. V corporation negotiates with R to obtain the right to operate an income tax return preparation outlet under a franchise from R. V pays an initial $100,000 franchise fee to R in exchange for the franchise agreement. In addition, V pays its outside counsel $4,000 to represent V during the negotiations with R. V also pays $2,000 to an industry consultant to advise V during the negotiations with R.

(ii) Under paragraph (d)(6)(i)(A) of this section, V's payment of $100,000 is an amount paid to another party to enter into an agreement with that party providing V the right to use tangible or intangible property. Accordingly, V must capitalize its $100,000 payment to R. The franchise agreement is a self-created amortizable section 197 intangible within the meaning of section 197(c). Accordingly, as provided in paragraph (f)(3) of this section, the 12-month rule contained in paragraph (f)(1) of this section does not apply.

(iii) V's payment of $4,000 to its outside counsel and $2,000 to the industry consultant are amounts paid to facilitate the creation of an intangible, as described in paragraph (e)(1)(i) of this section. Because V's aggregate transaction costs exceed $5,000, V's transaction costs are not de minimis within the meaning of paragraph (e)(4)(iii)(A) of this section. Accordingly, V must capitalize the $4,000 payment to its outside counsel and the $2,000 payment to the industry consultant under this section into the basis of the franchise, as provided in paragraph (g) of this section.

Example 3. Covenant not to compete. (i) On December 1, 2005, N corporation, a calendar year taxpayer, enters into a covenant not to compete with B, a key employee that is leaving the employ of N. The covenant not to compete is not entered into in connection with the acquisition of an interest in a trade or business. The covenant not to compete prohibits B from competing with N for a period of 9 months, beginning December 1, 2005. N pays B $25,000 in full consideration for B's agreement not to compete. In addition, N pays its outside counsel $6,000 to facilitate the creation of the covenant not to compete with B. N does not have a short taxable year in 2005 or 2006.

(ii) Under paragraph (d)(6)(i)(C) of this section, N's payment of $25,000 is an amount paid to another party to induce that party to enter into a covenant not to compete with N. However, because the covenant not to compete has a duration that does not extend beyond 12 months after the first date on which N realizes the rights attributable to its payment (i.e., December 1, 2005) or beyond the end of the taxable year following the taxable year in which payment is made, the 12-month rule contained in paragraph (f)(1) of this section applies. Accordingly, N is not required to capitalize its $25,000 payment to B or its $6,000 payment to facilitate the creation of the covenant not to compete.

Example 4. Demand-side management. (i) X corporation, a public utility engaged in generating and distributing electrical energy, provides programs to its customers to promote energy conservation and energy efficiency. These programs are aimed at reducing electrical costs to X's customers, building goodwill with X's customers, and reducing X's future operating and capital costs. X provides these programs without obligating any of its customers participating in the programs to purchase power from X in the future. Under these programs, X pays a consultant to help industrial customers design energy-efficient manufacturing processes, to conduct "energy efficiency audits" that serve to identify for customers inefficiencies in their energy usage patterns, and to provide cash allowances to encourage residential customers to replace existing appliances with more energy efficient appliances.

(ii) The amounts paid by X to the consultant are not amounts to acquire or create an intangible under paragraph (c) or (d) of this section or to facilitate such an acquisition or creation. In addition, the amounts do not create a separate and distinct intangible asset within the meaning of paragraph (b)(3) of this section. Accordingly, the amounts paid to the consultant are not required to be capitalized under this section. While the amounts may serve to reduce future operating and capital costs and create goodwill with customers, these benefits, without more, are not intangibles for which capitalization is required under this section.

Example 5. Business process re-engineering. (i) V corporation manufactures its products using a batch production system. Under this system, V continuously produces component parts of its various products and stockpiles these parts until they are needed in V's final assembly line. Finished goods are stockpiled awaiting orders from customers. V discovers that this process ties up significant amounts of V's capital in work-in-process and finished goods inventories. V hires B, a consultant, to advise V on improving the efficiency of its manufacturing operations. B recommends a complete re-engineering of V's manufacturing process to a process known as just-in-time manufacturing. Just-in-time manufacturing involves reconfiguring a manufacturing plant to a configuration of "cells" where each team in a cell performs the entire manufacturing process for a particular customer order, thus reducing inventory stockpiles.

(ii) V incurred three categories of costs to convert its manufacturing process to a just-in-time system. First, V paid B, a consultant, $250,000 in professional fees to implement the conversion of V's plant to a just-in-time system. Second, V paid C, a contractor, $100,000 to relocate and reconfigure V's manufacturing equipment from an assembly line layout to a configuration of cells. Third, V paid D, a consultant, $50,000 to train V's employees in the just-in-time manufacturing process.

(iii) The amounts paid by V to B, C, and D are not amounts to acquire or create an intangible under paragraph (c) or (d) of this section or to facilitate such an acquisition or creation. In addition, the amounts do not create a separate and distinct intangible asset within the meaning of paragraph (b)(3) of this section. Accordingly, the amounts paid to B, C, and D are not required to be capitalized under this section. While the amounts produce long term benefits to V in the form of reduced inventory stockpiles, improved product quality, and increased efficiency, these benefits, without more, are not intangibles for which capitalization is required under this section.

Example 6. Defense of business reputation. (i) X, an investment adviser, serves as the fund manager of a money market investment fund. X, like its competitors in the industry, strives to maintain a constant net asset value for its money market fund of $1.00 per share. During 2005, in the course of managing the fund assets, X incorrectly predicts the direction of market interest rates, resulting in significant investment losses to the fund. Due to these significant losses, X is faced with the prospect of reporting a net asset value that is less than $1.00 per share. X is not aware of any investment adviser in its industry that has ever reported a net asset value for its money market fund of less than $1.00 per share. X is concerned that reporting a net asset value of less than $1.00 per share will significantly harm its reputation as an investment adviser, and could lead to litigation by shareholders. X decides to contribute $2,000,000 to the fund in order to raise the net asset value of the fund to $1.00 per share. This contribution is not a loan to the fund and does not give X any ownership interest in the fund.

(ii) The $2,000,000 contribution is not an amount paid to acquire or create an intangible under paragraph (c) or (d) of this section or to facilitate such an acquisition or creation. In addition, the amount does not create a separate and distinct intangible asset within the meaning of paragraph (b)(3) of this section. Accordingly, the amount contributed to the fund is not required to be capitalized under this section. While the amount serves to protect the business reputation of the taxpayer and may protect the taxpayer from litigation by shareholders, these benefits, without more, are not intangibles for which capitalization is required under this section.

Example 7. Product launch costs. (i) R corporation, a manufacturer of pharmaceutical products, is required by law to obtain regulatory approval before selling its products. While awaiting regulatory approval on Product A, R pays to develop and implement a marketing strategy and an advertising campaign to raise consumer awareness of the purported need for Product A. R also pays to train health care professionals and other distributors in the proper use of Product A.

(ii) The amounts paid by R are not amounts paid to acquire or create an intangible under paragraph (c) or (d) of this section or to facilitate such an acquisition or creation. In addition, the amounts do not create a separate and distinct intangible asset within the meaning of paragraph (b)(3) of this section. Accordingly, R is not required to capitalize these amounts under this section. While the amounts may benefit R by creating consumer demand for Product A and increasing awareness of Product A among distributors, these benefits, without more, are not intangibles for which capitalization is required under this section.

Example 8. Stocklifting costs. (i) N corporation is a wholesale distributor of Brand A aftermarket automobile replacement parts. In an effort to induce a retail automobile parts supply store to stock only Brand A parts, N offers to replace all of the store's inventory of other branded parts with Brand A parts, and to credit the store for its cost of other branded parts. The store is under no obligation to continue stocking Brand A parts or to purchase a minimum volume of Brand A parts from N in the future.

(ii) The amount paid by N as a credit to the store for the cost of other branded parts is not an amount paid to acquire or create an intangible under paragraph (c) or (d) of this section or to facilitate such an acquisition or creation. In addition, the amount does not create a separate and distinct intangible asset within the meaning of paragraph (b)(3) of this section. Accordingly, N is not required to capitalize the amount under this section. While the amount may create a hope or expectation by N that the store will continue to stock Brand A parts, this benefit, without more, is not an intangible for which capitalization is required under this section.

(iii) Alternatively, assume that N agrees to credit the store for its cost of other branded parts in exchange for the store's agreement to purchase all of its inventory requirements for such parts from N for a period of at least 3 years. The amount paid by N as a credit to the store for the cost of other branded parts is an amount paid to induce the store to enter into an agreement providing R the right to provide property. Accordingly, R must capitalize its payment.

Example 9. Package design costs. (i) Z corporation manufactures and markets personal care products. Z pays $100,000 to a consultant to develop a package design for Z's newest product, Product A. Z also pays a fee to a government agency to obtain trademark and copyright protection on certain elements of the package design. Z pays outside legal counsel $10,000 for services rendered in preparing and filing the trademark and copyright applications and for other services rendered in securing the trademark and copyright protection.

(ii) The $100,000 paid by Z to the consultant for development of the package design is not an amount paid to acquire or create an intangible under paragraph (c) or (d) of this section or to facilitate such an acquisition or creation. In addition, as provided in paragraph (b)(3)(v) of this section, amounts paid to develop a package design are treated as amounts that do not create a separate and distinct intangible asset. Accordingly, Z is not required to capitalize the $100,000 payment under this section.

(iii) The amounts paid by Z to the government agency to obtain trademark and copyright protection are amounts paid to a government agency for a right granted by that agency. Accordingly, Z must capitalize the payment. In addition, the $10,000 paid by Z to its outside counsel is an amount paid to facilitate the creation of the trademark and copyright. Because the aggregate amounts paid to facilitate the transaction exceed $5,000, the amounts are not de minimis as defined in paragraph (e)(4)(iii)(A) of this section. Accordingly, Z must capitalize the $10,000 payment to its outside counsel under paragraph (b)(1)(v) of this section.

(iv) Alternatively, assume that Z acquires an existing package design for Product A as part of an acquisition of a trade or business that constitutes an applicable asset acquisition within the meaning of section 1060(c). Assume further that $100,000 of the consideration paid by N in the acquisition is properly allocable to the package design for Product A. Under paragraph (c)(1) of this section, Z must capitalize the $100,000 payment.

Example 10. Contract to provide services. (i) Q corporation, a financial planning firm, provides financial advisory services on a fee-only basis. During 2005, Q and several other financial planning firms submit separate bids to R corporation for a contract to become one of three providers of financial advisory services to R's employees. Q pays $2,000 to a printing company to develop and produce materials for its sales presentation to R's management. Q also pays $6,000 to travel to R's corporate headquarters to make the sales presentation, and $20,000 of salaries to its employees for services performed in preparing the bid and making the presentation to R's management. Q's bid is successful and Q enters into an agreement with R in 2005 under which Q agrees to provide financial advisory services to R's employees, and R agrees to pay Q's fee on behalf of each employee who chooses to utilize such services. R enters into similar agreements with two other financial planning firms, and R's employees may choose to use the services of any one of the three firms. Based on its past experience, Q reasonably expects to provide services to at least 5 percent of R's employees.

(ii) Q's agreement with R is not an agreement providing Q the right to provide services, as described in paragraph (d)(6)(i)(B) of this section. Under paragraph (d)(6)(iv) the agreement places no obligation on another person to request or pay for Q's services. Accordingly, Q is not required to capitalize any of the amounts paid in the process of pursuing the agreement with R.

Example 11. Mutual fund distributor. (i) D incurs costs to enter into a distribution agreement with M, a mutual fund. The initial term of the distribution agreement is two years, and afterwards must be approved annually by M. The distribution agreement can be terminated by either party on 60 days notice. Although distribution agreements are rarely terminated in the mutual fund industry, M is not economically compelled to continue D's distribution agreement. Under the distribution agreement, D has the exclusive right to sell shares of M and agrees to use its best efforts to solicit orders for the sale of shares of M. D sells shares in M directly to the general public as well as through brokers. When an investor places an order for M shares with a broker, D pays the broker a commission for selling the shares to the investor. Under the distribution agreement, D receives compensation from M in the form of 12b-1 fees (which equal a percentage of M's net asset value attributable to investors that have held their shares for up to 6 years) and contingent deferred sales charges (which are paid if the investor redeems the purchased shares within 6 years).

(ii) The distribution agreement is not an agreement providing D with the right to provide services, as described in paragraph (d)(6)(i)(B) of this section, because the distribution agreement can be terminated by M at will upon 60 days notice and M is not economically compelled to continue the distribution agreement. Accordingly, D is not required to capitalize the costs of creating (or facilitating the creation of) the distribution agreement under paragraphs (b)(1)(ii) or (v) of this section. In addition, as provided in paragraph (b)(3)(ii) of this section, amounts paid to create an agreement are treated as amounts that do not create a separate and distinct intangible asset. Accordingly, D also is not required to capitalize the costs of creating (or facilitating the creation of) the distribution agreement under paragraph (b)(1)(iii) or (v) of this section.

(iii) Under paragraph (b)(3)(iii), the broker commissions paid by D in performing services under the distribution agreement do not create (or facilitate the creation of) a separate and distinct intangible asset. In addition, the broker commissions do not create an intangible described in paragraph (d) of this section. Accordingly, D is not required to capitalize the broker commissions under this section.

(m) *Amortization.*—For rules relating to amortization of certain intangibles, see § 1.167(a)-3.

(n) *Intangible interests in land.*—[Reserved].

(o) *Effective date.*—This section applies to amounts paid or incurred on or after December 31, 2003.

(p) *Accounting method changes.*—(1) *In general.*—A taxpayer seeking to change a method of accounting to comply with this section must secure the consent of the Commissioner in accordance with the requirements of § 1.446-1(e). For the taxpayer's first taxable year ending on or after December 31, 2003, the taxpayer is granted the consent of the Commissioner to change its method of accounting to comply with this section, provided the taxpayer follows the administrative procedures issued under § 1.446-1(e)(3)(ii) for obtaining the Commissioner's automatic consent to a change in accounting method (for further guidance, for example, see Rev. Proc. 2002-9 (2002-1 C.B. 327) and § 601.601(d)(2)(ii)(b) of this chapter).

(2) *Scope limitations.*—Any limitations on obtaining the automatic consent of the Commissioner do not apply to a taxpayer seeking to change to a method of accounting to comply with this section for its first taxable year ending on or after December 31, 2003.

(3) *Section 481(a) adjustment.*—With the exception of a change to a pooling method authorized by this section, the section 481(a) adjustment for a change in method of accounting to comply with this section for a taxpayer's first taxable year ending on or after December 31, 2003, is determined by taking into account only amounts paid or incurred in taxable years ending on or after January 24, 2002. A taxpayer seeking to change to a pooling method authorized by this section on or after the effective date of these regulations must change to the method using a cut-off method. [Reg. § 1.263(a)-4.]

☐ [T.D. 9107, 12-31-2003.]

[Reg. § 1.263(a)-5]

§ 1.263(a)-5. Amounts paid or incurred to facilitate an acquisition of a trade or business, a change in the capital structure of a business entity, and certain other transactions.—(a) *General rule.*— A taxpayer must capitalize an amount paid to facilitate (within the meaning of paragraph (b) of this section) each of the following transactions, without regard to whether the transaction is comprised of a single step or a series of steps carried out as part of a single plan and without regard to whether gain or loss is recognized in the transaction:

(1) An acquisition of assets that constitute a trade or business (whether the taxpayer is the acquirer in the acquisition or the target of the acquisition).

(2) An acquisition by the taxpayer of an ownership interest in a business entity if, immediately after the acquisition, the taxpayer and the business entity are related within the meaning of section 267(b) or 707(b) (see § 1.263(a)-4 for rules requiring capitalization of amounts paid by the taxpayer to acquire an ownership interest in a business entity, or to facilitate the acquisition of an ownership interest in a business entity, where the taxpayer and the business entity are not related within the meaning of section 267(b) or 707(b) immediately after the acquisition).

(3) An acquisition of an ownership interest in the taxpayer (other than an acquisition by the taxpayer of an ownership interest in the taxpayer, whether by redemption or otherwise).

(4) A restructuring, recapitalization, or reorganization of the capital structure of a business entity (including reorganizations described in section 368 and distributions of stock by the taxpayer as described in section 355).

(5) A transfer described in section 351 or section 721 (whether the taxpayer is the transferor or transferee).

(6) A formation or organization of a disregarded entity.

(7) An acquisition of capital.

(8) A stock issuance.

(9) A borrowing. For purposes of this section, a borrowing means any issuance of debt, including an issuance of debt in an acquisition of capital or in a recapitalization. A borrowing also includes debt issued in a debt for debt exchange under § 1.1001-3.

(10) Writing an option.

(b) *Scope of facilitate.*—(1) *In general.*—Except as otherwise provided in this section, an amount is paid to facilitate a transaction described in paragraph (a) of this section if the amount is paid in the process of investigating or otherwise pursuing the transaction. Whether an amount is paid in the process of investigating or otherwise pursuing the transaction is determined based on all of the facts and circumstances. In determining whether an amount is paid to facilitate a transaction, the fact that the amount would (or would not) have been paid but for the transaction is relevant, but is not determinative. An amount paid to determine the value or price of a transaction is an amount paid in the process of investigating or otherwise pursuing the transaction. An amount paid to another party in exchange for tangible or intangible property is not an amount paid to facilitate the exchange. For example, the purchase price paid to the target of an asset acquisition in exchange for its assets is not an amount paid to facilitate the acquisition. Similarly, the purchase price paid by an acquirer to the target's shareholders in exchange for their stock in a stock acquisition is not an amount paid to facilitate the acquisition of the stock. See § 1.263(a)-1, § 1.263(a)-2, and § 1.263(a)-4 for rules requiring capitalization of the purchase price paid to acquire property.

(2) *Ordering rules.*—An amount paid in the process of investigating or otherwise pursuing both a transaction described in paragraph (a) of this section and an acquisition or creation of an intangible described in § 1.263(a)-4 is subject to the rules contained in this section, and not to the rules contained in § 1.263(a)-4. In addition, an amount required to be capitalized by § 1.263(a)-1, § 1.263(a)-2, or § 1.263(a)-4 does not facilitate a transaction described in paragraph (a) of this section.

(c) *Special rules for certain costs.*—(1) *Borrowing costs.*—An amount paid to facilitate a borrowing does not facilitate another transaction (other than the borrowing) described in paragraph (a) of this section.

(2) *Costs of asset sales.*—An amount paid by a taxpayer to facilitate a sale of its assets does not facilitate another transaction (other than the sale) described in paragraph (a) of this section. For example, where a target corporation, in preparation for a merger with an acquiring corporation, sells assets that are not desired by the acquiring corporation, amounts paid to facilitate the sale of the unwanted assets are not required to be capitalized as amounts paid to facilitate the merger.

(3) *Mandatory stock distributions.*—An amount paid in the process of investigating or otherwise pursuing a distribution of stock by a taxpayer to its shareholders does not facilitate a transaction described in paragraph (a) of this section if the divestiture of the stock (or of properties transferred to an entity whose stock is distributed) is required by law, regulatory mandate, or court order. A taxpayer is not required to capitalize (under this section or § 1.263(a)-4) an amount paid to organize (or facilitate the organization of) an entity if the entity is organized solely to receive properties that the taxpayer is required to divest by law, regulatory mandate, or court order and if the taxpayer distributes the stock of the entity to its shareholders. A taxpayer also is not required to capitalize (under this section or § 1.263(a)-4) an amount paid to transfer property to an entity if the taxpayer is required to divest itself of that property by law, regulatory mandate, or court order and if the stock of the recipient entity is distributed to the taxpayer's shareholders.

(4) *Bankruptcy reorganization costs.*—An amount paid to institute or administer a proceeding under Chapter 11 of the Bankruptcy Code by a taxpayer that is the debtor under the proceeding constitutes an amount paid to facilitate a reorganization within the meaning of paragraph (a)(4) of this section, regardless of the purpose for which the proceeding is instituted. For example, an amount paid to prepare and file a petition under Chapter 11, to obtain an extension of the exclusivity period under Chapter 11, to formulate plans of reorganization under Chapter 11, to analyze plans of reorganization formulated by another party in interest, or to contest or obtain approval of a plan of reorganization under Chapter 11 facilitates a reorganization within the meaning of this section. However, amounts specifically paid to formulate, analyze, contest or obtain approval of the portion of a plan of reorganization under Chapter 11 that resolves tort liabilities of the taxpayer do not facilitate a reorganization within the meaning of paragraph (a)(4) of this section if the amounts would have been treated as ordinary and necessary business expenses under section 162 had the bankruptcy proceeding not been instituted. In addition, an amount paid by the taxpayer to defend against the

commencement of an involuntary bankruptcy proceeding against the taxpayer does not facilitate a reorganization within the meaning of paragraph (a)(4) of this section. An amount paid by the debtor to operate its business during a Chapter 11 bankruptcy proceeding is not an amount paid to institute or administer the bankruptcy proceeding and does not facilitate a reorganization. Such amount is treated in the same manner as it would have been treated had the bankruptcy proceeding not been instituted.

(5) *Stock issuance costs of open-end regulated investment companies.*—Amounts paid by an open-end regulated investment company (within the meaning of section 851) to facilitate an issuance of its stock are treated as amounts that do not facilitate a transaction described in paragraph (a) of this section unless the amounts are paid during the initial stock offering period.

(6) *Integration costs.*—An amount paid to integrate the business operations of the taxpayer with the business operations of another does not facilitate a transaction described in paragraph (a) of this section, regardless of when the integration activities occur.

(7) *Registrar and transfer agent fees for the maintenance of capital stock records.*—An amount paid by a taxpayer to a registrar or transfer agent in connection with the transfer of the taxpayer's capital stock does not facilitate a transaction described in paragraph (a) of this section unless the amount is paid with respect to a specific transaction described in paragraph (a). For example, a taxpayer is not required to capitalize periodic payments to a transfer agent for maintaining records of the names and addresses of shareholders who trade the taxpayer's shares on a national exchange. By comparison, a taxpayer is required to capitalize an amount paid to the transfer agent for distributing proxy statements requesting shareholder approval of a transaction described in paragraph (a) of this section.

(8) *Termination payments and amounts paid to facilitate mutually exclusive transactions.*—An amount paid to terminate (or facilitate the termination of) an agreement to enter into a transaction described in paragraph (a) of this section constitutes an amount paid to facilitate a second transaction described in paragraph (a) of this section only if the transactions are mutually exclusive. An amount paid to facilitate a transaction described in paragraph (a) of this section is treated as an amount paid to facilitate a second transaction described in paragraph (a) of this section only if the transactions are mutually exclusive.

(d) *Simplifying conventions.*—(1) *In general.*—For purposes of this section, employee compensation (within the meaning of paragraph (d)(2) of this section), overhead, and de minimis costs (within the meaning of paragraph (d)(3) of this section) are treated as amounts that do not facilitate a transaction described in paragraph (a) of this section.

(2) *Employee compensation.*—(i) *In general.*—The term *employee compensation* means compensation (including salary, bonuses and commissions) paid to an employee of the taxpayer. For purposes of this section, whether an individual is an employee is determined in accordance with the rules contained in section 3401(c) and the regulations thereunder.

(ii) *Certain amounts treated as employee compensation.*—For purposes of this section, a guaranteed payment to a partner in a partnership is treated as employee compensation. For purposes of this section, annual compensation paid to a director of a corporation is treated as employee compensation. For example, an amount paid to a director of a corporation for attendance at a regular meeting of the board of directors (or committee thereof) is treated as employee compensation for purposes of this section. However, an amount paid to the director for attendance at a special meeting of the board of directors (or committee thereof) is not treated as employee compensation. An amount paid to a person that is not an employee of the taxpayer (including the employer of the individual who performs the services) is treated as employee compensation for purposes of this section only if the amount is paid for secretarial, clerical, or similar administrative support services (other than services involving the preparation and distribution of proxy solicitations and other documents seeking shareholder approval of a transaction described in paragraph (a) of this section). In the case of an affiliated group of corporations filing a consolidated federal income tax return, a payment by one member of the group to a second member of the group for services performed by an employee of the second member is treated as employee compensation if the services provided by the employee are provided at a time during which both members are affiliated.

(3) *De minimis costs.*—(i) *In general.*—The term *de minimis costs* means amounts (other than employee compensation and overhead) paid in the process of investigating or otherwise pursuing a transac-

tion described in paragraph (a) of this section if, in the aggregate, the amounts do not exceed $5,000 (or such greater amount as may be set forth in published guidance). If the amounts exceed $5,000 (or such greater amount as may be set forth in published guidance), none of the amounts are de minimis costs within the meaning of this paragraph (d)(3). For purposes of this paragraph (d)(3), an amount paid in the form of property is valued at its fair market value at the time of the payment.

(ii) *Treatment of commissions.*—The term *de minimis costs* does not include commissions paid to facilitate a transaction described in paragraph (a) of this section.

(4) *Election to capitalize.*—A taxpayer may elect to treat employee compensation, overhead, or de minimis costs paid in the process of investigating or otherwise pursuing a transaction described in paragraph (a) of this section as amounts that facilitate the transaction. The election is made separately for each transaction and applies to employee compensation, overhead, or de minimis costs, or to any combination thereof. For example, a taxpayer may elect to treat overhead and de minimis costs, but not employee compensation, as amounts that facilitate the transaction. A taxpayer makes the election by treating the amounts to which the election applies as amounts that facilitate the transaction in the taxpayer's timely filed original federal income tax return (including extensions) for the taxable year during which the amounts are paid. In the case of an affiliated group of corporations filing a consolidated return, the election is made separately with respect to each member of the group, and not with respect to the group as a whole. In the case of an S corporation or partnership, the election is made by the S corporation or by the partnership, and not by the shareholders or partners. An election made under this paragraph (d)(4) is revocable with respect to each taxable year for which made only with the consent of the Commissioner.

(e) *Certain acquisitive transactions.*—(1) *In general.*—Except as provided in paragraph (e)(2) of this section (relating to inherently facilitative amounts), an amount paid by the taxpayer in the process of investigating or otherwise pursuing a covered transaction (as described in paragraph (e)(3) of this section) facilitates the transaction within the meaning of this section only if the amount relates to activities performed on or after the earlier of—

(i) The date on which a letter of intent, exclusivity agreement, or similar written communication (other than a confidentiality agreement) is executed by representatives of the acquirer and the target; or

(ii) The date on which the material terms of the transaction (as tentatively agreed to by representatives of the acquirer and the target) are authorized or approved by the taxpayer's board of directors (or committee of the board of directors) or, in the case of a taxpayer that is not a corporation, the date on which the material terms of the transaction (as tentatively agreed to by representatives of the acquirer and the target) are authorized or approved by the appropriate governing officials of the taxpayer. In the case of a transaction that does not require authorization or approval of the taxpayer's board of directors (or appropriate governing officials in the case of a taxpayer that is not a corporation) the date determined under this paragraph (e)(1)(ii) is the date on which the acquirer and the target execute a binding written contract reflecting the terms of the transaction.

(2) *Exception for inherently facilitative amounts.*—An amount paid in the process of investigating or otherwise pursuing a covered transaction facilitates that transaction if the amount is inherently facilitative, regardless of whether the amount is paid for activities performed prior to the date determined under paragraph (e)(1) of this section. An amount is inherently facilitative if the amount is paid for—

(i) Securing an appraisal, formal written evaluation, or fairness opinion related to the transaction;

(ii) Structuring the transaction, including negotiating the structure of the transaction and obtaining tax advice on the structure of the transaction (for example, obtaining tax advice on the application of section 368);

(iii) Preparing and reviewing the documents that effectuate the transaction (for example, a merger agreement or purchase agreement);

(iv) Obtaining regulatory approval of the transaction, including preparing and reviewing regulatory filings;

(v) Obtaining shareholder approval of the transaction (for example, proxy costs, solicitation costs, and costs to promote the transaction to shareholders); or

(vi) Conveying property between the parties to the transaction (for example, transfer taxes and title registration costs).

(3) *Covered transactions.*—For purposes of this paragraph (e), the term *covered transaction* means the following transactions:

(i) A taxable acquisition by the taxpayer of assets that constitute a trade or business.

(ii) A taxable acquisition of an ownership interest in a business entity (whether the taxpayer is the acquirer in the acquisition or the target of the acquisition) if, immediately after the acquisition, the acquirer and the target are related within the meaning of section 267(b) or 707(b).

(iii) A reorganization described in section 368(a)(1)(A), (B), or (C) or a reorganization described in section 368(a)(1)(D) in which stock or securities of the corporation to which the assets are transferred are distributed in a transaction which qualifies under section 354 or 356 (whether the taxpayer is the acquirer or the target in the reorganization).

(f) *Documentation of success-based fees.*—An amount paid that is contingent on the successful closing of a transaction described in paragraph (a) of this section is an amount paid to facilitate the transaction except to the extent the taxpayer maintains sufficient documentation to establish that a portion of the fee is allocable to activities that do not facilitate the transaction. This documentation must be completed on or before the due date of the taxpayer's timely filed original federal income tax return (including extensions) for the taxable year during which the transaction closes. For purposes of this paragraph (f), documentation must consist of more than merely an allocation between activities that facilitate the transaction and activities that do not facilitate the transaction, and must consist of supporting records (for example, time records, itemized invoices, or other records) that identify—

(1) The various activities performed by the service provider;

(2) The amount of the fee (or percentage of time) that is allocable to each of the various activities performed;

(3) Where the date the activity was performed is relevant to understanding whether the activity facilitated the transaction, the amount of the fee (or percentage of time) that is allocable to the performance of that activity before and after the relevant date; and

(4) The name, business address, and business telephone number of the service provider.

(g) *Treatment of capitalized costs.*—(1) *Tax-free acquisitive transactions.*—[Reserved].

(2) *Taxable acquisitive transactions.*—(i) *Acquirer.*—In the case of an acquisition, merger, or consolidation that is not described in section 368, an amount required to be capitalized under this section by the acquirer is added to the basis of the acquired assets (in the case of a transaction that is treated as an acquisition of the assets of the target for federal income tax purposes) or the acquired stock (in the case of a transaction that is treated as an acquisition of the stock of the target for federal income tax purposes).

(ii) *Target.*—(A) *Asset acquisition.*—In the case of an acquisition, merger, or consolidation that is not described in section 368 and that is treated as an acquisition of the assets of the target for federal income tax purposes, an amount required to be capitalized under this section by the target is treated as a reduction of the target's amount realized on the disposition of its assets.

(B) *Stock acquisition.*—[Reserved].

(3) *Stock issuance transactions.*—[Reserved].

(4) *Borrowings.*—For the treatment of amounts required to be capitalized under this section with respect to a borrowing, see § 1.446-5.

(5) *Treatment of capitalized amounts by option writer.*—An amount required to be capitalized by an option writer under paragraph (a)(10) of this section is not currently deductible under section 162 or 212. Instead, the amount required to be capitalized generally reduces the total premium received by the option writer. However, other provisions of law may limit the reduction of the premium by the capitalized amount (for example, if the capitalized amount is never deductible by the option writer).

(h) *Application to accrual method taxpayers.*—For purposes of this section, the terms *amount paid* and *payment* mean, in the case of a taxpayer using an accrual method of accounting, a liability incurred (within the meaning of § 1.446-1(c)(1)(ii)). A liability may not be taken into account under this section prior to the taxable year during which the liability is incurred.

(i) [Reserved].

(j) *Coordination with other provisions of the Internal Revenue Code.*—Nothing in this section changes the treatment of an amount that is specifically provided for under any other provision of the Internal Revenue Code (other than section 162(a) or 212) or regulations thereunder.

(k) *Treatment of indirect payments.*—For purposes of this section, references to an amount paid to or by a party include an amount paid on behalf of that party.

(l) *Examples.*—The following examples illustrate the rules of this section:

Example 1. Costs to facilitate. Q corporation pays its outside counsel $20,000 to assist Q in registering its stock with the Securities and Exchange Commission. Q is not a regulated investment company within the meaning of section 851. Q's payments to its outside counsel are amounts paid to facilitate the issuance of stock. Accordingly, Q must capitalize its $20,000 payment under paragraph (a)(8) of this section (whether incurred before or after the issuance of the stock and whether or not the registration is productive of equity capital).

Example 2. Costs to facilitate. Q corporation seeks to acquire all of the outstanding stock of Y corporation. To finance the acquisition, Q must issue new debt. Q pays an investment banker $25,000 to market the debt to the public and pays its outside counsel $10,000 to prepare the offering documents for the debt. Q's payment of $35,000 facilitates a borrowing and must be capitalized under paragraph (a)(9) of this section. As provided in paragraph (c)(1) of this section, Q's payment does not facilitate the acquisition of Y, notwithstanding the fact that Q incurred the new debt to finance its acquisition of Y. See § 1.446-5 for the treatment of Q's capitalized payment.

Example 3. Costs to facilitate. (i) Z agrees to pay investment banker B $1,000,000 for B's services in evaluating four alternative transactions ($250,000 for each alternative): an initial public offering; a borrowing of funds; an acquisition by Z of a competitor; and an acquisition of Z by a competitor. Z eventually decides to pursue a borrowing and abandons the other options.

(ii) The $250,000 payment to evaluate the possibility of a borrowing is an amount paid in the process of investigating or otherwise pursuing a transaction described in paragraph (a)(9) of this section. Accordingly Z must capitalize that $250,000 payment to B. See § 1.446-5 for the treatment of Z's capitalized payment.

(iii) The $250,000 payment to evaluate the possibility of an initial public offering is an amount paid in the process of investigating or otherwise pursuing a transaction described in paragraph (a)(8) of this section. Accordingly, Z must capitalize that $250,000 payment to B under this section. Because the borrowing and the initial public offering are not mutually exclusive transactions, the $250,000 is not treated as an amount paid to facilitate the borrowing. When Z abandons the initial public offering, Z may recover under section 165 the $250,000 paid to facilitate the initial public offering.

(iv) The $500,000 paid by Z to evaluate the possibilities of an acquisition of Z by a competitor and an acquisition of a competitor by Z are amounts paid in the process of investigating or otherwise pursuing transactions described in paragraphs (a) and (e)(3) of this section. Accordingly, Z is only required to capitalize under this section the portion of the $500,000 payment that relates to inherently facilitative activities under paragraph (e)(2) of this section or to activities performed on or after the date determined under paragraph (e)(1) of this section. Because the borrowing and the possible acquisitions are not mutually exclusive transactions, no portion of the $500,000 is treated as an amount paid to facilitate the borrowing. When Z abandons the acquisition transactions, Z may recover under section 165 any portion of the $500,000 that was paid to facilitate the acquisitions.

Example 4. Corporate acquisition. (i) On February 1, 2005, R corporation decides to investigate the acquisition of three potential targets: T corporation, U corporation, and V corporation. R's consideration of T, U, and V represents the consideration of three distinct transactions, any or all of which R might consummate and has the financial ability to consummate. On March 1, 2005, R enters into an exclusivity agreement with T and stops pursuing U and V. On July 1, 2005, R acquires all of the stock of T in a transaction described in section 368. R pays $1,000,000 to an investment banker and $50,000 to its outside counsel to conduct due diligence on T, U, and V; determine the value of T, U, and V; negotiate and structure the transaction with T; draft the merger agreement; secure shareholder approval; prepare SEC filings; and obtain the necessary regulatory approvals.

(ii) Under paragraph (e)(1) of this section, the amounts paid to conduct due diligence on T, U and V prior to March 1, 2005 (the date of the exclusivity agreement) are not amounts paid to facilitate the acquisition of the stock of T, U or V and are not required to be capitalized under this section. However, the amounts paid to conduct due diligence on T on and after March 1, 2005, are amounts paid to facilitate the acquisition of the stock of T and must be capitalized under paragraph (a)(2) of this section.

(iii) Under paragraph (e)(2) of this section, the amounts paid to determine the value of T, negotiate and structure the transaction with T, draft the merger agreement, secure shareholder approval, prepare SEC filings, and obtain necessary regulatory approvals are inherently facilitative amounts paid to facilitate the acquisition of the stock of T and must be capitalized, regardless of whether those activities occur prior to, on, or after March 1, 2005.

(iv) Under paragraph (e)(2) of this section, the amounts paid to determine the value of U and V are inherently facilitative amounts paid to facilitate the acquisition of U or V and must be capitalized. Because the acquisition of U, V, and T are not mutually exclusive transactions, the costs that facilitate the acquisition of U and V do not facilitate the acquisition of T. Accordingly, the amounts paid to determine the value of U and V may be recovered under section 165 in the taxable year that R abandons the planned mergers with U and V.

Example 5. Corporate acquisition; employee bonus. Assume the same facts as in *Example 4*, except R pays a bonus of $10,000 to one of its corporate officers who negotiated the acquisition of T. As provided by paragraph (d)(1) of this section, Y is not required to capitalize any portion of the bonus paid to the corporate officer.

Example 6. Corporate acquisition; integration costs. Assume the same facts as in *Example 4*, except that, before and after the acquisition is consummated, R incurs costs to relocate personnel and equipment, provide severance benefits to terminated employees, integrate records and information systems, prepare new financial statements for the combined entity, and reduce redundancies in the combined business operations. Under paragraph (c)(6) of this section, these costs do not facilitate the acquisition of T. Accordingly, R is not required to capitalize any of these costs under this section.

Example 7. Corporate acquisition; compensation to target's employees. Assume the same facts as in *Example 4*, except that, prior to the acquisition, certain employees of T held unexercised options issued pursuant to T's stock option plan. These options granted the employees the right to purchase T stock at a fixed option price. The options did not have a readily ascertainable value (within the meaning of §1.83-7(b)), and thus no amount was included in the employees' income when the options were granted. As a condition of the acquisition, T is required to terminate its stock option plan. T therefore agrees to pay its employees who hold unexercised stock options the difference between the option price and the current value of T's stock in consideration of their agreement to cancel their unexercised options. Under paragraph (d)(1) of this section, T is not required to capitalize the amounts paid to its employees. See section 83 for the treatment of amounts received in cancellation of stock options.

Example 8. Asset acquisition; employee compensation. N corporation owns tangible and intangible assets that constitute a trade or business. M corporation purchases all the assets of N in a taxable transaction. Under paragraph (a)(1) of this section, M must capitalize amounts paid to facilitate the acquisition of the assets of N. Under paragraph (d)(1) of this section, no portion of the salaries of M's employees who work on the acquisition are treated as facilitating the transaction.

Example 9. Corporate acquisition; retainer. Y corporation's outside counsel charges Y $60,000 for services rendered in facilitating the friendly acquisition of the stock of Y corporation by X corporation. Y has an agreement with its outside counsel under which Y pays an annual retainer of $50,000. Y's outside counsel has the right to offset amounts billed for any legal services rendered against the annual retainer. Pursuant to this agreement, Y's outside counsel offsets $50,000 of the legal fees from the acquisition against the retainer and bills Y for the balance of $10,000. The $60,000 legal fee is an amount paid to facilitate the acquisition of an ownership interest in Y as described in paragraph (a)(3) of this section. Y must capitalize the full amount of the $60,000 legal fee.

Example 10. Corporate acquisition; antitrust defense costs. On March 1, 2005, V corporation enters into an agreement with X corporation to acquire all of the outstanding stock of X. On April 1, 2005, federal and state regulators file suit against V to prevent the acquisition of X on the ground that the acquisition violates antitrust laws. V enters into a consent agreement with regulators on May 1, 2005, that allows the acquisition to proceed, but requires V to hold separate the business operations of X pending the outcome of the antitrust suit and subjects V to possible divestiture. V acquires title to all of the outstanding stock of X on June 1, 2005. After June 1, 2005, the regulators pursue antitrust litigation against V seeking rescission of the acquisition. V pays $50,000 to its outside counsel for services rendered after June 1, 2005, to defend against the antitrust litigation. V ultimately prevails in the antitrust litigation. V's costs to defend the antitrust litigation are costs to facilitate its acquisition of the stock of X under paragraph (a)(2) of this section and must be capitalized. Although title to the shares of X passed to V prior to the date V incurred costs to defend the antitrust litigation, the amounts paid by V are paid in the process of pursuing the acquisition of the stock of X because the acquisition was not complete until the antitrust litigation was ultimately resolved. V must capitalize the $50,000 in legal fees.

Example 11. Corporate acquisition; defensive measures. (i) On January 15, 2005, Y corporation, a publicly traded corporation, becomes the target of a hostile takeover attempt by Z corporation. In an effort to defend against the takeover, Y pays legal fees to seek an injunction against the takeover and investment banking fees to locate a potential "white knight" acquirer. Y also pays amounts to complete a defensive recapitalization, and pays $50,000 to an investment banker for a fairness opinion regarding Z's initial offer. Y's efforts to enjoin the takeover and locate a white knight acquirer are unsuccessful, and on March 15, 2005, Y's board of directors decides to abandon its defense against the takeover and negotiate with Z in an effort to obtain the highest possible price for its shareholders. After Y abandons its defense against the takeover, Y pays an investment banker $1,000,000 for a second fairness opinion and for services rendered in negotiating with Z.

(ii) The legal fees paid by Y to seek an injunction against the takeover are not amounts paid in the process of investigating or otherwise pursuing the transaction with Z. Accordingly, these legal fees are not required to be capitalized under this section.

(iii) The investment banking fees paid to search for a white knight acquirer do not facilitate an acquisition of Y by a white knight because none of Y's costs with respect to a white knight were inherently facilitative amounts and because Y did not reach the date described in paragraph (e)(1) of this section with respect to a white knight. Accordingly, these amounts are not required to be capitalized under this section.

(iv) The amounts paid by Y to investigate and complete the recapitalization must be capitalized under paragraph (a)(4) of this section.

(v) The $50,000 paid to the investment bankers for a fairness opinion during Y's defense against the takeover and the $1,000,000 paid to the investment bankers after Y abandons its defense against the takeover are inherently facilitative amounts with respect to the transaction with Z and must be capitalized under paragraph (a)(3) of this section.

Example 12. Corporate acquisition; acquisition by white knight. (i) Assume the same facts as in *Example 11*, except that Y's investment bankers identify three potential white knight acquirers: U corporation, V corporation, and W corporation. Y pays its investment bankers to conduct due diligence on the three potential white knight acquirers. On March 15, 2005, Y's board of directors approves a tentative acquisition agreement under which W agrees to acquire all of the stock of Y, and the investment bankers stop due diligence on U and V. On June 15, 2005, W acquires all of the stock of Y.

(ii) Under paragraph (e)(1) of this section, the amounts paid to conduct due diligence on U, V, and W prior to March 15, 2005 (the date of board of directors' approval) are not amounts paid to facilitate the acquisition of the stock of Y and are not required to be capitalized under this section. However, the amounts paid to conduct due diligence on W on and after March 15, 2005, facilitate the acquisition of the stock of Y and are required to be capitalized.

Example 13. Corporate acquisition; mutually exclusive costs. (i) Assume the same facts as in *Example 11*, except that Y's investment banker finds W, a white knight. Y and W execute a letter of intent on March 10, 2005. Under the terms of the letter of intent, Y must pay W a $10,000,000 break-up fee if the merger with W does not occur. On April 1, 2005, Z significantly increases the amount of its offer, and Y decides to accept Z's offer instead of merging with W. Y pays its investment banker $500,000 for inherently facilitative costs with respect to the potential merger with W. Y also pays its investment banker $2,000,000 for due diligence costs with respect to the potential merger with W, $1,000,000 of which relates to services performed on or after March 10, 2005.

(ii) Y's $500,000 payment for inherently facilitative costs and Y's $1,000,000 payment for due diligence activities performed on or after March 10, 2005 (the date the letter of intent with W is entered into) facilitate the potential merger with W. Because Y could not merge with both W and Z, under paragraph (c)(8) of this section the $500,000 and $1,000,000 payments also facilitate the transaction between Y and Z. Accordingly, Y must capitalize the $500,000 and $1,000,000 payments as amounts that facilitate the transaction with Z.

(iii) Similarly, because Y could not merge with both W and Z, under paragraph (c)(8) of this section the $10,000,000 termination payment facilitates the transaction between Y and Z. Accordingly, Y must capitalize the $10,000,000 termination payment as an amount that facilitates the transaction with Z.

Example 14. Break-up fee; transactions not mutually exclusive. N corporation and U corporation enter into an agreement under which U would acquire all the stock or all the assets of N in exchange for U stock. Under the terms of the agreement, if either party terminates the agreement, the terminating party must pay the other party $10,000,000. U decides to terminate the agreement and pays N $10,000,000. Shortly thereafter, U acquires all the stock of V corporation, a competitor of N. U had the financial resources to have acquired both N and V. U's $10,000,000 payment does not facilitate U's acquisition of V. Accordingly, U is not required to capitalize the $10,000,000 payment under this section.

Example 15. Corporate reorganization; initial public offering. Y corporation is a closely held corporation. Y's board of directors authorizes an initial public offering of Y's stock to fund future growth. Y pays $5,000,000 in professional fees for investment banking services related to the determination of the offering price and legal services related to the development of the offering prospectus and the registration and issuance of stock. The investment banking and legal services are performed both before and after board authorization. Under paragraph (a)(8) of this section, the $5,000,000 is an amount paid to facilitate a stock issuance.

Example 16. Auction. (i) N corporation seeks to dispose of all of the stock of its wholly owned subsidiary, P corporation, through an auction process and requests that each bidder submit a non-binding purchase offer in the form of a draft agreement. Q corporation hires an investment banker to assist in the preparation of Q's bid to acquire P and to conduct a due diligence investigation of P. On July 1, 2005, Q submits its draft agreement. On August 1, 2005, N informs Q that it has accepted Q's offer, and presents Q with a signed letter of intent to sell all of the stock of P to Q. On August 5, 2005, Q's board of directors approves the terms of the transaction and authorizes Q to execute the letter of intent. Q executes a binding letter of intent with N on August 6, 2005.

(ii) Under paragraph (e)(1) of this section, the amounts paid by Q to its investment banker that are not inherently facilitative and that are paid for activities performed prior to August 5, 2005 (the date Q's board of directors approves the transaction) are not amounts paid to facilitate the acquisition of P. Amounts paid by Q to its investment banker for activities performed on or after August 5, 2005, and amounts paid by Q to its investment banker that are inherently facilitative amounts within the meaning of paragraph (e)(2) of this section are required to be capitalized under this section.

Example 17. Stock distribution. Z corporation distributes natural gas throughout state Y. The federal government brings an antitrust action against Z seeking divestiture of certain of Z's natural gas distribution assets. As a result of a court ordered divestiture, Z and the federal government agree to a plan of divestiture that requires Z to organize a subsidiary to receive the divested assets and to distribute the stock of the subsidiary to its shareholders. During 2005, Z pays $300,000 to various independent contractors for the following services: studying customer demand in the area to be served by the divested assets, identifying assets to be transferred to the subsidiary, organizing the subsidiary, structuring the transfer of assets to the subsidiary to qualify as a tax-free transaction to Z, and distributing the stock of the subsidiary to the stockholders. Under paragraph (c)(3) of this section, Z is not required to capitalize any portion of the $300,000 payments.

Example 18. Bankruptcy reorganization. (i) X corporation is the defendant in numerous lawsuits alleging tort liability based on X's role in manufacturing certain defective products. X files a petition for reorganization under Chapter 11 of the Bankruptcy Code in an effort to manage all of the lawsuits in a single proceeding. X pays its outside counsel to prepare the petition and plan of reorganization, to analyze adequate protection under the plan, to attend hearings before the Bankruptcy Court concerning the plan, and to defend against motions by creditors and tort claimants to strike the taxpayer's plan.

(ii) X's reorganization under Chapter 11 of the Bankruptcy Code is a reorganization within the meaning of paragraph (a)(4) of this section. Under paragraph (c)(4) of this section, amounts paid by X to its outside counsel to prepare, analyze or obtain approval of the portion of X's plan of reorganization that resolves X's tort liability do not facilitate the reorganization and are not required to be capitalized, provided that such amounts would have been treated as ordinary and necessary business expenses under section 162 had the bankruptcy proceeding not been instituted. All other amounts paid by X to its outside counsel for the services described above (including all amounts paid to prepare the bankruptcy petition) facilitate the reorganization and must be capitalized.

(m) *Effective date.*—This section applies to amounts paid or incurred on or after December 31, 2003.

(n) *Accounting method changes.*—(1) *In general.*—A taxpayer seeking to change a method of accounting to comply with this section must secure the consent of the Commissioner in accordance with the requirements of §1.446-1(e). For the taxpayer's first taxable year ending on or after December 31, 2003, the taxpayer is granted the consent of the Commissioner to change its method of accounting to comply with this section, provided the taxpayer follows the administrative procedures issued under §1.446-1(e)(3)(ii) for obtaining the Commissioner's automatic consent to a change in accounting method (for further guidance, for example, see Rev. Proc. 2002-9 (2002-1 C.B. 327) and §601.601(d)(2)(ii)(*b*) of this chapter).

(2) *Scope limitations.*—Any limitations on obtaining the automatic consent of the Commissioner do not apply to a taxpayer seeking to change to a method of accounting to comply with this section for its first taxable year ending on or after December 31, 2003.

(3) *Section 481(a) adjustment.*—The section 481(a) adjustment for a change in method of accounting to comply with this section for a taxpayer's first taxable year ending on or after December 31, 2003, is determined by taking into account only amounts paid or incurred in taxable years ending on or after January 24, 2002. [Reg. §1.263(a)-5.]

☐ [*T.D. 9107, 12-31-2003.*]

≫→ *Caution: Reg. §1.263(a)-6, below, as added by T.D. 9636, generally applies to tax years beginning on or after January 1, 2014; see Reg. §1.263(a)-6(c), below, for details and exceptions.*

[Reg. §1.263(a)-6.]

§1.263(a)-6. Election to deduct or capitalize certain expenditures.—(a) *In general.*—Under certain provisions of the Internal Revenue Code (Code), taxpayers may elect to treat capital expenditures as deductible expenses or as deferred expenses, or to treat deductible expenses as capital expenditures.

(b) *Election provisions.*—The sections referred to in paragraph (a) of this section include:

(1) Section 173 (circulation expenditures);

(2) Section 174 (research and experimental expenditures);

(3) Section 175 (soil and water conservation expenditures; endangered species recovery expenditures);

(4) Section 179 (election to expense certain depreciable business assets);

(5) Section 179A (deduction for clean-fuel vehicles and certain refueling property);

(6) Section 179B (deduction for capital costs incurred in complying with environmental protection agency sulfur regulations);

(7) Section 179C (election to expense certain refineries);

(8) Section 179D (energy efficient commercial buildings deduction);

(9) Section 179E (election to expense advanced mine safety equipment);

(10) Section 180 (expenditures by farmers for fertilizer);

(11) Section 181 (treatment of certain qualified film and television productions);

(12) Section 190 (expenditures to remove architectural and transportation barriers to the handicapped and elderly);

(13) Section 193 (tertiary injectants);

(14) Section 194 (treatment of reforestation expenditures);

(15) Section 195 (start-up expenditures);

(16) Section 198 (expensing of environmental remediation costs);

(17) Section 198A (expensing of qualified disaster expenses);

(18) Section 248 (organization expenditures of a corporation);

(19) Section 266 (carrying charges);

(20) Section 616 (development expenditures); and

(21) Section 709 (organization and syndication fees of a partnership).

(c) *Effective/applicability date.*—(1) *In general.*—This section applies to taxable years beginning on or after January 1, 2014. Except as provided in paragraphs (c)(2) and (c)(3) of this section, §1.263(a)-3 as contained in 26 CFR part 1 edition revised as of April 1, 2011, applies to taxable years beginning before January 1, 2014. For the effective dates of the enumerated election provisions, see those Code sections and the regulations under those sections.

(2) *Early application of this section.*—A taxpayer may choose to apply this section to taxable years beginning on or after January 1, 2012.

(3) *Optional application of TD 9564.*—A taxpayer may choose to apply §1.263(a)-6T as contained in TD 9564 (76 FR 81060) December 27, 2011, to taxable years beginning on or after January 1, 2012, and before January 1, 2014. [Reg. §1.263(a)-6.]

☐ [*T.D. 9636, 9-13-2013.*]

⟫⟫→ *Caution: Temporary Reg. §1.263(a)-6T, below, was removed by T.D. 9636, but a taxpayer may choose to apply Temporary Reg. §1.263(a)-6T to tax years beginning on or after January 1, 2012, and before January 1, 2014.*

[Reg. §1.263(a)-6T]

§1.263(a)-6T. Election to deduct or capitalize certain expenditures (Temporary).—(a) *In general.*—Under certain provisions of the Internal Revenue Code, taxpayers may elect to treat capital expenditures as deductible expenses or as deferred expenses, or to treat deductible expenses as capital expenditures.

(b) *Election provisions.*—The sections referred to in paragraph (a) of this section include:

(1) Section 173 (circulation expenditures);

(2) Section 174 (research and experimental expenditures);

(3) Section 175 (soil and water conservation expenditures; endangered species recovery expenditures);

(4) Section 179 (election to expenses certain depreciable business assets);

(5) Section 179A (deduction for clean-fuel vehicles and certain refueling property);

(6) Section 179B (deduction for capital costs incurred in complying with environmental protection agency sulfur regulations);

(7) Section 179C (election to expense certain refineries);

(8) Section 179D (energy efficient commercial buildings deduction);

(9) Section 179E (election to expense advanced mine safety equipment);

(10) Section 180 (expenditures by farmers for fertilizer);

(11) Section 181 (treatment of certain qualified film and television productions);

(12) Section 190 (expenditures to remove architectural and transportation barriers to the handicapped and elderly);

(13) Section 193 (tertiary injectants);

(14) Section 194 (treatment of reforestation expenditures);

(15) Section 195 (start-up expenditures);

(16) Section 198 (expensing of environmental remediation costs);

(17) Section 198A (expensing of qualified disaster expenses);

(18) Section 248 (organization expenditures of a corporation);

(19) Section 266 (carrying charges);

(20) Section 616 (development expenditures); and

(21) Section 709 (organization and syndication fees of a partnership).

(c) *Effective/applicability date.*—(1) *In general.*—This section applies to taxable years beginning on or after January 1, 2014. Section 1.263(a)-3 as contained in 26 CFR part 1 edition revised as of April 1, 2011, applies to taxable years beginning before January 1, 2014. For the effective dates of the enumerated election provisions, see those Internal Revenue Code sections and the regulations thereunder.

(2) *Optional early application.*—A taxpayer may choose to apply this section to taxable years beginning on or after January 1, 2012.

(d) *Expiration date.*—The applicability of this section expires on December 23, 2014. [Temporary Reg. §1.263(a)-6T.]

☐ [*T.D. 9564, 12-23-2011 (corrected 3-27-2012 and 12-14-2012). Removed by T.D. 9636, 9-13-2013.*]

[Reg. §1.263(b)-1]

§1.263(b)-1. Expenditures for advertising or promotion of good will.—See §1.162-14 for the rules applicable to a corporation which has elected to capitalize expenditures for advertising or the promotion of good will under the provisions of section 733 or section 451 of the Internal Revenue Code of 1939, in computing its excess profits tax credit under subchapter E, chapter 2, or subchapter D of chapter 1, of the Internal Revenue Code of 1939. [Reg. §1.263(b)-1.]

☐ [*T.D. 6313, 9-16-58.*]

[Reg. §1.263(c)-1]

§1.263(c)-1. Intangible drilling and development costs in the case of oil and gas wells.—For rules relating to the option to deduct as expenses intangible drilling and development costs in the case of oil and gas wells, see §1.612-4. [Reg. §1.263(c)-1.]

☐ [*T.D. 6313, 9-16-58.*]

[Reg. §1.263(e)-1]

§1.263(e)-1. Expenditures in connection with certain railroad rolling stock.—(a) *Allowance of deduction.*—(1) *Election.*—Under section 263(e), for any taxable year beginning after December 31, 1969, a taxpayer may elect to treat certain expenditures paid or incurred during such taxable year as deductible repairs under section 162 or 212. This election applies only to expenditures described in paragraph (c) of this section in connection with the rehabilitation of a unit of railroad rolling stock (as defined in paragraph (b)(2) of this section) used by a domestic common carrier by railroad (as defined in paragraph (b)(3) and (4) of this section). However, an election under section 263(e) may not be made with respect to expenditures in connection with any unit of railroad rolling stock for which an election under section 263(f) and the regulations thereunder is in effect. An election made under section 263(e) is an annual election which may be made with respect to one or more of the units of railroad rolling stock owned by the taxpayer.

(2) *Special 20 percent rule.*—Section 263(e) shall not apply if, under paragraph (d) of this section, expenditures paid or incurred during any period of 12 calendar months in connection with the rehabilitation of a unit exceed 20 percent of the basis (as defined in paragraph (b)(1) of this section) of such unit in the hands of the taxpayer. However, section 263(e) does not constitute a limit on the deduction of expenditures for repairs which are deductible without regard to such section. Accordingly, amounts otherwise deductible as repairs will continue to be deductible even though such amounts exceed 20 percent of the basis of the unit of railroad rolling stock in the hands of the taxpayer.

(3) *Time and manner of making election.*—(i) An election by a taxpayer under section 263(e) shall be made by a statement to that effect attached to its income tax return or amended income tax return for the taxable year for which the election is made if such return or amended return is filed no later than the time prescribed by law (including extensions thereof) for filing the return for the taxable year of election. An election under section 263(e) may be made with respect to one or more of the units of railroad rolling stock owned by the taxpayer. If an election is not made within the time and in the manner prescribed in this subparagraph, no election may be made (by the filing of an amended return or in any other manner) with respect to the taxable year.

(ii) If the taxpayer has filed a return on or before March 14, 1973, and has claimed a deduction under section 162 or 212 by reason of section 263(e), and if the taxpayer does not desire to make an election under section 263(e) for the taxable year with respect to which such return was filed, the taxpayer shall file an amended return for such taxable year on or before [the 90th day after such date of publication], and shall pay any additional tax due for such year. The taxpayer shall also file an amended return for each taxable year which is affected by the filing of an amended return under the preceding sentence and shall pay any additional tax due for such year. Nothing in this subdivision shall be construed as extending the time specified in section 6511 within which a claim for credit or refund may be filed.

(iii) If an election under section 263(e) was not made at the time the return for a taxable year was filed, and it is subsequently determined that an expenditure was erroneously treated as an expenditure which was not in connection with rehabilitation (as determined under paragraph (c) of this section), an election under section 263(e) may be made with respect to the unit of railroad rolling stock for which such expenditure was made for such taxable year, notwithstanding any provision in this subparagraph (3) to the contrary. Nothing in this subdivision shall be construed as extending the time specified in section 6511 within which a claim for credit or refund may be filed.

(iv) The statement required by subdivision (i) of this subparagraph shall include the following information:

(a) The total number of units of railroad rolling stock with respect to which an election is being made under section 263(e).

(b) The aggregate basis (as defined in paragraph (b)(1) of this section) of the units described in (a) of this subdivision (iv), and

(c) The total deduction being claimed under section 263(e) for the taxable year.

(b) *Definitions.*—(1) *Basis.*—(i) In general, for purposes of section 263(e) the basis of a unit of railroad rolling stock shall be the adjusted basis of such unit determined without regard to the adjustments provided in paragraphs (1), (2), and (3) of section 1016(a) and section 1017. Thus, the basis of property would generally be its cost without regard to adjustments to basis such as for depreciation or for capital improvements. If the basis of a unit in the hands of a transferee is determined in whole or in part by reference to its basis in the hands of the transferor, for example, by reason of the application of section 362 (relating to basis to corporations), 374 (relating to gain or loss not recognized in certain railroad reorganizations), or 723 (relating to the basis of property contributed to a partnership), then the basis of such unit in the hands of the transferor for purposes of section 263(e) shall be its basis for purposes of section 263(e) in the hands of the transferee. Similarly, when the basis of a unit of railroad rolling stock in the hands of the taxpayer is determined in whole or in part by reference to the basis of another unit, for example, by reason of the application of the first sentence of section 1033(c) (relating to involuntary conversions), then the basis of the latter unit for purposes of section 263(e) shall be the basis for purposes of section 263(e) of the former unit. The question whether a capital expenditure in connection with a unit of railroad rolling stock results in the retirement of such unit and the creation of another unit of railroad rolling stock shall be determined without regard to rules under the uniform system of accounts prescribed by the Interstate Commerce Commission.

(ii) For example, if a unit of railroad rolling stock has a cost to M of $10,000 and because of depreciation adjustments of $4,000 and capital expenditures of $3,000, such unit has an adjusted basis in the hands of M of $9,000, the basis for purposes of section 263(e) of such unit in the hands of M is $10,000. Further, if M transfers such unit to N in a transaction in which no gain or loss is recognized such as, for example, a transaction to which section 351(a) (relating to a transfer to a corporation controlled by the transferor) applies, the basis of such unit for purposes of section 263(e) is $10,000 in the hands of N.

(2) *Railroad rolling stock.*—For purposes of this section, the term "unit" or "unit of railroad rolling stock" means a unit of transportation equipment the expenditures for which are of a type chargeable (or in the case of property leased to a domestic common carrier by railroad, would be chargeable) to the equipment investment accounts in the uniform system of accounts for railroad companies prescribed by the Interstate Commerce Commission (49 CFR Part 1201), but only if (i) such unit exclusively moves on, moves under, or is guided by rail, and (ii) such unit is not a locomotive. Thus, for example, a unit of railroad rolling stock includes a box car, a gondola car, a passenger car, a car designed to carry truck trailers and containerized freight, a wreck crane, and a bunk car. However, such term does not include equipment which does not exclusively move on, move under, or is not exclusively guided by rail such as, for example, a barge, a tugboat, a container which is used on cars designed to carry containerized freight, a truck trailer, or an automobile. A locomotive is self-propelled equipment, the sole function of which is to push or pull railroad rolling stock. Thus, a self-propelled passenger or freight car is not a locomotive.

(3) *Domestic common carrier by railroad.*—The term "domestic common carrier by railroad" means a railroad subject to regulation under Part I of the Interstate Commerce Act (49 U.S.C. 1 et seq.) or a railroad which would be subject to regulation under Part I of the Interstate Commerce Act if it were engaged in interstate commerce.

(4) *Use.*—For purposes of this section, a unit of railroad rolling stock is not used by a domestic common carrier by railroad if it is owned by a person other than a domestic common carrier by railroad and (i) is exclusively used for transportation by the owner or (ii) is exclusively used for transportation by another person which is not a domestic common carrier by railroad. Thus, for example, a unit of railroad rolling stock which is owned by a person which is not a domestic common carrier by railroad and is leased to a manufacturing company by the owner is not a unit of railroad rolling stock used by a domestic common carrier by railroad.

(c) *Expenditures considered in connection with rehabilitation.*—For purposes of section 263(e) and this section, all expenditures which would be properly chargeable to capital account but for the application of section 263(e) or (f) shall be considered to be expenditures in connection with the rehabilitation of a unit of railroad rolling stock. Expenditures which are paid or incurred in connection with incidental repairs or maintenance of a unit of railroad rolling stock and which are deductible without regard to section 263(e) or (f) shall not be included in any determination or computation under section 263(e) and shall not be treated as paid or incurred in connection with the rehabilitation of a unit of railroad rolling stock for purposes of section 263(e). The determination of whether an item would be, but for section 263(e) or (f), properly chargeable to capital account shall be made in a manner consistent with the principles for classification of expenditures as between capital and expenses under the Internal Revenue Code. See, for example, §§ 1.162-4, 1.263(a)-1, 1.263(a)-2, and paragraph (b)(1) of this section and (iii) of § 1.446-1. An expenditure shall be classified as capital or as expense without regard to its classification under the uniform system of accounts prescribed by the Interstate Commerce Commission.

(d) *20-percent limitation.*—(1) *In general.*—No expenditures in connection with the rehabilitation of a unit of railroad rolling stock shall be treated as a deductible repair by reason of an election under section 263(e) if, during any period of 12 calendar months in which the month the expenditure is included falls, all such expenditures exceed an amount equal to 20 percent of the basis (as defined in paragraph (b)(1) of this section) of such unit in the hands of the taxpayer. All such expenditures shall be included in the computation of the 20-percent limitation even if such expenditures were deducted

under section 263(f) in either the preceding or succeeding taxable year. Solely for purposes of the 20-percent limitation in this paragraph, such expenditures shall be deemed to be included in the month in which a rehabilitation of the unit of railroad rolling stock is completed. For the requirement that expenditures treated as repairs solely by reason of an election under section 263(e) be deducted in the taxable year paid or incurred, see paragraph (a) of this section.

(2) *12-month period.*—For purposes of this section, any period of 12 calendar months shall consist of any 12 consecutive calendar months except that calendar months prior to the calendar month of January 1970 shall not be included in determining such period.

(3) *Period for certain corporate acquisitions.*—If a unit of railroad rolling stock to which section 263(e) applies is sold, exchanged, or otherwise disposed of in a transaction in which its basis in the hands of the transferee is determined in whole or in part by reference to its basis in the hands of the transferor (see paragraph (b)(1) of this section), calendar months during which such unit is in the hands of the transferor and in the hands of such transferee shall both be included in the calendar months used by the transferor and the transferee to determine any period of 12 calendar months for purposes of section 263(e).

(4) *Deduction allowed in year paid or incurred.*—If, based on the information available when the income tax return for a taxable year is filed, an expenditure paid or incurred in such taxable year would be deductible by reason of the application of section 263(e) but for the fact that it cannot be established whether the 20-percent limitation in subparagraph (1) of this paragraph will be exceeded, the expenditure shall be deducted for such taxable year. If by reason of the application of such 20-percent limitation it is subsequently determined that such expenditure is not deductible as a repair, an amended return shall be filed for the year in which such deduction was treated as a deductible repair and additional tax, if any, for such year shall be paid. Appropriate adjustment with respect to the taxpayer's tax liability for any other affected year shall be made. Nothing in this subparagraph shall be construed as extending the time specified in section 6511 within which a claim for credit or refund may be filed.

(e) *Recordkeeping requirements.*—(1) *In general.*—Such records as will enable the accurate determination of the expenditures which may be subject to the treatment provided in section 263(e) shall be maintained. No deduction shall be allowed under section 162 or 212 by reason of section 263(e) with respect to a unit unless the taxpayer substantiates by adequate records that expenditures in connection with such unit of railroad rolling stock meet the requirements and limitations of this section.

(2) *Separate records.*—A separate section 263(e) record shall be maintained for each unit with respect to which an election under section 263(e) is made. Such record shall—

(i) Identify the unit,

(ii) State the basis (as defined in paragraph (b)(1) of this section) and the date of acquisition of the unit,

(iii) Enumerate for each unit the amount of all expenditures incurred in connection with rehabilitation of such unit which would, but for section 263 (e) or (f), be properly chargeable to capital account (including expenditures incurred by the taxpayer in connection with rehabilitation of such unit undertaken by a person other than the taxpayer) regardless of whether such expenditures during any 12-month period exceed 20 percent of the basis of such unit,

(iv) Describe the nature of the work in connection with each expenditure, and

(v) Specify the calendar month in which the rehabilitation is completed and the taxable year in which each expenditure is paid or incurred.

A section 263(e) record need only be prepared for a unit of railroad rolling stock for the period beginning on the first day of the eleventh calendar month immediately preceding the month in which the rehabilitation of such unit is completed and ending on the last day of the eleventh calendar month immediately succeeding such month. No section 263(e) record need be prepared for calendar months before January 1970.

(3) *Records for certain expenditures.*—Expenditures determined to be incidental repairs and maintenance (referred to in paragraph (c) of this section) shall not be entered in the section 263(e) record. However, each taxpayer shall maintain records to reflect that such expenditures are properly deductible.

(4) *Convenience rule.*—In general, expenditures and information maintained in compliance with subparagraphs (1) and (2) of this paragraph shall be recorded in the section 263(e) record of the specific unit with respect to which such expenditures are incurred. However, when a group of units of the same type are rehabilitated in a single project and the expenditure for each unit in the project will

approximate the average expenditure per unit for the project, expenditures for the project may be aggregated without regard to the unit in the project with respect to which each expenditure is connected, and an amount equal to the aggregate expenditures for the project divided by the number of units in the project may be entered in the section 263(e) account of each unit in the project.

(f) *Examples.*—The provisions of this section may be illustrated by the following examples:

Example (1). M Corporation, a domestic common carrier by railroad, uses the calendar year as its taxable year. M owns and uses several gondola cars to which an election under section 263(e) applies for its taxable years 1970-1972. Gondola car # 1 has a basis (defined in paragraph (b)(1) of this section) of $10,000. No expenditures properly chargeable to the section 263(e) record are made on gondola car # 1 in 1970 and 1971, except in January 1971. In January 1971, M at a cost of $1,500 performed rehabilitation work on gondola car # 1. Such amount was properly entered in the section 263(e) record for gondola car # 1. Since the expenditures in such record do not exceed an amount equal to 20 percent of the basis of gondola car # 1 ($2,000) during any period of 12 calendar months in which January 1971 falls, the expenditures during January 1971 shall be treated as a deductible expense regardless of what the treatment would have been if section 263(e) had not been enacted.

Example (2). Assume the same facts as in example (1). Assume further that for 1970, 1971, and 1972, only the following expenditures in connection with rehabilitation which would, but for section 263(e), be properly chargeable to capital account were deemed included for gondola car # 2:

(a) December 1970	$1,500
(b) November 1971	600
(c) December 1971	400
(d) January 1972	1,050

Assume further that gondola car # 2 has a basis (as defined in paragraph (b)(1) of this section) equal to $10,000, that M files its tax return by September 15 following each taxable year, and that each rehabilitation was completed in the month in which expenditures in connection with it were incurred. Any expenditures in connection with each gondola car (# 1 or # 2) have no effect on the treatment of expenditures in connection with the other gondola car. With respect to gondola car # 2, the expenditures of December 1970 are treated as deductible repairs at the time M's income tax return for 1970 is filed because, based on the information available when the income tax return for 1970 is filed, such expenditure would be deductible by reason of application of section 263(e) but for the fact that it cannot be established whether the 20-percent limitation in paragraph (d)(1) of this section will be exceeded. Nevertheless, because such expenditures during the period of 12 calendar months including calendar months December 1970 and November 1971 exceed $2,000, the December 1970 rehabilitation expenditures are not subject to the provisions of section 263(e). Because such rehabilitation expenditures during the period of 12 calendar months including calendar months February 1971 and January 1972 exceed $2,000, rehabilitation expenditures in 1971 are not subject to the provisions of section 263(e). Similarly, the 1972 rehabilitation expenditures are not subject to the provisions of section 263(e). [Reg. § 1.263(e)-1.]

☐ [*T.D. 7257, 2-9-73.*]

[Reg. § 1.263(f)-1]

§ 1.263(f)-1. Reasonable repair allowance.—(a) For rules regarding the election of the repair allowance authorized by section 263(f), the definition of repair allowance property, and the conditions under which an election may be made, see paragraphs (d)(2) and (f) of § 1.167(a)-11. An election may be made under this section for a taxable year only if the taxpayer makes an election under § 1.167(a)-11 for such taxable year. [Reg. § 1.263(f)-1.]

☐ [*T.D. 7272, 4-20-73. Amended by T.D. 7593, 1-25-79.*]

[Reg. § 1.263A-0]

§ 1.263A-0. Outline of regulations under section 263A.—This section lists the paragraphs in § § 1.263A-1 through 1.263A-4 and § § 1.263A-7 through 1.263A-15 as follows:

§ 1.263A-1. Uniform capitalization of costs.
  (a) Introduction.
    (1) In general.
    (2) Effective dates.
    (3) General scope.
      (i) Property to which section 263A applies.
      (ii) Property produced.
      (iii) Property acquired for resale.
      (iv) Inventories valued at market.
      (v) Property produced in a farming business.

      (vi) Creative property.
      (vii) Property produced or property acquired for resale by foreign persons.
  (b) Exceptions.
    (1) Small business taxpayers.
    (2) Long-term contracts.
    (3) Costs incurred in certain farming businesses.
    (4) Costs incurred in raising, harvesting, or growing timber.
    (5) Qualified creative expenses.
    (6) Certain not-for-profit activities.
    (7) Intangible drilling and development costs.
    (8) Natural gas acquired for resale.
      (i) Cushion gas.
      (ii) Emergency gas.
    (9) Research and experimental expenditures.
    (10) Certain property that is substantially constructed.
    (11) Certain property provided incident to services.
      (i) In general.
      (ii) Definition of services.
      (iii) De minimis property provided incident to services.
    (12) De minimis rule for certain producers with total indirect costs of $200,000 or less.
    (13) Exception for the origination of loans.
  (c) General operation of section 263A.
    (1) Allocations.
    (2) Otherwise deductible.
    (3) Capitalize.
    (4) Recovery of capitalized costs.
    (5) Costs allocable only to property sold.
  (d) Definitions.
    (1) Self-constructed assets.
    (2) Section 471 costs.
      (i) In general.
      (ii) Inclusion of direct costs.
        (A) In general.
        (B) Allocation of direct costs.
      (iii) Alternative method to determine amounts of section 471 costs by using taxpayer's financial statement.
        (A) In general.
        (B) Book-to-tax adjustments.
        (C) Exclusion of certain financial statement items.
        (D) Changes in method of accounting.
        (E) Examples.
      (iv) De minimis rule exceptions for certain direct costs.
        (A) In general.
        (B) De minimis rule for certain direct labor costs.
        (C) De minimis rule for certain direct material costs.
        (D) Taxpayers using a historic absorption ratio.
        (E) Examples.
      (v) Safe harbor method for certain variances and under or over-applied burdens.
        (A) In general.
        (B) Consistency requirement.
        (C) Allocation of variances and under or over-applied burdens between production and preproduction costs under the modified simplified production method.
        (D) Allocation of variances and under or over-applied burdens between storage and handling costs absorption ratio and purchasing costs absorption ratio under the simplified resale method.
        (E) Method of accounting.
      (vi) Removal of section 471 costs.
      (vii) Method changes.
    (3) Additional section 263A costs.
      (i) In general.
      (ii) Negative adjustments.
        (A) In general.
        (B) Exception for certain taxpayers removing costs from section 471 costs.
        (C) No negative adjustments for cash or trade discounts.
        (D) No negative adjustments for certain expenses.
        (E) Consistency requirement for negative adjustments.
    (4) Section 263A costs.
    (5) Classification of costs.
    (6) Financial statement.
  (e) Types of costs subject to capitalization.
    (1) In general.
    (2) Direct costs.
      (i) Producers.
        (A) Direct material costs.
        (B) Direct labor costs.

☐ [*T.D.* 8482, 8-6-93. *Amended by T.D.* 8584, 12-28-94; *T.D.* 8728, 8-4-97; *T.D.* 8897, 8-18-2000; *T.D.* 9636, 9-13-2013, *T.D.* 9652, 1-10-2014, *T.D.* 9843, 11-19-2018 *and T.D.* 9942, 12-31-2020 (*corrected* 6-16-2021).]

[Reg. §1.263A-1]

§1.263A-1. Uniform capitalization of costs.—(a) *Introduction.*— (1) *In general.*—The regulations under §§1.263A-1 through 1.263A-6 provide guidance to taxpayers that are required to capitalize certain costs under section 263A. These regulations generally apply to all costs required to be capitalized under section 263A except for interest that must be capitalized under section 263A(f) and the regulations thereunder. Statutory or regulatory exceptions may provide that section 263A does not apply to certain activities or costs; however, those activities or costs may nevertheless be subject to capitalization requirements under other provisions of the Internal Revenue Code and regulations.

(2) *Applicability dates.*—(i) In general, this section and §§1.263A-2 and 1.263A-3 apply to costs incurred in taxable years beginning after December 31, 1993. In the case of property that is inventory in the hands of the taxpayer, however, these sections are applicable for taxable years beginning after December 31, 1993. The

small business taxpayer exception described in paragraph (b)(1) of this section and set forth in paragraph (j) of this section is applicable for taxable years beginning after December 31, 2017. Changes in methods of accounting necessary as a result of the rules in this section and §§ 1.263A-2 and 1.263A-3 must be made under terms and conditions prescribed by the Commissioner. Under these terms and conditions, the principles of § 1.263A-7 must be applied in revaluing inventory property.

(ii) For taxable years beginning before January 1, 1994, taxpayers must take reasonable positions on their federal income tax returns when applying section 263A. For purposes of this paragraph (a)(2)(iii), a reasonable position is a position consistent with the temporary regulations, revenue rulings, revenue procedures, notices, and announcements concerning section 263A applicable in taxable years beginning before January 1, 1994. See § 601.601(d)(2)(ii)(*b*) of this chapter.

(3) *General scope.*—(i) *Property to which section 263A applies.*—Taxpayers subject to section 263A must capitalize all direct costs and certain indirect costs properly allocable to—

(A) Real property and tangible personal property produced by the taxpayer; and

(B) Real property and personal property described in section 1221(1), which is acquired by the taxpayer for resale.

(ii) *Property produced.*—Taxpayers that produce real property and tangible personal property (producers) must capitalize all the direct costs of producing the property and the property's properly allocable share of indirect costs (described in paragraphs (e)(2)(i) and (3) of this section), regardless of whether the property is sold or used in the taxpayer's trade or business. See § 1.263A-2 for rules relating to producers.

(iii) *Property acquired for resale.*—Retailers, wholesalers, and other taxpayers that acquire property described in section 1221(1) for resale (resellers) must capitalize the direct costs of acquiring the property and the property's properly allocable share of indirect costs (described in paragraphs (e)(2)(ii) and (3) of this section). See § 1.263A-3 for rules relating to resellers. See also section 263A(b)(2)(B), which excepts from section 263A personal property acquired for resale by a small reseller.

(iv) *Inventories valued at market.*—Section 263A does not apply to inventories valued at market under either the market method or the lower of cost or market method if the market valuation used by the taxpayer generally equals the property's fair market value. For purposes of this paragraph (a)(3)(iv), the term fair market value means the price at which the taxpayer sells its inventory to its customers (e.g., as in the market value definition provided in § 1.471-4(b)) less, if applicable, the direct cost of disposing of the inventory. However, section 263A does apply in determining the market value of any inventory for which market is determined with reference to replacement cost or reproduction cost. See §§ 1.471-4 and 1.471-5.

(v) *Property produced in a farming business.*—Section 263A generally requires taxpayers engaged in a farming business to capitalize certain costs. See sections 263A(d) and 263A(e) and § 1.263A-4 for rules relating to taxpayers engaged in a farming business.

(vi) *Creative property.*—Section 263A generally requires taxpayers engaged in the production and resale of creative property to capitalize certain costs.

(vii) *Property produced or property acquired for resale by foreign persons.*—Section 263A generally applies to foreign persons.

(b) *Exceptions.*—(1) *Small business taxpayers.*—For taxable years beginning after December 31, 2017, see section 263A(i) and paragraph (j) of this section for an exemption for certain small business taxpayers from the requirements of section 263A.

(2) *Long-term contracts.*—Except for certain home construction contracts described in section 460(e)(1), section 263A does not apply to any property produced by the taxpayer pursuant to a long-term contract as defined in section 460(f), regardless of whether the taxpayer uses an inventory method to account for such production.

(3) *Costs incurred in certain farming businesses.*—See section 263A(d) for an exception for costs paid or incurred in certain farming businesses. See § 1.263A-4 for specific rules relating to taxpayers engaged in the trade or business of farming.

(4) *Costs incurred in raising, harvesting, or growing timber.*—See section 263A(c)(5) for an exception for costs paid or incurred in raising, harvesting, or growing timber and certain ornamental trees. See § 1.263A-4, however, for rules relating to taxpayers producing certain trees to which section 263A applies.

(5) *Qualified creative expenses.*—See section 263A(h) for an exception for qualified creative expenses paid or incurred by certain freelance authors, photographers, and artists.

(6) *Certain not-for-profit activities.*—See section 263A(c)(1) for an exception for property produced by a taxpayer for use by the taxpayer other than in a trade or business or an activity conducted for profit. This exception does not apply, however, to property produced by an exempt organization in connection with its unrelated trade or business activities.

(7) *Intangible drilling and development costs.*—See section 263A(c)(3) for an exception for intangible drilling and development costs. Additionally, section 263A does not apply to any amount allowable as a deduction under section 59(e) with respect to qualified expenditures under sections 263(c), 616(a), or 617(a).

(8) *Natural gas acquired for resale.*—Under this paragraph (b)(8), section 263A does not apply to any costs incurred by a taxpayer relating to natural gas acquired for resale to the extent such costs would otherwise be allocable to cushion gas.

(i) *Cushion gas.*—Cushion gas is the portion of gas stored in an underground storage facility or reservoir that is required to maintain the level of pressure necessary for operation of the facility. However, section 263A applies to costs incurred by a taxpayer relating to natural gas acquired for resale to the extent such costs are properly allocable to emergency gas.

(ii) *Emergency gas.*—Emergency gas is natural gas stored in an underground storage facility or reservoir for use during periods of unusually heavy customer demand.

(9) *Research and experimental expenditures.*—See section 263A(c)(2) for an exception for any research and experimental expenditure allowable as a deduction under section 174 or the regulations thereunder. Additionally, section 263A does not apply to any amount allowable as a deduction under section 59(e) with respect to qualified expenditures under section 174.

(10) *Certain property that is substantially constructed.*—Section 263A does not apply to any property produced by a taxpayer for use in its trade or business if substantial construction occurred before March 1, 1986.

(i) For purposes of this section, substantial construction is deemed to have occurred if the lesser of—

(A) 10 percent of the total estimated costs of construction; or

(B) The greater of $10 million or 2 percent of the total estimated costs of construction, was incurred before March 1, 1986.

(ii) For purposes of the provision in paragraph (b)(10)(i) of this section, the total estimated costs of construction shall be determined by reference to a reasonable estimate, on or before March 1, 1986, of such amount. Assume, for example, that on March 1, 1986, the estimated costs of constructing a facility were $150 million. Assume that before March 1, 1986, $12 million of construction costs had been incurred. Based on the above facts, substantial construction would be deemed to have occurred before March 1, 1986, because $12 million (the costs of construction incurred before such date) is greater than $10 million (the lesser of $15 million; or the greater of $10 million or $3 million). For purposes of this provision, construction costs are defined as those costs incurred after construction has commenced at the site of the property being constructed (unless the property will not be located on land and, therefore, the initial construction of the property must begin at a location other than the intended site). For example, in the case of a building, construction commences when work begins on the building, such as the excavation of the site, the pouring of pads for the building, or the driving of foundation pilings into the ground. Preliminary activities such as project engineering and architectural design do not constitute the commencement of construction, nor are such costs considered construction costs, for purposes of this paragraph (b)(10).

(11) *Certain property provided incident to services.*—(i) *In general.*—Under this paragraph (b)(11), section 263A does not apply to property that is provided to a client (or customer) incident to the provision of services by the taxpayer if the property provided to the client is—

(A) De minimis in amount; and

(B) Not inventory in the hands of the service provider.

(ii) *Definition of services.*—For purposes of this paragraph (b)(11), services is defined with reference to its ordinary and accepted meaning under federal income tax principles. In determining whether a taxpayer is a bona-fide service provider under this paragraph (b)(11), the nature of the taxpayer's trade or business and the facts and circumstances surrounding the taxpayer's trade or business activities must be considered. Examples of taxpayers qualifying as service providers under this paragraph include taxpayers performing services in the fields of health, law, engineering, architecture, accounting, actuarial science, performing arts, or consulting.

(iii) *De minimis property provided incident to services.*—In determining whether property provided to a client by a service provider is de minimis in amount, all facts and circumstances, such as the nature of the taxpayer's trade or business and the volume of its service activities in the trade or business, must be considered. A significant factor in making this determination is the relationship between the acquisition or direct materials costs of the property that is provided to clients and the price that the taxpayer charges its clients for its services and the property. For purposes of this paragraph (b)(11), if the acquisition or direct materials cost of the property provided to a client incident to the services is less than or equal to five percent of the price charged to the client for the services and property, the property is de minimis. If the acquisition or direct materials cost of the property exceeds five percent of the price charged for the services and property, the property may be de minimis if additional facts and circumstances so indicate.

(12) *De minimis rule for certain producers with total indirect costs of $200,000 or less.*—See §1.263A-2(b)(3)(iv) for a de minimis rule that treats producers with total indirect costs of $200,000 or less as having no additional section 263A costs (as defined in paragraph (d)(3) of this section) for purposes of the simplified production method.

(13) *Exception for the origination of loans.*—For purposes of section 263A(b)(2)(A), the origination of loans is not considered the acquisition of intangible property for resale. (But section 263A(b)(2)(A) does include the acquisition by a taxpayer of pre-existing loans from other persons for resale.)

(c) *General operation of section 263A.*—(1) *Allocations.*—Under section 263A, taxpayers must capitalize their direct costs and a properly allocable share of their indirect costs to property produced or property acquired for resale. In order to determine these capitalizable costs, taxpayers must allocate or apportion costs to various activities, including production or resale activities. After section 263A costs are allocated to the appropriate production or resale activities, these costs are generally allocated to the items of property produced or property acquired for resale during the taxable year and capitalized to the items that remain on hand at the end of the taxable year. See however, the simplified production method, the modified simplified production method, and the simplified resale method in §§1.263A-2(b) and (c) and 1.263A-3(d).

(2) *Otherwise deductible.*—(i) Any cost which (but for section 263A and the regulations thereunder) may not be taken into account in computing taxable income for any taxable year is not treated as a cost properly allocable to property produced or acquired for resale under section 263A and the regulations thereunder. Thus, for example, if a business meal deduction is limited by section 274(n) to 80 percent of the cost of the meal, the amount properly allocable to property produced or acquired for resale under section 263A is also limited to 80 percent of the cost of the meal.

(ii) The amount of any cost required to be capitalized under section 263A may not be included in inventory or charged to capital accounts or basis any earlier than the taxable year during which the amount is incurred within the meaning of §1.446-1(c)(1)(ii).

(3) *Capitalize.*—Capitalize means, in the case of property that is inventory in the hands of a taxpayer, to include in inventory costs and, in the case of other property, to charge to a capital account or basis.

(4) *Recovery of capitalized costs.*—Costs that are capitalized under section 263A are recovered through depreciation, amortization, cost of goods sold, or by an adjustment to basis at the time the property is used, sold, placed in service, or otherwise disposed of by the taxpayer. Cost recovery is determined by the applicable Internal Revenue Code and regulation provisions relating to use, sale, or disposition of property.

(5) *Costs allocable to property sold.*—A cost that is allocated under this section, §1.263A-2, or §1.263A-3 entirely to property sold must be included in cost of goods sold and may not be included in determining the cost of goods on hand at the end of the taxable year.

(d) *Definitions.*—(1) *In general.*—Except as otherwise provided in paragraphs (d)(2)(ii), (iv), (v), and (vi) of this section, for purposes of section 263A, a taxpayer's section 471 costs are the types of costs, other than interest, that a taxpayer capitalizes to property produced or property acquired for resale in its financial statement. Thus, although section 471 applies only to inventories, section 471 costs include any non-inventory costs, other than interest, that a taxpayer capitalizes to, or includes in acquisition or production costs of, prop-

erty produced or property acquired for resale in its financial statement. Except as otherwise provided in paragraph (d)(2)(iii) of this section, a taxpayer determines the amounts of section 471 costs by using the amounts of such costs that are incurred in the taxable year for federal income tax purposes.

(2) *Section 471 costs.*—(i) *In general.*—Except as otherwise provided in paragraphs (d)(2)(ii), (iv), (v), and (vi) of this section, for purposes of section 263A, a taxpayer's section 471 costs are the types of costs, other than interest, that a taxpayer capitalizes to property produced or property acquired for resale in its financial statement. Thus, although section 471 applies only to inventories, section 471 costs include any non-inventory costs, other than interest, that a taxpayer capitalizes to, or includes in acquisition or production costs of, property produced or property acquired for resale in its financial statement. Except as otherwise provided in paragraph (d)(2)(iii) of this section, a taxpayer determines the amounts of section 471 costs by using the amounts of such costs that are incurred in the taxable year for federal income tax purposes.

(ii) *Inclusion of direct costs.*—(A) *In general.*—Notwithstanding the last sentence of paragraph (g)(2) of this section, a taxpayer's section 471 costs must include all direct costs of property produced and property acquired for resale, whether or not a taxpayer capitalizes these costs to property produced or property acquired for resale in its financial statement. See paragraph (e)(2) of this section for a description of direct costs of property produced and property acquired for resale.

(B) *Allocation of direct costs.*—Except for any direct costs that are treated as additional section 263A costs under paragraphs (d)(2)(iv) and (v) of this section, a taxpayer's direct costs of property produced and property acquired for resale must be allocated using a method provided in paragraph (f) of this section.

(iii) *Alternative method to determine amounts of section 471 costs by using taxpayer's financial statement.*—(A) *In general.*—In lieu of determining the amounts of section 471 costs under paragraph (d)(2)(i) of this section, a taxpayer described in paragraph (d)(3)(ii)(B) of this section may determine the amounts of section 471 costs by using the amounts of such costs that are incurred in the taxable year in its financial statement using the taxpayer's financial statement methods of accounting if the taxpayer's financial statement is described in paragraph (d)(6)(i), (ii), or (iii) of this section. If the taxpayer's financial statement is described only in paragraph (d)(6)(iv) of this section, the taxpayer may not use the alternative method described in this paragraph (d)(2)(iii) and must use the method described in paragraph (d)(2)(i) of this section to determine its amounts of section 471 costs. A taxpayer using the alternative method described in this paragraph (d)(2)(iii) must remove all section 471 costs described in paragraph (d)(2)(vi) of this section, if any, by including negative adjustments in additional section 263A costs. A taxpayer using the alternative method described in this paragraph (d)(2)(iii) applies the method to all of its section 471 costs, including costs described under paragraphs (d)(2)(ii), (iv), (v), and (vi) of this section.

(B) *Book-to-tax adjustments.*—A taxpayer using the alternative method described in this paragraph (d)(2)(iii) must include as additional section 263A costs all negative and positive adjustments required to be made as a result of differences in the book and tax amounts of the taxpayer's section 471 costs, including adjustments for direct costs required to be added to section 471 costs under paragraph (d)(2)(ii) of this section, and costs removed from section 471 costs under paragraphs (d)(2)(vi) and (d)(3)(ii)(B) of this section. In addition, the taxpayer must include as additional section 263A costs all negative and positive adjustments required to be made as a result of differences in the book and tax amounts of section 471 costs that are treated as additional section 263A costs (for example, de minimis direct costs described in paragraph (d)(2)(iv) of this section and certain variances and under or over-applied burdens described in paragraph (d)(2)(v) of this section). For purposes of determining the negative and positive adjustments required to be made as a result of differences in book and tax amounts for a taxpayer using the burden rate or standard cost methods described in paragraph (f)(3) of this section, the taxpayer compares the actual amount of the cost incurred in the taxable year for federal income tax purposes to the actual amount of the cost incurred in the taxable year in its financial statement using the taxpayer's financial statement methods of accounting, regardless of how the taxpayer treats its variances or under or over-applied burdens.

(C) *Exclusion of certain financial statement items.*—A taxpayer that determines the amounts of section 471 costs under this paragraph (d)(2)(iii) may not include any financial statement write-downs, reserves, or other financial statement valuation adjustments when determining the amounts of its section 471 costs.

(D) *Changes in method of accounting.*—The use of this method to determine the amounts of section 471 costs under this paragraph (d)(2)(iii) is the adoption of, or a change in, a method of accounting under section 446 of the Internal Revenue Code.

(E) *Examples.*—The following examples illustrate this paragraph (d)(2)(iii):

(1) *Example 1—Alternative-method taxpayer using de minimis direct labor costs rule.* Taxpayer P uses the modified simplified production method described in §1.263A-2(c) and determines its amounts of section 471 costs by using the alternative method under paragraph (d)(2)(iii) of this section. Additionally, P uses the de minimis direct labor costs rule under paragraph (d)(2)(iv)(B) of this section. P does not capitalize vacation pay or holiday pay to property produced or property acquired for resale in its financial statement but does capitalize all other direct labor costs to such property in its financial statement. On its 2018 financial statement, P incurs $3,500,000 of total direct labor costs, including $110,000 of vacation pay costs and $10,000 of holiday pay costs. For federal income tax purposes, P incurs $150,000 of vacation pay costs and $18,000 of holiday pay costs in the taxable year. P's uncapitalized direct labor costs are $120,000 ($110,000 of vacation pay plus $10,000 of holiday pay). For purposes of the five percent test in paragraph (d)(2)(iv)(B) of this section, P's uncapitalized direct labor costs are 3.43% of total direct labor costs ($120,000 divided by $3,500,000). Accordingly, under paragraph (d)(2)(iv)(B) of this section, P includes $120,000 in its additional section 263A costs and excludes that amount from its section 471 costs in the taxable year. Additionally, pursuant to paragraph (d)(2)(iii)(B) of this section, P includes in additional section 263A costs a positive book-to-tax adjustment of $40,000 for vacation pay costs ($150,000 tax amount - $110,000 book amount) and a positive book-to-tax adjustment of $8,000 for holiday pay costs ($18,000 tax amount - $10,000 book amount).

(2) *Example 2—Alternative-method taxpayer with under and over-applied burdens that uses safe harbor rule for certain variances and under or over-applied burdens.* Taxpayer X uses the modified simplified production method described in §1.263A-2(c) and determines its amounts of section 471 costs by using the alternative method under paragraph (d)(2)(iii) of this section. In 2018, X uses a burden rate method for book purposes to allocate costs to Products A and B, and does not capitalize any under or over-applied burdens to property produced or property acquired for resale in its financial statement. X does not allocate costs to any other products using a burden rate method, and X does not allocate costs to any products using a standard cost method. On its 2018 financial statement, using X's burden rate, the total amount of predetermined indirect costs for Product A is $545,000 and the total amount of actual indirect costs incurred for Product A is $550,000; accordingly, X has an under-applied burden of $5,000 for Product A. For federal income tax purposes, the actual indirect costs incurred in 2018 for Product A is $560,000. Additionally, on its 2018 financial statement, using X's burden rate, the total amount of predetermined indirect costs for Product B is $250,000 and the total amount of actual indirect costs incurred for Product B is $225,000; accordingly, X has an over-applied burden of $25,000 for Product B. For federal income tax purposes, the actual indirect costs incurred in 2018 for Product B is $240,000. X uses the safe harbor rule for certain variances and under or over-applied burdens. Prior to the application of this safe harbor rule, X's total section 471 costs for 2018 for Products A and B (the only items to which X allocates costs using a standard cost method or burden rate method) are $2,000,000, which includes $550,000 actual indirect costs for Product A, $225,000 actual indirect costs for Product B, and $1,225,000 of other section 471 costs for Products A and B that are not allocated under X's burden rate method. For purposes of determining the amount of uncapitalized variances and uncapitalized under or over-applied burdens for the five percent test in paragraph (d)(2)(v)(A) of this section, X's under and over-applied burdens for Products A and B are treated as positive amounts. Consequently, the sum of X's uncapitalized variances and uncapitalized under or over-applied burdens is $30,000 ($5,000 under-applied burden for Product A plus $25,000 over-applied burden for Product B). Accordingly, under paragraph (d)(2)(v)(A) of this section, the sum of X's uncapitalized variances and uncapitalized under or over-applied burdens is 1.5% of X's total section 471 costs for all items to *which it allocates costs using a standard cost method or burden rate* method ($30,000 divided by $2,000,000), and X includes a positive $5,000 under-applied burden for Product A and a negative $25,000 over-applied burden for Product B in its additional section 263A costs, and excludes those amounts from its section 471 costs. Additionally, pursuant to paragraph (d)(2)(iii)(B) of this section, X includes in its additional section 263A costs a positive book-to-tax adjustment of $10,000 for Product A ($560,000 actual cost tax amount - $550,000 actual cost book amount) and a positive book-to-tax adjustment of $15,000 for Product B ($240,000 actual tax amount cost - $225,000 actual book amount cost) in the taxable year.

(iv) *De minimis rule exceptions for certain direct costs.*—(A) *In general.*—Notwithstanding paragraph (d)(2)(ii) of this section, a taxpayer that uses the simplified resale method, the simplified production method, or the modified simplified production method, and that does not capitalize certain direct costs to property produced or property acquired for resale in its financial statement (uncapitalized direct labor costs or uncapitalized direct material costs), may use either or both the de minimis direct labor costs rule or the de minimis direct material costs rule to include in additional section 263A costs, and exclude from section 471 costs, certain uncapitalized direct labor costs or uncapitalized direct material costs that are incurred in the taxable year as provided in paragraphs (d)(2)(iv)(B) and (C) of this section, respectively. The use of the de minimis rules described in paragraphs (d)(2)(iv)(B) and (C) of this section is the adoption of, or a change in, a method of accounting under section 446 of the Internal Revenue Code.

(B) *De minimis rule for certain direct labor costs.*—A taxpayer described in paragraph (d)(2)(iv)(A) of this section that uses the de minimis rule described in this paragraph (d)(2)(iv)(B) includes in additional section 263A costs, and excludes from section 471 costs, the sum of the amounts of all of those uncapitalized direct labor costs that are incurred in the taxable year, if that sum is less than five percent of total direct labor costs incurred in the taxable year (whether or not capitalized in the taxpayer's financial statement), or another amount specified in other published guidance (*see* §601.601(d)(2) of this chapter). For purposes of determining the amount of uncapitalized direct labor costs for this five percent test, any amounts that constitute a reduction to costs are treated as a positive amount. The amounts of uncapitalized direct labor costs used for the five percent test, and the amounts of uncapitalized direct labor costs included in additional section 263A costs under this paragraph (d)(2)(iv)(B), must not include amounts relating to basic compensation or overtime, or the types of costs included in the taxpayer's standard cost or burden rate methods used for section 471 costs (but see paragraphs (d)(2)(v) and (f)(3)(i)(C) of this section for special rules for certain variances and under or over-applied burdens).

(C) *De minimis rule for certain direct material costs.*—A taxpayer described in paragraph (d)(2)(iv)(A) of this section that uses the de minimis rule described in this paragraph (d)(2)(iv)(C) includes in additional section 263A costs, and excludes from section 471 costs, the sum of the amounts of all of those uncapitalized direct material costs that are incurred in the taxable year, if that sum is less than five percent of total direct material costs incurred in the taxable year (whether or not capitalized in the taxpayer's financial statement), or another amount specified in other published guidance (*see* §601.601(d)(2) of this chapter). For purposes of determining the amount of uncapitalized direct material costs for this five percent test, any amounts that constitute a reduction to costs, such as cash and trade discounts, are treated as a positive amount. The amounts of uncapitalized direct material costs used for the five percent test, and the amounts of uncapitalized direct material costs included in additional section 263A costs under this paragraph (d)(2)(iv)(C), must not include the types of costs included in the taxpayer's standard cost method used for section 471 costs (but see paragraphs (d)(2)(v) and (f)(3)(ii)(B) of this section for special rules for certain variances).

(D) *Taxpayers using a historic absorption ratio.*—A taxpayer that uses the historic absorption ratio provided in §1.263A-2(b)(4) or (c)(4) or §1.263A-3(d)(4), and that uses a de minimis rule described in paragraph (d)(2)(iv) of this section during its test period or updated test period, determines whether direct labor costs or direct material costs, as applicable, are included in any of its section 471 costs remaining on hand at year end during its qualifying period or extended qualifying period according to how those direct labor costs or direct material costs, respectively, are identified in at least two of the three years of the taxpayer's applicable test period or updated test period. If a taxpayer described in this paragraph (d)(2)(iv)(D) is required to revise any of its actual absorption ratios for its test period or updated test period as a result of a change in a method of accounting, the taxpayer determines whether direct labor costs or direct material costs, as applicable, are included in any of its section 471 costs on hand at year end during a qualifying period or extended qualifying period according to how those direct labor costs or direct material costs, respectively, are identified in the taxpayer's revised actual absorption ratios during its applicable test period or updated test period.

(E) *Examples.*—The following examples illustrate this paragraph (d)(2)(iv):

(1) *Example 1—Taxpayer using de minimis direct material costs rule.* Taxpayer R uses the modified simplified production method described in §1.263A-2(c) and the de minimis method of accounting

under paragraph (d)(2)(iv)(C) of this section. In 2018, R does not capitalize freight-in costs or trade discounts to property produced or property acquired for resale in its financial statement but does capitalize all other direct material costs to such property in its financial statement. R incurs total direct material costs of $3,105,000, which represents invoice price of $3,000,000 on goods purchased, plus $120,000 of freight-in costs, less $15,000 for trade discounts. For purposes of determining the amount of uncapitalized direct material costs for the five percent test in paragraph (d)(2)(iv)(C) of this section, R's trade discounts are treated as a positive amount. Consequently, R's uncapitalized direct material costs for purposes of the five percent test are $135,000 ($120,000 of freight-in plus $15,000 of trade discounts). Accordingly, under paragraph (d)(2)(iv)(C) of this section, R's uncapitalized direct material costs are 4.35% of total direct material costs ($135,000 divided by $3,105,000), and R includes a positive $120,000 of freight-in and a negative $15,000 of trade discounts in its additional section 263A costs and excludes those amounts from its section 471 costs in the taxable year.

(2) Example 2—Taxpayer using de minimis direct labor costs rule and historic absorption ratio. Taxpayer S uses the historic absorption ratio provided in §1.263A-2(c)(4). S uses the de minimis method of accounting under paragraph (d)(2)(iv)(B). S excludes certain uncapitalized direct labor costs from its section 471 costs (and includes them in additional section 263A costs) under paragraph (d)(2)(iv)(B) of this section in Years 1 and 3 of its applicable test period. Because S excluded direct labor costs from its section 471 costs in at least two of the three years of its applicable test period, S must exclude those same costs from its pre-production and production section 471 costs remaining on hand at year end during its qualifying period or extended qualifying period.

(v) Safe harbor method for certain variances and under or over-applied burdens.—(A) *In general.*—Notwithstanding paragraphs (d)(2)(i) and (ii), (f)(3)(i)(C), and (f)(3)(ii)(B) of this section, a taxpayer that uses the simplified resale method, the simplified production method, or the modified simplified production method, may use the safe harbor method described in this paragraph (d)(2)(v)(A) for all of its variances and under or over-applied burdens that are not capitalized to property produced or property acquired for resale in its financial statement (uncapitalized variances and uncapitalized under or over-applied burdens). A taxpayer using this safe harbor method must include in additional section 263A costs, and exclude from section 471 costs, the sum of the amounts of all of those uncapitalized variances and uncapitalized under or over-applied burdens for the taxable year, if that sum is less than five percent of the taxpayer's total section 471 costs for all items to which it allocates costs using a standard cost method or burden rate method, or another percentage specified in other published guidance (*see* §601.601(d)(2) of this chapter). If the sum of uncapitalized variances and uncapitalized under or over-applied burdens is not less than this five percent threshold, the taxpayer may not exclude such uncapitalized variances and uncapitalized under or over-applied burdens from section 471 costs, and must reallocate such uncapitalized variances and uncapitalized under or over-applied burdens to or among the units of property to which the costs are allocable in accordance with paragraphs (f)(3)(i)(C) and (f)(3)(ii)(B) of this section (but see paragraph (d)(2)(v)(B) of this section for a rule that a taxpayer using the safe harbor method described in this paragraph (d)(2)(v)(A) may not use the methods of accounting described in paragraphs (f)(3)(i)(C) and (f)(3)(ii)(B) of this section to treat certain uncapitalized variances and certain uncapitalized under or over-applied burdens as not allocable to property). For purposes of determining the amounts of uncapitalized variances and uncapitalized under or over-applied burdens for this five percent test, all variances and under or over-applied burdens are treated as positive amounts. Additionally, for purposes of this five percent test, a taxpayer's total section 471 costs for all items to which it allocates costs using a standard cost method or burden rate method are determined before application of the safe harbor method described in this paragraph (d)(2)(v)(A), and therefore this amount must reflect the actual amounts incurred by the taxpayer for those items during the taxable year, which includes variances and under or over-applied burdens. The variances described in this paragraph (d)(2)(v)(A) include any variances on cash or trade discounts, if those discounts are capitalized as part of the taxpayer's standard cost method used for section 471 costs.

(B) *Consistency requirement.*—A taxpayer using the safe harbor method described in paragraph (d)(2)(v)(A) of this section must use the method consistently for all items to which it allocates costs using a standard cost method or burden rate method and may not use the methods of accounting described in paragraphs (f)(3)(i)(C) and (f)(3)(ii)(B) of this section to treat its uncapitalized variances and uncapitalized under or over-applied burdens that are not significant in amount relative to the taxpayer's total indirect costs incurred with respect to production and resale activities for the year as not allocable to property produced or property acquired for resale.

(C) *Allocation of variances and under or over-applied burdens between production and preproduction costs under the modified simplified production method.*—In the case of a taxpayer using the modified simplified production method and the safe harbor method described in paragraph (d)(2)(v)(A) of this section, uncapitalized variances and uncapitalized under or over-applied burdens treated as additional section 263A costs under the safe harbor method must be allocated between production additional section 263A costs, as described in §1.263A-2(c)(3)(ii)(D)(*1*), and preproduction additional section 263A costs, as described in §1.263A-2(c)(3)(ii)(B)(*1*), using any reasonable method. In the case of a taxpayer using the modified simplified production method and the safe harbor method described in paragraph (d)(2)(v)(A) of this section, uncapitalized variances and uncapitalized under or over-applied burdens that are not excluded from section 471 costs must be allocated between production section 471 costs, as described in §1.263A-2(c)(3)(ii)(D)(*3*), and pre-production section 471 costs, as described in §1.263A-2(c)(3)(ii)(B)(*2*) based on the taxpayer's reallocation of such uncapitalized variances and uncapitalized under or over-applied burdens to or among the units of property to which the costs are allocable in accordance with paragraphs (f)(3)(i)(C) and (f)(3)(ii)(B) of this section, as described in paragraph (d)(2)(v)(A) of this section.

(D) *Allocation of variances and under or over-applied burdens between storage and handling costs absorption ratio and purchasing costs absorption ratio under the simplified resale method.*—In the case of a taxpayer using the simplified resale method, any uncapitalized variances and uncapitalized under or over-applied burdens treated as additional section 263A costs under the safe harbor method described in paragraph (d)(2)(v)(A) of this section must be allocated between storage and handling costs, as described in §1.263A-3(d)(3)(i)(D)(2), and current year's purchasing costs, as described in §1.263A-3(d)(3)(i)(E)(2), using any reasonable method.

(E) *Method of accounting.*—The use of the safe harbor method described in this paragraph (d)(2)(v) is the adoption of, or a change in, a method of accounting under section 446 of the Internal Revenue Code.

(vi) *Removal of section 471 costs.*—A taxpayer must remove those costs included in its section 471 costs that are not permitted to be capitalized under either paragraph (c)(2) or (j)(2)(ii) of this section and those costs included in its section 471 costs that are eligible for capitalization under paragraph (j)(2) of this section that the taxpayer does not elect to capitalize under section 263A. Except as otherwise provided in paragraph (d)(3)(ii)(B) of this section, a taxpayer must remove costs pursuant to this paragraph (d)(2)(vi) by adjusting its section 471 costs and may not remove the costs by including a negative adjustment in its additional section 263A costs. A taxpayer that removes costs pursuant to this paragraph (d)(2)(vi) by adjusting its section 471 costs must use a reasonable method that approximates the manner in which the taxpayer originally capitalized the costs to its property produced or property acquired for resale in its financial statement.

(vii) *Method changes.*—A taxpayer using the simplified production method, simplified resale method, or the modified simplified production method and that changes its financial statement practices for a cost in a manner that would change its section 471 costs is required to change its method of accounting for federal income tax purposes. A taxpayer may change its method of accounting for determining section 471 costs only with the consent of the Commissioner as required under section 446(e) and the corresponding regulations.

(3) *Additional section 263A costs.*—(i) *In general.*—Additional section 263A costs are the costs, other than interest, that are not included in a taxpayer's section 471 costs but that are required to be capitalized under section 263A. Additional section 263A costs generally do not include the direct costs that are required to be included in a taxpayer's section 471 costs under paragraph (d)(2)(ii) of this section; however, additional section 263A costs must include any direct costs excluded from section 471 costs under paragraphs (d)(2)(iv) and (v) of this section. For a taxpayer using the alternative method described in paragraph (d)(2)(iii) of this section, additional section 263A costs must also include any negative or positive adjustments required to be made as a result of differences in the book and tax amounts of the taxpayer's section 471 costs.

(ii) *Negative adjustments.*—(A) *In general.*—Except as otherwise provided by regulations or other published guidance (*see* §601.601(d)(2) of this chapter), a taxpayer may not include negative adjustments in additional section 263A costs. However, for a taxpayer using the alternative method described in paragraph (d)(2)(iii) of this section, see paragraph (d)(2)(iii)(B) of this section for negative or positive adjustments required to be made as a result of differences in the book and tax amounts of the taxpayer's section 471 costs.

(B) *Exception for certain taxpayers removing costs from section 471 costs.*—Notwithstanding paragraphs (d)(2)(vi) and (d)(3)(ii)(A) of this section, and except as otherwise provided in paragraphs (d)(3)(ii)(C) and (D) of this section, the following taxpayers may, but are not required to, include negative adjustments in additional section 263A costs to remove the taxpayer's section 471 costs that are described in paragraph (d)(2)(vi) of this section (costs that are not required to be, or are not permitted to be, capitalized under section 263A):

(1) A taxpayer using the simplified production method under §1.263A-2(b) if the taxpayer's (or its predecessor's) average annual gross receipts for the three previous taxable years (test period) do not exceed $50,000,000, or another amount specified in other published guidance (*see* §601.601(d)(2) of this chapter). The rules of §1.263A-1(j) apply for purposes of determining the amount of a taxpayer's gross receipts and the test period;

(2) A taxpayer using the modified simplified production method under §1.263A-2(c); and

(3) A taxpayer using the simplified resale method under §1.263A-3(d).

(C) *No negative adjustments for cash or trade discounts.*—A taxpayer may not include negative adjustments in additional section 263A costs for cash or trade discounts described in §1.471-3(b). However, see paragraph (d)(2)(iv)(C) of this section for a de minimis rule for certain direct material costs that may be included in additional section 263A costs and paragraph (d)(2)(v) of this section for certain variance amounts that may be included in additional section 263A costs.

(D) *No negative adjustments for certain expenses.*—A taxpayer may not include negative adjustments in additional section 263A costs for an amount which is of a type for which a deduction would be disallowed under section 162(c), (e), (f), or (g) and the regulations thereunder in the case of a business expense.

(E) *Consistency requirement for negative adjustments.*—A taxpayer that is permitted to include negative adjustments in additional section 263A costs to remove section 471 costs under paragraph (d)(3)(ii)(B) of this section and that includes negative adjustments to remove section 471 costs must use that method of accounting to remove all section 471 costs required to be removed under paragraph (d)(2)(vi) of this section.

(4) *Section 263A costs.*—Section 263A costs are defined as the costs that a taxpayer must capitalize under section 263A. Thus, section 263A costs are the sum of a taxpayer's section 471 costs, its additional section 263A costs, and interest capitalizable under section 263A(f).

(5) *Classification of costs.*—A taxpayer must classify section 471 costs, additional section 263A costs, and any permitted adjustments to section 471 or additional section 263A costs, using the narrower of the classifications of costs described in paragraphs (e)(2), (3), and (4) of this section, whether or not the taxpayer is required to maintain inventories, or the classifications of costs used by a taxpayer in its financial statement. If a cost is not described in paragraph (e)(2), (3), or (4) of this section, the cost is to be classified using the classification of costs used in the taxpayer's financial statement.

(6) *Financial statement.*—For purposes of section 263A, financial statement means the taxpayer's financial statement listed in paragraphs (d)(6)(i) through (iv) of this section that has the highest priority, including within paragraphs (d)(6)(ii) and (iv) of this section. The financial statements are, in descending priority:

(i) A financial statement required to be filed with the Securities and Exchange Commission (SEC) (the 10-K or the Annual Statement to Shareholders);

(ii) A certified audited financial statement that is accompanied by the report of an independent certified public accountant (or in the case of a foreign entity, by the report of a similarly qualified independent professional) that is used for:

(A) Credit purposes;

(B) Reporting to shareholders, partners, or similar persons; or

(C) Any other substantial non-tax purpose;

(iii) A financial statement (other than a tax return) required to be provided to the federal or a state government or any federal or state agency (other than the SEC or the Internal Revenue Service); or

(iv) A financial statement that is used for:

(A) Credit purposes;

(B) Reporting to shareholders, partners, or similar persons; or

(C) Any other substantial non-tax purpose.

(e) *Types of costs subject to capitalization.*—(1) *In general.*—Taxpayers subject to section 263A must capitalize all direct costs and certain indirect costs properly allocable to property produced or property acquired for resale. This paragraph (e) describes the types of costs subject to section 263A.

(2) *Direct costs.*—(i) *Producers.*—Producers must capitalize direct material costs and direct labor costs.

(A) *Direct material costs.*—Direct materials costs include the cost of those materials that become an integral part of specific property produced and those materials that are consumed in the ordinary course of production and that can be identified or associated with particular units or groups of units of property produced. For example, a cost described in §1.162-3, relating to the cost of a material or supply, may be a direct material cost.

(B) *Direct labor costs* include the costs of labor that can be identified or associated with particular units or groups of units of specific property produced. For this purpose, labor encompasses full-time and part-time employees, as well as contract employees and independent contractors. Direct labor costs include all elements of compensation other than employee benefit costs described in paragraph (e)(3)(ii)(D) of this section. Elements of direct labor costs include basic compensation, overtime pay, vacation pay, holiday pay, sick leave pay (other than payments pursuant to a wage continuation plan under section 105(d) as it existed prior to its repeal in 1983), shift differential, payroll taxes, and payments to a supplemental unemployment benefit plan.

(ii) *Resellers.*—Resellers must capitalize the acquisition costs of property acquired for resale. In the case of inventory, the acquisition cost is the cost described in §1.471-3(b).

(3) *Indirect costs.*—(i) *In general.*—(A) Indirect costs are defined as all costs other than direct material costs and direct labor costs (in the case of property produced) or acquisition costs (in the case of property acquired for resale). Taxpayers subject to section 263A must capitalize all indirect costs properly allocable to property produced or property acquired for resale. Indirect costs are properly allocable to property produced or property acquired for resale when the costs directly benefit or are incurred by reason of the performance of production or resale activities. Indirect costs may directly benefit or be incurred by reason of the performance of production or resale activities even if the costs are calculated as a percentage of revenue or gross profit from the sale of inventory, are determined by reference to the number of units of property sold, or are incurred only upon the sale of inventory. Indirect costs may be allocable to both production and resale activities, as well as to other activities that are not subject to section 263A. Taxpayers must make a reasonable allocation of indirect costs between production, resale, and other activities.

(B) *Example.*—The following example illustrates the provisions of this paragraph (e)(3)(i):

Example. (i) Taxpayer A manufactures tablecloths and other linens. A enters into a licensing agreement with Company L under which A may label its tablecloths with L's trademark if the tablecloths meet certain specified quality standards. In exchange for its right to use L's trademark, the licensing agreement requires A to pay L a royalty of $X for each tablecloth carrying L's trademark that A sells. The licensing agreement does not require A to pay L any minimum or lump-sum royalties.

(ii) The licensing agreement provides A with the right to use L's intellectual property, a trademark. The licensing agreement also requires A to conduct its production activities according to certain standards as a condition of exercising that right. Thus, A's right to use L's trademark under the licensing agreement is directly related to A's production of tablecloths. The royalties the licensing agreement requires A to pay for using L's trademark are the costs A incurs in exchange for these rights. Therefore, although A incurs royalty costs only when A sells a tablecloth carrying L's trademark, the royalty costs directly benefit production activities and are incurred by reason of production activities within the meaning of paragraph (e)(3)(i)(A) of this section.

(ii) *Examples of indirect costs required to be capitalized.*—The following are examples of indirect costs that must be capitalized to the extent they are properly allocable to property produced or property acquired for resale:

(A) *Indirect labor costs.*—Indirect labor costs include all labor costs (including the elements of labor costs set forth in paragraph (e)(2)(i) of this section) that cannot be directly identified or associated with particular units or groups of units of specific property produced or property acquired for resale (e.g., factory labor that is not direct labor). As in the case of direct labor, indirect labor encompasses full-time and part-time employees, as well as contract employees and independent contractors.

Reg. §1.263A-1(e)(3)(ii)(A)

(B) *Officers' compensation.*—Officers' compensation includes compensation paid to officers of the taxpayer.

(C) *Pension and other related costs.*—Pension and other related costs include contributions paid to or made under any stock bonus, pension, profit-sharing or annuity plan, or other plan deferring the receipt of compensation, whether or not the plan qualifies under section 401(a). Contributions to employee plans representing past services must be capitalized in the same manner (and in the same proportion to property currently being acquired or produced) as amounts contributed for current service.

(D) *Employee benefit expenses.*—Employee benefit expenses include all other employee benefit expenses (not described in paragraph (e)(3)(ii)(C) of this section) to the extent such expenses are otherwise allowable as deductions under chapter 1 of the Internal Revenue Code. These other employee benefit expenses include: worker's compensation; amounts otherwise deductible or allowable in reducing earnings and profits under section 404A; payments pursuant to a wage continuation plan under section 105(d) as it existed prior to its repeal in 1983; amounts includible in the gross income of employees under a method or arrangement of employer contributions or compensation that has the effect of a stock bonus, pension, profit-sharing or annuity plan, or other plan deferring receipt of compensation or providing deferred benefits; premiums on life and health insurance; and miscellaneous benefits provided for employees such as safety, medical treatment, recreational and eating facilities, membership dues, etc. Employee benefit expenses do not, however, include direct labor costs described in paragraph (e)(2)(i) of this section.

(E) *Indirect material costs.*—Indirect material costs include the cost of materials that are not an integral part of specific property produced and the cost of materials that are consumed in the ordinary course of performing production or resale activities that cannot be identified or associated with particular units of property. Thus, for example, a cost described in §1.162-3, relating to the cost of a material or supply, may be an indirect cost.

(F) *Purchasing costs.*—Purchasing costs include costs attributable to purchasing activities. See §1.263A-3(c)(3) for a further discussion of purchasing costs.

(G) *Handling costs.*—Handling costs include costs attributable to processing, assembling, repackaging and transporting goods, and other similar activities. See §1.263A-3(c)(4) for a further discussion of handling costs.

(H) *Storage costs.*—Storage costs include the costs of carrying, storing, or warehousing property. See §1.263A-3(c)(5) for a further discussion of storage costs.

(I) *Cost recovery.*—Cost recovery includes depreciation, amortization, and cost recovery allowances on equipment and facilities (including depreciation or amortization of self-constructed assets or other previously produced or acquired property to which section 263A or section 263 applies).

(J) *Depletion.*—Depletion includes allowances for depletion, whether or not in excess of cost. Depletion is, however, only properly allocable to property that has been sold (i.e., for purposes of determining gain or loss on the sale of the property).

(K) *Rent.*—Rent includes the cost of renting or leasing equipment, facilities, or land.

(L) *Taxes.*—Taxes include those taxes (other than taxes described in paragraph (e)(3)(iii)(F) of this section) that are otherwise allowable as a deduction to the extent such taxes are attributable to labor, materials, supplies, equipment, land, or facilities used in production or resale activities.

(M) *Insurance.*—Insurance includes the cost of insurance on plant or facility, machinery, equipment, materials, property produced, or property acquired for resale.

(N) *Utilities.*—Utilities include the cost of electricity, gas, and water.

(O) *Repairs and maintenance.*—Repairs and maintenance include the cost of repairing and maintaining equipment or facilities.

(P) *Engineering and design costs.*—Engineering and design costs include pre-production costs, such as costs attributable to research, experimental, engineering, and design activities (to the extent that such amounts are not research and experimental expenditures as described in section 174 and the regulations thereunder).

(Q) *Spoilage.*—Spoilage includes the costs of rework labor, scrap, and spoilage.

(R) *Tools and equipment.*—Tools and equipment include the costs of tools and equipment which are not otherwise capitalized.

(S) *Quality control.*—Quality control includes the costs of quality control and inspection.

(T) *Bidding costs.*—Bidding costs are costs incurred in the solicitation of contracts (including contracts pertaining to property acquired for resale) ultimately awarded to the taxpayer. The taxpayer must defer all bidding costs paid or incurred in the solicitation of a particular contract until the contract is awarded. If the contract is awarded to the taxpayer, the bidding costs become part of the indirect costs allocated to the subject matter of the contract. If the contract is not awarded to the taxpayer, bidding costs are deductible in the taxable year that the contract is awarded to another party, or in the taxable year that the taxpayer is notified in writing that no contract will be awarded and that the contract (or a similar or related contract) will not be rebid, or in the taxable year that the taxpayer abandons its bid or proposal, whichever occurs first. Abandoning a bid does not include modifying, supplementing, or changing the original bid or proposal. If the taxpayer is awarded only part of the bid (for example, the taxpayer submitted one bid to build each of two different types of products, and the taxpayer was awarded a contract to build only one of the two types of products), the taxpayer shall deduct the portion of the bidding costs related to the portion of the bid not awarded to the taxpayer. In the case of a bid or proposal for a multi-unit contract, all bidding costs must be included in the costs allocated to the subject matter of the contract awarded to the taxpayer to produce or acquire for resale any of such units. For example, where the taxpayer submits one bid to produce three similar turbines and the taxpayer is awarded a contract to produce only two of the three turbines, all bidding costs must be included in the cost of the two turbines. For purposes of this paragraph (e)(3)(ii)(T), a contract means—

(1) In the case of a specific unit of property, any agreement under which the taxpayer would produce or sell property to another party if the agreement is entered into before the taxpayer produces or acquires the specific unit of property to be delivered to the party under the agreement; and

(2) In the case of fungible property, any agreement to the extent that, at the time the agreement is entered into, the taxpayer has on hand an insufficient quantity of completed fungible items of such property that may be used to satisfy the agreement (plus any other production or sales agreements of the taxpayer).

(U) *Licensing and franchise costs.*—(1) Licensing and franchise costs include fees incurred in securing the contractual right to use a trademark, corporate plan, manufacturing procedure, special recipe, or other similar right associated with property produced or property acquired for resale. These costs include the otherwise deductible portion (such as amortization) of the initial fees incurred to obtain the license or franchise and any minimum annual payments and any royalties that are incurred by a licensee or a franchisee. These costs also include fees, payments, and royalties otherwise described in this paragraph (e)(3)(ii)(U) that a taxpayer incurs (within the meaning of section 461) only upon the sale of property produced or acquired for resale.

(2) If a taxpayer incurs (within the meaning of section 461) a fee, payment, or royalty described in this paragraph (e)(3)(ii)(U) only upon the sale of property produced or acquired for resale and the cost is required to be capitalized under this paragraph (e)(3), the taxpayer may properly allocate the cost entirely to property produced or acquired for resale by the taxpayer that has been sold.

(V) *Interest.*—Interest includes interest on debt incurred or continued during the production period to finance the production of real property or tangible personal property to which section 263A(f) applies.

(W) *Capitalizable service costs.*—Service costs that are required to be capitalized include capitalizable service costs and capitalizable mixed service costs as defined in paragraph (e)(4) of this section.

(iii) *Indirect costs not capitalized.*—The following indirect costs are not required to be capitalized under section 263A:

(A) *Selling and distribution costs.*—These costs are marketing, selling, advertising, and distribution costs.

(B) *Research and experimental expenditures.*—Research and experimental expenditures are expenditures described in section 174 and the regulations thereunder.

(C) *Section 179 costs.*—Section 179 costs are expenses for certain depreciable assets deductible at the election of the taxpayer under section 179 and the regulations thereunder.

(D) *Section 165 losses.*—Section 165 losses are losses under section 165 and the regulations thereunder.

(E) *Cost recovery allowances on temporarily idle equipment and facilities.*—(1) *In general.*—Cost recovery allowances on temporarily idle equipment and facilities include only depreciation, amortization, and cost recovery allowances on equipment and facilities that have been placed in service but are temporarily idle. Equipment and facilities are temporarily idle when a taxpayer takes them out of service for a finite period. However, equipment and facilities are not considered temporarily idle—

(i) During worker breaks, non-working hours, or on regularly scheduled non-working days (such as holidays or weekends);

(ii) During normal interruptions in the operation of the equipment or facilities;

(iii) When equipment is enroute to or located at a job site; or

(iv) When under normal operating conditions, the equipment is used or operated only during certain shifts.

(2) *Examples.*—The provisions of this paragraph (e)(3)(iii)(E) are illustrated by the following examples:

Example 1. Equipment operated only during certain shifts. Taxpayer A manufactures widgets. Although A's manufacturing facility operates 24 hours each day in three shifts, A only operates its stamping machine during one shift each day. Because A only operates its stamping machine during certain shifts, A's stamping machine is not considered temporarily idle during the two shifts that it is not operated.

Example 2. Facility shut down for retooling. Taxpayer B owns and operates a manufacturing facility. B closes its manufacturing facility for two weeks to retool its assembly line. B's manufacturing facility is considered temporarily idle during this two-week period.

(F) *Taxes assessed on the basis of income.*—Taxes assessed on the basis of income include only state, local, and foreign income taxes, and franchise taxes that are assessed on the taxpayer based on income.

(G) *Strike expenses.*—Strike expenses include only costs associated with hiring employees to replace striking personnel (but not wages of replacement personnel), costs of security, and legal fees associated with settling strikes.

(H) *Warranty and product liability costs.*—Warranty costs and product liability costs are costs incurred in fulfilling product warranty obligations for products that have been sold and costs incurred for product liability insurance.

(I) *On-site storage costs.*—On-site storage costs are storage and warehousing costs incurred by a taxpayer at an on-site storage facility, as defined in § 1.263A-3(c)(5)(ii)(A), with respect to property produced or property acquired for resale.

(J) *Unsuccessful bidding expenses.*—Unsuccessful bidding costs are bidding expenses incurred in the solicitation of contracts not awarded to the taxpayer.

(K) *Deductible service costs.*—Service costs that are not required to be capitalized include deductible service costs and deductible mixed service costs as defined in paragraph (e)(4) of this section.

(4) *Service costs.*—(i) *Introduction.*—This paragraph (e)(4) provides definitions and categories of service costs. Paragraph (g)(4) of this section provides specific rules for determining the amount of service costs allocable to property produced or property acquired for resale. In addition, paragraph (h) of this section provides a simplified method for determining the amount of service costs that must be capitalized.

(A) *Definition of service costs.*—Service costs are defined as a type of indirect costs (e.g., general and administrative costs) that can be identified specifically with a service department or function or that directly benefit or are incurred by reason of a service department or function.

(B) *Definition of service departments.*—Service departments are defined as administrative, service, or support departments that incur service costs. The facts and circumstances of the taxpayer's activities and business organization control whether a department is a service department. For example, service departments include personnel, accounting, data processing, security, legal, and other similar departments.

(ii) *Various service cost categories.*—(A) *Capitalizable service costs.*—Capitalizable service costs are defined as service costs that directly benefit or are incurred by reason of the performance of the production or resale activities of the taxpayer. Therefore, these ser-

vice costs are required to be capitalized under section 263A. Examples of service departments or functions that incur capitalizable service costs are provided in paragraph (e)(4)(iii) of this section.

(B) *Deductible service costs.*—Deductible service costs are defined as service costs that do not directly benefit or are not incurred by reason of the performance of the production or resale activities of the taxpayer, and therefore, are not required to be capitalized under section 263A. Deductible service costs generally include costs incurred by reason of the taxpayer's overall management or policy guidance functions. In addition, deductible service costs include costs incurred by reason of the marketing, selling, advertising, and distribution activities of the taxpayer. Examples of service departments or functions that incur deductible service costs are provided in paragraph (e)(4)(iv) of this section.

(C) *Mixed service costs.*—Mixed service costs are defined as service costs that are partially allocable to production or resale activities (capitalizable mixed service costs) and partially allocable to non-production or non-resale activities (deductible mixed service costs). For example, a personnel department may incur costs to recruit factory workers, the costs of which are allocable to production activities, and it may incur costs to develop wage, salary, and benefit policies, the costs of which are allocable to non-production activities.

(iii) *Examples of capitalizable service costs.*—Costs incurred in the following departments or functions are generally allocated among production or resale activities:

(A) The administration and coordination of production or resale activities (wherever performed in the business organization of the taxpayer).

(B) Personnel operations, including the cost of recruiting, hiring, relocating, assigning, and maintaining personnel records or employees.

(C) Purchasing operations, including purchasing materials and equipment, scheduling and coordinating delivery of materials and equipment to or from factories or job sites, and expediting and follow-up.

(D) Materials handling and warehousing and storage operations.

(E) Accounting and data services operations, including, for example, cost accounting, accounts payable, disbursements, and payroll functions (but excluding accounts receivable and customer billing functions).

(F) Data processing.

(G) Security services.

(H) Legal services.

(iv) *Examples of deductible service costs.*—Costs incurred in the following departments or functions are not generally allocated to production or resale activities:

(A) Departments or functions responsible for overall management of the taxpayer or for setting overall policy for all of the taxpayer's activities or trades or businesses, such as the board of directors (including their immediate staff), and the chief executive, financial, accounting, and legal officers (including their immediate staff) of the taxpayer, provided that no substantial part of the cost of such departments or functions benefits a particular production or resale activity.

(B) Strategic business planning.

(C) General financial accounting.

(D) General financial planning (including general budgeting) and financial management (including bank relations and cash management).

(E) Personnel policy (such as establishing and managing personnel policy in general; developing wage, salary, and benefit policies; developing employee training programs unrelated to particular production or resale activities; negotiating with labor unions; and maintaining relations with retired workers).

(F) Quality control policy.

(G) Safety engineering policy.

(H) Insurance or risk management policy (but not including bid or performance bonds or insurance related to activities associated with property produced or property acquired for resale).

(I) Environmental management policy (except to the extent that the costs of any system or procedure benefits a particular production or resale activity).

(J) General economic analysis and forecasting.

(K) Internal audit.

(L) Shareholder, public, and industrial relations.

(M) Tax services.

(N) Marketing, selling, or advertising.

(f) *Cost allocation methods.*—(1) *Introduction.*—This paragraph (f) sets forth various detailed or specific (facts-and-circumstances) cost allocation methods that taxpayers may use to allocate direct and indirect costs to property produced and property acquired for resale. Paragraph (g) of this section provides general rules for applying these allocation methods to various categories of costs (i.e., direct materials, direct labor, and indirect costs, including service costs). In addition, in lieu of a facts-and-circumstances allocation method, taxpayers may use the simplified methods provided in §§ 1.263A-2(b) and (c) and 1.263A-3(d) to allocate direct and indirect costs to eligible property produced or eligible property acquired for resale; see those sections for definitions of eligible property. Paragraph (h) of this section provides a simplified method for determining the amount of mixed service costs required to be capitalized to eligible property. The methodology set forth in paragraph (h) of this section for mixed service costs may be used in conjunction with either a facts-and-circumstances or a simplified method of allocating costs to eligible property produced or eligible property acquired for resale.

(2) *Specific identification method.*—A specific identification method traces costs to a cost objective, such as a function, department, activity, or product, on the basis of a cause and effect or other reasonable relationship between the costs and the cost objective.

(3) *Burden rate and standard cost methods.*—(i) *Burden rate method.*—(A) *In general.*—A burden rate method allocates an appropriate amount of indirect costs to property produced or property acquired for resale during a taxable year using predetermined rates that approximate the actual amount of indirect costs incurred by the taxpayer during the taxable year. Burden rates (such as ratios based on direct costs, hours, or similar items) may be developed by the taxpayer in accordance with acceptable accounting principles and applied in a reasonable manner. A taxpayer may allocate different indirect costs on the basis of different burden rates. Thus, for example, the taxpayer may use one burden rate for allocating the cost of rent and another burden rate for allocating the cost of utilities. Any periodic adjustment to a burden rate that merely reflects current operating conditions, such as increases in automation or changes in operation or prices, is not a change in method of accounting under section 446(e). A change, however, in the concept or base upon which such rates are developed, such as a change from basing the rates on direct labor hours to basing them on direct machine hours, is a change in method of accounting to which section 446(e) applies.

(B) *Development of burden rates.*—The following factors, among others, may be used in developing burden rates:

(1) The selection of an appropriate level of activity and a period of time upon which to base the calculation of rates reflecting operating conditions for purposes of the unit costs being determined.

(2) The selection of an appropriate statistical base, such as direct labor hours, direct labor dollars, machine hours, or a combination thereof, upon which to apply the overhead rate.

(3) The appropriate budgeting, classification, and analysis of expenses (for example, the analysis of fixed versus variable costs).

(C) *Operation of the burden rate method.*—The purpose of the burden rate method is to allocate an appropriate amount of indirect costs to production or resale activities through the use of predetermined rates intended to approximate the actual amount of indirect costs incurred. Accordingly, the proper use of the burden rate method under this section requires that any net negative or net positive difference between the total predetermined amount of costs allocated to property and the total amount of indirect costs actually incurred and required to be allocated to such property (i.e., the under or over-applied burden) must be treated as an adjustment to the taxpayer's ending inventory or capital account (as the case may be) in the taxable year in which such difference arises. However, if such adjustment is not significant in amount in relation to the taxpayer's total indirect costs incurred with respect to production or resale activities for the year, such adjustment need not be allocated to the property produced or property acquired for resale unless such allocation is made in the taxpayer's financial statement. The taxpayer must treat both positive and negative adjustments consistently.

(ii) *Standard cost method.*—(A) *In general.*—A standard cost method allocates an appropriate amount of direct and indirect costs to property produced by the taxpayer through the use of preestablished standard allowances, without reference to costs actually incurred during the taxable year. A taxpayer may use a standard cost method to allocate costs, provided variances are treated in accordance with the procedures prescribed in paragraph (f)(3)(ii)(B) of this section. Any periodic adjustment to standard costs that merely reflects current operating conditions, such as increases in automation or changes in operation or prices, is not a change in method of accounting under section 446(e). A change, however, in the concept or base upon which standard costs are developed is a change in method of accounting to which section 446(e) applies.

(B) *Treatment of variances.*—For purposes of this section, net positive overhead variance means the excess of total standard indirect costs over total actual indirect costs and net negative overhead variance means the excess of total actual indirect costs over total standard indirect costs. The proper use of a standard cost method requires that a taxpayer must reallocate to property a pro rata portion of any net negative or net positive overhead variances and any net negative or net positive direct cost variances. The taxpayer must apportion such variances to or among the property to which the costs are allocable. However, if such variances are not significant in amount relative to the taxpayer's total indirect costs incurred with respect to production and resale activities for the year, such variances need not be allocated to property produced or property acquired for resale unless such allocation is made in the taxpayer's financial statement. A taxpayer must treat both positive and negative variances consistently.

(4) *Reasonable allocation methods.*—A taxpayer may use the methods described in paragraph (f)(2) or (3) of this section if they are reasonable allocation methods within the meaning of this paragraph (f)(4). In addition, a taxpayer may use any other reasonable method to properly allocate direct and indirect costs among units of property produced or property acquired for resale during the taxable year. An allocation method is reasonable if, with respect to the taxpayer's production or resale activities taken as a whole—

(i) The total costs actually capitalized during the taxable year do not differ significantly from the aggregate costs that would be properly capitalized using another permissible method described in this section or in §§ 1.263A-2 and 1.263A-3, with appropriate consideration given to the volume and value of the taxpayer's production or resale activities, the availability of costing information, the time and cost of using various allocation methods, and the accuracy of the allocation method chosen as compared with other allocation methods;

(ii) The allocation method is applied consistently by the taxpayer; and

(iii) The allocation method is not used to circumvent the requirements of the simplified methods in this section or in § 1.263A-2, 1.263A-3, or the principles of section 263A.

(g) *Allocating categories of costs.*—(1) *Direct materials.*—Direct material costs (as defined in paragraph (e)(2) of this section) incurred during the taxable year must be allocated to the property produced or property acquired for resale by the taxpayer using the taxpayer's method of accounting for materials (e.g., specific identification; first-in, first-out (FIFO); or last-in, first-out (LIFO)), or any other reasonable allocation method (as defined under the principles of paragraph (f)(4) of this section).

(2) *Direct labor.*—Direct labor costs (as defined in paragraph (e)(2) of this section) incurred during the taxable year are generally allocated to property produced or property acquired for resale using a specific identification method, standard cost method, or any other reasonable allocation method (as defined under the principles of paragraph (f)(4) of this section). All elements of compensation, other than basic compensation, may be grouped together and then allocated in proportion to the charge for basic compensation. Further, a taxpayer is not treated as using an erroneous method of accounting if direct labor costs are treated as indirect costs under the taxpayer's allocation method, provided such costs are capitalized to the extent required by paragraph (g)(3) of this section.

(3) *Indirect costs.*—Indirect costs (as defined in paragraph (e)(3) of this section) are generally allocated to intermediate cost objectives such as departments or activities prior to the allocation of such costs to property produced or property acquired for resale. Indirect costs are allocated using either a specific identification method, a standard cost method, a burden rate method, or any other reasonable allocation method (as defined under the principles of paragraph (f)(4) of this section).

(4) *Service costs.*—(i) *In general.*—Service costs are a type of indirect costs that may be allocated using the same allocation methods available for allocating other indirect costs described in paragraph (g)(3) of this section. Generally, taxpayers that use a specific identification method or another reasonable allocation method must allocate service costs to particular departments or activities based on a factor or relationship that reasonably relates the service costs to the benefits received from the service departments or activities. For example, a reasonable factor for allocating legal services to particular departments or activities is the number of hours of legal services attributable to each department or activity. See paragraph (g)(4)(iv) of this section for other illustrations. Using reasonable factors or relationships, a taxpayer must allocate mixed service costs under a direct reallocation method described in paragraph (g)(4)(iii)(A) of this section, a step-allocation method described in paragraph (g)(4)(iii)(B) of this section, or any other reasonable allocation method (as defined under the principles of paragraph (f)(4) of this section).

(ii) *De minimis rule.*—For purposes of administrative convenience, if 90 percent or more of a mixed service department's costs are deductible service costs, a taxpayer may elect not to allocate any portion of the service department's costs to property produced or property acquired for resale. For example, if 90 percent of the costs of an electing taxpayer's industrial relations department benefit the taxpayer's overall policy-making activities, the taxpayer is not required to allocate any portion of these costs to a production activity. Under this election, however, if 90 percent or more of a mixed service department's costs are capitalizable service costs, a taxpayer must allocate 100 percent of the department's costs to the production or resale activity benefitted. For example, if 90 percent of the costs of an electing taxpayer's accounting department benefit the taxpayer's manufacturing activity, the taxpayer must allocate 100 percent of the costs of the accounting department to the manufacturing activity. An election under this paragraph (g)(4)(ii) applies to all of a taxpayer's mixed service departments and constitutes the adoption of a (or a change in) method of accounting under section 446 of the Internal Revenue Code.

(iii) *Methods for allocating mixed service costs.*—(A) *Direct reallocation method.*—Under the direct reallocation method, the total costs (direct and indirect) of all mixed service departments are allocated only to departments or cost centers engaged in production or resale activities and then from those departments to particular activities. This direct reallocation method ignores benefits provided by one mixed service department to other mixed service departments, and also excludes other mixed service departments from the base used to make the allocation.

(B) *Step-allocation method.*—(1) Under a step-allocation method, a sequence of allocations is made by the taxpayer. First, the total costs of the mixed service departments that benefit the greatest number of other departments are allocated to—

(i) Other mixed service departments;

(ii) Departments that incur only deductible service costs; and

(iii) Departments that exclusively engage in production or resale activities.

(2) A taxpayer continues allocating mixed service costs in the manner described in paragraph (g)(4)(iii)(B)(1) of this section (i.e., from the service departments benefitting the greatest number of departments to the service departments benefitting the least number of departments) until all mixed service costs are allocated to the types of departments listed in this paragraph (g)(4)(iii). Thus, a step-allocation method recognizes the benefits provided by one mixed service department to another mixed service department and also includes mixed service departments that have not yet been allocated in the base used to make the allocation.

(C) *Examples.*—The provisions of this paragraph (g)(4)(iii) are illustrated by the following examples:

Example 1. Direct reallocation method. (i) Taxpayer E has the following five departments: the Assembling Department, the Painting Department, and the Finishing Department (production departments), and the Personnel Department and the Data Processing Department (mixed service departments). E allocates the Personnel Department's costs on the basis of total payroll costs and the Data Processing Department's costs on the basis of data processing hours.

(ii) Under a direct reallocation method, E allocates the Personnel Department's costs directly to its Assembling, Painting, and Finishing Department, and not to its Data Processing department.

Department	Total Dept. Costs	Amount of Payroll Costs	Allocation Ratio	Amount Allocated
Personnel	$500,000	$50,000	—	<$500,000>
Data Proc'g	250,000	15,000	—	—
Assembling	250,000	15,000	15,000/285,000	26,315
Painting	1,000,000	90,000	90,000/285,000	157,895
Finishing	2,000,000	180,000	180,000/285,000	315,790
	$4,000,000	$350,000		

(iii) After E allocates the Personnel Department's costs, E then allocates the costs of its Data Processing Department in the same manner.

Department	Total Dept. Cost After Initial Allocation	Total Data Proc. Hours	Allocation Ratio	Amount Allocated	Total Dept. Cost After Final Allocation
Personnel	$0	2,000	—	—	$0
Data Proc'g	250,000	—	—	<$250,000>	
Assembling	276,315	2,000	2,000/10,000	50,000	326,315
Painting	1,157,895	0	0/10,000	0	1,157,895
Finishing	2,315,790	8,000	8,000/10,000	200,000	2,515,790
	$4,000,000	12,000			$4,000,000

Example 2. Step-allocation method. (i) Taxpayer F has the following five departments: the Manufacturing Department (a production department), the Marketing Department and the Finance Department (departments that incur only deductible service costs), the Personnel Department and the Data Processing Department (mixed service departments). F uses a step-allocation method and allocates the Personnel Department's costs on the basis of total payroll costs and the Data Processing Department's costs on the basis of data processing hours. F's Personnel Department benefits all four of F's other departments, while its Data Processing Department benefits only three departments. Because F's Personnel Department benefits the greatest number of other departments, F first allocates its Personnel Department's costs to its Manufacturing, Marketing, Finance and Data Processing departments, as follows:

Department	Total Cost of Dept.	Total Payroll Costs	Allocation Ratio	Amount Allocated
Personnel	$500,000	$50,000	—	<$500,000>
Data Proc'g	250,000	15,000	15,000/300,000	25,000
Finance	250,000	15,000	15,000/300,000	25,000
Marketing	1,000,000	90,000	90,000/300,000	150,000
Manufac'g	2,000,000	180,000	180,000/300,000	300,000
	$4,000,000	$350,000		

(ii) Under a step-allocation method, the denominator of F's allocation ratio includes the payroll costs of its Manufacturing, Marketing, Finance, and Data Processing departments.

(iii) Next, F allocates the costs of its Data Processing Department on the basis of data processing hours. Because the costs incurred by F's Personnel Department have already been allocated, no allocation is made to the Personnel Department.

Department	Total Dept. Cost After Initial Allocation	Total Data Proc. Hours	Allocation Ratio	Amount Allocated	Total Dept. Cost After Final Allocation
Personnel	$0	2,000	—	—	$0
Data Proc'g	275,000	—	—	<$275,000>	0
Finance	275,000	2,000	2,000/10,000	55,000	330,000
Marketing	1,150,000	0	0/10,000	0	1,150,000
Manufac'g	2,300,000	8,000	8,000/10,000	220,000	2,520,000
	$4,000,000	12,000			$4,000,000

Reg. §1.263A-1(g)(4)(iii)(C)

(iv) Under the second step of F's step-allocation method, the denominator of F's allocation ratio includes the data processing hours of its Manufacturing, Marketing, and Finance Departments, but does not include the data processing hours of its Personnel Department (the other mixed service department) because the costs of that department have previously been allocated.

(iv) *Illustrations of mixed service cost allocations using reasonable factors or relationships.*—This paragraph (g)(4)(iv) illustrates various reasonable factors and relationships that may be used in allocating different types of mixed service costs. Taxpayers, however, are permitted to use other reasonable factors and relationships to allocate mixed service costs. In addition, the factors or relationships illustrated in this paragraph (g)(4)(iv) may be used to allocate other types of service costs not illustrated in this paragraph (g)(4)(iv).

(A) *Security services.*—The costs of security or protection services must be allocated to each physical area that receives the services using any reasonable method applied consistently (e.g., the size of the physical area, the number of employees in the area, or the relative fair market value of assets located in the area).

(B) *Legal services.*—The costs of legal services are generally allocable to a particular production or resale activity on the basis of the approximate number of hours of legal service performed in connection with the activity, including research, bidding, negotiating, drafting, reviewing a contract, obtaining necessary licenses and permits, and resolving disputes. Different hourly rates may be appropriate for different services. In determining the number of hours allocable to any activity, estimates are appropriate, detailed time records are not required to be kept, and insubstantial amounts of services provided to an activity by senior legal staff (such as administrators or reviewers) may be ignored. Legal costs may also be allocated to a particular production or resale activity based on the ratio of the total direct costs incurred for the activity to the total direct costs incurred with respect to all production or resale activities. The taxpayer must also allocate directly to an activity the cost incurred for any outside legal services. Legal costs relating to general corporate functions are not required to be allocated to a particular production or resale activity.

(C) *Centralized payroll services.*—The costs of a centralized payroll department or activity are generally allocated to the departments or activities benefitted on the basis of the gross dollar amount of payroll processed.

(D) *Centralized data processing services.*—The costs of a centralized data processing department are generally allocated to all departments or activities benefitted using any reasonable basis, such as total direct data processing costs or the number of data processing hours supplied. The costs of data processing systems or applications developed for a particular activity are directly allocated to that activity.

(E) *Engineering and design services.*—The costs of an engineering or a design department are generally directly allocable to the departments or activities benefitted based on the ratio of the approximate number of hours of work performed with respect to the particular activity to the total number of hours of engineering or design work performed for all activities. Different services may be allocated at different hourly rates.

(F) *Safety engineering services.*—The costs of a safety engineering departments or activities generally benefit all of the taxpayer's activities and, thus, should be allocated using a reasonable basis, such as: the approximate number of safety inspections made in connection with a particular activity as a fraction of total inspections, the number of employees assigned to an activity as a fraction of total employees, or the total labor hours worked in connection with an activity as a fraction of total hours. However, in determining the allocable costs of a safety engineering department, costs attributable to providing a safety program relating only to a particular activity must be directly assigned to such activity. Additionally, the cost of a safety engineering department only responsible for setting safety policy and establishing safety procedures to be used in all of the taxpayer's activities is not required to be allocated.

(v) *Accounting method change.*—A change in the method or base used to allocate service costs (such as changing from an allocation base using direct labor costs to a base using direct labor hours), or a change in the taxpayer's determination of what functions or

departments of the taxpayer are to be allocated, is a change in method of accounting to which section 446(e) and the regulations thereunder apply.

(h) *Simplified service cost method.*—(1) *Introduction.*—This paragraph (h) provides a simplified method for determining capitalizable mixed service costs incurred during the taxable year with respect to eligible property (i.e., the aggregate portion of mixed service costs that are properly allocable to the taxpayer's production or resale activities).

(2) *Eligible property.*—(i) *In general.*—Except as otherwise provided in paragraph (h)(2)(ii) of this section, the simplified service cost method, if elected for any trade or business of the taxpayer, must be used for all production and resale activities of the trade or business associated with any of the following categories of property that are subject to section 263A:

(A) *Inventory property.*—Stock in trade or other property properly includible in the inventory of the taxpayer.

(B) *Non-inventory property held for sale.*—Non-inventory property held by a taxpayer primarily for sale to customers in the ordinary course of the taxpayer's trade or business.

(C) *Certain self-constructed assets.*—Self-constructed assets substantially identical in nature to, and produced in the same manner as, inventory property produced by the taxpayer or other property produced by the taxpayer and held primarily for sale to customers in the ordinary course of the taxpayer's trade or business.

(D) *Self-constructed tangible personal property produced on a routine and repetitive basis.*—(1) *In general.*—Self-constructed tangible personal property produced by the taxpayer on a routine and repetitive basis in the ordinary course of the taxpayer's trade or business. Self-constructed tangible personal property is produced by the taxpayer on a routine and repetitive basis in the ordinary course of the taxpayer's trade or business when units of tangible personal property (as defined in §1.263A-10(c)) are mass-produced, that is, numerous substantially identical assets are manufactured within a taxable year using standardized designs and assembly line techniques, and either the applicable recovery period of the property determined under section 168(c) is not longer than 3 years or the property is a material or supply that will be used and consumed within 3 years of being produced. For purposes of this paragraph (h)(2)(i)(D), the applicable recovery period of the assets will be determined at the end of the taxable year in which the assets are placed in service for purposes of §1.46-3(d). Subsequent changes to the applicable recovery period after the assets are placed in service will not affect the determination of whether the assets are produced on a routine and repetitive basis for purposes of this paragraph (h)(2)(i)(D).

(2) *Examples.*—The following examples illustrate this paragraph (h)(2)(i)(D):

Example 1. Y is a manufacturer of automobiles. During the taxable year Y produces numerous substantially identical dies and molds using standardized designs and assembly line techniques. The dies and molds have a 3-year applicable recovery period for purposes of section 168(c). Y uses the dies and molds to produce or process particular automobile components and does not hold them for sale. The dies and molds are produced on a routine and repetitive basis in the ordinary course of Y's business for purposes of this paragraph because the dies and molds are both mass-produced and have a recovery period of not longer than 3 years.

Example 2. Z is an electric utility that regularly manufactures and installs identical poles that are used in transmitting and distributing electricity. The poles have a 20-year applicable recovery period for purposes of section 168(c). The poles are not produced on a routine and repetitive basis in the ordinary course of Z's business for purposes of this paragraph because the poles have an applicable recovery period that is longer than 3 years.

(ii) *Election to exclude self-constructed assets.*—At the taxpayer's election, the simplified service cost method may be applied within a trade or business to only the categories of inventory property and non-inventory property held for sale described in paragraphs (h)(2)(i)(A) and (B) of this section. Taxpayers electing to exclude the self-constructed assets described in paragraphs (h)(2)(i)(C) and (D) of this section from application of the simplified service cost method must, however, allocate service costs to such property in accordance with paragraph (g)(4) of this section.

(3) *General allocation formula.*—(i) Under the simplified service cost method, a taxpayer computes its capitalizable mixed service costs using the following formula:

$$\text{Allocation ratio} \quad \times \quad \text{Total mixed service costs.}$$

(ii) A producer may elect one of two allocation ratios, the labor-based allocation ratio or the production cost allocation ratio. A reseller that satisfies the requirements for using the simplified resale method of § 1.263A-3(d) (whether or not that method is elected) may elect the simplified service cost method, but must use a labor-based allocation ratio. (See § 1.263A-3(d) for labor-based allocation ratios to be used in conjunction with the simplified resale method.) The allocation ratio used by a trade or business of a taxpayer is a method of accounting which must be applied consistently within the trade or business.

(4) *Labor-based allocation ratio.*—(i) The labor-based allocation ratio is computed as follows:

$$\frac{\text{Section 263A labor costs}}{\text{Total labor costs.}}$$

(ii) Section 263A labor costs are defined as the total labor costs (excluding labor costs included in mixed service costs) allocable to property produced and property acquired for resale under section 263A that are incurred in the taxpayer's trade or business during the taxable year. Total labor costs are defined as the total labor costs (excluding labor costs included in mixed service costs) incurred in the taxpayer's trade or business during the taxable year. Total labor costs include labor costs incurred in all parts of the trade or business (i.e., if the taxpayer has both property produced and property acquired for resale, the taxpayer must include labor costs from resale activities as well as production activities). For example, taxpayer G incurs $1,000 of total mixed service costs during the taxable year. G's section 263A labor costs are $5,000 and its total labor costs are $10,000. Under the labor-based allocation ratio, G's capitalizable mixed service costs are $500 (i.e., $1,000 x ($5,000 divided by $10,000)).

(5) *Production cost allocation ratio.*—(i) Producers may use the production cost allocation ratio, computed as follows:

$$\frac{\text{Section 263A production costs}}{\text{Total costs.}}$$

(ii) Section 263A production costs are defined as the total costs (excluding mixed service costs and interest) allocable to property produced (and property acquired for resale if the producer is also engaged in resale activities) under section 263A that are incurred in the taxpayer's trade or business during the taxable year. Total costs are defined as all costs (excluding mixed service costs and interest) incurred in the taxpayer's trade or business during the taxable year. Total costs include all direct and indirect costs allocable to property produced (and property acquired for resale if the producer is also engaged in resale activities) as well as all other costs of the taxpayer's trade or business, including, but not limited to: salaries and other labor costs of all personnel; all depreciation taken for federal income tax purposes; research and experimental expenditures; and selling, marketing, and distribution costs. Such costs do not include, however, taxes described in paragraph (e)(3)(iii)(F) of this section. For example, taxpayer H, a producer, incurs $1,000 of total mixed service costs in the taxable year. H's section 263A production costs are $10,000 and its total costs are $20,000. Under the production cost allocation ratio, H's capitalizable mixed service costs are $500 (i.e., $1,000 x ($10,000 divided by $20,000)).

(6) *Definition of total mixed service costs.*—Total mixed service costs are defined as the total costs incurred during the taxable year in all departments or functions of the taxpayer's trade or business that perform mixed service activities. See paragraph (e)(4)(ii)(C) of this section which defines mixed service costs. In determining the total mixed service costs of a trade or business, the taxpayer must include all costs incurred in its mixed service departments and cannot exclude any otherwise deductible service costs. For example, if the accounting department within a trade or business is a mixed service department, then in determining the total mixed service costs of the trade or business, the taxpayer cannot exclude the costs of personnel in the accounting department that perform services relating to non-production activities (e.g., accounts receivable or customer billing activities). Instead, the entire cost of the accounting department must be included in the total mixed service costs.

(7) *Costs allocable to more than one business.*—To the extent mixed service costs, labor costs, or other costs are incurred in more than one trade or business, the taxpayer must determine the amounts allocable to the particular trade or business for which the simplified service cost method is being applied by using any reasonable allocation method consistent with the principles of paragraph (f)(4) of this section.

(8) *De minimis rule.*—If the taxpayer elects to apply the de minimis rule of paragraph (g)(4)(ii) of this section to any mixed service department, the department is not considered a mixed service department for purposes of the simplified service cost method. Instead, the costs of such department are allocated exclusively to the particular activity satisfying the 90-percent test.

(9) *Separate election.*—A taxpayer may elect the simplified service cost method in conjunction with any other allocation method used at the trade or business level, including the simplified methods described in §§ 1.263A-2(b) and (c) and 1.263A-3(d). However, the election of the simplified service cost method must be made independently of the election to use those other simplified methods.

(i) [Reserved]

(j) *Exemption for certain small business taxpayers.*—(1) *In general.*—A taxpayer, other than a tax shelter prohibited from using the cash receipts and disbursements method of accounting under section 448(a)(3), that meets the gross receipts test under section 448(c) and § 1.448-2(c) (section 448(c) gross receipts test) for any taxable year (small business taxpayer) is not required to capitalize costs under section 263A to any real or tangible personal property produced, and any real or personal property described in section 1221(a)(1) acquired for resale, during that taxable year. This section 448(c) gross receipts test applies even if the taxpayer is not otherwise subject to section 448(a).

(2) *Application of the section 448(c) gross receipts test.*—(i) *In general.*—In the case of any taxpayer that is not a corporation or a partnership, and except as provided in paragraphs (j)(2)(ii) and (iii) of this section, the section 448(c) gross receipts test is applied in the same manner as if each trade or business of the taxpayer were a corporation or partnership.

(ii) *Gross receipts of individuals, etc.*—Except when the aggregation rules of section 448(c)(2) apply, the gross receipts of a taxpayer other than a corporation or partnership are the amount derived from all trades or businesses of such taxpayer. Amounts not related to a trade or business are excluded from the gross receipts of the taxpayer. For example, an individual taxpayer's gross receipts do not include inherently personal amounts, such as personal injury awards or settlements with respect to an injury of the individual taxpayer, disability benefits, Social Security benefits received by the taxpayer during the taxable year, and wages received as an employee that are reported on Form W-2.

(iii) *Partners and S corporation shareholders.*—Except when the aggregation rules of section 448(c)(2) apply, each partner in a partnership includes a share of the partnership's gross receipts in proportion to such partner's distributive share, as determined under section 704, of items of gross income that were taken into account by the partnership under section 703. Similarly, a shareholder of an S corporation includes such shareholder's *pro rata* share of S corporation gross receipts taken into account by the S corporation under section 1363(b).

(iv) *Examples.*—The operation of this paragraph (j) is illustrated by the following examples:

(A) *Example 1.*—Taxpayer A is an individual who operates two separate and distinct trades or business that are reported on Schedule C, *Profit or Loss from Business*, of A's Federal income tax return. For 2020, one trade or business has annual average gross receipts of $5 million, and the other trade or business has average annual gross receipts of $35 million. Under paragraph (j)(2)(ii) of this section, for 2020, neither of A's trades or businesses meets the gross receipts test of paragraph (j)(2) of this section ($5 million + $35 million = $40 million, which is greater than the inflation-adjusted gross receipts test amount for 2020, which is $26 million).

(B) *Example 2.*—Taxpayer B is an individual who operates three separate and distinct trades or business that are reported on Schedule C of B's Federal income tax return. For 2020, Business X is a retail store with average annual gross receipts of $15 million, Business Y is a dance studio with average annual gross receipts of $6 million, and Business Z is a car repair shop with average annual gross receipts of $12 million. Under paragraph (j)(2)(ii) of this section, B's gross receipts are the combined amount derived from all three of B's trades or businesses. Therefore, for 2020, X, Y and Z do not meet the gross receipts test of paragraph (j)(2)(i) of this section ($15 million + $6 million + $12 million = $33 million, which is greater than the inflation-adjusted gross receipts test amount for 2020, which is $26 million).

(3) *Change in method of accounting.*—(i) *In general.*—A change from applying the small business taxpayer exemption under paragraph (j) of this section to not applying the exemption under this paragraph (j), or *vice versa*, is a change in method of accounting under section 446(e) and §1.446-1(e). A taxpayer changing its method of accounting under paragraph (j) of this section may do so only with the consent of the Commissioner as required under section 446(e) and §1.446-1. In the case of any taxpayer required by this section to change its method of accounting for any taxable year, the change shall be treated as a change initiated by the taxpayer. For rules relating to the clear reflection of income and the pattern of consistent treatment of an item, see section 446 and §1.446-1. The amount of the net section 481(a) adjustment and the adjustment period necessary to implement a change in method of accounting required under this section are determined under §1.446-1(e) and the applicable administrative procedures to obtain the Commissioner's consent to change a method of accounting as published in the Internal Revenue Bulletin (see Revenue Procedure 2015-13 (2015-5 IRB 419) (or successor) (see also §601.601(d)(2) of this chapter).

(ii) *Automatic consent for certain method changes.*—Certain changes in method of accounting made under paragraph (j) of this section may be made under the procedures to obtain the automatic consent of the Commissioner to change a method of accounting. See Revenue Procedure 2015-13 (2015-5 IRB 419) (or successor) (see also §601.601(d)(2) of this chapter)). In certain situations, special terms and conditions may apply.

(k) *Special rules.*—(1) *Costs provided by a related person.*—(i) *In general.*—A taxpayer subject to section 263A must capitalize an arm's-length charge for any section 263A costs (e.g., costs of materials, labor, or services) incurred by a related person that are properly allocable to the property produced or property acquired for resale by the taxpayer. Both the taxpayer and the related person must account for the transaction as if an arm's-length charge had been incurred by the taxpayer with respect to its property produced or property acquired for resale. For purposes of this paragraph (j)(1)(i), a taxpayer is considered related to another person if the taxpayer and such person are described in section 482. Further, for purposes of this paragraph (j)(1)(i), arm's-length charge means the arm's-length charge (or other appropriate charge where permitted and applicable) under the principles of section 482. Any correlative adjustments necessary because of the arm's-length charge requirement of this paragraph (j)(1)(i) shall be determined under the principles of section 482.

(ii) *Exceptions.*—The provisions of paragraph (j)(1)(i) of this section do not apply if, and to the extent that—

(A) It would be inappropriate under the principles of section 482 for the Commissioner to adjust the income of the taxpayer or the related person with respect to the transaction at issue; or

(B) A transaction is accounted for under an alternative Internal Revenue Code section resulting in the capitalization (or deferral of the deduction) of the costs of the items provided by the related party and the related party does not deduct such costs earlier than the costs would have been deducted by the taxpayer if the costs were capitalized under section 263A. See §1.1502-13.

(2) *Optional capitalization of period costs.*—(i) *In general.*—Taxpayers are not required to capitalize indirect costs that do not directly benefit or are not incurred by reason of the production of property or acquisition of property for resale (i.e., period costs). A taxpayer may, however, elect to capitalize certain period costs if: the method is consistently applied; is used in computing beginning inventories, ending inventories, and cost of goods sold; and does not result in a material distortion of the taxpayer's income. A material distortion relates to the source, character, amount, or timing of the cost capitalized or any other item affected by the capitalization of the costs. Thus, for example, a taxpayer may not capitalize a period cost under

section 263A if capitalization would result in a material change in the computation of the foreign tax credit limitation under section 904. An election to capitalize a period cost is the adoption of (or a change in) a method of accounting under section 446 of the Internal Revenue Code.

(ii) *Period costs eligible for capitalization.*—The types of period costs eligible for capitalization under this paragraph (j)(2) include only the types of period costs (e.g., under paragraph (e)(3)(iii) of this section) for which some portion of the costs incurred is properly allocable to property produced or property acquired for resale in the year of the election. Thus, for example, marketing or advertising costs, no portion of which are properly allocable to property produced or property acquired for resale, do not qualify for elective capitalization under this paragraph (j)(2).

(3) *Trade or business application.*—Notwithstanding the references generally to taxpayer throughout this section and §§1.263A-2 and 1.263A-3, the methods of accounting provided under section 263A are to be elected and applied independently for each separate and distinct trade or business of the taxpayer in accordance with the provisions of section 446(d) and the regulations thereunder.

(4) *Transfers with a principal purpose of tax avoidance.*—The District Director may require appropriate adjustments to valuations of inventory and other property subject to section 263A if a transfer of property is made to another person for a principal purpose of avoiding the application of section 263A. Thus, for example, the District Director may require a taxpayer using the simplified production method of §1.263A-2(b) to apply that method to transferred inventories immediately prior to a transfer under section 351 if a principal purpose of the transfer is to avoid the application of section 263A.

(l) *Change in method of accounting.*—(1) *In general.*—A change in a taxpayer's treatment of mixed service costs to comply with paragraph (h)(2)(i)(D) of this section is a change in method of accounting to which the provisions of sections 446 and 481 and the regulations under those sections apply. See §1.263A-7. For a taxpayer's first taxable year ending on or after August 2, 2005, the taxpayer is granted the consent of the Commissioner to change its method of accounting to comply with paragraph (h)(2)(i)(D) of this section, provided the taxpayer follows the administrative procedures, as modified by paragraphs (k)(2) through (4) of this section, issued under §1.446-1(e)(3)(ii) for obtaining the Commissioner's automatic consent to a change in accounting method (for further guidance, for example, see Rev. Proc. 2002-9 (2002-1 CB 327), as modified and clarified by Announcement 2002-17 (2002-1 CB 561), modified and amplified by Rev. Proc. 2002-19 (2002-1 CB 696), and amplified, clarified, and modified by Rev. Proc. 2002-54 (2002-2 CB 432), and §601.601(d)(2)(ii)(b) of this chapter). For purposes of Form 3115, "Application for Change in Accounting Method," the designated number for the automatic accounting method change authorized by this paragraph (k) is "95." If Form 3115 is revised or renumbered, any reference in this section to that form is treated as a reference to the revised or renumbered form. Alternatively, notwithstanding the provisions of any administrative procedures that preclude a taxpayer from requesting the advance consent of the Commissioner to change a method of accounting that is required to be made pursuant to a published automatic change procedure, for its first taxable year ending on or after August 2, 2005, a taxpayer may request the advance consent of the Commissioner to change its method of accounting to comply with paragraph (h)(2)(i)(D) of this section, provided the taxpayer follows the administrative procedures, as modified by paragraphs (k)(2) through (5) of this section, for obtaining the advance consent of the Commissioner (for further guidance, for example, see Rev. Proc. 97-27 (1997-1 CB 680), as modified and amplified by Rev. Proc. 2002-19 (2002-1 CB 696), as amplified and clarified by Rev. Proc. 2002-54 (2002-2 CB 432), and §601.601(d)(2)(ii)(b) of this chapter). For the taxpayer's second and subsequent taxable years ending on or after August 2, 2005, requests to secure the consent of the Commissioner must be made under the administrative procedures, as modified by paragraphs (k)(3) and (4) of this section, for obtaining the Commissioner's advance consent to a change in accounting method.

(2) *Scope limitations.*—Any limitations on obtaining the automatic consent or advance consent of the Commissioner do not apply to a taxpayer seeking to change its method of accounting to comply with paragraph (h)(2)(i)(D) of this section for its first taxable year ending on or after August 2, 2005.

(3) *Audit protection.*—A taxpayer that changes its method of accounting in accordance with this paragraph (k) to comply with paragraph (h)(2)(i)(D) of this section does not receive audit protection if its method of accounting for mixed service costs is an issue under consideration at the time the application is filed with the national office.

(4) *Section 481(a) adjustment.*—A change in method of accounting to conform to paragraph (h)(2)(i)(D) of this section requires a section 481(a) adjustment. The section 481(a) adjustment period is two taxable years for a net positive adjustment for an accounting method change that is made to conform to paragraph (h)(2)(i)(D) of this section.

(5) *Time for requesting change.*—Notwithstanding the provisions of §1.446-1(e)(3)(i) and any contrary administrative procedure, a taxpayer may submit a request for advance consent to change its method of accounting to comply with paragraph (h)(2)(i)(D) of this section for its first taxable year ending on or after August 2, 2005, on or before the date that is 30 days after the end of the taxable year for which the change is requested.

(m) *Effective/applicability date.*—(1) *In general.*—Except as provided in (l)(2), (l)(3), and (l)(4) of this section, the effective dates for this section are provided in paragraph (a)(2) of this section.

(2) *Mixed service costs; self-constructed tangible personal property produced on a routine and repetitive basis.*—Paragraphs (h)(2)(i)(D), (k), and (l)(2) of this section apply for taxable years ending on or after August 2, 2005.

(3) *Costs allocable to property sold; indirect costs; licensing and franchise costs.*—Paragraphs (c)(5), (e)(3)(i), and (e)(3)(ii)(U) of this section apply for taxable years ending on or after January 13, 2014.

(4) *Materials and supplies.*—(i) *In general.*—The last sentence of paragraphs (e)(2)(i)(A) and (e)(3)(ii)(E) of this section, and paragraph (l)(4) of this section apply to amounts paid (to acquire or produce property) in taxable years beginning on or after January 1, 2014.

(ii) *Early application of this section.*—A taxpayer may choose to apply the last sentence of paragraphs (e)(2)(i)(A) and (e)(3)(ii)(E) of this section, and paragraph (l)(4) of this section to amounts paid (to acquire or produce property) in taxable years beginning on or after January 1, 2012.

(iii) *Optional application of TD 9564.*—A taxpayer may choose to apply §1.263A-1T(b)(14), the introductory phrase of §1.263A-1T(c)(4), the last sentence of §1.263A-1T(e)(2)(i)(A), the last sentence of §1.263A-1T(e)(3)(ii)(E), §1.263A-1T(l), and §1.263A-1T(m)(2), as these provisions are contained in TD 9564 (76 FR 81060) December 27, 2011, to amounts paid (to acquire or produce property) in taxable years beginning on or after January 1, 2012, and before January 1, 2014.

(5) *Definitions of section 471 costs and additional section 263A costs.*—Paragraphs (d)(2) and (3) of this section apply for taxable years beginning on or after November 20, 2018. For any taxable year that both begins before November 20, 2018 and ends after November 20, 2018, the IRS will not challenge return positions consistent with all of paragraphs (d)(2) and (3) of this section.

(6) *Exemption for certain small business taxpayers.*—The second and third sentence in paragraph (a)(2)(i), paragraphs (b)(1) and (j) of this section apply to taxable years beginning on or after January 5, 2021. However, for a taxable year beginning after December 31, 2017, and before January 5, 2021, a taxpayer may apply the paragraphs described in the first sentence of this paragraph (m)(6), provided that the taxpayer follows all the applicable rules contained in the regulations under section 263A for such taxable year and all subsequent taxable years. [Reg. §1.263A-1.]

☐ [*T.D. 8482, 8-6-93. Amended by T.D. 8559, 8-2-94; T.D. 8584, 12-28-94; T.D. 8597, 7-12-95; T.D. 8728, 8-4-97; T.D. 8729, 8-21-97; T.D. 8897, 8-18-2000 (corrected 10-13-2000); T.D. 9217, 8-2-2005; T.D. 9318, 3-28-2007; T.D. 9564, 12-23-2011; T.D. 9636, 9-13-2013 (corrected 7-18-2014); T.D. 9652, 1-10-2014, T.D. 9843, 11-19-2018 and T.D. 9942, 12-31-2020.*]

[Reg. §1.263A-2]

§1.263A-2. Rules relating to property produced by the taxpayer.—(a) *In general.*—Section 263A applies to real property and tangible personal property produced by a taxpayer for use in its trade or business or for sale to its customers. In addition, section 263A applies to property produced for a taxpayer under a contract with another party. The principal terms related to the scope of section 263A with respect to producers are provided in this paragraph (a). See §1.263A-1(b)(11) for an exception in the case of certain de minimis property provided to customers incident to the provision of services. For taxable years beginning after December 31, 2017, see §1.263A-1(j) for an exception in the case of a small business taxpayer that meets the gross receipts test of section 448(c) and §1.448-2(c)

(1) *Produce.*—(i) *In general.*—For purposes of section 263A, *produce* includes the following: construct, build, install, manufacture, develop, improve, create, raise, or grow.

(ii) *Ownership.*—(A) *General rule.*—Except as provided in paragraphs (a)(1)(ii)(B) and (C) of this section, a taxpayer is not considered to be producing property unless the taxpayer is considered an owner of the property produced under federal income tax principles. The determination as to whether a taxpayer is an owner is based on all of the facts and circumstances, including the various benefits and burdens of ownership vested with the taxpayer. A taxpayer may be considered an owner of property produced, even though the taxpayer does not have legal title to the property.

(B) *Property produced for the taxpayer under a contract.*—(1) *In general.*—Property produced for the taxpayer under a contract with another party is treated as property produced by the taxpayer to the extent the taxpayer makes payments or otherwise incurs costs with respect to the property. A taxpayer has made payment under this section if the transaction would be considered payment by a taxpayer using the cash receipts and disbursements method of accounting.

(2) *Definition of a contract.*—(i) *General rule.*—Except as provided under paragraph (a)(1)(ii)(B)(2)(ii) of this section, a contract is any agreement providing for the production of property if the agreement is entered into before the production of the property to be delivered under the contract is completed. Whether an agreement exists depends on all the facts and circumstances. Facts and circumstances indicating an agreement include, for example, the making of a prepayment, or an arrangement to make a prepayment, for property prior to the date of the completion of production of the property, or the incurring of significant expenditures for property of specialized design or specialized application that is not intended for self-use.

(ii) *Routine purchase order exception.*—A routine purchase order for fungible property is not treated as a contract for purposes of this section. An agreement will not be treated as a routine purchase order for fungible property, however, if the contractor is required to make more than *de minimis* modifications to the property to tailor it to the customer's specific needs, or if at the time the agreement is entered into, the customer knows or has reason to know that the contractor cannot satisfy the agreement within 30 days out of existing stocks and normal production of finished goods.

(C) *Home construction contracts.*—Section 263A applies to a home construction contract unless that contract will be completed within two years of the contract commencement date, and, for contracts entered into after December 31, 2017, in taxable years ending after December 31, 2017, the taxpayer meets the gross receipts test of section 448(c) and §1.448-2(c) for the taxable year in which such contract is entered into. Except as otherwise provided in this paragraph (a)(1)(ii)(C), section 263A applies to such a contract even if the contractor is not considered the owner of the property produced under the contract under Federal income tax principles.

(2) *Tangible personal property.*—(i) *General rule.*—In general, section 263A applies to the costs of producing tangible personal property, and not to the costs of producing intangible property. For example, section 263A applies to the costs manufacturers incur to produce goods, but does not apply to the costs financial institutions incur to originate loans.

(ii) *Intellectual or creative property.*—For purposes of determining whether a taxpayer producing intellectual or creative property is producing tangible personal property or intangible property, the term tangible personal property includes films, sound recordings, video tapes, books, and other similar property embodying words, ideas, concepts, images, or sounds by the creator thereof. Other similar property for this purpose generally means intellectual or creative property for which, as costs are incurred in producing the property, it is intended (or is reasonably likely) that any tangible medium in which the property is embodied will be mass distributed by the creator or any one or more third parties in a form that is not substantially altered. However, any intellectual or creative property that is embodied in a tangible medium that is mass distributed merely incident to the distribution of a principal product or good of the creator is not other similar property for these purposes.

(A) *Intellectual or creative property that is tangible personal property.*—Section 263A applies to tangible personal property defined in this paragraph (a)(2) without regard to whether such property is treated as tangible or intangible property under other sections of the Internal Revenue Code. Thus, for example, section 263A applies to the costs of producing a motion picture or researching and writing a book even though these assets may be considered intangible for other purposes of the Internal Revenue Code. Tangible personal property includes, for example, the following:

(1) *Books.*—The costs of producing and developing books (including teaching aids and other literary works) required to be capitalized under this section include costs incurred by an author in

researching, preparing, and writing the book. (However, see section 263A(h), which provides an exemption from the capitalization requirements of section 263A in the case of certain free-lance authors.) In addition, the costs of producing and developing books include prepublication expenditures incurred by publishers, including payments made to authors (other than commissions for sales of books that have already taken place), as well as costs incurred by publishers in writing, editing, compiling, illustrating, designing, and developing the books. The costs of producing a book also include the costs of producing the underlying manuscript, copyright, or license. (These costs are distinguished from the separately capitalizable costs of printing and binding the tangible medium embodying the book (e.g., paper and ink).) See § 1.174-2(a)(1), which provides that the term research or experimental expenditures does not include expenditures incurred for research in connection with literary, historical, or similar projects.

(2) *Sound recordings.*—A sound recording is a work that results from the fixation of a series of musical, spoken, or other sounds, regardless of the nature of the material objects, such as discs, tapes, or other phonorecordings, in which such sounds are embodied.

(B) *Intellectual or creative property that is not tangible personal property.*—Items that are not considered tangible personal property within the meaning of section 263A(b) and paragraph (a)(2)(ii) of this section include:

(1) *Evidences of value.*—Tangible personal property does not include property that is representative or evidence of value, such as stock, securities, debt instruments, mortgages, or loans.

(2) *Property provided incident to services.*—Tangible personal property does not include de minimis property provided to a client or customer incident to the provision of services, such as wills prepared by attorneys, or blueprints prepared by architects. See § 1.263A-1(b)(11).

(3) *Costs required to be capitalized by producers.*—(i) *In general.*—Except as specifically provided in section 263A (f) with respect to interest costs, producers must capitalize direct and indirect costs properly allocable to property produced under section 263A, without regard to whether those costs are incurred before, during, or after the production period (as defined in section 263A(f)(4)(B)).

(ii) *Pre-production costs.*—If property is held for future production, taxpayers must capitalize direct and indirect costs allocable to such property (e.g., purchasing, storage, handling, and other costs), even though production has not begun. If property is not held for production, indirect costs incurred prior to the beginning of the production period must be allocated to the property and capitalized if, at the time the costs are incurred, it is reasonably likely that production will occur at some future date. Thus, for example, a manufacturer must capitalize the costs of storing and handling raw materials before the raw materials are committed to production. In addition, a real estate developer must capitalize property taxes incurred with respect to property if, at the time the taxes are incurred, it is reasonably likely that the property will be subsequently developed.

(iii) *Post-production costs.*—Generally, producers must capitalize all indirect costs incurred subsequent to completion of production that are properly allocable to the property produced. Thus, for example, storage and handling costs incurred while holding the property produced for sale after production must be capitalized to the property to the extent properly allocable to the property. However, see § 1.263A-3(c) for exceptions.

(4) *Practical capacity concept.*—Notwithstanding any provision to the contrary, the use, directly or indirectly, of the practical capacity concept is not permitted under section 263A. For purposes of section 263A, the term practical capacity concept means any concept, method, procedure, or formula (such as the practical capacity concept described in § 1.471-11(d)(4)) whereunder fixed costs are not capitalized because of the relationship between the actual production at the taxpayer's production facility and the practical capacity of the facility. For purposes of this section, the practical capacity of a facility includes either the practical capacity or theoretical capacity of the facility, as defined in § 1.471-11(d)(4), or any similar determination of productive or operating capacity. The practical capacity concept may not be used with respect to any activity to which section 263A applies (i.e., production or resale activities). A taxpayer shall not be considered to be using the practical capacity concept solely because the taxpayer properly does not capitalize costs described in § 1.263A-1(e)(3)(iii)(E), relating to certain costs attributable to temporarily idle equipment.

(5) *Taxpayers required to capitalize costs under this section.*—This section generally applies to taxpayers that produce property. If a taxpayer is engaged in both production activities and resale activities, the taxpayer applies the principles of this section as if it read production or resale activities, and by applying appropriate principles from § 1.263A-3. If a taxpayer is engaged in both production and resale activities, the taxpayer may elect the simplified production method or the modified simplified production method provided in this section, but generally may not elect the simplified resale method discussed in § 1.263A-3(d). If elected, the simplified production method or the modified simplified production method must be applied to all eligible property produced and all eligible property acquired for resale by the taxpayer.

(b) *Simplified production method.*—(1) *Introduction.*—This paragraph (b) provides a simplified method for determining the additional section 263A costs properly allocable to ending inventories of property produced and other eligible property on hand at the end of the taxable year.

(2) *Eligible property.*—(i) *In general.*—Except as otherwise provided in paragraph (b)(2)(ii) of this section, the simplified production method, if elected for any trade or business of a producer, must be used for all production and resale activities associated with any of the following categories of property to which section 263A applies:

(A) *Inventory property.*—Stock in trade or other property properly includible in the inventory of the taxpayer.

(B) *Non-inventory property held for sale.*—Non-inventory property held by a taxpayer primarily for sale to customers in the ordinary course of the taxpayer's trade or business.

(C) *Certain self-constructed assets.*—Self-constructed assets substantially identical in nature to, and produced in the same manner as, inventory property produced by the taxpayer or other property produced by the taxpayer and held primarily for sale to customers in the ordinary course of the taxpayer's trade or business.

(D) *Self-constructed tangible personal property produced on a routine and repetitive basis.*—(1) *In general.*—Self-constructed tangible personal property produced by the taxpayer on a routine and repetitive basis in the ordinary course of the taxpayer's trade or business. Self-constructed tangible personal property is produced by the taxpayer on a routine and repetitive basis in the ordinary course of the taxpayer's trade or business when units of tangible personal property (as defined in § 1.263A-10(c)) are mass-produced, that is, numerous substantially identical assets are manufactured within a taxable year using standardized designs and assembly line techniques, and either the applicable recovery period of the property determined under section 168(c) is not longer than 3 years or the property is a material or supply that will be used and consumed within 3 years of being produced. For purposes of this paragraph (b)(2)(i)(D), the applicable recovery period of the assets will be determined at the end of the taxable year in which the assets are placed in service for purposes of § 1.46-3(d). Subsequent changes to the applicable recovery period after the assets are placed in service will not affect the determination of whether the assets are produced on a routine and repetitive basis for purposes of this paragraph (b)(2)(i)(D).

(2) *Examples.*—The following examples illustrate this paragraph (b)(2)(i)(D):

Example 1. Y is a manufacturer of automobiles. During the taxable year Y produces numerous substantially identical dies and molds using standardized designs and assembly line techniques. The dies and molds have a 3-year applicable recovery period for purposes of section 168(c). Y uses the dies and molds to produce or process particular automobile components and does not hold them for sale. The dies and molds are produced on a routine and repetitive basis in the ordinary course of Y's business for purposes of this paragraph because the dies and molds are both mass-produced and have a recovery period of not longer than 3 years.

Example 2. Z is an electric utility that regularly manufactures and installs identical poles that are used in transmitting and distributing electricity. The poles have a 20-year applicable recovery period for purposes of section 168(c). The poles are not produced on a routine and repetitive basis in the ordinary course of Z's business for purposes of this paragraph because the poles have an applicable recovery period that is longer than 3 years.

(ii) *Election to exclude self-constructed assets.*—At the taxpayer's election, the simplified production method may be applied within a trade or business to only the categories of inventory property and non-inventory property held for sale described in paragraphs (b)(2)(i)(A) and (B) of this section. Taxpayers electing to exclude the self-constructed assets, defined in paragraphs (b)(2)(i)(C) and (D) of this section, from application of the simplified production method must, however, allocate additional section 263A costs to such property in accordance with §1.263A-1(f).

(3) *Simplified production method without historic absorption ratio election.*—(i) *General allocation formula.*—(A) *In general.*—Except as

$$ \text{Absorption ratio} \qquad \times $$

(B) *Effect of allocation.*—The absorption ratio generally is multiplied by the section 471 costs remaining in ending inventory or otherwise on hand at the end of each taxable year in which the simplified production method is applied. The resulting product is the additional section 263A costs that are added to the taxpayer's ending section 471 costs to determine the section 263A costs that are capitalized. See, however, paragraph (b)(3)(iii) of this section for special rules applicable to LIFO taxpayers. Except as otherwise provided in

$$ \frac{\text{Add'l section 263A costs incurred during the taxable year}}{\text{Section 471 costs incurred during the taxable year.}} $$

(1) *Additional section 263A costs incurred during the taxable year.*—Additional section 263A costs incurred during the taxable year are defined as the additional section 263A costs described in §1.263A-1(d)(3) that a taxpayer incurs during its current taxable year.

(2) *Section 471 costs incurred during the taxable year.*—Section 471 costs incurred during the taxable year are defined as the section 471 costs described in §1.263A-1(d)(2) that a taxpayer incurs during its current taxable year.

(B) *Section 471 costs remaining on hand at year end.*—Section 471 costs remaining on hand at year end means the section 471 costs, as defined in §1.263A-1(d)(2), that a taxpayer incurs during its current taxable year which remain in its ending inventory or are otherwise on hand at year end. For LIFO inventories of a taxpayer, the section 471 costs remaining on hand at year end means the increment, if any, for the current year stated in terms of section 471 costs. See paragraph (b)(3)(iii) of this section.

(C) *Costs allocated to property sold.*—Additional section 263A costs incurred during the taxable year, as defined in paragraph (b)(3)(ii)(A)(1) of this section, section 471 costs incurred during the taxable year, as defined in paragraph (b)(3)(ii)(A)(2) of this section, and section 471 costs remaining on hand at year end, as defined in paragraph (b)(3)(ii)(B) of this section, do not include costs described in §1.263A-1(e)(3)(ii) or cost reductions described in §1.471-3(e) that a taxpayer properly allocates entirely to property that has been sold.

(iii) *LIFO taxpayers electing the simplified production method.*—(A) *In general.*—Under the simplified production method, a taxpayer using a LIFO method must calculate a particular year's index (e.g., under §1.472-8(e)) without regard to its additional section 263A costs. Similarly, a taxpayer that adjusts current-year costs by applicable indexes to determine whether there has been an inventory increment or decrement in the current year for a particular LIFO pool must disregard the additional section 263A costs in making that determination.

(B) *LIFO increment.*—If the taxpayer determines there has been an inventory increment, the taxpayer must state the amount of the increment in current-year dollars (stated in terms of section 471 costs). The taxpayer then multiplies this amount by the absorption ratio. The resulting product is the additional section 263A costs that

$$ \frac{\text{Add'l §263A costs incurred during 1994}}{\text{Section 471 costs incurred during 1994}} $$

(ii) Under the simplified production method, J determines the additional section 263A costs allocable to its ending inventory by

(iii) *J adds this $300,000 to the $3,000,000 of section 471 costs remaining in its ending inventory to calculate its total ending inventory of $3,300,000. The balance of J's additional section 263A costs incurred during 1994, $700,000, ($1,000,000 less $300,000) is taken into account in 1994 as part of J's cost of goods sold.

Example 2—LIFO inventory method (i) Taxpayer K uses a dollar-value LIFO inventory method. K's beginning inventory for 1994 is $2,500,000 (consisting of $2,000,000 of section 471 costs and $500,000 of additional section 263A costs). During 1994, K incurs $10,000,000 of section 471 costs and $1,000,000 of additional section 263A costs. K's 1994 LIFO increment is $1,000,000 ($3,000,000 of section 471 costs

otherwise provided in paragraph (b)(3)(iv) of this section, the additional section 263A costs allocable to eligible property remaining on hand at the close of the taxable year under the simplified production method are computed as follows:

Section 471 costs
remaining on hand
at year end.

this section or in §1.263A-1 or 1.263A-3, additional section 263A costs that are allocated to inventories on hand at the close of the taxable year under the simplified production method of this paragraph (b) are treated as inventory costs for all purposes of the Internal Revenue Code.

(ii) *Definitions.*—(A) *Absorption ratio.*—Under the simplified production method, the absorption ratio is determined as follows:

must be added to the taxpayer's increment for the year stated in terms of section 471 costs.

(C) *LIFO decrement.*—If the taxpayer determines there has been an inventory decrement, the taxpayer must state the amount of the decrement in dollars applicable to the particular year for which the LIFO layer has been invaded. The additional section 263A costs incurred in prior years that are applicable to the decrement are charged to cost of goods sold. The additional section 263A costs that are applicable to the decrement are determined by multiplying the additional section 263A costs allocated to the layer of the pool in which the decrement occurred by the ratio of the decrement (excluding additional section 263A costs) to the section 471 costs in the layer of that pool.

(iv) *De minimis rule for producers with total indirect costs of $200,000 or less.*—(A) *In general.*—If a producer using the simplified production method incurs $200,000 or less of total indirect costs in a taxable year, the additional section 263A costs allocable to eligible property remaining on hand at the close of the taxable year are deemed to be zero. Solely for purposes of this paragraph (b)(3)(iv), taxpayers are permitted to exclude any category of indirect costs (listed in §1.263A-1(e)(3)(iii)) that is not required to be capitalized (e.g., selling and distribution costs) in determining total indirect costs.

(B) *Related party and aggregation rules.*—In determining whether the producer incurs $200,000 or less of total indirect costs in a taxable year, the related party and aggregation rules of §1.263A-3(b)(3) are applied by substituting total indirect costs for gross receipts wherever gross receipts appears.

(v) *Examples.*—The provisions of this paragraph (b) are illustrated by the following examples.

Example 1—FIFO inventory method (i) Taxpayer J uses the FIFO method of accounting for inventories. J's beginning inventory for 1994 (all of which is sold during 1994) is $2,500,000 (consisting of $2,000,000 of section 471 costs and $500,000 of additional section 263A costs). During 1994, J incurs $10,000,000 of section 471 costs and $1,000,000 of additional section 263A costs. J's additional section 263A costs include capitalizable mixed service costs computed under the simplified service cost method as well as other allocable costs. J's section 471 costs remaining in ending inventory at the end of 1994 are $3,000,000. J computes its absorption ratio for 1994, as follows:

$$ = \frac{\$1,000,000}{\$10,000,000} = 10\% $$

multiplying the absorption ratio by the section 471 costs remaining in its ending inventory:

$$ \text{Add'l §263A costs} = 10\% \times \$3,000,000 = \$300,000. $$

in ending inventory less $2,000,000 of section 471 costs in beginning inventory).

(ii) To determine the additional section 263A costs allocable to its ending inventory, K multiplies the 10% absorption ratio ($1,000,000 additional section 263A costs divided by $10,000,000 of section 471 costs) by the $1,000,000 of LIFO increment. Thus, K's additional section 263A costs allocable to its ending inventory are $100,000 ($1,000,000 multiplied by 10%). This $100,000 is added to the $1,000,000 to determine a total 1994 LIFO increment of $1,100,000. K's ending inventory is $3,600,000 (its beginning inventory of $2,500,000 plus the $1,100,000 increment). The balance of K's additional section

263A costs incurred during 1994, $900,000 ($1,000,000 less $100,000), is taken into account in 1994 as part of K's cost of goods sold.

(iii) In 1995, K sells one-half of the inventory in its 1994 LIFO increment. K must include in its cost of goods sold for 1995 the amount of additional section 263A costs relating to this inventory, $50,000 (one-half of the additional section 263A costs capitalized in 1994 ending inventory, or $100,000).

$$\frac{\text{Additional § 263A costs incurred during 1994}}{\text{Section 471 costs incurred during 1994}}$$

1994:	Total	X	Y	Z
Ending section 471 costs	$3,000	$1,600	$600	$800
Additional section 263A costs (10%)	300	160	60	80
1994 ending inventory	$3,300	$1,760	$660	$880

(ii) During 1995, L incurs $2,000 of section 471 costs as shown below and $400 of additional section 263A costs. Moreover, L sells

$$\frac{\text{Additional § 263A costs incurred during 1995}}{\text{Section 471 costs incurred during 1995}}$$

1995:	Total	X	Y	Z
Beginning section 471 costs	$3,000	$1,600	$600	$800
1995 section 471 costs	2,000	1,500	300	200
Section 471 cost of goods sold	(1,000)	(300)	(300)	(400)
1995 ending section 471 costs	$4,000	$2,800	$600	$600
Consisting of:				
1994 layer	$2,800	$1,600	$600	$600
1995 layer	1,200	1,200	—	—
	$4,000	$2,800	$600	$600
Additional section 263A costs:				
1994 (10%)	$280	$160	$60	$60
1995 (20%)	240	240	—	—
	$520	$400	$60	$60
1995 ending inventory	$4,520	$3,200	$660	$660

(iii) In 1995, L experiences a $200 decrement in pool Z. Thus, L must charge the additional section 263A costs incurred in prior years applicable to the decrement to 1995's cost of goods sold. To do so, L determines a ratio by dividing the decrement by the section 471 costs in the 1994 layer ($200 divided by $800, or 25%). L then multiplies this ratio (25%) by the additional section 263A costs in the 1994 layer ($80) to determine the additional section 263A costs applicable to the decrement ($20). Therefore, $20 is taken into account by L in 1995 as part of its cost of goods sold ($80 multiplied by 25%).

(4) *Simplified production method with historic absorption ratio election.*—(i) *In general.*—This paragraph (b)(4) generally permits producers using the simplified production method to elect a historic absorption ratio in determining additional section 263A costs allocable to eligible property remaining on hand at the close of their taxable years. Except as provided in paragraph (b)(4)(v) of this

(2) Additional section 263A costs incurred during the test period are defined as the additional section 263A costs described in §1.263A-1(d)(3) that the taxpayer incurs during the test period described in paragraph (b)(4)(ii)(B) of this section.

(3) Section 471 costs incurred during the test period mean the section 471 costs described in §1.263A-1(d)(2) that the taxpayer incurs during the test period described in paragraph (b)(4)(ii)(B) of this section.

(4) Additional section 263A costs incurred during the test period, as defined in paragraph (b)(4)(ii)(A)(2) of this section, and section 471 costs incurred during the test period, as defined in paragraph (b)(4)(ii)(A)(3) of this section, do not include costs specifically described in §1.263A-1(e)(3)(ii) or cost reductions described in §1.471-3(e) that a taxpayer properly allocates entirely to property that has been sold.

(B) *Test period.*—(1) *In general.*—The test period is generally the three taxable-year period immediately prior to the taxable year that the historic absorption ratio is elected.

(2) *Updated test period.*—The test period begins again with the beginning of the first taxable year after the close of a qualifying period. This new test period, the updated test period, is the three

Example 3—LIFO pools (i) Taxpayer L begins its business in 1994 and adopts the LIFO inventory method. During 1994, L incurs $10,000 of section 471 costs and $1,000 of additional section 263A costs. At the end of 1994, L's ending inventory includes $3,000 of section 471 costs contained in three LIFO pools (X, Y, and Z) as shown below. Under the simplified production method, L computes its absorption ratio and inventory for 1994 as follows:

$$\frac{\$1,000}{\$10,000} = 10\%$$

goods from pools X, Y, and Z having a total cost of $1,000. L computes its absorption ratio and inventory for 1995:

$$\frac{\$400}{\$2,000} = 20\%$$

section, a taxpayer may only make a historic absorption ratio election if it has used the simplified production method for three or more consecutive taxable years immediately prior to the year of election and has capitalized additional section 263A costs using an actual absorption ratio (as defined under paragraph (b)(3)(ii) of this section) for its three most recent consecutive taxable years. This method is not available to a taxpayer that is deemed to have zero additional section 263A costs under paragraph (b)(3)(iv) of this section. The historic absorption ratio is used in lieu of an actual absorption ratio computed under paragraph (b)(3)(ii) of this section and is based on costs capitalized by a taxpayer during its test period. If elected, the historic absorption ratio must be used for each taxable year within the qualifying period described in paragraph (b)(4)(ii)(C) of this section.

(ii) *Operating rules and definitions.*—(A) *Historic absorption ratio.*—(1) The historic absorption ratio is equal to the following ratio:

$$\frac{\text{Add'l section 263A costs incurred during the test period}}{\text{Section 471 costs incurred during the test period.}}$$

taxable-year period beginning with the first taxable year after the close of the qualifying period as defined in paragraph (b)(4)(ii)(C) of this section.

(C) *Qualifying period.*—(1) *In general.*—A qualifying period includes each of the first five taxable years beginning with the first taxable year after a test period (or an updated test period).

(2) *Extension of qualifying period.*—In the first taxable year following the close of each qualifying period, (e.g., the sixth taxable year following the test period), the taxpayer must compute the actual absorption ratio under the simplified production method. If the actual absorption ratio computed for this taxable year (the recomputation year) is within one-half of one percentage point (plus or minus) of the historic absorption ratio used in determining capitalizable costs for the qualifying period (i.e., the previous five taxable years), the qualifying period is extended to include the recomputation year and the following five taxable years, and the taxpayer must continue to use the historic absorption ratio throughout the extended qualifying period. If, however, the actual absorption ratio computed for the recomputation year is not within one-half of one percentage point (plus or minus) of the historic absorption ratio, the taxpayer must use actual absorption ratios beginning with the recomputation year under the simplified production method and throughout the

updated test period. The taxpayer must resume using the historic absorption ratio (determined with reference to the updated test period) in the third taxable year following the recomputation year.

(iii) *Method of accounting.*—(A) *Adoption and use.*—The election to use the historic absorption ratio is a method of accounting. A taxpayer using the simplified production method may elect the historic absorption ratio in any taxable year if permitted under this paragraph (b)(4), provided the taxpayer has not obtained the Commissioner's consent to revoke the historic absorption ratio election within its prior six taxable years. The election is to be effected on a cut-off basis, and thus, no adjustment under section 481(a) is required or permitted. The use of a historic absorption ratio has no effect on other methods of accounting adopted by the taxpayer and used in conjunction with the simplified production method in determining its section 263A costs. Accordingly, in computing its actual absorption ratios, the taxpayer must use the same methods of accounting used in computing its historic absorption ratio during its most recent test period unless the taxpayer obtains the consent of the Commissioner. Finally, for purposes of this paragraph (b)(4)(iii), the recomputation of the historic absorption ratio during an updated test period and the change from a historic absorption ratio to an actual absorption ratio by reason of the requirements of this paragraph (b)(4) are not considered changes in methods of accounting under section 446(e) and, thus, do not require the consent of the Commissioner or any adjustments under section 481(a).

(B) *Revocation of election.*—A taxpayer may only revoke its election to use the historic absorption ratio with the consent of the Commissioner in a manner prescribed under section 446(e) and the regulations thereunder. Consent to the change for any taxable year that is included in the qualifying period (or an extended qualifying period) will be granted only upon a showing of unusual circumstances.

(iv) *Reporting and recordkeeping requirements.*—(A) *Reporting.*— A taxpayer making an election under this paragraph (b)(4) must attach a statement to its federal income tax return for the taxable year in which the election is made showing the actual absorption ratios determined under the simplified production method during its first test period. This statement must disclose the historic absorption ratio to be used by the taxpayer during its qualifying period. A similar statement must be attached to the federal income tax return for the first taxable year within any subsequent qualifying period (i.e., after an updated test period).

(B) *Recordkeeping.*—A taxpayer must maintain all appropriate records and details supporting the historic absorption ratio until the expiration of the statute of limitations for the last year for which the taxpayer applied the particular historic absorption ratio in determining additional section 263A costs capitalized to eligible property.

(v) *Transition rules.*—(A) *Transition to elect historic absorption ratio.*—Taxpayers will be permitted to elect a historic absorption ratio in their first, second, or third taxable year beginning after December 31, 1993, under such terms and conditions as may be prescribed by the Commissioner. Taxpayers are eligible to make an election under these transition rules whether or not they previously used the simplified production method. A taxpayer making such an election must recompute (or compute) its additional section 263A costs, and thus, its historic absorption ratio for its first test period as if the rules prescribed in this section and §§ 1.263A-1 and 1.263A-3 had applied throughout the test period.

(B) *Transition to revoke historic absorption ratio.*—Notwithstanding the requirements provided in paragraph (b)(4)(iii)(B) of this section regarding revocations of the historic absorption ratio during a qualifying period, a taxpayer will be permitted to revoke the historic absorption ratio in their first, second, or third taxable year ending on or after November 20, 2018, under such administrative procedures and with terms and conditions prescribed by the Commissioner.

(vi) *Example.*—The provisions of this paragraph (b)(4) are illustrated by the following example:

Example. (i) Taxpayer M uses the FIFO method of accounting for inventories and for 1994 elects to use the historic absorption ratio with the simplified production method. After recomputing its additional section 263A costs in accordance with the transition rules of paragraph (b)(4)(v) of this section, M identifies the following costs incurred during the test period:

1991:
> Add'l section 263A costs — $100
> Section 471 costs — $3,000

1992:
> Add'l section 263A costs — 200
> Section 471 costs — 4,000

1993:
> Add'l section 263A costs — 300
> Section 471 costs — 5,000

(ii) Therefore, M computes a 5% historic absorption ratio determined as follows:

$$\text{Historic absorption ratio} = \frac{\$100 + 200 + 300}{\$3,000 + 4,000 + 5,000} = \frac{\$600}{\$12,000} = 5\%$$

(iii) In 1994, M incurs $10,000 of section 471 costs of which $3,000 remain in inventory at the end of the year. Under the simplified production method using a historic absorption ratio, M determines the additional section 263A costs allocable to its ending inventory by multiplying its historic absorption ratio (5%) by the section 471 costs remaining in its ending inventory as follows:

Add'l section 263A costs = 5% × $3,000 = $150

(iv) To determine its ending inventory under section 263A, M adds the additional section 263A costs allocable to ending inventory to its section 471 costs remaining in ending inventory ($3,150 = $150 + $3,000). The balance of M's additional section 263A costs incurred during 1994 is taken into account in 1994 as part of M's cost of goods sold.

(v) M's qualifying period ends with the close of its 1998 taxable year. Therefore, 1999 is a recomputation year in which M must compute its actual absorption ratio. M determines its actual absorption ratio for 1999 to be 5.25% and compares that ratio to its historic absorption ratio (5.0%). Therefore, M must continue to use its historic absorption ratio of 5.0% throughout an extended qualifying period, 1999 through 2004 (the recomputation year and the following five taxable years).

(vi) If, instead, M's actual absorption ratio for 1999 were not between 4.5% and 5.5%, M's qualifying period would end and M would be required to compute a new historic absorption ratio with reference to an updated test period of 1999, 2000, and 2001. Once M's historic absorption ratio is determined for the updated test period, it would be used for a new qualifying period beginning in 2002.

(c) *Modified simplified production method.*—(1) *Introduction.*—This paragraph (c) provides a simplified method for determining the additional section 263A costs properly allocable to ending inventories of property produced and other eligible property on hand at the end of the taxable year.

(2) *Eligible property.*—(i) *In general.*—Except as otherwise provided in paragraph (c)(2)(ii) of this section, the modified simplified production method, if elected for any trade or business of a producer, must be used for all production and resale activities associated with any of the categories of property to which section 263A applies as described in paragraph (b)(2)(i) of this section.

(ii) *Election to exclude-self-constructed assets.*—A taxpayer using the modified simplified production method may elect to exclude self-constructed assets from application of the modified simplified production method by following the same rules applicable to a taxpayer using the simplified production method provided in paragraph (b)(2)(ii) of this section.

(3) *Modified simplified production method without historic absorption ratio election.*—(i) *General allocation formula.*—(A) *In general.*—Except as otherwise provided in paragraph (c)(3)(v) of this section, the additional section 263A costs allocable to eligible property remaining on hand at the close of the taxable year under the modified simplified production method are computed as follows:

$$\left(\begin{array}{c}\text{Pre-production absorption}\\ \text{ratio}\end{array} \times \begin{array}{c}\text{Pre-production section 471 costs}\\ \text{remaining on hand at year end}\end{array} \right) + \left(\text{Production absorption ratio} \times \begin{array}{c}\text{Production section 471 costs}\\ \text{remaining on hand at year}\\ \text{end}\end{array} \right)$$

(B) *Effect of allocation.*—The pre-production and production absorption ratios generally are multiplied by the pre-production and production section 471 costs, respectively, remaining in ending inventory or otherwise on hand at the end of each taxable year in which the modified simplified production method is applied. The sum of the resulting products is the additional section 263A costs that are added to the taxpayer's ending section 471 costs to determine the section 263A costs that are capitalized. See, however, paragraph (c)(3)(iv) of this section for special rules applicable to LIFO taxpayers. Except as otherwise provided in this section or in §1.263A-1 or §1.263A-3, additional section 263A costs that are allocated to inventories on hand at the close of the taxable year under the modified simplified production method of this paragraph (c) are treated as inventory costs for all purposes of the Internal Revenue Code.

(ii) *Definitions.*—(A) *Direct material costs.*—For purposes of paragraph (c) of this section, direct material costs has the same meaning as described in §1.263A-1(e)(2)(i)(A). For purposes of paragraph (c) of this section, direct material costs include property produced for the taxpayer under a contract with another party that are direct material costs for the taxpayer to be used in an additional production process of the taxpayer.

(B) *Pre-production absorption ratio.*—Under the modified simplified production method, the pre-production absorption ratio is determined as follows:

$$\frac{\text{Pre-production additional section 263A costs}}{\text{Pre-production section 471 costs}}$$

(1) *Pre-production additional section 263A costs.*—Pre-production additional section 263A costs are defined as the additional section 263A costs described in §1.263A-1(d)(3) that are pre-production costs, as described in paragraph (a)(3)(ii) of this section, that a taxpayer incurs during its current taxable year, including capitalizable mixed service costs allocable to pre-production additional section 263A costs, as described in paragraph (c)(3)(iii) of this section, that a taxpayer incurs during its current taxable year:

(i) Plus additional section 263A costs properly allocable to property acquired for resale that a taxpayer incurs during its current taxable year; and

(ii) Plus additional section 263A costs properly allocable to property produced for the taxpayer under a contract with another party that is treated as property produced by the taxpayer, as described in paragraph (a)(1)(ii)(B) of this section, that a taxpayer incurs during its current taxable year.

(2) *Pre-production section 471 costs.*—Pre-production section 471 costs are defined as the section 471 costs described in §1.263A-1(d)(2) that are direct material costs that a taxpayer incurs during its current taxable year plus the section 471 costs for property acquired for resale (*see* §1.263A-1(e)(2)(ii)) that a taxpayer incurs during its current taxable year, including property produced for the taxpayer under a contract with another party that is acquired for resale.

(C) *Pre-production section 471 costs remaining on hand at year end.*—Preproduction section 471 costs remaining on hand at year end means the pre-production section 471 costs, as defined in paragraph (c)(3)(ii)(B)(2) of this section, that a taxpayer incurs during its current taxable year which remain in its ending inventory or are otherwise on hand at year end, excluding the section 471 costs that are direct material costs that have entered or completed production at year end (for example, direct material costs in ending work-in-process inventory and ending finished goods inventory). For LIFO inventories of a taxpayer, see paragraph (c)(3)(iv) of this section.

(D) *Production absorption ratio.*—Under the modified simplified production method, the production absorption ratio is determined as follows:

$$\frac{(\text{Production additional section 263A costs} + \text{Residual pre-production additional section 263A costs})}{(\text{Production section 471 costs} + \text{Direct materials adjustment})}$$

(1) *Production additional section 263A costs.*—Production additional section 263A costs are defined as the additional section 263A costs described in §1.263A-1(d)(3) that are not pre-production additional section 263A costs, as defined in paragraph (c)(3)(ii)(B)(1) of this section, that a taxpayer incurs during its current taxable year, including capitalizable mixed service costs not allocable to pre-production additional section 263A costs, as described in paragraph (c)(3)(iii) of this section, that a taxpayer incurs during its current taxable year. For example, production additional section 263A costs include post-production costs, other than post-production costs included in section 471 costs, as described in paragraph (a)(3)(iii) of this section.

(2) *Residual pre-production additional section 263A costs.*—Residual preproduction additional section 263A costs are defined as the pre-production additional section 263A costs, as defined in paragraph (c)(3)(ii)(B)(1) of this section, that a taxpayer incurs during its current taxable year less the product of the pre-production absorption ratio, as determined in paragraph (c)(3)(ii)(B) of this section, and the preproduction section 471 costs remaining on hand at year end, as defined in paragraph (c)(3)(ii)(C) of this section.

(3) *Production section 471 costs.*—Production section 471 costs are defined as the section 471 costs described in §1.263A-1(d)(2) that a taxpayer incurs during its current taxable year less pre-production section 471 costs, as defined in paragraph (c)(3)(ii)(B)(2) of this section, that a taxpayer incurs during its current taxable year.

(4) *Direct materials adjustment.*—The direct materials adjustment is defined as the section 471 costs that are direct material costs, including property produced for a taxpayer under a contract with another party that are direct material costs for the taxpayer to be used in an additional production process of the taxpayer, that had not entered production at the beginning of the current taxable year:

(i) Plus the section 471 costs that are direct material costs incurred during the current taxable year (that is, direct material purchases); and

(ii) Less the section 471 costs that are direct material costs that have not entered production at the end of the current taxable year.

(E) *Production section 471 costs remaining on hand at year end.*—Production section 471 costs remaining on hand at year end means the section 471 costs, as defined in §1.263A-1(d)(2), that a taxpayer incurs during its current taxable year which remain in its ending inventory or are otherwise on hand at year end, less the preproduction section 471 costs remaining on hand at year end, as described in paragraph (c)(3)(ii)(C) of this section. For LIFO inventories of a taxpayer, see paragraph (c)(3)(iv) of this section.

(F) *Costs allocated to property sold.*—The terms defined in paragraph (c)(3)(ii) of this section do not include costs described in §1.263A-1(e)(2)(ii) or cost reductions described in §1.471-3(e) that a taxpayer properly allocates entirely to property that has been sold.

(iii) *Allocable mixed service costs.*—(A) *In general.*—If a taxpayer using the modified simplified production method determines its capitalizable mixed service costs using a method described in §1.263A-1(g)(4), the taxpayer must use a reasonable method to allocate the costs (for example, department or activity costs) between production and pre-production additional section 263A costs. If the taxpayer's §1.263A-1(g)(4) method allocates costs to a department or activity that is exclusively identified as production or pre-production, those costs must be allocated to production or preproduction additional section 263A costs, respectively.

(B) *Taxpayer using the simplified service cost method.*—If a taxpayer using the modified simplified production method determines its capitalizable mixed service costs using the simplified service cost method described in §1.263A-1(h), the amount of capitalizable mixed service costs, as computed using the general allocation formula in §1.263A-1(h)(3)(i), allocated to and included in pre-production additional section 263A costs in the absorption ratio described in paragraph (c)(3)(ii)(B) of this section is determined based on either of the following: the proportion of direct material costs to total section 471 costs that a taxpayer incurs during its current taxable year or the proportion of pre-production labor costs to total labor costs that a taxpayer incurs during its current taxable year. The taxpayer must include the capitalizable mixed service costs that are not allocated to pre-production additional section 263A costs in production additional section 263A costs in the absorption ratio described in paragraph (c)(3)(ii)(D) of this section. A taxpayer that allocates capitalizable mixed service costs based on labor under this paragraph (c)(3)(iii)(B) must exclude mixed service labor costs from both pre-production labor costs and total labor costs.

(C) *De minimis rule.*—Notwithstanding paragraphs (c)(3)(iii)(A) and (B) of this section, if 90 percent or more of a taxpayer's capitalizable mixed service costs determined under paragraph (c)(3)(iii)(A) or (B) of this section are allocated to preproduction additional section 263A costs or production additional section 263A costs, the taxpayer may elect to allocate 100 percent of its capitalizable mixed service costs to that amount. For example, if 90 percent of capitalizable mixed service costs are allocated to production additional section 263A costs based on the labor costs that are pre-production costs in total labor costs incurred in the taxpayer's trade or business during the taxable year, then 100 percent of capitalizable mixed service costs may be allocated to production additional section 263A costs. An election to allocate capitalizable mixed service costs under this paragraph (c)(3)(iii)(C) is the adoption of, or a change in, a method of accounting under section 446 of the Internal Revenue Code.

(iv) *LIFO taxpayers electing the modified simplified production method.*—(A) *In general.*—Under the modified simplified production method, a taxpayer using a LIFO method must calculate a particular year's index (for example, under §1.472-8(e)) without regard to its additional section 263A costs. Similarly, a taxpayer that adjusts current-year costs by applicable indexes to determine whether there has been an inventory increment or decrement in the current year for a particular LIFO pool must disregard the additional section 263A costs in making that determination.

(B) *LIFO increment.*—(1) *In general.*—If the taxpayer determines there has been an inventory increment, the taxpayer must state the amount of the increment in terms of section 471 costs in current-year dollars. The taxpayer then multiplies this amount by the combined absorption ratio, as defined in paragraph (c)(3)(iv)(B)(2) of this section. The resulting product is the additional section 263A costs that must be added to the taxpayer's increment in terms of section 471 costs in current-year dollars for the taxable year.

(2) *Combined absorption ratio defined.*—For purposes of paragraph (c)(3)(iv)(B)(1) of this section, the combined absorption ratio is the additional section 263A costs allocable to eligible property remaining on hand at the close of the taxable year, as described in paragraph (c)(3)(i)(A) of this section, determined on a non-LIFO basis, divided by the pre-production and production section 471 costs remaining on hand at year end, determined on a non-LIFO basis.

(C) *LIFO decrement.*—If the taxpayer determines there has been an inventory decrement, the taxpayer must state the amount of the decrement in dollars applicable to the particular year for which the LIFO layer has been invaded. The additional section 263A costs incurred in prior years that are applicable to the decrement are charged to cost of goods sold. The additional section 263A costs that are applicable to the decrement are determined by multiplying the additional section 263A costs allocated to the layer of the pool in which the decrement occurred by the ratio of the decrement, excluding additional section 263A costs, to the section 471 costs in the layer of that pool.

(v) *De minimis rule for producers with total indirect costs of $200,000 or less.*—Paragraph (b)(3)(iv) of this section, which provides that the additional section 263A costs allocable to eligible property remaining on hand at the close of the taxable year are deemed to be zero for producers with total indirect costs of $200,000 or less, applies to the modified simplified production method.

(vi) *Examples.*—The provisions of this paragraph (c) are illustrated by the following examples:

(A) *Example 1—FIFO inventory method.* (1) Taxpayer P uses the FIFO method of accounting for inventories valued at cost. P's beginning inventory for 2018 (all of which is sold during 2018) is $2,500,000, consisting of $500,000 of pre-production section 471 costs (including $400,000 of direct material costs and $100,000 of property acquired for resale), $1,500,000 of production section 471 costs, and $500,000 of additional section 263A costs. During 2018, P incurs $2,500,000 of pre-production section 471 costs (including $1,900,000 of direct material costs and $600,000 of property acquired for resale), $7,500,000 of production section 471 costs, $200,000 of pre-production additional section 263A costs, and $800,000 of production additional section 263A costs. P's additional section 263A costs include capitalizable mixed service costs under the simplified service cost method. P's pre-production and production section 471 costs remaining in ending inventory at the end of 2018 are $1,000,000 (including $800,000 of direct material costs and $200,000 of property acquired for resale) and $2,000,000, respectively. P computes its pre-production absorption ratio for 2018 under paragraph (c)(3)(ii)(B) of this section, as follows:

$$\frac{\text{Pre-production additional section 263A costs}}{\text{Pre-production section 471 costs}} = \frac{\$200,000}{\$2,500,000} = 8.00\%$$

(2) Under paragraph (c)(3)(ii)(D)(2) of this section, P's residual pre-production additional section 263A costs for 2018 are $120,000 ($200,000 of pre-production additional section 263A costs less $80,000 (the product of the 8% pre-production absorption ratio and the $1,000,000 of pre-production section 471 costs remaining on hand at year end)).

(3) Under paragraph (c)(3)(ii)(D)(4) of this section, P's direct materials adjustment for 2018 is $1,500,000 ($400,000 of direct material costs in beginning raw materials inventory, plus $1,900,000 of direct material costs incurred to acquire raw materials during the taxable year, less $800,000 direct material costs in ending raw materials inventory).

(4) P computes its production absorption ratio for 2018 under paragraph (c)(3)(ii)(D) of this section, as follows:

$$\frac{\text{(Production additional section 263A costs + Residual pre-production additional section 263A costs)}}{\text{(Production section 471 costs + Direct materials adjustment)}} = \frac{(\$800,000 + 120,000)}{(\$7,500,000 + 1,500,000)} = 10.22\%$$

(5) Under the modified simplified production method, P determines the additional section 263A costs allocable to its ending inventory under paragraph (c)(3)(i)(A) of this section by multiplying the pre-production absorption ratio by the pre-production section 471 costs remaining on hand at year end and the production absorption ratio by the production section 471 costs remaining on hand at year end, as follows:

Additional section 263A costs = (8% x $1,000,000)+(10.22% x $2,000,000) = $284,400

(6) P adds this $284,400 to the $3,000,000 of section 471 costs remaining on hand at year end to calculate its total ending inventory of $3,284,400. The balance of P's additional section 263A costs incurred during 2018, $715,600 ($1,000,000 less $284,400), is taken into account in 2018 as part of P's cost of goods sold.

(7) P's computation is summarized in the following table:

Beginning Inventory	Reference	Amount
Direct material costs	a	$ 400,000
Property acquired for resale	b	$ 100,000
Pre-production section 471 costs	c=a+b	$ 500,000
Production section 471 costs	d	$ 1,500,000
Additional section 263A costs	e	$ 500,000
Total	f=c+d+e	$ 2,500,000
Incurred During 2018		
Direct material costs	g	$ 1,900,000
Property acquired for resale	h	$ 600,000
Pre-production section 471 costs	i=g+h	$ 2,500,000
Production section 471 costs	j	$ 7,500,000
Pre-production additional section 263A costs	k	$ 200,000
Production additional section 263A costs	l	$ 800,000

Beginning Inventory	Reference	Amount
Total	m=i+j+k+l	$ 11,000,000
Ending inventory		
Direct material costs	n	$ 800,000
Property acquired for resale	o	$ 200,000
Pre-production section 471 costs	p=n+o	$ 1,000,000
Production section 471 costs	q	$ 2,000,000
Section 471 costs	r=p+q	$ 3,000,000
Additional section 263A costs allocable to ending inventory	s=v+z	$ 284,400
Total	t=r+s	$ 3,284,400
Modified Simplified Production Method		
Pre-production additional section 263A costs	k	$ 200,000
Pre-production section 471 costs	i	$ 2,500,000
Pre-production absorption ratio	u=k/i	8.00%
Pre-production section 471 costs remaining on hand at year end	p	$ 1,000,000
Pre-production additional section 263A costs allocable to ending inventory	v=u*p	$ 80,000
Production additional section 263A costs	l	$ 800,000
Residual pre-production additional section 263A costs	w=k-(u*p)	$ 120,000
Production section 471 costs	j	$ 7,500,000
Direct materials adjustment	x=a+g-n	$ 1,500,000
Production absorption ratio	y=(l+w)/(j+x)	10.22%
Production section 471 costs remaining on hand at year end	q	$ 2,000,000
Production additional section 263A costs allocable to ending inventory	z=y*q	$ 204,400
Summary		
Pre-production additional section 263A costs allocable to ending inventory	v	$ 80,000
Production additional section 263A costs allocable to ending inventory	z	$ 204,400
Additional section 263A costs allocable to ending inventory	s	$ 284,400
Section 471 costs	r	$ 3,000,000
Total Ending Inventory	t	$ 3,284,400

(B) *Example 2—FIFO inventory method with alternative method to determine amounts of section 471 costs.* (1) The facts are the same as in *Example 1* of paragraph (c)(3)(vi)(A) of this section, except that P uses the alternative method to determine amounts of section 471 costs by using its financial statement under §1.263A-1(d)(2)(iii) rather than tax amounts under §1.263A-1(d)(2)(i). In 2018, P's production section 471 costs exclude $40,000 of tax depreciation in excess of financial statement depreciation and include $50,000 of financial statement direct labor in excess of tax direct labor. These are P's only differences in its book and tax amounts.

(2) Under §1.263A-1(d)(2)(iii)(B), the positive $40,000 depreciation adjustment and the negative $50,000 direct labor adjustment must be included in additional section 263A costs. Accordingly, P's production additional section 263A costs are $790,000 ($800,000 plus $40,000 less $50,000).

(3) P computes its production absorption ratio for 2018 under paragraph (c)(3)(ii)(D) of this section, as follows:

$$\frac{(\text{Production additional section 263A costs} + \text{Residual pre-production additional section 263A costs})}{(\text{Production section 471 costs} + \text{Direct materials adjustment})} = \frac{(\$790,000 + 120,000)}{(\$7,500,000 + 1,500,000)} = 10.11\%$$

(4) Under the modified simplified production method, P determines the additional section 263A costs allocable to its ending inventory under paragraph (c)(3)(i)(A) of this section by multiplying the pre-production absorption ratio by the pre-production section 471 costs remaining on hand at year end and the production absorption ratio by the production section 471 costs remaining on hand at year end, as follows:
Additional section 263A costs = (8.00% x $1,000,000) + (10.11% x $2,000,000) = $282,200

(5) P adds this $282,200 to the $3,000,000 of section 471 costs remaining on hand at year end to calculate its total ending inventory of $3,282,200. The balance of P's additional section 263A costs incurred during 2018, $717,800 ($1,000,000 less $282,200), is taken into account in 2018 as part of P's cost of goods sold.

(C) *Example 3—LIFO inventory method.* (1) The facts are the same as in *Example 1* of paragraph (c)(3)(vi)(A) of this section, except that P uses a dollar-value LIFO inventory method rather than the FIFO method. P's 2018 LIFO increment is $1,500,000.

(2) Under paragraph (c)(3)(iv)(B)(1) of this section, to determine the additional section 263A costs allocable to its ending inventory, P multiplies the combined absorption ratio by the $1,500,000 of LIFO increment. Under paragraph (c)(3)(iv)(B)(2) of this section, the combined absorption ratio is 9.48% ($284,400 additional section 263A costs allocable to ending inventory, determined on a non-LIFO basis, divided by $3,000,000 of section 471 costs on hand at year end,

determined on a non-LIFO basis). Thus, P's additional section 263A costs allocable to its ending inventory are $142,200 ($1,500,000 multiplied by 9.48%). This $142,200 is added to the $1,500,000 to determine a total 2018 LIFO increment of $1,642,200. The balance of P's additional section 263A costs incurred during 2018, $857,800 ($1,000,000 less $142,200), is taken into account in 2018 as part of P's cost of goods sold.

(3) In 2019, P sells one-half of the inventory in its 2018 increment. P must include in its cost of goods sold for 2019 the amount of additional section 263A costs relating to this inventory, $71,100 (one-half of the $142,200 additional section 263A costs capitalized in 2018 ending inventory).

(D) *Example 4—Direct materials-based allocation of mixed service costs.* (1) Taxpayer R computes its capitalizable mixed service costs using the simplified service cost method described in §1.263A-1(h). During 2018, R incurs $200,000 of capitalizable mixed service costs, computed using the general allocation formula in §1.263A-1(h). During 2018, R also incurs $8,000,000 of total section 471 costs, including $2,000,000 of direct material costs.

(2) Under paragraph (c)(3)(iii)(B) of this section, R determines its capitalizable mixed service costs allocable to pre-production additional section 263A costs based on the proportion of direct material costs in total section 471 costs. R's direct material costs are 25% of total section 471 costs ($2,000,000 of direct material costs incurred during the year divided by $8,000,000 of total section 471 costs

incurred during the year). Thus, R allocates $50,000 (25% x $200,000) of mixed service costs to preproduction additional section 263A costs. R includes the remaining $150,000 ($200,000 less $50,000) of capitalizable mixed service costs as production additional section 263A costs.

(E) *Example 5—Labor-based allocation of mixed service costs. (1)* Taxpayer S computes its capitalizable mixed service costs using the simplified service cost method described in §1.263A-1(h). During 2018, S incurs $200,000 of capitalizable mixed service costs, computed using the general allocation formula in §1.263A-1(h). During 2018, S also incurs $10,000,000 of total labor costs (excluding any labor costs included in mixed service costs), including $1,000,000 of labor costs that are pre-production costs as described in paragraph (a)(3)(ii) of this section (excluding any labor costs included in mixed service costs).

(2) Under paragraph (c)(3)(iii)(B) of this section, S determines its capitalizable mixed service costs allocable to pre-production additional section 263A costs based on the proportion of labor costs that are pre-production costs in labor costs. S's pre-production labor costs are 10% of labor costs ($1,000,000 of labor costs incurred during the year that are pre-production costs (excluding any labor costs included in mixed service costs), divided by $10,000,000 of total labor costs incurred during the year (excluding any labor costs included in mixed service costs). Thus, S allocates $20,000 (10% x $200,000) of mixed service costs to pre-production additional section 263A costs. S includes the remaining $180,000 ($200,000 less $20,000) of capitalizable mixed service costs as production additional section 263A costs.

(F) *Example 6—De minimis rule for allocation of mixed service costs.* The facts are the same as in *Example 5* in paragraph (c)(3)(vi)(E) of this section, except that S uses the de minimis rule for mixed service costs in paragraph (c)(3)(iii)(C) of this section. Because 90% or more of S's capitalizable mixed service costs are allocated to production additional section 263A costs, under the de minimis rule, S allocates all $200,000 of capitalizable mixed service costs to production additional section 263A costs. None of the capitalizable mixed service costs are allocated to pre-production additional section 263A costs.

(4) *Modified simplified production method with historic absorption ratio election.—*(i) *In general.—*This paragraph (c)(4) generally permits taxpayers using the modified simplified production method to elect a historic absorption ratio in determining additional section 263A costs allocable to eligible property remaining on hand at the close of their taxable years. A taxpayer may only make a historic absorption ratio election under this paragraph (c)(4) if it has used the modified simplified production method for three or more consecutive taxable years immediately prior to the year of election and has capitalized additional section 263A costs using an actual pre-production absorption ratio, as defined in paragraph (c)(3)(ii)(B) of this section, and an actual production absorption ratio, as defined in paragraph (c)(3)(ii)(D) of this section, or an actual combined absorption ratio, as defined in paragraph (c)(3)(iv)(B)(2) of this section, for its three most recent consecutive taxable years. This method is not available to a taxpayer that is deemed to have zero additional section 263A costs under paragraph (c)(3)(v) of this section. The historic absorption ratio is used in lieu of the actual absorption ratios computed under paragraph (c)(3)(ii) of this section or the actual combined absorption ratio computed under paragraph (c)(3)(iv) and is based on costs capitalized by a taxpayer during its test period. If elected, the historic absorption ratio must be used for each taxable year within the qualifying period described in paragraph (b)(4)(ii)(C) of this section. Except as otherwise provided in this paragraph (c)(4), paragraph (b)(4) of this section applies to the historic absorption ratio election under the modified simplified production method.

(ii) *Operating rules and definitions.—*(A) *Pre-production historic absorption ratio.—*The pre-production historic absorption ratio is computed as follows:

Pre-production additional section 263A costs incurred during the test period

Pre-production section 471 costs incurred during the test period

---

(1) Pre-production additional section 263A costs incurred during the test period are defined as the pre-production additional section 263A costs described in paragraph (c)(3)(ii)(B)(1) of this section that the taxpayer incurs during the test period described in paragraph (b)(4)(ii)(B) of this section.

(2) Pre-production section 471 costs incurred during the test period are defined as the pre-production section 471 costs described in paragraph (c)(3)(ii)(B)(2) of this section that the taxpayer incurs during the test period described in paragraph (b)(4)(ii)(B) of this section.

(B) *Production historic absorption ratio.—*The production historic absorption ratio is computed as follows:

$$\left(\frac{\text{Production additional section 263A costs incurred during the test period}}{\text{Production section 471 costs incurred during the test period}} \right) + \left(\frac{\text{Residual pre-production additional section 263A costs incurred during the test period}}{\text{Direct materials adjustments made during the test period}} \right)$$

(1) Production additional section 263A costs incurred during the test period are defined as the production additional section 263A costs described in paragraph (c)(3)(ii)(D)(1) of this section that the taxpayer incurs during the test period described in paragraph (b)(4)(ii)(B) of this section.

(2) Residual pre-production additional section 263A costs incurred during the test period are defined as the residual pre-production additional section 263A costs described in paragraph (c)(3)(ii)(D)(2) of this section that the taxpayer incurs during the test period described in paragraph (b)(4)(ii)(B) of this section.

(3) Production section 471 costs incurred during the test period are defined as the production section 471 costs described in paragraph (c)(3)(ii)(D)(3) of this section that the taxpayer incurs during the test period described in paragraph (b)(4)(ii)(B) of this section.

(4) Direct materials adjustments made during the test period are defined as the direct materials adjustments described in paragraph (c)(3)(ii)(D)(4) of this section that the taxpayer incurs during the test period described in paragraph (b)(4)(ii)(B) of this section.

(iii) *LIFO taxpayers making the historic absorption ratio election.—*(A) *In general.—*Instead of the pre-production and production historic absorption ratios defined in paragraph (c)(4)(ii) of this section, a LIFO taxpayer making the historic absorption ratio election under the modified simplified production method calculates a combined historic absorption ratio based on costs the taxpayer capitalizes during its test period.

(B) *Combined historic absorption ratio.—*The combined historic absorption ratio is computed as follows:

Total allocable additional section 263A costs incurred during the test period

Total section 471 costs remaining on hand at each year end of the test period

---

(1) *Total allocable additional section 263A costs incurred during the test period.—*Total allocable additional section 263A costs incurred during the test period are the sum of the total additional section 263A costs allocable to eligible property on hand at year end as described in paragraph (c)(3)(i)(A) of this section, determined on a non-LIFO basis, for all taxable years in the test period.

(2) *Total section 471 costs remaining on hand at each year end of the test period.—*Total section 471 costs remaining on hand at each year end of the test period are the sum of the total pre-production section 471 costs remaining on hand at year end as described in paragraph (c)(3)(ii)(C) of this section and the total production section 471 costs remaining on hand at year end as described in paragraph (c)(3)(ii)(E) of this section, determined on a non-LIFO basis, for all taxable years in the test period.

(iv) *Extension of qualifying period.—*In the first taxable year following the close of each qualifying period (for example, the sixth taxable year following the test period), a taxpayer must compute the actual absorption ratios under paragraph (c)(3) of this section (pre-production and production absorption ratios or, for LIFO taxpayers, the combined absorption ratio). If the actual combined absorption ratio or both the actual pre-production and production absorption ratios, as applicable, computed for this taxable year (the recomputation year) is within one-half of one percentage point, plus or minus, of the corresponding historic absorption ratio or ratios used in determining capitalizable costs for the qualifying period (the previous five taxable years), the qualifying period is extended to include the recomputation year and the following five taxable years, and the taxpayer must continue to use the historic absorption ratio or ratios throughout the extended qualifying period. If, however, the actual combined historic absorption ratio or either the actual pre-production absorption ratio or production absorption ratio, as applicable, is not within one-half of one percentage point, plus or minus, of the corresponding historic absorption ratio, the taxpayer must use the actual combined absorption ratio or ratios beginning with the recomputation year and throughout the updated test period. The taxpayer must resume using the historic absorption ratio or ratios based on the updated test period in the third taxable year following the recomputation year.

Pre-production additional section 263A costs
Production additional section 263A costs
Pre-production section 471 costs
Production section 471 costs
Residual pre-production additional section 263A costs
Direct materials adjustments

(2) Under paragraph (c)(4)(ii)(A) of this section, S computes the pre-production historic absorption ratio as follows:

$$\frac{\text{Pre-production additional section 263A costs incurred during the test period}}{\text{Pre-production section 471 costs incurred during the test period}} = \frac{\$100 + 200 + 300}{\$2,000 + 2,500 + 3,000} = \frac{\$600}{\$7,500} = 8.00\%$$

(3) Under paragraph (c)(4)(ii)(B) of this section, S computes the production historic absorption ratio as follows:

$$\frac{(\text{Production additional section 263A costs incurred during the test period} + \text{Residual pre-production additional section 263A costs incurred during the test period})}{(\text{Production section 471 costs incurred during the test period} + \text{Direct materials adjustments made during the test period})}$$

$$= \frac{(\$200+350+450) + (60+136+220)}{(\$2,500+3,500+4,000)+(2,700+3,200+3,700)} = \frac{\$1,416}{\$19,600} = 7.22\%$$

(4) In 2021, S incurs $10,000 of section 471 costs of which $1,000 preproduction section 471 costs and $2,000 production 471 costs remain in ending inventory. Under the modified simplified production method using a historic absorption ratio, S determines the pre-production additional section 263A costs allocable to its ending inventory by multiplying its pre-production historic absorption ratio (8.00%) by the pre-production section 471 costs remaining on hand at year end ($1,000). Thus, S allocates $80 of pre-production additional section 263A costs to its ending inventory (8.00% x $1,000). S determines the production additional section 263A costs allocable to its ending inventory by multiplying its production historic absorption ratio (7.22%) by the production section 471 costs remaining on hand at year end ($2,000). Thus, S allocates $144 of production additional section 263A costs to its ending inventory (7.22% x $2,000).

(5) Under paragraph (c)(4)(i) of this section, S's total additional section 263A costs allocable to ending inventory in 2021 are $224,

Additional section 263A costs incurred during the taxable year allocable to ending inventory
Section 471 costs incurred during the taxable year that remain in ending inventory

(ii) In 2021, the LIFO value of S's increment is $1,500.

$$\frac{\text{Total allocable additional section 263A costs incurred during the test period}}{\text{Total section 471 costs remaining on hand at each year end of the test period}} = \frac{\$90 + 137 + 167}{\$1,000 + 1,400 + 2,100} = \frac{\$394}{\$4,500} = 8.76\%$$

(3) S's additional section 263A costs allocable to its 2021 LIFO increment are $131 ($1,500 beginning LIFO increment x 8.76% combined historic absorption ratio). S adds the $131 to the $1,500 LIFO increment to determine a total 2021 LIFO increment of $1,631.

(d) *Additional simplified methods for producers.*—The Commissioner may prescribe additional elective simplified methods by revenue ruling or revenue procedure.

(e) *Cross reference.*—See § 1.6001-1(a) regarding the duty of taxpayers to keep such records as are sufficient to establish the amount of gross income, deductions, etc.

(v) *Examples.*—The provisions of this paragraph (c)(4) are illustrated by the following examples:

(A) *Example 1—HAR and FIFO inventory method.* (1) Taxpayer S uses the FIFO method of accounting for inventories valued at cost and for 2021 elects to use the historic absorption ratio with the modified simplified production method. S identifies the following costs incurred during the test period:

	2018	2019	2020
	$ 100	$ 200	$ 300
	200	350	450
	2,000	2,500	3,000
	2,500	3,500	4,000
	60	136	220
	$2,700	$3,200	$3,700

which is the sum of the allocable pre-production additional section 263A costs ($80) and the allocable production additional section 263A costs ($144). S's ending inventory in 2021 is $3,224, which is the sum of S's additional section 263A costs allocable to ending inventory and S's section 471 costs remaining in ending inventory ($224 + $3,000). The balance of S's additional section 263A costs incurred during 2021 is taken into account in 2021 as part of S's cost of goods sold.

(B) *Example 2—HAR and LIFO inventory method.* (1)(i) The facts are the same as in *Example 1* in paragraph (c)(4)(v)(A) of this section, except that S uses a dollar-value LIFO inventory method rather than the FIFO method. S calculates additional section 263A costs incurred during the taxable year and allocable to ending inventory under paragraph (c)(4)(iii) of this section and identifies the following costs incurred during the test period:

	2018	2019	2020
	$90	$137	$167
	$1,000	$1,400	$2,100

(2) Under paragraph (c)(4)(iii) of this section, S computes a combined historic absorption ratio as follows:

(f) *Change in method of accounting.*—(1) *In general.*—A change in a taxpayer's treatment of additional section 263A costs to comply with paragraph (b)(2)(i)(D) of this section is a change in method of accounting to which the provisions of sections 446 and 481 and the regulations under those sections apply. See § 1.263A-7. For a taxpayer's first taxable year ending on or after August 2, 2005, the taxpayer is granted the consent of the Commissioner to change its method of accounting to comply with paragraph (b)(2)(i)(D) of this section, provided the taxpayer follows the administrative procedures, as modified by paragraphs (e)(2) through (4) of this section, issued under § 1.446-1(e)(3)(ii) for obtaining the Commissioner's automatic consent to a change in accounting method (for further guidance, for example, see Rev. Proc. 2002-9 (2002-1 CB 327), as modified and clarified by Announcement 2002-17 (2002-1 CB 561), modified and amplified by Rev. Proc. 2002-19 (2002-1 CB 696), and amplified, clarified, and modified by Rev. Proc. 2002-54 (2002-2 CB 432), and §601.601(d)(2)(ii)(b) of this chapter). For purposes of Form 3115, "Application for Change in Accounting Method," the designated number for the automatic accounting method change authorized by this paragraph (e) is "95." If Form 3115 is revised or renumbered, any reference in this section to that form is treated as a reference to the revised or renumbered form. Alternatively, notwithstanding the provisions of any administrative procedures that preclude a taxpayer from requesting the advance consent of the Commissioner to change a method of accounting that is required to be made pursuant to a published automatic change procedure, for its first taxable year ending on or after August 2, 2005, a taxpayer may request the advance consent of the Commissioner to change its method of accounting to comply with paragraph (b)(2)(i)(D) of this section, provided the taxpayer follows the administrative procedures, as modified by paragraphs (e)(2) through (5) of this section, for obtaining the advance consent of the Commissioner (for further guidance, for example, see Rev. Proc. 97-27 (1997-1 CB 680), as modified and amplified by Rev. Proc. 2002-19 (2002-1 CB 696), as amplified and clarified by Rev. Proc. 2002-54 (2002-2 CB 432), and §601.601(d)(2)(ii)(b) of this chapter). For the taxpayer's second and subsequent taxable years ending on or after August 2, 2005, requests to secure the consent of the Commissioner must be made under the administrative procedures, as modified by paragraphs (e)(3) and (4) of this section, for obtaining the Commissioner's advance consent to a change in accounting method.

(2) *Scope limitations.*—Any limitations on obtaining the automatic consent or advance consent of the Commissioner do not apply to a taxpayer seeking to change its method of accounting to comply with paragraph (b)(2)(i)(D) of this section for its first taxable year ending on or after August 2, 2005.

(3) *Audit protection.*—A taxpayer that changes its method of accounting in accordance with this paragraph (e) to comply with paragraph (b)(2)(i)(D) of this section does not receive audit protection if its method of accounting for additional section 263A costs is an issue under consideration at the time the application is filed with the national office.

(4) *Section 481(a) adjustment.*—A change in method of accounting to conform to paragraph (b)(2)(i)(D) of this section requires a section 481(a) adjustment. The section 481(a) adjustment period is two taxable years for a net positive adjustment for an accounting method change that is made to conform to paragraph (b)(2)(i)(D) of this section.

(5) *Time for requesting change.*—Notwithstanding the provisions of §1.446-1(e)(3)(i) and any contrary administrative procedure, a taxpayer may submit a request for advance consent to change its method of accounting to comply with paragraph (b)(2)(i)D) of this section for its first taxable year ending on or after August 2, 2005, on or before the date that is 30 days after the end of the taxable year for which the change is requested.

(g) *Applicability dates.*—(1) Paragraphs (b)(2)(i)(D), (e), and (f) of this section apply for taxable years ending on or after August 2, 2005.

(2) Paragraphs (b)(3)(ii)(C) and (b)(4)(ii)(A)(4) of this section apply for taxable years ending on or after January 13, 2014.

(3) Paragraph (c) of this section applies for taxable years beginning on or after November 20, 2018. For any taxable year that both begins before November 20, 2018 and ends after November 20, 2018, the IRS will not challenge return positions consistent with all of paragraphs (c) of this section.

(4) The rules set forth in the last sentence of the introductory text of paragraph (a) of this section and in paragraph (a)(1)(ii)(C) of this section apply for taxable years beginning on or after January 5, 2021. However, for a taxable year beginning after December 31, 2017, and before January 5, 2021, a taxpayer may apply the paragraphs described in the first sentence of this paragraph (g)(4), provided that the taxpayer follows all the applicable rules contained in the regulations under section 263A for such taxable year and all subsequent taxable years. [Reg. §1.263A-2.]

☐ [*T.D. 8482, 8-6-93. Amended by T.D. 8584, 12-28-94; T.D. 9217, 8-2-2005; T.D. 9318, 3-28-2007; T.D. 9652, 1-10-2014, T.D. 9843, 11-19-2018 and T.D. 9942, 12-31-2020.]*

[Reg. §1.263A-3]

§1.263A-3. Rules relating to property acquired for resale.— (a) *Capitalization rules for property acquired for resale.*—(1) *In general.*— Section 263A applies to real property and personal property described in section 1221(1) acquired for resale by a retailer, wholesaler, or other taxpayer (reseller). However, for taxable years beginning after December 31, 2017, a small business taxpayer, as defined in §1.263A-1(j), is not required to apply section 263A in that taxable year. For this purpose, personal property includes both tangible and intangible property. Property acquired for resale includes stock in trade of the taxpayer or other property which is includible in the taxpayer's inventory if on hand at the close of the taxable year, and property held by the taxpayer primarily for sale to customers in the ordinary course of the taxpayer's trade or business. See, however, §1.263A-1(b)(11) for an exception for certain de minimis property provided to customers incident to the provision of services.

(2) *Resellers with production activities.*—(i) *In general.*—Generally, a taxpayer must capitalize all direct costs and certain indirect costs associated with real property and tangible personal property it produces. See §1.263A-2(a). Thus, except as provided in paragraphs (a)(2)(ii) and (3) of this section, a reseller, including a small reseller, that also produces property must capitalize the additional section 263A costs associated with any property it produces.

(ii) *Exemption for certain small business taxpayers.*—For taxable years beginning after December 31, 2017, see §1.263A-1(j) for an exception in the case of a small business taxpayer that meets the gross receipts test of section 448(c) and §1.448-2(c).

(iii) *De minimis production activities.*—See paragraph (a)(5) of this section for rules relating to an exception for resellers with *de minimis* production activities.

(3) *Resellers with property produced under contract.*—Generally, property produced for a taxpayer under a contract (within the meaning of §1.263A-2(a)(1)(ii)(B)(2)) is treated as property produced by the taxpayer. See §1.263A-2(a)(1)(ii)(B). However, a small business taxpayer is not required to capitalize additional section 263A costs to personal property produced for it under contract with an unrelated person if the contract is entered into incident to the resale activities of the small business taxpayer and the property is sold to its customers. For purposes of this paragraph, persons are related if they are described in section 267(b) or 707(b).

(4) *Use of the simplified resale method.*—(i) *In general.*—Except as provided in paragraphs (a)(4)(ii) and (iii) of this section, a taxpayer may elect the simplified production method, as described in §1.263A-2(b), or the modified simplified production method, as described in §1.263A-2(c), but may not elect the simplified resale method, as described in paragraph (d) of this section, if the taxpayer is engaged in both production and resale activities with respect to the items of eligible property listed in §1.263A-2(b)(2).

(ii) *Resellers with de minimis production activities.*—A reseller otherwise permitted to use the simplified resale method in paragraph (d) of this section may use the simplified resale method if its production activities with respect to the items of eligible property listed in §1.263A-2(b)(2) are de minimis (within the meaning of paragraph (a)(5) of this section) and incident to its resale of personal property described in section 1221(1).

(iii) *Resellers with property produced under a contract.*—A reseller otherwise permitted to use the simplified resale method in paragraph (d) of this section may use the simplified resale method even though it has personal property produced for it (e.g., private label goods) under a contract with an unrelated person if the contract is entered into incident to its resale activities and the property is sold to its customers. For purposes of this paragraph (a)(4)(iii), persons are related if they are described in section 267(b) or 707(b).

(iv) *Application of simplified resale method.*—A taxpayer that uses the simplified resale method and has de minimis production activities incident to its resale activities or property produced under contract must capitalize all costs allocable to eligible property produced using the simplified resale method.

(5) *De minimis production activities.*—(i) *In general.*—In determining whether a taxpayer's production activities are *de minimis*, all facts and circumstances must be considered. For example, the taxpayer must consider the volume of the production activities in its trade or business. Production activities are presumed *de minimis* if—

(A) The gross receipts from the sale of the property produced by the reseller are less than 10 percent of the total gross receipts of the trade or business; and

(B) The labor costs allocable to the trade or business's production activities are less than 10 percent of the reseller's total labor costs allocable to its trade or business.

(ii) *Definition of gross receipts to determine de minimis production activities.*—Gross receipts has the same definition as for purposes of the gross receipts test under §1.448-2(c), except that gross receipts are measured at the trade-or-business level rather than at the single-employer level.

(iii) *Example: Reseller with de minimis production activities.*— Taxpayer N is in the retail grocery business. In 2019, N's average annual gross receipts for the three previous taxable years are greater than the gross receipts test of section 448(c). Thus, N is not exempt from the requirement to capitalize costs under section 263A. N's grocery stores typically contain bakeries where customers may purchase baked goods produced by N. N produces no other goods in its retail grocery business. N's gross receipts from its bakeries are 5 percent of the entire grocery business. N's labor costs from its bakeries are 3 percent of its total labor costs allocable to the entire grocery business. Because both ratios are less than 10 percent, N's production activities are *de minimis*. Further, because N's production activities are incident to its resale activities, N may use the simplified resale method, as provided in paragraph (a)(4)(ii) of this section.

(b) [Reserved]

(c) *Purchasing, handling, and storage costs.*—(1) *In general.*—Generally, §1.263A-1(e) describes the types of costs that must be capitalized by taxpayers. Resellers must capitalize the acquisition cost of property acquired for resale, as well as indirect costs described in §1.263A-1(e)(3), which are properly allocable to property acquired for resale. The indirect costs most often incurred by resellers are purchasing, handling, and storage costs. This paragraph (c) provides additional guidance regarding each of these categories of costs. As provided in §1.263A-1(e), this paragraph (c) also applies to producers incurring purchasing, handling, and storage costs.

(2) *Costs attributable to purchasing, handling, and storage.*—The costs attributable to purchasing, handling, and storage activities generally consist of direct and indirect labor costs (including the costs of pension plans and other fringe benefits); occupancy expenses including rent, depreciation, insurance, security, taxes, utilities and maintenance; materials and supplies; rent, maintenance, depreciation, and insurance of vehicles and equipment; tools; telephone; travel; and the general and administrative costs that directly benefit or are incurred by reason of the taxpayer's activities.

(3) *Purchasing costs.*—(i) *In general.*—Purchasing costs are costs associated with operating a purchasing department or office within a trade or business, including personnel costs (e.g., of buyers, assistant buyers, and clerical workers), relating to—

(A) The selection of merchandise;

(B) The maintenance of stock assortment and volume;

(C) The placement of purchase orders;

(D) The establishment and maintenance of vendor contacts; and

(E) The comparison and testing of merchandise.

(ii) *Determination of whether personnel are engaged in purchasing activities.*—The determination of whether a person is engaged in purchasing activities is based upon the activities performed by that person and not upon the person's title or job classification. Thus, for example, although an employee's job function may be described in such a way as to indicate activities outside the area of purchasing (e.g., a marketing representative), such activities must be analyzed on the basis of the activities performed by that employee. If a person performs both purchasing and non-purchasing activities, the taxpayer must reasonably allocate the person's labor costs between these activities. For example, a reasonable allocation is one based on the amount of time the person spends on each activity.

(A) *1/3-2/3 rule for allocating labor costs.*—A taxpayer may elect the 1/3-2/3 rule for allocating labor costs of persons performing both purchasing and non-purchasing activities. If elected, the taxpayer must allocate the labor costs of all such persons using the 1/3-2/3 rule. Under this rule—

(1) If less than one-third of a person's activities are related to purchasing, none of that person's labor costs are allocated to purchasing;

(2) If more than two-thirds of a person's activities are related to purchasing, all of that person's labor costs are allocated to purchasing; and

(3) In all other cases, the taxpayer must reasonably allocate labor costs between purchasing and non-purchasing activities.

(B) *Example.*—The application of paragraph (c)(3)(ii)(A) of this section may be illustrated by the following example:

Example. Taxpayer O is a reseller that employs three persons, A, B, and C, who perform both purchasing and non-purchasing activities. These persons spend the following time performing purchasing activities: A—25%; B—70%; and C—50%. Under the 1/3-2/3 rule, Taxpayer O treats none of A's labor costs as purchasing costs, all of B's labor costs as purchasing costs, and Taxpayer O allocates 50% of C's labor costs as purchasing costs.

(4) *Handling costs.*—(i) *In general.*—Handling costs include costs attributable to processing, assembling, repackaging, transporting, and other similar activities with respect to property acquired for resale, provided the activities do not come within the meaning of the term produce as defined in §1.263A-2(a)(1). Handling costs are generally required to be capitalized under section 263A. Under this paragraph (c)(4)(i), however, handling costs incurred at a retail sales facility (as defined in paragraph (c)(5)(ii)(B) of this section) with respect to property sold to retail customers at the facility are not required to be capitalized. Thus, for example, handling costs incurred at a retail sales facility to unload, unpack, mark, and tag goods sold to retail customers at the facility are not required to be capitalized. In addition, handling costs incurred at a dual-function storage facility (as defined in paragraph (c)(5)(ii)(G) of this section) with respect to property sold to customers from the facility are not required to be capitalized to the extent that the costs are incurred with respect to property sold in on-site sales. Handling costs attributable to property sold to customers from a dual-function storage facility in on-site sales are determined by applying the ratio in paragraph (c)(5)(iii)(B) of this section.

(ii) *Processing costs.*—Processing costs are the costs a reseller incurs in making minor changes or alterations to the nature or form of a product acquired for resale. Minor changes to a product include, for example, monogramming a sweater, altering a pair of pants, and other similar activities.

(iii) *Assembling costs.*—Generally, assembling costs are costs associated with incidental activities that are necessary in readying property for resale (e.g., attaching wheels and handlebars to a bicycle acquired for resale).

(iv) *Repackaging costs.*—Repackaging costs are the costs a taxpayer incurs to package property for sale to its customers.

(v) *Transportation costs.*—Generally, transportation costs are the costs a taxpayer incurs moving or shipping property acquired for resale. These costs include the cost of dispatching trucks; loading and unloading shipments; and sorting, tagging, and marking property. Transportation costs may consist of depreciation on trucks and equipment and the costs of fuel, insurance, labor, and similar costs. Generally, transportation costs required to be capitalized include costs incurred in transporting property—

(A) From the vendor to the taxpayer;

(B) From one of the taxpayer's storage facilities to another of its storage facilities;

(C) From the taxpayer's storage facility to its retail sales facility;

(D) From the taxpayer's retail sales facility to its storage facility; and

(E) From one of the taxpayer's retail sales facilities to another of its retail sales facilities.

(vi) *Costs not required to be capitalized as handling costs.*—(A) *Distribution costs.*—(1) *In general.*—Distribution costs are not required to be capitalized. Distribution costs are any transportation costs incurred outside a storage facility in delivering goods to a customer. For this purpose, any costs incurred on a loading dock are treated as incurred outside a storage facility.

(2) *Costs incurred in transporting goods to a related person.*—Distribution costs do not include costs incurred by a taxpayer in delivering goods to a related person. Thus, for example, when a taxpayer sells goods to a related person, the costs of transporting the goods are included in determining the basis of the goods that are sold, and hence in determining the resulting gain or loss from the sale, for all purposes of the Internal Revenue Code and the regulations thereunder. See, e.g., sections 267, 707, and 1502. For purposes of this provision, persons are related if they are described in section 267(b) or section 707(b).

(B) *Delivery of custom-ordered items.*—Generally, costs incurred in transporting goods from a taxpayer's storage facility to its retail sales facility must be capitalized. However, costs incurred outside a storage facility in delivering custom-ordered items to a retail sales facility are not required to be capitalized. For this purpose, any costs incurred on a loading dock are treated as incurred outside a storage facility. Delivery of custom-ordered items occurs when a taxpayer can demonstrate that a delivery to the taxpayer's retail sales facility is made to fill an identifiable order of a particular customer (placed by the customer before the delivery of the goods occurs) for the particular goods in question. Factors that may demonstrate the existence of a specific, identifiable delivery include the following—

(1) The customer has paid for the item in advance of the delivery;

(2) The customer has submitted a written order for the item;

(3) The item is not normally available at the retail sales facility for on-site customer purchases; and

(4) The item will be returned to the storage facility (and not held for sale at the retail sales facility) if the customer cancels an order.

(C) *Pick and pack costs.*—(1) *In general.*—Generally, handling costs incurred inside a storage or warehousing facility must be capitalized. However, costs attributable to pick and pack activities inside a storage or warehousing facility are not required to be capitalized. Pick and pack activities are activities undertaken in preparation for imminent shipment to a particular customer after the customer has ordered the specific goods in question. Examples of pick and pack activities include:

(i) Moving specific goods from a storage location in preparation for shipment to the customer;

(ii) Packing or repacking those goods for shipment to the customer; and

(iii) Staging those goods for shipment to the customer.

(2) *Activities that are not pick and pack activities.*—Pick and pack activities do not include:

(i) Unloading goods that are received for storage;

(ii) Checking the quantity and quality of goods received;

(iii) Comparing the quantity of goods received to the amounts ordered and preparing the receiving documents;

(iv) Moving the goods to their storage location, e.g., bins, racks, containers, etc.; and

(v) Storing the goods.

(3) *Costs not attributable to pick and pack activities.*—Occupancy costs, such as rent, depreciation, insurance, security, taxes, utilities, and maintenance costs properly allocable to the storage or warehousing facility, are not costs attributable to pick and pack activities.

(5) *Storage costs.*—(i) *In general.*—Generally, storage costs are capitalized under section 263A to the extent they are attributable to the operation of an off-site storage or warehousing facility (an off-site storage facility). However, storage costs attributable to the operation of an on-site storage facility (as defined in paragraph (c)(5)(ii)(A) of this section) are not required to be capitalized under section 263A. Storage costs attributable to a dual-function storage facility (as defined in paragraph (c)(5)(ii)(G) of this section) must be capitalized to the extent that the facility's costs are allocable to off-site storage.

(ii) *Definitions.*—(A) *On-site storage facility.*—An on-site storage facility is defined as a storage or warehousing facility that is physically attached to, and an integral part of, a retail sales facility.

(B) *Retail sales facility.*—(1) A retail sales facility is defined as a facility where a taxpayer sells merchandise exclusively to retail customers in on-site sales. For this purpose, a retail sales facility includes those portions of any specific retail site—

(i) Which are customarily associated with and are an integral part of the operations of that retail site;

(ii) Which are generally open each business day exclusively to retail customers;

(iii) On or in which retail customers normally and routinely shop to select specific items of merchandise; and

(iv) Which are adjacent to or in immediate proximity to other portions of the specific retail site.

(2) Thus, for example, two lots of an automobile dealership physically separated by an alley or an access road would generally be considered one retail sales facility, provided customers routinely shop on both of the lots to select the specific automobiles that they wish to acquire.

(C) *An integral part of a retail sales facility.*—A storage facility is considered an integral part of a retail sales facility when the storage facility is an essential and indispensable part of the retail sales facility. For example, if the storage facility is used exclusively for filling orders or completing sales at the retail sales facility, the *storage facility is an integral part of the retail sales facility.*

(D) *On-site sales.*—On-site sales are defined as sales made to retail customers physically present at a facility. For example, mail order and catalog sales are made to customers not physically present at the facility, and thus, are not on-site sales.

(E) *Retail customer.*—(1) *In general.*—A retail customer is defined as the final purchaser of the merchandise. A retail customer does not include a person who resells the merchandise to others, such as a contractor or manufacturer that incorporates the merchandise into another product for sale to customers.

(2) *Certain non-retail customers treated as retail customers.*—For purposes of this section, a non-retail customer is treated as a retail customer with respect to a particular facility if the following requirements are satisfied—

(i) The non-retail customer purchases goods under the same terms and conditions as are available to retail customers (e.g., no special discounts);

(ii) The non-retail customer purchases goods in the same manner as a retail customer (e.g., the non-retail customer may not place orders in advance and must come to the facility to examine and select goods);

(iii) Retail customers shop at the facility on a routine basis (i.e., on most business days), and no special days or hours are reserved for non-retail customers; and

(iv) More than 50 percent of the gross sales of the facility are made to retail customers.

(F) *Off-site storage facility.*—An off-site storage facility is defined as a storage facility that is not an on-site storage facility.

(G) *Dual-function storage facility.*—A dual-function storage facility is defined as a storage facility that serves as both an off-site storage facility and an on-site storage facility. For example, a dual-function storage facility would include a regional warehouse that serves the taxpayer's separate retail sales outlets and also contains a sales outlet therein. A dual-function storage facility also includes any facility where sales are made to retail customers in on-site sales and to—

(1) Retail customers in sales that are not on-site sales; or

(2) Other customers.

(iii) *Treatment of storage costs incurred at a dual-function storage facility.*—(A) *In general.*—Storage costs associated with a dual-function storage facility must be allocated between the off-site storage function and the on-site storage function. To the extent that the dual-function storage facility's storage costs are allocable to the off-site storage function, they must be capitalized. To the extent that the dual-function storage facility's storage costs are allocable to the on-site storage function, they are not required to be capitalized.

(B) *Dual-function storage facility allocation ratio.*—(1) *In general.*—Storage costs associated with a dual-function storage facility must be allocated between the off-site storage function and the on-site storage function using the ratio of—

(i) Gross on-site sales of the facility (i.e., gross sales of the facility made to retail customers visiting the premises in person and purchasing merchandise stored therein); to

(ii) Total gross sales of the facility. For this purpose, the total gross sales of the facility include the value of items shipped to other facilities of the taxpayer.

(2) *Illustration of ratio allocation.*—For example, if a dual-function storage facility's on-site sales are 40 percent of the total gross sales of the facility, then 40 percent of the facility's storage costs are allocable to the on-site storage function and are not required to be capitalized under section 263A.

(3) *Appropriate adjustments for other uses of a dual-function storage facility.*—Prior to computing the allocation ratio in paragraph (c)(5)(iii)(B) of this section, a taxpayer must apply the principles of paragraph (c)(5)(iv) of this section in determining the portion of the facility that is a dual-function storage facility (and the costs attributable to such portion).

(C) *De minimis 90-10 rule for dual-function storage facilities.*—If 90 percent or more of the costs of a facility are attributable to the on-site storage function, the entire storage facility is deemed to be an on-site storage facility. In contrast, if 10 percent or less of the costs of a storage facility are attributable to the on-site storage function, the entire storage facility is deemed to be an off-site storage facility.

(iv) *Costs not attributable to an off-site storage facility.*—To the extent that costs incurred at an off-site storage facility are not properly allocable to the taxpayer's storage function, the costs are not accounted for as off-site storage costs. For example, if a taxpayer has an office attached to its off-site storage facility where work unrelated to the storage function is performed, such as a sales office, costs associated with this office are not off-site storage costs. However, if a taxpayer uses a portion of an off-site storage facility in a manner related to the storage function, for example, to store equipment or supplies that are not offered for sale to customers, costs associated with this portion of the facility are off-site storage costs.

(v) *Examples.*—The provisions of this paragraph (c)(5) are illustrated by the following examples:

Example 1. Catalog or mail order center. Taxpayer P operates a mail order catalog business. As part of its business, P stores merchandise for shipment to customers who purchase the merchandise through orders placed by telephone or mail. P's storage facility is not an on-site storage facility because no on-site sales are made at the facility.

    Example 2. Pooled-stock facility. Taxpayer Q maintains a pooled-stock facility, which functions as a back-up regional storage facility for Q's retail sales outlets in the nearby area. Q's pooled stock facility is an off-site storage facility because it is neither physically attached to nor an integral part of a retail sales facility.

    Example 3. Wholesale warehouse. Taxpayer R operates a wholesale warehouse where wholesale sales are made to customers physically present at the facility. R's customers resell the goods they purchase from R to final retail customers. Because no retail sales are conducted at the facility, all storage costs attributable to R's wholesale warehouse must be capitalized.

    (d) *Simplified resale method.*—(1) *Introduction.*—This paragraph (d) provides a simplified method for determining the additional section

Combined absorption ratio

    (B) *Effect of allocation.*—The resulting product under the general allocation formula is the additional section 263A costs that are added to the taxpayer's ending section 471 costs to determine the section 263A costs that are capitalized.

    (C) *Definitions.*—(1) *Combined absorption ratio.*—The combined absorption ratio is defined as the sum of the storage and handling costs absorption ratio as defined in paragraph (d)(3)(i)(D) of this section and the purchasing costs absorption ratio as defined in paragraph (d)(3)(i)(E) of this section.

    (2) *Section 471 costs remaining on hand at year end.*—Section 471 costs remaining on hand at year end mean the section 471 costs, as defined in §1.263A-1(d)(2), that the taxpayer incurs during its current taxable year, which remain in its ending inventory or are otherwise on hand at year end. For LIFO inventories of a taxpayer, the section 471 costs remaining on hand at year end means the

263A costs properly allocable to property acquired for resale and other eligible property on hand at the end of the taxable year.

    (2) *Eligible property.*—Generally, the simplified resale method is only available to a trade or business exclusively engaged in resale activities. However, certain resellers with property produced as a result of de minimis production activities or property produced under contract may elect the simplified resale method, as described in paragraph (a)(4) of this section. Eligible property for purposes of the simplified resale method, therefore, includes any real or personal property described in section 1221(1) that is acquired for resale and any eligible property (within the meaning of §1.263A-2(b)(2)) that is described in paragraph (a)(4) of this section.

    (3) *Simplified resale method without historic absorption ratio election.*—(i) *General allocation formula.*—(A) *In general.*—Under the simplified resale method, the additional section 263A costs allocable to eligible property remaining on hand at the close of the taxable year are computed as follows:

$$\times \quad \frac{\text{Section 471 costs remaining on hand at}}{\text{year end.}}$$

increment, if any, for the current year stated in terms of section 471 costs. See paragraph (d)(3)(ii) of this section for special rules applicable to LIFO taxpayers. Except as otherwise provided in this section or in §1.263A-1 or 1.263A-2, additional section 263A costs that are allocated to inventories on hand at the close of the taxable year under the simplified resale method of this paragraph (d) are treated as inventory costs for all purposes of the Internal Revenue Code.

    (3) *Costs allocable to property sold.*—Section 471 costs remaining on hand at year end, as defined in paragraph (d)(3)(i)(C)(2) of this section, do not include costs that are specifically described in §1.263A-1(e)(3)(ii) or cost reductions described in §1.471-3(e) that a taxpayer properly allocates entirely to property that has been sold.

    (D) *Storage and handling costs absorption ratio.*
    (1) Under the simplified resale method, the storage and handling costs absorption ratio is determined as follows:

Current year's storage and handling costs

Beginning inventory plus current year's purchases.

    (2) Current year's storage and handling costs are defined as the total storage costs plus the total handling costs incurred during the taxable year that relate to the taxpayer's property acquired for resale and other eligible property. See paragraph (c) of this section, which discusses storage and handling costs. Storage and handling costs must include the amount of allocable mixed service costs as described in paragraph (d)(3)(i)(F) of this section. Beginning inventory in the denominator of the storage and handling costs absorption ratio refers to the section 471 costs of any property acquired for resale or other eligible property held by the taxpayer as of the beginning of the taxable year. Current year's purchases generally mean the taxpayer's section 471 costs incurred with respect to purchases of property acquired for resale during the current taxable year. In computing the denominator of the storage and handling costs absorption ratio, a taxpayer using a dollar-value LIFO method of accounting, must state beginning inventory amounts using the LIFO carrying value of the inventory and not current-year dollars.

    (3) Current year's storage and handling costs, beginning inventory, and current year's purchases, as defined in paragraph (d)(3)(i)(D)(2) of this section, do not include costs that are specifically described in §1.263A-1(e)(3)(ii) or cost reductions described in §1.471-3(e) that a taxpayer properly allocates entirely to property that has been sold.

    (E) *Purchasing costs absorption ratio.*—(1) Under the simplified resale method, the purchasing costs absorption ratio is determined as follows:

Labor costs allocable to activity

Total labor costs

    (2) Labor costs allocable to activity are defined as the total labor costs allocable to each particular activity (i.e., purchasing, handling, and storage), excluding labor costs included in mixed service costs. Total labor costs are defined as the total labor costs (excluding labor costs included in mixed service costs) that are incurred in the taxpayer's trade or business during the taxable year. See §1.263A-1(h)(6) for the definition of total mixed service costs.

    (ii) *LIFO taxpayers electing simplified resale method.*—(A) *In general.*—Under the simplified resale method, a taxpayer using a LIFO method must calculate a particular year's index (e.g., under §1.472-8(e)) without regard to its additional section 263A costs. Simi-

Current year's purchasing costs

Current year's purchases.

    (2) Current year's purchasing costs are defined as the total purchasing costs incurred during the taxable year that relate to the taxpayer's property acquired for resale and eligible property. See paragraph (c)(3) of this section, which discusses purchasing costs. Purchasing costs must include the amount of allocable mixed service costs determined in paragraph (d)(3)(i)(F) of this section. Current year's purchases generally mean the taxpayer's section 471 costs incurred with respect to purchases of property acquired for resale during the current taxable year.

    (3) Current year's purchasing costs and current year's purchases, as defined in paragraph (d)(3)(i)(E)(2) of this section, do not include costs that are specifically described in §1.263A-1(e)(3)(ii) or cost reductions described in §1.471-3(e) that a taxpayer properly allocates entirely to property that has been sold.

    (F) *Allocable mixed service costs.*—(1) If a taxpayer allocates its mixed service costs to purchasing costs, storage costs, and handling costs using a method described in §1.263A-1(g)(4), the taxpayer is not required to determine its allocable mixed service costs under this paragraph (d)(3)(i)(F). However, if the taxpayer uses the simplified service cost method, the amount of mixed service costs allocated to and included in purchasing costs, storage costs, and handling costs in the absorption ratios in paragraphs (d)(3)(i)(D) and (E) of this section is determined as follows:

Total mixed service costs.

$\times$

larly, a taxpayer that adjusts current-year costs by applicable indexes to determine whether there has been an inventory increment or decrement in the current year for a particular LIFO pool must disregard the additional section 263A costs in making that determination.

    (B) *LIFO increment.*—If the taxpayer determines there has been an inventory increment, the taxpayer must state the amount of the increment in current-year dollars (stated in terms of section 471 costs). The taxpayer then multiplies this amount by the combined absorption ratio. The resulting product is the additional section 263A costs that must be added to the taxpayer's increment for the year stated in terms of section 471 costs.

(C) *LIFO decrement.*—If the taxpayer determines there has been an inventory decrement, the taxpayer must state the amount of the decrement in dollars applicable to the particular year for which the LIFO layer has been invaded. The additional section 263A costs incurred in prior years that are applicable to the decrement are charged to cost of goods sold. The additional section 263A costs that are applicable to the decrement are determined by multiplying the additional section 263A costs allocated to the layer of the pool in which the decrement occurred by the ratio of the decrement (excluding additional section 263A costs) to the section 471 costs in the layer of that pool.

(iii) *Permissible variations of the simplified resale method.*—The following variations of the simplified resale method are permitted:

(A) The exclusion of beginning inventories from the denominator in the storage and handling costs absorption ratio formula in paragraph (d)(3)(i)(D) of this section; or

(B) Multiplication of the storage and handling costs absorption ratio in paragraph (d)(3)(i)(D) of this section by the total of section 471 costs included in a LIFO taxpayer's ending inventory (rather than just the increment, if any, experienced by the LIFO taxpayer during the taxable year) for purposes of determining capitalizable storage and handling costs.

$$\frac{\text{1994 purchasing costs}}{\text{1994 purchases}} = \frac{\$460,000 + \$40,000}{\$10,000,000}$$

$$= \frac{\$500,000}{\$10,000,000}$$

$$= 5.0\%$$

(iv) S computes its storage and handling costs absorption ratio for 1994 as follows:

$$\frac{\text{Storage and handling costs}}{\substack{\text{Beginning inventory}\\\text{plus 1994 purchases}}} = \frac{(\$110,000 + \$80,000) + (\$90,000 + \$80,000)}{\$2,000,000 + \$10,000,000}$$

$$= \frac{\$190,000 + \$170,000}{\$12,000,000}$$

$$= \frac{\$360,000}{\$12,000,000}$$

$$= 3.0\%$$

(v) S's combined absorption ratio is 8.0%, or the sum of the purchasing costs absorption ratio (5.0%) and the storage and handling costs absorption ratio (3.0%). Under the simplified resale method, S determines the additional section 263A costs allocable to its ending inventory by multiplying the combined absorption ratio by its section 471 costs with respect to current year's purchases remaining in ending inventory:

$$\text{Additional § 263A costs} = 8.0\% \times \$3,000,000 = \$240,000$$

(vi) S adds this $240,000 to the $3,000,000 of purchases remaining in its ending inventory to determine its total ending FIFO inventory of $3,240,000.

Example 2. LIFO inventory method. (i) Taxpayer T uses a dollar-value LIFO inventory method. T's beginning inventory for 1994 is $2,100,000 (consisting of $2,000,000 of section 471 costs and $100,000 of additional section 263A costs). During 1994, T makes purchases of $10,000,000. In addition, T incurs purchasing costs of $460,000, storage costs of $110,000, and handling costs of $90,000. T's 1994 LIFO increment is $1,000,000 ($3,000,000 of section 471 costs in ending inventory less $2,000,000 of section 471 costs in beginning inventory).

(ii) In 1994, T incurs $400,000 of total mixed service costs and $1,000,000 of total labor costs (excluding labor costs included in mixed service costs). In addition, T incurs the following labor costs (excluding labor costs included in mixed service costs): purchasing—$100,000, storage—$200,000, and handling—$200,000. Accordingly, the following mixed service costs must be included in purchasing costs, storage costs, and handling costs as capitalizable mixed service costs: purchasing—$40,000 ([$100,000 divided by $1,000,000] multiplied by $400,000); storage—$80,000 ([$200,000 divided by $1,000,000]multiplied by $400,000); and handling—$80,000 ([$200,000 divided by $1,000,000] multiplied by $400,000).

(iv) *Examples.*—The provisions of this paragraph (d)(3) are illustrated by the following examples:

Example 1. FIFO inventory method. (i) Taxpayer S uses the FIFO method of accounting for inventories. S's beginning inventory for 1994 (all of which was sold during 1994) was $2,100,000 (consisting of $2,000,000 of section 471 costs and $100,000 of additional section 263A costs). During 1994, S makes purchases of $10,000,000. In addition, S incurs purchasing costs of $460,000, storage costs of $110,000, and handling costs of $90,000. S's purchases (section 471 costs) remaining in ending inventory at the end of 1994 are $3,000,000.

(ii) In 1994, S incurs $400,000 of total mixed service costs and $1,000,000 of total labor costs (excluding labor costs included in mixed service costs). In addition, S incurs the following labor costs (excluding labor costs included in mixed service costs): purchasing—$100,000, storage—$200,000, and handling—$200,000. Accordingly, the following mixed service costs must be included in purchasing costs, storage costs, and handling costs as capitalizable mixed service costs: purchasing—$40,000 ([$100,000 divided by $1,000,000] multiplied by $400,000); storage—$80,000 ([$200,000 divided by $1,000,000]multiplied by $400,000); and handling—$80,000 ([$200,000 divided by $1,000,000] multiplied by $400,000).

(iii) S computes its purchasing costs absorption ratio for 1994 as follows:

(iii) Based on these facts, T determines that it has a combined absorption ratio of 8.0%. To determine the additional section 263A costs allocable to its ending inventory, T multiplies its combined absorption ratio (8.0%) by the $1,000,000 LIFO increment. Thus, T's additional section 263A costs allocable to its ending inventory are $80,000 ($1,000,000 multiplied by 3.0%). This $80,000 is added to the $1,000,000 to determine a total 1994 LIFO increment of $1,080,000. T's ending inventory is $3,180,000 (its beginning inventory of $2,100,000 plus the $1,080,000 increment).

(iv) In 1995, T sells one-half of the inventory in its 1994 LIFO increment. T must include in its cost of goods sold for 1995 the amount of additional section 263A costs relating to this inventory, i.e., one-half of the $80,000 additional section 263A costs capitalized in 1994 ending inventory, or $40,000.

Example 3. LIFO pools. (i) Taxpayer U begins its business in 1994, and adopts the LIFO inventory method. During 1994, U makes purchases of $10,000, and incurs $400 of purchasing costs, $350 of storage costs and $250 of handling costs. U's purchasing costs, storage costs, and handling costs include their proper allocable share of mixed service costs.

(ii) U computes its purchasing costs absorption ratio for 1994, as follows:

$$\frac{\text{1994 purchasing costs}}{\text{1994 purchases}} = \frac{\$400}{\$10,000}$$

$$= 4.0\%$$

(iii) U computes its storage and handling costs absorption ratio for 1994, as follows:

$$\frac{1994 \text{ storage and handling costs}}{\text{Beginning inventory plus 1994 purchases}} = \frac{\$350 + \$250}{\$0 + \$10,000}$$

$$= \frac{\$600}{\$10,000}$$

$$= 6.0\%$$

(iv) U's combined absorption ratio is 10%, or the sum of the purchasing costs absorption ratio (4.0%) and the storage and handling costs absorption ratio (6.0%). At the end of 1994, U's ending

inventory included $3,000 of current year purchases, contained in three LIFO pools (X, Y, and Z) as shown below. Under the simplified resale method, U computes its ending inventory for 1994 as follows:

1994:

	Total
Ending section 471 costs	$3,000
Additional section 263A costs (10%)	300
1994 Ending Inventory	$3,300

	X	Y	Z
	$1,600	$600	$800
	160	60	80
	$1,760	$660	$880

(v) During 1995, U makes purchases of $2,000 as shown below, and incurs $200 of purchasing costs, $325 of storage costs and $175 of handling costs. U's purchasing costs, storage costs, and handling costs include their proper share of mixed service costs. Moreover, U

sold goods from pools X, Y, and Z having a total cost of $1,000. U computes its ending inventory for 1995 as follows.

(vi) U computes its purchasing costs absorption ratio for 1995:

$$\frac{1995 \text{ purchasing costs}}{1995 \text{ purchases}} = \frac{\$200}{\$2,000}$$

$$= 10.0\%$$

(vii) U computes its storage and handling costs absorption ratio for 1995:

$$\frac{1995 \text{ storage and handling costs}}{\text{Beginning inventory plus 1995 purchases}} = \frac{\$325 + 175}{\$3,000 + 2,000}$$

$$= \frac{\$500}{\$5,000}$$

$$= 10.0\%$$

(viii) U's combined absorption ratio is 20.0%, or the sum of the purchasing costs absorption ratio (10.0%) and the storage and handling costs absorption ratio (10.0%).

1995:

	Total	X	Y	Z
Beginning section 471 costs	$3,000	$1,600	$600	$800
1995 section 471 costs	2,000	1,500	300	200
Section 471 cost of goods sold	(1,000)	(300)	(300)	(400)
1995 Ending Section 471 costs	$4,000	$2,800	$600	$600
Consisting of:				
1994 layer	$2,800	$1,600	$600	$600
1995 layer	1,200	1,200	—	—
	$4,000	$2,800	$600	$600
Additional section 263A costs:				
1994 (10%)	$280	$160	$60	$60
1995 (20%)	240	240	—	—
	$520	$400	$60	$60
1995 ending inventory	$4,520	$3,200	$660	$660

(ix) In 1995, U experiences a $200 decrement in Pool Z. Thus, U must charge the additional section 263A costs incurred in prior years applicable to the decrement to 1995's cost of goods sold. To do so, U determines a ratio by dividing the decrement by the section 471 costs in the 1994 layer ($200 divided by $800, or 25%). U then multiplies this ratio (25%) by the additional section 263A costs in the 1994 layer ($80) to determine the additional section 263A costs applicable to the decrement ($20). Therefore, $ 20 is taken into account by U in 1995 as part of its cost of goods sold ($80 multiplied by 25%).

(4) *Simplified resale method with historic absorption ratio election.*—(i) *In general.*—This paragraph (d)(4) permits resellers using the simplified resale method to elect a historic absorption ratio in determining additional section 263A costs allocable to eligible property

remaining on hand at the close of their taxable years. Except as provided in paragraph (d)(4)(v) of this section, a taxpayer may only make a historic absorption ratio election if it has used the simplified resale method for three or more consecutive taxable years immediately prior to the year of election. The historic absorption ratio is used in lieu of an actual combined absorption ratio computed under paragraph (d)(3)(i)(C)(1) of this section and is based on costs capitalized by a taxpayer during its test period. If elected, the historic absorption ratio must be used for the qualifying period described in paragraph (d)(4)(ii)(C) of this section.

(ii) *Operating rules and definitions.*—(A) *Historic absorption ratio.*—(1) The historic absorption ratio is equal to the following ratio:

$$\frac{\text{Add'l section 263A costs incurred during the test period}}{\text{Section 471 costs incurred during the test period.}}$$

Reg. §1.263A-3(d)(4)

(2) Additional section 263A costs incurred during the test period are defined as the sum of the products of the combined absorption ratios (defined in paragraph (d)(3)(i)(C)(*1*) of this section) multiplied by a taxpayer's section 471 costs incurred with respect to purchases, for each taxable year of the test period.

(3) Section 471 costs incurred during the test period mean the section 471 costs described in §1.263A-1(d)(2) that a taxpayer incurs generally with respect to its purchases during the test period described in paragraph (d)(4)(ii)(B) of this section.

(B) *Test period.*—*(1) In general.*—The test period is generally the three taxable-year period immediately prior to the taxable year that the historic absorption ratio is elected.

(2) Updated test period.—The test period begins again with the beginning of the first taxable year after the close of a qualifying period (as defined in paragraph (d)(4)(ii)(C) of this section). This new test period, the updated test period, is the three taxable-year period beginning with the first taxable year after the close of the qualifying period.

(C) *Qualifying period.*—*(1) In general.*—A qualifying period includes each of the first five taxable years beginning with the first taxable year after a test period (or updated test period).

(2) Extension of qualifying period.—In the first taxable year following the close of each qualifying period (e.g., the sixth taxable year following the test period), the taxpayer must compute the actual combined absorption ratio under the simplified resale method. If the actual combined absorption ratio computed for this taxable year (the recomputation year) is within one-half of one percentage point (plus or minus) of the historic absorption ratio used in determining capitalizable costs for the qualifying period (i.e., the previous five taxable years), the qualifying period must be extended to include the recomputation year and the following five taxable years, and the taxpayer must continue to use the historic absorption ratio throughout the extended qualifying period. If, however, the actual combined absorption ratio computed for the recomputation year is not within one-half of one percentage point (plus or minus) of the historic absorption ratio, the taxpayer must use actual combined absorption ratios beginning with the recomputation year under the simplified resale method and throughout the updated test period. The taxpayer must resume using the historic absorption ratio (determined with reference to the updated test period) in the third taxable year following the recomputation year.

(iii) *Method of accounting.*—(A) *Adoption and use.*—The election to use the historic absorption ratio is a method of accounting. A taxpayer using the simplified resale method may elect the historic absorption ratio in any taxable year if permitted under this paragraph (d)(4), provided the taxpayer has not obtained the Commissioner's consent to revoke the historic absorption ratio election within its prior six taxable years. The election is to be effected on a cut-off basis, and thus, no adjustment under section 481(a) is required or permitted. The use of a historic absorption ratio has no effect on other methods of accounting adopted by the taxpayer and used in conjunction with the simplified resale method in determining its section 263A costs. Accordingly, in computing its actual combined absorption ratios, the taxpayer must use the same methods of accounting used in computing its historic absorption ratio during its most recent test period unless the taxpayer obtains the consent of the Commissioner. Finally, for purposes of this paragraph (d)(4)(iii)(A), the recomputation of the historic absorption ratio during an updated test period and the change from a historic absorption ratio to an actual combined absorption ratio during an updated test period by reason of the requirements of this paragraph (d)(4) are not considered changes in methods of accounting under section 446(e) and,

thus, do not require the consent of the Commissioner or any adjustments under section 481(a).

(B) *Revocation of election.*—A taxpayer may only revoke its election to use the historic absorption ratio with the consent of the Commissioner in a manner prescribed under section 446(e) and the regulations thereunder. Consent to the change for any taxable year that is included in the qualifying period (or an extended qualifying period) will be granted only upon a showing of unusual circumstances.

(iv) *Reporting and recordkeeping requirements.*—(A) *Reporting.*—A taxpayer making an election under this paragraph (d)(4) must attach a statement to its federal income tax return for the taxable year in which the election is made showing the actual combined absorption ratios determined under the simplified resale method during its first test period. This statement must disclose the historic absorption ratio to be used by the taxpayer during its qualifying period. A similar statement must be attached to the federal income tax return for the first taxable year within any subsequent qualifying period (i.e., after an updated test period).

(B) *Recordkeeping.*—A taxpayer must maintain all appropriate records and details supporting the historic absorption ratio until the expiration of the statute of limitations for the last year for which the taxpayer applied the particular historic absorption ratio in determining additional section 263A costs capitalized to eligible property.

(v) *Transition rules.*—(A) *Transition to elect historic absorption ratio.*—Taxpayers will be permitted to elect a historic absorption ratio in their first, second, or third taxable year beginning after December 31, 1993, under such terms and conditions as may be prescribed by the Commissioner. Taxpayers are eligible to make an election under these transition rules whether or not they previously used the simplified resale method. A taxpayer making such an election must recompute (or compute) its additional section 263A costs, and thus, its historic absorption ratio for its first test period as if the rules prescribed in this section and §§1.263A-1 and 1.263A-2 had applied throughout the test period.

(B) *Transition to revoke historic absorption ratio.*—Notwithstanding the requirements provided in paragraph (d)(4)(iii)(B) of this section regarding revocations of the historic absorption ratio during a qualifying period, a taxpayer will be permitted to revoke the historic absorption ratio in their first, second, or third taxable year ending on or after November 20, 2018, under such administrative procedures and with terms and conditions prescribed by the Commissioner.

(vi) *Example.*—The provisions of this paragraph (d)(4) are illustrated by the following example:

Example. (i) Taxpayer V uses the FIFO method of accounting for inventories and in 1994 elects to use the historic absorption ratio with the simplified resale method. After recomputing its additional section 263A costs in accordance with the transition rules of paragraph (d)(4)(v) of this section, V identifies the following costs incurred during the test period:

1991:

> Add'l section 263A costs – $100
> Section 471 costs – $3,000

1992:

> Add'l section 263A costs – 200
> Section 471 costs – 4,000

1993:

> Add'l section 263A costs – 300
> Section 471 costs – 5,000

(ii) Therefore, V computes a 5% historic absorption ratio determined as follows:

$$\text{Historic absorption ratio} = \frac{\$100 + 200 + 300}{\$3,000 + 4,000 + 5,000} = \frac{\$600}{\$12,000} = 5\%$$

(iii) In 1994, V incurs $10,000 of section 471 costs of which $3,000 remain in inventory at the end of the year. Under the simplified resale method using a historic absorption ratio, V determines the

additional section 263A costs allocable to its ending inventory by multiplying its historic ratio (5%) by the section 471 costs remaining in its ending inventory:

$$\text{Add'l section 263A costs} = 5\% \times \$3,000 = \$150$$

(iv) To determine its ending inventory under section 263A, V adds the additional section 263A costs allocable to ending inventory to its section 471 costs remaining in ending inventory ($3,150 = $150 + $3,000). The balance of V's additional section 263A costs incurred during 1994 is taken into account in 1994 as part of V's cost of goods sold.

(v) V's qualifying period ends as of the close of its 1998 taxable year. Therefore, 1999 is a recomputation year in which V must compute its actual combined absorption ratio. V determines its actual

absorption ratio for 1999 to be 5.25% and compares that ratio to its historic absorption ratio (5.0%). Therefore, V must continue to use its historic absorption ratio of 5.0% throughout an extended qualifying period, 1999 through 2004 (the recomputation year and the following five taxable years).

(vi) If, instead, V's actual combined absorption ratio for 1999 were not between 4.5% and 5.5%, V's qualifying period would end and V would be required to compute a new historic absorption ratio with reference to an updated test period of 1999, 2000, and 2001.

Once V's historic absorption ratio is determined for the updated test period, it would be used for a new qualifying period beginning in 2002.

(5) *Additional simplified methods for resellers.*—The Commissioner may prescribe additional elective simplified methods by revenue ruling or revenue procedure.

(e) *Cross reference.*—See §1.6001-1(a) regarding the duty of taxpayers to keep such records as are sufficient to establish the amount of gross income, deductions, etc.

(f) *Applicability dates.*—(1) Paragraphs (d)(3)(i)(C)(3), (d)(3)(i)(D)(3), and (d)(3)(i)(E)(3) of this section apply for taxable years ending on or after January 13, 2014.

(2) The rules set forth in the second sentence of paragraph (a)(1) of this section, paragraphs (a)(2)(ii) and (iii) of this section, the third sentence of paragraph (a)(3) of this section, and paragraphs (a)(4)(ii) and (a)(5) of this section apply for taxable years beginning on or after January 5, 2021. However, for a taxable year beginning after December 31, 2017, and before January 5, 2021, a taxpayer may apply the paragraphs described in the first sentence of this paragraph (f)(2), provided the taxpayer follows all the applicable rules contained in the regulations under section 263A for such taxable year and all subsequent taxable years. [Reg. §1.263A-3.]

☐ [*T.D.* 8482, 8-6-93. *Amended by T.D.* 8559, 8-2-94; *T.D.* 9652, 1-10-2014, *and T.D.* 9843, 11-19-2018 *and T.D.* 9942, 12-31-2020.]

[Reg. §1.263A-4]

§1.263A-4. Rules for property produced in a farming business.—(a) *Introduction.*—(1) *In general.*—This section provides guidance with respect to the application of section 263A to property produced in a farming business as defined in paragraph (a)(5) of this section. Except as otherwise provided by the rules of this section, the general rules of §§1.263A-1 through 1.263A-3 and §§1.263A-7 through 1.263A-15 apply to property produced in a farming business. A taxpayer that engages in the raising or growing of any agricultural or horticultural commodity, including both plants and animals, is engaged in the production of property. Section 263A generally requires the capitalization of the direct costs and an allocable portion of the indirect costs that directly benefit or are incurred by reason of the production of this property. The direct and indirect costs of producing plants or animals generally include preparatory costs allocable to the plant or animal and preproductive period costs of the plant or animal. Except as provided in paragraphs (a)(2), (a)(3), and (e) of this section, taxpayers must capitalize the costs of producing all plants and animals unless the election described in paragraph (d) of this section is made.

(2) *Exception.*—(i) *In general.*—Section 263A does not apply to the costs of producing plants with a preproductive period of 2 years or less or the costs of producing animals in a farming business, if the taxpayer is not—

(A) A corporation or partnership required to use an accrual method of accounting (accrual method) under section 447 in computing its taxable income from farming; or

(B) A tax shelter prohibited from using the cash receipts and disbursements method of accounting (cash method) under section 448(a)(3).

(ii) *Tax shelter.*—(A) *In general.*—A farming business is considered a tax shelter, and thus a taxpayer prohibited from using the cash method under section 448(a)(3), if the farming business is—

(1) A farming syndicate as defined in section 461(k); or

(2) A tax shelter, within the meaning of section 6662(d)(2)(C)(iii).

(B) *Presumption.*—Marketed arrangements in which persons carry on farming activities using the services of a common managerial or administrative service will be presumed to have the principal purpose of tax avoidance, within the meaning of section 6662(d)(2)(C)(iii), if such persons prepay a substantial portion of their farming expenses with borrowed funds.

(iii) *Examples.*—The following examples illustrate the provisions of this paragraph (a)(2):

Example 1. Farmer A grows trees that have a preproductive period in excess of 2 years, and that produce an annual crop. Farmer A is not required by section 447 to use an accrual method or prohibited by section 448(a)(3) from using the cash method. Accordingly, *Farmer A qualifies for the exception described in this paragraph* (a)(2). Since the trees have a preproductive period in excess of 2 years, Farmer A must capitalize the direct costs and an allocable portion of the indirect costs that directly benefit or are incurred by reason of the production of the trees. Since the annual crop has a

preproductive period of 2 years or less, Farmer A is not required to capitalize the costs of producing the crops.

Example 2. Assume the same facts as *Example 1*, except that Farmer A is required by section 447 to use an accrual method or prohibited by 448(a)(3) from using the cash method. Farmer A does not qualify for the exception described in this paragraph (a)(2). Farmer A is required to capitalize the direct costs and an allocable portion of the indirect costs that directly benefit or are incurred by reason of the production of the trees and crops.

(3) *Exemption for certain small business taxpayers.*—For taxable years beginning after December 31, 2017, see §1.263A-1(j) for an exception in the case of a small business taxpayer that meets the gross receipts test of section 448(c) and §1.448-2(c).

(4) *Costs required to be capitalized or inventoried under another provision.*—The exceptions from capitalization provided in paragraphs (a)(2), (a)(3), (d) and (e) of this section do not apply to any cost that is required to be capitalized or inventoried under another Internal Revenue Code or regulatory provision, such as section 263 or 471.

(5) *Farming business.*—(i) *In general.*—A farming business means a trade or business involving the cultivation of land or the raising or harvesting of any agricultural or horticultural commodity. Examples include the trade or business of operating a nursery or sod farm; the raising or harvesting of trees bearing fruit, nuts, or other crops; the raising of ornamental trees (other than evergreen trees that are more than 6 years old at the time they are severed from their roots); and the raising, shearing, feeding, caring for, training, and management of animals. For purposes of this section, the term harvesting does not include contract harvesting of an agricultural or horticultural commodity grown or raised by another. Similarly, merely buying and reselling plants or animals grown or raised entirely by another is not raising an agricultural or horticultural commodity. A taxpayer is engaged in raising a plant or animal, rather than the mere resale of a plant or animal, if the plant or animal is held for further cultivation and development prior to sale. In determining whether a plant or animal is held for further cultivation and development prior to sale, consideration will be given to all of the facts and circumstances, including: the value added by the taxpayer to the plant or animal through agricultural or horticultural processes; the length of time between the taxpayer's acquisition of the plant or animal and the time that the taxpayer makes the plant or animal available for sale; and in the case of a plant, whether the plant is kept in the container in which purchased, replanted in the ground, or replanted in a series of larger containers as it is grown to a larger size.

(A) *Plant.*—A plant produced in a farming business includes, but is not limited to, a fruit, nut, or other crop bearing tree, an ornamental tree, a vine, a bush, sod, and the crop or yield of a plant that will have more than one crop or yield raised by the taxpayer. Sea plants are produced in a farming business if they are tended and cultivated as opposed to merely harvested.

(B) *Animal.*—An animal produced in a farming business includes, but is not limited to, any stock, poultry or other bird, and fish or other sea life raised by the taxpayer. Thus, for example, the term animal may include a cow, chicken, emu, or salmon raised by the taxpayer. Fish and other sea life are produced in a farming business if they are raised on a fish farm. A fish farm is an area where fish or other sea life are grown or raised as opposed to merely caught or harvested.

(ii) *Incidental activities.*—(A) *In general.*—A farming business includes processing activities that are normally incident to the growing, raising, or harvesting of agricultural or horticultural products. For example, a taxpayer in the trade or business of growing fruits and vegetables may harvest, wash, inspect, and package the fruits and vegetables for sale. Such activities are normally incident to the raising of these crops by farmers. The taxpayer will be considered to be in the trade or business of farming with respect to the growing of fruits and vegetables and the processing activities incident to their harvest.

(B) *Activities that are not incidental.*—Farming business does not include the processing of commodities or products beyond those activities that are normally incident to the growing, raising, or harvesting of such products.

(iii) *Examples.*—The following examples illustrate the provisions of this paragraph (a)(5):

Example 1. Individual A operates a retail nursery. Individual A has three categories of plants. The first category is comprised of plants that Individual A grows from seeds or cuttings. The second category is comprised of plants that Individual A purchases in containers and grows for a period of from several months to several years. Individual A replants some of these plants in the ground. The others are replanted in a series of larger containers as they grow. The third category is comprised of plants that are purchased by Individual A in containers. Individual A does not grow these plants to a larger size before making them available for resale. Instead, Individual A makes these plants available for resale, in the container in which purchased, shortly after receiving them. Thus, no value is added to these plants by Individual A through horticultural processes. Individual A also sells soil, mulch, chemicals, and yard tools. Individual A is producing property in the farming business with respect to the first two categories of plants because these plants are held for further cultivation and development prior to sale. The plants in the third category are not held for further cultivation and development prior to sale and, therefore, are not regarded as property produced in a farming business for purposes of section 263A. Accordingly, Individual A must account for the third category of plants, along with the soil, mulch, chemicals, and yard tools, as property acquired for resale.

Example 2. Individual B is in the business of growing and harvesting wheat and other grains. Individual B also processes grain that Individual B has harvested in order to produce breads, cereals, and other similar food products, which Individual B then sells to customers in the course of its business. Although Individual B is in the farming business with respect to the growing and harvesting of grain, Individual B is not in the farming business with respect to the processing of such grain to produce the food products.

Example 3. Individual C is in the business of raising poultry and other livestock. Individual C also operates a meat processing operation in which the poultry and other livestock are slaughtered, processed, and packaged or canned. The packaged or canned meat is sold to Individual C's customers. Although Individual C is in the farming business with respect to the raising of poultry and other livestock, Individual C is not in the farming business with respect to the slaughtering, processing, packaging, and canning of such animals to produce the food products.

(b) *Application of section 263A to property produced in a farming business.*—(1) *In general.*—Unless otherwise provided in this section, section 263A requires the capitalization of the direct costs and an allocable portion of the indirect costs that directly benefit or are incurred by reason of the production of any property in a farming business (including animals and plants without regard to the length of their preproductive period). Section 1.263A-1(e) describes the types of direct and indirect costs that generally must be capitalized by taxpayers under section 263A and paragraphs (b)(1)(i) and (ii) of this section provide specific examples of the types of costs typically incurred in the trade or business of farming. For purposes of this section, soil and water conservation expenditures that a taxpayer has elected to deduct under section 175 and fertilizer that a taxpayer has elected to deduct under section 180 are not subject to capitalization under section 263A, except to the extent these costs are required to be capitalized as a preproductive period cost of a plant or animal.

(i) *Plants.*—The costs of producing a plant typically required to be capitalized under section 263A include the costs incurred so that the plant's growing process may begin (preparatory costs), such as the acquisition costs of the seed, seedling, or plant, and the costs of planting, cultivating, maintaining, or developing the plant during the preproductive period (preproductive period costs). Preproductive period costs include, but are not limited to, management, irrigation, pruning, soil and water conservation (including costs that the taxpayer has elected to deduct under section 175), fertilizing (including costs that the taxpayer has elected to deduct under section 180), frost protection, spraying, harvesting, storage and handling, upkeep, electricity, tax depreciation and repairs on buildings and equipment used in raising the plants, farm overhead, taxes (except state and Federal income taxes), and interest required to be capitalized under section 263A(f).

(ii) *Animals.*—The costs of producing an animal typically required to be capitalized under section 263A include the costs incurred so that the animal's raising process may begin (preparatory costs), such as the acquisition costs of the animal, and the costs of raising or caring for such animal during the preproductive period (preproductive period costs). Preproductive period costs include, but are not limited to, management, feed (such as grain, silage, concentrates, supplements, haylage, hay, pasture and other forages), maintaining pasture or pen areas (including costs that the taxpayer has elected to deduct under sections 175 or 180), breeding, artificial insemination, veterinary services and medicine, livestock hauling, bedding, fuel, electricity, hired labor, tax depreciation and repairs on buildings and equipment used in raising the animals (for example, barns, trucks, and trailers), farm overhead, taxes (except state and Federal income taxes), and interest required to be capitalized under section 263A(f).

(2) *Preproductive period.*—(i) *Plant.*—(A) *In general.*—The preproductive period of property produced in a farming business means—

(1) In the case of a plant that will have more than one crop or yield (for example, an orange tree), the period before the first marketable crop or yield from such plant;

(2) In the case of the crop or yield of a plant that will have more than one crop or yield (for example, the orange), the period before such crop or yield is disposed of; or

(3) In the case of any other plant, the period before such plant is disposed of.

(B) *Applicability of section 263A.*—For purposes of determining whether a plant has a preproductive period in excess of 2 years, the preproductive period of plants grown in commercial quantities in the United States is based on the nationwide weighted average preproductive period for such plant. The Commissioner will publish a noninclusive list of plants with a nationwide weighted average preproductive period in excess of 2 years. In the case of other plants grown in commercial quantities in the United States, the nationwide weighted average preproductive period must be determined based on available statistical data. For all other plants, the taxpayer is required, at or before the time the seed or plant is acquired or planted, to reasonably estimate the preproductive period of the plant. If the taxpayer estimates a preproductive period in excess of 2 years, the taxpayer must capitalize the costs of producing the plant. If the estimate is reasonable, based on the facts in existence at the time it is made, the determination of whether section 263A applies is not modified at a later time even if the actual length of the preproductive period differs from the estimate. The actual length of the preproductive period will, however, be considered in evaluating the reasonableness of the taxpayer's future estimates. The nationwide weighted average preproductive period or the estimated preproductive period is only used for purposes of determining whether the preproductive period of a plant is greater than 2 years.

(C) *Actual preproductive period.*—The plant's actual preproductive period is used for purposes of determining the period during which a taxpayer must capitalize preproductive period costs with respect to a particular plant.

(1) *Beginning of the preproductive period.*—The actual preproductive period of a plant begins when the taxpayer first incurs costs that directly benefit or are incurred by reason of the plant. Generally, this occurs when the taxpayer plants the seed or plant. In the case of a taxpayer that acquires plants that have already been permanently planted, or plants that are tended by the taxpayer or another prior to permanent planting, the actual preproductive period of the plant begins upon acquisition of the plant by the taxpayer. In the case of the crop or yield of a plant that will have more than one crop or yield, the actual preproductive period begins when the plant has become productive in marketable quantities and the crop or yield first appears, for example, in the form of a sprout, bloom, blossom, or bud.

(2) *End of the preproductive period.*—(i) *In general.*—In the case of a plant that will have more than one crop or yield, the actual preproductive period ends when the plant first becomes productive in marketable quantities. In the case of any other plant (including the crop or yield of a plant that will have more than one crop or yield), the actual preproductive period ends when the plant, crop, or yield is sold or otherwise disposed of. Field costs, such as irrigating, fertilizing, spraying and pruning, that are incurred after the harvest of a crop or yield but before the crop or yield is sold or otherwise disposed of are not required to be included in the preproductive period costs of the harvested crop or yield because they do not benefit and are unrelated to the harvested crop or yield.

(ii) *Marketable quantities.*—A plant that will have more than one crop or yield becomes productive in marketable quantities once a crop or yield is produced in sufficient quantities to be harvested and marketed in the ordinary course of the taxpayer's business. Factors that are relevant to determining whether a crop or yield is produced in sufficient quantities to be harvested and marketed in the ordinary course include: whether the crop or yield is harvested that is more than *de minimis*, although it may be less than expected at the maximum bearing stage, based on a comparison of the quantities per acre harvested in the year in question to the quantities per acre expected to be harvested when the plant reaches full maturity; and whether the sales proceeds exceed the costs of harvest and make a reasonable contribution to an allocable share of farm expenses.

(D) *Examples.*—The following examples illustrate the provisions of this paragraph (b)(2):

Example 1. (i) Farmer A, a taxpayer that qualifies for the exception in paragraph (a)(2) of this section, grows plants that will have more than one crop or yield. The plants are grown in commercial quantities in the United States. Farmer A acquires 1 year-old plants by purchasing them from an unrelated party, Corporation B, and plants them immediately. The nationwide weighted average preproductive period of the plant is 4 years. The particular plants grown by Farmer A do not begin to produce in marketable quantities until 3 years and 6 months after they are planted by Farmer A.

(ii) Since the plants are deemed to have a preproductive period in excess of 2 years, Farmer A is required to capitalize the costs of producing the plants. See paragraphs (a)(2) and (b)(2)(i)(B) of this section. In accordance with paragraph (b)(2)(i)(C)(1) of this section, Farmer A must begin to capitalize the preproductive period costs when the plants are planted. In accordance with paragraph (b)(2)(i)(C)(2) of this section, Farmer A must continue to capitalize preproductive period costs to the plants until the plants begin to produce in marketable quantities. Thus, Farmer A must capitalize the preproductive period costs for a period of 3 years and 6 months (that is, until the plants are 4 years and 6 months old), notwithstanding the fact that the plants, in general, have a nationwide weighted average preproductive period of 4 years.

Example 2. (i) Farmer B, a taxpayer that qualifies for the exception in paragraph (a)(2) of this section, grows plants that will have more than one crop or yield. The plants are grown in commercial quantities in the United States. The nationwide weighted average preproductive period of the plant is 2 years and 5 months. Farmer B acquires 1 month-old plants by purchasing them from an unrelated party, Corporation B. Farmer B enters into a contract with Corporation B under which Corporation B will retain and tend the plants for 7 months following the sale. At the end of 7 months, Farmer B takes possession of the plants and plants them in the permanent orchard. The plants become productive in marketable quantities 1 year and 11 months after they are planted by Farmer B.

(ii) Since the plants are deemed to have a preproductive period in excess of 2 years, Farmer B is required to capitalize the costs of producing the plants. See paragraphs (a)(2) and (b)(2)(i)(B) of this section. In accordance with paragraph (b)(2)(i)(C)(1) of this section, Farmer B must begin to capitalize the preproductive period costs when the purchase occurs. In accordance with paragraph (b)(2)(i)(C)(2) of this section, Farmer B must continue to capitalize the preproductive period costs to the plants until the plants begin to produce in marketable quantities. Thus, Farmer B must capitalize the preproductive period costs of the plants for a period of 2 years and 6 months (the 7 months the plants are tended by Corporation B and the 1 year and 11 months after the plants are planted by Farmer B), that is, until the plants are 2 years and 7 months old, notwithstanding the fact that the plants, in general, have a nationwide weighted average preproductive period of 2 years and 5 months.

Example 3. (i) Assume the same facts as in *Example* 2, except that Farmer B acquires the plants by purchasing them from Corporation B when the plants are 8 months old and that the plants are planted by Farmer B upon acquisition.

(ii) Since the plants are deemed to have a preproductive period in excess of 2 years, Farmer B is required to capitalize the costs of producing the plants. See paragraphs (a)(2) and (b)(2)(i)(B) of this section. In accordance with paragraph (b)(2)(i)(C)(1) of this section, Farmer B must begin to capitalize the preproductive period costs when the plants are planted. In accordance with paragraph (b)(2)(i)(C)(2) of this section, Farmer B must continue to capitalize the preproductive period costs to the plants until the plants begin to produce in marketable quantities. Thus, Farmer B must capitalize the preproductive period costs of the plants for a period of 1 year and 11 months.

Example 4. (i) Farmer C, a taxpayer that qualifies for the exception in paragraph (a)(2) of this section, grows plants that will have more than one crop or yield. The plants are grown in commercial quantities in the United States. Farmer C acquires 1 month-old plants from an unrelated party and plants them immediately. The nationwide weighted average preproductive period of the plant is 2 years and 3 months. The particular plants grown by Farmer C begin to produce in marketable quantities 1 year and 10 months after they are planted by Farmer C.

(ii) Since the plants are deemed to have a nationwide weighted average preproductive period in excess of 2 years, Farmer C is required to capitalize the costs of producing the plants, notwithstanding the fact that the particular plants grown by Farmer C become productive in less than 2 years. See paragraph (b)(2)(i)(B) of this section. In accordance with paragraph (b)(2)(i)(C)(1) of this section, Farmer C must begin to capitalize the preproductive period costs when it plants the plants. In accordance with paragraph (b)(2)(i)(C)(2) of this section, Farmer C properly ceases capitalization of preproductive period costs when the plants become productive in marketable quantities (that is, 1 year and 10 months after they are planted, which is when they are 1 year and 11 months old).

Example 5. (i) Farmer D, a taxpayer that qualifies for the exception in paragraph (a)(2) of this section, grows plants that will have more than one crop or yield. The plants are not grown in commercial quantities in the United States. Farmer D acquires and plants the plants when they are 1 year old and estimates that they will become productive in marketable quantities 3 years after planting. Thus, at the time the plants are acquired and planted Farmer D reasonably estimates that the plants will have a preproductive period of 4 years. The actual plants grown by Farmer D do not begin to produce in marketable quantities until 3 years and 6 months after they are planted by Farmer D.

(ii) Since the plants have an estimated preproductive period in excess of 2 years, Farmer D is required to capitalize the costs of producing the plants. See paragraph (b)(2)(i)(B) of this section. In accordance with paragraph (b)(2)(i)(C)(1) of this section, Farmer D must begin to capitalize the preproductive period costs when it acquires and plants the plants. In accordance with paragraph (b)(2)(i)(C)(2) of this section, Farmer D must continue to capitalize the preproductive period costs until the plants begin to produce in marketable quantities. Thus, Farmer D must capitalize the preproductive period costs of the plants for a period of 3 years and 6 months (that is, until the plants are 4 years and 6 months old), notwithstanding the fact that Farmer D estimated that the plants would become productive after 4 years.

Example 6. (i) Farmer E, a taxpayer that qualifies for the exception in paragraph (a)(2) of this section grows plants from seed. The plants are not grown in commercial quantities in the United States. The plants do not have more than 1 crop or yield. At the time the seeds are planted Farmer E reasonably estimates that the plants will have a preproductive period of 1 year and 10 months. The actual plants grown by Farmer E are not ready for harvesting and disposal until 2 years and 2 months after the seeds are planted by Farmer E.

(ii) Because Farmer E's estimate of the preproductive period (which was 2 years or less) was reasonable at the time made based on the facts, Farmer E will not be required to capitalize the costs of producing the plants under section 263A, notwithstanding the fact that the actual preproductive period of the plants exceeded 2 years. See paragraph (b)(2)(i)(B) of this section. However, Farmer E must take the actual preproductive period of the plants into consideration when making future estimates of the preproductive period of such plants.

Example 7. (i) Farmer F, a calendar year taxpayer that does not qualify for the exception in paragraph (a)(2) of this section, grows trees that will have more than one crop. Farmer F acquires and plants the trees in April, Year 1. On October 1, Year 6, the trees become productive in marketable quantities.

(ii) The costs of producing the plant, including the preproductive period costs incurred by Farmer F on or before October 1, Year 6, are capitalized to the trees. Preproductive period costs incurred after October 1, Year 6, are capitalized to a crop when incurred during the preproductive period of the crop and deducted as a cost of maintaining the tree when incurred between the disposal of one crop and the appearance of the next crop. See paragraphs (b)(2)(i)(A), (b)(2)(i)(C)(1) and (b)(2)(i)(C)(2) of this section.

Example 8. (i) Farmer G, a taxpayer that qualifies for the exception in paragraph (a)(2) of this section, produces fig trees on 10 acres of land. The fig trees are grown in commercial quantities in the United States and have a nationwide weighted average preproductive period in excess of 2 years. Farmer G acquires and plants the fig trees in their permanent grove during Year 1. When the fig trees are mature, Farmer G expects to harvest 10x tons of figs per acre. At the end of Year 4, Farmer G harvests .5x tons of figs per acre that it sells for $100x. During Year 4, Former G incurs expenses related to the fig operation of: $50x to harvest the figs and transport them to market and other direct and indirect costs related to the fig operation in the amount of $1000x.

(ii) Since the fig trees have a preproductive period in excess of 2 years, Farmer G is required to capitalize the costs of producing the fig trees. See paragraphs (a)(2) and (b)(2)(i)(B) of this section. In accordance with paragraph (b)(2)(i)(C)(2) of this section, Farmer G must continue to capitalize preproductive period costs to the trees until they become productive in marketable quantities. The following factors weigh in favor of a determination that the fig trees did not become productive in Year 4: the quantity of harvested figs is *de minimis* based on the fact that the yield is only 5 percent of the expected yield at maturity and the proceeds from the sale of the figs are sufficient, after covering the costs of harvesting and transporting the figs, to cover only a negligible portion of the allocable farm expenses. Based on these facts and circumstances, the fig trees did not become productive in marketable quantities in Year 4.

(ii) *Animal.*—An animal's actual preproductive period is used to determine the period that the taxpayer must capitalize preproductive period costs with respect to a particular animal.

(A) *Beginning of the preproductive period.*—The preproductive period of an animal begins at the time of acquisition, breeding, or embryo implantation.

(B) *End of the preproductive period.*—In the case of an animal that will be used in the trade or business of farming (for example, a dairy cow), the preproductive period generally ends when the animal is (or would be considered) placed in service for purposes of section 168 (without regard to the applicable convention). However, in the case of an animal that will have more than one yield (for example, a breeding cow), the preproductive period ends when the animal produces (for example, gives birth to) its first yield. In the case of any other animal, the preproductive period ends when the animal is sold or otherwise disposed of.

(C) *Allocation of costs between animal and yields.*—In the case of an animal that will have more than one yield, the costs incurred after the beginning of the preproductive period of the first yield but before the end of the preproductive period of the animal must be allocated between the animal and the yield using any reasonable method. Any depreciation allowance on the animal may be allocated entirely to the yield. Costs incurred after the beginning of the preproductive period of the second yield, but before the first yield is weaned from the animal must be allocated between the first and second yield using any reasonable method. However, a taxpayer may elect to allocate these costs entirely to the second yield. An allocation method used by a taxpayer is a method of accounting that must be used consistently and is subject to the rules of section 446 and the regulations thereunder.

(c) *Inventory methods.*—(1) *In general.*—Except as otherwise provided, the costs required to be allocated to any plant or animal under this section may be determined using reasonable inventory valuation methods such as the farm-price method or the unit-livestock-price method. See §1.471-6. Under the unit-livestock-price method, unit prices must include all costs required to be capitalized under section 263A. A taxpayer using the unit-livestock-price method may elect to use the cost allocation methods in §1.263A-1(f) or 1.263A-2(b) to allocate its direct and indirect costs to the property produced in the business of farming. In such a situation, section 471 costs are the costs taken into account by the taxpayer under the unit-livestock-price method using the taxpayer's standard unit price as modified by this paragraph (c)(1). Tax shelters, as defined in paragraph (a)(2)(ii) of this section, that use the unit-livestock-price method for inventories must include in inventory the annual standard unit price for all animals that are acquired during the taxable year, regardless of whether the purchases are made during the last 6 months of the taxable year. Taxpayers required by section 447 to use an accrual method or prohibited by section 448(a)(3) from using the cash method that use the unit-livestock-price method must modify the annual standard price in order to reasonably reflect the particular period in the taxable year in which purchases of livestock are made, if such modification is necessary in order to avoid significant distortions in income that would otherwise occur through operation of the unit-livestock-price method.

(2) *Available for property used in a trade or business.*—The farm-price method or the unit-livestock-price method may be used by any taxpayer to allocate costs to any plant or animal under this section, regardless of whether the plant or animal is held or treated as inventory property by the taxpayer. Thus, for example, a taxpayer may use the unit-livestock-price method to account for the costs of raising livestock that will be used in the trade or business of farming (for example, a breeding animal or a dairy cow) even though the property in question is not inventory property.

(3) *Exclusion of property to which section 263A does not apply.*—Notwithstanding a taxpayer's use of the farm-price method with respect to farm property to which the provisions of section 263A apply, that taxpayer is not required, solely by such use, to use the farm-price method with respect to farm property to which the provisions of section 263A do not apply. Thus, for example, assume Farmer A raises fruit trees that have a preproductive period in excess of 2 years and to which the provisions of section 263A, therefore, apply. Assume also that Farmer A raises cattle is not required to use an accrual method by section 447 or prohibited from using the cash method by section 448(a)(3). Because Farmer A qualifies for the exception in paragraph (a)(2) of this section, Farmer A is not required to capitalize the costs of raising the cattle. Although Farmer A may use the farm-price method with respect to the fruit trees, Farmer A is not required to use the farm-price method with respect to the cattle. Instead, Farmer A's accounting for the cattle is determined under other provisions of the Code and regulations.

(d) *Election not to have section 263A apply under section 263A(d)(3).*—(1) *Introduction.*—This paragraph (d) permits certain taxpayers to make an election not to have the rules of this section apply to any plant produced in a farming business conducted by the electing taxpayer. Except as provided in paragraph (d)(5) and (6) of this section, the election is a method of accounting under section 446. An election made under section 263A(d)(3) and this paragraph (d) is revocable only with the consent of the Commissioner.

(2) *Availability of the election.*—The election described in this paragraph (d) is available to any taxpayer that produces plants in a farming business, except that no election may be made by a corporation, partnership, or tax shelter required to use an accrual method under section 447 or prohibited from using the cash method by section 448(a)(3). Moreover, the election does not apply to the costs of planting, cultivation, maintenance, or development of a citrus or almond grove (or any part thereof) incurred prior to the close of the fourth taxable year beginning with the taxable year in which the trees were planted in the permanent grove (including costs incurred prior to the permanent planting). If a citrus or almond grove is planted in more than one taxable year, the portion of the grove planted in any one taxable year is treated as a separate grove for purposes of determining the year of planting.

(3) *Time and manner of making the election.*—(i) *Automatic election.*—A taxpayer makes the election under this paragraph (d) by not applying the rules of section 263A to determine the capitalized costs of plants produced in a farming business and by applying the special rules in paragraph (d)(4) of this section on its original return for the first taxable year in which the taxpayer is otherwise required to capitalize section 263A costs. Thus, in order to be treated as having made the election under this paragraph (d), it is necessary to report both income and expenses in accordance with the rules of this paragraph (d) (for example, it is necessary to use the alternative depreciation system as provided in paragraph (d)(4)(ii) of this section). For example, a farmer who deducts costs that are otherwise required to be capitalized under section 263A but fails to use the alternative depreciation system under section 168(g)(2) for applicable property placed in service has not made an election under this paragraph (d) and is not in compliance with the provisions of section 263A.

(ii) *Nonautomatic election.*—Except as provided in paragraphs (d)(5) and (6) of this section, a taxpayer that does not make the election under this paragraph (d) as provided in paragraph (d)(3)(i) of this section must obtain the consent of the Commissioner to make the election by filing a Form 3115, *Application for Change in Method of Accounting,* in accordance with §1.446-1(e)(3).

(4) *Special rules.*—If the election under this paragraph (d) is made, the taxpayer is subject to the special rules in this paragraph (d)(4).

(i) *Section 1245 treatment.*—The plant produced by the taxpayer is treated as section 1245 property and any gain resulting from any disposition of the plant is recaptured (that is, treated as ordinary income) to the extent of the total amount of the deductions that, but for the election, would have been required to be capitalized with respect to the plant. In calculating the amount of gain that is recaptured under this paragraph (d)(4)(i), a taxpayer may use the farm-price method or another simplified method permitted under these regulations in determining the deductions that otherwise would have been capitalized with respect to the plant.

(ii) *Required use of alternative depreciation system.*—If the taxpayer or a related person makes an election under this paragraph (d), the alternative depreciation system (as defined in section 168(g)(2)) must be applied to all property used predominantly in any farming business of the taxpayer or related person and placed in service in any taxable year during which the election is in effect. The requirement to use the alternative depreciation system by reason of an election under this paragraph (d) will not prevent a taxpayer from making an election under section 179 to deduct certain depreciable business assets.

(iii) *Related person.*—(A) *In general.*—For purposes of this paragraph (d)(4), related person means—

(1) The taxpayer and members of the taxpayer's family;

(2) Any corporation (including an S corporation) if 50 percent or more of the stock (in value) is owned directly or indirectly (through the application of section 318) by the taxpayer or members of the taxpayer's family;

(3) A corporation and any other corporation that is a member of the same controlled group (within the meaning of section 1563(a)(1)); and

(4) Any partnership if 50 percent or more (in value) of the interests in such partnership is owned directly or indirectly by the taxpayer or members of the taxpayer's family.

(B) *Members of family.*—For purposes of this paragraph (d)(4)(iii), the terms "members of the taxpayer's family", and "members of family" (for purposes of applying section 318(a)(1)), means the spouse of the taxpayer (other than a spouse who is legally separated from the individual under a decree of divorce or separate maintenance) and any of the taxpayer's children (including legally adopted children) who have not reached the age of 18 as of the last day of the taxable year in question.

(5) *Revocation of section 263A(d)(3) election to permit exemption under section 263A(i).*—A taxpayer that elected under section 263A(d)(3) and paragraph (d)(3) of this section not to have section 263A apply to any plant produced in a farming business that wants to revoke its section 263A(d)(3) election, and in the same taxable year, apply the small business taxpayer exemption under section 263A(i) and §1.263A-1(j) may revoke the election in accordance with the applicable administrative guidance as published in the Internal Revenue Bulletin (*see* §601.601(d)(2)(ii)(b) of this chapter). A revocation of the taxpayer's section 263A(d)(3) election under this paragraph (d)(5) is not a change in method of accounting under sections 446 and 481 and §§1.446-1 and 1.481-1 through 1.481-5.

(6) *Change from applying exemption under section 263A(i) to making a section 263A(d)(3) election.*—A taxpayer whose method of accounting is to not capitalize costs under section 263A based on the exemption under section 263A(i), that becomes ineligible to use the exemption under section 263A(i), and is eligible and wants to elect under section 263A(d)(3) for this same taxable year to not capitalize costs under section 263A for any plant produced in the taxpayer's farming business, must make the election in accordance with the applicable administrative guidance as published in the Internal Revenue Bulletin (*see* §601.601(d)(2)(ii)(b) of this chapter). An election under section 263A(d)(3) made in accordance with this paragraph (d)(6) is not a change in method of accounting under sections 446 and 481 and §§1.446-1 and 1.481-1 through 1.481-5.

(7) *Examples.*—The following examples illustrate the provisions of this paragraph (d):
Example 1. (i) Farmer A, an individual, is engaged in the trade or business of farming. Farmer A grows apple trees that have a preproductive period greater than 2 years. In addition, Farmer A grows and harvests wheat and other grains. Farmer A elects under this paragraph (d) not to have the rules of section 263A apply to the costs of growing the apple trees.

(ii) In accordance with paragraph (d)(4) of this section, Farmer A is required to use the alternative depreciation system described in section 168(g)(2) with respect to all property used predominantly in any farming business in which Farmer A engages (including the growing and harvesting of wheat) if such property is placed in service during a year for which the election is in effect. Thus, for example, all assets and equipment (including trees and any equipment used to grow and harvest wheat) placed in service during a year for which the election is in effect must be depreciated as provided in section 168(g)(2).

Example 2. Assume the same facts as in *Example 1,* except that Farmer A and members of Farmer A's family (as defined in paragraph (d)(4)(iii)(B) of this section) also own 51 percent (in value) of the interests in Partnership P, which is engaged in the trade or business of growing and harvesting corn. Partnership P is a related person to Farmer A under the provisions of paragraph (d)(4)(iii) of this section. Thus, the requirements to use the alternative depreciation system under section 168(g)(2) also apply to any property used predominantly in a trade or business of farming which Partnership P places in service during a year for which an election made by Farmer A is in effect.

(e) *Exception for certain costs resulting from casualty losses.*—(1) *In general.*—Section 263A does not require the capitalization of costs that are attributable to the replanting, cultivating, maintaining, and developing of any plants bearing an edible crop for human consumption (including, but not limited to, plants that constitute a grove, orchard, or vineyard) that were lost or damaged while owned by the taxpayer by reason of freezing temperatures, disease, drought, pests, or other casualty (replanting costs). Such replanting costs may be incurred with respect to property other than the property on which the damage or loss occurred to the extent the acreage of the property with respect to which the replanting costs are incurred is not in excess of the acreage of the property on which the damage or loss occurred. This paragraph (e) applies only to the replanting of plants of the same type as those lost or damaged. This paragraph (e) applies to plants replanted on the property on which the damage or loss occurred or property of the same or lesser acreage in the United States irrespective of differences in density between the lost or damaged and replanted plants. Plants bearing crops for human consumption are those crops normally eaten or drunk by humans. Thus, for example, costs incurred with respect to replanting plants bearing

jojoba beans do not qualify for the exception provided in this paragraph (e) because that crop is not normally eaten or drunk by humans.

(2) *Ownership.*—Replanting costs described in paragraph (e)(1) of this section generally must be incurred by the taxpayer that owned the property at the time the plants were lost or damaged. Paragraph (e)(1) of this section will apply, however, to costs incurred by a person other than the taxpayer that owned the plants at the time of damage or loss if—

(i) The taxpayer that owned the plants at the time the damage or loss occurred owns an equity interest of more than 50 percent in such plants at all times during the taxable year in which the replanting costs are paid or incurred; and

(ii) Such other person owns any portion of the remaining equity interest and materially participates in the replanting, cultivating, maintaining, or developing of such plants during the taxable year in which the replanting costs are paid or incurred. A person will be treated as materially participating for purposes of this provision if such person would otherwise meet the requirements with respect to material participation within the meaning of section 2032A(e)(6).

(3) *Examples.*—The following examples illustrate the provisions of this paragraph (e):
Example 1. (i) Farmer A grows cherry trees that have a preproductive period in excess of 2 years and produce an annual crop. These cherries are normally eaten by humans. Farmer A grows the trees on a 100 acre parcel of land (parcel 1) and the groves of trees cover the entire acreage of parcel 1. Farmer A also owns a 150 acre parcel of land (parcel 2) that Farmer A holds for future use. Both parcels are in the United States. In 2000, the trees and the irrigation and drainage systems that service the trees are destroyed in a casualty (within the meaning of paragraph (e)(1) of this section). Farmer A installs new irrigation and drainage systems on parcel 1, purchases young trees (seedlings), and plants the seedlings on parcel 1.

(ii) The costs of the irrigation and drainage systems and the seedlings must be capitalized. In accordance with paragraph (e)(1) of this section, the costs of planting, cultivating, developing, and maintaining the seedlings during their preproductive period are not required to be capitalized by section 263A.

Example 2. (i) Assume the same facts as in *Example 1* except that Farmer A decides to replant the seedlings on parcel 2 rather than on parcel 1. Accordingly, Farmer A installs the new irrigation and drainage systems on 100 acres of parcel 2 and plants seedlings on those 100 acres.

(ii) The costs of the irrigation and drainage systems and the seedlings must be capitalized. Because the acreage of the related portion of parcel 2 does not exceed the acreage of the destroyed orchard on parcel 1, the costs of planting, cultivating, developing, and maintaining the seedlings during their preproductive period are not required to be capitalized by section 263A. See paragraph (e)(1) of this section.

Example 3. (i) Assume the same facts as in *Example 1* except that Farmer A replants the seedlings on parcel 2 rather than on parcel 1, and Farmer A additionally decides to expand its operations by growing 125 rather than 100 acres of trees. Accordingly, Farmer A installs new irrigation and drainage systems on 125 acres of parcel 2 and plants seedlings on those 125 acres.

(ii) The costs of the irrigation and drainage systems and the seedlings must be capitalized. The costs of planting, cultivating, developing, and maintaining 100 acres of the trees during their preproductive period are not required to be capitalized by section 263A. The costs of planting, cultivating, maintaining, and developing the additional 25 acres are, however, subject to capitalization under section 263A. See paragraph (e)(1) of this section.

(4) *Special rule for citrus and almond groves.*—(i) *In general.*—The exception in this paragraph (e) is available with respect to replanting costs of a citrus or almond grove incurred prior to the close of the fourth taxable year after replanting, notwithstanding the taxpayer's election to have section 263A not apply (described in paragraph (d) of this section).

(ii) *Example.*—The following example illustrates the provisions of this paragraph (e)(4):
Example. (i) Farmer A, an individual, is engaged in the trade or business of farming. Farmer A grows citrus trees that have a preproductive period of 5 years. Farmer A elects, under paragraph (d) of this section, not to have section 263A apply. This election, however, is unavailable with respect to the costs of producing a citrus grove incurred within the first 4 years beginning with the year the trees were planted. See paragraph (d)(2) of this section. In year 10, after the citrus grove has become productive in marketable quantities, the citrus grove is destroyed by a casualty within the meaning of paragraph (e)(1) of this section. In year 10, Farmer A acquires and

plants young citrus trees in the same grove to replace those destroyed by the casualty.

(ii) Farmer A must capitalize the costs of producing the citrus grove incurred before the close of the fourth taxable year beginning with the year in which the trees were permanently planted. As a result of the election not to have section 263A apply, Farmer A may deduct the preproductive period costs incurred in the fifth year. In year 10, Farmer A must capitalize the acquisition cost of the young trees. However, the costs of planting, cultivating, developing, and maintaining the young trees that replace those destroyed by the casualty are exempted from capitalization under this paragraph (e).

(5) *Special temporary rule for citrus plants lost by reason of casualty.*—Section 263A(d)(2)(A) provides that if plants bearing an edible crop for human consumption were lost or damaged while in the hands of the taxpayer by reason of freezing temperatures, disease, drought, pests, or casualty, section 263A does not apply to any costs of the taxpayer of replanting plants bearing the same type of crop (whether on the same parcel of land on which such lost or damaged plants were located or any other parcel of land of the same acreage in the United States). The rules of this paragraph (e)(5) apply to certain costs that are paid or incurred after December 22, 2017, and on or before December 22, 2027, to replant citrus plants after the loss or damage of citrus plants. Notwithstanding paragraph (e)(2) of this section, in the case of replanting citrus plants after the loss or damage of citrus plants by reason of freezing temperatures, disease, drought, pests, or casualty, section 263A does not apply to replanting costs paid or incurred by a taxpayer other than the owner described in section 263A(d)(2)(A) if—

(i) The owner described in section 263A(d)(2)(A) has an equity interest of not less than 50 percent in the replanted citrus plants at all times during the taxable year in which such amounts were paid or incurred and the taxpayer holds any part of the remaining equity interest; or

(ii) The taxpayer acquired the entirety of the equity interest in the land of that owner described in section 263A(d)(2)(A) and on which land the lost or damaged citrus plants were located at the time of such loss or damage, and the replanting is on such land.

(f) *Change in method of accounting.*—Except as provided in paragraphs (d)(5) and (6) of this section, any change in a taxpayer's method of accounting necessary to comply with this section is a change in method of accounting to which the provisions of sections 446 and 481 and §1.446-1 through 1.446-7 and §1.481-1 through §1.481-3 apply.

(g) *Applicability dates.*—(1) *In general.*—In the case of property that is not inventory in the hands of the taxpayer, this section is applicable to costs incurred after August 21, 2000 in taxable year ending after August 21, 2000. In the case of inventory property, this section is applicable to taxable years beginning after August 21, 2000.

(2) *Changes made by Tax Cuts and Jobs Act (Pub. L. No. 115-97).*— Paragraphs (a)(3), (d)(5), (d)(6), and (e)(5) of this section apply for taxable years beginning on or after January 5, 2021. However, for a taxable year beginning after December 31, 2017, and before January 5, 2021, a taxpayer may apply the paragraphs described in the first sentence of this paragraph (g)(2), provided that the taxpayer follows all the applicable rules contained in the regulations under section 263A for such taxable year and all subsequent taxable years. [Reg. §1.263A-4.]

☐ [*T.D. 8482, 8-6-93. Amended by T.D. 8897, 8-18-2000 (corrected 10-13-2000). and T.D. 9942, 12-31-2020 (corrected 6-16-2021).*]

[Reg. §1.263A-5]

§1.263A-5. Exception for qualified creative expenses incurred by certain free-lance authors, photographers, and artists.—[Reserved]

☐ [*T.D. 8482, 8-6-93.*]

[Reg. §1.263A-6]

§1.263A-6. Rules for foreign persons.—[Reserved]

☐ [*T.D. 8482, 8-6-93.*]

[Reg. §1.263A-7]

§1.263A-7. Changing a method of accounting under section 263A.—(a) *Introduction.*—(1) *Purpose.*—These regulations provide guidance to taxpayers changing their methods of accounting for costs subject to section 263A. The principal purpose of these regulations is to provide guidance regarding how taxpayers are to revalue property on hand at the beginning of the taxable year in which they change their method of accounting for costs subject to section 263A. Paragraph (c) of this section provides guidance regarding how items or costs included in beginning inventory in the year of change must be revalued. Paragraph (d) of this section provides guidance regarding

how non-inventory property should be revalued in the year of change.

(2) *Taxpayers that adopt a method of accounting under section 263A.*—Taxpayers may adopt a method of accounting for costs subject to section 263A in the first taxable year in which they engage in resale or production activities. For purposes of this section, the adoption of a method of accounting has the same meaning as provided in §1.446-1(e)(1). Taxpayers are not subject to the provisions of these regulations to the extent they adopt, as opposed to change, a method of accounting.

(3) *Taxpayers that change a method of accounting under section 263A.*—Taxpayers changing their method of accounting for costs subject to section 263A are subject to the revaluation and other provisions of this section. Taxpayers subject to these regulations include, but are not limited to—

(i) For taxable years beginning after December 31, 2017, resellers of real or personal property or producers of real or tangible personal property whose average annual gross receipts for the immediately preceding 3-taxable-year period, or lesser period if the taxpayer was not in existence for the three preceding taxable years, annualized as required, exceed the gross receipts test of section 448(c) and the accompanying regulations where the taxpayer was not subject to section 263A in the prior taxable year;

(ii) Resellers of real or personal property that are using a method that fails to comply with section 263A and desire to change to a method of accounting that complies with section 263A;

(iii) Producers of real or tangible personal property that are using a method that fails to comply with section 263A and desire to change to a method of accounting that complies with section 263A; and

(iv) Resellers and producers that desire to change from one permissible method of accounting for costs subject to section 263A to another permissible method.

(4) *Applicability dates.*—(i) *In general.*—The provisions of this section are effective for taxable years beginning on or after August 5, 1997. For taxable years beginning before August 5, 1997, the rules of §1.263A-7T contained in the 26 CFR part 1 edition revised as of April 1, 1997, as modified by other administrative guidance, will apply.

(ii) *Changes made by Tax Cuts and Jobs Act (Pub. L. No. 115-97).*—Paragraph (a)(3)(i) of this section applies to taxable years beginning on or after January 5. 2021. However, for a taxable year beginning after December 31, 2017, and before January 5, 2021, a taxpayer may apply the paragraph described in the first sentence of this paragraph (a)(4)(ii), provided that the taxpayer follows all the applicable rules contained in the regulations under section 263A for such taxable year and all subsequent taxable years.

(5) *Definition of change in method of accounting.*—For purposes of this section, a change in method of accounting has the same meaning as provided in §1.446-1(e)(2)(ii). Changes in method of accounting for costs subject to section 263A include changes to methods required or permitted by section 263A and the regulations thereunder. Changes in method of accounting may be described in the preceding sentence irrespective of whether the taxpayer's previous method of accounting resulted in the capitalization of more (or fewer) costs than the costs required to be capitalized under section 263A and the regulations thereunder, and irrespective of whether the taxpayer's previous method of accounting was a permissible method under the law in effect when the method was being used. However, changes in method of accounting for costs subject to section 263A do not include changes relating to factors other than those described therein. For example, a change in method of accounting for costs subject to section 263A does not include a change from one inventory identification method to another inventory identification method, such as a change from the last-in, first-out (LIFO) method to the first-in, first-out (FIFO) method, or vice versa, or a change from one inventory valuation method to another inventory valuation method under section 471, such as a change from valuing inventory at cost to valuing the inventory at cost or market, whichever is lower, or vice versa. In addition, a change in method of accounting for costs subject to section 263A does not include a change within the LIFO inventory method, such as a change from the double extension method to the link-chain method, or a change in the method used for determining the number of pools. Further, a change from the modified resale method set forth in Notice 89-67 (1989-1 C.B. 723), see §601.601(d)(2) of this chapter, to the simplified resale method set forth in §1.263A-3(d) is not a change in method of accounting within the meaning of §1.446-1(e)(2)(ii) and is therefore not subject to the provisions of this section. However, a change from the simplified resale method set forth in former §1.263A-1T(d)(4) to the simplified resale method set forth in §1.263A-3(c) is a change in method of accounting

within the meaning of §1.446-1(e)(2)(ii) and is subject to the provisions of this section.

(b) *Rules applicable to a change in method of accounting.*—(1) *General rules.*—All changes in method of accounting for costs subject to section 263A are subject to the rules and procedures provided by the Code, regulations, and administrative procedures applicable to such changes. The Internal Revenue Service has issued specific revenue procedures that govern certain accounting method changes for costs subject to section 263A. Where a specific revenue procedure is not applicable, changes in method of accounting for costs subject to section 263A are subject to the same rules and procedures that govern other accounting method changes. See Revenue Procedure 2015-13 (2015-5 IRB 419) and §601.601(d)(2) of this chapter.

(2) *Special rules.*—(i) *Ordering rules when multiple changes in method of accounting occur in the year of change.*—(A) *In general.*—A change in method of accounting for costs subject to section 263A is generally deemed to occur (including the computation of the adjustment under section 481(a)) before any other change in method of accounting is deemed to occur for that same taxable year.

(B) *Exceptions to the general ordering rule.*—(1) *Change from the LIFO inventory method.*—In the case of a taxpayer that is discontinuing its use of the LIFO inventory method in the same taxable year it is changing its method of accounting for costs subject to section 263A, the change from the LIFO method may be made before the change in method of accounting (and the computation of the corresponding adjustment under section 481 (a)) under section 263A is made.

(2) *Change from the specific goods LIFO inventory method.*— In the case of a taxpayer that is changing from the specific goods LIFO inventory method to the dollar-value LIFO inventory method in the same taxable year it is changing its method of accounting for costs subject to section 263A, the change from the specific goods LIFO inventory method may be made before the change in method of accounting under section 263A is made.

(3) *Change in overall method of accounting.*—In the case of a taxpayer that is changing its overall method of accounting from the cash receipts and disbursements method to an accrual method in the same taxable year it is changing its method of accounting for costs subject to section 263A, the taxpayer must change to an accrual method for capitalizable costs (see §1.263A-1(c)(2)(ii)) before the change in method of accounting (and the computation of the corresponding adjustment under section 481(a)) under section 263A is made.

(4) *Change in method of accounting for depreciation.*—In the case of a taxpayer that is changing its method of accounting for depreciation in the same taxable year it is changing its method of accounting for costs subject to section 263A and any portion of the depreciation is subject to section 263A, the change in method of accounting for depreciation must be made before the change in method of accounting (and the computation of the corresponding adjustment under section 481(a)) under section 263A is made.

(ii) *Adjustment required by section 481(a).*—In the case of any taxpayer required or permitted to change its method of accounting for any taxable year under section 263A and the regulations thereunder, the change will be treated as initiated by the taxpayer for purposes of the adjustment required by section 481(a). The taxpayer must take the net section 481(a) adjustment into account over the section 481(a) adjustment period as determined under the applicable administrative procedures issued under §1.446-1(e)(3)(ii) for obtaining the Commissioner's consent to a change in accounting method (for example, see Revenue Procedure 2015-13, 2015-5 IRB 419 (or successor)) (also see §601.601(d)(2) of this chapter)). This paragraph applies to taxable years ending on or after June 16, 2004.

(iii) *Base year.*—(A) *Need for a new base year.*—Certain dollar-value LIFO taxpayers (whether using double extension or link-chain) must establish a new base year when they revalue their inventories under section 263A.

(1) *Facts and circumstances revaluation method used.*—A dollar-value LIFO taxpayer that uses the facts and circumstances revaluation method is permitted, but not required, to establish a new base year.

(2) *3-year average method used.*—(i) *Simplified method not used.*—A dollar-value LIFO taxpayer using the 3-year average method but not the simplified production method or the simplified resale method to revalue its inventory is required to establish a new base year.

(ii) *Simplified method used.*—A dollar-value LIFO taxpayer using the 3-year average method and the simplified production method, the modified simplified production method, or the simplified resale method to revalue its inventory is permitted, but not required, to establish a new base year.

(B) *Computing a new base year.*—For purposes of determining future indexes, the year of change becomes the new base year (that is, the index at the beginning of the year of change generally must be 1.00) and all costs are restated in new base year costs for purposes of extending such costs in future years. However, when a new base year is established, costs associated with old layers retain their separate identity within the base year, with such layers being restated in terms of the new base year index. For example, for purposes of determining whether a particular layer has been invaded, each layer must retain its separate identity. Thus, if a decrement in an inventory pool occurs, layers accumulated in more recent years must be viewed as invaded first, in order of priority.

(c) *Inventory.*—(1) *Need for adjustments.*—When a taxpayer changes its method of accounting for costs subject to section 263A, the taxpayer generally must, in computing its taxable income for the year of change, take into account the adjustments required by section 481(a). The adjustments required by section 481(a) relate to revaluations of inventory property, whether the taxpayer produces the inventory or acquires it for resale. See paragraph (d) of this section in regard to the adjustments required by section 481(a) that relate to non-inventory property.

(2) *Revaluing beginning inventory.*—(i) *In general.*—If a taxpayer changes its method of accounting for costs subject to section 263A, the taxpayer must revalue the items or costs included in its beginning inventory in the year of change as if the new method (that is, the method to which the taxpayer is changing) had been in effect during all prior years. In revaluing inventory costs under this procedure, all of the capitalization provisions of section 263A and the regulations thereunder apply to all inventory costs accumulated in prior years. The necessity to revalue beginning inventory as if these capitalization rules had been in effect for all prior years includes, for example, the revaluation of costs or layers incurred in taxable years preceding the transition period to the full absorption method of inventory costing as described in §1.471-11(e), regardless of whether the taxpayer employed a cut-off method under those regulations. The difference between the inventory as originally valued using the former method (that is, the method from which the taxpayer is changing) and the inventory as revalued using the new method is equal to the amount of the adjustment required under section 481(a).

(ii) *Methods to revalue inventory.*—There are three methods available to revalue inventory. The first method, the facts and circumstances revaluation method, may be used by all taxpayers. Under this method, a taxpayer determines the direct and indirect costs that must be assigned to each item of inventory based on all the facts and circumstances. This method is described in paragraph (c)(2)(iii) of this section. The second method, the weighted average method, is available only in certain situations to taxpayers using the FIFO inventory method or the specific goods LIFO inventory method. This method is described in paragraph (c)(2)(iv) of this section. The third method, the 3-year average method, is available to all taxpayers using the dollar-value LIFO inventory method of accounting. This method is described in paragraph (c)(2)(v) of this section. The weighted average method and the 3-year average method revalue inventory through processes of estimation and extrapolation, rather than based on the facts and circumstances of a particular year's data. All three methods are available regardless of whether the taxpayer elects to use a simplified method to capitalize costs under section 263A.

(iii) *Facts and circumstances revaluation method.*—(A) *In general.*—Under the facts and circumstances revaluation method, a taxpayer generally is required to revalue inventories by applying the capitalization rules of section 263A and the regulations thereunder to the production and resale activities of the taxpayer, with the same degree of specificity as required of inventory manufacturers under the law immediately prior to the effective date of the Tax Reform Act of 1986 (Public Law 99-514, 100 Stat. 2085, 1986-3 C.B. (Vol. 1)). Thus, for example, with respect to any prior year that is relevant in determining the total amount of the revalued balance as of the beginning of the year of change, the taxpayer must analyze the production and resale data for that particular year and apply the rules and principles of section 263A and the regulations thereunder to determine the appropriate revalued inventory costs. However, under the facts and circumstances revaluation method, a taxpayer may utilize reasonable estimates and procedures in valuing inventory costs if—

(1) The taxpayer lacks, and is not able to reconstruct from its books and records, actual financial and accounting data which is required to apply the capitalization rules of section 263A and the regulations thereunder to the relevant facts and circumstances surrounding a particular item of inventory or cost; and

(2) The total amounts of costs for which reasonable estimates and procedures are employed are not significant in comparison to the total restated value (including costs previously capitalized under the taxpayer's former method) of the items or costs for the period in question.

(B) *Exception.*—A taxpayer that is not able to comply with the requirement of paragraph (c)(2)(iii)(A)(2) of this section because of the existence of a significant amount of costs that would require the use of estimates and procedures must revalue its inventories under the procedures provided in paragraph (c)(2)(iv) or (v) of this section.

(C) *Estimates and procedures allowed.*—The estimates and procedures of this paragraph (c)(2)(iii) include—

(1) The use of available information from more recent years to estimate the amount and nature of inventory costs applicable to earlier years; and

(2) The use of available information with respect to comparable items of inventory produced or acquired during the same year in order to estimate the costs associated with other items of inventory.

(D) *Use by dollar-value LIFO taxpayers.*—Generally, a dollar-value LIFO taxpayer must recompute its LIFO inventory for each taxable year that the LIFO inventory method was used.

(E) *Examples.*—The provisions of this paragraph (c)(2)(iii) are illustrated by the following three examples. The principles set forth in these examples are applicable both to production and resale activities and the year of change in all three examples is 1997. The examples read as follows:

Example 1. Taxpayer X lacks information for the years 1993 and earlier, regarding the amount of costs incurred in transporting finished goods from X's factory to X's warehouse and in storing those goods at the warehouse until their sale to customers. X determines that, for 1994 and subsequent years, these transportation and storage costs constitute 4 percent of the total costs of comparable goods under X's method of accounting for such years. Under this paragraph (c)(2)(iii), X may assume that transportation and storage costs for the years 1993 and earlier constitute 4 percent of the total costs of such goods.

Example 2. Assume the same facts as in *Example 1,* except that for the year 1993 and earlier, X used a different method of accounting for inventory costs whereunder significantly fewer costs were capitalized than amounts capitalized in later years. Thus, the application of transportation and storage based on a percentage of costs for 1994 and later years would not constitute a reasonable estimate for use in earlier years. X may use the information from 1994 and later years, if appropriate adjustments are made to reflect the differences in inventory costs for the applicable years, including, for example—

(i) Increasing the percentage of costs that are intended to represent transportation and storage costs to reflect the aggregate differences in capitalized amounts under the two methods of accounting; or

(ii) Taking the absolute dollar amount of transportation and storage costs for comparable goods in inventory and applying that amount (adjusted for changes in general price levels, where appropriate) to goods associated with 1993 and prior periods.

Example 3. Taxpayer Z lacks information for certain years with respect to factory administrative costs, subject to capitalization under section 263A and the regulations thereunder, incurred in the production of inventory in factory A. Z does have sufficient information to determine factory administrative costs with respect to production of inventory in factory B, wherein inventory items were produced during the same years as factory A. Z may use the information from factory B to determine the appropriate amount of factory administrative costs to capitalize as inventory costs for comparable items produced in factory A during the same years.

(iv) *Weighted average method.*—(A) *In general.*—A taxpayer using the FIFO method or the specific goods LIFO method of accounting for inventories may use the weighted average method as provided in this paragraph (c)(2)(iv) to estimate the change in the *amount of costs that must be allocated to* inventories for prior years. The weighted average method under this paragraph (c)(2)(iv) is only available to a taxpayer that lacks sufficient data to revalue its inventory costs under the facts and circumstances revaluation method provided for in paragraph (c)(2)(iii) of this section. Moreover, a taxpayer that qualifies for the use of the weighted average method under this paragraph (c)(2)(iv) must utilize such method only with respect to items or costs for which it lacks sufficient information to revalue under the facts and circumstances revaluation method. Particular items or costs must be revalued under the facts and circumstances revaluation method if sufficient information exists to make

such a revaluation. If a taxpayer lacks sufficient information to otherwise apply the weighted average method under this paragraph (c)(2)(iv) (for example, the taxpayer is unable to revalue the costs of any of its items in inventory due to a lack of information), then the taxpayer must use reasonable estimates and procedures, as described in the facts and circumstances revaluation method, to whatever extent is necessary to allow the taxpayer to apply the weighted average method.

(B) *Weighted average method for FIFO taxpayers.*—(1) *In general.*—This paragraph (c)(2)(iv)(B) sets forth the mechanics of the weighted average method as applicable to FIFO taxpayers. Under the weighted average method, an item in ending inventory for which sufficient data is not available for revaluation under section 263A and the regulations thereunder must be revalued by using the weighted average percentage increase or decrease with respect to such item for the earliest subsequent taxable year for which sufficient data is available. With respect to an item for which no subsequent data exists, such item must be revalued by using the weighted average percentage increase or decrease with respect to all reasonably comparable items in the taxpayer's inventory for the same year or the earliest subsequent taxable year for which sufficient data is available.

(2) *Example.*—The provisions of this paragraph (c)(2)(iv)(B) are illustrated by the following example. The principles set forth in this example are applicable both to production and resale activities and the year of change in the example is 1997. The example reads as follows:

Example. Taxpayer A manufactures bolts and uses the FIFO method to identify inventories. Under A's former method, A did not capitalize all of the costs required to be capitalized under section 263A. A maintains inventories of bolts, two types of which it no longer produces. Bolt A was last produced in 1994. The revaluation of the costs of Bolt A under this section for bolts produced in 1994 results in a 20 percent increase of the costs of Bolt A. A portion of the inventory of Bolt A, however, is attributable to 1993. A does not have sufficient data for revaluation of the 1993 cost for Bolt A. With respect to Bolt A, A may apply the 20 percent increase determined for 1994 to the 1993 production as an acceptable estimate. Bolt B was last produced in 1992 and no data exists that would allow revaluation of the inventory cost of Bolt B. The inventories of all other bolts for which information is available are attributable to 1994 and 1995. Revaluation of the costs of these other bolts using available data results in an average increase in inventory costs of 15 percent for 1994 production. With respect to Bolt B, the overall 15 percent increase for A's inventory for 1994 may be used in revaluing the cost of Bolt B.

(C) *Weighted average method for specific goods LIFO taxpayers.*—(1) *In general.*—This paragraph (c)(2)(iv)(C) sets forth the mechanics of the weighted average method as applicable to LIFO taxpayers using the specific goods method of valuing inventories. Under the weighted average method, the inventory layers with respect to an item for which data is available are revalued under this section and the increase or decrease in amount for each layer is expressed as a percentage of change from the cost in the layer as originally valued. A weighted average of the percentage of change for all layers for each type of good is computed and applied to all earlier layers for each type of good that lack sufficient data to allow for revaluation. In the case of earlier layers for which sufficient data exists, such layers are to be revalued using actual data. In cases where sufficient data is not available to make a weighted average estimate with respect to a particular item of inventory, a weighted average increase or decrease is to be determined using all other inventory items revalued by the taxpayer in the same specific goods grouping. This percentage increase or decrease is then used to revalue the cost of the item for which data is lacking. If the taxpayer lacks sufficient data to revalue any of the inventory items contained in a specific goods grouping, then the weighted average increase or decrease of substantially similar items (as determined by principles similar to the rules applicable to dollar-value LIFO taxpayers in § 1.472-8(b)(3)) must be applied in the revaluation of the items in such grouping. If insufficient data exists with respect to all the items in a specific goods grouping and to all items that are substantially similar (or such items do not exist), then the weighted average for all revalued items in the taxpayer's inventory must be applied in revaluing items for which data is lacking.

(2) *Example.*—The provisions of this paragraph (c)(2)(iv)(C) are illustrated by the following example. The principles set forth in this example are applicable both to production and resale activities and the year of change in the example is 1997. The example reads as follows:

Example. (i) Taxpayer M is a manufacturer that produces two different parts. Under M's former method, M did not capitalize all of the costs required to be capitalized under section 263A. Work-in-process inventory is recorded in terms of equivalent units of finished goods. M's records show the following at the end of 1996 under the specific goods LIFO inventory method:

LIFO
Product and layer

	Number	Cost	Carrying values
Product #1:			
1993	150	$5.00	$750
1994	100	6.00	600
1995	100	6.50	650
1996	50	7.00	350
			$2,350
Product #2:			
1993	200	$4.00	$800
1994	200	4.50	900
1995	100	5.00	500
1996	100	6.00	600
			$2,800

Total carrying value of Products #1 and #2
under M's former Method $5,150

(ii) M has sufficient data to revalue the unit costs of Product #1 using its new method for 1994, 1995 and 1996. These costs are: $7.00 in 1994, $7.75 in 1995, and $9.00 in 1996. This data for Product #1 results in a weighted average percentage change of 20.31 percent [(100 × ($7.00 – $6.00)) + (100 × ($7.75 – $6.50)) + (50 × ($9.00 – $7.00)) divided by (100 × $6.00) + (100 × $6.50) + (50 × $7.00)]. M has sufficient data to revalue the unit costs of Product #2 only in 1995 and 1996. These costs are: $6.00 in 1995 and $7.00 in 1996. This data for Product #2 results in a weighted average percentage change of 18.18 percent [(100 × ($6.00 – $5.00)) + (100 × ($7.00 – $6.00)) divided by (100 × $5.00) + (100 × $6.00)].

(iii) M can estimate its revalued costs for Product #1 for 1993 by applying the weighted average increase computed for Product #1 (20.31 percent) to the unit costs originally carried on M's records for 1993 under M's former method. The estimated revalued unit cost of Product #1 would be $6.02 ($5.00 × 1.2031). M estimates its revalued costs for Product #2 for 1993 and 1994 in a similar fashion. M applies the weighted average increase determined for Product #2 (18.18 percent) to the unit costs of $4.00 and $4.50 for 1993 and 1994 respectively. The revalued unit costs of Product #2 are $4.73 for 1993 ($4.00 × 1.1818) and $5.32 for 1994 ($4.50 × 1.1818).

(iv) M's inventory would be revalued as follows:

LIFO
Product and layer

	Number	Cost	Carrying values
Product #1:			
1993	150	$6.02	$903
1994	100	7.00	700
1995	100	7.75	775
1996	50	9.00	450
			$2,828
Product #2:			
1993	200	$4.73	$946
1994	200	5.32	1,064
1995	100	6.00	600
1996	100	7.00	700
			$3,310

Total value of Products #1 and #2
as revalued under M's new method $6,138

Total amount of adjustment required under
Section 481(a) [$6,138 – $5,150] $988

(D) *Adjustments to inventory costs from prior years.*—For special rules applicable when a revaluation using the weighted average method includes costs not incurred in prior years, see paragraph (c)(2)(v)(E) of this section.

(v) *3-year average method.*—(A) *In general.*—A taxpayer using the dollar-value LIFO method of accounting for inventories may revalue all existing LIFO layers of a trade or business based on the 3-year average method as provided in this paragraph (c)(2)(v). The 3-year average method is based on the average percentage change (the 3-year revaluation factor) in the current costs of inventory for each LIFO pool based on the three most recent taxable years for which the taxpayer has sufficient information (typically, the three most recent taxable years of such trade or business). The 3-year revaluation factor is applied to all layers for each pool in beginning inventory in the year of change. The 3-year average method is available to any dollar-value LIFO taxpayer that complies with the requirements of this paragraph (c)(2)(v) regardless of whether such taxpayer lacks sufficient data to revalue its inventory costs under the facts and circumstances revaluation method prescribed in paragraph (c)(2)(iii) of this section. The 3-year average method must be applied with respect to all inventory in a taxpayer's trade or business. A taxpayer *is not permitted to apply the method for the revaluation of some,* but not all, inventory costs on the basis of pools, business units, or other measures of inventory amounts that do not constitute a separate trade or business. Generally, a taxpayer revaluing its inventory using the 3-year average method must establish a new base year. See,

paragraph (b)(2)(iii)(A)(2)(*i*) of this section. However, a dollar-value LIFO taxpayer using the 3-year average method and either the simplified production method or the simplified resale method to revalue its inventory is permitted, but not required, to establish a new base year. See, paragraph (b)(2)(iii)(A)(2)(*ii*) of this section. If a taxpayer lacks sufficient information to otherwise apply the 3-year average method under this paragraph (c)(2)(v) (for example, the taxpayer is unable to revalue the costs of any of its LIFO pools for three years due to a lack of information), then the taxpayer must use reasonable estimates and procedures, as described in the facts and circumstances revaluation method under paragraph (c)(2)(iii) of this section, to whatever extent is necessary to allow the taxpayer to apply the 3-year average method.

(B) *Consecutive year requirement.*—Under the 3-year average method, if sufficient data is available to calculate the revaluation factor for more than three years, the taxpayer may use data from such additional years in determining the average percentage increase or decrease only if the additional years are consecutive to and prior to the year of change. The requirement under the preceding sentence to use consecutive years is applicable under this method regardless of whether any inventory costs in beginning inventory as of the year of change are viewed as incurred in, or attributable to, those consecutive years under the LIFO inventory method. Thus, the requirement to use data from consecutive years may result in using information from a year in which no LIFO increment occurred. For example, if a taxpayer is changing its method of accounting in 1997 and has sufficient data to revalue its inventory for the years 1991 through 1996, the taxpayer may calculate the revaluation factor using all six years. If, however, the taxpayer has sufficient data to revalue its inventory for the years 1990 through 1992, and 1994 through 1996, only the three years consecutive to the year of change, that is, 1994 through 1996, may be used in determining the revaluation factor. Similarly, for example, a taxpayer with LIFO increments in 1995, 1993, and 1992 may not calculate the revaluation factor based on the data from those years alone, but instead must use the data from consecutive years for which the taxpayer has information.

(C) *Example.*—The provisions of this paragraph (c)(2)(v) are illustrated by the following example. The principles set forth in this example are applicable both to production and resale activities and the year of change in the example is 1997. The example reads as follows:

Example. (i) Taxpayer G. a calendar year taxpayer, is a reseller that is required to change its method of accounting under section 263A. G will not use either the simplified production method or the simplified resale method. G adopted the dollar-value LIFO inventory method in 1991, using a single pool and the double extension method. G's beginning LIFO inventory as of January 1, 1997, computed using its former method, for the year of change is as follows:

	Base year costs	Index	LIFO carrying value
Base layer	$14,000	1.00	$14,000
1991 layer	4,000	1.20	4,800
1992 layer	5,000	1.30	6,500
1993 layer	2,000	1.35	2,700
1994 layer	0	1.40	0
1995 layer	4,000	1.50	6,000
1996 layer	5,000	1.60	8,000
Total	$34,000	—	$42,000

(ii) G is able to recompute total inventoriable costs incurred under its new method for the three preceding taxable years as follows:

	Current cost as recorded (former method)	Current cost as adjusted (new method)	Percentage change
1994	$35,000	$45,150	.29
1995	43,500	54,375	.25
1996	54,400	70,720	.30
Total	$132,900	$170,245	.28

(iii) Applying the average revaluation factor of .28 to each layer, G's inventory is restated as follows:

	Restated base year costs	Index	Restated LIFO carrying value
Base layer	$17,920	1.00	$17,920
1991 layer	5,120	1.20	6,144
1992 layer	6,400	1.30	8,320
1993 layer	2,560	1.35	3,456
1994 layer	0	1.40	0
1995 layer	5,120	1.50	7,680
1996 layer	6,400	1.60	10,240
Total	$43,520	—	$53,760

(iv) The adjustment required by section 481(a) is $11,760. This amount may be computed by multiplying the average percentage of .28 by the LIFO carrying value of G's inventory valued using its former method ($42,000). Alternatively, the adjustment required by section 481(a) may be computed by the difference between—

(A) The revalued costs of the taxpayer's inventory under its new method ($53,760), and

(B) The costs of the taxpayer's inventory using its former method ($42,000).

(v) In addition, the inventory as of the first day of the year of change (January 1, 1997) becomes the new base year cost for purposes of determining the LIFO index in future years. See, paragraphs (b)(2)(iii)(A)(2)(i) and (b)(2)(iii)(B) of this section. This requires that layers in years prior to the base year be restated in terms of the new base year index. The current year cost of G's inventory, as adjusted, is $70,720. Such cost must be apportioned to each layer in proportion to the restated base year cost of that layer to total restated base year costs ($43,520), as follows:

	Restated base year costs	Restated Index	Restated LIFO carrying value
Old base layer	$29,120	.615	$17,920
1991 layer	8,320	.738	6,144
1992 layer	10,400	.80	8,320
1993 layer	4,160	.831	3,456
1994 layer	0	—	0
1995 layer	8,320	.923	7,680
1996 layer	10,400	.985	10,240
Total	$70,720	—	$53,760

(D) *Short taxable years.*—A short taxable year is treated as a full 12 months.

(E) *Adjustments to inventory costs from prior years.*—*(1) General rule.*—*(i)* The use of the revaluation factor, based on current costs, to estimate the revaluation of prior inventory layers under the 3-year average method, as described in paragraph (c)(2)(v) of this section, may result in an allocation of costs that include amounts attributable to costs not incurred during the year in which the layer arose. To the extent a taxpayer can demonstrate that costs that contributed to the determination of the revaluation factor could not have affected a prior year, the revaluation factor as applied to that year may be adjusted under the restatement adjustment procedure, as described in paragraph (c)(2)(v)(F) of this section. The determination that a cost could not have affected a prior year must be made by a taxpayer only upon showing that the type of cost incurred during the years used to calculate the revaluation factor (revaluation years) was not present during such prior year. An item of cost will not be eligible for the restatement adjustment procedure simply because the cost varies in amount from year to year or the same type of cost is described or referred to by a different name from year to year. Thus, the restatement adjustment procedure allowed under paragraph (c)(2)(v)(F) of this section is not available in a prior year with respect to a particular cost if the same type of cost was incurred both in the revaluation years and in such prior year, although the amount of such cost and the name or description thereof may vary.

(ii) The provisions of this paragraph (c)(2)(v)(E) are also applicable to taxpayers using the weighted average method in revaluing inventories under paragraph (c)(2)(iv) of this section. Thus, to the extent a taxpayer can demonstrate that costs that contributed to the determination of the restatement of a particular year or item could not have affected a prior year or item, the taxpayer may adjust the revaluation of that prior year or item accordingly under the weighted average method. All the requirements and definitions, however, applicable to the restatement adjustment procedure under this paragraph (c)(2)(v)(E) fully apply to a taxpayer using the weighted average method to revalue inventories.

(2) *Examples of costs eligible for restatement adjustment procedure.*—The provisions of this paragraph (c)(2)(v)(E) are illustrated by the following four examples. The principles set forth in these examples are applicable both to production and resale activities and the year of change in the four examples is 1997. The examples read as follows:

Example 1. Taxpayer A is a reseller that introduced a defined benefit pension plan in 1994, and made the plan available to personnel whose labor costs were (directly or indirectly) properly allocable to resale activities. A determines the revaluation factor based on data available for the years 1994 through 1996, for which the pension plan was in existence. Based on these facts, the costs of the pension plan in the revaluation years are eligible for the restatement adjustment procedure for years prior to 1994.

Example 2. Assume the same facts as in *Example 1*, except that a defined contribution plan was available, during prior years, to personnel whose labor costs were properly allocable to resale activities. The defined contribution plan was terminated before the introduction of the defined benefit plan in 1994. Based on these facts, the costs of the defined benefit pension plan in the revaluation years are not eligible for the restatement adjustment procedure with respect to years for which the defined contribution plan existed.

Example 3. Taxpayer C is a manufacturer that established a security department in 1995 to patrol and safeguard its production and warehouse areas used in C's trade or business. Prior to 1995, C had not been required to utilize security personnel in its trade or business; C established the security department in 1995 in response to increasing vandalism and theft at its plant locations. Based on these facts, the costs of the security department are eligible for the restatement adjustment procedure for years prior to 1995.

Example 4. Taxpayer D is a reseller that established a payroll department in 1995 to process the company's weekly payroll. In the years 1991 through 1994, D engaged the services of an outside vendor to process the company's payroll. Prior to 1991, D's payroll processing was done by D's accounting department, which was responsible for payroll processing as well as for other accounting functions. Based on these facts, the costs of the payroll department are not eligible for the restatement adjustment procedure. D was incurring the same type of costs in earlier years as D was incurring in the payroll department in 1995 and subsequent years, although these costs were designated by a different name or description.

(F) *Restatement adjustment procedure.*—(1) *In general.*—(i) This paragraph (c)(2)(v)(F) provides a restatement adjustment procedure whereunder a taxpayer may adjust the restatement of inventory costs in prior taxable years in order to produce a different restated value than the value that would otherwise occur through application of the revaluation factor to such prior taxable years.

(ii) Under the restatement adjustment procedure as applied to a particular prior year, a taxpayer must determine the particular items of cost that are eligible for the restatement adjustment with respect to such prior year. The taxpayer must then recompute, using reasonable estimates and procedures, the total inventoriable costs that would have been incurred for each revaluation year under the taxpayer's former method and the taxpayer's new method by making appropriate adjustments in the data for such revaluation year to reflect the particular costs eligible for adjustment.

(iii) The taxpayer must then compute the total percentage change with respect to each revaluation year, using the revised estimates of total inventoriable costs for such year as described in paragraph (c)(2)(v)(F)(1)(ii) of this section. The percentage change must be determined by calculating the ratio of the revised total of the inventoriable costs for such revaluation year under the taxpayer's

new method to the revised total of the inventoriable costs for such revaluation year under the taxpayer's former method.

(iv) An average of the resulting percentage change for all revaluation years is then calculated, and the resulting average is applied to the prior year in issue.

(2) *Examples of restatement adjustment procedure.*—The provisions of this paragraph (c)(2)(v)(F) are illustrated by the following two examples. The principles set forth in these examples are applicable both to production and resale activities and the year of change in the two examples is 1997. The examples read as follows:

Example 1. Taxpayer A is a reseller that is eligible to make a restatement adjustment by reason of the costs of a defined benefit pension plan that was introduced in 1994, during the revaluation period. The revaluation factor, before adjustment of data to reflect the pension costs, is as provided in the example in paragraph (c)(2)(v)(C) of this section. Thus, for example, with respect to the year 1994, the total inventoriable costs under A's former method is $35,000, the total inventoriable costs under A's new method is $45,150, and the percentage change is .29. Under the method of accounting used by A during 1994 (the former method), none of the pension costs were included as inventoriable costs. Thus, under the restatement adjustment procedure, the total inventoriable cost under A's former method would remain at $35,000 if the pension plan had not been in existence. Similarly, A determines that the total inventoriable costs for 1994 under A's new method, if the pension plan had not been in existence, would have been $42,000. The restatement adjustment for 1994 determined under this paragraph (c)(2)(v)(F) would then be equal to .20 ([$42,000 – $35,000]/$35,000). A would make similar calculations with respect to 1995 and 1996. The average of such amounts for each of the three years in the revaluation period would then be determined as in the example in paragraph (c)(2)(v)(C) of this section. Such average would be used to revalue cost layers for years for which the pension plan was not in existence. Such revalued layers would then be viewed as restated in compliance with the requirements of this paragraph. With respect to cost layers incurred during years for which the pension plan was in existence, no adjustment of the revaluation factor would occur.

Example 2. Assume the same facts as in *Example 1*, except that a portion of the pension costs were included as inventoriable costs under the method used by A during 1994 (the former method). Under the restatement adjustment procedure, A determines that the total inventoriable costs for 1994 under the former method, if the pension plan had not been in existence, would have been $34,000. Similarly, A determines that the total inventoriable costs for 1994 under A's new method, if the pension plan had not been in existence, would have been $42,000. The restatement adjustment for 1994 determined under this paragraph (c)(2)(v)(F) would then be equal to .24 ([$42,000 – $34,000]/$34,000). A would make similar calculations with respect to 1995 and 1996. The average of such amounts for each of the three years in the revaluation period would then be determined as in the example in paragraph (c)(2)(v)(C) of this section. Such average would be used to revalue cost layers for years for which the pension plan was not in existence.

(3) *Intercompany items.*—(i) *Revaluing intercompany transactions.*—Pursuant to any change in method of accounting for costs subject to section 263A, taxpayers are required to revalue the amount of any intercompany item resulting from the sale or exchange of inventory property in an intercompany transaction to an amount equal to the intercompany item that would have resulted had the cost of goods sold for that inventory property been determined under the taxpayer's new method. The requirement of the preceding sentence applies with respect to both inventory produced by a taxpayer and inventory acquired by the taxpayer for resale. In addition, the requirements of this paragraph (c)(3) apply only to any intercompany item of the taxpayer as of the beginning of the year of change in method of accounting. See § 1.1502-13(b)(2)(ii). A taxpayer must revalue the amount of any intercompany item only if the inventory property sold in the intercompany transaction is held as inventory by a buying member as of the date the taxpayer changes its method of accounting under section 263A. Corresponding changes to the adjustment required under section 481(a) must be made with respect to any adjustment of the intercompany item required under this paragraph (c)(3). Moreover, the requirements of this paragraph (c)(3) apply regardless of whether the taxpayer has any items in beginning inventory as of the year of change in method of accounting. See § 1.1502-13 for the definition of intercompany transaction.

(ii) *Example.*—The provisions of this paragraph (c)(3) are illustrated by the following example. The principles set forth in this example are applicable both to production and resale activities and the year of change in the example is 1997. The example reads as follows:

Example. (i) Assume that S, a member of a consolidated group filing its federal income tax return on a calendar year, manufactures and sells inventory property to B, a member of the same consolidated group, in 1996. The sale between S and B is an intercompany transaction as defined under § 1.1502-13(b)(1). The gain from the intercompany transaction is an intercompany item to S under § 1.1502-13(b)(2). As of the beginning of the year of change in method of accounting (January 1, 1997), the inventory property is still held by B based on the particular inventory method of accounting used by B for federal income tax purposes (for example, the LIFO or FIFO inventory method). The property was sold by S to B in 1996 for $150; the cost of goods sold with respect to the property under the method in effect at the time the inventory was produced was $100, resulting in an intercompany item of $50 to S under § 1.1502-13. As of January 1, 1997, S still has an intercompany item of $50.

(ii) S is required to revalue the amount of its intercompany item to an amount equal to what the intercompany item would have been had the cost of goods sold for that inventory property been determined under S's new method. Assume that the cost of the inventory under this method would have been $110, had the method applied to S's manufacture of the property in 1996. Thus, S is required to revalue the amount of its intercompany item to $40 (that is, $150 less $110), necessitating a negative adjustment to the intercompany item of $10. Moreover, S is required to increase its adjustment under section 481(a) by $10 in order to prevent the omission of such amount by virtue of the decrease in the intercompany item.

(iii) *Availability of revaluation methods.*—In revaluing the amount of any intercompany item resulting from the sale or exchange of inventory property in an intercompany transaction to an amount equal to the intercompany item that would have resulted had the cost of goods sold for that inventory property been determined under the taxpayer's new method, a taxpayer may use the other methods and procedures otherwise properly available to that particular taxpayer in revaluing inventory under section 263A and the regulations thereunder, including, if appropriate, the various simplified methods provided in section 263A and the regulations thereunder and the various procedures described in this paragraph (c).

(4) *Anti-abuse rule.*—(i) *In general.*—Section 263A(i)(1) provides that the Secretary shall prescribe such regulations as may be necessary or appropriate to carry out the purposes of section 263A, including regulations to prevent the use of related parties, pass-thru entities, or intermediaries to avoid the application of section 263A and the regulations thereunder. One way in which the application of section 263A and the regulations thereunder would be otherwise avoided is through the use of entities described in the preceding sentence in such a manner as to effectively avoid the necessity to restate beginning inventory balances under the change in method of accounting required or permitted under section 263A and the regulations thereunder.

(ii) *Deemed avoidance of this section.*—(A) *Scope.*—For purposes of this paragraph (c), the avoidance of the application of section 263A and the regulations thereunder will be deemed to occur if a taxpayer using the LIFO method of accounting for inventories, transfers inventory property to a related corporation in a transaction described in section 351, and such transfer occurs:

(1) On or before the beginning of the transferor's taxable year beginning in 1987; and

(2) After September 18, 1986.

(B) *General rule.*—Any transaction described in paragraph (c)(4)(ii)(A) of this section will be treated in the following manner:

(1) Notwithstanding any provision to the contrary (for example, section 381), the transferee corporation is required to revalue the inventories acquired from the transferor under the provisions of this paragraph (c) relating to the change in method of accounting and the adjustment required by section 481(a), as if the inventories had never been transferred and were still in the hands of the transferor; and

(2) Absent an election as described in paragraph (c)(4)(iii) of this section, the transferee must account for the inventories acquired from the transferor by treating such inventories as if they were contained in the transferee's LIFO layer(s).

(iii) *Election to use transferor's LIFO layers.*—If a transferee described in paragraph (c)(4)(ii) of this section so elects, the transferee may account for the inventories acquired from the transferor by allocating such inventories to LIFO layers corresponding to the layers to which such properties were properly allocated by the transferor, prior to their transfer. The transferee must account for such inventories for all subsequent periods with reference to such layers to which the LIFO costs were allocated. Any such election is to be made on a statement attached to the timely filed federal income tax return of the transferee for the first taxable year for which section 263A and the regulations thereunder applies to the transferee.

(iv) *Tax avoidance intent not required.*—The provisions of paragraph (c)(4)(ii) of this section will apply to any transaction described therein, without regard to whether such transaction was consummated with an intention to avoid federal income taxes.

(v) *Related corporation.*—For purposes of this paragraph (c)(4), a taxpayer is related to a corporation if—

(A) the relationship between such persons is described in section 267(b)(1), or

(B) such persons are engaged in trades or businesses under common control (within the meaning of paragraphs (a) and (b) of section 52).

(d) *Non-inventory property.*—(1) *Need for adjustments.*—A taxpayer that changes its method of accounting for costs subject to section 263A with respect to non-inventory property must revalue the non-inventory property on hand at the beginning of the year of change as set forth in paragraph (d)(2) of this section, and compute an adjustment under section 481(a). The adjustment under section 481(a) will equal the difference between the adjusted basis of the property as revalued using the taxpayer's new method and the adjusted basis of the property as originally valued using the taxpayer's former method.

(2) *Revaluing property.*—A taxpayer must revalue its non-inventory property as of the beginning of the year of change in method of accounting. The facts and circumstances revaluation method of paragraph (c)(2)(iii) of this section must be used to revalue this property. In revaluing non-inventory property, however, the only additional section 263A costs that must be taken into account are those additional section 263A costs incurred after the later of December 31, 1986, or the date the taxpayer first becomes subject to section 263A, in taxable years ending after that date. See § 1.263A-1(d)(3) for the definition of additional section 263A costs. [Reg. § 1.263A-7.]

☐ [*T.D.* 8728, 8-4-97. *Amended by T.D.* 9131, 6-15-2004, *T.D.* 9843, 11-19-2018 *and T.D.* 9942, 12-31-2020.]

[Reg. § 1.263A-8]

§ 1.263A-8. Requirement to capitalize interest.—(a) *In general.*—(1) *General rule.*—Capitalization of interest under the avoided cost method described in § 1.263A-9 is required with respect to the production of designated property described in paragraph (b) of this section. However, a taxpayer, other than a tax shelter prohibited from using the cash receipts and disbursements method of accounting under section 448(a)(3), that meets the gross receipts test of section 448(c) for the taxable year is not required to capitalize costs, including interest, under section 263A. See § 1.263A-1(j)

(2) *Treatment of interest required to be capitalized.*—In general, interest that is capitalized under this section is treated as a cost of the designated property and is recovered in accordance with § 1.263A-1(c)(4). Interest capitalized by reason of assets used to produce designated property (within the meaning of § 1.263A-11(d)) is added to the basis of the designated property rather than the bases of the assets used to produce the designated property. Interest capitalized with respect to designated property that includes both components subject to an allowance for depreciation or depletion and components not subject to an allowance for depreciation or depletion is ratably allocated among, and is treated as a cost of, components that are subject to an allowance for depreciation or depletion.

(3) *Methods of accounting under section 263A(f).*—Except as otherwise provided, methods of accounting and other computations under §§ 1.263A-8 through 1.263A-15 are applied on a taxpayer, as opposed to a separate and distinct trade or business, basis.

(4) *Special definitions.*—(i) *Related person.*—Except as otherwise provided, for purposes of §§ 1.263A-8 through 1.263A-15, a person is related to a taxpayer if their relationship is described in section 267(b) or 707(b).

(ii) *Placed in service.*—For purposes of §§ 1.263A-8 through 1.263A-15, *placed in service* has the same meaning as set forth in § 1.46-3(d).

(b) *Designated property.*—(1) *In general.*—Except as provided in paragraphs (b)(3) and (b)(4) of this section, *designated property* means any property that is produced and that is either:

(i) Real property; or

(ii) Tangible personal property (as defined in § 1.263A-2(a)(2)) which meets any of the following criteria:

(A) Property with a class life of 20 years or more under section 168 (long-lived property), but only if the property is not property described in section 1221(1) in the hands of the taxpayer or a related person,

(B) Property with an estimated production period (as defined in § 1.263A-12) exceeding 2 years (2-year property), or

(C) Property with an estimated production period exceeding 1 year and an estimated cost of production exceeding $1,000,000 (1-year property).

(2) *Special rules.*—(i) *Application of thresholds.*—The thresholds described in paragraphs (b)(1)(ii)(A), (B), and (C) of this section are applied separately for each unit of property (as defined in §1.263A-10).

(ii) *Relevant activities and costs.*—For purposes of determining whether property is designated property, all activities and costs are taken into account if they are performed or incurred by, or for, the taxpayer or any related person and they directly benefit or are incurred by reason of the production of the property.

(iii) *Production period and cost of production.*—For purposes of applying the classification thresholds under paragraphs (b)(1)(ii)(B) and (C) of this section to a unit of property, the taxpayer is required, at the beginning of the production period, to reasonably estimate the production period and the total cost of production for the unit of property. The taxpayer must maintain contemporaneous written records supporting the estimates and classification. If the estimates are reasonable based on the facts in existence at the beginning of the production period, the taxpayer's classification of the property is not modified in subsequent periods, even if the actual length of the production period or the actual cost of production differs from the estimates. To be considered reasonable, estimates of the production period and the total cost of production must include anticipated expense and time for delay, rework, change orders, and technological, design or other problems. To the extent that several distinct activities related to the production of the property are expected to occur simultaneously, the period during which these distinct activities occur is not counted more than once. The bases of assets used to produce a unit of property (within the meaning of §1.263A-11(d)) and any interest that would be required to be capitalized if a unit of property were designated property are disregarded in making estimates of the total cost of production for purposes of this paragraph (b)(2)(iii).

(3) *Excluded property.*—Designated property does not include:

(i) Timber and evergreen trees that are more than 6 years old when severed from the roots, or

(ii) Property produced by the taxpayer for use by the taxpayer other than in a trade or business or an activity conducted for profit.

(4) *De minimis rule.*—(i) *In general.*—Designated property does not include property for which—

(A) The production period does not exceed 90 days; and

(B) The total production expenditures do not exceed $1,000,000 divided by the number of days in the production period.

(ii) *Determination of total production expenditures.*—For purposes of determining whether the condition of paragraph (b)(4)(i)(B) of this section is met with respect to property, the cost of land, the adjusted basis of property used to produce property, and interest that would be capitalized with respect to property if it were designated property are excluded from total production expenditures.

(c) *Definition of real property.*—(1) *In general.*—Real property includes land, unsevered natural products of land, buildings, and inherently permanent structures. Any interest in real property of a type described in this paragraph (c), including fee ownership, co-ownership, a leasehold, an option, or a similar interest is real property under this section. Real property includes the structural components of both buildings and inherently permanent structures, such as walls, partitions, doors, wiring, plumbing, central air conditioning and heating systems, pipes and ducts, elevators and escalators, and other similar property. Tenant improvements to a building that are inherently permanent or otherwise classified as real property within the meaning of this paragraph (c)(1) are real property under this section. However, property produced for sale that is not real property in the hands of the taxpayer or a related person, but that may be incorporated into real property by an unrelated buyer, is not treated as real property by the producing taxpayer (e.g., bricks, nails, paint, and windowpanes).

(2) *Unsevered natural products of land.*—Unsevered natural products of land include growing crops and plants, mines, wells, and other natural deposits. Growing crops and plants, however, are real property only if the preproductive period of the crop or plant exceeds 2 years.

(3) *Inherently permanent structures.*—Inherently permanent structures include property that is affixed to real property and that will ordinarily remain affixed for an indefinite period of time, such as swimming pools, roads, bridges, tunnels, paved parking areas and other pavements, special foundations, wharves and docks, fences,

inherently permanent advertising displays, inherently permanent outdoor lighting facilities, railroad tracks and signals, telephone poles, power generation and transmission facilities, permanently installed telecommunications cables, broadcasting towers, oil and gas pipelines, derricks and storage equipment, grain storage bins and silos. For purposes of this section, affixation to real property may be accomplished by weight alone. Property may constitute an inherently permanent structure even though it is not classified as a building for purposes of former section 48(a)(1)(B) and §1.48-1. Any property not otherwise described in this paragraph (c)(3) that constitutes other tangible property under the principles of former section 48(a)(1)(B) and §1.48-1(d) is treated for the purposes of this section as an inherently permanent structure.

(4) *Machinery.*—(i) *Treatment.*—A structure that is property in the nature of machinery or is essentially an item of machinery or equipment is not an inherently permanent structure and is not real property. In the case, however, of a building or inherently permanent structure that includes property in the nature of machinery as a structural component, the property in the nature of machinery is real property.

(ii) *Certain factors not determinative.*—A structure may be an inherently permanent structure, and not property in the nature of machinery or essentially an item of machinery, even if the structure is necessary to operate or use, supports, or is otherwise associated with, machinery.

(d) *Production.*—(1) *Definition of produce.*—Produce is defined as provided in section 263A(g) and §1.263A-2(a)(1)(i).

(2) *Property produced under a contract.*—(i) *Customer.*—A taxpayer is treated as producing any property that is produced for the taxpayer (the customer) by another party (the contractor) under a contract with the taxpayer or an intermediary. Property produced under a contract is designated property to the customer if it is real property or tangible personal property that satisfies the classification thresholds described in paragraph (b)(1)(ii) of this section. If property produced under a contract will become part of a unit of designated property produced by the customer in the customer's hands, the property produced under the contract is designated property to the customer.

(ii) *Contractor.*—Property produced under a contract is designated property to the contractor if it is real property, 2-year property, or 1-year property and the property produced under the contract is not excluded by reason of paragraph (d)(2)(v) of this section.

(iii) *Definition of a contract.*—For purposes of this paragraph (d)(2), *contract* has the same meaning as under §1.263A-2(a)(1)(ii)(B)(2).

(iv) *Determination of whether thresholds are satisfied.*—In the case of tangible personal property produced under a contract, the customer and the contractor each determine under this paragraph (d)(2), whether the property satisfies the classification thresholds described in paragraph (b)(1)(ii) of this section. Thus, tangible personal property may be designated property with respect to either, or both, the customer and the contractor. The provisions of paragraph (b)(2)(iii) of this section are modified as set forth in this paragraph (d)(2)(iv) for purposes of determining whether tangible personal property produced under a contract is 2-year property or 1-year property.

(A) *Customer.*—In determining a customer's estimated cost of production, the customer takes into account costs and payments that are reasonably expected to be incurred by the customer, but does not take into account costs incurred (or to be incurred) by an unrelated contractor. In determining the customer's estimated length of the production period, the production period is treated as beginning on the earlier of the date the contract is executed or the date that the customer's accumulated production expenditures for the unit are at least 5 percent of the customer's total estimated production expenditures for the unit. The customer, however, may elect to treat the production period as beginning on the date the sum of the accumulated production expenditures of the contractor (or contractors if more than one contractor is producing components for the unit of property) and of the customer are at least 5 percent of the customer's estimated production expenditures for the unit.

(B) *Contractor.*—In determining a contractor's estimated cost of production, the contractor takes into account only the costs that are reasonably expected to be incurred by the contractor, without any reduction for payments from the customer. In determining the contractor's estimated length of the production period, the production period is treated as beginning on the date the contractor's accumulated production expenditures (without any reduction for payments from the customer) are at least 5 percent of the contractor's total estimated accumulated production expenditures.

(v) *Exclusion for property subject to long-term contract rules.*—Property described in paragraph (b) of this section is designated property with respect to a contractor only if—

(A) The contract is not a long-term contract (within the meaning of section 460(f)); or

(B) The contract is a home construction contract (within the meaning of section 460(e)(6)(A)) with respect to which the requirements of section 460(e)(1)(B)(i) and (ii) are not met.

(3) *Improvements to existing property.*—(i) *In general.*—Any improvement to property described in §1.263(a)-1(b) constitutes the production of property. Generally, any improvement to designated property constitutes the production of designated property. An improvement is not treated as the production of designated property, however, if the de minimis exception described in paragraph (b)(4) of this section applies to the improvement. In addition, paragraph (d)(3)(iii) of this section provides an exception for certain improvements to tangible personal property. Incidental maintenance and repairs are not treated as improvements under this paragraph (d)(3). See §1.162-4.

(ii) *Real property.*—The rehabilitation or preservation of a standing building, the clearing of raw land prior to sale, and the drilling of an oil well are activities constituting improvements to real property and, therefore, the production of designated property. Similarly, the demolition of a standing building generally constitutes an activity that is an improvement to real property and, therefore, the production of designated property. See the exceptions, however, in paragraphs (b)(3) and (b)(4) of this section.

(iii) *Tangible personal property.*—If the taxpayer has treated a unit of tangible personal property as designated property under this section, an improvement to such property constitutes the production of designated property regardless of the remaining useful life of the improved property (or the improvement) and, except as provided in paragraph (b)(4) of this section, regardless of the estimated length of the production period or the estimated cost of the improvement. If the taxpayer has not treated a unit of tangible personal property as designated property under this section, an improvement to such property constitutes the production of designated property only if the improvement independently meets the classification thresholds described in paragraph (b)(1)(ii) of this section. [Reg. §1.263A-8.]

☐ [*T.D.* 8584, 12-28-94. *Amended by T.D.* 9942, 12-31-2020.]

[Reg. §1.263A-9]

§1.263A-9. The avoided cost method.—(a) *In general.*—(1) *Description.*—The avoided cost method described in this section must be used to calculate the amount of interest required to be capitalized under section 263A(f). Generally, any interest that the taxpayer theoretically would have avoided if accumulated production expenditures (as defined in §1.263A-11) had been used to repay or reduce the taxpayer's outstanding debt must be capitalized under the avoided cost method. The application of the avoided cost method does not depend on whether the taxpayer actually would have used the amounts expended for production to repay or reduce debt. Instead, the avoided cost method is based on the assumption that debt of the taxpayer would have been repaid or reduced without regard to the taxpayer's subjective intentions or to restrictions (including legal, regulatory, contractual, or other restrictions) against repayment or use of the debt proceeds.

(2) *Overview.*—(i) *In general.*—For each unit of designated property (within the meaning of §1.263A-8(b)), the avoided cost method requires the capitalization of—

(A) The traced debt amount under paragraph (b) of this section, and

(B) The excess expenditure amount under paragraph (c) of this section.

(ii) *Rules that apply in determining amounts.*—The traced debt and excess expenditure amounts are determined for each taxable year or shorter computation period (as defined in §1.263A-12) of a unit of designated property. Paragraph (d) of this section provides an election not to trace debt to specific units of designated property. Paragraph (f) of this section provides rules for selecting the computation period, for calculating averages, and for determining measurement dates within the computation period. Special rules are in paragraph (g) of this section.

(3) *Definitions of interest and incurred.*—Except as provided in the case of certain expenses that are treated as a substitute for interest under paragraphs (c)(2)(iii) and (g) (2)(iv) of this section, *interest* refers to all amounts that are characterized as interest expense under any provision of the Code, including, for example, sections 482, 483, 1272, 1274, and 7872. *Incurred* refers to the amount of interest that is properly accruable during the period of time in question determined

by taking into account the loan agreement and any applicable provisions of the Internal Revenue laws and regulations such as section 163, §1.446-2, and sections 1271 through 1275.

(4) *Definition of eligible debt.*—Except as provided in this paragraph (a)(4), *eligible debt* includes all outstanding debt (as evidenced by a contract, bond, debenture, note, certificate, or other evidence of indebtedness). Eligible debt does not include—

(i) Debt (or the portion thereof) bearing interest that is disallowed under a provision described in §1.163-8T(m)(7)(ii);

(ii) Debt, such as accounts payable and other accrued items, that bears no interest, except to the extent that such debt is traced debt (as defined in paragraph (b)(2) of this section);

(iii) Debt that is borrowed directly or indirectly from a person related to the taxpayer and that bears a rate of interest that is less than the applicable Federal rate in effect under section 1274(d) on the date of issuance;

(iv) Debt (or the portion thereof) bearing personal interest within the meaning of section 163(h)(2);

(v) Debt (or the portion thereof) bearing qualified residence interest within the meaning of section 163(h)(3);

(vi) Debt incurred by an organization that is exempt from Federal income tax under section 501(a), except to the extent interest on such debt is directly attributable to an unrelated trade or business of the organization within the meaning of section 512;

(vii) Reserves, deferred tax liabilities, and similar items that are not treated as debt for Federal income tax purposes, regardless of the extent to which the taxpayer's applicable financial accounting or other regulatory reporting principles require or support treating these items as debt;

(viii) Federal, State, and local income tax liabilities, deferred tax liabilities under section 453A, and hypothetical tax liabilities under the look-back method of section 460(b) or similar provisions; and

(ix) A purchase money obligation given by the lessor to the lessee (or a party that is related to the lessee) in a sale and leaseback transaction involving an agreement qualifying as a lease under §5c.168(f)(8)-1 through §5c.168(f)(8)-11 of this chapter. See §5c.168(f)(8)-1(e) *Example (2)* of this chapter.

(b) *Traced debt amount.*—(1) *General rule.*—Interest must be capitalized with respect to a unit of designated property in an amount (the traced debt amount) equal to the total interest incurred on the traced debt during each measurement period (as defined in paragraph (f)(2)(ii) of this section) that ends on a measurement date described in paragraph (f)(2)(iii) of this section. See the example in paragraph (b)(3) of this section. If any interest incurred on the traced debt is not taken into account for the taxable year that includes the measurement period because of a deferral provision, see paragraph (g)(2) of this section for the time and manner for capitalizing and recovering that amount. This paragraph (b)(1) does not apply if the taxpayer elects under paragraph (d) of this section not to trace debt.

(2) *Identification and definition of traced debt.*—On each measurement date described in paragraph (f)(2)(iii) of this section, the taxpayer must identify debt that is traced debt with respect to a unit of designated property. On each such date, traced debt with respect to a unit of designated property is the outstanding eligible debt (as defined in paragraph (a)(4) of this section) that is allocated, on that date, to accumulated production expenditures with respect to the unit of designated property under the rules of §1.163-8T. Traced debt also includes unpaid interest that has been capitalized with respect to such unit under paragraph (b)(1) of this section and that is included in accumulated production expenditures on the measurement date.

(3) *Example.*—The provisions of paragraphs (b)(1) and (b)(2) of this section are illustrated by the following example.

Example. Corporation X, a calendar year taxpayer, is engaged in the production of a single unit of designated property during 1995 (unit A). Corporation X adopts a taxable year computation period and quarterly measurement dates. Production of unit A starts on January 14, 1995, and ends on June 16, 1995. On March 31, 1995 and on June 30, 1995, Corporation X has outstanding a $1,000,000 loan that is allocated under the rules of §1.163-8T to production expenditures with respect to unit A. During the period January 1, 1995, through June 30, 1995, Corporation X incurs $50,000 of interest related to the loan. Under paragraph (b)(1) of this section, the $50,000 of interest Corporation X incurs on the loan during the period January 1, 1995, through June 30, 1995, must be capitalized with respect to unit A.

(c) *Excess expenditure amount.*—(1) *General rule.*—If there are accumulated production expenditures in excess of traced debt with respect to a unit of designated property on any measurement date described in paragraph (f)(2)(iii) of this section, the taxpayer must, for the computation period that includes the measurement date, capitalize with respect to the unit the excess expenditure amount calculated under this paragraph (c)(1). However, if the sum of the excess expenditure amounts for all units of designated property of a taxpayer exceeds the total interest described in paragraph (c)(2) of this section, only a prorata amount (as determined under paragraph (c)(7) of this section) of such interest must be capitalized with respect to each unit. For each unit of designated property, the excess expenditure amount for a computation period equals the product of—

(i) The average excess expenditures (as determined under paragraph (c)(5)(ii) of this section) for the unit of designated property for that period, and

(ii) The weighted average interest rate (as determined under paragraph (c)(5)(iii) of this section) for that period.

(2) *Interest required to be capitalized.*—With respect to an excess expenditure amount, interest incurred during the computation period is capitalized from the following sources and in the following sequence but not in excess of the excess expenditure amount for all units of designated property:

(i) Interest incurred on nontraced debt (as defined in paragraph (c)(5)(i) of this section);

(ii) Interest incurred on borrowings described in paragraph (a)(4)(iii) of this section (relating to certain borrowings from related persons); and

(iii) In the case of a partnership, guaranteed payments for the use of capital (within the meaning of section 707(c)) that would be deductible by the partnership if section 263A(f) did not apply.

(3) *Example.*—The provisions of paragraph (c)(1) and (2) of this section are illustrated by the following example.

Example. (i) P, a partnership owned equally by Corporation A and Individual B, is engaged in the construction of an office building during 1995. Average excess expenditures for the office building for 1995 are $2,000,000. When P was formed, A and B agreed that A would be entitled to an annual guaranteed payment of $70,000 in exchange for A's capital contribution. The only borrowing of P, A, and B for 1995 is a loan to P from an unrelated lender of $1,000,000 (loan #1). The loan is nontraced debt and bears interest at an annual rate of 10 percent. Thus, P's weighted average interest rate (determined under paragraph (c)(5)(iii) of this section) is 10 percent and interest incurred during 1995 is $100,000.

(ii) In accordance with paragraph (c)(1) of this section, the excess expenditure amount is $200,000 ($2,000,000 × 10%). The interest capitalized under paragraph (c)(2) of this section is $170,000 ($100,000 of interest plus $70,000 of guaranteed payments).

(4) *Treatment of interest subject to a deferral provision.*—If any interest described in paragraph (c)(2) of this section is not taken into account for the taxable year that includes the computation period because of a deferral provision described in paragraph (g)(1)(ii) of this section, paragraph (c)(2) of this section is first applied without regard to the amount of the deferred interest. After applying paragraph (c)(2) without regard to the deferred interest, if the amount of interest capitalized with respect to all units of designated property for the computation period is less than the amount that would have been capitalized if a deferral provision did not apply, see paragraph (g)(2) of this section for the time and manner for capitalizing and recovering the difference (the shortfall amount).

(5) *Definitions.*—(i) *Nontraced debt.*—(A) *Defined.*—Nontraced debt means all eligible debt on a measurement date other than any debt that is treated as traced debt with respect to any unit of designated property on that measurement date. For example, nontraced debt includes eligible debt that is allocated to expenditures that are not capitalized under section 263A(a) (e.g., expenditures deductible under section 174(a) or 263(c)). Similarly, even if eligible debt is allocated to a production expenditure for a unit of designated property, the debt is included in nontraced debt on measurement dates before the first or after the last measurement date for that unit of designated property. Thus, nontraced debt may include debt that was previously treated as traced debt or that will be treated as traced debt on a future measurement date.

(B) *Example.*—The provisions of paragraph (c)(5)(i)(A) of this section are illustrated by the following example.

Example. In 1995, Corporation X begins, but does not complete, the construction of two office buildings that are separate units of designated property as defined in §1.263A-10 (Property D and Property E). At the beginning of 1995, X borrows $2,500,000 (the $2,500,000 loan), which will be used exclusively to finance production expenditures for Property D. Although interest is paid currently, the entire principal amount of the loan remains outstanding at the end of 1995. Corporation X also has outstanding during all of 1995 a long-term loan with a principal amount of $2,000,000 (the $2,000,000 loan). The proceeds of the $2,000,000 loan were used exclusively to finance the production of Property C, a unit of designated property

that was completed in 1994. Under the rules of paragraph (b)(2) of this section, the portion of the $2,500,000 loan allocated to accumulated production expenditures for property D at each measurement date during 1995 is treated as traced debt for that measurement date. The excess, if any, of $2,500,000 over the amount treated as traced debt at each measurement date during 1995 is treated as nontraced debt for that measurement date, even though it is expected that the entire $2,500,000 will be treated as traced debt with respect to Property D on subsequent measurement dates as more of the proceeds of the loan are used to finance additional production expenditures. In addition, the entire principal amount of the $2,000,000 loan is treated as nontraced debt for 1995, even though it was treated as traced debt with respect to Property C in a previous period.

(ii) *Average excess expenditures.*—(A) *General rule.*—The average excess expenditures for a unit of designated property for a computation period are computed by—

(1) Determining the amount (if any) by which accumulated production expenditures exceed traced debt at each measurement date during the computation period; and

(2) Dividing the sum of these amounts by the number of measurement dates during the computation period.

(B) *Example.*—The provisions of paragraph (c)(5)(ii)(A) of this section are illustrated by the following example.

Example. Corporation X, a calendar year taxpayer, is engaged in the production of a single unit of designated property during 1995 (unit A). Corporation X adopts the taxable year as the computation period and quarterly measurement dates. The production period for unit A begins on January 14, 1995, and ends on June 16, 1995. On March 31, 1995, and on June 30, 1995, Corporation X has outstanding $1,000,000 of traced debt with respect to unit A. Accumulated production expenditures for unit A on March 31, 1995, are $1,400,000 and on June 30, 1995, are $1,600,000. Accumulated production expenditures in excess of traced debt for unit A on March 31, 1995, are $400,000 and on June 30, 1995, are $600,000. Average excess expenditures for unit A during 1995 are therefore $250,000 ([$400,000 + $600,000 + $0 + $0] 4).

(iii) *Weighted average interest rate.*—(A) *Determination of rate.*—The weighted average interest rate for a computation period is determined by dividing interest incurred on nontraced debt during the period by average nontraced debt for the period.

(B) *Interest incurred on nontraced debt.*—Interest incurred on nontraced debt during the computation period is equal to the total amount of interest incurred during the computation period on all eligible debt minus the amount of interest incurred during the computation period on traced debt. Thus, all interest incurred on nontraced debt during the computation period is included in the numerator of the weighted average interest rate, even if the underlying nontraced debt is repaid before the end of a measurement period and excluded from nontraced debt outstanding for measurement dates after repayment, in determining the denominator of the weighted average interest rate. However, see paragraph (g)(7) of this section for an election to treat eligible debt that is repaid within the 15-day period immediately preceding a quarterly measurement date as outstanding on that measurement date. See paragraph (a)(3) of this section for the definitions of interest and incurred.

(C) *Average nontraced debt.*—The average nontraced debt for a computation period is computed by—

(1) Determining the amount of nontraced debt outstanding on each measurement date during the computation period; and

(2) Dividing the sum of these amounts by the number of measurement dates during the computation period.

(D) *Special rules if taxpayer has no nontraced debt or rate is contingent.*—If the taxpayer does not have nontraced debt outstanding during the computation period, the weighted average interest rate for purposes of applying paragraphs (c)(1) and (c)(2) of this section is the highest applicable Federal rate in effect under section 1274(d) during the computation period. If interest is incurred at a rate that is contingent at the time the return for the year that includes the computation period is filed, the amount of interest is determined using the higher of the fixed rate of interest (if any) on the underlying debt or the applicable Federal rate in effect under section 1274(d) on the date of issuance.

(6) *Examples.*—The following examples illustrate the principles of this paragraph (c):

Example 1. (i) W, a calendar year taxpayer, is engaged in the production of a unit of designated property during 1995. For purposes of applying the avoided cost method of this section, W uses the taxable year as the computation period. During 1995, W's only debt is a $1,000,000 loan bearing interest at a rate of 7 percent from Y, a person that is related to W. Assuming the applicable Federal rate in effect under section 1274(d) on the date of issuance of the loan is 10 percent, the loan is not eligible debt under paragraph (a)(4) of this section. However, even though W has no eligible debt, W incurs $70,000 ($1,000,000 × 7%) of interest during the computation period. This interest is described in paragraph (c)(2) of this section and must be capitalized under paragraph (c)(1) of this section to the extent it does not exceed W's excess expenditure amount for the unit of property.

(ii) W determines, under paragraph (c)(5)(ii) of this section, that average excess expenditures for the unit of property are $600,000. Assuming the highest applicable Federal rate in effect under section 1274(d) during the computation period is 10 percent, W uses 10 percent as the weighted average interest rate for purposes of determining the excess expenditure amount. See paragraph (c)(5)(iii)(D) of this section. In accordance with paragraph (c)(1) of this section, the excess expenditure amount is therefore $60,000. Because this amount does not exceed the total amount of interest described in paragraph (c)(2) of this section ($70,000), W is required to capitalize $60,000 of interest with respect to the unit of designated property for the 1995 computation period.

Example 2. (i) Corporation X, a calendar year taxpayer, is engaged in the production of a single unit of designated property during 1995 (unit A). Corporation X adopts the taxable year as the computation period and quarterly measurement dates. Production of unit A begins in 1994 and ends on June 30, 1995. On March 31, 1995, and on June 30, 1995, Corporation X has outstanding $1,000,000 of eligible debt (loan #1) that is allocated under the rules of § 1.163-8T to production expenditures for unit A. During each of the first two quarters of 1995, $30,000 of interest is incurred on loan #1. The loan is repaid on July 1, 1995. Throughout 1995, Corporation X also has outstanding $2,000,000 of eligible debt (loan #2) which is not allocated under the rules of § 1.163-8T to the production of unit A. During 1995, $200,000 of interest is incurred on this nontraced debt. Accumulated production expenditures on March 31, 1995, are $1,400,000 and on June 30, 1995, are $1,600,000. Accumulated production expenditures in excess of traced debt on March 31, 1995, are $400,000 and on June 30, 1995, are $600,000.

(ii) Under paragraph (b)(1) of this section, the amount of interest capitalized with respect to traced debt is $60,000 ($30,000 for the measurement period ending March 31, 1995, and $30,000 for the measurement period ending June 30, 1995). Under paragraph (c)(5)(ii) of this section, average excess expenditures for unit A are $250,000 ([($1,400,000 − $1,000,000) + ($1,600,000 − $1,000,000) + $0 + $0] 4). Under paragraph (c)(5)(iii)(C) of this section, average nontraced debt is $2,000,000 ([$2,000,000 + $2,000,000 + $2,000,000 + $2,000,000] 4). Under paragraph (c)(5)(iii)(B) of this section, interest incurred on nontraced debt is $200,000 ($260,000 of interest incurred on all eligible debt less $60,000 of interest incurred on traced debt). Under paragraph (c)(5)(iii)(A) of this section, the weighted average interest rate is 10 percent ($200,000 $2,000,000). Under paragraph (c)(1) of this section, Corporation X capitalizes the excess expenditure amount of $25,000 ($250,000 × 10%), because it does not exceed the total amount of interest subject to capitalization under paragraph (c)(2) of this section ($200,000). Thus, the total interest capitalized with respect to unit A during 1995 is $85,000 ($60,000 + $25,000).

(7) *Special rules where the excess expenditure amount exceeds incurred interest.*—(i) *Allocation of total incurred interest to units.*—For a computation period in which the sum of the excess expenditure amounts under paragraph (c)(1) of this section for all units of designated property exceeds the total amount of interest (including deferred interest) available for capitalization, as determined under paragraph (c)(2) of this section, the amount of interest that is allocated to a unit of designated property is equal to the product of—

(A) The total amount of interest (including deferred interest) available for capitalization, as determined under paragraph (c)(2) of this section; and

(B) A fraction, the numerator of which is the average excess expenditures for the unit of designated property and the denominator of which is the sum of the average excess expenditures for all units of designated property.

(ii) *Application of related person rules to average excess expenditures.*—Certain excess expenditures must be taken into account by the persons (if any) required to capitalize interest with respect to production expenditures of the taxpayer under applicable related person rules. For each computation period, the amount of average excess expenditures that must be taken into account by such persons for each unit of the taxpayer's property is computed by—

(A) Determining, for the computation period, the amount (if any) by which the excess expenditure amount for the unit exceeds the amount of interest allocated to the unit under paragraph (c)(7)(i) of this section; and

(B) Dividing the excess by the weighted average interest rate for the period.

(iii) *Special rule for corporations.*—If a corporation is related to another person for the purposes of the applicable related party rules, the District Director upon examination may require that the corporation apply this paragraph (c)(7) and other provisions of the regulations by excluding deferred interest from the total interest available for capitalization.

(d) *Election not to trace debt.*—(1) *General rule.*—Taxpayers may elect not to trace debt. If the election is made, the average excess expenditures and weighted average interest rate under paragraph (c)(5) of this section are determined by treating all eligible debt as nontraced debt. For this purpose, debt specified in paragraph (a)(4)(ii) of this section (e.g., accounts payable) may be included in eligible debt, provided it would be treated as traced debt but for an election under this paragraph (d). The election not to trace debt is a method of accounting that applies to the determination of capitalized interest for all designated property of the taxpayer. The making or revocation of the election is a change in method of accounting requiring the consent of the Commissioner under section 446(e) and § 1.446-1(e).

(2) *Example.*—The provisions of paragraph (d)(1) of this section are illustrated by the following example.

Example. (i) Corporation X, a calendar year taxpayer, is engaged in the production of a single unit of designated property during 1995 (unit A). Corporation X adopts the taxable year as the computation period and quarterly measurement dates. At each measurement date (March 31, June 30, September 30, and December 31) Corporation X has the following outstanding indebtedness:

Noninterest-bearing accounts payable traced to unit A	$100,000
Noninterest-bearing accounts payable that are not traced to unit A	$300,000
Interest-bearing loans that are eligible debt within the meaning of paragraph (a)(4) of this section	$900,000

(ii) Corporation X elects under this paragraph (d) not to trace debt. Eligible debt at each measurement date for purposes of calculating the weighted average interest rate under paragraph (c)(5)(iii) of this section is $1,000,000 ($100,000 + $900,000).

(e) *Election to use external rate.*—(1) *In general.*—An eligible taxpayer may elect to use the highest applicable Federal rate (AFR) under section 1274(d) in effect during the computation period plus 3 percentage points (AFR plus 3) as a substitute for the weighted average interest rate determined under paragraph (c)(5)(iii) of this section. A taxpayer that makes this election may not use traced debt. The use of the AFR plus 3 as provided under this paragraph (e)(1) constitutes a method of accounting. A taxpayer makes the election to use the AFR plus 3 method by using the AFR plus 3 as the taxpayer's weighted average interest rate, and any change to the AFR plus 3 method by a taxpayer that has never previously used the method does not require the consent of the Commissioner. Any other change to or from the use of the AFR plus 3 method under this paragraph (e)(1) (other than by reason of a taxpayer ceasing to be an eligible taxpayer) is a change in method of accounting requiring the consent of the Commissioner under section 446(e) and § 1.446-1(e). All changes to or from the AFR plus 3 method are effected on a cut-off basis.

(2) *Eligible taxpayer.*—A taxpayer is an eligible taxpayer for a taxable year for purposes of this paragraph (e) if the average annual gross receipts of the taxpayer for the three previous taxable years do not exceed $10,000,000 (the $10,000,000 gross receipts test) and the taxpayer has met the $10,000,000 gross receipts test for all prior taxable years beginning after December 31, 1994. For purposes of this paragraph (e)(2), the principles of section 263A(b)(2)(B) and (C) and § 1.263A-3(b) apply in determining whether a taxpayer is an eligible taxpayer for a taxable year. A taxpayer is an eligible taxpayer for a taxable year for purposes of this paragraph (e) if the taxpayer is a small business taxpayer, as defined in § 1.263A-1(j).

(f) *Selection of computation period and measurement dates and application of averaging conventions.*—(1) *Computation period.*—(i) *In general.*—A taxpayer may (but is not required to) make the avoided cost calculation on the basis of a full taxable year. If the taxpayer uses the taxable year as the computation period, a single avoided cost calculation is made for each unit of designated property for the entire taxable year. If the taxpayer uses a computation period that is shorter than the full taxable year, an avoided cost calculation is made for each unit of designated property for each shorter computation period within the taxable year. If the taxpayer uses a shorter computation period, the computation period may not include portions of more than one taxable year and, except as provided in the case of short taxable years, each computation period within a taxable year must be the same length. In the case of a short taxable year, a taxpayer may treat a period shorter than the taxpayer's regular computation period as the first or last computation period, or as the only computation period for the year if the year is shorter than the taxpayer's regular computation period. A taxpayer must use the same computation periods for all designated property produced during a single taxable year.

(ii) *Method of accounting.*—The choice of a computation period is a method of accounting. Any change in the computation period is a change in method of accounting requiring the consent of the Commissioner under section 446(e) and § 1.446-1(e).

(iii) *Production period beginning or ending during the computation period.*—The avoided cost method applies to the production of a unit of designated property on the basis of a full computation period, regardless of whether the production period for the unit of designated property begins or ends during the computation period.

(2) *Measurement dates.*—(i) *In general.*—If a taxpayer uses the taxable year as the computation period, measurement dates must occur at quarterly or more frequent regular intervals. If the taxpayer uses computation periods that are shorter than the taxable year, measurement dates must occur at least twice during each computation period and at least four times during the taxable year (or consecutive 12-month period in the case of a short taxable year). The taxpayer must use the same measurement dates for all designated property produced during a computation period. Except in the case of a computation period that differs from the taxpayer's regular computation period by reason of a short taxable year (see paragraph (f)(1)(i) of this section), measurement dates must occur at equal intervals during each computation period that falls within a single taxable year. For any computation period that differs from the taxpayer's regular computation period by reason of a short taxable year, the measurement dates used by the taxpayer during that period must be consistent with the principles and purposes of section 263A(f). A taxpayer is permitted to modify the frequency of measurement dates from year to year.

(ii) *Measurement period.*—For purposes of this section, *measurement period* means the period that begins on the first day following the preceding measurement date and that ends on the measurement date.

(iii) *Measurement dates on which accumulated production expenditures must be taken into account.*—The first measurement date on which accumulated production expenditures must be taken into account with respect to a unit of designated property is the first measurement date following the beginning of the production period for the unit of designated property. The final measurement date on which accumulated production expenditures with respect to a unit of designated property must be taken into account is the first measurement date following the end of the production period for the unit of designated property. Accumulated production expenditures with respect to a unit of designated property must also be taken into account on all intervening measurement dates. See § 1.263A-12 to determine when the production period begins and ends.

#	Principal	Annual rate
1	$1,000,000	9%
2	2,000,000	11%

(ii) Based on the annual 9 percent rate of interest, Corporation X incurs $7,500 of interest during each month that Loan #1 is outstanding.

Measurement Date	Unit A	Unit B
March 31	$1,200,000	-0-
June 30	$1,800,000	$ 500,000
Sept. 30	-0-	$1,000,000

(iv) Corporation X must first determine the amount of interest incurred on traced debt and capitalize the interest incurred on this debt (the traced debt amount). Loan #1 is allocated to Unit A on the March 31 and June 30 measurement dates. Accordingly, Loan #1 is treated as traced debt with respect to unit A for the measurement periods beginning January 1 and ending June 30. The interest incurred on Loan #1 during the period that Loan #1 is treated as traced debt must be capitalized with respect to Unit A. Thus, $45,000 ($7,500 per month for 6 months) is capitalized with respect to Unit A.

(iv) *More frequent measurement dates.*—When in the opinion of the District Director more frequent measurement dates are necessary to determine capitalized interest consistent with the principles and purposes of section 263A(f) for a particular computation period, the District Director may require the use of more frequent measurement dates. If a significant segment of the taxpayer's production activities (the first segment) requires more frequent measurement dates than another significant segment of the taxpayer's production activities, the taxpayer may request a ruling from the Internal Revenue Service permitting, for a taxable year and all subsequent taxable years, a segregation of the two segments and, notwithstanding paragraph (f)(2)(i) of this section, the use of the more frequent measurement dates for only the first segment. The request for a ruling must be made in accordance with any applicable rules relating to submissions of ruling requests. The request must be filed on or before the due date (including extensions) of the original Federal income tax return for the first taxable year to which it will apply.

(3) *Examples.*—The following examples illustrate the principles of this paragraph (f):

Example 1. Corporation X, a calendar year taxpayer, is engaged in the production of designated property during 1995. Corporation X adopts the taxable year as the computation period and quarterly measurement dates. Corporation X must identify traced debt, accumulated production expenditures, and nontraced debt at each quarterly measurement date (March 31, June 30, September 30, and December 31). Under paragraph (c)(5)(ii) of this section, Corporation X must calculate average excess expenditures for each unit of designated property by determining the amount by which accumulated production expenditures exceed traced debt for each unit at the end of each quarter and dividing the sum of these amounts by four. Under paragraph (c)(5)(iii)(C) of this section, Corporation X must calculate average nontraced debt by determining the amount of nontraced debt outstanding at the end of each quarter and dividing the sum of these amounts by four.

Example 2. Corporation X, a calendar year taxpayer, is engaged in the production of designated property during 1995. Corporation X adopts a 6-month computation period with two measurement dates within each computation period. Corporation X must identify traced debt, accumulated production expenditures, and nontraced debt at each measurement date (March 31 and June 30 for the first computation period and September 30 and December 31 for the second computation period). Under paragraph (c)(5)(ii) of this section, Corporation X must, for each computation period, calculate average excess expenditures for each unit of designated property by determining the amount by which accumulated production expenditures exceed traced debt for each unit at each measurement date during the period and dividing the sum of these amounts by two. Under paragraph (c)(5)(iii)(C) of this section, Corporation X must calculate average nontraced debt for each computation period by determining the amount of nontraced debt outstanding at each measurement date during the period and dividing the sum of these amounts by two.

Example 3. (i) Corporation X, a calendar year taxpayer, is engaged in the production of two units of designated property during 1995. Production of Unit A starts in 1994 and ends on June 20, 1995. Production of Unit B starts on April 15, 1995, but does not end until 1996. Corporation X adopts the taxable year as its computation period and does not elect under paragraph (d) of this section not to trace debt. Corporation X uses quarterly measurement dates and pays all interest on eligible debt in the quarter in which the interest is incurred. During 1995, Corporation X has two items of eligible debt. The debt and the manner in which it is used are as follows:

Period outstanding	Use of proceeds
1/01-9/01	Unit A
6/01-12/31	Nontraced

(iii) Accumulated production expenditures at the end of each quarter during 1995 are as follows:

(v) Second, Corporation X must determine average excess expenditures for Unit A and Unit B. For Unit A, this amount is $250,000 ([$200,000 + $800,000 + $0 + $0] ÷ 4). For Unit B, this amount is $775,000 ([$0 + $500,000 + $1,000,000 + $1,600,000] ÷ 4).

(vi) Third, Corporation X must determine the weighted average interest rate and apply that rate to the average excess expenditures for Units A and B. The rate is equal to the total amount of interest incurred on nontraced debt (i.e., interest incurred on all eligible debt reduced by interest incurred on traced debt) divided by the average nontraced debt. The interest incurred on nontraced debt equals

$143,333 ([$1,000,000 × 9% × 8/12] + [$2,000,000 × 11% × 7/12] − $45,000). The average nontraced debt equals $1,500,000 ([$0 + $2,000,000 + $2,000,000 + $2,000,000] ÷ 4). The weighted average interest rate of 9.56 percent ($143,333 ÷ $1,500,000), is then applied to average excess expenditures for Units A and B. Accordingly, Corporation X capitalizes an additional $23,900 ($250,000 × 9.56%) with respect to Unit A and $74,090 ($775,000 × 9.56%) with respect to Unit B (the excess expenditure amounts).

(g) *Special rules.*—(1) *Ordering rules.*—(i) *Provisions preempted by section 263A(f).*—Interest must be capitalized under section 263A(f) before the application of section 163(d) (regarding the investment interest limitation), section 163(j) (regarding the limitation on business interest expense), section 266 (regarding the election to capitalize carrying charges), section 469 (regarding the limitation on passive losses), and section 861 (regarding the allocation of interest to United States sources). Any interest that is capitalized under section 263A(f) is not taken into account as interest under those sections. However, in applying section 263A(f) with respect to the excess expenditure amount, the taxpayer must capitalize all interest that is neither investment interest under section 163(d), business interest expense under section 163(j), nor passive interest under section 469 before capitalizing any interest that is either investment interest, business interest expense, or passive interest. Any interest that is not required to be capitalized after the application of section 263A(f) is then taken into account as interest subject to sections 163(d), 163(j), 266, 469, and 861. If, after the application of section 263A(f), interest is deferred under sections 163(d), 163(j), 266, or 469, that interest is not subject to capitalization under section 263A(f) in any subsequent taxable year.

(ii) *Deferral provisions applied before this section.*—Interest (including contingent interest) that is subject to a deferral provision described in this paragraph (g)(1)(ii) is subject to capitalization under section 263A(f) only in the taxable year in which it would be deducted if section 263A(f) did not apply. Deferral provisions include sections 163(e)(3), 267, 446, and 461, and all other deferral or limitation provisions that are not described in paragraph (g)(1)(i) of this section. In contrast to the provisions of paragraph (g)(1)(i) of this section, deferral provisions are applied before the application of section 263A(f).

(2) *Application of section 263A(f) to deferred interest.*—(i) *In general.*—This paragraph (g)(2) describes the time and manner of capitalizing and recovering the deferral amount. The deferral amount for any computation period equals the sum of—

(A) The amount of interest that is incurred on traced debt that is deferred during the computation period and is not deductible for the taxable year that includes the computation period because of a deferral provision described in paragraph (g)(1)(ii) of this section, and

(B) The shortfall amount described in paragraph (c)(4) of this section.

(ii) *Capitalization of deferral amount.*—The rules described in paragraph (g)(2)(iii) of this section apply to the deferral amount unless the taxpayer elects under paragraph (g)(2)(iv) of this section to capitalize substitute costs.

(iii) *Deferred capitalization.*—If the taxpayer does not elect under paragraph (g)(2)(iv) of this section to capitalize substitute costs, deferred interest to which the deferral amount is attributable (determined under any reasonable method) is capitalized in the year or years in which the deferred interest would have been deductible but for the application of section 263A(f) (the capitalization year). For this purpose, any interest that is deferred from a prior computation period is taken into account in subsequent capitalization years in the same order in which the interest was deferred. If a unit of designated property to which previously deferred interest relates is sold before the capitalization year, the deferred interest applicable to that unit of property is taken into account in the capitalization year and treated as if recovered from the sale of the property. If the taxpayer continues to hold, throughout the capitalization year, a unit of depreciable property to which previously deferred interest relates, the adjusted basis and applicable recovery percentages for the unit of property are redetermined for the capitalization year and subsequent years so that *the increase in basis is accounted for over the remaining recovery periods beginning with the capitalization year. See Example 2 of paragraph (g)(2)(v) of this section.

(iv) *Substitute capitalization.*—(A) *General rule.*—In lieu of deferred capitalization under paragraph (g)(2)(iii) of this section, the taxpayer may elect the substitute capitalization method described in this paragraph (g)(2)(iv). Under this method, the taxpayer capitalizes for the computation period in which interest is incurred and deferred (the deferral period) costs that would be deducted but for this paragraph (g)(2)(iv) (substitute costs). The taxpayer must capitalize an amount of substitute costs equal to the deferral amount for each

unit of designated property, or if less, a prorata amount (determined in accordance with the principles of paragraph (c)(7)(i) of this section) of the total substitute costs that would be deducted but for this paragraph (g)(2)(iv) during the deferral period. If the entire deferral amount is capitalized pursuant to this paragraph (g)(2)(iv) in the deferral period, any interest incurred and deferred in the deferral period is neither capitalized nor deducted during the deferral period and, unless subsequently capitalized as a substitute cost under this paragraph (g)(2)(iv), is deductible in the appropriate subsequent period without regard to section 263A(f).

(B) *Capitalization of amount carried forward.*—If the taxpayer has an insufficient amount of substitute costs in the deferral period, the amount by which substitute costs are insufficient with respect to each unit of designated property is a deferral amount carryforward to succeeding computation periods beginning with the next computation period. In any carryforward year, the taxpayer must capitalize an amount of substitute costs equal to the deferral amount carryforward or, if less, a prorata amount (determined in accordance with the principles of paragraph (c)(7)(i) of this section) of the total substitute costs that would be deducted during the carryforward year or years (the carryforward capitalization year) but for this paragraph (g)(2)(iv) (after applying the substitute cost method of this paragraph (g)(2)(iv) to the production of designated property in the carryforward period). If a unit of designated property to which the deferral amount carryforward relates is sold prior to the carryforward capitalization year, substitute costs applicable to that unit of property are taken into account in the carryforward capitalization year and treated as if recovered from the sale of the property. If the taxpayer continues to hold, throughout the capitalization year, a unit of depreciable property to which a deferral amount carryforward relates, the adjusted basis and applicable recovery percentages for the unit of property are redetermined for the carryforward capitalization year and subsequent years so that the increase in basis is accounted for over the remaining recovery periods beginning with the carryforward capitalization year. See Example 2 of paragraph (g)(2)(v) of this section.

(C) *Method of accounting.*—The substitute capitalization method under this paragraph (g)(2)(iv) is a method of accounting that applies to all designated property of the taxpayer. A change to or from the substitute capitalization method is a change in method of accounting requiring the consent of the Commissioner under section 446(e) and §1.446-1(e).

(v) *Examples.*—The following examples illustrate the application of the avoided cost method when interest is subject to a deferral provision:

Example 1. (i) Corporation X is a calendar year taxpayer and uses the taxable year as its computation period. During 1995, X is engaged in the construction of a warehouse which X will use in its storage business. The warehouse is completed and placed in service in December 1995. X's average excess expenditures for 1995 equal $1,000,000. Throughout 1995, X's only outstanding debt is nontraced debt of $900,000 and $1,200,000, bearing interest at 15 percent and 9 percent, respectively, per year. Of the $243,000 interest incurred during the year ([$900,000 × 15%] + [$1,200,000 × 9%] = [$135,000 + $108,000]), $75,000 is deferred under section 267(a)(2).

(ii) X must first determine the amount of interest required to be capitalized under paragraph (c)(1) of this section for 1995 (the deferral period) without applying section 267(a)(2). The weighted average interest rate is 11.6 percent ([$135,000 + $108,000] ÷ $2,100,000), and the excess expenditure amount under paragraph (c)(1) of this section is $116,000 ($1,000,000 × 11.6%). Under paragraph (c)(4) of this section, X must then determine the amount of interest that would be capitalized by applying paragraph (c)(2) of this section without regard to the amount of deferred interest. Disregarding deferred interest, the amount of interest available for capitalization is $168,000 ([$900,000 × 15%] + [$1,200,000 × 9%] − $75,000). Thus, the full excess expenditure amount ($116,000) is capitalized from interest that is not deferred under section 267(a)(2) and there is no shortfall amount.

Example 2. (i) The facts are the same as in Example 1, except that $140,000 of interest is deferred under section 267 (a)(2) in 1995. The taxpayer does not elect to use the substitute capitalization method. This interest is also deferred in 1996 but would be deducted in 1997 if section 263A(f) did not apply. As in Example 1, the excess expenditure amount is $116,000. However, the amount of interest available for capitalization after excluding the amount of deferred interest is $103,000 ([$900,000 × 15%] + [$1,200,000 × 9%] − $140,000). Thus, only $103,000 of interest is capitalized with respect to the warehouse in 1995. Since $116,000 of interest would be capitalized if section 267(a)(2) did not apply, the deferral amount determined under paragraphs (c)(2) and (g)(2)(i) of this section is $13,000 ($116,000 − $103,000), and $13,000 of deferred interest must be capitalized in the year in which it would be deducted if section 263A(f) did not apply.

(ii) The $140,000 of interest deferred under section 267(a)(2) in 1995 would be deducted in 1997 if section 263A(f) did not apply. X is therefore required to capitalize an additional $13,000 of interest with respect to the warehouse in 1997 and must redetermine its basis and recovery percentage.

(3) *Simplified inventory method.*—(i) *In general.*—This paragraph (g)(3) provides a simplified method of capitalizing interest expense with respect to designated property that is inventory. Under this method, the taxpayer determines beginning and ending inventory and cost of goods sold applying all other capitalization provisions, including, for example, the simplified production method of §1.263A-2(b), but without regard to the capitalization of interest with respect to inventory. The taxpayer must establish a separate capital asset, however, in an amount equal to the aggregate interest capitalization amount (as defined in paragraph (g)(3)(iii)(C) of this section). Under the simplified inventory method, increases in the aggregate interest capitalization amount from one year to the next generally are treated as reductions in interest expense, and decreases in the aggregate interest capitalization amount from one year to the next are treated as increases to cost of goods sold.

(ii) *Segmentation of inventory.*—(A) *General rule.*—Under the simplified inventory method, the taxpayer first separates its total ending inventory value into segments that are equal to the total ending inventory value divided by the inverse inventory turnover rate. Each inventory segment is then assigned an age starting with one year and increasing by one year for each additional segment. The inverse inventory turnover rate is determined by finding the average of beginning and ending inventory, dividing the average by the cost of goods sold for the year, and rounding the result to the nearest whole number. Beginning and ending inventory amounts are determined using total current cost of inventory for the year (rather than carrying value). Cost of goods sold, however, may be determined using either total current cost or the taxpayer's inventory method. In addition, for purposes of this paragraph (g)(3)(ii), current costs for a year (and, if applicable, the cost of goods sold for the year under the taxpayer's inventory method) are determined without regard to the capitalization of interest with respect to inventory.

(B) *Example.*—The provisions of paragraph (g)(3)(ii)(A) of this section are illustrated by the following example.

Example. X, a taxpayer using the FIFO inventory method, determines that total cost of goods sold for 1995 equals $900, and the cost of both beginning and ending inventory equals $3,000. Thus, X's inverse inventory turnover rate equals 3 (3.33 rounded to the nearest whole number). Total ending inventory of $3,000 is divided into three segments of $1,000 each. One segment is treated as 3-year-old inventory, one segment is treated as 2-year-old inventory, and one segment is treated as 1-year-old inventory.

(iii) *Aggregate interest capitalization amount.*—(A) *Computation period and weighed average interest rate.*—If a taxpayer elects the simplified inventory method, the taxpayer must use the taxable year as its computation period and use the weighted average interest rate determined under this paragraph (g)(3)(iii)(A) in determining the aggregate interest capitalization amount defined in paragraph (g)(3)(iii)(C) of this section and in determining the amount of interest capitalized with respect to any designated property that is not inventory. Under the simplified inventory method, the taxpayer determines the weighted average interest rate in accordance with paragraph (c)(5)(iii) of this section, treating all eligible debt (other than debt traced to noninventory property in the case of a taxpayer tracing debt) as nontraced debt (i.e., without tracing debt to inventory). A taxpayer that has elected under paragraph (e) of this section to use an external rate as a substitute for the weighted average interest rate determined under paragraph (c)(5)(iii) of this section uses the rate described in paragraph (e)(1) as the weighted average interest rate.

(B) *Computation of the tentative aggregate interest capitalization amount.*—The weighted average interest rate is compounded annually by the number of years assigned to a particular inventory segment to produce an interest factor (applicable interest factor) for that segment. The amounts determined by multiplying the value of each inventory segment by its applicable interest factor are then combined to produce a tentative aggregate interest capitalization amount.

(C) *Coordination with other interest capitalization computations.*—(1) *In general.*—If the tentative aggregate interest capitalization amount for a year exceeds the aggregate interest capitalization amount (defined in paragraph (g)(3)(iii)(D) of this section) as of the close of the preceding year, then, for purposes of applying the rules of paragraph (c)(7) of this section, the excess is treated as an excess

expenditure amount and the inventory to which the simplified inventory method of this paragraph (g)(3) applies is treated as a single unit of designated property. If, after these modifications, no paragraph (c)(7) interest allocation is necessary (i.e., the excess expenditure amounts for all units of designated property do not exceed the total amount of interest (including deferred interest) available for capitalization), the aggregate interest capitalization amount generally equals the tentative aggregate interest capitalization amount. If, on the other hand, a paragraph (c)(7) allocation is necessary, the tentative aggregate interest capitalization amount is generally adjusted to reflect the results of that allocation (i.e., the increase in the aggregate interest capitalization amount is limited to the amount of interest allocated to inventory, reduced, however, by any substitute costs that are capitalized with respect to inventory under applicable related party rules).

(2) *Deferred interest.*—In determining the aggregate interest capitalization amount, the tentative aggregate interest capitalization amount is adjusted (after the application of paragraph (c)(7) of this section) as appropriate to reflect the deferred interest rules of paragraph (g)(2) of this section. The tentative aggregate interest capitalization amount would be reduced, for example, by the amount of a taxpayer's deferred interest for a taxable year unless the taxpayer has elected the substitute capitalization method under paragraph (g)(2)(iv).

(3) *Other coordinating provisions.*—The Commissioner may prescribe, by revenue ruling or revenue procedure, additional provisions to coordinate the election and use of the simplified inventory method with other interest capitalization requirements and methods. See §601.601(d)(2)(ii)(b) of this chapter.

(D) *Treatment of increases or decreases in the aggregate interest capitalization amount.*—Except as otherwise provided in this paragraph (g)(3)(iii)(D), increases in the aggregate interest capitalization amount from one year to the next are treated as reductions in interest expense, and decreases in the aggregate interest capitalization amount from one year to the next are treated as increases to cost of goods sold. To the extent a taxpayer capitalizes substitute costs under either applicable related party rules or the deferred interest rules in paragraph (g)(2) of this section, increases in the aggregate interest capitalization amount are treated as reductions in applicable substitute costs, rather than interest expense.

(E) *Example.*—The provisions of this paragraph (g)(3)(iii) are illustrated by the following example.

Example. The facts are the same as in the example in paragraph (g)(3)(ii)(B) of this section, and, in addition X determines that its weighted average interest rate for 1995 is 10 percent. Additionally, assume that X has no deferred interest in 1995 or 1996 and no deferral amount carryforward to either 1995 or 1996. (See paragraph (g)(2) of this section.) Also assume that no allocation is necessary under paragraph (c)(7) of this section in either 1995 or 1996. Under the rules of paragraph (g)(3)(ii) of this section, X divides ending inventory into segments of $1,000 each. One segment is 1-year old inventory, one segment is 2-year old inventory, and one segment is 3-year old inventory. Under paragraph (g)(3)(iii)(B) of this section, X must compute the applicable interest factor for each segment. The applicable interest factor for the 1-year old inventory is not compounded. The applicable interest factor for the 2-year old inventory is compounded for 1 year. The applicable interest factor for the 3-year old inventory is compounded for 2 years. The interest factor applied to the 1-year old inventory segment is .1. The interest factor applied to the 2-year old inventory segment is .21 [(1.1 × 1.1) – 1]. The interest factor applied to the 3-year old inventory is .331 [(1.1 × 1.1 × 1.1) – 1]. Thus, the tentative aggregate interest capitalization amount for 1995 is $641 (1,000 × [.1 + .21 + .331]). Because X has no deferred interest in 1995, no deferral amount carryforward to 1995, and no required allocation under paragraph (c)(7) of this section in 1995, X's aggregate interest capitalization amount equals its $641 tentative aggregate interest capitalization amount. If, in 1996, X computes an aggregate interest capitalization amount of $750, the $109 increase in the amount from 1995 to 1996 would be treated as a reduction in interest expense for 1996.

(iv) *Method of accounting.*—The simplified inventory method is a method of accounting that must be elected for and applied to all inventory within a single trade or business of the taxpayer (within the meaning of section 446(d) and §1.446-1(d)). This method may be elected only if the inventory in that trade or business consists only of designated property and only if the taxpayer's inverse inventory turnover rate for that trade or business (as defined in paragraph (g)(3)(ii)(A) of this section) is greater than or equal to one. A change from or to the simplified inventory method is a change in method of accounting requiring the consent of the Commissioner under section 446(e) and §1.446-(1)(e).

(4) *Financial accounting method disregarded.*—The avoided cost method is applied under this section without regard to any financial or regulatory accounting principles for the capitalization of interest. For example, this section determines the amount of interest that must be capitalized without regard to Financial Accounting Standards Board (FASB) Statement Nos. 34, 71, and 90, issued by the Financial Accounting Standards Board, Norwalk, CT 06856-5116. Similarly, taxpayers are not permitted to net interest income and interest expense in determining the amount of interest that must be capitalized under this section with respect to certain restricted tax-exempt borrowings even though netting is permitted under FASB Statement No. 62.

(5) *Treatment of intercompany transactions.*—(i) *General rule.*—If interest capitalized under section 263A(f) by a member of a consolidated group (within the meaning of §1.1502-1(h)) with respect to a unit of designated property is attributable to a loan from another member of the group (the lending member), the intercompany transaction provisions of the consolidated return regulations do not apply to the lending member's interest income with respect to that loan, except as provided in paragraph (g)(5)(ii) of this section. For this purpose, the capitalized interest expense that is attributable to a loan from another member is determined under any method that reasonably reflects the principles of the avoided cost method, including the traced and nontraced concepts. For purposes of this paragraph (g)(5)(i) and paragraph (g)(5)(ii) of this section, in order for a method to be considered reasonable it must be consistently applied.

(ii) *Special rule for consolidated group with limited outside borrowing.*—If, for any year, the aggregate amount of interest income described in paragraph (g)(5)(i) of this section for all members of the group with respect to all units of designated property exceeds the total amount of interest that is deductible for that year by all members of the group with respect to debt of a member owed to nonmembers (group deductible interest) after applying section 263A(f), the intercompany transaction provisions of the consolidated return regulations are applied to the excess, and the amount of interest income that must be taken into account by the group under paragraph (g)(5)(i) of this section is limited to the amount of the group deductible interest. The amount to which the intercompany transaction provisions of the consolidated return regulations apply by reason of this paragraph (g)(5)(ii) is allocated among the lending members under any method that reasonably reflects each member's share of interest income described in paragraph (g)(5)(i) of this section. If a lending member has interest income that is attributable to more than one unit of designated property, the amount to which the intercompany transaction provisions of the consolidated return regulations apply by reason of this paragraph (g)(5)(ii) with respect to the member is allocated among the units in accordance with the principles of paragraph (c)(7)(i) of this section.

(iii) *Example.*—The provisions of paragraph (g)(5)(ii) of this section are illustrated by the following example.

Example. (i) P and S1 are the members of a consolidated group. In 1995, S1 begins and completes the construction of a shopping center and is required to capitalize interest with respect to the construction. S1's average excess expenditures for 1995 are $5,000,000. Throughout 1995, S1's only borrowings include a $6,000,000 loan from P bearing interest at an annual rate of 10 percent ($600,000 per year). Under the avoided cost method, S1 is required to capitalize interest in the amount of $500,000 ($600,000 ÷ $6,000,000 × $5,000,000).

(ii) P's only borrowing from unrelated lenders is a $2,000,000 loan bearing interest at an annual rate of 10 percent ($200,000 per year). Under the principles of paragraph (g)(5)(ii) of this section, because the aggregate amount of interest described in paragraph (g)(5)(i) of this section ($500,000) exceeds the aggregate amount of currently deductible interest of the group ($200,000), the intercompany transaction provisions of the consolidated return regulations apply to the excess of $300,000 and the amount of P's interest income that is subject to current inclusion by reason of paragraph (g)(5)(i) of this section is limited to $200,000.

(6) *Notional principal contracts and other derivatives.*—[Reserved]

(7) *15-day repayment rule.*—A taxpayer may elect to treat any eligible debt that is repaid within the 15-day period immediately preceding a quarterly measurement date as outstanding as of that measurement date for purposes of determining traced debt, average nontraced debt, and the weighted average interest rate. This election may be made or discontinued for any computation period and is not a method of accounting. [Reg. §1.263A-9.]

☐ [T.D. 8584, 12-28-94. *Amended by* T.D. 9129, 5-19-2004, T.D. 9179, 2-22-2005, T.D. 9905, 9-3-2020 *and* T.D. 9942, 12-31-2020.]

[Reg. §1.263A-10]

§1.263A-10. Unit of property.—(a) *In general.*—The unit of property as defined in this section is used as the basis to determine accumulated production expenditures under §1.263A-11 and the beginning and end of the production period under §1.263A-12. Whether property is 1-year or 2-year property under §1.263A-8(b)(1)(ii) is also determined separately with respect to each unit of property as defined in this section.

(b) *Units of real property.*—(1) *In general.*—A unit of real property includes any components of real property owned by the taxpayer or a related person that are functionally interdependent and an allocable share of any common feature owned by the taxpayer or a related person that is real property ever though the common feature does not meet the functional interdependence test. When the production period begins with respect to any functionally interdependent component or any common feature of the unit of real property, the production period has begun for the entire unit of real property. See, however, paragraph (b)(5) of this section for rules under which the costs of a common feature or benefitted property are excluded from accumulated production expenditures for one or more measurement dates. The portion of land included in a unit of real property includes land on which real property (including a common feature) included in the unit is situated, land subject to setback restrictions with respect to such property, and any other contiguous portion of the tract of land other than land that the taxpayer holds for a purpose unrelated to the unit being produced (e.g., investment purposes, personal use purposes, or specified future development as a separate unit of real property).

(2) *Functional interdependence.*—Components of real property produced by, or for, the taxpayer, for use by the taxpayer or a related person are functionally interdependent if the placing in service of one component is dependent on the placing in service of the other component by the taxpayer or a related person. In the case of property produced for sale, components of real property are functionally interdependent if they are customarily sold as a single unit. For example, the real property components of a single-family house (e.g., the land, foundation, and walls) are functionally interdependent. In contrast, components of real property that are expected to be separately placed in service or held for resale are not functionally interdependent. Thus, dwelling units within a multi-unit building that are separately placed in service or sold (within the meaning of §1.263A-12(d)(1)) are treated as functionally independent of any other units, even though the units are located in the same building.

(3) *Common features.*—For purposes of this section, a common feature generally includes any real property (as defined in §1.263A-8(c)) that benefits real property produced by, or for, the taxpayer or a related person, and that is not separately held for the production of income. A common feature need not be physically contiguous to the real property that it benefits. Examples of common features include streets, sidewalks, playgrounds, clubhouses, tennis courts, sewer lines, and cables that are not held for the production of income separately from the units of real property that they benefit.

(4) *Allocation of costs to unit.*—Except as provided in paragraph (b)(5) of this section, the accumulated production expenditures for a unit of real property include, in all cases, the costs that directly benefit, or are incurred by reason of the production of, the unit of real property. Accumulated production expenditures also include the adjusted basis of property used to produce the unit of real property. The accumulated costs of a common feature or land that benefits more than one unit of real property, or that benefits designated property and property other than designated property, is apportioned among the units of designated property, or among the designated property and property other than designated property, in determining accumulated production expenditures. The apportionment of the accumulated costs of the common feature (allocable share) or land (attributable land costs) generally may be made using any method that is applied on a consistent basis and that reasonably reflects the benefits provided. For example, an apportionment based on relative costs to be incurred, relative space to be occupied, or relative fair market values may be reasonable.

(5) *Treatment of costs when a common feature is included in a unit of real property.*—(i) *General rule.*—Except as provided in this paragraph (b)(5), the accumulated production expenditures of a unit of real property include the costs of functionally interdependent components (benefitted property) and an allocable share of the cost of common features throughout the entire production period of the unit. See §1.263A-12, relating to the production period of a unit of property.

(ii) *Production activity not undertaken on benefitted property.*—(A) *Direct production activity not undertaken.*—(1) *In general.*—The costs of land attributable to a benefitted property may be treated as not included in accumulated production expenditures for a unit of real property for measurement dates prior to the first date a production activity (direct production activity), including the clearing and grading of land, has been undertaken with respect to the land attributable to the benefitted property. Thus, the costs of land attributable to a benefitted property (as opposed to land attributable to the common features) with respect to which no direct production activities have been undertaken may be treated as not included in the accumulated production expenditures of a unit of real property even though a production activity has begun on a common feature allocable to the unit.

(2) Land attributable to a benefitted property.—For purposes of this paragraph (b)(5)(ii), land attributable to a benefitted property includes all land in the unit of real property that includes the benefitted property other than land for a common feature. (Thus, land attributable to a benefitted property does not include land attributable to a common feature.)

(B) Suspension of direct production activity after clearing and grading undertaken.—(1) General rule.—This paragraph (b)(5)(ii)(B) may be used to determine the accumulated production expenditures for a unit of real property, if the only production activity with respect to a benefitted property has been clearing and grading and no further direct production activity is undertaken with respect to the benefitted property for at least 120 consecutive days (i.e., direct production activity has ceased). Under this paragraph (b)(5)(ii)(B), the accumulated production expenditures attributable to a benefitted property qualifying under this paragraph (b)(5)(ii)(B) may be excluded from the accumulated production expenditures of the unit of real property even though production continues on a common feature allocable to the unit. For purposes of this paragraph (b)(5)(ii)(B), production activity is considered to occur during any time which would not qualify as a cessation of production activities under the suspension period rules of § 1.263A-12(g).

(2) Accumulated production expenditures.—If this paragraph (b)(5)(ii)(B) applies, accumulated production expenditures attributable to the benefitted property of the unit of real property may be treated as not included in the accumulated production expenditures for the unit starting with the first measurement period beginning after the first day of the 120 consecutive day period, but must be included in the accumulated production expenditures for the unit beginning in the measurement period in which direct production activity has resumed on the benefitted property. Accumulated production expenditures with respect to common features allocable to the unit of real property may not be excluded under this paragraph (b)(5)(ii)(B).

(iii) Common feature placed in service before the end of production of a benefitted property.—To the extent that a common feature with respect to which all production activities to be undertaken by, or for, a taxpayer or a related person are completed is placed in service before the end of the production period of a unit that includes an allocable share of the costs of the common feature, the costs of the common feature are not treated as included in accumulated production expenditures of the unit for measurement periods beginning after the date the common feature is placed in service.

(iv) Benefitted property sold before production completed on common feature.—If a unit of real property is sold before common features included in the unit are completed, the production period of the unit ends on the date of sale. Thus, common feature costs actually incurred and properly allocable to the unit as of the date of sale are excluded from accumulated production expenditures for measurement periods beginning after the date of sale. Common feature costs properly allocable to the unit and actually incurred after the sale are not taken into account in determining accumulated production expenditures.

(v) Benefitted property placed in service before production completed on common feature.—Where production activities remain to be undertaken on a common feature allocable to a unit of real property that includes benefitted property, the costs of the benefitted property are not treated as included in the accumulated production expenditures for the unit for measurement periods beginning after the date the benefitted property is placed in service and all production activities reasonably expected to be undertaken by, or for, the taxpayer or a related person with respect to the benefitted property are completed.

(6) Examples.—The principles of paragraph (b) of this section are illustrated by the following examples:

Example 1. B, an individual, is in the trade or business of constructing custom-built houses for sale. B owns a 10-acre tract upon which B intends to build four houses on 2-acre lots. In addition, on the remaining 2 acres B plans to construct a perimeter road that benefits the four houses and is not held for the production of income separately from the sale of the houses. In 1995, B begins constructing the perimeter road and clears the land for one house. Under the principles of paragraph (b)(1) of this section, each planned house (including attributable land) is part of a separate unit of real property (house unit). Under the principles of paragraph (b)(3) of this section, the perimeter road (including attributable land) constitutes a common feature with respect to each planned house (i.e., benefitted property). In accordance with paragraph (b)(1), the production period for all four house units begins when production commences on the perimeter road in 1995. In addition, under the principles of paragraph (b)(4) of this section, the accumulated production expenditures for the four house units include the allocable costs of the road. In addition, for the house with respect to which B has cleared the land, the accumulated production expenditures for the house unit include the land costs attributable to the house. See paragraph (b)(5)(i) of this section. However, the accumulated production expenditures for each of the three house units that include a house for which B has not yet undertaken a direct production activity do not include the land costs attributable to the house. See paragraph (b)(5)(ii) of this section.

Example 2. Assume the same facts as Example 1, except that B undertakes no further direct production activity with respect to the house for which the land was cleared for a period of at least 120 days but continues constructing the perimeter road during this period. In accordance with paragraph (b)(5)(ii)(B) of this section, B may exclude the accumulated production expenditures attributable to the benefitted property from the accumulated production expenditures of the house unit starting with the first measurement period that begins after the first day of the 120 consecutive day period. B must include the accumulated production expenditures attributable to the benefitted property in the accumulated production expenditures for the house unit beginning with the measurement period in which direct production resumes on the benefitted property. The house unit will continue to include the accumulated production expenditures attributable to the perimeter road during the period in which direct production activity was suspended on the benefitted property.

Example 3. (i) D, a corporation, is in the trade or business of developing commercial real property. D owns a 20-acre tract upon which D intends to build a shopping center with 150 stores. D intends to lease the stores. D will also provide on the 20 acres a 1500-car parking lot, which is not held by D for the production of income separately from the stores in the shopping center. Additionally, D will not produce any other common features as part of the project. D intends to complete the shopping center in phases and expects that each store will be placed in service independently of any other store.

(ii) Under paragraphs (b)(1) and (b)(2) of this section, each store (including attributable land) is part of a separate unit of real property (store unit). The 1500-car parking lot is a common feature benefitting each store, and D must include an allocable share of the parking lot in each store unit. See paragraphs (b)(1) and (b)(3). In accordance with paragraph (b)(5)(i), D includes in the accumulated production expenditures for each store unit during each store unit's production period: the costs capitalized with respect to the store (including attributable land costs in accordance with paragraph (b)(5) of this section) and an allocable share of the parking lot costs (including attributable land costs in accordance with paragraph (b)(5) of this section). Under paragraph (b)(4), the portion of the parking lot costs that is included in the accumulated production expenditures of a store unit is determined using a reasonable method of allocation.

Example 4. X, a real estate developer, begins a project to construct a condominium building and a convenience store for the benefit of the condominium. X intends to separately lease the convenience store. Because the convenience store is held for the production of income separately from the condominium units that it benefits, the convenience store is not a common feature with respect to the condominium building. Instead, the convenience store is a separate unit of property with a separate production period and for which a separate determination of accumulated production expenditures must be made.

Example 5. (i) In 1995, X, a real estate developer, begins a project consisting of a condominium building and a common swimming pool that is not held for the production of income separately from the condominium sales. The condominium building consists of 10 stories, and each story is occupied by a single condominium. Production of the swimming pool begins in January. No direct production activity is undertaken on any condominium until September, when direct production activity commences on each condominium. On December 31, 1995, 1 condominium that was completed in December has been sold, 3 condominiums that were completed in December have not been sold, and 6 condominiums are only partially complete; additionally, the swimming pool is completed. X is a calendar year taxpayer that uses a full taxable year as the computation period, and quarterly measurement dates.

(ii) Under paragraphs (b)(1) and (b)(2) of this section, each condominium (including attributable land) is part of a separate unit of real property. Under the principles of paragraph (b)(3) of this section, the swimming pool is a common feature with respect to each condominium and under paragraph (b)(4) of this section the cost of the swimming pool is allocated equally among the condominiums.

(iii) Under paragraph (b)(1) of this section, the production period of each of the 10 condominium units begins in January when production of the swimming pool begins. On X's March 31, 1995, and June 30, 1995, measurement dates, the accumulated production expenditures for each condominium unit include the allocable costs of the swimming pool, but not the land costs attributable to the condominium because no direct production activity has been undertaken on the condominium. See paragraph (b)(5)(ii)(A) of this section. On X's September 30, 1995, and December 31, 1995, measurement dates, the accumulated production expenditures for each unit include the allocable costs of the swimming pool, and the costs of the condominium (including attributable land costs) because a direct production activity has commenced on the condominium. See paragraph (b)(5)(i) of this section.

(iv) The production period for the condominium unit that includes the condominium that is sold as of the end of 1995 ends on the date the condominium is sold. See paragraph (b)(5)(iv) of this section. The production period of each unit that is ready to be held for sale ends when all production activities have been completed on the unit, in this case on December 31, 1995, the date that the swimming pool included in the unit is completed. See §1.263A-12(d). Accordingly, interest capitalization ceases for each such unit that is sold or ready to be held for sale as of the end of 1995 (including each unit's allocable share of the completed swimming pool).

(v) The production periods for the condominium units that include the condominiums that are only partially complete at the end of 1995 continue after 1995. The accumulated production expenditures for each partially completed condominium unit continue to include the costs of the condominium (including attributable land costs) in addition to the costs of an allocable share of the completed swimming pool (including attributable land costs).

Example 6. Assume the same facts as in Example 5, except that the swimming pool is only partially complete as of the end of 1995. Under these facts, X capitalizes no interest during 1996 for the 1 unit that includes the condominium sold during 1995 (including the costs of the allocable share of the swimming pool). See paragraph (b)(5)(iv) of this section. However, with respect to the 6 condominiums that are partially complete and the 3 condominiums that are completed but unsold, interest capitalization continues after the end of 1995. The accumulated production expenditures for each of these 9 units include the costs of an allocable share of the swimming pool. See paragraph (b)(5)(i) of this section. In determining the costs of an allocable share of the swimming pool included in the accumulated production expenditures for each of the 9 units, X includes all costs of the swimming pool properly allocable to each unit, including those costs incurred as of the date of the sale of unit 1 that may have been used under applicable administrative procedures (e.g., Rev. Proc. 92-29, 1992-1 C.B. 748) in determining the basis of unit 1 solely for purposes of computing gain or loss on the sale of unit 1. See §601.601(d)(2)(ii)(*b*) of this chapter.

Example 7. (i) Assume the same facts as in Example 5, except that X intends to lease rather than sell the condominiums and the completed swimming pool is placed in service for depreciation purposes on December 31, 1995. Additionally, assume that all 10 condominiums are partially completed at the end of 1995.

(ii) Under these facts, because the swimming pool is a common feature that is placed in service separately from the condominiums that it benefits, under paragraph (b)(5)(iii) of this section, the accumulated production expenditures of each of the condominium units do not include the costs of the allocable share of the swimming pool after 1995.

(c) *Units of tangible personal property.*—Components of tangible personal property are a single unit of property if the components are functionally interdependent. Components of tangible personal property that are produced by, or for, the taxpayer, for use by the taxpayer or a related person, are functionally interdependent if the placing in service of one component is dependent on the placing in service of the other component by the taxpayer or a related person. In the case of tangible personal property produced for sale, components of tangible personal property are functionally interdependent if they are customarily sold as a single unit. For example, if an aircraft manufacturer customarily sells completely assembled aircraft, the unit of property includes all components of a completely assembled aircraft. If the manufacturer also customarily sells aircraft engines separately, any engines that are reasonably expected to be sold separately are treated as single units of property.

(d) *Treatment of installations.*—If the taxpayer produces or is treated as producing any property that is installed on or in other property, the production activity and installation activity relating to each unit of property generally are not aggregated for purposes of this section. However, if the taxpayer is treated as producing and installing any property for use by the taxpayer or a related person or if the taxpayer enters into a contract requiring the taxpayer to install property for use by a customer, the production activity and installation activity are aggregated for purposes of this section. [Reg. §1.263A-10.]

☐ [T.D. 8584, 12-28-94.]

[Reg. §1.263A-11]

§1.263A-11. Accumulated production expenditures.—(a) *General rule.*—*Accumulated production expenditures* generally means the cumulative amount of direct and indirect costs described in section 263A(a) that are required to be capitalized with respect to the unit of property (as defined in §1.263A-10), including interest capitalized in prior computation periods, plus the adjusted bases of any assets described in paragraph (d) of this section that are used to produce the unit of property during the period of their use. Accumulated production expenditures may also include the basis of any property received by the taxpayer in a nontaxable transaction.

(b) *When costs are first taken into account.*—(1) *In general.*—Except as provided in paragraph (c)(1) of this section, costs are taken into account in the computation of accumulated production expenditures at the time and to the extent they would otherwise be taken into account under the taxpayer's method of accounting (e.g., after applying the requirements of section 461, including the economic performance requirement of section 461(h)). Costs that have been incurred and capitalized with respect to a unit of property prior to the beginning of the production period are taken into account as accumulated production expenditures beginning on the date on which the production period of the property begins (as defined in §1.263A-12(c)). Thus, for example, the cost of raw land acquired for development, the cost of a leasehold in mineral properties acquired for development, and the capitalized cost of planning and design activities are taken into account as accumulated production expenditures beginning on the first day of the production period. For purposes of determining accumulated production expenditures on any measurement date during a computation period, the interest required to be capitalized for the computation period is deemed to be capitalized on the day immediately following the end of the computation period. For any subsequent measurement dates and computation periods, that interest is included in accumulated production expenditures. If the cost of land or common features is allocated among planned units of property that are completed in phases, any portion of the cost properly allocated to completed units is not reallocated to any incomplete units of property.

(2) *Dedication rule for materials and supplies.*—The costs of raw materials, supplies, or similar items are taken into account as accumulated production expenditures when they are incurred and dedicated to production of a unit of property. *Dedicated* means the first date on which the raw materials, supplies, or similar items are specifically associated with the production of any unit of property, including by record, assignment to the specific job site, or physical incorporation. In contrast, in the case of a component or subassembly that is reasonably expected to be become a part of (e.g., be incorporated into) any unit of property, costs incurred (including dedicated raw materials) for the component or subassembly are taken into account as accumulated production expenditures during the production of any portion of the component or subassembly and prior to its connection with (e.g., incorporation into) any specific unit of property. For purposes of the preceding sentence, components and subassemblies must be aggregated at each measurement date in a reasonable manner that is consistent with the purposes of section 263A(f).

(c) *Property produced under a contract.*—(1) *Customer.*—If a unit of property produced under a contract is designated property under §1.263A-8(d)(2)(i) with respect to the customer, the customer's accumulated production expenditures include any payments under the contract that represent part of the purchase price of the unit of designated property or, to the extent costs are incurred earlier than payments are made (determined on a cumulative basis for each unit of designated property), any part of such price for which the requirements of section 461 have been satisfied. The customer has made a payment under this section if the transaction would be considered a payment by a taxpayer using the cash receipts and disbursements method of accounting. The customer's accumulated production expenditures also include any other costs incurred by the customer, such as interest, or any other direct or indirect costs that are required to be capitalized under section 263A(a) and the regulations thereunder with respect to the production of the unit of designated property.

(2) *Contractor.*—If a unit of property produced under a contract is designated property under §1.263A-8(d)(2)(ii) with respect to the contractor, the contractor must treat the cumulative amount of payments made by the customer under the contract attributable to the unit of property as a reduction in the contractor's accumulated production expenditures. The customer has made a payment under this section if the transaction would be considered a payment by a taxpayer using the cash receipts and disbursements method of accounting.

(d) *Property used to produce designated property.*—(1) *In general.*—Accumulated production expenditures include the adjusted bases (or portion thereof) of any equipment, facilities, or other similar assets, used in a reasonably proximate manner for the production of a unit of designated property during any measurement period in which the asset is so used. Examples of assets used in a reasonably proximate manner include machinery and equipment used directly or indirectly in the production process, such as assembly-line structures, cranes, bulldozers, and buildings. A taxpayer apportions the adjusted basis of an asset used in the production of more than one unit of designated property in a measurement period among such units of designated property using reasonable criteria corresponding to the use of the asset, such as machine hours, mileage, or units of production. If an asset used in a reasonably proximate manner for the production of a unit of designated property is temporarily idle (within the meaning of §1.263A-1(e)(3)(iii)(E)) for an entire measurement period, the adjusted basis of the asset is excluded from the accumulated production expenditures for the unit during that measurement period. Notwithstanding this paragraph (d)(1), the portion of the depreciation allowance for equipment, facilities, or any other asset that is capitalized with respect to a unit of designated property in accordance with §1.263A-1(e)(3)(ii)(I) is included in accumulated production expenditures without regard to the extent of use under this paragraph (d)(1) (i.e., without regard to whether the asset is used in a reasonably proximate manner for the production of the unit of designated property).

(2) *Example.*—The following example illustrates how the basis of an asset is allocated on the basis of time:

Example. In 1995, X uses a bulldozer exclusively to clear the land on several adjacent real estate development projects, A, B, and C. A, B, and C are treated as separate units of property under the principles of §1.263A-10. X decides to allocate the basis of the bulldozer among the three projects on the basis of time. At the end of the first quarter of 1995, the production period has commenced for all three projects. The bulldozer was operated for 30 hours on project A, 80 hours on project B, and 10 hours on project C, for a total of 120 hours for the entire period. For purposes of determining accumulated production expenditures as of the end of the first quarter, 1/4 of the adjusted basis of the bulldozer is allocated to project A, 2/3 to project B, and 1/12 to project C. Nonworking hours, regularly scheduled nonworking days, or other periods in which the bulldozer is temporarily idle (within the meaning of §1.263A-1(e)(3)(iii)(E)) during the measurement period are not taken into account in allocating the basis of the bulldozer.

(3) *Excluded equipment and facilities.*—The adjusted bases of equipment, facilities, or other assets that are not used in a reasonably proximate manner to produce a unit of property are not included in the computation of accumulated production expenditures. For example, the adjusted bases of equipment and facilities, including buildings and other structures, used in service departments performing administrative, purchasing, personnel, legal, accounting, or similar functions, are excluded from the computation of accumulated production expenditures under this paragraph (d)(3).

(e) *Improvements.*—(1) *General rule.*—If an improvement constitutes the production of designated property under §1.263A-8(d)(3), accumulated production expenditures with respect to the improvement consist of—

(i) All direct and indirect costs required to be capitalized with respect to the improvement,

(ii) In the case of an improvement to a unit of real property—

(A) An allocable portion of the cost of land, and

(B) For any measurement period, the adjusted basis of any existing structure, common feature, or other property that is not placed in service or must be temporarily withdrawn from service to complete the improvement (associated property) during any part of the measurement period if the associated property directly benefits the property being improved, the associated property directly benefits from the improvement, or the improvement was incurred by reason of the associated property. See, however, the de minimis rule under paragraph (e)(2) of this section that applies in the case of associated property.

(iii) In the case of an improvement to a unit of tangible personal property, the adjusted basis of the asset being improved if

that asset either is not placed in service or must be temporarily withdrawn from service to complete the improvement.

(2) *De minimis rule.*—For purposes of paragraph (e)(1)(ii) of this section, the total costs of all associated property for an improvement unit (associated property costs) are excluded from the accumulated production expenditures for the improvement unit during its production period if, on the date the production period of the unit begins, the taxpayer reasonably expects that at no time during the production period of the unit will the accumulated production expenditures for the unit, determined without regard to the associated property costs, exceed 5 percent of the associated property costs.

(f) *Mid-production purchases.*—If a taxpayer purchases a unit of property for further production, the taxpayer's accumulated production expenditures include the full purchase price of the property plus, in accordance with the principles of paragraph (e) of this section, additional direct and indirect costs incurred by the taxpayer.

(g) *Related person costs.*—The activities of a related person are taken into account in applying the classification thresholds under §1.263A-8(b)(1)(ii)(B) and (C), and in determining the production period of a unit of designated property under §1.263A-12. However, only those costs incurred by the taxpayer are taken into account in the taxpayer's accumulated production expenditures under this section because the related person includes its own capitalized costs in the related person's accumulated production expenditures with respect to any unit of designated property upon which the parties engage in mutual production activities. For purposes of the preceding sentence, the accumulated production expenditures of any property transferred to a taxpayer in a nontaxable transaction are treated as accumulated production expenditures incurred by the taxpayer.

(h) *Installation.*—If the taxpayer installs property that is purchased by the taxpayer, accumulated production expenditures include the cost of the property that is installed in addition to the direct and indirect costs of installation. [Reg. §1.263A-11.]

☐ [*T.D.* 8584, 12-28-94.]

[Reg. §1.263A-12]

§1.263A-12. Production period.—(a) *In general.*—Capitalization of interest is required under §1.263A-9 for computation periods (within the meaning of §1.263A-9(f)(1)) that include the production period of a unit of designated property. In contrast, section 263A(a) requires the capitalization of all other direct or indirect costs, such as insurance, taxes, and storage, that directly benefit or are incurred by reason of the production of property without regard to whether they are incurred during a period in which production activity occurs.

(b) *Related person activities.*—Activities performed and costs incurred by a person related to the taxpayer that directly benefit or are incurred by reason of the taxpayer's production of designated property are taken into account in determining the taxpayer's production period (regardless of whether the related person is performing only a service or is producing a subassembly or component that the related person is required to treat as an item of designated property). These activities and the related person's costs are also taken into account in determining whether tangible personal property produced by the taxpayer is 1-year or 2-year property under §1.263A-8(b)(1)(ii)(B) and (C).

(c) *Beginning of production period.*—(1) *In general.*—A separate production period is determined for each unit of property defined in §1.263A-10. The production period begins on the date that production of the unit of property begins.

(2) *Real property.*—The production period of a unit of real property begins on the first date that any physical production activity (as defined in paragraph (e) of this section) is performed with respect to a unit of real property. See §1.263A-10(b)(1). The production period of a unit of real property produced under a contract begins for the contractor on the date the contractor begins physical production activity on the property. The production period of a unit of real property produced under a contract begins for the customer on the date either the customer or the contractor begins physical production activity on the property.

(3) *Tangible personal property.*—The production period of a unit of tangible personal property begins on the first date by which the taxpayer's accumulated production expenditures, including planning and design expenditures, are at least 5 percent of the taxpayer's total estimated accumulated production expenditures for the property unit. Thus, the beginning of the production period is determined without regard to whether physical production activity has commenced. The production period of a unit of tangible personal property produced under a contract begins for the contractor when the contractor's accumulated production expenditures, without any re-

duction for payments from the customer, are at least 5 percent of the contractor's total estimated accumulated production expenditures. The production period for a unit of tangible personal property produced under a contract begins for the customer when the customer's accumulated production expenditures are at least 5 percent of the customer's total estimated accumulated production expenditures.

(d) *End of production period.*—(1) *In general.*—The production period for a unit of property produced for self use ends on the date that the unit is placed in service and all production activities reasonably expected to be undertaken by, or for, the taxpayer or a related person are completed. The production period for a unit of property produced for sale ends on the date that the unit is ready to be held for sale and all production activities reasonably expected to be undertaken by, or for, the taxpayer or a related person are completed. See, however, §1.263A-10(b)(5)(iv) providing an exception for common features in the case of a benefitted property that is sold. In the case of a unit of property produced under a contract, the production period for the customer ends when the property is placed in service by the customer and all production activities reasonably expected to be undertaken are complete (i.e., generally, no earlier than when the customer takes delivery). In the case of property that is customarily aged (such as tobacco, wine, or whiskey) before it is sold, the production period includes the aging period.

(2) *Special rules.*—The production period does not end for a unit of property prior to the completion of physical production activities by the taxpayer even though the property is held for sale or lease, since all production activities reasonably expected to be undertaken by the taxpayer with respect to such property have not in fact been completed. See, however, §1.263A-10(b)(5) regarding separation of certain common features.

(3) *Sequential production or delivery.*—The production period ends with respect to each unit of property (as defined in §1.263A-10) and its associated accumulated production expenditures as the unit of property is completed within the meaning of paragraph (d)(1) of this section, without regard to the production activities or costs of any other units of property. Thus, for example, in the case of separate apartments in a multi-unit building, each of which is a separate unit of property within the meaning of §1.263A-10, the production period ends for each separate apartment when it is ready to be held for sale or placed in service within the meaning of paragraph (d)(1) of this section. In the case of a single unit of property that merely undergoes separate and distinct stages of production, the production period ends at the same time (i.e., when all separate stages of production are completed with respect to the entire amount of accumulated production expenditures for the property).

(4) *Examples.*—The provisions of paragraph (d) of this section are illustrated by the following examples:

Example 1. E is engaged in the original construction of a high-rise office building with two wings. At the end of 1995, Wing #1, but not Wing #2, is placed in service. Moreover, at the end of 1995, all production activities reasonably expected to be undertaken on Wing #1 are completed. In accordance with §1.263A-10(b)(1), Wing #1 and Wing #2 are separate units of designated property. E may stop capitalizing interest on Wing #1 but not on Wing #2.

Example 2. F is in the business of constructing finished houses. F generally paints and finishes the interior of the house, although this does not occur until a potential buyer is located. Because F reasonably expects to undertake production activity (painting and finishing), the production period of each house does not end until these activities are completed.

(e) *Physical production activities.*—(1) *In general.*—The term *physical production activities* includes any physical activity that constitutes production within the meaning of §1.263A-8(d)(1). The production period begins and interest must be capitalized with respect to real property if any physical production activities are undertaken, whether alone or in preparation for the construction of buildings or other structures, or with respect to the improvement of existing structures. For example, the clearing of raw land constitutes the production of designated property, even if only cleared prior to resale.

(2) *Illustrations.*—The following is a partial list of activities any one of which constitutes a physical production activity with respect to the production of real property:

(i) Clearing, grading, or excavating of raw land;

(ii) Demolishing a building or gutting a standing building;

(iii) Engaging in the construction of infrastructure, such as roads, sewers, sidewalks, cables, and wiring;

(iv) Undertaking structural, mechanical, or electrical activities with respect to a building or other structure; or

(v) Engaging in landscaping activities.

(f) *Activities not considered physical production.*—The activities described in paragraphs (f)(1) and (f)(2) of this section are not considered physical production activities:

(1) *Planning and design.*—Soil testing, preparing architectural blueprints or models, or obtaining building permits.

(2) *Incidental repairs.*—Physical activities of an incidental nature that may be treated as repairs under §1.162-4.

(g) *Suspension of production period.*—(1) *In general.*—If production activities related to the production of a unit of designated property cease for at least 120 consecutive days (cessation period), a taxpayer may suspend the capitalization of interest with respect to the unit of designated property starting with the first measurement period that begins after the first day in which production ceases. The taxpayer must resume the capitalization of interest with respect to a unit beginning with the measurement period during which production activities resume. In addition, production activities are not considered to have ceased if they cease because of circumstances inherent in the production process, such as normal adverse weather conditions, scheduled plant shut-downs, or delays due to design or construction flaws, the obtaining of a permit or license, or the settlement of groundfill to construct property. Interest incurred on debt that is traced debt with respect to a unit of designated property during the suspension period is subject to capitalization with respect to the production of other units of designated property as interest on non-traced debt. See §1.263A-9(c)(5)(i) of this section. For applications of the avoided cost method after the end of the suspension period, the accumulated production expenditures for the unit include the balance of accumulated production expenditures as of the beginning of the suspension period, plus any additional capitalized costs incurred during the suspension period. No further suspension of interest capitalization may occur unless the requirements for a new suspension period are satisfied.

(2) *Special rule.*—If a cessation period spans more than one taxable year, the taxpayer may suspend the capitalization of interest with respect to a unit beginning with the first measurement period of the taxable year in which the 120-day period is satisfied.

(3) *Method of accounting.*—An election to suspend interest capitalization under paragraph (g)(1) of this section is a method of accounting that must be consistently applied to all units that satisfy the requirements of paragraph (g)(1) of this section. However, the special rule in paragraph (g)(2) of this section is applied on an annual basis to all units of an electing taxpayer that satisfy the requirements of paragraph (g)(2) of this section.

(4) *Example.*—The provisions of paragraph (g)(1) of this section are illustrated by the following example.

Example. (i) D, a calendar-year taxpayer, began production of a residential housing development on January 1, 1995. D, in applying the avoided cost method, chose a taxable year computation period and quarterly measurement dates. On April 10, 1995, all production activities ceased with respect to the units in the development until December 1, 1996. The cessation, which occurred for a period of at least 120 consecutive days, was not attributable to circumstances inherent in the production process. With respect to the units in the development, D incurred production expenditures of $2,000,000 from January 1, 1995 through April 10, 1995. D incurred interest of $100,000 on traced debt with respect to the units for the period beginning January 1, 1995, and ending June 30, 1995. D did not incur any production expenditures for the more than 20-month cessation beginning April 10, 1995, and ending December 1, 1996, but incurred $200,000 of production expenditures from December 1, 1996, through December 31, 1996.

(ii) D is required to capitalize the $100,000 interest on traced debt incurred during the two measurement periods beginning January 1, 1995, and ending June 30, 1995. Because D satisfied the 120-day rule under this paragraph (g), D is not required to capitalize interest with respect to the accumulated production expenditures for the units for the measurement period beginning July 1, 1995, and ending September 30, 1995, which is the first measurement period that begins after the date production activities ceased. D is required to resume interest capitalization with respect to the $ 2,300,000 (2,000,000 + 100,000 + 200,000) of accumulated production expenditures for the units for the measurement period beginning October 1, 1996, and ending December 31, 1996 (the measurement period during which production activities resume). Accordingly, D may suspend the capitalization of interest with respect to the units from July 1, 1995, through September 30, 1996. [Reg. §1.263A-12.]

□ [T.D. 8584, 12-28-94.]

[Reg. §1.263A-13]

§1.263A-13. Oil and gas activities.—(a) *In general.*—This section provides rules that are to be applied in tandem with §§1.263A-8 through 1.263A-12, 1.263A-14, and 1.263A-15 in capitalizing interest with respect to the development (within the meaning of section 263A(g)) of oil or gas property. For this purpose, oil or gas property consists of each separate operating mineral interest in oil or gas as defined in section 614(a), or, if a taxpayer makes an election under section 614(b), the aggregate of two or more separate operating mineral interests in oil or gas as described in section 614(b) (section 614 property). Thus, an oil or gas property is designated property unless the de minimis rule applies. A taxpayer must apply the rules in paragraph (c) of this section if the taxpayer cannot establish, at the beginning of the production period of the first well drilled on the property, a definite plan that identifies the number and location of other wells planned with respect to the property. If a taxpayer can establish such a plan at the beginning of the production period of the first well drilled on the property, the taxpayer may either apply the rules of paragraph (c) of this section or treat each of the planned wells as a separate unit and partition the leasehold acquisition costs and costs of common features based on the number of planned well units.

(b) *Generally applicable rules.*—(1) *Beginning of production period.*—(i) *Onshore activities.*—In the case of onshore oil or gas development activities, the production period for a unit begins on the first date physical site preparation activities (such as building an access road, leveling a site for a drilling rig, or excavating a mud pit) are undertaken with respect to the unit.

(ii) *Offshore activities.*—In the case of offshore development activities, the production period for a unit begins on the first date physical site preparation activities, other than activities undertaken with respect to expendable wells, are undertaken with respect to the unit. For purposes of the preceding sentence, the first physical site preparation activity undertaken with respect to a section 614 property is generally the first activity undertaken with respect to the anchoring of a platform (e.g., drilling to drive the piles). For purposes of this section, an expendable well is a well drilled solely to determine the location and delineation of offshore hydrocarbon deposits.

(2) *End of production period.*—The production period ends for a productive well unit on the date the well is placed in service and all production activities reasonably expected to be undertaken by, or for, the taxpayer or a related person are completed. See §1.263A-12(d).

(3) *Accumulated production expenditures.*—(i) *Costs included.*—Accumulated production expenditures for a well unit include the following costs (to the extent they are not intangible drilling and development costs allowable as a deduction under section 263(c), 263(i), or 291(b)(2)): the costs of acquiring the section 614 leasehold and the costs of taxes and similar items that are required to be capitalized under section 263A(a) with respect to the section 614 leasehold; the costs of real property associated with developing the section 614 property (e.g., casing); the basis of real property that constitutes a common feature within the meaning of §1.263A-10(b)(3); and the adjusted basis of property used to produce property (such as a mobile rig, drilling ship, or an offshore drilling platform).

(ii) *Improvement unit.*—To the extent section 614 costs are allocated to a well unit, the undepleted portion of those section 614 costs must also be included in the accumulated production expenditures for any improvement unit (within the meaning of §1.263A-8(d)(3)) with respect to that well unit.

(c) *Special rules when definite plan not established.*—(1) *In general.*—The special rules of this paragraph (c) must be applied by a taxpayer that cannot establish, at the beginning of the production period of the first well drilled on the property, a definite plan that identifies the number and location of the wells planned with respect to the property. A taxpayer that can establish such a plan is permitted, but not required, to apply the rules of this paragraph (c), provided the rules of this paragraph (c) are consistently applied for all the taxpayer's oil or gas properties for which a definite plan can be established.

(2) *Oil and gas units.*—(i) *First productive well unit.*—Until the first productive well is placed in service and all production activities reasonably expected to be undertaken by, or for, the taxpayer or a related person are completed, a first productive well unit includes the section 614 property and all real property associated with the development of the section 614 property. Thus, for example, a first productive well unit includes the section 614 property and real property associated with any nonproductive well drilled on the section 614 property on or before the date the first productive well is placed in service and all production activities reasonably expected to be undertaken by, or for, the taxpayer or a related person are com-

pleted. For purposes of this section, a productive well is a well that produces in commercial quantities. See paragraph (c)(5) of this section, which provides a special rule whereby the costs of a section 614 property and common feature costs for a section 614 property generally are included only in the accumulated production expenditures for the first productive well unit.

(ii) *Subsequent units.*—Generally, real property associated with each productive or nonproductive well with respect to which production activities begin after the date the first productive well is placed in service and all production activities reasonably expected to be undertaken by, or for, the taxpayer or a related person are completed, constitutes a unit of real property. Additionally, a productive or nonproductive well that is included in a first productive well unit and for which development continues after the date the first productive well is placed in service and all production activities reasonably expected to be undertaken by, or for, the taxpayer or a related person are completed, generally is treated as a separate unit of property after that date. See, however, paragraph (c)(5) of this section, which provides rules for the treatment of costs included in the accumulated production expenditures of a first productive well unit.

(3) *Beginning of production period.*—(i) *First productive well unit.*—The beginning of the production period of the first productive well unit is determined as provided in paragraph (b) of this section.

(ii) *Subsequent wells.*—In applying paragraph (b) of this section to subsequent well units (as described in paragraph (c)(2)(ii) of this section), any activities occurring prior to the date the production period ends for the first productive well unit are not taken into account in determining the beginning of the production period for the subsequent well units.

(4) *End of production period.*—The end of the production period for both the first productive well unit and subsequent productive well units is determined as provided in paragraph (b)(2) of this section. See §1.263A-12(d). Nonproductive wells included in the first productive well unit need not be plugged and abandoned for the production period to end for a first productive well unit.

(5) *Accumulated production expenditures.*—(i) *First productive well unit.*—The accumulated production expenditures for a first productive well unit include all costs incurred with respect to the section 614 property and associated real property at any time through the end of the production period for the first productive well unit. Thus, the costs of acquiring the section 614 property, the costs of taxes and similar items that are required to be capitalized under section 263A(a) with respect to the section 614 property, and the costs of common features, that are incurred at any time through the end of the production period of the first productive well unit (section 614 costs) are included in the accumulated production expenditures for the first productive well unit.

(ii) *Subsequent well unit.*—The accumulated production expenditures for a subsequent well do not include any costs included in the accumulated production expenditures for a first productive well unit. In the event that section 614 costs or common feature costs with respect to a section 614 property are incurred subsequent to the end of the production period of the first productive well unit, those common feature costs and undepleted section 614 costs are allocated among the accumulated production expenditures of wells being drilled as of the date such costs are incurred.

(6) *Allocation of interest capitalized with respect to first productive well unit.*—Interest attributable to any productive or nonproductive well included in the first productive well unit (within the meaning of paragraph (c)(2)(ii) of this section) is allocated among and capitalized to the basis of the property associated with the first productive well unit. See §1.263A-8(a)(2).

(7) *Example.*—The provisions of this paragraph (c) are illustrated by the following example.

Example. (i) Corporation Z, an oil company, acquired a section 614 property in an onshore tract, Tract B, for development. In 1995, Corporation Z began site preparation activities on Tract B and also commenced drilling Well 1 on Tract B. Corporation Z was unable to establish, as provided in paragraph (a) of this section, a definite plan identifying the number and location of other wells planned on Tract B. In 1996, Corporation Z began drilling Well 2. On May 1, 1997, Well 2, a productive well, was placed in service and all production activities reasonably expected to be undertaken with respect to Well 2 were completed. By that date, also, Well 1 was abandoned.

(ii) Well 2 is a first productive well (within the meaning of paragraph (c)(2)(i) of this section). Well 1 is a nonproductive well drilled prior to a first productive well. Under paragraph (c) of this section, Corporation Z must treat both Well 1 and Well 2 as part of the first productive well unit on the section 614 property. In accordance with paragraphs (c)(3) and (c)(4) of this section, the production period of the first productive well unit begins on the date physical site preparation activities are undertaken with respect to Well 1 in 1995 and ends on May 1, 1997, the date that Well 2 is placed in service and all production activities reasonably expected to be undertaken are completed. In accordance with paragraph (c)(5) of this section, the accumulated production expenditures for the first productive well unit include, among other capitalized costs, the entire section 614 property costs capitalized with respect to Tract B and all common feature costs incurred with respect to the section 614 property through May 1, 1997.

(iii) Any well that Corporation Z begins after May 1, 1997, is a separate unit of property. See paragraph (c)(2)(ii) of this section. Under paragraph (c)(3)(ii) of this section, the production period for any such well unit begins on the first day after May 1, 1997, on which Corporation Z undertakes physical site preparation activities with respect to the well unit. Moreover, Corporation Z does not include any of the section 614 property costs in the accumulated production expenditures for any well unit begun after May 1, 1997. [Reg. §1.1263A-13.]

☐ [T.D. 8584, 12-28-94.]

[Reg. §1.263A-14]

§1.263A-14. Rules for related persons.—Taxpayers must account for average excess expenditures allocated to related persons under applicable administrative pronouncements interpreting section 263A(f). See §601.601(d)(2)(ii)(b) of this chapter. [Reg. §1.263A-14.]

☐ [T.D. 8584, 12-28-94.]

[Reg. §1.263A-15]

§1.263A-15. Effective dates, transitional rules, and anti-abuse rule.—(a) *Effective dates.*—(1) Sections 1.263A-8 through 1.263A-15 generally apply to interest incurred in taxable years beginning on or after January 1, 1995. In the case of property that is inventory in the hands of the taxpayer, however, these sections are effective for taxable years beginning on or after January 1, 1995. Changes in methods of accounting necessary as a result of the rules in §§1.263A-8 through 1.263A-15 must be made under the terms and conditions prescribed by the Commissioner. Under these terms and conditions, the principles of §1.263A-7 must be applied in revaluing inventory property.

(2) For taxable years beginning before January 1, 1995, taxpayers must take reasonable positions on their federal income tax returns when applying section 263A(f). For purposes of this paragraph (a)(2), a reasonable position is a position consistent with the temporary regulations, revenue rulings, revenue procedures, notices, and announcements concerning section 263A applicable in taxable years beginning before January 1, 1995. See §601.601(d)(2)(ii)(b) of this chapter. For this purpose, Notice 88-99, 1988-2 C.B. 422, applies to taxable years beginning after August 17, 1988, in the case of inventory, and to interest incurred in taxable years beginning after August 17, 1988, in all other cases. Finally, under administrative procedures issued by the Commissioner, taxpayers may elect early application of §§1.263A-8 through 1.263A-15 to taxable years beginning on or after January 1, 1994, in the case of inventory property, and to interest incurred in taxable years beginning on or after January 1, 1994, in the case of property that is not inventory in the hands of the taxpayer.

(3) Section 1.263A-9(a)(4)(ix) generally applies to interest incurred in taxable years beginning on or after May 20, 2004. In the case of property that is inventory in the hands of the taxpayer, §1.263A-9(a)(4)(ix) applies to taxable years beginning on or after May 20, 2004. Taxpayers may elect to apply §1.263A-9(a)(4)(ix) to interest incurred in taxable years beginning on or after January 1, 1995, or, in the case of property that is inventory in the hands of the taxpayer, to taxable years beginning on or after January 1, 1995. A change in a taxpayer's treatment of interest to a method consistent with §1.263A-9(a)(4)(ix) is a change in method of accounting to which sections 446 and 481 apply.

(4) Section 1.263A-9(g)(1)(i) applies to taxable years beginning on or after November 13, 2020. However, taxpayers and their related parties, within the meaning of sections 267(b) and 707(b)(1), may choose to apply the rules of that section to a taxable year beginning after December 31, 2017, so long as the taxpayers and their related parties consistently apply the rules of the section 163(j) regulations (as defined in §1.163(j)-1(b)(37)), and, if applicable, §§1.381(c)(20)-1, 1.382-1, 1.382-2, 1.382-5, 1.382-6, 1.382-7, 1.383-0, 1.383-1, 1.469-9, 1.469-11, 1.704-1, 1.882-5, 1.1362-3, 1.1368-1, 1.1377-1, 1.1502-13, 1.1502-21, 1.1502-36, 1.1502-79, 1.1502-91 through 1.1502-99 (to the extent they effectuate the rules of §§1.382-2, 1.382-5, 1.382-6, and 1.383-1), and 1.1504-4, to that taxable year. The last sentence of each of §1.263A-8(a)(1) and §1.263A-9(e)(2) apply to taxable years beginning on or after January 5, 2021. However, for a taxable year beginning after December 31, 2017, and before January 5, 2021, a taxpayer may apply the last sentence of each of §1.263A-8(a)(1) and

§1.263A-9(e)(2), provided that the taxpayer follows all the applicable rules contained in the regulations under section 263A for such taxable year and all subsequent taxable years.

(5) The last sentence of each of §1.263A-8(a)(1) and §1.263A-9(e)(2) apply to taxable years beginning on or after January 5, 2021. However, for a taxable year beginning after December 31, 2017, and before January 5, 2021, a taxpayer may apply the last sentence of each of §1.263A-8(a)(1) and §1.263A-9(e)(2), provided that the taxpayer follows all the applicable rules contained in the regulations under section 263A for such taxable year and all subsequent taxable years.

(b) *Transitional rule for accumulated production expenditures.*—(1) *In general.*—Except as provided in paragraph (b)(2) of this section, costs incurred before the effective date of section 263A are included in accumulated production expenditures (within the meaning of §1.263A-11) with respect to noninventory property only to the extent those costs were required to be capitalized under section 263 when incurred and would have been taken into account in determining the amount of interest required to be capitalized under former section 189 (relating to the capitalization of real property interest and taxes) or pursuant to an election that was in effect under section 266 (relating to the election to capitalize certain carrying charges).

(2) *Property used to produce designated property.*—The basis of property acquired prior to 1987 and used to produce designated noninventory property after December 31, 1986, is included in accumulated production expenditures in accordance with §1.263A-11(d) without regard to whether the basis would have been taken into account under former section 189 or section 266.

(c) *Anti-abuse rule.*—The interest capitalization rules contained in §§1.263A-8 through 1.263A-15 must be applied by the taxpayer in a manner that is consistent with and reasonably carries out the purposes of section 263A(f). For example, in applying §1.263A-10, regarding the definition of a unit of property, taxpayers may not divide a single unit of property to avoid properly classifying the property as designated property. Similarly, taxpayers may not use loans in lieu of advance payments, tax-exempt parties, loan restructurings at measurement dates, or obligations bearing an unreasonable low rate of interest (even if such rate equals or exceeds the applicable Federal rate under section 1274(d)) to avoid the purposes of section 263A(f). For purposes of this paragraph (c), the presence of back-to-back loans with different rates of interest, and other uses of related parties to facilitate an avoidance of interest capitalization, evidences abuse. In such cases, the District Director may, based upon all the facts and circumstances, determine the amount of interest that must be capitalized in a manner that is consistent with and reasonably carries out the purposes of section 263A(f). [Reg. §1.263A-15.]

☐ [T.D. 8584, 12-28-94. *Amended by T.D. 8728, 8-4-97, T.D. 9179, 2-22-2005, T.D. 9905, 9-3-2020 and T.D. 9942, 12-31-2020 (corrected 6-16-2021).*]

[Reg. §1.264-1]

§1.264-1. Premiums on life insurance taken out in a trade or business.—(a) *When premiums are not deductible.*—Premiums paid by a taxpayer on a life insurance policy are not deductible from the taxpayer's gross income, even though they would otherwise be deductible as trade or business expenses, if they are paid on a life insurance policy covering the life of any officer or employee of the taxpayer, or any person (including the taxpayer) who is financially interested in any trade or business carried on by the taxpayer, when the taxpayer is directly or indirectly a beneficiary of the policy. For additional provisions relating to the nondeductibility of premiums paid on life insurance policies (whether under section 162 or any other section of the Internal Revenue Code), see section 262, relating to personal, living, and family expenses, and section 265, relating to expenses allocable to tax-exempt income.

(b) *When taxpayer is a beneficiary.*—If a taxpayer takes out a policy for the purpose of protecting himself from loss in the event of the death of the insured, the taxpayer is considered a beneficiary directly or indirectly under the policy. However, if the taxpayer is not a beneficiary under the policy, the premiums so paid will not be disallowed as deductions merely because the taxpayer may derive a benefit from the increased efficiency of the officer or employee insured. See section 162 and the regulations thereunder. A taxpayer is considered a beneficiary under a policy where, for example, he, as a principal member of a partnership, takes out an insurance policy on his own life irrevocably designating his partner as the sole beneficiary in order to induce his partner to retain his investment in the partnership. Whether or not the taxpayer is a beneficiary under a policy, the proceeds of the policy paid by reason of the death of the insured may be excluded from gross income whether the beneficiary is an individual or a corporation, except in the case of (1) certain transferees, as provided in section 101(a)(2); (2) portions of amounts of life insurance proceeds received at a date later than death under the provisions of section 101(d); and (3) life insurance policy proceeds which are includible in the gross income of a husband or wife under section 71 (relating to alimony) or section 682 (relating to income of an estate or trust in case of divorce, etc.). (See section 101(e).) For further reference, see, generally, section 101 and the regulations thereunder. [Reg. § 1.264-1.]

☐ [T.D. 6228, 4-17-57.]

[Reg. § 1.264-2]

§ 1.264-2. Single premium life insurance, endowment, or annuity contracts.—Amounts paid or accrued on indebtedness incurred or continued, directly or indirectly, to purchase or to continue in effect a single premium life insurance or endowment contract, or to purchase or to continue in effect a single premium annuity contract purchased (whether from the insurer, annuitant, or any other person) after March 1, 1954, are not deductible under section 163 or any other provision of chapter 1 of the Code. This prohibition applies even though the insurance is not on the life of the taxpayer and regardless of whether or not the taxpayer is the annuitant or payee of such annuity contract. A contract is considered a single premium life insurance, endowment, or annuity contract, for the purposes of this section, if substantially all the premiums on the contract are paid within four years from the date on which the contract was purchased, or if an amount is deposited after March 1, 1954, with the insurer for payment of a substantial number of future premiums on the contract. [Reg. § 1.264-2.]

☐ [T.D. 6228, 4-17-57.]

[Reg. § 1.264-3]

§ 1.264-3. Effective date; taxable years ending after March 1, 1954, subject to the Internal Revenue Code of 1939.—Pursuant to section 7851(a)(1)(C), the regulations prescribed in § 1.264-2, to the extent that they relate to amounts paid or accrued on indebtedness incurred or continued to purchase or carry a single premium annuity contract purchased after March 1, 1954, and to the extent they consider a contract a single premium life insurance, endowment, or annuity contract if an amount is deposited after March 1, 1954, with the insurer for payment of a substantial number of future premiums on the contract, shall also apply to taxable years beginning before January 1, 1954, and ending after March 1, 1954, and to taxable years beginning after December 31, 1953, and ending after March 1, 1954, but before August 17, 1954, although such years are subject to the Internal Revenue Code of 1939. [Reg. § 1.264-3.]

☐ [T.D. 6228, 4-17-57.]

[Reg. § 1.264-4]

§ 1.264-4. Other life insurance, endowment, or annuity contracts.—(a) *General rule.*—Except as otherwise provided in paragraphs (d) and (e) of this section, no deduction shall be allowed under section 163 or any other provision of chapter 1 of the Code for any amount (determined under paragraph (b) of this section) paid or accrued during the taxable year on indebtedness incurred or continued to purchase or continue in effect a life insurance, endowment, or annuity contract (other than a single premium contract or a contract treated as a single premium contract) if such indebtedness is incurred pursuant to a plan of purchase which contemplates the systematic direct or indirect borrowing of part or all of the increases in the cash value of such contract (either from the insurer or otherwise). For the purposes of the preceding sentence, the term "of purchase" includes the payment of part or all of the premiums on a contract, and not merely payment of the premium due upon initial issuance of the contract. The rule of this paragraph applies whether or not the taxpayer is the insured, payee, or annuitant under the contract. The rule of this paragraph does not apply to contracts purchased by the taxpayer on or before August 6, 1963, even though there is a substantial increase in premiums after such date. The rule of this paragraph does not apply to any amount paid or accrued on indebtedness incurred or continued to purchase or carry a single premium life insurance, endowment, or annuity contract (including a contract treated as a single premium contract); the treatment of such amounts is governed by § 1.264-2.

(b) *Determination of amount not allowed.*—The amount not allowed as a deduction under paragraph (a) of this section is determined with reference to the entire amount of borrowing to purchase or carry the contract, and is not limited with reference to the amount of borrowing of increases in the cash value. The rule of this paragraph may be illustrated by the following example:

Example. A, a calendar year taxpayer using the cash receipts and disbursements method of accounting, on January 1, 1964, purchases from a life insurance company a policy in the amount of $100,000 with an annual gross premium of $2,200. For the first policy year, A pays the annual premium by means other than by borrowing. For the

second, third, fourth, and fifth policy years, A continues the policy in effect by incurring indebtedness pursuant to a plan referred to in paragraph (a) of this section. The years and amounts applicable to the policy are as follows:

Years	Cumulative cash value of contract	Total loan outstanding	Interest paid at 4.8 percent
1964	$ 370	$ 0	$ 0
1965	2,175	2,200	105.60
1966	4,000	4,400	211.20
1967	5,865	6,600	316.80
1968	7,745	8,800	422.40

On these facts (assuming that none of the exceptions contained in paragraph (d) of this section are applicable), no deduction is allowed for the interest paid during the year 1968. Moreover, the interest deduction will be disallowed for the taxable years 1965 through 1967 if such taxable years are not closed by reason of the statute of limitations or other rule of law.

(c) *Special rules.*—For purposes of this section—

(1) *Determination of existence of a plan which contemplates systematic borrowing.*—(i) *In general.*—The determination of whether indebtedness is incurred or continued pursuant to a plan referred to in paragraph (a) of this section shall be made on the basis of all facts and circumstances in each case. Unless the taxpayer shows otherwise, in the case of borrowing in connection with premiums for more than three years, the existence of a plan referred to in paragraph (a) of this section will be presumed. The mere fact that a taxpayer does not borrow to pay a premium in a particular year does not in and of itself preclude the existence of a plan referred to in paragraph (a) of this section. A plan referred to in paragraph (a) of this section need not exist at the time the contract is entered into, but may come into existence at any time during the 7-year period following the taxpayer's purchase of the contract or following a substantial increase (referred to in paragraph (d)(1) of this section) in premiums on the contract.

(ii) *Premium attributable to more than one year.*—For purposes of subdivision (i) of this subparagraph, if the stated annual premiums due on a contract vary in amount, borrowing in connection with any premium, the amount of which exceeds the amount of any other premium, on such contract may be considered borrowing to pay premiums for more than one year. The preceding sentence shall not apply where the borrowing is in connection with a substantially increased premium within the meaning of paragraph (d)(1) of this section.

(2) *Direct or indirect.*—A plan referred to in paragraph (a) of this section may contemplate direct or indirect borrowing of increases in cash value of the contract directly or indirectly to pay premiums and may contemplate borrowing either from an insurance carrier, from a bank, or from any other person. Thus, for example, if a taxpayer borrows $100,000 from a bank and uses the funds to purchase securities, later borrows $100,000 from a second bank and uses the funds to repay the first bank, later sells the securities and uses the funds as a part of a plan referred to in paragraph (a) of this section to pay premiums on a contract of cash value life insurance, the deduction for interest paid in continuing the loan from the second bank shall not be allowed (assuming that none of the exceptions contained in paragraph (d) of this section are applicable). Moreover, a plan referred to in paragraph (a) of this section need not involve a pledge of the contract, but may contemplate unsecured borrowing or the use of other property.

(d) *Exceptions.*—No deduction shall be denied under paragraph (a) of this section with respect to any amount paid or accrued during a taxable year on indebtedness incurred or continued as part of a plan referred to in paragraph (a) of this section if any of the following exceptions apply.

(1) *The 7-year exception.*—(i) *In general.*—No part of 4 of the annual premiums due during the 7-year period (beginning with the date the first premium on the contract to which such plan relates was paid) is paid under such plan by means of indebtedness. For purposes of this exception, in the event of a substantial increase in any annual premium on a contract, a new 7-year period begins on the date such increased premium is paid. If premiums on a contract are payable other than on an annual basis (for example, monthly), the annual premium is the aggregate of premiums due for the year. See paragraph (c)(1)(ii) of this section for cases where one premium on a contract paid by means of indebtedness may be considered as more than one annual premium.

(ii) *Application of borrowings.*—For purposes of subdivision (i) of this subparagraph, if during a 7-year period referred to in such subdivision the taxpayer, directly or indirectly, borrows with respect to more than one annual premium on a contract, such borrowing shall be considered first attributable to the premium for the current policy year (within the meaning of subdivision (iii) of this subparagraph) and then attributable to premiums for prior policy years beginning with the most recent prior policy year (but not including any prior policy year to the extent that such taxpayer has indebtedness outstanding with respect to the premium for such prior policy year). If such borrowing exceeds the premiums paid for the current policy year and for prior policy years and the taxpayer has, with respect to the current policy year, deposited premiums in advance of the due date of such premiums, such excess borrowing shall be considered indebtedness incurred to carry the contract which is attributable to the premiums deposited for succeeding policy years beginning with the premium for the next succeeding policy year. The preceding sentence shall not apply to a single premium contract referred to in §1.264-2.

(iii) *Current policy year.*—For purposes of subdivision (ii) of this subparagraph, the term "current policy year" refers to the policy year which begins with or within the taxable year of the taxpayer.

(iv) *Illustrations.*—The provisions of subdivision (ii) of this subparagraph may be illustrated by the following examples:

Example (1). A, a calendar year taxpayer using the cash receipts and disbursements method of accounting, on January 1, 1964, purchases from a life insurance company a policy in the amount of $100,000 with an annual gross premium of $2,200. For the first four policy years, A initially pays the annual premium by means other than borrowing. On January 1, 1968, pursuant to a plan referred to in paragraph (a) of this section, A borrows $10,000 with respect to the policy. Such borrowing is considered first attributable to paying the premium for the year 1968 and then attributable to paying the premiums for the years 1967, 1966, 1965, and 1964 (in part). No deduction is allowed for the interest paid by A on the $10,000 indebtedness during the year 1968.

Example (2). The facts are the same as in example (1), except that on January 1, 1964, A pays the first annual premium and deposits an amount equal to the second and third annual premiums, all such amounts initially being paid or deposited by means other than borrowing. On January 1, 1965, A deposits an amount equal to the fourth, fifth, and sixth annual premiums, and borrows $4,400 pursuant to a plan referred to in paragraph (a) of this section. Such borrowing is considered attributable to the premiums paid for the policy years 1965 and 1964. On January 1, 1966, A deposits an amount equal to the seventh, eighth, and ninth annual premiums, and borrows $6,600 pursuant to such plan. Such borrowing is considered attributable to the premium paid for the policy year 1966 and deposited for the policy years 1967 and 1968. No deduction is allowed for interest paid by A on the $11,000 indebtedness during 1966. Moreover, the interest deduction will be disallowed for the taxable year 1965. However, if this contract is treated as a single premium contract under §1.264-2 (by reason of deposit with the insurer of an amount for payment of a substantial number of future premiums), the deduction for interest on indebtedness incurred or continued to purchase or carry the contract would be denied without reference to this section.

(2) *The $100 exception.*—The total amount paid or accrued during the taxable year by the taxpayer who has entered one or more plans referred to in paragraph (a) of this section for which (without regard to this subparagraph) no deduction would be allowable under paragraph (a) of this section does not exceed $100. Where the amount so paid or accrued during the taxable year exceeds $100, the entire amount shall be subject to the general rule of paragraph (a) of this section.

(3) *The unforeseen events exception.*—The amount is paid or accrued by the taxpayer on indebtedness incurred because of an unforeseen substantial loss of such taxpayer's income or an unforeseen substantial increase in such taxpayer's financial obligations. A loss of income or increase in financial obligations is not unforeseen, within the meaning of this subparagraph, if at the time of the purchase of the contract such event was or could have been foreseen. College education expenses are foreseeable; however, if college expenses substantially increase, then to the extent that such increases are unforeseen, this exception will apply. This exception applies only if the plan referred to in paragraph (a) of this section arises because of the unforeseen event. Thus, for example, if a taxpayer or his family incur substantial unexpected medical expenses or the taxpayer is laid off from his job, and for that reason systematically borrows against the cash value of a previously purchased contract, the deduction for the interest paid on the loan will not be denied, whether or not the loan is used to pay a premium on the contract.

(4) *The trade or business exception.*—The indebtedness is incurred by the taxpayer in connection with his trade or business. To be within this exception, the indebtedness must be incurred to finance business obligations rather than to finance cash value life insurance. Thus, if a taxpayer pledges a life insurance, endowment, or annuity contract as part of the collateral for a loan to finance the expansion of inventory or capital improvements for his business, no part of the deduction for interest on such loan will be denied under paragraph (a) of this section. Borrowing by a business taxpayer to finance business life insurance such as under so-called keyman, split dollar, or stock retirement plans is not considered to be incurred in connection with the taxpayer's trade or business within the meaning of this subparagraph. The determination of whether the indebtedness is incurred in connection with the taxpayer's trade or business, within the meaning of this exception, rather than to finance cash value life insurance shall be made on the basis of all the facts and circumstances. The provisions of this subparagraph may be illustrated by the following examples:

Example (1). Corporation M each year borrows substantial sums to carry on its business. Corporation M agrees to provide a retirement plan for its employees and purchases level premium life insurance to fund its obligation under the plan. The mere fact that M Corporation purchases a cash value life insurance policy will not cause its deduction for interest paid on its normal indebtedness to be denied even though the policy is later used as part of the collateral for its normal indebtedness.

Example (2). Corporation R has $200,000 of bonds outstanding and purchases cash value life insurance policies on several of its key employees. Such purchase by R Corporation will not, of itself, cause its deduction for interest on its bonded indebtedness to be denied. If, however, the premiums on the life insurance policies are $10,000 each year, the cash value increases by $8,000 each year, and R Corporation increases its indebtedness by $10,000 each year, its deduction for interest on such indebtedness will not be allowed under the rule of paragraph (a) of this section. On the other hand, the absence of such a directly parallel increase will not of itself establish that the deduction for interest is allowable.

(e) *Applicability of section.*—The rules of this section apply with respect to taxable years beginning after December 31, 1963, but only with respect to contracts purchased after August 6, 1963. With respect to contracts entered into on or before August 6, 1963, but purchased or acquired whether from the insurer, insured, or any other person (other than by gift, bequest, or inheritance, or in a transaction to which section 381(a) of the Code applies) after such date, the rules of this section apply after such purchase or acquisition. [Reg. §1.264-4.]

☐ [T.D. 6773, 11-23-64.]

[Reg. §1.265-1]

§1.265-1. **Expenses relating to tax-exempt income.**— (a) *Nondeductibility of expenses allocable to exempt income.*.—(1) No amount shall be allowed as a deduction under any provision of the Internal Revenue Code of 1954 for any expense or amount which is otherwise allowable as a deduction and which is allocable to a class or classes of exempt income other than a class or classes of exempt interest income.

(2) No amount shall be allowed as a deduction under section 212 (relating to expenses for production of income) for any expense or amount which is otherwise allowable as a deduction and which is allocable to a class or classes of exempt interest income.

(b) *Exempt income and nonexempt income.*—(1) As used in this section, the term "class of exempt income" means any class of income (whether or not any amount of income of such class is received or accrued) wholly exempt from the taxes imposed by subtitle A of the Code. For purposes of this section, a class of income which is considered as wholly exempt from the taxes imposed by subtitle A includes any class of income which is—

(i) Wholly excluded from gross income under any provision of subtitle A, or

(ii) Wholly exempt from the taxes imposed by subtitle A under the provisions of any other law.

(2) As used in this section the term "nonexempt income" means any income which is required to be included in gross income.

(c) *Allocation of expenses to a class or classes of exempt income.*— Expenses and amounts otherwise allowable which are directly allocable to any class or classes of exempt income shall be allocated thereto; and expenses and amounts directly allocable to any class or classes of nonexempt income shall be allocated thereto. If an expense or amount otherwise allowable is indirectly allocable to both a class of nonexempt income and a class of exempt income, a reasonable proportion thereof determined in the light of all the facts and circumstances in each case shall be allocated to each.

(d) *Statement of classes of exempt income; records.*—(1) A taxpayer receiving any class of exempt income or holding any property or engaging in any activity the income from which is exempt shall submit with his return as a part thereof an itemized statement, in detail, showing (i) the amount of each class of exempt income, and (ii) the amount of expenses and amounts otherwise allowable allocated to each such class (the amount allocated by apportionment being shown separately) as required by paragraph (c) of this section. If an item is apportioned between a class of exempt income and a class of nonexempt income, the statement shall show the basis of the apportionment. Such statement shall also recite that each deduction claimed in the return is not in any way attributable to a class of exempt income.

(2) The taxpayer shall keep such records as will enable him to make the allocations required by this section. See section 6001 and the regulations thereunder. [Reg. § 1.265-1.]

☐ [T.D. 6313, 9-16-58.]

[Reg. § 1.265-2]

§ 1.265-2. Interest relating to tax-exempt income.—(a) *In general.*—No amount shall be allowed as a deduction for interest on any indebtedness incurred or continued to purchase or carry obligations, the interest on which is wholly exempt from tax under subtitle A of the Code, such as municipal bonds, Panama Canal loan 3-percent bonds, or obligations of the United States, the interest on which is wholly exempt from tax under subtitle A, and which were issued after September 24, 1917, and not originally subscribed for by the taxpayer. Interest paid or accrued within the taxable year on indebtedness incurred or continued to purchase or carry (1) obligations of the United States issued after September 24, 1917, the interest on which is not wholly exempt from the taxes imposed under subtitle A of the Code, or (2) obligations of the United States issued after September 24, 1917, and originally subscribed for by the taxpayer, the interest on which is wholly exempt from the taxes imposed by subtitle A of the Code, is deductible. For rules as to the inclusion in gross income of interest on certain governmental obligations, see section 103 and the regulations thereunder.

(b) *Special rule for certain financial institutions.*—(1) No deduction shall be disallowed, for taxable years ending after February 26, 1964, under section 265(2) for interest paid or accrued by a financial institution which is a face-amount certificate company registered under the Investment Company Act of 1940 (15 U.S.C. 80a-1 and following) and which is subject to the banking laws of the State in which it is incorporated, on face-amount certificates (as defined in section 2(a)(15) of the Investment Company Act of 1940) issued by such institution and on amounts received for the purchase of such certificates to be issued by the institution, if the average amount of obligations, the interest on which is wholly exempt from the taxes imposed by subtitle A of the Code, held by such institution during the taxable year, does not exceed 15 percent of the average amount of the total assets of such institution during such year. See subparagraph (3) of this paragraph for treatment of interest paid or accrued on face-amount certificates where the figure is in excess of 15 percent. Interest expense other than that paid or accrued on face-amount certificates or on amounts received for the purchase of such certificates does not come within the rules of this paragraph.

(2) This subparagraph is prescribed under the authority granted the Secretary or his delegate under section 265(2) to prescribe regulations governing the determination of the average amount of tax-exempt obligations and of the total assets held during an institution's taxable year. The average amount of tax-exempt obligations held during an institution's taxable year shall be the average of the amounts of tax-exempt obligations held at the end of each month ending within such taxable year. The average amount of total assets for a taxable year shall be the average of the total assets determined at the beginning and end of the institution's taxable year. If the Commissioner, however, determines that any amount is not fairly representative of the average amount of tax-exempt obligations or total assets, as the case may be, held by such institution during such taxable year, then the Commissioner shall determine the amount which is fairly representative of the average amount of tax-exempt obligations or total assets, as the case may be. The percentage which the average amount of tax-exempt obligations is of the average amount of total assets is determined by dividing the average amount of tax-exempt obligations by the average amount of total assets, and multiplying by 100. The amount of tax-exempt obligations means that portion of the total assets of the institution which consists of obligations the interest on which is wholly exempt from tax under subtitle A of the Code, and valued at their adjusted basis, appropriately adjusted for amortization of premium or discount. Total assets means the sum of the money, plus the aggregate of the adjusted basis of the property other than money held by the taxpayer in good faith for the purpose of the business. Such adjusted basis for any asset is

its adjusted basis for determining gain upon sale or exchange for Federal income tax purposes.

(3) If the percentage computation required by subparagraph (2) of this paragraph results in a figure in excess of 15 percent for the taxable year, there is interest that does not come within the special rule for certain financial institutions contained in section 265(2). The amount of such interest is obtained by multiplying the total interest paid or accrued for the taxable year on face-amount certificates and on amounts received for the purchase of such certificates by the percentage figure equal to the excess of the percentage figure computed under subparagraph (2) of this paragraph over 15 percent. See paragraph (a) for the disallowance of interest on indebtedness incurred or continued to purchase or carry obligations the interest on which is wholly exempt from tax under subtitle A of the Code.

(4) Every financial institution claiming the benefits of the special rule for certain financial institutions contained in section 265(2) shall file with its return for the taxable year:

(i) A statement showing that it is a face-amount certificate company registered under the Investment Company Act of 1940 (15 U.S.C. 80a-1 and following) and that it is subject to the banking laws of the State in which it is incorporated.

(ii) A detailed schedule showing the computation of the average amount of tax-exempt obligations, the average amount of total assets of such institution, and the total amount of interest paid or accrued on face-amount certificates and on amounts received for the purchase of such certificates for the taxable year. [Reg. § 1.265-2.]

☐ [T.D. 6313, 9-16-58. *Amended by T.D. 6927, 9-18-67.*]

[Reg. § 1.265-3]

§ 1.265-3. Nondeductibility of interest relating to exempt-interest dividends.—(a) *In general.*—No deduction is allowed to a shareholder of a regulated investment company for interest on indebtedness that relates to exempt-interest dividends distributed by the company to the shareholder during the shareholder's taxable year.

(b) *Interest relating to exempt-interest dividends.*—(1) All or a portion of the interest on an indebtedness relates to exempt-interest dividends if the indebtedness is either incurred or continued to purchase or carry shares of stock of a regulated investment company that distributes exempt-interest dividends (as defined in section 852(b)(5) of the Code) to the holder of the shares during the shareholder's taxable year.

(2) To determine the amount of interest that relates to the exempt-interest dividends the total amount of interest paid or accrued on the indebtedness is multiplied by a fraction. The numerator of the fraction is the amount of exempt-interest dividends received by the shareholder. The denominator of the fraction is the sum of the exempt-interest dividends and taxable dividends received by the shareholder (excluding capital gain dividends received by the shareholder and capital gains required to be included in the shareholder's computation of long-term capital gains under section 852(b)(3)(D)). [Reg. § 1.265-3.]

☐ [T.D. 7601, 3-15-79.]

[Reg. § 1.266-1]

§ 1.266-1. Taxes and carrying charges chargeable to capital account and treated as capital items.—(a)(1) *In general.*—In accordance with section 266, items enumerated in paragraph (b)(1) of this section may be capitalized at the election of the taxpayer. Thus, taxes and carrying charges with respect to property of the type described in this section are chargeable to capital account at the election of the taxpayer, notwithstanding that they are otherwise expressly deductible under provisions of subtitle A of the Code. No deduction is allowable for any items so treated.

(2) See §§ 1.263A-8 through 1.263A-15 for rules regarding the requirement to capitalize interest, that apply prior to the application of this section. After applying §§ 1.263A-8 through 1.263A-15, a taxpayer may elect to capitalize interest under section 266 with respect to designated property within the meaning of § 1.263A-8(b), provided a computation under any provision of the Internal Revenue Code is not thereby materially distorted, including computations relating to the source of deductions.

(b) *Taxes and carrying charges.*—(1) The taxpayer may elect, as provided in paragraph (c) of this section, to treat the items enumerated in this subparagraph which are otherwise expressly deductible under the provisions of subtitle A of the Code as chargeable to capital account either as a component of original cost or other basis, for the purposes of section 1012, or as an adjustment to basis, for the purpose of section 1016(a)(1). The items thus chargeable to capital account are—

(i) In the case of unimproved and unproductive real property: Annual taxes, interest on a mortgage, and other carrying charges.

(ii) In the case of real property, whether improved or unimproved and whether productive or unproductive:

(a) Interest on a loan (but not theoretical interest of a taxpayer using his own funds),

(b) Taxes of the owner of such real property measured by compensation paid to his employees,

(c) Taxes of such owner imposed on the purchase of materials, or on the storage, use, or other consumption of materials, and

(d) Other necessary expenditures,

paid or incurred for the development of the real property or for the construction of an improvement or additional improvement to such real property, up to the time the development or construction work has been completed. The development or construction work with respect to which such items are incurred may relate to unimproved and unproductive real estate whether the construction work will make the property productive of income subject to tax (as in the case of a factory) or not (as in the case of a personal residence), or may relate to property already improved or productive (as in the case of a plant addition or improvement, such as the construction of another floor on a factory or the installation of insulation therein).

(iii) In the case of personal property:

(a) Taxes of an employer measured by compensation for services rendered in transporting machinery or other fixed assets to the plant or installing them therein,

(b) Interest on a loan to purchase such property or to pay for transporting or installing the same, and

(c) Taxes of the owner thereof imposed on the purchase of such property or on the storage, use, or other consumption of such property, paid or incurred up to the date of installation or the date when such property is first put into use by the taxpayer, whichever date is later.

(iv) Any other taxes and carrying charges with respect to property, otherwise deductible, which in the opinion of the Commissioner are, under sound accounting principles, chargeable to capital account.

(2) The sole effect of section 266 is to permit the items enumerated in subparagraph (1) of this paragraph to be chargeable to capital account notwithstanding that such items are otherwise expressly deductible under the provisions of subtitle A of the Code. An item not otherwise deductible may not be capitalized under section 266.

(3) In the absence of a provision in this section for treating a given item as a capital item, this section has no effect on the treatment otherwise accorded such item. Thus, items which are otherwise deductible are deductible notwithstanding the provisions of this section, and items which are otherwise treated as capital items are to be so treated. Similarly, an item not otherwise deductible is not made deductible by this section. Nor is the absence of a provision in this section for treating a given item as a capital item to be construed as withdrawing or modifying the right now given to the taxpayer under any other provisions of subtitle A of the Code, or of the regulations thereunder, to elect to capitalize or to deduct a given item.

(c) *Election to charge taxes and carrying charges to capital account.*—(1) If for any taxable year there are two or more items of the type described in paragraph (b)(1) of this section, which relate to the same project to which the election is applicable, the taxpayer may elect to capitalize any one or more of such items even though he does not elect to capitalize the remaining items or to capitalize items of the same type relating to other projects. However, if expenditures for several items of the same type are incurred with respect to a single project, the election to capitalize must, if exercised, be exercised as to all items of that type. For purposes of this section, a "project" means, in the case of items described in paragraph (b)(1)(ii) of this section, a particular development of, or construction of an improvement to, real property, and in the case of items described in paragraph (b)(1)(iii) of this section, the transportation and installation of machinery or other fixed assets.

(2)(i) An election with respect to an item described in paragraph (b)(1)(i) of this section is effective only for the year for which it is made.

(ii) An election with respect to an item described in—

(a) Paragraph (b)(1)(ii) of this section is effective until the development or construction work described in that subdivision has been completed.

(b) Paragraph (b)(1)(iii) of this section is effective until the later of either the date of installation of the property described in that subdivision, or the date when such property is first put into use by the taxpayer;

(c) Paragraph (b)(1)(iv) of this section is effective as determined by the Commissioner.

Thus, an item chargeable to capital account under this section must continue to be capitalized for the entire period described in this subdivision applicable to such election although such period may consist of more than one taxable year.

(3) If the taxpayer elects to capitalize an item or items under this section, such election shall be exercised by filing with the original return for the year for which the election is made a statement indicating the item or items (whether with respect to the same project or to different projects) which the taxpayer elects to treat as chargeable to capital account. Elections filed for taxable years beginning before January 1, 1954, and for taxable years ending before August 17, 1954, under section 24(a)(7) of the Internal Revenue Code of 1939, and the regulations thereunder, shall have the same effect as if they were filed under this section. See section 7807(b)(2).

(d) The following examples are illustrative of the application of the provisions of this section:

Example (1). In 1956 and 1957 A pays annual taxes and interest on a mortgage on a piece of real property. During 1956, the property is vacant and unproductive, but throughout 1957 A operates the property as a parking lot. A may capitalize the taxes and mortgage interest paid in 1956, but not the taxes and mortgage interest paid in 1957.

Example (2). In February 1957, B began the erection of an office building for himself. B in 1957, in connection with the erection of the building, paid $6,000 social security taxes, which in his 1957 return he elected to capitalize. B must continue to capitalize the social security taxes paid in connection with the erection of the building until its completion.

Example (3). Assume the same facts as in example (2) except that in November 1957, B also begins to build a hotel. In 1957 B pays $3,000 social security taxes in connection with the erection of the hotel. B's election to capitalize the social security taxes paid in erecting the office building started in February 1957 does not bind him to capitalize the social security taxes paid in erecting the hotel; he may deduct the $3,000 social security taxes paid in erecting the hotel.

Example (4). In 1957, M Corporation began the erection of a building for itself, which will take three years to complete. M Corporation in 1957 paid $4,000 social security taxes and $8,000 interest on a building loan in connection with this building. M Corporation may elect to capitalize the social security taxes although it deducts the interest charges.

Example (5). C purchases machinery in 1957 for use in his factory. He pays social security taxes on the labor for transportation and installation of the machinery, as well as interest on a loan to obtain funds to pay for the machinery and for transportation and installation costs. C may capitalize either the social security taxes or the interest, or both, up to the date of installation or until the machinery is first put into use by him, whichever date is later.

(e) *Allocation.*—If any tax or carrying charge with respect to property is in part a type of item described in paragraph (b) of this section and in part a type of item or items with respect to which no election to treat as a capital item is given, a reasonable proportion of such tax or carrying charge, determined in the light of all the facts and circumstances in each case, shall be allocated to each item. The rule of this paragraph may be illustrated by the following example:

Example. N Corporation, the owner of a factory in New York on which a new addition is under construction, in 1957 pays its general manager, B, a salary of $10,000 and also pays a New York State unemployment insurance tax of $81 on B's salary. B spends nine-tenths of his time in the general business of the firm and the remaining one-tenth in supervising the construction work. N Corporation treats as expenses $9,000 of B's salary, and charges the remaining $1,000 to capital account. N Corporation may elect to capitalize $8.10 of the $81 New York State unemployment insurance tax paid in 1957 since such tax is deductible under section 164. [Reg. § 1.266-1.]

□ [*T.D. 6313, 9-16-58. Amended by T.D. 6380, 5-26-59 and T.D. 8584, 12-28-94.*]

[Reg. § 1.267(a)-1]

§ 1.267(a)-1. Deductions disallowed.—(a) *Losses.*—Except in cases of distributions in corporate liquidations, no deduction shall be allowed for losses arising from direct or indirect sales or exchanges of property between persons who, on the date of the sale or exchange, are within any one of the relationships specified in section 267(b). See § 1.267(b)-1.

(b) *Unpaid expenses and interest*—(1) No deduction shall be allowed a taxpayer for trade or business expenses otherwise deductible under section 162, for expenses for production of income otherwise deductible under section 212, or for interest otherwise deductible under section 163—

(i) If, at the close of the taxpayer's taxable year within which such items are accrued by the taxpayer or at any time within 2½ months thereafter, both the taxpayer and the payee are persons within any one of the relationships specified in section 267(b) (see § 1.267(b)-1); and

(ii) If the payee is on the cash receipts and disbursements method of accounting with respect to such items of gross income for his taxable year in which or with which the taxable year of accrual by the debtor-taxpayer ends; and

(iii) If, within the taxpayer's taxable year within which such items are accrued by the taxpayer and 2¹/₂ months after the close thereof, the amount of such items is not paid and the amount of such items is not otherwise (under the rules of constructive receipt) includible in the gross income of the payee.

(2) The provisions of section 267(a)(2) and this paragraph do not otherwise affect the general rules governing the allowance of deductions under an accrual method of accounting. For example, if the accrued expenses or interest are paid after the deduction has become disallowed under section 267(a)(2), no deduction would be allowable for the taxable year in which payment is made, since an accrual item is deductible only in the taxable year in which it is properly accruable.

(3) The expenses and interest specified in section 267(a)(2) and this paragraph shall be considered as paid for purposes of that section to the extent of the fair market value on the date of issue of notes or other instruments of similar effect received in payment of such expenses or interest if such notes or other instruments were issued in such payment by the taxpayer within his taxable year or within 2¹/₂ months after the close thereof. The fair market value on the date of issue of such notes or other instruments of similar effect is includible in the gross income of the payee for the taxable year in which he receives the notes or other instruments.

(4) The provisions of this paragraph may be illustrated by the following example:

Example. A, an individual, is the holder and owner of an interest-bearing note of the M Corporation, all the stock of which was owned by him on December 31, 1956. A and the M Corporation uses an accrual method of accounting. A uses a combination of accounting methods permitted under section 446(c)(4) in which he uses the cash receipts and disbursements method in respect of items of gross income. The M Corporation does not pay any interest on the note to A during the calendar year 1956 or within 2¹/₂ months after the close of that year, nor does it credit any interest to A's account in such a manner that it is subject to his unqualified demand and thus is constructively received by him. M Corporation claims a deduction for the year 1956 for the interest accruing on the note in that year. Since A is on the cash receipts and disbursements method in respect of items of gross income, the interest is not includible in his return for the year 1956. Under the provisions of section 267(a)(2) and this paragraph, no deduction for such interest is allowable in computing the taxable income of the M Corporation for the taxable year 1956 or for any other taxable year. However, if the interest had actually been paid to A on or before March 15, 1957, or if it had been made available to A before that time (and thus had been constructively received by him), the M Corporation would be allowed to deduct the amount of the payment in computing its taxable income for 1956.

(c) *Scope of section.*—Section 267(a) requires that deductions for losses or unpaid expenses or interest described therein be disallowed even though the transaction in which such losses, expenses, or interest were incurred was a bona fide transaction. However, section 267 is not exclusive. No deduction for losses or unpaid expenses or interest arising in a transaction which is not bona fide will be allowed even though section 267 does not apply to the transaction. [Reg. § 1.267(a)-1.]

☐ [*T.D.* 6312, 9-10-58.]

[Reg. § 1.267(a)-2T]

§ 1.267(a)-2T. Temporary regulations; questions and answers arising under the Tax Reform Act of 1984 (Temporary).—(a) *Introduction.*—(1) *Scope.*—This section prescribes temporary question and answer regulations under section 267(a) and related provisions as amended by section 174 of the Tax Reform Act of 1984, Pub. L. No. 98-369.

(2) *Effective date.*—Except as otherwise provided by *Answer 2* or *Answer 3* in paragraph (c) of this section, the effective date set forth in section 174(c) of the Tax Reform Act of 1984 applies to this section.

(b) *Questions applying section 267(a)(2) and (b) generally.*—The following questions and answers deal with the application of section 267(a)(2) and (b) generally:

Question 1: Does section 267(a)(2) ever apply to defer the deduction of an otherwise deductible amount if the person to whom the payment is to be made properly uses the completed contract method of accounting with respect to such amount?

Answer 1: No. Section 267(a)(2) applies only if an otherwise deductible amount is owed to a related person under whose method of accounting such amount is not includible in income unless paid to such person. Regardless of when payment is made, an amount owed

to a contractor using the completed contract method of accounting is includible in the income of the contractor in accordance with § 1.451-3(d) in the year in which the contract is completed or in which certain disputes are resolved.

Question 2: Does section 267(a)(2) ever apply to defer the deduction of otherwise deductible original issue discount as defined in sections 163(e) and 1271 through 1275 ("the OID rules")?

Answer 2: No. Regardless of when payment is made, an amount owed to a lender that constitutes original issue discount is included in the income of the lender periodically in accordance with the OID rules. Similarly, section 267(a)(2) does not apply to defer an otherwise deductible amount to the extent section 467 or section 7872 requires periodic inclusion of such amount in the income of the person to whom payment is to be made, even though payment has not been made.

Question 3: Does section 267(a)(2) ever apply to defer the deduction of otherwise deductible unstated interest determined to exist under section 483?

Answer 3: Yes. If section 483 recharacterizes any amount as unstated interest and the other requirements of section 267(a)(2) are met, a deduction for such unstated interest will be deferred under section 267.

Question 4: Does section 267(a)(2) ever apply to defer the deduction of otherwise deductible cost recovery, depreciation, or amortization?

Answer 4: Yes, in certain cases. In general, section 267(a)(2) does not apply to defer the deduction of otherwise deductible cost recovery, depreciation, or amortization. Notwithstanding this general rule, if the other requirements of section 267(a)(2) are met, section 267(a)(2) does apply to defer deductions for cost recovery, depreciation, or amortization of an amount owed to a related person for interest or rent or for the performance or nonperformance of services, which amount the taxpayer payor capitalized or treated as a deferred expense (unless the taxpayer payor elected to capitalize or defer the amount and section 267(a)(2) would not have deferred the deduction of such amount if the taxpayer payor had not so elected). Amounts owed for services that may be subject to this provision include, for example, amounts owed for acquisition, development, or organizational services or for covenants not to compete. In applying this rule, payments made between persons described in any of the paragraphs of section 267(b) (as modified by section 267(e)) will be closely scrutinized to determine whether they are made in respect of capitalized costs (or costs treated as deferred expenses) that are subject to deferral under section 267(a)(2), or in respect of other capitalized costs not so subject.

Question 5: If a deduction in respect of an otherwise deductible amount is deferred by section 267(a)(2) and, prior to the time the amount is includible in the gross income of the person to whom payment is to be made, such person and the payor taxpayer cease to be persons specified in any of the paragraphs of section 267(b) (as modified by section 267(e)), is the deduction allowable as of the day on which the relationship ceases?

Answer 5: No. The deduction is not allowable until the day as of which the amount is includible in the gross income of the person to whom payment of the amount is made, even though the relationship ceases to exist at an earlier time.

Question 6: Do references in other sections to persons described in section 267(b) incorporate changes made to section 267(b) by section 174 of the Tax Reform Act of 1984?

Answer 6: Yes. References in other sections to persons described in section 267(b) take into account changes made to section 267(b) by section 174 of the Tax Reform Act of 1984 (without modification by section 267(e)(1)). For example, a transfer after December 31, 1983 (the effective date of the new section 267(b)(3) relationship added by the Tax Reform Act of 1984) of section 1245 class property placed in service before January 1, 1981, from one corporation to another corporation, 11 percent of the stock of which is owned by the first corporation, will not constitute recovery property (as defined in section 168) in the hands of the second corporation by reason of section 168(e)(4)(A)(i) and (D).

(c) *Questions applying section 267(a) to partnerships.*—The following questions and answers deal with the application of section 267(a) to partnerships:

Question 1: Does section 267(a) disallow losses and defer otherwise deductible amounts at the partnership (entity) level?

Answer 1: Yes. If a loss realized by a partnership from a sale or exchange of property is disallowed under section 267(a)(1), that loss shall not enter into the computation of the partnership's taxable income. If an amount that otherwise would be deductible by a partnership is deferred by section 267(a)(2), that amount shall not enter into the computation of the partnership's taxable income until the taxable year of the partnership in which falls the day on which the amount is includible in the gross income of the person to whom payment of the amount is made.

Question 2: Does section 267(a)(1) ever apply to disallow a loss if the sale or exchange giving rise to the loss is between two partnerships even though the two partnerships are not persons specified in any of the paragraphs of section 267(b)?

Answer 2: Yes. If the other requirements of section 267(a)(1) are met, section 267(a)(1) applies to such losses arising as a result of transactions entered into after December 31, 1984 between partnerships not described in any of the paragraphs of section 267(b) as follows, and §1.267(b)-1(b) does not apply. If the two partnerships have one or more common partners (*i.e.,* if any person owns directly, indirectly, or constructively any capital or profits interest in each of such partnerships), or if any partner in either partnership and one or more partners in the other partnership are persons specified in any of the paragraphs of section 267(b) (without modification by section 267(e)), a portion of the selling partnership's loss will be disallowed under section 267(a)(1). The amount disallowed under this rule is the greater of: (1) The amount that would be disallowed if the transaction giving rise to the loss had occurred between the selling partnership and the separate partners of the purchasing partnership (in proportion to their respective interests in the purchasing partnership); or (2) the amount that would be disallowed if such transaction had occurred between the separate partners of the selling partnership (in proportion to their respective interests in the selling partnership) and the purchasing partnership. Notwithstanding the general rule of this paragraph (c), *Answer 2,* no disallowance shall occur if the amount that would be disallowed pursuant to the immediately preceding sentence is less than 5 percent of the loss arising from the sale or exchange.

Question 3: Does section 267(a)(2) ever apply to defer an otherwise deductible amount if the taxpayer payor is a partnership and the person to whom payment of such amount is to be made is a partnership even though the two partnerships are not persons specified in any of the paragraphs of section 267(b) (as modified by section 267(e))?

Answer 3: Yes. If the other requirements of section 267(a)(2) are met, section 267(a)(2) applies to such amounts arising as a result of transactions entered into after December 31, 1984 between partnerships not described in any of the paragraphs of section 267(b) (as modified by section 267(e)) as follows, and §1.267(b)-1(b) does not apply. If the two partnerships have one or more common partners (*i.e.,* if any person owns directly, indirectly, or constructively any capital or profits interest in each of such partnerships), or if any partner in either partnership and one or more partners in the other partnership are persons specified in any of the paragraphs of section 267(b) (without modification by section 267(e)), a portion of the payor partnership's otherwise allowable deduction will be deferred under section 267(a)(2). The amount deferred under this rule is the greater of: (1) The amount that would be deferred if the transaction giving rise to the otherwise allowable deduction had occurred between the payor partnership and the separate partners of the payee partnership (in proportion to their respective interests in the payee partnership); or (2) the amount that would be deferred if such transaction had occurred between the separate partners of the payor partnership (in proportion to their respective interests in the payor partnership) and the payee partnership. Notwithstanding the general rule of this paragraph (c) *Answer 3,* no deferral shall occur if the amount that would be deferred pursuant to the immediately preceding sentence is less than 5 percent of the otherwise allowable deduction.

Example. On May 1, 1985, partnership AB enters into a transaction whereby it accrues an otherwise deductible amount to partnership AC. AC is on the cash receipts and disbursements method of accounting. A holds a 5 percent capital and profits interest in AB and a 49 percent capital and profits interest in AC, and A's interest in each item of the income, gain, loss, deduction, and credit of each partnership is 5 percent and 49 percent, respectively. B and C are not related. Notwithstanding that AB and AC are not persons specified in section 267(b), 49 percent of the deduction in respect of such amount will be deferred under section 267(a)(2). The result would be the same if A held a 49 percent interest in AB and a 5 percent interest in AC. However, if A held more than 50 percent of the capital or profits interest of either AB or AC, the entire deduction in respect of such amount would be deferred under section 267(a)(2).

Question 4: What does the phrase "incurred at an annual rate not in excess of 12 percent" mean as used in section 267(e)(5)(C)(ii)?

Answer 4: The phrase refers to interest that accrues but is not includible in the income of the person to whom payment is to be made during the taxable year of the payor. Thus, in determining whether the requirements of section 267(e)(5) (providing an exception to certain provisions of section 267 for certain expenses and interest of partnerships owning low income housing) are met with respect to a transaction, the requirement of section 267(e)(5)(C)(ii) will be satisfied, even though the total interest (both stated and unstated) paid or accrued in any taxable year of the payor taxpayer exceeds 12 percent, if the interest in excess of 12 percent per annum, compounded semi-annually, on the outstanding loan balance (princi-

pal and accrued but unpaid interest) is includible in the income of the person to whom payment is to be made no later than the last day of such taxable year of the payor taxpayer. [Temporary Reg. §1.267(a)-2T.]

☐ [*T.D.* 7991, 11-29-84.]

[Reg. §1.267(a)-3]

§1.267(a)-3. Deduction of amounts owed to related foreign persons.—(a) *Purpose and scope.*—This section provides rules under section 267(a)(2) and (3) governing when an amount owed to a related foreign person that is otherwise deductible under Chapter 1 may be deducted. Paragraph (b) of this section provides the general rules, and paragraph (c) of this section provides exceptions and special rules.

(b) *Deduction of amount owed to related foreign person.*—(1) *In general.*—Except as provided in paragraph (c) of this section, section 267(a)(3) requires a taxpayer to use the cash method of accounting with respect to the deduction of amounts owed to a related foreign person. An amount that is owed to a related foreign person and that is otherwise deductible under Chapter 1 thus may not be deducted by the taxpayer until such amount is paid to the related foreign person. For purposes of this section, a related foreign person is any person that is not a United States person within the meaning of section 7701(a)(30), and that is related (within the meaning of section 267(b)) to the taxpayer at the close of the taxable year in which the amount incurred by the taxpayer would otherwise be deductible. Section 267(f) defines "controlled group" for purposes of section 267(b) without regard to the limitations of section 1563(b). An amount is treated as paid for purposes of this section if the amount is considered paid for purposes of section 1441 or section 1442 (including an amount taken into account pursuant to section 884(f)).

(2) *Amounts covered.*—This section applies to otherwise deductible amounts that are of a type described in section 871(a)(1)(A), (B) or (D), or in section 881(a)(1), (2) or (4). The rules of this section also apply to interest that is from sources outside the United States. Amounts other than interest that are from sources outside the United States, and that are not income of a related foreign person effectively connected with the conduct by such related foreign person of a trade or business within the United States, are not subject to the rules of section 267(a)(2) or (3) or this section. See paragraph (c) of this section for rules governing the treatment of amounts that are income of a related foreign person effectively connected with the conduct of a trade or business within the United States by such related foreign person.

(3) *Change in method of accounting.*—A taxpayer that uses a method of accounting other than that required by the rules of this section must change its method of accounting to conform its method to the rules of this section. The taxpayer's change in method must be made pursuant to the rules of section 446(e), the regulations thereunder, and any applicable administrative procedures prescribed by the Commissioner. Because the rules of this section prescribe a method of accounting, these rules apply in the determination of a taxpayer's earnings and profits pursuant to §1.1312-6(a).

(4) *Examples.*—The provisions of this paragraph (b) may be illustrated by the following examples:

Example 1. (i) FC, a corporation incorporated in Country X, owns 100 percent of the stock of C, a domestic corporation. C uses the accrual method of accounting in computing its income and deductions, and is a calendar year taxpayer. In Year 1, C accrues an amount owed to FC for interest. C makes an actual payment of the amount owed to FC in Year 2.

(ii) Regardless of its source, the interest owed to FC is an amount to which this section applies. Pursuant to the rules of this paragraph (b), the amount owed to FC by C will not be allowable as a deduction in Year 1. Section 267 does not preclude the deduction of this amount in Year 2.

Example 2. (i) RS, a domestic corporation, is the sole shareholder of FSC, a foreign sales corporation. Both RS and FSC use the accrual method of accounting. In Year 1, RS accrues $z owed to FSC for commissions earned by FSC in Year 1. Pursuant to the foreign sales company provisions, sections 921 through 927, a portion of this amount, $x, is treated as effectively connected income of FSC from sources outside the United States. Accordingly, the rules of section 267(a)(3) and paragraph (b) of this section do not apply. See paragraph (c) of this section for the rules governing the treatment of amounts that are effectively connected income of FSC.

(ii) The remaining amount of the commission, $y, is classified as exempt foreign trade income under section 923(a)(3) and is treated as income of FSC from sources outside the United States that is not effectively connected income. This amount is one to which the provisions of this section do not apply, since it is an amount other than interest from sources outside the United States and is not effectively connected income. Therefore, a deduction for $y is allowable to RS as of the day on which it accrues the otherwise deductible amount, without regard to section 267(a)(2) and (a)(3) and the regulations thereunder.

(c) *Exceptions and special rules.*—(1) *Effectively connected income subject to United States tax.*—The provisions of section 267(a)(2) and the regulations thereunder, and not the provisions of paragraph (b) of this section, apply to an amount that is income of the related foreign person that is effectively connected with the conduct of a United States trade or business of such related foreign person. An amount described in this paragraph (c)(1) thus is allowable as a deduction as of the day on which the amount is includible in the gross income of the related foreign person as effectively connected income under sections 872(a)(2) or 882(b) (or, if later, as of the day on which the deduction would be so allowable but for section 267(a)(2)). However, this paragraph (c)(1) does not apply if the related foreign person is exempt from United States income tax on the amount owed, or is subject to a reduced rate of tax, pursuant to a treaty obligation of the United States (such as under an article relating to the taxation of business profits).

(2) *Items exempt from tax by treaty.*—Except with respect to interest, neither paragraph (b) of this section nor section 267(a)(2) applies to any amount that is income of a related foreign person with respect to which the related foreign person is exempt from United States taxation on the amount owed pursuant to a treaty obligation of the United States (such as under an article relating to the taxation of business profits). Interest that is effectively connected income of the related foreign person under sections 872(a)(2) or 882(b) is an amount covered by paragraph (c)(1) of this section. Interest that is not effectively connected income of the related foreign person is an amount covered by paragraph (b) of this section, regardless of whether the related foreign person is exempt from United States taxation on the amount owed pursuant to a treaty obligation of the United States.

(3) *Items subject to reduced rate of tax by treaty.*—Paragraph (b) of this section applies to amounts that are income of a related foreign person with respect to which the related foreign person claims a reduced rate of United States income tax on the amount owed pursuant to a treaty obligation of the United States (such as under an article relating to the taxation of royalties).

(4) *Certain amounts owed to certain controlled foreign corporations.*—An amount that is income of a related foreign person is exempt from the application of section 267(a)(3)(B)(i) if the related foreign person is a controlled foreign corporation that does not have any United States shareholders (as defined in section 951(b)) that own (within the meaning of section 958(a)) stock of the controlled foreign corporation. However, in this case, the amount is subject to the application of section 267(a)(3)(A) in the same manner as if the related foreign person were a foreign corporation that is not a controlled foreign corporation.

(d) *Effective date.*—The rules of this section are effective with respect to interest that is allowable as a deduction under chapter 1 (without regard to the rules of this section) in taxable years beginning after December 31, 1983, but are not effective with respect to interest that is incurred with respect to indebtedness incurred on or before September 29, 1983, or incurred after that date pursuant to a contract that was binding on that date and at all times thereafter (unless the indebtedness or the contract was renegotiated, extended, renewed, or revised after that date). Except as otherwise provided in this paragraph (d), the regulations in this section issued under section 267 apply to all other deductible amounts that are incurred after July 31, 1989, but do not apply to amounts that are incurred pursuant to a contract that was binding on September 29, 1983, and at all times thereafter (unless the contract was renegotiated, extended, renewed, or revised after that date). Paragraph (c)(2) of this section applies to payments accrued on or after October 22, 2004. For payments accrued before October 22, 2004, see §1.267(a)-3(c)(2), as contained in 26 CFR part 1, revised as of April 1, 2004. Paragraph (c)(4) of this section applies to payments accrued on or after October 1, 2019. For payments accrued before October 1, 2019, a taxpayer may apply paragraph (c)(4) of this section for payments accrued during the last taxable year of a foreign corporation beginning before January 1, 2018, and each subsequent taxable year of the foreign corporation, provided that the taxpayer and United States persons that are related (within the meaning of section 267 or 707) to the taxpayer consistently apply such paragraph with respect to all foreign corporations. For payments accrued before October 22, 2004, see §1.267(a)-3(c)(4), as contained in 26 CFR part 1, revised as of April 1, 2004. [Reg. §1.267(a)-3.]

□ [*T.D.* 8465, 12-31-92. *Amended by T.D.* 9908, 9-21-2020.]

Reg. §1.267(a)-3(c)(1)

§1.267(b)-1. Relationships.—(a) *In general.*—(1) The persons referred to in section 267(a) and §1.267(a)-1 are specified in section 267(b).

(2) Under section 267(b)(3), it is not necessary that either of the two corporations be a personal holding company or a foreign personal holding company for the taxable year in which the sale or exchange occurs or in which the expenses or interest are properly accruable, but either one of them must be such a company for the taxable year next preceding the taxable year in which the sale or exchange occurs or in which the expenses or interest are accrued.

(3) Under section 267(b)(9), the control of certain educational and charitable organizations exempt from tax under section 501 includes any kind of control, direct or indirect, by means of which a person in fact controls such an organization, whether or not the control is legally enforceable and regardless of the method by which the control is exercised or exercisable. In the case of an individual, control possessed by the individual's family, as defined in section 267(c)(4) and paragraph (a)(4) of §1.267(c)-1, shall be taken into account.

(b) *Partnerships.*—(1) Since section 267 does not include members of a partnership and the partnership as related persons, transactions between partners and partnerships do not come within the scope of section 267. Such transactions are governed by section 707 for the purposes of which the partnership is considered to be an entity separate from the partners. See section 707 and §1.707-1. Any transaction described in section 267(a) between a partnership and a person other than a partner shall be considered as occurring between the other person and the members of the partnership separately. Therefore, if the other person and a partner are within any one of the relationships specified in section 267(b), no deductions with respect to such transactions between the other person and the partnership shall be allowed—

(i) To the related partner to the extent of his distributive share of partnership deductions for losses or unpaid expenses or interest resulting from such transactions, and

(ii) To the other person to the extent the related partner acquires an interest in any property sold to or exchanged with the partnership by such other person at a loss, or to the extent of the related partner's distributive share of the unpaid expenses or interest payable to the partnership by the other person as a result of such transaction.

(2) The provisions of this paragraph may be illustrated by the following examples:

Example (1). A, an equal partner in the ABC partnership, personally owns all the stock of M Corporation. B and C are not related to A. The partnership and all the partners use an accrual method of accounting, and are on a calendar year. M Corporation uses the cash receipts and disbursements method of accounting and is also on a calendar year. During 1956 the partnership borrowed money from M Corporation and also sold property to M Corporation, sustaining a loss on the sale. On December 31, 1956, the partnership accrued its interest liability to the M Corporation and on April 1, 1957 (more than 2½ months after the close of its taxable year), it paid the M Corporation the amount of such accrued interest. Applying the rules of this paragraph, the transactions are considered as occurring between M Corporation and the partners separately. The sale and interest transactions considered as occurring between A and the M Corporation fall within the scope of section 267(a) and (b), but the transactions considered as occurring between partners B and C and the M Corporation do not. The latter two partners may, therefore, deduct their distributive shares of partnership deductions for the loss and the accrued interest. However, no deduction shall be allowed to A for his distributive shares of these partnership deductions. Furthermore, A's adjusted basis for his partnership interest must be decreased by the amount of his distributive share of such deductions. See section 705(a)(2).

Example (2). Assume the same facts as in example (1) of this subparagraph except that the partnership and all the partners use the cash receipts and disbursements method of accounting, and that M Corporation uses an accrual method. Assume further, that during 1956 M Corporation borrowed money from the partnership and that on a sale of property to the partnership during that year M Corporation sustained a loss. On December 31, 1956, the M Corporation accrued its interest liability on the borrowed money and on April 1, 1957 (more than 2½ months after the close of its taxable year) it paid the accrued interest to the partnership. The corporation's deduction for the accrued interest is not allowed to the extent of A's distributive share (one-third) of such interest income. M Corporation's deduction for the loss on the sale of the property to the partnership is not allowed to the extent of A's one-third interest in the purchased property. [Reg. §1.267(b)-1.]

□ [*T.D.* 6312, 9-10-58.]

[Reg. §1.267(c)-1]

§1.267(c)-1. Constructive ownership of stock.—(a) *In general.*—(1) The determination of stock ownership for purposes of section 267(b) shall be in accordance with the rules in section 267(c).

(2) For an individual to be considered under section 267(c)(2) as constructively owning the stock of a corporation which is owned, directly or indirectly, by or for members of his family it is not necessary that he own stock in the corporation either directly or indirectly. On the other hand, for an individual to be considered under section 267(c)(3) as owning the stock of a corporation owned either actually, or constructively under section 267(c)(1), by or for his partner, such individual must himself actually own, or constructively own under section 267(c)(1), stock of such corporation.

(3) An individual's constructive ownership, under section 267(c)(2) or (3), of stock owned directly or indirectly by or for a member of his family, or by or for his partner, is not to be considered as actual ownership of such stock, and the individual's constructive ownership of the stock is not to be attributed to another member of his family or to another partner. However, an individual's constructive ownership, under section 267(c)(1), of stock owned directly or indirectly by or for a corporation, partnership, estate, or trust shall be considered as actual ownership of the stock, and the individual's ownership may be attributed to a member of his family or to his partner.

(4) The family of an individual shall include only his brothers and sisters, spouse, ancestors, and lineal descendants. In determining whether any of these relationships exist, full effect shall be given to a legal adoption. The term "ancestors" includes parents and grandparents, and the term "lineal descendants" includes children and grandchildren.

(b) *Examples.*—The application of section 267(c) may be illustrated by the following examples:

Example (1). On July 1, 1957, A owned 75 percent, and AW, his wife, owned 25 percent, of the outstanding stock of the M Corporation. The M Corporation in turn owned 80 percent of the outstanding stock of the O Corporation. Under section 267(c)(1), A and AW are each considered as owning an amount of the O Corporation stock actually owned by M Corporation in proportion to their respective ownership of M Corporation stock. Therefore, A constructively owns 60 percent (75 percent of 80 percent) of the O Corporation stock and AW constructively owns 20 percent (25 percent of 80 percent) of such stock. Under the family ownership rule of section 267(c)(2), an individual is considered as constructively owning the stock actually owned by his spouse. A and AW, therefore, are each considered as constructively owning the M Corporation stock actually owned by the other. For the purpose of applying this family ownership rule, A's and AW's constructive ownership of O Corporation stock is considered as actual ownership under section 267(c)(5). Thus, A constructively owns the 20 percent of the O Corporation stock constructively owned by AW, and AW constructively owns the 60 percent of the O Corporation stock constructively owned by A. In addition, the family ownership rule may be applied to make AWF, AW's father, the constructive owner of the 25 percent of the M Corporation stock actually owned by AW. As noted above, AW's constructive ownership of 20 percent of the O Corporation stock is considered as actual ownership for purposes of applying the family ownership rule, and AWF is thereby considered the constructive owner of this stock also. However, AW's constructive ownership of the stock constructively and actually owned by A may not be considered as actual ownership for the purpose of again applying the family ownership rule to make AWF the constructive owner of these shares. The ownership of the stock in the M and O Corporations may be tabulated as follows:

Person	Stock ownership in M Corporation		Total under Section 267 Percent	Stock ownership in O Corporation		Total under Section 267 Percent
	Actual Percent	Constructive Percent		Actual Percent	Constructive Percent	
A	75	25	100	None	{60}{20}	80
AW (A's wife)	25	75	100	None	{20}{60}	80
AWF (AW's father)	None	25	25	None	20	20
M Corporation	...	...	...	80	None	80
O Corporation	None	None	None	...	...	...

Assuming that the M Corporation and the O Corporation make their income tax returns for calendar years, and that there was no distribution in liquidation of the M or O Corporation, and further assuming that either corporation was a personal holding company under section 542 for the calendar year 1956, no deduction is allowable with respect to losses from sales or exchanges of property made on July 1, 1957, between the two corporations. Moreover, whether or not either corporation was a personal holding company, no loss would be allowable on a sale or exchange between A or AW and either corporation. A deduction would be allowed, however, for a loss sustained in an arm's length sale or exchange between A and AWF, and between AWF and the M or O Corporation.

Example (2). On June 15, 1957, all of the stock of the N Corporation was owned in equal proportions by A and his partner, AP. Except in the case of distributions in liquidation by the N Corporation, no deduction is allowable with respect to losses from sales or exchanges of property made on June 15, 1957, between A and the N Corporation or AP and the N Corporation since each partner is considered as owning the stock owned by the other; therefore, each is considered as owning more than 50 percent in value of the outstanding stock of the N Corporation.

Example (3). On June 7, 1957, A owned no stock in X Corporation, but his wife, AW, owned 20 percent in value of the outstanding stock of X, and A's partner, AP, owned 60 percent in value of the outstanding stock of X. The partnership firm of A and AP owned no stock in X Corporation. The ownership of AW's stock is attributed to A, but not that of AP since A does not own any X Corporation stock either actually, or constructively under section 267(c)(1). A's constructive ownership of AW's stock is not the ownership required for the attribution of AP's stock. Therefore, deductions for losses from sales or exchanges of property made on June 7, 1957, between X Corporation and A or AW are allowable since neither person owned more than 50 percent in value of the outstanding stock of X, but deductions for losses from sales or exchanges between X Corporation and AP would not be allowable by section 267(a) (except for distributions in liquidation of X Corporation). [Reg. §1.267(c)-1.]

☐ [*T.D. 6312, 9-10-58.*]

[Reg. §1.267(d)-1]

§1.267(d)-1. Amount of gain where loss previously disallowed.—(a) *General rule.*—(1) If a taxpayer acquires property by purchase or exchange from a transferor who, on the transaction, sustained a loss not allowable as a deduction by reason of section 267(a)(1) (or by reason of section 24(b) of the Internal Revenue Code of 1939), then any gain realized by the taxpayer on a sale or other disposition of the property after December 31, 1953, shall be recognized only to the extent that the gain exceeds the amount of such loss as is properly allocable to the property sold or otherwise disposed of by the taxpayer.

(2) The general rule is also applicable to a sale or other disposition of property by a taxpayer when the basis of such property in the taxpayer's hands is determined directly or indirectly by reference to other property acquired by the taxpayer from a transferor through a sale or exchange in which a loss sustained by the transferor was not allowable. Therefore, section 267(d) applies to a sale or other disposition of property after a series of transactions if the basis of the property acquired in each transaction is determined by reference to the basis of the property transferred, and if the original property was acquired in a transaction in which a loss to a transferor was not allowable by reason of section 267(a)(1) (or by reason of section 24(b) of the Internal Revenue Code of 1939).

(3) The benefit of the general rule is available only to the original transferee but does not apply to any original transferee (for example, a donee or a person acquiring property from a decedent where the basis of property is determined under section 1014 or 1022) who acquired the property in any manner other than by purchase or exchange.

(4) The application of the provisions of this paragraph may be illustrated by the following examples:

Example (1). He sells to his wife, W, for $500, certain corporate stock with an adjusted basis for determining loss to him of $800. The loss of $300 is not allowable to H by reason of section 267(a)(1) and paragraph (a) of §1.267(a)-1. W later sells this stock for $1,000. Although W's realized gain is $500 ($1,000 minus $500, her basis), her recognized gain under section 267(d) is only $200, the excess of the realized gain of $500 over the loss of $300 not allowable to H. In determining capital gain or loss W's holding period commences on the date of the sale from H to W.

Example (2). Assume the same facts as in example (1) except that W later sells her stock for $300 instead of $1,000. Her recognized loss is $200 and not $500 since section 267(d) applies only to the nonrecognition of gain and does not affect basis.

Example (3). Assume the same facts as in example (1) except that W transfers her stock as a gift to X. The basis of the stock in the hands of X for the purpose of determining gain, under the provisions of section 1015, is the same as W's, or $500. If X later sells the stock for $1,000 the entire $500 gain is taxed to him.

Example (4). H sells to his wife, W, for $5,500, farmland, with an adjusted basis for determining loss to him of $8,000. The loss of $2,500 is not allowable to H by reason of section 267(a)(1) and paragraph (a) of §1.267(a)-1. W exchanges the farmland, held for investment purposes, with S, an unrelated individual, for two city lots, also held for investment purposes. The basis of the city lots in the hands of W ($5,500) is a substituted basis determined under section 1031(d) by reference to the basis of the farmland. Later W sells the city lots for $10,000. Although W's realized gain is $4,500 ($10,000 minus $5,500), her recognized gain under section 267(d) is only $2,000, the excess of the realized gain of $4,500 over the loss of $2,500 not allowable to H.

(b) *Determination of basis and gain with respect to divisible property.*— (1) *Taxpayer's basis.*—When the taxpayer acquires divisible property or property that consists of several items or classes of items by a purchase or exchange on which loss is not allowable to the transferor, the basis in the taxpayer's hands of a particular part, item, or class of such property shall be determined (if the taxpayer's basis for that part is not known) by allocating to the particular part, item, or class a portion of the taxpayer's basis for the entire property in the proportion that the fair market value of the particular part, item, or class bears to the fair market value of the entire property at the time of the taxpayer's acquisition of the property.

(2) *Taxpayer's recognized gain.*—Gain realized by the taxpayer on sales or other dispositions after December 31, 1953, of a part, item, or class of the property shall be recognized only to the extent that such gain exceeds the amount of loss attributable to such part, item, or class of property not allowable to the taxpayer's transferor on the latter's sale or exchange of such property to the taxpayer.

(3) *Transferor's loss not allowable.*—(i) The transferor's loss on the sale or exchange of a part, item, or class of the property to the taxpayer shall be the excess of the transferor's adjusted basis for determining loss on the part, item, or class of the property over the amount realized by the transferor on the sale or exchange of the part, item, or class. The amount realized by the transferor on the part, item, or class shall be determined (if such amount is not known) in the same manner that the taxpayer's basis for such part, item, or class is determined. See subparagraph (1) of this paragraph.

(ii) If the transferor's basis for determining loss on the part, item, or class cannot be determined, the transferor's loss on the particular part, item, or class transferred to the taxpayer shall be determined by allocating to the part, item, or class a portion of his loss on the entire property in the proportion that the fair market value of such part, item, or class bears to the fair market value of the entire property on the date of the taxpayer's acquisition of the entire property.

(4) *Examples.*—The application of the provisions of this paragraph may be illustrated by the following examples:

Example (1). During 1953, H sold class A stock which had cost him $1,100, and common stock which had cost him $2,000, to his wife W for a lump sum of $1,500. Under section 24(b)(1)(A) of the 1939 Code, the loss of $1,600 on the transaction was not allowable to H. At the time the stocks were purchased by W, the fair market value of class A stock was $900 and the fair market value of common stock was $600. In 1954, W sold the class A stock for $2,500. W's recognized gain is determined as follows:

Amount realized by W on sale of class A stock	$2,500
Less: Basis allocated to class A stock—$900/$1,500 × $1,500	900
Realized gain on transaction	1,600
Less: Loss sustained by H on sale of class A stock to W not allowable as a deduction:	
Basis to H of class A stock $1,100	

Amount realized by H on class A stock— $900/$1,500 × $1,500	900
Unallowable loss to H on sale of class A stock	200
Recognized gain on sale of Class A stock by W	1,400

Example (2). Assume the same facts as those stated in example (1) of this subparagraph except that H originally purchased both classes of stock for a lump sum of $3,100. The unallowable loss to H on the sale of all the stock to W is $1,600 ($3,100 minus $1,500). An exact determination of the unallowable loss sustained by H on sale to W of class A stock cannot be made because H's basis for class A stock cannot be determined. Therefore, a determination of the unallowable loss is made by allocating to class A stock a portion of H's loss on the entire property transferred to W in the proportion that the fair market value of class A stock at the time acquired by W ($900) bears to the fair market value of both classes of stock at that time ($1,500). The allocated portion is $900/$1,500 × $1,600, or $960. W's recognized gain is, therefore, $640 (W's realized gain of $1,600 minus $960).

(c) *Special rules.*—(1) Section 267(d) does not affect the basis of property for determining gain. Depreciation and other items which depend on such basis are also not affected.

(2) The provisions of section 267(d) shall not apply if the loss sustained by the transferor is not allowable to the transferor as a deduction by reason of section 1091, or section 118 of the Internal Revenue Code of 1939, which relate to losses from wash sales of stock or securities.

(3) In determining the holding period in the hands of the transferee of property received in an exchange with a transferor with respect to whom a loss on the exchange is not allowable by reason of section 267, section 1223(2) does not apply to include the period during which the property was held by the transferor. In determining such holding period, however, section 1223(1) may apply to include the period during which the transferee held the property which he exchanged where, for example, he exchanged a capital asset in a transaction which, as to him, was nontaxable under section 1031 and the property received in the exchange has the same basis as the property exchanged. [Reg. §1.267(d)-1.]

☐ [*T.D. 6312, 9-10-58. Amended by T.D. 9811, 1-18-2017.*]

[Reg. §1.267(d)-2]

§1.267(d)-2. Effective/applicability dates.—Pursuant to section 7851(a)(1)(C), the regulations prescribed in §1.267(d)-1, to the extent that they relate to determination of gain resulting from the sale or other disposition of property after December 31, 1953, with respect to which property a loss was not allowable to the transferor by reason of section 267(a)(1) (or by reason of section 24(b) of the Internal Revenue Code of 1939), shall also apply to taxable years beginning before January 1, 1954, and ending after December 31, 1953, and taxable years beginning after December 31, 1953, and ending before August 17, 1954, which years are subject to the Internal Revenue Code of 1939. The provisions of §1.267(d)-1(a)(3) relating to section 1022 are effective on and after January 19, 2017. [Reg. §1.267(d)-2.]

☐ [*T.D. 6312, 9-10-58. Amended by T.D. 9811, 1-18-2017.*]

[Reg. §1.267(f)-1]

§1.267(f)-1. Controlled groups.—(a) *In general.*—(1) *Purpose.*— This section provides rules under section 267(f) to defer losses and deductions from certain transactions between members of a controlled group (intercompany sales). The purpose of this section is to prevent members of a controlled group from taking into account a loss or deduction solely as the result of a transfer of property between a selling member (S) and a buying member (B).

(2) *Application of consolidated return principles.*—Under this section, S's loss or deduction from an intercompany sale is taken into account under the *timing* principles of §1.1502-13 (intercompany transactions between members of a consolidated group), treating the intercompany sale as an intercompany transaction. For this purpose:

(i) The matching and acceleration rules of §1.1502-13(c) and (d), the definitions and operating rules of §1.1502-13(b) and (j), and the simplifying rules of §1.1502-13(e)(1) apply with the adjustments in paragraphs (b) and (c) of this section to reflect that this section—

(A) Applies on a controlled group basis rather than consolidated group basis; and

(B) Generally affects only the *timing* of a loss or deduction, and not its *attributes* (e.g., its *source* and *character*) or the holding period of property.

(ii) The special rules under §1.1502-13(f) (stock of members) and (g) (obligations of members) apply under this section only to the extent the transaction is also an intercompany transaction to which §1.1502-13 applies.

(iii) Any election under §1.1502-13 to take items into account on a separate entity basis does not apply under this section. See §1.1502-13(e)(3).

(3) *Other law.*—The rules of this section apply in addition to other applicable law (including nonstatutory authorities). For example, to the extent a loss or deduction deferred under this section is from a transaction that is also an intercompany transaction under §1.1502-13(b)(1), attributes of the loss or deduction are also subject to recharacterization under §1.150213. See also, sections 269 (acquisitions to evade or avoid income tax) and 482 (allocations among commonly controlled taxpayers). Any loss or deduction taken into account under this section can be deferred, disallowed, or eliminated under other applicable law. See, for example, section 1091 (loss eliminated on wash sale).

(b) *Definitions and operating rules.*—The definitions in §1.1502-13(b) and the operating rules of §1.1502-13(j) apply under this section with appropriate adjustments, including the following:

(1) *Intercompany sale.*—An intercompany sale is a sale, exchange, or other transfer of property between members of a controlled group, if it would be an intercompany transaction under the principles of §1.1502-13, determined by treating the references to a consolidated group as references to a controlled group and by disregarding whether any of the members join in filing consolidated returns.

(2) *S's losses or deductions.*—Except to the extent the intercompany sale is also an intercompany transaction to which §1.1502-13 applies, S's losses or deductions subject to this section are determined on a separate entity basis. For example, the principles of §1.1502-13(b)(2)(iii) (treating certain amounts not yet recognized as items to be taken into account) do not apply. A loss or deduction is from an intercompany sale whether it is directly or indirectly from the intercompany sale.

(3) *Controlled group; member.*—For purposes of this section, a controlled group is defined in section 267(f). Thus, a controlled group includes a FSC (as defined in section 922) and excluded members under section 1563(b)(2), but does not include a DISC (as defined in section 992). Corporations remain members of a controlled group as long as they remain in a controlled group relationship with each other. For example, corporations become nonmembers with respect to each other when they cease to be in a controlled group relationship with each other, rather than by having a separate return year (described in §1.1502-13(j)(7)). Further, the principles of §1.1502-13(j)(6) (former common parent treated as continuation of group) apply to any corporation if, immediately before it becomes a nonmember, it is both the selling member and the owner of property with respect to which a loss or deduction is deferred (whether or not it becomes a member of a different controlled group filing consolidated or separate returns). Thus, for example, if S and B merge together in a transaction described in section 368(a)(1)(A), the surviving corporation is treated as the successor to the other corporation, and the controlled group relationship is treated as continuing.

(4) *Consolidated taxable income.*—References to consolidated taxable income (and consolidated tax liability) include references to the combined taxable income of the members (and their combined tax liability). For corporations filing separate returns, it ordinarily will not be necessary to actually combine their taxable incomes (and tax liabilities) because the taxable income (and tax liability) of one corporation does not affect the taxable income (or tax liability) of another corporation.

(c) *Matching and acceleration principles of §1.1502-13.*—(1) *Adjustments to the timing rules.*—Under this section, S's losses and deductions are deferred until they are taken into account under the timing principles of the matching and acceleration rules of §1.1502-13(c) and (d) with appropriate adjustments. For example, if S sells depreciable property to B at a loss, S's loss is deferred and taken into account under the principles of the matching rule of §1.1502-13(c) to reflect the difference between B's depreciation taken into account with respect to the property and the depreciation that B would take into account if S and B were divisions of a single corporation; if S and B subsequently cease to be in a controlled group relationship with each other, S's remaining loss is taken into account under the principles of the acceleration rule of §1.1502-13(d). For purposes of this section, the adjustments to §1.1502-13(c) and (d) include the following:

(i) *Application on controlled group basis.*—The matching and acceleration rules apply on a controlled group basis, rather than a consolidated group basis. Thus if S and B are wholly-owned members of a consolidated group and 21% of the stock of S is sold to an unrelated person, S's loss continues to be deferred under this section because S and B continue to be members of a controlled group even though S is no longer a member of the consolidated group. Similarly, S's loss would continue to be deferred if S and B remain in a controlled group relationship after both corporations become nonmembers of their former consolidated group.

(ii) *Different taxable years.*—If S and B have different taxable years, the taxable years that include a December 31 are treated as the same taxable years. If S or B has a short taxable year that does not include a December 31, the short year is treated as part of the succeeding taxable year that does include a December 31.

(iii) *Transfer to a section 267(b) or 707(b) related person.*—To the extent S's loss or deduction from an intercompany sale of property is taken into account under this section as a result of B's transfer of the property to a nonmember that is a person related to any member, immediately after the transfer, under sections 267(b) or 707(b), or as a result of S or B becoming a nonmember that is related to any member under section 267(b), the loss or deduction is taken into account but allowed only to the extent of any income or gain taken into account as a result of the transfer. The balance not allowed is treated as a loss referred to in section 267(d) if it is from a sale or exchange by B (rather than from a distribution).

(iv) *B's item is excluded from gross income or noncapital and nondeductible.*—To the extent S's loss would be redetermined to be a noncapital, nondeductible amount under the principles of §1.1502-13, but is not redetermined under paragraph (c)(2) of this section (which generally renders the attribute redetermination rule inapplicable to sales between members of a controlled group), S's loss continues to be deferred. For purposes of this paragraph, stock held by S, stock held by B, stock held by all members of S's consolidated group, stock held by any member of a controlled group of which S is a member that was acquired from a member of S's consolidated group, and stock issued by T to a member of the controlled group must be taken into account in determining whether a loss would be redetermined to be a noncapital, nondeductible amount under the principles of §1.1502-13. If the loss remains deferred, it is taken into account when S and B (including their successors) are no longer in a controlled group relationship. (If, however, the property is transferred to certain related persons, paragraph (c)(1)(iii) of this section will cause the loss to be permanently disallowed.) For example, if S sells all of the T stock to B at a loss (in a transaction that is treated as a sale or exchange for Federal income tax purposes), and T subsequently liquidates in an unrelated transaction that qualifies under section 332, S's loss is deferred until S and B are no longer in a controlled group relationship. Similarly, if S owns all of the T stock and sells 30 percent of T's stock to B at a loss (in a transaction that is treated as a sale or exchange for Federal income tax purposes), and T subsequently liquidates, S's loss on the sale is deferred until S and B (including their successors) are no longer in a controlled group relationship.

(v) *Circularity of references.*—References to deferral or elimination under the Internal Revenue Code or regulations do not include references to section 267(f) or this section. See, e.g., §1.1502-13(a)(4) (applicability of other law).

(2) *Attributes generally not affected.*—The matching and acceleration rules are not applied under this section to affect the attributes of S's intercompany item, or cause it to be taken into account before it is taken into account under S's separate entity method of accounting. However, the attributes of S's intercompany item may be redetermined, or an item may be taken into account earlier than under S's separate entity method of accounting, to the extent the transaction is also an intercompany transaction to which §1.1502-13 applies. Similarly, except to the extent the transaction is also an intercompany transaction to which §1.1502-13 applies, the matching and acceleration rules do not apply to affect the timing or attributes of B's corresponding items.

(d) *Intercompany sales of inventory involving foreign persons.*—(1) *General rule.*—Section 267(a)(1) and this section do not apply to an intercompany sale of property that is inventory (within the meaning of section 1221(1)) in the hands of both S and B, if—

(i) The intercompany sale is in the ordinary course of S's trade or business;

(ii) S or B is a foreign corporation; and

(iii) Any income or loss realized on the intercompany sale by S or B is not income or loss that is recognized as effectively connected with the conduct of a trade or business within the United States within the meaning of section 864 (unless the income is exempt from taxation pursuant to a treaty obligation of the United States).

(2) *Intercompany sales involving related partnerships.*—For purposes of paragraph (d)(1) of this section, a partnership and a foreign

corporation described in section 267(b)(10) are treated as members, provided that the income or loss of the foreign corporation is described in paragraph (d)(1)(iii) of this section.

(3) *Intercompany sales in ordinary course.*—For purposes of this paragraph (d), whether an intercompany sale is in the ordinary course of business is determined under all the facts and circumstances.

(e) *Treatment of a creditor with respect to a loan in nonfunctional currency.*—Sections 267(a)(1) and this section do not apply to an exchange loss realized with respect to a loan of nonfunctional currency if—

(1) The loss is realized by a member with respect to nonfunctional currency loaned to another member;

(2) The loan is described in §1.988-1(a)(2)(i);

(3) The loan is not in a hyperinflationary currency as defined in §1.988-1(f); and

(4) The transaction does not have as a significant purpose the avoidance of Federal income tax.

(f) *Receivables.*—If S acquires a receivable from the sale of goods or services to a nonmember at a gain, and S sells the receivable at fair market value to B, any loss or deduction of S from its sale to B is not deferred under this section to the extent it does not exceed S's income or gain from the sale to the nonmember that has been taken into account at the time the receivable is sold to B.

(g) *Earnings and profits.*—A loss or deduction deferred under this section is not reflected in S's earnings and profits before it is taken into account under this section. See, e.g., §§1.312-6(a), 1.312-7, and 1.1502-33(c)(2).

(h) *Anti-avoidance rule.*—If a transaction is engaged in or structured with a principal purpose to avoid the purposes of this section (including, for example, by avoiding treatment as an intercompany sale or by distorting the timing of losses or deductions), adjustments must be made to carry out the purposes of this section.

(i) [Reserved]

(j) *Examples.*—For purposes of the examples in this paragraph (j), unless otherwise stated, corporation P owns 75% of the only class of stock of subsidiaries S and B, X is a person unrelated to any member of the P controlled group, the taxable year of all persons is the calendar year, all persons use the accrual method of accounting, tax liabilities are disregarded, the facts set forth the only activity, and no member has a special status. If a member acts as both a selling member and a buying member (e.g., with respect to different aspects of a single transaction, or with respect to related transactions), the member is referred as to M (rather than as S or B). This section is illustrated by the following examples.

Example 1. Matching and acceleration rules. (a) *Facts.* S holds land for investment with a basis of $130. On January 1 of Year 1, S sells the land to B for $100. On a separate entity basis, S's loss is long-term capital loss. B holds the land for sale to customers in the ordinary course of business. On July 1 of Year 3, B sells the land to X for $110.

(b) *Matching rule.* Under paragraph (b)(1) of this section, S's sale of land to B is an intercompany sale. Under paragraph (c)(1) of this section, S's $30 loss is taken into account under the timing principles of the matching rule of §1.1502-13(c) to reflect the difference for the year between B's corresponding items taken into account and the recomputed corresponding items. If S and B were divisions of a single corporation and the intercompany sale were a transfer between the divisions, B would succeed to S's $130 basis in the land and would have a $20 loss from the sale to X in Year 3. Consequently, S takes no loss into account in Years 1 and 2, and takes the entire $30 loss into account in Year 3 to reflect the $30 difference in that year between the $10 gain B takes into account and its $20 recomputed loss. The attributes of S's intercompany items and B's corresponding items are determined on a separate entity basis. Thus, S's $30 loss is long-term capital loss and B's $10 gain is ordinary income.

(c) *Acceleration resulting from sale of B stock.* The facts are the same as in paragraph (a) of this *Example 1*, except that on July 1 of Year 3 P sells all of its B stock to X (rather than B's selling the land to X). Under paragraph (c)(1) of this section, S's $30 loss is taken into account under the timing principles of the acceleration rule of §1.1502-13(d) immediately before the effect of treating S and B as divisions of a single corporation cannot be produced. Because the effect cannot be produced once B becomes a nonmember, S takes its $30 loss into account in Year 3 immediately before B becomes a nonmember. S's loss is long-term capital loss.

(d) *Subgroup principles applicable to sale of S and B stock.* The facts are the same as in paragraph (a) of this *Example 1*, except that on July 1 of Year 3 P sells all of its S and B stock to X (rather than B's selling the land to X). Under paragraph (b)(3) of this section, S and B are considered to remain members of a controlled group as long as they

remain in a controlled group relationship with each other (whether or not in the original controlled group). P's sale of their stock does not affect the controlled group relationship of S and B with each other. Thus, S's loss is not taken into account as a result of P's sale of the stock. Instead, S's loss is taken into account based on subsequent events (e.g., B's sale of the land to a nonmember).

Example 2. Distribution of loss property. (a) *Facts.* S holds land with a basis of $130 and value of $100. On January 1 of Year 1, S distributes the land to P in a transaction to which section 311 applies. On July 1 of Year 3, P sells the land to X for $110.

(b) *No loss taken into account.* Under paragraph (b)(2) of this section, because P and S are not members of a consolidated group, §1.1502-13(f)(2)(iii) does not apply to cause S to recognize a $30 loss under the principles of section 311(b). Thus, S has no loss to be taken into account under this section. (If P and S were members of a consolidated group, §1.1502-13(f)(2)(iii) would apply to S's loss in addition to the rules of this section, and the loss would be taken into account in Year 3 as a result of P's sale to X.)

Example 3. Loss not yet taken into account under separate entity accounting method. (a) *Facts.* S holds land with a basis of $130. On January 1 of Year 1, S sells the land to B at a $30 loss but does not take into account the loss under its separate entity method of accounting until Year 4. On July 1 of Year 3, B sells the land to X for $110.

(b) *Timing.* Under paragraph (b)(2) of this section, S's loss is determined on a separate entity basis. Under paragraph (c)(1) of this section, S's loss is not taken into account before it is taken into account under S's separate entity method of accounting. Thus, although B takes its corresponding gain into account in Year 3, S has no loss to take into account until Year 4. Once S's loss is taken into account in Year 4, it is not deferred under this section because B's corresponding gain has already been taken into account. (If S and B were members of a consolidated group, S would be treated under §1.1502-13(b)(2)(iii) as taking the loss into account in Year 3.)

Example 4. Consolidated groups. (a) *Facts.* P owns all of the stock of S and B, and the P group is a consolidated group. S holds land for investment with a basis of $130. On January 1 of Year 1, S sells the land to B for $100. B holds the land for sale to customers in the ordinary course of business. On July 1 of Year 3, P sells 25% of B's stock to X. As a result of P's sale, B becomes a nonmember of the P consolidated group but S and B remain in a controlled group relationship with each other for purposes of section 267(f). Assume that if S and B were divisions of a single corporation, the items of S and B from the land would be ordinary by reason of B's activities.

(b) *Timing and attributes.* Under paragraph (a)(3) of this section, S's sale to B is subject to both §1.1502-13 and this section. Under §1.1502-13, S's loss is redetermined to be an ordinary loss by reason of B's activities. Under paragraph (b)(3) of this section, because S and B remain in a controlled group relationship with each other, the loss is not taken into account under the acceleration rule of §1.1502-13(d) as modified by paragraph (c) of this section. See §1.1502-13(a)(4). Nevertheless, S's loss is redetermined by §1.1502-13 to be an ordinary loss, and the character of the loss is not further redetermined under this section. Thus, the loss continues to be deferred under this section, and will be taken into account as ordinary loss based on subsequent events (e.g., B's sale of the land to a nonmember).

(c) *Resale to controlled group member.* The facts are the same as in paragraph (a) of this *Example 4*, except that P owns 75% of X's stock, and B resells the land to X (rather than P's selling any B stock). The results for S's loss are the same as in paragraph (b) of this *Example 4*. Under paragraph (b) of this section, X is also in a controlled group relationship, and B's sale to X is a second intercompany sale. Thus, S's loss continues to be deferred and is taken into account under this section as ordinary loss based on subsequent events (e.g., X's sale of the land to a nonmember).

Example 5. Intercompany sale followed by installment sale. (a) *Facts.* S holds land for investment with a basis of $13Ox. On January 1 of Year 1, S sells the land to B for $100x. B holds the land for investment. On July 1 of Year 3, B sells the land to X in exchange for X's $110x note. The note bears a market rate of interest in excess of the applicable Federal rate, and provides for principal payments of $55x in Year 4 and $55x in Year 5. Section 453A applies to X's note.

(b) *Timing and attributes.* Under paragraph (c) of this section, S's $30x loss is taken into account under the timing principles of the matching rule of §1.1502-13(c) to reflect the difference in each year between B's gain taken into account and its recomputed gain. Under section 453, B takes into account $5x of gain in Year 4 and in Year 5. Therefore, S takes $20x of its loss into account in Year 3 to reflect the $20x difference in that year between B's $0 loss taken into account and its $20x recomputed loss. In addition, S takes $5x of its loss into account in Year 4 and in Year 5 to reflect the $5x difference in each year between B's $5x gain taken into account and its $0 recomputed gain. Although S takes into account a loss and B takes into account a gain, the attributes of B's $10x gain are determined on a separate entity basis, and therefore the interest charge under section 453A(c) applies to B's $10x gain on the installment sale beginning in Year 3.

Example 6. Section 721 transfer to a related nonmember. (a) *Facts.* S owns land with a basis of $130. On January 1 of Year 1, S sells the land to B for $100. On July 1 of Year 3, B transfers the land to a partnership in exchange for a 40% interest in capital and profits in a transaction to which section 721 applies. P also owns a 25% interest in the capital and profits of the partnership.

(b) *Timing.* Under paragraph (c)(1)(iii) of this section, because the partnership is a nonmember that is a related person under sections 267(b) and 707(b), S's $30 loss is taken into account in Year 3, but only to the extent of any income or gain taken into account as a result of the transfer. Under section 721, no gain or loss is taken into account as a result of the transfer to the partnership, and thus none of S's loss is taken into account. Any subsequent gain recognized by the partnership with respect to the property is limited under section 267(d). (The results would be the same if the P group were a consolidated group, and S's sale to B were also subject to § 1.1502-13.)

Example 7. Receivables. (a) *Controlled group.* S owns goods with a $60 basis. In Year 1, S sells the goods to X for X's $100 note. The note bears a market rate of interest in excess of the applicable Federal rate, and provides for payment of principal in Year 5. S takes into account $40 of income in Year 1 under its method of accounting. In Year 2, the fair market value of X's note falls to $90 due to an increase in prevailing market interest rates, and S sells the note to B for its $90 fair market value.

(b) *Loss not deferred.* Under paragraph (f) of this section, S takes its $10 loss into account in Year 2. (If the sale were not at fair market value, paragraph (f) of this section would not apply and none of S's $10 loss would be taken into account in Year 2.)

(c) *Consolidated group.* Assume instead that P owns all of the stock of S and B, and the P group is a consolidated group. In Year 1, S sells to X goods having a basis of $90 for X's $100 note (bearing a market rate of interest in excess of the applicable Federal rate, and providing for payment of principal in Year 5), and S takes into account $10 of income in Year 1. In Year 2, S sells the receivable to B for its $85 fair market value. In Year 3, P sells 25% of B's stock to X. Although paragraph (f) of this section provides that $10 of S's loss (i.e., the extent to which S's $15 loss does not exceed its $10 of income) is not deferred under this section, S's entire $15 loss is subject to § 1.1502-13 and none of the loss is taken into account in Year 2 under the matching rule of § 1.1502-13(c). See paragraph (a)(3) of this section (continued deferral under § 1.1502-13). P's sale of B stock results in B becoming a nonmember of the P consolidated group in Year 3. Thus, S's $15 loss is taken into account in Year 3 under the acceleration rule of S1.1502-13(d). Nevertheless, B remains in a controlled group relationship with S and paragraph (f) of this section permits only $10 of S's loss to be taken into account in Year 3. See § 1.1502-13(a)(4) (continued deferral under section 267). The remaining $5 of S's loss continues to be deferred under this section and taken into account under this section based on subsequent events (e.g., B's collection of the note or P's sale of the remaining B stock to a nonmember).

Example 8. Selling member ceases to be a member. (a) *Facts.* P owns all of the stock of S and B, and the P group is a consolidated group. S has several historic assets, including land with a basis of $130 and value of $100. The land is not essential to the operation of S's business. On January 1 of Year 1, S sells the land to B for $100. On July 1 of Year 3, P transfers all of S's stock to newly formed X in exchange for a 20% interest in X stock as part of a transaction to which section 351 applies. Although X holds many other assets, a principal purpose for P's transfer is to accelerate taking S's $30 loss into account. P has no plan or intention to dispose of the X stock.

(b) *Timing.* Under paragraph (c) of this section, S's $30 loss ordinarily is taken into account immediately before P's transfer of the S stock, under the timing principles of the acceleration rule of § 1.1502-13(d). Although taking S's loss into account results in a $30 negative stock basis adjustment under § 1.1502-32, because P has no plan or intention to dispose of its X stock, the negative adjustment will not immediately affect taxable income. P's transfer accelerates a loss that otherwise would be deferred, and an adjustment under paragraph (h) of this section is required. Thus, S's loss is never taken into account, and S's stock basis and earnings and profits are reduced by $30 under § § 1.1502-32 and 1.1502-33 immediately before P's transfer of the S stock.

(c) *Nonhistoric assets.* Assume instead that, with a principal purpose to accelerate taking into account any further loss that may accrue in the value of the land without disposing of the land outside of the controlled group, P forms M with a $100 contribution on January 1 of Year 1 and S sells the land to M for $100. On December 1 of Year 1, when the value of the land has decreased to $90, M sells the land to B for $90. On July 1 of Year 3, while B still owns the land, P sells all of M's stock to X and M becomes a nonmember. Under paragraph (c) of this section, M's $10 loss ordinarily is taken into account under the timing principles of the acceleration rule of § 1.1502-13(d) immedi-

ately before M becomes a nonmember. (S's $30 loss is not taken into account under the timing principles of § 1.1502-13(c) or § 1.1502-13(d) as a result of M becoming a nonmember, but is taken into account based on subsequent events such as B's sale of the land to a nonmember or P's sale of the stock of S or B to a nonmember.) The land is not an historic asset of M and, although taking M's loss into account reduces P's basis in the M stock under § 1.1502-32, the negative adjustment only eliminates the $10 duplicate stock loss. Under paragraph (h) of this section, M's loss is never taken into account. M's stock basis, and the earnings and profits of M and P, are reduced by $10 under § § 1.1502-32 and 1.1502-33 immediately before P's sale of the M stock.

Example 9. Sale of stock by consolidated group member to controlled group member. (a) *Facts.* P1, a domestic corporation, owns 75% of the outstanding stock of P, the common parent of a consolidated group. P owns all of the outstanding stock of subsidiaries M and S, which are members of P's consolidated group. M and S each own 50% of the only class of stock of L, a nonmember life insurance company. On January 1 of Year 1, S sells 25% of L's stock to P1 for $50 cash. At the time of the sale, S's aggregate basis in the L shares transferred to P1 was $80, and S recognizes a $30 loss. On February 18 of Year 3, at a time when the L shares held by P1 are worth $60, L liquidates. As a result of the liquidation, P1 recognizes a $10 gain.

(b) *Timing.* Under paragraph (a)(2) of this section, S's loss on the sale of the L stock to P1 is deferred. Under paragraph (c)(1)(iv) of this section, upon the liquidation of L, to the extent S's loss would be redetermined to be a noncapital, nondeductible amount under the principles of § 1.1502-13, S's loss continues to be deferred. Under the principles of § 1.1502-13, S's loss is not redetermined to be a noncapital, nondeductible amount to the extent of P1's $10 of gain recognized. Accordingly, S takes into account $10 of loss as a result of the liquidation. In determining whether the remainder of S's $20 loss would be redetermined to be a noncapital, nondeductible amount, under paragraph (c)(1)(iv) of this section, stock held by P1, stock held by M, and stock held by S is taken into account. Accordingly, under the principles of § 1.1502- 13, the liquidation of L would be treated as a liquidation qualifying under section 332, and the remainder of S's loss would be redetermined to be a noncapital, nondeductible amount. Thus, under paragraph (c)(1)(iv), S's remaining $20 loss continues to be deferred until S and P1 are no longer in a controlled group relationship.

Example 10. Issuance of stock to controlled group member. (a) *Facts.* FP is a foreign corporation that owns all the stock of FS, a foreign corporation, and all the stock of P, a domestic corporation. P owns all of the single class of outstanding common stock of T. In Year 1, FS contributes cash to T in exchange for newly issued stock of T that constitutes 40 percent of T's outstanding stock. In Year 2, when the value of the T stock owned by P is less than its basis in P's hands, P sells all of its T stock to FP. In Year 3, in a transaction unrelated to the issuance of the T stock in Year 1, T converts under state law to a limited liability company that is treated as a partnership for Federal income tax purposes.

(b) *Timing.* Under paragraph (a) 2) of this section, P's loss on the sale of its T stock is deferred. Under paragraph (c)(1)(iv) of this section, upon the conversion of T, to the extent P's loss would be redetermined to be a noncapital, nondeductible amount under the principles of § 1.1502-13, P's loss continues to be deferred. In determining whether the loss would be redetermined to be a noncapital, nondeductible amount, stock held by FS (which was acquired from T) and stock held by FP (the buyer of the T stock from P and a member of P's controlled group) is taken into account. Accordingly, under the principles of § 1.1502-13 the deemed liquidation of T resulting from the conversion of T would be treated as a liquidation qualifying under section 332, and P's loss would be redetermined to be a noncapital, nondeductible amount. Thus, under paragraph (c)(1)(iv), P's loss continues to be deferred until P and FP are no longer in a controlled group relationship.

(k) *Cross-reference.*—For additional rules applicable to the disposition, deconsolidation, or transfer of the stock of members of consolidated groups, see § § 1.337(d)-2, 1.1502-13(f)(6), 1.1502-35 and 1.1502-36.

(l) *Effective dates.*—(1) *In general.*—This section applies with respect to transactions occurring in S's years beginning on or after July 12, 1995. If both this section and prior law apply to a transaction, or neither applies, with the result that items are duplicated, omitted, or eliminated in determining taxable income (or tax liability), or items are treated inconsistently, prior law (and not this section) applies to the transaction.

(2) *Avoidance transactions.*—This paragraph (l)(2) applies if a transaction is engaged in or structured on or after April 8, 1994, with a principal purpose to avoid the rules of this section (and instead to apply prior law). If this paragraph (l)(2) applies, appropriate adjustments must be made in years beginning on or after July 12, 1995, to

prevent the avoidance, duplication, omission, or elimination of any item (or tax liability), or any other inconsistency with the rules of this section.

(3) *Effective/applicability date.*—Paragraph (c)(1)(iv) of this section applies to a loss that continues to be deferred pursuant to that paragraph if the event that would cause the loss to be redetermined as a noncapital nondeductible amount under the principles of § 1.1502-13 occurs on or after April 16, 2012.

(4) *Prior law.*—For transactions occurring in S's years beginning before July 12, 1995, see the applicable regulations issued under sections 267 and 1502. See, e.g., §§ 1.267(f)-1, 1.267(f)-1T, 1.267(f)-2T, 1.267(f)-3, 1.1502-13, 1.1502-13T, 1.1502-14, 1.1502-14T, and 1.1502-31 (as contained in the 26 CFR part 1 edition revised as of April 1, 1995). [Reg. § 1.267(f)-1.]

☐ [*T.D. 8400, 3-16-92. Amended by T.D. 8597, 7-12-95; T.D. 8660, 3-11-96; T.D. 9048, 3-11-2003 T.D. 9187, 3-2-2005; T.D. 9254, 3-9-2006 T.D. 9424, 9-9-2008 and T.D. 9583, 4-13-2012.*]

[Reg. § 1.267A-1]

§ 1.267A-1. Disallowance of certain interest and royalty deductions.—(a) *Scope.*—This section and §§ 1.267A-2 through 1.267A-5 provide rules regarding when a deduction for any interest or royalty paid or accrued is disallowed under section 267A. Section 1.267A-2 describes hybrid and branch arrangements. Section 1.267A-3 provides rules for determining income inclusions and provides that certain amounts are not amounts for which a deduction is disallowed. Section 1.267A-4 provides an imported mismatch rule. Section 1.267A-5 sets forth definitions and special rules that apply for purposes of section 267A. Section 1.267A-6 illustrates the application of section 267A through examples. Section 1.267A-7 provides applicability dates.

(b) *Disallowance of deduction.*—This paragraph (b) sets forth the exclusive circumstances in which a deduction is disallowed under section 267A. Except as provided in paragraph (c) of this section, a specified party's deduction for any interest or royalty paid or accrued (the amount paid or accrued with respect to the specified party, a *specified payment*) is disallowed under section 267A to the extent that the specified payment is described in this paragraph (b). *See also* § 1.267A-5(b)(5) (treating structured payments as interest paid or accrued for purposes of section 267A and the regulations in this part under section 267A). A specified payment is described in this paragraph (b) to the extent that it is—

(1) A disqualified hybrid amount, as described in § 1.267A-2 (hybrid and branch arrangements);

(2) A disqualified imported mismatch amount, as described in § 1.267A-4 (payments offset by a hybrid deduction); or

(3) A specified payment for which the requirements of the anti-avoidance rule of § 1.267A-5(b)(6) are satisfied.

(c) *De minimis exception.*—Paragraph (b) of this section does not apply to a specified party for a taxable year in which the sum of the specified party's specified payments that but for this paragraph (c) would be described in paragraph (b) of this section is less than $50,000. For purposes of this paragraph (c), specified parties that are related (within the meaning of § 1.267A-5(a)(14)) are treated as a single specified party. [Reg. § 1.267(A)-1.]

☐ [*T.D. 9896, 4-7-2020.*]

[Reg. § 1.267A-2]

§ 1.267A-2. Hybrid and branch arrangements.—(a) *Payments pursuant to hybrid transactions.*—(1) *In general.*—If a specified payment is made pursuant to a hybrid transaction, then, subject to § 1.267A-3(b) (amounts included or includible in income), the payment is a disqualified hybrid amount to the extent that—

(i) A specified recipient of the payment does not include the payment in income, as determined under § 1.267A-3(a) (to such extent, a *no-inclusion*); and

(ii) The specified recipient's no-inclusion is a result of the payment being made pursuant to the hybrid transaction. For purposes of this paragraph (a)(1)(ii), the specified recipient's no-inclusion is a result of the specified payment being made pursuant to the hybrid transaction to the extent that the no-inclusion would not occur were the specified recipient's tax law to treat the payment as interest or a royalty, as applicable. See § 1.267A-6(c)(1) and (2) for examples illustrating the application of paragraph (a) of this section.

(2) *Definition of hybrid transaction.*—(i) *In general.*—The term *hybrid transaction* means any transaction, series of transactions, agreement, or instrument one or more payments with respect to which are treated as interest or royalties for U.S. tax purposes but are not so treated for purposes of the tax law of a specified recipient of the

payment. Examples of a hybrid transaction include an instrument a payment with respect to which is treated as interest for U.S. tax purposes but, for purposes of a specified recipient's tax law, is treated as a distribution with respect to equity or a recovery of principal with respect to indebtedness.

(ii) *Special rules.*—(A) *Long-term deferral.*—A specified payment is deemed to be made pursuant to a hybrid transaction if the taxable year in which a specified recipient of the payment takes the payment into account in income under its tax law (or, based on all the facts and circumstances, is reasonably expected to take the payment into account in income under its tax law) ends more than 36 months after the end of the taxable year in which the specified party would be allowed a deduction for the payment under U.S. tax law. In addition, if the tax law of a specified recipient of the specified payment does not impose an income tax, then such tax law does not cause the payment to be deemed to be made pursuant to a hybrid transaction under this paragraph (a)(2)(ii)(A). See § 1.267A-6(c)(8) for an example illustrating the application of this paragraph (a)(2)(ii)(A) in the context of the imported mismatch rule.

(B) *Royalties treated as payments in exchange for property under foreign law.*—In the case of a specified payment that is a royalty for U.S. tax purposes and for purposes of the tax law of a specified recipient of the payment is consideration received in exchange for property, the tax law of the specified recipient is not treated as causing the payment to be made pursuant to a hybrid transaction.

(C) *Coordination with disregarded payment rule.*—A specified payment is not considered made pursuant to a hybrid transaction if the payment is a disregarded payment, as described in paragraph (b)(2) of this section.

(3) *Payments pursuant to securities lending transactions, sale-repurchase transactions, or similar transactions.*—This paragraph (a)(3) applies if a specified payment is made pursuant to a repo transaction and is not regarded under a foreign tax law, but another amount connected to the payment (the *connected amount*) is regarded under such foreign tax law. For purposes of this paragraph (a)(3), a *repo transaction* means a transaction one or more payments with respect to which are treated as interest (as defined in § 1.267A-5(a)(12)) or a structured payment (as defined in § 1.267A-5(b)(5)(ii)) for U.S. tax purposes and that is a securities lending transaction or sale-repurchase transaction (including as described in § 1.861-2(a)(7)), or other similar transaction or series of related transactions in which legal title to property is transferred and the property (or similar property, such as securities of the same class and issue) is reacquired or expected to be reacquired. For example, this paragraph (a)(3) applies if a specified payment arising from characterizing a repo transaction of stock in accordance with its substance (that is, characterizing the specified payment as interest) is not regarded as such under a foreign tax law but an amount consistent with the form of the transaction (such as a dividend) is regarded under such foreign tax law. When this paragraph (a)(3) applies, the determination of the identity of a specified recipient of the specified payment under the foreign tax law is made with respect to the connected amount. In addition, if the specified recipient includes the connected amount in income (as determined under § 1.267A-3(a), by treating the connected amount as the specified payment), then the amount of the specified recipient's no-inclusion with respect to the specified payment is correspondingly reduced. Further, the principles of this paragraph (a)(3) apply to cases similar to repo transactions in which a foreign tax law does not characterize the transaction in accordance with its substance. See § 1.267A-6(c)(2) for an example illustrating the application of this paragraph (a)(3).

(4) *Payments pursuant to interest-free loans and similar arrangements.*—In the case of a specified payment that is interest for U.S. tax purposes, the following special rules apply:

(i) The payment is deemed to be made pursuant to a hybrid transaction to the extent that—

(A) Under U.S. tax law, the payment is imputed (for example, under section 482 or 7872, including because the instrument pursuant to which it is made is indebtedness but the terms of the instrument provide for an interest rate equal to or less than the risk-free rate or the rate on sovereign debt with similar terms in the relevant foreign currency); and

(B) A tax resident or taxable branch to which the payment is made does not take the payment into account in income under its tax law because such tax law does not impute any interest. The rules of paragraph (b)(4) of this section apply for purposes of determining whether the specified payment is made indirectly to a tax resident or taxable branch.

(ii) A tax resident or taxable branch the tax law of which causes the payment to be deemed to be made pursuant to a hybrid transaction under paragraph (a)(4)(i) of this section is deemed to be a specified recipient of the payment for purposes of paragraph (a)(1) of this section.

(b) *Disregarded payments.*—(1) *In general.*—Subject to §1.267A-3(b) (amounts included or includible in income), the excess (if any) of the sum of a specified party's disregarded payments for a taxable year over its dual inclusion income for the taxable year is a disqualified hybrid amount. See §1.267A-6(c)(3) and (4) for examples illustrating the application of paragraph (b) of this section.

(2) *Definition of disregarded payment.*—(i) *In general.*—The term *disregarded payment* means a specified payment to the extent that, under the tax law of a tax resident or taxable branch to which the payment is made, the payment is not regarded (for example, because under such tax law it is a payment involving a single taxpayer or members of a group) and, were the payment to be regarded (and treated as interest or a royalty, as applicable) under such tax law, the tax resident or taxable branch would include the payment in income, as determined under §1.267A-3(a).

(ii) *Special rules.*—(A) *Foreign consolidation and similar regimes.*—A disregarded payment includes a specified payment that, under the tax law of a tax resident or taxable branch to which the payment is made, is a payment that gives rise to a deduction or similar offset allowed to the tax resident or taxable branch (or group of entities that include the tax resident or taxable branch) under a foreign consolidation, fiscal unity, group relief, loss sharing, or any similar regime.

(B) *Certain payments of a U.S. taxable branch.*—In the case of a specified payment of a U.S. taxable branch, the payment is not a disregarded payment to the extent that under the tax law of the tax resident to which the payment is made the payment is otherwise taken into account. See paragraph (c)(2) of this section for an example of when an amount may be otherwise taken into account.

(C) *Coordination with other hybrid and branch arrangements.*—A disregarded payment does not include a deemed branch payment described in paragraph (c)(2) of this section, a specified payment pursuant to a repo transaction or similar transaction described in paragraph (a)(3) of this section, or a specified payment pursuant to an interest-free loan or similar transaction described in paragraph (a)(4) of this section.

(3) *Definition of dual inclusion income.*—(i) *In general.*—With respect to a specified party, the term *dual inclusion income* means the excess, if any, of—

(A) The sum of the specified party's items of income or gain for U.S. tax purposes that are included in the specified party's income, as determined under §1.267A-3(a) (by treating the items of income or gain as the specified payment; and, in the case of a specified party that is a CFC, by treating U.S. tax law as the CFC's tax law), to the extent the items of income or gain are included in the income of the tax resident or taxable branch to which the disregarded payments are made, as determined under §1.267A-3(a) (by treating the items of income or gain as the specified payment); over

(B) The sum of the specified party's items of deduction or loss for U.S. tax purposes (other than deductions for disregarded payments), to the extent the items of deduction or loss are allowable (or have been or will be allowable during a taxable year that ends no more than 36 months after the end of the specified party's taxable year) under the tax law of the tax resident or taxable branch to which the disregarded payments are made.

(ii) *Special rule for certain dividends.*—An item of income or gain of a specified party that is included in the specified party's income but not included in the income of the tax resident or taxable branch to which the disregarded payments are made is considered described in paragraph (b)(3)(i)(A) of this section to the extent that, under the tax resident's or taxable branch's tax law, the item is a dividend that would have been included in the income of the tax resident or taxable branch but for an exemption, exclusion, deduction, credit, or other similar relief particular to the item, provided that the party paying the item is not allowed a deduction or other tax benefit for it under its tax law. Similarly, an item of income or gain of a specified party that is included in the income of the tax resident or taxable branch to which the disregarded payments are made but not included in the specified party's income is considered described in paragraph (b)(3)(ii)(A) of this section to the extent that, under U.S. tax law, the item is a dividend that would have been included in the income of the specified party but for a dividends received deduction with respect to the dividend (for example, a deduction under section 245A(a)), provided that the party paying the item is not allowed a deduction or other tax benefit for it under its tax law. See §1.267A-6(c)(3)(iv) for an example illustrating the application of this paragraph (b)(3)(ii).

(4) *Payments made indirectly to a tax resident or taxable branch.*—A specified payment made to an entity an interest of which is directly or indirectly (determined under the rules of section 958(a) without regard to whether an intermediate entity is foreign or domestic, or under substantially similar rules under a tax resident's or taxable branch's tax law) owned by a tax resident or taxable branch is considered made to the tax resident or taxable branch to the extent that, under the tax law of the tax resident or taxable branch, the entity to which the payment is made is fiscally transparent (and all intermediate entities, if any, are also fiscally transparent).

(c) *Deemed branch payments.*—(1) *In general.*—If a specified payment is a deemed branch payment, then the payment is a disqualified hybrid amount if the tax law of the home office provides an exclusion or exemption for income attributable to the branch. See §1.267A-6(c)(4) for an example illustrating the application of this paragraph (c).

(2) *Definition of deemed branch payment.*—The term *deemed branch payment* means, with respect to a U.S. taxable branch that is a U.S. permanent establishment of a treaty resident eligible for benefits under an income tax treaty between the United States and the treaty country, any amount of interest or royalties allowable as a deduction in computing the business profits of the U.S. permanent establishment, to the extent the amount is deemed paid to the home office (or other branch of the home office), is not regarded (or otherwise taken into account) under the home office's tax law (or the other branch's tax law), and, were the payment to be regarded (and treated as interest or a royalty, as applicable) under the home office's tax law (or other branch's tax law), the home office (or other branch) would include the payment in income, as determined under §1.267A-3(a). An amount may be otherwise taken into account for purposes of this paragraph (c)(2) if, for example, under the home office's tax law a corresponding amount of interest or royalties is allocated and attributable to the U.S. permanent establishment and is therefore not deductible.

(d) *Payments to reverse hybrids.*—(1) *In general.*—If a specified payment is made to a reverse hybrid, then, subject to §1.267A-3(b) (amounts included or includible in income), the payment is a disqualified hybrid amount to the extent that—

(i) An investor, the tax law of which treats the reverse hybrid as not fiscally transparent, does not include the payment in income, as determined under §1.267A-3(a) (to such extent, a *no-inclusion*); and

(ii) The investor's no-inclusion is a result of the payment being made to the reverse hybrid. For purposes of this paragraph (d)(1)(ii), the investor's no-inclusion is a result of the specified payment being made to the reverse hybrid to the extent that the no-inclusion would not occur were the investor's tax law to treat the reverse hybrid as fiscally transparent (and treat the payment as interest or a royalty, as applicable). See §1.267A-6(c)(5) for an example illustrating the application of paragraph (d) of this section.

(2) *Definition of reverse hybrid.*—The term *reverse hybrid* means an entity (regardless of whether domestic or foreign) that is fiscally transparent under the tax law of the country in which it is created, organized, or otherwise established but not fiscally transparent under the tax law of an investor of the entity.

(3) *Payments made indirectly to a reverse hybrid.*—A specified payment made to an entity an interest of which is directly or indirectly (determined under the rules of section 958(a) without regard to whether an intermediate entity is foreign or domestic, or under substantially similar rules under a tax resident's or taxable branch's tax law) owned by a reverse hybrid is considered made to the reverse hybrid to the extent that, under the tax law of an investor of the reverse hybrid, the entity to which the payment is made is fiscally transparent (and all intermediate entities, if any, are also fiscally transparent).

(4) *Exception for inclusion by taxable branch in establishment country.*—Paragraph (d)(1) of this section does not apply to a specified payment made to a reverse hybrid to the extent that a taxable branch located in the country in which the reverse hybrid is created, organized, or otherwise established (and the activities of which are carried on by one or more investors of the reverse hybrid) includes the payment in income, as determined under §1.267A-3(a).

(e) *Branch mismatch payments.*—(1) *In general.*—If a specified payment is a branch mismatch payment, then, subject to §1.267A-3(b) (amounts included or includible in income), the payment is a disqualified hybrid amount to the extent that—

(i) A home office, the tax law of which treats the payment as income attributable to a branch of the home office, does not include the payment in income, as determined under §1.267A-3(a) (to such extent, a *no-inclusion*); and

(ii) The home office's no-inclusion is a result of the payment being a branch mismatch payment. For purposes of this paragraph (e)(1)(ii), the home office's no-inclusion is a result of the specified payment being a branch mismatch payment to the extent that the no-inclusion would not occur were the home office's tax law to treat the payment as income that is not attributable a branch of the home office (and treat the payment as interest or a royalty, as applicable). See §1.267A-6(c)(6) for an example illustrating the application of paragraph (e) of this section.

(2) *Definition of branch mismatch payment.*—The term *branch mismatch payment* means a specified payment for which the following requirements are satisfied:

(i) Under a home office's tax law, the payment is treated as income attributable to a branch of the home office; and

(ii) Either—

(A) The branch is not a taxable branch; or

(B) Under the branch's tax law, the payment is not treated as income attributable to the branch.

(f) *Relatedness or structured arrangement limitation.*—A specified recipient, a tax resident or taxable branch to which a specified payment is made, an investor, or a home office to which a specified payment is made is taken into account for purposes of paragraphs (a), (b), (d), and (e) of this section, respectively, only if the specified recipient, the tax resident or taxable branch, the investor, or the home office, as applicable, is related (as defined in §1.267A-5(a)(14)) to the specified party or is a party to a structured arrangement (as defined in §1.267A-5(a)(20)) pursuant to which the specified payment is made. [Reg. §1.267(A)-2.]

☐ [*T.D. 9896, 4-7-2020.*]

[Reg. §1.267A-3]

§1.267A-3. Income inclusions and amounts not treated as disqualified hybrid amounts.—(a) *Income inclusions.*—(1) *General rule.*—For purposes of section 267A, a tax resident or taxable branch includes in income a specified payment to the extent that, under the tax law of the tax resident or taxable branch—

(i) It takes the payment into account (or has taken the payment into account, or, based on all the facts and circumstances, is reasonably expected to take the payment into account during a taxable year that ends no more than 36 months after the end of the specified party's taxable year) in its income or tax base at the full marginal rate imposed on ordinary income (or, if different, the full marginal rate imposed on interest or a royalty, as applicable); and

(ii) The payment is not reduced or offset by an exemption, exclusion, deduction, credit (other than for withholding tax imposed on the payment), or other similar relief particular to such type of payment. Examples of such reductions or offsets include a participation exemption, a dividends received deduction, a deduction or exclusion with respect to a particular category of income (such as income attributable to a branch, or royalties under a patent box regime), a credit for underlying taxes paid by a corporation from which a dividend is received, and a recovery of basis with respect to stock or a recovery of principal with respect to indebtedness. A specified payment is not considered reduced or offset by a deduction or other similar relief particular to the type of payment if it is offset by a generally applicable deduction or other tax attribute, such as a deduction for depreciation or a net operating loss. For purposes of this paragraph (a)(1)(ii), a deduction may be treated as being generally applicable even if it arises from a transaction related to the specified payment (for example, if the deduction and payment are in connection with a back-to-back financing arrangement).

(2) *Coordination with foreign hybrid mismatch rules.*—Whether a tax resident or taxable branch includes in income a specified payment is determined without regard to any defensive or secondary rule contained in hybrid mismatch rules, if any, under the tax law of the tax resident or taxable branch. For purposes of this paragraph (a)(2), a defensive or secondary rule means a provision of hybrid mismatch rules that requires a tax resident or taxable branch to include an amount in income if a deduction for the amount is not disallowed under the payer's tax law. However, a defensive or secondary rule does not include a rule pursuant to which a participation exemption or similar relief particular to a dividend is inapplicable as to a dividend for which the payer is allowed a deduction or other tax benefit under its tax law. Thus, a defensive or secondary rule does not include a rule consistent with recommendation 2.1 in Chapter 2 of OECD/G-20, *Neutralising the Effects of Hybrid Mismatch Arrangements, Action 2: 2015 Final Report* (October 2015).

(3) *Inclusions with respect to reverse hybrids.*—With respect to a tax resident or taxable branch that is an investor of a reverse hybrid, whether the investor includes in income a specified payment made to the reverse hybrid is determined without regard to a distribution from the reverse hybrid (or the right to a distribution from the

reverse hybrid triggered by the payment). However, if the reverse hybrid distributes all of its income during a taxable year, then, for that year, the determination of whether an investor includes in income a specified payment made to the reverse hybrid is made with regard to one or more distributions from the reverse hybrid during the year, by treating a portion of the specified payment as relating to each distribution during the year. For purposes of this paragraph (a)(3), the portion of the specified payment that is considered to relate to a distribution is the lesser of—

(i) The specified payment multiplied by a fraction, the numerator of which is the amount of the distribution and the denominator of which is the aggregate amount of distributions from the reverse hybrid during the taxable year; and

(ii) The amount of the distribution multiplied by a fraction, the numerator of which is the specified payment and the denominator of which is the sum of all specified payments made to the reverse hybrid during the taxable year.

(4) *Inclusions with respect to certain payments pursuant to hybrid transactions.*—This paragraph (a)(4) applies to a specified payment that is interest and that is made pursuant to a hybrid transaction, to the extent that, under the tax law of a specified recipient of the payment, the payment is a recovery of basis with respect to stock or a recovery of principal with respect to indebtedness such that, but for this paragraph (a)(4), a no-inclusion would occur with respect to the specified recipient. In such a case, an amount that is a repayment of principal for U.S. tax purposes and that is or has been paid (or, based on all the facts and circumstances, is reasonably expected to be paid) by the specified party pursuant to the hybrid transaction (such amount, the *principal payment*) is, to the extent included in the income of the specified recipient, treated as correspondingly reducing the specified recipient's no-inclusion with respect to the specified payment. For purposes of this paragraph (a)(4), whether the specified recipient includes the principal payment in income is determined under paragraph (a)(1) of this section, by treating the principal payment as the specified payment and the taxable year period described in paragraph (a)(1) as being composed of taxable years of the specified recipient ending no more than 36 months after the end of the specified party's taxable year during which the specified payment is made (as opposed to, for example, being composed of taxable years of the specified recipient ending no more than 36 months after the end of the specified party's taxable year during which the principal payment is reasonably expected to be made). Moreover, once a principal payment reduces a no-inclusion with respect to a specified payment, it is not again taken into account for purposes of applying this paragraph (a)(4) to another specified payment. See §1.267A-6(c)(1)(vi) for an example illustrating the application of this paragraph (a)(4).

(5) *Deemed full inclusions and de minimis inclusions.*—A preferential rate, exemption, exclusion, deduction, credit, or similar relief particular to a type of payment that reduces or offsets 90 percent or more of the payment is considered to reduce or offset 100 percent of the payment. In addition, a preferential rate, exemption, exclusion, deduction, credit, or similar relief particular to a type of payment that reduces or offsets 10 percent or less of the payment is considered to reduce or offset none of the payment.

(b) *Certain amounts not treated as disqualified hybrid amounts to extent included or includible in income for U.S. tax purposes.*—(1) *In general.*—A specified payment, to the extent that but for this paragraph (b) it would be a disqualified hybrid amount (such amount, a *tentative disqualified hybrid amount*), is reduced under the rules of paragraphs (b)(2) through (4) of this section, as applicable. The tentative disqualified hybrid amount, as reduced under such rules, is the disqualified hybrid amount. See §1.267A-6(c)(3) and (7) for examples illustrating the application of paragraph (b) of this section.

(2) *Included in income of United States tax resident or U.S. taxable branch.*—A tentative disqualified hybrid amount is reduced to the extent that a specified recipient that is a tax resident of the United States or a U.S. taxable branch takes the tentative disqualified hybrid amount into account in determining its gross income.

(3) *Includible in income under section 951(a)(1)(A).*—A tentative disqualified hybrid amount is reduced to the extent that the tentative disqualified hybrid amount is received by a CFC and includible under section 951(a)(1)(A) (determined without regard to properly allocable deductions of the CFC, qualified deficits under section 952(c)(1)(B), and the earnings and profits limitation under §1.952-1(c)) in the gross income of a United States shareholder of the CFC. However, if the United States shareholder is a domestic partnership, then the amount includible under section 951(a)(1)(A) in the gross income of the United States shareholder reduces the tentative disqualified hybrid amount only to the extent that a tax resident of the United States would take into account the amount.

(4) *Includible in income under section 951A(a).*—A tentative disqualified hybrid amount is reduced to the extent that the tentative disqualified hybrid amount increases a United States shareholder's pro rata share of tested income (as determined under §§ 1.951A-1(d)(2) and 1.951A-2(b)(1)) with respect to a CFC, reduces the shareholder's pro rata share of tested loss (as determined under §§ 1.951A-1(d)(4) and 1.951A-2(b)(2)) of the CFC, or both. However, to the extent that a deduction for the tentative disqualified hybrid amount would be allowed to a tax resident of the United States or a U.S. taxable branch, or would be allowed to a CFC but would be allocated and apportioned to gross income of the CFC that is gross income taken into account in determining subpart F income (as described in section 952) or gross income that is effectively connected (or treated as effectively connected) with the conduct of a trade or business in the United States (as described in § 1.882-4(a)(1)), the reduction provided under this paragraph (b)(4) is equal to the reduction that would be provided under this paragraph (b)(4) but for this sentence multiplied by the difference of 100 percent and the percentage described in section 250(a)(1)(B).

(5) *Includible in income under section 1293.*—A tentative disqualified hybrid amount is reduced to the extent that the tentative disqualified hybrid amount is received by a qualified electing fund (as described in section 1295) and is includible under section 1293 in the gross income of a United States person that owns stock of that fund. However, if the United States person is a domestic partnership, then the amount includible under section 1293 in the gross income of the United States person reduces the tentative disqualified hybrid amount only to the extent that a tax resident of the United States would take into account the amount. [Reg. § 1.267(A)-3.]

□ [T.D. 9896, 4-7-2020.]

[Reg. § 1.267A-4]

§ 1.267A-4. Disqualified imported mismatch amounts.—(a) *Disqualified imported mismatch amounts.*—(1) *Rule.*—An imported mismatch payment is a disqualified imported mismatch amount to the extent that, under the set-off rules of paragraph (c) of this section, the income attributable to the payment is directly or indirectly offset by a hybrid deduction incurred by a foreign tax resident or foreign taxable branch that is related to the imported mismatch payer (or that is a party to a structured arrangement pursuant to which the payment is made). See § 1.267A-6(c)(8) through (12) for examples illustrating the application of this section.

(2) *Definitions of certain terms.*—The following definitions apply for purposes of this section:

(i) A *foreign tax resident* means a tax resident that is not a tax resident of the United States.

(ii) A *foreign taxable branch* means a taxable branch that is not a U.S. taxable branch.

(iii) An *imported mismatch payee* means, with respect to an imported mismatch payment, a foreign tax resident or foreign taxable branch that includes the payment in income, as determined under § 1.267A-3(a).

(iv) An *imported mismatch payer* means, with respect to an imported mismatch payment, the specified party.

(v) An *imported mismatch payment* means a specified payment to the extent that it is neither a disqualified hybrid amount nor included or includible in income in the United States. For purposes of this paragraph (a)(2)(v), a specified payment is included or includible in income in the United States to the extent that, if the payment were a tentative disqualified hybrid amount (as described in § 1.267A-3(b)(1)), it would be reduced under the rules of § 1.267A-3(b)(2) through (5).

(b) *Hybrid deduction.*—(1) *In general.*—A *hybrid deduction* means any of the following:

(i) A deduction allowed to a foreign tax resident or foreign taxable branch under its tax law for an amount paid or accrued that is interest (including an amount that would be a structured payment under the principles of § 1.267A-5(b)(5)(ii)) or royalty under such tax law, to the extent that a deduction for the amount would be disallowed if such tax law contained rules substantially similar to those under §§ 1.267A-1 through 1.267A-3 and 1.267A-5. Such a deduction is a hybrid deduction regardless of whether or how the amount giving rise to the deduction would be recognized under U.S. tax law.

(ii) A deduction allowed to a foreign tax resident or foreign taxable branch under its tax law with respect to equity (including deemed equity), such as a notional interest deduction (or similar deduction determined with respect to the foreign tax resident's or foreign taxable branch's equity). However, a deduction allowed to a foreign tax resident or foreign taxable branch with respect to equity is a hybrid deduction only to the extent that an investor of the foreign tax resident, or the home office of the foreign taxable branch, would include the amount in income if, for purposes of the investor's or

home office's tax law, the amount were interest paid by the foreign tax resident ratably (by value) with respect to the interests of the foreign tax resident, or interest paid by the foreign taxable branch to the home office. For purposes of this paragraph (b)(1)(ii), the rules of § 1.267A-3(a) apply to determine the extent that an investor or home office would include an amount in income, by treating the amount as the specified payment.

(2) *Special rules.*—(i) *Foreign tax law contains hybrid mismatch rules.*—In the case of a foreign tax resident or foreign taxable branch the tax law of which contains hybrid mismatch rules, only the following deductions allowed to the foreign tax resident or foreign taxable branch under its tax law are hybrid deductions:

(A) A deduction described in paragraph (b)(1)(i) of this section, to the extent that the deduction would be disallowed if the foreign tax resident's or foreign taxable branch's tax law—

(1) Contained a rule substantially similar to § 1.267A-2(a)(4) (payments pursuant to interest-free loans and similar arrangements); or

(2) Did not permit an inclusion in income in a third country to discharge the application of its hybrid mismatch rules as to the amount giving rise to the deduction when the amount is not included in income in another country as a result of a hybrid or branch arrangement.

(B) A deduction described in paragraph (b)(1)(ii) of this section (deductions with respect to equity).

(ii) *Dual inclusion income used to determine hybrid deductions arising from deemed branch payments in certain cases.*—In the case of a foreign taxable branch the tax law of which permits a loss of the foreign taxable branch to be shared with a tax resident or taxable branch (without regard to whether it is in fact so shared or whether there is a tax resident or taxable branch with which the loss can be shared), a deduction allowed to the foreign taxable branch for an amount that would be a deemed branch payment were such tax law to contain a provision substantially similar to § 1.267A-2(c) is a hybrid deduction to the extent of the excess (if any) of the sum of all such amounts over the foreign taxable branch's dual inclusion income (as determined under the principles of § 1.267A-2(b)(3)). The rule in this paragraph (b)(2)(ii) applies without regard to whether the tax law of the home office provides an exclusion or exemption for income attributable to the branch.

(iii) *Certain deductions are hybrid deductions only if allowed for an accounting period beginning on or after December 20, 2018.*—A deduction described in paragraph (b)(1)(ii) of this section (deductions with respect to equity), or a deduction that would be disallowed if the foreign tax resident's or foreign taxable branch's tax law contained a rule substantially similar to § 1.267A-2(a)(4) (payments pursuant to interest-free loans and similar arrangements), is a hybrid deduction only if allowed for an accounting period beginning on or after December 20, 2018.

(iv) *Certain deductions of a CFC are not hybrid deductions.*—A deduction that but for this paragraph (b)(2)(iv) would be a hybrid deduction is not a hybrid deduction to the extent that the amount paid or accrued giving rise to the deduction is—

(A) A disqualified hybrid amount (but subject to the special rule of paragraph (g) of this section); or

(B) Included or includible in income in the United States. For purposes of this paragraph (b)(2)(iv)(B), an amount is included or includible in income in the United States to the extent that, if the amount were a tentative disqualified hybrid amount (as described in § 1.267A-3(b)(1)), it would be reduced under the rules of § 1.267A-3(b)(2) through (5).

(v) *Loss carryovers.*—A hybrid deduction for a particular accounting period includes a loss carryover from another accounting period, but only to the extent that a hybrid deduction incurred in an accounting period ending on or after December 20, 2018, comprises the loss carryover.

(c) *Set-off rules.*—(1) *In general.*—In the order described in paragraph (c)(2) of this section, a hybrid deduction directly or indirectly offsets the income attributable to an imported mismatch payment to the extent that, under paragraph (c)(3) of this section, the payment directly or indirectly funds the hybrid deduction. The rules of paragraphs (c)(2) and (3) of this section are applied by taking into account the application of paragraph (c)(4) of this section (adjustments to ensure that amounts not taken into account more than once).

(2) *Ordering rules.*—The following ordering rules apply for purposes of determining the extent that a hybrid deduction directly or indirectly offsets income attributable to imported mismatch payments.

(i) First, the hybrid deduction offsets income attributable to a factually-related imported mismatch payment that directly or indirectly funds the hybrid deduction. For purposes of this paragraph (c)(2)(i), a *factually-related imported mismatch payment* means an imported mismatch payment that is made pursuant to a transaction, agreement, or instrument entered into pursuant to the same plan or series of related transactions that includes the transaction, agreement, or instrument pursuant to which the hybrid deduction is incurred, provided that a design of the plan or series of related transactions was for the hybrid deduction to offset income attributable to the payment (as determined under the principles of §1.267A-5(a)(20)(i), by treating the offset as the "hybrid mismatch" described in §1.267A-5(a)(20)(i)).

(ii) Second, to the extent remaining, the hybrid deduction offsets income attributable to an imported mismatch payment (other than a factually-related imported mismatch payment) that directly funds the hybrid deduction.

(iii) Third, to the extent remaining, the hybrid deduction offsets income attributable to an imported mismatch payment (other than a factually-related imported mismatch payment) that indirectly funds the hybrid deduction.

(3) *Funding rules.*—The following funding rules apply for purposes of determining the extent that an imported mismatch payment directly or indirectly funds a hybrid deduction.

(i) The imported mismatch payment directly funds a hybrid deduction to the extent that the imported mismatch payee incurs the hybrid deduction.

(ii) The imported mismatch payment indirectly funds a hybrid deduction to the extent that the imported mismatch payee is allocated the hybrid deduction, and provided that the imported mismatch payee is related to the imported mismatch payer (or is a party to a structured arrangement pursuant to which the imported mismatch payment is made).

(iii) The imported mismatch payee is allocated a hybrid deduction to the extent that the imported mismatch payee directly or indirectly makes a funded taxable payment to the foreign tax resident or foreign taxable branch that incurs the hybrid deduction.

(iv) An imported mismatch payee indirectly makes a funded taxable payment to the foreign tax resident or foreign taxable branch that incurs a hybrid deduction to the extent that a chain of funded taxable payments connects the imported mismatch payee, each intermediary foreign tax resident or foreign taxable branch, and the foreign tax resident or foreign taxable branch that incurs the hybrid deduction, and provided that each intermediary foreign tax resident or foreign taxable branch is related to the imported mismatch payer (or is a party to a structured arrangement pursuant to which the imported mismatch payment is made).

(v) The term *funded taxable payment* means an amount paid or accrued by a foreign tax resident or foreign taxable branch under its tax law (other than an amount that gives rise to a hybrid deduction), to the extent that—

(A) The amount is deductible (but, if such tax law contains hybrid mismatch rules, determined without regard to a provision substantially similar to this section);

(B) Another foreign tax resident or foreign taxable branch includes the amount in income, as determined under §1.267A-3(a) (by treating the amount as the specified payment); and

(C) The amount is neither a disqualified hybrid amount (but subject to the special rule of paragraph (g) of this section) nor included or includible in income in the United States. For purposes of this paragraph (c)(3)(v)(C), an amount is included or includible in income in the United States to the extent that, if the amount were a tentative disqualified hybrid amount (as described in §1.267A-3(b)(1)), it would be reduced under the rules of §1.267A-3(b)(2) through (5).

(vi) If a deduction or loss that is not incurred by a foreign tax resident or foreign taxable branch is directly or indirectly made available to offset income of the foreign tax resident or foreign taxable branch under its tax law, then, for purposes of this paragraph (c), the foreign tax resident or foreign taxable branch to which the deduction or loss is made available and the foreign tax resident or foreign taxable branch that incurs the deduction or loss are treated as a single foreign tax resident or foreign taxable branch. For example, if a deduction or loss of one foreign tax resident is made available to offset income of another foreign tax resident under a tax consolidation, fiscal unity, group relief, loss sharing, or any similar regime, then the foreign tax residents are treated as a single foreign tax resident for purposes of this paragraph (c).

(vii) An imported mismatch payee that directly makes a funded taxable payment to the foreign tax resident or foreign taxable branch that incurs a hybrid deduction is allocated the hybrid deduction before the hybrid deduction (to the extent remaining) is allocated to an imported mismatch payee that indirectly makes a funded

taxable payment to the foreign tax resident or foreign taxable branch that incurs the hybrid deduction.

(viii) An imported mismatch payee that, through a chain of funded taxable payments consisting of a particular number of funded taxable payments, indirectly makes a funded taxable payment to the foreign tax resident or foreign taxable branch that incurs a hybrid deduction is allocated the hybrid deduction before the hybrid deduction (to the extent remaining) is allocated to an imported mismatch payee that, through a chain of funded taxable payments consisting of a greater number of funded taxable payments, indirectly makes a funded taxable payment to the foreign tax resident or foreign taxable branch that incurs the hybrid deduction.

(4) *Adjustments to ensure amounts not taken into account more than once.*—To the extent that the income attributable to an imported mismatch payment is directly or indirectly offset by a hybrid deduction, the imported mismatch payment, the hybrid deduction, and, if applicable, each funded taxable payment comprising the chain of funded taxable payments connecting the imported mismatch payee, each intermediary foreign tax resident or foreign taxable branch, and the foreign tax resident or foreign taxable branch that incurs the hybrid deduction is correspondingly reduced; as a result, such amounts are not again taken into account under this section.

(d) *Calculations based on aggregate amounts during accounting period.*—For purposes of this section, amounts are determined on an accounting period basis. Thus, for example, the amount of imported mismatch payments made by an imported mismatch payer to a particular imported mismatch payee is equal to the aggregate amount of all such payments made by the imported mismatch payer during the accounting period.

(e) *Pro rata adjustments.*—Amounts are allocated on a pro rata basis if there would otherwise be more than one permissible manner in which to allocate the amounts. Thus, for example, if multiple imported mismatch payers make an imported mismatch payment to a single imported mismatch payee, the sum of such payments exceeds the hybrid deduction incurred by the imported mismatch payee, and the payments are not factually-related imported mismatch payments, then a pro rata portion of each imported mismatch payer's payment is considered to directly fund the hybrid deduction. See §1.267A-6(c)(9) and (12) for examples illustrating the application of this paragraph (e).

(f) *Special rules regarding manner in which this section is applied.*—(1) *Initial application of this section.*—This section is first applied without regard to paragraph (f)(2) of this section and by taking into account only the following hybrid deductions:

(i) A hybrid deduction described in paragraph (b)(1)(i) of this section, to the extent that—

(A) The deduction would be disallowed if the foreign tax resident's or foreign taxable branch's tax law contained a rule substantially similar to §1.267A-2(a)(4) (payments pursuant to interest-free loans and similar arrangements); or

(B) The paid or accrued amount giving rise to the deduction is included in income in a third country but is not included in income in another country as a result of a hybrid or branch arrangement.

(ii) A hybrid deduction described in paragraph (b)(1)(ii) of this section (deductions with respect to equity).

(2) *Subsequent application of this section takes into account certain amounts deemed to be imported mismatch payments.*—After this section is applied pursuant to the rules of paragraph (f)(1) of this section, the section is then applied by taking into account only hybrid deductions other than those described in paragraph (f)(1) of this section. In addition, when applying this section in the manner described in the previous sentence, for purposes of determining the extent to which the income attributable to an imported mismatch payment is directly or indirectly offset by a hybrid deduction, an amount paid or accrued by a foreign tax resident or foreign taxable branch that is not a specified party is deemed to be an imported mismatch payment (and such foreign tax resident or foreign taxable branch and a foreign tax resident or foreign taxable branch that includes the amount in income, as determined under §1.267A-3(a), by treating the amount as the specified payment, are deemed to be an imported mismatch payer and an imported mismatch payee, respectively) to the extent that—

(i) The tax law of such foreign tax resident or foreign taxable branch contains hybrid mismatch rules; and

(ii) The amount is subject to disallowance under a provision of the hybrid mismatch rules substantially similar to this section. See §1.267A-6(c)(10) and (12) for examples illustrating the application of paragraph (f)(2) of this section.

(g) *Special rule regarding extent to which a disqualified hybrid amount of a CFC prevents a hybrid deduction or a funded taxable payment.*—A disqualified hybrid amount of a CFC is taken into account for purposes of paragraph (b)(2)(iv)(A) or (c)(3)(v)(C) of this section (certain deductions not hybrid deductions or funded taxable payments to the extent the amount giving rise to the deduction is a disqualified hybrid amount) only to the extent of the excess (if any) of the disqualified hybrid amount over the sum of the amounts described in paragraphs (g)(1) through (3) of this section. See § 1.267A-6(c)(11) for an example illustrating the application of this paragraph (g).

(1) The disqualified hybrid amount to the extent that, if allowed as a deduction, it would be allocated and apportioned to residual CFC gross income (as described in § 1.951A-2(c)(5)(iii)(B)) of the CFC.

(2) The disqualified hybrid amount to the extent that, if allowed as a deduction, it would be allocated and apportioned (under the rules of section 954(b)(5)) to gross income that is taken into account in determining the CFC's subpart F income (as described in section 952 and § 1.952-1), multiplied by the difference of 100 percent and the percentage of stock (by value) of the CFC that, for purposes of sections 951 and 951A, is owned (within the meaning of section 958(a), and determined by treating a domestic partnership as foreign) by one or more tax residents of the United States that are United States shareholders of the CFC.

(3) The disqualified hybrid amount to the extent that, if allowed as a deduction, it would be allocated and apportioned (under the rules of § 1.951A-2(c)(3)) to gross tested income of the CFC (as described in section 951A(c)(2)(A) and § 1.951A-2(c)(1)), multiplied by the difference of 100 percent and the percentage of stock (by value) of the CFC that, for purposes of sections 951 and 951A, is owned (within the meaning of section 958(a), and determined by treating a domestic partnership as foreign) by one or more tax residents of the United States that are United States shareholders of the CFC. [Reg. § 1.267(A)-4.]

☐ [T.D. 9896, 4-7-2020.]

[Reg. § 1.267A-5]

§ 1.267A-5. Definitions and special rules.—(a) *Definitions.*—For purposes of §§ 1.267A-1 through 1.267A-7 the following definitions apply.

(1) The term *accounting period* means a taxable year, or a period of similar length over which, under a provision of hybrid mismatch rules substantially similar to § 1.267A-4, computations similar to those under § 1.267A-4 are made under a foreign tax law.

(2) The term *branch* means a taxable presence of a tax resident in a country other than its country of residence as determined under either the tax resident's tax law or such other country's tax law.

(3) The term *branch mismatch payment* has the meaning provided in § 1.267A-2(e)(2).

(4) The term *controlled foreign corporation* (or *CFC*) has the meaning provided in section 957.

(5) The term *deemed branch payment* has the meaning provided in § 1.267A-2(c)(2).

(6) The term *disregarded payment* has the meaning provided in § 1.267A-2(b)(2).

(7) The term *entity* means any person as described in section 7701(a)(1), including an entity that under §§ 301.7701-1 through 301.7701-3 of this chapter is disregarded as an entity separate from its owner, other than an individual.

(8) The term *fiscally transparent* means, with respect to an entity, fiscally transparent with respect to an item of income as determined under the principles of § 1.894-1(d)(3)(ii) and (iii), without regard to whether a tax resident (either the entity or interest holder in the entity) that derives the item of income is a resident of a country that has an income tax treaty with the United States. In addition, the following special rules apply with respect to an item of income received by an entity:

(i) The entity is fiscally transparent with respect to the item under the tax law of the country in which the entity is created, organized, or otherwise established if, under that tax law, the entity does not take the item into account in its income (without regard to whether such tax law requires an investor of the entity, wherever resident, to separately take into account on a current basis the investor's respective share of the item), and the effect under that tax law is that an investor of the entity is required to take the item into account in its income as if the item were realized directly from the source from which realized by the entity, whether or not distributed.

(ii) The entity is fiscally transparent with respect to the item under the tax law of an investor of the entity if, under that tax law, an investor of the entity takes the item into account in its income (without regard to whether such tax law requires the investor to separately take into account on a current basis the investor's respective share of the item) as if the item were realized directly from the source from which realized by the entity, whether or not distributed.

(iii) The entity is fiscally transparent with respect to the item under the tax law of the country in which the entity is created, organized, or otherwise established if—

(A) That tax law imposes a corporate income tax; and

(B) Under that tax law, neither the entity is required to take the item into account in its income nor an investor of the entity is required to take the item into account in its income as if the item were realized directly from the source from which realized by the entity, whether or not distributed.

(9) The term *home office* means a tax resident that has a branch.

(10) The term *hybrid mismatch rules* means rules, regulations, or other tax guidance substantially similar to section 267A, and includes rules the purpose of which is to neutralize the deduction/no-inclusion outcome of hybrid and branch mismatch arrangements. Examples of such rules would include rules based on, or substantially similar to, the recommendations contained in OECD/G-20, *Neutralising the Effects of Hybrid Mismatch Arrangements, Action 2: 2015 Final Report* (October 2015), and OECD/G-20, *Neutralising the Effects of Branch Mismatch Arrangements, Action 2: Inclusive Framework on BEPS* (July 2017).

(11) The term *hybrid transaction* has the meaning provided in § 1.267A-2(a)(2).

(12) The term *interest* means any amount described in paragraph (a)(12)(i) or (ii) of this section that is paid or accrued, or treated as paid or accrued, for the taxable year or that is otherwise designated as interest expense in paragraph (a)(12)(i) or (ii) of this section.

(i) *In general.*—Interest is an amount paid, received, or accrued as compensation for the use or forbearance of money under the terms of an instrument or contractual arrangement, including a series of transactions, that is treated as a debt instrument for purposes of section 1275(a) and § 1.1275-1(d), and not treated as stock under § 1.385-3, or an amount that is treated as interest under other provisions of the Internal Revenue Code (Code) or the regulations in this part. Thus, interest includes, but is not limited to, the following—

(A) Original issue discount (OID);

(B) Qualified stated interest, as adjusted by the issuer for any bond issuance premium;

(C) OID on a synthetic debt instrument arising from an integrated transaction under § 1.1275-6;

(D) Repurchase premium to the extent deductible by the issuer under § 1.163-7(c);

(E) Deferred payments treated as interest under section 483;

(F) Amounts treated as interest under a section 467 rental agreement;

(G) Forgone interest under section 7872;

(H) De minimis OID taken into account by the issuer;

(I) Amounts paid in connection with a sale-repurchase agreement treated as indebtedness under Federal tax principles;

(J) Redeemable ground rent treated as interest under section 163(c); and

(K) Amounts treated as interest under section 636.

(ii) *Swaps with significant nonperiodic payments.*—(A) *In general.*—Except as provided in paragraphs (a)(12)(ii)(B) and (C) of this section, a swap with significant nonperiodic payments is treated as two separate transactions consisting of an on-market, level payment swap and a loan. The loan must be accounted for by the parties to the contract independently of the swap. The time value component associated with the loan, determined in accordance with § 1.446-3(f)(2)(iii)(A), is recognized as interest expense to the payor.

(B) *Exception for cleared swaps.*—Paragraph (a)(12)(ii)(A) of this section does not apply to a cleared swap. The term *cleared swap* means a swap that is cleared by a derivatives clearing organization, as such term is defined in section 1a of the Commodity Exchange Act (7 U.S.C. 1a), or by a clearing agency, as such term is defined in section 3 of the Securities Exchange Act of 1934 (15 U.S.C. 78c), that is registered as a derivatives clearing organization under the Commodity Exchange Act or as a clearing agency under the Securities Exchange Act of 1934, respectively, if the derivatives clearing organization or clearing agency requires the parties to the swap to post and collect margin or collateral.

(C) *Exception for non-cleared swaps subject to margin or collateral requirements.*—Paragraph (a)(12)(ii)(A) of this section does not apply to a non-cleared swap that requires the parties to meet the margin or collateral requirements of a Federal regulator or that provides for margin or collateral requirements that are substantially similar to a cleared swap or a non-cleared swap subject to the margin or collateral requirements of a Federal regulator. For purposes of this paragraph (a)(12)(ii)(C), the term *Federal regulator* means the Securities and Exchange Commission (SEC), the Commodity Futures Trading Commission (CFTC), or a prudential regulator, as defined in section 1a(39) of the Commodity Exchange Act (7 U.S.C. 1a), as amended by section 721 of the Dodd-Frank Wall Street Reform and Consumer Protection Act of 2010, Public Law No. 111-203, 124 Stat. 1376, Title VII.

(13) The term *investor* means, with respect to an entity, any tax resident or taxable branch that directly or indirectly (determined under the rules of section 958(a) without regard to whether an intermediate entity is foreign or domestic, or under substantially similar rules under a tax resident's or taxable branch's tax law) owns an interest in the entity.

(14) The term *related* has the meaning provided in this paragraph (a)(14). A tax resident or taxable branch is related to a specified party if the tax resident or taxable branch is a related person within the meaning of section 954(d)(3), determined by treating the specified party as the "controlled foreign corporation" referred to in section 954(d)(3) and the tax resident or taxable branch as the "person" referred to in section 954(d)(3). In addition, for the purposes of this paragraph (a)(14), a tax resident that under §§ 301.7701-1 through 301.7701-3 of this chapter is disregarded as an entity separate from its owner for U.S. tax purposes, as well as a taxable branch, is treated as a corporation. *See also* § 1.954-1(f)(2)(iv)(B)(*1*) (neither section 318(a)(3), nor § 1.958-2(d) or the principles thereof, applies to attribute stock or other interests).

(15) The term *reverse hybrid* has the meaning provided in § 1.267A-2(d)(2).

(16) The term *royalty* includes amounts paid or accrued as consideration for the use of, or the right to use—

(i) Any copyright, including any copyright of any literary, artistic, scientific or other work (including cinematographic films and software);

(ii) Any patent, trademark, design or model, plan, secret formula or process, or other similar property (including goodwill); or

(iii) Any information concerning industrial, commercial or scientific experience, but does not include—

(A) Amounts paid or accrued for after-sales services;

(B) Amounts paid or accrued for services rendered by a seller to the purchaser under a warranty;

(C) Amounts paid or accrued for pure technical assistance; or

(D) Amounts paid or accrued for an opinion given by an engineer, lawyer or accountant.

(17) The term *specified party* means a tax resident of the United States, a CFC (other than a CFC with respect to which there is not a tax resident of the United States that, for purposes of sections 951 and 951A, owns (within the meaning of section 958(a), and determined by treating a domestic partnership as foreign) at least ten percent (by vote or value) of the stock of the CFC), and a U.S. taxable branch. Thus, an entity that is fiscally transparent for U.S. tax purposes is not a specified party, though an owner of the entity may be a specified party. For example, in the case of a payment by a partnership, a domestic corporation that is a partner of the partnership is a specified party and a deduction for its allocable share of the payment is subject to disallowance under section 267A.

(18) The term *specified payment* has the meaning provided in § 1.267A-1(b).

(19) The term *specified recipient* means, with respect to a specified payment, any tax resident that derives the payment under its tax law or any taxable branch to which the payment is attributable under its tax law (or any tax resident that, based on all the facts and circumstances, is reasonably expected to derive the payment under its tax law, or any taxable branch to which, based on all the facts and circumstances, the payment is reasonably expected to be attributable under its tax law). The principles of § 1.894-1(d)(1) apply for purposes of determining whether a tax resident derives (or is reasonably expected to derive) a specified payment under its tax law, without regard to whether the tax resident is a resident of a country that has an income tax treaty with the United States. There may be more than one specified recipient with respect to a specified payment.

(20) The terms *structured arrangement* and *party to a structured arrangement* have the meaning set forth in this paragraph (a)(20).

(i) *Structured arrangement.*—A structured arrangement means an arrangement with respect to which one or more specified payments would be a disqualified hybrid amount (or a disqualified imported mismatch amount) without regard to the relatedness limitation in § 1.267A-2(f) (or without regard to the phrase "that is related to the specified party" in § 1.267A-4(a)) (either such outcome, a *hybrid mismatch*), provided that, based on all the facts and circumstances (including the terms of the arrangement), the arrangement is designed to produce the hybrid mismatch. Facts and circumstances that indicate the arrangement is designed to produce the hybrid mismatch include the following:

(A) The hybrid mismatch is priced into the terms of the arrangement, including—

(*1*) The pricing of the arrangement is different from what the pricing would have been absent the hybrid mismatch;

(*2*) Features that alter the terms of the arrangement, including its return if the hybrid mismatch is no longer available; or

(*3*) A below-market return absent the tax effects or benefits resulting from the hybrid mismatch.

(B) The arrangement is marketed as tax-advantaged where some or all of the tax advantage derives from the hybrid mismatch.

(C) The arrangement is marketed to tax residents of a country the tax law of which enables the hybrid mismatch.

(ii) *Party to a structured arrangement.*—A party to a structured arrangement means a tax resident, a taxable branch, or an entity that participates in the structured arrangement. For purposes of this paragraph (a)(20)(ii), in the case of an entity, the entity's participation in a structured arrangement is imputed to its investors. However, a tax resident, a taxable branch or an entity (the *relevant party*) is considered to participate in the structured arrangement only if—

(A) The relevant party (or a related tax resident or taxable branch, determined under paragraph (a)(14) of this section by treating the relevant party as a specified party) could, based on all the facts and circumstances, reasonably be expected to be aware of the hybrid mismatch; and

(B) The relevant party or one or more of its investors (or a related tax resident or taxable branch, determined under paragraph (a)(14) of this section by treating the relevant party or an investor as a specified party) shares in the value of the tax benefit resulting from the hybrid mismatch.

(21) The term *tax law* of a country includes statutes, regulations, administrative or judicial rulings, and income tax treaties of the country. If a country has an income tax treaty with the United States that applies to taxes imposed by a political subdivision or other local authority of that country, then the tax law of the political subdivision or other local authority is deemed to be a tax law of a country. When used with respect to a tax resident or branch, tax law refers to—

(i) In the case of a tax resident, the tax law of the country or countries where the tax resident is resident; and

(ii) In the case of a branch, the tax law of the country where the branch is located.

(22) The term *taxable branch* means a branch that has a taxable presence under its tax law.

(23) The term *tax resident* means either of the following:

(i) A body corporate or other entity or body of persons liable to tax under the tax law of a country as a resident. For purposes of this paragraph (a)(23)(i), an entity that is created, organized, or otherwise established under the tax law of a country that does not impose a corporate income tax is treated as liable to tax under the tax law of such country as a resident if under the corporate or commercial laws of such country the entity is treated as a body corporate or a company. A body corporate or other entity or body of persons may be a tax resident of more than one country.

(ii) An individual liable to tax under the tax law of a country as a resident. An individual may be a tax resident of more than one country.

(24) The term *United States shareholder* has the meaning provided in section 951(b).

(25) The term *U.S. taxable branch* means a trade or business carried on in the United States by a tax resident of another country, except that if an income tax treaty applies, the term means a permanent establishment of a tax treaty resident eligible for benefits under an income tax treaty between the United States and the treaty country. Thus, for example, a U.S. taxable branch includes a U.S. trade or business of a foreign corporation taxable under section 882(a) or a U.S. permanent establishment of a tax treaty resident.

(b) *Special rules.*—For purposes of §§ 1.267A-1 through 1.267A-7, the following special rules apply.

(1) *Coordination with other provisions.*—(i) *In general.*—Except as provided in paragraph (b)(1)(ii) of this section, a specified payment is subject to section 267A after the application of any other applicable provisions of the Code and regulations in this part. Thus, the determination of whether a deduction for a specified payment is disallowed under section 267A is made with respect to the taxable year for which a deduction for the payment would otherwise be allowed for U.S. tax purposes. *See, for example*, sections 163(e)(3) and 267(a)(3) for rules that may defer the taxable year for which a deduction is allowed. *See also* § 1.882-5(a)(5) (providing that provisions that disallow interest expense apply after the application of § 1.882-5). In addition, provisions that characterize amounts paid or accrued as something other than interest or royalties, such as § 1.894-1(d)(2), govern the treatment of such amounts and therefore such amounts would not be treated as specified payments. Moreover, to the extent that a specified payment is not described in § 1.267A-1(b) when it is subject to section 267A, the payment is not again subject to section

267A at a later time. For example, if for the taxable year in which a specified payment is paid the payment is not described in §1.267A-1(b) but under section 163(j) a deduction for the payment is deferred, the payment is not again subject to section 267A in the taxable year for which section 163(j) no longer defers the deduction.

(ii) *Section 267A applied before certain provisions.*—In addition to the extent provided in any other applicable provision of the Code or regulations in this part, section 267A applies before the application of sections 163(j), 461(l), 465, and 469.

(iii) *Coordination with capitalization and recovery provisions.*—To the extent a specified payment is described in §1.267A-1(b), a deduction for the payment is considered permanently disallowed for all purposes of the Code and regulations in this part and, therefore, the payment is not taken into account for purposes of computing costs that are required to be capitalized and recovered through depreciation, amortization, cost of goods sold, adjustment to basis, or similar forms of recovery under any applicable provision of the Code or in regulations in this part. Thus, for example, to the extent an interest or royalty payment is a specified payment described in §1.267A-1(b), the payment is not capitalized and included in inventory cost or added to basis under section 263A. As an additional example, to the extent that a debt issuance cost is a specified payment described in §1.267A-1(b), it is neither capitalized under section 263 or the regulations in this part under section 263 nor recoverable under §1.446-5.

(iv) *Specified payments arising in taxable years beginning before January 1, 2018.*—Section 267A does not apply to a specified payment that is paid or accrued in a taxable year beginning before January 1, 2018, regardless of whether under a provision of the Code or regulations in this part (for example, section 267(a)(3)) a deduction for the payment is deferred to a taxable year beginning after December 31, 2017, or whether the payment is carried over to another taxable year and under another provision of the Code (for example, section 163(j)) is considered paid or accrued in such taxable year.

(2) *Foreign currency gain or loss.*—Except as set forth in this paragraph (b)(2), section 988 gain or loss is not taken into account under section 267A. Foreign currency gain or loss recognized with respect to a specified payment is taken into account under section 267A to the extent that a deduction for the specified payment is disallowed under section 267A, provided that the foreign currency gain or loss is described in §1.988-2(b)(4) (relating to exchange gain or loss recognized by the issuer of a debt instrument with respect to accrued interest) or §1.988-2(c) (relating to items of expense or gross income or receipts which are to be paid after the date accrued). If a deduction for a specified payment is disallowed under section 267A, then a proportionate amount of foreign currency loss under section 988 with respect to the specified payment is also disallowed, and a proportionate amount of foreign currency gain under section 988 with respect to the specified payment reduces the amount of the disallowance. For purposes of this paragraph (b)(2), the proportionate amount is the amount of the foreign currency gain or loss under section 988 with respect to the specified payment multiplied by a fraction, the numerator of which is the amount of the specified payment for which a deduction is disallowed under section 267A and the denominator of which is the total amount of the specified payment.

(3) *U.S. taxable branch payments.*—(i) *Amounts considered paid or accrued by a U.S. taxable branch.*—For purposes of section 267A, a U.S. taxable branch is considered to pay or accrue an amount of interest or royalty equal to either—

(A) The amount of interest or royalty allocable to effectively connected income of the U.S. taxable branch under section 873(a) or 882(c)(1), as applicable; or

(B) In the case of a U.S. taxable branch that is a U.S. permanent establishment of a treaty resident eligible for benefits under an income tax treaty between the United States and the treaty country, the amount of interest or royalty allowable in computing the business profits attributable to the U.S. permanent establishment.

(ii) *Treatment of U.S. taxable branch payments.*—(A) *Interest.*—Interest considered paid or accrued by a U.S. taxable branch of a foreign corporation under paragraph (b)(3)(i) of this section (the "U.S. taxable branch interest payment") is treated as a payment directly to the person to which the interest is payable, to the extent it is paid or accrued with respect to a liability described in §1.882-5(a)(1)(ii)(A) or (B) (resulting in directly allocable interest) or with respect to a U.S. booked liability, as described in §1.882-5(d)(2). If the U.S. taxable branch interest payment exceeds in the aggregate the interest paid or accrued on the U.S. taxable branch's directly allocable interest and interest paid or accrued on U.S. booked liabilities, the excess amount is treated as paid or accrued by the U.S. taxable branch on a pro-rata basis to the same persons and pursuant to the same terms that the home office paid or accrued interest,

excluding any directly allocable interest or interest paid or accrued on a U.S. booked liability. The rules of this paragraph (b)(3)(ii) for determining to whom interest is paid or accrued apply without regard to whether the U.S. taxable branch interest payment is determined under the method described in §1.882-5(b) through (d) or the method described in §1.882-5(e).

(B) *Royalties.*—Royalties considered paid or accrued by a U.S. taxable branch under paragraph (b)(3)(i) of this section are treated solely for purposes of section 267A as paid or accrued on a pro-rata basis by the U.S. taxable branch to the same persons and pursuant to the same terms that the home office paid or accrued such royalties.

(C) *Permanent establishments and interbranch payments.*—If a U.S. taxable branch is a permanent establishment in the United States, the principles of the rules in paragraphs (b)(3)(ii)(A) and (B) of this section apply with respect to interest and royalties allowed in computing the business profits of a treaty resident eligible for treaty benefits. This paragraph (b)(3)(ii)(C) does not apply to interbranch interest or royalty payments allowed as deduction under certain U.S. income tax treaties (as described in §1.267A-2(c)(2)).

(4) *Effect on earnings and profits.*—The disallowance of a deduction under section 267A does not affect whether the amount paid or accrued that gave rise to the deduction reduces earnings and profits of a corporation. However, for purposes of section 952(c)(1) and §1.952-1(c), a CFC's earnings and profits are not reduced by a specified payment a deduction for which is disallowed under section 267A, if a principal purpose of the transaction pursuant to which the payment is made is to reduce or limit the CFC's subpart F income.

(5) *Application to structured payments.*—(i) *In general.*—For purposes of section 267A and the regulations in this part under section 267A, a structured payment (as defined in paragraph (b)(5)(ii) of this section) is treated as interest. Thus, a structured payment is treated as subject to section 267A and the regulations in this part under section 267A to the same extent as if the payment were an amount of interest paid or accrued.

(ii) *Structured payment.*—A structured payment means any amount described in paragraph (b)(5)(ii)(A) or (B) of this section.

(A) *Substitute interest payments.*—A substitute interest payment described in §1.861-2(a)(7) is treated as a structured payment for purposes of section 267A, unless the payment relates to a sale-repurchase agreement or a securities lending transaction that is entered into by the payor in the ordinary course of the payor's business. This paragraph (b)(5)(ii)(A) does not apply to an amount described in paragraph (a)(12)(i)(I) of this section.

(B) *Amounts economically equivalent to interest.*—(1) *Principal purpose to reduce interest expense.*—Any expense or loss economically equivalent to interest is treated as a structured payment for purposes of section 267A if a principal purpose of structuring the transaction(s) is to reduce an amount incurred by the taxpayer that otherwise would have been described in paragraph (a)(12) or (b)(5)(ii)(A) of this section. For purposes of this paragraph (b)(5)(ii)(B)(1), the fact that the taxpayer has a business purpose for obtaining the use of funds does not affect the determination of whether the manner in which the taxpayer structures the transaction(s) is with a principal purpose of reducing the taxpayer's interest expense. In addition, the fact that the taxpayer has obtained funds at a lower pre-tax cost based on the structure of the transaction(s) does not affect the determination of whether the manner in which the taxpayer structures the transaction(s) is with a principal purpose of reducing the taxpayer's interest expense. For purposes of this paragraph (b)(5)(ii)(B), any expense or loss is economically equivalent to interest to the extent that the expense or loss is—

(i) Deductible by the taxpayer;

(ii) Incurred by the taxpayer in a transaction or series of integrated or related transactions in which the taxpayer secures the use of funds for a period of time;

(iii) Substantially incurred in consideration of the time value of money; and

(iv) Not described in paragraph (a)(12) or (b)(5)(ii)(A) of this section.

(2) *Principal purpose.*—Whether a transaction or a series of integrated or related transactions is entered into with a principal purpose described in paragraph (b)(5)(ii)(B)(1) of this section depends on all the facts and circumstances related to the transaction(s). A purpose may be a principal purpose even though it is outweighed by other purposes (taken together or separately). Factors to be taken into account in determining whether one of the taxpayer's principal purposes for entering into the transaction(s) include the taxpayer's normal borrowing rate in the taxpayer's functional currency, whether

the taxpayer would enter into the transaction(s) in the ordinary course of the taxpayer's trade or business, whether the parties to the transaction(s) are related persons (within the meaning of section 267(b) or 707(b)), whether there is a significant and bona fide business purpose for the structure of the transaction(s), whether the transactions are transitory, for example, due to a circular flow of cash or other property, and the substance of the transaction(s).

(6) *Anti-avoidance rule.*—A specified party's deduction for a specified payment is disallowed to the extent that both of the following requirements are satisfied:

(i) The payment (or income attributable to the payment) is not included in the income of a tax resident or taxable branch, as determined under §1.267A-3(a) (but without regard to the deemed full inclusion rule in §1.267A-3(a)(5)).

(ii) A principal purpose of the terms or structure of the arrangement (including the form and the tax laws of the parties to the arrangement) is to avoid the application of the regulations in this part under section 267A in a manner that is contrary to the purposes of section 267A and the regulations in this part under section 267A. [Reg. §1.267(A)-5.]

☐ [*T.D. 9896, 4-7-2020 (corrected 8-11-2020).*]

[Reg. §1.267A-6]

§1.267A-6. Examples.—(a) *Scope.*—This section provides examples that illustrate the application of §§1.267A-1 through 1.267A-5.

(b) *Presumed facts.*—For purposes of the examples in this section, unless otherwise indicated, the following facts are presumed:

(1) US1, US2, and US3 are domestic corporations that are tax residents solely of the United States.

(2) FW, FX, and FZ are bodies corporate established in, and tax residents of, Country W, Country X, and Country Z, respectively. They are not fiscally transparent under the tax law of any country. They are not specified parties.

(3) Under the tax law of each country, interest and royalty payments are deductible.

(4) The tax law of each country provides a 100 percent participation exemption for dividends received from non-resident corporations.

(5) The tax law of each country, other than the United States, provides an exemption for income attributable to a branch.

(6) Except as provided in paragraphs (b)(4) and (5) of this section, all amounts derived (determined under the principles of §1.894-1(d)(1)) by a tax resident, or attributable to a taxable branch, are included in income, as determined under §1.267A-3(a).

(7) Only the tax law of the United States contains hybrid mismatch rules.

(c) *Examples.*—(1) *Example 1. Payment pursuant to a hybrid financial instrument.*—(i) *Facts.* FX holds all the interests of US1. FX also holds an instrument issued by US1 that is treated as equity for Country X tax purposes and indebtedness for U.S. tax purposes (the FX-US1 instrument). On date 1, US1 pays $50x to FX pursuant to the instrument. The amount is treated as an excludible dividend for Country X tax purposes (by reason of the Country X participation exemption) and as interest for U.S. tax purposes.

(ii) *Analysis.* US1 is a specified party and thus a deduction for its $50x specified payment is subject to disallowance under section 267A. As described in paragraphs (c)(1)(ii)(A) through (C) of this section, the entire $50x payment is a disqualified hybrid amount under the hybrid transaction rule of §1.267A-2(a) and, as a result, a deduction for the payment is disallowed under §1.267A-1(b)(1).

(A) US1's payment is made pursuant to a hybrid transaction because a payment with respect to the FX-US1 instrument is treated as interest for U.S. tax purposes but not for purposes of Country X tax law (the tax law of FX, a specified recipient that is related to US1). *See* §1.267A-2(a)(2) and (f). Therefore, §1.267A-2(a) applies to the payment.

(B) For US1's payment to be a disqualified hybrid amount under §1.267A-2(a), a no-inclusion must occur with respect to FX. *See* §1.267A-2(a)(1)(i). As a consequence of the Country X participation exemption, FX includes $0 of the payment in income and therefore a $50x no-inclusion occurs with respect to FX. *See* §1.267A-3(a)(1). The result is the same regardless of whether, under the Country X participation exemption, the $50x payment is simply excluded from FX's taxable income or, instead, is reduced or offset by other means, such as a $50x dividends received deduction. *See* §1.267A-3(a)(1).

(C) Pursuant to §1.267A-2(a)(1)(ii), FX's $50x no-inclusion gives rise to a disqualified hybrid amount to the extent that it is a result of US1's payment being made pursuant to the hybrid transaction. FX's $50x no-inclusion is a result of the payment being made pursuant to the hybrid transaction because, were the payment to be treated as

interest for Country X tax purposes, FX would include $50x in income and, consequently, the no-inclusion would not occur.

(iii) *Alternative facts – multiple specified recipients.* The facts are the same as in paragraph (c)(1)(i) of this section, except that FX holds all the interests of FZ, which is fiscally transparent for Country X tax purposes, and FZ holds all of the interests of US1. Moreover, the FX-US1 instrument is held by FZ (rather than by FX) and US1 makes its $50x payment to FZ (rather than to FX); the payment is derived by FZ under its tax law and by FX under its tax law and, accordingly, both FZ and FX are specified recipients of the payment. Further, the payment is treated as interest for Country Z tax purposes and FZ includes it in income. For the reasons described in paragraph (c)(1)(ii) of this section, FX's no-inclusion causes the payment to be a disqualified hybrid amount. FZ's inclusion in income (regardless of whether Country Z has a low or high tax rate) does not affect the result, because the hybrid transaction rule of §1.267A-2(a) applies if any no-inclusion occurs with respect to a specified recipient of the payment as a result of the payment being made pursuant to the hybrid transaction.

(iv) *Alternative facts – preferential rate.* The facts are the same as in paragraph (c)(1)(i) of this section, except that for Country X tax purposes US1's payment is treated as a dividend subject to a 4% tax rate, whereas the marginal rate imposed on ordinary income is 20%. FX includes $10x of the payment in income, calculated as $50x multiplied by 0.2 (.04, the rate at which the particular type of payment (a dividend for Country X tax purposes) is subject to tax in Country X, divided by 0.2, the marginal tax rate imposed on ordinary income). *See* §1.267A-3(a)(1). Thus, a $40x no-inclusion occurs with respect to FX ($50x less $10x). The $40x no-inclusion is a result of the payment being made pursuant to the hybrid transaction because, were the payment to be treated as interest for Country X tax purposes, FX would include the entire $50x in income at the full marginal rate imposed on ordinary income (20%) and, consequently, the no-inclusion would not occur. Accordingly, $40x of US1's payment is a disqualified hybrid amount.

(v) *Alternative facts – no-inclusion not the result of hybridity.* The facts are the same as in paragraph (c)(1)(i) of this section, except that Country X has a pure territorial regime (that is, Country X only taxes income with a domestic source). Although US1's payment is pursuant to a hybrid transaction and a $50x no-inclusion occurs with respect to FX, FX's no-inclusion is not a result of the payment being made pursuant to the hybrid transaction. This is because if Country X tax law were to treat the payment as interest, FX would include $0 in income and, consequently, the $50x no-inclusion would still occur. Accordingly, US1's payment is not a disqualified hybrid amount. *See* §1.267A-2(a)(1)(ii). The result would be the same if Country X instead did not impose a corporate income tax.

(vi) *Alternative facts – indebtedness under both tax laws but different ordering rules give rise to hybrid transaction; reduction of no-inclusion by reason of inclusion of a principal payment.* The facts are the same as in paragraph (c)(1)(i) of this section, except that the FX-US1 instrument is indebtedness for both U.S. and Country X tax purposes. In addition, the $50x date 1 payment is treated as interest for U.S. tax purposes and a repayment of principal for Country X tax purposes. On date 1, based on all the facts and circumstances (including the terms of the FX-US1 instrument, the tax laws of the United States and Country X, and an absence of a plan pursuant to which FX would dispose of the FX-US1 instrument), it is reasonably expected that on date 2 (a date that is within 36 months after the end of the taxable year of US1 that includes date 1), US1 will pay a total of $200x to FX and that, for U.S. tax purposes, $25x will be treated as interest and $175x as a repayment of principal, and, for Country X tax purposes, $75x will be treated as interest (and included in FX's income) and $125x as a repayment of principal. US1's $50x specified payment is made pursuant to a hybrid transaction and, but for §1.267A-3(a)(4), a $50x no-inclusion would occur with respect to FX. *See* §§1.267A-2(a)(2) and 1.267A-3(a)(1). However, pursuant to §1.267A-3(a)(4), FX's inclusion in income with respect to $50x of the date 2 amount that is a repayment of principal for U.S. tax purposes is treated as correspondingly reducing FX's no-inclusion with respect to the specified payment. As a result, as to US1's $50x specified payment, a no-inclusion does not occur with respect to FX. *See* §1.267A-3(a)(4). Therefore, US1's $50x specified payment is not a disqualified hybrid amount. *See* §1.267A-2(a)(1)(i).

(2) *Example 2. Payment pursuant to a repo transaction.*—(i) *Facts.* FX holds all the interests of US1, and US1 holds all the interests of US2. On date 1, US1 and FX enter into a sale and repurchase transaction. Pursuant to the transaction, US1 transfers shares of preferred stock of US2 to FX in exchange for $1,000x, subject to a binding commitment of US1 to reacquire those shares on date 3 for an agreed price, which represents a repayment of the $1,000x plus a financing or time value of money return reduced by the amount of any distributions paid with respect to the preferred stock between dates 1 and 3 that are retained by FX. On date 2, US2 pays a $100x

dividend on its preferred stock to FX. For Country X tax purposes, FX is treated as owning the US2 preferred stock and therefore is the beneficial owner of the dividend. For U.S. tax purposes, the transaction is treated as a loan from FX to US1 that is secured by the US2 preferred stock. Thus, for U.S. tax purposes, US1 is treated as owning the US2 preferred stock and is the beneficial owner of the dividend. In addition, for U.S. tax purposes, US1 is treated as paying $100x of interest to FX (an amount corresponding to the $100x dividend paid by US2 to FX). Further, the marginal tax rate imposed on ordinary income under Country X tax law is 25%. Moreover, instead of a participation exemption, Country X tax law provides its tax residents a credit for underlying foreign taxes paid by a non-resident corporation from which a dividend is received; with respect to the $100x dividend received by FX from US2, the credit is $10x.

(ii) *Analysis.* US1 is a specified party and thus a deduction for its $100x specified payment is subject to disallowance under section 267A. As described in paragraphs (c)(2)(ii)(A) through (D) of this section, $40x of the payment is a disqualified hybrid amount under the hybrid transaction rule of §1.267A-2(a) and, as a result, $40x of the deduction is disallowed under §1.267A-1(b)(1).

(A) Although US1's $100x interest payment is not regarded under Country X tax law, a connected amount (US2's dividend payment) is regarded and derived by FX under such tax law. Thus, FX is considered a specified recipient with respect to US1's interest payment. *See* §1.267A-2(a)(3).

(B) US1's payment is made pursuant to a hybrid transaction because a payment with respect to the sale and repurchase transaction is treated as interest for U.S. tax purposes but not for purposes of Country X tax law (the tax law of FX, a specified recipient that is related to US1), which does not regard the payment. *See* §1.267A-2(a)(2) and (f). Therefore, §1.267A-2(a) applies to the payment.

(C) For US1's payment to be a disqualified hybrid amount under §1.267A-2(a), a no-inclusion must occur with respect to FX. *See* §1.267A-2(a)(1)(i). As a consequence of Country X tax law not regarding US1's payment, FX includes $0 of the payment in income and therefore a $100x no-inclusion occurs with respect to FX. *See* §1.267A-3(a). However, FX includes $60x of a connected amount (US2's dividend payment) in income, calculated as $100x (the amount of the dividend) less $40x (the portion of the connected amount that is not included in income in Country X due to the foreign tax credit, determined by dividing the amount of the credit, $10x, by 0.25, the tax rate in Country X). *See* §1.267A-3(a). Pursuant to §1.267A-2(a)(3), FX's inclusion in income with respect to the connected amount correspondingly reduces the amount of its no-inclusion with respect to US1's payment. Therefore, for purposes of §1.267A-2(a), FX's no-inclusion with respect to US1's payment is $40x ($100x less $60x). *See* §1.267A-2(a)(3).

(D) Pursuant to §1.267A-2(a)(1)(ii), FX's $40x no-inclusion gives rise to a disqualified hybrid amount to the extent that FX's no-inclusion is a result of US1's payment being made pursuant to the hybrid transaction. FX's $40x no-inclusion is a result of US1's payment being made pursuant to the hybrid transaction because, were the sale and repurchase transaction to be treated as a loan from FX to US1 for Country X tax purposes, FX would include US1's $100x interest payment in income (because it would not be entitled to a foreign tax credit) and, consequently, the no-inclusion would not occur.

(iii) *Alternative facts – structured arrangement.* The facts are the same as in paragraph (c)(2)(i) of this section, except that FX is a bank that is unrelated to US1. In addition, the sale and repurchase transaction is a structured arrangement and FX is a party to the structured arrangement. The result is the same as in paragraph (c)(2)(ii) of this section. That is, even though FX is not related to US1, it is taken into account with respect to the determinations under §1.267A-2(a) because it is a party to a structured arrangement pursuant to which the payment is made. *See* §1.267A-2(f).

(3) *Example 3. Disregarded payment.*—(i) *Facts.* FX holds all the interests of US1. For Country X tax purposes, US1 is a disregarded entity of FX. During taxable year 1, US1 pays $100x to FX pursuant to a debt instrument. The amount is treated as interest for U.S. tax purposes but is disregarded for Country X tax purposes as a transaction involving a single taxpayer. During taxable year 1, US1's only other items of income, gain, deduction, or loss are $125x of gross income (the entire amount of which is included in US1's income) and a $60x item of deductible expense. The $125x item of gross income is included in FX's income, and the $60x item of deductible expense is allowable for Country X tax purposes.

(ii) *Analysis.* US1 is a specified party and thus a deduction for its $100x specified payment is subject to disallowance under section 267A. As described in paragraphs (c)(3)(ii)(A) and (B) of this section, $35x of the payment is a disqualified hybrid amount under the disregarded payment rule of §1.267A-2(b) and, as a result, $35x of the deduction is disallowed under §1.267A-1(b)(1).

(A) US1's $100x payment is not regarded under the tax law of Country X (the tax law of FX, a related tax resident to which the payment is made) because under such tax law the payment involves a single taxpayer. *See* §1.267A-2(b)(2) and (f). In addition, were the tax law of Country X to regard the payment (and treat it as interest), FX would include it in income. Therefore, the payment is a disregarded payment to which §1.267A-2(b) applies. *See* §1.267A-2(b)(2).

(B) Under §1.267A-2(b)(1), the excess (if any) of US1's disregarded payments for taxable year 1 ($100x) over its dual inclusion income for the taxable year is a disqualified hybrid amount. US1's dual inclusion income for taxable year 1 is $65x, calculated as $125x (the amount of US1's gross income that is included in FX's income) less $60x (the amount of US1's deductible expenses, other than deductions for disregarded payments, that are allowable for Country X tax purposes). *See* §1.267A-2(b)(3). Therefore, $35x is a disqualified hybrid amount ($100x less $65x). *See* §1.267A-2(b)(1).

(iii) *Alternative facts – non-dual inclusion income arising from hybrid transaction.* The facts are the same as in paragraph (c)(3)(i) of this section, except that US1 holds all the interests of FZ (a specified party that is a CFC) and US1's only item of income, gain, deduction, or loss during taxable year 1 (other than the $100x payment to FX) is $80x paid to US1 by FZ pursuant to an instrument treated as indebtedness for U.S. and Country Z tax purposes and equity for Country X tax purposes (the US1-FZ instrument). The $80x is treated as interest for Country Z and U.S. tax purposes (the entire amount of which is included in US1's income) and is treated as an excludible dividend for Country X tax purposes (by reason of the Country X participation exemption). Paragraphs (c)(3)(iii)(A) and (B) of this section describe the extent to which the specified payments by FZ and US1, each of which is a specified party, are disqualified hybrid amounts.

(A) The hybrid transaction rule of §1.267A-2(a) applies to FZ's payment because the payment is made pursuant to a hybrid transaction, as a payment with respect to the US1-FZ instrument is treated as interest for U.S. tax purposes but not for purposes of Country X's tax law (the tax law of FX, a specified recipient that is related to FZ). As a consequence of the Country X participation exemption, an $80x no-inclusion occurs with respect to FX, and such no-inclusion is a result of the payment being made pursuant to the hybrid transaction. Thus, but for §1.267A-3(b), the entire $80x of FZ's payment would be a disqualified hybrid amount. However, because US1 (a tax resident of the United States that is also a specified recipient of the payment) takes the entire $80x payment into account in its gross income, no portion of the payment is a disqualified hybrid amount. *See* §1.267A-3(b)(2).

(B) The disregarded payment rule of §1.267A-2(b) applies to US1's $100x payment to FX, for the reasons described in paragraph (c)(3)(ii)(A) of this section. In addition, US1 has no dual inclusion income for taxable year 1 because, as a result of the Country X participation exemption, no portion of FZ's $80x payment to US1 (which is derived by FX under its tax law) is included in FX's income. *See* §§1.267A-2(b)(3) and 1.267A-3(a). Therefore, the entire $100x payment from US1 to FX is a disqualified hybrid amount, calculated as $100x (the amount of the payment) less $0 (the amount of dual inclusion income). *See* §1.267A-2(b)(1).

(iv) *Alternative facts – dual inclusion income despite participation exemption.* The facts are the same as in paragraph (c)(3)(iii) of this section, except that the US1-FZ instrument is treated as indebtedness for U.S. tax purposes and equity for Country Z and Country X tax purposes. In addition, the $80x paid to US1 by FZ is treated as interest for U.S. tax purposes (the entire amount of which is included in US1's income), a dividend for Country Z tax purposes (for which FZ is not allowed a deduction or other tax benefit), and an excludible dividend for Country X tax purposes (by reason of the Country X participation exemption). For the reasons described in paragraph (c)(3)(iii)(A) of this section, the hybrid transaction rule of §1.267A-2(a) applies to FZ's payment but no portion of the payment is a disqualified hybrid amount. In addition, the disregarded payment rule of §1.267A-2(b) applies to US1's $100x payment to FX, for the reasons described in paragraph (c)(3)(ii)(B) of this section. US1's dual inclusion income for taxable year 1 is $80x. This is because the $80x paid to US1 by FZ is included in US1's income and, although not included in FX's income, it is a dividend for Country X tax purposes that would have been included in FX's income but for the Country X participation exemption, and FZ is not allowed a deduction or other tax benefit for it under Country Z tax law. *See* §1.267A-2(b)(3)(ii). Therefore, $20x of US1's $100x payment is a disqualified hybrid amount ($100x less $80x). *See* §1.267A-2(b)(1).

(4) *Example 4. Payment allocable to a U.S. taxable branch.*—(i) *Facts.* FX1 and FX2 are foreign corporations that are bodies corporate established in and tax residents of Country X. FX1 holds all the interests of FX2, and FX1 and FX2 file a consolidated return under Country X tax law. FX2 has a U.S. taxable branch ("USB"). During taxable year 1, FX2 pays $50x to FX1 pursuant to an instrument (the "FX1-FX2 instrument"). The amount paid pursuant to the instrument

is treated as interest for U.S. tax purposes but, as a consequence of the Country X consolidation regime, is treated as a disregarded transaction between group members for Country X tax purposes. Also during taxable year 1, FX2 pays $100x of interest to an unrelated bank that is not a party to a structured arrangement (the instrument pursuant to which the payment is made, the "bank-FX2 instrument"). FX2's only other item of income, gain, deduction, or loss for taxable year 1 is $200x of gross income. Under Country X tax law, the $200x of gross income is attributable to USB, but is not included in FX2's income because Country X tax law exempts income attributable to a branch. Under U.S. tax law, the $200x of gross income is effectively connected income of USB. Further, under section 882(c)(1), $75x of interest is, for taxable year 1, allocable to USB's effectively connected income. USB has neither liabilities that are directly allocable to it, as described in § 1.882-5(a)(1)(ii)(A), nor U.S. booked liabilities, as defined in § 1.882-5(d)(2).

(ii) *Analysis.* USB is a specified party and thus any interest or royalty allowable as a deduction in determining its effectively connected income is subject to disallowance under section 267A. Pursuant to § 1.267A-5(b)(3)(i)(A), USB is treated as paying $75x of interest, and such interest is thus a specified payment. Of that $75x, $25x is treated as paid to FX1, calculated as $75x (the interest allocable to USB under section 882(c)(1)) multiplied by 1/3 ($50x, FX2's payment to FX1, divided by $150x, the total interest paid by FX2). *See* § 1.267A-5(b)(3)(ii)(A). As described in paragraphs (c)(4)(ii)(A) and (B) of this section, the $25x of the specified payment treated as paid by USB to FX1 is a disqualified hybrid amount under the disregarded payment rule of § 1.267A-2(b) and, as a result, a deduction for that amount is disallowed under § 1.267A-1(b)(1).

(A) USB's $25x payment to FX1 is not regarded under the tax law of Country X (the tax law of FX1, a related tax resident to which the payment is made) because under such tax law it is a disregarded transaction between group members. *See* § 1.267A-2(b)(2) and (f). In addition, were the tax law of Country X to regard the payment (and treat it as interest), FX1 would include it in income. Therefore, the payment is a disregarded payment to which § 1.267A-2(b) applies. *See* § 1.267A-2(b)(2).

(B) Under § 1.267A-2(b)(1), the excess (if any) of USB's disregarded payments for taxable year 1 ($25x) over its dual inclusion income for the taxable year is a disqualified hybrid amount. USB's dual inclusion income for taxable year 1 is $0. This is because, as a result of the Country X exemption for income attributable to a branch, no portion of USB's $200x item of gross income is included in FX2's income. *See* § 1.267A-2(b)(3). Therefore, the entire $25x of the specified payment treated as paid by USB to FX1 is a disqualified hybrid amount, calculated as $25x (the amount of the payment) less $0 (the amount of dual inclusion income). *See* § 1.267A-2(b)(1).

(iii) *Alternative facts – deemed branch payment.* The facts are the same as in paragraph (c)(4)(i) of this section, except that FX2 does not pay any amounts during taxable year 1 (thus, it does not pay the $50x to FX1 or the $100x to the bank). However, under an income tax treaty between the United States and Country X, USB is a U.S. permanent establishment and, for taxable year 1, $25x of royalties is allowable as a deduction in computing the business profits of USB and is deemed paid to FX2. Under Country X tax law, the $25x is not regarded. Accordingly, the $25x is a specified payment that is a deemed branch payment. *See* §§ 1.267A-2(c)(2) and 1.267A-5(b)(3)(i)(B). In addition, the entire $25x is a disqualified hybrid amount for which a deduction is disallowed because the tax law of Country X provides an exclusion or exemption for income attributable to a branch. *See* § 1.267A-2(c)(1).

(5) *Example 5. Payment to a reverse hybrid.*—(i) *Facts.* FX holds all the interests of US1 and FY, and FY holds all the interests of FV. FY is an entity established in Country Y, and FV is an entity established in Country V. FY is fiscally transparent for Country Y tax purposes but is not fiscally transparent for Country X tax purposes. FV is fiscally transparent for Country X tax purposes. On date 1, US1 pays $100x to FY. The payment is treated as interest for U.S. tax purposes and Country X tax purposes.

(ii) *Analysis.* US1 is a specified party and thus a deduction for its $100x specified payment is subject to disallowance under section 267A. As described in paragraphs (c)(5)(ii)(A) through (C) of this section, the entire $100x payment is a disqualified hybrid amount under the reverse hybrid rule of § 1.267A-2(d) and, as a result, a deduction for the payment is disallowed under § 1.267A-1(b)(1).

(A) US1's payment is made to a reverse hybrid because FY is fiscally transparent under the tax law of Country Y (the tax law of the country in which it is established) but is not fiscally transparent under the tax law of Country X (the tax law of FX, an investor that is related to US1). *See* § 1.267A-2(d)(2) and (f). Therefore, § 1.267A-2(d) applies to the payment. The result would be the same if the payment were instead made to FV. *See* § 1.267A-2(d)(3).

(B) For US1's payment to be a disqualified hybrid amount under § 1.267A-2(d), a no-inclusion must occur with respect to FX, an inves-

tor the tax law of which treats FY as not fiscally transparent. *See* § 1.267A-2(d)(1)(i). Because FX does not derive the $100x payment under Country X tax law (as FY is not fiscally transparent under such tax law), FX includes $0 of the payment in income and therefore a $100x no-inclusion occurs with respect to FX. *See* § 1.267A-3(a).

(C) Pursuant to § 1.267A-2(d)(1)(ii), FX's $100x no-inclusion gives rise to a disqualified hybrid amount to the extent that it is a result of US1's payment being made to the reverse hybrid. FX's $100x no-inclusion is a result of the payment being made to the reverse hybrid because, were FY to be treated as fiscally transparent for Country X tax purposes, FX would include $100x in income and, consequently, the no-inclusion would not occur. The result would be the same if Country X tax law instead viewed US1's payment as a dividend, rather than interest. *See* § 1.267A-2(d)(1)(ii).

(iii) *Alternative facts – inclusion under anti-deferral regime.* The facts are the same as in paragraph (c)(5)(i) of this section, except that, under a Country X anti-deferral regime, FX takes into account $100x attributable to the $100x payment received by FY. If under the rules of § 1.267A-3(a) FX includes the entire attributed amount in income (that is, if FX takes the amount into account in its income at the full marginal rate imposed on ordinary income and the amount is not reduced or offset by certain relief particular to the amount), then a no-inclusion does not occur with respect to FX. As a result, in such a case, no portion of US1's payment would be a disqualified hybrid amount under § 1.267A-2(d).

(iv) *Alternative facts – multiple investors.* The facts are the same as in paragraph (c)(5)(i) of this section, except that FX holds all the interests of FZ, which is fiscally transparent for Country X tax purposes; FZ holds all the interests of FY, which is fiscally transparent for Country Z tax purposes; and FZ includes the $100x payment in income. Thus, each of FZ and FX is an investor of FY, as each directly or indirectly holds an interest of FY. *See* § 1.267A-5(a)(13). A $100x no-inclusion occurs with respect to FX, an investor the tax law of which treats FY as not fiscally transparent. FX's no-inclusion is a result of the payment being made to the reverse hybrid because, were FY to be treated as fiscally transparent for Country X tax purposes, then FX would include $100x in income (as FZ is fiscally transparent for Country X tax purposes). Accordingly, FX's no-inclusion is a result of US1's payment being made to the reverse hybrid and, consequently, the entire $100x payment is a disqualified hybrid amount. However, if instead FZ were not fiscally transparent for Country X tax purposes, then FX's no-inclusion would not be a result of US1's payment being made to the reverse hybrid and, therefore, the payment would not be a disqualified hybrid amount under § 1.267A-2(d).

(v) *Alternative facts – portion of no-inclusion not the result of hybridity.* The facts are the same as in paragraph (c)(5)(i) of this section, except that the $100x is viewed as a royalty for U.S. tax purposes and Country X tax purposes, and Country X tax law contains a patent box regime that provides an 80% deduction with respect to certain royalty income. If the royalty payment would qualify for the Country X patent box deduction were FY to be treated as fiscally transparent for Country X tax purposes, then only $20x of FX's $100x no-inclusion would be the result of the payment being paid to a reverse hybrid, calculated as $100x (the no-inclusion with respect to FX that actually occurs) less $80x (the no-inclusion with respect to FX that would occur if FY were to be treated as fiscally transparent for Country X tax purposes). *See* § 1.267A-2(d)(1)(ii) and 1.267A-3(a)(1)(ii). Accordingly, in such a case, only $20x of US1's payment would be a disqualified hybrid amount under § 1.267A-2(d).

(vi) *Alternative facts – payment to a discretionary trust*—(A) *Facts.* The facts are the same as in paragraph (c)(5)(i) of this section, except that FY is a discretionary trust established in, and a tax resident of, Country Y (and as a result, FY is generally not fiscally transparent for Country Y tax purposes under the principles of § 1.894-1(d)(3)(ii)). In general, under Country Y tax law, FX, an investor of FY, is not required to separately take into account in its income US1's $100x payment received by FY; instead, FY is required to take the payment into account in its income. However, under the trust agreement, the trustee of FY may, with respect to certain items of income received by FY, allocate such an item to FY's beneficiary, FX. When this occurs, then, for Country Y tax purposes, FY does not take the item into account in its income, and FX is required to take the item into account in its income as if it received the item directly from the source from which realized by FY. For Country X tax purposes, FX in all cases does not take into account in its income any item of income received by FY. With respect to the $100x paid from US1 to FY, the trustee allocates the $100x to FX.

(B) *Analysis.* FY is fiscally transparent with respect to US1's $100x payment under the tax law of Country Y (the tax law of the country in which FY is established). *See* § 1.267A-5(a)(8)(i). In addition, FY is not fiscally transparent with respect to US1's $100x payment under the tax law of Country X (the tax law of FX, the investor of FY). *See* § 1.267A-5(a)(8)(ii). Thus, FY is a reverse hybrid with respect to the payment. *See* § 1.267A-2(d)(2) and (f). Therefore, for reasons similar to those discussed in paragraphs (c)(5)(ii)(B) and (C) of this section, the entire $100x payment is a disqualified hybrid amount.

(6) *Example 6. Branch mismatch payment.*—(i) *Facts.* FX holds all the interests of US1 and FZ. FZ owns BB, a Country B branch that gives rise to a taxable presence in Country B under Country Z tax law but not under Country B tax law. On date 1, US1 pays $50x to FZ. The amount is treated as a royalty for U.S. tax purposes and Country Z tax purposes. Under Country Z tax law, the amount is treated as income attributable to BB and, as a consequence of County Z tax law exempting income attributable to a branch, is excluded from FZ's income.

(ii) *Analysis.* US1 is a specified party and thus a deduction for its $50x specified payment is subject to disallowance under section 267A. As described in paragraphs (c)(6)(ii)(A) through (C) of this section, the entire $50x payment is a disqualified hybrid amount under the branch mismatch rule of §1.267A-2(e) and, as a result, a deduction for the payment is disallowed under §1.267A-1(b)(1).

(A) US1's payment is a branch mismatch payment because under Country Z tax law (the tax law of FZ, a home office that is related to US1) the payment is treated as income attributable to BB, and BB is not a taxable branch (that is, under Country B tax law, BB does not give rise to a taxable presence). *See* §1.267A-2(e)(2) and (f). Therefore, §1.267A-2(e) applies to the payment. The result would be the same if instead BB were a taxable branch and, under Country B tax law, US1's payment were treated as income attributable to FZ, the home office, and not BB. *See* §1.267A-2(e)(2).

(B) For US1's payment to be a disqualified hybrid amount under §1.267A-2(e), a no-inclusion must occur with respect to FZ. *See* §1.267A-2(e)(1)(i). As a consequence of the Country Z branch exemption, FZ includes $0 of the payment in income and therefore a $50x no-inclusion occurs with respect to FZ. *See* §1.267A-3(a).

(C) Pursuant to §1.267A-2(e)(1)(ii), FZ's $50x no-inclusion gives rise to a disqualified hybrid amount to the extent that it is a result of US1's payment being a branch mismatch payment. FZ's $50x no-inclusion is a result of the payment being a branch mismatch payment because, were the payment to not be treated as income attributable to BB for Country Z tax purposes, FZ would include $50x in income and, consequently, the no-inclusion would not occur.

(7) *Example 7. Reduction of disqualified hybrid amount for certain amounts includible in income.*—(i) *Facts.* US1 and FW hold 60% and 40%, respectively, of the interests of FX, and FX holds all the interests of FZ. Each of FX and FZ is a specified party that is a CFC. FX holds an instrument issued by FZ that it is treated as equity for Country X tax purposes and as indebtedness for U.S. tax purposes (the FX-FZ instrument). On date 1, FZ pays $100x to FX pursuant to the FX-FZ instrument. The amount is treated as a dividend for Country X tax purposes and as interest for U.S. tax purposes. In addition, pursuant to section 954(c)(6), the amount is not foreign personal holding company income of FX and, under section 951A, the amount is gross tested income (as described in §1.951A-2(c)(1)) of FX. Further, were FZ allowed a deduction for the amount, it would be allocated and apportioned to gross tested income (as described in §1.951A-2(c)(1)) of FZ. Lastly, Country X tax law provides an 80% participation exemption for dividends received from nonresident corporations and, as a result of such participation exemption, FX includes $20x of FZ's payment in income.

(ii) *Analysis.* FZ, a CFC, is a specified party and thus a deduction for its $100x specified payment is subject to disallowance under section 267A. But for §1.267A-3(b), $80x of FZ's payment would be a disqualified hybrid amount (such amount, a "tentative disqualified hybrid amount"). *See* §§1.267A-2(a) and 1.267A-3(b)(1). Pursuant to §1.267A-3(b), the tentative disqualified hybrid amount is reduced by $48x. *See* §1.267A-3(b)(4). The $48x is the tentative disqualified hybrid amount to the extent that it increases US1's pro rata share of tested income with respect to FX under section 951A (calculated as $80x multiplied by 60%). *See* §1.267A-3(b)(4). Accordingly, $32x of FZ's payment ($80x less $48x) is a disqualified hybrid amount under §1.267A-2(a) and, as a result, $32x of the deduction is disallowed under §1.267A-1(b)(1).

(iii) *Alternative facts – United States shareholder is a domestic partnership.* The facts are the same as in paragraph (c)(7)(i) of this section, except that US1 is a domestic partnership, 90% of the interests of which are held by US2 and the remaining 10% of which are held by an individual that is a nonresident alien (as defined in section 7701(b)(1)(B)). Thus, although each of US1 and US2 is a United States shareholder of FX, only US2 has a pro rata share of any tested item of FX. *See* §1.951A-1(e). In addition, $43.2x of the $80x tentative disqualified hybrid amount increases US2's pro rata share of the tested income of FX (calculated as $80x multiplied by 60% multiplied by 90%). Thus, $36.8x of FZ's payment ($80x less $43.2x) is a disqualified hybrid amount under §1.267A-2(a). *See* §1.267A-3(b)(4).

(8) *Example 8. Imported mismatch rule – direct offset.*—(i) *Facts.* FX holds all the interests of FW, and FW holds all the interests of US1. FX holds an instrument issued by FW that is treated as equity for Country X tax purposes and indebtedness for Country W tax purposes (the FX-FW instrument). FW holds an instrument issued by US1 that is treated as indebtedness for Country W and U.S. tax purposes (the FW-US1 instrument). In accounting period 1, FW pays $100x to FX pursuant to the FX-FW instrument. The amount is treated as an excludible dividend for Country X tax purposes (by reason of the Country X participation exemption) and as interest for Country W tax purposes. Also in accounting period 1, US1 pays $100x to FW pursuant to the FW-US1 instrument. The amount is treated as interest for Country W and U.S. tax purposes and is included in FW's income. The FX-FW instrument was not entered into pursuant to the same plan or series of related transactions pursuant to which the FW-US1 instrument was entered into.

(ii) *Analysis.* US1 is a specified party and thus a deduction for its $100x specified payment is subject to disallowance under section 267A. US1's $100x payment is neither a disqualified hybrid amount nor included or includible in income in the United States. *See* §1.267A-4(a)(2)(v). In addition, FW's $100x deduction is a hybrid deduction because it is a deduction allowed to FW that results from an amount paid that is interest under Country W tax law, and were Country W law to have rules substantially similar to those under §§1.267A-1 through 1.267A-3 and 1.267A-5, a deduction for the payment would be disallowed (because under such rules the payment would be pursuant to a hybrid transaction and FX's no-inclusion would be a result of the hybrid transaction). *See* §§1.267A-2(a) and 1.267A-4(b). Under §1.267A-4(a)(2), US1's payment is an imported mismatch payment, US1 is an imported mismatch payer, and FW (the foreign tax resident that includes the imported mismatch payment in income) is an imported mismatch payee. The imported mismatch payment is a disqualified imported mismatch amount to the extent that the income attributable to the payment is directly or indirectly offset by the hybrid deduction incurred by FW (a foreign tax resident that is related to US1). *See* §1.267A-4(a)(1). Under §1.267A-4(c)(1), the $100x hybrid deduction directly or indirectly offsets the income attributable to US1's imported mismatch payment to the extent that the payment directly or indirectly funds the hybrid deduction. The entire $100x of US1's payment directly funds the hybrid deduction because FW (the imported mismatch payee) incurs at least that amount of the hybrid deduction. *See* §1.267A-4(c)(3)(i). Accordingly, the entire $100x payment is a disqualified imported mismatch amount under §1.267A-4(a)(1) and, as a result, a deduction for the payment is disallowed under §1.267A-1(b)(2).

(iii) *Alternative facts – long-term deferral.* The facts are the same as in paragraph (c)(8)(i) of this section, except that the FX-FW instrument is treated as indebtedness for Country X and Country W tax purposes, and FW does not pay any amounts pursuant to the instrument during accounting period 1 In addition, under Country W tax law, FW is allowed to deduct interest under the FX-FW instrument as it accrues, whereas under Country X tax law FX does not take into account in its income interest under the FX-FW instrument until the interest is paid. Further, FW accrues $100x of interest during accounting period 1, and FW will not pay such amount to FX for more than 36 months after the end of accounting period 1. The results are the same as in paragraph (c)(8)(ii) of this section. That is, FW's $100x deduction for the accrued interest is a hybrid deduction, *see* §§1.267A-2(a), 1.267A-3(a), and 1.267A-4(b), and the income attributable to US1's $100x imported mismatch payment is offset by the hybrid deduction for the reasons described in paragraph (c)(8)(ii) of this section. As a result, a deduction for the payment is disallowed under §1.267A-1(b)(2). The result would be the same even if the FX-FW instrument is expected to be redeemed or capitalized before the $100x of interest is paid such that FX will never take into account in its income (and therefore will not include in income) the $100x of interest.

(iv) *Alternative facts – notional interest deduction.* The facts are the same as in paragraph (c)(8)(i) of this section, except that there is no FX-FW instrument and thus FW does not pay any amounts to FX during accounting period 1. However, during accounting period 1, FW is allowed a $100x notional interest deduction with respect to its equity under Country W tax law. Pursuant to §1.267A-4(b)(1)(ii), FW's notional interest deduction is a hybrid deduction. The results are the same as in paragraph (c)(8)(ii) of this section. That is, income attributable to US1's $100x imported mismatch payment is offset by FW's hybrid deduction for the reasons described in paragraph (c)(8)(ii) of this section. As a result, a deduction for the payment is disallowed under §1.267A-1(b)(2). The result would be the same if the tax law of Country W contains hybrid mismatch rules because FW's deduction is a deduction with respect to equity. *See* §1.267A-4(b)(2)(i).

(v) *Alternative facts – foreign hybrid mismatch rules prevent hybrid deduction.* The facts are the same as in paragraph (c)(8)(i) of this section, except that the tax law of Country W contains hybrid mismatch rules, and under such rules FW is not allowed a deduction for the $100x that it pays to FX pursuant to the FX-FW instrument. The $100x paid by FW therefore does not give rise to a hybrid deduction. See §1.267A-4(b). Accordingly, because the income attributable to US1's payment to FW is not directly or indirectly offset by a hybrid deduction, the payment is not a disqualified imported mismatch amount. Therefore, a deduction for the payment is not disallowed under §1.267A-1(b)(2).

(9) *Example 9. Imported mismatch rule – indirect offsets and pro rata allocations.*—(i) *Facts.* FX holds all the interests of FZ, and FZ holds all the interests of US1 and US2. FX has a Country B branch that, for Country X and Country B tax purposes, gives rise to a taxable presence in Country B and is therefore a taxable branch ("BB"). Under the Country B-Country X income tax treaty, BB is a permanent establishment entitled to deduct expenses properly attributable to BB for purposes of computing its business profits under the treaty. In addition, BB is deemed to pay a royalty to FX for the right to use intangibles developed by FX equal to cost plus y%. The deemed royalty is a deductible expense properly attributable to BB under the Country B-Country X income tax treaty. For Country X tax purposes, any transactions between BB and X are disregarded. The deemed royalty is $80x for accounting period 1. Country B tax law does not permit a loss of a taxable branch to be shared with a tax resident or another taxable branch. In addition, an instrument issued by FZ to FX is properly reflected as an asset on the books and records of BB (the FX-FZ instrument). The FX-FZ instrument is treated as indebtedness for Country X, Country Z, and Country B tax purposes. In accounting period 1, FZ pays $80x to FX pursuant to the FX-FZ instrument; the amount is treated as interest for Country X, Country Z, and Country B tax purposes, and is treated as income attributable to BB for Country X and Country B tax purposes (but, for Country X tax purposes, is excluded from FX's income as a consequence of the Country X exemption for income attributable to a branch). Further, in accounting period 1, US1 and US2 pay $60x and $40x, respectively, to FZ pursuant to instruments that are treated as indebtedness for Country Z and U.S. tax purposes; the amounts are treated as interest for Country Z and U.S. tax purposes and are included in FZ's income. Lastly, neither the instrument pursuant to which US1 pays the $60x nor the instrument pursuant to which US2 pays the $40x was entered into pursuant to a plan or series of related transactions that includes the transaction or agreement giving rise to BB's deduction for the deemed royalty.

(ii) *Analysis.* US1 and US2 are specified parties and thus deductions for their specified payments are subject to disallowance under section 267A. Neither of the payments is a disqualified hybrid amount, nor is either of the payments included or includible in income in the United States. See §1.267A-4(a)(2)(v). In addition, BB's $80x deduction for the deemed royalty is a hybrid deduction because it is a deduction allowed to BB that results from an amount paid that is treated as a royalty under Country B tax law (regardless of whether a royalty deduction would be allowed under U.S. law), and were Country B tax law to have rules substantially similar to those under §§1.267A-1 through 1.267A-3 and 1.267A-5, a deduction for the payment would be disallowed because under such rules the payment would be a deemed branch payment and Country X has an exclusion for income attributable to a branch. See §§1.267A-2(c) and 1.267A-4(b). Under §1.267A-4(a)(2), each of US1's and US2's payments is an imported mismatch payment, US1 and US2 are imported mismatch payers, and FZ (the foreign tax resident that includes the imported mismatch payments in income) is an imported mismatch payee. The imported mismatch payments are disqualified imported mismatch amounts to the extent that the income attributable to the payments is directly or indirectly offset by the hybrid deduction incurred by BB (a foreign taxable branch that is related to US1 and US2). See §1.267A-4(a). Under §1.267A-4(c)(1), the $80x hybrid deduction directly or indirectly offsets the income attributable to the imported mismatch payments to the extent that the payments directly or indirectly fund the hybrid deduction. Paragraphs (c)(9)(ii)(A) and (B) of this section describe the extent to which the imported mismatch payments directly or indirectly fund the hybrid deduction.

(A) Neither US1's nor US2's payment directly funds the hybrid deduction because FZ (the imported mismatch payee) does not incur the hybrid deduction. See §1.267A-4(c)(3)(i). To determine the extent to which the payments indirectly fund the hybrid deduction, the amount of the hybrid deduction that is allocated to FZ must be determined. See §1.267A-4(c)(3)(ii). FZ is allocated the hybrid deduction to the extent that it directly or indirectly makes a funded taxable payment to BB (the foreign taxable branch that incurs the hybrid deduction). See §1.267A-4(c)(3)(iii). The $80x that FZ pays pursuant to the FX-FZ instrument is a funded taxable payment of FZ to BB. See §1.267A-4(c)(3)(v). Therefore, because FZ makes a funded taxable payment to BB that is at least equal to the amount of the hybrid

deduction, FZ is allocated the entire amount of the hybrid deduction. See §1.267A-4(c)(3)(iii).

(B) But for US2's imported mismatch payment, the entire $60x of US1's imported mismatch payment would indirectly fund the hybrid deduction because FZ is allocated at least that amount of the hybrid deduction. See §1.267A-4(c)(3)(ii). Similarly, but for US1's imported mismatch payment, the entire $40x of US2's imported mismatch payment would indirectly fund the hybrid deduction because FZ is allocated at least that amount of the hybrid deduction. See §1.267A-4(c)(3)(ii). However, because the sum of US1's and US2's imported mismatch payments to FZ ($100x) exceeds the hybrid deduction allocated to FZ ($80x), pro rata adjustments must be made. See §1.267A-4(e). Thus, $48x of US1's imported mismatch payment is considered to indirectly fund the hybrid deduction, calculated as $80x (the amount of the hybrid deduction) multiplied by 60% ($60x, the amount of US1's imported mismatch payment to FZ, divided by $100x, the sum of the imported mismatch payments that US1 and US2 make to FZ). Similarly, $32x of US2's imported mismatch payment is considered to indirectly fund the hybrid deduction, calculated as $80x (the amount of the hybrid deduction) multiplied by 40% ($40x, the amount of US2's imported mismatch payment to FZ, divided by $100x, the sum of the imported mismatch payments that US1 and US2 make to FZ). Accordingly, $48x of US1's imported mismatch payment, and $32x of US2's imported mismatch payment, are disqualified imported mismatch amounts under §1.267A-4(a)(1) and, as a result, deductions for such amounts are disallowed under §1.267A-1(b)(2).

(iii) *Alternative facts – loss made available through foreign group relief regime.* The facts are the same as in paragraph (c)(9)(i) of this section, except that FZ holds all the interests in FZ2, a body corporate that is a tax resident of Country Z, FZ2 (rather than FZ) holds all the interests of US1 and US2, and US1 and US2 make their respective $60x and $40x payments to FZ2 (rather than to FZ). Further, in accounting period 1, a $10x loss of FZ is made available to offset income of FZ2 through a Country Z foreign group relief regime. Pursuant to §1.267A-4(c)(3)(vi), FZ and FZ2 are treated as a single foreign tax resident for purposes of §1.267A-4(c) because a loss that is not incurred by FZ2 (FZ's $10x loss) is made available to offset income of FZ2 under the Country Z group relief regime. Accordingly, the results are the same as in paragraph (c)(9)(ii) of this section. That is, by treating FZ and FZ2 as a single foreign tax resident for purposes of §1.267A-4(c), BB's hybrid deduction offsets the income attributable to US1's and US2's imported mismatch payments to the same extent as described in paragraph (c)(9)(ii) of this section.

(10) *Example 10. Imported mismatch rule – ordering rules and rule deeming certain payments to be imported mismatch payments.*—(i) *Facts.* FX holds all the interests of FW, and FW holds all the interests of US1, US2, and FZ. FZ holds all the interests of US3. FX transfers cash to FW in exchange for an instrument that is treated as equity for Country X tax purposes and indebtedness for Country W tax purposes (the FX-FW instrument). FW transfers cash to US1 in exchange for an instrument that is treated as indebtedness for Country W and U.S. tax purposes (the FW-US1 instrument). The FX-FW instrument and the FW-US1 instrument were entered into pursuant to a plan a design of which was for deductions incurred by FW pursuant to the FX-FW instrument to offset income attributable to payments by US1 pursuant to the FW-US1 instrument. In accounting period 1, FW pays $125x to FX pursuant to the FX-FW instrument; the amount is treated as an excludible dividend for Country X tax purposes (by reason of the Country X participation exemption regime) and as interest for Country W tax purposes. Also in accounting period 1, US1 pays $50x to FW pursuant to the FW-US1 instrument; US2 pays $50x to FW pursuant to an instrument treated as indebtedness for Country W and U.S. tax purposes (the FW-US2 instrument); US3 pays $50x to FZ pursuant to an instrument treated as indebtedness for Country Z and U.S. tax purposes (the FZ-US3 instrument); and FZ pays $50x to FW pursuant to an instrument treated as indebtedness for Country W and Country Z tax purposes (FW-FZ instrument). The amounts paid by US1, US2, US3, and FZ are treated as interest for purposes of the relevant tax laws and are included in the income of FW (in the case of US1's, US2's and FZ's payment) or FZ (in the case of US3's payment). Lastly, neither the FW-US2 instrument, the FW-FZ instrument, nor the FZ-US3 instrument was entered into pursuant to a plan or series of related transactions that includes the transaction pursuant to which the FX-FW instrument was entered into.

(ii) *Analysis.* US1, US2, and US3 are specified parties (but FZ is not a specified party, see §1.267A-5(a)(17)) and thus deductions for US1's, US2's, and US3's specified payments are subject to disallowance under section 267A. None of the specified payments is a disqualified hybrid amount, nor is any of the payments included or includible in income in the United States. See §1.267A-4(a)(2)(v). Under §1.267A-4(a)(2), each of the payments is an imported mismatch payment, US1, US2, and US3 are imported mismatch payers, and FW and FZ (the foreign tax residents that include the imported mismatch payments in income) are imported mismatch payees. The imported mismatch payments are disqualified imported mismatch amounts to the extent that the income attributable to the payments is directly or indirectly offset by FW's $125x hybrid deduction. *See* §1.267A-4(a)(1) and (b). Under §1.267A-4(c)(1), the $125x hybrid deduction directly or indirectly offsets the income attributable to the imported mismatch payments to the extent that the payments directly or indirectly fund the hybrid deduction. Paragraphs (c)(10)(ii)(A) through (C) of this section describe the extent to which the imported mismatch payments directly or indirectly fund the hybrid deduction and are therefore disqualified hybrid amounts for which a deduction is disallowed under §1.267A-1(b)(2).

(A) First, the $125x hybrid deduction offsets the income attributable to US1's imported mismatch payment, a factually-related imported mismatch payment that directly funds the hybrid deduction. *See* §1.267A-4(c)(2)(i). The entire $50x of US1's payment directly funds the hybrid deduction because FW (the imported mismatch payee) incurs at least that amount of the hybrid deduction. *See* §1.267A-4(c)(3)(i). Accordingly, the entire $50x of the payment is a disqualified imported mismatch amount under §1.267A-4(a)(1).

(B) Second, the remaining $75x hybrid deduction offsets the income attributable to US2's imported mismatch payment, a factually-unrelated imported mismatch payment that directly funds the remaining hybrid deduction. *See* §1.267A-4(c)(2)(ii). The entire $50x of US2's payment directly funds the remaining hybrid deduction because FW (the imported mismatch payee) incurs at least that amount of the remaining hybrid deduction. *See* §1.267A-4(c)(3)(i). Accordingly, the entire $50x of the payment is a disqualified imported mismatch amount under §1.267A-4(a)(1).

(C) Third, the remaining $25x hybrid deduction offsets the income attributable to US3's imported mismatch payment, a factually-unrelated imported mismatch payment that indirectly funds the remaining hybrid deduction. *See* §1.267A-4(c)(2)(iii). The imported mismatch payment indirectly funds the remaining hybrid deduction to the extent that FZ (the imported mismatch payee) is allocated the remaining hybrid deduction. *See* §1.267A-4(c)(3)(ii). FZ is allocated the remaining hybrid deduction to the extent that it directly or indirectly makes a funded taxable payment to FW (the tax resident that incurs the hybrid deduction). *See* §1.267A-4(c)(3)(iii). The $50x that FZ pays to FW pursuant to the FW-FZ instrument is a funded taxable payment of FZ to FW. *See* §1.267A-4(c)(3)(v). Therefore, because FZ makes a funded taxable payment to FW that is at least equal to the amount of the remaining hybrid deduction, FZ is allocated the remaining hybrid deduction. *See* §1.267A-4(c)(3)(iii). Accordingly, $25x of US3's payment indirectly funds the $25x remaining hybrid deduction and, consequently, $25x of US3's payment is a disqualified imported mismatch amount under §1.267A-4(a)(2).

(iii) *Alternative facts – amount deemed to be an imported mismatch payment.* The facts are the same as in paragraph (c)(10)(i) of this section, except that US1 is not a domestic corporation but instead is a body corporate that is only a tax resident of Country E (hereinafter, "FE") (thus, for purposes of this paragraph (c)(10)(iii), the FW-US1 instrument is instead issued by FE and is the "FW-FE instrument"). In addition, the tax law of Country E contains hybrid mismatch rules and the $50x FE pays to FW pursuant to the FW-FE instrument is subject to disallowance under a provision of the hybrid mismatch rules substantially similar to §1.267A-4. Pursuant to §1.267A-4(f)(2), the $50x that FE pays to FW pursuant to the FW-FE instrument is deemed to be an imported mismatch payment for purposes of determining the extent to which the income attributable to an imported mismatch payment is offset by FW's hybrid deduction (a hybrid deduction other than one described in §1.267A-4(f)(1)). The results are the same as in paragraphs (c)(10)(ii)(B) and (C) of this section. That is, by treating the $50x that FE pays to FW as an imported mismatch payment, and for reasons similar to those described in paragraphs (c)(10)(ii)(A) through (C) of this section, $50x of FW's $125x hybrid deduction offsets income attributable to FE's imported mismatch payment, $50x of the remaining $75x hybrid deduction offsets income attributable to US2's imported mismatch payment, and the remaining $25x hybrid deduction offsets income attributable to US3's imported mismatch payment. Accordingly, the entire $50x of US2's payment is a disqualified imported mismatch amount, and $25x of US3's payment is a disqualified imported mismatch amount.

(iv) *Alternative facts – amount deemed to be an imported mismatch payment and "waterfall" approach.* The facts are the same as in paragraph (c)(10)(i) of this section, except that FZ holds all of the interests of US3 indirectly through FE, a body corporate that is only a tax resident of Country E (hereinafter, "FE"), and US3 makes its $50x payment to FE (rather than to FZ); such amount is treated as interest for Country E tax purposes and is included in FE's income. In addition, during accounting period 1, FE pays $50x to FZ pursuant to an instrument; such amount is treated as interest for Country E and Country Z tax purposes, and is included in FZ's income. Further, the

tax law of Country E contains hybrid mismatch rules and the $50x FE pays to FZ pursuant to the instrument is subject to disallowance under a provision of the hybrid mismatch rules substantially similar to §1.267A-4. For purposes of determining the extent to which the income attributable to an imported mismatch payment is directly or indirectly offset by a hybrid deduction, the $50x that FE pays to FZ is deemed to be an imported mismatch payment (and FE and FZ are deemed to be an imported mismatch payer and imported mismatch payee, respectively). *See* §1.267A-4(f)(2). With respect to US1 and US2, the results are the same as described in paragraphs (c)(10)(ii)(A) and (B) of this section. No portion of US3's payment is a disqualified imported mismatch amount because, by treating the $50x that FE pays to FZ as an imported mismatch payment, the remaining $25x of FW's hybrid deduction offsets income attributable to FE's imported mismatch payment. This is because the remaining $25x of FW's hybrid deduction is indirectly funded solely by FE's imported mismatch payment (as opposed to also being funded by US3's imported mismatch payment), as FZ (the imported mismatch payee with respect to FE's payment) directly makes a funded taxable payment to FW, whereas FE (the imported mismatch payee with respect to US3's payment) indirectly makes a funded taxable payment to FW. *See* §1.267A-4(c)(3)(ii) through (v) and (vii).

(11) *Example 11. Imported mismatch rule – hybrid deduction of a CFC.*—(i) *Facts.* FX holds all the interests of US1, and FX and US1 hold 80% and 20%, respectively, of the interests of FZ, a specified party that is a CFC. US1 also holds all the interests of US2, and FX also holds all the interests of FY. FY is an entity established in Country Y, and is fiscally transparent for Country Y tax purposes but is not fiscally transparent for Country X tax purposes. In accounting period 1, US2 pays $100x to FZ pursuant to an instrument (the FZ-US2 instrument). The amount is treated as interest for U.S. tax purposes and Country Z tax purposes, and is included in FZ's income; in addition, for U.S. tax purposes, the amount is foreign personal holding company income of FZ. Also in accounting period 1, FZ pays $100x to FY pursuant to an instrument (the FY-FZ instrument). The amount is treated as interest for U.S. tax purposes and Country Z tax purposes, and none of the amount is included in FX's income. Under Country Z tax law, FZ is allowed a deduction for its entire $100x payment. Under §1.267A-2(d), the entire $100x of FZ's payment is a disqualified hybrid amount (by reason of being made to a reverse hybrid) and, as a result, a deduction for the payment is disallowed under §1.267A-1(b)(1); in addition, if a deduction were allowed for the $100x, it would be allocated and apportioned (under the rules of section 954(b)(5)) to gross subpart F income of FZ. Lastly, the FZ-US2 instrument was not entered into pursuant to a plan or series of related transactions that includes the transaction pursuant to which the FY-FZ instrument was entered into.

(ii) *Analysis.* US2 is a specified party and thus a deduction for its $100x specified payment is subject to disallowance under section 267A. As described in paragraphs (c)(11)(ii)(A) through (C) of this section, $80x of US2's payment is a disqualified imported mismatch amount for which a deduction is disallowed under §1.267A-1(b)(2).

(A) $80x of US2's specified payment is an imported mismatch payment, calculated as $100x (the amount of the payment) less $0 (the disqualified hybrid amount with respect to the payment) less $20 (the amount of the payment that is included or includible in income in the United States). *See* §1.267A-4(a)(2)(v). US2 is an imported mismatch payer and FZ (a foreign tax resident that includes the imported mismatch in income) is an imported mismatch payee. *See* §1.267A-4(a)(2).

(B) But for §1.267A-4(b)(2)(iv), the entire $100x deduction allowed to FZ under its tax law would be a hybrid deduction. *See* §§1.267A-2(d) and 1.267A-4(b)(1). However, pursuant to §1.267A-4(b)(2)(iv), only $80x of the deduction is a hybrid deduction, calculated as $100x (the deduction to the extent that it would be a hybrid deduction but for §1.267A-4(b)(2)(iv)) less $20x (the extent that FZ's payment giving rise to the deduction is a disqualified hybrid amount that is taken into account for purposes of §1.267A-4(b)(2)(iv)(A)), less $0 (the extent that FZ's payment giving rise to the deduction is included or includible in income in the United States). *See* §1.267A-4(b)(2)(iv). The $20x disqualified hybrid amount that is taken into account for purposes of §1.267A-4(b)(2)(iv)(A) is calculated as $100x (the extent that FZ's payment is a disqualified hybrid amount) less $80x ($100x, the disqualified hybrid amount to the extent that, if allowed as a deduction, it would be allocated and apportioned to gross subpart F income, multiplied by 80%, the difference of 100% and the percentage of the stock (by value) of FZ that is owned by US1)). *See* §1.267A-4(g).

(C) The $80x hybrid deduction offsets the income attributable to US2's imported mismatch payment, an imported mismatch payment that directly funds the hybrid deduction. *See* §1.267A-4(c)(2)(ii). The entire $80x of US2's imported mismatch payment directly funds the hybrid deduction because FZ (the imported mismatch payee) incurs at least that amount of the hybrid deduction. *See* §1.267A-4(c)(3)(i).

Accordingly, the entire $80x of US2's imported mismatch payment is a disqualified imported mismatch amount under § 1.267A-4(a)(1).

(12) *Example 12. Imported mismatch rule – application first with respect to certain hybrid deductions, then with respect to other hybrid deductions.*—(i) *Facts.* FX holds all the interests of FZ, and FZ holds all the interests of each of US1 and FE. The tax law of Country E contains hybrid mismatch rules. FX holds an instrument issued by FZ that is treated as equity for Country X tax purposes and indebtedness for Country Z tax purposes (the FX-FZ instrument). In accounting period 1, FZ pays $10x to FX pursuant to the FX-FZ instrument. The amount is treated as an excludible dividend for Country X tax purposes (by reason of the Country X participation exemption) and as interest for Country Z tax purposes. Also in accounting period 1, FZ is allowed a $90x notional interest deduction with respect to its equity under Country Z tax law. In addition, in accounting period 1, US1 pays $100x to FZ pursuant to an instrument (the FZ-US1 instrument); the amount is treated as interest for U.S. tax purposes and Country Z tax purposes, and is included in FZ's income. Further, in accounting period 1, FE pays $40x to FZ pursuant to an instrument (the FZ-FE instrument); the amount is treated as interest for Country E and Country Z tax purposes, is included in FZ's income, and is subject to disallowance under a provision of Country E hybrid mismatch rules substantially similar to § 1.267A-4. Lastly, neither the FZ-US1 instrument nor the FZ-FE instrument was entered into pursuant to a plan or series of related transactions that includes the transaction pursuant to which the FX-FZ instrument was entered into.

(ii) *Analysis.* US1 is a specified party and thus a deduction for its $100x specified payment is subject to disallowance under section 267A. As described in paragraphs (c)(12)(ii)(A) through (D) of this section, $92x of US1's payment is a disqualified imported mismatch amount for which a deduction is disallowed under § 1.267A-1(b)(2).

(A) The entire $100x of US1's specified payment is an imported mismatch payment. See § 1.267A-4(a)(2)(v). US1 is an imported mismatch payer and FZ (a foreign tax resident that includes the imported mismatch payment in income) is an imported mismatch payee. See § 1.267A-4(a)(2).

(B) FZ has $100x of hybrid deductions (the $10x deduction for the payment pursuant to the FX-FZ instrument plus the $90x notional interest deduction). See § 1.267A-4(b). Pursuant to § 1.267A-4(f)(1), § 1.267A-4 is first applied by taking into account only the $90x hybrid deduction consisting of the notional interest deduction; in addition, for purposes of applying § 1.267A-4 in this manner, FE's $40x payment is not treated as an imported mismatch payment. Thus, the $90x hybrid deduction offsets the income attributable to US1's imported mismatch payment, an imported mismatch payment that directly funds the hybrid deduction. See § 1.267A-4(c)(2)(ii). Moreover, $90x of US1's imported mismatch payment directly funds the hybrid deduction because FZ (the imported mismatch payee) incurs at least that amount of the hybrid deduction. See § 1.267A-4(c)(3)(i).

(C) Section § 1.267A-4 is next applied by taking into account only the $10x hybrid deduction consisting of the deduction for the payment pursuant to the FX-FZ instrument. See § 1.267A-4(f)(2). When applying § 1.267A-4 in this manner, and for purposes of determining the extent to which the income attributable to an imported mismatch payment is directly or indirectly offset by a hybrid deduction, FE's $40x payment is treated as an imported mismatch payment. See § 1.267A-4(f)(2). In addition, US1's imported mismatch payment is reduced from $100x to $10x. See § 1.267A-4(c)(4). But for FE's imported mismatch payment, the entire $10x of US1's imported mismatch payment would directly fund the $10x hybrid deduction because FZ incurred at least that amount of the hybrid deduction. See § 1.267A-4(c)(3)(i). Similarly, but for US1's imported mismatch payment, the entire $40x of FE's imported mismatch payment would directly fund the $10x hybrid deduction because FZ incurred at least that amount of the hybrid deduction. See § 1.267A-4(c)(3)(i). However, because the sum of US1's and FE's imported mismatch payments to FZ ($50x) exceeds the hybrid deduction incurred by FZ ($10x), pro rata adjustments must be made. See § 1.267A-4(e). Thus, $2x of US1's imported mismatch payment is considered to directly fund the hybrid deduction, calculated as $10x (the amount of the hybrid deduction) multiplied by 20% ($10x, the amount of US1's imported mismatch payment to FZ, divided by $50x, the sum of the imported mismatch payments that US1 and FE make to FZ). Similarly, $8x of FE's imported mismatch payment is considered to directly fund the hybrid deduction, calculated as $10x (the amount of the hybrid deduction) multiplied by 80% ($40x, the amount of FE's imported mismatch payment to FZ, divided by $50x, the sum of the imported mismatch payments that US1 and FE make to FZ). Accordingly, $2x of FZ's $10x hybrid deduction offsets income attributable to US1's $10x imported mismatch payment, and $8x of the hybrid deduction offsets income attributable to FE's $40x imported mismatch payment.

(D) Therefore, $92x of US1's imported mismatch payment is a disqualified imported mismatch amount, calculated as $90x (the amount that is a disqualified imported mismatch amount determined by applying § 1.267A-4 in the manner set forth in § 1.267A-4(f)(1)) plus $2x (the amount that is a disqualified imported mismatch amount determined by applying § 1.267A-4 in the manner set forth in § 1.267A-4(f)(2)). See § 1.267A-4(a)(1) and (f).

(iii) *Alternative facts – amount deemed to be an imported mismatch payment solely funds hybrid instrument deduction.* The facts are the same as in paragraph (c)(12)(i) of this section, except that FZ holds all of the interests of US1 indirectly through FE, and US1 makes its $100x payment to FE (rather than to FZ); such amount is treated as interest for U.S. and Country E tax purposes, and is included in FE's income. Moreover, FE pays $100x to FZ (rather than $40x); such amount is included in FZ's income, and is subject to disallowance under a provision of Country E hybrid mismatch rules substantially similar to § 1.267A-4. As described in paragraphs (c)(12)(iii)(A) through (D) of this section, $90x of US1's payment is a disqualified imported mismatch amount for which a deduction is disallowed under § 1.267A-1(b)(2).

(A) The entire $100x of US1's specified payment is an imported mismatch payment. See § 1.267A-4(a)(2)(v). US1 is an imported mismatch payer and FE (a foreign tax resident that includes the imported mismatch payment in income) is an imported mismatch payee. See § 1.267A-4(a)(2).

(B) FZ has $100x of hybrid deductions. See § 1.267A-4(b). Pursuant to § 1.267A-4(f)(1), § 1.267A-4 is first applied by taking into account only the $90x hybrid deduction consisting of the notional interest deduction; in addition, for purposes of applying § 1.267A-4 in this manner, FE's $100x payment is not treated as an imported mismatch payment. Thus, the $90x hybrid deduction offsets the income attributable to US1's imported mismatch payment, an imported mismatch payment that indirectly funds the hybrid deduction. See § 1.267A-4(c)(2)(iii). The imported mismatch payment indirectly funds the hybrid deduction because FE (the imported mismatch payee) is allocated the deduction, as FE makes a funded taxable payment (the $100x payment to FZ) that is at least equal to the amount of the deduction. See § 1.267A-4(c)(3)(ii), (iii), and (v).

(C) Section § 1.267A-4 is next applied by taking into account only the $10x hybrid deduction consisting of the deduction for the payment pursuant to the FX-FZ instrument. See § 1.267A-4(f)(2). For purposes of applying § 1.267A-4 in this manner, FE's $100x payment is reduced from $100x to $10x, and similarly US1's imported mismatch payment is reduced from $100x to $10x. See § 1.267A-4(c)(4). Further, FE's $10x payment is treated as an imported mismatch payment. See § 1.267A-4(f)(2). The entire $10x of FE's imported mismatch payment directly funds the hybrid deduction because FZ (the imported mismatch payee with respect to FE's imported mismatch payment) incurs at least that amount of the hybrid deduction. See § 1.267A-4(c)(3)(i). Accordingly, the $10x hybrid deduction offsets the income attributable to FE's imported mismatch payment, and none of the income attributable to US1's imported mismatch payment.

(D) Therefore, $90x of US1's imported mismatch payment is a disqualified imported mismatch amount, calculated as $90x (the amount that is a disqualified imported mismatch amount determined by applying § 1.267A-4 in the manner set forth in § 1.267A-4(f)(1)) plus $0 (the amount that is a disqualified imported mismatch amount determined by applying § 1.267A-4 in the manner set forth in § 1.267A-4(f)(2)). See § 1.267A-4(a)(1) and (f). [Reg. § 1.267(A)-6.]

☐ [*T.D.* 9896, 4-7-2020.]

[Reg. § 1.267A-7]

§ 1.267A-7. Applicability dates.—(a) *General rule.*—Except as provided in paragraph (b) of this section, §§ 1.267A-1 through 1.267A-6 apply to taxable years ending on or after December 20, 2018, provided that such taxable years begin after December 31, 2017. However, taxpayers may apply the regulations in §§ 1.267A-1 through 1.267A-6 in their entirety (including by taking into account paragraph (b) of this section) for taxable years beginning after December 31, 2017, and ending before December 20, 2018. In lieu of applying the regulations in §§ 1.267A-1 through 1.267A-6 (including paragraph (b) of this section), taxpayers may apply the provisions matching §§ 1.267A-1 through 1.267A-6 (including by taking into account the provision matching paragraph (b) of this section) from the Internal Revenue Bulletin (IRB) 2019-03 (https://www.irs.gov/pub/irs-irbs/irb19-03.pdf) in their entirety for all taxable years ending on or before April 8, 2020.

(b) *Special rules.*—The following special rules apply regarding applicability dates:

(1) Sections 1.267A-2(a)(4) (payments pursuant to interest-free loans and similar arrangements), (b) (disregarded payments), (c) (deemed branch payments), and (e) (branch mismatch transactions), 1.267A-4 (imported mismatch rule), and 1.267A-5(b)(5) (structured

payments), except as provided in paragraph (b)(5) of this section, apply to taxable years beginning on or after December 20, 2018.

(2) Section 1.267A-5(a)(20) (defining structured arrangement), as well as the portions of §§ 1.267A-1 through 1.267A-3 that relate to structured arrangements and that are not otherwise described in paragraph (b) of this section, apply to taxable years beginning on or after December 20, 2018. However, in the case of a specified payment made pursuant to an arrangement entered into before December 22, 2017, § 1.267A-5(a)(20), and the portions of §§ 1.267A-1 through 1.267A-3 that relate to structured arrangements and that are not otherwise described in paragraph (b) of this section, apply to taxable years beginning after December 31, 2020.

(3) Except as provided in paragraph (b)(4) of this section, the rules provided in § 1.267A-5(a)(12)(ii) (swaps with significant nonperiodic payments) apply to notional principal contracts entered into on or after April 8, 2021. However, taxpayers may apply the rules provided in § 1.267A-5(a)(12)(ii) to notional principal contracts entered into before April 8, 2021.

(4) For a notional principal contract entered into before April 8, 2021, the interest equivalent rules provided in § 1.267A-5(b)(5)(ii)(B) (applied without regard to the references to § 1.267A-5(a)(12)(ii)) apply to a notional principal contract entered into on or after April 8, 2020.

(5) Section 1.267A-5(b)(5)(ii)(B) (interest equivalent rules) applies to transactions entered into on or after April 8, 2020. [Reg. § 1.267(A)-7.]

☐ [*T.D.* 9896, 4-7-2020 (*corrected* 8-11-2020).]

[Reg. § 1.268-1]

§ 1.268-1. Items attributable to an unharvested crop sold with the land.—In computing taxable income no deduction shall be allowed in respect of items attributable to the production of an unharvested crop which is sold, exchanged, or involuntarily converted with the land and which is considered as property used in the trade or business under section 1231(b)(4). Such items shall be so treated whether or not the taxable year involved is that of the sale, exchange, or conversion of such crop and whether they are for expenses, depreciation, or otherwise. If the taxable year involved is not that of the sale, exchange, or conversion of such crop, a recomputation of the tax liability for such year shall be made; such recomputation should be in the form of an "amended return" if necessary. For the adjustments to basis as a result of such disallowance, see section 1016(a)(11) and the regulations thereunder. [Reg. § 1.268-1.]

☐ [*T.D.* 6252, 9-12-57.]

[Reg. § 1.269-1]

§ 1.269-1. Meaning and use of terms.—As used in section 269 and §§ 1.269-2 through 1.269-7—

(a) *Allowance.*—The term "allowance" refers to anything in the internal revenue laws which has the effect of diminishing tax liability. The term includes, among other things, a deduction, a credit, an adjustment, an exemption, or an exclusion.

(b) *Evasion or avoidance.*—The phrase "evasion or avoidance" is not limited to cases involving criminal penalties, or civil penalties for fraud.

(c) *Control.*—The term "control" means the ownership of stock possessing at least 50 percent of the total combined voting power of all classes of stock entitled to vote, or at least 50 percent of the total value of shares of all classes of stock of the corporation. For control to be "acquired on or after October 8, 1940", it is not necessary that all of such stock be acquired on or after October 8, 1940. Thus, if A, on October 7, 1940, and at all times thereafter, owns 40 percent of the stock of X Corporation and acquires on October 8, 1940, an additional 10 percent of such stock, an acquisition within the meaning of such phrase is made by A on October 8, 1940. Similarly, if B, on October 7, 1940, owns certain assets and transfers on October 8, 1940, such assets to a newly organized Y Corporation in exchange for all the stock of Y Corporation, an acquisition within the meaning of such phrase is made by B on October 8, 1940. If, under the facts stated in the preceding sentence, B is a corporation, all of whose stock is owned by Z Corporation, then an acquisition within the meaning of such phrase is also made by Z Corporation on October 8, 1940, as well as by the shareholders of Z Corporation taken as a group on such date, and by any of such shareholders if such shareholders as a group own 50 percent of the stock of Z on such date.

(d) *Person.*—The term "person" includes an individual, a trust, an estate, a partnership, an association, a company, or a corporation. [Reg. § 1.269-1.]

☐ [*T.D.* 6595, 4-13-62. *Amended by T.D.* 8388, 12-31-91.]

[Reg. § 1.269-2]

§ 1.269-2. Purpose and scope of section 269.—(a) *General.*—Section 269 is designed to prevent in the instances specified therein the use of the sections of the Internal Revenue Code providing deductions, credits, or allowances in evading or avoiding Federal income tax. See § 1.269-3.

(b) *Disallowance of deduction, credit, or other allowance.*—Under the Code, an amount otherwise constituting a deduction, credit, or other allowance becomes unavailable as such under certain circumstances. Characteristic of such circumstances are those in which the effect of the deduction, credit, or other allowance would be to distort the liability of the particular taxpayer when the essential nature of the transaction or situation is examined in the light of the basic purpose or plan which the deduction, credit, or other allowance was designed by the Congress to effectuate. The distortion may be evidenced, for example, by the fact that the transaction was not undertaken for reasons germane to the conduct of the business of the taxpayer, by the unreal nature of the transaction such as its sham character, or by the unreal or unreasonable relation which the deduction, credit, or other allowance bears to the transaction. The principle of law making an amount unavailable as a deduction, credit, or other allowance in cases in which the effect of making an amount so available would be to distort the liability of the taxpayer has been judicially recognized and applied in several cases. Included in these cases are *Gregory v. Helvering* (1935) (293 U.S. 465; Ct. D. 911, C.B. XIV-1, 193); *Griffiths v. Helvering* (1939) (308 U.S. 355; Ct. D. 1431, C.B. 1940-1, 136); *Higgins v. Smith* (1940) (308 U.S. 473; Ct. D. 1434, C.B. 1940-1, 127); and *J.D. & A.B. Spreckels Co. v. Commissioner* (1940) (41 B.T.A. 370). In order to give effect to such principle, but not in limitation thereof, several provisions of the Code, for example, section 267 and section 270, specify with some particularity instances in which disallowance of the deduction, credit, or other allowance is required. Section 269 is also included in such provisions of the Code. The principle of law and the particular sections of the Code are not mutually exclusive and in appropriate circumstances they may operate together or they may operate separately. See, for example, § 1.269-6. [Reg. § 1.269-2.]

☐ [*T.D.* 6595, 4-13-62.]

[Reg. § 1.269-3]

§ 1.269-3. Instances in which section 269(a) disallows a deduction, credit, or other allowance.—(a) *Instances of disallowance.*—Section 269 specifies two instances in which a deduction, credit, or other allowance is to be disallowed. These instances, described in paragraphs (1) and (2) of section 269(a), are those in which—

(1) Any person or persons acquire, or acquired on or after October 8, 1940, directly or indirectly, control of a corporation, or

(2) Any corporation acquires, or acquired on or after October 8, 1940, directly or indirectly, property of another corporation (not controlled, directly or indirectly, immediately before such acquisition by such acquiring corporation or its stockholders), the basis of which property in the hands of the acquiring corporation is determined by reference to the basis in the hands of the transferor corporation.

In either instance the principal purpose for which the acquisition was made must have been the evasion or avoidance of Federal income tax by securing the benefit of a deduction, credit, or other allowance which such other person, or persons, or corporation, would not otherwise enjoy. If this requirement is satisfied, it is immaterial by what method or by what conjunction of events the benefit was sought. Thus, an acquiring person or corporation can secure the benefit of a deduction, credit, or other allowance within the meaning of section 269 even though it is the acquired corporation that is entitled to such deduction, credit, or other allowance in the determination of its tax. If the purpose to evade or avoid Federal income tax exceeds in importance any other purpose, it is the principal purpose. This does not mean that only those acquisitions fall within the provisions of section 269 which would not have been made if the evasion or avoidance purpose was not present. The determination of the purpose for which an acquisition was made requires a scrutiny of the entire circumstances in which the transaction or course of conduct occurred, in connection with the tax result claimed to arise therefrom.

(b) *Acquisition of control; transactions indicative of purpose to evade or avoid tax.*—If the requisite acquisition of control within the meaning of paragraph (1) of section 269(a) exists, the transactions set forth in the following subparagraphs are among those which, in the absence of additional evidence to the contrary, ordinarily are indicative that the principal purpose for acquiring control was evasion or avoidance of Federal income tax:

(1) A corporation or other business enterprise (or the interest controlling such corporation or enterprise) with large profits acquires control of a corporation with current, past, or prospective credits, deductions, net operating losses, or other allowances and the acquisi-

tion is followed by such transfers or other action as is necessary to bring the deduction, credit, or other allowance into conjunction with the income (see further § 1.259-6). This subparagraph may be illustrated by the following example:

Example. Individual A acquires all of the stock of L Corporation which has been engaged in the business of operating retail drug stores. At the time of the acquisition, L Corporation has net operating loss carryovers aggregating $100,000 and its net worth is $100,000. After the acquisition, L Corporation continues to engage in the business of operating retail drug stores but the profits attributable to such business after the acquisition are not sufficient to absorb any substantial portion of the net operating loss carryovers. Shortly after the acquisition, individual A causes to be transferred to L Corporation the assets of a hardware business previously controlled by A which business produces profits sufficient to absorb a substantial portion of L Corporation's net operating loss carryovers. The transfer of the profitable business, which has the effect of using net operating loss carryovers to offset gains of a business unrelated to that which produced the losses, indicates that the principal purpose for which the acquisition of control was made is evasion or avoidance of Federal income tax.

(2) A person or persons organize two or more corporations instead of a single corporation in order to secure the benefit of multiple surtax exemptions (see section 11(c)) or multiple minimum accumulated earnings credits (see section 535(c)(2) and (3)).

(3) A person or persons with high earning assets transfer them to a newly organized controlled corporation retaining assets producing net operating losses which are utilized in an attempt to secure refunds.

(c) *Acquisition of property; transactions indicative of purpose to evade or avoid tax.*—If the requisite acquisition of property within the meaning of paragraph (2) of section 269(a) exists, the transactions set forth in the following subparagraphs are among those which, in the absence of additional evidence to the contrary, ordinarily are indicative that the principal purpose for acquiring such property was evasion or avoidance of Federal income tax:

(1) A corporation acquires property having in its hands an aggregate carryover basis which is materially greater than its aggregate fair market value at the time of such acquisition and utilizes the property to create tax-reducing losses or deductions.

(2) A subsidiary corporation, which has sustained large net operating losses in the operation of business X and which has filed separate returns for the taxable years in which the losses were sustained, acquires high earning assets, comprising business Y, from its parent corporation. The acquisition occurs at a time when the parent would not succeed to the net operating loss carryovers of the subsidiary if the subsidiary were liquidated, and the profits of business Y are sufficient to offset a substantial portion of the net operating loss carryovers attributable to business X (see further example (3) of § 1.269-6).

(d) *Ownership changes to which section 382(l)(5) applies; transactions indicative of purpose to evade or avoid tax.*—(1) *In general.*—Absent strong evidence to the contrary, a requisite acquisition of control or property in connection with an ownership change to which section 382(l)(5) applies is considered to be made for the principal purpose of evasion or avoidance of Federal income tax unless the corporation carries on more than an insignificant amount of an active trade or business during and subsequent to the title 11 or similar case (as defined in section 382(l)(5)(G)). The determination of whether the corporation carries on more than an insignificant amount of an active trade or business is made without regard to the continuity of business enterprise requirement set forth in § 1.368-1(d). The determination is based on all the facts and circumstances, including, for example, the amount of business assets that continue to be used, or the number of employees in the work force who continue employment, in an active trade or business (although not necessarily the historic trade or business). Where the corporation continues to utilize a significant amount of its business assets or work force, the requirement of carrying on more than an insignificant amount of an active trade or business may be met even though all trade or business activities temporarily cease for a period of time in order to address business exigencies.

(2) *Effective date.*—The presumption under paragraph (d) of this section applies to acquisitions of control or property effected pursuant to a plan of reorganization confirmed by a court in a title 11 or similar case (within the meaning of section 368(a)(3)(A)) after August 14, 1990.

(e) *Relationship of section 269 to 11 U.S.C. 1129(d).*—In determining for purposes of section 269 of the Internal Revenue Code whether an acquisition pursuant to a plan of reorganization in a case under title 11 of the United States Code was made for the principal purpose of evasion or avoidance of Federal income tax, the fact that a govern-

mental unit did not seek a determination under 11 U.S.C. 1129(d) is not taken into account and any determination by a court under 11 U.S.C. 1129(d) that the principal purpose of the plan is not avoidance of taxes is not controlling. [Reg. § 1.269-3.]

☐ [T.D. 6595, 4-13-62. *Amended by T.D.* 8388, 12-31-91.]

[Reg. § 1.269-4]

§ 1.269-4. **Power of district director to allocate deduction, credit, or allowance in part.**—The district director is authorized by section 269 (b) to allow a part of the amount disallowed by section 269(a), but he may allow such part only if and to the extent that he determines that the amount allowed will not result in the evasion or avoidance of Federal income tax for which the acquisition was made. The district director is also authorized to use other methods to give effect to part of the amount disallowed under section 269(a), but only to such extent as he determines will not result in the evasion or avoidance of Federal income tax for which the acquisition was made. Whenever appropriate to give proper effect to the deduction, credit, or other allowance, or such part of it which may be allowed, this authority includes the distribution, apportionment, or allocation of both the gross income and the deductions, credits, or other allowances the benefit of which was sought, between or among the corporations, or properties, or parts thereof, involved, and includes the disallowance of any such deduction, credit, or other allowance to any of the taxpayers involved. [Reg. § 1.269-4.]

☐ [T.D. 6595, 4-13-62.]

[Reg. § 1.269-5]

§ 1.269-5. **Time of acquisition of control.**—(a) *In general.*—For purposes of section 269, an acquisition of control occurs when one or more persons acquire beneficial ownership of stock possessing at least 50 percent of the total combined voting power of all classes of stock entitled to vote or at least 50 percent of the total value of shares of all classes of stock of the corporation.

(b) *Application of general rule to certain creditor acquisitions.*—(1) For purposes of section 269, creditors of an insolvent or bankrupt corporation (by themselves or in conjunction with other persons) acquire control of the corporation when they acquire beneficial ownership of the requisite amount of stock. Although insolvency or bankruptcy may cause the interests of creditors to predominate as a practical matter, creditor interests do not constitute beneficial ownership of the corporation's stock. Solely for purposes of section 269, creditors of a bankrupt corporation are treated as acquiring beneficial ownership of stock of the corporation no earlier than the time a bankruptcy court confirms a plan of reorganization.

(2) The provisions of this section are illustrated by the following example.

Example. Corporation L files a petition under chapter 11 of the Bankruptcy Code on January 5, 1987. A creditors' committee is formed. On February 22, 1987, and upon the request of the creditors, the bankruptcy court removes the debtor-in-possession from business management and operations and appoints a trustee. The trustee consults regularly with the creditors' committee in formulating both short-term and long-term management decisions. After three years, the creditors approve a plan of reorganization in which the outstanding stock of Corporation L is cancelled and its creditors receive shares of stock constituting all of the outstanding shares. The bankruptcy court confirms the plan of reorganization on March 23, 1990, and the plan is put into effect on May 25, 1990. For purposes of section 269, the creditors acquired control of Corporation L no earlier than March 23, 1990. Similarly, the determination of whether the creditors acquired control of Corporation L with the principal purpose of evasion or avoidance of Federal income tax is made by reference to the creditors' purposes as of no earlier than March 23, 1990. [Reg. § 1.269-5.]

☐ [T.D. 6595, 4-13-62. *Amended by T.D.* 8388, 12-31-91.]

[Reg. § 1.269-6]

§ 1.269-6. **Relationship of section 269 to section 382 before the Tax Reform Act of 1986.**—Section 269 and § § 1.269-1 through 1.269-5 may be applied to disallow a net operating loss carryover even though such carryover is not disallowed (in whole or in part) under section 382 and the regulations thereunder. This section may be illustrated by the following examples:

Example (1). L Corporation has computed its taxable income on a calendar year basis and has sustained heavy net operating losses for a number of years. Assume that A purchases all of the stock of L Corporation on December 31, 1955, for the principal purpose of utilizing its net operating loss carryovers by changing its business to a profitable new business. Assume further that A makes no attempt to revitalize the business of L Corporation during the calendar year 1956 and that during January 1957 the business is changed to an entirely new and profitable business. The carryovers will be disallowed under the provisions of section 269(a) without regard to the application of section 382.

Example (2). L Corporation has sustained heavy net operating losses for a number of years. In a merger under State law, P Corporation acquires all of the assets of L Corporation for the principal purpose of utilizing the net operating loss carryovers of L Corporation against the profits of P Corporation's business. As a result of the merger, the former stockholders of L Corporation own, immediately after the merger, 12 percent of the fair market value of the outstanding stock of P Corporation. If the merger qualifies as a reorganization to which section 381(a) applies, the entire net operating loss carryovers will be disallowed under the provisions of section 269(a) without regard to the application of section 382.

Example (3). L Corporation has been sustaining net operating losses for a number of years. P Corporation, a profitable corporation, on December 31, 1955, acquires all of the stock of L Corporation for the purpose of continuing and improving the operation of L Corporation's business. Under the provisions of sections 334(b)(2) and 381(a)(1), P Corporation would not succeed to L Corporation's net operating loss carryovers if L Corporation were liquidated pursuant to a plan of liquidation adopted within two years after the date of the acquisition. During 1956, P Corporation transfers a profitable business to L Corporation for the principal purpose of using the profits of such business to absorb the net operating loss carryovers of L Corporation. The transfer is such as to cause the basis of the transferred assets in the hands of L Corporation to be determined by reference to their basis in the hands of P Corporation. L Corporation's net operating loss carryovers will be disallowed under the provisions of section 269(a) without regard to the application of section 382. [Reg. §1.269-6.]

☐ *[T.D. 6595, 4-13-62. Amended by T.D. 8388, 12-31-91.]*

[Reg. §1.269-7]

§1.269-7. Relationship of section 269 to sections 382 and 383 after the Tax Reform Act of 1986.—Section 269 and §§1.269-1 through 1.269-5 may be applied to disallow a deduction, credit, or other allowance notwithstanding that the utilization or amount of a deduction, credit, or other allowance is limited or reduced under section 382 or 383 and the regulations thereunder. However, the fact that the amount of taxable income or tax that may be offset by a deduction, credit, or other allowance is limited under section 382(a) or 383 and the regulations thereunder is relevant to the determination of whether the principal purpose of an acquisition is the evasion or avoidance of Federal income tax. [Reg. §1.269-7.]

☐ *[T.D. 8388, 12-31-91.]*

[Reg. §1.269B-1]

§1.269B-1. Stapled foreign corporations.—(a) *Treatment as a domestic corporation.*—(1) *General rule.*—Except as otherwise provided, if a foreign corporation is a stapled foreign corporation within the meaning of paragraph (b)(1) of this section, such foreign corporation will be treated as a domestic corporation for U.S. Federal income tax purposes. Accordingly, for example, the worldwide income of such corporation will be subject to the tax imposed by section 11. For application of the branch profits tax under section 884, and application of sections 871(a), 881, 1441, and 1442 to dividends and interest paid by a stapled foreign corporation, see §§1.884-1(h) and 1.884-4(d).

(2) *Foreign owned exception.*—Paragraph (a)(1) of this section will not apply if a foreign corporation and a domestic corporation are stapled entities (as provided in paragraph (b) of this section) and such foreign and domestic corporations are foreign owned within the meaning of this paragraph (a)(2). A corporation will be treated as foreign owned if it is established to the satisfaction of the Commissioner that United States persons hold directly (or indirectly applying section 958(a)(2) and (3) and section 318(a)(4)) less than 50 percent of the total combined voting power of all classes of stock entitled to vote and less than 50 percent of the total value of the stock of such corporation. For the consequences of a stapled foreign corporation becoming or ceasing to be foreign owned, therefore converting its status as either a foreign or domestic corporation within the meaning of this paragraph (a)(2), see paragraph (c) of this section.

(b) *Definition of a stapled foreign corporation.*—(1) *General rule.*—A foreign corporation is a stapled foreign corporation if such foreign corporation and a domestic corporation are stapled entities. A foreign corporation and a domestic corporation are stapled entities if more than 50 percent of the aggregate value of each corporation's beneficial ownership consists of interests that are stapled. In the case of corporations with more than one class of stock, it is not necessary for a class of stock representing more than 50 percent of the beneficial ownership of the foreign corporation to be stapled to a class of stock

representing more than 50 percent of the beneficial ownership of the domestic corporation, provided that more than 50 percent of the aggregate value of each corporation's beneficial ownership (taking into account all classes of stock) are in fact stapled. Interests are stapled if a transferor of one or more interests in one entity is required, by form of ownership, restrictions on transfer, or other terms or conditions, to transfer interests in the other entity. The determination of whether interests are stapled for this purpose is based on the relevant facts and circumstances, including, but not limited to, the corporations' by-laws, articles of incorporation or association, and stock certificates, shareholder agreements, agreements between the corporations, and voting trusts with respect to the corporations. For the consequences of a foreign corporation becoming or ceasing to be a stapled foreign corporation (e.g., a corporation that is no longer foreign owned) under this paragraph (b)(1), see paragraph (c) of this section.

(2) *Related party ownership rule.*—For purposes of determining whether a foreign corporation is a stapled foreign corporation, the Commissioner may, at his discretion, treat interests that otherwise would be stapled interests as not being stapled if the same person or related persons (within the meaning of section 267(b) or 707(b)) hold stapled interests constituting more than 50 percent of the beneficial ownership of both corporations, and a principal purpose of the stapling of those interests is the avoidance of U.S. income tax. A stapling of interests may have a principal purpose of tax avoidance even though the tax avoidance purpose is outweighed by other purposes when taken together.

(3) *Example.*—The principles of paragraph (b)(1) of this section are illustrated by the following example:

Example. USCo, a domestic corporation, and FCo, a foreign corporation, are publicly traded companies, each having two classes of stock outstanding. USCo's class A shares, which constitute 75% of the value of all beneficial ownership in USCo, are stapled to FCo's class B shares, which constitute 25% of the value of all beneficial ownership in F Co. USCo's class B shares, which constitute 25% of the value of all beneficial ownership in USCo, are stapled to FCo class A shares, which constitute 75% of the value of all beneficial ownership in FCo. Because more than 50% of the aggregate value of the stock of each corporation is stapled to the stock of the other corporation, USCo and FCo are stapled entities within the meaning of section 269B(c)(2).

(c) *Changes in domestic or foreign status.*—The deemed conversion of a foreign corporation to a domestic corporation under section 269B is treated as a reorganization under section 368(a)(1)(F). Similarly, the deemed conversion of a corporation that is treated as a domestic corporation under section 269B to a foreign corporation is treated as a reorganization under section 368(a)(1)(F). For the consequences of a deemed conversion, including the closing of a corporation's taxable year, see §§1.367(a)-1(e), (f) and 1.367(b)-2(f).

(d) *Includible corporation.*—(1) Except as provided in paragraph (d)(2) of this section, a stapled foreign corporation treated as a domestic corporation under section 269B nonetheless is treated as a foreign corporation in determining whether it is an includible corporation within the meaning of section 1504(b). Thus, for example, a stapled foreign corporation is not eligible to join in the filing of a consolidated return under section 1501, and a dividend paid by such corporation is not a qualifying dividend under section 243(b), unless a valid section 1504(d) election is made with respect to such corporation.

(2) A stapled foreign corporation is treated as a domestic corporation in determining whether it is an includible corporation under section 1504(b) for purposes of applying §§1.904(i)-1 and 1.861-11T(d)(6).

(e) *U.S. treaties.*—(1) A stapled foreign corporation that is treated as a domestic corporation under section 269B may not claim an exemption from U.S. income tax or a reduction in U.S. tax rates by reason of any treaty entered into by the United States.

(2) The principles of this paragraph (e) are illustrated by the following example:

Example. FCo, a Country X corporation, is a stapled foreign corporation that is treated as a domestic corporation under section 269B. FCo qualifies as a resident of Country X pursuant to the income tax treaty between the United States and Country X. Under such treaty, the United States is permitted to tax business profits of a Country X resident only to the extent that the business profits are attributable to a permanent establishment of the Country X resident in the United States. While FCo earns income from sources within and without the United States, it does not have a permanent establishment in the United States within the meaning of the relevant treaty. Under paragraph (e)(1) of this section, however, FCo is subject to U.S. Federal income tax on its income as a domestic corporation without regard to the provisions of the U.S.- Country X treaty and therefore without regard to the fact that FCo has no permanent establishment in the United States.

(f) *Tax assessment and collection procedures.*—(1) *In general.*—(i) Any income tax imposed on a stapled foreign corporation by reason of its treatment as a domestic corporation under section 269B (whether such income tax is shown on the stapled foreign corporation's U.S. Federal income tax return or determined as a deficiency in income tax) shall be assessed as the income tax liability of such stapled foreign corporation.

(ii) Any income tax assessed as a liability of a stapled foreign corporation under paragraph (f)(1)(i) of this section shall be considered as having been properly assessed as an income tax liability of the stapled domestic corporation (as defined in paragraph (f)(4)(i) of this section) and all 10-percent shareholders of the stapled foreign corporation (as defined in paragraph (f)(4)(ii) of this section). The date of such deemed assessment shall be the date the income tax liability of the stapled foreign corporation was properly assessed. The Commissioner may collect such income tax from the stapled domestic corporation under the circumstances set forth in paragraph (f)(2) of this section and may collect such income tax from any 10-percent shareholders of the stapled foreign corporation under the circumstances set forth in paragraph (f)(3) of this section.

(2) *Collection from domestic stapled corporation.*—If the stapled foreign corporation does not pay its income tax liability that was properly assessed, the unpaid balance of such income tax or any portion thereof may be collected from the stapled domestic corporation, provided that the following conditions are satisfied—

(i) The Commissioner has issued a notice and demand for payment of such income tax to the stapled foreign corporation in accordance with § 301.6303-1 of this Chapter;

(ii) The stapled foreign corporation has failed to pay the income tax by the date specified in such notice and demand;

(iii) The Commissioner has issued a notice and demand for payment of such unpaid portion of such income tax to the stapled domestic corporation in accordance with § 301.6303-1 of this Chapter.

(3) *Collection from 10-percent shareholders of the stapled foreign corporation.*—The unpaid balance of the stapled foreign corporation's income tax liability may be collected from a 10-percent shareholder of the stapled foreign corporation, limited to each such shareholder's income tax liability as determined under paragraph (f)(4)(iv) of this section, provided the following conditions are satisfied—

(i) The Commissioner has issued a notice and demand to the stapled domestic corporation for the unpaid portion of the stapled foreign corporation's income tax liability, as provided in paragraph (f)(2)(iii) of this section;

(ii) The stapled domestic corporation has failed to pay the income tax by the date specified in such notice and demand;

(iii) The Commissioner has issued a notice and demand for payment of such unpaid portion of such income tax to such 10-percent shareholder of the stapled foreign corporation in accordance with § 301.6303-1 of this Chapter.

(4) *Special rules and definitions.*—For purposes of this paragraph (f), the following rules and definitions apply:

(i) *Stapled domestic corporation.*—A domestic corporation is a *stapled domestic corporation* with respect to a stapled foreign corporation if such domestic corporation and the stapled foreign corporation are stapled entities as described in paragraph (b)(1) of this section.

(ii) *10-percent shareholder.*—A *10-percent shareholder* of a stapled foreign corporation is any person that owned directly 10 percent or more of the total value or total combined voting power of all classes of stock in the stapled foreign corporation for any day of the stapled foreign corporation's taxable year with respect to which the income tax liability relates.

(iii) *10-percent shareholder in the case of indirect ownership of stapled foreign corporation stock.*—[Reserved].

(iv) *Determination of a 10-percent shareholder's income tax liability.*—The income tax liability of a 10-percent shareholder of a stapled foreign corporation, for the income tax of the stapled foreign corporation under section 269B and this section, is determined by assigning an equal portion of the total income tax liability of the stapled foreign corporation for the taxable year to each day in such corporation's taxable year, and then dividing that portion ratably among the shares outstanding for that day on the basis of the relative values of such shares. The liability of any 10-percent shareholder for this purpose is the sum of the income tax liability allocated to the shares held by such shareholder for each day in the taxable year.

(v) *Income tax.*—The term *income tax* means any income tax liability imposed on a domestic corporation under title 26 of the United States Code, including additions to tax, additional amounts, penalties, and interest related to such income tax liability.

(g) *Effective dates.*—(1) Except as provided in this paragraph (g), the provisions of this section are applicable for taxable years that begin after July 29, 2005.

(2) Paragraphs (d)(1) and (f) of this section (except as applied to the collection of tax from any 10-percent shareholder of a stapled foreign corporation that is a foreign person) are applicable beginning on—

(i) July 18, 1984, for any foreign corporation that became stapled to a domestic corporation after June 30, 1983; and

(ii) January 1, 1987, for any foreign corporation that was stapled to a domestic corporation as of June 30, 1983.

(3) Paragraph (d)(2) of this section is applicable for taxable years beginning after July 22, 2003, except that in the case of a foreign corporation that becomes stapled to a domestic corporation on or after July 22, 2003, paragraph (d)(2) of this section applies for taxable years ending on or after July 22, 2003.

(4) Paragraph (e) of this section is applicable beginning on July 18, 1984, except as provided in paragraph (g)(5) of this section.

(5) In the case of a foreign corporation that was stapled to a domestic corporation as of June 30, 1983, which was entitled to claim benefits under an income tax treaty as of that date, and which remains eligible for such treaty benefits, paragraph (e) of this section will not apply to such foreign corporation and for all purposes of the Internal Revenue Code such corporation will continue to be treated as a foreign entity. The prior sentence will continue to apply even if such treaty is subsequently modified by protocol, or superseded by a new treaty, so long as the stapled foreign corporation continues to be eligible to claim such treaty benefits. If the treaty benefits to which the stapled foreign corporation was entitled as of June 30, 1983, are terminated, then a deemed conversion of the foreign corporation to a domestic corporation shall occur pursuant to paragraph (c) of this section as of the date of such termination. [[Reg. § 1.269B-1.]

☐ [*T.D.* 9216, 7-28-2005. Amended by *T.D.* 9739, 9-18-2015.]

[Reg. § 301.269B-1]

§ 301.269B-1. Stapled foreign corporations.—In accordance with section 269B(a)(1), a stapled foreign corporation is subject to the same taxes that apply to a domestic corporation under Title 26 of the Internal Revenue Code. For provisions concerning taxes other than income for which the stapled foreign corporation is liable, apply the same rules as set forth in § 1.269B-1(a) through (f)(1)(i), and (g) of this Chapter, except that references to *income tax* shall be replaced with the term *tax*. In addition, for purposes of collecting those taxes solely from the stapled foreign corporation, the term *tax* means any tax liability imposed on a domestic corporation under Title 26 of the United States Code, including additions to tax, additional amounts, penalties, and interest related to that tax liability. [Reg. § 301.269B-1.]

☐ [*T.D.* 9216, 7-28-2005.]

[Reg. § 1.271-1]

§ 1.271-1. Debts owed by political parties.—(a) *General rule.*—In the case of a taxpayer other than a bank (as defined in section 581 and the regulations thereunder), no deduction shall be allowed under section 166 (relating to bad debts) or section 165(g) (relating to worthlessness of securities) by reason of the worthlessness of any debt, regardless of how it arose, owed by a political party. For example, it is immaterial that the debt may have arisen as a result of services rendered or goods sold or that the taxpayer included the amount of the debt in income. In the case of a bank, no deduction shall be allowed unless, under the facts and circumstances, it appears that the bad debt was incurred to or purchased by, or the worthless security was acquired by, the taxpayer in accordance with its usual commercial practices. Thus, if a bank makes a loan to a political party not in accordance with its usual commercial practices but solely because the president of the bank has been active in the party no bad debt deduction will be allowed with respect to the loan.

(b) *Definitions.*—(1) *Political party.*—For purposes of this section and § 1.276-1, the term "political party" means a political party (as commonly understood), a National, State, or local committee thereof, or any committee, association, or organization, whether incorporated or not, which accepts contributions (as defined in subparagraph (2) of this paragraph) or makes expenditures (as defined in subparagraph (3) of this paragraph) for the purpose of influencing or attempting to influence the election of presidential or vice-presidential electors, or the selection, nomination, or election of any individual to any Federal, State, or local elective public office, whether or not such individual or electors are selected, nominated, or elected. Accordingly, a political party includes a committee or other group which accepts contributions or makes expenditures for the purpose of promoting the nomination of an individual for an elective public office in a primary election, or in any convention, meeting, or caucus of a political party. It is immaterial whether the contributions or expenditures are accepted or made directly or indirectly. Thus, for example, a committee or other group is considered to be a political party if, although it does not expend any funds, it turns funds over to another organization which does expend funds for the purpose of attempting to influence the nomination of an individual for an elective public office. An organization which engages in activities which are truly nonpartisan in nature will not be considered a political party merely because it conducts activities with respect to an election campaign if, under all the facts and circumstances, it is clear that its efforts are not directed to the election of the candidates of any particular party or parties or to the selection, nomination or election of any particular candidate. For example, a committee or group will not be treated as a political party if it is organized merely to inform the electortte as to the identity and experience of all candidates involved, to present on a nonpreferential basis the issues or views of the parties or candidates as described by the parties or candidates, or to provide a forum in which thee candidates are freely invited on a nonpreferential basis to discuss or debate the issues.

(2) *Contributions.*—For purposes of this section and §1.276-1, the term "contributions" includes a gift, subscription, loan, advance, or deposit, of money or anything of value, and includes a contract, promise, or agreement to make a contribution, whether or not legally enforceable.

(3) *Expenditures.*—For purposes of this section and §1.276-1, the term "expenditures" includes a payment, distribution, loan, advance, deposit, or gift, of money or anything of value, and includes a contract, promise, or agreement to make an expenditure, whether or not legally enforceable. [Reg. §1.271-1.]

☐ [T.D. 6996, 1-17-69.]

[Reg. §1.272-1]

§1.272-1. Expenditures relating to disposal of coal or domestic iron ore.—(a) *Introduction.*—Section 272 provides special treatment for certain expenditures paid or incurred by a taxpayer in connection with a contract (hereafter sometimes referred to as a "coal royalty contract" or "iron ore royalty contract") for the disposal of coal or iron ore the gain or loss from which is treated under section 631(c) as a section 1231 gain or loss on the sale of coal or iron ore. See paragraph (e) of §1.631-3 for special rules relating to iron ore. The expenditures covered by section 272 are those which are attributable to the making and administering of such a contract or to the preservation of the economic interest retained under the contract. For examples of such expenditures, see paragraph (d) of this section. For a taxable year in which gross royalty income is realized under the contract of disposal, such expenditures shall not be allowed as a deduction. Instead, they are to be added to the adjusted depletion basis of the coal or iron ore disposed of in the taxable year in computing gain or loss under section 631(c). However, where no gross royalty income is realized under the contract of disposal in a particular taxable year, such expenditure shall be treated without regard to section 272.

(b) *In general.*—(1) Where the disposal of coal or iron ore is covered by section 631(c), the provisions of section 272 and this section shall be applicable for a taxable year in which there is income under the contract of disposal. (For purposes of section 272 and this section, the term "income" means gross amounts received or accrued which are royalties or bonuses in connection with a contract to which section 631(c) applies.) All expenditures paid or incurred by the taxpayer during the taxable year which are attributable to the making and administering of the contract disposing of the coal or iron ore and all expenditures paid or incurred during the taxable year in order to preserve the owner's economic interest retained under the contract shall be disallowed as deductions in computing taxable income for the taxable year. The sum of such expenditures and the adjusted depletion basis of the coal or iron ore disposed of in the taxable year shall be used in determining the amount of gain or loss with respect to the disposal. See §1.631-3. For special rule in case of loss, see paragraph (c) of this section. Section 272 and this section do not apply to capital expenditures, and such expenditures are not taken into account in computing gain or loss under section 631(c) except to the extent they are properly part of the depletable basis of the coal or iron ore.

(2) The expenditures covered under section 272 and this section are disallowed as a deduction only with respect to a taxable year in which income is realized under the coal royalty contract (or iron ore royalty contract) to which such expenditures are attributable. Where no income is realized under the contract in a taxable year, these expenditures shall be deducted as expenses for the production of income, or as a business expense, or they may be treated under section 266 (relating to taxes and carrying charges) if applicable.

(3) The provisions of section 272 and this section apply to a taxable year in which income frcm the disposal by the owner of coal or iron ore held by him for more than 1 year (6 months for taxable years beginning before 1977; 9 months for taxable years beginning in 1977) is subject to the provisions of subject 631(c) even though the actual mining of coal or iron ore under the coal royalty contract (or iron ore royalty contract) does not take place during the taxable year. Where the right under the contract to mine coal or iron ore for which advance payment has been made expires, terminates, or is abandoned before the coal or iron ore is mined, and paragraph (c) of §1.631-3 requires the owner to recompute his tax with respect to such payment, the recomputation must be made without applying the provisions of section 272 and this section.

(c) *Losses.*—If, in any taxable year, the expenditures referred to in section 272 and this section plus the adjusted depletion basis (as defined in paragraph (b)(2) of §1.631-3) of the coal or iron ore disposed of during the taxable year exceed the amount realized under the contract which is subject to section 631(c) during the taxable year, such excess shall be considered under section 1231 as a loss from the sale of property used in the trade or business and, to the extent not availed of as a reduction of gain under that section, shall be a loss deductible under section 165(a) (relating to the deduction of losses generally).

(d) *Examples of expenditures.*—(1) The expenditures referred to in section 272 include, but are not limited to, the following items, if such items are attributable to the making or administering of the contract or preserving the economic interest therein: Ad valorem taxes imposed by State or local authorities, costs of fire protection, costs of insurance (other than liability insurance), costs incurred in administering the contract (including costs of bookkeeping and technical supervision), interest on loans, expenses of flood control, legal and technical expenses, and expenses of measuring and checking quantities of coal or iron ore disposed of under the contract. Whether the interest on loans is attributable to the making or administering of the contract or preserving the economic interest therein will depend upon the use to which the borrowed monies are put.

(2) Any expenditure referred to in this section which is applicable to more than one coal royalty contract or iron ore royalty contract shall be reasonably apportioned to each of such contracts. Furthermore, if an expenditure applies only in part to the making or administering of the contract or the preservation of the economic interest, then only such part shall be treated under section 272. The apportionment of the expenditure shall be made on a reasonable basis. For example, where a taxpayer has other income (such as income from oil or gas royalties, rentals, right of way fees, interest, or dividends) as well as income under section 631(c), and where the salaries of some of its employees or other expenses relate to both classes of income, such expenses shall be allocated reasonably between the income subject to section 631(c) and the other income. Where a taxpayer has more than one coal royalty contract or iron ore royalty contract, expenditures under this section relating to a contract from which no income has been received in the taxable year may not be allocated to income from another contract from which income has been received in the taxable year.

(3) The taxpayer may have expenses which are not attributable even partly to making and administering a coal royalty contract or iron ore royalty contract or to the preservation of the economic interest retained under the contract and, accordingly, are not included in the expenditures described in section 272. These include such items as ad valorem taxes imposed by State or local authorities on property not covered by the contract, salaries, wages, or other expenses entirely incident to the ownership and protection of such property and depreciation of improvements thereon, fire insurance on such property, charitable contributions, and similar expenses unrelated to the making or to the administering of coal royalty contracts or iron ore royalty contracts or preserving the taxpayer's economic interest retained therein.

(e) *Nonapplication of section.*—For purposes of section 543, the provisions of section 272 shall have no application. For example, the taxpayer may, for the purposes of section 543(a)(3)(C) or the corresponding provisions of prior income tax laws, include in the sum of the deductions which are allowable under section 162 an amount paid to an attorney as compensation for legal services rendered in connection with the making of a coal royalty contract or iron ore royalty contract (assuming the expenditure otherwise qualifies under Section 162 as an ordinary and necessary expense incurred in the taxpayer's trade or business), even though such expenditure is disallowed as a deduction under section 272. [Reg. §1.272-1.]

☐ [T.D. 6281, 12-20-57. *Amended by T.D. 6841, 7-26-65 and T.D. 7728,* 10-31-80.]

[Reg. §1.273-1]

§1.273-1. Life or terminable interests.—(a) *In general.*—Amounts paid as income to the holder of a life or a terminable interest acquired by gift, bequest, or inheritance shall not be subject to any deduction for shrinkage (whether called by depreciation or any other name) in the value of such interest due to the lapse of time. In other words, the holder of such an interest so acquired may not set up the value of the expected future payments as corpus or principal and claim deduction for shrinkage or exhaustion thereof due to the passage of time. For the treatment generally of distributions to beneficiaries of an estate or trust, see Subparts A, B, C, and D (section 641 and following), Subchapter J, Chapter 1 of the Code, and the regulations thereunder. For basis of property acquired from a decedent and by gifts and transfers in trust, see sections 1014, 1015, and 1022, and the regulations thereunder.

(b) *Effective/applicability date.*—The provisions in this section are applicable for taxable years beginning on or after September 16, 1958. The provisions of this section relating to section 1022 are effective on and after January 19, 2017. [Reg. §1.273-1.]

☐ [*T.D. 6313, 9-16-58. Amended by T.D. 9811, 1-18-2017.*]

[Reg. §1.274-1]

§1.274-1. Disallowance of certain entertainment, gift and travel expenses.—Section 274 disallows in whole, or in part, certain expenditures for entertainment, gifts and travel which would otherwise be allowable under chapter 1 of the Code. The requirements imposed by section 274 are in addition to the requirements for deductibility imposed by other provisions of the Code. If a deduction is claimed for an expenditure for entertainment, gifts, or travel, the taxpayer must first establish that it is otherwise allowable as a deduction under chapter 1 of the Code before the provisions of section 274 become applicable. An expenditure for entertainment, to the extent it is lavish or extravagant, shall not be allowable as a deduction. The taxpayer should then substantiate such an expenditure in accordance with the rules under section 274(d). See §1.274-5. Section 274 is a disallowance provision exclusively, and does not make deductible any expense which is disallowed under any other provision of the Code. Similarly, section 274 does not affect the includability of an item in, or the excludability of an item from, the gross income of any taxpayer. For specific provisions with respect to the deductibility of expenditures: for an activity of a type generally considered to constitute entertainment, amusement, or recreation, and for a facility used in connection with such an activity, as well as certain travel expenses of a spouse, etc., see §1.274-2; for expenses for gifts, see §1.274-3; for expenses for foreign travel, see §1.274-4; for expenditures deductible without regard to business activity, see §1.274-6; and for treatment of personal portion of entertainment facility, see §1.274-7. [Reg. §1.274-1.]

☐ [*T.D. 6659, 6-24-63. Amended by T.D. 8666, 5-29-96.*]

[Reg. §1.274-2]

§1.274-2. Disallowance of deductions for certain expenses for entertainment, amusement, recreation, or travel.—(a) *General rules.*—(1) *Entertainment activity.*—Except as provided in this section, no deduction otherwise allowable under chapter 1 of the Code shall be allowed for any expenditure with respect to entertainment unless the taxpayer establishes—

(i) That the expenditure was directly related to the active conduct of the taxpayer's trade or business, or

(ii) In the case of an expenditure directly preceding or following a substantial and bona fide business discussion (including business meetings at a convention or otherwise), that the expenditure was associated with the active conduct of the taxpayer's trade or business.

Such deduction shall not exceed the portion of the expenditure directly related to (or in the case of an expenditure described in subdivision (ii) above, the portion of the expenditure associated with) the active conduct of the taxpayer's trade or business.

(2) *Entertainment facilities.*—(i) *Expenditures paid or incurred after December 31, 1978, and not with respect to a club.*—Except as provided in this section with respect to a club, no deduction otherwise allowable under chapter 1 of the Code shall be allowed for any expenditure paid or incurred after December 31, 1978, with respect to a facility used in connection with entertainment.

(ii) *Expenditures paid or incurred before January 1, 1979, with respect to entertainment facilities, or paid or incurred before January 1, 1994, with respect to clubs.*—(a) *Requirements for deduction.*—Except as provided in this section, no deduction otherwise allowable under chapter 1 of the Internal Revenue Code shall be allowed for any expenditure paid or incurred before January 1, 1979, with respect to a facility used in connection with entertainment, or for any expendi-

ture paid or incurred before January 1, 1994, with respect to a club used in connection with entertainment, unless the taxpayer establishes—

(1) That the facility or club was used primarily for the furtherance of the taxpayer's trade or business; and

(2) That the expenditure was directly related to the active conduct of that trade or business.

(b) *Amount of deduction.*—The deduction allowable under paragraph (a)(2)(ii)(a) of this section shall not exceed the portion of the expenditure directly related to the active conduct of the taxpayer's trade or business.

(iii) *Expenditures paid or incurred after December 31, 1993, with respect to a club.*—(a) *In general.*—No deduction otherwise allowable under chapter 1 of the Internal Revenue Code shall be allowed for amounts paid or incurred after December 31, 1993, for membership in any club organized for business, pleasure, recreation, or other social purpose. The purposes and activities of a club, and not its name, determine whether it is organized for business, pleasure, recreation, or other social purpose. Clubs organized for business, pleasure, recreation, or other social purpose include any membership organization if a principal purpose of the organization is to conduct entertainment activities for members of the organization or their guests or to provide members or their guests with access to entertainment facilities within the meaning of paragraph (e)(2) of this section. Clubs organized for business, pleasure, recreation, or other social purpose include, but are not limited to, country clubs, golf and athletic clubs, airline clubs, hotel clubs, and clubs operated to provide meals under circumstances generally considered to be conducive to business discussion.

(b) *Exceptions.*—Unless a principal purpose of the organization is to conduct entertainment activities for members or their guests or to provide members or their guests with access to entertainment facilities, business leagues, trade associations, chambers of commerce, boards of trade, real estate boards, professional organizations (such as bar associations and medical associations), and civic or public service organizations will not be treated as clubs organized for business, pleasure, recreation, or other social purpose.

(3) *Cross references.*—For definition of the term "entertainment," see paragraph (b)(1) of this section. For the disallowance of deductions for the cost of admission to a dinner or program any part of the proceeds of which inures to the use of a political party or political candidate, and cost of admission to an inaugural event or similar event identified with any political party or political candidate, see §1.276-1. For rules and definitions with respect to—

(i) "Directly related entertainment", see paragraph (c) of this section,

(ii) "Associated entertainment", see paragraph (d) of this section,

(iii) "Expenditures paid or incurred before January 1, 1979, with respect to entertainment facilities or before January 1, 1994, with respect to clubs", see paragraph (e) of this section, and

(iv) "Specific exceptions" to the disallowance rules of this section, see paragraph (f) of this section.

(b) *Definitions.*—(1) *Entertainment defined.*—(i) *In general.*—For purposes of this section, the term "entertainment" means any activity which is of a type generally considered to constitute entertainment, amusement, or recreation, such as entertaining at night clubs, cocktail lounges, theaters, country clubs, golf and athletic clubs, sporting events, and on hunting, fishing, vacation and similar trips, including such activity relating solely to the taxpayer or the taxpayer's family. The term "entertainment" may include an activity, the cost of which is claimed as a business expense by the taxpayer, which satisfies the personal, living, or family needs of any individual, such as providing food and beverages, a hotel suite, or an automobile to a business customer or his family. The term "entertainment" does not include activities which, although satisfying personal, living, or family needs of an individual, are clearly not regarded as constituting entertainment, such as (a) supper money provided by an employer to his employee working overtime, (b) a hotel room maintained by an employer for lodging of his employees while in business travel status, or (c) an automobile used in the active conduct of trade or business even though used for routine personal purposes such as commuting to and from work. On the other hand, the providing of a hotel room or an automobile by an employer to his employee who is on vacation would constitute entertainment of the employee.

(ii) *Objective test.*—An objective test shall be used to determine whether an activity is of a type generally considered to constitute entertainment. Thus, if an activity is generally considered to be entertainment, it will constitute entertainment for purposes of this section and section 274(a) regardless of whether the expenditure can also be described otherwise, and even though the expenditure relates to the taxpayer alone. This objective test precludes arguments such as that "entertainment" means only entertainment of others or that an expenditure for entertainment should be characterized as an expenditure for advertising or public relations. However, in applying this test the taxpayer's trade or business shall be considered. Thus, although attending a theatrical performance would generally be considered entertainment, it would not be so considered in the case of a professional theater critic, attending in his professional capacity. Similarly, if a manufacturer of dresses conducts a fashion show to introduce his products to a group of store buyers, the show would not be generally considered to constitute entertainment. However, if an appliance distributor conducts a fashion show for the wives of his retailers, the fashion show would be generally considered to constitute entertainment.

(iii) *Special definitional rules.*—*(a) In general.*—Except as otherwise provided in *(b)* or *(c)* of this subdivision, any expenditure which might generally be considered either for a gift or entertainment, or considered either for travel or entertainment, shall be considered an expenditure for entertainment rather than for a gift or travel.

(b) *Expenditures deemed gifts.*—An expenditure described in *(a)* of this subdivision shall be deemed for a gift to which this section does not apply if it is:

(1) An expenditure for packaged food or beverages transferred directly or indirectly to another person intended for consumption at a later time.

(2) An expenditure for tickets of admission to a place of entertainment transferred to another person if the taxpayer does not accompany the recipient to the entertainment unless the taxpayer treats the expenditure as entertainment. The taxpayer may change his treatment of such an expenditure as either a gift or entertainment at any time within the period prescribed for assessment of tax as provided in section 6501 of the Code and the regulations thereunder.

(3) Such other specific classes of expenditure generally considered to be for a gift as the Commissioner, in his discretion, may prescribe.

(c) *Expenditures deemed travel.*—An expenditure described in *(a)* of this subdivision shall be deemed for travel to which this section does not apply if it is:

(1) With respect to a transportation type facility (such as an automobile or an airplane), even though used on other occasions in connection with an activity of a type generally considered to constitute entertainment, to the extent the facility is used in pursuit of a trade or business for purposes of transportation not in connection with entertainment. See also paragraph (e)(3)(iii)(b) of this section for provisions covering non-entertainment expenditures with respect to such facilities.

(2) Such other specific classes of expenditure generally considered to be for travel as the Commissioner, in his discretion, may prescribe.

(2) *Other definitions.*—(i) *Expenditure.*—The term "expenditure" as used in this section shall include expenses paid or incurred for goods, services, facilities, and items (including items such as losses and depreciation).

(ii) *Expenses for production of income.*—For purposes of this section, any reference to "trade or business" shall include any activity described in section 212.

(iii) *Business associate.*—The term "business associate" as used in this section means a person with whom the taxpayer could reasonably expect to engage or deal in the active conduct of the taxpayer's trade or business such as the taxpayer's customer, client, supplier, employee, agent, partner, or professional adviser, whether established or prospective.

(c) *Directly related entertainment.*—(1) *In general.*—Except as otherwise provided in paragraph (d) of this section (relating to associated entertainment) or under paragraph (f) of this section (relating to business meals and other specific exceptions), no deduction shall be allowed for any expenditure for entertainment unless the taxpayer establishes that the expenditure was directly related to the active conduct of his trade or business within the meaning of this paragraph.

(2) *Directly related entertainment defined.*—Any expenditure for entertainment, if it is otherwise allowable as a deduction under chapter 1 of the Code, shall be considered directly related to the active conduct of the taxpayer's trade or business if it meets the requirements of any one of subparagraphs (3), (4), (5), or (6) of this paragraph.

(3) *Directly related in general.*—Except as provided in subparagraph (7) of this paragraph, an expenditure for entertainment shall be considered directly related to the active conduct of the taxpayer's

trade or business if it is established that it meets all of the requirements of subdivisions (i), (ii), (iii) and (iv) of this subparagraph.

(i) At the time the taxpayer made the entertainment expenditure (or committed himself to make the expenditure), the taxpayer had more than a general expectation of deriving some income or other specific trade or business benefit (other than the goodwill of the person or persons entertained) at some indefinite future time from the making of the expenditure. A taxpayer, however, shall not be required to show that income or other business benefit actually resulted from each and every expenditure for which a deduction is claimed.

(ii) During the entertainment period to which the expenditure related, the taxpayer actively engaged in a business meeting, negotiation, discussion, or other bona fide business transaction, other than entertainment, for the purpose of obtaining such income or other specific trade or business benefit (or, at the time the taxpayer made the expenditure or committed himself to the expenditure, it was reasonable for the taxpayer to expect that he would have done so, although such was not the case solely for reasons beyond the taxpayer's control).

(iii) In light of all the facts and circumstances of the case, the principal character or aspect of the combined business and entertainment to which the expenditure related was the active conduct of the taxpayer's trade or business (or at the time the taxpayer made the expenditure or committed himself to the expenditure, it was reasonable for the taxpayer to expect that the active conduct of trade or business would have been the principal character or aspect of the entertainment, although such was not the case solely for reasons beyond the taxpayer's control). It is not necessary that more time be devoted to business than to entertainment to meet this requirement. The active conduct of trade or business is considered not to be the principal character or aspect of combined business and entertainment activity on hunting or fishing trips or on yachts and other pleasure boats unless the taxpayer clearly establishes to the contrary.

(iv) The expenditure was allocable to the taxpayer and a person or persons with whom the taxpayer engaged in the active conduct of trade or business during the entertainment or with whom the taxpayer establishes he would have engaged in such active conduct of trade or business if it were not for circumstances beyond the taxpayer's control. For expenditures closely connected with directly related entertainment, see paragraph (d)(4) of this section.

(4) *Expenditures in clear business setting.*—An expenditure for entertainment shall be considered directly related to the active conduct of the taxpayer's trade or business if it is established that the expenditure was for entertainment occurring in a clear business setting directly in furtherance of the taxpayer's trade or business. Generally, entertainment shall not be considered to have occurred in a clear business setting unless the taxpayer clearly establishes that any recipient of the entertainment would have reasonably known that the taxpayer had no significant motive, in incurring the expenditure, other than directly furthering his trade or business. Objective rather than subjective standards will be determinative. Thus, entertainment which occurred under any circumstances described in subparagraph (7)(ii) of this paragraph ordinarily will not be considered as occurring in a clear business setting. Such entertainment will generally be considered to be socially rather than commercially motivated. Expenditures made for the furtherance of a taxpayer's trade or business in providing a "hospitality room" at a convention (described in paragraph (d)(3)(i)(b) of this section) at which goodwill is created through display or discussion of the taxpayer's products, will, however, be treated as directly related. In addition, entertainment of a clear business nature which occurred under circumstances where there was no meaningful personal or social relationship between the taxpayer and the recipients of the entertainment may be considered to have occurred in a clear business setting. For example, entertainment of business representatives and civic leaders at the opening of a new hotel or theatrical production, where the clear purpose of the taxpayer is to obtain business publicity rather than to create or maintain the goodwill of the recipients of the entertainment, would generally be considered to be in a clear business setting. Also, entertainment which has the principal effect of a price rebate in connection with the sale of the taxpayer's products generally will be considered to have occurred in a clear business setting. Such would be the case, for example, if a taxpayer owning a hotel were to provide occasional free dinners at the hotel for a customer who patronized the hotel.

(5) *Expenditures for services performed.*—An expenditure shall be considered directly related to the active conduct of the taxpayer's trade or business if it is established that the expenditure was made directly or indirectly by the taxpayer for the benefit of an individual (other than an employee), and if such expenditure was in the nature of compensation for services rendered or was paid as a prize or award which is required to be included in gross income under

section 74 and the regulations thereunder. For example, if a manufacturer of products provides a vacation trip for retailers of his products who exceed sales quotas, as a prize or award includible in gross income, the expenditure will be considered directly related to the active conduct of the taxpayer's trade or business.

(6) *Club dues, etc., allocable to business meals.*—An expenditure shall be considered directly related to the active conduct of the taxpayer's trade or business if it is established that the expenditure was with respect to a facility (as described in paragraph (e) of this section) used by the taxpayer for the furnishing of food or beverages under circumstances described in paragraph (f)(2)(i) of this section (relating to business meals and similar expenditures), to the extent allocable to the furnishing of such food or beverages. This paragraph (c)(6) applies to club dues paid or incurred before January 1, 1987.

(7) *Expenditures generally considered not directly related.*—Expenditures for entertainment, even if connected with the taxpayer's trade or business, will generally be considered not directly related to the active conduct of the taxpayer's trade or business, if the entertainment occurred under circumstances where there was little or no possibility of engaging in the active conduct of trade or business. The following circumstances will generally be considered circumstances where there was little or no possibility of engaging in the active conduct of a trade or business:

(i) The taxpayer was not present;

(ii) The distractions were substantial, such as—

(a) A meeting or discussion at night clubs, theaters, and sporting events, or during essentially social gatherings such as cocktail parties, or

(b) A meeting or discussion, if the taxpayer meets with a group which includes persons other than business associates, at places such as cocktail lounges, country clubs, golf and athletic clubs, or at vacation resorts.

An expenditure for entertainment in any such case is considered not to be directly related to the active conduct of the taxpayer's trade or business unless the taxpayer clearly establishes to the contrary.

(d) *Associated entertainment.*—(1) *In general.*—Except as provided in paragraph (f) of this section (relating to business meals and other specific exceptions) and subparagraph (4) of this paragraph (relating to expenditures closely connected with directly related entertainment), any expenditure for entertainment which is not directly related to the active conduct of the taxpayer's trade or business will not be allowable as a deduction unless—

(i) It was associated with the active conduct of trade or business as defined in subparagraph (2) of this paragraph, and

(ii) The entertainment directly preceded or followed a substantial and bona fide business discussion as defined in subparagraph (3) of this paragraph.

(2) *Associated entertainment defined.*—Generally, any expenditure for entertainment, if it is otherwise allowable under chapter 1 of the Code, shall be considered associated with the active conduct of the taxpayer's trade or business if the taxpayer establishes that he had a clear business purpose in making the expenditure, such as to obtain new business or to encourage the continuation of an existing business relationship. However, any portion of an expenditure allocable to a person who was not closely connected with a person who engaged in the substantial and bona fide business discussion (as defined in subparagraph (3)(i) of this paragraph) shall not be considered associated with the active conduct of the taxpayer's trade or business. The portion of an expenditure allocable to the spouse of a person who engaged in the discussion will, if it is otherwise allowable under chapter 1 of the Code, be considered associated with the active conduct of the taxpayer's trade or business.

(3) *Directly preceding or following a substantial and bona fide business discussion defined.*—(i) *Substantial and bona fide business discussion.*—(a) *In general.*—Whether any meeting, negotiation or discussion constitutes a "substantial and bona fide business discussion" within the meaning of this section depends upon the facts and circumstances of each case. It must be established, however, that the taxpayer actively engaged in a business meeting, negotiation, discussion, or other bona fide business transaction, other than entertainment, for the purpose of obtaining income or other specific trade or business benefit. In addition, it must be established that such a business meeting, negotiation, discussion, or transaction was substantial in relation to the entertainment. This requirement will be satisfied if the principal character or aspect of the combined entertainment and business activity was the active conduct of business. However, it is not necessary that more time be devoted to business than to entertainment to meet this requirement.

(b) *Meetings at conventions, etc.*—Any meeting officially scheduled in connection with a program at a convention or similar general assembly, or at a bona fide trade or business meeting sponsored and conducted by business or professional organizations, shall be considered to constitute a substantial and bona fide business discussion within the meaning of this section provided—

(1) *Expenses necessary to taxpayer's attendance.*—The expenses necessary to the attendance of the taxpayer at the convention, general assembly, or trade or business meeting, were ordinary and necessary within the meaning of section 162 or 212;

(2) *Convention program.*—The organization which sponsored the convention, or trade or business meeting had scheduled a program of business activities (including committee meetings or presentation of lectures, panel discussions, display of products, or other similar activities), and that such program was the principal activity of the convention, general assembly, or trade or business meeting.

(ii) *Directly preceding or following.*—Entertainment which occurs on the same day as a substantial and bona fide business discussion (as defined in subdivision (i) of this subparagraph) will be considered to directly precede or follow such discussion. If the entertainment and the business discussion do not occur on the same day, the facts and circumstances of each case are to be considered, including the place, date and duration of the business discussion, whether the taxpayer or his business associates are from out of town, and, if so, the date of arrival and departure, and the reasons the entertainment did not take place on the day of the business discussion. For example, if a group of business associates comes from out of town to the taxpayer's place of business to hold a substantial business discussion, the entertainment of such business guests and their wives on the evening prior to, or on the evening of the day following, the business discussion would generally be regarded as directly preceding or following such discussion.

(4) *Expenses closely connected with directly related entertainment.*—If any portion of an expenditure meets the requirements of paragraph (c)(3) of this section (relating to directly related entertainment in general), the remaining portion of the expenditure, if it is otherwise allowable under chapter 1 of the Code, shall be considered associated with the active conduct of the taxpayer's trade or business to the extent allocable to a person or persons closely connected with a person referred to in paragraph (c)(3)(iv) of this section. The spouse of a person referred to in paragraph (c)(3)(iv) of this section will be considered closely connected to such a person for purposes of this subparagraph. Thus, if a taxpayer and his wife entertain a business customer and the customer's wife under circumstances where the entertainment of the customer is considered directly related to the active conduct of the taxpayer's trade or business (within the meaning of paragraph (c)(3) of this section) the portion of the expenditure allocable to both wives will be considered associated with the active conduct of the taxpayer's trade or business under this subparagraph.

(e) *Expenditures paid or incurred before January 1, 1979, with respect to entertainment facilities or before January 1, 1994, with respect to clubs.*—(1) *In general.*—Any expenditure paid or incurred before January 1, 1979, with respect to a facility, or paid or incurred before January 1, 1994, with respect to a club, used in connection with entertainment shall not be allowed as a deduction except to the extent it meets the requirements of paragraph (a)(2)(ii) of this section.

(2) *Facilities used in connection with entertainment.*—(i) *In general.*—Any item of personal or real property owned, rented, or used by a taxpayer shall (unless otherwise provided under the rules of subdivision (ii) of this subparagraph) be considered to constitute a facility used in connection with entertainment if it is used during the taxable year for, or in connection with, entertainment (as defined in paragraph (b)(1) of this section). Examples of facilities which might be used for, or in connection with, entertainment include yachts, hunting lodges, fishing camps, swimming pools, tennis courts, bowling alleys, automobiles, airplanes, apartments, hotel suites, and homes in vacation resorts.

(ii) *Facilities used incidentally for entertainment.*—A facility used only incidentally during a taxable year in connection with entertainment, if such use is insubstantial, will not be considered a "facility used in connection with entertainment" for purposes of this section or for purposes of the record keeping requirements of section 274(d). See § 1.274-5(c)(6)(iii).

(3) *Expenditures with respect to a facility used in connection with entertainment.*—(i) *In general.*—The phrase "expenditures with respect to a facility used in connection with entertainment" includes depreciation and operating costs, such as rent and utility charges (for example, water or electricity), expenses for the maintenance, preservation or protection of a facility (for example, repairs, painting, insurance charges), and salaries or expenses for subsistence paid to

caretakers or watchmen. In addition, the phrase includes losses realized on the sale or other disposition of a facility.

(ii) *Club dues.*—(a) *Club dues paid or incurred before January 1, 1994.*—Dues or fees paid before January 1, 1994, to any social, athletic, or sporting club or organization are considered expenditures with respect to a facility used in connection with entertainment. The purposes and activities of a club or organization, and not its name, determine its character. Generally, the phrase *social, athletic, or sporting club or organization* has the same meaning for purposes of this section as that phrase had in section 4241 and the regulations thereunder, relating to the excise tax on club dues, prior to the repeal of section 4241 by section 301 of Pub. L. 89-44. However, for purposes of this section only, clubs operated solely to provide lunches under circumstances of a type generally considered to be conducive to business discussion, within the meaning of paragraph (f)(2)(i) of this section, will not be considered social clubs.

(b) *Club dues paid or incurred after December 31, 1993.*—See paragraph (a)(2)(iii) of this section with reference to the disallowance of deductions for club dues paid or incurred after December 31, 1993.

(iii) *Expenditures not with respect to a facility.*—The following expenditures shall not be considered to constitute expenditures with respect to a facility used in connection with entertainment—

(a) *Out of pocket expenditures.*—Expenses (exclusive of operating costs and other expenses referred to in subdivision (i) of this subparagraph) incurred at the time of an entertainment activity, even though in connection with the use of facility for entertainment purposes, such as expenses for food and beverages, or expenses for catering, or expenses for gasoline and fishing bait consumed on a fishing trip;

(b) *Non-entertainment expenditures.*—Expenses or items attributable to the use of a facility for other than entertainment purposes such as expenses for an automobile when not used for entertainment; and

(c) *Expenditures otherwise deductible.*—Expenses allowable as a deduction without regard to their connection with a taxpayer's trade or business such as taxes, interest, and casualty losses. The provisions of this subdivision shall be applied in the case of a taxpayer which is not an individual as if it were an individual. See also § 1.274-6.

(iv) *Cross reference.*—For other rules with respect to treatment of certain expenditures for entertainment-type facilities, see § 1.274-7.

(4) *Determination of primary use.*—(i) *In general.*—A facility used in connection with entertainment shall be considered as used primarily for the furtherance of the taxpayer's trade or business only if it is established that the primary use of the facility during the taxable year was for purposes considered ordinary and necessary within the meaning of sections 162 and 212 and the regulations thereunder. All of the facts and circumstances of each case shall be considered in determining the primary use of a facility. Generally, it is the actual use of the facility which establishes the deductibility of expenditures with respect to the facility; not its availability for use and not the taxpayer's principal purpose in acquiring the facility. Objective rather than subjective standards will be determinative. If membership entitles the member's entire family to use of a facility, such as a country club, their use will be considered in determining whether business use of the facility exceeds personal use. The factors to be considered include the nature of each use, the frequency and duration of use for business purposes as compared with other purposes, and the amount of expenditures incurred during use for business compared with amount of expenditures incurred during use for other purposes. No single standard of comparison, or quantitative measurement, as to the significance of any such factor, however, is necessarily appropriate for all classes or types of facilities. For example, an appropriate standard for determining the primary use of a country club during a taxable year will not necessarily be appropriate for determining the primary use of an airplane. However, a taxpayer shall be deemed to have established that a facility was used primarily for the furtherance of his trade or business if he establishes such *primary use in accordance with subdivision (ii) or (iii) of this subparagraph.* Subdivisions (ii) and (iii) of this subparagraph shall not preclude a taxpayer from otherwise establishing the primary use of a facility under the general provisions of this subdivision.

(ii) *Certain transportation facilities.*—A taxpayer shall be deemed to have established that a facility of a type described in this subdivision was used primarily for the furtherance of his trade or business if—

(a) *Automobiles.*—In the case of an automobile, the taxpayer establishes that more than 50 percent of mileage driven during the

taxable year was in connection with travel considered to be ordinary and necessary within the meaning of section 162 or 212 and the regulations thereunder.

(b) *Airplanes.*—In the case of an airplane, the taxpayer establishes that more than 50 percent of hours flown during the taxable year was in connection with travel considered to be ordinary and necessary within the meaning of section 162 or 212 and the regulations thereunder.

(iii) *Entertainment facilities in general.*—A taxpayer shall be deemed to have established that—

(a) A facility used in connection with entertainment, such as a yacht or other pleasure boat, hunting lodge, fishing camp, summer home or vacation cottage, hotel suite, country club, golf club or similar social, athletic, or sporting club or organization, bowling alley, tennis court, or swimming pool, or,

(b) A facility for employees not falling within the scope of section 274(e)(2) or (5)

was used primarily for the furtherance of his trade or business if he establishes that more than 50 percent of the total calendar days of use of the facility by, or under authority of, the taxpayer during the taxable year were days of business use. Any use of a facility (of a type described in this subdivision) during one calendar day shall be considered to constitute a "day of business use" if the primary use of the facility on such day was ordinary and necessary within the meaning of section 162 or 212 and the regulations thereunder. For the purposes of this subdivision, a facility shall be deemed to have been primarily used for such purposes on any one calendar day if the facility was used for the conduct of a substantial and bona fide business discussion (as defined in paragraph (d)(3)(i) of this section) notwithstanding that the facility may also have been used on the same day for personal or family use by the taxpayer or any member of the taxpayer's family not involving entertainment of others by, or under the authority of, the taxpayer.

(f) *Specific exceptions to application of this section.*—(1) *In general.*—The provisions of paragraphs (a) through (e) of this section (imposing limitations on deductions for entertainment expenses) are not applicable in the case of expenditures set forth in subparagraph (2) of this paragraph. Such expenditures are deductible to the extent allowable under Chapter 1 of the Code. This paragraph shall not be construed to affect the allowability or nonallowability of a deduction under section 162 or 212 and the regulations thereunder. The fact that an expenditure is not covered by a specific exception provided for in this paragraph shall not be determinative of the allowability or nonallowability of the expenditure under paragraphs (a) through (e) of this section. Expenditures described in subparagraph (2) of this paragraph are subject to the substantiation requirements of section 274(d) to the extent provided in § 1.274-5.

(2) *Exceptions.*—The expenditures referred to in subparagraph (1) of this paragraph are set forth in subdivisions (i) through (ix) of this subparagraph.

(i) *Business meals and similar expenditures paid or incurred before January 1, 1987.*—(a) *In general.*—Any expenditure for food or beverages furnished to an individual under circumstances of a type generally considered conducive to business discussion (taking into account the surroundings in which furnished, the taxpayer's trade, business, or income-producing activity, and the relationship to such trade, business or activity of the persons to whom the food or beverages are furnished) is not subject to the limitations on allowability of deductions provided for in paragraphs (a) through (e) of this section. There is no requirement that business actually be discussed for this exception to apply.

(b) *Surroundings.*—The surroundings in which the food or beverages are furnished must be such as would provide an atmosphere where there are no substantial distractions to discussion. This exception applies primarily to expenditures for meals and beverages served during the course of a breakfast, lunch or dinner meeting of the taxpayer and his business associates at a restaurant, hotel dining room, eating club or similar place not involving distracting influences such as a floor show. This exception also applies to expenditures for beverages served apart from meals if the expenditure is incurred in surroundings similarly conducive to business discussion, such as an expenditure for beverages served during the meeting of the taxpayer and his business associates at a cocktail lounge or hotel bar not involving distracting influences such as a floor show. This exception may also apply to expenditures for meals or beverages served in the taxpayer's residence on a clear showing that the expenditure was commercially rather than socially motivated. However, this exception, generally, is not applicable to any expenditure for meals or beverages furnished in circumstances where there are major distractions not conducive to business discussion, such as at night clubs, sporting events, large cocktail parties, sizeable social gatherings or other major distracting influences.

(c) Taxpayer's trade or business and relationship of persons entertained.—The taxpayer's trade, business, or income-producing activity and the relationship of the persons to whom the food or beverages are served to such trade, business or activity must be such as will reasonably indicate that the food or beverages were furnished for the primary purpose of furthering the taxpayer's trade or business and did not primarily serve a social or personal purpose. Such a business purpose would be indicated, for example, if a salesman employed by a manufacturing supply company meets for lunch during a normal business day with a purchasing agent for a manufacturer which is a prospective customer. Such a purpose would also be indicated if a life insurance agent meets for lunch during a normal business day with a client.

(d) Business programs.—Expenditures for business luncheons or dinners which are part of a business program, or banquets officially sponsored by business or professional associations, will be regarded as expenditures to which the exception of this subdivision (i) applies. In the case of such a business luncheon or dinner it is not always necessary that the taxpayer attend the luncheon or dinner himself. For example, if a dental equipment supplier purchased a table at a dental association banquet for dentists who are actual or prospective customers for his equipment, the cost of the table would not be disallowed under this section. See also paragraph (c)(4) of this section relating to expenditures made in a clear business setting.

(ii) Food and beverages for employees.—Any expenditure by a taxpayer for food and beverages (or for use of a facility in connection therewith) furnished on the taxpayer's business premises primarily for employees is not subject to the limitations on allowability of deductions provided for in paragraphs (a) through (e) of this section. This exception applies not only to expenditures for food or beverages furnished in a typical company cafeteria or an executive dining room, but also to expenditures with respect to the operation of such facilities. This exception applies even though guests are occasionally served in the cafeteria or dining room.

(iii) Certain entertainment and travel expenses treated as compensation.—(A) *In general.*—Any expenditure by a taxpayer for entertainment (or for use of a facility in connection therewith) or for travel described in section 274(m)(3), if an employee is the recipient of the entertainment or travel, is not subject to the limitations on allowability of deductions provided for in paragraphs (a) through (e) of this section to the extent that the expenditure is treated by the taxpayer—

(1) On the taxpayer's income tax return as originally filed, as compensation paid to the employee, and

(2) As wages to the employee for purposes of withholding under chapter 24 (relating to collection of income tax at source on wages).

(B) Expenses includible in income of persons who are not employees.—Any expenditure by a taxpayer for entertainment (or for use of a facility in connection therewith), or for travel described in section 274(m)(3), is not subject to the limitations on allowability of deductions provided for in paragraphs (a) through (e) of this section to the extent the expenditure is includible in gross income as compensation for services rendered, or as a prize or award under section 74, by a recipient of the expenditure who is not an employee of the taxpayer. The preceding sentence shall not apply to any amount paid or incurred by the taxpayer if such amount is required to be included (or would be so required except that the amount is less than $600) in any information return filed by such taxpayer under part III of subchapter A of chapter 61 and is not so included. See section 274(e)(9).

(C) Example.—The following example illustrates the provisions of this paragraph (f):

Example. If an employer rewards the employee (and the employee's spouse) with an expense paid vacation trip, the expense is deductible by the employer (if otherwise allowable under section 162 and the regulations thereunder) to the extent the employer treats the expenses as compensation and as wages. On the other hand, if a taxpayer owns a yacht which the taxpayer uses for the entertainment of business customers, the portion of salary paid to employee members of the crew which is allocable to use of the yacht for entertainment purposes (even though treated on the taxpayer's tax return as compensation and treated as wages for withholding tax purposes) would not come within this exception since the members of the crew were not recipients of the entertainment. If an expenditure of a type described in this subdivision properly constitutes a dividend paid to a shareholder or if it constitutes unreasonable compensation paid to an employee, nothing in this exception prevents disallowance of the expenditure to the taxpayer under other provisions of the Internal Revenue Code.

(iv) Reimbursed entertainment, food, or beverage expenses.—(A) *Introduction.*—In the case of any expenditure for entertainment, amusement, recreation, food, or beverages made by one person in performing services for another person (whether or not the other person is an employer) under a reimbursement or other expense allowance arrangement, the limitations on deductions in paragraphs (a) through (e) of this section and section 274(n)(1) apply either to the person who makes the expenditure or to the person who actually bears the expense, but not to both. If an expenditure of a type described in this paragraph (f)(2)(iv) properly constitutes a dividend paid to a shareholder, unreasonable compensation paid to an employee, a personal expense, or other nondeductible expense, nothing in this exception prevents disallowance of the expenditure to the taxpayer under other provisions of the Code.

(B) Reimbursement arrangements involving employees.—In the case of an employee's expenditure for entertainment, amusement, recreation, food, or beverages in performing services as an employee under a reimbursement or other expense allowance arrangement with a payor (the employer, its agent, or a third party), the limitations on deductions in paragraphs (a) through (e) of this section and section 274(n)(1) apply—

(1) To the employee to the extent the employer treats the reimbursement or other payment of the expense on the employer's income tax return as originally filed as compensation paid to the employee and as wages to the employee for purposes of withholding under chapter 24 (relating to collection of income tax at source on wages); or

(2) To the payor to the extent the reimbursement or other payment of the expense is not treated as compensation and wages paid to the employee in the manner provided in paragraph (f)(2)(iv)(B)(1) of this section (however, see paragraph (f)(2)(iv)(C) of this section if the payor receives a payment from a third party that may be treated as a reimbursement arrangement under that paragraph).

(C) Reimbursement arrangements involving persons that are not employees.—In the case of an expense for entertainment, amusement, recreation, food, or beverages of a person who is not an employee (referred to as an independent contractor) in performing services for another person (a client or customer) under a reimbursement or other expense allowance arrangement with the person, the limitations on deductions in paragraphs (a) through (e) of this section and section 274(n)(1) apply to the party expressly identified in an agreement between the parties as subject to the limitations. If an agreement between the parties does not expressly identify the party subject to the limitations, the limitations apply—

(1) To the independent contractor (which may be a payor described in paragraph (f)(2)(iv)(B) of this section) to the extent the independent contractor does not account to the client or customer within the meaning of section 274(d) and the associated regulations; or

(2) To the client or customer if the independent contractor accounts to the client or customer within the meaning of section 274(d) and the associated regulations. See also § 1.274-5.

(D) Reimbursement or other expense allowance arrangement.—The term *reimbursement or other expense allowance arrangement* means—

(1) For purposes of paragraph (f)(2)(iv)(B) of this section, an arrangement under which an employee receives an advance, allowance, or reimbursement from a payor (the employer, its agent, or a third party) for expenses the employee pays or incurs; and

(2) For purposes of paragraph (f)(2)(iv)(C) of this section, an arrangement under which an independent contractor receives an advance, allowance, or reimbursement from a client or customer for expenses the independent contractor pays or incurs if either—

(a) A written agreement between the parties expressly states that the client or customer will reimburse the independent contractor for expenses that are subject to the limitations on deductions in paragraphs (a) through (e) of this section and section 274(n)(1); or

(b) A written agreement between the parties expressly identifies the party subject to the limitations.

(E) Examples.—The following examples illustrate the application of this paragraph (f)(2)(iv).

Example 1. (i) Y, an employee, performs services under an arrangement in which L, an employee leasing company, pays Y a per diem allowance of $10x for each day that Y performs services for L's client, C, while traveling away from home. The per diem allowance is a reimbursement of travel expenses for food and beverages that Y pays in performing services as an employee. L enters into a written agreement with C under which C agrees to reimburse L for any substantiated reimbursements for travel expenses, including meals, that L pays to Y. The agreement does not expressly identify the party that is subject to the deduction limitations. Y performs services for C while traveling away from home for 10 days and provides L with substantiation that satisfies the requirements of section 274(d) of $100x of meal expenses incurred by Y while traveling away from home. L pays Y $100x to reimburse those expenses pursuant to their arrangement. L delivers a copy of Y's substantiation to C. C pays L $300x, which includes $200x compensation for services and $100x as reimbursement of L's payment of Y's travel expenses for meals. Neither L nor C treats the $100x paid to Y as compensation or wages.

(ii) Under paragraph (f)(2)(iv)(D)(1) of this section, Y and L have established a reimbursement or other expense allowance arrangement for purposes of paragraph (f)(2)(iv)(B) of this section. Because the reimbursement payment is not treated as compensation and wages paid to Y, under section 274(e)(3)(A) and paragraph (f)(2)(iv)(B)(1) of this section, Y is not subject to the section 274 deduction limitations. Instead, under paragraph (f)(2)(iv)(B)(2) of this section, L, the payor, is subject to the section 274 deduction limitations unless L can meet the requirements of section 274(e)(3)(B) and paragraph (f)(2)(iv)(C) of this section.

(iii) Because the agreement between L and C expressly states that C will reimburse L for substantiated reimbursements for travel expenses that L pays to Y, under paragraph (f)(2)(iv)(D)(2)(a) of this section, L and C have established a reimbursement or other expense allowance arrangement for purposes of paragraph (f)(2)(iv)(C) of this section. L accounts to C for C's reimbursement in the manner required by section 274(d) by delivering to C a copy of the substantiation L received from Y. Therefore, under section 274(e)(3)(B) and paragraph (f)(2)(iv)(C)(2) of this section, C and not L is subject to the section 274 deduction limitations.

Example 2. (i) The facts are the same as in *Example 1* except that, under the arrangements between Y and L and between L and C, Y provides the substantiation of the expenses directly to C, and C pays the per diem directly to Y.

(ii) Under paragraph (f)(2)(iv)(D)(1) of this section, Y and C have established a reimbursement or other expense allowance arrangement for purposes of paragraph (f)(2)(iv)(C) of this section. Because Y substantiates directly to C and the reimbursement payment was not treated as compensation and wages paid to Y, under section 274(e)(3)(A) and paragraph (f)(2)(iv)(C)(1) of this section Y is not subject to the section 274 deduction limitations. Under paragraph (f)(2)(iv)(C)(2) of this section, C, the payor, is subject to the section 274 deduction limitations.

Example 3. (i) The facts are the same as in *Example 1*, except that the written agreement between L and C expressly provides that the limitations of this section will apply to C.

(ii) Under paragraph (f)(2)(iv)(D)(2)(b) of this section, L and C have established a reimbursement or other expense allowance arrangement for purposes of paragraph (f)(2)(iv)(C) of this section. Because the agreement provides that the 274 deduction limitations apply to C, under section 274(e)(3)(B) and paragraph (f)(2)(iv)(C) of this section, C and not L is subject to the section 274 deduction limitations.

Example 4. (i) The facts are the same as in *Example 1*, except that the agreement between L and C does not provide that C will reimburse L for travel expenses.

(ii) The arrangement between L and C is not a reimbursement or other expense allowance arrangement within the meaning of section 274(e)(3)(B) and paragraph (f)(2)(iv)(D)(2) of this section. Therefore, even though L accounts to C for the expenses, L is subject to the section 274 deduction limitations.

(F) *Effective/applicability date.*—This paragraph (f)(2)(iv) applies to expenses paid or incurred in taxable years beginning after August 1, 2013.

(v) *Recreational expenses for employees generally.*—Any expenditure by a taxpayer for a recreational, social, or similar activity (or for use of a facility in connection therewith), primarily for the benefit of his employees generally, is not subject to the limitations on allowability of deductions provided for in paragraphs (a) through (e) of this section. This exception applies only to expenditures made primarily for the benefit of employees of the taxpayer other than employees who are officers, shareholders or other owners who own a 10-percent or greater interest in the business, or other highly compensated employees. For purposes of the preceding sentence, an employee shall be treated as owning any interest owned by a member of his family (within the meaning of section 267(c)(4) and the regulations thereunder). Ordinarily, this exception applies to usual employee benefit programs such as expenses of a taxpayer (*a*) in holding Christmas parties, annual picnics, or summer outings, for his employees generally, or (*b*) of maintaining a swimming pool, baseball diamond, bowling alley, or golf course available to his employees generally. Any expenditure for an activity which is made under circumstances which discriminate in favor of employees who are officers, shareholders or other owners, or highly compensated em-

ployees shall not be considered made primarily for the benefit of employees generally. On the other hand, an expenditure for an activity will not be considered outside of this exception merely because, due to the large number of employees involved, the activity is intended to benefit only a limited number of such employees at one time, provided the activity does not discriminate in favor of officers, shareholders, other owners, or highly compensated employees.

(vi) *Employee, stockholder, etc., business meetings.*—Any expenditure by a taxpayer for entertainment which is directly related to bona fide business meetings of the taxpayer's employees, stockholders, agents, or directors held principally for discussion of trade or business is not subject to the limitations on allowability of deductions provided for in paragraphs (a) through (e) of this section. For purposes of this exception, a partnership is to be considered a taxpayer and a member of a partnership is to be considered an agent. For example, an expenditure by a taxpayer to furnish refreshments to his employees at a bona fide meeting, sponsored by the taxpayer for the principal purpose of instructing them with respect to a new procedure for conducting his business would be within the provisions of this exception. A similar expenditure made at a bona fide meeting of stockholders of the taxpayer for the election of directors and discussion of corporate affairs would also be within the provisions of this exception. While this exception will apply to bona fide business meetings even though some social activities are provided, it will not apply to meetings which are primarily for social or nonbusiness purposes rather than for the transaction of the taxpayer's business. A meeting under circumstances where there was little or no possibility of engaging in the active conduct of trade or business (as described in paragraph (c)(7) of this section) generally will not be considered a business meeting for purposes of this subdivision. This exception will not apply to a meeting or convention of employees or agents, or similar meeting for directors, partners or others for the principal purpose of rewarding them for their services to the taxpayer. However, such a meeting or convention of employees might come within the scope of subdivisions (iii) or (v) of this subparagraph.

(vii) *Meetings of business leagues, etc.*—Any expenditure for entertainment directly related and necessary to attendance at bona fide business meetings or conventions of organizations exempt from taxation under section 501(c)(6) of the Code, such as business leagues, chambers of commerce, real estate boards, boards of trade, and certain professional associations, is not subject to the limitations on allowability of deductions provided in paragraphs (a) through (e) of this section.

(viii) *Items available to the public.*—Any expenditure by a taxpayer for entertainment (or for a facility in connection therewith) to the extent the entertainment is made available to the general public is not subject to the limitations on allowability of deductions provided for in paragraphs (a) through (e) of this section. Expenditures for entertainment of the general public by means of television, radio, newspapers and the like, will come within this exception, as will expenditures for distributing samples to the general public. Similarly, expenditures for maintaining private parks, golf courses and similar facilities, to the extent that they are available for public use, will come within this exception. For example, if a corporation maintains a swimming pool which it makes available for a period of time each week to children participating in a local public recreational program, the portion of the expense relating to such public use of the pool will come within this exception.

(ix) *Entertainment sold to customers.*—Any expenditure by a taxpayer for entertainment (or for use of a facility in connection therewith) to the extent the entertainment is sold to customers in a bona fide transaction for an adequate and full consideration in money or money's worth is not subject to the limitations on allowability of deductions provided for in paragraphs (a) through (e) of this section. Thus, the cost of producing night club entertainment (such as salaries paid to employees of night clubs and amounts paid to performers) for sale to customers or the cost of operating a pleasure cruise ship as a business will come within this exception.

(g) *Additional provisions of section 274—travel of spouse, dependent or others.*—Section 274(m)(3) provides that no deduction shall be allowed under this chapter (except section 217) for travel expenses paid or incurred with respect to a spouse, dependent, or other individual accompanying the taxpayer (or an officer or employee of the taxpayer) on business travel, unless certain conditions are met. As provided in section 274(m)(3), the term *other individual* does not include a business associate (as defined in paragraph (b)(2)(iii) of this section) who otherwise meets the requirements of sections 274(m)(3)(B) and (C). [Reg. § 1.274-2.]

☐ [*T.D. 6659*, 6-24-63. *Amended by T.D. 6996*, 1-17-69; *T.D. 8051*, 9-6-85; *T.D. 8601*, 7-18-95; *T.D. 8666*, 5-29-96 *and T.D. 9625*, 7-31-2013.]

[Reg. §1.274-3]

§1.274-3. Disallowance of deduction for gifts.—(a) *In general.*— No deduction shall be allowed under section 162 or 212 for any expense for a gift made directly or indirectly by a taxpayer to any individual to the extent that such expense, when added to prior expenses of the taxpayer for gifts made to such individual during the taxpayer's taxable year, exceeds $25.

(b) *Gift defined.*—(1) *In general.*—Except as provided in subparagraph (2) of this paragraph the term "gift", for purposes of this section, means any item excludable from the gross income of the recipient under section 102 which is not excludable from his gross income under any other provision of chapter 1 of the Code. Thus, a payment by an employer to a deceased employee's widow is not a gift, for purposes of this section, to the extent the payment constitutes an employee's death benefit excludable by the recipient under section 101(b). Similarly, a scholarship which is excludable from a recipient's gross income under section 117, and a prize or award which is excludable from a recipient's gross income under section 74(b), are not subject to the provisions of this section.

(2) *Items not treated as gifts.*—The term "gift", for purposes of this section, does not include the following:

(i) An item having a cost to the taxpayer not in excess of $4.00 on which the name of the taxpayer is clearly and permanently imprinted and which is one of a number of identical items distributed generally by such a taxpayer.

(ii) A sign, display rack, or other promotional material to be used on the business premises of the recipient, or the

(iii) In the case of a taxable year of a taxpayer ending on or after August 13, 1981, an item of tangible personal property which is awarded before January 1, 1987, to an employee of the taxpayer by reason of the employee's length of service (including an award upon retirement), productivity, or safety achievement, but only to the extent that—

(A) The cost of the item to the taxpayer does not exceed $400; or

(B) The item is a qualified plan award (as defined in paragraph (d) of this section); or

(iv) In the case of a taxable year of a taxpayer ending before August 13, 1981, an item of tangible personal property having a cost to the taxpayer not in excess of $100 which is awarded to an employee of the taxpayer by reason of the employee's length of service (including an award upon retirement) or safety achievement. For purposes of paragraphs (b)(2) (iii) and (iv), the term "tangible personal property" does not include cash or any gift certificate other than a nonnegotiable gift certificate conferring only the right to receive tangible personal property. Thus, for example, if a nonnegotiable gift certificate entitles an employee to choose between selecting an item of merchandise or receiving cash or reducing the balance due on his account with the issuer of the gift certificate, the gift certificate is not tangible personal property for purposes of this section. To the extent that an item is not treated as a gift for purposes of this section, the deductibility of the expense of the item is not governed by this section, and the taxpayer need not take such item into account in determining whether the $25 limitation on gifts to any individual has been exceeded. For example, if an employee receives by reason of his length of service a gift of an item of tangible personal property that costs the employer $450, the deductibility of only $50 ($450 minus $400) is governed by this section, and the employer takes the $50 into account for purposes of the $25 limitation on gifts to that employee. The fact that an item is wholly or partially excepted from the applicability of this section has no effect in determining whether the value of the item is includible in the gross income of the recipient. For rules relating to the taxability to the recipient of any item described in this subparagraph, see sections 61, 74, and 102 and the regulations thereunder. For rules relating to the deductibility of employee achievement awards awarded after December 31, 1986, see section 274(j).

(c) *Expense for a gift.*—For purposes of this section, the term "expense for a gift" means the cost of the gift to the taxpayer, other than incidental costs such as for customary engraving on jewelry, or for packaging, insurance, and mailing or other delivery. A related cost will be considered "incidental" only if it does not add substantial value to the gift. Although the cost of customary gift wrapping will be considered an incidental cost, the purchase of an ornamental basket for packaging fruit will not be considered an incidental cost of packaging if the basket has a value which is substantial in relation to the value of the fruit.

(d) *Qualified plan award.*—(1) *In general.*—Except as provided in subparagraph (2) of this paragraph the term "qualified plan award," for purposes of this section, means an item of tangible personal property that is awarded to an employee by reason of the employee's length of service (including retirement), productivity, or safety

achievement, and that is awarded pursuant to a permanent, written award plan or program of the taxpayer that does not discriminate as to eligibility or benefits in favor of employees who are officers, shareholders, or highly compensated employees. The "permanency" of an award plan shall be determined from all the facts and circumstances of the particular case, including the taxpayer's ability to continue to make the awards as required by the award plan. Although the taxpayer may reserve the right to change or to terminate an award plan, the actual termination of the award plan for any reason other than business necessity within a few years after it has taken effect may be evidence that the award plan from its inception was not a "permanent" award plan. Whether or not an award plan is discriminatory shall be determined from all the facts and circumstances of the particular case. An award plan may fail to qualify because it is discriminatory in its actual operation even though the written provisions of the award plan are not discriminatory.

(2) *Items not treated as qualified plan awards.*—The term "qualified plan award," for purposes of this section, does not include an item qualifying under paragraph (d)(1) of this section to the extent that the cost of the item exceeds $1,600. In addition, that term does not include any items qualifying under paragraph (d)(1) of this section if the average cost of all items (whether or not tangible personal property) awarded during the taxable year by the taxpayer under any plan described in paragraph (d)(1) of this section exceeds $400. The average cost of those items shall be computed by dividing (i) the sum of the costs for those items (including amounts in excess of the $1,600 limitation) by (ii) the total number of those items.

(e) *Gifts made indirectly to an individual.*—(1) *Gift to spouse or member of family.*—If a taxpayer makes a gift to the wife of a man who has a business connection with the taxpayer, the gift generally will be considered as made indirectly to the husband. However, if the wife has a bona fide business connection with the taxpayer independently of her relationship to her husband, a gift to her generally will not be considered as made indirectly to her husband unless the gift is intended for his eventual use or benefit. Thus, if a taxpayer makes a gift to a wife who is engaged with her husband in the active conduct of a partnership business, the gift to the wife will not be considered an indirect gift to her husband unless it is intended for his eventual use or benefit. The same rules apply to gifts to any other member of the family of an individual who has a business connection with the taxpayer.

(2) *Gift to corporation or other business entity.*—If a taxpayer makes a gift to a corporation or other business entity intended for the eventual personal use or benefit of an individual who is an employee, stockholder, or other owner of the corporation or business entity, the gift generally will be considered as made indirectly to such individual. Thus, if a taxpayer provides theater tickets to a closely held corporation for eventual use by any one of the stockholders of the corporation, and if such tickets are gifts, the gifts will be considered as made indirectly to the individual who eventually uses such ticket. On the other hand, a gift to a business organization of property to be used in connection with the business of the organization (for example, a technical manual) will not be considered as a gift to an individual, even though, in practice, the book will be used principally by a readily identifiable individual employee. A gift for the eventual personal use or benefit of some undesignated member of a large group of individuals generally will not be considered as made indirectly to the individual who eventually uses, or benefits from, such gifts unless, under the circumstances of the case, it is reasonably practicable for the taxpayer to ascertain the ultimate recipient of the gift. Thus, if a taxpayer provides several baseball tickets to a corporation for the eventual use by any one of a large number of employees or customers of the corporation, and if such tickets are gifts, the gifts generally will not be treated as made indirectly to the individuals who use such tickets.

(f) *Special rules.*—(1) *Partnership.*—In the case of a gift by a partnership, the $25 annual limitation contained in paragraph (a) of this section shall apply to the partnership as well as to each member of the partnership. Thus, in the case of a gift made by a partner with respect to the business of the partnership, the $25 limitation will be applied at the partnership level as well as at the level of the individual partner. Consequently, deductions for gifts made with respect to partnership business will not exceed $25 annually for each recipient, regardless of the number of partners.

(2) *Husband and wife.*—For purposes of applying the $25 annual limitation contained in paragraph (a) of this section, a husband and wife shall be treated as one taxpayer. Thus, in the case of gifts to an individual by a husband and wife, the spouses will be treated as one donor; and they are limited to a deduction of $25 annually for each recipient. This rule applies regardless of whether the husband and wife file a joint return or whether the husband and wife make separate gifts to an individual with respect to separate businesses.

Since the term "taxpayer" in paragraph (a)(1) of this section refers only to the donor of a gift, this special rule does not apply to treat a husband and wife as one individual where each is a recipient of a gift. See paragraph (e) (1) of this section.

(g) *Cross reference.*—For rules with respect to whether this section or § 1.274-2 applies, see § 1.274-2(b)(1)(iii). [Reg. § 1.274-3.]

☐ [*T.D. 6659, 6-24-63. Amended by T.D. 8230, 9-19-88.*]

[Reg. § 1.274-4]

§ 1.274-4. Disallowance of certain foreign travel expenses.— (a) *Introductory.*—Section 274(c) and this section impose certain restrictions on the deductibility of travel expenses incurred in the case of an individual who, while traveling outside the United States away from home in the pursuit of trade or business (hereinafter termed "business activity"), engages in substantial personal activity not attributable to such trade or business (hereinafter termed "nonbusiness activity"). Section 274(c) and this section are limited in their application to individuals (whether or not an employee or other person traveling under a reimbursement or other expense allowance arrangement) who engage in nonbusiness activity while traveling outside the United States away from home, and do not impose restrictions on the deductibility of travel expenses incurred by an employer or client under an advance, reimbursement, or other arrangement with the individual who engages in nonbusiness activity. For purposes of this section, the term "United States" includes only the States and the District of Columbia, and any reference to "trade or business" or "business activity" includes any activity described in section 212. For rules governing the determination of travel outside the United States away from home, see paragraph (e) of this section. For rules governing the disallowance of travel expense to which this section applies, see paragraph (f) of this section.

(b) *Limitations on application of section.*—The restrictions on deductibility of travel expenses contained in paragraph (f) of this section are applicable only if—

(1) The travel expense is otherwise deductible under section 162 or 212 and the regulations thereunder.

(2) The travel expense is for travel outside the United States away from home which exceeds 1 week (as determined under paragraph (c) of this section), and

(3) The time outside the United States away from home attributable to nonbusiness activity (as determined under paragraph (d) of this section) constitutes 25 percent or more of the total time on such travel.

(c) *Travel in excess of one week.*—This section does not apply to an expense of travel unless the expense is for travel outside the United States away from home which exceeds 1 week. For purposes of this section, 1 week means 7 consecutive days. The day in which travel outside the United States away from home begins shall not be considered, but the day in which such travel ends shall be considered, in determining whether a taxpayer is outside the United States away from home for more than 7 consecutive days. For example, if a taxpayer departs on travel outside the United States away from home on a Wednesday morning and ends such travel the following Wednesday evening, he shall be considered as being outside the United States away from home only 7 consecutive days. In such a case, this section would not apply because the taxpayer was not outside the United States away from home for more than 7 consecutive days. However, if the taxpayer travels outside the United States away from home for more than 7 consecutive days, both the day such travel begins and the day such travel ends shall be considered a "business day" or a "nonbusiness day", as the case may be, for purposes of determining whether nonbusiness activity constituted 25 percent or more of travel time under paragraph (d) of this section and for purposes of allocating expenses under paragraph (f) of this section. For purposes of determining whether travel is outside the United States away from home, see paragraph (e) of this section.

(d) *Nonbusiness activity constituting 25 percent or more of travel time.*—(1) *In general.*—This section does not apply to any expense of travel outside the United States away from home unless the portion of time outside the United States away from home attributable to nonbusiness activity constitutes 25 percent or more of the total time on such travel.

(2) *Allocation on per day basis.*—The total time traveling outside the United States away from home will be allocated on a day-by-day basis to (i) days of business activity or (ii) days of nonbusiness activity (hereinafter termed "business days" or "nonbusiness days" respectively) unless the taxpayer establishes that a different method of allocation more clearly reflects the portion of time outside the United States away from home which is attributable to nonbusiness activity. For purposes of this section, a day spent outside the United States away from home shall be deemed entirely a business day even though spent only in part on business activity if the taxpayer establishes—

(i) *Transportation days.*—That on such day the taxpayer was traveling to or returning from a destination outside the United States away from home in the pursuit of trade or business. However, if for purposes of engaging in nonbusiness activity, the taxpayer while traveling outside the United States away from home does not travel by a reasonably direct route, only that number of days shall be considered business days as would be required for the taxpayer, using the same mode of transportation, to travel to or return from the same destination by a reasonably direct route. Also if, while so traveling, the taxpayer interrupts the normal course of travel by engaging in substantial diversions for nonbusiness reasons of his own choosing only that number of days shall be considered business days as equals the number of days required for the taxpayer, using the same mode of transportation, to travel to or return from the same destination without engaging in such diversion. For example, if a taxpayer residing in New York departs on an evening on a direct flight to Quebec for a business meeting to be held in Quebec the next morning, for purposes of determining whether nonbusiness activity constituted 25 percent or more of his travel time, the entire day of his departure shall be considered a business day. On the other hand, if a taxpayer travels by automobile from New York to Quebec to attend a business meeting and while enroute spends 2 days in Ottawa and 1 day in Montreal on nonbusiness activities of his personal choice, only that number of days outside the United States shall be considered business days as would have been required for the taxpayer to drive by a reasonably direct route to Quebec, taking into account normal periods for rest and meals.

(ii) *Presence required.*—That on such day his presence outside the United States away from home was required at a particular place for a specific and bona fide business purpose. For example, if a taxpayer is instructed by his employer to attend a specific business meeting, the day of the meeting shall be considered a business day even though, because of the scheduled length of the meeting, the taxpayer spends more time during normal working hours of the day on nonbusiness activity than on business activity.

(iii) *Days primarily business*—That during hours normally considered to be appropriate for business activity, his principal activity on such day was the pursuit of trade or business.

(iv) *Circumstances beyond control.*—That on such day he was prevented from engaging in the conduct of trade or business as his principal activity due to circumstances beyond his control.

(v) *Weekends, holidays, etc.*—That such day was a Saturday, Sunday, legal holiday, or other reasonably necessary standby day which intervened during that course of the taxpayer's trade or business while outside the United States away from home which the taxpayer endeavored to conduct with reasonable dispatch. For example, if a taxpayer travels from New York to London to take part in business negotiations beginning on a Wednesday and concluding on the following Tuesday, the intervening Saturday and Sunday shall be considered business days whether or not business is conducted on either of such days. Similarly, if in the above case the meetings which concluded on Tuesday evening were followed by business meetings with another business group in London on the immediately succeeding Thursday and Friday, the intervening Wednesday will be deemed a business day. However if at the conclusion of the business meetings on Friday, the taxpayer stays in London for an additional week for personal purposes, the Saturday and Sunday following the conclusion of the business meeting will not be considered business days.

(e) *Domestic travel excluded.*—(1) *In general.*—For purposes of this section, travel outside the United States away from home does not include any travel from one point in the United States to another point in the United States. However, travel which is not from one point in the United States to another point in the United States shall be considered travel outside the United States. If a taxpayer travels from a place within the United States to a place outside the United States, the portion, if any, of such travel which is from one point in the United States to another point in the United States is to be disregarded for purposes of determining—

(i) Whether the taxpayer's travel outside the United States away from home exceeds 1 week (see paragraph (c) of this section),

(ii) Whether the time outside the United States away from home attributable to nonbusiness activity constitutes 25 percent or more of the total time of such travel (see paragraph (d) of this section), or

(iii) The amount of travel expense subject to the allocation rules of this section (see paragraph (f) of this section).

(2) *Determination of travel from one point in the United States to another point in the United States.*—In the case of the following means of transportation, travel from one point in the United States to another point in the United States shall be determined as follows—

(i) *Travel by public transportation.*—In the case of travel by public transportation, any place in the United States at which the vehicle makes a scheduled stop for the purpose of adding or discharging passengers shall be considered a point in the United States.

(ii) *Travel by private automobile.*—In the case of travel by private automobile, any such travel which is within the United States shall be considered travel from one point in the United States to another point in the United States.

(iii) *Travel by private airplane.*—In the case of travel by private airplane, any flight, whether or not constituting the entire trip, where both the takeoff and the landing are within the United States shall be considered travel from one point in the United States to another point in the United States.

(3) *Examples.*—The provisions of subparagraph (2) may be illustrated by the following examples:

Example (1). Taxpayer A flies from Los Angeles to Puerto Rico with a brief scheduled stopover in Miami for the purpose of adding and discharging passengers and A returns by airplane nonstop to Los Angeles. The travel from Los Angeles to Miami is considered travel from one point in the United States to another point in the United States. The travel from Miami to Puerto Rico and from Puerto Rico to Los Angeles is not considered travel from one point in the United States to another point in the United States and, thus, is considered to be travel outside the United States away from home.

Example (2). Taxpayer B travels by train from New York to Montreal. The travel from New York to the last place in the United States where the train is stopped for the purpose of adding or discharging passengers is considered to be travel from one point in the United States to another point in the United States.

Example (3). Taxpayer C travels by automobile from Tulsa to Mexico City and back. All travel in the United States is considered to be travel from one point in the United States to another point in the United States.

Example (4). Taxpayer D flies nonstop from Seattle to Juneau. Although the flight passes over Canada, the trip is considered to be travel from one point in the United States to another point in the United States.

Example (5). If in example (4) above, the airplane makes a scheduled landing in Vancouver, the time spent in traveling from Seattle to Juneau is considered to be travel outside the United States away from home. However, the time spent in Juneau is not considered to be travel outside the United States away from home.

(f) *Application of disallowance rules.*—(1) *In general.*—In the case of expense for travel outside the United States away from home by an individual to which this section applies, except as otherwise provided in subparagraph (4) or (5) of this paragraph, no deduction shall be allowed for that amount of travel expense specified in subparagraph (2) or (3) of this paragraph (whichever is applicable) which is obtained by multiplying the total of such travel expense by a fraction—

(i) The numerator of which is the number of nonbusiness days during such travel, and

(ii) The denominator of which is the total number of business days and nonbusiness days during such travel.

For determination of "business days" and "nonbusiness days", see paragraph (d)(2) of this section.

(2) *Nonbusiness activity at, near, or beyond business destination.*—If the place at which the individual engages in nonbusiness activity (hereinafter termed "nonbusiness destination") is at, near, or beyond the place to which he travels in the pursuit of a trade or business (hereinafter termed "business destination"), the amount of travel expense referred to in subparagraph (1) of this paragraph shall be the amount of travel expense, otherwise allowable as a deduction under section 162 or section 212, which would have been incurred in traveling from the place where travel outside the United States away from home begins to the business destination, and returning. Thus, if the individual travels from New York to London on business, and then takes a vacation in Paris before returning to New York, the amount of the travel expense subject to allocation is the expense which would have been incurred in traveling from New York to London and returning.

(3) *Nonbusiness activity on the route to or from business destination.*—If the nonbusiness destination is on the route to or from the business destination, the amount of the travel expense referred to in subparagraph (1) of this paragraph shall be the amount of travel expense, otherwise allowable as a deduction under section 162 or

212, which would have been incurred in traveling from the place where travel outside the United States away from home begins to the nonbusiness destination and returning. Thus, if the individual travels on business from Chicago to Rio de Janeiro, Brazil with a scheduled stop in New York for the purpose of adding and discharging passengers, and while enroute stops in Caracas, Venezuela for a vacation and returns to Chicago from Rio de Janeiro with another scheduled stop in New York for the purpose of adding and discharging passengers, the amount of travel expense subject to allocation is the expense which would have been incurred in traveling from New York to Caracas and returning.

(4) *Other allocation method.*—If taxpayer establishes that a method other than allocation on a day-by-day basis (as determined under paragraph (d)(2) of this section) more clearly reflects the portion of time outside the United States away from home which is attributable to nonbusiness activity, the amount of travel expense for which no deduction shall be allowed shall be determined by such other method.

(5) *Travel expense deemed entirely allocable to business activity.*—Expenses of travel shall be considered allocable in full to business activity, and no portion of such expense shall be subject to disallowance under this section, if incurred under circumstances provided for in subdivision (i) or (ii) of this subparagraph.

(i) *Lack of control over travel.*—Expenses of travel otherwise deductible under section 162 or 212 shall be considered fully allocable to business activity if, considering all the facts and circumstances, the individual incurring such expenses did not have substantial control over the arranging of the business trip. A person who is required to travel to a business destination will not be considered to have substantial control over the arranging of the business trip merely because he has control over the timing of the trip. Any individual who travels on behalf of his employer under a reimbursement or other expense allowance arrangement shall be considered not to have had substantial control over the arranging of his business trip, provided the employee is not—

(a) A managing executive of the employer for whom he is traveling (and for this purpose the term "managing executive" includes only an employee who, by reason of his authority and responsibility, is authorized, without effective veto procedures, to decide upon the necessity for his business trip), or

(b) Related to his employer within the meaning of section 267(b) but for this purpose the percentage referred to in section 267(b)(2) shall be 10 percent.

(ii) *Lack of major consideration to obtain a vacation.*—Any expense of travel, which qualifies for deduction under section 162 or 212, shall be considered fully allocable to business activity if the individual incurring such expenses can establish that, considering all the facts and circumstances, he did not have a major consideration, in determining to make the trip, of obtaining a personal vacation or holiday. If such a major consideration were present, the provisions of subparagraphs (1) through (4) of this paragraph shall apply. However, if the trip were primarily personal in nature, the traveling expenses to and from the destination are not deductible even though the taxpayer engages in business activities while at such destination. See paragraph (b) of §1.162-2.

(g) *Examples.*—The application of this section may be illustrated by the following examples:

Example (1). Individual A flew from New York to Paris where he conducted business for 1 day. He spent the next 2 days sightseeing in Paris and then flew back to New York. The entire trip, including 2 days for travel en route, took 5 days. Since the time outside the United States away from home during the trip did not exceed 1 week, the disallowance rules of this section do not apply.

Example (2). Individual B flew from Tampa to Honolulu (from one point in the United States to another point in the United States) for a business meeting which lasted 3 days and for personal matters which took 10 days. He then flew to Melbourne, Australia where he conducted business for 2 days and went sightseeing for 1 day. Immediately thereafter he flew back to Tampa, with a scheduled landing in Honolulu for the purpose of adding and discharging passengers. Although the trip exceeded 1 week, the time spent outside the United States away from home, including 2 days for traveling from Honolulu to Melbourne and return, was 5 days. Since the time outside the United States away from home during the trip did not exceed 1 week, the disallowance rules of this section do not apply.

Example (3). Individual C flew from Los Angeles to New York where he spent 5 days. He then flew to Brussels where he spent 14 days on business and 5 days on personal matters. He then flew back to Los Angeles by way of New York. The entire trip, including 4 days for travel en route, took 28 days. However, the 2 days spent traveling from Los Angeles to New York and return, and the 5 days spent in

New York are not considered travel outside the United States away from home and, thus, are disregarded for purposes of this section. Although the time spent outside the United States away from home exceeded 1 week, the time outside the United States away from home attributable to nonbusiness activities (5 days out of 21) was less than 25 percent of the total time outside the United States away from home during the trip. Therefore, the disallowance rules of this section do not apply.

Example (4). D, an employee of Y Company, who is neither a managing executive of, nor related to, Y Company within the meaning of paragraph (f)(5)(i) of this section, traveled outside the United States away from home on behalf of his employer and was reimbursed by Y for his traveling expense to and from the business destination. The trip took more than a week and D took advantage of the opportunity to enjoy a personal vacation which exceeded 25 percent of the total time on the trip. Since D, traveling under a reimbursement arrangement, is not a managing executive of, or related to, Y Company, he is not considered to have substantial control over the arranging of the business trip, and the travel expenses shall be considered fully allocable to business activity.

Example (5). E, a managing executive and principal shareholder of X Company, travels from New York to Stockholm, Sweden, to attend a series of business meetings. At the conclusion of the series of meetings, which last 1 week, E spends 1 week on a personal vacation in Stockholm. If E establishes either that he did not have substantial control over the arranging of the trip or that a major consideration in his determining to make the trip was not to provide an opportunity for taking a personal vacation, the entire travel expense to and from Stockholm shall be considered fully allocable to business activity.

Example (6). F, a self-employed professional man, flew from New York to Copenhagen, Denmark, to attend a convention sponsored by a professional society. The trip lasted 3 weeks, of which 2 weeks were spent on vacation in Europe. F generally would be regarded as having substantial control over arranging his business trip. Unless F can establish that obtaining a vacation was not a major consideration in determining to make the trip, the disallowance rules of this section apply.

Example (7). Taxpayer G flew from Chicago to New York where he spent 6 days on business. He then flew to London where he conducted business for 2 days. G then flew to Paris for a 5 day vacation after which he flew back to Chicago, with a scheduled landing in New York for the purpose of adding and discharging passengers. G would not have made the trip except for the business he had to conduct in London. The travel outside the United States away from home, including 2 days for travel en route, exceeded a week and the time devoted to nonbusiness activities was not less than 25 percent of the total time on such travel. The 2 days spent traveling from Chicago to New York and return, and the 6 days spent in New York are disregarded for purposes of determining whether the travel outside the United States away from home exceeded a week and whether the time devoted to nonbusiness activities was less than 25 percent of the total time outside the United States away from home. If G is unable to establish either that he did not have substantial control over the arranging of the business trip or that an opportunity for taking a personal vacation was not a major consideration in his determining to make the trip, 5/9ths (5 days devoted to nonbusiness activities out of a total 9 days outside the United States away from home on the trip) of the expenses attributable to transportation and food from New York to London and from London to New York will be disallowed (unless G establishes that a different method of allocation more clearly reflects the portion of time outside the United States away from home which is attributable to nonbusiness activity).

(h) *Cross reference.*—For rules with respect to whether an expense is travel or entertainment, see paragraph (b)(1)(iii) of §1.274-2. [Reg. §1.274-4.]

☐ [T.D. 6659, 6-24-63. Amended by T.D. 6758, 9-9-64.]

[Reg. §1.274-5]

§1.274-5. Substantiation requirements.—(a) and (b) [Reserved] For further guidance, see §1.274-5T(a) and (b).

(c) *Rules of substantiation.*—(1) [Reserved].—For further guidance, see §1.274-5T(c)(1).

(2) *Substantiation by adequate records.*—(i) and (ii) [Reserved] For further guidance, see §1.274-5T(c)(2)(i) and (ii).

(iii) *Documentary evidence.*—(A) Except as provided in paragraph (c)(2)(iii)(B), documentary evidence, such as receipts, paid bills, or similar evidence sufficient to support an expenditure, is required for—

(1) Any expenditure for lodging while traveling away from home, and

(2) Any other expenditure of $75 or more except, for transportation charges, documentary evidence will not be required if not readily available.

(B) The Commissioner, in his or her discretion, may prescribe rules waiving the documentary evidence requirements in circumstances where it is impracticable for such documentary evidence to be required. Ordinarily, documentary evidence will be considered adequate to support an expenditure if it includes sufficient information to establish the amount, date, place, and the essential character of the expenditure. For example, a hotel receipt is sufficient to support expenditures for business travel if it contains the following: name, location, date, and separate amounts for charges such as for lodging, meals, and telephone. Similarly, a restaurant receipt is sufficient to support an expenditure for a business meal if it contains the following: name and location of the restaurant, the date and amount of the expenditure, the number of people served, and, if a charge is made for an item other than meals and beverages, an indication that such is the case. A document may be indicative of only one (or part of one) element of an expenditure. Thus, a cancelled check, together with a bill from the payee, ordinarily would establish the element of cost. In contrast, a cancelled check drawn payable to a named payee would not by itself support a business expenditure without other evidence showing that the check was used for a certain business purpose.

(iv) and (v) [Reserved] For further guidance, see §1.274-5T(c)(2)(iv) and (v).

(3) through (7) [Reserved] For further guidance, see §1.274-5T(c)(3) through (7).

(d) and (e) [Reserved] For further guidance, see §1.274-5T(d) and (e).

(f) *Reporting and substantiation of expenses of certain employees for travel, entertainment, gifts, and with' respect to listed property.*—(1) through (3) [Reserved] For further guidance, see §1.274-5T(f)(1) through (3).

(4) *Definition of an adequate accounting to the employer.*—(i) *In general.*—For purposes of this paragraph (f) an *adequate accounting* means the submission to the employer of an account book, diary, log, statement of expense, trip sheet, or similar record maintained by the employee in which the information as to each element of an expenditure or use (described in paragraph (b) of this section) is recorded at or near the time of the expenditure or use, together with supporting documentary evidence, in a manner that conforms to all the adequate records requirements of paragraph (c)(2) of this section. An adequate accounting requires that the employee account for all amounts received from the employer during the taxable year as advances, reimbursements, or allowances (including those charged directly or indirectly to the employer through credit cards or otherwise) for travel, entertainment, gifts, and the use of listed property. The methods of substantiation allowed under paragraph (c)(4) or (c)(5) of this section also will be considered to be an adequate accounting if the employer accepts an employee's substantiation and establishes that such substantiation meets the requirements of paragraph (c)(4) or (c)(5). For purposes of an adequate accounting, the method of substantiation allowed under paragraph (c)(3) of this section will not be permitted.

(ii) *Procedures for adequate accounting without documentary evidence.*—The Commissioner may, in his or her discretion, prescribe rules under which an employee may make an adequate accounting to an employer by submitting an account book, log, diary, etc., alone, without submitting documentary evidence.

(iii) *Employer.*—For purposes of this section, the term *employer* includes an agent of the employer or a third party payor who pays amounts to an employee under a reimbursement or other expense allowance arrangement.

(5) [Reserved].—For further guidance, see §1.274-5T(f)(5).

(g) *Substantiation by reimbursement arrangements or per diem, mileage, and other traveling allowances.*—(1) *In general.*—The Commissioner may, in his or her discretion, prescribe rules in pronouncements of general applicability under which allowances for expenses described in paragraph (g)(2) of this section will, if in accordance with reasonable business practice, be regarded as equivalent to substantiation by adequate records or other sufficient evidence, for purposes of paragraph (c) of this section, of the amount of the expenses and as satisfying, with respect to the amount of the expenses, the requirements of an adequate accounting to the employer for purposes of paragraph (f)(4) of this section. If the total allowance received exceeds the deductible expenses paid or incurred by the employee, such excess must be reported as income on the employee's return. See paragraph (j)(1) of this section relating to the substantiation of meal expenses while traveling away from home, and paragraph (j)(2) of this section relating to the substantiation of expenses for the business use of a vehicle.

(2) *Allowances for expenses described.*—An allowance for expenses is described in this paragraph (g)(2) if it is a—

(i) Reimbursement arrangement covering ordinary and necessary expenses of traveling away from home (exclusive of transportation expenses to and from destination);

(ii) Per diem allowance providing for ordinary and necessary expenses of traveling away from home (exclusive of transportation costs to and from destination); or,

(iii) Mileage allowance providing for ordinary and necessary expenses of local transportation and transportation to, from, and at the destination while traveling away from home.

(h) [Reserved].—For further guidance, see § 1.274-5T(h).

(i) [Reserved].

(j) *Authority for optional methods of computing certain expenses.*—(1) *Meal expenses while traveling away from home.*—The Commissioner may establish a method under which a taxpayer may use a specified amount or amounts for meals while traveling away from home in lieu of substantiating the actual cost of meals. The taxpayer will not be relieved of the requirement to substantiate the actual cost of other travel expenses as well as the time, place, and business purpose of the travel. See paragraphs (b)(2) and (c) of this section.

(2) *Use of mileage rates for vehicle expenses.*—The Commissioner may establish a method under which a taxpayer may use mileage rates to determine the amount of the ordinary and necessary expenses of using a vehicle for local transportation and transportation to, from, and at the destination while traveling away from home in lieu of substantiating the actual costs. The method may include appropriate limitations and conditions in order to reflect more accurately vehicle expenses over the entire period of usage. The taxpayer will not be relieved of the requirement to substantiate the amount of each business use (i.e., the business mileage), or the time and business purpose of each use. See paragraphs (b)(2) and (c) of this section.

(3) *Incidental expenses while traveling away from home.*—The Commissioner may establish a method under which a taxpayer may use a specified amount or amounts for incidental expenses paid or incurred while traveling away from home in lieu of substantiating the actual cost of incidental expenses. The taxpayer will not be relieved of the requirement to substantiate the actual cost of other travel expenses as well as the time, place, and business purpose of the travel.

(k) *Exceptions for qualified nonpersonal use vehicles.*—(1) *In general.*—The substantiation requirements of section 274(d) and this section do not apply to any qualified nonpersonal use vehicle (as defined in paragraph (k)(2) of this section).

(2) *Qualified nonpersonal use vehicle.*—(i) *In general.*—For purposes of section 274(d) and this section, the term *qualified nonpersonal use vehicle* means any vehicle which, by reason of its nature (that is, design), is not likely to be used more than a de minimis amount for personal purposes.

(ii) *List of vehicles.*—Vehicles which are qualified nonpersonal use vehicles include the following:

(A) Clearly marked police, fire, and public safety officer vehicles (as defined and to the extent provided in paragraph (k)(3) of this section).

(B) Ambulances used as such or hearses used as such.

(C) Any vehicle designed to carry cargo with a loaded gross vehicle weight over 14,000 pounds.

(D) Bucket trucks (cherry pickers).

(E) Cement mixers.

(F) Combines.

(G) Cranes and derricks.

(H) Delivery trucks with seating only for the driver, or only for the driver plus a folding jump seat.

(I) Dump trucks (including garbage trucks).

(J) Flatbed trucks.

(K) Forklifts.

(L) Passenger buses used as such with a capacity of at least 20 passengers.

(M) Qualified moving vans (as defined in paragraph (k)(4) of this section).

(N) Qualified specialized utility repair trucks (as defined in paragraph (k)(5) of this section).

(O) Refrigerated trucks.

(P) School buses (as defined in section 4221(d)(7)(c)).

(Q) Tractors and other special purpose farm vehicles.

(R) Unmarked vehicles used by law enforcement officers (as defined in paragraph (k)(6) of this section) if the use is officially authorized.

(S) Such other vehicles as the Commissioner may designate.

(3) *Clearly marked police, fire, or public safety officer vehicles.*—A police, fire, or public safety officer vehicle is a vehicle, owned or leased by a governmental unit, or any agency or instrumentality thereof, that is required to be used for commuting by a police officer, fire fighter, or public safety officer (as defined in section 402(l)(4)(C) of this chapter) who, when not on a regular shift, is on call at all times, provided that any personal use (other than commuting) of the vehicle outside the limit of the police officer's arrest powers or the fire fighter's or public safety officer's obligation to respond to an emergency is prohibited by such governmental unit. A police, fire, or public safety officer vehicle is clearly marked if, through painted insignia or words, it is readily apparent that the vehicle is a police, fire, or public safety officer vehicle. A marking on a license plate is not a clear marking for purposes of this paragraph (k).

(4) *Qualified moving van.*—The term *qualified moving van* means any truck or van used by a professional moving company in the trade or business of moving household or business goods if—

(i) No personal use of the van is allowed other than for travel to and from a move site (or for de minimis personal use, such as a stop for lunch on the way between two move sites);

(ii) Personal use for travel to and from a move site is an irregular practice (that is, not more than five times a month on average); and

(iii) Personal use is limited to situations in which it is more convenient to the employer, because of the location of the employee's residence in relation to the location of the move site, for the van not to be returned to the employer's business location.

(5) *Qualified specialized utility repair truck.*—The term *qualified specialized utility repair truck* means any truck (not including a van or pickup truck) specifically designed and used to carry heavy tools, testing equipment, or parts if—

(i) The shelves, racks, or other permanent interior construction which has been installed to carry and store such heavy items is such that it is unlikely that the truck will be used more than a de minimis amount for personal purposes; and

(ii) The employer requires the employee to drive the truck home in order to be able to respond in emergency situations for purposes of restoring or maintaining electricity, gas, telephone, water, sewer, or steam utility services.

(6) *Unmarked law enforcement vehicles.*—(i) *In general.*—The substantiation requirements of section 274(d) and this section do not apply to officially authorized uses of an unmarked vehicle by a "law enforcement officer". To qualify for this exception, any personal use must be authorized by the Federal, State, county, or local governmental agency or department that owns or leases the vehicle and employs the officer, and must be incident to law enforcement functions, such as being able to report directly from home to a stakeout or surveillance site, or to an emergency situation. Use of an unmarked vehicle for vacation or recreation trips cannot qualify as an authorized use.

(ii) *Law enforcement officer.*—The term *law enforcement officer* means an individual who is employed on a full-time basis by a governmental unit that is responsible for the prevention or investigation of crime involving injury to persons or property (including apprehension or detention of persons for such crimes), who is authorized by law to carry firearms, execute search warrants, and to make arrests (other than merely a citizen's arrest), and who regularly carries firearms (except when it is not possible to do so because of the requirements of undercover work). The term "law enforcement officer" may include an arson investigator if the investigator otherwise meets the requirements of this paragraph (k)(6)(ii), but does not include Internal Revenue Service special agents.

(7) *Trucks and vans.*—The substantiation requirements of section 274(d) and this section apply generally to any pickup truck or van, unless the truck or van has been specially modified with the result that it is not likely to be used more than a de minimis amount for personal purposes. For example, a van that has only a front bench for seating, in which permanent shelving that fills most of the cargo area has been installed, that constantly carries merchandise or equipment, and that has been specially painted with advertising or the company's name, is a vehicle not likely to be used more than a de minimis amount for personal purposes.

(8) *Examples.*—The following examples illustrate the provisions of paragraph (k)(3) and (6) of this section:

Example 1. Detective C, who is a "law enforcement officer" employed by a state police department, headquartered in City M, is provided with an unmarked vehicle (equipped with radio communication) for use during off-duty hours because C must be able to communicate with headquarters and be available for duty at any time (for example, to report to a surveillance or crime site). The police department generally has officially authorized personal use of the vehicle by C but has prohibited use of the vehicle for recreational purposes or for personal purposes outside the state. Thus, C's use of the vehicle for commuting between headquarters or a surveillance site and home and for personal errands is authorized personal use as described in paragraph (k)(6)(i) of this section. With respect to these authorized uses the vehicle is not subject to the substantiation requirements of section 274(d) and the value of these uses is not included in C's gross income.

Example 2. Detective T is a "law enforcement officer" employed by City M. T is authorized to make arrests only within M's city limits. T, along with all other officers of the force, is ordinarily on duty for eight hours each work day and on call during the other sixteen hours. T is provided with the use of a clearly marked police vehicle in which T is required to commute to his home in City M. The police department's official policy regarding marked police vehicles prohibits its personal use (other than commuting) of the vehicles outside the city limits. When not using the vehicle on the job, T uses the vehicle only for commuting, personal errands on the way between work and home, and personal errands within City M. All use of the vehicle by T conforms to the requirements of paragraph (k)(3) of this section. Therefore, the value of that use is excluded from T's gross income as a working condition fringe and the vehicle is not subject to the substantiation requirements of section 274(d).

Example 3. Director C is employed by City M as the director of the City's rescue squad and is provided with a vehicle for use in responding to emergencies. Director C is trained in rescue activity and has the legal authority and legal responsibility to engage in rescue activity. The city's rescue squad is not a part of City M's police or fire departments. The director's vehicle is a sedan which is painted with insignia and words identifying the vehicle as being owned by the City's rescue squad. C, when not on a regular shift, is on call at all times. The City's official policy regarding clearly marked public safety officer vehicles prohibits personal use (other than for commuting) of the vehicle outside of the limits of the public safety officer's obligation to respond to an emergency. When not using the vehicle to respond to emergencies, City M authorizes C to use the vehicle only for commuting, personal errands on the way between work and home, and personal errands within the limits of C's obligation to respond to emergencies. With respect to these authorized uses, the vehicle is not subject to the substantiation requirements of section 274(d) and the value of these uses is not includable in C's gross income.

Example 4. Coroner D is employed by County N to investigate and determine the cause, time, and manner of certain deaths occurring in the County. Coroner D also safeguards the property of the deceased, notifies the next of kin, conducts inquests, and arranges for the burial of indigent persons. D is provided with a vehicle for use by County N. The vehicle is to be used in County N business and for commuting. Personal use other than for commuting purposes is forbidden. D is trained in rescue activity but has no legal authority or legal responsibility to engage in rescue activity. D's vehicle is a sedan which is painted with insignia and words identifying it as a County N vehicle. D, when not on a regular shift, is on call at all times. D does not satisfy the criteria of a public safety officer under 28 C.F.R. § 32.3 (2008). Thus, D's vehicle cannot qualify as a clearly marked public safety officer vehicle. Accordingly, business use of the vehicle is subject to the substantiation requirements of section 274(d), and the value of any personal use of the vehicle, such as commuting, is includable in D's gross income.

(l) *Definitions.*—For purposes of section 274(d) and this section, the terms *automobile* and *vehicle* have the same meanings as prescribed in § 1.61-21(d)(1)(ii) and (e)(2), respectively. Also, for purposes of section 274(d) and this section, the terms *employer*, *employee* and *personal use* have the same meanings as prescribed in § 1.274-6T(e).

(m) *Effective date.*—This section applies to expenses paid or incurred after December 31, 1997. However, paragraph (j)(3) of this section applies to expenses paid or incurred after September 30, 2002, and paragraph (k) applies to clearly marked public safety officer vehicles, as defined in § 1.274-5(k)(3), only with respect to uses occurring after May 19, 2010. [Reg. § 1.274-5.]

☐ [*T.D.* 8864, 1-21-2000 (*corrected* 3-22-2000). *Amended by T.D.* 9020, 11-8-2002; *T.D.* 9064, 6-30-2003 *and T.D.* 9483, 5-18-2010.]

⋙→ *Caution: Reg. §1.274-5A, below, applies to tax years beginning before January 1, 1986.*

[Reg. § 1.274-5A]

§ 1.274-5A. Substantiation requirements.—(a) *In general.*—No deduction shall be allowed for any expenditure or item with respect to—

(1) Traveling away from home (including meals and lodging) deductible under section 162 or 212.

(2) Any activity which is of a type generally considered to constitute entertainment, amusement, or recreation, or with respect to a facility used in connection with such an activity, including the items specified in section 274(e), or

(3) Gifts defined in section 274,

unless the taxpayer substantiates such expenditure as provided in paragraph (c) of this section. This limitation supersedes with respect to any such expenditure the doctrine of *Cohan v. Commissioner* (C.C.A. 2d 1930) 39 F. 2d 540. The decision held that where the evidence indicated a taxpayer incurred deductible travel or entertainment expenses but the exact amount could not be determined, the court should make a close approximation and not disallow the deduction entirely. Section 274(d) contemplates that no deduction shall be allowed a taxpayer for such expenditures on the basis of such approximations or unsupported testimony of the taxpayer. For purposes of this section, the term "entertainment" means entertainment, amusement, or recreation, and use of a facility therefor; and the term "expenditure" includes expenses and items (including items such as losses and depreciation).

(b) *Elements of an expenditure.*—(1) *In general.*—Section 274(d) and this section contemplate that no deduction shall be allowed for any expenditure for travel, entertainment, or a gift unless the taxpayer substantiates the following elements for each such expenditure:

(i) Amount;

(ii) Time and place of travel or entertainment (or use of a facility with respect to entertainment), or date and description of a gift:

(iii) Business purpose; and

(iv) Business relationship to the taxpayer of each person entertained, using an entertainment facility or receiving a gift.

(2) *Travel.*—The elements to be proved with respect to an expenditure for travel are—

(i) *Amount.*—Amount of each separate expenditure for traveling away from home, such as cost of transportation or lodging, except that the daily cost of the traveler's own breakfast, lunch, and dinner and of expenditures incidental to such travel may be aggregated, if set forth in reasonable categories, such as for meals, for gasoline and oil, and for taxi fares;

(ii) *Time.*—Dates of departure and return for each trip away from home, and number of days away from home spent on business;

(iii) *Place.*—Destinations or locality of travel, described by name of city or town or other similar designation; and

(iv) *Business purpose.*—Business reason for travel or nature of the business benefit derived or expected to be derived as a result of travel.

(3) *Entertainment in general.*—Elements to be proved with respect to an expenditure for entertainment are—

(i) *Amount.*—Amount of each separate expenditure for entertainment, except that such incidental items as taxi fares or telephone calls may be aggregated on a daily basis;

(ii) *Time.*—Date of entertainment;

(iii) *Place.*—Name, if any, address or location, and designation of type of entertainment, such as dinner or theater, in such information is not apparent from the designation of the place;

(iv) *Business purpose.*—Business reason for the entertainment or nature of business benefit derived or expected to be derived as a result of the entertainment and, except in the case of business meals described in section 274(e)(1), the nature of any business discussion or activity;

(v) *Business relationship.*—Occupation or other information relating to the person or persons entertained, including name, title, or other designation, sufficient to establish business relationship to the taxpayer.

(4) *Entertainment directly preceding or following a substantial and bona fide business discussion.*—If a taxpayer claims a deduction for entertainment directly preceding or following a substantial and bona fide business discussion on the ground that such entertainment was associated with the active conduct of the taxpayer's trade or business,

>>> *Caution: Reg. §1.274-5A, below, applies to tax years beginning before January 1, 1986.*

the elements to be proved with respect to such expenditure, in addition to those enumerated in subparagraph (3)(i), (ii), (iii), and (v) of this paragraph, are—

(i) *Time.*—Date and duration of business discussion;

(ii) *Place.*—Place of business discussion;

(iii) *Business purpose.*—Nature of business discussion, and business reason for the entertainment or nature of business benefit derived or expected to be derived as the result of the entertainment;

(iv) *Business relationship.*—Identification of those persons entertained who participated in the business discussion.

(5) *Gifts.*—Elements to be proved with respect to an expenditure for a gift are—

(i) *Amount.*—Cost of the gift to the taxpayer;

(ii) *Time.*—Date of the gift;

(iii) *Description.*—Description of the gift;

(iv) *Business purpose.*—Business reason for the gift or nature of business benefit derived or expected to be derived as a result of the gift; and

(v) *Business relationship.*—Occupation or other information relating to the recipient of the gift, including name, title, or other designation, sufficient to establish business relationship to the taxpayer.

(c) *Rules for substantiation.*—(1) *In general.*—A taxpayer must substantiate each element of an expenditure (described in paragraph (b) of this section) by adequate records or by sufficient evidence corroborating his own statement except as otherwise provided in this section. Section 274(d) contemplates that a taxpayer will maintain and produce such substantiation as will constitute clear proof of an expenditure for travel, entertainment, or gifts referred to in section 274. A record of the elements of an expenditure made at or near the time of the expenditure, supported by sufficient documentary evidence, has a high degree of credibility not present with respect to a statement prepared subsequent thereto when generally there is a lack of accurate recall. Thus, the corroborative evidence required to support a statement not made at or near the time of the expenditure must have a high degree of probative value to elevate such statement and evidence to the level of credibility reflected by a record made at or near the time of the expenditure supported by sufficient documentary evidence. The substantiation requirements of section 274(d) are designed to encourage taxpayers to maintain the records, together with documentary evidence, as provided in subparagraph (2) of this paragraph. To obtain a deduction for an expenditure for travel, entertainment, or gifts, a taxpayer must substantiate, in accordance with the provisions of this paragraph, each element of such an expenditure.

(2) *Substantiation by adequate records.*—(i) *In general.*—To meet the "adequate records" requirements of section 274(d), a taxpayer shall maintain an account book, diary, statement of expense or similar record (as provided in subdivision (ii) of this subparagraph) and documentary evidence (as provided in subdivision (iii) of this subparagraph) which, in combination, are sufficient to establish each element of an expenditure specified in paragraph (b) of this section. It is not necessary to record information in an account book, diary, statement of expense or similar record which duplicates information reflected on a receipt so long as such account book and receipt complement each other in an orderly manner.

(ii) *Account book, diary, etc.*—An account book, diary, statement of expense or similar record must be prepared or maintained in such manner that each recording of an element of an expenditure is made at or near the time of the expenditure.

(a) *Made at or near the time of the expenditure.*—For purposes of this section, the phrase "made at or near the time of the expenditure" means the elements of an expenditure are recorded at a time when, in relation to the making of an expenditure, the taxpayer has full present knowledge of each element of the expenditure, such as the amount, time, place and business purpose of the expenditure and business relationship to the taxpayer of any person entertained. An expense account statement which is a transcription of an account book, diary, or similar record prepared or maintained in accordance with the provisions of this subdivision shall be considered a record prepared or maintained in the manner prescribed in the preceding sentence if such expense account statement is submitted by an employee to his employer or by an independent contractor to his client or customers in the regular course of good business practice.

(b) *Substantiation of business purpose.*—In order to constitute an adequate record of business purpose within the meaning of section 274(d) and this subparagraph, a written statement of business purpose generally is required. However, the degree of substantiation necessary to establish business purpose will vary depending upon the facts and circumstances of each case. Where the business purpose of an expenditure is evident from the surrounding facts and circumstances, a written explanation of such business purpose will not be required. For example, in the case of a salesman calling on customers on an established sales route, a written explanation of the business purpose of such travel ordinarily will not be required. Similarly, in the case of a business meal described in section 274(e)(1), if the business purpose of such meal is evident from the business relationship to the taxpayer of the persons entertained and other surrounding circumstances, a written explanation of such business purpose will not be required.

(c) *Confidential information.*—If any information relating to the elements of an expenditure, such as place, business purpose or business relationship, is of a confidential nature, such information need not be set forth in the account book, diary, statement of expense or similar record, provided such information is recorded at or near the time of the expenditure and is elsewhere available to the district director to substantiate such element of the expenditure.

(iii) *Documentary evidence.*—Documentary evidence, such as receipts, paid bills, or similar evidence sufficient to support an expenditure shall be required for—

(a) Any expenditure for lodging while traveling away from home, and

(b) Any other expenditure of $25 or more, except, for transportation charges, documentary evidence will not be required if not readily available,

provided, however, that the Commissioner, in his discretion, may prescribe rules waiving such requirements in circumstances where he determines it is impracticable for such documentary evidence to be required. Ordinarily, documentary evidence will be considered adequate to support an expenditure if it includes sufficient information to establish the amount, date, place, and the essential character of the expenditure. For example, a hotel receipt is sufficient to support expenditures for business travel if it contains the following: name, location, date, and separate amounts for charges such as for lodging, meals, and telephone. Similarly, a restaurant receipt is sufficient to support an expenditure for a business meal if it contains the following: name and location of the restaurant, the date and amount of the expenditure, and, if a charge is made for an item other than meals and beverages, an indication that such is the case. A document may be indicative of only one (or part of one) element of an expenditure. Thus, a cancelled check, together with a bill from the payee, ordinarily would establish the element of cost. In contrast, a cancelled check drawn payable to a named payee would not by itself support a business expenditure without other evidence showing that the check was used for a certain business purpose.

(iv) *Retention of documentary evidence.*—The Commissioner may, in his discretion, prescribe rules under which an employer may dispose of documentary evidence submitted to him by employees who are required to, and do, make an adequate accounting to the employer (within the meaning of paragraph (e)(4) of this section) if the employer maintains adequate accounting procedures with respect to such employees (within the meaning of paragraph (e)(5) of this section).

(v) *Substantial compliance.*—If a taxpayer has not fully substantiated a particular element of an expenditure, but the taxpayer establishes to the satisfaction of the district director that he has substantially complied with the "adequate records" requirements of this subparagraph with respect to the expenditure, the taxpayer may be permitted to establish such element by evidence which the district director shall deem adequate.

(3) *Substantiation by other sufficient evidence.*—If a taxpayer fails to establish to the satisfaction of the district director that he has substantially complied with the "adequate records" requirements of subparagraph (2) of this paragraph with respect to an element of an expenditure, then, except as otherwise provided in this paragraph, the taxpayer must establish such element—

(i) By his own statement, whether written or oral, containing specific information in detail as to such element; and

(ii) By other corroborative evidence sufficient to establish such element.

If such element is the description of a gift, or the cost, time, place, or date of an expenditure, the corroborative evidence shall be direct evidence, such as a statement in writing or the oral testimony of persons entertained or other witness setting forth detailed informa-

>>>→ *Caution: Reg. §1.274-5A, below, applies to tax years beginning before January 1, 1986.*

tion about such element, or the documentary evidence described in subparagraph (2) of this paragraph. If such element is either the business relationship to the taxpayer of persons entertained or the business purpose of an expenditure, the corroborative evidence may be circumstantial evidence.

(4) *Substantiation in exceptional circumstances.*—If a taxpayer establishes that, by reason of the inherent nature of the situation in which an expenditure was made—

(i) He was unable to obtain evidence with respect to an element of the expenditure which conforms fully to the "adequate records" requirements of subparagraph (2) of this paragraph,

(ii) He is unable to obtain evidence with respect to such element which conforms fully to the "other sufficient evidence" requirements of subparagraph (3) of this paragraph, and

(iii) He has presented other evidence, with respect to such element, which possesses the highest degree of probative value possible under the circumstances,

such other evidence shall be considered to satisfy the substantiation requirements of section 274(d) and this paragraph.

(5) *Loss of records due to circumstances beyond control of taxpayer.*—Where the taxpayer establishes that the failure to produce adequate records is due to the loss of such records through circumstances beyond the taxpayer's control, such as destruction by fire, flood, earthquake, or other casualty, the taxpayer shall have a right to substantiate a deduction by reasonable reconstruction of his expenditures.

(6) *Special rules.*—(i) *Separate expenditure.*—(a) *In general.*—For the purposes of this section, each separate payment by the taxpayer shall ordinarily be considered to constitute a separate expenditure. However, concurrent or repetitious expenses of a similar nature occurring during the course of a single event shall be considered a single expenditure. To illustrate the above rules, where a taxpayer entertains a business guest at dinner and thereafter at the theater, the payment for dinner shall be considered to constitute one expenditure and the payment for the tickets for the theater shall be considered to constitute a separate expenditure. Similarly, if during a day of business travel a taxpayer makes separate payments for breakfast, lunch, and dinner, he shall be considered to have made three separate expenditures. However, if during entertainment at a cocktail lounge the taxpayer pays separately for each serving of refreshments, the total amount expended for the refreshments will be treated as a single expenditure. A tip may be treated as a separate expenditure.

(b) *Aggregation.*—Except as otherwise provided in this section, the account book, diary, statement of expense, or similar record required by subparagraph (2) (ii) of this paragraph shall be maintained with respect to each separate expenditure and not with respect to aggregate amounts for two or more expenditures. Thus, each expenditure for such items as lodging and air or rail travel shall be recorded as a separate item and not aggregated. However, at the option of the taxpayer, amounts expended for breakfast, lunch, or dinner, may be aggregated. A tip or gratuity which is related to an underlying expense may be aggregated with such expense. For other provisions permitting recording of aggregate amounts in an account book, diary, statement of expense or similar record see paragraph (b) (2) (i) and (b) (3) of this section (relating to incidental costs of travel and entertainment).

(ii) *Allocation of expenditure.*—For purposes of this section, if a taxpayer has established the amount of an expenditure, but is unable to establish the portion of such amount which is attributable to each person participating in the event giving rise to the expenditure, such amount shall ordinarily be allocated to each participant on a pro rata basis, if such determination is material. Accordingly, the total number of persons for whom a travel or entertainment expenditure is incurred must be established in order to compute the portion of the expenditure allocable to each such person.

(iii) *Primary use of a facility.*—Section 274(a)(1)(B) and (2)(C) denies a deduction for any expenditure paid or incurred before January 1, 1979, with respect to a facility, or paid or incurred at any time with respect to a club, used in connection with an entertainment activity unless the taxpayer establishes that the facility (including a club) was used primarily for the furtherance of his trade or business. A determination whether a facility before January 1, 1979, or a club at any time was used primarily for the furtherance of the taxpayer's trade or business will depend upon the facts and circumstances of each case. In order to establish that a facility was used primarily for the furtherance of his trade or business, the taxpayer shall maintain records of the use of the facility, the cost of using the facility, mileage or its equivalent (if appropriate), and such other information as shall

tend to establish such primary use. Such records of use shall contain—

(a) For each use of the facility claimed to be in furtherance of the taxpayer's trade or business, the elements of an expenditure specified in paragraph (b) of this section, and

(b) For each use of the facility not in furtherance of the taxpayer's trade or business, an appropriate description of such use, including cost, date, number of persons entertained, nature of entertainment and, if applicable, information such as mileage or its equivalent. A notation such as "personal use" or "family use" would, in the case of such use, be sufficient to describe the nature of entertainment.

If a taxpayer fails to maintain adequate records concerning a facility which is likely to serve the personal purposes of the taxpayer, it shall be presumed that the use of such facility was primarily personal.

(iv) *Additional information.*—In a case where it is necessary to obtain additional information, either—

(a) To clarify information contained in records, statements, testimony, or documentary evidence submitted by a taxpayer under the provisions of paragraph (c)(2) or (c)(3) of this section, or

(b) To establish the reliability of accuracy of such records, statements, testimony, or documentary evidence, the district director may, notwithstanding any other provision of this section, obtain such additional information as he determines necessary to properly implement the provisions of section 274 and the regulations thereunder by personal interview or otherwise.

(7) *Specific exceptions.*—Except as otherwise prescribed by the Commissioner, substantiation otherwise required by this paragraph is not required for—

(i) Expenses described in section 274(e)(2) relating to food and beverages for employees, section 274(e)(3) relating to expenses treated as compensation, section 274(e)(8) relating to items available to the public, and section 274(e)(9) relating to entertainment sold to customers, and

(ii) Expenses described in section 274(e)(5) relating to recreational, etc., expenses for employees, except that a taxpayer shall keep such records or other evidence as shall establish that such expenses were for activities (or facilities used in connection therewith) primarily for the benefit of employees other than employees who are officers, shareholders or other owners (as defined in section 274(e)(5)), or highly compensated employees.

(d) *Disclosure on returns.*—The Commissioner may, in his discretion, prescribe rules under which any taxpayer claiming a deduction for entertainment, gifts, or travel or any other person receiving advances, reimbursements, or allowances for such items, shall make disclosure on his tax return with respect to such items. The provisions of this paragraph shall apply notwithstanding the provisions of paragraph (e) of this section.

(e) *Reporting and substantiation of expenses of certain employees for travel, entertainment, and gifts.*—(1) *In general.*—The purpose of this paragraph is to provide rules for reporting and substantiation of certain expenses paid or incurred by taxpayers in connection with the performance of services as employees. For purposes of this paragraph, the term "business expenses" means ordinary and necessary expenses for travel, entertainment, or gifts which are deductible under section 162, and the regulations thereunder, to the extent not disallowed by section 274(c). Thus, the term "business expenses" does not include personal, living or family expenses disallowed by section 262 or travel expenses disallowed by section 274(c), and advances, reimbursements or allowances for such expenditures must be reported as income by the employee.

(2) *Reporting of expenses for which the employee is required to make an adequate accounting to his employer.*—(i) *Reimbursements equal to expenses.*—For purposes of computing tax liability, an employee need not report on his tax return business expenses for travel, transportation, entertainment, gifts, and similar purposes, paid or incurred by him solely for the benefit of his employer for which he is required to, and does, make an adequate accounting to his employer (as defined in subparagraph (4) of this paragraph) and which are charged directly or indirectly to the employer (for example, through credit cards) or for which the employee is paid through advances, reimbursements, or otherwise, provided that the total amount of such advances, reimbursements, and charges is equal to such expenses.

(ii) *Reimbursements in excess of expenses.*—In case the total of the amounts charged directly or indirectly to the employer or received from the employer as advances, reimbursements, or otherwise, exceeds the business expenses paid or incurred by the employee and the employee is required to, and does, make an adequate accounting to his employer for such expenses, the em-

>>> *Caution: Reg. §1.274-5A, below, applies to tax years beginning before January 1, 1986.*

ployee must include such excess (including amounts received for expenditures not deductible by him) in income.

(iii) *Expense in excess of reimbursements.*—If an employee incurs deductible business expenses on behalf of his employer which exceed the total of the amounts charged directly or indirectly to the employer and received from the employer as advances, reimbursements, or otherwise, and the employee wishes to claim a deduction for such excess, he must—

(a) Submit a statement as part of his tax return showing all of the information required by subparagraph (3) of this paragraph, and,

(b) Maintain such records and supporting evidence as will substantiate each element of an expenditure (described in paragraph (b) of this section) in accordance with paragraph (c) of this section.

(3) *Reporting of expenses for which the employee is not required to make an adequate accounting to his employer.*—If the employee is not required to make an adequate accounting to his employer for his business expenses or, though required, fails to make an adequate accounting for such expenses, he must submit, as a part of his tax return, a statement showing the following information:

(i) The total of all amounts received as advances or reimbursements from his employer, including amounts charged directly or indirectly to the employer through credit cards or otherwise; and

(ii) The nature of his occupation, the number of days away from home on business, and the total amount of business expenses paid or incurred by him (including those charged directly or indirectly to the employer through credit cards or otherwise) broken down into such categories as transportation, meals and lodging while away from home overnight, entertainment, gifts, and other business expenses.

In addition, he must maintain such records and supporting evidence as will substantiate each element of an expenditure (described in paragraph (b) of this section) in accordance with paragraph (c) of this section.

(4) *Definition of an "adequate accounting" to the employer.*—For purposes of this paragraph an adequate accounting means the submission to the employer of an account book, diary, statement of expense, or similar record maintained by the employee in which the information as to each element of an expenditure (described in paragraph (b) of this section) is recorded at or near the time of the expenditure, together with supporting documentary evidence, in a manner which conforms to all the "adequate records" requirements of paragraph (c)(2) of this section. An adequate accounting requires that the employee account for all amounts received from his employer during the taxable year as advances, reimbursements, or allowances (including those charged directly or indirectly to the employer through credit cards or otherwise) for travel, entertainment, and gifts. The methods of substantiation allowed under paragraph (c)(4) or (c)(5) of this section also will be considered to be an adequate accounting if the employer accepts an employee's substantiation and establishes that such substantiation meets the requirements of such paragraph (c)(4) or (c)(5). For purposes of an adequate accounting the method of substantiation allowed under paragraph (c)(3) of this section will not be permitted.

(5) *Substantiation of expenditures by certain employees.*—An employee who makes an adequate accounting to his employer within the meaning of this paragraph will not again be required to substantiate such expense account information except in the following cases:

(i) An employee whose business expenses exceed the total of amounts charged to his employer and amounts received through advances, reimbursements or otherwise and who claims a deduction on his return for such excess;

(ii) An employee who is related to his employer within the meaning of section 267(b) but for this purpose the percentage referred to in section 267(b)(2) shall be 10 percent; and

(iii) Employees in cases where it is determined that the accounting procedures used by the employer for the reporting and substantiation of expenses by such employees are not adequate, or where it cannot be determined that such procedures are adequate. The district director will determine whether the employer's accounting procedures are adequate by considering the facts and circumstances of each case, including the use of proper internal controls. For example, an employer should require that an expense account must be verified and approved by a responsible person other than the person incurring such expenses. Accounting procedures will be considered inadequate to the extent that the employer does not require an adequate accounting from his employees as defined in subparagraph (4) of this paragraph, or does not maintain such substantiation. To the extent an employer fails to maintain adequate accounting

procedures he will thereby obligate his employees to separately substantiate their expense account information.

(f) *Substantiation by reimbursement arrangements or per diem, mileage, and other traveling allowances.*—The Commissioner may, in his discretion, prescribe rules under which—

(1) Reimbursement arrangements covering ordinary and necessary expenses of traveling away from home (exclusive of transportation expenses to and from destination),

(2) Per diem allowances providing for ordinary and necessary expenses of traveling away from home (exclusive of transportation costs to and from destination), and

(3) Mileage allowances provided for ordinary and necessary expenses of transporation while traveling away from home,

will, if in accordance with reasonable business practice, be regarded as equivalent to substantiation by adequate records or other sufficient evidence for purposes of paragraph (c) of this section of the amount of such traveling expenses and as satisfying, with respect to the amount of such traveling expenses, the requirements of an adequate accounting to the employer for purposes of paragraph (e)(4) of this section. If the total travel allowance received exceeds the deductible traveling expenses paid or incurred by the employee, such excess must be reported as income on the employee's return. See paragraph (h) in this section relating to the substantiation of meal expenses while traveling.

(g) *Reporting and substantiation of certain reimbursements of persons other than employees.*—(1) *In general.*—The purpose of this paragraph is to provide rules for the reporting and substantiation of certain expenses for travel, entertainment, and gifts paid or incurred by one person (hereinafter termed "independent contractor") in connection with services performed for another person other than an employer (hereinafter termed "client or customer") under a reimbursement or other expense allowance arrangement with such client or customer. For purposes of this paragraph, the term "business expenses" means ordinary and necessary expenses for travel, entertainment, or gifts which are deductible under section 162, and the regulations thereunder, to the extent not disallowed by section 274(c). Thus, the term "business expenses" does not include personal, living or family expenses disallowed by section 262 or travel expenses disallowed by section 274(c), and reimbursements for such expenditures must be reported as income by the independent contractor. For purposes of this paragraph, the term "reimbursements" means advances, allowances, or reimbursements received by an independent contractor for travel, entertainment, or gifts, in connection with the performance by him of services for his client or customer, under a reimbursement or other expense allowance arrangement with his client or customer, and includes amounts charged directly or indirectly to the client or customer through credit card systems or otherwise. See paragraph (h) of this section relating to the substantiation of meal expenses while traveling.

(2) *Substantiation by independent contractors.*—An independent contractor shall substantiate, with respect to his reimbursements, each element of an expenditure (described in paragraph (b) of this section) in accordance with the requirements of paragraph (c) of this section; and, to the extent he does not so substantiate, he shall include such reimbursements in income. An independent contractor shall so substantiate a reimbursement for entertainment regardless of whether he accounts (within the meaning of subparagraph (3) of this paragraph) for such entertainment.

(3) *Accounting to a client or customer under section 274(e)(4)(B).*—Section 274(e)(4)(B) provides that section 274(a) (relating to disallowance of expenses for entertainment) shall not apply to expenditures for entertainment for which an independent contractor has been reimbursed if the independent contractor accounts to his client or customer to the extent provided by section 274(d). For purposes of section 274(e)(4)(B), an independent contractor shall be considered to account to his client or customer for an expense paid or incurred under a reimbursement or other expense allowance arrangement with his client or customer if, with respect to such expense for entertainment, he submits to his client or customer adequate records or other sufficient evidence conforming to the requirements of paragraph (c) of this section.

(4) *Substantiation by client or customer.*—A client or customer shall not be required to substantiate, in accordance with the requirements of paragraph (c) of this section, reimbursements to an independent contractor for travel and gifts, or for entertainment unless the independent contractor has accounted to him (within the meaning of section 274(e)(4)(B) and subparagraph (3) of this paragraph) for such entertainment. If an independent contractor has so accounted to a client or customer for entertainment, the client or customer shall substantiate each element of the expenditure (as described in para-

>>>→ *Caution: Reg. §1.274-5A, below, applies to tax years beginning before January 1, 1986.*

graph (b) of this section) in accordance with the requirements of paragraph (c) of this section.

(h) *Authority for an optional method of computing meal expenses while traveling.*—The Commissioner may establish a method under which a taxpayer may elect to use a specified amount or amounts for meals while traveling in lieu of substantiating the actual cost of meals. The taxpayer would not be relieved of substantiating the actual cost of other travel expenses as well as the time, place, and business purpose of the travel. See paragraphs (b)(2) and (c) of this section.

(i) *Effective date.*—(1) *In general.*—Section 274(d) and this section apply with respect to taxable years ending after December 31, 1962, but only with respect to periods after that date.

(2) *Certain meal expenses.*—Paragraph (h) of this section is effective for expenses paid or incurred after December 31, 1982 [Reg. §1.274-5A.]

☐ [T.D. 6630, 12-27-62. Amended by T.D. 7226, 12-14-72, T.D. 7909, 9-6-83 and T.D. 8051, 9-6-85. Redesignated by T.D. 8715, 3-24-97.]

[Reg. §1.274-5T]

§1.274-5T. Substantiation requirements (temporary).—(a) *In general.*—For taxable years beginning on or after January 1, 1986, no deduction or credit shall be allowed with respect to—

(1) Traveling away from home (including meals and lodging),

(2) Any activity which is of a type generally considered to constitute entertainment, amusement, or recreation, or with respect to a facility used in connection with such an activity, including the items specified in section 274(e),

(3) Gifts defined in section 274(b), or

(4) Any listed property (as defined in section 280F(d)(4) and §1.280F-6T(b)),
unless the taxpayer substantiates each element of the expenditure or use (as described in paragraph (b) of this section) in the manner provided in paragraph (c) of this section. This limitation supersedes the doctrine founded in *Cohan v. Commissioner,* 39 F.2d 540 (2d Cir. 1930). The decision held that, where the evidence indicated a taxpayer incurred deductible travel or entertainment expenses but the exact amount could not be determined, the court should make a close approximation and not disallow the deduction entirely. Section 274(d) contemplates that no deduction or credit shall be allowed a taxpayer on the basis of such approximations or unsupported testimony of the taxpayer. For purposes of this section, the term "entertainment" means entertainment, amusement, or recreation, and use of a facility therefor; and the term "expenditure" includes expenses and items (including items such as loss and depreciation).

(b) *Elements of an expenditure or use.*—(1) *In general.*—Section 274(d) and this section contemplate that no deduction or credit shall be allowed for travel, entertainment, a gift, or with respect to listed property unless the taxpayer substantiates the requisite elements of each expenditure or use as set forth in this paragraph (b).

(2) *Travel away from home.*—The elements to be proved with respect to an expenditure for travel away from home are—

(i) *Amount.*—Amount of each separate expenditure for traveling away from home, such as cost of transportation or lodging, except that the daily cost of the traveler's own breakfast, lunch, and dinner and of expenditures incidental to such travel may be aggregated, if set forth in reasonable categories, such as for meals, for gasoline and oil, and for taxi fares;

(ii) *Time.*—Dates of departure and return for each trip away from home, and number of days away from home spent on business;

(iii) *Place.*—Destinations or locality of travel, described by name of city or town or other similar designation; and

(iv) *Business purpose.*—Business reason for travel or nature of the business benefit derived or expected to be derived as a result of travel.

(3) *Entertainment in general.*—The elements to be proved with respect to an expenditure for entertainment are—

(i) *Amount.*—Amount of each separate expenditure for entertainment, except that such incidental items as taxi fares or telephone calls may be aggregated on a daily basis;

(ii) *Time.*—Date of entertainment;

(iii) *Place.*—Name, if any, address or location, and designation of type of entertainment, such as dinner or theater, if such information is not apparent from the designation of the place;

(iv) *Business purpose.*—Business reason for the entertainment or nature of business benefit derived or expected to be derived as a result of the entertainment and, except in the case of business meals described in section 274(e)(1), the nature of any business discussion or activity;

(v) *Business relationship.*—Occupation or other information relating to the person or persons entertained, including name, title, or other designation, sufficient to establish business relationship to the taxpayer.

(4) *Entertainment directly preceding or following a substantial and bona fide business discussion.*—If a taxpayer claims a deduction for entertainment directly preceding or following a substantial and bona fide business discussion on the ground that such entertainment was associated with the active conduct of the taxpayer's trade or business, the elements to be proved with respect to such expenditure, in addition to those enumerated in paragraph (b)(3)(i), (ii), (iii), and (v) of this section are—

(i) *Time.*—Date and duration of business discussion;

(ii) *Place.*—Place of business discussion;

(iii) *Business purpose.*—Nature of business discussion, and business reason for the entertainment or nature of business benefit derived or expected to be derived as the result of the entertainment;

(iv) *Business relationship.*—Identification of those persons entertained who participated in the business discussion.

(5) *Gifts.*—The elements to be proved with respect to an expenditure for a gift are—

(i) *Amount.*—Cost of the gift to the taxpayer;

(ii) *Time.*—Date of the gift;

(iii) *Description.*—Description of the gift;

(iv) *Business purpose.*—Business reason for the gift or nature of business benefit derived or expected to be derived as a result of the gift; and

(v) *Business relationship.*—Occupation or other information relating to the recipient of the gift, including name, title, or other designation, sufficient to establish business relationship to the taxpayer.

(6) *Listed property.*—The elements to be proved with respect to any listed property are—

(i) *Amount.*—(A) *Expenditures.*—The amount of each separate expenditure with respect to an item of listed property, such as the cost of acquisition, the cost of capital improvements, lease payments, the cost of maintenance and repairs, or other expenditures, and

(B) *Uses.*—The amount of each business/investment use (as defined in §1.280F-6T(d)(3) and (e)), based on the appropriate measure (i.e., mileage for automobiles and other means of transportation and time for other listed property, unless the Commissioner approves an alternative method), and the total use of the listed property for the taxable period.

(ii) *Time.*—Date of the expenditure or use with respect to listed property, and

(iii) *Business or investment purpose.*—The business purpose for an expenditure or use with respect to any listed property (*see* §1.274-5T(c)(6)(i)(B) and (C) for special rules for the aggregation of expenditures and business use and §1.280F-6T(d)(2) for the distinction between qualified business use and business/investment use). *See also* §1.274-5T(e) relating to the substantiation of business use of employer-provided listed property and §1.274-6T for special rules for substantiating the business/investment use of certain types of listed property.

(c) *Rules of substantiation.*—(1) *In general.*—Except as otherwise provided in this section and §1.274-6T, a taxpayer must substantiate each element of an expenditure or use (described in paragraph (b) of this section) by adequate records or by sufficient evidence corroborating his own statement. Section 274(d) contemplates that a taxpayer will maintain and produce such substantiation as will constitute proof of each expenditure or use referred to in section 274. Written evidence has considerably more probative value than oral evidence alone. In addition, the probative value of written evidence is greater the closer in time it relates to the expenditure or use. A contemporaneous log is not required, but a record of the elements of an expenditure or of a business use of listed property made at or near the time of the expenditure or use, supported by sufficient documentary evidence, has a high degree of credibility not present with respect to a statement prepared subsequent thereto when generally there is a lack of accurate recall. Thus, the corroborative evidence required to support a statement not made at or near the time of the expenditure or use must have a high degree of probative value to elevate such statement and evidence to the level of credibility reflected by a record made at or near the time of the expenditure or use supported by sufficient documentary evidence. The substantiation requirements of section 274(d) are designed to encourage taxpayers to maintain the records, together with documentary evidence, as provided in paragraph (c)(2) of this section.

(2) *Substantiation by adequate records.*—(i) *In general.*—To meet the "adequate records" requirements of section 274(d), a taxpayer shall maintain an account book, diary, log, statement of expense, trip sheets, or similar record (as provided in paragraph (c)(2)(ii) of this section), and documentary evidence (as provided in paragraph (c)(2)(iii) of this section) which, in combination, are sufficient to establish each element of an expenditure or use specified in paragraph (b) of this section. It is not necessary to record information in an account book, diary, log, statement of expense, trip sheet, or similar record which duplicates information reflected on a receipt so long as the account book, etc., and receipt complement each other in an orderly manner.

(ii) *Account book, diary, etc.*—An account book, diary, log, statement of expense, trip sheet, or similar record must be prepared or maintained in such manner that each recording of an element of an expenditure or use is made at or near the time of the expenditure or use.

(A) *Made at or near the time of the expenditure or use.*—For purposes of this section, the phrase "made at or near the time of the expenditure or use" means the elements of an expenditure or use are recorded at a time when, in relation to the use or making of an expenditure, the taxpayer has full present knowledge of each element of the expenditure or use, such as the amount, time, place, and business purpose of the expenditure and business relationship. An expense account statement which is a transcription of an account book, diary, log, or similar record prepared or maintained in accordance with the provisions of this paragraph (c)(2)(ii) shall be considered a record prepared or maintained in the manner prescribed in the preceding sentence if such expense account statement is submitted by an employee to his employer or by an independent contractor to his client or customer in the regular course of good business practice. For example, a log maintained on a weekly basis, which accounts for use during the week, shall be considered a record made at or near the time of such use.

(B) *Substantiation of business purpose.*—In order to constitute an adequate record of business purpose within the meaning of section 274(d) and this paragraph (c)(2), a written statement of business purpose generally is required. However, the degree of substantiation necessary to establish business purpose will vary depending upon the facts and circumstances of each case. Where the business purpose is evident from the surrounding facts and circumstances, a written explanation of such business purpose will not be required. For example, in the case of a salesman calling on customers on an established sales route, a written explanation of the business purpose of such travel ordinarily will not be required. Similarly, in the case of a business meal described in section 274(e)(1), if the business purpose of such meal is evident from the business relationship to the taxpayer of the persons entertained and other surrounding circumstances, a written explanation of such business purpose will not be required.

(C) *Substantiation of business use of listed property.*—(1) *Degree of substantiation.*—In order to constitute an adequate record (within the meaning of section 274(d) and this paragraph (c)(2)(ii)), which substantiates business/investment use of listed property (as defined in § 1.280F-6T(d)(3)), the record must contain sufficient information as to each element of every business/investment use. However, the level of detail required in an adequate record to substantiate business/investment use may vary depending upon the facts and circumstances. For example, a taxpayer who uses a truck for both business and personal purposes and whose only business use of a truck is to make deliveries to customers on an established route may satisfy the adequate record requirement by recording the total number [of] miles driven during the taxable year, the length of the delivery route once, and the date of each trip at or near the time of the trips. Alternatively, the taxpayer may establish the date of each trip with a receipt, record of delivery, or other documentary evidence.

(2) *Written record.*—Generally, an adequate record must be written. However, a record of the business use of listed property, such as a computer or automobile, prepared in a computer memory

device with the aid of a logging program will constitute an adequate record.

(D) *Confidential information.*—If any information relating to the elements of an expenditure or use, such as place, business purpose, or business relationship, is of a confidential nature, such information need not be set forth in the account book, diary, log, statement of expense, trip sheet, or similar record, provided such information is recorded at or near the time of the expenditure or use and is elsewhere available to the district director to substantiate such element of the expenditure or use.

(iii) [Reserved].—For further guidance, see § 1.274-5(c)(2)(iii).

(iv) *Retention of written evidence.*—The Commissioner may, in his discretion, prescribe rules under which an employer may dispose of the adequate records and documentary evidence submitted to him by employees who are required to, and do, make an adequate accounting to the employer (within the meaning of paragraph (f)(4) of this section) if the employer maintains adequate accounting procedures with respect to such employees (within the meaning of paragraph (f)(5) of this section).

(v) *Substantial compliance.*—If a taxpayer has not fully substantiated a particular element of an expenditure or use, but the taxpayer establishes to the satisfaction of the district director that he has substantially complied with the "adequate records" requirements of this paragraph (c)(2) with respect to the expenditure or use, the taxpayer may be permitted to establish such element by evidence which the district director shall deem adequate.

(3) *Substantiation by other sufficient evidence.*—(i) *In general.*—If a taxpayer fails to establish to the satisfaction of the district director that he has substantially complied with the "adequate records" requirements of paragraph (c)(2) of this section with respect to an element of an expenditure or use, then, except as otherwise provided in this paragraph, the taxpayer must establish such element—

(A) By his own statement, whether written or oral, containing specific information in detail as to such element; and

(B) By other corroborative evidence sufficient to establish such element.

If such element is the description of a gift, or the cost or amount, time, place, or date of an expenditure or use, the corroborative evidence shall be direct evidence, such as a statement in writing or the oral testimony of persons entertained or other witnesses setting forth detailed information about such element, or the documentary evidence described in paragraph (c)(2) of this section. If such element is either the business relationship to the taxpayer of persons entertained, or the business purpose of an expenditure, the corroborative evidence may be circumstantial evidence.

(ii) *Sampling.*—(A) *In general.*—Except as provided in paragraph (c)(3)(ii)(B) of this section, a taxpayer may maintain an adequate record for portions of a taxable year and use that record to substantiate the business/investment use of listed property for all or a portion of the taxable year if the taxpayer can demonstrate by other evidence that the periods for which an adequate record is maintained are representative of the use for the taxable year or a portion thereof.

(B) *Exception for pooled vehicles.*—The sampling method of paragraph (c)(3)(ii)(A) of this section may not be used to substantiate the business/investment use of an automobile or other vehicle of an employer that is made available for use by more than one employee for all or a portion of a taxable year.

(C) *Examples.*—The following examples illustrate this paragraph (c)(3)(ii).

Example (1). A, a sole proprietor and calendar year taxpayer, operates an interior decorating business out of her home. A uses an automobile for local business travel to visit the homes or offices of clients, to meet with suppliers and other subcontractors, and to pick up and deliver certain items to clients when feasible. There is no other business use of the automobile but A and other members of her family also use the automobile for personal purposes. A maintains adequate records for the first three months of 1986 that indicate that 75 percent of the use of the automobile was in A's business. Invoices from subcontractors and paid bills indicate that A's business continued at approximately the same rate for the remainder of 1986. If other circumstances do not change (e.g., A does not obtain a second car for exclusive use in her business), the determination that the business/investment use of the automobile for the taxable year is 75 percent is based on sufficient corroborative evidence.

Example (2). The facts are the same as in example (1), except that A maintains adequate records during the first week of every month, which indicate that 75 percent of the use of the automobile is in A's business. The invoices from A's business indicate that A's business continued at the same rate during the subsequent weeks of each month so that A's weekly records are representative of each month's business use of the automobile. Thus, the determination that the business/investment use of the automobile for the taxable year is 75 percent is based on sufficient corroborative evidence.

Example (3). B, a sole proprietor and calendar year taxpayer, is a salesman in a large metropolitan area for a company that manufactures household products. For the first three weeks of each month, B uses his own automobile occasionally to travel within the metropolitan area on business. During these three weeks, B's use of the automobile for business purposes does not follow a consistent pattern from day to day or week to week. During the fourth week of each month, B delivers to his customers all the orders taken during the previous month. B's use of his automobile for business purposes, as substantiated by adequate records, is 70 percent of the total use during that fourth week. In this example, a determination based on the records maintained during that fourth week that the business/investment use of the automobile for the taxable year is 70 percent is not based on sufficient corroborative evidence because use during this week is not representative of use during other periods.

(iii) *Special rules.*—See §1.274-6T for special rules for substantiation by sufficient corroborating evidence with respect to certain listed property.

(4) *Substantiation in exceptional circumstances.*—If a taxpayer establishes that, by reason of the inherent nature of the situation—

(i) He was unable to obtain evidence with respect to an element of the expenditure or use which conforms fully to the "adequate records" requirements of paragraph (c)(2) of this section,

(ii) He is unable to obtain evidence with respect to such element which conforms fully to the "other sufficient evidence" requirements of paragraph (c)(3) of this section, and

(iii) He has presented other evidence, with respect to such element, which possesses the highest degree of probative value possible under the circumstances, such other evidence shall be considered to satisfy the substantiation requirements of section 274(d) and this paragraph.

(5) *Loss of records due to circumstances beyond control of the taxpayer.*—Where the taxpayer establishes that the failure to produce adequate records is due to the loss of such records through circumstances beyond the taxpayer's control, such as destruction by fire, flood, earthquake, or other casualty, the taxpayer shall have a right to substantiate a deduction by reasonable reconstruction of his expenditures or use.

(6) *Special rules.*—(i) *Separate expenditure or use.*—(A) *In general.*—For the purposes of this section, each separate payment or use by the taxpayer shall ordinarily be considered to constitute a separate expenditure. However, concurrent or repetitious expenses or uses may be substantiated as a single item. To illustrate the above rules, where a taxpayer entertains a business guest at dinner and thereafter at the theater, the payment for dinner shall be considered to constitute one expenditure and the payment for the tickets for the theater shall be considered to constitute a separate expenditure. Similarly, if during a day of business travel a taxpayer makes separate payments for breakfast, lunch, and dinner, he shall be considered to have made three separate expenditures. However, if during entertainment at a cocktail lounge the taxpayer pays separately for each serving of refreshments, the total amount expended for the refreshments will be treated as a single expenditure. A tip may be treated as a separate expenditure.

(B) *Aggregation of expenditures.*—Except as otherwise provided in this section, the account book, diary, log, statement of expense, trip sheet, or similar record required by paragraph (c)(2)(ii) of this section shall be maintained with respect to each separate expenditure and not with respect to aggregate amounts for two or more expenditures. Thus, each expenditure for such items as lodging and air or rail travel shall be recorded as a separate item and not aggregated. However, at the option of the taxpayer, amounts expended for breakfast, lunch, or dinner, may be aggregated. A tip or gratuity which is related to an underlying expense may be aggregated with such expense. In addition, amounts expended in connection with the use of listed property during a taxable year, such as for gasoline or repairs for an automobile, may be aggregated. If these expenses are aggregated, the taxpayer must establish the date and amount, but need not prove the business purpose of each expenditure. Instead, the taxpayer may prorate the expenses based on the total business use of the listed property. For other provisions permitting recording of aggregate amounts in an account book, diary, log, statement of expense, trip sheet, or similar record, see paragraphs (b)(2)(i) and (b)(3) of this section (relating to incidental costs of travel and entertainment).

(C) *Aggregation of business use.*—Uses which may be considered part of a single use, for example, a round trip or uninterrupted

business use, may be accounted for by a single record. For example, use of a truck to make deliveries at several different locations which begins and ends at the business premises and which may include a stop at the business premises in between two deliveries may be accounted for by a single record of miles driven. In addition, use of a passenger automobile by a salesman for a business trip away from home over a period of time may be accounted for by a single record of miles traveled. De minimis personal use (such as a stop for lunch on the way between two business stops) is not an interruption of business use.

(ii) *Allocation of expenditure.*—For purposes of this section, if a taxpayer has established the amount of an expenditure, but is unable to establish the portion of such amount which is attributable to each person participating in the event giving rise to the expenditure, such amount shall be allocated ordinarily to each participant on a pro rata basis, if such determination is material. Accordingly, the total number of persons for whom a travel or entertainment expenditure is incurred must be established in order to compute the portion of the expenditure allocable to each such person.

(iii) *Primary use of a facility.*—Section 274(a)(1)(B) and (2)(C) deny a deduction for any expenditure paid or incurred before January 1, 1979, with respect to a facility, or paid or incurred before January 1, 1994, with respect to a club, used in connection with an entertainment activity unless the taxpayer establishes that the facility (including a club) was used primarily for the furtherance of the taxpayer's trade or business. A determination whether a facility before January 1, 1979, or a club before January 1, 1994, was used primarily for the furtherance of the taxpayer's trade or business will depend upon the facts and circumstances of each case. In order to establish that a facility was used primarily for the furtherance of his trade or business, the taxpayer shall maintain records of the use of the facility, the cost of using the facility, mileage or its equivalent (if appropriate), and such other information as shall tend to establish such primary use. Such records of use shall contain—

(A) For each use of the facility claimed to be in furtherance of the taxpayer's trade or business, the elements of an expenditure specified in paragraph (b)(3) of this section, and

(B) For each use of the facility not in furtherance of the taxpayer's trade or business, an appropriate description of such use, including cost, date, number of persons entertained, nature of entertainment and, if applicable, information such as mileage or its equivalent. A notation such as "personal use" or "family use" would, in the case of such use, be sufficient to describe the nature of entertainment.

If a taxpayer fails to maintain adequate records concerning a facility which is likely to serve the personal purposes of the taxpayer, it shall be presumed that the use of such facility was primarily personal.

(iv) *Additional information.*—In a case where it is necessary to obtain additional information, either—

(A) To clarify information contained in records, statements, testimony, or documentary evidence submitted by a taxpayer under the provisions of paragraph (c)(2) or (c)(3) of this section, or

(B) To establish the reliability or accuracy of such records, statements, testimony, or documentary evidence,

the district director may, notwithstanding any other provision of this section, obtain such additional information by personal interview or otherwise as he determines necessary to implement properly the provisions of section 274 and the regulations thereunder.

(7) *Specific exceptions.*—Except as otherwise prescribed by the Commissioner, substantiation otherwise required by this paragraph is not required for—

(i) Expenses described in section 274(e)(2) relating to food and beverages for employees, section 274(e)(3) relating to expenses treated as compensation, section 274(e)(8) relating to items available to the public, and section 274(e)(9) relating to entertainment sold to customers, or

(ii) Expenses described in section 274(e)(5) relating to recreational, etc., expenses for employees, except that a taxpayer shall keep such records or other evidence as shall establish that such expenses were for activities (or facilities used in connection therewith) primarily for the benefit of employees other than employees who are officers, shareholders or other owners (as defined in section 274(e)(5)), or highly compensated employees.

(d) *Disclosure on returns.*—(1) *In general.*—The Commissioner may, in his discretion, prescribe rules under which any taxpayer claiming a deduction or credit for entertainment, gifts, travel, or with respect to listed property, or any other person receiving advances, reimbursements, or allowances for such items, shall make disclosure on his tax return with respect to such items. The provisions of this paragraph shall apply notwithstanding the provisions of paragraph (f) of this section.

(2) *Business use of passenger automobiles and other vehicles.*—(i) On returns for taxable years beginning after December 31, 1984, taxpayers that claim a deduction or credit with respect to any vehicle are required to answer certain questions providing information about the use of the vehicle. The information required on the tax return relates to mileage (total, business, commuting, and other personal mileage), percentage of business use, date placed in service, use of other vehicles, after-work use, whether the taxpayer has evidence to support the business use claimed on the return, and whether or not the evidence is written.

(ii) Any employer that provides the use of a vehicle to an employee must obtain information from the employee sufficient to complete the employer's tax return. Any employer that provides more than five vehicles to its employees need not include any information on its return. The employer, instead, must obtain the information from its employees, indicate on its return that it has obtained the information, and retain the information received. Any employer—

(A) That can satisfy the requirements of §1.274-6T(a)(2), relating to vehicles not used for personal purposes,

(B) That can satisfy the requirements of §1.274-6T(a)(3), relating to vehicles not used for personal purposes other than commuting, or

(C) That treats all use of vehicles by employees as personal use

need not obtain information with respect to those vehicles, but instead must indicate on its return that it has vehicles exempt from the requirements of this paragraph (d)(2).

(3) *Business use of other listed property.*—On returns for taxable years beginning after December 31, 1984, taxpayers that claim a deduction or credit with respect to any listed property other than a vehicle (for example, a yacht, airplane, or certain computers) are required to provide the following information:

(i) The date that the property was placed in service,

(ii) The percentage of business use,

(iii) Whether evidence is available to support the percentage of business use claimed on the return, and

(iv) Whether the evidence is written.

(e) *Substantiation of the business use of listed property made available by an employer for use by an employee.*—(1) *Employee.*—(i) *In general.*—An employee may not exclude from gross income as a working condition fringe any amount of the value of the availability of listed property provided by an employer to the employee, unless the employee substantiates for the period of availability the amount of the exclusion in accordance with the requirements of section 274(d) and either this section or §1.274-6T.

(ii) *Vehicles treated as used entirely for personal purposes.*—If an employer includes the value of the availability of a vehicle (as defined in §1.61-21(e)(2)) in an employee's gross income without taking into account any exclusion for a working condition fringe allowable under section 132 and the regulations thereunder with respect to the vehicle, the employee must substantiate any deduction claimed under §§1.162-25 and 1.162-25T for the business/investment use of the vehicle in accordance with the requirements of section 274(d) and either this section or §1.274-6T.

(2) *Employer.*—(i) *In general.*—An employer substantiates its business/investment use of listed property by showing either—

(A) That, based on evidence that satisfies the requirements of section 274(d) or statements submitted by employees that summarize such evidence, all or a portion of the use of the listed property is by employees in the employer's trade or business and, if any employee used the property for personal purposes, the employer included an appropriate amount in the employee's income, or

(B) In the case of a vehicle, the employer treats all use by employees as personal use and includes an appropriate amount in the employees' income.

(ii) *Reliance on employee records.*—For purposes of substantiating the business/investment use of listed property that an employer provides to an employee and for purposes of the information required by paragraph (d)(2) and (3) of this section, the employer may rely on adequate records maintained by the employee or on the employee's own statement if corroborated by other sufficient evidence unless the employer knows or has reason to know that the statement, records, or other evidence are not accurate. The employer must retain a copy of the adequate records maintained by the employee or the other sufficient evidence, if available. Alternatively, the employer may rely on a statement submitted by the employee that provides sufficient information to allow the employer to determine the business/investment use of the property unless the employer knows or has reason to know that the statement is not based on adequate records or on the employee's own statement corroborated by other sufficient evidence. If the employer relies on the employee's state-

ment, the employer must retain only a copy of the statement. The employee must retain a copy of the adequate records or other evidence.

(f) *Reporting and substantiation of expenses of certain employees for travel, entertainment, gifts, and with respect to listed property.*—(1) *In general.*—The purpose of this paragraph is to provide rules for reporting and substantiation of certain expenses paid or incurred by employees in connection with the performance of services as employees. For purposes of this paragraph, the term "business expenses" means ordinary and necessary expenses for travel, entertainment, gifts, or with respect to listed property which are deductible under section 162, and the regulations thereunder, to the extent not disallowed by sections 262, 274(c), and 280F. Thus, the term "business expenses" does not include personal, living, or family expenses disallowed by section 262, travel expenses disallowed by section 274(c), or cost recovery deductions and credits with respect to listed property disallowed by section 280F(d)(3) because the use of such property is not for the convenience of the employer and required as a condition of employment. Except as provided in paragraph (f)(2), advances, reimbursements, or allowances for such expenditures must be reported as income by the employee.

(2) *Reporting of expenses for which the employee is required to make an adequate accounting to his employer.*—(i) *Reimbursements equal to expenses.*—For purposes of computing tax liability, an employee need not report on his tax return business expenses for travel, transportation, entertainment, gifts, or with respect to listed property, paid or incurred by him solely for the benefit of his employer for which he is required to, and does, make an adequate accounting to his employer (as defined in paragraph (f)(4) of this section) and which are charged directly or indirectly to the employer (for example, through credit cards) or for which the employee is paid through advances, reimbursements, or otherwise, provided that the total amount of such advances, reimbursements, and charges is equal to such expenses.

(ii) *Reimbursements in excess of expenses.*—In case the total of the amounts charged directly or indirectly to the employer or received from the employer as advances, reimbursements, or otherwise, exceeds the business expenses paid or incurred by the employee and the employee is required to, and does, make an adequate accounting to his employer for such expenses, the employee must include such excess (including amounts received for expenditures not deductible by him) in income.

(iii) *Expenses in excess of reimbursement.*—If an employee incurs deductible business expenses on behalf of his employer which exceed the total of the amounts charged directly or indirectly to the employer and received from the employer as advances, reimbursements, or otherwise, and the employee makes an adequate accounting to his employer, the employee must be able to substantiate any deduction for such excess with such records and supporting evidence as will substantiate each element of an expenditure (described in paragraph (b) of this section) in accordance with paragraph (c) of this section.

(3) *Reporting of expenses for which the employee is not required to make an adequate accounting to his employer.*—If the employee is not required to make an adequate accounting to his employer for his business expenses or, though required, fails to make an adequate accounting for such expenses, he must submit, as a part of his tax return, the appropriate form issued by the Internal Revenue Service for claiming deductions for employee business expenses (e.g., Form 2106, Employee Business Expenses, for 1985) and provide the information requested on that form, including the information required by paragraph (d)(2) and (3) of this section if the employee's business expenses are with respect to the use of listed property. In addition, the employee must maintain such records and supporting evidence as will substantiate each element of an expenditure or use (described in paragraph (b) of this section) in accordance with paragraph (c) of this section.

(4) [Reserved].—For further guidance, see §1.274-5(f)(4).

(5) *Substantiation of expenditures by certain employees.*—An employee who makes an adequate accounting to his employer within the meaning of this paragraph will not again be required to substantiate such expense account information except in the following cases:

(i) An employee whose business expenses exceed the total of amounts charged to his employer and amounts received through advances, reimbursements or otherwise and who claims a deduction on his return for such excess,

(ii) An employee who is related to his employer within the meaning of section 267(b), but for this purpose the percentage referred to in section 267(b)(2) shall be 10 percent, and

(iii) Employees in cases where it is determined that the accounting procedures used by the employer for the reporting and substantiation of expenses by such employees are not adequate, or where it cannot be determined that such procedures are adequate. The district director will determine whether the employer's accounting procedures are adequate by considering the facts and circumstances of each case, including the use of proper internal controls. For example, an employer should require that an expense account be verified and approved by a reasonable person other than the person incurring such expenses. Accounting procedures will be considered inadequate to the extent that the employer does not require an adequate accounting from his employees as defined in paragraph (f)(4) of this section, or does not maintain such substantiation. To the extent an employer fails to maintain adequate accounting procedures he will thereby obligate his employees to substantiate separately their expense account information.

(g) [Reserved].—For further guidance, see §1.274-5(g).

(h) *Reporting and substantiation of certain reimbursements of persons other than employees.*—(1) *In general.*—The purpose of this paragraph is to provide rules for the reporting and substantiation of certain expenses for travel, entertainment, gifts, or with respect to listed property paid or incurred by one person (hereinafter termed "independent contractor") in connection with services performed for another person other than an employer (hereinafter termed "client or customer") under a reimbursement or other expense allowance arrangement with such client or customer. For purposes of this paragraph, the term "business expenses" means ordinary and necessary expenses for travel, entertainment, gifts, or with respect to listed property which are deductible under section 162, and the regulations thereunder, to the extent not disallowed by sections 262 and 274(c). Thus, the term "business expenses" does not include personal, living, or family expenses disallowed by section 262 or travel expenses disallowed by section 274(c), and reimbursements for such expenditures must be reported as income by the independent contractor. For purposes of this paragraph, the term "reimbursements" means advances, allowances, or reimbursements received by an independent contractor for travel, entertainment, gifts, or with respect to listed property in connection with the performance by him of services for his client or customer, under a reimbursement or other expense allowance arrangement with his client or customer, and includes amounts charged directly or indirectly to the client or customer through credit card systems or otherwise. *See* paragraph (j) of this section relating to the substantiation of meal expenses while traveling away from home.

(2) *Substantiation by independent contractors.*—An independent contractor shall substantiate, with respect to his reimbursements, each element of an expenditure (described in paragraph (b) of this section) in accordance with the requirements of paragraph (c) of this section; and, to the extent he does not so substantiate, he shall include such reimbursements in income. An independent contractor shall so substantiate a reimbursement for entertainment regardless of whether he accounts (within the meaning of paragraph (d)(3) of this section) for such entertainment.

(3) *Accounting to a client or customer under section 274(e)(4)(B).*—Section 274(e)(4)(B) provides that section 274(a) (relating to disallowance of expenses for entertainment) shall not apply to expenditures for entertainment for which an independent contractor has been reimbursed if the independent contractor accounts to his client or customer, to the extent provided by section 274(d). For purposes of section 274(e)(4)(B), an independent contractor shall be considered to account to his client or customer for an expense paid or incurred under a reimbursement or other expense allowance arrangement with his client or customer if, with respect to such expense for entertainment, he submits to his client or customer adequate records or other sufficient evidence conforming to the requirements of paragraph (c) of this section.

(4) *Substantiation by client or customer.*—A client or customer shall not be required to substantiate, in accordance with the requirements of paragraph (c) of this section, reimbursements to an independent contractor for travel and gifts, or for entertainment unless the independent contractor has accounted to him (within the meaning of section 274(e)(4)(B) and paragraph (h)(3) of this section) for such entertainment. If an independent contractor has so accounted to a client or customer for entertainment, the client or customer shall substantiate each element of the expenditure (as described in paragraph (b) of this section) in accordance with the requirements of paragraph (c) of this section.

(i) [Reserved].

(j) [Reserved]. For further guidance, see §1.274-5(j).

(k) and (l) [Reserved]. For further guidance, see §1.274-5(k) and (l).

(m) *Effective date.*—Section 274(d), as amended by the Tax Reform Act of 1984 and Public Law 99-44, and this section (except as pro-vided in paragraph (d)(2) and (3) of this section) apply with respect to taxable years beginning after December 31, 1985. Section 274(d) and this section apply to any deduction or credit claimed in a taxable year beginning after December 31, 1985, with respect to any listed property, regardless of the taxable year in which the property was placed in service. However, except as provided in §1.132-5(h) with respect to qualified nonpersonal use vehicles, the substantiation requirements of section 274(d) and this section do not apply to the determination of an employee's working condition fringe exclusion or to the determination under §1.162-25(b) of an employee's deduction before the date that those requirements apply, under this paragraph (m), to the employer, if the employer is taxable. Paragraph (j)(3) of this section applies to expenses paid or incurred after September 30, 2002. [Temporary Reg. §1.274-5T.]

☐ [T.D. 8061, 10-31-85. *Amended by* T.D. 8063, 12-18-85; T.D. 8276, 12-7-89; T.D. 8451, 12-4-92; T.D. 8601, 7-18-95; T.D. 8715, 3-24-97; T.D. 8864, 1-21-2000; T.D. 9020, 11-8-2002; T.D. 9064, 6-30-2003 and T.D. 9483, 5-18-2010.]

[Reg. §1.274-6]

§1.274-6. **Expenditures deductible without regard to trade or business or other income producing activity.**—The provisions of §§1.274-1 through 1.274-5, inclusive, do not apply to any deduction allowable to the taxpayer without regard to its connection with the taxpayer's trade or business or other income producing activity. Examples of such items are interest, taxes such as real property taxes, and casualty losses. Thus, if a taxpayer owned a fishing camp, the taxpayer could still deduct mortgage interest and real property taxes in full even if deductions for its use are not allowable under section 274(a) and §1.274-2. In the case of a taxpayer which is not an individual, the provisions of this section shall be applied as if it were an individual. Thus, if a corporation sustains a casualty loss on an entertainment facility used in its trade or business, it could deduct the loss even though deductions for the use of the facility are not allowable. [Reg. §1.274-6.]

☐ [T.D. 6659, 6-24-63. *Amended by* T.D. 8051, 9-6-85.]

[Reg. §1.274-6T]

§1.274-6T. **Substantiation with respect to certain types of listed property for taxable years beginning after 1985 (temporary).**—(a) *Written policy statements as to vehicles.*—(1) *In general.*—Two types of written policy statements satisfying the conditions described in paragraph (a)(2) and (3) of this section, if initiated and kept by an employer to implement a policy of no personal use, or no personal use except for commuting, of a vehicle provided by the employer, qualify as sufficient evidence corroborating the taxpayer's own statement and therefore will satisfy the employer's substantiation requirements under section 274(d). Therefore, the employer need not keep a separate set of records for purposes of the employer's substantiation requirements under section 274(d) with respect to use of a vehicle satisfying these written policy statement rules. A written policy statement adopted by a governmental unit as to employee use of its vehicles is eligible for these exceptions to the section 274(d) substantiation rules. Thus, a resolution of a city council or a provision of state law or a state constitution would qualify as a written policy statement, as long as the conditions described in paragraph (a)(2) and (3) of this section are met.

(2) *Vehicles not used for personal purposes.*—(i) *Employers.*—A policy statement that prohibits personal use by an employee satisfies an employer's substantiation requirements under section 274(d) if all the following conditions are met—

(A) The vehicle is owned or leased by the employer and is provided to one or more employees for use in connection with the employer's trade or business,

(B) When the vehicle is not used in the employer's trade or business, it is kept on the employer's business premises, unless it is temporarily located elsewhere, for example, for maintenance or because of a mechanical failure,

(C) No employee using the vehicle lives at the employer's business premises,

(D) Under a written policy of the employer, neither an employee, nor any individual whose use would be taxable to the employee, may use the vehicle for personal purposes, except for de minimis personal use (such as a stop for lunch between two business deliveries), and

(E) The employer reasonably believes that, except for de minimis use, neither the employee, nor any individual whose use would be taxable to the employee, uses the vehicle for any personal purpose.

There must also be evidence that would enable the Commissioner to determine whether the use of the vehicle meets the preceding five conditions.

(ii) *Employees.*—An employee, in lieu of substantiating the business/investment use of an employer-provided vehicle under §1.274-5T, may treat all use of the vehicle as business/investment use if the following conditions are met—

(A) The vehicle is owned or leased by the employer and is provided to one or more employees for use in connection with the employer's trade or business,

(B) When the vehicle is not used in the employer's trade or business, it is kept on the employer's business premises, unless it is temporarily located elsewhere, for example, for maintenance or because of a mechanical failure,

(C) No employee using the vehicle lives at the employer's business premises,

(D) Under a written policy of the employer, neither the employee, nor any individual whose use would be taxable to the employee, may use the vehicle for personal purposes, except for de minimis personal use (such as a stop for lunch between two business deliveries), and

(E) Except for de minimis personal use, neither the employee, nor any individual whose use would be taxable to the employee, uses the vehicle for any personal purpose.

There must also be evidence that would enable the Commissioner to determine whether the use of the vehicle meets the preceding five conditions.

(3) *Vehicles not used for personal purposes other than commuting.*—(i) *Employers.*—A policy statement that prohibits personal use by an employee, other than commuting, satisfies an employer's substantiation requirements under section 274(d) if all the following conditions are met—

(A) The vehicle is owned or leased by the employer and is provided to one or more employees for use in connection with the employer's trade or business and is used in the employer's trade or business,

(B) For bona fide noncompensatory business reasons, the employer requires the employee to commute to and/or from work in the vehicle,

(C) The employer has established a written policy under which neither the employee, nor any individual whose use would be taxable to the employee, may use the vehicle for personal purposes, other than for commuting or de minimis personal use (such as a stop for a personal errand on the way between a business delivery and the employee's home),

(D) The employer reasonably believes that, except for de minimis personal use, neither the employee, nor any individual whose use would be taxable to the employee, uses the vehicle for any personal purpose other than commuting,

(E) The employee required to use the vehicle for commuting is not a control employee (as defined in §1.61-21(f)(5) and (6)) required to use an automobile (as defined in §1.61-21(d)(1)(ii)) and

(F) The employer accounts for the commuting use by including in the employee's gross income the commuting value provided in §1.61-21(f)(3) (to the extent not reimbursed by the employee).

There must be evidence that would enable the Commissioner to determine whether the use of the vehicle met the preceding six conditions.

(ii) *Employees.*—An employee, in lieu of substantiating the business/investment use of an employer-provided vehicle under §1.274-5T, may substantiate any exclusion allowed under section 132 for a working condition fringe by including in income the commuting value of the vehicle (determined by the employer pursuant to §1.61-21(f)(3)) if all the following conditions are met:

(A) The vehicle is owned or leased by the employer and is provided to one or more employees for use in connection with the employer's trade or business and is used in the employer's trade or business,

(B) For bona fide noncompensatory business reasons, the employer requires the employee to commute to and/or from work in the vehicle,

(C) Under a written policy of the employer, neither the employee, nor any individual whose use would be taxable to the employee, may use the vehicle for personal purposes, other than for commuting or de minimis personal use (such as a stop for a personal errand on the way between a business delivery and the employee's home),

(D) Except for de minimis personal use, neither the employee, nor any individual whose use would be taxable to the employee, uses the vehicle for any personal purpose other than commuting,

(E) The employee required to use the vehicle for commuting is not a control employee (as defined in §1.61-21(f)(5) and (6) required to use an automobile (as defined in §1.61-21(d)(1)(ii), and

(F) The employee includes in gross income the commuting value determined by the employer as provided in §1.61-21(f)(3) (to the extent that the employee does not reimburse the employer for the commuting use).

There must also be evidence that would enable the Commissioner to determine whether the use of the vehicle met the preceding six conditions.

(b) *Vehicles used in connection with the business of farming.*—(1) *In general.*—If, during a taxable year or shorter period, a vehicle, not otherwise described in section 274(i), §1.274-5T(k), or paragraph (a)(2) or (3) of this section, is owned or leased by an employer and used during most of a normal business day directly in connection with the business of farming (as defined in paragraph (b)(2) of this section), the employer, in lieu of substantiating the use of the vehicle as prescribed in §1.274-5T(b)(6)(i)(B), may determine any deduction or credit with respect to the vehicle as if the business/investment use (as defined in §1.280F-6T(d)(3)(i)) and the qualified business use (as defined in §1.280F-6T(d)(2)) of the vehicle in the business of farming for the taxable year or shorter period were 75 percent plus that percentage, if any, attributable to an amount included in an employee's gross income. If the vehicle is also available for personal use by employees, the employer must include the value of that personal use in the gross income of the employees, allocated among them in the manner prescribed in §1.132-5(g).

(2) *Directly in connection with the business of farming.*—The phrase "directly in connection with the business of farming" means that the vehicle must be used directly in connection with the business of operating a farm (i.e., cultivating land or raising or harvesting any agricultural or horticultural commodity, or the raising, shearing, feeding, caring for, training, and management of animals) or incidental thereto (for example, trips to the feed and supply store).

(3) *Substantiation by employees.*—If an employee is provided with the use of a vehicle to which this paragraph (b) applies, the employee may, in lieu of substantiating the business/investment use of the vehicle in the manner prescribed in §1.274-5T, substantiate any exclusion allowed under section 132 for a working condition fringe as if the business/investment use of the vehicle were 75 percent, plus that percentage, if any, determined by the employer to be attributable to the use of the vehicle by individuals other than the employee, provided that the employee includes in gross income the amount determined by the employer as includible in the employee's gross income. See §1.132-5(g)(3) for examples illustrating the allocation of use of a vehicle among employees.

(c) *Vehicles treated as used entirely for personal purposes.*—An employer may satisfy the substantiation requirements under section 274(d) for a taxable year or shorter period with respect to the business use of a vehicle that is provided to an employee by including the value of the availability of the vehicle during the relevant period in the employee's gross income without any exclusion for a working condition fringe with respect to the vehicle and, if required, by withholding any taxes. Under these circumstances, the employer's business/investment use of the vehicle during the relevant period is 100 percent. The employer's qualified business use of the vehicle is dependent upon the relationship of the employee to the employer (see §1.280F-6T(d)(2)).

(d) *Limitation.*—If a taxpayer chooses to satisfy the substantiation requirements of section 274(d) and §1.274-5T by using one of the methods prescribed in paragraphs (a)(2) or (3), (b), or (c) of this section and files a return with the Internal Revenue Service for a taxable year consistent with such choice, the taxpayer may not later use another of these methods. Similarly, if a taxpayer chooses to satisfy the substantiation requirements of section 274(d) in the manner prescribed in §1.274-5T and files a return with the Internal Revenue Service for a taxable year consistent with such choice, the taxpayer may not later use a method prescribed in paragraph (a)(2) or (3), (b), or (c) of this section. This rule applies to an employee for purposes of substantiating any working condition fringe exclusion as well as to an employer. For example, if an employee excludes on his federal income tax return for a taxable year 90 percent of the value of the availability of an employer-provided automobile on the basis of records that allegedly satisfy the "adequate records" requirement of §1.274-5T(c)(2), and that requirement is not satisfied, then the employee may not satisfy the substantiation requirements of section 274(d) for the taxable year by any method prescribed in this section, but may present other corroborative evidence as prescribed in §1.274-5T(c)(3).

(e) *Definitions.*—(1) *In general.*—The definitions provided in this paragraph (e) apply for purposes of section 274(d), §1.274-5T, and this section.

(2) *Employer and employee.*—The terms "employer" and "employee" include the following:

(i) A sole proprietor shall be treated as both an employer and employee,

(ii) A partnership shall be treated as an employer of its partners, and

(iii) A partner shall be treated as an employee of the partnership.

(3) *Automobile.*—The term "automobile" has the same meaning as prescribed in §1.61-21(d)(1)(ii).

(4) *Vehicle.*—The term "vehicle" has the same meaning as prescribed in §1.61-21(e)(2).

(5) *Personal use.*—"Personal use" by an employee of an employer-provided vehicle includes use in any trade or business other than the trade or business of being the employee of the employer providing the vehicle.

(f) *Effective date.*—This section is effective for taxable years beginning after December 31, 1985. [Temporary Reg. §1.274-6T.]

☐ [*T.D. 8061*, 10-31-85. *Amended by T.D. 8063*, 12-18-85 *and T.D. 9849*, 3-11-2019.]

[Reg. §1.274-7]

§1.274-7. Treatment of certain expenditures with respect to entertainment-type facilities.—If deductions are disallowed under §1.274-2 with respect to any portion of a facility, such portion shall be treated as an asset which is used for personal, living, and family purposes (and not as an asset used in a trade or business). Thus, the basis of such a facility will be adjusted for purposes of computing depreciation deductions and determining gain or loss on the sale of such facility in the same manner as other property (for example, a residence) which is regarded as used partly for business and partly for personal purposes. [Reg. §1.274-7.]

☐ [*T.D. 6659*, 6-24-63.]

[Reg. §1.274-8]

§1.274-8. Effective/applicability date.—Except as provided in §§1.274-2(a), 1.274-2(e), 1.274-2(f)(2)(iv)(F), and 1.274-5, §§1.274-1 through 1.274-7 apply to taxable years ending after December 31, 1962. [Reg. §1.274-8.]

☐ [*T.D. 6659*, 6-24-63. *Amended by T.D. 8051*, 9-6-85 *and T.D. 9625*, 7-31-2013.]

[Reg. §5e.274-8]

§5e.274-8. Travel Expenses of Members of Congress (Temporary).—(a) *In general.*—Members of Congress (including any Delegate and Resident Commissioner) who are away from home within the meaning of section 162(a), in the Washington, D.C. area, may elect in accordance with paragraph (f) to deduct an amount described in paragraph (c) as living expenses, without substantiation. A Member who elects under this section may not deduct any amount for the living expenses described in paragraph (b). A Member who does not make an election under this section must substantiate his expenses for living in Washington, D.C. in accordance with section 274 and §1.274-5.

(b) *Living expenses covered.*—The amount allowed to be deducted without substantiation, pursuant to this section, for costs incurred for living in the Washington, D.C. area represents amounts expended for meals, lodging, and other incidental expenses. Meals include the actual cost of the food and expenses incident to the preparation and serving thereof. Lodging includes amounts paid for rent, care of premises, utilities, insurance and depreciation of household furnishings owned by the Member. In the case of a Member who lives in a residence owned by him in the Washington, D.C. area, the cost of lodging also includes depreciation on such residence. Other incidental expenses include laundry, cleaning, and local transportation. Local transportation includes travel within a 50 mile radius of Washington, D.C., whether by private automobile, taxicab or other transportation for hire. Interest and taxes on personal property will not be considered expenses to be included within this paragraph.

(c)(1) *Amounts allowed without substantiation.*—The amount that may be deducted pursuant to section 162 and these regulations is an amount equal to the product of the number of Congressional days in the taxable year, multiplied by the designated amount. The designated amount is—

(i) In the case of a Member who deducts interest and taxes attributable to the ownership of a personal residence in the Washington, D.C. area, two-thirds of the maximum amount of actual subsistence for Washington, D.C. payable pursuant to 5 U.S.C. 5702(c), or

(ii) In the case of a Member not described in paragraph (c)(1)(i), the maximum amount of actual subsistence for Washington, D.C. payable pursuant to 5 U.S.C. 5702(c).

A Member who incurs interest and taxes on his residence in the Washington, D.C. area may forego the deduction of such amounts and use the designated amount prescribed by paragraph (c)(1)(ii).

(2) If a Member, who lives in a residence owned by him in the Washington, D.C. area, chooses to deduct amounts prescribed in paragraph (c)(1), the Member must treat as an adjustment to the basis of such residence an amount equal to 20 percent of the maximum amount of actual subsistence multiplied by the number of Congressional days. Such adjustments will be considered a proper adjustment for exhaustion, wear, and tear under this subtitle.

(d) *Congressional days.*—The number of Congressional days with respect to a Member is the number of days in the taxable year less the number of days in periods in which the Member's Congressional chamber was not in session for 5 consecutive days or more (including Saturday and Sunday). The number of days with respect to a Member is determined without regard to whether or not the Member was in the Washington, D.C. area on such days.

(e) *Other deductible amounts.*—This section does not preclude the deduction of otherwise allowable expenses for travel fares (other than local travel in the Washington, D.C.), long distance telephone and telegraph, and travel expenses incurred other than in the Washington, D.C. area. However, such expenses are subject to the substantiation requirements of section 274.

(f) *Election.*—To elect to deduct the amounts prescribed by this section, a Member must attach to his return for the taxable year a statement indicating, (1) that the deduction for travel expenses while living in the Washington, D.C. area are computed pursuant to §5e.274-8, and (2) whether a separate deduction is being taken for interest and taxes paid or incurred with respect to the personal residence of the Member if in the Washington, D.C. area.

(g) *Effective date.*—This section is effective for taxable year beginning after December 31, 1980.

(h) *Examples.*—The following examples are based on a calendar from a Final Edition of the Calendar of the United States, House of Representatives and History of Legislation. The marked days indicate days the House of Representatives was in session.

198X

JANUARY
Sun	M	Tu	W	Th	F	Sat
		1	2	3	4	5
6	7	8	9	10	11	12
13	14	15	16	17	18	19
20	21	22	23	24	25	26
27	28	29	30	31		

JULY
Sun	M	Tu	W	Th	F	Sat
		1	2	3	4	5
6	7	8	9	10	11	12
13	14	15	16	17	18	19
20	21	22	23	24	25	26
27	28	29	30	31		

FEBRUARY
Sun	M	Tu	W	Th	F	Sat
					1	2
3	4	5	6	7	8	9
10	11	12	13	14	15	16
17	18	19	20	21	22	23
24	25	26	27	28	29	

AUGUST
Sun	M	Tu	W	Th	F	Sat
					1	2
3	4	5	6	7	8	9
10	11	12	13	14	15	16
17	18	19	20	21	22	23
24	25	26	27	28	29	30
31						

MARCH
Sun	M	Tu	W	Th	F	Sat
						1
2	3	4	5	6	7	8
9	10	11	12	13	14	15
16	17	18	19	20	21	22
23	24	25	26	27	28	29
30	31					

SEPTEMBER
Sun	M	Tu	W	Th	F	Sat
	1	2	3	4	5	6
7	8	9	10	11	12	13
14	15	16	17	18	19	20
21	22	23	24	25	26	27
28	29	30				

APRIL
Sun	M	Tu	W	Th	F	Sat
		1	2	3	4	5
6	7	8	9	10	11	12
13	14	15	16	17	18	19
20	21	22	23	24	25	26
27	28	29	30			

OCTOBER
Sun	M	Tu	W	Th	F	Sat
		1	2	3	4
5	6	7	8	9	10	11
12	13	14	15	16	17	18
19	20	21	22	23	24	25
26	27	28	29	30	31	

MAY
Sun	M	Tu	W	Th	F	Sat
				1	2	3
4	5	6	7	8	9	10
11	12	13	14	15	16	17
18	19	20	21	22	23	24
25	26	27	28	29	30	31

NOVEMBER
Sun	M	Tu	W	Th	F	Sat
						1
2	3	4	5	6	7	8
9	10	11	12	13	14	15
16	17	18	19	20	21	22
23	24	25	26	27	28	29
30						

JUNE
Sun	M	Tu	W	Th	F	Sat
1	2	3	4	5	6	7
8	9	10	11	12	13	14
15	16	17	18	19	20	21
22	23	24	25	26	27	28
29	30					

DECEMBER
Sun	M	Tu	W	Th	F	Sat
	1	2	3	4	5	6
7	8	9	10	11	12	13
14	15	16	17	18	19	20
21	22	23	24	25	26	27
28	29	30	31			

Example (1). In determining the number of Congressional days for 198X for which the designated amount may be computed, the number of days in such year is reduced by 125 days determined as follows:

5 days	February 14-18
12 days	April 3-14
5 days	May 23-27
18 days	July 3-20
16 days	August 2-17
5 days	August 29-September 2
40 days	October 3-November 11
9 days	November 22-November 30
15 days	December 17-December 31
125	

Thus for 198X (a leap year) a typical Member of the House of Representatives will have 241 (366 − 125) Congressional days.

Example (2). On August 1, Z, a calendar year taxpayer is elected to the Congress to fill the unexpired term of Member Y. In determining the number of Congressional days, Z may only consider the number of days during the year for which he was a Member of Congress. For Z the number of Congressional days is 68.

Example (3). Member X, a calendar year taxpayer, owns his own home in Washington, D.C., where he lives with his family. While in Washington, D.C. Member X is away from home within the meaning of section 162(a). X maintains no records attributable to his expenses in Washington, D.C. X has been a Member of Congress for the entire year. The maximum amount of subsistence for Washington, D.C. for 198X is $75. X may deduct for 198X $18,075 (241 days × $75) attributable to expenses while away from home in Washington, D.C. Even if X maintained records as to living expenses in Washington, D.C., X may choose to deduct $18,075 as the total amount attributable to living expenses in Washington, D.C. If X deducts $18,075 X may not

Reg. §5e.274-8(h)

deduct any interest and taxes under section 163 or 164 attributable to the residence in Washington, D.C.

Example (4). Member C, a calendar year taxpayer owns his own home in Washington, D.C., where he lives with his family. While in Washington, D.C. Member C is away from home within the meaning of section 162(a). C can establish that he paid $12,000 as interest on a mortgage and $3,000 in local real estate taxes. C has been a Member of Congress for the entire year. C may choose to deduct $12,050 (241 days × [²/₃ × $75]) attributable to expenses in Washington, D.C. Further, C may deduct under sections 163 and 164 $12,000 of interest and $3,000 of taxes respectively.

Example (5). Assume the same facts as in Example (4). In addition, on March 15, 16, and 17, Member C travels to New York City to deliver a speech for which he receives an honorarium which he includes in income. C receives no additional amounts for travel reimbursement. While in New York City C incurs $350 for 3 nights lodging at a hotel and $150 for meals. In addition to the amounts deductible pursuant to this section, C may deduct the $500 as travel expenses. Such deduction is subject to the substantiation rules of section 274.

Example (6). Assume the same facts as example (5). Member C receives, in addition to the honorarium, $600 reimbursement for travel expenses. C must include the $600 in income and may deduct the travel expenses he incurred. [Temporary Reg. § 5e.274-8.]

☐ [*T.D. 7802, 1-15-82.*]

[Reg. § 1.274-9]

§ 1.274-9. Entertainment provided to specified individuals.— (a) *In general.—*Paragraphs (e)(2) and (e)(9) of section 274 provide exceptions to the disallowance of section 274(a) for expenses for entertainment, amusement, or recreation activities, or for an entertainment facility. In the case of a specified individual (as defined in paragraph (b) of this section), the exceptions of paragraphs (e)(2) and (e)(9) of section 274 apply only to the extent that the expenses do not exceed the amount of the expenses treated as compensation (under section 274(e)(2)) or as income (under section 274(e)(9)) to the specified individual. The amount disallowed is reduced by any amount that the specified individual reimburses a taxpayer for the entertainment.

(b) *Specified individual defined.—*(1) A specified individual is an individual who is subject to section 16(a) of the Securities Act of 1934 in relation to the taxpayer, or an individual who would be subject to section 16(a) if the taxpayer were an issuer of equity securities referred to in that section. Thus, for example, a specified individual is an officer, director, or more than 10 percent owner of a corporation taxed under subchapter C or subchapter S or a personal service corporation. A specified individual includes every individual who—

(i) Is the direct or indirect beneficial owner of more than 10 percent of any class of any registered equity (other than an exempted security);

(ii) Is a director or officer of the issuer of the security;

(iii) Would be the direct or indirect beneficial owner of more than 10 percent of any class of a registered security if the taxpayer were an issuer of equity securities; or

(iv) Is comparable to an officer or director of an issuer of equity securities.

(2) For partnership purposes, a specified individual includes any partner that holds more than a 10 percent equity interest in the partnership, or any general partner, officer, or managing partner of a partnership.

(3) For purposes of this section, *officer* has the same meaning as in 17 CFR § 240.16a-1(f).

(4) A specified individual includes a director or officer of a tax-exempt entity.

(5) A specified individual of a taxpayer includes a specified individual of a party related to the taxpayer within the meaning of section 267(b) or section 707(b).

(c) *Specified individual treated as recipient of entertainment provided to others.—*For purposes of section 274(a), a specified individual is treated as the recipient of entertainment provided to another individual because of the relationship of the other individual to the specified individual if the entertainment is a fringe benefit to the specified individual under section 61(a)(1) (without regard to any exclusions from gross income). Thus, expenses allocable to entertainment provided to the other individual are attributed to the specified individual for purposes of determining the amount of disallowed expenses.

(d) *Entertainment use of aircraft by specified individuals.—*For rules relating to entertainment use of aircraft by specified individuals, see § 1.274-10.

(e) *Effective/applicability date.—*This section applies to taxable years beginning after August 1, 2012. [Reg. § 1.274-9.]

☐ [*T.D. 9597, 7-31-2012.*]

[Reg. § 1.274-10]

§ 1.274-10. Special rules for aircraft used for entertainment.— (a) *Use of an aircraft for entertainment.—*(1) *In general.—*Section 274(a) disallows a deduction for certain expenses for entertainment, amusement, or recreation activities, or for an entertainment facility. Under section 274(a) and this section, no deduction otherwise allowable under chapter 1 is allowed for expenses for the use of a taxpayer-provided aircraft for entertainment, except as provided in paragraph (a)(2) of this section.

(2) *Exceptions.—*(i) *In general.—*Paragraph (a)(1) of this section does not apply to deductions for expenses for business entertainment air travel or to deductions for expenses that meet the exceptions of section 274(e), § 1.274-2(f), and this section. Section 274(e)(2) and (e)(9) provides certain exceptions to the disallowance of section 274(a) for expenses for goods, services, and facilities for entertainment, recreation, or amusement.

(ii) *Expenses treated as compensation.—*(A) *Employees who are not specified individuals.—*Section 274(e), § 1.274-2(a) through (d), and paragraph (a)(1) of this section, in accordance with section 274(e)(2)(A), do not apply to expenses for entertainment air travel provided to an employee who is not a specified individual to the extent that a taxpayer—

(1) Properly treats the expenses relating to the recipient of entertainment as compensation to an employee under chapter 1 and as wages to the employee for purposes of chapter 24; and

(2) Treats the proper amount as compensation to the employee under § 1.61-21.

(B) *Persons who are not employees and are not specified individuals.—*Section 274(a), § 1.274-2(a) through (d), and paragraph (a)(1) of this section, in accordance with section 274(e)(9), do not apply to expenses for entertainment air travel provided to a person who is not an employee and is not a specified individual to the extent that the expenses are includible in the income of that person. This exception does not apply to any amount paid or incurred by the taxpayer that is required to be included in any information return filed by the taxpayer under part III of subchapter A of chapter 61 and is not so included.

(C) *Specified individuals.—*Section 274(a), § 1.274-2(a) through (d), and paragraph (a)(1) of this section, in accordance with section 274(e)(2)(B), do not apply to expenses for entertainment air travel of a specified individual to the extent that the amount of the expenses do not exceed the sum of—

(1) The amount treated as compensation to or included in the income of the specified individual in the manner specified under paragraph (a)(2)(ii)(A)(1) of this section (if the specified individual is an employee) or under paragraph (a)(2)(ii)(B) of this section (if the specified individual is not an employee); and

(2) Any amount the specified individual reimburses the taxpayer.

(iii) *Travel on regularly scheduled commercial airlines.—*Section 274(a), § 1.274-2(a) through (d), and paragraph (a)(1) of this section do not apply to expenses for entertainment air travel that a taxpayer that is a commercial passenger airline provides to specified individuals of the taxpayer on the taxpayer's regularly scheduled flights on which at least 90 percent of the seats are available for sale to the public to the extent the expenses are includible in the income of the recipient of the entertainment in the manner specified under paragraph (a)(2)(ii)(A)(1) of this section (if the specified individual is an employee) or under paragraph (a)(2)(ii)(B) of this section (if the specified individual is not an employee).

(b) *Definitions.—*The definitions in this paragraph (b) apply for purposes of this section.

(1) *Entertainment.—*For the definition of *entertainment* for purposes of this section, see § 1.274-2(b)(1). Entertainment does not include personal travel that is not for entertainment purposes. For example, travel to attend a family member's funeral is not entertainment.

(2) *Entertainment air travel.—Entertainment air travel* is any travel aboard a taxpayer-provided aircraft for entertainment purposes.

(3) *Business entertainment air travel.—Business entertainment air travel* is any entertainment air travel aboard a taxpayer-provided aircraft that is directly related to the active conduct of the taxpayer's trade or business or related to an expenditure directly preceding or following a substantial and bona fide business discussion and associated with the active conduct of the taxpayer's trade or business. See § 1.274-2(a)(1)(i) and (ii). Air travel is not business entertainment air travel merely because a taxpayer-provided aircraft is used for the travel as a result of a bona fide security concern under § 1.132-5(m).

(4) *Taxpayer-provided aircraft.*—A *taxpayer-provided aircraft* is any aircraft owned by, leased to, or chartered to, a taxpayer or any party related to the taxpayer (within the meaning of section 267(b) or section 707(b)).

(5) *Specified individual.*—For rules relating to the definition of a specified individual, see § 1.274-9.

(c) *Amount disallowed.*—Except as otherwise provided, the amount disallowed under this section for an entertainment flight by a specified individual is the amount of expenses allocable to the entertainment flight of the specified individual under paragraph (e)(2), (e)(3), or (f)(3) of this section, reduced (but not below zero) by the amount the taxpayer treats as compensation or reports as income under paragraph (a)(2)(ii)(C)(1) of this section to the specified individual, plus any amount the specified individual reimburses the taxpayer.

(d) *Expenses subject to disallowance under this section.*—(1) *Definition of expenses.*—In determining the amount of expenses subject to disallowance under this section, a taxpayer must include all of the expenses of operating the aircraft, including all fixed and variable expenses the taxpayer deducts in the taxable year. These expenses include, but are not limited to, salaries for pilots, maintenance personnel, and other personnel assigned to the aircraft; meal and lodging expenses of flight personnel; take-off and landing fees; costs for maintenance flights; costs of on-board refreshments, amenities and gifts; hangar fees (at home or away); management fees; costs of fuel, tires, maintenance, insurance, registration, certificate of title, inspection, and depreciation; interest on debt secured by or properly allocated (within the meaning of § 1.163-8T) to an aircraft; and all costs paid or incurred for aircraft leased or chartered to the taxpayer.

(2) *Leases or charters to third parties.*—Expenses allocable to a lease or charter of a taxpayer's aircraft to an unrelated (as determined under section 267(b) or 707(b)) third-party in a bona-fide business transaction for adequate and full consideration are excluded from the definition of expenses in paragraph (d)(1) of this section. Only expenses allocable to the lease or charter period are excluded under this paragraph (d)(2).

(3) *Straight-line method permitted for determining depreciation disallowance under this section.*—(i) *In general.*—In lieu of the amount of depreciation deducted in the taxable year, solely for purposes of paragraph (d)(1) of this section, a taxpayer may elect to treat as its depreciation deduction the amount that would result from using the straight-line method of depreciation over the class life (as defined by section 168(i)(1) and using the applicable convention under section 168(d)) of an aircraft, even if the taxpayer uses a different methodology to calculate depreciation for the aircraft under other sections of the Internal Revenue Code (for example, section 168). If the property qualifies for the additional first-year depreciation deduction provided by, for example, section 168(k), 168(n), 1400L(b), or 1400N(d), depreciation for purposes of this straightline election is determined on the unadjusted depreciable basis (as defined in § 1.168(b)-1(a)(3)) of the property. However, the amount of depreciation disallowed as a result of this paragraph (d)(3) for any taxable year cannot exceed a taxpayer's allowable depreciation for that taxable year. For purposes of this section, a taxpayer that elects to use the straight-line method and class life under this paragraph (d)(3) for any aircraft it operates must use that methodology for all depreciable aircraft it operates and must continue to use the methodology for the entire period the taxpayer uses any depreciable aircraft.

(ii) *Aircraft placed in service in earlier taxable years.*—The amount of depreciation for purposes of this paragraph (d)(3) for aircraft placed in service in taxable years before the taxable year of the election is determined by applying the straight-line method of depreciation to the unadjusted depreciable basis (or, for property acquired in an exchange to which section 1031 applies, the basis of the aircraft as determined under section 1031(d)) and over the class life (using the applicable convention under section 168(d)) of the aircraft as though the taxpayer used that methodology from the year the aircraft was placed in service.

(iii) *Manner of making and revoking election.*—A taxpayer makes the election under this paragraph (d)(3) by filing an income tax return for the taxable year that determines the taxpayer's expenses for purposes of paragraph (d)(1) of this section by computing depreciation under this paragraph (d)(3). A taxpayer may revoke an election only for compelling circumstances upon consent of the Commissioner by private letter ruling.

(4) *Aggregation of aircraft.*—(i) *In general.*—A taxpayer may aggregate the expenses of aircraft of similar cost profiles for purposes of calculating disallowed expenses under paragraph (c) of this section.

(ii) *Similar cost profiles.*—Aircraft are of similar cost profiles if their operating costs per mile or per hour of flight are comparable.

Aircraft must have the same engine type (jet or propeller) and the same number of engines to have similar cost profiles. Other factors to be considered in determining whether aircraft have similar cost profiles include, but are not limited to, maximum take-off weight, payload, passenger capacity, fuel consumption rate, age, maintenance costs, and depreciable basis.

(5) *Authority for establishing safe harbors for determining expenses.*—The Commissioner may establish in published guidance, see § 601.601(d)(2) of this chapter, one or more safe harbor methods under which a taxpayer may determine the amount of expenses paid or incurred for entertainment flights.

(e) *Allocation of expenses.*—(1) *General rule.*—For purposes of determining the expenses allocated to entertainment air travel of a specified individual under paragraph (a)(2)(ii)(C) of this section, a taxpayer must use either the occupied seat hours or miles method of paragraph (e)(2) of this section or the flight-by-flight method of paragraph (e)(3) of this section. A taxpayer must use the chosen method for all flights of all aircraft for the taxable year.

(2) *Occupied seat hours or miles method.*—(i) *In general.*—The occupied seat hours or miles method determines the amount of expenses allocated to a particular entertainment flight of a specified individual based on the occupied seat hours or miles for an aircraft for the taxable year. Under this method, a taxpayer may choose to use either occupied seat hours or miles for the taxable year to determine the amount of expenses allocated to entertainment flights of specified individuals, but must use occupied seat hours or miles consistently for all flights of all aircraft for the taxable year.

(ii) *Computation under the occupied seat hours or miles method.*—The amount of expenses allocated to an entertainment flight taken by a specified individual is computed under the occupied seat hours or miles method by determining—

(A) The total expenses for the year under paragraph (d) of this section for the aircraft or group of aircraft (if aggregated under paragraph (d)(4) of this section), as applicable;

(B) The number of occupied seat hours or miles for the taxable year for the aircraft or group of aircraft by totaling the occupied seat hours or miles of all flights in the taxable year flown by the aircraft or group of aircraft, as applicable. The occupied seat hours or miles for a flight is the number of hours or miles flown for the flight multiplied by the number of seats occupied on that flight. For example, a flight of 6 hours with three passengers results in 18 occupied seat hours;

(C) The cost per occupied seat hour or mile for the aircraft or group of aircraft, as applicable, by dividing the total expenses under paragraph (e)(2)(ii)(A) of this section by the total number of occupied seat hours or miles under paragraph (e)(2)(ii)(B) of this section; and

(D) The amount of expenses allocated to an entertainment flight taken by a specified individual by multiplying the number of hours or miles of the flight by the cost per occupied hour or mile for that aircraft or group of aircraft, as applicable, as determined under paragraph (e)(2)(ii)(C) of this section.

(iii) *Allocation of expenses of multi-leg trips involving both business and entertainment legs.*—A taxpayer that uses the occupied seat hours or miles allocation method must allocate the expenses of a trip by a specified individual that involves at least one segment for business and one segment for entertainment between the business travel and the entertainment travel unless none of the expenses for the entertainment segment are disallowed. The entertainment cost of a multi-leg trip is the total cost of the flights (by occupied seat hours or miles) minus the cost of the flights that would have been taken without the entertainment segment or segments.

(iv) *Examples.*—The following examples illustrate the provisions of this paragraph (e)(2):

Example 1. (i) A taxpayer-provided aircraft is used for Flights 1, 2, and 3, of 5 hours, 5 hours, and 4 hours, respectively, during the Taxpayer's taxable year. Each flight carries four passengers. On Flight 1, none of the passengers is a specified individual. On Flight 2, passengers A and B are specified individuals traveling for entertainment purposes and passengers C and D are not specified individuals. For Flight 2, Taxpayer treats $1,200 as compensation to A, and B reimburses Taxpayer $500. On Flight 3, all four passengers (A, B, E, and F) are specified individuals traveling for entertainment purposes. For Flight 3, Taxpayer treats $1,300 each as compensation to A, B, E, and F. Taxpayer incurs $56,000 in expenses for the operation of the aircraft for the taxable year. The aircraft is operated for 56 occupied seat hours for the period (four passengers times 5 hours (20 occupied seat hours) for Flight 1, plus four passengers times 5 hours (20 occupied seat hours) for Flight 2, plus four passengers times 4 hours (16 occupied seat hours) for Flight 3. The cost per occupied seat hour is $1,000 ($56,000/56 hours).

(ii) For purposes of determining the amount disallowed (to the extent not treated as compensation or reimbursed) for entertainment provided to specified individuals, $5,000 ($1,000 X 5 hours) each is allocable to A and B for Flight 2, and $4,000 ($1,000 X 4 hours) each is allocable to A, B, E, and F for Flight 3.

(iii) For Flight 2, because Taxpayer treats $1,200 as compensation to A, and B reimburses Taxpayer $500, Taxpayer may deduct $1,700 of the cost of Flight 2 allocable to A and B. The deduction for the remaining $8,300 cost allocable to entertainment provided to A and B on Flight 2 is disallowed (for A, $5,000 less the $1,200 treated as compensation, and for B, $5,000 less the $500 reimbursed).

(iv) For Flight 3, because Taxpayer treats $1,300 each as compensation to A, B, E, and F, Taxpayer may deduct $5,200 of the cost of Flight 3. The deduction for the remaining $10,800 cost allocable to entertainment provided to A, B, E, and F on Flight 3 is disallowed ($4,000 less the $1,300 treated as compensation to each specified individual).

Example 2. (i) G, a specified individual, is the sole passenger on an aircraft that makes three flights. First, G travels on a two-hour flight from City A to City B for business purposes. G then travels on a three-hour flight from City B to City C for entertainment purposes, and returns from City C to City A on a four-hour flight. G's flights have resulted in nine occupied seat hours (two for the first segment, plus three for the second segment, plus four for the third segment). If G had returned directly to City A from City B, the flights would have resulted in four occupied seat hours.

(ii) Under paragraph (e)(2)(iii) of this section, five occupied seat hours are allocable to G's entertainment (nine total occupied seat hours minus the four occupied seat hours that would have resulted if the travel had been a roundtrip business trip without the entertainment segment). If Taxpayer's cost per occupied seat hour for the year is $1,000, $5,000 is allocated to G's entertainment use of the aircraft ($1,000 X five occupied seat hours). The amount disallowed is $5,000 minus the total of any amount the Taxpayer treats as compensation to G plus any amount that G reimburses Taxpayer.

(3) *Flight-by-flight method.*—(i) *In general.*—The flight-by-flight method determines the amount of expenses allocated to a particular entertainment flight of a specified individual on a flight-by-flight basis by allocating expenses to individual flights and then to a specified individual traveling for entertainment purposes on that flight.

(ii) *Allocation of expenses.*—A taxpayer using the flight-by-flight method must combine all expenses (as defined in paragraph (d)(1) of this section) for the taxable year for the aircraft or group of aircraft (if aggregated under paragraph (d)(4) of this section), as applicable, and divide the total amount of expenses by the number of flight hours or miles for the taxable year for that aircraft or group of aircraft, as applicable, to determine the cost per hour or mile. Expenses are allocated to each flight by multiplying the number of miles for the flight by the cost per mile or the number of hours for the flight by the cost per hour. The expenses for the flight then are allocated to the passengers on the flight per capita. Thus, if five passengers are traveling on a flight, and the total expense allocated to the flight is $10,000, the expense allocable to each passenger is $2,000.

(f) *Special rules.*—(1) *Determination of basis.*—(i) If any deduction for depreciation is disallowed under this section, the rules of §1.274-7 apply. In that case, the basis of an aircraft is not reduced for the amount of depreciation disallowed under this section.

(ii) The provisions of this paragraph (f)(1) are illustrated by the following examples:

Example 1. (i) B Co. is a calendar-year taxpayer that owns an aircraft not used in commercial or contract carrying of passengers or freight. The aircraft is placed in service on July 1 of Year 1 and has an unadjusted depreciable basis of $1,000,000. The class life of the aircraft for depreciation purposes is 6 years. For determining depreciation under section 168, B Co. uses the optional depreciation table that corresponds with the general depreciation system, the 200 percent declining balance method of depreciation, a 5-year recovery period, and the half-year convention. For determining the depreciation disallowance for each year under paragraph (d)(3) of this section, B Co. elects to use the straight-line method of depreciation and the class life of 6 years and, therefore, uses the optional depreciation table for purposes of section 168 that corresponds with the straight-line method of depreciation, a recovery period of 6 years, and the half-year convention. In each year, the aircraft entertainment use subject to disallowance under this section is 10 percent of the total use.

(ii) B Co. calculates the depreciation and basis of the aircraft as follows:

	200 Percent Declining Balance Depreciation Amount	Straight Line Depreciation Amount	Depreciation Disallowance Under Section 274	Depreciation Deduction	§1.274-7 Basis of Aircraft	Suspended Basis
Year 1	200,000	83,300	8,330. (.10 X 83,300)	191,670 (200,000 minus 8,330)	808,330 (1,000,000 minus 191,670)	8,330
Year 2	320,000	166,700	16,670 (.10 X 166,700)	303,330 (320,000 minus 16,670)	505,000 (808,330 minus 303,330)	25,000 (8,300 plus 16,670)
Year 3	192,000	166,700	16,670 (.10 X 166,700)	175,330 (192,000 minus 16,670)	329,670 (505,000 minus 175,330)	41,670 (25,000 plus 16,670)
Year 4	115,200	166,700	16,670 (.10 X 166,700)	98,530 (115,200 minus 16,670)	231,140 (329,670 minus 98,530)	58,340 (41,670 plus 16,670)
Year 5	115,200	166,600	16,660 (.10 X 166,600)	98,540 (115,200 minus 16,660)	132,600 (231,140 minus 98,540)	75,000 (58,340 plus 16,660)
Year 6	57,600	166,700	16,670 (.10 X 166,700)	40,930 (57,600 minus 16,670)	91,670 (132,600 minus 40,930)	91,670 (75,000 plus 16,670)
Year 7		83,300	8,330 (.10 X 83,300)		91,670	91,670

(iii) In Year 7, there is no further deduction for depreciation of the aircraft, therefore, under paragraph (d)(3) of this section, no depreciation expense is disallowed. Under §1.274-7 and this paragraph (f)(1), basis is not reduced for disallowed depreciation. Therefore, at the end of Year 7, the basis of the aircraft for purposes of §1.274-7 is $91,670, which is the total amount of disallowed deprecia-

tion in Years 1 through 6. B Co.'s deductions for depreciation total $908,330, which added to $91,670 equals $1,000,000.

Example 2. (i) The facts are the same as in *Example 1*, except that B Co. does not elect to use the straight-line method of depreciation under paragraph (d)(3) of this section until Year 3.

(ii) B Co. calculates the depreciation and basis of the aircraft as follows:

	200 Percent Declining Balance Depreciation Amount	Straight Line Depreciation Amount	Depreciation Disallowance Under Section 274	Depreciation Deduction	§1.274-7 Basis of Aircraft	Suspended Basis
Year 1	200,000		20,000 (.10 X 200,000)	180,000	820,000 (1,000,000 minus 180,000)	20,000
Year 2	320,000		32,000 (.10 X 320,000)	288,000 (320,000 minus 32,000)	532,000 (820,000 minus 288,000)	52,000 (20,000 plus 32,000)
Year 3	192,000	166,700	16,670 (.10 X 166,700)	175,330 (192,000 minus 16,670)	356,670 (532,000 minus 175,330)	68,670 (52,000 plus 16,670)
Year 4	115,200	166,700	16,670 (.10 X 166,700)	98,530 (115,200 minus 16,670)	258,140 (356,670 minus 98,530)	85,340 (68,670 plus 16,670)

	200 Percent Declining Balance Depreciation Amount	Straight Line Depreciation Amount	Depreciation Disallowance Under Section 274	Depreciation Deduction	§1.274-7 Basis of Aircraft	Suspended Basis
Year 5	115,200	166,600	16,660 (.10 X 166,600)	98,540 (115,200 minus 16,660)	159,600 (258,140 minus 98,540)	102,000 (85,340 plus 16,660)
Year 6	57,600	166,700	16,670 (.10 X 166,700)	40,930 (57,600 minus 16,670)	118,670 (159,600 minus 40,930)	118,670 (102,000 plus 16,670)
Year 7		83,300	8,330 (.10 X 83,300)	0	118,670	118,670

(iii) In Year 7, there is no further deduction for depreciation of the aircraft, therefore, under paragraph (d)(3) of this section, no depreciation expense is disallowed. Under §1.274-7 and this paragraph (f)(1), basis is not reduced for disallowed depreciation. Therefore, at the end of Year 7, the basis of the aircraft for purposes of §1.274-7 is $118,670, which is the total amount of disallowed depreciation in Years 1 through 6. B Co.'s deductions for depreciation total $881,330, which added to $118,670 equals $1,000,000.

(2) *Pro rata disallowance.*—(i) The amount of disallowed expenses, and any amounts reimbursed or treated as compensation, under this section are applied on a pro rata basis to all of the categories of expenses subject to disallowance under this section.

(ii) The provisions of this paragraph (f)(2) are illustrated by the following example:

Example. (i) C Co. owns an aircraft that it uses for business and other purposes. The expenses of operating the aircraft in the current year total $1,000,000. This amount includes $250,000 for depreciation (25 percent of total expenses).

(ii) In the same year, the aircraft entertainment use subject to disallowance under this section is 20 percent of the total use and C Co. treats $80,000 as compensation to specified individuals. Thus, the amount of the disallowance under this section is $120,000 ($1,000,000 X 20 percent) ($200,000) less $80,000).

(iii) Under paragraph (f)(2) of this section, C Co. may calculate the amount by which a category of expense, such as depreciation, is disallowed by multiplying the total disallowance of $120,000 by the ratio of the amount of the expense to total expenses. Thus, $30,000 of the $120,000 total disallowed expenses is depreciation ($250,000/$1,000,000 (25 percent) X $120,000).

(iv) The result is the same if C Co. separately calculates the amount of depreciation in total disallowed expenses and in the amount treated as compensation and nets the result. Depreciation is 25 percent of total expenses, thus, the amount of depreciation in disallowed expenses is $50,000 (25 percent X $200,000 total disallowed expenses) and the amount of depreciation treated as compensation is $20,000 (25 percent X $80,000). Disallowed depreciation is $50,000 less $20,000, or $30,000.

(3) *Deadhead flights.*—(i) For purposes of this section, an aircraft returning without passengers after discharging passengers or flying without passengers to pick up passengers (deadheading) is treated as having the same number and character of passengers as the leg of the trip on which passengers are aboard for purposes of allocating expenses under paragraphs (e)(2) or (e)(3) of this section. For example, when an aircraft travels from point A to point B and then back to point A, and one of the legs is a deadhead flight, for determination of disallowed expenses, the aircraft is treated as having made both legs of the trip with the same passengers aboard for the same purposes.

(ii) When a deadhead flight does not occur within a roundtrip flight, but occurs between two unrelated flights involving more than two destinations (such as an occupied flight from point A to point B, followed by a deadhead flight from point B to point C, and then an occupied flight from point C to point A), the allocation of passengers and expenses to the deadhead flight occurring between the two occupied trips must be based solely on the number of passengers on board for the two occupied legs of the flight, the character of the travel of the passengers on board (entertainment or nonentertainment) and the length in hours or miles of the two occupied legs of the flight.

(iii) The provisions of this paragraph (f)(3) are illustrated by the following examples:

Example 1. (i) Aircraft flies from City A to City B, a 6-hour trip, with 12 passengers aboard. Eight of the passengers are traveling for business and four of the passengers are specified individuals traveling for entertainment purposes. The aircraft flies empty (deadheads) from City B to City C, a 4-hour trip. At City C it picks up 12 passengers, six of whom are traveling for business and six of whom are specified individuals traveling for entertainment purposes, for a 2-hour trip to City A. The taxpayer uses the occupied seat hour method of allocating expenses.

(ii) The two legs of the trip on which the aircraft is occupied comprise 96 occupied seat hours (12 passengers X 6 hours (72) for the first leg plus 12 passengers X 2 hours (24) for the third leg). Sixty occupied seat hours are for business (8 passengers X 6 hours (48) for

the first leg plus 6 passengers X 2 (12) hours for the third leg) and 36 occupied seat hours are for entertainment purposes (4 passengers X 6 hours (24) for the first leg plus 6 passengers X 2 (12) hours for the third leg). Dividing the 36 occupied seat entertainment hours by 96 total occupied seat hours, 37.5 percent of the total occupied seat hours of the two occupied flights are for entertainment.

(iii) The 4-hour deadhead leg comprises one-third of the total flight time of 12 hours. Therefore, the deadhead flight is deemed to have provided one-third of the total 96 occupied seat hours, or 32 occupied seat hours (96 X 1/3 = 32). Of the 32 deemed occupied seat hours, 37.5 percent, or 12 deemed occupied seat hours, are treated as entertainment under paragraph (f)(3)(ii) of this section. The 32 deemed occupied seat hours for the deadhead flight are included in the calculation under paragraph (e)(2)(ii)(B) of this section and expenses are allocated under paragraph (e)(2)(ii)(D) of this section to the 12 deemed occupied seat hours treated as entertainment.

Example 2. (i) The facts are the same as for *Example 1*, but the taxpayer uses the flight-by-flight method of allocation.

(ii) Of the 24 passengers on the occupied flights, 10 passengers, or 41.7 percent, are traveling for entertainment purposes. If the annual cost per flight hour calculated under paragraph (e)(3)(ii) of this section is $1,000, $4,000 is allocated to the 4-hour deadhead leg. Under paragraph (f)(3)(ii) of this section, 41.7 percent of the $4,000, or $1,667, is treated as an expense for entertainment. The calculation of the cost per mile or hour for the year under paragraph (e)(3)(ii) of this section includes the expenses and number of miles or hours flown for the deadhead leg.

(g) *Effective/applicability date.*—This section applies to taxable years beginning after August 1, 2012. [Reg. §1.274-10.]

☐ [T.D. 9597, 7-31-2012.]

[Reg. §1.274-11]

§1.274-11. Disallowance of deductions for certain entertainment, amusement, or recreation expenditures paid or incurred after December 31, 2017.—(a) *In general.*—Except as provided in this section, no deduction otherwise allowable under chapter 1 of the Internal Revenue Code (Code) is allowed for any expenditure with respect to an activity that is of a type generally considered to be entertainment, or with respect to a facility used in connection with an entertainment activity. For this purpose, dues or fees to any social, athletic, or sporting club or organization are treated as items with respect to facilities and, thus, are not deductible. In addition, no deduction otherwise allowable under chapter 1 of the Code is allowed for amounts paid or incurred for membership in any club organized for business, pleasure, recreation, or other social purpose.

(b) *Definitions.*—(1) *Entertainment.*—(i) *In general.*—For section 274 purposes, the term *entertainment* means any activity which is of a type generally considered to constitute entertainment, amusement, or recreation, such as entertaining at bars, theaters, country clubs, golf and athletic clubs, sporting events, and on hunting, fishing, vacation and similar trips, including such activity relating solely to the taxpayer or the taxpayer's family. These activities are treated as entertainment under this section, subject to the objective test, regardless of whether the expenditure for the activity is related to or associated with the active conduct of the taxpayer's trade or business. The term *entertainment* may include an activity, the cost of which otherwise is a business expense of the taxpayer, which satisfies the personal, living, or family needs of any individual, such as providing a hotel suite or an automobile to a business customer or the customer's family. The term *entertainment* does not include activities which, although satisfying personal, living, or family needs of an individual, are clearly not regarded as constituting entertainment, such as the providing of a hotel room maintained by an employer for lodging of employees while in business travel status or an automobile used in the active conduct of a trade or business even though used for routine personal purposes such as commuting to and from work. On the other hand, the providing of a hotel room or an automobile by an employer to an employee who is on vacation would constitute entertainment of the employee.

(ii) *Food or beverages.*—Under this section, the term *entertainment* does not include food or beverages unless the food or beverages are provided at or during an entertainment activity. Food or beverages provided at or during an entertainment activity generally are treated as part of the entertainment activity. However, in the case of food or beverages provided at or during an entertainment activity, the food or beverages are not considered entertainment if the food or beverages are purchased separately from the entertainment, or the cost of the food or beverages is stated separately from the cost of the entertainment on one or more bills, invoices, or receipts. The amount charged for food or beverages on a bill, invoice, or receipt must reflect the venue's usual selling cost for those items if they were to be purchased separately from the entertainment or must approximate the reasonable value of those items. If the food or beverages are not purchased separately from the entertainment, or the cost of the food or beverages is not stated separately from the cost of the entertainment on one or more bills, invoices, or receipts, no allocation between entertainment and food or beverage expenses may be made and, except as further provided in this section and section 274(e), the entire amount is a nondeductible entertainment expenditure under this section and section 274(a).

(iii) *Objective test.*—An objective test is used to determine whether an activity is of a type generally considered to be entertainment. Thus, if an activity is generally considered to be entertainment, it will be treated as entertainment for purposes of this section and section 274(a) regardless of whether the expenditure can also be described otherwise, and even though the expenditure relates to the taxpayer alone. This objective test precludes arguments that *entertainment* means only entertainment of others or that an expenditure for entertainment should be characterized as an expenditure for advertising or public relations. However, in applying this test the taxpayer's trade or business is considered. Thus, although attending a theatrical performance generally would be considered entertainment, it would not be so considered in the case of a professional theater critic attending in a professional capacity. Similarly, if a manufacturer of dresses conducts a fashion show to introduce its products to a group of store buyers, the show generally would not be considered entertainment. However, if an appliance distributor conducts a fashion show, the fashion show generally would be considered to be entertainment.

(2) *Expenditure.*—The term *expenditure* as used in this section includes amounts paid or incurred for goods, services, facilities, and other items, including items such as losses and depreciation.

(3) *Expenditures for production of income.*—For purposes of this section, any reference to *trade or business* includes an activity described in section 212.

(c) *Exceptions.*—Paragraph (a) of this section does not apply to any expenditure described in section 274(e)(1), (2), (3), (4), (5), (6), (7), (8), or (9).

(d) *Examples.*—The following examples illustrate the application of paragraphs (a) and (b) of this section. In each example, assume that the taxpayer is engaged in a trade or business for purposes of section 162 and that neither the taxpayer nor any business associate is engaged in a trade or business that relates to the entertainment activity. Also assume that none of the exceptions under section 274(e) and paragraph (c) of this section apply.

(1) *Example 1.*—Taxpayer A invites, B, a business associate, to a baseball game to discuss a proposed business deal. A purchases tickets for A and B to attend the game. The baseball game is entertainment as defined in §1.274-11(b)(1) and thus, the cost of the game tickets is an entertainment expenditure and is not deductible by A.

(2) *Example 2.*—The facts are the same as in paragraph (d)(1) of this section (*Example 1*), except that A also buys hot dogs and drinks for A and B from a concession stand. The cost of the hot dogs and drinks, which are purchased separately from the game tickets, is not an entertainment expenditure and is not subject to the disallowance under §1.274-11(a) and section 274(a)(1). Therefore, A may deduct 50 percent of the expenses associated with the hot dogs and drinks purchased at the game if the expenses meet the requirements of section 162 and §1.274-12.

(3) *Example 3.*—Taxpayer C invites D, a business associate, to a basketball game. C purchases tickets for C and D to attend the game in a suite, where they have access to food and beverages. The cost of the basketball game tickets, as stated on the invoice, includes the food or beverages. The basketball game is entertainment as defined in §1.274-11(b)(1), and, thus, the cost of the game tickets is an entertainment expenditure and is not deductible by C. The cost of the food and beverages, which are not purchased separately from the game tickets, is not stated separately on the invoice. Thus, the cost of the food and beverages is an entertainment expenditure that is subject to disallowance under section 274(a)(1) and paragraph (a) of

this section, and C may not deduct the cost of the tickets or the food and beverages associated with the basketball game.

(4) *Example 4.*—The facts are the same as in paragraph (d)(3) of this section (*Example 3*), except that the invoice for the basketball game tickets separately states the cost of the food and beverages and reflects the venue's usual selling price if purchased separately. As in paragraph (d)(3) of this section (*Example 3*), the basketball game is entertainment as defined in §1.274-11(b)(1), and, thus, the cost of the game tickets, other than the cost of the food and beverages, is an entertainment expenditure and is not deductible by C. However, the cost of the food and beverages, which is stated separately on the invoice for the game tickets and reflects the venue's usual selling price of the food and beverages if purchased separately, is not an entertainment expenditure and is not subject to the disallowance under section 274(a)(1) and paragraph (a) of this section. Therefore, C may deduct 50 percent of the expenses associated with the food and beverages provided at the game if the expenses meet the requirements of section 162 and §1.274-12.

(e) *Applicability date.*—This section applies for taxable years that begin on or after October 9, 2020. [Reg. §1.274-11.]

☐ [*T.D. 9925, 10-2-2020.*]

[Reg. §1.274-12]

§1.274-12. Limitation on deductions for certain food or beverage expenses paid or incurred after December 31, 2017.—(a) *Food or beverage expenses.*—(1) *In general.*—Except as provided in this section, no deduction is allowed for the expense of any food or beverages provided by the taxpayer (or an employee of the taxpayer) unless—

(i) The expense is not lavish or extravagant under the circumstances;

(ii) The taxpayer, or an employee of the taxpayer, is present at the furnishing of such food or beverages; and

(iii) The food or beverages are provided to the taxpayer or a business associate.

(2) *Only 50 percent of food or beverage expenses allowed as deduction.*—Except as provided in this section, the amount allowable as a deduction for any food or beverage expense described in paragraph (a)(1) of this section may not exceed 50 percent of the amount of the expense that otherwise would be allowable.

(3) *Examples.*—The following examples illustrate the application of paragraph (a)(1) and (2) of this section. In each example, assume that the food or beverage expenses are ordinary and necessary expenses under section 162(a) that are paid or incurred during the taxable year in carrying on a trade or business and are not lavish or extravagant under the circumstances. Also assume that none of the exceptions in paragraph (c) of this section apply.

(i) *Example 1.*—Taxpayer A takes client B out to lunch. Under section 274(k) and (n) and paragraph (a) of this section, A may deduct 50 percent of the food or beverage expenses.

(ii) *Example 2.*—Taxpayer C takes employee D out to lunch. Under section 274(k) and (n) and paragraph (a) of this section, C may deduct 50 percent of the food or beverage expenses.

(iii) *Example 3.*—Taxpayer E holds a business meeting at a hotel during which food and beverages are provided to attendees. Expenses for the business meeting, other than the cost of food and beverages, are not subject to the deduction limitations in section 274 and are deductible if they meet the requirements for deduction under section 162. Under section 274(k) and (n) and paragraph (a) of this section, E may deduct 50 percent of the food and beverage expenses.

(iv) *Example 4.*—The facts are the same as in paragraph (a)(3)(iii) of this section (*Example 3*), except that all the attendees of the meeting are employees of E. Expenses for the business meeting, other than the cost of food and beverages, are not subject to the deduction limitations in section 274 and are deductible if they meet the requirements for deduction under section 162. Under section 274(k) and (n) and paragraph (a) of this section, E may deduct 50 percent of the food and beverage expenses. The exception in section 274(e)(5) does not apply to food and beverage expenses under section 274(k) and (n).

(4) *Special rules for travel meals.*—(i) *In general.*—Food or beverage expenses paid or incurred while traveling away from home in pursuit of a trade or business generally are subject to the deduction limitations in section 274(k) and (n) and paragraph (a)(1) and (2) of this section, as well as the substantiation requirements in section 274(d). In addition, travel expenses generally are subject to the limitations in section 274(m)(1), (2), and (3).

(ii) *Substantiation.*—Except as provided in this section, no deduction is allowed for the expense of any food or beverages paid or incurred while traveling away from home in pursuit of a trade or business unless the taxpayer meets the substantiation requirements in section 274(d).

(iii) *Travel meal expenses of spouse, dependent or others.*—No deduction is allowed under chapter 1 of the Internal Revenue Code (Code), except under section 217 for certain members of the Armed Forces of the United States, for the expense of any food or beverages paid or incurred with respect to a spouse, dependent, or other individual accompanying the taxpayer, or an officer or employee of the taxpayer, on business travel, unless—

(A) The spouse, dependent, or other individual is an employee of the taxpayer;

(B) The travel of the spouse, dependent, or other individual is for a bona fide business purpose of the taxpayer; and

(C) The expenses would otherwise be deductible by the spouse, dependent or other individual.

(D) *Example.*—The following example illustrates the application of paragraph (a)(4)(iii) of this section:

(1) *Example.* Taxpayer F, a sole proprietor, and Taxpayer F's spouse travel from New York to Boston to attend a series of business meetings related to F's trade or business. F's spouse is not an employee of F, does not travel to Boston for a bona fide business purpose of F, and the expenses would not otherwise be deductible. While in Boston, F and F's spouse go out to dinner. Under section 274(m)(3) and paragraph (a)(4)(iii) of this section, the expenses associated with the food and beverages consumed by F's spouse are not deductible. Therefore, the cost of F's spouse's dinner is not deductible. F may deduct 50 percent of the expense associated with the food and beverages F consumed while on business travel if F meets the requirements in sections 162 and 274, including section 274(k) and (d).

(2) [Reserved]

(b) *Definitions.*—Except as otherwise provided in this section, the following definitions apply for purposes of section 274(k) and (n), § 1.274-11(b)(1)(ii) and (d), and this section:

(1) *Food or beverages.*—*Food or beverages* means all food and beverage items, regardless of whether characterized as meals, snacks, or other types of food and beverages, and regardless of whether the food and beverages are treated as *deminimis* fringes under section 132(e).

(2) *Food or beverage expenses.*—*Food or beverage expenses* mean the full cost of food or beverages, including any delivery fees, tips, and sales tax. In the case of employer-provided meals furnished at an eating facility on the employer's business premises, *food or beverage expenses* do not include expenses for the operation of the eating facility such as salaries of employees preparing and serving meals and other overhead costs.

(3) *Business associate.*—*Business associate* means a person with whom the taxpayer could reasonably expect to engage or deal in the active conduct of the taxpayer's trade or business such as the taxpayer's customer, client, supplier, employee, agent, partner, or professional adviser, whether established or prospective.

(4) *Independent contractor.*—For purposes of the reimbursement or other expense allowance arrangements described in paragraph (c)(2)(ii) of this section, *independent contractor* means a person who is not an employee of the payor.

(5) *Client or customer.*—For purposes of the reimbursement or other expense allowance arrangements described in paragraph (c)(2)(ii) of this section, client or *customer* of an independent contractor means a person who receives services from an independent contractor and enters into a reimbursement or other expense allowance arrangement with the independent contractor.

(6) *Payor.*—For purposes of the reimbursement or other expense allowance arrangements described in paragraph (c)(2)(ii) of this section, *payor* means a person that enters into a reimbursement or other expense allowance arrangement with an employee and may include an employer, its agent, or a third party.

(7) *Reimbursement or other expense allowance arrangement.*—For purposes of the reimbursement or other expense allowance arrangements described in paragraph (c)(2)(ii) of this section, *reimbursement or other expense allowance arrangement* means—

(i) For purposes of paragraph (c)(2)(ii)(B) of this section, an arrangement under which an employee receives an advance, allowance, or reimbursement from a payor for expenses the employee pays or incurs; and

(ii) For purposes of paragraph (c)(2)(ii)(C) of this section, an arrangement under which an independent contractor receives an advance, allowance, or reimbursement from a client or customer for expenses the independent contractor pays or incurs if either—

(A) A written agreement between the parties expressly states that the client or customer will reimburse the independent contractor for expenses that are subject to the limitations on deductions described in paragraph (a) of this section; or

(B) A written agreement between the parties expressly identifies the party subject to the limitations.

(8) *Primarily consumed.*—For purposes of paragraph (c)(2)(iv) of this section, *primarily consumed* means greater than 50 percent of actual or reasonably estimated consumption.

(9) *General public.*—For purposes of paragraph (c)(2)(iv) of this section, the *general public* includes, but is not limited to, customers, clients, and visitors. The *general public* does not include employees, partners, 2-percent shareholders of S corporations (as defined in section 1372(b)), or independent contractors of the taxpayer. Also, the guests on an exclusive list of guests are not the *general public.*

(c) *Exceptions.*—(1) *In general.*—The limitations on the deduction of food or beverage expenses in paragraph (a) of this section do not apply to any expense described in paragraph (c)(2) of this section. These expenses are deductible to the extent allowable under chapter 1 of the Code (chapter 1).

(2) *Exceptions.*—(i) *Expenses treated as compensation.*— (A) *Expenses includible in income of persons who are employees and are not specified individuals.*—In accordance with section 274(e)(2)(A), and except as provided in paragraph (c)(2)(i)(D) of this section, an expense paid or incurred by a taxpayer for food or beverages, if an employee who is not a specified individual is the recipient of the food or beverages, is not subject to the deduction limitations in paragraph (a) of this section to the extent that the taxpayer—

(1) Properly treats the expense relating to the recipient of food or beverages as compensation to an employee under chapter 1 and as wages to the employee for purposes of chapter 24 of the Code (chapter 24).; and

(2) Treats the proper amount as compensation to the employee under § 1.61-21.

(B) *Expenses includible in income of persons who are not employees and are not specified individuals.*—In accordance with section 274(e)(9), and except as provided in paragraph (c)(2)(i)(D) of this section, an expense paid or incurred by a taxpayer for food or beverages is not subject to the deduction limitations in paragraph (a) of this section to the extent that the expenses are properly included in income as compensation for services rendered by, or as a prize or award under section 74 to, a recipient of the expense who is not an employee of the taxpayer and is not a specified individual. The preceding sentence does not apply to any amount paid or incurred by the taxpayer if the amount is required to be included, or would be so required except that the amount is less than $600, in any information return filed by such taxpayer under part III of subchapter A of chapter 61 of the Code and is not so included.

(C) *Specified Individuals.*—In accordance with section 274(e)(2)(B), in the case of a specified individual (as defined in section 274(e)(2)(B)(ii)), the deduction limitations in paragraph (a) of this section do not apply to an expense for food or beverages of the specified individual to the extent that the amount of the expense does not exceed the sum of—

(1) The amount treated as compensation to the specified individual under chapter 1 and as wages to the specified individual for purposes of chapter 24 (if the specified individual is an employee) or as compensation for services rendered by, or as a prize or award under section 74 to, a recipient of the expense (if the specified individual is not an employee); and

(2) Any amount the specified individual reimburses the taxpayer.

(D) *Expenses for which an amount is excluded from income or is less than the proper amount.*—Notwithstanding paragraphs (c)(2)(i)(A) and (B) of this section, in the case of an expense paid or incurred by a taxpayer for food or beverages for which an amount is wholly or partially excluded from a recipients' income under any section of subtitle A of the Code (other than because the amount is reimbursed by the recipient), or for which an amount included in compensation and wages to an employee (or as income to a nonemployee) is less than the amount required to be included under § 1.61-21, the deduction limitations in paragraph (a) of this section do not apply to the extent that the amount of the expense does not exceed the sum of—

(1) The amount treated as compensation to the employee under chapter 1 (or as income to a nonemployee) and as wages to the employee for purposes of chapter 24; and

(2) Any amount the recipient reimburses the taxpayer.

(E) Examples.—The following examples illustrate the application of paragraph (c)(2)(i) of this section. In each example, assume that the food or beverage expenses are ordinary and necessary expenses under section 162(a) that are paid or incurred during the taxable year in carrying on a trade or business.

(1) Example 1.—Employer G provides food and beverages to its non-specified individual employees without charge at a company cafeteria on its premises. The food and beverages do not meet the definition of a *de minimis* fringe under section 132(e). Thus, G treats the full fair market value of the food and beverage expenses as compensation and wages, and properly determines this amount under §1.61-21. Under section 274(e)(2) and paragraph (c)(2)(i)(A) of this section, the expenses associated with the food and beverages provided to the employees are not subject to the 50 percent deduction limitation in paragraph (a) of this section. Thus, G may deduct 100 percent of the food and beverage expenses.

(2) Example 2.—The facts are the same as in paragraph (c)(2)(i)(E)(1) of this section (*Example 1*), except that each employee pays $8 per day for the food and beverages. The fair market value of the food and beverages is $10 per day, per employee. G incurs $9 per day, per employee for the food and beverages. G treats the food and beverage expenses as compensation and wages, and properly determines the amount of the inclusion under §1.61-21 to be $2 per day, per employee ($10 fair market value - $8 reimbursed by the employee = $2). Therefore, under paragraph (c)(2)(i)(A) of this section, G may deduct 100 percent of the food and beverage expenses, or $9 per day, per employee.

(3) Example 3.—Employer H provides meals to its employees without charge. The meals are properly excluded from the employees' income under section 119 as meals provided for the convenience of the employer. Under §1.61-21(b)(1), an employee must include in gross income the amount by which the fair market value of a fringe benefit exceeds the sum of the amount, if any, paid for the benefit by or on behalf of the recipient, and the amount, if any, specifically excluded from gross income by some other section of subtitle A of the Code. Because the entire value of the employees' meals is excluded from the employees' income under section 119, the fair market value of the fringe benefit does not exceed the amount excluded from gross income under subtitle A of the Code, so there is nothing to be included in the employees' income under §1.61-21. Thus, the exception in section 274(e)(2) and paragraph (c)(2)(i) of this section does not apply and, assuming no other exceptions provided under section 274(n)(2) and paragraph (c)(2) of this section apply, H may deduct only 50 percent of the expenses for the food and beverages provided to employees. In addition, the limitations in section 274(k)(1) and paragraph (a)(1) of this section apply because none of the exceptions in section 274(k)(2) and paragraph (c)(2) of this section apply.

(ii) *Reimbursed food or beverage expenses.*—(A) *In general.*—In accordance with section 274(e)(3), in the case of expenses for food or beverages paid or incurred by one person in connection with the performance of services for another person, whether or not the other person is an employer, under a reimbursement or other expense allowance arrangement, the deduction limitations in paragraph (a) of this section apply either to the person who makes the expenditure or to the person who actually bears the expense, but not to both. If an expense of a type described in paragraph (c)(2)(ii) of this section properly constitutes a dividend paid to a shareholder, unreasonable compensation paid to an employee, a personal expense, or other nondeductible expense, nothing in this exception prevents disallowance of the deduction to the taxpayer under other provisions of the Code.

(B) *Reimbursement arrangements involving employees.*—In the case of expenses paid or incurred by an employee for food or beverages in performing services as an employee under a reimbursement or other expense allowance arrangement with a payor, the limitations on deductions in paragraph (a) of this section apply—

(1) To the employee to the extent the employer treats the reimbursement or other payment of the expense on the employer's income tax return as originally filed as compensation paid to the employee and as wages to the employee for purposes of withholding under chapter 24 relating to collection of income tax at source on wages; or

(2) To the payor to the extent the reimbursement or other payment of the expense is not treated as compensation and wages paid to the employee in the manner provided in paragraph (c)(2)(ii)(B)(1) of this section. However, see paragraph (c)(2)(ii)(C) of this section if the payor receives a payment from a third party that may be treated as a reimbursement arrangement under this paragraph.

(C) *Reimbursement arrangements involving persons that are not employees.*—In the case of expenses for food or beverages paid or incurred by an independent contractor in connection with the performance of services for a client or customer under a reimbursement or other expense allowance arrangement with the independent contractor, the limitations on deductions in paragraph (a) of this section apply to the party expressly identified in an agreement between the parties as subject to the limitations. If an agreement between the parties does not expressly identify the party subject to the limitations, then the deduction limitations in paragraph (a) of this section apply—

(1) To the independent contractor (which may be a payor) to the extent the independent contractor does not account to the client or customer within the meaning of section 274(d); or

(2) To the client or customer if the independent contractor accounts to the client or customer within the meaning of section 274(d).

(D) *Section 274(d) substantiation.*—If the reimbursement or other expense allowance arrangement involves persons who are not employees and the agreement between the parties does not expressly identify the party subject to the limitations on deductions in paragraph (a) of this section, the limitations on deductions in paragraph (a) of this section apply to the independent contractor unless the independent contractor accounts to the client or customer with substantiation that satisfies the requirements of section 274(d).

(E) *Examples.*—The following examples illustrate the application of paragraph (c)(2)(ii) of this section.

(1) Example 1.—(i) Employee I performs services under an arrangement in which J, an employee leasing company, pays I a per diem allowance of $10x for each day that I performs services for J's client, K, while traveling away from home. The per diem allowance is a reimbursement of travel expenses for food or beverages that I pays in performing services as an employee. J enters into a written agreement with K under which K agrees to reimburse J for any substantiated reimbursements for travel expenses, including meal expenses, that J pays to I. The agreement does not expressly identify the party that is subject to the limitations on deductions in paragraph (a) of this section. I performs services for K while traveling away from home for 10 days and provides J with substantiation that satisfies the requirements of section 274(d) of $100x of meal expenses incurred by I while traveling away from home. J pays I $100x to reimburse those expenses pursuant to their arrangement. I delivers a copy of I's substantiation to K. K pays J $300x, which includes $200x compensation for services and $100x as reimbursement of J's payment of I's travel expenses for meals. Neither J nor K treats the $100x paid to I as compensation or wages.

(ii) Under paragraph (b)(7)(i) of this section, I and J have established a reimbursement or other expense allowance arrangement for purposes of paragraph (c)(2)(ii)(B) of this section. Because the reimbursement payment is not treated as compensation and wages paid to I, under section 274(e)(3)(A) and paragraph (c)(2)(ii)(B)(1) of this section, I is not subject to the limitations on deductions in paragraph (a) of this section. Instead, under paragraph (c)(2)(ii)(B)(2) of this section, J, the payor, is subject to limitations on deductions in paragraph (a) of this section unless J can meet the requirements of section 274(e)(3)(B) and paragraph (c)(2)(ii)(C) of this section.

(iii) Because the agreement between J and K expressly states that K will reimburse J for substantiated reimbursements for travel expenses that J pays to I, under paragraph (b)(7)(ii)(A) of this section, J and K have established a reimbursement or other expense allowance arrangement for purposes of paragraph (c)(2)(ii)(C) of this section. J accounts to K for K's reimbursement in the manner required by section 274(d) by delivering to K a copy of the substantiation J received from I. Therefore, under section 274(e)(3)(B) and paragraph (c)(2)(ii)(C)(2) of this section, K and not J is subject to the deduction limitations in paragraph (a) of this section.

(2) Example 2.—(i) The facts are the same as in paragraph (c)(2)(ii)(E)(1) of this section (*Example 1*) except that under the arrangements between I and J and between J and K, I provides the substantiation of the expenses directly to K, and K pays the per diem directly to I.

(ii) Under paragraph (b)(7)(i) of this section, I and K have established a reimbursement or other expense allowance arrangement for purposes of paragraph (c)(2)(ii)(C) of this section. Because I substantiates directly to K and the reimbursement payment was not treated as compensation and wages paid to I, under section 274(e)(3)(A) and paragraph (c)(2)(ii)(C)(1) of this section, I is not subject to the limitations on deductions in paragraph (a) of this section. Under paragraph (c)(2)(ii)(C)(2) of this section, K, the payor, is subject to the limitations on deductions in paragraph (a) of this section.

(3) Example 3.—*(i)* The facts are the same as in·paragraph (c)(2)(ii)(E)(1) of this section (*Example 1*), except that the written agreement between J and K expressly provides that the limitations of this section will apply to K.

(ii) Under paragraph (b)(7)(ii)(B) of this section, J and K have established a reimbursement or other expense allowance arrangement for purposes of paragraph (c)(2)(ii)(C) of this section. Because the agreement provides that the 274 deduction limitations apply to K, under section 274(e)(3)(B) and paragraph (c)(2)(ii)(C) of this section, K and not J is subject to the limitations on deductions in paragraph (a) of this section.

(4) Example 4.—*(i)* The facts are the same as in (c)(2)(ii)(E)(1) of this section (*Example 1*), except that the agreement between J and K does not provide that K will reimburse J for travel expenses.

(ii) The arrangement between J and K is not a reimbursement or other expense allowance arrangement within the meaning of section 274(e)(3)(B) and paragraph (b)(7)(ii) of this section. Therefore, even though J accounts to K for the expenses, J is subject to the limitations on deductions in paragraph (a) of this section.

(iii) Recreational expenses for employees.—*(A) In general.*—In accordance with section 274(e)(4), any food or beverage expense paid or incurred by a taxpayer for a recreational, social, or similar activity, primarily for the benefit of a taxpayer's employees (other than employees who are highly compensated employees (within the meaning of section 414(q))) is not subject to the deduction limitations in paragraph (a) of this section. For purposes of this paragraph (c)(2)(iii), an employee owning less than a 10-percent interest in the taxpayer's trade or business is not considered a shareholder or other owner, and for such purposes an employee is treated as owning any interest owned by a member of the employee's family (within the meaning of section 267(c)(4)). Any expense for food or beverages that is made under circumstances which discriminate in favor of highly compensated employees is not considered to be made primarily for the benefit of employees generally. An expense for food or beverages is not to be considered outside of the exception of this paragraph (c)(2)(iii) merely because, due to the large number of employees involved, the provision of food or beverages is intended to benefit only a limited number of employees at one time, provided the provision of food or beverages does not discriminate in favor of highly compensated employees. This exception applies to expenses paid or incurred for events such as holiday parties, annual picnics, or summer outings. This exception does not apply to expenses for meals the value of which is excluded from employees' income under section 119 because the meals are provided for the convenience of the employer and are therefore not primarily for the benefit of the taxpayer's employees.

(B) Examples.—The following examples illustrate the application of this paragraph (c)(2)(iii). In each example, assume that the food or beverage expenses are ordinary and necessary expenses under section 162(a) that are paid or incurred during the taxable year in carrying on a trade or business.

(1) Example 1.—Employer L invites all employees to a holiday party in a hotel ballroom that includes a buffet dinner and an open bar. Under section 274(e)(4), this paragraph (c)(2)(iii), and §1.274-11(c), the cost of the party, including food and beverage expenses, is not subject to the deduction limitations in paragraph (a) of this section because the holiday party is a recreational, social, or similar activity primarily for the benefit of non-highly compensated employees. Thus, L may deduct 100 percent of the cost of the party.

(2) Example 2.—The facts are the same as in paragraph (c)(2)(iii)(B)(1) of this section (*Example 1*), except that Employer L invites only highly-compensated employees to the holiday party, and the invoice provided by the hotel lists the costs for food and beverages separately from the cost of the rental of the ballroom. The costs reflect the venue's usual selling price for food or beverages. The exception in this paragraph (c)(2)(iii) does not apply to the rental of the ballroom or the food and beverage expenses because L invited only highly-compensated employees to the holiday party. However, under §1.274-11(b)(1)(ii), the food and beverage expenses are not treated as entertainment. Therefore, L is not subject to the full disallowance for its separately stated food and beverage expense under section 274(a)(1) and §1.274-11(a). Unless another exception in section 274(n)(2) and paragraph (c)(2) of this section applies, L may deduct only 50 percent of the food and beverage costs under paragraph (a)(2) of this section. In addition, the limitations in section 274(k)(1) and paragraph (a)(1) of this section apply because none of the exceptions in section 274(k)(2) and paragraph (c)(2) of this section apply.

(3) Example 3.—Employer M provides free coffee, soda, bottled water, chips, donuts, and other snacks in a break room available to all employees. A break room is not a recreational, social, or similar activity primarily for the benefit of the employees, even if some socializing related to the food and beverages provided occurs. Thus, the exception in section 274(e)(4) and this paragraph (c)(2)(iii) does not apply and unless another exception in section 274(n)(2) and paragraph (c)(2) of this section applies, M may deduct only 50 percent of the expenses for food and beverages provided in the break room under paragraph (a)(2) of this section. In addition, the limitations in section 274(k)(1) and paragraph (a)(1) of this section apply because none of the exceptions in section 274(k)(2) and paragraph (c)(2) of this section apply.

(4) Example 4.—Employer N has a written policy that employees in a certain medical services-related position must be available for emergency calls due to the nature of the position that requires frequent emergency responses. Because these emergencies can and do occur during meal periods, N furnishes food and beverages to employees in this position without charge in a cafeteria on N's premises. N excludes food and beverage expenses from the employees' income as meals provided for the convenience of the employer excludable under section 119. Because these food and beverages are furnished for the employer's convenience, and therefore are not primarily for the benefit of the employees, the exception in section 274(e)(4) and this paragraph (c)(2)(iii) does not apply, even if some socializing related to the food and beverages provided occurs. Further, the exception in section 274(e)(2) and paragraph (c)(2)(i) of this section does not apply. Thus, unless another exception in section 274(n)(2) and paragraph (c)(2) of this section applies, N may deduct only 50 percent of the expenses for food and beverages provided to employees in the cafeteria under paragraph (a)(2) of this section. In addition, the limitations in section 274(k)(1) and paragraph (a)(1) of this section apply because none of the exceptions in section 274(k)(2) and paragraph (c)(2) of this section apply.

(5) Example 5.—Employer 0 invites an employee and a client to dinner at a restaurant. Because it is the birthday of the employee, 0 orders a special dessert in celebration. Because the meal is a business meal, and therefore not primarily for the benefit of the employee, the exception in section 274(e)(4) and this paragraph (c)(2)(iii) does not apply, even though an employee social activity in the form of a birthday celebration occurred during the meal. Thus, unless another exception in section 274(n)(2) and paragraph (c)(2) of this section applies, 0 may deduct only 50 percent of the meal expense. In addition, the limitations in section 274(k)(1) and paragraph (a)(1) of this section apply because none of the exceptions in section 274(k)(2) and paragraph (c)(2) of this section apply.

(iv) Items available to the public.—*(A) In general.*—In accordance with section 274(e)(7), any expense paid or incurred by a taxpayer for food or beverages to the extent the food or beverages are made available to the general public is not subject to the deduction limitations in paragraph (a) of this section. If a taxpayer provides food or beverages to employees, this exception applies to the entire amount of expenses for those food or beverages if the same type of food or beverages is provided to, and are primarily consumed by, the general public.

(B) Examples.—The following examples illustrate the application of this paragraph (c)(2)(iv). In each example, assume that the food and beverage expenses are ordinary and necessary expenses under section 162(a) that are paid or incurred during the taxable year in carrying on a trade or business.

(1) Example 1.—Employer P is a real estate agent and provides refreshments at an open house for a home available for sale to the public. The refreshments are consumed by P's employees, potential buyers of the property, and other real estate agents. Under section 274(e)(7) and this paragraph (c)(2)(iv), the expenses associated with the refreshments are not subject to the deduction limitations in paragraph (a) of this section if P determines that over 50 percent of the food and beverages are actually or reasonably estimated to be consumed by potential buyers and other real estate agents. If more than 50 percent of the food and beverages are not actually or reasonably estimated to be consumed by the general public, only the costs attributable to the food and beverages provided to the general public are excepted under section 274(e)(7) and this paragraph (c)(2)(iv). In addition, the limitations in section 274(k)(1) and paragraph (a)(1) of this section apply to the expenses associated with the refreshments that are not excepted under section 274(e)(7) and this paragraph (c)(2)(iv).

(2) Example 2.—Employer Q is an automobile service center and provides refreshments in its waiting area. The refreshments are consumed by Q's employees and customers, and Q reasonably estimates that more than 50 percent of the refreshments are

consumed by customers. Under section 274(e)(7) and this paragraph (c)(2)(iv), the expenses associated with the refreshments are not subject to the deduction limitations provided for in paragraph (a) of this section because the food and beverages are primarily consumed by customers. Thus, Q may deduct 100 percent of the food and beverage expenses.

(3) *Example 3.*—Employer R operates a summer camp open to the general public for children and provides breakfast and lunch, as part of the fee to attend camp, both to camp counselors, who are employees, and to camp attendees, who are customers. There are 20 camp counselors and 100 camp attendees. The same type of meal is available to each counselor and attendee, and attendees consume more than 50 percent of the food and beverages. Under section 274(e)(7) and this paragraph (c)(2)(iv), the expenses associated with the food and beverages are not subject to the deduction limitations in paragraph (a) of this section, because over 50 percent of the food and beverages are consumed by camp attendees and the food and beverages are therefore primarily consumed by the general public. Thus, R may deduct 100 percent of the food and beverage expenses.

(4) *Example 4.*—Employer S provides food and beverages to its employees without charge at a company cafeteria on its premises. Occasionally, customers or other visitors also eat without charge in the cafeteria. The occasional consumption of food and beverages at the company cafeteria by customers and visitors is less than 50 percent of the total amount of food and beverages consumed at the cafeteria. Therefore, the food and beverages are not primarily consumed by the general public, and only the costs attributable to the food and beverages provided to the general public are excepted under section 274(e)(7) and this paragraph (c)(2)(iv). In addition, the limitations in section 274(k)(1) and paragraph (a)(1) of this section apply to the expenses associated with the food and beverages that are not excepted under section 274(e)(7) and this paragraph (c)(2)(iv).

(v) *Goods or services sold to customers.*—(A) *In general.*—In accordance with section 274(e)(8), an expense paid or incurred for food or beverages, to the extent the food or beverages are sold to customers in a bona fide transaction for an adequate and full consideration in money or money's worth, is not subject to the deduction limitations in paragraph (a) of this section. However, *money or money's worth* does not include payment through services provided. Under this paragraph (c)(2)(v), a restaurant or catering business may deduct 100 percent of its costs for food or beverage items, purchased in connection with preparing and providing meals to its paying customers, which are also consumed at the worksite by employees who work in the employer's restaurant or catering business. In addition, for purposes of this paragraph (c)(2)(v), the term *customer* includes anyone, including an employee of the taxpayer, who is sold food or beverages in a bona fide transaction for an adequate and full consideration in money or money's worth.

(B) *Example.*—The following example illustrates the application of this paragraph (c)(2)(v):

Example. Employer T operates a restaurant. T provides food and beverages to its food service employees before, during, and after their shifts for no consideration. Under section 274(e)(8) and this paragraph (c)(2)(v), the expenses associated with the food and beverages provided to the employees are not subject to the 50 percent deduction limitation in paragraph (a) of this section because the restaurant sells food and beverages to customers in a bona fide transaction for an adequate and full consideration in money or money's worth. Thus, T may deduct 100 percent of the food and beverage expenses.

(d) *Applicability date.*—This section applies for taxable years that begin on or after October 9, 2020. [Reg. § 1.274-12.]

☐ [*T.D.* 9925, 10-2-2020.]

[Reg. § 1.274-13]

§ 1.274-13. Disallowance of deductions for certain qualified transportation fringe expenditures.—(a) *In general.*—Except as provided in this section, no deduction otherwise allowable under chapter 1 of the *Internal Revenue Code* (Code) is allowed for any expense of any qualified transportation fringe as defined in paragraph (b)(1) of this section.

(b) *Definitions.*—The following definitions apply for purposes of this section:

(1) *Qualified transportation fringe.*—The term *qualified transportation fringe* means any of the following provided by an employer to an employee:

(i) Transportation in a commuter highway vehicle if such transportation is in connection with travel between the employee's residence and place of employment (as described in sections 132(f)(1)(A) and 132(f)(5)(B));

(ii) Any transit pass (as described in sections 132(f)(1)(B) and 132(f)(5)(A)); or

(iii) Qualified parking (as described in sections 132(f)(1)(C) and 132(f)(5)(c)).

(2) *Employee.*—The term *employee* means a common law employee or other statutory employee, such as an officer of a corporation, who is currently employed by the taxpayer. See § 1.132-9 Q/A-5. Partners, 2-percent shareholders of S corporations (as defined in section 1372(b)), sole proprietors, and independent contractors are not employees of the taxpayer for purposes of this section. See § 1.132-9 Q/A-24.

(3) *General public.*—(i) *In general.*—The term *general public* includes, but is not limited to, customers, clients, visitors, individuals delivering goods or services to the taxpayer, students of an educational institution, and patients of a health care facility. The term general public does not include individuals that are employees, partners, 2-percent shareholders of S corporations (as defined in section 1372(b)), sole proprietors, or independent contractors of the taxpayer. Also, an exclusive list of guests of a taxpayer is not the general public. Parking spaces that are available to the general public but empty are treated as provided to the general public. Parking spaces that are used to park vehicles owned by the general public while the vehicles await repair or service by the taxpayer are also treated as provided to the general public.

(ii) *Multi-tenant building.*—If a taxpayer owns or leases space in a multi-tenant building, the term *general public* includes employees, partners, 2-percent shareholders of S corporations (as defined in section 1372(b)), sole proprietors, independent contractors, clients, or customers of unrelated tenants in the building.

(4) *Parking facility.*—The term *parking facility* includes indoor and outdoor garages and other structures, as well as parking lots and other areas, where a taxpayer provides qualified parking (as defined in section 132(f)(5)(C)) to one or more of its employees. The term *parking facility* may include one or more parking facilities but does not include parking spaces on or near property used by an employee for residential purposes.

(5) *Geographic location.*—The term *geographic location* means contiguous tracts or parcels of land owned or leased by the taxpayer. Two or more tracts or parcels of land are contiguous if they share common boundaries or would share common boundaries but for the interposition of a road, street, railroad, stream, or similar property. Tracts or parcels of land which touch only at a common corner are not contiguous.

(6) *Total parking spaces.*—The term *total parking spaces* means the total number of parking spaces, or the taxpayer's portion thereof, in the parking facility.

(7) *Reserved employee spaces.*—The term *reserved employee spaces* means the spaces in the parking facility, or the taxpayer's portion thereof, exclusively reserved for the taxpayer's employees. Employee spaces in the parking facility, or portion thereof, may be exclusively reserved for employees by a variety of methods, including, but not limited to, specific signage (for example, "Employee Parking Only") or a separate facility or portion of a facility segregated by a barrier to entry or limited by terms of access. Inventory/unusable spaces are not included in *reserved employee spaces.*

(8) *Reserved nonemployee spaces.*—The term *reserved nonemployee spaces* means the spaces in the parking facility, or the taxpayer's portion thereof, exclusively reserved for nonemployees. Such parking spaces may include, but are not limited to, spaces reserved exclusively for visitors, customers, partners, sole proprietors, 2-percent shareholders of S corporations (as defined in section 1372(b)), vendor deliveries, and passenger loading/unloading. Nonemployee spaces in the parking facility, or portion thereof, may be exclusively reserved for nonemployees by a variety of methods, including, but not limited to, specific signage (for example, "Customer Parking Only") or a separate facility, or portion of a facility, segregated by a barrier to entry or limited by terms of access. Inventory/unusable spaces are not included in *reserved nonemployee spaces.*

(9) *Inventory/unusable spaces.*—The term *inventory/unusable spaces* means the spaces in the parking facility, or the taxpayer's portion thereof, exclusively used or reserved for inventoried vehicles, qualified nonpersonal use vehicles described in § 1.274-5(k), or other fleet vehicles used in the taxpayer's business, or that are otherwise not usable for parking by employees or the general public. Examples of such parking spaces include, but are not limited to, parking spaces for vehicles that are intended to be sold or leased at a car dealership or car rental agency, parking spaces for vehicles owned by an electric

utility used exclusively to maintain electric power lines, or parking spaces occupied by trash dumpsters (or similar property). Taxpayers may use any reasonable methodology to determine the number of inventory/unusable spaces in the parking facility. A reasonable methodology may include using the average of monthly inventory counts.

(10) *Available parking spaces.*—The term *available parking spaces* means the total parking spaces, less reserved employee spaces and less inventory/unusable spaces, that are available to employees and the general public.

(11) *Primary use.*—The term *primary use* means greater than 50 percent of actual or estimated usage of the available parking spaces in the parking facility.

(12) *Total parking expenses.*—(i) *In general.*—The term *total parking expenses* means all expenses of the taxpayer related to total parking spaces in a parking facility including, but not limited to, repairs, maintenance, utility costs, insurance, property taxes, interest, snow and ice removal, leaf removal, trash removal, cleaning, landscape costs, parking lot attendant expenses, security, and rent or lease payments or a portion of a rent or lease payment (if not broken out separately). A taxpayer may use any reasonable methodology to allocate mixed parking expenses to a parking facility. A deduction for an allowance for depreciation on a parking facility owned by a taxpayer and used for parking by the taxpayer's employees is an allowance for the exhaustion, wear and tear, and obsolescence of property, and not included in *total parking expenses* for purposes of this section. Expenses paid or incurred for nonparking facility property, including items related to property next to the parking facility, such as landscaping or lighting, also are not included in *total parking expenses.*

(ii) *Optional rule for allocating certain mixed parking expenses.*—A taxpayer may choose to allocate 5 percent of any the following mixed parking expenses to a parking facility: lease or rental agreement expenses, property taxes, interest expense, and expenses for utilities and insurance.

(13) *Mixed parking expense.*—The term *mixed parking expense* means a single expense amount paid or incurred by a taxpayer that includes both parking facility and nonparking facility expenses for a property that a taxpayer owns or leases.

(14) *Peak demand period.*—(i) *In general.*—The term *peak demand period* refers to the period of time on a typical business day during the taxable year when the greatest number of the taxpayer's employees are utilizing parking spaces in the taxpayer's parking facility. If a taxpayer's employees work in shifts, the *peak demand period* would take into account the shift during which the largest number of employees park in the taxpayer's parking facility. However, a brief transition period during which two shifts overlap in their use of parking spaces, as one shift of employees is getting ready to leave and the next shift is reporting to work, may be disregarded. Taxpayers may use any reasonable methodology to determine the total number of spaces used by employees during the *peak demand period* on a typical business day. A reasonable methodology may include periodic inspections or employee surveys.

(ii) *Optional rule for federally declared disasters.*—If a taxpayer owns or leases a parking facility that is located in a federally declared disaster area, as defined in section 165(i)(5), the taxpayer may choose to identify a typical business day for the taxable year in which the disaster occurred by reference to a typical business day in that taxable year prior to the date that the taxpayer's operations were impacted by the federally declared disaster. Alternatively, a taxpayer may choose to identify a typical business day during the month(s) of the taxable year in which the disaster occurred by reference to a typical business day during the same month(s) of the taxable year immediately preceding the taxable year in which the disaster first occurred. For purposes of applying the optional rule for federally declared disasters, the taxable year in which the disaster occurs is determined without regard to whether an election under section 165(i) is made with respect to the disaster.

(c) *Optional aggregation rule for calculating total parking spaces; taxpayer owned or leased parking facilities.*—For purposes of determining total parking spaces in calculating the disallowance of deductions for qualified transportation fringe parking expenses under the general rule in paragraph (d)(2)(i) of this section, the primary use methodology in paragraph (d)(2)(ii)(B) of this section, or the cost per space methodology in paragraph (d)(2)(ii)(C) of this section, a taxpayer that owns or leases more than one parking facility in a single geographic location may aggregate the number of spaces in those parking facilities. For example, parking spaces at an office park or an industrial complex in the geographic location may be aggregated. However, a taxpayer may not aggregate parking spaces in parking facilities that are in different geographic locations. A taxpayer that chooses to aggregate its parking spaces under this paragraph (c) must determine its total parking expenses, including the allocation of mixed parking expenses, as if the aggregated parking spaces constitute one parking facility.

(d) *Calculation of disallowance of deductions for qualified transportation fringe expenses.*—(1) *Taxpayer pays a third party for parking qualified transportation fringe.*—If a taxpayer pays a third party an amount for its employees' parking qualified transportation fringe, the section 274(a)(4) disallowance generally is calculated as the taxpayer's total annual cost of employee parking qualified transportation fringes paid to the third party.

(2) *Taxpayer provides parking qualified transportation fringe at a parking facility it owns or leases.*—If a taxpayer owns or leases all or a portion of one or more parking facilities where its employees park, the section 274(a)(4) disallowance may be calculated using the general rule in paragraph (d)(2)(i) of this section or any of the simplified methodologies in paragraph (d)(2)(ii) of this section. A taxpayer may choose to use the general rule or any of the following methodologies for each taxable year and for each parking facility.

(i) *General rule.*—A taxpayer that uses the general rule in this paragraph (d)(2)(i) must calculate the disallowance of deductions for qualified transportation fringe parking expenses for each employee receiving the qualified transportation fringe based on a reasonable interpretation of section 274(a)(4). A taxpayer that uses the general rule in this paragraph (d)(2)(i) may use the aggregation rule in paragraph (c) of this section for determining total parking spaces. An interpretation of section 274(a)(4) is not reasonable unless the taxpayer applies the following rules when calculating the disallowance under this paragraph (d)(2)(i).

(A) *A taxpayer must not use value to determine expense.*—A taxpayer may not use the value of employee parking to determine expenses allocable to employee parking that is either owned or leased by the taxpayer because section 274(a)(4) disallows a deduction for the expense of providing a qualified transportation fringe, regardless of its value.

(B) *A taxpayer must not deduct expenses related to reserved employee spaces.*—A taxpayer must determine the allocable portion of total parking expenses that relate to any reserved employee spaces. No deduction is allowed for the parking expenses that relate to reserved employee spaces.

(C) *A taxpayer must not improperly apply the exception for qualified parking made available to the public.*—A taxpayer must not improperly apply the exception in section 274(e)(7) or paragraph (e)(2)(ii) of this section to parking facilities, for example, by treating a parking facility regularly used by employees as available to the general public merely because the general public has access to the parking facility.

(ii) *Additional simplified methodologies.*—Instead of using the general rule in paragraph (d)(2)(i) of this section for a taxpayer owned or leased parking facility, a taxpayer may use a simplified methodology under paragraph (d)(2)(ii)(A), (B), or (C) of this section.

(A) *Qualified parking limit methodology.*—A taxpayer that uses the qualified parking limit methodology in this paragraph (d)(2)(ii)(A) must calculate the disallowance of deductions for qualified transportation fringe parking expenses by multiplying the total number of spaces used by employees during the peak demand period, or the total number of taxpayer's employees, by the section 132(f)(2) monthly per employee limitation on exclusion (adjusted for inflation), for each month in the taxable year. The result is the amount of the taxpayer's expenses that are disallowed under section 274(a)(4). In applying this methodology, a taxpayer calculates the disallowed amount as required under this paragraph (d)(2)(ii)(A), regardless of the actual amount of the taxpayer's total parking expenses. This methodology may be used only if the taxpayer includes the value of the qualified transportation fringe in excess of the sum of the amount, if any, paid by the employee for the qualified transportation fringe and the applicable statutory monthly limit in section 132(f)(2) as compensation paid to the employee under chapter 1 of the Code (chapter 1) and as wages to the employee for purposes of withholding under chapter 24 of the Code (chapter 24), relating to collection of Federal income tax at source on wages. In addition, the exception to the disallowance for amounts treated as employee compensation provided for in section section 274(e)(2) and in paragraph (e)(2)(i) of this section cannot be applied to reduce a section 274(a)(4) disallowance calculated using this methodology. A taxpayer using this methodology may not use the aggregation rule in paragraph (c) of this section.

(B) *Primary use methodology.*—A taxpayer that uses the primary use methodology in this paragraph (d)(2)(ii)(B) must use the following four-step methodology to calculate the disallowance of deductions for qualified transportation fringe parking expenses for each parking facility for which the taxpayer uses the primary use methodology. A taxpayer using this methodology may use the aggregation rule in paragraph (c) of this section for determining total parking spaces.

(1) *Step 1 - Calculate the disallowance for reserved employee spaces.*—A taxpayer must identify the total parking spaces in the parking facility, or the taxpayer's portion thereof, exclusively reserved for the taxpayer's employees. The taxpayer must then determine the percentage of reserved employee spaces in relation to total parking spaces and multiply that percentage by the taxpayer's total parking expenses for the parking facility. The product is the amount of the deduction for total parking expenses that is disallowed under section 274(a)(4) for reserved employee spaces. There is no disallowance for reserved employee spaces if the following conditions are met:

(i) The primary use (as defined in paragraphs (b)(11) and (d)(2)(ii)(B)(2) of this section) of the available parking spaces is to provide parking to the general public;

(ii) There are five or fewer reserved employee spaces in the parking facility; and

(iii) The reserved employee spaces are 5 percent or less of the total parking spaces.

(2) *Step 2 - Determine the primary use of available parking spaces.*—A taxpayer must identify the available parking spaces in the parking facility and determine whether their primary use is to provide parking to the general public. If the primary use of the available parking spaces in the parking facility is to provide parking to the general public, then total parking expenses allocable to available parking spaces at the parking facility are excepted from the section 274(a)(4) disallowance by the general public exception under section 274(e)(7) and paragraph (e)(2)(ii) of this section. Primary use of available parking spaces is based on the number of available parking spaces used by employees during the peak demand period.

(3) *Step 3 - Calculate the allowance for reserved nonemployee spaces.*—If the primary use of a taxpayer's available parking spaces is not to provide parking to the general public, the taxpayer must identify the number of available parking spaces in the parking facility, or the taxpayer's portion thereof, exclusively reserved for nonemployees. A taxpayer that has no reserved nonemployee spaces may proceed to Step 4 in paragraph (d)(2)(ii)(B)(4) of this section. If the taxpayer has reserved nonemployee spaces, it may determine the percentage of reserved nonemployee spaces in relation to remaining total parking spaces and multiply that percentage by the taxpayer's remaining total parking expenses. The product is the amount of the deduction for remaining total parking expenses that is not disallowed because the spaces are not available for employee parking.

(4) *Step 4 - Determine remaining use of available parking spaces and allocable expenses.*—If a taxpayer completes Steps 1 - 3 in paragraph (d)(2)(ii)(B) of this section and has any remaining total parking expenses not specifically categorized as deductible or nondeductible, the taxpayer must reasonably allocate such expenses by determining the total number of available parking spaces used by employees during the peak demand period.

(C) *Cost per space methodology.*—A taxpayer using the cost per space methodology in this paragraph (d)(2)(ii)(C) must calculate the disallowance of deductions for qualified transportation fringe parking expenses by multiplying the cost per space by the number of total parking spaces used by employees during the peak demand period. The product is the amount of the deduction for total parking expenses that is disallowed under section 274(a)(4). A taxpayer may calculate cost per space by dividing total parking expenses by total parking spaces. This calculation may be performed on a monthly basis. A taxpayer using this methodology may use the aggregation rule in paragraph (c) of this section for determining total parking spaces.

(3) *Expenses for transportation in a commuter highway vehicle or transit pass.*—If a taxpayer pays a third party an amount for its employees' commuter highway vehicle or a transit pass qualified transportation fringe, the section 274(a)(4) disallowance generally is equal to the taxpayer's total annual cost of employee commuter highway vehicle or a transit pass qualified transportation fringes paid to the third party. If a taxpayer provides transportation in a commuter highway vehicle or transit pass qualified transportation fringes in kind directly to its employees, the taxpayer must calculate the disallowance of deductions for expenses for such fringes based on a reasonable interpretation of section 274(a)(4). However, a taxpayer may not use the value of the qualified commuter highway vehicle or transit pass fringe to the employee to determine expenses allocable to such fringe because section 274(a)(4) disallows a deduction for the expense of providing a qualified transportation fringe, regardless of its value to the employee.

(e) *Specific exceptions to disallowance of deduction for qualified transportation fringe expenses.*—(1) *In general.*—The provisions of section 274(a)(4) and paragraph (a) of this section (imposing limitations on deductions for qualified transportation fringe expenses) are not applicable in the case of expenditures set forth in paragraph (e)(2) of this section. Such expenditures are deductible to the extent allowable under chapter 1 of the Code. This paragraph (e) cannot be construed to affect whether a deduction under section 162 or 212 is allowed or allowable. The fact that an expenditure is not covered by a specific exception provided for in this paragraph (e) is not determinative of whether a deduction for the expenditure is disallowed under section 274(a)(4) and paragraph (a) of this section.

(2) *Exceptions to disallowance.*—The expenditures referred to in paragraph (e)(1) of this section are set forth in paragraphs (e)(2)(i) through (iii) of this section.

(i) *Certain qualified transportation fringe expenses treated as compensation.*—(A) *Expenses includible in income of persons who are employees and are not specified individuals.*—In accordance with section 274(e)(2)(A), and except as provided in paragraph (e)(2)(i)(C) of this section, an expense paid or incurred by a taxpayer for a qualified transportation fringe, if an employee who is not a specified individual is the recipient of the qualified transportation fringe, is not subject to the disallowance of deductions provided for in paragraph (a) of this section to the extent that the taxpayer—

(1) Properly treats the expense relating to the recipient of the qualified transportation fringe as compensation to an employee under chapter 1 and as wages to the employee for purposes of chapter 24; and

(2) Treats the proper amount as compensation to the employee under §1.61-21.

(B) *Specified Individuals.*—In accordance with section 274(e)(2)(B), in the case of a specified individual (as defined in section 274(e)(2)(B)(ii)), the disallowance of deductions provided for in paragraph (a) of this section does not apply to an expense for a qualified transportation fringe of the specified individual to the extent that the amount of the expense does not exceed the sum of—

(1) The amount treated as compensation to the specified individual under chapter 1 and as wages to the specified individual for purposes of chapter 24; and

(2) Any amount the specified individual reimburses the taxpayer.

(C) *Expenses for which an amount is excluded from income or is less than the proper amount.*—Notwithstanding paragraph (e)(2)(i)(A) of this section, in the case of an expense paid or incurred by a taxpayer for a qualified transportation fringe for which an amount is wholly or partially excluded from a recipient's income under subtitle A of the Code (other than because the amount is reimbursed by the recipient), or for which an amount included in compensation and wages to an employee is less than the amount required to be included under §1.61-21, the disallowance of deductions provided for in paragraph (a) of this section does not apply to the extent that the amount of the expense does not exceed the sum of—

(1) The amount treated as compensation to the recipient under chapter 1 and as wages to the recipient for purposes of chapter 24; and

(2) Any amount the recipient reimburses the taxpayer.

(ii) *Expenses for transportation in a commuter highway vehicle, transit pass, or parking made available to the public.*—Under section 274(e)(7) and this paragraph (e)(2)(ii), any expense paid or incurred by a taxpayer for transportation in a commuter highway vehicle, a transit pass, or parking that otherwise qualifies as a qualified transportation fringe is not subject to the disallowance of deductions provided for in paragraph (a) of this section to the extent that such transportation, transit pass, or parking is made available to the general public. With respect to parking, this exception applies to the entire amount of the taxpayer's parking expense, less any expenses specifically attributable to employees (for example, expenses allocable to reserved employee spaces), if the primary use of the parking is by the general public. If the primary use of the parking is not by the general public, this exception applies only to the costs attributable to the parking used by the general public.

(iii) *Expenses for transportation in a commuter highway vehicle, transit pass, or parking sold to customers.*—Under section 274(e)(8) and this paragraph (e)(2)(iii), any expense paid or incurred by a taxpayer for transportation in a commuter highway vehicle, a transit pass, or parking that otherwise qualifies as a qualified transportation fringe to the extent such transportation, transit pass, or parking is sold to customers in a bona fide transaction for an adequate and full consideration in money or money's worth, is not subject to the disallowance of deductions provided for in paragraph (a) of this section. For purposes of this paragraph (e)(2)(iii), the term *customer* includes an employee of the taxpayer who purchases transportation in a commuter highway vehicle, a transit pass, or parking in a bona fide transaction for an adequate and full consideration in money or money's worth. If in a bona fide transaction, the adequate and full consideration for qualified parking is zero, the exception in this paragraph (e)(2)(iii) applies even though the taxpayer does not actually sell the parking to its employees. To apply the exception in this case, the taxpayer bears the burden of proving that the fair market value of the qualified parking is zero. However, solely for purposes of this paragraph (e)(2)(iii), a taxpayer will be treated as satisfying this burden if the qualified parking is provided in a rural, industrial, or remote area in which no commercial parking is available and an individual other than an employee ordinarily would not pay to park in the parking facility.

(f) *Examples.*—The following examples illustrate the provisions of this section related to parking expenses for qualified transportation fringes. For each example, unless otherwise stated, assume the parking expenses are otherwise deductible expenses paid or incurred during the 2020 taxable year; all or some portion of the expenses relate to a qualified transportation fringe under section 132(f); the section 132(f)(2) monthly per employee limitation on an employee's exclusion is $270; the fair market value of the qualified parking is not $0; all taxpayers are calendar-year taxpayers; and the length of the 2020 taxable year is 12 months.

(1) *Example 1.*—Taxpayer A pays B, a third party who owns a parking garage adjacent to A's place of business, $100 per month per parking space for each of A's 10 employees to park in B's garage, or $12,000 for parking in 2020 (($100 x 10) x 12 = $12,000). The $100 per month paid for each of A's 10 employees for parking is excludible from the employees' gross income under section 132(a)(5), and none of the exceptions in section 274(e) or paragraph (e) of this section are applicable. Thus, the entire $12,000 is subject to the section 274(a)(4) disallowance under paragraphs (a) and (d)(1) of this section.

(2) *Example 2.*—(i) Assume the same facts as in paragraph (f)(1) of this section (*Example 1*), except A pays B $300 per month for each parking space, or $36,000 for parking for 2020 (($300 x 10) x 12 = $36,000). Of the $300 per month paid for parking for each of 10 employees, $270 is excludible under section 132(a)(5) for 2020 and none of the exceptions in section 274(e) or paragraph (e) of this section are applicable to this amount. A properly treats the excess amount of $30 ($300 - $270) per employee per month as compensation and wages. Thus, $32,400 (($270 x 10) x 12 = $32,400) is subject to the section 274(a)(4) disallowance under paragraphs (a) and (d)(1) of this section.

(ii) The excess amount of $30 per employee per month is not excludible under section 132(a)(5). As a result, the exceptions in section 274(e)(2) and paragraph (e)(2)(i) of this section are applicable to this amount. Thus, $3,600 ($36,000 - $32,400 = $3,600) is not subject to the section 274(a)(4) disallowance and remains deductible.

(3) *Example 3.*—(i) Taxpayer C leases from a third party a parking facility that includes 200 parking spaces at a rate of $500 per space, per month in 2020. C's annual lease payment for the parking spaces is $1,200,000 ((200 x $500) x 12 = $1,200,000). The number of available parking spaces used by C's employees during the peak demand period is 200.

(ii) C uses the qualified parking limit methodology described in paragraph (d)(2)(ii)(A) of this section to determine the disallowance under section 274(a)(4). Under this methodology, the section 274(a)(4) disallowance is calculated by multiplying the number of available parking spaces used by employees during the peak demand period, 200, the section 132(f)(2) monthly per employee limitation on exclusion, $270, and 12, the number of months in the applicable taxable year. The amount subject to the section 274(a)(4) disallowance is $648,000 (200 x $270 x 12 = $648,000). This amount is excludible from C's employees' gross incomes under section 132(a)(5) and none of the exceptions in section 274(e) or paragraph (e) of this section are applicable to this amount. The excess $552,000 ($1,200,000 - $648,000) for which C is not disallowed a deduction under 274(a)(4) is included in C's employees' gross incomes because it exceeds the section 132(f)(2) monthly per employee limitation on exclusion.

(4) *Example 4.*—(i) *Facts.* Taxpayer D, a big box retailer, owns a surface parking facility adjacent to its store. D incurs $10,000 of total parking expenses for its store in the 2020 taxable year. D's parking facility has 510 spaces that are used by its customers, employees, and its fleet vehicles. None of D's parking spaces are reserved. The number of available parking spaces used by D's employees during

the peak demand period is 50. Approximately 30 nonreserved parking spaces are empty during D's peak demand period. D's fleet vehicles occupy 10 parking spaces.

(ii) *Methodology.* D uses the primary use methodology in paragraph (d)(2)(ii)(B) of this section to determine the amount of parking expenses that are disallowed under section 274(a)(4).

(iii) *Step 1.* Because none of D's parking spaces are exclusively reserved for employees, there is no amount to be specifically allocated to reserved employee spaces under paragraph (d)(2)(ii)(B)(1) of this section.

(iv) *Step 2.* D's number of available parking spaces is the total parking spaces reduced by the number of reserved employee spaces and inventory/unusable spaces or 500 (510 – 0 –10 = 500). The number of available parking spaces used by D's employees during the peak demand period is 50. Of the 500 available parking spaces, 450 are used to provide parking to the general public, including the 30 empty nonreserved parking spaces that are treated as provided to the general public. The primary use of D's available parking spaces is to provide parking to the general public because 90% (450 / 500 = 90%) of the available parking spaces are used by the general public under paragraph (d)(2)(ii)(B)(2) of this section. Because the primary use of the available parking spaces is to provide parking to the general public, the exception in section 274(e)(7) and paragraph (e)(2)(ii) of this section applies and none of the $10,000 of total parking expenses is subject to the section 274(a)(4) disallowance.

(5) *Example 5.*—(i) *Facts.* Taxpayer E, a manufacturer, owns a surface parking facility adjacent to its plant. E incurs $10,000 of total parking expenses in 2020. E's parking facility has 500 spaces that are used by its visitors and employees. E reserves 25 of these spaces for nonemployee visitors. The number of available parking spaces used by E's employees during the peak demand period is 400.

(ii) *Methodology.* E uses the primary use methodology in paragraph (d)(2)(ii)(B) of this section to determine the amount of parking expenses that are disallowed under section 274(a)(4).

(iii) *Step 1.* Because none of E's parking spaces are exclusively reserved for employees, there is no amount to be specifically allocated to reserved employee spaces under paragraph (d)(2)(ii)(B)(1) of this section.

(iv) *Step 2.* The primary use of E's parking facility is not to provide parking to the general public because 80% (400 / 500 = 80%) of the available parking spaces are used by its employees. Thus, expenses allocable to those spaces are not excepted from the section 274(a) disallowance by section 274(e)(7) and paragraph (e)(2)(ii) of this section under the primary use test in paragraph (d)(2)(ii)(B)(2) of this section.

(v) *Step 3.* Because 5% (25 / 500 = 5%) of E's available parking spaces are reserved nonemployee spaces, up to $9,500 ($10,000 x 95% = $9,500) of E's total parking expenses are subject to the section 274(a)(4) disallowance under this step as provided in paragraph (d)(2)(ii)(B)(3) of this section. The remaining $500 ($10,000 x 5% = $500) of expenses allocable to reserved nonemployee spaces is excepted from the section 274(a) disallowance and continues to be deductible.

(vi) *Step 4.* E must reasonably determine the employee use of the remaining parking spaces by using the number of available parking spaces used by E's employees during the peak demand period and determine the expenses allocable to employee parking spaces under paragraph (d)(2)(ii)(B)(4) of this section.

(6) *Example 6.*—(i) *Facts.* Taxpayer F, a manufacturer, owns a surface parking facility adjacent to its plant. F incurs $10,000 of total parking expenses in 2020. F's parking facility has 500 spaces that are used by its visitors and employees. F reserves 50 spaces for management. All other employees park in nonreserved spaces in F's parking facility; the number of available parking spaces used by F's employees during the peak demand period is 400. Additionally, F reserves 10 spaces for nonemployee visitors.

(ii) *Methodology.* F uses the primary use methodology in paragraph (d)(2)(ii)(B) of this section to determine the amount of parking expenses that are disallowed under section 274(a)(4).

(iii) *Step 1.* Because F reserved 50 spaces for management, $1,000 ((50 / 500) x $10,000 = $1,000) is the amount of total parking expenses that is nondeductible for reserved employee spaces under section 274(a)(4) and paragraphs (a) and (d)(2)(ii)(B)(1) of this section. None of the exceptions in section 274(e) or paragraph (e) of this section are applicable to this amount.

(iv) *Step 2.* The primary use of the remainder of F's parking facility is not to provide parking to the general public because 89% (400 / 450 = 89%) of the available parking spaces in the facility are used by its employees. Thus, expenses allocable to these spaces are not excepted from the section 274(a)(4) disallowance by section 274(e)(7) and paragraph (e)(2)(ii) of this section under the primary use test in paragraph (d)(2)(ii)(B)(2) of this section.

(v) *Step 3.* Because 2% (10 / 450 = 2.22%) of F's available parking spaces are reserved nonemployee spaces, the $180 allocable to those spaces (($10,000 - $1,000) x 2%) is not subject to the *section 274(a)(4)* disallowance and continues to be deductible under paragraph (d)(2)(ii)(B)(3) of this section.

(vi) *Step 4.* F must reasonably determine the employee use of the remaining parking spaces by using the number of available parking spaces used by F's employees during the peak demand period and determine the expenses allocable to employee parking spaces under paragraph (d)(2)(ii)(B)(4) of this section.

(7) *Example 7.*—(i) *Facts.* Taxpayer G, a financial services institution, owns a multi-level parking garage adjacent to its office building. G incurs $10,000 of total parking expenses in 2020. G's parking garage has 1,000 spaces that are used by its visitors and employees. However, one floor of the parking garage is segregated by an electronic barrier that can only be accessed with a card provided by G to its employees. The segregated parking floor contains 100 spaces. The other floors of the parking garage are not used by employees for parking during the peak demand period.

(ii) *Methodology.* G uses the primary use methodology in paragraph (d)(2)(ii)(B) of this section to determine the amount of parking expenses that are disallowed under section 274(a)(4).

(iii) *Step 1.* Because G has 100 reserved spaces for employees, $1,000 ((100 / 1,000) x $10,000 = $1,000) is the amount of total parking expenses that is nondeductible for reserved employee spaces under section 274(a)(4) and paragraph (d)(2)(ii)(B)(*1*) of this section. None of the exceptions in section 274(e) or paragraph (e) of this section are applicable to this amount.

(iv) *Step 2.* The primary use of the available parking spaces in G's parking facility is to provide parking to the general public because 100% (900 / 900 = 100%) of the available parking spaces are used by the public. Thus, expenses allocable to those spaces, $9,000, are excepted from the section 274(a)(4) disallowance by section 274(e)(7) and paragraph (e)(2)(ii) of this section under the primary use test in paragraph (d)(2)(ii)(B)(2).

(8) *Example 8.*—(i) *Facts.* Taxpayer H, an accounting firm, leases a parking facility adjacent to its office building. H incurs $10,000 of total parking expenses related to the lease payments in 2020. H's leased parking facility has 100 spaces that are used by its clients and employees. None of the parking spaces are reserved. The number of available parking spaces used by H's employees during the peak demand period is 60.

(ii) *Methodology.* H uses the primary use methodology in paragraph (d)(2)(ii)(B) of this section to determine the amount of parking expenses that are disallowed under section 274(a)(4).

(iii) *Step 1.* Because none of H's leased parking spaces are exclusively reserved for employees, there is no amount to be specifically allocated to reserved employee spaces under paragraph (d)(2)(ii)(B)(*1*) of this section.

(iv) *Step 2.* The primary use of H's leased parking facility under paragraph (d)(2)(ii)(B)(2) of this section is not to provide parking to the general public because 60% (60/100 = 60%) of the lot is used by its employees. Thus, H may not utilize the general public exception from the section 274(a)(4) disallowance provided by section 274(e)(7) and paragraph (e)(2)(ii) of this section.

(v) *Step 3.* Because none of H's parking spaces are exclusively reserved for nonemployees, there is no amount to be specifically allocated to reserved nonemployee spaces under paragraph (d)(2)(ii)(B)(3) of this section.

(vi) *Step 4.* H must reasonably determine the use of the parking spaces and the related expenses allocable to employee parking. Because the number of available parking spaces used by H's employees during the peak demand period is 60, H reasonably determines that 60% (60 / 100 = 60%) of H's total parking expenses or $6,000 ($10,000 x 60% = $6,000) is subject to the section 274(a)(4) disallowance under paragraph (d)(2)(ii)(B)(4) of this section.

(9) *Example 9.*—(i) *Facts.* Taxpayer I, a large manufacturer, owns multiple parking facilities adjacent to its manufacturing plant, warehouse, and office building at its complex in the city of X. All of I's tracts or parcels of land at its complex in city X are located in a single geographic location. I owns parking facilities in other cities. I incurs $50,000 of total parking expenses related to the parking facilities at its complex in city X in 2020. I's parking facilities at its complex in city X have 10,000 total parking spaces that are used by its visitors and employees of which 500 are reserved for management. All other spaces at parking facilities in I's complex in city X are nonreserved. The number of nonreserved spaces used by I's employees other than management during the peak demand period at I's parking facilities in city X is 8,000.

(ii) *Methodology.* I uses the primary use methodology in paragraph (d)(2)(ii)(B) of this section to determine the amount of parking expenses that are disallowed under section 274(a)(4). I chooses to apply the aggregation rule in paragraph (c) of this section to aggregate all parking facilities in the geographic location that comprises its complex in city X. However, I may not aggregate parking facilities in other cities with its parking facilities in city X because they are in different geographic locations.

(iii) *Step 1.* Because 500 spaces are reserved for management, $2,500 ((500 / 10,000) x $50,000 = $2,500) is the amount of total parking expenses that is nondeductible for reserved employee spaces for I's parking facilities in city X under section 274(a)(4) and paragraphs (a) and (d)(2)(ii)(B)(*1*) of this section.

(iv) *Step 2.* The primary use of the remainder of I's parking facility is not to provide parking to the general public because 84% (8,000 / 9,500 = 84%) of the available parking spaces in the facility are used by its employees. Thus, expenses allocable to these spaces are not excepted from the section 274(a)(4) disallowance by section 274(e)(7) or paragraph (e)(2)(ii) of this section under the primary use test in paragraph (d)(2)(ii)(B)(2) of this section.

(v) *Step 3.* Because none of I's parking spaces in its parking facilities in city X are exclusively reserved for nonemployees, there is no amount to be specifically allocated to reserved nonemployee spaces under paragraph (d)(2)(ii)(B)(3) of this section.

(vi) *Step 4.* I must reasonably determine the use of the remaining parking spaces and the related expenses allocable to employee parking for its parking facilities in city X. Because the number of available parking spaces used by I's employees during the peak demand period in city X during an average workday is 8,000, I reasonably determines that 84.2% (8,000 / 9,500 = 84.2%) of I's remaining parking expense or $39,900 (($50,000 - $2,500) x 84% = $39,900) is subject to the section 274(a)(4) disallowance under paragraph (d)(2)(ii)(B)(4) of this section.

(10), *Example 10.*—(i) Taxpayer J, a manufacturer, owns a parking facility and incurs the following mixed parking expenses (along with other parking expenses): property taxes, utilities, insurance, security expenses, and snow removal expenses. In accordance with paragraph (b)(12)(i) and (i) of this section, J determines its total parking expenses by allocating 5% of its property tax, utilities, and insurance expenses to its parking facility. J uses a reasonable methodology to allocate to its parking facility an applicable portion of its security and snow removal expenses. J determines that it incurred $100,000 of total parking expenses in 2020. J's parking facility has 500 spaces that are used by its visitors and employees. The number of total parking spaces used by J's employees during the peak demand period is 475.

(ii) J uses the cost per space methodology described in paragraph (d)(2)(ii)(C) of this section to determine the amount of parking expenses that are disallowed under section 274(a)(4). Under this methodology, J multiplies the cost per space by the number of total parking spaces used by J's employees during the peak demand period. J calculates the cost per space by dividing total parking expenses by the number of total parking spaces ($100,000 / 500 = $200). J determines that $95,000 ($200 x 475 = $95,000) of J's total parking expenses is subject to the section 274(a)(4) disallowance and none of the exceptions in section 274(e) or paragraph (e) of this section are applicable.

(11) *Example 11.*—Taxpayer K operates an industrial plant with a parking facility in a rural area in which no commercial parking is available. K provides qualified parking at the plant to its employees free of charge. Further, an individual other than an employee ordinarily would not consider paying any amount to park in the plant's parking facility. Although K does not charge its employees for the qualified parking, the exception in section 274(e)(8) and this paragraph (e)(3)(iii) will apply to K's total parking expenses if in a bona fide transaction, the adequate and full consideration for the qualified parking is zero. In order to treat the adequate and full consideration as zero, K bears the burden of proving that the parking has no objective value. K is treated as satisfying this burden because the parking is provided in a rural area in which no commercial parking is available and in which an individual other than an employee ordinarily would not consider paying any amount to park in the parking facility. Therefore, the exception in paragraph (e)(2)(iii) of this section applies to K's total parking expenses and a deduction for the expenses is not disallowed by reason of section 274(a)(4).

(g) *Applicability date.*—This section applies to taxable years beginning on or after December 16, 2020. However, taxpayers may choose to apply §1.274-13(b)(14)(ii) to taxable years ending after December 31, 2019. [Reg. §1.274-13.]

□ [*T.D.* 9939, 12-15-2020 (*corrected* 4-27-2021).]

[Reg. §1.274-14]

§1.274-14. Disallowance of deductions for certain transportation and commuting benefit expenditures.—(a) *General rule.*—Except as provided in this section, no deduction is allowed for any expense incurred for providing any transportation, or any payment or reimbursement, to an employee of the taxpayer in connection with travel between the employee's residence and place of employment. The disallowance is not subject to the exceptions provided in section 274(e). The disallowance applies regardless of whether the travel between the employee's residence and place of employment includes more than one mode of transportation, and regardless of whether the taxpayer provides, or pays or reimburses the employee for, all modes of transportation used during the trip. For example, the disallowance applies if an employee drives a personal vehicle to a location where a different mode of transportation is used to complete the trip to the place of employment, even though the taxpayer may not incur any expense for the portion of travel in the employee's personal vehicle. The rules in section 274(l) and this section do not apply to business expenses under section 162(a)(2) paid or incurred while traveling away from home. The rules in section 274(l) and this section also do not apply to any expenditure for any qualified transportation fringe (as defined in section 132(f)) provided to an employee of the taxpayer. All qualified transportation fringe expenses are required to be analyzed under section 274(a)(4) and §1.274-13

(b) *Exception.*—The disallowance for the deduction for expenses incurred for providing any transportation or commuting in paragraph (a) of this section does not apply if the transportation or commuting expense is necessary for ensuring the safety of the employee. The transportation or commuting expense is necessary for ensuring the safety of the employee if unsafe *conditions*, as described in §1.61-21(k)(5), exist for the employee.

(c) *Definitions.*—The following definitions apply for purposes of this section:

(1) *Employee.*—The term *employee* means an employee of the taxpayer as defined in section 3121(d)(1) and (2) (that is, officers of a corporate taxpayer and employees of the taxpayer under the common law rules).

(2) *Residence.*—The term *residence* means a residence as defined in §1.121-1(b)(1). An employee's residence is not limited to the employee's principal residence.

(3) *Place of employment.*—The term *place of employment* means the employee's regular or principal (if more than one regular) place of business. An employee's place of employment does not include temporary or occasional places of employment. An employee must have at least one regular or principal place of business.

(d) *Applicability date.*—This section applies to taxable years beginning on or after December 16, 2020. [Reg. §1.274-14.]

☐ [T.D. 9939, 12-15-2020.]

[Reg. §1.275-1]

§1.275-1. Deduction denied in case of certain taxes.—For description of the taxes for which a deduction is denied under section 275, see paragraphs (a), (b), (c), (d), (e), and (h) of §1.164-2. [Reg. §1.275-1.]

☐ [T.D. 6780, 12-21-64. Amended by T.D. 7767, 2-3-81.]

[Reg. §1.276-1]

§1.276-1. Disallowance of deductions for certain indirect contributions to political parties.—(a) *In general.*—Notwithstanding any other provision of law, no deduction shall be allowed for income tax purposes in respect of any amount paid or incurred after March 15, 1966, in a taxable year of the taxpayer beginning after December 31, 1965, for any expenditure to which paragraph (b)(1), (c), (d), or (e) of this section is applicable. Section 276 is a disallowance provision exclusively and does not make deductible any expenses which are not otherwise allowed under the Code. For certain other rules in respect of deductions for expenditures for political purposes, see §§1.162-15(b), 1.162-20, and 1.271-1.

(b) *Advertising in convention program.*—(1) *General rule.*—(i) Except as provided in subparagraph (2) of this paragraph, no deduction shall be allowed for an expenditure for advertising in a convention program of a political party. For purposes of this subparagraph it is immaterial who publishes the convention program or to whose use the proceeds of the program inure (or are intended to inure). A convention program is any written publication (as defined in paragraph (c) of this section) which is distributed or displayed in connection with or at a political convention, conclave, or meeting. Under certain conditions payments to a committee organized for the purpose of bringing a political convention to an area are deductible under paragraph (b) of §1.162-15. This rule is not affected by the provisions of this section. For example, such payments may be deductible notwithstanding the fact that the committee purchases from a political party the right to publish a pamphlet in connection

with a convention and that the deduction of costs of advertising in the pamphlet is prohibited under this section.

(ii) The application of the provisions of this subparagraph may be illustrated by the following example:

Example. M Corporation publishes the convention program of the Y political party for a convention not described in subparagraph (2) of this paragraph. The corporation makes no payment of any kind to or on behalf of the party or any of its candidates and no part of the proceeds of the publication and sale of the program inures directly or indirectly to the benefit of any political party or candidate. P Corporation purchases an advertisement in the program. P Corporation may not deduct the cost of such advertisement.

(2) *Amounts paid or incurred on or after January 1, 1968, for advertising in programs of certain national political conventions.*—(i) Subject to the limitations in subdivision (ii) of this subparagraph, a deduction may be allowed for any amount paid or incurred on or after January 1, 1968, for advertising in a convention program of a political party distributed in connection with a convention held for the purpose of nominating candidates for the offices of President and Vice President of the United States, if the proceeds from the program are actually used solely to defray the costs of conducting the convention (or are set aside for such use at the next convention of the party held for such purpose) and if the amount paid or incurred for the advertising is reasonable. If such amount is not reasonable or if any part of the proceeds is used for a purpose other than that of defraying such convention costs, no part of the amount is deductible. Whether or not an amount is reasonable shall be determined in light of the business the taxpayer may expect to receive either directly as a result of the advertising or as a result of the convention being held in an area in which the taxpayer has a principal place of business. For these purposes, an amount paid or incurred for advertising will not be considered as reasonable if it is greater than the amount which would be paid for comparable advertising in a comparable convention program of a nonpolitical organization. Institutional advertising (*e.g.*, advertising of a type not designed to sell specific goods or services to persons attending the convention) is not advertising which may be expected to result directly in business for the taxpayer sufficient to make the expenditures reasonable. Accordingly, an amount spent for institutional advertising in a convention program may be deductible only if the taxpayer has a principal place of business in the area where the convention is held. An official statement made by a political party after a convention as to the use made of the proceeds from its convention program shall constitute prima facie evidence of such use.

(ii) No deduction may be taken for any amount described in this subparagraph which is not otherwise allowable as a deduction under section 162, relating to trade or business expenses. Therefore, in order for any such amount to be deductible, it must first satisfy the requirements of section 162, and, in addition, it must also satisfy the more restrictive requirements of this subparagraph.

(c) *Advertising in publication other than convention program.*—No deduction shall be allowed for an expenditure for advertising in any publication other than a convention program if any part of the proceeds of such publication directly or indirectly inures (or is intended to inure) to or for the use of a political party or a political candidate. For purposes of this paragraph, a publication includes a book, magazine, pamphlet, brochure, flier, almanac, newspaper, newsletter, handbill, billboard, menu, sign, scorecard, program, announcement, radio or television program or announcement, or any similar means of communication. For the definition of inurement of proceeds to a political party or a political candidate, see paragraph (f)(3) of this section.

(d) *Admission to dinner or program.*—No deduction shall be allowed for an expenditure for admission to any dinner or program, if any part of the proceeds of such event directly or indirectly inures (or is intended to inure) to or for the use of a political party or a political candidate. For purposes of this paragraph, a dinner or program includes a gala, dance, ball, theatrical or film presentation, cocktail or other party, picnic, barbecue, sporting event, brunch, tea, supper, auction, bazaar, reading, speech, forum, lecture, fashion show, concert, opening, meeting, gathering, or any similar event. For the definition of inurement of proceeds to a political party or a political candidate and of admission to a dinner or program, see paragraph (f) of this section.

(e) *Admission to inaugural event.*—(1) No deduction shall be allowed for an expenditure for admission to an inaugural ball, inaugural gala, inaugural parade, or inaugural concert, or to any similar event (such as a dinner or program, as defined in paragraph (d) of this section), in connection with the inauguration or installation in office of any official, or any equivalent event for an unsuccessful candidate, if the event is identified with a political party or a political candidate. For purposes of this paragraph, the sponsorship of the event and the use to which the proceeds of the event are or may be put are irrelevant, except insofar as they may tend to identify the event with a political party or a political candidate. For the definition of admission to an inaugural event, see paragraph (f)(4) of this section.

(2) The application of the provisions of this paragraph may be illustrated by the following example:

Example. An inaugural reception for A, a prominent member of Y party who has been recently elected judge of the municipal court of F city, is held with the proceeds going to the city treasury. The price of admission to such affair is not deductible.

(f) *Definitions.*—(1) *Political party.*—For purposes of this section the term "political party" has the same meaning as that provided for in paragraph (b)(1) of § 1.271-1.

(2) *Political candidate.*—For purposes of this section, the term "political candidate" is to be construed in accordance with the purpose of section 276 to deny tax deductions for certain expenditures which may be used directly or indirectly to finance political campaigns. The term includes a person who, at the time of the event or publication with respect to which the deduction is being sought, has been selected or nominated by a political party for any elective office. It also includes an individual who is generally believed, under the facts and circumstances at the time of the event or publication, by the persons making expenditures in connection therewith to be an individual who is or who in the reasonably foreseeable future will be seeking selection, nomination, or election to any public office. For purposes of the preceding sentence, the facts and circumstances to be considered include, but are not limited to, the purpose of the event or publication and the disposition to be made of the proceeds. In the absence of evidence to the contrary it shall be presumed that persons making expenditures in connection with an event or publication generally believe that an incumbent of an elective public office will run for reelection to his office or for election to some other public office.

(3) *Inurement of proceeds to political party or political candidate.*—(i) *In general.*—Subject to the special rules presented in subdivision (iii) of this subparagraph (relating to a political candidate), proceeds directly or indirectly inure to or for the use of a political party or a political candidate (a) if the party or candidate may order the disposition of any part of such proceeds, regardless of what use is actually made thereof, or (b) if any part of such proceeds is utilized by any person for the benefit of the party or candidate. These conditions are equally applicable in determining whether the proceeds are intended to inure. Accordingly, it is immaterial whether the event or publication operates at a loss if, had there been a profit, any part of the proceeds would have inured to or for the use of a political party or a political candidate. Moreover, it shall be presumed that where a dinner, program, or publication is sponsored by or identified with a political party or political candidate, the proceeds of such dinner, program, or publication directly or indirectly inure (or are intended to inure) to or for the use of the party or candidate. On the other hand, proceeds are not considered to directly or indirectly inure to the benefit of a political party or political candidate if the benefit derived is so remote as to be negligible or merely a coincidence of the relationship of a political candidate to a trade or business profiting from an expenditure of funds. For example, the proceeds of expenditures made by a taxpayer in the ordinary course of his trade or business for advertising in a publication, such as a newspaper or magazine, are not considered as inuring to the benefit of a political party or political candidate merely because the publication endorses a particular political candidate or candidates of a particular political party, the publisher independently contributes to the support of political party or candidate out of his own personal funds, or the principal stockholder of the publishing firm is a candidate for public office.

(ii) *Proceeds to political party.*—If a political party may order the disposition of any part of the proceeds of a publication or event described in paragraph (c) or (d) of this section, such proceeds inure to the use of the party regardless of what the proceeds are to be used for or that their use is restricted to a particular purpose unrelated to the election of specific candidates for public office. Accordingly, where a political party holds a dinner for the purpose of raising funds to be used in a voter registration drive, voter education program, or nonprofit political research program, partisan or nonpartisan, the proceeds are considered to directly or indirectly inure to or for the use of the political party. Proceeds may inure to or for the use of a political party even though they are to be used for purposes which may not be directly related to any particular election (such as to pay office rent for its permanent quarters, salaries to permanent employees, or utilities charges, or to pay the cost of an event such as a dinner or program as defined in paragraph (d) of this section).

(iii) *Proceeds to political candidate.*—Proceeds directly or indirectly inure (or are intended to inure) to or for the use of a political candidate if, in addition to meeting the conditions described in subdivision (i) of this subparagraph, (a) some part of the proceeds is or may be used directly or indirectly for the purpose of furthering his candidacy for selection, nomination, or election to any elective public office, and (b) they are not received by him in the ordinary course of a trade or business (other than the trade or business of holding public office). Proceeds may so inure whether or not the expenditure sought to be deducted was paid or incurred before the commencement of political activities with respect to the selection, nomination, or election referred to in (a) of this subdivision, or after such selection, nomination, or election has been made or has taken place. For example, proceeds of an event which may be used by an individual who, under the facts and circumstances at the time of the event, the persons making expenditures in connection therewith generally believe will in the reasonably foreseeable future run for a public office, and which may be used in furtherance of such individual's candidacy, generally will be deemed to inure (or to be intended to inure) to or for the use of a political candidate for the purpose of furthering such individual's candidacy. Or, as another example, proceeds of an event occurring after an election, which may be used by a candidate in that election to repay loans incurred in directly or indirectly furthering his candidacy, or in reimbursement of expenses incurred in directly or indirectly furthering his candidacy, will be deemed to directly or indirectly inure (or to be intended to inure) to or for the use of a political candidate for the purpose of furthering his candidacy. For purposes of this subdivision, if the proceeds received by a candidate exceed substantially the fair market value of the goods furnished or services rendered by him, the proceeds are not received by the candidate in the ordinary course of his trade or business.

(iv) The application of the provisions of this subparagraph may be illustrated by the following examples:

Example (1). Corporation O pays the Y political party $100,000 per annum for the right to publish the Y News, and retains the entire proceeds from the sale of the publication. Amounts paid or incurred for advertising in the Y News are not deductible because a part of the proceeds thereof indirectly inures to or for the use of a political party.

Example (2). The X political party holds a highly publicized ball honoring one of its active party members and admission tickets are offered to all. The guest of honor is a prominent national figure and a former incumbent of a high public office. The price of admission is designed to cover merely the cost of entertainment, food, and the ballroom, and all proceeds are paid to the hotel where the function is held, with the political party bearing the cost of any deficit. No deduction may be taken for the price of admission to the ball since the proceeds thereof inure to or for the use of a political party.

Example (3). Taxpayer A, engaged in a trade or business, purchases a number of tickets for admission to a fund raising affair held on behalf of political candidate B. The funds raised by this affair can be used by B for the purpose of furthering his candidacy. These expenditures are not deductible by A notwithstanding that B donates the proceeds of the affair to a charitable organization.

Example (4). A, an individual taxpayer who publishes a newspaper, is a candidate for elective public office. X Corporation advertises its products in A's newspaper, paying substantially more than the normal rate for such advertising. X Corporation may not deduct any portion of the cost of that advertising.

(4) *Admission to dinners, programs, inaugural events.*—For purposes of this section, the cost of admission to a dinner, program, or inaugural event includes all charges, whether direct or indirect, for attendance and participation at such function. Thus, for example, amounts spent to be eligible for door prizes, for the privilege of sitting at the head table, or for transportation furnished as part of such an event, or any separate charges for food or drink, are amounts paid for admission. [Reg. § 1.276-1.]

□ [*T.D.* 6996, 1-17-69. *Amended by T.D.* 7010, 4-30-69.]

[Reg. § 1.278-1]

§ 1.278-1. Capital expenditures incurred in planning and developing citrus and almond groves.—(a) *General rule.*—(1)(i) Except as provided in subparagraph (a)(iii) of this paragraph and paragraph (b) of this section, there shall be charged to capital account any amount (allowable as a deduction without regard to section 278 or this section) which is attributable to the planting, cultivation, maintenance, or development of any citrus or almond grove (or part thereof), and which is incurred before the close of the fourth taxable year beginning with the taxable year in which the trees were planted. For purposes of section 278 and this section, such an amount shall be considered as "incurred" in accordance with the taxpayer's regular tax accounting method used in reporting income and expenses connected with the citrus or almond grove operation. For purposes of this paragraph, the portion of a citrus or almond grove planted in 1 taxable year shall be treated separately from the portion of such grove planted in another taxable year. The provisions of section 278 and this section apply to taxable years beginning after December 31, 1969, in the case of a citrus grove, and to taxable years beginning after January 12, 1971, in the case of an almond grove.

(ii) The provisions of this subparagraph may be illustrated by the following examples:

Example (1). T, a fiscal year taxpayer, plants a citrus grove 5 weeks before the close of his taxable year ending in 1971. T is required to capitalize any amount (allowable as a deduction without regard to section 278 or this section) attributable to the planting, cultivation, maintenance, or development of such grove until the close of his taxable year ending in 1974.

Example (2). Assume the same facts as in example (1), except that T plants one portion of such grove 5 weeks before the close of his taxable year ending in 1971 and another portion of such grove at the beginning of his taxable year ending in 1972. The required capitalization period for expenses attributable to the first portion of such grove shall run until the close of T's taxable year ending in 1974. The required capitalization period for expenses attributable to the second portion of such grove shall run until the close of T's taxable year ending in 1975.

(2)(i) For purposes of section 278 and this section a "citrus grove" is defined as one or more trees of the rue family, often thorny and bearing large fruit with hard, usually thick peel and pulpy flesh, such as the orange, grapefruit, lemon, lime, citron, tangelo, and tangerine.

(ii) For purposes of section 278 and this section, an "almond grove" is defined as one or more of the species *Prunus amygdalus*.

(iii) An amount attributable to the cultivation, maintenance, or development of a citrus or almond grove (or part thereof) shall include, but shall not be limited to, the following developmental or cultural practices expenditures: Irrigation, cultivation, pruning, fertilizing, management fees, frost protection, spraying, and upkeep of the citrus or almond grove. The provisions of section 278(a) and this paragraph shall apply to expenditures for fertilizer and related materials notwithstanding the provisions of section 180, but shall not apply to expenditures attributable to real estate taxes or interest, to soil and water conservation expenditures allowable as a deduction under section 175, or to expenditures for clearing land allowable as a deduction under section 182. Further, the provisions of section 278(a) and this paragraph apply only to expenditures allowable as deductions without regard to section 278 and have no application to expenditures otherwise chargeable to capital account, such as the cost of the land and preparatory expenditures incurred in connection with the citrus or almond grove.

(iv) For purposes of section 278 and this section, a citrus or almond tree shall be considered to be "planted" on the date on which the tree is placed in the permanent grove from which production is expected.

(3)(i) The period during which expenditures described in section 278(a) and this paragraph are required to be capitalized shall, once determined, be unaffected by a sale or other disposition of the citrus or almond grove. Such period shall, in all cases, be computed by reference to the taxable years of the owner of the grove at the time that the citrus or almond trees were planted. Therefore, if a citrus or almond grove subject to the provisions of section 278 or this paragraph is sold or otherwise transferred by the original owner of the grove before the close of his fourth taxable year beginning with the taxable year in which the trees were planted, expenditures described in section 278(a) or this paragraph made by the purchaser or other transferee of the citrus or almond grove from the date of his acquisition until the close of the original holder's fourth such taxable year are required to be capitalized.

(ii) The provisions of this subparagraph may be illustrated by the following example:

Example. T, a fiscal year taxpayer, plants a citrus grove at the beginning of his taxable year ending in 1971. At the beginning of his taxable year ending in 1972, T sells the grove to X. The required period during which expenditures described in section 278(a) are required to be capitalized runs from the date on which T planted the grove until the end of T's taxable year ending in 1974. Therefore, X must capitalize any such expenditures made by him from the time he purchased the grove from T until the end of T's taxable year ending in 1974.

(b) *Exceptions.*—(1) Paragraph (a) of this section shall not apply to amounts allowable as deductions (*without regard to section 278 or this section*) and attributable to a citrus or almond grove (or part thereof) which is replanted by a taxpayer after having been lost or damaged (while in the hands of such taxpayer) by reason of freeze, disease, drought, pests, or casualty.

(2)(i) Paragraph (a) of this section shall not apply to amounts allowable as deductions (without regard to section 278 or this section), and attributable to a citrus grove (or part thereof) which was planted or replanted prior to December 30, 1969, or to an almond grove (or part thereof) which was planted or replanted prior to December 30, 1970.

(ii) The provisions of this subparagraph may be illustrated by the following examples:

Example (1). T, a fiscal year taxpayer with a taxable year of July 1, 1969, through June 30, 1970, plants a citrus grove on August 1, 1969. Since the grove was planted prior to December 30, 1969, no expenses incurred with respect to the grove shall be subject to the provisions of paragraph (a).

Example (2). Assume the same facts as in example (1), except that T plants the grove on March 1, 1970. Since the grove was planted after December 30, 1969, all amounts allowable as deductions (without regard to section 278 or this section) and attributable to the grove shall be subject to the provisions of paragraph (a). However, since paragraph (a) applies only to taxable years beginning after December 31, 1969, T must capitalize only those amounts incurred during his taxable years ending in 1971, 1972, and 1973. [Reg. § 1.278.1.]

☐ [*T.D. 7098, 3-17-71. Amended by T.D. 7136, 8-10-71.*]

[Reg. § 1.279-1]

§ 1.279-1. General rule; purpose.—An obligation issued to provide a consideration directly or indirectly for a corporate acquisition, although constituting a debt under section 385, may have characteristics which make it more appropriate that the participation in the corporation which the obligation represents be treated for purposes of the deduction of interest as if it were a stockholder interest rather than a creditors interest. To deal with such cases, section 279 imposes certain limitations on the deductibility of interest paid or incurred on obligations which have certain equity characteristics and are classified as corporate acquisition indebtedness. Generally, section 279 provides that no deduction will be allowed for any interest paid or incurred by a corporation during the taxable year with respect to its corporate acquisition indebtedness to the extent such interest exceeds $5 million. However, the $5 million limitation is reduced by the amount of interest paid or incurred on obligations issued under the circumstances described in section 279(a)(2) but are not corporate acquisition indebtedness. Section 279(b) provides that an obligation will be corporate acquisition indebtedness if it was issued under certain circumstances and meets the four tests enumerated therein. Although an obligation may satisfy the conditions referred to in the preceding sentence, it may still escape classification as corporate acquisition indebtedness if the conditions are described in sections 279(d)(3), (4), and (5), 279(f), or 279(i) are present. However, no inference should be drawn from the rules of section 279 as to whether a particular instrument labeled a bond, debenture, note, or other evidence of indebtedness is in fact a debt. Before the determination as to whether the deduction for payments pursuant to an obligation as described in this section is to be disallowed, the obligation must first qualify as debt in accordance with section 385. If the obligation is not debt under section 385, it will be unnecessary to apply section 279 to any payments pursuant to such obligation. [Reg. § 1.279-1.]

☐ [*T.D. 7262, 3-2-73.*]

[Reg. § 1.279-2]

§ 1.279-2. Amount of disallowance of interest on corporate acquisition indebtedness.—(a) *In general.*—Under section 279(a), no deduction is allowed for any interest paid or incurred by a corporation during the taxable year with respect to its corporate acquisition indebtedness to the extent that such interest exceeds—

(1) $5 million, reduced by

(2) The amount of interest paid or incurred by such corporation during such year on any obligation issued after December 31, 1967, to provide consideration directly or indirectly for an acquisition described in section 279(b)(1) but which is not corporate acquisition indebtedness. Such an obligation is not corporate acquisition indebtedness if it—

(i) Was issued prior to October 10, 1969, or

(ii) Was issued after October 9, 1969, but does not meet any one or more of the tests of section 279(b)(2), (3), or (4), or

(iii) Was originally deemed to be corporate acquisition indebtedness but is no longer so treated by virtue of the application of paragraphs (3) or (4) of section 279(d), or

(iv) Is specifically excluded from treatment as corporate acquisition indebtedness by virtue of sections 279(d)(5), (f), or (i).

The computation of the amount by which the $5 million limitation described in this paragraph is to be reduced with respect to any taxable year is to be made as of the last day of the taxable year in which an acquisition described in section 279(b)(1) occurs. In no case shall the $5 million limitation be reduced below zero.

(b) *Certain terms defined.*—When used in section 279 and the regulations thereunder—

(1) The term "issued" includes the giving of a note or other evidence of indebtedness to a bank or other lender as well as an issuance of a bond or debenture. In the case of obligations which are registered with the Securities and Exchange Commission, the date of issue is the date on which the issue is first offered to the public. In the case of obligations which are not so registered, the date of issue is the date on which the obligation is sold to the first purchaser.

(2) The term "interest" includes both stated interest and unstated interest (such as original issue discount as defined in paragraph (a)(1) of § 1.163-4 and amounts treated as interest under section 483).

(3) The term "money" means cash and its equivalent.

(4) The term "control" shall have the meaning assigned to such term by section 368(c).

(5) The term "affiliated group" shall have the meaning assigned to such term by section 1504(a), except that all corporations other than the acquired corporation shall be treated as includible corporations (without any exclusion under section 1504(b)) and the acquired corporation shall not be treated as an includible corporation. This definition shall apply whether or not some or all of the members of the affiliated group file a consolidated return.

(c) *Examples.*—The provisions of paragraph (a) of this section may be illustrated by the following examples:

Example (1). On March 4, 1973, X Corporation, a calendar year taxpayer, issues an obligation which satisfies the test of section 279(b)(1) but fails to satisfy either of the tests of section 279(b)(2) or (3). Since at least one of the tests of section 279(b) is not satisfied the obligation is not corporate acquisition indebtedness. However, since the test of section 279(b)(1) is satisfied, the interest on the obligation will reduce the $5 million limitation provided by section 279(a)(1).

Example (2). On January 1, 1969, X Corporation, a calendar year taxpayer, issues an obligation, which satisfies all the tests of section 279(b), requiring it to pay $3.5 million of interest each year. Since the obligation was issued before October 10, 1969, the obligation cannot be corporate acquisition indebtedness, and a deduction for the $3.5 million of interest attributable to such obligation is not subject to disallowance under section 279(a). However, since the obligation was issued after December 31, 1967, in an acquisition described in section 279(b)(1), under section 279(a)(2) the $3.5 million of interest attributable to such obligation reduces the $5 million limitation provided by section 279(a)(1) to $1.5 million.

Example (3). Assume the same facts as in example (2). Assume further that on January 11, 1970, X Corporation issues more obligations which are classified as corporate acquisition indebtedness and which require X Corporation to pay $4 million of interest each year. For 1970 the amount of interest paid or accrued on corporate acquisition indebtedness, which may be deducted is $1.5 million ($5 million maximum provided by section 279(a)(1) less $3.5 million, the reduction required under section 279(a)(2)). Thus, $2.5 million of the $4 million interest incurred on a corporate acquisition indebtedness is subject to disallowance under section 279(a) for the taxable year 1970.

Example (4). Assume the same facts as in example (3). Assume further that on the last day of each of the taxable years 1971, 1972, and 1973 of X Corporation neither of the conditions described in section 279(b)(4) was present.

Under these circumstances, such obligations for all taxable years after 1973 are not corporate acquisition indebtedness under section 279(d)(4). Therefore, the $2.5 million of interest previously not deductible is now deductible for all taxable years after 1973. Although such obligations are no longer treated as corporate acquisition indebtedness, the interest attributable thereto must be applied in further reduction of the $5 million limitation. The $5 million limitation of section 279(a)(1) is therefore reduced to zero. While the limitation is at the zero level any interest paid or incurred on corporate acquisition indebtedness will be disallowed. [Reg. § 1.279-2.]

☐ [*T.D.* 7262, 3-2-73.]

[Reg. § 1.279-3]

§ 1.279-3. Corporate acquisition indebtedness.—(a) *Corporate acquisition indebtedness.*—For purposes of section 279, the term "corporate acquisition indebtedness" means any obligation evidenced by a bond, debenture, note, or certificate or other evidence of indebtedness issued after October 9, 1969, by a corporation (referred to in section 279 and the regulations thereunder as "issuing corporation") if the obligation is issued to provide consideration directly or indirectly for the acquisition of stock in, or certain assets of, another corporation (as described in paragraph (b) of this § 1.279-3), is "subordinated" (as described in paragraph (c) of this § 1.279-3), is "convertible" (as described in paragraph (d) of this § 1.279-3), and satisfies either the ratio of debt to equity test (as described in paragraph (f) of

§ 1.279-5) or the projected earnings test (as described in paragraph (d) of § 1.279-5).

(b) *Acquisition of stock or assets.*—(1) Section 279(b)(1) describes one of the tests to be satisfied if an obligation is to be classified as corporate acquisition indebtedness. Under section 279(b)(1), the obligation must be issued to provide consideration directly or indirectly for the acquisition of—

(i) Stock (whether voting or nonvoting) in another corporation (referred to in section 279 and the regulations thereunder as "acquired corporation"), or

(ii) Assets of another corporation (referred to in section 279 and the regulations thereunder as "acquired corporation") pursuant to a plan under which at least two-thirds (in value) of all the assets (excluding money) used in trades or businesses carried on by such corporation are acquired.

The fact that the corporation that issues the obligation is not the same corporation that acquires the acquired corporation does not prevent the application of section 279. For example, if X Corporation acquires all the stock of Y Corporation through the utilization of an obligation of Z Corporation, a wholly owned subsidiary of X Corporation, this section will apply.

(2) *Direct or indirect consideration.*—Obligations are issued to provide direct consideration for an acquisition within the meaning of section 279(b)(1) where the obligations are issued to the shareholders of an acquired corporation in exchange for stock in such acquired corporation or where the obligations are issued to the acquired corporation in exchange for its assets. The application of the provisions of this subsection relating to indirect consideration for an acquisition of stock or assets depends upon the facts and circumstances surrounding the acquisition and the issuance of the obligations. Obligations are issued to provide indirect consideration for an acquisition of stock or assets within the meaning of section 279(b)(1) where (i) at the time of the issuance of the obligations the issuing corporation anticipated the acquisition of such stock or assets and the obligations would not have been issued if the issuing corporation had not so anticipated such acquisition, or where (ii) at the time of the acquisition the issuing corporation foresaw or reasonably should have foreseen that it would be required to issue obligations, which it would not have otherwise been required to issue if the acquisition had not occurred, in order to meet its future economic needs.

(3) *Stock acquisition.*—(i) For purposes of section 279, an acquisition in which the issuing corporation issues an obligation to provide consideration directly or indirectly for the acquisition of stock in the acquired corporation shall be treated as a stock acquisition within the meaning of section 279(b)(1)(A). Where the stock of one corporation is acquired from another corporation and such stock constitutes at least two-thirds (in value) of all the assets (excluding money) of the latter corporation, such acquisition shall be deemed an asset acquisition as described in section 279(b)(1)(B) and subparagraph (4) of this section. If the issuing corporation acquires less than two-thirds (in value) of all the assets (excluding money) used in trades or businesses carried on by the acquired corporation within the meaning of section 279(b)(1)(B) and subparagraph (4) of this paragraph and such assets include stock of another corporation, the acquisition of such stock is a stock acquisition within the meaning of section 279(b)(1)(A) and of this subparagraph. In such a case the amount of the obligation which is characterized as corporate acquisition indebtedness shall bear the same relationship to the total amount of the obligation issued as the fair market value of the stock acquired bears to the total of the fair market value of the assets acquired and stock acquired, as of the date of acquisition. For rules with respect to acquisitions of stock, where the total amount of stock of the acquired corporation held by the issuing corporation never exceeded 5 percent of the total combined voting power of all classes of stock of the acquired corporation entitled to vote, see § 1.279-4(b)(1).

(ii) If the issuing corporation acquired stock of an acquired corporation in an acquisition described in section 279(b)(1)(A), and liquidated the acquired corporation under section 334(b)(2) and the regulations thereunder before the last day of the taxable year in which such stock acquisition is made, such obligation issued to provide consideration directly or indirectly to acquire such stock of the acquired corporation shall be considered as issued in an acquisition described in section 279(b)(1)(B).

(4) *Asset acquisition.*—(i) For purposes of section 279, an acquisition in which the issuing corporation issues an obligation to provide consideration directly or indirectly for the acquisition of assets of an acquired corporation pursuant to a plan under which at least two-thirds of the gross value of all the assets (excluding money) used in trades and businesses carried on by such acquired corporation are acquired shall be treated as an asset acquisition within the meaning of section 279(b)(1)(B). For purposes of section 279(b)(1)(B), the gross value of any acquired asset shall be its fair market value as of the day

of its acquisition. In determining the fair market value of an asset, no reduction shall be made for any liabilities, mortgages, liens, or other encumbrances to which the asset or any part thereof may be subjected. For purposes of this subparagraph, an asset which has been actually used in the trades and businesses of a corporation but which is temporarily not being used in such trades and businesses shall be treated as if it is being used in such manner. For purposes of this paragraph, the day of acquisition will be determined by reference to the facts and circumstances surrounding the transaction.

(ii) For purposes of the two-thirds test described in section 279(b)(1)(B), the stock of any corporation which is controlled by the acquired corporation shall be considered as an asset used in the trades and businesses of such acquired corporation.

(5) *Certain nontaxable transactions.*—(i) Under section 279(e), an acquisition of stock of a corporation of which the issuing corporation is in control in a transaction in which gain or loss is not recognized shall be deemed an acquisition described in section 279(b)(1)(A) only if immediately before such transaction the acquired corporation was in existence, and the issuing corporation was not in control of such corporation. If the issuing corporation is a member of an affiliated group, then in accordance with section 279(g), the affiliated group shall be treated as the issuing corporation. Thus, any stock of the acquired corporation, owned by members of the affiliated group, shall be aggregated in determining whether the issuing corporation was in control of the acquired corporation.

(ii) The $5 million limitation provided by section 279(a)(1) is not reduced by the interest on an obligation issued in a transaction which, under section 279(e), is deemed not to be an acquisition described in section 279(b)(1).

(iii) The provisions of this subparagraph may be illustrated by the following examples:

Example (1). On January 1, 1973, W Corporation, a calendar year taxpayer, issues to the public 10,000 ten year convertible bonds each with a principal of $1,000 for $9 million. On June 6, 1973, W Corporation transfers the $9 million proceeds of such bond issue to X Corporation in exchange for X Corporation's common stock in a transaction that satisfies the provisions of section 315(a). On December 31, 1973, W Corporation's ratio of debt to equity is 1½ to 1 and its projected earnings exceed three times the annual interest to be paid or incurred. Immediately prior to the transaction between the two corporations W Corporation owned no stock in X Corporation which had been in existence for several years. However, immediately after this transaction W Corporation is in control of X Corporation. Since X Corporation, the acquired corporation, was in existence and W Corporation, the issuing corporation, was not in control of X Corporation immediately before the section 351 transaction (a transaction in which gain or loss is not recognized) and since W Corporation is now in control of X Corporation, the acquisition of X Corporation's common stock by W Corporation is not protected from treatment as an acquisition described in section 279(b)(1)(A). However, the obligation will not be deemed to be corporate acquisition indebtedness since the test of section 279(b)(4) is not met. The interest on the obligation will reduce the $5 million limitation of section 279(a).

Example (2). Assume the facts are the same as described in example (1), except that X Corporation was not in existence prior to June 6, 1973, but rather is newly created by W Corporation on such date. Since X Corporation, the acquired corporation, was not in existence before June 6, 1973, the date on which W Corporation, the issuing corporation, acquired control of X Corporation in a transaction on which gain or loss is not recognized, the acquisition is not deemed to be an acquisition described in section 279(b)(1)(A). Thus, under the provisions of subdivision (ii) of this subparagraph, the $5 million limitation provided by section 279(a)(1) will not be reduced by the yearly interest incurred on the convertible bonds issued by W Corporation.

Example (3). Assume that the facts are the same as described in example (1), except that W Corporation was in control of X Corporation immediately before the transaction. Since W Corporation was in control of X Corporation immediately before the section 351(a) transaction and is in control of X Corporation after such transaction, the result will be the same as in example (2).

(c) *Subordinated obligation.*—(1) *In general.*—An obligation which is issued to provide consideration for an acquisition described in section 279(b)(1) is subordinated within the meaning of section 279(b)(2) if it is either—

(i) Subordinated to the claims of trade creditors of the issuing corporation generally, or

(ii) Expressly subordinated in right of payment to the payment of any substantial amount of unsecured indebtedness, where outstanding or subsequently issued, of the issuing corporation, irrespective of whether such subordination relates to payment of interest, or principal, or both. In applying section 279(b)(2) and this paragraph in any case where the issuing corporation is a member of an affiliated group of corporations, the affiliated group shall be treated as the issuing corporation.

(2) *Expressly subordinated obligation.*—In applying subparagraph (1)(ii) of this paragraph, an obligation is considered expressly subordinated whether the terms of the subordination are provided in the evidence of indebtedness itself, or in another agreement between the parties to such obligation. An obligation shall be considered to be expressly subordinated within the meaning of subparagraph (1)(ii) of this paragraph if such obligation by its terms can become subordinated in right of payment to the payment of any substantial amount of unsecured indebtedness which is outstanding or which may be issued subsequently. However, an obligation shall not be considered expressly subordinated if such subordination occurs solely by operation of law, such as in the case of bankruptcy laws. For purposes of this paragraph, the term "substantial amount of unsecured indebtedness" means an amount of unsecured indebtedness equal to 5 percent or more of the face amount of the obligations issued within the meaning of section 279(b)(1).

(d) *Convertible obligation.*—An obligation which is issued to provide consideration directly or indirectly for an acquisition described in section 279(b)(1) is convertible within the meaning of section 279(b)(3) if it is either—

(1) Convertible directly or indirectly into stock of the issuing corporation, or

(2) Part of an investment unit or other arrangement which includes, in addition to such bond or other evidence of indebtedness, an option to acquire directly or indirectly stock in the issuing corporation. Stock warrants or convertible preferred stock included as part of an investment unit constitute options within the meaning of the preceding sentence. Indebtedness is indirectly convertible if the conversion feature gives the holder the right to convert into another bond of the issuing corporation which is then convertible into the stock of the issuing corporation.

In any case where the corporation which in fact issues an obligation to provide consideration for an acquisition described in section 279(b)(1) is a member of an affiliated group, the provisions of section 279(b)(3) and this paragraph are deemed satisfied if the stock into which either the obligation or option which is part of an investment unit or other arrangement is convertible, directly or indirectly, is stock of any member of the affiliated group.

(e) *Ratio of debt to equity and projected earnings test.*—For rules with respect to the application of section 279(b)(4) (relating to the ratio of debt to equity and the ratio of projected earnings to annual interest to be paid or incurred), see paragraphs (d), (e), and (f) of § 1.279-5.

(f) *Certain obligations issued after October 9, 1969.*—(1) *In general.*—Under section 279(i), an obligation shall not be corporate acquisition indebtedness if such obligation is issued after October 9, 1969, to provide consideration for the acquisition of—

(i) Stock or assets pursuant to a binding written contract which was in effect on October 9, 1969, and at all times thereafter before such acquisition, or

(ii) Stock in any corporation where the issuing corporation, on October 9, 1969, and at all times thereafter before such acquisition, owned at least 50 percent of the total combined voting power of all classes of stock entitled to vote of the acquired corporation.

Subdivision (ii) of this subparagraph shall cease to apply when (at any time on or after October 9, 1969) the issuing corporation has acquired control of the acquired corporation. The interest attributable to any obligation which satisfies the conditions stated in the first sentence of this subparagraph shall reduce the $5 million limitation of section 279(a)(1).

(2) *Examples.*—The provisions of this paragraph may be illustrated by the following examples:

Example (1). On September 5, 1969, M Corporation, a calendar year taxpayer, entered into a binding written contract with N Corporation to purchase 20 percent of the voting stock of N Corporation. The contract was in effect on October 9, 1969, and at all times thereafter before the acquisition of the stock on January 1, 1970. Pursuant to such contract M Corporation issued on January 1, 1970, to N Corporation an obligation which satisfies the tests of section 279(b) requiring it to pay $1 million of interest each year. However, under the provisions of subparagraph (1)(i) of this paragraph, such obligation is not corporate acquisition indebtedness since it was issued to provide consideration for the acquisition of stock pursuant to a binding written contract which was in effect on October 9, 1969, and at all times thereafter before such acquisition. The $1 million of yearly interest on the obligation reduces the $5 million limitation provided for in section 279(a)(1) to $4 million since such interest is attributable to an obligation which was issued to provide consideration for the acquisition of stock in an acquired corporation.

Example (2). On October 9, 1969, O Corporation, a calendar year taxpayer, owned 50 percent of the total combined voting power of all classes of stock entitled to vote of P Corporation. P Corporation has no other class of stock. On January 1, 1970, while still owning such voting stock O Corporation issued to the shareholders of P Corporation to provide consideration for an additional 40 percent of P Corporation's voting stock an obligation which satisfied the tests of section 279(b) requiring it to pay $4 million of interest each year. Hence, O Corporation acquired control of P Corporation, and the provisions of subparagraph (1)(ii) of this paragraph ceased to apply to O Corporation. Thus, 75 percent of the obligation issued by O Corporation to provide consideration for the stock of P Corporation is not corporate acquisition indebtedness (that is, of the 40 percent of the voting stock of P Corporation which was acquired, only 30 percent was needed to give O Corporation control). Since 25 percent of the obligation is corporate acquisition indebtedness, $1 million of interest attributable to such obligation is subject to disallowance under section 279(a) for the taxable year 1970. The remaining $3 million of interest attributable to the obligation will reduce the $5 million limitation provided by in section 279(a)(1).

(g) *Exemptions for certain acquisitions of foreign corporations.*—(1) *In general.*—Under section 279(f), the term "corporate acquisition indebtedness" does not include any indebtedness issued to any person to provide consideration directly or indirectly for the acquisition of stock in, or assets of, any foreign corporation substantially all the income of which, for the 3-year period ending with the date of such acquisition or for such part of such period as the foreign corporation was in existence, is from sources without the United States. The interest attributable to any obligation excluded from treatment as corporate acquisition indebtedness by reason of this paragraph shall reduce the $5 million limitation of [section] 279(a)(1).

(2) *Foreign corporation.*—For purposes of this paragraph, the term "foreign corporation" shall have the same meaning as in section 7701(a)(5).

(3) *Income from sources without the United States.*—For purposes of this paragraph, the term "income from sources without the United States" shall be determined in accordance with sections 862 and 863. If more than 80 percent of a foreign corporation's gross income is derived from sources without the United States, such corporation shall be considered to be deriving substantially all of its income from sources without the United States. [Reg. § 1.279-3.]

☐ [T.D. 7262, 3-2-73.]

[Reg. § 1.279-4]

§ 1.279-4. Special rules.—(a) *Special 3-year rule.*—Under section 279(d)(4), if an obligation which has been deemed to be corporate acquisition indebtedness for any taxable year would not be such indebtedness for each of any 3 consecutive taxable years thereafter if the ratio of debt to equity and the ratio of projected earnings to annual interest to be paid or incurred of section 279(b)(4) were applied as of the close of each of such 3 years, then such obligation shall not be corporate acquisition indebtedness for all later taxable years after such 3 consecutive taxable years. The test prescribed by section 279(b)(4) shall be applied as of the close of any taxable year whether or not the issuing corporation issues any obligation to provide consideration for an acquisition described in section 279(b)(1) in such taxable year. Thus, for example, if a corporation, reporting income on a calendar year basis, has an obligation outstanding as of December 31, 1975, which was classified as a corporate acquisition indebtedness as of the close of 1972 and such obligation would not have been classified as corporate acquisition indebtedness as of the close of 1973, 1974, and 1975 because neither of the conditions of section 279(b)(4) were present as of such dates, then such obligation shall not be corporate acquisition indebtedness for 1976 and all taxable years thereafter. Such obligation shall not be reclassified as corporate acquisition indebtedness in any taxable year following 1975, even if the issuing corporation issues more obligations (whether or not found to be corporate acquisition indebtedness) in such later years to provide consideration for the acquisition of additional stock in, or assets of, the same acquired corporation with respect to which the original obligation was issued. The interest attributable to such obligation shall reduce the $5 million limitation provided by section 279(a)(1) for 1976 and all taxable years thereafter.

(b) *Five percent stock rule.*—(1) *In general.*—Under section 279(d)(5), if an obligation issued to provide consideration for an acquisition of stock in another corporation meets the tests of section 279(b), such obligation shall be corporate acquisition for a taxable year only if at sometime after October 9, 1969, and before the close of such year the issuing corporation owns or has owned 5 percent or more of the total combined voting power of all classes of stock entitled to vote in the acquired corporation. If the issuing corporation is a member of an affiliated group, then in accordance with section 279(g) the affiliated group shall be treated as the issuing corporation. Thus, any stock of the acquired corporation owned by members of the affiliated group shall be aggregated to determine if the percentage limitation provided by this subparagraph is exceeded. Once an obligation is deemed to be corporate acquisition indebtedness, such obligation will continue to be deemed corporate acquisition indebtedness for all taxable years thereafter unless the provisions of section 279(d)(3) or (4) apply, notwithstanding the fact that the issuing corporation owns less than 5 percent of the combined voting power of all classes of stock entitled to vote of the acquired corporation in any or all taxable years thereafter.

(2) *Examples.*—The provisions of this paragraph may be illustrated by the following examples:

Example (1). Corporation Y uses the calendar year as its taxable year and has only one class of stock outstanding. On June 1, 1972, X Corporation which is also a calendar year taxpayer and which has never been a shareholder of Y Corporation acquires from the shareholders of Y Corporation 4 percent of the stock of Y Corporation in exchange for obligations which satisfy the conditions of section 279(b). At no time during 1972 does X Corporation own 5 percent or more of the stock of Y Corporation. Accordingly, under the provisions of subparagraph (1) of this paragraph, for 1972 the obligations issued by X Corporation to provide consideration for the acquisition of Y Corporation's stock do not constitute corporate acquisition indebtedness.

Example (2). Assume the same facts as in example (1). Assume further that on February 24, 1973, X Corporation acquires from the shareholders of Y Corporation an additional 7 percent of the stock of Y Corporation in exchange for obligations which satisfy all of the tests of section 279(b). On December 28, 1973, X Corporation sells all of its stock in Y Corporation. For 1973, the obligations issued by X Corporation in 1972 and in 1973 constitute corporate acquisition indebtedness since X Corporation at some time after October 9, 1969, and before the close of 1973 owned 5 percent or more of the voting stock of Y Corporation. Furthermore, such obligations shall be corporate acquisition indebtedness for all taxable years thereafter unless the special provisions of section 279(d)(3) or (4) could apply.

(c) *Changes in obligation.*—(1) *In general.*—Under section 279(h), for purposes of section 279—

(i) Any extension, renewal or refinancing of an obligation evidencing a preexisting indebtedness shall not be deemed to be the issuance of a new obligation, and

(ii) Any obligation which is corporate acquisition indebtedness of the issuing corporation is also corporate acquisiton indebtedness of any corporation which in any transaction or by operation of law assumes liability for such obligation or becomes liable for such obligation as guarantor, endorser, or indemnitor.

(2) *Examples.*—The provisions of this paragraph may be illustrated by the following examples:

Example (1). On January 1, 1971, X Corporation, which files its return on the basis of a calendar year, issues an obligation, which satisfies the tests of section 279(b), and is deemed to be corporate acquisition indebtedness. On January 1, 1973, an agreement is concluded between X Corporation and the holder of the obligation whereby the maturity date of such obligation is extended until December 31, 1979. Under the provisions of subparagraph (1)(i) of this paragraph such extended obligation is not deemed to be a new obligation, and still constitutes corporate acquisition indebtedness.

Example (2). On June 12, 1971, X Corporation, a calendar year taxpayer, issued convertible and subordinated obligations to acquire the stock of Z Corporation. The obligations were deemed corporate acquisition indebtedness on December 31, 1971. On March 4, 1973, X Corporation and Y Corporation consolidated to form XY Corporation in accordance with state law. Corporation XY is liable for the obligations issued by X Corporation by operation of law and the obligations continue to be corporate acquisition indebtedness. In 1975 XY Corporation exchanges its own nonconvertible obligations for the obligations X Corporation issued. The obligations of XY Corporation issued in exchange for those of X Corporation will be deemed to be corporate acquisition indebtedness [Reg. § 1.279-4.]

☐ [T.D. 7262, 3-2-73.]

[Reg. § 1.279-5]

§ 1.279-5. Rules for application of section 279(b).—(a) *Taxable years to which applicable.*—(1) *First year of disallowance.*—Under section 279(d)(1), the deduction of interest on any obligation shall not be disallowed under section 279(a) before the first taxable year of the issuing corporation as of the last day of which the application of either section 279(b)(4)(A) or (B) results in such obligation being classified as corporate acquisition indebtedness. See section 279(c)(1) and paragraph (b)(2) of this section for the time when an obligation is subjected to the test of section 279(b)(4).

(2) *General rule for succeeding years.*—Under section 279(d)(2), except as provided in paragraphs (3), (4), and (5) of section 279(d), if an obligation is determined to be corporate acquisition indebtedness as of the last day of any taxable year of the issuing corporation, such obligation shall be corporate acquisition indebtedness for such taxable year and all subsequent taxable years.

(b) *Time of determination.*—(1) *In general.*—The determination of whether an obligation meets the conditions of section 279(b)(1), (2), and (3) shall be made as of the day on which the obligation is issued.

(2) *Ratio of debt to equity, projected earnings, and annual interest to be paid or incurred.*—(i) Under section 279(c)(1), the determination of whether an obligation meets the conditions of section 279(b)(4) is first to be made as of the last day of the taxable year of the issuing corporation in which it issues the obligation to provide consideration directly or indirectly for an acquisition described in section 279(b)(1) of stock in, or assets of, the acquired corporation. An obligation which is not corporate acquisition indebtedness only because it does not satisfy the test of section 279(b)(4) in the taxable year of the issuing corporation in which the obligation is issued for stock in, or assets of, the acquired corporation may be subjected to the test of section 279(b)(4) again. A retesting will occur in any subsequent taxable year of the issuing corporation in which the issuing corporation issues any obligation to provide consideration directly or indirectly for an acquisition described in section 279(b)(1) with respect to the same acquired corporation, irrespective of whether such subsequent obligation is itself classified as corporate acquisition indebtedness. If the issuing corporation is a member of an affiliated group, then in accordance with section 279(g) the affiliated group shall be treated as the issuing corporation. Thus, if any member of the affiliated group issues an obligation to acquire additional stock in, or assets of, the acquired corporation, this paragraph shall apply.

(ii) For purposes of section 279(b)(4) and this paragraph, in any case where the issuing corporation is a member of an affiliated group (see section 279(g) and § 1.279-6 for rules regarding application of section 279 to certain affiliated groups) which does not file a consolidated return and all the members of which do not have the same taxable year, determinations with respect to the ratio of debt to equity of, and projected earnings of, and annual interest to be paid or incurred by, any member of the affiliated group shall be made as of the last day of the taxable year of the corporation which in fact issues the obligation to provide consideration for an acquisition described in section 279(b)(1).

(3) *Redetermination where control or substantially all the properties have been acquired.*—Under section 279(d)(3), if an obligation is determined to be corporate acquisition indebtedness as of the close of a taxable year of the issuing corporation in which section 279(c)(3)(A)(i) (relating to the projected earnings of the issuing corporation only) applied, but would not be corporate acquisition indebtedness if the determination were made as of the close of the first taxable year of such corporation thereafter in which section 279(c)(3)(A)(ii) (relating to the projected earnings of both the issuing corporation and the acquired corporation) could apply, such obligation shall be considered not to be corporate acquisition indebtedness for such later taxable year and all taxable years thereafter. Where an obligation ceases to be corporate acquisition indebtedness as a result of the application of this paragraph, the interest on such obligation shall not be disallowed under section 279(a) as a deduction for the taxable year in which the obligation ceases to be corporate acquisition indebtedness and all taxable years thereafter. However, under section 279(a)(2) the interest paid or incurred on such obligation which is allowed as a deduction will reduce the $5 million limitation provided by section 279(a)(1).

(4) *Examples.*—The provisions of this paragraph may be illustrated by the following examples:

Example (1). In 1971, X Corporation, which files its Federal income tax return on the basis of a calendar year, issues its obligations to provide consideration for the acquisition of 15 percent of the voting stock of both Y Corporation and Z Corporation. Y Corporation and Z Corporation each have only one class of stock. When issued, such obligations satisfied the tests prescribed in section 279(b)(1), (2), and (3) and would have constituted corporate acquisition indebtedness but for the test prescribed in section 279(b)(4). On December 31, 1971, the application of section 279(b)(4) results in X Corporation's obligations issued in 1971 not being treated as corporate acquisitions indebtedness for that year.

Example (2). Assume the same facts as in example (1), except that in 1972, X Corporation issues more obligations which come within the tests of section 279(b)(1), (2), and (3) to acquire an additional 10 percent of the voting stock of Y Corporation. No stock of Z Corporation is acquired after 1971. The application of section 279(b)(4)(B) (relating to the projected earnings of X Corporation) as of the end of

1972 results in the obligations issued in 1972 to provide consideration for the acquisition of the stock of Y Corporation being treated as corporate acquisition indebtedness. Since X Corporation during 1972 did issue obligations to acquire more stock of Y Corporation, under the provisions of section 279(c)(1) and subparagraph (2) of this paragraph the obligations issued by X Corporation in 1971 to acquire stock in Y Corporation are again tested to determine whether the test of section 279(b)(4) with respect to such obligations is satisfied for 1972. Thus, since such obligations issued by X Corporation to acquire Y Corporation's stock in 1971 previously came within the provisions of section 279(b)(1), (2), and (3) and the projected earnings test of section 279(b)(4)(B) is satisfied for 1972, all of such obligations are to be deemed to constitute corporate acquisition indebtedness for 1972 and subsequent taxable years. The obligations issued in 1971 to acquire stock in Z Corporation continue not to constitute corporate acquisition indebtedness.

Example (3). Assume the same facts as in examples (1) and (2). In 1973, X Corporation issues more obligations which come within the tests of section 279(b)(1), (2), and (3) to acquire more stock (but not control) in Y Corporation. On December 31, 1973, it is determined with respect to X Corporation that neither of the conditions described in section 279(b)(4) are present. Thus, the obligations issued in 1973 do not constitute corporate acquisition indebtedness. However, the obligations issued in 1971 and 1972 by X Corporation to acquire stock in Y Corporation continue to be treated as corporate acquisition indebtedness.

Example (4). Assume the same facts as in example (3), except that X Corporation acquires control of Y Corporation in 1973. Since X Corporation has acquired control of Y Corporation, the average annual earnings (as defined in section 279(c)(3)(b)) and the annual interest to be paid or incurred (as provided by section 279(c)(4)) of both X Corporation and Y Corporation under section 279(c)(3)(A)(ii) are taken into account in computing for 1973 the ratio of projected earnings to annual interest to be paid or incurred described in section 279(b)(4)(B). Assume further that after applying section 279(b)(4)(B) the obligations issued in 1973 escape treatment as corporate acquisition indebtedness for 1973. Under section 279(d)(3), all of the obligations issued by X Corporation to acquire stock in Y Corporation in 1971 and 1972 are removed from classification as corporate acquisition indebtedness for 1973 and all subsequent taxable years.

Example (5). In 1975, M Corporation, which files its federal income tax return on the basis of a calendar year, issues its obligations to acquire 30 percent of the voting stock of N Corporation. N Corporation has only one class of stock. Such obligations satisfy the tests prescribed in section 279(b)(1), (2), and (3). Additionally, as of the close of 1975, M Corporation's ratio of debt to equity exceeds the ratio of 2 to 1 and its projected earnings do not exceed 3 times the annual interest to be paid or incurred. The obligations issued by M Corporation are corporate acquisition indebtedness for 1975 since all the provisions of section 279(b) are satisfied. In 1976 M Corporation issues its obligations to acquire from the shareholders of N Corporation an additional 60 percent of the voting stock of N Corporation, thereby acquiring control of N Corporation. However, with respect to the obligations issued by M Corporation in 1975, there is no redetermination under section 279(d)(3) and subparagraph (3) of this paragraph as to whether such obligations may escape classification as corporate acquisition indebtedness because in 1975 it was the ratio of debt to equity test which caused such obligations to be corporate acquisition indebtedness. If in 1975, M Corporation met the conditions of section 279(b)(4) solely because of the ratio of projected earnings to annual interest to be paid or incurred described in section 279(b)(4)(B), its obligation issued in 1975 could be retested in 1976.

(c) *Acquisition of stock or assets of several corporations.*—An issuing corporation which acquires stock in, or assets of, more than one corporation during any taxable year must apply the tests described in section 279(b)(1), (2), and (3) separately with respect to each obligation issued to provide consideration for the acquisition of stock in, or assets of, each such acquired corporation. Thus, if an acquisition is made with obligations of the issuing corporation that satisfy the tests described in section 279(b)(2) and (3) and obligations that fail to satisfy such tests, only those obligations satisfying such tests need be further considered to determine whether they constitute corporate acquisition indebtedness. Those obligations which meet the test of section 279(b)(1) but which are not deemed corporate acquisition indebtedness shall be taken into account for purposes of determining the reduction in the $5 million limitation of section 279(a)(1).

(d) *Ratio of debt to equity and projected earnings.*—(1) *In general.*—One of the four tests to determine whether an obligation constitutes corporate acquisition indebtedness is contained in section 279(b)(4). An obligation will meet the test of section 279(b)(4) if, as of a day determined under section 279(c)(1) and paragraph (b)(2) of this section, either—

(i) the ratio of debt to equity (as defined in paragraph (f) of this section) of the issuing corporation exceeds 2 to 1, or

(ii) the projected earnings (as defined in subparagraph (2) of this paragraph) of the issuing corporation, or of both the issuing corporation and acquired corporation in any case where subparagraph (2)(ii) of this paragraph is applicable, do not exceed 3 times the annual interest to be paid or incurred (as defined in paragraph (e) of this section) by such issuing corporation, or, where applicable, by such issuing corporation and acquired corporation. Where paragraphs (d)(2)(ii) and (e)(1)(ii) of this section are applicable in computing projected earnings and annual interest to be paid or incurred, 100 percent of the acquired corporation's projected earnings and annual interest to be paid or incurred shall be included in such computation, even though less than all of the stock or assets of the acquired corporation have been acquired.

(2) *Projected earnings.*—The term "projected earnings" means the "average annual earnings" (as defined in subparagraph (3) of this paragraph) of—

(i) The issuing corporation only, if subdivision (ii) of this subparagraph does not apply, or

(ii) Both the issuing corporation and the acquired corporation, in any case where the issuing corporation as of the close of its taxable year has acquired control, or has acquired substantially all of the properties, of the acquired corporation.

For purposes of subdivision (ii) of this subparagraph, an acquisition of "substantially all of the properties" of the acquired corporation means the acquisition of assets representing at least 90 percent of the fair market value of the net assets and at least 70 percent of the fair market value of the gross assets held by the acquired corporation immediately prior to the acquisition.

(3) *Average annual earnings.*—(i) The term "average annual earnings" referred to in subparagraph (2) of this paragraph is, for any corporation, the amount of its earnings and profits for any 3-year period ending with the last day of a taxable year of the issuing corporation in which it issues any obligation to provide consideration for an acquisition described in section 279(b)(1), computed without reduction for—

(a) Interest paid or incurred,

(b) Depreciation or amortization allowed under chapter 1 of the Code,

(c) Liability for tax under chapter 1 of the Code, and

(d) Distributions to which section 301(c)(1) apply (other than such distributions from the acquired corporation to the issuing corporation),

and reduced to an annual average for such 3-year period. For the rules to determine the amount of earnings and profits of any corporation, see section 312 and the regulations thereunder.

(ii) Except as provided for in subdivision (iii) of this subparagraph, for purposes of subdivision (i) of this subparagraph in the case of any corporation, the earnings and profits for such 3-year period shall be reduced to an annual average by dividing such earnings and profits by 36 and multiplying the quotient by 12. If a corporation was not in existence during the entire 36-month period as of the close of the taxable year referred to in subdivision (i) of this subparagraph, its average annual earnings shall be determined by dividing its earnings and profits for the period of its existence by the number of whole calendar months in such period and multiplying the quotient by 12.

(iii) Where the issuing corporation acquires substantially all of the properties of an acquired corporation, the computation of earnings and profits of such acquired corporation shall be made for the period of such corporation beginning with the first day of the 3-year period of the issuing corporation and ending with the last day prior to the date on which substantially all of the properties were acquired. In determining the number of whole calendar months for such acquired corporation where the period for determining its earnings and profits includes two months which are not whole calendar months and the total number of days in such two fractional months exceed 30 days, the number of whole calendar months for such period shall be increased by one. Where the number of days in the two fractional months total 30 days or less such fractional months shall be disregarded. After the number of whole calendar months is determined, the calculation for average annual earnings shall be made in the same manner as described in the last sentence of subdivision (ii) of this subparagraph.

(e) *Annual interest to be paid or incurred.*—(1) *In general.*—For purposes of section 279(b)(4)(B), the term "annual interest to be paid or incurred" means—

(i) If subdivision (ii) of this subparagraph does not apply, the annual interest to be paid or incurred by the issuing corporation only, for the taxable year beginning immediately after the day described in section 279(c)(1), determined by reference to its total indebtedness outstanding as of such day, or

(ii) If projected earnings are determined under paragraph (d)(2)(ii) of this section, the annual interest to be paid or incurred by both the issuing corporation and the acquired corporation for one year beginning immediately after the day described in section 279(c)(1), determined by reference to their combined total indebtedness outstanding as of such day. However, where the issuing corporation acquires substantially all of the properties of the acquired corporation, the annual interest to be paid or incurred will be determined by reference to the total indebtedness outstanding of the issuing corporation only (including any indebtedness it assumed in the acquisition) as of the day described in section 279(c)(1).

The term "annual interest to be paid or incurred" refers to both actual interest and unstated interest. Such unstated interest includes original issue discount as defined in paragraph (a)(1) of § 1.163-4 and amounts treated as interest under section 483. For purposes of this paragraph and paragraph (f) of this section (relating to the ratio of debt to equity), the indebtedness of any corporation shall be determined in accordance with generally accepted accounting principles. Thus, for example, the indebtedness of a corporation includes short-term liabilities, such as accounts payable to suppliers, as well as long-term indebtedness. Contingent liabilities, such as those arising out of discounted notes, the assignment of accounts receivable, or the guarantee of the liability of another, shall be included in the determination of the indebtedness of a corporation if the contingency is likely to become a reality. In addition, the indebtedness of a corporation includes obligations issued by the corporation, secured only by property of the corporation, and with respect to which the corporation is not personally liable. See section 279(g) and § 1.279-6 for rules with respect to the computation of annual interest to be paid or incurred in regard to members of an affiliated group of corporations.

(2) *Examples.*—The provisions of these paragraphs may be illustrated by the following examples:

Example (1). Corporation X's earnings and profits calculated in accordance with section 279(c)(3)(B) for 1972, 1971, and 1970 respectively were $29 million, $23 million, and $20 million. The interest to be paid or incurred during the calendar year of 1973 as determined by reference to the issuing corporation's total outstanding indebtedness as of December 31, 1972, was $10 million. By dividing the sum of the earnings and profits for the three years by 36 (the number of whole calendar months in the 3-year period) and multiplying the quotient by 12, the average annual earnings for X Corporation is $24 million. Since the projected earnings of X Corporation do not exceed by 3 times the annual interest to be paid or incurred (they exceed by only 2.4 times), one of the circumstances described in section 279(b)(4) is present.

Example (2). On March 1, 1972, W Corporation acquires substantially all of the properties of Z Corporation in exchange for W Corporation's bonds which satisfy the tests of section 279(b)(2) and (3). W Corporation files its income tax returns on the basis of fiscal years ending June 30. Z Corporation, which was formed on September 1, 1969, is a calendar year taxpayer. The earnings and profits of W Corporation for the last three fiscal years ending June 30, 1972, calculated in accordance with the provisions of section 279(c)(3)(B) were $300 million, $400 million, and $380 million, respectively. The average annual earnings of W Corporation is $360 million ($1,080 million ÷ 36 × 12). The earnings and profits of Z Corporation calculated in accordance with the provisions of section 279(c)(3)(B) were $4 million for the period of September 1, 1969 to December 31, 1969, $10 million and $14 million for the calendar years of 1970 and 1971, respectively, and $2 million for the period of January 1, 1972, through February 29, 1972, or a total of $30 million. To arrive at the average annual earnings, the sum of the earnings and profits, $30 million, must be divided by 30 (the number of whole calendar months that Z Corporation was in existence during W Corporation's 3-year period ending with [the] day prior to the date substantially all the assets were acquired) and the quotient is multiplied by 12, which results in an average annual earnings of $12 million ($30 million ÷ 30 × 12) for Z Corporation. The combined average annual earnings of W Corporation and Z Corporation is $372 million. The interest for the fiscal year ending June 30, 1973, to be paid or incurred by W Corporation on its outstanding indebtedness as of June 30, 1972, is $110 million. Since the projected earnings exceed the annual interest to be paid or incurred by more than 3 times, the obligation will not be corporate acquisition indebtedness, unless the issuing corporation's debt to equity ratio exceeds 2 to 1.

(f) *Ratio of debt to equity.*—(1) *In general.*—The condition described in section 279(b)(4)(A) is present if the ratio of debt to equity of the issuing corporation exceeds 2 to 1. Under section 279(c)(2), the term "ratio of debt to equity" means the ratio which the total indebtedness of the issuing corporation bears to the sum of its money and all its other assets (in an amount equal to adjusted basis for determining gain) less such total indebtedness. For the meaning of the term "indebtedness", see paragraph (e)(1) of this section. See section 279(g) and §1.279-6 for rules with respect to the computation of the ratio of debt to equity in regard to an affiliated group of corporations.

(2) *Examples.*—The provisions of section 279(b)(4)(A) and this paragraph may be illustrated by the following example:

Example (1). On June 1, 1971, X Corporation, which files its federal income tax returns on a calendar year basis, issues an obligation for $45 million to the shareholders of Y Corporation to provide consideration for the acquisition of all of the stock of Y Corporation. Such obligation has the characteristics of corporate acquisition indebtedness described in section 279(b)(2) and (3). The projected earnings of X Corporation and Y Corporation exceed 3 times the annual interest to be paid or incurred by those corporations and, accordingly, the condition described in section 279(b)(4)(B) is not present. Also, on December 31, 1971, X Corporation has total assets with an adjusted basis of $150 million (including the newly acquired stock of Y Corporation having a basis of $45 million) and total indebtedness of $90 million. Hence, X Corporation's equity is $60 million computed by subtracting its $90 million of total indebtedness from its $150 million of total assets. Since X Corporation's ratio of debt to equity of 1.5 to 1 ($90 million of total indebtedness over $60 million equity) does not exceed 2 to 1, the condition described in section 279(b)(4)(A) is not present. Therefore, X Corporation's obligation for $45 million is not corporate acquisition indebtedness because on December 31, 1971, neither of the conditions specified in section 279(b)(4) existed.

(g) *Special rules for banks and lending or finance companies.*—(1) *Debt to equity and projected earnings.*—Under section 279(c)(5), with respect to any corporation which is a bank (as defined in section 581) or is primarily engaged in a lending or finance business, the following rules are to be applied:

(i) In determining under paragraph (f) of this section the ratio of debt to equity of such corporation (or of the affiliated group of which such corporation is a member), the total indebtedness of such corporation (and the assets of such corporation) shall be reduced by an amount equal to the total indebtedness owed to such corporation which arises out of the banking business of such corporation, or out of the lending or finance business of such corporation, as the case may be;

(ii) In determining under paragraph (e) of this section the annual interest to be paid or incurred by such corporation (or by the issuing corporation and acquired corporation referred to in section 279(c)(4)(B) or by the affiliated group of corporations of which such corporation is a member), the amount of such interest (determined without regard to this subparagraph) shall be reduced by an amount which bears the same ratio to the amount of such interest as the amount of the reduction for the taxable year under subdivision (i) of this subparagraph bears to the total indebtedness of such corporation; and

(iii) In determining under section 279(c)(3)(B) the average annual earnings, the amount of the earnings and profits for the 3-year period shall be reduced by the sum of the reductions under subdivision (ii) of this subparagraph for such period.

For purposes of this paragraph, the term "lending or finance business" means a business of making loans or purchasing or discounting accounts receivable, notes, or installment obligations. Additionally, the rules stated in this paragraph regarding the application of the ratio of debt to equity, the determination of the annual interest to be paid or incurred, and the determination of the average annual earnings also apply if the bank or lending or finance company is a member of an affiliated group of corporations. However, the rules are to be applied only for purposes of determining the debt, equity, projected earnings and annual interest of the bank or lending or finance company which then are taken into account in determining the debt to equity ratio and ratio of projected earnings to annual interest to be paid or incurred by the affiliated group as a whole. Thus, these rules are to be applied to reduce the bank's or lending or finance corporation's indebtedness, annual interest to be paid or incurred, and average annual earnings which are taken into account with respect to the group, but are not to reduce the indebtedness of, annual interest to be paid or incurred by, and average annual earnings of, any corporation in the affiliated group which is not a bank or a lending or finance company. In determining whether any corporation which is a member of an affiliated group is primarily engaged in a lending or finance business, only the activities of such corporation, and not those of the whole group, are to be taken into account. See §1.279-6 for the application of section 279 to certain affiliated groups of corporations.

(2) *Examples.*—The provisions of this paragraph may be illustrated by the following examples:

Example (1). As of the close of the taxable year, X Bank has a total indebtedness of $100 million, total assets of $115 million, and $80 million is owed to X Bank by its customers. Bank X's indebtedness is $20 million ($100 million total indebtedness less $80 million owed to the X Bank by its customers) and its assets are $35 million ($115 million total assets less $80 million owed to the bank by its customers). If its annual interest to be paid or incurred is $5 million, such amount is reduced by $4 million

$$\left(\text{\$5 million interest to be paid or incurred} \times \frac{\$ 80 \text{ million owed to X Bank by its customers}}{\$100 \text{ million total indebtedness.}}\right)$$

Thus, X Bank's annual interest to be paid or incurred is $1 million.

Example (2). Assume the same facts as in example (1). X Bank has earnings and profits of $23 million for the 3-year period used to determine projected earnings. In computing the average annual earnings, the $23 million amount will be reduced by $12 million (three times the $4 million reduction of interest in example (1), assuming that the reduction was the same for each year). Thus X Bank's earnings and profits for such 3-year period are $11 million ($23 million total earnings and profits less $12 million reduction).

[Reg. §1.279-5.]

☐ [T.D. 7262, 3-2-73. *Amended by* T.D. 9264, 5-26-2006.]

[Reg. §1.279-6]

§1.279-6. Application of section 279 to certain affiliated groups.—(a) *In general.*—Under section 279(g), in any case in which the issuing corporation is a member of an affiliated group, the application of section 279 shall be determined by treating all of the members of the affiliated group in the aggregate as the issuing corporation, except that the ratio of debt to equity of, projected earnings of, and the annual interest to be paid or incurred by any corporation (other than the issuing corporation determined without regard to this paragraph) shall be included in the determinations required under section 279(b)(4) as of any day only if such corporation is a member of the affiliated group on such day, and, in determining projected earnings of such corporation under section 279(c)(3), there shall be taken into account only the earnings and profits of such corporation for the period during which it was a member of the affiliated group. The total amount of an affiliated member's assets, indebtedness, projected earnings, and interest to be paid or incurred will enter into the computation required by this section, irrespective of any minority ownership in such member.

(b) *Aggregate money and other assets.*—In determining the aggregate money and all the other assets of the affiliated group, the money and all the other assets of each member of such group shall be separately computed and such separately computed amounts shall be added together, except that adjustments shall be made, as follows:

(1) There shall be eliminated from the aggregate money and all the other assets of the affiliated group intercompany receivables as of the date described in section 279(c)(1);

(2) There shall be eliminated from the total assets of the affiliated group any amount which represents stock ownership in any member of such group;

(3) In any case where gain or loss is not recognized on transactions between members of an affiliated group under paragraph (d)(3) of this section, the basis of any asset involved in such transaction shall be the transferor's basis;

(4) The basis of property in a transaction to which §1.1502-13 applies is the basis of the property determined under that section; and

(5) There shall be eliminated from the money and all the other assets of the affiliated group any other amount which, if included, would result in a duplication of amounts in the aggregate money and all the other assets of the affiliated group.

(c) *Aggregate indebtedness.*—For purposes of applying section 279(c), in determining the aggregate indebtedness of an affiliated group of corporations the total indebtedness of each member of such group shall be separately determined, and such separately determined amounts shall be added together, except that there shall be eliminated from such total indebtedness as of the date described in section 279(c)(1)—

(1) The amount of intercompany accounts payable,

(2) The amount of intercompany bonds or other evidences of indebtedness, and

(3) The amount of any other indebtedness which, if included, would result in a duplication of amounts in the aggregate indebtedness of such affiliated group.

(d) *Aggregate projected earnings.*—In the case of an affiliated group of corporations (whether or not such group files a consolidated return under section 1501), the aggregate projected earnings of such group shall be computed by separately determining the projected earnings of each member of such group under paragraph (d) of §1.279-5, and then adding together such separately determined amounts, except that—

(1) A dividend (a distribution which is described in section 301(c)(1) other than a distribution described in section 243(c)(1)) distributed by one member to another member shall be eliminated, and

(2) In determining the earnings and profits of any member of an affiliated group, there shall be eliminated any amount of interest income received or accrued, and of interest expense paid or incurred, which is attributable to intercompany indebtedness,

(3) No gain or loss shall be recognized in any transaction between members of the affiliated group, and

(4) Members of an affiliated group who file a consolidated return shall not apply the provisions of section 1.1502-18 dealing with inventory adjustments in determining earnings and profits for purposes of this section.

(e) *Aggregate interest to be paid or incurred.*—For purposes of section 279(c)(4), in determining the aggregate annual interest to be paid or incurred by an affiliated group of corporations, the annual interest to be paid or incurred by each member of such affiliated group shall be separately calculated under paragraph (e) of §1.279-5, and such separately calculated amounts shall be added together, except that any amount of annual interest to be paid or incurred on any intercompany indebtedness shall be eliminated from such aggregate interest. [Reg. §1.279-6.]

☐ [*T.D. 7262, 3-2-73. Amended by T.D. 8560, 8-12-94 and T.D. 8597, 7-12-95.*]

[Reg. §1.279-7]

§1.279-7. Effect on other provisions.—Under section 279(j), no inference is to be drawn from any provision in section 279 and the regulations thereunder that any instrument designated as a bond, debenture, note, or certificate or other evidence of indebtedness by its issuer represents an obligation or indebtedness of such issuer in applying any other provision of this title. Thus, for example, an instrument, the interest on which is not subject to disallowance under section 279 could, under section 385 and the regulations thereunder, be found to constitute a stock interest, so that any amounts paid or payable thereon would not be deductible. [Reg. §1.279-7.]

☐ [*T.D. 7262, 3-2-73.*]

[Reg. §1.280B-1]

§1.280B-1. Demolition of structures.—(a) *In general.*—Section 280B provides that, in the case of the demolition of any structure, no deduction otherwise allowable under chapter 1 of subtitle A shall be allowed to the owner or lessee of such structure for any amount expended for the demolition or any loss sustained on account of the demolition, and that the expenditure or loss shall be treated as properly chargeable to the capital account with respect to the land on which the demolished structure was located.

(b) *Definition of structure.*—For purposes of section 280B, the term *structure* means a building, as defined in §1.48-1(e)(1), including the structural components of that building, as defined in §1.48-1(e)(2).

(c) *Effective date.*—This section is effective for demolitions commencing on or after December 30, 1997. [Reg. §1.280B-1.]

☐ [*T.D. 8745, 12-29-97.*]

[Reg. §1.280C-1]

§1.280C-1. Disallowance of certain deductions for wage or salary expenses.—If an employer is entitled to a credit under section 44B, it must reduce its deduction for wage or salary expenses paid or incurred in the year the credit is earned by the amount allowable as credit (determined without regard to the provisions of section 53). In the case in which wages and salaries are capitalized, the amount subject to depreciation must be reduced by an amount equal to the amount of the credit (determined without regard to the provisions of section 53) in determining the depreciation deduction. If the employer is an organization that is under common control (as described in §1.52-1), it must reduce its deduction for wage or salary expenses by the amount of the credit that it is allowed under subsection (a) or (b) of section 52. The deduction for wage and salary expenses must be reduced in the year the new jobs credit is earned, even if the

employer is unable to use the credit in that year because of the limitations imposed by section 53. [Reg. §1.280C-1.]

☐ [*T.D. 7553, 7-20-78. Amended by T.D. 7921, 11-18-83.*]

[Reg. §1.280C-3]

§1.280C-3. Disallowance of certain deductions for qualified clinical testing expenses when section 28 credit is allowable.—(a) *In general.*—If a taxpayer is entitled to a credit under section 28 for qualified clinical testing expenses (as defined in section 28(b)), it must reduce the amount of any deduction for qualified clinical testing expenses paid or incurred in the year the credit is earned by the amount allowable as credit for such expenses (determined without regard to section 28(d)(2)).

(b) *Capitalization of qualified clinical testing expenses.*—In a case in which qualified clinical testing expenses are capitalized, the amount chargeable to the capital account for a taxable year must be reduced by the excess of the amount of the credit allowable for the taxable year under section 28 (determined without regard to section 28(d)(2)) over the amount allowable as a deduction for qualified clinical testing expenses (determined without regard to paragraph (a) of this section) for the taxable year. See section 174 and the regulations thereunder.

(c) *Controlled group of corporations: organizations under common control.*—In the case of a taxpayer described in paragraph (d)(5) of §1.28-1 of this chapter (relating to controlled groups of corporations and organizations under common control), paragraphs (a) and (b) of this section shall be applied in accordance with the rules prescribed for aggregation of expenditures under that paragraph.

(d) *Example.*—The following example illustrates the application of paragraphs (a) and (b) of this section:

Example. A incurs $1,000 in clinical testing expenses for which a $500 credit is allowable under section 28. A also elects under section 174 of the Code to amortize these expenses over a 5-year period beginning in the year the credit is claimed. Under paragraph (a), the current year amortization deduction of $200 ($1,000 ÷ 5) is disallowed. Moreover, the amount which would otherwise be capitalized, $800, is reduced by the excess of the amount of the section 28 credit claimed for the taxable year over the amount of the allowable section 174 amortization deduction for the taxable year, or $300 ($500 – $200). Thus, the amount chargeable to the capital account for the taxable year is $500 ($800 – $300). A is entitled to amortize $500 over the remaining amortization period resulting in a deduction of $125 for each of the remaining four years. [Reg. §1.280C-3.]

☐ [*T.D. 8232, 9-30-88.*]

[Reg. §1.280C-4]

§1.280C-4. Credit for increasing research activities.—(a) *In general.*—An election under section 280C(c)(3) to have the provisions of section 280C(c)(1) and (c)(2) not apply and elect the reduced research credit under section 280C(c)(3)(B) shall be made on Form 6765, "Credit for Increasing Research Activities" (or any successor form). In order for the election to be effective, the Form 6765 must clearly indicate the taxpayer's intent to make the section 280C(c)(3) election, and must be filed with an original return for the taxable year filed on or before the due date (including extensions) for filing the income tax return for such year, regardless of whether any research credits are claimed on the original return. An election, once made for any taxable year, is irrevocable for that taxable year.

(b) *Controlled groups of corporations; trades or businesses under common control.*—(1) *In general.*—A member of a controlled group of corporations (within the meaning of section 41(f)(5)), or a trade or business which is treated as being under common control with other trades or businesses (within the meaning of section 41(f)(1)(B)), may make the election under section 280C(c)(3). However, only the common parent (within the meaning of §1.1502-77(a)(1)(i)) of a consolidated group may make the election on behalf of the members of a consolidated group. A member or trade or business shall make the election on Form 6765 and by the time prescribed in paragraph (a) of this section.

(2) *Example.*—The following example illustrates an application of paragraph (b) of this section: A, B, and C, all of which are calendar year taxpayers, are members of a controlled group of corporations (within the meaning of section 41(f)(5)). A, B, and C each attach a statement to the 2012 Form 6765, "Credit for Increasing Research Activities," showing A and C were the only members of the controlled group to have qualified research expenses when calculating the group credit. A and C report their allocated portions of the group credit on the 2012 Form 6765 and B reports no research credit on Form 6765. Pursuant to paragraph (a) of this section, A and B, but not C, each make an election for the reduced credit under section

280C(c)(3)(B) on the 2012 Form 6765. In December 2013, B determines it had qualified research expenses in 2012 resulting in an increased group credit. On an amended 2012 Form 6765, A, B, and C each report their allocated portions of the group credit. B reports its credit as a regular credit under section 41(a) and reduces the credit under section 280C(c)(3)(B). C may not reduce its credit under section 280C(c)(3)(B) because C did not make an election for the reduced credit with its original return.

(c) *Effective/applicability date.*—(1) This section applies to taxable years ending on or after July 27, 2011.

(2) *Taxable years beginning after December 31, 2011.*—Paragraphs (b)(2) and (c)(2) and (3) of this section apply to taxable years beginning on or after April 2, 2018. For taxable years ending before April 2, 2018, see §1.280C-4T as contained in 26 CFR part 1, as revised April 1, 2017.

(3) *For taxable years ending before January 1, 2012.*—See §1.280C-4 as contained in 26 CFR part 1, revised April 1, 2014. [Reg. §1.280C-4.]

☐ [*T.D. 8282, 1-23-90. Amended by T.D. 9539, 7-26-2011. T.D. 9717, 4-2-2015 and T.D. 9832, 3-27-2018.*]

§1.280F-2T	§1.280F-3T	§1.280F-4T
(a)	(b)	(d)(2)
(d)(1)	(d)(1)	
(d)(8)		
(d)(10)		

Sections 1.280F-2T(f) and 1.280F-4T(b) also provide special rules for improvements to passenger automobiles and other listed property that qualify as capital expenditures.

(c) *Effective dates.*—(1) *In general.*—This section and §§1.280F-2T through 1.280F-6 apply to property placed in service or leased after June 18, 1984, in taxable years ending after that date. Section 1.280F-7 applies to property leased after December 31, 1986, in taxable years ending after that date.

(2) *Exception.*—This section and §§1.280F-2T through 1.280F-6 shall not apply to any property—

(i) Acquired pursuant to a binding contract in effect on June 18, 1984, and at all times thereafter, or under construction by the taxpayer on that date, but only if the property is placed in service before January 1, 1985 (January 1, 1987, in the case of 15-year real property), or

(ii) Leased pursuant to a binding contract in effect on June 18, 1984, and at all times thereafter, but only if the lessee first uses such property under the lease before January 1, 1985 (January 1, 1987, in the case of 15-year real property).

(3) *Leased passenger automobiles.*—Section 1.280F-5T(e) generally applies to passenger automobiles leased after April 2, 1985, and before January 1, 1987, in taxable years ending after April 2, 1985. If §1.280F-5T(e) does not apply to a passenger automobile, *see* paragraph (c)(1) and (2) of this section. Section 1.280F-7(a) applies to passenger automobiles leased after December 31, 1986, in taxable years ending after that date. [Temporary Reg. §1.280F-1T.]

☐ [*T.D. 7986, 10-19-84. Amended by T.D. 8061, 10-31-85; T.D. 8218, 8-5-88; T.D. 8473, 4-9-93 and T.D. 9133, 6-24-2004.*]

[Reg. §1.280F-2T]

§1.280F-2T. Limitations on recovery deductions and the investment tax credit for certain passenger automobiles (Temporary).—
(a) *Limitation on amount of investment tax credit.*—(1) *General rule.*—The amount of the investment tax credit determined under section 46(a) for any passenger automobile shall not exceed $1,000. For a passenger automobile placed in service after December 31, 1984, the $1,000 amount shall be increased by the automobile price inflation adjustment (as defined in section 280F(d)(7)) for the calendar year in which the automobile is placed in service.

(2) *Election of reduced investment tax credit.*—If the taxpayer elects under section 48(q)(4) to reduce the amount of the investment tax credit in lieu of adjusting the basis of the passenger automobile under section 48(q)(1), the amount of the investment tax credit for any passenger automobile shall not exceed two-thirds of the amount determined under paragraph (a)(1) of this section.

(b) *Limitations on allowable recovery deductions.*—(1) *Recovery deduction for year passenger automobile is placed in service.*—For the taxable year that a taxpayer places a passenger automobile in service, the allowable recovery deduction under section 168(a) shall not exceed

[Reg. §1.280F-1T]

§1.280F-1T. Limitations on investment tax credit and recovery deductions under section 168 for passenger automobiles and certain other listed property; overview of regulations (Temporary).—
(a) *In general.*—Section 280F(a) limits the amount of investment tax credit determined under section 46(a) and recovery deductions under section 168 for passenger automobiles. Section 280F(b) denies the investment tax credit and requires use of the straight line method of recovery for listed property that is not predominantly used in a qualified business use. In certain circumstances, section 280F(b) requires the recapture of an amount of cost recovery deductions previously claimed by the taxpayer. Section 280F(c) provides that lessees are to be subject to restrictions substantially equivalent to those imposed on owners of such property under section 280F(a) and (b). Section 280F(d) provides definitions and special rules; note that section 280F(d)(2) and (3) apply with respect to all listed property, even if the other provisions of section 280F do not affect the treatment of the property.

(b) *Key to Code provisions.*—The following table identifies the provisions of section 280F under which regulations are provided, and lists each provision below with its corresponding regulation section:

§§1.280F-5T and 1.280F-7	§1.280F-6
(c)	(d)(3)
	(d)(4)
	(d)(5)
	(d)(6)

$4,000. See paragraph (b)(3) of this section for the adjustment to this limitation.

(2) *Recovery deduction for remaining taxable years during the recovery period.*—For any taxable year during the recovery period remaining after the year that the property is placed in service, the allowable recovery deduction under section 168(a) shall not exceed $6,000. See paragraph (b)(3) of this section for the adjustment to this limitation.

(3) *Adjustment to limitation by reason of automobile price inflation adjustment.*—The limitations on the allowable recovery deductions prescribed in paragraph (b)(1) and (2) of this section are increased by the automobile price inflation adjustment (as defined in section 280F(d)(7)) for the calendar year in which the automobile is placed in service.

(4) *Coordination with section 179.*—For the purposes of section 280F(a) and this section, any deduction allowable under section 179 (relating to the election to expense certain depreciable trade or business assets) is treated as if that deduction were a recovery deduction under section 168. Thus, the amount of the section 179 deduction is subject to the limitations described in paragraph (b)(1) and (2) of this section.

(c) *Disallowed recovery deductions allowed for years subsequent to the recovery period.*—(1) *In general.*—(i) Except as otherwise provided in this paragraph (c), the "unrecovered basis" (as defined in paragraph (c)(1)(ii) of this section) of any passenger automobile is treated as a deductible expense in the first taxable year succeeding the end of the recovery period.

(ii) The term "unrecovered basis" means the excess (if any) of—

(A) The unadjusted basis (as defined in section 168(d)(1)(A), except that there is no reduction by reason of an election to expense a portion of the basis under section 179) of the passenger automobile, over

(B) The amount of the recovery deductions (including any section 179 deduction elected by the taxpayer) which would have been allowable for taxable years in the recovery period (determined after the application of section 280F(a) and paragraph (b) of this section and as if all use during the recovery period were use described in section 168(c)(1)).

(2) *Special rule when taxpayer elects to use the section 168(b)(3) optional recovery percentages.*—If the taxpayer elects to use the optional recovery percentages under section 168(b)(3) or must use the straight line method over the earnings and profits life (as defined and described in §1.280F-3T(f)), the second succeeding taxable year after the end of the recovery period is treated as the first succeeding taxable year after the end of the recovery period for purposes of this paragraph (c) because of the half-year convention. For example, assume a calendar-year taxpayer places in service on July 1, 1984, a passenger automobile (*i.e.*, 3-year recovery property) and elects under section 168(b)(3) to recover its cost over 5 years using the straight line optional percentages. Based on these facts, calendar year 1990 is

treated as the first succeeding taxable year after the end of the recovery period.

(3) *Deduction limited to $6,000 for any taxable year.*—The amount that may be treated as a deductible expense under this paragraph (c) in the first taxable year succeeding the recovery period shall not exceed $6,000. Any excess shall be treated as an expense for the succeeding taxable years. However, in no event may any deduction in a succeeding taxable year exceed $6,000. The limitation on amounts deductible as an expense under this paragraph (c) with respect to any passenger automobile is increased by the automobile price inflation adjustment (as defined in section 280F(d)(7)) for the calendar year in which such automobile is placed in service.

(4) *Deduction treated as a section 168 recovery deduction.*—Any amount allowable as an expense in a taxable year after the recovery period by reason of this paragraph (c) shall be treated as a recovery deduction allowable under section 168. However, a deduction is allowable by reason of this paragraph (c) with respect to any passenger automobile for a taxable year only to the extent that a deduction under section 168 would be allowable with respect to the automobile for that year. For example, no recovery deduction is allowable for a year during which a passenger automobile is disposed of or is used exclusively for personal purposes.

(d) *Additional reduction in limitations by reason of personal use of passenger automobile or by reason of a short taxable year.*—See paragraph (i) of this section for rules regarding the additional reduction in the limitations prescribed by paragraphs (a) through (c) of this section by reason of the personal use of a passenger automobile or by reason of a short taxable year.

(e) *Examples.*—The provisions of paragraphs (a) through (c) of this section may be illustrated by the following examples. For purposes of these examples, assume that all taxpayers use the calendar year and that no short taxable years are involved.

Example (1). (i) On July 1, 1984, B purchases for $45,000 and places in service a passenger automobile which is 3-year recovery property under section 168. In 1984, B does not elect under section 179 to expense a portion of the cost of the automobile. The automobile is used exclusively in B's business during taxable years 1984 through 1990.

(ii) The maximum amount of B's investment tax credit is $1,000 (*i.e.,* the lesser of $1,000 or .06 × $45,000). B's unadjusted basis for purposes of section 168 is $44,500 (*i.e.,* $45,000 reduced under section 48(q)(1) by $500). B selects the use of the accelerated recovery percentages under section 168(b)(1).

(iii) The maximum amount of B's recovery deduction for 1984 is $4,000 (*i.e.,* the lesser of $4,000 or .25 × $44,500); for 1985, $6,000 (*i.e.,* the lesser of $6,000 or .38 × $44,500); and for 1986, $6,000 (*i.e.,* the lesser of $6,000 or .37 × $44,500).

(iv) At the beginning of taxable year 1987, B's unrecovered basis in the automobile is $28,500 (*i.e.,* $44,500 – $16,000). Under paragraph (c) of this section, B may expense $6,000 of the unrecovered basis in the automobile in 1987. This expense is treated as a recovery deduction under section 168. For taxable years 1988 through 1990, B may deduct $6,000 of the unrecovered basis per year. At the beginning of 1991, B's unrecovered basis in the automobile is $4,500. During that year, B disposes of the automobile. B is not allowed a deduction for 1991 because no deduction would be allowable under section 168 based on these facts.

Example (2). (i) On July 1, 1984, C purchases for $50,000 and places in service a passenger automobile which is 3-year recovery property under section 168. The automobile is used exclusively in C's business during taxable years 1984 through 1992. In 1984, C does not elect under section 179 to expense a portion of the automobile's cost. C elects under section 48(q)(4) to take a reduced investment tax credit in lieu of the section 48(q)(1) basis adjustment.

(ii) The maximum amount of C's investment tax credit is $666.67 (*i.e.,* the lesser of $^2/_3$ of $1,000 or .04 × $50,000). C's unadjusted basis for purposes of section 168 is $50,000. C elects to use the optional recovery percentages under section 168(b)(3) based on a 5-year recovery period.

(iii) The maximum amount of C's recovery deduction for 1984 is $4,000 (*i.e.,* the lesser of $4,000 or .10 × $50,000); for taxable years 1985 through 1988, $6,000 per year (*i.e.,* the lesser of $6,000 or .20 × $50,000). C's recovery deduction for 1989 is $5,000 (*i.e.,* the lesser of .10 × $50,000 or $6,000).

(iv) At the beginning of taxable year 1990, C's unrecovered basis in the automobile is $17,000. Under paragraph (c) of this section, C may expense $6,000 of the unrecovered basis in the automobile in 1990. This expense is treated as a recovery deduction under section 168. For taxable years 1991 and 1992, C may deduct $6,000, and $5,000, respectively of the unrecovered basis per year.

Example (3). Assume the same facts as in example (2), except that C disposes of the passenger automobile on July 1, 1990. Under paragraph (c) of this section, C is not allowed a deduction for 1990 or for any succeeding taxable year because no deduction would be allowable under section 168 based on these facts.

Example (4). (i) On July 1, 1984, G purchases for $15,000 and places in service a passenger automobile which is 3-year recovery property under section 168. The automobile is used exclusively in G's business during taxable years 1984 through 1987. In 1984, G elects under Section 179 to expense $5,000 of the cost of the property.

(ii) The maximum amount of G's investment tax credit is $600 (*i.e.,* the lesser of .06 × $10,000 or $1,000).

(iii) G's unadjusted basis for purposes of section 168 is $9,700 (*i.e.,* $15,000 minus the sum of $5,000 (the amount of the expense elected under section 179) and $300 (one-half of the investment tax credit under section 48(q)(1))). Under paragraph (b)(4) of this section, the allowable deduction under section 179 is treated as a recovery deduction under section 168 for purposes of this section. Thus, the maximum amount of G's section 179 deduction is $4,000 (*i.e.,* the lesser of $4,000 or $5,000 + .25 × $9,700). G is entitled to no further recovery deduction under section 168 for 1984. The amount of G's 1985 and 1986 recovery deductions are $3,686 (*i.e.,* the lesser of .38 × $9,700 or $6,000) and $3,589 (*i.e.,* the lesser of .37 × $9,700 or $6,000), respectively. At the beginning of 1987, G's unrecovered basis in the automobile is $3,425 (*i.e.,* $14,700 – $11.275). Under paragraph (c) of this section, G may expense the remaining $3,425 in 1987.

Example (5). (i) On July 1, 1984, D purchases for $55,000 and places in service a passenger automobile which is 3-year recovery property under section 168. The automobile is used exclusively in D's business during taxable years 1984 through 1993. In 1984, D elects under section 179 to expense $5,000 of the cost of the property.

(ii) The maximum amount of D's investment tax credit is $1,000 (*i.e.,* the lesser of $1,000 or .06 × $50.000).

(iii) D's unadjusted basis for purposes of section 168 is $49,500 (*i.e.,* $55,000 minus the sum of $5,000 (the amount of the expense elected under section 179) and $500 (one-half of the investment tax credit under section 49(q)(1))). Under paragraph (b)(4) of this section, the allowance deduction under section 179 is treated as a recovery deduction under section 168 for purposes of this section. Thus, the maximum amount of D's section 179 deduction is $4,000 (*i.e.,* the lesser of $4,000 or $5,000 + .25 × $49,500). D is entitled to no further recovery deduction under section 168 for 1984. The maximum amount of D's 1985 recovery deduction is $6,000 (*i.e.,* the lesser of $6,000 or .38 × $49,500); and for 1986, $6,000 (*i.e.,* the lesser of $6,000 or .37 of $49,500).

(iv) At the beginning of 1987, D's unrecovered basis is $38,500. D may expense the remaining unrecovered basis at the rate of $6,000 per year through 1992 and $2,500 in 1993.

Example (6). Assume the same facts as in example (5), except that in 1993, D uses the automobile only 60 percent in his business. Under paragraph (c)(4) of this section, for 1993, D may expense $1,500 (*i.e.,* .60 × $2,500). D is entitled to no further deductions with respect to the automobile in any later year.

Example (7). (i) On July 1, 1984, F purchases for $44,500 and places in service a passenger automobile which is 3-year recovery property under section 168. The automobile is used exclusively in F's business during taxable years 1984 through 1992. In 1984, F elects under section 179 to expense $5,000 of the cost of the property.

(ii) F elects under section 48(q)(4) to take a reduced investment tax credit in lieu of the section 48(q)(1) basis adjustment. The maximum amount of F's investment tax credit is $666.67 (*i.e.,* the lesser of $^2/_3$ of $1,000 or .04 × $39,500).

(iii) F's unadjusted basis for purposes of section 168 is $39,500 (*i.e.,* $44,500 – $5,000 (the amount of the expense elected under section 179)). F elects to use the optional recovery percentage under section 168(b)(3) based on a 5-year recovery period. Under paragraph (b)(4) of this section, the allowable section 179 deduction is treated as a recovery deduction under section 168 for purposes of this section. Thus, the maximum amount of F's section 179 deduction is $4,000 (*i.e.,* the lesser of $4,000 or $5,000 + .10 × $39,500). F is entitled to no further recovery deduction under section 168 for 1984. The maximum amounts of F's recovery deductions for 1985 through 1988 are $6,000 per year (*i.e.,* the lesser of $6,000 or .20 × $39,500). F's recovery deduction for 1989 (the first taxable year after the 5-year recovery period but the sixth recovery year for purposes of section 168) is $3,950 (*i.e.,* the lesser of .10 × $39,500 or $6,000).

(iv) Under paragraph (c), taxable year 1990 is considered to be the first taxable year succeeding the end of the recovery period. At the beginning of taxable year 1990, F's unrecovered basis in the automobile is $12,550 (*i.e.,* $44,500 – $31,950). Under paragraph (c), F may expense $6,000 of his unrecovered basis in the automobile in 1990 and in 1991. This expense is treated as a recovery deduction under section 168. For taxable year 1992, F may expense the remaining $550 of his unrecovered basis in the automobile.

Reg. §1.280F-2T(e)

(f) *Treatment of improvements that qualify as capital expenditures.*—An improvement to a passenger automobile that qualifies as a capital expenditure under section 263 is treated as a new item of recovery property placed in service in the year the improvement is made. However, the limitations in paragraph (b) of this section on the amount of recovery deductions allowable are determined by taking into account as a whole both the improvement and the property of which the improvement is a part. If that improvement also qualifies as an investment in new section 38 property under section 48(b) and §1.48-2(b)(2), the limitation in paragraph (a)(1) of this section on the amount of the investment tax credit for that improvement is determined by taking into account any investment tax credit previously allowed for the passenger automobile (including any prior improvement considered part of the passenger automobile). Thus, the maximum credit allowable for the automobile (including the improvement) will be $1,000 (or $2/3$ of $1,000, in the case of an election to take a reduced credit under section 48(q)(4)) (adjusted under section 280F(d)(7) to reflect the automobile price inflation adjustment for the year the property of which the improvement is a part is placed in service).

(g) *Treatment of section 1031 or section 1033 transactions.*—(1) *Treatment of exchanged passenger automobile.*—For a taxable year in which a transaction described in section 1031 or section 1033 occurs, the unadjusted basis of an exchanged or converted passenger automobile shall cease to be taken into account in determining any recovery deductions allowable under section 168 as of the beginning of the taxable year in which the exchange or conversion occurs. Thus, no recovery deduction is allowable for the exchanged or converted automobile in the year of the exchange or conversion.

(2) *Treatment of acquired passenger automobile.*—(i) *In general.*—The acquired automobile is treated as new property placed in service in the year of the exchange (or in the replacement year) and that year is its first recovery year.

(ii) *Limitations on recovery deductions.*—If the exchanged (or converted) automobile was acquired after the effective date of section 280F (as set out in §1.280F-1(c)), the basis of that automobile as determined under section 1031(d) or section 1033(b) (whichever is applicable) must be reduced for purposes of computing recovery deductions with respect to the acquired automobile (but not for purposes of determining the amount of the investment tax credit and gain or loss on the sale or other disposition of the property) by the excess (if any) of—

(A) The sum of the amounts that would have been allowable as recovery deductions with respect to the exchanged (or converted) automobile during taxable years preceding the year of the exchange (or conversion) if all of the use of the automobile during those years was use described in section 168(c), over

(B) The sum of the amounts allowable as recovery deductions during those years.

(3) *Examples.*—The provisions of this paragraph (g) may be illustrated by the following examples:

Example (1). (i) In 1982, F purchases and places in service a passenger automobile which is 3-year recovery property under section 168. The automobile is used exclusively in F's business.

(ii) On July 1, 1984, F exchanges the passenger automobile and $1,000 cash for a new passenger automobile ("like kind" property). Under paragraph (g)(1) of this section, no recovery deduction is allowed in 1984 for the exchanged automobile. Any investment tax credit claimed with respect to that automobile is subject to recapture under section 47.

(iii) F's basis in the acquired property (as determined under section 1031(d)) and F's qualified investment are $20,000. Under the provisions of paragraph (g)(2)(i) of this section, the acquired property is treated as new recovery property placed in service in 1984 to the extent of the full $20,000 of basis. The maximum amount of F's investment tax credit is limited to $1,000 (i.e., the lesser of $1,000 or .06 × $20,000). Cost recovery deductions are computed pursuant to paragraph (b) of this section.

Example (2). (i) On July 1, 1984, E purchases for $30,000 and places in service a passenger automobile which is 3-year recovery property under section 168. In 1984, E's business use percentage is 80 percent and such use constitutes his total business/investment use.

(ii) E elects under section 48(q)(4) to take a reduced investment tax credit in lieu of the section 48(q)(1) basis adjustment. The maximum amount of E's investment tax credit is $533.33 (i.e., the lesser of $2/3$ of $1,000 × .80 or .80 × .04 × $30,000).

(iii) E's unadjusted basis for purposes of section 168 is $30,000. E *selects the use of the accelerated recovery percentages under section* 168(b)(1). The maximum amount of E's recovery deduction for 1984 is $3,200 (i.e., the lesser of .80 × $4,000 or .80 × .25 × $30,000).

(iv) On June 10, 1985, E exchanges the passenger automobile and $1,000 cash for a new passenger automobile ("like kind" property).

Under paragraph (g)(1) of this section, no recovery deduction is allowable in 1985 for the exchanged automobile. The investment tax credit claimed is subject to recapture under section 47. Under paragraph (g)(2)(ii) of this section, E's basis in the acquired property for purposes of computing recovery deductions under section 280F is $27,000 (i.e., $27,800 (section 1031(d) basis) − $800). The acquired automobile is used exclusively in F's business during taxable years 1985 through 1988. Under paragraph (g)(2) of this section, the acquired property is treated as new recovery property placed in service in 1985. Assume that the automobile price inflation adjustment (as described under section 280F(d)(7)) is zero. E's qualifying investment in the property, as determined under §1.46-3(c)(1), is $27,800. The maximum amount of E's investment tax credit is $1,000 (i.e., the lesser of $1,000 or .06 × $27,800). E's unadjusted basis for purposes of section 168 is $26,500 (i.e., $27,000 reduced under section 48(q)(1) by $500). Cost recovery deductions are computed pursuant to paragraph (b) of this section.

(h) *Other nonrecognition transactions.*—[Reserved]

(i) *Limitation under this section applies before other limitations.*—(1) *Personal use.*—The limitations imposed upon the maximum amount of the allowable investment tax credit and the allowable recovery deductions (as described in paragraphs (a) through (c) of this section) must be adjusted during any taxable year in which a taxpayer makes any use of a passenger automobile other than for business/investment use (as defined in §1.280F-6(d)(3)). The limitations on the amount of the allowable investment tax credit (as described in paragraph (a) of this section) and the allowable cost recovery deductions (as described in paragraphs (b) and (c) of this section) are redetermined by multiplying the limitations by the percentage of business/investment use (determined on an annual basis) during the taxable year.

(2) *Short taxable year.*—The limitations imposed upon the maximum amount of the allowable recovery deductions (as described in paragraphs (a) through (c) of this section) must be adjusted during any taxable year in which a taxpayer has a short taxable year. In this case, the limitation is adjusted by multiplying the limitation that would have been applied if the taxable year were not a short taxable year by a fraction, the numerator of which is the number of months and part-months in the short taxable year and the denominator of which is 12.

(3) *Examples.*—The provisions of this paragraph (i) may be illustrated by the following examples:

Example (1). On July 1, 1984, A purchases and places in service a passenger automobile and uses it 80 percent for business/investment use during 1984. Under paragraph (i)(1) of this section, the maximum amount of the investment tax credit that A may claim for the automobile is $800 (i.e., .80 × $1,000).

Example (2). Assume the same facts as in example (1), except that A elects under section 48(q)(4) to take a reduced investment tax credit in lieu of the section 48(q)(1) basis adjustment. Under paragraph (i)(1) of this section, the maximum amount of the investment tax credit that A may claim for the automobile is $533.33 (i.e., .80 × $2/3$ × $1,000).

Example (3). On July 1, 1984, B purchases and places in service a passenger automobile and uses it 60 percent for business/investment use during 1984. Under paragraph (i)(1) of this section, the maximum amount of the investment tax credit that B may claim for the automobile is $600 (i.e., .60 × $1,000). B uses the car 70 percent for business/investment use during 1985 and 80 percent during 1986. Under paragraph (i)(1) of this section, the maximum amount of recovery deductions that B may claim for 1984, 1985, and 1986 are $2,400 (i.e., .60 × $4,000), $4,200 (i.e., .70 × $6,000), and $4,800 (i.e., .80 × $6,000), respectively.

Example (4). Assume the same facts as in example (3) with the added facts that B's unrecovered basis at the beginning of 1987 is $6,000 and that B uses the automobile 85 percent for business/investment use during 1987. Under paragraph (i)(1) of this section, the maximum amount that B may claim as an expense for 1987 is $5,100 (i.e., .85 × $6,000).

Example (5). On August 1, 1984, C purchases and places in service a passenger automobile and uses it exclusively for business. Taxable year 1984 for C is a short taxable year which consists of 6 months. Under paragraph (i)(2) of this section, the maximum amount that C may claim as a recovery deduction for 1984 is $2,000 (i.e., 6/12 × $4,000).

Example (6). Assume the same facts as in example (5), except that C uses the passenger automobile 70 percent for business/investment use during 1984. Under paragraph (i)(1) and (2) of this section, the maximum amount that C may claim as a recovery deduction for 1984 is $1,400 (i.e., .70 × 6/12 × $4,000). [Temporary Reg. §1.280F-2T.]

☐ [*T.D. 7986*, 10-19-84. *Amended by T.D. 9133*, 6-24-2004.]

Reg. §1.280F-2T(f)

[Reg. §1.280F-3T]

§1.280F-3T. Limitations on recovery deductions and the investment tax credit when the business use percentage of listed property is not greater than 50 percent (Temporary).—(a) *In general.*—Section 280F(b), generally, imposes limitations with respect to the amount allowable as an investment tax credit under section 46(a) and the amount allowable as a recovery deduction under section 168 in the case of listed property (as defined in §1.280F-6(b)) if certain business use of the property (referred to as "qualified business use") does not exceed 50 percent during a taxable year. "Qualified business use" generally means use in a trade or business, rather than use in an investment or other activity conducted for the production of income within the meaning of section 212. See §1.280F-6(d) for the distinction between "business/investment use" and "qualified business use."

(b) *Limitation on the amount of investment tax credit.*—(1) *Denial of investment tax credit when business use percentage not greater than 50 percent.*—Listed property is not treated as section 38 property to any extent unless the business use percentage (as defined in section 280F(d)(6) and §1.280F-6(d)(1)) is greater than 50 percent. For example, if a taxpayer uses listed property in a trade or business in the taxable year in which it is placed in service, but the business use percentage is not greater than 50 percent, no investment tax credit is allowed for that listed property. If, in the taxable year in which listed property is placed in service, the only business/investment use (as defined in §1.280F-6(d)(3)) of that property is qualified business use (as defined in §1.280F-6(d)(2)(i)), and the business use percentage is 55 percent, the investment tax credit is allowed for the 55 percent of the listed property that is treated as section 38 property. The credit allowed is unaffected by any increase in the business use percentage in a subsequent taxable year.

(2) *Recapture of investment tax credit.*—Listed property ceases to be section 38 property to the extent that the business/investment use (as defined in §1.280F-6(d)(3)) for any taxable year is less than the business/investment use for the taxable year in which the property is placed in service. See §1.47-2(c). If the business use percentage (as defined in §1.280F-6(d)(1)) of listed property is greater than 50 percent for the taxable year in which the property is placed in service, and less than or equal to 50 percent for any subsequent taxable year, that property ceases to be section 38 property in its entirety in that subsequent taxable year. Under §1.47-1(c)(1)(ii)(*b*), the property (or a portion thereof) is treated as ceasing to be section 38 property on the first day of the taxable year in which the cessation occurs.

(c) *Limitation on the method of cost recovery under section 168 when business use of property not greater than 50 percent.*—(1) *Year of acquisition.*—If any listed property (as defined in §1.280F-6(b)) is not predominantly used in a qualified business use (as defined in §1.280F-6(d)(4)) in the year it is acquired, the recovery deductions allowed under section 168 for the property for that taxable year and for succeeding taxable years are to be determined using the straight line method over its earnings and profits life (as defined in paragraph (f) of this section). Additionally, the taxpayer is not entitled to make any election under section 179 with respect to the property for that year.

(2) *Subsequent years.*—If any listed property is not subject to paragraph (c)(1) of this section because such property is predominantly used in a qualified business use (as defined in §1.280F-6(d)(4)) during the year it is acquired but is not predominantly used in a qualified business use during a subsequent taxable year, the rules of this paragraph (c)(2) apply. In such a case, the taxpayer must determine the recovery deductions allowed under section 168 for the taxable year that the listed property is not predominantly used in a qualified business use and for any subsequent taxable year as if such property was not predominantly used in a qualified business use in the year in which it was acquired and there had been no section 179 election with respect to the property. Thus, the recovery deductions allowable under section 168 for the remaining taxable years are computed by determining the applicable recovery percentage that would apply if the taxpayer had used the straight line method over the property's earnings and profits life beginning with the year the property was placed in service.

(3) *Effect of rule on recovery property that is not listed property.*—The mandatory use of the straight line method over the property's earnings and profits life under paragraph (d)(1) and (2) of this section does not have any effect on the proper method of cost recovery for other recovery property of that same class placed in service in the same taxable year by the taxpayer and does not constitute an election to use an optional recovery period under section 168(b)(3).

(d) *Recapture of excess recovery deductions claimed.*—(1) *In general.*—If paragraph (c)(2) of this section is applicable, any excess depreciation (as defined in paragraph (d)(2) of this section) must be included in the taxpayer's gross income and added to the property's adjusted basis for the first taxable year in which the property is not predominantly used in a qualified business use (as defined in §1.280F-6(d)(4)).

(2) *Definition of "excess depreciation".*—For purposes of this section, the term "excess depreciation" means the excess (if any) of—

(i) The amount of the recovery deductions allowable with respect to the property for taxable years before the first taxable year in which the property was not predominantly used in a qualified business use, over

(ii) The amount of the recovery deductions which would have been allowable for those years if the property had not been predominantly used in a qualified business use for the year it was acquired and there had been no section 179 election with respect to the property.

For purposes of paragraph (d)(2)(i), any deduction allowable under section 179 (relating to the election to expense certain depreciable trade or business assets) is treated as if that deduction was a recovery deduction under section 168.

(3) *Recordkeeping requirement.*—A taxpayer must be able to substantiate the use of any listed property, as prescribed in section 274(d)(4) and §1.274-5T or §1.274-5T, for any taxable year for which recapture under section 280F(b)(3) and paragraph (d)(1) and (2) of this section may occur even if the taxpayer has fully depreciated (or expensed) the listed property in a prior year. For example, in the case of 3-year recovery property, the taxpayer shall maintain a log, journal, etc. for six years even though the taxpayer fully depreciated the property in the first three years.

(e) *Earnings and profits life.*—(1) *Definition.*—The earnings and profits life with respect to any listed property is generally the following:

In the case of:	The applicable recovery period is:
3-year property	5 years
5-year property	12 years
10-year property	25 years
18-year real property and low-income housing	40 years
15-year public utility property	35 years

However, if the recovery period applicable to any recovery property under section 168 is longer than the above assigned recovery period, such longer recovery period shall be used. For example, generally, the recovery period for recovery property used predominantly outside the United States is the property's present class life (as defined in section 168(g)(2)). In many cases, a property's present class life is longer than the recovery period assigned to the property under the above table. Pursuant to this paragraph (e)(1), the property's recovery period is its present class life.

(2) *Applicable recovery percentages.*—If the applicable recovery period is determined pursuant to the table prescribed in paragraph (e)(1) of this section, the applicable recovery percentage is:

(i) For property other than 18-year real property or low-income housing:

If the recovery year is:	And the recovery period is:			
	5	12	25	35
1	10	4	2	1
2	20	9	4	3
3	20	9	4	3
4	20	9	4	3
*[5]	[20]	[9]	[4]	[3]

If the recovery year is:	5 / 10	12	25	35
[6]5 ..	10	8	4	3
7		8	4	3
8		8	4	3
9		8	4	3
10		8	4	3
11		8	4	3
12		8	4	3
13		4	4	3
14			4	3
15			4	3
16			4	3
17			4	3
18			4	3
19			4	3
20			4	3
21			4	3
22			4	3
23			4	3
24			4	3
25			4	3
26			2	3
27				3
28				3
29				3
30				3
31				3
32				2
33				2
34				2
35				2
36				1

* Bracketed percentages were omitted from the regulation as originally promulgated from the Treasury Department. The correct figures were obtained from Table XVI of IRS Pub. 534 (Rev. Dec. 186).—CCH.

    (ii) For 18-year real property: [Reserved]
    (iii) For low-income housing: [Reserved]

    (f) *Examples.*—The provisions of this section may be illustrated by the following examples. For purposes of these examples, assume that all taxpayers use the calendar year and that no short taxable years are involved.

    Example (1). On July 1, 1984, B purchases for $50,000 and places in service an item of listed property (other than a passenger automobile) which is 3-year recovery property under section 168. For the first taxable year that the property is in service, B uses the property 40 percent in a trade or business, 40 percent for the production of income, and 20 percent for personal purposes. Although B's total business/investment use is greater than 50 percent, the business use percentage for that taxable year is only 40 percent. Under paragraph (b)(1) of this section, no investment tax credit is allowed for the property.

    Example (2). (i) On January 1, 1985, C purchases for $40,000 and places in service an item of listed property (other than a passenger automobile) that is 3-year recovery property under section 168. Seventy percent of the use of the property is in C's trade or business and 30 percent of the use is for personal purposes. C does not elect a reduced investment tax credit under section 48(q)(4). The amount of C's investment tax credit is $1,680 (*i.e.*, $40,000 × .10 × .70).

    (ii) In addition, in 1986, only 55 percent of the use of the property is in C's trade or business and 45 percent of the use is for personal purposes. Under paragraph (b)(2) of this section, the property ceases to be section 38 property to the extent that the use in a trade or business decreased below 70 percent. As a result, a portion of the investment tax credit must be recaptured as an increase in tax liability for 1986 under the rules of section 47 (relating to the recapture of investment tax credit). See section 47(a)(5) and §1.47-2(e) for rules relating to the computation of the recapture amount.

    Example (3). On July 1, 1984, B purchases and places in service an item of listed property (other than a passenger automobile) that is 3-year recovery property. B elects to take a reduced investment tax credit under section 48(q)(4). In 1984, B uses the property exclusively in his business. Assume that B's 1984 allowable recovery deduction is $12,500. In 1985 and 1986, the property is not predominantly used in a qualified business use. The investment tax credit claimed is subject to recapture in full under section 47 in 1985 since the property ceases to be section 38 property in its entirety on January 1, 1985. Under paragraph (c)(2) of this section, B must treat the property for 1985 and subsequent taxable years as if he recovered its cost over a 5-year recovery period (*i.e.*, its earnings and profits life) using the straight line method (with the half-year convention) from the time it was placed in service. Therefore, taxable year 1985 is treated as the property's second recovery year (of its 5-year recovery period) and

the applicable recovery deduction using the straight line method must be used to determine the recovery deduction. Under paragraph (d) of this section, B must recapture any excess depreciation claimed for taxable year 1984. If B had used the straight line method over a 5-year recovery period his recovery deduction for 1984 would have been $5,000. Under paragraph (d)(2) of this section, B's excess depreciation is $7,500 (*i.e.*, $12,500 − $5,000) and that amount must be included in B's 1985 gross income and added to the property's basis. The taxable years 1986 through 1989 are the property's second through sixth recovery years, respectively, of such property's 5-year recovery period.

    Example (4). Assume the same facts as in example (3), except that in 1986 B uses the property exclusively in his business. B is entitled to no investment tax credit with respect to the property in 1986 and must continue to recover the property's cost over a 5-year recovery period using the straight line method.

    Example (5). On July 1, 1984, H purchases and places in service listed property (other than a passenger automobile) which is 3-year recovery property under section 168. H selects the use of the accelerated recovery percentages under section 168. In 1984 through 1986, H uses the property exclusively for business. In 1987, the property is not predominantly used in a qualified business use. Under paragraph (c)(2) of this section, H must compute his 1987 and subsequent taxable year's recovery deductions using the straight line method over a 5-year recovery period with 1987 treated as the fourth recovery year. Under paragraph (d) of this section, H must recapture any excess depreciation claimed for taxable years 1984 through 1986 even though by 1987 the full cost of the property had already been recovered.

    Example (6). Assume the same facts as in example (5), except that H uses the property exclusively for personal purposes in 1987. Under paragraph (d) of this section, H must recapture any excess depreciation claimed for taxable years 1984 through 1986. H is entitled to no cost recovery deduction under the 5-year straight line method for 1987. Assume further that in 1988 H uses the property 70 percent in his business. Thus, H's business use percentage for that year is 70 percent. Under paragraph (c)(2) of this section, H must compute his 1988 cost recovery deduction using the straight line method over a 5-year recovery period with 1988 treated as the fifth recovery year.

    Example (7). (i) On July 1, 1984, F purchases for $70,000 and places in service listed property (other than a passenger automobile) which is 3-year recovery property under section 168. F's business use percentage for 1984 through 1986 is 60 percent. F elects under section 179 to expense $5,000 of the cost of the property.

    (ii) F elects a reduced investment tax credit under section 48(q)(4). The maximum amount of F's investment tax credit is $1,560 (*i.e.*, $65,000 × .04 × .60).

Reg. §1.280F-3T(e)(2)(ii)

(iii) F's unadjusted basis for purposes of section 168 is $65,000 (*i.e.*, $70,000 reduced by the $5,000 section 179 expense). F selects the use of the accelerated recovery percentages under section 168 (b)(1). F's recovery deduction for 1984 is $9,750 (*i.e.*, $65,000 × .25 × .60).

(iv) In 1985, the property is not predominantly used in a qualified business use. The investment tax credit claimed is subject to recapture in full under section 47 in 1985 since the property ceases to be section 38 property in its entirety on January 1, 1985. Under paragraph (c)(2) of this section, F must treat the property for 1985 and subsequent taxable years as if he recovered its cost over a 5-year recovery period (*i.e.*, its earnings and profits life) using the straight line method (with the half year convention) from the time it was placed in service. Under paragraph (d) of this section, F must recapture any excess depreciation claimed for taxable year 1984. F's excess depreciation is $10,500 [*i.e.*, ($65,000 × .25 × .60 + $5,000) − ($70,000 × .10 × .60)]. This amount must be included in F's 1985 gross income and added to the property's adjusted basis.

Example (8). (i) On July 1, 1984, G purchases for $60,000 and places in service a passenger automobile which is 3-year recovery property under section 168.

(ii) In 1984, G's business use percentage is 80 percent and such use constitutes his total business/investment use. G elects under section 48(q)(4) to take a reduced investment tax credit in lieu of the basis adjustment under section 48(q)(1). The maximum amount of G's investment tax credit is $533.33 (*i.e.*, the lesser of .80 × ²/₃ × $1,000 or $60,000 × .80 × .04).

(iii) In 1984, G does not elect under section 179 to expense a portion of the automobile's cost. G selects the use of the accelerated recovery percentages under section 168. G's unadjusted basis for purposes of section 168 is $60,000. The maximum amount of G's 1984 recovery deduction is $3,200 (*i.e.*, the lesser of .80 × $4,000 or .80 × .25 × $60,000).

(iv) In 1985, G's business use percentage is 80 percent and such use constitutes his total business/investment use. The maximum amount of G's 1985 recovery deduction is $4,800 (*i.e.*, the lesser of .80 × $6,000 or .80 × .38 × $60,000).

(v) In 1986, G's business use percentage is 45 percent and such use constitutes his total business/investment use. Under paragraph (b)(2) of this section, as a result of the decline in business use percentage to 50 percent or less, the automobile ceases to be section 38 property in its entirety and G must recapture (pursuant to §§ 1.47-1(c) and 1.47-2(e) the investment tax credit previously claimed. Since G's business use percentage in 1986 is not greater than 50 percent, under the provisions of paragraph (d) of this section, G must recompute (for recapture purposes) his recovery deductions for 1984 and 1985 using the straight line method over a 5-year recovery period (*i.e.*, earnings and profits life for 3-year recovery property using the half-year convention) to determine if any excess depreciation must be included in his 1986 taxable income. G's recomputed recovery deductions for 1984 and 1985 are $3,200 (*i.e.*, the lesser of .80 × $4,000 or .80 × .10 × $60,000), and $4,800 (*i.e.*, the lesser of .80 × $6,000 or .80 × .20 × $60,000), respectively. G does not have to recapture any excess depreciation since his recovery deductions for 1984 and 1985 computed using the straight line method over a 5-year recovery period are the same as the amounts actually claimed during those years.

(vi) Under paragraph (c)(2) of this section, for 1986 and succeeding taxable years G must compute his remaining recovery deductions using the straight line method over a 5-year recovery period beginning with the third recovery year. The maximum amount of G's 1986 recovery deduction is $2,700 (*i.e.*, the lesser of .45 × $6,000 or .45 × .20 × $60,000). For taxable years 1987 through 1993, G's business use percentage is 55 percent and such use constitutes his total business/investment use. G's 1987 and 1988 recovery deductions are $3,300 per year (*i.e.*, the lesser of .55 × $6,000 or .55 × .20 × $60,000). For taxable year 1989 (the last recovery year), G's recovery deduction is $3,300 (*i.e.*, .55 × .10 × $60,000 or .55 × $6,000).

(vii) As of the beginning of 1990, G will have claimed a total of $20,600 of recovery deductions. Under § 1.280F-2T(c), G may expense his remaining unrecovered basis (up to a certain amount per year) in the first succeeding taxable year after the end of the recovery period and in taxable years thereafter. If G had used his automobile for 100 percent business use in taxable years 1984 through 1989, G could have claimed a *recovery deduction of $4,000 in 1984* and a recovery deduction of $6,000 in each of those remaining years. At the beginning of 1990, therefore, G's unrecovered basis (as defined in section 280F(d)(8)) is $26,000 (*i.e.*, $60,000 − $34,000). The maximum amount of G's 1990 recovery deduction is $3,300 (*i.e.*, .55 × $6,000). At the beginning of 1991, G's unrecovered basis is $20,000 (*i.e.*, $26,000 adjusted under section 280F(d)(2) and § 1.280F-4T(a) to account for the amount that would have been claimed in 1990 for 100 percent business/investment use during that year). The maximum amount of G's 1991 recovery deduction is $3,300 (*i.e.*, .55 × $6,000) and his unrecovered basis as of the beginning of 1992 is $14,000 (*i.e.*, $20,000 −

$6,000). In 1992, G disposes of the automobile. G is not allowed a recovery deduction for 1992. [Temporary Reg. § 1.280F-3T.]

☐ [*T.D.* 7986, 10-19-84. *Amended by T.D.* 8061, 10-31-85 *and T.D.* 9133, 6-24-2004.]

[Reg. § 1.280F-4T]

§ 1.280F-4T. Special rules for listed property (Temporary).—(a) *Limitations on allowable recovery deductions in subsequent taxable years.*—(1) *Subsequent taxable years affected by reason of personal use in prior years.*—For purposes of computing the amount of the recovery deduction for "listed property" for a subsequent taxable year, the amount that would have been allowable as a recovery deduction during an earlier taxable year if all of the use of the property was use described in section 168(c) is treated as the amount of the recovery deduction allowable during that earlier taxable year. The preceding sentence applies with respect to all earlier taxable years, beginning with the first taxable year in which some or all use of the "listed property" is use described in section 168(c). For example, on July 1, 1984, B purchases and places in service listed property (other than a passenger automobile) which is 5-year recovery property under section 168. B selects the use of the accelerated percentages under section 168. B's business/investment use of the property (all of which is qualified business use as defined in section 280F(d)(6)(B) and § 1.280F-6(d)(2)) in 1984 through 1988 is 80 percent, 80 percent, 70 percent, 60 percent, and 55 percent, respectively, and B claims recovery deductions for those years based on those percentages. B's qualified business use for the property for 1989 and taxable years thereafter increases to 100 percent. Pursuant to this rule, B may not claim a recovery deduction in 1989 (or for any subsequent taxable year) for the increase in business use because there is no adjusted basis remaining to be recovered for cost recovery purposes after 1988.

(2) *Special rule for passenger automobiles.*—In the case of a passenger automobile that is subject to the limitations of § 1.280F-2T, the amount treated as the amount that would have been allowable as a recovery deduction if all of the use of the automobile was use described in section 168(c) shall not exceed $4,000 for the year the passenger automobile is placed in service and $6,000 for each succeeding taxable year (adjusted to account for the automobile price inflation adjustment, if any, under section 280F(d)(7) and for a short taxable year under § 1.280F-2T(i)(2)). See § 1.280F-3T(g) *Example (8).*

(b) *Treatment of improvements that qualify as capital expenditures.*—(1) *In general.*—In the case of any improvement that qualifies as a capital expenditure under section 263 made to any listed property other than a passenger automobile, the rules of this paragraph (b) apply. See § 1.280F-2T(f) for the treatment of an improvement made to a passenger automobile.

(2) *Investment tax credit allowed for the improvement.*—If the improvement qualifies as an investment in new section 38 property under section 48(b) and 1.48-2(b), the investment tax credit for that improvement is limited by paragraph (b)(1) of § 1.280F-3T, as applied to the item of listed property as a whole.

(3) *Cost recovery of the improvement.*—The improvement is treated as a new item of recovery property. The method of cost recovery with respect to that improvement is limited by § 1.280F-3T(c), as applied to the item of listed property as a whole. [Temporary Reg. § 1.280F-4T.]

☐ [*T.D.* 7986, 10-19-84. *Amended by T.D.* 9133, 6-24-2004.]

[Reg. § 1.280F-5T]

§ 1.280F-5T. Leased property (Temporary).—(a) *In general.*—Except as otherwise provided in this section, the limitation on cost recovery deductions and the investment tax credit provided in section 280F(a) and (b) and §§ 1.280F-2T and 1.280F-3T do not apply to any listed property leased or held for leasing by any person regularly engaged in the business of leasing listed property. If a person is not regularly engaged in the business of leasing listed property, the limitations on cost recovery deductions and the investment tax credit provided in section 280F and §§ 1.280F-2T and 1.280F-3T apply to such property leased or held for leasing by such person. The special rules for lessees set out in this section apply with respect to all lessees of listed property, even those whose lessors are not regularly engaged in the business of leasing listed property. For rules on determining inclusion amounts with respect to passenger automobiles, see paragraphs (d), (e) and (g) of this section, and see § 1.280F-7(a). For rules on determining inclusion amounts with respect to other listed property, see paragraphs (f) and (g) of this section, and see § 1.280F-7(b).

(b) *Section 48(d) election.*—If a lessor elects under section 48(d) with respect to any listed property to treat the lessee as having acquired such property, the amount of the investment tax credit allowed to the lessee is subject to the limitation prescribed in § 1.280F-3T(b)(1) and (2). If a lessor elects under section 48(d) with respect to any passenger automobile to treat the lessee as having acquired such automobile, the amount of the investment tax credit allowed to the lessee is also subject to the limitations prescribed in §1.280F-2T(a) and (i).

(c) *Regularly engaged in the business of leasing.*—For purposes of paragraph (a) of this section, a person shall be considered regularly engaged in the business of leasing listed property only if contracts to lease such property are entered into with some frequency over a continuous period of time. The determination shall be made on the basis of the facts and circumstances in each case, taking into account the nature of the person's business in its entirety. Occasional or incidental leasing activity is insufficient. For example, a person leasing only one passenger automobile during a taxable year is not regularly engaged in the business of leasing automobiles. In addition, an employer that allows an employee to use the employer's property for personal purposes and charges such employee for the use of the property is not regularly engaged in the business of leasing with respect to the property used by the employee.

(d) *Inclusions in income of lessees of passenger automobiles leased after June 18, 1984, and before April 3, 1985.*—(1) *In general.*—If a taxpayer leases a passenger automobile after June 18, 1984, but before April 3, 1985, for each taxable year (except the last taxable year) during which the taxpayer leases the automobile, the taxpayer must include in gross income an inclusion amount (prorated for the number of days of the lease term included in that taxable year), determined under this paragraph (d)(1), and multiplied by the business/investment use (as defined in §1.280F-6(d)(3)(i)) for the particular taxable year. The inclusion amount—

(i) Is 7.5 percent of the excess (if any) of the automobile's fair market value over $16,500 for each of the first three taxable years during which a passenger automobile, which is leased after June 18, 1984, and before April 3, 1985, is leased.

(ii) Is 6 percent of the excess (if any) of the automobile's fair market value over $22,500 for the fourth taxable year during which a passenger automobile is leased.

(iii) Is 6 percent of the excess (if any) of the automobile's fair market value over $28,500 for the fifth taxable year during which a passenger automobile is leased.

(iv) Is 6 percent of the excess (if any) of the automobile's fair market value over $34,500 for the sixth taxable year during which a passenger automobile is leased.

For the seventh and subsequent taxable years during which a passenger automobile is leased, the inclusion amount is 6 percent of the excess (if any) of the automobile's fair market value over the sum of (A) $16,500 and (B) $6,000 multiplied by the number of such taxable years in excess of three years. See paragraph (g)(2) of this section for the definition of fair market value.

(2) *Additional inclusion amount when less than predominant use in a qualified business use.*—(i) If a passenger automobile is not used predominantly in a qualified business use during a taxable year, the lessee must add to gross income in the first taxable year that the automobile is not so used (and only in that year) an inclusion amount determined under this paragraph (d)(2). This inclusion amount is in addition to the amount required to be included in gross income under paragraph (d)(1) of this section.

(ii) If the fair market value (as defined in paragraph (h)(2) of this section) of the automobile is greater than $16,500, the inclusion amount is determined by multiplying the average of the business/investment use (as defined in paragraph (h)(3) of this section) by the appropriate dollar amount from the table in paragraph (d)(2)(iii) of this section. If the fair market value (as defined in paragraph (h)(2) of this section) of the automobile is $16,500 or less, the inclusion amount is the product of the fair market value of the automobile, the average business/investment use, and the applicable percentage from the table in paragraph (d)(2)(iv) of this section.

(iii) The dollar amount is determined under the following table:

If a passenger automobile is not predominantly used in a qualified business use during—	The dollar amount is:			
	Lease term (years)			
	1	*2*	*3*	*4 or more*
The first year of the leased term	$350	$700	$1,350	$1,850
The second taxable year of the lease term	—	—	650	1,250
The third taxable year of the lease term	—	—	—	650

(iv) The applicable percentage is determined under the following table:

If a passenger automobile is not predominantly used in a qualified business use during—	The applicable percentage is:			
	Lease term (years)			
	1	*2*	*3*	*4 or more*
The first taxable year of the lease term	3.0 %	6.00 %	10.20 %	13.2 %
The second taxable year of the lease term	—	1.25	6.20	10.4
The third taxable year of the lease term	—	—	2.25	6.5
The fourth taxable year of the lease term	—	—	—	1.7
The fifth taxable year of the lease term	—	—	—	0.5

(e) *Inclusions in income of lessees of passenger automobiles leased after April 2, 1985 and before January 1, 1987.*—(1) *In general.*—For any passenger automobile that is leased after April 2, 1985, and before January 1, 1987, for each taxable year (except the last taxable year) during which the taxpayer leases the automobile, the taxpayer must include in gross income an inclusion amount determined under subparagraphs (2) through (5) of this paragraph (e). Additional inclusion amounts when a passenger automobile is not used predominantly in a qualified business use during a taxable year are determined under paragraph (e)(6) of this section. *See* paragraph (h)(2) of this section for the definition of fair market value.

(2) *Fair market value not greater than $50,000: years one through three.*—For any passenger automobile that has a fair market value not

greater than $50,000, the inclusion amount for each of the first three taxable years during which the automobile is leased is determined as follows:

(i) For the appropriate range of fair market values in the table in paragraph (e)(2)(iv) of this section, select the dollar amount from the column for the quarter of the taxable year in which the automobile is first used under the lease,

(ii) Prorate the dollar amount for the number of days of the lease term included in the taxable year, and

(iii) Multiply the prorated dollar amount by the business/investment use for the taxable year.

(iv) DOLLAR AMOUNTS: YEARS 1-3

Fair Market Value		Taxable year quarter			
Greater than	*But not greater than*	*Fourth*	*Third*	*Second*	*First*
$11,250	$11,500	$8	$7	$6	$6
11,500	11,750	24	21	19	17
11,750	12,000	40	35	32	29
12,000	12,250	56	49	44	40
12,250	12,500	72	64	57	52
12,500	12,750	88	78	70	63
12,750	13,000	104	92	83	75
13,000	13,250	120	106	95	86
13,250	13,500	144	128	115	104
13,500	13,750	172	153	137	124
13,750	14,000	200	177	159	145
14,000	14,250	228	202	182	165

Fair Market Value Greater than	But not greater than	Fourth	Taxable year quarter Third	Second	First
14,250	14,500	256	227	204	185
14,500	14,750	284	252	226	206
14,750	15,000	312	277	249	226
15,000	15,250	340	302	271	246
15,250	15,500	369	327	293	266
15,500	15,750	397	352	316	287
15,750	16,000	425	377	338	307
16,000	16,250	453	402	360	327
16,250	16,500	481	426	383	348
16,500	16,750	509	451	405	368
16,750	17,000	537	476	428	388
17,000	17,500	579	514	461	419
17,500	18,000	635	563	506	459
18,000	18,500	691	613	550	500
18,500	19,000	748	663	595	541
19,000	19,500	804	713	640	581
19,500	20,000	860	763	685	622
20,000	20,500	916	812	729	662
20,500	21,000	972	862	774	703
21,000	21,500	1028	912	819	744
21,500	22,000	1084	962	863	784
22,000	23,000	1169	1036	930	845
23,000	24,000	1281	1136	1020	926
24,000	25,000	1393	1236	1109	1007
25,000	26,000	1506	1335	1199	1089
26,000	27,000	1618	1435	1288	1170
27,000	28,000	1730	1534	1377	1251
28,000	29,000	1842	1634	1467	1332
29,000	30,000	1955	1734	1556	1413
30,000	31,000	2067	1833	1646	1495
31,000	32,000	2179	1933	1735	1576
32,000	33,000	2292	2032	1824	1657
33,000	34,000	2404	2132	1914	1738
34,000	35,000	2516	2232	2003	1819
35,000	36,000	2629	2331	2093	1901
36,000	37,000	2741	2431	2182	1982
37,000	38,000	2853	2530	2271	2063
38,000	39,000	2965	2630	2361	2144
39,000	40,000	3078	2730	2450	2225
40,000	41,000	3190	2829	2540	2307
41,000	42,000	3302	2929	2629	2388
42,000	43,000	3415	3028	2718	2469
43,000	44,000	3527	3128	2808	2550
44,000	45,000	3639	3228	2897	2631
45,000	46,000	3752	3327	2987	2713
46,000	47,000	3864	3427	3076	2794
47,000	48,000	3976	3526	3165	2875
48,000	49,000	4088	3626	3255	2956
49,000	50,000	4201	3726	3344	3037

(3) *Fair market value not greater than $50,000: years four through six.*—For any passenger automobile that has a fair market value greater than $18,000, but not greater than $50,000, the inclusion amount for the fourth, fifth, and sixth taxable years during which the automobile is leased is determined as follows:

(i) For the appropriate range of fair market values in the table in paragraph (e)(3)(iv) of this section, select the dollar amount from the column for the taxable year in which the automobile is used under the lease,

(ii) Prorate the dollar amount for the number of days of the lease term included in the taxable year, and

(iii) Multiply this dollar amount by the business/investment use for the taxable year.

(iv) *DOLLAR AMOUNTS: YEARS 4-6*

Fair Market Value Greater than	But not greater than	Year 4	Year 5	Year 6
$18,000	$18,500	$15	—	—
18,500	19,000	45	—	—
19,000	19,500	75	—	—
19,500	20,000	105	—	—
20,000	20,500	135	—	—
20,500	21,000	165	—	—
21,000	21,500	195	—	—
21,500	22,000	225	—	—
22,000	23,000	270	—	—
23,000	24,000	330	$42	—
24,000	25,000	390	102	—
25,000	26,000	450	162	—
26,000	27,000	510	222	—

Fair Market Value Greater than	But not greater than	Year 4	Year 5	Year 6
27,000	28,000	570	282	—
28,000	29,000	630	342	$54
29,000	30,000	690	402	114
30,000	31,000	750	462	174
31,000	32,000	810	522	234
32,000	33,000	870	582	294
33,000	34,000	930	642	354
34,000	35,000	990	702	414
35,000	36,000	1050	762	474
36,000	37,000	1110	822	534
37,000	38,000	1170	882	594
38,000	39,000	1230	942	654
39,000	40,000	1290	1002	714
40,000	41,000	1350	1062	774
41,000	42,000	1410	1122	834
42,000	43,000	1470	1182	894
43,000	44,000	1530	1242	954
44,000	45,000	1590	1302	1014
45,000	46,000	1650	1362	1074
46,000	47,000	1710	1422	1134
47,000	48,000	1770	1482	1194
48,000	49,000	1830	1542	1254
49,000	50,000	1890	1602	1314

(4) *Fair market value greater than $50,000: years one through six.*—(i) For any passenger automobile that has a fair market value greater than $50,000, the inclusion amount for the first six taxable years during which the automobile is leased is determined as follows:

Reg. §1.280F-5T(e)(4)(i)

(A) Determine the dollar amount by using the appropriate formula in paragraph (e)(4)(ii) of this section,

(B) Prorate the dollar amount for the number of days of the lease term included in the taxable year, and

(C) Multiply this dollar amount by the business/investment use for the taxable year.

(ii) The dollar amount is computed as follows:

(A) If the automobile is first used under the lease in the fourth quarter of a taxable year, the dollar amount for each of the first three taxable years during which the automobile is leased is the sum of—

(1) $124, and

(2) 11 percent of the excess of the automobile's fair market value over $13,200.

(B) If the automobile is first used under the lease in the third quarter of a taxable year, the dollar amount for each of the first three taxable years during which the automobile is leased is the sum of—

(1) $110, and

(2) 10 percent of the excess of the automobile's fair market value over $13,200.

(C) If the automobile is first used under the lease in the second quarter of a taxable year, the dollar amount for each of the first three taxable years during which the automobile is leased is the sum of—

(1) $100, and

(2) 9 percent of the excess of the automobile's fair market value over $13,200.

(D) If the automobile is first used under the lease in the first quarter of a taxable year, the dollar amount for each of the first three taxable years during which the automobile is leased is the sum of—

(1) $90, and

(2) 8 percent of the excess of the automobile's fair market value over $13,200.

(E) For the fourth taxable year during which the automobile is leased, the dollar amount is 6 percent of the excess of the automobile's fair market value over $18,000.

(F) For the fifth taxable year during which the automobile is leased, the dollar amount is 6 percent of the excess of the automobile's fair market value over $22,800.

If a passenger automobile is not predominantly used in a qualified business use during—

The first taxable year of the lease term	
The second taxable year of the lease term	
The third taxable year of the lease term	

(iv) The applicable percentage is determined under the following table:

If a passenger automobile is not predominantly used in a qualified business use during—

The first taxable year of the lease term	
The second taxable year of the lease term	
The third taxable year of the lease term	
The fourth taxable year of the lease term	
The fifth taxable year of the lease term	

(f) *Inclusions in income of lessees of listed property other than passenger automobiles.*—(1) *In general.*—If listed property other than a passenger automobile is not used predominantly in a qualified business use in any taxable year in which such property is leased, the lessee must add an inclusion amount to gross income in the first taxable year in which such property is not so predominantly used (and only in that year). This inclusion amount is determined under paragraph (f)(2) of this section for property leased after June 18, 1984, and before January 1, 1987. The inclusion amount is determined under § 1.280F-7(b) for property leased after December 31, 1986.

(2) *Inclusion amount for property leased after June 18, 1984, and before January 1, 1987.*—The inclusion amount for property leased

(G) For the sixth taxable year during which the automobile is leased, the dollar amount is 6 percent of the excess of the automobile's fair market value over $27,600.

(5) *Seventh and subsequent taxable years.*—(i) For any passenger automobile that has a fair market value less than or equal to $32,400, the inclusion amount for the seventh and subsequent taxable years during which the automobile is leased is zero.

(ii) For any passenger automobile that has a fair market value greater than $32,400, the inclusion amount for the seventh and subsequent taxable years during which the automobile is leased is 6 percent of—

(A) The excess (if any) of the automobile's fair market value, over

(B) The sum of—

(1) $13,200 and

(2) $4,800 multiplied by the number of taxable years in excess of three years.

(6) *Additional inclusion amount when less than predominant use in a qualified business use.*—(i) If a passenger automobile, which is leased after April 2, 1985, and before January 1, 1987, is not predominantly used in a qualified business use during a taxable year, the lessee must add to gross income in the first taxable year that the automobile is not so used (and only in that year) an inclusion amount determined under this paragraph (e)(6). This inclusion amount is in addition to the amount required to be included in gross income under paragraph (e)(2), (3), (4), and (5) of this section.

(ii) If the fair market value (as defined in paragraph (h)(2) of this section) of the automobile is greater than $11,250, the inclusion amount is determined by multiplying the average of the business/investment use (as defined in paragraph (h)(3) of this section) by the appropriate dollar amount from the table in paragraph (e)(6)(iii) of this section. If the fair market value of the automobile is $11,250 or less, the inclusion amount is the product of the fair market value of the automobile, the average business/investment use, and the applicable percentage from the table in paragraph (e)(6)(iv) of this section.

(iii) The dollar amount is determined under the following table:

The dollar amount is:
Lease Term (years)

1	2	3	4 or more
$350	$700	$1150	$1500
—	150	700	1200
—	—	250	750

The applicable percentage
Lease Term (years)

	1	2	3	4 or more
The first taxable year of the lease term	3.0	6.0	10.2	13.2
The second taxable year of the lease term		1.25	6.2	10.4
The third taxable year of the lease term			2.25	6.5
The fourth taxable year of the lease term				1.7
The fifth taxable year of the lease term				0.5

after June 18, 1984, and before January 1, 1987, is the product of the following amounts:

(i) The fair market value (as defined in paragraph (h)(2) of this section) of the property,

(ii) The average business/investment use (as defined in paragraph (h)(3) of this section), and

(iii) The applicable percentage (as determined under paragraph (f)(3) of this section).

(3) *Applicable percentages.*—The applicable percentages for 3-, 5-, and 10-year recovery property are determined according to the following tables:

(i) In the case of 3-year recovery property:

Reg. §1.280F-5T(e)(4)(i)(A)

For the first taxable year in which the business use percentage is 50 percent
or less, the applicable percentage for such taxable year is:

Taxable year during lease term	1	2	3	4	5	6 and later
For a lease term of:						
1 year	3.0 %					
2 years	6.0	1.25 %				
3 years	10.2	6.2	2.25 %			
4 or more years	13.2	10.4	6.5 %	1.7 %	0.5 %	0

(ii) In the case of 5-year recovery property:

For the first taxable year in which the business use percentage is 50 percent
or less, the applicable percentage for such taxable year is:

Taxable year during lease term	1	2	3	4	5	6	7	8	9	10	11	12
For a lease term of:												
1 year	2.7 %											
2 years	5.3	1.2 %										
3 years	9.9	6.1	1.6 %									
4 years	14.4	11.1	7.3	2.3 %								
5 years	18.4	15.7	12.4	8.2	3.0 %							
6 or more years	21.8	19.6	16.7	13.5	9.6	5.25 %	4.4 %	3.6 %	2.8 %	1.8 %	1.0 %	0 %

(iii) In the case of 10-year recovery property:

For the first taxable year in which the business use percentage is 50 percent
or less, the applicable percentage for such taxable year is:

Taxable year during lease term	1	2	3	4	5	6	7	8	9	10	11	12	13	14	15
For a lease term of:															
1 year	2.5 %														
2 years	5.1	.6 %													
3 years	9.8	5.6	1.0 %												
4 years	14.0	10.3	6.2	1.4 %											
5 years	17.9	14.5	10.9	6.7	1.8 %										
6 years	21.3	18.3	15.1	11.4	7.1	2.1 %									
7 years	21.9	19.0	15.9	12.4	8.4	3.9	2.4 %								
8 years	22.4	19.6	16.7	13.4	9.7	5.5	4.5	2.7 %							
9 years	22.9	20.2	17.4	14.3	10.9	7.0	6.4	5.1	3.0 %						
10 years	23.5	20.9	18.2	15.2	11.9	8.3	8.1	7.2	5.7	3.3 %					
11 years	23.9	21.4	18.8	16.0	12.8	9.3	9.4	8.9	7.7	5.9	3.1 %				
12 years	24.3	21.9	19.3	16.5	13.4	10.1	10.3	10.0	9.3	7.8	5.5	2.9 %			
13 years	24.7	22.2	19.7	16.9	14.0	10.7	11.1	11.0	10.4	9.2	7.4	5.2	2.7 %		
14 years	25.0	22.5	20.1	17.3	14.4	11.1	11.6	11.7	11.3	10.3	8.8	6.9	4.8	2.5 %	
15 or more years	25.3	22.8	20.3	17.5	14.7	11.5	12.0	12.2	11.9	11.1	9.8	8.2	6.5	4.5	2.3 %

(g) *Special rules applicable to inclusions in income of lessees.*—This paragraph (g) applies to the inclusions in gross income of lessees prescribed under paragraphs (d)(2), (e)(6), or (f) of this section, or prescribed under §1.280F-7(b).

(1) *Lease term commences within 9 months of the end of lessee's taxable year.*—If—

(i) The lease term commences within 9 months before the close of the lessee's taxable year,

(ii) The property is not predominantly used in a qualified business use during that portion of the taxable year, and

(iii) The lease term continues into the lessee's subsequent taxable year,

then the inclusion amount is added to gross income in the lessee's subsequent taxable year and the amount is determined by taking into account the average of the business/investment use for both taxable years and the applicable percentage for the taxable year in which the lease term begins (or, in the case of a passenger automobile with a fair market value greater than $16,500, the appropriate dollar amount for the taxable year in which the lease term begins).

(2) *Lease term less than one year.*—If the lease term is less than one year, the amount which must be added to gross income is an amount that bears the same ratio to the inclusion amount determined before the application of this paragraph (g)(2) as the number of days in the lease term bears to 365.

(3) *Maximum inclusion amount.*—The inclusion amount shall not exceed the sum of all deductible amounts in connection with the use of the listed property properly allocable to the lessee's taxable year in which the inclusion amount must be added to gross income.

(h) *Definitions.*—(1) *Lease term.*—In determining the term of any lease for purposes of this section, the rules of section 168(i)(3)(A) shall apply.

(2) *Fair market value.*—For purposes of this section, the fair market value of listed property is such value on the first day of the lease term. If the capitalized cost of listed property is specified in the lease agreement, the lessee shall treat such amount as the fair market value of the property.

(3) *Average business/investment use.*—For purposes of this section, the average business/investment use of any listed property is the average of the business/investment use for the first taxable year in which the business use percentage is 50 percent or less and all preceding taxable years in which such property is leased. See paragraph (g)(1) of this section for special rule when lease term commences within 9 months before the end of the lessee's taxable year.

(i) *Examples.*—This section may be illustrated by the following examples.

Example (1). On January 1, 1985, A, a calendar year taxpayer, leases and places in service a passenger automobile with a fair market value of $55,000. The lease is to be for a period of four years. During taxable years 1985 and 1986, A uses the automobile exclusively in a trade or business. Under paragraph (d)(1) of this section, A must include in gross income in both 1985 and 1986, $2887.50 (*i.e.*, ($55,000 − $16,500) × 7.5%).

Example (2). The facts are the same as in example (1), and in addition, A uses the automobile only 45 percent in a trade or business during 1987. Under paragraph (d)(1) of this section for 1987, A must include in gross income $1299.38 (*i.e.*, ($55,000 − $16,500) × 7.5% × 45%). In addition, under paragraph (d)(2) of this section, A must

Reg. §1.280F-5T(i)

also include in gross income in 1987, $530.85 (*i.e.,* $650 × 81.67%, average business/investment use).

Example (3). On August 1, 1985, B, a calendar year taxpayer, leases and places in service an item of listed property which is 5-year recovery property, with a fair market value of $10,000. The lease is to be for a period of 5 years. B's qualified business use of the property is 40 percent in 1985, 100 percent in 1986, and 90 percent in 1987. Under paragraphs (f)(1) and (g)(1) of this section, before the application of paragraph (g)(3) of this section, B must include in gross income in 1986, $1288.00 (*i.e.,* $10,000 × 70% × 18.4%, the product of the fair market value, the average business use for both taxable years, and the applicable percentage for year one from the table in paragraph (f)(3)(ii) of this section).

Example (4). On October 1, 1985, C, a calendar year taxpayer, leases and places in service an item of listed property which is 3-year recovery property with a fair market value of $15,000. The lease term is 6 months (ending March 31, 1986) during which C uses the property 45 percent in a trade or business, the only business/investment use. Under paragraphs (f)(1) and (g)(1) and (2) of this section, before the application of paragraph (g)(3) of this section, C must include in gross income in 1986, $100.97 (*i.e.,* $15,000 × 45% × 3% × 182/365, the product of the fair market value, the average business use for both taxable years, and the applicable percentage for year one from the table in paragraph (f)(3)(i) of this section, prorated for the length of the lease term).

Example (5). On July 15, 1985, A, a calendar year taxpayer, leases and places in service a passenger automobile with a fair market value of $45,300. The lease is for a period of 5 years, during which A uses the automobile exclusively in a trade or business. Under paragraph (e)(2) and (3) of this section, for taxable years 1985 through 1989, A must include the following amounts in gross income:

Taxable year	Dollar amount	Proration	Business use	Inclusion
1985 . . .	$3327	170/365	100%	$1550
1986 . . .	3327	365/365	100%	3327
1987 . . .	3327	365/365	100%	3327
1988 . . .	1650	366/366	100%	1650
1989 . . .	1362	365/365	100%	1362

Example (6). The facts are the same as in example (1), except that A uses the automobile only 45 percent in a trade or business during 1987 through 1990. Under § 1.280F-5T(e)(6), A must include in gross income for taxable year 1987, the first taxable year in which the automobile is not used predominantly in a trade or business, an additional amount based on the average business/investment use for taxable years 1985 through 1987. For taxable years 1985 through 1989, A must include the following amounts in gross income:

Taxable year	Dollar amount	Proration	Business use	Inclusion
1985 . . .	$3327	170/365	100.00%	$1550
1986 . . .	3327	365/365	100.00%	3327
1987 . . .	3327	365/365	45.00%	1497
	750		81.67%	612
1988 . . .	1650	366/366	45.00%	743
1989 . . .	1362	365/365	45.00%	613

[Temporary Reg. § 1.280F-5T.]

☐ [*T.D. 7986, 10-19-84. Amended by T.D. 8061, 10-31-85; T.D. 8218, 8-5-88; T.D. 8473, 4-9-93 and T.D. 9133, 6-24-2004.*]

[Reg. § 1.280F-6]

§ 1.280F-6. Special rules and definitions.—(a) *Deductions of employee.*—(1) *In general.*—Employee use of listed property shall not be treated as business/investment use (as defined in paragraph (d)(3) of this section) for purposes of determining the amount of any recovery deduction allowable (including any deduction under section 179) to the employee unless that use is for the convenience of the employer and required as a condition of employment.

(2) *"Convenience of the employer" and "condition of employment" requirements.*—(i) *In general.*—The terms "convenience of the employer" and "condition of employment" generally have the same meaning for purposes of section 280F as they have for purpose of section 119 (relating to the exclusion from gross income for meals or lodging furnished for the convenience of the employer).

(ii) *"Condition of employment".*—In order to satisfy the "condition of employment" requirement, the use of the property must be required in order for the employee to perform the duties of his or her employment properly. Whether the use of the property is so required depends on all the facts and circumstances. Thus, the employer need not explicitly require the employee to use the property. Similarly, a mere statement by the employer that the use of the property is a condition of employment is not sufficient.

(iii) *"Convenience of employer".*—[Reserved]

(3) *Employee use.*—For purposes of this section, the term "employee use" means any use in connection with the performance of services by the employee as an employee.

(4) *Examples.*—The principles of this paragraph are illustrated in the following examples:

Example (1). A is employed as a courier with W, which provides local courier services. A owns and uses a motorcycle to deliver packages to downtown offices for W. W does not provide delivery vehicles and explicitly requires all of its couriers to own a car or motorcycle for use in their employment with the company. A's use of the motorcycle for delivery purposes is for the convenience of W and is required as a condition of employment.

Example (2). B is an inspector for X, a construction company with many construction sites in the local area. B is required to travel to the various construction sites on a regular basis; B uses her automobile to make these trips. Although X does not furnish B an automobile, X does not explicitly require B to use her own automobile. However, X reimburses B for any costs she incurs in traveling to the various job sites. B's use of her automobile in her employment is for the convenience of X and is required as a condition of employment.

Example (3). Assume the same facts as in example (2), except that X makes an automobile available to B who chooses to use her own automobile and receive reimbursement. B's use of her own automobile is not for the convenience of X and is not required as a condition of employment.

Example (4). C is a pilot for Y, a small charter airline. Y requires its pilots to obtain x hours of flight time annually in addition to the number of hours of flight time spent with the airline. Pilots can usually obtain these hours by flying with a military reserve unit or by flying part-time with another airline. C owns his own airplane. C's use of his airplane to obtain the required flight hours is not for the convenience of the employer and is not required as a condition of employment.

Example (5). D is employed as an engineer with Z, an engineering contracting firm. D occasionally takes work home at night rather than working late in the office. D owns and uses a computer which is virtually identical to the one she uses at the office to complete her work at home. D's use of the computer is not for the convenience of her employer and is not required as a condition of employment.

(b) *Listed property.*—(1) *In general.*—Except as otherwise provided in paragraph (b)(5) of this section, the term "listed property" means—

(i) Any passenger automobile (as defined in paragraph (c) of this section),

(ii) Any other property used as a means of transportation (as defined in paragraph (b)(2) of this section),

(iii) Any property of a type generally used for purposes of entertainment, recreation, or amusement, and

(iv) Any computer or peripheral equipment (as defined in section 168(i)(2)(B)), and

(v) Any other property specified in paragraph (b)(4) of this section.

(2) *"Means of transportation".*—(i) *In general.*—Except as otherwise provided in paragraph (b)(2)(ii) of this section, property used as a "means of transportation" includes trucks, buses, trains, boats, airplanes, motorcycles, and any other vehicles for transporting persons or goods.

(ii) *Exception.*—The term "listed property" does not include any vehicle that is a qualified nonpersonal use vehicle as defined in section 274(i) and § 1.274-5(k).

(3) *Property used for entertainment, etc.*—(i) *In general.*—Property of a type generally used for purposes of entertainment, recreation, or amusement includes property such as photographic, phonographic, communication, and video recording equipment.

(ii) *Exception.*—The term "listed property" does not include any photographic, phonographic, communication, or video recording equipment of a taxpayer if the equipment is used either exclusively at the taxpayer's regular business establishment or in connection with the taxpayer's principal trade or business.

(iii) *Regular business establishment.*—The regular business establishment of an employee is the regular business establishment of the employer of the employee. For purposes of this paragraph (b)(3), a portion of a dwelling unit is treated as a regular business establishment if the requirements of section 280A(c)(1) are met with respect to that portion.

(4) *Other property.*—[Reserved]

(5) *Exception for computers.*—The term "listed property" shall not include any computer (including peripheral equipment) used exclu-

sively at a regular business establishment. For purposes of the preceding sentence, a portion of a dwelling unit shall be treated as a regular business establishment if (and only if) the requirements of section 280A(c)(1) are met with respect to that portion.

(c) *Passenger automobile.*—(1) *In general.*—Except as provided in paragraph (c)(3) of this section, the term "passenger automobile" means any 4-wheeled vehicle which is—

(i) Manufactured primarily for use on public streets, roads, and highways, and

(ii) Rated at 6,000 pounds gross vehicle weight or less.

(2) *Parts, etc. of automobile.*—The term "passenger automobile" includes any part, component, or other item that is physically attached to the automobile or is traditionally included in the purchase price of an automobile. The term does not include repairs that are not capital expenditures within the meaning of section 263.

(3) *Exception for certain vehicles.*—The term "passenger automobile" shall not include any—

(i) Ambulance, hearse, or combination ambulance-hearse used by the taxpayer directly in a trade or business,

(ii) Vehicle used by the taxpayer directly in the trade or business of transporting persons or property for compensation or hire, or

(iii) Truck or van that is a qualified nonpersonal use vehicle as defined under §1.274-5T(k).

(d) *Business use percentage.*—(1) *In general.*—The term "business use percentage" means the percentage of the use of any listed property which is qualified business use as described in paragraph (d)(2) of this section.

(2) *Qualified business use.*—(i) *In general.*—Except as provided in paragraph (d)(2)(ii) of this section, the term "qualified business use" means any use in a trade or business of the taxpayer. The term "qualified business use" does not include use for which a deduction is allowable under section 212. Whether the amount of qualified business use exceeds 50 percent is determinative of whether the investment tax credit and the accelerated percentages under section 168 are available for listed property (or must be recaptured). See §1.280F-3T.

(ii) *Exception for certain use by 5-percent owners and related persons.*—(A) *In general.*—The term "qualified business use" shall not include—

(1) Leasing property to any 5-percent owner or related person,

(2) Use of property provided as compensation for the performance of services by a 5-percent owner or related person, or

(3) Use of property provided as compensation for the performance of services by any person not described in paragraph (d)(2)(ii)(A)(2) of this section unless an amount is properly reported by the taxpayer as income to such person and, where required, there was withholding under chapter 24.

Paragraph (d)(2)(ii)(A)(1) of this section shall apply only to the extent that the use of the listed property is by an individual who is a related party or a 5-percent owner with respect to the owner or lessee of the property.

(B) *Special rule for aircraft.*—Paragraph (d)(2)(ii)(A) of this section shall not apply with respect to any aircraft if at least 25 percent of the total use of the aircraft during the taxable year consists of qualified business use not described in paragraph (d)(2)(ii)(A).

(C) *Definitions.*—For purposes of this paragraph—

(1) *5-percent owner.*—The term "5-percent owner" means any person who is a 5-percent owner with respect to the taxpayer (as defined in section 416(i)(1)(B)(i)).

(2) *Related person.*—The term "related person" means any person related to the taxpayer (within the meaning of section 267(b)).

(3) *Business/investment use.*—(i) *In general.*—The term "business/investment use" means the total business or investment use of listed property that may be taken into account for purposes of computing (without regard to section 280F(b)) the percentage of cost recovery deduction for a passenger automobile or other listed property for the taxable year. Whether the accelerated percentages under section 168 (as opposed to use of the straight line method of cost recovery) are available with respect to listed property or must be recaptured is determined, however, by reference to qualified business use (as defined in paragraph (d)(2) of this section) rather than by reference to business/investment use. Whether a particular use of property is a business or investment use shall generally be determined under the rules of section 162 or 212.

(ii) *Entertainment use.*—The use of listed property for entertainment, recreation, or amusement purposes shall be treated as business use to the extent that expenses (other than interest and property tax expenses) attributable to that use are deductible after application of section 274.

(iii) *Employee use.*—See paragraph (a) of this section for requirements to be satisfied for employee use of listed property to be considered business/investment use of the property.

(iv) *Use of taxpayer's automobile by another person.*—Any use of the taxpayer's automobile by another person shall not be treated, for purposes of section 280F, as use in a trade or business under section 162 unless that use—

(A) Is directly connected with the business of the taxpayer,

(B) Is properly reported by the taxpayer as income to the other person and, where required, there was withholding under chapter 24, or

(C) Results in a payment of fair market rent.

For purposes of this paragraph (d)(4)(iv)(C), payment to the owner of the automobile in connection with such use is treated as the payment of rent.

(4) *Predominantly used in qualified business use.*—(i) *Definition.*—Property is predominantly used in a qualified business use for any taxable year if the business use percentage (as defined in paragraph (d)(1) of this section) is greater than 50 percent.

(ii) *Special rule for transfers at death.*—Property does not cease to be used predominantly in a qualified business use by reason of a transfer at death.

(iii) *Other dispositions of property.*—[Reserved]

(5) *Examples.*—The following examples illustrate the principles set forth in this paragraph.

Example (1). E uses a home computer 50 percent of the time to manage her investments. The computer is listed property within the meaning of section 280F(d)(4). E also uses the computer 40 percent of the time in her part-time consumer research business. Because E's business use percentage for the computer does not exceed 50 percent, the computer is not predominantly used in a qualified business use for the taxable year. Her aggregate business/investment use for purposes of determining the percent of the total allowable straight line depreciation that she can claim is 90 percent.

Example (2). Assume that E in example (1) uses the computer 30 percent of the time to manage her investments and 60 percent of the time in her consumer research business. E's business use percentage exceeds 50 percent. Her aggregate business/investment use for purposes of determining her allowable investment tax credit and cost recovery deductions is 90 percent.

Example (3). F is the proprietor of a plumbing contracting business. F's brother is employed with F's company. As part of his compensation, F's brother is allowed to use one of the company automobiles for personal use. The use of the company automobiles by F's brother is not a qualified business use because F and F's brother are related parties within the meaning of section 267(b).

Example (4). F, in example (3), allows employees unrelated to him to use company automobiles as part of their compensation. F, however, does not include the value of these automobiles in the employees' gross income and F does not withhold with respect to the use of these automobiles. The use of the company automobiles by the employees in this case is not business/investment use.

Example (5). X Corporation owns several automobiles which its employees use for business purposes. The employees are also allowed to take the automobiles home at night. However, the fair market value of the use of the automobile for any personal purpose, *e.g.*, commuting to work, is reported by X as income to the employee and is withheld upon by X. The use of the automobile by the employee, even for personal purposes, is a qualified business use with respect to X.

(e) *Method of allocating use of property.*—(1) *In general.*—For purposes of section 280F, the taxpayer shall allocate the use of any listed property that is used for more than one purpose during the taxable year to the various uses in the manner prescribed in paragraph (e)(2) and (3) of this section.

(2) *Passenger automobiles and other means of transportation.*—In the case of a passenger automobile or any other means of transportation, the taxpayer shall allocate the use of the property on the basis of mileage. Thus, the percentage of use in a trade or business for the year shall be determined by dividing the number of miles the vehicle is driven for purposes of that trade or business during the year by the total number of miles the vehicle is driven during the year for any purpose.

Reg. §1.280F-6(e)(2)

(3) *Other listed property.*—In the case of other listed property, the taxpayer shall allocate the use of that property on the basis of the most appropriate unit of time the property is actually used (rather than merely being available for use). For example, the percentage of use of a computer in a trade or business for a taxable year is determined by dividing the number of hours the computer is used for business purposes during the year by the total number of hours the computer is used for any purpose during the year.

(f) *Effective date.*—(1) *In general.*—Except as provided in paragraph (f)(2) of this section, this section applies to property placed in service by a taxpayer on or after July 7, 2003. For regulations applicable to property placed in service before July 7, 2003, see §1.280F-6T as in effect prior to July 7, 2003 (§1.280F-6T as contained in 26 CFR part 1, revised as of April 1, 2003).

(2) *Property placed in service before July 7, 2003.*—The following rules apply to property that is described in paragraph (c)(3)(iii) of this section, was placed in service by the taxpayer before July 7, 2003, and was treated by the taxpayer as a passenger automobile under §1.280F-6T as in effect prior to July 7, 2003 (pre-effective date vehicle):

(i) Except as provided in paragraphs (f)(2)(ii), (iii), and (iv) of this section, a pre-effective date vehicle will be treated as a passenger automobile to which section 280F(a) applies.

(ii) A pre-effective date vehicle will be treated as property to which section 280F(a) does not apply if the taxpayer adopts that treatment in determining depreciation deductions on the taxpayer's original return for the year in which the vehicle is placed in service.

(iii) A pre-effective date vehicle will be treated, to the extent provided in this paragraph (f)(2)(iii), as property to which section 280F(a) does not apply if the taxpayer adopts that treatment on an amended Federal tax return in accordance with this paragraph (f)(2)(iii). This paragraph (f)(2)(iii) applies only if, on or before December 31, 2004, the taxpayer files, for all applicable taxable years, amended Federal tax returns (or qualified amended returns, if applicable (for further guidance, see Rev. Proc. 94-69 (1994-2 C.B. 804) and §601.601(d)(2)(ii)(*b*) of this chapter)) treating the vehicle as property to which section 280F(a) does not apply. The applicable taxable years for this purpose are the taxable year in which the vehicle was placed in service by the taxpayer (or, if the period of limitation for assessment under section 6501 has expired for such year or any subsequent year (a closed year), the first taxable year following the most recent closed year) and all subsequent taxable years in which the vehicle was treated on the taxpayer's return as property to which section 280F(a) applies. If the earliest applicable taxable year is not the year in which the vehicle was placed in service, the adjusted depreciable basis of the property as of the beginning of the first applicable taxable year is recovered over the remaining recovery period. If the remaining recovery period as of the beginning of the first applicable taxable year is less than 12 months, the entire adjusted depreciable basis of the property as of the beginning of the first applicable taxable year is recovered in that year.

(iv) A pre-effective date vehicle will be treated, to the extent provided in this paragraph (f)(2)(iv), as property to which section 280F(a) does not apply if the taxpayer adopts that treatment on Form 3115, Application for Change in Accounting Method, in accordance with this paragraph (f)(2)(iv). The taxpayer must follow the applicable administrative procedures issued under §1.446-1(e)(3)(ii) for obtaining the Commissioner's automatic consent to a change in method of accounting (for further guidance, for example, see Rev. Proc. 2002-9 (2002-1 C.B. 327) and §601.601(d)(2)(ii)(*b*) of this chapter). If the taxpayer files a Form 3115 treating the vehicle as property to which section 280F(a) does not apply, the taxpayer will be permitted to treat the change as a change in method of accounting under section 446(e) of the Internal Revenue Code and to take into account the section 481 adjustment resulting from the method change. For purposes of Form 3115, the designated number for the automatic accounting method change authorized for this paragraph (f)(2)(iv) is 89. [Reg. §1.280F-6.]

☐ [*T.D. 7986,* 10-19-84. *Amended by T.D. 8009,* 2-15-85; *T.D. 8061,* 10-31-85; *T.D. 9069,* 7-3-2003. *Redesignated and amended by T.D. 9133,* 6-24-2004. *Amended by T.D. 9483,* 5-18-2010.]

[Reg. §1.280F-7]

§1.280F-7. Property leased after December 31, 1986.—(a) *Inclusions in income of lessees of passenger automobiles leased after December 31, 1986.*—(1) *In general.*—If a taxpayer leases a passenger automobile after December 31, 1986, the taxpayer must include in gross income an inclusion amount determined under this paragraph (a) for each taxable year during which the taxpayer leases the automobile. This paragraph (a) applies only to passenger automobiles for which the taxpayer's lease term begins after December 31, 1986. See §§1.280F-5T(d) and 1.280F-5T(e) for rules on determining inclusion amounts for passenger automobiles for which the taxpayer's lease term begins before January 1, 1987. See §1.280F-5T(h)(2) for the definition of fair market value.

(2) *Inclusion Amount.*—For any passenger automobile leased after December 31, 1986, the inclusion amount for each taxable year during which the automobile is leased is determined as follows:

(i) For the appropriate range of fair market values in the applicable table, select the dollar amount from the column for the taxable year in which the automobile is used under the lease (but for the last taxable year during any lease that does not begin and end in the same taxable year, use the dollar amount for the *preceding* taxable year).

(ii) Prorate the dollar amount for the number of days of the lease term included in the taxable year.

(iii) Multiply the prorated dollar amount by the business/investment use (as defined in §1.280F-6(d)(3)(i)) for the taxable year.

(iv) The following table is the applicable table in the case of a passenger automobile leased after December 31, 1986, and before January 1, 1989:

DOLLAR AMOUNTS FOR AUTOMOBILES WITH A LEASE TERM BEGINNING
IN CALENDAR YEAR 1987 OR 1988

Fair Market Value of Automobile		Taxable Year During Lease				
Over	Not Over	1st	2nd	3rd	4th	5 and Later
$12,800	$13,100	$2	$5	$7	$8	$9
13,100	13,400	6	14	20	24	28
13,400	13,700	10	23	34	41	47
13,700	14,000	15	32	47	57	65
14,000	14,300	19	41	61	73	84
14,300	14,600	23	50	74	89	103
14,600	14,900	27	59	88	105	122
14,900	15,200	31	68	101	122	140
15,200	15,500	35	77	115	138	159
15,500	15,800	40	87	128	154	178
15,800	16,100	44	96	142	170	196
16,100	16,400	48	105	155	186	215
16,400	16,700	52	114	169	203	234
16,700	17,000	56	123	182	219	253
17,000	17,500	62	135	200	240	277
17,500	18,000	69	150	223	267	309
18,000	18,500	76	166	246	294	340
18,500	19,000	83	181	268	321	371
19,000	19,500	90	196	291	348	402
19,500	20,000	97	211	313	375	433
20,000	20,500	104	226	336	402	465
20,500	21,000	111	242	358	429	496
21,000	21,500	117	257	381	456	527
21,500	22,000	124	272	403	483	558
22,000	23,000	135	295	437	524	605
23,000	24,000	149	325	482	578	667

DOLLAR AMOUNTS FOR AUTOMOBILES WITH A LEASE TERM BEGINNING
IN CALENDAR YEAR 1987 OR 1988

Fair Market Value of Automobile		Taxable Year During Lease				
Over	Not Over	1st	2nd	3rd	4th	5 and Later
24,000	25,000	163	356	527	632	729
25,000	26,000	177	386	572	686	792
26,000	27,000	190	416	617	740	854
27,000	28,000	204	447	662	794	917
28,000	29,000	218	477	707	848	979
29,000	30,000	232	507	752	902	1,041
30,000	31,000	246	538	797	956	1,104
31,000	32,000	260	568	842	1,010	1,166
32,000	33,000	274	599	887	1,064	1,228
33,000	34,000	288	629	933	1,118	1,291
34,000	35,000	302	659	978	1,172	1,353
35,000	36,000	316	690	1,023	1,226	1,415
36,000	37,000	329	720	1,068	1,280	1,478
37,000	38,000	343	751	1,113	1,334	1,540
38,000	39,000	357	781	1,158	1,388	1,602
39,000	40,000	371	811	1,203	1,442	1,665
40,000	41,000	385	842	1,248	1,496	1,727
41,000	42,000	399	872	1,293	1,550	1,789
42,000	43,000	413	902	1,338	1,604	1,852
43,000	44,000	427	933	1,383	1,658	1,914
44,000	45,000	441	963	1,428	1,712	1,976
45,000	46,000	455	994	1,473	1,766	2,039
46,000	47,000	468	1,024	1,518	1,820	2,101
47,000	48,000	482	1,054	1,563	1,874	2,164
48,000	49,000	496	1,085	1,608	1,928	2,226
49,000	50,000	510	1,115	1,653	1,982	2,288
50,000	51,000	524	1,146	1,698	2,036	2,351
51,000	52,000	538	1,176	1,743	2,090	2,413
52,000	53,000	552	1,206	1,788	2,144	2,475
53,000	54,000	566	1,237	1,834	2,198	2,538
54,000	55,000	580	1,267	1,879	2,252	2,600
55,000	56,000	594	1,297	1,924	2,306	2,662
56,000	57,000	607	1,328	1,969	2,360	2,725
57,000	58,000	621	1,358	2,014	2,414	2,787
58,000	59,000	635	1,389	2,059	2,468	2,849
59,000	60,000	649	1,419	2,104	2,522	2,912
60,000	62,000	670	1,465	2,171	2,603	3,005
62,000	64,000	698	1,525	2,262	2,711	3,130
64,000	66,000	726	1,586	2,352	2,819	3,255
66,000	68,000	753	1,647	2,442	2,927	3,379
68,000	70,000	781	1,708	2,532	3,035	3,504
70,000	72,000	809	1,768	2,622	3,143	3,629
72,000	74,000	837	1,829	2,712	3,251	3,753
74,000	76,000	865	1,890	2,802	3,359	3,878
76,000	78,000	892	1,951	2,892	3,468	4,003
78,000	80,000	920	2,012	2,982	3,576	4,128
80,000	85,000	969	2,118	3,140	3,765	4,346
85,000	90,000	1,038	2,270	3,365	4,035	4,658
90,000	95,000	1,108	2,422	3,590	4,305	4,969
95,000	100,000	1,177	2,574	3,816	4,575	5,281
100,000	110,000	1,282	2,802	4,154	4,980	5,749
110,000	120,000	1,421	3,105	4,604	5,520	6,372
120,000	130,000	1,560	3,409	5,055	6,060	6,996
130,000	140,000	1,699	3,713	5,505	6,600	7,619
140,000	150,000	1,838	4,017	5,956	7,140	8,243
150,000	160,000	1,977	4,321	6,406	7,680	8,866
160,000	170,000	2,116	4,625	6,857	8,221	9,490
170,000	180,000	2,255	4,929	7,307	8,761	10,113
180,000	190,000	2,394	5,232	7,758	9,301	10,737
190,000	200,000	2,533	5,536	8,208	9,841	11,360

(v) The applicable table in the case of a passenger automobile first leased after December 31, 1988, will be contained in a revenue ruling or revenue procedure published in the Internal Revenue Bulletin.

(3) *Example.*—The following example illustrates the application of this paragraph (a):

Example. On April 1, 1987, A, a calendar year taxpayer, leases and places in service a passenger automobile with a fair market value of $31,500. The lease is to be for a period of three years. During taxable years 1987 and 1988, A uses the automobile exclusively in a trade or business. During 1989 and 1990, A's business/investment use is 45 percent. The appropriate dollar amounts from the table in paragraph (a)(2)(iv) of this section are $260 for 1987 (first taxable year during the lease), $568 for 1988 (second taxable year during the lease), $842 for 1989 (third taxable year during the lease), and $842 for 1990. Since 1990 is the last taxable year during the lease, the dollar amount for the preceding year (the third year) is used, rather than the dollar amount for the fourth year. For taxable years 1987 through 1990, A's inclusion amounts are determined as follows:

Tax year	Dollar amount	Proration	Business use	Inclusion amount
1987	$260	275/365	100%	$196
1988	$568	366/366	100%	$568
1989	$842	365/365	45%	$379
1990	$842	90/365	45%	$ 93

(b) *Inclusions in income of lessees of listed property (other than passenger automobiles) leased after December 31, 1986.*—(1) *In general.*—If listed property other than a passenger automobile is not used predominantly in a qualified business use in any taxable year in which such property is leased, the lessee must add an inclusion amount to gross income in the first taxable year in which such property is not so predominantly used (and only in that year). This year is the first taxable year in which the business use percentage (as defined in §1.280F-6(d)(1)) of the property is 50 percent or less. This inclusion amount is determined under this paragraph (b) for property for which the taxpayer's lease term begins after December 31, 1986 (and under §1.280F-5T(f) for property for which the taxpayer's lease term begins before January 1, 1987). See also §1.280F-5T(g).

(2) *Inclusion amount.*—The inclusion amount for any listed property (other than a passenger automobile) leased after December 31, 1986, is the sum of the amounts determined under subdivisions (i) and (ii) of this subparagraph (2).

(i) The amount determined under this subdivision (i) is the product of the following amounts:

(A) The fair market value (as defined in §1.280F-5T(h)(2)) of the property,

(B) The business/investment use (as defined in §1.280F-6(d)(3)(i)) for the first taxable year in which the business use percentage (as defined in §1.280F-6(d)(1)) is 50 percent or less, and

(C) The applicable percentage from the following table:

Type of Property	First Taxable Year During Lease in Which Business Use Percentage Is 50% or Less											
	1	2	3	4	5	6	7	8	9	10	11	12 & Later
Property with a Recovery Period of Less Than 7 Years under the Alternative Depreciation System (Such as Computers, Trucks and Airplanes)	2.1%	-7.2%	-19.8%	-20.1%	-12.4%	-12.4%	-12.4%	-12.4%	-12.4%	-12.4%	-12.4%	-12.4%
Property with a 7- to 10-Year Recovery Period under the Alternative Depreciation System (Such as Recreation Property)	3.9%	-3.8%	-17.7%	-25.1%	-27.8%	-27.2%	-27.1%	-27.6%	-23.7%	-14.7%	-14.7%	-14.7%
Property with a Recovery Period of More Than 10 Years under the Alternative Depreciation System (Such as Certain Property with No Class Life)	6.6%	-1.6%	-16.9%	-25.6%	-29.9%	-31.1%	-32.8%	-35.1%	-33.3%	-26.7%	-19.7%	-12.2%

Reg. §1.280F-7(b)(2)(i)(C)

(ii) The amount determined under this subdivision (ii) is the product of the following amounts:

(A) The fair market value of the property,

(B) The average of the business/investment use for all taxable years (in which such property is leased) that precede the first taxable year in which the business use percentage is 50 percent or less, and

(C) The applicable percentage from the following table:

Type of Property	First Taxable Year During Lease in Which Business Use Percentage Is 50% or Less											
	1	2	3	4	5	6	7	8	9	10	11	12 & Later
Property with a Recovery Period of Less Than 7 Years under the Alternative Depreciation System (Such as Computers, Trucks and Airplanes)	0.0%	10.0%	22.0%	21.2%	12.7%	12.7%	12.7%	12.7%	12.7%	12.7%	12.7%	12.7%
Property with a 7- to 10-Year Recovery Period under the Alternative Depreciation System (Such as Recreation Property)	0.0%	9.3%	23.8%	31.3%	33.8%	32.7%	31.6%	30.5%	25.0%	15.0%	15.0%	15.0%
Property with a Recovery Period of More Than 10 Years under the Alternative Depreciation System (Such as Certain Property with No Class Life)	0.0%	10.1%	26.3%	35.4%	39.6%	40.2%	40.8%	41.4%	37.5%	29.2%	20.8%	12.5%

(3) *Example.*—The following example illustrates the application of this paragraph (b):

Example. On February 1, 1987, B, a calendar year taxpayer, leases and places in service a computer with a fair market value of $3,000. The lease is to be for a period of two years. B's qualified business use of the property, which is the only business/investment use, is 80 percent in taxable year 1987, 40 percent in taxable year 1988, and 35 percent in taxable year 1989. B must add an inclusion amount to gross income for taxable year 1988, the first taxable year in which B does not use the computer predominantly for business (*i.e.*, the first taxable year in which B's business use percentage is 50 percent or less). Since 1988 is the second taxable year during the lease, and since the computer has a 5-year recovery period under the General and Alternative Depreciation Systems, the applicable percentage from the table in subdivision (i) of paragraph (b)(2) is –7.2%, and the applicable percentage from the table in subdivision (ii) is 10%. B's inclusion amount is $154, which is the sum of the amounts determined under subdivisions (i) and (ii) of subparagraph (b)(2) of this paragraph. The amount determined under subdivision (i) is – $86 [$3,000 × 40% × (–7.2%)], and the amount determined under subdivision (ii) is $240 [$3,000 × 80% × 10%]. [Reg. § 1.280F-7.]

☐ [*T.D. 8218, 8-5-88. Amended by T.D. 8298, 4-11-90. Redesignated by T.D. 8473, 4-9-93. Amended by T.D. 9133, 6-24-2004.]*

[Reg. § 1.280G-1]

§ 1.280G-1. Golden parachute payments.—The following questions and answers relate to the treatment of golden parachute payments under section 280G of the Internal Revenue Code of 1986, as added by section 67 of the Tax Reform Act of 1984 (Public Law No. 98-369; 98 Stat. 585) and amended by section 1804(j) of the Tax Reform Act of 1986 (Public Law No. 99-514; 100 Stat. 2807), section 1018(d)(6)-(8) of the Technical and Miscellaneous Revenue Act of 1988 (Public Law No. 100-647; 102 Stat. 3581), and section 1421 of the Small Business Job Protection Act of 1996 (Public Law No. 104-188; 110 Stat. 1755). The following is a table of contents of subjects in this section:

Overview

Q-1: What is the effect of Internal Revenue Code section 280G?

A-1: (a) Section 280G disallows a deduction for any excess parachute payment paid or accrued. For rules relating to the imposition of a nondeductible 20-percent excise tax on the recipient of any excess parachute payment, see Internal Revenue Code sections 4999, 275(a)(6), and 3121(v)(2)(A).

(b) The disallowance of a deduction under section 280G is not contingent on the imposition of the excise tax under section 4999. The imposition of the excise tax under section 4999 is not contingent on the disallowance of a deduction under section 280G. Thus, for example, because the imposition of the excise tax under section 4999 is not contingent on the disallowance of a deduction under section 280G, a payee may be subject to the 20-percent excise tax under section 4999 even though the disallowance of the deduction for the excess parachute payment may not directly affect the federal taxable income of the payor.

Q-2: What is a parachute payment for purposes of section 280G?

A-2: (a) The term *parachute payment* means any payment (other than an exempt payment described in Q/A-5) that—

(1) Is in the nature of compensation;

(2) Is made or is to be made to (or for the benefit of) a disqualified individual;

(3) Is contingent on a change—

(i) In the ownership of a corporation;

(ii) In the effective control of a corporation; or

(iii) In the ownership of a substantial portion of the assets of a corporation; and

(4) Has (together with other payments described in paragraphs (a)(1), (2), and (3) of this A-2 with respect to the same disqualified individual) an aggregate present value of at least 3 times the individual's base amount.

(b) Hereinafter, a change referred to in paragraph (a)(3) of this A-2 is generally referred to as a change in ownership or control. For a discussion of the application of paragraph (a)(1), see Q/A-11 through Q/A-14; paragraph (a)(2), Q/A-15 through Q/A-21; paragraph (a)(3), Q/A-22 through Q/A-29; and paragraph (a)(4), Q/A-30 through Q/A-36.

(c) The term *parachute payment* also includes any payment in the nature of compensation to (or for the benefit of) a disqualified individual that is pursuant to an agreement that violates a generally enforced securities law or regulation. This type of parachute payment is referred to in this section as a securities violation parachute payment. See Q/A-37 for the definition and treatment of securities violation parachute payments.

Q-3: What is an excess parachute payment for purposes of section 280G?

A-3: The term *excess parachute payment* means an amount equal to the excess of any parachute payment over the portion of the base amount allocated to such payment. Subject to certain exceptions and limitations, an excess parachute payment is reduced by any portion of the payment which the taxpayer establishes by clear and convincing evidence is reasonable compensation for personal services actually rendered by the disqualified individual before the date of the change in ownership or control. For a discussion of the nonreduction of a securities violation parachute payment by reasonable compensation, see Q/A-37. For a discussion of the computation of excess parachute payments and their reduction by reasonable compensation, see Q/A-38 through Q/A-44.

Q-4: What is the effective date of section 280G and this section?

A-4: In general, section 280G applies to payments under agreements entered into or renewed after June 14, 1984. Section 280G also applies to certain payments under agreements entered into on or before June 14, 1984, and amended or supplemented in significant relevant respect after that date. This section applies to any payment that is contingent on a change in ownership or control and the change in ownership or control occurs on or after January 1, 2004. For a discussion of the application of the effective date, see Q/A-47 and Q/A-48.

Exempt Payments

Q-5: Are some types of payments exempt from the definition of the term *parachute payment*?

A-5: (a) Yes, the following five types of payments are exempt from the definition of *parachute payment*—

(1) Payments with respect to a small business corporation (described in Q/A-6 of this section);

(2) Certain payments with respect to a corporation no stock in which is readily tradeable on an established securities market (or otherwise) (described in Q/A-6 of this section);

(3) Payments to or from a qualified plan (described in Q/A-8 of this section);

(4) Certain payments made by a corporation undergoing a change in ownership or control that is described in any of the following sections of the Internal Revenue Code: section 501(c) (but only if such organization is subject to an express statutory prohibition against inurement of net earnings to the benefit of any private shareholder or individual, or if the organization is described in section 501(c)(1) or section 501(c)(21)), section 501(d), or section 529, collectively referred to as *tax-exempt organizations* (described in Q/A-6 of this section); and

(5) Certain payments of reasonable compensation for services to be rendered on or after the change in ownership or control (described in Q/A-9 of this section).

(b) Deductions for payments exempt from the definition of *parachute payment* are not disallowed by section 280G, and such exempt payments are not subject to the 20-percent excise tax of section 4999. In addition, such exempt payments are not taken into account in applying the 3-times-base-amount test of Q/A-30 of this section.

Q-6: Which payments with respect to a corporation referred to in paragraph (a)(1), (a)(2), or (a)(4) of Q/A-5 of this section are exempt from the definition of *parachute payment*?

A-6: (a) The term *parachute payment* does not include—

(1) Any payment to a disqualified individual with respect to a corporation which (immediately before the change in ownership or control) would qualify as a small business corporation (as defined in section 1361(b) but without regard to section 1361(b)(1)(C) thereof), without regard to whether the corporation had an election to be treated as a corporation under section 1361 in effect on the date of the change in ownership or control;

(2) Any payment to a disqualified individual with respect to a corporation (other than a small business corporation described in paragraph (a)(1) of this A-6) if—

(i) Immediately before the change in ownership or control, no stock in such corporation was readily tradeable on an established securities market or otherwise; and

(ii) The shareholder approval requirements described in Q/A-7 of this section are met with respect to such payment; or

(3) Any payment to a disqualified individual made by a corporation which is a tax-exempt organization (as defined in paragraph (a)(4) of Q/A-5 of this section), but only if the corporation meets the definition of a tax-exempt organization both immediately before and immediately after the change in ownership or control.

(b) For purposes of paragraph (a)(1) of this A-6, the members of an affiliated group are not treated as one corporation.

(c) The requirements of paragraph (a)(2)(i) of this A-6 are not met with respect to a corporation if a substantial portion of the assets of any entity consists (directly or indirectly) of stock in such corporation and any ownership interest in such entity is readily tradeable on an established securities market or otherwise. For this purpose, such stock constitutes a substantial portion of the assets of an entity if the total fair market value of the stock is equal to or exceeds one third of the total gross fair market value of all of the assets of the entity. For this purpose, *gross fair market value* means the value of the assets of the entity, determined without regard to any liabilities associated with such assets. If a corporation is a member of an affiliated group (which group is treated as one corporation under A-46 of this section), the requirements of paragraph (a)(2)(i) of this A-6 are not met if any stock in any member of such group is readily tradeable on an established securities market or otherwise.

(d) For purposes of paragraph (a)(2)(i) of this A-6, the term *stock* does not include stock described in section 1504(a)(4) if the payment does not adversely affect the redemption and liquidation rights of any shareholder owning such stock.

(e) For purposes of paragraph (a)(2)(i) of this A-6, stock is treated as readily tradeable if it is regularly quoted by brokers or dealers making a market in such stock.

(f) For purposes of paragraph (a)(2)(i) of this A-6, the term *established securities market* means an established securities market as defined in §1.897-1(m).

(g) The following examples illustrate the application of this exemption:

Example 1. A small business corporation (within the meaning of paragraph (a)(1) of this A-6) operates two businesses. The corporation sells the assets of one of its businesses, and these assets represent a substantial portion of the assets of the corporation. Because of the sale, the corporation terminates its employment relationship with persons employed in the business the assets of which are sold. Several of these employees are highly-compensated individuals to whom the owners of the corporation make severance payments in excess of 3 times each employee's base amount. Since the corporation is a small business corporation immediately before the change in ownership or control, the payments are not parachute payments.

Example 2. Assume the same facts as in *Example 1*, except that the corporation is not a small business corporation within the meaning of paragraph (a)(1) of this A-6. If no stock in the corporation is readily tradeable on an established securities market (or otherwise) immediately before the change in ownership or control and the shareholder approval requirements described in Q/A-7 of this section are met, the payments are not parachute payments.

Example 3. Stock of Corporation S is owned by Corporation P, stock in which is readily tradeable on an established securities market. The Corporation S stock equals or exceeds one third of the total gross fair market value of the assets of Corporation P, and thus, represents a substantial portion of the assets of Corporation P. Corporation S makes severance payments to several of its highly-compensated individuals that are parachute payments under section 280G and Q/A-2 of this section. Because stock in Corporation P is readily tradeable on an established securities market, the payments are not exempt from the definition of *parachute payments* under this A-6.

Example 4. A is a corporation described in section 501(c)(3), and accordingly, its net earnings are prohibited from inuring to the benefit of any private shareholder or individual. A transfers substantially all of its assets to another corporation resulting in a change in ownership or control. Contingent on the change in ownership or control, A makes a payment that, but for the potential application of the exemption described in A-5(a)(4), would constitute a *parachute payment*. However, one or more aspects of the transaction that constitutes the change in ownership or control causes A to fail to be described in section 501(c)(3). Accordingly, A fails to meet the definition of a *tax-exempt organization* both immediately before and immediately after the change in ownership or control, as required by this A-6. As a result, the payment made by A that was contingent on the change in ownership or control is not exempt from the definition of *parachute payment* under this A-6.

Example 5. B is a corporation described in section 501(c)(15). B does not meet the definition of a *tax-exempt organization* because section 501(c)(15) does not expressly prohibit inurement of B's net earnings to the benefit of any private shareholder or individual. Accordingly, if B has a change in ownership or control and makes a payment that would otherwise meet the definition of a *parachute payment*, such payment is not exempt from the definition of the term *parachute payment* for purposes of this A-6.

Q-7: How are the shareholder approval requirements referred to in paragraph (a)(2)(ii) of Q/A-6 of this section met?

A-7: (a) *General rule.* The shareholder approval requirements referred to in paragraph (a)(2)(ii) of Q/A-6 of this section are met with respect to any payment if—

(1) Such payment is approved by more than 75 percent of the voting power of all outstanding stock of the corporation entitled to vote (as described in this A-7) immediately before the change in ownership or control; and

(2) Before the vote, there was adequate disclosure to all persons entitled to vote (as described in this A-7) of all material facts concerning all material payments which (but for Q/A-6 of this section) would be parachute payments with respect to a disqualified individual.

(b) *Voting requirements*—(1) *General rule.* The vote described in paragraph (a)(1) of this A-7 must determine the right of the disqualified individual to receive the payment, or, in the case of a payment made before the vote, the right of the disqualified individual to retain the payment. Except as otherwise provided in this A-7, the normal voting rules of the corporation are applicable. Thus, for example, an optionholder is generally not permitted to vote for purposes of this A-7. For purposes of this A-7, the vote can be on less than the full amount of the payment(s) to be made. Shareholder approval can be a single vote on all payments to any one disqualified individual, or on all payments to more than one disqualified individual. The total payment(s) submitted for shareholder approval, however, must be separately approved by the shareholders. The requirements of this paragraph (b)(1) are not satisfied if approval of the change in ownership or control is contingent, or otherwise conditioned, on the approval of any payment to a disqualified individual that would be a parachute payment but for Q/A-6 of this section.

(2) *Special rule.* A vote to approve the payment does not fail to be a vote of the outstanding stock of the corporation entitled to vote immediately before the change in ownership or control merely because the determination of the shareholders entitled to vote on the payment is based on the shareholders of record as of any day within the six-month period immediately prior to and ending on date of the change in ownership or control, provided the disclosure requirements described in paragraph (c) of this A-7 are met.

(3) *Entity shareholder.* (i) Approval of a payment by any shareholder that is not an individual (an entity shareholder) generally must be made by the person authorized by the entity shareholder to approve the payment. See paragraph (b)(4) of this A-7 if the person so authorized by the entity shareholder is a disqualified individual who would receive a parachute payment if the shareholder approval requirements of this A-7 are not met.

(ii) However, if a substantial portion of the assets of an entity shareholder consists (directly or indirectly) of stock in the corporation undergoing the change in ownership or control, approval of the payment by that entity shareholder must be made by a separate vote of the persons who hold, immediately before the change in ownership or control, more than 75 percent of the voting power of the entity shareholder entitled to vote. The preceding sentence does not apply if the value of the stock of the corporation owned, directly or indirectly, by or for the entity shareholder does not exceed 1 percent of the total value of the outstanding stock of the corporation undergoing a change in ownership or control. Where approval of a payment by an entity shareholder must be made by a separate vote of the owners of the entity shareholder, the normal voting rights of the entity shareholder determine which owners shall vote. For purposes of this (b)(3)(ii), stock represents a substantial portion of the assets of an entity shareholder if the total fair market value of the stock held by the entity shareholder in the corporation undergoing the change in ownership or control is equal to or exceeds one third of the total gross fair market value of all of the assets of the entity shareholder. For this purpose, *gross fair market value* means the value of the assets of the entity, determined without regard to any liabilities associated with such assets.

(4) *Disqualified individuals and attribution of stock ownership.* In determining the persons entitled to vote referred to in paragraph (a)(1) or (b)(3) of this A-7, stock that would otherwise be entitled to vote is not counted as outstanding stock and is not considered in determining whether the more than 75 percent vote has been obtained under this A-7 if the stock is actually owned or constructively owned under section 318(a) by or for a disqualified individual who receives (or is to receive) payments that would be parachute payments if the shareholder approval requirements described in paragraph (a) of this A-7 are not met. Likewise, stock is not counted as outstanding stock if the owner is considered under section 318(a) to own any part of the stock owned directly or indirectly by or for a disqualified individual described in the preceding sentence. In addition, if the person authorized to vote the stock of an entity shareholder is a disqualified individual who would receive a parachute payment if the shareholder approval requirements described in this A-7 are not met, such person is not permitted to vote such shares, but the entity shareholder is permitted to appoint an equity interest holder in the entity shareholder, or in the case of a trust another person eligible to vote on behalf of the trust, to vote the otherwise eligible shares. However, if all persons who hold voting power in the corporation undergoing the change in ownership or control are disqualified individuals or related persons described in this paragraph (b)(4), then such stock is counted as outstanding stock and votes by such persons are considered in determining whether the more than 75 percent vote has been obtained.

(c) *Adequate disclosure.* To be adequate disclosure for purposes of paragraph (a)(2) of this A-7, disclosure must be full and truthful disclosure of the material facts and such additional information as is necessary to make the disclosure not materially misleading at the time the disclosure is made. Disclosure of such information must be made to every shareholder of the corporation entitled to vote under this A-7. For each disqualified individual, material facts that must be disclosed include, but are not limited to, the event triggering the payment or payments, the total amount of the payments that would be parachute payments if the shareholder approval requirements described in paragraph (a) of this A-7 are not met, and a brief description of each payment (*e.g.*, accelerated vesting of options, bonus, or salary). An omitted fact is considered a material fact if there is a substantial likelihood that a reasonable shareholder would consider it important.

(d) *Corporation without shareholders.* If a corporation does not have shareholders, the exemption described in Q/A-6(a)(2) of this section and the shareholder approval requirements described in this A-7 do not apply. Solely for purposes of this paragraph (d), a shareholder

does not include a member in an association, joint stock company, or insurance company.

(e) *Examples.* The following examples illustrate the application of this A-7:

Example 1. Corporation S has two shareholders—Corporation P, which owns 76 percent of the stock of Corporation S, and A, a disqualified individual who would receive a parachute payment if the shareholder approval requirements of this A-7 are not met. No stock of Corporation P or S is readily tradeable on an established securities market (or otherwise). The value of the stock of Corporation S equals or exceeds one third of the gross fair market value of the assets of Corporation P, and thus, represents a substantial portion of the assets of Corporation P. All of the stock of Corporation S is sold to Corporation M. Contingent on the change in ownership of Corporation S, severance payments are made to certain officers of Corporation S in excess of 3 times each officer's base amount. If the payments are approved by a separate vote of the persons who hold, immediately before the sale, more than 75 percent of the voting power of the outstanding stock entitled to vote of Corporation P and the disclosure rules of paragraph (a)(2) of this A-7 are complied with, the shareholder approval requirements of this A-7 are met, and the payments are exempt from the definition of *parachute payment* pursuant to A-6 of this section.

Example 2. (i) Stock of Corporation X, none of which is traded on an established market, is acquired by Corporation Y. In the voting ballot concerning the sale, the Corporation X shareholders are asked to vote either "yes" on the sale and "yes" to paying parachute payments to A, a disqualified individual with respect to Corporation A, or "no" on the sale and "no" to paying parachute payments to A.

(ii) Because the approval of the change in ownership or control is conditioned on the approval of the payments to A, the shareholder approval requirements of this A-7 are not satisfied. If the payments are made to A, the payments are not exempt from the definition of *parachute payment* pursuant to Q/A-6 of this section.

(iii) Assume the same facts as in paragraph (i) of this *Example 2*, except that the acquisition agreement between Corporation X and Corporation Y states that the acquisition is approved only if there are no parachute payments made to A. If the shareholder approval and the disclosure requirements described in this A-7 are met, the payments will not be parachute payments. Alternatively, if the shareholders do not approve the payments, the payments can not be made (or retained). Thus, the transaction is not conditioned on the approval of the parachute payments. If the payments are made and the requirements of this A-7 are met, the payments are exempt from the definition of *parachute payment* pursuant to Q/A-6 of this section.

Example 3. Corporation M is wholly owned by Partnership P. No interest in either M or P is readily tradeable on an established securities market (or otherwise). The value of the stock of Corporation M equals or exceeds one third of the gross fair market value of the assets of Partnership P, and thus, represents a substantial portion of the assets of Partnership P. Corporation M undergoes a change in ownership or control. Partnership P has one general partner and 200 limited partners. The general partner is not a disqualified individual. None of the limited partners are entitled to vote on issues involving the management of the partnership investments. If the payments that would be parachute payments if shareholder approval requirements of this A-7 are not met are approved by the general partner and the disclosure rules of paragraph (a)(2) of this A-7 are complied with, the shareholder approval requirements of this A-7 are met, and the payments are exempt from the definition of *parachute payment* pursuant to A-6 of this section.

Example 4. Corporation A has several shareholders including X and Y, who are disqualified individuals with respect to Corporation A and would receive parachute payments if the shareholder approval requirements of this A-7 are not met. No stock of Corporation A is readily tradeable on an established securities market (or otherwise). Corporation A undergoes a change in ownership or control. Contingent on the change in ownership or control, severance payments are payable to X and Y that are in excess of 3 times each individual's base amount. To determine whether the shareholder approval requirements of paragraph (a)(1) of this A-7 are satisfied regarding the payments to X and Y, the stock of X and Y is not considered outstanding, and X and Y are not entitled to vote.

Example 5. Assume the same facts as in *Example 4*, except that after adequate disclosure of all material facts (within the meaning of paragraph (a)(2) of this A-7) to all shareholders entitled to vote, 60 percent of the shareholders who are entitled to vote approve the payments to X and Y. Because more than 75 percent of the shareholders holding outstanding stock who were entitled to vote did not approve the payments to X and Y, the payments cannot be made.

Example 6. Assume the same facts as in *Example 4* except that disclosure of all the material facts (within the meaning of paragraph (a)(2) of this A-7) regarding the payments to X and Y is made to two of Corporation A's shareholders, who collectively own 80 percent of

Corporation A's stock entitled to vote and approve the payment. Both shareholders approve the payments. Assume further that no adequate disclosure of the material facts regarding the payments to X and Y is made to other Corporation A shareholders who are entitled to vote within the meaning of this A-7. Notwithstanding that 80 percent of the shareholders entitled to vote approve the payments, because disclosure regarding the payments to X and Y is not made to all of Corporation A's shareholders who were entitled to vote, the disclosure requirements of paragraph (a)(2) of this A-7 are not met, and the payments are not exempt from the definition of *parachute payment* pursuant to Q/A-6.

Example 7. Corporation C has three shareholders—Partnership, which owns 20 percent of the stock of Corporation C; A, an individual who owns 60 percent of the stock of Corporation C; and B, an individual who owns 20 percent of Corporation C. Stock of Corporation C does not represent a substantial portion of the assets of Partnership. No interest in either Partnership or Corporation C is readily tradeable on an established securities market (or otherwise). P, a one-third partner in Partnership, is a disqualified individual with respect to Corporation C. Corporation C undergoes a change in ownership or control. Contingent on the change, a severance payment is payable to P in excess of 3 times P's base amount. To determine the persons who are entitled to vote referred to in paragraph (a)(1) of this A-7, one-third of the stock held by Partnership is not considered outstanding stock. If P is the person authorized by Partnership to approve the payment, none of the shares of Partnership are considered outstanding stock. However, Partnership is permitted to appoint an equity interest holder in Partnership (who is not a disqualified individual who would receive a parachute payment if the requirements of this A-7 are not met), to vote the two-thirds of the shares held by Partnership that are otherwise entitled to be voted.

Example 8. X, Y, and Z are all employees and disqualified individuals with respect to Corporation E. No stock in Corporation E is readily tradeable on an established securities market (or otherwise). Each individual has a base amount of $100,000. Corporation E undergoes a change in ownership or control. Contingent on the change, a severance payment of $400,000 is payable to X; $600,000 is payable to Y; and $1,000,000 is payable to Z. Corporation E provides each Corporation E shareholder entitled to vote (as determined under this A-7) with a ballot listing and describing the payments of $400,000 to X; $600,000 to Y; and $1,000,000 to Z and the triggering event that generated the payments. Next to each name and corresponding amount on the ballot, Corporation E requests approval (with a "yes" and "no" box) of each total payment to be made to each individual and states that if the payment is not approved the payment will not be made. Adequate disclosure, within the meaning of this A-7 is made to each shareholder entitled to vote under this A-7. More than 75 percent of the Corporation E shareholders who are entitled to vote under paragraph (a)(1) of this A-7 approve each payment to each individual. The shareholder approval requirements of this A-7 are met, and the payments are exempt from the definition of *parachute payment* pursuant to A-6 of this section.

Example 9. Assume the same facts as in *Example 8* except that the ballot does not request approval of each total payment to each individual separately. Instead, the ballot states that $2,000,000 in payments will be made to X, Y, and Z and requests approval of the $2,000,000 payments. Assuming the triggering event and amount of the payments to X, Y, and Z are separately described to the shareholders entitled to vote under this A-7, the shareholder approval requirements of paragraph (a)(1) of this A-7 are met, and the payments are exempt from the definition of *parachute payment* pursuant to A-6 of this section.

Example 10. B, an employee of Corporation X, is a disqualified individual with respect to Corporation X. Stock of Corporation X is not readily tradeable on an established securities market (or otherwise). Corporation X undergoes a change in ownership or control. B's base amount is $205,000. Under B's employment agreement with Corporation X, in the event of a change in ownership or control, B's stock options will vest and B will receive severance and bonus payments. Contingent on the change in ownership or control, B's stock options with a fair market value of $500,000 immediately vest, $200,000 of which is contingent on the change, and B will receive a $200,000 bonus payment and a $400,000 severance payment. Corporation X distributes a ballot to every shareholder of Corporation X *who immediately before the change is entitled to vote* as described in this A-7. The ballot contains adequate disclosure of all material facts and lists the following payments to be made to B: the contingent payment of $200,000 attributable to options, a $200,000 bonus payment, and a $400,000 severance payment. The ballot requests shareholder approval of the $200,000 bonus payment to B and states that whether or not the $200,000 bonus payment is approved, B will receive $200,000 attributable to options and a $400,000 severance payment. More than 75 percent of the shareholders entitled to vote as described by this A-7 approve the $200,000 bonus payment to B. The shareholder approval requirements of this A-7 are met, and the

$200,000 payment is exempt from the definition of *parachute payment* pursuant to A-6 of this section.

Q-8: Which payments under a qualified plan are exempt from the definition of *parachute payment*?

A-8: The term *parachute payment* does not include any payment to or from—

(a) A plan described in section 401(a) which includes a trust exempt from tax under section 501(a);

(b) An annuity plan described in section 403(a);

(c) A simplified employee pension (as defined in section 408(k)); or

(d) A simple retirement account (as defined in section 408(p)).

Q-9: Which payments of reasonable compensation are exempt from the definition of *parachute payment*?

A-9: Except in the case of securities violation parachute payments, the term *parachute payment* does not include any payment (or portion thereof) which the taxpayer establishes by clear and convincing evidence is reasonable compensation for personal services to be rendered by the disqualified individual on or after the date of the change in ownership or control. See Q/A-37 of this section for the definition and treatment of securities violation parachute payments. See Q/A-40 through Q/A-44 of this section for rules on determining amounts of reasonable compensation.

Payor of Parachute Payments

Q-10: Who may be the payor of parachute payments?

A-10: Parachute payments within the meaning of Q/A-2 of this section may be paid, directly or indirectly, by—

(i) The corporation referred to in paragraph (a)(3) of Q/A-2 of this section;

(ii) A person acquiring ownership or effective control of that corporation or ownership of a substantial portion of that corporation's assets; or

(iii) Any person whose relationship to such corporation or other person is such as to require attribution of stock ownership between the parties under section 318(a).

Payments in the Nature of Compensation

Q-11: What types of payments are in the nature of compensation?

A-11: (a) *General rule.* For purposes of this section, all payments—in whatever form—are payments in the nature of compensation if they arise out of an employment relationship or are associated with the performance of services. For this purpose, the performance of services includes holding oneself out as available to perform services and refraining from performing services (such as under a covenant not to compete or similar arrangement). Payments in the nature of compensation include (but are not limited to) wages and salary, bonuses, severance pay, fringe benefits, life insurance, pension benefits, and other deferred compensation (including any amount characterized by the parties as interest thereon). A payment in the nature of compensation also includes cash when paid, the value of the right to receive cash (including the value of accelerated vesting under Q/A-24(c)), or a transfer of property. However, payments in the nature of compensation do not include attorney's fees or court costs paid or incurred in connection with the payment of any amount described in paragraphs (a)(1), (2), and (3) of Q/A-2 of this section or a reasonable rate of interest accrued on any amount during the period the parties contest whether a payment will be made.

(b) *When payment is considered to be made.* Except as otherwise provided in A-11 through Q/A-13 of this section, a payment in the nature of compensation is considered made (and is subject to the excise tax under section 4999) in the taxable year in which it is includible in the disqualified individual's gross income or, in the case of fringe benefits and other benefits excludible from income, in the taxable year the benefits are received.

(c) *Prepayment rule.* Notwithstanding the general rule described in paragraph (b) of this A-11, a disqualified individual may, in the year of the change in ownership or control, or any later year, prepay the excise tax under section 4999, provided that the payor and disqualified individual treat the payment of the excise tax consistently and the payor satisfies its obligations under section 4999(c) in the year of prepayment. The prepayment of the excise tax for purposes of section 4999 must be based on the present value of the excise tax that would be due in the year the excess parachute payment would actually be paid (calculated using the discount rate equal to 120 percent of the applicable Federal rate (determined under section 1274(d) and regulations thereunder; see Q/A-32)). For purposes of projecting the future value of a payment that provides for interest to be credited at a variable interest rate, it is permissible to make a reasonable assumption regarding this variable rate. A disqualified individual is not required to adjust the excise tax paid under this paragraph (c) merely because the interest rates in the future are not the same as the rate used for purposes of projecting the future value of the payment. However, a disqualified individual may not apply this paragraph (c) of this A-11 to a payment to be made in cash if the present value of the payment would be considered not reasonably ascertainable under section 3121(v) and § 31.3121(v)(2)-1(e)(4) of this Chapter or to a payment related to health benefits or coverage. The Commissioner may provide additional guidance regarding the applicability of this paragraph (c) to certain payments in published guidance of general applicability under § 601.601(d)(2) of this Chapter.

(d) *Transfers of property.* Transfers of property are treated as payments for purposes of this A-11. See Q/A-12 of this section for rules on determining when such payments are considered made and the amount of such payments. See Q/A-13 of this section for special rules on transfers of stock options.

(e) The following example illustrates the principles of this A-11:

Example. D is a disqualified individual with respect to Corporation X. D has a base amount of $100,000 and is entitled to receive two parachute payments, one of $200,000 and the other of $400,000. A change in ownership or control of Corporation X occurs on May 1, 2005, and the $200,000 payment is made to D at the time of the change in ownership or control. The $400,000 payment is to be made on October 1, 2010. Corporation X and D agree that D will prepay the excise tax and X will satisfy its obligations under section 4999(c) with respect to the $400,000 payment. Using discount rate determined under Q/A-32, Corporation X and D determine that the present value of the $400,000 payment is $300,000 on the date of the change in ownership or control. The portions of the base amount allocated to these payments are $40,000 (($200,000/$500,000) × $100,000) and $60,000 (($300,000/$500,000) × $100,000), respectively. Thus, the amount of the first excess parachute payment is $160,000 ($200,000 – $40,000) and that of the second excess parachute payment is $340,000 ($400,000 – $60,000). The excise tax on the $400,000 payment is $68,000 ($340,000 × 20 percent). Assume the present value (calculated in accordance with paragraph (c) of this A-11) of $68,000 is $50,000. To prepay the excise tax due on the $400,000 payment, Corporation X must satisfy its obligations under section 4999 with respect to the $50,000, in addition to the $32,000 withholding required with respect to the $200,000 payment.

Q-12: If a property transfer to a disqualified individual is a payment in the nature of compensation, when is the payment considered made (or to be made), and how is the amount of the payment determined?

A-12: (a) Except as provided in this A-12 and Q/A-13 of this section, a transfer of property is considered a payment made (or to be made) in the taxable year in which the property transferred is includible in the gross income of the disqualified individual under section 83 and the regulations thereunder. Thus, in general, such a payment is considered made (or to be made) when the property is transferred (as defined in § 1.83-3(a)) to the disqualified individual and becomes substantially vested (as defined in § 1.83-3(b) and (j)) in such individual. The amount of the payment is determined under section 83 and the regulations thereunder. Thus, in general, the amount of the payment is equal to the excess of the fair market value of the transferred property (determined without regard to any lapse restriction, as defined in § 1.83-3(i)) at the time that the property becomes substantially vested, over the amount (if any) paid for the property.

(b) An election made by a disqualified individual under section 83(b) with respect to transferred property will not apply for purposes of this A-12. Thus, even if such an election is made with respect to a property transfer that is a payment in the nature of compensation, for purposes of this section, the payment is generally considered made (or to be made) when the property is transferred to and becomes substantially vested in such individual.

(c) See Q/A-13 of this section for rules on applying this A-12 to transfers of stock options.

(d) The following example illustrates the principles of this A-12:

Example. On January 1, 2006, Corporation M gives to A, a disqualified individual, a bonus of 100 shares of Corporation M stock in connection with the performance of services to Corporation M. Under the terms of the bonus arrangement A is obligated to return the Corporation M stock to Corporation M unless the earnings of Corporation M double by January 1, 2009, or there is a change in ownership or control of Corporation M before that date. A's rights in the stock are treated as substantially nonvested (within the meaning of § 1.83-3(b)) during that period because A's rights in the stock are subject to a substantial risk of forfeiture (within the meaning of § 1.83-3(c)) and are nontransferable (within the meaning of § 1.83-3(d)). On January 1, 2008, a change in ownership or control of Corporation M occurs. On that day, the fair market value of the Corporation M stock is $250 per share. Because A's rights in the Corporation M stock become substantially vested (within the meaning of § 1.83-3(b)) on that day, the payment is considered made on that day, and the amount of the payment for purposes of this section is equal to $25,000 (100 × $250). See Q/A-38 through 41 for rules relating to the reduction of the excess parachute payment by the portion of the payment which is established to be reasonable com-

pensation for personal services actually rendered before the date of a change in ownership or control.

Q-13: How are transfers of statutory and nonstatutory stock options treated?

A-13: (a) For purposes of this section, an option (including an option to which section 421 applies) is treated as property that is transferred when the option becomes vested (regardless of whether the option has a readily ascertainable fair market value as defined in § 1.83-7(b)). For purposes of this A-13, *vested* means substantially vested within the meaning of § 1.83-3(b) and (j) or the right to the payment is not otherwise subject to a substantial risk of forfeiture within the meaning of section 83(c). Thus, for purposes of this section, the vesting of such an option is treated as a payment in the nature of compensation. The value of an option at the time the option vests is determined under all the facts and circumstances in the particular case. Factors relevant to such a determination include, but are not limited to: the difference between the option's exercise price and the value of the property subject to the option at the time of vesting; the probability of the value of such property increasing or decreasing; and the length of the period during which the option can be exercised. Thus, an option is treated as a payment in the nature of compensation on the date of grant or vesting, as applicable, without regard to whether such option has an ascertainable fair market value. For purposes of this A-13, valuation may be determined by any method prescribed by the Commissioner in published guidance of general applicability under § 601.601(d)(2) of this Chapter.

(b) Any money or other property transferred to the disqualified individual on the exercise, or as consideration on the sale or other disposition, of an option described in paragraph (a) of this A-13 after the time such option vests is not treated as a payment in the nature of compensation to the disqualified individual under Q/A-11 of this section. Nonetheless, the amount of the otherwise allowable deduction under section 162 or 212 with respect to such transfer is reduced by the amount of the payment described in paragraph (a) of this A-13 treated as an excess parachute payment.

Q-14: Are payments in the nature of compensation reduced by consideration paid by the disqualified individual?

A-14: Yes, to the extent not otherwise taken into account under Q/A-12 and Q/A-13 of this section, the amount of any payment in the nature of compensation is reduced by the amount of any money or the fair market value of any property (owned by the disqualified individual without restriction) that is (or will be) transferred by the disqualified individual in exchange for the payment. For purposes of the preceding sentence, the fair market value of property is determined as of the date the property is transferred by the disqualified individual.

Disqualified Individuals

Q-15: Who is a disqualified individual?

A-15: (a) For purposes of this section, an individual is a disqualified individual with respect to a corporation if, at any time during the *disqualified individual determination period* (as defined in Q/A-20 of this section), the individual is an employee or independent contractor of the corporation and is, with respect to the corporation—

(1) A shareholder (but see Q/A-17 of this section);

(2) An officer (see Q/A-18 of this section); or

(3) A highly-compensated individual (see Q/A-19 of this section).

(b) For purposes of this A-15, a director is a disqualified individual with respect to a corporation if, at any time during the *disqualified individual determination period*, the director is, with respect to the corporation, a shareholder (see Q/A -17 of this section), an officer (see Q/A-18 of this section), or a highly-compensated individual (see Q/A -19 of this section).

(c) For purposes of this A-15, an individual who is an employee or independent contractor of a corporation other than the corporation undergoing a change in ownership or control is disregarded for purposes of determining who is a disqualified individual if such individual is employed by the corporation undergoing the change in ownership or control only on the last day of the disqualified individual determination period. Thus, for example, assume that E is an employee of Corporation X, that Y is acquired by Corporation X, and that Y undergoes a change in ownership or control. If E becomes an employee of Y on the date of the acquisition, in determining the disqualified individuals with respect to Y, E is disregarded under this paragraph (c).

Q-16: Is a personal service corporation treated as an individual?

A-16: (a) Yes. For purposes of this section, a personal service corporation (as defined in section 269A(b)(1)), or a noncorporate entity that would be a personal service corporation if it were a corporation, is treated as an individual.

(b) The following example illustrates the principles of this A-16:

Example. Corporation N, a personal service corporation (as defined in section 269A(b)(1)), has a single individual as its sole shareholder and employee. Corporation N performs personal services for Corporation M. The compensation paid to Corporation N by Corporation M puts Corporation N within the group of highly-compensated individuals of Corporation M as determined under A-19 of this section. Thus, Corporation N is treated as a highly-compensated individual with respect to Corporation M.

Q-17: Are all shareholders of a corporation considered sharehold-ers for purposes of paragraphs (a)(1) and (b) of Q/A-15 of this section?

A-17: (a) No. Only an individual who owns stock of a corporation with a fair market value that exceeds 1 percent of the fair market value of the outstanding shares of all classes of the corporation's stock is treated as a disqualified individual with respect to the corporation by reason of stock ownership. An individual who owns a lesser amount of stock may, however, be a disqualified individual with respect to the corporation if such individual is an officer (see Q/A-18) or highly-compensated individual (see Q/A-19) with respect to the corporation.

(b) For purposes of determining the amount of stock owned by an individual for purposes of paragraph (a) of this A-17, the construc-tive ownership rules of section 318(a) apply. Stock underlying a vested option is considered owned by an individual who holds the vested option (and the stock underlying an unvested option is not considered owned by an individual who holds the unvested option). For purposes of the preceding sentence, however, if the option is exercisable for stock that is not substantially vested (as defined by §§ 1.83-3(b) and (j)), the stock underlying the option is not treated as owned by the individual who holds the option. Solely for purposes of determining the amount of stock owned by an individual for purposes of this A-17, mutual and cooperative corporations are treated as having stock.

(c) The following examples illustrates the principles of this A-17:

Example 1. E, an employee of Corporation A, received options under Corporation A's Stock Option Plan. E's stock options vest three years after the date of grant. E is not an officer or highly compensated individual during the disqualified individual determi-nation period. E does not own, and is not considered to own under section 318, any other Corporation A stock. Two years after the options are granted to E, all of Corporation A's stock is acquired by Corporation B. Under Corporation A's Stock Option Plan, E's options are converted to Corporation B options and the vesting schedule remains the same. Under paragraph (b) of this A-17, the stock under-lying the unvested options held by E on the date of the change in ownership or control is not considered owned by E. Because E is not considered to own Corporation A stock with a fair market value exceeding 1 percent of the total fair market value of all of the outstanding shares of all classes of Corporation A and E is not an officer or highly-compensated individual during the disqualified individual determination period, E is not a disqualified individual within the meaning of Q&A-15 of this section with respect to Corpo-ration A.

Example 2. Assume the same facts as in *Example 1*, except that Corporation A's Stock Option Plan provides that all unvested op-tions will vest immediately on a change in ownership or control. Under paragraph (b) of this A-17, the stock underlying the options that vest on the change in ownership or control is considered owned by E. If the stock considered owned by E exceeds 1 percent of the total fair market value of all of the outstanding shares of all classes of Corporation A stock (including for this purpose, all stock owned or constructively owned by all shareholders, provided that no share of stock is counted more than once), E is a disqualified individual within the meaning of Q/A-15 of this section with respect to Corpo-ration A.

Example 3. Assume the same facts as in *Example 1* except that E received nonstatutory stock options that are exercisable for stock subject to a substantial risk of forfeiture under section 83. Assume further that under Corporation A's Stock Option Plan, the nonstatu-tory options will vest on a change in ownership or control. Under paragraph (b) of this A-17, E is not considered to own the stock underlying the options that vest on the change in ownership or control because the options are exercisable for stock subject to a substantial risk of forfeiture within the meaning of section 83. Be-cause E is not considered to own Corporation A stock with a fair market value exceeding 1 percent of the total fair market value of all of the outstanding shares of all classes of Corporation A stock and E is not an officer or highly compensated individual during the dis-qualified individual determination period, E is not a disqualified individual within the meaning of Q/A-15 of this section with respect to Corporation A.

Q-18: Who is an officer?

A-18: (a) For purposes of this section, whether an individual is an officer with respect to a corporation is determined on the basis of all the facts and circumstances in the particular case (such as the source of the individual's authority, the term for which the individual is elected or appointed, and the nature and extent of the individual's

duties). Any individual who has the title of officer is presumed to be an officer unless the facts and circumstances demonstrate that the individual does not have the authority of an officer. However, an individual who does not have the title of officer may nevertheless be considered an officer if the facts and circumstances demonstrate that the individual has the authority of an officer. Generally, the term officer means an administrative executive who is in regular and continued service. The term officer implies continuity of service and excludes those employed for a special and single transaction.

(b) An individual who is an officer with respect to any member of an affiliated group that is treated as one corporation pursuant to Q/A-46 of this section is treated as an officer of such one corporation.

(c) No more than 50 employees (or, if less, the greater of 3 employ-ees, or 10 percent of the employees (rounded up to the nearest integer)) of the corporation (in the case of an affiliated group treated as one corporation, each member of the affiliated group) are treated as disqualified individuals with respect to a corporation by reason of being an officer of the corporation. For purposes of the preceding sentence, the number of employees of the corporation is the greatest number of employees the corporation has during the disqualified individual determination period (as defined in Q/A-20 of this sec-tion). If the number of officers of the corporation exceeds the number of employees who may be treated as officers under the first sentence of this paragraph (c), then the employees who are treated as officers for purposes of this section are the highest paid 50 employees (or, if less, the greater of 3 employees, or 10 percent of the employees (rounded up to the nearest integer)) of the corporation when ranked on the basis of compensation (as determined under Q/A-21 of this section) paid during the disqualified individual determination period.

(d) In determining the total number of employees of a corporation for purposes of this A-18, employees are not counted if they normally work less than 17½ hours per week (as defined in section 414(q)(5)(B) and the regulations thereunder) or if they normally work during not more than 6 months during any year (as defined in section 414(q)(5)(C) and the regulations thereunder). However, an employee who is not counted for purposes of the preceding sentence may still be an officer.

Q-19: Who is a highly-compensated individual?

A-19: (a) For purposes of this section, a highly-compensated indi-vidual with respect to a corporation is any individual who is, or would be if the individual were an employee, a member of the group consisting of the lesser of the highest paid 1 percent of the employees of the corporation (rounded up to the nearest integer), or the highest paid 250 employees of the corporation, when ranked on the basis of compensation (as determined under Q/A-21 of this section) earned during the disqualified individual determination period (as defined in Q/A-20 of this section). For purposes of the preceding sentence, the number of employees of the corporation is the greatest number of employees the corporation has during the disqualified individual determination period (as defined in Q/A-20 of this section). How-ever, no individual whose annualized compensation during the dis-qualified individual determination period is less than the amount described in section 414(q)(1)(B)(i) for the year in which the change in ownership or control occurs will be treated as a highly-compensated individual.

(b) An individual who is not an employee of the corporation is not treated as a highly-compensated individual with respect to the cor-poration on account of compensation received for performing ser-vices (such as brokerage, legal, or investment banking services) in connection with a change in ownership or control of the corporation, if the services are performed in the ordinary course of the individ-ual's trade or business and the individual performs similar services for a significant number of clients unrelated to the corporation.

(c) The total number of employees of a corporation for purposes of this A-19 is determined in accordance with Q/A-18(d) of this section. However, an employee who is not counted for purposes of the preceding sentence may still be a highly-compensated individual.

Q-20: What is the disqualified individual determination period?

A-20: The disqualified individual determination period is the twelve-month period prior to and ending on the date of the change in ownership or control of the corporation.

Q-21: How is *compensation* defined for purposes of determining who is a disqualified individual?

A-21: (a) For purposes of determining who is a disqualified indi-vidual, the term *compensation* means the compensation which was earned by the individual for services performed for the corporation with respect to which the change in ownership or control occurs (changed corporation), for a predecessor entity, or for a related entity. Such compensation is determined without regard to sections 125, 132(f)(4), 402(e)(3), and 402(h)(1)(B). Thus, for example, compen-sation includes elective or salary reduction contributions to a cafete-ria plan, cash or deferred arrangement or tax-sheltered annuity, and amounts credited under a nonqualified deferred compensation plan.

(b) For purposes of this A-21, a predecessor entity is any entity which, as a result of a merger, consolidation, purchase or acquisition of property or stock, corporate separation, or other similar business transaction transfers some or all of its employees to the changed corporation or to a related entity or to a predecessor entity of the changed corporation. The term *related entity* includes—

(1) All members of a controlled group of corporations (as defined in section 414(b)) that includes the changed corporation or a predecessor entity;

(2) All trades or businesses (whether or not incorporated) that are under common control (as defined in section 414(c)) if such group includes the changed corporation or a predecessor entity;

(3) All members of an affiliated service group (as defined in section 414(m)) that includes the changed corporation or a predecessor entity; and

(4) Any other entities required to be aggregated with the changed corporation or a predecessor entity pursuant to section 414(o) and the regulations thereunder (except leasing organizations as defined in section 414(n)).

(c) For purposes of Q/A-18 and Q/A-19 of this section, compensation that was contingent on the change in ownership or control and that was payable in the year of the change is not treated as compensation.

Contingent on Change in Ownership or Control

Q-22: When is a payment contingent on a change in ownership or control?

A-22: (a) In general, a payment is treated as contingent on a change in ownership or control if the payment would not, in fact, have been made had no change in ownership or control occurred, even if the payment is also conditioned on the occurrence of another event. A payment generally is treated as one which would not, in fact, have been made in the absence of a change in ownership or control unless it is substantially certain, at the time of the change, that the payment would have been made whether or not the change occurred. (But see Q/A-23 of this section regarding payments under agreements entered into after a change in ownership or control.) A payment that becomes vested as a result of a change in ownership or control is not treated as a payment which was substantially certain to have been made whether or not the change occurred. For purposes of this A-22, *vested* means the payment is substantially vested within the meaning of §1.83-3(b) and (j) or the right to the payment is not otherwise subject to a substantial risk of forfeiture as defined by section 83(c).

(b)(1) For purposes of paragraph (a), a payment is treated as contingent on a change in ownership or control if—

(i) The payment is contingent on an event that is closely associated with a change in ownership or control;

(ii) A change in ownership or control actually occurs; and

(iii) The event is materially related to the change in ownership or control.

(2) For purposes of paragraph (b)(1)(i) of this A-22, a payment is treated as contingent on an event that is closely associated with a change in ownership or control unless it is substantially certain, at the time of the event, that the payment would have been made whether or not the event occurred. An event is considered closely associated with a change in ownership or control if the event is of a type often preliminary or subsequent to, or otherwise closely associated with, a change in ownership or control. For example, the following events are considered closely associated with a change in the ownership or control of a corporation: The onset of a tender offer with respect to the corporation; a substantial increase in the market price of the corporation's stock that occurs within a short period (but only if such increase occurs prior to a change in ownership or control); the cessation of the listing of the corporation's stock on an established securities market; the acquisition of more than 5 percent of the corporation's stock by a person (or more than one person acting as a group) not in control of the corporation; the voluntary or involuntary termination of the disqualified individual's employment; a significant reduction in the disqualified individual's job responsibilities; and a change in ownership or control as defined in the disqualified individual's employment agreement (or elsewhere) that does not meet the definition of a change in ownership or control described in Q/A-27, 28, or 29 of this section. Whether other events are treated as closely associated with a change in ownership or control is based on all the facts and circumstances of the particular case.

(3) For purposes of determining whether an event (as described in paragraph (b)(2) of this A-22) is materially related to a change in ownership or control, the event is presumed to be materially related to a change in ownership or control if such event occurs within the period beginning one year before and ending one year after the date of the change in ownership or control. If such event occurs outside of the period beginning one year before and ending one year after the date of change in ownership or control, the event is presumed not

materially related to the change in ownership or control. A payment does not fail to be contingent on a change in ownership or control merely because it is also contingent on the occurrence of a second event (without regard to whether the second event is closely associated with or materially related to a change in ownership or control). Similarly, a payment that is treated as contingent on a change in ownership or control because it is contingent on a closely associated event does not fail to be treated as contingent on a change in ownership or control merely because it is also contingent on the occurrence of a second event (without regard to whether the second event is closely associated with or materially related to a change in ownership or control).

(c) A payment that would in fact have been made had no change in ownership or control occurred is treated as contingent on a change in ownership or control if the change in ownership or control (or the occurrence of an event that is closely associated with and materially related to a change in ownership or control within the meaning of paragraph (b)(1) of this A-22), accelerates the time at which the payment is made. Thus, for example, if a change in ownership or control accelerates the time of payment of deferred compensation that is vested without regard to the change in ownership or control, the payment may be treated as contingent on the change. See Q/A-24 of this section regarding the portion of a payment that is so treated. See also Q/A-8 of this section regarding the exemption for certain payments under qualified plans and Q/A-40 of this section regarding the treatment of a payment as reasonable compensation.

(d) A payment is treated as contingent on a change in ownership or control even if the employment or independent contractor relationship of the disqualified individual is not terminated (voluntarily or involuntarily) as a result of the change.

(e) The following examples illustrate the principles of this A-22:

Example 1. A corporation grants a stock appreciation right to a disqualified individual, A, more than one year before a change in ownership or control. After the stock appreciation right vests and becomes exercisable, a change in ownership or control of the corporation occurs, and A exercises the right. Assuming neither the granting nor the vesting of the stock appreciation right is contingent on a change in ownership or control, the payment made on exercise is not contingent on the change in ownership or control.

Example 2. A contract between a corporation and B, a disqualified individual, provides that a payment will be made to B if the corporation undergoes a change in ownership or control and B's employment with the corporation is terminated at any time over the succeeding 5 years. Eighteen months later, a change in the ownership of the corporation occurs. Two years after the change in ownership, B's employment is terminated and the payment is made to B. Because it was not substantially certain that the corporation would have made the payment to B on B's termination of employment if there had not been a change in ownership, the payment is treated as contingent on the change in ownership under paragraph (a) of this A-22. This is true even though B's termination of employment is presumed not to be, and in fact may not be, materially related to the change in ownership or control.

Example 3. A contract between a corporation and C, a disqualified individual, provides that a payment will be made to C if C's employment is terminated at any time during the succeeding 3 years (without regard to whether or not there is a change in ownership or control). Eighteen months after the contract is entered into, a change in the ownership or control of the corporation occurs. Six months after the change in ownership or control, C's employment is terminated and the payment is made to C. Termination of employment is considered an event closely associated with a change in ownership or control. Because the termination occurred within one year after the date of the change in ownership or control, the termination of C's employment is presumed to be materially related to the change in ownership or control under paragraph (b)(3) of this A-22. If this presumption is not successfully rebutted, the payment will be treated as contingent on the change in ownership or control under paragraph (b) of this A-22.

Example 4. A contract between a corporation and a disqualified individual, D, provides that a payment will be made to D upon the onset of a tender offer for shares of the corporation's stock. A tender offer is made on December 1, 2008, and the payment is made to D. Although the tender offer is unsuccessful, it leads to a negotiated merger with another entity on June 1, 2009, which results in a change in the ownership or control of the corporation. It was not substantially certain, at the time of the onset of the tender offer, that the payment would have been made had no tender offer taken place. The onset of a tender offer is considered closely associated with a change in ownership or control. Because the tender offer occurred within one year before the date of the change in ownership or control of the corporation, the onset of the tender offer is presumed to be materially related to the change in ownership or control. If this presumption is not rebutted, the payment will be treated as contingent on the change in ownership or control. If no change in ownership or control had occurred, the payment would not be treated as contingent on a change in ownership or control; however, the payment still could be a parachute payment under Q/A-37 of this section if the contract violated a generally enforced securities law or regulation.

Example 5. A contract between a corporation and a disqualified individual, E, provides that a payment will be made to E if the corporation's level of product sales or profits reaches a specified level. At the time the contract was entered into, the parties had no reason to believe that such an increase in the corporation's level of product sales or profits would be preliminary or subsequent to, or otherwise closely associated with, a change in ownership or control of the corporation. Eighteen months later, a change in the ownership or control of the corporation occurs and within one year after the date of the change of ownership or control, the corporation's level of product sales or profits reaches the specified level. Under these facts and circumstances (and in the absence of contradictory evidence), the increase in product sales or profits of the corporation is not an event closely associated with the change in ownership or control of the corporation. Accordingly, even if the increase is materially related to the change in ownership or control, the payment will not be treated as contingent on a change in ownership or control.

Q-23: May a payment be treated as contingent on a change in ownership or control if the payment is made under an agreement entered into after the change?

A-23: (a) No. Payments are not treated as contingent on a change in ownership or control if they are made (or are to be made) pursuant to an agreement entered into after the change (a post-change agreement). For this purpose, an agreement that is executed after a change in ownership or control pursuant to a legally enforceable agreement that was entered into before the change is considered to have been entered into before the change. (See Q/A-9 of this section regarding the exemption for reasonable compensation for services rendered on or after a change in ownership or control.) If an individual has a right to receive a payment that would be a parachute payment if made under an agreement entered into prior to a change in ownership or control (pre-change agreement) and gives up that right as bargained-for consideration for benefits under a post-change agreement, the agreement is treated as a post-change agreement only to the extent the value of the payments under the agreement exceed the value of the payments under the pre-change agreement. To the extent payments under the agreement have the same value as the payments under the pre-change agreement, such payments retain their character as parachute payments subject to this section.

(b) The following examples illustrate the principles of this A-23:

Example 1. Assume that a disqualified individual is an employee of a corporation. A change in ownership or control of the corporation occurs, and thereafter the individual enters into an employment agreement with the acquiring company. Because the agreement is entered into after the change in ownership or control occurs, payments to be made under the agreement are not treated as contingent on the change.

Example 2. Assume the same facts as in *Example 1*, except that the agreement between the disqualified individual and the acquiring company is executed after the change in ownership or control, pursuant to a legally enforceable agreement entered into before the change. Payments to be made under the agreement may be treated as contingent on the change in ownership or control pursuant to Q/A-22 of this section. However, see Q/A-9 of this section regarding the exemption from the definition of parachute payment for certain amounts of reasonable compensation.

Example 3. Assume the same facts as in *Example 1*, except that prior to the change in ownership or control, the individual and corporation enter into an agreement under which the individual will receive parachute payments in the event of a change in ownership or control of the corporation. After the change, the individual agrees to give up the right to payments under the pre-change agreement that would be parachute payments if made, in exchange for compensation under a new agreement with the acquiring corporation. Because the individual gave up the right to parachute payments under the pre-change agreement in exchange for other payments under the post-change agreement, payments in an amount equal to the parachute payments under the pre-change agreement are treated as contingent on the change in ownership or control under this A-23. Because the post-change agreement was entered into after the change, payments in excess of this amount are not treated as parachute payments.

Q-24: If a payment is treated as contingent on a change in ownership or control, is the full amount of the payment so treated?

A-24: (a)(1) *General rule.* Yes. If the payment is a transfer of property, the amount of the payment is determined under Q/A-12 or Q/A-13 of this section. For all other payments, the amount of the payment is determined under Q/A-11 of this section. However, in certain circumstances, described in paragraphs (b) and (c) of this A-24, only a portion of the payment is treated as contingent on the

change. Paragraph (b) of this A-24 applies to a payment that is vested, without regard to the change in ownership or control, and is treated as contingent on the change in ownership or control because the change accelerates the time at which the payment is made. Paragraph (c) of this A-24 applies to a payment that becomes vested as a result of the change in ownership or control if, without regard to the change in ownership or control, the payment was contingent only on the continued performance of services for the corporation for a specified period of time and if the payment is attributable, at least in part, to services performed before the date the payment becomes vested. Paragraph (b) or (c) does not apply to any payment (or portion thereof) if the payment is treated as contingent on the change in ownership or control pursuant to Q/A-25 of this section. For purposes of this A-24, *vested* has the same meaning as provided in Q/A-22(a).

(2) *Reduction by reasonable compensation.* The amount of a payment under paragraph (a)(1) of this A-24 is reduced by any portion of such payment that the taxpayer establishes by clear and convincing evidence is reasonable compensation for personal services rendered by the disqualified individual on or after the date of the change of control. See Q/A-9 and Q/A-38 through 44 of this section for rules concerning reasonable compensation. The portion of an amount treated as contingent under paragraph (b) or (c) of this A-24 may not be reduced by reasonable compensation.

(b) *Vested payments.* This paragraph (b) applies if a payment is vested, without regard to the change in ownership or control, and is treated as contingent on the change in ownership or control because the change accelerates the time at which the payment is made. In such a case, the portion of the payment, if any, that is treated as contingent on the change in ownership or control is the amount by which the amount of the accelerated payment exceeds the present value of the payment absent the acceleration. If the value of such a payment absent the acceleration is not reasonably ascertainable, and the acceleration of the payment does not significantly increase the present value of the payment absent the acceleration, the present value of the payment absent the acceleration is treated as equal to the amount of the accelerated payment. If the value of the payment absent the acceleration is not reasonably ascertainable, but the acceleration significantly increases the present value of the payment, the future value of such payment is treated as equal to the amount of the accelerated payment. For rules on determining present value, see paragraph (e) of this A-24, Q/A-32, and Q/A-33 of this section.

(c)(1) *Nonvested payments.* This paragraph (c) applies to a payment that becomes vested as a result of the change in ownership or control to the extent that—

(i) Without regard to the change in ownership or control, the payment was contingent only on the continued performance of services for the corporation for a specified period of time; and

(ii) The payment is attributable, at least in part, to the performance of services before the date the payment is made or becomes certain to be made.

(2) The portion of the payment subject to paragraph (c) of this A-24 that is treated as contingent on the change in ownership or control is the amount described in paragraph (b) of this A-24, plus an amount, as determined in paragraph (c)(4) of this A-24, to reflect the lapse of the obligation to continue to perform services. In no event can the portion of the payment treated as contingent on the change in ownership or control under this paragraph (c) exceed the amount of the accelerated payment, or, if the payment is not accelerated, the present value of the payment.

(3) For purposes of this paragraph (c) of this A-24, the acceleration of the vesting of a stock option or the lapse of a restriction on restricted stock is considered to significantly increase the value of a payment.

(4) The amount reflecting the lapse of the obligation to continue to perform services (described in paragraph (c)(2) of this A-24) is 1 percent of the amount of the accelerated payment multiplied by the number of full months between the date that the individual's right to receive the payment is vested and the date that, absent the acceleration, the payment would have been vested. This paragraph (c)(4) applies to the accelerated vesting of a payment in the nature of compensation even if the time at which the payment is made is not accelerated. In such a case, the amount reflecting the lapse of the obligation to continue to perform services is 1 percent of the present value of the future payment multiplied by the number of full months between the date that the individual's right to receive the payment is vested and the date that, absent the acceleration, the payment would have been vested.

(d) *Application of this A-24 to certain payments.*—(1) *Benefits under a nonqualified deferred compensation plan.* In the case of a payment of benefits under a nonqualified deferred compensation plan, paragraph (b) of this A-24 applies to the extent benefits under the plan are vested without regard to the change in ownership or control. Paragraph (c) of this A-24 applies to the extent benefits under the plan become vested as a result of the change in ownership or control and are attributable, at least in part, to the performance of services prior to vesting. Any other payment of benefits under a nonqualified deferred compensation plan is a payment in the nature of compensation subject to the general rule of paragraph (a) of this A-24 and the rules in Q/A-11 of this section.

(2) *Employment agreements.* The general rule of paragraph (a) of this A-24 (and not the rules in paragraphs (b) or (c)) applies to the payment of amounts due under an employment agreement on a termination of employment or a change in ownership or control that otherwise would be attributable to the performance of services (or refraining from the performance of services) during any period that begins after the date of termination of employment or change in ownership or control, as applicable. For purposes of this paragraph (d)(2) of this A-24, an employment agreement means an agreement between an employee or independent contractor and employer or service recipient which describes, among other things, the amount of compensation or remuneration payable to the employee or independent contractor. See Q/A-42(b) and 44 of this section for the treatment of the remaining amounts of salary under an employment agreement.

(3) *Vesting due to an event other than services.* Neither paragraph (b) nor (c) of this A-24 applies to a payment if (without regard to the change in ownership or control) vesting of the payment depends on an event other than the performance of services, such as the attainment of a performance goal, and the event does not occur prior to the change in ownership or control. In such circumstances, the full amount of the accelerated payment is treated as contingent on the change in ownership or control under paragraph (a) of this A-24. However, see Q/A-39 of this section for rules relating to the reduction of the excess parachute payment by the portion of the payment which is established to be reasonable compensation for personal services actually rendered before the date of a change in ownership or control.

(e) *Present value.* For purposes of this A-24, the present value of a payment is determined as of the date on which the accelerated payment is made.

(f) *Examples.* The following examples illustrate the principles of this A-24:

Example 1. (i) Corporation maintains a qualified plan and a nonqualified supplemental retirement plan (SERP) for its executives. Benefits under the SERP are not paid to participants until retirement. E, a disqualified individual with respect to Corporation, has a vested account balance of $500,000 under the SERP. A change in ownership or control of Corporation occurs. The SERP provides that in the event of a change in ownership or control, all vested accounts will be paid to SERP participants.

(ii) Because E was vested in $500,000 of benefits under the SERP prior to the change in ownership or control and the change merely accelerated the time at which the payment was made to E, only a portion of the payment, as determined under paragraph (b) of this A-24, is treated as contingent on the change. Thus, the portion of the payment that is treated as contingent on the change is the amount by which the amount of the accelerated payment ($500,000) exceeds the present value of the payment absent the acceleration.

(iii) Assume the same facts as in paragraph (i) of this *Example 1,* except that E's account balance of $500,000 is not vested. Instead, assume that E will vest in E's account balance of $500,000 in 2 years if E continues to perform services for the next 2 years. Assume further that the SERP provides that all unvested SERP benefits vest immediately on a change in ownership or control and are paid to the participants. Because the vesting of the SERP payment, without regard to the change, depends only on the performance of services for a specified period of time and the payment is attributable, in part, to the performance of services before the change in ownership or control, only a portion of the $500,000 payment, as determined under paragraph (c) of this A-24, is treated as contingent on the change. The portion of the payment that is treated as contingent on the change is the lesser of the amount of the accelerated payment or the amount by which the accelerated payment exceeds the present value of the payment absent the acceleration, plus an amount to reflect the lapse of the obligation to continue to perform services.

(iv) Assume the same facts as in paragraph (i) of this *Example 1,* except that in addition to the pay out of the vested account balance of $500,000 on the change in ownership or control, an additional $70,000 will be credited to E's account and included in the payment to E. Because the $500,000 was vested without regard to the change in ownership or control, paragraph (b) of this A-24 applies to the $500,000 payment. Because the $70,000 is not vested, without regard *to the change, and is not attributable to the performance of services* prior to the change, the entire $70,000 payment is contingent on the change in ownership or control under paragraph (a) of this A-24.

(v) Assume the same facts as in paragraph (i) of this *Example 1,* except that the benefit under the SERP is calculated using a percent-

age of final average compensation multiplied by years of service. If, contingent on the change in ownership or control, E is credited with additional years of service, an adjustment to final average compensation, or an increase in the applicable percentage, any increase in the benefit payable under the SERP is not attributable to the performance of services prior to the change, and the entire increase in the benefit is contingent on the change in ownership or control under paragraph (a) of this A-24.

Example 2. As a result of a change in the effective control of a corporation D, a disqualified individual with respect to the corporation, receives accelerated payment of D's vested account balance in a nonqualified deferred compensation account plan. Actual interest and other earnings on the plan assets are credited to each account as earned before distribution. Investment of the plan assets is not restricted in such a manner as would prevent the earning of a market rate of return on the plan assets. The date on which D would have received D's vested account balance absent the change in ownership or control is uncertain, and the rate of earnings on the plan assets is not fixed. Thus, the amount of the payment absent the acceleration is not reasonably ascertainable. Under these facts, acceleration of the payment does not significantly increase the present value of the payment absent the acceleration, and the present value of the payment absent the acceleration is treated as equal to the amount of the accelerated payment. Accordingly, no portion of the payment is treated as contingent on the change.

Example 3. (i) On January 15, 2006, a corporation and a disqualified individual, F, enter into a contract providing for a retention bonus of $500,000 to be paid to F on January 15, 2011. The payment of the bonus will be forfeited by F if F does not remain employed by the corporation for the entire 5-year period. However, the contract provides that the full amount of the payment will be made immediately on a change in ownership or control of the corporation during the 5-year period. On January 15, 2009, a change in ownership or control of the corporation occurs and the full amount of the payment ($500,000) is made on that date to F. Under these facts, the payment of $500,000 was contingent only on F's performance of services for a specified period and is attributable, in part, to the performance of services before the change in ownership or control. Therefore, only a portion of the payment, as determined under paragraph (c) of this A-24 is treated as contingent on the change. The portion of the payment that is treated as contingent on the change is the amount by which the amount of the accelerated payment (i.e., $500,000, the amount paid to the individual because of the change in ownership) exceeds the present value of the payment that was expected to have been made absent the acceleration (i.e., $406,838, the present value on January 15, 2009, of a $500,000 payment on January 15, 2011), plus $115,000 (1 percent × 23 months × $500,000) which is the amount reflecting the lapse of the obligation to continue to perform services. Accordingly, the amount of the payment treated as contingent on the change in ownership or control is $208,162, the sum of $93,162 ($500,000 − $406,838) + $115,000). This result does not change if F actually remains employed until the end of the 5-year period.

(ii) Assume the same facts as in paragraph (i) of this *Example 3,* except that the retention bonus will vest on the change in ownership or control, but will not be paid until January 15, 2011 (the original date in the contract). Because the payment of $500,000 was contingent only on F's performance of services for a specified period and is attributable, in part, to the performance of services before the change in ownership or control, only a portion of the $500,000 payment is treated as contingent on the change in ownership or control as determined under paragraph (c) of this A-24. Because there is accelerated vesting of the bonus, the portion of the payment treated as contingent on the change is the amount described in paragraph (b) of this A-27, which is $0 under these facts, plus an amount reflecting the lapse of the obligation to continue to perform services which is $93,573 (1 percent × 23 months × $406,838 (the present value of a $500,000 payment).

Example 4. (i) On January 15, 2006, a corporation gives to a disqualified individual, in connection with her performance of services to the corporation, a bonus of 1,000 shares of the corporation's stock. Under the terms of the bonus arrangement, the individual is obligated to return the stock to the corporation if she terminates her employment for any reason prior to January 15, 2011. However, if there is a change in the ownership or effective control of the corporation prior to January 15, 2011, she ceases to be obligated to return the stock. The individual's rights in the stock are treated as substantially nonvested (within the meaning of §1.83-3(b) and (j)) during that period. On January 15, 2009, a change in the ownership of the corporation occurs. On that day, the fair market value of the stock is $500,000.

(ii) Under these facts, the payment was contingent only on performance of services for a specified period and is attributable, in part, to the performance of services before the change in ownership or control. Thus, only a portion of the payment, as determined under paragraph (c) of this A-24, is treated as contingent on the change in ownership or control. The portion of the payment that is treated as contingent on the change is the amount by which the present value of the accelerated payment on January 15, 2009 ($500,000), exceeds the present value of the payment that was expected to have been made on January 15, 2011, plus an amount reflecting the lapse of the obligation to continue to perform services. At the time of the change, it cannot be reasonably ascertained what the value of the stock would have been on January 15, 2011. The acceleration of the lapse of a restriction on stock is treated as significantly increasing the value of the payment. Therefore, the value of such stock on January 15, 2011, is deemed to be $500,000, the amount of the accelerated payment. The present value on January 15, 2009, of a $500,000 payment to be made on January 15, 2011, is $406,838. Thus, the portion of the payment treated as contingent on the change is $208,162, the sum of $93,162 ($500,000 – $406,838), plus $115,000 (1 percent × 23 months × $500,000), the amount reflecting the lapse of the obligation to continue to perform services.

Example 5. (i) On January 15, 2006, a corporation grants to a disqualified individual nonqualified stock options to purchase 30,000 shares of the corporation's stock. The options will be forfeited by the individual if he fails to perform personal services for the corporation until January 15, 2009. The options will, however, vest in the individual at an earlier date if there is a change in ownership or control of the corporation. On January 16, 2008, a change in the ownership or control of the corporation occurs and the options become vested in the individual. The value of the options on January 16, 2008, determined in accordance with Q/A-13, is $600,000.

(ii) The payment of the options to purchase 30,000 shares was contingent only on performance of services for the corporation until January 15, 2009, and is attributable, in part, to the performance of services before the change in ownership or control. Therefore, only a portion of the payment is treated as contingent on the change. The portion of the payment that is treated as contingent on the change is the amount by which the accelerated payment on January 16, 2008 ($600,000) exceeds the present value on January 16, 2008, of the payment that was expected to have been made on January 15, 2009, absent the acceleration, plus an amount reflecting the lapse of the obligation to continue to perform services. At the time of the change, it cannot be reasonably ascertained what the value of the options would have been on January 15, 2009. The acceleration of vesting in the options is treated as significantly increasing the value of the payment. Therefore, the value of such options on January 15, 2009, is deemed to be $600,000, the amount of the accelerated payment. The present value on January 16, 2008, of a $600,000 payment to be made on January 15, 2009, is $549,964. Thus, the portion of the payment treated as contingent on the change is $116,036, the sum of $50,036 ($600,000 – $549,964), plus an amount reflecting the lapse of the obligation to continue to perform services which is $66,000 (1 percent × 11 months × $600,000).

Example 6. (i) Assume the same facts as in *Example 5*, except that the options become vested periodically (absent a change in ownership or control), with one-third of the options vesting on January 15, 2007, 2008, and 2009, respectively. Thus, options to purchase 20,000 shares vest independently of the January 16, 2008, change in ownership or control and the options to purchase the remaining 10,000 shares vest as a result of the change in ownership or control.

(ii) The payment of the options to purchase 10,000 shares was contingent only on performance of services for the corporation until January 15, 2009, and is attributable, in part, to the performance of services before the change in ownership or control. Therefore, only a portion of the payment as determined under paragraph (c) of this A-24 is treated as contingent on the change in ownership or control. The portion of the payment that is treated as contingent on the change in ownership or control is the amount by which the accelerated payment on January 16, 2008 ($200,000) exceeds the present value on January 16, 2008, of the payment that was expected to have been made on January 15, 2009, absent the acceleration, plus an amount reflecting the lapse of the obligation to perform services. At the time of the change in ownership or control, it cannot be reasonably ascertained what the value of the options would have been on January 15, 2009. The acceleration of vesting in the options is treated as significantly increasing the value of the payment. Therefore, the value of such options on January 15, 2009, is deemed to be $200,000, the amount of the accelerated payment. The present value on January 16, 2008, of a $200,000 payment to be made on January 15, 2009, is $183,328.38. Thus, the portion of the payment treated as contingent on the change is $38,671.62, the sum of $16,671.62 ($200,000 – $183,328.38), plus an amount reflecting the lapse of the obligation to continue to perform services which is $22,000 (1 percent × 11 months × $200,000).

Example 7. Assume the same facts as in *Example 5*, except that the option agreement provides that the options will vest either on the corporation's level of profits reaching a specified level, or if earlier, on the date on which there is a change in ownership or control of the corporation. The corporation's level of profits do not reach the speci-

fied level prior to January 16, 2008. In such case, the full amount of the payment, $600,000, is treated as contingent on the change in ownership or control under paragraph (a) of this A-24. Because the payment was not contingent only on the performance of services for the corporation for a specified period, the rules of paragraph (b) and (c) of this A-24 do not apply. See Q/A-39 of this section for rules relating to the reduction of the excess parachute payment by the portion of the payment which is established to be reasonable compensation for personal services actually rendered before the date of a change in ownership or control.

Example 8. On January 1, 2005 E, a disqualified individual with respect to Corporation X, enters into an employment agreement with Corporation X under which E will be paid wages of $200,000 each year during the 5-year employment agreement. The employment agreement provides that if a change in ownership or control of Corporation X occurs, E will be paid the present value of the remaining salary under the employment agreement. On January 1, 2006, a change in ownership or control of Corporation X occurs, E is terminated, and E receives a payment of the present value of $200,000 for each of the 4 years remaining under the employment agreement. Because the payment represents future salary under an employment agreement (i.e., amounts otherwise attributable to the performance of services for periods that begin after the termination of employment), the general rule of paragraph (a) of this A-24 applies to the payment and not the rules of paragraphs (b) and (c) of this A-24. See Q/A-42(c) and 44 of this section for the treatment of the remaining payments under an employment agreement.

Presumption That Payment Is Contingent on Change

Q-25: Is there a presumption that certain payments are contingent on a change in ownership or control?

A-25: Yes, for purposes of this section, any payment is presumed to be contingent on such a change unless the contrary is established by clear and convincing evidence if the payment is made pursuant to—

(a) An agreement entered into within one year before the date of a change in ownership or control; or

(b) An amendment that modifies a previous agreement in any significant respect, if the amendment is made within one year before the date of a change in ownership or control. In the case of an amendment described in paragraph (b) of this A-25, only the portion of any payment that exceeds the amount of such payment that would have been made in the absence of the amendment is presumed, by reason of the amendment, to be contingent on the change in ownership or control.

Q-26: How may the presumption described in Q/A-25 of this section be rebutted?

A-26: (a) To rebut the presumption described in Q/A-25 of this section, the taxpayer must establish by clear and convincing evidence that the payment is not contingent on the change in ownership or control. Whether the payment is contingent on such change is determined on the basis of all the facts and circumstances of the particular case. Factors relevant to such a determination include, but are not limited to, the content of the agreement or amendment and the circumstances surrounding the execution of the agreement or amendment, such as whether it was entered into at a time when a takeover attempt had commenced and the degree of likelihood that a change in ownership or control would actually occur. However, even if the presumption is rebutted with respect to an agreement, some or all of the payments under the agreement may still be contingent on the change in ownership or control pursuant to Q/A-22 of this section.

(b) In the case of an agreement described in Q/A-25 of this section, clear and convincing evidence that the agreement is one of the three following types will generally rebut the presumption that payments under the agreement are contingent on the change in ownership or control—

(1) A *nondiscriminatory employee plan or program* as defined in paragraph (c) of this A-26;

(2) A contract between a corporation and an individual that replaces a prior contract entered into by the same parties more than one year before the change in ownership or control, if the new contract does not provide for increased payments (apart from normal increases attributable to increased responsibilities or cost of living adjustments), accelerate the payment of amounts due at a future time, or modify (to the individual's benefit) the terms or conditions under which payments will be made; or

(3) A contract between a corporation and an individual who did not perform services for the corporation prior to the one year period before the change in ownership or control occurs, if the contract does not provide for payments that are significantly different in amount, timing, terms, or conditions from those provided under contracts entered into by the corporation (other than contracts that themselves were entered into within one year before the change in ownership or control and in contemplation of the change) with individuals performing comparable services.

Reg. §1.280G-1

(c) For purposes of this section, the term *nondiscriminatory employee plan or program* means: a group term life insurance plan that meets the requirements of section 79(d); a self insured medical reimbursement plan that meets the requirements of section 105(h); a cafeteria plan (within the meaning of section 125); an educational assistance program (within the meaning of section 127); a dependent care assistance program (within the meaning of section 129); a no-additional-cost service (within the meaning of section 132(b)) or qualified employee discount (within the meaning of section 132(c)); a qualified retirement planning services program under section 132(m); an adoption assistance program (within the meaning of section 137); and such other items as provided by the Commissioner in published guidance of general applicability under § 601.601(d)(2). Payments under certain other plans are exempt from the definition of *parachute payment* under Q/A-8 of this section.

(d) The following examples illustrate the application of the presumption:

Example 1. A corporation and a disqualified individual who is an employee of the corporation enter into an employment contract. The contract replaces a prior contract entered into by the same parties more than one year before the change in ownership or control and the new contract does not provide for any increased payments other than a cost of living adjustment, does not accelerate the payment of amounts due at a future time, and does not modify (to the individual's benefit) the terms or conditions under which payments will be made. Clear and convincing evidence of these facts rebuts the presumption described in A-25 of this section. However, payments under the contract still may be contingent on the change in ownership or control pursuant to Q/A-22 of this section.

Example 2. Assume the same facts as in *Example 1*, except that the contract is entered into after a tender offer for the corporation's stock had commenced and it was likely that a change in ownership or control would occur and the contract provides for a substantial bonus payment to the individual upon his signing the contract. The individual has performed services for the corporation for many years, but previous employment contracts between the corporation and the individual did not provide for a similar signing bonus. One month after the contract is entered into, a change in the ownership or control of the corporation occurs. All payments under the contract are presumed to be contingent on the change in ownership or control even though the bonus payment would have been legally required even if no change had occurred. Clear and convincing evidence of these facts rebuts the presumption described in A-25 of this section with respect to all of the payments under the contract with the exception of the bonus payment (which is treated as contingent on the change). However, payments other than the bonus under the contract still may be contingent on the change in ownership or control pursuant to Q/A-22 of this section.

Example 3. A corporation and a disqualified individual, who is an employee of the corporation, enter into an employment contract within one year of a change in ownership or control of the corporation. Under the contract, in the event of a change in ownership or control and subsequent termination of employment, certain payments will be made to the individual. A change in ownership or control occurs, but the individual is not terminated until 2 years after the change in ownership or control. If clear and convincing evidence does not rebut the presumption described in A-25 of this section, because the payment is made pursuant to an agreement entered into within one year of the date of the change in ownership or control, the payment is presumed contingent on the change under A-25 of this section. This is true even though A's termination of employment is presumed not to be materially related to the change in ownership or control under Q/A-22 of this section.

Change in Ownership or Control

Q-27: When does a change in the ownership of a corporation occur?

A-27: (a) For purposes of this section, a change in the ownership of a corporation occurs on the date that any one person, or more than one person acting as a group (as defined in paragraph (b) of this A-27), acquires ownership of stock of the corporation that, together with stock held by such person or group, has more than 50 percent of the total fair market value or total voting power of the stock of such corporation. However, if any one person, or more than one person acting as a group, is considered to own more than 50 percent of the total fair market value or total voting power of the stock of a corporation, the acquisition of additional stock by the same person or persons is not considered to cause a change in the ownership of the corporation (or to cause a change in the effective control of the corporation (within the meaning of Q/A-28 of this section)). An increase in the percentage of stock owned by any one person, or persons acting as a group, as a result of a transaction in which the corporation acquires its stock in exchange for property will be treated as an acquisition of stock for purposes of this section. This A-27

applies only when there is a transfer of stock of a corporation (or issuance of stock of a corporation) and stock in such corporation remains outstanding after the transaction. (See Q/A-29 for rules regarding the transfer of assets of a corporation.)

(b) For purposes of paragraph (a) of this A-27, persons will not be considered to be acting as a group merely because they happen to purchase or own stock of the same corporation at the same time, or as a result of the same public offering. However, persons will be considered to be acting as a group if they are owners of a corporation that enters into a merger, consolidation, purchase or acquisition of stock, or similar business transaction with the corporation. If a person, including an entity shareholder, owns stock in both corporations that enter into a merger, consolidation, purchase or acquisition of stock, or similar transaction, such shareholder is considered to be acting as a group with other shareholders in a corporation only with respect to the ownership in that corporation prior to the transaction giving rise to the change and not with respect to the ownership interest in the other corporation.

(c) For purposes of this A-27 (and Q/A-28 and 29), section 318(a) applies to determine stock ownership. Stock underlying a vested option is considered owned by the individual who holds the vested option (and the stock underlying an unvested option is not considered owned by the individual who holds the unvested option). For purposes of the preceding sentence, however, if the option is exercisable for stock that is not substantially vested (as defined by sections 1.83-3(b) and (j)), the stock underlying the option is not treated as owned by the individual who holds the option. In addition, mutual and cooperative corporations are treated as having stock for purposes of this A-27.

(d) The following examples illustrate the principles of this A-27:

Example 1. Corporation M has owned stock with a fair market value equal to 19 percent of the value of the stock of Corporation N (an otherwise unrelated corporation) for many years prior to 2006. Corporation M acquires additional stock with a fair market value equal to 15 percent of the value of the stock of Corporation N on January 1, 2006, and an additional 18 percent on February 21, 2007. As of February 21, 2007, Corporation M has acquired stock with a fair market value greater than 50 percent of the value of the stock of Corporation N. Thus, a change in the ownership of Corporation N is considered to occur on February 21, 2007 (assuming that Corporation M did not have effective control of Corporation N immediately prior to the acquisition on that date).

Example 2. All of the corporation's stock is owned by the founders of the corporation. The board of directors of the corporation decides to offer shares of the corporation to the public. After the public offering, the founders of the corporation own a total of 40 percent of the corporation's stock, and members of the public own 60 percent. If no one person (or more than one person acting as a group) owns more than 50 percent of the corporation's stock (by value or voting power) after the public offering, there is no change in the ownership of the corporation.

Example 3. Corporation P merges into Corporation O (a previously unrelated corporation). In the merger, the shareholders of Corporation P receive Corporation O stock in exchange for their Corporation P stock. Immediately after the merger, the former shareholders of Corporation P own stock with a fair market value equal to 60 percent of the value of the stock of Corporation O, and the former shareholders of Corporation O own stock with a fair market value equal to 40 percent of the value of the stock of Corporation O. The former shareholders of Corporation P will be treated as acting as a group in their acquisition of Corporation O stock. Thus, a change in the ownership of Corporation O occurs on the date of the merger. See Q/A-29, *Example 3*, regarding whether there is a change in ownership or control of P.

Example 4. Assume the same facts as in *Example 3*, except that immediately after the change, the former shareholders of Corporation P own stock with a fair market value of 51 percent of the value of Corporation O stock and the former shareholders of Corporation O own stock with a fair market value equal to 49 percent of the value of Corporation O stock. Assume further that prior to the merger several Corporation O shareholders also owned Corporation P stock (overlapping shareholders). In the merger, those O shareholders received additional O stock by virtue of their ownership of P stock with a fair market value of 5 percent of the value of Corporation O stock. Including the O stock attributable to the P shares, the O shareholders hold 54 percent of O after the transaction. However, those overlapping shareholders that owned both Corporation O stock and Corporation P stock prior to the merger are treated as acting as a group with the Corporation O shareholders only with respect to their ownership interest in Corporation O prior to the transaction. Therefore, because the Corporation O shareholders owned 49 percent of the value of Corporation O stock, a change in the ownership of Corporation O occurs on the date of the merger. See Q/A-29, *Example 3*, regarding whether there is a change in ownership or control of P.

Example 5. A, an individual, owns stock with a fair market value equal to 20 percent of the value of the stock of Corporation Q. On January 1, 2007, Corporation Q acquires in a redemption for cash all of the stock held by shareholders other than A. Thus, A is left as the sole shareholder of Corporation O. A change in ownership of Corporation O is considered to occur on January 1, 2007 (assuming that A did not have effective control of Corporation Q immediately prior to the redemption).

Example 6. Assume the same facts as in *Example 5*, except that A owns stock with a fair market value equal to 51 percent of the value of all the stock of Corporation Q immediately prior to the redemption. There is no change in the ownership of Corporation Q as a result of the redemption.

Q-28: When does a change in the effective control of a corporation occur?

A-28: (a) Notwithstanding that a corporation has not undergone a change in ownership under Q/A-27, for purposes of this section, a change in the effective control of a corporation is presumed to occur on the date that either—

(1) Any one person, or more than one person acting as a group (as determined under paragraph (e) of this A-28), acquires (or has acquired during the 12-month period ending on the date of the most recent acquisition by such person or persons) ownership of stock of the corporation possessing 20 percent or more of the total voting power of the stock of such corporation; or

(2) A majority of members of the corporation's board of directors is replaced during any 12-month period by directors whose appointment or election is not endorsed by a majority of the members of the corporation's board of directors prior to the date of the appointment or election.

(b) The presumption of paragraph (a) of this A-28 may be rebutted by establishing that such acquisition or acquisitions of the corporation's stock, or such replacement of the majority of the members of the corporation's board of directors, does not transfer the power to control (directly or indirectly) the management and policies of the corporation from any one person (or more than one person acting as a group) to another person (or group). For purposes of this section, in the absence of an event described in paragraph (a) (1) or (2) of this A-28, a change in the effective control of a corporation is presumed not to have occurred.

(c) In no event does a change in effective control under this A-28 occur in any transaction in which either of the two corporations involved in the transaction has a change in ownership or control under Q/A-27 or 29 of this section. Thus, for example, assume Corporation P transfers more than one-third of the total gross fair market value of its assets to Corporation O in exchange for 20 percent of O's stock. Because P has undergone a change in ownership of a substantial portion of its assets under Q/A-29 of this section, O does not have a change in effective control under Q/A-28.

(d) If any one person, or more than one person acting as a group, is considered to effectively control a corporation (within the meaning of this A-28), the acquisition of additional control of the corporation by the same person or persons is not considered to cause a change in the effective control of the corporation (or to cause a change in the ownership of the corporation within the meaning of Q/A-27 of this section).

(e) For purposes of this A-28, persons will not be considered to be acting as a group merely because they happen to purchase or own stock of the same corporation at the same time, or as a result of the same public offering. However, persons will be considered to be acting as a group if they are owners of a corporation that enters into a merger, consolidation, purchase or acquisition of stock, or similar business transaction with the corporation. If a person, including an entity shareholder, owns stock in both corporations that enter into a merger, consolidation, purchase or acquisition of stock, or similar transaction, such shareholder is considered to be acting as a group with other shareholders in a corporation only with respect to the ownership in that corporation prior to the transaction giving rise to the change and not with respect to the ownership interest in the other corporation.

(f) For purposes of determining stock ownership, see Q/A-27(c).

(g) The following examples illustrate the principles of this A-28:

Example 1. Shareholder A acquired the following percentages of the voting stock of Corporation M (an otherwise unrelated corporation) on the following dates: 16 percent on January 1, 2005; 10 percent on January 10, 2006; 8 percent on February 10, 2006; 11 percent on March 1, 2007; and 8 percent on March 10, 2007. Thus, on March 10, 2007, A owns a total of 53 percent of M's voting stock. Because A did not acquire 20 percent or more of M's voting stock during any 12-month period, there is no presumption of a change in effective control pursuant to paragraph (a)(1) of this A-28. In addition, under these facts there is a presumption that no change in the effective control of Corporation M occurred. If this presumption is not rebutted (and thus no change in effective control of Corporation M is treated as

occurring prior to March 10, 2007), a change in the ownership of Corporation M is treated as having occurred on March 10, 2007 (pursuant to Q/A-27 of this section) because A had acquired more than 50 percent of Corporation M's voting stock as of that date.

Example 2. A minority group of shareholders of a corporation opposes the practices and policies of the corporation's current board of directors. A proxy contest ensues. The minority group presents its own slate of candidates for the board at the next annual meeting of the corporation's shareholders, and candidates of the minority group are elected to replace a majority of the current members of the board. A change in the effective control of the corporation is presumed to have occurred on the date the election of the new board of directors becomes effective.

Q-29: When does a change in the ownership of a substantial portion of a corporation's assets occur?

A-29: (a) For purposes of this section, a change in the ownership of a substantial portion of a corporation's assets occurs on the date that any one person, or more than one person acting as a group (as determined in paragraph (c) of this A-29), acquires (or has acquired during the 12-month period ending on the date of the most recent acquisition by such person or persons) assets from the corporation that have a total gross fair market value equal to or more than one-third of the total gross fair market value of all of the assets of the corporation immediately prior to such acquisition or acquisitions. For this purpose, *gross fair market value* means the value of the assets of the corporation, or the value of the assets being disposed of, determined without regard to any liabilities associated with such assets. This A-29 applies in any situation other than one involving the transfer of stock (or issuance of stock) in a parent corporation and stock in such corporation remains outstanding after the transaction. Thus, this A-29 applies to the sale of stock in a subsidiary (when that subsidiary is treated as a single corporation with the parent pursuant to Q/A-46) and to mergers involving the creation of a new corporation or with respect to the corporation that is not surviving entity.

(b)(1) There is no change in ownership or control under this A-29 when there is a transfer to an entity that is controlled by the shareholders of the transferring corporation immediately after the transfer, as provided in this paragraph (b). A transfer of assets by a corporation is not treated as a change in the ownership of such assets if the assets are transferred to—

(i) A shareholder of the corporation (immediately before the asset transfer) in exchange for or with respect to its stock;

(ii) An entity, 50 percent or more of the total value or voting power of which is owned, directly or indirectly, by the corporation;

(iii) A person, or more than one person acting as a group, that owns, directly or indirectly, 50 percent or more of the total value or voting power of all the outstanding stock of the corporation; or

(iv) An entity, at least 50 percent of the total value or voting power is owned, directly or indirectly, by a person described in paragraph (b)(1)(iii) of this A-29.

(2) For purposes of paragraph (b) and except as otherwise provided, a person's status is determined immediately after the transfer of the assets. For example, a transfer to a corporation in which the transferor corporation has no ownership interest before the transaction, but which is a majority-owned subsidiary of the transferor corporation after the transaction is not treated as a change in the ownership of the assets of the transferor corporation.

(c) For purposes of this A-29, persons will not be considered to be acting as a group merely because they happen to purchase assets of the same corporation at the same time, or as a result of the same public offering. However, persons will be considered to be acting as a group if they are owners of a corporation that enters into a merger, consolidation, purchase or acquisition of assets, or similar business transaction with the corporation. If a person, including an entity shareholder, owns stock in both corporations that enter into a merger, consolidation, purchase or acquisition of stock, or similar transaction, such shareholder is considered to be acting as a group with other shareholders in a corporation only to the extent of the ownership in that corporation prior to the transaction giving rise to the change and not with respect to the ownership interest in the other corporation.

(d) For purposes of determining stock ownership, see Q/A-27(c).

(e) The following examples illustrate the principles of this A-29:

Example 1. Corporation M acquires assets having a gross fair market value of $500,000 from Corporation N (an unrelated corporation) on January 1, 2006. The total gross fair market value of Corporation N's assets immediately prior to the acquisition was $3 million. Since the value of the assets acquired by Corporation M is less than one-third of the total gross fair market value of Corporation N's total assets immediately prior to the acquisition, the acquisition does not represent a change in the ownership of a substantial portion of Corporation N's assets.

Example 2. Assume the same facts as in *Example 1*. Also assume that on November 1, 2006, Corporation M acquires from Corporation N additional assets having a fair market value of $700,000. Thus, Corporation M has acquired from Corporation N assets worth a total of $1.2 million during the 12-month period ending on November 1, 2006. Since $1.2 million is more than one-third of the total gross fair market value of all of Corporation N's assets immediately prior to the earlier of these acquisitions ($3 million), a change in the ownership of a substantial portion of Corporation N's assets is considered to have occurred on November 1, 2006.

Example 3. (i) All of the assets of Corporation P are transferred to Corporation O (an unrelated corporation). In exchange, the shareholders of Corporation P receive Corporation O stock. Immediately after the transfer, the former shareholders of Corporation P own 60 percent of the fair market value of the outstanding stock of Corporation O and the former shareholders of Corporation O own 40 percent of the fair market value of the outstanding stock of Corporation O. Because Corporation O is an entity more than 50 percent of the fair market value of the outstanding stock of which is owned by the former shareholders of Corporation P (based on ownership of Corporation P prior the change), the transfer of assets is not treated as a change in ownership of a substantial portion of the assets of Corporation P. However, a change in the ownership (within the meaning of Q/A-27) of Corporation O occurs.

(ii) The result in paragraph (i) would be the same if immediately after the change, the former shareholders of Corporation P own stock with a fair market value of 51 percent of the value of Corporation O stock because Corporation O is an entity more than 50 percent of the fair market value of the outstanding stock of which is owned by the former shareholders of Corporation P. See Q/A-27, *Example 4*, regarding whether there is a change in ownership or control of O.

Example 4. Corporation P sells all of the stock of its wholly-owned subsidiary, S, to Corporation Y. The fair market value of the affiliated group, determined without regard to its liabilities, is $210 million. The fair market value of S, determined without regard to its liabilities, is $80 million. Because there is a change in more than one-third of the gross fair market value of the total assets of the affiliated group, there is a change in the ownership of a substantial portion of the assets of the affiliated group.

Three-Times-Base-Amount Test for Parachute Payments

Q-30: Are all payments that are in the nature of compensation, are made to a disqualified individual, and are contingent on a change in ownership or control, parachute payments?

A-30: (a) No. To determine whether such payments are parachute payments, they must be tested against the individual's *base amount* (as defined in Q/A-34 of this section). To do this, the aggregate present value of all payments in the nature of compensation that are made or to be made to (or for the benefit of) the same disqualified individual and are contingent on the change in ownership or control must be determined. If this aggregate present value equals or exceeds the amount equal to 3 times the individual's base amount, the payments are parachute payments. If this aggregate present value is less than the amount equal to 3 times the individual's base amount, no portion of the payment is a parachute payment. See Q/A-31, Q/A-32, and Q/A-33 of this section for rules on determining present value. Parachute payments that are securities violation parachute payments are not included in the foregoing computation if they are not contingent on a change in ownership or control. See Q/A-37 of this section for the definition and treatment of securities violation parachute payments.

(b) The following examples illustrate the principles of this A-30:

Example 1. A is a disqualified individual with respect to Corporation M. A's base amount is $100,000. Payments in the nature of compensation that are contingent on a change in the ownership or control of Corporation M totaling $400,000 are made to A on the date of the change in ownership or control. The payments are parachute payments because they have an aggregate present value at least equal to 3 times A's base amount of $100,000 (3 × $100,000 = $300,000).

Example 2. Assume the same facts as in *Example 1*, except that the payments contingent on the change in the ownership or control of Corporation M total $290,000. Because the payments do not have an aggregate present value at least equal to 3 times A's base amount, no portion of the payments is a parachute payment.

Q-31: As of what date is the present value of a payment determined?

A-31: (a) Except as provided in this section, the present value of a payment is determined as of the date on which the change in ownership or control occurs, or, if a payment is made prior to such date, the date on which the payment is made.

(b)(1) For purposes of determining whether a payment is a parachute payment, if a payment in the nature of compensation is the right to receive payments in a year (or years) subsequent to the year of the change in ownership or control, the value of the payment is the present value of such payment (or payments) calculated in accor-

dance with Q/A-32 of this section and based on reasonable actuarial assumptions.

(2) If the payment in the nature of compensation is an obligation to provide health care, then for purposes of this A-31 and for applying the 3-times-base-amount test under Q/A-30 of this section, the present value of such obligation should be calculated in accordance with generally accepted accounting principles. For purposes of Q/A-30 and this A-31, the obligation to provide health care is permitted to be measured by projecting the cost of premiums for purchased health care insurance, even if no health care insurance is actually purchased. If the obligation to provide health care is made in coordination with a health care plan that the corporation makes available to a group, then the premiums used for this purpose may be group premiums.

Q-32: What discount rate is to be used to determine present value?

A-32: For purposes of this section, present value generally is determined by using a discount rate equal to 120 percent of the applicable Federal rate (determined under section 1274(d) and the regulations thereunder) compounded semiannually. The applicable Federal rate to be used for this purpose is the Federal rate that is in effect on the date as of which the present value is determined, using the period until the payment would have been made without regard to the change in ownership or control as the term of the debt instrument under section 1274(d). See Q/A-24 and 31 of this section. However, for any payment, the corporation and the disqualified individual may elect to use the applicable Federal rate that is in effect on the date that the contract which provides for the payment is entered into, if such election is made in the contract.

Q-33: If the present value of a payment to be made in the future is contingent on an uncertain future event or condition, how is the present value of the payment determined?

A-33: (a) In certain cases, it may be necessary to apply the 3-times-base-amount test of Q/A-30 of this section, or to allocate a portion of the base amount to a payment described in paragraphs (a)(1), (2), and (3) of Q/A-2 of this section, at a time when the aggregate present value of all such payments cannot be determined with certainty because the time, amount, or right to receive one or more such payments is contingent on the occurrence of an uncertain future event or condition. For example, a disqualified individual's right to receive a payment may be contingent on the involuntary termination of such individual's employment with the corporation. In such a case, it must be reasonably estimated whether the payment will be made. If it is reasonably estimated that there is a 50-percent or greater probability that the payment will be made, the full amount of the payment is considered for purposes of the 3-times-base-amount test and the allocation of the base amount. Conversely, if it is reasonably estimated that there is a less than 50-percent probability that the payment will be made, the payment is not considered for either purpose.

(b) If the estimate made under paragraph (a) of this A-33 is later determined to be incorrect, the 3-times-base-amount test described in Q/A-30 of this section must be reapplied (and the portion of the base amount allocated to previous payments must be reallocated (if necessary) to such payments) to reflect the actual time and amount of the payment. Whenever the 3-times-base-amount test is applied (or whenever the base amount is allocated), the aggregate present value of the payments received or to be received by the disqualified individual is redetermined as of the date described in A-31 of this section, using the discount rate described in A-32 of this section. This redetermination may affect the amount of any excess parachute payment for a prior taxable year. Alternatively, if, based on the application of the 3-times-base-amount test without regard to the payment described in paragraph (a) of this A-33, a disqualified individual is determined to have an excess parachute payment or payments, then the 3- times-base-amount test does not have to be reapplied when a payment described in paragraph (a) of this A-33 is made (or becomes certain to be made) if no base amount is allocated to such payment.

(c) To the extent provided in published guidance of general applicability under §601.601(d)(2) of this Chapter, an initial estimate of the value of an option subject to Q/A-13 of this section is permitted be made, with the valuation subsequently re-determined, and the three-times-base-amount test reapplied.

(d) The following examples illustrate the principles of this A-33:

Example 1. A, a disqualified individual with respect to Corporation M, has a base amount of $100,000. Under A's employment agreement with Corporation M, A is entitled to receive a payment in the nature of compensation in the amount of $250,000 contingent on a change in ownership or control of Corporation M. In addition, the agreement provides that if A's employment is terminated within 1 year after the change in ownership or control, A will receive an additional payment in the nature of compensation in the amount of $150,000, payable 1 year after the date of the change in ownership or control. A change in ownership or control of Corporation M occurs and A receives the first payment of $250,000. Corporation M reasonably estimates that there is a 50-percent probability that, as a result of the change, A's employment will be terminated within 1 year of the date of the change. For purposes of applying the 3- times-base-amount test (and if the first payment is determined to be a parachute payment, for purposes of allocating a portion of A's base amount to that payment), because M reasonably estimates that there is a 50-percent or greater probability that, as a result of the change, A's employment will be terminated within 1 year of the date of the change, Corporation M must assume that the $150,000 payment will be made to A as a result of the change in ownership or control. The present value of the additional payment is determined under Q/A-31 and Q/A-32 of this section.

Example 2. Assume the same facts as in *Example 1,* except that Corporation M reasonably estimates that there is a less than 50-percent probability that, as a result of the change, A's employment will be terminated within 1 year of the date of the change. For purposes of applying the 3-times-base-amount test, because Corporation M reasonably estimates that there is a less than 50-percent probability that, as a result of the change, A's employment will be terminated within 1 year of the date of the change, Corporation M must assume that the $150,000 payment will not be made to A as a result of the change in ownership or control.

Example 3. B, a disqualified individual with respect to Corporation P, has a base amount of $200,000. Under B's employment agreement with Corporation P, if there is a change in ownership or control of Corporation P, B will receive a severance payment of $600,000 and a bonus payment of $400,000. In addition, the agreement provides that if B's employment is terminated within 1 year after the change, B will receive an additional payment in the nature of compensation of $500,000. A change in ownership or control of Corporation P occurs, and B receives the $600,000 and $400,000 payments. At the time of the change in ownership or control, Corporation P reasonably estimates that there is a less than 50-percent probability that B's employment will be terminated within 1 year of the change. For purposes of applying the 3-times-base-amount test, because Corporation P reasonably estimates that there is a less than 50-percent probability that B's employment will be terminated within 1 year of the date of the change, Corporation P assumes that the $500,000 payment will not be made to B. Eleven months after the change in ownership or control, B's employment is terminated, and the $500,000 payment is made to B. Because B was determined to have excess parachute payments without regard to the $500,000 payment, the 3-times-base-amount test is not reapplied and the base amount is not reallocated to include the $500,000 payment. The entire $500,000 payment is treated as an excess parachute payment.

Q-34: What is the base amount?

A-34: (a) The base amount of a disqualified individual is the average annual compensation for services performed for the corporation with respect to which the change in ownership or control occurs (or for a predecessor entity or a related entity as defined in Q/A-21 of this section) which was includible in the gross income of such individual for taxable years in the base period (including amounts that were excluded under section 911), or which would have been includible in such gross income if such person had been a United States citizen or resident. See Q/A-35 of this section for the definition of base period and for examples of base amount computations.

(b) If the base period of a disqualified individual includes a short taxable year or less than all of a taxable year, compensation for such short or incomplete taxable year must be annualized before determining the average annual compensation for the base period. In annualizing compensation, the frequency with which payments are expected to be made over an annual period must be taken into account. Thus, any amount of compensation for such a short or incomplete taxable year that represents a payment that will not be made more often than once per year is not annualized.

(c) Because the base amount includes only compensation that is includible in gross income, the base amount does not include certain items that constitute parachute payments. For example, payments in the form of excludible fringe benefits are not included in the base amount but may be treated as parachute payments.

(d) The base amount includes the amount of compensation included in income under section 83(b) during the base period. See Q/A-35 for the definition of *base period.*

(e) The following example illustrates the principles of this A-34:

Example. A disqualified individual, D, receives an annual salary of $500,000 per year during the 5-year base period. D defers $100,000 of D's salary each year under the corporation's nonqualified deferred compensation plan. D's base amount is $400,000 ($400,000 × (5/5)).

Q-35: What is the base period?

A-35: (a) The base period of a disqualified individual is the most recent 5 taxable years of the individual ending before the date of the change in ownership or control. For this purpose, the date of the change in ownership or control is the date the corporation exper-

iences one of the events described in Q/A-27, Q/A-28, or Q/A-29 of this section. However, if the disqualified individual was not an employee or independent contractor of the corporation with respect to which the change in ownership or control occurs (or a predecessor entity or a related entity as defined in Q/A-21 of this section) for this entire 5-year period, the individual's base period is the portion of such 5-year period during which the individual performed personal services for the corporation or predecessor entity or related entity.

(b) The following examples illustrate the principles of Q/A-34 of this section and this Q/A-35:

Example 1. A disqualified individual, D, was employed by a corporation for 2 years and 4 months preceding the taxable year in which a change in ownership or control of the corporation occurs. D's includible compensation income from the corporation was $30,000 for the 4-month period, $120,000 for the first full year, and $150,000 for the second full year. D's base amount is $120,000, ((3 × $30,000) + $120,000 + $150,000)/3.

Example 2. Assume the same facts as in *Example 1,* except that D also received a $60,000 signing bonus when D's employment with the corporation commenced at the beginning of the 4-month period. D's base amount is $140,000, (($60,000 + (3 × $30,000)) + $120,000 + $150,000)/3. Since the bonus will not be paid more often than once per year, the amount of the bonus is not increased in annualizing D's compensation for the 4-month period.

Example 3. E is a disqualified individual with respect to Corporation X who was not an employee or independent contractor for the full 5-year base period. In 2004 and 2005, E is a director of X and receives $30,000 per year for E's services. In 2006, E becomes an officer of X. E's includible compensation from Corporation X is $250,000 for 2006 and 2007, and $300,000 for 2008. In 2008, X undergoes a change in ownership or control. E's base amount is $140,000 ((2 × $250,000) + (2 × $30,000)/4).

Q-36: How is the base amount determined in the case of a disqualified individual who did not perform services for the corporation (or a predecessor entity or a related entity as defined in Q/A-21 of this section), prior to the individual's taxable year in which the change in ownership or control occurs?

A-36: (a) In such a case, the individual's base amount is the annualized compensation for services performed for the corporation (or a predecessor entity or related entity) which—

(1) Was includible in the individual's gross income for that portion, prior to such change, of the individual's taxable year in which the change occurred (including amounts that were excluded under section 911), or would have been includible in such gross income if such person had been a United States citizen or resident;

(2) Was not contingent on the change in ownership or control; and

(3) Was not a securities violation parachute payment.

(b) The following examples illustrate the principles of this A-36:

Example 1. On January 1, 2006, A, an individual whose taxable year is the calendar year, enters into a 4-year employment contract with Corporation M as an officer of the corporation. A has not previously performed services for Corporation M (or any predecessor entity or related entity as defined in Q/A-21 of this section). Under the employment contract, A is to receive an annual salary of $120,000 for each of the 4 years that he remains employed by Corporation M with any remaining unpaid balance to be paid immediately in the event that A's employment is terminated without cause. On July 1, 2006, after A has received compensation of $60,000, a change in the ownership or control of Corporation M occurs. Because of the change, A's employment is terminated without cause, and he receives a payment of $420,000. It is established by clear and convincing evidence that the $60,000 in compensation is not contingent on the change in ownership or control, but the presumption that the $420,000 payment is contingent on the change is not rebutted. Thus, the payment of $420,000 is treated as contingent on the change in ownership or control of Corporation M. In this case, A's base amount is $120,000 (2 × $60,000). Since the present value of the payment which is contingent on the change in ownership of Corporation M ($420,000) is more than 3 times A's base amount of $120,000 (3 × $120,000 = $360,000), the payment is a parachute payment.

Example 2. Assume the same facts as in *Example 1,* except that A also receives a signing bonus of $50,000 from Corporation M on January 1, 2006. It is established by clear and convincing evidence that the bonus is not contingent on the change in ownership or control. When the change in ownership or control occurs on July 1, 2006, A has received compensation of $110,000 (the $50,000 bonus plus $60,000 in salary). In this case, A's base amount is $170,000 ($50,000 + (2 × $60,000)). Because the $50,000 bonus will not be paid more than once per year, the amount of the bonus is not increased in annualizing A's compensation. The present value of the potential parachute payment ($420,000) is less than 3 times A's base amount of $170,000 (3 × $170,000 = $510,000), and therefore no portion of the payment is a parachute payment.

Securities Violation Parachute Payments

Q-37: Must a payment be contingent on a change in ownership or control in order to be a parachute payment?

A-37: (a) No, the term *parachute payment* also includes any payment (other than a payment exempted under Q/A-6 or Q/A-8 of this section) that is in the nature of compensation and is to (or for the benefit of) a disqualified individual, if such payment is a securities violation payment. A securities violation payment is a payment made or to be made—

(1) Pursuant to an agreement that violates any generally enforced Federal or state securities laws or regulations; and

(2) In connection with a potential or actual change in ownership or control.

(b) A violation is not taken into account under paragraph (a)(1) of this A-37 if it is merely technical in character or is not materially prejudicial to shareholders or potential shareholders. Moreover, a violation will be presumed not to exist unless the existence of the violation has been determined or admitted in a civil or criminal action (or an administrative action by a regulatory body charged with enforcing the particular securities law or regulation) which has been resolved by adjudication or consent. Parachute payments described in this A-37 are referred to in this section as securities violation payments.

(c) Securities violation parachute payments that are not contingent on a change in ownership or control within the meaning of Q/A-22 of this section are not taken into account in applying the 3-times-base-amount test of Q/A-30 of this section. Such payments are considered parachute payments regardless of whether such test is met with respect to the disqualified individual (and are included in allocating base amount under Q/A-38 of this section). Moreover, the amount of a securities violation parachute payment treated as an excess parachute payment shall not be reduced by the portion of such payment that is reasonable compensation for personal services actually rendered before the date of a change in ownership or control if such payment is not contingent on such change. Likewise, the amount of a securities violation parachute payment includes the portion of such payment that is reasonable compensation for personal services to be rendered on or after the date of a change in ownership or control if such payment is not contingent on such change.

(d) The rules in paragraph (b) of this A-37 also apply to securities violation parachute payments that are contingent on a change in ownership or control if the application of these rules results in greater total excess parachute payments with respect to the disqualified individual than would result if the payments were treated simply as payments contingent on a change in ownership or control (and hence were taken into account in applying the 3-times-base-amount test and were reduced by, or did not include, any applicable amount of reasonable compensation).

(e) The following examples illustrate the principles of this A-37:

Example 1. A, a disqualified individual with respect to Corporation M, receives two payments in the nature of compensation that are contingent on a change in the ownership or control of Corporation M. The present value of the first payment is equal to A's base amount and is not a securities violation parachute payment. The present value of the second payment is equal to 1.5 times A's base amount and is a securities violation parachute payment. Neither payment includes any reasonable compensation. If the second payment is treated simply as a payment contingent on a change in ownership or control, the amount of A's total excess parachute payments is zero because the aggregate present value of the payments does not equal or exceed 3 times A's base amount. If the second payment is treated as a securities violation parachute payment subject to the rules of paragraph (b) of this A-37, the amount of A's total excess parachute payments is 0.5 times A's base amount. Thus, the second payment is treated as a securities violation parachute payment.

Example 2. Assume the same facts as in *Example 1*, except that the present value of the first payment is equal to 2 times A's base amount. If the second payment is treated simply as a payment contingent on a change in ownership or control, the total present value of the payments is 3.5 times A's base amount, and the amount of A's total excess parachute payments is 2.5 times A's base amount. If the second payment is treated as a securities violation parachute payment, the amount of A's total excess parachute payments is 0.5 times A's base amount. Thus, the second payment is treated simply as a payment contingent on a change in ownership or control.

Example 3. B, a disqualified individual with respect to Corporation N, receives two payments in the nature of compensation that are contingent on a change in the control of Corporation N. The present value of the first payment is equal to 4 times B's base amount and is a securities violation parachute payment. The present value of the second payment is equal to 2 times B's base amount and is not a securities violation parachute payment. B establishes by clear and convincing evidence that the entire amount of the first payment is reasonable compensation for personal services to be rendered after the change in ownership or control. If the first payment is treated simply as a payment contingent on a change in ownership or control, it is exempt from the definition of *parachute payment* pursuant to Q/A-9 of this section. Thus, the amount of B's total excess parachute payment is zero because the present value of the second payment does not equal or exceed three times B's base amount. However, if the first payment is treated as a securities violation parachute payment, the amount of B's total excess parachute payments is 3 times B's base amount. Thus, the first payment is treated as a securities violation parachute payment.

Example 4. Assume the same facts as in *Example 3*, except that B does not receive the second payment and B establishes by clear and convincing evidence that the first payment is reasonable compensation for services actually rendered before the change in the control of Corporation N. If the payment is treated simply as a payment contingent on a change in ownership or control, the amount of B's excess parachute payment is zero because the amount treated as an excess parachute payment is reduced by the amount that B establishes as reasonable compensation. However, if the payment is treated as a securities violation parachute payment, the amount of B's excess parachute payment is 3 times B's base amount. Thus, the payment is treated as a securities violation parachute payment.

Computation and Reduction of Excess Parachute Payments

Q-38: How is the amount of an excess parachute payment computed?

A-38: (a) The amount of an excess parachute payment is the excess of the amount of any parachute payment over the portion of the disqualified individual's base amount that is allocated to such payment. For this purpose, the portion of the base amount allocated to any parachute payment is the amount that bears the same ratio to the base amount as the present value of such parachute payment bears to the aggregate present value of all parachute payments made or to be made to (or for the benefit of) the same disqualified individual. Thus, the portion of the base amount allocated to any parachute payment is determined by multiplying the base amount by a fraction, the numerator of which is the present value of such parachute payment and the denominator of which is the aggregate present value of all such payments. See Q/A-31, Q/A-32, and Q/A-33 of this section for rules on determining present value and Q/A-34 of this section for the definition of *base amount*.

(b) The following example illustrates the principles of this A-38:

Example. An individual with a base amount of $100,000 is entitled to receive two parachute payments, one of $200,000 and the other of $400,000. The $200,000 payment is made at the time of the change in ownership or control, and the $400,000 payment is to be made at a future date. The present value of the $400,000 payment is $300,000 on the date of the change in ownership or control. The portions of the base amount allocated to these payments are $40,000 (($200,000/$500,000) × $100,000) and $60,000 (($300,000/$500,000) × $100,000), respectively. Thus, the amount of the first excess parachute payment is $160,000 ($200,000 − $40,000) and that of the second is $340,000 ($400,000 − $60,000).

Q-39: May the amount of an excess parachute payment be reduced by reasonable compensation for personal services actually rendered before the change in ownership or control?

A-39: (a) Generally, yes. Except in the case of payments treated as securities violation parachute payments or when the portion of a payment that is treated as contingent on the change in ownership or control is determined under paragraph (b) or (c) of Q/A-24 of this section, the amount of an excess parachute payment is reduced by any portion of the payment that the taxpayer establishes by clear and convincing evidence is reasonable compensation for personal services actually rendered by the disqualified individual before the date of the change in ownership or control. Services reasonably compensated for by payments that are not parachute payments (for example, because the payments are not contingent on a change in ownership or control and are not securities violation parachute payments, or because the payments are exempt from the definition of parachute payment under Q/A-6 through Q/A-9 of this section) are not taken into account for this purpose. The portion of any parachute payment that is established as reasonable compensation is first reduced by the portion of the disqualified individual's base amount that is allocated to such parachute payment; any remaining portion of the parachute payment established as reasonable compensation then reduces the excess parachute payment.

(b) The following examples illustrate the principles of this A-39:

Example 1. Assume that a parachute payment of $600,000 is made to a disqualified individual, and the portion of the individual's base amount that is allocated to the parachute payment is $100,000. Also assume that $300,000 of the $600,000 parachute payment is established as reasonable compensation for personal services actually rendered by the disqualified individual before the date of the change in ownership or control. Before the reasonable compensation is taken into account, the amount of the excess parachute payment is $500,000 ($600,000 – $100,000). In reducing the excess parachute payment by reasonable compensation, the portion of the parachute payment that is established as reasonable compensation ($300,000) is first reduced by the portion of the disqualified individual's base amount that is allocated to the parachute payment ($100,000), and the remainder ($200,000) then reduces the excess parachute payment. Thus, in this case, the excess parachute payment of $500,000 is reduced by $200,000 of reasonable compensation.

Example 2. Assume the same facts as in *Example 1*, except that the full amount of the $600,000 parachute payment is established as reasonable compensation. In this case, the excess parachute payment of $500,000 is reduced to zero by $500,000 of reasonable compensation. As a result, no portion of any deduction for the payment is disallowed by section 280G, and no portion of the payment is subject to the 20-percent excise tax of section 4999.

Determination of Reasonable Compensation

Q-40: How is it determined whether payments are reasonable compensation?

A-40: (a) In general, whether payments are reasonable compensation for personal services actually rendered, or to be rendered, by the disqualified individual is determined on the basis of all the facts and circumstances of the particular case. Factors relevant to such a determination include, but are not limited to, the following—

(1) The nature of the services rendered or to be rendered;

(2) The individual's historic compensation for performing such services; and

(3) The compensation of individuals performing comparable services in situations where the compensation is not contingent on a change in ownership or control.

(b) For purposes of section 280G, reasonable compensation for personal services includes reasonable compensation for holding oneself out as available to perform services and refraining from performing services (such as under a covenant not to compete).

Q-41: Is any particular type of evidence generally considered clear and convincing evidence of reasonable compensation for personal services?

A-41: Yes. A showing that payments are made under a nondiscriminatory employee plan or program (as defined in Q/A-26 of this section) generally is considered to be clear and convincing evidence that the payments are reasonable compensation. This is true whether the personal services for which the payments are made are actually rendered before, or are to be rendered on or after, the date of the change in ownership or control. Q/A-46 of this section (relating to the treatment of an affiliated group as one corporation) does not apply for purposes of this A-41. No determination of reasonable compensation is needed for payments under qualified plans to be exempt from the definition of *parachute payment* under Q/A-8 of this section.

Q-42: Is any particular type of evidence generally considered clear and convincing evidence of reasonable compensation for personal services to be rendered on or after the date of a change in ownership or control?

A-42: (a) Yes, if payments are made or to be made to (or on behalf of) a disqualified individual for personal services to be rendered on or after the date of a change in ownership or control, a showing of the following generally is considered to be clear and convincing evidence that the payments are reasonable compensation for services to be rendered on or after the date of the change in ownership or control—

(1) The payments were made or are to be made only for the period the individual actually performs such personal services; and

(2) If the individual's duties and responsibilities are substantially the same after the change in ownership or control, the individual's annual compensation for such services is not significantly greater than such individual's annual compensation prior to the change in ownership or control, apart from normal increases attributable to increased responsibilities or cost of living adjustments. If the scope of the individual's duties and responsibilities are not substantially the same, the annual compensation after the change is not significantly greater than the annual compensation customarily paid by the employer or by comparable employers to persons performing comparable services. However, except as provided in paragraph (b) and (c) of this A-42, such clear and convincing evidence will not exist if the individual does not, in fact, perform the services contemplated in exchange for the compensation.

(b) Generally, an agreement under which the disqualified individual must refrain from performing services (e.g., a covenant not to compete) is an agreement for the performance of personal services for purposes of this A-42 to the extent that it is demonstrated by clear and convincing evidence that the agreement substantially constrains the individual's ability to perform services and there is a reasonable likelihood that the agreement will be enforced against the individual.

In the absence of clear and convincing evidence, payments under the agreement are treated as severance payments under Q/A-44 of this section.

(c) If the employment of a disqualified individual is involuntarily terminated before the end of a contract term and the individual is paid damages for breach of contract, a showing of the following factors generally is considered clear and convincing evidence that the payment is reasonable compensation for personal services to be rendered on or after the date of change in ownership or control—

(1) The contract was not entered into, amended, or renewed in contemplation of the change in ownership or control;

(2) The compensation the individual would have received under the contract would have qualified as reasonable compensation under section 162;

(3) The damages do not exceed the present value (determined as of the date of receipt) of the compensation the individual would have received under the contract if the individual had continued to perform services for the employer until the end of the contract term;

(4) The damages are received because an offer to provide personal services was made by the disqualified individual but was rejected by the employer (including involuntary termination or constructive discharge); and

(5) The damages are reduced by mitigation. Mitigation will be treated as occurring when such damages are reduced (or any payment of such damages is returned) to the extent of the disqualified individual's earned income (within the meaning of section 911(d)(2)(A)) during the remainder of the period in which the contract would have been in effect. See Q/A-44 of this section for rules regarding damages for a failure to make severance payments.

(d) The following examples illustrate the principles of this A-42:

Example 1. A, a disqualified individual, has a three-year employment contract with Corporation M, a publicly traded corporation. Under this contract, A is to receive a salary for $100,000 for the first year of the contract and, for each succeeding year, an annual salary that is 10 percent higher than the prior year's salary. During the third year of the contract, Corporation N acquires all the stock of Corporation M. Prior to the change in ownership, Corporation N arranges to retain A's services by entering into an employment contract with A that is essentially the same as A's contract with Corporation M. Under the new contract, Corporation N is to fulfill Corporation M's obligations for the third year of the old contract, and, for each of the succeeding years, pay A an annual salary that is 10 percent higher than A's prior year's salary. Amounts are payable under the new contract only for the portion of the contract term during which A remains employed by Corporation N. A showing of the facts described above (and in the absence of contradictory evidence) is regarded as clear and convincing evidence that all payments under the new contract are reasonable compensation for personal services to be rendered on or after the date of the change in ownership. Therefore, the payments under this agreement are exempt from the definition of *parachute payment* pursuant to Q/A-9 of this section.

Example 2. Assume the same facts as in *Example 1*, except that A does not perform the services described in the new contract, but receives payment under the new contract. Because services were not rendered after the change, the payments under this contract are not exempt from the definition of *parachute payment* pursuant to Q/A-9 of this section.

Example 3. Assume the same facts as in *Example 1*, except that under the new contract A agrees to perform consulting services to Corporation N, when and if Corporation N requires A's services. Assume further that when Corporation N does not require A's services, the contract provides that A must not perform services for any other competing company. Corporation N previously enforced similar contracts against former employees of Corporation N. Because A is substantially constrained under this contract and Corporation N is reasonably likely to enforce the contract against A, the agreement is an agreement for the performance of services under paragraph (b) of this A-42. Assuming the requirements of paragraph (a) of this A-42 are met and there is clear and convincing evidence that all payments under the new contract are reasonable compensation for personal services to be rendered on or after the date of the change in ownership, the payments under this contract are exempt from the definition of *parachute payment* pursuant to Q/A-9 of this section.

Example 4. Assume the same facts as in *Example 1*, except that instead of agreeing not to compete with Corporation N, under the new agreement A agrees not to disparage either Corporation M or Corporation N. Because the nondisparagement agreement does not substantially constrain A's ability to perform services, no amount of the payments under this contract are reasonable compensation for the nondisparagement agreement.

Example 5. Assume the same facts as in *Example 1*, except that the employment contract with Corporation N does not provide that amounts are payable under the contract only for the portion of the term for which A remains employed by Corporation N. Shortly after the change in ownership, and despite A's request to remain employed by Corporation N, A's employment with Corporation N is involuntarily terminated. Shortly thereafter, A obtains employment with Corporation O. A commences a civil action against Corporation N, alleging breach of the employment contract. In settlement of the litigation, A receives an amount equal to the present value of the compensation A would have received under the contract with Corporation N, reduced by the amount of compensation A otherwise receives from Corporation O during the period that the contract would have been in effect. A showing of the facts described above (and in the absence of contradictory evidence) is regarded as clear and convincing evidence that the amount A receives as damages is reasonable compensation for personal services to be rendered on or after the date of the change in ownership. Therefore, the amount received by A is exempt from the definition of *parachute payment* pursuant to Q/A-9 of this section.

Q-43: Is any particular type of payment generally considered reasonable compensation for personal services actually rendered before the date of a change in ownership or control?

A-43: Yes, payments of compensation earned before the date of a change in ownership or control generally are considered reasonable compensation for personal services actually rendered before the date of a change in ownership or control if they qualify as reasonable compensation under section 162.

Q-44: May severance payments be treated as reasonable compensation?

A-44: (a) No, severance payments are not treated as reasonable compensation for personal services actually rendered before, or to be rendered on or after, the date of a change in ownership or control. Moreover, any damages paid for a failure to make severance payments are not treated as reasonable compensation for personal services actually rendered before, or to be rendered on or after, the date of such change. For purposes of this section, the term *severance payment* means any payment that is made to (or for the benefit of) a disqualified individual on account of the termination of such individual's employment prior to the end of a contract term, but does not include any payment that otherwise would be made to (or for the benefit of) such individual on the termination of such individual's employment, whenever occurring.

(b) The following example illustrates the principles of this A-44:

Example. A, a disqualified individual, has a three-year employment contract with Corporation X. Under the contract, A will receive a salary of $200,000 for the first year of the contract, and for each succeeding year, an annual salary that is $100,000 higher than the previous year. In the event of A's termination of employment following a change in ownership or control, the contract provides that A will receive the remaining salary due under the employment contract. At the beginning of the second year of the contract, Corporation Y acquires all of the stock of Corporation X, A's employment is terminated, and A receives $700,000 ($300,000 for the second year of the contract plus $400,000 for the third year of the contract) representing the remaining salary due under the employment contract. Because the $700,000 payment is treated as a severance payment, it is not reasonable compensation for personal services on or after the date of the change in ownership or control. Thus, the full amount of the $700,000 is a parachute payment.

Miscellaneous Rules

Q-45: How is the term *corporation* defined?

A-45: For purposes of this section, the term *corporation* has the meaning prescribed by section 7701(a)(3) and § 301.7701-2(b) of this Chapter. For example, a *corporation*, for purposes of this section, includes a publicly traded partnership treated as a corporation under section 7704(a); an entity described in § 301.7701-3(c)(1)(v)(A) of this Chapter; a real estate investment trust under section 856(a); a corporation that has mutual or cooperative (rather than stock) ownership, such as a mutual insurance company, a mutual savings bank, or a cooperative bank (as defined in section 7701(a)(32)), and a foreign corporation as defined under section 7701(a)(5).

Q-46: How is an affiliated group treated?

A-46: For purposes of this section, and except as otherwise provided in this section, all members of the same affiliated group (as defined in section 1504, determined without regard to section 1504(b)) are treated as one corporation. Rules affected by this treatment of an affiliated group include (but are not limited to) rules relating to exempt payments of certain corporations (Q/A-6, Q/A-7 of this section (except as provided therein)), payor of parachute payments (Q/A-10 of this section), disqualified individuals (Q/A-15 through Q/A-21 of this section (except as provided therein)), rebuttal of the presumption that payments are contingent on a change (Q/A-26 of this section (except as provide therein)), change in ownership or control (Q/A-27, 28, and 29 of this section), and reasonable compensation (Q/A-42, 43, and 44 of this section).

Effective Date

Q-47: What is the general effective date of section 280G?

A-47: (a) Generally, section 280G applies to payments under agreements entered into or renewed after June 14, 1984. Any agreement that is entered into before June 15, 1984, and is renewed after June 14, 1984, is treated as a new contract entered into on the day the renewal takes effect.

(b) For purposes of paragraph (a) of this A-47, a contract that is terminable or cancellable unconditionally at will by either party to the contract without the consent of the other, or by both parties to the contract, is treated as a new contract entered into on the date any such termination or cancellation, if made, would be effective. However, a contract is not treated as so terminable or cancellable if it can be terminated or cancelled only by terminating the employment relationship or independent contractor relationship of the disqualified individual.

(c) Section 280G applies to payments under a contract entered into on or before June 14, 1984, if the contract is amended or supplemented after June 14, 1984, in significant relevant respect. For this purpose, a *supplement* to a contract is defined as a new contract entered into after June 14, 1984, that affects the trigger, amount, or time of receipt of a payment under an existing contract.

(d)(1) Except as otherwise provided in paragraph (e) of this A-47, a contract is considered to be amended or supplemented in significant relevant respect if provisions for payments contingent on a change in ownership or control (parachute provisions), or provisions in the nature of parachute provisions, are added to the contract, or are amended or supplemented to provide significant additional benefits to the disqualified individual. Thus, for example, a contract generally is treated as amended or supplemented in significant relevant respect if it is amended or supplemented—

(i) To add or modify, to the disqualified individual's benefit, a change in ownership or control trigger;

(ii) To increase amounts payable that are contingent on a change in ownership or control (or, where payment is to be made under a formula, to modify the formula to the disqualified individual's advantage); or

(iii) To accelerate, in the event of a change in ownership or control, the payment of amounts otherwise payable at a later date.

(2) For purposes of paragraph (a) of this A-47, a payment is not treated as being accelerated in the event of a change in ownership or control if the acceleration does not increase the present value of the payment.

(e) A contract entered into on or before June 14, 1984, is not treated as amended or supplemented in significant relevant respect merely by reason of normal adjustments in the terms of employment relationship or independent contractor relationship of the disqualified individual. Whether an adjustment in the terms of such a relationship is considered normal for this purpose depends on all of the facts and circumstances of the particular case. Relevant factors include, but are not limited to, the following—

(1) The length of time between the adjustment and the change in ownership or control;

(2) The extent to which the corporation, at the time of the adjustment, viewed itself as a likely takeover candidate;

(3) A comparison of the adjustment with historical practices of the corporation;

(4) The extent of overlap between the group receiving the benefits of the adjustment and those members of that group who are the beneficiaries of pre-June 15, 1984, parachute contracts; and

(5) The size of the adjustment, both in absolute terms and in comparison with the benefits provided to other members of the group receiving the benefits of the adjustment.

Q-48: What is the effective date of this section?

A-48: This section applies to any payments that are contingent on a change in ownership or control if the change in ownership or control occurs on or after January 1, 2004. Taxpayers may rely on these regulations after August 4, 2003, for the treatment of any parachute payment.

[Reg. § 1.280G-1.]

☐ [T.D. 9083, 8-1-2003 (*corrected* 10-10-2003).]

[Reg. § 1.280H-0T]

§ 1.280H-0T. Table of contents (temporary).—This section lists the captions that appear in the temporary regulations under section 280H.

§ 1.280H-1T. Limitation on certain amounts paid to employee-owners by personal service corporations electing alternative taxable years (temporary).

(a) Introduction.

(b) Limitations on certain deductions of a personal service corporation.

(1) In general.

(2) Carryover of nondeductible amounts.

(3) Disallowance inapplicable for certain purposes.

(4) Definition of applicable amount.

    (i) In general.

    (ii) Special rule for certain indirect payments.

    (iii) Examples.

(c) Minimum distribution requirement.

    (1) Determination of whether requirement satisfied.

    (i) In general.

    (ii) Employee-owner defined.

    (2) Preceding year test.

    (i) In general.

    (ii) Example.

    (3) 3-year average test.

    (i) In general.

    (ii) Applicable percentage.

    (iii) Adjusted taxable income.

       (A) In general.

       (B) Determination of adjusted taxable income for the deferral period of the applicable election year.

       (C) NOL carryovers.

       (D) Examples.

(d) Maximum deductible amount.

    (1) In general.

    (2) Example.

(e) Special rules and definition.

    (1) Newly organized personal service corporations.

    (2) Existing corporations that become personal service corporations.

    (3) Disallowance of NOL carryback.

    (4) Deferral period.

    (5) Examples.

(f) Effective date.

[Temporary Reg. § 1.280H-0T.]

☐ [*T.D. 8205, 5-24-88.*]

[Reg. § 1.280H-1T]

§ 1.280H-1T. Limitation on certain amounts paid to employee-owners by personal service corporations electing alternative taxable years (temporary).—(a) *Introduction.*—This section applies to any taxable year that a personal service corporation has a section 444 election in effect (an "applicable election year"). For purposes of this section, the term "personal service corporation" has the same meaning given such term in § 1.441-3(c).

(b) *Limitation on certain deductions of personal service corporations.*— (1) *In general.*—If, for any applicable election year, a personal service corporation does not satisfy the minimum distribution requirement in paragraph (c) of this section, the deduction otherwise allowable under chapter 1 of the Internal Revenue Code of 1986 (the Code) for applicable amounts, as defined in paragraph (b)(4) of this section, shall not exceed the maximum deductible amount, as defined in paragraph (d) of this section.

(2) *Carryover of nondeductible amounts.*—Any amount not allowed as a deduction in an applicable election year under paragraph (b)(1) of this section shall be allowed as a deduction in the succeeding taxable year.

(3) *Disallowance inapplicable for certain purposes.*—The disallowance of deductions under paragraph (b)(1) of this section shall not apply for purposes of subchapter G of chapter 1 of the Code (relating to corporations used to avoid income tax on shareholders) nor for determining whether the compensation of employee-owners is reasonable. Thus, for example, in determining whether a personal service corporation is subject to the accumulated earnings tax imposed by section 531, deductions disallowed under paragraph (b)(1) of this section are treated as allowed in computing accumulated taxable income.

(4) *Definition of applicable amount.*—(i) *In general.*—For purposes of section 280H and the regulations thereunder, the term "applicable amount" means, with respect to a taxable year, any amount that is otherwise deductible by a personal service corporation in such year and includible at any time, directly or indirectly, in the gross income of a taxpayer that during such year is an employee-owner. Thus, an amount includible in the gross income of an employee-owner will be considered an applicable amount even though such employee owns no stock of the corporation on the date the employee includes the amount in income. See example (1) in paragraph (b)(4)(iii) of this section.

(ii) *Special rule for certain indirect payments.*—For purposes of paragraph (b)(4)(i) of this section, amounts are indirectly includible

in the gross income of an employee-owner of a personal service corporation that has made a section 444 election (an electing personal service corporation) if the amount is includible in the gross income of—

    (A) The spouse (other than a spouse who is legally separated from the partner or shareholder under a decree of divorce or separate maintenance) or child (under age 14) of such employee-owner, or

    (B) A corporation more than 50 percent (measured by fair market value) of which is owned in the aggregate by employee-owners (and individuals related under paragraph (b)(4)(ii)(A) of this section to such employee-owners), of the electing personal service corporation, or

    (C) A partnership more than 50 percent of the profits and capital of which is owned by employee-owners (and individuals related under paragraph (b)(4)(ii)(A) of this section to such employee-owners) of the electing personal service corporation, or

    (D) A trust more than 50 percent of the beneficial ownership of which is owned in the aggregate by employee-owners (and individuals related under paragraph (b)(4)(ii)(A) of this section to any such employee-owners), of the electing personal service corporation.

For purposes of this paragraph (b)(4)(ii), ownership by any person described in this paragraph (b)(4)(ii) shall be treated as ownership by the employee-owners of the electing personal service corporation. Paragraph (b)(4)(ii)(B) of this section will not apply if the corporation has made a section 444 election to use the same taxable year as that of the electing personal service corporation. Similarly, paragraph (b)(4)(ii)(C) of this section will not apply if the partnership has made a section 444 election to use the same taxable year as that of the electing personal service corporation. Notwithstanding the general effective date provision of paragraph (f) of this section, this paragraph (b)(4)(ii) is effective for amounts deductible on or after June 1, 1988.

(iii) *Examples.*—The provisions of paragraph (b)(4) of this section may be illustrated by the following examples.

Example (1). A is an employee of P, an accrual basis personal service corporation with a taxable year ending September 30. P makes a section 444 election for its taxable year beginning October 1, 1987. On October 1, 1987, A owns no stock of P; however, on March 31, 1988, A acquires 10 of the 200 outstanding shares of P stock. During the period October 1, 1987 to March 31, 1988, A earned $40,000 of compensation as an employee of P. During the period April 1, 1988 to September 30, 1988, A earned $60,000 of compensation as an employee-owner of P. If paragraph (b) of this section does not apply, P would deduct for its taxable year ended September 30, 1988, the $100,000 earned by A during such year. Based upon these facts, the $100,000 otherwise deductible amount is considered an applicable amount under this section.

Example (2). I1 and I2, calendar-year individuals, are employees of PSC1, a personal service corporation that has historically used a taxable year ending January 31. I1 and I2 also own all the stock, and are employees, of PSC2, a calendar-year personal service corporation. For its taxable years beginning February 1, 1987, 1988, and 1989, PSC1 has a section 444 election in effect to use a January 31 taxable year. During its taxable years beginning February 1, 1986, 1987, and 1988, PSC1 deducted $10,000, $11,000, and $12,000, respectively, that was included in PSC2's gross income. Furthermore, of the $12,000 deducted by PSC1 for its taxable year beginning February 1, 1988, $7,000 was deducted during the period June 1, 1988 to January 31, 1989. Pursuant to paragraph (b)(4)(ii)(B) of this section, the $7,000 deducted by PSC1 on or after June 1, 1988, and included in PSC2's gross income is considered an applicable amount for PSC1's taxable year beginning February 1, 1988. Amounts deducted by PSC1 prior to June 1, 1988, are not subject to paragraph (b)(4)(ii)(B) of this section.

Example (3). The facts are the same as in example (2), except that for its taxable years beginning February 1, 1987, 1988, and 1989, PSC2 has a section 444 election in effect to use a January 31 taxable year. Since both PSC1 and PSC2 have the same taxable year and both have section 444 elections in effect, paragraph (b)(4)(ii)(B) of this section does not apply to the $7,000 deducted by PSC1 for its taxable year beginning February 1, 1988.

(c) *Minimum distribution requirement.*—(1) *Determination of whether requirement satisfied.*—(i) *In general.*—A personal service corporation meets the minimum distribution requirement of this paragraph (c) for an applicable election year if, during the deferral period of such taxable year, the applicable amounts (determined without regard to paragraph (b)(2) of this section) for all employee-owners in the aggregate equal or exceed the lesser of—

    (A) The amount determined under the "preceding year test" (see paragraph (c)(2) of this section), or

(B) The amount determined under the "3-year average test" (see paragraph (c)(3) of this section).

The following example illustrates the application of this paragraph (c)(1)(i).

Example. Q, an accrual-basis personal service corporation, makes a section 444 election to retain a year ending January 31 for its taxable year beginning February 1, 1987. Q has 4 employee-owners, B, C, D, and E. For Q's applicable election year beginning February 1, 1987 and ending January 31, 1988, B earns $6,000 a month plus a $45,000 bonus on January 15, 1988; C earns $5,000 a month plus a $40,000 bonus on January 15, 1988; D and E each earn $4,500 a month plus a $4,000 bonus on January 15, 1988. Q meets the minimum distribution requirement for such applicable election year if the applicable amounts during the deferral period (*i.e.*, $220,000) equal or exceed the amount determined under the preceding year test or the 3-year average test.

(ii) *Employee-owner defined.*—For purposes of section 280H and the regulations thereunder, a person is an employee-owner of a corporation for a taxable year if—

(A) On any day of the corporation's taxable year, the person is an employee of the corporation or performs personal services for or on behalf of the corporation, even if the legal form of that person's relationship to the corporation is that of an independent contractor, and

(B) On any day of the corporation's taxable year, the person owns any outstanding stock of the corporation.

(2) *Preceding year test.*—(i) *In general.*—The amount determined under the preceding year test is the product of—

(A) The applicable amounts during the taxable year preceding the applicable election year (the "preceding taxable year"), divided by the number of months (but not less than one) in the preceding taxable year, multiplied by

(B) The number of months in the deferral period of the applicable election year.

(ii) *Example.*—The provisions of paragraph (c)(2) of this section may be illustrated by the following example.

Example. R, a personal service corporation, has historically used a taxable year ending January 31. For its taxable year beginning February 1, 1987, R makes a section 444 election to retain its January 31 taxable year. R is an accrual basis taxpayer and has one employee-owner, F. For R's taxable year ending January 31, 1987, F earns $5,000 a month plus a $40,000 bonus on January 15, 1987. The amount determined under the preceding year test for R's applicable election year beginning February 1, 1987 is $91,667 ($100,000, the applicable amounts during R's taxable year ending January 31, 1987, divided by 12, the number of months in R's taxable year ending January 31, 1987, multiplied by 11, the number of months in R's deferral period for such year).

(3) *3-year average test.*—(i) *In general.*—The amount determined under the 3-year average test is the applicable percentage multiplied by the adjusted taxable income for the deferral period of the applicable election year.

(ii) *Applicable percentage.*—The term "applicable percentage" means the percentage (not in excess of 95 percent) determined by dividing—

(A) The applicable amounts during the 3 taxable years of the corporation (or, if fewer, the taxable years the corporation has been in existence) immediately preceding the applicable election year, by

(B) The adjusted taxable income of such corporation for such 3 taxable years (or, if fewer, the taxable years of existence).

(iii) *Adjusted taxable income.*—(A) *In general.*—The term "adjusted taxable income" means taxable income determined without regard to applicable amounts.

(B) *Determination of adjusted taxable income for the deferral period of the applicable election year.*—Adjusted taxable income for the deferral period of the applicable election year equals the adjusted taxable income that would result if the personal service corporation filed an income tax return for the deferral period of the applicable election year under its normal method of accounting. However, a personal service corporation may make a reasonable estimate of such amount.

(C) *NOL carryovers.*—For purposes of determining adjusted taxable income for any period, any NOL carryover shall be reduced by the amount of such carryover that is attributable to the deduction of applicable amounts. The portion of the NOL carryover attributable to the deduction of applicable amounts is the difference between the NOL carryover computed with the deduction of such amounts and the NOL carryover computed without the deduction of such

amounts. For purposes of determining the adjusted taxable income for the deferral period, an NOL carryover to the applicable election year, reduced as provided in this paragraph (c)(3)(iii)(C), shall be allowed first against the income of the deferral period.

(D) *Examples.*—The provisions of this paragraph (c)(3)(iii) may be illustrated by the following examples.

Example (1). S is a personal service corporation that has historically used a taxable year ending January 31. For its taxable year beginning February 1, 1987, S makes a section 444 election to retain its taxable year ending January 31. S does not satisfy the minimum distribution requirement for its first applicable election year, and the applicable amounts for that year exceed the maximum deductible amount by $54,000. Under paragraph (b)(2) of this section, the $54,000 excess is carried over to S's taxable year beginning February 1, 1988. Furthermore, if S continues its section 444 election for its taxable year beginning February 1, 1988, and desires to use the 3-year average test provided in this paragraph for such year, pursuant to paragraph (c)(3)(iii)(A) of this section the $54,000 will not be allowed to reduce adjusted taxable income for such year. See also section 280H(e) regarding the disallowance of net operating loss carrybacks to (or from) any taxable year of a corporation personal service election under section 444 applies.

Example (2). T, a personal service corporation with a section 444 election in effect, is determining whether it satisfies the 3-year average test for its second applicable election year. T had a net operating loss (NOL) for its first applicable election year of $45,000. The NOL resulted from $150,000 of gross income less the sum of $96,000 of salary, $45,000 of other expenses, and $54,000 of deductible applicable amounts. Pursuant to paragraph (c)(3)(iii)(C) of this section, the entire amount of the $45,000 NOL is attributable to applicable amounts since the applicable amounts deducted in arriving at the NOL (*i.e.*, $54,000) were greater than the NOL (*i.e.*, $45,000). Thus, for purposes of computing the adjusted taxable income for the deferral period of T's second applicable election year, the NOL carryover to that year is $0 ($45,000 NOL less $45,000 amount of NOL attributable to applicable amounts).

(d) *Maximum deductible amount.*—(1) *In general.*—For purposes of this section, the term "maximum deductible amount" means the sum of—

(i) The applicable amounts during the deferral period of the applicable election year, plus

(ii) An amount equal to the product of—

(A) The amount determined under paragraph (d)(1)(i) of this section divided by the number of months in the deferral period of the applicable election year, multiplied by

(B) The number of months in the nondeferral period of the applicable election year.

For purposes of the preceding sentence, the term "nondeferral period" means the portion of the applicable election year that occurs after the portion of such year constituting the deferral period.

(2) *Example.*—The provisions of paragraph (d)(1) of this section may be illustrated by the following example.

Example. U, an accrual basis personal service corporation with a taxable year ending January 31, makes a section 444 election to retain a year ending January 31 for its taxable year beginning February 1, 1987. For its applicable election year beginning February 1, 1987, U does not satisfy the minimum distribution requirement in paragraph (c) of this section. Furthermore, U has 3 employee-owners, G, H, and I. G and H have been employee-owners of U for 10 years. Although I has been an employee of U for 4 years, I did not become an employee-owner until December 1, 1987, when I acquired 5 of the 20 outstanding shares of U stock. For U's applicable election year beginning February 1, 1987, G earns $5,000 a month plus a $40,000 bonus on January 15, 1988, and H and I each earn $4,000 a month plus a $32,000 bonus on January 15, 1988. Thus, the total of the applicable amounts during the deferral period of the applicable election year beginning February 1, 1987 is $143,000. Based on these facts, U's deduction for applicable amounts is limited to $156,000, determined as follows—$143,000 (applicable amounts during the deferral period) plus $13,000 (applicable amounts during the deferral period, divided by the number of months in the deferral period, multiplied by the number of months in the nondeferral period).

(e) *Special rules and definition.*—(1) *Newly organized personal service corporations.*—A personal service corporation is deemed to satisfy the preceding year test and the 3-year average test for the first year of the corporation's existence.

(2) *Existing corporations that become personal service corporations.*— If an existing corporation becomes a personal service corporation and makes a section 444 election, the determination of whether the corporation satisfies the preceding year test and the 3-year average test is made by treating the corporation as though it were a personal service

corporation for each of the 3 years preceding the applicable election year.

(3) *Disallowance of NOL carryback.*—No net operating loss carryback shall be allowed to (or from) any applicable election year of a personal service corporation.

(4) *Deferral period.*—For purposes of section 280H and the regulations thereunder, the term "deferral period" has the same meaning as under §1.444-1T(b)(4).

(5) *Examples.*—The provisions of this paragraph (e) may be illustrated by the following examples.

Example (1). V is a personal service corporation with a taxable year ending September 30. V makes a section 444 election for its taxable year beginning October 1, 1987, and incurs a net operating loss (NOL) for such year. Because an NOL is not allowed to be carried back from an applicable election year, V may not carry back the NOL from its first applicable election year to reduce its 1985, 1986, or 1987 taxable income.

Example (2). W, a personal service corporation, commences operations on July 1, 1990. Furthermore, for its taxable year beginning July 1, 1990, W makes a section 444 election to use a year ending September 30. Pursuant to paragraph (e)(1) of this section, W satisfies the preceding year test and the 3-year average test for its first year in existence. Thus, W may deduct, without limitation under this section, any applicable amounts for its taxable year beginning July 1, 1990.

Example (3). The facts are the same as in example (2). For its taxable year beginning October 1, 1990, W incurs an NOL and is not a personal service corporation. Furthermore, W desires to carry back the NOL to its preceding taxable year (a year that was an applicable election year). Pursuant to paragraph (e)(3) of this section, W may not carry back an NOL "to" its taxable year beginning July 1, and ending September 30, 1990, because such year was an applicable election year.

(f) *Effective date.*—The provisions of this section are effective for taxable years beginning after December 31, 1986. [Temporary Reg. §1.280H-1T.]

☐ [*T.D.* 8205, 5-24-88. *Amended by T.D.* 8996, 5-16-2002.]

Terminal Railroad Corporations and Their Shareholders

[Reg. §1.281-1]

§1.281-1. In general.—Section 281 provides special rules for the computation of the taxable incomes of a terminal railroad corporation and its shareholders when the terminal railroad corporation, as a result of taking related terminal income into account, reduces a charge which was made or which would be made for related terminal services furnished to a railroad corporation. Section 281 and paragraphs (a) and (b) of §1.281-2 provide that the "reduced amount" described in paragraph (c) of §1.281-2 is not includible in gross income of the terminal railroad corporation, is not treated as a dividend or other distribution to its railroad shareholders, and is not treated as an amount paid or incurred by the railroad shareholders to the terminal railroad corporation. Section 281 and paragraph (a)(2) of §1.281-2 provide that no deduction otherwise allowable to a terminal railroad corporation shall be disallowed as a result of the "reduced amount" described in paragraph (c) of §1.281-2. Section 1.281-3 defines the terms "terminal railroad corporation", "related terminal income", "related terminal services", "agreement", and "railroad corporation". Section 1.281-4 describes the effective dates and special rules for application of section 281 to taxable years ending before October 23, 1962. [Reg. §1.281-1.]

☐ [*T.D.* 7356, 5-30-75.]

[Reg. §1.281-2]

§1.281-2. Effect of section 281 upon the computation of taxable income.—(a) *Computation of taxable income of terminal railroad corporations.*—(1) *Income not considered received or accrued.*—A terminal railroad corporation (as defined in paragraph (a) of §1.281-3) shall not be considered to have received or accrued the "reduced amount" described in paragraph (c) of this section in the computation of its taxable income. Thus, income is not to be considered accrued or actually or constructively received by a terminal railroad corporation where, in the manner described in paragraph (c) of this section, (i) a charge which would be made to any railroad corporation for related terminal service is not made, or (ii) a portion of any liability payable by any railroad corporation with respect to related terminal services is discharged.

(2) *Deduction not disallowed.*—In the computation of the taxable income of a terminal railroad corporation, a deduction relating to a "reduced amount", described in paragraph (c) of this section, which is otherwise allowable to it under chapter 1 of the Code (without regard to sec. 277) shall not be disallowed by reason of section 281. Thus, deductions for expenses attributable to services rendered to a shareholder are not to be disallowed to a terminal railroad corporation merely because, in the manner described in paragraph (c) of this section, (i) a charge which would be made to any railroad corporation for related terminal services is not made, or (ii) a portion of any liability payable by any railroad corporation with respect to related terminal services is discharged. To the extent that section 281 applies to a deduction relating to a "reduced amount", such deduction shall not be disallowed under section 277.

(b) *Computation of taxable income of shareholders.*—(1) *Income not considered received or accrued.*—A shareholder of a terminal railroad corporation shall not be considered to have received or accrued any "reduced amount" (described in paragraph (c) of this section) in the computation of the shareholder's taxable income. Thus a dividend is not to be considered actually or constructively received by a shareholder of a terminal railroad corporation merely because, in the

manner described in paragraph (c) of this section, (i) a charge which would be made to the shareholder or any other railroad corporation for related terminal services is not made, or (ii) a portion of any liability payable by it or any other railroad corporation with respect to related terminal services is discharged.

(2) *Expenses not considered paid or incurred.*—In the computation of the taxable income of a shareholder of a terminal railroad corporation, the shareholder shall not be considered to have paid or incurred any "reduced amount" (described in paragraph (c) of this section). Thus, a shareholder of the terminal railroad corporation may not deduct as an expense for related terminal services (as defined in paragraph (c) of §1.281-3) an amount in excess of the net cost to it of such services.

(c) *Amounts to which section 281 applies.*—(1) *Reduced amount.*—For purposes of this section, the term "reduced amount" means, subject to the limitation of paragraph (c)(4) of this section, the amount by which—

(i) A charge which would be made by a terminal railroad corporation for its taxable year for related terminal services provided to a railroad corporation; or

(ii) A liability of a railroad corporation, resulting from a charge made by a terminal railroad corporation for its taxable year, with respect to related terminal services provided by the terminal railroad corporation, is reduced by reason of the terminal railroad corporation's taking into account, pursuant to an agreement (as defined in paragraph (d) of §1.281-3), related terminal income (as defined in paragraph (b) of §1.281-3) received or accrued (without regard to section 281) during such taxable year.

(2) *Charge which would be made.*—For purposes of this section, a "charge which would be made" by a terminal railroad corporation is the amount that would be charged to any railroad corporation for related terminal services provided if the terminal railroad corporation made the charge without taking related terminal income into account.

(3) *Reduction resulting from related terminal income.*—For purposes of subparagraph (1) of this section, a charge or a liability is reduced by taking related terminal income into account to the extent that—

(i) Related terminal income is received or accrued (without regard to section 281) by the terminal railroad corporation for its taxable year in which the charge or liability is reduced; and

(ii) The charge or liability in question would have been larger than it is had such income not been received or accrued (without regard to section 281).

The reduction must be made (directly or indirectly) on the books of the terminal railroad corporation, and in fact, for the same taxable year for which the charge would be made or for which the liability is incurred. The reduction of the charge or liability must be taken into account by the terminal railroad corporation in ascertaining the income, profit, or loss for such taxable year for the purpose of reports to shareholders and the Interstate Commerce Commission, and for credit purposes.

(4) *Limitation.*—To the extent that a reduced amount (as described in paragraph (c)(1) of this section but without regard to the limitation under this subparagraph) would operate either to create or to increase a net operating loss for the terminal railroad corporation, this section shall not apply. Therefore, if a portion of a liability is discharged (in the manner described in this paragraph) and the

discharged portion of the liability exceeds an amount equal to the terminal railroad corporation's gross income minus the deductions allowed by chapter 1 of the Code (computed with regard to the modifications specified in section 172(d) but without regard to section 281 and this section), then section 281 and this section shall not apply to such excess. The limitation described in this subparagraph shall apply only to taxable years of terminal railroad corporations ending after October 23, 1962.

(d) *Examples.*—The provisions of this section may be illustrated by the following examples. In these examples, references to "before the application of section 281", "after the application of section 281", "taxable income", and "allowable deductions" take no account of section 277, which may apply to deductions to which section 281 does not apply.

Example (1).—(i) *Facts.*—The T Company is a terminal railroad corporation which charges its three equal shareholders, the X, Y, and Z railroad corporations, a rental calculated monthly on a wheelage or use basis for the use of its services and facilities. The T Company and each of its shareholders report income on the calendar year basis. A written lease agreement to which all of the shareholders were parties was entered into in 1947. The agreement provides that at the end of each year the liabilities of each of the shareholders resulting from charges for rental obligations with respect to related terminal services shall be reduced by the shareholder's one-third share of the net income from each source of revenue that produced income (computed before reduction for Federal income taxes). For the calendar year 1973, the T Company's charges to its shareholders include the following charges for related terminal services: $35,000 to the X Company, $25,000 to the Y Company, and $20,000 to the Z Company. Thus, prior to reduction, total shareholder liabilities to the T Company for related terminal services are $80,000 at the end of 1973. The T Company's net income from all sources (before reduction of liabilities pursuant to the 1947 agreement and before reduction for Federal income taxes) and its taxable income, before the application of section 281, for 1973 are $36,000 determined as follows:

Source	Gross income	Allowable deductions	Income (or Loss)
Related terminal services performed:			
For shareholders	$80,000	$65,000	$15,000
For nonshareholders	46,000	37,000	9,000
Related terminal income	126,000	102,000	24,000
Nonrelated terminal income	30,000	18,000	12,000
Total	156,000	120,000	36,000

The liability of each shareholder is, pursuant to the agreement, discharged in part by the T Company crediting $12,000 against the rental due from each shareholder for a total discharge of liabilities of $36,000 (the net income from all sources), resulting in net shareholder liabilities owing to the T Company at the end of 1973 of $44,000 ($80,000 less $36,000): $23,000 from the X Company, $13,000 from the Y Company, and $8,000 from the Z Company.

(ii) *Effect on terminal railroad corporation.*—The reduced amount to which this section applies is $24,000 (related terminal income of $9,000 from nonshareholders and $15,000 from shareholders). Thus, to the extent of $24,000, the T Company is not considered to have received or accrued income from the discharged liabilities of $36,000. Similarly, to the extent of the same $24,000, the T Company is not disallowed deductions for expenses merely by reason of the dis-

charge. The T Company's taxable income for 1973 after application of section 281 is $12,000, computed as follows:

Gross income ($156,000 less $24,000)	$132,000
Less allowable deductions	120,000
Taxable income	12,000

(iii) *Effect on shareholders.*—The reduced amount of $24,000 shall not be deemed to constitute either a dividend to the shareholders of the T Company or an expense paid or incurred by them. Thus, under the facts described, neither the X Company, the Y Company, nor the Z Company shall be considered to have received or accrued a dividend of $8,000, or to have paid or incurred an expense of $8,000. Assuming the X Company's taxable income for 1973 before the application of section 281 would have been $43,200, computed in the following manner, its taxable income for 1973 after the application of section 281 is $50,000, determined as follows:

	Before the application of sec. 281	After the application of sec. 281
Gross income:		
From sources other than T Co.	$146,000	$146,000
Dividend considered received because of T Co.'s discharge of liabilities of $12,000	12,000	4,000
Total	158,000	150,000
Less allowable deductions:		
From sources other than T Co.	$69,600	$69,600
85 percent dividend received deduction under sec. 243 attributable to dividend considered received because of T Co.'s discharge of liabilities	10,200	3,400
Expenses for accrued charges for related terminal services performed by T Co.	35,000	27,000
	114,800	100,000
Taxable income	43,200	50,000

Example (2).—Assume the same facts as in example (1), except that the charges to each of the shareholders for related terminal services for 1973 were as follows: $35,000 to the X Company, $40,000 to the Y Company, and $5,000 to the Z Company. Assume further that the Z Company, prior to the reduction in liabilities at the end of 1973, owed the T Company an additional $4,000 resulting from charges for 1972 for related terminal services and $6,000 resulting from the purchase of equipment. Since only $21,000 (X Company $8,000, Y Company $8,000, Z Company $5,000) of the liabilities which were discharged resulted from charges made for 1973 for related terminal services, the reduced amount to which this section applies is $21,000 (instead of $24,000 as in example (1)). Thus, the T Company's taxable

income for 1973 would be $15,000 ($36,000 less $21,000 reduced amount) and the amount which shall be considered not to have been received or accrued as a dividend nor paid or incurred as an expense of each shareholder is $8,000 for the X Company, $8,000 for the Y Company, and $5,000 for the Z Company.

Example (3).—Assume the same facts as in example (1), except that the allowable deductions with respect to nonrelated terminal activities were $39,000 instead of $18,000. The T Company's net income from all sources (before reduction for Federal income taxes) and its taxable income, before the application of section 281, is therefore $15,000, determined as follows:

Source	Gross income	Allowable deductions	Income (or loss)
Related terminal income	$126,000	$102,000	$24,000
Nonrelated terminal income	30,000	39,000	(9,000)
Total	156,000	141,000	15,000

The liability of each shareholder is nevertheless discharged in part, pursuant to the agreement, by the T Company crediting $8,000 against the rental due from each shareholder for a total discharge of

liabilities of $24,000 (the net income from each source of revenue that produced income). Assume further that none of the modifications specified in section 172(d) apply. If the limitation under paragraph (c)(4) of this section were not applied, the reduced amount for the purposes of this section would be $24,000, and the operation of this section would result in a net operating loss of $9,000, since the allowable deductions of $141,000 would exceed the gross income of $132,000 ($156,000 less discharged liabilities of $24,000) by that amount. Because of the limitation under paragraph (c)(4) of this section, however, $9,000 is not included in the reduced amount to which this section applies. Accordingly, the reduced amount is $15,000 (instead of $24,000 as in example (1)). Thus, the T Company's taxable income for 1973 would be zero ($15,000 less the $15,000 reduced amount), and the amount which each shareholder shall be considered not to have received or accrued as a dividend nor paid or incurred as an expense is $5,000.

Example (4).—Assume the same facts as in example (1), except that under the agreement income from the terminal parking lot would not reduce the shareholders' liabilities. Assume further that such income amounted to $3,000 of the total related terminal income of $24,000 for the taxable year 1973. The liability of each shareholder therefore is discharged by crediting $11,000 against its rental due for a total discharge of liabilities of $33,000. The reduced amount to which this section applies is $21,000 ($24,000 less $3,000) since only to the extent of $21,000 would there have been no such reduction under the agreement if there were no related terminal income.

Example (5).—Assume the same facts as in example (1), except that, pursuant to the agreement, the A Company, a nonshareholder railroad corporation, is to have its liabilities resulting from charges for rental obligations reduced equally with each of the shareholders. Assume further that the T Company's charges to the A Company for the calendar year 1973 included $15,000 for related terminal services and that the liability of each shareholder and the A Company is discharged in part pursuant to the agreement by the T Company

Source		
Related terminal services performed:		
For shareholders		
For nonshareholders		
Related terminal income		
Nonrelated terminal income from nonshareholders		
Total		

For the calendar year 1973, The TR company's charges to its shareholders are $23,000 ($30,000 less $7,000) to the M company, $13,000 ($20,000 less $7,000) to the N company, and $8,000 ($15,000 less $7,000) to the O company for a total of $44,000 for related terminal services.

(ii) *Effect on terminal railroad corporation.*—The reduced amount to which this section applies is $9,000. The TR company is not considered to have received or accrued income of $9,000 (related terminal income) merely because the charge of $21,000 (net income from all sources other than shareholders) was not made. Similarly, to the extent of $9,000, the TR company is not disallowed deductions for expenses merely because the full cost of services was not charged. The TR company's taxable income for 1973 after application of section 281, is $12,000, computed as follows:

Gross income ($141,000 less $9,000 charges not made)	$132,000
Less allowable deductions	120,000
Taxable income	$12,000

(iii) *Effect on shareholders.*—Neither the M company, the N company, nor the O company shall be considered to have received or accrued a dividend of $3,000 nor to have paid or incurred an expense of $3,000 merely by reason of the reduced charges. Thus, assuming the M company's taxable income for 1973 before the application of section 281 would have been $47,450, computed in the following manner, its taxable income for 1973 after the application of section 281 is $50,000, determined as follows:

	Before the application of sec. 281	After the application of sec. 281
Gross income:		
From sources other than TR Co.	$146,000	$146,000
Dividend considered received because of TR Co.'s reduction of charges	7,000	4,000
Total	$153,000	$150,000
Less allowable deductions:		
From sources other than ETR Co. . . .	$69,600	$69,600
85 percent dividend received deduction under sec. 243 attributable to dividend considered received because of TR Co.'s reduction of charges	5,950	3,400

crediting $9,000 against the rental due from each. The reduced amount to which this section applies is $24,000. Thus, the T Company's taxable income for 1973 is $12,000, and each shareholder shall not be considered to have received or accrued as a dividend nor paid or incurred as an expense $6,000 ($24,000/$36,000 × $9,000) merely because of the discharge of its own liability. Similarly, each shareholder shall not be considered to have received or accrued as a dividend nor paid or incurred as an expense $2,000 (^{1}/3 × ($24,000/$36,000 × $9,000)) merely because of the discharge of the liability of the A Company. Section 281 does not apply to the determination of the tax consequences of the transaction to the A Company. Similarly, the section does not apply to the determination of the tax consequences to the shareholders resulting from that portion of the discharge of the liability of the A Company which is attributable to the application of income which is not related terminal income ($3,000). Hence, such consequences shall be determined under the sections of the Internal Revenue Code which govern in the absence of section 281.

Example (6).—(i) *Facts.*—The TR Company is a terminal railroad corporation with three equal shareholders, the M, N, and O Railroad Corporations. The TR Company and each of its shareholders report income on the calendar year basis. Pursuant to a written agreement entered into in 1947 to which all shareholders were parties, the TR Company makes one annual charge to each of the three shareholders at the end of each year for the difference between the cost of operations, allocated on a wheelage or user basis for the use of its services and facilities provided to the shareholder during the year, and one-third of its net income from all other sources (computed before reduction for Federal income taxes). The TR Company's taxable income, before the application of section 281, for 1973 is $21,000 determined as follows:

	Gross income	Allowable deductions	Income (or loss)
Related terminal services performed:			
For shareholders	$65,000	$65,000	0
For nonshareholders	46,000	37,000	$9,000
Related terminal income	111,000	102,000	9,000
Nonrelated terminal income from nonshareholders	30,000	18,000	12,000
Total	$141,000	$120,000	$21,000
Expenses for accrued charges for related terminal services performed by TR Co.	30,000		27,000
	105,550		100,000
Taxable income	47,450		50,000

[Reg. §1.281-2.]

☐ [T.D. 7356, 5-30-75.]

[Reg. §1.281-3]

§1.281-3. Definitions.—(a) *Terminal railroad corporation.*—The term "terminal railroad corporation" means a corporation which, in the taxable year, meets all of the following conditions:

(1) The corporation and each of its shareholders must be domestic corporations. Thus, all of the shareholders of the corporation, as well as the corporation itself, must be corporations which were organized or created in the United States, including only the States and the District of Columbia, or under the law of the United States or of any State or territory.

(2) All of the shareholders must be railroad corporations which are subject to part I of the Interstate Commerce Act. Thus, if any shareholder of the corporation, regardless of the class or percentage of stock owned, is not subject to the jurisdiction of the Interstate Commerce Commission under part I of that act, the corporation cannot qualify as a terminal railroad corporation.

(3) The corporation must not be a member of an affiliated group of corporations (as defined in section 1504) other than as a common parent corporation. For this purpose it is immaterial whether or not the affiliated group has ever made a consolidated income tax return. Thus, if the X railroad corporation owns 80 percent of all of the outstanding stock of the Y railroad corporation, the X railroad corporation may qualify, but the Y railroad corporation cannot qualify, as a terminal railroad corporation.

(4) The primary business of the corporation must be that of providing to domestic railroad corporations subject to part I of the Interstate Commerce Act and to the shippers and passengers of such railroad corporations one or more of the following facilities or services: (i) Railroad terminal facilities, (ii) railroad switching facilities, (iii) railroad terminal services, or (iv) railroad switching services. The designated facilities and services include the furnishing of terminal trackage, the operation of stockyards or a union passenger or freight station, and the operation of railroad bridges and ferries. The providing of the designated facilities includes the leasing of those facilities. A corporation shall be considered as having established that its

primary business is that of providing the designated facilities and services if more than 50 percent of its gross income (computed without regard to section 281, and excluding dividends and gains and losses from the disposition of capital assets or property described in section 1231(b)) for the taxable year is derived from those sources. The fact that income from a service or facility is included within the definition of related terminal income is immaterial for purposes of determining whether that service or facility is one which is designated in this subparagraph. Thus, although income from the operation of a commuter railroad line may be related terminal income, a corporation whose primary business is the operation of that facility is not a terminal railroad corporation, since its primary business is not the providing of the designated facilities or services.

(5) A substantial part of the services rendered by the corporation for the taxable year must be rendered to one or more of its shareholders. For purposes of this requirement, providing the use of facilities shall be considered the rendering of services.

(6) Each shareholder of the corporation must compute its taxable income on the basis of a taxable year which either begins or ends on the same day as the taxable year of the corporation.

(b) *Related terminal income.*—(1) *In general.*—Related terminal income is, generally, the type of income normally earned from the operation of a railroad terminal. The term "related terminal income" means the taxable income (computed without regard to sections 172, 277, or 281) which the terminal railroad corporation derives for the taxable year from the sources enumerated in paragraph (b)(2) of this section. Related terminal income must be derived from direct provision of the specified facilities or services by the terminal corporation itself. Thus, income consisting of rent from a lease of a terminal facility by a terminal corporation to a railroad user would qualify; but dividends from a corporation in which the terminal corporation owned stock and which provided such facilities or services to others would not qualify. The term does not include gain or loss derived from the sale, exchange, or other disposition of capital assets or section 1231 assets, whether or not section 1245 or section 1250 applies to part or all of that gain. For example, the term does not apply to gain from the sale of a terminal building or terminal equipment. All direct and indirect expenses and other deductible items attributable to related terminal services or facilities shall be deducted in determining related terminal income. Attribution shall be determined in accordance with customary railroad accounting practices accepted by the Interstate Commerce Commission, except that interest paid with respect to the indebtedness of a terminal railroad corporation shall be deducted from related terminal income to the extent that the proceeds from the indebtedness were directly or indirectly applied to facilities or activities producing such income. The district director may either accept the use of the taxpayer's method of determining the application of the proceeds of all indebtedness of such corporation or prescribe the use of another method which, under all the facts and circumstances, appears to reflect more accurately the probable application of such proceeds.

(2) *Sources of related terminal income.*—The term "related terminal income" includes only income derived from one or more of the following sources:

(i) From services or facilities of a character ordinarily and regularly provided by terminal railroad corporations for railroad corporations or for the employees, passengers, or shippers of railroad corporations. Whether the services or facilities are of a character ordinarily and regularly provided by terminal railroad corporations is to be determined by accepted industry practice. The fact that nonterminal businesses may also provide such services or facilities is immaterial. However, there must be a direct relationship between the service or facility provided and the operation of the terminal, including the operation of its trackage and switching facilities. Thus, the term "related terminal income" includes income derived from operating or leasing switching facilities and terminal facilities, such as income from charges to railroad corporations for the use of a union passenger or freight station. Also included for this purpose is income derived from charges to railroad shippers, including express companies and freight forwarders, for the use of sheds or warehouses, even though not directly intended for railroad use. The term includes income derived from leasing or operating restaurants, drugstores, barbershops, newsstands, ticket agencies, banking facilities, car rental facilities, or other similar facilities for passengers, in waiting rooms or along passenger concourses. Similarly, the term includes income derived from operating or leasing passenger parking facilities, and from renting taxicab space, located on or adjacent to the terminal premises. Although the term does include income derived from the operation of a small hotel operated primarily for and usually occupied primarily by the employees of the railroad corporations, it does not include income derived from the operation of a hotel for passengers or other persons.

(ii) From any railroad corporation for services or facilities provided by the terminal railroad corporation in connection with railroad operations. A service or a facility is provided in connection with railroad operations if it is of a character ordinarily and regularly availed of by railroad corporations. For purposes of this subdivision, the income must be derived from railroad corporations. Thus, in addition to the income derived from sources described in paragraph (b)(2)(i) of this section, the term "related terminal income" includes income derived from switching facilities or leasing to any railroad corporation, or operating for the benefit of such corporation, a beltline or bypass railroad leading to or from the terminal premises. Also included are income derived from the rental of office space (whether or not services are provided to the occupants) in the terminal building to any railroad corporation for that corporation's administrative or operating divisions, and income derived from tolls charged to any railroad corporation for the use of a railroad bridge or ferry.

(iii) From the use by persons other than railroad corporations of a portion of a facility, or of a service, which is used primarily for railroad purposes. A facility or service issued primarily for railroad purposes if the predominant reason for its continued operation or provision is the furnishing of facilities or services described in either subdivision (i) or (ii) of this subparagraph. The determination required by this subdivision is to be made independently for each separate facility or service. Two substantial portions of a single structure may be considered separate facilities, depending upon the respective uses made of each. Moreover, any substantial addition, constructed after October 23, 1962, to a facility shall be considered a separate facility. The term "related terminal income" includes income produced by operating a commuter service or by renting tracks and facilities for a commuter service to an independent operator. The term also includes the sale or rental of advertising space at a terminal facility. If the conditions described in this subdivision are satisfied, the term "related terminal income" may include income which has no connection with the operation of the terminal. Thus, if a terminal railroad corporation operates a railroad bridge primarily to provide railroad corporations a means of crossing a river and the lower level of the bridge contains a roadway for similar use by automobiles, the term includes income derived from the tolls charged to the automobiles for the use of the bridge roadway. However, upon the discontinuance of operations of the railroad level of the bridge, the term would cease to include the automobile tolls. If excess steam from a steam plant operated primarily to supply steam to the terminal is sold to another business in the neighborhood, the term would include the income derived from such sale. However, because an oil or gas well or a mine constitutes a separate facility, the term "related terminal income" does not include income derived in any form from a deposit of oil, natural gas, or any other mineral located on property owned or leased by the terminal railroad corporation.

Similarly, while the term includes income derived from the rental of a small number of offices located in the terminal building (whether or not the lessees are railroad corporations), it does not include income derived from the leasing or operation, for the use of the general public, of a large number of offices or a large number of rooms for lodging, whether or not the space is physically part of the same structure as the terminal. Moreover, the term does not include income derived from the rental of offices to the general public in an addition to the terminal building constructed after October 23, 1962, unless the addition is primarily used for railroad purposes and the offices rented to the general public do not constitute a separate facility in the addition. Whether or not income from the addition is determined to be related terminal income, the income from the small number of offices which were included in the terminal building before the addition was constructed shall continue to be related terminal income.

(iv) From the United States in payment for facilities or services in connection with mail handling. The income must be derived directly from the U.S. Government, or any agency thereof (including for this purpose the U.S. Postal Service), through the receipt of payments for mail-handling facilities or services. Thus, the term would include income derived from the rental of space for a post office for use by the general public on the terminal premises or from the sorting of mail in a railroad box car.

(3) *Illustration.*—The provisions of this paragraph may be illustrated by the following example:

Example.—For its calendar year 1973, the R Company, a terminal railroad corporation, has taxable income of $36,000, before the application of section 281 and taking no account of section 277, determined as follows:

Gross income:

Switching charges	$50,000
Express companies	2,000
Commuter line	4,000

U.S. mail handling	4,000
Railroad bridge tolls:	
From railroads	2,000
From automobiles	1,000
Total	3,000
Station and train charges	47,000
Terminal parking lot	4,000
Rent from terminal building:	
Passenger facilities (ground level)	8,000
Offices leased to railroads (2d floor)	3,000
Offices leased to others (2d floor)	1,000
Hotel open to public (3d through 6th floors) . .	14,000
Total	26,000
Interest received from bond investments	1,500
Dividends received from wholly owned subsidiary .	
. . . .	10,000
Amount realized from sale of equipment	6,000
Less:	
Adjusted basis	1,000
Expenses of sale	500
	1,500
	4,500
	156,000
Allowable deductions:	
Dividend received deduction	8,500
Interest paid:	
On loan for hotel furnishings	1,500
On loan for rolling stock	2,000
	3,500
Maintenance, depreciation, management and other	
expenses:	
Attributable to hotel	3,000
Attributable to parking lot	1,000
Attributable to U.S. mail handling	1,000
All other	98,000
	103,000
Loss from sale of securities	3,000
Charitable contribution	500
Net operating loss deduction	1,500
	120,000
Taxable income before the application of sec. 281 .	36,000

The R Co.'s related terminal income for 1973 is $24,000, computed as follows:

Taxable income (before the application of sec. 281)	36,000
Less:	
Dividend received	10,000
Minus dividend received deduction	8,500
	1,500
Interest received	1,500
Amount realized from sale of equipment	6,000
Less:	
Adjusted basis	1,000
Expense of sale	500
	1,500
	4,500
Hotel income	14,000
Less:	
Interest paid on loan for hotel	1,500
Other hotel expenses	3,000
	4,500
	9,500
	17,000
	19,000
Add:	
Loss from sale of securities	3,000
Charitable contribution	500
Net operating loss deduction	1,500
	5,000
Related terminal income	24,000

(c) *Related terminal services.*—The term "related terminal services" means only the services or the use of facilities, provided by the terminal railroad corporation, which are taken into account in computing related terminal income. Thus, the term includes the providing of terminal and switching services, the furnishing of terminal and switching facilities including the furnishing of terminal trackage, and the operation of bridges and ferries for railroad purposes. For exam-

ple, upon the facts of the example in the preceding paragraph, the charges for related terminal services are $126,000, determined as follows:

Switching charges	$50,000
Express companies	2,000
Commuter line	4,000
U.S. mail handling	4,000
Railroad bridge tolls	3,000
Station and train charges	47,000
Terminal parking lot	4,000
Rent from:	
Passenger facilities	8,000
Offices	4,000
Total	126,000

(d) *Agreement.*—As used in section 281 and § 1.281-2 the term "agreement" means a written contract, entered into before the beginning of the terminal railroad corporation's taxable year in question, to which all shareholders of the terminal railroad corporation are parties. The fact that other railroad corporations or persons are also parties will not disqualify an agreement. Section 281 applies only if, and to the extent that, the reduction of the liability or charge that would be made, as described in paragraph (c) of § 1.281-2, results from the agreement. Thus, where the other conditions of the statute are met, section 281 applies if a written agreement, to which all of the shareholders were parties and which was entered into prior to the beginning of the terminal railroad corporation's taxable year, provides that the net revenues of the terminal railroad corporation are to be applied as a reduction of what would otherwise be the charge for the taxable year for related terminal services provided to the shareholders. Similarly, section 281 applies, where its other requirements are fulfilled, if the agreement provides that the net revenues are to be credited against rental obligations resulting from related terminal services furnished to shareholders. However, section 281 does not apply where the agreement provides that the net revenues are to be divided among the shareholders and distributed to them in cash or held subject to their unconditional right of withdrawal instead of being applied to the computation of charges, or in reduction of liabilities incurred, for related terminal services.

(e) *Railroad corporation.*—For purposes of section 281, § 1.281-2, and this section, the term "railroad corporation" means any corporation (regardless of whether it is a shareholder of the terminal railroad corporation) that is engaged as a common carrier in the furnishing or sale of transportation by railroad, or is a lessor of railroad equipment or facilities. For purposes of the preceding sentence, a corporation is a lessor of railroad equipment or facilities only if (1) it is subject to part I of the Interstate Commerce Act, (2) substantially all of its railroad properties have been leased to a railroad corporation or corporations, (3) each lease is for a term of more than 20 years, and (4) 80 percent or more of its gross income for the taxable year is derived from such lease. [Reg. § 1.281-3.]

☐ [*T.D.* 7356, 5-30-75.]

[Reg. § 1.281-4]

§ 1.281-4. Taxable years affected.—(a) *In general.*—Except as provided in paragraph (b) of this section, the provisions of section 281 and §§ 1.281-2 and 1.281-3 shall apply to all taxable years to which either the Internal Revenue Code of 1954 or the Internal Revenue Code of 1939 apply.

(b) *Taxable years ending before October 23, 1962.*—(1)(i) In the case of a taxable year of a terminal railroad corporation ending before October 23, 1962, section 281 (a) shall apply only to the extent that the terminal railroad corporation (a) computed its taxable income on its return for such taxable year as if the "reduced amount", described in paragraph (c) of § 1.281-2, were not received or accrued, and (b) did not decrease its otherwise allowable deductions for such taxable year on account of that "reduced amount". Similarly, in the case of a taxable year of a shareholder of a terminal railroad corporation ending before October 23, 1962, section 281(b) shall apply only to the extent that such shareholder computed its taxable income on its return for such taxable year as if the shareholder had neither received or accrued as a dividend nor paid or incurred as an expense the "reduced amount" described in paragraph (c) of § 1.281-2. Such return must have been filed on or before the due date (including the period of any extension of time) for filing the return for the applicable taxable year. The fact that an amended return or claim for refund or credit of overpayment was subsequently filed, or a deficiency subsequently assessed, based upon a computation of taxable income which is inconsistent with the manner in which the taxable income was computed on the timely filed return, is immaterial.

(ii) The provisions of this paragraph may be illustrated by the following examples:

Example (1).—The G Company is a terminal railroad corporation which in 1960 reduced the liabilities resulting from charges to its shareholders, pursuant to a 1947 written agreement, by its income from nonshareholder sources. For the calendar year 1960, the G Company's related terminal income was $24,000, of which $3,000 is attributable to income from the United States in payment for facilities and services in connection with mail handling. Although the shareholders' liabilities were reduced by $24,000 as a result of taking related terminal income earned during the taxable year into account, on its timely filed 1960 income tax return the G Company treated the $3,000 of liabilities which were reduced on account of income from mail handling as gross income received or accrued during the year. Assuming that the provisions of § 1.281-2 otherwise apply, their application to the determination of the 1960 tax liability of the G Company shall not extend to the entire "reduced amount" of $24,000, but shall be limited to $21,000 of that amount.

Example (2).—Assume the same facts as in example (1), and the following additional facts. The G Company had three shareholders in 1960, and an equal discharge of liability of $8,000 resulted for each of them on account of related terminal income. Each shareholder treated, on its timely filed 1960 income tax return, $1,000 of its liabilities, which were so reduced and were attributable to income from the United States in payment for facilities and services in connection with mail handling, as if it had received $1,000 from the G Company as a dividend and paid that $1,000 to the G Company for services. Each shareholder treated the remaining $7,000 of its liabilities which were so reduced as if the liabilities which were reduced had never been incurred. Assuming that the provisions of § 1.281-2 otherwise apply, each shareholder shall not be considered to have received or accrued as a dividend, nor to have paid or incurred as an expense $7,000 (instead of $8,000).

(2) For any taxable year of a terminal railroad corporation ending before October 23, 1962, a claim for refund or credit of overpayment of income tax based upon section 281 may be filed, even though such refund or credit of overpayment was otherwise barred by

operation of any law or rule of law on October 23, 1962, subject to the conditions set forth in paragraph (b)(2)(i) through (v) of this section.

(i) The claim for refund or credit of overpayment must not have been barred by a closing agreement (under either section 3760 of the Internal Revenue Code of 1939 or section 7121 of the Internal Revenue Code of 1954), or by a compromise (under section 3761 of the Internal Revenue Code of 1939 or section 7122 of the Internal Revenue Code of 1954);

(ii) The claim for refund or credit of overpayment shall be allowed only to the extent that the overpayment of income tax results from the recomputation of the terminal railroad corporation's taxable income in the manner described in paragraph (a) of § 1.281-2;

(iii) The claim for refund or credit of the overpayment must have been filed prior to October 23, 1963;

(iv) The claim for refund or credit of overpayment shall be allowed only to the extent that the manner in which the terminal railroad corporation's taxable income is recomputed is the manner in which the terminal railroad corporation's taxable income was computed on its timely filed income tax return for such taxable year; and

(v) Each railroad corporation which was a shareholder of the terminal railroad corporation during such taxable year must consent in writing to the assessment, within such period as may be agreed upon with the district director, of any deficiency for any year (even though assessment of the deficiency would otherwise be prevented by the operation of any law or rule of law at the time of filing the consent) to the extent that—

(A) The deficiency is attributable to the recomputation of the shareholder's taxable income in the manner described in paragraph (b) of § 1.281-2, and

(B) The deficiency results from the shareholder's allocable portion of the "reduced amount" (described in paragraph (c) of § 1.281-2) which gives rise to the refund or credit granted to the terminal railroad corporation under this subparagraph. [Reg. § 1.281-4.]

☐ [*T.D.* 7356, 5-30-75.]

[The next page is 30,401.]

30,401

CORPORATE DISTRIBUTIONS AND ADJUSTMENTS
Distributions by Corporations
See p. 20,601 for regulations not amended to reflect law changes

[Reg. §1.301-1]

§1.301-1. Rules applicable with respect to distributions of money and other property.—(a) *General.*—Section 301 provides the general rule for the treatment of distributions made in taxable years beginning after December 31, 1986, of property by a corporation to a shareholder with respect to its stock. The term *property* is defined in section 317(a). Except as otherwise provided in chapter 1 of the Internal Revenue Code (Code), such distributions are treated as provided in section 301(c). Under section 301(c), distributions may be included in gross income to the extent the amount distributed is considered a dividend under section 316, applied against and reduces the adjusted basis of the stock, treated as gain from the sale or exchange of property, or exempt from Federal income tax in the case of certain distributions out of increase in value accrued before March 1, 1913. The amount of a distribution to which section 301 applies is determined in accordance with the provisions of section 301(b). The basis of property received in a distribution to which section 301 applies is the fair market value of the property, as provided in section 301(d).

(b) *Amount of distribution and determination of fair market value.*—The amount of a distribution to which section 301 applies is the amount of money received in the distribution, plus the fair market value of other property received in the distribution. The fair market value of any property distributed is determined as of the date of the distribution.

(c) *Time of inclusion in gross income and time of determination of fair market value.*—A distribution made by a corporation to its shareholders is included in the gross income of the distributees when the cash or other property is unqualifiedly made subject to their demands, without regard to whether such date is the same as that on which the corporation made the distribution. For example, if a corporation distributes a taxable dividend in property on December 30, 2021, that is received by, or unqualifiedly made subject to the demands of, its shareholders on January 3, 2022, the amount to be included in the gross income of the shareholders will be the fair market value of such property on December 30, 2021, determined under paragraph (b) of this section, although such amount will not be includible in the gross income of the shareholders until January 3, 2022.

(d) *Application of section to shareholders.*—Section 301 is not applicable to an amount paid by a corporation to a shareholder unless the amount is paid to the shareholder in the shareholder's capacity as such.

(e) *Example.*—Corporation M, formed in 1998, has never been an acquiring corporation in a transaction to which section 381(a) applies. On January 1, 2021, A, an individual, owned all of the stock of Corporation M, consisting of a single share with an adjusted basis of $2,000. During 2021, A received distributions from Corporation M totaling $30,000, consisting of $10,000 in cash and listed securities having a basis in the hands of Corporation M and a fair market value on the date distributed of $20,000. Corporation M's taxable year is the calendar year. As of December 31, 2020, Corporation M had accumulated earnings and profits in the amount of $26,000, and it had no earnings and profits and no deficit for 2021. Of the $30,000 received by A, $26,000 is treated as an ordinary dividend; of the remaining $4,000, $2,000 is applied against and reduces the adjusted basis of A's stock under section 301(c)(2), and the $2,000 in excess of the adjusted basis of A's stock is treated as gain from the sale or exchange of property under section 301(c)(3)(A). If A immediately sells the stock in Corporation M, the basis for determining gain or loss on the sale will be zero.

(f) *Reduction for liabilities.*—(1) *General rule.*—For purposes of section 301(b)(2), no reduction in the amount of a distribution is made for the amount of any liability, except to the extent the liability is assumed by the shareholder within the meaning of section 357(d).

(2) *No reduction below zero.*—Any reduction pursuant to paragraph (f)(1) of this section does not cause the amount of the distribution to be reduced below zero.

(3) *Applicability dates.*—(i) *In general.*—This paragraph (f) applies to distributions occurring after January 4, 2001.

(ii) *Retroactive application.*—For distributions made on or before January 4, 2001, see §1.301-1(g) as contained in 26 CFR part 1 revised April 1, 2021.

(g) *Basis.*—The basis of property received in a distribution to which section 301 applies is the fair market value of such property. See paragraph (b) of this section.

(h) *Transfers for less than fair market value.*—If property is transferred by a corporation to a shareholder for an amount less than its fair market value in a sale or exchange, such shareholder is treated as having received a distribution to which section 301 applies. In such case, the amount of the distribution is the excess of the fair market value of the property over the amount paid for such property at the time of the transfer. For example, on January 3, 2021, A, a shareholder of Corporation X, purchased property from X for $20 when the fair market value of such property was $100. The amount of the distribution to A determined under section 301(b) is $80.

(i) [Reserved]

(j) *Transactions treated as distributions.*—A distribution to shareholders with respect to their stock is within the terms of section 301, although it takes place at the same time as another transaction, if the distribution is in substance a separate transaction (whether or not connected in a formal sense). This situation is most likely to occur in the case of a recapitalization, a reincorporation, or a merger of a corporation with a newly organized corporation having substantially no property. For example, if a corporation having only common stock outstanding exchanges one share of newly issued common stock and one bond with a principal amount of $10 for each share of outstanding common stock, the distribution of the bond will be a distribution of property (to the extent of its fair market value) to which section 301 applies, even though the exchange of common stock for common stock may be pursuant to a plan of reorganization under the terms of section 368(a)(1)(E) (recapitalization) and may result in the shareholder not recognizing any gain or loss on the exchange by reason of section 354.

(k) *Cancellation of indebtedness.*—The cancellation of indebtedness of a shareholder by a corporation is treated as a distribution of property.

(l) *Cross-references.*—For certain rules relating to adjustments to earnings and profits and for determining the extent to which a distribution is a dividend, see sections 312 and 316 of the Code and the regulations in this part under sections 312 and 316.

(m) *Split-dollar and other life insurance arrangements.*—(1) *Split-dollar life insurance arrangements.*—(i) *Distribution of economic benefits.*—The provision by a corporation to its shareholder pursuant to a split-dollar life insurance arrangement, as defined in §1.61-22(b)(1) or (2), of economic benefits described in §1.61-22(d), or of amounts described in §1.61-22(e), is treated as a distribution of property, the amount of which is determined under §1.61-22(d) and (e), respectively.

(ii) *Distribution of entire contract or undivided interest therein.*—A transfer (within the meaning of §1.61-22(c)(3)) of the ownership of a life insurance contract (or an undivided interest therein) that is part of a split-dollar life insurance arrangement is a distribution of property, the amount of which is determined pursuant to §1.61-22(g)(1) and (2).

(2) *Other life insurance arrangements.*—A payment by a corporation on behalf of a shareholder of premiums on a life insurance contract or an undivided interest therein that is owned by the shareholder constitutes a distribution of property, even if such payment is not part of a split-dollar life insurance arrangement under §1.61-22(b).

(3) *When distribution is made*—(i) *In general.*—Except as provided in paragraph (m)(3)(ii) of this section, paragraph (c) of this section applies to determine when a distribution described in paragraph (m)(1) or (2) of this section is taken into account by a shareholder.

(ii) *Exception.*—Notwithstanding paragraph (c) of this section, a distribution described in paragraph (m)(1)(ii) of this section is treated as made by a corporation to its shareholder at the time that the life insurance contract, or an undivided interest therein, is transferred (within the meaning of §1.61-22(c)(3)) to the shareholder.

(4) *Applicability date.*—(i) *General rule.*—This paragraph (m) applies to split-dollar and other life insurance arrangements entered into after September 17, 2003. For purposes of this paragraph (m)(4),

a split-dollar life insurance arrangement is entered into as determined under § 1.61-22(j)(1)(ii).

(ii) *Modified arrangements treated as new arrangements.*—If a split-dollar life insurance arrangement entered into on or before September 17, 2003, is materially modified (within the meaning of § 1.61-22(j)(2)) after September 17, 2003, the arrangement is treated as a new arrangement entered into on the date of the modification.

(n) *Applicability date.*—Paragraphs (a) through (c), (e), (g), and (h) of this section apply to distributions under section 301 made after September 22, 2021.

☐ [*T.D.* 6152, 12-2-55. *Amended by T.D.* 6752, 9-8-64; *T.D.* 7084, 1-7-71; *T.D.* 7209, 10-3-72; *T.D.* 7283, 8-2-73; *T.D.* 7293, 11-27-73; *T.D.* 7587, 1-4-79; *T.D.* 8474, 4-26-93; *T.D.* 8586, 1-9-95; *T.D.* 8924, 1-3-2001; *T.D.* 8964, 9-26-2001, *T.D.* 9092, 9-11-2003 and *T.D.* 9954, 9-21-2021.]

[Reg. §1.302-1]

§1.302-1. General.—(a) Under section 302(d), unless otherwise provided in subchapter C, chapter 1 of the Code, a distribution in redemption of stock shall be treated as a distribution of property to which section 301 applies if the distribution is not within any of the provisions of section 302(b). A distribution in redemption of stock shall be considered a distribution in part or full payment in exchange for the stock under section 302(a) provided paragraph (1), (2), (3), or (4) of section 302(b) applies. Section 318(a) (relating to constructive ownership of stock) applies to all redemptions under section 302 except that in the termination of a shareholder's interest certain limitations are placed on the application of section 318(a)(1) by section 302(c)(2). The term "redemption of stock" is defined in section 317(b). Section 302 does not apply to that portion of any distribution which qualifies as a distribution in partial liquidation under section 346. For special rules relating to redemption of stock to pay death taxes see section 303. For special rules relating to redemption of section 306 stock see section 306. For special rules relating to redemption of stock in partial or complete liquidation see section 331.

(b) If, in connection with a partial liquidation under the terms of section 346, stock is redeemed in an amount in excess of the amount specified by section 331(a)(2), section 302(b) shall first apply as to each shareholder to which it is applicable without limitation because of section 331(a)(2). That portion of the total distribution which is used in all redemptions from specific shareholders which are within the terms of section 302(a) shall be excluded in determining the application of sections 346 and 331(a)(2). For example, Corporation X has $50,000 which is attributable to the sale of one of two active businesses and which, if distributed in redemption of stock, would qualify as a partial liquidation under the terms of section 346(b). Corporation X distributes $60,000 to its shareholders in redemption of stock, $20,000 of which is in redemption of all of the stock of shareholder A within the meaning of section 302(b)(3). The $20,000 distributed in redemption of the stock of shareholder A will be excluded in determining the application of sections 346 and 331(a)(2). The entire $60,000 will be treated as in part or full payment for stock ($20,000 qualifying under section 302(a) and $40,000 qualifying under sections 346 and 331(a)(2)). [Reg. §1.302-1.]

☐ [*T.D.* 6152, 12-2-55.]

[Reg. §1.302-2]

§1.302-2. Redemptions not taxable as dividends.—(a) *In general.*—The fact that a redemption fails to meet the requirements of paragraph (2), (3) or (4) of section 302(b) shall not be taken into account in determining whether the redemption is not essentially equivalent to a dividend under section 302(b)(1). See, however, paragraph (b) of this section. For example, if a shareholder owns only nonvoting stock of a corporation which is not section 306 stock and which is limited and preferred as to dividends and in liquidation, and one-half of such stock is redeemed, the distribution will ordinarily meet the requirements of paragraph (1) of section 302(b) but will not meet the requirements of paragraph (2), (3) or (4) of such section. The determination of whether or not a distribution is within the phrase "essentially equivalent to a dividend" (that is, having the same effect as a distribution without any redemption of stock) shall be made without regard to the earnings and profits of the corporation at the time of the distribution. For example, if A owns all the stock of a corporation and the corporation redeems part of his stock at a time when it has no earnings and profits, the distribution shall be treated as a distribution under section 301 pursuant to section 302(d).

(b) *Redemption not essentially equivalent to a dividend.*—(1) *In general.*—The question whether a distribution in redemption of stock of a shareholder is not essentially equivalent to a dividend under section 302(b)(1) depends upon the facts and circumstances of each case. One of the facts to be considered in making this determination is the constructive stock ownership of such shareholder under section 318(a). All distributions in pro rata redemptions of a part of the stock of a corporation generally will be treated as distributions under section 301 if the corporation has only one class of stock outstanding. However, for distributions in partial liquidation, see section 302(e). The redemption of all of one class of stock (except section 306 stock) either at one time or in a series of redemptions generally will be considered as a distribution under section 301 if all classes of stock outstanding at the time of the redemption are held in the same proportion. Distributions in redemption of stock may be treated as distributions under section 301 regardless of the provisions of the stock certificate and regardless of whether all stock being redeemed was acquired by the stockholders from whom the stock was redeemed by purchase or otherwise.

(2) *Statement.*—Unless § 1.331-1(d) applies, every significant holder that transfers stock to the issuing corporation in exchange for property from such corporation must include on or with such holder's return for the taxable year of such exchange a statement entitled, "STATEMENT PURSUANT TO § 1.302-2(b)(2) BY [INSERT NAME AND TAXPAYER IDENTIFICATION NUMBER (IF ANY) OF TAXPAYER], A SIGNIFICANT HOLDER OF THE STOCK OF [INSERT NAME AND EMPLOYER IDENTIFICATION NUMBER (IF ANY) OF ISSUING CORPORATION]." If a significant holder is a controlled foreign corporation (within the meaning of section 957), each United States shareholder (within the meaning of section 951(b)) with respect thereto must include this statement on or with its return. The statement must include—

(i) The fair market value and basis of the stock transferred by the significant holder to the issuing corporation; and

(ii) A description of the property received by the significant holder from the issuing corporation.

(3) *Definitions.*—For purposes of this section:

(i) Significant holder means any person that, immediately before the exchange—

(A) Owned at least five percent (by vote or value) of the total outstanding stock of the issuing corporation if the stock owned by such person is publicly traded; or

(B) Owned at least one percent (by vote or value) of the total outstanding stock of the issuing corporation if the stock owned by such person is not publicly traded.

(ii) Publicly traded stock means stock that is listed on—

(A) A national securities exchange registered under section 6 of the Securities Exchange Act of 1934 (15 U.S.C. 78f); or

(B) An interdealer quotation system sponsored by a national securities association registered under section 15A of the Securities Exchange Act of 1934 (15 U.S.C. 78o-3).

(iii) Issuing corporation means the corporation that issued the shares of stock, some or all of which were transferred by a significant holder to such corporation in the exchange described in paragraph (b)(2) of this section.

(4) *Cross reference.*—See section 6043 of the Internal Revenue Code for requirements relating to a return by a liquidating corporation.

(c) *Basis adjustments.*—In any case in which an amount received in redemption of stock is treated as a distribution of a dividend, proper adjustment of the basis of the remaining stock will be made with respect to the stock redeemed. (For adjustments to basis required for certain redemptions of corporate shareholders that are treated as extraordinary dividends, see section 1059 and the regulations thereunder.) The following examples illustrate the application of this rule:

Example (1). A, an individual, purchased all of the stock of Corporation X for $100,000. In 1955 the corporation redeems half of the stock for $150,000, and it is determined that this amount constitutes a dividend. The remaining stock of Corporation X held by A has a basis of $100,000.

Example (2). H and W, husband and wife, each own half of the stock of Corporation X. All of the stock was purchased by H for $100,000 cash. In 1950 H gave one-half of the stock to W, the stock transferred having a value in excess of $50,000. In 1955 all of the stock of H is redeemed for $150,000, and it is determined that the distribution to H in redemption of his shares constitutes the distribution of a dividend. Immediately after the transaction, W holds the remaining stock of Corporation X with a basis of $100,000.

Example (3). The facts are the same as in Example (2) with the additional facts that the outstanding stock of Corporation X consists of 1,000 shares and all but 10 shares of the stock of H is redeemed. Immediately after the transaction, H holds 10 shares of the stock of Corporation X with a basis of $50,000, and W holds 500 shares with a basis of $50,000.

(d) *Effective/applicability date.*— Paragraphs (b)(2), (b)(3) and (b)(4) of this section apply to any taxable year beginning on or after May 30, 2006. However, taxpayers may apply paragraphs (b)(2), (b)(3) and (b)(4) of this section to any original Federal income tax return (including any amended return filed on or before the due date (including extensions) of such original return) timely filed on or after May 30, 2006. For taxable years beginning before May 30, 2006, see §1.302-2 as contained in 26 CFR part 1 in effect on April 1, 2006. [Reg. §1.302-2.]

☐ [*T.D. 6152, 12-2-55. Amended by T.D. 8724, 7-15-97; T.D. 9264, 5-26-2006 and T.D. 9329, 6-13-2007.*]

[Reg. §1.302-3]

§1.302-3. Substantially disproportionate redemption.— (a) Section 302(b)(2) provides for the treatment of an amount received in redemption of stock as an amount received in exchange for such stock if—

(1) Immediately after the redemption the shareholder owns less than 50 percent of the total combined voting power of all classes of stock as provided in section 302(b)(2)(B),

(2) The redemption is a substantially disproportionate redemption within the meaning of section 302(b)(2)(C), and

(3) The redemption is not pursuant to a plan described in section 302(b)(2)(D).

Section 318(a) (relating to constructive ownership of stock) shall apply both in making the disproportionate redemption test and in determining the percentage of stock ownership after the redemption. The requirements under section 302(b)(2) shall be applied to each shareholder separately and shall be applied only with respect to stock which is issued and outstanding in the hands of the shareholders. Section 302(b)(2) only applies to a redemption of voting stock or to a redemption of both voting stock and other stock. Section 302(b)(2) does not apply to the redemption solely of nonvoting stock (common or preferred). However, if a redemption is treated as an exchange to a particular shareholder under the terms of section 302(b)(2), such section will apply to the simultaneous redemption of nonvoting preferred stock (which is not section 306 stock) owned by such shareholder and such redemption will also be treated as an exchange. Generally, for purposes of this section, stock which does not have voting rights until the happening of an event, such as a default in the payment of dividends on preferred stock, is not voting stock until the happening of the specified event. Subsection 302(b)(2)(D) provides that a redemption will not be treated as substantially disproportionate if made pursuant to a plan the purpose or effect of which is a series of redemptions which result in the aggregate in a distribution which is not substantially disproportionate. Whether or not such a plan exists will be determined from all the facts and circumstances.

(b) The application of paragraph (a) of this section is illustrated by the following example:

Example. Corporation M has outstanding 400 shares of common stock of which A, B, C and D each own 100 shares or 25 percent. No stock is considered constructively owned by A, B, C or D under section 318. Corporation M redeems 55 shares from A, 25 shares from B, and 20 shares from C. For the redemption to be disproportionate as to any shareholder, such shareholder must own after the redemptions less than 20 percent (80 percent of 25 percent) of the 300 shares of stock then outstanding. After the redemptions, A owns 45 shares (15 percent), B owns 75 shares (25 percent), and C owns 80 shares (26²/₃ percent). The distribution is disproportionate only with respect to A. [Reg. §1.302-3.]

☐ [*T.D. 6152, 12-2-55.*]

[Reg. §1.302-4]

§1.302-4. Termination of shareholder's interest.— Section 302(b)(3) provides that a distribution in redemption of all of the stock of the corporation owned by a shareholder shall be treated as a distribution in part or full payment in exchange for the stock of such shareholder. In determining whether all of the stock of the shareholder has been redeemed, the general rule of section 302(c)(1) requires that the rules of constructive ownership provided in section 318(a) shall apply. Section 302(c)(2), however, provides that section 318(a)(1) (relating to constructive ownership of stock owned by members of a family) shall not apply where the specific requirements of section 302(c)(2) are met. The following rules shall be applicable in determining whether the specific requirements of section 302(c)(2) are met:

(a) *Statement.—*The agreement specified in section 302(c)(2)(A)(iii) shall be in the form of a statement entitled, "STATEMENT PURSUANT TO SECTION 302(c)(2)(A)(iii) BY [INSERT NAME AND TAXPAYER IDENTIFICATION NUMBER (IF ANY) OF TAXPAYER OR RELATED PERSON, AS THE CASE MAY BE], A DISTRIBUTEE (OR RELATED PERSON) OF [INSERT NAME AND EMPLOYER IDENTIFICATION NUMBER (IF ANY) OF DISTRIBUTING CORPORATION]." The distributee must include such statement on or with the distributee's first return for the taxable year in which the distribution described in section 302(b)(3) occurs. If the distributee is a controlled

foreign corporation (within the meaning of section 957), each United States shareholder (within the meaning of section 951(b)) with respect thereto must include this statement on or with its return. The distributee must represent in the statement—

(1) THE DISTRIBUTEE (OR RELATED PERSON) HAS NOT ACQUIRED, OTHER THAN BY BEQUEST OR INHERITANCE, ANY INTEREST IN THE CORPORATION (AS DESCRIBED IN SECTION 302(c)(2)(A)(i)) SINCE THE DISTRIBUTION; and

(2) THE DISTRIBUTEE (OR RELATED PERSON) WILL NOTIFY THE INTERNAL REVENUE SERVICE OF ANY ACQUISITION, OTHER THAN BY BEQUEST OR INHERITANCE, OF SUCH AN INTEREST IN THE CORPORATION WITHIN 30 DAYS AFTER THE ACQUISITION, IF THE ACQUISITION OCCURS WITHIN 10 YEARS FROM THE DATE OF THE DISTRIBUTION.

(b) *Substantiation information.—*The distributee who files an agreement under section 302(c)(2)(A)(iii) shall retain copies of income tax returns and any other records indicating fully the amount of tax which would have been payable had the redemption been treated as a distribution subject to section 301.

(c) *Stock of parent, subsidiary or successor corporation redeemed.—*If stock of a parent corporation is redeemed, section 302(c)(2)(A), relating to acquisition of an interest in the corporation within 10 years after termination shall be applied with reference to an interest both in the parent corporation and any subsidiary of such parent corporation. If stock of a parent corporation is sold to a subsidiary in a transaction described in section 304, section 302(c)(2)(A) shall be applicable to the acquisition of an interest in such subsidiary corporation or in the parent corporation. If stock of a subsidiary corporation is redeemed, section 302(c)(2)(A) shall be applied with reference to an interest both in such subsidiary corporation and its parent. Section 302(c)(2)(A) shall also be applied with respect to an interest in a corporation which is a successor corporation to the corporation the interest in which has been terminated.

(d) *Redeemed shareholder as creditor.—*For the purpose of section 302(c)(2)(A)(i), a person will be considered to be a creditor only if the rights of such person with respect to the corporation are not greater or broader in scope than necessary for the enforcement of his claim. Such claim must not in any sense be proprietary and must not be subordinate to the claims of general creditors. An obligation in the form of a debt may thus constitute a proprietary interest. For example, if under the terms of the instrument the corporation may discharge the principal amount of its obligation to a person by payments, the amount or certainty of which are dependent upon the earnings of the corporation, such a person is not a creditor of the corporation. Furthermore, if under the terms of the instrument the rate of purported interest is dependent upon earnings, the holder of such instrument may not, in some cases, be a creditor.

(e) *Acquisition of assets pursuant to creditor's rights.—*In the case of a distributee to whom section 302(b)(3) is applicable, who is a creditor after such transaction, the acquisition of the assets of the corporation in the enforcement of the rights of such creditor shall not be considered an acquisition of an interest in the corporation for purposes of section 302(c)(2) unless stock of the corporation, its parent corporation, or, in the case of a redemption of stock of a parent corporation, of a subsidiary of such corporation is acquired.

(f) *Constructive ownership rules applicable.—*In determining whether an entire interest in the corporation has been terminated under section 302(b)(3), under all circumstances paragraphs (2), (3), (4), and (5) of section 318(a) (relating to constructive ownership of stock) shall be applicable.

(g) *Avoidance of Federal income tax.—*Section 302(c)(2)(B) provides that section 302(c)(2)(A) shall not apply—

(1) If any portion of the stock redeemed was acquired directly or indirectly within the 10-year period ending on the date of the distribution by the distributee from a person, the ownership of whose stock would (at the time of distribution) be attributable to the distributee under section 318(a), or

(2) If any person owns (at the time of the distribution) stock, the ownership of which is attributable to the distributee under section 318(a), such person acquired any stock in the corporation directly or indirectly from the distributee within the 10-year period ending on the date of the distribution, and such stock so acquired from the distributee is not redeemed in the same transaction,

unless the acquisition (described in (1) of this paragraph) or the disposition by the distributee (described in subparagraph (2)) did not have as one of its principal purposes the avoidance of Federal income tax. A transfer of stock by the transferor, within the 10-year period ending on the date of the distribution, to a person whose stock would be attributable to the transferor shall not be deemed to have as one of its principal purposes the avoidance of Federal income tax merely because the transferee is in a lower income tax bracket than the transferor.

(h) *Effective/applicability date.*—Paragraph (a) of this section applies to any taxable year beginning on or after May 30, 2006. However, taxpayers may apply paragraph (a) of this section to any original Federal income tax return (including any amended return filed on or before the due date (including extensions) of such original return) timely filed on or after May 30, 2006. For taxable years beginning before May 30, 2006, see § 1.302-4 as contained in 26 CFR part 1 in effect on April 1, 2006. [Reg. § 1.302-4.]

☐ [*T.D. 6152, 12-2-55. Amended by T.D. 6969, 8-22-68; T.D. 7535, 3-14-78; T.D. 9264, 5-26-2006 and T.D. 9329, 6-13-2007.*]

[Reg. § 1.303-1]

§ 1.303-1. General.—Section 303 provides that in certain cases a distribution in redemption of stock, the value of which is included in determining the value of the gross estate of a decedent, shall be treated as a distribution in full payment in exchange for the stock so redeemed. [Reg. § 1.303-1.]

☐ [*T.D. 6152, 12-2-55.*]

[Reg. § 1.303-2]

§ 1.303-2. Requirements.—(a) Section 303 applies only where the distribution is with respect to stock of a corporation the value of whose stock in the gross estate of the decedent for Federal estate tax purposes is an amount in excess of (1) 35 percent of the value of the gross estate of such decedent, or (2) 50 percent of the taxable estate of such decedent. For the purposes of such 35 percent and 50 percent requirements, stock of two or more corporations shall be treated as the stock of a single corporation if more than 75 percent in value of the outstanding stock of each such corporation is included in determining the value of the decedent's gross estate. For the purpose of the 75 percent requirement, stock which, at the decedent's death, represents the surviving spouse's interest in community property shall be considered as having been included in determining the value of the decedent's gross estate.

(b) For the purpose of section 303(b)(2)(A)(i), the term "gross estate" means the gross estate as computed in accordance with section 2031 (or, in the case of the estate of a decedent nonresident not a citizen of the United States, in accordance with section 2103). For the purpose of section 303(b)(2)(A)(ii), the term "taxable estate" means the taxable estate as computed in accordance with section 2051 (or, in the case of the estate of a decedent non-resident not a citizen of the United States, in accordance with section 2106). In case the value of an estate is determined for Federal estate tax purposes under section 2032 (relating to alternate valuation), then, for purposes of section 303(b)(2), the value of the gross estate, the taxable estate, and the stock shall each be determined on the applicable date prescribed in section 2032.

(c)(1) In determining whether the estate of the decedent is comprised of stock of a corporation of sufficient value to satisfy the percentage requirements of section 303(b)(2)(A) and section 303(b)(2)(B), the total value, in the aggregate, of all classes of stock of the corporation includible in determining the value of the gross estate is taken into account. A distribution under section 303(a) may be in redemption of the stock of the corporation includible in determining the value of the gross estate, without regard to the class of such stock.

(2) The above may be illustrated by the following example:

Example. The gross estate of the decedent has a value of $1,000,000, the taxable estate is $700,000, and the sum of the death taxes and funeral and administration expenses is $275,000. Included in determining the gross estate of the decedent is stock of three corporations which, for Federal estate tax purposes, is valued as follows:

Corporation A:
Common stock	$100,000
Preferred stock	100,000

Corporation B:
Common stock	50,000
Preferred stock	350,000

Corporation C:
Common stock	200,000

The stock of Corporation A and Corporation C included in the estate of the decedent constitutes all of the outstanding stock of both corporations. The stock of Corporation A and the stock of Corporation C, treated as the stock of a single corporation under section 303(b)(2)(B), has a value in excess of $350,000 (35 percent of the gross estate or 50 percent of the taxable estate). Likewise, the stock of

Corporation B has a value in excess of $350,000. The distribution by one or more of the above corporations, within the period prescribed in section 303(b)(1), of amounts not exceeding, in the aggregate, $275,000, in redemption of preferred stock or common stock of such corporation or corporations, will be treated as in full payment in exchange for the stock so redeemed.

(d) If stock includible in determining the value of the gross estate of a decedent is exchanged for new stock, the basis of which is determined by reference to the basis of the old stock, the redemption of the new stock will be treated the same under section 303 as the redemption of the old stock would have been. Thus, section 303 shall apply with respect to a distribution in redemption of stock received by the estate of a decedent (1) in connection with a reorganization under section 368, (2) in a distribution or exchange under section 355 (or so much of section 356 as relates to section 355), (3) in an exchange under section 1036 or (4) in a distribution to which section 305(a) applies. Similarly, a distribution in redemption of stock will qualify under section 303, notwithstanding the fact that the stock redeemed is section 306 stock to the extent that the conditions of section 303 are met.

(e) Section 303 applies to distributions made after the death of the decedent and (1) before the expiration of the 3-year period of limitations for the assessment of estate tax provided in section 6501(a) (determined without the application of any provisions of law extending or suspending the running of such period of limitations), or within 90 days after the expiration of such period, or (2) if a petition for redetermination of a deficiency in such estate tax has been filed with the Tax Court within the time prescribed in section 6213, at any time before the expiration of 60 days after the decision of the Tax Court becomes final. The extension of the period of distribution provided in section 303(b)(1)(B) has reference solely to bona fide contests in the Tax Court and will not apply in the case of a petition for redetermination of a deficiency which is initiated solely for the purpose of extending the period within which section 303 would otherwise be applicable.

(f) While section 303 will most frequently have application in the case where stock is redeemed from the executor or administrator of an estate, the section is also applicable to distributions in redemption of stock included in the decedent's gross estate and held at the time of the redemption by any person who acquired the stock by any of the means comprehended by Part III, Subchapter A, Chapter 11 of the Code, including the heir, legatee, or donee of the decedent, a surviving joint tenant, surviving spouse, appointee, or taker in default of appointment, or a trustee of a trust created by the decedent. Thus, section 303 may apply with respect to a distribution in redemption of stock from a donee to whom the decedent has transferred stock in contemplation of death where the value of such stock is included in the decedent's gross estate under section 2035. Similarly, section 303 may apply to the redemption of stock from a beneficiary of the estate to whom an executor has distributed the stock pursuant to the terms of the will of the decedent. However, section 303 is not applicable to the case where stock is redeemed from a stockholder who has acquired the stock by gift or purchase from any person to whom such stock has passed from the decedent. Nor is section 303 applicable to the case where stock is redeemed from a stockholder who has acquired the stock from the executor in satisfaction of a specific monetary bequest.

(g)(1) The total amount of the distributions to which section 303 may apply with respect to redemptions of stock included in the gross estate of a decedent may not exceed the sum of the estate, inheritance, legacy, and succession taxes (including any interest collected as a part of such taxes) imposed because of the decedent's death and the amount of funeral and administration expenses allowable as deductions to the estate. Where there is more than one distribution in redemption of stock described in section 303(b)(2) during the period of time prescribed in section 303(b)(1), the distributions shall be applied against the total amount which qualifies for treatment under section 303 in the order in which the distributions are made. For this purpose, all distributions in redemption of such stock shall be taken into account, including distributions which under another provision of the Code are treated as in part or full payment in exchange for the stock redeemed.

(2) Subparagraph (1) of this paragraph may be illustrated by the following example:

Example. (i) The gross estate of the decedent has a value of $800,000, the taxable estate is $500,000, and the sum of the death taxes and funeral and administrative expenses is $225,000. Included in determining the gross estate of the decedent is the stock of a corporation which for Federal estate tax purposes is valued at $450,000. During the first year of administration, one-third of such stock is distributed to a legatee and shortly thereafter this stock is redeemed by the corporation for $150,000. During the second year of administration, another one-third of such stock includible in the estate is redeemed for $150,000.

(ii) The first distribution of $150,000 is applied against the amount that qualifies for treatment under section 303, regardless of whether the first distribution was treated as in payment in exchange for stock under section 302(a). Thus, only $75,000 of the second distribution may be treated as in full payment in exchange for stock under section 303. The tax treatment of the remaining $75,000 would be determined under other provisions of the Code.

(h) For the purpose of section 303, the Federal estate tax or any other estate, inheritance, legacy, or succession tax shall be ascertained after the allowance of any credit, relief, discount, refund, remission or reduction of tax. [Reg. § 1.303-2.]

☐ [T.D. 6152, 12-2-55. Amended by T.D. 6724, 4-20-64 and T.D. 7346, 3-6-75.]

[Reg. § 1.303-3]

§1.303-3. Application of other sections.—(a) The sole effect of section 303 is to exempt from tax as a dividend a distribution to which such section is applicable when made in redemption of stock includible in a decedent's gross estate. Such section does not, however, in any other manner affect the principles set forth in sections 302 and 306. Thus, if stock of a corporation is owned equally by A, B, and the C Estate, and the corporation redeems one-half of the stock of each shareholder, the determination of whether the distributions to A and B are essentially equivalent to dividends shall be made without regard to the effect which section 303 may have upon the taxability of the distribution to the C Estate.

(b) See section 304 relative to redemption of stock through the use of related corporations. [Reg. § 1.303-3.]

☐ [T.D. 6152, 12-2-55.]

[Reg. § 1.304-1]

§1.304-1. General.—(a) Except as provided in paragraph (b) of this section, section 304 is applicable where a shareholder sells stock of one corporation to a related corporation as defined in section 304. Sales to which section 304 is applicable shall be treated as redemptions subject to sections 302 and 303.

(b) In the case of—

(1) Any acquisition of stock described in section 304 which occurred before June 22, 1954, and

(2) Any acquisition of stock described in section 304 which occurred on or after June 22, 1954, and on or before December 31, 1958, pursuant to a contract entered into before June 22, 1954,

the extent to which the property received in return for such acquisition shall be treated as a dividend shall be determined as if the Internal Revenue Code of 1939 continued to apply in respect of such acquisition and as if the Internal Revenue Code of 1954 had not been enacted. See section 391. In cases to which this paragraph applies, the basis of the stock received by the acquiring corporation shall be determined as if the Internal Revenue Code of 1939 continued to apply in respect of such acquisition and as if the Internal Revenue Code of 1954 had not been enacted. [Reg. § 1.304-1.]

☐ [T.D. 6152, 12-2-55. Amended by T.D. 6533, 1-18-61.]

[Reg. § 1.304-2]

§1.304-2. Acquisition by related corporation (other than subsidiary).—(a) If a corporation, in return for property, acquires stock of another corporation from one or more persons, and the person or persons from whom the stock was acquired were in control of both such corporations before the acquisition, then such property shall be treated as received in redemption of stock of the acquiring corporation. The stock received by the acquiring corporation shall be treated as a contribution to the capital of such corporation. See section 362(a) for determination of the basis of such stock. The transferor's basis for his stock in the acquiring corporation shall be increased by the basis of stock surrendered by him. (But see below in this paragraph for subsequent reductions of basis in certain cases.) As to each person transferring stock, the amount received shall be treated as a distribution of property under section 302(d), unless as to such person such amount is to be treated as received in exchange for the stock under the terms of section 302(a) or section 303. In applying section 302(b), reference shall be had to the shareholder's ownership of stock in the issuing corporation and not to his ownership of stock in the acquiring corporation (except for purposes of applying section 318(a)). In determining control and applying section 302(b), section 318(a) (relating to the constructive ownership of stock) shall be applied without regard to the 50-percent limitation contained in section 318(a)(2)(C) and (3)(C). A series of redemptions referred to in section 302(b)(2)(D) shall include acquisitions by either of the corporations of stock of the other and stock redemptions by both corporations. If section 302(d) applies to the surrender of stock by a shareholder, his basis for his stock in the acquiring corporation after the transaction (increased as stated above in this paragraph) shall not be decreased except as provided in section 301. If section 302(d) does not apply, the property

received shall be treated as received in a distribution in payment in exchange for stock of the acquiring corporation under section 302(a), which stock has a basis equal to the amount by which the shareholder's basis for his stock in the acquiring corporation was increased on account of the contribution to capital as provided for above in this paragraph. Accordingly, such amount shall be applied in reduction of the shareholder's basis for his stock in the acquiring corporation. Thus, the basis of each share of the shareholder's stock in the acquiring corporation will be the same as the basis of such share before the entire transaction. The holding period of the stock which is considered to have been redeemed shall be the same as the holding period of the stock actually surrendered.

(b) In any case in which two or more persons, in the aggregate, control two corporations, section 304(a)(1) will apply to sales by such persons of stock in either corporation to the other (whether or not made simultaneously) provided the sales by each of such persons are related to each other. The determination of whether the sales are related to each other shall be dependent upon the facts and circumstances surrounding all of the sales. For this purpose, the fact that the sales may occur during a period of one or more years (such as in the case of a series of sales by persons who together control each of such corporations immediately prior to the first of such sales and immediately subsequent to the last of such sales) shall be disregarded, provided the other facts and circumstances indicate related transactions.

(c) The application of section 304(a)(1) may be illustrated by the following examples:

Example (1). Corporation X and corporation Y each have outstanding 200 shares of common stock. One-half of the stock of each corporation is owned by an individual, A, and one-half by another individual, B, who is unrelated to A. On or after August 31, 1964, A sells 30 shares of corporation X stock to corporation Y for $50,000, such stock having an adjusted basis of $10,000 to A. After the sale, A is considered as owning corporation X stock as follows: (i) 70 shares directly, and (ii) 15 shares constructively, since by virtue of his 50-percent ownership of Y he constructively owns 50 percent of the 30 shares owned directly by Y. Since A's percentage of ownership of X's voting stock after the sale (85 out of 200 shares, or 42.5%) is not less than 80 percent of his percentage of ownership of X's voting stock before the sale (100 out of 200 shares, or 50%), the transfer is not "substantially disproportionate" as to him as provided in section 302(b)(2). Under these facts, and assuming that section 302(b)(1) is not applicable, the entire $50,000 is treated as a dividend to A to the extent of the earnings and profits of corporation Y. The basis of the corporation X stock to corporation Y is $10,000, its adjusted basis to A. The amount of $10,000 is added to the basis of the stock of corporation Y in the hands of A.

Example (2). The facts are the same as in example (1) except that A sells 80 shares of corporation X stock to corporation Y, and the sale occurs before August 31, 1964. After the sale, A is considered as owning corporation X stock as follows: (i) 20 shares directly, and (ii) 90 shares indirectly, since by virtue of his 50-percent ownership of Y he constructively owns 50 percent of the 80 shares owned directly by Y and 50 percent of the 100 shares attributed to Y because they are owned by Y's stockholder, B. Since after the sale A owns a total of more than 50 percent of the voting power of all of the outstanding stock of X (110 out of 200 shares, or 55%), the transfer is not "substantially disproportionate" as to him as provided in section 302(b)(2).

Example (3). Corporation X and corporation Y each have outstanding 100 shares of common stock. A, an individual, owns one-half the stock of each corporation. B owns one-half the stock of corporation X, and C owns one-half the stock of corporation Y. A, B, and C are unrelated. A sells 30 shares of the stock of corporation X to corporation Y for $50,000, such stock having an adjusted basis of $10,000 to him. After the sale, A is considered as owning 35 shares of the stock of corporation X (20 shares directly and 15 constructively because one-half of the 30 shares owned by corporation Y are attributed to him). Since before the sale he owned 50 percent of the stock of corporation X and after the sale he owned directly and constructively only 35 percent of such stock, the redemption is substantially disproportionate as to him pursuant to the provisions of section 302(b)(2). He, therefore, realizes a gain of $40,000 ($50,000 minus $10,000). If the stock surrendered is a capital asset, such gain is long-term or short-term capital gain depending on the period of time that such stock was held. The basis to A for the stock of corporation Y is not changed as a result of the entire transaction. The basis to corporation Y for the stock of corporation X is $50,000, i.e., the basis of the transferor ($10,000), increased in the amount of gain recognized to the transferor ($40,000) on the transfer.

Example (4). Corporation X and corporation Y each have outstanding 100 shares of common stock. H, an individual, W, his wife, S, his son, and G, his grandson, each own 25 shares of stock of each corporation. H sells all of his 25 shares of stock of corporation X to corporation Y. Since both before and after the transaction H owned directly and constructively 100 percent of the stock of corporation X, and assuming that section 302(b)(1) is not applicable, the amount received by him for his stock of corporation X is treated as a dividend to him to the extent of the earnings and profits of corporation Y. [Reg. § 1.304-2.]

☐ [*T.D. 6152*, 12-2-55. *Amended by T.D. 6533*, 1-18-61 *and T.D. 6969*, 8-22-68.]

[Reg. § 1.304-3]

§ 1.304-3. Acquisition by a subsidiary.—(a) If a subsidiary acquires stock of its parent corporation from a shareholder of the parent corporation, the acquisition of such stock shall be treated as though the parent corporation had redeemed its own stock. For the purpose of this section, a corporation is a parent corporation if it meets the 50 percent ownership requirements of section 304(c). The determination whether the amount received shall be treated as an amount received in payment in exchange for the stock shall be made by applying section 303, or by applying section 302(b) with reference to the stock of the issuing parent corporation. If such distribution would have been treated as a distribution of property (pursuant to section 302(d) under section 301, the entire amount of the selling price of the stock shall be treated as a dividend to the seller to the extent of the earnings and profits of the parent corporation determined as if the distribution had been made to it of the property that the subsidiary exchanged for the stock. In such cases, the transferor's basis for his remaining stock in the parent corporation will be determined by including the amount of the basis of the stock of the parent corporation sold to the subsidiary.

(b) Section 304(a)(2) may be illustrated by the following example:

Example. Corporation M has outstanding 100 shares of common stock which are owned as follows: B, 75 shares, C, son of B, 20 shares, and D, daughter of B, 5 shares. Corporation M owns the stock of Corporation X. B sells his 75 shares of Corporation M stock to Corporation X. Under section 302(b)(3) this is a termination of B's entire interest in Corporation M and the full amount received from the sale of his stock will be treated as payment in exchange for this stock, provided he fulfills the requirements of section 302(c)(2) (relating to an acquisition of an interest in the corporations). [Reg. § 1.304-3.]

☐ [*T.D. 6152*, 12-2-55.]

[Reg. § 1.304-4]

§ 1.304-4. Special rules for the use of related corporations to avoid the application of section 304.—(a) *Scope and purpose.*—This section applies to determine the amount of a property distribution constituting a dividend (and the source thereof) under section 304(b)(2), for certain transactions involving controlled corporations. The purpose of this section is to prevent the avoidance of the application of section 304 to a controlled corporation.

(b) *Amount and source of dividend.*—For purposes of determining the amount constituting a dividend (and source thereof) under section 304(b)(2), the following rules shall apply:

(1) *Deemed acquiring corporation.*—A corporation (deemed acquiring corporation) shall be treated as acquiring for property the stock of a corporation (issuing corporation) acquired for property by another corporation (acquiring corporation) that is controlled by the deemed acquiring corporation, if a principal purpose for creating, organizing, or funding the acquiring corporation by any means (including through capital contributions or debt) is to avoid the application of section 304 to the deemed acquiring corporation. See paragraph (c) *Example 1* of this section for an illustration of this paragraph.

(2) *Deemed issuing corporation.*—The acquiring corporation shall be treated as acquiring for property the stock of a corporation (deemed issuing corporation) controlled by the issuing corporation if, in connection with the acquisition for property of stock of the issuing corporation by the acquiring corporation, the issuing corporation acquired stock of the deemed issuing corporation with a principal purpose of avoiding the application of section 304 to the deemed issuing corporation. See paragraph (c) *Example 2* of this section for an illustration of this paragraph.

(c) *Examples.*—The rules of this section are illustrated by the following examples:

Example 1. (i) *Facts.* P, a domestic corporation, wholly owns CFC1, a controlled foreign corporation with substantial accumulated earnings and profits. CFC1 is organized in Country X, which imposes a high rate of tax on the income of CFC1. P also wholly owns CFC2, a controlled foreign corporation with accumulated earnings and profits of $200x. CFC2 is organized in Country Y, which imposes a low rate of tax on the income of CFC2. P wishes to own all of its foreign corporations in a direct chain and to repatriate the cash of CFC2. In

order to avoid having to obtain Country X approval for the acquisition of CFC1 (a Country X corporation) by CFC2 (a Country Y corporation) and to avoid the dividend distribution from CFC2 to P that would result if CFC2 were the acquiring corporation, P causes CFC2 to form CFC3 in Country X and to contribute $100x to CFC3. CFC3 then acquires all of the stock of CFC1 from P for $100x.

(ii) *Result.* Because a principal purpose for creating, organizing, or funding CFC3 (acquiring corporation) is to avoid the application of section 304 to CFC2 (deemed acquiring corporation), under paragraph (b)(1) of this section, for purposes of determining the amount of the $100x distribution constituting a dividend (and source thereof) under section 304(b)(2), CFC2 shall be treated as acquiring the stock of CFC1 (issuing corporation) from P for $100x. As a result, P receives a $100x distribution out of the earnings and profits of CFC2 to which section 301(c)(1) applies.

Example 2. (i) *Facts.* P, a domestic corporation, wholly owns CFC1, a controlled foreign corporation with substantial accumulated earnings and profits. The CFC1 stock has a basis of $100x. CFC1 is organized in Country X. P also wholly owns CFC2, a controlled foreign corporation with zero accumulated earnings and profits. CFC2 is organized in Country Y. P wishes to own all of its foreign corporations in a direct chain and to repatriate the cash of CFC2. In order to avoid having to obtain Country X approval for the acquisition of CFC1 (a Country X corporation) by CFC2 (a Country Y corporation) and to avoid a dividend distribution from CFC1 to P, P forms a new corporation (CFC3) in Country X and transfers the stock of CFC1 to CFC3 in exchange for CFC3 stock. P then transfers the stock of CFC3 to CFC2 in exchange for $100x.

(ii) *Result.* Because a principal purpose for the transfer of the stock of CFC1 (deemed issuing corporation) by P to CFC3 (issuing corporation) is to avoid the application of section 304 to CFC1, under paragraph (b)(2) of this section, for purposes of determining the amount of the $100x distribution constituting a dividend (and source thereof) under section 304(b)(2), CFC2 (acquiring corporation) shall be treated as acquiring the stock of CFC1 from P for $100x. As a result, P receives a $100x distribution out of the earnings and profits of CFC1 to which section 301(c)(1) applies.

(d) *Effective/applicability date.*—This section applies to acquisitions of stock occurring on or after December 29, 2009. [Reg. § 1.304-4.]

☐ [*T.D. 9477*, 12-29-2009. *Amended by T.D. 9606*, 12-21-2012.]

[Reg. § 1.304-5]

§ 1.304-5. Control.—(a) *Control requirement in general.*—Section 304(c)(1) provides that, for purposes of section 304, control means the ownership of stock possessing at least 50 percent of the total combined voting power of all classes of stock entitled to vote or at least 50 percent of the total value of shares of all classes of stock. Section 304(c)(3) makes section 318(a) (relating to constructive ownership of stock), as modified by section 304(c)(3)(B), applicable to section 304 for purposes of determining control under section 304(c)(1).

(b) *Effect of section 304(c)(2)(B).*—(1) *In general.*—In determining whether the control test with respect to both the issuing and acquiring corporations is satisfied, section 304(a)(1) considers only the person or persons that—

(i) Control the issuing corporation before the transaction;

(ii) Transfer issuing corporation stock to the acquiring corporation for property; and

(iii) Control the acquiring corporation thereafter.

(2) *Application.*—Section 317 defines property to include money, securities, and any other property except stock (or stock rights) in the distributing corporation. However, section 304(c)(2)(B) provides a special rule to extend the relevant group of persons to be tested for control of both the issuing and acquiring corporations to include the person or persons that do not acquire property, but rather solely stock from the acquiring corporation in the transaction. Section 304(c)(2)(B) provides that if two or more persons in control of the issuing corporation transfer stock of such corporation to the acquiring corporation, and if the transferors are in control of the acquiring corporation after the transfer, the person or persons in control of each corporation include each of those transferors. Because the purpose of section 304(c)(2)(B) is to include in the relevant control group the person or persons that retain or acquire acquiring corporation stock in the transaction, only the person or persons transferring stock of the issuing corporation that retain or acquire any proprietary interest in the acquiring corporation are taken into account for purposes of applying section 304(c)(2)(B).

(3) *Example.*—This section may be illustrated by the following example.

Example. (a) A, the owner of 20% of T's only class of stock, transfers that stock to P solely in exchange for all of the P stock. Pursuant to the same transaction, P, solely in exchange for cash, acquires the remaining 80% of the T stock from T's other shareholder, B, who is unrelated to A and P.

(b) Although A and B together were in control of T (the issuing corporation) before the transaction and A and B each transferred T stock to P (the acquiring corporation), sections 304(a)(1) and (c)(2)(B) do not apply to B because B did not retain or acquire any proprietary interest in P in the transaction. Section 304(a)(1) also does not apply to A because A (or any control group of which A was a member) did not control T before the transaction and P after the transaction.

(c) *Effective date.*—This section is effective January 20, 1994. [Reg. §1.304-5.]

☐ [*T.D.* 8515, 1-12-94.]

[Reg. §1.304-6]

§1.304-6. Amount constituting a dividend.— [Reserved]

☐ [*T.D.* 9761, 4-4-2016.]

[Reg. §1.304-7]

§1.304-7. Certain acquisitions by foreign acquiring corporations.—(a) *Scope.*—This section provides rules regarding the application of section 304(b)(5)(B) to an acquisition of stock described in section 304 by an acquiring corporation that is foreign (foreign acquiring corporation). Paragraph (b) of this section provides the rule for determining which earnings and profits are taken into account for purposes of applying section 304(b)(5)(B). Paragraph (c) of this section provides rules addressing the use of a partnership, option (or similar interest), or other arrangement. Paragraph (d) of this section provides examples that illustrate the rules of this section. Paragraph (e) of this section provides the applicability date.

(b) *Earnings and profits taken into account.*—For purposes of applying section 304(b)(5)(B), only the earnings and profits of the foreign acquiring corporation are taken into account in determining whether more than 50 percent of the dividends arising from the acquisition (determined without regard to section 304(b)(5)(B)) would neither be subject to tax under chapter 1 of subtitle A of the Internal Revenue Code for the taxable year in which the dividends arise (subject to tax) nor be includible in the earnings and profits of a controlled foreign corporation (includible by a controlled foreign corporation). For purposes of this section, a controlled foreign corporation has the meaning provided in section 957 and without regard to section 953(c), determined without applying subparagraphs (A), (B), and (C) of section 318(a)(3) so as to consider a United States person as owning stock which is owned by a person who is not a United States person.

(c) *Use of a partnership, option (or similar interest), or other arrangement.*—If a partnership, option (or similar interest), or other arrangement, is used with a principal purpose of avoiding the application of this section (for example, to treat a transferor as a controlled foreign corporation), then the partnership, option (or similar interest), or other arrangement will be disregarded for purposes of applying this section.

(d) *Examples.*—The following examples illustrate the rules of this section. For purposes of the examples, assume the following facts in addition to the facts stated in the examples:

(1) FA is a foreign corporation that is not a controlled foreign corporation;

(2) FA wholly owns DT, a domestic corporation;

(3) DT wholly owns FS1, a controlled foreign corporation; and

(4) No portion of a dividend from FS1 would be treated as from sources within the United States under section 861.

Example 1—(i) *Facts.* DT has earnings and profits of $51x, and FS1 has earnings and profits of $49x. FA transfers DT stock with a fair market value of $100x to FS1 in exchange for $100x of cash.

(ii) *Analysis.* Under section 304(a)(2), the $100x of cash is treated as a distribution in redemption of the stock of DT. The redemption of the DT stock is treated as a distribution to which section 301 applies pursuant to section 302(d), which ordinarily would be sourced first from FS1 under section 304(b)(2)(A). Without regard to the application of section 304(b)(5)(B), more than 50 percent of the dividend arising from the acquisition, taking into account only the earnings and profits of FS1 pursuant to paragraph (b) of this section, would neither be subject to tax nor includible by a controlled foreign corporation. In particular, no portion of a dividend from FS1 would be subject to tax or includible by a controlled foreign corporation, Accordingly, section 304(b)(5)(B) and paragraph (b) of this section apply to the transaction, and no portion of the distribution of $100x is treated under section 301(c)(1) as a dividend out of the earnings and profits of FS1. Furthermore, the $100x of cash is treated as a dividend to the extent of the earnings and profits of DT ($51x).

Example 2—(i) *Facts.* FA and DT own 40 percent and 60 percent, respectively, of the capital and profits interests of PRS, a foreign partnership. PRS wholly owns FS2, a controlled foreign corporation.

The FS2 stock has a fair market value of $100x. FS1 has earnings and profits of $150x. PRS transfers all of its FS2 stock to FS1 in exchange for $100x of cash. DT enters into a gain recognition agreement that complies with the requirements set forth in section 4.01 of Notice 2012-15, 2012-9 I.R.B 424, with respect to the portion (60 percent) of the FS2 stock that DT is deemed to transfer to FS1 in an exchange described in section 367(a)(1). See §1.367(a)-1T(c)(3)(i)(A).

(ii) *Analysis.* Under section 304(a)(1), PRS and FS1 are treated as if PRS transferred its FS2 stock to FS1 in an exchange described in section 351(a) solely for FS1 stock, and, in turn, FS1 redeemed such FS1 stock in exchange for $100x of cash. The redemption of the FS1 stock is treated as a distribution to which section 301 applies pursuant to section 302(d). Without regard to the application of section 304(b)(5)(B), more than 50 percent of a dividend arising from the acquisition, taking into account only the earnings and profits of FS1 pursuant to paragraph (b) of this section, would be subject to tax. In particular, 60 percent of a dividend from FS1 would be included in DT's distributive share of PRS's partnership income and therefore would be subject to tax. Accordingly, section 304(b)(5)(B) does not apply, and the entire distribution of $100x is treated under section 301(c)(1) as a dividend out of the earnings and profits of FS1.

(e) *Applicability date.*—This section applies to acquisitions that are completed on or after September 22, 2014. [Reg. §1.304-7.]

☐ [*T.D.* 9834, 7-11-2018.]

[Reg. §1.305-1]

§1.305-1. Stock dividends.—(a) *In general.*—Under section 305, a distribution made by a corporation to its shareholders in its stock or in rights to acquire its stock is not included in gross income except as provided in section 305(b) and the regulations promulgated under the authority of section 305(c). A distribution made by a corporation to its shareholders in its stock or rights to acquire its stock which would not otherwise be included in gross income by reason of section 305 shall not be so included merely because such distribution was made out of Treasury stock or consisted of rights to acquire Treasury stock. See section 307 for rules as to basis of stock and stock rights acquired in a distribution.

(b) *Amount of distribution.*—(1) In general, where a distribution of stock or rights to acquire stock of a corporation is treated as a distribution of property to which section 301 applies by reason of section 305(b), the amount of the distribution, in accordance with section 301(b) and §1.301-1, is the fair market value of such stock or rights on the date of distribution. See example (1) of §1.305-2(b).

(2) Where a corporation which regularly distributes its earnings and profits, such as a regulated investment company, declares a dividend pursuant to which the shareholders may elect to receive either money or stock of the distributing corporation of equivalent value, the amount of the distribution of the stock received by any shareholder electing to receive stock will be considered to equal the amount of the money which could have been received instead. See example (2) of §1.305-2(b).

(3) For rules for determining the amount of the distribution where certain transactions, such as changes in conversion ratios or periodic redemptions, are treated as distributions under section 305(c), see examples (6), (8), (9), and (15) of §1.305-3(e).

(c) *Adjustment in purchase price.*—A transfer of stock (or rights to acquire stock) or an increase or decrease in the conversion ratio or redemption price of stock which represents an adjustment of the price to be paid by the distributing corporation in acquiring property (within the meaning of section 317(a)) is not within the purview of section 305 because it is not a distribution with respect to its stock. For example, assume that on January 1, 1970, pursuant to a reorganization, corporation X acquires all the stock of corporation Y solely in exchange for its convertible preferred class B stock. Under the terms of the class B stock, its conversion ratio is to be adjusted in 1976 under a formula based upon the earnings of corporation Y over the 6-year period ending on December 31, 1975. Such an adjustment in 1976 is not covered by section 305.

(d) *Definitions.*—(1) For purposes of this section and §§1.305-2 through 1.305-7, the term "stock" includes rights or warrants to acquire such stock.

(2) For purposes of §§1.305-2 through 1.305-7, the term "shareholder" includes a holder of rights or warrants or a holder of convertible securities. [Reg. §1.305-1.]

☐ [*T.D.* 6152, 12-2-55. *Amended by T.D.* 7281, 7-11-73.]

[Reg. §1.305-2]

§1.305-2. Distributions in lieu of money.—(a) *In general.*—Under section 305(b)(1), if any shareholder has the right to an election or option with respect to whether a distribution shall be made either in money or any other property, or in stock or rights to acquire stock of the distributing corporation, then, with respect to all shareholders, the distribution of stock or rights to acquire stock is treated as a distribution of property to which section 301 applies regardless of—

(1) Whether the distribution is actually made in whole or in part in stock or in stock rights;

(2) Whether the election or option is exercised or exercisable before or after the declaration of the distribution;

(3) Whether the declaration of the distribution provides that the distribution will be made in one medium unless the shareholder specifically requests payment in the other;

(4) Whether the election governing the nature of the distribution is provided in the declaration of the distribution or in the corporate charter or arises from the circumstances of the distribution; or

(5) Whether all or part of the shareholders have the election.

(b) *Examples.*—The application of section 305(b)(1) may be illustrated by the following examples:

Example (1). (i) Corporation X declared a dividend payable in additional shares of its common stock to the holders of its outstanding common stock on the basis of two additional shares for each share held on the record date but with the provision that, at the election of any shareholder made within a specified period prior to the distribution date, he may receive one additional share for each share held on the record date plus $12 principal amount of securities of corporation Y owned by corporation X. The fair market value of the stock of corporation X on the distribution date was $10 per share. The fair market value of $12 principal amount of securities of corporation Y on the distribution date was $11 but such securities had a cost basis to corporation X of $9.

(ii) The distribution to all shareholders of one additional share of stock of corporation X (with respect to which no election applies) for each share outstanding is not a distribution to which section 301 applies.

(iii) The distribution of the second share of stock of corporation X to those shareholders who do not elect to receive securities of corporation Y is a distribution of property to which section 301 applies, whether such shareholders are individuals or corporations. The amount of the distribution to which section 301 applies is $10 per share of stock of corporation X held on the record date (the fair market value of the stock of corporation X on the distribution date).

(iv) The distribution of securities of corporation Y in lieu of the second share of stock of corporation X to the shareholders of corporation X whether individuals or corporations, who elect to receive such securities, is also a distribution of property to which section 301 applies.

(v) In the case of the individual shareholders of corporation X who elect to receive such securities, the amount of the distribution to which section 301 applies is $11 per share of stock of corporation X held on the record date (the fair market value of the $12 principal amount of securities of corporation Y on the distribution date).

(vi) In the case of the corporate shareholders of corporation X electing to receive such securities, the amount of the distribution to which section 301 applies is $9 per share of stock of corporation X held on the record date (the basis of the securities of corporation Y in the hands of corporation X).

Example (2). On January 10, 1970, corporation X, a regulated investment company, declared a dividend of $1 per share on its common stock payable on February 11, 1970, in cash or in stock of corporation X of equivalent value determined as of January 22, 1970, at the election of the shareholder made on or before January 22, 1970. The amount of the distribution to which section 301 applies is $1 per share whether the shareholder elects to take cash or stock and whether the shareholder is an individual or a corporation. Such amount will also be used in determining the dividend paid deduction of corporation X and the reduction in earnings and profits of corporation X. [Reg. § 1.305-2.]

☐ [*T.D. 6152, 12-2-55. Amended by T.D. 6476, 6-3-60; T.D. 6990, 1-10-69; T.D. 7004, 2-7-69 and T.D. 7281, 7-11-73.*]

[Reg. § 1.305-3]

§ 1.305-3. Disproportionate distributions.—(a) *In general.*—Under section 305(b)(2), a distribution (including a deemed distribution) by a corporation of its stock or rights to acquire its stock is treated as a distribution of property to which section 301 applies if the distribution (or a series of distributions of which such distribution is one) has the result of (1) the receipt of money or other property by some *shareholders*, and (2) an increase in the proportionate interests of other shareholders in the assets or earnings and profits of the corporation. Thus, if a corporation has two classes of common stock outstanding and cash dividends are paid on one class and stock dividends are paid on the other class, the stock dividends are treated as distributions to which section 301 applies.

(b) *Special rules.*—(1) As used in section 305(b)(2), the term "a series of distributions" encompasses all distributions of stock made or deemed made by a corporation which have the result of a receipt of cash or property by some shareholders and an increase in the proportionate interests of other shareholders.

(2) In order for a distribution of stock to be considered as one of a series of distributions it is not necessary that such distribution be pursuant to a plan to distribute cash or property to some shareholders and to increase the proportionate interests of other shareholders. It is sufficient if there is an actual or deemed distribution of stock (of which such distribution is one) and as a result of such distribution or distributions some shareholders receive cash or property and other shareholders increase their proportionate interests. For example, if a corporation pays quarterly stock dividends to one class of common shareholders and annual cash dividends to another class of common shareholders the quarterly stock dividends constitute a series of distributions of stock having the result of the receipt of cash or property by some shareholders and an increase in the proportionate interests of other shareholders. This is so whether or not the stock distributions and the cash distributions are steps in an overall plan or are independent and unrelated. Accordingly, all the quarterly stock dividends are distributions to which section 301 applies.

(3) There is no requirement that both elements of section 305(b)(2) (*i.e.*, receipt of cash or property by some shareholders and an increase in proportionate interests of other shareholders) occur in the form of a distribution or series of distributions as long as the result of a distribution or distributions of stock is that some shareholders' proportionate interests increase and other shareholders in fact receive cash or property. Thus, there is no requirement that the shareholders receiving cash or property acquire the cash or property by way of a corporate distribution with respect to their shares, so long as they receive such cash or property in their capacity as shareholders, if there is a stock distribution which results in a change in the proportionate interests of some shareholders and other shareholders receive cash or property. However, in order for a distribution of property to meet the requirements of section 305(b)(2), such distribution must be made to a shareholder in his capacity as a shareholder, and must be a distribution to which section 301, 356(a)(2), 871(a)(1)(A), 881(a)(1), 852(b), or 857(b) applies. (Under section 305(d)(2), the payment of interest to a holder of a convertible debenture is treated as a distribution of property to a shareholder for purposes of section 305(b)(2).) For example if a corporation makes a stock distribution to its shareholders, and, pursuant to a prearranged plan with such corporation, a related corporation purchases such stock from those shareholders who want cash, in a transaction to which section 301 applies by virtue of section 304, the requirements of section 305(b)(2) are satisfied. In addition, a distribution of property incident to an isolated redemption of stock (for example, pursuant to a tender offer) will not cause section 305(b)(2) to apply even though the redemption distribution is treated as a distribution of property to which section 301, 871(a)(1)(A), 881(a)(1), or 356(a)(2) applies.

(4) Where the receipt of cash or property occurs more than 36 months following a distribution or series of distributions of stock, or where a distribution or series of distributions of stock is made more than 36 months following the receipt of cash or property, such distribution or distributions will be presumed not to result in the receipt of cash or property by some shareholders and an increase in the proportionate interest of other shareholders, unless the receipt of cash or property and the distribution or series of distributions of stock are made pursuant to a plan. For example, if, pursuant to a plan, a corporation pays cash dividends to some shareholders on January 1, 1971 and increases the proportionate interests of other shareholders on March 1, 1974, such increases in proportionate interests are distributions to which section 301 applies.

(5) In determining whether a distribution or a series of distributions has the result of a disproportionate distribution, there shall be treated as outstanding stock of the distributing corporation (i) any right to acquire such stock (whether or not exercisable during the taxable year), and (ii) any security convertible into stock of the distributing corporation (whether or not convertible during the taxable year).

(6) In cases where there is more than one class of stock outstanding, each class of stock is to be considered separately in determining whether a shareholder has increased his proportionate interest in the assets or earnings and profits of a corporation. The individual shareholders of a class of stock will be deemed to have an increased interest if the class of stock as a whole has an increased interest in the corporation.

(c) *Distributions of cash in lieu of fractional shares.*—(1) Section 305(b)(2) will not apply if—

(i) A corporation declares a dividend payable in stock of the corporation and distributes cash in lieu of fractional shares to which shareholders would otherwise be entitled, or

(ii) Upon a conversion of convertible stock or securities a corporation distributes cash in lieu of fractional shares to which shareholders would otherwise be entitled.

Provided the purpose of the distribution of cash is to save the corporation the trouble, expense, and inconvenience of issuing and transferring fractional shares (or scrip representing fractional shares), or issuing full shares representing the sum of fractional shares, and not to give any particular group of shareholders an increased interest in the asset or earnings and profits of the corporation. For purposes of paragraph (c)(1)(i) of this section, if the total amount of cash distributed in lieu of fractional shares is 5 percent or less of the total fair market value of the stock distributed (determined as of the date of declaration), the distribution shall be considered to be for such valid purpose.

(2) In a case to which subparagraph (1) of this paragraph applies, the transaction will be treated as though the fractional shares were distributed as part of the stock distribution and then were redeemed by the corporation. The treatment of the cash received by a shareholder will be determined under section 302.

(d) *Adjustment in conversion ratio.*—(1)(i) Except as provided in subparagraph (2) of this paragraph, if a corporation has convertible stock or convertible securities outstanding (upon which it pays or is deemed to pay dividends or interest in money or other property) and distributes a stock dividend (or rights to acquire such stock) with respect to the stock into which the convertible stock or securities are convertible, an increase in proportionate interest in the assets or earnings and profits of the corporation by reason of such stock dividend shall be considered to have occurred unless a full adjustment in the conversion ratio or conversion price to reflect such stock dividend is made. Under certain circumstances, however, the application of an adjustment formula which in effect provides for a "credit" where stock is issued for consideration in excess of the conversion price may not satisfy the requirement for a "full adjustment". Thus, if under a "conversion price" antidilution formula the formula provides for a "credit" where stock is issued for consideration in excess of the conversion price (in effect as an offset against any decrease in the conversion price which would otherwise be required when stock is subsequently issued for consideration below the conversion price) there may still be an increase in proportionate interest by reason of a stock dividend after application of the formula, since any downward adjustment of the conversion price that would otherwise be required to reflect the stock dividend may be offset, in whole or in part, by the effect of prior sales made at prices above the conversion price. On the other hand, if there were no prior sales of stock above the conversion price then a full adjustment would occur upon the application of such an adjustment formula and there would be no change in proportionate interest. Similarly, if consideration is to be received in connection with the issuance of stock, such as in the case of a rights offering or a distribution of warrants, the fact that such consideration is taken into account in making the antidilution adjustment will not preclude a full adjustment. See paragraph (b) of the example in this subparagraph for a case where the application of an adjustment formula with a cumulative feature does not result in a full adjustment and where a change in proportionate interest therefore occurs. See paragraph (c) for a case where the application of an adjustment formula with a cumulative feature does result in a full adjustment and where no change in proportionate interest therefore occurs. See paragraph (d) for an application of an antidilution formula in the case of a rights offering. See paragraph (e) for a case where the application of a noncumulative type adjustment formula will in all cases prevent a change in proportionate interest from occurring in the case of a stock dividend, because of the omission of the cumulative feature.

(ii) The principles of this subparagraph may be illustrated by the following example:

Example. (a) Corporation S has two classes of securities outstanding, convertible debentures and common stock. At the time of issuance of the debentures the corporation had 100 shares of common stock outstanding. Each debenture is interest-paying and is convertible into common stock at a conversion price of $2. The debenture's conversion price is subject to reduction pursuant to the following formula:

(Number of common shares outstanding at date of issue of debentures times initial conversion price)

plus

(Consideration received upon issuance of additional common shares)

divided by

(Number of common shares outstanding at date of issue of debentures)

plus

(Number of additional common shares issued)

Under the formula, common stock dividends are treated as an issue of common stock for zero consideration. If the computation results in

a figure which is less than the existing conversion price the conversion price is reduced. However, under the formula, the existing conversion price is never increased. The formula works upon a cumulative basis since the numerator includes the consideration received upon the issuance of all common shares subsequent to the issuance of the debentures, and the reduction effected by the formula because of a sale or issuance of common stock below the existing conversion price is thus limited by any prior sales made above the existing conversion price.

(b) In 1972 corporation S sells 100 common shares at $3 per share. In 1973 the corporation declares a stock dividend of 20 shares to all holders of common stock. Under the antidilution formula no adjustment will be made to the conversion price of the debentures to reflect the stock dividend to common stockholders since the prior sale of common stock in excess of the conversion price in 1972 offsets the reduction in the conversion price which would otherwise result, as follows:

$$100 \times \$2 + \$300 \div 100 + 120 = \frac{\$500}{220} = \$2.27$$

Since $2.27 is greater than the existing conversion price of $2 no adjustment is required. As a result, there is an increase in proportionate interest of the common stockholders by reason of the stock dividend and the additional shares of common stock will be treated, pursuant to section 305(b)(2), as a distribution of property to which section 301 applies.

(c) Assume the same facts as above, but instead of selling 100 common shares at $3 per share in 1972, assume corporation S sold no shares. Application of the antidilution formula would give rise to an adjustment in the conversion price as follows:

$$100 \times \$2 + \$0 \div 100 + 20 = \frac{\$200}{220} = \$1.67$$

The conversion price, being reduced from $2 to $1.67, fully reflects the stock dividend distributed to the common stockholders. Hence, the distribution of common stock is not treated under section 305(b)(2) as one to which section 301 applies because the distribution does not increase the proportionate interests of the common shareholders as a class.

(d) Corporation S distributes to its shareholders rights entitling the shareholders to purchase a total of 20 shares at $1 per share. Application of the antidilution formula would produce an adjustment in the conversion price as follows:

$$100 \times \$2 + 20 \times \$1 \div 100 + 20 = \frac{\$220}{120} = \$1.83$$

The conversion price, being reduced from $2 to $1.83, fully reflects the distribution of rights to purchase stock at a price lower than the conversion price. Hence, the distribution of the rights is not treated under section 305(b)(2) as one to which section 301 applies because the distribution does not increase the proportionate interests of the common shareholders as a class.

(e) Assume the same facts as in (b) above, but instead of using a "conversion price" antidilution formula which operates on a cumulative basis, assume corporation S has employed a formula which operates as follows with respect to all stock dividends: The conversion price in effect at the opening of business on the day following the dividend record date is reduced by multiplying such conversion price by a fraction the numerator of which is the number of shares of common stock outstanding at the close of business on the record date and the denominator of which is the sum of such shares so outstanding and the number of shares constituting the stock dividend. Under such a formula the following adjustment would be made to the conversion price upon the declaration of a stock dividend of 20 shares in 1973:

$$200 \div 200 + 20 = \frac{200}{220} \times \$2 = \$1.82$$

The conversion price, being reduced from $2 to $1.82, fully reflects the stock dividend distributed to the common stockholders. Hence, the distribution of common stock is not treated under section 305(b)(2) as one to which section 301 applies because the distribution does not increase the proportionate interests of the common shareholders as a class.

(2)(i) A distributing corporation either must make the adjustment required by subparagraph (1) of this paragraph as of the date of the distribution of the stock dividend, or must elect (in the manner provided in subdivision (iii) of this subparagraph) to make such adjustment within the time provided in subdivision (ii) of this subparagraph.

(ii) If the distributing corporation elects to make such adjustment, such adjustment must be made no later than the earlier of (a) 3

Reg. §1.305-3(d)(2)(ii)

years after the date of the stock dividend, or *(b)* that date as of which the aggregate stock dividends for which adjustment of the conversion ratio has not previously been made total at least 3 percent of the issued and outstanding stock with respect to which such stock dividends were distributed.

(iii) The election provided by subdivision (ii) of this subparagraph shall be made by filing with the income tax return for the taxable year during which the stock dividend is distributed—

(a) A statement that an adjustment will be made as provided by that subdivision, and

(b) A description of the antidilution provisions under which the adjustment will be made.

(3) Notwithstanding the preceding subparagraph, if a distribution has been made before July 12, 1973, and the adjustment required by subparagraph (1) or the election to make such adjustment was not made before such date, the adjustment or the election to make such adjustment, as the case may be, shall be considered valid if made no later than 15 days following the date of the first annual meeting of the shareholders after July 12, 1973, or July 12, 1974, whichever is earlier. If the election is made within such period, and if the income tax return has been filed before the time of such election, the statement of adjustment and the description of the antidilution provisions required by subparagraph (2)(iii) shall be filed with the Internal Revenue Service Center with which the income tax return was filed.

(4) See § 1.305-7(b) for a discussion of antidilution adjustments in connection with the application of section 305(c) in conjunction with section 305(b).

(e) *Examples.*—The application of section 305(b)(2) to distributions of stock and section 305(c) to deemed distributions of stock may be illustrated by the following examples:

Example 1. Corporation X is organized with two classes of common stock, class A and class B. Each share of stock is entitled to share equally in the assets and earnings and profits of the corporation. Dividends may be paid in stock or in cash on either class of stock without regard to the medium of payment of dividends on the other class. A dividend is declared on the class A stock payable in additional shares of class A stock and a dividend is declared on class B stock payable in cash. Since the class A shareholders as a class will have increased their proportionate interests in the assets and earnings and profits of the corporation and the class B shareholders will have received cash, the additional shares of class A stock are distributions of property to which section 301 applies. This is true even with respect to those shareholders who may own class A stock and class B stock in the same proportion.

Example 2. Corporation Y is organized with two classes of stock, class A common, and class B, which is nonconvertible and limited and preferred as to dividends. A dividend is declared upon the class A stock payable in additional shares of class A stock and a dividend is declared on the class B stock payable in cash. The distribution of class A stock is not one to which section 301 applies because the distribution does not increase the proportionate interests of the class A shareholders as a class.

Example 3. Corporation K is organized with two classes of stock, class A common, and class B, which is nonconvertible preferred stock. A dividend is declared upon the class A stock payable in shares of class B stock and a dividend is declared on the class B stock payable in cash. Since the class A shareholders as a class have an increased interest in the assets and earnings and profits of the corporation, the stock distribution is treated as a distribution to which section 301 applies. If, however, a dividend were declared upon the class A stock payable in a new class of preferred stock that is subordinated in all respects to the class B stock, the distribution would not increase the proportionate interests of the class A shareholders in the assets or earnings and profits of the corporation and would not be treated as a distribution to which section 301 applies.

Example 4. (i) Corporation W has one class of stock outstanding, class A common. The corporation also has outstanding interest paying securities convertible into class A common stock which have a fixed conversion ratio that is not subject to a full adjustment in the event stock dividends or rights are distributed to the class A shareholders. Corporation W distributes to the class A shareholders rights to acquire additional shares of class A stock. During the year, interest is paid on the convertible securities.

(ii) The stock rights and convertible securities are considered to be outstanding stock of the corporation and the distribution increases the proportionate interests of the class A shareholders in the assets and earnings and profits of the corporation. Therefore, the distribution is treated as a distribution to which section 301 applies. The same result would follow if, instead of convertible securities, the corporation had outstanding convertible stock. If, however, the conversion ratio of the securities or stock were fully adjusted to reflect the distribution of rights to the class A shareholders, the rights to

acquire class A stock would not increase the proportionate interests of the class A shareholders in the assets or earnings and profits of the corporation and would not be treated as a distribution to which section 301 applies.

Example 5. (i) Corporation S is organized with two classes of stock, class A common and class B convertible preferred. The class B is fully protected against dilution in the event of a stock dividend or stock split with respect to the class A stock; however, no adjustment in the conversion ratio is required to be made until the stock dividends equal 3 percent of the common stock issued and outstanding on the date of the first such stock dividend except that such adjustment must be made no later than 3 years after the date of the stock dividend. Cash dividends are paid annually on the class B stock.

(ii) Corporation S pays a 1 percent stock dividend on the class A stock in 1973. In 1974, another 1 percent stock dividend is paid and in 1975 another 1 percent stock dividend is paid. The conversion ratio of the class B stock is increased in 1975 to reflect the three stock dividends paid on the class A stock. The distributions of class A stock are not distributions to which section 301 applies because they do not increase the proportionate interests of the class A shareholders in the assets or earnings and profits of the corporation.

Example 6. (i) Corporation M is organized with two classes of stock outstanding, class A and class B. Each class B share may be converted, at the option of the holder, into class A shares. During the first year, the conversion ratio is one share of class A stock for each share of class B stock. At the beginning of each subsequent year, the conversion ratio is increased by 0.05 share of class A stock for each share of class B stock. Thus, during the second year, the conversion ratio would be 1.05 shares of class A stock for each share of class B stock, during the third year, the ratio would be 1.10 shares, etc.

(ii) M pays an annual cash dividend on the class A stock. At the beginning of the second year, when the conversion ratio is increased to 1.05 shares of class A stock for each share of class B stock, a distribution of 0.05 shares of class A stock is deemed made under section 305(c) with respect to each share of class B stock, since the proportionate interests of the class B shareholders in the assets or earnings and profits of M are increased and the transaction has the effect described in section 305(b)(2). Accordingly, sections 305(b)(2) and 301 apply to the transaction.

Example 7. (i) Corporation N has two classes of stock outstanding, class A and class B. Each class B share is convertible into class A stock. However, in accordance with a specified formula, the conversion ratio is decreased each time a cash dividend is paid on the class B stock to reflect the amount of the cash dividend. The conversion ratio is also adjusted in the event that cash dividends are paid on the class A stock to increase the number of class A shares into which the class B shares are convertible to compensate the class B shareholders for the cash dividend paid on the class A stock.

(ii) In 1972, a $1 cash dividend per share is declared and paid on the class B stock. On the date of payment, the conversion ratio of the class B stock is decreased. A distribution of stock is deemed made under section 305(c) to the class A shareholders, since the proportionate interest of the class A shareholders in the assets or earnings and profits of the corporation is increased and the transaction has the effect described in section 305(b)(2). Accordingly, sections 305(b)(2) and 301 apply to the transaction.

(iii) In the following year a cash dividend is paid on the class A stock and none is paid on the class B stock. The increase in conversion rights of the class B shares is deemed to be a distribution under section 305(c) to the class B shareholders since their proportionate interest in the assets or earnings and profits of the corporation is increased and since the transaction has the effect described in section 305(b)(2). Accordingly, sections 305(b)(2) and 301 apply to the transaction.

Example 8. Corporation T has 1,000 shares of stock outstanding. C owns 100 shares. Nine other shareholders each owns 100 shares. Pursuant to a plan for periodic redemptions, T redeems up to 5 percent of each shareholder's stock each year. During the year, each of the nine other shareholders has five shares of his stock redeemed for cash. Thus, C's proportionate interest in the assets and earnings and profits of T is increased. Assuming that the cash received by the nine other shareholders is taxable under section 301, C is deemed under section 305(c) to have received a distribution under section 305(b)(2) of 5.25 shares of T stock to which section 301 applies. The amount of C's distribution is measured by the fair market value of the number of shares which would have been distributed to C had the corporation sought to increase his interest by 0.47 percentage points (C owned 10 percent of the T stock immediately before the redemption and 10.47 percent immediately thereafter) and the other shareholders continued to hold 900 shares (i.e.,

(a) $\dfrac{100}{955}$ = 10.47% (percent of C's ownership after redemption);

(b) $\dfrac{100 + X}{1000 + X}$ = $\begin{array}{l}10.47\%; X = 5.25 \text{ (additional}\\ \text{shares considered to be}\\ \text{distributed to C)).}\end{array}$

Since in computing the amount of additional shares deemed to be distributed to C the redemption of shares is disregarded, the redemption of shares will be similarly disregarded in determining the value of the stock of the corporation which is deemed to be distributed. Thus, in the example, 1,005.25 shares of stock are considered as outstanding after the redemption. The value of each share deemed to be distributed to C is then determined by dividing the 1,005.25 shares into the aggregate fair market value of the actual shares outstanding (955) after the redemption.

Example 9. (i) Corporation O has a stock redemption program under which, instead of paying out earnings and profits to its shareholders in the form of dividends, it redeems the stock of its shareholders up to a stated amount which is determined by the earnings and profits of the corporation. If the stock tendered for redemption exceeds the stated amount, the corporation redeems the stock on a pro rata basis up to the stated amount.

(ii) During the year corporation O offers to distribute $10,000 in redemption of its stock. At the time of the offering, corporation O has 1,000 shares outstanding of which E and F each owns 150 shares and G and H each own 350 shares. The corporation redeems 15 shares from E and 35 shares from G. F and H continue to hold all of their stock.

(iii) F and H have increased their proportionate interests in the assets and earnings and profits of the corporation. Assuming that the cash E and G receive is taxable under section 301, F will be deemed under section 305(c) to have received a distribution under section 305(b)(2) of 16.66 shares of stock to which section 301 applies and H will be deemed under section 305(c) to have received a distribution under section 305(b)(2) of 38.86 shares of stock to which section 301 applies. The amount of the distribution to F and H is measured by the number of shares which would have been distributed to F and H had the corporation sought to increase the interest of F by 0.79 percentage points (F owned 15 percent of the stock immediately before the redemption and 15.79 percent immediately thereafter) and the interest of H by 1.84 percentage points (H owned 35 percent of the stock immediately before the redemption and 36.84 percent immediately thereafter) and E and G had continued to hold 150 shares and 350 shares, respectively (*i.e.,*

(a) $\dfrac{150}{950} + \dfrac{350}{950}$ = $\begin{array}{l}52.63\% \text{ (percent of}\\ \text{F and H's ownership}\\ \text{after redemption);}\end{array}$

(b) $\dfrac{500 + y}{1000 + y}$ = $\begin{array}{l}52.63\%; y = 55.52 \text{ (additional}\\ \text{shares considered to be}\\ \text{distributed to F and H);}\end{array}$

(c)(1) $\dfrac{150}{500} \times 55.52$ = $\begin{array}{l}16.66 \text{ (shares}\\ \text{considered to be}\\ \text{distributed to F);}\end{array}$

(2) $\dfrac{350}{500} \times 55.52$ = $\begin{array}{l}38.86 \text{ (shares}\\ \text{considered to be}\\ \text{distributed to H)).}\end{array}$

Since in computing the amount of additional shares deemed to be distributed to F and H the redemption of shares is disregarded, the redemption of shares will be similarly disregarded in determining the value of the stock of the corporation which is deemed to be distributed. Thus, in the example, 1,055.52 shares of stock are considered as outstanding after the redemption. The value of each share deemed to be distributed to F and H is then determined by dividing the 1,055.52 shares into the aggregate fair market value of the actual shares outstanding (950) after the redemption.

Example 10. Corporation P has 1,000 shares of stock outstanding. T owns 700 shares of the P stock and G owns 300 shares of the P stock. In a single and isolated redemption to which section 301 applies, the corporation redeems 150 shares of T's stock. Since this is an isolated redemption and is not a part of a periodic redemption plan, G is not treated as having received a deemed distribution under section 305(c) to which sections 305(b)(2) and 301 apply even though he has an increased proportionate interest in the assets and earnings and profits of the corporation.

Example 11. Corporation Q is a large corporation whose sole class of stock is widely held. However, the four largest shareholders are officers of the corporation and each owns 8 percent of the outstanding stock. In 1974, in a distribution to which section 301 applies, the corporation redeems 1.5 percent of the stock from each of the four largest shareholders in preparation for their retirement. From 1970 through 1974, the corporation distributes annual stock dividends to its shareholders. No other distributions were made to these shareholders. Since the 1974 redemptions are isolated and are not part of a plan for periodically redeeming the stock of the corporation, the shareholders receiving stock dividends will not be treated as having

received a distribution under section 305(b)(2) even though they have an increased proportionate interest in the assets and earnings and profits of the corporation and whether or not the redemptions are treated as distributions to which section 301 applies.

Example 12. Corporation R has 2,000 shares of class A stock outstanding. Five shareholders own 300 shares each and five shareholders own 100 shares each. In preparation for the retirement of the five major shareholders, corporation R, in a single and isolated transaction, has a recapitalization in which each share of class A stock may be exchanged either for five shares of new class B nonconvertible preferred stock plus 0.4 share of new class C common stock, or for two shares of new class C common stock. As a result of the exchanges, each of the five major shareholders receives 1,500 shares of class B nonconvertible preferred stock and 120 shares of class C common stock. The remaining shareholders each receives 200 shares of class C common stock. None of the exchanges are within the purview of section 305.

Example 13. Corporation P is a widely-held company whose shares are listed for trading on a stock exchange. P distributes annual cash dividends to its shareholders. P purchases shares of its common stock directly from small stockholders (holders of record of 100 shares or less) or through brokers where the holders may not be known at the time of purchase. Where such purchases are made through brokers, they are pursuant to the rules and regulations of the Securities and Exchange Commission. The shares are purchased for the purpose of issuance to employee stock investment plans, to holders of convertible stock or debt, to holders of stock options, or for future acquisitions. Provided the purchases are not pursuant to a plan to increase the proportionate interest of some shareholders and distribute property to other shareholders, thus the remaining shareholders of P are not treated as having received a deemed distribution under section 305 to which section 305(b)(2) and 301 apply, even though they have an increased proportionate interest in the assets and earnings and profits of the corporation.

Example 14. Corporation U is a large manufacturing company whose products are sold through independent dealers. In order to assist individuals who lack capital to become dealers, the corporation has an established investment plan under which it provides 75 percent of the capital necessary to form a dealership corporation and the individual dealer provides the remaining 25 percent. Corporation U receives class A stock and a note representing its 75 percent interest. The individual dealer receives class B stock representing his 25 percent interest. The class B stock is nonvoting until all the class A shares are redeemed. At least 70 percent of the earnings and profits of the dealership corporation must be used each year to retire the note and to redeem the class A stock. The class A stock is redeemed at a fixed price. The individual dealer has no control over the redemption of stock and has no right to have his stock redeemed during the period the plan is in existence. U's investment is thus systematically eliminated and the individual becomes the sole owner of the dealership corporation. Since this type of plan is akin to a security arrangement, the redemptions of the class A stock will not be deemed under section 305(c) as distributions taxable under sections 305(b)(2) and 301 during the years in which the class A stock is redeemed.

Example 15. (i) *Facts.* Corporation V is organized with two classes of stock, class A common and class B convertible preferred. The class B stock is issued for $100 per share and is convertible at the holder's option into class A at a fixed ratio that is not subject to full adjustment in the event stock dividends or rights are distributed to the class A shareholders. The class B stock pays no dividends but it is mandatorily redeemable in 10 years for $200. Under sections 305(c) and 305(b)(4), the entire redemption premium (i.e., the excess of the redemption price over the issue price) is deemed to be a distribution of preferred stock on preferred stock which is taxable as a distribution of property under section 301. This amount is considered to be distributed over the 10-year period under principles similar to the principles of section 1272(a). During the year, the corporation declares a dividend on the class A stock payable in additional shares of class A stock.

(ii) *Analysis.* The distribution on the class A stock is a distribution to which sections 305(b)(2) and 301 apply since it increases the proportionate interests of the class A shareholders in the assets and earnings and profits of the corporation and the class B shareholders have received property (i.e., the constructive distribution described above). If, however, the conversion ratio of the class B stock were subject to full adjustment to reflect the distribution of stock to class A shareholders, the distribution of stock dividends on the class A stock would not increase the proportionate interest of the class A shareholders in the assets and earnings and profits of the corporation and such distribution would not be a distribution to which section 301 applies.

(iii) *Effective date.* This *Example 15* applies to stock issued on or after December 20, 1995. For previously issued stock, see §1.305-3(e) *Example (15)* (as contained in the 26 CFR part 1 edition revised April 1, 1995). [Reg. §1.305-3.]

Reg. §1.305-3(e)

☐ [T.D. 6152, 12/2/55. *Amended by T.D. 6990, 1/10/69, T.D. 7004, 2-7-69, T.D. 7281, 7-11-73, T.D. 7329, 10-11-74 and T.D. 8643, 12-20-95.*]

[Reg. §1.305-4]

§1.305-4. Distributions of common and preferred stock.—(a) *In general.*—Under section 305(b)(3), a distribution (or a series of distributions) by a corporation which results in the receipt of preferred stock (whether or not convertible into common stock) by some common shareholders and the receipt of common stock by other common shareholders is treated as a distribution of property to which section 301 applies. For the meaning of the term "a series of distributions", see subparagraphs (1) through (6) of §1.305-3(b).

(b) *Examples.*—The application of section 305(b)(3) may be illustrated by the following examples:

Example (1). Corporation X is organized with two classes of common stock, class A and class B. Dividends may be paid in stock or in cash on either class of stock without regard to the medium of payment of dividends on the other class. A dividend is declared on the class A stock payable in additional shares of class A stock and a dividend is declared on class B stock payable in newly authorized class C stock which is nonconvertible and limited and preferred as to dividends. Both the distribution of class A shares and the distribution of new class C shares are distributions to which section 301 applies.

Example (2). Corporation Y is organized with one class of stock, class A common. During the year the corporation declares a dividend on the class A stock payable in newly authorized class B preferred stock which is convertible into class A stock no later than 6 months from the date of distribution at a price that is only slightly higher than the market price of class A stock on the date of distribution. Taking into account the dividend rate, redemption provisions, the marketability of the convertible stock, and the conversion price, it is reasonable to anticipate that within a relatively short period of time some shareholders will exercise their conversion rights and some will not. Since the distribution can reasonably be expected to result in the receipt of preferred stock by some common shareholders and the receipt of common stock by other common shareholders, the distribution is a distribution of property to which section 301 applies. [Reg. §1.305-4.]

☐ [T.D. 7281, 7-11-73.]

[Reg. §1.305-5]

§1.305-5. Distributions on preferred stock.—(a) *In general.*—Under section 305(b)(4), a distribution by a corporation of its stock (or rights to acquire its stock) made (or deemed made under section 305(c)) with respect to its preferred stock is treated as a distribution of property to which section 301 applies unless the distribution is made with respect to convertible preferred stock to take into account a stock dividend, stock split, or any similar event (such as the sale of stock at less than the fair market value pursuant to a rights offering) which would otherwise result in the dilution of the conversion right. For purposes of the preceding sentence, an adjustment in the conversion ratio of convertible preferred stock made solely to take into account the distribution by a closed-end regulated investment company of a capital gain dividend with respect to the stock into which such stock is convertible shall not be considered a "similar event". The term "preferred stock" generally refers to stock which, in relation to other classes of stock outstanding, enjoys certain limited rights and privileges (generally associated with specified dividend and liquidation priorities) but does not participate in corporate growth to any significant extent. The distinguishing feature of "preferred stock" for the purposes of section 305(b)(4) is not its privileged position as such, but that such privileged position is limited and that such stock does not participate in corporate growth to any significant extent. However, a right to participate which lacks substance will not prevent a class of stock from being treated as preferred stock. Thus, stock which enjoys a priority as to dividends and on liquidation but which is entitled to participate, over and above such priority, with another less privileged class of stock in earnings and profits and upon liquidation, may nevertheless be treated as preferred stock for purposes of section 305 if, taking into account all the facts and circumstances, it is reasonable to anticipate at the time a distribution is made (or is deemed to have been made) with respect to such stock that there is little or no likelihood of such stock actually participating in current and anticipated earnings and upon liquidation beyond its preferred interest. Among the facts and circumstances to be considered are the prior and anticipated earnings per share, the cash dividends per share, the book value per share, the extent of preference and of *participation of each class,* both absolutely and relative to each other, and any other facts which indicate whether or not the stock has a real and meaningful probability of actually participating in the earnings and growth of the corporation. The determination of whether stock is preferred for purposes of section 305 shall be made without regard to any right to convert such stock into another class of stock of the corporation. The term "preferred stock", however, does not include convertible debentures.

(b) *Redemption premium.*—(1) *In general.*—If a corporation issues preferred stock that may be redeemed under the circumstances described in this paragraph (b) at a price higher than the issue price, the difference (the redemption premium) is treated under section 305(c) as a constructive distribution (or series of constructive distributions) of additional stock on preferred stock that is taken into account under principles similar to the principles of section 1272(a). However, constructive distribution treatment does not result under this paragraph (b) if the redemption premium does not exceed a de minimis amount, as determined under the principles of section 1273(a)(3). For purposes of this paragraph (b), preferred stock that may be acquired by a person other than the issuer (the third person) is deemed to be redeemable under the circumstances described in this paragraph (b), and references to the issuer include the third person, if—

(i) this paragraph (b) would apply to the stock if the third person were the issuer; and

(ii) either—

(A) the acquisition of the stock by the third person would be treated as a redemption for federal income tax purposes (under section 304 or otherwise); or

(B) the third person and the issuer are members of the same affiliated group (having the meaning for this purpose given the term by section 1504(a), except that section 1504(b) shall not apply) and a principal purpose of the arrangement for the third person to acquire the stock is to avoid the application of section 305 and paragraph (b)(1) of this section.

(2) *Mandatory redemption or holder put.*—Paragraph (b)(1) of this section applies to stock if the issuer is required to redeem the stock at a specified time or the holder has the option (whether or not currently exercisable) to require the issuer to redeem the stock. However, paragraph (b)(1) of this section will not apply if the issuer's obligation to redeem or the holder's ability to require the issuer to redeem is subject to a contingency that is beyond the legal or practical control of either the holder or the holders as a group (or through a related party within the meaning of section 267(b) or 707(b)), and that, based on all of the facts and circumstances as of the issue date, renders remote the likelihood of redemption. For purposes of this paragraph, a contingency does not include the possibility of default, insolvency, or similar circumstances, or that a redemption may be precluded by applicable law which requires that the issuer have a particular level of capital, surplus, or similar items. A contingency also does not include an issuer's option to require earlier redemption of the stock. For rules applicable if stock may be redeemed at more than one time, see paragraph (b)(4) of this section.

(3) *Issuer call.*—(i) *In general.*—Paragraph (b)(1) of this section applies to stock by reason of the issuer's right to redeem the stock (even if the right is immediately exercisable), but only if, based on all of the facts and circumstances as of the issue date, redemption pursuant to that right is more likely than not to occur. However, even if redemption is more likely than not to occur, paragraph (b)(1) of this section does not apply if the redemption premium is solely in the nature of a penalty for premature redemption. A redemption premium is not a penalty for premature redemption unless it is a premium paid as a result of changes in economic or market conditions over which neither the issuer nor the holder has legal or practical control.

(ii) *Safe harbor.*—For purposes of this paragraph (b)(3), redemption pursuant to an issuer's right to redeem is not treated as more likely than not to occur if—

(A) The issuer and the holder are not related within the meaning of section 267(b) or 707(b) (for purposes of applying sections 267(b) and 707(b) (including section 267(f)(1)), the phrase "20 percent" shall be substituted for the phrase "50 percent");

(B) There are no plans, arrangements, or agreements that effectively require or are intended to compel the issuer to redeem the stock (disregarding, for this purpose, a separate mandatory redemption obligation described in paragraph (b)(2) of this section); and

(C) Exercise of the right to redeem would not reduce the yield of the stock, as determined under principles similar to the principles of section 1272(a) and the regulations under sections 1271 through 1275.

(iii) *Effect of not satisfying safe harbor.*—The fact that a redemption right is not described in paragraph (b)(3)(ii) of this section does not affect the determination of whether a redemption pursuant to the right to redeem is more likely than not to occur.

(4) *Coordination of multiple redemption provisions.*—If stock may be redeemed at more than one time, the time and price at which

redemption is most likely to occur must be determined based on all of the facts and circumstances as of the issue date. Any constructive distribution under paragraph (b)(1) of this section will result only with respect to the time and price identified in the preceding sentence. However, if redemption does not occur at that identified time, the amount of any additional premium payable on any later redemption date, to the extent not previously treated as distributed, is treated as a constructive distribution over the period from the missed call or put date to that later date, to the extent required under the principles of this paragraph (b).

(5) *Consistency.*—The issuer's determination as to whether there is a constructive distribution under this paragraph (b) is binding on all holders of the stock, other than a holder that explicitly discloses that its determination as to whether there is a constructive distribution under this paragraph (b) differs from that of the issuer. Unless otherwise prescribed by the Commissioner, the disclosure must be made on a statement attached to the holder's timely filed federal income tax return for the taxable year that includes the date the holder acquired the stock. The issuer must provide the relevant information to the holder in a reasonable manner. For example, the issuer may provide the name or title and either the address or telephone number of a representative of the issuer who will make available to holders upon request the information required for holders to comply with this provision of this paragraph (b).

(c) *Cross reference.*—For rules for applying sections 305(b)(4) and 305(c) to recapitalizations, see § 1.305-7(c).

(d) *Examples.*—The applications of sections 305(b)(4) and 305(c) may be illustrated by the following examples:

Example 1. (i) Corporation T has outstanding 1,000 shares of $100 par 5-percent cumulative preferred stock and 10,000 shares of no-par common stock. The corporation is 4 years in arrears on dividends to the preferred shareholders. The issue price of the preferred stock is $100 per share. Pursuant to a recapitalization under section 368(a)(1)(E), the preferred shareholders exchange their preferred stock, including the right to dividend arrearages, on the basis of one old preferred share for 1.20 newly authorized class A preferred shares. Immediately following the recapitalization, the new class A shares are traded at $100 per share. The class A shares are entitled to a liquidation preference of $100. The preferred shareholders have increased their proportionate interest in the assets or earnings and profits of corporation T since the fair market value of 1.20 shares of class A preferred stock ($120) exceeds the issue price of the old preferred stock ($100). Accordingly, the preferred shareholders are deemed under section 305(c) to receive a distribution in the amount of $20 on each share of old preferred stock and the distribution is one to which sections 305(b)(4) and 301 apply.

(ii) The same result would occur if the fair market value of the common stock immediately following the recapitalization were $20 per share and each share of preferred stock were exchanged for one share of the new class A preferred stock and one share of common stock.

Example 2. Corporation A, a publicly held company whose stock is traded on a securities exchange (or in the over-the-counter-market) has two classes of stock outstanding, common and cumulative preferred. Each share of preferred stock is convertible into .75 shares of common stock. There are no dividend arrearages. At the time of issue of the preferred stock, there was no plan or prearrangement by which it was to be exchanged for common stock. The issue price of the preferred stock is $100 per share. In order to retire the preferred stock, corporation A recapitalizes in a transaction to which section 368(a)(1)(E) applies and each share of preferred stock is exchanged for one share of common stock. Immediately after the recapitalization the common stock has a fair market value of $110 per share. Notwithstanding the fact that the fair market value of the common stock received in the exchange (determined immediately following the recapitalization) exceeds the issue price of the preferred stock surrendered, the recapitalization is not deemed under section 305(c) to result in a distribution to which sections 305(b)(4) and 301 apply since the recapitalization is not pursuant to a plan to periodically increase a shareholder's proportionate interest in the assets or earnings and profits and does not involve dividend arrearages.

Example 3. Corporation V is organized with two classes of stock, 1,000 shares of class A common and 1,000 shares of class B convertible preferred. Each share of class B stock may be converted into two shares of class A stock. Pursuant to a recapitalization under section 368(a)(1)(E), the 1,000 shares of class A stock are surrendered in exchange for 500 shares of new class A common and 500 shares of newly authorized class C common. The conversion right of class B stock is changed to one share of class A stock and one share of class C stock for each share of class B stock. The change in the conversion right is not deemed under section 305(c) to be a distribution on preferred stock to which sections 305(b)(4) and 301 apply.

Example 4—(i) *Facts.* Corporation X is a domestic corporation with only common stock outstanding. In connection with its acquisition of Corporation T, X issues 100 shares of its 4% preferred stock to the shareholders of T, who are unrelated to X both before and after the transaction. The issue price of the preferred stock is $40 per share. Each share of preferred stock is convertible at the shareholder's election into three shares of X common stock. At the time the preferred stock is issued, the X common stock has a value of $10 per share. The preferred stock does not provide for its mandatory redemption or for redemption at the option of the holder. It is callable at the option of X at any time beginning three years from the date of issuance for $100 per share. There are no other plans, arrangements, or agreements that effectively require or are intended to compel X to redeem the stock.

(ii) *Analysis.* The preferred stock is described in the safe harbor rule of paragraph (b)(3)(ii) of this section because X and the former shareholders of T are unrelated, there are no plans, arrangements, or agreements that effectively require or are intended to compel X to redeem the stock, and calling the stock for $100 per share would not reduce the yield of the preferred stock. Therefore, the $60 per share call premium is not treated as a constructive distribution to the shareholders of the preferred stock under paragraph (b) of this section.

Example 5—(i) *Facts*—(A) Corporation Y is a domestic corporation with only common stock outstanding. On January 1, 1996, Y issues 100 shares of its 10% preferred stock to a holder. The holder is unrelated to Y both before and after the stock issuance. The issue price of the preferred stock is $100 per share. The preferred stock is—

(1) Callable at the option of Y on or before January 1, 2001, at a price of $105 per share plus any accrued but unpaid dividends; and

(2) Mandatorily redeemable on January 1, 2006, at a price of $100 per share plus any accrued but unpaid dividends.

(B) The preferred stock provides that if Y fails to exercise its option to call the preferred stock on or before January 1, 2001, the holder will be entitled to appoint a majority of Y's directors. Based on all of the facts and circumstances as of the issue date, Y is likely to have the legal and financial capacity to exercise its right to redeem. There are no other facts and circumstances as of the issue date that would affect whether Y will call the preferred stock on or before January 1, 2001.

(ii) *Analysis.* Under paragraph (b)(3)(i) of this section, paragraph (b)(1) of this section applies because, by virtue of the change of control provision and the absence of any contrary facts, it is more likely than not that Y will exercise its option to call the preferred stock on or before January 1, 2001. The safe harbor rule of paragraph (b)(3)(ii) of this section does not apply because the provision that failure to call will cause the holder to gain control of the corporation is a plan, arrangement, or agreement that effectively requires or is intended to compel Y to redeem the preferred stock. Under paragraph (b)(4) of this section, the constructive distribution occurs over the period ending on January 1, 2001. Redemption is most likely to occur on that date, because that is the date on which the corporation minimizes the rate of return to the holder while preventing the holder from gaining control. The de minimis exception of paragraph (b)(1) of this section does not apply because the $5 per share difference between the redemption price and the issue price exceeds the amount determined under the principles of section 1273(a)(3) (5 × .0025 × $105 = $1.31). Accordingly, $5 per share, the difference between the redemption price and the issue price, is treated as a constructive distribution received by the holder on an economic accrual basis over the five-year period ending on January 1, 2001, under principles similar to the principles of section 1272(a).

Example 6. Corporation A, a publicly held company whose stock is traded on a securities exchange (or in the over-the-counter market) has two classes of stock outstanding, common and preferred. The preferred stock is nonvoting and nonconvertible, limited and preferred as to dividends, and has a fixed liquidation preference. There are no dividend arrearages. At the time of issue of the preferred stock, there was no plan or prearrangement by which it was to be exchanged for common stock. In order to retire the preferred stock, corporation A recapitalizes in a transaction to which section 368(a)(1)(E) applies and the preferred stock is exchanged for common stock. The transaction is not deemed to be a distribution under section 305(c) and sections 305(b) and 301 do not apply to the transaction. The same result would follow if the preferred stock was exchanged in any reorganization described in section 368(a)(1) for a new preferred stock having substantially the same market value and having no greater call price or liquidation preference than the old preferred stock, whether the new preferred stock has voting rights or is convertible into common stock of corporation A at a fixed ratio subject to change solely to take account of stock dividends, stock splits, or similar transactions with respect to the stock into which the preferred stock is convertible.

Example 7—(i) *Facts*—(A) Corporation Z is a domestic corporation with only common stock outstanding. On January 1, 1996, Z issues

100 shares of its 10% preferred stock to C, an individual unrelated to Z both before and after the stock issuance. The issue price of the preferred stock is $100 per share. The preferred stock is—

(1) Not callable for a period of 5 years from the issue date;

(2) Callable at the option of Z on January 1, 2001, at a price of $110 per share plus any accrued but unpaid dividends;

(3) Callable at the option of Z on July 1, 2002, at a price of $120 per share plus any accrued but unpaid dividends; and

(4) Mandatorily redeemable on January 1, 2004, at a price of $150 per share plus any accrued but unpaid dividends.

(B) There are no other plans, arrangements, or agreements between Z and C concerning redemption of the stock. Moreover, there are no other facts and circumstances as of the issue date that would affect whether Z will call the preferred stock on either January 1, 2001, or July 1, 2002.

(ii) *Analysis.* This stock is described in paragraph (b)(2) of this section because it is mandatorily redeemable. It is also potentially described in paragraph (b)(3)(i) of this section because it is callable at the option of the issuer. The safe harbor rule of paragraph (b)(3)(ii) of this section does not apply to the option to call on January 1, 2001, because the call would reduce the yield of the stock when compared to the yield produced by the January 1, 2004, mandatory redemption feature. Moreover, absent any other facts indicating a contrary result, the fact that redemption on January 1, 2001, would produce the lowest yield indicates that redemption is most likely to occur on that date. Under paragraph (b)(4) of this section, paragraph (b)(1) of this section applies with respect to the issuer's right to call on January 1, 2001, because redemption is most likely to occur on January 1, 2001, for $110 per share. The de minimis exception of paragraph (b)(1) of this section does not apply because the $10 per share difference between the redemption price payable in 2001 and the issue price exceeds the amount determined under the principles of section 1273(a)(3) (5 × .0025 × $110 = $1.38). Accordingly, $10 per share, the difference between the redemption price and the issue price, is treated as a constructive distribution received by the holder on an economic accrual basis over the five-year period ending January 1, 2001, under principles similar to the principles of section 1272(a).

(iii) *Coordination rules*—(A) If Z does not exercise its option to call the preferred stock on January 1, 2001, paragraph (b)(4) of this section provides that the principles of paragraph (b) of this section must be applied to determine if any remaining constructive distribution occurs. Under paragraphs (b)(3)(i) and (b)(4) of this section, paragraph (b)(1) of this section applies because, absent any other facts indicating a contrary result, the fact that redemption on July 1, 2002, would produce a lower yield than the yield produced by the mandatory redemption feature indicates that redemption on that date is most likely to occur. The safe harbor rule of paragraph (b)(3)(ii) of this section does not apply to the option to call on July 1, 2002, because, as of January 1, 2001, a call by Z on July 1, 2002, for $120 would reduce the yield of the stock. The de minimis exception of paragraph (b)(1) of this section does not apply because the $10 per share difference between the redemption price and the issue price (revised as of the missed call date as provided by paragraph (b)(4) of this section) exceeds the amount determined under the principles of section 1273(a)(3) (1 × .0025 × $120 = $.30). Accordingly, the $10 per share of additional redemption premium that is payable on July 1, 2002, is treated as a constructive distribution received by the holder on an economic accrual basis over the period between January 1, 2001, and July 1, 2002, under principles similar to the principles of section 1272(a).

(B) If Z does not exercise its second option to call the preferred stock on July 1, 2002, then the $30 additional redemption premium that is payable on January 1, 2004, is treated as a constructive distribution under paragraphs (b)(2) and (b)(1) of this section. The de minimis exception of paragraph (b)(1) of this section does not apply because the $30 per share difference between the redemption price and the issue price (revised as of the second missed call date) exceeds the amount determined under the principles of section 1273(a)(3) (1 × .0025 × $150 = $.38). The holder is treated as receiving the constructive distribution on an economic accrual basis over the period between July 1, 2002, and January 1, 2004, under principles similar to the principles of section 1272(a).

Example 8—(i) *Facts.* The facts are the same as in paragraph (i) of *Example 7*, except that, based on all of the facts and circumstances as of the issue date (including an expected lack of funds on the part of Z), it is unlikely that Z will exercise the right to redeem on either January 1, 2001, or July 1, 2002.

(ii) *Analysis.* The safe harbor rule of paragraph (b)(3)(ii) of this section does not apply to the option to call on either January 1, 2001, or July 1, 2002, because each call would reduce the yield of the stock. Under paragraph (b)(3)(i) of this section, neither option to call is more likely than not to occur, because, based on all of the facts and circumstances as of the issue date (including an expected lack of funds on the part of Z), it is not more likely than not that Z will

exercise either option. However, the $50 per share redemption premium that is payable on January 1, 2004, is treated as a constructive distribution under paragraphs (b)(1) and (2) of this section, regardless of whether Z is anticipated to have sufficient funds to redeem on that date, because Z is required to redeem the stock on that date. The de minimis exception of paragraph (b)(1) of this section does not apply because the $50 per share difference between the redemption price and the issue price exceeds the amount determined under the principles of section 1273(a)(3) (8 × .0025 × $150 = $3).

Example 9. Corporation Q is organized with 10,000 shares of class A stock and 1,000 shares of class B stock. The terms of the class B stock require that the class B have a preference of $5 per share with respect to dividends and $100 per share with respect to liquidation. In addition, upon a distribution of $10 per share to the class A stock, class B participates equally in any additional dividends. The terms also provide that upon liquidation the class B stock participates equally after the class A stock receives $100 per share. Corporation Q has no accumulated earnings and profits. In 1971 it earned $10,000, the highest earnings in its history. The corporation is in an industry in which it is reasonable to anticipate a growth in earnings of 5 percent per year. In 1971 the book value of corporation O's assets totalled $100,000. In that year the corporation paid a dividend of $5 per share to the class B stock and $.50 per share to the class A. In 1972 the corporation had no earnings and in lieu of a $5 dividend distributed one share of class B stock for each outstanding share of class B. No distribution was made to the class A stock. Since, in 1972, it was not reasonable to anticipate that the class B stock would participate in the current and anticipated earnings and growth of the corporation beyond its preferred interest, the class B stock is preferred stock and the distribution of class B shares to the class B shareholders is a distribution to which sections 305(b)(4) and 301 apply.

Example 10. Corporation P is organized with 10,000 shares of class A stock and 1,000 shares of class B stock. The terms of the class B stock require that the class B have a preference of $5 per share with respect to dividends and $100 per share with respect to liquidation. In addition, upon a distribution of $5 per share to the class A stock, class B participates equally in any additional dividends. The terms also provide that upon liquidation the class B stock participates equally after the class A receives $100 per share. Corporation P has accumulated earnings and profits of $100,000. In 1971 it earned $75,000. The corporation is in an industry in which it is reasonable to anticipate a growth in earnings of 10 percent per year. In 1971 the book value of corporation P's assets totalled $5 million. In that year the corporation paid a dividend of $5 per share to the class B stock, $5 per share to the class A stock, and it distributed an additional $1 per share to both class A and class B stock. In 1972 the corporation had earnings of $82,500. In that year it paid a dividend of $5 per share to the class B stock and $5 per share to the class A stock. In addition, the corporation declared stock dividends of one share of class B stock for every 10 outstanding shares of class B and one share of class A stock for every 10 outstanding shares of class A. Since, in 1972, it was reasonable to anticipate that both the class B stock and the class A stock would participate in the current and anticipated earnings and growth of the corporation beyond their preferred interests, neither class is preferred stock and the stock dividends are not distributions to which section 305(b)(4) applies.

(e) *Effective date.*—The rules of paragraph (b) of this section and *Examples 4, 5, 7,* and *8* of paragraph (d) of this section apply to stock issued on or after December 20, 1995. For rules applicable to previously issued stock, see §1.305-5(b) and (d) *Examples (4), (5),* and *(7)* (as contained in the 26 CFR part 1 edition revised April 1, 1995). Although the rules of paragraph (b) of this section and the revised examples do not apply to stock issued before December 20, 1995, the rules of sections 305(c)(1), (2), and (3) apply to stock described therein issued on or after October 10, 1990, except as provided in section 11322(b)(2) of the Revenue Reconciliation Act of 1990 (Public Law 101-508 Stat.). Moreover, except as provided in section 11322(b)(2) of the Revenue Reconciliation Act of 1990 (Public Law 101-508 Stat.), with respect to stock issued on or after October 10, 1990, and issued before December 20, 1995, the economic accrual rule of section 305(c)(3) will apply to the entire call premium on stock that is not described in paragraph (b)(2) of this section if the premium is considered to be unreasonable under the principles of §1.305-5(b) (as contained in the 26 CFR part 1 edition revised April 1, 1995). A call premium described in the preceding sentence will be accrued over the period of time during which the preferred stock cannot be called for redemption. [Reg. §1.305-5.]

☐ [*T.D. 7281,* 7-11-73. *Amended by T.D. 7329,* 10-11-74 *and T.D. 8643,* 12-20-95.]

[Reg. §1.305-6]

§1.305-6. Distributions of convertible preferred.—(a) *In general.*—(1) Under section 305(b)(5), a distribution by a corporation of its convertible preferred stock or rights to acquire such stock made or considered as made with respect to its stock is treated as a distribution of property to which section 301 applies unless the corporation establishes that such distribution will not result in a disproportionate distribution as described in § 1.305-3.

(2) The distribution of convertible preferred stock is likely to result in a disproportionate distribution when both of the following conditions exist: (i) The conversion right must be exercised within a relatively short period of time after the date of distribution of the stock; and (ii) taking into account such factors as the dividend rate, the redemption provisions, the marketability of the convertible stock, and the conversion price, it may be anticipated that some shareholders will exercise their conversion rights and some will not. On the other hand, where the conversion right may be exercised over a period of many years and the dividend rate is consistent with market conditions at the time of distribution of the stock, there is no basis for predicting at what time and the extent to which the stock will be converted and it is unlikely that a disproportionate distribution will result.

(b) *Examples.*—The application of section 305(b)(5) may be illustrated by the following examples:

Example (1). Corporation Z is organized with one class of stock, class A common. During the year the corporation declares a dividend on the class A stock payable in newly authorized class B preferred stock which is convertible into class A stock for a period of 20 years from the date of issuance. Assuming dividend rates are normal in light of existing conditions so that there is no basis for predicting the extent to which the stock will be converted, these circumstances will ordinarily be sufficient to establish that a disproportionate distribution will not result since it is impossible to predict the extent to which the class B stock will be converted into class A stock. Accordingly, the distribution of class B stock is not one to which section 301 applies.

Example (2). Corporation X is organized with one class of stock, class A common. During the year the corporation declares a dividend on the class A stock payable in newly authorized redeemable class C preferred stock which is convertible into class A common stock no later than 4 months from the date of distribution at a price slightly higher than the market price of class A stock on the date of distribution. By prearrangement with corporation X, corporation Y, an insurance company, agrees to purchase class C stock from any shareholder who does not wish to convert. By reason of this prearrangement, it is anticipated that the shareholders will either sell the class C stock to the insurance company (which expects to retain the shares for investment purposes) or will convert. As a result, some of the shareholders exercise their conversion privilege and receive additional shares of class A stock, while other shareholders sell their class C stock to corporation Y and receive cash. The distribution is a distribution to which section 301 applies since it results in the receipt of property by some shareholders and an increase in the proportionate interests of other shareholders. [Reg. § 1.305-6.]

☐ [*T.D. 7281, 7-11-73.*]

[Reg. § 1.305-7]

§ 1.305-7. Certain transactions treated as distributions.—(a) *In general.*—Under section 305(c), a change in conversion ratio, a change in redemption price, a difference between redemption price and issue price, a redemption which is treated as a distribution to which section 301 applies, or any transaction (including a recapitalization) having a similar effect on the interest of any shareholder may be treated as a distribution with respect to any shareholder whose proportionate interest in the earnings and profits or assets of the corporation is increased by such change, difference, redemption, or similar transaction. In general, such change, difference, redemption, or similar transaction will be treated as a distribution to which sections 305(b) and 301 apply where—

(1) The proportionate interest of any shareholder in the earnings and profits or assets of the corporation deemed to have made such distribution is increased by such change, difference, redemption, or similar transaction; and

(2) Such distribution has the result described in paragraph (2), (3), (4), or (5) of section 305(b).
Where such change, difference, redemption, or similar transaction is treated as a distribution under the provisions of this section, such distribution will be deemed made with respect to any shareholder whose interest in the earnings and profits or assets of the distributing corporation is increased thereby. Such distribution will be deemed to be a distribution of the stock of such corporation made by the corporation to such shareholder with respect to his stock. Depending upon the facts presented, the distribution may be deemed to be made in common or preferred stock. For example, where a redemption premium exists with respect to a class of preferred stock under the circumstances described in § 1.305-5(b) and the other requirements of this section are also met, the distribution will be deemed made with

respect to such preferred stock, in stock of the same class. Accordingly, the preferred shareholders are considered under sections 305(b)(4) and 305(c) to have received a distribution of preferred stock to which section 301 applies. See the examples in § § 1.305-3(e) and 1.305-5(d) for further illustrations of the application of section 305(c).

(b) *Antidilution provisions.*—(1) For purposes of applying section 305(c) in conjunction with section 305(b), a change in the conversion ratio or conversion price of convertible preferred stock (or securities), or in the exercise price of rights or warrants, made pursuant to a bona fide, reasonable, adjustment formula (including, but not limited to, either the so-called "market price" or "conversion price" type of formulas) which has the effect of preventing dilution of the interest of the holders of such stock (or securities) will not be considered to result in a deemed distribution of stock. An adjustment in the conversion ratio or price to compensate for cash or property distributions to other shareholders that are taxable under section 301, 356(a)(2), 871(a)(1)(A), 881(a)(1), 352(b), or 857(b) will not be considered as made pursuant to a bona fide adjustment formula.

(2) The principles of this paragraph may be illustrated by the following example:

Example. (i) Corporation U has two classes of stock outstanding, class A and class B. Each class B share is convertible into class A stock. In accordance with a bona fide, reasonable, antidilution provision, the conversion price is adjusted if the corporation transfers class A stock to anyone for a consideration that is below the conversion price.

(ii) The corporation sells class A stock to the public at the current market price but below the conversion price. Pursuant to the antidilution provision, the conversion price is adjusted downward. Such a change in conversion price will not be deemed to be a distribution under section 305(c) for the purposes of section 305(b).

(c) *Recapitalizations.*—(1) A recapitalization (whether or not an isolated transaction) will be deemed to result in a distribution to which section 305(c) and this section apply if—

(i) It is pursuant to a plan to periodically increase a shareholder's proportionate interest in the assets or earnings and profits of the corporation, or

(ii) A shareholder owning preferred stock with dividends in arrears exchanges his stock for other stock and, as a result, increases his proportionate interest in the assets or earnings and profits of the corporation. An increase in a preferred shareholder's proportionate interest occurs in any case where the fair market value or the liquidation preference, whichever is greater, of the stock received in the exchange (determined immediately following the recapitalization), exceeds the issue price of the preferred stock surrendered.

(2) In a case to which subparagraph (1)(ii) of this paragraph applies, the amount of the distribution deemed under section 305(c) to result from the recapitalization is the lesser of (i) the amount by which the fair market value or the liquidation preference, whichever is greater, of the stock received in the exchange (determined immediately following the recapitalization) exceeds the issue price of the preferred stock surrendered, or (ii) the amount of the dividends in arrears.

(3) For purposes of applying subparagraphs (1) and (2) of this paragraph with respect to stock issued before July 12, 1973, the term "issue price of the preferred stock surrendered" shall mean the greater of the issue price or the liquidation preference (not including dividends in arrears) of the stock surrendered.

(4) For an illustration of the application of this paragraph, see example (12) of § 1.305-3(e) and examples (1), (2), (3), and (6) of § 1.305-5(d).

(5) For rules relating to redemption premiums on preferred stock, see § 1.305-5(b) [Reg. § 1.305-7.]

☐ [*T.D. 7281, 7-11-73. Amended by T.D. 8643, 12-20-95.*]

[Reg. § 1.305-8]

§ 1.305-8. Effective dates.—(a) *In general.*—Section 421(b) of the Tax Reform Act of 1969 (83 Stat. 515) provides as follows:

"(b) *Effective dates.* (1) Except as otherwise provided in this subsection, the amendment made by subsection (a) shall apply with respect to distributions (or deemed distributions) made after January 10, 1969, in taxable years ending after such date.

"(2)(A) Section 305(b)(2) of the Internal Revenue Code of 1954 (as added by subsection (a)) shall not apply to a distribution (or deemed distribution) of stock made before January 1, 1991, with respect to stock (i) outstanding on January 10, 1969, (ii) issued pursuant to a contract binding on January 10, 1969, on the distributing corporation, (iii) which is additional stock of that class of stock which (as of January 10, 1969) had the largest fair market value of all classes of stock of the corporation (taking into account only stock outstanding on January 10, 1969, or issued pursuant to a contract binding on January 10, 1969), (iv) described in subparagraph (C)(iii), or (v) issued in a prior distribution described in clause (i), (ii), (iii), or (iv).

"(B) Subparagraph (A) shall apply only if—

"(i) The stock as to which there is a receipt of property was outstanding on January 10, 1969 (or was issued pursuant to a contract binding on January 10, 1969, on the distributing corporation), and

"(ii) If such stock and any stock described in subparagraph (A)(i) were also outstanding on January 10, 1968, a distribution of property was made on or before January 10, 1969, with respect to such stock, and a distribution of stock was made on or before January 10, 1969, with respect to such stock described in subparagraph (A)(i).

"(C) Subparagraph (A) shall cease to apply when at any time after October 9, 1969, the distributing corporation issues any of its stock (other than in a distribution of stock with respect to stock of the same class) which is not—

"(i) Nonconvertible preferred stock,

"(ii) Additional stock of that class of stock which meets the requirements of subparagraph (A)(iii), or

"(iii) Preferred stock which is convertible into stock which meets the requirements of subparagraph (A)(iii) at a fixed conversion ratio which takes account of all stock dividends and stock splits with respect to the stock into which such convertible stock is convertible.

"(D) For purposes of this paragraph, the term 'stock' includes rights to acquire such stock.

"(3) In cases to which Treasury Decision 6990 (promulgated January 10, 1969) would not have applied, in applying paragraphs (1) and (2) April 22, 1969, shall be substituted for January 10, 1969.

"(4) Section 305(b)(4) of the Internal Revenue Code of 1954 (as added by subsection (a)) shall not apply to any distribution (or deemed distribution) with respect to preferred stock (including any increase in the conversion ratio of convertible stock) made before January 1, 1991, pursuant to the terms relating to the issuance of such stock which were in effect on January 10, 1969.

"(5) With respect to distributions made or considered as made after January 10, 1969, in taxable years ending after such date, to the extent that the amendment made by subsection (a) does not apply by reason of paragraph (2), (3), or (4) of this subsection, section 305 of the Internal Revenue Code of 1954 (as in effect before the amendment made by subsection (a)) shall continue to apply."

(b) *Rules of application.*—(1) The rules contained in section 421(b)(2) of the Tax Reform Act of 1969 (83 Stat. 615), hereinafter called "the Act", shall apply with respect to the application of section 305(b)(2), section 305(b)(3), and 305(b)(5). Thus, for example, section 305(b)(5) of the Code will not apply to a distribution of convertible preferred stock made before January 1, 1991, with respect to stock outstanding on January 10, 1969 (or which was issued pursuant to a contract binding on the distributing corporation on January 10, 1969), provided the distribution is pursuant to the terms relating to the issuance of such stock which were in effect on January 10, 1969.

(2)(i) For purposes of section 421(b)(2)(A), (B)(i), and (C) of the Act, stock is considered as outstanding on January 10, 1969, if it could be acquired on such date or some future date by the exercise of a right or conversion privilege in existence on such date (including a right or conversion privilege with respect to stock issued pursuant to a contract binding, on January 10, 1969, on the distributing corporation). Thus, if on January 10, 1969, corporation X has outstanding 1,000 shares of class A common stock and 3,000 shares of class B common stock which are convertible on a one-to-one basis into class A stock, corporation X is considered for purposes of section 421(b)(2)(A), (B)(i), and (C) of the Act to have outstanding on January 10, 1969, 4,000 shares of class A stock (1,000 shares actually outstanding and 3,000 shares that could be acquired by the exercise of the conversion privilege contained in the class B stock) and 3,000 shares of class B stock.

(ii) For the purposes of section 421(b)(2)(A) (other than for the purpose of determining under section 421(b)(2)(A)(iii) that class of stock which as of January 10, 1969, had the largest fair market value of all classes of stock of the corporation), (B)(i), and (C) of the Act, stock will be considered as outstanding on January 10, 1969, if it is issued pursuant to a conversion privilege contained in stock issued, mediately or immediately, as a stock dividend with respect to stock outstanding on January 10, 1969.

(3) If, after applying subparagraph (2) of this paragraph, the *class of stock which as of January 10, 1969, had the largest fair market* value of all classes of stock of the corporation is a class of stock which is convertible into another class of nonconvertible stock, then for purposes of section 421(b)(2)(C)(ii) of the Act stock issued upon conversion of any such convertible stock (whether or not outstanding

on January 10, 1969) into stock of such other class shall be deemed to be stock which meets the requirements of section 421(b)(2)(A)(iii) of the Act.

(4) For purposes of section 421(b) of the Act, stock of a corporation held in its treasury will not be considered as outstanding and a distribution of such stock will be considered to be an issuance of such stock on the date of distribution. Stock of a parent corporation held by its subsidiary is not considered treasury stock.

(5) The following stock shall not be taken into account for purposes of applying section 421(b)(2)(B)(i) of the Act: (i) Stock issued after January 10, 1969, and before October 10, 1969 (other than stock which was issued pursuant to a contract binding on January 10, 1969, on the distributing corporation); (ii) stock described in section 421(b)(2)(C)(i), (ii), or (iii) of the Act; and (iii) stock issued, mediately or immediately, as a stock dividend with respect to stock of the same class outstanding on January 10, 1969. For example, if on June 1, 1970, corporation Y issues additional stock of that class of stock which as of January 10, 1969, had the largest fair market value of all classes of stock of the corporation, such additional stock will not be taken into account for the purpose of meeting the requirement under section 421(b)(2)(B)(i) of the Act that the stock as to which there is a receipt of property must have been outstanding on January 10, 1969, and thus subparagraph (A) of section 421(b)(2) of the Act will not, where otherwise applicable, cease to apply.

(6) Section 421(b)(2)(A) of the Act, if otherwise applicable, will not cease to apply if the distributing corporation issues after October 9, 1969, securities which are convertible into stock that meets the requirements of section 421(b)(2)(A)(iii) of the Act at a fixed conversion ratio which takes account of all stock dividends and stock splits with respect to the stock into which the securities are convertible.

(7) Under section 421(b)(4) of the Act, section 305(b)(4) does not apply to any distribution (or deemed distribution) by a corporation with respect to preferred stock made before January 1, 1991, if such distribution is pursuant to the terms relating to the issuance of such stock which were in effect on January 10, 1969. For example, if as of January 10, 1969, a corporation had followed the practice of paying stock dividends on preferred stock (or of periodically increasing the conversion ratio of convertible preferred stock) or if the preferred stock provided for a redemption price in excess of the issue price, then section 305(b)(4) would not apply to any distribution of stock made (or which would be considered made if section 305(b)(4) applied) before January 1, 1991, pursuant to such practice.

(8) If section 421(b)(2) is not applicable and, for that reason, a distribution (or deemed distribution) is treated as a distribution to which section 301 applies by virtue of the application of section 305(b)(2), (b)(3), or (b)(5), it is irrelevant that, by reason of the application of section 421(b)(4) of such Act, section 305(b)(4) is not applicable to the distribution. [Reg. §1.305-8.]

☐ [*T.D.* 7281, 7-11-73.]

[Reg. §1.306-1]

§1.306-1. **General.**—(a) Section 306 provides, in general, that the proceeds from the sale or redemption of certain stock (referred to as "section 306 stock") shall be treated either as ordinary income or as a distribution of property to which section 301 applies. Section 306 stock is defined in section 306(c) and is usually preferred stock received either as a nontaxable dividend or in a transaction in which no gain or loss is recognized. Section 306(b) lists certain circumstances in which the special rules of section 306(a) shall not apply.

(b)(1) If a shareholder sells or otherwise disposes of section 306 stock (other than by redemption or within the exceptions listed in section 306(b)), the entire proceeds received from such disposition shall be treated as ordinary income to the extent that the fair market value of the stock sold, on the date distributed to the shareholder, would have been a dividend to such shareholder had the distributing corporation distributed cash in lieu of stock. Any excess of the amount received over the sum of the amount treated as ordinary income plus the adjusted basis of the stock disposed of shall be treated as gain from the sale of a capital asset or noncapital asset as the case may be. No loss shall be recognized. No reduction of earnings and profits results from any disposition of stock other than a redemption. The term "disposition" under section 306(a)(1) includes, among other things, pledges of stock under certain circumstances, particularly where the pledgee can look only to the stock itself as its security.

(2) Section 306(a)(1) may be illustrated by the following examples:

Example (1). On December 15, 1954, A and B owned equally all of the stock of Corporation X which files its income tax return on a calendar year basis. On that date Corporation X distributed pro rata 100 shares of preferred stock as a dividend on its outstanding common stock. On December 15, 1954, the preferred stock had a fair market value of $10,000. On December 31, 1954, the earnings and profits of Corporation X were $20,000. The 50 shares of preferred stock so distributed to A had an allocated basis to him of $10 per share or a total of $500 for the 50 shares. Such shares had a fair market value of $5,000 when issued. A sold the 50 shares of preferred stock on July 1, 1955, for $6,000. Of this amount $5,000 will be treated as ordinary income; $500 ($6,000 minus $5,500) will be treated as gain from the sale of a capital or noncapital asset as the case may be.

Example (2). The facts are the same as in example 1 except that A sold his 50 shares of preferred stock for $5,100. Of this amount $5,000 will be treated as ordinary income. No loss will be allowed. There will be added back to the basis of the common stock of Corporation X with respect to which the preferred stock was distributed, $400, the allocated basis of $500 reduced by the $100 received.

Example (3). The facts are the same as in example 1 except that A sold 25 of his shares of preferred stock for $2,600. Of this amount $2,500 will be treated as ordinary income. No loss will be allowed. There will be added back to the basis of the common stock of Corporation X with respect to which the preferred stock was distributed, $150, the allocated basis of $250 reduced by the $100 received.

(c) The entire amount received by a shareholder from the redemption of section 306 stock shall be treated as a distribution of property under section 301. See also section 303 (relating to distribution in redemption of stock to pay death taxes). [Reg. § 1.306-1.]

☐ [T.D. 6152, 12-2-55. *Amended by T.D. 7556, 8-2-78.*]

[Reg. § 1.306-2]

§ 1.306-2. Exceptions.—(a) If a shareholder terminates his entire stock interest in a corporation—

(1) By a sale or other disposition within the requirements of section 306(b)(1)(A), or

(2) By redemption under section 302(b)(3) (through the application of section 306(b)(1)(B)),

the amount received from such disposition shall be treated as an amount received in part or full payment for the stock sold or redeemed. In the case of a sale, only the stock interest need be terminated. In determining whether an entire stock interest has been terminated under section 306(b)(1)(A), all of the provisions of section 318(a) (relating to constructive ownership of stock) shall be applicable. In determining whether a shareholder has terminated his entire interest in a corporation by a redemption of his stock under section 302(b)(3), all of the provisions of section 318(a) shall be applicable unless the shareholder meets the requirements of section 302(c)(2) (relating to termination of all interest in the corporation). If the requirements of section 302(c)(2) are met, section 318(a)(1) (relating to members of a family) shall be inapplicable. Under all circumstances paragraphs (2), (3), (4), and (5) of section 318(a) shall be applicable.

(b) Section 306(a) does not apply to—

(1) Redemptions of section 306 stock pursuant to a partial or complete liquidation of a corporation to which part (section 331 and following), subchapter C, chapter 1 of the Code applies,

(2) Exchanges of section 306 stock solely for stock in connection with a reorganization or in an exchange under section 351, 355, or section 1036 (relating to exchanges of stock for stock in the same corporation) to the extent that gain or loss is not recognized to the shareholder as the result of the exchange of the stock (see paragraph (d) of § 1.306-3 relative to the receipt of other property), and

(3) A disposition or redemption, if it is established to the satisfaction of the Commissioner that the distribution, and the disposition or redemption, was not in pursuance of a plan having as one of its principal purposes the avoidance of Federal income tax. However, in the case of a prior or simultaneous disposition (or redemption) of the stock with respect to which the section 306 stock disposed of (or redeemed) was issued, it is not necessary to establish that the distribution was not in pursuance of such a plan. For example, in the absence of such a plan and of any other facts the first sentence of this subparagraph would be applicable to the case of dividends and isolated dispositions of section 306 stock by minority shareholders. Similarly, in the absence of such a plan and of any other facts, if a shareholder received a distribution of 100 shares of section 306 stock on his holdings of 100 shares of voting common stock in a corporation and sells his voting common stock before he disposes of his section 306 stock, the subsequent disposition of his section 306 stock would not ordinarily be considered a disposition one of the principal purposes of which is the avoidance of Federal income tax. [Reg. § 1.306-2.]

☐ [T.D. 6152, 12-2-55. *Amended by T.D. 6969, 8-22-68.*]

[Reg. § 1.306-3]

§ 1.306-3. Section 306 stock defined.—(a) For the purpose of subchapter C, chapter 1 of the Code, the term "section 306 stock" means stock which meets the requirements of section 306(c)(1). Any class of stock distributed to a shareholder in a transaction in which no amount is includible in the income of the shareholder or no gain or loss is recognized may be section 306 stock, if a distribution of money

by the distributing corporation in lieu of such stock would have been a dividend in whole or in part. However, except as provided in section 306(g), if no part of a distribution of money by the distributing corporation in lieu of such stock would have been a dividend, the stock distributed will not constitute section 306 stock.

(b) For the purpose of section 306, rights to acquire stock shall be treated as stock. Such rights shall not be section 306 stock if no part of the distribution would have been a dividend if money had been distributed in lieu of the rights. When stock is acquired by the exercise of rights which are treated as section 306 stock, the stock acquired is section 306 stock. Upon the disposition of such stock (other than by redemption or within the exceptions listed in section 306(b)), the proceeds received from the disposition shall be treated as ordinary income to the extent that the fair market value of the stock rights, on the date distributed to the shareholder, would have been a dividend to the shareholder had the distributing corporation distributed cash in lieu of stock rights. Any excess of the amount realized over the sum of the amount treated as ordinary income plus the adjusted basis of the stock shall be treated as gain from the sale of the stock.

(c) Section 306(c)(1)(A) provides that section 306 stock is any stock (other than common issued with respect to common) distributed to the shareholder selling or otherwise disposing thereof if, under section 305(a) (relating to distributions of stock and stock rights) any part of the distribution was not included in the gross income of the distributee.

(d) Section 306(c)(1)(B) includes in the definition of section 306 stock any stock except common stock, which is received by a shareholder in connection with a reorganization under section 368 or in a distribution or exchange under section 355 (or so much of section 356 as relates to section 355) provided the effect of the transaction is substantially the same as the receipt of a stock dividend, or the stock is received in exchange for section 306 stock. If, in a transaction to which section 356 is applicable, a shareholder exchanges section 306 stock for stock and money or other property, the entire amount of such money and of the fair market value of the other property (not limited to the gain recognized) shall be treated as a distribution of property to which section 301 applies. Common stock received in exchange for section 306 stock in a recapitalization shall not be considered section 306 stock. Ordinarily, section 306 stock includes stock which is not common stock received in pursuance of a plan of reorganization (within the meaning of section 368(a)) or received in a distribution or exchange to which section 355 (or so much of section 356 as relates to section 355) applies if cash received in lieu of such stock would have been treated as a dividend under section 356(a)(2) or would have been treated as a distribution to which section 301 applies by virtue of section 356(b) or section 302(d). The application of the preceding sentence is illustrated by the following examples:

Example (1). Corporation A, having only common stock outstanding, is merged in a statutory merger (qualifying as a reorganization under section 368(a)) with Corporation B. Pursuant to such merger, the shareholders of Corporation A received both common and preferred stock in Corporation B. The preferred stock received by such shareholders is section 306 stock.

Example (2). X and Y each own one-half of the 2,000 outstanding shares of preferred stock and one-half of the 2,000 outstanding shares of common stock of Corporation C. Pursuant to a reorganization within the meaning of section 368(a)(1)(E) (recapitalization) each shareholder exchanges his preferred stock for preferred stock of a new issue which is not substantially different from the preferred stock previously held. Unless the preferred stock exchanged was itself section 306 stock the preferred stock received is not section 306 stock.

(e) Section 306(c)(1)(C) includes in the definition of section 306 stock any stock (except as provided in section 306(c)(1)(B)) the basis of which in the hands of the person disposing of such stock, is determined by reference to section 306 stock held by such shareholder or any other person. Under this paragraph common stock can be section 306 stock. Thus, if a person owning section 306 stock in Corporation A transfers it to Corporation B which is controlled by him in exchange for common stock of Corporation B in a transaction to which section 351 is applicable, the common stock so received by him would be section 306 stock and subject to the provisions of section 306(a) on its disposition. In addition, the section 306 stock transferred is section 306 stock in the hands of Corporation B, the transferee. Section 306 stock transferred by gift remains section 306 stock in the hands of the donee. Stock received in exchange for section 306 stock under section 1036(a) (relating to exchange of stock for stock in the same corporation) or under so much of section 1031(b) as relates to section 1036(a) becomes section 306 stock and acquires, for purposes of section 306, the characteristics of the section 306 stock exchanged. The entire amount of the fair market value of the other property received in such transaction shall be considered as received upon a disposition (other than a redemption) to which section 306(a) applies. Section 306 stock ceases to be so classified if the basis of such stock is determined by reference to its fair market value on the date of the decedent-stockholder's death under section 1014 or the optional valuation date under section 2032. Section 306 stock continues to be so classified if the basis of such stock is determined under section 1022.

(f) If section 306 stock which was distributed with respect to common stock is exchanged for common stock in the same corporation (whether or not such exchange is pursuant to a conversion privilege contained in section 306 stock), such common stock shall not be section 306 stock. This paragraph applies to exchanges not coming within the purview of section 306(c)(1)(B). Common stock which is convertible into stock other than common stock or into property, shall not be considered common stock. It is immaterial whether the conversion privilege is contained in the stock or in some type of collateral agreement.

(g) If there is a substantial change in the terms and conditions of any stock, then, for the purpose of this section—

(1) The fair market value of such stock shall be the fair market value at the time of distribution or the fair market value at the time of such change, whichever is higher;

(2) Such stock's ratable share of the amount which would have been distributed in lieu of stock shall be determined by reference to the time of distribution or by reference to the time of such change, whichever ratable share is higher; and

(3) Section 306(c)(2) shall be inapplicable if there would have been a dividend to any extent if money had been distributed in lieu of the stock either at the time of the distribution or at the time of such change.

(h) When section 306 stock is disposed of, the amount treated under section 306(a)(1)(A) as ordinary income will, for the purposes of Part I, subchapter N, chapter 1 of the Code, be treated as derived from the same source as would have been the source if money had been received from the corporation as a dividend at the time of the distribution of such stock. If the amount is determined to be derived from sources within the United States, the amount shall be considered to be fixed or determinable annual or periodic gains, profits, and income within the meaning of section 871(a) or section 881(a), relating, respectively, to the tax on nonresident alien individuals and on foreign corporations not engaged in business in the United States.

(i) Section 306 shall be inapplicable to stock received before June 22, 1954, and to stock received on or after June 22, 1954, in transactions subject to the provisions of the Internal Revenue Code of 1939. [Reg. § 1.306-3.]

☐ *[T.D. 6152, 12-2-55. Amended by T.D. 7281, 7-11-73, T.D. 7556, 8-2-78 and T.D. 9811, 1-18-2017.]*

[Reg. § 1.306-4]

§ 1.306-4. Effective/applicability date.—The provisions of §§ 1.306-1 through 1.306-3 are applicable on or after June 22, 1954. The provisions of § 1.306-3 relating to section 1022 are effective on and after January 19, 2017. [Reg. § 1.306-4.]

☐ *[T.D. 9811, 1-18-2017.]*

[Reg. § 1.307-1]

§ 1.307-1. General.—(a) If a shareholder receives stock or stock rights as a distribution on stock previously held and under section 305 such distribution is not includible in gross income then, except as provided in section 307(b) and § 1.307-2, the basis of the stock with respect to which the distribution was made shall be allocated between the old and new stocks or rights in proportion to the fair market values of each on the date of distribution. If a shareholder receives stock or stock rights as a distribution on stock previously held and pursuant to section 305 part of the distribution is not includible in gross income, then (except as provided in section 307(b) and § 1.307-2) the basis of the stock with respect to which the distribution is made shall be allocated between (1) the old stock and (2) that part of the new stock or rights which is not includible in gross income, in proportion to the fair market values of each on the date of distribution. The date of distribution in each case shall be the date the stock or the rights are distributed to the stockholder and not the record date. The general rule will apply with respect to stock rights only if such rights are exercised or sold.

(b) The application of paragraph (a) of this section is illustrated by the following example:

Example. A taxpayer in 1947 purchased 100 shares of common stock at $100 per share and in 1954 by reason of the ownership of such stock acquired 100 rights entitling him to subscribe to 100 additional *shares of such stock at $90 a share. Immediately after the issuance of the rights, each of the shares of stock in respect of which the rights were acquired had a fair market value, ex-rights, of $110 and the rights had a fair market value of $19 each. The basis of the rights and the common stock for the purpose of determining the basis for gain

or loss on a subsequent sale or exercise of the rights or a sale of the old stock is computed as follows:

100 (shares) × $100	=	$10,000, cost of old stock (stock in respect of which the rights were acquired).
100 (shares) × $110	=	$11,000, market value of old stock.
100 (rights) × $ 19	=	$ 1,900, market value of rights.
11,000/12,900 of $10,000	=	$ 8,527.13, cost of old stock apportioned to such stock.
1,900/12,900 of $10,000	=	$ 1,472.87, cost of old stock apportioned to rights.

If the rights are sold, the basis for determining gain or loss will be $14.7287 per right. If the rights are exercised, the basis of the new stock acquired will be the subscription price paid therefor ($90) plus the basis of the rights exercised ($14.7287 each) or $104.7287 per share. The remaining basis of the old stock for the purpose of determining gain or loss on a subsequent sale will be $85.2713 per share. [Reg. § 1.307-1.]

☐ *[T.D. 6152, 12-2-55.]*

[Reg. § 1.307-2]

§ 1.307-2. Exception.—The basis of rights to buy stock which are excluded from gross income under section 305(a), shall be zero if the fair market value of such rights on the date of distribution is less than 15 percent of the fair market value of the old stock on that date, unless the shareholder elects to allocate part of the basis of the old stock to the rights as provided in paragraph (a) of § 1.307-1. The election shall be made by a shareholder with respect to all the rights received by him in a particular distribution in respect of all the stock of the same class owned by him in the issuing corporation at the time of such distribution. Such election to allocate basis to rights shall be in the form of a statement attached to the shareholder's return for the year in which the rights are received. This election, once made, shall be irrevocable with respect to the rights for which the election was made. Any shareholder making such an election shall retain a copy of the election and of the tax return with which it was filed, in order to substantiate the use of an allocated basis upon a subsequent disposition of the stock acquired by exercise. [Reg. § 1.307-2.]

☐ *[T.D. 6152, 12-2-55.]*

[Reg. § 1.312-1]

§ 1.312-1. Adjustment to earnings and profits reflecting distributions by corporations.—(a) In general, on the distribution of property by a corporation with respect to its stock, its earnings and profits (to the extent thereof) shall be decreased by—

(1) The amount of money,

(2) The principal amount of the obligations of such corporation issued in such distribution, and

(3) The adjusted basis of other property.

For special rule with respect to distributions to which section 312(e) applies, see § 1.312-5.

(b) The adjustment provided in section 312(a)(3) and paragraph (a)(3) of this section with respect to a distribution of property (other than money or its own obligations) shall be made notwithstanding the fact that such property has appreciated or depreciated in value since acquisition.

(c) The application of paragraphs (a) and (b) of this section may be illustrated by the following examples:

Example (1). Corporation A distributes to its sole shareholder property with a value of $10,000 and a basis of $5,000. It has $12,500 in earnings and profits. The reduction in earnings and profits by reason of such distribution is $5,000. Such is the reduction even though the amount of $10,000 is includible in the income of the shareholder (other than a corporation) as a dividend.

Example (2). The facts are the same as in example (1) above except that the property has a basis of $15,000 and the earnings and profits of the corporation are $20,000. The reduction in earnings and profits is $15,000. Such is the reduction even though only the amount of $10,000 is includible in the income of the shareholder as a dividend.

(d) In the case of a distribution of stock or rights to acquire stock a portion of which is includible in income by reason of section 305(b), the earnings and profits shall be reduced by the fair market value of such portion. No reduction shall be made if a distribution of stock or rights to acquire stock is not includible in income under the provisions of section 305.

(e) No adjustment shall be made in the amount of the earnings and profits of the issuing corporation upon a disposition of section 306 stock unless such disposition is a redemption. [Reg. § 1.312-1.]

☐ *[T.D. 6152, 12-2-55.]*

[Reg. §1.312-2]

§1.312-2. Distributions of inventory assets.—Section 312(b) provides for the increase and the decrease of the earnings and profits of a corporation which distributes, with respect to its stock, inventory assets as defined in section 312(b)(2), where the fair market value of such assets exceeds their adjusted basis. The rules provided in section 312(b) (relating to distributions of certain inventory assets) shall be applicable without regard to the method used in computing inventories for the purpose of the computation of taxable income. Section 312(b) does not apply to distributions described in section 312(e). [Reg. §1.312-2.]

☐ [*T.D.* 6152, 12-2-55.]

[Reg. §1.312-3]

§1.312-3. Liabilities.—The amount of any reductions in earnings and profits described in section 312(a) or (b) shall be (a) reduced by the amount of any liability to which the property distributed was subject and by the amount of any other liability of the corporation assumed by the shareholder in connection with such distribution, and (b) increased by the amount of gain recognized to the corporation under section 311(b), (c), or (d), or under section 341(f), 617(d), 1245(a), 1250(a), 1251(c), 1252(a), or 1254(a). [Reg. §1.312-3.]

☐ [*T.D.* 6152, 12-2-55. *Amended by T.D.* 6832, 7-6-65, *T.D.* 7084, 1-7-71; *T.D.* 7209, 10-3-72 *and T.D.* 8586, 1-9-95.]

[Reg. §1.312-4]

§1.312-4. Examples of adjustments provided in section 312(c).—The adjustments provided in section 312(c) may be illustrated by the following examples:

Example (1). On December 2, 1954, Corporation X distributed to its sole shareholder, A, an individual, as a dividend in kind a vacant lot which was not an inventory asset. On that date, the lot had a fair market value of $5,000 and was subject to a mortgage of $2,000. The adjusted basis of the lot was $3,100. The amount of the earnings and profits was $10,000. The amount of the dividend received by A is $3,000 ($5,000, the fair market value, less $2,000, the amount of the mortgage) and the reduction in the earnings and profits of Corporation X is $1,100 ($3,100, the basis, less $2,000, the amount of mortgage).

Example (2). The facts are the same as in example (1) above with the exception that the amount of the mortgage to which the property was subject was $4,000. The amount of the dividend received by A is $1,000, and there is no reduction in the earnings and profits of the corporation as a result of the distribution (disregarding such reduction as may result from an increase in tax to Corporation X because of gain resulting from distribution). There is a gain of $900 recognized to Corporation X, the difference between the basis of the property ($3,100) and the amount of the mortgage ($4,000), under section 311(c) and an increase in earnings and profits of $900.

Example (3). Corporation A, having accumulated earnings and profits of $100,000, distributed in kind to its shareholders, not in liquidation, inventory assets which had a basis to it on the "Lifo" method (section 472) of $46,000 and on the basis of cost or market (section 471) of $50,000. The inventory had a fair market value of $55,000 and was subject to a liability of $35,000. This distribution results in a net decrease in earnings and profits of Corporation A of $11,000, (without regard to any tax on Corporation A) computed as follows:

"Fifo" basis of inventory	$50,000	
Less: "Lifo" basis of inventory	46,000	
Gain recognized—addition to earnings and profits (section 311(b))		$ 4,000
Adjustment to earnings and profits required by section 312(b)(1)(A):		
Fair market value of inventory	$55,000	
Less: "Lifo" basis plus adjustment under section 311(b)	50,000	5,000
Total increase in earnings and profits		$ 9,000
Decrease in earnings and profits—under section 312(b)(1)(B)(i)	$55,000	
Less: Liability assumed	35,000	
Net amount of distribution (decrease in earnings)		20,000
Net decrease in earnings and profits		$11,000

[Reg. §1.312-4.]

☐ [*T.D.* 6152, 12-2-55.]

[Reg. §1.312-5]

§1.312-5. Special rule for partial liquidations and certain redemptions.—The part of the distribution properly chargeable to capital account within the provisions of section 312(e) shall not be considered a distribution of earnings and profits within the meaning of section 301 for the purpose of determining taxability of subsequent distributions by the corporation. [Reg. §1.312-5.]

☐ [*T.D.* 6152, 12-2-55.]

[Reg. §1.312-6]

§1.312-6. Earnings and profits.—(a) In determining the amount of earnings and profits (whether of the taxable year, or accumulated since February 28, 1913, or accumulated before March 1, 1913) due consideration must be given to the facts, and, while mere bookkeeping entries increasing or decreasing surplus will not be conclusive, the amount of the earnings and profits in any case will be dependent upon the method of accounting properly employed in computing taxable income (or net income, as the case may be). For instance, a corporation keeping its books and filing its income tax returns under subchapter E, chapter 1 of the Code, on the cash receipts and disbursements basis may not use the accrual basis in determining earnings and profits; a corporation computing income on the installment basis as provided in section 453 shall, with respect to the installment transactions, compute earnings and profits on such basis; and an insurance company subject to taxation under section 831 shall exclude from earnings and profits that portion of any premium which is unearned under the provisions of section 832(b)(4) and which is segregated accordingly in the unearned premium reserve.

(b) Among the items entering into the computation of corporate earnings and profits for a particular period are all income exempted by statute, income not taxable by the Federal Government under the Constitution, as well as all items includible in gross income under section 61 or corresponding provisions of prior revenue acts. Gains and losses within the purview of section 1002 or corresponding provisions of prior revenue acts are brought into the earnings and profits at the time and to the extent such gains and losses are recognized under that section. Interest on State bonds and certain other obligations, although not taxable when received by a corporation, is taxable to the same extent as other dividends when distributed to shareholders in the form of dividends.

(c)(1) In the case of a corporation in which depletion or depreciation is a factor in the determination of income, the only depletion or depreciation deductions to be considered in the computation of the total earnings and profits are those based on cost or other basis without regard to March 1, 1913, value. In computing the earnings and profits for any period beginning after February 28, 1913, the only depletion or depreciation deductions to be considered are those based on (i) cost or other basis, if the depletable or depreciable asset was acquired subsequent to February 28, 1913, or (ii) adjusted cost or March 1, 1913, value, whichever is higher, if acquired before March 1, 1913. Thus, discovery or percentage depletion under all revenue acts for mines and oil and gas wells is not to be taken into consideration in computing the earnings and profits of a corporation. Similarly, where the basis of property in the hands of a corporation is a substituted basis, such basis, and not the fair market value of the property at the time of the acquisition by the corporation, is the basis for computing depletion and depreciation for the purpose of determining earnings and profits of the corporation.

(2) The application of subparagraph (1) of this paragraph may be illustrated by the following example:

Example. Oil producing property which A had acquired in 1949 at a cost of $28,000 was transferred to Corporation Y in December 1951, in exchange for all of its capital stock. The fair market value of the stock and of the property as of the date of the transfer was $247,000. Corporation Y, after four years' operation, effected in 1955 a cash distribution to A in the amount of $165,000. In determining the extent to which the earnings and profits of Corporation Y available for dividend distributions have been increased as the result of production and sale of oil, the depletion to be taken into account is to be computed upon the basis of $28,000 established in the nontaxable exchange in 1951 regardless of the fair market value of the property or of the stock issued in exchange therefor.

(d) A loss sustained for a year before the taxable year does not affect the earnings and profits of the taxable year. However, in determining the earnings and profits accumulated since February 28, 1913, the excess of a loss sustained for a year subsequent to February 28, 1913, over the undistributed earnings and profits accumulated since February 28, 1913, and before the year for which the loss was sustained, reduces surplus as of March 1, 1913, to the extent of such excess. If the surplus as of March 1, 1913, was sufficient to absorb such excess, distributions to shareholders after the year of the loss are out of earnings and profits accumulated since the year of the loss to the extent of such earnings.

(e) With respect to the effect on the earnings and profits accumulated since February 28, 1913, of distributions made on or after January 1, 1916, and before August 6, 1917, out of earnings or profits accumulated before March 1, 1913, which distributions were specifically declared to be out of earnings and profits accumulated before March 1, 1913, see section 31(b) of the Revenue Act of 1916, as amended by section 1211 of the Revenue Act of 1917 (40 Stat. 336). [Reg. § 1.312-6.].

☐ [T.D. 6152, 12-2-55.]

[Reg. § 1.312-7]

§ 1.312-7. Effect on earnings and profits of gain or loss realized after February 28, 1913.—(a) In order to determine the effect on earnings and profits of gain or loss realized from the sale or other disposition (after February 28, 1913) of property by a corporation, section 312(f)(1) prescribes certain rules for—

(1) The computation of the total earnings and profits of the corporation of most frequent application in determining invested capital; and

(2) The computation of earnings and profits of the corporation for any period beginning after February 28, 1913, of most frequent application in determining the source of dividend distributions.

Such rules are applicable whenever under any provision of subtitle A of the Code it is necessary to compute either the total earnings and profits of the corporation or the earnings and profits for any period beginning after February 28, 1913. For example, since the earnings and profits accumulated after February 28, 1913, or the earnings and profits of the taxable year, are earnings and profits for a period beginning after February 28, 1913, the determination of either must be in accordance with the regulations prescribed by this section, for the ascertainment of earnings and profits for any period beginning after February 28, 1913. Under subparagraph (1) of this paragraph, such gain or loss is determined by using the adjusted basis (under the law applicable to the year in which the sale or other disposition was made) for determining gain, but disregarding value as of March 1, 1913. Under subparagraph (2) of this paragraph, there is used such adjusted basis for determining gain, giving effect to the value as of March 1, 1913, whenever applicable. In both cases the rules are the same as those governing depreciation and depletion in computing earnings and profits (see § 1.312-6). Under both subparagraphs (1) and (2) of this paragraph, the adjusted basis is subject to the limitations of the third sentence of section 312(f)(1) requiring the use of adjustments proper in determining earnings and profits. The proper adjustments may differ under section 312(f)(1)(A) and (B) depending upon the basis to which the adjustments are to be made. If the application of section 312(f)(1)(B) results in a loss and if the application of section 312(f)(1)(A) to the same transaction reaches a different result, then the loss under section 312(f)(1)(B) will be subject to the adjustment thereto required by section 312(g)(2). (See § 1.312-9.)

(b)(1) The gain or loss so realized increases or decreases the earnings and profits to, but not beyond, the extent to which such gain or loss was recognized in computing taxable income (or net income, as the case may be) under the law applicable to the year in which such sale or disposition was made. As used in this paragraph, the term "recognized" has reference to that kind of realized gain or loss which is recognized for income tax purposes by the statute applicable to the year in which the gain or loss was realized. For example, see section 356. A loss (other than a wash sale loss with respect to which a deduction is disallowed under the provisions of section 1091 or corresponding provisions of prior revenue laws) may be recognized though not allowed as a deduction (by reason, for example, of the operation of sections 267 and 1211 and corresponding provisions of prior revenue laws) but the mere fact that it is not allowed does not prevent decrease in earnings and profits by the amount of such disallowed loss. Wash sale losses, however, disallowed under section 1091 and corresponding provisions of prior revenue laws, are deemed nonrecognized losses and do not reduce earnings or profits. The "recognized" gain or loss for the purpose of computing earnings and profits is determined by applying the recognition provisions to the realized gain or loss computed under the provisions of section 312(f)(1) as distinguished from the realized gain or loss used in computing taxable income (or net income, as the case may be).

(2) The application of subparagraph (1) of this paragraph may be illustrated by the following examples:

Example (1). Corporation X on January 1, 1952, owned stock in Corporation Y which it had acquired from Corporation Y in December 1951, in an exchange transaction in which no gain or loss was recognized. The adjusted basis to Corporation X of the property exchanged by it for the stock in Corporation Y was $30,000. The fair market value of the stock in Corporation Y when received by Corporation X was $930,000. On April 9, 1955, Corporation X made a cash distribution of $900,000 and, except for the possible effect of the transaction in 1951, had no earnings or profits accumulated after February 28, 1913, and had no earnings or profits for the taxable year. The amount of $900,000 representing the excess of the fair market value of the stock of Corporation Y over the adjusted basis of the property exchanged therefor was not recognized gain to Corporation X under the provisions of section 112 of the Internal Revenue Code of 1939. Accordingly, the earnings and profits of Corporation X are not increased by $900,000, the amount of the gain realized but not recognized in the exchange, and the distribution was not a taxable dividend. The basis in the hands of Corporation Y of the property acquired by it from Corporation X is $30,000. If such property is thereafter sold by Corporation Y, gain or loss will be computed on such basis of $30,000, and earnings and profits will be increased or decreased accordingly.

Example (2). On January 2, 1910, Corporation M acquired nondepreciable property at a cost of $1,000. On March 1, 1913, the fair market value of such property in the hands of Corporation M was $2,200. On December 31, 1952, Corporation M transfers such property to Corporation N in exchange for $1,900 in cash and all Corporation N's stock, which has a fair market value of $1,100. For the purpose of computing the total earnings and profits of Corporation M, the gain on such transaction is $2,000 (the sum of $1,900 in cash and stock worth $1,100 minus $1,000, the adjusted basis for computing gain, determined without regard to March 1, 1913, value), $1,900 of which is recognized under section 356, since this was the amount of money received, although for the purpose of computing net income the gain is only $800 (the sum of $1,900 in cash and stock worth $1,100, minus $2,200, the adjusted basis for computing gain determined by giving effect to March 1, 1913, value). Such earnings and profits will therefore be increased by $1,900. In computing the earnings and profits of Corporation M for any period beginning after February 28, 1913, however, the gain arising from the transaction, like the taxable gain, is only $800, all of which is recognized under section 112(c) of the Internal Revenue Code of 1939, the money received being in excess of such amount. Such earnings and profits will therefore be increased by only $800 as a result of the transaction. For increase in that part of the earnings and profits consisting of increase in value of property accrued before, but realized on or after March 1, 1913, see § 1.312-9.

Example (3). On July 31, 1955, Corporation R owned oil-producing property acquired after February 28, 1913, at a cost of $200,000, but having an adjusted basis (by reason of taking percentage depletion) of $100,000 for determining gain. However, the adjusted basis of such property to be used in computing gain or loss for the purpose of earnings and profits is, because of the provisions of the third sentence of section 312(f)(1), $150,000. On such day Corporation R transferred such property to Corporation S in exchange for $25,000 in cash and all of the stock of Corporation S, which had a fair market value of $100,000. For the purpose of computing taxable income, Corporation R has realized a gain of $25,000 as a result of this transaction, all of which is recognized under section 356. For the purpose of computing earnings and profits, however, Corporation R has realized a loss of $25,000, none of which is recognized owing to the provisions of section 356(c). The earnings and profits of Corporation R are therefore neither increased nor decreased as a result of the transaction. The adjusted basis of the Corporation S stock in the hands of Corporation R for purposes of computing earnings and profits, however, will be $125,000 (though only $100,000 for the purpose of computing taxable income), computed as follows:

Basis of property transferred	$200,000
Less money received on exchange	25,000
Plus gain or minus loss recognized on exchange	None
Basis of stock	$175,000
Less adjustments (same as those used in determining adjusted basis of property transferred)	$50,000
Adjusted basis of stock	$125,000

If, therefore, Corporation R should subsequently sell the Corporation S stock for $100,000, a loss of $25,000 will again be realized for the purpose of computing earnings and profits, all of which will be recognized and will be applied to decrease the earnings and profits of Corporation R.

(c)(1) The third sentence of section 312(f)(1) provides for cases in which the adjustments, prescribed in section 1016, to the basis indicated in section 312(f)(1)(A) or (B), as the case may be, differ from the adjustments to such basis proper for the purpose of determining earnings or profits. The adjustments provided by such third sentence reflect the treatment provided by §§ 1.312-6 and 1.312-15 relative to cases where the deductions for depletion and depreciation in computing taxable income (or net income, as the case may be) differ from the deductions proper for the purpose of computing earnings and profits.

(2) The effect of the third sentence of section 312(f)(1) may be illustrated by the following examples:

Example (1). Corporation X purchased on January 2, 1931, an oil lease at a cost of $10,000. The lease was operated only for the years 1931 and 1932. The deduction for depletion in each of the years 1931 and 1932 amounted to $2,750, of which amount $1,750 represented percentage depletion in excess of depletion based on cost. The lease was sold in 1955 for $15,000. Under section 1016(a)(2), in determining the gain or loss from the sale of the property, the basis must be adjusted for cost depletion of $1,000 in 1931 and percentage depletion of $2,750 in 1932. However, the adjustment of such basis, proper for the determination of earnings and profits, is $1,000 for each year, or $2,000. Hence, the cost is to be adjusted only to the extent of $2,000, leaving an adjusted basis of $8,000 and the earnings and profits will be increased by $7,000, and not by $8,750. The difference of $1,750 is equal to the amount by which the percentage depletion for the year 1932 ($2,750) exceeds the depletion on cost for that year ($1,000) and has already been applied in the computation of earnings and profits for the year 1932 by taking into account only $1,000 instead of $2,750 for depletion in the computation of such earnings and profits. (See § 1.316-1.)

Example (2). If, in example (1), above, the property, instead of being sold, is exchanged in a transaction described in section 1031 for like property having a fair market value of $7,750 and cash of $7,250, then the increase in earnings and profits amounts to $7,000, that is, $15,000 ($7,750 plus $7,250) minus the basis of $8,000. However, in computing taxable income of Corporation X, the gain is $8,750, that is, $15,000 minus $6,250 ($10,000 less depletion of $3,750), of which only $7,250 is recognized because the recognized gain cannot exceed the sum of money received in the transaction. See section 1031(b) and the corresponding provisions of prior revenue laws. If, however, the cash received was only $2,250 and the value of the property received was $12,750, then the increase in earnings and profits would be $2,250, that amount being the gain recognized under section 1031.

Example (3). On January 1, 1973, corporation X purchased for $10,000 a depreciable asset with an estimated useful life of 20 years and no salvage value. In computing depreciation on the asset, corporation X used the declining balance method with a rate twice the straight line rate. On December 31, 1976, the asset was sold for $9,000. Under section 1016(a)(2), the basis of the asset is adjusted for depreciation allowed for the years 1973 through 1976, or a total of $3,439. Thus, X realizes a gain of $2,439 (the excess of the amount realized, $9,000, over the adjusted basis, $6,561). However, the proper adjustment to basis for the purpose of determining earnings and profits is only $2,000, i.e., the total amount which, under § 1.312-15, was applied in the computation of earnings and profits for the years 1973-76. Hence, upon sale of the asset, earnings and profits are increased by only $1,000, i.e., the excess of the amount realized, $9,000, over the adjusted basis for earnings and profits purposes, $8,000.

(d) For adjustment and allocation of the earnings and profits of the transferor as between the transferor and the transferee in cases where the transfer of property by one corporation to another corporation results in the nonrecognition in whole or in part of gain or loss, see § 1.312-10; and see section 381 for earnings and profits of successor corporations in certain transactions. [Reg. § 1.312-7.]

☐ [*T.D. 6152, 12-2-55. Amended by T.D. 7221, 11-20-72.*]

[Reg. § 1.312-8]

§ 1.312-8. Effect on earnings and profits of receipt of tax-free distributions requiring adjustment or allocation of basis of stock.— (a) In order to determine the effect on earnings and profits, where a corporation receives (after February 28, 1913) from a second corporation a distribution which (under the law applicable to the year in which the distribution was made) was not a taxable dividend to the shareholders of the second corporation, section 312(f) prescribes certain rules. It provides that the amount of such distribution shall not increase the earnings and profits of the first or receiving corporation in the following cases: (1) No such increase shall be made in respect of the part of such distribution which (under the law applicable to the year in which the distribution was made) is directly applied in *reduction of the basis of the stock in respect of which the distribution was made* and (2) no such increase shall be made if (under the law applicable to the year in which the distribution was made) the distribution causes the basis of the stock in respect of which the distribution was made to be allocated between such stock and the property received (or such basis would but for section 307(b) be so allocated). Where, therefore, the law (applicable to the year in which the distribution was made, as, for example, a distribution in 1934 from earnings and profits accumulated before March 1, 1913) requires that the amount of such distribution shall be applied against and reduce the basis of the stock with respect to which the distribution

was made, there is no increase in the earnings and profits by reason of the receipt of such distribution. Similarly, where there is received by a corporation a distribution from another corporation in the form of a stock dividend and the law applicable to the year in which such distribution was made requires the allocation, as between the old stock and the stock received as a dividend, of the basis of the old stock (or such basis would but for section 307(b) be so allocated), then there is no increase in the earnings and profits by reason of the receipt of such stock dividend even though such stock dividend constitutes income within the meaning of the sixteenth amendment to the Constitution.

(b) The principles set forth in paragraph (a) of this section may be illustrated by the following examples:

Example (1). Corporation X in 1955 distributed to Corporation Y, one of its shareholders, $10,000 which was out of earnings or profits accumulated before March 1, 1913, and did not exceed the adjusted basis of the stock in respect of which the distribution was made. This amount of $10,000 was, therefore, a tax-free distribution and under the provisions of section 301(c)(2) must be applied against and reduce the adjusted basis of the stock in respect of which the distribution was made. The earnings and profits of Corporation Y are not increased by reason of the receipt of this distribution.

Example (2). Corporation Z in 1955 had outstanding common and preferred stock of which Corporation Y held 100 shares of the common and no preferred. The stock had a cost basis to Corporation Y of $100 per share, or a total cost of $10,000. In December of that year it received a dividend of 100 shares of the preferred stock of Corporation Z. Such distribution is a stock dividend which, under section 305, was not taxable and was accordingly not included in the gross income of Corporation Y. The original cost of $10,000 is allocated to the 200 shares of Corporation Z none of which has been sold or otherwise disposed of by Corporation Y. See section 307 and § 1.307-1. The earnings and profits of Corporation Y are not increased by reason of the receipt of such stock dividend. [Reg. § 1.312-8.]

☐ [*T.D. 6152, 12-2-55.*]

[Reg. § 1.312-9]

§ 1.312-9. Adjustments to earnings and profits reflecting increase in value accrued before March 1, 1913.—(a) In order to determine, for the purpose of ascertaining the source of dividend distributions, that part of the earnings and profits which is represented by increase in value of property accrued before, but realized on or after, March 1, 1913, section 312(g) prescribes certain rules.

(b)(1) Section 312(g)(1) sets forth the general rule with respect to computing the increase to be made in that part of the earnings and profits consisting of increase in value of property accrued before, but realized on or after, March 1, 1913.

(2) The effect of section 312(g)(1) may be illustrated by the following examples:

Example (1). Corporation X acquired nondepreciable property before March 1, 1913, at a cost of $10,000. Its fair market value as of March 1, 1913, was $12,000 and it was sold in 1955 for $15,000. The increase in earnings and profits based on the value as of March 1, 1913, representing earnings and profits accumulated since February 28, 1913, is $3,000. If the basis is determined without regard to the value as of March 1, 1913, there would be an increase in earnings and profits of $5,000. The difference of $2,000 ($5,000 minus $3,000) represents the increase to be made in that part of the earnings and profits of Corporation X consisting of the increase in value of property accrued before, but realized on or after, March 1, 1913.

Example (2). Corporation Y acquired depreciable property in 1908 at a cost of $100,000. Assuming no additions or betterments, and that the depreciation sustained before March 1, 1913, was $10,000, the adjusted cost as of that date was $90,000. Its fair market value as of March 1, 1913, was $94,000 and on February 28, 1955, it was sold for $25,000. For the purpose of determining gain from the sale, the basis of the property is the fair market value of $94,000 as of March 1, 1913, adjusted for depreciation for the period subsequent to February 28, 1913, computed on such fair market value. If the amount of the depreciation deduction allowed after February 28, 1913, and properly allowable for each of such years to the date of the sale in 1955 is the aggregate sum of $81,467, the adjusted basis for determining gain in 1955 ($94,000 less $81,467) is $12,533 and the gain would be $12,467 ($25,000 less $12,533). The increase in earnings and profits accumulated since February 28, 1913, by reason of the sale, based on the value as of March 1, 1913, adjusted for depreciation, is $12,467. If the depreciation since February 28, 1913, had been based on the adjusted cost of $90,000 ($100,000 less $10,000) instead of the March 1, 1913, value of $94,000, the depreciation sustained from that date to the date of sale would have been $78,000 instead of $81,467 and the actual gain on the sale based on the cost of $100,000 adjusted by depreciation on such cost to $12,000 ($100,000 reduced by the sum of $10,000 and $78,000) would be $13,000 ($25,000 less $12,000). If the adjusted basis of the property was determined without regard to the value as of March 1, 1913, there would be an increase in earnings and profits of $13,000. The difference of $533 ($13,000 minus $12,467) represents the increase to be made in that part of the earnings and profits of Corporation Y consisting of the increase in value of property accrued before, but realized on or after, March 1, 1913 (assuming that the proper increase in such surplus had been made each year for the difference between depreciation based on cost and the depreciation based on March 1, 1913, value). Thus, the total increase in that part of earnings and profits consisting of the increase in value of property accrued before, but realized on or after, March 1, 1913, is $4,000 ($94,000 less $90,000).

(c)(1) Section 312(g)(2) is an exception to the general rule in section 312(g)(1) and also operates as a limitation on the application of section 312(f). It provides that, if the application of section 312(f)(1)(B) to a sale or other disposition after February 28, 1913, results in a loss which is to be applied in decrease of earnings and profits for any period beginning after February 28, 1913, then, notwithstanding section 312(f) and in lieu of the rule provided in section 312(g)(1), the amount of such loss so to be applied shall be reduced by the amount, if any, by which the adjusted basis of the property used in determining the loss, exceeds the adjusted basis computed without regard to the fair market value of the property on March 1, 1913. If the amount so applied in reduction of the loss exceeds such loss, the excess over such loss shall increase that part of the earnings and profits consisting of increase in value of property accrued before, but realized on or after March 1, 1913.

(2) The application of section 312(g)(2) may be illustrated by the following examples:

Example (1). Corporation Y acquired nondepreciable property before March 1, 1913, at a cost of $8,000. Its fair market value as of March 1, 1913, was $13,000, and it was sold in 1955 for $10,000. The application of section 312(f)(1)(B) would result in a loss from the sale in 1955 to be applied in decrease of earnings and profits for that year. Section 312(g)(2), however, applies and the loss of $3,000 is reduced by the amount by which the adjusted basis of $13,000 exceeds the cost of $8,000 (the adjusted basis computed without regard to the value on March 1, 1913), namely, $5,000. The amount of the loss is, accordingly, reduced from $3,000 to zero and there is no decrease in earnings and profits of Corporation Y for the year 1955 as a result of the sale. The amount applied in reduction of the decrease, namely, $5,000, exceeds $3,000. Accordingly, as a result of the sale the excess of $2,000 increases that part of the earnings and profits of Corporation Y consisting of increase in value of property accrued before, but realized on or after March 1, 1913.

Example (2). Corporation Z acquired nondepreciable property before March 1, 1913, at a cost of $10,000. Its fair market value as of March 1, 1913, was $12,000, and it was sold in 1955 for $8,000. Under section 312(f)(1)(B) the adjusted basis would be $12,000 and there would be a loss of $4,000. The application of section 312(f)(1)(B) would result in a loss from the sale in 1955 to be applied in decrease of earnings and profits for that year. Section 312(g)(2), however, applies and the loss of $4,000 is reduced by the amount by which the adjusted basis of $12,000 exceeds the cost of $10,000 (the adjusted basis computed without regard to the value on March 1, 1913), namely, $2,000. The amount of the loss is, accordingly, reduced from $4,000 to $2,000 and the decrease in earnings and profits of Corporation Z for the year 1955 as a result of the sale is $2,000 instead of $4,000. The amount applied in reduction of the decrease, namely, $2,000, does not exceed $4,000. Accordingly, as a result of the sale there is no increase in that part of the earnings and profits of Corporation Z consisting of increase in value of property accrued before, but realized on or after, March 1, 1913. [Reg. § 1.312-9.]

☐ [T.D. 6152, 12-2-55.]

[Reg. § 1.312-10]

§ 1.312-10. Allocation of earnings in certain corporate separations.—(a) If one corporation transfers part of its assets constituting an active trade or business to another corporation in a transaction to which section 368(a)(1)(D) applies and immediately thereafter the stock and securities of the controlled corporation are distributed in a distribution or exchange to which section 355 (or so much of section 356 as relates to section 355) applies, the earnings and profits of the distributing corporation immediately before the transaction shall be allocated between the distributing corporation and the controlled corporation. In the case of a newly created controlled corporation, such allocation generally shall be made in proportion to the fair market value of the business or businesses (and interests in any other properties) retained by the distributing corporation and the business or businesses (and interests in any other properties) of the controlled *corporation immediately after the transaction.* In a proper case, allocation shall be made between the distributing corporation and the controlled corporation in proportion to the net basis of the assets transferred and of the assets retained or by such other method as may be appropriate under the facts and circumstances of the case.

The term "net basis" means the basis of the assets less liabilities assumed or liabilities to which such assets are subject. The part of the earnings and profits of the taxable year of the distributing corporation in which the transaction occurs allocable to the controlled corporation shall be included in the computation of the earnings and profits of the first taxable year of the controlled corporation ending after the date of the transaction.

(b) If a distribution or exchange to which section 355 applies (or so much of section 356 as relates to section 355) is not in pursuance of a plan meeting the requirements of a reorganization as defined in section 368(a)(1)(D), the earnings and profits of the distributing corporation shall be decreased by the lesser of the following amounts:

(1) The amount by which the earnings and profits of the distributing corporation would have been decreased if it had transferred the stock of the controlled corporation to a new corporation in a reorganization to which section 368(a)(1)(D) applied and immediately thereafter distributed the stock of such new corporation or,

(2) The net worth of the controlled corporation. (For this purpose the term "net worth" means the sum of the bases of all of the properties plus cash minus all liabilities.)

If the earnings and profits of the controlled corporation immediately before the transaction are less than the amount of the decrease in earnings and profits of the distributing corporation (including a case in which the controlled corporation has a deficit) the earnings and profits of the controlled corporation, after the transaction, shall be equal to the amount of such decrease. If the earnings and profits of the controlled corporation immediately before the transaction are more than the amount of the decrease in the earnings and profits of the distributing corporation, they shall remain unchanged.

(c) In no case shall any part of a deficit of a distributing corporation within the meaning of section 355 be allocated to a controlled corporation. [Reg. § 1.312-10.]

☐ [T.D. 6152, 12-2-55.]

[Reg. § 1.312-11]

§ 1.312-11. Effect on earnings and profits of certain other tax-free exchanges, tax-free distributions, and tax-free transfers from one corporation to another.—(a) In a transfer described in section 381(a), the acquiring corporation, as defined in § 1.381(a)-1(b)(2), and only that corporation, succeeds to the earnings and profits of the distributor or transferor corporation (within the meaning of § 1.381(a)-1(a)). Except as provided in § 1.312-10, in all other cases in which property is transferred from one corporation to another, no allocation of the earnings and profits of the transferor is made to the transferee.

(b) The general rule provided in section 316 that every distribution is made out of earnings or profits to the extent thereof and from the most recently accumulated earnings or profits does not apply to:

(1) The distribution, in pursuance of a plan of reorganization, by or on behalf of a corporation a party to the reorganization, or in a transaction subject to section 355, to its shareholders—

(i) Of stock or securities in such corporation or in another corporation a party to the reorganization in any taxable year beginning before January 1, 1934, without the surrender by the distributees of stock or securities in such corporation (see section 112(g) of the Revenue Act of 1932 (47 Stat. 197)); or

(ii) Of stock (other than preferred stock) in another corporation which is a party to the reorganization without the surrender by the distributees of stock in the distributing corporation if the distribution occurs after October 20, 1951, and is subject to section 112(b)(11) of the Internal Revenue Code of 1939; or

(iii) Of stock or securities in such corporation or in another corporation a party to the reorganization in any taxable year beginning before January 1, 1939, or on or after such date, in exchange for its stock or securities in a transaction to which section 112(b)(3) of the Internal Revenue Code of 1939 was applicable; or

(iv) Of stock or securities in such corporation or in another corporation in exchange for its stock or securities in a transaction subject to section 354 or 355,

if no gain to the distributees from the receipt of such stock or securities was recognzied by law.

(2) The distribution in any taxable year (beginning before January 1, 1939, or on or after such date) of stock or securities, or other property or money, to a corporation in complete liquidation of another corporation, under the circumstances described in section 112(b)(6) of the Revenue Act of 1936 (49 Stat. 1679), the Revenue Act of 1938 (52 Stat. 485), of the Internal Revenue Code of 1939, or section 332 of the Internal Revenue Code of 1954.

(3) The distribution in any taxable year (beginning after December 31, 1939 [1938]), of stock or securities, or other property or money, in the case of an exchange or distribution described in section 371 of the Internal Revenue Code of 1939 or in section 1081 of the Internal Revenue Code of 1954 (relating to exchanges and distributions in obedience to orders of the Securities and Exchange Commis-

sion), if no gain to the distributee from the receipt of such stock, securities, or other property or money was recognized by law.

(4) A stock dividend which was not subject to tax in the hands of the distributee because either it did not constitute income to him within the meaning of the sixteenth amendment to the Constitution or because exempt to him under section 115(f) of the Revenue Act of 1934 (48 Stat. 712) or a corresponding provision of a prior revenue act, or section 305 of the Code.

(5) The distribution, in a taxable year of the distributee beginning after December 31, 1931, by or on behalf of an insolvent corporation, in connection with a section 112(b)(10) reorganization under the Internal Revenue Code of 1939, or in a transaction subject to section 371 of the Internal Revenue Code of 1954, of stock or securities in a corporation organized or made use of to effectuate the plan of reorganization, if under section 112(I) of the Internal Revenue Code of 1939 or sections 371 of the Internal Revenue Code of 1954 no gain to the distributee from the receipt of such stock or securities was recognized by law.

(c) A distribution described in paragraph (b) of this section does not diminish the earnings or profits of any corporation. In such cases, the earnings or profits remain intact and available for distribution as dividends by the corporation making such distribution, or by another corporation to which the earnings or profits are transferred upon such reorganization or other exchange. In the case, however, of amounts distributed in liquidation (other than a tax-free liquidation or reorganization described in paragraph (b)(1), (2), (3), or (5) of this section) the earnings or profits of the corporation making the distribution are diminished by the portion of such distribution properly chargeable to earnings or profits accumulated after February 28, 1913, after first deducting from the amount of such distribution the portion thereof allocable to capital account.

(d) For the purposes of this section, the terms "reorganization" and "party to the reorganization" shall, for any taxable year beginning before January 1, 1934, have the meanings assigned to such terms in section 112 of the Revenue Act of 1932 (47 Stat. 196); for any taxable year beginning after December 31, 1933, and before January 1, 1936, have the meanings assigned to such terms in section 112 of the Revenue Act of 1934 (48 Stat. 704); for any taxable year beginning after December 31, 1935, and before January 1, 1938, have the meanings assigned to such terms in section 112 of the Revenue Act of 1936 (49 Stat. 1678); for any taxable year beginning after December 31, 1937, and before January 1, 1939, have the meanings assigned to such terms in section 112 of the Revenue Act of 1938 (52 Stat. 485); and for any taxable year beginning after December 31, 1938, and ending before June 22, 1954, providing no election is made under section 393(b)(2) of the Internal Revenue Code of 1954, have the meanings assigned to such terms in section 112(g)(1) of the Internal Revenue Code of 1939.

(e) *Effective/applicability date.*—Paragraph (a) of this section applies to transactions occurring on or after November 10, 2014. [Reg. § 1.312-11.]

☐ [*T.D.* 6152, 12-2-55. *Amended by T.D.* 6476, 6-30-60 *and T.D.* 9700, 11-7-2014.]

[Reg. § 1.312-12]

§ 1.312-12. Distributions of proceeds of loans guaranteed by the United States.—(a) The provisions of section 312(j) are applicable with respect to a loan, any portion of which is guaranteed by an agency of the United States Government without regard to the percentage of such loan subject to such guarantee.

(b) The application of section 312(j) is illustrated by the following example:

Example. Corporation A borrowed $1,000,000 for the purpose of construction of an apartment house, the cost and adjusted basis of which was $900,000. This loan was guaranteed by an agency of the United States Government. One year after such loan was made and after the completion of construction of the building (but before such corporation had received any income) it distributed $100,000 cash to its shareholders. The earnings and profits of the taxable year of such corporation are increased (pursuant to section 312(j)) by $100,000 immediately prior to such distribution and are decreased by $100,000 immediately after such distribution. Such decrease, however, does *not reduce the earnings and profits below zero.* Two years later, it has no accumulated earnings and has earnings of the taxable year of $100,000. Before it has made any payments on the loan, it distributes $200,000 to its shareholders. The earnings and profits of the taxable year of the corporation ($100,000) are increased by $100,000, the excess of the amount of the guaranteed loan over the adjusted basis of the apartment house (calculated without adjustment for depreciation). The entire amount of each distribution is treated as a distribution out of earnings and profits and, accordingly, as a taxable dividend. [Reg. § 1.312-12.]

☐ [*T.D.* 6152, 12-2-55.]

[Reg. § 1.312-13]

§ 1.312-13. [Reserved]

[Reg. § 1.312-14]

§ 1.312-14. [Reserved]

[Reg. § 1.312-15]

§ 1.312-15. Effect of depreciation on earnings and profits.—(a) *Depreciation for taxable years beginning after June 30, 1972.*—(1) *In general.*—Except as provided in subparagraph (2) of this paragraph and paragraph (c) of this section, for purposes of computing the earnings and profits of a corporation (including a real estate investment trust as defined in section 856) for any taxable year beginning after June 30, 1972, the allowance for depreciation (and amortization, if any) shall be deemed to be the amount which would be allowable for such year if the straight line method of depreciation had been used for all property for which depreciation is allowable for each taxable year beginning after June 30, 1972. Thus, for taxable years beginning after June 30, 1972, in determining the earnings and profits of a corporation, depreciation must be computed under the straight line method, notwithstanding that in determining taxable income the corporation uses an accelerated method of depreciation described in subparagraph (A), (B), or (C) of section 312(m)(2) or elects to amortize the basis of property under section 169, 184, 187, or 188, or any similar provision. See § 1.168(k)-1(f)(7) with respect to the treatment of the additional first year depreciation deduction allowable under section 168(k) for qualified property or 50-percent bonus depreciation property, and § 1.1400L(b)-1(f)(7) with respect to the treatment of the additional first year depreciation deduction allowable under section 1400L(b) for qualified New York Liberty Zone property, for purposes of computing the earnings and profits of a corporation. Further, see § 1.168(k)-2(g)(7) with respect to the treatment of the additional first year depreciation deduction allowable under section 168(k), as amended by the Tax Cuts and Jobs Act, Public Law 115-97 (131 Stat. 2054 (December 22, 2017)), for purposes of computing the earnings and profits of a corporation.

(2) *Exception.*—(i) If, for any taxable year beginning after June 30, 1972, a method of depreciation is used by a corporation in computing taxable income which the Secretary or his delegate has determined results in a reasonable allowance under section 167(a) and which is not a declining balance method of depreciation (described in § 1.167(b)-2), the sum of the years-digits methods (described in § 1.167(b)-3), or any other method allowed solely by reason of the application of subsection (b)(4) or (j)(1)(C) of section 167, then the adjustment to earnings and profits for depreciation for such year shall be determined under the method so used (in lieu of the straight line method).

(ii) The Commissioner has determined that the "unit of production" (see § 1.167(b)-0 (b)), and the "machine hour" methods of depreciation, when properly used under appropriate circumstances, meet the requirements of subdivision (i) of this subparagraph. Thus, the adjustment to earnings and profits for depreciation (for the taxable year for which either of such methods is properly used under appropriate circumstances) shall be determined under whichever of such methods is used to compute taxable income.

(3) *Determinations under straight line method.*—(i) In the case of property with respect to which an allowance for depreciation is claimed in computing taxable income, the determination of the amount which would be allowable under the straight line method shall be based on the manner in which the corporation computes depreciation in determining taxable income. Thus, if an election under § 1.167(a)-11 is in effect with respect to the property, the amount of depreciation which would be allowable under the straight line method shall be determined under § 1.167(a)-11(g)(3). On the other hand, if property is not depreciated under the provisions of § 1.167(a)-11, the amount of depreciation which would be allowable under the straight line method shall be determined under § 1.167(b)-1. Any election made under section 167(f), with respect to reducing the amount of salvage value taken into account in computing the depreciation allowance for certain property, or any convention adopted under § 1.167(a)-10(b) or § 1.167(a)-11(c)(2), with respect to additions and retirements from multiple asset accounts, which is used in computing depreciation for taxable income shall be used in computing depreciation for earnings and profits purposes.

(ii) In the case of property with respect to which an election to amortize is in effect under section 169, 184, 187, or 188, or any similar provision, the amount which would be allowable under the straight line method of depreciation shall be determined under the provisions of § 1.167(b)-1. Thus, the cost or other basis of the property, less its estimated salvage value, is to be deducted in equal annual amounts over the period of the estimated useful life of the property. In computing the amount of depreciation for earnings and profits purposes, a taxpayer may utilize the provisions of section 167(f) (relating to the reduction in the amount of salvage value taken into account in computing the depreciation allowance for certain property) and any convention which could have been adopted for such property under § 1.167(a)-10(b) (relating to additions and retirements from multiple asset accounts).

(b) *Transitional rules.*—(1) *Depreciation.*—If, for the taxable year which includes June 30, 1972, (i) the allowance for depreciation of any property is computed under a method other than the straight line method or a method described in paragraph (a)(2) of this section, and (ii) paragraph (a)(1) of this section applies to such property for the first taxable year beginning after June 30, 1972, then adjustments to earnings and profits for depreciation of such property for taxable years beginning after June 30, 1972, shall be determined as if the corporation changed to the straight line method with respect to such property as of the first day of the first taxable year beginning after June 30, 1972. Thus, if an election under § 1.167(a)-11 is in effect with respect to the property, the change shall be made under the provisions of § 1.167(a)-11(c)(1)(iii), except that no statement setting forth the vintage accounts for which the change is made shall be furnished with the income tax return of the year of change if the change is only for purposes of computing earnings and profits. In all other cases, the unrecovered cost or other basis of the property (less a reasonable estimate for salvage) as of such first day shall be recovered through equal annual allowances over the estimated remaining useful life determined in accordance with the circumstances existing at that time. See paragraph (a)(3)(i) of this section for rules relating to the applicability of section 167(f) in determining salvage value.

(2) *Amortization.*—If, for the taxable year which includes June 30, 1971, the basis of any property is amortized under section 169, 184, 187 or 188, or any similar provision, then adjustments to earnings and profits for depreciation or amortization of such property for taxable years beginning after June 30, 1972, shall be determined as if the unrecovered cost or other basis of the property (less a reasonable estimate for salvage) as of the first day of the first taxable year beginning after June 30, 1972, were recovered through equal annual allowances over the estimated remaining useful life of the property determined in accordance with the circumstances existing at that time. See paragraph (a)(3)(ii) of this section for rules relating to the applicability of section 167(f).

(c) *Certain foreign corporations.*—Paragraphs (a) and (b) of this section shall not apply in computing the earnings and profits of a foreign corporation for any taxable year for which less than 20 percent of the gross income from all sources of such corporation is derived from sources within the United States.

(d) *Books and records.*—Wherever different methods of depreciation are used for taxable income and earnings and profits purposes, records shall be maintained which show the depreciation taken for earnings and profits purposes each year and which will allow computation of the adjusted basis of the property in each account using the depreciation taken for earnings and profits purposes.

(e) *Applicability date of qualified property.*—The last sentence of paragraph (a)(1) of this section applies to the taxpayer's taxable years ending on or after September 24, 2019. However, a taxpayer may choose to apply the last sentence in paragraph (a)(1) of this section for the taxpayer's taxable years ending on or after September 28, 2017. A taxpayer may rely on the last sentence in paragraph (a)(1) of this section in regulation project REG-104397-18 (2018-41 I.R.B. 558) (see § 601.601(d)(2)(ii)(*b*) of this chapter) for the taxpayer's taxable years ending on or after September 28, 2017, and ending before the taxpayer's taxable year that includes September 24, 2019. [Reg. § 1.312-15.]

☐ [*T.D. 7221, 11-20-72. Amended by T.D. 9283, 8-28-2006 and T.D. 9874, 9-17-2019.*]

[Reg. § 1.316-1]

§ 1.316-1. Dividends.—(a)(1) The term "dividend" for the purpose of subtitle A of the Code (except when used in subchapter L, chapter 1 of the Code, in any case where the reference is to dividends and similar distributions of insurance companies paid to policyholders as such) comprises any distribution of property as defined in section 317 in the ordinary course of business, even though extraordinary in amount, made by a domestic or foreign corporation to its shareholders out of either—

(i) Earnings and profits accumulated since February 28, 1913, or

(ii) Earnings and profits of the taxable year computed without regard to the amount of the earnings and profits (whether of such year or accumulated since February 28, 1913) at the time the distribution was made.

The earnings and profits of the taxable year shall be computed as of the close of such year, without diminution by reason of any distributions made during the taxable year. For the purpose of determining whether a distribution constitutes a dividend, it is unnecessary to ascertain the amount of the earnings and profits accumulated since February 28, 1913, if the earnings and profits of the taxable year are equal to or in excess of the total amount of the distributions made within such year.

(2) Where a corporation distributes property to its shareholders on or after June 22, 1954, the amount of the distribution which is a dividend to them may not exceed the earnings and profits of the distributing corporation.

(3) The rule of (2) above may be illustrated by the following example:

Example. X and Y, individuals, each own one-half of the stock of Corporation A which has earnings and profits of $10,000. Corporation A distributes property having a basis of $6,000 and a fair market value of $16,000 to its shareholders, each shareholder receiving property with a basis of $3,000 and with a fair market value of $8,000 in a distribution to which section 301 applies. The amount taxable to each shareholder as a dividend under section 301(c) is $5,000.

(b)(1) In the case of a corporation which, under the law applicable to the taxable year in which a distribution is made, is a personal holding company or which, for the taxable year in respect of which a distribution is made under section 563 (relating to dividends paid within 2½ months after the close of the taxable year), or section 547 (relating to deficiency dividends), or corresponding provisions of a prior income tax law, was under the applicable law a personal holding company, the term "dividend", in addition to the meaning set forth in the first sentence of section 316, also means a distribution to its shareholders as follows: A distribution within a taxable year of the corporation, or of a shareholder, is a dividend to the extent of the corporation's undistributed personal holding company income (determined under section 545 without regard to distributions under section 316(b)(2)) for the taxable year in which, or, in the case of a distribution under section 563 or section 547, the taxable year in respect of which, the distribution was made. This subparagraph does not apply to distributions in partial or complete liquidation of a personal holding company. In the case of certain complete liquidations of a personal holding company see subparagraph (2) of this paragraph.

(2) In the case of a corporation which, under the law applicable to the taxable year in which a distribution is made, is a personal holding company or which, for the taxable year in respect of which a distribution is made under section 563, or section 547, or corresponding provisions of a prior income tax law, was under the applicable law a personal holding company, the term "dividend", in addition to the meaning set forth in the first sentence of section 316, also means, in the case of a complete liquidation occurring within 24 months after the adoption of a plan of liquidation, a distribution of property to its shareholders within such period, but—

(i) Only to the extent of the amounts distributed to distributees other than corporate shareholders, and

(ii) Only to the extent that the corporation designates such amounts as a dividend distribution and duly notifies such distributees in accordance with subparagraph (5) of this paragraph, but

(iii) Not in excess of the sum of such distributees' allocable share of the undistributed personal holding company income for such year (determined under section 545 without regard to sections 562(b) and 316(b)(2)(B)).

Section 316(b)(2)(B) and this subparagraph apply only to distributions made in any taxable year of the distributing corporation beginning after December 31, 1963. The amount designated with respect to a noncorporate distributee may not exceed the amount actually distributed to such distributee. For purposes of determining a noncorporate distributee's gain or loss on liquidation, amounts distributed in complete liquidation to such distributee during a taxable year are reduced by the amounts designated as a dividend with respect to such distributee for such year. For purposes of section 333(e)(1), a shareholder's ratable share of the earnings and profits of the corporation accumulated after February 28, 1913, shall be reduced by the amounts designated as a dividend with respect to such shareholder (even though such designated amounts are distributed during the one-month period referred to in section 333).

(3) For purposes of subparagraph (2)(iii) of this paragraph—

(i) Except as provided in subdivision (ii) of this subparagraph, the sum of the noncorporate distributees' allocable share of undistributed personal holding company income for the taxable year in which, or in respect of which, the distribution was made (computed without regard to sections 562(b) or 316(b)(2)(B)) shall be determined by multiplying such undistributed personal holding company income by the ratio which the aggregate value of the stock held by all noncorporate shareholders immediately before the record date of the last liquidating distribution in such year bears to the total value of all stock outstanding on such date. For rules applicable in a case where the distributing corporation has more than one class of stock, see subdivision (iii) of this subparagraph.

(ii) If more than one liquidating distribution was made during the year, and if, after the record date of the first distribution but before the record date of the last distribution, there was a change in the relative shareholdings as between noncorporate shareholders and corporate shareholders, then the sum of the noncorporate distributees' allocable share of undistributed personal holding company income for the taxable year in which, or in respect of which, the distributions were made (computed without regard to sections 562(b) and 316(b)(2)(B)) shall be determined as follows:

(a) First, allocate the corporation's undistributed personal holding company income among the distributions made during the taxable year by reference to the ratio which the aggregate amount of each distribution bears to the total amount of all distributions during such year;

(b) Second, determine the noncorporate distributees' allocable share of the corporation's undistributed personal holding company income for each distribution by multiplying the amount determined under (a) of this subdivision (ii) for each distribution by the ratio which the aggregate value of the stock held by all noncorporate shareholders immediately before the record date of such distribution bears to the total value of all stock outstanding on such date; and

(c) Last, determine the sum of the noncorporate distributees' allocable share of the corporation's undistributed personal holding company income for all such distributions.

For rules applicable in a case where the distributing corporation has more than one class of stock, see subdivision (iii) of this subparagraph.

(iii) Where the distributing corporation has more than one class of stock—

(a) The undistributed personal holding company income for the taxable year in which, or in respect of which, the distribution was made shall be treated as a fund from which dividends may properly be paid and shall be allocated between or among the classes of stock in a manner consistent with the dividend rights of such classes under local law and the pertinent governing instruments, such as, for example, the distributing corporation's articles or certificate of incorporation and by-laws;

(b) The noncorporate distributees' allocable share of the undistributed personal holding company income for each class of stock shall be determined separately in accordance with the rules set forth in subdivisions (i) or (ii) of this subparagraph, as if each class of stock were the only class of stock outstanding; and

(c) The sum of the noncorporate distributees' allocable share of the undistributed personal holding company income for the taxable year in which, or in respect of which, the distribution was made shall be the sum of the noncorporate distributees' allocable share of the undistributed personal holding company income for all classes of stock.

(iv) For purposes of this subparagraph, in any case where the record date of a liquidating distribution cannot be ascertained, the record date of the distribution shall be the date on which the liquidating distribution was actually made.

(4) The amount designated as a dividend to a noncorporate distributee for any taxable year of the distributing corporation may not exceed an amount equal to the sum of the noncorporate distributees' allocable share of undistributed personal holding company income (as determined under subparagraph (3) of this paragraph) for such year multiplied by the ratio which the aggregate value of the stock held by such distributee immediately before the record date of the liquidating distribution or, if the record date cannot be ascertained, immediately before the date on which the liquidating distribution was actually made, bears to the aggregate value of outstanding stock held by all noncorporate distributees on such date. In any case where more than one liquidating distribution is made during the taxable year, the aggregate amount which may be designated as a dividend to a noncorporate distributee for such year may not exceed the aggregate of the amounts determined by applying the principle of the preceding sentence to the amounts determined under subparagraph (3)(ii)(a) and (b) of this paragraph for each distribution. Where the distributing corporation has more than one class of stock, the limitation on the amount which may be designated as a dividend to a noncorporate distributee for any taxable year shall be determined by applying the rules of this subparagraph separately with respect to the noncorporate distributees' allocable share of the undistributed personal holding company income for each class of stock (as determined under subparagraph (3)(iii)(a) and (b) of this paragraph).

(5) A corporation may designate as a dividend to a shareholder all or part of a distribution in complete liquidation described in section 316(b)(2)(B) and this paragraph by:

(i) Claiming a dividends paid deduction for such amount in its return for the year in which, or in respect of which, the distribution is made,

(ii) Including such amount as a dividend in Form 1099 filed in respect of such shareholder pursuant to section 6042(a) and the regulations thereunder and in a written statement of dividend payments furnished to such shareholder pursuant to section 6042(c) and §1.6042-4, and

(iii) Indicating on the written statement of dividend payments furnished to such shareholder the amount included in such statement which is designated as a dividend under section 316(b)(2)(B) and this paragraph.

If a corporation complies with the procedure prescribed in the preceding sentence, it satisfies both the designation and notification requirements of section 316(b)(2)(B)(ii) and paragraph (b)(2)(ii) of this section. An amount designated as a dividend shall not be included as a distribution in liquidation on Form 1099L filed pursuant to §1.6043-2 (relating to returns of information respecting distributions in liquidation). If a corporation designates a dividend in accordance with this subparagraph, it shall attach to the return in which it claims a deduction for such designated dividend a schedule indicating all facts necessary to determine the sum of the noncorporate distributees' allocable share of undistributed personal holding company income (determined in accordance with subparagraph (3) of this paragraph) for the year in which, or in respect of which, the distribution is made.

(c) Except as provided in section 316(b)(1), the term "dividend" includes any distribution of property to shareholders to the extent made out of accumulated or current earnings and profits. See, however, section 331 (relating to distributions in complete or partial liquidation), section 301(e) (relating to distributions by personal service corporations), section 302(b) (relating to redemptions treated as amounts received from the sale or exchange of stock), and section 303 (relating to distributions in redemption of stock to pay death taxes). See also section 305(b) for certain distributions of stock or stock rights treated as distributions of property.

(d) In the case of a corporation which, under the law applicable to the taxable year in respect of which a distribution is made under section 860 (relating to deficiency dividends), was a regulated investment company (within the meaning of section 851), or a real estate investment trust (within the meaning of section 856), the term "dividend", in addition to the meaning set forth in paragraphs (a) and (b) of section 316, means a distribution of property to its shareholders which constitutes a "deficiency dividend" as defined in section 860(f).

(e) The application of section 316 may be illustrated by the following examples:

Example (1). At the beginning of the calendar year 1955, Corporation M had an operating deficit of $200,000 and the earnings and profits for the year amounted to $100,000. Beginning on March 16, 1955, the corporation made quarterly distributions of $25,000 during the taxable year to its shareholders. Each distribution is a taxable dividend in full, irrespective of the actual or the pro rata amount of the earnings and profits on hand at any of the dates of distribution, since the total distributions made during the year ($100,000) did not exceed the total earnings and profits of the year ($100,000).

Example (2). At the beginning of the calendar year 1955, Corporation N, a personal holding company, had no accumulated earnings and profits. During that year it made no earnings and profits but, due to the disallowance of certain deductions, its undistributed personal holding company income (determined under section 545 without regard to distributions under section 316(b)(2)) was $16,000. It distributed to shareholders on December 15, 1955, $15,000, and on February 1, 1956, $1,000, the latter amount being claimed as a deduction under section 563 in its personal holding company schedule for 1955 filed with its return for 1955 on March 15, 1956. Both distributions are taxable dividends in full, since they do not exceed the undistributed personal holding company income (determined without regard to such distributions) for 1955, the taxable year in which the distribution of $15,000 was made and with respect to which the distribution of $1,000 was made. It is immaterial whether Corporation N is a personal holding company for the taxable year 1956 or whether it had any income for that year.

Example (3). In 1959, a deficiency in personal holding company tax was established against Corporation O for the taxable year 1955 in the amount of $35,500 based on an undistributed personal holding company income of $42,000. Corporation O complied with the provisions of section 547 and in December 1959 distributed $42,000 to its stockholders as "deficiency dividends." The distribution of $42,000 is a taxable dividend since it does not exceed $42,000 (the undistributed personal holding company income for 1955, the taxable year with respect to which the distribution was made). It is immaterial whether Corporation O is a personal holding company for the taxable year 1959 or whether it had any income for that year.

Example (4). At the beginning of the taxable year 1955, Corporation P, a personal holding company had a deficit in earnings and profits of $200,000. During that year it made earnings and profits of $90,000. For that year, however, it had an undistributed personal holding income (determined under section 545 without regard to distributions under section 316(b)(2)) of $80,000. During such taxable year it distributed to its shareholders $100,000. The distribution of $100,000 is a taxable dividend to the extent of $90,000 since its earnings and profits for that year, $90,000, exceed $80,000, the undistributed personal holding company income determined without regard to such distribution.

Example (5). Corporation O, a calendar year taxpayer, is completely liquidated on December 31, 1964, pursuant to a plan of liquidation adopted July 1, 1964. No distributions in liquidation were made pursuant to the plan of liquidation adopted July 1, 1964, until the distribution in complete liquidation on December 31, 1964. Corporation O has undistributed personal holding company income of $300,000 for the year 1964 (computed without regard to section 562(b) or section 316(b)(2)(B)). On December 31, 1964, immediately before the record date of the distribution in complete liquidation, individual A owns 200 shares of corporation O's outstanding stock and corporation P owns the remaining 100 shares of outstanding stock. All shares are equal in value. The noncorporate distributees' allocable share of undistributed personal holding company income for 1964 is $200,000

$$\left(\frac{200 \text{ shares}}{300 \text{ shares}} \times \$300,000 \right)$$

$$\left(\frac{50 \text{ preferred shares}}{100 \text{ preferred shares}} \times \$1,000 + \right.$$

If at least $26,500 is distributed to B in the liquidation, then corporation Q may designate $26,500 to B as a dividend in accordance with paragraph (b)(5) of this section, and, if such amount is designated, then B must treat $26,500 as a dividend to which section 301 applies.

Example (7). In 1979, a deficiency of $46,000 in the tax on real estate investment trust taxable income is established against corporation R for the taxable year 1977, based on an increase in real estate investment trust taxable income of $100,000. Corporation R complied with the provisions of section 860 and in December 1979 distributed to its stockholders $100,000, which qualified as "deficiency dividends" under section 860. The distribution of $100,000 is a taxable dividend. It is immaterial whether corporation R is a real estate investment trust for the taxable year 1979 or whether it had accumulated or current earnings and profits in 1979. See section 316(b)(3). [Reg. §1.316-1.]

☐ [*T.D.* 6152, 12-2-55. *Amended by T.D.* 6625, 12-18-62, *T.D.* 6949, 4-8-68, *T.D.* 7767, 2-3-81 and *T.D.* 7936, 1-17-84.]

[Reg. §1.316-2]

§1.316-2. Sources of distribution in general.—(a) For the purpose of income taxation every distribution made by a corporation is made out of earnings and profits to the extent thereof and from the most recently accumulated earnings and profits. In determining the source of a distribution, consideration should be given first, to the earnings and profits of the taxable year; second, to the earnings and profits accumulated since February 28, 1913, only in the case where, and to the extent that, the distributions made during the taxable year are not regarded as out of the earnings and profits of that year; third, to the earnings and profits accumulated before March 1, 1913, only after all the earnings and profits of the taxable year and all the earnings and profits accumulated since February 28, 1913, have been distributed; and, fourth, to sources other than earnings and profits only after the earnings and profits have been distributed.

(b) If the earnings and profits of the taxable year (computed as of the close of the year without diminution by reason of any distribu-

If at least $200,000 is distributed to A in the liquidation, then corporation O may designate $200,000 to A as a dividend in accordance with paragraph (b)(5) of this section, and, if such amount is designated, then A must treat $200,000 as a dividend to which section 301 applies. For an example of the treatment of the distribution to corporation P see paragraph (b)(2)(iii) of §1.562-1.

Example (6). Corporation Q, a calendar year taxpayer, is completely liquidated on December 31, 1964, pursuant to a plan of liquidation adopted July 1, 1964. No distributions in liquidation were made pursuant to the plan of liquidation adopted July 1, 1964, until the distribution in complete liquidation on December 31, 1964. Corporation Q has undistributed personal holding company income of $40,000 for the year 1964 (computed without regard to section 562(b) or section 316(b)(2)(B)). On December 31, 1964, immediately before the record date of the distribution in complete liquidation, corporation Q has outstanding 300 shares of common stock and 100 shares of noncumulative preferred stock. Corporation Q's articles of incorporation provide that the preferred stock is entitled to dividends of $10 per share per year. Of corporation Q's stock, individual B owns 200 shares of the common stock and 50 shares of the preferred stock, and corporation R owns all remaining shares. All of the common shares are equal in value, and all of the preferred shares are equal in value. No dividends had been paid on the preferred stock during the year 1964. Of the $40,000 of undistributed personal holding company income, $1,000 must be allocated to the preferred stock because of the rights of the holders of such stock, under Q's articles of incorporation, to receive that amount in dividends for the year 1964. The noncorporate distributees' allocable share of undistributed personal holding company income for 1964 is $26,500

$$\left. \frac{200 \text{ common shares}}{300 \text{ common shares}} \times \$39,000 \right).$$

tions made during the year and without regard to the amount of earnings and profits at the time of the distribution) are sufficient in amount to cover all the distributions made during that year, then each distribution is a taxable dividend. See §1.316-1. If the distributions made during the taxable year exceed the earnings and profits of such year, then that proportion of each distribution which the total of the earnings and profits of the year bears to the total distributions made during the year shall be regarded as out of the earnings and profits of that year. The portion of each such distribution which is not regarded as out of earnings and profits of the taxable year shall be considered a taxable dividend to the extent of the earnings and profits accumulated since February 28, 1913, and available on the date of the distribution. In any case in which it is necessary to determine the amount of earnings and profits accumulated since February 28, 1913, and the actual earnings and profits to the date of a distribution within any taxable year (whether beginning before January 1, 1936, or, in the case of an operating deficit, on or after that date) cannot be shown, the earnings and profits for the year (or accounting period, if less than a year) in which the distribution was made shall be prorated to the date of the distribution not counting the date on which the distribution was made.

(c) The provisions of the section may be illustrated by the following example:

Example. At the beginning of the calendar year 1955, Corporation M had $12,000 in earnings and profits accumulated since February 28, 1913. Its earnings and profits for 1955 amounted to $30,000. During the year it made quarterly cash distributions of $15,000 each. Of each of the four distributions made, $7,500 (that portion of $15,000 which the amount of $30,000, the total earnings and profits of the taxable year, bears to $60,000, the total distributions made during the year) was paid out of the earnings and profits of the taxable year; and of the first and second distributions, $7,500 and $4,500, respectively, were paid out of the earnings and profits accumulated after February 28, 1913, and before the taxable year, as follows:

Distributions during 1955		Portion out of earnings and profits of the taxable year	Portion out of earnings accumulated since Feb. 28, 1913, and before the taxable year	Taxable amount of each distribution
Date	Amount			
March 10	$15,000	$7,500	$7,500	$15,000
June 10	15,000	7,500	4,500	12,000
September 10	15,000	7,500	. . .	7,500
December 10	15,000	7,500	. . .	7,500
Total amount taxable as dividends				42,000

(d) Any distribution by a corporation out of earnings and profits accumulated before March 1, 1913, or out of increase in value of property accrued before March 1, 1913 (whether or not realized by sale or other disposition, and, if realized, whether before, on, or after March 1, 1913), is not a dividend within the meaning of subtitle A of the Code.

(e) A reserve set up out of gross income by a corporation and maintained for the purpose of making good any loss of capital assets on account of depletion or depreciation is not a part of surplus out of which ordinary dividends may be paid. A distribution made from a depletion or a depreciation reserve based upon the cost or other basis of the property will not be considered as having been paid out of earnings and profits, but the amount thereof shall be applied against and reduce the cost or other basis of the stock upon which declared. If such a distribution is in excess of the basis, the excess shall be taxed as a gain from the sale or other disposition of property as provided in section 301(c)(3)(A). A distribution from a depletion reserve based upon discovery value to the extent that such reserve represents the excess of the discovery value over the cost or other basis for determining gain or loss, is, when received by the shareholders, taxable as an ordinary dividend. The amount by which a corporation's percentage depletion allowance for any year exceeds depletion sustained on cost or other basis, that is, determined without regard to discovery or percentage depletion allowances for the year of distribution or prior years, constitutes a part of the corporation's "earnings and profits accumulated after February 28, 1913," within the meaning of section 316, and, upon distribution to shareholders, is taxable to them as a dividend. A distribution made from that portion of a depletion reserve based upon a valuation as of March 1, 1913, which is in excess of the depletion reserve based upon cost, will not be considered as having been paid out of earnings and profits, but the amount of the distribution shall be applied against and reduce the cost or other basis of the stock upon which declared. See section 301. No distribution, however, can be made from such a reserve until all the earnings and profits of the corporation have first been distributed. [Reg. § 1.316-2.]

☐ [T.D. 6152, 12-2-55. *Amended by T.D. 9914, 10-19-2020.*]

[Reg. § 1.317-1]

§ 1.317-1. Property defined.—The term "property", for purposes of Part 1, subchapter C, chapter 1 of the Code, means any property (including money, securities, and indebtedness to the corporation) other than stock, or rights to acquire stock, in the corporation making the distribution. [Reg. § 1.317-1.]

☐ [T.D. 6152, 12-2-55.]

[Reg. § 1.318-1]

§ 1.318-1. Constructive ownership of stock; introduction.—(a) For the purposes of certain provisions of chapter 1 of the Code, section 318(a) provides that stock owned by a taxpayer includes stock constructively owned by such taxpayer under the rules set forth in such section. An individual is considered to own the stock owned, directly or indirectly, by or for his spouse (other than a spouse who is legally separated from the individual under a decree of divorce or separate maintenance), and by or for his children, grandchildren, and parents. Under section 318(a)(2) and (3), constructive ownership rules are established for partnerships and partners, estates and beneficiaries, trusts and beneficiaries, and corporations and stockholders. If any person has an option to acquire stock, such stock is considered as owned by such person. The term "option" includes an option to acquire such an option and each of a series of such options.

(b) In applying section 318(a) to determine the stock ownership of any person for any one purpose—

(1) A corporation shall not be considered to own its own stock by reason of section 318(a)(3)(C);

(2) In any case in which an amount of stock owned by any person may be included in the computation more than one time, such stock shall be included only once, in the manner in which it will impute to the person concerned the largest total stock ownership; and

(3) In determining the 50-percent requirement of section 318(a)(2)(C) and (3)(C) all of the stock owned actually and constructively by the person concerned shall be aggregated. [Reg. § 1.318-1.]

☐ [T.D. 6152, 12-2-55. *Amended by T.D. 6598, 4-25-62, T.D. 6621, 11-30-62 and T.D. 6969, 8-22-68.*]

[Reg. § 1.318-2]

§ 1.318-2. Application of general rules.—(a) The application of paragraph (b) of § 1.318-1 may be illustrated by the following examples:

Example (1). H, an individual owns all of the stock of Corporation A. Corporationo A is not considered to own the stock owned by H in Corporation A.

Example (2). H, an individual, his wife, W, and his son, S, each own one-third of the stock of the Green Corporation. For purposes of determining the amount of stock owned by H, W, or S for the purpose of section 318(a)(2)(C) and (3)(C), the amount of stock held by the other members of the family shall be added pursuant to paragraph (b)(3) of § 1.318-1 in applying the 50-percent requirement of such section. H, W, or S, as the case may be, is for this purpose deemed to own 100 percent of the stock of the Green Corporation.

(b) The application of section 318(a)(1), relating to members of a family, may be illustrated by the following example:

Example. An individual, H, his wife, W, his son, S, and his grandson (S's son), G, own the 100 outstanding shares of stock of a corporation, each owning 25 shares. H, W, and S are each considered as owning 100 shares. G is considered as owning only 50 shares, that is, his own and his father's.

(c) The application of section 318(a)(2) and (3), relating to partnerships, trusts and corporations, may be illustrated by the following examples:

Example (1). A, an individual, has a 50 percent interest in a partnership. The partnership owns 50 of the 100 outstanding shares of stock of a corporation, the remaining 50 shares being owned by A. The partnership is considered as owning 100 shares. A is considered as owning 75 shares.

Example (2). A testamentary trust owns 25 of the outstanding 100 shares of stock of a corporation. A, an individual, who holds a vested remainder in the trust having a value, computed actuarially equal to 4 percent of the value of the trust property, owns the remaining 75 shares. Since the interest of A in the trust is a vested interest rather than a contingent interest (whether or not remote), the trust is considered as owning 100 shares. A is considered as owning 76 shares.

Example (3). The facts are the same as in (2), above, except that A's interest in the trust is a contingent remainder. A is considered as owning 76 shares. However, since A's interest in the trust is a remote contingent interest, the trust is not considered as owning any of the shares owned by A.

Example (4). A and B, unrelated individuals, own 70 percent and 30 percent, respectively, in value of the stock of Corporation M. Corporation M owns 50 of the 100 outstanding shares of stock of Corporation O, the remaining 50 shares being owned by A. Corporation M is considered as owning 100 shares of Corporation O, and A is considered as owning 85 shares.

Example (5). A and B, unrelated individuals, own 70 percent and 30 percent, respectively, of the stock of corporation M. A, B, and corporation M all own stock of corporation O. Since B owns less than 50 percent in value of the stock of corporation M, neither B nor corporation M constructively owns the stock of corporation O owned by the other. However, for purposes of certain sections of the Code, such as sections 304 and 856(d), the 50-percent limitation of section 318(a)(2)(C) and (3)(C) is disregarded or is reduced to less than 30 percent. For such purposes, B constructively owns his proportionate share of the stock of corporation O owned directly by corporation M, and corporation M constructively owns the stock of corporation O owned by B. [Reg. § 1.318-2.]

☐ [T.D. 6152, 12-2-55. *Amended by T.D. 6969, 8-22-68.*]

[Reg. § 1.318-3]

§ 1.318-3. Estates, trusts, and options.—(a) For the purpose of applying section 318(a), relating to estates, property of a decedent shall be considered as owned by his estate if such property is subject to administration by the executor or administrator for the purpose of paying claims against the estate and expenses of administration notwithstanding that, under local law, legal title to such property vests in the decedent's heirs, legatees or devisees immediately upon death. The term "beneficiary" includes any person entitled to receive property of a decedent pursuant to a will or pursuant to laws of descent and distribution. A person shall no longer be considered a beneficiary of an estate when all the property to which he is entitled has been received by him, when he no longer has a claim against the estate arising out of having been a beneficiary, and when there is only a remote possibility that it will be necessary for the estate to seek the return of property or to seek payment from him by contribution or otherwise to satisfy claims against the estate or expenses of administration. When, pursuant to the preceding sentence, a person ceases to be a beneficiary, stock owned by him shall not thereafter be considered owned by the estate, and stock owned by the estate shall not thereafter be considered owned by him. The application of section 318(a) relating to estates may be illustrated by the following examples:

Example (1). (a) A decedent's estate owns 50 of the 100 outstanding shares of stock of corporation X. The remaining shares are owned by three unrelated individuals, A, B and C, who together own the entire interest in the estate. A owns 12 shares of stock of corporation X directly and is entitled to 50 percent of the estate. B owns 18 shares directly and has a life estate in the remaining 50 percent of the estate.

C owns 20 shares directly and also owns the remainder interest after B's life estate.

(b) If section 318(a)(5)(C) applies (see paragraph (c)(3) of §1.318-4), the stock of corporation X is considered to be owned as follows: the estate is considered as owning 80 shares, 50 shares directly, 12 shares constructively through A, and 18 shares constructively through B; A is considered as owning 37 shares, 12 shares directly, and 25 shares constructively (50 percent of the 50 shares owned directly by the estate); B is considered as owning 43 shares, 18 shares directly and 25 shares constructively (50 percent of the 50 shares owned directly by the estate); C is considered as owning 20 shares directly and no shares constructively. C is not considered a beneficiary of the estate under section 318(a) since he has no direct present interest in the property held by the estate nor in the income produced by such property.

(c) If section 318(a)(5)(C) does not apply, A is considered as owning nine additional shares (50 percent of the 18 shares owned constructively by the estate through B), and B is considered as owning six additional shares (50 percent of the 12 shares owned constructively by the estate through A).

Example (2). Under the will of A, Blackacre is left to B for life, remainder to C, an unrelated individual. The residue of the estate consisting of stock of a corporation is left to D. B and D are beneficiaries of the estate under section 318(a). C is not considered a beneficiary since he has no direct present interest in Blackacre nor in the income produced by such property. The stock owned by the estate is considered as owned proportionately by B and D.

(b) For the purpose of section 318(a)(2)(B) stock owned by a trust will be considered as being owned by its beneficiaries only to the extent of the interest of such beneficiaries in the trust. Accordingly, the interest of income beneficiaries, remainder beneficiaries, and other beneficiaries will be computed on an actuarial basis. Thus, if a trust owns 100 percent of the stock of Corporation A, and if, on an actuarial basis, W's life interest in the trust is 15 percent, Y's life interest is 25 percent, and Z's remainder interest is 60 percent, under this provision W will be considered to be the owner of 15 percent of the stock of Corporation A, Y will be considered to be the owner of 25 percent of such stock, and Z will be considered to be the owner of 60 percent of such stock. The factors and methods prescribed in §20.2031-7 of this chapter (Estate Tax Regulations) for use in ascertaining the value of an interest in property for estate tax purposes shall be used in determining a beneficiary's actuarial interest in a trust for purposes of this section. See §20.2031-7 of this chapter (Estate Tax Regulations) for examples illustrating the use of these factors and methods.

(c) The application of section 318(a) relating to options may be illustrated by the following example:

Example. A and B, unrelated individuals, own all of the 100 outstanding shares of stock of a corporation, each owning 50 shares. A has an option to acquire 25 of B's shares and has an option to acquire a further option to acquire the remaining 25 of B's shares. A is

considered as owning the entire 100 shares of stock of the corporation. [Reg. §1.318-3.]

☐ *[T.D. 6152, 12-2-55. Amended by T.D. 6462, 5-5-60 and T.D. 6969, 8-22-68.]*

[Reg. §1.318-4]

§1.318-4. Constructive ownership as actual ownership; exceptions.—(a) *In general.*—Section 318(a)(5)(A) provides that, except as provided in section 318(a)(5)(B) and (C), stock constructively owned by a person by reason of the application of section 318(a)(1), (2), (3), or (4) shall be considered as actually owned by such person for purposes of applying section 318(a)(1), (2), (3), and (4). For example, if a trust owns 50 percent of the stock of corporation X, stock of corporation Y owned by corporation X which is attributed to the trust may be further attributed to the beneficiaries of the trust.

(b) *Constructive family ownership.*—Section 318(a)(5)(B) provides that stock constructively owned by an individual by reason of ownership by a member of his family shall not be considered as owned by him for purposes of making another family member the constructive owner of such stock under section 318(a)(1). For example, if F and his two sons, A and B, each own one-third of the stock of a corporation, under section 381(a)(1), A is treated as owning constructively the stock owned by his father but is not treated as owning the stock owned by B. Section 318(a)(5)(B) prevents the attribution of the stock of one brother through the father to the other brother, an attribution beyond the scope of section 318(a)(1) directly.

(c) *Reattribution.*—(1) Section 318(a)(5)(C) provides that stock constructively owned by a partnership, estate, trust, or corporation by reason of the application of section 318(a)(3) shall not be considered as owned by it for purposes of applying section 318(a)(2) in order to make another the constructive owner of such stock. For example, if two unrelated individuals are beneficiaries of the same trust, stock held by one which is attributed to the trust under section 318(a)(3) is not reattributed from the trust to the other beneficiary. However, stock constructively owned by reason of section 318(a)(2) may be reattributed under section 318(a)(3). Thus, for example, if all the stock of corporations X and Y is owned by A, stock of corporation Z held by X is attributed to Y through A.

(2) Section 318(a)(5)(C) does not prevent reattribution under section 318(a)(2) of stock constructively owned by an entity under section 318(a)(3) if the stock is also constructively owned by the entity under section 318(a)(4). For example, if individuals A and B are beneficiaries of a trust and the trust has an option to buy stock from A, B is considered under section 318(a)(2)(B) as owning a proportionate part of such stock.

(3) Section 318(a)(5)(C) is effective on and after August 31, 1964, except that for purposes of sections 302 and 304 it does not apply with respect to distributions in payment for stock acquisitions or redemptions if such acquisitions or redemptions occurred before August 31, 1964. [Reg. §1.318-4.]

☐ *[T.D. 6152, 12-2-55. Amended by T.D. 6969, 8-22-68.]*

Corporate Liquidations

[Reg. §1.331-1]

§1.331-1. Corporate liquidations.—(a) *In general.*—Section 331 contains rules governing the extent to which gain or loss is recognized to a shareholder receiving a distribution in complete or partial liquidation of a corporation. Under section 331(a)(1), it is provided that amounts distributed in complete liquidation of a corporation shall be treated as in full payment in exchange for the stock. Under section 331(a)(2), it is provided that amounts distributed in partial liquidation of a corporation shall be treated as in full or part payment in exchange for the stock. For this purpose, the term "partial liquidation" shall have the meaning ascribed in section 346. If section 331 is applicable to the distribution of property by a corporation, section 301 (relating to the effects on a shareholder of distributions of property) has no application other than to a distribution in complete liquidation to which section 316(b)(2)(B) applies. See paragraph (b)(2) of §1.316-1.

(b) *Gain or loss.*—The gain or loss to a shareholder from a distribution in partial or complete liquidation is to be determined under section 1001 by comparing the amount of the distribution with the cost or other basis of the stock. The gain or loss will be recognized to the extent provided in section 1002 and will be subject to the provisions of parts I, II, and III (section 1201 and following), subchapter P, *chapter 1 of the Code.*

(c) *Recharacterization.*—A liquidation which is followed by a transfer to another corporation of all or part of the assets of the liquidating corporation or which is preceded by such a transfer may, however, have the effect of the distribution of a dividend or of a transaction in

which no loss is recognized and gain is recognized only to the extent of "other property." See sections 301 and 356.

(d) *Reporting requirement.*—(1) *General rule.*—Every significant holder that transfers stock to the issuing corporation in exchange for property from such corporation must include on or with such holder's return for the year of such exchange the statement described in paragraph (d)(2) of this section unless—

(i) The property is part of a distribution made pursuant to a corporate resolution reciting that the distribution is made in complete liquidation of the corporation; and

(ii) The issuing corporation is completely liquidated and dissolved within one year after the distribution.

(2) *Statement.*—If required by paragraph (d)(1) of this section, a significant holder must include on or with such holder's return a statement entitled, "STATEMENT PURSUANT TO §1.331-1(d) BY [INSERT NAME AND TAXPAYER IDENTIFICATION NUMBER (IF ANY) OF TAXPAYER], A SIGNIFICANT HOLDER OF THE STOCK OF [INSERT NAME AND EMPLOYER IDENTIFICATION NUMBER (IF ANY) OF ISSUING CORPORATION]." If a significant holder is a controlled foreign corporation (within the meaning of section 957), each United States shareholder (within the meaning of section 951(b)) with respect thereto must include this statement on or with its return. The statement must include—

(i) The fair market value and basis of the stock transferred by the significant holder to the issuing corporation; and

(ii) A description of the property received by the significant holder from the issuing corporation.

(3) *Definitions.*—For purposes of this section:

(i) Significant holder means any person that, immediately before the exchange—

(A) Owned at least five percent (by vote or value) of the total outstanding stock of the issuing corporation if the stock owned by such person is publicly traded; or

(B) Owned at least one percent (by vote or value) of the total outstanding stock of the issuing corporation if the stock owned by such person is not publicly traded.

(ii) Publicly traded stock means stock that is listed on—

(A) A national securities exchange registered under section 6 of the Securities Exchange Act of 1934 (15 U.S.C. 78f); or

(B) An interdealer quotation system sponsored by a national securities association registered under section 15A of the Securities Exchange Act of 1934 (15 U.S.C. 78o-3).

(iii) Issuing corporation means the corporation that issued the shares of stock, some or all of which were transferred by a significant holder to such corporation in the exchange described in paragraph (d)(1) of this section.

(4) *Cross reference.*—See section 6043 of the Code for requirements relating to a return by a liquidating corporation.

(e) *Example.*—The provisions of this section may be illustrated by the following example:

Example. A, an individual who makes his income tax returns on the calendar year basis, owns 20 shares of stock of the P Corporation, a domestic corporation, 10 shares of which were acquired in 1951 at a cost of $1,500 and the remainder of 10 shares in December 1954 at a cost of $2,900. He receives in April 1955 a distribution of $250 per share in complete liquidation, or $2,500 on the 10 shares acquired in 1951, and $2,500 on the 10 shares acquired in December 1954. The gain of $1,000 on the shares acquired in 1951 is a long-term capital gain to be treated as provided in parts I, II, and III (section 1201 and following), subchapter P, chapter 1 of the Code. The loss of $400 on the shares acquired in 1954 is a short-term capital loss to be treated as provided in parts I, II, and III (section 1201 and following), subchapter P, chapter 1 of the Code.

(f) *Effective/applicability date.*—Paragraph (d) of this section applies to any taxable year beginning on or after May 30, 2006. However, taxpayers may apply paragraph (d) of this section to any original Federal income tax return (including any amended return filed on or before the due date (including extensions) of such original return) timely filed on or after May 30, 2006. For taxable years beginning before May 30, 2006, see §1.331-1 as contained in 26 CFR part 1 in effect on April 1, 2006. [Reg. §1.331-1.]

☐ [*T.D.* 6152, 12-2-55. *Amended by T.D.* 6949, 4-8-68; *T.D.* 9264, 5-26-2006 *and T.D.* 9329, 6-13-2007.]

[Reg. §1.332-1]

§1.332-1. Distributions in liquidation of subsidiary corporation; general.—Under the general rule prescribed by section 331 for the treatment of distributions in liquidation of a corporation, amounts received by one corporation in complete liquidation of another corporation are treated as in full payment in exchange for stock in such other corporation, and gain or loss from the receipt of such amounts is to be determined as provided in section 1001. Section 332 excepts from the general rule property received, under certain specifically described circumstances, by one corporation as a distribution in complete liquidation of the stock of another corporation and provides for the nonrecognition of gain or loss in those cases which meet the statutory requirements. Section 367 places a limitation on the application of section 332 in the case of foreign corporations. See section 334(b) for the basis for determining gain or loss from the subsequent sale of property received upon complete liquidations such as described in this section. See section 453(d)(4)(A) relative to distribution of installment obligations by subsidiary. [Reg. §1.332-1.]

☐ [*T.D.* 6152, 12-2-55.]

[Reg. §1.332-2]

§1.332-2. Requirements for nonrecognition of gain or loss.—
(a) The nonrecognition of gain or loss under section 332 is limited to the receipt of property by a corporation that is the actual owner of stock (in the liquidating corporation) meeting the requirements of section 1504(a)(2). The recipient corporation must have been the owner of the specified amount of such stock on the date of the adoption of the plan of liquidation and have continued so to be at all times until the receipt of the property. If the recipient corporation does not continue qualified with respect to the ownership of stock of the liquidating corporation and if the failure to continue qualified occurs at any time prior to the completion of the transfer of all the property, the provisions for the nonrecognition of gain or loss do not apply to any distribution received under the plan.

(b) Section 332 applies only to those cases in which the recipient corporation receives at least partial payment for the stock which it owns in the liquidating corporation. If section 332 is not applicable, see section 165(g) relative to allowance of losses on worthless securities.

(c) To constitute a distribution in complete liquidation within the meaning of section 332, the distribution must be (1) made by the liquidating corporation in complete cancellation or redemption of all of its stock in accordance with a plan of liquidation, or (2) one of a series of distributions in complete cancellation or redemption of all its stock in accordance with a plan of liquidation. Where there is more than one distribution, it is essential that a status of liquidation exist at the time the first distribution is made under the plan and that such status continue until the liquidation is completed. Liquidation is completed when the liquidating corporation and the receiver or trustees in liquidation are finally divested of all the property (both tangible and intangible). A status of liquidation exists when the corporation ceases to be a going concern and its activities are merely for the purpose of winding up its affairs, paying its debts and distributing any remaining balance to its shareholders. A liquidation may be completed prior to the actual dissolution of the liquidating corporation. However, legal dissolution of the corporation is not required. Nor will the mere retention of a nominal amount of assets for the sole purpose of preserving the corporation's legal existence disqualify the transaction. (See 26 CFR (1939) 39.22(a)-20 (Regulations 118).)

(d) If a transaction constitutes a distribution in complete liquidation within the meaning of the Internal Revenue Code of 1954 and satisfies the requirements of section 332, it is not material that it is otherwise described under the local law. If a liquidating corporation distributes all of its property in complete liquidation and if pursuant to the plan for such complete liquidation a corporation owning the specified amount of stock in the liquidating corporation receives property constituting amounts distributed in complete liquidation within the meaning of the Code and also receives other property attributable to shares not owned by it, the transfer of the property to the recipient corporation shall not be treated, by reason of the receipt of such other property, as not being a distribution (or one of a series of distributions) in complete cancellation or redemption of all of the stock of the liquidating corporation within the meaning of section 332, even though for purposes of those provisions relating to corporate reorganizations the amount received by the recipient corporation in excess of its ratable share is regarded as acquired upon the issuance of its stock or securities in a tax-free exchange as described in section 361 and the cancellation or redemption of the stock not owned by the recipient corporation is treated as occurring as a result of a tax-free exchange described in section 354.

(e) The application of these rules may be illustrated by the following example:

Example. On September 1, 1954, the M Corporation had outstanding capital stock consisting of 3,000 shares of common stock, par value $100 a share, and 1,000 shares of preferred stock, par value $100 a share, which preferred stock was limited and preferred as to dividends and had no voting rights. On that date, and thereafter until the date of dissolution of the M Corporation, the O Corporation owned 2,500 shares of common stock of the M Corporation. By statutory merger consummated on October 1, 1954, pursuant to a plan of liquidation adopted on September 1, 1954, the M Corporation was merged into the O Corporation, the O Corporation under the plan issuing stock which was received by the other holders of the stock of the M Corporation. The receipt by the O Corporation of the properties of the M Corporation is a distribution received by the O Corporation in complete liquidation of the M Corporation within the meaning of section 332, and no gain or loss is recognized as the result of the receipt of such properties.

(f) *Applicability date.*—The first sentence of paragraph (a) of this section applies to plans of complete liquidation adopted after March 28, 1985, except as specified in section 1804(e)(6)(B)(ii) and (iii) of Pub. L. 99-514. [Reg. §1.332-2.]

☐ [*T.D.* 6152, 12-2-55. *Amended by T.D.* 9759, 3-25-2016.]

[Reg. §1.332-3]

§1.332-3. Liquidations completed within one taxable year.—If in a liquidation completed within one taxable year pursuant to a plan of complete liquidation, distributions in complete liquidation are received by a corporation which owns the specified amount of stock in the liquidating corporation and which continues qualified with respect to the ownership of such stock until the transfer of all the property within such year is completed (see paragraph (a) of §1.332-2), then no gain or loss shall be recognized with respect to the distributions received by the recipient corporation. In such case no waiver or bond is required of the recipient corporation under section 332. [Reg. §1.332-3.]

☐ [*T.D.* 6152, 12-2-55.]

[Reg. §1.332-4]

§1.332-4. Liquidations covering more than one taxable year.—
(a) If the plan of liquidation is consummated by a series of distributions extending over a period of more than one taxable year, the nonrecognition of gain or loss with respect to the distributions in liquidation shall, in addition to the requirements of §1.332-2, be subject to the following requirements:

(1) In order for the distribution in liquidation to be brought within the exception provided in section 332 to the general rule for computing gain or loss with respect to amounts received in liquidation of a corporation, the entire property of the corporation shall be transferred in accordance with a plan of liquidation, which plan shall include a statement showing the period within which the transfer of the property of the liquidating corporation to the recipient corporation is to be completed. The transfer of all the property under the liquidation must be completed within three years from the close of the taxable year during which is made the first of the series of distributions under the plan.

(2) For each of the taxable years which falls wholly or partly within the period of liquidation, the recipient corporation shall, at the time of filing its return, file with the district director of internal revenue a waiver of the statute of limitations on assessment. The waiver shall be executed on such form as may be prescribed by the Commissioner and shall extend the period of assessment of all income and profits taxes for each such year to a date not earlier than one year after the last date of the period for assessment of such taxes for the last taxable year in which the transfer of the property of such liquidating corporation to the controlling corporation may be completed in accordance with section 332. Such waiver shall also contain such other terms with respect to assessment as may be considered by the Commissioner to be necessary to insure the assessment and collection of the correct tax liability for each year within the period of liquidation.

(3) For each of the taxable years which falls wholly or partly within the period of liquidation, the recipient corporation may be required to file a bond, the amount of which shall be fixed by the district director. The bond shall contain all terms specified by the Commissioner, including provisions unequivocally assuring prompt payment of the excess of income and profits taxes (plus penalty, if any, and interest) as computed by the district director without regard to the provisions of sections 332 and 334(b) over such taxes computed with regard to such provisions, regardless of whether such excess may or may not be made the subject of a notice of deficiency under section 6212 and regardless of whether it may or may not be assessed. Any bond required under section 332 shall have such surety or sureties as the Commissioner may require. However, see 6 U.S.C.15, providing that where a bond is required by law or regulations, in lieu of surety or sureties there may be deposited bonds or notes of the United States. Only surety companies holding certificates of authority from the Secretary as acceptable sureties on Federal bonds will be approved as sureties. The bonds shall be executed in triplicate so that the Commissioner, the taxpayer, and the surety or the depository may each have a copy. On and after September 1, 1953, the functions of the Commissioner with respect to such bonds shall be performed by the district director for the internal revenue district in which the return was filed and any bond filed on or after such date shall be filed with such district director.

(b) Pending the completion of the liquidation, if there is a compliance with paragraph (a)(1), (2), and (3) of this section and §1.332-2 with respect to the nonrecognition of gain or loss, the income and profits tax liability of the recipient corporation for each of the years covered in whole or in part by the liquidation shall be determined without the recognition of any gain or loss on account of the receipt of the distributions in liquidation. In such determination, the basis of the property or properties received by the recipient corporation shall be determined in accordance with section 334(b). However, if the transfer of the property is not completed within the three-year period allowed by section 332 or if the recipient corporation does not continue qualified with respect to the ownership of stock of the liquidating corporation as required by that section, gain or loss shall be recognized with respect to each distribution and the tax liability for each of the years covered in whole or in part by the liquidation shall be recomputed without regard to the provisions of section 332 or section 334(b) and the amount of any additional tax due upon such recomputation shall be promptly paid. [Reg. §1.332-4.]

☐ *[T.D. 6152, 12-2-55.]*

[Reg. §1.332-5]

§1.332-5. Distributions in liquidation as affecting minority interests.—Upon the liquidation of a corporation in pursuance of a plan of complete liquidation, the gain or loss of minority shareholders shall be determined without regard to section 332, since it does not apply to that part of distributions in liquidation received by minority shareholders. [Reg. §1.332-5.]

☐ *[T.D. 6152, 12-2-55.]*

[Reg. §1.332-6]

§1.332-6. Records to be kept and information to be filed with return.—(a) *Statement filed by recipient corporation.—*If any recipient corporation received a liquidating distribution from the liquidating corporation pursuant to a plan (whether or not that recipient corporation has received or will receive other such distributions from the liquidating corporation in other tax years as part of the same plan) during the current tax year, such recipient corporation must include a statement entitled, "STATEMENT PURSUANT TO SECTION 332 BY [INSERT NAME AND EMPLOYER IDENTIFICATION NUMBER (IF ANY) OF TAXPAYER], A CORPORATION RECEIVING A LIQUIDATING DISTRIBUTION," on or with its return for such year. If any recipient corporation is a controlled foreign corporation (within the meaning of section 957), each United States shareholder (within the meaning of section 951(b)) with respect thereto must include this statement on or with its return. The statement must include—

(1) The name and employer identification number (if any) of the liquidating corporation;

(2) The date(s) of all distribution(s) (whether or not pursuant to the plan) by the liquidating corporation during the current tax year;

(3) The fair market value and basis of assets of the liquidating corporation that have been or will be transferred to any recipient corporation, aggregated as follows:

(i) Importation property distributed in a loss importation transaction, as defined in §1.362-3(c)(2) and (3) (except that "section 332 liquidation" is substituted for "section 362 transaction"), respectively;

(ii) Property with respect to which gain or loss was recognized on the distribution;

(iii) Property not described in paragraph (a)(3)(i) or (ii) of this section;

(4) The date and control number of any private letter ruling(s) issued by the Internal Revenue Service in connection with the liquidation;

(5) The following representation: THE PLAN OF COMPLETE LIQUIDATION WAS ADOPTED ON [INSERT DATE (mm/dd/yyyy)]; and

(6) A representation by such recipient corporation either that—

(i) THE LIQUIDATION WAS COMPLETED ON [INSERT DATE (mm/dd/yyyy)]; or

(ii) THE LIQUIDATION IS NOT COMPLETE AND THE TAXPAYER HAS TIMELY FILED [INSERT EITHER FORM 952, "Consent To Extend the Time to Assess Tax Under Section 332(b)," OR NUMBER AND NAME OF THE SUCCESSOR FORM].

(b) *Filings by the liquidating corporation.—*The liquidating corporation must timely file Form 966, "Corporate Dissolution or Liquidation," (or its successor form) and its final Federal corporate income tax return. See also section 6043 of the Code.

(c) *Definitions.—*For purposes of this section:

(1) Plan means the plan of complete liquidation within the meaning of section 332.

(2) Recipient corporation means the corporation described in section 332(b)(1).

(3) Liquidating corporation means the corporation that makes a distribution of property to a recipient corporation pursuant to the plan.

(4) Liquidating distribution means a distribution of property made by the liquidating corporation to a recipient corporation pursuant to the plan.

(d) *Substantiation information.—*Under §1.6001-1(e), taxpayers are required to retain their permanent records and make such records available to any authorized Internal Revenue Service officers and employees. In connection with a liquidation described in this section, these records should specifically include information regarding the amount, basis, and fair market value of all distributed property, and relevant facts regarding any liabilities assumed or extinguished as part of such liquidation.

(e) *Effective/applicability date.—*This section applies to any taxable year beginning on or after May 30, 2006. However, taxpayers may apply this section to any original Federal income tax return (including any amended return filed on or before the due date (including extensions) of such original return) timely filed on or after May 30, 2006. For taxable years beginning before May 30, 2006, see §1.332-6 as contained in 26 CFR part 1 in effect on April 1, 2006. Paragraph (a)(3) of this section applies with respect to liquidations under section

332 occurring on or after March 28, 2016, and also with respect to liquidations under section 332 occurring before such date as a result of an entity classification election under §301.7701-3 of this chapter filed on or after March 28, 2016, unless such liquidation is pursuant to a binding agreement that was in effect prior to March 28, 2016 and at all times thereafter. [Reg. §1.332–6.]

☐ [*T.D. 9329, 6-13-2007. Amended by T.D. 9759, 3-25-2016.*]

[Reg. §1.332-7]

§1.332-7. Indebtedness of subsidiary to parent.—If section 332(a) is applicable to the receipt of the subsidiary's property in complete liquidation, then no gain or loss shall be recognized to the subsidiary upon the transfer of such properties even though some of the properties are transferred in satisfaction of the subsidiary's indebtedness to its parent. See section 337(b)(1). However, any gain or loss realized by the parent corporation on such satisfaction of indebtedness, shall be recognized to the parent corporation at the time of the liquidation. For example, if the parent corporation purchased its subsidiary's bonds at a discount and upon liquidation of the subsidiary the parent corporation receives payment for the face amount of such bonds, gain shall be recognized to the parent corporation. Such gain shall be measured by the difference between the cost or other basis of the bonds to the parent and the amount received in payment of the bonds. [Reg. §1.332-7.]

☐ [*T.D. 6152, 12-2-55. Amended by T.D. 9759, 3-25-2016.*]

[Reg. §1.332-8]

§1.332-8. Recognition of gain on liquidation of certain holding companies.—(a) *Definition of controlled foreign corporation.*—For purposes of section 332(d)(3), a controlled foreign corporation has the meaning provided in section 957, determined without applying section 318(a)(3)(A), (B), and (C) so as to consider a United States person as owning stock which is owned by a person who is not a United States person.

(b) *Applicability date.*—This section applies to distributions in complete liquidation occurring on or after October 1, 2019, and to distributions in complete liquidation occurring before October 1, 2019, that result from an entity classification election made under §301.7701-3 of this chapter that is filed on or after October 1, 2019. For distributions in complete liquidation occurring before October 1, 2019, other than distributions in complete liquidation occurring before October 1, 2019, that result from an entity classification election made under §301.7701-3 of this chapter that is filed on or after October 1, 2019, a taxpayer may apply this section to distributions in complete liquidation occurring during the last taxable year of a distributee foreign corporation beginning before January 1, 2018, and each subsequent taxable year of the foreign corporation, provided that the taxpayer and United States persons that are related (within the meaning of section 267 or 707) to the taxpayer consistently apply this section with respect to all foreign corporations. [Reg. §1.332-8.]

☐ [*T.D. 9908, 9-21-2020.*]

[Reg. §1.334-1]

§1.334-1. Basis of property received in liquidations.—(a) *In general.*—Section 334 sets forth rules for determining a distributee's basis in property received in a distribution in complete liquidation of a corporation. The general rule is set forth in section 334(a) and provides that, if property is received in a distribution in complete liquidation of a corporation and if gain or loss is recognized on the receipt of the property, then the distributee's basis in the property is the fair market value of the property at the time of the distribution. However, if property is received in a complete liquidation to which section 332 applies, including property received in satisfaction of an indebtedness described in section 337(b)(1), see section 334(b)(1) and paragraph (b) of this section.

(b) *Liquidations under section 332.*—(1) *General rule.*—Except as otherwise provided in paragraph (b)(2) or (3) of this section, if a corporation (P) meeting the ownership requirements of section 332(b)(1) receives property from a subsidiary (S) in a complete liquidation to which section 332 applies (section 332 liquidation), including property received in a transfer in satisfaction of indebtedness that satisfies the requirements of section 337(b)(1), P's basis in the property received is the same as S's basis in the property immediately before the property was distributed. However, see §1.460-4(k)(3)(iv)(B)(2) for rules relating to adjustments to the basis of certain contracts accounted for using a long-term contract method of accounting that are acquired in a section 332 liquidation.

(2) *Basis in property with respect to which gain or loss was recognized.*—Except as otherwise provided in Subtitle A of the Internal Revenue Code (Code) and this subchapter of the Income Tax Regulations, if S recognizes gain or loss on the distribution of property to P

in a section 332 liquidation, P's basis in that property is the fair market value of the property at the time of the distribution. Section 334(b)(1)(A) (certain tax-exempt distributions under section 337(b)(2)); see also, for example, §1.367(e)-2(b)(3)(i).

(3) *Basis in importation property received in loss importation transaction.*—(i) *Purpose.*—The purpose of section 334(b)(1)(B) and this paragraph (b)(3) is to modify the application of this section to prevent P from importing a net built-in loss in a transaction described in section 332. See paragraph (b)(3)(iii)(A) of this section for definitions of terms used in this paragraph (b)(3).

(ii) *Determination of basis.*—Notwithstanding paragraph (b)(1) of this section, if a section 332 liquidation is a loss importation transaction, P's basis in each importation property received from S in the liquidation is an amount that is equal to the value of the property. The basis of property received in a section 332 liquidation that is not importation property received in a loss importation transaction is determined under generally applicable basis rules without regard to whether the liquidation also involves the receipt of importation property in a loss importation transaction.

(iii) *Operating rules.*—(A) *In general.*—For purposes of section 334(b)(1)(B) and this paragraph (b)(3), the provisions of §1.362-3 (basis of importation property received in a loss importation transaction) apply, adjusted as appropriate to apply to section 332 liquidations. Thus, when used in this paragraph (b)(3), the terms "importation property," "loss importation transaction," and "value" have the same meaning as in §1.362-3(c)(2), (3), and (4), respectively, except that "the section 332(b)(1) distributee corporation" is substituted for "Acquiring" and "section 332 liquidation" is substituted for "section 362 transaction." Similarly, when gain or loss on property would be owned or treated as owned by multiple persons, the provisions of §1.362-3(d)(2) apply to tentatively divide the property in applying this section, substituting "section 332 liquidation" for "section 362 transaction" and making such other adjustments as necessary.

(B) *Time for making determinations.*—For purposes of section 334(b)(1)(B) and this paragraph (b)(3)—

(1) *P's basis in distributed property.*—P's basis in each property S distributes to P in the section 332 liquidation is determined immediately after S distributes each such property;

(2) *Value of distributed property.*—The value of each property S distributes to P in the section 332 liquidation is determined immediately after S distributes the property;

(3) *Importation property.*—The determination of whether each property distributed by S is importation property is made as of the time S distributes each such property;

(4) *Loss importation transaction.*—The determination of whether a section 332 liquidation is a loss importation transaction is made immediately after S makes the final liquidating distribution to P.

(C) *Effect of basis determination under this paragraph (b)(3).*—(1) *Determination by reference to transferor's basis.*—A determination of basis under section 334(b)(1)(B) and this paragraph (b)(3) is a determination by reference to the transferor's basis, including for purposes of sections 1223(2) and 7701(a)(43). However, solely for purposes of applying section 755, a determination of basis under this paragraph (b)(3) is treated as a determination not by reference to the transferor's basis.

(2) *Not tax-exempt income or noncapital, nondeductible expense.*—The application of this paragraph (b)(3) does not give rise to an item treated as tax-exempt income under §1.1502-32(b)(2)(ii) or as a noncapital, nondeductible expense under §1.1502-32(b)(2)(iii)

(3) *No effect on earnings and profits.*—Any determination of basis under this paragraph (b)(3) does not reduce or otherwise affect the calculation of the all earnings and profits amount provided in §1.367(b)-2(d).

(iv) *Examples.*—The examples in this paragraph (b)(3)(iv) illustrate the application of section 334(b)(1)(B) and the provisions of this paragraph (b)(3). Unless the facts indicate otherwise, the examples use the following nomenclature and assumptions: USP is a domestic corporation that has not elected to be an S corporation within the meaning of section 1361(a)(1); FC, CFC1, and CFC2 are controlled foreign corporations within the meaning of section 957(a), which are not engaged in a U.S. trade or business, have no U.S. real property interests, and have no other relationships, activities, or interests that would cause their property to be subject to any tax imposed under subtitle A of the Code (federal income tax); there is no applicable income tax treaty; and all persons and transactions are unrelated. All other relevant facts are set forth in the examples:

Example 1. Basic application of this paragraph (b)(3). (i) *Distribution of importation property in a loss importation transaction.* (A) *Facts.* USP owns the sole outstanding share of FC stock. FC owns three assets, A1 (basis $40, value $50), A2 (basis $120, value $30), and A3 (basis $140, value $20). On Date 1, FC distributes A1, A2, and A3 to USP in a complete liquidation that qualifies under section 332.

(B) *Importation property.* Under §1.362-3(d)(2), the fact that any gain or loss recognized by a CFC may affect an income inclusion under section 951(a) does not alone cause gain or loss recognized by the CFC to be treated as taken into account in determining a federal income tax liability for purposes of this section. Thus, if FC had sold either A1, A2, or A3 immediately before the transaction, no gain or loss recognized on the sale would have been taken into account in determining a federal income tax liability. Further, if USP had sold A1, A2, or A3 immediately after the transaction, USP would take into account any gain or loss recognized on the sale in determining its federal income tax liability. Therefore, A1, A2, and A3 are all importation properties. See paragraph (b)(3)(iii)(A) of this section and §1.362-3(c)(2).

(C) *Loss importation transaction.* Immediately after the distribution, USP's aggregate basis in the importation properties, A1, A2, and A3, would, but for section 334(b)(1)(B) and this section, be $300 ($40 + $120 + $140) and the properties' aggregate value would be $100 ($50 + $30 + $20). Therefore, the importation properties' aggregate basis would exceed their aggregate value and the distribution is a loss importation transaction. See paragraph (b)(3)(iii)(A) of this section and §1.362-3(c)(3).

(D) *Basis of importation property distributed in loss importation transaction.* Because the importation properties, A1, A2, and A3, were transferred in a loss importation transaction, the basis in each of the importation properties received is equal to its value immediately after FC distributes the property. Accordingly, USP's basis in A1 is $50; USP's basis in A2 is $30; and USP's basis in A3 is $20.

(ii) *Distribution of both importation and non-importation property in a loss importation transaction.* (A) *Facts.* The facts are the same as in paragraph (i)(A) of this *Example 1* except that FC is engaged in a U.S. trade or business and A3 is used in that U.S. trade or business.

(B) *Importation property.* A1 and A2 are importation properties for the reasons set forth in paragraph (i)(B) of this *Example 1.* However, if FC had sold A3 immediately before the transaction, FC would take into account any gain or loss recognized on the sale in determining its federal income tax liability. Therefore, A3 is not importation property. See paragraph (b)(3)(iii)(A) of this section and §1.362-3(c)(2).

(C) *Loss importation transaction.* Immediately after the distribution, USP's aggregate basis in the importation properties, A1 and A2, would, but for section 334(b)(1)(B) and this section, be $160 ($40 + $120). Further, the properties' aggregate value would be $80 ($50 + $30). Therefore, the importation properties' aggregate basis would exceed their aggregate value and the distribution is a loss importation transaction. See paragraph (b)(3)(iii)(A) of this section and §1.362-3(c)(3).

(D) *Basis of importation property distributed in loss importation transaction.* Because the importation properties, A1 and A2, were transferred in a loss importation transaction, the basis in each of the importation properties received is equal to its value immediately after FC distributes the property. Accordingly, USP's basis in A1 is $50 and USP's basis in A2 is $30.

(E) *Basis of other property.* Because A3 is not importation property distributed in a loss importation transaction, USP's basis in A3 is determined under generally applicable basis rules. Accordingly, USP's basis in A3 is $140, the adjusted basis that FC had in the property immediately before the distribution. See section 334(b)(1).

(iii) *FC not wholly owned.* The facts are the same as in paragraph (i)(A) of this *Example 1* except that USP owns only 80% of the sole outstanding class of FC stock and the remaining 20% is owned by individual X. Further, on Date 1 and pursuant to the plan of liquidation, FC distributes A1 and A2 to USP and A3 to X. A1 and A2 are importation properties, the distribution to USP is a loss importation transaction, and USP's bases in A1 and A2 are equal to their value ($50 and $30, respectively) for the reasons set forth in paragraphs (ii)(C) and (D) of this *Example 1.* Under section 334(a), X's basis in A3 is $20.

(iv) *Importation property, no net built in loss.* (A) *Facts.* The facts are the same as in paragraph (i)(A) of this *Example 1* except that the value of A2 is $230.

(B) *Importation property.* A1, A2, and A3, are importation properties for the reasons set forth in paragraph (i)(B) of this *Example 1.*

(C) *Loss importation transaction.* Immediately after the distribution, USP's aggregate basis in the importation properties, A1, A2, and A3, would, but for section 334(b)(1)(B) and this section, be $300 ($40

+ $120 + $140). However, the properties' aggregate value would also be $300 ($50 + $230 + $20). Therefore, the importation properties' aggregate basis would not exceed their aggregate value and the distribution is not a loss importation transaction. See paragraph (b)(3)(iii)(A) of this section and §1.362-3(c)(3).

(D) *Basis of importation property not distributed in loss importation transaction.* Because the importation properties, A1, A2, and A3, were not distributed in a loss importation transaction, the basis of each of the importation properties is determined under the generally applicable basis rules. Accordingly, immediately after the distribution, USP's basis in A1 is $40, USP's basis in A2 is $120, and USP's basis in A3 is $140, the adjusted bases that FC had in the properties immediately before the distribution. See section 334(b)(1).

(v) *CFC stock as importation property distributed in loss importation transaction.* (A) *Facts.* USP owns the sole outstanding share of FC stock. FC owns the sole outstanding share of CFC1 stock (basis $80, value $100) and the sole outstanding share of CFC2 stock (basis $100, value $5). On Date 1, FC distributes its shares of CFC1 and CFC2 stock to USP in a complete liquidation that qualifies under section 332.

(B) *Importation property.* No special rule applies to the treatment of property that is the stock of a CFC. Thus, if FC had sold either the CFC1 share or the CFC2 share immediately before the transaction, no gain or loss recognized on the sale would have been taken into account in determining a federal income tax liability. Further, if USP had sold either the CFC1 share or the CFC2 share immediately after the transaction, USP would take into account any gain or loss recognized on the sale in determining its federal income tax liability. Thus, the CFC1 share and the CFC2 share are importation property. See paragraph (b)(3)(iii)(A) of this section and §1.362-3(c)(2).

(C) *Loss importation transaction.* Immediately after the distribution, USP's aggregate basis in importation property (the CFC1 share and the CFC2 share) would, but for section 334(b)(1)(B) and this section, be $180 ($80 + $100) and the shares' aggregate value is $105 ($100 + $5). Therefore, the importation property's aggregate basis would exceed their aggregate value and the distribution is a loss importation transaction. See paragraph (b)(3)(iii)(A) of this section and §1.362-3(c)(3).

(D) *Basis of importation property distributed in loss importation transaction.* Because the importation property (the CFC1 share and the CFC2 share) was transferred in a loss importation transaction, USP's basis in each of the shares received is equal to its value immediately after FC distributes the shares. Accordingly, USP's basis in the CFC1 share is $100 and USP's basis in the CFC2 share is $5.

Example 2. Multiple step liquidation. (i) *Facts.* USP owns the sole outstanding share of FC stock. On January 1 of year 1, FC adopts a plan of liquidation. FC makes the following distributions to USP in a transaction that qualifies as a complete liquidation under section 332. In year 1, FC distributes A1 and, immediately before the distribution, FC's basis in A1 is $100 and A1's value is $120. In Year 2, FC distributes A2, and, immediately before the distribution, FC's basis in A2 is $100 and A2's value is $120. In year 3, in its final liquidating distribution, FC distributes A3 and, immediately before the distribution, FC's basis in A3 is $100 and A3's value is $120. As of the time of the final distribution, USP had depreciated the bases of A1 and A2 to $90 and $95, respectively; the value of A1 had appreciated to $160; and, the value of A2 has declined to $0.

(ii) *Importation property.* If FC had sold either A1, A2, or A3 immediately before it was distributed, no gain or loss recognized on the sale would have been taken into account in determining a federal income tax liability. Further, if USP had sold either A1, A2, or A3 immediately after it was distributed, USP would take into account any gain or loss recognized on the sale in determining its federal income tax liability. Therefore, A1, A2, and A3 are all importation properties. See paragraph (b)(3)(iii)(A) of this section and §1.362-3(c)(2).

(iii) *Loss importation transaction.* Immediately after it was distributed, USP's basis in each of the importation properties, A1, A2, and A3, would, but for section 334(b)(1)(B) and this section, have been $100. Further, immediately after each such property was distributed, its value was $120. Thus, the properties' aggregate basis, $300, would not have exceeded the properties' aggregate value, $360. Accordingly, the distribution is not a loss importation transaction irrespective of the fact that, when the liquidation was completed, the properties' aggregate basis was $285 and the properties' aggregate value was $280. See paragraph (b)(3)(iii)(B) of this section and §1.362-3(c)(3).

(iv) *Basis of importation property not distributed in loss importation transaction.* Because the importation properties, A1, A2, and A3, were not distributed in a loss importation transaction, the basis of each of the importation properties is determined under the generally applicable basis rules. Accordingly, USP takes each of the properties with a basis of $100 and, immediately after the final distribution, has an adjusted basis of $90 in A1 (USP's $100 basis less the $10 depreciation), $95 in A2 (USP's $100 basis less the $5 depreciation), and $100 in A3. See section 334(b).

(c) *Applicability date.*—This section applies with respect to liquidations occurring on or after March 28, 2016, and also with respect to liquidations occurring before such date as a result of an entity classification election under §301.7701-3 of this chapter filed on or after March 28, 2016, unless such liquidation is pursuant to a binding agreement that was in effect prior to March 28, 2016 and at all times thereafter. In addition, taxpayers may apply this section to any section 332 liquidation occurring after October 22, 2004. [Reg. §1.334-1.]

☐ [T.D. 6152, 12-2-55. *Amended by* T.D. 6298, 6-23-58; T.D. 7231, 12-21-72; *T.D.* 8474, 4-26-93, T.D. 8995, 5-14-2002 *and T.D.* 9759, 3-25-2016.]

[Reg. §1.336-0]

§1.336-0. Table of contents.—This section lists captions contained in §§1.336-1, 1.336-2, 1.336-3, 1.336-4, and 1.336-5.

(5) Recently purchased stock; recently disposed stock.

(6) Nonrecently purchased stock; nonrecently disposed stock.

(c) Gain recognition election.

(1) In general.

(2) 80-percent purchaser.

(3) Non-80-percent purchaser.

(4) Gain recognition election statement.

(d) Examples.

§ 1.336-5 Effective/applicability date.

[Reg. § 1.336-0.]

☐ [T.D. 9619, 5-10-2013.]

[Reg. § 1.336-1]

§ 1.336-1. General principles, nomenclature, and definitions for a section 336(e) election.—(a) *Overview.*—(1) *In general.*—Section 336(e) authorizes the promulgation of regulations under which, in certain circumstances, a sale, exchange, or distribution of the stock of a corporation may be treated as an asset sale. This section and §§ 1.336-2 through 1.336-5 provide the rules for and consequences of making such election. This section provides the definitions and nomenclature. Generally, except to the extent inconsistent with section 336(e), the results of section 336(e) should coincide with those of section 338(h)(10). Accordingly, to the extent not inconsistent with section 336(e) or these regulations, the principles of section 338 and the regulations under section 338 apply for purposes of these regulations. For example, § 1.338(h)(10)-1(d)(8), concerning the availability of the section 453 installment method, may apply with respect to section 336(e).

(2) *Consistency rules.*—In general, the principles of § 1.338-8, concerning asset and stock consistency, apply with respect to section 336(e). However, for this purpose, the application of § 1.338-8(b)(1) is modified such that § 1.338-8(b)(1)(iii) applies to an asset if the asset is owned, immediately after its acquisition and on the disposition date, by a person or by a related person (as defined in § 1.336-1(b)(12)) to a person that acquires, by sale, exchange, distribution, or any combination thereof, five percent or more, by value, of the stock of target in the qualified stock disposition.

(b) *Definitions.*—For purposes of §§ 1.336-1 through 1.336-5 (except as otherwise provided):

(1) *Seller.*—The term *seller* means any domestic corporation that makes a qualified stock disposition of stock of another corporation. Seller includes both a transferor and a distributor of target stock. Generally, all members of a consolidated group that dispose of target stock are treated as a single seller. See § 1.336-2(g)(2).

(2) *Purchaser.*—The term *purchaser* means one or more persons that acquire or receive the stock of another corporation in a qualified stock disposition. A purchaser includes both a transferee and a distributee of target stock.

(3) *Target; S corporation target; old target; new target.*—The term *target* means any domestic corporation the stock of which is sold, exchanged, or distributed in a qualified stock disposition. An *S corporation target* is a target that is an S corporation immediately before the disposition date; any other target is a *non-S corporation target.* Except as the context otherwise requires, a reference to target includes a reference to an S corporation target. In the case of a transaction not described in section 355(d)(2) or (e)(2), *old target* refers to target for periods ending on or before the close of target's disposition date and *new target* refers to target for subsequent periods. In the case of a transaction described in section 355(d)(2) or (e)(2), *old target* refers to target for periods ending on or before the disposition date as well as for subsequent periods.

(4) *S corporation shareholders.*—*S corporation shareholders* are the S corporation target's shareholders. Unless otherwise provided, a reference to S corporation shareholders refers both to S corporation shareholders who dispose of and those who do not dispose of their S corporation target stock.

(5) *Disposed of; disposition.*—(i) *In general.*—The term *disposed of* refers to a transfer of stock in a disposition. The term *disposition* means any sale, exchange, or distribution of stock, but only if —

(A) The basis of the stock in the hands of the purchaser is not determined in whole or in part by reference to the adjusted basis of such stock in the hands of the person from whom the stock is acquired, is not determined under section 1014(a) (relating to property acquired from a decedent), or is not determined under section 1022 (relating to the basis of property acquired from certain decedents who died in 2010);

(B) Except as provided in paragraph (b)(5)(ii) of this section, the stock is not sold, exchanged, or distributed in a transaction to which section 351, 354, 355, or 356 applies and is not sold, exchanged, or distributed in any transaction described in regulations in which the transferor does not recognize the entire amount of the gain or loss realized in the transaction; and

(C) The stock is not sold, exchanged, or distributed to a related person.

(ii) *Exception for disposition of stock in certain section 355 transactions.*—Notwithstanding paragraph (b)(5)(i)(B) of this section, a distribution of stock to a person who is not a related person in a transaction in which the full amount of stock gain would be recognized pursuant to section 355(d)(2) or (e)(2) shall be considered a disposition.

(iii) *Transactions with related persons.*—In determining whether stock is sold, exchanged, or distributed to a related person, the principles of section 338(h)(3)(C) and § 1.338-3(b)(3) shall apply.

(iv) *No consideration paid.*—Stock in target may be considered disposed of if, under general principles of tax law, seller is considered to sell, exchange, or distribute stock of target notwithstanding that no amount may be paid for (or allocated to) the stock.

(v) *Disposed of stock reacquired by certain persons.*—Stock disposed of by seller to another person under this section that is reacquired by seller or a member of seller's consolidated group during the 12-month disposition period shall not be considered as disposed of. Similarly, stock disposed of by an S corporation shareholder to another person under this section that is reacquired by the S corporation shareholder or by a person related (within the meaning of paragraph (b)(12) of this section) to the S corporation shareholder during the 12-month disposition period shall not be considered as disposed of.

(6) *Qualified stock disposition.*—(i) *In general.*—The term *qualified stock disposition* means any transaction or series of transactions in which stock meeting the requirements of section 1504(a)(2) of a domestic corporation is either sold, exchanged, or distributed, or any combination thereof, by another domestic corporation or by the S corporation shareholders in a disposition, within the meaning of paragraph (b)(5) of this section, during the 12-month disposition period.

(ii) *Overlap with qualified stock purchase.*—(A) *In general.*—Except as provided in paragraph (b)(6)(ii)(B) of this section, a transaction satisfying the definition of a qualified stock disposition under paragraph (b)(6)(i) of this section, which also qualifies as a qualified stock purchase (as defined in section 338(d)(3)), will not be treated as a qualified stock disposition.

(B) *Exception.*—If, as a result of the deemed sale of old target's assets pursuant to a section 336(e) election, there would be, but for paragraph (b)(6)(ii)(A) of this section, a qualified stock disposition of the stock of a subsidiary of target, then paragraph (b)(6)(ii)(A) shall not apply to the disposition of the stock of the subsidiary.

(7) *12-month disposition period.*—The term *12-month disposition period* means the 12-month period beginning with the date of the first sale, exchange, or distribution of stock included in a qualified stock disposition.

(8) *Disposition date.*—The term *disposition date* means, with respect to any corporation, the first day on which there is a qualified stock disposition with respect to the stock of such corporation.

(9) *Disposition date assets.*—*Disposition date assets* are the assets of target held at the beginning of the day after the disposition date (but see § 1.338-1(d) (regarding certain transactions on the disposition date)).

(10) *Domestic corporation.*—The term *domestic corporation* has the same meaning as in § 1.338-2(c)(9).

(11) *Section 336(e) election.*—A section 336(e) election is an election to apply section 336(e) to target. A section 336(e) election is made by making an election for target under § 1.336-2(h).

(12) *Related persons.*—Two persons are related if stock of a corporation owned by one of the persons would be attributed under section 318(a), other than section 318(a)(4), to the other. However, neither section 318(a)(2)(A) nor section 318(a)(3)(A) apply to attribute stock ownership from a partnership to a partner, or from a partner to a partnership, if such partner owns, directly or indirectly, interests representing less than five percent of the value of the partnership.

(13) *Liquidation.*—Any reference to a liquidation is treated as a reference to the transfer described in § 1.336-2(b)(1)(iii) notwithstanding its ultimate characterization for Federal income tax purposes.

(14) *Deemed asset disposition.*—The deemed sale of old target's assets is, without regard to its characterization for Federal income tax purposes, referred to as the deemed asset disposition.

(15) *Deemed disposition tax consequences.*—Deemed disposition tax consequences refers to, in the aggregate, the Federal income tax consequences (generally, the income, gain, deduction, and loss) of the deemed asset disposition. Deemed disposition tax consequences also refers to the Federal income tax consequences of the transfer of a particular asset in the deemed asset disposition.

(16) *80-percent purchaser.*—An 80-percent purchaser is any purchaser that, after application of the attribution rules of section 318(a), other than section 318(a)(4), owns 80 percent or more of the voting power or value of target stock.

(17) *Recently disposed stock.*—The term *recently disposed stock* means any stock in target that is not held by seller, a member of seller's consolidated group, or an S corporation shareholder immediately after the close of the disposition date and that was disposed of by seller, a member of seller's consolidated group, or an S corporation shareholder during the 12-month disposition period.

(18) *Nonrecently disposed stock.*—The term *nonrecently disposed stock* means stock in target that is held on the disposition date by a purchaser or a person related (as described in § 1.336-1(b)(12)) to the purchaser who owns, on the disposition date, with the application of section 318(a), other than section 318(a)(4), at least 10 percent of the total voting power or value of the stock of target and that is not recently disposed stock.

(c) *Nomenclature.*—For purposes of §§ 1.336-1 through 1.336-5, except as otherwise provided, Parent, Seller, Target, Sub, S Corporation Target, and Target Subsidiary are domestic corporations and A, B, C, and D are individuals, none of whom are related to Parent, Seller, Target, Sub, S Corporation Target, Target Subsidiary, or each other. [Reg. § 1.336-1.]

☐ [*T.D. 9619, 5-10-2013. Amended by T.D. 9811, 1-18-2017.*]

[Reg. § 1.336-2]

§ 1.336-2. Availability, mechanics, and consequences of section 336(e) election.—(a) *Availability of election.*—A section 336(e) election is available if seller or S corporation shareholder(s) dispose of stock of another corporation (target) in a qualified stock disposition (as defined in § 1.336-1(b)(6)). A section 336(e) election is irrevocable. A section 336(e) election is not available for transactions described in section 336(e) that do not constitute qualified stock dispositions.

(b) *Deemed transaction.*—(1) *Dispositions not described in section 355(d)(2) or (e)(2).*—(i) *Old target—deemed asset disposition.*—(A) *In general.*—This paragraph (b)(1) provides the Federal income tax consequences of a section 336(e) election made with respect to a qualified stock disposition not described, in whole or in part, in section 355(d)(2) or (e)(2). For the Federal income tax consequences of a section 336(e) election made with respect to a qualified stock disposition described, in whole or in part, in section 355(d)(2) or (e)(2), see paragraph (b)(2) of this section. In general, if a section 336(e) election is made, seller (or S corporation shareholders) are treated as not having sold, exchanged, or distributed the stock disposed of in the qualified stock disposition. Instead, old target is treated as selling its assets to an unrelated person in a single transaction at the close of the disposition date (but before the deemed liquidation described in paragraph (b)(1)(iii) of this section) in exchange for the aggregate deemed asset disposition price (ADADP) as determined under § 1.336-3. ADADP is allocated among the disposition date assets in the same manner as the aggregate deemed sale price (ADSP) is allocated under §§ 1.338-6 and 1.338-7 in order to determine the amount realized from each of the sold assets. Old target realizes the deemed disposition tax consequences from the deemed asset disposition before the close of the disposition date while old target is owned by seller or the S corporation shareholders. If old target is an S corporation target, old target's S election continues in effect through the close of the disposition date (including the time of the deemed asset disposition and the deemed liquidation) notwithstanding section 1362(d)(2)(B). Also, if old target is an S corporation target (but *not a qualified subchapter S subsidiary*), any direct or indirect subsidiaries of old target that old target has elected to treat as qualified subchapter S subsidiaries under section 1361(b)(3) remain qualified subchapter S subsidiaries through the close of the disposition date.

(B) *Gains and losses.*—(1) *Gains.*—Except as provided in § 1.338(h)(10)-1(d)(8) (regarding the installment method), old target shall recognize all of the gains realized on the deemed asset disposition.

(2) *Losses.*—(i) *In general.*—Except as provided in paragraphs (b)(1)(i)(B)(2)(*ii*), (*iii*), and (*iv*) of this section, old target shall recognize all of the losses realized on the deemed asset disposition.

(ii) *Stock distributions.*—Notwithstanding paragraphs (b)(1)(i)(A) and (b)(1)(iii)(A) of this section, for purposes of determining the amount of target's losses that are disallowed on the deemed asset disposition, seller is still treated as selling, exchanging, or distributing its target stock disposed of in the 12-month disposition period. If target's losses realized on the deemed sale of all of its assets exceed target's gains realized (a net loss), the portion of such net loss attributable to a distribution of target stock during the 12-month disposition period is disallowed. The total amount of disallowed loss and the allocation of disallowed loss is determined in the manner provided in paragraphs (b)(1)(i)(B)(2)(*iii*) and (*iv*) of this section.

(iii) *Amount and allocation of disallowed loss.*—The total disallowed loss pursuant to paragraph (b)(1)(i)(B)(2)(*ii*) of this section shall be determined by multiplying the net loss realized on the deemed asset disposition by the disallowed loss fraction. The numerator of the disallowed loss fraction is the value of target stock, determined on the disposition date, distributed by seller during the 12-month disposition period, whether or not a part of the qualified stock disposition (for example, stock distributed to a related person), and the denominator of the disallowed loss fraction is the sum of the value of target stock, determined on the disposition date, disposed of by sale or exchange in the qualified stock disposition during the 12-month disposition period and the value of target stock, determined on the disposition date, distributed by seller during the 12-month disposition period, whether or not a part of the qualified stock disposition. The amount of the disallowed loss allocated to each asset disposed of in the deemed asset disposition is determined by multiplying the total amount of the disallowed loss by the loss allocation fraction. The numerator of the loss allocation fraction is the amount of loss realized with respect to the asset and the denominator of the loss allocation fraction is the sum of the amount of losses realized with respect to each loss asset disposed of in the deemed asset disposition. To the extent old target's losses from the deemed asset disposition are not disallowed under this paragraph, such losses may be disallowed under other provisions of the Internal Revenue Code or general principles of tax law, in the same manner as if such assets were actually sold to an unrelated person.

(iv) *Tiered targets.*—If an asset of target is the stock of a subsidiary corporation of target for which a section 336(e) election is made, any gain or loss realized on the deemed sale of the stock of the subsidiary corporation is disregarded in determining the amount of disallowed loss. For purposes of determining the amount of disallowed loss on the deemed asset disposition by a subsidiary of target for which a section 336(e) election is made, the amount of subsidiary stock deemed sold in the deemed asset disposition of target's assets multiplied by the disallowed loss fraction with respect to the corporation that is deemed to have disposed of stock of the subsidiary is considered to have been distributed. In determining the disallowed loss fraction with respect to the deemed asset disposition of any subsidiary of target, disregard any sale, exchange, or distribution of its stock that was made after the disposition date if such stock was included in the deemed asset disposition of the corporation deemed to have disposed of the subsidiary stock.

(3) *Examples.*—The following examples illustrate this paragraph (b)(1)(i)(B).

Example 1. (i) *Facts.* Parent owns 60 of the 100 outstanding shares of the common stock of Seller, Seller's only class of stock outstanding. The remaining 40 shares of the common stock of Seller are held by shareholders unrelated to Seller or each other. Seller owns 95 of the 100 outstanding shares of Target common stock, and all 100 shares of Target preferred stock that is described in section 1504(a)(4). The remaining 5 shares of Target common stock are owned by A. On January 1 of Year 1, Seller sells 72 shares of Target common stock to B for $3,520. On July 1 of Year 1, Seller distributes 12 shares of Target common stock to Parent and 8 shares to its unrelated shareholders in a distribution described in section 301. Seller retains 3 shares of Target common stock and all 100 shares of Target preferred stock immediately after July 1. The value of Target common stock on July 1 is $60 per share. The value of Target preferred stock on July 1 is $36 per share. Target has three assets, Asset 1, a Class IV asset, with a basis of $1,776 and a fair market value of $2,000, Asset 2, a Class V asset, with a basis of $2,600 and a fair market value of $2,750, and Asset 3, a Class V asset, with a basis of $3,900 and a fair market value of $3,850. Seller incurred no selling costs on the sale of the 72 shares of Target common stock to B. Target has no liabilities. A section 336(e) election is made.

(ii) *Consequences—Deemed Asset Sale.* Because at least 80 percent ((72 + 8)/100) of Target stock, other than stock described in section 1504(a)(4), was disposed of (within the meaning of § 1.336-1(b)(5)) by Seller during the 12-month disposition period, a qualified stock disposition occurred. July 1 of Year 1, the first day on which there was a qualified stock disposition with respect to Target stock, is the disposition date. Accordingly, pursuant to the section 336(e) election, for Federal income tax purposes, Seller generally is not treated as selling the 72 shares of Target common stock sold to B or distributing the 8 shares of Target common stock distributed to its unrelated shareholders. However, Seller is still treated as distributing the 12 shares of Target common stock distributed to Parent because Seller and Parent are related persons within the meaning of § 1.336-1(b)(12) and accordingly the 12 shares are not part of the qualified stock disposition. Target is treated as if, on July 1, it sold all of its assets to an unrelated person in exchange for the ADADP, $8,000, which is allocated $2,000 to Asset 1, $2,500 to Asset 2, and $3,500 to Asset 3 (see *Example 1* of § 1.336-3(g) for the determination and allocation of ADADP).

(iii) *Consequences—Amount and Allocation of Disallowed Loss.* Old Target realized a net loss of $276 on the deemed asset disposition ($224 gain realized on Asset 1, $100 loss realized on Asset 2, and $400 loss realized on Asset 3). However, 20 shares of Target common stock were distributed by Seller during the 12-month disposition period (8 shares distributed to Seller's unrelated shareholders in the qualified stock disposition plus 12 shares distributed to Parent that were not part of the qualified stock disposition). Therefore, because there was a net loss realized on the deemed asset disposition and a portion of the stock of Target was distributed during the 12-month disposition period, a portion of the loss on the deemed sale of each of Target's loss assets is disallowed. The total amount of disallowed loss equals $60 ($276 net loss realized on the deemed disposition of Assets 1, 2, and 3 multiplied by the disallowed loss fraction, the numerator of which is $1,200, the value on July 1, the disposition date, of the 20 shares of Target common stock distributed during the 12-month disposition period, and the denominator of which is $5,520, the sum of $4,320, the value on July 1 of the 72 shares of Target common stock sold to B and $1,200, the value on July 1 of the 20 shares of Target common stock distributed during the 12-month disposition period). The portion of the disallowed loss allocated to Asset 2 is $12 ($60 total disallowed loss multiplied by the loss allocation fraction, the numerator of which is $100, the loss realized on the deemed disposition of Asset 2 and the denominator of which is $500, the sum of the losses realized on the deemed disposition of Assets 2 and 3). The portion of the disallowed loss allocated to Asset 3 is $48 ($60 total disallowed loss multiplied by the loss allocation fraction, the numerator of which is $400, the loss realized on the deemed disposition of Asset 3 and the denominator of which is $500, the sum of the losses realized on the deemed disposition of Assets 2 and 3). Accordingly, Old Target recognizes $224 of gain on Asset 1, recognizes $88 of loss on Asset 2 (realized loss of $100 less allocated disallowed loss of $12), and recognizes $352 of loss on Asset 3 (realized loss of $400 less allocated disallowed loss of $48) or a recognized net loss of $216 on the deemed asset disposition.

Example 2. (i) *Facts.* The facts are the same as in *Example 1* except that Asset 2 is the stock of Target Subsidiary, a corporation of which Target owns 100 of the 110 shares of common stock, the only outstanding class of Target Subsidiary stock. The remaining 10 shares of Target Subsidiary stock are owned by D. The value of Target Subsidiary stock on July 1 is $27.50 per share. Target Subsidiary has two assets, Asset 4, a Class IV asset, with a basis of $800 and a fair market value of $1,000, and Asset 5, a Class IV asset, with a basis of $2,200 and a fair market value of $2,025. Target Subsidiary has no liabilities. A section 336(e) election with respect to Target Subsidiary is also made.

(ii) *Consequences—Target.* The ADADP on the deemed sale of Target's assets is determined and allocated in the same manner as in *Example 1*. However, Target's loss realized on the deemed sale of Target Subsidiary is disregarded in determining the amount of disallowed loss on the deemed asset disposition of Target's assets. Thus, the net loss is only $176 ($224 gain realized on Asset 1 and $400 loss realized on Asset 3), and the amount of disallowed loss equals $38.26 ($176 net loss multiplied by the disallowed loss fraction with respect to Target stock, $1,200/$5,520). The entire disallowed loss is allocated to Asset 3.

(iii) *Consequences—Target Subsidiary.* The deemed sale of the stock of Target Subsidiary is disregarded and instead Target Subsidiary is deemed to sell all of its assets to an unrelated person. The ADADP on the deemed asset disposition of Target Subsidiary is $2,750, which is allocated $909 to Asset 4 and $1,841 to Asset 5 (see *Example 2* of § 1.336-3(g) for the determination and allocation of ADADP). Old Target Subsidiary realized $109 of gain on Asset 4 and realized $359 of loss on Asset 5 in the deemed asset disposition. Although Old Target Subsidiary realized a net loss of $250 on the deemed asset disposition ($109 gain on Asset 4 and $359 loss on Asset 5), a portion of this net loss is disallowed because a portion of Target stock was distributed during the 12-month disposition period. For purposes of determining the amount of disallowed loss on the

deemed sale of the assets of Target Subsidiary, the portion of the 100 shares of Target Subsidiary stock deemed sold by Target pursuant to the section 336(e) election for Target Subsidiary multiplied by the disallowed loss fraction with respect to Target stock is treated as having been distributed. Thus, for purposes of determining the amount of disallowed loss on the deemed asset disposition of Target Subsidiary's assets, 21.74 shares of Target Subsidiary stock (100 shares of Target Subsidiary stock owned by Target multiplied by the disallowed loss fraction with respect to Target stock, $1,200/$5,520) are treated as having been distributed by Target during the 12-month disposition period. The total amount of disallowed loss with respect to the deemed asset disposition of Target Subsidiary's assets equals $54 ($250 net loss realized on the deemed disposition of Assets 4 and 5 multiplied by the disallowed loss fraction with respect to Target Subsidiary, the numerator of which is $598, the value on July 1, the disposition date, of the 21.74 shares of Target Subsidiary stock deemed distributed during the 12-month disposition period (21.74 shares × $27.50) and the denominator of which is $2,750 (the sum of $2,152, the value on July 1 of the 78.26 shares of Target Subsidiary stock deemed sold in the qualified stock disposition pursuant to the section 336(e) election for Target Subsidiary (78.26 shares × $27.50) and $598, the value on July 1 of the 21.74 shares of Target Subsidiary stock deemed distributed during the 12-month disposition period)). (The 10 shares of Target Subsidiary owned by D are not part of the qualified stock disposition and therefore are not included in the denominator of the disallowed loss fraction.) All of the disallowed loss is allocated to Asset 5, the only loss asset. Accordingly, Old Target Subsidiary recognizes $109 of gain on Asset 4 and recognizes $305 of loss on Asset 5 (realized loss of $359 less disallowed loss of $54) or a net loss of $196 on the deemed asset disposition.

Example 3. (i) *Facts.* The facts are the same as in *Example 2* except that on August 1 of Year 1, Target sells 50 of its shares of Target Subsidiary stock and distributes the remaining 50 shares.

(ii) *Consequences.* Because the 100 shares of Target Subsidiary stock that were sold and distributed on August 1 were deemed disposed of on July 1 in the deemed asset disposition of Target, the August 1 sale and distribution of Target Subsidiary stock are disregarded in determining the amount of disallowed loss. Accordingly, the consequences are the same as in *Example 2*.

(C) *Tiered targets.*—In the case of parent-subsidiary chains of corporations making section 336(e) elections, the deemed asset disposition of a higher-tier subsidiary is considered to precede the deemed asset disposition of a lower-tier subsidiary.

(ii) *New target—deemed purchase.*—New target is treated as acquiring all of its assets from an unrelated person in a single transaction at the close of the disposition date (but before the deemed liquidation) in exchange for an amount equal to the adjusted grossed-up basis (AGUB) as determined under § 1.336-4. New target allocates the consideration deemed paid in the transaction in the same manner as new target would under § § 1.338-6 and 1.338-7 in order to determine the basis in each of the purchased assets. If new target qualifies as a small business corporation within the meaning of section 1361(b) and wants to be an S corporation, a new election under section 1362(a) must be made. Notwithstanding paragraph (b)(1)(iii) of this section (deemed liquidation of old target), new target remains liable for the tax liabilities of old target (including the tax liability for the deemed disposition tax consequences). For example, new target remains liable for the tax liabilities of the members of any consolidated group that are attributable to taxable years in which those corporations and old target joined in the same consolidated return. See § 1.1502-6(a).

(iii) *Old target and seller—deemed liquidation.*—(A) *In general.*— If old target is an S corporation, S corporation shareholders (whether or not they sell or exchange their stock) take their pro rata share of the deemed disposition tax consequences into account under section 1366 and increase or decrease their basis in target stock under section 1367. Old target and seller (or S corporation shareholders) are treated as if, before the close of the disposition date, after the deemed asset disposition described in paragraph (b)(1)(i)(A) of this section, and while target is owned by seller or S corporation shareholders, old target transferred all of the consideration deemed received from new target in the deemed asset disposition to seller or S corporation shareholders, any S corporation election for old target terminated, and old target ceased to exist. The transfer from old target to seller or S corporation shareholders is characterized for Federal income tax purposes in the same manner as if the parties had actually engaged in the transactions deemed to occur because of this section and taking into account other transactions that actually occurred or are deemed to occur. For example, the transfer may be treated as a distribution in pursuance of a plan of reorganization, a distribution in complete cancellation or redemption of all of its stock, one of a series of distributions in complete cancellation or redemption of all of its stock in accordance with a plan of liquidation, or part of a circular flow of cash. In most cases, the transfer will be treated as a distribution in complete liquidation to which sections 331 or 332 and sections 336 or 337 apply.

(B) *Tiered targets.*—In the case of parent-subsidiary chains of corporations making section 336(e) elections, the deemed liquidation of a lower-tier subsidiary corporation is considered to precede the deemed liquidation of a higher-tier subsidiary.

(iv) *Seller—distribution of target stock.*—In the case of a distribution of target stock in a qualified stock disposition, seller (the distributor) is deemed to purchase from an unrelated person, on the disposition date, immediately after the deemed liquidation of old target, the amount of stock distributed in the qualified stock disposition (new target stock) and to have distributed such new target stock to its shareholders. Seller recognizes no gain or loss on the distribution of such stock.

(v) *Seller—retention of target stock.*—If seller or an S corporation shareholder retains any target stock after the disposition date, seller or the S corporation shareholder is treated as purchasing the stock so retained from an unrelated person (new target stock) on the day after the disposition date for its fair market value. The holding period for the retained stock starts on the day after the disposition date. For purposes of this paragraph (b)(1)(v), the fair market value of all of the target stock equals the grossed-up amount realized on the sale, exchange, or distribution of recently disposed stock of target (see § 1.336-3(c)).

(2) *Dispositions described in section 355(d)(2) or (e)(2).*—(i) *Old target—deemed asset disposition.*—(A) *In general.*—This paragraph (b)(2) provides the Federal income tax consequences of a section 336(e) election made with respect to a qualified stock disposition resulting, in whole or in part, from a disposition described in section 355(d)(2) or (e)(2). Old target is treated as selling its assets to an unrelated person in a single transaction at the close of the disposition date in exchange for the ADADP as determined under § 1.336-3. ADADP is allocated among the disposition date assets in the same manner as ADSP is allocated under §§ 1.338-6 and 1.338-7 in order to determine the amount realized from each of the sold assets. Old target realizes the deemed disposition tax consequences from the deemed asset disposition before the close of the disposition date while old target is owned by seller.

(1) *Old target not deemed to liquidate.*—In general, unlike a section 338(h)(10) election or a section 336(e) election made with respect to a qualified stock disposition not described, in whole or in part, in section 355(d)(2) or (e)(2), old target is not deemed to liquidate after the deemed asset disposition.

(2) *Exception.*—If an election is made under § 1.1502-13(f)(5)(ii)(E), then solely for purposes of § 1.1502-13(f)(5)(ii)(C), immediately after the deemed asset disposition of old target, old target is deemed to liquidate into seller.

(B) *Gains and losses.*—(1) *Gains.*—Except as provided in § 1.338(h)(10)-1(d)(8) (regarding the installment method), old target shall recognize all of the gains realized on the deemed asset disposition.

(2) *Losses.*—(i) *In general.*—Except as provided in paragraphs (b)(2)(i)(B)(2)(ii), (iii), and (iv) of this section, old target shall recognize all of the losses realized on the deemed asset disposition.

(ii) *Stock distributions.*—If target's losses realized on the deemed sale of all of its assets exceed target's gains realized (a net loss), the portion of such net loss attributable to a distribution of target stock during the 12-month disposition period is disallowed. The total amount of disallowed loss and the allocation of disallowed loss is determined in the manner provided in paragraphs (b)(2)(i)(B)(2)(iii) and (iv) of this section.

(iii) *Amount and allocation of disallowed loss.*—The total disallowed loss pursuant to paragraph (b)(2)(i)(B)(2)(ii) of this section shall be determined by multiplying the net loss realized on the deemed asset disposition by the disallowed loss fraction. The numerator of the disallowed loss fraction is the value of target stock, determined on the disposition date, distributed by seller during the 12-month disposition period, whether or not a part of the qualified stock disposition (for example, stock distributed to a related person), and the denominator of the disallowed loss fraction is the sum of the value of target stock, determined on the disposition date, disposed of by sale or exchange in the qualified stock disposition during the 12-month disposition period and the value of target stock, determined on the disposition date, distributed by seller during the 12-month disposition period, whether or not a part of the qualified

stock disposition. The amount of the disallowed loss allocated to each asset disposed of in the deemed asset disposition is determined by multiplying the total amount of the disallowed loss by the loss allocation fraction. The numerator of the loss allocation fraction is the amount of loss realized with respect to the asset and the denominator of the loss allocation fraction is the sum of the amount of losses realized with respect to each loss asset disposed of in the deemed asset disposition. To the extent old target's losses from the deemed asset disposition are not disallowed under this paragraph, such losses may be disallowed under other provisions of the Internal Revenue Code or general principles of tax law, in the same manner as if such assets were actually sold to an unrelated person.

(iv) *Tiered targets.*—If an asset of target is the stock of a subsidiary corporation of target for which a section 336(e) election is made, any gain or loss realized on the deemed sale of the stock of the subsidiary corporation is disregarded in determining the amount of disallowed loss. For purposes of determining the amount of disallowed loss on the deemed asset disposition by a subsidiary of target for which a section 336(e) election is made, see paragraph (b)(1)(i)(B)(2) of this section.

(3) *Examples.*—The following examples illustrate this paragraph (b)(2)(i)(B).

Example 1. (i) *Facts.* Seller owns 90 of the 100 outstanding shares of Target common stock, the only class of Target stock outstanding. The remaining 10 shares of Target common stock are owned by C. On January 1 of Year 1, Seller sells 10 shares of Target common stock to D for $910. On July 1, in an unrelated transaction, Seller distributes its remaining 80 shares of Target common stock to its unrelated shareholders in a distribution described in section 355(d)(2) or (e)(2). On July 1, the value of Target common stock is $100 per share. Target has three assets, Asset 1 with a basis of $1,220, Asset 2 with a basis of $3,675, and Asset 3 with a basis of $5,725. Seller incurred no selling costs on the sale of the 10 shares of Target common stock to D. Target has no liabilities. A section 336(e) election is made.

(ii) *Consequences.* Because at least 80 percent of Target stock ((10 + 80)/100) was disposed of (within the meaning of § 1.336-1(b)(5)) by Seller during the 12-month disposition period, a qualified stock disposition occurred. July 1 of Year 1, the first day on which there was a qualified stock disposition with respect to Target, is the disposition date. Accordingly, pursuant to the section 336(e) election, for Federal income tax purposes, Target is treated as if, on July 1, it sold all of its assets to an unrelated person in exchange for the ADADP, $9,900, as determined under § 1.336-3. Assume that the ADADP is allocated $2,000 to Asset 1, $3,300 to Asset 2, and $4,600 to Asset 3 under § 1.336-3. Old Target realized a net loss of $720 on the deemed asset disposition ($780 gain realized on Asset 1, $375 loss realized on Asset 2, and $1,125 loss realized on Asset 3). However, because a portion of Target stock was distributed during the 12-month disposition period and there was a net loss on the deemed asset disposition, a portion of the loss on each of the loss assets is disallowed. The total amount of disallowed loss equals $640 ($720 net loss realized on the deemed disposition of Assets 1, 2, and 3 multiplied by the disallowed loss fraction, the numerator of which is $8,000, the value on July 1, the disposition date, of the 80 shares of Target common stock distributed by Seller during the 12-month disposition period, and the denominator of which is $9,000, the sum of $1,000, the value on July 1 of the 10 shares of Target common stock sold to D, and $8,000, the value on July 1 of the 80 shares of Target common stock distributed by Seller during the 12-month disposition period). The portion of the disallowed loss allocated to Asset 2 is $160 ($640 total disallowed loss on the deemed asset disposition multiplied by the loss allocation fraction, the numerator of which is $375, the loss realized on the deemed disposition of Asset 2, and the denominator of which is $1,500, the sum of the losses realized on the deemed disposition of Assets 2 and 3). The portion of the disallowed loss allocated to Asset 3 is $480 ($640 total disallowed loss on the deemed asset disposition multiplied by the loss allocation fraction, the numerator of which is $1,125, the loss realized on the deemed disposition of Asset 3, and the denominator of which is $1,500, the sum of the losses realized on the deemed disposition of Assets 2 and 3). Accordingly, Old Target recognizes $780 of gain on Asset 1, recognizes $215 of loss on Asset 2 (realized loss of $375 less allocated disallowed loss of $160), and recognizes $645 of loss on Asset 3 (realized loss of $1,125 less allocated disallowed loss of $480) or a recognized net loss of $80 on the deemed asset disposition.

Example 2. (i) *Facts.* The facts are the same as in *Example 1* except that Asset 2 is 100 shares of common stock of Target Subsidiary, a wholly-owned subsidiary of Target. The value of Target Subsidiary common stock on July 1 is $40 per share. Target Subsidiary has two assets, Asset 4 with a basis of $500 and Asset 5 with a basis of $3,000. Target Subsidiary has no liabilities. A section 336(e) election is also made with respect to Target Subsidiary.

(ii) *Consequences—Target.* The ADADP on the deemed sale of Target's assets is determined and allocated in the same manner as in *Example 1.* However, Old Target's loss realized on the deemed sale of Target Subsidiary is disregarded in determining the amount of the disallowed loss on the deemed asset disposition of Old Target's assets. Thus, the realized net loss is only $345 ($780 gain on Asset 1 and $1,125 loss on Asset 3), and the amount of disallowed loss equals $307, the $345 realized net loss multiplied by the disallowed loss fraction with respect to Target stock, $8,000/$9,000. The entire disallowed loss is allocated to Asset 3. Accordingly, Old Target recognizes $780 of gain on Asset 1 and recognizes $818 of loss on Asset 3 (realized loss of $1,125 less allocated disallowed loss of $307) or a recognized net loss of $38 on the deemed asset disposition.

(iii) *Consequences—Target Subsidiary.* Because the deemed sale of Target Subsidiary is not a transaction described in section 355(d)(2) or (e)(2), the tax consequences of the deemed sale of Target Subsidiary are determined under paragraph (b)(1) of this section and not this paragraph (b)(2). The deemed sale of the stock of Target Subsidiary is disregarded and instead Target Subsidiary is deemed to sell all of its assets to an unrelated person. The ADADP on the deemed asset disposition of Target Subsidiary as determined under § 1.336-3 is $3,300. Assume that the ADADP is allocated $900 to Asset 4 and $2,400 to Asset 5 under § 1.336-3. Old Target Subsidiary realized a net loss of $200 on the deemed asset disposition ($400 gain realized on Asset 4 and $600 loss realized on Asset 5). However, because a portion of Target stock was distributed during the 12-month disposition period, for purposes of determining the amount of disallowed loss on the deemed sale of the assets of Target Subsidiary, the portion of the 100 shares of Target Subsidiary stock deemed sold pursuant to the section 336(e) election for Target Subsidiary multiplied by the disallowed loss fraction with respect to Target stock are treated as having been distributed. Thus, for purposes of determining the amount of disallowed loss on the deemed asset disposition of Target Subsidiary's assets, 88.89 shares of Target Subsidiary common stock (100 shares owned by Target multiplied by the disallowed loss fraction with respect to Target stock, $8,000/$9,000) are treated as distributed during the 12-month disposition period. The total amount of disallowed loss with respect to the deemed asset disposition of Target Subsidiary's assets equals $177.78 ($200 net loss realized on the deemed disposition of Assets 4 and 5 multiplied by the disallowed loss fraction with respect to Target Subsidiary, the numerator of which is $3,556, the value on July 1, the disposition date, of the 88.89 shares of Target Subsidiary common stock deemed distributed during the 12-month disposition period (88.89 shares × $40) and the denominator of which is $4,000 (the sum of $444, the value on July 1 of the 11.11 shares of Target Subsidiary common stock deemed sold in the qualified stock disposition pursuant to the section 336(e) election for Target Subsidiary (11.11 shares × $40) and $3,556, the value on July 1 of the 88.89 shares of Target Subsidiary common stock deemed distributed during the 12-month disposition period)). All of the disallowed loss is allocated to Asset 5, the only loss asset. Accordingly, Old Target Subsidiary recognizes $400 of gain on Asset 4 and recognizes $422.22 of loss on Asset 5 (realized loss of $600 less allocated disallowed loss of $177.78) or a recognized net loss of $22.22 on the deemed asset disposition.

(C) *Tiered targets.*—In the case of parent-subsidiary chains of corporations making section 336(e) elections, the deemed asset disposition of a higher-tier subsidiary is considered to precede the deemed asset disposition of a lower-tier subsidiary.

(ii) *Old target—deemed purchase.*—(A) *In general.*—Immediately after the deemed asset disposition described in paragraph (b)(2)(i)(A) of this section, old target is treated as acquiring all of its assets from an unrelated person in a single, separate transaction at the close of the disposition date (but before the distribution described in paragraph (b)(2)(iii)(A) of this section) in exchange for an amount equal to the AGUB as determined under § 1.336-4. Old target allocates the consideration deemed paid in the transaction in the same manner as new target would under § § 1.338-6 and 1.338-7 in order to determine the basis in each of the purchased assets.

(B) *Tiered targets.*—In the case of parent-subsidiary chains of corporations making section 336(e) elections with respect to a qualified stock disposition described, in whole or in part, in section 355(d)(2) or (e)(2), old target's deemed purchase of all its assets is considered to precede the deemed asset disposition of a lower-tier subsidiary.

(C) *Application of section 197(f)(9), section 1091, and other provisions to old target.*—Solely for purposes of section 197(f)(9), section 1091, and any other provision designated in the Internal Revenue Bulletin by the Internal Revenue Service (see § 601.601(d)(2)(ii) of this chapter), old target, in its capacity as seller of assets in the deemed asset disposition described in paragraph (b)(2)(i)(A) of this section, shall be treated as a separate and distinct taxpayer from, and

unrelated to, old target in its capacity as acquirer of assets in the deemed purchase described in paragraph (b)(2)(ii)(A) of this section and for subsequent periods.

(iii) *Seller—distribution of target stock.*—(A) *In general.*—Immediately after old target's deemed purchase of its assets described in paragraph (b)(2)(ii) of this section, seller is treated as distributing the stock of old target actually distributed to its shareholders in the qualified stock disposition. No gain or loss is recognized by seller on the distribution. Additionally, if stock of target is sold, exchanged, or distributed outside of the section 355 transaction but still as part of a qualified stock disposition described, in whole or in part, in section 355(d)(2) or (e)(2), no gain or loss is recognized by seller on such sale, exchange, or distribution.

(B) *Tiered targets.*—In the case of parent-subsidiary chains of corporations making section 336(e) elections with respect to a qualified stock disposition described, in whole or in part, in section 355(d)(2) or (e)(2), the Federal income tax consequences of the section 336(e) election for a subsidiary of target shall be determined under paragraph (b)(1) of this section unless the stock of the subsidiary of target is actually disposed of in a qualified stock disposition described, in whole or in part, in section 355(d)(2) or (e)(2). The deemed liquidation of a lower-tier subsidiary pursuant to paragraph (b)(1)(iii) of this section is considered to precede the deemed liquidation of a higher-tier subsidiary. The deemed liquidation of the highest tier subsidiary of target is considered to precede the distribution of old target stock described in paragraph (b)(2)(iii)(A) of this section.

(iv) *Seller—retention of target stock.*—If seller retains any target stock after the disposition date, seller is treated as having disposed of the old target stock so retained, on the disposition date, in a transaction in which no gain or loss is recognized, and then, on the day after the disposition date, purchasing the stock so retained from an unrelated person for its fair market value. The holding period for the retained stock starts on the day after the disposition date. For purposes of this paragraph (b)(2)(iv), the fair market value of all of the target stock equals the grossed-up amount realized on the sale, exchange, or distribution of recently disposed stock of target (see § 1.336-3(c)).

(v) *Qualification under section 355.*—Old target's deemed sale of all its assets to an unrelated person and old target's deemed purchase of all its assets from an unrelated person will not cause the distribution of old target to fail to satisfy the requirements of section 355. Similarly, any deemed transactions under paragraph (b)(1) or (b)(2) of this section that a subsidiary of target is treated as engaging in will not cause the distribution of old target to fail to satisfy the requirements of section 355. For purposes of applying section 355(a)(1)(D), seller is treated as having disposed of any stock disposed of in the qualified stock disposition on the date seller actually sold, exchanged, or distributed such stock. Further, seller's deemed disposition of retained old target stock under paragraph (b)(2)(iv) of this section is disregarded for purposes of applying section 355(a)(1)(D).

(vi) *Earnings and profits.*—The earnings and profits of seller and target shall be determined pursuant to § 1.312-10 and, if applicable, § 1.1502-33(e). For this purpose, target will not be treated as a newly created controlled corporation and any increase or decrease in target's earnings and profits pursuant to the deemed asset disposition will increase or decrease, as the case may be, target's earnings and profits immediately before the allocation described in § 1.312-10.

(c) *Purchaser.*—Generally, the making of a section 336(e) election will not affect the Federal income tax consequences to which purchaser would have been subject with respect to the acquisition of target stock if a section 336(e) election was not made. Thus, notwithstanding § § 1.336-2(b)(1)(i)(A), 1.336-2(b)(1)(iv), and 1.336-2(b)(2)(iii)(A), purchaser will still be treated as having purchased, received in an exchange, or received in a distribution, the stock of target so acquired on the date actually acquired. However, see section 1223(1)(B) with respect to the holding period for stock acquired pursuant to a distribution qualifying under section 355 (or so much of section 356 that relates to section 355). The Federal income tax consequences of the deemed asset disposition and liquidation of target may affect purchaser's consequences. For example, if seller distributes the stock of target to its shareholders in a qualified stock disposition for which a section 336(e) election is made, any increase in seller's earnings and profits as a result of old target's deemed asset disposition and liquidation into seller may increase the amount of a distribution to the shareholders constituting a dividend under section 301(c)(1).

(d) *Minority shareholders.*—(1) *In general.*—This paragraph (d) describes the treatment of shareholders of old target other than seller, a member of seller's consolidated group, and S corporation shareholders (whether or not they sell or exchange their stock of target). A shareholder to which this paragraph (d) applies is referred to as a minority shareholder.

(2) *Sale, exchange, or distribution of target stock by a minority shareholder.*—A minority shareholder recognizes gain or loss (as permitted under the general principles of tax law) on its sale, exchange, or distribution of target stock.

(3) *Retention of target stock by a minority shareholder.*—A minority shareholder who retains its target stock does not recognize gain or loss under this section with respect to its shares of target stock. The minority shareholder's basis and holding period for that target stock are not affected by the section 336(e) election. Notwithstanding this treatment of the minority shareholder, if a section 336(e) election is made, target will still be treated as disposing of all of its assets in the deemed asset disposition.

(e) *Treatment consistent with an actual asset disposition.*—Except as otherwise provided, no provision in this section shall produce a Federal income tax result under subtitle A of the Internal Revenue Code that would not occur if the parties had actually engaged in the transactions deemed to occur because of this section, taking into account other transactions that actually occurred or are deemed to occur. See §1.338-1(a)(2) regarding the application of other rules of law.

(f) *Treatment of target under other provisions of the Internal Revenue Code.*—The provisions §1.338-1(b) apply with respect to the treatment of new target after a section 336(e) election, treating any reference to section 338 or 338(h)(10) as a reference to section 336(e).

(g) *Special rules.*—(1) *Target as two corporations.*—Although target is a single corporation under corporate law, if a section 336(e) election is made, then, except with respect to a distribution described in section 355(d)(2) or (e)(2) and as provided in §1.338-1(b)(2), two separate corporations, old target and new target, generally are considered to exist for purposes of subtitle A of the Internal Revenue Code.

(2) *Treatment of members of a consolidated group.*—For purposes of §§1.336-1 through 1.336-5, all members of seller's consolidated group are treated as a single seller, regardless of which member or members actually dispose of any stock. Accordingly, any dispositions of stock made by members of the same consolidated group shall be treated as made by one corporation, and any stock owned by members of the same consolidated group and not disposed of will be treated as stock retained by seller.

(3) *International provisions.*—(i) *Source and foreign tax credit.*—The principles of section 338(h)(16) apply to section 336(e) elections for targets with foreign operations to ensure that the source and foreign tax credit limitation are properly determined.

(ii) *Allocation of foreign income taxes.*—(A) *General rule.*—Except as provided in paragraph (g)(3)(ii)(B) of this section, if a section 336(e) election is made for target and target's taxable year under foreign law (if any) does not close at the end of the disposition date, foreign income tax as defined in §1.960-1(b) (other than a withholding tax as defined in section 901(k)(1)(B)) paid or accrued by new target with respect to such foreign taxable year is allocated between old target and new target. If there is more than one section 336(e) election with respect to target during target's foreign taxable year, foreign income tax paid or accrued with respect to that foreign taxable year is allocated among all old targets and new targets. The allocation is made based on the respective portions of the taxable income (as determined under foreign law) for the foreign taxable year that are attributable under the principles of §1.1502-76(b) to the period of existence of each old target and new target during the foreign taxable year.

(B) *Foreign income taxes imposed on partnerships and disregarded entities.*—If a section 336(e) election is made for target and target holds an interest in a disregarded entity (as described in §301.7701-2(c)(2)(i) of this chapter) or partnership, the rules of §1.901-2(f)(4) and (5) apply to determine the person who is considered for Federal income tax purposes to pay foreign income tax imposed at the entity level on the income of the disregarded entity or partnership.

(iii) *Disallowance of foreign tax credits under section 901(m).*—For rules that may apply to disallow foreign tax credits by reason of a section 336(e) election, see section 901(m) and §§1.901(m)-1 through 1.901(m)-8.

(h) *Making the section 336(e) election.*—(1) *Consolidated group.*—If seller(s) and target are members of the same consolidated group, a section 336(e) election is made by completing the following requirements:

(i) Seller(s) and target must enter into a written, binding agreement, on or before the due date (including extensions) of the consolidated group's consolidated Federal income tax return for the taxable year that includes the disposition date, to make a section 336(e) election;

(ii) The common parent of the consolidated group must retain a copy of the written agreement;

(iii) The common parent of the consolidated group must attach the section 336(e) election statement, described in paragraphs (h)(5) and (6) of this section, to the group's timely filed (including extensions) consolidated Federal income tax return for the taxable year that includes the disposition date; and

(iv) The common parent of the consolidated group must provide a copy of the section 336(e) election statement to target on or before the due date (including extensions) of the consolidated group's consolidated Federal income tax return.

(2) *Non-consolidated/non-S corporation target.*—If target is neither a member of the same consolidated group as seller nor an S corporation, a section 336(e) election is made by completing the following requirements:

(i) Seller and target must enter into a written, binding agreement, on or before the due date (including extensions) of seller's or target's Federal income tax return for the taxable year that includes the disposition date, whichever is earlier, to make a section 336(e) election;

(ii) Seller and target each must retain a copy of the written agreement; and

(iii) Seller and target each must attach the section 336(e) election statement, described in paragraphs (h)(5) and (6) of this section, to its timely filed (including extensions) Federal income tax return for the taxable year that includes the disposition date. However, seller's section 336(e) election statement may disregard paragraph (h)(6)(xii) of this section (concerning a gain recognition election).

(3) *S corporation target.*—A section 336(e) election for an S corporation target is made by completing the following requirements:

(i) All of the S corporation shareholders, including those who do not dispose of any stock in the qualified stock disposition, and the S corporation target must enter into a written, binding agreement, on or before the due date (including extensions) of the Federal income tax return of the S corporation target for the taxable year that includes the disposition date, to make a section 336(e) election;

(ii) S corporation target must retain a copy of the written agreement; and

(iii) S corporation target must attach the section 336(e) election statement, described in paragraphs (h)(5) and (6) of this section, to its timely filed (including extensions) Federal income tax return for the taxable year that includes the disposition date.

(4) *Tiered targets.*—In the case of parent-subsidiary chains of corporations making section 336(e) elections, in order to make a section 336(e) election for a lowertier target (target subsidiary), the requirements described in paragraph (h)(1) or (h)(2),of this section, whichever is applicable to the qualified stock disposition of target subsidiary, must be satisfied. The written agreement described in paragraph (h)(1) or (h)(2) of this section for the section 336(e) election with respect to target subsidiary may be either a separate written agreement between target subsidiary and the corporation deemed to dispose of the stock of target subsidiary or may be included in the written agreement between seller(s) (or the S corporation shareholders) and target.

(5) *Section 336(e) election statement.*—(i) *In general.*—The section 336(e) election statement must be entitled "THIS IS AN ELECTION UNDER SECTION 336(e) TO TREAT THE DISPOSITION OF THE STOCK OF [insert name and employer identification number of target] AS A DEEMED SALE OF SUCH CORPORATION'S ASSETS." The section 336(e) election statement must include the information described in paragraph (h)(6) of this section. The relevant information for each S corporation shareholder and, notwithstanding paragraph (g)(2) of this section, each consolidated group member that disposes of or retains target stock must be set forth individually, not in the aggregate.

(ii) *Target subsidiaries.*—In the case of a section 336(e) election for a target subsidiary, a separate statement must be filed for each target subsidiary. In preparing the section 336(e) election statement with respect to a target subsidiary, any reference to seller in paragraph (h)(6) of this section should be considered a reference to the corporation deemed to dispose of the stock of the target subsidiary and any reference to target in paragraphs (h)(5)(i) and (h)(6) of this section should be considered a reference to the target subsidiary.

(6) *Contents of section 336(e) election statement.*—The section 336(e) election statement must include:

(i) The name, address, taxpayer identifying number (TIN), taxable year, and state of incorporation (if any) of the seller(s) or the S corporation shareholder(s);

(ii) The name, address, employer identification number (EIN), taxable year, and state of incorporation of the common parent, if any, of seller(s);

(iii) The name, address, EIN, taxable year, and state of incorporation of target;

(iv) The name, address, TIN, taxable year, and state of incorporation (if any) of any 80-percent purchaser;

(v) The name, address, TIN, taxable year, and state of incorporation (if any) of any purchaser that holds nonrecently disposed stock within the meaning of §1.336-1(b)(18);

(vi) The disposition date;

(vii) The percentage of target stock that was disposed of by each seller or S corporation shareholder in the qualified stock disposition;

(viii) The percentage of target stock that was disposed of by each seller or S corporation shareholder in the qualified stock disposition on or before the disposition date;

(ix) A statement regarding whether target realized a net loss on the deemed asset disposition;

(x) If target realized a net loss on the deemed asset disposition, a statement regarding whether any stock of target or that of any higher-tier corporation up through the highest-tier corporation for which a section 336(e) election was made by any seller(s) or S corporation shareholder(s) was distributed during the 12-month disposition period. If so, also provide a statement regarding whether any stock of target or that of any higher-tier corporation up through the highest-tier corporation for which a section 336(e) election was made was actually sold or exchanged (rather than deemed sold in a deemed asset disposition) by any seller(s) or S corporation shareholder(s) in a qualified stock disposition;

(xi) The percentage of target stock that was retained by each seller or S corporation shareholder after the disposition date;

(xii) The name, address, and TIN of any purchaser that made a gain recognition election pursuant to §1.336-4(c). A copy of the gain recognition election statement must be retained by the filer of the section 336(e) election statement designated as the appropriate party in §1.336-4(c)(3); and

(xiii) A statement that each of the seller(s) or S corporation shareholder(s) (as applicable) and target have executed a written, binding agreement to make a section 336(e) election.

(7) *Asset Allocation Statement.*—Old target and new target must report information concerning the deemed sale of target's assets on Form 8883, "Asset Allocation Statement Under Section 338," (making appropriate adjustments to report the results of the section 336(e) election), or on any successor form prescribed by the Internal Revenue Service, in accordance with forms, instructions, or other appropriate guidance provided by the Internal Revenue Service. In addition, in the case of a section 336(e) election as the result of a transaction described in section 355(d)(2) or (e)(2), old target should file two Forms 8883, (or successor forms), one in its capacity as the seller of the assets in the deemed asset disposition described in paragraph (b)(2)(i) of this section and one in its capacity as the purchaser of the assets in the deemed purchase described in paragraph (b)(2)(ii) of this section.

(8) *Examples.*—The following examples illustrate the provisions of paragraph (h) of this section.

Example 1. (i) *Facts.* Seller owns all of the stock of Target and Target owns all of the stock of Target Subsidiary. Seller is the common parent of a consolidated group that includes Target. However, Target Subsidiary is not included in the consolidated group pursuant to section 1504(a)(3). On Date 1, Seller sells 80 percent of its Target stock to A and distributes the remaining 20 percent of Target stock to Seller's unrelated shareholders.

(ii) *Making of election for Target.* Because Seller and Target are members of a consolidated group, in order to make a section 336(e) election for the qualified stock disposition of Target, the requirements of paragraph (h)(1) of this section must be satisfied. On or before the due date of Seller group's consolidated Federal income tax return that includes Date 1, Seller and Target must enter into a written, binding agreement to make a section 336(e) election; Seller must retain a copy of the written agreement; Seller must attach the section 336(e) election statement to the group's timely filed consolidated return for the taxable year that includes Date 1, and Seller must provide a copy of the section 336(e) election statement to Target on or *before the due date (including extensions) of the consolidated return.*

(iii) *Making of election for Target Subsidiary.* Because Target and Target Subsidiary do not join in the filing of a consolidated Federal income tax return and Target Subsidiary is not an S corporation, in order to make a section 336(e) election for the qualified stock disposi-

tion of Target Subsidiary, the requirements of paragraph (h)(2) of this section must be satisfied. On or before the due date of Seller group's consolidated Federal income tax return that includes Date 1, or Target Subsidiary's Federal income tax return that includes Date 1, whichever is earlier, either Target Subsidiary must join in the written agreement described in paragraph (ii) of this *Example 1* to make a section 336(e) election with respect to the qualified stock disposition of Target Subsidiary or Target and Target Subsidiary must enter into a separate written, binding agreement to make a section 336(e) election with respect to the qualified stock disposition of Target Subsidiary; Seller (as agent of the consolidated group that includes Target) and Target Subsidiary each must retain a copy of the written agreement; and Seller (as agent of the consolidated group that includes Target) and Target Subsidiary each must attach the section 336(e) election statement with respect to the qualified stock disposition of Target Subsidiary to its timely filed Federal income tax return for the taxable year that includes Date 1. In preparing the section 336(e) election statement, paragraph (i) of the statement should include the relevant information for Target, paragraph (ii) of the statement should include the relevant information for Seller, paragraph (iii) of the statement should include the relevant information for Target Subsidiary, paragraphs (vii) through (xi) of the statement should provide information for both Seller's actual sale and distribution of Target stock as well as information for Target's deemed sale of Target Subsidiary stock, and paragraph (xiii) of the statement should include a statement that Seller, Target, and Target Subsidiary, or Target and Target Subsidiary, whichever is appropriate, have executed a written, binding agreement to make a section 336(e) election with respect to the qualified stock disposition of Target Subsidiary.

Example 2. (i) *Facts.* A and B each own 45 percent and C owns the remaining 10 percent of the stock of S Corporation Target, an S corporation. S Corporation Target owns 80 percent of the stock of Target Subsidiary and D owns the remaining 20 percent. On Date 1, A and B each sell all of their S Corporation Target stock to an unrelated individual. C retains his 10 percent of the stock of S Corporation Target.

(ii) *Making of election for S Corporation Target.* Because S Corporation Target is an S Corporation Target, in order to make a section 336(e) election for the qualified stock disposition of S Corporation Target, the requirements of paragraph (h)(3) of this section must be satisfied. On or before the due date of S Corporation Target's Federal income tax return that includes Date 1, A, B, C, and S Corporation Target must enter into a written, binding agreement to make a section 336(e) election; S Corporation Target must retain a copy of the written agreement; and S Corporation Target must attach the section 336(e) election statement to its timely filed Federal income tax return for the taxable year that includes Date 1.

(iii) *Making of election for Target Subsidiary.* Because Target Subsidiary is neither a member of the same consolidated group as S Corporation Target nor is an S corporation, in order to make a section 336(e) election for the qualified stock disposition of Target Subsidiary, the requirements of paragraph (h)(2) of this section must be satisfied. On or before the due date of S Corporation Target's Federal income tax return that includes Date 1, or Target Subsidiary's Federal income tax return that includes Date 1, whichever is earlier, either Target Subsidiary must join in the written agreement described in paragraph (ii) of this *Example 2* to make a section 336(e) election with respect to the qualified stock disposition of Target Subsidiary or S Corporation Target and Target Subsidiary must enter into a separate written, binding agreement to make a section 336(e) election with respect to the qualified stock disposition of Target Subsidiary; S Corporation Target and Target Subsidiary each must retain a copy of the written agreement; and S Corporation Target and Target Subsidiary each must attach the section 336(e) election statement to its timely filed Federal income tax return for the taxable year that includes Date 1. In preparing the section 336(e) election statement, paragraph (i) of the statement should include the relevant information for S Corporation Target, paragraph (iii) of the statement should include the relevant information for Target Subsidiary, paragraphs (vii) through (xi) of the statement should provide information for both A's and B's actual sale and C's actual retention of S Corporation Target stock as well as information for S Corporation Target's deemed sale of Target Subsidiary stock, and paragraph (xiii) of the statement should include a statement that A, B, C, S Corporation Target, and Target Subsidiary, or S Corporation Target and Target Subsidiary, whichever is appropriate, have executed a written, binding agreement to make a section 336(e) election with respect to the qualified stock disposition of Target Subsidiary.

(i) [Reserved]

(j) *Protective section 336(e) election.*—Taxpayers may make a protective election under section 336(e) in connection with a transaction. Such an election will have no effect if the transaction does not constitute a qualified stock disposition, as defined in §1.336-1(b)(6), but will otherwise be binding and irrevocable.

(k) *Examples.*—The following examples illustrate the provisions of this section.

Example 1. Sale of 100 percent of Target stock. (i) *Facts.* Parent owns all 100 shares of Target's only class of stock. Target's only assets are two parcels of land. Parcel 1 has a basis of $5,000 and Parcel 2 has a basis of $4,000. Target has no liabilities. On July 1 of Year 1, Parent sells all 100 shares of Target stock to A for $100 per share. Parent incurs no selling costs and A incurs no acquisition costs. On July 1, the value of Parcel 1 is $7,000 and the value of Parcel 2 is $3,000. A section 336(e) election is made.

(ii) *Consequences.* The sale of Target stock constitutes a qualified stock disposition. July 1 of Year 1 is the disposition date. Accordingly, pursuant to the section 336(e) election, for Federal income tax purposes, rather than treating Parent as selling the stock of Target to A, the following events are deemed to occur. Target is treated as if, on July 1, it sold all of its assets to an unrelated person in exchange for the ADADP of $10,000, which is allocated $7,000 to Parcel 1 and $3,000 to Parcel 2 (see §§ 1.336-3 and 1.338-6 for determination of amount and allocation of ADADP). Target recognizes gain of $2,000 on Parcel 1 and loss of $1,000 on Parcel 2. New Target is then treated as acquiring all its assets from an unrelated person in a single transaction in exchange for the amount of the AGUB of $10,000, which is allocated $7,000 to Parcel 1 and $3,000 to Parcel 2 (see §§ 1.336-4, 1.338-5, and 1.338-6 for determination of amount and allocation of AGUB). Old Target is treated as liquidating into Parent immediately thereafter, distributing the $10,000 deemed received in exchange for Parcel 1 and Parcel 2 in a transaction qualifying under section 332. Parent recognizes no gain or loss on the liquidation. A's basis in New Target stock is $100 per share, the amount paid for the stock.

Example 2. Sale of 80 percent of Target stock. (i) *Facts.* The facts are the same as in Example 1 except that Parent only sells 80 shares of its Target stock to A and retains the other 20 shares.

(ii) *Consequences.* The results are the same as in *Example 1* except that Parent also is treated as purchasing from an unrelated person on July 2, the day after the disposition date, the 20 shares of Target stock (New Target stock) not sold to A, for their fair market value as determined under § 1.336-2(b)(1)(v) of $2,000 ($100 per share).

Example 3. Distribution of 100 percent of Target stock. (i) *Facts.* The facts are the same as in *Example 1* except that instead of on July 1 Parent selling 100 shares of Target stock to A, Parent distributes 100 shares to its shareholders, all of whom are unrelated to Parent, in a transaction that does not qualify under section 355. The value of Target stock on July 1 is $100 per share.

(ii) *Consequences.* The distribution of Target stock constitutes a qualified stock disposition. July 1 of Year 1 is the disposition date. Accordingly, pursuant to the section 336(e) election, for Federal income tax purposes, rather than treating Parent as distributing the stock of Target to its shareholders, the following events are deemed to occur. Target is treated as if, on July 1, it sold all of its assets to an unrelated person in exchange for the ADADP of $10,000, which is allocated $7,000 to Parcel 1 and $3,000 to Parcel 2 (see §§ 1.336-3 and 1.338-6 for determination of amount and allocation of ADADP). Target recognizes gain of $2,000 on Parcel 1 and loss of $1,000 on Parcel 2. Because Target's losses realized on the deemed asset disposition do not exceed Target's gains realized on the deemed asset disposition, Target can recognize all of the losses from the deemed asset disposition (see § 1.336-2(b)(1)(i)(B)). New Target is then treated as acquiring all its assets from an unrelated person in a single transaction in exchange for the amount of the AGUB of $10,000, which is allocated $7,000 to Parcel 1 and $3,000 to Parcel 2 (see §§ 1.336-4, 1.338-5, and 1.338-6 for determination of amount and allocation of AGUB). Old Target is treated as liquidating into Parent immediately thereafter, distributing the $10,000 deemed received in exchange for Parcel 1 and Parcel 2 in a transaction qualifying under section 332. Parent recognizes no gain or loss on the liquidation. On July 1, immediately after the deemed liquidation of Target, Parent is deemed to purchase from an unrelated person 100 shares of New Target stock and distribute those New Target shares to its shareholders. Parent recognizes no gain or loss on the deemed distribution of the shares under § 1.336-2(b)(1)(iv). The shareholders receive New Target stock as a distribution pursuant to section 301 and their basis in New Target stock received is its fair market value pursuant to section 301(d).

Example 4. Distribution of 80 percent of Target stock. (i) *Facts.* The facts are the same as in *Example 3* except that Parent distributes only 80 shares of Target stock to its shareholders and retains the other 20 shares.

(ii) *Consequences.* The results are the same as in *Example 3* except that Parent is treated as purchasing on July 1 only 80 shares of New Target stock and as distributing only 80 shares of New Target stock to its shareholders and then as purchasing (and retaining) on July 2, the day after the disposition date, 20 shares of New Target stock at their fair market value as determined under § 1.336-2(b)(1)(v), $2,000 ($100 per share).

Example 5. Part sale, part distribution. (i) *Facts.* Parent owns all 100 shares of Target's only class of stock. Target has two assets, both of which are buildings used in its business. Building 1 has a basis of $6,000 and Building 2 has a basis of $5,100. Target has no liabilities. On January 1 of Year 1, Parent sells 50 shares of Target to A for $88 per share. Parent incurred no selling costs with respect to the sale of Target stock and A incurred no acquisition costs with respect to the purchase. On July 1 of Year 1, when the value of Target stock is $120 per share, Parent distributes 30 shares of Target to Parent's unrelated shareholders. Parent retains the remaining 20 shares. On July 1, the value of Building 1 is $7,800 and the value of Building 2 is $4,200. A section 336(e) election is made.

(ii) *Consequences.* Because the sale of the 50 shares and the distribution of the 30 shares occurred within a 12-month disposition period, the 80 shares of Target stock sold and distributed were disposed of in a qualified stock disposition. July 1 of Year 1 is the disposition date. On July 1, Target is treated as if it sold its assets to an unrelated person in exchange for the ADADP, $10,000 ($8,000 ((50 shares × $88) + (30 shares × $120)) / .80 ($9,600 (80 shares × $120) / $12,000 (100 shares × $120))), which is allocated to Buildings 1 and 2 in proportion to their fair market values, $6,500 to Building 1 and $3,500 to Building 2 (see §§ 1.336-3 and 1.338-6 for determination of amount and allocation of ADADP). Target realizes a gain of $500 on the deemed sale of Building 1 ($6,500 - $6,000). Target realizes a loss of $1,600 on the deemed sale of Building 2 ($3,500 - $5,100). Target recognizes all of its gains on the deemed asset disposition. However, because 30 shares of Target stock were distributed during the 12-month disposition period and there was a net loss of $1,100 realized on the deemed disposition of Buildings 1 and 2, $413 of the loss on the deemed sale is disallowed (see § 1.336-2(b)(1)(i)(B)(2) for the determination of the disallowed loss amount). New Target is then treated as acquiring all its assets from an unrelated person in a single transaction in exchange for the amount of the AGUB, $10,000 ($8,000 ((50 shares × $88) + (30 shares × $120)) × 1.25 ((100 - 0) / 80)), which is allocated to Buildings 1 and 2 in proportion to their fair market values, $6,500 to Building 1 and $3,500 to Building 2 (see §§ 1.336-4, 1.338-5, and 1.338-6 for determination of amount and allocation of AGUB). Old Target is treated as liquidating into Parent immediately after the deemed asset disposition, distributing the $10,000 deemed received in exchange for its assets in a transaction qualifying under section 332. Parent recognizes no gain or loss on the liquidation. Parent is then deemed to purchase 30 shares of New Target stock from an unrelated person on July 1, and to distribute those 30 New Target shares to its shareholders. Parent recognizes no gain or loss on the deemed distribution of the 30 shares under § 1.336-2(b)(1)(iv). Parent is then deemed to purchase (and retain) on July 2, the day after the disposition date, 20 shares of New Target stock at their fair market value as determined under § 1.336-2(b)(1)(v), $2,000 ($100 per share(20 shares multiplied by $100 fair market value per share ($10,000 grossed-up amount realized on the sale and distribution of 80 shares of target stock divided by 100 shares)). A is treated as having purchased the 50 shares of New Target stock on January 1 of Year 1 at a cost of $88 per share, the same as if no section 336(e) election had been made. Parent's shareholders are treated as receiving New Target stock on July 1 of Year 1 as a distribution pursuant to section 301 and their basis in New Target stock received is $120 per share, its fair market value, pursuant to section 301(d), the same as if no section 336(e) election had been made.

Example 6. Sale of Target stock by consolidated group members. (i) *Facts.* Parent owns all of the stock of Sub and 50 of the 100 outstanding shares of Target stock. Sub owns the remaining 50 shares of Target stock. Target's assets have an aggregate basis of $9,000. Target has no liabilities. Parent, Sub, and Target file a consolidated Federal income tax return. On February 1 of Year 1, Parent sells 30 shares of its Target stock to A for $2,400. On March 1 of Year 1, Sub sells all 50 shares of its Target stock to B for $5,600. Neither Parent nor Sub incurred any selling costs. Neither A nor B incurred any acquisition costs. A section 336(e) election is made.

(ii) *Consequences.* Because Parent and Sub are members of the same consolidated group, their sale of Target stock is treated as made by one seller (see paragraph (g)(2) of this section), and the sales of Target stock constitute a qualified stock disposition. March 1 of Year 1 is the disposition date. For Federal income tax purposes, Parent and Sub are not treated as selling the stock of Target to A and B, respectively. Instead, the following events are deemed to occur. Old Target is treated as if, on March 1, it sold all its assets to unrelated person in exchange for the ADADP, $10,000 (see § 1.336-3 for determination of ADADP), recognizing a net gain of $1,000. New Target is then treated as acquiring all its assets from an unrelated person in a single transaction in exchange for the amount of the AGUB, $10,000 (see §§ 1.336-4 and 1.338-5 for the determination of AGUB). Old Target is treated as liquidating into Parent and Sub immediately thereafter, distributing the $10,000 deemed received in exchange for its assets in a transaction qualifying under section 332 (see §1.1502-34). Neither Parent nor Sub recognizes gain or loss on the liquidation. Parent is then treated as purchasing from an unrelated person on March 2, the day after the disposition date, the 20 shares of Target stock (New Target stock) retained for their fair market value as determined under §1.336-2(b)(1)(v), $2,000 ($100 per share). A is treated as having purchased 30 shares of New Target stock on February 1 of Year 1 at a cost of $2,400 ($80 per share), the same as if no section 336(e) election had been made. B is treated as having purchased 50 shares of New Target stock on March 1 of Year 1 at a cost of $5,600 ($112 per share), the same as if no section 336(e) election had been made.

Example 7. Sale of Target stock by non-consolidated group members. (i) *Facts.* The facts are the same as in *Example 6* except that Parent, Sub, and Target do not join in the filing of a consolidated Federal income tax return.

.(ii) *Consequences.* Because Parent and Sub do not join in the filing of a consolidated Federal income tax return and no single seller sells, exchanges, or distributes Target stock meeting the requirements of section 1504(a)(2), the transaction does not constitute a qualified stock disposition. The section 336(e) election made with respect to the disposition of Target stock has no effect.

Example 8. Distribution of 80 percent of Target stock in complete redemption of a greater-than-50-percent shareholder. (i) *Facts.* A and B own 51 and 49 shares, respectively, of Seller's only class of stock. Seller owns all 100 shares of Target's only class of stock. Seller distributes 80 shares of Target stock to A in complete redemption of A's 51 shares of Seller in a transaction that does not qualify under section 355. A section 336(e) election is made.

(ii) *Consequences.* Prior to the redemption, Seller and A would be related persons because, under section 318(a)(2)(C), any stock of a corporation that is owned by Seller would be attributed to A because A owns 50 percent or more of the value of the stock of Seller. However, for purposes of §§1.336-1 through 1.336-5, the determination of whether Seller and A are related is made immediately after the redemption of A's stock. See §§1.336-1(b)(5)(iii) and 1.338-3(b)(3)(ii)(A). After the redemption, A no longer owns any stock of Seller. Accordingly, A and Seller are not related persons, as defined in §1.336-1(b)(12), and the distribution of Target stock constitutes a qualified stock disposition. For Federal income tax purposes, rather than Seller distributing the stock of Target to A, the following is deemed to occur. Old Target is treated as if it sold its assets to an unrelated person. New Target is then treated as acquiring all its assets from an unrelated person in a single transaction. Immediately thereafter, Old Target is treated as liquidating into Seller in a transaction qualifying under section 332. Seller recognizes no gain or loss on the liquidation. Seller is then treated as purchasing 80 shares of New Target stock from an unrelated person and then distributing the 80 shares of New Target stock to A in exchange for A's 51 shares of Seller stock. Seller recognizes no gain or loss on the distribution of New Target stock pursuant to §1.336-2(b)(1)(iv). Seller is then treated as purchasing from an unrelated person on the day after the disposition date the 20 shares of Target stock (New Target stock) retained for their fair market value as determined under §1.336-2(b)(1)(v). The Federal income tax consequences to A are the same as if no section 336(e) election had been made.

Example 9. Pro-rata distribution of 80 percent of Target stock. (i) *Facts.* A and B own 60 and 40 shares, respectively, of Seller's only class of stock. Seller owns all 100 shares of Target's only class of stock. Seller distributes 48 shares of Target stock to A and 32 shares of Target stock to B in a transaction that does not qualify under section 355. A section 336(e) election is made.

(ii) *Consequences.* Any stock of a corporation that is owned by Seller would be attributed to A under section 318(a)(2)(C) because, after the distribution, A owns 50 percent or more of the value of the stock of Seller. Therefore, after the distribution, A and Seller are related persons, as defined in §1.336-1(b)(12), and the distribution of Target stock to A is not a disposition. Because only 32 percent of Target stock was sold, exchanged, or distributed to unrelated persons, there has not been a qualified stock disposition. Accordingly, the section 336(e) election made with respect to the distribution of Target stock has no effect. [Reg. §1.336-2.]

☐ [*T.D. 9619, 5-10-2013 (corrected 8-27-2013). Amended by T.D. 9959, 12-28-2021.*]

[Reg. §1.336-3]

§1.336-3. Aggregate deemed asset disposition price; various aspects of taxation of the deemed asset disposition.—(a) *Scope.*—This section provides rules under section 336(e) to determine the aggregate deemed asset disposition price (ADADP) for target. ADADP is the amount for which old target is deemed to have sold all of its assets in the deemed asset disposition. ADADP is allocated among target's assets in the same manner as the aggregate deemed sale price (ADSP) is allocated under §1.338-6 to determine the amount for which each asset is deemed to have been sold. If a subsequent

increase or decrease is required under general principles of tax law with respect to an element of ADADP, the redetermined ADADP is allocated among target's assets in the same manner as redetermined ADSP is allocated under §1.338-7.

(b) *Determination of ADADP.*—(1) *General rule.*—ADADP is the sum of—

    (i) The grossed-up amount realized on the sale, exchange, or distribution of recently disposed stock of target; and

    (ii) The liabilities of old target.

(2) *Time and amount of ADADP.*—(i) *Original determination.*—ADADP is initially determined at the beginning of the day after the disposition date of target. General principles of tax law apply in determining the timing and amount of the elements of ADADP.

(ii) *Redetermination of ADADP.*—ADADP is redetermined at such time and in such amount as an increase or decrease would be required, under general principles of tax law, for the elements of ADADP. For example, ADADP is redetermined because of an increase or decrease in the amount realized on the sale or exchange of recently disposed stock of target or because liabilities not originally taken into account in determining ADADP are subsequently taken into account. Increases or decreases with respect to the elements of ADADP result in the reallocation of ADADP among target's assets in the same manner as ADSP under §1.338-7.

(c) *Grossed-up amount realized on the disposition of recently disposed stock of target.*—(1) *Determination of amount.*—The grossed-up amount realized on the disposition of recently disposed stock of target is an amount equal to—

    (i) The sum of —

    (A) With respect to recently disposed of stock of target that is not distributed in the qualified stock disposition, the amount realized on the sale or exchange of such recently disposed stock of target, determined as if seller or S corporation shareholders were required to use old target's accounting methods and characteristics and the installment method were not available and determined without regard to the selling costs taken into account under paragraph (c)(1)(iii) of this section, and

    (B) With respect to recently disposed of stock of target that is distributed in the qualified stock disposition, the fair market value of such recently disposed stock of target determined on the date of each distribution;

    (ii) Divided by the percentage of target stock (by value, determined on the disposition date) attributable to the recently disposed stock;

    (iii) Less the selling costs incurred by seller or S corporation shareholders in connection with the sale or exchange of recently disposed stock that reduce its amount realized on the sale or exchange of the stock (for example, brokerage commissions and any similar costs to sell the stock).

(2) *Example.*—The following example illustrates this paragraph (c):

Example. Target has two classes of stock outstanding, voting common stock and preferred stock described in section 1504(a)(4). Seller owns all 100 shares of each class of stock. On March 1 of Year 1, Seller sells 10 shares of Target voting common stock to A for $75. On April 1 of Year 2, Seller distributes 15 shares of Target voting common stock with a fair market value of $120 to B. On May 1 of Year 2, Seller distributes 10 shares of Target voting common stock with a fair market value of $110 to C. On July 1 of Year 2, Seller sells 55 shares of Target voting common stock to D for $550. On July 1 of Year 2, the fair market value of all the Target voting common stock is $1,000 ($10 per share) and the fair market value of all the preferred stock is $600 ($6 per share). Seller incurs $20 of selling costs with respect to the sale to A and $60 of selling costs with respect to the sale to D. The grossed-up amount realized on the sale, exchange, or distribution of recently disposed stock of Target is calculated as follows: The sum of the amount realized on the sale or exchange of recently disposed stock sold or exchanged (without regard to selling costs) and the fair market value of the recently disposed stock distributed is $780 ($120 + $110 + $550) (the 10 shares sold to A on March 1 of Year 1 is not recently disposed stock because it was not disposed of during the 12-month disposition period). The percentage of Target stock by value on the disposition date attributable to recently disposed stock equals 50% ($800 (80 shares of recently disposed stock × $10, the fair market value of each share of Target common stock on the disposition date) / $1,600 ($1,000 (the total value of Target's common stock on the disposition date) + $600 (the total value of Target's preferred stock on the disposition date))). The grossed-up amount realized equals $1,500 (($780/.50) - $60 selling costs).

(d) *Liabilities of old target.*—(1) *In general.*—In general, the liabilities of old target are measured as of the beginning of the day after the disposition date. However, if a target for which a section 336(e) election is made engages in a transaction outside the ordinary course of business on the disposition date after the event resulting in the qualified stock disposition of target or a higher-tier corporation, target and all persons related thereto (either before or after the qualified stock disposition) under section 267(b) or section 707 must treat the transaction for all Federal income tax purposes as occurring at the beginning of the day following the transaction and after the deemed disposition by old target. In order to be taken into account in ADADP, a liability must be a liability of target that is properly taken into account in amount realized under general principles of tax law that would apply if old target had sold its assets to an unrelated person for consideration that included the discharge of its liabilities. See §1.1001-2(a). Such liabilities may include liabilities for the tax consequences resulting from the deemed asset disposition.

(2) *Time and amount of liabilities.*—The time for taking into account liabilities of old target in determining ADADP and the amount of the liabilities taken into account is determined as if old target had sold its assets to an unrelated person for consideration that included the discharge of the liabilities by the unrelated person. For example, if no amount of a target liability is properly taken into account in amount realized as of the beginning of the day after the disposition date, the liability is not initially taken into account in determining ADADP, but it may be taken into account at some later date.

(e) *Deemed disposition tax consequences.*—Gain or loss on each asset in the deemed asset disposition is computed by reference to the ADADP allocated to that asset. ADADP is allocated in the same manner as is ADSP under §1.338-6. Although deemed disposition tax consequences may increase or decrease ADADP by creating or reducing a tax liability, the amount of the tax liability itself may be a function of the size of the deemed disposition tax consequences. Thus, these determinations may require trial and error computations.

(f) *Other rules apply in determining ADADP.*—ADADP may not be applied in such a way as to contravene other applicable rules. For example, a capital loss cannot be applied to reduce ordinary income in calculating the tax liability on the deemed asset disposition for purposes of determining ADADP.

(g) *Examples.*—The following examples illustrate this section.

Example 1. (i) *Facts.* The facts are the same as in *Example 1* of §1.336-2(b)(1)(i)(B)(3), that is, Parent owns 60 of the 100 outstanding shares of the common stock of Seller, Seller's only class of stock outstanding. The remaining 40 shares of the common stock of Seller are held by shareholders unrelated to Seller or each other. Seller owns 95 of the 100 outstanding shares of Target common stock, and all 100 shares of Target preferred stock that is described in section 1504(a)(4). The remaining 5 shares of Target common stock are owned by A. On January 1 of Year 1, Seller sells 72 shares of Target common stock to B for $3,520. On July 1 of Year 1, Seller distributes 12 shares of Target common stock to Parent and 8 shares to its unrelated shareholders in a distribution described in section 301. Seller retains 3 shares of Target common stock and all 100 shares of Target preferred stock immediately after July 1. The value of Target common stock on July 1 is $60 per share. The value of Target preferred stock on July 1 is $36 per share. Target has three assets, Asset 1, a Class IV asset, with a basis of $1,776 and a fair market value of $2,000, Asset 2, a Class V asset, with a basis of $2,600 and a fair market value of $2,750, and Asset 3, a Class V asset, with a basis of $3,900 and a fair market value of $3,850. Seller incurred no selling costs on the sale of the 72 shares of Target common stock to B. Target has no liabilities. A section 336(e) election is made.

(ii) *Determination of ADADP.* The ADADP on the deemed asset disposition of Target is determined as follows. The grossed-up amount realized on the sale, exchange, or distribution of recently disposed stock of Target is $8,000, the sum of $3,520, the amount realized on the sale to B of the 72 shares of Target common stock and $480, the fair market value on the date distributed of the 8 shares of Target common stock distributed to Seller's unrelated shareholders in the qualified stock disposition, divided by .50, the percentage of Target stock by value, determined on the disposition date, attributable to the recently disposed stock ($4,800 (80 shares of Target common stock disposed of in the qualified stock disposition × $60, the value of a share of Target common stock on the disposition date) divided by $9,600 ((100, the total number of shares of Target common stock × $60, the value of a share of Target common stock on the disposition date) + (100, the total number of shares of Target preferred stock × $36, the value of a share of Target preferred stock on the disposition date))), minus $0, Seller's selling costs in connection with the sale of the 72 shares of Target common stock sold to B. The $8,000 grossed-up amount realized on the sale, exchange, or distribution of recently disposed stock of Target is then added to the liabilities of Old Target, $0, to arrive at the ADADP, $8,000.

(iii) *Allocation of ADADP.* The ADADP of $8,000 is allocated first to Asset 1, the Class IV asset, but not in excess of Asset 1's fair market value, $2,000. The remaining ADADP of $6,000 is allocated between Assets 2 and 3, both Class V assets, in proportion to their fair market values, but not in excess of their fair market values. Because the total fair market value of Assets 2 and 3, $6,600, exceeds the ADADP remaining after allocation of a portion of the ADADP to Asset 1, the $6,000 remaining ADADP is allocated to Assets 2 and 3 in proportion to their respective fair market values. Accordingly, $2,500 is allocated to Asset 2 ($6,000 × ($2,750/($2,750 + $3,850))) and $3,500 is allocated to Asset 3 ($6,000 × ($3,850/($2,750 + $3,850))).

Example 2. (i) *Facts.* The facts are the same as in *Example 1* except that Asset 2 is the stock of Target Subsidiary, a corporation of which Target owns 100 of the 110 shares of common stock, the only outstanding class of Target Subsidiary stock. The remaining 10 shares of Target Subsidiary stock are owned by D. The value of Target Subsidiary stock on July 1 is $27.50 per share. Target Subsidiary has two assets, Asset 4, a Class IV asset, with a basis of $800 and a fair market value of $1,000, and Asset 5, a Class IV asset, with a basis of $2,200 and a fair market value of $2,025. Target Subsidiary has no liabilities. A section 336(e) election with respect to Target Subsidiary is also made.

(ii) *Determination of ADADP.* The ADADP on the deemed asset disposition of Target Subsidiary is determined as follows. The grossed-up amount realized on the sale, exchange, or distribution of recently disposed stock of Target Subsidiary is $2,750, ($2,500 ADADP allocable to Asset 2, the 100 shares of the stock of Target Subsidiary owned by Target, divided by .909, the percentage of Target Subsidiary stock by value, determined on the disposition date, attributable to the recently disposed stock ($2,750 (100 shares of the stock of Target Subsidiary deemed disposed in the qualified stock disposition × $27.50, the value of a share of Target Subsidiary stock on the disposition date) divided by $3,025 (110, the total number of shares of Target Subsidiary stock × $27.50, the value of a share of Target Subsidiary stock on the disposition date)), minus $0, Seller's selling costs in connection with the deemed sale of the 100 shares of Target Subsidiary stock). The $2,750 grossed-up amount realized on the sale, exchange, or distribution of recently disposed stock of Target Subsidiary is then added to the liabilities of Old Target Subsidiary, $0, to arrive at the ADADP of Target Subsidiary, $2,750.

(iii) *Allocation of ADADP.* Because Assets 4 and 5 are each assets of the same class, and the total fair market value of Assets 4 and 5 exceeds the $2,750 ADADP of Target Subsidiary, the $2,750 ADADP is allocated to Assets 4 and 5 in proportion to their respective fair market values. Accordingly, $909 is allocated to Asset 4 ($2,750 × ($1,000/($1,000 + $2,025))) and $1,341 is allocated to Asset 5 ($2,750 × ($2,025/($1,000 + $2,025))).

Example 3. (i) Seller owns all 100 of the outstanding shares of the common stock of Target, the only class of Target stock outstanding. On January 1 of Year 1, Seller sells 10 shares of Target stock to A for $6,000 ($600 per share). On August 1 of Year 1, Seller distributes the remaining 90 shares of Target stock to its unrelated shareholders in a transaction described in section 355(d)(2) or (e)(2). The value of Target stock on August 1 is $560 per share. Target has two assets, Asset 1, which is stock in trade of Target, a Class IV asset, with a basis of $15,000 and a value of $50,000, and Asset 2, which is stock in a publicly traded, unrelated corporation, a Class II asset, with a basis of $38,000 and a value of $16,000. Target has no liabilities other than any liabilities for Federal tax on account of the deemed asset disposition. Assume Target's Federal tax rate for any gain or income on the deemed asset disposition is 34 percent. Seller had no selling costs in connection with its sale of the 10 shares of Target stock. A section 336(e) election is made.

(ii) Because at least 80 percent of Target stock was disposed of (within the meaning of §1.336-1(b)(5)) by Seller during the 12-month disposition period, a qualified stock disposition occurred. August 1 of Year 1 is the disposition date. Accordingly, pursuant to the section 336(e) election, for Federal income tax purposes, Target is treated as if, on August 1, it sold all of its assets to an unrelated person in exchange for the ADADP.

(iii) Under these facts, although a portion of the qualified stock disposition was the result of a stock distribution, because the grossed-up amount realized on the disposition of recently disposed stock of Target, $56,400 (($6,000 + ($560 × 90))/1) exceeds Target's total basis in its assets, none of the losses realized on the deemed asset disposition are disallowed under §1.336-2(b)(2)(i)(B)(2). Because the grossed-up amount realized on the disposition of recently disposed stock of Target exceeds the value of Asset 2, the ADADP allocated to Asset 2 equals the value of Asset 2, $16,000, and Target realizes a $22,000 loss on the deemed disposition of Asset 2. None of this loss is disallowed under section 1091. See §1.336-2(b)(2)(ii)(C). Accordingly, Target recognizes a $22,000 loss on the deemed disposition of Asset 2.

(iv) The ADADP allocated to Asset 1 is determined as follows (for purposes of this *Example 3*, TotADADP is the total ADADP for the deemed asset disposition, A1ADADP is the tentative amount of the total ADADP allocated to Asset 1, A2ADADP is the amount of the total ADADP allocated to Asset 2, G is the grossed-up amount realized on the disposition of recently disposed stock of Target, L is Target's liabilities other than Target's tax liability for the deemed disposition tax consequences, TR is the applicable tax rate, and B1 is the adjusted basis of Asset 1 and B2 is the adjusted basis of Asset 2):

TotADADP = G + L + (TR × (TotADADP -B1 - B2))

A1ADADP = TotADADP - A2ADADP

A2ADADP = $16,000

A1ADADP = TotADADP - $16,000

G = ($6,000 + ($560 × 90))/1

G = $56,400

TotADADP = $56,400 + 0 + (.34 × (TotADADP - $15,000 - $38,000))

TotADADP = $56,400 + .34TotADADP - $18,020 .66TotADADP = $38,380

TotADADP = $58,152

A1ADADP = $42,152

(v) Because A1ADADP, $42,152, does not exceed the value of Asset 1, $50,000, the entire A1ADADP is allocated to Asset 1. Old Target thus realizes and recognizes a gain of $27,152 on the deemed disposition of Asset 1 ($42,152 - $15,000). [Reg. § 1.336-3.]

☐ [T.D. 9619, 5-10-2013.]

[Reg. § 1.336-4]

§ 1.336-4. Adjusted grossed-up basis.—(a) *Scope.*—Except as provided in paragraphs (b) and (c) of this section or as the context otherwise requires, the principles of paragraphs (b) through (g) of § 1.338-5 apply in determining the adjusted grossed-up basis (AGUB) for target and the consequences of a gain recognition election. AGUB is the amount for which new target is deemed to have purchased all of its assets in the deemed purchase under § 1.336-2(b)(1)(ii) or the amount for which old target is deemed to have purchased all of its assets in the deemed purchase under § 1.336-2(b)(2)(ii). AGUB is allocated among target's assets in accordance with § 1.338-6 to determine the price at which the assets are deemed to have been purchased. If a subsequent increase or decrease with respect to an element of AGUB is required under general principles of tax law, redetermined AGUB is allocated among target's assets in accordance with § 1.338-7.

(b) *Modifications to the principles in § 1.338-5.*—Solely for purposes of applying § § 1.336-1 through 1.336-4, the principles of § 1.338-5 are modified as follows—

(1) *Purchasing corporation; purchaser.*—Any reference to the *purchasing corporation* shall be treated as a reference to a purchaser, as defined in § 1.336-1(b)(2).

(2) *Acquisition date; disposition date.*—Any reference to the *acquisition date* shall be treated as a reference to the disposition date, as defined in § 1.336-1(b)(8).

(3) *Section 338 election; section 338(h)(10) election; section 336(e) election.*—Any reference to a *section 338 election* or a *section 338(h)(10) election* shall be treated as a reference to a section 336(e) election, as defined in § 1.336-1(b)(11).

(4) *New target; old target.*—In the case of a disposition described in section 355(d)(2) or (e)(2), any reference to *new target* shall be treated as a reference to *old target* in its capacity as the purchaser of assets pursuant to the section 336(e) election.

(5) *Recently purchased stock; recently disposed stock.*—Any reference to *recently purchased stock* shall be treated as a reference to recently disposed stock, as defined in § 1.336-1(b)(17). In the case of a distribution of stock, for purposes of determining the purchaser's grossed-up basis of recently disposed stock, the purchaser's basis in recently disposed stock shall be deemed to be such stock's fair market value on the date it was acquired.

(6) *Nonrecently purchased stock; nonrecently disposed stock.*—Any reference to *nonrecently purchased stock* shall be treated as a reference to nonrecently disposed stock, as defined in § 1.336-1(b)(18).

(c) *Gain recognition election.*—(1) *In general.*—Any holder of nonrecently disposed stock of target may make a gain recognition election. The gain recognition election is irrevocable. Each owner of nonrecently disposed stock determines its basis amount, and therefore the gain recognized pursuant to the gain recognition election, by applying § § 1.338-5(c) and 1.338-5(d)(3)(ii) by reference to its own recently disposed stock and nonrecently disposed stock, and not by reference to all recently disposed stock and nonrecently disposed stock.

(2) *80-percent purchaser.*—If a section 336(e) election is made for target, any 80-percent purchaser and all persons related to the 80-percent purchaser are automatically deemed to have made a gain recognition election for its nonrecently disposed target stock.

(3) *Non-80-percent purchaser.*—If not automatically deemed made under paragraph (c)(2) of this section, a gain recognition election is made by a non-80-percent purchaser providing, on or before the due date for filing the section 336(e) election statement by the appropriate party, a gain recognition election statement, as described in paragraph (c)(4) of this section, to the appropriate party. If seller and target are members of the same consolidated group, seller is the appropriate party and the common parent of the consolidated group must retain the gain recognition election statement. If seller and target are members of the same affiliated group but do not join in the filing of a consolidated Federal income tax return, or if target is an S corporation, target is the appropriate party and target must retain the gain recognition election statement. If a non-80-percent purchaser makes a gain recognition election, all related persons to the non-80-percent purchaser must also make a gain recognition election. Otherwise, the gain recognition election for the non-80-percent purchaser will have no effect.

(4) *Gain recognition election statement.*—A gain recognition election statement must include the following declarations (or substantially similar declarations):

(i) [Insert name, address, and taxpayer identifying number of person for whom gain recognition election is actually being made] has elected to recognize gain under § 1.336-4(c) with respect to [his, hers, or its] nonrecently disposed stock.

(ii) [Insert name of person for whom gain recognition election is actually being made] agrees to report any gain under the gain recognition election on [his, hers, or its] Federal income tax return (including an amended return, if necessary) for the taxable year that includes the disposition date of [insert name and employer identification number of target].

(d) *Examples.*—The following examples illustrate the provisions of this section.

Example 1. On January 1 of Year 1, Seller owns 85 shares of Target stock, A owns 8 shares, B owns 4 shares, and C owns the remaining 3 shares. Each of A's 8 shares, B's 4 shares, and C's 3 shares have a $5 basis. Assume that Target has no liabilities. On July 1 of Year 2, Seller sells 70 shares of Target stock to A for $10 per share. On September 1 of Year 2, Seller sells 5 shares of Target stock to B and 5 shares of Target stock to C for $14 per share. A section 336(e) election is made. A does not make a gain recognition election. A incurs $25 of acquisition costs and B and C each incur $10 of acquisition costs in connection with their respective Year 2 purchases. These costs are capitalized in the basis of Target stock. September 1 of Year 2 is the disposition date. Because A owns at least 10 percent of Target stock on September 1, the disposition date, and A's original 8 shares of Target stock owned on January 1 of Year 1 were not disposed of in the qualified stock disposition, A's original 8 shares of Target stock are nonrecently disposed stock. Although B's original 4 shares and C's original 3 shares were not disposed of in the qualified stock disposition, because neither B nor C owns, with the application of section 318(a), other than section 318(a)(4), at least 10 percent of the total voting power or value of Target stock on the disposition date, their original shares are not nonrecently disposed stock. The grossed-up basis of recently disposed Target stock is $1,011, determined as follows: The purchasers' (A, B, and C) aggregate basis in the recently disposed target stock, determined without regard to acquisition costs, is $840 ((70 × $10) + (5 × $14) + (5 × $14)). This amount is multiplied by a fraction, the numerator of which is 100 minus 8, the percentage of Target stock that is nonrecently disposed stock, and the denominator of which is 80, the percentage of Target stock attributable to recently disposed stock ($840 × 92/80 = $966). This amount is then increased by the $45 of acquisition costs incurred by A, B, and C to arrive at the $1,011 grossed-up basis of recently disposed Target stock ($966 + $45 = $1,011). New Target's AGUB is $1,051, the sum of $1,011, the grossed-up basis of recently disposed Target stock and $40 (8 × $5), A's basis in his nonrecently disposed Target stock.

Example 2. The facts are the same as in *Example 1* except that A makes a gain recognition election. Pursuant to the gain recognition election, A is treated as if he sold on September 1 of Year 2, the disposition date, his 8 shares of nonrecently disposed Target stock for the basis amount, and A's basis in nonrecently disposed target stock immediately after the deemed sale is the basis amount. A's basis amount equals his basis in his recently disposed Target stock without regard to acquisition costs, $700 (70 × $10), multiplied by a fraction, the numerator of which is 100 minus 8, the percentage of Target stock, by value, determined on the disposition date, which is A's nonrecently disposed Target stock, and the denominator of which is 70, the percentage of Target stock, by value, determined on the disposition date, which is A's recently disposed stock, which is then multiplied by a fraction, the numerator of which is 8, the percentage of Target stock, by value, determined on the disposition date, attributable to A's nonrecently disposed Target stock and the denominator of which is 100 minus the numerator amount. Accordingly, A's basis amount is $80 ($700 × 92/70 × 8/92). A therefore recognizes gain of $40 under the gain recognition election ($80 basis amount minus A's $40 basis in his nonrecently disposed stock prior to the gain recognition election). New Target's AGUB is $1,091, the sum of $1,011, the grossed-up basis of all recently disposed Target stock and $80, A's basis in his nonrecently disposed Target stock pursuant to the gain recognition election.

Example 3. (i) The facts are the same as in *Example 3* of §1.336-3(g), that is, Seller owns all 100 of the outstanding shares of the common stock of Target, the only class of Target stock outstanding. On January 1 of Year 1, Seller sells 10 shares of Target stock to A for $6,000 ($600 per share). On August 1 of Year 1, Seller distributes the remaining 90 shares of Target stock to its unrelated shareholders in a transaction described in section 355(d)(2) or (e)(2). The value of Target stock on August 1 is $560 per share. Target has two assets, Asset 1, which is stock in trade of Target, a Class IV asset, with a basis of $15,000 and a value of $50,000, and Asset 2, which is stock in a publicly traded, unrelated corporation, a Class II asset, with a basis of $38,000 and a value of $16,000. Target has no liabilities other than any liabilities for Federal tax on account of the deemed asset disposition. Assume Target's Federal tax rate for any gain or income on the deemed asset disposition is 34 percent. Seller had no selling costs in connection with its sale of the 10 shares of Target stock. A section 336(e) election is made. In addition, A incurred $100 of acquisition costs with respect to the purchase of the 10 shares of Target stock. Target's AGUB in the assets deemed acquired pursuant to §1.336-2(b)(2)(ii)(B) is determined as follows (for purposes of this *Example 3*, GRD is the grossed-up basis of recently disposed stock, BND is the basis in nonrecently disposed stock, TotL is Target's total liabilities, including Target's tax liability, and X is the A's total acquisition costs):

AGUB = GRD + BND + TotL

GRD = ($6,000 + ($560 × 90)) × ((100 - 0) / 100) + X

GRD = ($6,000 + $50,400) × (100/100) + $100

GRD = $56,500

BND = $0

TotL = .34 × ($27,152 (Target's gain recognized on deemed disposition of Asset 1) - $22,000 (Target's loss recognized on deemed disposition of Asset 2)) (see *Example 3* of §1.336-3(g) for determination of Target's gain and loss recognized on deemed disposition of Assets 1 and 2)

TotL = $1,752

AGUB = $56,500 + $0 + $1,752

AGUB = $58,252

(ii) The AGUB allocated to Asset 2 is $16,000, the value of Asset 2. Because the excess of the total AGUB, $58,252, over the portion of the AGUB allocated to Asset 2, $16,000, does not exceed the value of Asset 1, the AGUB allocated to Asset 1 is such excess, $42,252. [Reg. §1.336-4.]

☐ [*T.D.* 9619, 5-10-2013.]

[Reg. §1.336-5]

§1.336-5. Applicability dates.—Except as otherwise provided in this section, the provisions of §§1.336-1 through 1.336-4 apply to any qualified stock disposition for which the disposition date is on or after May 15, 2013. The provisions of §1.336-1(b)(5)(i)(A) relating to section 1022 apply on and after January 19, 2017. The provisions of §1.336-2(g)(3)(ii) and (iii) apply to foreign income taxes paid or accrued in taxable years beginning on or after December 28, 2021. [Reg. §1.336-5.]

☐ [*T.D.* 9619, 5-10-2013. *Amended by T.D.* 9811, 1-18-2017 *and T.D.* 9959, 12-28-2021.]

[Reg. §1.337-1]

§1.337-1. Nonrecognition for property distributed to parent in complete liquidation of subsidiary.—(a) *General rule.*—If sections 332(a) and 337 are applicable with respect to the receipt of a subsidiary's property in complete liquidation, no gain or loss is recognized to the liquidating subsidiary with respect to such property (including property distributed with respect to indebtedness, see section 337(b)(1) and §1.332-7), except as provided in section 337(b)(2) (distributions to certain tax-exempt distributees), section 367(e)(2) (distributions to foreign corporations), and section 897(d) (distributions of U.S. real property interests by foreign corporations).

(b) *Applicability date.*—This section applies to any taxable year beginning on or after March 28, 2016. [Reg. §1.337-1.]

☐ [*T.D.* 9759, 3-25-2016.]

[Reg. §1.337(d)-1]

§1.337(d)-1. Transitional loss limitation rule.—(a) *Loss limitation rule for transitional subsidiary.*—(1) *General rule.*—No deduction is allowed for any loss recognized by a member of a consolidated group with respect to the disposition of stock of a transitional subsidiary. However, for transactions involving loss shares of subsidiary stock occurring on or after September 17, 2008, see §1.1502-36. Further, this section does not apply to a transaction that is subject to §1.1502-36.

(2) *Allowable loss.*—(i) *In general.*—Paragraph (a)(1) of this section does not apply to the extent the taxpayer establishes that the loss is not attributable to the recognition of built-in gain by any transitional subsidiary on the disposition of an asset (including stock and securities) after January 6, 1987.

(ii) *Statement of allowable loss.*—Paragraph (a)(2)(i) of this section applies only if a separate statement entitled "ALLOWABLE LOSS UNDER SECTION 1.337(d)-1(a)" is filed with the taxpayer's return for the year of the stock disposition. If the separate statement is required to be filed with a return the due date (including extensions) of which is before January 16, 1991, or with a return due (including extensions) after January 15, 1991 but filed before that date, the statement may be filed with an amended return for the year of the disposition or with the taxpayer's first subsequent return the due date (including extensions) of which is after January 15, 1991.

(iii) *Contents of statement.*—The statement required under paragraph (a)(2)(ii) of this section must contain—

(A) The name and employer identification number (E.I.N.) of the transitional subsidiary.

(B) The basis of the stock of the transitional subsidiary immediately before the disposition

(C) The amount realized on the disposition.

(D) The amount of the deduction not disallowed under paragraph (a)(1) of this section by reason of this paragraph (a)(2).

(E) The amount of loss disallowed under paragraph (a)(1) of this section.

(3) *Coordination with loss deferral and other disallowance rules.*—For purposes of this section, the rules of §1.1502-20(a)(3) apply, with appropriate adjustments to reflect differences between the approach of this section and that of §1.1502-20.

(4) *Definitions.*—For purposes of this section—

(i) The definitions in §1.1502-1 apply.

(ii) "Transitional subsidiary" means any corporation that became a subsidiary of the group (whether or not the group was a consolidated group) after January 6, 1987. Notwithstanding the preceding sentence, a subsidiary is not a transitional subsidiary if the subsidiary (and each predecessor) was a member of the group at all times after the subsidiary's (and each predecessor's) organization.

(iii) "Built-in gain" of a transitional subsidiary means gain attributable, directly or indirectly, in whole or in part, to any excess of value over basis, determined immediately before the transitional subsidiary became a subsidiary, with respect to any asset owned directly or indirectly by the transitional subsidiary at that time.

(iv) "Disposition" means any event in which gain or loss is recognized, in whole or in part.

(v) "Value" means fair market value.

(5) *Examples.*—For purposes of the examples in this section, unless otherwise stated, the group files consolidated returns on a calendar year basis, the facts set forth the only corporate activity, and all sales and purchases are with unrelated buyers or sellers. The basis of each asset is the same for determining earnings and profits adjustments and taxable income. Tax liability and its effect on basis, value, and earnings and profits are disregarded. "Investment adjustment system" means the rules of §1.1502-32. The principles of this paragraph (a) are illustrated by the following examples:

Example (1). Loss attributable to recognized built-in gain. (i) P buys all the stock of T for $100 on February 1, 1987, and T becomes a member of the P group. T has an asset with a value of $100 and basis of $0. T sells the asset in 1989 and recognizes $100 of built-in gain on the sale (*i.e.*, the asset's value exceeded its basis by $100 at the time T became a member of the P group). Under the investment adjustment system, P's basis in the T stock increases to $200. P sells all the stock of T on December 31, 1989, and recognizes a loss of $100. Under paragraph (a)(1) of this section, no deduction is allowed to P for the $100 loss.

(ii) Assume that, after T sells its asset but before P sells the T stock, T issues additional stock to unrelated persons and ceases to be a member of the P group. P then sells all its stock of T in 1997. Although T ceases to be a subsidiary within the meaning of §1.1502-1, T continues to be a transitional subsidiary within the meaning of this section. Consequently, under paragraph (a)(1) of this section, no deduction is allowed to P for its $100 loss.

Example (2). Loss attributable to post-acquisition loss. P buys all the stock of T for $100 on February 1, 1987, and T becomes a member of the P group. T has $50 cash and an asset with $50 of built-in gain. During 1988, T retains the asset but loses $40 of the cash. The P group is unable to use the loss, and the loss becomes a net operating loss carryover attributable to T. Under the investment adjustment system, P's basis in the stock of T remains $100. P sells all the stock of T on December 31, 1988, for $60 and recognizes a $40 loss. Under paragraph (a)(2)(i) of this section, P establishes that it did not dispose of the built-in gain asset. None of P's loss is disallowed under paragraph (a)(1) if P satisfies the requirements of paragraph (a)(2)(ii) of this section.

Example (3). Stacking rules—postacquisition loss offsets postacquisition gain. (i) P buys all the stock of T for $100 on February 1, 1987, and T becomes a member of the P group. T has 2 assets. Asset 1 has a basis and value of $50, and asset 2 has a basis of $0 and a value of $50. During 1989, asset 1 declines in value to $0, and T sells asset 2 for $50, and reinvests the proceeds in asset 3. The value of asset 3 appreciates to $90. Under the investment adjustment system, P's basis in the stock of T increases from $100 to $150 as a result of the gain recognized on the sale of asset 2 but is unaffected by the unrealized post-acquisition decline in the value of asset 1. On December 31, 1989, P sells all the stock of T for $90 and recognizes a $60 loss.

(ii) Although T incurred a $50 post-acquisition loss of built-in gain because of the decline in the value of asset 1, T also recognized $50 of built-in gain. Under paragraph (a)(2) of this section, any loss on the sale of stock is treated first as attributable to recognized built-in gain. Thus, for purposes of determining under paragraph (a)(2) of this section whether P's $60 loss on the disposition of the T stock is attributable to the recognition of built-in gain on the disposition of an asset, T's unrealized post-acquisition gain of $40 offsets $40 of the $50 of unrealized post-acquisition loss. Therefore, $50 of the $60 loss is attributable to the recognition of built-in gain on the disposition of an asset and is disallowed under paragraph (a)(1) of this section.

Example (4). Stacking rules—built-in loss offsets built-in gain. (i) P buys all the stock of T for $50 on February 1, 1987, and T becomes a member of the P group. T has 2 assets. Asset 1 has a basis of $50 and a value of $0, and asset 2 has a basis of $0 and a value of $50. During 1989, T sells asset 1 for $0 and asset 2 for $50, and reinvests the $50 proceeds in asset 3. The value of asset 3 declines to $40. Under the investment adjustment system, P's basis in the stock of T remains $50 as a result of the offsetting gain and loss recognized on the sale of assets 1 and 2 and is unaffected by the unrealized post-acquisition decline in the value of asset 3. On December 31, 1989, P sells all the stock of T for $40 and recognizes a $10 loss.

(ii) Although T recognized a $50 built-in gain on the sale of asset 2, T also recognized a $50 built-in loss on the sale of asset 1. For purposes of determining under paragraph (a)(2) of this section whether P's $10 loss on the disposition of the T stock is attributable to the recognition of built-in gain on the disposition of an asset, T's recognized built-in gain is offset by its recognized built-in loss. Thus none of P's $10 loss is attributable to the recognition of built-in gain on the disposition of an asset.

(iii) The result would be the same if, instead of a $50 built-in loss in asset 2, T has a $50 net operating loss carryover when P buys the T stock, and the net operating loss carryover is used to offset the built-in gain.

Example (5). Outside basis partially corresponds to inside basis. (i) Individual A owns all the stock of T, for which A has a basis of $60. On February 1, 1987, T owns 1 asset with a basis of $0 and a value of $100, P acquires all the stock of T from A in an exchange to which section 351(a) applies, and T becomes a member of the P group. P has a carryover basis of $60 in the T stock. During 1988, T sells the asset and recognizes $100 of gain. Under the investment adjustment system, P's basis in the T stock increases from $60 to $160. T reinvests the $100 proceeds in another asset, which declines in value to $90. On January 1, 1989, P sells all the stock of T for $90 and recognizes a loss of $70.

(ii) Although P's basis in the T stock was increased by $100 as a result of the recognition of built-in gain on the disposition of T's asset, only $60 of the $70 loss on the sale of the stock is attributable under paragraph (a)(2) of this section to the recognition of built-in gain from the disposition of the asset. (Had T's asset not declined in value to $90, the T stock would have been sold for $100, and a $60 loss would have been attributable to the recognition of the built-in gain.) Therefore, $60 of the $70 loss is disallowed under paragraph (a)(2), and $10 is not disallowed if P satisfies the requirements of paragraph (a)(2). If P had sold the stock of T for $95 because T's other assets had unrealized appreciation of $5, $60 of the $65 loss would still be attributable to T's recognition of built-in gain on the disposition of assets.

Example (6). Creeping acquisition. P owns 60 percent of the stock of S on January 6, 1987. On February 1, 1987, P buys an additional 20 percent of the stock of S, and S becomes a member of the P group. P sells all the S stock on March 1, 1989 and recognizes a loss of $100. All 80 percent of the stock of S owned by P is subject to the rules of this section and, under paragraph (a)(1) and (2) of this section, P is not allowed to deduct the $100 loss, except to the extent P establishes the loss is not attributable to the recognition by S of built-in gain on the disposition of assets.

Example (7). Effect of post-acquisition appreciation. P buys all the stock of T for $100, and T becomes a member of the P group. T has an asset with a basis of $0 and a value of $100. T sells the asset for $100. Under the investment adjustment system, P's basis in the T stock increases to $200. T reinvests the proceeds of the sale in an asset that appreciates in value to $180. Five years after the sale, P sells all the stock of T for $180 and recognizes a $20 loss. Under paragraph (a)(1) of this section, no deduction is allowed to P for the $20 loss.

Example (8). Deferred loss and recognized gain. (i) P is the common parent of a consolidated group, S is a wholly owned subsidiary of P, and T is a wholly owned subsidiary of S. S purchased all of the T stock on February 1, 1987 for $100, and T has an asset with a basis of $40 and a value of $100. T sells the asset for $100, recognizing $60 of gain. Under the investment adjustment system, S's basis in the T stock increases from $100 to $160. S sells its T stock to P for $100 in a deferred intercompany transaction, recognizing a $60 loss that is deferred under section 267(f) and § 1.1502-13. P subsequently sells all the stock of T for $100 to X, a member of the same controlled group (as defined in section 267(f)) as P but not a member of the P consolidated group.

(ii) Under paragraph (a)(3) of this section, the application of paragraph (a)(1) of this section to S's $60 loss is deferred, because S's loss is deferred under section 267(f) and § 1.1502-13. Although P's sale of the T stock to X would cause S's deferred loss to be taken into account under § 1.1502-13, § 1.267(f)-1 provides that the loss is not taken into account because X is a member of the same controlled group as P and S. Nevertheless, under paragraph (a)(3) of this section, because the T stock ceases to be owned by a member of the P consolidated group, S's deferred loss is disallowed immediately before the sale and is never taken into account under section 267(f).

(b) *Indirect disposition of transitional subsidiary.*—(1) *Loss limitation rule for transitional parent.*—No deduction is allowed for any loss recognized by a member of a consolidated group with respect to the disposition of stock of a transitional parent.

(2) *Allowable loss.*—(i) *In general.*—Paragraph (b)(1) of this section does not apply to the extent the taxpayer establishes that the loss exceeds the amount that would be disallowed under paragraph (a) of this section if each highest tier transitional subsidiary's stock in which the transitional parent has a direct or indirect interest had been sold immediately before the disposition of the transitional parent's stock. In applying the preceding sentence, appropriate adjustments shall be made to take into account circumstances where less than all the stock of a transitional parent owned by members of a consolidated group is disposed of in the same transaction, or the stock of a transitional subsidiary or a transitional parent is directly owned by more than 1 member.

(ii) *Statement of allowable loss.*—Paragraph (b)(2)(i) of this section applies only if a separate statement entitled "ALLOWABLE LOSS UNDER SECTION 1.337(d)-1(b)" is filed with the taxpayer's return for the year of the stock disposition. If the separate statement is required to be filed with a return the due date (including extensions) of which is before January 16, 1991, or with a return due (including extensions) after January 15, 1991 but filed before that date, the statement may be filed with an amended return for the year of the disposition or with the taxpayer's first subsequent return the due date (including extensions) of which is after January 15, 1991.

(iii) *Contents of statement.*—The statement required under paragraph (b)(2)(ii) of this section must contain—

(A) The name and employer identification number (E.I.N.) of the transitional parent.

(B) The basis of the stock of the transitional parent immediately before the disposition.

(C) The amount realized on the disposition.

(D) The amount of the deduction not disallowed under paragraph (b)(1) of this section by reason of this paragraph (b)(2).

(E) The amount of loss disallowed under paragraph (b)(1) of this section.

(3) *Coordination with loss deferral and other disallowance rules.*—For purposes of this section, the rules of § 1.1502-20(a)(3) apply, with appropriate adjustments to reflect differences between the approach of this section and that of § 1.1502-20.

(4) *Definitions.*—For purposes of this section—

(i) "Transitional parent" means any subsidiary, other than a transitional subsidiary, that owned at any time after January 6, 1987, a direct or indirect interest in the stock of a corporation that is a transitional subsidiary.

(ii) "Highest tier transitional subsidiary" means the transitional subsidiary (or subsidiaries) in which the transitional parent has a direct or indirect interest and that is the highest transitional subsidiary (or subsidiaries) in a chain of members.

(5) *Examples.*—The principles of this paragraph (b) are illustrated by the following examples:

Example (1). Ownership of chain of transitional subsidiaries. (i) P forms S with $200 on January 1, 1985, and S becomes a member of the P group. On February 1, 1987, S buys all the stock of T, and T buys all the stock of T1, and both T and T1 become members of the P group. On January 1, 1988, P sells all the stock of S and recognizes a $90 loss on the sale.

(ii) Under paragraph (a)(4)(ii) of this section, both T and T1 are transitional subsidiaries, because they became members of the P group after January 6, 1987. Under paragraph (b)(4)(i) of this section, S is a transitional parent, because it owns a direct interest in stock of transitional subsidiaries and is not itself a transitional subsidiary.

(iii) Under paragraph (b)(1) and (2) of this section, because S is a transitional parent, no deduction is allowed to P for its $90 loss except to the extent the loss exceeds the amount of S's loss that would have been disallowed if S had sold all the stock of T, S's highest tier transitional subsidiary, immediately before P's sale of all the S stock. Assume all the T stock would have been sold for a $90 loss and that all the loss would be attributable to the recognition of built-in gain from the disposition of assets. Because in that case $90 of loss would be disallowed, all of P's loss on the sale of the S stock is disallowed under paragraph (b).

Example (2). Ownership of brother-sister transitional subsidiaries. (i) P forms S with $200 on January 1, 1985, and S becomes a member of the P group. On February 1, 1987, S buys all the stock of both T and T1, and T and T1 become members of the P group. On January 1, 1988, P sells all the stock of S and recognizes a $90 loss on the sale.

(ii) Under paragraph (b)(1) and (2) of this section, no deduction is allowed to P for its $90 loss except to the extent P establishes that the loss exceeds the amount of S's stock losses that would be disallowed if S sold all the stock of T and T1, S's highest tier transitional subsidiaries, immediately before P's sale of all the S stock. Assume that all the T stock would have been sold for a $50 loss, all the T1 stock for a $40 loss, and that the entire amount of each loss would be attributable to the recognition of built-in gain on the disposition of assets. Because $90 of loss would be disallowed with respect to the sale of S's T and T1 stock, P's $90 loss on the sale of all the S stock is disallowed under paragraph (b).

(c) *Successors.*—(1) *General rule.*—This section applies, to the extent necessary to effectuate the purposes of this section, to—

(i) Any property owned by a member or former member, the basis of which is determined, directly or indirectly, in whole or in part, by reference to the basis in a subsidiary's stock, and

(ii) Any property owned by any other person whose basis in the property is determined, directly or indirectly, in whole or in part, by reference to a member's (or former member's) basis in a subsidiary's stock.

(2) *Examples.*—The principles of this paragraph (c) are illustrated by the following examples:

Example (1). Merger into grandfathered subsidiary. P, the common parent of a group, owns all the stock of T, a transitional subsidiary. On January 1, 1989, T merges into S, a wholly owned subsidiary of P that is not a transitional subsidiary. Under paragraph (c)(1) of this section, all the stock of S is treated as stock of a transitional subsidiary. As a result, no deduction is allowed for any loss recognized by P on the disposition of any S stock, except to the extent the P group establishes under paragraph (a)(2) that the loss is not attributable to the recognition of built-in gain on the disposition of assets of T.

Example (2). Nonrecognition exchange of transitional stock. (i) P, the common parent of a group, owns all the stock of T, a transitional subsidiary. On January 1, 1989, P transfers the stock of T to X, a corporation that is not a member of the P group, in exchange for 20 percent of its stock in a transaction to which section 351(a) applies. T and X file separate returns.

(ii) Under paragraph (c)(1) of this section, all the stock of X owned by P is treated as stock of a transitional subsidiary because P's basis for the X stock is determined by reference to its basis for the T stock. As a result, no deduction is allowed to P for any loss recognized on the disposition of the X stock, except to the extent permitted under paragraph (a) of this section.

(iii) Under paragraph (c)(1), X is treated as a member subject to paragraph (a) of this section with respect to the T stock because X's

basis for the stock is determined by reference to P's basis for the stock. Moreover, all of the T stock owned by X continues to be stock of a transitional subsidiary. As a result, no deduction is allowed to X for any loss recognized on the disposition of any T stock, except to the extent permitted under paragraph (a) of this section.

(d) *Investment adjustments and earnings and profits.*—(1) *In general.*—For purposes of determining investment adjustments under §1.1502-32 and earnings and profits under §1.1502-33(c) with respect to a member of a consolidated group that owns stock in a subsidiary, any deduction that is disallowed under this section is treated as a loss arising and absorbed by the member in the tax year in which the disallowance occurs.

(2) *Example.*—(i) In 1986, P forms S with a contribution of $100, and S becomes a member of the P group. On February 1, 1987, S buys all the stock of T for $100. T has an asset with a basis of $0 and a value of $100. In 1988, T sells the asset for $100. Under the investment adjustment system, S's basis in the T stock increases to $200, P's basis in the S stock increases to $200, and P's earnings and profits and S's earnings and profits increase by $100. In 1989, S sells all of the T stock for $100, and S's recognized loss of $100 is disallowed under paragraph (a)(1) of this section.

(ii) Under paragraph (d)(1) of this section, S's earnings and profits for 1989 are reduced by $100, the amount of the loss disallowed under paragraph (a)(1). As a result, P's basis in the S stock is reduced from $200 to $100 under the investment adjustment system. P's earnings and profits for 1989 are correspondingly reduced by $100.

(e) *Effective dates.*—(1) *General rule.*—This section applies with respect to dispositions after January 6, 1987. For dispositions on or after November 19, 1990, however, this section applies only if the stock was deconsolidated (as that term is defined in §1.337(d)-2(b)(2)) before November 19, 1990, and only to the extent the disposition is not subject to §1.337(d)-2 or §1.1502-20.

(2) *Binding contract rule.*—For purposes of this paragraph (e), if a corporation became a subsidiary pursuant to a binding written contract entered into before January 6, 1987, and in continuous effect until the corporation became a subsidiary, or a disposition was pursuant to a binding written contract entered into before March 9, 1990, and in continuous effect until the disposition, the date the contract became binding shall be treated as the date the corporation became a subsidiary or as the date of disposition.

(3) *Application of §1.1502-20T to certain transactions.*—(i) *In general.*—If a group files the certification described in paragraph (e)(3)(ii) of this section, it may apply §1.1502-20T (as contained in the CFR edition revised as of April 1, 1990), to all of its members with respect to all dispositions and deconsolidations by the certifying group to which §1.1502-20T otherwise applied by its terms occurring—

(A) On or after March 9, 1990 (but only if not pursuant to a binding contract described in §1.337(d)-1T(e)(2) (as contained in the CFR edition revised as of April 1, 1990) that was entered into before March 9, 1990); and

(B) Before November 19, 1990 (or thereafter, if pursuant to a binding contract described in §1.1502-20T(g)(3) that was entered into on or after March 9, 1990 and before November 19, 1990).

The certification under this paragraph (e)(3)(i) with respect to the application of §1.1502-20T to any transaction described in this paragraph (e)(3)(i) may not be withdrawn and, if the certification is filed, §1.1502-20T must be applied to all such transactions on all returns (including amended returns) on which such transactions are included.

(ii) *Time and manner of filing certification.*—The certification described in paragraph (e)(3)(i) of this section must be made in a separate statement entitled "[insert name and employer identification number of common parent] HEREBY CERTIFIES UNDER SECTION 1.337(d)-1(e)(3) THAT THE GROUP OF WHICH IT IS THE COMMON PARENT IS APPLYING §1.1502-20T TO ALL TRANSACTIONS TO WHICH THAT SECTION OTHERWISE APPLIED BY ITS TERMS." The statement must be signed by the common parent and filed with the group's income tax return for the taxable year of the first disposition or deconsolidation to which the certification applies. If the separate statement required under this paragraph (e)(3) is to be filed with a return the due date (including extensions) of which is before November 16, 1991, the statement may be filed with an amended return for the year of the disposition or deconsolidation that is filed within 180 days after September 13, 1991. Any other filings required under §1.1502-20T, such as the statement required under §1.1502-20T(f)(5), may be made with the amended return, regardless of whether §1.1502-20T permits such filing by amended return. [Reg. §1.337(d)-1.]

□ [*T.D.* 8319, 11-19-90. *Amended by T.D.* 8364, 9-13-91; *T.D.* 8560, 8-12-94; *T.D.* 8597, 7-12-95 *and T.D.* 9424, 9-9-2008.]

[Reg. §1.337(d)-2]

§1.337(d)-2. Loss limitation rules.—(a) *Loss disallowance.*—(1) *General rule.*—No deduction is allowed for any loss recognized by a member of a consolidated group with respect to the disposition of stock of a subsidiary. However, for transactions involving loss shares of subsidiary stock occurring on or after September 17, 2008, see § 1.1502-36. Further, this section does not apply to a transaction that is subject to § 1.1502-36.

(2) *Definitions.*—For purposes of this section:

(i) The definitions in § 1.1502-1 apply.

(ii) *Disposition* means any event in which gain or loss is recognized, in whole or in part.

(3) *Coordination with loss deferral and other disallowance rules.*—For purposes of this section, the rules of § 1.1502-20(a)(3) apply, with appropriate adjustments to reflect differences between the approach of this section and that of § 1.1502-20.

(4) *Netting.*—Paragraph (a)(1) of this section does not apply to loss with respect to the disposition of stock of a subsidiary, to the extent that, as a consequence of the same plan or arrangement, gain is taken into account by members with respect to stock of the same subsidiary having the same material terms. If the gain to which this paragraph applies is less than the amount of the loss with respect to the disposition of the subsidiary's stock, the gain is applied to offset loss with respect to each share disposed of as a consequence of the same plan or arrangement in proportion to the amount of the loss deduction that would have been disallowed under paragraph (a)(1) of this section with respect to such share before the application of this paragraph (a)(4). If the same item of gain could be taken into account more than once in limiting the application of paragraphs (a)(1) and (b)(1) of this section, the item is taken into account only once.

(b) *Basis reduction on deconsolidation.*—(1) *General rule.*—If the basis of a member of a consolidated group in a share of stock of a subsidiary exceeds its value immediately before a deconsolidation of the share, the basis of the share is reduced at that time to an amount equal to its value. If both a disposition and a deconsolidation occur with respect to a share in the same transaction, paragraph (a) of this section applies and, to the extent necessary to effectuate the purposes of this section, this paragraph (b) applies following the application of paragraph (a) of this section.

(2) *Deconsolidation.*—*Deconsolidation* means any event that causes a share of stock of a subsidiary that remains outstanding to be no longer owned by a member of any consolidated group of which the subsidiary is also a member.

(3) *Value.*—*Value* means fair market value.

(4) *Netting.*—Paragraph (b)(1) of this section does not apply to reduce the basis of stock of a subsidiary, to the extent that, as a consequence of the same plan or arrangement, gain is taken into account by members with respect to stock of the same subsidiary having the same material terms. If the gain to which this paragraph applies is less than the amount of basis reduction with respect to shares of the subsidiary's stock, the gain is applied to offset basis reduction with respect to each share deconsolidated as a consequence of the same plan or arrangement in proportion to the amount of the reduction that would have been required under paragraph (b)(1) of this section with respect to such share before the application of this paragraph (b)(4).

(c) *Allowable loss.*—(1) *Application.*—This paragraph (c) applies with respect to stock of a subsidiary only if a separate statement entitled *§ 1.337(d)-2(c) statement* is included with the return in accordance with paragraph (c)(3) of this section.

(2) *General rule.*—Loss is not disallowed under paragraph (a)(1) of this section and basis is not reduced under paragraph (b)(1) of this section to the extent the taxpayer establishes that the loss or basis is not attributable to the recognition of built-in gain, net of directly related expenses, on the disposition of an asset (including stock and securities). Loss or basis may be attributable to the recognition of built-in gain on the disposition of an asset by a prior group. For purposes of this section, gain recognized on the disposition of an asset is built-in gain to the extent attributable, directly or indirectly, in whole or in part, to any excess of value over basis that is reflected, *before the disposition of the asset*, in the basis of the share, directly or indirectly, in whole or in part, after applying section 1503(e) and other applicable provisions of the Internal Revenue Code and regulations. Federal income taxes may be directly related to built-in gain recognized on the disposition of an asset only to the extent of the

excess (if any) of the group's income tax liability actually imposed under Subtitle A of the Internal Revenue Code for the taxable year of the disposition of the asset over the group's income tax liability for the taxable year redetermined by not taking into account the built-in gain recognized on the disposition of the asset. For this purpose, the group's income tax liability actually imposed and its redetermined income tax liability are determined without taking into account the foreign tax credit under section 27(a) of the Internal Revenue Code.

(3) *Contents of statement and time of filing.*—The statement required under paragraph (c)(1) of this section must be included with or as part of the taxpayer's return for the year of the disposition or deconsolidation and must contain—

(i) The name and employer identification number (E.I.N.) of the subsidiary; and

(ii) The amount of the loss not disallowed under paragraph (a)(1) of this section by reason of this paragraph (c) and the amount of basis not reduced under paragraph (b)(1) of this section by reason of this paragraph (c).

(4) *Example.*—The principles of paragraphs (a), (b), and (c) of this section are illustrated by the examples in § § 1.337(d)-1(a)(5) and 1.1502-20(a)(5) (other than *Examples 3, 4, and 5*) and (b), with appropriate adjustments to reflect differences between the approach of this section and that of § 1.1502-20, and by the following example. For purposes of the examples in this section, unless otherwise stated, the group files consolidated returns on a calendar year basis, the facts set forth the only corporate activity, and all sales and purchases are with unrelated buyers or sellers. The basis of each asset is the same for determining earnings and profits adjustments and taxable income. Tax liability and its effect on basis, value, and earnings and profits are disregarded. *Investment adjustment system* means the rules of § 1.1502-32. The example reads as follows:

Example. Loss offsetting built-in gain in a prior group. (i) P buys all the stock of T for $50 in Year 1, and T becomes a member of the P group. T has 2 assets. Asset 1 has a basis of $50 and a value of $0, and asset 2 has a basis of $0 and a value of $50. T sells asset 2 during Year 3 for $50 and recognizes a $50 gain. Under the investment adjustment system, P's basis in the T stock increased to $100 as a result of the recognition of gain. In Year 5, all of the stock of P is acquired by the P1 group, and the former members of the P group become members of the P1 group. T then sells asset 1 for $0, and recognizes a $50 loss. Under the investment adjustment system, P's basis in the T stock decreases to $50 as a result of the loss. T's assets decline in value from $50 to $40. P then sells all the stock of T for $40 and recognizes a $10 loss.

(ii) P's basis in the T stock reflects both T's unrecognized gain and unrecognized loss with respect to its assets. The gain T recognizes on the disposition of asset 2 is built-in gain with respect to both the P and P1 groups for purposes of paragraph (c)(2) of this section. In addition, the loss T recognizes on the disposition of asset 1 is built-in loss with respect to the P and P1 groups for purposes of paragraph (c)(2) of this section. T's recognition of the built-in loss while a member of the P1 group offsets the effect on T's stock basis of T's recognition of the built-in gain while a member of the P group. Thus, P's $10 loss on the sale of the T stock is not attributable to the recognition of built-in gain, and the loss is therefore not disallowed under paragraph (c)(2) of this section.

(iii) The result would be the same if, instead of having a $50 built-in loss in asset 1 when it becomes a member of the P group, T has a $50 net operating loss carryover and the carryover is used by the P group.

(d) *Successors.*—For purposes of this section, the rules and examples of § 1.1502-20(d) apply, with appropriate adjustments to reflect differences between the approach of this section and that of § 1.1502-20.

(e) *Anti-avoidance rules.*—For purposes of this section, the rules and examples of § 1.1502-20(e) apply, with appropriate adjustments to reflect differences between the approach of this section and that of § 1.1502-20.

(f) *Investment adjustments.*—For purposes of this section, the rules and examples of § 1.1502-20(f) apply, with appropriate adjustments to reflect differences between the approach of this section and that of § 1.1502-20.

(g) *Effective dates.*—This section applies with respect to dispositions and deconsolidations on or after March 3, 2005. In addition, this section applies to dispositions and deconsolidations for which an election is made under § 1.1502-20(i)(2) to determine allowable loss under this section. If loss is recognized because stock of a subsidiary became worthless, the disposition with respect to the stock is treated as occurring on the date the stock became worthless. For dispositions and deconsolidations after March 6, 2002 and before March 3, 2005, see § 1.337(d)-2T as contained in the 26 CFR part 1 in effect on March 2, 2005. [Reg. § 1.337(d)-2.]

☐ [*T.D. 8364, 9-13-91. Amended by T.D. 8560, 8-12-94; T.D. 8597, 7-12-95; T.D. 8984, 3-7-2002; T.D. 9187, 3-2-2005 and T.D. 9424, 9-9-2008.*]

[Reg. § 1.337(d)-3]

§ 1.337(d)-3. Gain recognition upon certain partnership transactions involving a partner's stock.—(a) *Purpose.*—The purpose of this section is to prevent corporate taxpayers from using a partnership to circumvent gain required to be recognized under section 311(b) or section 336(a). The rules of this section, including the determination of the amount of gain, must be applied in a manner that is consistent with and reasonably carries out this purpose.

(b) *In general.*—This section applies when a partnership, either directly or indirectly, owns, acquires, or distributes Stock of the Corporate Partner (within the meaning of paragraph (c)(2) of this section). Under paragraphs (d) or (e) of this section, a Corporate Partner (within the meaning of paragraph (c)(1) of this section) is required to recognize gain when a transaction has the effect of the Corporate Partner acquiring or increasing an interest in its own stock in exchange for appreciated property in a manner that contravenes the purpose of this section as set forth in paragraph (a) of this section. Paragraph (f) of this section sets forth exceptions under which a Corporate Partner does not recognize gain.

(c) *Definitions.*—The following definitions apply for purposes of this section:

(1) *Corporate Partner.*—A *Corporate Partner* is a person that is classified as a corporation for federal income tax purposes and holds or acquires an interest in a partnership.

(2) *Stock of the Corporate Partner.*—(i) *In general.*—With respect to a Corporate Partner, *Stock of the Corporate Partner* includes the Corporate Partner's stock, or other equity interests, including options, warrants, and similar interests, in the Corporate Partner or a corporation that controls the Corporate Partner within the meaning of section 304(c) (except that section 318(a)(1) and (3) shall not apply). *Stock of the Corporate Partner* also includes interests in any entity to the extent that the value of the interest is attributable to Stock of the Corporate Partner.

(ii) *Affiliated partner exception.*—Stock of the Corporate Partner does not include any stock or other equity interests held or acquired by a partnership if all interests in the partnership's capital and profits are held by members of an affiliated group as defined in section 1504(a) that includes the Corporate Partner.

(3) *Section 337(d) Transaction.*—A *Section 337(d) Transaction* is a transaction (or series of transactions) that has the effect of an exchange by a Corporate Partner of its interest in appreciated property for an interest in Stock of the Corporate Partner owned, acquired, or distributed by a partnership. For example, a Section 337(d) Transaction may occur when —

(i) A Corporate Partner contributes appreciated property to a partnership that owns Stock of the Corporate Partner;

(ii) A partnership acquires Stock of the Corporate Partner;

(iii) A partnership that owns Stock of the Corporate Partner distributes appreciated property to a partner other than a Corporate Partner;

(iv) A partnership distributes Stock of the Corporate Partner to the Corporate Partner; or

(v) A partnership agreement is amended in a manner that increases a Corporate Partner's interest in Stock of the Corporate Partner (including in connection with a contribution to, or distribution from, a partnership).

(4) *Gain Percentage.*—A Corporate Partner's *Gain Percentage* equals a fraction, the numerator of which is the Corporate Partner's interest (by value) in appreciated property effectively exchanged for Stock of the Corporate Partner under the test described in paragraphs (d)(1) and (2) of this section, and the denominator of which is the Corporate Partner's interest (by value) in that appreciated property immediately before the Section 337(d) Transaction. Paragraph (d) of this section requires a partnership to multiply the Gain Percentage by the Corporate Partner's aggregate gain in appreciated property to determine gain recognized under this section.

(d) *Deemed redemption rule.*—(1) *In general.*—A Corporate Partner in a partnership that engages in a Section 337(d) Transaction recognizes gain at the time, and to the extent, that the Corporate Partner's interest in appreciated property (other than Stock of the Corporate Partner) is reduced in exchange for an increased interest in Stock of the Corporate Partner, as determined under paragraph (d)(2) of this

section. This section does not apply to the extent a transaction has the effect of an exchange by a Corporate Partner of non-appreciated property for Stock of the Corporate Partner, or has the effect of an exchange by a Corporate Partner for property other than Stock of the Corporate Partner.

(2) *Corporate Partner's interest in partnership property.*—The Corporate Partner's interest with respect to both Stock of the Corporate Partner and the appreciated property that is the subject of the exchange is determined based on all facts and circumstances, including the allocation and distribution rights set forth in the partnership agreement. The Corporate Partner's interest in an identified share of Stock of the Corporate Partner will never be less than the Corporate Partner's largest interest (by value) in that share of Stock of the Corporate Partner that was taken into account when the partnership previously determined whether there had been a Section 337(d) Transaction with respect to such share (regardless of whether the Corporate Partner recognized gain in the earlier transaction). See *Example 7* of paragraph (h) of this section. However, this limitation will not apply if any reduction in the Corporate Partner's interest in the identified share of Stock of the Corporate Partner occurred as part of a plan or arrangement to circumvent the purpose of this section. See *Example 8* of paragraph (h) of this section.

(3) *Amount and character of gain recognized on the exchange.*—(i) *Amount of gain.*—The amount of gain the Corporate Partner recognizes under paragraph (d)(1) of this section equals the product of the Corporate Partner's Gain Percentage and the gain from the appreciated property that is the subject of the exchange that the Corporate Partner would recognize if, immediately before the Section 337(d) Transaction, all assets of the partnership and any assets contributed to the partnership in the Section 337(d) Transaction were sold in a fully taxable transaction for cash in an amount equal to the fair market value of such property (taking into account section 7701(g)), reduced, but not below zero, by any gain the Corporate Partner is required to recognize with respect to the appreciated property in the Section 337(d) Transaction under any other provision of this chapter. This gain is computed taking into account allocations of tax items applying the principles of section 704(c), including any remedial allocations under § 1.704-3(d), and also taking into account any basis adjustments including adjustments made pursuant to section 743(b).

(ii) *Character of gain.*—The character of the gain that the Corporate Partner recognizes under paragraph (d)(1) of this section from the appreciated property that is the subject of the exchange shall be the character of the gain that the Corporate Partner would recognize if, immediately before the Section 337(d) Transaction, the Corporate Partner had disposed of the appreciated property that is the subject of the exchange in a fully taxable transaction for cash in an amount equal to the fair market value of such property (taking into account section 7701(g)).

(4) *Basis adjustments.*—(i) *Corporate Partner's basis in the partnership interest.*—The basis of the Corporate Partner's interest in the partnership is increased by the amount of gain that the Corporate Partner recognizes under this paragraph (d).

(ii) *Partnership's basis in partnership property.*—The partnership's adjusted tax basis in the appreciated property that is treated as the subject of the exchange under this paragraph (d) is increased by the amount of gain recognized with respect to that property by the Corporate Partner as a result of that exchange, regardless of whether the partnership has an election in effect under section 754. For basis recovery purposes, this basis increase is treated as property that is placed in service by the partnership in the taxable year of the Section 337(d) Transaction.

(e) *Distribution of Stock of the Corporate Partner.*—(1) *In general.*—This paragraph (e) applies to distributions to the Corporate Partner of Stock of the Corporate Partner to which section 732(f) does not apply and that have previously been the subject of a Section 337(d) Transaction or become the subject of a Section 337(d) Transaction as a result of the distribution. Upon the distribution of Stock of the Corporate Partner to the Corporate Partner, paragraph (d) of this section will apply as though immediately before the distribution the partners amended the partnership agreement to allocate to the Corporate Partner a 100 percent interest in that portion of the Stock of the Corporate Partner that is distributed, and to allocate an appropriately reduced interest in other partnership property away from the Corporate Partner.

(2) *Basis rules.*—(i) *Basis allocation on distributions of stock and other property.*—If, as part of the same transaction, a partnership distributes Stock of the Corporate Partner and other property (other than cash) to the Corporate Partner, see § 1.732-1(c)(1)(iii) for a rule allocating basis first to the Stock of the Corporate Partner before the distribution of the other property.

(ii) *Computation of basis.*—For purposes of determining the basis of property distributed to a partner in a transaction that includes the distribution of Stock of the Corporate Partner (other than the basis of the Corporate Partner in its own stock), the basis of the partner's remaining partnership interest, and the partnership's basis in undistributed Stock of the Corporate Partner, and for purposes of computing gain under paragraph (e)(3) of this section, the partnership's basis of Stock of the Corporate Partner distributed to the partner equals the greater of—

(A) The partnership's basis of that distributed Stock of the Corporate Partner immediately before the distribution; or

(B) The fair market value of that distributed Stock of the Corporate Partner immediately before the distribution less the partner's allocable share of gain from all of the Stock of the Corporate Partner if the partnership sold all of its assets in a fully taxable transaction for cash in an amount equal to the fair market value of such property (taking into account section 7701(g)) immediately before the distribution.

(iii) *Section 732(f) basis reduction.*—For purposes of determining the amount of the decrease to the basis of property held by a distributed corporation pursuant to section 732(f), the amount of this decrease shall be reduced by the amount of gain that a Corporate Partner has recognized under this section in the same Section 337(d) Transaction or in a prior Section 337(d) Transaction involving the property.

(3) *Gain recognition.*—The Corporate Partner will recognize gain on a distribution of Stock of the Corporate Partner to the Corporate Partner to the extent that the partnership's adjusted basis in the distributed Stock of the Corporate Partner (as determined under paragraph (e)(2)(ii) of this section) immediately before the distribution exceeds the Corporate Partner's adjusted basis in its partnership interest immediately after the distribution.

(f) *Exceptions.*—(1) *De minimis rule.*—(i) *In general.*—Unless Stock of the Corporate Partner is acquired as part of a plan to circumvent the purpose of this section, this section does not apply to a Corporate Partner if at the time that the partnership acquires Stock of the Corporate Partner or at the time of a revaluation event as described in §1.704-1(b)(2)(iv)(f) (without regard to whether or not the partnership revalues its assets)—

(A) The Corporate Partner and any persons related to the Corporate Partner under section 267(b) or section 707(b) own in the aggregate less than 5 percent of the partnership;

(B) The partnership holds Stock of the Corporate Partner with a value of less than 2 percent of the partnership's gross assets (including the Stock of the Corporate Partner); and

(C) The partnership has never, at any point in time, held in the aggregate—

(1) Stock of the Corporate Partner with a fair market value greater than $1,000,000; or

(2) More than 2 percent of any particular class of Stock of the Corporate Partner.

(ii) *De minimis rule ceases to apply.*—If a partnership satisfies the conditions of the de minimis rule of paragraph (f)(1) of this section upon an acquisition of Stock of the Corporate Partner or revaluation event as described in §1.704-1(b)(2)(iv)(f), but later fails to satisfy the conditions of the de minimis rule upon a subsequent acquisition or revaluation event, then solely for purposes of paragraph (d) of this section, the Corporate Partner may compute its gain on the subsequent acquisition or revaluation event as if it had already recognized gain at the previous event. Neither the Corporate Partner nor the partnership increases its basis by the gain the Corporate Partner would have recognized if the de minimis rule of paragraph (f)(1) of this section did not apply to the prior acquisition or revaluation event.

(2) *Certain dispositions of stock.*—Unless acquired as part of a plan to circumvent the purpose of this section, this section does not apply to Stock of the Corporate Partner that —

(i) Is disposed of (by sale or distribution) by the partnership before the due date (including extensions) of its federal income tax return for the taxable year during which the Stock of the Corporate Partner is acquired (or for the taxable year in which the Corporate Partner becomes a partner, whichever is applicable); and

(ii) Is not distributed to the Corporate Partner or a corporation that controls the Corporate Partner within the meaning of section 304(c), except that section 318(a)(1) and (3) shall not apply.

(g) *Tiered partnerships.*—The rules of this section shall apply to tiered partnerships in a manner that is consistent with the purpose set forth in paragraph (a) of this section.

(h) *Examples.*—The following examples illustrate the principles of this section. All amounts in the following examples are reported in millions of dollars:

Example 1. Deemed redemption rule – contribution of Stock of the Corporate Partner. (i) In Year 1, X, a corporation, and A, an individual, form partnership AX as equal partners in all respects. X contributes Asset 1 with a fair market value of $100 and a basis of $20. A contributes X stock, which is Stock of the Corporate Partner, with a basis and fair market value of $100.

(ii) Because A and X are equal partners in AX in all respects, the partnership formation causes X's interest in X stock to increase from $0 to $50 and its interest in Asset 1 to decrease from $100 to $50. Thus, the partnership formation is a Section 337(d) Transaction because the formation has the effect of an exchange by X of $50 of Asset 1 for $50 of X stock.

(iii) X must recognize gain under paragraph (d) of this section with respect to Asset 1 to prevent the circumvention of section 311(b) principles. X's gain equals the product of X's Gain Percentage and the gain from Asset 1 that X would recognize (decreased, but not below zero, by any gain that X recognized with respect to Asset 1 in the Section 337(d) Transaction under any other provision of this chapter) if, immediately before the Section 337(d) Transaction, all assets were sold in a fully taxable transaction for cash in an amount equal to the fair market value of such property. If Asset 1 had been sold in a fully taxable transaction immediately before the formation of partnership AX, X's allocable share of gain would have been $80. X's Gain Percentage is 50 percent (equal to a fraction, the numerator of which is X's $50 interest in Asset 1 effectively exchanged for X stock, and the denominator of which is X's $100 interest in Asset 1 immediately before the Section 337(d) Transaction). Thus, X recognizes $40 of gain ($80 multiplied by 50 percent) under the deemed redemption rule in paragraph (d) of this section. Under paragraph (d)(4)(i) of this section, X's basis in its AX partnership interest increases from $20 to $60. Under paragraph (d)(4)(ii) of this section, AX's basis in Asset 1 increases from $20 to $60 because Asset 1 is the appreciated property treated as the subject of the exchange.

Example 2. Deemed redemption rule – contribution of stock in a corporation that controls the Corporate Partner. (i) In Year 1, X, a corporation, and A, an individual, form partnership AX as equal partners in all respects. X contributes Asset 1 with a fair market value of $100 and a basis of $20. A contributes stock in P, with a basis and fair market value of $100. P is the sole owner of X. P's interest in X constitutes 10 percent of P's total assets.

(ii) Because P controls X within the meaning of section 304(c), stock in P is Stock of the Corporate Partner under paragraph (c)(2)(i) of this section.

(iii) Because A and X are equal partners in AX in all respects, the partnership formation causes X's interest in Stock of the Corporate Partner stock to increase from $0 to $50 and its interest in Asset 1 to decrease from $100 to $50. Thus, the partnership formation is a Section 337(d) Transaction because the formation has the effect of an exchange by X of $50 of Asset 1 for $50 of Stock of the Corporate Partner.

(iv) X must recognize gain under paragraph (d) of this section with respect to Asset 1 to prevent the circumvention of section 311(b) principles. X's gain equals the product of X's Gain Percentage and the gain from Asset 1 that X would recognize (decreased, but not below zero, by any gain that X recognized with respect to Asset 1 in the Section 337(d) Transaction under any other provision of this chapter) if, immediately before the Section 337(d) Transaction, all assets were sold in a fully taxable transaction for cash in an amount equal to the fair market value of such property. If Asset 1 had been sold in a fully taxable transaction immediately before the formation of partnership AX, X's allocable share of gain would have been $80. X's Gain Percentage is 50 percent (equal to a fraction, the numerator of which is X's $50 interest in Asset 1 effectively exchanged for Stock of the Corporate Partner, and the denominator of which is X's $100 interest in Asset 1 immediately before the Section 337(d) Transaction). Thus, X recognizes $40 of gain ($80 multiplied by 50 percent) under the deemed redemption rule in paragraph (d) of this section. Under paragraph (d)(4)(i) of this section, X's basis in its AX partnership interest increases from $20 to $60. Under paragraph (d)(4)(ii) of this section, AX's basis in Asset 1 increases from $20 to $60 because Asset 1 is the appreciated property treated as the subject of the exchange.

Example 3. Distribution of Stock of the Corporate Partner – pro rata distribution. (i) The facts are the same as in *Example 1(i)* of this paragraph (h). AX liquidates in Year 9, when Asset 1 and the X stock each have a fair market value of $200. X and A each receive 50 percent of Asset 1 and 50 percent of the X stock in the liquidation. At the time AX liquidates, X's basis in its AX partnership interest is $60 and A's basis in its AX partnership interest is $100.

(ii) When AX liquidates, X's interests in its stock and in Asset 1 do not change. Thus, the liquidation is not a Section 337(d) Transaction because it does not have the effect of an exchange by X of appreciated property for Stock of the Corporate Partner.

(iii) Paragraph (e) of this section applies because the distributed X stock was the subject of a previous Section 337(d) Transaction and because section 732(f) does not apply. Under §1.732-1(c)(1)(iii), the distribution to X of X stock is deemed to immediately precede the distribution of 50 percent of Asset 1 to X for purposes of determining X's basis in the distributed property. For purposes of determining X's basis in Asset 1 and X's gain on distribution, the basis of the distributed X stock is treated as $50, the greater of $50 (50 percent of the stock's $100 basis in the hands of the partnership), or $50, the fair market value of that distributed X stock ($100) less X's allocable share of gain from the distributed X stock if AX had sold all of its assets in a fully taxable transaction for cash in an amount equal to the fair market value of such property immediately before the distribution ($50). Thus, X reduces its basis in its partnership interest by $50 prior to the distribution of Asset 1. Accordingly, X's basis in the distributed portion of Asset 1 is $10. Because AX's basis in the distributed X stock immediately before the distribution ($50) does not exceed X's basis in its AX partnership interest immediately before the distribution ($60), X recognizes no gain under paragraph (e)(3) of this section.

Example 4. Distribution of Stock of the Corporate Partner – non pro rata distribution. (i) The facts are the same as *Example 3(i)* of this paragraph (h), except that when AX liquidates, X receives 75 percent of the X stock and 25 percent of Asset 1 and A receives 25 percent of the X stock and 75 percent of Asset 1.

(ii) The liquidation of AX causes X's interest in X stock to increase from $100 to $150 and its interest in Asset 1 to decrease from $100 to $50. Thus, AX's liquidating distributions of X stock and Asset 1 to X are a Section 337(d) Transaction because the distributions have the effect of an exchange by X of $50 of Asset 1 for $50 of X stock.

(iii)(A) X must recognize gain with respect to Asset 1 to prevent the circumvention of section 311(b) principles. Under paragraph (e)(1) of this section, paragraph (d) of this section is applied as if X and A amended the AX partnership agreement to allocate to X a 100 percent interest in the distributed portion of the X stock. X must recognize gain equal to the product of X's Gain Percentage and the gain from Asset 1 that X would have recognized (decreased, but not below zero, by any gain X recognized with respect to Asset 1 in the Section 337(d) Transaction under any other provision of this chapter) if, immediately before the Section 337(d) Transaction, AX had sold all of its assets in a fully taxable transaction for cash in an amount equal to the fair market value of such property.

(B) If Asset 1 had been sold in a fully taxable transaction immediately before the amendment of the AX partnership agreement, X's allocable share of gain would have been $90, or the sum of X's $40 remaining gain under section 704(c) and $50 of the $100 post-contribution appreciation. X's Gain Percentage is 50 percent (equal to a fraction, the numerator of which is X's $50 interest in Asset 1 effectively exchanged for X stock, and the denominator of which is X's $100 interest in Asset 1 immediately before the Section 337(d) Transaction). Thus, X recognizes $45 of gain ($90 multiplied by 50 percent) under the deemed redemption rule in paragraph (d) of this section. Under paragraph (d)(4)(i) of this section, X's basis in its AX partnership interest increases from $60 to $105. Under paragraph (d)(4)(ii) of this section, AX's basis in Asset 1 increases from $60 to $105 because Asset 1 is the appreciated property treated as the subject of the exchange.

(iv)(A) Paragraph (e) of this section applies because the distributed X stock was the subject of a previous Section 337(d) Transaction and because section 732(f) does not apply. Under §1.732-1(c)(1)(iii), AX is treated as first distributing the X stock to X before the distribution of 25 percent of Asset 1. For purposes of determining X's basis in Asset 1 and X's gain on distribution, the basis of the distributed X stock is treated as $100, the greater of $75 (75 percent of the stock's $100 basis in the hands of the partnership) or $100, the fair market value of the distributed X stock ($150) less X's allocable share of gain if the partnership had sold all of the X stock immediately before the distribution for cash in an amount equal to its fair market value ($50). Thus, X will reduce its basis in its partnership interest by $100 prior to the distribution of Asset 1. Accordingly, X's basis in the distributed portion of Asset 1 is $5. Because AX's basis in the distributed X stock immediately before the distribution as computed for purposes of this section ($100) does not exceed X's basis in its AX partnership interest immediately before the distribution ($105), X recognizes no additional gain under paragraph (e)(3) of this section.

(B) For purposes of determining A's basis in Asset 1 and A's gain on distribution, the basis of the distributed X stock is treated as $25, the greater of $25 (25 percent of the stock's $100 basis in the hands of the partnership) or $0, the fair market value of the distributed X stock ($50) less A's allocable share of gain if the partnership had sold all of the X stock immediately before the distribution for cash in an amount equal to its fair market value ($50). Thus, A will reduce its basis in its

partnership interest by $25 prior to the distribution of Asset 1. Accordingly, A's basis in the distributed portion of Asset 1 is $75. Because AX's basis in the distributed X stock immediately before the distribution as computed for purposes of this section ($100) does not exceed A's basis in its AX partnership interest immediately before the distribution ($100), A recognizes no additional gain under paragraph (e)(3) of this section.

Example 5. Deemed redemption rule – subsequent purchase of Stock of the Corporate Partner. The facts are the same as *Example 1(i)* of this paragraph (h), except that A contributes cash of $100 instead of X stock. In a later year, when the value of Asset 1 has not changed, AX uses the contributed cash to purchase X stock for $100. AX's purchase of X stock has the effect of an exchange by X of appreciated property for X stock, and thus, is a Section 337(d) Transaction. X must recognize gain at the time, and to the extent, that X's share of appreciated property (other than X stock) is reduced in exchange for X stock. Thus, the consequences of the partnership's purchase of X stock are the same as those described in *Example 1(ii)* and *(iii)* of this paragraph (h), resulting in X recognizing $40 of gain.

Example 6. Change in allocation ratios – amendment of partnership agreement. (i) The facts are the same as *Example 3(i)* of this paragraph (h), except that in Year 9, AX does not liquidate, and the AX partnership agreement is amended to allocate to X 80 percent of the income, gain, loss, and deduction from the X stock and to allocate to A 80 percent of the income, gain, loss, and deduction from Asset 1. If AX had sold the partnership assets immediately before the change to the partnership agreement, X would have been allocated $90 of gain from Asset 1 and $50 of gain from the X stock.

(ii) The amendment to the AX partnership agreement causes X's interest in its stock to increase from $100 (50 percent of the stock value immediately before the amendment of the agreement) to $160 (80 percent of stock value immediately following amendment of agreement) and its interest in Asset 1 to decrease from $100 to $40. Thus, the amendment of the partnership agreement is a Section 337(d) Transaction because the amendment has the effect of an exchange by X of $60 of Asset 1 for $60 of its stock.

(iii) X must recognize gain equal to the product of X's Gain Percentage and the gain from Asset 1 that X would have recognized (decreased, but not below zero, by any gain X recognized with respect to Asset 1 in the Section 337(d) Transaction under any other provision of this chapter) if, immediately before the Section 337(d) Transaction, AX had sold all of its assets in a fully taxable transaction for cash in an amount equal to the fair market value of such property. If Asset 1 had been sold in a fully taxable transaction immediately before the amendment of the AX partnership agreement, X's allocable share of gain would have been $90, or the sum of X's $40 remaining gain under section 704(c) and 50 percent of the $100 post-contribution appreciation. X's Gain Percentage is 60 percent (equal to a fraction, the numerator of which is X's $60 interest in Asset 1 effectively exchanged for X stock, and the denominator of which is X's $100 interest in Asset 1 immediately before the Section 337(d) Transaction). Thus, X recognizes $54 of gain ($90 multiplied by 60 percent) under the deemed redemption rule in paragraph (d) of this section. Under paragraph (d)(4)(i) of this section, X's basis in its AX partnership interest increases from $60 to $114. Under paragraph (d)(4)(ii) of this section, AX's basis in Asset 1 increases from $60 to $114 because Asset 1 is the appreciated property treated as the subject of the exchange.

Example 7. Change in allocation ratios – admission and exit of a partner. (i) The facts are the same as *Example 1(i)* of this paragraph (h). In addition, in Year 2, when the values of Asset 1 and the X stock have not changed, B contributes $100 of cash to AX in exchange for a one-third interest in the partnership. Upon the admission of B as a partner, X's interest in Asset 1 decreases from $50 to $33.33, and its interest in B's contributed cash increases. B's admission is not a Section 337(d) Transaction because it does not have the effect of an exchange by X of its interest in Asset 1 for X stock. Accordingly, X does not recognize gain under paragraph (d) of this section.

(ii) In Year 9, when the values of Asset 1 and the X stock have not changed, the partnership distributes $50 of cash and 50 percent of Asset 1 (valued at $50) to B in liquidation of B's interest. X and A are equal partners in all respects after the distribution. Upon the liquidation of B's interest, X's interest in Asset 1 decreases from $33.33 to $25, and its interest in X stock increases from $33.33 to $50. AX's liquidation of B's interest has the effect of an exchange by X of appreciated property for X stock, and thus, is a Section 337(d) Transaction.

(iii) Pursuant to paragraph (d)(2) of this section, X's interest in X stock and other appreciated property held by the partnership is determined based on all facts and circumstances, including allocation and distribution rights in the partnership agreement. However, paragraph (d)(2) of this section also requires that X's interest in its stock for purposes of paragraph (d) will never be less than the Corporate Partner's largest interest (by value) in those shares of Stock of the

Corporate Partner taken into account when the partnership previously determined whether there had been a Section 337(d) Transaction (regardless of whether the Corporate Partner recognized gain in the earlier transaction). Although X's interest in X stock increases to $50 upon AX's liquidation of B's interest, X's largest interest previously taken into account under paragraph (d)(1) of this section was $50. Thus, X's interest in its stock is not considered to be increased, and X therefore recognizes no gain under paragraph (d) of this section, provided that the transactions did not occur as part of a plan or arrangement to circumvent the purpose of this section.

Example 8. Change in allocation ratios – plan to circumvent purpose of this section. (i) In Year 1, X, a corporation, and A, an individual, contribute $99 and $1, respectively, to newly-formed partnership AX, with X receiving a 99 percent interest in AX and A receiving a 1 percent interest in AX. AX borrows $100,000 from a third-party lender and uses the proceeds to purchase X stock, which is Stock of the Corporate Partner. Later, as part of a plan or arrangement to circumvent the purposes of this section, A contributes $99,999 of cash, which AX uses to repay the loan, and X contributes Asset 1 with a fair market value of $99,901 and basis of $20,000. After these contributions, A and X are equal partners in AX in all respects.

(ii) Pursuant to paragraph (d)(2) of this section, X's interest in X stock and other appreciated property held by the partnership is determined based on all facts and circumstances, including allocation and distribution rights in the partnership agreement. Generally, pursuant to paragraph (d)(2) of this section, X's interest in X stock for purposes of paragraph (d) of this section will never be less than the Corporate Partner's largest interest (by value) in those shares of Stock of the Corporate Partner taken into account when the partnership previously determined whether there had been a Section 337(d) Transaction (regardless of whether the Corporate Partner recognized gain in the earlier transaction). This limitation does not apply, however, if the reduction in X's interest in X's stock occurred as part of a plan or arrangement to circumvent the purpose of this section. Because the transactions described in this example are part of a plan or arrangement to circumvent the purpose of this section, the limitation in paragraph (d)(2) of this section does not apply. Accordingly, the deemed redemption rule under paragraph (d) of this section applies to the transactions with the consequences described in *Example 1(iii)* of this paragraph (h), resulting in X recognizing $39,950.50 of gain.

Example 9. Tiered partnership. (i) In Year 1, X, a corporation, and A, an individual, form partnership UTP. X contributes Asset 1 with a fair market value of $80 and a basis of $0 in exchange for an 80 percent interest in UTP. A contributes $20 of cash in exchange for a 20 percent interest in UTP. UTP and B, an individual, form partnership LTP as equal partners. UTP contributes Asset 1 and $20 of cash. B contributes X stock, which is Stock of the Corporate Partner, with a basis and fair market value of $100.

(ii) Pursuant to paragraph (g) of this section, the rules of this section shall apply to tiered partnerships in a manner that is consistent with the purpose set forth in paragraph (a) of this section. Pursuant to paragraph (d)(1) of this section, if X is in a partnership that engages in a Section 337(d) Transaction, X must recognize gain at the time, and to the extent, that X's share of appreciated property is reduced in exchange for X stock. The formation of LTP causes X's interest in X stock to increase from $0 to $40 and its interest in Asset 1 to decrease from $64 to $32. Thus, LTP's formation is a Section 337(d) Transaction because the formation has the effect of an exchange by X of $32 of Asset 1 for $32 of X stock.

(iii) X must recognize gain with respect to Asset 1 to prevent the circumvention of section 311(b) principles. X must recognize gain equal to the product of X's Gain Percentage and the gain from Asset 1 (decreased, but not below zero, by any gain X recognized with respect to Asset 1 in the Section 337(d) Transaction under any other provision of this chapter) that X would recognize if, immediately before the Section 337(d) Transaction, all assets were sold in a fully taxable transaction for cash in an amount equal to the fair market value of such property. If Asset 1 had been sold in a fully taxable transaction immediately before LTP's formation, X's allocable share of gain would have been $80 pursuant to section 704(c). X's Gain Percentage is 50 percent (equal to a fraction, the numerator of which is X's $32 interest in Asset 1 effectively exchanged for X stock, and the denominator of which is X's $64 interest in Asset 1 immediately before the Section 337(d) Transaction). Thus, X recognizes $40 of gain ($80 multiplied by 50 percent) under the deemed redemption rule in paragraph (d) of this section. Under paragraphs (d)(4)(i) and (ii) of this section, X's basis in its UTP partnership interest increases from $0 to $40, UTP's basis in its LTP partnership interest increases from $20 to $60, and LTP's basis in Asset 1 increases from $0 to $40 pursuant to paragraph (g) of this section.

(i) *Applicability date.*—This section applies to transactions occurring on or after June 12, 2015. [Reg. § 1.337(d)-3.]

☐ [*T.D.* 9833, 6-7-18.]

§ 1.337(d)-4. Taxable to tax-exempt.—(a) *Gain or loss recognition.*—(1) *General rule.*—Except as provided in paragraph (b) of this section, if a taxable corporation transfers all or substantially all of its assets to one or more tax-exempt entities, the taxable corporation must recognize gain or loss immediately before the transfer as if the assets transferred were sold at their fair market values. But see section 267 and paragraph (d) of this section concerning limitations on the recognition of loss.

(2) *Change in corporation's tax status treated as asset transfer.*—Except as provided in paragraphs (a)(3) and (b) of this section, a taxable corporation's change in status to a tax-exempt entity will be treated as if it transferred all of its assets to a tax-exempt entity immediately before the change in status becomes effective in a transaction to which paragraph (a)(1) of this section applies. For example, if a state, a political subdivision thereof, or an entity any portion of whose income is excluded from gross income under section 115, acquires the stock of a taxable corporation and thereafter any of the taxable corporation's income is excluded from gross income under section 115, the taxable corporation will be treated as if it transferred all of its assets to a tax-exempt entity immediately before the stock acquisition.

(3) *Exceptions for certain changes in status.*—(i) *To whom available.*—Paragraph (a)(2) of this section does not apply to the following corporations—

(A) A corporation previously tax-exempt under section 501(a) which regains its tax-exempt status under section 501(a) within three years from the later of a final adverse adjudication on the corporation's tax exempt status, or the filing by the corporation, or by the Secretary or his delegate under section 6020(b), of a federal income tax return of the type filed by a taxable corporation;

(B) A corporation previously tax-exempt under section 501(a) or that applied for but did not receive recognition of exemption under section 501(a) before January 15, 1997, if such corporation is tax-exempt under section 501(a) within three years from January 28, 1999;

(C) A newly formed corporation that is tax-exempt under section 501(a) (other than an organization described in section 501(c)(7)) within three taxable years from the end of the taxable year in which it was formed;

(D) A newly formed corporation that is tax-exempt under section 501(a) as an organization described in section 501(c)(7) within seven taxable years from the end of the taxable year in which it was formed;

(E) A corporation previously tax-exempt under section 501(a) as an organization described in section 501(c)(12), which, in a given taxable year or years prior to again becoming tax-exempt, is a taxable corporation solely because less than 85 percent of its income consists of amounts collected from members for the sole purpose of meeting losses and expenses; if, in a taxable year, such a corporation would be a taxable corporation even if 85 percent or more of its income consists of amounts collected from members for the sole purpose of meeting losses and expenses (a non-85 percent violation), paragraph (a)(3)(i)(A) of this section shall apply as if the corporation became a taxable corporation in its first taxable year that a non-85 percent violation occurred; or

(F) A corporation previously taxable that becomes tax-exempt under section 501(a) as an organization described in section 501(c)(15) if during each taxable year in which it is described in section 501(c)(15) the organization is the subject of a court supervised rehabilitation, conservatorship, liquidation, or similar state proceeding; if such a corporation continues to be described in section 501(c)(15) in a taxable year when it is no longer the subject of a court supervised rehabilitation, conservatorship, liquidation, or similar state proceeding, paragraph (a)(2) of this section shall apply as if the corporation first became tax-exempt for such taxable year.

(ii) *Application for recognition.*—An organization is deemed to have or regain tax-exempt status within one of the periods described in paragraph (a)(3)(i)(A), (B), (C), or (D) of this section if it files an application for recognition of exemption with the Commissioner within the applicable period and the application either results in a determination by the Commissioner or a final adjudication that the organization is tax-exempt under section 501(a) during any part of the applicable period. The preceding sentence does not require the filing of an application for recognition of exemption by any organization not otherwise required, such as by § 1.501(a)-1, § 1.505(c)-1T, and § 1.508-1(a), to apply for recognition of exemption.

(iii) *Anti-abuse rule.*—This paragraph (a)(3) does not apply to a corporation that, with a principal purpose of avoiding the application of paragraph (a)(1) or (a)(2) of this section, acquires all or substantially all of the assets of another taxable corporation and then changes its status to that of a tax-exempt entity.

(4) *Related transactions.*—This section applies to any series of related transactions having an effect similar to any of the transactions to which this section applies.

(b) *Exceptions.*—Paragraph (a) of this section does not apply to—

(1) Any assets transferred to a tax-exempt entity to the extent that the assets are used in an activity the income from which is subject to tax under section 511(a) (referred to hereinafter as a "section 511(a) activity"). However, if assets used to any extent in a section 511(a) activity are disposed of by the tax-exempt entity, then, notwithstanding any other provision of law (except section 1031 or section 1033), any gain (not in excess of the amount not recognized by reason of the preceding sentence) shall be included in the tax-exempt entity's unrelated business taxable income. To the extent that the tax-exempt entity ceases to use the assets in a section 511(a) activity, the entity will be treated for purposes of this paragraph (b)(1) as having disposed of the assets on the date of the cessation for their fair market value. For purposes of paragraph (a)(1) of this section and this paragraph (b)(1)—

(i) If during the first taxable year following the transfer of an asset or the corporation's change to tax-exempt status the asset will be used by the tax-exempt entity partly or wholly in a section 511(a) activity, the taxable corporation will recognize an amount of gain or loss that bears the same ratio to the asset's built-in gain or loss as 100 percent reduced by the percentage of use for such taxable year in the section 511(a) activity bears to 100 percent. For purposes of determining the gain or loss, if any, to be recognized, the taxable corporation may rely on a written representation from the tax-exempt entity estimating the percentage of the asset's anticipated use in a section 511(a) activity for such taxable year, using a reasonable method of allocation, unless the taxable corporation has reason to believe that the tax-exempt entity's representation is not made in good faith;

(ii) If for any taxable year the percentage of an asset's use in a section 511(a) activity decreases from the estimate used in computing gain or loss recognized under paragraph (b)(1)(i) of this section, adjusted for any decreases taken into account under this paragraph (b)(1)(ii) in prior taxable years, the tax-exempt entity shall recognize an amount of gain or loss that bears the same ratio to the asset's built-in gain or loss as the percentage point decrease in use in the section 511(a) activity for the taxable year bears to 100 percent;

(iii) If property on which all or a portion of the gain or loss is not recognized by reason of the first sentence of paragraph (b)(1) of this section is disposed of in a transaction that qualifies for nonrecognition treatment under section 1031 or section 1033, the tax-exempt entity must treat the replacement property as remaining subject to paragraph (b)(1) of this section to the extent that the exchanged or involuntarily converted property was so subject;

(iv) The tax-exempt entity must use the same reasonable method of allocation for determining the percentage that it uses the assets in a section 511(a) activity as it uses for other tax purposes, such as determining the amount of depreciation deductions. The tax-exempt entity also must use this same reasonable method of allocation for each taxable year that it holds the assets; and

(v) An asset's built-in gain or loss is the amount that would be recognized under paragraph (a)(1) of this section except for this paragraph (b)(1);

(2) Any transfer of assets to the extent gain or loss otherwise is recognized by the taxable corporation on the transfer. See, for example, sections 336, 337(b)(2), 367, and 1001;

(3) Any transfer of assets to the extent the transaction qualifies for nonrecognition treatment under section 1031 or section 1033; or

(4) Any forfeiture of a taxable corporation's assets in a criminal or civil action to the United States, the government of a possession of the United States, a state, the District of Columbia, the government of a foreign country, or a political subdivision of any of the foregoing; or any expropriation of a taxable corporation's assets by the government of a foreign country.

(c) *Definitions.*—For purposes of this section:

(1) *Taxable corporation.*—A *taxable corporation* is any corporation that is not a tax-exempt entity as defined in paragraph (c)(2) of this section.

(2) *Tax-exempt entity.*—A *tax-exempt entity* is—

(i) Any entity that is exempt from tax under section 501(a) or section 529;

(ii) A charitable remainder annuity trust or charitable remainder unitrust as defined in section 664(d);

(iii) The United States, the government of a possession of the United States, a state, the District of Columbia, the government of a foreign country, or a political subdivision of any of the foregoing;

(iv) An Indian Tribal Government as defined in section 7701(a)(40), a subdivision of an Indian Tribal Government determined in accordance with section 7871(d), or an agency or instrumentality of an Indian Tribal Government or subdivision thereof;

(v) An Indian Tribal Corporation organized under section 17 of the Indian Reorganization Act of 1934, 25 U.S.C. 477, or section 3 of the Oklahoma Welfare Act, 25 U.S.C. 503;

(vi) An international organization as defined in section 7701(a)(18);

(vii) An entity any portion of whose income is excluded under section 115; or

(viii) An entity that would not be taxable under the Internal Revenue Code for reasons substantially similar to those applicable to any entity listed in this paragraph (c)(2) unless otherwise explicitly made exempt from the application of this section by statute or by action of the Commissioner.

(3) *Substantially all.*—The term *substantially all* has the same meaning as under section 368(a)(1)(C).

(d) *Loss limitation rule.*—For purposes of determining the amount of gain or loss recognized by a taxable corporation on the transfer of its assets to a tax-exempt entity under paragraph (a) of this section, if assets are acquired by the taxable corporation in a transaction to which section 351 applied or as a contribution to capital, or assets are distributed from the taxable corporation to a shareholder or another member of the taxable corporation's affiliated group, and in either case such acquisition or distribution is made as part of a plan a principal purpose of which is to recognize loss by the taxable corporation on the transfer of such assets to the tax-exempt entity, the losses recognized by the taxable corporation on such assets transferred to the tax-exempt entity will be disallowed. For purposes of the preceding sentence, the principles of section 336(d)(2) apply.

(e) *Effective date.*—This section is applicable to transfers of assets as described in paragraph (a) of this section occurring after January 28, 1999, unless the transfer is pursuant to a written agreement which is (subject to customary conditions) binding on or before January 28, 1999. [Reg. § 1.337(d)-4.]

☐ [*T.D. 8802,* 12-28-98.]

[Reg. § 1.337(d)-5]

§ 1.337(d)-5. Old transitional rules imposing tax on property owned by a C corporation that becomes property of a RIC or REIT.—(a) *Treatment of C corporations.*—(1) *Scope.*—This section applies to the net built-in gain of C corporation assets that become assets of a RIC or REIT by—

(i) The qualification of a C corporation as a RIC or REIT; or

(ii) The transfer of assets of a C corporation to a RIC or REIT in a transaction in which the basis of such assets are determined by reference to the C corporation's basis (a carryover basis).

(2) *Net built-in gain.*—Net built-in gain is the excess of aggregate gains (including items of income) over aggregate losses.

(3) *General rule.*—Unless an election is made pursuant to paragraph (b) of this section, the C corporation will be treated, for all purposes including recognition of net built-in gain, as if it had sold all of its assets at their respective fair market values on the deemed liquidation date described in paragraph (a)(7) of this section and immediately liquidated.

(4) *Loss.*—Paragraph (a)(3) of this section shall not apply if its application would result in the recognition of net built-in loss.

(5) *Basis adjustment.*—If a corporation is subject to corporate-level tax under paragraph (a)(3) of this section, the bases of the assets in the hands of the RIC or REIT will be adjusted to reflect the recognized net built-in gain. This adjustment is made by taking the C corporation's basis in each asset, and, as appropriate, increasing it by the amount of any built-in gain attributable to that asset, or decreasing it by the amount of any built-in loss attributable to that asset.

(6) *Exception.*—(i) *In general.*—Paragraph (a)(3) of this section does not apply to any C corporation that—

(A) Immediately prior to qualifying to be taxed as a RIC was subject to tax as a C corporation for a period not exceeding one taxable year; and

(B) Immediately prior to being subject to tax as a C corporation was subject to the RIC tax provisions for a period of at least one taxable year.

(ii) *Additional requirement.*—The exception described in paragraph (a)(6)(i) of this section applies only to assets acquired by the corporation during the year when it was subject to tax as a C corporation in a transaction that does not result in its basis in the asset being determined by reference to a corporate transferor's basis.

(7) *Deemed liquidation date.*—(i) *Conversions.*—In the case of a C corporation that qualifies to be taxed as a RIC or REIT, the deemed liquidation date is the last day of its last taxable year before the taxable year in which it qualifies to be taxed as a RIC or REIT.

(ii) *Carryover basis transfers.*—In the case of a C corporation that transfers property to a RIC or REIT in a carryover basis transaction, the deemed liquidation date is the day before the date of the transfer.

(b) *Section 1374 treatment.*—(1) *In general.*—Paragraph (a) of this section will not apply if the transferee RIC or REIT elects (as described in paragraph (b)(3) of this section) to be subject to the rules of section 1374, and the regulations thereunder. The electing RIC or REIT will be subject to corporate-level taxation on the built-in gain recognized during the 10-year period on assets formerly held by the transferor C corporation. The built-in gains of electing RICs and REITs, and the corporate-level tax imposed on such gains, are subject to rules similar to the rules relating to net income from foreclosure property of REITs. See sections 857(a)(1)(A)(ii), and 857(b)(2)(B), (D), and (E). An election made under this paragraph (b) shall be irrevocable.

(2) *Ten-year recognition period.*—In the case of a C corporation that qualifies to be taxed as a RIC or REIT, the 10-year recognition period described in section 1374(d)(7) begins on the first day of the RIC's or REIT's taxable year for which the corporation qualifies to be taxed as a RIC or REIT. In the case of a C corporation that transfers property to a RIC or REIT in a carryover basis transaction, the 10-year recognition period begins on the day the assets are acquired by the RIC or REIT.

(3) *Making the election.*—A RIC or REIT validly makes a section 1374 election with the following statement: "[Insert name and employer identification number of electing RIC or REIT] elects under paragraph (b) of this section to be subject to the rules of section 1374 and the regulations thereunder with respect to its assets which formerly were held by a C corporation, [insert name and employer identification number of the C corporation, if different from name and employer identification number of RIC or REIT]." This statement must be signed by an official authorized to sign the income tax return of the RIC or REIT and attached to the RIC's or REIT's Federal income tax return for the first taxable year in which the assets of the C corporation become assets of the RIC or REIT.

(c) *Special rule.*—In cases where the first taxable year in which the assets of the C corporation become assets of the RIC or REIT ends after June 10, 1987 but before March 8, 2000, the section 1374 election may be filed with the first Federal income tax return filed by the RIC or REIT after March 8, 2000.

(d) *Effective date.*—In the case of carryover basis transactions involving the transfer of property of a C corporation to a RIC or REIT, the regulations apply to transactions occurring on or after June 10, 1987, and before January 2, 2002. In the case of a C corporation that qualifies to be taxed as a RIC or REIT, the regulations apply to such qualifications that are effective for taxable years beginning on or after June 10, 1987, and before January 2, 2002. However, RICs and REITs that are subject to section 1374 treatment under this section may not rely on paragraph (b)(1) of this section, but must apply paragraphs (c)(1)(i), (c)(2)(i), (c)(2)(ii), and (c)(3) of §1.337(d)-6, with respect to built-in gains and losses recognized in taxable years beginning on or after January 2, 2002. In lieu of applying this section, taxpayers may rely on §1.337(d)-6 to determine the tax consequences (for all taxable years) of any conversion transaction. For transactions and qualifications that occur on or after January 2, 2002, see §1.337(d)-7. [Reg. §1.337(d)-5.]

☐ [T.D. 8872, 2-4-2000. *Amended by* T.D. 8975, 12-31-2001. *Redesignated and amended by* T.D. 9047, 3-13-2003.]

[Reg. §1.337(d)-6]

§1.337(d)-6. New transitional rules imposing tax on property owned by a C corporation that becomes property of a RIC or REIT.—(a) *General rule.*—(1) *Property owned by a C corporation that becomes property of a RIC or REIT.*—If property owned by a C corporation (as defined in paragraph (a) (2) (i) of this section) becomes the property of a RIC or REIT (the converted property) in a conversion transaction (as defined in paragraph (a)(2)(ii) of this section), then deemed sale treatment will apply as described in paragraph (b) of this section, unless the RIC or REIT elects section 1374 treatment with respect to the conversion transaction as provided in paragraph (c) of this section. See paragraph (d) of this section for exceptions to this paragraph (a).

(2) *Definitions.*—(i) *C corporation.*—For purposes of this section, the term *C corporation* has the meaning provided in section 1361(a)(2) except that the term does not include a RIC or REIT.

(ii) *Conversion transaction.*—For purposes of this section, the term *conversion transaction* means the qualification of a C corporation as a RIC or REIT or the transfer of property owned by a C corporation to a RIC or REIT.

(b) *Deemed sale treatment.*—(1) *In general.*—If property owned by a C corporation becomes the property of a RIC or REIT in a conversion transaction, then the C corporation recognizes gain and loss as if it sold the converted property to an unrelated party at fair market value on the deemed sale date (as defined in paragraph (b)(3) of this section). This paragraph (b) does not apply if its application would result in the recognition of a net loss. For this purpose, *net loss* is the excess of aggregate losses over aggregate gains (including items of income), without regard to character.

(2) *Basis adjustment.*—If a corporation recognizes a net gain under paragraph (b)(1) of this section, then the converted property has a basis in the hands of the RIC or REIT equal to the fair market value of such property on the deemed sale date.

(3) *Deemed sale date.*—(i) *RIC or REIT qualifications.*—If the conversion transaction is a qualification of a C corporation as a RIC or REIT, then the deemed sale date is the end of the last day of the C corporation's last taxable year before the first taxable year in which it qualifies to be taxed as a RIC or REIT.

(ii) *Other conversion transactions.*—If the conversion transaction is a transfer of property owned by a C corporation to a RIC or REIT, then the deemed sale date is the end of the day before the day of the transfer.

(4) *Example.*—The rules of this paragraph (b) are illustrated by the following example:

Example. Deemed sale treatment on merger into RIC. (i) X, a calendar-year taxpayer, has qualified as a RIC since January 1, 1991. On May 31, 1994, Y, a C corporation and calendar-year taxpayer, transfers all of its property to X in a transaction that qualifies as a reorganization under section 368(a)(1)(C). X does not elect section 1374 treatment under paragraph (c) of this section and chooses not to rely on §1.337(d)-5. As a result of the transfer, Y is subject to deemed sale treatment under this paragraph (b) on its tax return for the short taxable year ending May 31, 1994. On May 31, 1994, Y's only assets are Capital Asset, which has a fair market value of $100,000 and a basis of $40,000 as of the end of May 30, 1994, and $50,000 cash. Y also has an unrestricted net operating loss carryforward of $12,000 and accumulated earnings and profits of $50,000. Y has no taxable income for the short taxable year ending May 31, 1994, other than gain recognized under this paragraph (b). In 1997, X sells Capital Asset for $110,000. Assume the applicable corporate tax rate is 35%.

(ii) Under this paragraph (b), Y is treated as if it sold the converted property (Capital Asset and $50,000 cash) at fair market value on May 30, 1994, recognizing $60,000 of gain ($150,000 amount realized – $90,000 basis). Y must report the gain on its tax return for the short taxable year ending May 31, 1994. Y may offset this gain with its $12,000 net operating loss carryforward and will pay tax of $16,800 (35% of $48,000).

(iii) Under section 381, X succeeds to Y's accumulated earnings and profits. Y's accumulated earnings and profits of $50,000 increase by $60,000 and decrease by $16,800 as a result of the deemed sale. Thus, the aggregate amount of subchapter C earnings and profits that must be distributed to satisfy section 852(a)(2)(B) is $93,200 ($50,000 + $60,000 – $16,800). X's basis in Capital Asset is $100,000. On X's sale of Capital Asset in 1997, X recognizes $10,000 of gain, which is taken into account in computing X's net capital gain for purposes of section 852(b)(3).

(c) *Election of section 1374 treatment.*—(1) *In general.*—(i) *Property owned by a C corporation that becomes property of a RIC or REIT.*—Paragraph (b) of this section does not apply if the RIC or REIT that was formerly a C corporation or that acquired property from a C corporation makes the election described in paragraph (c)(4) of this section. A RIC or REIT that makes such an election will be subject to tax on the net built-in gain in the converted property under the rules of section 1374 and the regulations thereunder, as modified by this paragraph (c), as if the RIC or REIT were an S corporation.

(ii) *Property subject to the rules of section 1374 owned by a RIC, REIT, or S corporation that becomes property of a RIC or REIT.*—If property subject to the rules of section 1374 owned by a RIC, a REIT, or an S corporation (the predecessor) becomes the property of a RIC or REIT (the successor) in a continuation transaction, the rules of section 1374 apply to the successor to the same extent that the predecessor was subject to the rules of section 1374 with respect to such property, and the 10-year recognition period of the successor with respect to such property is reduced by the portion of the 10-year recognition period of the predecessor that expired before the date of the continuation transaction. For this purpose, a continuation transaction means the qualification of the predecessor as a RIC or REIT or the transfer of property from the predecessor to the successor in a transaction in which the successor's basis in the transferred property is determined, in whole or in part, by reference to the predecessor's basis in that property.

(2) *Modification of section 1374 treatment.*—(i) *Net recognized built-in gain for REITs.*—(A) *Prelimitation amount.*—The prelimitation amount determined as provided in §1.1374-2(a)(1) is reduced by the portion of such amount, if any, that is subject to tax under section 857(b)(4), (5), (6), or (7). For this purpose, the amount of a REIT's recognized built-in gain that is subject to tax under section 857(b)(5) is computed as follows:

(1) Where the tax under section 857(b)(5) is computed by reference to section 857(b)(5)(A), the amount of a REIT's recognized built-in gain that is subject to tax under section 857(b)(5) is the tax imposed by section 857(b)(5) multiplied by a fraction the numerator of which is the amount of recognized built-in gain (without regard to recognized built-in loss and recognized built-in gain from prohibited transactions) that is not derived from sources referred to in section 856(c)(2) and the denominator of which is the gross income (without regard to gross income from prohibited transactions) of the REIT that is not derived from sources referred to in section 856(c)(2).

(2) Where the tax under section 857(b)(5) is computed by reference to section 857(b)(5)(B), the amount of a REIT's recognized built-in gain that is subject to tax under section 857(b)(5) is the tax imposed by section 857(b)(5) multiplied by a fraction the numerator of which is the amount of recognized built-in gain (without regard to recognized built-in loss and recognized built-in gain from prohibited transactions) that is not derived from sources referred to in section 856(c)(3) and the denominator of which is the gross income (without regard to gross income from prohibited transactions) of the REIT that is not derived from sources referred to in section 856(c)(3).

(B) *Taxable income limitation.*—The taxable income limitation determined as provided in §1.1374-2(a)(2) is reduced by an amount equal to the tax imposed under sections 857(b)(5), (6), and (7).

(ii) *Loss carryforwards, credits and credit carryforwards.*—(A) *Loss carryforwards.*—Consistent with paragraph (c)(1)(i) of this section, net operating loss carryforwards and capital loss carryforwards arising in taxable years for which the corporation that generated the loss was not subject to subchapter M of chapter 1 of the Internal Revenue Code are allowed as a deduction against net recognized built-in gain to the extent allowed under section 1374 and the regulations thereunder. Such loss carryforwards must be used as a deduction against net recognized built-in gain for a taxable year to the greatest extent possible before such losses can be used to reduce other investment company taxable income for purposes of section 852(b) or other real estate investment trust taxable income for purposes of section 857(b) for that taxable year.

(B) *Credits and credit carryforwards.*—Consistent with paragraph (c)(1)(i) of this section, minimum tax credits and business credit carryforwards arising in taxable years for which the corporation that generated the credit was not subject to subchapter M of chapter 1 of the Internal Revenue Code are allowed to reduce the tax imposed on net recognized built-in gain under this paragraph (c) to the extent allowed under section 1374 and the regulations thereunder. Such credits and credit carryforwards must be used to reduce the tax imposed under this paragraph (c) on net recognized built-in gain for a taxable year to the greatest extent possible before such credits and credit carryforwards can be used to reduce the tax, if any, on other investment company taxable income for purposes of section 852(b) or on other real estate investment trust taxable income for purposes of section 857(b) for that taxable year.

(iii) *10-year recognition period.*—In the case of a conversion transaction that is a qualification of a C corporation as a RIC or REIT, the 10-year recognition period described in section 1374(d)(7) begins on the first day of the RIC's or REIT's first taxable year. In the case of other conversion transactions, the 10-year recognition period begins on the day the property is acquired by the RIC or REIT.

(3) *Coordination with subchapter M rules.*—(i) *Recognized built-in gains and losses subject to subchapter M.*—Recognized built-in gains and losses of a RIC or REIT are included in computing investment company taxable income for purposes of section 852(b)(2), real estate investment trust taxable income for purposes of section 857(b)(2), capital gains for purposes of sections 852(b)(3) and 857(b)(3), gross income derived from sources within any foreign country or possession of the United States for purposes of section 853, and the dividends paid deduction for purposes of sections 852(b)(2)(D), 852(b)(3)(A), 857(b)(2)(B), and 857(b)(3)(A). In computing such income and deduction items, capital loss carryforwards and net operating loss carryforwards that are used by the RIC or REIT to reduce recognized built-in gains are allowed as a deduction, but only to the extent that they are otherwise allowable as a deduction against such income under the Internal Revenue Code (including section 852(b)(2)(B)).

(ii) *Treatment of tax imposed.*—The amount of tax imposed under this paragraph (c) on net recognized built-in gain for a taxable year is treated as a loss sustained by the RIC or the REIT during such taxable year. The character of the loss is determined by allocating the tax proportionately (based on recognized built-in gain) among the items of recognized built-in gain included in net recognized built-in gain. With respect to RICs, the tax imposed under this paragraph (c) on net recognized built-in gain is treated as attributable to the portion of the RIC's taxable year occurring after October 31.

(4) *Making the section 1374 election.*—(i) *In general.*—A RIC or REIT makes a section 1374 election with the following statement: "[Insert name and employer identification number of electing RIC or REIT] elects under §1.337-6(c) to be subject to the rules of section 1374 and the regulations thereunder with respect to its property that formerly was held by a C corporation, [insert name and employer identification number of the C corporation, if different from name and employer identification number of the RIC or REIT]." However, a RIC or REIT need not file an election under this paragraph (c), but will be deemed to have made such an election if it can demonstrate that it informed the Internal Revenue Service prior to January 2, 2002 of its intent to make a section 1374 election. An election under this paragraph (c) is irrevocable.

(ii) *Time for making the election.*—An election under this paragraph (c) may be filed by the RIC or REIT with any Federal income tax return filed by the RIC or REIT on or before September 15, 2003, provided that the RIC or REIT has reported consistently with such election for all periods.

(5) *Example.*—The rules of this paragraph (c) are illustrated by the following example:

Example. Section 1374 treatment on REIT election. (i) X, a C corporation that is a calendar-year taxpayer, elects to be taxed as a REIT on its 1994 tax return, which it files on March 15, 1995. As a result, X is a REIT for its 1994 taxable year and would be subject to deemed sale treatment under paragraph (b) of this section but for X's timely election of section 1374 treatment under this paragraph (c). X chooses not to rely on §1.337(d)-5. As of the beginning of the 1994 taxable year, X's property consisted of Real Property, which is not section 1221(a)(1) property and which had a fair market value of $100,000 and an adjusted basis of $80,000, and $25,000 cash. X also had accumulated earnings and profits of $25,000, unrestricted capital loss carryforwards of $3,000, and unrestricted business credit carryforwards of $2,000. On July 1, 1997, X sells Real Property for $110,000. For its 1997 taxable year, X has no other income or deduction items. Assume the highest corporate tax rate is 35%.

(ii) Upon its election to be taxed as a REIT, X retains its $80,000 basis in Real Property and its $25,000 accumulated earnings and profits. X retains its $3,000 of capital loss carryforwards and its $2,000 of business credit carryforwards. To satisfy section 857(a)(2)(B), X must distribute $25,000, an amount equal to its earnings and profits accumulated in non-REIT years, to its shareholders by the end of its 1994 taxable year.

(iii) Upon X's sale of Real Property in 1997, X recognizes gain of $30,000 ($110,000 – $80,000). X's recognized built-in gain for purposes of applying section 1374 is $20,000 ($100,000 fair market value as of the beginning of X's first taxable year as a REIT – $80,000 basis). Because X's $30,000 of net income for the 1997 taxable year exceeds the net recognized built-in gain of $20,000, the taxable income limitation does not apply. X, therefore, has $20,000 net recognized built-in gain for the year. Assuming that X has not used its $3,000 of capital loss carryforwards in a prior taxable year and that their use is allowed under section 1374(b)(2) and §1.1374-5, X is allowed a $3,000 deduction against the $20,000 net recognized built-in gain. X would owe tax of $5,950 (35% of $17,000) on its net recognized built-in gain, except that X may use its $2,000 of business credit carryforwards to reduce this tax, assuming that X has not used the credit carryforwards in a prior taxable year and that their use is allowed under section 1374(b)(3) and §1.1374-6. Thus, X owes tax of $3,950 under this paragraph (c).

(iv) For purposes of subchapter M of chapter 1 of the Internal Revenue Code, X's earnings and profits for the year increase by $26,050 ($30,000 capital gain on the sale of Real Property – $3,950 tax under this paragraph (c)). For purposes of section 857(b)(2) and (b)(3), X's net capital gain for the year is $23,050 ($30,000 capital gain reduced by $3,000 capital loss carryforward and further reduced by $3,950 tax).

(d) *Exceptions.*—(1) *Gain otherwise recognized.*—Paragraph (a) of this section does not apply to any conversion transaction to the extent that gain or loss otherwise is recognized on such conversion transaction. See, for example, sections 336, 351(b), 351(e), 356, 357(c), 367, 368(a)(2)(F), and 1001.

(2) *Re-election of RIC or REIT status.*—(i) *Generally.*—Except as provided in paragraphs (d)(2)(ii) and (iii) of this section, paragraph (a)(1) of this section does not apply to any corporation that—

(A) Immediately prior to qualifying to be taxed as a RIC or REIT was subject to tax as a C corporation for a period not exceeding two taxable years; and

(B) Immediately prior to being subject to tax as a C corporation was subject to tax as a RIC or REIT for a period of at least one taxable year.

(ii) *Property acquired from another corporation while a C corporation.*—The exception described in paragraph (d)(2)(i) of this section does not apply to property acquired by the corporation while it was subject to tax as a C corporation from any person in a transaction that results in the acquirer's basis in the property being determined by reference to a C corporation's basis in the property.

(iii) *RICs and REITs previously subject to section 1374 treatment.*—If the RIC or REIT had property subject to paragraph (c) of this section before the RIC or REIT became subject to tax as a C corporation as described in paragraph (d)(2)(i) of this section, then paragraph (c) of this section applies to the RIC or REIT upon its requalification as a RIC or REIT, except that the 10-year recognition period with respect to such property is reduced by the portion of the 10-year recognition period that expired before the RIC or REIT became subject to tax as a C corporation and by the period of time that the corporation was subject to tax as a C corporation.

(e) *Effective date.*—This section applies to conversion transactions that occur on or after June 10, 1987, and before January 2, 2002. In lieu of applying this section, taxpayers generally may apply §1.337(d)-5 to determine the tax consequences (for all taxable years) of any conversion transaction that occurs on or after June 10, 1987 and before January 2, 2002, except that RICs and REITs that are subject to section 1374 treatment with respect to a conversion transaction may not rely on §1.337(d)-5(b)(1), but must apply paragraphs (c)(1)(i), (c)(2)(i), (c)(2)(ii), and (c)(3) of this section, with respect to built-in gains and losses recognized in taxable years beginning on or after January 2, 2002. Taxpayers are not prevented from relying on §1.337(d)-5 merely because they elect section 1374 treatment in the manner described in paragraph (c)(4) of this section instead of in the manner described in §1.337(d)-5(b)(3) and (c). For conversion transactions that occur on or after January 2, 2002, see §1.337(d)-7. [Reg. §1.337(d)-6.]

☐ [*T.D. 9047, 3-13-2003.*]

[Reg. §1.337(d)-7]

§1.337(d)-7. Tax on property owned by a C corporation that becomes property of a RIC or REIT.—(a) *General rule.*—(1) *Property owned by a C corporation that becomes property of a RIC or a REIT.*—If property owned by a C corporation (as defined in paragraph (a)(2)(i) of this section) becomes the property of a RIC or a REIT in a conversion transaction (as defined in paragraph (a)(2)(ii) of this section), then section 1374 treatment will apply as described in paragraph (b) of this section, unless the C corporation elects, or is treated as electing, deemed sale treatment with respect to the conversion transaction as provided in paragraph (c) of this section. See paragraph (d) of this section for exceptions to this paragraph (a).

(2) *Definitions.*—For purposes of this section:

(i) *C corporation.*—The term *C corporation* has the meaning provided in section 1361(a)(2) except that the term does not include a RIC or a REIT.

(ii) *Conversion transaction.*—The term *conversion transaction* means the qualification of a C corporation as a RIC or REIT or the transfer of property owned by a C corporation to a RIC or a REIT.

(iii) *RIC.*—The term *RIC* means a regulated investment company within the meaning of section 851(a).

(iv) *REIT.*—The term *REIT* means a real estate investment trust within the meaning of section 856(a).

(v) *S corporation.*—The term *S corporation* has the meaning provided in section 1361(a)(1).

(vi) *Section 355 distribution.*—The term *section 355 distribution* means any distribution to which section 355 (or so much of section 356 as relates to section 355) applies, including a distribution on which the distributing corporation recognizes gain pursuant to sections 355(d) or 355(e).

(vii) *Converted property.*—The term *converted property* means—

(A) Property owned by a C corporation that becomes the property of a RIC or a REIT; and

(B) Any other property of a RIC or a REIT the basis of which is determined, directly or indirectly, in whole or in part, by reference to the basis of property described in paragraph (a)(2)(vii)(A) of this section.

(viii) *Distribution property.*—The term *distribution property* means—

(A) Property owned immediately after a section 355 distribution by the distributing corporation, a controlled corporation (as those terms are defined in section 355(a)(1)), or a member of a separate affiliated group (as defined in section 355(b)(3)(B)) of which the distributing corporation or a controlled corporation is the common parent (but no formulation of the step transaction doctrine will be used to determine whether property acquired after the distribution is distribution property pursuant to this paragraph (a)(2)(viii)(A)); and

(B) Property with a basis determined, directly or indirectly, in whole or in part, by reference to property described in paragraph (a)(2)(viii)(A) of this section.

(b) *Section 1374 treatment.*—(1) *In general.*—(i) *Property owned by a C corporation that becomes property of a RIC or REIT.*—If property owned by a C corporation becomes the property of a RIC or REIT in a conversion transaction, then the RIC or REIT will be subject to tax on the net built-in gain in the converted property under the rules of section 1374 and the regulations thereunder, as modified by this paragraph (b), as if the RIC or REIT were an S corporation.

(ii) *Property subject to the rules of section 1374 owned by a RIC, REIT, or S corporation that becomes property of a RIC or REIT.*—If property subject to the rules of section 1374 owned by a RIC, a REIT, or an S corporation (the predecessor) becomes the property of a RIC or REIT (the successor) in a continuation transaction, the rules of section 1374 apply to the successor to the same extent that the predecessor was subject to the rules of section 1374 with respect to such property, and the recognition period of the successor with respect to such property is reduced by the portion of the recognition period of the predecessor that expired before the date of the continuation transaction. For this purpose, a continuation transaction means the qualification of the predecessor as a RIC or REIT or the transfer of property from the predecessor to the successor in a transaction in which the successor's basis in the transferred property is determined, in whole or in part, by reference to the predecessor's basis in that property.

(2) *Modification of section 1374 treatment.*—(i) *Net recognized built-in gain for REITs.*—(A) *Prelimitation amount.*—The prelimitation amount determined as provided in §1.1374-2(a)(1) is reduced by the portion of such amount, if any, that is subject to tax under section 857(b)(4), (5), (6), or (7). For this purpose, the amount of a REIT's recognized built-in gain that is subject to tax under section 857(b)(5) is computed as follows:

(1) Where the tax under section 857(b)(5) is computed by reference to section 857(b)(5)(A), the amount of a REIT's recognized built-in gain that is subject to tax under section 857(b)(5) is the tax imposed by section 857(b)(5) multiplied by a fraction the numerator of which is the amount of recognized built-in gain (without regard to recognized built-in loss and recognized built-in gain from prohibited transactions) that is not derived from sources referred to in section 856(c)(2) and the denominator of which is the gross income (without regard to gross income from prohibited transactions) of the REIT that is not derived from sources referred to in section 856(c)(2).

(2) Where the tax under section 857(b)(5) is computed by reference to section 857(b)(5)(B), the amount of a REIT's recognized built-in gain that is subject to tax under section 857(b)(5) is the tax imposed by section 857(b)(5) multiplied by a fraction the numerator of which is the amount of recognized built-in gain (without regard to recognized built-in loss and recognized built-in gain from prohibited transactions) that is not derived from sources referred to in section 856(c)(3) and the denominator of which is the gross income (without regard to gross income from prohibited transactions) of the REIT that is not derived from sources referred to in section 856(c)(3).

(B) *Taxable income limitation.*—The taxable income limitation determined as provided in §1.1374-2(a)(2) is reduced by an amount equal to the tax imposed under section 857(b)(5), (6), and (7).

(ii) *Loss carryforwards, credits and credit carryforwards.*—(A) *Loss carryforwards.*—Consistent with paragraph (b)(1)(i) of this section, net operating loss carryforwards and capital loss carryforwards arising in taxable years for which the corporation that generated the loss was not subject to subchapter M of chapter 1 of the Internal Revenue Code are allowed as a deduction against net recognized built-in gain to the extent allowed under section 1374 and the regulations thereunder. Such loss carryforwards must be used as a deduction against net recognized built-in gain for a taxable year to the greatest extent possible before such losses can be used to reduce other investment company taxable income for purposes of section 852(b) or other real estate investment trust taxable income for purposes of section 857(b) for that taxable year.

(B) *Credits and credit carryforwards.*—Consistent with paragraph (b)(1)(i) of this section, minimum tax credits and business credit carryforwards arising in taxable years for which the corporation that generated the credit was not subject to subchapter M of chapter 1 of the Internal Revenue Code are allowed to reduce the tax imposed on net recognized built-in gain under this paragraph (b) to the extent allowed under section 1374 and the regulations thereunder. Such credits and credit carryforwards must be used to reduce the tax imposed under this paragraph (b) on net recognized built-in gain for a taxable year to the greatest extent possible before such credits and credit carryforwards can be used to reduce the tax, if any, on other investment company taxable income for purposes of section 852(b) or on other real estate investment trust taxable income for purposes of section 857(b) for that taxable year.

(iii) *Recognition period.*—For purposes of applying the rules of section 1374 and the regulations thereunder, as modified by paragraph (b) of this section, the term *recognition period* means the *recognition period* described in section 1374(d)(7), beginning—

(A) In the case of a conversion transaction that is a qualification of a C corporation as a RIC or a REIT, on the first day of the RIC's or the REIT's first taxable year; and

(B) In the case of other conversion transactions, on the day the RIC or the REIT acquires the property.

(3) *Coordination with subchapter M rules.*—(i) *Recognized built-in gains and losses subject to subchapter M.*—Recognized built-in gains and losses of a RIC or REIT are included in computing investment company taxable income for purposes of section 852(b)(2), real estate investment trust taxable income for purposes of section 857(b)(2), capital gains for purposes of sections 852(b)(3) and 857(b)(3), gross income derived from sources within any foreign country or possession of the United States for purposes of section 853, and the dividends paid deduction for purposes of sections 852(b)(2)(D), 852(b)(3)(A), 857(b)(2)(B), and 857(b)(3)(A). In computing such income and deduction items, capital loss carryforwards and net operating loss carryforwards that are used by the RIC or REIT to reduce recognized built-in gains are allowed as a deduction, but only to the extent that they are otherwise allowable as a deduction against such income under the Internal Revenue Code (including section 852(b)(2)(B)).

(ii) *Treatment of tax imposed.*—The amount of tax imposed under this paragraph (b) on net recognized built-in gain for a taxable year is treated as a loss sustained by the RIC or the REIT during such taxable year. The character of the loss is determined by allocating the tax proportionately (based on recognized built-in gain) among the items of recognized built-in gain included in net recognized built-in gain. With respect to RICs, the tax imposed under this paragraph (b) on net recognized built-in gain is treated as attributable to the portion of the RIC's taxable year occurring after October 31.

(4) *Section 355 distribution following a conversion transaction.*—(i) *In general.*—If a REIT is described in paragraph (f)(1) of this section and the related section 355 distribution (as defined in paragraph (f)(1)(i) of this section) follows a conversion transaction, then for the taxable year in which the related section 355 distribution occurs, § 1.1374-2(a)(1) and (2) (as modified by paragraph (b)(2)(i) of this section) do not apply, and the REIT's net recognized built-in gain for such taxable year is the amount of its net unrealized built-in gain limitation (as defined in § 1.1374-2(a)(3)) for such taxable year.

(ii) *Basis adjustment.*—(A) *In general.*—If a REIT recognizes gain under paragraph (b)(4)(i) of this section, the aggregate basis of the converted property held by the REIT at the end of the taxable year in which the related section 355 distribution occurs shall be increased by an amount equal to the amount of gain so recognized, increased by the amount of the REIT's recognized built-in loss for such taxable year, and reduced by the amount of the REIT's recognized built-in gain and recognized built-in gain carryover for such taxable year.

(B) *Allocation of basis increase.*—The aggregate increase in basis by reason of paragraph (b)(4)(ii)(A) of this section shall be allocated among the converted property in proportion to their respective built-in gains on the date of the conversion transaction.

(5) *Example.*—The rules of this paragraph (b) are illustrated by the following example:

Example. Section 1374 treatment on REIT election. (i) X, a C corporation that is a calendar-year taxpayer, elects to be taxed as a REIT on its 2004 tax return, which it files on March 15, 2005. As a result, X is a REIT for its 2004 taxable year and is subject to section 1374 treatment under this paragraph (b). X does not elect deemed sale treatment under paragraph (c) of this section. As of the beginning of the 2004 taxable year, X's property consisted of Real Property, which is not section 1221(a)(1) property and which had a fair market value of $100,000 and an adjusted basis of $80,000, and $25,000 cash. X also had accumulated earnings and profits of $25,000, unrestricted capital loss carryforwards of $3,000, and unrestricted business credit carryforwards of $2,000. On July 1, 2007, X sells Real Property for $110,000. For its 2007 taxable year, X has no other income or deduction items. Assume the highest corporate tax rate is 35%.

(ii) Upon its election to be taxed as a REIT, X retains its $80,000 basis in Real Property and its $25,000 accumulated earnings and profits. X retains its $3,000 of capital loss carryforwards and its $2,000 of business credit carryforwards. To satisfy section 857(a)(2)(B), X must distribute $25,000, an amount equal to its earnings and profits accumulated in non-REIT years, to its shareholders by the end of its 2004 taxable year.

(iii) Upon X's sale of Real Property in 2007, X recognizes gain of $30,000 ($110,000 – $80,000). X's recognized built-in gain for purposes of applying section 1374 is $20,000 ($100,000 fair market value as of the beginning of X's first taxable year as a REIT – $80,000 basis). Because X's $30,000 of net income for the 2007 taxable year exceeds the net recognized built-in gain of $20,000, the taxable income limitation does not apply. X, therefore, has $20,000 net recognized built-in gain for the year. Assuming that X has not used its $3,000 of capital loss carryforwards in a prior taxable year and that their use is allowed under section 1374(b)(2) and § 1.1374-5, X is allowed a $3,000 deduction against the $20,000 net recognized built-in gain. X would owe tax of $5,950 (35% of $17,000) on its net recognized built-in gain, except that X may use its $2,000 of business credit carryforwards to reduce the tax, assuming that X has not used the credit carryforwards in a prior taxable year and that their use is allowed under section 1374(b)(3) and § 1.1374-6. Thus, X owes tax of $3,950 under this paragraph (b).

(iv) For purposes of subchapter M of chapter 1 of the Internal Revenue Code, X's earnings and profits for the year increase by $26,050 ($30,000 capital gain on the sale of Real Property – $3,950 tax under this paragraph (b)). For purposes of section 857(b)(2) and (b)(3), X's net capital gain for the year is $23,050 ($30,000 capital gain reduced by $3,000 capital loss carryforward and further reduced by $3,950 tax).

(c) *Election of deemed sale treatment.*—(1) *In general.*—Paragraph (b) of this section does not apply if the C corporation that qualifies as a RIC or a REIT or transfers property to a RIC or a REIT makes the election described in paragraph (c)(5) of this section or is treated as making such election under paragraph (c)(6) of this section, except to the extent permitted by paragraph (c)(6)(ii) of this section. A C corporation that makes, or that is treated as making, such an election recognizes gain and loss as if it sold the converted property to an unrelated party at fair market value on the deemed sale date (as defined in paragraph (c)(3) of this section). See paragraph (c)(4) of this section concerning limitations on the use of loss in computing gain. Paragraph (c) of this section does not apply if its application would result in the recognition of a net loss. For this purpose, net loss is the excess of aggregate losses over aggregate gains (including items of income), without regard to character.

(2) *Basis adjustment.*—If a corporation recognizes a net gain under paragraph (c)(1) of this section, then the converted property has a basis in the hands of the RIC or REIT equal to the fair market value of such property on the deemed sale date.

(3) *Deemed sale date.*—(i) *RIC or REIT qualifications.*—If the conversion transaction is a qualification of a C corporation as a RIC or REIT, then the deemed sale date is the end of the last day of the C corporation's last taxable year before the first taxable year in which it qualifies to be taxed as a RIC or REIT.

(ii) *Other conversion transactions.*—If the conversion transaction is a transfer of property owned by a C corporation to a RIC or REIT, then the deemed sale date is the end of the day before the day of the transfer.

(4) *Anti-stuffing rule.*—A C corporation must disregard converted property in computing gain or loss recognized on the conversion transaction under this paragraph (c), if—

(i) The converted property was acquired by the C corporation in a transaction to which section 351 applied or as a contribution to capital;

(ii) Such converted property had an adjusted basis immediately after its acquisition by the C corporation in excess of its fair market value on the date of acquisition; and

(iii) The acquisition of such converted property by the C corporation was part of a plan a principal purpose of which was to reduce gain recognized by the C corporation in connection with the conversion transaction. For purposes of this paragraph (c)(4), the principles of section 336(d)(2) apply.

(5) *Making the deemed sale election.*—A C corporation (or a partnership to which the principles of this section apply under paragraph (e) of this section) makes the deemed sale election with the following statement: "[Insert name and employer identification number of electing corporation or partnership] elects deemed sale treatment under § 1.337(d)-7(c) with respect to its property that was converted to property of, or transferred to, a RIC or REIT, [insert name and employer identification number of the RIC or REIT, if different from the name and employer identification number of the C corporation or partnership]." This statement must be attached to the Federal income tax return of the C corporation or partnership for the taxable year in which the deemed sale occurs. An election under this paragraph (c) is irrevocable.

(6) *Conversion transaction following a section 355 distribution.*—(i) *In general.*—Except as provided in paragraph (c)(6)(ii) of this section, a C corporation described in paragraph (f)(1) of this section is treated as having made the election under paragraph (c)(5) of this section with respect to a conversion transaction if the conversion transaction occurs following the related section 355 distribution (as defined in paragraph (f)(1)(i) of this section) and the C corporation has not made such an election.

(ii) *Limitation.*—A C corporation treated as having made the election under paragraph (c)(5) of this section as a result of paragraph (c)(6)(i) of this section is not treated as having made the election with respect to property that the taxpayer establishes is not distribution property with respect to the related section 355 distribution. For purposes of this paragraph (c)(6)(ii), any property with an adjusted basis in excess of its fair market value as of the date of the conversion transaction will not be treated as distribution property unless the taxpayer establishes that it owned such asset immediately after the related section 355 distribution. Paragraph (b) of this section will apply to property with respect to which the taxpayer is not treated as having made the election under paragraph (c)(5) of this section as a result of this paragraph (c)(6)(ii).

(7) *Examples.*—The rules of this paragraph (c) are illustrated by the following examples:

Example 1. Deemed sale treatment on merger into RIC. (i) X, a calendar-year taxpayer, has qualified as a RIC since January 1, 2001. On May 31, 2004, Y, a C corporation and calendar-year taxpayer, transfers all of its property to X in a transaction that qualifies as a reorganization under section 368(a)(1)(C). As a result of the transfer, Y would be subject to section 1374 treatment under paragraph (b) of this section but for its timely election of deemed sale treatment under this paragraph (c). As a result of such election, Y is subject to deemed sale treatment on its tax return for the short taxable year ending May 31, 2004. On May 31, 2004, Y's only assets are Capital Asset, which has a fair market value of $100,000 and a basis of $40,000 as of the end of May 30, 2004, and $50,000 cash. Y also has an unrestricted net operating loss carryforward of $12,000 and accumulated earnings and profits of $50,000. Y has no taxable income for the short taxable year ending May 31, 2004, other than gain recognized under this paragraph (c). In 2007, X sells Capital Asset for $110,000. Assume the applicable corporate tax rate is 35%.

(ii) Under this paragraph (c), Y is treated as if it sold the converted property (Capital Asset and $50,000 cash) at fair market value on May 30, 2004, recognizing $60,000 of gain ($150,000 amount realized – $90,000 basis). Y must report the gain on its tax return for the short taxable year ending May 31, 2004. Y may offset this gain with its $12,000 net operating loss carryforward and will pay tax of $16,800 (35% of $48,000).

(iii) Under section 381, X succeeds to Y's accumulated earnings and profits. Y's accumulated earnings and profits of $50,000 increase by $60,000 and decrease by $16,800 as a result of the deemed sale. Thus, the aggregate amount of subchapter C earnings and profits that must be distributed to satisfy section 852(a)(2)(B) is $93,200 ($50,000 + $60,000 – $16,800). X's basis in Capital Asset is $100,000. On X's sale of Capital Asset in 2007, X recognizes $10,000 of gain which is taken into account in computing X's net capital gain for purposes of section 852(b)(3).

Example 2. Loss limitation. (i) Assume the facts are the same as those described in *Example 1*, but that, prior to the reorganization, a shareholder of Y contributed to Y a capital asset, Capital Asset 2, which has a fair market value of $10,000 and a basis of $20,000, in a section 351 transaction.

(ii) Assuming that Y's acquisition of Capital Asset 2 was made pursuant to a plan a principal purpose of which was to reduce the amount of gain that Y would recognize in connection with the

conversion transaction, Capital Asset 2 would be disregarded in computing the amount of Y's net gain on the conversion transaction.

(d) *Exceptions.*—(1) *Gain otherwise recognized.*—Paragraph (a)(1) of this section does not apply to any conversion transaction to the extent that gain or loss otherwise is recognized on such conversion transaction by the C corporation that either qualifies as a RIC or a REIT or that transfers property to a RIC or REIT. See, for example, sections 311(b), 336(a), 351(b), 351(e), 356, 357(c), 367, 368(a)(2)(F), 1001, 1031(b), and 1033(a)(2).

(2) *Re-election of RIC or REIT status.*—(i) *Generally.*—Except as provided in paragraphs (d)(2)(ii) and (iii) of this section, paragraph (a)(1) of this section does not apply to any corporation that—

(A) Immediately prior to qualifying to be taxed as a RIC or REIT was subject to tax as a C corporation for a period not exceeding two taxable years; and

(B) Immediately prior to being subject to tax as a C corporation was subject to tax as a RIC or REIT for a period of at least one taxable year.

(ii) *Property acquired from another corporation while a C corporation.*—The exception described in paragraph (d)(2)(i) of this section does not apply to property acquired by the corporation while it was subject to tax as a C corporation from any person in a transaction that results in the acquirer's basis in the property being determined by reference to a C corporation's basis in the property.

(iii) *RICs and REITs previously subject to section 1374 treatment.*—If the RIC or REIT had property subject to paragraph (b) of this section before the RIC or REIT became subject to tax as a C corporation as described in paragraph (d)(2)(i) of this section, then paragraph (b) of this section applies to the RIC or REIT upon its requalification as a RIC or REIT, except that the recognition period with respect to such property is reduced by the portion of the recognition period that expired before the RIC or REIT became subject to tax as a C corporation and by the period of time that the corporation was subject to tax as a C corporation.

(3) *Special rules for like-kind exchanges and involuntary conversions.*—(i) *In general.*—Paragraph (a)(1) of this section does not apply to a conversion transaction to the extent that a C corporation transfers property with a built-in gain to a RIC or REIT, and the C corporation's gain is not recognized by reason of either section 1031 or 1033.

(ii) *Clarification regarding exchanged property previously subject to section 1374 treatment.*—Notwithstanding paragraph (d)(3)(i) of this section, if, in a transaction described in paragraph (d)(3)(i) of this section, a RIC or REIT surrenders property that was subject to section 1374 treatment immediately prior to the transaction, the rules of section 1374(d)(6) will apply to continue section 1374 treatment to the replacement property acquired by the RIC or REIT in the transaction.

(iii) *Examples.*—The rules of this paragraph (d)(3) are illustrated by the following examples. In each of the examples, X is a REIT, Y is a C corporation, and X and Y are not related.

Example 1. Section 1031(a) exchange. (i) *Facts.* X owned a building that it leased for commercial use (Property A). Y owned a building leased for commercial use (Property B). On January 1, Year 3, Y transferred Property B to X in exchange for Property A in a nonrecognition transaction under section 1031(a). Immediately before the exchange, Properties A and B each had a value of $100, X had an adjusted basis of $60 in Property A, Y had an adjusted basis of $70 in Property B, and X was not subject to section 1374 treatment with respect to Property A.

(ii) *Analysis.* The transfer of property (Property B) by Y (a C corporation) to X (a REIT) is a conversion transaction within the meaning of paragraph (a)(2)(ii) of this section. The conversion transaction is a nonrecognition transaction under section 1031(a) as to Y; thus, Y does not recognize any of its $30 gain. Therefore, the conversion transaction is not subject to paragraph (a)(1) of this section by reason of paragraph (d)(3)(i) of this section.

Example 2. Section 1031(a) exchange of section 1374 property. (i) *Facts.* The facts are the same as in *Example 1*, except that X had acquired Property A in a conversion transaction in Year 2, and immediately before the Year 3 exchange X was subject to section 1374 treatment with respect to $25 of net built-in gain in Property A.

(ii) *Analysis.* The Year 3 transfer of Property B by Y to X is a conversion transaction within the meaning of paragraph (a)(2)(ii) of this section. The conversion transaction is a nonrecognition transaction under section 1031(a) as to Y; thus, Y does not recognize any of its $30 gain. Therefore, the Year 3 transfer is not subject to paragraph (a)(1) of this section by reason of paragraph (d)(3)(i) of this section. However, X had been subject to section 1374 treatment with respect to $25 of net built-in gain in Property A immediately before the Year 3 transfer, and X's basis in Property B is determined (in whole or in part) by reference to its adjusted basis in Property A. Accordingly, the rules of section 1374(d)(6) apply and X is subject to section 1374 treatment on Property B with respect to the $25 net built-in gain. See paragraph (d)(3)(ii) of this section.

Example 3. Section 1031(b) exchange. (i) *Facts.* The facts are the same as in *Example 1*, except that immediately before the Year 3 exchange Property A had a value of $92, and X transferred Property A and $8 to Y in exchange for Property B in a nonrecognition transaction under section 1031(b).

(ii) *Analysis.* The transfer of Property B by Y to X is a conversion transaction within the meaning of paragraph (a)(2)(ii) of this section. Pursuant to section 1031(b), Y recognizes $8 of its gain. Paragraph (a)(1) of this section does not apply to the transaction to the extent of the $8 gain recognized by Y by reason of paragraph (d)(1) of this section, or to the extent of the $22 gain realized but not recognized by Y by reason of paragraph (d)(3)(i) of this section.

Example 4. Section 1033(a) involuntary conversion of property held by a C corporation transferor. (i) *Facts.* Y owned uninsured, improved property (Property 1) that was involuntarily converted (within the meaning of section 1033(a)) in a fire. Y sold Property 1 for $100 to X, which owned an adjacent property and wanted Property 1 for use as a parking lot. Y had a $70 basis in Property 1 immediately before the sale. Y elected to defer gain recognition under section 1033(a)(2), and purchased qualifying replacement property (Property 2) for $100 from an unrelated party prior to the expiration of the period described in section 1033(a)(2)(B).

(ii) *Analysis.* The transfer of Property 1 by Y to X is a conversion transaction within the meaning of paragraph (a)(2)(ii) of this section. The conversion transaction (combined with Y's purchase of Property 2) is a nonrecognition transaction under section 1033(a) as to Y; thus, Y does not recognize any of its $30 gain. Therefore, the conversion transaction is not subject to paragraph (a)(1) of this section by reason of paragraph (d)(3)(i) of this section.

Example 5. Section 1033(a) involuntary conversion of property held by a REIT. (i) *Facts.* X owned property (Property 1). On January 1, Year 2, Property 1 had a fair market value of $100 and a basis of $70, and X was not subject to section 1374 treatment with respect to Property 1. On that date, when Property 1 was under a threat of condemnation, X sold Property 1 to an unrelated party for $100 (First Transaction). X elected to defer gain recognition under section 1033(a)(2), and purchased qualifying replacement property (Property 2) for $100 from Y (Second Transaction) prior to the expiration of the period described in section 1033(a)(2)(B).

(ii) *Analysis.* The transfer of Property 2 by Y to X in the Second Transaction is a conversion transaction within the meaning of paragraph (a)(2)(ii) of this section. The Second Transaction (combined with the First Transaction) is a nonrecognition transaction under section 1033(a) as to X, but not as to Y. Assume no nonrecognition provision applied to Y; thus, Y recognized gain or loss on its sale of Property 2 in the Second Transaction, and the Second Transaction is not subject to paragraph (a)(1) of this section by reason of paragraph (d)(1) of this section.

(4) *Special rule if C corporation is a tax-exempt entity.*—Paragraph (a)(1) of this section does not apply to a conversion transaction in which the C corporation that owned the converted property is a tax-exempt entity described in § 1.337(d)-4(c)(2) to the extent that gain (if any) would not be subject to tax under Title 26 of the United States Code if a deemed sale election under paragraph (c)(5) of this section were made.

(e) *Special rule for partnerships.*—(1) *In general.*—The principles of this section apply to property transferred by a partnership to a RIC or REIT to the extent of any gain or loss in the converted property that would be allocated directly or indirectly, through one or more partnerships, to a C corporation if the partnership sold the converted property to an unrelated party at fair market value on the deemed sale date (as defined in paragraph (c)(3) of this section). If the partnership were to elect deemed sale treatment under paragraph (c) of this section in lieu of section 1374 treatment under paragraph (b) of this section with respect to such transfer, then any net gain recognized by the partnership on the deemed sale must be allocated to the C corporation partner, but does not increase the capital account of any partner. Any adjustment to the partnership's basis in the RIC or REIT stock as a result of deemed sale treatment under paragraph (c) of this section shall constitute an adjustment to the basis of that stock with respect to the C corporation partner only. The principles of section 743 apply to such basis adjustment.

(2) *Example; Transfer by partnership of property to REIT.*—(i) *Facts.*—PRS, a partnership for Federal income tax purposes, has three partners: TE, a C corporation (within the meaning of paragraph (a)(2)(i) of this section) that is also a tax-exempt entity (within the meaning of § 1.337(d)-4(c)(2)), owns 50 percent of the capital and profits of PRS; A, an individual, owns 30 percent of the capital and profits of PRS; and Y, a C corporation (within the meaning of

paragraph (a)(2)(i) of this section, owns the remaining 20 percent. PRS owns a building that it leases for commercial use (Property 1). On January 1, Year 2, when PRS has an adjusted basis in Property 1 of $100 and Property 1 has a fair market value of $500, PRS transfers Property 1 to X, a REIT, in exchange for stock of X in an exchange described in section 351. PRS does not elect deemed sale treatment under paragraph (c) of this section. TE would not be subject to tax with respect to any gain that would be allocated to it if PRS had sold Property 1 to an unrelated party at fair market value.

(ii) *Analysis.*—The transfer of Property 1 by PRS to X is a conversion transaction within the meaning of paragraph (a)(2)(ii) of this section to the extent of any gain or loss that would be allocated to any C corporation partner if PRS sold Property 1 at fair market value to an unrelated party on the deemed sale date. TE and Y are C corporations, but A is not a C corporation within the meaning of paragraph (a)(2)(i) of this section. Therefore, the transfer of Property 1 by PRS to X is a conversion transaction within the meaning of paragraph (a)(2)(ii) of this section to the extent of the gain in Property 1 that would be allocated to TE and Y. Pursuant to paragraph (d)(4) of this section, paragraph (a)(1) of this section does not apply to the extent of the gain that would be allocated to TE if PRS had sold Property 1 to an unrelated party at fair market value on the deemed sale date. If PRS were to sell Property 1 to an unrelated party at fair market value on the deemed sale date, PRS would allocate $80 of built-in gain to Y. Thus, X is subject to section 1374 treatment on Property 1 with respect to $80 of built-in gain.

(f) *Conversion transaction preceding or following a section 355 distribution.*—(1) *In general.*—A C corporation or a REIT is described in this paragraph (f)(1) if—

(i) The C corporation or the REIT engages in a conversion transaction involving a REIT during the twenty-year period beginning on the date that is ten years before the date of a section 355 distribution (the *related section 355 distribution*); and

(ii) The C corporation or the REIT engaging in the related section 355 distribution is either—

(A) The distributing corporation or the controlled corporation, as those terms are defined in section 355(a)(1); or

(B) A member of the separate affiliated group (as defined in section 355(b)(3)(B)) of the distributing corporation or the controlled corporation.

(2) *Predecessors and successors.*—For purposes of this paragraph (f), any reference to a controlled corporation, a distributing corporation, or a member of the separate affiliated group of a distributing corporation or a controlled corporation includes a reference to any predecessor or successor of such corporation. Successors include corporations which succeed to and take into account items described in section 381(c) of the distributing corporation or the controlled corporation. Predecessors include corporations having such items to which the distributing corporation or the controlled corporation succeeded and took into account.

(3) *Exclusion of certain conversion transactions.*—A C corporation or a REIT is not described in paragraph (f)(1) of this section if—

(i) The distributing corporation and the controlled corporation are both REITs immediately after the related section 355 distribution (including by reason of elections under section 856(c)(1) made after the related section 355 distribution that are effective before the related section 355 distribution) and at all times during the two years thereafter;

(ii) Section 355(h)(1) does not apply to the related section 355 distribution by reason of section 355(h)(2)(B); or

(iii) The related section 355 distribution occurred before December 7, 2015, or is described in a ruling request referred to in section 311(c) of Division Q of the Consolidated Appropriations Act, 2016, Public Law 114-113, 129 Stat. 2422.

(g) *Effective/Applicability date.*—(1) *In general.*—Except as provided in paragraph (g)(2) of this section, this section applies to conversion transactions that occur on or after January 2, 2002. For conversion transactions that occurred on or after June 10, 1987, and before January 2, 2002, see § § 1.337(d)-5 and 1.337(d)-6.

(2) *Special rules.*—(i) *Conversion transactions occurring on or after August 2, 2013 and certain prior conversion transactions.*—Paragraphs (a)(2)(i) through (v), (d)(1), (d)(3), (d)(4), and (e) of this section apply to conversion transactions that occur on or after August 2, 2013. However, taxpayers may apply paragraphs (a)(2)(i) through (v), (d)(1), (d)(3), (d)(4), and (e) of this section to conversion transactions that occurred before August 2, 2013. For conversion transactions that occurred on or after January 2, 2002 and before August 2, 2013, see § 1.337(d)-7 as contained in 26 CFR part 1 in effect on April 1, 2013.

(ii) *Conversion transactions occurring on or after June 7, 2019, and certain prior conversion transactions.*—Paragraphs (a)(1), (a)(2)(vi), (vii), and (viii), (b)(4), (c)(1) and (6), and (f) of this section apply to conversion transactions occurring on or after June 7, 2019, and to conversion transactions and related section 355 distributions for which the conversion transaction occurs before, and the related section 355 distribution occurs on or after, June 7, 2019. For conversion transactions that occurred on or after June 7, 2016, and before June 7, 2019 (other than conversion transactions and related section 355 distributions for which the conversion transaction occurs before, and the related section 355 distribution occurs on or after, June 7, 2019), see §§1.337(d)-7 and 1.337(d)-7T as contained in 26 CFR part 1 in effect on April 1, 2019.

(iii) *Recognition period.*—Paragraphs (b)(1)(ii) and (d)(2)(iii) of this section apply to conversion transactions that occur on or after August 8, 2016. Paragraph (b)(2)(iii) of this section applies to conversion transactions that occur after February 17, 2017. For conversion transactions that occurred on or after August 8, 2016 and on or before February 17, 2017, see §1.337(d)-7T(b)(2)(iii) in effect on August 8, 2016. However, taxpayers may apply paragraph (b)(2)(iii) of this section to conversion transactions that occurred on or after August 8, 2016 and on or before February 17, 2017. For conversion transactions that occurred on or after January 2, 2002 and before August 8, 2016, see §1.337(d)-7 as contained in 26 CFR part 1 in effect on April 1, 2016. [Reg. §1.337(d)-7.]

☐ [*T.D. 9047, 3-13-2003. Amended by T.D. 9626, 8-1-2013, T.D. 9770, 6-7-2016, T.D. 9810, 1-17-2017 and T.D. 9862, 6-3-2019.*]

[Reg. §1.338-0]

§1.338-0. Outline of topics.—This section lists the captions contained in the regulations under section 338 as follows:

☐ [*T.D. 8940,* 2-12-2001. *Amended by T.D. 9158,* 9-15-2004; *T.D. 9257,* 4-7-2006; *T.D. 9264,* 5-26-2006; *T.D. 9329,* 6-13-2007; *T.D. 9358,* 9-10-2007; *T.D. 9377,* 1-22-2008 *and T.D. 9619,* 5-10-2013.]

[Reg. §1.338-1]

§1.338-1. General principles; status of old target and new target.—(a) *In general.*—(1) *Deemed transaction.*—Elections are available under section 338 when a purchasing corporation acquires the stock of another corporation (the target) in a qualified stock purchase. One type of election, under section 338(g), is available to the purchasing corporation. Another type of election, under section 338(h)(10), is, in more limited circumstances, available jointly to the purchasing corporation and the sellers of the stock. (Rules concerning eligibility for these elections are contained in §§1.338-2, 1.338-3, and 1.338(h)(10)-1.) However, if, as a result of the deemed purchase of old target's assets pursuant to a section 336(e) election, there would be both a qualified stock purchase and a qualified stock disposition (as defined in §1.336-1(b)(6)) of the stock of a subsidiary of target, neither a section 338(g) election nor a section 338(h)(10) election may be made with respect to the qualified stock purchase of the subsidiary. Instead, a section 336(e) election may be made with respect to such purchase. See §1.336-1(b)(6)(ii). Although target is a single corporation under corporate law, if a section 338 election is made, then two separate corporations, old target and new target, generally are considered to exist for purposes of subtitle A of the Internal Revenue Code. Old target is treated as transferring all of its assets to an unrelated person in exchange for consideration that includes the discharge of its liabilities (see §1.1001-2(a)), and new target is treated as acquiring all of its assets from an unrelated person in exchange for consideration that includes the assumption of those liabilities. (Such transaction is, without regard to its characterization for Federal income tax purposes, referred to as the deemed asset sale and the income tax consequences thereof as the deemed sale tax consequences.) If a section 338(h)(10) election is made, old target is deemed to liquidate following the deemed asset sale.

(2) *Application of other rules of law.*—Other rules of law apply to determine the tax consequences to the parties as if they had actually engaged in the transactions deemed to occur under section 338 and the regulations thereunder except to the extent otherwise provided in those regulations. See also §1.338-6(c)(2). Other rules of law may characterize the transaction as something other than or in addition to a sale and purchase of assets; however, the transaction between old and new target must be a taxable transaction. For example, if the target is an insurance company for which a section 338 election is made, the deemed asset sale results in an assumption reinsurance transaction for the insurance contracts deemed transferred from old target to new target. See, generally, §1.817-4(d), and for special rules regarding the acquisition of insurance company targets, §1.338-11. See also §1.367(a)-8(k)(13) for a rule applicable to gain recognition agreements (filed under §§1.367(a)-3(b)(1)(ii) and 1.367(a)-8) and deemed asset sales as a result of an election under section 338(g).

(3) *Overview.*—Definitions and special nomenclature and rules for making the section 338 election are provided in §1.338-2. Qualification for the section 338 election is addressed in §1.338-3. The amount for which old target is treated as selling all of its assets (the aggregate deemed sale price, or ADSP) is addressed in §1.338-4. The amount for which new target is deemed to have purchased all its assets (the adjusted grossed-up basis, or AGUB) is addressed in §1.338-5. Section 1.338-6 addresses allocation both of ADSP among the assets old target is deemed to have sold and of AGUB among the assets new target is deemed to have purchased. Section 1.338-7 addresses allocation of ADSP or AGUB when those amounts subsequently change. Asset and stock consistency are addressed in §1.338-8. International aspects of section 338 are covered in §1.338-9. Rules for the filing of returns are provided in §1.338-10. Section 1.338-11 provides special rules for insurance company targets. Eligibility for and treatment of section 338(h)(10) elections is addressed in §1.338(h)(10)-1.

(b) *Treatment of target under other provisions of the Internal Revenue Code.*—(1) *General rule for subtitle A.*—Except as provided in this section, new target is treated as a new corporation that is unrelated to old target for purposes of subtitle A of the Internal Revenue Code. Thus—

(i) New target is not considered related to old target for purposes of section 168 and may make new elections under section 168 without taking into account the elections made by old target; and

(ii) New target may adopt, without obtaining prior approval from the Commissioner, any taxable year that meets the requirements of section 441 and any method of accounting that meets the requirements of section 446. Notwithstanding §1.441-1T(b)(2), a new target may adopt a taxable year on or before the last day for making

the election under section 338 by filing its first return for the desired taxable year on or before that date.

(2) *Exceptions for subtitle A.*—New target and old target are treated as the same corporation for purposes of—

(i) The rules applicable to employee benefit plans (including those plans described in sections 79, 104, 105, 106, 125, 127, 129, 132, 137, and 220), qualified pension, profit-sharing, stock bonus and annuity plans (sections 401(a) and 403(a)), simplified employee pensions (section 408(k)), tax qualified stock option plans (sections 422 and 423), welfare benefit funds (sections 419, 419A, 512(a)(3), and 4976), voluntary employees' beneficiary associations (section 501(c)(9) and the regulations thereunder), and tax on excess tax-exempt organization executive compensation (section 4960) and the regulations in part 53 under section 4960;

(ii) Sections 1311 through 1314 (relating to the mitigation of the effect of limitations), if a section 338(h)(10) election is not made for target;

(iii) Section 108(e)(5) (relating to the reduction of purchase money debt);

(iv) Section 45A (relating to the Indian Employment Credit), section 51 (relating to the Work Opportunity Credit), section 51A (relating to the Welfare to Work Credit), and section 1396 (relating to the Empowerment Zone Act);

(v) Sections 401(h) and 420 (relating to medical benefits for retirees);

(vi) Section 414 (relating to definitions and special rules); and

(vii) Section 846(e) (relating to an election to use an insurance company's historical loss payment pattern).

(viii) Any other provision designated in the Internal Revenue Bulletin by the Internal Revenue Service. See §601.601(d)(2)(ii) of this chapter. See, for example, §1.10C1-3(e)(4)(i)(F) providing that an election under section 338 does not result in the substitution of a new obligor on target's debt. See also, for example, §1.1502-77(c)(8), providing that an election under section 338 does not result in a deemed termination of target's existence for purposes of the rules applicable to the agent for a consolidated group.

(3) *General rule for other provisions of the Internal Revenue Code.*—Except as provided in the regulations under section 338 or in the Internal Revenue Bulletin by the Internal Revenue Service (see §601.601(d)(2)(ii) of this chapter), new target is treated as a continuation of old target for purposes other than subtitle A of the Internal Revenue Code. For example—

(i) New target is liable for old target's Federal income tax liabilities, including the tax liability for the deemed sale tax consequences and those tax liabilities of the other members of any consolidated group that included old target that are attributable to taxable years in which those corporations and old target joined in the same consolidated return (see §1.1502-6(a));

(ii) Wages earned by the employees of old target are considered wages earned by such employees from new target for purposes of sections 3101 and 3111 (Federal Insurance Contributions Act) and section 3301 (Federal Unemployment Tax Act); and

(iii) Old target and new target must use the same employer identification number.

(c) *Anti-abuse rule.*—(1) *In general.*—The rules of this paragraph (c) apply for purposes of applying the regulations under sections 336(e), 338, and 1060. The Commissioner is authorized to treat any property (including cash) transferred by old target in connection with the transactions resulting in the application of the residual method (and not held by target at the close of the acquisition date) as, nonetheless, property of target at the close of the acquisition date if the property so transferred is, within 24 months after the deemed asset sale, owned by new target, or is owned, directly or indirectly, by a member of the affiliated group of which new target is a member and continues after the acquisition date to be held or used primarily in connection with one or more of the activities of new target. In addition, the Commissioner is authorized to treat any property (including cash) transferred to old target in connection with the transactions resulting in the application of the residual method (and held by target at the close of the acquisition date) as, nonetheless, not being property of target at the close of the acquisition date if the property so transferred is, within 24 months after the deemed asset sale, not owned by new target but owned, directly or indirectly, by a member of the affiliated group of which new target is a member, or owned by new target but held or used primarily in connection with an activity conducted, directly or indirectly, by another member of the affiliated group of which new target is a member in combination with other property retained by or acquired, directly or indirectly, from the transferor of the property (or a member of the same affiliated group) to old target. For purposes of this paragraph (c)(1), an interest in an entity is considered held or used in connection with an activity if property of the entity is so held or used. The authority of the

Commissioner under this paragraph (c)(1) includes the making of any appropriate correlative adjustments (avoiding, to the extent possible, the duplication or omission of any item of income, gain, loss, deduction, or basis).

(2) *Examples.*—The following examples illustrate this paragraph (c):

Example 1. Prior to a qualified stock purchase under section 338, target transfers one of its assets to a related party. The purchasing corporation then purchases the target stock and also purchases the transferred asset from the related party. After its purchase of target, the purchasing corporation and target are members of the same affiliated group. A section 338 election is made. Under an arrangement with the purchaser, the separately transferred asset is used primarily in connection with target's activities. Applying the anti-abuse rule of this paragraph (c), the Commissioner may consider target to own the transferred asset for purposes of applying the residual method under section 338.

Example 2. T owns all the stock of T1. T1 leases intellectual property to T, which T uses in connection with its own activities. P, a purchasing corporation, wishes to buy the T-T1 chain of corporations. P, in connection with its planned purchase of the T stock, contracts to consummate a purchase of all the stock of T1 on March 1 and of all the stock of T on March 2. Section 338 elections are thereafter made for both T and T1. Immediately after the purchases, P, T and T1 are members of the same affiliated group. T continues to lease the intellectual property from T1 and that is the primary use of the intellectual property. Thus, an asset of T, the T1 stock, was removed from T's own assets prior to the qualified stock purchase of the T stock, T1's own assets are used after the deemed asset sale in connection with T's own activities, and the T1 stock is after the deemed asset sale owned by P, a member of the same affiliated group of which T is a member. Applying the anti-abuse rule of this paragraph (c), the Commissioner may, for purposes of application of the residual method under section 338 both to T and to T1, consider P to have bought only the stock of T, with T at the time of the qualified stock purchases of both T and T1 (the qualified stock purchase of T1 being triggered by the deemed sale under section 338 of T's assets) owning T1. The Commissioner accordingly would allocate consideration to T's assets as though the T1 stock were one of those assets, and then allocate consideration within T1 based on the amount allocated to the T1 stock at the T level.

(d) *Next day rule for post-closing transactions.*—If a target corporation for which an election under section 338 is made engages in a transaction outside the ordinary course of business on the acquisition date after the event resulting in the qualified stock purchase of the target or a higher tier corporation, the target and all persons related thereto (either before or after the qualified stock purchase) under section 267(b) or section 707 must treat the transaction for all Federal income tax purposes as occurring at the beginning of the day following the transaction and after the deemed purchase by new target.

(e) *Effective/applicability date.*—Paragraphs (a)(1) and (c)(1) of this section are applicable to any qualified stock disposition for which the disposition date (as defined in §1.336-1(b)(8)) is on or after May 15, 2013. [Reg. §1.338-1.]

☐ [*T.D. 8940, 2-12-2001. Amended by T.D. 9002, 6-27-2002; T.D. 9257, 4-7-2006; T.D. 9377, 1-22-2008; T.D. 9446, 2-9-2009; T.D. 9619, 5-10-2013; T.D. 9715, 3-31-2015; T.D. 9932, 12-28-2020 and T.D. 9938, 1-15-2021.]*

[Reg. §1.338-2]

§1.338-2. Nomenclature and definitions; mechanics of the section 338 election.—(a) *Scope.*—This section prescribes rules relating to elections under section 338.

(b) *Nomenclature.*—For purposes of the regulations under section 338 (except as otherwise provided):

(1) T is a domestic target corporation that has only one class of stock outstanding. Old T refers to T for periods ending on or before the close of T's acquisition date; new T refers to T for subsequent periods.

(2) P is the purchasing corporation.

(3) The P group is an affiliated group of which P is a member.

(4) P1, P2, etc., are domestic corporations that are members of the P group.

(5) T1, T2, etc., are domestic corporations that are target affiliates of T. These corporations (T1, T2, etc.) have only one class of stock outstanding and may also be targets.

(6) S is a domestic corporation (unrelated to P and B) that owns T prior to the purchase of T by P. (S is referred to in cases in which it is appropriate to consider the effects of having all of the outstanding stock of T owned by a domestic corporation.)

(7) A, a U.S. citizen or resident, is an individual (unrelated to P and B) who owns T prior to the purchase of T by P. (A is referred to in cases in which it is appropriate to consider the effects of having all of the outstanding stock of T owned by an individual who is a U.S. citizen or resident. Ownership of T by A and ownership of T by S are mutually exclusive circumstances.)

(8) B, a U.S. citizen or resident, is an individual (unrelated to T, S, and A) who owns the stock of P.

(9) F, used as a prefix with the other terms in this paragraph (b), connotes foreign, rather than domestic, status. For example, FT is a foreign corporation (as defined in section 7701(a)(5)) and FA is an individual other than a U.S. citizen or resident.

(10) CFC, used as a prefix with the other terms in this paragraph (b) referring to a corporation, connotes a controlled foreign corporation (as defined in section 957, taking into account section 953(c)). A corporation identified with the prefix F may be a controlled foreign corporation. (The prefix CFC is used when the corporation's status as a controlled foreign corporation is significant.)

(c) *Definitions.*—For purposes of the regulations under section 338 (except as otherwise provided):

(1) *Acquisition date.*—The term *acquisition date* has the same meaning as in section 338(h)(2).

(2) *Acquisition date assets.*—*Acquisition date assets* are the assets of the target held at the beginning of the day after the acquisition date (but see §1.338-1(d) (regarding certain transactions on the acquisition date)).

(3) *Affiliated group.*—The term *affiliated group* has the same meaning as in section 338(h)(5). Corporations are affiliated on any day they are members of the same affiliated group.

(4) *Common parent.*—The term *common parent* has the same meaning as in section 1504.

(5) *Consistency period.*—The *consistency period* is the period described in section 338(h)(4)(A) unless extended pursuant to §1.338-8(j)(1).

(6) *Deemed asset sale.*—The *deemed asset sale* is the transaction described in §1.338-1(a)(1) that is deemed to occur for purposes of subtitle A of the Internal Revenue Code if a section 338 election is made.

(7) *Deemed sale tax consequences.*—*Deemed sale tax consequences* refers to, in the aggregate, the Federal income tax consequences (generally, the income, gain, deduction, and loss) of the deemed asset sale. Deemed sale tax consequences also refers to the Federal income tax consequences of the transfer of a particular asset in the deemed asset sale.

(8) *Deemed sale return.*—The *deemed sale return* is the return on which target's deemed sale tax consequences are reported that does not include any other items of target. Target files a deemed sale return when a section 338 election (but not a section 338(h)(10) election) is filed for target and target is a member of a selling group (defined in paragraph (c)(16) of this section) that files a consolidated return for the period that includes the acquisition date. See §1.338-10. If target is an S corporation for the period that ends on the day before the acquisition date and a section 338 election (but not a section 338(h)(10) election) is filed for target, see §1.338-10(a)(3).

(9) *Domestic corporation.*—A *domestic corporation* is a corporation—

(i) That is domestic within the meaning of section 7701(a)(4) or that is treated as domestic for purposes of subtitle A of the Internal Revenue Code (e.g., to which an election under section 953(d) or 1504(d) applies); and

(ii) That is not a DISC, a corporation described in section 1248(e), or a corporation to which an election under section 936 applies.

(10) *Old target's final return.*—*Old target's final return* is the income tax return of old target for the taxable year ending at the close of the acquisition date that includes the deemed sale tax consequences. However, if a deemed sale return is filed for old target, the deemed sale return is considered old target's final return.

(11) *Purchasing corporation.*—The term *purchasing corporation* has the same meaning as in section 338(d)(1). The purchasing corporation may also be referred to as purchaser. Unless otherwise provided, any reference to the purchasing corporation is a reference to all members of the affiliated group of which the purchasing corporation is a member. See sections 338(h)(5) and (8). Also, unless otherwise provided, any reference to the purchasing corporation is, with respect to a deemed purchase of stock under section 338(a)(2), a reference to

new target with respect to its own deemed purchase of stock in another target.

(12) *Qualified stock purchase.*—The term *qualified stock purchase* has the same meaning as in section 338(d)(3).

(13) *Related persons.*—Two persons are related if stock in a corporation owned by one of the persons would be attributed under section 318(a) (other than section 318(a)(4)) to the other.

(14) *Section 338 election.*—A *section 338 election* is an election to apply section 338(a) to target. A section 338 election is made by filing a statement of section 338 election pursuant to paragraph (d) of this section. The form on which this statement is filed is referred to in the regulations under section 338 as the Form 8023, "Elections Under Section 338 For Corporations Making Qualified Stock Purchases."

(15) *Section 338(h)(10) election.*—A *section 338(h)(10) election* is an election to apply section 338(h)(10) to target. A section 338(h)(10) election is made by making a joint election for target under §1.338(h)(10)-1 on Form 8023.

(16) *Selling group.*—The *selling group* is the affiliated group (as defined in section 1504) eligible to file a consolidated return that includes target for the taxable period in which the acquisition date occurs. However, a selling group is not an affiliated group of which target is the common parent on the acquisition date.

(17) *Target; old target; new target.*—*Target* is the target corporation as defined in section 338(d)(2). *Old target* refers to target for periods ending on or before the close of target's acquisition date. *New target* refers to target for subsequent periods.

(18) *Target affiliate.*—The term *target affiliate* has the same meaning as in section 338(h)(6) (applied without section 338(h)(6)(B)(i)). Thus, a corporation described in section 338(h)(6)(B)(i) is considered a target affiliate for all purposes of section 338. If a target affiliate is acquired in a qualified stock purchase, it is also a target.

(19) *12-month acquisition period.*—The *12-month acquisition period* is the period described in section 338(h)(1), unless extended pursuant to §1.338-8(j)(2).

(d) *Time and manner of making election.*—The purchasing corporation makes a section 338 election for target by filing a statement of section 338 election on Form 8023 in accordance with the instructions to the form. The section 338 election must be made not later than the 15th day of the 9th month beginning after the month in which the acquisition date occurs. A section 338 election is irrevocable. See §1.338(h)(10)-1(c)(2) for section 338(h)(10) elections.

(e) *Special rules for foreign corporations or DISCs.*—(1) *Elections by certain foreign purchasing corporations.*—(i) *General rule.*—A qualifying foreign purchasing corporation is not required to file a statement of section 338 election for a qualifying foreign target before the earlier of 3 years after the acquisition date and the 180th day after the close of the purchasing corporation's taxable year within which a triggering event occurs.

(ii) *Qualifying foreign purchasing corporation.*—A purchasing corporation is a *qualifying foreign purchasing corporation* only if, during the acquisition period of a qualifying foreign target, all the corporations in the purchasing corporation's affiliated group are foreign corporations that are not subject to United States tax.

(iii) *Qualifying foreign target.*—A target is a *qualifying foreign target* only if target and its target affiliates are foreign corporations that, during target's acquisition period, are not subject to United States tax (and will not become subject to United States tax during such period because of a section 338 election). A target affiliate is taken into account for purposes of the preceding sentence only if, during target's 12-month acquisition period, it is or becomes a member of the affiliated group that includes the purchasing corporation.

(iv) *Triggering event.*—A *triggering event* occurs in the taxable year of the qualifying foreign purchasing corporation in which either that corporation or any corporation in its affiliated group becomes subject to United States tax.

(v) *Subject to United States tax.*—For purposes of this paragraph (e)(1), a foreign corporation is considered subject to United States tax—

(A) For the taxable year for which that corporation is required under §1.6012-2(g) (other than §1.6012-2(g)(2)(i)(B)(2)) to file a United States income tax return; or

(B) For the period during which that corporation is a controlled foreign corporation, a passive foreign investment company for which an election under section 1295 is in effect, a foreign

investment company, or a foreign corporation the stock ownership of which is described in section 552(a)(2).

(2) *Acquisition period.*—For purposes of this paragraph (e), the term *acquisition period* means the period beginning on the first day of the 12-month acquisition period and ending on the acquisition date.

(3) *Statement of section 338 election may be filed by United States shareholders in certain cases.*—The United States shareholders (as defined in section 951(b)) of a foreign purchasing corporation that is a controlled foreign corporation (as defined in section 957 (taking into account section 953(c))) may file a statement of section 338 election on behalf of the purchasing corporation if the purchasing corporation is not required under §1.6012-2(g) (other than §1.6012-2(g)(2)(i)(B)(2)) to file a United States income tax return for its taxable year that includes the acquisition date. Form 8023 must be filed as described in the form and its instructions and also must be attached to the Form 5471, "Information Returns Of U.S. Persons With Respect To Certain Foreign Corporations," filed with respect to the purchasing corporation by each United States shareholder for the purchasing corporation's taxable year that includes the acquisition date (or, if paragraph (e)(1)(i) of this section applies to the election, for the purchasing corporation's taxable year within which it becomes a controlled foreign corporation). The provisions of §1.964-1(c) (including §1.964-1(c)(7)) do not apply to an election made by the United States shareholders.

(4) *Notice requirement for U.S. persons holding stock in foreign target.*—(i) *General rule.*—If a target subject to a section 338 election was a controlled foreign corporation, a passive foreign investment company, or a foreign personal holding company at any time during the portion of its taxable year that ends on its acquisition date, the purchasing corporation must deliver written notice of the election (and a copy of Form 8023, its attachments and instructions) to—

(A) Each U.S. person (other than a member of the affiliated group of which the purchasing corporation is a member (the purchasing group member)) that, on the acquisition date of the foreign target, holds stock in the foreign target; and

(B) Each U.S. person (other than a purchasing group member) that sells stock in the foreign target to a purchasing group member during the foreign target's 12-month acquisition period.

(ii) *Limitation.*—The notice requirement of this paragraph (e)(4) applies only where the section 338 election for the foreign target affects income, gain, loss, deduction, or credit of the U.S. person described in paragraph (e)(4)(i) of this section under section 551, 951, 1248, or 1293.

(iii) *Form of notice.*—The notice to U.S. persons must be identified prominently as a notice of section 338 election and must—

(A) Contain the name, address, and employer identification number (if any) of, and the country (and, if relevant, the lesser political subdivision) under the laws of which are organized the purchasing corporation and the relevant target (i.e., the target the stock of which the particular U.S. person held or sold under the circumstances described in paragraph (e)(4)(i) of this section);

(B) Identify those corporations as the purchasing corporation and the foreign target, respectively; and

(C) Contain the following declaration (or a substantially similar declaration):

THIS DOCUMENT SERVES AS NOTICE OF AN ELECTION UNDER SECTION 338 FOR THE ABOVE CITED FOREIGN TARGET THE STOCK OF WHICH YOU EITHER HELD OR SOLD UNDER THE CIRCUMSTANCES DESCRIBED IN TREASURY REGULATIONS SECTION 1.338-2(e)(4). FOR POSSIBLE UNITED STATES FEDERAL INCOME TAX CONSEQUENCES UNDER SECTION 551, 951, 1248, OR 1293 OF THE INTERNAL REVENUE CODE OF 1986 THAT MAY APPLY TO YOU, SEE TREASURY REGULATIONS SECTION 1.338-9(b). YOU MAY BE REQUIRED TO ATTACH THE INFORMATION ATTACHED TO THIS NOTICE TO CERTAIN RETURNS.

(iv) *Timing of notice.*—The notice required by this paragraph (e)(4) must be delivered to the U.S. person on or before the later of the 120th day after the acquisition date of the particular target or the day on which Form 8023 is filed. The notice is considered delivered on the date it is mailed to the proper address (or an address similar enough to complete delivery), unless the date it is mailed cannot be reasonably determined. The date of mailing will be determined under the rules of section 7502. For example, the date of mailing is the date of U.S. postmark or the applicable date recorded or marked by a designated delivery service.

(v) *Consequence of failure to comply.*—A statement of section 338 election is not valid if timely notice is not given to one or more U.S. persons described in this paragraph (e)(4). If the form of notice fails to comply with all requirements of this paragraph (e)(4), the

Reg. §1.338-2(e)(4)(v)

section 338 election is valid, but the waiver rule of §1.338-10(b)(1) does not apply.

(vi) *Good faith effort to comply.*—The purchasing corporation will be considered to have complied with this paragraph (e)(4), even though it failed to provide notice or provide timely notice to each person described in this paragraph (e)(4), if the Commissioner determines that the purchasing corporation made a good faith effort to identify and provide timely notice to those U.S. persons. [Reg. §1.338-2.]

☐ [*T.D.* 8940, 2-12-2001.]

[Reg. §1.338-3]

§1.338-3. Qualification for the section 338 election.—(a) *Scope.*—This section provides rules on whether certain acquisitions of stock are qualified stock purchases and on other miscellaneous issues under section 338.

(b) *Rules relating to qualified stock purchases.*—(1) *Purchasing corporation requirement.*—An individual cannot make a qualified stock purchase of target. Section 338(d)(3) requires, as a condition of a qualified stock purchase, that a corporation purchase the stock of target. If an individual forms a corporation (new P) to acquire target stock, new P can make a qualified stock purchase of target if new P is considered for tax purposes to purchase the target stock. Facts that may indicate that new P does not purchase the target stock include new P's merging downstream into target, liquidating, or otherwise disposing of the target stock following the purported qualified stock purchase.

(2) *Purchase.*—The term *purchase* has the same meaning as in section 338(h)(3). Stock in a target (or target affiliate) may be considered purchased if, under general principles of tax law, the purchasing corporation is considered to own stock of the target (or target affiliate) meeting the requirements of section 1504(a)(2), notwithstanding that no amount may be paid for (or allocated to) the stock.

(3) *Acquisitions of stock from related corporations.*—(i) *In general.*—Stock acquired by a purchasing corporation from a related corporation (R) is generally not considered acquired by purchase. See section 338(h)(3)(A)(iii).

(ii) *Time for testing relationship.*—For purposes of section 338(h)(3)(A)(iii), a purchasing corporation is treated as related to another person if the relationship specified in section 338(h)(3)(A)(iii) exists—

(A) In the case of a single transaction, immediately after the purchase of target stock;

(B) In the case of a series of acquisitions otherwise constituting a qualified stock purchase within the meaning of section 338(d)(3), immediately after the last acquisition in such series; and

(C) In the case of a series of transactions effected pursuant to an integrated plan to dispose of target stock, immediately after the last transaction in such series.

(iii) *Cases where section 338(h)(3)(C) applies—acquisitions treated as purchases.*—If section 338(h)(3)(C) applies and the purchasing corporation is treated as acquiring stock by purchase from R, solely for purposes of determining when the stock is considered acquired, target stock acquired from R is considered to have been acquired by the purchasing corporation on the day on which the purchasing corporation is first considered to own that stock under section 318(a) (other than section 318(a)(4)).

(iv) *Examples.*—The following examples illustrate this paragraph (b)(3):

Example 1. (i) S is the parent of a group of corporations that are engaged in various businesses. Prior to January 1, Year 1, S decided to discontinue its involvement in one line of business. To accomplish this, S forms a new corporation, Newco, with a nominal amount of cash. Shortly thereafter, on January 1, Year 1, S transfers all the stock of the subsidiary conducting the unwanted business (T) to Newco in exchange for 100 shares of Newco common stock and a Newco promissory note. Prior to January 1, Year 1, S and Underwriter (U) had entered into a binding agreement pursuant to which U would purchase 60 shares of Newco common stock from S and then sell those shares in an Initial Public Offering (IPO). On January 6, Year 1, the IPO closes.

(ii) Newco's acquisition of T stock is one of a series of transactions undertaken pursuant to one integrated plan. The series of transactions ends with the closing of the IPO and the transfer of all the shares of stock in accordance with the agreements. Immediately after the last transaction effected pursuant to the plan, S owns 40 percent of Newco, which does not give rise to a relationship described in section 338(h)(3)(A)(iii). See §1.338-3(b)(3)(ii)(C). Accord-

ingly, S and Newco are not related for purposes of section 338(h)(3)(A)(iii).

(iii) Further, because Newco's basis in the T stock is not determined by reference to S's basis in the T stock and because the transaction is not an exchange to which section 351, 354, 355, or 356 applies, Newco's acquisition of the T stock is a purchase within the meaning of section 338(h)(3).

Example 2. (i) On January 1 of Year 1, P purchases 75 percent in value of the R stock. On that date, R owns 4 of the 100 shares of T stock. On June 1 of Year 1, R acquires an additional 16 shares of T stock. On December 1 of Year 1, P purchases 70 shares of T stock from an unrelated person and 12 of the 20 shares of T stock held by R.

(ii) Of the 12 shares of T stock purchased by P from R on December 1 of Year 1, 3 of those shares are deemed to have been acquired by P on January 1 of Year 1, the date on which 3 of the 4 shares of T stock held by R on that date were first considered owned by P under section 318(a)(2)(C) (i.e., 4 × .75). The remaining 9 shares of T stock purchased by P from R on December 1 of Year 1 are deemed to have been acquired by P on June 1 of Year 1, the date on which an additional 12 of the 20 shares of T stock owned by R on that date were first considered owned by P under section 318(a)(2)(C) (i.e., (20 × .75) – 3). Because stock acquisitions by P sufficient for a qualified stock purchase of T occur within a 12-month period (i.e., 3 shares constructively on January 1 of Year 1, 9 shares constructively on June 1 of Year 1, and 70 shares actually on December 1 of Year 1), a qualified stock purchase is made on December 1 of Year 1.

Example 3. (i) On February 1 of Year 1, P acquires 25 percent in value of the R stock from B (the sole shareholder of P). That R stock is not acquired by purchase. See section 338(h)(3)(A)(iii). On that date, R owns 4 of the 100 shares of T stock. On June 1 of Year 1, P purchases an additional 25 percent in value of the R stock, and on January 1 of Year 2, P purchases another 25 percent in value of the R stock. On June 1 of Year 2, R acquires an additional 16 shares of the T stock. On December 1 of Year 2, P purchases 68 shares of the T stock from an unrelated person and 12 of the 20 shares of the T stock held by R.

(ii) Of the 12 shares of the T stock purchased by P from R on December 1 of Year 2, 2 of those shares are deemed to have been acquired by P on June 1 of Year 1, the date on which 2 of the 4 shares of the T stock held by R on that date were first considered owned by P under section 318(a)(2)(C) (i.e., 4 × .5). For purposes of this attribution, the R stock need not be acquired by P by purchase. See section 338(h)(1). (By contrast, the acquisition of the T stock by P from R does not qualify as a purchase unless P has acquired at least 50 percent in value of the R stock by purchase. Section 338(h)(3)(C)(i).) Of the remaining 10 shares of the T stock purchased by P from R on December 1 of Year 2, 1 of those shares is deemed to have been acquired by P on January 1 of Year 2, the date on which an additional 1 share of the 4 shares of the T stock held by R on that date was first considered owned by P under section 318(a)(2)(C) (i.e., (4 × .75) – 2). The remaining 9 shares of the T stock purchased by P from R on December 1 of Year 2, are deemed to have been acquired by P on June 1 of Year 2, the date on which an additional 12 shares of the T stock held by R on that date were first considered owned by P under section 318(a)(2)(C) (i.e., (20 × .75) – 3). Because a qualified stock purchase of T by P is made on December 1 of Year 2 only if all 12 shares of the T stock purchased by P from R on that date are considered acquired during a 12-month period ending on that date (so that, in conjunction with the 68 shares of the T stock P purchased on that date from the unrelated person, 80 of T's 100 shares are acquired by P during a 12-month period) and because 2 of those 12 shares are considered to have been acquired by P more than 12 months before December 1 of Year 2 (i.e., on June 1 of Year 1), a qualified stock purchase is not made. (Under §1.338-8(j)(2), for purposes of applying the consistency rules, P is treated as making a qualified stock purchase of T if, pursuant to an arrangement, P purchases T stock satisfying the requirements of section 1504(a)(2) over a period of more than 12 months.)

Example 4. Assume the same facts as in *Example 3*, except that on February 1 of Year 1, P acquires 25 percent in value of the R stock by purchase. The result is the same as in *Example 3*.

(4) *Acquisition date for tiered targets.*—(i) *Stock sold in deemed asset sale.*—If an election under section 338 is made for target, old target is deemed to sell target's assets and new target is deemed to acquire those assets. Under section 338(h)(3)(B), new target's deemed purchase of stock of another corporation is a purchase for purposes of section 338(d)(3) on the acquisition date of target. If new target's deemed purchase causes a qualified stock purchase of the other corporation and if a section 338 election is made for the other corporation, the acquisition date for the other corporation is the same as the acquisition date of target. However, the deemed sale and purchase of the other corporation's assets is considered to take place after the deemed sale and purchase of target's assets.

(ii) *Example.*—The following example illustrates this paragraph (b)(4):

Example. A owns all of the T stock. T owns 50 of the 100 shares of X stock. The other 50 shares of X stock are owned by corporation Y, which is unrelated to A, T, or P. On January 1 of Year 1, P makes a qualified stock purchase of T from A and makes a section 338 election for T. On December 1 of Year 1, P purchases the 50 shares of X stock held by Y. A qualified stock purchase of X is made on December 1 of Year 1, because the deemed purchase of 50 shares of X stock by new T because of the section 338 election for T and the actual purchase of 50 shares of X stock by P are treated as purchases made by one corporation. Section 338(h)(8). For purposes of determining whether those purchases occur within a 12-month acquisition period as required by section 338(d)(3), T is deemed to purchase its X stock on T's acquisition date, i.e., January 1 of Year 1.

(5) *Effect of redemptions.*—(i) *General rule.*—Except as provided in this paragraph (b)(5), a qualified stock purchase is made on the first day on which the percentage ownership requirements of section 338(d)(3) are satisfied by reference to target stock that is both—

(A) Held on that day by the purchasing corporation; and

(B) Purchased by the purchasing corporation during the 12-month period ending on that day.

(ii) *Redemptions from persons unrelated to the purchasing corporation.*—Target stock redemptions from persons unrelated to the purchasing corporation that occur during the 12-month acquisition period are taken into account as reductions in target's outstanding stock for purposes of determining whether target stock purchased by the purchasing corporation in the 12-month acquisition period satisfies the percentage ownership requirements of section 338(d)(3).

(iii) *Redemptions from the purchasing corporation or related persons during 12-month acquisition period.*—(A) *General rule.*—For purposes of the percentage ownership requirements of section 338(d)(3), a redemption of target stock during the 12-month acquisition period from the purchasing corporation or from any person related to the purchasing corporation is not taken into account as a reduction in target's outstanding stock.

(B) *Exception for certain redemptions from related corporations.*—A redemption of target stock during the 12-month acquisition period from a corporation related to the purchasing corporation is taken into account as a reduction in target's outstanding stock to the extent that the redeemed stock would have been considered purchased by the purchasing corporation (because of section 338(h)(3)(C)) during the 12-month acquisition period if the redeemed stock had been acquired by the purchasing corporation from the related corporation On the day of the redemption. See paragraph (b)(3) of this section.

(iv) *Examples.*—The following examples illustrate this paragraph (b)(5):

Example 1. QSP on stock purchase date; redemption from unrelated person during 12-month period. A owns all 100 shares of T stock. On January 1 of Year 1, P purchases 40 shares of the T stock from A. On July 1 of Year 1, T redeems 25 shares from A. On December 1 of Year 1, P purchases 20 shares of the T stock from A. P makes a qualified stock purchase of T on December 1 of Year 1, because the 60 shares of T stock purchased by P within the 12-month period ending on that date satisfy the 80-percent ownership requirements of section 338(d)(3) (i.e., 60/75 shares), determined by taking into account the redemption of 25 shares.

Example 2. QSP on stock redemption date; redemption from unrelated person during 12-month period. The facts are the same as in *Example 1,* except that P purchases 60 shares of T stock on January 1 of Year 1 and none on December 1 of Year 1. P makes a qualified stock purchase of T on July 1 of Year 1, because that is the first day on which the T stock purchased by P within the preceding 12-month period satisfies the 80-percent ownership requirements of section 338(d)(3) (i.e., 60/75 shares), determined by taking into account the redemption of 25 shares.

Example 3. Redemption from purchasing corporation not taken into account. On December 15 of Year 1, T redeems 30 percent of its stock from P. The redeemed stock was held by P for several years and constituted P's total interest in T. On December 1 of Year 2, P purchases the remaining T stock from A. P does not make a qualified stock purchase of T on December 1 of Year 2. For purposes of the 80-percent ownership requirements of section 338(d)(3), the redemption of P's T stock on December 15 of Year 1 is not taken into account as a reduction in T's outstanding stock.

Example 4. Redemption from related person taken into account. On January 1 of Year 1, P purchases 60 of the 100 shares of X stock. On that date, X owns 40 of the 100 shares of T stock. On April 1 of Year 1, T redeems X's T stock and P purchases the remaining 60 shares of T stock from an unrelated person. For purposes of the 80-percent ownership requirements of section 338(d)(3), the redemption of the T stock from X (a person related to P) is taken into account as a reduction in T's outstanding stock. If P had purchased the 40 redeemed shares from X on April 1 of Year 1, all 40 of the shares would have been considered purchased (because of section 338(h)(3)(C)(i)) during the 12-month period ending on April 1 of Year 1 (24 of the 40 shares would have been considered purchased by P on January 1 of Year 1 and the remaining 16 shares would have been considered purchased by P on April 1 of Year 1). See paragraph (b)(3) of this section. Accordingly, P makes a qualified stock purchase of T on April 1 of Year 1, because the 60 shares of T stock purchased by P on that date satisfy the 80-percent ownership requirements of section 338(d)(3) (i.e., 60/60 shares), determined by taking into account the redemption of 40 shares.

(c) *Effect of post-acquisition events on eligibility for section 338 election.*—(1) *Post-acquisition elimination of target.*—(i) The purchasing corporation may make an election under section 338 for target even though target is liquidated on or after the acquisition date. If target liquidates on the acquisition date, the liquidation is considered to occur on the following day and immediately after new target's deemed purchase of assets. The purchasing corporation may also make an election under section 338 for target even though target is merged into another corporation, or otherwise disposed of by the purchasing corporation provided that, under the facts and circumstances, the purchasing corporation is considered for tax purposes as the purchaser of the target stock. See § 1.338(h)(10)-1(c)(2) for special rules concerning section 338(h)(10) elections in certain multi-step transactions.

(ii) The following examples illustrate this paragraph (c)(1):

Example 1. On January 1 of Year 1, P purchases 100 percent of the outstanding common stock of T. On June 1 of Year 1, P sells the T stock to an unrelated person. Assuming that P is considered for tax purposes as the purchaser of the T stock, P remains eligible, after June 1 of Year 1, to make a section 338 election for T that results in a deemed asset sale of T's assets on January 1 of Year 1.

Example 2. On January 1 of Year 1, P makes a qualified stock purchase of T. On that date, T owns the stock of T1. On March 1 of Year 1, T sells the T1 stock to an unrelated person. On April 1 of Year 1, P makes a section 338 election for T. Notwithstanding that the T1 stock was sold on March 1 of Year 1, the section 338 election for T on April 1 of Year 1 results in a qualified stock purchase by T of T1 on January 1 of Year 1. See paragraph (b)(4)(i) of this section.

(2) *Post-acquisition elimination of the purchasing corporation.*—An election under section 338 may be made for target after the acquisition of assets of the purchasing corporation by another corporation in a transaction described in section 381(a), provided that the purchasing corporation is considered for tax purposes as the purchaser of the target stock. The acquiring corporation in the section 381(a) transaction may make an election under section 338 for target.

(d) *Consequences of post-acquisition elimination of target where section 338 election not made.*—(1) *Scope.*—The rules of this paragraph (d) apply to the transfer of target assets to the purchasing corporation (or another member of the same affiliated group as the purchasing corporation) (the transferee) following a qualified stock purchase of target stock, if the purchasing corporation does not make a section 338 election for target. Notwithstanding the rules of this paragraph (d), section 354(a) (and so much of section 356 as relates to section 354) cannot apply to any person other than the purchasing corporation or another member of the same affiliated group as the purchasing corporation unless the transfer of target assets is pursuant to a reorganization as determined without regard to this paragraph (d).

(2) *Continuity of interest.*—By virtue of section 338, in determining whether the continuity of interest requirement of § 1.368-1(b) is satisfied on the transfer of assets from target to the transferee, the purchasing corporation's target stock acquired in the qualified stock purchase represents an interest on the part of a person who was an owner of the target's business enterprise prior to the transfer that can be continued in a reorganization.

(3) *Control requirement.*—By virtue of section 338, the acquisition of target stock in the qualified stock purchase will not prevent the purchasing corporation from qualifying as a shareholder of the target transferor for the purpose of determining whether, immediately after the transfer of target assets, a shareholder of the transferor is in control of the corporation to which the assets are transferred within the meaning of section 368(a)(1)(D).

(4) *Solely for voting stock requirement.*—By virtue of section 338, the acquisition of target stock in the qualified stock purchase for consideration other than voting stock will not prevent the subsequent transfer of target assets from satisfying the solely for voting stock requirement for purposes of determining if the transfer of target assets qualifies as a reorganization under section 368(a)(1)(C).

Reg. § 1.338-3(d)(4)

(5) *Example.*—The following example illustrates this paragraph (d):

Example. (i) *Facts.* P, T, and X are domestic corporations. T and X each operate a trade or business. A and K, individuals unrelated to P, own 85 and 15 percent, respectively, of the stock of T. P owns all of the stock of X. The total adjusted basis of T's property exceeds the sum of T's liabilities plus the amount of liabilities to which T's property is subject. P purchases all of A's T stock for cash in a qualified stock purchase. P does not make an election under section 338(g) with respect to its acquisition of T stock. Shortly after the acquisition date, and as part of the same plan, T merges under applicable state law into X in a transaction that, but for the question of continuity of interest, satisfies all the requirements of section 368(a)(1)(A). In the merger, all of T's assets are transferred to X. P and K receive X stock in exchange for their T stock. P intends to retain the stock of X indefinitely.

(ii) *Status of transfer as a reorganization.* By virtue of section 338, for the purpose of determining whether the continuity of interest requirement of §1.368-1(b) is satisfied, P's T stock acquired in the qualified stock purchase represents an interest on the part of a person who was an owner of T's business enterprise prior to the transfer that can be continued in a reorganization through P's continuing ownership of X. Thus, the continuity of interest requirement is satisfied and the merger of T into X is a reorganization within the meaning of section 368(a)(1)(A). Moreover, by virtue of section 338, the requirement of section 368(a)(1)(D) that a target shareholder control the transferee immediately after the transfer is satisfied because P controls X immediately after the transfer. In addition, all of T's assets are transferred to X in the merger and P and K receive the X stock exchanged therefor in pursuance of the plan of reorganization. Thus, the merger of T into X is also a reorganization within the meaning of section 368(a)(1)(D).

(iii) *Treatment of T and X.* Under section 361(a), T recognizes no gain or loss in the merger. Under section 362(b), X's basis in the assets received in the merger is the same as the basis of the assets in T's hands. X succeeds to and takes into account the items of T as provided in section 381.

(iv) *Treatment of P.* By virtue of section 338, the transfer of T assets to X is a reorganization. Pursuant to that reorganization, P exchanges its T stock solely for stock of X, a party to the reorganization. Because P is the purchasing corporation, section 354 applies to P's exchange of T stock for X stock in the merger of T into X. Thus, P recognizes no gain or loss on the exchange. Under section 358, P's basis in the X stock received in the exchange is the same as the basis of P's T stock exchanged therefor.

(v) *Treatment of K.* Because K is not the purchasing corporation (or an affiliate thereof), section 354 cannot apply to K's exchange of T stock for X stock in the merger of T into X unless the transfer of T's assets is pursuant to a reorganization as determined without regard to this paragraph (d). Under general principles of tax law applicable to reorganizations, the continuity of interest requirement is not satisfied because P's stock purchase and the merger of T into X are pursuant to an integrated transaction in which A, the owner of 85 percent of the stock of T, received solely cash in exchange for A's T stock. See, e.g., §1.368-1(e)(1)(i); *Yoc Heating v. Commissioner*, 61 T.C. 168 (1973); *Kass v. Commissioner*, 60 T.C. 218 (1973), aff'd, 491 F.2d 749 (3d Cir. 1974). Thus, the requisite continuity of interest under §1.368-1(b) is lacking and section 354 does not apply to K's exchange of T stock for X stock. K recognizes gain or loss, if any, pursuant to section 1001(c) with respect to its T stock.

[Reg. §1.338-3.]

☐ [*T.D. 8940, 2-12-2001 (corrected 3-29-2001). Amended by T.D. 9071, 7-8-2003 and T.D. 9271, 7-3-2006.*]

[Reg. §1.338-4]

§1.338-4. Aggregate deemed sale price; various aspects of taxation of the deemed asset sale.—(a) *Scope.*—This section provides rules under section 338(a)(1) to determine the aggregate deemed sale price (ADSP) for target. ADSP is the amount for which old target is deemed to have sold all of its assets in the deemed asset sale. ADSP is allocated among target's assets in accordance with §1.338-6 to determine the amount for which each asset is deemed to have been sold. When a subsequent increase or decrease is required under general principles of tax law with respect to an element of ADSP, the redetermined ADSP is allocated among target's assets in accordance with §1.338-7. This §1.338-4 also provides rules regarding the recognition of gain or loss on the deemed sale of target affiliate stock. Notwithstanding section 338(h)(6)(B)(ii), stock held by a target affiliate in a foreign corporation or in a corporation that is a DISC or that is described in section 1248(e) is not excluded from the operation of section 338.

(b) *Determination of ADSP.*—(1) *General rule.*—ADSP is the sum of—

(i) The grossed-up amount realized on the sale to the purchasing corporation of the purchasing corporation's recently purchased target stock (as defined in section 338(b)(6)(A)); and

(ii) The liabilities of old target.

(2) *Time and amount of ADSP.*—(i) *Original termination.*—ADSP is initially determined at the beginning of the day after the acquisition date of target. General principles of tax law apply in determining the timing and amount of the elements of ADSP.

(ii) *Redetermination of ADSP.*—ADSP is redetermined at such time and in such amount as an increase or decrease would be required, under general principles of tax law, for the elements of ADSP. For example, ADSP is redetermined because of an increase or decrease in the amount realized for recently purchased stock or because liabilities not originally taken into account in determining ADSP are subsequently taken into account. Increases or decreases with respect to the elements of ADSP result in the reallocation of ADSP among target's assets under §1.338-7.

(iii) *Example.*—The following example illustrates this paragraph (b)(2):

Example. In Year 1, T, a manufacturer, purchases a customized delivery truck from X with purchase money indebtedness having a stated principal amount of $100,000. P acquires all of the stock of T in Year 3 for $700,000 and makes a section 338 election for T. Assume T has no liabilities other than its purchase money indebtedness to X. In Year 4, when T is neither insolvent nor in a title 11 case, T and X agree to reduce the amount of the purchase money indebtedness to $80,000. Assume further that the reduction would be a purchase price reduction under section 108(e)(5). T and X's agreement to reduce the amount of the purchase money indebtedness would not, under general principles of tax law that would apply if the deemed asset sale had actually occurred, change the amount of liabilities of old target taken into account in determining its amount realized. Accordingly, ADSP is not redetermined at the time of the reduction. See §1.338-5(b)(2)(iii) *Example 1* for the effect on AGUB.

(c) *Grossed-up amount realized on the sale to the purchasing corporation of the purchasing corporation's recently purchased target stock.*—(1) *Determination of amount.*—The grossed-up amount realized on the sale to the purchasing corporation of the purchasing corporation's recently purchased target stock is an amount equal to—

(i) The amount realized on the sale to the purchasing corporation of the purchasing corporation's recently purchased target stock determined as if the selling shareholder(s) were required to use old target's accounting methods and characteristics and the installment method were not available and determined without regard to the selling costs taken into account under paragraph (c)(1)(iii) of this section;

(ii) Divided by the percentage of target stock (by value, determined on the acquisition date) attributable to that recently purchased target stock;

(iii) Less the selling costs incurred by the selling shareholders in connection with the sale to the purchasing corporation of the purchasing corporation's recently purchased target stock that reduce their amount realized on the sale of the stock (e.g., brokerage commissions and any similar costs to sell the stock).

(2) *Example.*—The following example illustrates this paragraph (c):

Example. T has two classes of stock outstanding, voting common stock and preferred stock described in section 1504(a)(4). On March 1 of Year 1, P purchases 40 percent of the outstanding T stock from S1 for $500, 20 percent of the outstanding T stock from S2 for $225, and 20 percent of the outstanding T stock from S3 for $275. On that date, the fair market value of all the T voting common stock is $1,250 and the preferred stock $750. S1, S2, and S3 incur $40, $35, and $25 respectively of selling costs. S1 continues to own the remaining 20 percent of the outstanding T stock. The grossed-up amount realized on the sale to P of P's recently purchased T stock is calculated as follows: The total amount realized (without regard to selling costs) is $1,000 (500 + 225 + 275). The percentage of T stock by value on the acquisition date attributable to the recently purchased T stock is 50% (1,000/(1,250 + 750)). The selling costs are $100 (40 + 35 + 25). The grossed-up amount realized is $1,900 (1,000/.5 − 100).

(d) *Liabilities of old target.*—(1) *In general.*—In general, the liabilities of old target are measured as of the beginning of the day after the acquisition date. (But see §1.338-1(d) (regarding certain transactions on the acquisition date).) In order to be taken into account in ADSP, a liability must be a liability of target that is properly taken into account in amount realized under general principles of tax law that would apply if old target had sold its assets to an unrelated person for consideration that included the discharge of its liabilities. See §1.1001-2(a). Such liabilities may include liabilities for the tax consequences resulting from the deemed sale.

(2) *Time and amount of liabilities.*—The time for taking into account liabilities of old target in determining ADSP and the amount of the liabilities taken into account is determined as if old target had sold its assets to an unrelated person for consideration that included the discharge of the liabilities by the unrelated person. For example, if no amount of a target liability is properly taken into account in amount realized as of the beginning of the day after the acquisition date, the liability is not initially taken into account in determining ADSP (although it may be taken into account at some later date).

(e) *Deemed sale tax consequences.*—Gain or loss on each asset in the deemed sale is computed by reference to the ADSP allocated to that asset. ADSP is allocated under the rules of § 1.338-6. Though deemed sale tax consequences may increase or decrease ADSP by creating or reducing a tax liability, the amount of the tax liability itself may be a function of the size of the deemed sale tax consequences. Thus, these determinations may require trial and error computations.

(f) *Other rules apply in determining ADSP.*—ADSP may not be applied in such a way as to contravene other applicable rules. For example, a capital loss cannot be applied to reduce ordinary income in calculating the tax liability on the deemed sale for purposes of determining ADSP.

(g) *Examples.*—The following examples illustrate this section. For purposes of the examples in this paragraph (g), unless otherwise stated, T is a calendar year taxpayer that files separate returns and that has no loss, tax credit, or other carryovers to Year 1. Depreciation for Year 1 is not taken into account. T has no liabilities other than the Federal income tax liability resulting from the deemed asset sale, and the T shareholders have no selling costs. Assume that T's tax rate for any ordinary income or net capital gain resulting from the deemed sale of assets is 34 percent and that any capital loss is offset by capital gain. On July 1 of Year 1, P purchases all of the stock of T and makes a section 338 election for T. The examples are as follows:

Example 1. One class. (i) On July 1 of Year 1, T's only asset is an item of section 1245 property with an adjusted basis to T of $50,400, a recomputed basis of $80,000, and a fair market value of $100,000. P purchases all of the T stock for $75,000, which also equals the amount

realized for the stock determined as if the selling shareholder(s) were required to use old target's accounting methods and characteristics.

(ii) ADSP is determined as follows (for purposes of this section (g), G is the grossed-up amount realized on the sale to P of P's recently purchased T stock, L is T's liabilities other than T's tax liability for the deemed sale tax consequences, T_R is the applicable tax rate, and B is the adjusted basis of the asset deemed sold):

$$ADSP = G + L + T_R \times (ADSP - B)$$
$$ADSP = (\$75,000/1) + \$0 + .34 \times (ADSP - \$50,400)$$
$$ADSP = \$75,000 + .34ADSP - \$17,136$$
$$.66ADSP = \$57,864$$
$$ADSP = \$87,672.72$$

(iii) Because ADSP for T ($87,672.72) does not exceed the fair market value of T's asset ($100,000), a Class V asset, T's entire ADSP is allocated to that asset. Thus, T's deemed sale results in $37,272.72 of taxable income (consisting of $29,600 of ordinary income and $7,672.72 of capital gain).

(iv) The facts are the same as in paragraph (i) of this *Example 1*, except that on July 1 of Year 1, P purchases only 80 of the 100 shares of T stock for $60,000. The grossed-up amount realized on the sale to P of P's recently purchased T stock (G) is $75,000 ($60,000/.8). Consequently, ADSP and the deemed sale tax consequences are the same as in paragraphs (ii) and (iii) of this *Example 1*.

(v) The facts are the same as in paragraph (i) of this *Example 1*, except that T also has goodwill (a Class VII asset) with an appraised value of $10,000. The results are the same as in paragraphs (ii) and (iii) of this *Example 1*. Because ADSP does not exceed the fair market value of the Class V asset, no amount is allocated to the Class VII asset (goodwill).

Example 2. More than one class. (i) P purchases all of the T stock for $140,000, which also equals the amount realized for the stock determined as if the selling shareholder(s) were required to use old target's accounting methods and characteristics. On July 1 of Year 1, T has liabilities (not including the tax liability for the deemed sale tax consequences) of $50,000, cash (a Class I asset) of $10,000, actively traded securities (a Class II asset) with a basis of $4,000 and a fair market value of $10,000, goodwill (a Class VII asset) with a basis of $3,000, and the following Class V assets:

Asset	Basis	FMV	Ratio of asset FMV to total Class V FMV
Land	$5,000	$35,000	.14
Building	10,000	50,000	.20
Equipment A (Recomputed basis $80,000)	5,000	90,000	.36
Equipment B (Recomputed basis $20,000)	10,000	75,000	.30
Totals	$30,000	$250,000	1.00

(ii) ADSP exceeds $20,000. Thus, $10,000 of ADSP is allocated to the cash and $10,000 to the actively traded securities. The amount allocated to an asset (other than a Class VII asset) cannot exceed its fair market value (however, the fair market value of any property subject to nonrecourse indebtedness is treated as being not less than the amount of such indebtedness; see § 1.338-6(a)(2)). See § 1.338-6(c)(1) (relating to fair market value limitation).

(iii) The portion of ADSP allocable to the Class V assets is preliminarily determined as follows (in the formula, the amount allocated to the Class I assets is referred to as I and the amount allocated to the Class II assets as II):

$$ADSP_V = (G - (I + II)) + L + T_R \times [(II - B_{II}) + (ADSP_V - B_V)]$$
$$ADSP_V = (\$140,000 - (\$10,000 + \$10,000)) + \$50,000 + .34 \times [(\$10,000 - \$4,000) + (ADSP_V - (\$5,000 + \$10,000 + \$5,000 + \$10,000))]$$
$$ADSP_V = \$161,840 + .34\ ADSP_V$$
$$.66\ ADSP_V = \$161,840$$
$$ADSP_V = \$245,212.12$$

(iv) Because, under the preliminary calculations of ADSP, the amount to be allocated to the Class I, II, III, IV, V, and VI assets does not exceed their aggregate fair market value, no ADSP amount is allocated to goodwill. Accordingly, the deemed sale of the goodwill

results in a capital loss of $3,000. The portion of ADSP allocable to the Class V assets is finally determined by taking into account this loss as follows:

$$ADSP_V = (G - (I + II)) + L + T_R \times [(II - B_{II}) + (ADSP_V - B_V) + (ADSP_{VII} - B_{VII})]$$
$$ADSP_V = (\$140,000 - (\$10,000 + \$10,000)) + \$50,000 + .34 \times [(\$10,000 - \$4,000) + (ADSP_V - \$30,000) + (\$0 - \$3,000)]$$
$$ADSP_V = \$160,820 + .34\ ADSP_V$$
$$.66\ ADSP_V = \$160,820$$
$$ADSP_V = \$243,666.67$$

(v) The allocation of $ADSP_V$ among the Class V assets is in proportion to their fair market values, as follows:

Asset	ADSP	Gain
Land	$34,113.33	$29,113.33 (capital gain)
Building	48,733.34	38,733.34 (capital gain)

Reg. § 1.338-4(g)

Asset	ADSP	Gain
Equipment A	87,720.00	82,720.00 (75,000 ordinary income 7,720 capital gain)
Equipment B	73,100.00	63,100.00 (10,000 ordinary income 53,100 capital gain)
Totals	$243,666.67	$213,666.67

Example 3. More than one class. (i) The facts are the same as in *Example 2*, except that P purchases the T stock for $150,000, rather than $140,000. The amount realized for the stock determined as if the selling shareholder(s) were required to use old target's accounting methods and characteristics is also $150,000.

(ii) As in *Example 2*, ADSP exceeds $20,000. Thus, $10,000 of ADSP is allocated to the cash and $10,000 to the actively traded securities.

(iii) The portion of ADSP allocable to the Class V assets as preliminarily determined under the formula set forth in paragraph (iii) of

$$ADSP = G + L + T_R \times [(II - B_{II}) + (V - B_V) + (ADSP - (I + II + V + B_{VII}))]$$
$$ADSP = \$150,000 + \$50,000 + .34 \times [(\$10,000 - \$4,000) + (\$250,000 - \$30,000) + (ADSP - (\$10,000 + \$10,000 + \$250,000 + \$3,000))]$$
$$ADSP = \$200,000 + .34 ADSP - \$15,980$$
$$.66 ADSP = \$184,020$$
$$ADSP = \$278,818.18$$

(v) Because ADSP as determined exceeds the aggregate fair market value of the Class I, II, III, IV, V, and VI assets, the $250,000 amount preliminarily allocated to the Class V assets is appropriate. Thus, the amount of ADSP allocated to Class V assets equals their aggregate fair market value ($250,000), and the allocated ADSP amount for each Class V asset is its fair market value. Further, because there are no Class VI assets, the allocable ADSP amount for the Class VII asset (goodwill) is $8,818.18 (the excess of ADSP over the aggregate ADSP amounts for the Class I, II, III, IV, V and VI assets).

Example 4. Amount allocated to T1 stock. (i) The facts are the same as in *Example 2*, except that T owns all of the T1 stock (instead of the building), and T1's only asset is the building. The T1 stock and the building each have a fair market value of $50,000, and the building has a basis of $10,000. A section 338 election is made for T1 (as well as T), and T1 has no liabilities other than the tax liability for the deemed sale tax consequences. T is the common parent of a consolidated group filing a final consolidated return described in § 1.338-10(a)(1).

(ii) ADSP exceeds $20,000. Thus, $10,000 of ADSP is allocated to the cash and $10,000 to the actively traded securities.

(iii) Because T does not recognize any gain on the deemed sale of the T1 stock under paragraph (h)(2) of this section, appropriate adjustments must be made to reflect accurately the fair market value of the T and T1 assets in determining the allocation of ADSP among T's Class V assets (including the T1 stock). In preliminarily calculating ADSPv in this case, the T1 stock can be disregarded and, because T owns all of the T1 stock, the T1 asset can be treated as a T asset. Under this assumption, ADSPV is $243,666.67. See paragraph (iv) of *Example 2*.

(iv) Because the portion of the preliminary ADSP allocable to Class V assets ($243,666.67) does not exceed their fair market value ($250,000), no amount is allocated to Class VII assets for T. Further, this amount ($243,666.67) is allocated among T's Class V assets in proportion to their fair market values. See paragraph (v) of *Example 2*. Tentatively, $48,733.34 of this amount is allocated to the T1 stock.

(v) The amount tentatively allocated to the T1 stock, however, reflects the tax incurred on the deemed sale of the T1 asset equal to $13,169.34 (.34 × ($48,733.34 - $10,000)). Thus, the ADSP allocable to the Class V assets of T, and the ADSP allocable to the T1 stock, as preliminarily calculated, each must be reduced by $13,169.34. Consequently, these amounts, respectively, are $230,497.33 and $35,564.00. In determining ADSP for T1, the grossed-up amount realized on the deemed sale to new T of new T1's recently purchased T1 stock is $35,564.00.

(vi) The facts are the same as in paragraph (i) of this *Example 4*, except that the T1 building has a $12,500 basis and a $62,500 value, all of the outstanding T1 stock has a $62,500 value, and T owns 80 percent of the T1 stock. In preliminarily calculating ADSPv, the T1 stock can be disregarded but, because T owns only 80 percent of the T1 stock, only 80 percent of T1 asset basis and value should be taken into account in calculating T's ADSP. By taking into account 80 percent of these amounts, the remaining calculations and results are the same as in paragraphs (ii), (iii), (iv), and (v) of this *Example 4*, except that the grossed-up amount realized on the sale of the recently purchased T1 stock is $44,455.00 ($35,564.00/0.8).

Example 2 is $260,363.64. The amount allocated to the Class V assets cannot exceed their aggregate fair market value ($250,000). Thus, preliminarily, the ADSP amount allocated to Class V assets is $250,000.

(iv) Based on the preliminary allocation, the ADSP is determined as follows (in the formula, the amount allocated to the Class I assets is referred to as I, the amount allocated to the Class II assets as II, and the amount allocated to the Class V assets as V):

(h) *Deemed sale of target affiliate stock.*—(1) *Scope.*—This paragraph (h) prescribes rules relating to the treatment of gain or loss realized on the deemed sale of stock of a target affiliate when a section 338 election (but not a section 338(h)(10) election) is made for the target affiliate. For purposes of this paragraph (h), the definition of domestic corporation in §1.338-2(c)(9) is applied without the exclusion therein for DISCs, corporations described in section 1248(e), and corporations to which an election under section 936 applies.

(2) *In general.*—Except as otherwise provided in this paragraph (h), if a section 338 election is made for target, target recognizes no gain or loss on the deemed sale of stock of a target affiliate having the same acquisition date and for which a section 338 election is made if—

(i) Target directly owns stock in the target affiliate satisfying the requirements of section 1504(a)(2);

(ii) Target and the target affiliate are members of a consolidated group filing a final consolidated return described in § 1.338-10(a)(1); or

(iii) Target and the target affiliate file a combined return under § 1.338-10(a)(4).

(3) *Deemed sale of foreign target affiliate by a domestic target.*—A domestic target recognizes gain or loss on the deemed sale of stock of a foreign target affiliate. For the proper treatment of such gain or loss, see, e.g., sections 1246, 1248, 1291 et seq., and 338(h)(16) and § 1.338-9.

(4) *Deemed sale producing effectively connected income.*—A foreign target recognizes gain or loss on the deemed sale of stock of a foreign target affiliate to the extent that such gain or loss is effectively connected (or treated as effectively connected) with the conduct of a trade or business in the United States.

(5) *Deemed sale of insurance company target affiliate electing under section 953(d).*—A domestic target recognizes gain (but not loss) on the deemed sale of stock of a target affiliate that has in effect an election under section 953(d) in an amount equal to the lesser of the gain realized or the earnings and profits described in section 953(d)(4)(B).

(6) *Deemed sale of DISC target affiliate.*—A foreign or domestic target recognizes gain (but not loss) on the deemed sale of stock of a target affiliate that is a DISC or a former DISC (as defined in section 992(a)) in an amount equal to the lesser of the gain realized or the amount of accumulated DISC income determined with respect to such stock under section 995(c). Such gain is included in gross income as a dividend as provided in sections 995(c)(2) and 996(g).

(7) *Anti-stuffing rule.*—If an asset the adjusted basis of which exceeds its fair market value is contributed or transferred to a target affiliate as transferred basis property (within the meaning of section 7701(a)(43)) and a purpose of such transaction is to reduce the gain (or increase the loss) recognized on the deemed sale of such target affiliate's stock, the gain or loss recognized by target on the deemed sale of stock of the target affiliate is determined as if such asset had not been contributed or transferred.

(8) *Examples.*—The following examples illustrate this paragraph (h):

Example 1. (i) P makes a qualified stock purchase of T and makes a section 338 election for T. T's sole asset, all of the T1 stock, has a basis of $50 and a fair market value of $150. T's deemed purchase of the T1 stock results in a qualified stock purchase of T1 and a section 338 election is made for T1. T1's assets have a basis of $50 and a fair market value of $150.

(ii) T realizes $100 of gain on the deemed sale of the T1 stock, but the gain is not recognized because T directly owns stock in T1 satisfying the requirements of section 1504(a)(2) and a section 338 election is made for T1.

(iii) T1 recognizes gain of $100 on the deemed sale of its assets.

Example 2. The facts are the same as in *Example 1,* except that P does not make a section 338 election for T1. Because a section 338 election is not made for T1, the $100 gain realized by T on the deemed sale of the T1 stock is recognized.

Example 3. (i) P makes a qualified stock purchase of T and makes a section 338 election for T. T owns all of the stock of T1 and T2. T's deemed purchase of the T1 and T2 stock results in a qualified stock purchase of T1 and T2 and section 338 elections are made for T1 and T2. T1 and T2 each own 50 percent of the vote and value of T3 stock. The deemed purchases by T1 and T2 of the T3 stock result in a qualified stock purchase of T3 and a section 338 election is made for T3. T is the common parent of a consolidated group and all of the deemed asset sales are reported on the T group's final consolidated return. See § 1.338-10(a)(1).

(ii) Because T, T1, T2 and T3 are members of a consolidated group filing a final consolidated return, no gain or loss is recognized by T, T1 or T2 on their respective deemed sales of target affiliate stock.

Example 4. (i) T's sole asset, all of the FT1 stock, has a basis of $25 and a fair market value of $150. FT1's sole asset, all of the FT2 stock, has a basis of $75 and a fair market value of $150. FT1 and FT2 each have $50 of accumulated earnings and profits for purposes of section 1248(c) and (d). FT2's assets have a basis of $125 and a fair market value of $150, and their sale would not generate subpart F income under section 951. The sale of the FT2 stock or assets would not generate income effectively connected with the conduct of a trade or business within the United States. FT1 does not have an election in effect under section 953(d) and neither FT1 nor FT2 is a passive foreign investment company.

(ii) P makes a qualified stock purchase of T and makes a section 338 election for T. T's deemed purchase of the FT1 stock results in a qualified stock purchase of FT1 and a section 338 election is made for M. Similarly, FT1's deemed purchase of the FT2 stock results in a qualified stock purchase of FT2 and a section 338 election is made for FT2.

(iii) T recognizes $125 of gain on the deemed sale of the FT1 stock under paragraph (h)(3) of this section. FT1 does not recognize $75 of gain on the deemed sale of the FT2 stock under paragraph (h)(2) of this section. FT2 recognizes $25 of gain on the deemed sale of its assets. The $125 gain T recognizes on the deemed sale of the FT1 stock is included in T's income as a dividend under section 1248, because FT1 and FT2 have sufficient earnings and profits for full recharacterization ($50 of accumulated earnings and profits in FT1, $50 of accumulated earnings and profits in FT2, and $25 of deemed sale earnings and profits in FT2). Section 1.338-9(b). For purposes of sections 901 through 908, the source and foreign tax credit limitation basket of $25 of the recharacterized gain on the deemed sale of the FT1 stock is determined under section 338(h)(16).

[Reg. § 1.338-4.]

☐ [*T.D. 8940, 2-12-2001.*]

[Reg. § 1.338-5]

§ 1.338-5. Adjusted grossed-up basis.—(a) *Scope.*—This section provides rules under section 338(b) to determine the adjusted grossed-up basis (AGUB) for target. AGUB is the amount for which new target is deemed to have purchased all of its assets in the deemed purchase under section 338(a)(2). AGUB is allocated among target's assets in accordance with § 1.338-6 to determine the price at which the assets are deemed to have been purchased. When a subsequent increase or decrease with respect to an element of AGUB is required under general principles of tax law, redetermined AGUB is allocated among target's assets in accordance with § 1.338-7.

(b) *Determination of AGUB.*—(1) *General rule.*—AGUB is the sum of—

(i) The grossed-up basis in the purchasing corporation's recently purchased target stock;

(ii) The purchasing corporation's basis in nonrecently purchased target stock; and

(iii) The liabilities of new target.

(2) *Time and amount of AGUB.*—(i) *Original determination.*—AGUB is initially determined at the beginning of the day after the acquisition date of target. General principles of tax law apply in determining the timing and amount of the elements of AGUB.

(ii) *Redetermination of AGUB.*—AGUB is redetermined at such time and in such amount as an increase or decrease would be required, under general principles of tax law, with respect to an element of AGUB. For example, AGUB is redetermined because of an increase or decrease in the amount paid or incurred for recently purchased stock or nonrecently purchased stock or because liabilities not originally taken into account in determining AGUB are subsequently taken into account. An increase or decrease to one element of AGUB also may cause an increase or decrease to another element of AGUB. For example, if there is an increase in the amount paid or incurred for recently purchased stock after the acquisition date, any increase in the basis of nonrecently purchased stock because a gain recognition election was made is also taken into account when AGUB is redetermined. Increases or decreases with respect to the elements of AGUB result in the reallocation of AGUB among target's assets under § 1.338-7.

(iii) *Examples.*—The following examples illustrate this paragraph (b)(2):

Example 1. In Year 1, T, a manufacturer, purchases a customized delivery truck from X with purchase money indebtedness having a stated principal amount of $100,000. P acquires all of the stock of T in Year 3 for $700,000 and makes a section 338 election for T. Assume T has no liabilities other than its purchase money indebtedness to X. In Year 4, when T is neither insolvent nor in a title 11 case, T and X agree to reduce the amount of the purchase money indebtedness to $80,000. Assume that the reduction would be a purchase price reduction under section 108(e)(5). T and X's agreement to reduce the amount of the purchase money indebtedness would, under general principles of tax law that would apply if the deemed asset sale had actually occurred, change the amount of liabilities of old target taken into account in determining its basis. Accordingly, AGUB is redetermined at the time of the reduction. See paragraph (e)(2) of this section. Thus the purchase price reduction affects the basis of the truck only indirectly, through the mechanism of § § 1.338-6 and 1.338-7. See § 1.338-4(b)(2)(iii) *Example* for the effect on ADSP.

Example 2. T, an accrual basis taxpayer, is a chemical manufacturer. In Year 1, T is obligated to remediate environmental contamination at the site of one of its plants. Assume that all the events have occurred that establish the fact of the liability and the amount of the liability can be determined with reasonable accuracy but economic performance has not occurred with respect to the liability within the meaning of section 461(h). P acquires all of the stock of T in Year 1 and makes a section 338 election for T. Assume that, if a corporation unrelated to T had actually purchased T's assets and assumed T's obligation to remediate the contamination, the corporation would not satisfy the economic performance requirements until Year 5. Under section 461(h), the assumed liability would not be treated as incurred and taken into account in basis until that time. The incurrence of the liability in Year 5 under the economic performance rules is an increase in the amount of liabilities properly taken into account in basis and results in the redetermination of AGUB. (Respecting ADSP, compare § 1.461-4(d)(5), which provides that economic performance occurs for old T as the amount of the liability is properly taken into account in amount realized on the deemed asset sale. Thus ADSP is not redetermined when new T satisfies the economic performance requirements.)

(c) *Grossed-up basis of recently purchased stock.*—The purchasing corporation's grossed-up basis of recently purchased target stock (as defined in section 338(b)(6)(A)) is an amount equal to—

(1) The purchasing corporation's basis in recently purchased target stock at the beginning of the day after the acquisition date determined without regard to the acquisition costs taken into account in paragraph (c)(3) of this section;

(2) Multiplied by a fraction, the numerator of which is 100 minus the number that is the percentage of target stock (by value, determined on the acquisition date) attributable to the purchasing corporation's nonrecently purchased target stock, and the denominator of which is the number equal to the percentage of target stock (by value, determined on the acquisition date) attributable to the purchasing corporation's recently purchased target stock;

(3) Plus the acquisition costs the purchasing corporation incurred in connection with its purchase of the recently purchased stock that are capitalized in the basis of such stock (e.g., brokerage commissions and any similar costs incurred by the purchasing corporation to acquire the stock).

(d) *Basis of nonrecently purchased stock; gain recognition election.*—(1) *No gain recognition election.*—In the absence of a gain recognition election under section 338(b)(3) and this section, the purchasing corporation retains its basis in the nonrecently purchased stock.

(2) *Procedure for making gain recognition election.*—A gain recognition election may be made for nonrecently purchased stock of target (or a target affiliate) only if a section 338 election is made for target (or the target affiliate). The gain recognition election is made by attaching a gain recognition statement to a timely filed Form 8023 for target. The gain recognition statement must contain the information specified in the form and its instructions. The gain recognition election is irrevocable. If a section 338(h)(10) election is made for target, see § 1.338(h)(10)-1(d)(1) (providing that the purchasing corporation is automatically deemed to have made a gain recognition election for its nonrecently purchased T stock).

(3) *Effect of gain recognition election.*—(i) *In general.*—If the purchasing corporation makes a gain recognition election, then for all purposes of the Internal Revenue Code—

(A) The purchasing corporation is treated as if it sold on the acquisition date the nonrecently purchased target stock for the basis amount determined under paragraph (d)(3)(ii) of this section; and

(B) The purchasing corporation's basis on the acquisition date in nonrecently purchased target stock immediately following the deemed sale in paragraph (d)(3)(i)(A) of this section is the basis amount.

(ii) *Basis amount.*—The basis amount is equal to the amount in paragraphs (c)(1) and (2) of this section (the purchasing corporation's grossed-up basis in recently purchased target stock at the beginning of the day after the acquisition date determined without regard to the acquisition costs taken into account in paragraph (c)(3) of this section) multiplied by a fraction the numerator of which is the percentage of target stock (by value, determined on the acquisition date) attributable to the purchasing corporation's nonrecently purchased target stock and the denominator of which is 100 percent minus the numerator amount. Thus, if target has a single class of outstanding stock, the purchasing corporation's basis in each share of nonrecently purchased target stock after the gain recognition election is equal to the average price per share of the purchasing corporation's recently purchased target stock.

(iii) *Losses not recognized.*—Only gains (unreduced by losses) on the nonrecently purchased target stock are recognized.

(iv) *Stock subject to election.*—The gain recognition election applies to—

(A) All nonrecently purchased target stock; and

(B) Any nonrecently purchased stock in a target affiliate having the same acquisition date as target if such target affiliate stock is held by the purchasing corporation on such date.

(e) *Liabilities of new target.*—(1) *In general.*—The liabilities of new target are the liabilities of target as of the beginning of the day after the acquisition date (but see § 1.338-1(d)(regarding certain transactions on the acquisition date)). In order to be taken into account in AGUB, a liability must be a liability of target that is properly taken into account in basis under general principles of tax law that would apply if new target had acquired its assets from an unrelated person for consideration that included discharge of the liabilities of that unrelated person. Such liabilities may include liabilities for the tax consequences resulting from the deemed sale.

(2) *Time and amount of liabilities.*—The time for taking into account liabilities of old target in determining AGUB and the amount of the liabilities taken into account is determined as if new target had acquired its assets from an unrelated person for consideration that included the discharge of its liabilities.

(3) *Interaction with deemed sale tax consequences.*—In general, see § 1.338-4(e). Although ADSP and AGUB are not necessarily linked, if an increase in the amount realized for recently purchased stock of target is taken into account after the acquisition date, and if the tax on the deemed sale tax consequences is a liability of target, any increase in that liability is also taken into account in redetermining AGUB.

(f) *Adjustments by the Internal Revenue Service.*—In connection with the examination of a return, the Commissioner may increase (or decrease) AGUB under the authority of section 338(b)(2) and allocate such amounts to target's assets under the authority of section 338(b)(5) so that AGUB and the basis of target's assets properly reflect the cost to the purchasing corporation of its interest in target's assets. Such items may include distributions from target to the purchasing corporation, capital contributions from the purchasing corporation to target during the 12-month acquisition period, or acquisitions of target stock by the purchasing corporation after the acquisition date from minority shareholders. See also § 1.338-1(d) (regarding certain transactions on the acquisition date).

(g) *Examples.*—The following examples illustrate this section. For purposes of the examples in this paragraph (g), T has no liabilities other than the tax liability for the deemed sale tax consequences, T shareholders incur no costs in selling the T stock, and P incurs no costs in acquiring the T stock. The examples are as follows:

Example 1. (i) Before July 1 of Year 1, P purchases 10 of the 100 shares of T stock for $5,000. On July 1 of Year 2, P purchases 80 shares of T stock for $60,000 and makes a section 338 election for T. As of July 1 of Year 2, T's only asset is raw land with an adjusted basis to T of $50,400 and a fair market value of $100,000. T has no loss or tax credit carryovers to Year 2. T's marginal tax rate for any ordinary income or net capital gain resulting from the deemed asset sale is 34 percent. The 10 shares purchased before July 1 of Year 1 constitute nonrecently purchased T stock with respect to P's qualified stock purchase of T stock on July 1 of Year 2.

(ii) The ADSP formula as applied to these facts is the same as in § 1.338-4(g) *Example 1.* Accordingly, the ADSP for T is $87,672.72. The existence of nonrecently purchased T stock is irrelevant for purposes of the ADSP formula, because that formula treats P's nonrecently purchased T stock in the same manner as T stock not held by P.

(iii) The total tax liability resulting from T's deemed asset sale, as calculated under the ADSP formula, is $12,672.72.

(iv) If P does not make a gain recognition election, the AGUB of new T's assets is $85,172.72, determined as follows (in the following formula below, GRP is the grossed-up basis in P's recently purchased T stock, BNP is P's basis in nonrecently purchased T stock, L is T's liabilities, and X is P's acquisition costs for the recently purchased T stock):

$$AGUB = GRP + BNP + L + X$$
$$AGUB = \$60,000 \times [(1 - .1)/.8] + \$5,000 + \$12,672.72 + 0$$
$$AGUB = \$85,172.72$$

(v) If P makes a gain recognition election, the AGUB of new T's assets is $87,672.72, determined as follows:

$$AGUB = \$60,000 \times [(1 - .1)/.8] + \$60,000 \times [(1 - .1)/.8] \times [.1/(1 - .1)] + \$12,672.72$$
$$AGUB = \$87,672.72$$

(vi) The calculation of AGUB if P makes a gain recognition election may be simplified as follows:

$$AGUB = \$60,000/.8 + \$12,672.72$$
$$AGUB = \$87,672.72$$

(vii) As a result of the gain recognition election, P's basis in its nonrecently purchased T stock is increased from $5,000 to $7,500 (i.e., $60,000 \times [(1 - .1)/.8] \times [.1/(1 - .1)]$). Thus, P recognizes a gain in Year 2 with respect to its nonrecently purchased T stock of $2,500 (i.e., $7,500 - $5,000).

Example 2. On January 1 of Year 1, P purchases one-third of the T stock. On March 1 of Year 1, T distributes a dividend to all of its shareholders. On April 15 of Year 1, P purchases the remaining T stock and makes a section 338 election for T. In appropriate circumstances, the Commissioner may decrease the AGUB of T to take into account the payment of the dividend and properly reflect the fair market value of T's assets deemed purchased.

Example 3. (i) T's sole asset is a building worth $100,000. At this time, T has 100 shares of stock outstanding. On August 1 of Year 1, P purchases 10 of the 100 shares of T stock for $8,000. On June 1 of Year 2, P purchases 50 shares of T stock for $50,000. On June 15 of Year 2, P contributes a tract of land to the capital of T and receives 10 additional shares of T stock as a result of the contribution. Both the basis and fair market value of the land at that time are $10,800. On June 30 of Year 2, P purchases the remaining 40 shares of T stock for $40,000 and makes a section 338 election for T. The AGUB of T is $108,800.

(ii) To prevent the shifting of basis from the contributed property to other assets of T, the Commissioner may allocate $10,800 of the AGUB to the land, leaving $98,000 to be allocated to the building. See paragraph (f) of this section. Otherwise, applying the allocation rules of § 1.338-6 would, on these facts, result in an allocation to the recently contributed land of an amount less than its value of $10,800, with the difference being allocated to the building already held by T.

(h) *Effective/applicability date.*—Paragraph (d)(3)(ii) of this section is applicable to any qualified stock purchase or qualified stock disposition (as defined in § 1.336-1(b)(6)) for which the acquisition date or disposition date (as defined in § 1.336-1(b)(8)), respectively, is on or after May 15, 2013. [Reg. § 1.338-5.]

☐ [*T.D.* 8940, 2-12-2001. *Amended by T.D.* 9619, 5-10-2013.]

[Reg. § 1.338-6]

§ 1.338-6. Allocation of ADSP and AGUB among target assets.—(a) *Scope.*—(1) *In general.*—This section prescribes rules for allocating ADSP and AGUB among the acquisition date assets of a target for which a section 338 election is made.

(2) *Fair market value.*—(i) *In general.*—Generally, the fair market value of an asset is its gross fair market value (i.e., fair market value determined without regard to mortgages, liens, pledges, or other

liabilities). However, for purposes of determining the amount of old target's deemed sale tax consequences, the fair market value of any property subject to a nonrecourse indebtedness will be treated as being not less than the amount of such indebtedness. (For purposes of the preceding sentence, a liability that was incurred because of the acquisition of the property is disregarded to the extent that such liability was not taken into account in determining old target's basis in such property.)

(ii) *Transaction costs.*—Transaction costs are not taken into account in allocating ADSP or AGUB to assets in the deemed sale (except indirectly through their effect on the total ADSP or AGUB to be allocated).

(iii) *Internal Revenue Service authority.*—In connection with the examination of a return, the Internal Revenue Service may challenge the taxpayers determination of the fair market value of any asset by any appropriate method and take into account all factors, including any lack of adverse tax interests between the parties.

(b) *General rule for allocating ADSP and AGUB.*—(1) *Reduction in the amount of consideration for Class I assets.*—Both ADSP and AGUB, in the respective allocation of each, are first reduced by the amount of Class I assets. Class I assets are cash and general deposit accounts (including savings and checking accounts) other than certificates of deposit held in banks, savings and loan associations, and other depository institutions. If the amount of Class I assets exceeds AGUB, new target will immediately realize ordinary income in an amount equal to such excess. The amount of ADSP or AGUB remaining after the reduction is to be allocated to the remaining acquisition date assets.

(2) *Other assets.*—(i) *In general.*—Subject to the limitations and other rules of paragraph (c) of this section, ADSP and AGUB (as reduced by the amount of Class I assets) are allocated among Class II acquisition date assets of target in proportion to the fair market values of such Class II assets at such time, then among Class III assets so held in such proportion, then among Class IV assets so held in such proportion, then among Class V assets so held in such proportion, then among Class VI assets so held in such proportion, and finally to Class VII assets. If an asset is described below as includible in more than one class, then it is included in such class with the lower or lowest class number (for instance, Class III has a lower class number than Class IV).

(ii) *Class II assets.*—Class II assets are actively traded personal property within the meaning of section 1092(d)(1) and §1.1092(d)-1 (determined without regard to section 1092(d)(3)). In addition, Class II assets include certificates of deposit and foreign currency even if they are not actively traded personal property. Class II assets do not include stock of target affiliates, whether or not of a class that is actively traded, other than actively traded stock described in section 1504(a)(4). Examples of Class II assets include U.S. government securities and publicly traded stock.

(iii) *Class III assets.*—Class III assets are assets that the taxpayer marks to market at least annually for Federal income tax purposes and debt instruments (including accounts receivable). However, Class III assets do not include—

(A) Debt instruments issued by persons related at the beginning of the day following the acquisition date to the target under section 267(b) or 707;

(B) Contingent debt instruments subject to §1.1275-4, §1.483-4, or section 988, unless the instrument is subject to the noncontingent bond method of §1.1275-4(b) or is described in §1.988-2(b)(2)(i)(B) (2); and

(C) Debt instruments convertible into the stock of the issuer or other property.

(iv) *Class IV assets.*—Class IV assets are stock in trade of the taxpayer or other property of a kind that would properly be included in the inventory of taxpayer if on hand at the close of the taxable year, or property held by the taxpayer primarily for sale to customers in the ordinary course of its trade or business.

(v) *Class V assets.*—Class V assets are all assets other than Class I, II, III, IV, VI, and VII assets.

(vi) *Class VI assets.*—Class VI assets are all section 197 intangibles, as defined in section 197, except goodwill and going concern value.

(vii) *Class VII assets.*—Class VII assets are goodwill and going concern value (whether or not the goodwill or going concern value qualifies as a section 197 intangible).

(3) *Other items designated by the Internal Revenue Service.*—Similar items may be added to any class described in this paragraph (b) by designation in the Internal Revenue Bulletin by the Internal Revenue Service (see §601.601(d)(2) of this chapter).

(c) *Certain limitations and other rules for allocation to an asset.*—(1) *Allocation not to exceed fair market value.*—The amount of ADSP or AGUB allocated to an asset (other than Class VII assets) cannot exceed the fair market value of that asset at the beginning of the day after the acquisition date.

(2) *Allocation subject to other rules.*—The amount of ADSP or AGUB allocated to an asset is subject to other provisions of the Internal Revenue Code or general principles of tax law in the same manner as if such asset were transferred to or acquired from an unrelated person in a sale or exchange. For example, if the deemed asset sale is a transaction described in section 1056(a) (relating to basis limitation for player contracts transferred in connection with the sale of a franchise), the amount of AGUB allocated to a contract for the services of an athlete cannot exceed the limitation imposed by that section. As another example, section 197(f)(5) applies in determining the amount of AGUB allocated to an amortizable section 197 intangible resulting from an assumption-reinsurance transaction.

(3) *Special rule for allocating AGUB when purchasing corporation has nonrecently purchased stock.*—(i) *Scope.*—This paragraph (c)(3) applies if at the beginning of the day after the acquisition date—

(A) The purchasing corporation holds nonrecently purchased stock for which a gain recognition election under section 338(b)(3) and §1.338-5(d) is not made; and

(B) The hypothetical purchase price determined under paragraph (c)(3)(ii) of this section exceeds the AGUB determined under §1.338-5(b).

(ii) *Determination of hypothetical purchase price.*—Hypothetical purchase price is the AGUB that would result if a gain recognition election were made.

(iii) *Allocation of AGUB.*—Subject to the limitations in paragraphs (c)(1) and (2) of this section, the portion of AGUB (after reduction by the amount of Class I assets) to be allocated to each Class II, III, IV, V, VI, and VII asset of target held at the beginning of the day after the acquisition date is determined by multiplying—

(A) The amount that would be allocated to such asset under the general rules of this section were AGUB equal to the hypothetical purchase price; by

(B) A fraction, the numerator of which is actual AGUB (after reduction by the amount of Class I assets) and the denominator of which is the hypothetical purchase price (after reduction by the amount of Class I assets).

(4) *Liabilities taken into account in determining amount realized on subsequent disposition.*—In determining the amount realized on a subsequent sale or other disposition of property deemed purchased by new target, §1.1001-2(a)(3) shall not apply to any liability that was taken into account in AGUB.

(5) *Allocation to certain nuclear decommissioning funds.*—(i) *General rule.*—For purposes of allocating ADSP or AGUB among the acquisition date assets of a target (and for no other purpose), a taxpayer may elect to treat a nonqualified nuclear decommissioning fund (as defined in paragraph (c)(5)(ii) of this section) of the target as if—

(A) Such fund were an entity classified as a corporation;

(B) The stock of the corporation were among the acquisition date assets of the target and a Class V asset;

(C) The corporation owned the assets of the fund;

(D) The corporation bore the responsibility for decommissioning one or more nuclear power plants to the extent assets of the fund are expected to be used for that purpose; and

(E) A section 338(h)(10) election were made for the corporation (regardless of whether the requirements for a section 338(h)(10) election are otherwise satisfied).

(ii) *Definition of nonqualified nuclear decommissioning fund.*—A nonqualified nuclear decommissioning fund means a trust, escrow account, Government fund or other type of agreement—

(A) That is established in writing by the owner or licensee of a nuclear generating unit for the exclusive purpose of funding the decommissioning of one or more nuclear power plants;

(B) That is described to the Nuclear Regulatory Commission in a report described in 10 CFR 50.75(b) as providing assurance that funds will be available for decommissioning;

(C) That is not a Nuclear Decommissioning Reserve Fund, as described in section 468A;

(D) That is maintained at all times in the United States; and

(E) The assets of which are to be used only as permitted by 10 CFR 50.82(a)(8).

(iii) *Availability of election.*—P may make the election described in this paragraph (c)(5) regardless of whether the selling consolidated group (or the selling affiliate or the S corporation shareholders) also makes the election. In addition, the selling consolidated group (or the selling affiliate or the S corporation shareholders) may make the election regardless of whether P also makes the election. If T is an S corporation, all of the S corporation shareholders, including those that do not sell their stock, must consent to the election for the election to be effective as to any S corporation shareholder.

(iv) *Time and manner of making election.*—The election described in this paragraph (c)(5) is made by taking a position on an original or amended tax return for the taxable year of the qualified stock purchase that is consistent with having made the election. Such tax return must be filed no later than the later of 30 days after the date on which the section 338 election is due or the day the original tax return for the taxable year of the qualified stock purchase is due (with extensions).

(v) *Irrevocability of election.*—An election made pursuant to this paragraph (c)(5) is irrevocable.

(vi) *Effective/applicability date.*—This paragraph (c)(5) applies to qualified stock purchases occurring on or after September 11, 2007. For qualified stock purchases occurring before September 11, 2007 and on or after September 15, 2004, see § 1.338-6T as contained in 26 CFR Part 1 in effect on April 1, 2007. For qualified stock purchases occurring before September 15, 2004, see § 1.338-6 as contained in 26 CFR Part 1 in effect on April 1, 2004.

(d) *Examples.*—The following examples illustrate §§ 1.338-4, 1.338-5, and this section:

Asset Class	Asset	Fair market value
I	Cash	$200 *
II	Portfolio of actively traded securities	300
III	Accounts receivable	600
IV	Inventory	300
V	Building	800
V	Land	200
V	Investment in T1	450
	Total	$2,850

_____

* Amount

(vi) Under paragraph (b)(1) of this section, the amount of ADSP and AGUB allocable to T's Class II, III, IV, and V assets is reduced by the amount of cash to $2,800, i.e., $3,000 – $200. $300 of ADSP and of AGUB is then allocated to actively traded securities. $600 of ADSP and of AGUB is then allocated to accounts receivable. $300 of ADSP and of AGUB is then allocated to the inventory. Since the remaining amount of ADSP and of AGUB is $1,600 (i.e., $3,000 – ($200 + $300 + $600 + $300)), an amount which exceeds the sum of the fair market values of T's Class V assets, the amount of ADSP and of AGUB allocated to each Class V asset is its fair market value:

Building	800
Land	200
Investment in T1	450
Total	$1,450

(vii) T has no Class VI assets. The amount of ADSP and of AGUB allocated to T's Class VII assets (goodwill and going concern value) is $150, i.e., $1,600 – $1,450.

Asset Class	Asset	Fair Market Value
I	Cash	$ 50 *
IV	Inventory	200
VI	Patent	350
	Total	$600

_____

* Amount.

(xiii) The amount of ADSP and of AGUB allocable to T1's Class IV and VI assets is first reduced by the $50 of cash.

(xiv) Because the remaining amount of ADSP and of AGUB ($570) is an amount which exceeds the fair market value of T1's only Class IV asset, the inventory, the amount allocated to the inventory is its fair market value ($200). After that, the remaining amount of ADSP and of AGUB ($370) exceeds the fair market value of T1's only Class VI asset, the patent. Thus, the amount of ADSP and of AGUB allocated to the patent is its fair market value ($350).

(xv) The amount of ADSP and of AGUB allocated to T1's Class VII assets (goodwill and going concern value) is $20, i.e., $570 – $550.

Grossed-up basis of recently purchased stock as determined under § 1.338-5(c) ($1,600 × (1 – .2)/.8)	$1,600
Basis of nonrecently purchased stock	100
Liabilities	1,000
AGUB	$2,700

(iv) Since P holds nonrecently purchased stock, the hypothetical purchase price of the T stock must be computed and is determined as follows:

Example 1. (i) T owns 90 percent of the outstanding T1 stock. P purchases 100 percent of the outstanding T stock for $2,000. There are no acquisition costs. P makes a section 338 election for T and, as a result, T1 is considered acquired in a qualified stock purchase. A section 338 election is made for T1. The grossed-up basis of the T stock is $2,000 (i.e., $2,000 × 1/1).

(ii) The liabilities of T as of the beginning of the day after the acquisition date (including the tax liability for the deemed sale tax consequences) that would, under general principles of tax law, properly be taken into account at that time, are as follows:

Liabilities (nonrecourse mortgage plus unsecured liabilities)	$700
Taxes Payable	300
Total	$1,000

(iii) The AGUB of T is determined as follows:

Grossed-up basis	$2,000
Total liabilities.................................	1,000
AGUB	$3,000

(iv) Assume that ADSP is also $3,000.

(v) Assume that, at the beginning of the day after the acquisition date, T's cash and the fair market values of T's Class II, III, IV, and V assets are as follows:

(viii) The grossed-up basis of the T1 stock is $500, i.e., $450 × 1/.9.

(ix) The liabilities of T1 as of the beginning of the day after the acquisition date (including the tax liability for the deemed sale tax consequences) that would, under general principles of tax law, properly be taken into account at that time, are as follows:

General Liabilities	$100
Taxes Payable	20
Total	$120

(x) The AGUB of T1 is determined as follows:

Grossed-up basis of T1 Stock	$500
Liabilities	120
AGUB	$620

(xi) Assume that ADSP is also $620.

(xii) Assume that at the beginning of the day after the acquisition date, T1's cash and the fair market values of its Class IV and VI assets are as follows:

Example 2. (i) Assume that the facts are the same as in *Example 1* except that P has, for five years, owned 20 percent of T's stock, which has a basis in P's hands at the beginning of the day after the acquisition date of $100, and P purchases the remaining 80 percent of T's stock for $1,600. P does not make a gain recognition election under section 338(b)(3).

(ii) Under § 1.338-5(c), the grossed-up basis of recently purchased T stock is $1,600, i.e., $1,600 × (1 – .2)/.8.

(iii) The AGUB of T is determined as follows:

Grossed-up basis of recently purchased stock as determined under §1.338-5(c) ($1,600 × (1 − .2)/.8) $1,600
Basis of nonrecently purchased stock as if the gain recognition election under §1.338-5(d)(2) had been made ($1,600 × .2/(1 − .2)) 400
Liabilities 1,000

Total $3,000

(v) Since the hypothetical purchase price ($3,000) exceeds the AGUB ($2,700) and no gain recognition election is made under section 338(b)(3), AGUB is allocated under paragraph (c)(3) of this section.

(vi) First, an AGUB amount equal to the hypothetical purchase price ($3,000) is allocated among the assets under the general rules of this section. The allocation is set forth in the column below entitled *Original Allocation*. Next, the allocation to each asset in Class II through Class VII is multiplied by a fraction having a numerator equal to the actual AGUB reduced by the amount of Class I assets ($2,700 − $200 = $2,500) and a denominator equal to the hypothetical purchase price reduced by the amount of Class I assets ($3,000 − $200 = $2,800), or 2,500/2,800. This produces the *Final Allocation*:

Class	Asset	Original Allocation	Final Allocation
I	Cash	$200	$200
II	Portfolio of actively traded securities	300	268 *
III	Accounts receivable	600	536
IV	Inventory	300	268
V	Building	800	714
V	Land	200	178
V	Investment in T1	450	402
VII	Goodwill and going concern value	150	134
	Total	$3,000	$2,700

* All numbers rounded for convenience.

[Reg. §1.338-6.]

☐ [T.D. 8940, 2-12-2001 (*corrected* 3-29-2001). *Amended by* T.D. 9158, 9-15-2004 *and* T.D. 9358, 9-10-2007.]

[Reg. §1.338-7]

§1.338-7. Allocation of redetermined ADSP and AGUB among target assets.—(a) *Scope.*—ADSP and AGUB are redetermined at such time and in such amount as an increase or decrease would be required under general principles of tax law for the elements of ADSP or AGUB. This section provides rules for allocating redetermined ADSP or AGUB.

(b) *Allocation of redetermined ADSP and AGUB.*—When ADSP or AGUB is redetermined, a new allocation of ADSP or AGUB is made by allocating the redetermined ADSP or AGUB amount under the rules of §1.338-6. If the allocation of the redetermined ADSP or AGUB amount under §1.338-6 to a given asset is different from the original allocation to it, the difference is added to or subtracted from the original allocation to the asset, as appropriate. (See paragraph (d) of this section for new target's treatment of the amount so allocated.) Amounts allocable to an acquisition date asset (or with respect to a disposed-of acquisition date asset) are subject to all the asset allocation rules (for example, the fair market value limitation in §1.338-6(c)(1)) as if the redetermined ADSP or AGUB were the ADSP or AGUB on the acquisition date.

(c) *Special rules for ADSP.*—(1) *Increases or decreases in deemed sale tax consequences taxable notwithstanding old target ceases to exist.*—To the extent general principles of tax law would require a seller in an actual asset sale to account for events relating to the sale that occur after the sale date, target must make such an accounting. Target is not precluded from realizing additional deemed sale tax consequences because the target is treated as a new corporation after the acquisition date.

(2) *Procedure for transactions in which section 338(h)(10) is not elected.*—(i) *Deemed sale tax consequences included in new target's return.*—If an election under section 338(h)(10) is not made, any additional deemed sale tax consequences of old target resulting from an increase or decrease in the ADSP are included in new target's income tax return for new target's taxable year in which the increase or decrease is taken into account. For example, if after the acquisition date there is an increase in the allocable ADSP of section 1245 property for which the recomputed basis (but not the adjusted basis) exceeds the portion of the ADSP allocable to that particular asset on the acquisition date, the additional gain is treated as ordinary income to the extent it does not exceed such excess amount. See paragraph (c)(2)(ii) of this section for the special treatment of old target's carryovers and carrybacks. Although included in new target's income tax return, the deemed sale tax consequences are separately accounted for as an item of old target and may not be offset by income, gain, deduction, loss, credit, or other amount of new target. The amount of tax on income of old target resulting from an increase or decrease in the ADSP is determined as if such deemed sale tax consequences had been recognized in old target's taxable year ending at the close of the acquisition date. However, because the income resulting from the increase or decrease in ADSP is reportable in new target's taxable year of the increase or decrease, not in old target's taxable year ending at the close of the acquisition date, there is not a resulting underpayment of tax in that past taxable year of old target for purposes of calculation of interest due.

(ii) *Carryovers and carrybacks.*—(A) *Loss carryovers to new target taxable years.*—A net operating loss or net capital loss of old target may be carried forward to a taxable year of new target, under the principles of section 172 or 1212, as applicable, but is allowed as a deduction only to the extent of any recognized income of old target for such taxable year, as described in paragraph (c)(2)(i) of this section. For this purpose, however, taxable years of new target are not taken into account in applying the limitations in section 172(b)(1) or 1212(a)(1)(B) (or other similar limitations). In applying sections 172(b) and 1212(a)(1), only income, gain, loss, deduction, credit, and other amounts of old target are taken into account. Thus, if old target has an unexpired net operating loss at the close of its taxable year in which the deemed asset sale occurred that could be carried forward to a subsequent taxable year, such loss may be carried forward until it is absorbed by old target's income.

(B) *Loss carrybacks to taxable years of old target.*—An ordinary loss or capital loss accounted for as a separate item of old target under paragraph (c)(2)(i) of this section may be carried back to a taxable year of old target under the principles of section 172 or 1212, as applicable. For this purpose, taxable years of new target are not taken into account in applying the limitations in section 172(b) or 1212(a) (or other similar limitations).

(C) *Credit carryovers and carrybacks.*—The principles described in paragraphs (c)(2)(ii)(A) and (B) of this section apply to carryovers and carrybacks of amounts for purposes of determining the amount of a credit allowable under part IV, subchapter A, chapter 1 of the Internal Revenue Code. Thus, for example, credit carryovers of old target may offset only income tax attributable to items described in paragraph (c)(2)(i) of this section.

(3) *Procedure for transactions in which section 338(h)(10) is elected.*—If an election under section 338(h)(10) is made, any changes in the deemed sale tax consequences caused by an increase or decrease in the ADSP are accounted for in determining the taxable income (or other amount) of the member of the selling consolidated group, the selling affiliate, or the S corporation shareholders to which such income, loss, or other amount is attributable for the taxable year in which such increase or decrease is taken into account.

(d) *Special rules for AGUB.*—(1) *Effect of disposition or depreciation of acquisition date assets.*—If an acquisition date asset has been disposed of, depreciated, amortized, or depleted by new target before an amount is added to the original allocation to the asset, the increased amount otherwise allocable to such asset is taken into account under general principles of tax law that apply when part of the cost of an asset not previously taken into account in basis is paid or incurred after the asset has been disposed of, depreciated, amortized, or depleted. A similar rule applies when an amount is subtracted from the original allocation to the asset. For purposes of the preceding sentence, an asset is considered to have been disposed of to the extent that its allocable portion of the decrease in AGUB would reduce its basis below zero.

(2) *Section 38 property.*—Section 1.47-2(c) applies to a reduction in basis of section 38 property under this section.

(e) *Examples.*—The following examples illustrate this section. Any amount described in the following examples is exclusive of interest. For rules characterizing deferred contingent payments as principal or interest, see §§ 1.483-4, 1.1274-2(g), and 1.1275-4(c). The examples are as follows:

Asset Class	Asset	
V	Building	$100
V	Stock of X (not a target)	200
	Total	$300

(B) T has no liabilities other than a contingent liability that would not be taken into account under general principles of tax law in an asset sale between unrelated parties when the buyer assumed the liability or took property subject to it.

(ii)(A) On September 1, 2000, P purchases all of the outstanding stock of T for $270 and makes a section 338 election for T. The grossed-up basis of the T stock and T's AGUB are both $270. The AGUB is ratably allocated among T's Class V assets in proportion to their fair market values as follows:

Asset	Basis
Building ($270 × 100/300)	$90
Stock ($270 × 200/300)	180
Total	$270

(B) No amount is allocated to the Class VII assets. New T is a calendar year taxpayer. Assume that the X stock is a capital asset in the hands of new T.

Asset	
Building	
X Stock	
Goodwill and going concern value	
Total	

(vi) Since the X stock was disposed of before the contingent liability was properly taken into account for tax purposes, no amount of the increase in AGUB attributable to such stock may be allocated to any T asset. Rather, such amount ($20) is allowed as a capital loss to T for the taxable year 2002 under the principles of *Arrowsmith v. Commissioner*, 344 U.S. 6 (1952). In addition, the $10 increase in AGUB allocated to the building and the $30 increase in AGUB allocated to

Asset Class	Asset		Basis
V	Machinery		$150
V	Land		250
VII	Goodwill and going concern value		100
	Total		$500

(ii) On September 30, 2004, P filed a claim against the selling shareholders of T in a court of appropriate jurisdiction alleging fraud in the sale of the T stock.

(iii) On January 1, 2007, the former shareholders refund $140 of the purchase price to P in a settlement of the lawsuit. Assume that, under general principles of tax law, both the seller and the buyer properly take into account such refund when paid. Assume also that the refund has no effect on the tax liability for the deemed sale tax consequences. This refund results in a decrease of T's ADSP and AGUB of $140, from $500 to $360.

(iv) The redetermined ADSP and AGUB of $360 is allocated among T's acquisition date assets. Because ADSP and AGUB do not exceed the fair market value of the Class V assets, the ADSP and AGUB amounts are allocated to the Class V assets in proportion to their fair market values at the beginning of the day after the acquisition date. Thus, $135 ($150 × ($360/($150 + $250))) is allocated to the machinery and $225 ($250 × ($360/($150 + $250))) is allocated to the land. Accordingly, the basis of the machinery is reduced by $15 ($150 original allocation – $135 redetermined allocation) and the basis of the land is reduced by $25 ($250 original allocation – $225 redetermined allocation). No amount is allocated to the Class VII assets. Accordingly, the basis of the goodwill and going concern value is reduced by $100 ($100 original allocation – $0 redetermined allocation).

(v) Assume that, as a result of deductions under section 168, the adjusted basis of the machinery immediately before the decrease in

Example 1. (i)(A) T's assets other than goodwill and going concern value, and their fair market values at the beginning of the day after the acquisition date, are as follows:

	Fair Market Value

(iii) On January 1, 2001, new T sells the X stock and uses the proceeds to purchase inventory.

(iv) Pursuant to events on June 30, 2002, the contingent liability of old T is at that time properly taken into account under general principles of tax law. The amount of the liability is $60.

(v) T's AGUB increases by $60 from $270 to $330. This $60 increase in AGUB is first allocated among T's acquisition date assets in accordance with the provisions of §1.338-6. Because the redetermined AGUB for T ($330) exceeds the sum of the fair market values at the beginning of the day after the acquisition date of the Class V acquisition date assets ($300), AGUB allocated to those assets is limited to those fair market values under §1.338-6(c)(1). As there are no Class VI assets, the remaining AGUB of $30 is allocated to goodwill and going concern value (Class VII assets). The amount of increase in AGUB allocated to each acquisition date asset is determined as follows:

Original AGUB	Redetermined AGUB	Increase
$90	$100	$10
180	200	20
0	30	30
$270	$330	$60

the goodwill and going concern value are treated as basis redeterminations in 2002. See paragraph (d)(1) of this section.

Example 2. (i) On January 1, 2002, P purchases all of the outstanding stock of T and makes a section 338 election for T. Assume that ADSP and AGUB of T are both $500 and are allocated among T's acquisition date assets as follows:

AGUB is zero. The machinery is treated as if it were disposed of before the decrease is taken into account. In 2007, T recognizes income of $15, the character of which is determined under the principles of *Arrowsmith v. Commissioner* and the tax benefit rule. No adjustment to the basis of T's assets is made for any tax paid on this amount. Assume also that, as a result of amortization deductions, the adjusted basis of the goodwill and going concern value immediately before the decrease in AGUB is $40. A similar adjustment to income is made in 2007 with respect to the $60 of previously amortized goodwill and going concern value.

(vi) In summary, the basis of T's acquisition date assets, as of January 1, 2007, is as follows:

Asset	Basis
Machinery	$0
Land	225
Goodwill and going concern value	0

Example 3. (i) Assume that the facts are the same as §1.338-6(d) *Example 2* except that the recently purchased stock is acquired for $1,600 plus additional payments that are contingent upon T's future earnings. Assume that, under general principles of tax law, such later payments are properly taken into account when paid. Thus, T's AGUB, determined as of the beginning of the day after the acquisition date (after reduction by T's cash of $200), is $2,500 and is allocated among T's acquisition date assets under §1.338-6(c)(3)(iii) as follows:

Class	Asset	Final Allocation
I	Cash	$200
II	Portfolio of actively traded securities	268 *
III	Accounts receivable	536
IV	Inventory	268
V	Building	714
V	Land	178
V	Investment in T1	402
VII	Goodwill and going concern value	134
	Total	$2,700

_____

* All numbers rounded for convenience.

(ii) At a later point in time, P pays an additional $200 for its recently purchased T stock. Assume that the additional consideration paid would not increase T's tax liability for the deemed sale tax consequences.

Grossed-up basis of recently purchased stock as determined under § 1.338-5(c) ($1,800 × (1 − .2)/.8) $1,800
Basis of nonrecently purchased stock as if the gain recognition election under § 1.338-5(d)(2) had been made ($1,800 × .2/(1 − .2)) 450
Liabilities 1,000

Total $3,250

(v) Since the redetermined hypothetical purchase price ($3,250) exceeds the redetermined AGUB ($2,900) and no gain recognition election was made under section 338(b)(3), the rules of § 1.338-6(c)(3)(iii) are reapplied using the redetermined hypothetical purchase price and the redetermined AGUB.

(vi) First, an AGUB amount equal to the redetermined hypothetical purchase price ($3,250) is allocated among the assets under the

Class	Asset	Hypothetical Allocation	Final Allocation
I	Cash	$200	$200
II	Portfolio of actively traded securities	300	266 *
III	Accounts receivable	600	531
IV	Inventory	300	266
V	Building	800	708
V	Land	200	177
V	Investment in T1	450	398
VII	Goodwill and going concern value	400	354
	Total	$3,250	$2,900

_____

* All numbers rounded for convenience.

(vii) As illustrated by this example, reapplying § 1.338-6(c)(3) results in a basis increase for some assets and a basis decrease for other

Asset	Original (c)(3) allocation	Redetermined (c)(3) allocation	Increase (decrease)
Portfolio of actively traded securities	$268	$266	$(2)
Accounts receivable	536	531	(5)
Inventory	268	266	(2)
Building	714	708	(6)
Land	178	177	(1)
Investment in T1	402	398	(4)
Goodwill and going concern value	134	354	220
Total	$2,500	$2,700	$200

Example 4. (i) On January 1, 2001, P purchases all of the outstanding T stock and makes a section 338 election for T. P pays $700 of cash and promises also to pay a maximum $300 of contingent consideration at various times in the future. Assume that, under general principles of tax law, such later payments are properly taken into

(iii) T's AGUB increases by $200, from $2,700 to $2,900. This $200 increase in AGUB is accounted for in accordance with the provisions of § 1.338-6(c)(3)(iii).

(iv) The hypothetical purchase price of the T stock is redetermined as follows:

(see table above right)

general rules of § 1.338-6. The allocation is set forth in the column below entitled _Hypothetical Allocation_. Next, the allocation to each asset in Class II through Class VII is multiplied by a fraction with a numerator equal to the actual redetermined AGUB reduced by the amount of Class I assets ($2,900 − $200 = $2,700) and a denominator equal to the redetermined hypothetical purchase price reduced by the amount of Class I assets ($3,250 − $200 = $3,050), or 2,700/3,050. This produces the _Final Allocation_:

(see table above right)

assets. The amount of redetermined AGUB allocated to each acquisition date asset is determined as follows:

(see table above right)

account by P when paid. Assume also, however, that the current fair market value of the contingent payments is reasonably ascertainable. The fair market value of T's assets (other than goodwill and going concern value) as of the beginning of the following day is as follows:

Asset Class	Assets	Fair market value
V	Equipment	$200
V	Non-actively traded securities	100
V	Building	500
	Total	$800

(ii) T has no liabilities. The AGUB is $700. In calculating ADSP, assume that, under § 1.1001-1, the current amount realized attributable to the contingent consideration is $200. ADSP is therefore $900 ($700 cash plus $200).

(iii) (A) The AGUB of $700 is ratably allocated among T's Class V acquisition date assets in proportion to their fair market values as follows:

Asset	Basis
Equipment ($700 × 200/800)	$175.00
Non-actively traded securities ($700 × 100/800)	87.50
Building ($700 × 500/800)	437.50
Total	$700.00

(B) No amount is allocated to goodwill or going concern value.

Asset	Basis
Equipment	$200
Non-actively traded securities	100
Building	500
Total	$800

(B) The remaining ADSP, $100, is allocated to goodwill and going concern value (Class VII).

(v) P and T file a consolidated return for 2001 and each following year with P as the common parent of the affiliated group.

(vi) In 2004, a contingent amount of $120 is paid by P. For old T, this payment has no effect on ADSP, because the payment is ac-

Asset	Original AGUB	Redetermined AGUB	Increase
Equipment	$175.00	$200.00	$25.00
Land	87.50	100.00	12.50
Building	437.50	500.00	62.50
Goodwill and going concern value	0.00	20.00	20.00
Total	$700.00	$820.00	$120.00

[Reg. §1.338-7.]

☐ [T.D. 8940, 2-12-2001.]

[Reg. §1.338-8]

§1.338-8. Asset and stock consistency.—(a) *Introduction.*—(1) *Overview.*—This section implements the consistency rules of sections 338(e) and (f). Under this section, no election under section 338 is deemed made or required with respect to target or any target affiliate. Instead, the person acquiring an asset may have a carryover basis in the asset.

(2) *General application.*—The consistency rules generally apply if the purchasing corporation acquires an asset directly from target during the target consistency period and target is a subsidiary in a consolidated group. In such a case, gain from the sale of the asset is reflected under the investment adjustment provisions of the consolidated return regulations in the basis of target stock and may reduce gain from the sale of the stock. See §1.1502-32 (investment adjustment provisions). Under the consistency rules, the purchasing corporation generally takes a carryover basis in the asset, unless a section 338 election is made for target. Similar rules apply if the purchasing corporation acquires an asset directly from a lower-tier target affiliate if gain from the sale is reflected under the investment adjustment provisions in the basis of target stock.

(3) *Extensions of the general rules.*—If an arrangement exists, paragraph (f) of this section generally extends the carryover basis rule to certain cases in which the purchasing corporation acquires assets indirectly from target (or a lower-tier target affiliate). To prevent avoidance of the consistency rules, paragraph (j) of this section also may extend the consistency period or the 12-month acquisition period and may disregard the presence of conduits.

(4) *Application where certain dividends are paid.*—Paragraph (g) of this section extends the carryover basis rule to certain cases in which dividends are paid to a corporation that is not a member of the same consolidated group as the distributing corporation. Generally, this rule applies where a 100 percent dividends received deduction is used in conjunction with asset dispositions to achieve an effect similar to that available under the investment adjustment provisions of the consolidated return regulations.

(5) *Application to foreign target affiliates.*—Paragraph (h) of this section extends the carryover basis rule to certain cases involving target affiliates that are controlled foreign corporations.

(6) *Stock consistency.*—This section limits the application of the stock consistency rules to cases in which the rules are necessary to prevent avoidance of the asset consistency rules. Following the general treatment of a section 338(h)(10) election, a sale of a corporation's stock is treated as a sale of the corporation's assets if a section 338(h)(10) election is made. Because gain from this asset sale may be reflected in the basis of the stock of a higher-tier target, the carryover basis rule may apply to the assets.

(iv)(A) The ADSP of $900 is ratably allocated among T's Class V acquisition date assets in proportion to their fair market values as follows:

counted for as a separate transaction. We have assumed that, under general principles of tax law, the payment is properly taken into account by P at the time made. Therefore, in 2004, there is an increase in new T's AGUB of $120. The amount of the increase allocated to each acquisition date asset is determined as follows:

(b) *Consistency for direct acquisitions.*—(1) *General rule.*—The basis rules of paragraph (d) of this section apply to an asset if—

(i) The asset is disposed of during the target consistency period;

(ii) The basis of target stock, as of the target acquisition date, reflects gain from the disposition of the asset (see paragraph (c) of this section); and

(iii) The asset is owned, immediately after its acquisition and on the target acquisition date, by a corporation that acquires stock of target in the qualified stock purchase (or by an affiliate of an acquiring corporation).

(2) *Section 338(h)(10) elections.*—For purposes of this section, if a section 338(h)(10) election is made for a corporation acquired in a qualified stock purchase—

(i) The acquisition is treated as an acquisition of the corporation's assets (see §1.338(h)(10)-1); and

(ii) The corporation is not treated as target.

(c) *Gain from disposition reflected in basis of target stock.*—For purposes of this section:

(1) *General rule.*—Gain from the disposition of an asset is reflected in the basis of a corporation's stock if the gain is taken into account under §1.1502-32, directly or indirectly, in determining the basis of the stock, after applying section 1503(e) and other provisions of the Internal Revenue Code.

(2) *Gain not reflected if section 338 election made for target.*—Gain from the disposition of an asset that is otherwise reflected in the basis of target stock as of the target acquisition date is not considered reflected in the basis of target stock if a section 338 election is made for target.

(3) *Gain reflected by reason of distributions.*—Gain from the disposition of an asset is not considered reflected in the basis of target stock merely by reason of the receipt of a distribution from a target affiliate that is not a member of the same consolidated group as the distributee. See paragraph (g) of this section for the treatment of dividends eligible for a 100 percent dividends received deduction.

(4) *Controlled foreign corporations.*—For a limitation applicable to gain of a target affiliate that is a controlled foreign corporation, *see* paragraph (h)(2) of this section.

(5) *Gain recognized outside the consolidated group.*—Gain from the disposition of an asset by a person other than target or a target affiliate is not reflected in the basis of a corporation's stock unless the person is a conduit, as defined in paragraph (j)(4) of this section.

(d) *Basis of acquired assets.*—(1) *Carryover basis rule.*—If this paragraph (d) applies to an asset, the asset's basis immediately after its acquisition is, for all purposes of the Internal Revenue Code, its adjusted basis immediately before its disposition.

(2) *Exceptions to carryover basis rule for certain assets.*—The carryover basis rule of paragraph (d)(1) of this section does not apply to the following assets—

(i) Any asset disposed of in the ordinary course of a trade or business (see section 338(e)(2)(A));

(ii) Any asset the basis of which is determined wholly by reference to the adjusted basis of the asset in the hands of the person that disposed of the asset (see section 338(e)(2)(B));

(iii) Any debt or equity instrument issued by target or a target affiliate (*see* paragraph (h)(3) of this section for an exception relating to the stock of a target affiliate that is a controlled foreign corporation);

(iv) Any asset the basis of which immediately after its acquisition would otherwise be less than its adjusted basis immediately before its disposition; and

(v) Any asset identified by the Internal Revenue Service in a revenue ruling or revenue procedure.

(3) *Exception to carryover basis rule for de minimis assets.*—The carryover basis rules of this section do not apply to an asset if the asset is not disposed of as part of the same arrangement as the acquisition of target and the aggregate amount realized for all assets otherwise subject to the carryover basis rules of this section does not exceed $250,000.

(4) *Mitigation rule.*—(i) *General rule.*—If the carryover basis rules of this section apply to an asset and the asset is transferred to a domestic corporation in a transaction to which section 351 applies or as a contribution to capital and no gain is recognized, the transferor's basis in the stock of the transferee (but not the transferee's basis in the asset) is determined without taking into account the carryover basis rules of this section.

(ii) *Time for transfer.*—This paragraph (d)(4) applies only if the asset is transferred before the due date (including extensions) for the transferor's income tax return for the year that includes the last date for which a section 338 election may be made for target.

(e) *Examples.*—(1) *In general.*—For purposes of the examples in this section, unless otherwise stated, the basis of each asset is the same for determining earnings and profits and taxable income, the exceptions to paragraph (d)(1) of this section do not apply, the taxable year of all persons is the calendar year, and the following facts apply: S is the common parent of a consolidated group that includes T, T1, T2, and T3; S owns all of the stock of T and T3; and T owns all of the stock of T1, which owns all of the stock of T2. B is unrelated to the S group and owns all of the stock of P, which owns all of the stock of P1. Y and Y1 are partnerships that are unrelated to the S group but may be related to the P group. Z is a corporation that is not related to any of the other parties.

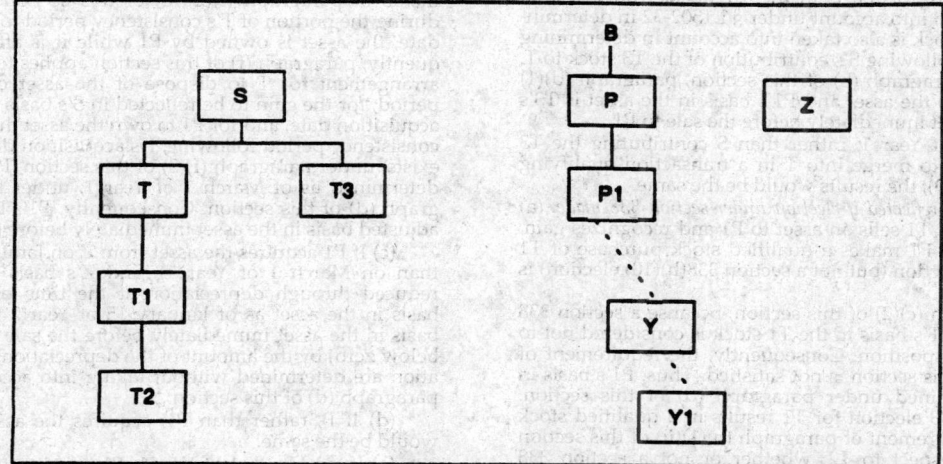

(2) *Direct acquisitions.*—Paragraphs (b), (c), and (d) of this section may be illustrated by the following examples:

Example 1. Asset acquired from target by purchasing corporation. (a) On February 1 of Year 1, T sells an asset to P1 and recognizes gain. T's gain from the disposition of the asset is taken into account under §1.1502-32 in determining S's basis in the T stock. On January 1 of Year 2, P1 makes a qualified stock purchase of T from S. No section 338 election is made for T.

(b) T disposed of the asset during its consistency period, gain from the asset disposition is reflected in the basis of the T stock as of T's acquisition date (January 1 of Year 2), and the asset is owned both immediately after the asset disposition (February 1 of Year 1) and on T's acquisition date by P1, the corporation that acquired T stock in the qualified stock purchase. Consequently, under paragraph (b) of this section, paragraph (d)(1) of this section applies to the asset and P1's basis in the asset is T's adjusted basis in the asset immediately before the sale to P1.

Example 2. Gain from section 338(h)(10) election reflected in stock basis. (a) On February 1 of Year 1, P1 makes a qualified stock purchase of T2 from T1. A section 338(h)(10) election is made for T2 and T2 recognizes gain on each of its assets. T2's gain is taken into account under §1.1502-32 in determining S's basis in the T stock. On January 1 of Year 2, P1 makes a qualified stock purchase of T from S. No section 338 election is made for T.

(b) Under paragraph (b)(2) of this section, the acquisition of the T2 stock is treated as an acquisition of T2's assets on February 1 of Year 1, because a section 338(h)(10) election is made for T2. The gain recognized by T2 under section 338(h)(10) is reflected in S's basis in the T stock as of T's acquisition date. Because the other requirements of paragraph (b) of this section are satisfied, paragraph (d)(1) of this section applies to the assets and new T2's basis in its assets is old T2's adjusted basis in the assets immediately before the disposition.

Example 3. Corporation owning asset ceases affiliation with corporation purchasing target before target acquisition date. (a) On February 1 of Year 1, T sells an asset to P1 and recognizes gain. On December 1 of Year 1, P disposes of all of the P1 stock while P1 still owns the asset. On January 1 of Year 2, P makes a qualified stock purchase of T from S. No section 338 election is made for T.

(b) Immediately after T's disposition of the asset, the asset is owned by P1 which is affiliated on that date with P, the corporation that acquired T stock in the qualified stock purchase. However, the asset is owned by a corporation (P1) that is no longer affiliated with P on T's acquisition date. Although the other requirements of paragraph (b) of this section are satisfied, the requirements of paragraph (b)(1)(iii) of this section are not satisfied. Consequently, the basis rules of paragraph (d) of this section do not apply to the asset by reason of P1's acquisition.

(c) If P acquires all of the Z stock and P1 transfers the asset to Z on or before T's acquisition date (January 1 of Year 2), the asset is owned by an affiliate of P both on February 1 of Year 1 (P1) and on January 1 of Year 2 (Z). Consequently, all of the requirements of paragraph (b) of this section are satisfied and paragraph (d)(1) of this section applies to the asset and P1's basis in the asset is T's adjusted basis in the asset immediately before the sale to P1.

Example 4. Gain reflected in stock basis notwithstanding offsetting loss or distribution. (a) On April 1 of Year 1, T sells an asset to P1 and recognizes gain. In Year 1, T distributes an amount equal to the gain. On March 1 of Year 2, P makes a qualified stock purchase of T from S. No section 338 election is made for T.

(b) Although, as a result of the distribution, there is no adjustment with respect to the T stock under §1.1502-32 for Year 1, T's gain from the disposition of the asset is considered reflected in the basis in the T stock. The gain is considered to have been taken into account under §1.1502-32 in determining the adjustments to S's basis in the T stock because S's basis in the T stock is different from what it would have been had there been no gain.

(c) If T distributes an amount equal to the gain on February 1 of Year 2, rather than in Year 1, the results would be the same because

S's basis in the T stock is different from what it would have been had there been no gain. If the distribution in Year 2 is by reason of an election under § 1.1502-32(f)(2), the results would be the same.

(d) If, in Year 1, T does not make a distribution and the S group does not file a consolidated return, but, in Year 2, the S group does file a consolidated return and makes an election under § 1.1502-32(f)(2) for T, the results would be the same. S's basis in the T stock is different from what it would have been had there been no gain. Paragraph (c)(3) of this section (gain not considered reflected by reason of distributions) does not apply to the deemed distribution under the election because S and T are members of the same consolidated group. If T distributes an amount equal to the gain in Year 2 and no election is made under § 1.1502-32(f)(2), the results would be the same.

(e) If, in Year 1, T incurs an unrelated loss in an amount equal to the gain, rather than distributing an amount equal to the gain, the results would be the same because the gain is taken into account under § 1.1502-32 in determining S's basis in the T stock.

Example 5. Gain of a target affiliate reflected in stock basis after corporate reorganization. (a) On February 1 of Year 1, T sells an asset to P1 and recognizes gain. On March 1 of Year 1, S contributes the T3 stock to T in a transaction qualifying under section 351. On January 15 of Year 2, P1 makes a qualified stock purchase of T from S. No section 338 election is made for T.

(b) T3's gain from the asset sale is taken into account under § 1.1502-32 in determining S's basis in the T3 stock. Under section 358, the gain that is taken into account under § 1.1502-32 in determining S's basis in the T3 stock is also taken into account in determining S's basis in the T stock following S's contribution of the T3 stock to T. Consequently, under paragraph (b) of this section, paragraph (d)(1) of this section applies to the asset and P1's basis in the asset is T3's adjusted basis in the asset immediately before the sale to P1.

(c) If on March 1 of Year 1, rather than S contributing the T3 stock to T, S causes T3 to merge into T in a transaction qualifying under section 368(a)(1)(D), the results would be the same.

Example 6. Gain not reflected if election under section 338 made. (a) On February 1 of Year 1, T1 sells an asset to P1 and recognizes gain. On January 1 of Year 2, P1 makes a qualified stock purchase of T1 from T. A section 338 election (but not a section 338(h)(10) election) is made for T1.

(b) Under paragraph (c)(2) of this section, because a section 338 election is made for T1, T's basis in the T1 stock is considered not to reflect gain from the disposition. Consequently, the requirement of paragraph (b)(1)(ii) of this section is not satisfied. Thus, P1's basis in the asset is not determined under paragraph (d) of this section. Although the section 338 election for T1 results in a qualified stock purchase of T2, the requirement of paragraph (b)(1)(ii) of this section is not satisfied with respect to T2, whether or not a section 338 election is made for T2.

(c) If, on January 1 of Year 2, P1 makes a qualified stock purchase of T from S and a section 338 election for T, rather than T1, S's basis in the T stock is considered not to reflect gain from T1's disposition of the asset. However, the section 338 election for T results in a qualified stock purchase of T1. Because the gain is reflected in T's basis in the T1 stock, the requirements of paragraph (b) of this section are satisfied. Consequently, P1's basis in the asset is determined under paragraph (d)(1) of this section unless a section 338 election is also made for T1.

(f) *Extension of consistency to indirect acquisitions.*—(1) *Introduction.*—If an arrangement exists (see paragraph (j)(5) of this section), this paragraph (f) generally extends the consistency rules to indirect acquisitions that have the same effect as direct acquisitions. For example, this paragraph (f) applies if, pursuant to an arrangement, target sells an asset to an unrelated person who then sells the asset to the purchasing corporation.

(2) *General rule.*—This paragraph (f) applies to an asset if, pursuant to an arrangement—

(i) The asset is disposed of during the target consistency period;

(ii) The basis of target stock as of, or at any time before, the target acquisition date reflects gain from the disposition of the asset; and

(iii) The asset ownership requirements of paragraph (b)(1)(iii) of this section are not satisfied, but the asset is owned, at any time during the portion of the target consistency period following the target acquisition date, by—

(A) A corporation—

(1) The basis of whose stock, as of, or at any time before, the target acquisition date, reflects gain from the disposition of the asset; and

(2) That is affiliated, at any time during the target consistency period, with a corporation that acquires stock of target in the qualified stock purchase; or

(B) A corporation that at the time it owns the asset is affiliated with a corporation described in paragraph (f)(2)(iii)(A) of this section.

(3) *Basis of acquired assets.*—If this paragraph (f) applies to an asset, the principles of the basis rules of paragraph (d) of this section apply to the asset as of the date, following the disposition with respect to which gain is reflected in the basis of target's stock, that the asset is first owned by a corporation described in paragraph (f)(2)(iii) of this section. If the principles of the carryover basis rule of paragraph (d)(1) of this section apply to an asset, the asset's basis also is reduced (but not below zero) by the amount of any reduction in its basis occurring after the disposition with respect to which gain is reflected in the basis of target's stock.

(4) *Examples.*—This paragraph (f) may be illustrated by the following examples:

Example 1. Acquisition of asset from unrelated party by purchasing corporation. (a) On February 1 of Year 1, T sells an asset to Z and recognizes gain. On February 15 of Year 1, P1 makes a qualified stock purchase of T from S. No section 338 election is made for T. P1 buys the asset from Z on March 1 of Year 1, before Z has reduced the basis of the asset through depreciation or otherwise.

(b) Paragraph (b) of this section does not apply to the asset because the asset ownership requirements of paragraph (b)(1)(iii) of this section are not satisfied. However, the asset ownership requirements of paragraph (f)(2)(iii) of this section are satisfied because, during the portion of T's consistency period following T's acquisition date, the asset is owned by P1 while it is affiliated with T. Consequently, paragraph (f) of this section applies to the asset if there is an arrangement for T to dispose of the asset during T's consistency period, for the gain to be reflected in S's basis in the T stock as of T's acquisition date, and for P1 to own the asset during the portion of T's consistency period following T's acquisition date. If the arrangement exists, under paragraph (f)(3) of this section, P1's basis in the asset is determined as of March 1 of Year 1, under the principles of paragraph (d) of this section. Consequently, P1's basis in the asset is T's adjusted basis in the asset immediately before the sale to Z.

(c) If P1 acquires the asset from Z on January 15 of Year 2 (rather than on March 1 of Year 1), and Z's basis in the asset has been reduced through depreciation at the time of the acquisition, P1's basis in the asset as of January 15 of Year 2 would be T's adjusted basis in the asset immediately before the sale to Z, reduced (but not below zero) by the amount of the depreciation. Z's basis and depreciation are determined without taking into account the basis rules of paragraph (d) of this section.

(d) If P, rather than P1, acquires the asset from Z, the results would be the same.

(e) If, on March 1 of Year 1, P1 acquires the Z stock, rather than acquiring the asset from Z, paragraph (f) of this section would apply to the asset if an arrangement exists. However, under paragraph (f)(3) of this section, Z's basis in the asset would be determined as of February 1 of Year 1, the date the asset is first owned by a corporation (Z) described in paragraph (f)(2)(iii) of this section. Consequently, Z's basis in the asset as of February 1 of Year 1, determined under the principles of paragraph (d) of this section, would be T's adjusted basis in the asset immediately before the sale to Z.

Example 2. Acquisition of asset from target by target affiliate. (a) On February 1 of Year 1, T contributes an asset to T1 in a transaction qualifying under section 351 and in which T recognizes gain under section 351(b) that is deferred under § 1.1502-13. On March 1 of Year 1, P1 makes a qualified stock purchase of T from S and, pursuant to § 1.1502-13, the deferred gain is taken into account by T immediately before T ceases to be a member of the S group. No section 338 election is made for T.

(b) Paragraph (b) of this section does not apply to the asset because the asset ownership requirements of paragraph (b)(1)(iii) of this section are not satisfied.

(c) T1 is not described in paragraph (f)(2)(iii)(A) of this section because the basis of the T1 stock does not reflect gain from the disposition of the asset. Although, under section 358(a)(1)(B)(ii), T's basis in the T1 stock is increased by the amount of the gain, the gain is not taken into account directly or indirectly under § 1.1502-32 in determining T's basis in the T1 stock.

(d) T1 is described in paragraph (f)(2)(iii)(B) of this section because, during the portion of T's consistency period following T's acquisition date, T1 owns the asset while it is affiliated with T, a corporation described in paragraph (f)(2)(iii)(A) of this section. Consequently, paragraph (f) of this section applies to the asset if there is an arrangement. Under paragraph (j)(5) of this section, the fact that, at the time T1 acquires the asset from T, T1 is related (within the meaning of section 267(b)) to T indicates that an arrangement exists.

Example 3. Acquisition of asset from target and indirect acquisition of target stock. (a) On February 1 of Year 1, T sells an asset to P1 and recognizes gain. On March 1 of Year 1, Z makes a qualified stock purchase of T from S. No section 338 election is made for T. On January 1 of Year 2, P1 acquires the T stock from Z other than in a qualified stock purchase.

(b) The asset ownership requirements of paragraph (b)(1)(iii) of this section are not satisfied because the asset was never owned by Z, the corporation that acquired T stock in the qualified stock purchase (or by a corporation that was affiliated with Z at the time it owned the asset). However, because the asset is owned by P1 while it is affiliated with T during the portion of T's consistency period following T's acquisition date, paragraph (f) of this section applies to the asset if there is an arrangement. If there is an arrangement, the principles of the carryover basis rule of paragraph (d)(1) of this section apply to determine P1's basis in the asset unless Z makes a section 338 election for T. See paragraph (c)(2) of this section.

(c) If P1 also makes a qualified stock purchase of T from Z, the results would be the same. If there is an arrangement, the principles of the carryover basis rule of paragraph (d)(1) of this section apply to determine P1's basis in the asset unless Z makes a section 338 election for T. However, these principles apply to determine P1's basis in the asset if P1, but not Z, makes a section 338 election for T. The basis of the T stock no longer reflects, as of T's acquisition date by P1, the gain from the disposition of the asset.

(d) Assume Z purchases the T stock other than in a qualified stock purchase and P1 makes a qualified stock purchase of T from Z. Paragraph (b) of this section does not apply to the asset because gain from the disposition of the asset is not reflected in the basis of T's stock as of T's acquisition date (January 1 of Year 2). However, because the gain is reflected in S's basis in the T stock before T's acquisition date and the asset is owned by P1 while it is affiliated with T during the portion of T's consistency period following T's acquisition date, paragraph (f) of this section applies to the asset if there is an arrangement. If there is an arrangement, the principles of the carryover basis rule of paragraph (d)(1) of this section apply to determine P1's basis in the asset even if P1 makes a section 338 election for T. The basis of the T stock no longer reflects, as of T's acquisition date, the gain from the disposition of the asset.

Example 4. Asset acquired from target affiliate by corporation that becomes its affiliate. (a) On February 1 of Year 1, T1 sells an asset to P1 and recognizes gain. On February 15 of Year 1, Z makes a qualified stock purchase of T from S. No section 338 election is made for T. On June 1 of Year 1, P1 acquires the T1 stock from T, other than in a qualified stock purchase.

(b) The asset ownership requirements of paragraph (b)(1)(iii) of this section are not satisfied because the asset was never owned by Z, the corporation that acquired T stock in the qualified stock purchase (or by a corporation that was affiliated with Z at the time it owned the asset).

(c) P1 is not described in paragraph (f)(2)(iii)(A) of this section because gain from the disposition of the asset is not reflected in the basis of the P1 stock.

(d) P1 is described in paragraph (f)(2)(iii)(B) of this section because the asset is owned by P1 while P1 is affiliated with T1 during the portion of T's consistency period following T's acquisition date. T1 becomes affiliated with Z, the corporation that acquired T stock in the qualified stock purchase, during T's consistency period, and, as of T's acquisition date, the basis of T1's stock reflects gain from the disposition of the asset. Consequently, paragraph (f) of this section applies to the asset if there is an arrangement.

Example 5. De minimis rules. (a) On February 1 of Year 1, T sells an asset to P and recognizes gain. On February 15 of Year 1, T1 sells an asset to Z and recognizes gain. The aggregate amount realized by T and T1 on their respective sales of assets is not more than $250,000. On March 1 of Year 1, T3 sells an asset to P and recognizes gain. On April 1 of Year 1, P makes a qualified stock purchase of T from S. No section 338 election is made for T. On June 1 of Year 1, P1 buys from Z the asset sold by T1.

(b) Under paragraph (b) of this section, the basis rules of paragraph (d) of this section apply to the asset sold by T. Under paragraph (f) of this section, the principles of the basis rules of paragraph (d) of this section apply to the asset sold by T1 if there is an arrangement. Because T3's gain is not reflected in the basis of the T stock, the basis rules of this section do not apply to the asset sold by T3.

(c) The de minimis rule of paragraph (d)(3) of this section applies to an asset if the asset is not disposed of as part of the same arrangement as the acquisition of T and the aggregate amount realized for all assets otherwise subject to the carryover basis rules does not exceed $250,000. The aggregate amount realized by T and T1 does not exceed $250,000. (The asset sold by T3 is not taken into account for purposes of the de minimis rule.) Thus, the de minimis rule applies to the asset sold by T if the asset is not disposed of as part of the same arrangement as the acquisition of T.

(d) If, under paragraph (f) of this section, the principles of the carryover basis rules of paragraph (d)(1) of this section otherwise

apply to the asset sold by T1 because of an arrangement, the de minimis rules of this section do not apply to the asset because of the arrangement.

(e) Assume on June 1 of Year 1, Z acquires the T1 stock from T, other than in a qualified stock purchase, rather than P1 buying the T1 asset, and paragraph (f) of this section applies because there is an arrangement. Because the asset was disposed of and the T1 stock was acquired as part of the arrangement, the de minimis rules of this section do not apply to the asset.

(g) *Extension of consistency if dividends qualifying for 100 percent dividends received deduction are paid.*—(1) *General rule for direct acquisitions from target.*—Unless a section 338 election is made for target, the basis rules of paragraph (d) of this section apply to an asset if—

(i) Target recognizes gain (whether or not deferred) on disposition of the asset during the portion of the target consistency period that ends on the target acquisition date;

(ii) The asset is owned, immediately after the asset disposition and on the target acquisition date, by a corporation that acquires stock of target in the qualified stock purchase (or by an affiliate of an acquiring corporation); and

(iii) During the portion of the target consistency period that ends on the target acquisition date, the aggregate amount of dividends paid by target, to which section 243(a)(3) applies, exceeds the greater of—

(A) $250,000; or

(B) 125 percent of the yearly average amount of dividends paid by target, to which section 243(a)(3) applies, during the three calendar years immediately preceding the year in which the target consistency period begins (or, if shorter, the period target was in existence).

(2) *Other direct acquisitions having same effect.*—The basis rules of paragraph (d) of this section also apply to an asset if the effect of a transaction described in paragraph (g)(1) of this section is achieved through any combination of disposition of assets and payment of dividends to which section 243(a)(3) applies (or any other dividends eligible for a 100 percent dividends received deduction). See paragraph (h)(4) of this section for additional rules relating to target affiliates that are controlled foreign corporations.

(3) *Indirect acquisitions.*—The principles of paragraph (f) of this section also apply for purposes of this paragraph (g).

(4) *Examples.*—This paragraph (g) may be illustrated by the following examples:

Example 1. Asset acquired from target paying dividends to which section 243(a)(3) applies. (a) The S group does not file a consolidated return. In Year 1, Year 2, and Year 3, T pays dividends to S to which section 243(a)(3) applies of $200,000, $250,000, and $300,000, respectively. On February 1 of Year 4, T sells an asset to P and recognizes gain. On January 1 of Year 5, P makes a qualified stock purchase of T from S. No section 338 election is made for T. During the portion of T's consistency period that ends on T's acquisition date, T pays S dividends to which section 243(a)(3) applies of $1,000,000.

(b) Under paragraph (g)(1) of this section, paragraph (d) of this section applies to the asset. T recognizes gain on disposition of the asset during the portion of T's consistency period that ends on T's acquisition date, the asset is owned by P immediately after the disposition and on T's acquisition date, and T pays dividends described in paragraph (g)(1)(iii) of this section. Consequently, under paragraph (d)(1) of this section, P's basis in the asset is T's adjusted basis in the asset immediately before the sale to P.

(c) If T is a controlled foreign corporation, the results would be the same if T pays dividends in the amount described in paragraph (g)(1)(iii) of this section that qualify for a 100 percent dividends received deduction. See sections 243(e) and 245.

(d) If S and T3 file a consolidated return in which T, T1, and T2 do not join, the results would be the same because the dividends paid by T are still described in paragraph (g)(1)(iii) of this section.

(e) If T, T1, and T2 file a consolidated return in which S and T3 do not join, the results would be the same because the dividends paid by T are still described in paragraph (g)(1)(iii) of this section.

Example 2. Asset disposition by target affiliate achieving same effect. (a) The S group does not file a consolidated return. On February 1 of Year 1, T2 sells an asset to P and recognizes gain. T pays dividends to S described in paragraph (g)(1)(iii) of this section. On January 1 of Year 2, P makes a qualified stock purchase of T from S. No section 338 election is made for T.

(b) Paragraph (g)(1) of this section does not apply to the asset because T did not recognize gain on the disposition of the asset. However, under paragraph (g)(2) of this section, because the asset disposition by T2 and the dividends paid by T achieve the effect of a transaction described in paragraph (g)(1) of this section, the carryover basis rule of paragraph (d)(1) of this section applies to the asset.

The effect was achieved because T2 is a lower-tier affiliate of T and the dividends paid by T to S reduce the value to S of T and its lower-tier affiliates.

(c) If T2 is a controlled foreign corporation, the results would be the same because T2 is a lower-tier affiliate of T and the dividends paid by T to S reduce the value to S of T and its lower-tier affiliates.

(d) If P buys an asset from T3, rather than T2, the asset disposition and the dividends do not achieve the effect of a transaction described in paragraph (g)(1) of this section because T3 is not a lower-tier affiliate of T. Thus, the basis rules of paragraph (d) of this section do not apply to the asset. The results would be the same whether or not P also acquires the T3 stock (whether or not in a qualified stock purchase).

Example 3. Dividends by target affiliate achieving same effect. (a) The S group does not file a consolidated return. On February 1 of Year 1, T1 sells an asset to P and recognizes gain. On January 1 of Year 2, P makes a qualified stock purchase of T from S. No section 338 election is made for T. T does not pay dividends to S described in paragraph (g)(1)(iii) of this section. However, T1 pays dividends to T that would be described in paragraph (g)(1)(iii) of this section if T1 were a target.

(b) Paragraph (g)(1) of this section does not apply to the asset because T did not recognize gain on the disposition of the asset and did not pay dividends described in paragraph (g)(1)(iii) of this section. Further, paragraph (g)(2) of this section does not apply because the dividends paid by T1 to T do not reduce the value to S of T and its lower-tier affiliates.

(c) If both S and T own T1 stock and T1 pays dividends to S that would be described in paragraph (g)(1)(iii) of this section if T1 were a target, paragraph (g)(2) of this section would apply because the dividends paid by T1 to S reduce the value to S of T and its lower-tier affiliates. If T, rather than T1, sold the asset to P, the results would be the same. Further, if T and T1 pay dividends to S that, only when aggregated, would be described in paragraph (g)(1)(iii) of this section (if they were all paid by T), the results would be the same.

Example 4. Gain reflected by reason of dividends. (a) S and T file a consolidated return in which T1 and T2 do not join. On February 1 of Year 1, T1 sells an asset to P and recognizes gain. On January 1 of Year 2, P makes a qualified stock purchase of T from S. No section 338 election is made for T. T1 pays dividends to T that would be described in paragraph (g)(1)(iii) of this section if T1 were a target.

(b) The requirements of paragraph (b) of this section are not satisfied because, under paragraph (c)(3) of this section, gain from T1's sale is not reflected in S's basis in the T stock by reason of the dividends paid by T1 to T.

(c) Although the dividends paid by T1 to T do not reduce the value to S of T and its lower-tier affiliates, paragraph (g)(2) of this section applies because the dividends paid by T1 to T are taken into account under §1.1502-32 in determining S's basis in the T stock. Consequently, the carryover basis rule of paragraph (d)(1) of this section applies to the asset.

(h) *Consistency for target affiliates that are controlled foreign corporations.*—(1) *In general.*—This paragraph (h) applies only if target is a domestic corporation. For additional rules that may apply with respect to controlled foreign corporations, see paragraph (g) of this section. The definitions and nomenclature of §1.338-2(b) and (c) and paragraph (e) of this section apply for purposes of this section.

(2) *Income or gain resulting from asset dispositions.*—(i) *General rule.*—Income or gain of a target affiliate that is a controlled foreign corporation from the disposition of an asset is not reflected in the basis of target stock under paragraph (c) of this section unless the income or gain results in an inclusion under section 951(a)(1)(A), 951(a)(1)(C), 1291 or 1293.

(ii) *Basis of controlled foreign corporation stock.*—If, by reason of paragraph (h)(2)(i) of this section, the carryover basis rules of this section apply to an asset, no increase in basis in the stock of a controlled foreign corporation under section 961(a) or 1293(d)(1), or under regulations issued pursuant to section 1297(b)(5), is allowed to target or a target affiliate to the extent the increase is attributable to income or gain described in paragraph (h)(2)(i) of this section. A similar rule applies to the basis of any property by reason of which the stock of the controlled foreign corporation is considered owned under section 958(a)(2) or 1297(a).

(iii) *Operating rule.*—For purposes of this paragraph (h)(2)—

(A) If there is an income inclusion under section 951 (a)(1)(A) or (C), the shareholder's income inclusion is first attributed to the income or gain of the controlled foreign corporation from the disposition of the asset to the extent of the shareholder's pro rata share of such income or gain; and

(B) Any income or gain under section 1293 is first attributed to the income or gain from the disposition of the asset to the extent of the shareholder's pro rata share of the income or gain.

(iv) *Increase in asset or stock basis.*—(A) If the carryover basis rules under paragraph (h)(2)(i) of this section apply to an asset, and the purchasing corporation disposes of the asset to an unrelated party in a taxable transaction and recognizes and includes in its U.S. gross income or the U.S. gross income of its shareholders the greater of the income or gain from the disposition of the asset by the selling controlled foreign corporation that was reflected in the basis of the target stock under paragraph (c) of this section, or the gain recognized on the asset by the purchasing corporation on the disposition of the asset, then the purchasing corporation or the target or a target affiliate, as appropriate, shall increase the basis of the selling controlled foreign corporation stock subject to paragraph (h)(2)(ii) of this section, as of the date of the disposition of the asset by the purchasing corporation, by the amount of the basis increase that was denied under paragraph (h)(2)(i) of this section. The preceding sentence shall apply only to the extent that the controlled foreign corporation stock is owned (within the meaning of section 958(a)) by a member of the purchasing corporation's affiliated group.

(B) If the carryover basis rules under paragraph (h)(2)(i) of this section apply to an asset, and the purchasing corporation or the target or a target affiliate, as appropriate, disposes of the stock of the selling controlled foreign corporation to an unrelated party in a taxable transaction and includes in its U.S. gross income or the U.S. gross income of its shareholders the greater of the gain equal to the basis increase that was denied under paragraph (h)(2)(ii) of this section, or the gain recognized in the stock by the purchasing corporation or by the target or a target affiliate, as appropriate, on the disposition of the stock, then the purchasing corporation or by the target or a target affiliate, as appropriate, shall increase the basis of the asset, as of the date of the disposition of the stock of the selling controlled foreign corporation by the purchasing corporation or by the target or a target affiliate, as appropriate, by the amount of the basis increase that was denied pursuant to paragraph (h)(2)(i) of this section. The preceding sentence shall apply only to the extent that the asset is owned (within the meaning of section 958(a)) by a member of the purchasing corporation's affiliated group.

(3) *Stock issued by target affiliate that is a controlled foreign corporation.*—The exception to the carryover basis rules of this section provided in paragraph (d)(2)(iii) of this section does not apply to stock issued by a target affiliate that is a controlled foreign corporation. After applying the carryover basis rules of this section to the stock, the basis in the stock is increased by the amount treated as a dividend under section 1248 on the disposition of the stock (or that would have been so treated but for section 1291), except to the extent the basis increase is attributable to the disposition of an asset in which a carryover basis is taken under this section.

(4) *Certain distributions.*—(i) *General rule.*—In the case of a target affiliate that is a controlled foreign corporation, paragraph (g) of this section applies with respect to the target affiliate by treating any reference to a dividend to which section 243(a)(3) applies as a reference to any amount taken into account under §1.1502-32 in determining the basis of target stock that is—

(A) A dividend;

(B) An amount treated as a dividend under section 1248 (or that would have been so treated but for section 1291); or

(C) An amount included in income under section 951(a)(1)(B).

(ii) *Basis of controlled foreign corporation stock.*—If the carryover basis rules of this section apply to an asset, the basis in the stock of the controlled foreign corporation (or any property by reason of which the stock is considered owned under section 958(a)(2)) is reduced (but not below zero) by the sum of any amounts that are treated, solely by reason of the disposition of the asset, as a dividend, amount treated as a dividend under section 1248 (or that would have been so treated but for section 1291), or amount included in income under section 951(a)(1)(B). For this purpose, any dividend, amount treated as a dividend under section 1248 (or that would have been so treated but for section 1291), or amount included in income under section 951(a)(1)(B) is considered attributable first to earnings and profits resulting from the disposition of the asset.

(iii) *Increase in asset or stock basis.*—(A) If the carryover basis rules under paragraphs (g) and (h)(4)(i) of this section apply to an asset, and the purchasing corporation disposes of the asset to an unrelated party in a taxable transaction and recognizes and includes in its U.S. gross income or the U.S. gross income of its shareholders the greater of the gain equal to the basis increase denied in the asset pursuant to paragraphs (g) and (h)(4)(i) of this section, or the gain recognized on the asset by the purchasing corporation on the disposition of the asset, then the purchasing corporation or the target or a target affiliate, as appropriate, shall increase the basis of the selling controlled foreign corporation stock subject to paragraph (h)(4)(ii) of this section, as of the date of the disposition of the asset by the purchasing corporation, by the amount of the basis reduction under paragraph (h)(4)(ii) of this section. The preceding sentence shall apply only to the extent that the controlled foreign corporation stock is owned (within the meaning of section 958(a)) by a member of the purchasing corporation's affiliated group.

(B) If the carryover basis rules under paragraphs (g) and (h)(4)(i) of this section apply to an asset, and the purchasing corporation or the target or a target affiliate, as appropriate, disposes of the stock of the selling controlled foreign corporation to an unrelated party in a taxable transaction and recognizes and includes in its U.S. gross income or the U.S. gross income of its shareholders the greater of the amount of the basis reduction under paragraph (h)(4)(ii) of this section, or the gain recognized in the stock by the purchasing corporation or by the target or a target affiliate, as appropriate, on the disposition of the stock, then the purchasing corporation shall increase the basis of the asset, as of the date of the disposition of the stock of the selling controlled foreign corporation by the purchasing corporation or by the target or a target affiliate, as appropriate, by the amount of the basis increase that was denied pursuant to paragraphs (g) and (h)(4)(i) of this section. The preceding sentence shall apply only to the extent that the asset is owned (within the meaning of section 958(a)) by a member of the purchasing corporation's affiliated group.

(5) *Examples.*—This paragraph (h) may be illustrated by the following examples:

Example 1. Stock of target affiliate that is a CFC. (a) The S group files a consolidated return; however, T2 is a controlled foreign corporation. On December 1 of Year 1, T1 sells the T2 stock to P and recognizes gain. On January 2 of Year 2, P makes a qualified stock purchase of T from S. No section 338 election is made for T.

(b) Under paragraph (b)(1) of this section, paragraph (d) of this section applies to the T2 stock. Under paragraph (h)(3) of this section, paragraph (d)(2)(iii) of this section does not apply to the T2 stock. Consequently, paragraph (d)(1) of this section applies to the T2 stock. However, after applying paragraph (d)(1) of this section, P's basis in the T2 stock is increased by the amount of T1's gain on the sale of the T2 stock that is treated as a dividend under section 1248. Because P has a carryover basis in the T2 stock, the T2 stock is not considered purchased within the meaning of section 338(h)(3) and no section 338 election may be made for T2.

Example 2. Stock of target affiliate CFC; inclusion under subpart F. (a) The S group files a consolidated return; however, T2 is a controlled foreign corporation. On December 1 of Year 1, T2 sells an asset to P and recognizes subpart F income that results in an inclusion in T1's gross income under section 951(a)(1)(A). On January 2 of Year 2, P makes a qualified stock purchase of T from S. No section 338 election is made for T.

(b) Because gain from the disposition of the asset results in an inclusion under section 951(a)(1)(A), the gain is reflected in the basis of the T stock as of T's acquisition date. See paragraph (h)(2)(i) of this section. Consequently, under paragraph (b)(1) of this section, paragraph (d)(1) of this section applies to the asset. In addition, under paragraph (h)(2)(ii) of this section, T1's basis in the T2 stock is not increased under section 961(a) by the amount of the inclusion that is attributable to the sale of the asset.

(c) If, in addition to making a qualified stock purchase of T, P acquires the T2 stock from T1 on January 1 of Year 2, the results are the same for the asset sold by T2. In addition, under paragraph (h)(2)(ii) of this section, T1's basis in the T2 stock is not increased by the amount of the inclusion that is attributable to the gain on the sale of the asset. Further, under paragraph (h)(3) of this section, paragraph (d)(1) of this section applies to the T2 stock. However, after applying paragraph (d)(1) of this section, P's basis in the T2 stock is increased by the amount of T1's gain on the sale of the T2 stock that is treated as a dividend under section 1248. Finally, because P has a carryover basis in the T2 stock, the T2 stock is not considered purchased within the meaning of section 338(h)(3) and no section 338 election may be made for T2.

(d) If P makes a qualified stock purchase of T2 from T1, rather than of T from S, and T1's gain on the sale of T2 is treated as a dividend under section 1248, under paragraph (h)(1) of this section, paragraphs (h)(2) and (3) of this section do not apply because there is no target that is a domestic corporation. Consequently, the carryover basis rules of paragraph do not apply to the asset sold by T2 or the T2 stock.

Example 3. Gain reflected by reason of section 1248 dividend; gain from non-subpart F asset. (a) The S group files a consolidated return; however, T2 is a controlled foreign corporation. In Years 1 through 4, T2 does not pay any dividends to T1 and no amount is included in T1's income under section 951(a)(1)(B). On December 1 of Year 4, T2 sells an asset with a basis of $400,000 to P for $900,000. T2's gain of $500,000 is not subpart F income. On December 15 of Year 4, T1 sells T2, in which it has a basis of $600,000, to P for $1,600,000. Under section 1248, $800,000 of T1's gain of $1,000,000 is treated as a

dividend. However, in the absence of the sale of the asset by T2 to P, only $300,000 would have been treated as a dividend under section 1248. On December 30 of Year 4, P makes a qualified stock purchase of T1 from T. No section 338 election is made for T1.

(b) Under paragraph (h)(4) of this section, paragraph (g)(2) of this section applies by reference to the amount treated as a dividend under section 1248 on the disposition of the T2 stock. Because the amount treated as a dividend is taken into account in determining T's basis in the T1 stock under §1 150232, the sale of the T2 stock and the deemed dividend have the effect of a transaction described in paragraph (g)(1) of this section. Consequently, paragraph (d)(1) of this section applies to the asset sold by T2 to P and P's basis in the asset is $400,000 as of December 1 of Year 4.

(c) Under paragraph (h)(3) of this section, paragraph (d)(1) of this section applies to the T2 stock and P's basis in the T2 stock is $600,000 as of December 15 of Year 4. Under paragraphs (h)(3) and (4)(ii) of this section, however, P's basis in the T2 stock is increased by $300,000 (the amount of T1's gain treated as a dividend under section 1248 ($800,000), other than the amount treated as a dividend solely as a result of the sale of the asset by T2 to P ($500,000)) to $900,000.

(i) [Reserved]

(j) *Anti-avoidance rules.*—For purposes of this section—

(1) *Extension of consistency period.*—The target consistency period is extended to include any continuous period that ends on, or begins on, any day of the consistency period during which a purchasing corporation, or any person related, within the meaning of section 267(b) or 707(b)(1), to a purchasing corporation, has an arrangement—

(i) To purchase stock of target; or

(ii) To own an asset to which the carryover basis rules of this section apply, taking into account the extension.

(2) *Qualified stock purchase and 12-month acquisition period.*—The 12-month acquisition period is extended if, pursuant to an arrangement, a corporation acquires by purchase stock of another corporation satisfying the requirements of section 1504(a)(2) over a period of more than 12 months.

(3) *Acquisitions by conduits.*—(i) *Asset ownership.*—(A) *General rule.*—A corporation is treated as owning any portion of an asset attributed to the corporation from a conduit under section 318(a) (treating any asset as stock for this purpose), for purposes of—

   (1) The asset ownership requirements of this section; and

   (2) Determining whether a controlled foreign corporation is a target affiliate for purposes of paragraph (h) of this section.

(B) *Application of carryover basis rule.*—If the basis rules of this section apply to the asset, the basis rules of this section apply to the entire asset (not just the portion for which ownership is attributed).

(ii) *Stock acquisitions.*—(A) *Purchase by conduit.*—A corporation is treated as purchasing stock of another corporation attributed to the corporation from a conduit under section 318(a) on the day the stock is purchased by the conduit. The corporation is not treated as purchasing the stock, however, if the conduit purchased the stock more than two years before the date the stock is first attributed to the corporation.

(B) *Purchase of conduit by corporation.*—If a corporation purchases an interest in a conduit (treating the interest as stock for this purpose), the corporation is treated as purchasing on that date any stock owned by a conduit on that date and attributed to the corporation under section 318(a) with respect to the interest in the conduit that was purchased.

(C) *Purchase of conduit by conduit.*—If a conduit (the *first conduit*) purchases an interest in a second conduit (treating the interest as stock for this purpose), the first conduit is treated as purchasing on that date any stock owned by a conduit on that date and attributed to the first conduit under section 318(a) with respect to the interest in the second conduit that was purchased.

(4) *Conduit.*—A person (other than a corporation) is a conduit as to a corporation if—

(i) The corporation would be treated under section 318(a)(2)(A) and (B) (attribution from partnerships, estates, and trusts) as owning any stock owned by the person; and

(ii) The corporation, together with its affiliates, would be treated as owning an aggregate of at least 50 percent of the stock owned by the person.

(5) *Existence of arrangement.*—The existence of an arrangement is determined under all the facts and circumstances. For an arrangement to exist, there need not be an enforceable, written, or uncondi-

tional agreement, and all the parties to the transaction need not have participated in each step of the transaction. One factor indicating the existence of an arrangement is the participation of a related party. For this purpose, persons are related if they are related within the meaning of section 267(b) or 707(b)(1).

(6) *Predecessor and successor.*—(i) *Persons.*—A reference to a person (including target, target affiliate, and purchasing corporation) includes, as the context may require, a reference to a predecessor or successor. For this purpose, a predecessor is a transferor or distributor of assets to a person (the successor) in a transaction—

    (A) To which section 381(a) applies; or

    (B) In which the successor's basis for the assets is determined, directly or indirectly, in whole or in part, by reference to the basis of the transferor or distributor.

(ii) *Assets.*—A reference to an asset (the first asset) includes, as the context may require, a reference to any asset the basis of which is determined, directly or indirectly, in whole or in part, by reference to the first asset.

(7) *Examples.*—This paragraph (j) may be illustrated by the following examples:

Example 1. Asset owned by conduit treated as owned by purchaser of target stock. (a) P owns a 60-percent interest in Y. On March 1 of Year 1, T sells an asset to Y and recognizes gain. On January 1 of Year 2, P makes a qualified stock purchase of T from S. No section 338 election is made for T.

(b) Under paragraph (j)(4) of this section, Y is a conduit with respect to P. Consequently, under paragraph (j)(3)(i)(A) of this section, P is treated as owning 60% of the asset on March 1 of Year 1 and January 1 of Year 2. Because P is treated as owning part or all of the asset both immediately after the asset disposition and on T's acquisition date, paragraph (b) of this section applies to the asset. Consequently, paragraph (d)(1) of this section applies to the asset and Y's basis in the asset is T's adjusted basis in the asset immediately before the sale to Y.

Example 2. Corporation whose stock is owned by conduit treated as affiliate. (a) P owns an 80-percent interest in Y. Y owns all of the stock of Z. On March 1 of Year 1, T sells an asset to Z and recognizes gain. On January 1 of Year 2, P makes a qualified stock purchase of T from S. No section 338 election is made for T.

(b) Under paragraph (j)(4) of this section, Y is a conduit with respect to P. Consequently, under paragraph (j)(3)(i)(A) of this section, P is treated as owning 80% of the Z stock and Z is therefore treated as an affiliate of P for purposes of applying the asset ownership requirements of paragraph (b)(1)(iii) of this section. Because Z, an affiliate of P, owns the asset both immediately after the asset disposition and on T's acquisition date, paragraph (b) of this section applies to the asset, and the asset's basis is determined under paragraph (d) of this section.

(c) If, instead of owning an 80-percent interest in Y, P owned a 79-percent interest in Y, Z would not be treated as an affiliate of P and paragraph (b) of this section would not apply to the asset.

Example 3. Qualified stock purchase by reason of stock purchase by conduit. (a) P owns a 90-percent interest in Y. Y owns a 60-percent interest in Y1. On February 1 of Year 2, T sells an asset to P and recognizes gain. On January 1 of Year 3, P purchases 70% of the T stock from S and Y1 purchases the remaining 30% of the T stock from S.

(b) Under paragraph (j)(3)(ii)(A) of this section, P is treated as purchasing on January 1 of Year 3, the 16.2% of the T stock that is attributed to P from Y and Y1 under section 318(a). Thus, for purposes of this section, P is treated as making a qualified stock purchase of T on January 1 of Year 3, paragraph (b) of this section applies to the asset, and the asset's basis is determined under paragraph (d) of this section. However, because P is not treated as having made a qualified stock purchase of T for purposes of making an election under section 338, no election can be made for T.

(c) If Y1 purchases 20% of the T stock from S on December 1 of Year 1, rather than 30% on January 1 of Year 3, P would be treated as purchasing 10.8% of the T stock on December 1 of Year 1. Thus, if paragraph (j)(2) of this section (relating to extension of the 12-month acquisition period) does not apply, P would not be treated as making a qualified stock purchase of T, because P is not treated as purchasing T stock satisfying the requirements of section 1504(a)(2) within a 12-month period.

Example 4. Successor asset. (a) On February 1 of Year 1, T sells stock of X to P1 and recognizes gain. On December 1 of Year 1, P1 exchanges its X stock for stock in new X in a reorganization qualifying under section 368(a)(1)(F). On January 1 of Year 2, P1 makes a qualified stock purchase of T from S. No section 338 election is made for T.

(b) The asset ownership requirements of paragraph (b)(1)(iii) of this section are satisfied because, under paragraph (j)(6)(ii) of this

section, P1 is treated as owning the X stock on T's acquisition date. P1 is treated as owning the X stock on that date because P1 owns the new X stock and P1's basis in the new X stock is determined by reference to P1's basis in the X stock. Consequently, under paragraph (d)(1) of this section, P1's basis in the X stock on February 1 of Year 1 is T's adjusted basis in the X stock immediately before the sale to P1. [Reg. §1.338-8.]

☐ [*T.D. 8515, 1-12-94. Amended by T.D. 8597, 7-12-95 and T.D. 8710, 1-22-97. Redesignated by T.D. 8858, 1-5-2000. Amended by T.D. 8940, 2-12-2001.*]

[Reg. §1.338-9]

§1.338-9. International aspects of section 338.—(a) *Scope.*—This section provides guidance regarding international aspects of section 338. As provided in §1.338-2(c)(18), a foreign corporation, a DISC, or a corporation for which a section 936 election has been made is considered a target affiliate for all purposes of section 338. In addition, stock described in section 338(h)(6)(B)(ii) held by a target affiliate is not excluded from the operation of section 338.

(b) *Application of section 338 to foreign targets.*—(1) *In general.*—For purposes of subtitle A, the deemed sale tax consequences, as defined in §1.338-2(c)(7), of a foreign target for which a section 338 election is made (FT), and the corresponding earnings and profits, are taken into account in determining the taxation of FT and FT's direct and indirect shareholders. See, however, section 338(h)(16). For example, the income and earnings and profits of FT are determined, for purposes of sections 551, 951, 1248, and 1293, by taking into account the deemed sale tax consequences.

(2) *Ownership of FT stock on the acquisition date.*—A person who transfers FT stock to the purchasing corporation on FT's acquisition date is considered to own the transferred stock at the close of FT's acquisition date. See, e.g., §1.951-1(f) (relating to determination of holding period for purposes of sections 951 through 964). If on the acquisition date the purchasing corporation owns a block of FT stock that was acquired before FT's acquisition date, the purchasing corporation is considered to own such block of stock at the close of the acquisition date.

(3) *Carryover FT stock.*—(i) *Definition.*—FT stock is carryover FT stock if—

    (A) FT was a controlled foreign corporation within the meaning of section 957 (taking into account section 953(c)) at any time during the portion of the 12-month acquisition period that ends on the acquisition date; and

    (B) Such stock is owned as of the beginning of the day after FT's acquisition date by a person other than a purchasing corporation, or by a purchasing corporation if the stock is nonrecently purchased and is not subject to a gain recognition election under §1.338-5(d).

(ii) *Carryover of earnings and profits.*—The earnings and profits of old FT (and associated foreign taxes) attributable to the carryover FT stock (adjusted to reflect deemed sale tax consequences) carry over to new FT solely for purposes of—

    (A) Characterizing an actual distribution with respect to a share of carryover FT stock as a dividend;

    (B) Characterizing gain on a post-acquisition date transfer of a share of carryover FT stock as a dividend under section 1248 (if such section is otherwise applicable);

    (C) Characterizing an investment of earnings in United States property as income under sections 951(a)(1)(B) and 956 (if such sections are otherwise applicable); and

    (D) Determining foreign taxes deemed paid under sections 902 and 960 with respect to the amount treated as a dividend or income by virtue of this paragraph (b)(3)(ii) (subject to the operation of section 338(h)(16)).

(iii) *Cap on carryover of earnings and profits.*—The amount of earnings and profits of old FT taken into account with respect to a share of carryover FT stock is limited to the amount that would have been included in gross income of the owner of such stock as a dividend under section 1248 if—

    (A) The shareholder transferred that share to the purchasing corporation on FT's acquisition date for a consideration equal to the fair market value of that share on that date; or

    (B) In the case of nonrecently purchased FT stock treated as carryover FT stock, a gain recognition election under section 338(b)(3)(A) applied to that share. For purposes of the preceding sentence, a shareholder that is a controlled foreign corporation is considered to be a United States person, and the principle of section 1248(c)(2)(D)(ii) (concerning a United States person's indirect ownership of stock in a foreign corporation) applies in determining the correct holding period.

(iv) *Post-acquisition date distribution of old FT earnings and profits.*—A post-acquisition date distribution with respect to a share of carryover FT stock is considered to be derived first from earnings and profits derived after FT's acquisition date and then from earnings and profits derived on or before FT's acquisition date.

(v) *Old FT earnings and profits unaffected by post-acquisition date deficits.*—The carryover amount for a share of carryover FT stock is not reduced by deficits in earnings and profits incurred by new FT. This rule applies for purposes of determining the amount of foreign taxes deemed paid regardless of the fact that there are no accumulated earnings and profits. For example, a distribution by new FT with respect to a share of carryover FT stock is treated as a dividend by the distributee to the extent of the carryover amount for that share notwithstanding that new FT has no earnings and profits.

(vi) *Character of FT stock as carryover FT stock eliminated upon disposition.*—A share of FT stock is not considered carryover FT stock after it is disposed of provided that all gain realized on the transfer is recognized at the time of the transfer, or that, if less than all of the realized gain is recognized, the recognized amount equals or exceeds the remaining carryover amount for that share.

(4) *Passive foreign investment company stock.*—Stock that is owned as of the beginning of the day after FT's acquisition date by a person other than a purchasing corporation, or by a purchasing corporation if the FT stock is nonrecently purchased stock not subject to a gain recognition election under §1.338-5(d), is treated as passive foreign investment company stock to the extent provided in section 1297(b)(1).

(c) *Dividend treatment under section 1248(e).*—The principles of this paragraph (b) apply to shareholders of a domestic corporation subject to section 1248(e).

(d) *Allocation of foreign income taxes.*—(1) *In general.*—Except as provided in paragraph (d)(3) of this section, if a section 338 election is made for target (whether foreign or domestic), and target's taxable year under foreign law (if any) does not close at the end of the acquisition date, foreign income tax as defined in §1.901-2(a)) (other than a withholding tax as defined in section 901(k)(1)(B)) paid or accrued by new target with respect to such foreign taxable year is allocated between old target and new target. If there is more than one section 338 election with respect to target during target's foreign taxable year, foreign income tax paid or accrued with respect to that foreign taxable year is allocated among all old targets and new targets. The allocation is made based on the respective portions of the taxable income (as determined under foreign law) for the foreign taxable year that are attributable under the principles of §1.1502-76(b) to the period of existence of each old target and new target during the foreign taxable year.

(2) *Foreign income taxes imposed on partnerships and disregarded entities.*—If a section 338 election is made for target and target holds an interest in a disregarded entity (as described in §301.7701-2(c)(2)(i) of this chapter) or partnership, the rules of §1.901-2(f)(4) and (5) apply to determine the person who is considered for Federal income tax purposes to pay foreign income tax imposed at the entity level on the income of the disregarded entity or partnership.

(3) *Disallowance of foreign tax credits under section 901(m).*—For rules that may apply to disallow foreign tax credits by reason of a section 338 election, see section 901(m) and §§1.901(m)-1 through 1.901(m)-8.

(4) *Applicability date.*—This paragraph (d) applies to foreign income taxes paid or accrued in taxable years beginning on or after December 28, 2021.

(e) *Operation of section 338(h)(16).*—[Reserved]

(f) *Examples.*—(1) Except as otherwise provided, all corporations use the calendar year as the taxable year, have no earnings and profits (or deficit) accumulated for any taxable year, and have only one class of outstanding stock.

(2) This section may be illustrated by the following examples:

Example 1. Gain recognition election for carryover FT stock. (a) A has owned 90 of the 100 shares of CFCT stock since CFCT was organized on March 13, 1989. P has owned the remaining 10 shares of CFCT stock since CFCT was organized. Those 10 shares constitute nonrecently purchased stock in P's hands within the meaning of section 338(b)(6)(B). On November 1, 1994, P purchases A's 90 shares of CFCT stock for $90,000 and makes a section 338 election for CFCT.

P also makes a gain recognition election under section 338(b)(3)(A) and §1.338-5(d).

(b) CFCT's earnings and profits for its short taxable year ending on November 1, 1994, are $50,000, determined without taking into account the deemed asset sale. Assume A recognizes gain of $81,000 on the sale of the CFCT stock. Further, assume that CFCT recognizes gain of $40,000 by reason of its deemed sale of assets under section 338(a)(1).

(c) A's sale of CFCT stock to F is a transfer to which section 1248 and paragraphs (b)(1) and (2) of this section apply. For purposes of applying section 1248(a) to A, the earnings and profits of CFCT for its short taxable year ending on November 1, 1994, are $90,000 (the earnings and profits for that taxable year as determined under §1.1248-2(e) ($50,000) plus earnings from the deemed sale ($40,000)). Thus, A's entire gain is characterized as a dividend under section 1248 (but see section 338(h)(16)).

(d) Assume that P recognizes a gain of $9,000 with respect to the 10 shares of nonrecently purchased CFCT stock by reason of the gain recognition election. Because P is treated as selling the nonrecently purchased stock for all purposes of the Internal Revenue Code, section 1248 applies. Thus, under §1.1248-2(e), $9,000 of the $90,000 of earnings and profits for 1994 are attributable to the block of 10 shares of CFCT stock deemed sold by P at the close of November 1, 1994 ($90,000 × 10/100). Accordingly, P's entire gain on the deemed sale of 10 shares of CFCT stock is included under section 1248(a) in P's gross income as a dividend (but see section 338(h)(16)).

Example 2. No gain recognition election for carryover FT stock. (a) Assume the same facts as in *Example 1*, except that P does not make a gain recognition election.

(b) The 10 shares of nonrecently purchased CFCT stock held by P is carryover FT stock under paragraph (b)(3) of this section. Accordingly, the earnings and profits (and attributable foreign taxes) of old CFCT carry over to new CFCT solely for purposes of that block of 10 shares. The amount of old CFCT's earnings and profits taken into account with respect to that block in the event, for example, of a distribution by new CFCT with respect to that block is the amount of the section 1248 dividend that P would have recognized with respect to that block had it made a gain recognition election under section 338(b)(3)(A). Under the facts of *Example 1*, P would have recognized a gain of $9,000 with respect to that block, all of which would have been a section 1248 dividend ($90,000 × 10/100). Accordingly, the carryover amount for the block of 10 shares of nonrecently purchased CFCT stock is $9,000.

Example 3. Sale of controlled foreign corporation stock prior to and on the acquisition date. (a) X and Y, both U.S. corporations, have each owned 50% of the CFCT stock since 1986. Among CFCT's assets are assets the sale of which would generate subpart F income. On December 31, 1994, X sells its CFCT stock to P. On June 30, 1995, Y sells its CFCT stock to P. P makes a section 338 election for CFCT. In both 1994 and 1995, CFCT has subpart F income resulting from operations.

(b) For taxable year 1994, X and Y are United States shareholders on the last day of CFCT's taxable year, so pursuant to section 951(a)(1)(A) each must include in income its pro rata share of CFCT's subpart F income for 1994. Because P's holding period in the CFCT stock acquired from X does not begin until January 1, 1995, P is not a United States shareholder on the last day of 1994 for purposes of section 951(a)(1)(A) (see §1.951-1(f)). X must then determine the extent to which section 1248 recharacterizes its gain on the sale of CFCT stock as a dividend.

(c) For the short taxable year ending June 30, 1995, Y is considered to own the CFCT stock sold to P at the close of CFCT's acquisition date. Because the acquisition date is the last day of CFCT's taxable year, Y and P are United States shareholders on the last day of CFCT's taxable year. Pursuant to section 951(a)(1)(A), each must include its pro rata share of CFCT's subpart F income for the short taxable year ending June 30, 1995. This includes any income generated on the deemed sale of CFCT's assets. Y must then determine the extent to which section 1248 recharacterizes its gain on the sale of the CFCT stock as a dividend, taking into account any increase in CFCT's earnings and profits due to the deemed sale of assets.

Example 4. Acquisition of control for purposes of section 951 prior to the acquisition date. FS owns 100% of the FT stock. On July 1, 1994, P buys 60% of the FT stock. On December 31, 1994, P buys the remaining 40% of the FT stock and makes a section 338 election for FT. For tax year 1994, FT has earnings and profits of $1,000 (including earnings resulting from the deemed sale). The section 338 election results in $500 of subpart F income. As a result of the section 338 election, P must include in gross income the following amount under section 951(a)(1)(A) (see §1.951-[1](b)(2)):

FT's subpart F income for 1994	$500.00
Less: reduction under section 951(a)(2)(A) for period (1-1-94 through 7-1-94) during which FT is not a controlled foreign corporation ($500 × 182/365)	249.32
Subpart F income as limited by section 951 (a)(2)(A)	$250.68
P's pro rata share of subpart F income as determined under section 951(a)(2)(A) (60% × 250.68)	$150.41

Example 5. Coordination with section 936. (a) T is a corporation for which a section 936 election has been made. P makes a qualified stock purchase of T and makes a section 338 election for T.

(b) T's deemed sale of assets under section 338 constitutes a sale for purposes of subtitle A of the Internal Revenue Code, including section 936(a)(1)(A)(ii). To the extent that the assets deemed sold are used in the conduct of an active trade or business in a possession for purposes of section 936(a)(1)(A)(i), and assuming all the other conditions of section 936 are satisfied, the income from the deemed sale qualifies for the credit granted by section 936(a). The source of income from the deemed sale is determined as if the assets had actually been sold and is not affected for purposes of section 936 by section 338(h)(16).

(c) Because new T is treated a new corporation for purposes of subtitle A of the Internal Revenue Code, the three year testing period in section 936(a)(2)(A) begins again for new T on the day following T's acquisition date. Thus, if the character or source of old T's gross income disqualified it for the credit under section 936, a fresh start is allowed by a section 338 election. [Reg. §1.338-9.]

☐ [*T.D. 8515, 1-12-94. Redesignated by T.D. 8858, 1-5-2000. Amended by T.D. 8940, 2-12-2001 and T.D. 9959, 12-28-2021 (corrected 7-26-2022).*]

[Reg. §1.338-10]

§1.338-10. Filing of returns.—(a) *Returns including tax liability from deemed asset sale.*—(1) *In general.*—Except as provided in paragraphs (a)(2) and (3) of this section, any deemed sale tax consequences are reported on the final return of old target filed for old target's taxable year that ends at the close of the acquisition date. Paragraphs (a)(2), (3) and (4) of this section do not apply to elections under section 338(h)(10). If old target is the common parent of an affiliated group, the final return may be a consolidated return (any such consolidated return must also include any deemed sale tax consequences of any members of the consolidated group that are acquired by the purchasing corporation on the same acquisition date as old target).

(2) *Old target's final taxable year otherwise included in consolidated return of selling group.*—(i) *General rule.*—If the selling group files a consolidated return for the period that includes the acquisition date, old target is disaffiliated from that group immediately before the deemed asset sale and must file a deemed sale return separate from the group, which includes only the deemed sale tax consequences and the carryover items specified in paragraph (a)(2)(iii) of this section. The deemed asset sale occurs at the close of the acquisition date and is the last transaction of old target and the only transaction reported on the separate return. Except as provided in §1.338-1(d) (regarding certain transactions on the acquisition date), any transactions of old target occurring on the acquisition date other than the deemed asset sale are included in the selling group's consolidated return. A deemed sale return includes a combined deemed sale return as defined in paragraph (a)(4) of this section.

(ii) *Separate taxable year.*—The deemed asset sale included in the deemed sale return under this paragraph (a)(2) occurs in a separate taxable year, except that old target's taxable year of the sale and the consolidated year of the selling group that includes the acquisition date are treated as the same year for purposes of determining the number of years in a carryover or carryback period.

(iii) *Carryover and carryback of tax attributes.*—Target's attributes may be carried over to, and carried back from, the deemed sale return under the rules applicable to a corporation that ceases to be a member of a consolidated group.

(iv) *Old target is a component member of purchasing corporation's controlled group.*—For purposes of its deemed sale return, target is a component member of the controlled group of corporations including the purchasing corporation unless target is treated as an excluded member under section 1563(b)(2).

(3) *Old target is an S corporation.*—If target is an S corporation for the period that ends on the day before the acquisition date and a section 338 election (but not a section 338(h)(10) election) is filed for target, old target files a return as a C corporation reflecting its activities on the acquisition date, including target's deemed sale. See section 1362(d)(2). For purposes of this return, target is a component member of the controlled group of corporations including the

purchasing corporation unless target is treated as an excluded member under section 1563(b)(2).

(4) *Combined deemed sale return.*—(i) *General rule.*—Under section 338(h)(15), a combined deemed sale return (combined return) may be filed for all targets from a single selling consolidated group (as defined in §1.338(h)(10)-1(b)(3)) that are acquired by the purchasing corporation on the same acquisition date and that otherwise would be required to file separate deemed sale returns. The combined return must include all such targets. For example, T and T1 may be included in a combined return if—

(A) T and T1 are directly owned subsidiaries of S;

(B) S is the common parent of a consolidated group; and

(C) P makes qualified stock purchases of T and T1 on the same acquisition date.

(ii) *Gain and loss offsets.*—Gains and losses recognized on the deemed asset sales by targets included in a combined return are treated as the gains and losses of a single target. In addition, loss carryovers of a target that were not subject to the separate return limitation year restrictions (SRLY restrictions) of the consolidated return regulations while that target was a member of the selling consolidated group may be applied without limitation to the gains of other targets included in the combined return. If, however, a target has loss carryovers that were subject to the SRLY restrictions while that target was a member of the selling consolidated group, the use of those losses in the combined return continues to be subject to those restrictions, applied in the same manner as if the combined return were a consolidated return. A similar rule applies, when appropriate, to other tax attributes.

(iii) *Procedure for filing a combined return.*—A combined return is made by filing a single corporation income tax return in lieu of separate deemed sale returns for all targets required to be included in the combined return. The combined return reflects the deemed asset sales of all targets required to be included in the combined return. If the targets included in the combined return constitute a single affiliated group within the meaning of section 1504(a), the income tax return is signed by an officer of the common parent of that group. Otherwise, the return must be signed by an officer of each target included in the combined return. Rules similar to the rules in §1.1502-75(j) apply for purposes of preparing the combined return. The combined return must include a statement entitled, "ELECTION TO FILE A COMBINED RETURN UNDER SECTION 338(h)(15)." The statement must include—

(A) The name, address, and employer identification number of each target required to be included in the combined return; and

(B) The following declaration: EACH TARGET IDENTIFIED IN THIS ELECTION TO FILE A COMBINED RETURN CONSENTS TO THE FILING OF A COMBINED RETURN.

(iv) *Consequences of filing a combined return.*—Each target included in a combined return is severally liable for any tax associated with the combined return. See §1.338-1(b)(3).

(5) *Deemed sale excluded from purchasing corporation's consolidated return.*—Old target may not be considered a member of any affiliated group that includes the purchasing corporation with respect to its deemed asset sale.

(6) *Due date for old target's final return.*—(i) *General rule.*—Old target's final return is generally due on the 15th day of the third calendar month following the month in which the acquisition date occurs. See section 6072 (time for filing income tax returns).

(ii) *Application of §1.1502-76(c).*—(A) *In general.*—Section 1.1502-76(c) applies to old target's final return if old target was a member of a selling group that did not file consolidated returns for the taxable year of the common parent that precedes the year that includes old target's acquisition date. If the selling group has not filed a consolidated return that includes old target's taxable period that ends on the acquisition date, target may, on or before the final return due date (including extensions), either—

(1) File a deemed sale return on the assumption that the selling group will file the consolidated return; or

(2) File a return for so much of old target's taxable period as ends at the close of the acquisition date on the assumption that the consolidated return will not be filed.

(B) *Deemed extension.*—For purposes of applying § 1.1502-76(c)(2), an extension of time to file old target's final return is considered to be in effect until the last date for making the election under section 338.

(C) *Erroneous filing of deemed sale return.*—If, under this paragraph (a)(6)(ii), target files a deemed sale return but the selling group does not file a consolidated return, target must file a substituted return for old target not later than the due date (including extensions) for the return of the common parent with which old target would have been included in the consolidated return. The substituted return is for so much of old target's taxable year as ends at the close of the acquisition date. Under § 1.1502-76(c)(2), the deemed sale return is not considered a return for purposes of section 6011 (relating to the general requirement of filing a return) if a substituted return must be filed.

(D) *Erroneous filing of return for regular tax year.*—If, under this paragraph (a)(6)(ii), target files a return for so much of old target's regular taxable year as ends at the close of the acquisition date but the selling group files a consolidated return, target must file an amended return for old target not later than the due date (including extensions) for the selling group's consolidated return. (The amended return is a deemed sale return.)

(E) *Last date for payment of tax.*—If either a substituted or amended final return of old target is filed under this paragraph (a)(6)(ii), the last date prescribed for payment of tax is the final return due date (as defined in paragraph (a)(6)(i) of this section).

(7) *Examples.*—The following examples illustrate this paragraph (a):

Example 1. (i) S is the common parent of a consolidated group that includes T. The S group files calendar year consolidated returns. At the close of June 30 of Year 1, P makes a qualified stock purchase of T from S. P makes a section 338 election for T, and T's deemed asset sale occurs as of the close of T's acquisition date (June 30).

(ii) T is considered disaffiliated for purposes of reporting the deemed sale tax consequences. Accordingly, T is included in the S group's consolidated return through T's acquisition date except that the tax liability for the deemed sale tax consequences is reported in a separate deemed sale return of T. Provided that T is not treated as an excluded member under section 1563(b)(2), T is a component member of P's controlled group for the taxable year of the deemed asset sale, and the taxable income bracket amounts available in calculating tax on the deemed sale return must be limited accordingly.

(iii) If P purchased the stock of T at 10 a.m. on June 30 of Year 1, the results would be the same. See paragraph (a)(2)(i) of this section.

Example 2. The facts are the same as in *Example 1*, except that the S group does not file consolidated returns. T must file a separate return for its taxable year ending on June 30 of Year 1, which return includes the deemed asset sale.

(b) *Waiver.*—(1) *Certain additions to tax.*—An addition to tax or additional amount (addition) under subchapter A of chapter 68 of the Internal Revenue Code arising on or before the last day for making the election under section 338 because of circumstances that would not exist but for an election under section 338 is waived if—

(i) Under the particular statute the addition is excusable upon a showing of reasonable cause; and

(ii) Corrective action is taken on or before the last day.

(2) *Notification.*—The Internal Revenue Service should be notified at the time of correction (e.g., by attaching a statement to a return that constitutes corrective action) that the waiver rule of this paragraph (b) is being asserted.

(3) *Elections or other actions required to be specified on a timely filed return.*—(i) *In general.*—If paragraph (b)(1) of this section applies or would apply if there were an underpayment, any election or other action that must be specified on a timely filed return for the taxable period covered by the late filed return described in paragraph (b)(1) of this section is considered timely if specified on a late-filed return filed on or before the last day for making the election under section 338.

(ii) *New target in purchasing corporation's consolidated return.*—If new target is includible for its first taxable year in a consolidated return filed by the affiliated group of which the purchasing corporation is a member on or before the last day for making the election under section 338, any election or other action that must be specified in a timely filed return for new target's first taxable year (but which is not specified in the consolidated return) is considered timely if specified in an amended return filed on or before such last day, at the place where the consolidated return was filed.

(4) *Examples.*—The following examples illustrate this paragraph (b):

Example 1. T is an unaffiliated corporation with a tax year ending March 31. At the close of September 20 of Year 1, P makes a qualified stock purchase of T. P does not join in filing a consolidated return. P makes a section 338 election for T on or before June 15 of Year 2, which causes T's taxable year to end as of the close of September 20 of Year 1. An income tax return for T's taxable period ending on September 20 of Year 1 was due on December 15 of Year 1. Additions to tax for failure to file a return and to pay tax shown on a return will not be imposed if T's return is filed and the tax paid on or before June 15 of Year 2. (This waiver applies even if the acquisition date coincides with the last day of T's former taxable year, i.e., March 31 of Year 2.) Interest on any underpayment of tax for old T's short taxable year ending September 20 of Year 1 runs from December 15 of Year 1. A statement indicating that the waiver rule of this paragraph is being asserted should be attached to T's return.

Example 2. Assume the same facts as in *Example 1.* Assume further that new T adopts the calendar year by filing, on or before June 15 of Year 2, its first return (for the period beginning on September 21 of Year 1 and ending on December 31 of Year 1) indicating that a calendar year is chosen. See § 1.338-1(b)(1). Any additions to tax or amounts described in this paragraph (b) that arise because of the late filing of a return for the period ending on December 31 of Year 1 are waived, because they are based on circumstances that would not exist but for the section 338 election. Notwithstanding this waiver, however, the return is still considered due March 15 of Year 2, and interest on any underpayment runs from that date.

Example 3. Assume the same facts as in *Example 2*, except that T's former taxable year ends on October 31. Although prior to the election old T had a return due on January 15 of Year 2 for its year ending October 31 of Year 1, that return need not be filed because a timely election under section 338 was made. Instead, old T must file a final return for the period ending on September 20 of Year 1, which is due on December 15 of Year 1.

(c) *Effective/applicability date.*—Paragraph (a)(4)(iii) of this section applies to any taxable year beginning on or after May 30, 2006. However, taxpayers may apply paragraph (a)(4)(iii) of this section to any original Federal income tax return (including any amended return filed on or before the due date (including extensions) of such original return) timely filed on or after May 30, 2006. For taxable years beginning before May 30, 2006, see § 1.338-10 as contained in 26 CFR part 1 in effect on April 1, 2006. [Reg. § 1.338-10.]

☐ [T.D. 8940, 2-12-2001. Amended by T.D. 9264, 5-26-2006 and T.D. 9329, 6-13-2007.]

[Reg. § 1.338-11]

§ 1.338-11. Effect of section 338 election on insurance company targets.—(a) *In general.*—This section provides rules that apply when an election under section 338 is made for a target that is an insurance company. The rules in this section apply in addition to those generally applicable upon the making of an election under section 338. In the case of a conflict between the provisions of this section and other provisions of the Internal Revenue Code or regulations, the rules set forth in this section determine the Federal income tax treatment of the parties and the transaction when a section 338 election is made for an insurance company target.

(b) *Computation of ADSP and AGUB.*—(1) *Reserves taken into account as a liability.*—Old target's tax reserves are the reserves for Federal income tax purposes for any insurance, annuity, and reinsurance contracts deemed sold by old target to new target in the deemed asset sale. The amount of old target's tax reserves is the amount that is properly taken into account by old target for the contracts at the close of the taxable year that includes the deemed sale tax consequences (before giving effect to the deemed asset sale and assumption reinsurance transaction). Old target's tax reserves are a liability of old target taken into account in determining ADSP under § 1.338-4 and a liability of new target taken into account in determining AGUB under § 1.338-5.

(2) *Allocation of ADSP and AGUB to specific insurance contracts.*—For purposes of allocating AGUB and ADSP under §§ 1.338-6 and 1.338-7, the fair market value of a specific insurance, reinsurance or annuity contract or group of insurance, reinsurance or annuity contracts (*insurance contracts*) is the amount of the ceding commission a willing reinsurer would pay a willing ceding company in an arm's length transaction for the reinsurance of the contracts if the gross reinsurance premium for the contracts were equal to old target's tax reserves for the contracts. See § 1.197-2(g)(5) for rules concerning the treatment of the amount allocable to insurance contracts acquired in the deemed asset sale.

(c) *Application of assumption reinsurance principles.*—(1) *In general.*—If a target is an insurance company, the deemed sale of insurance contracts is treated for Federal income tax purposes as an assumption reinsurance transaction between old target, as the reinsured or ceding company, and new target, as the reinsurer or acquiring company, at the close of the acquisition date. The Federal income tax treatment of the assumption reinsurance transaction is determined under the applicable provisions of subchapter L, chapter 1, subtitle A of the Internal Revenue Code, as modified by the rules set forth in this section.

(2) *Reinsurance premium.*—Old target is deemed to pay a gross amount of premium in the assumption reinsurance transaction equal to the amount of old target's tax reserves for the insurance contracts that are acquisition date assets (*acquired contracts*). New target is deemed to receive a reinsurance premium in the amount of old target's tax reserves for the acquired contracts. See paragraph (d) of this section for circumstances in which new target is deemed to receive additional premium. See § 1.817-4(d)(2) for old target's and new target's treatment of the premium.

(3) *Ceding commission.*—Old target is deemed to receive a ceding commission in an amount equal to the amount of ADSP allocated to the acquired contracts, as determined under §§ 1.338-6 and 1.338-7 and paragraph (b) of this section. New target is deemed to pay a ceding commission in an amount equal to the amount of AGUB allocated to the acquired contracts, as determined under §§ 1.338-6 and 1.338-7 and paragraph (b) of this section. See § 1.817-4(d)(2) for old target's and new target's treatment of the ceding commission.

(4) *Examples.*—The following examples illustrate this paragraph (c):

Example 1. (i) *Facts.* On January 1, 2003, T, an insurance company, has the following assets with the following fair market values: $10 cash, $30 of securities, $10 of equipment, a life insurance contract having a value, under paragraph (b)(2) of this section, of $17, and goodwill and going concern value. T has tax reserves of $50 and no other liabilities. On January 1, 2003, P purchases all of the stock of T for $16 and makes a section 338 election for T. For purposes of the capitalization requirements of section 848, assume new T has $20 of general deductions in its first taxable year ending on December 31, 2003, and earns no other premiums during the year.

(ii) *Analysis.* (A) For Federal income tax purposes, the section 338 election results in a deemed sale of the assets of old T to new T. Old T's ADSP is $66 ($16 amount realized for the T stock plus $50 liabilities). New T's AGUB also is $66 ($16 basis for the T stock plus $50 liabilities). See paragraph (b)(1) of this section. Each of the AGUB and ADSP is allocated under the residual method of § 1.338-6 to determine the purchase or sale price of each asset transferred. Each of the AGUB and ADSP is allocated as follows: $10 to cash (Class I), $30 to the securities (Class II), $10 to equipment (Class V), $16 to the life insurance contract (Class VI), and $0 to goodwill and going concern value (Class VII).

(B) Under section 1001, old T's amount realized for the securities is $30 and for the equipment is $10. As a result of the deemed asset sale, there is an assumption reinsurance transaction between old T (as ceding company) and new T (as reinsurer) at the close of the acquisition date for the life insurance contract issued by old T. See paragraph (c)(1) of this section. Although the assumption reinsurance transaction results in a $50 decrease in old T's reserves, which is taxable income to old T, the reinsurance premium paid by old T is deductible by old T. Under paragraph (c)(2) of this section, old T is deemed to pay a reinsurance premium equal to the reserve for the life insurance contract immediately before the deemed asset sale ($50) and is deemed to receive a ceding commission from new T. Under paragraph (c)(3) of this section, the portion of the ADSP allocated to the life insurance contract is $16; thus, the ceding commission is $16. Old T, therefore, is deemed to pay new T a reinsurance premium of $34 ($50 – $16 = $34). Old T also has $34 of net negative consideration for purposes of section 848. See paragraph (f) of this section for rules relating to the effect of a section 338 election on the capitalization of amounts under section 848.

(C) New T obtains an initial basis of $30 in the securities and $10 in the equipment. New T is deemed to receive a reinsurance premium from old T in an amount equal to the $50 of reserves for the life insurance contract and to pay old T a $16 ceding commission for the contract. See paragraphs (c)(2) and (3) of this section. Accordingly, new T includes $50 of premium in income and deducts $50 for its increase in reserves. For purposes of section 848, new T has $34 of net positive consideration for the deemed assumption reinsurance transaction. Because the only contract involved in the deemed assumption reinsurance transaction is a life insurance contract, new T must capitalize $2.62 ($34 × 7.7% = $2.62) under section 848. New T will amortize the $2.62 as provided under section 848. New T's adjusted basis in the life insurance contract, which is an amortizable section 197 intangible, is $13.38, the excess of the $16 ceding commission over the $2.62 capitalized under section 848. See section 197 and § 1.197-2(g)(5). New T deducts the $2.62 of the ceding commission

that is not amortizable under section 197 because it is reflected in the amount capitalized under section 848 and also deducts the remaining $17.38 of its general deductions.

Example 2. (i) *Facts.* Assume the same facts as in *Example 1*, except the life insurance contract has a value of $0 and the fair market value of T's securities are $60. Thus, to reinsure the contract in an arm's length transaction, T would have to pay the reinsurer a reinsurance premium in excess of T's $50 of tax reserves for the contract.

(ii) *Analysis.* (A) For Federal income tax purposes, the section 338 election results in a deemed sale of the assets of old T to new T. Old T's ADSP is $66 ($16 amount realized for the T stock plus $50 liabilities). New T's AGUB also is $66 ($16 basis for the T stock plus $50 liabilities). See paragraph (b)(1) of this section. Each of the AGUB and ADSP is allocated under the residual method of § 1.338-6 to determine the purchase or sale price of each asset transferred. Each of the AGUB and ADSP is allocated as follows: $10 to cash (Class I), $56 to the securities (Class II), $0 to the equipment (Class V), $0 to the life insurance contract (Class VI), and $0 to goodwill and going concern value (Class VII).

(B) Under section 1001, old T's amount realized for the securities is $56 and for the equipment is $0. As a result of the deemed asset sale, there is an assumption reinsurance transaction between old T (as ceding company) and new T (as reinsurer) at the close of the acquisition date for the life insurance contract issued by old T. See paragraph (c)(1) of this section. Although the assumption reinsurance transaction results in a $50 decrease in old T's reserves, which is taxable income to old T, the reinsurance premium deemed paid by old T to new T is deductible by old T. Under paragraph (c)(2) of this section, old T is deemed to pay a reinsurance premium equal to the reserve for the life insurance contract immediately before the deemed asset sale ($50), and is deemed to receive from new T a ceding commission equal to the amount of AGUB allocated to the life insurance contract ($0), as provided in paragraph (c)(3) of this section. Old T also has $50 of net negative consideration for purposes of section 848. See paragraph (f) of section for rules relating to the effect of a section 338 election on capitalization amounts under section 848.

(C) New T obtains an initial basis of $56 in the securities (with a fair market value of $60) and $0 in the equipment (with a fair market value of $10). New T is deemed to receive a reinsurance premium from old T in an amount equal to the $50 of reserves for the life insurance contract. Accordingly, new T includes $50 of premium in income and deducts $50 for its increase in reserves. For purposes of section 848, new T has $50 of net positive consideration for the deemed assumption reinsurance transaction. Because the only contract involved in the assumption reinsurance transaction is a life insurance contract, new T must capitalize $3.85 ($50 × 7.7%) under section 848 from the transaction and deducts the remaining $16.15 of its general deductions. Because new T allocates $0 of the AGUB to the insurance contract, no amount is amortizable under section 197 with respect to the insurance contract. See § 1.338-11T(d) for rules on adjustments required if new T increases its reserves for, or reinsures at a loss, the acquired life insurance contract.

(d) *Reserve increases by new target after the deemed asset sale.*—(1) *In general.*—If in new target's first taxable year or any subsequent year, new target increases its reserves for any acquired contracts, new target is treated as receiving an additional premium, which is computed under paragraph (d)(3) of this section, in the assumption reinsurance transaction described in paragraph (c)(1) of this section. New target includes the additional premium in gross income for the taxable year in which new target increases its reserves for acquired contracts. New target's increase in reserves for the insurance contracts acquired in the deemed asset sale is a liability of new target not originally taken into account in determining AGUB that is subsequently taken into account. Thus, AGUB is increased by the amount of the additional premium included in new target's gross income. See §§ 1.338-5(b)(2)(ii) and 1.338-7. Old target has no deduction under this paragraph (d) and makes no adjustments under §§ 1.338-4(b)(2)(ii) and 1.338-7.

(2) *Exception.*—New target is not treated as receiving additional premium under paragraph (d)(1) of this section if it is under state receivership as of the close of the taxable year for which the increase in reserves occurs.

(3) *Amount of additional premium.*—(i) *In general.*—The additional premium taken into account under this paragraph (d) is an amount equal to the sum of the positive amounts described in paragraphs (d)(3)(ii) through (iv) of this section. However, the additional premium cannot exceed the limitation described in paragraph (d)(4) of this section.

(ii) *Increases in unpaid loss reserves.*—The positive amount with respect to unpaid loss reserves is computed using the formula $A/B \times (C - [D + E])$ where—

(A) A equals old target's discounted unpaid losses (determined under section 846) included in AGUB under paragraph 11(b)(1) of this section;

(B) B equals old target's undiscounted unpaid losses (determined under section 846(b)(1)) as of the close of the acquisition date;

(C) C equals new target's undiscounted unpaid losses (determined under section 846(b)(1)) at the end of the taxable year that are attributable to losses incurred by old target on or before acquisition date;

(D) D (which may be a negative number) equals old target's undiscounted unpaid losses as of the close of the acquisition date, reduced by the cumulative amount of losses, loss adjustment expenses, and reinsurance premiums paid by new target through the end of the taxable year for losses incurred by old target on or before the acquisition date; and

(E) E equals the amount obtained by dividing the cumulative amount of reserve increases taken into account under this paragraph (d) in prior taxable years by A/B.

(iii) *Increases in section 807(c) reserves.*—The positive amount with respect to the items referred to in section 807(c) other than discounted unpaid loss reserves is the sum of the net increases in such items that are required to be taken into account under section 807(f).

(iv) *Increases in other reserves.*—The positive amount with respect to reserves other than discounted unpaid loss reserves and other items referred to in section 807(c) is the net increase of those reserves due to changes in estimate, methodology, or other assumptions used to compute the reserves (including the adoption by new target of a methodology or assumptions different from those used by old target).

(4) *Limitation on additional premium.*—The additional premium taken into account by new target under paragraph (d)(1) of this section is limited to the excess, if any, of—

(i) The fair market value of old target's assets acquired by new target in the deemed asset sale (other than Class VI and Class VII assets); over

(ii) The AGUB allocated to those assets (including increases in AGUB allocated to those assets as the result of reserve increases by new target in prior taxable years).

(5) *Treatment of additional premium under section 848.*—If a portion of the positive amounts described in paragraphs (d)(3)(ii) and (iii) of this section are attributable to an increase in reserves for specified insurance contracts (as defined in section 848(e)), new target takes an allocable portion of the additional premium in determining its specified policy acquisition expenses under section 848(c) for the taxable year of the reserve increase.

(6) *Examples.*—The following examples illustrate this paragraph (d):

Example 1. (i) *Facts.* On January 1, 2006, P purchases all of the stock of T, a non-life insurance company, for $120 and makes a section 338 election for T. On the acquisition date, old T has total reserve liabilities under state law of $725, consisting of undiscounted unpaid losses of $625 and unearned premiums of $100. Old T's tax reserves on the acquisition date are $580, which consist of discounted unpaid losses (as defined in section 846) of $500 and unearned premiums (as computed under section 832(b)(4)(B)) of $80. Old T has Class I through Class V assets with a fair market value of $800. Old T also has a Class VI asset with a fair market value of $75, consisting of the future profit stream of certain insurance contracts. During 2006, new T makes loss and loss adjustment expense payments of $200 with respect to the unpaid losses incurred by old T before the acquisition date. As of December 31, 2006, new T reports undiscounted unpaid losses of $475 attributable to losses incurred before the acquisition date. The related amount of discounted unpaid losses (as defined in section 846) for those losses is $390.

(ii) *Computation and allocation of AGUB.* Under $1.338-5 and paragraph (b)(1) of this section, as of the acquisition date, AGUB is $700, reflecting the sum of the amount paid for old T's stock ($120) and the tax reserves assumed by new T in the transaction ($580). The fair market value of old T's Class I through V assets is $800, whereas the AGUB available for such assets under $1.338-6 is $700. There is no AGUB available for old T's Class VI assets, even though such assets have a fair market value of $75 on the acquisition date.

(iii) *Adjustments for increases in reserves for unpaid losses.* Under paragraph (d) of this section, new T must determine whether there are any amounts by which it increased its unpaid loss reserves that will be treated as an additional premium and an increase in AGUB. New T applies the formula of paragraph (d)(3) of this section, where A equals $500, B equals $625, C equals $475, D equals $425 ($625 - $200), and E equals $0. Under this formula, new T is treated as having increased its reserves for discounted unpaid losses attributa-

ble to losses incurred by old T by $40 ($500/$625 × ($475 – [$425+0]). The limitation under paragraph (d)(5) of this section based on the difference between the fair market value of old T's Class I through Class V assets and the AGUB allocated to such assets is $100. Accordingly, new T includes an additional premium of $40 in gross income for 2006, and increases the AGUB allocated to old T's Class I through Class V assets to reflect this additional premium.

Example 2. (i) *Facts.* Assume the same facts as in *Example 1.* Further assume that during 2007 new T deducts total loss and loss expense payments of $375 with respect to losses incurred by old T before the acquisition date. On December 31, 2007, new T reports undiscounted unpaid losses of $150 with respect to losses incurred before the acquisition date. The related amount of discounted unpaid losses (as defined in section 846) for those unpaid losses is $125.

(ii) *Analysis.* New T must determine whether any amounts by which it increased its unpaid losses during 2007 will be treated as an additional premium in paragraph (d)(3) of this section. New T applies the formula under paragraph (d)(3) of this section, where A equals $500, B equals $625, C equals $150, D equals $50 ($625 - $575), and E equals $50 ($40 divided by .8). In paragraph (d)(3) of this section, new T is treated as increasing its reserves for discounted unpaid losses by $40 during 2007 with respect to losses incurred by old T ($500/$625 × ($150 - [$50 + $50]). New T determines the limitation of paragraph (d)(5) of this section by comparing the $800 fair market value of the Class I through V assets on the acquisition date to the $740 AGUB allocated to such assets (which includes the $40 addition to AGUB included during 2006). Thus, new T recognizes $40 of additional premium as a result of the increase in reserves during 2007, and adjusts the AGUB allocable to the Class I through V assets acquired from old T to reflect such additional premium.

Example 3. (i) *Facts.* The facts are the same as *Example 2,* except that on January 1, 2008, new T reinsures the outstanding liability with respect to losses incurred by old T before the acquisition date through a portfolio reinsurance transaction with R, another non-life insurance company. R agrees to assume any remaining liability relating to losses incurred by old T before the acquisition date in exchange for a reinsurance premium of $200. Accordingly, as of December 31, 2008, new T reports no undiscounted unpaid losses with respect to losses incurred by old T before the acquisition date.

(ii) *Analysis.* New T must determine whether any amount by which it increased its unpaid loss reserves will be treated as an additional premium under paragraph (d) of this section. New T applies the formula of paragraph (d)(3) of this section, where A equals $500, B equals $625, C equals $0, and D equals -$150 ($625 - ($575 + $200), and E equals $100 ($80 divided by .8). Thus, new T is treated as having increased its discounted unpaid losses by $40 in 2008 with respect to losses incurred by old T before the acquisition date ($500/$625 × (0 - [-$150 + $100]). New T includes this positive amount in gross income, subject to the limitation of paragraph (d)(4) of this section. The limitation of paragraph (d)(4) of this section equals $20, which is computed by comparing the $800 fair market value of the Class I through V assets acquired from old T with the $780 AGUB allocated to such assets (which includes the $40 addition to AGUB in 2006 and the $40 addition to AGUB in 2007). Thus, New T includes $20 in additional premium, and increases the AGUB allocated to the Class I through V assets acquired from old T by $20. As a result of these adjustments, the limitation under paragraph (d)(4) of this section is reduced to zero.

(7) *Effective/applicability date.*—(i) *In general.*—This section applies to increases to reserves made by new target after a deemed asset sale occurring on or after April 10, 2006.

(ii) *Application to pre-effective date increases to reserves.*—If either new target makes an election under §1.338(i)-1(c)(2) or old target makes an election under §1.338(i)-1(c)(3) to apply the rules of this section, in whole, to a qualified stock purchase occurring before April 10, 2006, then the rules contained in this section shall apply in whole to the qualified stock purchase.

(iii) *Application of paragraphs (d)(2) and (3) of this section.*—Paragraphs (d)(2) and (3) of this section apply to taxable years beginning after October 13, 2020 For taxable years beginning on or before such date, see paragraph (d) of this section as contained in 26 CFR part 1 revised as of April 1, 2020.

(e) *Effect of section 338 election on section 846(e) election.*—(1) *In general.*—New target and old target are treated as the same corporation for purposes of an election by old target to use its historical loss payment pattern under section 846(e). See §1.338-1(b)(2)(vii). Therefore, if old target has a section 846(e) election in effect on the acquisition date, new target will continue to use the historical loss payment pattern of old target to discount unpaid losses incurred in accident years covered by the election, unless new target elects to revoke the section 846(e) election. In addition, new target may consider old target's historical loss payment pattern when determining whether to make the section 846(e) election for a determination year that includes or is subsequent to the acquisition date.

(2) *Revocation of existing section 846(e) election.*—New target may revoke old target's section 846(e) election to use its historical loss payment pattern to discount unpaid losses. If new target elects to revoke old target's section 846(e) election, new target will use the industry-wide patterns determined by the Secretary to discount unpaid losses incurred in accident years beginning on or after the acquisition date through the subsequent determination year. New target may revoke old target's section 846(e) election by attaching a statement to new target's original tax return for its first taxable year.

(f) *Effect of section 338 election on old target's capitalization amounts under section 848.*—(1) *Determination of net consideration for specified insurance contracts.*—For purposes of applying section 848 and §1.848-2(f) to the deemed assumption reinsurance transaction, old target's net consideration (either positive or negative) for each category of specified insurance contracts is an amount equal to—

    (i) The allocable portion of the ceding commission (if any) relating to contracts in that category; less

    (ii) The amount by which old target's tax reserves for contracts in that category has been reduced as a result of the deemed assumption reinsurance transaction.

(2) *Determination of capitalization amount.*—Except as provided in §1.381(c)(22)-1(b)(13)—

    (i) If, after the deemed asset sale, old target has an amount otherwise required to be capitalized under section 848 for the taxable year or an unamortized balance of specified policy acquisition expenses from prior taxable years, then old target deducts such remaining amount or unamortized balance as an expense incurred in the taxable year that includes the deemed sale tax consequences; and

    (ii) If, after the deemed asset sale, the negative capitalization amount resulting from the reinsurance transaction exceeds the amount that old target can deduct under section 848(f)(1), then old target's capitalization amount is treated as zero at the close of the taxable year that includes the deemed sale tax consequences.

(3) *Section 381 transactions.*—For transactions described in section 381, see §1.381(c)(22)-1(b)(13).

(g) *Effect of section 338 election on policyholders surplus account.*—Except as specifically provided in §1.381(c)(22)-1(b)(7), the deemed asset sale effects a distribution of old target's policyholders surplus account to the extent the grossed-up amount realized on the sale to the purchasing corporation of the purchasing corporation's recently purchased target stock (as defined in §1.338-4(c)) exceeds old target's shareholders surplus account under section 815(c).

(h) *Effect of section 338 election on section 847 special estimated tax payments.*—If old target had elected to claim an additional deduction under section 847 for the taxable year that includes the deemed sale tax consequences or any earlier years, the amount remaining in old target's special loss discount account under section 847(3) must be reduced to the extent it relates to contracts transferred to new target and the amount of such reduction must be included in old target's gross income for the taxable year that includes the deemed sale tax consequences. Old target may apply the balance of its special estimated tax account as a credit against any tax resulting from such inclusion in gross income. Any special estimated tax payments remaining after this credit are voided and, therefore, are not available for credit or refund. Under section 847(1), new target is permitted to claim a section 847 deduction for losses incurred before the deemed asset sale, subject to the general requirement that new target makes timely special estimated tax payments equal to the tax benefit resulting from this deduction. See §1.381(c)(22)-1(c)(14) regarding the carryover of the special loss discount account attributable to contracts transferred in a section 381 transaction. [Reg. §1.338-11.]

☐ [*T.D. 9257, 4-7-2006. Amended by T.D. 9377, 1-22-2008 and T.D. 9911, 10-9-2020.*]

[Reg. §1.338(h)(10)-1]

§1.338(h)(10)-1. Deemed asset sale and liquidation.—(a) *Scope.*—This section prescribes rules for qualification for a section 338(h)(10) election and for making a section 338(h)(10) election. This section also prescribes the consequences of such election. The rules of this section are in addition to the rules of §§1.338-1 through 1.338-10 and, in appropriate cases, apply instead of the rules of §§1.338-1 through 1.338-10.

(b) *Definitions.*—(1) *Consolidated target.*—A *consolidated target* is a target that is a member of a consolidated group within the meaning of §1.1502-1(h) on the acquisition date and is not the common parent of the group on that date.

(2) *Selling consolidated group.*—A *selling consolidated group* is the consolidated group of which the consolidated target is a member on the acquisition date.

(3) *Selling affiliate; affiliated target.*—A *selling affiliate* is a domestic corporation that owns on the acquisition date an amount of stock in a domestic target, which amount of stock is described in section 1504(a)(2), and does not join in filing a consolidated return with the target. In such case, the target is an *affiliated target.*

(4) *S corporation target.*—An *S corporation target* is a target that is an S corporation immediately before the acquisition date.

(5) *S corporation shareholders.*—*S corporation shareholders* are the S corporation target's shareholders. Unless otherwise indicated, a reference to S corporation shareholders refers both to S corporation shareholders who do and those who do not sell their target stock.

(6) *Liquidation.*—Any reference in this section to a liquidation is treated as a reference to the transfer described in paragraph (d)(4) of this section notwithstanding its ultimate characterization for Federal income tax purposes.

(c) *Section 338(h)(10) election.*—(1) *In general.*—A section 338(h)(10) election may be made for T if P acquires stock meeting the requirements of section 1504(a)(2) from a selling consolidated group, a selling affiliate, or the S corporation shareholders in a qualified stock purchase.

(2) *Availability of section 338(h)(10) election in certain multi-step transactions.*—Notwithstanding anything to the contrary in §1.338-3(c)(1)(i), a section 338(h)(10) election may be made for T where P's acquisition of T stock, viewed independently, constitutes a qualified stock purchase and, after the stock acquisition, T merges or liquidates into P (or another member of the affiliated group that includes P), whether or not, under relevant provisions of law, including the step transaction doctrine, the acquisition of the T stock and the merger or liquidation of T qualify as a reorganization described in section 368(a). If a section 338(h)(10) election is made in a case where the acquisition of T stock followed by a merger or liquidation of T into P qualifies as a reorganization described in section 368(a), for all Federal tax purposes, P's acquisition of T stock is treated as a qualified stock purchase and is not treated as part of a reorganization described in section 368(a).

(3) *Simultaneous joint election requirement.*—A section 338(h)(10) election is made jointly by P and the selling consolidated group (or the selling affiliate or the S corporation shareholders) on Form 8023 in accordance with the instructions to the form. S corporation shareholders who do not sell their stock must also consent to the election. The section 338(h)(10) election must be made not later than the 15th day of the 9th month beginning after the month in which the acquisition date occurs.

(4) *Irrevocability.*—A section 338(h)(10) election is irrevocable. If a section 338(h)(10) election is made for T, a section 338 election is deemed made for T.

(5) *Effect of invalid election.*—If a section 338(h)(10) election for T is not valid, the section 338 election for T is also not valid.

(d) *Certain consequences of section 338(h)(10) election.*—For purposes of subtitle A of the Internal Revenue Code (except as provided in §1.338-1(b)(2)), the consequences to the parties of making a section 338(h)(10) election for T are as follows:

(1) *P.*—P is automatically deemed to have made a gain recognition election for its nonrecently purchased T stock, if any. The effect of a gain recognition election includes a taxable deemed sale by P on the acquisition date of any nonrecently purchased target stock. See §1.338-5(d).

(2) *New T.*—The AGUB for new T's assets is determined under §1.338-5 and is allocated among the acquisition date assets under §§1.338-6 and 1.338-7. Notwithstanding paragraph (d)(4) of this section (deemed liquidation of old T), new T remains liable for the tax liabilities of old T (including the tax liability for the deemed sale tax consequences). For example, new T remains liable for the tax liabilities of the members of any consolidated group that are attributable to taxable years in which those corporations and old T joined in the same consolidated return. See §1.1502-6(a).

(3) *Old T—deemed sale.*—(i) *In general.*—Old T is treated as transferring all of its assets to an unrelated person in exchange for consideration that includes the discharge of its liabilities in a single transaction at the close of the acquisition date (but before the deemed liquidation). See §1.338-1(a) regarding the tax characterization of the deemed asset sale. Except as provided in §1.338(h)(10)-1(d)(8) (regarding the installment method), old T recognizes all of the gain

realized on the deemed transfer of its assets in consideration for the ADSP. ADSP for old T is determined under §1.338-4 and allocated among the acquisition date assets under §§1.338-6 and 1.338-7. Old T realizes the deemed sale tax consequences from the deemed asset sale before the close of the acquisition date while old T is a member of the selling consolidated group (or owned by the selling affiliate or owned by the S corporation shareholders). If T is an affiliated target, or an S corporation target, the principles of §§1.338-2(c)(10) and 1.338-10(a)(1), (5), and (6)(i) apply to the return on which the deemed sale tax consequences are reported. When T is an S corporation target, T's S election continues in effect through the close of the acquisition date (including the time of the deemed asset sale and the deemed liquidation) notwithstanding section 1362(d)(2)(B). Also, when T is an S corporation target (but not a qualified subchapter S subsidiary), any direct and indirect subsidiaries of T which T has elected to treat as qualified subchapter S subsidiaries under section 1361(b)(3) remain qualified subchapter S subsidiaries through the close of the acquisition date.

(ii) *Tiered targets.*—In the case of parent-subsidiary chains of corporations making elections under section 338(h)(10), the deemed asset sale of a parent corporation is considered to precede that of its subsidiary. See §1.338-3(b)(4)(i).

(4) *Old T and selling consolidated group, selling affiliate, or S corporation shareholders—deemed liquidation; tax characterization.*—(i) *In general.*—Old T is treated as if, before the close of the acquisition date, after the deemed asset sale in paragraph (d)(3) of this section, and while old T is a member of the selling consolidated group (or owned by the selling affiliate or owned by the S corporation shareholders), it transferred all of its assets to members of the selling consolidated group, the selling affiliate, or S corporation shareholders and ceased to exist. The transfer from old T is characterized for Federal income tax purposes in the same manner as if the parties had actually engaged in the transactions deemed to occur because of this section and taking into account other transactions that actually occurred or are deemed to occur. For example, the transfer may be treated as a distribution in pursuance of a plan of reorganization, a distribution in complete cancellation or redemption of all its stock, one of a series of distributions in complete cancellation or redemption of all its stock in accordance with a plan of liquidation, or part of a circular flow of cash. In most cases, the transfer will be treated as a distribution in complete liquidation to which section 336 or 337 applies.

(ii) *Tiered targets.*—In the case of parent-subsidiary chains of corporations making elections under section 338(h)(10), the deemed liquidation of a subsidiary corporation is considered to precede the deemed liquidation of its parent.

(5) *Selling consolidated group, selling affiliate, or S corporation shareholders.*—(i) *In general.*—If T is an S corporation target, S corporation shareholders (whether or not they sell their stock) take their pro rata share of the deemed sale tax consequences into account under section 1366 and increase or decrease their basis in T stock under section 1367. Members of the selling consolidated group, the selling affiliate, or S corporation shareholders are treated as if, after the deemed asset sale in paragraph (d)(3) of this section and before the close of the acquisition date, they received the assets transferred by old T in the transaction described in paragraph (d)(4)(i) of this section. In most cases, the transfer will be treated as a distribution in complete liquidation to which section 331 or 332 applies.

(ii) *Basis and holding period of T stock not acquired.*—A member of the selling consolidated group (or the selling affiliate or an S corporation shareholder) retaining T stock is treated as acquiring the stock so retained on the day after the acquisition date for its fair market value. The holding period for the retained stock starts on the day after the acquisition date. For purposes of this paragraph, the fair market value of all of the T stock equals the grossed-up amount realized on the sale to P of P's recently purchased target stock. See §1.338-4(c).

(iii) *T stock sale.*—Members of the selling consolidated group (or the selling affiliate or S corporation shareholders) recognize no gain or loss on the sale or exchange of T stock included in the qualified stock purchase (although they may recognize gain or loss on the T stock in the deemed liquidation).

(6) *Nonselling minority shareholders other than nonselling S corporation shareholders.*—(i) *In general.*—This paragraph (d)(6) describes the treatment of shareholders of old T other than the following: members of the selling consolidated group, the selling affiliate, S corporation shareholders (whether or not they sell their stock), and P. For a description of the treatment of S corporation shareholders, see paragraph (d)(5) of this section. A shareholder to which this paragraph (d)(6) applies is called a minority shareholder.

(ii) *T stock sale.*—A minority shareholder recognizes gain or loss on the shareholder's sale or exchange of T stock included in the qualified stock purchase.

(iii) *T stock not acquired.*—A minority shareholder does not recognize gain or loss under this section with respect to shares of T stock retained by the shareholder. The shareholder's basis and holding period for that T stock is not affected by the section 338(h)(10) election.

(7) *Consolidated return of selling consolidated group.*—If P acquires T in a qualified stock purchase from a selling consolidated group—

(i) The selling consolidated group must file a consolidated return for the taxable period that includes the acquisition date;

(ii) A consolidated return for the selling consolidated group for that period may not be withdrawn on or after the day that a section 338(h)(10) election is made for T; and

(iii) Permission to discontinue filing consolidated returns cannot be granted for, and cannot apply to, that period or any of the immediately preceding taxable periods during which consolidated returns continuously have been filed.

(8) *Availability of the section 453 installment method.*—Solely for purposes of applying sections 453, 453A, and 453B, and the regulations thereunder (the installment method) to determine the consequences to old T in the deemed asset sale and to old T (and its shareholders, if relevant) in the deemed liquidation, the rules in paragraphs (d)(1) through (7) of this section are modified as follows:

(i) *In deemed asset sale.*—Old T is treated as receiving in the deemed asset sale new T installment obligations, the terms of which are identical (except as to the obligor) to P installment obligations issued in exchange for recently purchased stock of T. Old T is treated as receiving in cash all other consideration in the deemed asset sale other than the assumption of, or taking subject to, old T liabilities. For example, old T is treated as receiving in cash any amounts attributable to the grossing-up of amount realized under §1.338-4(c). The amount realized for recently purchased stock taken into account in determining ADSP is adjusted (and, thus, ADSP is redetermined) to reflect the amounts paid under an installment obligation for the stock when the total payments under the installment obligation are greater or less than the amount realized.

(ii) *In deemed liquidation.*—Old T is treated as distributing in the deemed liquidation the new T installment obligations that it is treated as receiving in the deemed asset sale. The members of the selling consolidated group, the selling affiliate, or the S corporation shareholders are treated as receiving in the deemed liquidation the new T installment obligations that correspond to the P installment obligations they actually received individually in exchange for their recently purchased stock. The new T installment obligations may be recharacterized under other rules. See for example §1.453-11(a)(2) which, in certain circumstances, treats the new T installment obligations deemed distributed by old T as if they were issued by new T in exchange for the stock in old T owned by members of the selling consolidated group, the selling affiliate, or the S corporation shareholders. The members of the selling consolidated group, the selling affiliate, or the S corporation shareholders are treated as receiving all other consideration in the deemed liquidation in cash.

(9) *Treatment consistent with an actual asset sale.*—No provision in section 338(h)(10) or this section shall produce a Federal income tax result under subtitle A of the Internal Revenue Code that would not occur if the parties had actually engaged in the transactions deemed to occur because of this section and taking into account other transactions that actually occurred or are deemed to occur. See, however, §1.338-1(b)(2) for certain exceptions to this rule.

(e) *Examples.*—The following examples illustrate the provisions of this section:

Example 1. (i) S1 owns all of the T stock and T owns all of the stock of T1 and T2. S1 is the common parent of a consolidated group that includes T, T1, and T2. P makes a qualified stock purchase of all of the T stock from S1. S1 joins with P in making a section 338(h)(10) election for T and for the deemed purchase of T1. A section 338 election is not made for T2.

(ii) S1 does not recognize gain or loss on the sale of the T stock and T does not recognize gain or loss on the sale of the T1 stock because section 338(h)(10) elections are made for T and T1. Thus, for example, gain or loss realized on the sale of the T or T1 stock is not taken into account in earnings and profits. However, because a section 338 election is not made for T2, T must recognize any gain or loss realized on the deemed sale of the T2 stock. See §1.338-4(h).

(iii) The results would be the same if S1, T, T1, and T2 are not members of any consolidated group, because S1 and T are selling affiliates.

Example 2. (i) S and T are solvent corporations. S owns all of the outstanding stock of T. S and P agree to undertake the following transaction: T will distribute half its assets to S, and S will assume half of T's liabilities. Then, P will purchase the stock of T from S. S and P will jointly make a section 338(h)(10) election with respect to the sale of T. The corporations then complete the transaction as agreed.

(ii) Under section 338(a), the assets present in T at the close of the acquisition date are deemed sold by old T to new T. Under paragraph (d)(4) of this section, the transactions described in paragraph (d) of this section are treated in the same manner as if they had actually occurred. Because S and P had agreed that, after T's actual distribution to S of part of its assets, S would sell T to P pursuant to an election under section 338(h)(10), and because paragraph (d)(4) of this section deems T subsequently to have transferred all its assets to its shareholder, T is deemed to have adopted a plan of complete liquidation under section 332. T's actual transfer of assets to S is treated as a distribution pursuant to that plan of complete liquidation.

Example 3. (i) S1 owns all of the outstanding stock of both T and S2. All three are corporations. S1 and P agree to undertake the following transaction. T will transfer substantially all of its assets and liabilities to S2, with S2 issuing no stock in exchange therefor, and retaining its other assets and liabilities. Then, P will purchase the stock of T from S1. S1 and P will jointly make a section 338(h)(10) election with respect to the sale of T. The corporations then complete the transaction as agreed.

(ii) Under section 338(a), the remaining assets present in T at the close of the acquisition date are deemed sold by old T to new T. Under paragraph (d)(4) of this section, the transactions described in this section are treated in the same manner as if they had actually occurred. Because old T transferred substantially all of its assets to S2, and is deemed to have distributed all its remaining assets and gone out of existence, the transfer of assets to S2, taking into account the related transfers, deemed and actual, qualifies as a reorganization under section 368(a)(1)(D). Section 361(c)(1) and not section 332 applies to T's deemed liquidation.

Example 4. (i) T owns two assets: an actively traded security (Class II) with a fair market value of $100 and an adjusted basis of $100, and inventory (Class IV) with a fair market value of $100 and an adjusted basis of $100. T has no liabilities. S is negotiating to sell all the stock in T to P for $100 cash and contingent consideration. Assume that under generally applicable tax accounting rules, P's adjusted basis in the T stock immediately after the purchase would be $100, because the contingent consideration is not taken into account. Thus, under

Assets	Basis
Land	$50,000
Equipment	30,000
Total	$80,000

(iii) Under paragraph (d)(3) of this section, old T has gain on the deemed sale of $40,000 (consisting of $16,667 of capital gain and $23,333 of ordinary income).

(iv) Under paragraph (d)(5)(iii) of this section, S1 recognizes no gain or loss upon its sale of the old T stock to P. S1 also recognizes no gain or loss upon the deemed liquidation of T. See paragraph (d)(4) of this section and section 332.

(v) P's basis in new T stock is P's cost for the stock, $80,000. See section 1012.

(vi) Under § 1.338-5, the AGUB for new T is $120,000, i.e., P's cost for the old T stock ($80,000) plus T's liability ($40,000). This AGUB is allocated as basis among the new T assets under §§ 1.338-6 and 1.338-7.

Example 6. (i) The facts are the same as in *Example 5*, except that S1 sells 80 percent of the old T stock to P for $64,000, rather than 100 percent of the old T stock for $80,000.

(ii) The consequences to P, T, and S1 are the same as in *Example 5*, except that:

(A) P's basis for its 80-percent interest in the new T stock is P's $64,000 cost for the stock. See section 1012.

(B) Under § 1.338-5, the AGUB for new T is $120,000 (i.e., $64,000/.8 + $40,000 + $0).

(C) Under paragraph (d)(4) of this section, S1 recognizes no gain or loss with respect to the retained stock in T. See section 332.

(D) Under paragraph (d)(5)(ii) of this section, the basis of the T stock retained by S1 is $16,000 (i.e., $120,000 − $40,000 (the ADSP amount for the old T assets over the sum of new T's liabilities immediately after the acquisition date) × .20 (the proportion of T stock retained by S1)).

Example 7. (i) The facts are the same as in *Example 6*, except that K, a shareholder unrelated to T or P, owns the 20 percent of the T stock

the rules of § 1.338-5, AGUB would be $100. Under the allocation rules of § 1.338-6, the entire $100 would be allocated to the Class II asset, the actively traded security, and no amount would be allocated to the inventory. P, however, plans immediately to cause T to sell the inventory, but not the actively traded security, so it requests that, prior to the stock sale, S cause T to create a new subsidiary, Newco, and contribute the actively traded security to the capital of Newco. Because the stock in Newco, which would not be actively traded, is a Class V asset, under the rules of § 1.338-6 $100 of AGUB would be allocated to the inventory and no amount of AGUB would be allocated to the Newco stock. Newco's own AGUB, $0 under the rules of § 1.338-5, would be allocated to the actively traded security. When P subsequently causes T to sell the inventory, T would realize no gain or loss instead of realizing gain of $100.

(ii) Assume that, if the T stock had not itself been sold but T had instead sold both its inventory and the Newco stock to P, T would for tax purposes be deemed instead to have sold both its inventory and actively traded security directly to P, with P deemed then to have created Newco and contributed the actively traded security to the capital of Newco. Section 338, if elected, generally recharacterizes a stock sale as a deemed sale of assets. However, paragraph (d)(9) of this section states, in general, that no provision of section 338(h)(10) or the regulations thereunder shall produce a Federal income tax result under subtitle A of the Internal Revenue Code that would not occur if the parties had actually engaged in the transactions deemed to occur by virtue of the section 338(h)(10) election, taking into account other transactions that actually occurred or are deemed to occur. Hence, the deemed sale of assets under section 338(h)(10) should be treated as one of the inventory and actively traded security themselves, not of the inventory and Newco stock. The anti-abuse rule of § 1.338-1(c) does not apply, because the substance of the deemed sale of assets is a sale of the inventory and the actively traded security themselves, not of the inventory and the Newco stock. Otherwise, the anti-abuse rule might apply.

Example 5. (i) T, a member of a selling consolidated group, has only one class of stock, all of which is owned by S1. On March 1 of Year 2, S1 sells its T stock to P for $80,000, and joins with P in making a section 338(h)(10) election for T. There are no selling costs or acquisition costs. On March 1 of Year 2, T owns land with a $50,000 basis and $75,000 fair market value and equipment with a $30,000 adjusted basis, $70,000 recomputed basis, and $60,000 fair market value. T also has a $40,000 liability. S1 pays old T's allocable share of the selling group's consolidated tax liability for Year 2 including the tax liability for the deemed sale tax consequences (a total of $13,600).

(ii) ADSP of $120,000 ($80,000 + $40,000 + 0) is allocated to each asset as follows:

FMV	Fraction	Allocable ADSP
$75,000	5/9	$66,667
60,000	4/9	53,333
$135,000	1	$120,000

that is not acquired by P in the qualified stock purchase. K's basis in its T stock is $5,000.

(ii) The consequences to P, T, and S1 are the same as in *Example 6*.

(iii) Under paragraph (d)(6)(iii) of this section, K recognizes no gain or loss, and K's basis in its T stock remains at $5,000.

Example 8. (i) The facts are the same as in *Example 5*, except that the equipment is held by T1, a wholly-owned subsidiary of T, and a section 338(h)(10) election is also made for T1. The T1 stock has a fair market value of $60,000. T1 has no assets other than the equipment and no liabilities. S1 pays old T's and old T1's allocable shares of the selling group's consolidated tax liability for Year 2 including the tax liability for T and T1's deemed sale tax consequences.

(ii) ADSP for T is $120,000, allocated $66,667 to the land and $53,333 to the stock. Old T's deemed sale results in $16,667 of capital gain on its deemed sale of the land. Under paragraph (d)(5)(iii) of this section, old T does not recognize gain or loss on its deemed sale of the T1 stock. See section 332.

(iii) ADSP for T1 is $53,333 (i.e., $53,333 + $0 + $0). On the deemed sale of the equipment, T1 recognizes ordinary income of $23,333.

(iv) Under paragraph (d)(5)(iii) of this section, S1 does not recognize gain or loss upon its sale of the old T stock to P.

Example 9. (i) The facts are the same as in *Example 8*, except that P already owns 20 percent of the T stock, which is nonrecently purchased stock with a basis of $6,000, and that P purchases the remaining 80 percent of the T stock from S1 for $64,000.

(ii) The results are the same as in *Example 8*, except that under paragraph (d)(1) of this section and § 1.338-5(d), P is deemed to have made a gain recognition election for its nonrecently purchased T stock. As a result, P recognizes gain of $10,000 and its basis in the nonrecently purchased T stock is increased from $6,000 to $16,000. P's basis in all the T stock is $80,000 (i.e., $64,000 + $16,000). The computations are as follows:

(A) P's grossed-up basis for the recently purchased T stock is $64,000 (i.e., $64,000 (the basis of the recently purchased T stock) × (1 − .2)/(.8) (the fraction in section 338(b)(4))).

(B) P's basis amount for the nonrecently purchased T stock is $16,000 (i.e., $64,000 (the grossed-up basis in the recently purchased T stock) × (.2)/(1.0 − .2) (the fraction in section 338(b)(3)(B))).

(C) The gain recognized on the nonrecently purchased stock is $10,000 (i.e., $16,000 − $6,000).

Example 10. (i) T is an S corporation whose sole class of stock is owned 40 percent each by A and B and 20 percent by C. T, A, B, and C all use the cash method of accounting. A and B each has an adjusted basis of $10,000 in the stock. C has an adjusted basis of $5,000 in the stock. A, B, and C hold no installment obligations to which section 453A applies. On March 1 of Year 1, A sells its stock to P for $40,000 in cash and B sells its stock to P for a $25,000 note issued by P and real estate having a fair market value of $15,000. The $25,000 note, due in full in Year 7, is not publicly traded and bears adequate stated interest. A and B have no selling expenses. T's sole asset is real estate, which has a value of $110,000 and an adjusted basis of $35,000. Also, T's real estate is encumbered by long-outstanding purchase-money indebtedness of $10,000. The real estate does not have built-in gain subject to section 1374. A, B, and C join with P in making a section 338(h)(10) election for T.

(ii) Solely for purposes of application of sections 453, 453A, and 453B, old T is considered in its deemed asset sale to receive back from new T the $25,000 note (considered issued by new T) and $75,000 of cash (total consideration of $80,000 paid for all the stock sold, which is then divided by .80 in the grossing-up, with the resulting figure of $100,000 then reduced by the amount of the installment note). Absent an election under section 453(d), gain is reported by old T under the installment method.

(iii) In applying the installment method to old T's deemed asset sale, the contract price for old T's assets deemed sold is $100,000, the $110,000 selling price reduced by the indebtedness of $10,000 to which the assets are subject. (The $110,000 selling price is itself the sum of the $80,000 grossed-up in paragraph (ii) above to $100,000 and the $10,000 liability.) Gross profit is $75,000 ($110,000 selling price − old T's basis of $35,000). Old T's gross profit ratio is 0.75 (gross profit of $75,000 ÷ $100,000 contract price). Thus, $56,250 (0.75 × the $75,000 cash old T is deemed to receive in Year 1) is Year 1 gain attributable to the sale, and $18,750 ($75,000 − $56,250) is recovery of basis.

(iv) In its liquidation, old T is deemed to distribute the $25,000 note to B, since B actually sold the stock partly for that consideration. To the extent of the remaining liquidating distribution to B, it is deemed to receive, along with A and C, the balance of old T's liquidating assets in the form of cash. Under section 453(h), B, unless it makes an election under section 453(d), is not required to treat the receipt of the note as a payment for the T stock; P's payment of the $25,000 note in Year 7 to B is a payment for the T stock. Because section 453(h) applies to B, old T's deemed liquidating distribution of the note is, under section 453B(h), not treated as a taxable disposition by old T.

(v) Under section .1366, A reports 40 percent, or $22,500, of old T's $56,250 gain recognized in Year 1. Under section 1367, this increases A's $10,000 adjusted basis in the T stock to $32,500. Next, in old T's deemed liquidation, A is considered to receive $40,000 for its old T shares, causing it to recognize an additional $7,500 gain in Year 1.

(vi) Under section 1366, B reports 40 percent, or $22,500, of old T's $56,250 gain recognized in Year 1. Under section 1367, this increases B's $10,000 adjusted basis in its T stock to $32,500. Next, in old T's deemed liquidation, B is considered to receive the $25,000 note and $15,000 of other consideration. Applying section 453, including section 453(h), to the deemed liquidation, B's selling price and contract price are both $40,000. Gross profit is $7,500 ($40,000 selling price − B's basis of $32,500). B's gross profit ratio is 0.1875 (gross profit of $7,500 ÷ $40,000 contract price). Thus, $2,812.50 (0.1875 × $15,000) is Year 1 gain attributable to the deemed liquidation. In Year 7, when the $25,000 note is paid, B has $4,687.50 (0.1875 × $25,000) of additional gain.

(vii) Under section 1366, C reports 20 percent, or $11,250, of old T's $56,250 gain recognized in Year 1. Under section 1367, this increases C's $5,000 adjusted basis in its T stock to $16,250. Next, in old T's deemed liquidation, C is considered to receive $20,000 for its old T shares, causing it to recognize an additional $3,750 gain in Year 1. Finally, under paragraph (d)(5)(ii) of this section, C is considered to acquire its stock in T on the day after the acquisition date for $20,000 (fair market value = grossed-up amount realized of $100,000 × 20%). C's holding period in the stock deemed received in new T begins at that time.

Example 11. Stock acquisition followed by upstream merger-without section 338(h)(10) election. (i) P owns all the stock of Y, a newly formed subsidiary. S owns all the stock of T. Each of P, S, T and Y is a

domestic corporation. P acquires all of the T stock in a statutory merger of Y into T, with T surviving. In the merger, S receives consideration consisting of 50% P voting stock and 50% cash. Viewed independently of any other step, P's acquisition of T stock constitutes a qualified stock purchase. As part of the plan that includes P's acquisition of the T stock, T subsequently merges into P. Viewed independently of any other step, T's merger into P qualifies as a liquidation described in section 332. Absent the application of paragraph (c)(2) of this section, the step transaction doctrine would apply to treat P's acquisition of the T stock and T's merger into P as an acquisition by P of T's assets in a reorganization described in section 368(a). P and S do not make a section 338(h)(10) election with respect to P's purchase of the T stock.

(ii) Because P and S do not make an election under section 338(h)(10) for T, P's acquisition of the T stock and T's merger into P is treated as part of a reorganization described in section 368(a).

Example 12. Stock acquisition followed by upstream merger-with section 338(h)(10) election. (i) The facts are the same as in *Example 11* except that P and S make a joint election under section 338(h)(10) for T.

(ii) Pursuant to paragraph (c)(2) of this section, as a result of the election under section 338(h)(10), for all Federal tax purposes, P's acquisition of the T stock is treated as a qualified stock purchase and P's acquisition of the T stock is not treated as part of a reorganization described in section 368(a).

Example 13. Stock acquisition followed by brother-sister merger-with section 338(h)(10) election. (i) The facts are the same as in *Example 12*, except that, following P's acquisition of the T stock, T merges into X, a domestic corporation that is a wholly owned subsidiary of P. Viewed independently of any other step, T's merger into X qualifies as a reorganization described in section 368(a). Absent the application of paragraph (c)(2) of this section, the step transaction doctrine would apply to treat P's acquisition of the T stock and T's merger into X as an acquisition by X of T's assets in a reorganization described in section 368(a).

(ii) Pursuant to paragraph (c)(2) of this section, as a result of the election under section 338(h)(10), for all Federal tax purposes, P's acquisition of T stock is treated as a qualified stock purchase and P's acquisition of T stock is not treated as part of a reorganization described in section 368(a).

Example 14. Stock acquisition that does not qualify as a qualified stock purchase followed by upstream merger. (i) The facts are the same as in *Example 11*, except that, in the statutory merger of Y into T, S receives only P voting stock.

(ii) Pursuant to § 1.338-3(c)(1)(i) and paragraph (c)(2) of this section, no election under section 338(h)(10) can be made with respect to P's acquisition of the T stock because, pursuant to relevant provisions of law, including the step transaction doctrine, that acquisition followed by T's merger into P is treated as a reorganization described in section 368(a)(1)(A), and that acquisition, viewed independently of T's merger into P, does not constitute a qualified stock purchase under section 338(d)(3). Accordingly, P's acquisition of the T stock and T's merger into P is treated as a reorganization described in section 368(a).

(f) *Inapplicability of provisions.*—The provisions of section 6043, § 1.331-1(d) and § 1.332-6 (relating to information returns and record-keeping requirements for corporate liquidations) do not apply to the deemed liquidation of old T under paragraph (d)(4) of this section.

(g) *Required information.*—The Commissioner may exercise the authority granted in section 338(h)(10)(C)(iii) to require provision of any information deemed necessary to carry out the provisions of section 338(h)(10) by requiring submission of information on any tax reporting form.

(h) *Effective date.*—This section is applicable to stock acquisitions occurring on or after July 5, 2006. For stock acquisitions occurring before July 5, 2006, see § 1.338(h)(10)-1T as contained in the edition of 26 CFR part 1, revised as of April 1, 2006. [Reg. § 1.338(h)(10)-1.]

☐ [T.D. 8940, 2-12-2001. *Amended by T.D. 9071, 7-8-2003; T.D. 9264, 5-26-2006; T.D. 9271, 7-3-2006 and T.D. 9329, 6-13-2007.*]

[Reg. § 1.338(i)-1]

§ 1.338(i)-1. Effective/applicability date.—(a) *In general.*—The provisions of §§ 1.338-1 through 1.338-7, 1.338-10 and 1.338(h)(10)-1 apply to any qualified stock purchase occurring after March 15, 2001. For rules applicable to qualified stock purchases on or before March 15, 2001, see §§ 11.338-1T through 1.338-7T, 1.338-10T, 1.338(h)(10)-1T and 1.338(i)-1T in effect prior to March 16, 2001 (see 26 CFR part 1 revised April 1, 2000).

(b) *Section 338(h)(10) elections for S corporation targets.*—The requirements of §§ 1.338(h)(10)-1T(c)(2) and 1.338(h)(10)-1(c)(2) that S corporation shareholders who do not sell their stock must also consent to an election under section 338(h)(10) will not invalidate an otherwise valid election made on the September 1997 revision of Form 8023, "Elections Under Section 338 For Corporations Making Qualified Stock Purchases," not signed by the nonselling shareholders, provided that the S corporation and all of its shareholders (including nonselling shareholders) report the tax consequences consistently with the results under section 338(h)(10).

(c) *Section 338 elections for insurance company targets.*—(1) *In general.*—The rules of §1.338-11 apply to qualified stock purchases occurring on or after April 10, 2006.

(2) *New target election for retroactive application.*—(i) *Availability of election.*—New target may make an irrevocable election to apply the rules in §1.338-11 (including the applicable provisions in §§1.197-2(g)(5), 381(c)(22)-1, and 846) in whole, but not in part, to a qualified stock purchase occurring before April 10, 2006 for which a section 338 election is made, provided that new target's first taxable year and all subsequent affected taxable years are years for which an assessment of deficiency or a refund for overpayment is not prevented by any law or rule of law. In the case of a section 338 election for which a section 338(h)(10) election is made (or a section 338 election for a foreign target), new target may make the election to apply the regulations retroactively without regard to whether old target makes the election. In the case of a section 338 election for a domestic target for which no section 338(h)(10) election is made, new target may make the election to apply the regulations retroactively only if old target also makes the election. Paragraph (c)(2)(ii) of this section prescribes the time and manner of the election for new target.

(ii) *Time and manner of making the election for new target.*—New target may make an election described in paragraph (c)(2)(i) of this section by attaching a statement to its original or amended income tax return for its first taxable year. The statement must be entitled "Election to Retroactively Apply the Rules in §1.338-11 (including the applicable provisions in §§1.197-2(g)(5), 1.381(c)(22)-1 and 846) in whole to a transaction completed before April 10, 2006" and must include the following information—

(A) The name and E.I.N. for new target; and

(B) The following declaration (or a substantially similar declaration): New target has amended its income tax returns for its first taxable year and for all affected subsequent years to reflect the rules in §1.338-11 (including the applicable provisions in §§1.197-2(g)(5), 1.381(c)(22)-1 and 846). All other parties whose income tax liabilities are affected by new target's election have amended their income tax returns for all affected years to reflect the rules in §1.338-11 (including the applicable provisions in §§1.197-2(g)(5), 1.381(c)(22)-1 and 846).

(3) *Old target election for retroactive application.*—(i) *Availability of election.*—Old target may make an irrevocable election to apply the rules in §§1.338-11 (including the applicable provisions in §§1.197-2(g)(5), 1.381(c)(22)-1 and 846) in whole, but not in part, to a qualified stock purchase occurring before April 10, 2006 for which a section 338 election is made, provided that old target's taxable year that includes the deemed sale tax consequences and all subsequent affected taxable years are years for which an assessment of deficiency or a refund for overpayment is not prevented by any law or rule of law. In the case of a section 338 election for which a section 338(h)(10) election is made (or a section 338 election for a foreign target), old target may make the election to apply the regulations retroactively without regard to whether new target makes the election. In the case of a section 338 election for a domestic target for which no section 338(h)(10) election is made, old target may make the election to apply the regulations retroactively only if new target also makes the election. Paragraph (c)(3)(ii) of this section prescribes the time and manner of the election for old target.

(ii) *Time and manner of making the election for old target.*—Old target may make an election described in paragraph (c)(3)(i) of this section by attaching a statement to each affected party's original or amended income tax return for the taxable year that includes the deemed sale tax consequences. The statement must be entitled "Election to Retroactively Apply the Rules in §1.338-11 (including the applicable provisions in §§1.197-2(g)(5), 1.381(c)(22)-1 and 846) to a transaction completed before April 10, 2006" and must include the following information—

(A) The name and E.I.N. for old target; and

(B) The following declaration (or a substantially similar declaration): Old target has amended its income tax returns for the taxable year that includes the deemed sale tax consequences and for all affected subsequent years to reflect the rules in §§1.338-11 (including the applicable provisions in §§1.197-2(g)(5), 1.381(c)(22)-1 and 846). All other parties whose income tax liabilities are affected by old target's election have amended their income tax returns for all affected years to reflect the rules in §1.338-11 (including the applica-

ble provisions in §§1.197-2(g)(5), 1.381(c)(22)-1 and 846). [Reg. §1.338(i)-1.]

☐ [T.D. 8940, 2-12-2001. *Amended by* T.D. 9257, 4-7-2006 *and* T.D. 9377, 1-22-2008.]

[Reg. §1.346-1]

§1.346-1. **Partial liquidation.**—(a) *General.*—This section defines a partial liquidation. If amounts are distributed in partial liquidation such amounts are treated under section 331(a)(2) as received in part or full payment in exchange for the stock. A distribution is treated as in partial liquidation of a corporation if:

(1) The distribution is one of a series of distributions in redemption of all the stock of the corporation pursuant to a plan of complete liquidation or

(2) The distribution:

(i) Is not essentially equivalent to a dividend,

(ii) Is in redemption of a part of the stock of the corporation pursuant to a plan, and

(iii) Occurs within the taxable year in which the plan is adopted or within the succeeding taxable year.

An example of a distribution which will qualify as a partial liquidation under subparagraph (2) of this paragraph and section 346(a) is a distribution resulting from a genuine contraction of the corporate business such as the distribution of unused insurance proceeds recovered as a result of a fire which destroyed part of the business causing a cessation of a part of its activities. On the other hand, the distribution of funds attributable to a reserve for an expansion program which has been abandoned does not qualify as a partial liquidation within the meaning of section 346(a). A distribution to which section 355 applies (or so much of section 356 as relates to section 355) is not a distribution in partial liquidation within the meaning of section 346(a).

(b) *Special requirements on termination of business.*—A distribution which occurs within the taxable year in which the plan is adopted or within the succeeding taxable year and which meets the requirements of subsection (b) of section 346 falls within paragraph (a)(2) of this section and within section 346(a)(2). The requirements which a distribution must meet to fall within subsection (b) of section 346 are:

(1) Such distribution is attributable to the corporation's ceasing to conduct, or consists of assets of, a trade or business which has been actively conducted throughout the five-year period immediately before the distribution, which trade or business was not acquired by the corporation within such period in a transaction in which gain or loss was recognized in whole or in part, and

(2) Immediately after such distribution by the corporation it is actively engaged in the conduct of a trade or business, which trade or business was actively conducted throughout the five-year period ending on the date of such distribution and was not acquired by the corporation within such period in a transaction in which gain or loss was recognized in whole or in part.

A distribution shall be treated as having been made in partial liquidation pursuant to section 346(b) if it consists of the proceeds of the sale of the assets of a trade or business which has been actively conducted for the five-year period and has been terminated, or if it is a distribution in kind of the assets of such a business, or if it is a distribution in kind of some of the assets of such a business and of the proceeds of the sale of the remainder of the assets of such a business. In general, a distribution which will qualify under section 346(b) may consist of, *but is not limited to*—

(i) Assets (other than inventory or property described in subdivision (ii) of this subparagraph) used in the trade or business throughout the five-year period immediately before the distribution (for this purpose an asset shall be considered used in the trade or business during the period of time the asset which it replaced was so used), or

(ii) Proceeds from the sale of assets described in (i), and, in addition,

(iii) The inventory of such trade or business or property held primarily for sale to customers in the ordinary course of business, if:

(a) The items constituting such inventory or such property were substantially similar to the items constituting such inventory or property during the five-year period immediately before the distribution, and

(b) The quantity of such items on the date of distribution was not substantially in excess of the quantity of similar items regularly on hand in the conduct of such business during such five-year period, or

(iv) Proceeds from the sale of inventory or property described in subdivision (iii) of this subparagraph, if such inventory or property is sold in bulk in the course of termination of such trade or business and if with respect to such inventory the conditions of subdivision (iii) (a) and (b) of this subparagraph would have been met had such inventory or property been distributed on the date of such sale.

(c) *Active conduct of a trade or business.*—For the purpose of section 346(b)(1), a corporation shall be deemed to have actively conducted a trade or business immediately before the distribution, if:

(1) In the case of a business the assets of which have been distributed in kind, the business was operated by such corporation until the date of distribution, or

(2) In the case of a business the proceeds of the sale of the assets of which are distributed, such business was actively conducted until the date of sale and the proceeds of such sale were distributed as soon thereafter as reasonably possible.

The term "active conduct of a trade or business" shall have the same meaning in this section as in paragraph (c) of §1.355-1. [Reg. §1.346-1.]

☐ [*T.D.* 6152, 12-2-55.]

[Reg. §1.346-2]

§1.346-2. Treatment of certain redemptions.—If a distribution in a redemption of stock qualifies as a distribution in part or full payment in exchange for the stock under both section 302(a) and this section, then only this section shall be applicable. None of the limitations of Section 302 shall be applicable to such redemption. [Reg. §1.346-2.]

☐ [*T.D.* 6152, 12-2-55.]

[Reg. §1.346-3]

§1.346-3. Effect of certain sales.—The determination of whether assets sold in connection with a partial liquidation are sold by the distributing corporation or by the shareholder is a question of fact to be determined under the facts and circumstances of each case. [Reg. §1.346-3.]

☐ [*T.D.* 6152, 12-2-55.]

[The next page is 31,801.]

Corporate Organizations and Reorganizations

See p. 20,601 for regulations not amended to reflect law changes

[Reg. §1.351-1]

§1.351-1. Transfer to corporation controlled by transferor.—
(a) *In general.*—(1) *Nonrecognition of gain or loss.*—Section 351(a) provides, in general, for the nonrecognition of gain or loss upon the transfer by one or more persons of property to a corporation solely in exchange for stock of such corporation if, immediately after the exchange, such person or persons are in control of the corporation to which the property was transferred. As used in section 351, the phrase "one or more persons" includes individuals, trusts, estates, partnerships, associations, companies, or corporations (see section 7701(a)(1)). To be in control of the transferee corporation, such person or persons must own immediately after the transfer stock possessing at least 80 percent of the total combined voting power of all classes of stock entitled to vote and at least 80 per cent of the total number of shares of all other classes of stock of such corporation (see section 368(c)). In determining control under this section, the fact that any corporate transferor distributes part or all of the stock which it receives in the exchange to its shareholders shall not be taken into account. The phrase "immediately after the exchange" does not necessarily require simultaneous exchanges by two or more persons, but comprehends a situation where the rights of the parties have been previously defined and the execution of the agreement proceeds with an expedition consistent with orderly procedure. For purposes of this section, stock rights and stock warrants are not included in the term *stock*. In addition, for purposes of this section—

(i) Stock will not be treated as issued for property if it is issued for services rendered or to be rendered to or for the benefit of the issuing corporation; and

(ii) Stock will not be treated as issued for property if it is issued for property which is of relatively small value in comparison to the value of the stock already owned (or to be received for services) by the person who transferred such property and the primary purpose of the transfer is to qualify under this section the exchanges of property by other persons transferring property.

(2) *Application.*—The application of section 351(a) is illustrated by the following examples:

Example (1). C owns a patent right worth $25,000 and D owns a manufacturing plant worth $75,000. C and D organize the R Corporation with an authorized capital stock of $100,000. C transfers his patent right to the R Corporation for $25,000 of its stock and D transfers his plant to the new corporation for $75,000 of its stock. No gain or loss to C or D is recognized.

Example (2). B owns certain real estate which cost him $50,000 in 1930, but which has a fair market value of $200,000 in 1955. He transfers the property to the N Corporation in 1955 for 78 percent of each class of stock of the corporation having a fair market value of $200,000, the remaining 22 percent of the stock of the corporation having been issued by the corporation in 1940 to other persons for cash. B realized a taxable gain of $150,000 on this transaction.

Example (3). E, an individual, owns property with a basis of $10,000 but which has a fair market value of $18,000. E also had rendered services valued at $2,000 to Corporation F. Corporation F has outstanding 100 shares of common stock all of which are held by G. Corporation F issues 400 shares of its common stock (having a fair market value of $20,000) to E in exchange for his property worth $18,000 and in compensation for the services he has rendered worth $2,000. Since immediately after the transaction, E owns 80 percent of the outstanding stock of Corporation F, no gain is recognized upon the exchange of the property for the stock. However, E realized $2,000 of ordinary income as compensation for services rendered to Corporation F.

(3) *Underwritings of stock.*—(i) *In general.*—For the purpose of section 351, if a person acquires stock of a corporation from an underwriter in exchange for cash in a qualified underwriting transaction, the person who acquires stock from the underwriter is treated as transferring cash directly to the corporation in exchange for stock of the corporation and the underwriter is disregarded. A qualified underwriting transaction is a transaction in which a corporation issues stock for cash in an underwriting in which either the underwriter is an agent of the corporation or the underwriter's ownership of the stock is transitory.

(ii) *Effective date.*—This paragraph (a)(3) is effective for qualified underwriting transactions occurring on or after May 1, 1996.

(b) *Multiple transferors.*—(1) *Disproportionate transfers.*—When property is transferred to a corporation by two or more persons in exchange for stock, as described in paragraph (a) of this section, and the stock received is disproportionate to the transferor's prior interest in such property, the entire transaction will be given tax effect in accordance with its true nature, and the transaction may be treated as if the stock had first been received in proportion and then some of such stock had been used to make gifts (section 2501 and following), to pay compensation (sections 61(a)(1) and 83(a)), or to satisfy obligations of the transferor of any kind.

(2) *Application.*—The application of paragraph (b)(1) of this section may be illustrated as follows:

Example (1). Individuals A and B, father and son, organize a corporation with 100 shares of common stock to which A transfers property worth $8,000 in exchange for 20 shares of stock, and B transfers property worth $2,000 in exchange for 80 shares of stock. No gain or loss will be recognized under section 351. However, if it is determined that A in fact made a gift to B, such gift will be subject to tax under section 2501 and following. Similarly, if B had rendered services to A (such services having no relation to the assets transferred or to the business of the corporation) and the disproportion in the amount of stock received constituted the payment of compensation by A to B, B will be taxable upon the fair market value of the 60 shares of stock received as compensation for services rendered, and A will realize gain or loss upon the difference between the basis to him of the 60 shares and their fair market value at the time of the exchange.

Example (2). Individuals C and D each transferred, to a newly organized corporation, property having a fair market value of $4,500 in exchange for the issuance by the corporation of 45 shares of its capital stock to each transferor. At the same time, the corporation issued to E, an individual, 10 shares of its capital stock in payment for organizational and promotional services rendered by E for the benefit of the corporation. E transferred no property to the corporation. C and D were under no obligation to pay for E's services. No gain or loss is recognized to C or D. E received compensation taxable as ordinary income to the extent of the fair market value of the 10 shares of stock received by him.

(c)(1) The general rule of section 351 does not apply, and consequently gain or loss will be recognized, where property is transferred to an investment company after June 30, 1967. A transfer of property after June 30, 1967, will be considered to be a transfer to an investment company if—

(i) The transfer results, directly or indirectly, in diversification of the transferors' interests, and

(ii) The transferee is (*a*) a regulated investment company, (*b*) a real estate investment trust, or (*c*) a corporation more than 80 percent of the value of whose assets (excluding cash and nonconvertible debt obligations from consideration) are held for investment and are readily marketable stocks or securities, or interests in regulated investment companies or real estate investment trusts.

(2) The determination of whether a corporation is an investment company shall ordinarily be made by reference to the circumstances in existence immediately after the transfer in question. However, where circumstances change thereafter pursuant to a plan in existence at the time of the transfer, this determination shall be made by reference to the later circumstances.

(3) Stocks and securities will be considered readily marketable if (and only if) they are part of a class of stock or securities which is traded on a securities exchange or traded or quoted regularly in the over-the-counter market. For purposes of subparagraph (1)(ii)(*c*) of this paragraph, the term "readily marketable stocks or securities" includes convertible debentures, convertible preferred stock, warrants, and other stock rights if the stock for which they may be converted or exchanged is readily marketable. Stocks and securities will be considered to be held for investment unless they are (i) held primarily for sale to customers in the ordinary course of business, or (ii) used in the trade or business of banking, insurance, brokerage, or a similar trade or business.

(4) In making the determination required under subparagraph (1)(ii)(*c*) of this paragraph, stock and securities in subsidiary corporations shall be disregarded and the parent corporation shall be deemed to own its ratable share of its subsidiaries' assets. A corporation shall be considered a subsidiary if the parent owns 50 percent or more of (i) the combined voting power of all classes of stock entitled to vote, or (ii) the total value of shares of all classes of stock outstanding.

(5) A transfer ordinarily results in the diversification of the transferors' interests if two or more persons transfer nonidentical assets to a corporation in the exchange. For this purpose, if any transaction involves one or more transfers of nonidentical assets which, taken in the aggregate, constitute an insignificant portion of the total value of assets transferred, such transfers shall be disregarded in determining whether diversification has occurred. If there is only one transferor (or two or more transferors of identical assets)

to a newly organized corporation, the transfer will generally be treated as not resulting in diversification. If a transfer is part of a plan to achieve diversification without recognition of gain, such as a plan which contemplates a subsequent transfer, however delayed, of the corporate assets (or of the stock or securities received in the earlier exchange) to an investment company in a transaction purporting to qualify for nonrecognition treatment, the original transfer will be treated as resulting in diversification.

(6)(i) For purposes of paragraph (c)(5) of this section, a transfer of stocks and securities will not be treated as resulting in a diversification of the transferors' interests if each transferor transfers a diversified portfolio of stocks and securities. For purposes of this paragraph(c)(6), a portfolio of stocks and securities is diversified if it satisfies the 25 and 50-percent tests of section 368(a)(2)(F)(ii), applying the relevant provisions of section 368(a)(2)(F). However, Government securities are included in total assets for purposes of the denominator of the 25 and 50-percent tests (unless the Government securities are acquired to meet the 25 and 50-percent tests), but are not treated as securities of an issuer for purposes of the numerator of the 25 and 50-percent tests.

(ii) Paragraph (c)(6)(i) of this section is effective for transfers completed on or after May 2, 1996. Transfers of diversified (within the meaning of paragraph (c)(6)(i) of this section), but nonidentical, portfolios of stocks and securities completed before May 2, 1996, may be treated either—

(A) Consistent with paragraph (c)(6)(i) of this section; or

(B) As resulting in diversification of the transferors' interests.

(7) The application of subparagraph (5) of this paragraph may be illustrated as follows:

Example (1). Individuals A, B, and C organize a corporation with 101 shares of common stock. A and B each transfers to it $10,000 worth of the only class of stock of corporation X, listed on the New York Stock Exchange, in exchanges for 50 shares of stock. C transfers $200 worth of readily marketable securities in corporation Y for one share of stock. In determining whether or not diversification has occurred, C's participation in the transaction will be disregarded. There is, therefore, no diversification, and gain or loss will not be recognized.

Example (2). A, together with 50 other transferors, organizes a corporation with 100 shares of stock. A transfers $10,000 worth of stock in corporation X, listed on the New York Stock Exchange, in exchange for 50 shares of stock. Each of the other 50 transferors transfers $200 worth of readily marketable securities in corporations other than X in exchange for one share of stock. In determining whether or not diversification has occurred, all transfers will be taken into account. Therefore, diversification is present, and gain or loss will be recognized.

(d) *Applicability date.*—Paragraphs (a)(1) and (b)(1) of this section apply to transfers after October 2, 1989, for tax years ending after such date, except as specified in section 7203(c)(2) and (3) of Public Law 101-239. [Reg. § 1.351-1.]

☐ [*T.D.* 6152, 12-2-55. *Amended by T.D.* 6942, 12-28-67; *T.D.* 8663, 5-1-96, T.D. 8665, 4-30-96 *and T.D.* 9759, 3-25-2016.]

[Reg. § 1.351-2]

§1.351-2. Receipt of property.—(a) If an exchange would be within the provisions of section 351(a) if it were not for the fact that the property received in exchange consists not only of property permitted by such subsection to be received without the recognition of gain, but also of other property or money, then the gain, if any, to the recipient shall be recognized, but in an amount not in excess of the sum of such money and the fair market value of such other property. No loss to the recipient shall be recognized.

(b) See section 357 and the regulations pertaining to that section for applicable rules as to the treatment of liabilities as "other property" in cases subject to section 351, where another party to the exchange assumes a liability, or acquires property subject to a liability.

(c) See sections 358 and 362 and the regulations pertaining to those sections for applicable rules with respect to the determination of the basis of stock, securities, or other property received in exchanges subject to section 351.

(d) See part 1 (section 301 and following), subchapter C, chapter 1 of the Code, and the regulations thereunder for applicable rules with respect to the taxation of dividends where a distribution by a corporation of its stock or securities in connection with an exchange subject to section 351(a) has the effect of the distribution of a taxable dividend.

(e) See § 1.356-7(a) for the applicability of the definition of nonqualified preferred stock in section 351(g)(2) for stock issued prior to June 9, 1997, and for stock issued in transactions occurring after June 8, 1997, that are described in section 1014(f)(2) of the Taxpayer Relief

Act of 1997, Public Law 105-34 (111 Stat. 788, 921). See § 1.356-7(c) for the treatment of preferred stock received in certain exchanges for common or preferred stock described in section 351(g)(2)(C)(i)(II). [Reg. § 1.351-2.]

☐ [*T.D.* 6152, 12-2-55. *Amended by T.D.* 8904, 9-29-2000.]

[Reg. § 1.351-3]

§1.351-3. Records to be kept and information to be filed.—
(a) *Significant transferor.*—Every significant transferor must include a statement entitled, "STATEMENT PURSUANT TO §1.351-3(a) BY [INSERT NAME AND TAXPAYER IDENTIFICATION NUMBER (IF ANY) OF TAXPAYER], A SIGNIFICANT TRANSFEROR," on or with such transferor's income tax return for the taxable year of the section 351 exchange. If a significant transferor is a controlled foreign corporation (within the meaning of section 957), each United States shareholder (within the meaning of section 951(b)) with respect thereto must include this statement on or with its return. The statement must include—

(1) The name and employer identification number (if any) of the transferee corporation;

(2) The date(s) of the transfer(s) of assets;

(3) The fair market value and basis of the property transferred by such transferor in the exchange, determined immediately before the transfer and aggregated as follows:

(i) Importation property transferred in a loss importation transaction, as defined in § 1.362-3(c)(2) and (3), respectively;

(ii) Loss duplication property as defined in § 1.362-4(g)(1);

(iii) Property with respect to which any gain or loss was recognized on the transfer (without regard to whether such property is also identified in paragraph (a)(3)(i) or (ii) of this section); and

(iv) Property not described in paragraph (a)(3)(i), (ii), or (iii) of this section.

(4) The date and control number of any private letter ruling(s) issued by the Internal Revenue Service in connection with the section 351 exchange.

(b) *Transferee corporation.*—Except as provided in paragraph (c) of this section, every transferee corporation must include a statement entitled, "STATEMENT PURSUANT TO §1.351-3(b) BY [INSERT NAME AND EMPLOYER IDENTIFICATION NUMBER (IF ANY) OF TAXPAYER], A TRANSFEREE CORPORATION," on or with its income tax return for the taxable year of the exchange. If the transferee corporation is a controlled foreign corporation (within the meaning of section 957), each United States shareholder (within the meaning of section 951(b)) with respect thereto must include this statement on or with its return. The statement must include—

(1) The name and taxpayer identification number (if any) of every significant transferor;

(2) The date(s) of the transfer(s) of assets;

(3) The fair market value and basis of property received in the exchange, determined immediately before the transfer and aggregated as follows:

(i) Importation property transferred in a loss importation transaction, as defined in § 1.362-3(c)(2) and (3), respectively;

(ii) Loss duplication property as defined in § 1.362-4(g)(1);

(iii) Property with respect to which any gain or loss was recognized on the transfer (without regard to whether such property is also identified in paragraph (b)(3)(ii) of this section);

(iv) Property not described in paragraph (b)(3)(i), (ii), or (iii) of this section; and

(4) The date and control number of any private letter ruling(s) issued by the Internal Revenue Service in connection with the section 351 exchange.

(c) *Exception for certain transferee corporations.*—The transferee corporation is not required to file a statement under paragraph (b) of this section if all of the information that would be included in the statement described in paragraph (b) of this section is included in any statement(s) described in paragraph (a) of this section that is attached to the same return for the same section 351 exchange.

(d) *Definitions.*—For purposes of this section:

(1) Significant transferor means a person that transferred property to a corporation and received stock of the transferee corporation in an exchange described in section 351 if, immediately after the exchange, such person—

(i) Owned at least five percent (by vote or value) of the total outstanding stock of the transferee corporation if the stock owned by such person is publicly traded, or

(ii) Owned at least one percent (by vote or value) of the total outstanding stock of the transferee corporation if the stock owned by such person is not publicly traded.

(2) Publicly traded stock means stock that is listed on—

(i) A national securities exchange registered under section 6 of the Securities Exchange Act of 1934 (15 U.S.C. 78f); or

(ii) An interdealer quotation system sponsored by a national securities association registered under section 15A of the Securities Exchange Act of 1934 (15 U.S.C. 78o-3).

(e) *Substantiation information.*—Under §1.6001-1(e), taxpayers are required to retain their permanent records and make such records available to any authorized Internal Revenue Service officers and employees. In connection with the exchange described in this section, these records should specifically include information regarding the amount, basis, and fair market value of all transferred property, and relevant facts regarding any liabilities assumed or extinguished as part of such exchange.

(f) *Effective/applicability date.*—This section applies to any taxable year beginning on or after May 30, 2006. However, taxpayers may apply this section to any original Federal income tax return (including any amended return filed on or before the due date (including extensions) of such original return) timely filed on or after May 30, 2006. For taxable years beginning before May 30, 2006, see §1.351-3 as contained in 26 CFR part 1 in effect on April 1, 2006. Paragraphs (a)(3) and (b)(3) of this section apply with respect to exchanges under section 351 occurring on or after March 28, 2016, and also with respect to exchanges under section 351 occurring before such date as a result of an entity classification election under §301.7701-3 of this chapter filed on or after March 28, 2016, unless such exchange is pursuant to a binding agreement that was in effect prior to March 28, 2016 and at all times thereafter. [Reg. §1.351–3.]

☐ [*T.D. 9329, 6-13-2007. Amended by T.D. 9759, 3-25-2016.*]

[Reg. §1.354-1]

§1.354-1. Exchanges of stock and securities in certain reorganizations.—(a) Section 354 provides that under certain circumstances no gain or loss is recognized to a shareholder who surrenders his stock in exchange for other stock or to a security holder who surrenders his securities in exchange for stock. Section 354 also provides that under certain circumstances a security holder may surrender securities and receive securities in the same principal amount or in a lesser principal amount without the recognition of gain or loss to him. The exchanges to which section 354 applies must be pursuant to a plan of reorganization as provided in section 368(a) and the stock and securities surrendered as well as the stock and securities received must be those of a corporation which is a party to the reorganization. Section 354 does not apply to exchanges pursuant to a reorganization described in section 368(a)(1)(D) unless the transferor corporation—

(1) Transfers all or substantially all of its assets to a single corporation, and

(2) Distributes all of its remaining properties (if any) and the stock, securities and other properties received in the exchange to its shareholders or security holders in pursuance of the plan of reorganization. The fact that properties retained by the transferor corporation, or received in exchange for the properties transferred in the reorganization, are used to satisfy existing liabilities not represented by securities and which were incurred in the ordinary course of business before the reorganization does not prevent the application of section 354 to an exchange pursuant to a plan of reorganization defined in section 368(a)(1)(D).

(b) Except as provided in section 354(c) and (d), section 354 is not applicable to an exchange of stock or securities if a greater principal amount of securities is received than the principal amount of securities the recipient surrenders, or if securities are received and the recipient surrenders no securities. See, however, section 356 and regulations pertaining to such section. See also section 306 with respect to the receipt of preferred stock in a transaction to which section 354 is applicable.

(c) An exchange of stock or securities shall be subject to section 354(a)(1) even though—

(1) Such exchange is not pursuant to a plan of reorganization described in section 368(a), and

(2) The principal amount of the securities received exceeds the principal amount of the securities surrendered or if securities are received and no securities are surrendered—

if such exchange is pursuant to a plan of reorganization for a railroad corporation as defined in section 77(m) of the Bankruptcy Act (11 U.S.C. 205(m)) and is approved by the Interstate Commerce Commission under section 77 of such Act or under section 20b of the Interstate Commerce Act (49 U.S.C. 20b) as being in the public interest. Section 354 is not applicable to such exchanges if there is received property other than stock or securities. See, however, section 356 and regulations pertaining to such section.

(d) The rules of section 354 may be illustrated by the following examples:

Example 1. Pursuant to a reorganization under section 368(a) to which Corporations T and W are parties, A, a shareholder in Corporation T, surrenders all his common stock in Corporation T in exchange for common stock of Corporation W. No gain or loss is recognized to A.

Example 2. Pursuant to a reorganization under section 368(a) to which Corporations X and Y (which are not railroad corporations) are parties, B, a shareholder in Corporation X, surrenders all his stock in X for stock and securities in Y. Section 354 does not apply to this exchange. See, however, section 356.

Example 3. C, a shareholder in Corporation Z (which is not a railroad corporation), surrenders all his stock in Corporation Z in exchange for securities in Corporation Z. Whether or not this exchange is in connection with a recapitalization under section 368(a)(1)(E), section 354 does not apply. See, however, section 302.

Example 4. The facts are the same as in *Example 3* of this paragraph (d), except that C receives solely rights to acquire stock in Corporation Z. Section 354 does not apply.

(e) Except as provided in §1.356-6, for purposes of section 354, the term *securities* includes rights issued by a party to the reorganization to acquire its stock. For purposes of this section and section 356(d)(2)(B), a right to acquire stock has no principal amount. For this purpose, rights to acquire stock has the same meaning as it does under sections 305 and 317(a). Other Internal Revenue Code provisions governing the treatment of rights to acquire stock may also apply to certain exchanges occurring in connection with a reorganization. See, for example, sections 83 and 421 through 424 and the regulations thereunder. This paragraph (e) applies to exchanges occurring on or after March 9, 1998.

(f) See §1.356-7(a) and (b) for the treatment of nonqualified preferred stock (as defined in section 351(g)(2)) received in certain exchanges for nonqualified preferred stock or preferred stock. See §1.356-7(c) for the treatment of preferred stock received in certain exchanges for common or preferred stock described in section 351(g)(2)(C)(i)(II). [Reg. §1.354-1.]

☐ [*T.D. 6152, 12-2-55. Amended by T.D. 7616, 5-7-79; T.D. 8752, 1-5-98; T.D. 8882, 5-15-2000 and T.D. 8904, 9-29-2000.*]

[Reg. §1.355-0]

§1.355-0. Outline of sections.—In order to facilitate the use of §§1.355-1 through 1.355-8, this section lists the major paragraphs in those sections as follows:

§1.355-1 Distribution of stock and securities of a controlled corporation.
  (a) Effective date of certain sections.
  (b) Application of section.

§1.355-2 Limitations.
  (a) Property distributed.
  (b) Independent business purpose.
   (1) Independent business purpose requirement.
   (2) Corporate business purpose.
   (3) Business purpose for distribution.
   (4) Business purpose as evidence of nondevice.
   (5) Examples.
  (c) Continuity of interest requirement.
   (1) Requirement.
   (2) Examples.
  (d) Device for distribution of earnings and profits.
   (1) In general.
   (2) Device factors.
    (i) In general.
    (ii) Pro rata distribution.
    (iii) Subsequent sale or exchange of stock.
     (A) In general.
     (B) Sale or exchange negotiated or agreed upon before the distribution.
     (C) Sale or exchange not negotiated or agreed upon before the distribution.
     (D) Negotiated or agreed upon before the distribution.
     (E) Exchange in pursuance of a plan of reorganization.
    (iv) Nature and use of assets.
     (A) In general.
     (B) Assets not used in a trade or business meeting the requirement of section 355(b).
     (C) Related function.
   (3) Nondevice factors.
    (i) In general.
    (ii) Corporate business purpose.
    (iii) Distributing corporation publicly traded and widely held.
    (iv) Distribution to domestic corporate shareholders.

☐ [*T.D.* 8238, 1-5-89. *Amended by T.D.* 8913, 12-19-2000; *T.D.* 8960, 8-2-2001; *T.D.* 8988, 4-23-2002 (*corrected* 5-31-2002); *T.D.* 9198, 4-18-2005; *T.D.* 9264, 5-26-2006; *T.D.* 9329, 6-13-2007; *T.D.* 9435, 12-12-2008, *T.D.* 9548, 10-19-2011, *T.D.* 9805, 12-16-2016 *and T.D.* 9888, 12-16-2019.]

[Reg. §1.355-1]

§1.355-1. Distribution of stock and securities of a controlled corporation.—(a) *Effective/applicability date of certain sections.*—Except as otherwise provided, this section and §§1.355-2 through 1.355-4 apply to transactions occurring after February 6, 1989. For transactions occurring on or before that date, see 26 CFR 1.355-1 through 1.355-4 (revised as of April 1, 1987). This section and §§1.355-2 through 1.355-4, other than §1.355-2(g) and (i), do not reflect the amendments to section 355 made by the Revenue Act of 1987, the Technical and Miscellaneous Revenue Act of 1988, and the Tax Technical Corrections Act of 2007. For the applicability date of §§1.355-2(g), 1.355-5, 1.355-6, and 1.355-7, see §§1.355-2(i), 1.355-5(e), 1.355-6(g), and 1.355-7(k), respectively.

(b) *Application of section.*—Section 355 provides for the separation, without recognition of gain or loss to (or the inclusion in income of) the shareholders and security holders, of one or more existing businesses formerly operated, directly or indirectly, by a single corporation (the "distributing corporation"). It applies only to the separation of existing businesses that have been in active operation for at least five years (or a business that has been in active operation for at least five years into separate businesses), and which, in general, have been owned, directly or indirectly, for at least five years by the distributing corporation. A separation is achieved through the distribution by the distributing corporation of stock, or stock and securities, of one or more subsidiaries (the "controlled corporations") to its shareholders with respect to its stock or to its security holders in exchange for its securities. The controlled corporations may be preexisting or newly created subsidiaries. Throughout the regulations under section 355, the term "distribution" refers to a distribution by the distributing corporation of stock, or stock and securities, of one or more controlled corporations, unless the context indicates otherwise. Section 355 contemplates the continued operation of the business or businesses existing prior to the separation. See §1.355-4 for types of distributions that may qualify under section 355, including pro-rata distributions and non-pro-rata distributions.

(c) *Stock rights.*—Except as provided in §1.356-6, for purposes of section 355, the term *securities* includes rights issued by the distributing corporation or the controlled corporation to acquire the stock of that corporation. For purposes of this section and section 356(d)(2)(B), a right to acquire stock has no principal amount. For this purpose, rights to acquire stock has the same meaning as it does under sections 305 and 317(a). Other Internal Revenue Code provisions governing the treatment of rights to acquire stock may also apply to certain distributions occurring in connection with a transaction described in section 355. See, for example, sections 83 and 421 through 424 and the regulations thereunder. This paragraph (c) applies to distributions occurring on or after March 9, 1998.

(d) *Nonqualified preferred stock.*—See §1.356-7(a) and (b) for the treatment of nonqualified preferred stock (as defined in section 351(g)(2)) received in certain exchanges for (or in certain distributions with respect to) nonqualified preferred stock or preferred stock. See §1.356-7(c) for the treatment of the receipt of preferred stock in certain exchanges for (or in certain distributions with respect to) common or preferred stock described in section 351(g)(2)(C)(i)(II). [Reg. §1.355-1.]

☐ [*T.D.* 6152, 12-2-55. *Amended by T.D.* 8238, 1-4-89; *T.D.* 8752, 1-5-98; *T.D.* 8882, 5-15-2000; *T.D.* 8904, 9-29-2000; *T.D.* 9435, 12-12-2008 (*corrected* 1-16-2009) *and T.D.* 9548, 10-19-2011.]

[Reg. §1.355-2]

§1.355-2. Limitations.—(a) *Property distributed.*—Section 355 applies to a distribution only if the property distributed consists solely of stock, or stock and securities, of a controlled corporation. If additional property (including an excess principal amount of securities received over securities surrendered) is received, see section 356.

(b) *Independent business purpose.*—(1) *Independent business purpose requirement.*—Section 355 applies to a transaction only if it is carried out for one or more corporate business purposes. A transaction is carried out for a corporate business purpose if it is motivated, in whole or substantial part, by one or more corporate business purposes. The potential for the avoidance of Federal taxes by the distributing or controlled corporations (or a corporation controlled by either) is relevant in determining the extent to which an existing corporate business purpose motivated the distribution. The principal reason for this business purpose requirement is to provide nonrecognition treatment only to distributions that are incident to readjustments of corporate structures required by business exigencies and that effect only readjustments of continuing interests in property under modified corporate forms. This business purpose requirement is independent of the other requirements under section 355.

(2) *Corporate business purpose.*—A corporate business purpose is a real and substantial non-Federal tax purpose germane to the business of the distributing corporation, the controlled corporation, or the affiliated group (as defined in §1.355-3(b)(4)(iv)) to which the distributing corporation belongs. A purpose of reducing non-Federal taxes is not a corporate business purpose if (i) the transaction will effect a reduction in both Federal and non-Federal taxes because of similarities between Federal tax law and the tax law of the other jurisdiction and (ii) the reduction of Federal taxes is greater than or substantially coextensive with the reduction of non-Federal taxes. See examples (7) and (8) of paragraph (b)(5) of this section. A shareholder purpose (for

example, the personal planning purposes of a shareholder) is not a corporate business purpose. Depending upon the facts of a particular case, however, a shareholder purpose for a transaction may be so nearly coextensive with a corporate business purpose as to preclude any distinction between them. In such a case, the transaction is carried out for one or more corporate business purposes. See example (2) of paragraph (b)(5) of this section.

(3) *Business purpose for distribution.*—The distribution must be carried out for one or more corporate business purposes. See example (3) of paragraph (b)(5) of this section. If a corporate business purpose can be achieved through a nontaxable transaction that does not involve the distribution of stock of a controlled corporation and which is neither impractical nor unduly expensive, then, for purposes of paragraph (b)(1) of this section, the separation is not carried out for that corporate business purpose. See examples (3) and (4) of paragraph (b)(5) of this section. For rules with respect to the requirement of a business purpose for a transfer of assets to a controlled corporation in connection with a reorganization described in section 368(a)(1)(D), see § 1.368-1(b).

(4) *Business purpose as evidence of nondevice.*—The corporate business purpose or purposes for a transaction are evidence that the transaction was not used principally as a device for the distribution of earnings and profits within the meaning of section 355(a)(1)(B). See paragraph (d)(3)(ii) of this section.

(5) *Examples.*—The provisions of this paragraph (b) may be illustrated by the following examples:

Example (1). Corporation X is engaged in the production, transportation, and refining of petroleum products. In 1985, X acquires all of the properties of corporation Z, which is also engaged in the production, transportation, and refining of petroleum products. In 1991, as a result of antitrust litigation, X is ordered to divest itself of all of the properties acquired from Z. X transfers those properties to new corporation Y and distributes the stock of Y pro rata to X's shareholders. In view of the divestiture order, the distribution is carried out for a corporate business purpose. See paragraph (b)(1) of this section.

Example (2). Corporation X is engaged in two businesses: the manufacture and sale of furniture and the sale of jewelry. The businesses are of equal value. The outstanding stock of X is owned equally by unrelated individuals A and B. A is more interested in the furniture business, while B is more interested in the jewelry business. A and B decide to split up the businesses and go their separate ways. A and B anticipate that the operations of each business will be enhanced by the separation because each shareholder will be able to devote his undivided attention to the business in which he is more interested and more proficient. Accordingly, X transfers the jewelry business to new corporation Y and distributes the stock of Y to B in exchange for all of B's stock in X. The distribution is carried out for a corporate business purpose, notwithstanding that it is also carried out in part for shareholder purposes. See paragraph (b)(2) of this section.

Example (3). Corporation X is engaged in the manufacture and sale of toys and the manufacture and sale of candy. The shareholders of X wish to protect the candy business from the risks and vicissitudes of the toy business. Accordingly, X transfers the toy business to new corporation Y and distributes the stock of Y to X's shareholders. Under applicable law, the purpose of protecting the candy business from the risks and vicissitudes of the toy business is achieved as soon as X transfers the toy business to Y. Therefore, the distribution is not carried out for a corporate business purpose. See paragraph (b)(3) of this section.

Example (4). Corporation X is engaged in a regulated business in State T. X owns all of the stock of corporation Y, a profitable corporation that is not engaged in a regulated business. Commission C sets the rates that X may charge its customers, based on its total income. C has recently adopted rules according to which the total income of a corporation includes the income of a business if, and only if, the business is operated, directly or indirectly, by the corporation. Total income, for this purpose, includes the income of a wholly owned subsidiary corporation but does not include the income of a parent or "brother/sister" corporation. Under C's new rule, X's total income includes the income of Y, with the result that X has suffered a reduction of the rates that it may charge its customers. It would not be impractical or unduly expensive to create in a nontaxable transaction (such as a transaction qualifying under section 351) a holding company to hold the stock of X and Y. X distributes the stock of Y to X's shareholders. The distribution is not carried out for the purpose of increasing the rates that X may charge its customers because that purpose could be achieved through a nontaxable transaction, the creation of a holding company, that does not involve the distribution of stock of a controlled corporation and which is neither impractical nor unduly expensive. See paragraph (b)(3) of this section.

Example (5). The facts are the same as in example (4), except that C has recently adopted rules according to which the total income of a corporation includes not only the income included in example (3), but also the income of any member of the affiliated group to which the corporation belongs. In order to avoid a reduction in the rates that it may charge its customers, X distributes the stock of Y to X's shareholders. The distribution is carried out for a corporate business purpose. See paragraph (b)(3) of this section.

Example (6). (i) Corporation X owns all of the one class of stock of corporation Y. X distributes the stock of Y pro rata to its five shareholders, all of whom are individuals, for the sole purpose of enabling X and/or Y to elect to become an S corporation. The distribution does not meet the corporate business purpose requirement. See paragraph (b)(1) and (2) of this section.

(ii) The facts are the same as in Example (6)(i), except that the business of Y is operated as a division of X. X transfers this division to new corporation Y and distributes the stock of Y pro rata to its shareholders, all of whom are individuals, for the sole purpose of enabling X and/or Y to elect to become an S corporation. The distribution does not meet the corporate business purpose requirement. See paragraph (b)(1) and (2) of this section.

Example (7). The facts are the same as in example (6)(i), except that the distribution is made to enable X to elect to become an S corporation both for Federal tax purposes and for purposes of the income tax imposed by State M. State M has tax law provisions similar to subchapter S of the Internal Revenue Code of 1986. An election to be an S corporation for Federal tax purposes will effect a substantial reduction in Federal taxes that is greater than the reduction of State M taxes pursuant to an election to be an S corporation for State M purposes. The purpose of reducing State M taxes is not a corporate business purpose. The distribution does not meet the corporate business purpose requirement. See paragraph (b)(1) and (2) of this section.

Example (8). The facts are the same as Example (7), except that the distribution also is made to enable A, a key employee of Y, to acquire stock of Y without investing in X. A is considered to be critical to the success of Y and he has indicated that he will seriously consider leaving the company if he is not given the opportunity to purchase a significant amount of stock of Y. As a matter of state law, Y could not issue stock to the employee while it was a subsidiary of X. As in Example (7), the purpose of reducing State M taxes is not a corporate business purpose. In order to determine whether the issuance of stock to the key employee, in fact, motivated the distribution of the Y stock, the potential avoidance of Federal taxes is a relevant factor to take into account. If the facts and circumstances establish that the distribution was substantially motivated by the need to issue stock to the employee, the distribution will meet the corporate business purpose requirement.

(c) *Continuity of interest requirement.*—(1) *Requirement.*—Section 355 applies to a separation that effects only a readjustment of continuing interests in the property of the distributing and controlled corporations. In this regard section 355 requires that one or more persons who, directly or indirectly, were the owners of the enterprise prior to the distribution or exchange own, in the aggregate, an amount of stock establishing a continuity of interest in each of the modified corporate forms in which the enterprise is conducted after the separation. This continuity of interest requirement is independent of the other requirements under section 355.

(2) *Examples.*

Example (1). For more than five years, corporation X has been engaged directly in one business, and indirectly in a different business through its wholly owned subsidiary, S. The businesses are equal in value. At all times, the outstanding stock of X has been owned equally by unrelated individuals A and B. For valid business reasons, A and B cause X to distribute all of the stock of S to B in exchange for all of B's stock in X. After the transaction, A owns all the stock of X and B owns all the stock of S. The continuity of interest requirement is met because one or more persons who were the owners of X prior to the distribution (A and B) own, in the aggregate, an amount of stock establishing a continuity of interest in each of X and S after the distribution.

Example (2). Assume the same facts as in Example (1), except that pursuant to a plan to acquire a stock interest in X without acquiring, directly or indirectly, an interest in S, C purchased one-half of the X stock owned by A and immediately thereafter X distributed all of the S stock to B in exchange for all of B's stock in X. After the transactions, A owns 50 percent of X and B owns 100 percent of S. The distribution by X of all of the stock of S to B in exchange for all of B's stock in X will satisfy the continuity of interest requirement for section 355 because one or more persons who were the owners of X prior to the distribution (A and B) own, in the aggregate, an amount of stock establishing a continuity of interest in each of X and S after the distribution.

Example (3). Assume the same facts as in Example (1) and (2), except that C purchased all of the X stock owned by A. After the transactions, neither A nor B own any of the stock of X, and B owns all the stock of S. The continuity of interest requirement is not met because the owners of X prior to the distribution (A and B) do not, in the aggregate, own an amount of stock establishing a continuity of interest in each of X and S after the distribution, *i.e.*, although A and B collectively have retained 50 percent of their equity interest in the former combined enterprise, they have failed to continue to own the minimum stock interest in the distributing corporation, X, that would be required in order to meet the continuity of interest requirement.

Example (4). Assume the same facts as in Examples (1) and (2), except that C purchased 80 percent of the X stock owned by A. After the transactions, A owns 20 percent of the stock of X, B owns no X stock, and B owns 100 percent of the S stock. The continuity of interest requirement is not met because the owners of X prior to the distribution (A and B) do not, in the aggregate, have a continuity of interest in each of X and S after the distribution, *i.e.*, although A and B collectively have retained 60 percent of their equity interest in the former combined enterprise, the 20 percent interest of A in X is less than the minimum equity interest in the distributing corporation, X, that would be required in order to meet the continuity of interest requirement.

(d) *Device for distribution of earnings and profits.*—(1) *In general.*—Section 355 does not apply to a transaction used principally as a device for the distribution of the earnings and profits of the distributing corporation, the controlled corporation, or both (a "device"). Section 355 recognizes that a tax-free distribution of the stock of a controlled corporation presents a potential for tax avoidance by facilitating the avoidance of the dividend provisions of the Code through the subsequent sale or exchange of stock of one corporation and the retention of the stock of another corporation. A device can include a transaction that effects a recovery of basis. In this paragraph (d), "exchange" includes transactions, such as redemptions, treated as exchanges under the Code. Generally, the determination of whether a transaction was used principally as a device will be made from all of the facts and circumstances, including, but not limited to, the presence of the device factors specified in paragraph (d)(2) of this section ("evidence of device"), and the presence of the nondevice factors specified in paragraph (d)(3) of this section ("evidence of nondevice"). However, if a transaction is specified in paragraph (d)(5) of this section, then it is ordinarily considered not to have been used principally as a device.

(2) *Device factors.*—(i) *In general.*—The presence of any of the device factors specified in this subparagraph (2) is evidence of device. The strength of this evidence depends on the facts and circumstances.

(ii) *Pro rata distribution.*—A distribution that is pro rata or substantially pro rata among the shareholders of the distributing corporation presents the greatest potential for the avoidance of the dividend provisions of the Code and, in contrast to other types of distributions, is more likely to be used principally as a device. Accordingly, the fact that a distribution is pro rata or substantially pro rata is evidence of device.

(iii) *Subsequent sale or exchange of stock.*—(A) *In general.*—A sale or exchange of stock of the distributing or the controlled corporation after the distribution (a "subsequent sale or exchange") is evidence of device. Generally, the greater the percentage of the stock sold or exchanged after the distribution, the stronger the evidence of device. In addition, the shorter the period of time between the distribution and the sale or exchange, the stronger the evidence of device.

(B) *Sale or exchange negotiated or agreed upon before the distribution.*—A subsequent sale or exchange pursuant to an arrangement negotiated or agreed upon before the distribution is substantial evidence of device.

(C) *Sale or exchange not negotiated or agreed upon before the distribution.*—A subsequent sale or exchange not pursuant to an arrangement negotiated or agreed upon before the distribution is evidence of device.

(D) *Negotiated or agreed upon before the distribution.*—For purposes of this subparagraph (2), a sale or exchange is always pursuant to an arrangement negotiated or agreed upon before the distribution if enforceable rights to buy or sell existed before the distribution. If a sale or exchange was discussed by the buyer and the seller before the distribution and was reasonably to be anticipated by both parties, then the sale or exchange will ordinarily be considered to be pursuant to an arrangement negotiated or agreed upon before the distribution.

(E) *Exchange in pursuance of a plan of reorganization.*—For purposes of this subparagraph (2), if stock is exchanged for stock in pursuance of a plan of reorganization, and either no gain or loss or only an insubstantial amount of gain is recognized on the exchange, then the exchange is not treated as a subsequent sale or exchange, but the stock received in the exchange is treated as the stock surrendered in the exchange. For this purpose, gain treated as a dividend pursuant to sections 356(a)(2) and 316 shall be disregarded.

(iv) *Nature and use of assets.*—(A) *In general.*—The determination of whether a transaction was used principally as a device will take into account the nature, kind, amount, and use of the assets of the distributing and the controlled corporations (and corporations controlled by them) immediately after the transaction.

(B) *Assets not used in a trade or business meeting the requirement of section 355(b).*—The existence of assets that are not used in a trade or business that satisfies the requirements of section 355(b) is evidence of device. For this purpose, assets that are not used in a trade or business that satisfies the requirements of section 355(b) include, but are not limited to, cash and other liquid assets that are not related to the reasonable needs of a business satisfying such section. The strength of the evidence of device depends on all the facts and circumstances, including, but not limited to, the ratio for each corporation of the value of assets not used in a trade or business that satisfies the requirements of section 355(b) to the value of its business that satisfies such requirements. A difference in the ratio described in the preceding sentence for the distributing and controlled corporation is ordinarily not evidence of device if the distribution is not pro rata among the shareholders of the distributing corporation and such difference is attributable to a need to equalize the value of the stock distributed and the value of the stock or securities exchanged by the distributees.

(C) *Related function.*—There is evidence of device if a business of either the distributing or controlled corporation (or a corporation controlled by it) is (1) a "secondary business" that continues as a secondary business for a significant period after the separation, and (2) can be sold without adversely affecting the business of the other corporation (or a corporation controlled by it). A secondary business is a business of either the distributing or controlled corporation, if its principal function is to serve the business of the other corporation (or a corporation controlled by it). A secondary business can include a business transferred to a newly-created subsidiary or a business which serves a business transferred to a newly-created subsidiary. The activities of the secondary business may consist of providing property or performing services. Thus, in example (11) of § 1.355-3(c), evidence of device would be presented if the principal function of the coal mine (satisfying the requirements of the steel business) continued after the separation and the coal mine could be sold without adversely affecting the steel business. Similarly, in example (10) of § 1.355-3(c), evidence of device would be presented if the principal function of the sales operation after the separation is to sell the output from the manufacturing operation and the sales operation could be sold without adversely affecting the manufacturing operation.

(3) *Nondevice factors.*—(i) *In general.*—The presence of any of the nondevice factors specified in this subparagraph (3) is evidence of nondevice. The strength of this evidence depends on all of the facts and circumstances.

(ii) *Corporate business purpose.*—The corporate business purpose for the transaction is evidence of nondevice. The stronger the evidence of device (such as the presence of the device factors specified in paragraph (d)(2) of this section), the stronger the corporate business purpose required to prevent the determination that the transaction was used principally as a device. Evidence of device presented by the transfer or retention of assets not used in a trade or business that satisfies the requirements of section 355(b) can be outweighed by the existence of a corporate business purpose for those transfers or retentions. The assessment of the strength of a corporate business purpose will be based on all of the facts and circumstances, including, but not limited to, the following factors:

(A) The importance of achieving the purpose to the success of the business;

(B) The extent to which the transaction is prompted by a person not having a proprietary interest in either corporation, or by other outside factors beyond the control of the distributing corporation; and

(C) The immediacy of the conditions prompting the transaction.

(iii) *Distributing corporation publicly traded and widely held.*—The fact that the distributing corporation is publicly traded and has no shareholder who is directly or indirectly the beneficial owner of more than five percent of any class of stock is evidence of nondevice.

(iv) *Distribution to domestic corporate shareholders.*—The fact that the stock of the controlled corporation is distributed to one or more domestic corporations that, if section 355 did not apply, would be entitled to a deduction under section 243(a)(1) available to corporations meeting the stock ownership requirements of section 243(c), or a deduction under section 243(a)(2) or (3) or 245(b) is evidence of nondevice.

(4) *Examples.*—The provisions of paragraph (d)(1) through (3) of this section may be illustrated by the following examples:

Example (1). Individual A owns all of the stock of corporation X, which is engaged in the warehousing business. X owns all of the stock of corporation Y, which is engaged in the transportation business. X employs individual B, who is extremely knowledgeable of the warehousing business in general and the operations of X in particular. B has informed A that he will seriously consider leaving the company if he is not given the opportunity to purchase a significant amount of stock of X. Because of his knowledge and experience, the loss of B would seriously damage the business of X. B cannot afford to purchase any significant amount of stock of X as long as X owns Y. Accordingly, X distributes the stock of Y to A and A subsequently sells a portion of his X stock to B. However, X could have issued additional shares to B sufficient to give B an equivalent ownership interest in X. There is no other evidence of device or evidence of nondevice. In light of the fact that X could have issued additional shares to B, the sale of X stock by A is substantial evidence of device. The transaction is considered to have been used principally as a device. See paragraph (d)(1), (2)(ii), (iii)(A), (B) and (D), and (3)(i) and (ii) of this section.

Example (2). Corporation X owns and operates a fast food restaurant in State M and owns all of the stock of corporation Y, which owns and operates a fast food restaurant in State N. X and Y operate their businesses under franchises granted by D and E, respectively. X owns cash and marketable securities that exceed the reasonable needs of its business but whose value is small relative to the value of its business. E has recently changed its franchise policy and will no longer grant or renew franchises to subsidiaries (or other members of the same affiliated group) of corporations operating businesses under franchises granted by its competitors. Thus, Y will lose its franchise if it remains a subsidiary of X. The franchise is about to expire. Accordingly, X distributes the stock of Y pro rata among X's shareholders. X retains its business and transfers cash and marketable securities to Y in an amount proportional to the value of Y's business. There is no other evidence of device or evidence of nondevice. The transfer by X to Y and the retention by X of cash and marketable securities is relatively weak evidence of device because after the transfer X and Y hold cash and marketable securities in amounts proportional to the values of their businesses. The fact that the distribution is pro rata is evidence of device. A strong corporate business purpose is relatively strong evidence of nondevice. Accordingly, the transaction is considered not to have been used principally as a device. See paragraph (d)(1), (2)(ii), (iv)(A), and (B) and (3)(i) and (ii)(A), (B), and (C) of this section.

Example (3). Corporation X is engaged in a regulated business in State M and owns all of the stock of corporation Y, which is not engaged in a regulated business in State M. State M has recently amended its laws to provide that affiliated corporations operating in M may not conduct both regulated and unregulated businesses. X transfers cash not related to the reasonable needs of the business of X or Y to Y and then distributes the stock of Y pro rata among X's shareholders. As a result of the transfer of cash, the ratio of the value of its assets not used in a trade or business that satisfies the requirements of section 355(b) to the value of its business is substantially greater for Y than for X. There is no other evidence of device or evidence of nondevice. The transfer of cash by X to Y is relatively strong evidence of device because after the transfer Y holds disproportionately many assets that are not used in a trade or business that satisfies the requirements of section 355(b). The fact that the distribution is pro rata is evidence of device. The strong business purpose is relatively strong evidence of nondevice, but it does not pertain to the transfer. Accordingly, the transaction is considered to have been used principally as a device. See paragraph (d)(1), (2)(ii), (iv)(A) and (B), and (3)(i) and (ii) of this section.

Example (4). The facts are the same as in example (3), except that, instead of transferring cash to Y, X purchases operating assets unrelated to the business of Y and transfers them to Y prior to the distribution. There is no other evidence of device or evidence of nondevice. The transaction is considered to have been used principally as a device. See paragraph (d)(1), (2)(ii), (iv)(A) and (B), and (3)(i) and (ii) of this section.

(5) *Transactions ordinarily not considered as a device.*—(i) *In general.*—This subparagraph (5) specifies three distributions that ordinarily do not present the potential for tax avoidance described in paragraph (d)(1) of this section. Accordingly, such distributions are ordinarily considered not to have been used principally as a device, notwithstanding the presence of any of the device factors described in paragraph (d)(2) of this section. A transaction described in paragraph (d)(5)(iii) or (iv) of this section is not protected by this subparagraph (5) from a determination that it was used principally as a device if it involves the distribution of the stock of more than one controlled corporation and facilitates the avoidance of the dividend provisions of the Code through the subsequent sale or exchange of stock of one corporation and the retention of the stock of another corporation.

(ii) *Absence of earnings and profits.*—A distribution is ordinarily considered not to have been used principally as a device if—

(A) The distributing and controlled corporations have no accumulated earnings and profits at the beginning of their respective taxable years,

(B) The distributing and controlled corporations have no current earnings and profits as of the date of the distribution, and

(C) No distribution of property by the distributing corporation immediately before the separation would require recognition of gain resulting in current earnings and profits for the taxable year of the distribution.

(iii) *Section 303(a) transactions.*—A distribution is ordinarily considered not to have been used principally as a device if, in the absence of section 355, with respect to each shareholder distributee, the distribution would be a redemption to which section 303(a) applied.

(iv) *Section 302(a) transactions.*—A distribution is ordinarily considered not to have been used principally as a device if, in the absence of section 355, with respect to each shareholder distributee, the distribution would be a redemption to which section 302(a) applied. For purposes of the preceding sentence, section 302(c)(2)(A)(ii) and (iii) shall not apply.

(v) *Examples.*—The provisions of this subparagraph (5) may be illustrated by the following examples:

Example (1). The facts are the same as in example (3) of paragraph (d)(4) of this section, except that X and Y had no accumulated earnings and profits at the beginning of its taxable year, X and Y have no current earnings and profits as of the date of the distribution, and no distribution of property by X immediately before the separation would require recognition of gain that would result in earnings and profits for the taxable year of the distribution. The transaction is considered not to have been used principally as a device. See paragraph (d)(5)(i) and (ii) of this section.

Example (2). Corporation X is engaged in three businesses: a hotel business, a restaurant business, and a rental real estate business. Individuals A, B, and C own all of the stock of X. X transfers the restaurant business to new corporation Y and transfers the rental real estate business to new corporation Z. X then distributes the stock of Y and Z pro rata between B and C in exchange for all of their stock in X. In the absence of section 355, the distribution would be a redemption to which section 302(a) applied. Since this distribution involves the stock of more than one controlled corporation and facilitates the avoidance of the dividend provisions of the Code through the subsequent sale or exchange of stock in one corporation and the retention of the stock of another corporation, it is not protected by paragraph (d)(5)(i) and (iv) of this section from a determination that it was used principally as a device. Thus, the determination of whether the transaction was used principally as a device must be made from all the facts and circumstances, including the presence of the device factors and nondevice factors specified in paragraph (d)(2) and (3) of this section.

(e) *Stock and securities distributed.*—(1) *In general.*—Section 355 applies to a distribution only if the distributing corporation distributes—

(i) All of the stock and securities of the controlled corporation that it owns, or

(ii) At least an amount of the stock of the controlled corporation that constitutes control as defined in section 368(c). In such a case, all, or any part, of the securities of the controlled corporation may be distributed, and paragraph (e)(2) of this section shall apply.

(2) *Additional rules.*—Where a part of either the stock or the securities of the controlled corporation is retained under paragraph (e)(1)(ii) of this section, it must be established to the satisfaction of the Commissioner that the retention by the distributing corporation was not in pursuance of a plan having as one of its principal purposes the avoidance of Federal income tax. Ordinarily, the corporate business purpose or purposes for the distribution will require the distribution of all of the stock and securities of the controlled corporation. If the distribution of all of the stock and securities of a controlled corporation would be treated to any extent as a distribu-

tion of "other property" under section 356, this fact tends to establish that the retention of stock or securities is in pursuance of a plan having as one of its principal purposes the avoidance of Federal income tax.

(f) *Principal amount of securities.*—(1) *Securities received.*—Section 355 does not apply to a distribution if, with respect to any shareholder or security holder, the principal amount of securities received exceeds the principal amount of securities surrendered, or securities are received but no securities are surrendered. In such cases, see section 356.

(2) *Only stock received.*—If only stock is received in a distribution to which section 355(a)(1)(A) applies, the principal amount of the securities surrendered, if any, and the par value or stated value of the stock surrendered, if any, are not relevant to the application of that section.

(g) *Recently acquired controlled stock under section 355(a)(3)(B).*—(1) *Other property.*—Except as provided in paragraph (g)(2) of this section, for purposes of section 355(a)(1)(A), section 355(c), and so much of section 356 as relates to section 355, stock of a controlled corporation acquired by the DSAG in a taxable transaction (as defined in paragraph (g)(4) of this section) within the five-year period ending on the date of the distribution (pre-distribution period) shall not be treated as stock of the controlled corporation but shall be treated as "other property." Transfers of controlled corporation stock that is owned by the DSAG immediately before and immediately after the transfer are disregarded and are not acquisitions for purposes of this paragraph (g)(1).

(2) *Exceptions.*—Paragraph (g)(1) of this section does not apply to an acquisition of stock of the controlled corporation—

(i) If the controlled corporation is a DSAG member at any time after the acquisition (but prior to the distribution); or

(ii) Described in §1.355-3(b)(4)(iii).

(3) *DSAG.*—For purposes of this paragraph (g), a *DSAG* is the distributing corporation's separate affiliated group (the affiliated group which would be determined under section 1504(a) if such corporation were the common parent and section 1504(b) did not apply) that consists of the distributing corporation as the common parent and all corporations affiliated with the distributing corporation through stock ownership described in section 1504(a)(1)(B) (regardless of whether the corporations are includible corporations under section 1504(b)). For purposes of paragraph (g)(1) of this section, any reference to the DSAG is a reference to the distributing corporation if it is not the common parent of a separate affiliated group.

(4) *Taxable transaction.*—(i) *Generally.*—For purposes of this paragraph (g), a *taxable transaction* is a transaction in which gain or loss was recognized in whole or in part.

(ii) *Dunn Trust and predecessor issues.*—[Reserved].

(5) *Examples.*—The following examples illustrate this paragraph (g). Assume that C, D, P, and S are corporations, X is an unrelated individual, each of the transactions is unrelated to any other transaction and, but for the issue of whether C stock is treated as "other property" under section 355(a)(3)(B), the distributions satisfy all of the requirements of section 355. No inference should be drawn from any of these examples as to whether any requirements of section 355 other than section 355(a)(3)(B), as specified, are satisfied. Furthermore, the following definitions apply:

(i) *Purchase* is an acquisition that is a taxable transaction.

(ii) *Section 368(c) stock* is stock constituting control within the meaning of section 368(c).

(iii) *Section 1504(a)(2) stock* is stock meeting the requirements of section 1504(a)(2).

Example 1. Hot stock. For more than five years, D has owned section 368(c) stock but not section 1504(a)(2) stock of C. In year 6, D purchases additional C stock from X. However, D does not own section 1504(a)(2) stock of C after the year 6 purchase. If D distributes all of its C stock within five years after the year 6 purchase, for purposes of section 355(a)(1)(A), section 355(c), and so much of section 356 as relates to section 355, the C stock purchased in year 6 would be treated as "other property." See paragraph (g)(1) of this section.

Example 2. C becomes a DSAG member. For more than five years, D has owned section 368(c) stock but not section 1504(a)(2) stock of C. In year 6, D purchases additional C stock from X such that D's *total ownership* of C is section 1504(a)(2) stock. If D distributes all of its C stock within five years after the year 6 purchase, the distribution of the C stock purchased in year 6 would not be treated as "other property" because C becomes a DSAG member. See paragraph (g)(2)(i) of this section. The result would be the same if D did not

own any C stock prior to year 6 and D purchased all of the C stock in year 6. See paragraph (g)(2)(i) of this section. Similarly, if D did not own any C stock prior to year 6, D purchased 20 percent of the C stock in year 6, and then acquired all of the remaining C stock in year 7, the C stock purchased in year 6 and the C stock acquired in year 7 (even if purchased) would not be treated as "other property" because C becomes a DSAG member. See paragraph (g)(2)(i) of this section.

Example 3. Intra-SAG transaction. For more than five years, D has owned all of the stock of S. D and S, in the aggregate, have owned section 368(c) stock but not section 1504(a)(2) stock of C. Therefore, D and S are DSAG members. In year 6, D purchases S's C stock. If D distributes all of its C stock within five years after the year 6 purchase, the distribution of the C stock purchased in year 6 would not be treated as "other property". D's purchase of the C stock from S is disregarded for purposes of paragraph (g)(1) of this section because that C stock was owned by the DSAG immediately before and immediately after the purchase. See paragraph (g)(1) of this section.

Example 4. Affiliate exception. For more than five years, P has owned 90 percent of the sole outstanding class of the stock of D and a portion of the stock of C, and X has owned the remaining 10 percent of the D stock. Throughout this period, D has owned section 368(c) stock but not section 1504(a)(2) stock of C. In year 6, D purchases P's C stock. However, D does not own section 1504(a)(2) stock of C after the year 6 purchase. If D distributes all of its C stock to X in exchange for X's D stock within five years after the year 6 purchase, the distribution of the C stock purchased in year 6 would not be treated as "other property" because the C stock was purchased from a member (P) of the affiliated group (as defined in §1.355-3(b)(4)(iv)) of which D is a member, and P did not purchase that C stock within the pre-distribution period. See paragraph (g)(2)(ii) of this section.

(h) *Active conduct of a trade or business.*—Section 355 applies to a distribution only if the requirements of §1.355-3 (relating to the active conduct of a trade or business) are satisfied.

(i) *Effective/applicability date.*—Paragraphs (g)(1) through (g)(5) of this section apply to distributions occurring after October 20, 2011. For rules regarding distributions occurring on or before October 20, 2011, see §1.355-2T(i), as contained in 26 CFR part 1, revised as of April 1, 2011. [Reg. §1.355-2.]

☐ [T.D. 6152, 12-2-55. *Amended by* T.D. 8238, 1-4-89; T.D. 9435, 12-12-2008 *and* T.D. 9548, 10-19-2011.]

[Reg. §1.355-3]

§1.355-3. Active conduct of a trade or business.—(a) *General requirements.*—(1) *Application of section 355.*—Under section 355(b)(1), a distribution of stock, or stock and securities, of a controlled corporation qualifies under section 355 only if—

(i) The distributing and the controlled corporations are each engaged in the active conduct of a trade or business immediately after the distribution (section 355(b)(1)(A)), or

(ii) Immediately before the distribution, the distributing corporation had no assets other than stock or securities of the controlled corporations, and each of the controlled corporations is engaged in the active conduct of a trade or business immediately after the distribution (section 355(b)(1)(B)). A de minimis amount of assets held by the distributing corporation shall be disregarded for purposes of this paragraph (a)(1)(ii).

(2) *Examples.*—Paragraph (a)(1) of this section may be illustrated by the following examples:

Example (1). Prior to the distribution, corporation X is engaged in the active conduct of a trade or business and owns all of the stock of corporation Y, which also is engaged in the active conduct of a trade or business. X distributes all of the stock of Y to X's shareholders, and each corporation continues the active conduct of its trade or business. The active business requirement of section 355(b)(1)(A) is satisfied.

Example (2). The facts are the same as in example (1), except that X transfers all of its assets other than the stock of Y to a new corporation in exchange for all of the stock of the new corporation and then distributes the stock of both controlled corporations to X's shareholders. The active business requirement of section 355(b)(1)(B) is satisfied.

(b) *Active conduct of a trade or business defined.*—(1) *In general.*—Section 355(b)(2) provides rules for determining whether a corporation is treated as engaged in the active conduct of a trade or business for purposes of section 355(b)(1). Under section 355(b)(2)(A), a corporation is treated as engaged in the active conduct of a trade or business if it is itself engaged in the active conduct of a trade or business or if substantially all of its assets consist of the stock, or stock and securities, of a corporation or corporations controlled by it (immediately after the distribution) each of which is engaged in the active conduct of a trade or business.

(2) *Active conduct of a trade or business immediately after distribution.*—(i) *In general.*—For purposes of section 355(b), a corporation shall be treated as engaged in the "active conduct of a trade or business" immediately after the distribution if the assets and activities of the corporation satisfy the requirements and limitations described in paragraph (b)(2)(ii), (iii), and (iv) of this section.

(ii) *Trade or business.*—A corporation shall be treated as engaged in a trade or business immediately after the distribution if a specific group of activities are being carried on by the corporation for the purpose of earning income or profit, and the activities included in such group include every operation that forms a part of, or a step in, the process of earning income or profit. Such group of activities ordinarily must include the collection of income and the payment of expenses.

(iii) *Active conduct.*—For purposes of section 355(b), the determination whether a trade or business is actively conducted will be made from all of the facts and circumstances. Generally, the corporation is required itself to perform active and substantial management and operational functions. Generally, activities performed by the corporation itself do not include activities performed by persons outside the corporation, including independent contractors. A corporation may satisfy the requirements of this subdivision (iii) through the activities that it performs itself, even though some of its activities are performed by others. Separations of real property all or substantially all of which is occupied prior to the distribution by the distributing or the controlled corporation (or by any corporation controlled directly or indirectly by either of those corporations) will be carefully scrutinized with respect to the requirements of section 355(b) and this §1.355-3.

(iv) *Limitations.*—The active conduct of a trade or business does not include—

(A) The holding for investment purposes of stock, securities, land, or other property, or

(B) The ownership and operation (including leasing) of real or personal property used in a trade or business, unless the owner performs significant services with respect to the operation and management of the property.

(3) *Active conduct for five-year period preceding distribution.*—Under section 355(b)(2)(B), a trade or business that is relied upon to meet the requirements of section 355(b) must have been actively conducted throughout the five-year period ending on the date of the distribution. For purposes of this subparagraph (3)—

(i) activities which constitute a trade or business under the tests described in paragraph (b)(2) of this section shall be treated as meeting the requirement of the preceding sentence if such activities were actively conducted throughout the 5-year period ending on the date of distribution, and

(ii) the fact that a trade or business underwent change during the five-year period preceding the distribution (for example, by the addition of new or the dropping of old products, changes in production capacity, and the like) shall be disregarded, provided that the changes are not of such a character as to constitute the acquisition of a new or different business. In particular, if a corporation engaged in the active conduct of one trade or business during that five-year period purchased, created, or otherwise acquired another trade or business in the same line of business, then the acquisition of that other business is ordinarily treated as an expansion of the original business, all of which is treated as having been actively conducted during that five-year period, unless that purchase, creation, or other acquisition effects a change of such a character as to constitute the acquisition of a new or different business.

(4) *Special rules for acquisition of a trade or business (Prior to the Revenue Act of 1987 and Technical and Miscellaneous Revenue Act of 1988).*—(i) *In general.*—Under section 355(b)(2)(C), a trade or business relied upon to meet the requirements of section 355(b) must not have been acquired by the distributing corporation, the controlled corporation, or another member of the affiliated group during the five-year period ending on the date of the distribution unless it was acquired in a transaction in which no gain or loss was recognized. Similarly, under section 355(b)(2)(D), the trade or business must not have been indirectly acquired by any of those corporations (or a predecessor in interest of any of those corporations) during that five-year period in a transaction in which gain or loss was recognized in whole or in part and which consisted of the acquisition of control of the corporation directly engaged in the trade or business, or the indirect acquisition of control of that corporation through the direct or indirect acquisition of control of one or more other corporations. A trade or business acquired, directly or indirectly, within the five-year period ending on the date of the distribution in a transaction in which the basis of the assets acquired was not determined in whole or in part by reference to the transferor's basis does not qualify under

section 355(b)(2), even though no gain or loss was recognized by the transferror.

(ii) *Example.*—Paragraph (b)(4)(i) of this section may be illustrated by the following example:

Example. In 1985, corporation X, which operates a business and has cash and other liquid assets, purchases all of the stock of corporation Y, which is engaged in the active conduct of a trade or business. Later in the same year, X merges into Y in a "downstream" statutory merger. In 1986, Y transfers the business assets formerly owned by X to a new subsidiary, corporation Z, and then distributes the stock of Z to Y's shareholders. Section 355 does not apply to the distribution of the stock of Z because the trade or business of Y was indirectly acquired by X, a predecessor in interest of Y, during the five-year period preceding the distribution.

(iii) *Gain or loss recognized in certain transactions.*—The requirements of section 355(b)(2)(C) and (D) are intended to prevent the direct or indirect acquisition of a trade or business by a corporation in anticipation of a distribution by the corporation of that trade or business in a distribution to which section 355 would otherwise apply. A direct or indirect acquisition of a trade or business by one member of an affiliated group from another member of the group is not the type of transaction to which section 355(b)(2)(C) and (D) is intended to apply. Therefore, in applying section 355(b)(2)(C) or (D), such an acquisition, even though taxable, shall be disregarded.

(iv) *Affiliated group.*—For purposes of this subparagraph (4), the term "affiliated group" means an affiliated group as defined in section 1504(a) (without regard to section 1504(b)), except that the term "stock" includes nonvoting stock described in section 1504(a)(4).

(5) *Special rules for acquisition of a trade or business (After the Revenue Act of 1987 and Technical and Miscellaneous Revenue Act of 1988).*—[Reserved]

(c) *Examples.*—The following examples illustrate section 355(b)(2)(A) and (B) and paragraph (b)(1), (2), and (3) of this section. However, a transaction that satisfies these active business requirements will qualify under section 355 only if it satisfies the other requirements of section 355(a) and (b).

Example (1). Corporation X is engaged in the manufacture and sale of soap and detergents and also owns investment securities. X transfers the investment securities to new subsidiary Y and distributes the stock of Y to X's shareholders. Y does not satisfy the requirements of section 355(b) because the holding of investment securities does not constitute the active conduct of a trade or business. See paragraph (b)(2)(iv)(A) of this section.

Example (2). Corporation X owns, manages, and derives rental income from an office building and also owns vacant land. X transfers the land to new subsidiary Y and distributes the stock of Y to X's shareholders. Y will subdivide the land, install streets and utilities, and sell the developed lots to various homebuilders. Y does not satisfy the requirements of section 355(b) because no significant development activities were conducted with respect to the land during the five-year period ending on the date of the distribution. See paragraph (b)(3) of this section.

Example (3). Corporation X owns land on which it conducts a ranching business. Oil has been discovered in the area, and it is apparent that oil may be found under the land on which the ranching business is conducted. X has engaged in no significant activities in connection with its mineral rights. X transfers its mineral rights to new subsidiary Y and distributes the stock of Y to X's shareholders. Y will actively pursue the development of the oil producing potential of the property. Y does not satisfy the requirements of section 355(b) because X engaged in no significant exploitation activities with respect to the mineral rights during the five-year period ending on the date of the distribution. See paragraph (b)(3) of this section.

Example (4). For more than five years, corporation X has conducted a single business of constructing sewage disposal plants and other facilities. X transfers one half of its assets to new subsidiary Y. These assets include a contract for the construction of a sewage disposal plant in State M, construction equipment, cash, and other tangible assets. X retains a contract for the construction of a sewage disposal plant in State N, construction equipment, cash, and other intangible assets. X then distributes the stock of Y to one of X's shareholders in exchange for all of his stock of X. X and Y both satisfy the requirements of section 355(b). See paragraph (b)(3)(i) of this section.

Example (5). For the past six years, corporation X has owned and operated two factories devoted to the production of edible pork skins. The entire output of one factory is sold to one customer, C, while the output of the second factory is sold to C and a number of other customers. To eliminate errors in packaging, X opens a new factory. Thereafter, orders from C are processed and packaged at the two original factories, while the new factory handles only orders from other customers. Eight months after opening the new factory, X transfers it and related business assets to new subsidiary Y and distributes the stock of Y to X's shareholders. X and Y both satisfy the requirements of section 355(b). See paragraph (b)(3)(i) and (ii) of this section.

Example (6). Corporation X has owned and operated a men's retail clothing store in the downtown area of the City of G for nine years and has owned and operated another men's retail clothing store in a suburban area of G for seven years. X transfers the store building, fixtures, inventory, and other assets related to the operations of the suburban store to new subsidiary Y. X also transfers to Y the delivery trucks and delivery personnel that formerly served both stores. Henceforth, X will contract with a local public delivery service to make its deliveries. X retains the warehouses that formerly served both stores. Henceforth, Y will lease warehouse space from an unrelated public warehouse company. X then distributes the stock of Y to X's shareholders. X and Y both satisfy the requirements of section 355(b). See paragraph (b)(3)(i) of this section.

Example (7). For the past nine years, corporation X has owned and operated a department store in the downtown area of the City of G. Three years ago, X acquired a parcel of land in a suburban area of G and constructed a new department store on it. X transfers the suburban store and related business assets to new subsidiary Y and distributes the stock of Y to X's shareholders. After the distribution, each store has its own manager and is operated independently of the other store. X and Y both satisfy the requirements of section 355(b). See paragraph (b)(3)(i) and (ii) of this section.

Example (8). For the past six years, corporation X has owned and operated hardware stores in several states. Two years ago, X purchased all of the assets of a hardware store in State M, where X had not previously conducted business. X transfers the State M store and related business assets to new subsidiary Y and distributes the stock of Y to X's shareholders. After the distribution, the State M store has its own manager and is operated independently of the other stores. X and Y both satisfy the requirements of section 355(b). See paragraph (b)(3)(i) and (ii) of this section.

Example (9). For the past eight years, corporation X has engaged in the manufacture and sale of household products. Throughout this period, X has maintained a research department for use in connection with its manufacturing activities. The research department has 30 employees actively engaged in the development of new products. X transfers the research department to new subsidiary Y and distributes the stock of Y to X's shareholders. After the distribution, Y continues its research operations on a contractual basis with several corporations, including X. X and Y both satisfy the requirements of section 355(b). See paragraph (b)(3)(i) of this section. The result in this example is the same if, after the distribution, Y continues its research operations but furnishes its services only to X. See paragraph (b)(3)(i) of this section. However, see § 1.355-2(d)(2)(iv)(C) (related function device factor) for possible evidence of device.

Example (10). For the past six years, corporation X has processed and sold meat products. X derives income from no other source. X separates the sales function from the processing function by transferring the business assets related to the sales function and cash for working capital to new subsidiary Y. X then distributes the stock of Y to X's shareholders. After the distribution, Y purchases for resale the meat products processed by X. X and Y both satisfy the requirements of section 355(b). See paragraph (b)(3)(i) of this section. However, see § 1.355-2(d)(2)(iv)(C) (related function device factor) for possible evidence of device.

Example (11). For the past eight years, corporation X has been engaged in the manufacture and sale of steel and steel products. X owns all of the stock of corporation Y, which, for the past six years, has owned and operated a coal mine for the sole purpose of supplying X's coal requirements in the manufacture of steel. X distributes the stock of Y to X's shareholders. X and Y both satisfy the requirements of section 355(b). See paragraph (b)(3)(i) of this section. However, see § 1.355-2(d)(2)(iv)(C) (related function device factor) for possible evidence of device.

Example (12). For the past seven years, corporation X, a bank, has owned an eleven-story office building, the ground floor of which X has occupied in the conduct of its banking business. The remaining ten floors are rented to various tenants. Throughout this seven-year period, the building has been managed and maintained by employees of the bank. X transfers the building to new subsidiary Y and distributes the stock of Y to X's shareholders. Henceforth, Y will manage the building, negotiate leases, seek new tenants, and repair and maintain the building. X and Y both satisfy the requirements of section 355(b). See paragraph (b)(3) of this section.

Example (13). For the past nine years, corporation X, a bank, has owned a two-story building, the ground floor and one half of the second floor of which X has occupied in the conduct of its banking business. The other half of the second floor has been rented as storage space to a neighboring retail merchant. X transfers the build-

ing to new subsidiary Y and distributes the stock of Y to X's shareholders. After the distribution, X leases from Y the space in the building that it formerly occupied. Under the lease, X will repair and maintain its portion of the building and pay property taxes and insurance. Y does not satisfy the requirements of section 355(b) because it is not engaged in the active conduct of a trade or business immediately after the distribution. See paragraph (b)(2)(iv)(A) of this section. This example does not address the question of whether the activities of X with respect to the building prior to the separation would constitute the active conduct of a trade or business. [Reg. § 1.355-3.]

☐ [T.D. 6152, 12-2-55. *Amended by T.D. 8238, 1-5-89.*]

[Reg. § 1.355-4]

§ 1.355-4. Non pro rata distributions, etc.—Section 355 provides for nonrecognition of gain or loss with respect to a distribution whether or not (a) the distribution is pro rata with respect to all of the shareholders of the distributing corporation, (b) the distribution is pursuant to a plan of reorganization within the meaning of section 368(a)(1)(D), or (c) the shareholder surrenders stock in the distributing corporation. Under section 355, the stock of a controlled corporation may consist of common stock or preferred stock. (See, however, section 306 and the regulations thereunder.) Section 355 does not apply, however, if the substance of a transaction is merely an exchange between shareholders or security holders of stock or securities in one corporation for stock or securities in another corporation. For example, if two individuals, A and B, each own directly 50 percent of the stock of corporation X and 50 percent of the stock of corporation Y, section 355 would not apply to a transaction in which A and B transfer all of their stock of X and Y to a new corporation Z, for all of the stock of Z, and Z then distributes the stock of X to A and the stock of Y to B. [Reg. § 1.355-4.]

☐ [T.D. 6152, 12-2-55. *Amended by T.D. 8238, 1-5-89.*]

[Reg. § 1.355-5]

§ 1.355-5. Records to be kept and information to be filed.—(a) *Distributing corporation.*—(1) *In general.*—Every corporation that makes a distribution (the distributing corporation) of stock or securities of a controlled corporation, as described in section 355 (or so much of section 356 as relates to section 355), must include a statement entitled, "STATEMENT PURSUANT TO § 1.355-5(a) BY [INSERT NAME AND EMPLOYER IDENTIFICATION NUMBER (IF ANY) OF TAXPAYER], A DISTRIBUTING CORPORATION," on or with its return for the year of the distribution. If the distributing corporation is a controlled foreign corporation (within the meaning of section 957), each United States shareholder (within the meaning of section 951(b)) with respect thereto must include this statement on or with its return. The statement must include—

(i) The name and employer identification number (if any) of the controlled corporation;

(ii) The name and taxpayer identification number (if any) of every significant distributee;

(iii) The date of the distribution of the stock or securities of the controlled corporation;

(iv) The aggregate fair market value and basis, determined immediately before the distribution or exchange, of the stock, securities, or other property (including money) distributed by the distributing corporation in the transaction; and

(v) The date and control number of any private letter ruling(s) issued by the Internal Revenue Service in connection with the transaction.

(2) *Special rule when an asset transfer precedes a stock distribution.*— If the distributing corporation transferred property to the controlled corporation in a transaction described in section 351 or 368, as part of a plan to then distribute the stock or securities of the controlled corporation in a transaction described in section 355 (or so much of section 356 as relates to section 355), then, unless paragraph (a)(1)(v) of this section applies, the distributing corporation must also include on or with its return for the year of the distribution the statement required by § 1.351-3(a) or 1.368-3(a). If the distributing corporation is a controlled foreign corporation (within the meaning of section 957), each United States shareholder (within the meaning of section 951(b)) with respect thereto must include the statement required by § 1.351-3(a) or 1.368-3(a) on or with its return.

(b) *Significant distributee.*—Every significant distributee must include a statement entitled, "STATEMENT PURSUANT TO § 1.355-5(b) BY [INSERT NAME AND TAXPAYER IDENTIFICATION NUMBER (IF ANY) OF TAXPAYER], A SIGNIFICANT DISTRIBUTEE," on or with such distributee's return for the year in which such distribution is received. If a significant distributee is a controlled foreign corporation (within the meaning of section 957), each United States shareholder (within the meaning of section 951(b)) with respect thereto must include this statement on or with its return. The statement must include—

(1) The names and employer identification numbers (if any) of the distributing and controlled corporations;

(2) The date of the distribution of the stock or securities of the controlled corporation; and

(3) The aggregate basis, determined immediately before the exchange, of any stock or securities transferred by the significant distributee in the exchange, and the aggregate fair market value, determined immediately before the distribution or exchange, of the stock, securities or other property (including money) received by the significant distributee in the distribution or exchange.

(c) *Definitions.*—For purposes of this section:

(1) Significant distributee means—

(i) A holder of stock of a distributing corporation that receives, in a transaction described in section 355 (or so much of section 356 as relates to section 355), stock of a corporation controlled by the distributing corporation if, immediately before the distribution or exchange, such holder—

(A) Owned at least five percent (by vote or value) of the total outstanding stock of the distributing corporation if the stock owned by such holder is publicly traded; or

(B) Owned at least one percent (by vote or value) of the stock of the distributing corporation if the stock owned by such holder is not publicly traded; or

(ii) A holder of securities of a distributing corporation that receives, in a transaction described in section 355 (or so much of section 356 as relates to section 355), stock or securities of a corporation controlled by the distributing corporation if, immediately before the distribution or exchange, such holder owned securities in such distributing corporation with a basis of $1,000,000 or more.

(2) Publicly traded stock means stock that is listed on—

(i) A national securities exchange registered under section 6 of the Securities Exchange Act of 1934 (15 U.S.C. 78f); or

(ii) An interdealer quotation system sponsored by a national securities association registered under section 15A of the Securities Exchange Act of 1934 (15 U.S.C. 78o-3).

(d) *Substantiation information.*—Under § 1.6001-1(e), taxpayers are required to retain their permanent records and make such records available to any authorized Internal Revenue Service officers and employees. In connection with the distribution or exchange described in this section, these records should specifically include information regarding the amount, basis, and fair market value of all property distributed or exchanged, and relevant facts regarding any liabilities assumed or extinguished as part of such distribution or exchange.

(e) *Effective/applicability date.*—This section applies to any taxable year beginning on or after May 30, 2006. However, taxpayers may apply this section to any original Federal income tax return (including any amended return filed on or before the due date (including extensions) of such original return) timely filed on or after May 30, 2006. For taxable years beginning before May 30, 2006, see § 1.355-5 as contained in 26 CFR part 1 in effect on April 1, 2006. [Reg. § 1.355-5.]

☐ [*T.D. 9329, 6-13-2007.*]

[Reg. § 1.355-6]

§ 1.355-6. Recognition of gain on certain distributions of stock or securities in controlled corporation.—(a) *Conventions.*—(1) *Examples.*—For purposes of the examples in this section, unless otherwise stated, assume that P, S, T, X, Y, N, HC, D, D1, D2, D3, and C are corporations, A and B are individuals, shareholders are not treated as one person under section 355(d)(7), stock has been owned for more than five years and section 355(d)(6) and paragraph (e)(4) of this section do not apply, no election under section 338 (if available) is made, and all transactions described are respected under general tax principles, including the step transaction doctrine. No inference should be drawn from any example as to whether any requirements of section 355 other than those of section 355(d), as specified, are satisfied.

(2) *Five-year period.*—For purposes of this section, the term five-year period means the five-year period (determined after applying section 355(d)(6) and paragraph (e)(4) of this section) ending on the date of the distribution, but in no event beginning earlier than October 10, 1990.

(3) *Distributing securities.*—For purposes of determining if stock of any controlled corporation received in the distribution is disqualified stock described in section 355(d)(3)(B)(ii)(II) (relating to a distribution of controlled corporation stock on any securities in the distributing corporation acquired by purchase during the five-year

period), references in this section to stock of a corporation that is or becomes a distributing corporation includes securities of the corporation. Similarly, a reference to stock in paragraph (c)(4) of this section (relating to a plan or arrangement) includes securities.

(4) *Marketable securities.*—Unless otherwise stated, any reference in this section to marketable stock includes marketable securities.

(b) *General rules and purposes of section 355(d).*—(1) *Disqualified distributions in general.*—In the case of a disqualified distribution, any stock or securities in the controlled corporation shall not be treated as qualified property for purposes of section 355(c)(2) or 361(c)(2). In general, a disqualified distribution is any distribution to which section 355 (or so much of section 356 as relates thereto) applies if, immediately after the distribution—

(i) Any person holds disqualified stock in the distributing corporation that constitutes a 50 percent or greater interest in such corporation; or

(ii) Any person holds disqualified stock in the controlled corporation (or, if stock of more than one controlled corporation is distributed, in any controlled corporation) that constitutes a 50 percent or greater interest in such corporation.

(2) *Disqualified stock.*—(i) *In general.*—Disqualified stock is—

(A) Any stock in the distributing corporation acquired by purchase during the five-year period; and

(B) Any stock in any controlled corporation—

(*1*) Acquired by purchase during the five-year period; or

(*2*) Received in the distribution to the extent attributable to distributions on any stock in the distributing corporation acquired by purchase during the five-year period.

(ii) *Purchase.*—For the definition of a purchase for purposes of section 355(d) and this section, see section 355(d)(5) and paragraph (d) of this section.

(iii) *Exceptions.*—(A) *Purchase eliminated.*—Stock (or an interest in another entity) that is acquired by purchase (including stock (or another interest) that is treated as acquired by purchase under paragraph (e)(2), (3), or (4) of this section) ceases to be acquired by that purchase if (and when) the basis resulting from the purchase is eliminated. For purposes of this paragraph (b)(2)(iii), basis resulting from the purchase is basis in the stock (or in an interest in another entity) that is directly purchased during the five-year period or that is treated as acquired by purchase during such period under paragraph (e)(2), (3), or (4) of this section.

(B) *Deemed purchase eliminated.*—Stock (or an interest in another entity) that is deemed purchased under section 355(d)(8) or paragraph (e)(1) of this section shall cease to be treated as purchased if (and when) the basis resulting from the purchase that effects the deemed purchase is eliminated.

(C) *Elimination of basis.*—(*1*) *General rule.*—Basis in the stock of a corporation (or in an interest in another entity) is eliminated if (and when) it would no longer be taken into account by any person in determining gain or loss on a sale or exchange of any stock of such corporation (or an interest in the other entity). Basis is not eliminated, however, if it is allocated between stock of two corporations under § 1.358-2(a).

(*2*) *Special rule for transferred and exchanged basis property.*—Basis of stock (or an interest in another entity) resulting from a purchase (the first purchase) is eliminated if (and when) such stock (or other interest) is subsequently transferred to another person in an exchange or other transfer to which paragraph (e)(2) or (3) of this section applies (the second purchase). The elimination of basis in stock (or in another interest) resulting from the first purchase, however, does not eliminate the basis resulting from the second purchase in the stock (or other interest) that is treated as acquired by purchase by the acquirer in a transaction to which paragraph (e)(2) of this section applies or by the person making the exchange in a transaction to which paragraph (e)(3) of this section applies.

(*3*) *Special rule for split-offs and splitups.*—Under section 355(d)(3)(B)(ii) and paragraph (b)(2)(i)(B)(2) of this section, disqualified stock includes controlled corporation stock received in exchange for distributing corporation stock acquired by purchase. Solely for purposes of determining whether controlled corporation stock received in a distribution in exchange for distributing corporation stock is disqualified stock described in that section and paragraph immediately after the distribution, paragraph (b)(2)(iii)(C)(2) of this section does not apply to the exchange to eliminate basis resulting from a purchase of that distributing corporation stock (notwithstanding that paragraph (e)(3) of this section applies to the exchange).

(D) *Special rule if basis allocated between two corporations.*—If the shareholder of a distributing corporation, pursuant to § 1.358-2, allocates basis resulting from a purchase between the stock of two or more corporations then, following such allocation, the determination of whether such basis has been eliminated shall be made separately with respect to the stock of each such corporation.

(3) *Certain distributions not disqualified distributions because purposes of section 355(d) not violated.*—(i) *In general.*—Notwithstanding the provisions of section 355(d)(2) and this paragraph (b), a distribution is not a disqualified distribution if the distribution does not violate the purposes of section 355(d) as provided in this paragraph (b)(3). A distribution does not violate the purposes of section 355(d) if the effect of the distribution is neither—

(A) To increase ownership (combined direct and indirect) in the distributing corporation or any controlled corporation by a disqualified person; nor

(B) To provide a disqualified person with a purchased basis in the stock of any controlled corporation.

(ii) *Disqualified person.*—A disqualified person is any person (taking into account section 355(d)(7) and paragraph (c)(4) of this section) that, immediately after a distribution, holds (directly or indirectly under section 355(d)(8) and paragraph (e)(1) of this section) disqualified stock in the distributing corporation or controlled corporation that—

(A) The person—

(1) Acquired by purchase under section 355(d)(5) or (8) and paragraphs (d) and (e) of this section during the five-year period, or

(2) Received in the distribution to the extent attributable to distributions on any stock in the distributing corporation acquired by purchase under section 355(d)(5) or (8) and paragraphs (d) and (e) of this section by that person during the five-year period; and

(B) Constitutes a 50 percent or greater interest in such corporation (under section 355(d)(4) and paragraph (c) of this section).

(iii) *Purchased basis.*—In general, a purchased basis is basis in controlled corporation stock that is disqualified stock. However, basis in controlled corporation stock that is disqualified stock will not be treated as purchased basis if the controlled corporation stock and any distributing corporation stock with respect to which the controlled corporation stock is distributed are treated as acquired by purchase solely under the attribution rules of section 355(d)(8) and paragraph (e)(1) of this section. The prior sentence will not apply, however, if the distributing corporation stock is treated as acquired by purchase under the attribution rules as a result of the acquisition of an interest in a partnership (the purchased partnership), and following the distribution, the controlled corporation stock is directly held by the purchased partnership (or a chain of partnerships that includes the purchased partnership).

(iv) *Increase in interest because of payment of cash in lieu of fractional shares.*—Any increase in direct or indirect ownership in the distributing corporation or any controlled corporation by a disqualified person because of a payment of cash in lieu of issuing fractional shares will be disregarded for purposes of paragraph (b)(3)(i)(A) of this section if the payment of the cash is solely to avoid the expense and inconvenience of issuing fractional share interests, and does not represent separately bargained for consideration.

(v) *Other exceptions.*—The Commissioner may provide by guidance published in the Internal Revenue Bulletin that other distributions are not disqualified distributions because they do not violate the purposes of section 355(d).

(vi) *Examples.*—The following examples illustrate this paragraph (b)(3):

Example 1. Stock distributed in spin-off; no purchased basis. D owns all of the stock of D1, and D1 owns all the stock of C. A purchases 60 percent of the D stock for cash. Within five years of A's purchase, D1 distributes the C stock to D. A is treated as having purchased 60 percent of the stock of both D1 and C on the date A purchases 60 percent of the D stock under the attribution rules of section 355(d)(8) and paragraph (e)(1) of this section. The C stock received by D is attributable to a distribution on purchased D1 stock under section 355(d)(3)(B)(ii). Accordingly, the D1 and C stock each is disqualified stock under section 355(d)(3) and paragraph (b)(2) of this section, and A is a disqualified person under paragraph (b)(3)(ii) of this section. However, the purposes of section 355(d) under paragraph (b)(3)(i) of this section are not violated. A did not increase direct or indirect ownership in D1 or C. In addition, D's basis in the C stock is not a purchased basis under paragraph (b)(3)(iii) of this section because both the D1 and the C stock are treated as acquired by purchase solely under the attribution rules of section 355(d)(8) and paragraph (e)(1) of this section. Accordingly, D1's distribution of the C stock to D is not a disqualified distribution under section 355(d)(2) and paragraph (b)(1) of this section.

Example 2. Stock distributed in spin-off; purchased basis. The facts are the same as *Example 1*, except that D immediately further distributes the C stock to its shareholders (including A) pro rata. The D and C stock each is disqualified stock under section 355(d)(3) and paragraph (b)(2) of this section, and A is a disqualified person under paragraph (b)(3)(ii) of this section. The purposes of section 355(d) under paragraph (b)(3)(i) of this section are violated. A did not increase direct or indirect ownership in D or C. However, A's basis in the C stock is a purchased basis under paragraph (b)(3)(iii) of this section because the D stock is not treated as acquired by purchase solely under the attribution rules of section 355(d)(8) and paragraph (e)(1) of this section. Accordingly, the further distribution is a disqualified distribution under section 355(d)(2) and paragraph (b)(1) of this section.

Example 3. Stock distributed in split-off with ownership increase; purchased basis. The facts are the same as *Example 1*, except that D immediately further distributes the C stock to A in exchange for A's purchased stock in D. The C stock received by A is attributable to a distribution on purchased D stock under section 355(d)(3)(B)(ii), and A's basis in the C stock is determined by reference to the adjusted basis of A's purchased D stock under paragraph (e)(3) of this section. (Under paragraph (b)(2)(iii)(B)(3) of this section, the basis resulting from A's purchase of D stock is not eliminated solely for purposes of determining if the C stock acquired by A is disqualified stock immediately after the distribution, notwithstanding that paragraph (e)(3) of this section applies to the exchange.) Accordingly, the D stock and the C stock each is disqualified stock under section 355(d)(3) and paragraph (b)(2) of this section, and A is a disqualified person under paragraph (b)(3)(ii) of this section. The purposes of section 355(d) under paragraph (b)(3)(i) of this section are violated because A increased its ownership in C from a 60 percent indirect interest to a 100 percent direct interest, and because A's basis in the C stock is a purchased basis under paragraph (b)(3)(iii) of this section. Accordingly, the further distribution is a disqualified distribution under section 355(d)(2) and paragraph (b)(1) of this section.

Example 4. Stock distributed in spin-off; purchased basis. D1 owns all the stock of C. D purchases all of the stock of D1 for cash Within five years of D's purchase of D1, P acquires all of the stock of D1 from D in a section 368(a)(i)(B) reorganization that is not a reorganization under section 368(a)(1)(A) by reason of section 368(a)(2)(E), and D1 distributes all of its C stock to P. P is treated as having acquired the D1 stock by purchase on the date D acquired it under the transferred basis rule of section 355(d)(5)(C) and paragraph (e)(2) of this section. P is treated as having purchased all of the C stock on the date D purchased the D1 stock under the attribution rules of section 355(d)(8) and paragraph (e)(1) of this section, and the C stock received by P is attributable to a distribution on purchased D1 stock under section 355(d)(3)(B)(ii). Accordingly, the D1 and C stock each is disqualified stock under section 355(d)(3) and paragraph (b)(2) of this section, and P is a disqualified person under paragraph (b)(3)(ii) of this section. The purposes of section 355(d) under paragraph (b)(3)(i) of this section are violated. P did not increase direct or indirect ownership in D1 or C. However, P's basis in the C stock is a purchased basis under paragraph (b)(3)(iii) of this section because the D1 stock is not treated as acquired by purchase solely under the attribution rules of section 355(d)(8) and paragraph (e)(1) of this section. Accordingly, D1's distribution of the C stock to P is a disqualified distribution under section 355(d)(2) and paragraph (b)(1) of this section.

Example 5. Stock distributed in split-off with ownership increase; no purchased basis. P owns 50 percent of the stock of D, the remaining D stock is owned by unrelated persons, D owns all the stock of C, and A purchases all of the P stock from the P shareholders. Within five years of A's purchase, D distributes all of the C stock to P in exchange for P's D stock. A is treated as having purchased 50 percent of the stock of both D and C on the date A purchases the P stock under the attribution rules of section 355(d)(8) and paragraph (e)(1) of this section. The C stock received by P is attributable to a distribution on purchased D stock under section 355(d)(3)(B)(ii). Accordingly, the D stock and the C stock each is disqualified stock under section 355(d)(3) and paragraph (b)(2) of this section, and A is a disqualified person under paragraph (b)(3)(ii) of this section. The purposes of section 355(d) under paragraph (b)(3)(i) of this section are violated because, even though P's basis in the C stock is not a purchased basis under paragraph (b)(3)(iii) of this section, A increased its direct or indirect ownership in C from a 50 percent indirect interest to a 100 percent indirect interest. Accordingly, D's distribution of the C stock to P is a disqualified distribution under section 355(d)(2) and paragraph (b)(1) of this section.

Example 6. Stock distributed in split-off with no ownership increase; no purchased basis. A purchases all of the stock of T. T later merges into D in a section 368(a)(1)(A) reorganization and A exchanges its purchased T stock for 60 percent of the stock of D. D owns all of the stock of D1 and D2, D1 and D2 each owns 50 percent of the stock of D3, and D3 owns all of the stock of C. Within five years of A's purchase of the T stock, D3 distributes the C stock to D1 in exchange for all of D1's D3 stock. A is treated as having acquired 60 percent of the D stock by purchase on the date A purchases the T stock under paragraph (e)(3) of this section. A is treated as having purchased 60 percent of the stock of D1, D2, D3, and C on the date A purchases the T stock under the attribution rules of section 355(d)(8) and paragraph (e)(1) of this section. The C stock received by D1 is attributable to a distribution on purchased D3 stock under section 355(d)(3)(B)(ii). Accordingly, the D3 stock and the C stock each is disqualified stock under section 355(d)(3) and paragraph (b)(2) of this section, and A is a disqualified person under paragraph (b)(3)(ii) of this section. However, the purposes of section 355(d) under paragraph (b)(3)(i) of this section are not violated. A did not increase direct or indirect ownership in D3 or C, and D1's basis in the C stock is not a purchased basis under paragraph (b)(3)(iii) of this section because the D3 stock is treated as acquired by purchase solely under the attribution rules of section 355(d)(8) and paragraph (e)(1) of this section. Accordingly, D3's distribution of the C stock to D1 is not a disqualified distribution under section 355(d)(2) and paragraph (b)(1) of this section.

Example 7. Purchased basis eliminated by liquidation; stock distributed in spin-off. P owns 30 percent of the stock of D, D owns all of the stock of D1, and D1 owns all of the stock of C. P purchases the remaining 70 percent of the D stock for cash. Within five years of P's purchase, P liquidates D in a transaction qualifying under sections 332 and 337(a), and D1 then distributes the stock of C to P. Prior to the liquidation, P is treated as having purchased 70 percent of the stock of D1 and C on the date P purchases the D stock under the attribution rules of section 355(d)(8)(B) and paragraph (e)(1) of this section. After the liquidation, however, under paragraph (b)(2)(iii) of this section, P is not treated as having acquired by purchase the D1 or the C stock under section 355(d)(8)(B) and paragraph (e)(1) of this section because P's basis in the D stock is eliminated in the liquidation of D. Under section 334(b)(1), P's basis in the D1 stock is determined by reference to D's basis in the D1 stock and not by reference to P's basis in D. Paragraph (d)(2)(i)(B) of this section does not treat the D1 stock as newly purchased in P's hands because no gain or loss was recognized by D in the liquidation. Accordingly, neither the D1 stock nor the C stock is disqualified stock under section 355(d)(3) and paragraph (b)(2) of this section in P's hands, and the distribution is not a disqualified distribution under section 355(d)(2) and paragraph (b)(1) of this section.

Example 8. Purchased basis eliminated by upstream merger; stock distributed in spin-off. D owns all of the stock of D1, and D1 owns all of the stock of C. P purchases 60 percent of the D stock for cash. Within five years of P's purchase, D merges into P in a section 368(a)(1)(A) reorganization, with the D shareholders other than P receiving solely P stock in exchange for their D stock, and D1 then distributes the stock of C to P. Prior to the merger, P is treated as having purchased 60 percent of the stock of D1 and C on the date P purchases the D stock under the attribution rules of section 355(d)(8) and paragraph (e)(1) of this section. After the merger, however, under paragraph (b)(2)(iii) of this section, P is not treated as having acquired by purchase the D1 or the C stock under section 355(d)(8)(B) and paragraph (e)(1) of this section because P's basis in the D stock is eliminated in the merger. Under section 362(b), P's basis in the D1 stock is determined by reference to D's basis in the D1 stock and not by reference to P's basis in D. Paragraph (d)(2)(i)(B) of this section does not treat the D1 stock as newly purchased in P's hands because no gain or loss was recognized by D in the merger. Accordingly, neither the D1 stock nor the C stock is disqualified stock under section 355(d)(3) and paragraph (b)(2) of this section in P's hands, and the distribution is not a disqualified distribution under section 355(d)(2) and paragraph (b)(1) of this section.

Example 9. Purchased basis eliminated by distribution; stock distributed in spin-off. A purchases all the stock of C for cash on Date 1. D acquires all of the stock of C from A in a section 368(a)(1)(B) reorganization that is not a reorganization under section 368(a)(1)(A) by reason of section 368(A)(1)(E). A receives ten percent of the D stock in the transaction. The remaining D stock is owned by B. Within five years of A's purchase of the C stock, D distributes all the stock of C pro rata to A and B. Under the transferred basis rule of paragraph (e)(2) of this section, D is treated as having purchased all of the C stock on the date A acquired it. Under the exchanged basis rule of paragraph (e)(3) of this section, A is treated as having purchased its D stock on Date 1 and A is treated as having purchased ten percent of the C stock on Date 1 under the attribution rules of section 355(d)(8) and paragraph (e)(3) of this section. Moreover, under paragraph (b)(2)(iii)(C) of this section, A's basis in the C stock resulting from A's Date 1 purchase of C stock is eliminated. After the distribution, A's and B's bases in their C stock are determined by reference to the bases of their D stock under § 1.358-2(a)(2) (and not by reference to D's basis in the C stock). D's basis in the stock of C resulting from its deemed purchase of that stock under paragraph (e)(2) of this section is eliminated by the distribution of the C stock because it would no

longer be taken into account by any person in determining gain or loss on the sale of C stock. Therefore, the C stock distributed to A and B is not disqualified stock as a result of D's purchase of C. However, A's basis in its D stock resulting from its deemed purchase of that stock under paragraph (e)(3) of this section is not eliminated. Therefore, A's ten percent interest in the stock of D is disqualified stock. Furthermore, A's ten percent interest in the stock of C is disqualified stock because the distribution of the C stock is attributable to A's D stock that was acquired by purchase. However, there has not been a disqualified distribution because no person, immediately after the distribution, holds disqualified stock in either D or C that constitutes a 50 percent or greater interest in such corporation.

Example 10. Allocation of purchased basis analyzed separately. (i) P owns all the stock of D. D purchases all the stock of D1 for cash on Date 1. D1 owns all the stock of C (which owns all the stock of C1) and S. Within five years of Date 1, D1 distributes all the stock of C to D. The D1 and C stock each is disqualified stock under section 355(d)(3) and paragraph (b)(2) of this section, and D is a disqualified person under paragraph (b)(3)(ii) of this section. The purposes of section 355(d) under paragraph (b)(3)(i) of this section are violated. D did not increase direct or indirect ownership in D1 or C. However, D's basis in the C stock is a purchased basis under paragraph (b)(3)(iii) of this section because the D1 stock is not treated as acquired by purchase solely under the attribution rules of section 355(d)(8) and paragraph (e)(1) of this section. Accordingly, the distribution is a disqualified distribution under section 355(d) and paragraph (b)(1) of this section. D's basis in the D1 stock is allocated pursuant to § 1.358-2 between the D1 stock and the C stock. Therefore, under paragraph (e)(4) of this section, the C stock is deemed to be acquired by purchase on Date 1, the date D purchased all the stock of D1. If thereafter, and within five years of Date 1, C were to distribute all the stock of C1 to D, that distribution would also be a disqualified distribution because cf D's deemed purchase of the stock of C.

(ii) Following the distribution of the stock of C by D1, and within five years of Date 1, D distributes all the stock of D1 to P. Under paragraph (b)(2)(iii)(D) of this section, the determination of whether D's basis in D1 has been eliminated shall be made without regard to D's allocated basis in C. After the distribution, P's basis in the D1 stock is determined by reference to its basis in its D stock under § 1.358-2(a)(2) (and not by reference to D's basis in the D1 stock). D's basis in the D1 stock resulting from the purchase of that stock is eliminated by the distribution of the D1 stock because it would no longer be taken into account by any person in determining gain or loss on the sale of D1 stock. Therefore, the D1 stock distributed to P is not disqualified stock as a result of D's purchase of D1. Moreover, a subsequent distribution of the S stock by D1 to P would not be a disqualified distribution because both the D1 and S stock would cease to be treated as purchased when D's basis in D1 has been eliminated.

(4) *Anti-avoidance rule.*—(i) *In general.*—Notwithstanding any provision of section 355(d) or this section, the Commissioner may treat any distribution as a disqualified distribution under section 355(d)(2) and paragraph (b)(1) of this section if the distribution or another transaction or transactions are engaged in or structured with a principal purpose to avoid the purposes of section 355(d) or this section with respect to the distribution. Without limiting the preceding sentence, the Commissioner may determine that the existence of a related person, intermediary, pass-through entity, or similar person (an intermediary) should be disregarded, in whole or in part, if the intermediary is formed or availed of with a principal purpose to avoid the purposes of section 355(d) or this section.

(ii) *Example.*—The following example illustrates this paragraph (b)(4):

Example. Post-distribution redemption. B wholly owns D, which wholly owns C. With a principal purpose to avoid the purposes of section 355(d), A, B, D, and C engage in the following transactions. A purchases 45 of 100 shares of the only class of D stock. Within five years after A's purchase, D distributes all of its 100 shares in C to A and B pro rata. D then redeems 20 shares of B's D stock, and C redeems 20 shares of B's C stock. After the redemption, A owns 45 shares and B owns 35 shares in each of D and C. Under paragraph (b)(4)(i) of this section, the Commissioner may treat A as owning disqualified stock in D and C that constitutes a 50 percent or greater interest in D and C immediately after the distribution. Under that treatment, the distribution is a disqualified distribution under section 355(d)(2) and paragraph (b)(1) of this section.

(c) *Whether a person holds a 50 percent or greater interest.*—(1) *In general.*—Under section 355(d)(4), 50 percent or greater interest means stock possessing at least 50 percent of the total combined voting power of all classes of stock entitled to vote or at least 50 percent of the total value of shares of all classes of stock.

(2) *Valuation.*—For purposes of section 355(d)(4) and this section, all shares of stock within a single class are considered to have the same value. But see paragraph (c)(3)(vii)(A) of this section (determination of whether it is reasonably certain that an option will be exercised).

(3) *Effect of options, warrants, convertible obligations, and other similar interests.*—(i) *Application.*—This paragraph (c)(3) provides rules to determine when an option is treated as exercised for purposes of section 355(d) (other than section 355(d)(6)). Except as provided in this paragraph (c)(3), an option is not treated as exercised for purposes of section 355(d). This paragraph (c)(3) does not affect the determination of whether an instrument is an option or stock under general principles of tax law (such as substance over form).

(ii) *General rule.*—In determining whether a person has acquired by purchase a 50 percent or greater interest under section 355(d)(4), an option to acquire stock (as described in paragraphs (c)(3)(v) and (vi) of this section) that has not been exercised when a distribution occurs is treated as exercised on the date it was issued or most recently transferred if—

(A) Its exercise (whether by itself or in conjunction with the deemed exercise of one or more other options) would cause a person to become a disqualified person; and

(B) Immediately after the distribution, it is reasonably certain (as described in paragraph (c)(3)(vii) of this section) that the option will be exercised.

(iii) *Options deemed newly issued and substituted options.*—(A) *Exchange, adjustment, or alteration of existing option.*—For purposes of this paragraph (c)(3), each of the following is treated as a new issuance or transfer of an existing option only if it materially increases the likelihood that an option will be exercised—

(1) An exchange of an option for another option or options;

(2) An adjustment to the terms of an option (including an adjustment pursuant to the terms of the option);

(3) An adjustment to the terms of the underlying stock (including an adjustment pursuant to the terms of the stock);

(4) A change to the capital structure of the issuing corporation; and

(5) An alteration to the fair market value of issuing corporation stock through an asset transfer (other than regular, ordinary dividends) or through any other means.

(B) *Certain compensatory options.*—An option described in paragraph (c)(3)(vi)(B)(2) of this section is treated as issued on the date it becomes transferable.

(C) *Substituted options.*—If an option (existing option) is exchanged for another option or options (substituted option or options) and paragraph (c)(3)(iii)(A) of this section does not apply to treat such exchange as a new issuance or transfer of the existing option, the substituted option or options will be treated as issued or most recently transferred on the date that the existing option was issued or most recently transferred.

(iv) *Effect of treating an option as exercised.*—(A) *In general.*—For purposes of section 355(d), an option that is treated as exercised under this paragraph (c)(3) is treated as exercised both for purposes of determining the percentage of the voting power of stock owned by the holder and for purposes of determining the percentage of the value of stock owned by the holder.

(B) *Stock purchase agreement or similar arrangement.*—If a stock purchase agreement or similar arrangement is deemed exercised, the purchaser is treated as having purchased the stock under the terms of the agreement or arrangement as though all covenants had been satisfied and all contingencies met. The agreement or arrangement is deemed to have been exercised as of the date it is entered into or most recently assigned.

(v) *Instruments treated as options.*—For purposes of this paragraph (c)(3), except to the extent provided in paragraph (c)(3)(vi) of this section, the following are treated as options: A call option, warrant, convertible obligation, the conversion feature of convertible stock, put option, redemption agreement (including a right to cause the redemption of stock), notional principal contract (as defined in §1.446-3(c)) that provides for the payment of amounts in stock, stock purchase agreement or similar arrangement, or any other instrument that provides for the right to purchase, issue, redeem, or transfer stock (including an option on an option).

(vi) *Instruments generally not treated as options.*—For purposes of this paragraph (c)(3), the following are not treated as options, unless issued, transferred, or listed with a principal purpose to avoid the application of section 355(d) or this section:

(A) *Escrow, pledge, or other security agreements.*—An option that is part of a security arrangement in a typical lending transaction (including a purchase money loan), if the arrangement is subject to customary commercial conditions. For this purpose, a security arrangement includes, for example, an agreement for holding stock in escrow or under a pledge or other security agreement, or an option to acquire stock contingent upon a default under a loan.

(B) *Compensatory options.*—(1) *General rule.*—An option to acquire stock in a corporation with customary terms and conditions, provided to an employee, director, or independent contractor in connection with the performance of services for the corporation or a person related to it under section 355(d)(7)(A) (and that is not excessive by reference to the services performed) and that—

(i) Is nontransferable within the meaning of §1.83-3(d); and

(ii) Does not have a readily ascertainable fair market value as defined in §1.83-7(b).

(2) *Exception.*—Paragraph (c)(3)(vi)(B)(1) of this section ceases to apply to an option that becomes transferable.

(C) *Certain stock conversion features.*—The conversion feature of convertible stock, provided that—

(1) The stock is not convertible for at least five years after issuance or transfer; and

(2) The terms of the conversion feature do not require the tender of any consideration other than the stock being converted.

(D) *Options exercisable only upon death, disability, mental incompetency, or separation from service.*—Any option entered into between stockholders of a corporation (or a stockholder and the corporation) with respect to the stock of either stockholder that is exercisable only upon the death, disability, mental incompetency of the stockholder, or, in the case of stock acquired in connection with the performance of services for the corporation or a person related to it under section 355(d)(7)(A) (and that is not excessive by reference to the services performed), the stockholder's separation from service.

(E) *Rights of first refusal.*—A bona fide right of first refusal regarding the corporation's stock with customary terms, entered into between stockholders of a corporation (or between the corporation and a stockholder).

(F) *Other enumerated instruments.*—Any other instruments specified in regulations, a revenue ruling, or a revenue procedure. See §601.601(d)(2) of this chapter.

(vii) *Reasonably certain that the option will be exercised.*—(A) *In general.*—The determination of whether, immediately after the distribution, an option is reasonably certain to be exercised is based on all the facts and circumstances. In applying the previous sentence, the fair market value of stock underlying an option is determined by taking into account control premiums and minority and blockage discounts.

(B) *Stock purchase agreement or similar arrangement.*—A stock purchase agreement or similar arrangement is treated as reasonably certain to be exercised if the parties' obligations to complete the transaction are subject only to reasonable closing conditions.

(viii) *Examples.*—The following examples illustrate this paragraph (c)(3):

Example 1. D owns all of the stock of C. A purchases 40 percent of D's only class of stock and an option to purchase D stock from D, that if deemed exercised, would result in A owning a total of 60 percent of the stock of D. Assume that no control premium or minority or blockage discount applies to the D stock underlying the option. The option permits A to acquire the D stock at $30 per share, and D's stock has a fair market value of $27 per share on the date the option is issued. The option is subject to no contingencies or restrictive covenants, may be exercised within five years after its issuance, and is not described in paragraph (c)(3)(vi) of this section (regarding instruments generally not treated as options). Within five years of A's purchase of the D stock and option, D distributes the stock of its subsidiary C pro rata and A receives 40 percent of the C stock in the distribution. Immediately after the distribution, D's stock has a fair market value of $30 per share and C's stock has a fair market value of $15 per share. At the time of the distribution, A exchanges A's option for an option to purchase 20 percent of the D stock at $20 per share and an option to purchase 20 percent of the C stock at $10 per share. The exchange of the options in D for options in D and C did not materially increase the likelihood that the options would be exercised. Nonetheless, based on all the facts and circumstances, it is reasonably certain, immediately after the distribution, that A will exercise its options. Under paragraph (c)(3)(iii)(C) of this section, the substituted options are treated as issued on the date the original option was issued. Accordingly, the options are treated as exercised by A on the date that A purchased the original option. A is treated as owning 60 percent of the D stock and 60 percent of the C stock that is disqualified stock, and the distribution is a disqualified distribution under section 355(d)(2) and paragraph (b)(1) of this section.

Example 2. D owns all of the stock of C. A purchases 37 percent of D's only class of stock. B owns 38 percent of the D stock, and the remaining 25 percent is owned by 20 individuals, each of whom owns less than five percent of D's stock. A purchases an option to purchase an additional 14 percent of the D stock from shareholders other than B for $50 per share. The option is subject to no contingencies or restrictive covenants, may be exercised within five years after its issuance, and is not described in paragraph (c)(3)(vi) of this section. Within five years of A's purchase of the option and 37 percent interest in D, D distributes the stock of its subsidiary C pro rata and A receives 37 percent of the C stock in the distribution. At the time of the distribution, A exchanges its option for an option to purchase 14 percent of the D stock at $25 per share and an option to purchase 14 percent of the C stock at $25 per share. Assume that, although a shareholder that owned no D or C stock would pay only $20 per share for D or C stock immediately after the distribution, a shareholder in A's position would pay $30 per share for 14 percent of the stock of D or C because of the control premium which attaches to the shares. The control premium is taken into account under paragraph (c)(3)(vii)(A) of this section to determine whether A is reasonably certain to exercise the options. The exchange of the options in D for options in D and C did not materially increase the likelihood that the options would be exercised. Nonetheless, based on all the facts and circumstances, it is reasonably certain, immediately after the distribution, that A will exercise its options. Under paragraph (c)(3)(iii)(C) of this section, the substituted options are treated as issued on the date the original option was issued. Accordingly, the options are treated as exercised by A on the date that A purchased the original option. Under paragraph (c)(2) of this section, all shares of D and C are considered to have the same value to determine the amount of stock A is treated as purchasing under the options. A is treated as owning 51 percent of the D stock and 51 percent of the C stock that is disqualified stock, and the distribution is a disqualified distribution under section 355(d)(2).

(4) *Plan or arrangement.*—(i) *In general.*—Under section 355(d)(7)(B), if two or more persons act pursuant to a plan or arrangement with respect to acquisitions of stock in the distributing corporation or controlled corporation, those persons are treated as one person for purposes of section 355(d).

(ii) *Understanding.*—For purposes of section 355(d)(7)(B), two or more persons who are (or will after an acquisition become) shareholders (or are treated as shareholders under paragraph (c)(3)(ii) of this section) act pursuant to a plan or arrangement with respect to an acquisition of stock only if they have a formal or informal understanding among themselves to make a coordinated acquisition of stock. A principal element in determining if such an understanding exists is whether the investment decision of each person is based on the investment decision of one or more other existing or prospective shareholders. However, the participation by creditors in formulating a plan for an insolvency workout or a reorganization in a title 11 or similar case (whether as members of a creditors' committee or otherwise) and the receipt of stock by creditors in satisfaction of indebtedness pursuant to the workout or reorganization do not cause the creditors to be considered as acting pursuant to a plan or arrangement.

(iii) *Examples.*—The following examples illustrate paragraph (c)(4)(ii) of this section:

Example 1. D has 1,000 shares of common stock outstanding. A group of 20 unrelated individuals who previously owned no D stock (the Group) agree among themselves to acquire 50 percent or more of D's stock. The Group is not a person under section 7701(a)(1). Subsequently, pursuant to their understanding, the members of the Group purchase 600 shares of D common stock from the existing D shareholders (a total of 60 percent of the D stock), with each member purchasing 30 shares. Under paragraph (c)(4)(ii) of this section, the members of the Group have a formal or informal understanding among themselves to make a coordinated acquisition of stock. Their interests are therefore aggregated under section 355(d)(7)(B), and they are treated as one person that purchased 600 shares of D's stock for purposes of section 355(d).

Example 2. D has 1,000 shares of outstanding stock owned by unrelated individuals. D's management is concerned that D may become subject to a takeover bid. In separate meetings, D's management meets with potential investors who own no stock and are friendly to management to convince them to acquire D's stock based on an understanding that D will assemble a group that in the aggregate will acquire more than 50 percent of D's stock. Subsequently, 15 of these investors each purchases four percent of D's outstanding stock. Under paragraph (c)(4)(ii) of this section, the 15

investors have a formal or informal understanding among themselves to make a coordinated acquisition of stock. Their interests are therefore aggregated under section 355(d)(7)(B), and they are treated as one person that purchased 600 shares of D stock for purposes of section 355(d).

Example 3. (i) D has 1,000 shares of outstanding stock owned by unrelated individuals. An investment advisor advises its clients that it believes D's stock is undervalued and recommends that they acquire D stock. Acting on the investment advisor's recommendation, 20 unrelated individuals each purchases 30 shares of the outstanding D stock. Each client's decision was not based on the investment decisions made by one or more other clients. Because there is no formal or informal understanding among the clients to make a coordinated acquisition of D stock, their interests are not aggregated under section 355(d)(7)(B) and they are treated as making separate purchases.

(ii) The facts are the same as in paragraph (i) of this *Example 3*, except that the investment advisor is also the underwriter (without regard to whether it is a firm commitment or best efforts underwriting) for a primary or secondary offering of D stock. The result is the same.

(iii) The facts are the same as in paragraph (i) of this *Example 3*, except that, instead of an investment advisor recommending that clients purchase D stock, the trustee of several trusts qualified under section 401(a) sponsored by unrelated corporations causes each trust to purchase the D stock. The result is the same, provided that the trustee's investment decision made on behalf of each trust was not based on the investment decision made on behalf of one or more of the other trusts.

(iv) *Exception.*—(A) *Subsequent disposition.*—If two or more persons do not act pursuant to a plan or arrangement within the meaning of this paragraph (c)(4) with respect to an acquisition of stock in a corporation (the first corporation), a subsequent acquisition in which such persons exchange their stock in the first corporation for stock in another corporation (the second corporation) in a transaction in which the basis of the second corporation's stock in the hands of such persons is determined in whole or in part by reference to the basis of their stock in the first corporation, will not result in such persons being treated as one person, even if the acquisition of the second corporation's stock is pursuant to a plan or arrangement.

(B) *Example.*—The following example illustrates this paragraph (c)(4)(iv):

Example. In an initial public offering of D stock on Date 1, 100 investors independently purchase one percent each of the D stock. Two years later, D merges into P (in a reorganization described in section 368(a)(1)(A)) and, pursuant to the plan of reorganization, the D shareholders exchange their D stock for 50 percent of the stock of P. The D shareholders approve the plan by a two-thirds vote, as required by state law. Under section 358(a), each shareholder's basis in its P stock is determined by reference to the basis of the D stock it purchased. Under paragraph (e)(3) of this section, the former D shareholders are treated as purchasing their P stock on Date 1. The investors do not become a single person under paragraph (c)(4) of this section with respect to the deemed purchase of the P stock on Date 1 by virtue of their acquisition of the P stock pursuant to the merger on Date 2.

(d) *Purchase.*—(1) *In general.*—(i) *Definition of purchase under section 355(d)(5)(A).*—Under section 355(d)(5)(A), except as otherwise provided in section 355(d)(5)(B) and (C), a *purchase* means any acquisition, but only if—

(A) The basis of the property acquired in the hands of the acquirer is not determined—

(1) In whole or in part by reference to the adjusted basis of such property in the hands of the person from whom acquired; or

(2) Under section 1014(a) or 1022; and

(B) The property is not acquired in an exchange to which section 351, 354, 355, or 356 applies.

(ii) *Section 355 distributions.*—Paragraph (d)(1)(i)(B) of this section includes all section 355 distributions, whether in exchange (in whole or in part) for stock or pro rata.

(iii) *Example.*—The following example illustrates this paragraph (d)(1):

Example. Section 304(a)(1) acquisition. A, who owns all of the stock of P and T, sells the T stock to P for cash. The T stock is not marketable stock under section 355(d)(5)(B)(ii) and paragraph (d)(3)(ii) of this section. A is treated under section 304(a)(1) as receiving a distribution in redemption of the P stock. Under section 302(d). the deemed redemption is treated as a section 301 distribution. Assume that under sections 304(b)(2) and 301 (c)(1), all of the distribution is a dividend. A and P are treated in the same manner as if A had transferred the T stock to P in exchange for stock of P in a transaction to which section 351(a) applies, and P had then redeemed the stock P was treated as issuing in the transaction. Under section 362(a), P's basis in the T stock is determined by reference to A's adjusted basis in the T stock, and there is no basis increase in the T stock because A recognizes no gain on the deemed transfer. Accordingly, P's acquisition of the T stock from A is not a purchase by P under section 355(d)(5)(A)(i)(I) and paragraphs (d)(1)(i)(A)(*1*) and (d)(2)(i)(B) of this section.

(2) *Exceptions to definition of purchase under section 355(d)(5)(A).*—The following acquisitions are not treated as purchases under section 355(d)(5)(A):

(i) *Acquisition of stock in a transaction which includes other property or money.*—(A) *Transferors and shareholders of transferor or distributing corporations.*—(1) *In general.*—An acquisition of stock permitted to be received by a transferor of property without the recognition of gain under section 351(a), or permitted to be received without the recognition of gain under section 354, 355, or 356 is not a purchase to the extent section 358(a)(1) applies to determine the recipient's basis in the stock received, whether or not the recipient recognizes gain under section 351(b) or 356. But see paragraph (e)(3) of this section (interest received in exchange for purchased interest in exchanged basis transaction treated as purchased).

(2) *Exception.*—To the extent there is received in the exchange or distribution, in addition to stock described in paragraph (d)(2)(i)(A)(*1*) of this section, stock that is other property under section 351(b) or 356(a)(1), the stock is treated as purchased on the date of the exchange or distribution for purposes of section 355(d).

(B) *Transferee corporations.*—(1) *In general.*—An acquisition of stock by a corporation is not a purchase to the extent section 334(b) or 362(a) or (b) applies to determine the corporation's basis in the stock received. But see section 355(d)(5)(C) and paragraph (e)(2) of this section (purchased property transferred in transferred basis transaction is treated as purchased by transferee).

(2) *Exception.*—If a corporation acquires stock, the stock is treated as purchased on the date of the stock acquisition for purposes of section 355(d)—

(i) If the liquidating corporation recognizes gain or loss with respect to the transferred stock as described in section 334(b)(1); or

(ii) To the extent the basis of the transferred stock is increased through the recognition of gain by the transferor under section 362(a) or (b).

(C) *Examples.*—The following examples illustrate this paragraph (d)(2)(i):

Example 1. (i) A owns all the stock of T. T merges into D in a transaction qualifying under section 368(a)(1)(A), with A exchanging all of the T stock for D stock and $100 cash. Under section 356(a)(1), A recognizes $100 of the realized gain on the transaction. Under section 358(a)(1), A's basis in the D stock equals A's basis in the T stock, decreased by the $100 received and increased by the gain recognized, also $100. Under paragraph (d)(2)(i)(A) of this section, A is not treated as having purchased the D stock for purposes of section 355(d)(5).

(ii) The facts are the same as in paragraph (i) of this *Example 1*, except that rather than D stock and $100 cash, A receives D stock and stock in C, a corporation not a party to the reorganization, with a fair market value of $100. Under section 358(a)(2), A's basis in the C stock is its fair market value, or $100. Under paragraph (d)(2)(i)(A)(*2*) of this section, A is treated as having purchased the C stock, but not the D stock, for purposes of section 355(d)(5).

Example 2. A purchases all of the stock of D, which is not marketable stock, on Date 1 for $90. Within five years of A's purchase, on Date 2, A contributes the D stock to P in exchange for P stock worth $90 and $10 cash in a transaction qualifying under section 351. A recognizes a gain of $10 as a result of the transfer. Under section 362(a), P's basis in D is $100. P is treated as having purchased 90 percent ($90 worth) of the D stock on Date 1 under section 355(d)(5)(C) and paragraph (e)(2) of this section and as having purchased 10 percent ($10 worth) of the D stock on Date 2 under paragraph (d)(2)(i)(B)(*2*)(*ii*) of this section.

(ii) *Acquisition of stock in a distribution to which section 305(a) applies.*—An acquisition of stock in a distribution qualifying under section 305(a) is not a purchase to the extent section 307(a) applies to determine the recipient's basis. However, to the extent the distribution is of rights to acquire stock, see paragraph (c)(3) of this section for rules regarding options, warrants, convertible obligations, and other similar interests.

(iii) *Section 1036(a) exchange.*—An exchange of stock qualifying under section 1036(a) is not a purchase by either party to the exchange to the extent the basis of the property acquired equals that of the property exchanged under section 1031(d).

(iv) *Section 338 elections.*—(A) *In general.*—Stock acquired in a qualified stock purchase with respect to which a section 338 election (or a section 338(h)(10) election) is made is not treated as a purchase for purposes of section 355(d)(5)(A). However, any stock (or an interest in another entity) held by old target that is treated as purchased by new target is treated as acquired by purchase for purposes of section 355(d)(5)(A) unless a section 338 election or section 338(h)(10) election also is made for that stock. See § 1.338-2T(c) for the definitions of section 338 election, section 338(h)(10) election, old target, and new target.

(B) *Example.*—The following example illustrates this paragraph (d)(2)(iv):

Example. T owns all of the stock of S and no other assets. X acquires all of the T stock from the T shareholders for cash and makes an election under section 338. Under section 338(a) and (b), T, as Old T, is treated as having sold all of its assets at fair market value and purchased the assets as a new corporation, New T, as of the beginning of the day after the acquisition date. Under paragraph (d)(2)(iv)(A) of this section, X is not treated as having purchased the T stock. Absent a section 338 election or a section 338(h)(10) election with respect to S, New T is treated as having purchased all of the S stock under section 355(d)(5)(A).

(v) *Partnership distributions.*—(A) *Section 732(b).*—An acquisition of stock (or an interest in another entity) in a liquidation of a partner's interest in a partnership in which basis is determined pursuant to section 732(b) is a purchase at the time of the liquidation.

(B) *Section 734(b).*—If the adjusted basis of stock (or an interest in another entity) held by a partnership is increased under section 734(b), a proportionate amount of the stock (or other interest) will be treated as purchased at the time of the basis adjustment, determined by reference to the amount of the basis adjustment (but not in excess of the fair market value of the stock (or other interest) at the time of the adjustment) over the fair market value of the stock (or other interest) at the time of the adjustment.

(3) *Certain section 351 exchanges treated as purchases.*—(i) *In general.*—(A) *Treatment of stock received by transferor.*—Under section 355(d)(5)(B), a purchase includes any acquisition of property in an exchange to which section 351 applies to the extent the property is acquired in exchange for any cash or cash item, any marketable stock, or any debt of the transferor. The property treated as acquired by purchase is the property received by the transferor in the exchange.

(B) *Multiple classes of stock.*—If the transferor in a transaction described in section 355(d)(5)(B) receives stock or securities of more than one class, or receives both stock and securities, then the amount of stock or securities purchased is determined in a manner that corresponds to the allocation of basis to the stock or securities under section 358. See § 1.358-2(b).

(ii) *Cash item, marketable stock.*—For purposes of section 355(d)(5)(B) and this paragraph (d)(3), either or both of the terms cash item and marketable stock include personal property within the meaning of section 1092(d)(1) and § 1.1092(d)-1, without giving effect to section 1092(d)(3).

(iii) *Exception for certain acquisitions.*—(A) *In general.*—Except to the extent provided in paragraph (e)(3) of this section (interest received in exchange for purchased interest in exchanged basis transaction treated as purchased), an acquisition of stock in a corporation in a section 351 transaction by one or more persons in exchange for an amount of stock in another corporation (the transferred corporation) that meets the requirements of section 1504(a)(2) is not a purchase by the transferor or transferors, regardless of whether the stock of the transferred corporation is marketable stock under section 355(d)(5)(B)(ii) and paragraph (d)(3)(ii) of this section.

(B) *Example.*—The following example illustrates this paragraph (d)(3)(iii):

Example. D's two classes of stock, voting common and nonvoting preferred, are both widely held and publicly traded. The nonvoting preferred stock is stock described in section 1504(a)(4). Assume that all of the D stock is marketable stock under section 355(d)(5)(B)(ii) and paragraph (d)(3)(ii) of this section. D's board of directors proposes that, for valid business purposes, D's common stock should be held by a holding company, HC, but its preferred stock should not be transferred to HC. As proposed, the D common shareholders exchange their D stock solely for HC common stock in a section 351(a) transaction. The D preferred shareholders retain their stock. HC acquires an amount of D stock that meets the requirements of section 1504(a)(2). Although the D common stock was marketable stock in the hands of the D shareholders immediately before the transfer, and the D nonvoting preferred stock is marketable stock after the transfer, the D shareholders are not treated as having acquired the HC stock by purchase (except to the extent the exchanged basis rule of paragraph (e)(3) of this section may apply to treat HC stock as purchased on the date the exchanged D stock was purchased).

(iv) *Exception for assets transferred as part of an active trade or business.*—(A) *In general.*—Except to the extent provided in paragraph (e)(3) of this section, an acquisition not described in paragraph (d)(3)(iii) of this section of stock in exchange for any cash or cash item, any marketable stock, or any debt of the transferor in a section 351 transaction is not a purchase if—

(1) The transferor is engaged in the active conduct of a trade or business under paragraph (d)(3)(iv)(B) of this section and the transferred items (including debt incurred in the ordinary course of the trade or business) are used in the trade or business;

(2) The transferred items do not exceed the reasonable needs of the trade or business under paragraph (d)(3)(iv)(C) of this section;

(3) The transferor transfers the items as part of the trade or business; and

(4) The transferee continues the active conduct of the trade or business.

(B) *Active conduct of a trade or business.*—For purposes of this paragraph (d)(3)(iv), whether, with respect to the trade or business at issue, the transferor and transferee are engaged in the active conduct of a trade or business is determined under § 1.355-3(b)(2) and (3), except that—

(1) Conduct is tested before the transfer (with respect to the transferor) and after the transfer (with respect to the transferee) rather than immediately after a distribution; and

(2) The trade or business need not have been conducted for five years before its transfer, but it must have been conducted for a sufficient period of time to establish that it is a viable and ongoing trade or business.

(C) *Reasonable needs of the trade or business.*—For purposes of this paragraph (d)(3)(iv), the reasonable needs of the trade or business include only the amount of cash or cash items, marketable stock, or debt of the transferor that a prudent business person apprised of all relevant facts would consider necessary for the present and reasonably anticipated future needs of the business. Transferred items may be considered necessary for reasonably anticipated future needs only if the transferor and transferee have specific, definite, and feasible plans for their use. Those plans must require that items intended for anticipated future needs rather than present needs be used as expeditiously as possible consistent with the business purpose for retention of the items. Future needs are not reasonably anticipated if they are uncertain or vague or where the execution of the plan for their use is substantially postponed. The reasonable needs of a trade or business are generally its needs at the time of the transfer of the business including the items. However, for purposes of applying section 355(d) to a distribution, events and conditions after the transfer and through the date immediately after the distribution (including whether plans for the use of transferred items have been consummated or substantially postponed) may be considered to determine whether at the time of the transfer the items were necessary for the present and reasonably anticipated future needs of the business.

(D) *Consideration of all facts and circumstances.*—All facts and circumstances are considered in determining whether this paragraph (d)(3)(iv) applies.

(E) *Successive transfers.*—A transfer of assets does not fail to meet the requirements of paragraph (d)(3)(iv)(A)(4) of this section solely because the transferee transfers the assets directly (or indirectly through other members) to another member of the transferee's affiliated group, as defined in § 1.355-3(b)(4)(iv) (the final transferee), if the requirements of paragraphs (d)(3)(iv)(A)(1), (2), (3) and (4) of this section would be met if the transferor had transferred the assets directly to the final transferee.

(v) *Exception for transfer between members of the same affiliated group.*—(A) *In general.*—Except to the extent provided in paragraph (e)(3) of this section, an acquisition of stock (whether actual or constructive) not described in paragraphs (d)(3)(iii) and (iv) of this section in exchange for any cash or cash item, marketable stock, or debt of the transferor in a section 351 transaction is not a purchase if—

(1) The transferor corporation or corporations and the transferee corporation (whether formed in the transaction or already existing) are members of the same affiliated group as defined in

section 1504(a) before the section 351 transaction (if the transferee corporation is in existence before the transaction);

(2) The cash or cash item, marketable stock or debt of the transferor are not included in assets that are acquired (or treated as acquired) by the transferor (or another member of the transferor's affiliated group) from a nonmember in a related transaction in which section 362(a) or (b) applies to determine the basis in the acquired assets; and

(3) The transferor corporation or corporations, the transferee corporation, and any distributed controlled corporation of the transferee corporation do not cease to be members of such affiliated group in any transaction pursuant to a plan that includes the section 351 transaction (including any distribution of a controlled corporation by the transferee corporation). But see paragraph (b)(4) of this section where the transfer is made for a principal purpose to avoid the purposes of section 355(d).

(B) *Examples.*—The following examples illustrate this paragraph (d)(3)(v):

Example 1. Publicly traded P has wholly owned S since 1990. S is engaged in the telecommunications business and the business of computer software development. S is developing new software for use in the managed health care industry. Over a period of four years beginning on January 31, 2000, P contributes a substantial amount of cash to S solely for the purpose of funding the software development. On completion of the software in January of 2004, 60 percent of the value of the S stock is attributable to the cash contributions made within the last four years. The P group's primary lender requires that S separately incorporate the software and related assets and distribute the new subsidiary to P as a condition of providing required funding to market the Software. Accordingly, on February 1, 2004, S forms N, contributes the software and related assets to N, and distributes all of the N stock to P in a transaction intended to qualify under section 355(a). P, S, and N will not leave the affiliated group in any transaction related to the cash contributions. Under paragraph (d)(3)(v)(A) of this section, P's cash contributions to S are not treated as purchases of additional S stock, and the distribution of N from S to P is not a disqualified distribution under section 355(d)(2) and paragraph (b)(1) of this section.

Example 2. On Date 1, P contributes cash to its subsidiary S with a principal purpose to increase its stock basis in S. Sixty percent of the value of P's S stock is attributable to the cash contribution. Under paragraph (b)(4) of this section (anti-avoidance rule), 60 percent of the S stock is treated as purchased under section 355(d)(5)(B), notwithstanding paragraph (d)(3)(v)(A) of this section. Accordingly, any distribution of a subsidiary of S to P within the five-year period after Date 1 will be a disqualified distribution, regardless of whether P, S, and any distributed S subsidiary remain affiliated after the distribution and any transactions related to the cash contribution.

(4) *Triangular asset reorganizations.*—(i) *Definition.*—A *triangular asset reorganization* is a reorganization that qualifies under—

(A) Section 368(a)(1)(A) or (G) by reason of section 368(a)(2)(D);

(B) Section 368(a)(1)(A) by reason of section 368(a)(2)(E) (regardless of whether section 368(a)(3)(E) applies), unless the transaction also qualifies as either a section 351 transfer or a reorganization under section 368(a)(1)(B); or

(C) Section 368(a)(1)(C), and stock of the controlling corporation rather than the acquiring corporation is exchanged for the acquired corporation's properties.

(ii) *Treatment.*—Notwithstanding section 355(d)(5)(A), for purposes of section 355(d), the controlling corporation in a triangular asset reorganization is treated as having—

(A) Acquired the assets of the acquired corporation (and as having assumed any liabilities assumed by the controlling corporation's subsidiary corporation or to which the acquired corporation's assets were subject (the acquired liabilities)) in a transaction in which the controlling corporation's basis in the acquired corporation's assets was determined under section 362(b); and

(B) Transferred the acquired assets and acquired liabilities to its subsidiary corporation in a section 351 transfer.

(iii) *Example.*—The following example illustrates this paragraph (d)(4):

Example. Forward triangular reorganization. P forms S with $25 of cash and T merges into S in a reorganization qualifying under section 368(a)(1)(A) by reason of section 368(a)(2)(D) in which the T shareholders receive $70 of P stock and $15 of cash in exchange for their T stock. T is not a common parent of a consolidated group of corporations. The remaining $10 of cash with which P formed S will not be used in the acquired business. T's assets consist only of assets part of and used in its business with a value of $80, and $5 of cash that is not part of or used in T's business. T has no liabilities. S will use T's business assets in T's business (which will become S's business), but will invest the $5 of cash in an unrelated passive investment. Under paragraph (d)(4)(ii) of this section, P is treated as acquiring the T assets in a transaction in which P's basis in the T assets was determined under section 362(b) and contributing them to S in a section 351 transfer. Under paragraph (d)(3)(v) of this section, $10 (of the total $25) of cash contributed by P to S upon S's formation is not treated as a purchase of S stock. The $15 (of the total $25) of cash contributed by P to S upon S's formation that is paid to T's shareholders is not treated as a purchase of S stock. The exception in paragraph (d)(3)(v) of this section does not apply to the $5 of cash from T's business because P is treated as having acquired T's assets in a related transaction in which section 362(b) applies to determine P's basis in such assets. Accordingly, P is treated under section 355(d)(5)(B) and paragraph (d)(3)(iv) of this section as having purchased $5 of the S stock, but is not deemed to have purchased the remaining $80 of the S stock.

(5) *Reverse triangular reorganizations other than triangular asset reorganizations.*—(i) *In general.*—Except as provided in paragraph (d)(5)(ii) of this section, if a transaction qualifies as a reorganization under section 368(a)(1)(A) by reason of section 368(a)(2)(E) and also as either a reorganization under section 368(a)(1)(B) or a section 351 transfer, then either section 355(d)(5)(B) (and paragraphs (d)(3)(i) through (iv) of this section) or 355(d)(5)(C) (and paragraph (e)(2) of this section) applies. Regardless of which method the controlling corporation employs to determine its basis in the surviving corporation stock under §1.358-6(c)(2)(ii) or §1.1502-30(b), the total amount of surviving corporation stock treated as purchased by the controlling corporation will equal the higher of—

(A) The amount of surviving corporation stock that would be treated as purchased (on the date of the deemed section 351 transfer) by the controlling corporation if the controlling corporation acquired the surviving corporation's assets and assumed its liabilities in a transaction in which the controlling corporation's basis in the surviving corporation assets was determined under section 362(b), and then transferred the acquired assets and liabilities to the surviving corporation in a section 351 transfer (see §§1.358-6(c)(1) and (2)(ii)(A), and 1.1502-30(b)); or

(B) The amount of surviving corporation stock that would be treated as purchased (on the date the surviving corporation shareholders purchased their surviving corporation stock) if the controlling corporation acquired the stock of the surviving corporation in a transaction in which the basis in the surviving corporation's stock was determined under section 362(b) (see §§1.358-6(c)(2)(ii)(B) and 1.1502-30(b).

(ii) *Letter ruling and closing agreement.*—If a controlling corporation obtains a letter ruling and enters into a closing agreement under section 7121 in which it agrees to determine its basis in surviving corporation stock under §1.358-6(c)(2)(ii)(A), or under §1.1502-30(b) by applying §1.358-6(c)(2)(ii)(A) (deemed asset acquisition and transfer by controlling corporation), then section 355(d)(5)(B) and paragraphs (d)(3)(i) through (iv) of this section apply, and section 355(d)(5)(C) and paragraph (e)(2) of this section do not apply. If a controlling corporation obtains a letter ruling and enters into a closing agreement under section 7121 under which it agrees to determine its basis in surviving corporation stock under §1.358-6(c)(2)(ii)(B), or under §1.1502-30(b) by applying §1.358-6(c)(2)(ii)(B) (deemed stock acquisition), then section 355(d)(5)(C) and paragraph (e)(2) of this section apply, and section 355(d)(5)(B) and paragraphs (d)(3)(i) through (iv) of this section do not apply.

(iii) *Example.*—The following example illustrates this paragraph (d)(5):

Example. Reverse triangular reorganization; purchase. (i) A purchases 60 percent of the stock of D on Date 1. D owns no cash items, marketable stock, or transferor debt, but holds cash that is not part of or used in D's trade or business under paragraph (d)(3)(iv) of this section and that represents 20 percent of D's value. On Date 2, P forms S, and S merges into D in a reorganization qualifying under section 368(a)(1)(B) and under section 368(a)(1)(A) by reason of section 368(a)(2)(E). In the reorganization, P acquires all of the D stock in exchange solely for P stock. After Date 2, and within five years after Date 1, D distributes its wholly owned subsidiary C to P. P does not obtain a letter ruling and enter into a closing agreement under paragraph (d)(5)(ii) of this section. P would acquire 20 percent of the D stock by purchase on Date 2 under paragraph (d)(5)(i)(A) of this section by operation of section 355(d)(5)(B) and paragraph (d)(3)(iv) of this section. The exception in paragraph (d)(3)(v) of this section does not apply because D was not affiliated with P before the transaction in which the section 351 transfer is deemed to occur and D's assets are treated as acquired by P in a related transaction in which section 362(b) applies to determine P's basis in the D assets. P would acquire 60 percent of the D stock by purchase on Date 1 under

paragraph (d)(5)(i)(B) of this section because, under the transferred basis rule of section 355(d)(5)(C) and paragraph (e)(2) of this section, P is treated as though P purchased the D stock on the date A purchased it. Accordingly, under paragraph (d)(5)(i) of this section, P is treated as acquiring the higher amount (60 percent) by purchase on Date 1. D's distribution of C to P is a disqualified distribution under section 355(d)(2) and paragraph (b)(1) of this section. In addition, A is treated as acquiring the P stock by purchase on Date 1 under paragraph (e)(3) of this section because A's basis in the P stock is determined by reference to A's basis in the D stock.

(ii) The facts are the same as in paragraph (i) of this *Example,* except that P obtains a letter ruling and enters into a closing agreement under which it agrees to determine its basis in the D stock under §1.358-6(c)(2)(ii)(A). Under paragraph (d)(5)(ii) of this section, section 355(d)(5)(B) (and paragraphs (d)(3)(i) through (iv) of this section) applies, and section 355(d)(5)(C) (and paragraph (e)(2) of this section) does not apply. Accordingly, P is treated as acquiring only 20 percent of the D stock by purchase on Date 2. D's distribution of C to P is not a disqualified distribution under section 355(d)(2) and paragraph (b)(1) of this section.

(6) *Treatment of group structure changes.*—(i) *In general.*—Notwithstanding section 355(d)(5)(A), for purposes of section 355(d), if a corporation succeeds another corporation as the common parent of a consolidated group in a group structure change to which §1.1502-31 applies, the new common parent is treated as having acquired the assets and assumed the liabilities of the former common parent in a transaction in which the new common parent's basis in the former common parent's assets was determined under section 362(b), and then transferred the acquired assets and liabilities to the former common parent (or, if the former common parent does not survive, to the new common parent's subsidiary) in a section 351 transfer, with the new common parent and former common parent being treated as not in the same affiliated group at the time of the transfer for purposes of applying paragraph (d)(3)(v) of this section (notwithstanding §1.1502-31(c)(2)).

(ii) *Adjustments to basis of higher-tier members.*—A higher-tier member that indirectly owns all or part of the former common parent's stock after a group structure change is treated as having purchased the stock of an immediate subsidiary to the extent that the higher-tier member's basis in the subsidiary is increased under §1.1502-31(d)(4).

(iii) *Example.*—The following example illustrates this paragraph (d)(6):

Example. P is the common parent of a consolidated group, and T is the common parent of another group. P has owned S for more than five years, and the fair market value of the S stock is $50. T's assets consist only of non-marketable stock of direct and indirect wholly owned subsidiaries with a value of $50, assets used in its business with a value of $50, and $50 of marketable stock that is not part of or used in T's business. T has no liabilities. T merges into S with the T shareholders receiving solely P stock with a value of $150 in exchange for their T stock in a section 368(a)(2)(D) reorganization. S will use T's business assets in T's business (which will become S's business), but will hold the $50 of marketable stock for investment purposes. Assume that the transaction is a reverse acquisition under §1.1502-75(d)(3) because the T shareholders, as a result of owning T stock, own more than 50 percent of the value of P's stock immediately after the transaction. Thus, the transaction is a group structure change under §1.1502-33(f)(1). Under paragraph (d)(6) of this section, P is treated as having acquired the assets of T in a transaction in which P's basis in the T assets was determined under section 362(b), and then transferred the acquired assets to S in a section 351 transfer, with P and T being treated as not in the same affiliated group at the time of the transfer solely for purposes of paragraph (d)(3)(v) of this section. The exception in paragraph (d)(3)(v) of this section (transfers within an affiliated group) does not apply. Accordingly, P is treated under section 355(d)(5)(B) and paragraph (d)(3)(iv) of this section as having purchased $50 of the S stock (attributable to the marketable stock), but is not deemed to have purchased the remaining $150 of the S stock.

(7) *Special rules for triangular asset reorganizations, other reverse triangular reorganizations, and group structure changes.*—The amount of acquiring subsidiary, surviving corporation, or former common parent stock that is treated as purchased under paragraph (c)(4), (5)(i)(A), or (6) of this section (by operation of section 355(d)(5)(B) and paragraphs (d)(3)(i) through (iv) of this section) is adjusted to reflect any basis adjustment under—

(i) Section 1.358-6(c)(2)(i)(B) and (C) (reduction of basis adjustment in reverse triangular reorganization where controlling corporation acquires less than all of the surviving corporation stock), §1.1502-30(b) (applying §1.358-6(c)(2)(i)(B) and (C) to a consolidated group), and §1.1502-31(d)(2)(ii) (reduction of basis adjustment in group structure change where new common parent acquires less than all of the former common parent stock); or

(ii) Section 1.358-6(d) (reduction of basis adjustment in any triangular reorganization to the extent controlling corporation does not provide consideration), §1.1502-30(b) (applying §1.358-6(d) (except §1.358-6(d)(2)) to a consolidated group), and §1.1502-31(d)(1) (reduction of basis adjustment in group structure change to the extent new common parent does not provide consideration).

(e) *Deemed purchase and timing rules.*—(1) *Attribution and aggregation.*—(i) *In general.*—Under section 355(d)(8)(B), if any person acquires by purchase an interest in any entity, and the person is treated under section 355(d)(8)(A) as holding any stock by reason of holding the interest, the stock shall be treated as acquired by purchase on the later of the date of the purchase of the interest in the entity or the date the stock is acquired by purchase by such entity.

(ii) *Purchase of additional interest.*—If a person and an entity are treated as a single person under section 355(d)(7), and the person later purchases an additional interest in the entity, the person is treated as purchasing on the date of the later purchase the amount of stock attributed from the entity to the person under section 355(d)(8)(A) as a result of the additional interest.

(iii) *Purchase between persons treated as one person.*—If two persons are treated as one person under section 355(d)(7), and one later purchases stock from the other, the date of the later purchase is used for purposes of determining when the five-year period commences.

(iv) *Purchase by a person already treated as holding stock under section 355(d)(8)(A).*—If a person who is already treated as holding stock under section 355(d)(8)(A) later directly purchases such stock, the date of the later direct purchase is used for purposes of determining when the five-year period commences.

(v) *Examples.*—The following examples illustrate this paragraph (e)(1):

Example 1. On Date 1, A purchases 10 percent of the stock of P, which has held 100 percent of the stock of T for more than five years at the time of A's purchase. A is deemed to have purchased 10 percent of P's T stock on Date 1. If A later purchases an additional 41 percent of the stock of P on Date 2, A is deemed to have purchased an additional 41 percent of P's T stock on Date 2. Because A and P are now related persons under section 267(b), they are treated as one person under section 355(d)(7)(A), and A is treated as owning all of P's T stock. A is treated as acquiring 51 percent of the T stock by purchase at the times of A's respective purchases of P stock on Date 1 and Date 2. The remaining 49 percent of T stock is treated as acquired when P acquired the T stock, more than five years before Date 1. If P distributes T after Date 2 and within five years after Date 1, the distribution will be a disqualified distribution under section 355(d)(2) and paragraph (b)(1) of this section.

Example 2. A has owned 60 percent of the stock of P for more than five years, and P has owned 40 percent of the stock of T for more than five years. A and P are treated as one person, and A is treated as owning 40 percent of the stock of T for more than five years. If P later purchases an additional 20 percent of the stock of T on Date 1, A is treated as acquiring by purchase the additional 20 percent of T stock on Date 1. If A then purchases an additional 10 percent of the stock of P on Date 2, under paragraph (e)(1)(i) of this section, A is deemed to have purchased on Date 2 an additional four percent of the T stock (10 percent of the 40 percent that P originally owned). In addition, even though A and P were already treated as one person under section 355(d)(7)(A), A also is deemed to have purchased two percent of the T stock on Date 2 (10 percent of the 20 percent of the T stock that it was treated as purchasing on Date 1). A is still treated as owning all 60 percent of the T stock owned by P. However, of the 60 percent, A is treated as having purchased 18 percent of the T stock on Date 1 and 6 percent of the T stock on Date 2, for a total of 24 percent purchased stock.

Example 3. A purchases a 20 percent interest in partnership M on Date 1. M has owned 30 percent of the stock and 25 percent of the securities of P for more than five years. P has owned 40 percent of the stock and 100 percent of the securities of T for more than five years. Under section 318(a)(2)(C) as modified by section 355(d)(8)(A), M is deemed to own 12 percent of the stock (30 percent of the 40 percent P owns) and 30 percent of the securities (30 percent of the 100 percent P owns) of T. Under sections 318(a)(2)(A) and 355(d)(8)(B), A is deemed to have purchased 2.4 percent of the stock (20 percent of the 12 percent M is deemed to own) and 6 percent of the securities (20 percent of the 30 percent M is deemed to own) of T on Date 1. Similarly, A is deemed to have purchased 6 percent of the stock (20 percent of the 30 percent M owns) and five percent of the securities (20 percent of the 25 percent M owns) of P on Date 1. If M later purchases an additional 10 percent of P stock on Date 2, M is deemed to have purchased four percent of the stock (10 percent of the 40

percent P owns) and 10 percent of the securities (10 percent of the 100 percent P owns) of T on Date 2. A is deemed to have purchased two percent of the stock of P on Date 2 (20 percent of the 10 percent M purchased). A is also deemed to have purchased 0.8 percent of the stock (20 percent of the four percent M is deemed to have purchased) and two percent of the securities (20 percent of the 10 percent M is deemed to have purchased) of T on Date 2.

Example 4. A and B are brother and sister. For more than five years, A has owned 75 percent of the stock of P, and B has owned 25 percent of the stock of P. A and B are treated as one person under section 267(b), and the stock of each is treated as purchased on the date it was purchased by A and B, respectively. If B later purchases 50 percent of the P stock from A on Date 1, A and B are still treated as one person. However, under paragraph (e)(3)(iii) of this section, the 50 percent of P stock that B purchased from A is treated as purchased on Date 1.

(2) *Transferred basis rule.*—If any person acquires property from another person who acquired the property by purchase (determined with regard to section 355(d)(5) and paragraphs (d) and (e)(2), (3) and (4) of this section, but without regard to section 355(d)(8) and paragraph (e)(1) of this section), and the adjusted basis of the property in the hands of the acquirer is determined in whole or in part by reference to the adjusted basis of the property in the hands of the other person, the acquirer is treated as having acquired the property by purchase on the date it was so acquired by the other person. The rule in this paragraph (e)(2) applies, for example, where stock of a corporation acquired by purchase is subsequently acquired in a section 351 transfer or a reorganization qualifying under section 368(a)(1)(B), but does not apply if the stock of a former common parent is acquired in a group structure change to which §1.1502-31 applies. But see paragraph (d)(2)(i)(B)(2) of this section for situations where the stock is treated as purchased on the date of a transfer.

(3) *Exchanged basis rule.*—(i) *In general.*—If any person acquires an interest in an entity (the first interest) by purchase (determined with regard to section 355(d)(5) and paragraphs (d) and (e)(2), (3) and (4) of this section, but without regard to section 355(d)(8) and paragraph (e)(1) of this section), and the first interest is exchanged for an interest in the same or another entity (the second interest) where the adjusted basis of the second interest is determined in whole or in part by reference to the adjusted basis of the first interest, then the second interest is treated as having been purchased on the date the first interest was purchased. The rule in this paragraph (e)(3) applies only to exchanges that are not otherwise treated as purchases under section 355(d)(5) and paragraph (d) of this section. The rule in this paragraph (e)(3) applies, for example, where stock of a corporation acquired by purchase is subsequently exchanged for other stock in a section 351,354, or 1036(a) exchange. But see paragraph (d)(2)(i)(A)(2) of this section for situations where the stock is treated as purchased on the date of an exchange or distribution.

(ii) *Example.*—The following example illustrates this paragraph (e)(3):

Example. A purchases 50 percent of the stock of T on Date 1. On Date 2, T merges into D in a section 368(a)(1)(A) reorganization, with A exchanging all of the T stock solely for stock of D. Under section 358(a), A's basis in the D stock is determined by reference to the basis of the T stock it purchased. Accordingly, A is treated as having purchased the D stock on Date 1, and has a purchased basis in the D stock under paragraph (b)(3)(iii) of this section.

(4) *Certain section 355 or section 305 distributions.*—(i) *Section 355.*—If a distributing corporation distributes any stock of a controlled corporation with respect to recently purchased distributing stock in a distribution that qualifies under section 355 (or so much of section 356 as relates to section 355), such controlled corporation stock is deemed to be acquired by purchase by the distributee on the date the distributee acquired the recently purchased distributing stock. Recently purchased distributing stock is stock in the distributing corporation acquired by purchase (determined with regard to section 355(d)(5) and paragraphs (d) and (e)(2), (3), and (4) of this section, but without regard to section 355(d)(8) and paragraph (e)(1) of this section) by the distributee during the five-year period with respect to that distribution.

(ii) *Section 305.*—If a corporation distributes its stock in a distribution that qualifies under section 305(a), the stock received in the distribution (to the extent section 307(a) applies to determine the recipient's basis) is deemed to be acquired by purchase by the recipient on the date (if any) that the recipient acquired by purchase (determined with regard to section 355(d)(5) and paragraphs (d) and (e)(2), (3), and (4) of this section), the stock with respect to which the distribution is made.

(5) *Substantial diminution of risk.*—(i) *In general.*—If section 355(d)(6) applies to any stock for any period, the running of any five-

year period set forth in section 355(d)(3) is suspended during such period.

(ii) *Property to which suspension applies.*—Section 355(d)(6) applies to any stock for any period during which the holder's risk of loss with respect to such stock, or with respect to any portion of the activities of the corporation, is (directly or indirectly) substantially diminished by an option, a short sale, any special class of stock, or any other device or transaction.

(iii) *Risk of loss substantially diminished.*—Whether a holder's risk of loss is substantially diminished under section 355(d)(6) and paragraph (e)(5)(ii) of this section will be determined based on all facts and circumstances relating to the stock, the corporate activities, and arrangements for holding the stock.

(iv) *Special class of stock.*—For purposes of section 355(d)(6) and paragraph (e)(5)(ii) of this section, the term special class of stock includes a class of stock that grants particular rights to, or bears particular risks for, the holder or the issuer with respect to the earnings, assets, or attributes of less than all the assets or activities of a corporation or any of its subsidiaries. The term includes, for example, tracking stock and stock (or any related instruments or arrangements) the terms of which provide for the distribution (whether or not at the option of any party or in the event of any contingency) of any controlled corporation or other specified assets to the holder or to one or more persons other than the holder.

(f) *Duty to determine stockholders.*—(1) *In general.*—In determining whether section 355(d) applies to a distribution of controlled corporation stock, a distributing corporation must determine whether a disqualified person holds its stock or the stock of any distributed controlled corporation. This paragraph (f) provides rules regarding this determination and the extent to which a distributing corporation must investigate whether a disqualified person holds stock.

(2) *Deemed knowledge of contents of securities filings.*—A distributing corporation is deemed to have knowledge of the existence and contents of all schedules, forms, and other documents filed with or under the rules of the Securities and Exchange Commission, including without limitation any Schedule 13D or 13G (or any similar schedules) and amendments, with respect to any relevant corporation.

(3) *Presumption as to securities filings.*—Absent actual knowledge to the contrary, in determining whether section 355(d) applies to a distribution, a distributing corporation may presume, with respect to stock that is reporting stock (while such stock is reporting stock), that every shareholder or other person required to file a schedule, form, or other document with or under the rules of the Securities and Exchange Commission as of a given date has filed the schedule, form, or other document as of that date and that the contents of filed schedules, forms, or other documents are accurate and complete. Reporting stock is stock that is described in Rule 13d-1(i) of Regulation 13D (17 CFR 240.13d-1(i)) (or any rule or regulation to generally the same effect) promulgated by the Securities and Exchange Commission under the Securities Exchange Act of 1934 (15 U.S.C. 78a et seq.).

(4) *Presumption as to less-than-five-percent shareholders.*—Absent actual knowledge (or deemed knowledge under paragraph (f)(2) of this section) immediately after the distribution to the contrary with regard to a particular shareholder, a distributing corporation may presume that no less-than-five-percent shareholder of a corporation acquired stock or securities by purchase under section 355(d)(5) or (8) and paragraphs (d) and (e) of this section during the five-year period. For purposes of this paragraph (f), a less-than-five-percent shareholder is a person that, at no time during the five-year period, holds directly (or by application of paragraph (c)(3)(ii) of this section, but not by application of section 355(d)(7) or (8)) stock possessing five percent or more of the total combined voting power of all classes of stock entitled to vote or the total value of shares of all classes of stock of a corporation. However, this presumption does not apply to any less-than-five-percent shareholder that, at any time during the five-year period—

(i) Is related under section 355(d)(7)(A) to a shareholder in the corporation that is at any time during the five-year period, not a less-than-five-percent shareholder;

(ii) Acted pursuant to a plan or arrangement, with respect to acquisitions of the corporation's stock or securities under section 355(d)(7)(B) and paragraph (c)(4) of this section, with a shareholder in the corporation that is, at any time during the five-year period, not a less-than-five-percent shareholder; or

(iii) Holds stock or securities that is attributed under section 355(d)(8)(A) to a shareholder in the corporation that is, at any time during the five-year period, not a less-than-five-percent shareholder.

(5) *Examples.*—The following examples illustrate this paragraph (f):

Example 1. Publicly traded corporation; no schedules filed. D is a widely held and publicly traded corporation with a single class of reporting stock and no other class of stock. Assume that applicable federal law requires any person that directly holds five percent or more of the D stock to file a schedule with the Securities and Exchange Commission within 10 days after an acquisition. D distributes its wholly owned subsidiary C pro rata. D determines that no schedule, form, or other document has been filed with respect to its stock or the stock of any other relevant corporation during the five-year period or within 10 days after the distribution. Immediately after the distribution, D has no knowledge that any of its shareholders are (or were at any time during the five-year period) not less-than-five-percent shareholders, or that any particular shareholder acquired D stock by purchase under section 355(d)(5) or (8) and paragraphs (d) and (e) of this section during the five-year period. Under paragraph (f)(3) of this section, D may presume it has no shareholder that is or was not a less-than-five-percent shareholder during the five-year period due to the absence of any filed schedules, forms, or other documents. Under paragraph (f)(4) of this section, D may presume that none of its less-than-five-percent shareholders acquired D's stock by purchase during the five-year period. Accordingly, D may presume that section 355(d) does not apply to the distribution of C.

Example 2. Publicly traded corporation; schedule filed. The facts are the same as those in *Example 1*, except that D determines that, as of 10 days after the distribution, only one schedule has been filed with respect to its stock. That schedule discloses that X acquired 15 percent of the D stock one year before the distribution. Absent contrary knowledge, D may rely on the presumptions in paragraph (f)(3) of this section and so may presume that X is its only shareholder that is or was not a less-than-five-percent shareholder during the five-year period. D may not rely on the presumption in paragraph (f)(4) of this section with respect to X. In addition, D may not rely on the presumption in paragraph (f)(4) of this section with respect to any less-than-five-percent shareholder that, at any time during the five-year period, is related to X under section 355(d)(7)(A), acted pursuant to a plan or arrangement with X under section 355(d)(7)(B) and paragraph (c)(4) of this section with respect to acquisitions of D stock, or holds stock that is attributed to X under section 355(d)(8)(A). Accordingly, under paragraph (f)(1) of this section, to determine whether section 355(d) applies, D must determine: whether X acquired its directly held D stock by purchase under section 355(d)(5) and paragraphs (d) and (e)(2) and (3) of this section during the five-year period; whether X is treated as having purchased any additional D stock under section 355(d)(8) and paragraph (e)(1) of this section during the five-year period; and whether X is related to, or acquired its D stock pursuant to a plan or arrangement with, one or more of D's other shareholders during the five-year period under section 355(d)(7)(A) or (B) and paragraph (c)(4) of this section, and if so, whether those shareholders acquired their D stock by purchase under section 355(d)(5) or (8) and paragraphs (d) and (e) of this section during the five-year period.

Example 3. Acquisition of publicly traded corporation. The facts are the same as those in *Example 1*, except that P acquires all of the D stock in a section 368(a)(1)(B) reorganization that is not also a reorganization under section 368(a)(1)(A) by reason of section 368(a)(2)(E), and D distributes C to P one year later. Because D was widely held, P applies statistical sampling procedures that involve less than 50% of D's outstanding shares, to estimate the basis of all shares acquired, instead of surveying each shareholder. Under the deemed purchase rule of section 355(d)(5)(C) and paragraph (e)(2) of this section, P is treated as having acquired the D stock by purchase on the date the D shareholders acquired the D stock by purchase. Even though D has no less-than-five-percent shareholder immediately after the distribution, D may rely on the presumptions in paragraphs (f)(3) and (4) of this section to determine whether and to what extent the D stock is treated as purchased during the five-year period in P's hands under the deemed purchase rule of section 355(d)(5)(C) and paragraph (e)(2) of this section. Accordingly, D may presume that section 355(d) does not apply to the distribution of C to P. This result would not change even if the statistical sampling that involves less than 50 percent of D's outstanding shares indicated that more than 50% of D's shares were acquired by purchase during the five-year period.

Example 4. Non-publicly traded corporation. D is owned by 20 shareholders and has a single class of stock that is not reporting stock. D knows that A owns 40 percent of the D stock, and D does not know that any other shareholder has owned as much as five percent of the D stock at any time during the five-year period. D may not rely on the presumption in paragraph (f)(3) of this section because its stock is not reporting stock. D may not rely on the presumption in paragraph (f)(4) of this section with respect to A. In addition, D may not rely on the presumption in paragraph (f)(4) of this section for any less-than-five-percent shareholder that, at any time during the five-year period, is related to A under section 355(d)(7)(A), acted pursuant to a plan or arrangement with A under section 355(d)(7)(B) and paragraph (c)(4) of this section with respect to acquisitions of D stock, or holds stock that is attributed to A under section 355(d)(8)(A). D may rely on the presumption in paragraph (f)(4) of this section for less-than-five-percent shareholders that during the five-year period are not related to A, did not act pursuant to a plan or arrangement with A, and do not hold stock attributed to A. Accordingly, under paragraph (f)(1) of this section, to determine whether section 355(d) applies, D must determine: that A is its only shareholder that is (or was at any time during the five-year period) not a less-than-five-percent shareholder; whether A acquired its directly held D stock by purchase under section 355(d)(5) and paragraphs (d) and (e)(2) and (3) of this section during the five-year period; whether A is treated as having purchased any additional D stock under section 355(d)(8) and paragraph (e)(1) of this section during the five-year period; and whether A is related to, or acquired its D stock pursuant to a plan or arrangement with, one or more of D's other shareholders during the five-year period under section 355(d)(7)(A) or (B) and paragraph (c)(4) of this section, and if so, whether those shareholders acquired their D stock by purchase under section 355(d)(5) or (8) and paragraphs (d) and (e) of this section during the five-year period.

(g) *Effective/applicability dates.*—This section applies to distributions occurring after December 20, 2000, except that they do not apply to any distributions occurring pursuant to a written agreement that is (subject to customary conditions) binding on December 20, 2000, and at all later times. The provisions of paragraph (d)(1)(i)(A)(2) of this section relating to section 1022 are effective on and after January 19, 2017. [Reg. § 1.355-6.]

☐ [*T.D.* 8238, 1-5-89. *Amended by T.D.* 8913, 12-19-2000 (*corrected* 2-5-2001) *and T.D.* 9811, 1-18-2017.]

[Reg. § 1.355-7]

§ 1.355-7. Recognition of gain on certain distributions of stock or securities in connection with an acquisition.—(a) *In general.*—Except as provided in section 355(e) and in this section, section 355(e) applies to any distribution—

(1) To which section 355 (or so much of section 356 as relates to section 355) applies; and

(2) That is part of a plan (or series of related transactions) (hereinafter, plan) pursuant to which 1 or more persons acquire directly or indirectly stock representing a 50-percent or greater interest in the distributing corporation (Distributing) or any controlled corporation (Controlled).

(b) *Plan.*—(1) *In general.*—Whether a distribution and an acquisition are part of a plan is determined based on all the facts and circumstances. The facts and circumstances to be considered in demonstrating whether a distribution and an acquisition are part of a plan include, but are not limited to, the facts and circumstances set forth in paragraphs (b)(3) and (4) of this section. In general, the weight to be given each of the facts and circumstances depends on the particular case. Whether a distribution and an acquisition are part of a plan does not depend on the relative number of facts and circumstances set forth in paragraph (b)(3) that evidence that a distribution and an acquisition are part of a plan as compared to the relative number of facts and circumstances set forth in paragraph (b)(4) that evidence that a distribution and an acquisition are not part of a plan.

(2) *Certain post-distribution acquisitions.*—In the case of an acquisition (other than involving a public offering) after a distribution, the distribution and the acquisition can be part of a plan only if there was an agreement, understanding, arrangement, or substantial negotiations regarding the acquisition or a similar acquisition at some time during the two-year period ending on the date of the distribution. In the case of an acquisition (other than involving a public offering) after a distribution, the existence of an agreement, understanding, arrangement, or substantial negotiations regarding the acquisition or a similar acquisition at some time during the two-year period ending on the date of the distribution tends to show that the distribution and the acquisition are part of a plan. See paragraph (b)(3)(i) of this section. However, all facts and circumstances must be considered to determine whether the distribution and the acquisition are part of a plan. For example, in the case of an acquisition (other than involving a public offering) after a distribution, if the distribution was motivated in whole or substantial part by a corporate business purpose (within the meaning of § 1.355-2(b)) other than a business purpose to facilitate the acquisition or a similar acquisition of Distributing or Controlled (see paragraph (b)(4)(v) of this section) and would have occurred at approximately the same time and in similar form regardless of whether the acquisition or a similar acqui-

sition was effected (see paragraph (b)(4)(vi) of this section), the taxpayer may be able to establish that the distribution and the acquisition are not part of a plan.

(3) *Plan factors.*—Among the facts and circumstances tending to show that a distribution and an acquisition are part of a plan are the following:

(i) In the case of an acquisition (other than involving a public offering) after a distribution, at some time during the two-year period ending on the date of the distribution, there was an agreement, understanding, arrangement, or substantial negotiations regarding the acquisition or a similar acquisition. The weight to be accorded this fact depends on the nature, extent, and timing of the agreement, understanding, arrangement, or substantial negotiations. The existence of an agreement, understanding, or arrangement at the time of the distribution is given substantial weight.

(ii) In the case of an acquisition involving a public offering after a distribution, at some time during the two-year period ending on the date of the distribution, there were discussions by Distributing or Controlled with an investment banker regarding the acquisition or a similar acquisition. The weight to be accorded this fact depends on the nature, extent, and timing of the discussions.

(iii) In the case of an acquisition (other than involving a public offering) before a distribution, at some time during the two-year period ending on the date of the acquisition, there were discussions by Distributing or Controlled with the acquirer regarding a distribution. The weight to be accorded this fact depends on the nature, extent, and timing of the discussions. In addition, in the case of an acquisition (other than involving a public offering) before a distribution, the acquirer intends to cause a distribution and, immediately after the acquisition, can meaningfully participate in the decision regarding whether to make a distribution.

(iv) In the case of an acquisition involving a public offering before a distribution, at some time during the two-year period ending on the date of the acquisition, there were discussions by Distributing or Controlled with an investment banker regarding a distribution. The weight to be accorded this fact depends on the nature, extent, and timing of the discussions.

(v) In the case of an acquisition either before or after a distribution, the distribution was motivated by a business purpose to facilitate the acquisition or a similar acquisition.

(4) *Non-plan factors.*—Among the facts and circumstances tending to show that a distribution and an acquisition are not part of a plan are the following:

(i) In the case of an acquisition involving a public offering after a distribution, during the two-year period ending on the date of the distribution, there were no discussions by Distributing or Controlled with an investment banker regarding the acquisition or a similar acquisition.

(ii) In the case of an acquisition after a distribution, there was an identifiable, unexpected change in market or business conditions occurring after the distribution that resulted in the acquisition that was otherwise unexpected at the time of the distribution.

(iii) In the case of an acquisition (other than involving a public offering) before a distribution, during the two-year period ending on the date of the earlier to occur of the acquisition or the first public announcement regarding the distribution, there were no discussions by Distributing or Controlled with the acquirer regarding a distribution. Paragraph (b)(4)(iii) of this section does not apply to an acquisition where the acquirer intends to cause a distribution and, immediately after the acquisition, can meaningfully participate in the decision regarding whether to make a distribution.

(iv) In the case of an acquisition before a distribution, there was an identifiable, unexpected change in market or business conditions occurring after the acquisition that resulted in a distribution that was otherwise unexpected.

(v) In the case of an acquisition either before or after a distribution, the distribution was motivated in whole or substantial part by a corporate business purpose (within the meaning of § 1.355-2(b)) other than a business purpose to facilitate the acquisition or a similar acquisition.

(vi) In the case of an acquisition either before or after a distribution, the distribution would have occurred at approximately the same time and in similar form regardless of the acquisition or a similar acquisition.

(c) *Operating rules.*—The operating rules contained in this paragraph (c) apply for all purposes of this section.

(1) *Internal discussions and discussions with outside advisors evidence of business purpose.*—Discussions by Distributing or Controlled with outside advisors and internal discussions may be indicative of one or more business purposes for the distribution and the relative importance of such purposes.

(2) *Takeover defense.*—If Distributing engages in discussions with a potential acquirer regarding an acquisition of Distributing or Controlled and distributes Controlled stock intending, in whole or substantial part, to decrease the likelihood of the acquisition of Distributing or Controlled by separating it from another corporation that is likely to be acquired, Distributing will be treated as having a business purpose to facilitate the acquisition of the corporation that was likely to be acquired.

(3) *Effect of distribution on trading in stock.*—The fact that the distribution made all or a part of the stock of Controlled available for trading or made Distributing's or Controlled's stock trade more actively is not taken into account in determining whether the distribution and an acquisition of Distributing or Controlled stock were part of a plan.

(4) *Consequences of section 355(e) disregarded for certain purposes.*— For purposes of determining the intentions of the relevant parties under this section, the consequences of the application of section 355(e), and the existence of any contractual indemnity by Controlled for tax resulting from the application of section 355(e) caused by an acquisition of Controlled, are disregarded.

(5) *Multiple acquisitions.*—All acquisitions of stock of Distributing or Controlled that are considered to be part of a plan with a distribution pursuant to paragraph (b) of this section will be aggregated for purposes of the 50-percent test of paragraph (a)(2) of this section.

(d) *Safe harbors.*—(1) *Safe Harbor I.*—A distribution and an acquisition occurring after the distribution will not be considered part of a plan if—

(i) The distribution was motivated in whole or substantial part by a corporate business purpose (within the meaning of § 1.355-2(b)), other than a business purpose to facilitate an acquisition of the acquired corporation (Distributing or Controlled); and

(ii) The acquisition occurred more than six months after the distribution and there was no agreement, understanding, arrangement, or substantial negotiations concerning the acquisition or a similar acquisition during the period that begins one year before the distribution and ends six months thereafter.

(2) *Safe Harbor II.*—(i) *In general.*—A distribution and an acquisition occurring after the distribution will not be considered part of a plan if—

(A) The distribution was not motivated by a business purpose to facilitate the acquisition or a similar acquisition;

(B) The acquisition occurred more than six months after the distribution and there was no agreement, understanding, arrangement, or substantial negotiations concerning the acquisition or a similar acquisition during the period that begins one year before the distribution and ends six months thereafter; and

(C) No more than 25 percent of the stock of the acquired corporation (Distributing or Controlled) was either acquired or the subject of an agreement, understanding, arrangement, or substantial negotiations during the period that begins one year before the distribution and ends six months thereafter.

(ii) *Special rule.*—For purposes of paragraph (d)(2)(i)(C) of this section, acquisitions of stock that are treated as not part of a plan pursuant to Safe Harbor VII, Safe Harbor VIII, or Safe Harbor IX are disregarded.

(3) *Safe Harbor III.*—If an acquisition occurs after a distribution, there was no agreement, understanding, or arrangement concerning the acquisition or a similar acquisition at the time of the distribution, and there was no agreement, understanding, arrangement, or substantial negotiations concerning the acquisition or a similar acquisition within one year after the distribution, the acquisition and the distribution will not be considered part of a plan.

(4) *Safe Harbor IV.*—(i) *In general.*—A distribution and an acquisition (other than involving a public offering) occurring before the distribution will not be considered part of a plan if the acquisition occurs before the date of the first disclosure event regarding the distribution.

(ii) *Special rules.*—(A) Paragraph (d)(4)(i) of this section does not apply to a stock acquisition if the acquirer or a coordinating group of which the acquirer is a member is a controlling shareholder or a ten-percent shareholder of the acquired corporation (Distributing or Controlled) at any time during the period beginning immediately after the acquisition and ending on the date of the distribution.

(B) Paragraph (d)(4)(i) of this section does not apply to an acquisition that occurs in connection with a transaction in which the aggregate acquisitions are of stock possessing 20 percent or more of the total voting power of the stock of the acquired corporation (Distributing or Controlled) or stock having a value of 20 percent or more of the total value of the stock of the acquired corporation (Distributing or Controlled).

(5) *Safe Harbor V.*—(i) *In general.*—A distribution that is pro rata among the Distributing shareholders and an acquisition (other than involving a public offering) of Distributing stock occurring before the distribution will not be considered part of a plan if—

(A) The acquisition occurs after the date of a public announcement regarding the distribution; and

(B) There were no discussions by Distributing or Controlled with the acquirer regarding a distribution on or before the date of the first public announcement regarding the distribution.

(ii) *Special rules.*—(A) Paragraph (d)(5)(i) of this section does not apply to a stock acquisition if the acquirer or a coordinating group of which the acquirer is a member is a controlling shareholder or a ten-percent shareholder of Distributing at any time during the period beginning immediately after the acquisition and ending on the date of the distribution.

(B) Paragraph (d)(5)(i) of this section does not apply to an acquisition that occurs in connection with a transaction in which the aggregate acquisitions are of stock possessing 20 percent or more of the total voting power of the stock of Distributing or stock having a value of 20 percent or more of the total value of the stock of Distributing.

(6) *Safe Harbor VI.*—A distribution and an acquisition involving a public offering occurring before the distribution will not be considered part of a plan if the acquisition occurs before the date of the first disclosure event regarding the distribution in the case of an acquisition of stock that is not listed on an established market immediately after the acquisition, or before the date of the first public announcement regarding the distribution in the case of an acquisition of stock that is listed on an established market immediately after the acquisition.

(7) *Safe Harbor VII.*—(i) *In general.*—An acquisition (other than involving a public offering) of Distributing or Controlled stock that is listed on an established market is not part of a plan if, immediately before or immediately after the transfer, none of the transferor, the transferee, and any coordinating group of which either the transferor or the transferee is a member is—

(A) The acquired corporation (Distributing or Controlled);

(B) A corporation that the acquired corporation (Distributing or Controlled) controls within the meaning of section 368(c);

(C) A member of a controlled group of corporations within the meaning of section 1563 of which the acquired corporation (Distributing or Controlled) is a member;

(D) A controlling shareholder of the acquired corporation (Distributing or Controlled); or

(E) A ten-percent shareholder of the acquired corporation (Distributing or Controlled).

(ii) *Special rules.*—(A) Paragraph (d)(7)(i) of this section does not apply to a transfer of stock by or to a person if the corporation the stock of which is being transferred knows, or has reason to know, that the person or a coordinating group of which such person is a member intends to become a controlling shareholder or a ten-percent shareholder of the acquired corporation (Distributing or Controlled) at any time after the acquisition and before the date that is two years after the distribution.

(B) If a transfer of stock to which paragraph (d)(7)(i) of this section applies results immediately, or upon a subsequent event or the passage of time, in an indirect acquisition of voting power by a person other than the transferee, paragraph (d)(7)(i) of this section does not prevent an acquisition of stock (with the voting power such stock represents after the transfer to which paragraph (d)(7)(i) of this section applies) by such other person from being treated as part of a plan.

(8) *Safe Harbor VIII.*—(i) *In general.*—If, in a transaction to which section 83 or section 421(a) or (b) applies, stock of Distributing or Controlled is acquired by a person in connection with such person's performance of services as an employee, director, or independent contractor for Distributing, Controlled, a related person, a corporation the assets of which Distributing, Controlled, or a related person acquires in a reorganization under section 368(a), or a corporation that acquires the assets of Distributing or Controlled in such a reorganization (and the stock acquired is not excessive by reference to the services performed), the acquisition and the distribution will not be considered part of a plan. For purposes of this paragraph (d)(8)(i), a related person is a person related to Distributing or Controlled under section 355(d)(7)(A).

(ii) *Special rule.*—Paragraph (d)(8)(i) of this section does not apply to a stock acquisition if the acquirer or a coordinating group of which the acquirer is a member is a controlling shareholder or a ten-percent shareholder of the acquired corporation (Distributing or Controlled) immediately after the acquisition.

(9) *Safe Harbor IX.*—(i) *In general.*—If stock of Distributing or Controlled is acquired by a retirement plan of Distributing or Controlled (or a retirement plan of any other person that is treated as the same employer as Distributing or Controlled under section 414(b), (c), (m), or (o)) that qualifies under section 401(a) or 403(a), the acquisition and the distribution will not be considered part of a plan.

(ii) *Special rule.*—Paragraph (d)(9)(i) of this section does not apply to the extent that the stock acquired pursuant to acquisitions by all of the qualified plans of the persons described in paragraph (d)(9)(i) of this section during the four-year period beginning two years before the distribution, in the aggregate, represents more than ten percent of the total combined voting power of all classes of stock entitled to vote, or more than ten percent of the total value of shares of all classes of stock, of the acquired corporation (Distributing or Controlled).

(e) *Options, warrants, convertible obligations, and other similar interests.*—(1) *Treatment of options.*—(i) *General rule.*—For purposes of this section, if stock of Distributing or Controlled is acquired pursuant to an option that is written by Distributing, Controlled, or a person that is a controlling shareholder of Distributing or Controlled at the time the option is written, or that is acquired by a person that is a controlling shareholder of Distributing or Controlled immediately after the option is written, the option will be treated as an agreement, understanding, or arrangement to acquire the stock on the earliest of the following dates: the date that the option is written, if the option was more likely than not to be exercised as of such date; the date that the option is transferred if, immediately before or immediately after the transfer, the transferor or transferee was Distributing, Controlled, a corporation that Distributing or Controlled controls within the meaning of section 368(c), a member of a controlled group of corporations within the meaning of section 1563 of which Distributing or Controlled is a member, or a controlling shareholder or a ten-percent shareholder of Distributing or Controlled and the option was more likely than not to be exercised as of such date; and the date that the option is modified in a manner that materially increases the likelihood of exercise, if the option was more likely than not to be exercised as of such date; provided, however, if the writing, transfer, or modification had a principal purpose of avoiding section 355(e), the option will be treated as an agreement, understanding, arrangement, or substantial negotiations to acquire the stock on the date of the distribution. The determination of whether an option was more likely than not to be exercised is based on all the facts and circumstances, taking control premiums and minority and blockage discounts into account in determining the fair market value of stock underlying an option.

(ii) *Agreement, understanding, or arrangement to write, transfer, or modify an option.*—If there is an agreement, understanding, or arrangement to write an option, the option will be treated as written on the date of the agreement, understanding, or arrangement. If there is an agreement, understanding, or arrangement to transfer an option, the option will be treated as transferred on the date of the agreement, understanding, or arrangement. If there is an agreement, understanding, or arrangement to modify an option in a manner that materially increases the likelihood of exercise, the option will be treated as so modified on the date of the agreement, understanding, or arrangement.

(iii) *Substantial negotiations related to options.*—If an option is treated as an agreement, understanding, or arrangement to acquire the stock on the date that the option is written, substantial negotiations to acquire the option will be treated as substantial negotiations to acquire the stock subject to such option. If an option is treated as an agreement, understanding, or arrangement to acquire the stock on the date that the option is transferred, substantial negotiations regarding the transfer of the option will be treated as substantial negotiations to acquire the stock subject to such option. If an option is treated as an agreement, understanding, or arrangement to acquire the stock on the date that the option is modified in a manner that materially increases the likelihood of exercise, substantial negotiations regarding such modifications to the option will be treated as substantial negotiations to acquire the stock subject to such option.

(2) *Stock acquired pursuant to options.*—For purposes of this section, if an option is issued for cash, the terms of the acquisition of the option and the terms of the option are established by the corporation the stock of which is subject to the option (Distributing or Controlled) or the writer with the involvement of one or more investment bankers, and the potential acquirers of the option have no opportunity to negotiate the terms of the acquisition of the option or the terms of the option, then an acquisition pursuant to such option shall be treated as an acquisition involving a public offering occurring after the

distribution if the option is exercised after the distribution or an acquisition involving a public offering before a distribution if the option is exercised before the distribution. Otherwise, an acquisition pursuant to an option shall be treated as an acquisition not involving a public offering.

(3) *Instruments treated as options.*—For purposes of this section, except to the extent provided in paragraph (e)(4) of this section, call options, warrants, convertible obligations, the conversion feature of convertible stock, put options, redemption agreements (including rights to cause the redemption of stock), any other instruments that provide for the right or possibility to issue, redeem, or transfer stock (including an option on an option), or any other similar interests are treated as options.

(4) *Instruments generally not treated as options.*—For purposes of this section, the following are not treated as options unless (in the case of paragraphs (e)(4)(i), (ii), and (iii) of this section) written, transferred (directly or indirectly), modified, or listed with a principal purpose of avoiding the application of section 355(e) or this section.

(i) *Escrow, pledge, or other security agreements.*—An option that is part of a security arrangement in a typical lending transaction (including a purchase money loan), if the arrangement is subject to customary commercial conditions. For this purpose, a security arrangement includes, for example, an agreement for holding stock in escrow or under a pledge or other security agreement, or an option to acquire stock contingent upon a default under a loan.

(ii) *Options exercisable only upon death, disability, mental incompetency, or separation from service.*—Any option entered into between shareholders of a corporation (or a shareholder and the corporation) that is exercisable only upon the death, disability, or mental incompetency of the shareholder, or, in the case of stock acquired in connection with the performance of services for the corporation or a person related to it under section 355(d)(7)(A) (and that is not excessive by reference to the services performed), the shareholder's separation from service.

(iii) *Rights of first refusal.*—A bona fide right of first refusal regarding the corporation's stock with customary terms, entered into between shareholders of a corporation (or between the corporation and a shareholder).

(iv) *Other enumerated instruments.*—Any other instrument the Commissioner may designate in revenue procedures, notices, or other guidance published in the Internal Revenue Bulletin (see § 601.601(d)(2) of this chapter).

(f) *Multiple controlled corporations.*—Only the stock or securities of a controlled corporation in which one or more persons acquire directly or indirectly stock representing a 50-percent or greater interest as part of a plan involving the distribution of that corporation will be treated as not qualified property under section 355(e)(1) if—

(1) The stock or securities of more than one controlled corporation are distributed in distributions to which section 355 (or so much of section 356 as relates to section 355) applies; and

(2) One or more persons do not acquire, directly or indirectly, stock representing a 50-percent or greater interest in Distributing pursuant to a plan involving any of those distributions.

(g) *Valuation.*—Except as provided in paragraph (e)(1)(i) of this section, for purposes of section 355(e) and this section, all shares of stock within a single class are considered to have the same value. Thus, control premiums and minority and blockage discounts within a single class are not taken into account.

(h) *Definitions.*—For purposes of this section, the following definitions shall apply:

(1) *Agreement, understanding, arrangement, or substantial negotiations.*—(i) An agreement, understanding, or arrangement generally requires either—

(A) an agreement, understanding, or arrangement by one or more officers or directors acting on behalf of Distributing or Controlled, by controlling shareholders of Distributing or Controlled, or by another person or persons with the implicit or explicit permission of one or more of such officers, directors, or controlling shareholders, with the acquirer or with a person or persons with the implicit or explicit permission of the acquirer; or

(B) an agreement, understanding, or arrangement by an acquirer that is a controlling shareholder of Distributing or Controlled immediately after the acquisition that is the subject of the agreement, understanding, or arrangement, or by a person or persons with the implicit or explicit permission of such acquirer, with the transferor or with a person or persons with the implicit or explicit permission of the transferor.

(ii) In the case of an acquisition by a corporation, an agreement, understanding, or arrangement with the acquiring corporation generally requires an agreement, understanding, or arrangement with one or more officers or directors acting on behalf of the acquiring corporation, with controlling shareholders of the acquiring corporation, or with another person or persons with the implicit or explicit permission of one or more of such officers, directors, or controlling shareholders.

(iii) Whether an agreement, understanding, or arrangement exists depends on the facts and circumstances. The parties do not necessarily have to have entered into a binding contract or have reached agreement on all significant economic terms to have an agreement, understanding, or arrangement. However, an agreement, understanding, or arrangement clearly exists if a binding contract to acquire stock exists.

(iv) Substantial negotiations in the case of an acquisition (other than involving a public offering) generally require discussions of significant economic terms, e.g., the exchange ratio in a reorganization, either—

(A) by one or more officers or directors acting on behalf of Distributing or Controlled, by controlling shareholders of Distributing or Controlled, or by another person or persons with the implicit or explicit permission of one or more of such officers, directors, or controlling shareholders, with the acquirer or with a person or persons with the implicit or explicit permission of the acquirer; or

(B) if the acquirer is a controlling shareholder of Distributing or Controlled immediately after the acquisition that is the subject of substantial negotiations, by the acquirer or by a person or persons with the implicit or explicit permission of the acquirer, with the transferor or with a person or persons with the implicit or explicit permission of the transferor.

(v) In the case of an acquisition (other than involving a public offering) by a corporation, substantial negotiations generally require discussions of significant economic terms with one or more officers or directors acting on behalf of the acquiring corporation, or with controlling shareholders of the acquiring corporation, or with another person or persons with the implicit or explicit permission of one or more of such officers, directors, or controlling shareholders.

(vi) In the case of an acquisition involving a public offering, the existence of an agreement, understanding, arrangement, or substantial negotiations will be based on discussions by one or more officers or directors acting on behalf of Distributing or Controlled, by controlling shareholders of Distributing or Controlled, or by another person or persons with the implicit or explicit permission of one or more of such officers, directors, or controlling shareholders, with an investment banker.

(2) *Controlled corporation.*—A controlled corporation is a corporation the stock of which is distributed in a distribution to which section 355 (or so much of section 356 as relates to section 355) applies.

(3) *Controlling shareholder.*—(i) A controlling shareholder of a corporation the stock of which is listed on an established market is a five-percent shareholder who actively participates in the management or operation of the corporation. For purposes of this paragraph (h)(3)(i), a corporate director will be treated as actively participating in the management of the corporation.

(ii) A controlling shareholder of a corporation the stock of which is not listed on an established market is any person that owns stock possessing voting power representing a meaningful voice in the governance of the corporation. For purposes of determining whether a person owns stock possessing voting power representing a meaningful voice in the governance of the corporation, the person shall be treated as owning the stock that such person owns actually and constructively under the rules of section 318 (without regard to section 318(a)(4)). In addition, if the exercise of an option (whether by itself or in conjunction with the deemed exercise of one or more other options) would cause the holder to own stock possessing voting power representing a meaningful voice in the governance of the corporation, then the option will be treated as exercised.

(iii) If a distribution precedes an acquisition, Controlled's controlling shareholders immediately after the distribution and Distributing are included among Controlled's controlling shareholders at the time of the distribution.

(4) *Coordinating group.*—A coordinating group includes two or more persons that, pursuant to a formal or informal understanding, join in one or more coordinated acquisitions or dispositions of stock of Distributing or Controlled. A principal element in determining if such an understanding exists is whether the investment decision of each person is based on the investment decision of one or more other existing or prospective shareholders. A coordinating group is treated as a single shareholder for purposes of determining whether the

coordinating group is treated as a controlling shareholder, a five-percent shareholder, or a ten-percent shareholder.

(5) *Disclosure event.*—A disclosure event regarding the distribution means any communication by an officer, director, controlling shareholder, or employee of Distributing, Controlled, or a corporation related to Distributing or Controlled, or an outside advisor of any of those persons (where such advisor makes the communication on behalf of such person), regarding the distribution, or the possibility thereof, to the acquirer or any other person (other than an officer, director, controlling shareholder, or employee of Distributing, Controlled, or a corporation related to Distributing or Controlled, or an outside advisor of any of those persons). For purposes of this paragraph (h)(5), a corporation is related to Distributing or Controlled if it is a member of an affiliated group (as defined in section 1504(a) without regard to section 1504(b)) that includes either Distributing or Controlled or it is a member of a qualified group (as defined in § 1.368-1(d)(4)(ii)) that includes either Distributing or Controlled.

(6) *Discussions.*—Discussions by Distributing or Controlled generally require discussions by one or more officers or directors acting on behalf of Distributing or Controlled, by controlling shareholders of Distributing or Controlled, or by another person or persons with the implicit or explicit permission of one or more of such officers, directors, or controlling shareholders. Discussions with the acquirer generally require discussions with the acquirer or with a person or persons with the implicit or explicit permission of the acquirer. In the case of an acquisition by a corporation, discussions with the acquiring corporation generally require discussions with one or more officers or directors acting on behalf of the acquiring corporation, with controlling shareholders of the acquiring corporation, or with another person or persons with the implicit or explicit permission of one or more of such officers, directors, or controlling shareholders.

(7) *Established market.*—An established market is—

(i) A national securities exchange registered under section 6 of the Securities Exchange Act of 1934 (15 U.S.C. 78f);

(ii) An interdealer quotation system sponsored by a national securities association registered under section 15A of the Securities Act of 1934 (15 U.S.C. 78o-3); or

(iii) Any additional market that the Commissioner may designate in revenue procedures, notices, or other guidance published in the Internal Revenue Bulletin (see § 601.601(d)(2) of this chapter).

(8) *Five-percent shareholder.*—A person will be considered a five-percent shareholder of a corporation the stock of which is listed on an established market if the person owns five percent or more of any class of stock of the corporation whose stock is transferred. For purposes of determining whether a person owns five percent or more of any class of stock of the corporation whose stock is transferred, the person shall be treated as owning the stock that such person owns actually and constructively under the rules of section 318 (without regard to section 318(a)(4)). In addition, if the exercise of an option (whether by itself or in conjunction with the deemed exercise of one or more other options) would cause the holder to become a five-percent shareholder, then the option will be treated as exercised. Absent actual knowledge that a person is a five-percent shareholder, a corporation can rely on Schedules 13D and 13G (or any similar schedules) filed with the Securities and Exchange Commission to identify its five-percent shareholders.

(9) *Implicit permission.*—A corporation is treated as having the implicit permission of its shareholders when it engages in discussions or negotiations, or enters into an agreement, understanding, or arrangement.

(10) *Public announcement.*—A public announcement regarding the distribution means any communication by Distributing or Controlled regarding Distributing's intention to effect the distribution where the communication is generally available to the public.

(11) *Public offering.*—An acquisition involving a public offering means an acquisition of stock for cash where the terms of the acquisition are established by the acquired corporation (Distributing or Controlled) or the seller with the involvement of one or more investment bankers and the potential acquirers have no opportunity to negotiate the terms of the acquisition. For example, a public offering includes an underwritten offering of registered stock for cash.

(12) *Similar acquisition (not involving a public offering).*—In general, an actual acquisition (other than involving a public offering) is similar to another potential acquisition if the actual acquisition effects a direct or indirect combination of all or a significant portion of the same business operations as the combination that would have been effected by such other potential acquisition. Thus, an actual acquisition may be similar to another acquisition even if the timing or terms of the actual acquisition are different from the timing or terms of the

other acquisition. For example, an actual acquisition of Distributing by shareholders of another corporation in connection with a merger of such other corporation with and into Distributing is similar to another acquisition of Distributing by merger into such other corporation or into a subsidiary of such other corporation. However, in general, an actual acquisition (other than involving a public offering) is not similar to another acquisition if the ultimate owners of the business operations with which Distributing or Controlled is combined in the actual acquisition are substantially different from the ultimate owners of the business operations with which Distributing or Controlled was to be combined in such other acquisition.

(13) *Similar acquisition involving a public offering.*—(i) *One public offering.*—In general, an actual acquisition involving a public offering may be similar to a potential acquisition involving a public offering, even though there are changes in the terms of the stock, the class of stock being offered, the size of the offering, the timing of the offering, the price of the stock, or the participants in the offering.

(ii) *More than one public offering.*—More than one actual acquisition involving a public offering may be similar to a potential acquisition involving a public offering. If there is an actual acquisition involving a public offering (the first public offering) that is the same as, or similar to, a potential acquisition involving a public offering, then another actual acquisition involving a public offering (the second public offering) cannot be similar to the potential acquisition unless the purpose of the second public offering is similar to that of the potential acquisition and occurs close in time to the first public offering.

(iii) *Potential acquisition involving a public offering.*—For purposes of paragraph (h)(13)(i) and (ii) of this section, as the context may require, a potential acquisition involving a public offering means a potential acquisition involving a public offering that was discussed by Distributing or Controlled with an investment banker, that motivated the distribution, or that was the subject of an agreement, understanding, arrangement, or substantial negotiations.

(14) *Ten-percent shareholder.*—A person will be considered a ten-percent shareholder of a corporation the stock of which is listed on an established market if the person owns, actually or constructively under the rules of section 318 (without regard to section 318(a)(4)), ten percent or more of any class of stock of the corporation whose stock is transferred. A person will be considered a ten-percent shareholder of a corporation the stock of which is not listed on an established market if the person owns stock possessing ten percent or more of the total voting power of the stock of the corporation whose stock is transferred or stock having a value equal to ten percent or more of the total value of the stock of the corporation whose stock is transferred. For purposes of determining whether a person owns ten percent or more of the total voting power or value of the stock of the corporation whose stock is transferred, the person shall be treated as owning the stock that such person owns actually and constructively under the rules of section 318 (without regard to section 318(a)(4)). In addition, if the exercise of an option (whether by itself or in conjunction with the deemed exercise of one or more other options) would cause the holder to become a ten-percent shareholder, then the option will be treated as exercised. Absent actual knowledge that a person is a ten-percent shareholder, a corporation the stock of which is listed on an established market can rely on Schedules 13D and 13G (or any similar schedules) filed with the Securities and Exchange Commission to identify its ten-percent shareholders.

(i) [Reserved]

(j) *Examples.*—The following examples illustrate paragraphs (a) through (h) of this section. Throughout these examples, assume that Distributing (D) owns all of the stock of Controlled (C). Assume further that D distributes the stock of C in a distribution to which section 355 applies and to which section 355(d) does not apply. Unless otherwise stated, assume the corporations do not have controlling shareholders. No inference should be drawn from any example concerning whether any requirements of section 355 other than those of section 355(e) are satisfied. The examples are as follows:

Example 1. Unwanted assets. (i) D is in business 1. C is in business 2. D is relatively small in its industry. D wants to combine with X, a larger corporation also engaged in business 1. X and D begin negotiating for X to acquire D, but X does not want to acquire C. To facilitate the acquisition of D by X, D agrees to distribute all the stock of C pro rata before the acquisition. Prior to the distribution, D and X enter into a contract for D to merge into X subject to several conditions. One month after D and X enter into the contract, D distributes C and, on the day after the distribution, D merges into X. As a result of the merger, D's former shareholders own less than 50 percent of the stock of X.

(ii) The issue is whether the distribution of C and the merger of D into X are part of a plan. No Safe Harbor applies to this acquisition.

To determine whether the distribution of C and the merger of D into X are part of a plan, D must consider all the facts and circumstances, including those described in paragraph (b) of this section.

(iii) The following tends to show that the distribution of C and the merger of D into X are part of a plan: X and D had an agreement regarding the acquisition during the two-year period ending on the date of the distribution (paragraph (b)(3)(i) of this section), and the distribution was motivated by a business purpose to facilitate the merger (paragraph (b)(3)(v) of this section). Because the merger was agreed to at the time of the distribution, the fact described in paragraph (b)(3)(i) of this section is given substantial weight.

(iv) None of the facts and circumstances listed in paragraph (b)(4) of this section, tending to show that a distribution and an acquisition are not part of a plan, exist in this case.

(v) The distribution of C and the merger of D into X are part of a plan under paragraph (b) of this section.

Example 2. Public offering. (i) D's managers, directors, and investment banker discuss the possibility of offering D stock to the public. They decide a public offering of 20 percent of D's stock with D as a stand-alone corporation would be in D's best interest. One month later, to facilitate a stock offering by D of 20 percent of its stock, D distributes all the stock of C pro rata to D's shareholders. D issues new shares amounting to 20 percent of its stock to the public in a public offering seven months after the distribution.

(ii) The issue is whether the distribution of C and the public offering by D are part of a plan. No Safe Harbor applies to this acquisition. Safe Harbor VII, relating to public trading, does not apply to public offerings (see paragraph (d)(7)(i) of this section). To determine whether the distribution of C and the public offering by D are part of a plan, D must consider all the facts and circumstances, including those described in paragraph (b) of this section.

(iii) The following tends to show that the distribution of C and the public offering by D are part of a plan: D discussed the public offering with its investment banker during the two-year period ending on the date of the distribution (paragraph (b)(3)(ii) of this section), and the distribution was motivated by a business purpose to facilitate the public offering (paragraph (b)(3)(v) of this section).

(iv) None of the facts and circumstances listed in paragraph (b)(4) of this section, tending to show that a distribution and an acquisition are not part of a plan, exist in this case.

(v) The distribution of C and the public offering by D are part of a plan under paragraph (b) of this section.

Example 3. Hot market. (i) D is a widely-held corporation the stock of which is listed on an established market. D announces a distribution of C and distributes C pro rata to D's shareholders. By contract, C agrees to indemnify D for any imposition of tax under section 355(e) caused by the acts of C. The distribution is motivated by a desire to improve D's access to financing at preferred customer interest rates, which will be more readily available if D separates from C. At the time of the distribution, although neither D nor C has been approached by any potential acquirer of C, it is reasonably certain that soon after the distribution either an acquisition of C will occur or there will be an agreement, understanding, arrangement, or substantial negotiations regarding an acquisition of C. Corporation Y acquires C in a merger described in section 368(a)(1)(A) by reason of section 368(a)(2)(E) within six months after the distribution. The C shareholders receive less than 50 percent of the stock of Y in the exchange.

(ii) The issue is whether the distribution of C and the acquisition of C by Y are part of a plan. No Safe Harbor applies to this acquisition. Under paragraph (b)(2) of this section, because prior to the distribution neither D nor C and Y had an agreement, understanding, arrangement, or substantial negotiations regarding the acquisition or a similar acquisition, the distribution of C by D and the acquisition of C by Y are not part of a plan under paragraph (b) of this section.

Example 4. Unexpected opportunity. (i) D, the stock of which is listed on an established market, makes a public announcement that it will distribute all the stock of C pro rata to D's shareholders. After the public announcement but before the distribution, widely-held X becomes available as an acquisition target. There were no discussions by D or C with X before the date of the public announcement. D negotiates with X and X merges into D before the distribution. In the merger, X's shareholders receive ten percent of D's stock. D distributes the stock of C pro rata within six months after the acquisition of X. No shareholder of X was a controlling shareholder or a ten-percent shareholder of D at any time during the period beginning immediately after the merger and ending on the date of the distribution

(ii) The issue is whether the acquisition of X by D and the distribution of C are part of a plan. Safe Harbor V applies to this acquisition because the distribution is pro rata among D's shareholders, the acquisition occurs after the date of a public announcement regarding the distribution, there were no discussions by D or C with X on or before the date of the public announcement, no acquirer was a controlling shareholder or a ten-percent shareholder of D during the period beginning immediately after the merger and ending on the date of the distribution, and not more than 20 percent of D's stock was acquired by the X shareholders in the merger.

Example 5. Vote shifting transaction. (i) D is in business 1. C is in business 2. D wants to combine with X, which is also engaged in business 1. The stock of X is closely held. X and D begin negotiating for D to acquire X, but the X shareholders do not want to acquire an indirect interest in C. To facilitate the acquisition of X by D, D agrees to distribute all the stock of C pro rata before the acquisition of X. D and X enter into a contract for X to merge into D subject to several conditions. Among those conditions is that D will amend its corporate charter to provide for two classes of stock: Class A and Class B. Under all circumstances, each share of Class A stock will be entitled to ten votes in the election of each director on D's board of directors. Upon issuance, each share of Class B stock will be entitled to ten votes in the election of each director on D's board of directors; however, a disposition of such share by its original holder will result in such share being entitled to only one vote, rather than ten votes, in the election of each director. Immediately after the merger, the Class B shares will be listed on an established market. One month after D and X enter into the contract, D distributes C. Immediately after the distribution, the shareholders of D exchange their D stock for the new Class B shares. On the day after the distribution, X merges into D. In the merger, the former shareholders of X exchange their X stock for Class A shares of D. Immediately after the merger, D's historic shareholders own stock of D representing 51 percent of the total combined voting power of all classes of stock of D entitled to vote and more than 50 percent of the total value of all classes of stock of D. During the 30-day period following the merger, none of the Class A shares are transferred, but a number of D's historic shareholders sell their Class B stock of D in public trading with the result that, at the end of that 30-day period, the Class A shares owned by the former X shareholders represent 52 percent of the total combined voting power of all classes of stock of D entitled to vote.

(ii) *X acquisition.* (A) The issue is whether the distribution of C and the merger of X into D are part of a plan. No Safe Harbor applies to this acquisition. To determine whether the distribution of C and the merger of X into D are part of a plan, D must consider all the facts and circumstances, including those described in paragraph (b) of this section.

(B) The following tends to show that the distribution of C and the merger of X into D are part of a plan: X and D had an agreement regarding the acquisition during the two-year period ending on the date of the distribution (paragraph (b)(3)(i) of this section), and the distribution was motivated by a business purpose to facilitate the merger (paragraph (b)(3)(v) of this section). Because the merger was agreed to at the time of the distribution, the fact described in paragraph (b)(3)(i) of this section is given substantial weight.

(C) None of the facts and circumstances listed in paragraph (b)(4) of this section, tending to show that a distribution and an acquisition are not part of a plan, exist in this case.

(D) The distribution of C and the merger of X into D are part of a plan under paragraph (b) of this section.

(iii) *Public trading of Class B shares.* (A) Assuming that each of the transferors and the transferees of the Class B stock of D in public trading is not one of the prohibited transferors or transferees listed in paragraph (d)(7)(i), Safe Harbor VII will apply to the acquisitions of the Class B stock during the 30-day period following the merger such that the distribution and those acquisitions will not be treated as part of a plan. However, to the extent that those acquisitions result in an indirect acquisition of voting power by a person other than the acquirer of the transferred stock, Safe Harbor VII does not prevent the acquisition of the D stock (with the voting power such stock represents after those acquisitions) by the former X shareholders from being treated as part of a plan.

(B) To the extent that the transfer of the Class B shares causes the voting power of D to shift to the Class A stock acquired by the former X shareholders, such shifted voting power will be treated as attributable to the stock acquired by the former X shareholders as part of a plan that includes the distribution and the X acquisition.

Example 6. Acquisition not involving a public offering that is not similar. (i) D, X, and Y are each corporations the stock of which is publicly traded and widely held. Each of D, X, and Y is engaged in the manufacture and sale of trucks. C is engaged in the manufacture and sale of buses. D and X engage in substantial negotiations concerning X's acquisition of the stock of D from the D shareholders in exchange for stock of X. D and X do not reach an agreement regarding that acquisition. Three months after D and X first began negotiations *regarding that acquisition, D distributes* the stock of C pro rata to its shareholders. Three months after the distribution, Y acquires the stock of D from the D shareholders in exchange for stock of Y. The ultimate owners of Y are substantially different from the ultimate owners of X.

(ii) Although both X and Y engage in the manufacture and sale of trucks, X's truck business and Y's truck business are not the same business operations. Therefore, because Y's acquisition of D does not effect a combination of the same business operations as X's acquisition of D would have effected, and because the ultimate owners of Y are substantially different from the ultimate owners of X, Y's acquisition of D is not similar to X's potential acquisition of D that was the subject of earlier negotiations.

Example 7. Acquisition not involving a public offering that is similar. (i) D is engaged in the business of writing custom software for several industries (industries 1 through 6). The software business of D related to industries 4, 5, and 6 is significant relative to the software business of D related to industries 3, 4, 5, and 6. X, an unrelated corporation, is engaged in the business of writing software and the business of manufacturing and selling hardware devices. X's business of writing software is significant relative to its total businesses. X and D engage in substantial negotiations regarding X's acquisition of D stock from the D shareholders in exchange for stock of X. Because X does not want to acquire the software businesses related to industries 1 and 2, these negotiations relate to an acquisition of D stock where D owns the software businesses related only to industries 3, 4, 5, and 6. Thereafter, D concludes that the intellectual property licenses central to the software business related to industries 1 and 2 are not transferable and that a separation of the software business related to industry 3 from the software business related to industry 2 is not desirable. One month after D begins negotiating with X, D contributes the software businesses related to industries 4, 5, and 6 to C, and distributes the stock of C pro rata to its shareholders. In addition, X sells its hardware businesses for cash. After the distribution, C and X negotiate for X's acquisition of the C stock from the C shareholders in exchange for X stock, and X acquires the stock of C.

(ii) Although D and C are different corporations, C does not own the custom software business related to industry 3, and X sold its hardware business prior to the acquisition of C, because X's acquisition of C involves a combination of a significant portion of the same business operations as the combination that would have been effected by the acquisition of D that was the subject of negotiations between D and X, X's acquisition of C is the same as, or similar to, X's potential acquisition of D that was the subject of earlier negotiations.

Example 8. Acquisitions involving public offerings with different purposes. (i) D's managers, directors, and investment banker discuss the possibility of offering D stock to the public for the purpose of funding the acquisition of the assets of X. They decide a public offering of 20 percent of D's stock with D as a stand-alone corporation would allow D to raise the capital needed to effect the acquisition of X's assets. One month later, to facilitate a stock offering by D of 20 percent of its stock, D distributes all the stock of C pro rata to D's shareholders. Two months after the distribution, D issues new shares amounting to 20 percent of its stock to the public in a public offering (the first public offering). Four months after the distribution, D acquires the assets of X. Seven months after the distribution, D's managers, directors, and investment banker discuss the possibility of offering D stock to the public solely for the purpose of funding the acquisition of the assets of Y, a corporation unrelated to X. One year after the distribution, D issues new shares amounting to 40 percent of its stock to the public in a public offering (the second public offering). One month after the second public offering, D acquires the assets of Y.

(ii) The first public offering is the same as the potential acquisition that D's managers, directors, and investment banker discussed prior to the distribution. The purpose of the second public offering (funding the acquisition of the assets of Y) is not similar to that of the potential acquisition (funding the acquisition of the assets of X). Therefore, the second public offering is not similar to the potential acquisition.

Example 9. Acquisitions involving public offerings that are close in time. (i) D's managers, directors, and investment banker discuss the possibility of offering D stock to the public for the purpose of raising funds for general corporate purposes. They decide a public offering of 20 percent of D's stock with D as a stand-alone corporation would allow D to raise such funds. One month later, to facilitate a stock offering by D of 20 percent of its stock, D distributes all the stock of C pro rata to D's shareholders. Two months after the distribution, D issues new shares amounting to 20 percent of its stock to the public in a public offering (the first public offering). After the first public offering, D's managers, directors, and investment banker discuss the possibility of another offering of D stock to the public for the purpose of raising additional funds for general corporate purposes. Eight months after the distribution, D issues new shares amounting to ten percent of its stock to the public in a public offering (the second public offering).

(ii) The first public offering is the same as the potential acquisition that D's managers, directors, and investment banker discussed prior to the distribution. The purpose of the second public offering (raising funds for general corporate purposes) is the same as that of the potential acquisition. In addition, the second public offering is close in time to the first public offering. Therefore, the second public offering is similar to the potential acquisition.

Example 10. Acquisitions involving public offerings that are not close in time. The facts are the same as those in *Example 9*, except that the second public offering occurs fourteen months after the distribution. Although the purpose of the second public offering is the same as that of the potential acquisition, the second public offering is not close in time to the first public offering. Therefore, the second public offering is not similar to the potential acquisition.

(k) *Effective dates.*—This section applies to distributions occurring after April 19, 2005. For distributions occurring on or before April 19, 2005, and after April 26, 2002, see §1.355-7T as contained in 26 CFR part 1 revised as of April 1, 2003; however, taxpayers may apply these regulations, in whole, but not in part, to such distributions. For distributions occurring on or before April 26, 2002, and after August 3, 2001, see §1.355-7T as contained in 26 CFR part 1 revised as of April 1, 2002; however, taxpayers may apply, in whole, but not in part, either these regulations or §1.355-7T as contained in 26 CFR part 1 revised as of April 1, 2003, to such distributions. For distributions occurring on or before August 3, 2001, and after April 16, 1997, taxpayers may apply, in whole, but not in part, either these regulations or §1.355-7T as contained in 26 CFR part 1 revised as of April 1, 2003, to such distributions. [Reg. §1.355-7.]

☐ [T.D. 9198, 4-18-2005.]

[Reg. §1.355-8]

§1.355-8. Definition of predecessor and successor and limitations on gain recognition under section 355(e) and section 355(f).— (a) *In general.*—(1) *Scope.*—For purposes of section 355(e), this section provides rules under section 355(e)(4)(D) to determine whether a corporation is treated as a predecessor or successor of a distributing corporation (Distributing) or a controlled corporation (Controlled) with respect to a distribution by Distributing of stock (or stock and securities) of Controlled that qualifies under section 355(a) (or so much of section 356 as relates to section 355) (Distribution). This section also provides rules limiting the amount of Distributing's gain recognized under section 355(e) on a Distribution if section 355(e) applies to an acquisition by one or more persons, as part of a Plan, of stock that in the aggregate represents a 50-percent or greater interest (Planned 50-percent Acquisition) of a Predecessor of Distributing, or a Planned 50-percent Acquisition of Distributing. In addition, this section provides rules regarding the application of section 336(e) to a Distribution to which this section applies. This section also provides rules regarding the application of section 355(f) to a Distribution in certain cases.

(2) *Overview.*—(i) *Purposes and conceptual overview.*—Paragraph (a)(3) of this section summarizes the two principal purposes of this section and sets forth a brief conceptual overview of the scenarios in which a corporation may be a Predecessor of Distributing.

(ii) *References to and definitions of terms used in this section.*—Paragraph (a)(4) of this section provides rules regarding references to the terms *Distributing, Controlled, Distribution, Plan,* and *Plan Period* for purposes of section 355(e), §1.355-7, and this section. Paragraph (a)(5) of this section lists the terms used in this section and indicates where each term is defined. Paragraph (b) of this section defines the term *Predecessor of Distributing* and several related terms. Paragraph (c) of this section defines the terms *Predecessor of Controlled, Successor* (of Distributing or Controlled), and *Section 381 Transaction.*

(iii) *Special rules and examples.*—Paragraph (d) of this section provides guidance with regard to acquisitions and deemed acquisitions of stock if there is a Predecessor of Distributing or a Successor of either Distributing or Controlled. Paragraph (e) of this section provides two rules that may limit the amount of Distributing's gain on a Distribution if there is a Predecessor of Distributing, as well as an overall gain limitation. Paragraph (e) of this section also provides guidance with respect to the application of section 336(e). Regardless of whether there is a Predecessor of Distributing, Predecessor of Controlled, or Successor of either Distributing or Controlled, paragraph (f) of this section provides a special rule relating to section 355(e)(2)(C), which provides that section 355(e) does not apply to certain transactions within an Expanded Affiliated Group. Paragraph (g) of this section provides rules coordinating the application of section 355(f) with the rules of this section. Paragraph (h) of this section contains examples that illustrate the rules of this section.

(3) *Purposes of section; Predecessor of Distributing overview.*—(i) *Purposes.*—The rules in this section have two principal purposes. The first is to ensure that section 355(e) applies to a Distribution if, as part of a Plan, some of the assets of a Predecessor of Distributing are transferred directly or indirectly to Controlled without full recogni-

tion of gain, and the Distribution accomplishes a division of the assets of the Predecessor of Distributing. The second is to ensure that section 355(e) applies when there is a Planned 50-percent Acquisition of a Successor of Distributing or Successor of Controlled. The rules of this section must be interpreted and applied in a manner that is consistent with and reasonably carries out the purposes of this section.

(ii) *Predecessor of Distributing overview.*—The term Predecessor of Distributing is defined in paragraph (b) of this section. Only a Potential Predecessor can be a Predecessor of Distributing. See paragraph (b)(1)(i) of this section. A Potential Predecessor can be a Predecessor of Distributing only if, as part of a Plan, the Distribution accomplishes a division of the assets of the Potential Predecessor. See paragraph (b)(1)(iii) of this section. Accordingly, in the absence of that Plan, a Predecessor of Distributing cannot exist for purposes of section 355(e). The detailed rules set forth in paragraph (b) of this section provide that a Potential Predecessor the assets of which are divided as part of a Plan may be a Predecessor of Distributing in either of the following two scenarios:

(A) *Relevant Property transferred to Controlled.*—As part of the Plan, one or more of the Potential Predecessor's assets were transferred to Controlled in one or more tax-deferred transactions prior to the Distribution.

(B) *Relevant Property includes Controlled Stock.*—The Potential Predecessor's assets included Controlled stock that, as part of the Plan, was transferred to Distributing in one or more tax-deferred transactions prior to the Distribution.

(4) *References.*—(i) *References to Distributing or Controlled.*—For purposes of section 355(e), except as otherwise provided in this section, any reference to Distributing or Controlled includes, as the context may require, a reference to any Predecessor of Distributing or any Predecessor of Controlled, respectively, or any Successor of Distributing or Controlled, respectively. However, except as otherwise provided in this section, a reference to a Predecessor of Distributing or to a Successor of Distributing does not include a reference to Distributing, and a reference to a Predecessor of Controlled or to a Successor of Controlled does not include a reference to Controlled.

(ii) *References to Plan or Distribution.*—Except as otherwise provided in this section, references to a *Plan* in this section are references to a plan within the meaning of §1.355-7. References to a distribution in §1.355-7 include a reference to a Distribution and other related pre-Distribution transactions that together effect a division of the assets of a Predecessor of Distributing. In determining whether a Distribution and a Planned 50-percent Acquisition of a Predecessor of Distributing, Distributing (including any Successor thereof), or Controlled (including any Successor thereof) are part of a Plan, the rules of §1.355-7 apply. In applying those rules, references to Distributing or Controlled in §1.355-7 generally include references to any Predecessor of Distributing and any Successor of Distributing, or any Successor of Controlled, as appropriate. However, with regard to any possible Planned 50-percent Acquisition of a Predecessor of Distributing, any agreement, understanding, arrangement, or substantial negotiations with regard to the acquisition of the stock of the Predecessor of Distributing is analyzed under §1.355-7 with regard to the actions of officers or directors of Distributing or Controlled, controlling shareholders (as defined in §1.355-7(h)(3)) of Distributing or Controlled, or a person acting with permission of one of those parties. For purposes of the preceding sentence, references in §1.355-7 to Distributing do not include references to a Predecessor of Distributing. Therefore, the actions of officers, directors, or controlling shareholders of a Predecessor of Distributing, or of a person acting with the implicit or explicit permission of one of those parties, are not considered unless those parties otherwise would be treated as acting on behalf of Distributing or Controlled under §1.355-7 (for example, if a Predecessor of Distributing is a controlling shareholder of Distributing).

(iii) *Plan Period.*—For purposes of this section, the term *Plan Period* means the period that ends immediately after the Distribution and begins on the earliest date on which any pre-Distribution step that is part of the Plan is agreed to or understood, arranged, or substantially negotiated by one or more officers or directors acting on behalf of Distributing or Controlled, by controlling shareholders of Distributing or Controlled, or by another person or persons with the implicit or explicit permission of one or more of such officers, directors, or controlling shareholders. For purposes of the preceding sentence, references to Distributing and Controlled do not include references to any Predecessor of Distributing, Predecessor of Controlled, or Successor of Distributing or Controlled.

(5) *List of definitions.*—This section uses the following terms, which are defined where indicated—

(i) *Acquiring Owner.*—Paragraph (d)(1)(i) of this section.

(ii) *Controlled.*—Paragraph (a)(1) of this section.

(iii) *Distributing.*—Paragraph (a)(1) of this section.

(iv) *Distributing Gain Limitation Rule.*—Paragraph (e)(1)(ii) of this section.

(v) *Distribution.*—Paragraph (a)(1) of this section.

(vi) *Division of Relevant Property Requirement.*—Paragraph (b)(1)(iii) of this section.

(vii) *Expanded Affiliated Group.*—Paragraph (b)(2)(ii)(B) of this section.

(viii) *Hypothetical Controlled.*—Paragraph (e)(2)(i) of this section.

(ix) *Hypothetical D/355(e) Reorganization.*—Paragraph (e)(2)(i) of this section.

(x) *Plan.*—Paragraph (a)(4)(ii) of this section.

(xi) *Plan Period.*—Paragraph (a)(4)(iii) of this section.

(xii) *Planned 50-percent Acquisition.*—Paragraph (a)(1) of this section.

(xiii) *POD Gain Limitation Rule.*—Paragraph (e)(1)(ii) of this section.

(xiv) *Potential Predecessor.*—Paragraph (b)(2)(ii)(A) of this section.

(xv) *Predecessor of Controlled.*—Paragraph (c)(1) of this section.

(xvi) *Predecessor of Distributing.*—Paragraph (b)(1) of this section.

(xvii) *Reflection of Basis Requirement.*—Paragraph (b)(1)(ii)(B) of this section.

(xviii) *Relevant Equity.*—Paragraph (b)(2)(iv)(A) of this section.

(xix) *Relevant Property.*—Paragraph (b)(2)(iv)(A) of this section.

(xx) *Relevant Property Requirement.*—Paragraph (b)(1)(ii)(A) of this section.

(xxi) *Section 381 Transaction.*—Paragraph (c)(3) of this section.

(xxii) *Separated Property.*—Paragraph (b)(2)(vii) of this section.

(xxiii) *Statutory Recognition Amount.*—Paragraph (e)(1)(i) of this section.

(xxiv) *Substitute Asset.*—Paragraph (b)(2)(vi)(A) of this section.

(xxv) *Successor.*—Paragraph (c)(2)(i) of this section.

(xxvi) *Successor Transaction.*—Paragraph (c)(2)(i) of this section.

(xxvii) *Underlying Property.*—Paragraph (b)(2)(viii) of this section.

(b) *Predecessor of Distributing.*—(1) *Definition.*—(i) *In general.*—For purposes of section 355(e), a Potential Predecessor is a predecessor of Distributing (Predecessor of Distributing) if, taking into account the special rules of paragraph (b)(2) of this section—

(A) Both pre-Distribution requirements of paragraph (b)(1)(ii) of this section are satisfied; and

(B) The post-Distribution requirement of paragraph (b)(1)(iii) of this section is satisfied.

(ii) *Pre-Distribution requirements.*—(A) *Relevant Property requirement.*—The requirement set forth in this paragraph (b)(1)(ii)(A) (Relevant Property Requirement) is satisfied if, before the Distribution, and as part of a Plan, either—

(1) Any Controlled stock distributed in the Distribution was directly or indirectly acquired (or deemed acquired under the rules set forth in paragraph (b)(2)(x) of this section) by Distributing in exchange for any direct or indirect interest in Relevant Property—

(i) That is held directly or indirectly by Controlled *immediately before the Distribution;* and

(ii) The gain on which (if any) was not recognized in full at any point during the Plan Period; or

(2) Any Controlled stock that is distributed in the Distribution is Relevant Property of the Potential Predecessor.

(B) *Reflection of basis requirement.*—The requirement set forth in this paragraph (b)(1)(ii)(B) (Reflection of Basis Requirement) is satisfied if any Controlled stock that satisfies the Relevant Property Requirement—

(1) Either—

(i) Had a basis prior to the Distribution that was determined in whole or in part by reference to the basis of any Separated Property; or

(ii) Is Relevant Property of the Potential Predecessor; and

(2) During the Plan Period prior to the Distribution, was neither distributed in a distribution to which section 355(e) applied nor transferred in a transaction in which the gain (if any) on that Controlled stock was recognized in full.

(iii) *Post-Distribution requirement.*—The requirement set forth in this paragraph (b)(1)(iii) (Division of Relevant Property Requirement) is satisfied if, immediately after the Distribution, and as part of a Plan, direct or indirect ownership of the Potential Predecessor's Relevant Property has been divided between Controlled on the one hand, and Distributing or the Potential Predecessor (or a successor to the Potential Predecessor) on the other hand. For purposes of this paragraph (b)(1)(iii), if Controlled stock that is distributed in the Distribution is Relevant Property of a Potential Predecessor, then Controlled is deemed to have received Relevant Property of the Potential Predecessor.

(2) *Additional definitions and rules related to paragraph (b)(1) of this section.*—(i) *References to Distributing and Controlled.*—For purposes of the Relevant Property Requirement, the Reflection of Basis Requirement, and the Division of Relevant Property Requirement, references to Distributing and Controlled do not include references to any Predecessor of Distributing, Predecessor of Controlled, or Successor of Distributing or Controlled.

(ii) *Potential Predecessor.*—(A) *Potential Predecessor definition.*—The term *Potential Predecessor* means a corporation, other than Distributing or Controlled, if—

(1) As part of a Plan, the corporation transfers property to a Potential Predecessor, Distributing, or a member of the same Expanded Affiliated Group as Distributing in a Section 381 Transaction; or

(2) Immediately after completion of the Plan, the corporation is a member of the same Expanded Affiliated Group as Distributing.

(B) *Expanded Affiliated Group definition.*—The term *Expanded Affiliated Group* means an affiliated group (as defined in section 1504 without regard to section 1504(b)).

(iii) *Successors of Potential Predecessors.*—For purposes of the Division of Relevant Property Requirement, if a Potential Predecessor transfers property in a Section 381 Transaction to a corporation (other than Distributing or Controlled) during the Plan Period, the corporation is a successor to the Potential Predecessor.

(iv) *Relevant Property; Relevant Equity.*—(A) *In general.*—Except as otherwise provided in this paragraph (b)(2)(iv) or in paragraph (b)(2)(v) of this section, the term *Relevant Property* means any property that was held, directly or indirectly, by the Potential Predecessor during the Plan Period. The term *Relevant Equity* means Relevant Property that is an equity interest in a corporation or a partnership.

(B) *Property held by Distributing.*—Except as provided in paragraph (b)(2)(iv)(C) of this section, property held directly or indirectly by Distributing (including Controlled stock) is Relevant Property of a Potential Predecessor only to the extent that the property was transferred directly or indirectly to Distributing during the Plan Period, and it was Relevant Property of the Potential Predecessor before the direct or indirect transfer(s). For example, if during the Plan Period a subsidiary corporation of a Potential Predecessor merges into Controlled in a reorganization under section 368(a)(1)(A) and (2)(D), and, as a result, the Potential Predecessor directly or indirectly owns Distributing stock received in the merger, the subsidiary's assets held by Controlled are Relevant Property of that Potential Predecessor.

(C) *F reorganizations.*—For purposes of paragraph (b)(2)(iv)(B) of this section, the transferor and transferee in any reorganization described in section 368(a)(1)(F) (F reorganization) are treated as a single corporation. Therefore, for example, Relevant Property acquired during the Plan Period by a corporation that is a transferor (as to a later F reorganization) is treated as having been acquired directly (and from the same source) by the transferee (as to the later F reorganization) during the Plan Period. In addition, any transfer (or deemed transfer) of assets to Distributing in an F reorganization will not cause the transferred assets to be treated as Relevant Property.

(v) *Stock of Distributing as Relevant Property.*—(A) *In general.*—For purposes of the Division of Relevant Property Requirement, except as provided in paragraph (b)(2)(v)(B) of this section, stock of Distributing is not Relevant Property (and thus is not Relevant Equity) to the extent that the Potential Predecessor becomes, as part of a Plan, the direct or indirect owner of that stock as the result of the transfer to Distributing of direct or indirect interests in the Potential Predecessor's Relevant Property. For example, stock of Distributing is not Relevant Property if it is acquired by a Potential Predecessor as part of a Plan in an exchange to which section 351(a) applies.

(B) *Certain reorganizations.*—For purposes of the Division of Relevant Property Requirement, stock of Distributing is Relevant Property (and thus Relevant Equity) to the extent that the Potential Predecessor becomes, as part of the Plan, the direct or indirect owner of that stock as the result of a transaction described in section 368(a)(1)(E).

(vi) *Substitute Asset.*—(A) *In general.*—Subject to paragraph (b)(2)(vi)(B) of this section, the term *Substitute Asset* means any property that is held directly or indirectly by Distributing during the Plan Period and was received, during the Plan Period, in exchange for Relevant Property that was acquired directly or indirectly by Distributing if all gain on the transferred Relevant Property is not recognized on the exchange. For example, property received by Controlled in exchange for Relevant Property in a transaction qualifying under section 1031 is a Substitute Asset. In addition, stock received by Distributing in a distribution qualifying under section 305(a) or section 355(a) on Relevant Equity is a Substitute Asset.

(B) *Controlled stock received by Distributing.*—(1) *In general.*—Except as provided in paragraph (b)(2)(vi)(B)(2) of this section, stock of Controlled received in exchange for a direct or indirect transfer of Relevant Property by Distributing is not a Substitute Asset.

(2) *Exception.*—If the basis in Controlled stock received or deemed received in an exchange described in paragraph (b)(2)(vi)(B)(1) of this section is determined in whole or in part by reference to the basis of Relevant Equity the issuer of which ceases to exist for Federal income tax purposes under the Plan, that Controlled stock constitutes a Substitute Asset. See paragraph (b)(2)(x) of this section.

(C) *Treatment as Relevant Property.*—For purposes of this section, a Substitute Asset is treated as Relevant Property with the same ownership and transfer history as the Relevant Property for which (or with respect to which) it was received.

(vii) *Separated Property.*—The term *Separated Property* means each item of Relevant Property that is described in the Relevant Property Requirement (regardless of whether the fair market value of the Relevant Property exceeds its adjusted basis). However, if Relevant Equity is Separated Property, Underlying Property associated with that Relevant Equity is not treated as Separated Property. In addition, if Distributing directly or indirectly acquires Relevant Equity in a transaction in which gain is recognized in full, Underlying Property associated with that Relevant Equity is not treated as Separated Property.

(viii) *Underlying Property.*—The term *Underlying Property* means property directly or indirectly held by a corporation or partnership any equity interest in which is Relevant Equity.

(ix) *Multiple Predecessors of Distributing.*—If there are multiple Potential Predecessors that satisfy the pre-Distribution requirements and post-Distribution requirement of paragraph (b)(1) of this section, each of those Potential Predecessors is a Predecessor of Distributing. For example, a Potential Predecessor that transfers property to a Predecessor of Distributing without full recognition of gain (and that otherwise meets the requirements of paragraph (b)(1) of this section) is also a Predecessor of Distributing if the applicable transfer occurred as part of a Plan that existed at the time of such transfer.

(x) *Deemed exchanges.*—For purposes of paragraph (b)(1)(ii) of this section (regarding the Relevant Property Requirement and the Reflection of Basis Requirement) and paragraph (b)(2)(vi) of this section (regarding Substitute Assets), Distributing is treated as acquiring Controlled stock in exchange for a direct or indirect interest in Relevant Property if the basis of Distributing in that Controlled stock, immediately after a transfer of the Relevant Property, is determined in whole or in part by reference to the basis of that Relevant Property immediately before the transfer. For example, if a corporation transfers Relevant Property to Controlled in exchange for Distributing stock in a transaction that qualifies as a reorganization under section 368(a)(1)(C), then, for purposes of paragraphs (b)(1)(ii)

and (b)(2)(vi) of this section, Distributing is treated as acquiring Controlled stock in exchange for a direct or indirect interest in Relevant Property. See § 1.358-6(c)(1).

(c) *Additional definitions.*—(1) *Predecessor of Controlled.*—Solely for purposes of applying paragraph (f) of this section, a corporation is a predecessor of Controlled (Predecessor of Controlled) if, before the Distribution, it transfers property to Controlled in a Section 381 Transaction as part of a Plan. Other than for the purpose described in the preceding sentence, no corporation can be a Predecessor of Controlled. If multiple corporations satisfy the requirements of this paragraph (c)(1), each of those corporations is a Predecessor of Controlled. For example, a corporation that transfers property to a Predecessor of Controlled in a Section 381 Transaction is also a Predecessor of Controlled if the Section 381 Transaction occurred as part of a Plan that existed at the time of such transaction.

(2) *Successors.*—(i) *In general.*—For purposes of section 355(e), a successor (Successor) of Distributing or of Controlled is a corporation to which Distributing or Controlled, respectively, transfers property in a Section 381 Transaction after the Distribution (Successor Transaction).

(ii) *Determination of Successor status.*—More than one corporation may be a Successor of Distributing or Controlled. For example, if Distributing transfers property to another corporation (X) in a Section 381 Transaction, and X transfers property to another corporation (Y) in a Section 381 Transaction, then each of X and Y is a Successor of Distributing. In this case, the determination of whether Y is a Successor of Distributing is made after the determination of whether X is a Successor of Distributing.

(3) *Section 381 Transaction.*—The term *Section 381 Transaction* means a transaction to which section 381 applies.

(d) *Special acquisition rules.*—(1) *Deemed acquisitions of stock in Section 381 Transactions.*—(i) *Rule.*—This paragraph (d)(1)(i) applies to each shareholder of the acquiring corporation immediately before a Section 381 Transaction (Acquiring Owner). Each Acquiring Owner is treated for purposes of this section as acquiring, in the Section 381 Transaction, stock representing an interest in the distributor or transferor corporation, to the extent that the Acquiring Owner's interest in the acquiring corporation immediately after the Section 381 Transaction exceeds the Acquiring Owner's direct or indirect interest in the distributor or transferor corporation immediately before the Section 381 Transaction.

(ii) *Example.*—The example set forth in this paragraph (d)(1)(ii) illustrates the application of the deemed acquisition rule in paragraph (d)(1)(i) of this section. Assume that A held all of the stock of Distributing, Distributing held a 25-percent interest in a Predecessor of Distributing, and A held no direct interest, or other indirect interest, in the Predecessor of Distributing immediately before a Section 381 Transaction in which the Predecessor of Distributing transfers its assets to Distributing. In the Section 381 Transaction, the Predecessor of Distributing's shareholders (other than Distributing) collectively receive a 10-percent interest in Distributing (reducing A's interest in Distributing to 90 percent). Under paragraph (d)(1)(i) of this section, A is treated as acquiring in the Section 381 Transaction stock representing a 65-percent interest in the Predecessor of Distributing. This is because A's 90-percent interest in Distributing (the acquiring corporation in the Section 381 Transaction) immediately after the Section 381 Transaction exceeds A's 25-percent interest (held indirectly through Distributing) in the Predecessor of Distributing (the transferor corporation in the Section 381 Transaction) immediately before the Section 381 Transaction by 65 percent. Similarly, each Acquiring Owner of a Successor of Distributing is treated as acquiring, in the Successor Transaction, stock of Distributing, to the extent that the Acquiring Owner's interest in the Successor of Distributing immediately after the Successor Transaction exceeds the Acquiring Owner's direct or indirect interest in Distributing immediately before the Successor Transaction.

(2) *Deemed acquisitions of stock after Section 381 Transactions.*—For purposes of this section, after a Section 381 Transaction (including a Successor Transaction), an acquisition of stock of an acquiring corporation (including a deemed stock acquisition under paragraph (d)(1)(i) of this section) is treated also as an acquisition of an interest in the stock of the distributor or transferor corporation. For example, an acquisition of the stock of Distributing that occurs after a Section 381 Transaction is treated not only as an acquisition of the stock of Distributing, but also as an acquisition of the stock of any Predecessor of Distributing whose assets were acquired by Distributing in the prior Section 381 Transaction. Similarly, an acquisition of the stock of a Successor of Distributing that occurs after the Successor Transaction is treated not only as an acquisition of the stock of the Successor of Distributing, but also as an acquisition of the stock of Distributing.

(3) Separate counting for Distributing and each Predecessor of Distributing.—The measurement of whether one or more persons have acquired stock of any specific corporation in a Planned 50-percent Acquisition is made separately from the measurement of any potential Planned 50-percent Acquisition of any other corporation. Therefore, there may be a Planned 50-percent Acquisition of a Predecessor of Distributing even if there is no Planned 50-percent Acquisition of Distributing. Similarly, there may be a Planned 50-percent Acquisition of Distributing even if there is no Planned 50-percent Acquisition of a Predecessor of Distributing.

(e) Special rules for limiting gain recognition.—(1) Overview.—(i) Gain limitation.—This paragraph (e) provides rules that limit the amount of gain that must be recognized by Distributing by reason of section 355(e) to an amount that is less than the amount that Distributing otherwise would be required to recognize under section 355(c)(2) or section 361(c)(2) (Statutory Recognition Amount) in certain cases involving one or more Predecessors of Distributing.

(ii) Multiple Planned 50-percent Acquisitions.—If there are Planned 50-percent Acquisitions of multiple corporations (for example, two Predecessors of Distributing), Distributing must recognize the Statutory Recognition Amount with respect to each such corporation, subject to the limitations in paragraph (e)(2) of this section relating to a Planned 50-percent Acquisition of a Predecessor of Distributing (POD Gain Limitation Rule) and paragraph (e)(3) of this section relating to a Planned 50-percent Acquisition of Distributing (Distributing Gain Limitation Rule), if applicable. The POD Gain Limitation Rule and the Distributing Gain Limitation Rule are applied separately to the Planned 50-percent Acquisition of each such corporation to determine the amount of gain required to be recognized.

(iii) Statutory Recognition Amount limit; Section 336(e).—Paragraph (e)(4) of this section sets forth an overall gain limitation based on the Statutory Recognition Amount. Paragraph (e)(5) of this section clarifies the availability of an election under section 336(e) with regard to certain Distributions.

(2) Planned 50-percent Acquisition of a Predecessor of Distributing.—(i) In general.—If there is a Planned 50-percent Acquisition of a Predecessor of Distributing, the amount of gain recognized by Distributing by reason of section 355(e) as a result of the Planned 50-percent Acquisition is limited to the amount of gain, if any, that Distributing would have recognized if, immediately before the Distribution, Distributing had engaged in the following transaction: Distributing transferred all Separated Property received from the Predecessor of Distributing to a newly formed corporation (Hypothetical Controlled) in exchange solely for stock of Hypothetical Controlled in a reorganization under section 368(a)(1)(D) and then distributed the stock of Hypothetical Controlled to the shareholders of Distributing in a transaction to which section 355(e) applied (Hypothetical D/355(e) Reorganization). The computation in this paragraph (e)(2)(i) is applied regardless of whether Distributing actually directly held the Separated Property.

(ii) Operating rules.—For purposes of applying paragraph (e)(2)(i) of this section, the following rules apply:

(A) Separated Property other than Controlled stock.—Each of the basis and the fair market value of Separated Property other than stock of Controlled treated as transferred by Distributing to a Hypothetical Controlled in a Hypothetical D/355(e) Reorganization equals the basis and the fair market value, respectively, of such property in the hands of Controlled immediately before the Distribution.

(B) Controlled stock that is Separated Property.—Each of the basis and the fair market value of the stock of Controlled that is Separated Property treated as transferred by Distributing to a Hypothetical Controlled in a Hypothetical D/355(e) Reorganization equals the basis and the fair market value, respectively, of such stock in the hands of Distributing immediately before the Distribution.

(C) Anti-duplication rule.—A Predecessor of Distributing's Separated Property is taken into account for purposes of applying this paragraph (e)(2) only to the extent such property was not taken into account by Distributing in a Hypothetical D/355(e) Reorganization with respect to another Predecessor of Distributing. Further, appropriate adjustments must be made to prevent other duplicative inclusions of section 355(e) gain under this paragraph (e) reflecting the same economic gain.

(3) Planned 50-percent Acquisition of Distributing.—This paragraph (e)(3) applies if there is a Planned 50-percent Acquisition of Distributing. In that case, the amount of gain recognized by Distributing by reason of section 355(e) as a result of the Planned 50-percent Acquisition is limited to the excess, if any, of the Statutory Recognition Amount over the amount of gain, if any, that Distributing would

have been required to recognize under paragraphs (e)(1)(ii) and (e)(2) of this section if there had been a Planned 50-percent Acquisition of every Predecessor of Distributing, but not of Distributing or Controlled. For purposes of this paragraph (e)(3), references to Distributing are not references to a Predecessor of Distributing.

(4) Gain recognition limited to Statutory Recognition Amount.—The sum of the amounts required to be recognized by Distributing under section 355(e) (taking into account the POD Gain Limitation Rule and the Distributing Gain Limitation Rule) with regard to a single Distribution cannot exceed the Statutory Recognition Amount. In addition, Distributing may choose not to apply the POD Gain Limitation Rule or the Distributing Gain Limitation Rule to a Distribution, and instead may recognize the Statutory Recognition Amount. Distributing indicates its choice to apply the preceding sentence by reporting the Statutory Recognition Amount on its original or amended Federal income tax return for the year of the Distribution.

(5) Section 336(e) election.—Distributing is not eligible to make a section 336(e) election (as defined in § 1.336-1(b)(11)) with respect to a Distribution to which this section applies unless Distributing would, absent the making of a section 336(e) election, recognize the Statutory Recognition Amount with respect to the Distribution (taking into account the POD Gain Limitation Rule and the Distributing Gain Limitation Rule) without regard to the final two sentences of paragraph (e)(4) of this section. See § § 1.336-1 through 1.336-5 for additional requirements with regard to a section 336(e) election.

(f) Predecessor or Successor as a member of the affiliated group.—For purposes of section 355(e)(2)(C), if a corporation transfers its assets to a member of the same Expanded Affiliated Group in a Section 381 Transaction, the transferor will be treated as continuing in existence within the same Expanded Affiliated Group.

(g) Inapplicability of section 355(f) to certain intra-group Distributions.—(1) In general.—Section 355(f) does not apply to a Distribution if there is a Planned 50-percent Acquisition of a Predecessor of Distributing (but not of Distributing, Controlled, or their Successors), except as provided in paragraph (g)(2) of this section. Therefore, except as provided in paragraph (g)(2) of this section, section 355 (or so much of section 356 as relates to section 355) and the regulations under sections 355 and 356, including the POD Gain Limitation Rule, apply, without regard to section 355(f), to a Distribution within an affiliated group (as defined in section 1504(a)) if the Distribution and the Planned 50-percent Acquisition of the Predecessor of Distributing are part of a Plan. For purposes of this paragraph (g)(1), references to a Distribution (and Distributing and Controlled) include references to a distribution (and Distributing and Controlled) to which section 355 would apply but for the application of section 355(f).

(2) Alternative application of section 355(f).—Distributing may choose not to apply paragraph (g)(1) of this section to each Distribution (that occurs under a Plan) to which section 355(f) would otherwise apply absent paragraph (g)(1) of this section. Instead, Distributing may apply section 355(f) to all such Distributions according to its terms, but only if all members of the same Expanded Affiliated Group report consistently the Federal income tax consequences of the Distributions that are part of the Plan (determined without regard to section 355(f)). In such a case, neither the POD Gain Limitation Rule nor the Distributing Gain Limitation Rule is available with regard to any applicable Distribution. Distributing indicates its choice to apply section 355(f) consistently to all applicable Distributions by reporting the Federal income tax consequences of each Distribution in accordance with section 355(f) on its Federal income tax return for the year of the Distribution.

(h) Examples.—The following examples illustrate the principles of this section. Unless the facts indicate otherwise, assume throughout these examples that: Distributing (D) owns all the stock of Controlled (C), and none of the shares of C held by D has a built-in loss; D distributes the stock of C in a Distribution to which section 355(d) does not apply; X, Y, and Z are individuals; each of D, D1, C, P, P1, P2, and R is a corporation having one class of stock outstanding, and none is a member of a consolidated group; and each transaction that is part of a Plan defined in this section is respected as a separate transaction under general Federal income tax principles. No inference should be drawn from any example concerning whether any requirements of section 355 are satisfied other than those of section 355(e) or whether any general Federal income tax principles (including the step transaction doctrine) are implicated by the example:

(1) Example 1: Predecessor of D and Planned 50-Percent Acquisition of P—(i) Facts. X owns 100% of the stock of P, which holds multiple assets. Y owns 100% of the stock of D. The following steps occur as part of a Plan: P merges into D in a reorganization under section 368(a)(1)(A). Immediately after the merger, X and Y own 10% and 90%, respectively, of the stock of D. D then contributes to C one of the assets (Asset 1) acquired from P in the merger. At the time of the

contribution, Asset 1 has a basis of $40x and a fair market value of $110x. In exchange for Asset 1, D receives additional C stock and $10x. D distributes the stock of C (but not the cash) to X and Y, pro rata. The contribution and Distribution constitute a reorganization under section 368(a)(1)(D), and D recognizes $10x of gain under section 361(b) on the contribution. Immediately before the Distribution, taking into account the $10x of gain recognized by D on the contribution, Asset 1 has an adjusted basis of $50x under section 362(b) and a fair market value of $110x, and the stock of C held by D has a basis of $100x and a fair market value of $200x.

(ii) *Analysis*—(A) *P is a Predecessor of D.* Under paragraph (b)(1) of this section, P is a Predecessor of D. First, P is a Potential Predecessor because, as part of a Plan, P transferred property to D in a Section 381 Transaction. See paragraph (b)(2)(ii)(A)(*1*) of this section. Second, both of the pre-Distribution requirements and the post-Distribution requirement are satisfied. The Relevant Property Requirement is satisfied because, immediately before the Distribution and as part of a Plan, C holds P Relevant Property (Asset 1) the gain on which was not recognized in full at any point during the Plan Period, and some of the C stock distributed in the Distribution was acquired by D in exchange for Asset 1. See paragraph (b)(1)(ii)(A)(*1*) of this section. The Reflection of Basis Requirement is satisfied because that C stock had a basis prior to the Distribution that was determined in whole or in part by reference to the basis of Separated Property (Asset 1), and was neither distributed in a distribution to which section 355(e) applied nor transferred in a transaction in which the gain on that C stock was recognized in full during the Plan Period prior to the Distribution. See paragraph (b)(1)(ii)(B) of this section. The Division of Relevant Property Requirement is satisfied because immediately after the Distribution, D continues to hold Relevant Property of P, and therefore, as part of a Plan, P's Relevant Property has been divided between C and D. See paragraph (b)(1)(iii) of this section.

(B) *Planned 50-percent Acquisition of P.* Under paragraph (d)(1)(i) of this section, Y is treated as acquiring stock representing 90% of the voting power and value of P as a result of the merger of P into D. Accordingly, there has been a Planned 50-percent Acquisition of P.

(C) *Gain limited.* Without regard to the limitations in paragraph (e) of this section, D would be required to recognize $100x of gain ($200x of aggregate fair market value minus $100x of aggregate basis of the C stock held by D), the Statutory Recognition Amount described in section 361(c)(2). However, under the POD Gain Limitation Rule, D's gain recognized by reason of the Planned 50-percent Acquisition of P will not exceed $60x, an amount equal to the amount of gain D would have recognized had D transferred Asset 1 (Separated Property) to a newly formed corporation (C1) solely for C1 stock and distributed the C1 stock to D's shareholders in a Hypothetical D/355(e) Reorganization. See paragraph (e)(2)(i) of this section. For purposes of the computation in this paragraph (h)(1)(ii)(C), the basis and fair market value of Asset 1 equal the basis and fair market value of Asset 1 in the hands of C immediately before the Distribution. See paragraph (e)(2)(ii)(A) of this section. Under section 361(c)(2), D would recognize $60x of gain, an amount equal to the gain in the hypothetical C1 stock (excess of the $110x fair market value over the $50x basis). Therefore, D recognizes $60x of gain (in addition to the $10x of gain recognized under section 361(b)).

(iii) *Plan not in existence at time of acquisition of Potential Predecessor's property.* The facts are the same as in paragraph (h)(1)(i) of this section (*Example 1*) except that the merger of P into D occurred before the existence of a Plan. Even though D transferred P property (Asset 1) to C, Asset 1 was not Relevant Property of P because P did not hold Asset 1 during the Plan Period. See paragraphs (b)(2)(iv) and (a)(4)(iii) of this section. Because Asset 1 is not Relevant Property, D did not receive C stock distributed in the Distribution in exchange for Relevant Property when it contributed Asset 1 to C, none of the distributed C stock had a basis prior to the Distribution that was determined in whole or in part by reference to the basis of Separated Property, and C did not hold Relevant Property immediately before the Distribution. Further, Relevant Property of P has not been divided. Therefore, P is not a Predecessor of D.

(2) *Example 2: Planned 50-percent Acquisition of D, but not Predecessor of D*—(i) *Facts.* X owns 100% of the stock of P, which holds multiple assets. Y owns 100% of the stock of D. The following steps occur as part of a Plan: P merges into D in a reorganization under section 368(a)(1)(A). Immediately after the merger, X and Y own 90% and 10%, respectively, of the stock of D. D then contributes to C one of the assets (Asset 1) acquired from P in the merger. In exchange for Asset 1, D receives additional C stock. D distributes the stock of C to X and Y, pro rata. The contribution and Distribution constitute a reorganization under section 368(a)(1)(D). Immediately before the Distribution, Asset 1 has a basis of $50x and a fair market value of $110x, and the stock of C held by D has a basis of $120x and a fair market value of $200x.

(ii) *Analysis*—(A) *P is a Predecessor of D.* Under paragraph (b)(1) of this section, P is a Predecessor of D. First, P is a Potential Predecessor

because, as part of a Plan, P transferred property to D in a Section 381 Transaction. See paragraph (b)(2)(ii)(A)(*1*) of this section. Second, both of the pre-Distribution requirements and the post-Distribution requirement are satisfied. The Relevant Property Requirement is satisfied because, immediately before the Distribution and as part of a Plan, C holds P Relevant Property (Asset 1) the gain on which was not recognized in full at any point during the Plan Period, and some of the C stock distributed in the Distribution was acquired by D in exchange for Asset 1. See paragraph (b)(1)(ii)(A)(*1*) of this section. The Reflection of Basis Requirement is satisfied because that C stock had a basis prior to the Distribution that was determined in whole or in part by reference to the basis of Separated Property (Asset 1), and was neither distributed in a distribution to which section 355(e) applied nor transferred in a transaction in which the gain on that C stock was recognized in full during the Plan Period prior to the Distribution. See paragraph (b)(1)(ii)(B) of this section. The Division of Relevant Property Requirement is satisfied because immediately after the Distribution, D continues to hold Relevant Property of P, and therefore, as part of a Plan, P's Relevant Property has been divided between C and D. See paragraph (b)(1)(iii) of this section.

(B) *Planned 50-percent Acquisition of D.* Under paragraph (d)(1)(i) of this section, Y is treated as acquiring stock representing 10% of the voting power and value of P as a result of the merger of P into D. The 10% acquisition of P stock does not cause section 355(e) gain recognition or cause application of the POD Gain Limitation Rule because there has not been a Planned 50-percent Acquisition of P. X acquires 90% of the voting power and value of D as a result of the merger of P into D. Accordingly, there has been a Planned 50-percent Acquisition of D. This Planned 50-percent Acquisition implicates section 355(e) and results in gain recognition, subject to the rules of paragraph (e) of this section.

(C) *Gain limited.* Without regard to the limitations in paragraph (e) of this section, D would be required to recognize $80x of gain ($200x of fair market value minus $120x of basis of the C stock held by D), the Statutory Recognition Amount described in section 361(c)(2). However, under the Distributing Gain Limitation Rule, D's gain recognized by reason of the Planned 50-percent Acquisition of D will not exceed $20x, the excess of the Statutory Recognition Amount ($80x) over the amount of gain that D would have been required to recognize under the POD Gain Limitation Rule if there had been a Planned 50-percent Acquisition of P but not D or C ($60x). See paragraph (e)(3) of this section. The hypothetical gain limitation under the POD Gain Limitation Rule equals the amount D would have recognized had it transferred Asset 1 (Separated Property) to a newly formed corporation (C1) solely for stock and distributed the C1 stock in a Hypothetical D/355(e) Reorganization. See paragraph (e)(2)(i) of this section. Under section 361(c)(2), D would recognize $60x of gain, an amount equal to the gain in the hypothetical C1 stock (excess of the $110x fair market value over the $50x basis). Therefore, D recognizes $20x of gain ($80x - $60x).

(3) *Example 3: Predecessor of D owns C stock*—(i) *Facts.* X owns 100% of the stock of P, which holds multiple assets, including Asset 2. Y owns 100% of the stock of D. P owns 35% of the stock of C (Block 1), and D owns the remaining 65% of the C stock (Block 2). The following steps occur as part of a Plan: P merges into D in a reorganization under section 368(a)(1)(A), and D immediately thereafter distributes all of the C stock to X and Y pro rata. Immediately after the merger, X and Y own 10% and 90%, respectively, of the D stock, and, prior to the Distribution, D owns Block 1 with a basis of $30x and a fair market value of $35x, and Block 2 with a basis of $10x and a fair market value of $65x. D continues to hold Asset 2.

(ii) *Analysis*—(A) *P is a Predecessor of D.* Under paragraph (b)(1) of this section, P is a Predecessor of D. First, P is a Potential Predecessor because, as part of a Plan, P transferred property to D in a Section 381 Transaction. See paragraph (b)(2)(ii)(A)(*1*) of this section. Second, both of the pre-Distribution requirements and the post-Distribution requirement are satisfied. The Relevant Property Requirement is satisfied because some of the C stock distributed in the Distribution (Block 1) was Relevant Property of P. See paragraph (b)(1)(ii)(A)(*2*) of this section. The Reflection of Basis Requirement is satisfied because Block 1 of the C stock is Relevant Property of P, and was neither distributed in a distribution to which section 355(e) applied nor transferred in a transaction in which the gain on that C stock was recognized in full during the Plan Period prior to the Distribution. See paragraph (b)(1)(ii)(B) of this section. The Division of Relevant Property Requirement is satisfied because some of the C stock distributed in the Distribution was Relevant Property of P, and therefore C is deemed to have received Relevant Property of P, and D continues to hold Relevant Property of P immediately after the Distribution. See paragraph (b)(1)(iii) of this section. Therefore, as part of a Plan, P's Relevant Property has been divided between C and D.

(B) *Planned 50-percent Acquisition of P.* Under paragraph (d)(1)(i) of this section, Y is treated as acquiring stock representing 90% of the voting power and value of P as a result of the merger of P into D. Accordingly, there has been a Planned 50-percent Acquisition of P.

(C) *Gain limited*. Without regard to the limitations in paragraph (e) of this section, D would be required to recognize $60x of gain ($100x of fair market value minus $40x of basis of the C stock held by D), the Statutory Recognition Amount under section 355(c)(2). However, under the POD Gain Limitation Rule, D's gain recognized by reason of the Planned 50-percent Acquisition of P will not exceed $5x, an amount equal to the amount D would have recognized had it transferred Block 1 of the C stock (Separated Property) to a newly formed corporation (C1) solely for stock and distributed the C1 stock to D shareholders in a Hypothetical D/355(e) Reorganization. See paragraph (e)(2)(i) of this section. Because Relevant Equity (Block 1 of the C stock) is Separated Property, Underlying Property associated with that Relevant Equity is not treated as Separated Property. See paragraph (b)(2)(vii) of this section. For purposes of the computation in this paragraph (h)(3)(ii)(C), the basis and fair market value of the Block 1 C stock equal its basis and fair market value in the hands of D immediately before the Distribution. See paragraph (e)(2)(ii)(A) of this section. Under section 361(c)(2), D would recognize $5x of gain, an amount equal to the gain in the hypothetical C1 stock ($35x fair market value - $30x basis). Therefore, D recognizes $5x of gain.

(4) *Example 4: C stock as Substitute Asset*—(i) *Facts*. X owns 100% of the stock of P, which owns multiple assets, including 100% of the stock of R and Asset 2. Y owns 100% of the stock of D. The following steps occur as part of a Plan: P merges into D in a reorganization under section 368(a)(1)(A) (P-D reorganization). Immediately after the merger, X and Y own 10% and 90%, respectively, of the stock of D. D then causes R to transfer all of its assets to C and liquidate in a reorganization under section 368(a)(1) (R-C reorganization). At the time of the P-D reorganization, the R stock has a basis of $40x and a fair market value of $110x. D distributes the stock of C to X and Y, pro rata. D continues to directly hold Asset 2. Immediately before the Distribution, the C stock held by D that was deemed received in the R-C reorganization (Block 1) has a basis of $40x and a fair market value of $110x, and all of the stock of C held by D has a basis of $100x and a fair market value of $200x.

(ii) *Analysis*—(A) *P is a Predecessor of D.* Under paragraph (b)(1) of this section, P is a Predecessor of D. First, P is a Potential Predecessor because, as part of a Plan, P transferred property to D in a Section 381 Transaction. See paragraph (b)(2)(ii)(A)(*1*) of this section. Second, both pre-Distribution requirements and the post-Distribution requirement are satisfied. The Relevant Property Requirement is satisfied because, for the following two reasons, some of the C stock distributed in the Distribution (Block 1) was Relevant Property of P. D is treated as acquiring Block 1 of the C stock in exchange for a direct or indirect interest in R stock (that is, Relevant Property) in the R-C reorganization because the basis of D in that C stock immediately after a transfer of the R stock (in the liquidation of R) is determined in whole or in part by reference to the basis of the R stock immediately before the transfer. See paragraph (b)(2)(x) of this section. Further, because the basis in Block 1 of the C stock is determined in whole or in part by reference to the basis of Relevant Equity (the R stock) the issuer of which ceases to exist for Federal income tax purposes under the Plan, Block 1 of the C stock is a Substitute Asset, and is therefore treated as Relevant Property with the same ownership and transfer history as the R stock. See paragraph (b)(2)(vi)(B)(*2*) of this section. The Reflection of Basis Requirement is satisfied because Block 1 of the C stock is Relevant Property of P, and was neither distributed in a distribution to which section 355(e) applied nor transferred in a transaction in which the gain on that C stock was recognized in full during the Plan Period prior to the Distribution. See paragraph (b)(1)(ii)(B) of this section. The Division of Relevant Property Requirement is satisfied because some of the C stock distributed in the Distribution was Relevant Property of P, and therefore C is deemed to have received Relevant Property of P, and immediately after the Distribution, D continues to hold Asset 2, which is Relevant Property of P. See paragraph (b)(1)(iii) of this section. Therefore, as part of a Plan, P's Relevant Property has been divided between C and D.

(B) *Planned 50-percent Acquisition of P.* Under paragraph (d)(1)(i) of this section, Y is treated as acquiring stock representing 90% of the voting power and value of P as a result of the P-D reorganization. Accordingly, there has been a Planned 50-percent Acquisition of P.

(C) *Gain limited*. Without regard to the limitations in paragraph (e) of this section, D would be required to recognize $100x of gain ($200x of fair market value minus $100x of basis of all C stock held by D), the Statutory Recognition Amount described in section 355(c)(2). However, under the POD Gain Limitation Rule, D's gain recognized by reason of the Planned 50-percent Acquisition of P will not exceed $70x, an amount equal to the amount D would have recognized had it transferred Block 1 of the C stock (Separated Property) to a newly formed corporation (C1) solely for stock and distributed the C1 stock to D shareholders in a Hypothetical D/355(e) Reorganization. See paragraph (e)(2)(i) of this section. Because Relevant Equity (Block 1 of the C stock) is Separated Property, Underlying Property associated with that Relevant Equity is not treated as Separated Property. See

paragraph (b)(2)(vii) of this section. Under section 361(c)(2), D would recognize $70x of gain, an amount equal to the gain in the hypothetical C1 stock (excess of the $110x fair market value over the $40x basis). Therefore, D recognizes $70x of gain.

(5) *Example 5: Section 351 transaction*—(i) *Facts*. X owns 100% of the stock of P, which holds multiple assets, including Asset 1, Asset 2, and Asset 3. Y owns 100% of the stock of D. The following steps occur as part of a Plan: P transfers Asset 1 and Asset 2 to D and Y transfers property to D in an exchange qualifying under section 351. Immediately after the exchange, P and Y own 10% and 90%, respectively, of the stock of D. D then contributes Asset 1 to C in exchange for additional C stock. D distributes all of the stock of C to P and Y, pro rata. D continues to directly hold Asset 2, and P continues to directly hold Asset 3. The contribution and Distribution constitute a reorganization under section 368(a)(1)(D). Immediately before the Distribution, Asset 1 has a basis of $40x and a fair market value of $110x, and the stock of C held by D has a basis of $100x and a fair market value of $200x. Following the Distribution, and as part of the same Plan, Z acquires 51% of the P stock.

(ii) *Analysis*—*P is not a Predecessor of D.* Under paragraph (b)(1) of this section, P is not a Predecessor of D. P is not a Potential Predecessor because P did not transfer property to a Potential Predecessor, D, or a member of the same Expanded Affiliated Group as D in a Section 381 Transaction and P is not a member of the same Expanded Affiliated Group as D immediately after completion of the Plan. See paragraph (b)(2)(ii) of this section. Thus, P cannot be a Predecessor of D. See paragraph (b)(1)(i) of this section.

(6) *Example 6: Section 351 transaction after an acquisition of P*—(i) *Facts*. X owns 100% of the stock of P, which holds multiple assets, including Asset 1 and Asset 2. Y owns 100% of the stock of D, D owns 100% of the stock of D1, and D1 owns 100% of the stock of C. D files a consolidated return for the affiliated group of which it is the common parent. The following steps occur as part of a Plan: D acquires 100% of the stock of P from X. P transfers Asset 1 and Asset 2 to D1 for D1 stock in an exchange qualifying under section 351. See § 1.1502-34. D1 contributes Asset 1 to C in exchange for additional C stock. D1 distributes all of the stock of C to D in exchange for D1 stock (First Distribution). D then distributes all of the stock of C to Y (Second Distribution). D1 continues to directly hold Asset 2. Immediately before the First Distribution, Asset 1 has a basis of $10x and a fair market value of $60x, and the stock of C held by D1 has a basis of $100x and a fair market value of $200x.

(ii) *Analysis*—(A) *P is a Predecessor of D1.* Under paragraph (b)(1) of this section, P is a Predecessor of D1. First, P is a Potential Predecessor of D1 because P is a member of the same Expanded Affiliated Group as D1 immediately after completion of the Plan. See paragraph (b)(2)(ii)(A)(*2*) of this section. The Relevant Property Requirement is satisfied because, immediately before the First Distribution and as part of a Plan, C holds P Relevant Property (Asset 1) the gain on which was not recognized in full at any point during the Plan Period, and some of the C stock distributed in the First Distribution was acquired by D1 in exchange for Asset 1. See paragraph (b)(1)(ii)(A)(*1*) of this section. The Reflection of Basis Requirement is satisfied because that C stock had a basis prior to the First Distribution that was determined in whole or in part by reference to the basis of Separated Property (Asset 1), and was neither distributed in a distribution to which section 355(e) applied nor transferred in a transaction in which the gain on that C stock was recognized in full prior to the First Distribution. See paragraph (b)(1)(ii)(B) of this section. The Division of Relevant Property Requirement is satisfied because immediately after the First Distribution, each of C, on the one hand, and P or D1, on the other hand, continues to hold Relevant Property of P, and therefore, as part of a Plan, P's Relevant Property has been divided between C and D1. See paragraph (b)(1)(iii) of this section.

(B) *Planned 50-percent Acquisition of P.* D has acquired stock representing 100% of the voting power and value of P. Accordingly, there has been a Planned 50-percent Acquisition of P.

(C) *Gain on First Distribution.* Because there is a Planned 50-percent Acquisition of a Predecessor of Distributing (but not of Distributing, Controlled, or their Successors), section 355(e) will not apply to the First Distribution unless D and D1 choose to have section 355(f) apply. See paragraph (g) of this section. As a result, section 355, including the POD Gain Limitation Rule, will apply to the First Distribution. Under the POD Gain Limitation Rule, D1's gain recognized by reason of the Planned 50-percent Acquisition of P will not exceed $50x, an amount equal to the amount D1 would have recognized had it transferred Asset 1 (Separated Property) to a newly formed corporation (C1) solely for stock and distributed the C1 stock to D1 shareholders in a Hypothetical D/355(e) Reorganization. See paragraph (e)(2)(i) of this section. Under section 361(c)(2), D1 would recognize $50x of gain, an amount equal to the gain in the hypothetical C1 stock (excess of the $60x fair market value over the $10x basis). Therefore, D1 recognizes $50x of gain. Under paragraph (g)(2) of this section, however, D and D1 may choose to apply section 355(f) to the

First Distribution as an exception to the general application of paragraph (g)(1) of this section. By application of section 355(f), section 355 (including the POD Gain Limitation Rule) would not apply to the First Distribution. Therefore, D1 would be required to recognize $100x of gain (excess of the $200x fair market value over the $100x basis of C stock held by D1) under section 311(b), and D would be treated under section 302(d) as receiving a distribution of $200x to which section 301 applies.

(D) *P is not a Predecessor of D.* Under paragraph (b)(1) of this section, P is not a Predecessor of D. First, P is a Potential Predecessor of D because P is a member of the same Expanded Affiliated Group as D immediately after completion of the Plan. See paragraph (b)(2)(ii)(A)(2) of this section. However, although the Relevant Property Requirement is satisfied, the Reflection of Basis Requirement is not satisfied. The Relevant Property Requirement is satisfied because, immediately before the Second Distribution and as part of a Plan, C holds P Relevant Property (Asset 1) the gain on which was not recognized in full at any point during the Plan Period, and some of the C stock distributed in the Second Distribution was indirectly acquired by D in exchange for Asset 1. See paragraph (b)(1)(ii)(A)(1) of this section. However, regardless of whether D and D1 choose under paragraph (g)(2) of this section to have section 355(f) apply to the First Distribution, the Reflection of Basis Requirement cannot be satisfied. If section 355(f) applies to the First Distribution, then all of the C stock will have been transferred in a transaction in which the gain on the C stock was recognized in full during the Plan Period prior to the Second Distribution. If section 355(f) does not apply to the First Distribution, then all of the C stock will have been transferred in a distribution to which section 355(e) applied during the Plan Period prior to the Second Distribution. Because not all of the pre-Distribution and post-Distribution requirements are satisfied, P cannot be a Predecessor of D.

(7) *Example 7: Sequential Predecessors*—(i) *Facts.* X owns 100% of P1, which holds multiple assets, including Asset 1 and Asset 2. Y owns 100% of P2, which holds Asset 3, and Z owns 100% of D. The following steps occur as part of a Plan: P1 merges into P2 in a reorganization under 368(a)(1)(A) (P1-P2 reorganization). Immediately after the merger, X and Y own 10% and 90%, respectively, of the stock of P2. P2 then merges into D in a reorganization under 368(a)(1)(A) (P2-D reorganization). Immediately after the merger, X, Y, and Z own 1%, 9%, and 90%, respectively, of the stock of D. D then contributes Asset 1 to C in exchange for additional C stock, and retains Asset 2 and Asset 3. D distributes all of the stock of C to X, Y, and Z, pro rata. Immediately before the Distribution, Asset 1 has a basis of $40x and a fair market value of $100x, and the stock of C held by D has a basis of $100x and a fair market value of $200x.

(ii) *Analysis*—(A) *P2 is a Predecessor of D.* Under paragraph (b)(1) of this section, P2 is a Predecessor of D. First, P2 is a Potential Predecessor because, as part of a Plan, P2 transferred property to D in a Section 381 Transaction. See paragraph (b)(2)(ii)(A)(1) of this section. Second, both pre-Distribution requirements and the post-Distribution requirement are satisfied. The Relevant Property Requirement is satisfied because, immediately before the Distribution and as part of a Plan, C holds P2 Relevant Property (Asset 1) the gain on which was not recognized in full at any point during the Plan Period, and some of the C stock distributed in the Distribution was acquired by D in exchange for Asset 1. See paragraph (b)(1)(ii)(A)(1) of this section. The Reflection of Basis Requirement is satisfied because that C stock had a basis prior to the Distribution that was determined in whole or in part by reference to the basis of Separated Property (Asset 1), and was neither distributed in a distribution to which section 355(e) applied nor transferred in a transaction in which the gain on that C stock was recognized in full during the Plan Period prior to the Distribution. See paragraph (b)(1)(ii)(B) of this section. The Division of Relevant Property Requirement is satisfied because immediately after the Distribution, D continues to hold P2 Relevant Property (Asset 2 and Asset 3), and therefore, as part of a Plan, P2's Relevant Property has been divided between C and D. See paragraph (b)(1)(iii) of this section.

(B) *P1 is a Predecessor of D.* Under paragraph (b)(1) of this section, P1 is a Predecessor of D. First, P1 is a Potential Predecessor because, as part of a Plan, P1 transferred property to a Potential Predecessor (P2) in a Section 381 Transaction. See paragraph (b)(2)(ii)(A)(1) of this section. Second, both pre-Distribution requirements and the post-Distribution requirement are satisfied. The Relevant Property Requirement is satisfied because, immediately before the Distribution and as part of a Plan, C holds P1 Relevant Property (Asset 1) the gain on which was not recognized in full at any point during the Plan Period, and some of the C stock distributed in the Distribution was acquired by D in exchange for Asset 1. See paragraph (b)(1)(ii)(A)(1) of this section. The Reflection of Basis Requirement is satisfied because that C stock had a basis prior to the Distribution that was determined in whole or in part by reference to the basis of Separated Property (Asset 1), and was neither distributed in a distribution to which section 355(e) applied nor transferred in a transaction in which

the gain on that C stock was recognized in full during the Plan Period prior to the Distribution. See paragraph (b)(1)(ii)(B) of this section. The Division of Relevant Property Requirement is satisfied because immediately after the Distribution, D continues to hold Relevant Property of P1 (Asset 2) and therefore, as part of a Plan, P1's Relevant Property has been divided between C and D. See paragraph (b)(1)(iii) of this section.

(C) *Planned 50-percent Acquisitions of P1 and P2.* Under paragraph (d)(1)(i) of this section, Y is treated as acquiring stock representing 90% of the voting power and value of P1 as a result of the P1-P2 merger. In addition, under paragraph (d)(1)(i) of this section, Z is treated as acquiring stock representing 90% of the voting power and value of P2 in the P2-D merger. Accordingly, there have been Planned 50-percent Acquisitions of P1 and P2.

(D) *Gain limited.* Without regard to the limitations in paragraph (e) of this section, D would be required to recognize $100x of gain ($200x of aggregate fair market value minus $100x of aggregate basis of the C stock held by D), the Statutory Recognition Amount described in section 361(c)(2), because there have been Planned 50-percent Acquisitions of P1 and P2, both Predecessors of D. However, under paragraph (e) of this section, D's gain recognized by reason of the Planned 50-percent Acquisitions of P1 and P2 will not exceed $60x, an amount equal to the amount D would have recognized had it transferred Asset 1 (Separated Property) to a newly formed corporation (C1) solely for stock and distributed the C1 stock to D shareholders in a Hypothetical D/355(e) Reorganization. Under section 361(c)(2), D would recognize $60x, an amount equal to the gain in the hypothetical C1 stock (excess of the $100x fair market value over the $40x basis). Paragraph (e)(1)(ii) of this section provides that if there are Planned 50-percent Acquisitions of multiple corporations, Distributing must recognize the Statutory Recognition Amount with respect to each such corporation, subject to the POD Gain Limitation Rule and the Distributing Gain Limitation Rule, if applicable. In this case, the POD Gain Limitation Rule limits the amount of gain required to be recognized by D with respect to each of the Planned 50-percent Acquisitions of P1 and P2 to $60x. See paragraph (e)(2)(i) of this section. Ordinarily, each $60x limitation would be added together, and the total gain limitation provided by paragraph (e) of this section would be $120x. However, the anti-duplication rule set forth in paragraph (e)(2)(ii)(C) of this section provides that, for purposes of applying the POD Gain Limitation Rule, a Predecessor of Distributing's Separated Property is taken into account only to the extent such property was not taken into account with respect to another Predecessor of Distributing. Thus, Asset 1 may not be taken into account more than once in determining the total gain limitation. Therefore, D recognizes $60x of gain.

(8) *Example 8: Multiple Predecessors of D*—(i) *Facts.* X owns 100% of the stock of P1, which holds multiple assets, including Asset 1 and Asset 3. Y owns 100% of the stock of P2, which holds multiple assets, including Asset 2 and Asset 4. Z owns 100% of the stock of D. The following steps occur as part of a Plan: each of P1 and P2 merges into D in a reorganization under section 368(a)(1)(A). Immediately after the mergers, each of X and Y owns 10%, and Z owns 80%, of the stock of D. D then contributes to C Asset 1 (acquired from P1), and Asset 2 (acquired from P2). In exchange for Asset 1 and Asset 2, D receives additional C stock. D distributes the stock of C to X, Y, and Z, pro rata. D's contribution of Asset 1 and Asset 2 and the Distribution constitute a reorganization under section 368(a)(1)(D). D continues to hold Asset 3 and Asset 4. Immediately before the Distribution, Asset 1 has a basis of $50x and a fair market value of $110x, Asset 2 has a basis of $70x and a fair market value of $90x, and the stock of C held by D has a basis of $130x and a fair market value of $220x.

(ii) *Analysis*—(A) *P1 and P2 are Predecessors of D.* Under paragraph (b)(1) of this section, each of P1 and P2 is a Predecessor of D. First, each of P1 and P2 is a Potential Predecessor because, as part of a Plan, each of P1 and P2 transferred property to D in a Section 381 Transaction. See paragraph (b)(2)(ii)(A)(1) of this section. Second, both pre-Distribution requirements and the post-Distribution requirement are satisfied. The Relevant Property Requirement is satisfied because, immediately before the Distribution and as part of a Plan, C holds P1 Relevant Property (Asset 1) and P2 Relevant Property (Asset 2), the gain on each of which was not recognized in full at any point during the Plan Period, and some of the C stock distributed in the Distribution was acquired by D in exchange for each of Asset 1 and Asset 2. See paragraph (b)(1)(ii)(A)(1) of this section. The Reflection of Basis Requirement is satisfied because that C stock had a basis prior to the Distribution that was determined in whole or in part by reference to the basis of Separated Property (Asset 1 and Asset 2, respectively), and was neither distributed in a distribution to which section 355(e) applied nor transferred in a transaction in which the gain on that C stock was recognized in full during the Plan Period prior to the Distribution. See paragraph (b)(1)(ii)(B) of this section. The Division of Relevant Property Requirement is satisfied because immediately after the Distribution, D continues to hold Relevant Property of P1 and P2, and therefore, as part of a Plan, each of P1's and P2's Relevant Property has been divided between C and D. See paragraph (b)(1)(iii) of this section.

(B) *Planned 50-percent Acquisitions of P1 and P2.* Under paragraph (d)(1)(i) of this section, Z is treated as acquiring stock representing 80% of the voting power and value of each of P1 and P2 as a result of the mergers of P1 and P2 into D. Accordingly, there have been Planned 50-percent Acquisitions of P1 and P2.

(C) *Gain limited.* Without regard to the limitations in paragraph (e) of this section, D would be required to recognize $90x of gain ($220x of fair market value minus $130x of basis of the C stock held by D), the Statutory Recognition Amount under section 361(c)(2). However, under the POD Gain Limitation Rule, D's gain recognized by reason of the Planned 50-percent Acquisition of P1 will not exceed $60x ($110x fair market value minus $50x basis), an amount equal to the amount D would have recognized had it transferred Asset 1 (Separated Property) to a newly formed corporation (C1) solely for stock and distributed the C1 stock to D shareholders in a Hypothetical D/355(e) Reorganization. See paragraph (e)(2)(ii) of this section. In addition, under the POD Gain Limitation Rule, D's gain recognized by reason of the deemed acquisition of P2 stock will not exceed $20x ($90x fair market value minus $70x basis), an amount equal to the amount D would have recognized had it transferred Asset 2 (Separated Property) to a second newly formed corporation (C2) solely for stock and distributed the C2 stock to D shareholders in a Hypothetical D/355(e) Reorganization. See paragraph (e)(2)(i) of this section. Therefore, D recognizes $80x of gain ($60x + $20x). See paragraph (e)(1)(ii) of this section.

(9) *Example 9: Successor of C*—(i) *Facts.* X owns 100% of the stock of each of D and R. The following steps occur as part of a Plan: D distributes all of its C stock to X. Immediately before the Distribution, D's C stock has a basis of $10x and a fair market value of $30x. C then merges into R in a reorganization under section 368(a)(1)(D). Immediately after the merger, X owns all of the R stock. As part of the same Plan, Z acquires 51% of the stock of R from X.

(ii) *Analysis*—(A) *R is a Successor of C.* Under paragraph (c)(2)(i) of this section, R is a Successor of C because, after the Distribution, C transfers property to R in a Section 381 Transaction.

(B) *Planned 50-percent Acquisition of C.* Under paragraph (d)(2) of this section, Z's acquisition of stock of R is treated as an acquisition of stock of C. Therefore, Z is treated as acquiring 51% of the stock of C. Accordingly, there has been a Planned 50-percent Acquisition of C.

(C) *Gain not limited.* Section 355(e) applies to the Distribution because there has been a Planned 50-percent Acquisition of C. Neither the POD Gain Limitation Rule nor the Distributing Gain Limitation Rule applies because there has been no Planned 50-percent Acquisition of a Predecessor of D, and no Planned 50-percent Acquisition of D. Therefore, D recognizes $20x of gain ($30x fair market value minus $10x basis of the C stock held by D) under section 355(c)(2).

(10) *Example 10: Multiple Successors*—(i) *Facts.* X owns 100% of the stock of both D and R. Y owns 100% of the stock of S. The following steps occur as part of a Plan: D distributes all of the C stock to X. Immediately after the Distribution, D merges into R in a reorganization under section 368(a)(1)(A) (D-R merger). Following the D-R merger, R merges into S in a reorganization under section 368(a)(1)(A) (R-S merger). Immediately after the R-S merger, X and Y own 10% and 90%, respectively, of the S stock. Immediately before the Distribution, D's C stock has a basis of $10x and a fair market value of $30x.

(ii) *Analysis*—(A) *R and S are Successors of D.* Under paragraph (c)(2)(i) of this section, R is a Successor of D because, after the Distribution, D transfers property to R in a Section 381 Transaction. Under paragraph (c)(2)(ii) of this section, S is also a Successor of D because R (a Successor of D) transfers property to S in a Section 381 Transaction.

(B) *Planned 50-percent Acquisition of D.* Under paragraph (d)(1)(i) of this section, there is no deemed acquisition of D stock as a result of the D-R merger because X wholly owns the stock of D before the

merger and wholly owns the stock of R after the merger. Under paragraph (d)(1)(i) of this section, Y is treated as acquiring stock representing 90% of the voting power and value of R (a Successor of D) as a result of the R-S merger. Under paragraph (d)(2) of this section, an acquisition of R stock is also treated as an acquisition of D stock. Accordingly, there has been a Planned 50-percent Acquisition of D.

(C) *Gain not limited.* Section 355(e) applies to the Distribution because there has been a Planned 50-percent Acquisition of D. The POD Gain Limitation Rule does not apply because there has been no Planned 50-percent Acquisition of a Predecessor of D. The Distributing Gain Limitation Rule applies because there has been a Planned 50-percent Acquisition of D. However, the gain limitation under the Distributing Gain Limitation Rule equals the Statutory Recognition Amount, because there is no Predecessor of D (and thus no Separated Property). Therefore, D recognizes $20x of gain ($30x fair market value minus $10x basis of the C stock held by D) under section 355(c)(2).

(i) *Applicability date.*—This section applies to Distributions occurring after December 15, 2019. For Distributions occurring on or before December 15, 2019, see §1.355-8T as contained in 26 CFR part 1 revised as of April 1, 2019. [Reg. §1.355-8.]

☐ [*T.D.* 9888, 12-16-2019 (*corrected* 3-16-2020).]

[Reg. §1.356-1]

§1.356-1. Receipt of additional consideration in connection with an exchange.—(a) If in any exchange to which the provisions of section 354 or section 355 would apply except for the fact that there is received by the shareholders or security holders other property (in addition to property permitted to be received without recognition of gain by such sections) or money, then—

(1) The gain, if any, to the taxpayer shall be recognized in an amount not in excess of the sum of the money and the fair market value of the other property, but,

(2) The loss, if any, to the taxpayer from the exchange or distribution shall not be recognized to any extent.

(b) For purposes of computing the gain, if any, recognized pursuant to section 356 and paragraph (a)(1) of this section, to the extent the terms of the exchange specify the other property or money that is received in exchange for a particular share of stock or security surrendered or a particular class of stock or securities surrendered, such terms shall control provided that such terms are economically reasonable. To the extent the terms of the exchange do not specify the other property or money that is received in exchange for a particular share of stock or security surrendered or a particular class of stock or securities surrendered, a pro rata portion of the other property and money received shall be treated as received in exchange for each share of stock and security surrendered, based on the fair market value of such surrendered share of stock or security.

(c) If the distribution of such other property or money by or on behalf of a corporation has the effect of the distribution of a dividend, then there shall be chargeable to each distributee (either an individual or a corporation)—

(1) As a dividend, such an amount of the gain recognized as is not in excess of the distributee's ratable share of the undistributed earnings and profits of the corporation accumulated after February 28, 1913, and

(2) As a gain from the exchange of property, the remainder of the gain so recognized.

(d) The rules of this section may be illustrated by the following examples:

Example 1. In an exchange to which the provisions of section 356 apply and to which section 354 would apply but for the receipt of property not permitted to be received without the recognition of gain or loss, A (either an individual or a corporation), received the following in exchange for a share of stock having an adjusted basis to A of $85:

One share of stock worth	$100
Cash	25
Other property (basis $25) fair market value	50
Total fair market value of consideration received	$175
Adjusted basis of stock surrendered in exchange	$85
Total gain	90
Gain to be recognized, limited to cash and other property received	$75
A's pro rata share of earnings and profits accumulated after February 28, 1913 (taxable dividend)	$30
Remainder to be treated as a gain from the exchange of property	45

Example 2. If, in *Example 1,* A's stock had an adjusted basis to A of $200, A would have realized a loss of $25 on the exchange, which loss would not be recognized.

Example 3. (i) *Facts.* J, an individual, acquired 10 shares of Class A stock of Corporation X on Date 1 for $3 each and 10 shares of Class B stock of Corporation X on Date 2 for $9 each. On Date 3, Corporation Y acquires the assets of Corporation X in a reorganization under section 368(a)(1)(A). Pursuant to the terms of the plan of reorganization, J surrenders all of J's shares of Corporation X stock for 10 shares of Corporation Y stock and $100 of cash. On the date of the exchange, the fair market value of each share of Class A stock of Corporation X is $10, the fair market value of each share of Class B stock of Corporation X is $10, and the fair market value of each share of Corporation Y stock is $10. The terms of the exchange do not specify that shares of Corporation Y stock or cash are received in exchange for particular shares of Class A stock or Class B stock of Corporation X.

(ii) *Analysis.* Under paragraph (b) of this section, because the terms of the exchange do not specify that the cash is received in exchange for shares of Class A or Class B stock of Corporation X, a pro rata portion of the cash received is treated as received in exchange for each share of Class A stock of Corporation X and each share of Class B stock of Corporation X based on the fair market value of the surrendered shares. Therefore, J is treated as receiving shares of Corporation Y stock with a fair market value of $50 and $50 of cash in exchange for its shares of Class A stock of Corporation X and shares of Corporation Y stock with a fair market value of $50 and $50 of cash in exchange for its shares of Class B stock of Corporation X. J realizes a gain of $70 on the exchange of shares of Class A stock, $50 of which is recognized under section 356 and paragraph (a) of this section, and J realizes a gain of $10 on the exchange of shares of Class B stock of Corporation X, all of which is recognized under section 356 and paragraph (a) of this section. Assuming that J's gain recognized is not treated as a dividend under section 356(a)(2), such gain shall be treated as gain from the exchange of property.

Example 4. (i) *Facts.* The facts are the same as in *Example 3,* except that the terms of the plan of reorganization specify that J receives 10 shares of stock of Corporation Y in exchange for J's shares of Class A stock of Corporation X and $100 of cash in exchange for J's shares of Class B stock of Corporation X.

(ii) *Analysis.* Under paragraph (b) of this section, because the terms of the exchange specify that J receives 10 shares of stock of Corporation Y in exchange for J's shares of Class A stock of Corporation X and $100 of cash in exchange for J's shares of Class B stock of Corporation X and such terms are economically reasonable, such terms control. J realizes a gain of $70 on the exchange of shares of Class A stock, none of which is recognized under section 356 and paragraph (a) of this section, and J realizes a gain of $10 on the exchange of shares of Class B stock of Corporation X, all of which is recognized under section 356 and paragraph (a) of this section.

(e) Section 301(b)(1)(B) and section 301(d)(2) do not apply to a distribution of "other property" to a corporate shareholder if such distribution is within the provisions of section 356.

(f) See §1.301-1(j) for certain transactions that are not within the scope of section 356.

(g) This section applies to exchanges and distributions of stock and securities occurring on or after January 23, 2006. [Reg. §1.356-1.]

☐ [*T.D.* 6152, 12-2-55. *Amended by T.D.* 9244, 1-23-2006 *and T.D.* 9954, 9-21-2021.]

[Reg. §1.356-2]

§1.356-2. Receipt of additional consideration not in connection with an exchange.—(a) If, in a transaction to which section 355 would apply except for the fact that a shareholder (individual or corporate) receives property permitted by section 355 to be received without the recognition of gain, together with other property or money, without the surrender of any stock or securities of the distributing corporation, then the sum of the money and the fair market value of the other property as of the date of the distribution shall be treated as a distribution of property to which the rules of section 301 (other than section 301(b) and section 301(d) apply. See section 358 for determination of basis of such other property.

(b) Paragraph (a) of this section may be illustrated by the following examples:

Example (1). Individuals A and B each own 50 of the 100 outstanding shares of common stock of Corporation X. Corporation X owns all of the stock of Corporation Y, 100 shares. Corporation X distributes to each shareholder 50 shares of the stock of Corporation Y plus $100 cash without requiring the surrender of any shares of its own

stock. The $100 cash received by each is treated as a distribution of property to which the rules of section 301 apply.

Example (2). If, in the above example, Corporation X distributes 50 shares of stock of Corporation Y to A and 30 shares of such stock plus $100 cash to B without requiring the surrender of any of its own stock, the amount of cash received by B is treated as a distribution of property to which the rules of section 301 apply. [Reg. §1.356-2.]

☐ [*T.D.* 6152, 12-2-55.]

[Reg. §1.356-3]

§1.356-3. Rules for treatment of securities as "other property".—(a) As a general rule, for purposes of section 356, the term "other property" includes securities. However, it does not include securities permitted under section 354 or section 355 to be received tax free. Thus, when securities are surrendered in a transaction to which section 354 or section 355 is applicable, the characterization of the securities received as "other property" does not include securities received where the principal amount of such securities does not exceed the principal amount of securities surrendered in the transaction. If a greater principal amount of securities is received in an exchange described in section 354 (other than subsection (c) or (d) thereof) or section 355 over the principal amount of securities surrendered, the term "other property" includes the fair market value of such excess principal amount as of the date of the exchange. If no securities are surrendered in exchange, the term "other property" includes the fair market value, as of the date of receipt, of the entire principal amount of the securities received.

(b) Except as provided in §1.356-6, for purposes of this section, a right to acquire stock that is treated as a security for purposes of section 354 or 355 has no principal amount. Thus, such right is not *other property* when received in a transaction to which section 356 applies (regardless of whether securities are surrendered in the exchange). This paragraph (b) applies to transactions occurring on or after March 9, 1998.

(c) In the examples in this paragraph (c), *stock* means common stock and *warrants* means rights to acquire common stock. The following examples illustrate the rules of paragraph (a) of this section:—

Example 1. A, an individual, exchanged 100 shares of stock for 100 shares of stock and a security in the principal amount of $1,000 with a fair market value of $990. The amount of $990 is treated as "other property."

Example 2. B, an individual, exchanged 100 shares of stock and a security in the principal amount of $1,000 for 300 shares of stock and a security in the principal amount of $1,500. The security had a fair market value on the date of receipt of $1,575. The fair market value of the excess principal amount, or $525, is treated as "other property."

Example 3. C, an individual, exchanged a security in a principal amount of $1,000 for 100 shares of stock and a security in the principal amount of $900. No part of the security received is treated as "other property."

Example 4. D, an individual, exchanged a security in the principal amount of $1,000 for 100 shares of stock and a security in the principal amount of $1,200 with a fair market value of $1,100. The fair market value of the excess principal amount, or $183.33, is treated as "other property."

Example 5. E, an individual, exchanged a security in the principal amount of $1,000 for another security in the principal amount of $1,200 with a fair market value of $1,080. The fair market value of the excess principal amount, or $180, is treated as "other property."

Example 6. F, an individual, exchanged a security in the principal amount of $1,000 for two different securities each in the principal amount of $750. One of the securities had a fair market value of $750, the other had a fair market value of $600. One-third of the fair market value of each security ($250 and $200) is treated as "other property."

Example 7. G, an individual, exchanged stock for stock and a warrant. The warrant had no principal amount. Thus, G received no excess principal amount within the meaning of section 356(d).

Example 8. H, an individual, exchanged a warrant for stock and a warrant. The warrants had no principal amount. Thus, H received no excess principal amount within the meaning of section 356(d).

Example 9. I, an individual, exchanged a warrant for stock and a debt security. The warrant had no principal amount. The debt security had a $100 principal amount. I received $100 of excess principal amount within the meaning of section 356(d).

[Reg. §1.356-3.]

☐ [*T.D.* 6152, 12-2-55. *Amended by T.D.* 7616, 5-7-79; *T.D.* 8752, 1-5-98 *and T.D.* 8882, 5-15-2000.]

[Reg. § 1.356-4]

§ 1.356-4. Exchanges for section 306 stock.—If, in a transaction to which section 356 is applicable, other property or money is received in exchange for section 306 stock, an amount equal to the fair market value of the property plus the money, if any, shall be treated as a distribution of property to which section 301 is applicable. The determination of whether section 306 stock is surrendered for other property (including money) is a question of fact to be decided under all of the circumstances of each case. Ordinarily, the other property (including money) received will first be treated as received in exchange for any section 306 stock owned by a shareholder prior to such transaction. For example, if a shareholder who owns a share of common stock (having a basis to him of $100) and a share of preferred stock which is section 306 stock (having a basis to him of $100) surrenders both shares in a transaction to which section 356 is applicable for one share of common stock having a fair market value of $80 and one $100 bond having a fair market value of $100, the bond will be deemed received in exchange for the section 306 stock and it will be treated as a distribution to which section 301 is applicable to the extent of its entire fair market value ($100). [Reg. § 1.356-4.]

☐ [*T.D.* 6152, 12-2-55.]

[Reg. § 1.356-5]

§ 1.356-5. Transactions involving gift or compensation.—With respect to transactions described in sections 354, 355, or 356, but which—

(a) Result in a gift, see section 2501 and following, and the regulations pertaining thereto, or

(b) Have the effect of the payment of compensation, see section 61(a)(1), and the regulations pertaining thereto. [Reg. § 1.356-5.]

☐ [*T.D.* 6152, 12-2-55.]

[Reg. § 1.356-6]

§ 1.356-6. Rules for treatment of nonqualified preferred stock as other property.—(a) *In general.*—For purposes of §§ 1.354-1(e), 1.355-1(c), and 1.356-3(b), the terms *stock* and *securities* do not include—

(1) Nonqualified preferred stock, as defined in section 351(g)(2), received in exchange for (or in a distribution with respect to) stock, or a right to acquire stock, other than nonqualified preferred stock; or

(2) A right to acquire such nonqualified preferred stock, received in exchange for (or in a distribution with respect to) stock, or a right to acquire stock, other than nonqualified preferred stock.

(b) *Exceptions.*—The following exceptions apply:

(1) *Certain recapitalizations.*—Paragraph (a) of this section does not apply in the case of a recapitalization under section 368(a)(1)(E) of a family-owned corporation as described in section 354(a)(2)(C)(ii)(II).

(2) *Transition rule.*—Paragraph (a) of this section does not apply to a transaction described in section 1014(f)(2) of the Taxpayer Relief Act of 1997 (111 Stat. 921).

(c) *Effective date.*—This section applies to nonqualified preferred stock, or a right to acquire such stock, received in connection with a transaction occurring on or after March 9, 1998. [Reg. § 1.356-6.]

☐ [*T.D.* 8753, 1-5-98. *Redesignated by T.D.* 8882, 5-15-2000.]

[Reg. § 1.356-7]

§ 1.356-7. Rules for treatment of nonqualified preferred stock and other preferred stock received in certain transactions.—(a) *Stock issued prior to effective date.*—Stock described in section 351(g)(2) is nonqualified preferred stock (NQPS) regardless of the date on which the stock is issued. However, sections 351(g), 354(a)(2)(C), 355(a)(3)(D), 356(e), and 1036(b) do not apply to any transaction occurring prior to June 9, 1997, or to any transaction occurring after June 8, 1997, that is described in section 1014(f)(2) of the Taxpayer Relief Act of 1997, Public Law 105-34 (111 Stat. 788, 921). For purposes of this section, preferred stock that is not NQPS is referred to as Qualified Preferred Stock (QPS).

(b) *Receipt of preferred stock in exchange for (or distribution on) substantially identical preferred stock.*—(1) *General rule.*—For purposes of sections 354(a)(2)(C)(i), 355(a)(3)(D), and 356(e)(2), preferred stock is QPS, even though it is described in section 351(g)(2), if it is received in exchange for (or in a distribution with respect to) preferred stock (the original preferred stock) that is QPS, provided—

(i) The original preferred stock is QPS solely because, on its issue date, either a right or obligation described in clause (i), (ii), or (iii) of section 351(g)(2)(A) was not exercisable until after a 20-year period beginning on the issue date, or the right or obligation was

exercisable within the 20-year period beginning on the issue date but was subject to a contingency which made remote the likelihood of the redemption or purchase, or the issuer's (or a related party's) right to redeem or purchase the stock was not more likely than not to be exercised within a 20-year period beginning on the issue date, or because of any combination of these reasons; and

(ii) The stock received is substantially identical to the original preferred stock.

(2) *Substantially identical.*—The stock received is substantially identical to the original preferred stock if—

(i) The stock received does not contain any term or terms that, in relation to any term or terms of the original preferred stock, either decrease the period in which a right or obligation described in clause (i), (ii), or (iii) of section 351(g)(2)(A) can be exercised, or increase the likelihood that such a right or obligation will be exercised, or accelerate the timing of the returns from the stock instrument, including the timing of actual or deemed dividends or other distributions received on the stock; and

(ii) As a result of the exchange or distribution, exercise of the right or obligation does not become more likely than not to occur within a 20-year period beginning on the issue date of the original preferred stock.

(3) *Treatment of stock received.*—The stock received will continue to be treated as QPS in subsequent transactions involving such stock, and the principles of this paragraph (b) apply to such transactions as though the stock received is the original preferred stock issued on the same date as the original preferred stock.

(c) *Stock transferred for services.*—For purposes of sections 351(g)(1), 354(a)(2)(C)(i), 355(a)(3)(D), and 356(e)(2), preferred stock containing a right or obligation described in clause (i), (ii) or (iii) of section 351(g)(2)(A) that is exercisable only upon the holder's separation from service from the issuer or a related person (as described in section 351(g)(3)(B)) will be treated as transferred in connection with the performance of services (and representing reasonable compensation) within the meaning of section 351(g)(2)(C)(i)(II), if such preferred stock is received in exchange for (or in a distribution with respect to) existing stock containing a similar right or obligation (exercisable only upon separation from service) and the existing stock was transferred in connection with the performance of services for the issuer or a related person (and represented reasonable compensation when transferred). In applying the rules relating to NQPS, the preferred stock received will continue to be treated as transferred in connection with the performance of services (and representing reasonable compensation) in subsequent transactions involving such stock, and the principles of this paragraph (c) apply to such transactions.

(d) *Rights to acquire stock.*—For purposes of § 1.356-6, the principles of paragraphs (a), (b), and (c) of this section apply.

(e) *Examples.*—In the examples in this paragraph (e), T and P are corporations, A is a shareholder of T, and A surrenders and receives (in addition to the stock exchanged in the examples) common stock in the reorganizations described. The following examples illustrate paragraphs (a), (b), and (c) of this section:

Example 1. In 1995, A transfers property to T and receives T preferred stock that is described in section 351(g)(2) in a transaction under section 351. In 2002, pursuant to a reorganization under section 368(a)(1)(B), A surrenders the T preferred stock in exchange for P NQPS. Under paragraph (a) of this section, the T preferred stock issued to A in 1995 is NQPS. However, because section 351(g) does not apply to transactions occurring before June 9, 1997, the T NQPS was not "other property" within the meaning of section 351(b) when issued in 1995. Under sections 354(a)(2)(C) and 356(e)(2), the P NQPS received by A in 2002 is not "other property" within the meaning of section 356(a)(1)(B) because it is received in exchange for NQPS.

Example 2. T issues QPS to A on January 1, 2000 that is not NQPS solely because the holder cannot require T to redeem the stock until January 1, 2022. In 2007, pursuant to a reorganization under section 368(a)(1)(A) in which T merges into P, A surrenders the T preferred stock in exchange for P preferred stock with terms that are identical to the terms of the T preferred stock, including the term that the holder cannot require the redemption of the stock until January 1, 2022. Because the P stock and the T stock have identical terms, and because the redemption did not become more likely than not to occur within the 20-year period that begins on January 1, 2000 (which is the issue date of the T preferred stock) as a result of the exchange, under paragraph (b) of this section, the P preferred stock received by A is treated as QPS. Thus, the P preferred stock received is not "other property" within the meaning of section 356(a)(1)(B).

Example 3. The facts are the same as in *Example 2,* except that, in addition, in 2010, pursuant to a recapitalization of P under section 368(a)(1)(E), A exchanges the P preferred stock above for P NQPS that permits the holder to require P to redeem the stock in 2020. Under paragraph (b) of this section, the P preferred stock surrendered by A is treated as QPS. Because the P preferred stock received by A in the recapitalization is not substantially identical to the P preferred stock surrendered, the P preferred stock received by A is not treated as QPS. Thus, the P preferred stock received is "other property" within the meaning of section 356(a)(1)(B).

Example 4. T issues preferred stock to A on January 1, 2000 that permits the holder to require T to redeem the stock on January 1, 2018, or at any time thereafter, but which is not NQPS solely because, as of the issue date, the holder's right to redeem is subject to a contingency that makes remote the likelihood of redemption on or before January 1, 2020. In 2007, pursuant to a reorganization under section 368(a)(1)(A) in which T merges into P, A surrenders the T preferred stock in exchange for P preferred stock with terms that are identical to the terms of the T preferred stock. Immediately before the exchange, the contingency to which the holder's right to cause redemption of the T stock is subject makes remote the likelihood of redemption before January 1, 2020, but the P stock, although subject to the same contingency, is more likely than not to be redeemed before January 1, 2020. Because, as a result of the exchange of T stock for P stock, the exercise of the redemption right became more likely than not to occur within the 20-year period beginning on the issue date of the T preferred stock, the P preferred stock received by A is not substantially identical to the T stock surrendered, and is not treated as QPS. Thus, the P preferred stock received is "other property" within the meaning of section 356(a)(1)(B).

Example 5. The facts are the same as in *Example 4*, except that, immediately before the merger of T into P in 2007, the contingency to which the holder's right to cause redemption of the T stock is subject makes it more likely than not that the T stock will be redeemed before January 1, 2020. Because exercise of the redemption right did not become more likely than not to occur within the 20-year period beginning on the issue date of the T preferred stock as a result of the exchange, the P preferred stock received by A is substantially identical to the T stock surrendered, and is treated as QPS. Thus, the P preferred stock received is not "other property" within the meaning of section 356(a)(1)(B).

Example 6. A is an employee of T. In connection with A's performance of services for T, T transfers to A in 2000 an amount of T common stock that represents reasonable compensation. The T common stock contains a term granting A the right to require T to redeem the common stock, but only upon A's separation from service from T. In 2005, pursuant to a reorganization under section 368(a)(1)(A) in which T merges into P, A receives, in exchange for A's T common stock, P preferred stock granting a similar redemption right upon A's separation from P's service. Under paragraph (c) of this section, the P preferred stock received by A is treated as transferred in connection with the performance of services (and representing reasonable compensation) within the meaning of section 351(g)(2)(C)(i)(II). Thus, the P preferred stock received by A is QPS.

(f) *Effective dates.*—This section applies to transactions occurring on or after October 2, 2000. [Reg. § 1.356-7.]

☐ [T.D. 8904, 9-29-2000.]

[Reg. § 1.357-1]

§ 1.357-1. Assumption of liability.—(a) *General rule.*—Section 357(a) does not affect the rule that liabilities assumed are to be taken into account for the purpose of computing the amount of gain or loss realized under section 1001 upon an exchange. Section 357(a) provides, subject to the exceptions and limitations specified in section 357(b) and (c), that:

(1) Liabilities assumed are not to be treated as "other property or money" for the purpose of determining the amount of realized gain which is to be recognized under section 351, 361, 371, or 374, if the transactions would, but for the receipt of "other property or money" have been exchanges of the type described in any one of such sections; and

(2) If the only type of consideration received by the transferor in addition to that permitted to be received by section 351, 361, 371, or 374, consists of an assumption of liabilities, the transaction, if otherwise qualified, will be deemed to be within the provisions of section 351, 361, 371, or 374.

(b) *Application of general rule.*—The application of paragraph (a) of this section may be illustrated by the following example:

Example. A, an individual, transfers to a controlled corporation property with an adjusted basis of $10,000 in exchange for stock of the corporation with a fair market value of $8,000, $3,000 cash, and the assumption by the corporation of indebtedness of A amounting to $4,000. A's gain is $5,000, computed as follows:

Stock received, fair market value	$8,000
Cash received	3,000
Liability assumed by transferee	4,000
Total consideration received	15,000
Less: Adjusted basis of property transferred	10,000
Gain realized	$5,000

Assuming that the exchange falls within section 351 as a transaction in which the gain to be recognized is limited to "other property or money" received, the gain recognized to A will be limited to the $3,000 cash received, since, under the general rule of section 357(a), the assumption of the $4,000 liability does not constitute "other property."

(c) *Tax avoidance purpose.*—The benefits of section 357(a) do not extend to any exchange involving an assumption of liabilities where it appears that the principal purpose of the taxpayer with respect to such assumption was to avoid Federal income tax on the exchange, or, if not such purpose, was not a bona fide business purpose. In such cases, the total amount of liabilities assumed or acquired pursuant to such exchange (and not merely a particular liability with respect to which the tax avoidance purpose existed) shall, for the purpose of determining the amount of gain to be recognized upon the exchange in which the liabilities are assumed or acquired, be treated as money received by the taxpayer upon the exchange. Thus, if in the example set forth in paragraph (b) of this section, the principal purpose of the assumption of the $4,000 liability was to avoid tax on the exchange, or was not a bona fide business purpose, then the amount of gain recognized would be $5,000. In any suit or proceeding where the burden is on the taxpayer to prove that an assumption of liabilities is not to be treated as "other property or money" under section 357, which is the case if the Commissioner determines that the taxpayer's purpose with respect thereto was a purpose to avoid Federal income tax on the exchange or was not a bona fide business purpose, and the taxpayer contests such determination by litigation, the taxpayer must sustain such burden by the clear preponderance of the evidence. Thus, the taxpayer must prove his case by such a clear preponderance of all the evidence that the absence of a purpose to avoid Federal income tax on the exchange, or the presence of a bona fide business purpose, is unmistakable. [Reg. § 1.357-1.]

☐ [T.D. 6152, 12-2-55. Amended by T.D. 6528, 1-18-61.]

[Reg. § 1.357-2]

§ 1.357-2. Liabilities in excess of basis.—(a) Section 357(c) provides in general that in an exchange to which section 351 (relating to a transfer to a corporation controlled by the transferor) is applicable, or to which section 361 (relating to the nonrecognition of gain or loss to corporations) is applicable by reason of a section 368(a)(1)(D) reorganization, if the sum of the amount of liabilities assumed plus the amount of liabilities to which the property is subject exceeds the total of the adjusted basis of the property transferred pursuant to such exchange, then such excess shall be considered as a gain from the sale or exchange of a capital asset or of property which is not a capital asset as the case may be. Thus, if an individual transfers, under section 351, properties having a total basis in his hands of $20,000, one of which has a basis of $10,000 but is subject to a mortgage of $30,000, to a corporation controlled by him, such individual will be subject to tax with respect to $10,000, the excess of the amount of the liability over the total adjusted basis of all the properties in his hands. The same result will follow whether or not the liability is assumed by the transferee. The determination of whether a gain resulting from the transfer of capital assets is long-term or short-term capital gain shall be made by reference to the holding period to the transferor of the assets transferred. An exception to the general rule of section 357(c) is made (1) for any exchange as to which under section 357(b) (relating to assumption of liabilities for tax-avoidance purposes) the entire amount of the liabilities is treated as money received and (2) for an exchange to which section 371 (relating to reorganizations in certain receivership and bankruptcy proceedings) or section 374 (relating to gain or loss not recognized in certain railroad reorganizations) is applicable.

(b) The application of paragraph (a) of this section may be illustrated by the following examples:

Example (1). If all such assets transferred are capital assets and if half the assets (ascertained by reference to their fair market value at the time of the transfer) have been held for less than 1 year (6 months for taxable years beginning before 1977; 9 months for taxable years beginning in 1977) and the remaining half for more than 1 year (6 months for taxable years beginning before 1977; 9 months for taxable years beginning in 1977), half the excess of the amount of the liability over the total of the adjusted basis of the property transferred pursuant to the exchange shall be treated as short-term capital gain, and the remaining half shall be treated as long-term capital gain.

Example (2). If half of the assets (ascertained by reference to their fair market value at the time of the transfer) transferred are capital assets and half are assets other than capital assets, then half of the excess of the amount of the liability over the total of the adjusted basis of the property transferred pursuant to the exchange shall be treated as capital gain, and the remaining half shall be treated as gain from the sale or exchange of assets other than capital assets. [Reg. § 1.357-2.]

☐ [*T.D. 6152, 12-2-55. Amended by T.D. 6528, 1-18-61 and by T.D. 7728, 10-31-80.*]

[Reg. § 1.358-1]

§ 1.358-1. Basis to distributees.—(a) In the case of an exchange to which section 354 or 355 applies in which, under the law applicable to the year in which the exchange is made, only nonrecognition property is received, immediately after the transaction, the sum of the basis of all of the stock and securities received in the transaction shall be the same as the basis of all the stock and securities in such corporation surrendered in the transaction, allocated in the manner described in § 1.358-2. In the case of a distribution to which section 355 applies in which, under the law applicable to the year in which the distribution is made, only nonrecognition property is received, immediately after the transaction, the sum of the basis of all of the stock and securities with respect to which the distribution is made plus the basis of all stock and securities received in the distribution with respect to such stock and securities shall be the same as the basis of the stock and securities with respect to which the distribution is made immediately before the transaction, allocated in the manner described in § 1.358-2. In the case of an exchange to which section 351 or 361 applies in which, under the law applicable to the year in which the exchange was made, only nonrecognition property is received, the basis of all the stock and securities received in the exchange shall be the same as the basis of all property exchanged therefor. If in an exchange or distribution to which section 351, 356, or 361 applies both nonrecognition property and "other property" are received, the basis of all the property except "other property" held after the transaction shall be determined as described in the preceding three sentences decreased by the sum of the money and the fair market value of the "other property" (as of the date of the transaction) and increased by the sum of the amount treated as a dividend (if any) and the amount of the gain recognized on the exchange, but the term gain as here used does not include any portion of the recognized gain that was treated as a dividend. In any case in which a taxpayer transfers property with respect to which loss is recognized, such loss shall be reflected in determining the basis of the property received in the exchange. The basis of the "other property" is its fair market value as of the date of the transaction. See § 1.460-4(k)(3)(iv)(A) for rules relating to stock basis adjustments required where a contract accounted for using a long-term contract method of accounting is transferred in a transaction described in section 351 or a reorganization described in section 368(a)(1)(D) with respect to which the requirements of section 355 (or so much of section 356 as relates to section 355) are met.

(b) The application of paragraph (a) of this section may be illustrated by the following example:

Example. A purchased a share of stock in Corporation X in 1935 for $150. Since that date A has received distributions out of other than earnings and profits (as defined in section 316) totaling $60, so that A's adjusted basis for the stock is $90. In a transaction qualifying under section 356, A exchanged this share for one share in Corporation Y, worth $100, cash in the amount of $10, and other property with a fair market value of $30. The exchange had the effect of the distribution of a dividend. A's ratable share of the earnings and profits of Corporation X accumulated after February 28, 1913, was $5. A realized a gain of $50 on the exchange, but the amount recognized is limited to $40, the sum of the cash received and the fair market value of the other property. Of the gain recognized, $5 is taxable as a dividend, and $35 is taxable as a gain from the exchange of property. The basis to A of the one share of stock of Corporation Y is $90, that is, the adjusted basis of the one share of stock of Corporation X ($90), decreased by the sum of the cash received ($10) and the fair market value of the other property received ($30) and increased by the sum of the amount treated as a dividend ($5) and the amount treated as a gain from the exchange of property ($35). The basis of the other property received is $30.

(c) This section applies to exchanges and distributions of stock and securities occurring on or after January 23, 2006. [Reg. § 1.358-1.]

☐ [*T.D. 6152, 12-2-55. Amended by T.D. 6533, 1-18-61; T.D. 7616, 5-7-79; T.D. 8995, 5-14-2002 and T.D. 9244, 1-23-2006 (corrected 4-12-2006 and 10-25-2006).*]

[Reg. § 1.358-2]

§ 1.358-2. Allocation of basis among nonrecognition property.—(a) *Allocation of basis in exchanges or distributions to which section 354, 355, or 356 applies.*—(1) As used in this paragraph the term *stock* means stock which is not "other property" under section 356. The term *securities* means securities (including, where appropriate, fractional parts of securities) which are not "other property" under section 356. Stock, or securities, as the case may be, which differ either because they are in different corporations or because the rights attributable to them differ (although they are in the same corporation) are considered different classes of stock or securities, as the case may be, for purposes of this section.

(2)(i) If a shareholder or security holder surrenders a share of stock or a security in an exchange under the terms of section 354, 355, or 356, the basis of each share of stock or security received in the exchange shall be the same as the basis of the share or shares of stock or security or securities (or allocable portions thereof) exchanged therefor (as adjusted under § 1.358-1). If more than one share of stock or security is received in exchange for one share of stock or one security, the basis of the share of stock or security surrendered shall be allocated to the shares of stock or securities received in the exchange in proportion to the fair market value of the shares of stock or securities received. If one share of stock or security is received in exchange for more than one share of stock or security or if a fraction of a share of stock or security is received, then the basis of the shares of stock or securities surrendered must be allocated to the shares of stock or securities (or allocable portions thereof) received in a manner that reflects, to the greatest extent possible, that a share of stock or security received is received in respect of shares of stock or securities that were acquired on the same date and at the same price. To the extent it is not possible to allocate basis in this manner, the basis of the shares of stock or securities surrendered must be allocated to the shares of stock or securities (or allocable portions thereof) received in a manner that minimizes the disparity in the holding periods of the surrendered shares of stock or securities whose basis is allocated to any particular share of stock or security received.

(ii) If a shareholder or security holder surrenders a share of stock or a security in an exchange under the terms of section 354, 355, or 356, and receives shares of stock or securities of more than one class, or receives "other property" or money in addition to shares of stock or securities, then, to the extent the terms of the exchange specify that shares of stock or securities of a particular class or "other property" or money is received in exchange for a particular share of stock or security or a particular class of stock or securities, for purposes of applying the rules of this section, such terms shall control provided such terms are economically reasonable. To the extent the terms of the exchange do not specify that shares of stock or securities of a particular class or "other property" or money is received in exchange for a particular share of stock or security or a particular class of stock or securities, then, for purposes of applying the rules of paragraph (a)(2)(i) of this section, a pro rata portion of the shares of stock and securities of each class received and a pro rata portion of the "other property" and money received shall be treated as received in exchange for each share of stock and security surrendered, based on the fair market value of the stock and securities surrendered.

(iii)(A) For purposes of this section, if a shareholder or security holder surrenders a share of stock or a security in a transaction under the terms of section 354 (or so much of section 356 as relates to section 354) in which the shareholder or security holder receives no property or property (including property permitted by section 354 to be received without the recognition of gain or "other property" or money) with a fair market value less than that of the stock or securities surrendered in the transaction:

(1) Such shareholder or security holder shall be treated as receiving the stock, securities, other property, and money actually received by the shareholder or security holder in the transaction and an amount of stock of the issuing corporation (as defined in § 1.368-1(b)) that has a value equal to the excess of the value of the stock or securities the shareholder or security holder surrendered in the transaction over the value of the stock, securities, other property, and money the shareholder or security holder actually received in the transaction. If the shareholder owns only one class of stock of the issuing corporation the receipt of which would be consistent with the economic rights associated with each class of stock of the issuing corporation, the stock deemed received by the shareholder pursuant to the previous sentence shall be stock of such class. If the shareholder owns multiple classes of stock of the issuing corporation the receipt of which would be consistent with the economic rights associated with each class of stock of the issuing corporation, the stock

deemed received by the shareholder shall be stock of each such class owned by the shareholder immediately prior to the transaction, in proportion to the value of the stock of each such class owned by the shareholder at that time. The basis of each share of stock or security of the issuing corporation deemed received and actually received shall be determined under the rules of this section. If and to the extent necessary to reflect the actual ownership of the issuing corporation immediately after the exchange to which section 354 (or so much of section 356 as relates to section 354) applies, an appropriate amount of the stock of the issuing corporation treated as issued to the shareholder or security holder in the exchange is deemed further transferred in accordance with § 1.368-2(l) to reflect the actual ownership of the issuing corporation. Paragraph (a)(2)(iii)(A)(2) of this section is only applied to any shareholder of the issuing corporation after all of the deemed transfers pursuant to § 1.368-2(l) are completed. The transferred shares' basis shall be adjusted for all deemed transfers required by § 1.368-2(l).

(2) A direct shareholder of the issuing corporation that receives the shares deemed issued as part of the transaction, as described in paragraph (a)(2)(iii)(A)(1) of this section, shall then be treated as surrendering all of its shares of stock and securities in the issuing corporation, including those shares of stock or securities held immediately prior to the transaction, those shares of stock or securities actually received in the transaction, and those shares of stock deemed received as described in paragraph (a)(2)(iii)(A)(1) of this section, in a reorganization under section 368(a)(1)(E) in exchange for the shares of stock and securities of the issuing corporation that the shareholder or security holder actually holds immediately after the transaction. The basis of each share of stock and security deemed received in the reorganization under section 368(a)(1)(E) shall be determined under the rules of this section.

(B) For purposes of this section, if an actual shareholder of the issuing corporation is deemed to receive a nominal share of stock of the issuing corporation as provided in § 1.368-2(l), then that shareholder must, after allocating and adjusting the basis of the nominal share in accordance with the rules of this section and § 1.358-1, designate the share of stock of the issuing corporation that it owns to which the basis, if any, of the nominal share will attach. If the shareholder does not actually own any shares of stock in the issuing corporation immediately after the exchange to which section 354 (or so much of section 356 as relates to section 354) applies, the nominal share of stock of the issuing corporation received by the shareholder in the exchange is deemed further transferred in accordance with § 1.368-2(l) without applying the designation rule set forth in the first sentence of this paragraph until it is transferred to a person that actually owns stock in the issuing corporation. The transferred share's basis shall be adjusted for all deemed transfers required by § 1.368-2(l).

(iv) If a shareholder or security holder receives one or more shares of stock or one or more securities in a distribution under the terms of section 355 (or so much of section 356 as relates to section 355), the basis of each share of stock or security of the distributing corporation (as defined in § 1.355-1(b)), as adjusted under § 1.358-1, shall be allocated between the share of stock or security of the distributing corporation with respect to which the distribution is made and the share or shares of stock or security or securities (or allocable portions thereof) received with respect to the share of stock or security of the distributing corporation in proportion to their fair market values. If one share of stock or security is received with respect to more than one share of stock or security or if a fraction of a share of stock or security is received, then the basis of each share of stock or security of the distributing corporation must be allocated to the shares of stock or securities (or allocable portions thereof) received in a manner that reflects that, to the greatest extent possible, a share of stock or security received is received with respect to shares of stock or securities acquired on the same date and at the same price. To the extent it is not possible to allocate basis in this manner, the basis of each share of stock or security of the distributing corporation must be allocated to the shares of stock or securities (or allocable portions thereof) received in a manner that minimizes the disparity in the holding periods of the shares of stock or securities with respect to which such shares of stock or securities are received.

(v) If a shareholder or security holder receives shares of stock or securities of more than one class, or receives "other property" or money in addition to stock or securities in a distribution under the terms of section 355 (or so much of section 356 as relates to section 355), then, to the extent the terms of the distribution specify that shares of stock or securities of a particular class or "other property" or money is received with respect to a particular share of stock or security of the distributing corporation or a particular class of stock or securities of the distributing corporation, for purposes of applying the rules of this section, such terms shall control provided that such terms are economically reasonable. To the extent the terms of the distribution do not specify that shares of stock or securities of a particular class or "other property" or money is received with respect

to a particular share of stock or security of the distributing corporation or a particular class of stock or securities of the distributing corporation, then, for purposes of applying the rules of this section, a pro rata portion of the shares of stock and securities of each class received and a pro rata portion of the "other property" and money received shall be treated as received with respect to each share of stock and security of the distributing corporation with respect to which the distribution is made, based on the fair market value of each such share of stock or security.

(vi) If a share of stock or a security is received in exchange for, or with respect to, more than one share of stock or security and such shares or securities were acquired on different dates or at different prices, the share of stock or security received shall be divided into segments based on the relative fair market values of the shares of stock or securities surrendered in exchange for such share or security or the relative fair market values of the shares of stock or securities with respect to which the share of stock or security is received in a distribution under the terms of section 355 (or so much of section 356 as relates to section 355)). Each segment shall have a basis determined under the rules of paragraph (a)(2) of this section and a corresponding holding period.

(vii) If a shareholder or security holder that purchased or acquired shares of stock or securities in a corporation on different dates or at different prices exchanges such shares of stock or securities under the terms of section 354, 355, or 356, or receives a distribution of shares of stock or securities under the terms of section 355 (or so much of section 356 as relates to section 355), and the shareholder or security holder is not able to identify which particular share of stock or security (or allocable portion of a share of stock or security) is received (or deemed received) in exchange for, or with respect to, a particular share of stock or security, the shareholder or security holder may designate which share of stock or security is received in exchange for, or with respect to, a particular share of stock or security, provided that such designation is consistent with the terms of the exchange or distribution (or an exchange deemed to have occurred pursuant to paragraph (a)(2)(iii) of this section), and the other rules of this section. In the case of an exchange under the terms of section 354 or 356 (including a deemed exchange as a result of the application of paragraph (a)(2)(iii) of this section), the designation must be made on or before the first date on which the basis of a share of stock or a security received (or deemed received in the reorganization under section 368(a)(1)(E) in the case of a transaction to which paragraph (a)(2)(iii) of this section applies) is relevant. In the case of an exchange or distribution under the terms of section 355 (or so much of section 356 as relates to section 355), the designation must be made on or before the first date on which the basis of a share of stock or a security of the distributing corporation or the controlled corporation (as defined in § 1.355-1(b)) is relevant. The basis of the shares or securities received in an exchange under the terms of section 354 or section 356, for example, is relevant when such shares or securities are sold or otherwise transferred. The designation will be binding for purposes of determining the Federal tax consequences of any sale or transfer of, or distribution with respect to, the shares or securities received. If the shareholder fails to make a designation in a case in which the shareholder is not able to identify which share of stock is received in exchange for, or with respect to, a particular share of stock, then the shareholder will not be able to identify which shares are sold or transferred for purposes of determining the basis of property sold or transferred under section 1012 and § 1.1012-1(c) and, instead, will be treated as selling or transferring the share received in respect of the earliest share purchased or acquired.

(viii) This paragraph (a)(2) shall not apply to determine the basis of a share of stock or security received by a shareholder or security holder in an exchange described in both section 351 and either section 354 or 356, if, in connection with the exchange—

(A) The shareholder or security holder exchanges property for stock or securities in an exchange to which neither section 354 nor section 356 applies;

(B) The shareholder or security holder exchanges property for stock or securities in a transaction for which an election to apply section 362(e)(2)(C) is in effect; or

(C) Liabilities of the shareholder or security holder are assumed.

(ix) This paragraph (a)(2) shall apply to determine the basis of a share of stock or security received by a shareholder or security holder in an exchange described in both section 1036 and section 354 or section 356.

(b) *Allocation of basis in exchanges to which section 351 or 361 applies.*—(1) As used in this paragraph (b), the term *stock* refers only to stock which is not "other property" under section 351 or 361 and the term *securities* refers only to securities which are not "other property" under section 351 or 361.

(2) If in an exchange to which section 351 or 361 applies property is transferred to a corporation and the transferor receives stock

or securities of more than one class or receives both stock and securities, then the basis of the property transferred (as adjusted under §1.358-1) shall be allocated among all of the stock and securities received in proportion to the fair market values of the stock of each class and the securities of each class.

(c) *Examples.*—The application of paragraphs (a) and (b) of this section is illustrated by the following examples:

Example 1. (i) *Facts.* J, an individual, acquired 20 shares of Corporation X stock on Date 1 for $3 each and 10 shares of Corporation X stock on Date 2 for $6 each. On Date 3, Corporation Y acquires the assets of Corporation X in a reorganization under section 368(a)(1)(A). Pursuant to the terms of the plan of reorganization, J receives 2 shares of Corporation Y stock in exchange for each share of Corporation X stock. Therefore, J receives 60 shares of Corporation Y stock. Pursuant to section 354, J recognizes no gain or loss on the exchange. J is not able to identify which shares of Corporation Y stock are received in exchange for each share of Corporation X stock.

(ii) *Analysis.* Under paragraph (a)(2)(i) of this section, J has 40 shares of Corporation Y stock each of which has a basis of $1.50 and is treated as having been acquired on Date 1 and 20 shares of Corporation Y stock each of which has a basis of $3 and is treated as having been acquired on Date 2. Under paragraph (a)(2)(vii) of this section, on or before the date on which the basis of a share of Corporation Y stock received becomes relevant, J may designate which of the shares of Corporation Y stock have a basis of $1.50 and which have a basis of $3.

Example 2. (i) *Facts.* The facts are the same as in *Example 1*, except that instead of receiving 2 shares of Corporation Y stock in exchange for each share of Corporation X stock, J receives 11/2 shares of Corporation Y stock in exchange for each share of Corporation X stock. Therefore, J receives 45 shares of Corporation Y stock. Again, J is not able to identify which shares (or portions of shares) of Corporation Y stock are received in exchange for each share of Corporation X stock.

(ii) *Analysis.* Under paragraph (a)(2)(i) of this section, J has 30 shares of Corporation Y stock each of which has a basis of $2 and is treated as having been acquired on Date 1 and 15 shares of Corporation Y stock each of which has a basis of $4 and is treated as having been acquired on Date 2. Under paragraph (a)(2)(vii) of this section, on or before the date on which the basis of a share of Corporation Y stock received becomes relevant, J may designate which of the shares of Corporation Y stock received have a basis of $2 and which have a basis of $4.

Example 3. (i) *Facts.* J, an individual, acquired 10 shares of Class A stock of Corporation X on Date 1 for $3 each, 10 shares of Class A stock of Corporation X on Date 2 for $9 each, and 10 shares of Class B stock of Corporation X on Date 3 for $3 each. On Date 4, J surrenders all of J's shares of Class A stock in exchange for 20 shares of new Class C stock and 20 shares of new Class D stock in a reorganization under section 368(a)(1)(E). Pursuant to section 354, J recognizes no gain or loss on the exchange. On the date of the exchange, the fair market value of each share of Class A stock is $6, the fair market value of each share of Class C stock is $2, and the fair market value of each share of Class D stock is $4. The terms of the exchange do not specify that shares of Class C stock or shares of Class D stock of Corporation X are received in exchange for particular shares of Class A stock of Corporation X.

(ii) *Analysis.* Under paragraph (a)(2)(ii) of this section, because the terms of the exchange do not specify that shares of Class C stock or shares of Class D stock of Corporation X are received in exchange for particular shares of Class A stock of Corporation X, a pro rata portion of the shares of Class C stock and shares of Class D stock received will be treated as received in exchange for each share of Class A stock based on the fair market value of the surrendered shares of Class A stock. Therefore, J is treated as receiving one share of Class C stock and one share of Class D stock in exchange for each share of Class A stock. Under paragraph (a)(2)(i) of this section, J has 10 shares of Class C stock, each of which has a basis of $1 and is treated as having been acquired on Date 1 and 10 shares of Class C stock, each of which has a basis of $3 and is treated as having been acquired on Date 2. In addition, J has 10 shares of Class D stock, each of which has a basis of $2 and is treated as having been acquired on Date 1 and 10 shares of Class D stock, each of which has a basis of $6 and is treated as having been acquired on Date 2. J's basis in each share of Class B stock remains $3. Under paragraph (a)(2)(vii) of this section, on or before the date on which the basis of a share of Class C stock or Class D stock received becomes relevant, J may designate which of the shares of Class C stock have a basis of $1 and which have a basis of $3, and which of the shares of Class D stock have a basis of $2 and which *have a basis of $6.*

Example 4. (i) *Facts.* J, an individual, acquired 10 shares of Class A stock of Corporation X on Date 1 for $2 each, 10 shares of Class A stock of Corporation X on Date 2 for $4 each, and 20 shares of Class B stock of Corporation X on Date 3 for $6 each. On Date 4, Corporation

Y acquires the assets of Corporation X in a reorganization under section 368(a)(1)(A). Pursuant to the terms of the plan of reorganization, J surrenders all of J's shares of Corporation X stock for 40 shares of Corporation Y stock and $200 of cash. On the date of the exchange, the fair market value of each share of Class A stock of Corporation X is $10, the fair market value of each share of Class B stock of Corporation X is $10, and the fair market value of each share of Corporation Y stock is $5. The terms of the exchange do not specify that shares of Corporation Y stock or cash are received in exchange for particular shares of Class A stock or Class B stock of Corporation X.

(ii) *Analysis.* Under paragraph (a)(2)(ii) of this section and under §1.356-1(b), because the terms of the exchange do not specify that shares of Corporation Y stock or cash are received in exchange for particular shares of Class A stock or Class B stock of Corporation X, a pro rata portion of the shares of Corporation Y stock and cash received will be treated as received in exchange for each share of Class A stock and Class B stock of Corporation X surrendered based on the fair market value of such stock. Therefore, J is treated as receiving one share of Corporation Y stock and $5 of cash in exchange for each share of Class A stock of Corporation X and one share of Corporation Y stock and $5 of cash in exchange for each share of Class B stock of Corporation X. J realizes a gain of $140 on the exchange of shares of Class A stock of Corporation X, $100 of which is recognized under §1.356-1(a). J realizes a gain of $80 on the exchange of Class B stock of Corporation X, all of which is recognized under §1.356-1(a). Under paragraph (a)(2)(i) of this section, J has 10 shares of Corporation Y stock, each of which has a basis of $2 and is treated as having been acquired on Date 1, 10 shares of Corporation Y stock, each of which has a basis of $4 and is treated as having been acquired on Date 2, and 20 shares of Corporation Y stock, each of which has a basis of $5 and is treated as having been acquired on Date 3. Under paragraph (a)(2)(vii) of this section, on or before the date on which the basis of a share of Corporation Y stock received becomes relevant, J may designate which of the shares of Corporation Y stock received have a basis of $2, which have a basis of $4, and which have a basis of $5.

Example 5. (i) *Facts.* The facts are the same as in *Example 4*, except that the terms of the plan of reorganization specify that J receives 40 shares of stock of Corporation Y in exchange for J's shares of Class A stock of Corporation X and $200 of cash in exchange for J's shares of Class B stock of Corporation X.

(ii) *Analysis.* Under paragraph (a)(2)(ii) of this section and under §1.356-1(b), because the terms of the exchange specify that J receives 40 shares of stock of Corporation Y in exchange for J's shares of Class A stock of Corporation X and $200 of cash in exchange for J's shares of Class B stock of Corporation X and such terms are economically reasonable, such terms control. J realizes a gain of $140 on the exchange of shares of Class A stock of Corporation X, none of which is recognized under §1.356-1(a). J realizes a gain of $80 on the exchange of shares of Class B stock of Corporation X, all of which is recognized under §1.356-1(a). Under paragraph (a)(2)(i) of this section, J has 20 shares of Corporation Y stock, each of which has a basis of $1 and is treated as having been acquired on Date 1, and 20 shares of Corporation Y stock, each of which has a basis of $2 and is treated as having been acquired on Date 2. Under paragraph (a)(2)(vii) of this section, on or before the date on which the basis of a share of Corporation Y stock received becomes relevant, J may designate which of the shares of Corporation Y stock received have a basis of $1 and which have a basis of $2.

Example 6. (i) *Facts.* J, an individual, acquired 10 shares of stock of Corporation X on Date 1 for $2 each, and a security issued by Corporation X to J on Date 2 with a principal amount of $100 and a basis of $100. On Date 3, Corporation Y acquires the assets of Corporation X in a reorganization under section 368(a)(1)(A). Pursuant to the terms of the plan of reorganization, J surrenders all of J's shares of Corporation X stock in exchange for 10 shares of Corporation Y stock and surrenders J's Corporation X security in exchange for a Corporation Y security. On the date of the exchange, the fair market value of each share of stock of Corporation X is $10, the fair market value of J's Corporation X security is $100, the fair market value of each share of Corporation Y stock is $10, and the fair market value and principal amount of the Corporation Y security received by J is $100.

(ii) *Analysis.* Under paragraph (a)(2)(ii) of this section and under §1.354-1(a), because the terms of the exchange specify that J receives 10 shares of stock of Corporation Y in exchange for J's shares of Class A stock of Corporation X and a Corporation Y security in exchange for its Corporation X security and such terms are economically reasonable, such terms control. Pursuant to section 354, J recognizes no gain on either exchange. Under paragraph (a)(2)(i) of this section, J has 10 shares of Corporation Y stock, each of which has a basis of $2 and is treated as having been acquired on Date 1, and a security that has a basis of $100 and is treated as having been acquired on Date 2.

Example 7. (i) *Facts.* J, an individual, acquired 10 shares of Corporation X stock on Date 1 for $2 each and 10 shares of Corporation X stock on Date 2 for $5 each. On Date 3, Corporation Y acquires the stock of Corporation X in a reorganization under section 368(a)(1)(B). Pursuant to the terms of the plan of reorganization, J receives one share of Corporation Y stock in exchange for every 2 shares of Corporation X stock. Pursuant to section 354, J recognizes no gain or loss on the exchange. J is not able to identify which portion of each share of Corporation Y stock is received in exchange for each share of Corporation X stock.

(ii) *Analysis*. Under paragraph (a)(2)(i) of this section, J has 5 shares of Corporation Y stock each of which has a basis of $4 and is treated as having been acquired on Date 1 and 5 shares of Corporation Y stock each of which has a basis of $10 and is treated as having been acquired on Date 2. Under paragraph (a)(2)(vii) of this section, on or before the date on which the basis of a share of Corporation Y stock received becomes relevant, J may designate which of the shares of Corporation Y stock received have a basis of $4 and which have a basis of $10.

Example 8. (i) *Facts*. The facts are the same as in *Example 7*, except that, in addition to transferring the stock of Corporation X to Corporation Y, J transfers land to Corporation Y. In addition, after the transaction, J owns stock of Corporation Y satisfying the requirements of section 368(c). J's transfer of the Corporation X stock to Corporation Y is an exchange described in sections 351 and 354. J's transfer of land to Corporation Y is an exchange described in section 351.

(ii) *Analysis*. Under paragraph (a)(2)(viii) of this section, because neither section 354 nor section 356 applies to the transfer of land to Corporation Y, the rules of paragraph (a)(2) of this section do not apply to determine J's basis in the Corporation Y stock received in the transaction.

Example 9. (i) *Facts*. J, an individual, acquired 10 shares of Corporation X stock on Date 1 for $3 each and 10 shares of Corporation X stock on Date 2 for $6 each. On Date 3, Corporation Z, a newly formed, wholly owned subsidiary of Corporation Y, merges with and into Corporation X with Corporation X surviving. As part of the plan of merger, J receives one share of Corporation Y stock in exchange for each share of Corporation X stock. In connection with the transaction, Corporation Y assumes a liability of J. In addition, after the transaction, J owns stock of Corporation Y satisfying the requirements of section 368(c). J's transfer of the Corporation X stock to Corporation Y is an exchange described in sections 351 and 354.

(ii) *Analysis*. Under paragraph (a)(2)(viii) of this section, because, in connection with the transfer of the Corporation X stock to Corporation Y, Corporation Y assumed a liability of J, the rules of paragraph (a)(2) of this section do not apply to determine J's basis in the Corporation Y stock received in the transaction.

Example 10. (i) *Facts*. Each of Corporation X and Corporation Y has a single class of stock outstanding, all of which is owned by J, an individual. J acquired 100 shares of Corporation X stock on Date 1 for $1 each and 100 shares of Corporation Y stock on Date 2 for $2 each. On Date 3, Corporation Y acquires the assets of Corporation X in a reorganization under section 368(a)(1)(D). Pursuant to the terms of the plan of reorganization, J surrenders J's 100 shares of Corporation X stock but does not receive any additional Corporation Y stock. Immediately before the effective time of the reorganization, the fair market value of each share of Corporation X stock and each share of Corporation Y stock is $1. Pursuant to section 354, J recognizes no gain or loss.

(ii) *Analysis*. Under paragraph (a)(2)(iii) of this section, J is deemed to have received shares of Corporation Y stock with an aggregate fair market value of $100 in exchange for J's Corporation X shares. Given the number of outstanding shares of stock of Corporation Y and their value immediately before the effective time of the reorganization, J is deemed to have received 100 shares of stock of Corporation Y in the reorganization. Under paragraph (a)(2)(i) of this section, each of those shares has a basis of $1 and is treated as having been acquired on Date 1. Then, the stock of Corporation Y is deemed to be recapitalized in a reorganization under section 368(a)(1)(E) in which J receives 100 shares of Corporation Y stock in exchange for those shares of Corporation Y stock that J held immediately prior to the reorganization and those shares J is deemed to have received in the reorganization. Under paragraph (a)(2)(i), immediately after the reorganization, J holds 50 shares of Corporation Y stock each of which has a basis of $2 and is treated as having been acquired on Date 1 and 50 shares of *Corporation Y stock each of which has a basis of $4 and is treated as* having been acquired on Date 2. Under paragraph (a)(2)(vii) of this section, on or before the date on which the basis of any share of J's Corporation Y stock becomes relevant, J may designate which of the shares of Corporation Y have a basis of $2 and which have a basis of $4.

Example 11. (i) *Facts*. Corporation X has a single class of stock outstanding, all of which is owned by J, an individual. J acquired 100 shares of Corporation X stock on Date 1 for $1 each. Corporation Y has two classes of stock outstanding, common stock and nonvoting preferred stock. On Date 2, J acquired 100 shares of Corporation Y

common stock for $2 each and 100 shares of Corporation Y preferred stock for $4 each. On Date 3, Corporation Y acquires the assets of Corporation X in a reorganization under section 368(a)(1)(D). Pursuant to the terms of the plan of reorganization, J surrenders J's 100 shares of Corporation X stock but does not receive any additional Corporation Y stock. Immediately before the effective time of the reorganization, the fair market value of each share of Corporation X stock is $10, the fair market value of each share of Corporation Y common stock is $10, and the fair market value of each share of Corporation Y preferred stock is $20. Pursuant to section 354, J recognizes no gain or loss.

(ii) *Analysis*. Under paragraph (a)(2)(iii) of this section, J is deemed to have received shares of Corporation Y stock with an aggregate fair market value of $1,000 in exchange for J's Corporation X shares. Consistent with the economics of the transaction and the rights associated with each class of stock of Corporation Y owned by J, J is deemed to receive additional shares of Corporation Y common stock. Because the value of the common stock indicates that the liquidation preference associated with the Corporation Y preferred stock could be satisfied even if the reorganization did not occur, it is not appropriate to deem the issuance of additional Corporation Y preferred stock. Given the number of outstanding shares of common stock of Corporation Y and their value immediately before the effective time of the reorganization, J is deemed to have received 100 shares of common stock of Corporation Y in the reorganization. Under paragraph (a)(2)(i) of this section, each of those shares has a basis of $1 and is treated as having been acquired on Date 1. Then, the common stock of Corporation Y is deemed to be recapitalized in a reorganization under section 368(a)(1)(E) in which J receives 100 shares of Corporation Y common stock in exchange for those shares of Corporation Y common stock that J held immediately prior to the reorganization and those shares of Corporation Y common stock that J is deemed to have received in the reorganization. Under paragraph (a)(2)(i), immediately after the reorganization, J holds 50 shares of Corporation Y common stock, each of which has a basis of $2 and is treated as having been acquired on Date 1, and 50 shares of Corporation Y common stock, each of which has a basis of $4 and is treated as having been acquired on Date 2. Under paragraph (a)(2)(vii) of this section, on or before the date on which the basis of any share of J's Corporation Y common stock becomes relevant, J may designate which of those shares have a basis of $2 and which have a basis of $4.

Example 12. (i) *Facts*. J, an individual, acquired 5 shares of Corporation X stock on Date 1 for $4 each and 5 shares of Corporation X stock on Date 2 for $8 each. Corporation X owns all of the outstanding stock of Corporation Y. The fair market value of the stock of Corporation X is $1800. The fair market value of the stock of Corporation Y is $900. In a distribution to which section 355 applies, Corporation X distributes all of the stock of Corporation Y pro rata to its shareholders. No stock of Corporation X is surrendered in connection with the distribution. In the distribution, J receives 2 shares of Corporation Y stock with respect to each share of Corporation X stock. Pursuant to section 355, J recognizes no gain or loss on the receipt of the shares of Corporation Y stock. J is not able to identify which share of Corporation Y stock is received in respect of each share of Corporation X stock.

(ii) *Analysis*. Under paragraph (a)(2)(iv) of this section, because J receives 2 shares of Corporation Y stock with respect to each share of Corporation X stock, the basis of each share of Corporation X stock is allocated between such share of Corporation X stock and two shares of Corporation Y stock in proportion to the fair market value of those shares. Therefore, each of the 5 shares of Corporation X stock acquired on Date 1 will have a basis of $2 and each of the 10 shares of Corporation Y stock received with respect to those shares will have a basis of $1. In addition, each of the 5 shares of Corporation X stock acquired on Date 2 will have a basis of $4 and each of the 10 shares of Corporation Y stock received with respect to those shares will have a basis of $2. Under paragraph (a)(2)(vii) of this section, on or before the date on which the basis of a share of Corporation Y stock received becomes relevant, J may designate which of the shares of Corporation Y stock have a basis of $1 and which have a basis of $2.

Example 13. (i) *Facts*. J, an individual, acquired 20 shares of Corporation X stock on Date 1 for $2 each and 20 shares of Corporation X stock on Date 2 for $4 each. Corporation X has 80 shares of stock outstanding. Corporation X owns 40 shares of stock of Corporation Y, which represents all of the outstanding stock of Corporation Y. The fair market value of the stock of Corporation X is $80. The fair market value of the stock of Corporation Y is $40. Corporation X distributes all of the stock of Corporation Y in a transaction to which section 355 applies. In the transaction, J surrenders 20 shares of stock of Corporation X in exchange for 20 shares of stock of Corporation Y. J retains 20 shares of Corporation X stock. Pursuant to section 355, J recognizes no gain or loss on the receipt of the shares of Corporation Y stock. J is not able to identify which shares of Corporation X stock are surrendered. In addition, J is not able to identify which shares of Corporation Y stock are received in exchange for each surrendered share of Corporation X stock.

(ii) *Analysis.* Under paragraph (a)(2)(i) of this section, J has 20 shares of Corporation Y stock each of which is treated as received in exchange for one share of Corporation X stock. The basis of the 20 shares of Corporation X stock that are retained by J will remain unchanged. Under paragraph (a)(2)(vii) of this section, on or before the date on which the basis of a share of Corporation X or Corporation Y stock becomes relevant, J may designate which shares of Corporation X stock J surrendered in the exchange and which share of the Corporation Y stock received is received for each share of Corporation X stock surrendered. Therefore, it is possible that a share of Corporation Y stock would have a basis of $2 and be treated as having been acquired on Date 1, or would have a basis of $4 and be treated as having been acquired on Date 2.

Example 14. (i) Facts. J, an individual, acquired 10 shares of Corporation X stock on Date 1 for $3 each, 10 shares of Corporation X stock on Date 2 for $18 each, 10 shares of Corporation X stock on Date 3 for $6 each, and 10 shares of Corporation X stock on Date 4 for $9 each. On Date 5, Corporation Y acquires the assets of Corporation X in a reorganization under section 368(a)(1)(A). Pursuant to the terms of the plan of reorganization, J receives a 3/4 share of Corporation Y stock in exchange for each share of Corporation X stock. Therefore, J receives 30 shares of Corporation X stock. Pursuant to section 354, J recognizes no gain or loss on the exchange. J is not able to identify which shares of Corporation Y stock are received in exchange for each share (or portions of shares) of Corporation X stock.

(ii) *Analysis.* Under paragraph (a)(2)(i) of this section, J has 7 shares of Corporation Y stock each of which has a basis of $4 and is treated as having been acquired on Date 1, 7 shares of Corporation Y stock each of which has a basis of $24 and is treated as having been acquired on Date 2, 7 shares of Corporation Y stock each of which has a basis of $8 and is treated as having been acquired on Date 3, and 7 shares of Corporation Y stock each of which has a basis of $12 and is treated as having been acquired on Date 4. In addition, J has two shares of Corporation Y stock, each of which is divided into two equal segments under paragraph (a)(2)(vi) of this section. The first of those two shares has one segment with a basis of $2 that is treated as having been acquired on Date 1 and a second segment with a basis of $12 that is treated as having been acquired on Date 2. The second of those two shares has one segment with a basis of $4 that is treated as having been acquired on Date 3 and a second segment with a basis of $6 that is treated as having been acquired on Date 4. Under paragraph (a)(2)(vii), on or before the date on which a share of Corporation Y stock received becomes relevant, J may designate which of the shares of Corporation Y stock have a basis of $4, which have a basis of $24, which have a basis of $8, which have a basis of $12, and which share has a split basis of $2 and $12, and which share has a split basis of $4 and $6.

Example 15. (i) *Facts.* Each of Corporation X and Corporation Y has a single class of stock outstanding, all of which is owned by J, an individual. J purchased 100 shares of Corporation X stock on Date 1 for $1.50 each, resulting in J having an aggregate basis in the stock of Corporation X of $150. On Date 2, Corporation Y acquires the assets of Corporation X for $100 of cash, their fair market value, in a transaction described in § 1.368-2(l). Pursuant to the terms of the exchange, Corporation X does not receive any Corporation Y stock. Corporation X distributes the $100 of cash to J and retains no assets.

(ii) *Analysis.* Pursuant to § 1.368-2(l), Corporation Y will be deemed to issue a nominal share of Corporation Y stock to Corporation X in addition to the $100 of cash actually exchanged for the Corporation X assets. Corporation X will then be deemed to distribute the nominal share of Corporation Y stock to J in addition to the $100 of cash actually distributed to J. Pursuant to § 1.368-2(l), J, the actual shareholder of Corporation Y, the issuing corporation, is deemed to receive the nominal share of Corporation Y stock described in § 1.368-2(l). J will have a basis of $50 in the nominal share of Corporation Y stock under section 358(a)(1). Therefore, under paragraph (a)(2)(iii)(B) of this section, J must designate a share of Corporation Y stock to which J's basis of $50 in the nominal share of Corporation Y stock will attach.

Example 16. (i) *Facts.* Each of Corporation X and Corporation Y has a single class of stock outstanding, all of which is owned by Corporation P. Corporation T has a single class of stock outstanding, all of which is owned by Corporation X. The corporations do not join in the filing of a consolidated return. Corporation X purchased 100 shares of Corporation T stock on Date 1 for $1.50 each, resulting in Corporation X having an aggregate basis in the stock of Corporation T of $150. On Date 2, Corporation Y acquires the assets of Corporation T for $100 of cash, their fair market value, in a transaction described in § 1.368-2(l). Pursuant to the terms of the exchange, Corporation T does not receive any Corporation Y stock. Corporation T distributes the $100 of cash to Corporation X and retains no assets.

(ii) *Analysis.* Pursuant to § 1.368-2(l), Corporation Y will be deemed to issue a nominal share of Corporation Y stock to Corporation T in addition to the $100 of cash actually exchanged for the Corporation T assets. Corporation T will be deemed to distribute the nominal share of Corporation Y stock to Corporation X in addition to the $100 of cash actually distributed. Corporation X will have a basis of $50 in the nominal share of Corporation Y stock under section 358(a). However, Corporation X is not an actual shareholder of Corporation Y, the issuing corporation. Therefore, Corporation X cannot designate any share of Corporation Y stock under paragraph (a)(2)(iii)(B) of this section to which the basis of the nominal share of Corporation Y stock will attach and Corporation X will be deemed to distribute the nominal share of Corporation Y stock to Corporation P as required by § 1.368-2(l). Corporation X does not recognize the loss on the deemed distribution of the nominal share to Corporation P under section 311(a). Corporation P's basis in the nominal share it receives is zero, its fair market value, under section 301(d). Under paragraph (a)(2)(iii)(B) of this section, Corporation P must designate a share of Corporation Y stock to which the nominal share's zero basis will attach.

(d) *Effective/applicability date.*—This section generally applies to exchanges and distributions of stock and securities occurring on or after January 23, 2006. However, paragraph (a)(2)(iii) and Examples 15 and 16 of paragraph (c) of this section apply to exchanges and distributions of stock and securities occurring on or after November 12, 2014. See § 1.358-2T(a)(2)(iii) and § 1.358-2T(c), Examples 15 and 16, as contained in 26 CFR part 1, revised April 1, 2014, for exchanges and distributions of stock and securities occurring on or after November 21, 2011 and before November 12, 2014; see § 1.358-2(a)(2)(iii), as contained in 26 CFR part 1, revised as of April 1, 2011, for exchanges and distributions of stock and securities occurring on or after January 23, 2006 and before November 21, 2011. [Reg. § 1.358-2.]

☐ [T.D. 6152, 12-2-55. *Amended by* T.D. 7616, 5-7-79; T.D. 8648, 12-20-95; T.D. 9244, 1-23-2006 (corrected 4-12-2006 and 10-25-2006); T.D. 9475, 12-17-2009; T.D. 9558, 11-18-2011; T.D. 9633, 8-30-2013 *and* T.D. 9702, 11-10-2014.]

[Reg. § 1.358-3]

§ 1.358-3. Treatment of assumption of liabilities.—(a) For purposes of section 358, where a party to the exchange assumes a liability of a distributee or acquires from him property subject to a liability, the amount of such liability is to be treated as money received by the distributee upon the exchange, whether or not the assumption of liabilities resulted in a recognition of gain or loss to the taxpayer under the law applicable to the year in which the exchange was made.

(b) The application of paragraph (a) of this section may be illustrated by the following examples:

Example (1). A, an individual, owns property with an adjusted basis of $100,000 on which there is a purchase money mortgage of $25,000. On December 1, 1954, A organizes Corporation X to which he transfers the property in exchange for all the stock of Corporation X and the assumption by Corporation X of the mortgage. The capital stock of the Corporation X has a fair market value of $150,000. Under sections 351 and 357, no gain or loss is recognized to A. The basis in A's hands of the stock of Corporation X is $75,000, computed as follows:

Adjusted basis of property transferred	$100,000
Less: Amount of money received (amount of liabilities assumed)	25,000
Basis of Corporation X stock to A	$75,000

Example (2). A, an individual, owns property with an adjusted basis of $25,000 on which there is a mortgage of $50,000. On December 1, 1954, A organizes Corporation X to which he transfers the property in exchange for all the stock of Corporation X and the assumption by Corporation X of the mortgage. The stock of Corporation X has a fair market value of $50,000. Under sections 351 and 357, gain is recognized to A in the amount of $25,000. The basis in A's hands of the stock of Corporation X is zero, computed as follows:

Adjusted basis of property transferred	$25,000
Less: Amount of money received (amount of liabilities)	−50,000
Plus: Amount of gain recognized to taxpayer	$25,000
Basis of Corporation X stock to A	$0

☐ [T.D. 6152, 12-2-55.]

[Reg. §1.358-4]

§1.358-4. Exceptions.—(a) *Plan of reorganization adopted after October 22, 1968.*—In the case of a plan or reorganization adopted after October 22, 1968, section 358 does not apply in determining the basis of property acquired by a corporation in connection with such reorganization by the exchange of its stock or securities (or by the exchange of stock or securities of a corporation which is in control of the acquiring corporation) as the consideration in whole or in part for the transfer of the property to it. See section 362 and the regulations pertaining to that section for rules relating to basis to corporations of property acquired in such cases.

(b) *Plan of reorganization adopted before October 23, 1968.*—In the case of a plan of reorganization adopted before October 23, 1968, section 358 does not apply in determining the basis of property acquired by a corporation in connection with such reorganization by the issuance of stock or securities of such corporation (or by the issuance of stock or securities of another corporation which is in control of such corporation) as the consideration in whole or in part for the transfer of the property to it. The term "issuance of stock or securities" includes any transfer of stock or securities, including stock or securities which were purchased or were acquired as a contribution to capital. See section 362 and the regulations pertaining to that section for rules relating to basis to corporations of property acquired in such cases. [Reg. §1.358-4.]

□ [*T.D. 6152, 12-2-55; Amended by T.D. 7422, 6-25-76.*]

[Reg. §1.358-5]

§1.358-5. Special rules for assumption of liabilities.—(a) *In general.*—Section 358(h)(2)(B) does not apply to an exchange occurring on or after May 9, 2008.

(b) *Effective/Applicability date.*—For exchanges occurring on or after June 24, 2003, and before May 9, 2008, see §1.358-5T as contained in 26 CFR part 1 in effect on April 1, 2007. [Reg. §1.358-5.]

□ [*T.D. 9397, 5-8-2008.*]

[Reg. §1.358-6]

§1.358-6. Stock basis in certain triangular reorganizations.—(a) *Scope.*—This section provides rules for computing the basis of a controlling corporation in the stock of a controlled corporation as the result of certain reorganizations involving the stock of the controlling corporation as described in paragraph (b) of this section. The rules of this section are in addition to rules under other provisions of the Internal Revenue Code and principles of law. See, e.g., section 1001 for the recognition of gain or loss by the controlled corporation on the exchange of property for the assets or stock of a target corporation in a reorganization described in section 368. See also sections 362(e)(1) and 362(e)(2) for further adjustments to basis that may be necessary under either or both of those sections.

(b) *Triangular reorganizations.*—(1) *Nomenclature.*—For purposes of this section—

(i) *P* is a corporation—

(A) That is a party to a reorganization,

(B) That is in control (within the meaning of section 368(c)) of another party to the reorganization, and

(C) Whose stock is transferred pursuant to the reorganization.

(ii) *S* is a corporation—

(A) That is a party to the reorganization, and

(B) That is controlled by *P*.

(iii) *T* is a corporation that is another party to the reorganization.

(2) *Definitions of triangular reorganizations.*—This section applies to the following reorganizations (which are referred to collectively as *triangular reorganizations*):

(i) *Forward triangular merger.*—A forward triangular merger is a statutory merger of *T* and *S*, with *S* surviving, that qualifies as a reorganization under section 368(a)(1)(A) or (G) by reason of the application of section 368(a)(2)(D).

(ii) *Triangular C reorganization.*—A triangular C reorganization is an acquisition by *S* of substantially all of *T*'s assets in exchange for *P* stock in a transaction that qualifies as a reorganization under section 368(a)(1)(C).

(iii) *Reverse triangular merger.*—A reverse triangular merger is a statutory merger of *S* and *T*, with *T* surviving, that qualifies as a reorganization under section 368(a)(1)(A) by reason of the application of section 368(a)(2)(E).

(iv) *Triangular B reorganization.*—A triangular B reorganization is an acquisition by *S* of *T* stock in exchange for *P* stock in a transaction that qualifies as a reorganization under section 368(a)(1)(B).

(v) *Triangular G reorganization.*—A triangular G reorganization is an acquisition by S (other than by statutory merger) of substantially all of T's assets in a title 11 or similar case in exchange for P stock in a transaction that qualifies as a reorganization under section 368(a)(1)(G) by reason of the application of section 368(a)(2)(D).

(c) *General rules.*—Subject to the special rule provided in paragraph (d) of this section, *P*'s basis in the stock of *S* or *T*, as applicable, as a result of a triangular reorganization, is adjusted under the following rules—

(1) *Forward triangular merger or triangular C reorganization.*—(i) *In general.*—In a forward triangular merger or a triangular C reorganization *P*'s basis in its *S* stock is adjusted as if—

(A) *P* acquired the *T* assets acquired by *S* in the reorganization (and *P* assumed any liabilities which *S* assumed or to which the *T* assets acquired by *S* were subject) directly from *T* in a transaction in which *P*'s basis in the *T* assets was determined under section 362(b); and

(B) *P* transferred the *T* assets (and liabilities which *S* assumed or to which the *T* assets acquired by *S* were subject) to *S* in a transaction in which *P*'s basis in *S* stock was determined under section 358.

(ii) *Limitation.*—If, in applying section 358, the amount of *T* liabilities assumed by *S* or to which the *T* assets acquired by *S* are subject equals or exceeds *T*'s aggregate adjusted basis in its assets, the amount of the adjustment under paragraph (c)(1)(i) of this section is zero. *P* recognizes no gain under section 357(c) as a result of a triangular reorganization.

(2) *Reverse triangular merger.*—(i) *In general.*—(A) *Treated as a forward triangular merger.*—Except as otherwise provided in this paragraph (c)(2), *P*'s basis in its *T* stock acquired in a reverse triangular merger equals its basis in its *S* stock immediately before the transaction adjusted as if *T* had merged into *S* in a forward triangular merger to which paragraph (c)(1) of this section applies.

(B) *Allocable share.*—If *P* acquires less than all of the *T* stock in the transaction, the basis adjustment described in paragraph (c)(2)(i)(A) of this section is reduced in proportion to the percentage of *T* stock not acquired in the transaction. The percentage of *T* stock not acquired in the transaction is determined by taking into account the fair market value of all classes of *T* stock.

(C) *Special rule if P owns T stock before the transaction.*—Solely for purposes of paragraphs (c)(2)(i)(A) and (B) of this section, if *P* owns *T* stock before the transaction, *P* may treat that stock as acquired in the transaction or not, without regard to the form of the transaction.

(ii) *Reverse triangular merger that qualifies as a section 351 transfer or section 368(a)(1)(B) reorganization.*—Notwithstanding paragraph (c)(2)(i) of this section, if a reorganization qualifies as both a reverse triangular merger and as a section 351 transfer or as both a reverse triangular merger and a reorganization under section 368(a)(1)(B), *P* can—

(A) Determine the basis in its *T* stock as if paragraph (c)(2)(i) of this section applies; or

(B) Determine the basis in the *T* stock acquired as if *P* acquired such stock from the former *T* shareholders in a transaction in which *P*'s basis in the *T* stock was determined under section 362(b).

(3) *Triangular B reorganization.*—In a triangular B reorganization *P*'s basis in its *S* stock is adjusted as if—

(i) *P* acquired the *T* stock acquired by *S* in the reorganization directly from the *T* shareholders in a transaction in which *P*'s basis in the *T* stock was determined under section 362(b); and

(ii) *P* transferred the *T* stock to *S* in a transaction in which *P*'s basis in its *S* stock was determined under section 358.

(4) *Examples.*—The rules of this paragraph (c) are illustrated by the following examples. For purposes of these examples, P, S, and T are domestic corporations, the property transferred is not importation property within the meaning of §1.362-3(c)(2) or loss duplication property within the meaning of §1.362-4(g)(1), P and S do not file consolidated returns, P owns all of the shares of the only class of S stock, the P stock exchanged in the transaction satisfies the requirements of the applicable triangular reorganization provisions, and the facts set forth the only corporate activity.

Example 1. Forward triangular merger. (a) *Facts.* T has assets with an aggregate basis of $60 and fair market value of $100 and no liabilities. Pursuant to a plan, P forms S with $5 cash (which S retains), and T merges into S. In the merger, the T shareholders receive P stock worth $100 in exchange for their T stock. The transaction is a reorganization to which sections 368(a)(1)(A) and (a)(2)(D) apply.

(b) *Basis adjustment.* Under §1.358-6(c) (1), *P*'s $5 basis in its *S* stock is adjusted as if *P* acquired the *T* assets acquired by *S* in the reorganization directly from *T* in a transaction in which *P*'s basis in the *T* assets was determined under section 362(b). Under section 362(b), *P* would have an aggregate basis of $60 in the *T* assets. *P* is then treated as if it transferred the *T* assets to *S* in a transaction in which *P*'s basis in the *S* stock was determined under section 358. Under section 358, *P*'s $5 basis in its *S* stock would be increased by the $60 basis in the *T* assets deemed transferred. Consequently, *P* has a $65 basis in its *S* stock as a result of the reorganization.

(c) *Use of pre-existing S.* The facts are the same as paragraph (a) of this *Example 1*, except that *S* is an operating company with substantial assets that has been in existence for several years. *P* has a $110 basis in the *S* stock. Under §1.358-6(c)(1), *P*'s $110 basis in its *S* stock is increased by the $60 basis in the *T* assets deemed transferred. Consequently, *P* has a $170 basis in its *S* stock as a result of the reorganization.

(d) *Mixed consideration.* The facts are the same as paragraph (a) of this *Example 1*, except that the *T* shareholders receive *P* stock worth $80 and $20 cash from *P*. Under section 358, *P*'s $5 basis in its *S* stock is increased by the $60 basis in the *T* assets deemed transferred. Consequently, *P* has a $65 basis in its *S* stock as a result of the reorganization.

(e) *Liabilities.* The facts are the same as paragraph (a) of this *Example 1*, except that *T*'s assets are subject to $50 of liabilities, and the *T* shareholders receive $50 of *P* stock in exchange for their *T* stock. Under section 358, *P*'s basis in its *S* stock is increased by the $60 basis in the *T* assets deemed transferred and decreased by the $50 of liabilities to which the *T* assets acquired by *S* are subject. Consequently, *P* has a net basis adjustment of $10, and a $15 basis in its *S* stock as a result of the reorganization.

(f) *Liabilities in excess of basis.* The facts are the same as in paragraph (a) of this *Example 1*, except that *T*'s assets are subject to liabilities of $90, and the *T* shareholders receive $10 of *P* stock in exchange for their *T* stock in the reorganization. Under §1.358-6(c)(1)(ii), the adjustment under §1.358-6(c) is zero if the amount of the liabilities which *S* assumed or to which the *T* assets acquired by *S* are subject exceeds the aggregate adjusted basis in *T*'s assets. Consequently, *P* has no adjustment in its *S* stock, and *P* has a $5 basis in its *S* stock as a result of the reorganization.

Example 2. Reverse triangular merger. (a) *Facts. T* has assets with an aggregate basis of $60 and a fair market value of $100 and no liabilities. *P* has a $110 basis in its *S* stock. Pursuant to a plan, *S* merges into *T* with *T* surviving. In the merger, the *T* shareholders receive $10 cash from *P* and *P* stock worth $90 in exchange for their *T* stock. The transaction is a reorganization to which sections 368(a)(1)(A) and (a)(2)(E) apply.

(b) *Basis adjustment.* Under §1.358-6(c)(2)(i)(A), *P*'s basis in the *T* stock acquired is *P*'s $110 basis in its *S* stock before the transaction, adjusted as if *T* had merged into *S* in a forward triangular merger to which §1.358-6(c)(1) applies. In such a case, *P*'s $110 basis in its *S* stock before the transaction would have been increased by the $60 basis of the *T* assets deemed transferred. Consequently, *P* has a $170 basis in its *T* stock immediately after the transaction.

(c) *Reverse triangular merger that also qualifies under section 368(a)(1)(B).* The facts relating to *T* are the same as in paragraph (a) of this *Example 2. P*, however, forms *S* pursuant to the plan of reorganization. The *T* shareholders receive $100 worth of *P* stock (and no cash) in exchange for their *T* stock. The *T* shareholders have an aggregate basis in their *T* stock of $85 immediately before the reorganization. The reorganization qualifies as both a reverse triangular merger and a reorganization under section 368(a)(1)(B). Under §1.358-6(c)(2)(ii), *P* may determine its basis in its *T* stock either as if §1.358-6(c)(2)(i) applied to the *T* stock acquired, or as if *P* acquired the *T* stock from the former *T* shareholders in a transaction in which *P*'s basis in the *T* stock was determined under section 362(b). Accordingly, *P* may determine a basis in its *T* stock of $60 (*T*'s net asset basis) or $85 (the *T* shareholders' aggregate basis in the *T* stock immediately before the reorganization).

(d) *Allocable share in a reverse triangular merger.* The facts are the same as in paragraph (a) of this *Example 2*, except that X, a 10% shareholder of *T*, does not participate in the transaction. The remaining *T* shareholders receive $10 cash from *P* and *P* stock worth $80 for their *T* stock. *P* owns 90% of the *T* stock after the transaction. Under §1.358-6(c)(2)(i)(A), *P*'s basis in its *T* stock is *P*'s $110 basis in its *S* stock before the reorganization, adjusted as if *T* had merged into *S* in a forward triangular merger. In such a case, *P*'s basis would have been adjusted by the $60 basis in the *T* assets deemed transferred. Under §1.358-6(c)(2)(i)(B), however, the basis adjustment determined under §1.358-6(c)(2)(i)(A) is reduced in proportion to the percentage

of *T* stock not acquired by *P* in the transaction. The percentage of *T* stock not acquired in the transaction is 10%. Therefore, *P* reduces its $60 basis adjustment by 10%, resulting in a net basis adjustment of $54. Consequently, *P* has a $164 basis in its *T* stock as a result of the transaction.

(e) *P's ownership of T stock.* The facts are the same as in paragraph (a) of this *Example 2*, except that *P* owns 10% of the *T* stock before the transaction. *P*'s basis in that *T* stock is $8. All the *T* shareholders other than *P* surrender their *T* stock for $10 cash from *P* and *P* stock worth $80. *P* does not surrender the stock in the transaction. Under §1.358-6(c)(i)(C), *P* may treat its *T* stock owned before the transaction as acquired in the transaction or not. If *P* treats that *T* stock as acquired in the transaction, *P*'s basis in that *T* stock and the *T* stock actually acquired in the transaction equals *P*'s $110 basis in its *S* stock before the transaction, adjusted by the $60 basis of the *T* assets deemed transferred, for a total basis of $170. If *P* treats its *T* stock as not acquired, *P* retains its $8 pre-transaction basis in that stock. *P*'s basis in its other *T* shares equals *P*'s $110 basis in its *S* stock before the transaction, adjusted by $54 (the $60 basis in the *T* assets deemed transferred, reduced by 10%), for a total basis of $164 in those shares. See §1.358-6(c)(2)(i)(A) and (B). Consequently, if *P* treats its *T* shares as not acquired, *P*'s total basis in all of its *T* shares is $172.

Example 3. Triangular B reorganization. (a) *Facts. T* has assets with a fair market value of $100 and no liabilities. The *T* shareholders have an aggregate basis in their *T* stock of $85 immediately before the reorganization. Pursuant to a plan, *P* forms *S* with $5 cash and *S* acquires all of the *T* stock in exchange for $100 of *P* stock. The transaction is a reorganization to which section 368(a)(1)(B) applies.

(b) *Basis adjustment.* Under §1.358-6(c)(3), *P* adjusts its $5 basis in its *S* stock by treating *P* as if it acquired the *T* stock acquired by *S* in the reorganization directly from the *T* shareholders in exchange for the *P* stock in a transaction in which *P*'s basis in the *T* stock was determined under section 362(b). Under section 362(b), *P* would have an aggregate basis of $85 in the *T* stock received by *S* in the reorganization. *P* is then treated as if it transferred the *T* stock to *S* in a transaction in which *P*'s basis in the *S* stock was determined under section 358. Under section 358, *P*'s basis in its *S* stock would be increased by the $85 basis in the *T* stock deemed transferred. Consequently, *P* has a $90 basis in its *S* stock as a result of the reorganization.

(d) *Special rule for consideration not provided by P.*—(1) *In general.*—The amount of *P*'s adjustment to basis in its *S* or *T* stock, as applicable, described in paragraph (c) of this section is decreased by the fair market value of any consideration (including *P* stock in which gain or loss is recognized, see §1.1032-2(c)) that is exchanged in the reorganization and that is not provided by P pursuant to the plan of reorganization. This paragraph (d) does not apply to the amount of *T* liabilities assumed by *S* or to which the *T* assets acquired by *S* are subject under paragraph (c)(1) of this section (or deemed assumed or taken subject to by *S* under paragraph (c)(2)(i) of this section).

(2) *Limitation.*—*P* makes no adjustment to basis under this section if the decrease required under paragraph (d)(1) of this section equals or exceeds the amount of the adjustment described in paragraph (c) of this section.

(3) *Example.*—The rules of this paragraph (d) are illustrated by the following example. For purposes of this example, *P*, *S*, and *T* are domestic corporations, *P* and *S* do not file consolidated returns, *P* owns all of the only class of *S* stock, the *P* stock exchanged in the transaction satisfies the requirements of the applicable triangular reorganization provisions, and the facts set forth the only corporate activity.

Example. (a) *Facts. T* has assets with an aggregate basis of $60 and fair market value of $100 and no liabilities. *S* is an operating company with substantial assets that has been in existence for several years. *P* has a $100 basis in its *S* stock. Pursuant to a plan, *T* merges into *S* and the *T* shareholders receive $70 of *P* stock provided by *P* pursuant to the plan and $30 of cash provided by *S* in exchange for their *T* stock. The transaction is a reorganization to which sections 368(a)(1)(A) and (a)(2)(D) apply.

(b) *Basis adjustment.* Under §1.358-6(c)(1), *P*'s $100 basis in its *S* stock is increased by the $60 basis in the *T* assets deemed transferred. Under §1.358-6(d)(1), the $60 adjustment is decreased by the $30 of cash provided by *S* in the reorganization. Consequently, *P* has a net adjustment of $30 in its *S* stock, and *P* has a $130 basis in its *S* stock as a result of the reorganization.

(c) *Appreciated asset.* The facts are the same as in paragraph (a) of this *Example*, except that in the reorganization *S* provides an asset with a $20 adjusted basis and $30 fair market value instead of $30 of cash. The basis results are the same as in paragraph (b) of this *Example*. In addition S recognizes $10 of gain under section 1001 on its disposition of the asset in the reorganization.

(d) *Depreciated asset.* The facts are the same as in paragraph (c) of this *Example*, except that S has a $60 adjusted basis in the asset. The basis results are the same as in paragraph (b) of this *Example*. In addition, S recognizes $30 of loss under section 1001 on its disposition of the asset in the reorganization.

(e) *P stock.* The facts are the same as in paragraph (a) of this *Example*, except that in the reorganization S provides P stock with a fair market value of $30 instead of $30 of cash. S acquired the P stock in an unrelated transaction several years before the reorganization. S has a $20 adjusted basis in the P stock. The basis results are the same as in paragraph (b) of this *Example*. In addition, S recognizes $10 of gain on its disposition of the P stock in the reorganization. See § 1.1032-2(c).

(e) *Cross-references.*—(1) *Triangular reorganizations involving members of a consolidated group.*—For rules relating to stock basis adjustments made as a result of a triangular reorganization in which P and S, or P and T, as applicable, are, or become, members of a consolidated group, see § 1.1502-30. However, if a transaction is a group structure change, stock basis adjustments are determined under § 1.1502-31 and not under § 1.1502-30, even if the transaction also qualifies as a reorganization otherwise subject to § 1.1502-30.

(2) *Triangular reorganizations involving certain foreign corporations.*—For rules relating to stock basis adjustments made as a result of triangular reorganizations involving certain foreign corporations, see § § 1.367(b)-4(b), 1.367(b)-10, and 1.367(b)-13.

(f) *Effective/applicability dates.*—(1) *General rule.*—Except as otherwise provided in this paragraph (f), this section applies to triangular reorganizations occurring on or after December 23, 1994.

(2) *Special rule for reverse triangular mergers.*—For a reverse triangular merger occurring before December 23, 1994, P may—

(i) Determine the basis in its T stock as if paragraph (c) (2) (i) of this section applied; or

(ii) Determine the basis in its T stock acquired as if P acquired such stock from the former T shareholders in a transaction in which P's basis in the T stock was determined under section 362(b).

(3) *Triangular G reorganization and special rule for triangular reorganizations involving members of a consolidated group.*—Paragraph (e)(1) of this section shall apply to triangular reorganizations occurring on or after September 17, 2008. However, taxpayers may apply paragraph (b)(2)(v) of this section to triangular reorganizations occurring before September 17, 2008 and on or after December 23, 1994.

(4) *Triangular reorganizations involving importation property acquired in loss importation transaction or loss duplication transaction; triangular reorganizations involving certain foreign corporations.*—Paragraphs (a) and (e)(2) of this section apply to triangular reorganizations occurring after October 22, 2004 unless effected to a binding agreement that was in effect prior to that date and at all times thereafter. [Reg. § 1.358-6.]

☐ [*T.D. 8648*, 12-20-95. *Amended by T.D. 9243*, 1-23-2006, *T.D. 9424*, 9-9-2008 (*corrected* 10-17-2008) *and T.D. 9759*, 3-25-2016.]

[Reg. § 1.358-7]

§ 1.358-7. Transfers by partners and partnerships to corporations.—(a) *Transfers by partners of partnership interests.*—For purposes of section 358(h), a transfer of a partnership interest to a corporation is treated as a transfer of the partner's share of each of the partnership's assets and an assumption by the corporation of the partner's share of partnership liabilities (including section 358(h) liabilities, as defined in paragraph (d) of this section). See paragraph (e) *Example 2* of this section.

(b) *Transfers by partnerships.*—If a corporation assumes a section 358(h) liability from a partnership in an exchange to which section 358(a) applies, then, for purposes of applying section 705 (determination of basis of partner's interest) and § 1.704-1(b), any reduction, under section 358(h)(1), in the partnership's basis in corporate stock received in the transaction is treated as an expenditure of the partnership described in section 705(a)(2)(B). See paragraph (e) *Example 1* of this section. This expenditure must be allocated among the partners in accordance with section 704(b) and (c) and § 1.752-7(c). If a partner's share of the reduction, under section 358(h)(1), in the partnership's basis in corporate stock exceeds the partner's basis in the partnership interest, then the partner recognizes gain equal to the excess, which is treated as gain from the sale or exchange of a partnership interest. This paragraph does not apply to the extent that § 1.752-7(j)(4) applies to the assumption of the § 1.752-7 liability by the corporation.

(c) *Assumption of section 358(h) liability by partnership followed by transfer of partnership interest or partnership property to a corporation—trade or business exception.*—Where a partnership assumes a section 358(h) liability from a partner and, subsequently, the partner transfers all or part of the partner's partnership interest to a corporation in an exchange to which section 358(a) applies, then, for purposes of applying section 358(h)(2), the section 358(h) liability is treated as associated only with the contribution made to the partnership by that partner. See paragraph (e) *Example 2* of this section. Similar rules apply where a partnership assumes a section 358(h) liability of a partner and a corporation subsequently assumes that section 358(h) liability from the partnership in an exchange to which section 358(a) applies.

(d) *Section 358(h) liabilities defined.*—For purposes of this section, section 358(h) liabilities are liabilities described in section 358(h)(3).

(e) *Examples.*—The following examples illustrate the provisions of this section. Assume, for purposes of these examples, that the obligation assumed by the corporation does not reduce the shareholder's basis in the corporate stock under section 358(d). The examples are as follows:

Example 1. Transfer of partnership property to corporation. In 2004, in an exchange to which section 351(a) applies, PRS, a cash basis taxpayer, transfers $2,000,000 cash to Corporation X, also a cash basis taxpayer, in exchange for Corporation X shares and the assumption by Corporation X of $1,000,000 of accounts payable incurred by PRS. At the time of the exchange, PRS has two partners, A, a 90% partner, who has a $2,000,000 basis in the PRS interest, and B, a 10% partner, who has a $50,000 basis in the PRS interest. Assume that, under section 358(h)(1), PRS's basis in the Corporation X stock is reduced by the accounts payable assumed by Corporation X ($1,000,000). Under paragraph (b) of this section, A's and B's bases in PRS must be reduced, but not below zero, by their respective shares of the section 358(h)(1) basis reduction. If either partner's share of the section 358(h)(1) basis reduction exceeds the partner's basis in the partnership interest, then the partner recognizes gain equal to the excess. A's share of the section 358(h) basis reduction is $900,000 (90% of $1,000,000). Therefore, A's basis in the PRS interest is reduced to $1,100,000 ($2,000,000 - $900,000). B's share of the section 358(h) basis reduction is $100,000 (10% of $1,000,000). Because B's share of the section 358(h) basis reduction ($100,000) exceeds B's basis in the PRS interest ($50,000), B's basis in the PRS interest is reduced to $0 and B recognizes $50,000 of gain. This gain is treated as gain from the sale of the PRS interest.

Example 2. Transfer of partnership interest to corporation. In 2004, A contributes undeveloped land with a value and basis of $4,000,000 in exchange for a 50% interest in PRS and an assumption by PRS of $2,000,000 of pension liabilities from a separate business that A conducts. A's basis in the PRS interest immediately after the contribution is A's basis in the land, $4,000,000, unreduced by the amount of the pension liabilities. PRS develops the land as a landfill. Before PRS has economically performed with respect to the pension liabilities, A transfers A's interest in PRS to Corporation X, in an exchange to which section 351 applies. At the time of the exchange, the value of A's PRS interest is $2,000,000, A's basis in PRS is $4,000,000, and A has no share of partnership liabilities other than the pension liabilities. For purposes of applying section 358(h), the transfer of the PRS interest to Corporation X is treated as a transfer to Corporation X of A's share of PRS assets and an assumption by Corporation X of A's share of the pension liabilities of PRS ($2,000,000). Because the pension liabilities were not assumed by PRS from A in an exchange in which the trade or business associated with the liability was transferred to PRS, the transfer of the PRS interest to Corporation X is not excepted from section 358(h) under section 358(h)(2). See paragraph (c) of this section. Under section 358(h), A's basis in the Corporation X stock is reduced by the $2,000,000 of pension liabilities.

(f) *Effective date.*—This section applies to assumptions of liabilities by a corporation occurring on or after June 24, 2003. [Reg. § 1.358-7.]

☐ [*T.D. 9207*, 5-23-2005.]

[Reg. § 1.361-1]

§ 1.361-1. Nonrecognition of gain or loss to corporations.—Section 361 provides the general rule that no gain or loss shall be recognized if a corporation, a party to a reorganization, exchanges property in pursuance of the plan of reorganization solely for stock or securities in another corporation, a party to the reorganization. This provision includes only stock and securities received in connection with a reorganization defined in section 368(a). It also includes nonvoting stock and securities in a corporation, a party to a reorganization, received in a transaction to which section 368(a)(1)(C) is applicable only by reason of section 368(a)(2)(B). [Reg. § 1.361-1.]

☐ [*T.D. 6152*, 12-2-55.]

[Reg. §1.362-1]

§1.362-1. Basis to corporations.—(a) *In general.*—Section 362 provides, as a general rule, that if property was acquired on or after June 22, 1954, by a corporation (1) in connection with a transaction to which section 351 (relating to transfer of property to corporation controlled by transferor) applies, (2) as paid-in surplus or as a contribution to capital, or (3) in connection with a reorganization to which part III, subchapter C, chapter 1 of the Code applies, then the basis shall be the same as it would be in the hands of the transferor, increased in the amount of gain recognized to the transferor on such transfer. (See also §1.362-2.) See §1.460-4(k)(3)(iv)(B)(2) for rules relating to adjustments to the basis of certain contracts accounted for using a long-term contract method of accounting that are acquired in certain transfers described in section 351 and certain reorganizations described in section 368(a).

(b) *Exceptions.*—(1) In the case of a plan of reorganization adopted after October 22, 1968, section 362 does not apply if the property acquired in connection with such reorganization consists of stock or securities in a corporation a party to the reorganization, unless acquired by the exchange of stock or securities of the transferee (or of a corporation which is in control of the transferee) as the consideration in whole or in part for the transfer.

(2) In the case of a plan of reorganization adopted before October 23, 1968, section 362 does not apply if the property acquired in connection with such reorganization consists of stock or securities in a corporation a party to the reorganization, unless acquired by the issuance of stock or securities of the transferee (or, in the case of transactions occurring after December 31, 1963, of a corporation which is in control of the transferee) as the consideration in whole or in part for the transfer. The term "issuance of stock or securities" includes any transfer of stock or securities, including stock or securities which were purchased or were acquired as a contribution to capital. [Reg. §1.362-1.]

☐ [*T.D. 6152, 12-2-55. Amended by T.D. 7422, 6-25-76 and T.D. 8995,* 5-14-2002.]

[Reg. §1.362-2]

§1.362-2. Certain contributions to capital.—The following regulations shall be used in the application of section 362(c):

(a) Property deemed to be acquired with contributed money shall be that property, if any, the acquisition of which was the purpose motivating the contribution;

(b) In the case of an excess of the amount of money contributed over the cost of the property deemed to be acquired with such money (as defined in (a) above) such excess shall be applied to the reduction of the basis (but not below zero) of other properties held by the corporation, on the last day of the 12-month period beginning on the day the contribution is received, in the following order—

(1) All property of a character subject to an allowance for depreciation (not including any properties as to which a deduction for amortization is allowable),

(2) Property with respect to which a deduction for amortization is allowable,

(3) Property with respect to which a deduction for depletion is allowable under section 611 but not under section 613, and

(4) All other remaining properties.
The reduction of the basis of each of the properties within each of the above categories shall be made in proportion to the relative bases of such properties.

(c) With the consent of the Commissioner, the taxpayer may, however, have the basis of the various units of property within a particular category adjusted in a manner different from the general rule set forth in paragraph (b) of this section. Variations from such rule may, for example, involve adjusting the basis of only certain units of the taxpayer's property within a given category. A request for variations from the general rule should be filed by the taxpayer with its return for the taxable year for which the transfer of the property has occurred. [Reg. §1.362-2.]

☐ [*T.D. 6152, 12-2-55.*]

[Reg. §1.362-3]

§1.362-3. Basis of importation property acquired in loss importation transaction.—(a) *Purpose.*—The purpose of section 362(e)(1) and this section is to modify the application of section 362(a) (section 351 transfers, contributions to capital, or paid-in surplus) and section 362(b) (reorganizations) to prevent a corporation (Acquiring) from importing a net built-in loss in a transaction described in either section. See paragraph (c) of this section for definitions of terms used in this section.

(b) *Basis determinations under this section.*—(1) *Basis of importation property received in loss importation transaction.*—Notwithstanding the general rules of section 362(a) and (b), Acquiring's basis in importation property (as defined in paragraph (c)(2) of this section) acquired in a loss importation transaction (as defined in paragraph (c)(3) of this section) is equal to the value of the property immediately after the transaction.

(2) *Adjustment to basis of subsidiary stock in triangular reorganizations.*—If a corporation (P) computes its basis in stock of a subsidiary (whether S or T) under §1.358-6 (stock basis in certain triangular reorganizations), P's basis in property treated as acquired by P in §1.358-6(c) is determined under section 362(e)(1) and this section to the extent such property, if actually acquired by P, would be importation property acquired in a loss importation transaction. See §1.358-6(c)(1)(i)(A), (c)(2)(ii)(B), and (c)(3)(i). The subsidiary's basis in the property actually acquired in the transaction is determined under applicable law (including this section), without regard to the amount of any adjustment to P's basis in the subsidiary's stock. Thus, the basis of the property in S's or T's hands may differ from the amount of the adjustment to P's basis in its stock of S or T.

(3) *Acquiring's basis in other property transferred.*—In general, Acquiring's basis in property received in a section 362 transaction (as defined in paragraph (c)(1) of this section) that is not determined under section 362(e)(1) and this section is determined under section 362(a) or section 362(b). However, if the transaction is described in section 362(a) (without regard to whether it is also described in any other section), further adjustment may be required under section 362(e)(2). See §1.362-4.

(4) *Other effects of basis determination under this section.*—(i) *Determination by reference to transferor's basis.*—A determination of basis under this section is a determination by reference to the transferor's basis, including for purposes of sections 1223(2) and 7701(a)(43). However, solely for purposes of applying section 755, a determination of basis under this section is treated as a determination not by reference to the transferor's basis.

(ii) *Not tax-exempt income or noncapital, nondeductible expense.*—The application of this section does not give rise to an item treated as tax-exempt income under §1.1502-32(b)(2)(ii) or as a noncapital, nondeductible expense under §1.1502-32(b)(2)(iii).

(iii) *No effect on earnings and profits.*—Any determination of basis under this section does not reduce or otherwise affect the calculation of the all earnings and profits amount provided in §1.367(b)-2(d).

(c) *Definitions.*—For purposes of this section, the following definitions apply:

(1) *Section 362 transaction.*—The term *section 362 transaction* means any transaction described in section 362(a) or in section 362(b).

(2) *Importation property.*—(i) *General rule.*—The term *importation property* means any property (including separate portions determined under paragraph (d)(4) of this section and separate portions of property tentatively divided under paragraph (e)(2) of this section) with respect to which—

(A) Any gain or loss that would be recognized on its sale by the transferor immediately before the transaction (the transferor's hypothetical sale) would not be subject to tax imposed under any provision of subtitle A of the Internal Revenue Code (federal income tax) (taking into account the provisions of paragraph (d) of this section); and

(B) Any gain or loss that would be recognized on its sale by Acquiring immediately after the transaction (Acquiring's hypothetical sale) would be subject to federal income tax (taking into account the provisions of paragraph (d) of this section).

(ii) *Special rules for applying this paragraph (c)(2).*—See paragraph (d) of this section for rules for determining whether gain or loss on a hypothetical sale would be taken into account in determining a federal income tax liability and paragraph (e) of this section for rules applicable when more than one person would take such gain or loss into account.

(3) *Loss importation transaction.*—The term *loss importation transaction* means any section 362 transaction in which Acquiring's aggregate basis in all importation property received from all transferors in the transaction would exceed the aggregate value of such property immediately after the transaction. For this purpose, Acquiring's basis in property received is determined without regard to this section or section 362(e)(2).

(4) *Value.*—(i) *General rule.*—The term *value* means fair market value.

(ii) *Special rule for transfers of partnership interests.*—Notwithstanding the general rule in paragraph (c)(4)(i) of this section, when referring to a partnership interest, for purposes of this section, the term *value* means the sum of the cash that Acquiring would receive for the interest, assuming an exchange between a willing buyer and a willing seller (neither being under any compulsion to buy or sell and both having reasonable knowledge of relevant facts), increased by any § 1.752-1 liabilities (as defined in § 1.752-1(a)(4)) of the partnership allocated to Acquiring with regard to such transferred interest under section 752 immediately after the transfer to Acquiring. If a partnership has elected under section 754, or if section 743(b) would require a downward basis adjustment to the partnership property, the partnership must apply the rules of § 1.743-1 to determine the amount of the basis adjustment to the partnership property.

(d) *Rules for determining whether gain or loss would be taken into account in determining a federal income tax liability.*—(1) *General rule.*—In general, any gain or loss that would be recognized on a hypothetical sale described in paragraph (c)(2) of this section is considered to be subject to federal income tax if, taking into account all relevant facts and circumstances, such gain or loss would affect or be taken into account in determining the federal income tax liability of the transferor or Acquiring, respectively. This determination is made without regard to whether such person has or would have any actual federal income tax liability for the taxable year of the transaction.

(2) *Look-through rule in the case of certain pass-through entities.*—Notwithstanding the general rule in paragraph (d)(1) of this section, the determination of whether any gain or loss on a hypothetical sale would be treated as subject to federal income tax is made by reference to the person that would be required to include such gain or loss in its taxable income if the hypothetical seller is—

(i) A trust treated as owned by its grantors or others (see section 671);

(ii) A partnership (see section 701); or

(iii) An S corporation (see sections 1363 and 1366).

(3) *Controlled foreign corporation (CFC), passive foreign investment company (PFIC).*—For purposes of this section, gain or loss that would be recognized by a CFC (as defined in section 957(a)) or a PFIC (as defined in section 1297(a)) is not deemed taken into account in determining a federal income tax liability solely because it could affect an inclusion under section 951(a) or section 1293(a).

(4) *Special rule for debt-financed property subject to section 512.*—If property is debt-financed property (as defined in section 514(b)) owned by an organization subject to the unrelated business income tax described in section 511(a)(2) and, as a result, a portion of any gain or loss on a sale of the property would be included in unrelated taxable business income (UBTI) under section 512, such property is treated as divided into separate portions in proportion to the amount of such gain or loss that would be includible in UBTI. The rules of paragraph (e) of this section apply to determine the characterization of such portions (as includible in the determination of a federal income tax liability or not), and the tax treatment and consequences of the transaction in which such portions are transferred.

(5) *Look-through treatment in the case of certain avoidance transactions.*—(i) *Application of this paragraph (d)(5).*—This paragraph (d)(5) applies if—

(A) The transferor is a domestic entity that is a trust (other than a trust described in paragraph (d)(2)(i) of this section), estate, regulated investment company (as defined in section 851(a)), a real estate investment trust (as defined in section 856(a)), or a cooperative (as described in section 1381); and

(B) The transferor transfers, directly or indirectly, property that was transferred to or acquired by it as part of a plan (whether of transferor, Acquiring, or any other person) to avoid the application of section 362(e)(1) and this section to a section 362 transaction.

(ii) *Effect of application of this paragraph (d)(5).*—Notwithstanding paragraph (d)(1) of this section, if a transferor is described in both paragraphs (d)(5)(i)(A) and (B) of this section—

(A) The transferor is treated as though it distributes the proceeds of the hypothetical sale (which, for this purpose, are presumed to be an amount greater than zero);

(B) To the fullest extent possible under the transferor's organizing instrument, the deemed distribution is treated as made to a distributee or distributees that would not take distributions from the transferor into account in determining a federal income tax liability; and

(C) The determination of whether the gain or loss on the hypothetical sale is treated as subject to federal income tax is made by reference to the deemed distributee or distributees.

(iii) *Tiered entities.*—If a deemed distributee is an entity described in paragraph (d)(5)(i)(A) of this section, the determination of whether gain or loss on the hypothetical sale is taken into account in determining a federal income tax liability is made by treating the

deemed distributee, and any successive such deemed distributees, as a transferor and applying the rules in paragraphs (d)(5)(i) and (ii) of this section to its deemed distribution (and to all successive deemed distributions), until no deemed distributee or successive deemed distributee is an entity described in paragraph (d)(5)(i)(A) of this section.

(e) *Special rules for gain or loss that would be taken into account by multiple persons.*—(1) *In general.*—If gain or loss from a disposition of property would be includible in income by more than one person, the property is treated as tentatively divided into separate portions in proportion to the amount of gain or loss recognized with respect to the property that would be allocated to each such person. If an entity's organizing instrument specially allocates gain and loss, the tentative division of property under this paragraph (e) must reflect the manner in which gain or loss on the disposition of such property would be allocated under the terms of the organizing instrument and any applicable rules of law, taking into account the net gain or loss actually recognized by the entity in that tax year.

(2) *Application of section.*—The rules of this section apply independently to each tentatively divided portion to determine if the portion is importation property. Each tentatively divided portion that is determined to be importation property is included with all other importation property in the determination of whether the transaction is a loss importation transaction.

(3) *Acquiring's basis in property tentatively divided into separate portions.*—Immediately after the application of section 362(e)(1) and this section and before the application of section 362(e)(2), each property treated as tentatively divided into separate portions for purposes of applying section 362(e)(1) and this section ceases to be treated as tentatively divided and Acquiring has a single, undivided basis in such property that is equal to the sum of—

(i) The value of each tentatively divided portion that is importation property, if the transaction is a loss importation transaction; and

(ii) Acquiring's basis in each tentatively divided portion that is not importation property received in a loss importation transaction, as determined under section 362(a) or section 362(b), as applicable, and without regard to any potential application of section 362(e)(2).

(f) *Examples.*—The examples in this paragraph (f) illustrate the application of section 362(e)(1) and the provisions of this section. Unless otherwise indicated, the examples use the following nomenclature and assumptions: A and B are U.S. citizens. DC, DC1, and P are domestic corporations that have not elected to be S corporations within the meaning of section 1361(a)(1) and that are not members of a consolidated group. F is a foreign individual. FP is a foreign partnership. FC, FC1, and FC2 are foreign corporations. Unless the facts indicate otherwise, the foreign individuals, corporations, and partnerships are not engaged in a U.S. trade or business, have no U.S. real property interests, and have no other relationships, activities, or interests that would cause them, their shareholders, their partners, or their property to be subject to federal income tax. There is no applicable income tax treaty, all persons' tax years are calendar years, and all persons and transactions are unrelated unless the facts indicate otherwise.

Example 1. Basic application of section. (i) *Section 351 transfer of importation property in a loss importation transaction.* (A) *Facts.* FC owns three assets, A1 (basis $40, value $150), A2 (basis $120, value $30), and A3 (basis $140, value $20). On Date 1, FC transfers A1, A2, and A3 to DC in a transaction to which section 351 applies.

(B) *Importation property.* If FC had sold A1, A2, or A3 immediately before the transaction, no gain or loss recognized on the sale would have been taken into account in determining a federal income tax liability. Further, if DC had sold A1, A2, or A3 immediately after the transaction, DC would take into account any gain or loss recognized on the sale in determining its federal income tax liability. Therefore, A1, A2, and A3 are all importation properties. See paragraph (c)(2) of this section.

(C) *Loss importation transaction.* FC's transfer of A1, A2, and A3 is a section 362 transaction. Furthermore, but for section 362(e)(1) and this section and section 362(e)(2), DC's aggregate basis in the importation properties, A1, A2, and A3, would be $300 ($40 + $120 + $140) under section 362(a) and the properties' aggregate value would be $200 ($150 + $30 + $20). Therefore, the importation properties' aggregate basis would exceed their aggregate value and the transaction is a loss importation transaction. See paragraph (c)(3) of this section.

(D) *Application of section 362(e)(1) and this section to importation property received in loss importation transaction.* Because the importation properties, A1, A2, and A3, were transferred in a loss importation transaction, paragraph (b)(1) of this section applies and DC's basis in A1, A2, and A3 will each be equal to the property's value ($150, $30, and $20, respectively) immediately after the transfer.

Reg. § 1.362-3(f)

(E) *Basis of property received in transaction.* Following the application of section 362(e)(1) and this section, the provisions of section 362(e)(2) must be taken into account because the transfer is a section 362(a) transaction. Taking into account the application of section 362(e)(1) and this section, DC's aggregate basis in the transferred properties would not exceed their aggregate value immediately after the transfer. Therefore, FC does not have a net built-in loss, FC's transfer is not a loss duplication transaction, and section 362(e)(2) does not apply to this transaction. DC's bases in A1, A2, and A3, as determined under paragraph (i)(D) of this *Example 1*, are $150, $30, and $20, respectively. Under section 358(a), FC receives the DC stock with a basis of $300 (the sum of FC's bases in A1, A2, and A3 immediately before the exchange).

(ii) *Reorganization.* The facts are the same as in paragraph (i)(A) of this *Example 1* except that, instead of transferring property to DC in a section 351 exchange, FC merges with and into DC in a transaction described in section 368(a)(1)(A). The analysis and results are the same as set forth in paragraphs (i)(B), (C), and (D) of this *Example 1*. However, the analysis in paragraph (i)(E) of this *Example 1* does not apply to these facts because the transaction is not subject to 362(e)(2) and §1.362-4. Under section 358(a), FC's shareholders will take the DC stock with a basis determined by reference to their FC stock basis.

(iii) *FC's property used in U.S. trade or business.* (A) *Facts.* The facts are the same as in paragraph (i)(A) of this *Example 1*, except that FC is engaged in a U.S. trade or business and uses all the properties in that U.S. trade or business. In this case, none of the properties would be importation property because FC would take any gain or loss on the disposition of the properties into account in determining its federal income tax liability. Accordingly, this section does not apply to the transaction.

(B) *Basis of property received in transaction.* Following the application of section 362(e)(1) and this section, the provisions of section 362(e)(2) must be taken into account because the transfer is a section 362(a) transaction. Taking into account the application of section 362(e)(1) and this section but without taking into account the provisions of section 362(e)(2), DC's aggregate basis in the transferred properties would be $300 ($40 + $120 + $140) under section 362(a) and the properties' aggregate value immediately after the transfer would be $200 ($150 + $30 + $20). Therefore, FC has a net built-in loss and FC's transfer of A1, A2, and A3 is a loss duplication transaction. Accordingly, under the general rule of section 362(e)(2), FC's $100 net built-in loss ($300 aggregate basis over $200 aggregate value) would be allocated proportionately (by the amount of built-in loss in each property) to reduce DC's basis in the loss properties, A2 and A3. See §1.362-4. As a result, DC's basis in A2 would be $77.14 ($120 basis under section 362(a) reduced by $42.86, A2's proportionate share of FC's net built-in loss, computed as $90/$210 x $100) and DC's basis in A3 would be $82.86 ($140 basis under section 362(a) reduced by $57.14, A3's proportionate share of FC's net built-in loss, computed as $120/$210 x $100). However, if FC and DC were to elect under section 362(e)(2)(C) to apply the $100 basis reduction to FC's basis in the DC stock received in the transaction, DC's bases in A2 and A3 would remain their section 362(a) bases of $120 and $140, respectively. Under section 362(a), DC's basis in A1 is $40 (irrespective of whether the section 362(e)(2)(C) election is made). If FC and DC do not make a section 362(e)(2)(C) election, FC's basis in the DC stock received in the exchange will be $300; if FC and DC do make the election, FC's basis in the DC stock will be $200 ($300 - $100 net built-in loss). See §1.362-4(b).

Example 2. Multiple transferors. (i) *Facts.* The facts are the same as in paragraph (i)(A) of *Example 1* of this paragraph (f), except that FC only owns A1 (basis $40, value $150) and A2 (basis $120, value $30) and F owns A3 (basis $140, value $20). On Date 1, FC transfers A1 and A2, and F transfers A3, to DC in a single transaction described in section 351.

(ii) *Importation property.* A1 and A2 are importation properties for the reasons set forth in paragraph (i)(B) of *Example 1* of this paragraph (f). A3 is also an importation property because, if F had sold A3 immediately before the transaction, no gain or loss recognized on the sale would have been taken into account in determining a federal income tax liability, and, further, if DC had sold A3 immediately after the transaction, DC would take into account any gain or loss recognized on the sale in determining its federal income tax liability.

(iii) *Loss importation transaction.* The transfers by FC and F are a section 362 transaction. The transaction is a loss importation transaction for the reasons set forth in paragraph (i)(C) of *Example 1* of this paragraph (f) (notwithstanding that one of the transferors, FC, did not transfer a net built-in loss). See paragraph (c)(3) of this section.

(iv) *Application of section 362(e)(1) and this section to importation property received in loss importation transaction.* Because the importation properties, A1, A2, and A3, were transferred in a loss importation transaction, paragraph (b)(1) of this section applies and DC's basis in A1, A2, and A3 will each be equal to the property's value ($150, $30, and $20, respectively) immediately after the transfer.

(v) *Basis of property received in transaction.* Following the application of section 362(e)(1) and this section, the provisions of section 362(e)(2) must be taken into account because the transfer is a section 362(a) transaction. The application of section 362(e)(2) is determined separately for each transferor. See §1.362-4(b). Taking into account the application of section 362(e)(1) and this section, neither DC's aggregate basis in FC's properties nor DC's basis in F's property would exceed the properties' respective values immediately after the transaction. Therefore neither FC nor F has a net built-in loss, neither transfer is a loss duplication transaction, and section 362(e)(2) does not apply to either transfer. DC's bases in A1, A2, and A3, as determined under paragraph (iv) of this *Example 2*, are $150, $30, and $20, respectively. Under section 358(a), FC's basis in the DC stock received is $160 ($40 + $120) and F's basis in the DC stock received in the exchange is $140.

Example 3. Transfer of importation and non-importation property. (i) *Facts.* As in paragraph (i) of *Example 2*, FC owns A1 (basis $40, value $150) and A2 (basis $120, value $30), and F owns A3 (basis $140, value $20). In addition, A2 is a U.S. real property interest as defined in section 897(c)(1). On Date 1, FC transfers A1 and A2, and F transfers A3, to DC in a single transaction described in section 351.

(ii) *Importation property.* A1 and A3 are importation properties for the reasons set forth in paragraph (i)(B) of *Example 1* and paragraph (ii) of *Example 2* of this paragraph (f), respectively. However, A2 is not importation property because, if FC had sold A2 immediately before the transaction, FC would take into account any gain or loss recognized on the sale in determining its federal income tax liability.

(iii) *Loss importation transaction.* FC's and F's transfer is a section 362 transaction. Furthermore, but for section 362(e)(1) and this section and section 362(e)(2), DC's aggregate basis in the importation properties, A1 and A3, would be $180 ($40 + $140) and the properties' aggregate value would be $170 ($150 + $20) immediately after the transaction. Therefore, the importation properties' aggregate basis would exceed their aggregate value immediately after the transaction, and the transfer is a loss importation transaction.

(iv) *Application of section 362(e)(1) and this section to importation property received in loss importation transaction.* Because the importation properties, A1 and A3, were transferred in a loss importation transaction, paragraph (b)(1) of this section applies and DC's basis in A1 and in A3 will each be equal to the property's value ($150 and $20, respectively) immediately after the transfer.

(v) *Basis of property received in transaction.* Following the application of section 362(e)(1) and this section, the provisions of section 362(e)(2) must be taken into account because the transfer is a section 362(a) transaction. The application of section 362(e)(2) is determined separately for each transferor. See §1.362-4(b).

(A) *FC's transfer.* Taking into account the application of section 362(e)(1) and this section but without taking into account the provisions of section 362(e)(2), DC would have an aggregate basis of $270 in the transferred properties ($150 in A1, as determined under paragraph (iv) of this *Example 3*, plus $120 in A2, determined under section 362(a)), and the properties would have an aggregate value of $180 ($150 + $30) immediately after the transfer. Therefore, FC has a net built-in loss and FC's transfer of A1 and A2 is a loss duplication transaction. Accordingly, under the general rule of section 362(e)(2), FC's $90 net built-in loss ($270 aggregate basis to DC over $180 aggregate value) would be allocated proportionately to reduce DC's basis in the loss property transferred by FC. As a result, FC's entire net built-in loss would be allocated to A2, the only loss property transferred by FC, and DC's basis in A2 would be $30 ($120 basis under section 362(a) reduced by $90 net built-in loss). However, if FC and DC were to elect under section 362(e)(2)(C) to apply the $90 basis reduction to FC's basis in the DC stock received in the transaction, DC's basis in A2 would remain its section 362(a) basis of $120. DC's basis in A1 is $150 as determined under paragraph (iv) of this *Example 3* (irrespective of whether the section 362(e)(2)(C) election is made). If FC and DC do not make a section 362(e)(2)(C) election, FC's basis in the DC stock received in the exchange will be $160; if FC and DC do make the election, FC's basis in the DC stock will be $70 ($160 - $90 net built-in loss). See §1.362-4.

(B) *F's transfer of A3.* Taking into account the application of section 362(e)(1) and this section, DC's basis in A3, the property transferred by F, would not exceed its value immediately after the transfer. Therefore, F does not have a built-in loss, F's transfer is not a loss duplication transaction, and section 362(e)(2) does not apply to F's transfer. DC's basis in A3, as determined under paragraph (iv) of this *Example 3*, is $20. Under section 358(a), F receives the DC stock with a basis of $140.

Example 4. Multiple transferors of non-importation properties. (i) *Facts.* DC1 owns A1 (basis $40, value $150). In addition, as in *Example 3* of this paragraph (f), FC owns A2 (basis $120, value $30), a U.S. real property interest as defined in section 897(c)(1), and F owns A3 (basis $140, value $20). On Date 1, DC1 transfers A1, FC transfers A2, and F transfers A3, to DC in a single transaction described in section 351.

(ii) *Importation property.* A2 is not importation property and A3 is importation property for the reasons set forth in paragraph (ii) of *Example 3* and paragraph (i)(B) of *Example 1* of this paragraph (f), respectively. A1 is not importation property because, if DC1 had sold A2 immediately before the transaction, DC1 would take into account any gain or loss recognized on the sale in determining its federal income tax liability.

(iii) *Loss importation transaction.* The transfer of A1, A2, and A3 is a section 362 transaction. Furthermore, but for section 362(e)(1) and this section and section 362(e)(2), DC's basis in importation property, A3, would be $140 and the value of the property would be $20 immediately after the transaction. Therefore, the importation property's basis would exceed value and the transfer is a loss importation transaction.

(iv) *Application of section 362(e)(1) and this section to importation property received in loss importation transaction.* Because the importation property, A3, was transferred in a loss importation transaction, section 362(e)(1) and paragraph (b)(1) of this section apply and DC's basis in A3 will be equal to A3's $20 value immediately after the transfer.

(v) *Basis of property received in transaction.* Following the application of section 362(e)(1) and this section, the provisions of section 362(e)(2) must be taken into account because the transfer is a section 362(a) transaction. The application of section 362(e)(2) is determined separately for each transferor. See § 1.362-4.

(A) *DC1's transfer.* Taking into account the application of section 362(e)(1) and this section, DC's basis in A1 ($40 under section 362(a)) would not exceed its value immediately after the transfer. Therefore, DC1 does not have a net built-in loss, DC1's transfer is not a loss duplication transaction, and section 362(e)(2) does not apply to DC1's transfer. DC's basis in A1, determined under section 362(a), is $40. Under section 358(a), DC1 receives the DC stock with a basis of $40.

(B) *FC's transfer.* Taking into account the application of section 362(e)(1) and this section, but without taking into account the provisions of section 362(e)(2), DC would have a section 362(a) basis of $120 in A2, which would exceed A2's $30 value immediately after the transfer. Therefore, FC has a net built-in loss and FC's transfer of A2 is a loss duplication transaction. Accordingly, under the general rule of section 362(e)(2), FC's $90 net built-in loss (DC's $120 basis in A2 over A2's $30 value) would be applied to reduce DC's basis in A2, the only loss property transferred by FC. As a result, DC's basis in A2 would be $30 ($120 basis under section 362(a), reduced by the $90 net built-in loss). However, if FC and DC were to elect under section 362(e)(2)(C) to apply the $90 basis reduction to FC's basis in the DC stock received in the transaction, DC's basis in A2 would be its $120 basis determined under section 362(a). If FC and DC do not make a section 362(e)(2)(C) election, FC's basis in the DC stock received in the exchange will be $120; if FC and DC do make the election, FC's basis in the DC stock will be $30 ($120 - $90). See § 1.362-4.

(C) *F's transfer.* F's transfer of A3 is a transaction described in section 362(a). However, taking into account the application of section 362(e)(1) and this section, DC's basis in A3 ($20) would not exceed its value immediately after the transfer. Therefore, F does not have a built-in loss, F's transfer is not a loss duplication transaction, and section 362(e)(2) does not apply to F's transfer. DC's basis in A3, as determined under paragraph (iv) of this *Example 4*, is $20. Under section 358(a), F receives the DC stock with a basis of $140.

Example 5. Partnership transactions. (i) *Transfer by foreign partnership, foreign and domestic partners.* (A) *Facts.* A and F are equal partners in FP. FP owns A1 (basis $100, value $70). Under the terms of the FP partnership agreement, FP's items of income, gain, deduction, and loss are allocated equally between A and F. Section 704(c) does not apply with respect to the partnership property. FP transfers A1 to DC in a transfer to which section 351 applies. No election is made under section 362(e)(2)(C).

(B) *Importation property.* If FP had sold A1 immediately before the transaction, any gain or loss recognized on the sale would be allocated to and includible by A and F equally under the partnership agreement. Thus, under paragraph (d)(2) of this section, A1 is treated as tentatively divided into two equal portions, one treated as owned by A and one treated as owned by F. If FP had sold A1 immediately before the transaction, any gain or loss recognized on the portion *treated as owned by A* would have been taken into account in determining a federal income tax liability (A's); thus A's tentatively divided portion of A1 is not importation property. However, no gain or loss recognized on the tentatively divided portion treated as owned by F would have been taken into account in determining a federal income tax liability. Further, if DC had sold A1 immediately after the transaction, any gain or loss recognized on the sale would have been taken into account in determining a federal income tax liability (DC's); thus, F's tentatively divided portion of A1 is importation property.

(C) *Loss importation transaction.* FP's transfer of A1 is a section 362 transaction. Furthermore, but for section 362(e)(1) and this section

and section 362(e)(2), DC's basis in the importation property, F's portion of A1, would be $50 under section 362(a) and the property's value would be $35 immediately after the transaction. Therefore, the importation property's basis would exceed its value and the transfer is a loss importation transaction.

(D) *Application of section 362(e)(1) and this section to importation property received in loss importation transaction.* Because the importation property, F's tentatively divided portion of A1, was transferred in a loss importation transaction, section 362(e)(1) and paragraph (b)(1) of this section apply and DC's basis in F's portion of A1 will be equal to its $35 value.

(E) *Basis of property received in transaction.* Following the application of section 362(e)(1) and this section, the provisions of section 362(e)(2) must be taken into account because the transfer is a section 362(a) transaction. Taking into account the application of section 362(e)(1) and this section but without taking into account the provisions of section 362(e)(2), DC's aggregate basis in A1 would be $85 (the sum of the $35 basis in F's tentatively divided portion of A1, as determined under paragraph (i)(D) of this *Example 5*, and the $50 basis in A's tentatively divided portion of A1, determined under section 362(a), see paragraphs (d)(2) and (e)(3) of this section) and A1's value immediately after the transfer would be $70. Therefore, FP has a net built-in loss and FP's transfer of A1 is a loss duplication transaction. Accordingly, under the general rule of section 362(e)(2), FP's $15 net built-in loss ($85 basis over $70 value) would be allocated to reduce DC's basis in the loss asset, A1, the only loss property transferred by FP. As a result, DC's basis in A1 would be $70 ($85 basis under section 362(a) and this section, reduced by the $15 net built-in loss). Under section 358, FP's basis in the DC stock received in the exchange will be $100. See § 1.362-4.

(ii) *Transfer with election to apply section 362(e)(2)(C).* The facts are the same as in paragraph (i)(A) of this *Example 5*, except that FP and DC elect to apply section 362(e)(2)(C) to reduce FP's basis in the DC stock received in the exchange. The analysis and results are the same as in paragraphs (i)(B), (C), (D), and (E) of this *Example 5*, except that the $15 reduction to DC's basis in A1 is not made and, as a result, DC's basis in A1 remains $85, and FP's basis in the DC stock received in the exchange is reduced from $100 to $85. The $15 reduction to FP's basis in DC stock reduces A's basis in its FP interest under section 705(a)(2)(B). See § 1.362-4(e)(1).

(iii) *Transfer by domestic partnership.* The facts are the same as in paragraph (i)(A) of this *Example 5* except that FP is a domestic partnership. The analysis and results are the same as in paragraphs (i)(B), (C), (D), and (E) of this *Example 5*.

(iv) *Transfer of interest in partnership with liability.* (A) *Facts.* F and two other individuals are equal partners in FP. F's basis in its partnership interest is $247. F's share of FP's § 1.752-1 liabilities (as defined in § 1.752-1(a)(4)) is $150. F transfers his partnership interest to DC in a transaction to which section 351 applies. If DC were to sell the FP interest immediately after the transfer, DC would receive $100 in cash or other property. In addition, taking into account the rules under § 1.752-4, DC's share of FP's § 1.752-1 liabilities (as defined in § 1.752-1(a)(4)) is $145 immediately after the transfer.

(B) *Importation property.* If F had sold his partnership interest immediately before the transaction, no gain or loss recognized on the sale would have been taken into account in determining a federal income tax liability. Further, if DC had sold the partnership interest immediately after the transaction, any gain or loss recognized on the sale would have been taken into account in determining a federal income tax liability. Therefore, F's partnership interest is importation property.

(C) *Loss importation transaction.* F's transfer is a section 362 transaction. However, but for section 362(e)(1) and this section and section 362(e)(2), DC's basis in the importation property, the partnership interest, determined under section 362(a) and taking into account the rules under section 752, would be $242 (F's $247 basis reduced by F's $150 share of FP liabilities and increased by DC's $145 share of FP liabilities) and, under paragraph (c)(4)(ii) of this section, the value of the FP interest would be $245 (the sum of $100, the cash DC would receive if DC immediately sold the partnership interest, and $145, DC's share of the § 1.752-1 liabilities (as defined in § 1.752-1(a)(4)) under section 752 immediately after the transfer to DC). Therefore, the importation property's basis ($242) would not exceed its value ($245), and the transfer is not a loss importation transaction.

(D) *Basis in property received in transaction.* Following the application of section 362(e)(1) and this section, the provisions of section 362(e)(2) must be taken into account because the transfer is a section 362(a) transaction. As described in paragraph (iv)(C) of this *Example 5*, taking into account the application of section 362(e)(1) and this section, DC's basis in the partnership interest would not exceed its value. Therefore, under § 1.362-4, F does not have a net built-in loss, the transfer is not a loss duplication transaction, and section 362(e)(2) does not apply to the transfer. DC's basis in F's partnership interest is $242, determined under sections 362(a) and 752. Under section 358, taking into account the rules under section 752, F's basis in the DC stock received in the exchange is $97 ($247 reduced by F's $150 share of FP liabilities). If FP had elected under section 754, or if section 743(b) required a downward basis adjustment to the partnership property, FP would apply the rules of § 1.743-1 to determine the amount of the basis adjustment to the partnership property.

Example 6. Transactions involving tax-exempt entities. (i) *Exempt transferor.* (A) *Facts.* InsCo is a benevolent life insurance association of a purely local character exempt from federal income tax under section 501(a) because it is described in section 501(c)(12). InsCo owns shares of stock of DC1 (basis $100, value $70) for investment purposes, which are not debt-financed property (as defined in section 514). On December 31, Year 1, InsCo transfers the DC1 stock to DC in exchange for DC stock in a transaction to which section 351 applies. No election is made under section 362(e)(2)(C).

(B) *Importation property.* If InsCo had sold the DC1 stock immediately before the transaction, any gain or loss realized would be excluded from UBTI under section 512(b)(5), and thus no gain or loss recognized on the sale would have been taken into account in determining federal income tax liability. Further, if DC had sold the DC1 stock immediately after the transaction, any gain or loss recognized on the sale would have been taken into account in determining federal income tax liability. Therefore, the DC1 stock is importation property.

(C) *Loss importation transaction.* InsCo's transfer is a section 362 transaction. Furthermore, but for section 362(e)(1) and this section and section 362(e)(2), DC's basis in importation property, the DC1 stock, would be $100, and the stock's value would be $70 immediately after the transaction. Therefore, the importation property's basis would exceed its value and the transfer is a loss importation transaction.

(D) *Application of section 362(e)(1) and this section to importation property received in loss importation transaction.* Because the importation property, the DC1 stock, was transferred in a loss importation transaction, paragraph (b)(1) of this section applies and DC's basis in the stock will be equal to its $70 value.

(E) *Basis of property received in transaction.* Following the application of section 362(e)(1) and this section, the provisions of section 362(e)(2) must be taken into account because the transfer is a section 362(a) transaction. Taking into account the application of section 362(e)(1) and this section, DC's basis in the DC1 stock does not exceed its value immediately after the transaction. Therefore, InsCo does not have a net built-in loss, InsCo's transfer is not a loss duplication transaction, and section 362(e)(2) has no application to the transaction. DC's basis in the DC1 stock, as determined under paragraph (i)(D) of this *Example 6,* is $70. Under section 358, InsCo's basis in the DC stock received in the exchange will be $100.

(ii) *Transferor loses tax-exempt status.* (A) *Facts.* The facts are the same as in paragraph (i)(A) of this *Example 6* except that InsCo fails to be described in section 501(c)(12) in Year 1.

(B) *Importation property.* If InsCo had sold the DC1 stock immediately before the transaction, any gain or loss recognized on the sale would have been taken into account in determining a federal income tax liability. Therefore, the DC1 stock is not importation property and this section does not apply to the transaction.

(C) *Basis of property received in transaction.* Following the application of section 362(e)(1) and this section, the provisions of section 362(e)(2) must be taken into account because the transfer is a section 362(a) transaction. Taking into account the application of section 362(e)(1) and this section but without taking into account the provisions of section 362(e)(2), DC would have a section 362(a) basis of $100 in the stock, which would exceed its value of $70 immediately after the transfer. Therefore, InsCo has a net built-in loss and InsCo's transfer of the DC1 stock is a loss duplication transaction. Accordingly, under the general rule of section 362(e)(2), InsCo's $30 net built-in loss ($100 basis over $70 value) would be allocated to reduce DC's basis in the loss asset, the DC1 stock, the only loss property transferred by InsCo. As a result, DC's basis in the DC1 stock would be $70 ($100 basis under section 362(a), reduced by the $30 net built-in loss). Under section 358, InsCo's basis in the DC stock received in the exchange will be $100.

(iii) *Transfer of property that is subject to unrelated business tax.* (A) *Facts.* The facts are the same as in paragraph (i)(A) of this *Example 6* except that, on December 31, Year 1, instead of the DC1 stock, InsCo transfers A1 (basis $200, value $150) to DC. A1 is real property that InsCo owned from January 1 to December 31 of Year 1. During the entirety of this period, A1's basis was $200, and in the twelve months prior to December 31, Year 1, the highest amount of outstanding principal indebtedness on A1 was $40. For purposes of the UBTI rules under *section 512, A1 is debt-financed property within the* meaning of section 514(b).

(B) *Importation property.* If InsCo had sold A1 immediately before the transaction, 20 percent of any gain or loss recognized on that sale (that is, $40 of acquisition indebtedness on A1 divided by A1's $200

basis in Year 1) would, under sections 512 and 514, be includible in UBTI at the end of Year 1, and 80 percent would not. Thus, under paragraph (d)(4) of this section, A1 is treated as tentatively divided into two portions, one reflecting the gain or loss that would be taken into account in determining a federal income tax liability in InsCo's hands immediately before the transfer (the 20 percent portion) and one that would not (the 80 percent portion). Further, if DC sold A1 immediately after the transfer, any gain or loss on both portions would be taken into account in determining a federal income tax liability. Accordingly, the 20 percent portion is not importation property, but the 80 percent portion is.

(C) *Loss importation transaction.* InsCo's transfer of A1 is a section 362 transaction. Furthermore, but for section 362(e)(1) and this section and section 362(e)(2), DC's basis in the importation property, the 80 percent portion of A1, would be $160 (80 percent of InsCo's $200 basis) under section 362(a) and the property's value would be $120 (80% of A1's $120 value) immediately after the transaction. Therefore, the importation property's basis would exceed its value and the transfer is a loss importation transaction.

(D) *Application of section 362(e)(1) and this section to importation property received in loss importation transaction.* Because the importation property, the 80 percent portion of A1, was transferred in a loss importation transaction, section 362(e)(1) and paragraph (b)(1) of this section apply and DC's basis in that portion of A1 will be equal to its $120 value.

(E) *Basis of property received in transaction.* Following the application of section 362(e)(1) and this section, the provisions of section 362(e)(2) must be taken into account because the transfer is a section 362(a) transaction. Taking into account the application of section 362(e)(1) and this section but without taking into account the provisions of section 362(e)(2), DC's aggregate basis in A1 would be $160 (the sum of the $120 basis in the 80 percent importation portion of A1, as determined under paragraph (iii)(D) of this *Example 6,* and the $40 basis in the 20 percent portion of A1 that is not importation property, determined under section 362(a). See paragraph (e)(3) of this section). Further, A1's value immediately after the transfer would be $150. Therefore, InsCo has a net built-in loss in A1, and InsCo's transfer of A1 is a loss duplication transaction. Accordingly, under the general rule of section 362(e)(2), InsCo's $10 net built-in loss ($160 basis over $150 value) would be allocated to reduce DC's basis in the loss asset, A1, the only loss property transferred by InsCo. As a result, DC's basis in A1 would be $150 ($160 basis under section 362(a) and this section, reduced by the $10 net built-in loss). Under section 358, InsCo's basis in the DC stock received in the exchange will be $200. See § 1.362-4.

(iv) *Transfer with election to apply section 362(e)(2)(C).* The facts are the same as in paragraph (iii)(A) of this *Example 6,* except that InsCo and DC elect to apply section 362(e)(2)(C) to reduce InsCo's basis in the DC stock received in the exchange. The analysis and results are the same as in paragraphs (iii)(B), (C), (D), and (E) of this *Example 6,* except that the $10 reduction to DC's basis in A1 is not made and, as a result, DC's basis in A1 remains $160; however, InsCo's basis in the DC stock received in the exchange is reduced from $200 to $190.

Example 7. Transactions involving CFCs. (i) *Transfer by CFC.* (A) *Facts.* FC is a CFC with 100 shares of stock outstanding. A owns 60 of the shares and F owns the remaining 40 shares. FC owns two assets, A1 (basis $70, value $100), which is used in the conduct of a U.S. trade or business, and A2 (basis $100, value $75), which is not used in the conduct of a U.S. trade or business. FC transfers both assets to DC in a transaction to which section 351 applies.

(B) *Importation property.* If FC had sold A1 immediately before the transaction, any gain or loss recognized on the sale would have been taken into account in determining a federal income tax liability (FC's). See section 882(a). Therefore, A1 is not importation property. If FC had sold A2 immediately before the transaction, FC would not take the gain or loss recognized into account in determining its federal income tax liability, but the gain or loss could be taken into account in determining a section 951 inclusion to FC's U.S. shareholders. However, under paragraph (d)(3) of this section, gain or loss is not deemed taken into account in determining a federal income tax liability solely because it could affect an inclusion under section 951(a). Further, if DC had sold A2 immediately after the transaction, any gain or loss recognized on the sale would have been taken into account in determining a federal income tax liability. Therefore, A2 is importation property.

(C) *Loss importation transaction.* FC's transfer is a section 362 transaction. Furthermore, but for section 362(e)(1) and this section and section 362(e)(2), DC's basis in the importation property, A2, would be $100 and the property's value would be $75 immediately after the transaction. Therefore, the importation property's basis would exceed its value and the transfer is a loss importation transaction.

(D) *Application of section 362(e)(1) and this section to importation property received in loss importation transaction.* Because the importation property, A2, was transferred in a loss importation transaction, paragraph (b)(1) of this section applies and DC's basis in A2 will be equal to A2's $75 value immediately after the transfer.

(E) *Basis of property received in transaction.* Following the application of section 362(e)(1) and this section, the provisions of section 362(e)(2) must be taken into account because the transfer is a section 362(a) transaction. Taking into account the application of section 362(e)(1) and this section but without taking into account the provisions of section 362(e)(2), DC would have an aggregate basis of $145 in the transferred properties ($70 in A1, determined under section 362(a), plus $75 in A2, determined under this section) and the properties would have an aggregate value of $175 ($100 + $75) immediately after the transfer. Therefore, FC does not have a net built-in loss, FC's transfer is not a loss duplication transaction, and section 362(e)(2) does not apply to the transaction. DC's basis in A1 will be $70, determined under section 362(a), and DC's basis in A2 will be $75, as determined under paragraph (i)(D) of this *Example 7.* Under the general rule in section 358(a), FC receives the DC stock with a basis of $170 ($70 attributable to A1 plus $100 attributable to A2).

(ii) *Transfer of CFC stock.* (A) *Facts.* The facts are the same as in paragraph (i)(A) of this *Example 7,* except that A transfers its 60 shares of FC stock (basis $80, value $105) and F transfers its 40 shares of FC stock (basis $100, value $70) to DC in an exchange that qualifies under section 351.

(B) *Importation property.* If A had sold its FC shares immediately before the transaction, any gain or loss recognized on the sale would have been taken into account in determining a federal income tax liability (A's). Therefore, A's FC shares are not importation property. However, if F had sold its FC shares immediately before the transaction, no gain or loss recognized on the sale would have been taken into account in determining a federal income tax liability. Further, if DC had sold F's FC shares immediately after the transaction, any gain or loss recognized on the sale would have been taken into account in determining a federal income tax liability. Therefore, F's FC shares are importation property.

(C) *Loss importation transaction.* The transfer of the FC shares is a section 362 transaction. Furthermore, but for section 362(e)(1) and this section and section 362(e)(2), DC's aggregate basis in the importation property, F's shares of FC stock, would be $100 under section 362(a) and the shares' aggregate value would be $70. Therefore, the importation property's aggregate basis would exceed its aggregate value, and the transfer is a loss importation transaction.

(D) *Application of section 362(e)(1) and this section to importation property received in loss importation transaction.* Because the importation property, F's shares of FC stock, was transferred in a loss importation transaction, paragraph (b)(1) of this section applies and DC's aggregate basis in the shares will be equal to their $70 aggregate value immediately after the transfer.

(E) *Basis of property received in transaction.* Following the application of section 362(e)(1) and this section, the provisions of section 362(e)(2) must be taken into account because the transfer is a section 362(a) transaction. The application of section 362(e)(2) is determined separately for each transferor. See §1.362-4(b).

(1) *A's transfer.* Taking into account the application of section 362(e)(1) and this section, DC's aggregate basis in the shares ($80 under section 362(a)) would not exceed the shares' value ($105) immediately after the transaction. Therefore A does not have a built-in loss, A's transfer is not a loss duplication transaction, and section 362(e)(2) does not apply to A's transfer. DC's aggregate basis in A's shares, determined under section 362(a), is $80. Under section 358(a), A receives the DC stock with a basis of $80.

(2) *F's transfer.* Taking into account the application of section 362(e)(1) and this section, DC's aggregate basis in the shares would not exceed their value immediately after the transaction. Therefore, F does not have a built-in loss, F's transfer is not a loss duplication transaction, and section 362(e)(2) does not apply to F's transfer. DC's aggregate basis in F's shares, as determined under paragraph (ii)(D) of this *Example 7,* is $70. Under section 358(a), F receives the DC stock with a basis of $100.

Example 8. Property subject to withholding tax. (i) *Facts.* FC owns a share of DC1 stock (basis $100, value $70) as an investment. FC receives dividends on the share that are subject to federal withholding tax of 30 percent of the amount received under section 881(a); under section 1442(a), DC1 must withhold tax on the dividends paid. FC transfers the DC1 share to DC in a transaction to which section 351 applies.

(ii) *Importation property.* Although any dividends received with respect to the DC1 stock were subject to withholding tax, if FC had sold the share of stock of DC1, no gain or loss recognized on the sale would have been taken into account in determining a federal income tax liability. See section 865(a)(2). Further, if DC had sold the share of DC1 stock immediately after the transaction, any gain or loss recognized on the sale would be taken into account in determining federal income tax liability. Therefore, the share of DC1 stock is importation property.

(iii) *Loss importation transaction.* FC's transfer is a section 362 transaction. Furthermore, but for section 362(e)(1) and this section and section 362(e)(2), DC's basis in the importation property, the share of DC1 stock, would be $100 and the share's value would be $70 immediately after the transaction. Therefore, the share's basis would exceed its value and the transfer is a loss importation transaction.

(iv) *Application of section 362(e)(1) and this section to importation property received in loss importation transaction.* Because the importation property, the DC1 share, was transferred in a loss importation transaction, paragraph (b)(1) of this section applies and DC's basis in the share will be equal to the share's $70 value.

(v) *Basis of property received in transaction.* Following the application of section 362(e)(1) and this section, the provisions of section 362(e)(2) must be taken into account because the transfer is a section 362(a) transaction. Taking into account the application of section 362(e)(1) and this section, DC's basis in the DC1 share would not exceed the share's value immediately after the transaction. Therefore, FC does not have a net built-in loss, FC's transfer is not a loss duplication transaction, and section 362(e)(2) does not apply to the transaction. DC's basis in the DC1 share, as determined under paragraph (iv) of this *Example 8,* is $70. Under section 358, FC's basis in the DC stock received in the exchange will be $100.

Example 9. Property transferred in triangular reorganization. (i) *Foreign subsidiary.* (A) *Facts.* P owns the sole outstanding share of stock of FC (basis $1), FC1 owns the sole outstanding share of FC2 (basis $100), and FC2 owns one asset, A1 (basis $100, value $20). In a forward triangular merger described in §1.358-6(b)(2)(i), FC2 merges with and into FC, and FC1 receives shares of P stock in exchange for its FC2 stock. The forward triangular merger is a transaction described in section 368(a)(2)(D) and, therefore, in section 362(b).

(B) *Determining P's basis in its FC share.* Pursuant to §1.358-6, for purposes of determining the adjustment to P's basis in its FC shares, P is treated as though it first received A1 in a transaction in which its basis in A1 would be determined under section 362(b) and then it transferred A1 to FC in a transaction in which P's basis in its FC stock would be determined under section 358.

(1) *P's deemed acquisition and transfer of A1.* If FC2 had sold A1 for its value immediately before the deemed transaction, no gain or loss recognized on the sale would have been taken into account in determining a federal income tax liability. If P had sold A1 immediately after the deemed transaction, any gain or loss recognized on the sale would have been taken into account in determining a federal income tax liability (P's). Therefore, with respect to P's deemed acquisition, A1 is importation property. Furthermore, immediately after the deemed transaction, P's basis in A1, but for section 362(e)(1) and this section and section 362(e)(2), would be $100 and A1's value is $20. Therefore, the importation property's basis would exceed its value and the transfer is a loss importation transaction. Accordingly, P's deemed basis in A1 will be equal to A1's $20 value.

(2) *P's FC stock basis.* As a result of P's deemed transfer of A1 to FC (and applying the principles of §1.367(b)-13), P's basis in its FC stock is increased by its $20 deemed basis in A1. Accordingly, following the transaction, P's basis in its share of FC stock will be $21 (the sum of its original $1 basis and the $20 adjustment for the deemed transfer of A1).

(C) *FC's basis in A1.* FC's basis in A1 is determined under the rules of this section without regard to the determination of P's adjustment to its basis in FC stock. If FC2 had sold A1 for its value immediately before the transaction, no gain or loss recognized on the sale would have been taken into account in determining a federal income tax liability. However, if FC had sold A1 immediately after the transaction, no gain or loss recognized on the sale would have been taken into account in determining a federal income tax liability, so A1 is not importation property. Accordingly, this section will not apply to the transaction. Although there is a net built-in loss in A1, the transaction is not described in section 362(a), and so section 362(e)(2) and §1.362-4 will not apply to the transaction. Thus, under section 362(b), FC's basis in A1 will be $100.

(D) *FC1's basis in P stock.* Under section 358, FC1's basis in the P stock it receives in the exchange will be $100.

(ii) *Property transferred to U.S. subsidiary in triangular reorganization.* (A) *Facts.* The facts are the same as in paragraph (i)(A) of this *Example 9,* except that P also owns the sole outstanding share of DC (basis $1) and, instead of merging into FC, FC2 merged into DC.

(B) *Determining P's basis in its DC share.* As determined under paragraph (i)(B)(2) of this *Example 9,* P's basis in its DC share is $21, the sum of its original $1 basis plus the $20 adjustment for the deemed transfer of A1.

(C) *DC's basis in A1.* If FC2 had sold A1 for its value immediately before the transaction, no gain or loss recognized on the sale would have been taken into account in determining a federal income tax liability. However, if DC had sold A1 immediately after the transaction, any gain or loss recognized on the sale would have been taken into account in determining a federal income tax liability, so A1 is importation property with respect to DC. Furthermore, immediately after the transaction, DC's basis in A1, but for section 362(e)(1) and this section and section 362(e)(2), would be $100 and A1's value is $20. Therefore, the importation property's basis would exceed its value and the transfer is a loss importation transaction. Accordingly, DC's basis in A1 will be $20, A1's value immediately after the transaction.

(D) *FC1's basis in P stock.* Under section 358, FC1's basis in the P stock it receives in the exchange is $100.

(g) *Applicability date.*—This section applies with respect to any transaction occurring on or after March 28, 2016, and also with respect to any transaction occurring before such date as a result of an entity classification election under §301.7701-3 of this chapter filed on or after March 28, 2016, unless such transaction is pursuant to a binding agreement that was in effect prior to March 28, 2016 and at all times thereafter. In addition, taxpayers may apply this section to any transaction occurring after October 22, 2004. [Reg. §1.362-3.]

⬜ [T.D. 9759, 3-25-2016.]

[Reg. §1.362-4]

§1.362-4. Basis of loss duplication property.—(a) *Purpose and scope.*—(1) *In general.*—The purpose of section 362(e)(2) and this section is to prevent the duplication of net loss in transfers to which section 351 applies, capital contributions, and paid-in surplus (each, a section 362(a) transaction). See paragraph (g) of this section for definitions of terms used in this section.

(2) *Intercompany transactions.*—For rules relating to the application of section 362(e)(2) to transfers between members of a consolidated group on or after October 22, 2004, see §1.1502-80(h).

(b) *Basis determinations under section 362(e)(2) and this section.*—Notwithstanding section 362(a), if a corporation (Acquiring) receives loss duplication property (as defined in paragraph (g)(1) of this section) from a person (Transferor) in a loss duplication transaction (as defined in paragraph (g)(2) of this section), Acquiring's basis in such property is equal to the basis of the property determined without regard to section 362(e)(2) and this section (as described in paragraph (g)(1)(ii) of this section), reduced by the property's allocable portion of Transferor's net built-in loss (as defined in paragraph (g)(3) of this section). If more than one Transferor transfers property to a corporation in a section 362(a) transaction, whether and the extent to which section 362(e)(2) and this section apply is determined separately for each Transferor.

(c) *Exceptions and special rules.*—(1) *Transactions in which net built-in loss is eliminated without recognition.*—Section 362(e)(2) does not apply to a transaction to the extent that—

(i) Without recognizing gain or loss, Transferor distributes the Acquiring stock received in the transaction; and

(ii) Upon completion of the transaction, no person holds Acquiring stock or any other asset with a basis determined, in whole or in part, by reference to Transferor's basis in the distributed Acquiring stock.

(2) *Certain transactions outside of the United States.*—Section 362(e)(2) does not apply to a transaction if—

(i) Neither Transferor nor Acquiring is a U.S. person (as defined in section 7701(a)(30)), a person otherwise required to file a U.S. return for the year of the transaction, a controlled foreign corporation (CFC, as defined in paragraph (g)(7) of this section), or a controlled foreign partnership (CFP, as defined in paragraph (g)(9) of this section) on the date of the transaction;

(ii) The transfer occurs more than two years prior to the date of any event described in paragraph (d)(3)(ii)(E), (F), or (G) of this section; and

(iii) The original transaction and the event or events described in paragraph (d)(3)(ii)(E), (F), or (G) of this section were not entered into with a view to reducing or avoiding the Federal income tax liability of any person by avoiding the application of section 362(e)(2) and this section to the original transaction.

(3) *Other effects of basis determination under this section.*—(i) *Determination by reference to transferor's basis.*—A determination of basis under this section is a determination by reference to the transferor's basis, including for purposes of sections 755, 1223(2), and 7701(a)(43).

(ii) *Treatment as tax-exempt income or noncapital, nondeductible expense.*—A determination of basis under paragraph (b) of this section does not give rise to an item treated as a noncapital, nondeductible expense under §1.1502-32(b)(2)(iii). However, a determination of basis under paragraph (d) of this section does give rise to an item treated as a noncapital, nondeductible expense under §1.1502-32(b)(2)(iii).

(d) *Election to reduce Transferor's stock basis instead of Acquiring's asset basis.*—(1) *In general.*—In lieu of making the basis reductions otherwise required under paragraph (b) of this section, Transferor and Acquiring may elect to reduce Transferor's basis in Acquiring stock that is received in the transaction without the recognition of gain or loss (the section 362(e)(2)(C) election). The section 362(e)(2)(C) election may be made protectively and will have no effect to the extent that property transferred in the transaction is determined not to be subject to section 362(e)(2) and this section. However, the election is irrevocable once it is made. A section 362(e)(2)(C) election is made and effective if—

(i) Prior to the filing of a Section 362(e)(2)(C) Statement (described in paragraph (d)(3)(i) of this section), Transferor and Acquiring enter into a written, binding agreement to elect to apply section 362(e)(2)(C); and

(ii) The Section 362(e)(2)(C) Statement is filed in accordance with the provisions of paragraph (d)(3) of this section.

(2) *Effect of section 362(e)(2)(C) election.*—If a section 362(e)(2)(C) election is made and in effect—

(i) An amount equal to the portion of Transferor's net built-in loss (as defined in paragraph (g)(3) of this section) that would otherwise be applied to reduce asset basis under paragraph (b) of this section is allocated among the Acquiring shares received or deemed received in the exchange (in proportion to the value of such shares) and applied to reduce Transferor's basis (determined without regard to section 362(e)(2) and this section) in each such share; and

(ii) Acquiring's basis in loss duplication property received from Transferor in the transaction is not determined under section 362(e)(2) and this section.

(3) *Section 362(e)(2)(C) Statement.*—(i) *Form and contents of statement.*—The Section 362(e)(2)(C) Statement is to be titled "Section 362(e)(2)(C) Statement." The Section 362(e)(2)(C) Statement must—

(A) Identify (by name and tax identification number, if any) Transferor and Acquiring;

(B) State that Transferor and Acquiring have entered into a written, binding agreement to elect to apply section 362(e)(2)(C) as required in paragraph (d)(1)(i) of this section; and

(C) State the date of the transaction (or, if the transaction includes transfers on more than one date, then the dates of all transfers) to which the election applies.

(ii) *Filing the Section 362(e)(2)(C) Statement.*—In general, the Section 362(e)(2)(C) Statement is filed by the person or entity described in the applicable paragraph of this paragraph (d)(3)(ii). Thus, if Transferor is a partnership, S corporation, trust (including a subpart E trust), or other pass-through entity, or Acquiring is an S corporation, the entity (and not the partners, shareholders, or other persons having an interest in the entity or its property) is the person that must file the Section 362(e)(2)(C) Statement, without regard to whether such entity is foreign or domestic. However, in the case of a CFC or CFP, the controlling U.S. shareholders of the CFC or the reporting U.S. partners of the CFP, respectively, file the Section 362(e)(2)(C) Statement.

(A) *Transferor is a person required to file a U.S. return.*—If Transferor is a person required to file a U.S. return for the year of the transfer, Transferor must include the Section 362(e)(2)(C) Statement on or with its timely filed (including extensions) original U.S. return for the taxable year in which the transfer occurred.

(B) *Transferor is a CFC or CFP and not required to file a U.S. return.*—If paragraph (d)(3)(ii)(A) of this section does not apply and Transferor is either a CFC or a CFP on the date of the transfer, all of Transferor's controlling U.S. shareholders (in the case of a CFC) or all of Transferor's reporting U.S. partners (in the case of a CFP) must include the Section 362(e)(2)(C) Statement on or with their timely filed (including extensions) original U.S. returns for their taxable years in which the transfer occurred.

(C) *Transferor is not a person required to file a U.S. return, a CFC, or a CFP, but Acquiring is required to file U.S. return.*—If paragraphs (d)(3)(ii)(A) and (B) of this section do not apply and Acquiring is a person required to file a U.S. return for the year of the transfer, Acquiring must include the Section 362(e)(2)(C) Statement on or with its timely filed (including extensions) original U.S. return for the taxable year in which the transfer occurred.

(D) *Transferor is not a person required to file a U.S. return, a CFC, or a CFP, Acquiring is not required to file a U.S. return, but Acquiring is a CFC.*—If paragraphs (d)(3)(ii)(A) through (C) of this section do not apply and Acquiring is a CFC on the date of the transfer, all of Acquiring's controlling U.S. shareholders must include the Section 362(e)(2)(C) Statement on or with their timely filed (including extensions) original U.S. returns for their taxable years in which the transfer occurred.

(E) *Neither Transferor nor Acquiring is a person required to file a U.S. return, a CFC, or a CFP, but Transferor later becomes a person required to file a U.S. return, a CFC, or a CFP.*—If paragraphs (d)(3)(ii)(A) through (D) of this section do not apply and Transferor becomes a person required to file a U.S. return, a CFC, or a CFP, Transferor (if required to file a U.S. return), all of Transferor's controlling U.S. shareholders (if Transferor becomes a CFC not otherwise required to file a U.S. return), or all of Transferor's reporting U.S. partners (if Transferor becomes a CFP not otherwise required to file a U.S. return) must include the Section 362(e)(2)(C) Statement on or with their timely filed (including extensions) original U.S. returns for their taxable years in which an event described in this paragraph (d)(3)(ii)(E) first occurs. For purposes of this paragraph (d)(3)(ii)(E), the term Transferor includes any person holding property with a basis determined directly or indirectly by reference to Transferor's basis in the Acquiring stock received in the transaction.

(F) *Transferor is not and does not become a person required to file a U.S. return, a CFC, or a CFP, Acquiring is not, but later becomes either a person required to file a U.S. return, a CFC, or a CFP.*—If paragraphs (d)(3)(ii)(A) through (E) of this section do not apply and Acquiring becomes a person required to file a U.S. return, a CFC, or a CFP, Acquiring (if required to file a U.S. return), all of Acquiring's controlling U.S. shareholders (if Acquiring becomes a CFC not otherwise required to file a U.S. return), or all of Acquiring's reporting U.S. partners (if Acquiring becomes a CFP not otherwise required to file a U.S. return) must include the Section 362(e)(2)(C) Statement on or with their timely filed (including extensions) original U.S. returns for their taxable years in which an event described in this paragraph (d)(3)(ii)(F) first occurs. For purposes of this paragraph (d)(3)(ii)(F), the term Acquiring includes any person holding property with a basis determined directly or indirectly by reference to Acquiring's basis in loss duplication property received in the transaction.

(G) *Transferor and Acquiring are not and do not become a person required to file a U.S. return, a CFC, or a CFP, but the basis of the loss duplication property or Acquiring stock later becomes relevant for Federal tax purposes.*—If paragraphs (d)(3)(ii)(A) through (F) of this section do not apply and, in a transferred basis transaction, a person required to file a U.S. return, a CFC, or a CFP acquires either loss duplication property or Acquiring stock that was received in the loss duplication transaction, or any property the basis of which is determined in whole or in part by reference to any such property or stock, all such persons (or, in the case of a CFC or CFP not required to file a U.S. return, all the controlling U.S. shareholders or all the reporting U.S. partners, as applicable) must include the Section 362(e)(2)(C) Statement on or with their timely filed (including extensions) original U.S. returns for their first taxable year(s) in which there occurs an event or events described in this paragraph (d)(3)(ii)(G).

(e) *Transfers by partnerships and S corporations.*—(1) *Transfers by partnerships.*—If a partnership transfers property in a loss duplication transaction with respect to which a section 362(e)(2)(C) election is made, the resulting reduction to the partnership's basis in the Acquiring stock received in exchange for the loss duplication property is treated as an expenditure of the partnership described in section 705(a)(2)(B).

(2) *Transfers by S corporations.*—If an S corporation transfers property in a loss duplication transaction with respect to which a section 362(e)(2)(C) election is made, the resulting reduction to the S corporation's basis in the Acquiring stock received in exchange for the loss duplication property is treated as an expense of the S corporation described in section 1367(a)(2)(D).

(f) *Transfers to S corporations.*—If a person transfers property to an S corporation in a loss duplication transaction, any resulting reduction under section 362(e)(2) and this section to the S corporation's basis in the property received is not treated as an expense of the S corporation described in section 1367(a)(2)(D).

(g) *Definitions.*—For purposes of section 362(e)(2) and this section—

(1) *Loss duplication property* is any property—

(i) That is transferred by Transferor to Acquiring in a loss duplication transaction (as defined in paragraph (g)(2) of this section); and

(ii) That Acquiring would take with a basis in excess of value immediately after the transaction; for this purpose, the basis Acquiring would take in the property is determined immediately after the transaction and without regard to section 362(e)(2) and this section, but otherwise taking into account all applicable provisions of law, including, without limitation, section 362(e)(1).

(2) A *loss duplication transaction* is a section 362(a) transaction in which Acquiring's aggregate basis in the property received from Transferor would, but for section 362(e)(2) and this section, exceed

the aggregate value of such property immediately after the transaction. For this purpose—

(i) A transaction is a section 362(a) transaction if it is described in section 362(a) without regard to whether it is also described in any other provision of the Internal Revenue Code (Code), including, without limitation, section 362(b); and

(ii) Acquiring's aggregate basis in the property received from Transferor is determined immediately after the transaction and without regard to section 362(e)(2) and this section, but otherwise taking into account all applicable provisions of law, including, without limitation, section 362(e)(1).

(3) *Transferor's net built-in loss* is the excess of—

(i) Acquiring's aggregate basis (determined under paragraph (g)(2)(ii) of this section) in all property received from Transferor in a loss duplication transaction, over

(ii) The aggregate value of such property immediately after the transaction.

(4) A property's *built-in loss* is the excess of Acquiring's basis in the property (determined as described in paragraph (g)(1)(ii) of this section) over the property's value (determined immediately after the transaction).

(5) A property's *allocable portion of Transferor's net built-in loss* is the portion of Transferor's net built-in loss that bears the same ratio to Transferor's net built-in loss that the property's built-in loss bears to the aggregate built-in losses reflected in the bases of loss duplication property transferred by Transferor in the transaction.

(6) A *U.S. return* is a return of income under section 6012 or an information return under Subtitle F, Chapter 61, Subchapter A, Part III of the Code (sections 6031 and following) or the regulations thereunder, that the taxpayer is unconditionally required to file. Thus, the term does not include elective forms or statements that are required to be filed only to obtain a particular tax treatment, including forms filed to make an election or to reduce or avoid withholding by a person not otherwise required to file a U.S. return (as described in this paragraph (g)(6)) (for example, a notice of nonrecognition under § 1.1445-2(d)).

(7) A *controlled foreign corporation* (CFC) is any corporation described in section 957 or section 953(c).

(8) A *controlling U.S. shareholder* is any person that is treated as a controlling U.S. shareholder under § 1.964-1(c)(5) because such person either owns a direct interest in the CFC or is treated as owning an interest in the CFC by reason of section 318(a)(2) (attribution from partnerships, estates, trusts, and corporations).

(9) A *controlled foreign partnership* (CFP) is any partnership treated as a controlled foreign partnership for purposes of section 6038.

(10) A *reporting U.S. partner* is any partner of a CFP that is required to file an information return with respect to the CFP pursuant to section 6038 or the regulations thereunder, without regard to § 1.6038-3(c) or (j). In addition, in applying the constructive ownership rules of § 1.6038-3(b)(4), the term "nonresident alien" is replaced by the term "individual."

(11) The term *stock* means both Acquiring stock and Acquiring securities received by Transferor in the transaction if gain or loss on the receipt of the stock or securities is not recognized in whole or in part.

(12) *Value.*—(i) *General rule.*—The term *value* means fair market value.

(ii) *Special rule for transfers of partnership interests.*—Notwithstanding the general rule in paragraph (g)(12)(i) of this section, when referring to a partnership interest, for purposes of section 362(e)(2) and this section, the term *value* means the sum of the cash that Acquiring would receive for the interest, assuming an exchange between a willing buyer and a willing seller (neither being under any compulsion to buy or sell and both having reasonable knowledge of relevant facts), increased by any § 1.752-1 liabilities (as defined in § 1.752-1(a)(4)) of the partnership allocated to Acquiring with regard to such transferred interest under section 752 immediately after the transfer to Acquiring. See § 1.743-1 regarding the application of section 743(b) following a section 362(e) basis reduction.

(h) *Examples.*—The examples in this paragraph (h) illustrate the application of section 362(e)(2) and the provisions of this section. Unless the facts otherwise indicate, the examples use the following nomenclature and assumptions: X, Y, P, S, S1, and S2 are domestic corporations; A and B are U.S. individuals; FC1 and FC2 are foreign corporations and are not engaged in a U.S. trade or business, have no U.S. real property interests, and have no other relationships, activities, or interests that would cause them, their shareholders, or their property to be subject to tax imposed under any provision of subtitle A of the Internal Revenue Code (federal income tax); there is no applicable income tax treaty; PRS is a domestic partnership; no election is made under section 362(e)(2)(C); and the transferred property is not importation property (as defined in § 1.362-3(c)(2)) and the transfers are not loss importation transactions (as defined in § 1.362-3(c)(3)), so that the basis of no property is determined under section 362(e)(1). All persons and transactions are unrelated unless the facts indicate otherwise, all taxpayers are on a calendar tax year, and all other relevant facts are set forth in the examples. See § 1.362-3(f) for additional examples illustrating the application of section 362(e)(2) and this section, including to transactions that are subject to section 362(e)(2), and section 362(e)(1).

Example 1. Transfer described in section 351. (i) *Basic application of section.* (A) *Facts.* A owns Asset 1 (basis $90, value $60) and Asset 2 (basis $110, value $120). In a transaction to which section 351 applies, A transfers Asset 1 and Asset 2 to X in exchange for a single outstanding share of X stock representing all the outstanding X stock immediately after the transaction.

(B) *Analysis.* (1) *Loss duplication transaction.* A's transfer of Asset 1 and Asset 2 is a section 362(a) transaction. But for section 362(e)(2) and this section, X's aggregate basis in those assets would be $200 ($90 + $110), which would exceed the aggregate value of the assets $180 ($60 + $120) immediately after the transaction. Accordingly, the transfer is a loss duplication transaction and A has a net built-in loss of $20 ($200 - $180).

(2) *Identifying loss duplication property.* But for section 362(e)(2) and this section, X's basis in Asset 1 would be $90, which would exceed Asset 1's $60 value immediately after the transaction. Accordingly, Asset 1 is loss duplication property. But for section 362(e)(2) and this section, X's basis in Asset 2 would be $110, which would not exceed Asset 2's $120 value immediately after the transaction. Accordingly, Asset 2 is not loss duplication property.

(C) *Basis in loss duplication property.* X's basis in Asset 1 is $70, computed as its $90 basis under section 362(a) reduced by A's $20 net built-in loss.

(D) *Basis in other property.* Under section 362(a), X has a transferred basis of $110 in Asset 2. Under section 358(a), A has an exchanged basis of $200 in the X stock it receives in the transaction.

(ii) *Section 362(e)(2)(C) election.* The facts are the same as in paragraph (i)(A) of this *Example 1*, except that A and X make an election under section 362(e)(2)(C). Under paragraph (d)(2)(i) of this section, A reduces its basis in the X stock, as determined without regard to section 362(e)(2) and this section, by the amount of A's net built-in loss that would have been applied to reduce X's basis in Asset 1 had the section 362(e)(2)(C) election not been made. In addition, no reduction is made to X's basis in Asset 1, as determined without regard to section 362(e)(2) and this section. As a result, A's basis in the X stock is $180 ($200 - $20), X's basis in Asset 1 is $90, and X's basis in Asset 2 is $110.

Example 2. Transfer described in both section 351 and section 368(a)(1)(B). (i) *Basic application of section.* (A) *Facts.* P owns the sole outstanding share of S1 stock and the ten outstanding shares of S2 stock. In a transaction to which section 351 applies and that is described in section 368(a)(1)(B), P transfers its ten S2 shares to S1 in exchange for an additional ten shares of S1 voting stock. At the time of the transfer, P has a basis of $10 each in five of its S2 shares (Shares 1 - 5) and a basis of $5 each in its other five S2 shares (Shares 6 - 10), and the value of each share is $7.

(B) *Analysis.* (1) *Loss duplication transaction.* P's transfer of the S2 shares is a section 362(a) transaction notwithstanding that it is also a transaction described in section 368(a)(1)(B) and therefore section 362(b). But for section 362(e)(2) and this section, S1's aggregate basis in the S2 shares would be $75 ($10 × 5, or $50, for Shares 1-5 + $5 × 5, or $25, for Shares 6-10). Thus, S1's $75 aggregate basis in the shares would exceed the aggregate value of the shares, $70 ($7 × 10 shares), immediately after the transaction. Accordingly, the transfer is a loss duplication transaction and P has a net built-in loss of $5 ($75 - $70).

(2) *Identifying loss duplication property.* But for section 362(e)(2) and this section, S1's basis in each of Shares 1-5 would be $10, which would exceed each share's $7 value immediately after the transaction. Accordingly, Shares 1-5 are each loss duplication property. But for section 362(e)(2) and this section, S1's basis in each of Shares 6-10 would be $5, which would not exceed each share's $7 value immediately after the transaction. Accordingly, Shares 6-10 are not loss duplication property.

(C) *Basis in loss duplication property.* S1's basis in each of Shares 1 - 5 is $9, computed as its $10 basis (determined without regard to section 362(e)(2) and this section) reduced by $1, the share's allocable portion (1/5) of P's net built-in loss ($5).

(D) *Basis in other property.* Under section 362(a), S1 has a transferred basis of $5 in each of Shares 6 - 10. Under section 358(a), P has an exchanged basis in the ten S1 shares it receives in the exchange ($10 *in each of the five S1 shares received in exchange for Shares* 1-5 and $5 in each of the five S1 shares received in exchange for Shares 5 - 10).

(ii) *Section 362(e)(2)(C) election.* The facts are the same as in paragraph (i)(A) of this *Example 2*, except that an election under section 362(e)(2)(C) is made to reduce P's basis in the shares of S1 stock

received in the exchange. Under paragraph (d)(2)(i) of this section, P reduces its basis in the S1 stock by $5, the amount of P's net built-in loss that S1's basis in the S2 shares would have been reduced under section 362(e)(2) and this section had the section 362(e)(2)(C) election not been made, and no reduction is made to S1's basis in the S2 stock (as determined without regard to section 362(e)(2) and this section). Because an election is being made under section 362(e)(2)(C), P's basis in the new S1 shares is not determined under the general rule of § 1.358-2(a)(2)(i) (under which P's basis in each new S1 share would be equal to the basis of the S2 share transferred in exchange for the S1 share). Section 1.358-2(a)(2)(viii)(B). Accordingly, P's basis in each new S1 share will be $7, the share's allocable portion of P's $75 aggregate basis in the S2 shares transferred in the transaction (or, $7.50 per share), reduced under paragraph (d)(2)(i) of this section by the $5 that would have been applied to reduce S1's basis in the S2 shares had the section 362(e)(2)(C) election not been made (or $.50 per share). Under paragraph (d)(2)(ii) of this section and section 362(a), S1 receives five shares of the S2 stock with a basis of $10 each and five shares of the S2 stock with a basis of $5 each.

Example 3. Transfer described in both section 351 and section 368(a)(1)(A), multiple transferors, elimination of duplicated loss. (i) *Facts.* A owns Asset 1 (basis $120, value $130) and all the outstanding shares of X stock. B owns all the outstanding shares of Y stock (basis $150). Y owns Asset 2 (basis $250, value $210). Pursuant to a single plan, A transfers Asset 1 to X in exchange for additional X shares and, in a transaction qualifying as a reorganization described in section 368(a)(1)(A), Y merges with and into X. In the merger, B receives X stock with a basis equal to B's basis in its Y stock immediately before the merger. A's transfer of Asset 1 to X in exchange for X stock and Y's transfer of Asset 2 to X in the merger are both transactions to which section 351 applies. Notwithstanding that the transfers by A and Y are pursuant to a single plan forming one transaction, section 362(e)(2) and this section apply to each transferor separately.

(ii) *Application of section to A's transfer of Asset 1.* A's transfer of Asset 1 is a section 362(a) transaction. But for section 362(e)(2) and this section, X's basis in Asset 1 would be $120, which would not exceed Asset 1's $130 value immediately after the transaction. Accordingly, A's transfer of Asset 1 is not a loss duplication transaction notwithstanding that, taking both A's transfer and Y's transfer into account, X has an aggregate net loss in Asset 1 and Asset 2. Because Asset 1 is not received in a loss duplication transaction, it is not loss duplication property and section 362(e)(2) and this section do not apply to A's transfer of Asset 1.

(iii) *Application of section to Y's transfer of Asset 2.* (A) *Analysis.* (1) *Loss duplication transaction.* Y's transfer of Asset 2 to X is a section 362(a) transaction, notwithstanding that it is also a transaction described in section 368(a)(1)(A) and therefore section 362(b). But for section 362(e)(2) and this section, X's basis in Asset 2 would be $250, which would exceed Asset 2's $210 value immediately after the transaction. Accordingly, Y's transfer is a loss duplication transaction and Y has a net built-in loss of $40.

(2) *Identifying loss duplication property.* But for section 362(e)(2) and this section, X's basis in Asset 2 would be $250, which would exceed Asset 2's $210 value immediately after the transaction. Accordingly, Asset 2 is loss duplication property.

(B) *Basis in loss duplication property.* Although Asset 2 is loss duplication property, section 362(e)(2) does not apply to Y's transfer of Asset 2 to X because Y distributes all of the X stock received in the exchange without recognizing gain or loss, and, upon completion of the transaction, no person will hold the X stock or any other asset with a basis determined in whole or in part by reference to Y's basis in such stock. Accordingly, under paragraph (c)(1) of this section, X's basis in Asset 2 is not determined under section 362(e)(2) and this section. Thus, under section 362(a), X's basis in Asset 2 is $250.

(iv) *Basis in other property.* Under section 358, A's basis in the X stock received in exchange for Asset 1 is $120 and B's basis in the X stock received in the merger is $150. Under section 362(a), X's basis in Asset 1 is $120.

Example 4. Transfer described in both section 351 and section 368(a)(1)(D), followed by a distribution qualifying under section 355. (i) *Basic transaction.* (A) *Facts.* A and B each own one of the two outstanding shares of X common stock. X's assets include Asset 1 (basis $120, value $70), Asset 2 (basis $160, value $110), and Asset 3 (basis $220, value $240). In a transaction to which section 351 applies and that is described in section 368(a)(1)(D), X transfers Asset 1, Asset 2, and Asset 3 to Y in exchange for all the Y stock; then, in a distribution that qualifies under section 355, X distributes all the Y stock received in the exchange to A in exchange for all of A's X stock. Under section 361(c)(1), X does not recognize gain or loss as a result of the distribution of all the Y stock.

(B) *Analysis.* (1) *Loss duplication transaction.* X's transfer of Asset 1, Asset 2, and Asset 3 is a section 362(a) transaction. But for section 362(e)(2) and this section, Y's aggregate basis in those assets would be $500 ($120 + $160 + $220). The aggregate value of the assets immediately after the transaction is $420 ($70 + $110 + $240). Thus, Y's aggregate basis in the assets would exceed the aggregate value of the assets immediately after the transaction. Accordingly, the transfer is a loss duplication transaction and X has a net built-in loss of $80 ($500 - $420).

(2) *Identifying loss duplication property.* But for section 362(e)(2) and this section, Y's basis in Asset 1 would be $120, which would exceed Asset 1's $70 value immediately after the transaction. Accordingly, Asset 1 is loss duplication property. But for section 362(e)(2) and this section, Y's basis in Asset 2 would be $160, which would exceed Asset 2's $110 value immediately after the transaction. Accordingly, Asset 2 is also loss duplication property. But for section 362(e)(2) and this section, Y's basis in Asset 3 would be $220 and would therefore not exceed Asset 3's $240 value immediately after the transaction. Accordingly, Asset 3 is not loss duplication property.

(C) *Basis in loss duplication property.* Although Asset 1 and Asset 2 are each loss duplication property, X will distribute the Y stock received in exchange for Asset 1 and Asset 2 without recognition of gain or loss, and, upon completion of the transaction, no person will hold the Y stock received by X or any other asset with a basis determined in whole or in part by reference to X's basis in the Y stock received in the exchange. (A's basis in the Y stock will be determined by reference to his basis in his X stock.) Accordingly, under paragraph (c)(1) of this section, Y's bases in Asset 1 and Asset 2 are determined under section 362(a) and not under section 362(e)(2) and this section. Thus, Y's basis in Asset 1 is $120 and Y's basis in Asset 2 is $160.

(D) *Basis in other property.* Under section 358, A's basis in the Y stock received in exchange for his X stock is determined by reference to his basis in his X stock surrendered. Under section 362(a), Y's basis in Asset 3 is $220.

(ii) *Section 355(e).* (A) *Facts.* The facts are the same as in paragraph (i)(A) of this *Example 4*, except that, after the section 355 distribution, Y is acquired pursuant to a plan (within the meaning of § 1.355-7), resulting in the application of section 355(e) to the transactions.

(B) *Analysis.* Because section 361(c)(2), and not section 361(c)(1), will apply to X's distribution of Y stock, X will not qualify for nonrecognition treatment on the distribution of the Y stock. As a result, paragraph (c)(1) of this section does not apply to the transaction, and Y's bases in Asset 1 and Asset 2, the loss duplication property, are determined under section 362(e)(2) and this section. Asset 1 has a built-in loss of $50 ($120 - $70), and Asset 2 has a built-in loss of $50 ($160 - $110). Thus, Asset 1's allocable portion of X's net built-in loss is $40 ($50/$100 × $80), and Asset 2's allocable portion of X's net built-in loss is $40 ($50/$100 × $80). Accordingly, Y receives Asset 1 with a basis of $80 ($120 - $40) and Asset 2 with a basis of $120 ($160 - $40).

(iii) *Retained stock and securities.* (A) *Facts.* The facts are the same as in paragraph (i)(A) of this *Example 4*, except that X transfers Asset 1, Asset 2, and Asset 3 to Y in exchange for Y stock and Y securities, each constituting half of the consideration. In addition, for a valid business purpose, X retains Y stock and Y securities each worth 1 percent of the total consideration.

(B) *Analysis.* Paragraph (c)(1) of this section applies only to the extent that stock received in a transaction is distributed without recognition of gain or loss. Thus, section 362(e)(2) and this section apply to the extent that property was exchanged for the retained Y stock and Y securities (2 percent of the total). Accordingly, Y reduces its basis in Asset 1 and in Asset 2, the loss duplication property, by $1.60 (two percent of X's $80 net built-in loss). Asset 1 has a built-in loss of $50 ($120 - $70), and Asset 2 has a built-in loss of $50 ($160 - $110). Thus, Asset 1's allocable portion of X's net built-in loss is $.80 ($50/$100 × $1.60), and Asset 2's allocable portion of X's net built-in loss is $.80 ($50/$100 × $1.60). As a result, Y receives Asset 1 with a basis of $119.20 ($120 - $.80) and Asset 2 with a basis of $159.20 ($160 - $.80).

(iv) *Retained stock and securities with a section 362(e)(2)(C) election.* (A) *Facts.* The facts are the same as in paragraph (iii)(A) of this *Example 4*, except that an election under section 362(e)(2)(C) is made to reduce X's bases in its retained Y stock and retained Y securities.

(B) *Analysis.* Under paragraph (d)(2)(i) of this section, X reduces its basis in the retained Y stock and the retained Y securities (determined without regard to section 362(e)(2) and this section) by $1.60, *the portion of X's $80 net built-in loss that would have been applied* to reduce Y's basis in the transferred assets had the election to apply section 362(e)(2)(C) not been made. (Because the value of the Y stock and the value of the Y securities are equal, X's $500 basis in the transferred property would be allocated equally between the Y stock and the Y securities, $250 to each, under § 1.358-2(b)(2), and the retained Y stock and Y securities have a basis of $2.50 each (one percent of $250).) For the reasons set forth in paragraph (iii)(B) of this *Example 4*, Y would have been required to reduce its basis in the transferred assets by $1.60. Accordingly, X must reduce its aggregate basis in the retained Y stock and Y securities by $1.60. Under para-

graph (d)(2)(i) of this section, the $1.60 basis reduction is allocated and applied to reduce X's bases in the retained Y stock and Y securities in proportion to the value of each. Because X retained Y stock and Y securities with equal values, X holds each of the retained Y stock and securities with an adjusted basis of $1.70 ($2.50 - $.80). Under paragraph (d)(2)(ii) of this section, Y receives Asset 1 with a basis of $120, Asset 2 with a basis of $160, and Asset 3 with a basis of $220.

Example 5. Transfer of liabilities. (i) *Liabilities described in section 358(d)(1).* (A) *Basic application of section, no section 362(e)(2)(C) election.* (1) *Facts.* A owns Asset 1 (basis $800, value $700). A also has a $200 liability that has been taken into account for tax purposes and is thus described in section 358(d)(1), and not in sections 357(c)(3), 358(d)(2), and 358(h)(1). A transfers Asset 1 to X in exchange for a single outstanding share of X stock representing all the outstanding X stock immediately after the transaction and X's assumption of the liability. The transfer is a transaction to which section 351 applies.

(2) *Analysis.* (i) *Loss duplication transaction.* A's transfer of Asset 1 is a section 362(a) transaction. But for section 362(e)(2) and this section, X's basis in Asset 1 would be $800, which would exceed Asset 1's $700 value immediately after the transaction. Accordingly, the transfer is a loss duplication transaction and A has a net built-in loss of $100 ($800 - $700).

(ii) *Identifying loss duplication property.* But for section 362(e)(2) and this section, X's basis in Asset 1 would be $800, which would exceed the $700 value of Asset 1 immediately after the transaction. Accordingly, Asset 1 is loss duplication property.

(3) *Basis in loss duplication property.* X's basis in Asset 1 is $700, computed as its $800 basis determined under section 362(a) reduced by A's $100 net built-in loss.

(4) *Basis in other property.* Under sections 358(a) and (d)(1), A's basis in the X stock is $600 ($800 basis in property transferred - $200 liability assumed).

(B) *Section 362(e)(2)(C) election.* The facts are the same as in paragraph (i)(A)(1) of this *Example 5*, except that A and X make an election under section 362(e)(2)(C). In this case, A's $100 net built-in loss that would have been applied to reduce X's basis in Asset 1 is applied to reduce A's basis in the X stock received. As a result, A's basis in the X stock is $500 ($600, as determined in paragraph (i)(A)(4) of this *Example 5*, reduced by $100) and X's basis in Asset 1 is $800.

(ii) *Contingent liabilities described in section 358(h)(1), section 358(h)(2)(A) exception applies.* (A) *Facts.* The facts are the same as in paragraph (i)(A)(1) of this Example 5, except that A's liability (valued at $200) has not been taken into account for tax purposes and is described in sections 358(d)(2) and 358(h)(1). However, Asset 1 is a trade or business and the liability is associated with the trade or business; as a result, the liability is described in section 358(h)(2)(A) and is excepted from the general rule of section 358(h)(1).

(B) *Analysis.* For the reasons set forth in paragraph (i)(A)(2) of this *Example 5*, A's transfer of Asset 1 is a loss duplication transaction, A has a net built-in loss of $100, and Asset 1 is loss duplication property.

(C) *Basis in loss duplication property.* For the reasons set forth in paragraph (i)(A)(3) of this *Example 5*, X's basis in Asset 1 is $700.

(D) *Basis in other property.* A's basis in the X stock is $800 under sections 358(a), 358(d)(2), and 358(h)(2)(A).

(E) *Section 362(e)(2)(C) election.* The facts are the same as in paragraph (ii)(A) of this *Example 5*, except that A and X make an election under section 362(e)(2)(C). In this case, A's $100 net built-in loss that would have applied to reduce X's basis in Asset 1 is applied to reduce A's basis in the X stock received. As a result, A's basis in the X stock is $700 ($800, as determined in paragraph (ii)(D) of this *Example 5*, reduced by $100). X's basis in Asset 1 is $800.

Example 6. Section 351 transfer with boot. (i) *Basic transaction.* (A) *Facts.* A owns Asset 1 (basis $80, value $100) and Asset 2 (basis $30, value $25). In a transaction to which section 351 applies, A transfers Asset 1 and Asset 2 to X in exchange for 10 shares of X stock and $25.

(B) *Analysis.* (1) *Loss duplication transaction.* A's transfer of Asset 1 and Asset 2 is a section 362(a) transaction. But for section 362(e)(2) and this section, X's aggregate basis in those assets would be $130, computed as follows. Under section 362(a), a corporation's basis in property acquired in a transaction to which section 351 applies is the same as the property's basis in the hands of the transferor, increased by any gain recognized to the transferor on such transfer. Under section 351(b), gain (but not loss) is recognized to the extent a transferor in a section 351 exchange receives other property or money in addition to the stock permitted to be received without the recognition of gain. To determine the amount of gain recognized under section 351(b), the consideration is allocated proportionately (by value) among the transferred properties. A's gain on the transfer is therefore computed as follows: Asset 1 reflects 80 percent of the value transferred ($100/$125) and Asset 2 reflects 20 percent of the value transferred ($25/$125). Thus, 80 percent of the stock (eight shares) and the cash ($20) are treated as being received in exchange for Asset 1 and 20 percent of the stock (two shares) and the cash ($5) are treated as being received in exchange for Asset 2. Thus, under section 351(b), A recognizes $20 of gain for the cash received in exchange for Asset 1, but A recognizes no loss for the amount received for Asset 2. As a result, under section 362(a), X would have a basis of $100 in Asset 1 and $30 in Asset 2. Thus, X's aggregate basis in the assets would be $130, which exceeds the $125 aggregate value of the assets ($100 + $25)). The transfer is a loss duplication transaction and A has a net built-in loss of $5 ($130 - $125).

(2) *Identifying loss duplication property.* But for section 362(e)(2) and this section, X's basis in Asset 1 would be $100 (A's $80 basis increased by A's $20 gain recognized), which would not exceed Asset 1's $100 value immediately after the transaction. Accordingly, Asset 1 is not loss duplication property. But for section 362(e)(2) and this section, X's basis in Asset 2 would be $30, which would exceed Asset 2's $25 value immediately after the transaction. Accordingly, Asset 2 is loss duplication property.

(C) *Basis in loss duplication property.* X's basis in Asset 2 is $25, computed as its $30 basis under section 362(a) reduced by A's $5 net built-in loss.

(D) *Basis in other property.* Under section 362(a), X's basis in Asset 1 is $100 (A's $80 basis increased by the $20 gain recognized). Under section 358, A's basis in the X stock is $105 (the sum of its $80 basis in Asset 1, its $30 basis in Asset 2, and its $20 gain recognized, reduced by the $25 cash received in the exchange).

(ii) *Section 362(e)(2)(C) election.* The facts are the same as in paragraph (i)(A) of this *Example 6*, except that A and X elect to reduce A's stock basis under section 362(e)(2)(C). Under paragraph (d)(2)(i) of this section, A reduces its $105 basis in the X stock by $5, the amount of A's net built-in loss of that would have been applied to reduce X's basis in Asset 2 had the section 362(e)(2)(C) election not been made. As a result, A's basis in the X stock is $100, and X's basis in Asset 2 is $30.

Example 7. Section 304 sale of built-in loss stock. (i) *Basic transaction.* (A) *Facts.* A owns all the stock of X (basis $90, value $60) and all the stock of Y. A sells all his X stock to Y for $60. Under section 304, A is treated as though he transferred the X stock to Y in exchange for Y stock in a transaction to which section 351 applies. Then, Y is treated as redeeming the Y stock it was treated as having issued to A in the deemed section 351 transaction.

(B) *Analysis.* (1) *Loss duplication transaction.* A's deemed transfer of X stock to Y is a section 362(a) transaction. But for section 362(e)(2) and this section, Y's aggregate basis in the X stock would be $90, which would exceed the X stock's value of $60 immediately after the transaction. Accordingly, the transfer is a loss duplication transaction and A has a net built-in loss of $30.

(2) *Identifying loss duplication property.* But for section 362(e)(2) and this section, Y's basis in the X stock would be $90, which would exceed the X stock's $60 value immediately after the transaction. Accordingly, the X stock is loss duplication property.

(C) *Basis in loss duplication property.* Y's basis in the X stock is $60, its $90 basis determined without regard to section 362(e)(2) and this section, reduced by A's $30 net built-in loss.

(D) *Basis in other property.* Under section 358(a), A has an exchanged basis of $90 in the Y stock he is deemed to receive in the exchange; the effect of the deemed redemption of that stock is then determined under section 302.

(ii) *Section 362(e)(2)(C) election.* The facts are the same as in paragraph (i)(A) of this *Example 7*, except that the parties elect to reduce A's stock basis under section 362(e)(2)(C). For the reasons set forth in paragraphs (i)(B) and (C) of this *Example 7*, Y's basis in the X stock would be reduced by $30. Accordingly, A's basis in the deemed-issued Y stock is $60, his $90 basis otherwise determined under section 358(a) reduced by the $30 that would have been applied to reduce Y's basis in the X stock under section 362(e)(2) and this section; the effect of the deemed redemption of that stock is then determined under section 302. Y's basis in the X stock is $90.

Example 8. Transactions involving partnerships. (i) *Transfer by a partnership.* (A) *Basic application of section.* (1) *Facts.* PRS owns Asset 1 (basis $100, value $70). PRS contributes Asset 1 to X in a transaction to which section 351 applies.

(2) *Analysis.* (i) *Loss duplication transaction.* PRS's transfer of Asset 1 is a section 362(a) transaction. But for section 362(e)(2) and this section, X's basis in Asset 1 would be $100, which would exceed Asset 1's $70 value immediately after the transaction. Accordingly, the transfer is a loss duplication transaction and PRS has a net built-in loss of $30 ($100 - $70).

(ii) *Identifying loss duplication property.* But for section 362(e)(2) and this section, X's basis in Asset 1 would be $100 which would exceed Asset 1's $70 value immediately after the transaction. Accordingly, Asset 1 is loss duplication property.

(3) *Basis in loss duplication property.* X's basis in Asset 1 is $70, computed as its $100 basis under section 362(a) reduced by PRS's $30 net built-in loss.

(4) *Basis in other property.* Under section 358(a), PRS has an exchanged basis of $100 in the X stock it receives in the exchange.

(B) *Section 362(e)(2)(C) election.* The facts are the same as in paragraph (i)(A)(1) of this *Example 8*, except that PRS and X elect to reduce PRS's stock basis under section 362(e)(2)(C). In this case, PRS's $30 net built-in loss (as determined in paragraph (i)(A)(2)(i) of this *Example 8*) that would have been applied to reduce X's basis in Asset 1 is applied to reduce PRS's basis in the X stock received. As a result, PRS's basis in the X stock is $70 ($100 - $30) and X's basis in Asset 1 is $100. The $30 reduction to PRS's basis in the X stock is treated as an expenditure of PRS under section 705(a)(2)(B) and paragraph (e)(1) of this section. As a result, the partners of PRS must reduce their bases in their PRS interests.

(ii) *Transfer of interest in partnership with liability.* (A) *Basic application of section.* (1) *Facts.* A and two other individuals are equal partners in PRS. A's basis in its partnership interest is $247. A's share of PRS's §1.752-1 liabilities (as defined in §1.752-1(a)(4)) is $145. A transfers his partnership interest to X in a transaction to which section 351 applies. PRS has no election in effect under section 754. If X were to sell the PRS interest immediately after the transfer, X would receive $100 in cash or other property. In addition, assume that, taking into account the rules under §1.752-4, X's share of PRS's §1.752-1 liabilities (as defined in §1.752-1(a)(4)) is $150 immediately after the transfer.

(2) *Analysis.* (i) *Loss duplication transaction.* A's transfer of its PRS interest is a section 362(a) transaction. But for section 362(e)(2) and this section, X's basis in the PRS interest, would be $252 (A's basis of $247, reduced by A's $145 share of PRS liabilities, increased by X's $150 share of PRS liabilities) and, under paragraph (g)(12)(ii) of this section, the value of the PRS interest would be $250 (the sum of $100, the cash X would receive if X immediately sold the interest, and $150, X's share of the §1.752-1 liabilities (as defined in §1.752-1(a)(4)) under section 752 immediately after the transfer to X). Therefore, the transfer is a loss duplication transaction and A has a net built-in loss of $2 ($252 - $250).

(ii) *Identifying loss duplication property.* But for section 362(e)(2) and this section, X's basis in the PRS interest would be $252, which would exceed the PRS interest's $250 value immediately after the transaction. Accordingly, the PRS interest is loss duplication property.

(3) *Basis in loss duplication property.* X's basis in the PRS interest is $250, computed as its $252 basis under section 362(a), taking into account the rules under section 752, reduced by A's $2 net built-in loss.

(4) *Basis in other property.* Under section 358, taking into account the rules under section 752, A has a basis of $102 ($247 reduced by A's $145 share of PRS liabilities) in the X stock he receives in the transaction.

(B) *Section 362(e)(2)(C) election.* The facts are the same as in paragraph (i)(A) of this *Example 8*, except that A and X make an election under section 362(e)(2)(C). Under paragraph (d)(2)(i) of this section, A reduces his basis in the X stock, as determined without regard to section 362(e)(2) and this section, by the amount of A's net built-in loss that would have been applied to reduce X's basis in the PRS interest had the section 362(e)(2)(C) election not been made. In addition, no reduction is made to X's basis in the PRS interest, as determined without regard to section 362(e)(2) and this section. As a result, A's basis in the X stock is $100 ($102 - $2) and X's basis in the PRS interest is $252.

(C) *Transfer of partnership interest with liability, not loss duplication transaction.* The facts are the same as in paragraph (ii)(A)(1) of this *Example 8*, except that A's share of PRS's §1.752-1 liabilities (as defined in §1.752-1(a)(4)) is $155. But for section 362(e)(2) and this section, X's basis in the PRS interest would be $242 (A's basis of $247, reduced by A's $155 share of PRS liabilities, increased by X's $150 share of PRS liabilities), which would not exceed the PRS interest's $250 value immediately after the transaction. Accordingly, A's transfer of the PRS interest is not a loss duplication transaction and section 362(e)(2) and this section have no application to the transaction. Under section 362(a), X's basis in the PRS interest is $242 and, under section 358, taking into account the rules under section 752, A has a basis of $92 ($247 reduced by A's $155 share of PRS liabilities) in the X stock he receives in the transaction.

Example 9. Transactions involving S Corporations. (i) *Transfer by S Corporation.* (A) *No section 362(e)(2)(C) election.* (1) *Facts.* S, an S corporation as defined in section 1361(a)(1), owns Asset 1 (basis $100, value $70). S transfers Asset 1 to X in exchange for a single outstanding share of X stock representing all the outstanding X stock immediately after the transaction. S does not elect to treat X as a qualified subchapter S subsidiary. The transaction is one to which section 351 applies.

(2) *Analysis.* (i) *Loss duplication transaction.* S's transfer of Asset 1 is a section 362(a) transaction. But for section 362(e)(2) and this section, X's basis in Asset 1 would be $100, which would exceed Asset 1's $70 value immediately after the transaction. Accordingly, the transfer is a loss duplication transaction and S has a net built-in loss of $30 ($100 - $70).

(ii) *Identifying loss duplication property.* But for section 362(e)(2) and this section, X's basis in Asset 1 would be $100, which would exceed Asset 1's $70 value immediately after the transaction. Accordingly, Asset 1 is loss duplication property.

(iii) *Basis in loss duplication property.* X's basis in Asset 1 is $70, computed as its $100 basis under section 362(a) reduced by S's $30 net built-in loss.

(iv) *Basis in other property.* Under section 358(a), S has an exchanged basis of $100 in the X stock it receives in the exchange.

(B) *Section 362(e)(2)(C) election.* The facts are the same as in paragraph (i)(A)(*1*) of this *Example 9*, except that S and X elect to reduce S's stock basis under section 362(e)(2). In this case, S's $30 built-in loss (as determined in paragraph (i)(A)(2)(*i*) of this *Example 9*) that would have been applied to reduce X's basis in Asset 1 is applied to reduce S's basis in the X stock received. As a result, S's basis in the X stock is $70 ($100 - $30) and X's basis in Asset 1 is $100. The $30 reduction to S's basis in the X stock is treated as an expense of S under section 1367(a)(2)(D) and paragraph (e)(2) of this section. As a result, the shareholders of S must reduce their bases in their S stock.

(ii) *Transfer to S Corporation.* (A) *Basic application of section.* (1) *Facts.* A owns Asset 1 (basis $90, value $60) and Asset 2 (basis $110, value $120). In a transaction to which section 351 applies, A transfers Asset 1 and Asset 2 to S, an S corporation as defined in section 1361(a)(1), in exchange for a single share of S stock representing all the outstanding S stock immediately after the transaction.

(2) *Analysis.* (i) *Loss duplication transaction.* A's transfer of Asset 1 and Asset 2 is a section 362(a) transaction. But for section 362(e)(2) and this section, S's aggregate basis in those assets would be $200 ($90 + $110), which would exceed the aggregate value of the assets $180 ($60 + $120) immediately after the transaction. Accordingly, the transfer is a loss duplication transaction and A has a net built-in loss of $20 ($200 - $180).

(ii) *Identifying loss duplication property.* But for section 362(e)(2) and this section, S's basis in Asset 1 would be $90, which would exceed Asset 1's $60 value immediately after the transaction. As a result, Asset 1 is loss duplication property. But for section 362(e)(2) and this section, S's basis in Asset 2 would be $110, which would not exceed Asset 2's $120 value immediately after the transaction. As a result, Asset 2 is not loss duplication property.

(3) *Basis in loss duplication property.* S's basis in Asset 1 is $70, computed as its $90 basis under section 362(a) reduced by S's $20 net built-in loss. The $20 reduction to S's basis in Asset 1 does not require a reduction to A's basis in its S stock under section 1367(a)(2)(D). See paragraph (f) of this section.

(4) *Basis in other property.* Under section 362(a), S has a transferred basis of $110 in Asset 2. Under section 358(a), A has a basis of $200 in the S stock it receives in the exchange.

(B) *Section 362(e)(2)(C) election.* (1) *Application of section to transaction.* The facts are the same as in paragraph (ii)(A)(*1*) of this *Example 9*, except that A and S elect to reduce A's stock basis under section 362(e)(2)(C). In this case, A's $20 built-in loss (as determined in paragraph (ii)(A)(2) of this *Example 9*) that would have been applied to reduce S's basis in Asset 1 is applied to reduce A's basis in the S stock received. As a result, A's basis in the S stock is $180 ($200 - $20), S's basis in Asset 1 is $90, and S's basis in Asset 2 is $110.

(2) *Tax consequences of subsequent disposition of transferred assets.* The facts are the same as in paragraph (ii)(B)(*1*) of this *Example 9* except that, in addition, the year after the transaction, S sells Asset 1 (basis $90, value $60) and Asset 2 (basis $110, value $120) for $180, recognizing the $20 net built-in loss. The loss is allocated to A and reduces A's basis in the S stock from $180 to $160 under section 1367(a)(2)(B). If A then sells its S stock for its $180 value, A will recognize a gain of $20.

Example 10. Triangular reorganizations. (i) *Facts.* P owns all the stock of S1 and X owns all the stock of S2. In a merger described in section 368(a)(2)(D), S2 merges with and into S1, and X receives stock of P in exchange for its S2 stock. S2 has a net built-in loss in its assets acquired by S1 in the transaction.

(ii) *Analysis.* The reorganization is not a section 362(a) transaction, notwithstanding that, under §1.358-6(c), P is treated as acquiring and then transferring S2's assets to S1 for purposes of determining P's adjustment to its basis in its S1 stock. Accordingly, S1's basis in the property acquired in the transaction is not determined under section 362(a) and this section; it is determined under section 362(b).

Example 11. Transfers of importation property with non-importation property. (i) *Single transferor, loss importation transaction.* (A) *Facts.* FC1 transfers Asset 1 (basis $80, value $50), Asset 2 (basis $120, value

$110), and Asset 3 (basis $32, value $40) to DC in a transaction to which section 351 applies. Asset 1 is not importation property within the meaning of §1.362-3(c)(2). Asset 2 and Asset 3 are importation property within the meaning of §1.362-3(c)(2).

(B) *Application of section 362(e)(1).* Immediately after the transfer, and without regard to section 362(e)(1) or section 362(e)(2) and this section, DC's aggregate basis in importation property (Asset 2 and Asset 3) would be $152. The aggregate value of the importation property immediately after the transfer is $150. Accordingly, the transaction is a loss importation transaction within the meaning of §1.362-3(c)(3) and, under section 362(e)(1), DC's bases in Asset 2 and Asset 3 would equal the value of each, $110 and $40, respectively.

(C) *Application of section 362(e)(2) and this section.* (1) *Analysis.* (i) *Loss duplication transaction.* FC1's transfer of Asset 1, Asset 2, and Asset 3 is a transaction described in section 362(a). But for section 362(e)(2) and this section, DC's aggregate basis in those assets would be $230 ($80 under section 362(a) + $110 +$40 under section 362(e)(1)), which would exceed the aggregate value of the assets $200 ($50 + $110 +$40) immediately after the transaction. Accordingly, the transfer is a loss duplication transaction and FC1 has a net built-in loss of $30 ($230 - $200).

(ii) *Identifying loss duplication property.* But for section 362(e)(2) and this section, DC's basis in Asset 1 would be $80, which would exceed Asset 1's $50 value immediately after the transaction. Accordingly, Asset 1 is loss duplication property. But for section 362(e)(2) and this section, DC's basis in Asset 2 would be $110, which would not exceed Asset 2's $110 value immediately after the transaction. Accordingly, Asset 2 is not loss duplication property. But for section 362(e)(2) and this section, DC's basis in Asset 3 would be $40, which would not exceed Asset 3's $40 value immediately after the transaction. Accordingly, Asset 3 is not loss duplication property.

(D) *Basis in loss duplication property.* DC's basis in Asset 1 is $50, computed as its $80 basis under section 362(a) reduced by FC1's $30 net built-in loss.

(E) *Basis in other property.* Under section 362(e)(1), DC's basis in Asset 2 is $110 and DC's basis in Asset 3 is $40. Under section 358(a), FC1 has an exchanged basis of $232 in the DC stock it receives in the transaction.

(ii) *Multiple transferors, no importation of loss.* (A) *Facts.* The facts are the same as paragraph (i)(A) of this *Example 11*, except that, in addition, FC2 transfers Asset 4 (basis $100, value $150) to DC as part of the same transaction. Asset 4 is importation property within the meaning of §1.362-3(c)(2).

(B) *Application of section 362(e)(1).* Immediately after the transfer, and without regard to section 362(e)(1) or section 362(e)(2) and this section, DC's aggregate basis in importation property (Asset 2, Asset 3, and Asset 4) would be $252 ($120 + $32 + $100). The aggregate value of the importation property immediately after the transfer is $300 ($110 + $40 + $150). Accordingly, the transaction is not a loss importation transaction within the meaning of §1.362-3(c)(3) and DC's bases in the importation property is not determined under section 362(e)(1).

(C) *Application of section 362(e)(2) and this section.* Notwithstanding that the transfers by FC1 and FC2 are pursuant to a single plan forming one transaction, section 362(e)(2) and this section apply to each transferor separately.

(1) *Application of section to FC1.* (i) *Loss duplication transaction.* FC1's transfer of Asset 1, Asset 2, and Asset 3 is a transaction described in section 362(a). But for section 362(e)(2) and this section, DC's aggregate basis in those assets would be $232 ($80 + $120 +$32), which would exceed the aggregate value of the assets $200 ($50 + $110 + $40) immediately after the transaction. Accordingly, the transfer is a loss duplication transaction and FC1 has a net built-in loss of $32 ($232 - $200).

(ii) *Identifying loss duplication property.* But for section 362(e)(2) and this section, DC's basis in Asset 1 would be $80, which would exceed Asset 1's $50 value immediately after the transaction. Accordingly, Asset 1 is loss duplication property. But for section 362(e)(2) and this section, DC's basis in Asset 2 would be $120, which would exceed Asset 2's $110 value immediately after the transaction. Accordingly, Asset 2 is also loss duplication property. But for section 362(e)(2) and this section, DC's basis in Asset 3 would be $32, which would not exceed Asset 3's $40 value immediately after the transaction. Accordingly, Asset 3 is not loss duplication property.

(iii) *Basis in loss duplication property.* DC's basis in Asset 1 is $56, computed as its $80 basis under section 362(a) reduced by $24, its allocable portion of FC1's $32 net built-in loss ($30/40 x $32). DC's basis in Asset 2 is $112, computed as its $120 basis under section 362(a) reduced by $8, its allocable portion of FC1's $40 net built-in loss ($10/$40 x $32).

(iv) *Basis in other property.* Under section 358(a), FC1 has an exchanged basis of $232 in the DC stock it receives in the transaction.

(2) *Application of section to FC2.* FC2's transfer of Asset 3 is not a loss duplication transaction because Asset 3's value exceeds its basis

immediately after the transaction. Accordingly, under section 362(a), DC's basis in Asset 3 is $100.

Example 12. Section 362(e)(2)(C) elections with respect to transfers between persons that are not required to file a U.S. return and that are not CFCs or CFPs. (i) *Basic application of section.* On June 30, Year 1, FC1 transfers Asset 1 to FC2 in a transaction to which section 351 applies (the original transfer) and that is therefore a section 362(a) transaction. But for section 362(e)(2) and this section, FC2's basis in Asset 1 (determined immediately after the transfer, taking into account all applicable law, including section 362(e)(1)) exceeds the value of Asset 1 immediately after the transaction. Accordingly, the transaction is a loss duplication transaction and Asset 1 is loss duplication property. FC1 and FC2 executed a written, binding agreement to apply section 362(e)(2)(C) at some point before any Section 362(e)(2)(C) Statement is filed. However, the transfer was not entered into with a view to reducing or avoiding the Federal income tax liability of any person by avoiding the application of section 362(e)(2) and this section; further, no event described in paragraph (d)(3)(ii)(E), (F), or (G) of this section occurs prior to June 30, Year 3. As a result, under paragraph (c)(2) of this section, section 362(e)(2) and this section do not apply to the transfer. Accordingly, FC2's basis in Asset 1 is determined under section 362(a), no section 362(e)(2)(C) election can be made, and any protective filing of a Section 362(e)(2)(C) Statement will have no effect.

(ii) *Loss duplication property later acquired by a person required to file U.S. return.* The facts are the same as in paragraph (i) of this *Example 12*, except that, in addition, on January 1, Year 2, FC2 transfers Asset 1 to DC in an exchange to which section 351 applies. FC2's transfer is an event described in paragraph (d)(3)(ii)(G) of this section. As a result, paragraph (c)(2) does not except the original transfer from the application of section 362(e)(2) and this section. Under paragraph (d)(3)(ii)(G) of this section, DC must include the Section 362(e)(2)(C) Statement for the original transfer on or with its Year 2 U.S. return in order for that election to be effective. The result would be the same if, instead of FC2 transferring Asset 1 to DC, FC1 transferred its FC2 stock to DC in an exchange to which section 351 applies. (Further, if an asset transferred by FC1 or FC2 to DC is a loss asset immediately after its transfer to DC, DC's basis in that asset may be subject to section 362(e)(1).)

(iii) *Party to exchange later becomes a person required to file U.S. return.* The facts are the same as in paragraph (i) of this *Example 12*, except that, in addition, on January 1, Year 2, FC2 becomes engaged in a U.S. business. FC2's becoming engaged in a U.S. business is an event described in paragraph (d)(3)(ii)(F) of this section because it will cause FC2 to become a person required to file a U.S. return. As a result, paragraph (c)(2) of this section does not except the transfer from the application of section 362(e)(2) and this section. Under paragraph (d)(3)(ii)(F) of this section, FC2 must include the Section 362(e)(2)(C) Statement for the original transfer on or with its Year 2

U.S. return in order for the section 362(e)(2)(C) election for the original transfer to be effective.

(iv) *Statement not filed with respect to designated event.* The facts are the same as in paragraph (iii) of this *Example 12*, except that, in addition, FC1 became engaged in a U.S. trade or business on October 31, Year 1 and as a result became a person required to file a U.S. return, an event described in paragraph (d)(3)(ii)(E) of this section. As a result, paragraph (c)(2) of this section does not except the transfer from the application of section 362(e)(2) and this section. Further, in order for the election to be effective, FC1 must file the Section 362(e)(2)(C) Statement on or with its Year 1 U.S. return. See paragraph (d)(3)(ii)(E) of this section. A statement filed by FC2 on or with its Year 2 U.S. return has no effect. Thus, if FC1 does not file the statement, the election does not become effective and basis is determined under the general rule of section 362(e)(2).

(v) *Nonrecognition transfer of loss duplication property outside United States, transferee later becomes engaged in U.S. trade or business.* The facts are the same as in paragraph (i) of this *Example 12*, except that, in addition, on December 31, Year 1, FC2 transfers Asset 1 to FC3 in a transferred basis transaction. In Year 2, FC3 becomes engaged in a U.S. trade or business and as a result becomes a person required to file a U.S. return; Asset 1 is not used in or connected with the U.S. trade or business or otherwise subject to Federal income tax. FC3's becoming engaged in a U.S. trade or business is an event described in paragraph (d)(3)(ii)(F) of this section because FC3, a person who holds loss duplication property with a basis determined by FC2's basis in the property, will be required to file a U.S. return as a result of its becoming engaged in a U.S. business. As a result, paragraph (c)(2) of this section does not except the transfer from the application of section 362(e)(2) and this section. Under paragraph (d)(3)(ii)(F) of this section, FC3 must include the Section 362(e)(2)(C) Statement for the original transfer on or with its Year 2 U.S. return in order for the section 362(e)(2)(C) election for the original transfer to be effective.

(i) [Reserved].

(j) *Effective/applicability date.*—This section applies to transactions occurring after September 3, 2013, unless effected pursuant to a binding agreement that was in effect prior to September 3, 2013, and at all times thereafter. In addition, taxpayers may apply these regulations to transactions occurring after October 22, 2004. The introductory text and *Example 11* of paragraph (h) of this section apply with respect to transactions occurring on or after March 28, 2016, and also with respect to transactions occurring before such date as a result of an entity classification election under §301.7701-3 of this chapter filed on or after March 28, 2016, unless such transaction is pursuant to a binding agreement that was in effect prior to March 28, 2016 and at all times thereafter. In addition, taxpayers may apply such provisions to any transaction occurring after October 22, 2004. [Reg. §1.362-4.]

☐ [*T.D. 9424,* 9-9-2008. *Amended by T.D. 9633,* 8-30-2013 *and T.D. 9759,* 3-25-2016.]

⟫→ *Caution: The Treasury Department has identified Reg. §1.367(a)-0, as added by T.D. 9803, as a significant tax regulation that imposes an undue financial burden on U.S. taxpayers and/or adds undue complexity to the federal tax laws, pursuant to Executive Order 13789 (issued April 21, 2017) (Notice 2017-38, I.R.B. 2017-30). In a subsequent report, issued October 4, 2017, Treasury recommended planned actions that would reduce the burden of these regulations.*

[Reg. §1.367(a)-0]

§1.367(a)-0. Table of contents.—This section lists the paragraphs contained in §§1.367(a)-1 through 1.367(a)-8.

(m) Receipt of boot in nonrecognition transactions.

(1) Dispositions of transferred stock or securities.

(2) Dispositions of assets of transferred corporation.

(n) Special rules for distributions with respect to stock.

(1) Certain dividend equivalent redemptions treated as dispositions.

(2) Gain recognized under section 301(c)(3).

(o) Dispositions or other events that terminate or reduce the amount of gain subject to the gain recognition agreement.

(1) Taxable disposition of stock of the transferee foreign corporation.

(2) Gain recognized in connection with certain nonrecognition transactions.

(3) Gain recognized under section 301(c)(3).

(4) Dispositions of substantially all of the assets of a domestic transferred corporation.

(5) Certain distributions or transfers of transferred stock or securities to U.S. persons.

⋙→ Caution: *The Treasury Department has identified Reg. §1.367(a)-1, as amended by T.D. 9803, as a significant tax regulation that imposes an undue financial burden on U.S. taxpayers and/or adds undue complexity to the federal tax laws, pursuant to Executive Order 13789 (issued April 21, 2017) (Notice 2017-38, I.R.B. 2017-30). In a subsequent report, issued October 4, 2017, Treasury recommended planned actions that would reduce the burden of these regulations.*

[Reg. §1.367(a)-1]

§1.367(a)-1. Transfers to foreign corporations subject to section 367(a): In general.—(a) *Scope.*—Section 367(a)(1) provides the general rule concerning certain transfers of property by a United States person (referred to at times in this section as the "U.S. person" or "U.S. transferor") to a foreign corporation. Paragraph (b) of this section provides general rules explaining the effect of section 367(a)(1). Paragraph (c) of this section describes transfers of property that are described in section 367(a)(1). Paragraph (d) of this section provides definitions that apply for purposes of sections 367(a) and (d) and the regulations thereunder. Paragraphs (e) and (f) of this section provide rules that apply to certain reorganizations described in section 368(a)(1)(F). Paragraph (g) of this section provides dates of applicability. For rules concerning the reporting requirements under section 6038B for certain transfers of property to a foreign corporation, see §1.6038B-1.

(b) *General rules.*—(1) *Foreign corporation not considered a corporation for purposes of certain transfers.*—If a U.S. person transfers property to a foreign corporation in connection with an exchange described in section 351, 354, 356, or 361, then, pursuant to section 367(a)(1), the foreign corporation will not be considered to be a corporation for purposes of determining the extent to which gain is recognized on the transfer. Section 367(a)(1) denies nonrecognition treatment only to transfers of items of property on which gain is realized. Thus, the amount of gain recognized because of section 367(a)(1) is unaffected by the transfer of items of property on which loss is realized (but not recognized).

(2) *Cases in which foreign corporate status is not disregarded.*—For circumstances in which section 367(a)(1) does not apply to a U.S. transferor's transfer of property to a foreign corporation, and thus the foreign corporation is considered to be a corporation, see §§1.367(a)-2, 1.367(a)-3, and 1.367(a)-7.

(3) *Determination of value.*—In cases in which a U.S. transferor's transfer of property to a foreign corporation constitutes a controlled transaction as defined in §1.482-1(i)(8), the value of the property transferred is determined in accordance with section 482 and the regulations thereunder.

(4) *Character, source, and adjustments.*—(i) *In general.*—If a U.S. person is required to recognize gain under section 367 upon a transfer of property to a foreign corporation, then —

(A) The character and source of such gain are determined as if the property had been disposed of in a taxable exchange with the transferee foreign corporation (unless otherwise provided by regulation); and

(B) Appropriate adjustments to earnings and profits, basis, and other affected items will be made according to otherwise applicable rules, taking into account the gain recognized under section 367(a)(1). For purposes of applying section 362, the foreign corporation's basis in the property received is increased by the amount of gain recognized by the U.S. transferor under section 367(a) and the regulations issued pursuant to that section. To the extent the regulations provide that the U.S. transferor recognizes gain with respect to a particular item of property, the foreign corporation increases its basis in that item of property by the amount of such gain recognized. For example, §§1.367(a)-2, 1.367(a)-3, and 1.367(a)-4 provide that gain is recognized with respect to particular items of property. To the

extent the regulations do not provide that gain recognized by the U.S. transferor is with respect to a particular item of property, such gain is treated as recognized with respect to items of property subject to section 367(a) in proportion to the U.S. transferor's gain realized in such property, after taking into account gain recognized with respect to particular items of property transferred under any other provision of section 367(a). For example, §1.367(a)-6 provides that branch losses must be recaptured by the recognition of gain realized on the transfer but does not associate the gain with particular items of property. See also §1.367(a)-1(c)(3) for rules concerning transfers by partnerships or of partnership interests.

(C) The transfer will not be recharacterized for U.S. Federal tax purposes solely because the U.S. person recognizes gain in connection with the transfer under section 367(a)(1). For example, if a U.S. person transfers appreciated stock or securities to a foreign corporation in an exchange described in section 351, the transfer is not recharacterized as other than an exchange described in section 351 solely because the U.S. person recognizes gain in the transfer under section 367(a)(1).

(ii) *Example.*—The rules of this paragraph (b)(4) are illustrated by the following example.

Example. Domestic corporation DC transfers inventory with a fair market value of $ 1 million and adjusted basis of $ 800,000 to foreign corporation FC in exchange for stock of FC that is described in section 351(a). Title passes within the United States. Pursuant to section 367(a), DC is required to recognize gain of $200,000 upon the transfer. Under the rule of this paragraph (b)(4), the gain is treated as ordinary income (sections 1201 and 1221) from sources within the United States (section 861) arising from a taxable exchange with FC. Appropriate adjustments to earnings and profits, basis, etc., will be made as if the transfer were subject to section 351. Thus, for example, DC's basis in the FC stock received, and FC's basis in the transferred inventory, will each be increased by the $200,000 gain recognized by DC, pursuant to sections 358(a)(1) and 362(a), respectively.

(5) *Treatment of certain property as subject to section 367(d).*—A U.S. transferor may apply section 367(d) and §1.367(d)-1, rather than section 367(a) and the regulations thereunder, to a transfer of property to a foreign corporation that otherwise would be subject to section 367(a), provided that the property is not eligible property, as defined in §1.367(a)-2(b) but determined without regard to §1.367(a)-2(c). A U.S. transferor and any other U.S. transferor that is related (within the meaning of section 267(b) or 707(b)(1)) to the U.S. transferor must consistently apply this paragraph (b)(5) to all property described in this paragraph (b)(5) that is transferred to one or more foreign corporations pursuant to a plan. A U.S. transferor applies the provisions of this paragraph (b)(5) in the form and manner set forth in §1.6038B-1(d)(1)(iv) and (v).

(c)(1) through (c)(3)(i) reserved. For further guidance, see §1.367(a)-1T(c)(1) through (c)(3)(i).

(ii) *Transfer of partnership interest treated as transfer of proportionate share of assets.*—(A) *In general.*—If a U.S. person transfers an interest as a partner in a partnership (whether foreign or domestic) in an exchange described in section 367(a)(1), then that person is treated as having transferred a proportionate share of the property of the partnership in an exchange described in section 367(a)(1). Accordingly, the applicability of the exception to section 367(a)(1) provided in §1.367(a)-2 is determined with reference to the property of the partnership rather than the partnership interest itself. A U.S. person's

(6) Dispositions or other event following certain intercompany transactions.

(7) Expropriations under foreign law.

(p) Relief for certain failures to file or failures to comply that are not willful.

(1) In general.

(2) Procedures for establishing that a failure to file or failure to comply was not willful.

(3) Examples.

(q) Examples.

(1) Presumed facts and references.

(2) Examples.

(r) Effective/applicability date.

(1) General rule.

(2) Applicability to transfers occurring before March 13, 2009.

(3) Applicability to requests for relief submitted before November 19, 2014.

[Reg. §1.367(a)-0.]

□ [T.D. 9803, 12-15-2016.]

proportionate share of partnership property is determined under the rules and principles of sections 701 through 761 and the regulations thereunder.

(c)(3)(i)(A) *Example* through (7) reserved. For further guidance, see § 1.367(a)-1T(c)(3)(i)(A) *Example* through (7).

(d) *Definitions.*—The following definitions apply for purposes of sections 367(a) and (d) and the regulations thereunder.

(1) *United States person.*—The term "United States person" includes those persons described in section 7701(a)(30). The term includes a citizen or resident of the United States, a domestic partnership, a domestic corporation, and any estate or trust other than a foreign estate or trust. (For definitions of these terms, see section 7701 and the regulations thereunder.) For purposes of this section, an individual with respect to whom an election has been made under section 6013(g) or (h) is considered to be a resident of the United States while such election is in effect. A nonresident alien or a foreign corporation will not be considered a United States person because of its actual or deemed conduct of a trade or business within the United States during a taxable year.

(2) *Foreign corporation.*—The term "foreign corporation" has the meaning set forth in section 7701(a)(3) and (5) and § 301.7701-5.

(3) *Transfer.*—For purposes of section 367 and regulations thereunder, the term "transfer" means any transaction that constitutes a transfer for purposes of section 332, 351, 354, 355, 356, or 361, as applicable. A person's entering into a cost sharing arrangement under § 1.482-7 or acquiring rights to intangible property under such an arrangement shall not be considered a transfer of property described in section 367(a)(1). See § 1.6038B-1T(b)(4) for the date on which the transfer is considered to be made.

(4) *Property.*—For purposes of section 367 and the regulations thereunder, the term "property" means any item that constitutes property for purposes of section 351, 354, 355, 356, or 361, as applicable.

(5) *Intangible property.*—The term "intangible property" means either property described in section 936(h)(3)(B) or property to which a U.S. person applies section 367(d) pursuant to paragraph (b)(5) of this section, but does not include property described in section 1221(a)(3) or a working interest in oil and gas property.

(6) *Operating intangibles.*—An operating intangible is any property described in section 936(h)(3)(B) of a type not ordinarily licensed or otherwise transferred in transactions between unrelated parties for consideration contingent upon the licensee's or transferee's use of the property. Examples of operating intangibles may include longterm purchase or supply contracts, surveys, studies, and customer lists.

(e) *Close of taxable year in certain section 368(a)(1)(F) reorganizations.*—If a domestic corporation is the transferor corporation in a reorganization described in section 368(a)(1)(F) after March 30, 1987,

in which the acquiring corporation is a foreign corporation, then the taxable year of the transferor corporation shall end with the close of the date of the transfer and the taxable year of the acquiring corporation shall end with the close of the date on which the transferor's taxable year would have ended but for the occurrence of the transfer. With regard to the consequences of the closing of the taxable year, see section 381 and the regulations thereunder.

(f) *Exchanges under sections 354(a) and 361(a) in certain section 368(a)(1)(F) reorganizations.*—(1) *Rule.*—In every reorganization under section 368(a)(1)(F), where the transferor corporation is a domestic corporation, and the acquiring corporation is a foreign corporation, there is considered to exist—

(i) A transfer of assets by the transferor corporation to the acquiring corporation under section 361(a) in exchange for stock (or stock and securities) of the acquiring corporation and the assumption by the acquiring corporation of the transferor corporation's liabilities;

(ii) A distribution of the stock (or stock and securities) of the acquiring corporation by the transferor corporation to the shareholders (or shareholders and security holders) of the transferor corporation; and

(iii) An exchange by the transferor corporation's shareholders (or shareholders and security holders) of their stock (or stock and securities) of the transferor corporation for stock (or stock and securities) of the acquiring corporation under section 354(a).

(2) *Rule applies regardless of whether a continuance under applicable law.*—For purposes of paragraph (f)(1) of this section, it shall be immaterial that the applicable foreign or domestic law treats the acquiring corporation as a continuance of the transferor corporation.

(g) *Effective/applicability dates.*—(1) through (3) [Reserved]. For further guidance, *see* § 1.367(a)-1T(g)(1) through (3).

(4) The rules in paragraphs (b)(4)(i)(B) and (b)(4)(i)(C) of this section apply to transfers occurring on or after April 18, 2013. For guidance with respect to paragraph (b)(4)(i)(B) of this section before April 18, 2013, see 26 CFR part 1 revised as of April 1, 2012. The rules in paragraph (e) of this section apply to transactions occurring on or after March 31, 1987. The rules in paragraph (f) of this section apply to transactions occurring on or after January 1, 1985.

(5) Paragraphs (a), (b)(1) through (b)(4)(i)(B), (b)(4)(ii) through (b)(5), (c)(3)(ii)(A), (d) introductory text through (d)(2), (d)(4) through (d)(6) of this section apply to transfers occurring on or after September 14, 2015, and to transfers occurring before September 14, 2015, resulting from entity classification elections made under § 301.7701-3 that are filed on or after September 14, 2015. For transfers occurring before this section is applicable, see §§ 1.367(a)-1 and 1.367(a)-1T as contained in 26 CFR part 1 revised as of April 1, 2016. [Reg. § 1.367(a)-1.]

□ [T.D. 9441, 12-31-2008. *Amended by T.D. 9568, 12-16-2011, T.D. 9614, 3-18-2013, T.D. 9739, 9-18-2015 and T.D. 9803, 12-15-2016 (corrected 11-14-2017).]*

⟫⟫→ *Caution: The Treasury Department has identified Temporary Reg. §1.367(a)-1T, as amended by T.D. 9803, as a significant tax regulation that imposes an undue financial burden on U.S. taxpayers and/or adds undue complexity to the federal tax laws, pursuant to Executive Order 13789 (issued April 21, 2017) (Notice 2017-38, I.R.B. 2017-30). In a subsequent report, issued October 4, 2017, Treasury recommended planned actions that would reduce the burden of these regulations.*

[Reg. §1.367(a)-1T]

§1.367(a)-1T. Transfers to foreign corporations subject to section 367(a): In general (temporary).—(a) [Reserved].

(b) *General rules.*—(1) [Reserved].

(2) [Reserved].

(3) [Reserved].

(4) *Character, source, and adjustments.*—(i) *In general.*—If a U.S. person is required to recognize gain under section 367 upon a transfer of property to a foreign corporation, then—

(A) [Reserved].

(B) [Reserved]. For further guidance see § 1.367(a)-1(b)(4)(i)(B).

(C) [Reserved]. For further guidance see § 1.367(a)-1(b)(4)(i)(C).

(ii) [Reserved].

(5) [Reserved].

(c) *Transfers described in section 367(a)(1).*—(1) *In general.*—A transfer described in section 367 (a)(1) is any transfer of property by a U.S. person to a foreign corporation pursuant to an exchange described in section 332, 351, 354, 355, 356, or 361. Section 367(a)(1) applies to such a transfer whether it is made directly, indirectly, or constructively. Indirect or constructive transfers that are described in section 367(a)(1) include the transfers described in subparagraphs (2) through (7) of this paragraph (c).

(2) *Indirect transfers in certain reorganizations.*—[Reserved.] For further guidance, see § 1.367(a)-3(d).

(3) *Indirect transfers involving partnerships and interests therein.*—(i) *Transfer by partnership treated as transfer by partners.*—(A) *In general.*—If a partnership (whether foreign or domestic) transfers property to a foreign corporation in an exchange described in section 367(a)(1), then a U.S. person that is a partner in the partnership shall be treated as having transferred a proportionate share of the property in an exchange described in section 367(a)(1). A U.S. person's proportionate share of partnership property shall be determined under the rules and principles of section 701 through 761 and the regulations thereunder. The rule of this paragraph (c)(3)(i)(A) is illustrated by the following example.

Example. P is a partnership having five equal general partners, two of whom are United States persons. P transfers property to F, a foreign corporation, in connection with an exchange described in section 351. The exchange includes an indirect transfer of property by the partners to F. The transfers of property attributable to those partners who are United States persons, that is, 40 percent of each asset transferred to F, are transfers described in section 367(a)(1). The gain (if any) recognized on the transfer of 40 percent of each asset to F is attributable to the two partners who are United States persons.

(B) *Special adjustments to basis.*—If a U.S. person is treated under the rule of this paragraph (c)(3)(i) as having transferred a proportionate share of the property of a partnership in an exchange described in section 367(a), and is therefore required to recognize gain upon the transfer, then—

(1) The U.S. person's basis in the partnership shall be increased by the amount of gain recognized by him;

(2) Solely for purposes of determining the basis of the partnership in the stock of the transferee foreign corporation, the U.S. person shall be treated as having newly acquired an interest in the partnership (for an amount equal to the gain recognized), permitting the partnership to make an optional adjustment to basis pursuant to sections 743 and 754; and

(3) The transferee foreign corporation's basis in the property acquired from the partnership shall be increased by the amount of gain recognized by U.S. persons under this paragraph (c)(3)(i).

(ii) *Transfer of partnership interest treated as transfer of proportionate share of assets.*—(A) [Reserved].

(B) *Special adjustments to basis.*—If a U.S. person is treated under the rule of paragraph (c)(3)(ii)(A) of this section as having transferred a proportionate share of the property of a partnership in an exchange described in section 367(a), and is therefore required to recognize gain upon the transfer, then—

(1) The U.S. person's basis in the stock of the transferee foreign corporation shall be increased by the amount of gain so recognized by that person;

(2) The transferee foreign corporation's basis in the transferred partnership interest shall be increased by the amount of gain recognized by the U.S. person; and

(3) Solely for purposes of determining the partnership's basis in the property held by it, the U.S. person shall be treated as having newly acquired an interest in the partnership (for an amount equal to the gain recognized), permitting the partnership to make an optional adjustment to basis pursuant to sections 743 and 754.

(C) *Limited partnership interest.*—The transfer by a U.S. person of an interest in a partnership shall not be subject to the rules of paragraph (c)(3)(ii)(A) and (B) if—

(1) The interest transferred is a limited partnership interest; and

(2) Such interest is regularly traded on an established securities market.
Instead, the transfer of such an interest shall be treated in the same manner as a transfer of stock or securities. Thus, the consequences of such a transfer shall be determined under the rules of §1.367(a)-3. For purposes of this section, a limited partnership interest is an interest as a limited partner in a partnership that is organized under the laws of any State of the United States or the District of Columbia. Whether such an interest is regularly traded on an established securities market shall be determined under the provisions of paragraph (c)(3)(ii)(D) of this section.

(D) *Regularly traded on an established securities market.*—(1) *Established securities market.*—For purposes of this paragraph (c)(3)(ii), an established securities market is—

(i) A national securities exchange which is registered under section 6 of the Securities Exchange Act of 1934 (15 USC 78f);

(ii) A foreign national securities exchange which is officially recognized, sanctioned, or supervised by governmental authority; and

(iii) An over-the-counter market. An over-the-counter market is any market reflected by the existence of an inter-dealer quotation system. An inter-dealer quotation system is any system of general circulation to brokers and dealers which regularly disseminates quotations of stock and securities by identified brokers or dealers, other than by quotation sheets which are prepared and distributed by a broker or dealer in the regular course of business and which contain only quotations of such broker or dealer.

(2) *Regularly traded.*—A class of interest that is traded on an established securities market is considered to be regularly traded if it is regularly quoted by brokers or dealers making a market in such interests. A class of interests shall be presumed to be regularly traded if the entity has a total of 500 or more interest-holders.

(4) *Transfers by trusts and estates.*—(i) *In general.*—For purposes of section 367(a), a transfer of property by an estate or trust shall be

treated as a transfer by the entity itself and not as an indirect transfer by its beneficiaries. Thus, a transfer of property by a foreign trust or estate (as defined in section 7701(a)(31)) is not described in section 367(a)(1), regardless of whether the beneficiaries of the trust or estate are U.S. persons. Similarly, a transfer of property by a domestic trust or estate may be described in section 367(a)(1), regardless of whether the beneficiaries of the trust or estate are foreign persons.

(ii) *Grantor trusts.*—A transfer of a portion or all of the assets of a foreign or domestic trust to a foreign corporation in an exchange described in section 367(a)(1) is considered a transfer by any U.S. person who is treated as the owner of any such portion or all of the assets of the trust under sections 671 through 679.

(5) *Termination of election under section 1504(d).*—Section 367(a) applies to the constructive reorganization and transfer of property from a domestic corporation to a foreign corporation that occurs upon the termination of an election under section 1504(d), which permits the treatment of certain contiguous country corporations as domestic corporations. The rule of this paragraph (c)(5) is illustrated by the following example.

Example. Domestic corporation Y previously made a valid election under section 1504(d) to have its wholly owned Canadian subsidiary, C, treated as a domestic corporation. On July 1, 1986, C fails to continue to qualify for the election under section 1504(d). A constructive reorganization described in section 368(a)(1)(D) occurs. The resulting constructive transfer of assets by "domestic" corporation C to Canadian corporation C upon the termination of the election is a transfer of property described in section 367(a)(1).

(6) *Changes in classification of an entity.*—If a foreign entity is classified as an entity other than an association taxable as a corporation for United States tax purposes, and subsequently a change is made in the governing documents, articles, or agreements of the entity so that the entity is thereafter classified as an association taxable as a corporation, the change in classification is considered a transfer of property to a foreign corporation in connection with an exchange described in section 351. For purposes of section 367(a)(1), the transfer of property is considered as made by the persons determined under the rules set forth in paragraph (c)(3) of this section, with respect to partnerships, and paragraph (c)(4)(i) or (ii), with respect to trusts and estates, and the rules of such paragraphs apply in determining whether a transfer described in section 367(a)(1) has been made.

(7) *Contributions to capital.*—For rules with respect to the treatment of a contribution to the capital of a foreign corporation as a transfer described in section 367(a)(1), see section 367(c)(2) and the regulations thereunder.

(d) [Reserved].

(1) [Reserved].

(2) [Reserved].

(3) [Reserved]. For further guidance, see §1.367(a)-1(d)(3).

(4) [Reserved].

(5) [Reserved].

(6) [Reserved].

(e) [Reserved]. For further guidance, *see* §1.367(a)-1(e).

(f) [Reserved]. For further guidance, *see* §1.367(a)-1(f).

(g) *Effective date of certain sections.*—(1) *In general.*—Except as specifically provided to the contrary elsewhere in these sections, §§1.367(a)-1T through 1.367-6T apply to transfers occurring after December 31, 1984.

(2) *Private rulings.*—The taxpayer may rely on a private ruling under section 367(a) received by him before June 16, 1986.

(3) *Certain indirect transfers.*—Sections 1.367(a)-1T(c)(2)(i) and (iii) and 1.367(a)-1T(c)(3) apply to transfers made after June 16, 1986. For transfers made before that date, see 26 CFR §1.367(a)-1(b) (revised as of April 1, 1986).

(4) [Reserved]. For further guidance see §1.367(a)-1(g)(4). [Temporary Reg. §1.367(a)-1T.]

☐ [*T.D. 8087, 5-15-86. Amended by T.D. 8280, 1-12-90; T.D. 8770, 6-18-98; T.D. 9441, 12-31-2008; T.D. 9568, 12-16-2011, T.D. 9614, 3-18-2013, T.D. 9739, 9-18-2015 and T.D. 9803, 12-15-2016.*]

⫸⫸⫸ **Caution:** *The Treasury Department has identified Reg. §1.367(a)-2, as amended by T.D. 9803, as a significant tax regulation that imposes an undue financial burden on U.S. taxpayers and/or adds undue complexity to the federal tax laws, pursuant to Executive Order 13789 (issued April 21, 2017) (Notice 2017-38, I.R.B. 2017-30). In a subsequent report, issued October 4, 2017, Treasury recommended planned actions that would reduce the burden of these regulations.*

[Reg. §1.367(a)-2]

§1.367(a)-2. Exception for transfers of property for use in the active conduct of a trade or business.—(a) *Scope and general rule.*—(1) *Scope.*—Paragraph (a)(2) of this section provides the general exception to section 367(a)(1) for certain property transferred for use in

the active conduct of a trade or business. Paragraph (b) of this section describes property that is eligible for the exception provided in paragraph (a)(2) of this section. Paragraph (c) of this section describes property that is not eligible for the exception provided in paragraph (a)(2) of this section. Paragraph (d) of this section provides general rules, and paragraphs (e) through (h) of this section provide special rules, for determining whether property is used in the active conduct of a trade or business outside of the United States. Paragraph (i) of this section is reserved. Paragraph (j) of this section provides relief for certain failures to comply with the reporting requirements under paragraph (a)(2)(iii) of this section that are not willful. Paragraph (k) of this section provides dates of applicability. The rules of this section do not apply to a transfer of stock or securities in an exchange subject to § 1.367(a)-3.

(2) *General rule.*—Except as otherwise provided in §§ 1.367(a)-4, 1.367(a)-6, and 1.367(a)-7, section 367(a)(1) does not apply to property transferred by a United States person (U.S. transferor) to a foreign corporation if—

(i) The property constitutes eligible property;

(ii) The property is transferred for use by the foreign corporation in the active conduct of a trade or business outside of the United States, as determined under paragraph (d), (e), (f), (g), or (h) of this section, as applicable; and

(iii) The U.S. transferor complies with the reporting requirements of section 6038B and the regulations thereunder.

(b) *Eligible property.*—Except as provided in paragraph (c) of this section, eligible property means—

(1) Tangible property;

(2) A working interest in oil and gas property; and

(3) A financial asset. For purposes of this section, a financial asset is—

(i) A cash equivalent;

(ii) A security within the meaning of section 475(c)(2), without regard to the last sentence of section 475(c)(2) (referencing section 1256) and without regard to section 475(c)(4), but excluding an interest in a partnership;

(iii) A commodities position described in section 475(e)(2)(B), 475(e)(2)(C), or 475(e)(2)(D); and

(iv) A notional principal contract described in § 1.446-3(c)(1).

(c) *Exception for certain property.*—Notwithstanding paragraph (b) of this section, property described in paragraph (c)(1), (2), (3), or (4) of this section does not constitute eligible property.

(1) *Inventory.*—Stock in trade of the taxpayer or other property of a kind which would properly be included in the inventory of the taxpayer if on hand at the close of the taxable year, or property held by the taxpayer primarily for sale to customers in the ordinary course of its trade or business (including raw materials and supplies, partially completed goods, and finished products).

(2) *Installment obligations, etc.*—Installment obligations, accounts receivable, or similar property, but only to the extent that the principal amount of any such obligation has not previously been included by the taxpayer in its taxable income.

(3) *Nonfunctional currency, etc.*—(i) *In general.*—Property that gives rise to a section 988 transaction of the taxpayer described in section 988(c)(1)(A) through (C), without regard to section 988(c)(1)(D) and (E), or that would give rise to such a section 988 transaction if it were acquired, accrued, entered into, or disposed of directly by the taxpayer.

(ii) *Limitation of gain required to be recognized.*—If section 367(a)(1) applies to a transfer of property described in paragraph (c)(3)(i) of this section, then the gain required to be recognized is limited to the gain realized as part of the same transaction upon the transfer of property described in paragraph (c)(3)(i) of this section, less any loss realized as part of the same transaction upon the transfer of property described in paragraph (c)(3)(i) of this section. This limitation applies in lieu of the rule in § 1.367(a)-1(b)(1). No loss is recognized with respect to property described in this paragraph (c)(3).

(4) *Certain leased tangible property.*—Tangible property with respect to which the transferor is a lessor at the time of the transfer, unless either the foreign corporation is the lessee at the time of the transfer or the foreign corporation will lease the property to third persons.

(d) *Active conduct of a trade or business outside the United States.*—(1) *In general.*—Except as provided in paragraphs (e), (f), (g), and (h) of this section, to determine whether property is transferred for use by the foreign corporation in the active conduct of a trade or business outside of the United States, four factual determinations must be made:

(i) What is the trade or business of the foreign corporation (see paragraph (d)(2) of this section);

(ii) Do the activities of the foreign corporation constitute the active conduct of that trade or business (see paragraph (d)(3) of this section);

(iii) Is the trade or business conducted outside of the United States (see paragraph (d)(4) of this section); and

(iv) Is the transferred property used or held for use in the trade or business (see paragraph (d)(5) of this section)?

(2) *Trade or business.*—Whether the activities of the foreign corporation constitute a trade or business is determined based on all the facts and circumstances. In general, a trade or business is a specific unified group of activities that constitute (or could constitute) an independent economic enterprise carried on for profit. For example, the activities of a foreign selling subsidiary could constitute a trade or business if they could be independently carried on for profit, even though the subsidiary acts exclusively on behalf of, and has operations fully integrated with, its parent corporation. To constitute a trade or business, a group of activities must ordinarily include every operation which forms a part of, or a step in, a process by which an enterprise may earn income or profit. In this regard, one or more of such activities may be carried on by independent contractors under the direct control of the foreign corporation. (However, see paragraph (d)(3) of this section.) The group of activities must ordinarily include the collection of income and the payment of expenses. If the activities of the foreign corporation do not constitute a trade or business, then the exception provided by this section does not apply, regardless of the level of activities carried on by the corporation. The following activities are not considered to constitute by themselves a trade or business for purposes of this section:

(i) Any activity giving rise to expenses that would be deductible only under section 212 if the activities were carried on by an individual; or

(ii) The holding for one's own account of investments in stock, securities, land, or other property, including casual sales thereof.

(3) *Active conduct.*—Whether a trade or business is actively conducted by the foreign corporation is determined based on all the facts and circumstances. In general, a corporation actively conducts a trade or business only if the officers and employees of the corporation carry out substantial managerial and operational activities. A corporation may be engaged in the active conduct of a trade or business even though incidental activities of the trade or business are carried out on behalf of the corporation by independent contractors. In determining whether the officers and employees of the corporation carry out substantial managerial and operational activities, however, the activities of independent contractors are disregarded. On the other hand, the officers and employees of the corporation are considered to include the officers and employees of related entities who are made available to and supervised on a day-to-day basis by, and whose salaries are paid by (or reimbursed to the lending related entity by), the foreign corporation. See paragraph (d)(6) of this section for the standard that applies to determine whether a trade or business that produces rents or royalties is actively conducted. The rule of this paragraph (d)(3) is illustrated by the following example.

Example. X, a domestic corporation, and Y, a foreign corporation not related to X, transfer property to Z, a newly formed foreign corporation organized for the purpose of combining the research activities of X and Y. Z contracts all of its operational and research activities to Y for an arm's-length fee. Z's activities do not constitute the active conduct of a trade or business.

(4) *Outside of the United States.*—Whether the foreign corporation conducts a trade or business outside of the United States is determined based on all the facts and circumstances. Generally, the primary managerial and operational activities of the trade or business must be conducted outside the United States and immediately after the transfer the transferred assets must be located outside the United States. Thus, the exception provided by this section would not apply to the transfer of the assets of a domestic business to a foreign corporation if the domestic business continued to operate in the United States after the transfer. In such a case, the primary operational activities of the business would continue to be conducted in the United States. Moreover, the transferred assets would be located in the United States. However, it is not necessary that every item of property transferred be used outside of the United States. As long as the primary managerial and operational activities of the trade or business are conducted outside of the United States and substantially all of the transferred assets are located outside the United States, incidental items of transferred property located in the United States may be considered to have been transferred for use in the active conduct of a trade or business outside of the United States.

(5) *Use in the trade or business.*—Whether property is used or held for use by the foreign corporation in a trade or business is determined based on all the facts and circumstances. In general,

property is used or held for use in the foreign corporation's trade or business if it is—

(i) Held for the principal purpose of promoting the present conduct of the trade or business;

(ii) Acquired and held in the ordinary course of the trade or business; or

(iii) Otherwise held in a direct relationship to the trade or business. Property is considered held in a direct relationship to a trade or business if it is held to meet the present needs of that trade or business and not its anticipated future needs. Thus, property will not be considered to be held in a direct relationship to a trade or business if it is held for the purpose of providing for future diversification into a new trade or business, future expansion of trade or business activities, future plant replacement, or future business contingencies.

(6) *Active leasing and licensing.*—For purposes of paragraph (d)(3) of this section, whether a trade or business that produces rents or royalties is actively conducted is determined under the principles of section 954(c)(2)(A) and the regulations thereunder, but without regard to whether the rents or royalties are received from an unrelated party. See §§ 1.954-2(c) and (d).

(e) *Special rules for certain property to be leased.*—(1) *Leasing business of the foreign corporation.*—Except as otherwise provided in this paragraph (e), tangible property that will be leased to another person by the foreign corporation will be considered to be transferred for use by the foreign corporation in an active trade or business outside the United States only if—

(i) The foreign corporation's leasing of the property constitutes the active conduct of a leasing business, as determined under paragraph (d)(6) of this section;

(ii) The lessee of the property is not expected to, and does not, use the property in the United States; and

(iii) The foreign corporation has a need for substantial investment in assets of the type transferred.

(2) *De minimis leasing by the foreign corporation.*—Tangible property that will be leased to another person by the foreign corporation but that does not satisfy the conditions of paragraph (e)(1) of this section will, nevertheless, be considered to be transferred for use in the active conduct of a trade or business if either—

(i) The property transferred will be used by the foreign corporation in the active conduct of a trade or business but will be leased during occasional brief periods when the property would otherwise be idle, such as an airplane leased during periods of excess capacity; or

(ii) The property transferred is real property located outside the United States and—

(A) The property will be used primarily in the active conduct of a trade or business of the foreign corporation; and

(B) Not more than ten percent of the square footage of the property will be leased to others.

(3) *Aircraft and vessels leased in foreign commerce.*—For purposes of satisfying paragraph (e)(1) of this section, an aircraft or vessel, including component parts such as an engine leased separately from the aircraft or vessel, that will be leased to another person by the foreign corporation will be considered to be transferred for use in the active conduct of a trade or business if—

(i) The employees of the foreign corporation perform substantial managerial and operational activities of leasing aircraft or vessels outside the United States; and

(ii) The leased property is predominantly used outside the United States, as determined under § 1.954-2(c)(2)(v).

(f) *Special rules for oil and gas working interests.*—(1) *In general.*—A working interest in oil and gas property will be considered to be transferred for use in the active conduct of a trade or business if—

(i) The transfer satisfies the conditions of paragraph (f)(2) or (f)(3) of this section;

(ii) At the time of the transfer, the foreign corporation has no intention to farm out or otherwise transfer any part of the transferred working interest; and

(iii) During the first three years after the transfer there are no farmouts or other transfers of any part of the transferred working interest as a result of which the foreign corporation retains less than a 50-percent share of the transferred working interest.

(2) *Active use of working interest.*—A working interest in oil and gas property that satisfies the conditions in paragraphs (f)(1)(ii) and (iii) of this section will be considered to be transferred for use in the active conduct of a trade or business if—

(i) The U.S. transferor is regularly and substantially engaged in exploration for and extraction of minerals, either directly or

through working interests in joint ventures, other than by reason of the property that is transferred;

(ii) The terms of the working interest transferred were actively negotiated among the joint venturers;

(iii) The working interest transferred constitutes at least a five percent working interest;

(iv) Before and at the time of the transfer, through its own employees or officers, the U.S. transferor was regularly and actively engaged in—

(A) Operating the working interest, or

(B) Analyzing technical data relating to the activities of the venture;

(v) Before and at the time of the transfer, through its own employees or officers, the U.S. transferor was regularly and actively involved in decision making with respect to the operations of the venture, including decisions relating to exploration, development, production, and marketing; and

(vi) After the transfer, the foreign corporation will for the foreseeable future satisfy the requirements of subparagraphs (iv) and (v) of this paragraph (f)(2).

(3) *Start-up operations.*—A working interest in oil and gas property that satisfies the conditions in paragraphs (f)(1)(ii) and (iii) of this section but that does not satisfy all the requirements of paragraph (f)(2) of this section will, nevertheless, be considered to be transferred for use in the active conduct of a trade or business if—

(i) The working interest was acquired by the U.S. transferor immediately before the transfer and for the specific purpose of transferring it to the foreign corporation;

(ii) The requirements of paragraphs (f)(2)(ii) and (iii) of this section are satisfied; and

(iii) The foreign corporation will for the foreseeable future satisfy the requirements of paragraph (f)(2)(iv) and (v) of this section.

(4) *Other applicable rules.*—A working interest in oil and gas property that is not described in paragraph (f)(1) of this section may nonetheless qualify for the exception to section 367(a)(1) contained in this section depending upon the facts and circumstances.

(g) *Property retransferred by the foreign corporation.*—(1) *General rule.*—Property will not be considered to be transferred for use in the active conduct of a trade or business outside of the United States if—

(i) At the time of the transfer, it is reasonable to believe that, in the reasonably foreseeable future, the foreign corporation will sell or otherwise dispose of any material portion of the property other than in the ordinary course of business; or

(ii) Except as provided in paragraph (g)(2) of this section, the foreign corporation receives the property in an exchange described in section 367(a)(1), and, as part of the same transaction, transfers the property to another person. For purposes of the preceding sentence, a subsequent transfer within six months of the initial transfer will be considered to be part of the same transaction, and a subsequent transfer more than six months after the initial transfer may be considered to be part of the same transaction under step-transaction principles.

(2) *Exception.*—Notwithstanding paragraph (g)(1) of this section, the active conduct exception provided by this section shall apply to the initial transfer if—

(i) The initial transfer is followed by one or more subsequent transfers described in section 351 or 721; and

(ii) Each subsequent transferee is either a partnership in which the preceding transferor is a general partner or a corporation in which the preceding transferor owns common stock; and

(iii) The ultimate transferee uses the property in the active conduct of a trade or business outside the United States.

(h) *Compulsory transfers of property.*—Property is presumed to be transferred for use in the active conduct of a trade or business outside of the United States, if—

(1) The property was previously in use in the country in which the foreign corporation is organized; and

(2) The transfer is either:

(i) Legally required by the foreign government as a necessary condition of doing business; or

(ii) Compelled by a genuine threat of immediate expropriation by the foreign government.

(i) [Reserved].

(j) *Failure to comply with reporting requirements of section 6038B.*—(1) *Failure to comply.*—For purposes of the exception to the application of section 367(a)(1) provided in paragraph (a)(2) of this section, a failure to comply with the reporting requirements of section 6038B and the regulations thereunder (failure to comply) has the meaning set forth in § 1.6038B-1(f)(2).

(2) *Relief for certain failures to comply that are not willful.*—(i) *In general.*—A failure to comply described in paragraph (j)(1) of this section will be deemed not to have occurred for purposes of satisfying the requirements of this section if the taxpayer demonstrates that the failure was not willful using the procedure set forth in this paragraph (j)(2). For this purpose, willful is to be interpreted consistent with the meaning of that term in the context of other civil penalties, which would include a failure due to gross negligence, reckless disregard, or willful neglect. Whether a failure to comply was a willful failure will be determined by the Director of Field Operations, Cross Border Activities Practice Area, Large Business & International (or any successor to the roles and responsibilities of such position, as appropriate) (Director) based on all the facts and circumstances. The taxpayer must submit a request for relief and an explanation as provided in paragraph (j)(2)(ii)(A) of this section. Although a taxpayer whose failure to comply is determined not to be willful will not be subject to gain recognition under this section, the taxpayer will be subject to a penalty under section 6038B if the taxpayer fails to demonstrate that the failure was due to reasonable cause and not willful neglect. See §1.6038B-1(b)(1) and (f). The determination of whether the failure to comply was willful under this section has no effect on any request for relief made under §1.6038B-1(f).

(ii) *Procedures for establishing that a failure to comply was not willful.*—(A) *Time and manner of submission.*—A taxpayer's statement that the failure to comply was not willful will be considered only if, promptly after the taxpayer becomes aware of the failure, an amended return is filed for the taxable year to which the failure relates that includes the information that should have been included with the original return for such taxable year or that otherwise complies with the rules of this section, and that includes a written statement explaining the reasons for the failure to comply. The amended return must be filed with the Internal Revenue Service at the location where the taxpayer filed its original return. The taxpayer

may submit a request for relief from the penalty under section 6038B as part of the same submission. See §1.6038B-1(f).

(B) *Notice requirement.*—In addition to the requirements of paragraph (j)(2)(ii)(A) of this section, the taxpayer must comply with the notice requirements of this paragraph (j)(2)(ii)(B). If any taxable year of the taxpayer is under examination when the amended return is filed, a copy of the amended return and any information required to be included with such return must be delivered to the Internal Revenue Service personnel conducting the examination. If no taxable year of the taxpayer is under examination when the amended return is filed, a copy of the amended return and any information required to be included with such return must be delivered to the Director.

(3) For illustrations of the application of the willfulness standard of this paragraph (j), see the examples in §1.367(a)-8(p)(3).

(4) Paragraph (j) applies to requests for relief submitted on or after November 19, 2014.

(k) *Effective/applicability dates.*—(1) *In general.*—Except as provided in paragraphs (j)(4) and (k)(2) of this section, the rules of this section apply to transfers occurring on or after September 14, 2015, and to transfers occurring before September 14, 2015, resulting from entity classification elections made under §301.7701-3 that are filed on or after September 14, 2015. For transfers occurring before this section is applicable, see §§1.367(a)-2, -2T, -4, -4T, -5, and -5T as contained in 26 CFR part 1 revised as of April 1, 2016.

(2) *Foreign currency exception.*—Notwithstanding paragraph (c)(3)(i) of this section, §1.367(a)-5T(d)(2) as contained in 26 CFR part 1 revised as of April 1, 2016, applies to transfers of property denominated in a foreign currency occurring before December 16, 2016, other than transfers occurring before that date resulting from entity classification elections made under §301.7701-3 that are filed on or after that date. [Reg. §1.367(a)-2.]

☐ [T.D. 9525, 5-5-2011. *Amended by T.D. 9704, 11-18-2014 and T.D. 9803, 12-15-2016.*]

⟫→ *Caution: The Treasury Department has identified Reg. §1.367(a)-3, as amended by T.D. 9803, as a significant tax regulation that imposes an undue financial burden on U.S. taxpayers and/or adds undue complexity to the federal tax laws, pursuant to Executive Order 13789 (issued April 21, 2017) (Notice 2017-38, I.R.B. 2017-30). In a subsequent report, issued October 4, 2017, Treasury recommended planned actions that would reduce the burden of these regulations.*

[Reg. §1.367(a)-3]

§1.367(a)-3. Treatment of transfers of stock or securities to foreign corporations.—(a) *In general.*—(1) *Overview.*—This section provides rules concerning the transfer of stock or securities by a U.S. person to a foreign corporation in an exchange described in section 367(a)(1). In general, a transfer of stock or securities (including an indirect stock transfer described in paragraph (d) of this section) by a U.S. person to a foreign corporation that is described in section 351, 354 (including a section 354 exchange pursuant to a reorganization described in section 368(a)(1)(B)), 356, or section 361(a) or (b) is subject to section 367(a)(1). Therefore, gain is recognized on such a transfer unless one of the exceptions set forth in paragraph (a)(2) of this section (regarding general exceptions for certain exchanges of stock or securities), paragraph (b) of this section (regarding transfers of foreign stock or securities), paragraph (c) of this section (regarding transfers of domestic stock or securities), or paragraph (e) of this section (regarding transfers of stock or securities in a section 361 exchange) applies to the transfer. For rules applicable when, pursuant to section 304(a)(1), a U.S. person is treated as transferring stock of a domestic or foreign corporation to a foreign corporation in exchange for stock of such foreign corporation in a transaction to which section 351(a) applies, see §1.367(a)-9T.

(2) *Exceptions for certain exchanges of stock or securities.*—Unless otherwise provided, the following exchanges are not subject to section 367(a)(1) and therefore gain is not recognized under section 367(a)(1).

(i) *Section 368(a)(1)(E) reorganizations.*—In an exchange under section 354 or 356, a U.S. person exchanges stock or securities of a foreign corporation in a reorganization described in section 368(a)(1)(E).

(ii) *Certain section 368(a)(1) asset reorganizations.*—In an exchange under section 354 or 356, a U.S. person exchanges stock or securities of a domestic or foreign corporation pursuant to an asset reorganization that is not treated as an indirect stock transfer under paragraph (d) of this section. See paragraph (d)(3) *Example 16* of this section. For purposes of this section, an *asset reorganization* is defined as a reorganization described in section 368(a)(1) involving a transfer of property under section 361.

(iii) *Certain reorganizations described in sections 368(a)(1)(A) and (a)(2)(E).*—If, in an exchange described in section 361, a domestic merging corporation transfers stock of a controlling corporation to a

foreign surviving corporation in a reorganization described in section 368(a)(1)(A) and (a)(2)(E), the stock of the controlling corporation transferred in such section 361 exchange is not subject to section 367(a)(1) if the stock of the controlling corporation is provided to the merging corporation by the controlling corporation pursuant to the plan of reorganization. However, a section 361 exchange of other property, including stock of the controlling corporation not provided by the controlling corporation pursuant to the plan of reorganization, by the domestic merging corporation to the foreign surviving corporation pursuant to such a reorganization is described in section 367(a)(1) and therefore subject to section 367(a)(1) unless an exception to section 367(a)(1) applies.

(iv) *Certain triangular reorganizations described in §1.367(b)-10.*—If, in an exchange under section 354 or 356, one or more U.S. persons exchange stock or securities of T (as defined in §1.358-6(b)(1)(iii)) in connection with a transaction described in §1.367(b)-10 (applying to certain acquisitions of parent stock or securities for property in triangular reorganizations), section 367(a)(1) shall not apply to such U.S. persons with respect to the exchange of the stock or securities of T if the condition specified in this paragraph (iv) is satisfied. The condition specified in this paragraph (iv) is that the amount of gain in the T stock or securities that would otherwise be recognized under section 367(a)(1) (without regard to any exceptions thereto) pursuant to the indirect stock transfer rules of paragraph (d) of this section is less than the sum of the amount of the deemed distribution under §1.367(b)-10 treated as a dividend under section 301(c)(1) and the amount of such deemed distribution treated as gain from the sale or exchange of property under section 301(c)(3). See §1.367(b)-10(a)(2)(iii) (providing a similar rule that excludes certain transactions from the application of §1.367(b)-10).

(3) *Cross-references.*—For rules regarding other indirect or constructive transfers of stock or securities subject to section 367(a)(1) (unless an exception applies) see §1.367(a)-1(c). For additional rules regarding a transfer of stock or securities in an exchange described in section 361(a) or (b), see §1.367(a)-7. For special basis and holding period rules involving foreign corporations that are parties to certain triangular reorganizations under section 368(a)(1), see §1.367(b)-13. For additional rules relating to certain nonrecognition exchanges involving a foreign corporation, see section 367(b) and the regulations under that section. For rules regarding reporting requirements with respect to transfers described under section 367(a), see section 6038B and the regulations thereunder. For rules related to expatriated entities, see section 7874 and the regulations thereunder.

(b) *Transfers of stock or securities of foreign corporations.*—(1) *General rule.*—Except as provided in paragraph (e) of this section, a transfer of stock or securities of a foreign corporation by a U.S. person to a foreign corporation that would otherwise be subject to section 367(a)(1) under paragraph (a) of this section will not be subject to section 367(a)(1) if either—

(i) *Less than 5-percent shareholder.*—The U.S. person owns less than five percent (applying the attribution rules of section 318, as modified by section 958(b)) of both the total voting power and the total value of the stock of the transferee foreign corporation immediately after the transfer; or

(ii) *5-percent shareholder.*—The U.S. person enters into a five-year gain recognition agreement with respect to the transferred stock or securities as provided in §1.367(a)-8.

(2) *Certain transfers subject to sections 367(a) and (b).*—(i) *In general.*—A transfer of stock or securities described in section 367(a) or the regulations thereunder as well as in section 367(b) or the regulations thereunder shall be subject concurrently to sections 367(a) and (b) and the respective regulations thereunder, except as provided in paragraph (b)(2)(i)(A) through (C) of this section. See paragraph (d)(3) *Examples 11* and 14 of this section.

(A) Section 367(b) and the regulations thereunder shall not apply if a foreign corporation is not treated as a corporation under section 367(a)(1). See the example in paragraph (b)(2)(ii) of this section and paragraph (d)(3) *Example 14* of this section.

(B) If a foreign corporation transfers assets to a domestic corporation in a transaction to which §1.367(b)-3(a) and (b) and the indirect stock transfer rules of paragraph (d) of this section apply, and all the earnings and profits amount attributable to the stock of an exchanging shareholder under §1.367(b)-3(b) is greater than the amount of gain in such stock subject to section 367(a) pursuant to the indirect stock transfer rules of paragraph (d) of this section, then the rules of section 367(b), and not the rules of section 367(a), shall apply to the exchange. See paragraph (d)(3) *Example 15* of this section.

(C) [Reserved]. For further guidance, see §1.367(a)-3T(b)(2)(i)(C).

(ii) *Example.*—The following example illustrates the provisions of this paragraph (b)(2):

Example. (i) Facts. DC, a domestic corporation, owns all of the stock of FC1, a controlled foreign corporation within the meaning of section 957(a). DC's basis in the stock of FC1 is $50, and the value of such stock is $100. The section 1248 amount with respect to such stock is $30. FC2, also a foreign corporation, is owned entirely by foreign individuals who are not related to DC or FC1. In a reorganization described in section 368(a)(1)(B), FC2 acquires all of the stock of FC1 from DC in exchange for 20 percent of the voting stock of FC2. FC2 is not a controlled foreign corporation after the reorganization.

(ii) *Result without gain recognition agreement.* Under the provisions of this paragraph (b), if DC fails to enter into a gain recognition agreement, DC is required to recognize in the year of the transfer the $50 of gain that it realized upon the transfer, $30 of which will be treated as a dividend under section 1248.

(iii) *Result with gain recognition agreement.* If DC enters into a gain recognition agreement under §1.367(a)-8 with respect to the transfer of FC1 stock, the exchange will also be subject to the provisions of section 367(b) and the regulations thereunder to the extent that it is not subject to tax under section 367(a)(1). In such case, DC will be required to recognize the section 1248 amount of $30 on the exchange of FC1 for FC2 stock. See §1.367(b)-4(b). The deemed dividend of $30 recognized by DC will increase its basis in the FC1 stock exchanged in the transaction and, therefore, the basis of the FC2 stock received in the transaction. The remaining gain of $20 realized by DC (otherwise recognizable under section 367(a)) in the exchange of FC1 stock will not be recognized if DC enters into a gain recognition agreement with respect to the transfer. (The result would be unchanged if, for example, the exchange of FC1 stock for FC2 stock qualified as a section 351 exchange, or as an exchange described in both sections 351 and 368(a)(1)(B).)

(c) *Transfers of stock or securities of domestic corporations.*—(1) *General rule.*—Except as provided in paragraph (e) of this section, a transfer of stock or securities of a domestic corporation by a U.S. person to a foreign corporation that would otherwise be subject to section 367(a)(1) under paragraph (a) of this section will not be subject to section 367(a)(1) if the domestic corporation the stock or securities of which are transferred (referred to as the U.S. target company) complies with the reporting requirements in paragraph (c)(6) of this section and if each of the following four conditions is met:

(i) Fifty percent or less of both the total voting power and the total value of the stock of the transferee foreign corporation is received in the transaction, in the aggregate, by U.S. transferors (*i.e.*, the

amount of stock received does not exceed the 50-percent ownership threshold).

(ii) Fifty percent or less of each of the total voting power and the total value of the stock of the transferee foreign corporation is owned, in the aggregate, immediately after the transfer by U.S. persons that are either officers or directors of the U.S. target company or that are five-percent target shareholders (as defined in paragraph (c)(5)(iii) of this section) (*i.e.*, there is no control group). For purposes of this paragraph (c)(1)(ii), any stock of the transferee foreign corporation owned by U.S. persons immediately after the transfer will be taken into account, whether or not it was received in the exchange for stock or securities of the U.S. target company.

(iii) Either—

(A) The U.S. person is not a five-percent transferee shareholder (as defined in paragraph (c)(5)(ii) of this section); or

(B) The U.S. person is a five-percent transferee shareholder and enters into a five-year agreement to recognize gain with respect to the U.S. target company stock or securities it exchanged in the form provided in §1.367(a)-8; and

(iv) The active trade or business test (as defined in paragraph (c)(3) of this section) is satisfied.

(2) *Ownership presumption.*—For purposes of paragraph (c)(1) of this section, persons who transfer stock or securities of the U.S. target company in exchange for stock of the transferee foreign corporation are presumed to be U.S. persons. This presumption may be rebutted in accordance with paragraph (c)(7) of this section.

(3) *Active trade or business test.*—(i) *In general.*—The tests of this paragraph (c)(3), collectively referred to as the active trade or business test, are satisfied if:

(A) The transferee foreign corporation or any qualified subsidiary (as defined in paragraph (c)(5)(vii) of this section) or any qualified partnership (as defined in paragraph (c)(5)(viii) of this section) is engaged in an active trade or business outside the United States, within the meaning of §1.367(a)-2(d)(2), (3) and (4), for the entire 36-month period immediately before the transfer;

(B) At the time of the transfer, neither the transferors nor the transferee foreign corporation (and, if applicable, the qualified subsidiary or qualified partnership engaged in the active trade or business) have an intention to substantially dispose of or discontinue such trade or business; and

(C) The substantiality test (as defined in paragraph (c)(3)(iii) of this section) is satisfied.

(ii) *Special rules.*—For purposes of paragraphs (c)(3)(i)(A) and (B) of this section, the following special rules apply:

(A) The transferee foreign corporation, a qualified subsidiary, or a qualified partnership will be considered to be engaged in an active trade or business for the entire 36-month period preceding the exchange if it acquires at the time of, or any time prior to, the exchange a trade or business that has been active throughout the entire 36-month period preceding the exchange. This special rule shall not apply, however, if the acquired active trade or business assets were owned by the U.S. target company or any affiliate (within the meaning of section 1504(a) but excluding the exceptions contained in section 1504(b) and substituting "50 percent" for "80 percent" where it appears therein) at any time during the 36-month period prior to the acquisition. Nor will this special rule apply if the principal purpose of such acquisition is to satisfy the active trade or business test.

(B) An active trade or business does not include the making or managing of investments for the account of the transferee foreign corporation or any affiliate (within the meaning of section 1504(a) but excluding the exceptions contained in section 1504(b) and substituting "50 percent" for "80 percent" where it appears therein). (This paragraph (c)(3)(ii)(B) shall not create any inference as to the scope of §1.367(a)-2(d)(2) and (3) for other purposes.)

(iii) *Substantiality test.*—(A) *General rule.*—A transferee foreign corporation will be deemed to satisfy the substantiality test if, at the time of the transfer, the fair market value of the transferee foreign corporation is at least equal to the fair market value of the U.S. target company.

(B) *Special rules for transferee foreign corporation value.*—(1) For purposes of paragraph (c)(3)(iii)(A) of this section, the value of the transferee foreign corporation shall include assets acquired outside the ordinary course of business by the transferee foreign corporation within the 36-month period preceding the exchange only if either—

(i) Both—

(A) At the time of the exchange, such assets or, as applicable, the proceeds thereof, do not produce, and are not held for the production of, passive income as defined in section 1297(b); and

(B) Such assets are not acquired for the principal purpose of satisfying the substantiality test; or

(ii) Such assets consist of the stock of a qualified subsidiary or an interest in a qualified partnership. See paragraph (c)(3)(iii)(B)(2) of this section.

(2) For purposes of paragraph (c)(3)(iii)(A) of this section, the value of the transferee foreign corporation shall not include the value of the stock of any qualified subsidiary or the value of any interest in a qualified partnership, held directly or indirectly, to the extent that such value is attributable to assets acquired by such qualified subsidiary or partnership outside the ordinary course of business and within the 36-month period preceding the exchange unless those assets satisfy the requirements in paragraph (c)(3)(iii)(B)(1) of this section.

(3) For purposes of paragraph (c)(3)(iii)(A) of this section, the value of the transferee foreign corporation shall not include the value of assets received within the 36-month period prior to the acquisition, notwithstanding the special rule in paragraph (c)(3)(iii)(B)(1) of this section, if such assets were owned by the U.S. target company or an affiliate (within the meaning of section 1504(a) but without the exceptions under section 1504(b) and substituting "50 percent" for "80 percent" where it appears therein) at any time during the 36-month period prior to the transaction.

(C) *Special rule for U.S. target company value.*—For purposes of §1.367(a)-3(c)(3)(iii)(A), the fair market value of the U.S. target company includes the aggregate amount of non-ordinary course distributions (NOCDs) made by the U.S. target company. To calculate the aggregate value of NOCDs, the principles of §1.7874-10, including the rule regarding predecessors in §1.7874-10(e) and the rule regarding a deemed distribution of stock in certain cases in §1.7874-10(g), apply. However, this paragraph (c)(3)(iii)(C) does not apply if the principles of the de minimis exception in §1.7874-10(d) are satisfied.

(4) *Special rules.*—(i) *Treatment of partnerships.*—For purposes of this paragraph (c), if a partnership (whether domestic or foreign) owns stock or securities in the U.S. target company or the transferee foreign corporation, or transfers stock or securities in an exchange described in section 367(a), each partner in the partnership, and not the partnership itself, is treated as owning and as having transferred, or as owning, a proportionate share of the stock or securities. See §1.367(a)-1(c)(3).

(ii) *Treatment of options.*—For purposes of this paragraph (c), one or more options (or an interest similar to an option) will be treated as exercised and thus will be counted as stock for purposes of determining whether the 50percent threshold is exceeded or whether a control group exists if a principal purpose of the issuance or the acquisition of the option (or other interest) was the avoidance of the general rule contained in section 367(a)(1).

(iii) *U.S. target has a vestigial ownership interest in transferee foreign corporation.*—In cases where, immediately after the transfer, the U.S. target company owns, directly or indirectly (applying the attribution rules of sections 267(c)(1) and (5)), stock of the transferee foreign corporation, that stock will not in any way be taken into account (and, thus, will not be treated as outstanding) in determining whether the 50-percent threshold under paragraph (c)(1)(i) of this section is exceeded or whether a control group under paragraph (c)(1)(ii) of this section exists.

(iv) *Attribution rule.*—Except as otherwise provided in this section, the rules of section 318, as modified by the rules of section 958(b), shall apply for purposes of determining the ownership or receipt of stock, securities or other property under this paragraph (c).

(5) *Definitions.*—(i) *Ownership statement.*—An ownership statement is a statement, signed under penalties of perjury, stating—

(A) The identity and taxpayer identification number, if any, of the person making the statement;

(B) That the person making the statement is not a U.S. person (as defined in paragraph (c)(5)(iv) of this section);

(C) That the person making the statement either—

(1) Owns less than 1 percent of the total voting power and total value of a U.S. target company the stock of which is described in Rule 13d-1(d) of Regulation 13D (17 CFR 240.13d-1(d)) (or any rule or regulation to generally the same effect) promulgated by the Securities and Exchange Commission under the Securities and Exchange Act of 1934 (15 USC 78m), and such person did not acquire the stock with a principal purpose to enable the U.S. transferors to satisfy the requirement contained in paragraph (c)(1)(i) of this section; or

(2) Is not related to any U.S. person to whom the stock or securities owned by the person making the statement are attributable

under the rules of section 958(b), and did not acquire the stock with a principal purpose to enable the U.S. transferors to satisfy the requirement contained in paragraph (c)(1)(i) of this section;

(D) The citizenship, permanent residence, home address, and U.S. address, if any, of the person making the statement; and

(E) The ownership such person has (by voting power and by value) in the U.S. target company prior to the exchange and the amount of stock of the transferee foreign corporation (by voting power and value) received by such person in the exchange.

(ii) *Five-percent transferee shareholder.*—A five-percent transferee shareholder is a person that owns at least five percent of either the total voting power or the total value of the stock of the transferee foreign corporation immediately after the transfer described in section 367(a)(1). For special rules involving cases in which stock is held by a partnership, see paragraph (c)(4)(i) of this section.

(iii) *Five-percent target shareholder and certain other 5-percent shareholders.*—A five-percent target shareholder is a person that owns at least five percent of either the total voting power or the total value of the stock of the U.S. target company immediately prior to the transfer described in section 367(a)(1). If the stock of the U.S. target company (or any company through which stock of the U.S. target company is owned indirectly or constructively) is described in Rule 13d-1(d) of Regulation 13D (17 CFR 240.13d-1(d)) (or any rule or regulation to generally the same effect), promulgated by the Securities and Exchange Commission under the Securities Exchange Act of 1934 (15 USC 78m), then, in the absence of actual knowledge to the contrary, the existence or absence of filings of Schedule 13-D or 13-G (or any similar schedules) may be relied upon for purposes of identifying five-percent target shareholders (or a five-percent shareholder of a corporation which itself is a five-percent shareholder of the U.S. target company). For special rules involving cases in which U.S. target company stock is held by a partnership, see paragraph (c)(4)(i) of this section.

(iv) *U.S. person.*—For purposes of this section, a U.S. person is defined by reference to §1.367(a)-1(d)(1). For application of the rules of this section to stock or securities owned or transferred by a partnership that is a U.S. person, however, see paragraph (c)(4)(i) of this section.

(v) *U.S. transferor.*—A U.S transferor is a U.S. person (as defined in paragraph (c)(5)(iv) of this section) that transfers stock or securities of one or more U.S. target companies in exchange for stock of the transferee foreign corporation in an exchange described in section 367.

(vi) *Transferee foreign corporation.*—Except as provided in paragraph (d)(2)(i)(B) of this section, a transferee foreign corporation is the foreign corporation whose stock is received in the exchange by U.S. persons.

(vii) *Qualified subsidiary.*—A qualified subsidiary is a foreign corporation whose stock is at least 80-percent owned (by total voting power and total value), directly or indirectly, by the transferee foreign corporation. However, a corporation will not be treated as a qualified subsidiary if it was affiliated with the U.S. target company (within the meaning of section 1504(a) but without the exceptions under section 1504(b) and substituting "50 percent" for "80 percent" where it appears therein) at any time during the 36-month period prior to the transfer. Nor will a corporation be treated as a qualified subsidiary if it was acquired by the transferee foreign corporation at any time during the 36-month period prior to the transfer for the principal purpose of satisfying the active trade or business test, including the substantiality test.

(viii) *Qualified partnership.*—(A) Except as provided in paragraph (c)(5)(viii)(B) or (C) of this section, a qualified partnership is a partnership in which the transferee foreign corporation—

(1) Has active and substantial management functions as a partner with regard to the partnership business; or

(2) Has an interest representing a 25 percent or greater interest in the partnership's capital and profits.

(B) A partnership is not a qualified partnership if the U.S. target company or any affiliate of the U.S. target company (within the meaning of section 1504(a) but without the exceptions under section 1504(b) and substituting "50 percent" for "80 percent" where it appears therein) held a 5 percent or greater interest in the partnership's capital and profits at any time during the 36-month period prior to the transfer.

(C) A partnership is not a qualified partnership if the transferee foreign corporation's interest was acquired by that corporation at any time during the 36-month period prior to the transfer for the principal purpose of satisfying the active trade or business test, including the substantiality test.

(6) *Reporting requirements of U.S. target company.*—(i) In order for a U.S. person that transfers stock or securities of a domestic corporation to qualify for the exception provided by this paragraph (c) to the general rule under section 367(a)(1), in cases where 10 percent or more of the total voting power or the total value of the stock of the U.S. target company is transferred by U.S. persons in the transaction, the U.S. target company must comply with the reporting requirements contained in this paragraph (c)(6). The U.S. target company must attach to its timely filed U.S. income tax return for the taxable year in which the transfer occurs a statement titled "Section 367(a)—Reporting of Cross-Border Transfer Under Reg. § 1.367(a)-3(c)(6)," signed under penalties of perjury by an officer of the corporation to the best of the officer's knowledge and belief, disclosing the following information—

(A) A description of the transaction in which a U.S. person or persons transferred stock or securities in the U.S. target company to the transferee foreign corporation in a transfer otherwise subject to section 367(a)(1);

(B) The amount (specified as to the percentage of the total voting power and the total value) of stock of the transferee foreign corporation received in the transaction, in the aggregate, by persons who transferred stock or securities of the U.S. target company. For additional information that may be required to rebut the ownership presumption of paragraph (c)(2) of this section in cases where more than 50 percent of either the total voting power or the total value of the stock of the transferee foreign corporation is received in the transaction, in the aggregate, by persons who transferred stock or securities of the U.S. target company, see paragraph (c)(7) of this section;

(C) The amount (if any) of transferee foreign corporation stock owned directly or indirectly (applying the attribution rules of sections 267(c)(1) and (5)) immediately after the exchange by the U.S. target company;

(D) A statement that there is no control group within the meaning of paragraph (c)(1)(ii) of this section;

(E) A list of U.S. persons who are officers, directors or five-percent target shareholders and the percentage of the total voting power and the total value of the stock of the transferee foreign corporation owned by such persons both immediately before and immediately after the transaction; and

(F) A statement that includes the following—

(1) A statement that the active trade or business test described in paragraph (c)(3) of this section is satisfied by the transferee foreign corporation and a description of such business;

(2) A statement that on the day of the transaction, there was no intent on the part of the transferors or the transferee foreign corporation (or any qualified subsidiary or any qualified partnership, if relevant) to substantially dispose of or discontinue its active trade or business; and

(3) A statement that the substantiality test described in paragraph (c)(3)(iii) of this section is satisfied, and documentation that such test is satisfied, including the value of the transferee foreign corporation and the value of the U.S. target company on the day of the transfer, and either one of the following—

(i) A statement demonstrating that the value of the transferee foreign corporation 36 months prior to the acquisition, plus the value of any assets described in paragraph (c)(3)(iii)(B) of this section (including stock) acquired by the transferee foreign corporation within the 36-month period, less the amount of any liabilities acquired during that period, equals or exceeds the value of the U.S. target company on the acquisition date; or

(ii) A statement demonstrating that the value of the transferee foreign corporation on the date of the acquisition, reduced by the value of any assets not described in paragraph (c)(3)(iii)(B) of this section (including stock) acquired by the transferee foreign corporation within the 36-month period, equals or exceeds the value of the U.S. target company on the date of the acquisition.

(ii) Except as provided in paragraph (f) of this section, for purposes of this paragraph (c)(6), a U.S. income tax return will be considered timely filed if it is filed on or before the last date prescribed for filing (taking into account any extensions of time therefor) for the taxable year in which the transfer occurs.

(7) *Ownership statements.*—To rebut the ownership presumption of paragraph (c)(2) of this section, the U.S. target company must obtain ownership statements (described in paragraph (c)(5)(i) of this section) from a sufficient number of persons that transfer U.S. target company stock or securities in the transaction that are not U.S. persons to demonstrate that the 50-percent threshold of paragraph (c)(1)(i) of this section is not exceeded. In addition, the U.S. target company must attach to its timely filed U.S. income tax return (as described in paragraph (c)(6)(ii) of this section) for the taxable year in which the transfer occurs a statement, titled "Section 367(a) -Compilation of Ownership Statements under Reg. § 1.367(a)-3(c)," signed

under penalties of perjury by an officer of the corporation, disclosing the following information:

(i) The amount (specified as to the percentage of the total voting power and the total value) of stock of the transferee foreign corporation received, in the aggregate, by U.S. transferors;

(ii) The amount (specified as to the percentage of total voting power and total value) of stock of the transferee foreign corporation received, in the aggregate, by foreign persons that filed ownership statements;

(iii) A summary of the information tabulated from the ownership statements, including—

(A) The names of the persons that filed ownership statements stating that they are not U.S. persons;

(B) The countries of residence and citizenship of such persons; and

(C) Each of such person's ownership (by voting power and by value) in the U.S. target company prior to the exchange and the amount of stock of the transferee foreign corporation (by voting power and value) received by such persons in the exchange.

(8) *Certain transfers in connection with performance of services.*—Section 367(a)(1) shall not apply to a domestic corporation's transfer of its own stock or securities in connection with the performance of services, if the transfer is considered to be to a foreign corporation solely by reason of § 1.83-6(d)(1). The transfer may still, however, be reportable under section 6038B. See § 1.6038B-1(b)(2)(i)(A)(4) and (b)(2)(i)(B)(4).

(9) *Private letter ruling option.*—The Internal Revenue Service may, in limited circumstances, issue a private letter ruling to permit the taxpayer to qualify for an exception to the general rule under section 367(a)(1) if—

(i) A taxpayer is unable to satisfy all of the requirements of paragraph (c)(3) of this section relating to the active trade or business test of paragraph (c)(1)(iv) of this section, but such taxpayer meets all of the other requirements contained in paragraphs (c)(1)(i) through (c)(1)(iii) of this section, and such taxpayer is substantially in compliance with the rules set forth in paragraph (c)(3) of this section; or

(ii) A taxpayer is unable to satisfy any requirement of paragraph (c)(1) of this section due to the application of paragraph (c)(4)(iv) of this section. Notwithstanding the preceding sentence, in no event will the Internal Revenue Service rule on the issue of whether the principal purpose of an acquisition was to satisfy the active trade or business test, including the substantiality test.

(10) *Examples.*—This paragraph (c) may be illustrated by the following examples:

Example 1. Ownership presumption. (i) FC, a foreign corporation, issues 51 percent of its stock to the shareholders of S, a domestic corporation, in exchange for their S stock, in a transaction described in section 367(a)(1).

(ii) Under paragraph (c)(2) of this section, all shareholders of S who receive stock of FC in the exchange are presumed to be U.S. persons. Unless this ownership presumption is rebutted, the condition set forth in paragraph (c)(1)(i) of this section will not be satisfied, and the exception in paragraph (c)(1) of this section will not be available. As a result, all U.S. persons that transferred S stock will recognize gain on the exchange. To rebut the ownership presumption, S must comply with the reporting requirements contained in paragraph (c)(7) of this section, obtaining ownership statements (described in paragraph (c)(5)(i) of this section) from a sufficient number of non-U.S. persons who received FC stock in the exchange to demonstrate that the amount of FC stock received by U.S. persons in the exchange does not exceed 50 percent.

Example 2. Filing of gain recognition agreement. (i) The facts are the same as in *Example 1*, except that FC issues only 40 percent of its stock to the shareholders of S in the exchange. FC satisfies the active trade or business test of paragraph (c)(1)(iv) of this section. A, a U.S. person, owns 10 percent of S's stock immediately before the transfer. All other shareholders of S own less than five percent of its stock. None of S's officers or directors owns any stock in FC immediately after the transfer. A will own 15 percent of the stock of FC immediately after the transfer, 4 percent received in the exchange, and the balance being stock in FC that A owned prior to and independent of the transaction. No S shareholder besides A owns five percent or more of FC immediately after the transfer. The reporting requirements under paragraph (c)(6) of this section are satisfied.

(ii) The condition set forth in paragraph (c)(1)(i) of this section is satisfied because, even after application of the presumption in paragraph (c)(2) of this section, U.S. transferors could not receive more than 50 percent of FC's stock in the transaction. There is no control group because five-percent target shareholders and officers and directors of S do not, in the aggregate, own more than 50 percent of the stock of FC immediately after the transfer (A, the sole five-percent target shareholder, owns 15 percent of the stock of FC immediately after the transfer, and no officers or directors of S own any stock of FC immediately after the transfer). Therefore, the condition set forth in paragraph (c)(1)(ii) of this section is satisfied. The facts assume that the condition set forth in paragraph (c)(1)(iv) of this section is satisfied. Thus, U.S. persons that are not five-percent transferee shareholders will not recognize gain on the exchange of S shares for FC shares. A, a five-percent transferee shareholder, will not be required to include in income any gain realized on the exchange in the year of the transfer if he files a 5-year gain recognition agreement (GRA) and complies with section 6038B.

Example 3. Control group. (i) The facts are the same as in *Example 2*, except that B, another U.S. person, is a 5-percent target shareholder, owning 25 percent of S's stock immediately before the transfer. B owns 40 percent of the stock of FC immediately after the transfer, 10 percent received in the exchange, and the balance being stock in FC that B owned prior to and independent of the transaction.

(ii) A control group exists because A and B, each a five-percent target shareholder within the meaning of paragraph (c)(5)(iii) of this section, together own more than 50 percent of FC immediately after the transfer (counting both stock received in the exchange and stock owned prior to and independent of the exchange). As a result, the condition set forth in paragraph (c)(1)(ii) of this section is not satisfied, and all U.S. persons (not merely A and B) who transferred S stock will recognize gain on the exchange.

Example 4. Partnerships. (i) The facts are the same as in *Example 3*, except that B is a partnership (domestic or foreign) that has five equal partners, only two of whom, X and Y, are U.S. persons. Under paragraph (c)(4)(i) of this section, X and Y are treated as the owners and transferors of 5 percent each of the S stock owned and transferred by B and as owners of 8 percent each of the FC stock owned by B immediately after the transfer. U.S. persons that are five-percent target shareholders thus own a total of 31 percent of the stock of FC immediately after the transfer (A's 15 percent, plus X's 8 percent, plus Y's 8 percent).

(ii) Because no control group exists, the condition in paragraph (c)(1)(ii) of this section is satisfied. The conditions in paragraphs (c)(1)(i) and (iv) of this section also are satisfied. Thus, U.S. persons that are not five-percent transferee shareholders will not recognize gain on the exchange of S shares for FC shares. A, X, and Y, each a five-percent transferee shareholder, will not be required to include in income in the year of the transfer any gain realized on the exchange if they file 5-year GRAs and comply with section 6038B.

(11) *Applicability date of this paragraph (c).*—(i) *In general.*—Except as otherwise provided, this paragraph (c) applies to transfers occurring after January 29, 1997. A U.S. person exchanges stock or securities of a corporation (the acquired corporation) for stock or securities of a foreign corporation that controls the acquiring corporation in a reorganization described in either sections 368(a)(1)(A) and (a)(2)(D), or in sections 368(a)(1)(G) and (a)(2)(D). See paragraph (d)(3) *Example 1* of this section for an example of a reorganization described in sections 368(a)(1)(A) and (a)(2)(D) involving domestic acquired and acquiring corporations, and see paragraph (d)(3) *Example 10* of this section for an example involving a domestic acquired corporation and a foreign acquiring corporation.

(ii) *Applicability date of certain provisions of this paragraph (c).*—The first and second sentence of paragraph (c)(3)(iii)(C) of this section apply to transfers completed on or after September 22, 2014. The third sentence of paragraph (c)(3)(iii)(C) of this section applies to transfers completed on or after November 19, 2015. Taxpayers may, however, elect to apply the third sentence of paragraph (c)(3)(iii)(C) of this section to transfers completed on or after September 22, 2014, and before November 19, 2015.

(d) *Indirect stock transfers in certain nonrecognition transfers.*—(1) *In general.*—For purposes of this section, a U.S. person who exchanges, under section 354 (or section 356) stock or securities in a domestic or foreign corporation for stock or securities in a foreign corporation (or in a domestic corporation in control of a foreign acquiring corporation in a triangular section 368(a)(1)(B) reorganization) in connection with a transaction described in paragraphs (d)(1)(i) through (v) of this section (or who is deemed to make such an exchange under paragraph (d)(1)(vi) of this section) shall, except as provided in paragraph (d)(2)(vii) of this section, be treated as having made an indirect transfer of such stock or securities to a foreign corporation that is subject to the rules of this section, including, for example, the requirement, where applicable, that the U.S. transferor enter into a gain recognition agreement to preserve nonrecognition treatment under section 367(a). If the U.S. person exchanges stock or securities of a foreign corporation, see also section 367(b) and the regulations thereunder. For examples of the concurrent application of the indirect stock transfer rules under section 367(a) and the rules of section 367(b), see paragraph (d)(3) *Examples 14* and *15* of this section. For purposes of this paragraph (d), if a corporation acquiring assets in an asset reorganization transfers all or a portion of such assets to a

corporation controlled (within the meaning of section 368(c)) by the acquiring corporation as part of the same transaction, the subsequent transfer of assets to the controlled corporation will be referred to as a controlled asset transfer. See section 368(a)(2)(C).

(i) *Mergers described in sections 368(a)(1)(A) and (a)(2)(D) and reorganizations described in sections 368(a)(1)(G) and (a)(2)(D).*—A U.S. person exchanges stock or securities of a corporation (the acquired corporation) for stock or securities of a foreign corporation that controls the acquiring corporation in a reorganization described in either sections 368(a)(1)(A) and (a)(2)(D), or in sections 368(a)(1)(G) and (a)(2)(D). See paragraph (d)(3) *Example 1* of this section for an example of a reorganization described in sections 368(a)(1)(A) and (a)(2)(D) involving domestic acquired and acquiring corporations, and see paragraph (d)(3) *Example 10* of this section for an example involving a domestic acquired corporation and a foreign acquiring corporation.

(ii) *Mergers described in sections 368(a)(1)(A) and (a)(2)(E).*—A U.S. person exchanges stock or securities of a corporation (the acquiring corporation) for stock or securities in a foreign corporation that controls the acquired corporation in a reorganization described in sections 368(a)(1)(A) and (a)(2)(E). See paragraph (d)(3) *Example 2* of this section for an example of a reorganization described in sections 368(a)(1)(A) and (a)(2)(E) involving domestic acquired and acquiring corporations, and see paragraph (d)(3) *Example 11* of this section for an example involving a domestic acquired corporation and a foreign acquiring corporation.

(iii) *Triangular reorganizations described in section 368(a)(1)(B).*—(A) A U.S. person exchanges stock or securities of the acquired corporation for voting stock or securities of a foreign corporation that is in control (as defined in section 368(c)) of the acquiring corporation in a reorganization described in section 368(a)(1)(B). See paragraph (d)(3) *Example 5* of this section.

(B) A U.S. person exchanges stock or securities of the acquired corporation for voting stock or securities of a domestic corporation that is in control (as defined in section 368(c)) of a foreign acquiring corporation in a reorganization described in section 368(a)(1)(B). See paragraph (d)(3) *Example 5A* of this section.

(iv) *Triangular reorganizations described in section 368(a)(1)(C).*—A U.S. person exchanges stock or securities of a corporation (the acquired corporation) for voting stock or securities of a foreign corporation that controls the acquiring corporation in a reorganization described in section 368(a)(1)(C). See, e.g., paragraph (d)(3) *Example 6* of this section (for an example of a triangular section 368(a)(1)(C) reorganization involving domestic acquired and acquiring corporations), and paragraph (d)(3) *Example 8* of this section (for an example involving a domestic acquired corporation and a foreign acquiring corporation). If the acquired corporation is a foreign corporation, see paragraph (d)(3) *Example 14* of this section, and section 367(b) and the regulations thereunder.

(v) *Transfers of assets to subsidiaries in certain section 368(a)(1) reorganizations.*—A U.S. person exchanges stock or securities of a corporation (the acquired corporation) for stock or securities of a foreign acquiring corporation in an asset reorganization (other than a triangular section 368(a)(1)(C) reorganization described in paragraph (d)(1)(iv) of this section, a reorganization described in sections 368(a)(1)(A) and (a)(2)(D) or sections 368(a)(1)(G) and (a)(2)(D) described in paragraph (d)(1)(i) of this section, a reorganization described in sections 368(a)(1)(A) and (a)(2)(E) described in paragraph (d)(1)(ii) of this section, or a same-country section 368(a)(1)(F) reorganization) that is followed by a controlled asset transfer. For purposes of this section, a same-country section 368(a)(1)(F) reorganization is a reorganization described in section 368(a)(1)(F) in which both the acquired corporation and the acquiring corporation are foreign corporations and are created or organized under the laws of the same foreign country. In the case of a transaction described in this paragraph (d)(1)(v) in which some but not all of the assets of the acquired corporation are transferred in a controlled asset transfer, the transaction shall be considered to be an indirect transfer of stock or securities subject to this paragraph (d) only to the extent of the assets so transferred. The remaining assets shall be treated as having been transferred by the acquired corporation in an asset transfer rather than an indirect stock transfer, and, if the acquired corporation is a domestic corporation, such asset transfer shall be subject to the other provisions of section 367, including sections 367(a)(1), (3), and (5), and (d). See paragraph (d)(3) *Examples 6A* and *6B* of this section.

(vi) *Successive transfers of property to which section 351 applies.*—A U.S. person transfers property (other than stock or securities) to a foreign corporation in an exchange described in section 351, and all or a portion of such assets transferred to the foreign corporation by such person are, in connection with the same transaction, transferred to a second corporation that is controlled by the foreign corporation in one or more exchanges described in section 351. For purposes of this paragraph (d)(1) and §1.367(a)-8, the initial transfer by the U.S. person shall be deemed to be a transfer of stock described in section 354. (Any assets transferred to the foreign corporation that are not transferred by the foreign corporation to a second corporation shall be treated as a transfer of assets subject to the general rules of section 367, including sections 367(a)(1), (3), (5) and (d), and not as an indirect stock transfer under the rules of this paragraph (d).) See, e.g., paragraph (d)(3) *Example 13* and *Example 13A* of this section.

(2) *Special rules for indirect transfers.*—If a U.S. person is considered to make an indirect transfer of stock or securities described in paragraph (d)(1) of this section, the rules of this section and §1.367(a)-8 shall apply to the transfer. For purposes of applying the rules of this section and §1.367(a)-8:

(i) *Transferee foreign corporation.*—(A) *General rule.*—Except as provided in paragraph (d)(2)(i)(B) of this section, the transferee foreign corporation shall be the foreign corporation that issues stock or securities to the U.S. person in the exchange.

(B) *Special rule for triangular reorganizations described in paragraph (d)(1)(iii)(B) of this section.*—In the case of a triangular reorganization described in paragraph (d)(1)(iii)(B) of this section, the transferee foreign corporation shall be the foreign acquiring corporation. See paragraph (d)(3) *Example 5A* of this section.

(ii) *Transferred corporation.*—The transferred corporation shall be the acquiring corporation, except as provided in this paragraph (d)(2)(ii). In the case of a triangular section 368(a)(1)(B) reorganization described in paragraph (d)(1)(iii) of this section, the transferred corporation shall be the acquired corporation. In the case of an indirect stock transfer described in paragraph (d)(1)(i), (ii), or (iv) of this section followed by a controlled asset transfer, or an indirect stock transfer described in paragraph (d)(1)(v) of this section, the transferred corporation shall be the controlled corporation to which the assets are transferred. In the case of successive section 351 transfers described in paragraph (d)(1)(vi) of this section, the transferred corporation shall be the corporation to which the assets are transferred in the final section 351 transfer. The transferred property shall be the stock or securities of the transferred corporation, as appropriate under the circumstances.

(iii) *Amount of gain.*—For purposes of determining the amount of gain that a U.S. person is required to include in income as a result of a triggering event, see §1.367(a)-8(c)(1)(i).

(iv) *Gain recognition agreements involving multiple parties.*—The U.S. person's agreement to recognize gain, as provided in §1.367(a)-8, shall include appropriate provisions consistent with the principles of §1.367(a)-8. See *Examples 5* and *5A* of this section and §1.367(a)-8(j)(9).

(v) *Determination of whether substantially all of the transferred corporation's assets are disposed of.*—For purposes of applying §1.367(a)-8(j)(2)(i) to determine whether substantially all of the assets of the transferred corporation have been disposed of, the following assets shall be taken into account (but only if such assets are not fully taxable under section 367 in the taxable year that includes the indirect transfer)—

(A) In the case of a reorganization described in paragraph (d)(1)(i) of this section (a reorganization described in sections 368(a)(1)(A) and (a)(2)(D) or sections 368(a)(1)(G) and (a)(2)(D)) or a reorganization described in paragraph (d)(1)(iv) of this section (a triangular section 368(a)(1)(C) reorganization), the assets of the acquired corporation;

(B) In the case of a sections 368(a)(1)(A) and (a)(2)(E) reorganization described in paragraph (d)(1)(ii) of this section, the assets of the acquiring corporation immediately prior to the transaction;

(C) In the case of an asset reorganization followed by a controlled asset transfer, as described in paragraph (d)(1)(v) of this section, the assets of the acquired corporation that are transferred to the corporation controlled by the acquiring corporation;

(D) In the case of a triangular reorganization described in section 368(a)(1)(C) followed by a controlled asset transfer, a reorganization described in sections 368(a)(1)(A) and (a)(2)(D) followed by a controlled asset transfer, or a reorganization described in sections 368(a)(1)(G) and (a)(2)(D) followed by a controlled asset transfer, the assets of the acquired corporation including those transferred to the corporation controlled by the acquiring corporation;

(E) In the case of a reorganization described in sections 368(a)(1)(A) and (a)(2)(E) followed by a controlled asset transfer, the assets of the acquiring corporation including those transferred to the corporation controlled by the acquiring corporation; and

(F) In the case of successive section 351 exchanges described in paragraph (d)(1)(vi) of this section, the assets that are both

transferred initially to the foreign corporation, and transferred by the foreign corporation to a second corporation.

(vi) *Coordination between asset transfer rules and indirect stock transfer rules.*—(A) *General rule.*—Except as otherwise provided in this paragraph (d)(2)(vi), if, pursuant to any of the transactions described in paragraph (d)(1) of this section, a U.S. person transfers (or is deemed to transfer) assets to a foreign corporation in an exchange described in section 351 or section 361, the rules of section 367, including sections 367(a)(1), (a)(3), and (a)(5), as well as section 367(d), and the regulations thereunder shall apply prior to the application of the rules of this section.

(B) *Exceptions.*—(1) If a transaction is described in paragraph (d)(2)(vi)(A) of this section, section 367(a) and (d) will not apply to the extent a domestic corporation (domestic acquired corporation) transfers assets to a foreign corporation (foreign acquiring corporation) in an asset reorganization, and those assets (re-transferred assets) are transferred to a domestic corporation (domestic controlled corporation) in a controlled asset transfer, provided that each of the following conditions is satisfied:

(i) The domestic controlled corporation's adjusted basis in the re-transferred assets is not greater than the domestic acquired corporation's adjusted basis in those assets. For this purpose, any increase in basis in the re-transferred assets that results because the domestic acquired corporation recognized gain or income with respect to the re-transferred assets in the transaction is not taken into account.

(ii) The domestic acquired corporation includes a statement described in paragraph (d)(2)(vi)(C) of this section with its timely filed U.S. income tax return for the taxable year of the transfer; and

(iii) The requirements of paragraphs (c)(1)(i), (ii), and (iv) and (c)(6) of this section are satisfied with respect to the indirect transfer of stock in the domestic acquired corporation.

(2) Sections 367(a) and (d) shall not apply to transfers described in paragraph (d)(1)(vi) of this section if a U.S. person transfers assets to a foreign corporation in a section 351 exchange, to the extent that such assets are transferred by such foreign corporation to a domestic corporation in another section 351 exchange, but only if the domestic transferee's adjusted basis in the assets is not greater than the adjusted basis that the U.S. person had in such assets. Any increase in adjusted basis in the assets that results because the U.S. person recognized gain or income with respect to such assets in the initial section 351 exchange is not taken into account for purposes of determining whether the domestic transferee's adjusted basis in the assets is not greater than the U.S. person's adjusted basis in such assets. This paragraph (d)(2)(vi)(B)(2) will not, however, apply to an exchange described in section 351 that is also an exchange described in section 361(a) or (b). An exchange described in section 351 that is also an exchange described in section 361(a) or (b) is only eligible for the exception in paragraph (d)(2)(vi)(B)(1) of this section.

(C) *Required statement.*—The statement required by paragraph (d)(2)(vi)(B)(1)(ii) of this section shall be entitled "Required Statement under §1.367(a)-3(d) for Assets Transferred to a Domestic Corporation" and shall be signed under penalties of perjury by an authorized officer of the domestic acquired corporation and by an authorized officer of the foreign acquiring corporation. The required statement shall contain a certification that, if the foreign acquiring corporation disposes of any stock of the domestic controlled corporation in a transaction described in paragraph (d)(2)(vi)(D) of this section, the domestic acquired corporation shall recognize gain as described in paragraph (d)(2)(vi)(E) of this section. The domestic acquired corporation (or the foreign acquiring corporation on behalf of the domestic acquired corporation) shall file a U.S. income tax return (or an amended U.S. tax return, as the case may be) for the year of the transfer reporting such gain.

(D) *Gain recognition transaction.*—(1) A transaction described in this paragraph (d)(2)(vi)(D) is one where a principal purpose of the transfer by the domestic acquired corporation is the avoidance of U.S. tax that would have been imposed on the domestic acquired corporation on the disposition of the re-transferred assets. A transfer may have a principal purpose of tax avoidance even though the tax avoidance purpose is outweighed by other purposes when taken together.

(2) For purposes of paragraph (d)(2)(vi)(D)(1) of this section, a transaction is deemed to have a principal purpose of tax avoidance if the foreign acquiring corporation disposes of any stock of the domestic controlled corporation (whether in a recognition or non-recognition transaction) within 2 years of the transfer described in paragraph (d)(2)(vi)(A) of this section. The rule in this paragraph (d)(2)(vi)(D)(2) shall not apply if the domestic acquired corporation (or the foreign acquiring corporation on behalf of the domestic acquired corporation) demonstrates to the satisfaction of the Com-

missioner that the avoidance of U.S. tax was not a principal purpose of the transaction. For this purpose, a disposition by the foreign acquiring corporation of stock of the domestic controlled corporation more than 5 years after completion of the transfer described in paragraph (d)(2)(vi)(A) of this section is deemed to not have a principal purpose of tax avoidance.

(E) *Amount of gain recognized and other matters.*—(1) In the case of a transaction described in paragraph (d)(2)(vi)(D) of this section, solely for purposes of this paragraph (d)(2)(vi)(E), the domestic acquired corporation shall be treated as if, immediately prior to the transfer described in paragraph (d)(2)(vi)(A) of this section, it transferred the re-transferred assets, including any intangible assets, directly to a domestic corporation in exchange for stock of such domestic corporation in a transaction that is treated as a section 351 exchange, and immediately sold such stock to an unrelated party for its fair market value in a sale in which it shall recognize gain, if any (but not loss). Any gain recognized by the domestic acquired corporation pursuant to this paragraph (d)(2)(vi)(E) will increase the basis that the foreign acquiring corporation has in the stock of the domestic controlled corporation immediately before the transaction described in paragraph (d)(2)(vi)(D) of this section, but will not increase the basis of the re-transferred assets held by the domestic controlled corporation. Section 1.367(d)-1T(g)(6) shall not apply with respect to any intangible property included in the re-transferred assets described in this paragraph.

(2) If additional tax is required to be paid as a result of a transaction described in paragraph (d)(2)(vi)(D) of this section, then interest must be paid on that amount at rates determined under section 6621 with respect to the period between the date prescribed for filing the domestic acquired corporation's income tax return for the year of the transfer and the date on which the additional tax for that year is paid.

(F) *Examples.*—For illustrations of the rules in paragraph (d)(2)(vi) of this section, see paragraph (d)(3) *Examples 6B, 6C, 9,* and *13A* of this section.

(vii) *Change in status of a domestic acquired corporation to a foreign corporation.*—(A) A U.S. person that exchanges stock or securities of a domestic corporation for stock or securities of a foreign corporation under section 354 (or section 356) will be treated for purposes of this section as having made an indirect stock transfer of the stock or securities of a foreign corporation (and not of a domestic corporation) to a foreign corporation under paragraph (b) of this section (but not paragraph (c) of this section), if the acquired domestic corporation is a subsidiary member (within the meaning of §1.1502-1(c)) of a consolidated group (within the meaning of §1.1502-1(h)) immediately before the transaction, and if the transaction is either of the following:

(1) Described in paragraph (d)(1)(i) or (iv) of this section, but only if the acquiring corporation is foreign. See paragraph (d)(3) *Examples 8, 9, 10* and *12* of this section.

(2) Described in paragraph (d)(1)(v) of this section, but only to the extent the controlled asset transfer is to a foreign corporation. See paragraph (d)(3) *Example 6A* of this section.

(B) The rules of paragraph (d)(2)(vii)(A) of this section will not apply to the extent assets transferred to the foreign acquiring corporation in a transaction described in paragraph (d)(2)(vii)(A)(1) of this section, or assets transferred to a foreign corporation in a controlled asset transfer in a transaction described in paragraph (d)(2)(vii)(A)(2) of this section, are retransferred to a domestic controlled corporation in one or more successive transfers as part of the same transaction. See paragraph (d)(3) *Example 9* of this section.

(3) *Examples.*—The rules of this paragraph (d) and §1.367(a)-8 are illustrated by the following examples. For purposes of these examples, assume section 7874 does not apply.

Example 1. Section 368(a)(1)(A)/(a)(2)(D) reorganization—(i) *Facts.* F, a foreign corporation, owns all the stock of Newco, a domestic corporation. A, a domestic corporation, owns all of the stock of W, also a domestic corporation. A and W file a consolidated Federal income tax return. A does not own any stock in F (applying the attribution rules of section 318, as modified by section 958(b)). In a reorganization described in sections 368(a)(1)(A) and (a)(2)(D), *Newco acquires all of the assets of W, and A receives 40% of the stock of F in an exchange described in section 354.*

(ii) *Result.* Pursuant to paragraph (d)(1)(i) of this section, the reorganization is subject to the indirect stock transfer rules. F is treated as the transferee foreign corporation, and Newco is treated as the transferred corporation. Provided that the requirements of paragraph (c)(1) of this section are satisfied, including the requirement that A enter into a five-year gain recognition agreement as described in §1.367(a)-8, A's exchange of W stock for F stock under section 354 will not be subject to section 367(a)(1). If F disposes (within the meaning of §1.367(a)-8(j)(1)) of all (or a portion) of Newco's stock

within the five-year term of the agreement (and A has not made a valid election under §1.367(a)-8(c)(2)(vi)), A is required to file an amended return for the year of the transfer and include in income, with interest, the gain realized but not recognized on the initial section 354 exchange. If A has made a valid election under §1.367(a)-8(c)(2)(vi) to include the amount subject to the gain recognition agreement in the year of the triggering event, A would instead include the gain on its tax return for the taxable year that includes the triggering event, together with interest.

Example 1A. Transferor is a subsidiary in consolidated group—(i) *Facts.* The facts are the same as in *Example 1,* except that A is owned by P, a domestic corporation, and for the taxable year in which the transaction occurred, P, A and W filed a consolidated Federal income tax return.

(ii) *Result.* Even though A is the U.S. transferor, P is required under §1.367(a)-8(d)(3) and (e)(1)(i) to enter into the gain recognition agreement and comply with the requirements under §1.367(a)-8. If A leaves the P group, the gain recognition agreement would be triggered pursuant to §1.367(a)-8(j)(5), unless the exception provided under §1.367(a)-8(k)(10) applies.

Example 2. Section 368(a)(1)(A)/(a)(2)(E) reorganization—(i) *Facts.* The facts are the same as in *Example 1,* except that Newco merges into W and Newco receives stock of W which it distributes to F in a reorganization described in sections 368(a)(1)(A) and (a)(2)(E). Pursuant to the reorganization, A receives 40 percent of the stock of F in an exchange described in section 354.

(ii) *Result.* The consequences of the transfer are similar to those described in *Example 1.* Pursuant to paragraph (d)(1)(ii) of this section, A is considered to have transferred its W stock to F pursuant to the indirect stock transfer rules. F is treated as the transferee foreign corporation, and W is treated as the transferred corporation. Provided that the requirements of paragraph (c)(1) of this section are satisfied, including the requirement that A enter into a five-year gain recognition agreement as described in §1.367(a)-8, A's exchange of W stock for F stock under section 354 will not be subject to section 367(a)(1).

Example 3. Taxable transaction pursuant to indirect stock transfer rules—(i) *Facts.* The facts are the same as in *Example 1,* except that A receives 55 percent of either the total voting power or the total value of the stock of F in the transaction.

(ii) *Result.* A is required to include in income in the year of the exchange the amount of gain realized on such exchange. See paragraph (c)(1)(i) of this section. If A fails to include the income on its timely-filed return, A will also be liable for the penalty under section 6038B (together with interest and other applicable penalties) unless A's failure to include the income is due to reasonable cause and not willful neglect. See §1.6038B-1(f).

Example 4. Disposition by U.S. transferred corporation of substantially all of its assets—(i) *Facts.* The facts are the same as in *Example 1,* except that, during the third year of the gain recognition agreement, Newco disposes of substantially all (as described in §1.367(a)-8(j)(2)(i)) of the assets described in paragraph (d)(2)(v)(A) of this section for cash and recognizes currently all of the gain realized on the disposition.

(ii) *Result.* Under §1.367(a)-8(j)(2), the gain recognition agreement is generally triggered when the transferred corporation disposes of substantially all of its assets. However, under the special rule contained in §1.367(a)-8(o)(4), because A owned an amount of stock in W described in section 1504(a)(2) immediately before the transaction, and Newco, the transferred corporation, is a domestic corporation, the gain recognition agreement is terminated and has no further effect.

Example 5. Triangular section 368(a)(1)(B) reorganization—(i) *Facts.* F, a foreign corporation, owns all the stock of S, a domestic corporation. U, a domestic corporation, owns all of the stock of Y, also a domestic corporation. U does not own any of the stock of F (applying the attribution rules of section 318, as modified by section 958(b)). In a triangular reorganization described in section 368(a)(1)(B) and paragraph (d)(1)(iii)(A) of this section, S acquires all the stock of Y, and U receives 10% of the voting stock of F.

(ii) *Result.* U's exchange of Y stock for F stock will not be subject to section 367(a)(1), provided that all of the requirements of paragraph (c)(1) are satisfied, including the requirement that U enter into a five-year gain recognition agreement. For purposes of this section, F is treated as the transferee foreign corporation and Y is treated as the transferred corporation. See paragraphs (d)(2)(i) and (ii) of this section. Under §1.367(a)-8(j)(9), the gain recognition agreement would be triggered if F sold all or a portion of the stock of S.

Example 5A. Triangular section 368(a)(1)(B) reorganization—(i) *Facts.* The facts are the same as in *Example 5,* except that F is a domestic corporation and S is a foreign corporation.

(ii) *Result.* U's exchange of Y stock for stock of F, a domestic corporation in control of S, the foreign acquiring corporation, is treated as an indirect transfer of Y stock to a foreign corporation under paragraph (d)(1)(iii)(B) of this section. U's exchange of Y stock for F stock will not be subject to section 367(a)(1) provided that all of the requirements of paragraph (c)(1) of this section are satisfied, including the requirement that U enter into a five-year gain recognition agreement. In satisfying the 50 percent or less ownership requirements of paragraphs (c)(1)(i) and (ii) of this section, U's indirect ownership of S stock (through its direct ownership of F) will determine whether the requirement of paragraph (c)(1)(i) of this section is satisfied and will be taken into account in determining whether the requirement of paragraph (c)(1)(ii) of this section is satisfied. See paragraph (c)(4)(iv) of this section. For purposes of this section, S is treated as the transferee foreign corporation (see paragraph (d)(2)(i)(B) of this section). If Y sold substantially all of its assets (within the meaning of section 368(a)(1)(C)), the gain recognition agreement would be terminated because U owned an amount of stock in Y described in section 1504(a)(2) immediately before the transaction and Y is a domestic corporation. See § 1.367(a)-8(o)(4).

Example 6. Triangular section 368(a)(1)(C) reorganization—(i) *Facts.* F, a foreign corporation, owns all of the stock of R, a domestic corporation that operates an historical business. V, a domestic corporation, owns all of the stock of Z, also a domestic corporation. V does not own any of the stock of F (applying the attribution rules of section 318 as modified by section 958(b)). In a triangular reorganization described in section 368(a)(1)(C) (and paragraph (d)(1)(iv) of this section), R acquires all of the assets of Z, and V receives 30% of the voting stock of F.

(ii) *Result.* The consequences of the transfer are similar to those described in *Example 1*; V is required to enter into a 5-year gain recognition agreement under § 1.367(a)-8 to secure nonrecognition treatment under section 367(a). Under paragraphs (d)(2)(i) and (ii) of this section, F is treated as the transferee foreign corporation and R is treated as the transferred corporation. In determining whether, in a later transaction, R has disposed of substantially all of its assets under § 1.367(a)-8(j)(2)(i), see paragraph (d)(2)(v)(A) of this section.

Example 6A. Section 368(a)(1)(C) reorganization followed by a controlled asset transfer—(i) *Facts.* The facts are the same as in *Example 6*, except that the transaction is structured as a section 368(a)(1)(C) reorganization with Z transferring its assets to F, followed by a controlled asset transfer, and R is a foreign corporation. The following additional facts are present. Z has 3 businesses: Business A with a basis of $10 and a value of $50, Business B with a basis of $10 and a value of $40, and Business C with a basis of $10 and a value of $30. V and Z file a consolidated Federal income tax return and V has a basis of $30 in the Z stock, which has a value of $120. Assume that Businesses A and B consist solely of assets that will satisfy the section 367(a)(3) active trade or business exception; none of Business C's assets will satisfy the exception. Z transfers all 3 businesses to F in exchange for 30 percent of the F stock, which Z distributes to V pursuant to a section 368(a)(1)(C) reorganization. F then contributes Businesses B and C to R in a controlled asset transfer.

(ii) *Result.* The transfer of the Business A assets by Z to F does not constitute an indirect stock transfer under paragraph (d) of this section, and, subject to the conditions and requirements of section 367(a)(5) and § 1.367(a)-7(c), the Business A assets qualify for the section 367(a)(3) active trade or business exception and are not subject to section 367(a)(1). The transfer of the Business B and C assets by Z to F must first be tested under sections 367(a)(1), (a)(3), and (a)(5). Z recognizes $20 of gain on the outbound transfer of the Business C assets, as those assets do not qualify for an exception to section 367(a)(1). Subject to the conditions and requirements of section 367(a)(5) and § 1.367(a)-7(c), the Business B assets qualify for the active trade or business exception under section 367(a)(3). Pursuant to paragraphs (d)(1) and (d)(2)(vii)(A)(2) of this section, V is deemed to transfer the stock of a foreign corporation in a section 354 exchange subject to the rules of paragraphs (b) and (d) of this section. V must enter into the gain recognition agreement in the amount of $30 to preserve Z's nonrecognition treatment with respect to its transfer of Business B assets. Under paragraphs (d)(2)(i) and (d)(2)(ii) of this section, F is the transferee foreign corporation and R is the transferred corporation.

Example 6B. Section 368(a)(1)(C) reorganization followed by a controlled asset transfer to a domestic controlled corporation—(i) *Facts.* The facts are the same as in paragraph (d)(3), *Example 6A*, of this section, except that R is a domestic corporation.

(ii) *Result.* As in paragraph (d)(3), *Example 6A*, of this section, the outbound transfer of the Business A assets to F is not affected by the rules of § 1.367-3(d) and is subject to the general rules under section 367. Subject to the conditions and requirements of section 367(a)(5) and § 1.367(a)-7(c), the Business A assets qualify for the section 367(a)(3) active trade or business exception and are not subject to section 367(a)(1). The Business B and C assets are part of an indirect stock transfer under § 1.367-3(d), but must first be tested under section 367(a) and (d). The Business B assets qualify for the active trade or business exception under section 367(a)(3); the Business C assets do not. However, pursuant to paragraph (d)(2)(vi)(B)(1) of this section, the Business B and C assets are not subject to section 367(a)

or (d), provided that the basis of the Business B and C assets in the hands of R is not greater than the basis of the assets in the hands of Z, the requirements of paragraphs (c)(1)(i), (ii), and (iv) and (c)(6) of this section are satisfied, and Z attaches a statement described in paragraphs (d)(2)(vi)(C) of this section to its U.S. income tax return for the taxable year of the transfer. V also is deemed to make an indirect transfer of Z stock under the rules of paragraph (d) of this section to the extent the assets are transferred to R. To preserve nonrecognition treatment, and assuming the other requirements of paragraph (c) of this section are satisfied, V must enter into a gain recognition agreement in the amount of $50, which equals the aggregate gain in the Business B and C assets, because the transfer of those assets by Z was not taxable under section 367(a)(1) and constitute an indirect stock transfer.

Example 6C. Section 368(a)(1)(C) reorganization followed by a controlled asset transfer to a domestic controlled corporation—(i) *Facts.* The facts are the same as in paragraph (d)(3), *Example 6B*, of this section, except that Z is owned by U.S. individuals, none of whom qualify as five-percent target shareholders with respect to Z within the meaning of paragraph (c)(5)(iii) of this section. The following additional facts are present. No U.S. persons that are either officers or directors of Z own any stock of F immediately after the transfer. F is engaged in an active trade or business outside the United States that satisfies the test set forth in paragraph (c)(3) of this section.

(ii) *Result.* The Business A assets transferred to F are not retransferred to R and therefore Z's transfer of these assets is not subject to the rules of paragraph (d) of this section. However, gain must be recognized on the transfer of those assets under section 367(a)(1) because the section 367(a)(3) active trade or business exception is inapplicable pursuant to section 367(a)(5) and § 1.367(a)-7(b). The Business B and C assets are part of an indirect stock transfer under paragraph (d) of this section, but must first be tested with respect to Z under section 367(a) and (d), as provided in paragraph (d)(2)(vi) of this section. The transfer of the Business B assets (which otherwise would satisfy the section 367(a)(3) active trade or business exception) generally is subject to section 367(a)(1) pursuant to section 367(a)(5) and § 1.367(a)-7(b). The transfer of the Business C assets generally is subject to section 367(a)(1) because these assets do not qualify for the active trade or business exception under section 367(a)(3). However, pursuant to paragraph (d)(2)(vi)(B) of this section, the transfer of the Business B and C assets is not subject to sections 367(a)(1) and (d), provided the basis of the Business B and C assets in the hands of R is no greater than the basis in the hands of Z and certain other requirements are satisfied. Z may avoid immediate gain recognition under section 367(a) and (d) on the transfers of the Business B and Business C assets to F if, pursuant to paragraph (d)(2)(vi)(B) of this section, the indirect transfer of Z stock satisfies the requirements of paragraphs (c)(1)(i), (ii), and (iv) and (c)(6) of this section, and Z attaches a statement described in paragraph (d)(2)(vi)(C) of this section to its U.S. income tax return for the taxable year of the transfer. In general, the statement must contain a certification that, if F disposes of the stock of R (in a recognition or nonrecognition transaction) and a principal purpose of the transfer is the avoidance of U.S. tax that would have been imposed on Z on the disposition of the Business B and C assets transferred to R, then Z (or F on behalf of Z) will file a return (or amended return as the case may be) recognizing gain ($50), as if, immediately prior to the reorganization, Z transferred the Business B and C assets to a domestic corporation in exchange for stock in a transaction treated as a section 351 exchange and immediately sold such stock to an unrelated party for its fair market value. A transaction is deemed to have a principal purpose of U.S. tax avoidance if F disposes of R stock within two years of the transfer, unless Z (or F on behalf of Z) can rebut the presumption to the satisfaction of the Commissioner. See paragraph (d)(2)(vi)(D)(2) of this section. With respect to the indirect transfer of Z stock, assume the requirements of paragraphs (c)(1)(i), (ii), and (iv) of this section are satisfied. Thus, assuming Z attaches the statement described in paragraph (d)(2)(vi)(C) of this section to its U.S. income tax return and satisfies the reporting requirements of paragraph (c)(6) of this section, the transfer of Business B and C assets is not subject to immediate gain recognition under section 367(a) or (d).

Example 7. Triangular section 368(a)(1)(C) reorganization followed by 351 exchange—(i) *Facts.* The facts are the same as in *Example 6*, except that, during the fourth year of the gain recognition agreement, R transfers substantially all of the assets received from Z to K, a wholly-owned domestic subsidiary of R, in an exchange described in section 351.

(ii) *Result.* The disposition by R, the transferred corporation, of substantially all of its assets would terminate the gain recognition agreement if the assets were disposed of in a taxable transaction because V owned an amount of stock in Z described in section 1504(a)(2) immediately before the transaction, and R is a domestic corporation. See § 1.367(a)-8(o)(4). Because the assets were transferred in an exchange to which section 351 applies, such transfer does not trigger the gain recognition agreement if V complies with the requirements contained in §1.367(a)-8(k)(4). See also paragraph (d)(2)(iv) of this section. To determine whether substantially all of the assets are disposed of, any assets of Z that were transferred by Z to R and then contributed by R to K are taken into account.

Example 7A. Triangular section 368(a)(1)(C) reorganization followed by section 351 exchange with foreign transferee—(i) *Facts.* The facts are the same as in *Example 7* except that K is a foreign corporation.

(ii) *Result.* This transfer of assets by R to K must be analyzed to determine its effect upon the gain recognition agreement, and such transfer is also an outbound transfer of assets that is taxable under section 367(a)(1) unless the active trade or business exception under section 367(a)(3) applies. If the transfer is fully taxable under section 367(a)(1), the transfer is treated as if the transferred company, R, sold substantially all of its assets. Thus, the gain recognition agreement would terminate because V owned an amount of stock in Z described in section 1504(a)(2) immediately before the transaction, and R is a domestic corporation. See §1.367(a)-8(o)(4). If each asset transferred qualifies for nonrecognition treatment under section 367(a)(3) and the regulations thereunder (which require, under §1.367(a)-2(a)(2)(iii), the transferor to comply with the reporting requirements under section 6038B), the result is the same as in *Example 7*. If a portion of the assets transferred qualify for nonrecognition treatment under section 367(a)(3) and a portion are taxable under section 367(a)(1) (but such portion does not result in the disposition of substantially all of the assets), the gain recognition agreement will not be triggered if such information is reported as required under §1.367(a)-8(g) and V satisfies the requirements contained in §1.367(a)-8(k)(4).

Example 8. Concurrent application of asset transfer and indirect stock transfer rules in consolidated return setting—(i) *Facts.* Assume the same facts as in *Example 6*, except that R is a foreign corporation and V and Z file a consolidated return for Federal income tax purposes. The properties of Z consist of Business A assets, with an adjusted basis of $50 and fair market value of $90, and Business B assets, with an adjusted basis of $50 and a fair market value of $110. Assume that the Business A assets do not qualify for the active trade or business exception under section 367(a)(3), but that the Business B assets do qualify for the exception. V's basis in the Z stock is $100, and the value of such stock is $200.

(ii) *Result.* Under paragraph (d)(2)(vi), the assets of Businesses A and B that are transferred to R must be tested under sections 367(a)(3) and (a)(5) prior to consideration of the indirect stock transfer rules of this paragraph (d). Thus, Z must recognize $40 of income under section 367(a)(1) on the outbound transfer of Business A assets. Subject to the conditions and requirements of section 367(a)(5) and §1.367(a)-7(c), the Business B assets qualify for the active trade or business exception under section 367(a)(3). Under §1.1502-32, because V and Z file a consolidated return, V's basis in its Z stock increases from $100 to $140 as a result of Z's $40 gain. Pursuant to paragraphs (d)(1) and (d)(2)(vii)(A)(1) of this section, V is deemed to transfer the stock of a foreign corporation to F in a section 354 exchange subject to the rules of paragraphs (b) and (d) of this section, and therefore must enter into a gain recognition agreement in the amount of $60 (the gain realized but not recognized by V in the stock of Z after the $40 basis adjustment). If F sells a portion of its stock in R during the term of the agreement, V will be required to recognize a portion of the $60 gain subject to the agreement. To determine whether R disposes of substantially all of its assets (under §1.367(a)-8(j)(2)(i)), only the Business B assets will be considered (because the transfer of the Business A assets was taxable to Z under section 367). See paragraph (d)(2)(v)(A) of this section.

Example 8A. Concurrent application without consolidated returns—(i) *Facts.* The facts are the same as in *Example 8*, except that V and Z do not file consolidated income tax returns.

(ii) *Result.* Z would still recognize $40 of gain on the transfer of its Business A assets, and the Business B assets would still qualify for the active trade or business exception under section 367(a)(3). However, V's basis in its stock of Z would not be increased by the amount of Z's gain. V's indirect transfer of stock will be taxable unless V enters into a gain recognition agreement (as described in §1.367(a)-8) for the $100 of gain realized but not recognized with respect to the stock of Z.

Example 8B. Concurrent application with individual U.S. shareholder—(i) *Facts.* The facts are the same as in *Example 8*, except that V is an individual U.S. citizen.

(ii) *Result.* Under section 367(a)(5) and §1.367(a)-7(b), the active trade or business exception under section 367(a)(3) does not apply to Z's transfer of assets to R. Thus, Z's transfer of assets to R would be fully taxable under section 367(a)(1). Z would recognize $100 of income. V's basis in its stock of Z is not increased by this amount. V is taxable with respect to its indirect transfer of its Z stock unless V enters into a gain recognition agreement in the amount of the $100, the gain realized but not recognized with respect to its Z stock.

Example 8C. Concurrent application with nonresident alien shareholder—(i) *Facts.* The facts are the same as in *Example 8*, except that V is a nonresident alien.

(ii) *Result.* Under section 367(a)(5) and §1.367(a)-7(b), the active trade or business exception under section 367(a)(3) does not apply to Z's transfer of assets to R. Thus, Z has $100 of gain with respect to the Business A and B assets. Because V is a nonresident alien, however, V is not subject to section 367(a) with respect to its indirect transfer of Z stock.

Example 9. Indirect stock transfer by reason of a controlled asset transfer—(i) *Facts.* The facts are the same as in paragraph (d)(3), *Example 8*, of this section, except that R transfers the Business A assets to M, a wholly owned domestic subsidiary of R, in a controlled asset transfer. In addition, V's basis in its Z stock is $90.

(ii) *Result.* Pursuant to paragraph (d)(2)(vi)(B) of this section, sections 367(a) and (d) do not apply to Z's transfer of the Business A assets to R if M's basis in the Business A assets is not greater than the basis of the assets in the hands of Z, the requirements of paragraphs (c)(1)(i), (ii), and (iv) and (c)(6) of this section are satisfied, and Z includes a statement described in paragraph (d)(2)(vi)(C) of this section with its U.S. income tax return for the taxable year of the transfer. Subject to the conditions and requirements of section 367(a)(5) and §1.367(a)-7(c), Z's transfer of the Business B assets to R (which are not re-transferred to M) qualifies for the active trade or business exception under section 367(a)(3). Pursuant to paragraphs (d)(1) and (d)(2)(vii)(A)(1) of this section, V is generally deemed to transfer the stock of a foreign corporation to F in a section 354 exchange subject to the rules of paragraphs (b) and (d) of this section, including the requirement that V enter into a gain recognition agreement and comply with the requirements of §1.367(a)-8. However, pursuant to paragraph (d)(2)(vii)(B) of this section, paragraph (d)(2)(vii)(A) of this section does not apply to the extent of the transfer of business A assets by R to M, a domestic corporation. As a result, to the extent of the business A assets transferred by R to M, V is deemed to transfer the stock of Z (a domestic corporation) to F in a section 354 exchange subject to the rules of paragraphs (c) and (d) of this section. Thus, with respect to V's indirect transfer of stock of a domestic corporation to F, such transfer is not subject to gain recognition under section 367(a)(1) if the requirements of paragraph (c) of this section are satisfied, including the requirement that V enter into a gain recognition agreement (separate from the gain recognition agreement described above with respect to the deemed transfer of stock of a foreign corporation to F) and comply with the requirements of §1.367(a)-8. Under paragraphs (d)(2)(i) and (ii) of this section, the transferee foreign corporation is F and the transferred corporation is R (with respect to the transfer of stock of a foreign corporation) and M (with respect to the transfer of stock of a domestic corporation). Pursuant to paragraph (d)(2)(iv) of this section, a disposition by F of the stock of R would trigger both gain recognition agreements. In addition, a disposition by R of the stock of M would trigger the gain recognition agreement filed with respect to the transfer of the stock of a domestic corporation. To determine whether there is a triggering event under §1.367(a)-8(j)(2)(i) for the gain recognition agreement filed with respect to the transfer of stock of the domestic corporation, the Business A assets in M must be considered. To determine whether there is such a triggering event for the gain recognition agreement filed with respect to the transfer of stock of the foreign corporation, the Business B assets in R must be considered.

Example 10. Concurrent application of asset transfer and indirect stock transfer rules in section 368(a)(1)(A)/(a)(2)(D) reorganization—(i) *Facts.* The facts are the same as in *Example 8*, except that R acquires all of the assets of Z in a reorganization described in sections 368(a)(1)(A) and (a)(2)(D). Pursuant to the reorganization, V receives 30 percent of the stock of F in a section 354 exchange.

(ii) *Result.* The consequences of the transaction are similar to those in *Example 8*. The assets of Businesses A and B that are transferred to R must be tested under section 367(a) and (d) prior to the consideration of the indirect stock transfer rules of this paragraph (d). Subject to the conditions and requirements of section 367(a)(5) and §1.367(a)-7(c), the Business B assets qualify for the active trade or business exception under section 367(a)(3). Because the Business A assets do not qualify for the exception, Z must recognize $40 of gain under section 367(a) on the transfer of Business A assets to R. Further, because V and Z file a consolidated return, V's basis in the stock of Z is increased from $100 to $140 as a result of Z's $40 gain. Pursuant to paragraphs (d)(1) and (d)(2)(vii)(A)(1) of this section, V is deemed to transfer the stock of a foreign corporation to F in a section 354 exchange subject to the rules of paragraph (b) and (d) of this section. V's indirect transfer of foreign stock will be taxable under section 367(a) unless V enters into a gain recognition agreement in the amount of $60 ($200 value of Z stock less $140 adjusted basis).

Example 11. Concurrent application of section 367(a) and (b) in section 368(a)(1)(A)/(a)(2)(E) reorganization—(i) *Facts.* F, a foreign corporation, owns all the stock of D, a domestic corporation. V, a domestic corporation, owns all the stock of Z, a foreign corporation.

V has a basis of $100 in the stock of Z which has a fair market value of $200. D is an operating corporation with assets valued at $100 with a basis of $60. In a reorganization described in sections 368(a)(1)(A) and (a)(2)(E), D merges into Z, and V exchanges its Z stock for 55 percent of the outstanding F stock.

(ii) *Result.* Under paragraph (d)(1)(ii) of this section, V is treated as indirectly transferring Z stock to F. V must recognize gain on its indirect transfer of Z stock to F under section 367(a) (and section 1248 will be applicable) if V does not enter into a gain recognition agreement with respect to the indirect stock transfer in accordance with §1.367(a)-8. Under paragraph (b)(2) of this section, if V enters into a gain recognition agreement with respect to the indirect stock transfer, the exchange will be subject to the provisions of section 367(b) and the regulations pursuant to such section as well as section 367(a). Under §1.367(b)-4(b), however, no income inclusion is required because, immediately after the exchange, F and Z are controlled foreign corporations with respect to which V is a section 1248 shareholder. Under paragraphs (d)(2)(i) and (d)(2)(ii) of this section, the transferee foreign corporation is F, and the transferred corporation is Z (the acquiring corporation). If F disposes (within the meaning of §1.367(a)-8(j)(1)) of all (or a portion) of Z stock within the term of the gain recognition agreement, V must either file an amended return for the year of the indirect stock transfer and include in income, with interest, the gain realized but not recognized on the initial exchange or if a valid election under §1.367(a)-8(c)(2)(vi) was made, currently recognize the gain and pay the related interest. Under paragraph (d)(2)(v)(B) of this section, to determine whether, for purposes of the gain recognition agreement, Z (the transferred corporation) disposes of substantially all of its assets, only the assets held by Z immediately before the transaction are taken into account. Because D is wholly owned by F, a foreign corporation, the control requirement of section 367(a)(5) and §1.367(a)-7(c)(1) cannot be satisfied. Therefore, section 367(a)(5) and §1.367(a)-7(b) preclude the application of the active trade or business exception under section 367(a)(3) to any property transferred by D to Z. Thus, under section 367(a)(1), D must recognize the gross amount of gain in each asset transferred to Z, or $40.

Example 12. Concurrent application of direct and indirect stock transfer rules—(i) *Facts.* F, a foreign corporation, owns all of the stock of O, also a foreign corporation. D, a domestic corporation, owns all of the stock of E, also a domestic corporation, which owns all of the stock of N, also a domestic corporation. Prior to the transactions described in this *Example 12*, D, E and N filed a consolidated income tax return. D has a basis of $100 in the stock of E, which has a fair market value of $160. The N stock has a fair market value of $100, and E has a basis of $60 in such stock. In addition to the stock of N, E owns the assets of Business X. The assets of Business X have a fair market value of $60, and E has a basis of $50 in such assets. Assume that the Business X assets qualify for nonrecognition treatment under section 367(a)(3). D does not own any stock in F (applying the attribution rules of section 318 as modified by section 958(b)). In a triangular reorganization described in section 368(a)(1)(C) and paragraph (d)(1)(iv) of this section, O acquires all of the assets of E, and D exchanges its stock in E for 40% of the voting stock of F.

(ii) *Result.* E's transfer of its assets, including the N stock, must be tested under the general rules of section 367(a) before consideration of D's indirect transfer of the stock of E. Subject to the conditions and requirements of section 367(a)(5) and §1.367(a)-7(c), the active trade or business exception under section 367(a)(3) applies to E's transfer of Business X assets. E's transfer of its N stock could qualify for nonrecognition treatment if D satisfies the requirements in §1.367(a)-3(e)(3). O is the transferee foreign corporation; N is the transferred corporation. Pursuant to paragraphs (d)(1) and (d)(2)(vii)(A)(1) of this section, D is deemed to transfer the stock of a foreign corporation to F in a section 354 exchange subject to the rules of paragraphs (b) and (d) of this section, and therefore may enter into a gain recognition agreement for such indirect stock transfer as provided in paragraph (b) of this section and §1.367(a)-8. As to this transfer, F is the transferee foreign corporation; O is the transferred corporation. The amount of the gain recognition agreement is $60.

Example 13. Successive section 351 exchanges—(i) *Facts.* D, a domestic corporation, owns all the stock of X, a controlled foreign corporation that operates an historical business, which owns all the stock of Y, a controlled foreign corporation that also operates an historical business. The properties of D consist of Business A assets, with an adjusted basis of $50 and a fair market value of $90, and Business B assets, with an adjusted basis of $50 and a fair market value of $110. Assume that the Business B assets qualify for the exception under section 367(a)(3) and §1.367(a)-2(g)(2), but that the Business A assets do not qualify for the exception. In an exchange described in section 351, D transfers the assets of Businesses A and B to X, and, in connection with the same transaction, X transfers the assets of Business B to Y in another exchange described in section 351.

(ii) *Result.* Under paragraph (d)(1)(vi) of this section, this transaction is treated as an indirect stock transfer for purposes of section

367(a), but the transaction is not recharacterized for purposes of section 367(b). Moreover, under paragraph (d)(2)(vi) of this section, the assets of Businesses A and B that are transferred to X must be tested under section 367(a)(3). The Business A assets, which were not transferred to Y, are subject to the general rules of section 367(a), and not the indirect stock transfer rules described in this paragraph (d). D must recognize $40 of income on the outbound transfer of Business A assets. The transfer of the Business B assets is subject to both the asset transfer rules (under section 367(a)(3)) and the indirect stock transfer rules of this paragraph (d) and §1.367(a)-8. Thus, D's transfer of the Business B assets will not be subject to section 367(a)(1) if D enters into a five-year gain recognition agreement with respect to the stock of Y. Under paragraphs (d)(2)(i) and (ii) of this section, X will be treated as the transferee foreign corporation and Y will be treated as the transferred corporation for purposes of applying the terms of the agreement. If X sells all or a portion of the stock of Y during the term of the agreement, D will be required to recognize a proportionate amount of the $60 gain that was realized by D on the initial transfer of the Business B assets.

Example 13A. Successive section 351 exchanges with ultimate domestic transferee—(i) *Facts.* The facts are the same as in *Example 13*, except that Y is a domestic corporation.

(ii) *Result.* As in *Example 13*, D must recognize $40 of income on the outbound transfer of the Business A assets. Although the Business B assets qualify for the exception under section 367(a)(3) (and end up in U.S. corporate solution, in Y), the $60 of gain realized on the Business B assets is nevertheless taxable under paragraphs (c)(1) and (d)(1)(vi) of this section because the transaction is considered to be a transfer by D of stock of a domestic corporation, Y, in which D receives more than 50 percent of the stock of the transferee foreign corporation, X. A gain recognition agreement is not permitted.

Example 14. Concurrent application of indirect stock transfer rules and section 367(b)—(i) *Facts.* F, a foreign corporation, owns all of the stock of Newco, which is also a foreign corporation. P, a domestic corporation, owns all of the stock of S, a foreign corporation that is a controlled foreign corporation within the meaning of section 957(a). P's basis in the stock of S is $50 and the value of S is $100. The section 1248 amount with respect to S stock is $30. In a reorganization described in section 368(a)(1)(C) (and paragraph (d)(1)(iv) of this section), Newco acquires all of the properties of S, and P exchanges its stock in S for 49 percent of the stock of F.

(ii) *Result.* P's exchange of S stock for F stock under section 354 will be taxable under section 367(a) (and section 1248 will be applicable) if P fails to enter into a 5-year gain recognition agreement in accordance with §1.367(a)-8. Under paragraph (b)(2) of this section, if P enters into a gain recognition agreement, the exchange will be subject to the provisions of section 367(b) and the regulations thereunder as well as section 367(a). Under §1.367(b)-4(b) of this chapter, P must recognize the section 1248 amount of $30 because P exchanged stock of a controlled foreign corporation, S, for stock of a foreign corporation that is not a controlled foreign corporation, F. The indirect stock transfer rules do not apply with respect to section 367(b). The deemed dividend of $30 recognized by P will increase P's basis in the F stock received in the transaction, and F's basis in the Newco stock. Thus, the amount of the gain recognition agreement is $20 ($50 gain realized on the transfer less the $30 inclusion under section 367(b)). Under paragraphs (d)(2)(i) and (ii) of this section, F is treated as the transferee foreign corporation and Newco is the transferred corporation.

Example 14A. Triangular section 368(a)(1)(C) reorganization involving foreign acquired corporation—(i) *Facts.* Assume the same facts as in *Example 14*, except that P receives 51 percent of the stock of F.

(ii) *Result.* P may still enter into a gain recognition agreement to avoid taxation under section 367(a). Assuming §1.367(b)-4(b) does not apply, there is no income inclusion under section 367(b), and the amount of the gain recognition agreement is $50.

Example 15. Concurrent application of indirect stock transfer rules and section 367(b)—(i) *Facts.* F, a foreign corporation, owns all of the stock of Newco, a domestic corporation. P, a domestic corporation, owns all of the stock of FC, a foreign corporation. P's basis in the stock of FC is $50 and the value of FC stock is $100. The all earnings and profits amount with respect to the FC stock held by P is $60. See §1.367(b)-2(d). In a reorganization described in sections 368(a)(1)(A) and (a)(2)(D) (and paragraph (d)(1)(i) of this section), Newco acquires all of the properties of FC, and P exchanges its stock in FC for 20 percent of the stock in F.

(ii) *Result.* P's section 354 exchange is considered an indirect stock transfer under paragraph (d)(1)(i) of this section. Further, because the assets of FC were acquired by Newco, a domestic corporation, in an asset reorganization, the transaction is within §1.367(b)-3(a) and (b). Because the transactions is subject to §1.367(b)-3 and the indirect stock rules of paragraph (d) of this section, and because the all earnings and profits amount with respect to the FC stock exchanged by P ($60) is greater than the gain in such stock subject to section 367(a) ($50), the section 367(b) rules (and not the section 367(a) rules) apply to the exchange. See § 1.367(a)-3(b)(2)(i)(B). Under the rules of section 367(b), P must include in income the all earnings and profits amount of $60 with respect to its FC stock. See § 1.367(b)-3. Alternatively, if P's all earnings and profits amount with respect to its FC stock were $30 (which is less than the gain in such stock subject to section 367(a) ($50)), section 367(b) and the regulations thereunder would not apply if there is gain recognition under section 367(a). Thus, if P failed to enter into a 5-year gain recognition agreement in accordance with § 1.367(a)-8, then P would recognize $50 of gain under section 367(a) and there would be no income inclusion under section 367(b). If, instead, P enters into a 5-year gain recognition agreement under § 1.367(a)-8, thereby avoiding immediate gain recognition on the entire $50 of section 367(a) gain, P is required to include in income the all earnings and profits amount of $30. In such a case, P will adjust its basis in the FC stock pursuant to § 1.367(b)-2(e)(3)(ii) and enter into a gain recognition agreement in the amount of $20.

Example 16. Direct asset reorganization not subject to stock transfer rules—(i) *Facts.* D is a domestic corporation that owns all the stock of F1 and F2, both foreign corporations. In a reorganization described in section 368(a)(1)(D), F2 acquires all of the assets of F1, and D receives 30 percent of the stock of F2 in an exchange described in section 354.

(ii) *Result.* The section 368(a)(1)(D) reorganization is not an indirect stock transfer described in paragraph (d) of this section. Moreover, the section 354 exchange by D of F1 stock for F2 stock is not an exchange described under section 367(a). See paragraph (a)(2)(ii) of this section.

(e) *Transfers of stock or securities by a domestic corporation to a foreign corporation in a section 361 exchange.*—(1) *Overview.*—(i) *Scope and definitions.*—This paragraph (e) applies to a domestic corporation (U.S. transferor) that transfers stock or securities of a domestic or foreign corporation (transferred stock or securities) to a foreign corporation (foreign acquiring corporation) in a section 361 exchange. Except as otherwise provided in this paragraph (e), paragraphs (b) and (c) of this section do not apply to the U.S. transferor's transfer of the transferred stock or securities in the section 361 exchange. For purposes of this paragraph (e), the definitions of control group, control group member, and non-control group member in § 1.367(a)-7(f)(1), ownership interest percentage in § 1.367(a)-7(f)(7), section 361 exchange in § 1.367(a)-7(f)(8), and U.S. transferor shareholder in § 1.367(a)-7(f)(13), apply.

(ii) *Ordering rules.*—Except as otherwise provided, this paragraph (e) applies to the transfer of the transferred stock or securities in the section 361 exchange prior to the application of any other provision of section 367 to such transfer. Furthermore, any gain recognized (including gain treated as a deemed dividend pursuant to section 1248(a)) by the U.S. transferor under this paragraph (e) shall be taken into account for purposes of applying any other provision of section 367 (including § § 1.367(a)-6, 1.367(a)-7, and 1.367(b)-4) to the transfer of the transferred stock or securities.

(2) *General rule.*—Except as provided in paragraph (e)(3) of this section, the transfer by the U.S. transferor of the transferred stock or securities to the foreign acquiring corporation in the section 361 exchange shall be subject to section 367(a)(1), and therefore the U.S. transferor shall recognize any gain (but not loss) realized with respect to the transferred stock or securities. Realized gain is recognized pursuant to the prior sentence notwithstanding that the transfer is described in any other nonrecognition provision enumerated in section 367(a)(1) (such as section 351 or 354).

(3) *Exception.*—The general rule of paragraph (e)(2) of this section shall not apply if the conditions of paragraphs (e)(3)(i), (ii), and (iii) of this section are satisfied.

(i) The conditions set forth in § 1.367(a)-7(c) are satisfied with respect to the section 361 exchange.

(ii) If the transferred stock or securities are of a domestic corporation, the U.S. target company (as defined in paragraph (c)(1) of this section) complies with the reporting requirements of paragraph (c)(6) of this section, and the conditions of paragraphs (c)(1)(i), (ii), and (iv) of this section are satisfied with respect to the transferred stock or securities.

(iii) If the U.S. transferor owns (applying the attribution rules of section 318, as modified by section 958(b)) five percent or more of the total voting power or the total value of the stock of the transferee foreign corporation immediately after the transfer of the transferred stock or securities in the section 361 exchange, then the conditions set forth in paragraphs (e)(3)(iii)(A), (B), and (C) of this section are satisfied.

(A) Except as otherwise provided in this paragraph (e)(3)(iii)(A), each U.S. transferor shareholder that is a qualified U.S. person (as defined in paragraph (e)(6)(vii) of this section) owning

(applying the attribution rules of section 318, as modified by section 958(b)) five percent or more of the total voting power or the total value of the stock of the transferee foreign corporation immediately after the reorganization enters into a gain recognition agreement that satisfies the conditions of paragraph (e)(6) of this section and § 1.367(a)-8. A U.S. transferor shareholder is not required to enter into a gain recognition agreement pursuant to this paragraph if the amount of gain that would be subject to the gain recognition agreement (as determined under paragraph (e)(6)(i) of this section) is zero.

(B) With respect to non-control group members that are not described in paragraph (e)(3)(iii)(A) of this section, the U.S. transferor recognizes gain equal to the product of the aggregate ownership interest percentage of such non-control group members multiplied by the gain realized by the U.S. transferor on the transfer of the transferred stock or securities.

(C) With respect to each control group member that is not described in paragraph (e)(3)(iii)(A) of this section, the U.S. transferor recognizes gain equal to the product of the ownership interest percentage of such control group member multiplied by the gain realized by the U.S. transferor on the transfer of the transferred stock or securities.

(4) *Application of certain rules at U.S. transferor-level.*—For purposes of paragraphs (c)(5)(iii) and (e)(3)(ii) and (iii) of this section, ownership of the stock of the transferee foreign corporation is determined by reference to stock owned by the U.S. transferor immediately after the transfer of the transferred stock or securities to the foreign acquiring corporation in the section 361 exchange, but prior to and without taking into account the U.S. transferor's distribution under section 361(c)(1) of the stock received.

(5) *Transferee foreign corporation.*—(i) *General rule.*—Except as provided in paragraph (e)(5)(ii) of this section, the transferee foreign corporation for purposes of applying paragraph (e) of this section and § 1.367(a)-8 shall be the foreign corporation that issues stock or securities to the U.S. transferor in the section 361 exchange.

(ii) *Special rule for triangular asset reorganizations involving the receipt of stock or securities of a domestic corporation.*—In the case of a triangular asset reorganization described in § 1.358-6(b)(2)(i), (ii), or (iii) or (b)(2)(v) (triangular asset reorganization) in which the U.S. transferor receives stock or securities of a domestic corporation that is in control (within the meaning of section 368(c)) of the foreign acquiring corporation, the transferee foreign corporation shall be the foreign acquiring corporation.

(6) *Special requirements for gain recognition agreements.*—A gain recognition agreement filed by a U.S. transferor shareholder pursuant to paragraph (e)(3)(iii)(A) of this section is, in addition to the terms and conditions of § 1.367(a)-8, subject to the conditions of this paragraph (e)(6).

(i) The amount of gain subject to the gain recognition agreement shall equal the product of the ownership interest percentage of the U.S. transferor shareholder multiplied by the gain realized by the U.S. transferor on the transfer of the transferred stock or securities, reduced (but not below zero) by the sum of the amounts described in paragraphs (e)(6)(i)(A),(B), (C), and (D) of this section.

(A) Gain recognized by the U.S. transferor with respect to the transferred stock or securities under section 367(a)(1) (including any portion treated as a deemed dividend under section 1248(a)) that is attributable to such U.S. transferor shareholder pursuant to § 1.367(a)-7(c)(2) or (e)(5).

(B) A deemed dividend included in the income of the U.S. transferor with respect to the transferred stock under § 1.367(b)-4(b)(1)(i) that is attributable to such U.S. transferor shareholder pursuant to § 1.367(a)-7(e)(4).

(C) If the U.S. transferor shareholder is subject to an election under § 1.1248(f)-2(c)(1), a deemed dividend included in the income of the U.S. transferor pursuant to § 1.1248(f)-2(c)(3) that is attributable to the U.S. transferor shareholder.

(D) If the U.S. transferor shareholder is not subject to an election under § 1.1248(f)-2(c)(1), the hypothetical section 1248 amount (as defined in § 1.1248(f)-(c)(4)) with respect to the stock of each foreign corporation transferred in the section 361 exchange attributable to the U.S. transferor shareholder.

(ii) The gain recognition agreement shall include the election described in § 1.367(a)-8(c)(2)(vi).

(iii) The gain recognition agreement shall designate the U.S. transferor shareholder as the U.S. transferor for purposes of § 1.367(a)-8.

(iv) If the transfer of the transferred stock or securities in the section 361 exchange is pursuant to a triangular asset reorganization, the gain recognition agreement shall include appropriate provisions that are consistent with the principles of § 1.367(a)-8 for gain recognition agreements involving multiple parties. See § 1.367(a)-8(j)(9).

(v) The gain recognition agreement shall not be eligible for termination upon a taxable disposition pursuant to §1.367(a)-8(o)(1) unless the value of the stock or securities received by the U.S. transferor shareholder in exchange for the stock or securities of the U.S. transferor under section 354 or 356 is at least equal to the amount of gain subject to the gain recognition agreement filed by such U.S. transferor shareholder.

(vi) Except as otherwise provided in this paragraph (e)(6)(vi), if gain is subsequently recognized by the U.S. transferor shareholder under the terms of the gain recognition agreement pursuant to §1.367(a)-8(c)(1)(i), the increase in stock basis provided under §1.367(a)-8(c)(4)(i) with respect to the stock received by the U.S. transferor shareholder shall not exceed the amount of the stock basis adjustment made pursuant to §1.367(a)-7(c)(3) with respect to the stock received by the U.S. transferor shareholder. This paragraph (e)(6)(vi) shall not apply if the U.S. transferor shareholder and the U.S. transferor are members of the same consolidated group at the time of the reorganization.

(vii) For purposes of this section, a qualified U.S. person means a U.S. person, as defined in §1.367(a)-1T(d)(1), but for this purpose does not include domestic partnerships, regulated investment companies (as defined in section 851(a)), real estate investment trusts (as defined in section 856(a)), and S corporations (as defined in section 1361(a)).

(7) *Gain subject to section 1248(a)*.—If the U.S. transferor recognizes gain under paragraphs (e)(3)(iii)(B) or (C) of this section with respect to transferred stock that is stock in a foreign corporation to which section 1248(a) applies, then the portion of such gain treated as a deemed dividend under section 1248(a) is the product of the amount of the gain multiplied by the section 1248(a) ratio. The section 1248(a) ratio is the ratio of the amount that would be treated as a deemed dividend under section 1248(a) if all the gain in the transferred stock were recognized to the amount of gain realized in all the transferred stock.

(8) *Examples*.—The following examples illustrate the provisions of paragraph (e) of this section. Except as otherwise indicated: US1, US2, and UST are domestic corporations that are not members of a consolidated group; X is a United States citizen; US1, US2, and X are unrelated parties; CFC1, CFC2, and FA are foreign corporations; each corporation described herein has a single class of stock issued and outstanding and a tax year ending on December 31; the section 1248 amount (within the meaning of §1.367(b)-2(c)) with respect to the stock of CFC1 and CFC2 is zero; Asset A is section 367(a) property that, but for the application of section 367(a)(5), would qualify for the active foreign trade or business exception under §1.367(a)-2T; the requirements of §1.367(a)-7(c)(2) through (5) are satisfied with respect to a section 361 exchange; the provisions of §1.367(a)-6T (regarding branch loss recapture) are not applicable; and none of the foreign corporations in the examples is a surrogate foreign corporation (within the meaning of section 7874) as a result of the transactions described in the examples because one or more of the conditions of section 7874(a)(2)(B) is not satisfied.

Example 1. U.S. transferor owns less than 5% of stock of transferee foreign corporation—(i) *Facts*. US1, US2, and X own 80%, 5%, and 15%, respectively, of the stock of UST with a fair market value of $160x, $10x, and $30x, respectively. UST has two assets, Asset A and 100% of the stock of CFC1. UST has no liabilities. Asset A has a $150x basis and $100x fair market value (as defined in §1.367(a)-7(f)(3)), and the CFC1 stock has a $0x basis and $100x fair market value. UST transfers Asset A and the CFC1 stock to FA solely in exchange for $200x of FA voting stock in a reorganization described in section 368(a)(1)(C). UST's transfer of Asset A and the CFC1 stock to FA qualifies as a section 361 exchange. UST distributes the stock received in the section 361 exchange to US1, US2, and X pursuant to the plan of reorganization, and liquidates. US1 receives $160x of FA stock, US2 receives $10x of FA stock, and X receives $30x of FA stock in exchange for the UST stock. Immediately after the transfer of Asset A and the CFC1 stock to FA in the section 361 exchange, but prior to and without taking into account UST's distribution of the FA stock pursuant to section 361(c)(1), UST does not own (applying the attribution rules of section 318, as modified by section 958(b)) five percent or more of the total voting power or the total value of the stock of FA.

(ii) *Result*—(A) UST's transfer of the CFC1 stock to FA in the section 361 exchange is subject to the provisions of this paragraph (e), and this paragraph (e) applies to the transfer of the CFC1 stock prior to the application of any other provision of section 367 to such transfer. See paragraphs (e)(1)(i) and (ii) of this section. Pursuant to the general rule of paragraph (e)(2) of this section, UST must recognize the gain realized of $100x on the transfer of the CFC1 stock (computed as the excess of the $100x fair market value over the $0x basis) unless the requirements for the exception provided in paragraph (e)(3) of this section are satisfied. In this case, the requirements of paragraph (e)(3) are satisfied. First, the requirement

of paragraph (e)(3)(i) of this section is satisfied because the control requirement of §1.367(a)-7(c)(1) is satisfied, and a stated assumption is that the requirements of §1.367(a)-7(c)(2) through (5) will be satisfied. The control requirement is satisfied because US1 and US2, each a control group member, own in the aggregate 85% of the stock of UST immediately before the reorganization. Second, the requirement of paragraph (e)(3)(ii) of this section is not applicable because that paragraph applies to the transfer of stock of a domestic corporation and CFC1 is a foreign corporation. Third, paragraph (e)(3)(iii) of this section is not applicable because immediately after the section 361 exchange, but prior to and without taking into account UST's distribution of the FA stock pursuant to section 361(c)(1), UST does not own (applying the attribution rules of section 318, as modified by section 958(b)) 5% or more of the total voting power or the total value of the stock of FA. See paragraph (e)(4) of this section. Accordingly, UST does not recognize the $100x of gain realized in the CFC1 stock pursuant to this section.

(B) In order to meet the requirements of §1.367(a)-7(c)(2)(i), UST must recognize gain equal to the portion of the inside gain (as defined in §1.367(a)-7(f)(5)) attributable to non-control group members (X), or $7.50x. The $7.50x of gain is computed as the product of the inside gain ($50x) multiplied by X's ownership interest percentage in UST (15%). Pursuant to §1.367(a)-7(f)(5), the $50x of inside gain is the amount by which the aggregate fair market value ($200x) of the section 367(a) property (as defined in §1.367(a)-7(f)(10), or Asset A and the CFC1 stock) exceeds the sum of the inside basis ($150x) of such property and the product of the section 367(a) percentage (as defined in §1.367(a)-7(f)(9), or 100%) multiplied by UST's deductible liabilities (as defined in §1.367(a)-7(f)(2), or $0x). Pursuant to §1.367(a)-7(f)(4), the inside basis equals the aggregate basis of the section 367(a) property transferred in the section 361 exchange ($150x), increased by any gain or deemed dividends recognized by UST with respect to the section 367(a) property under section 367 ($0x), but not including the $7.50x of gain recognized by UST under §1.367(a)-7(c)(2)(i). Pursuant to §1.367(a)-7(e)(1), the $7.50x of gain recognized by UST is treated as recognized with respect to the CFC1 stock and Asset A in proportion to the amount of gain realized in each. However, because there is no gain realized by UST with respect to Asset A, all $7.50x of the gain is allocated to the CFC1 stock. Furthermore, FA's basis in the CFC1 stock, as determined under section 362 is increased by the $7.50x of gain recognized by UST. See §1.367(a)-1(b)(4)(i)(B).

(C) The requirement to recognize gain under §1.367(a)-7(c)(2)(ii) is not applicable because the portion of the inside gain attributable to US1 and US2 (control group members) can be preserved in the stock received by each such shareholder. As described in paragraph (ii)(B) of this *Example 1*, the inside gain is $50x. US1's attributable inside gain of $40x (equal to the product of $50x inside gain multiplied by US1's 80% ownership interest percentage, reduced by $0x, the sum of the amounts described in §1.367(a)-7(c)(2)(ii)(A)(1) through (3)) does not exceed $160x (equal to the product of the section 367(a) percentage of 100% multiplied by $160x fair market value of FA stock received by US1). Similarly, US2's attributable inside gain of $2.50x (equal to the product of $50x inside gain multiplied by US2's 5% ownership interest percentage, reduced by $0x, the sum of the amounts described in §1.367(a)-7(c)(2)(ii)(A)(1) through (3)) does not exceed $10x (equal to the product of the section 367(a) percentage of 100% multiplied by $10x fair market value of FA stock received by US2).

(D) Each control group member (US1 and US2) must separately compute any required adjustment to stock basis under §1.367(a)-7(c)(3).

Example 2. U.S. transferor owns 5% or more of the stock of the transferee foreign corporation—(i) *Facts*. The facts are the same as in paragraph (e), *Example 1*, of this section except that immediately after the section 361 exchange, but prior to and without taking into account UST's distribution of the FA stock pursuant to section 361(c)(1), UST owns (applying the attribution rules of section 318, as modified by section 958(b)) 5% or more of the total voting power or value of the stock of FA. Furthermore, immediately after the reorganization, US1 and X (but not US2) each own (applying the attribution rules of section 318, as modified by section 958(b)) five percent or more of the total voting power or value of the stock of FA.

(ii) *Result*—(A) As is the case with paragraph (e), *Example 1*, of this section, UST's transfer of the CFC1 stock to FA in the section 361 exchange is subject to the provisions of this paragraph (e), and this paragraph (e) applies to the transfer of the CFC1 stock prior to the application of any other provision of section 367 to such transfer. See paragraphs (e)(1)(i) and (ii) of this section. In addition, UST must recognize the gain realized of $100x on the transfer of the CFC1 stock (computed as the excess of the $100x fair market value over the $0x basis) unless the requirements for the exception provided in paragraph (e)(3) of this section are satisfied. For the same reasons provided in *Example 1*, the requirement in paragraph (e)(3)(i) of this section is satisfied and the requirement of paragraph (e)(3)(ii) of this section is not applicable.

(B) Unlike paragraph (e), *Example 1*, of this section, however, UST owns 5% or more of the voting power or value of the stock of FA immediately after the transfer of the CFC1 stock in the section 361 exchange, but prior to and without taking into account UST's distribution of the FA stock under section 361(c)(1). As a result, paragraph (e)(3)(iii) of this section is applicable to the section 361 exchange of the CFC1 stock. Accordingly, in order to meet the requirements of paragraph (e)(3)(iii)(A) of this section US1 and X must enter into gain recognition agreements that satisfy the requirements of paragraph (e)(6) of this section and §1.367(a)-8. See paragraph (ii)(G) of this *Example 2* for the computation of the amount of gain subject to each gain recognition agreement.

(C) In order to meet the requirements of paragraph (e)(3)(iii)(C) of this section, UST must recognize $5x of gain attributable to US2 (computed as the product of the $100x of gain realized with respect to the transfer of the CFC1 stock multiplied by the 5% ownership interest percentage of US2). The $5x of gain recognized is not included in the computation of inside basis (see §1.367(a)-7(f)(4)(i)), but reduces (but not below zero) the amount of gain recognized by UST pursuant to §1.367(a)-7(c)(2)(ii) that is attributable to US2. Furthermore, FA's basis in the CFC1 stock as determined under section 362 is increased for the $5x of gain recognized. See §1.367(a)-1(b)(4)(i)(B). Assuming US1 and X enter into the gain recognition agreements described in paragraph (ii)(B) of this *Example 2*, and UST recognizes the $5x of gain described in this example, the requirements of paragraph (e)(3) of this section are satisfied and, accordingly, UST does not recognize the remaining $95x of gain realized in the CFC1 stock pursuant to this section.

(D) As described in paragraph (ii)(B) of *Example 1* of this paragraph (e), UST must recognize $7.50x of gain pursuant to §1.367(a)-7(c)(2)(i), the amount of the $50x of inside gain attributable to X. Pursuant to §1.367(a)-7(e)(1), the $7.50x of gain recognized by UST is treated as recognized with respect to the CFC1 stock and Asset A in proportion to the amount of gain realized in each. However, because there is no gain realized by UST with respect to Asset A, all $7.50x of the gain is allocated to the CFC1 stock. Furthermore, FA's basis in the CFC1 stock as determined under section 362 is increased for the $7.50x of gain recognized. See §1.367(a)-1(b)(4)(i)(B).

(E) As described in paragraph (ii)(C) of *Example 1* of this paragraph (e), the requirement to recognize gain pursuant to §1.367(a)-7(c)(2)(ii) is not applicable because the attributable inside gain of US1 and US2 can be preserved in the stock received by each shareholder. However, if UST were required to recognize gain pursuant to §1.367(a)-7(c)(2)(ii) for inside gain attributable to US2 (for example, if US2 received solely cash rather than FA stock in the reorganization), the amount of such gain would be reduced (but not below zero) by the amount of gain recognized by UST pursuant to paragraph (e)(3)(iii)(C) of this section that is attributable to US2 (computed as $5x in paragraph (ii)(C) of this *Example 2*). See §1.367(a)-7(c)(2)(ii)(A)(*1*).

(F) Each control group member (US1 and US2) must separately compute any required adjustment to stock basis under §1.367(a)-7(c)(3).

(G) The amount of gain subject to the gain recognition agreement filed by each of US1 and X is determined pursuant to paragraph (e)(6)(i) of this section. With respect to US1, the amount of gain subject to the gain recognition agreement is $80x. The $80x is computed as the product of US1's ownership interest percentage (80%) multiplied by the gain realized by UST in the CFC1 stock as determined prior to taking into account the application of any other provision of section 367 ($100x), reduced by the sum of the amounts described in paragraphs (e)(6)(i)(A) through (D) of this section attributable to US1 ($0x). With respect to X, the amount of gain subject to the gain recognition agreement is $7.50x. The $7.50x is computed as the product of X's ownership interest percentage (15%) multiplied by the gain realized by UST in the CFC1 stock as determined prior to taking into account the application of any other provision of section 367 ($100x), reduced by the sum of the amounts described in paragraphs (e)(6)(i)(A) through (D) of this section attributable to X ($7.50x, as computed in paragraph (ii)(D) of this *Example 2*).

(H) In order the meet the requirements of paragraph (e)(6)(ii) of this section, each gain recognition agreement must include the election described in §1.367(a)-8(c)(2)(vi). Furthermore, pursuant to paragraph (e)(6)(iii) of this section, US1 and X must be designated as the U.S. transferor on their respective gain recognition agreements for purposes of §1.367(a)-8.

Example 3. U.S. transferor owns 5% or more of the stock of the transferee foreign corporation; interaction with section 1248(f)—(i) *Facts.* US1, US2, and X own 50%, 30%, and 20%, respectively, of the stock of UST. The UST stock owned by US1 has a $180x basis and $200x fair market value; the UST stock owned by US2 has a $100x basis and

$120x fair market value; and the UST stock owned by X has a $80x fair market value. UST owns Asset A, and all the stock of CFC1 and CFC2. UST has no liabilities. Asset A has a $10x basis and $200x fair market value. The CFC1 stock is a single block of stock (as defined in §1.1248(f)-1(c)(2)) with a $20x basis, $40x fair market value, and $30x of earnings and profits attributable to it for purposes of section 1248 (with the result that the section 1248 amount (as defined in §1.1248(f)-1(c)(9)) is $20x). The CFC2 stock is also a single block of stock with a $30x basis, $160x fair market value, and $150x of earnings and profits attributable to it for purposes of section 1248 (with the result that the section 1248 amount is $130x). On December 31, Year 3, in a reorganization described in section 368(a)(1)(D), UST transfers the CFC1 stock, CFC2 stock, and Asset A to FA in exchange for 60 shares of FA stock with a $400x fair market value. UST's transfer of the CFC1 stock, CFC2 stock, and Asset A to FA in exchange for the 60 shares of FA stock qualifies as a section 361 exchange. UST distributes the FA stock received in the section 361 exchange to US1, US2, and X pursuant to section 361(c)(1). US1, US2, and X exchange their UST stock for 30, 18, and 12 shares, respectively, of FA stock pursuant to section 354. Immediately after the reorganization, FA has 100 shares of stock outstanding, and US1 and US2 are each a section 1248 shareholder with respect to FA.

(ii) *Result*—(A) UST's transfer of the CFC1 stock and CFC2 stock to FA in the section 361 exchange is subject to the provisions of this paragraph (e), and this paragraph (e) applies to the transfer of the CFC1 stock and CFC2 stock prior to the application of any other provision of section 367 to such transfer. See paragraphs (e)(1)(i) and (ii) of this section. Pursuant to the general rule of paragraph (e)(2) of this section, UST must recognize the gain realized of $20x on the transfer of the CFC1 stock (the excess of $40x fair market value over $20x basis) and the gain realized of $130x on the transfer of the CFC2 stock (the excess of $160x fair market value over $30x basis), subject to the application of section 1248(a), unless the requirements for the exception provided in paragraph (e)(3) of this section are satisfied. In this case, the requirement of paragraph (e)(3)(i) of this section is satisfied because the control requirement of §1.367(a)-7(c)(1) is satisfied, and a stated assumption is that the requirements of §1.367(a)-7(c)(2) through (5) will be satisfied. The control requirement is satisfied because US1 and US2, each a control group member, own in the aggregate 80% of the UST stock immediately before the reorganization. The requirement of paragraph (e)(3)(ii) of this section is not applicable because paragraph (e)(3)(ii) applies to the transfer of stock of a domestic corporation, and CFC1 and CFC2 are foreign corporations. UST owns 5% or more of the total voting power or value of the stock of FA (60%, or 60 of the 100 shares of FA stock outstanding) immediately after the transfer of the CFC1 stock and CFC2 stock in the section 361 exchange, but prior to and without taking into account UST's distribution of the FA stock under section 361(c)(1). As a result, paragraph (e)(3)(iii) of this section is applicable to the section 361 exchange of the CFC1 stock and CFC2 stock. US1, US2, and X each own (applying the attribution rules of section 318, as modified by section 958(b)) 5% or more of the total voting power or value of the FA stock immediately after the reorganization, or 30%, 18%, and 12%, respectively. Accordingly, in order to meet the requirements of paragraph (e)(3)(iii)(A) of this section, US1 and US2 must enter into gain recognition agreements with respect to the CFC1 stock and CFC2 stock that satisfy the requirements of paragraph (e)(6) of this section and §1.367(a)-8. X is not required to enter into a gain recognition agreement because the amount of gain that would be subject to the gain recognition agreement is zero. See paragraph (ii)(J) of this *Example 3* for the computation of the amount of gain subject to each gain recognition agreement. Assuming US1 and US2 enter into the gain recognitions agreements described above, the requirements of paragraph (e)(3) of this section are satisfied and accordingly, UST does not recognize the gain realized of $20x in the stock of CFC1 or the gain realized of $130x in the stock of CFC2 pursuant to this section.

(B) UST's transfer of the CFC1 stock and CFC2 stock to FA pursuant to the section 361 exchange is subject to §1.367(b)-4(b)(1)(i), which applies prior to the application of §1.367(a)-7(c). See paragraph (e)(1) of this section. UST (the exchanging shareholder) is a U.S. person and a section 1248 shareholder with respect to CFC1 and CFC2 (each a foreign acquired corporation). However, UST is not required to include in income as a deemed dividend the section 1248 amount with respect to the CFC1 stock ($20x) or CFC2 stock ($130x) under §1.367(b)-4(b)(1)(i) because, immediately after UST's section 361 exchange of the CFC1 stock and CFC2 stock for FA stock (and before the distribution of the FA stock to US1, US2, and X under section 361(c)(1), FA, CFC1, and CFC2 are controlled foreign corporations as to which UST is a section 1248 shareholder. See §1.367(b)-4(b)(1)(ii)(A). However, if UST were required to include in income as a deemed dividend the section 1248 amount with respect to the CFC1 stock or CFC2 stock (for example, if FA were not a controlled foreign corporation), such deemed dividend would be taken into account prior to the application of §1.367(a)-7(c). Furthermore, because US1, US2, and X are all persons described in paragraph (e)(3)(iii)(A) of this section, any such deemed dividend would increase inside basis. See § 1.367(a)-7(f)(4).

(C) In order to meet the requirements of § 1.367(a)-7(c)(2)(i), UST must recognize gain equal to the portion of the inside gain attributable to non-control group members (X), or $68x. The $68x of gain is computed as the product of the inside gain ($340x) multiplied by X's ownership interest percentage in UST (20%), reduced (but not below zero) by $0x, the sum of the amounts described in § 1.367(a)-7(c)(2)(i)(A) through (C). Pursuant to § 1.367(a)-7(f)(5), the $340x of inside gain is the amount by which the aggregate fair market value ($400x) of the section 367(a) property (Asset A, CFC1 stock, and CFC2 stock) exceeds the sum of the inside basis ($60x) and $0x (the product of the section 367(a) percentage (100%) multiplied by UST's deductible liabilities ($0x)). Pursuant to § 1.367(a)-7(f)(4), the inside basis equals the aggregate basis of the section 367(a) property transferred in the section 361 exchange ($60x), increased by any gain or deemed dividends recognized by UST with respect to the section 367(a) property under section 367 ($0x), but not including the $68x of gain recognized by UST under § 1.367(a)-7(c)(2)(i). Under § 1.367(a)-7(e)(1), the $68x gain recognized is treated as being with respect to the CFC1 stock, CFC2 stock, and Asset A in proportion to the amount of gain realized by UST on the transfer of the property. The amount treated as recognized with respect to the CFC1 stock is $4x ($68x gain multiplied by $20x/$340x). The amount treated as recognized with respect to the CFC2 stock is $26x ($68x gain multiplied by $130x/$340x). The amount treated as recognized with respect to Asset A is $38x ($68x gain multiplied by $190x/$340x). Under section 1248(a), UST must include in gross income as a dividend the $4x gain recognized with respect to the CFC1 stock and the $26x gain recognized with respect to CFC2 stock. Furthermore, FA's basis in the CFC1 stock, CFC2 stock, and Asset A, as determined under section 362, is increased by the amount of gain recognized by UST with respect to such property. See § 1.367(a)-1(b)(4)(i)(B). Thus, FA's basis in the CFC1 stock is $24x ($20x increased by $4x of gain), the CFC2 stock is $56x ($30x increased by $26x of gain), and Asset A is $48x ($10x increased by $38x of gain).

(D) The requirement to recognize gain under § 1.367(a)-7(c)(2)(ii) is not applicable because the portion of the inside gain attributable to US1 and US2 (control group members) can be preserved in the stock received by each such shareholder. As described in paragraph (ii)(C) of this Example 3, the inside gain is $340x. US1's attributable inside gain of $170x (equal to the product of $340x inside gain multiplied by US1's 50% ownership interest percentage, reduced by $0x, the sum of the amounts described in § 1.367(a)-7(c)(2)(ii)(A)(1) through (3)) does not exceed $200x (equal to the product of the section 367(a) percentage of 100% multiplied by $200x fair market value of FA stock received by US1). Similarly, US2's attributable inside gain of $102x (equal to the product of $340x inside gain multiplied by US2's 30% ownership interest percentage, reduced by $0x, the sum of the amounts described in § 1.367(a)-7(c)(2)(ii)(A)(1) through (3)) does not exceed $120x (equal to the product of the section 367(a) percentage of 100% multiplied by $120x fair market value of FA stock received by US2).

(E) Each control group member (US1 and US2) separately computes any required adjustment to stock basis under § 1.367(a)-7(c)(3). US1's section 358 basis in the FA stock received of $180x (equal to US1's basis in the UST stock exchanged) is reduced to preserve the attributable inside gain with respect to US1, less any gain recognized with respect to US1 under § 1.367(a)-7(c)(2)(ii). Because UST does not recognize gain on the section 361 exchange with respect to US1 under § 1.367(a)-7(c)(2)(ii) (as determined in paragraph (ii)(D) of this Example 3), the attributable inside gain of $170x with respect to US1 is not reduced under § 1.367(a)-7(c)(3)(i)(A). US1's outside gain (as defined in § 1.367(a)-7(f)(6)) in the FA stock is $20x, the product of the section 367(a) percentage (100%) multiplied by the $20x gain (equal to the difference between $200x fair market value and $180x section 358 basis in the FA stock). Thus, US1's $180x section 358 basis in the FA stock must be reduced by $150x (the excess of $170x attributable inside gain, reduced by $0x, over $20x outside gain) to $30x. Similarly, US2's section 358 basis in the FA stock received of $100x (equal to US2's basis in the UST stock exchanged) is reduced to preserve the attributable inside gain with respect to US2, less any gain recognized with respect to US2 under § 1.367(a)-7(c)(2)(ii). Because UST does not recognize gain on the section 361 exchange with respect to US2 under § 1.367(a)-7(c)(2)(ii) (as determined in paragraph (ii)(D) of this Example 3), the attributable inside gain of $102x with respect to US2 is not reduced under § 1.367(a)-7(c)(3)(i)(A). US2's outside gain in the FA stock is $20x, the product of the section 367(a) percentage (100%) multiplied by the $20x gain (equal to the difference between $120x fair market value and $100x section 358 basis in FA stock). Thus, US2's $100x section 358 basis in the FA stock must be reduced by $82x (the excess of $102x attributable inside gain, reduced by $0x, over $20x outside gain) to $18x.

(F) UST's distribution of the FA stock to US1, US2, and X under section 361(c)(1) (new stock distribution) is subject to § 1.1248(f)-1(b)(3). Except as provided in § 1.1248(f)-2(c), under § 1.1248(f)-1(b)(3) UST must include in gross income as a dividend the total section 1248(f) amount (as defined in § 1.1248(f)-1(c)(14)). The total section 1248(f) amount is $120x, the sum of the section 1248(f) amount (as defined in § 1.1248(f)-1(c)(10)) with respect to the CFC1 stock ($16x) and CFC2 stock ($104x). The $16x section 1248(f) amount with respect to the CFC1 stock is the amount that UST would have included in income as a dividend under § 1.367(b)-4(b)(1)(i) with respect to the CFC1 stock if the requirements of § 1.367(b)-4(b)(1)(ii)(A) had not been satisfied ($20x), reduced by the amount of gain recognized by UST under § 1.367(a)-7(c)(2) allocable to the CFC1 stock and treated as a dividend under section 1248(a) ($4x, as described in paragraph (ii)(C) of this Example 3). Similarly, the section 1248(f) amount with respect to the CFC2 stock is $104x ($130x reduced by $26x).

(G) If, however, UST along with US1 and US2 (each a section 1248 shareholder of FA immediately after the distribution) elect to apply the provisions of § 1.1248(f)-2(c) (as provided in § 1.1248(f)-2(c)(1)), the amount that UST is required to include in income as a dividend under § 1.1248(f)-1(b)(3) ($120x total section 1248(f) amount as computed in paragraph (ii)(F) of this Example 3) is reduced by the sum of the portions of the section 1248(f) amount with respect to the CFC1 stock and CFC2 stock that is attributable (under the rules of § 1.1248(f)-2(d)) to the FA stock distributed to US1 and US2. Assume that the election is made to apply § 1.1248(f)-2(c).

(1) Under § 1.1248(f)-2(d)(1), the portion of the section 1248(f) amount with respect to the CFC1 stock that is attributed to the 30 shares of FA stock distributed to US1 is equal to the hypothetical section 1248 amount (as defined in § 1.1248(f)-1(c)(4)) with respect to the CFC1 stock that is attributable to US1's ownership interest percentage in UST. US1's hypothetical section 1248 amount with respect to the CFC1 stock is the amount that UST would have included in income as a deemed dividend under § 1.367(b)-4(b)(1)(i) with respect to the CFC1 stock if the requirements of § 1.367(b)-4(b)(1)(ii)(A) had not been satisfied ($20x) and that would be attributable to US1's ownership interest percentage in UST (50%), reduced by the amount of gain recognized by UST under § 1.367(a)-7(c)(2) attributable to US1 and allocable to the CFC1 stock, but only to the extent such gain is treated as a dividend under section 1248(a) ($0x, as described in paragraphs (ii)(C) and (D) of this Example 3). Thus, US1's hypothetical section 1248 amount with respect to the CFC1 stock is $10x ($20x multiplied by 50%, reduced by $0x). The $10x hypothetical section 1248 amount is attributed pro rata (based on relative values) among the 30 shares of FA stock distributed to US1, and the attributable share amount (as defined in § 1.1248(f)-2(d)(1)) is $.33x ($10x/30 shares). Similarly, US1's hypothetical section 1248 amount with respect to the CFC2 stock is $65x ($130x multiplied by 50%, reduced by $0x), and the attributable share amount is $2.17x ($65x/30 shares). Similarly, US2's hypothetical section 1248 amount with respect to the CFC1 stock is $6x ($20x multiplied by 30%, reduced by $0x), and the attributable share amount is also $.33x ($6x/18 shares). Finally, US2's hypothetical section 1248 amount with respect to the CFC2 stock is $39x ($130x multiplied by 30%, reduced by $0x), and the attributable share amount is also $2.17x ($39x/18 shares). Thus, the sum of the portion of the section 1248(f) amount with respect to the CFC1 stock and CFC2 stock attributable to shares of stock of FA distributed to US1 and US2 is $120x ($10x plus $65x plus $6x plus $39x).

(2) If the shares of FA stock are divided into portions, § 1.1248(f)-2(d)(2) applies to attribute the attributable share amount to portions of shares of FA stock distributed to US1 and US2. Under § 1.1248(f)-2(c)(2) each share of FA stock received by US1 (30 shares) and US2 (18 shares) is divided into three portions, one attributable to the single block of stock of CFC1, one attributable to the single block of stock of CFC2, and one attributable to Asset A. Thus, the attributable share amount of $.33x with respect to the CFC1 stock is attributed to the portion of each of the 30 shares and 18 shares of FA stock received by US1 and US2, respectively, that relates to the CFC1 stock. Similarly, the attributable share amount of $2.17x with respect to the CFC2 stock is attributed to the portion of each of the 30 shares and 18 shares of FA stock received by US1 and US2, respectively, that relates to the CFC2 stock.

(3) The total section 1248(f) amount ($120x) that UST is otherwise required to include in gross income as a dividend under § 1.1248(f)-1(b)(3) is reduced by $120x, the sum of the portions of the section 1248(f) amount with respect to the CFC1 stock and CFC2 stock that are attributable to the shares of FA stock distributed to US1 and US2. Thus, the amount DC is required to include in gross income as a dividend under § 1.1248(f)-1(b)(3) is $0x ($120x reduced by $120x).

(H) As stated in paragraph (ii)(G)(2) of this Example 3, under § 1.1248(f)-2(c)(2) each share of FA stock received by US1 (30 shares) and US2 (18 shares) is divided into three portions, one attributable to the CFC1 stock, one attributable to the CFC2 stock, and one attributable to Asset A. Under §1.1248(f)-2(c)(4)(i), the basis of each portion is the product of US1's and US2's section 358 basis in the share of FA stock multiplied by the ratio of the section 362 basis of the property (CFC1 stock, CFC2 stock, or Asset A, as applicable) received by FA in the section 361 exchange to which the portion relates, to the aggregate section 362 basis of all property received by FA in the section 361 exchange. Under §1.1248(f)-2(c)(4)(ii), the fair market value of each portion is the product of the fair market value of the share of FA stock multiplied by the ratio of the fair market value of the property (CFC1 stock, CFC2 stock, or Asset A, as applicable) to which the portion relates, to the aggregate fair market value of all property received by FA in the section 361 exchange. The section 362 basis of the CFC1 stock, CFC2 stock, and Asset A is $24x, $56x, and $48x, respectively, for an aggregate section 362 basis of $128x. See paragraph (ii)(C) of this *Example 3*. The fair market value of the CFC1 stock, CFC2 stock, and Asset A is $40x, $160x, and $200x, for an aggregate fair market value of $400x. Furthermore, US1's 30 shares of FA stock have an aggregate fair market value of $200x and section 358 basis of $30x (resulting in aggregate gain of $170x), and US2's 18 shares of FA stock have an aggregate fair market value of $120x and section 358 basis of $18x (resulting in aggregate gain of $102x). See paragraph (ii)(E) of this *Example 3*.

(1) With respect to US1's 30 shares of FA stock, the portions attributable to the CFC1 stock have an aggregate basis of $5.63x ($30x multiplied by $24x/$128x) and fair market value of $20x ($200x multiplied by $40x/$400x), resulting in aggregate gain in such portions of $14.38x (or $.48x gain in each such portion of the 30 shares). The portions attributable to the CFC2 stock have an aggregate basis of $13.13x ($30x multiplied by $56x/$128x) and fair market value of $80x ($200x multiplied by $160x/$400x), resulting in aggregate gain in such portions of $66.88x (or $2.23x in each such portion of the 30 shares). The portions attributable to Asset A have an aggregate basis of $11.25x ($30x multiplied by $48x/$128x) and fair market value of $100x ($200x multiplied by $200x/$400x), resulting in aggregate gain in such portions of $88.75x (or $2.96x in each such portion of the 30 shares). Thus, the aggregate gain in all the portions of the 30 shares is $170x ($14.38x plus $66.88x plus $88.75x).

(2) With respect to US2's 18 shares of FA stock, the portions attributable to the CFC1 stock have an aggregate basis of $3.38x ($18x multiplied by $24x/$128x) and fair market value of $12x ($120x multiplied by $40x/$400x), resulting in aggregate gain in such portions of $8.63x (or $.48x in each such portion of the 18 shares). The portions attributable to the CFC2 stock have an aggregate basis of $7.88x ($18x multiplied by $56x/$128x) and fair market value of $48x ($120x multiplied by $160x/$400x), resulting in aggregate gain of $40.13x (or $2.23x in each such portion of the 18 shares). The portions attributable to Asset A have an aggregate basis of $6.75x ($18x multiplied by $48x/$128x) and fair market value of $60x ($120x multiplied by $200x/$400x), resulting in aggregate gain of $53.25x (or $2.96x in each such portion of the 18 shares). Thus, the aggregate gain in all the portions of the 18 shares is $102x ($8.63x plus $40.13x plus $53.25x).

(3) Under §1.1248-8(b)(2)(iv), the earnings and profits of CFC1 attributable to the portions of US1's 30 shares of FA stock that relate to the CFC1 stock is $15x (the product of US1's 50% ownership interest percentage in UST multiplied by $30x of earnings and profits attributable to the CFC1 stock before the section 361 exchange, reduced by $0x of dividend included in UST's income with respect to the CFC1 stock under section 1248(a) attributable to US1). The earnings and profits of CFC2 attributable to the portions of US1's 30 shares of FA stock that relate to the CFC2 stock is $75x (the product of US1's 50% ownership interest percentage in UST multiplied by $150x of earnings and profits attributable to the CFC2 stock before the section 361 exchange, reduced by $0x of dividend included in UST's income with respect to the CFC2 stock under section 1248(a) attributable to US1). Similarly, the earnings and profits of CFC1 attributable to the portions of US2's 18 shares of FA stock that relate to the CFC1 stock is $9x (the product of US2's 30% ownership interest percentage in UST multiplied by $30x of earnings and profits attributable to the CFC1 stock before the section 361 exchange, reduced by $0x of dividend included in UST's income with respect to the CFC1 stock under section 1248(a) attributable to US2). Finally, the earnings and profits of CFC2 attributable to the portions of US2's 18 shares of FA stock that relate to the CFC2 stock is $45x (the product of US2's 30% ownership interest percentage in UST multiplied by $150x of earnings and profits attributable to the CFC2 stock before the section 361 exchange, reduced by $0x of dividend included in UST's income with respect to the CFC2 stock under section 1248(a) attributable to US2).

(I) Under §1.1248(f)-2(c)(3), neither US1 nor US2 is required to reduce the aggregate section 358 basis in the portions of their respective shares of FA stock, and UST is not required to include in gross income any additional deemed dividend.

(1) US1 is not required to reduce the aggregate section 358 basis of the portions of its 30 shares of FA stock that relate to the CFC1 stock because the $10x section 1248(f) amount with respect to the CFC1 stock attributable to the portions of the shares of FA stock received by US1 (as computed in paragraph (ii)(G) of this *Example 3*) does not exceed US1's postdistribution amount (as defined in §1.1248(f)-1(c)(6), or $14.38x) in those portions. The $14.38x postdistribution amount equals the amount that US1 would be required to include in income as a dividend under section 1248(a) with respect to such portion if it sold the 30 shares of FA stock immediately after the distribution in a transaction in which all realized gain is recognized, without taking into account basis adjustments or income inclusions under §1.1248(f)-2(c)(3) ($20x fair market value, $5.63x basis, and $15x earnings and profits attributable to the portions for purposes of section 1248). Similarly, US1 is not required to reduce the aggregate section 358 basis of the portions of its 30 shares of FA stock that relate to the CFC2 stock because the $65x section 1248(f) amount with respect to the CFC2 stock attributable to the portions of the shares of FA stock received by US1 (as computed in paragraph (ii)(G) of this *Example 3*) does not exceed US1's postdistribution amount ($66.88x) in those portions. The $66.88x postdistribution amount equals the amount that US1 would be required to include in income as a dividend under section 1248(a) with respect to such portion if it sold the 30 shares of FA stock immediately after the distribution in a transaction in which all realized gain is recognized, without taking into account basis adjustments or income inclusions under §1.1248(f)-2(c)(3) ($80x fair market value, $13.13x basis, and $75x earnings and profits attributable to the portions for purposes of section 1248).

(2) US2 is not required to reduce the aggregate section 358 basis of the portions of its 18 shares of FA stock that relate to the CFC1 stock because the $6x section 1248(f) amount with respect to the CFC1 stock attributable to the portions of the shares of FA stock received by US2 (as computed in paragraph (ii)(G) of this *Example 3*) does not exceed US2's postdistribution amount ($8.63x) in those portions. The $8.63x postdistribution amount equals the amount that US2 would be required to include in income as a dividend under section 1248(a) with respect to such portion if it sold the 18 shares of FA stock immediately after the distribution in a transaction in which all realized gain is recognized, without taking into account basis adjustments or income inclusions under §1.1248(f)-2(c)(3) ($12x fair market value, $3.38x basis, and $9x earnings and profits attributable to the portions for purposes of section 1248). Similarly, US2 is not required to reduce the aggregate section 358 basis of the portions of its 18 shares of FA stock that relate to the CFC2 stock because the $39x section 1248(f) amount with respect to the CFC2 stock attributable to the portions of the shares of FA stock received by US2 (as computed in paragraph (ii)(G) of this *Example 3*) does not exceed US1's postdistribution amount ($40.13x) in those portions. The $40.13x postdistribution amount equals the amount that US2 would be required to include in income as a dividend under section 1248(a) with respect to such portion if it sold the 18 shares of FA stock immediately after the distribution in a transaction in which all realized gain is recognized, without taking into account basis adjustments or income inclusions under §1.1248(f)-2(c)(3) ($48x fair market value, $7.88x basis, and $45x earnings and profits attributable to the portions for purposes of section 1248).

(J) The amount of gain subject to the gain recognition agreement filed by each of US1 and US2 is determined pursuant to paragraph (e)(6)(i) of this section. The amount of gain subject to the gain recognition agreement filed by US1 with respect to the stock of CFC1 and CFC2 is $10x and $65x, respectively. The $10x and $65x are computed as the product of US1's ownership interest percentage (50%) multiplied by the gain realized by UST in the CFC1 stock ($20x) and CFC2 stock ($130x), respectively, as determined prior to taking into account the application of any other provision of section 367, reduced by the sum of the amounts described in paragraphs (e)(6)(i)(A) through (D) of this section with respect to the CFC1 stock and CFC2 stock attributable to US1 ($0x with respect to the CFC1 stock, and $0x with respect to the CFC2 stock). The amount of gain subject to the gain recognition agreement filed by US2 with respect to the stock of CFC1 and CFC2 is $6x and $39x, respectively. The $6x and $39x are computed as the product of US2's ownership interest percentage (30%) multiplied by the gain realized by UST in the CFC1 stock ($20x) and CFC2 stock ($130x), respectively, as determined prior to taking into account the application of any other provision of section 367, reduced by the sum of the amounts described in paragraphs (e)(6)(i)(A) through (D) of this section with respect to the CFC1 stock and CFC2 stock attributable to US2 ($0x with respect to the CFC1 stock, and $0x with respect to the CFC2 stock). X is not required to enter into a gain recognition agreement because the amount of gain that would be subject to the gain recognition agreement is $0x with respect to the CFC1 stock, and $0x with respect to the CFC2 stock, computed as X's ownership percentage (20%) multiplied by the gain realized in the stock of CFC1 ($20x multiplied by 20%, or $4x) and CFC2 ($130x multiplied by 20%, or $26x), reduced by the amount of gain recognized by UST with respect to the stock of

CFC1 and CFC2 that is attributable to X pursuant to § 1.367(a)-7(c)(2) ($4x and $26x, respectively, as determined in paragraph (ii)(C) of this *Example 3*). Pursuant to paragraph (e)(6)(ii) of this section, each gain recognition agreement must include the election described in § 1.367(a)-8(c)(2)(vi). Furthermore, pursuant to paragraph (e)(6)(iii) of this section, US1 and US2 must be designated as the U.S. transferor on their respective gain recognition agreements for purposes of § 1.367(a)-8.

(9) *Illustration of rules.*—For rules relating to certain distributions of stock of a foreign corporation by a domestic corporation, see section 1248(f) and §§ 1.1248(f)-1 through 1.1248(f)-3.

(f) *Failure to file statements.*—(1) *Failure to file.*—For purposes of the exceptions to the application of section 367(a)(1) provided in paragraphs (c) and (d)(2)(vi)(B) of this section, there is a failure to file a statement described in paragraph (c)(6), (c)(7), or (d)(2)(vi)(C) of this section (failure to file) if the statement is not filed with a timely filed U.S. income tax return or is not completed in all material respects.

(2) *Relief for certain failures to file that are not willful.*—(i) *In general.*—A failure to file described in paragraph (f)(1) of this section will be deemed not to have occurred for purposes of satisfying the requirements of the applicable regulation if the taxpayer demonstrates that the failure was not willful using the procedure set forth in this paragraph (f)(2). For this purpose, willful is to be interpreted consistent with the meaning of that term in the context of other civil penalties, which would include a failure due to gross negligence, reckless disregard, or willful neglect. Whether a failure to file was a willful failure will be determined by the Director of Field Operations International, Large Business & International (or any successor to the roles and responsibilities of such position, as appropriate) (Director) based on all the facts and circumstances. The taxpayer must submit a request for relief and an explanation as provided in paragraph (f)(2)(ii)(A) of this section. Although a taxpayer whose failure to file is determined not to be willful will not be subject to gain recognition under this section, the taxpayer will be subject to a penalty under section 6038B if the taxpayer fails to satisfy the reporting requirements, if any, under that section and does not demonstrate that the failure was due to reasonable cause and not willful neglect. See § 1.6038B-1(b) and (f). The determination of whether the failure to file was willful under this section has no effect on any request for relief made under § 1.6038B-1(f).

(ii) *Procedures for establishing that a failure to file was not willful.*—(A) *Time and manner of submission.*—A taxpayer's statement that the failure to file was not willful will be considered only if, promptly after the taxpayer becomes aware of the failure, an amended return is filed for the taxable year to which the failure relates that includes the information that should have been included with the original return for such taxable year or that otherwise complies with the rules of this section, and that includes a written statement explaining the reasons for the failure to file. The amended return must be filed with the Internal Revenue Service at the location where the taxpayer filed its original return. The taxpayer may submit a request for relief from the penalty under section 6038B as part of the same submission. See § 1.6038B-1(f).

(B) *Notice requirement.*—In addition to the requirements of paragraph (f)(2)(ii)(A) of this section, the taxpayer must comply with the notice requirements of this paragraph (f)(2)(ii)(B). If any taxable year of the taxpayer is under examination when the amended return is filed, a copy of the amended return and any information required to be included with such return must be delivered to the Internal Revenue Service personnel conducting the examination. If no taxable year of the taxpayer is under examination when the amended return is filed, a copy of the amended return and any information required to be included with such return must be delivered to the Director.

(3) For illustrations of the application of the willfulness standard of this paragraph (f), see the examples in § 1.367(a)-8(p)(3).

(g) *Effective/applicability dates.*—(1) *Rules of applicability.*—(i) Except as otherwise provided in this paragraph (g), the rules in paragraphs (a), (b), and (d) of this section apply to transfers occurring on or after July 20, 1998.

(ii) The following rules apply to transactions occurring on or after January 23, 2006—

(A) The rules in paragraphs (a) and (d) of this section, as they apply to section 368(a)(1)(A) reorganizations (including reorganizations described in section 368(a)(2)(D) or (E)) involving a foreign *acquiring or foreign acquired corporation;*

(B) The rules in paragraph (b)(2)(i)(B) of this section;

(C) The rules in paragraph (d) of this section, as they apply to section 368(a)(1)(G) reorganizations (including reorganizations described in section 368(a)(2)(D));

(D) The rules of paragraph (d)(1) and (d)(2)(iv), as they relate to exchanges by a U.S. person of securities of an acquired corporation for voting stock or securities of a foreign corporation in control of the acquiring corporation in a triangular section 368(a)(1)(B) reorganization;

(E) The rules in paragraph (d)(1) and (d)(2)(iv) of this section, as they relate to exchanges by a U.S. person of stock or securities of an acquired corporation for voting stock or securities of a domestic corporation in control of the foreign acquiring corporation in a triangular section 368(a)(1)(B) reorganization; and

(F) The rules in paragraph (d)(2)(vii) of this section.

(iii) The rules of paragraph (a) of this section that apply to transfers of securities in a section 354 or 356 exchange (pursuant to a section 368(a)(1)(E) reorganization or an asset reorganization that is not treated as an indirect stock transfer) that is not subject to section 367(a) apply only to transfers occurring after January 5, 2005 (although taxpayers may apply such provision to transfers of securities occurring on or after July 20, 1998, and on or before January 5, 2005, if done consistently to all transactions).

(iv) The rules in paragraph (d)(1)(v) of this section apply to:

(A) A reorganization described in section 368(a)(1)(C) followed by a controlled asset transfer if such reorganization occurs on or after July 20, 1998;

(B) A reorganization described in section 368(a)(1)(D) followed by a controlled asset transfer if such reorganization occurs after December 9, 2002 (for additional guidance concerning such reorganizations that occur on or after July 20, 1998 and on or before December 9, 2002, see Rev. Rul. 2002-85 (2002-2 C.B. 986) and § 601.601(d)(2) of this chapter); and

(C) A reorganization described in section 368(a)(1)(A), (F), or (G) followed by a controlled asset transfer if such reorganization occurs on or after January 23, 2006.

(v) The rules of paragraph (d)(2)(vi) of this section apply only to transactions occurring on or after January 23, 2006. See § 1.367(a)-3(d)(2)(vi), as contained in 26 CFR Part 1 revised as of April 1, 2005, for transactions occurring on or after July 20, 1998 and before January 23, 2006.

(A) Except as provided in paragraphs (g)(1)(v)(B) of this section and § 1.367(a)–§ 3T(g)(1)(ix), the rules of paragraph (d)(2)(vi) of this section apply only to transactions occurring on or after January 23, 2006. See § 1.367(a)–§ 3(d)(2)(vi), as contained in 26 CFR part 1 revised as of April 1, 2005, for transactions occurring on or after July 20, 1998, and before January 23, 2006.

(B)(1) For purposes of paragraph (d)(2)(vi)(B)(1) of this section as contained in 26 CFR part 1 revised as of April 1, 2007, except as provided in paragraph (g)(1)(v)(B)(3) of this section, the following conditions must be satisfied for transactions occurring on or after December 28, 2007, and before March 18, 2013: The conditions and requirements of section 367(a)(5) and paragraph (g)(1)(v)(B)(2) of this section must be satisfied with respect to the domestic acquired corporation's transfer of assets to the foreign acquiring corporation and those conditions and requirements apply before the application of the exception under paragraph (d)(2)(vi)(B)(1) of this section as contained in 26 CFR part 1 revised as of April 1, 2007.

(2) The domestic acquired corporation is controlled (within the meaning of section 368(c)) by five or fewer (but at least one) domestic corporations (controlling domestic corporations) immediately before the reorganization, appropriate basis adjustments under section 367(a)(5) are made to the stock received by the controlling domestic corporations in the reorganization, and any other conditions as provided in regulations under section 367(a)(5) are satisfied. For purposes of determining whether the domestic acquired corporation is controlled by five or fewer domestic corporations, all members of the same affiliated group within the meaning of section 1504 are treated as one corporation. Any adjustments to stock basis required under section 367(a)(5) must be made to the stock received by the controlling domestic corporation in the reorganization so the appropriate amount of built-in gain in the property transferred by the domestic acquired corporation to the foreign acquiring corporation in the section 361 exchange is reflected in the stock received. The basis adjustment requirement cannot be satisfied by adjusting the basis in stock of the foreign acquiring corporation held by the controlling domestic corporation before the reorganization. To the extent the appropriate amount of built-in gain in the property transferred by the domestic acquired corporation to the foreign acquiring corporation in the section 361 exchange cannot be preserved in the stock received by the controlling domestic corporation in the reorganization, the domestic acquired corporation's transfer of property to the foreign acquiring corporation is subject to section section 367(a) and (d).

(3) For transactions occurring on or after August 19, 2008, and before March 18, 2013, the following condition also applies: To the extent any of the retransferred assets constitute property to which section 367(d) applies, the exception under paragraph (d)(2)(iv)(B)(1)

of this section, as contained in 26 CFR part 1 revised as of April 1, 2007, applies only if the property to which section 367(d) applies is treated as property subject to section 367(a) for purposes of satisfying the conditions and requirements of section 367(a)(5).

(vi) With respect to certain transfers of domestic stock or securities, the rules in paragraph (c) of this section are generally applicable for transfers occurring after January 29, 1997. See §1.367(a)-3(c)(11). For transition rules regarding certain transfers of domestic stock or securities after December 16, 1987, and before January 30, 1997, and transfers of foreign stock or securities after December 16, 1987, and before July 20, 1998, see paragraph (j) of this section.

(vii)(A) Except as provided in this paragraph (g)(1)(vii), the rules of paragraph (e) of this section apply to transfers of stock or securities occurring on or after April 17, 2013. For matters covered in this section for periods before April 17, 2013, but on or after March 13, 2009, see §1.367(a)-3(e) as contained in 26 CFR part 1 revised as of April 1, 2012. For matters covered in this section for periods before March 13, 2009, but on or after March 7, 2007, see §1.367(a)-3T(e) as contained in 26 CFR part 1 revised as of April 1, 2007. For matters covered in this section for periods before March 7, 2007, but on or after July 20, 1998, see §1.367(a)-8(f)(2)(i) as contained in 26 CFR part 1 revised as of April 1, 2006.

(B) Taxpayers may apply the rules of §1.367(a)-3(e) to transfers occurring before March 13, 2009 and during a taxable year for which the period of limitations on assessments under section 6501(a) has not closed, if done consistently to all such transfers occurring during each taxable year. A taxpayer applies the rules of §1.367(a)-3(e) to transfers occurring before March 13, 2009 and during a taxable year for which the period of limitations on assessments under section 6501(a) has not closed, by including the gain recognition agreement, annual certification, or other information filing, that is required as a result of the rules of §1.367(a)-3(e) applying to such a transfer, with an amended tax return for the taxable year in which the transfer occurs that is filed on or before August 10, 2009. A taxpayer that wishes to apply the rules of §1.367(a)-3(e) to transfers occurring before March 13, 2009 and during a taxable year for which the period of limitations on assessments under section 6501(a) has not closed but that fails to meet the filing requirement described in the preceding sentence must request relief for reasonable cause for such failure as provided in §1.367(a)-8.

(viii) Paragraph (a)(2)(iv) of this section applies to exchanges occurring on or after May 17, 2011. For exchanges that occur prior to May 17, 2011, see §1.367(a)-3T(b)(2)(i)(C) as contained in 26 CFR part 1 revised as of April 1, 2011.

(ix) Paragraphs (d)(2)(vi)(B)(1)(i) and (iii), (d)(2)(vi)(B)(2), and (d)(3), *Examples 6B, 6C,* and *9* of this section apply to transfers that occur on or after March 18, 2013. See paragraphs (d)(2)(vi)(B)(1)(i) and (iii), (d)(2)(vi)(B)(2), and (d)(3), *Examples 6B, 6C,* and *9* of this section, as contained in 26 CFR part 1 revised as of April 1, 2012, for transfers that occur on or after January 23, 2006, and before March 18, 2013. Paragraph (d)(2)(vi)(B)(1)(ii) of this section applies to statements that are required to be filed on or after November 19, 2014. See paragraph (d)(2)(vi)(B)(1)(ii) of this section, as contained in 26 CFR part 1 revised as of April 1, 2014, for statements required to be filed on or after March 18, 2013, and before November 19, 2014.

(x) Paragraphs (c)(6)(ii) and (f) of this section apply to statements that are required to be filed on or after November 19, 2014, as well as to requests for relief submitted on or after November 19, 2014.

(2) *Election.*—Notwithstanding paragraphs (g)(1) and (j) of this section, taxpayers may, by timely filing an original or amended return, elect to apply paragraphs (b) and (d) of this section to all transfers of foreign stock or securities occurring after December 16, 1987, and before July 20, 1998, except to the extent that a gain recognition agreement has been triggered prior to July 20, 1998. If an election is made under this paragraph (g)(2), the provisions of §1.367(a)-3T(g) (see 26 CFR part 1, revised April 1, 1998) shall apply, and, for this purpose, the term *substantial portion* under §1.367(a)-3T(g)(3)(iii) (see 26 CFR part 1, revised April 1, 1998) shall be interpreted to mean *substantially all* as defined in section 368(a)(1)(C). In addition, if such an election is made, the taxpayer must apply the rules under section 367(b) and the regulations thereunder to any transfers occurring within that period as if the election to apply §1.367(a)-3(b) and (d) to transfers occurring within that period had not been made, except that in the case of an exchange described in section 351 the taxpayer must apply section 367(b) and the regulations thereunder as if the exchange was described in §7.367(b)-7 of this chapter (as in effect before February 23, 2000; see 26 CFR part 1, revised as of April 1, 1999). For example, if a U.S. person, pursuant to a section 351 exchange, transfers stock of a controlled foreign corporation in which it is a United States shareholder but does not receive back stock of a controlled foreign corporation in which it is a United States shareholder, the U.S. person must include in income under §7.367(b)-7 of this chapter (as in effect

before February 23, 2000; see 26 CFR part 1, revised as of April 1, 1999) the section 1248 amount attributable to the stock exchanged (to the extent that the fair market value of the stock exchanged exceeds its adjusted basis). Such inclusion is required even though §7.367(b)-7 of this chapter (as in effect before February 23, 2000; see 26 CFR part 1, revised as of April 1, 1999), by its terms, did not apply to section 351 exchanges.

(h) *Former 10-year gain recognition agreements.*—If a taxpayer elects to apply the rules of this section to all prior transfers occurring after December 16, 1987, any 10-year gain recognition agreement that remains in effect (has not been triggered in full) on July 20, 1998 will be considered by the Internal Revenue Service to be a 5-year gain recognition agreement with a duration of five full taxable years following the close of the taxable year of the initial transfer.

(i) [Reserved].

(j) *Transition rules regarding certain transfers of domestic or foreign stock or securities after December 16, 1987, and prior to July 20, 1998.*— (1) *Scope.*—Transfers of domestic stock or securities described under section 367(a) that occurred after December 16, 1987, and prior to April 17, 1994, and transfers of foreign stock or securities described under section 367(a) that occur after December 16, 1987, and prior to July 20, 1998 are subject to the rules contained in section 367(a) and the regulations thereunder, as modified by the rules contained in paragraph (j)(2) of this section. For transfers of domestic stock or securities described under section 367(a) that occurred after April 17, 1994 and before January 30, 1997, see Temporary Income Regulations under section 367(a) in effect at the time of the transfer (§1.367(a)-3T(a) and (c), 26 CFR part 1, revised April 1, 1996) and paragraph (c)(11) of this section. For transfers of domestic stock or securities described under section 367(a) that occur after January 29, 1997, see §1.367(a)-3(c).

(2) *Transfers of domestic or foreign stock or securities: additional substantive rules.*—(i) *Rule for less than 5-percent shareholders.*—Unless paragraph (j)(2)(iii) of this section applies (in the case of domestic stock or securities) or paragraph (j)(2)(iv) of this section applies (in the case of foreign stock or securities), a U.S. transferor that transfers stock or securities of a domestic or foreign corporation in an exchange described in section 367(a) and owns less than 5 percent of both the total voting power and the total value of the stock of the transferee foreign corporation immediately after the transfer (taking into account the attribution rules of section 958) is not subject to section 367(a)(1) and is not required to enter into a gain recognition agreement.

(ii) *Rule for 5-percent shareholders.*—Unless paragraph (j)(2)(iii) or (iv) of this section applies, a U.S. transferor that transfers domestic or foreign stock or securities in an exchange described in section 367(a) and owns at least 5 percent of either the total voting power or the total value of the stock of the transferee foreign corporation immediately after the transfer (taking into account the attribution rules under section 958) may qualify for nonrecognition treatment by filing a gain recognition agreement in accordance with §1.367(a)-3T(g) in effect prior to July 20, 1998 (see 26 CFR part 1, revised April 1, 1998) for a duration of 5 or 10 years. The duration is 5 years if the U.S. transferor (5-percent shareholder) determines that all U.S. transferors, in the aggregate, own less than 50 percent of both the total voting power and the total value of the transferee foreign corporation immediately after the transfer. The duration is 10 years in all other cases. See, however, §1.367(a)-3(h). If a 5-percent shareholder fails to properly enter into a gain recognition agreement, the exchange is taxable to such shareholder under section 367(a)(1).

(iii) *Gain recognition agreement option not available to controlling U.S. transferor if U.S. stock or securities are transferred.*—Notwithstanding the provisions of paragraph (j)(2)(ii) of this section, in no event will any exception to section 367(a)(1) apply to the transfer of stock or securities of a domestic corporation where the U.S. transferor owns (applying the attribution rules of section 958) more than 50 percent of either the total voting power or the total value of the stock of the transferee foreign corporation immediately after the transfer (i.e., the use of a gain recognition agreement to qualify for nonrecognition treatment is unavailable in this case).

(iv) *Loss of United States shareholder status in the case of a transfer of foreign stock.*—Notwithstanding the provisions of paragraphs (j)(2)(i) and (ii) of this section, in no event will any exception to section 367(a)(1) apply to the transfer of stock of a foreign corporation in which the U.S. transferor is a United States shareholder (as defined in §7.367(b)-2(b) of this chapter (as in effect before February 23, 2000; see 26 CFR part 1, revised as of April 1, 1999) or section 953(c)) unless the U.S. transferor receives back stock in a controlled foreign corporation (as defined in section 953(c), section 957(a) or section 957(b)) as to which the U.S. transferor is a United States shareholder immediately after the transfer.

(k) [Reserved]. For further guidance, see §1.367-3T(k). [Reg. §1.367(a)-3.]

☐ [*T.D. 8702, 12-27-96. Amended by T.D. 8770, 6-18-98 (corrected 3-31-99); T.D. 8850, 12-27-99; T.D. 8862, 1-21-2000; T.D. 9243, 1-23-2006; T.D. 9250, 2-17-2006; T.D. 9311, 2-1-2007 T.D. 9400,* 5-23-2008; *T.D. 9446, 2-9-2009 (corrected 3-26-2009); T.D. 9444, 2-10-2009; T.D. 9526, 5-17-2011; T.D. 9614, 3-18-2013 (corrected 8-19-2020); T.D. 9615, 3-18-2013; T.D. 9704, 11-18-2014; T.D. 9760, 3-18-2016; T.D. 9761, 4-4-2016; T.D. 9803, 12-15-2016 and T.D. 9834, 7-11-2018.*]

⟫→ *Caution: The Treasury Department has identified Reg. §1.367(a)-4, as amended by T.D. 9803, as a significant tax regulation that imposes an undue financial burden on U.S. taxpayers and/or adds undue complexity to the federal tax laws, pursuant to Executive Order 13789 (issued April 21, 2017) (Notice 2017-38, I.R.B. 2017-30). In a subsequent report, issued October 4, 2017, Treasury recommended planned actions that would reduce the burden of these regulations.*

[Reg. §1.367(a)-4]

§1.367(a)-4. Special rule applicable to U.S. depreciated property.—(a) *Depreciated property used in the United States.*—(1) *In general.*—A U.S. person that transfers U.S. depreciated property (as defined in paragraph (a)(2) of this section) to a foreign corporation in an exchange described in section 367(a)(1), must include in its gross income for the taxable year in which the transfer occurs ordinary income equal to the gain realized that would have been includible in the transferor's gross income as ordinary income under section 617(d)(1), 1245(a), 1250(a), 1252(a), 1254(a), or 1255(a), whichever is applicable, if at the time of the transfer the U.S. person had sold the property at its fair market value. Recapture of depreciation under this paragraph (a) is required regardless of whether the exception to section 367(a)(1) provided by §1.367(a)-2(a)(2) applies to the transfer of the U.S. depreciated property. However, the transfer of the U.S. depreciated property may qualify for the exception with respect to realized gain that is not included in ordinary income pursuant to this paragraph (a).

(2) *U.S. depreciated property.*—U.S. depreciated property subject to the rules of this paragraph (a) is any property that—

(i) Is either mining property (as defined in section 617(f)(2)), section 1245 property (as defined in section 1245(a)(3)), section 1250 property (as defined in section 1250(c)), farm land (as defined in section 1252(a)(2)), section 1254 property (as defined in section 1254(a)(3)), or section 126 property (as defined in section 1255(a)(2)); and

(ii) Has been used in the United States or has been described in section 168(g)(4) before its transfer.

(3) *Property used within and without the United States.*—(i) If U.S. depreciated property has been used partly within and partly without the United States, then the amount required to be included in ordinary income pursuant to this paragraph (a) is reduced to an amount determined in accordance with the following formula:

$$\text{Full recapture amount} \times \frac{\text{U.S use}}{\text{Total use}}$$

(ii) For purposes of the fraction in paragraph (a)(3)(i) of this section, the "full recapture amount" is the amount that would otherwise be included in the transferor's income under paragraph (a)(1) of this section. "U.S. use" is the number of months that the property either was used within the United States or has been described in section 168(g)(4), and was subject to depreciation by the transferor or a related person. "Total use" is the total number of months that the property was used (or available for use), and subject to depreciation, by the transferor or a related person. For purposes of this paragraph (a)(3), property is not considered to have been in use outside of the United States during any period in which such property was, for purposes of section 168, treated as property not used predominantly outside the United States pursuant to section 168(g)(4). For purposes of this paragraph (a)(3), the term "related person" has the meaning set forth in §1.367(d)-1(h).

(b) *Effective/applicability dates.*—The rules of this section apply to transfers occurring on or after September 14, 2015, and to transfers occurring before September 14, 2015, resulting from entity classification elections made under §301.7701-3 that are filed on or after September 14, 2015. For transfers occurring before this section is applicable, see §§1.367(a)-4 and 1.367(a)-4T as contained in 26 CFR part 1 revised as of April 1, 2016. [Reg. §1.367(a)-4.]

☐ [*T.D. 9525, 5-5-2011. Amended by T.D. 9803, 12-15-2016.*]

⟫→ *Caution: The Treasury Department has identified Reg. §1.367(a)-5, as amended by T.D. 9803, as a significant tax regulation that imposes an undue financial burden on U.S. taxpayers and/or adds undue complexity to the federal tax laws, pursuant to Executive Order 13789 (issued April 21, 2017) (Notice 2017-38, I.R.B. 2017-30). In a subsequent report, issued October 4, 2017, Treasury recommended planned actions that would reduce the burden of these regulations.*

[Reg. §1.367(a)-5]

§1.367(a)-5. [Reserved].

☐ [*T.D. 9525, 5-5-2011. Removed and reserved by T.D. 9803, 12-15-2016.*]

⟫→ *Caution: The Treasury Department has identified Reg. §1.367(a)-6, as amended by T.D. 9803, as a significant tax regulation that imposes an undue financial burden on U.S. taxpayers and/or adds undue complexity to the federal tax laws, pursuant to Executive Order 13789 (issued April 21, 2017) (Notice 2017-38, I.R.B. 2017-30). In a subsequent report, issued October 4, 2017, Treasury recommended planned actions that would reduce the burden of these regulations.*

[Reg. §1.367(a)-6]

§1.367(a)-6. Transfer of foreign branch with previously deducted losses.—(a) through (b)(1) [Reserved]. For further guidance, see §1.367(a)-6T(a) through (b)(1).

(b)(2) *No active conduct exception.*—The rules of this paragraph (b) apply regardless of whether any of the assets of the foreign branch satisfy the active trade or business exception of §1.367(a)-2(a)(2).

(c)(1) [Reserved]. For further guidance, see §1.367(a)-6T(c)(1).

(2) *Gain limitation.*—The gain required to be recognized under paragraph (b)(1) of this section will not exceed the aggregate amount of gain realized on the transfer of all branch assets (without regard to the transfer of any assets on which loss is realized but not recognized).

(3) [Reserved].

(4) *Transfers of certain intangible property.*—Gain realized on the transfer of intangible property (computed with reference to the fair market value of the intangible property as of the date of the transfer) that is an asset of a foreign branch is taken into account in computing the limitation on loss recapture under paragraph (c)(2) of this section. For rules relating to the crediting of gain recognized under this section against income deemed to arise by operation of section 367(d), see §1.367(d)-1(g)(3).

(d) through (i) [Reserved]. For further guidance, see §1.367(a)-6T(d) through (i).

(j) *Effective/applicability dates.*—The rules of this section apply to transfers occurring on or after September 14, 2015, and to transfers occurring before September 14, 2015, resulting from entity classification elections made under §301.7701-3 that are filed on or after September 14, 2015. For transfers occurring before this section is applicable, see §1.367(a)-6T as contained in 26 CFR part 1 revised as of April 1, 2016. [Reg. §1.367(a)-6.]

☐ [*T.D. 9760, 3-18-2016. Amended by T.D. 9803, 12-15-2016.*]

>>>→ *Caution: The Treasury Department has identified Temporary Reg. §1.367(a)-6T, as amended by T.D. 9803, as a significant tax regulation that imposes an undue financial burden on U.S. taxpayers and/or adds undue complexity to the federal tax laws, pursuant to Executive Order 13789 (issued April 21, 2017) (Notice 2017-38, I.R.B. 2017-30). In a subsequent report, issued October 4, 2017, Treasury recommended planned actions that would reduce the burden of these regulations.*

[Reg. §1.367(a)-6T]

§1.367(a)-6T. Transfer of foreign branch with previously deducted losses (temporary).—(a) *In general.*—This section provides special rules relating to the transfer of the assets of a foreign branch with previously deducted losses. Paragraph (b) of this section provides generally that such losses must be recaptured by the recognition of the gain realized on the transfer. Paragraph (c) of this section sets forth rules concerning the character of, and limitations on, the gain required to be recognized. Paragraph (d) of this section defines the term "previously deducted losses." Paragraph (e) of this section describes certain reductions that are made to the previously deducted losses before they are taken into income under this section. Finally, paragraph (g) of this section defines the term "foreign branch."

(b) *Recognition of gain required.*—**(1)** *In general.*—If a U.S. person transfers any assets of a foreign branch to a foreign corporation in an exchange described in section 367(a)(1), then the transferor shall recognize gain equal to—

(i) The sum of the previously deducted branch ordinary losses as defined and reduced in paragraphs (d) and (e) of this section; and

(ii) The sum of the previously deducted branch capital losses as defined and reduced in paragraphs (d) and (e) of this section.

(2) [Reserved].

(c) *Special rules concerning gain recognized.*—**(1)** *Character and source of gain.*—The gain described in paragraph (b)(1)(i) of this section shall be treated as ordinary income of the transferor, and the gain described in paragraph (b)(1)(ii) of this section shall be treated as long-term capital gain of the transferor. Gain that is recognized pursuant to the rules of this section shall be treated as income from sources outside the United States. Such recognized gain shall be treated as foreign oil and gas extraction income (as defined in section 907) in the same proportion that previously deducted foreign oil and gas extraction losses bore to the total amount of previously deducted losses.

(2) [Reserved].

(3) *Foreign goodwill and going concern value.*—For purposes of this section, the assets of a foreign branch shall include foreign goodwill and going concern value related to the business of the foreign branch, as defined in §1.367(a)-1T(d)(5)(iii). Thus, gain realized upon the transfer of the foreign goodwill or going concern value of a foreign branch to a foreign corporation will be taken into account in computing the limitation on loss recapture under paragraph (c)(2) of this section.

(4) [Reserved].

(d) *Previously deducted losses.*—**(1)** *In general.*—This paragraph (d) provides rules for determining, for purposes of paragraph (b)(1) of this section, the previously deducted losses of a foreign branch any of whose assets are transferred to a foreign corporation in an exchange described in section 367(a)(1). Initially, the two previously deducted losses of a foreign branch for a taxable year are the total ordinary loss ("previously deducted branch ordinary loss") and the total capital loss ("previously deducted branch capital loss") that were realized by the foreign branch in that taxable year (a "branch loss year") prior to the transfer and that were or will be reflected on a U.S. income tax return of the transferor. The previously deducted branch ordinary loss for each branch loss year is reduced by expired net ordinary losses under paragraph (d)(2) of this section, while the previously deducted capital loss for each loss year is reduced by expired net capital losses under paragraph (d)(3) of this section. For each branch loss year, the remaining previously deducted branch ordinary loss and the remaining previously deducted branch capital loss are then reduced, proceeding from the first branch loss year to the last branch loss year, to reflect expired foreign tax credits under paragraph (d)(4) of this section. The reductions are made in the order of the taxable years in which the foreign tax credits arose. Finally, similar reductions are made to reflect expired investment credits under paragraph (d)(5) of this section.

(2) *Reduction by expired net ordinary loss.*—**(i)** *In general.*—The previously deducted branch ordinary loss for each branch loss year shall be reduced under this paragraph (d)(2) by the amount of any expired net ordinary loss with respect to that branch loss year. Expired net ordinary losses arising in years other than the branch loss year shall reduce the previously deducted branch ordinary loss for the branch loss year only to the extent that the previously deducted branch ordinary loss exceeds the net operating loss, if any, incurred by the transferor in the branch loss year. The previously deducted branch ordinary losses shall be reduced proceeding from the first branch loss year to the last branch loss year. For each branch loss year, expired net operating losses shall be applied to reduce the previously deducted branch ordinary loss for that year in the order in which the expired net ordinary losses arose.

(ii) *Existence of expired net ordinary loss.*—An expired net ordinary loss exists with respect to a branch loss year to the extent that—

(A) The transferor incurred a net operating loss (within the meaning of section 172(c));

(B) That net operating loss arose in the branch loss year or was available for carryover or carryback to the branch loss year under section 172(b)(1);

(C) That net operating loss has neither given rise to a net operating loss deduction (within the meaning of section 172(a)) for any taxable year prior to the year of the transfer, nor given rise to a reduction of any previously deducted branch ordinary loss (pursuant to paragraph (d)(2) of this section) of any foreign branch of the transferor upon a previous transfer to a foreign corporation; and

(D) The period during which the transferor may claim a net operating loss deduction with respect to that net operating loss has expired.

(3) *Reduction by expired net capital loss.*—**(i)** *In general.*—The previously deducted branch capital loss for each branch loss year shall be reduced under this paragraph (d)(3) by the amount of any expired net capital loss with respect to that branch loss year. Expired net capital losses arising in years other than the branch loss year shall reduce the previously deducted branch capital loss for the branch loss year only to the extent that the previously deducted branch capital loss exceeds the net capital loss, if any, incurred by the transferor in the branch loss year. The previously deducted branch capital losses shall be reduced proceeding from the first branch loss year to the last branch loss year. For each branch loss year, expired net capital losses shall be applied to reduce the previously deducted branch capital loss for that year in the order in which the expired net capital losses arose.

(ii) *Existence of expired net capital loss.*—An expired net capital loss exists with respect to a branch loss year to the extent that—

(A) The transferor incurred a net capital loss (within the meaning of section 1222(10));

(B) That net capital loss arose in the branch loss year or was available for carryover or carryback to the branch loss year under section 1212;

(C) That net capital loss has neither been allowed for any taxable year prior to the year of the transfer, nor given rise to a reduction of any previously deducted branch capital loss (pursuant to paragraph (d)(3) of this section) of any foreign branch of the transferor upon any previous transfer to a foreign corporation; and

(D) The period during which the transferor may claim a capital loss deduction with respect to that net capital loss has expired.

(4) *Reduction for expired foreign tax credits.*—**(i)** *In general.*—The previously deducted branch ordinary loss and the previously deducted branch capital loss for each branch loss year remaining after the reductions described in paragraph (d)(2) and (3) of this section shall be further reduced under this paragraph (d)(4) proportionately by the amount of any expired foreign tax credit loss equivalent with respect to that branch loss year. The previously deducted branch losses shall be reduced proceeding from the first branch loss year to the last branch loss year. For each branch loss year, expired foreign tax credit loss equivalents shall be applied to reduce the previously deducted branch loss for the year in the order in which the expired foreign tax credits arose.

(ii) *Existence of foreign tax credit loss equivalent.*—A foreign tax credit loss equivalent exists with respect to a branch loss year if—

(A) The transferor paid, accrued, or is deemed under section 902 or 960 to have paid creditable foreign taxes in a taxable year;

(B) The creditable foreign taxes were paid, accrued, or deemed paid in the branch loss year or were available for carryover or carryback to the branch loss year under section 904(c);

(C) No foreign tax credit with respect to the foreign taxes paid, accrued, or deemed paid has been taken because of the operation of section 904(a) or similar limitations provided by the Code or an applicable treaty, and such taxes have not given rise to a reduction (pursuant to this paragraph (d)(5)) of any previously deducted branch loss of the foreign branch for a prior taxable year or of any previously deducted branch losses of any foreign branch of the transferor upon a prior transfer to a foreign corporation; and

(D) The period during which the transferor may claim a foreign tax credit for the foreign taxes paid, accrued, or deemed paid has expired.

(iii) *Amount of foreign tax credit loss equivalent.*—The amount of the foreign tax credit loss equivalent for the branch loss year with respect to the creditable foreign taxes described in paragraph (d)(4)(ii) of this section is the amount of those creditable foreign taxes divided by the highest rate of tax to which the transferor was subject in the loss year.

(5) *Reduction for expired investment credits.*—(i) *In general.*—The previously deducted branch ordinary loss and the previously deducted branch capital loss for each branch loss year shall be further reduced under this paragraph (d)(5) proportionately by the amount of any expired investment credit loss equivalent with respect to that branch year. The previously deducted branch losses shall be reduced proceeding from the first branch loss year to the last branch loss year. For each branch loss year, expired investment credit loss equivalents shall be applied to reduce the previously deducted branch loss for that year in the order in which the expired investment credits were earned.

(ii) *Existence of investment credit loss equivalent.*—An investment credit loss equivalent exists with respect to a branch loss year if—

(A) The transferor earned an investment credit (within the meaning of section 46(a)) in a taxable year;

(B) The investment credit was earned in the branch loss year or was available for carryover or carryback to the branch loss year under section 39;

(C) The investment credit earned by the transferor in the credit year has been denied by section 38(a) or by similar provisions of the Code and has not given rise to a reduction (pursuant to this paragraph (d)(5)) of any previously deducted branch loss of the foreign branch for a preceding taxable year or of the previously deducted losses of any foreign branch of the transferor upon any previous transfer to a foreign corporation; and

(D) The period during which the transferor may claim the investment credit has expired.

(iii) *Amount of investment tax credit loss equivalent.*—The amount of the investment credit loss equivalent for the branch loss year with respect to the investment credit described in paragraph (d)(5)(ii) of this section is 85 percent of the amount of that investment credit divided by the highest rate of tax to which the transferor was subject in the loss year.

(e) *Amounts that reduce previously deducted losses subject to recapture.*—(1) *In general.*—This paragraph (e) describes five amounts that reduce the sum of the previously deducted branch ordinary losses and the sum of the previously deducted branch capital losses before they are taken into income under paragraph (b) of this section. Amounts representing ordinary income shall be applied to reduce first the sum of the previously deducted branch ordinary losses to the extent thereof, and then the sum of the previously deducted branch

capital losses to the extent thereof. Similarly, amounts representing capital gains shall be applied to reduce first the sum of the previously deducted branch capital losses and then the sum of the previously deducted branch ordinary losses.

(2) *Taxable income.*—The previously deducted losses shall be reduced by any taxable income of the foreign branch recognized through the close of the taxable year of the transfer, whether before or after any taxable year in which losses were incurred.

(3) *Amounts currently recaptured under section 904(f)(3).*—The previously deducted losses shall be reduced by the amount recognized under section 904(f)(3) on account of the transfer.

(4) [Reserved.]

(5) *Amounts previously recaptured under section 904(f)(3).*—(i) *In general.*—The previously deducted branch losses shall be reduced by the portion of any amount recognized under section 904(f)(3) upon a previous transfer of property that was attributable to the losses of the foreign branch, provided that the amount did not reduce any gain otherwise required to be recognized under section 367(a)(3)(C) and this section (or Revenue Ruling 78-201, 1978-1 C.B. 91).

(ii) *Portion attributable to the losses of the foreign branch.*—(A) *Branch property.*—The full amount recognized under section 904(f)(3) upon a previous transfer of property of the branch shall be treated as attributable to the losses of the foreign branch.

(B) *Non-branch property.*—The portion of the amount previously recognized under section 904(f)(3) upon a transfer of non-branch property that was attributable to the losses of the foreign branch shall be the sum, over the taxable years in which the transferor sustained an overall foreign loss some portion of which was recaptured on the disposition, of the recaptured portions of those overall foreign losses after multiplication by the following fraction:

$$\frac{\text{Losses of the foreign branch for the year}}{\text{All foreign losses for the year}}$$

For purposes of this fraction, the term "losses of the foreign branch for the year" means the losses of the foreign branch that were taken into account under section 904(f)(2) in determining the amount of the transferor's overall foreign loss for the year, and the term "all foreign losses for the year" means all of the losses of the transferor that were taken into account under section 904(f)(2).

(6) *Amounts previously recognized under the rules of this section.*—The previously deducted losses shall be reduced by the amounts previously recognized under the rules of this section upon a previous transfer of assets of the foreign branch.

(f) *Example.*—The rules of paragraphs (b) through (e) of this section are illustrated by the following example.

Example. (i) *Facts.* X, a U.S. corporation, is a calendar year taxpayer. On January 1, 1981, X established a branch in foreign country A to manufacture and sell X's products in country A. On July 1, 1986, X organized corporation Y, a country A subsidiary, and transferred to Y all of the assets of its country A branch, including goodwill and going concern value. During the period from January 1, 1981, through July 1, 1986, X's country A branch earned income and incurred losses in the following amounts:

Country A branch

Year	Ordinary income (loss)	Capital gain (loss)
1981	(200)	0
1982	(300)	(100)
1983	(400)	0
1984	200	0
1985	(100)	0
1986	50	0

At the time of the transfer of X's country A branch assets to Y, those assets had a fair market value of $2,500 and an adjusted basis of $1,000. For each of the assets, fair market value exceeded adjusted basis. X had no net capital loss or unused investment credit during any taxable year relevant to the transfer. In 1984, X incurred a net operating loss of $400, $200 of which was carried back to prior years. An additional $50 of the 1984 net operating loss was carried over to 1985. The remaining $150 of the 1984 net operating loss was not used in any year prior to the transfer. In 1979, X paid creditable foreign taxes of $330 that could not be claimed as a credit in that year or any earlier year because of section 904. Of those foreign taxes, $100 were carried over and claimed as a credit in 1983, but the remaining $230 were not used in any year prior to the transfer. X was not required to recognize any gain under section 904(f)(3) on account of the 1986 transfer or any prior transfer. X was not required to recognize gain upon the transfer under section 367(a) (other than by reason of the provisions of this section).

(ii) *Previously deducted losses.* The previously deducted losses of X's country A branch are $575 of ordinary losses and $25 of capital losses, computed as follows: Initially, the branch has previously deducted ordinary losses of $1,000 ($200 + $300 + $400 + $100), and previously deducted capital losses of $100. (See paragraph (d)(1) of this section.)

(iii) *Expired losses and credits.* Under the facts of this example, there are no reductions for expired net ordinary losses or expired net capital losses under paragraph (d)(2) or (3) of this section. However, the previously deducted losses are reduced proceeding from the first branch loss year to the last branch loss year to reflect the expired foreign tax credit from 1979. The amount of the foreign tax credit loss equivalent with respect to 1981 is $500 ($230 / .46). It reduces the previously deducted losses for 1981 proportionately. Thus, the previously deducted ordinary loss for 1981 is reduced from $200 to $0. (See paragraph (d)(4) of this section.) The amount of the foreign tax credit loss equivalent with respect to 1982 is $300 ($500 – $200, i.e., $138 / .46). (See paragraph (d)(4)(ii)(C) of this section.) It reduces the previously deducted losses for 1982 proportionately. Thus, the previously deducted ordinary loss for 1982 is reduced from $300 to $75, and the previously deducted capital loss for 1982 is reduced from $100 to $25.

(iv) *Further reductions.* The previously deducted ordinary losses of $575 and the previously deducted capital losses of $25 are reduced by the taxable income earned by the branch prior to the date of the transfer ($250). (See paragraph (e)(2) of this section.) Since that income was ordinary income, it is applied first to reduce the previously deducted ordinary losses of $575 to $325. (See paragraph (e)(1) of this section.)

(v) *Recapture.* Since the gain realized by X upon its transfer of the branch assets to Y exceeds the sum of the previously deducted branch losses as defined and reduced above ($325 + $25), the limitation in paragraph (c)(2) of this section does not apply. Thus, X is required to recognize $325 of ordinary income and $25 of long-term capital gain upon the transfer. (See paragraph (b) and (c)(1) of this section.)

(g) *Definition of foreign branch.*—(1) *In general.*—For purposes of this section, the term "foreign branch" means an integral business operation carried on by a U.S. person outside the United States. Whether the activities of a U.S. person outside the United States constitute a foreign branch operation must be determined under all the facts and circumstances. Evidence of the existence of a foreign branch includes, but is not limited to, the existence of a separate set of books and records, and the existence of an office or other fixed place of business used by employees or officers of the U.S. person in carrying out business activities outside the United States. Activities outside the United States shall be deemed to constitute a foreign branch for purposes of this section if the activities constitute a permanent establishment under the terms of a treaty between the United States and the country in which the activities are carried out. Any U.S. person may be treated as having a foreign branch for purposes of this section, whether that person is a corporation, partnership, trust, estate, or individual.

(2) *More than one branch.*—If a U.S. person carries on more than one branch operation outside the United States, then the rules of this section must be separately applied with respect to each foreign branch that is transferred to a foreign corporation. Thus, the previously deducted losses of one branch may not be offset, for purposes of determining the gain required to be recognized under the rules of this section, by the income of another branch that is also transferred to a foreign corporation. Similarly, the losses of one branch shall not be recaptured upon a transfer of the assets of a separate branch. Whether the foreign activities of a U.S. person are carried out through more than one branch must be determined under all of the facts and circumstances. In general, a separate branch exists if a particular group of activities is sufficiently integrated to constitute a single business that could be operated as an independent enterprise. For purposes of determining the combination of activities that constitute a branch operation as defined in this paragraph (g), the nominal relationship among those activities shall not be controlling. Factors suggesting that nominally separate business operations constitute a single foreign branch include a substantial identity of products, customers, operational facilities, operational processes, accounting and record-keeping functions, management, employees, distribution channels, or sales and purchasing forces. For examples of the applica-

tion of the principles of this paragraph (g)(2), see Revenue Ruling 81-82, 1981-1 C.B. 127.

(3) *Consolidated group.*—For purposes of this section, the activities of each of two domestic corporations outside the United States will be considered to constitute a single foreign branch if—

(i) The two corporations are members of the same consolidated group of corporations; and

(ii) The activities of the two corporations in the aggregate would constitute a single foreign branch if conducted by a single corporation.

Notwithstanding the preceding rule of this paragraph (g)(3), gains of a foreign branch of a domestic corporation arising in a year in which that corporation did not file a consolidated return with a second domestic corporation shall not be applied to reduce the previously deducted losses of a foreign branch of the second corporation (but may be applied to reduce such losses of the foreign branch of the first corporation) upon the transfer of the two branches to a foreign corporation, even though the two domestic corporations file a consolidated return for the year in which the transfer occurs and the two branches are considered at that time to constitute a single foreign branch. For an example of the application of the principles of this paragraph (g)(3), see Revenue Ruling 81-89, 1981-1 C.B. 129.

(4) *Property not transferred.*—A U.S. transferor's failure to transfer any property of a foreign branch shall be irrelevant to the determination of the previously deducted losses of the branch subject to recapture under the rules of this section. Thus, if the activities with respect to untransferred property constituted a part of the branch operation under the rules of this paragraph (g), then the losses generated by those activities shall be subject to recapture, notwithstanding the failure to transfer the property. For an example of the application of the principles of this paragraph (g)(4), see Revenue Ruling 80-247, 1980-2 C.B. 127, relating to property abandoned by the U.S. transferor.

(h) *Anti-abuse rule.*—If—

(1) A U.S. person transfers property of a foreign branch to a domestic corporation for a principal purpose of avoiding the effect of this section; and

(2) The domestic corporation thereafter transfers the property of the foreign branch to a foreign corporation,

then, solely for purposes of this section, that U.S. person shall be treated as having transferred the property of the branch directly to the foreign corporation. A U.S. person shall be presumed to have transferred property of a foreign branch for a principal purpose of avoiding the effect of this section if the property is transferred to the domestic corporation less than two years prior to the domestic corporation's transfer of the property to a foreign corporation. This presumption may be rebutted by clear evidence that the subsequent transfer of the property was not contemplated at the time of the initial transfer to the domestic corporation and that avoidance of the effect of this section was not a principal purpose for the transaction. A transfer may have more than one principal purpose.

(i) *Basis adjustments.*—Basis adjustments reflecting gain recognized pursuant to this section shall be made as described in § 1.367(a)-1T(b)(4)(ii).

(j) [Reserved]. [Temporary Reg. § 1.367(a)-6T]

☐ [*T.D.* 8087, 5-15-86. *Amended by T.D.* 9615, 3-18-2013, *T.D.* 9760, 3-18-2016 *and T.D.* 9803, 12-15-2016.]

⟫⟫→ *Caution: The Treasury Department has identified Reg. § 1.367(a)-7, as amended by T.D. 9803, as a significant tax regulation that imposes an undue financial burden on U.S. taxpayers and/or adds undue complexity to the federal tax laws, pursuant to Executive Order 13789 (issued April 21, 2017) (Notice 2017-38, I.R.B. 2017-30). In a subsequent report, issued October 4, 2017, Treasury recommended planned actions that would reduce the burden of these regulations.*

[Reg. § 1.367(a)-7]

§ 1.367(a)-7. Outbound transfers of property described in section 361(a) or (b).—(a) *Scope and purpose.*—This section provides rules under section 367(a)(5) that apply to the transfer of certain property (including stock or securities) by a domestic corporation (U.S. transferor) to a foreign corporation (foreign acquiring corporation) in a section 361 exchange. This section applies only to the transfer of section 367(a) property. See section 367(d) for rules applicable to transfers of section 367(d) property. Paragraph (b) of this section provides the general rule requiring the recognition of gain on the transfer of section 367(a) property, while paragraph (c) of this section provides an elective exception to the general rule that is available if certain requirements are satisfied. Paragraph (d) of this section provides rules for applying the elective exception to a section 361 exchange followed by successive distributions to which section 355 applies. Paragraph (e) of this section provides rules for recognizing gain on section 367(a) property, not willful relief provisions, an anti-abuse rule, and special rules that take into account income inclusions under § 1.367(b)-4 and gain recognition under § 1.367(a)-6. Paragraph

(f) of this section provides definitions, and paragraph (g) of this section provides examples. Paragraph (h) of this section provides applicable cross-references, paragraph (i) of this section is reserved, and paragraph (j) of this section provides effective/applicability dates.

(b) *General rule.*—(1) *Nonrecognition exchanges enumerated in section 367(a)(1).*—Except to the extent provided in paragraphs (b)(2) and (c) of this section, the exceptions to section 367(a)(1) provided in section 367(a) and the regulations under that section do not apply to a transfer of section 367(a) property by a U.S. transferor to a foreign acquiring corporation in a section 361 exchange, and the U.S. transferor shall recognize any gain (but not loss) realized with respect to the section 367(a) property under section 367(a)(1). Realized gain is recognized pursuant to the prior sentence notwithstanding the application of any other nonrecognition provision enumerated in section 367(a)(1) to the transfer (such as section 351 or 354).

(2) *Nonrecognition exchanges not enumerated in section 367(a)(1).*—To the extent a transfer of items of property described in paragraph

(b)(1) of this section also qualifies for nonrecognition under a provision that is not enumerated in section 367(a)(1) (such as section 1036), the U.S. transferor recognizes gain or loss realized on the transfer of such items of property, but the amount of loss recognized on the property shall not exceed the amount of gain recognized on the property. See section 337(d).

(c) *Elective exception.*—Except to the extent provided in paragraph (d) of this section, paragraph (b) of this section does not apply to the transfer of section 367(a) property by a U.S. transferor to a foreign acquiring corporation in a section 361 exchange if the conditions of paragraphs (c)(1), (c)(2), (c)(3), and (c)(4) of this section are satisfied, and an election to apply the exception provided by this paragraph (c) is made in the manner provided by paragraph (c)(5) of this section. If this paragraph (c) applies to the section 361 exchange, see, for example, §§ 1.367(a)-2, 1.367(a)-3, 1.367(a)-4, or 1.367(a)-6, as applicable, for additional requirements that must be satisfied in order for the U.S. transferor to not recognize gain under section 367(a)(1) on the transfer of section 367(a) property in the section 361 exchange. Nothing in this section provides for the nonrecognition of gain not otherwise permitted under another provision of the Internal Revenue Code (Code) or the regulations.

(1) *Control.*—Immediately before the reorganization, the U.S. transferor is controlled (within the meaning of section 368(c)) by five or fewer, but at least one, control group members. For illustrations of this rule, see paragraph (g) of this section, *Example 4* and *Example 5.*

(2) *Gain recognition.*—(i) *Non-control group members.*—The U.S. transferor recognizes gain equal to the product of the inside gain multiplied by the aggregate ownership interest percentage of all non-control group members, reduced (but not below zero) by the sum of the amounts described in paragraphs (c)(2)(i)(A), (c)(2)(i)(B), and (c)(2)(i)(C) of this section.

(A) Gain recognized with respect to stock or securities under § 1.367(a)-3(e)(3)(iii)(B) (including any portion treated as a deemed dividend under section 1248(a));

(B) Gain recognized with respect to stock or securities under § 1.367(a)-6 (including any portion treated as a deemed dividend under section 1248(a)) attributable to non-control group members (as determined pursuant to § 1.367(a)-7(e)(5)); and

(C) A deemed dividend included in income under § 1.367(b)-4 attributable to non-control group members (as determined pursuant to § 1.367(a)-7(e)(4)).

(ii) *Control group members.*—With respect to each control group member, the U.S. transferor recognizes gain equal to the amount, if any, by which the amount described in paragraph (c)(2)(ii)(A) of this section exceeds the amount described in paragraph (c)(2)(ii)(B) of this section.

(A) The product of the inside gain multiplied by such control group member's ownership interest percentage, reduced (but not below zero) by the sum of the amounts described in paragraphs (c)(2)(ii)(A)(*1*), (c)(2)(ii)(A)(*2*), and (c)(2)(ii)(A)(*3*) of this section (attributable inside gain).

(*1*) Gain recognized with respect to stock or securities under § 1.367(a)-3(e)(3)(iii)(C) (including any portion treated as a deemed dividend under section 1248(a)) attributable to the control group member;

(*2*) Gain recognized with respect to stock or securities under § 1.367(a)-6 (including any portion treated as a deemed dividend under section 1248(a)) attributable to the control group member (as determined pursuant to § 1.367(a)-7(e)(5)); and

(*3*) A deemed dividend included in income under § 1.367(b)-4 attributable to the control group member (as determined pursuant to § 1.367(a)-7(e)(4)).

(B) The product of the section 367(a) percentage multiplied by the fair market value of the stock received by the U.S. transferor in the section 361 exchange and distributed to the control group member under section 354, 355, or 356.

(iii) *Illustration of rules.*—For an illustration of gain recognition under paragraph (c)(2)(i) of this section, see paragraph (g) of this section, *Example 1.* For an illustration of gain recognition under paragraph (c)(2)(ii) of this section, see paragraph (g) of this section, *Example 2.*

(3) *Basis adjustments required for control group members.*—(i) *General rule.*—Except as provided in paragraph (c)(3)(iv) of this section, if there is any attributable inside gain (determined under paragraph (c)(2)(ii)(A) of this section) with respect to a control group member, then such control group member's aggregate basis in the stock received in exchange for (or with respect to, as applicable) stock or securities of the U.S. transferor under section 354, 355, or 356, as determined under section 358 and the regulations under that section

(section 358 basis), is reduced by the amount in paragraph (c)(3)(i)(A), (c)(3)(i)(B), or (c)(3)(i)(C) of this section, as applicable.

(A) If the control group member has outside gain, the amount, if any, by which the attributable inside gain, reduced by any gain recognized by the U.S. transferor with respect to the control group member under paragraph (c)(2)(ii) of this section, exceeds the control group member's outside gain.

(B) If the control group member has outside loss, the amount, if any, by which the attributable inside gain, reduced by any gain recognized by the U.S. transferor with respect to the control group member under paragraph (c)(2)(ii) of this section, exceeds the control group member's outside loss (for this purpose, treating the outside loss as a negative amount).

(C) If the control group member has no outside gain or outside loss, the amount of the attributable inside gain, reduced by any gain recognized by the U.S. transferor with respect to the control group member under paragraph (c)(2)(ii) of this section.

(ii) *Stock received in the section 361 exchange.*—This paragraph (c)(3) applies only to stock received by the U.S. transferor in the section 361 exchange and distributed to the control group member in exchange for (or with respect to, as applicable) stock or securities of the U.S. transferor.

(iii) *Pro rata adjustments.*—The section 358 basis of each share of stock received by the control group member must be reduced pro rata based on the relative section 358 basis of all shares of stock received by the control group member.

(iv) *Successive distributions to which section 355 applies.*—Paragraph (c)(3) of this section does not apply to a control group member that distributes the stock of a foreign acquiring corporation received from the U.S. transferor in a distribution satisfying the requirements of section 355 (section 355 distribution) that is in connection with a transaction described in paragraph (d) of this section (relating to successive section 355 distributions). If paragraph (c)(3) of this section does not apply to a control group member pursuant to this paragraph (c)(3)(iv), then paragraph (c)(3) of this section shall apply to the final distributee (as defined in paragraph (d) of this section) that receives the stock of the foreign acquiring corporation in the final section 355 distribution described in paragraph (d) of this section.

(v) *Illustration of rules.*—For illustrations of the adjustment to stock basis under paragraph (c)(3)(i) of this section, see paragraph (g) of this section, *Example 1* and *Example 2*, § 1.367(a)-3(e)(8), *Example 3*, and § 1.1248(f)-2(e), *Example 3.* For an illustration of the adjustment to stock basis under paragraph (c)(3)(iii) of this section, see paragraph (g) of this section, *Example 3.*

(4) *Agreement to amend or file a U.S. income tax return.*—(i) *General rule.*—Except as provided in paragraph (c)(4)(ii) of this section, the U.S. transferor complies with the requirements of § 1.6038B-1(c)(6)(iii), relating to the requirement to report gain that was not recognized by the U.S. transferor upon certain subsequent dispositions by the foreign acquiring corporation of section 367(a) property received from the U.S. transferor in the section 361 exchange.

(ii) *Exception.*—To the extent section 367(a) property transferred in the section 361 exchange is subject to § 1.367(a)-3(e) (relating to transfers of stock or securities by a domestic corporation to a foreign corporation in a section 361 exchange), § 1.6038B-1(c)(6)(iii) does not apply with respect to the transfer of that property.

(5) *Election and reporting requirements.*—(i) *General rule.*—The U.S. transferor and each control group member elect to apply the provisions of paragraph (c) of this section in the manner provided under paragraph (c)(5)(ii) or (c)(5)(iii) of this section, as applicable, and by entering into a written agreement described in paragraph (c)(5)(iv) of this section. If a control group member distributes the stock of the foreign acquiring corporation received from the U.S. transferor in a section 355 distribution that is in connection with a transaction described in paragraph (d) of this section, the final distributee that receives that stock in the final section 355 distribution elects to apply the provisions of this paragraph (c) and enters into the written agreement instead of the control group member. For this purpose, the term *control group member* will be replaced by the term *final distributee,* as appropriate.

(ii) *Control group member.*—(A) *Time and manner of making election.*—Each control group member elects to apply the provisions of paragraph (c) of this section by including a statement (in the form and with the content specified in paragraph (c)(5)(ii)(B) of this section) on or with a timely filed return for the taxable year in which the reorganization occurs. If the control group member is a member of a consolidated group but is not the common parent of the consolidated group, the common parent makes the election on behalf of the control group member.

(B) *Form and content of election statement.*—The statement must be entitled, "ELECTION TO APPLY EXCEPTION UNDER §1.367(a)-7(c)," and set forth:

(1) The name and taxpayer identification number (if any) of the control group member, the U.S. transferor, the foreign acquiring corporation and, in the case of a triangular reorganization (within the meaning of §1.358-6(b)(2)), the corporation that controls the foreign acquiring corporation; the control group member's ownership interest percentage in the U.S. transferor; and the percentage of voting stock and non-voting stock of the U.S. transferor owned by the control group member for purposes of satisfying the control requirement of paragraph (c)(1) of this section;

(2) If the control group member is a member of a consolidated group but is not the common parent, the name and taxpayer identification number of the common parent;

(3) The amount of the adjustment (if any) to stock basis required under paragraph (c)(3) of this section, the resulting adjusted basis in the stock, and the fair market value of the stock, or if no stock was received, indicate no stock was received; and

(4) The date on which the written agreement described in paragraph (c)(5)(iv) of this section was entered into.

(iii) *Statement by U.S. transferor.*—The U.S. transferor elects to apply the provisions of paragraph (c) of this section in the form and manner set forth in §1.6038B-1(c)(6)(ii).

(iv) *Written agreement.*—The U.S. transferor and each control group member must enter into a written agreement satisfying the conditions of this paragraph on or before the due date (including extensions) for the U.S. transferor's tax return for the taxable year in which the reorganization occurs. Each party to the agreement must retain the original or a copy of the agreement in the manner specified by §1.6001-1(e). Each party to the agreement must provide a copy of the agreement to the Internal Revenue Service within 30 days of the receipt of a request for the copy of the agreement. The written agreement must—

(A) State the document constitutes an agreement entered into pursuant to paragraph (c)(5) of this section;

(B) Identify the U.S. transferor, the foreign acquiring corporation, the corporation that controls the foreign acquiring corporation (in the case of a triangular reorganization within the meaning of §1.358-6(b)(2)), and each control group member, and provide the taxpayer identification number (if any) for each corporation;

(C) State the amount of gain (if any) recognized by the U.S. transferor under paragraph (c)(2) of this section; and

(D) With respect to each control group member, state the amount of the adjustment (if any) to stock basis required under paragraph (c)(3) of this section, the resulting adjusted basis in the stock, and the fair market value of the stock. Alternatively, if a control group member did not receive any stock, indicate that no stock was received.

(d) *Section 361 exchange followed by successive distributions to which section 355 applies.*—If the U.S. transferor distributes stock of the foreign acquiring corporation received in the section 361 exchange to a control group member in a section 355 distribution and, as part of a plan or series of related transactions, that stock is further distributed in one or more successive section 355 distributions, paragraph (c) of this section can apply to the section 361 exchange only to the extent each subsequent section 355 distribution is to a member of the affiliated group (within the meaning of section 1504) that includes the U.S. transferor immediately before the reorganization. In that case, each affiliated group member that receives stock of the foreign acquiring corporation in the final section 355 distribution (final distributee) is subject to the requirements of paragraphs (c)(3) and (c)(5) of this section. If this paragraph (d) applies, then for purposes of applying paragraphs (c)(3), (c)(5) or (e)(2) of this section the term *control group member* is replaced by the term *final distributee*, as appropriate.

(e) *Other rules.*—(1) *Section 367(a) property with respect to which gain is recognized.*—Except as otherwise provided in this paragraph (e)(1), gain recognized by the U.S. transferor pursuant to paragraph (c)(2) of this section will be treated as recognized with respect to the section 367(a) property transferred in the section 361 exchange in proportion to the amount of gain realized by the U.S. transferor on the transfer of each item of section 367(a) property. This paragraph (e)(1) will be applied after taking into account any gain or deemed dividends (including any deemed dividends under section 1248(a)) recognized by the U.S. transferor on the transfer of the section 367(a) property in the section 361 exchange pursuant to all other provisions of sections 367(a) and (b) and the regulations under that section. See, for example, §§1.367(a)-2, 1.367(a)-3(e), 1.367(a)-4, 1.367(a)-6, and 1.367(b)-4.

If the U.S. transferor recognizes gain (including gain treated as a deemed dividend under section 1248(a)) pursuant to §1.367(a)-3(e)(3)(iii)(B) or (e)(3)(iii)(C) with respect to stock or securities transferred in the section 361 exchange, the realized gain in such stock or securities shall not be taken into account for purposes of applying this paragraph (e)(1) to gain recognized under paragraph (c)(2) of this section attributable to U.S. transferor shareholders described in §1.367(a)-3(e)(3)(iii)(B) or (e)(3)(iii)(C). Accordingly, gain recognized under paragraph (c)(2) attributable to such U.S. transferor shareholders shall not be treated as recognized with respect to such stock or securities under this paragraph. Furthermore, to the extent gain recognized by the U.S. transferor under paragraph (c)(2) is treated as recognized with respect to stock in a foreign corporation transferred in the section 361 exchange to which section 1248(a) applies, the portion of such gain treated as a deemed dividend under section 1248(a) is the product of the amount of the gain multiplied by the ratio of the amount that would be treated as a deemed dividend under section 1248(a) if all gain in the transferred stock were recognized under §1.367(a)-7(b) and the amount of gain realized in the transferred stock. See §1.367(a)-1(b)(4) for additional rules on the character, source, and adjustments relating to gain recognized under section 367(a)(1), and §1.367(b)-2(e) for rules on the timing, treatment, and effect of amounts included in income as deemed dividends pursuant to regulations under section 367(b).

(2) *Relief for certain failures to comply that are not willful.*—(i) *In general.*—A control group member or U.S. transferor's failure to comply with any requirement of this section will be deemed not to have occurred for purposes of satisfying the requirements of this section if the control group member or U.S. transferor (or the foreign acquiring corporation on behalf of the U.S. transferor), as applicable, demonstrates that the failure was not willful using the procedure set forth in paragraph (e)(2)(ii) of this section. For this purpose, willful is to be interpreted consistent with the meaning of that term in the context of other civil penalties, which would include a failure due to gross negligence, reckless disregard, or willful neglect. Whether the failure to comply was a willful failure will be determined by the Director of Field Operations, Cross Border Activities Practice Area of Large Business & International (or any successor to the roles and responsibilities of such person) (Director) based on all the facts and circumstances. The control group member or U.S. transferor (or the foreign acquiring corporation on behalf of the U.S. transferor), as applicable, must submit a request for relief and an explanation as provided in paragraph (e)(2)(ii) of this section. Although a US transferor whose failure to comply is determined not to be willful will not be subject to gain recognition under this section, the U.S. transferor will be subject to a penalty under section 6038B if the U.S. transferor fails to demonstrate that the failure was due to reasonable cause and not willful neglect. See §1.6038B-1(b) and (f). The determination of whether the failure to comply was willful under this section has no effect on any request for relief made under §1.6038B-1(f).

(ii) *Procedures for establishing that a failure to comply was not willful.*—(A) *Time and manner of submission.*—A control group member or U.S. transferor's statement that the failure to comply was not willful will be considered only if, promptly after the control group member or U.S. transferor, as applicable, becomes aware of the failure, an amended return is filed for the taxable year to which the failure relates that includes the information that should have been included with the original return for such taxable year or that otherwise complies with the rules of this section, and that includes a written statement explaining the reasons for the failure to comply. The amended return must be filed with the Internal Revenue Service at the location where the taxpayer filed its original return. The U.S. transferor may submit a request for relief from the penalty under section 6038B as part of the same submission. See §1.6038B-1(f).

(B) *Notice requirement.*—In addition to the requirements of paragraph (e)(2)(ii)(A) of this section, a control group member or U.S. transferor, as applicable, must comply with the notice requirements of this paragraph (e)(2)(ii)(B). If any taxable year of the control group member or U.S. transferor, as applicable, is under examination when the amended return is filed, a copy of the amended return and any information required to be included with such return must be delivered to the Internal Revenue Service personnel conducting the examination. If no taxable year of the control group member or U.S transferor, as applicable, is under examination when the amended return is filed, a copy of the amended return and any information required to be included with such return must be delivered to the Director.

(iii) For illustrations of the application of the willfulness standard of this paragraph (e)(2), see the examples in §1.367(a)-8(p)(3).

(3) *Anti-abuse rule.*—Any property of the U.S. transferor acquired with a principal purpose of affecting any determination under this section (including, for example, the section 367(a) percentage,

inside gain, or inside basis) shall not be taken in account for purposes of any determination under this section. Nothing in this paragraph (e)(3) constitutes a limitation on or modification to judicial doctrines, including step-transaction or substance-over-form.

(4) *Certain income inclusions under §1.367(b)-4.*—(i) *Income inclusion attributable to U.S. transferor shareholder described in §1.367(a)-3(e)(3)(iii)(A).*—If pursuant to §1.367(a)-3(e)(3)(iii)(B) or (e)(3)(iii)(C) the U.S. transferor is required to recognize gain on the transfer of foreign stock (all or a portion of which is treated as a deemed dividend under section 1248(a)), and if pursuant to §1.367(b)-4(b)(1)(i) the U.S. transferor is also required to include in income as a deemed dividend the section 1248 amount (within the meaning of §1.367(b)-2(c)) in the foreign stock, then the section 1248 amount included in income under §1.367(b)-4(b)(1)(i) is attributable to each U.S. transferor shareholder described in §1.367(a)-3(e)(3)(iii)(A) pursuant to this paragraph (e)(4)(i). The portion of the section 1248 amount attributable to each U.S. transferor shareholder described in §1.367(a)-3(e)(3)(iii)(A) is the portion of the section 1248 amount that bears the same ratio as such U.S. transferor shareholder's ownership interest percentage bears to the aggregate ownership interest percentage of all U.S. transferor shareholders described in §1.367(a)-3(e)(3)(iii)(A).

(ii) *Ordering rules for determining section 1248 amount.*—The section 1248 amount (within the meaning of §1.367(b)-2(c)) included in income as a deemed dividend under §1.367(b)-4(b)(1)(i) is determined after taking into account any gain recognized under §§1.367(a)-3(e)(3)(iii)(B) or (e)(3)(iii)(C) or 1.367(a)-6 that is treated as a deemed dividend under section 1248(a). See §1.367(a)-3(e)(7) and paragraph (e)(5)(ii) of this section for rules to determine the amount of gain recognized under §§1.367(a)-3(e)(3)(iii)(B) or (e)(3)(iii)(C) or 1.367(a)-6, respectively, that is treated as a deemed dividend under section 1248(a).

(5) *Certain gain under §1.367(a)-6.*—(i) *Gain attributable to U.S. transferor shareholder described in §1.367(a)-3(e)(3)(iii)(A).*—If pursuant to §1.367(a)-3(e)(3)(iii)(B) or (e)(3)(iii)(C), the U.S. transferor is required to recognize gain on the transfer of stock or securities, and if pursuant to §1.367(a)-6 the U.S. transferor is also required to recognize gain, then gain recognized under §1.367(a)-6 (including any portion treated as a deemed dividend under section 1248(a)) to the extent treated as recognized with respect to the stock or securities, is attributable to each U.S. transferor shareholder described in §1.367(a)-3(e)(3)(iii)(A) pursuant to this paragraph (e)(5)(i). The portion of the gain (including any portion treated as a deemed dividend under section 1248(a)) that is attributable to each U.S. transferor shareholder described in §1.367(a)-3(e)(3)(iii)(A) is the portion of the gain that bears the same ratio as such U.S. transferor shareholder's ownership interest percentage bears to the aggregate ownership interest percentage of all U.S. transferor shareholders described in §1.367(a)-3(e)(3)(iii)(A).

(ii) *Gain subject to section 1248(a).*—If the U.S. transferor recognizes gain under §1.367(a)-6 with respect to transferred stock that is stock in a foreign corporation to which section 1248(a) applies, the portion of such gain treated as a deemed dividend under section 1248(a) is determined after taking into account any gain recognized under §1.367(a)-3(e)(3)(iii)(B) or (e)(3)(iii)(C) and the amount of such gain treated as a deemed dividend under section 1248(a) pursuant to §1.367(a)-3(e)(7).

(f) *Definitions.*—The following definitions apply for purposes of this section:

(1) *Control group, control group member, and non-control group member.*—(i) *General rule.*—Except as provided in paragraph (f)(1)(ii) of this section, the *control group* is the group of five or fewer, but at least one, domestic corporations that controls (within the meaning of section 368(c)) the U.S. transferor immediately before the reorganization. If the U.S. transferor is owned directly by more than five domestic corporations immediately before the reorganization, but some combination of five or fewer domestic corporations controls the U.S. transferor, the U.S. transferor must designate the five or fewer domestic corporations that comprise the control group on Form 926, "Return by a U.S. Transferor of Property to a Foreign Corporation." For purposes of identifying the control group, members of an affiliated group (within the meaning of section 1504) are treated as a single corporation. Except as provided in paragraph (f)(1)(ii) of this section, a *control group member* is a domestic corporation that is part of the control group. A *non-control group member* is a shareholder of the U.S. transferor immediately before the reorganization that is not a control group member.

(ii) *Exception for certain entities.*—Regulated investment companies (as defined in section 851(a)), real estate investment trusts (as defined in section 856(a)), and S corporations (as defined in section 1361(a)) cannot be control group members.

(2) *Deductible liability* is any liability of the U.S. transferor that is assumed in the section 361 exchange if payment of the liability would give rise to a deduction.

(3) *Fair market value* is the fair market value determined without regard to mortgages, liens, pledges, or other liabilities. For this purpose, the fair market value of any property subject to a nonrecourse indebtedness shall be treated as being not less than the amount of any nonrecourse indebtedness to which such property is subject.

(4) *Inside basis* is the aggregate basis of the section 367(a) property transferred by the U.S. transferor in the section 361 exchange and, except as otherwise provided in this paragraph (f)(4), increased by any gain recognized or any deemed dividend included in income by the U.S. transferor under section 367 on the transfer of the section 367(a) property in the section 361 exchange, but not including any gain recognized under paragraph (c)(2) of this section. If the U.S. transferor transfers stock or securities and recognizes gain under §1.367(a)-3(e)(3)(iii)(B) or (e)(3)(iii)(C) with respect to such stock or securities, then inside basis is not increased for gain recognized or deemed dividends included in income that are described in paragraph (f)(4)(i), (f)(4)(ii), or (f)(4)(iii) of this section.

(i) Gain recognized under §1.367(a)-3(e)(3)(iii)(B) or (e)(3)(iii)(C) (including any portion treated as a deemed dividend under section 1248(a));

(ii) Gain recognized under §1.367(a)-6 (including any portion treated as a deemed dividend under section 1248(a)) attributable to U.S. transferor shareholders described in §1.367(a)-3(e)(3)(iii)(A) (as determined pursuant to §1.367(a)-7(e)(5));

(iii) A deemed dividend included in income under §1.367(b)-4(b) attributable to U.S. transferor shareholders described in §1.367(a)-3(e)(3)(iii)(A) (as determined pursuant to §1.367(a)-7(e)(4)).

(5) *Inside gain* is the amount (but not below zero) by which the aggregate fair market value of the section 367(a) property transferred in the section 361 exchange exceeds the sum of:

(i) The inside basis; and

(ii) The product of the section 367(a) percentage multiplied by the aggregate deductible liabilities of the U.S. transferor.

(6) *Outside gain or loss* is the product of the section 367(a) percentage multiplied by the difference between—

(i) The aggregate fair market value of the stock received by a control group member in exchange for (or with respect to, as applicable) stock or securities of the U.S. transferor under section 354, 355, or 356, and

(ii) The control group member's aggregate section 358 basis (as defined in paragraph (c)(3) of this section) in such stock received, determined without regard to any adjustment to that basis under paragraph (c)(3) of this section.

(7) *Ownership interest percentage* is the ratio of the fair market value of the stock in the U.S. transferor owned by a shareholder to the fair market value of all of the outstanding stock of the U.S. transferor. Except as provided in this paragraph (f)(7), the ownership interest percentage of a shareholder is determined immediately before the reorganization. For purposes of determining the ownership interest percentage with respect to each shareholder, however, the numerator and denominator of the fraction are first reduced as described in this paragraph (f)(7). The numerator is reduced (but not below zero) by any distributions by the U.S. transferor of money or other property (within the meaning of section 356) to such shareholder pursuant to the plan of reorganization, but only to the extent such money or other property is not provided by the foreign acquiring corporation in exchange for property of the U.S. transferor acquired in the section 361 exchange. Furthermore, the denominator of the fraction is reduced (but not below zero) by all such distributions by the U.S. transferor to all shareholders. For illustrations of this definition, see paragraph (g) of this section, *Example 4* and *Example 5*.

(8) *Section 361 exchange* is an exchange described in section 361(a) or (b).

(9) *Section 367(a) percentage* is the ratio of the aggregate fair market value of the section 367(a) property transferred by the U.S. transferor in the section 361 exchange to the aggregate fair market value of all property transferred by the U.S. transferor in the section 361 exchange.

(10) *Section 367(a) property.*—Except as provided in paragraph (e)(3) of this section, *section 367(a) property* is any property, as defined in §1.367(a)-1(d)(4), other than section 367(d) property.

(11) Section 367(d) property is intangible property as defined in §1.367(a)-1(d)(5).

(12) *Timely filed return* is a U.S. income tax return filed on or before the due date set forth in section 6072(b), including any extensions of time to file the return granted under section 6081.

(13) *U.S. transferor shareholder* is a person that is either a control group member or a non-control group member.

(g) *Examples.*—The rules of this section are illustrated by the examples set forth in this paragraph (g). See also § 1.367(a)-3(e)(8), *Example 2* and *Example 3*. The analysis of the following examples is limited to a discussion of issues under this section. Unless otherwise indicated, for purposes of the following examples: DP1, DP2, and DC are domestic corporations that do not join in the filing of a consolidated return and none of which is a regulated investment company, a real estate investment trust, or an S corporation; FP and FA are foreign corporations created or organized under the laws of Country B and are unrelated to DP1, DP2, and DC; each corporation has a single class of stock outstanding; each share of stock of DC owned by a shareholder of DC has an identical stock basis; Business A consists solely of section 367(a) property whose fair market value exceeds its basis and that, but for the application of this section, would qualify for the active foreign trade or business exception under § 1.367(a)-2; the fair market value of any FA stock received in a reorganization is equal to the fair market value of property exchanged therefor; FA is not a surrogate foreign corporation for purposes of section 7874 because one or more of the conditions of section 7874(a)(2)(B) is not satisfied; DC has no liabilities; DP1 and DP2 satisfy the requirements of paragraph (c)(5) of this section, and DC satisfies the requirements of § 1.6038B-1(c)(6)(ii).

Example 1. Tainted assets and non-control group ownership. (i) *Facts.* DP1, DP2, and FP own 50%, 30%, and 20%, respectively, of the outstanding stock of DC. DP1 and DP2 are members of the same affiliated group within the meaning of section 1504. DP1's DC stock has a $120x basis and $100x fair market value. DP2's DC stock has a $50x basis and a $60x fair market value. DC owns inventory with a $40x basis and a $100x fair market value. DC also owns Business A (excluding the inventory) with a $10x basis and $100x fair market value. In a reorganization described in section 368(a)(1)(F), DC transfers the inventory and Business A to FA, a newly formed corporation, in exchange for all of the outstanding stock of FA. DC's transfer of the inventory and Business A to FA qualifies as a section 361 exchange. DP1, DP2, and FP exchange the DC stock for a proportionate amount of FA stock pursuant to section 354.

(ii) *Result.* (A) Under section 367(a)(3)(B)(i), DC must recognize $60x gain ($100x fair market value less $40x basis) on the transfer of the inventory to FA. The basis of the inventory in the hands of FA is increased by the gain recognized of $60x (that is, increased from $40x to $100x). See § 1.367(a)-1(b)(4)(i)(B). Under section 367(a)(5) and paragraph (b) of this section, DC's transfer of Business A to FA is subject to the general rule of section 367(a)(1). As a result, DC must also generally recognize $90x gain ($100x fair market value less $10x basis) on the transfer of Business A to FA notwithstanding the application of section 361 (or any other nonrecognition provision enumerated in section 367(a)(1)). However, if the conditions and requirements of paragraph (c) of this section are met, DC's transfer of Business A to FA would qualify for the active foreign trade or business exception provided by section 367(a)(3) and § 1.367(a)-2.

(B) The requirement of paragraph (c)(1) of this section is satisfied because DC is controlled (within the meaning of section 368(c)) by five or fewer domestic corporations immediately before the reorganization (in this case, by a single domestic corporation because DP1 and DP2 together own 80% of the stock of DC). DP1 and DP2 are treated as a single domestic corporation for this purpose under paragraph (f)(1)(i) of this section because DP1 and DP2 are members of the same affiliated group.

(C) Paragraph (c)(2)(i) of this section would be satisfied only if DC recognizes $18x gain on the transfer of Business A, which is the amount of inside gain attributable to FP, a non-control group member. The $18x gain equals the product of the inside gain ($90x) multiplied by FP's ownership interest percentage (20%) in DC, reduced by $0x (the sum of the amounts described in paragraphs (c)(2)(i)(A) through (c)(2)(i)(C) of this section). Under paragraph (f)(5) of this section, the $90x inside gain is the amount by which the aggregate fair market value ($200x) of the section 367(a) property (inventory and Business A) exceeds $110x, the sum of the inside basis of $110x and the product of the section 367(a) percentage (100%) multiplied by the deductible liabilities of DC ($0x). Under paragraph (f)(4) of this section, the inside basis equals the $50x aggregate basis of the section 367(a) property transferred in the section 361 exchange, increased by the $60x gain recognized by DC on the transfer of the inventory to FA, but not by the $18x gain recognized by DC under paragraph (c)(2)(i) of this section attributable to FP. The section 367(a) percentage is 100% because the only assets transferred are the inventory and Business A, which are section 367(a) property. Under paragraph (e)(1) of this section, the $18x gain recognized under paragraph (c)(2)(i) of this section is treated as recognized with respect to Business A. FA's basis in Business A as determined under section 362 is increased for the $18x gain recognized. See § 1.367(a)-1(b)(4)(i)(B).

(D) Paragraph (c)(2)(ii) of this section is not applicable with respect to either DP1 or DP2 because the attributable inside gain with respect to each such shareholder can be preserved in the FA stock received. As stated in paragraph (ii)(C) of this *Example 1*, the amount of the inside gain is $90x. The attributable inside gain with respect to DP1 of $45x (equal to the product of $90x inside gain multiplied by DP1's 50% ownership interest percentage, reduced by $0x (the sum of the amounts described in paragraphs (c)(2)(ii)(A)(1) through (c)(2)(ii)(A)(3) of this section)) does not exceed $100x (equal to the product of the section 367(a) percentage of 100% multiplied by $100x fair market value of FA stock received by DP1). Similarly, the attributable inside gain with respect to DP2 of $27x (equal to the product of $90x inside gain multiplied by DP2's 30% ownership interest percentage, reduced by $0x (the sum of the amounts described in paragraphs (c)(2)(ii)(A)(1) through (c)(2)(ii)(A)(3) of this section)) does not exceed $60x (equal to the product of the section 367(a) percentage of 100% multiplied by $60x fair market value of FA stock received by DP2).

(E) Each control group member (DP1 and DP2) separately computes any required adjustment to stock basis under paragraph (c)(3) of this section. DP1's section 358 basis in the FA stock received of $120x (the amount of DP1's basis in the DC stock exchanged) is reduced to preserve the attributable inside gain with respect to DP1, less any gain recognized with respect to DP1 under paragraph (c)(2)(ii) of this section. Because DC does not recognize gain on the section 361 exchange with respect to DP1 under paragraph (c)(2)(ii) of this section (as determined in paragraph (ii)(D) of this *Example 1*), the attributable inside gain of $45x with respect to DP1 is not reduced under paragraph (c)(3)(i)(B) of this section. DP1's outside loss in the FA stock is $20x, the product of the section 367(a) percentage of 100% multiplied by $20x loss (equal to the difference between $100x fair market value and $120x section 358 basis in FA stock). Thus, DP1's $120x section 358 basis in the FA stock must be reduced by $65x (excess of $45x, reduced by $0x, over $20x outside loss) to $55x.

(F) DP2's aggregate section 358 basis in the FA stock received of $50x (the amount of DP2's basis in the DC stock exchanged) is reduced to preserve the attributable inside gain with respect to DP2, less any gain recognized with respect to DP2 under paragraph (c)(2)(ii) of this section. Because DC does not recognize gain on the section 361 exchange with respect to DP2 (as determined in paragraph (ii)(D) of this *Example 1*), the attributable inside gain of $27x with respect to DP2 is not reduced under paragraph (c)(3)(i)(A) of this section. DP2's outside gain in the FA stock is $10x, the product of the section 367(a) percentage of 100% multiplied by $10x gain (equal to the difference between $60x fair market value and $50x section 358 basis in FA stock). Thus, DP2's $50x section 358 basis in the FA stock must be reduced by $17x (excess of $27x, reduced by $0x, over the $10x outside gain) to $33x.

(G) Paragraph (c)(4) of this section would be satisfied only if DC complies with the requirements of § 1.6038B-1(c)(6)(iii), including filing with its timely filed return for the year of the reorganization a statement agreeing to file an amended return reporting the gain realized but not recognized on the section 361 exchange in certain cases if a significant amount of the section 367(a) property received in the section 361 exchange is disposed of, directly or indirectly, in one or more related transactions within the prescribed 60-month period.

Example 2. Triangular reorganization involving an exchange of section 367(a) property for foreign stock and cash. (i) *Facts.* (A) DP1 wholly owns DC. DP1 and DC file a consolidated return. DP1's DC stock has a $170x basis and $200x fair market value. DC owns Business A, which has a $10x basis and $200x fair market value. FP wholly owns FA.

(B) In a triangular reorganization described in section 368(a)(1)(A) by reason of section 368(a)(2)(D), DC transfers Business A to FA in exchange for $180x of FP stock and $20x cash. DC's transfer of Business A to FA qualifies as a section 361 exchange. DP1 exchanges its DC stock for $180x of FP stock and $20x cash pursuant to section 356. The triangular reorganization constitutes an indirect stock transfer under § 1.367(a)-3(d)(1)(i), and DP1 properly files a gain recognition agreement under § 1.367(a)-8 with respect to the transfer. See also § 1.367(a)-3(d)(2)(vii).

(ii) *Result.* (A) Under section 367(a)(5) and paragraph (b) of this section, DC's transfer of Business A to FA is subject to the general rule of section 367(a)(1). As a result, DC must generally recognize $190x gain ($200x fair market value less $10x basis) on the transfer of Business A to FA notwithstanding the application of section 361 (or any other nonrecognition exchange enumerated in section 367(a)(1)). However, if the requirements of paragraph (c) of this section are satisfied, DC's transfer of Business A to FA would qualify for the active foreign trade or business exception provided in section 367(a)(3) and § 1.367(a)-2.

(B) The requirement of paragraph (c)(1) of this section is satisfied because DC is controlled (within the meaning of section 368(c)) by five or fewer domestic corporations immediately before the reorganization (in this case, by a single domestic corporation, DP1).

(C) DC is not required to recognize gain under paragraph (c)(2)(i) of this section because, immediately before the reorganization, DC is wholly owned by DP1, a control group member. In addition, DP1's ownership interest percentage is 100%. Paragraph (c)(2)(ii) of this section would be satisfied only if DC recognizes $10x gain, computed as the amount by which the attributable inside gain with respect to DP1 of $190x (the product of $190x inside gain multiplied by DP1's ownership interest percentage of 100%, reduced by $0x (the sum of the amounts in paragraphs (c)(2)(ii)(A)(1) through (c)(2)(ii)(A)(3) of this section)) exceeds $180x (the product of the section 367(a) percentage of 100% multiplied by $180x fair market value of FP stock received by DP1). Under paragraph (f)(5) of this section, the $190x inside gain is the amount by which the $200x aggregate fair market value of Business A exceeds $10x (the sum of the inside basis of $10x and the product of the section 367(a) percentage (100%) multiplied by the deductible liabilities of DC ($0x)). Under paragraph (f)(4) of this section, the inside basis equals the $10x aggregate basis of the section 367(a) property transferred in the section 361 exchange (not increased by the $10x gain recognized by DC under paragraph (c)(2)(ii) of this section). The section 367(a) percentage is 100% because the only asset transferred is Business A, which is section 367(a) property. Under § 1.1502-32(b)(2), DP1 increases the basis of its DC stock by the $10x gain recognized, that is, from $170x to $180x. Under paragraph (e)(1) of this section, the $10x gain recognized under paragraph (c)(2)(ii) of this section is treated as recognized with respect to Business A. FA's basis in Business A as determined under section 362 is increased for the $10x gain recognized. See § 1.367(a)-1(b)(4)(i)(B).

(D) Paragraph (c)(3) of this section would be satisfied only if DP1's section 358 basis in the FP stock is reduced by the amount by which the attributable inside gain with respect to DP1, reduced by any gain recognized by DC with respect to DP1 under paragraph (c)(2)(ii) of this section, exceeds DP1's outside gain in the FP stock. DP1's section 358 basis in the FP stock is $180x, computed as $180x basis in DC stock, as determined in paragraph (ii)(C) of this *Example 2*, decreased by $20x cash received and increased by $20x gain recognized under section 356 (such amount equal to the lesser of the $20x cash received and the $20x gain in the DC stock, computed as $200x fair market value less $180x basis). Because DC recognizes $10x gain on the section 361 exchange with respect to DP1 under paragraph (c)(2)(ii) of this section as determined in paragraph (ii)(C) of this *Example 2*, the $190x attributable inside gain with respect to DP1 is reduced by $10x to $180x under paragraph (c)(3)(i)(C) of this section. DP1's outside gain in the FP stock is $0x, the product of the section 367(a) percentage of 100% multiplied by $0x gain (the difference between $180x fair market value and $180x section 358 basis in FP stock). Thus, DP1's section 358 basis in the FP stock ($180x) must be reduced by $180x ($190x attributable inside gain reduced by $10x) to $0x.

(E) Paragraph (c)(4)(i) of this section would be satisfied only if DC complies with the requirements of § 1.6038B-1(c)(6)(iii), including filing with its tax return for the year of the reorganization a statement agreeing to file an amended return reporting the gain on the section 361 exchange in certain cases if a significant amount of the section 367(a) property received in the section 361 exchange is disposed of, directly or indirectly, in one or more related transactions within the prescribed 60-month period.

Example 3. Adjustment to basis of multiple blocks of stock; transfer of section 367(d) property. (i) *Facts.* (A) DP1 wholly owns DC. One half of DP1's shares of stock in DC, each with an identical basis, has an aggregate basis of $60x and fair market value of $100x (Block 1). The other one half of DP's shares of stock in DC, each with an identical basis, has an aggregate basis of $120x and fair market value of $100x (Block 2). DC owns Business A ($15x basis and $150x fair market value) (excluding the patent) and a patent ($0x basis and $50x fair market value). The patent is section 367(d) property.

(B) In a reorganization described in section 368(a)(1)(F), DC transfers Business A and the patent to FA, a newly formed corporation, in exchange for 2 shares of FA stock. DC's transfer of Business A and the patent to FA qualifies as a section 361 exchange. DP1 exchanges Block 1 and Block 2 for the two shares of FA stock pursuant to section 354. Pursuant to § 1.358-2(a)(2)(i), one share of the FA stock corresponds to Block 1 (Share 1) and the other share of FA stock corresponds to Block 2 (Share 2). The basis of Share 1 and Share 2 correspond to the basis of Block 1 and Block 2, respectively.

(ii) *Result.* (A) Under section 367(a)(5) and paragraph (b) of this section, DC's transfer of Business A to FA is subject to the general rule of section 367(a)(1). As a result, DC must generally recognize $135x of gain on the transfer of Business A to FA notwithstanding the application of section 361 (or any other nonrecognition exchange described in section 367(a)(1)). However, if the requirements of paragraph (c) of this section are met, DC's transfer of Business A to FA *would qualify for the active foreign trade or business exception* provided in section 367(a)(3). For rules applicable to DC's transfer of the patent to FA, see section 367(d).

(B) The requirement of paragraph (c)(1) of this section is satisfied because DC is controlled (within the meaning of section 368(c) by

five or fewer domestic corporations immediately before the reorganization (in this case, by a single domestic corporation, DP1).

(C) Paragraph (c)(2)(i) of this section is not applicable because, immediately before the reorganization, DC is wholly owned by DP1, a control group member. In addition, DP1's ownership interest percentage is 100%. Paragraph (c)(2)(ii) of this section is not applicable because the attributable inside gain with respect to DP1 can be preserved in the FA stock received. The attributable inside gain with respect to DP1 of $135x (equal to the product of $135x inside gain multiplied by DP1's 100% ownership interest percentage, reduced by $0x (the sum of the amounts in paragraphs (c)(2)(ii)(A)(1) through (c)(2)(ii)(A)(3) of this section)) does not exceed $150x (equal to the product of the section 367(a) percentage of 75% multiplied by $200x fair market value of FA stock received by DP1). Under paragraph (f)(5) of this section, the $135x inside gain is the amount by which the aggregate fair market value of Business A ($150x) exceeds $15x, the sum of the inside basis of Business A ($15x) and the product of the section 367(a) percentage (75%) multiplied by the deductible liabilities of DC ($0x). Under paragraph (f)(4) of this section, the inside basis equals the $15x aggregate basis of the section 367(a) property transferred in the exchange. The section 367(a) percentage of 75% is equal to the ratio of the fair market value of the section 367(a) property ($150x for Business A) to the fair market value of all the property transferred ($200x, the sum of $150x for Business A and $50x for the patent).

(D) Under paragraph (c)(3) of this section, DP1's aggregate section 358 basis of $180x in the stock of FA (computed as the sum of $60x basis in Share 1 and $120x basis in Share 2) is reduced by the amount by which the attributable inside gain with respect to DP1, reduced by any gain recognized by DC with respect to DP1 under paragraph (c)(2)(ii) of this section, exceeds DP1's outside gain in the FP stock received. Because DC recognizes no gain on the section 361 exchange with respect to DP1 under paragraph (c)(2)(ii) of this section as determined in paragraph (ii)(C) of this *Example 3*, the $135x attributable inside gain with respect to DP1 is not reduced under paragraph (c)(3)(i)(A) of this section. DP1's outside gain in Share 1 and Share 2 in the aggregate is $15x, the product of the section 367(a) percentage of 75% multiplied by $20x (the difference between $200x aggregate fair market value and $180x aggregate section 358 basis in the FA stock received by DP1). Thus, DP1's section 358 basis in the FA stock ($180x) must be reduced by $120x (the excess of $135x attributable inside gain, reduced by $0x, over $15x outside gain) to $60x.

(E) Under paragraph (c)(3)(iii) of this section, the $120x reduction to basis is allocated between Share 1 and Share 2 based on the relative section 358 basis of each share. Therefore, the basis in Share 1 is reduced by $40x ($120x multiplied by $60x/$180x). As adjusted, DP1's basis in Share 1 is $20x ($60x less $40x). The basis in Share 2 is reduced by $80x ($120x multiplied by $120x/$180x). As adjusted, DP1's basis in Share 2 is $40x ($120x less $80x).

(F) Paragraph (c)(4)(i) of this section would be satisfied only if DC complies with the requirements of § 1.6038B-1(c)(6)(iii), including filing with its tax return for the year of the reorganization, a statement agreeing to file an amended return reporting the gain realized but not recognized on the section 361 exchange in certain cases if a significant amount of the section 367(a) property received in the section 361 exchange is disposed of, directly or indirectly, in one or more related transactions within the prescribed 60-month period.

Example 4. Control requirement and ownership interest percentage; nonqualified property provided by foreign acquiring corporation. (i) *Facts.* DP1 and FP own 80% and 20%, respectively, of the outstanding stock of DC. DC owns Business A with a basis of $0x and $100x fair market value. DP1's DC stock has a fair market value of $80x, and FP's DC stock has a fair market value of $20x. In a reorganization described in section 368(a)(1)(D), DC transfers Business A to FA in exchange for $80x of FA stock and $20x cash. DC's transfer of Business A to FA qualifies as a section 361 exchange. DP1 exchanges its $80x of DC stock for $60x of FA stock and $20x cash, and FP exchanges its $20x of DC stock for $20x of FA stock.

(ii) *Result.* (A) The requirement of paragraph (c)(1) of this section is satisfied because DC is controlled (within the meaning of section 368(c)) by five or fewer domestic corporations immediately before the reorganization (in this case, by a single domestic corporation, DP1). The fact that the $20x cash is distributed solely to DP1 does not change the analysis of the control requirement. The control requirement is determined immediately before the reorganization and is not affected by distributions of property.

(B) Pursuant to paragraph (f)(7) of this section, the ownership interest percentages of DP1 and FP immediately before the reorganization are 80% ($80x/($80x + $20x)) and 20% ($20x/($80x + $20x)), respectively. The fact that the $20x of cash is distributed solely to DP1 does not change this result. The distribution of the $20x of cash is not taken into account for purposes of the ownership interest percentage computation because the $20x of cash distributed by DC is provided by FA to DC in the section 361 exchange.

Example 5. Control requirement and ownership interest percentage; non-qualified property provided by U.S. transferor. (i) *Facts.* The facts are the same as in *Example 4*, except as follows. Business A has a fair market value of $80x (and not $100x) and DC also owns inventory with a basis of $0x and fair market value of $20x. DC transfers Business A, but not the inventory, to FA in exchange for $80x of FA stock. DP1 exchanges its $80x of DC stock for $60x of FA stock and the $20x of inventory, and FP exchanges its $20x of DC stock for $20x of FA stock.

(ii) *Result.* (A) The requirement of paragraph (c)(1) of this section is satisfied because DC is controlled (within the meaning of section 368(c)) by five or fewer domestic corporations immediately before the reorganization (in this case, by a single domestic corporation, DP1). The fact that the $20x of inventory is not transferred to FA, but is instead distributed solely to DP1, does not change the analysis of the control requirement. The control requirement is determined immediately before the reorganization, and is not affected by distributions of property.

(B) Pursuant to the general rule of paragraph (f)(7) of this section, the ownership interest percentages of DP1 and FP immediately before the reorganization would be 80% ($80x/($80x + $20x)) and 20% ($20x/($80x + $20x)), respectively. In this case, however, the distribution of the $20x inventory to DP1 is taken into account for purposes of computing the ownership interest percentage of DP1 and FP because the inventory is not provided by FA to DC in the section 361 exchange. With respect to DP1, the numerator of the ownership interest percentage computation is $60x, computed as the fair market value of DC stock owned by DP1 immediately before the reorganization but reduced by the fair market value of the inventory distributed to DP1 ($80x less $20x). With respect to FP, the numerator of the ownership interest percentage computation is $20x, the fair market value of the DC stock owned by FP immediately before the reorganization. With respect to both DP1 and FP, the denominator of the ownership interest percentage computation is $80x, computed as the fair market value of all DC stock immediately before the reorganization, but reduced by the fair market value of the inventory distributed to DP1 ($100x, less $20x). Accordingly, the ownership interest percentage of DP1 is 75% ($60x/$80x), and the ownership interest percentage of FP is 25% ($20x/$80x).

(h) *Applicable cross-references.*—For rules relating to the character, source, and adjustments resulting from gain recognized by a U.S. transferor under section 367(a), see §1.367(a)-1(b)(4). For rules relating to transfers of stock or securities in a section 361 exchange, see §1.367(a)-3(e). For rules relating to the acquisition of the stock or assets of a foreign corporation by another foreign corporation, see §1.367(b)-4. For rules relating to transfers of section 367(d) property by a U.S. transferor to a foreign corporation, see section 367(d). For rules relating to distributions of stock of a foreign corporation by a domestic corporation under section 355 or 361, see §§1.367(b)-5, 1.367(e)-1, and 1.1248(f)-1 through 1.1248(f)-3. For additional rules relating to certain reporting requirements of a U.S. transferor, see §1.6038B-1. For rules regarding expatriated entities, see section 7874 and the regulations under that section.

(i) [Reserved].

(j) *Effective/applicability dates.*—(1) *In general.*—Except for paragraph (e)(2) of this section, and as provided in paragraph (j)(2) of this section, this section applies to transfers occurring on or after April 18, 2013. Paragraph (e)(2) applies to requests for relief submitted on or after November 19, 2014. Paragraph (e)(2) of this section also applies to requests for relief submitted before November 19, 2014 if the statute of limitations on the assessment of tax has not expired for any year to which the request relates and the control group member or U.S. transferor, as applicable, resubmits the request under paragraph (e)(2) of this section and notes, on the request, that the request is being submitted pursuant to the third sentence of this paragraph (j). See paragraph (e)(2) of this section, as contained in 26 CFR part 1 revised as of April 1, 2014, for requests for relief submitted after April 17, 2013, and before November 19, 2014, that are not resubmitted under paragraph (e)(2) of this section.

(2) *Section 367(d) property.*—The definition provided in paragraph (f)(11) of this section applies to transfers occurring on or after September 14, 2015, and to transfers occurring before September 14, 2015, resulting from entity classification elections made under §301.7701-3 that are filed on or after September 14, 2015. For transfers occurring before this section is applicable, see §1.367(a)-7 as contained in 26 CFR part 1 revised as of April 1, 2016. [Reg. §1.367(a)-7.]

☐ [T.D. 9614, 3-18-2013 (*corrected* 8-19-2020). *Amended by* T.D. 9704, 11-18-2014, T.D. 9760, 3-18-2016 and T.D. 9803, 12-15-2016.]

⋙→ Caution: The Treasury Department has identified Reg. §1.367(a)-8, as amended by T.D. 9803, as a significant tax regulation that imposes an undue financial burden on U.S. taxpayers and/or adds undue complexity to the federal tax laws, pursuant to Executive Order 13789 (issued April 21, 2017) (Notice 2017-38, I.R.B. 2017-30). In a subsequent report, issued October 4, 2017, Treasury recommended planned actions that would reduce the burden of these regulations.

[Reg. §1.367(a)-8]

§1.367(a)-8. Gain recognition agreement requirements.—(a) *Scope.*—This section provides the terms and conditions for a gain recognition agreement entered into by a United States person pursuant to §1.367(a)-3(b) through (e) in connection with a transfer of stock or securities to a foreign corporation pursuant to an exchange that would otherwise be subject to section 367(a)(1). Paragraph (b) of this section provides definitions and special rules. Paragraphs (c) through (h) of this section identify the form, content, and other conditions of a gain recognition agreement. Paragraph (i) of this section is reserved. Paragraph (j) of this section identifies certain events that may require gain to be recognized under a gain recognition agreement. Paragraph (k) of this section provides exceptions for certain events that would otherwise require gain to be recognized under a gain recognition agreement. Paragraph (l) of this section is reserved. Paragraph (m) of this section provides rules that require gain to be recognized under a gain recognition agreement in connection with certain events to which an exception under paragraph (k) of this section otherwise applies. Paragraph (n) of this section provides special rules in the case of a distribution of property with respect to stock to which section 301 applies. Paragraph (o) of this section provides rules for certain transactions that terminate or reduce the amount of gain subject to a gain recognition agreement. Paragraph (p) of this section provides relief for certain failures to file an initial gain recognition agreement (as defined in paragraph (b)(1)(vi) of this section) or to comply with the requirements of this section with respect to a gain recognition agreement (as described in paragraph (c) of this section). Paragraph (q) of this section provides examples that illustrate the rules of the section. Paragraph (r) of this section provides effective dates for the provisions of this section.

(b) *Definitions and special rules.*—The following definitions and special rules apply for purposes of this section.

(1) *Definitions.*—(i) *Asset reorganization.*—(A) *General rule.*—Except as provided in paragraph (b)(1)(i)(B) of this section, an *asset reorganization* is a reorganization described in section 368(a)(1) that involves an exchange of property described in section 361(a) or (b) (a section 361 exchange).

(B) *Exceptions.*—An asset reorganization does not include the following:

(1) A reorganization described in section 368(a)(1)(D) or (G) if the requirements of section 354(b)(1)(A) and (B) are not met.

(2) For purposes of paragraphs (j)(2)(ii)(B), (k)(6)(ii), and (k)(6)(iii) of this section, a triangular asset reorganization. For rules applicable to a triangular asset reorganization, see paragraph (k)(7) of this section.

(ii) A *consolidated group* has the meaning set forth in §1.1502-1(h).

(iii) *Disposition.*—Except as provided in this paragraph (b)(1)(iii), a *disposition* includes any transfer that would constitute a disposition for any purpose of the Internal Revenue Code. A disposition includes an indirect disposition of the stock of the transferred corporation as described in §1.367(a)-3(d). Except as provided in paragraph (n)(1) of this section, a disposition does not include the receipt of a distribution of property with respect to stock to which section 301 applies (including by reason of section 302(d)). See paragraphs (n)(2) and (o)(3) of this section for rules that apply if gain is recognized under section 301(c)(3). A complete or partial disposition by installment sale (under section 453) shall be treated as a disposition in the year of the installment sale.

(iv) A *gain recognition agreement document* means any agreement, statement, schedule, or form required to be filed under this section, including an initial gain recognition agreement (as defined in paragraph (b)(1)(vi) of this section), a new gain recognition agreement described in paragraph (c)(5) of this section, a Form 8838 extending the period of limitations on assessment of tax described in paragraph (f) of this section, and an annual certification described in paragraph (g) of this section.

(v) A *gain recognition event* is an event described in paragraphs (j) through (o) of this section that requires gain to be recognized under a gain recognition agreement.

(vi) An *initial gain recognition agreement* means the gain recognition agreement entered into under paragraph (c) of this section with respect to the initial transfer.

(vii) The *initial transfer* means a transfer of stock or securities (transferred stock or securities) to a foreign corporation pursuant to an exchange that would otherwise be subject to section 367(a)(1) but with respect to which a gain recognition agreement is entered into by a United States person pursuant to §1.367(a)-3(b) through (e).

(viii) An *intercompany item* has the meaning set forth in §1.1502-13(b)(2).

(ix) An *intercompany transaction* has the meaning set forth in §1.1502-13(b)(1).

(x) A *nonrecognition transaction* has the meaning set forth in section 7701(a)(45). In addition, a nonrecognition transaction includes an exchange described in section 351(b) or 356 even if all gain realized in the exchange is recognized.

(xi) The terms *P, S,* and *T* have the meanings set forth in §1.358-6(b)(1)(i), (ii), and (iii), respectively.

(xii) The determination of whether *substantially all* of the assets of the transferred corporation have been disposed of is based on all the facts and circumstances.

(xiii) A *timely filed return* means a Federal income tax return filed on or before the last date prescribed for filing (taking into account any extensions of time therefor) such return.

(xiv) *Transferee foreign corporation.*—Except as provided in this paragraph (b)(1)(xiv), the *transferee foreign corporation* is the foreign corporation to which the transferred stock or securities are transferred in an initial transfer. In the case of an indirect stock transfer, the transferee foreign corporation has the meaning set forth in §1.367(a)-3(d)(2)(i). The transferee foreign corporation also includes a corporation designated as the transferee foreign corporation in the case of a new gain recognition agreement entered into under this section.

(xv) *Transferred corporation.*—Except as provided in this paragraph (b)(1)(xv), the *transferred corporation* is the corporation the stock or securities of which are transferred in the initial transfer. In the case of an indirect stock transfer, the transferred corporation has the meaning set forth in §1.367(a)-3(d)(2)(ii). The transferred corporation also includes a corporation designated as the transferred corporation in the case of a new gain recognition agreement entered into under this section.

(xvi) A *triangular asset reorganization* is a reorganization described in §1.358-6(b)(2)(i), (ii), (iii), or (v).

(xvii) The *U.S. transferor* is the United States person (as defined in §1.367(a)-1(d)(1)) that transfers the transferred stock or securities to the transferee foreign corporation in the initial transfer. For purposes of determining the U.S. transferor in the case of a transfer by a partnership, see §1.367(a)-1(c)(3)(i). The *U.S. transferor* also includes the United States person designated as the U.S. transferor in the case of a new gain recognition agreement entered into under this section including, for example, under paragraph (k)(14) of this section.

(2) *Special rules.*—(i) *Stock deemed received or transferred.*—References to stock received include stock deemed received (for example, pursuant to section 367(c)(2)). References to a transfer of stock or securities include a deemed transfer of stock or securities.

(ii) *Stock of the transferee foreign corporation.*—References to stock of the transferee foreign corporation includes any stock of the transferee foreign corporation the basis of which is determined, in whole or in part, by reference to the basis of the stock of the transferee foreign corporation received by the U.S. transferor in the initial transfer.

(iii) *Transferred stock or securities.*—References to transferred stock or securities includes any stock or securities of the transferred corporation the basis of which is determined, in whole or in part, by reference to the basis of the stock or securities transferred in the initial transfer.

(c) *Gain recognition agreement.*—(1) *Terms of agreement.*—(i) *General rule.*—Except as provided in this paragraph (c)(1)(i), if a gain recognition event occurs during the period beginning on the date of the initial transfer and ending as of the close of the fifth full taxable year (not less than 60 months) following the close of the taxable year in which the initial transfer occurs (GRA term), the U.S. transferor must include in income the gain realized but not recognized on the initial transfer by reason of entering into the gain recognition agreement. In the case of a gain recognition event that occurs as a result of a partial disposition of stock, securities, or a partnership interest, as applicable, the U.S. transferor is required to recognize a proportionate amount of the gain subject to the gain recognition agreement, determined based on the fair market value of the stock, securities, or

partnership interest, as applicable, disposed of (measured at the time of the partial disposition) as compared to the fair market value of all the stock, securities, or partnership interest, as applicable (measured at the time of the partial disposition). If the U.S. transferor must recognize gain under this paragraph as a result of an event described in paragraph (m) or (n) of this section, see those paragraphs to determine the amount of the gain that must be recognized. The amount of gain subject to the gain recognition agreement shall be reduced by the amount of gain recognized under this paragraph. If the amount of gain subject to the gain recognition agreement is reduced to zero, the gain recognition agreement shall terminate without further effect.

(ii) *Ordering rule for gain recognized under multiple gain recognition agreements.*—If a gain recognition event occurs that requires gain to be recognized under multiple gain recognition agreements, gain shall first be recognized under the gain recognition agreement that relates to the earliest initial transfer, then under the gain recognition agreement that relates to the immediately following initial transfer and so forth until the appropriate amount of gain has been recognized under each gain recognition agreement. The amount of gain recognized under a gain recognition agreement shall be determined after taking into account, as appropriate, any increase to basis (including the basis of the transferred stock or securities) under paragraph (c)(4) of this section resulting from gain recognized under another gain recognition agreement. For an illustration of this ordering rule, see paragraph (q)(2)(vi) of this section.

(iii) *Taxable year in which gain is reported.*—(A) *Year of initial transfer.*—Except as provided in paragraph (c)(1)(iii)(B) of this section, the U.S. transferor must report any gain recognized under paragraph (c)(1)(i) of this section on an amended Federal income tax return for the taxable year of the initial transfer. The amended return must be filed on or before the 90th day following the date on which the gain recognition event occurs.

(B) *Year of gain recognition event.*—If an election under paragraph (c)(2)(vi) of this section is made with the gain recognition agreement or if paragraph (c)(5)(ii) of this section applies to the gain recognition agreement, the U.S. transferor must report any gain recognized under paragraph (c)(1)(i) of this section on its Federal income tax return for the taxable year during which the gain recognition event occurs. If an election under paragraph (c)(2)(vi) of this section is made with the gain recognition agreement or if paragraph (c)(5)(ii) of this section applies to the gain recognition agreement but the U.S. transferor does not report the gain recognized on its Federal income tax return for the taxable year during which the gain recognition event occurs, the Commissioner may require the U.S. transferor to report the gain on an amended Federal income tax return for the taxable year during which the initial transfer occurred.

(iv) *Offsets.*—No special limitations apply with respect to offsetting gain recognized under paragraph (c)(1)(i) of this section with net operating losses, capital losses, credits against tax, or similar items.

(v) *Payment and reporting of interest.*—Interest must be paid on any additional tax due with respect to gain recognized by the U.S. transferor under paragraph (c)(1)(i) of this section. Any interest due shall be determined based on the rates under section 6621 for the period between the date that was prescribed for filing the Federal income tax return of the U.S. transferor for the year of the initial transfer and the date on which the additional tax due is paid. If paragraph (c)(1)(iii)(B) of this section applies, any interest due must be included with the payment of tax due with the Federal income tax return of the U.S. transferor for the taxable year during which the gain recognition event occurs (or should reduce the amount of any refund due to the U.S. transferor for such taxable year). A schedule entitled "Calculation of Section 367 Tax and Interest" that separately identifies and calculates any additional tax and interest due must be included with the Federal income tax return on which any interest due is reported.

(2) *Content of gain recognition agreement.*—The gain recognition agreement must be entitled "GAIN RECOGNITION AGREEMENT UNDER §1.367(a)-8" and include the information described in paragraphs (c)(2)(i) through (viii) of this paragraph with the corresponding paragraph numbers. The information required under this paragraph (c)(2) and paragraph (c)(3) of this section must be included in the gain recognition agreement as filed.

(i) A statement that the document constitutes an agreement by the U.S. transferor to recognize gain in accordance with the requirements of this section.

(ii) A description of the transferred stock or securities and other information as required in paragraph (c)(3) of this section.

(iii) A statement that the U.S. transferor agrees to comply with all the conditions and requirements of this section, including to recognize gain under the gain recognition agreement in accordance with paragraph (c)(1)(i) of this section, to extend the period of limitations on assessment of tax as provided in paragraph (f) of this section, to file the certification described in paragraph (g) of this section, and, as provided in paragraph (j)(8) of this section, to treat a failure to comply (as described in paragraph (j)(8) of this section) as extending the period of limitations on assessment of tax for the taxable year in which gain is required to be reported.

(iv) A statement that arrangements have been made to ensure that the U.S. transferor is informed of any events that affect the gain recognition agreement, including triggering events or other gain recognition events.

(v) In the case of a new gain recognition agreement filed under this section—

(A) A description of the event (such as a triggering event) and the applicable exception, if any, that gave rise to the new gain recognition agreement (such as a triggering event exception), including the date of the event and the name, address, and taxpayer identification number (if any) of each person that is a party to the event;

(B) As applicable, a description of the class, amount, and characteristics of the stock, securities or partnership interest received in the transaction; and

(C) As applicable, a calculation of the amount of gain that remains subject to the new gain recognition agreement as a result of the application of paragraph (m), (n), or (o) of this section.

(vi) A statement whether the U.S. transferor elects to include in income any gain recognized under paragraph (c)(1)(i) of this section in the taxable year during which a gain recognition event occurs. See paragraph (c)(5)(ii) of this section for a rule that requires, in certain cases, for the gain recognized pursuant to a new gain recognition agreement to be included in income during the taxable year in which the gain recognition event occurs.

(vii) A statement whether a gain recognition event has occurred during the taxable year of the initial transfer.

(viii) A statement describing any disposition of assets of the transferred corporation during such taxable year other than in the ordinary course of business.

(3) *Description of transferred stock or securities and other information.*—The gain recognition agreement shall include the following:

(i) A description of the transferred stock or securities including—

(A) The type or class, amount, and characteristics of the transferred stock or securities;

(B) A calculation of the amount of the built-in gain in the transferred stock or securities that are subject to the gain recognition agreement, reflecting the basis and fair market value on the date of the initial transfer;

(C) The amount of any gain recognized by the U.S. transferor on the initial transfer; and

(D) The percentage (by voting power and value) that the transferred stock (if any) represents of the total stock outstanding of the transferred corporation on the date of the initial transfer.

(ii) The name, address, place of incorporation, and taxpayer identification number (if any) of the transferred corporation.

(iii) The date on which the U.S. transferor acquired the transferred stock or securities.

(iv) The name, address and place of incorporation of the transferee foreign corporation, and a description of the stock or securities received by the U.S. transferor in the initial transfer, including the percentage of stock (by vote and value) of the transferee foreign corporation received in such exchange.

(v) If the initial transfer is described in § 1.367(a)-3(e), a statement that the conditions of section 367(a)(5) and any regulations under that section have been satisfied, and a description of any adjustments to the basis of the stock received in the transaction or other adjustments made pursuant to section 367(a)(5) and any regulations under that section.

(vi) If the transferred corporation is domestic, a statement describing the application of section 7874 to the transaction, and indicating that the requirements of § 1.367(a)-3(c)(1) are satisfied.

(vii) *If the transferred corporation is foreign,* a statement indicating whether the U.S. transferor was a section 1248 shareholder (as defined in § 1.367(b)-2(b)) of the transferred corporation immediately before the initial transfer, and whether the U.S. transferor is a section 1248 shareholder with respect to the transferee foreign corporation immediately after the initial transfer, and whether any reporting requirements or other rules contained in regulations under section 367(b) are applicable, and, if so, whether they have been satisfied.

(viii) If the initial transfer involves a transfer by a partnership (see § 1.367(a)-1(c)(3)(i)) or a transfer of a partnership interest (see section 367(a)(4) and § 1.367(a)-1(c)(3)(ii)) a complete description of the transfer, including a description of the partners in the partnership.

(ix) If the transaction involved the transfer of property other than the transferred stock or securities and the transaction was subject to the indirect stock transfer rules of § 1.367(a)-3(d), a statement indicating whether—

(A) The reporting requirements under section 6038B have been satisfied with respect to the transfer of such other property;

(B) Whether gain was recognized under section 367(a)(1);

(C) Whether section 367(d) applied to the transfer of such property; and

(D) Whether the other property transferred qualified for the active foreign trade or business exception under section 367(a)(3).

(4) *Basis adjustments for gain recognized.*—The following basis adjustments shall be made if gain is recognized under paragraph (c)(1)(i) of this section.

(i) *Stock or securities of transferee foreign corporation.*—The basis of the stock or securities, as applicable, of the transferee foreign corporation received by the U.S. transferor in the initial transfer shall be increased as of the date of the initial transfer by the amount of gain recognized.

(ii) *Transferred stock or securities.*—The basis of the transferred stock or securities shall be increased as of the date of the initial transfer by the amount of the gain recognized.

(iii) *Other appropriate adjustments.*—The basis of other stock, securities, or a partnership interest shall be increased, as appropriate, in accordance with the principles of this paragraph (c)(4). Under no circumstances shall the basis of stock, securities, or of a partnership interest held by a U.S. person that does not recognize gain under paragraph (c)(1)(i) of this section be increased under this paragraph (c)(4). In addition, under no circumstances shall the basis of any property be increased by the amount of any additional tax due or interest paid with respect to such tax, nor shall the basis of the assets of the transferred corporation be increased as a result of gain recognized by the U.S. transferor under paragraph (c)(1)(i) of this section.

(iv) *Cross-reference.*—See paragraphs (q)(2)(i), (ii), (iii), and (v) of this section for illustrations of the rules of this paragraph (c)(4). See also § 1.367(a)-1(b)(4) for rules that determine the increase to basis of property resulting from the application of section 367(a).

(5) *Terms and conditions of a new gain recognition agreement.*—(i) *General rule.*—A new gain recognition agreement entered into pursuant to this section shall replace the existing gain recognition agreement, which shall terminate without further effect. The term of the new gain recognition agreement shall be the remaining term of the existing gain recognition agreement. The amount of gain subject to the new gain recognition agreement shall equal the amount of gain subject to the existing gain recognition agreement, reduced by any gain recognized under paragraph (c)(1)(i) of this section with respect to the existing gain recognition agreement by reason of the gain recognition event that gives rise to the new gain recognition agreement. The new gain recognition agreement shall, as applicable, be subject to the conditions and requirements of this section to the same extent as the existing gain recognition agreement. For example, a triggering event with respect to the new gain recognition agreement will generally include a disposition of the transferred stock or securities or of substantially all the assets of the transferred corporation. If, however, the transferred stock is canceled or redeemed pursuant to the disposition or other event that gives rise to the new gain recognition agreement (for example, pursuant to a liquidation where the transferee foreign corporation is the corporate distributee (within the meaning of section 334(b)(2)), or an asset reorganization where the transferee foreign corporation is the acquiring corporation) the transferred stock is not subject to the new gain recognition agreement.

(ii) *Special rule for inclusion of gain.*—If the U.S. transferor with respect to the new gain recognition agreement is not the U.S. transferor with respect to the existing gain recognition agreement, or a member of the consolidated group of which the U.S. transferor with respect to the existing gain recognition agreement was a member on the date of the initial transfer, then any gain recognized under paragraph (c)(1)(i) of this section with respect to the new gain recognition agreement must be included in income in the taxable year during which the gain recognition event occurs.

(6) *Cross-reference.*—For gain recognition agreements entered into pursuant to certain outbound asset reorganizations, see § 1.367(a)-3(e)(6).

(d) *Filing requirements.*—(1) *General rule.*—An initial gain recognition agreement must be timely filed in order for the U.S. transferor to avoid recognizing gain under section 367(a)(1) with respect to the transferred stock or securities by reason of the applicable exceptions provided under §1.367(a)-3. Except as provided in paragraph (p) of this section, an initial gain recognition agreement is timely filed only if—

(i) The initial gain recognition agreement and any other gain recognition agreement document required to be filed with the initial gain recognition agreement are included with a timely filed return of the U.S. transferor for the taxable year during which the initial transfer occurs; and

(ii) Each gain recognition agreement document identified in paragraph (d)(1)(i) of this section is completed in all material respects.

(2) *Special requirements.*—(i) *New gain recognition agreement.*—A new gain recognition agreement entered into under this section must be included with the timelyfiled return of the U.S. transferor (as identified in the new gain recognition agreement) for the taxable year during which the disposition or event that requires the new gain recognition agreement occurs. If the new gain recognition agreement is entered into by the U.S. transferor that entered into the existing gain recognition agreement, the new gain recognition agreement is in lieu of the annual certification otherwise required for such taxable year under paragraph (g) of this section with respect to the existing gain recognition agreement.

(ii) *Multiple events within a taxable year.*—Except as otherwise provided in this paragraph (d)(2)(ii), if the initial transfer and one or more dispositions or other events (even if a triggering event exception applies) that affect the gain recognition agreement entered into by the U.S. transferor with respect to the initial transfer occur within the same taxable year of such U.S. transferor, or if multiple dispositions or other events occur in a taxable year of the U.S. transferor that does not include the initial transfer, only one gain recognition agreement is required to be entered into and included with the timely-filed return of the U.S. transferor for such taxable year. The gain recognition agreement must describe the initial transfer and/or each disposition or other event that affects the gain recognition agreement (even if a triggering event exception applies). This paragraph does not apply, however, if any such disposition or other event requires a new gain recognition agreement to be entered into by a United States person other than the U.S. transferor with respect to the initial transfer or that entered into the existing gain recognition agreement, as applicable.

(3) *Common parent as agent for U.S. transferor.*—If the U.S. transferor is a member but not the common parent of a consolidated group, the common parent of the consolidated group is the agent for the U.S. transferor under §1.1502-77(a)(1). Thus, the common parent must file the gain recognition agreement on behalf of the U.S. transferor. References in this section to the timely-filed return of the U.S. transferor include the timely-filed return of the consolidated group of which the U.S. transferor is a member, as applicable.

(e) *Signatory.*—(1) *General rule.*—The gain recognition agreement must be signed under penalties of perjury by an agent of the U.S. transferor that is authorized to sign under a general or specific power of attorney, or by the appropriate party based on the category of the U.S. transferor described in this paragraph (e)(1).

(i) If the U.S. transferor is a corporation but not a member of a consolidated group, a responsible officer of the U.S. transferor. If the U.S. transferor is a member of a consolidated group, a responsible officer of the common parent of the consolidated group.

(ii) If the U.S. transferor is an individual, the individual.

(iii) If the U.S. transferor is a trust or estate, a trustee, executor, or equivalent fiduciary of the U.S. transferor.

(iv) In a bankruptcy case under Title 11, United States Code, a debtor in possession or trustee.

(2) *Signature requirement.*—The inclusion of an unsigned copy of the gain recognition agreement with the timely-filed return of the U.S. transferor shall satisfy the signature requirement of paragraph (e)(1) of this section if the U.S. transferor retains the original signed gain recognition agreement in the manner specified by §1.6001-1(e).

(f) *Extension of period of limitations on assessments of tax.*—(1) *General rule.*—In connection with the filing of a gain recognition agreement, the U.S. transferor must extend the period of limitations on assessments of tax with respect to the gain realized but not recognized on the initial transfer through the close of the eighth full taxable year following the taxable year during which the initial transfer occurs. The U.S. transferor extends the period of limitations by filing Form 8838 "Consent to Extend the Time to Assess Tax Under Section 367—Gain Recognition Agreement." The Form 8838 must be signed by a person authorized to sign the gain recognition agreement under paragraph (e)(1) of this section.

(2) *New gain recognition agreement.*—If a new gain recognition agreement is entered into under this section, the U.S. transferor must

extend the period of limitations on assessments of tax on the initial transfer through the close of the eighth full taxable year following the taxable year during which the initial transfer occurs, consistent with paragraph (f)(1) of this section, unless the U.S. transferor with respect to the new gain recognition agreement is the U.S. transferor with respect to the existing gain recognition agreement, or a member of the consolidated group of which the U.S. transferor with respect to the existing gain recognition agreement was a member on the date of the initial transfer.

(g) *Annual certification.*—Except as provided in paragraph (d)(2)(i) of this section, the U.S. transferor must include with its timely-filed return for each of the five full taxable years following the taxable year of the initial transfer a certification (annual certification) that includes the information described in paragraphs (g)(1) through (3) of this section, as appropriate. The annual certification must be signed by a person authorized under paragraph (e)(1) of this section to sign the gain recognition agreement for the initial transfer. The inclusion of an unsigned copy of the annual certification with the relevant timely-filed return of the U.S. transferor shall satisfy the signature requirement of paragraph (e)(1) of this section provided the U.S. transferor retains the original signed certification in the manner specified by §1.6001-1(e).

(1) A statement of whether a gain recognition event has or has not occurred during such taxable year. If a gain recognition event has occurred during such taxable year, the annual certification must state:

(i) The amount of gain subject to the gain recognition agreement at the time of the gain recognition event;

(ii) The amount of gain recognized under the gain recognition agreement by reason of the gain recognition event; and

(iii) A calculation of the reduction to the amount of gain subject to the gain recognition agreement by reason of the gain recognition event (for example, in the case of a gain recognition event described in paragraph (n)(2) of this section).

(2) A complete description of any event occurring during such taxable year that has terminated or reduced the amount of gain subject to the gain recognition agreement (for example, an event described in paragraph (o) of this section), including a calculation of any reduction to the amount of gain subject to the gain recognition agreement.

(3) A statement describing any disposition of assets of the transferred corporation during the taxable year not in the ordinary course of business.

(h) *Use of security.*—The U.S. transferor may be required to furnish a bond or other security that satisfies the requirements of §301.7101-1 if the Area Director, Field Examination, Small Business/Self Employed or the Director of Field Operations, Large and Mid-Size Business (Director) determines that such security is necessary to ensure the payment of any tax on the gain realized, but not recognized, upon the initial transfer. Such bond or security generally will be required only if the transferred stock or securities are a principal asset of the U.S. transferor and the Director has reason to believe that a disposition of the stock or securities may be contemplated.

(i) [Reserved.]

(j) *Triggering events.*—Except as provided in this section, if an event described in paragraphs (j)(1) through (10) of this section (triggering event) occurs during the GRA term, the U.S. transferor must recognize gain under the gain recognition agreement in accordance with paragraph (c)(1)(i) of this section. This paragraph (j) generally requires the U.S. transferor to recognize gain (and pay applicable interest with respect to any additional tax due as provided in paragraph (c)(1)(v) of this section) under the gain recognition agreement to the extent the transferred stock or securities are disposed of, directly or indirectly. This paragraph (j) also requires the U.S. transferor to recognize gain under the gain recognition agreement in certain cases where it is not appropriate for the gain recognition agreement to continue. See paragraph (k) of this section for exceptions available for certain events that would otherwise constitute triggering events under this paragraph (j). See paragraph (o) of this section for certain events that terminate or reduce the amount of gain subject to a gain recognition agreement.

(1) *Disposition of transferred stock or securities.*—A complete or partial disposition of the transferred stock or securities. See paragraph (q)(2)(ii) of this section for an illustration of the rule of this paragraph (j)(1).

(2) *Disposition of substantially all of the assets of the transferred corporation.*—(i) *General rule.*—Except as provided in paragraph (j)(2)(ii) of this section, a disposition in one or more related transactions of substantially all of the assets of the transferred corporation (including stock or securities in a subsidiary corporation or a partner-

ship interest). If the transferred corporation is domestic, see paragraph (o)(4) of this section.

(ii) *Exceptions.*—For purposes of paragraph (j)(2)(i) of this section, the following dispositions shall be disregarded—

(A) Dispositions of property described in section 1221(a)(1) occurring in the ordinary course of business;

(B) An exchange of stock or securities described in section 354 that is pursuant to an asset reorganization; and

(C) An exchange of stock by a corporate distributee (as defined in section 334(b)(2)) pursuant to a complete liquidation to which section 332 applies.

(3) *Disposition of certain partnership interests.*—If the initial transfer occurs by reason of the transfer of a partnership interest, a complete or partial disposition of such partnership interest. See section 367(a)(4) and § 1.367(a)-1(c)(3)(ii).

(4) *Disposition of stock of the transferee foreign corporation.*—A complete or partial disposition of the stock of the transferee foreign corporation received by the U.S. transferor in the initial transfer. For purposes of this section, an individual U.S. transferor that loses U.S. citizenship or ceases to be a lawful permanent resident of the United States (within the meaning of section 7701(b)(6)) shall be treated as disposing of all the stock of the transferee foreign corporation received in the initial transfer as of the date before the loss of such status.

(5) *Deconsolidation.*—A U.S. transferor that is a member of a consolidated group ceases to be a member of the consolidated group, other than by reason of an acquisition of the assets of the U.S. transferor in a transaction to which section 381(a) applies, or by reason of the U.S. transferor joining another consolidated group as part of the same transaction.

(6) *Consolidation.*—A U.S. transferor becomes a member of a consolidated group, including a U.S. transferor that is a member of a consolidated group and that becomes a member of another consolidated group.

(7) *Death of an individual; trust or estate ceases to exist.*—A U.S. transferor that is an individual dies, or a U.S. transferor that is a trust or estate ceases to exist.

(8) *Failure to comply.*—A U.S. transferor fails to comply in any material respect with any requirement of this section, or the terms of the gain recognition agreement as described in paragraph (c)(1) of this section. A failure to comply under this paragraph (j)(8) will extend the period of limitations on assessment of tax for the taxable year in which gain is required to be reported until the close of the third full taxable year ending after the date on which the U.S. transferor furnishes to the Director of Field Operations, Cross Border Activities Practice Area of Large Business & International (or any successor to the roles and responsibilities of such person) (Director) the information that should have been provided under this section. Except as provided in paragraph (p) of this section, for purposes of this paragraph (j)(8), a failure to comply includes—

(i) If there is a gain recognition event in a taxable year, a failure to report gain or pay any additional tax or interest due under the terms of the gain recognition agreement; and

(ii) A failure to file a gain recognition agreement document, other than an initial gain recognition agreement or a document required to be filed with the initial gain recognition agreement. For this purpose, there is a failure to file a gain recognition agreement document if—

(A) The gain recognition agreement document is not timely filed as required under this section, or

(B) The gain recognition agreement document is not completed in all material respects.

(9) *Gain recognition agreement filed in connection with indirect stock transfers and certain triangular asset reorganizations.*—With respect to a gain recognition agreement entered into in connection with an indirect stock transfer (as defined in § 1.367(a)-3(d)), or a triangular asset reorganization described in § 1.367(a)-3(e)(6)(iv), an indirect disposition of the transferred stock or securities. For example, in the case of an indirect stock transfer described in § 1.367(a)-3(d)(1)(iii)(A), a complete or partial disposition of the stock of the acquiring corporation.

(10) *Gain recognition agreement filed pursuant to paragraph (k)(14) of this section.*—In the case of a gain recognition agreement entered into pursuant to paragraph (k)(14) of this section, in addition to any disposition or other event described in paragraphs (j)(1) through (9) of this section,—

(i) Any disposition or other event identified as a triggering event in a new gain recognition agreement as required under paragraph (k)(14)(iii) of this section; and

(ii) Any disposition or other event that is inconsistent with the principles of paragraph (k) of this section including, for example, an indirect disposition of the transferred stock or securities.

(k) *Triggering event exceptions.*—Notwithstanding paragraph (j) of this section, a disposition or other event described in paragraphs (k)(1) through (14) of this section shall not constitute a triggering event. This paragraph (k) generally provides exceptions for certain dispositions that constitute nonrecognition transactions but only if, immediately after the disposition, a U.S. transferor retains, as applicable, a direct or indirect interest in the transferred stock or securities, or in the assets of the transferred corporation, and a new gain recognition agreement is entered into with respect to the initial transfer in accordance with this paragraph (k). Notwithstanding the application of this paragraph (k), if a gain recognition event described under paragraphs (m) and (n) of this section occurs during the GRA term the U.S. transferor may be required to recognize gain under the gain recognition agreement in accordance with paragraph (c)(1)(i) of this section. See paragraph (o) of this section which provides that, notwithstanding paragraph (j) of this section, certain dispositions or other events shall instead terminate or reduce the amount of gain subject to a gain recognition agreement.

(1) *Transfers of stock of the transferee foreign corporation to a corporation or partnership.*—A disposition of stock of the transferee foreign corporation received in the initial transfer pursuant to an exchange to which section 351, 354 (but only in a reorganization described in section 368(a)(1)(B) that is not a triangular reorganization), 361 (but only in a divisive reorganization to which section 355 applies), or 721 applies, shall not constitute a triggering event if a new gain recognition agreement is entered into in accordance with paragraphs (k)(1)(i) through (iv) of this section, as applicable. In the case of an exchange to which section 354 applies that is pursuant to a triangular reorganization described in section 368(a)(1)(B), see paragraph (k)(14) of this section and paragraph (q)(2)(iv) of this section.

(i) In the case of an exchange to which section 351 or 354 applies in which stock of a foreign acquiring corporation is received, the U.S. transferor includes with the new gain recognition agreement a statement that a complete or partial disposition of the stock of the foreign acquiring corporation received in the exchange shall constitute a triggering event. The principles of paragraph (o)(1)(i) or (ii), as appropriate, shall be applied to determine whether a subsequent complete or partial disposition of the stock of the foreign acquiring corporation received in the exchange shall instead terminate or reduce the amount of the new gain recognition agreement.

(ii) In the case of an exchange to which section 351 or 354 applies in which stock of a domestic acquiring corporation is received, the domestic acquiring corporation enters into the new gain recognition agreement, which must designate the domestic acquiring corporation as the U.S. transferor for purposes of this section. For an illustration of the rule provided by this paragraph (k)(1)(ii), see paragraph (q)(2)(iii) of this section.

(iii) In the case of a section 361 exchange that is pursuant to a divisive reorganization to which section 355 applies and in which stock of a domestic corporation (domestic controlled corporation) is received, the domestic controlled corporation enters into the new gain recognition agreement, which must designate the domestic controlled corporation as the U.S. transferor for purposes of this section. For an illustration of the rule provided by this paragraph (k)(1)(iii), see paragraph (q)(2)(xi) of this section.

(iv) In the case of an exchange to which section 721 applies, the U.S. transferor includes with the new gain recognition agreement a statement that a complete or partial disposition of the partnership interest received in the exchange shall constitute a triggering event for purposes of the new gain recognition agreement.

(2) *Complete liquidation of U.S. transferor under sections 332 and 337.*—A distribution by the U.S. transferor of the stock of the transferee foreign corporation received in the initial transfer to which section 337 applies, that is pursuant to a complete liquidation under section 332, shall not constitute a triggering event if the corporate distributee (as defined in section 334(b)(2)) is a domestic corporation (domestic corporate distributee) and the domestic corporate distributee enters into a new gain recognition agreement. The new gain recognition agreement must designate the domestic corporate distributee as the U.S. transferor for purposes of this section.

(3) *Transfers of transferred stock or securities to a corporation or partnership.*—A disposition of the transferred stock or securities pursuant to an exchange to which section 351, 354 (but only in a reorganization described in section 368(a)(1)(B)), or 721 applies, shall not constitute a triggering event if the U.S. transferor enters in to a new gain recognition agreement that provides that the dispositions described in paragraphs (k)(3)(i) and (ii) of this section shall constitute triggering events for purposes of the new gain recognition agreement.

Reg. § 1.367(a)-8(k)(3)

(i) A complete or partial disposition of the stock, securities, or partnership interest (as applicable) received in exchange for the transferred stock or securities.

(ii) Any other event that is inconsistent with the principles of this paragraph (k), including the indirect disposition of the transferred stock or securities.

(4) *Transfers of substantially all of the assets of the transferred corporation.*—A disposition of substantially all of the assets of the transferred corporation pursuant to an exchange to which section 351, 354 (but only in a reorganization described in section 368(a)(1)(B)), or 721 applies, shall not constitute a triggering event if the U.S. transferor enters into a new gain recognition agreement that provides that a complete or partial disposition of the stock, securities, or partnership interest (as applicable) received in exchange for the assets shall constitute a triggering event for purposes of the new gain recognition agreement.

(5) *Recapitalizations and section 1036 exchanges.*—A complete or partial disposition of the transferred stock or securities, or of the stock of the transferee foreign corporation received in the initial transfer, pursuant to a reorganization described under section 368(a)(1)(E), or pursuant to a transaction to which section 1036 applies, shall not constitute a triggering event if the U.S. transferor enters into a new gain recognition agreement.

(6) *Certain asset reorganizations.*—(i) *Stock of transferee foreign corporation.*—If stock of the transferee foreign corporation received in the initial transfer is transferred to a domestic acquiring corporation in a section 361 exchange that is pursuant to an asset reorganization, the exchanges made pursuant to the asset reorganization shall not constitute triggering events if the domestic acquiring corporation enters into a new gain recognition agreement that designates the domestic acquiring corporation as the U.S. transferor for purposes of this section. For an illustration of the rule provided by this paragraph (k)(6), see paragraph (q)(2)(v) of this section. If the acquiring corporation is foreign, see paragraph (k)(14) of this section and paragraph (q)(2)(vi) of this section.

(ii) *Transferred stock or securities.*—If the transferred stock or securities are transferred to a foreign acquiring corporation in a section 361 exchange that is pursuant to an asset reorganization, the exchanges made pursuant to the asset reorganization shall not constitute triggering events if the U.S. transferor enters into a new gain recognition agreement that designates the foreign acquiring corporation as the transferee foreign corporation for purposes of this section. For an illustration of the rule provided by this paragraph, see paragraph (q)(2)(vii) of this section. If the transfer is to a domestic acquiring corporation, or is pursuant to a triangular asset reorganization, see paragraph (k)(14) or (o)(5) of this section.

(iii) *Assets of transferred corporation.*—If substantially all of the assets of the transferred corporation are transferred to a foreign or domestic acquiring corporation in a section 361 exchange that is pursuant to an asset reorganization, the exchanges made pursuant to the asset reorganization shall not constitute triggering events if the U.S. transferor enters into a new gain recognition agreement that, unless the acquiring corporation is the transferee foreign corporation, designates the acquiring corporation as the transferred corporation for purposes of this section. Only the assets of the transferred corporation received by the acquiring corporation shall be treated as assets of the transferred corporation for purposes of this section (for example, only such assets will be taken into account for purposes of paragraph (j)(2) of this section). For an illustration of the rule provided by this paragraph, see paragraph (q)(2)(viii) of this section. If the transferred corporation is domestic, see section 367(a)(1) and (a)(5), and paragraph (o)(4) of this section. If the transfer is pursuant to a triangular asset reorganization, see paragraph (k)(14) of this section.

(7) *Certain triangular reorganizations.*—(i) *Transferee foreign corporation.*—If substantially all of the assets of the transferee foreign corporation are transferred to a foreign acquiring corporation in a section 361 exchange that is pursuant to a triangular asset reorganization, the exchanges made pursuant to the reorganization shall not constitute triggering events if a new gain recognition agreement is entered into in accordance with paragraphs (k)(7)(i)(A) through (C) of this section. If the acquiring corporation is domestic, see paragraph (k)(14) of this section. For rules that apply to gain recognition agreements entered into as a result of an indirect stock transfer, see § 1.367(a)-3(d)(2)(iv) and paragraph (j)(9) of this section.

(A) If P is foreign, the new gain recognition agreement *designates* P as the transferee foreign corporation and includes a statement that the U.S. transferor agrees to treat a complete or partial disposition of the S stock held by P as a triggering event.

(B) Except as provided in paragraph (k)(7)(i)(C) of this section, if P is domestic, P enters into the new gain recognition agree-

ment that designates P as the U.S. transferor and S as the transferee foreign corporation.

(C) If the triangular asset reorganization is described in section 368(a)(1)(A) by reason of section 368(a)(2)(E) and the transferee foreign corporation is the merged corporation, the U.S. transferor enters into the new gain recognition agreement and designates the surviving corporation as the transferee foreign corporation.

(ii) *Transferred corporation.*—If substantially all of the assets of the transferred corporation are transferred in a section 361 exchange pursuant to a triangular asset reorganization, the exchanges made pursuant to the reorganization shall not constitute triggering events if the U.S. transferor enters into a new gain recognition agreement in accordance with paragraph (k)(7)(ii)(A) of this section and, as applicable, paragraph (k)(7)(ii)(B) or (C) of this section.

(A) The new gain recognition agreement includes a statement that the U.S. transferor agrees to treat a complete or partial disposition of the P stock received in the reorganization as a triggering event.

(B) If the triangular asset reorganization is described in section 368(a)(1)(C), or section 368(a)(1)(A) or (G) by reason of section 368(a)(2)(D), the new gain recognition agreement includes a statement that the U.S. transferor agrees to treat a complete or partial disposition of the S stock held by P as a triggering event.

(C) If the triangular asset reorganization is described in section 368(a)(1)(A) by reason of section 368(a)(2)(E) and the transferred corporation is the merged corporation, the new gain recognition agreement includes a statement that the U.S. transferor agrees to treat a complete or partial disposition of the stock of the surviving corporation as a triggering event.

(8) *Complete liquidation of transferred corporation.*—A distribution of substantially all of the assets of the transferred corporation to which section 337 applies, and the related exchange of the transferred stock to which section 332 applies, shall not constitute triggering events, if the U.S. transferor enters into a new gain recognition agreement. If the transferred corporation is domestic, see § 1.367(e)-2 and paragraph (o)(4) of this section. See paragraph (q)(2)(ix) of this section for an illustration of the rules provided in this paragraph (k)(8).

(9) *Death of U.S. transferor.*—The death of a U.S. transferor shall not constitute a triggering event if the person winding up the affairs of the U.S. transferor—

(i) Retains sufficient assets of the U.S. transferor to satisfy any possible Federal tax liability of the U.S. transferor under the gain recognition agreement for the duration of the extended period of limitations on assessments of tax on the gain realized but not recognized in the initial transfer;

(ii) Provides security as required under paragraph (h) of this section for any possible Federal tax liability of the U.S. transferor under the gain recognition agreement; or

(iii) Obtains a ruling from the Internal Revenue Service providing for one or more successors to the U.S. transferor under the gain recognition agreement.

(10) *Deconsolidation.*—A deconsolidation of the U.S. transferor shall not constitute a triggering event if the U.S. transferor enters into a new gain recognition agreement.

(11) *Consolidation.*—A consolidation of the U.S. transferor shall not constitute a triggering event if the U.S. transferor enters into a new gain recognition agreement. See paragraph (d)(3) of this section.

(12) *Intercompany transactions.*—(i) *General rule.*—If, pursuant to an intercompany transaction, the U.S. transferor disposes of stock of the transferee foreign corporation received in the initial transfer, this paragraph (k)(12) applies to such disposition to the extent the intercompany transaction creates an intercompany item that is not taken into account in the taxable year during which the intercompany transaction occurs. To the extent this paragraph (k)(12) applies, the disposition shall not constitute a triggering event, and the U.S. transferor shall remain subject to the gain recognition agreement if the conditions of paragraphs (k)(12)(i)(A) and (B) of this section are satisfied. To the extent the intercompany transaction does not create an intercompany item see, for example, paragraph (k)(1) and paragraph (q)(2)(xx) of this section. See paragraph (o)(6) of this section for the effect on a gain recognition agreement when an intercompany item from an intercompany transaction to which this paragraph (k)(12)(i) applies is taken into account.

(A) At the time of the disposition, the basis of the stock of the transferee foreign corporation received in the initial transfer that is disposed of in the intercompany transaction is not greater than the sum of the amounts described in paragraphs (k)(12)(i)(A)(1) through (3) of this section. If only a portion of the stock of the transferee foreign corporation received in the initial transfer is disposed of, then the basis of such stock shall be compared with a proportionate amount (measured by value as determined at the time of the disposition) of the amounts described in paragraph (k)(12)(i)(A)(1) through (3) of this section. To satisfy the basis condition of this paragraph (k)(12)(i)(A), the U.S. transferor may reduce the basis of the stock of the transferee foreign corporation received in the initial transfer that is disposed of in the intercompany transaction in accordance with the principles of paragraph (o)(1)(iii) of this section.

    (1) The aggregate basis of the transferred stock or securities at the time of the initial transfer;

    (2) The amount of any increase to the basis of the transferred stock or securities by reason of gain recognized by the U.S. transferor on the initial transfer; and

    (3) The amount of any increase to the basis of the stock disposed of by reason of an income inclusion by the U.S. transferor with respect to such stock (for example, pursuant to section 961(a)).

    (B) The annual certification filed with respect to the existing gain recognition agreement for the taxable year during which the intercompany transaction occurs includes a complete description of the intercompany transaction and a schedule illustrating how the basis condition of paragraph (k)(12)(i)(A) of this section is satisfied.

    (ii) *Certain dispositions following intercompany transaction.*—A subsequent disposition of stock of the transferee foreign corporation that is transferred in an intercompany transaction to which the exception provided by paragraph (k)(12)(i) of this section applies shall not constitute a triggering event if—

    (A) The stock is transferred to a member of the consolidated group that includes the U.S. transferor immediately after the disposition, and

    (B) The annual certification filed with respect to the existing gain recognition agreement for the taxable year during which the subsequent disposition occurs includes a complete description of the disposition.

    (13) *Deemed asset sales pursuant to section 338(g) elections.*—A deemed sale of the assets of the transferred corporation or the transferee foreign corporation as a result of an election under section 338(g) shall not constitute a triggering event. This paragraph does not apply to the sale of the stock of the target corporation (within the meaning of section 338(d)(2)) with respect to which such election is made.

    (14) *Other dispositions or events.*—A disposition or other event that would constitute a triggering event, without regard to this paragraph (k)(14), shall not constitute a triggering event if the conditions of paragraph (k)(14)(i) through (iii) of this section, as applicable, are satisfied. See paragraphs (q)(2)(iv), (vi), (x), (xii), (xvii), (xxi), and (xxiii) of this section for illustrations of the rules provided by this paragraph (k)(14).

    (i) The disposition qualifies as a nonrecognition transaction.

    (ii) Immediately after the disposition or other event, a U.S. transferor retains a direct or indirect interest in the transferred stock or securities or, as applicable, in substantially all of the assets of the transferred corporation (for example, in a case where the transferred corporation has been liquidated pursuant to section 332). If, as a result of the disposition or other event, a foreign corporation acquires the transferred stock or securities or, as applicable, substantially all the assets of the transferred corporation, the condition of this paragraph (k)(14)(ii) is satisfied only if the U.S. transferor owns at least five percent (applying the attribution rules of section 318, as modified by section 958(b) but without applying section 318(a)(3)(A), (B), and (C) so as to consider the U.S. transferor as owning stock which is owned by a person who is not a United States person) of the total voting power and the total value of the outstanding stock of such foreign corporation.

    (iii) A new gain recognition agreement is entered into by the U.S. transferor described in paragraph (k)(14)(ii) of this section that includes—

    (A) An explanation of why this paragraph (k)(14) applies to the disposition or other event; and

    (B) A description of each subsequent disposition or other event that would constitute a triggering event, other than those described in paragraph (j) of this section, with respect to the new gain recognition agreement based on the principles of paragraphs (j) and (k) of this section including, for example, an indirect disposition of the transferred stock or securities.

    (l) [Reserved.]

    (m) *Receipt of boot in nonrecognition transactions.*—(1) *Dispositions of transferred stock or securities.*—Notwithstanding paragraph (k) of this section, if gain is required to be recognized (not including any gain that would be treated as a dividend under section 356(a)(2)) in connection with a disposition of the transferred stock or securities to which an exception under paragraph (k) of this section otherwise applies (triggering event exception), the U.S. transferor shall recognize gain under paragraph (c)(1)(i) of this section equal to the amount of gain required to be recognized in connection with the disposition, but not in excess of the amount of gain subject to the gain recognition agreement. For purposes of this paragraph (m)(1), the amount of gain required to be recognized in connection with the disposition shall be determined before taking into account any increase to the basis of the transferred stock or securities under paragraph (c)(4)(ii) of this section. See paragraph (q)(2)(xiii) of this section, for an illustration of the rule provided by this paragraph (m)(1).

    (2) *Dispositions of assets of transferred corporation.*—If gain is required to be recognized (not including any gain that would be treated as a dividend under section 356(a)(2)) in connection with a disposition of substantially all of the assets of the transferred corporation to which a triggering event exception otherwise applies, the U.S. transferor shall recognize gain under paragraph (c)(1)(i) of this section equal to the amount of gain required to be recognized in connection with the disposition, but not in excess of the amount of gain subject to the gain recognition agreement.

    (n) *Special rules for distributions with respect to stock.*—(1) *Certain dividend equivalent redemptions treated as dispositions.*—A redemption of the transferred stock or of stock of the transferee foreign corporation received in the initial transfer that is treated by reason of section 302(d) as a distribution of property to which section 301 applies shall constitute a disposition for purposes of this section unless the U.S. transferor enters into a new gain recognition agreement that includes appropriate provisions to account for the redemption. For an illustration of the rule of this paragraph (n)(1), see paragraph (q)(2)(xiv) of this section.

    (2) *Gain recognized under section 301(c)(3).*—If gain is required to be recognized under section 301(c)(3) with respect to the transferred stock, the U.S. transferor shall recognize gain under the gain recognition agreement in accordance with paragraph (c)(1)(i) of this section in an amount equal to the gain required to be recognized under section 301(c)(3), but not in excess of the amount of gain subject to the gain recognition agreement. For this purpose, the amount of gain required to be recognized under section 301(c)(3) shall be determined before taking into account any increase in the basis of the transferred stock under paragraph (c)(4)(ii) of this section.

    (o) *Dispositions or other events that terminate or reduce the amount of gain subject to the gain recognition agreement.*—Notwithstanding paragraph (j) of this section, the following dispositions or other events shall not constitute triggering events but instead shall terminate or reduce the amount of gain subject to the gain recognition agreement.

    (1) *Taxable disposition of stock of the transferee foreign corporation.*—(i) *Complete disposition.*—Except as otherwise provided in this paragraph (o)(1)(i), if the U.S. transferor disposes of all the stock of the transferee foreign corporation received in the initial transfer in a transaction in which all gain realized is recognized and included in taxable income during the taxable year of the disposition, the gain recognition agreement shall terminate without further effect if, at the time of the disposition, the aggregate basis of such stock is not greater than the sum of the amounts described in paragraphs (o)(1)(i)(A) through (C) of this section. This paragraph shall not apply to a disposition of stock of the transferee foreign corporation pursuant to an intercompany transaction to which paragraph (k)(12) of this section applies. This paragraph shall also not apply to an individual U.S. transferor that loses U.S. citizenship or ceases to be a lawful permanent resident of the United States (within the meaning of section 7701(b)(6)).

    (A) The aggregate basis of the transferred stock or securities at the time of the initial transfer;

    (B) The amount of any increase to the basis of the transferred stock or securities by reason of gain recognized by the U.S. transferor on the initial transfer; and

    (C) The amount of any increase to the basis of the stock disposed of by reason of an income inclusion by the U.S. transferor with respect to such stock (for example, pursuant to section 961(a)).

    (ii) *Partial dispositions.*—A partial disposition by the U.S. transferor of the stock of the transferee foreign corporation received in the initial transfer in a transaction otherwise described in paragraph (o)(1)(i) of this section shall reduce the amount of gain subject to the gain recognition agreement based on the relative fair market value of the stock disposed of (measured at the time of the disposition) compared to the fair market value of all of the stock of the transferee foreign corporation received in the initial transfer (measured at the time of the disposition). For determining whether the basis condition of paragraph (o)(1)(i) of this section is satisfied in the case of a partial disposition, the aggregate basis of the stock disposed of is compared to a proportionate amount (based on fair market value, as measured at the time of the partial disposition) of the amounts described in paragraphs (o)(1)(i)(A) through (C) of this section. For an illustration of the rules of this paragraph (o)(1)(ii), see paragraph (q)(2)(xv) of this section, of this section.

(iii) *Reduction of stock basis.*—For purposes of satisfying the basis condition of paragraph (o)(1)(i) or (ii) of this section, the U.S. transferor may reduce the aggregate basis of the stock of the transferee foreign corporation received in the initial transfer, effective immediately before the disposition. For an illustration of the rules of this paragraph (o)(1)(iii), see paragraph (q)(2)(xvi) of this section, of this section. The U.S. transferor reduces the basis of the stock of the transferee foreign corporation by including a statement with the timely-filed return of the U.S. transferor for the taxable year in which the disposition occurs, entitled "Election to Reduce Stock Basis Under § 1.367(a)-8(o)(1)(iii)" and that includes—

(A) A description, including the date, of the disposition;

(B) A description of the stock of the transferee foreign corporation disposed of and the basis adjustments made under this paragraph (o)(1)(iii); and

(C) The fair market value of all the stock of the transferee foreign corporation held by the U.S. transferor at the time of the disposition.

(2) *Gain recognized in connection with certain nonrecognition transactions.*—If the U.S. transferor recognizes gain in connection with a complete or partial disposition of stock of the transferee foreign corporation received in the initial transfer that is described in paragraph (k) of this section, and the basis condition of paragraph (o)(1)(i) or (ii) of this section, as applicable, is satisfied with the respect to such disposition, the amount of gain subject to the new gain recognition agreement filed under paragraph (k) of this section as a result of such disposition shall equal the amount of gain subject to the existing gain recognition agreement reduced by the amount of gain recognized by the U.S. transferor on the disposition. If the U.S. transferor recognizes gain in connection with a complete or partial disposition of the stock of the transferee foreign corporation received in the initial transfer that is described in paragraph (k) of this section, and the condition of paragraph (o)(1)(i) or (ii) of this section, as applicable, is satisfied with the respect to the disposition, but a new gain recognition agreement is not filed with respect to such disposition so that a triggering event exception does not apply to the disposition, the amount of gain required to be recognized by the U.S. transferor under the existing gain recognition agreement shall be reduced by the amount of the gain recognized on the disposition.

(3) *Gain recognized under section 301(c)(3).*—If the U.S. transferor recognizes gain under section 301(c)(3) with respect to the stock of the transferee foreign corporation received in the initial transfer, the amount of gain subject to the gain recognition agreement shall be reduced by the amount of such recognized gain.

(4) *Dispositions of substantially all of the assets of a domestic transferred corporation.*—Except as otherwise provided in this paragraph (o)(4), the gain recognition agreement shall terminate without further effect if substantially all of the assets of the transferred corporation are disposed of in a transaction in which all gain realized is recognized and included in taxable income during the taxable year of the disposition, but only if, at the time of the initial transfer, the U.S. transferor owned stock in the transferred corporation satisfying the requirements of section 1504(a)(2) and the U.S. transferor and the transferred corporation were members of the same consolidated group. If the initial transfer was part of an indirect stock transfer, the gain recognition agreement shall terminate without further effect if substantially all of the assets of the transferred corporation (taking into account § 1.367(a)-3(d)(2)(v)) are disposed of in a transaction in which all gain realized is recognized and included in taxable income during the taxable year of the disposition, but only if at the time of the initial transfer the U.S. transferor owned stock in the transferred corporation satisfying the requirements of section 1504(a)(2) (for example, in the case of a reorganization described in section 368(a)(1)(A) by reason of section 368(a)(2)(E)) and the U.S. transferor and the transferred corporation were members of the same consolidated group.

(5) *Certain distributions or transfers of transferred stock or securities to U.S. persons.*—To the extent a distribution or transfer of the transferred stock or securities satisfies the conditions of paragraphs (o)(5)(i) through (iii) of this section, the gain recognition agreement shall terminate without further effect, or the amount of gain subject to the gain recognition agreement shall be reduced, as appropriate.

(i) *Distributions or transfers described in section 337, 355, or 361.*—The transferred stock or securities are distributed or transferred pursuant to a transaction described in paragraph (o)(5)(i)(A) through (D) of this section, as appropriate.

(A) A distribution described in section 337 that is pursuant to a complete liquidation described in section 332. See paragraph (q)(2)(xviii) of this section, for an illustration of the rule provided by this paragraph (o)(5)(i)(A).

(B) A distribution to which section 355 applies. See paragraph (q)(2)(xix) of this section, for an illustration of the rule provided by this paragraph (o)(5)(i)(B).

(C) A section 361 exchange that is pursuant to an asset reorganization. See paragraph (q)(2)(xxii) of this section, for an illustration of the rule provided by this paragraph (o)(5)(i)(C).

(D) A distribution to which section 361(c) applies that is pursuant to an asset reorganization. See paragraph (q)(2)(xxii) of this section, for an illustration of the rule provided by this paragraph (o)(5)(i)(D).

(ii) *Qualified recipient.*—The recipient of the transferred stock or securities in the relevant transaction described in paragraph (o)(5)(i) of this section (qualified recipient) is—

(A) The U.S. transferor;

(B) A member of the consolidated group that includes the U.S. transferor immediately after the transaction; or

(C) An individual that is a United States person.

(iii) *Basis requirement.*—(A) *General rule.*—Immediately after the relevant transaction described in paragraph (o)(5)(i) of this section, the aggregate basis of the transferred stock or securities received by the qualified recipient is not greater than the aggregate basis of such stock or securities at the time of the initial transfer (as adjusted for gain recognized by the U.S. transferor on the initial transfer attributable to such stock or securities). For this purpose, the basis of the transferred stock in the hands of the qualified recipient shall be determined without regard to any basis attributable to income inclusions with respect to the stock (for example, under section 961(a)). In the case of a distribution to which section 355 applies, any adjustments to basis under § 1.367(b)-5(c) shall be made before determining whether the basis condition of this paragraph is satisfied.

(B) *Election to reduce basis in transferred stock or securities.*—If the basis condition of paragraph (o)(5)(iii)(A) of this section is not satisfied, each qualified recipient may reduce the basis of the transferred stock or securities received in the transaction to the extent necessary to satisfy the basis condition. A qualified recipient reduces the basis of the transferred stock or securities by including a statement with its timely-filed return for the taxable year during which the distribution or transfer occurs entitled "Election to Reduce Stock Basis Under § 1.367(a)-8(o)(5)(iii)(B)" and that includes—

(1) A complete description and the date of the distribution or transfer;

(2) The fair market value of the transferred stock or securities received by the qualified recipient in the transaction; and

(3) The basis of the transferred stock or securities received by the qualified recipient immediately before and after the basis reduction.

(6) *Dispositions or other event following certain intercompany transactions.*—If, subsequent to an intercompany transaction to which paragraph (k)(12) of this section applies, a disposition or other event occurs that requires the U.S. transferor to take into account the intercompany item related to the intercompany transaction (under the provisions of § 1.1502-13), the gain recognition agreement shall terminate without further effect or the amount of gain subject to the gain recognition agreement shall be reduced based on the principles of paragraph (o)(1)(i) or (ii) of this section, as appropriate. For an illustration of the rules of this paragraph (o)(6), see paragraph (q)(2)(xx) of this section.

(7) *Expropriations under foreign law.*—The amount of gain subject to the gain recognition agreement shall be reduced to the extent the stock or securities of the transferee foreign corporation received in the initial transfer, the transferred stock or securities, or substantially all the assets of the transferred corporation, are expropriated, seized, or subjected to a similar taking of such property by the government of a foreign country, any political subdivision thereof, or any agency or instrumentality of the foregoing. Principles similar to those of paragraph (o)(1)(i) or (o)(1)(ii) of this paragraph, as relevant, shall be applied to determine the amount of the reduction.

(p) *Relief for certain failures to file or failures to comply that are not willful.*—(1) *In general.*—This paragraph (p) provides relief if there is a failure to file an initial gain recognition agreement as required under paragraph (d)(1) of this section (failure to file), or a failure to comply that is a triggering event under paragraph (j)(8) of this section (failure to comply). A failure to file or failure to comply will be deemed not to have occurred for purposes of paragraph (d)(1) of this section or paragraph (j)(8) of this section if the U.S. transferor demonstrates that the failure was not willful using the procedure set forth in this paragraph (p). For this purpose, willful is to be interpreted consistent with the meaning of that term in the context of other civil penalties, which would include a failure due to gross negligence, reckless disregard, or willful neglect. Whether a failure to file or failure to comply was willful will be determined by the Director (as described in paragraph (j)(8) of this section) based on all the facts and circumstances. The U.S. transferor must submit a request for relief and an explanation as provided in paragraph (p)(2)(i) of this section. Although a U.S. transferor whose failure to file or failure to comply is determined not to be willful will not be subject to gain recognition under paragraph (b), (c), or (e) of § 1.367(a)-3 or paragraph (c)(1) of this section, as applicable, the U.S. transferor will be subject to a penalty under section 6038B if the U.S. transferor fails to satisfy the reporting requirements under that section and does not demonstrate that the failure was due to reasonable cause and not willful neglect. See § 1.6038B-1(b)(2) and (f). The determination of whether the failure to file or failure to comply was willful under this section has no effect on any request for relief made under § 1.6038B-1(f).

(2) *Procedures for establishing that a failure to file or failure to comply was not willful.*—(i) *Time and manner of submission.*—A U.S. transferor's statement that a failure to file or failure to comply was not willful will be considered only if, promptly after the U.S. transferor becomes aware of the failure, an amended return is filed for the taxable year to which the failure relates that includes the information that should have been included with the original return for such taxable year or that otherwise complies with the rules of this section, and that includes a written statement explaining the reasons for the failure to file or failure to comply. The U.S. transferor must file, with the amended return, a Form 8838 extending the period of limitations on assessment of tax with respect to the gain realized but not recognized on the initial transfer to the later of: the close of the eighth full taxable year following the taxable year during which the initial transfer occurred (date one); or the close of the third full taxable year ending after the date on which the required information is provided to the Director (date two). However, the U.S. transferor is not required to file a Form 8838 with the amended return if both date one is later than date two and a Form 8838 was previously filed extending the period of limitations on assessment of tax with respect to the gain realized but not recognized on the initial transfer to date one. If a Form 8838 is not required to be filed with the amended return pursuant to the previous sentence, a copy of the previously filed Form 8838 must be filed with the amended return. The amended return and either a Form 8838 or a copy of the previously filed Form 8838, as the case may be, must be filed with the Internal Revenue Service at the location where the U.S. transferor filed its original return. The U.S. transferor may submit a request for relief from the penalty under section 6038B as part of the same submission. See § 1.6038B-1(f).

(ii) *Notice requirement.*—In addition to the requirements of paragraph (p)(2)(i) of this section, the U.S. transferor must comply with the notice requirements of this paragraph (p)(2)(ii). If any taxable year of the U.S. transferor is under examination when the amended return is filed, a copy of the amended return and any information required to be included with such return must be delivered to the Internal Revenue Service personnel conducting the examination. If no taxable year of the U.S. transferor is under examination when the amended return is filed, a copy of the amended return and any information required to be included with such return must be delivered to the Director.

(3) *Examples.*—The following examples illustrate the application of this paragraph (p). All of the examples are based solely on the following facts and any additional facts stated in the particular example. DC, a domestic corporation, wholly owns FS and FA, each a foreign corporation. In Year 1, pursuant to a transaction qualifying both as an exchange under section 351 and a reorganization under section 368(a)(1)(B), DC transferred all the FS stock to FA solely in exchange for voting stock of FA (FS Transfer). The fair market value of the FS stock exceeded DC's tax basis in the stock at the time of the FS transfer. Absent the application of section 367 to the transaction, DC's exchange of the FS stock for the stock of FA qualified as a tax-free exchange under sections 351(a) and section 354. Immediately after the transaction, both FA and FS were controlled foreign corporations (as defined in section 957). Furthermore, DC was a section 1248 shareholder (as defined in § 1.367(b)-2(b)) with respect to FA and FS, and a 5-percent shareholder with respect to FA for purposes of § 1.367(a)-3(b)(ii). Thus, DC was required to recognize gain under section 367(a)(1) by reason of the FS Transfer unless DC timely filed an initial gain recognition agreement (GRA) as required by paragraph (d)(1) of this section and complies in all material respects with the requirements of this section throughout the term of the GRA. The application of section 6038B is not addressed in these examples. DC may be subject to a penalty under section 6038B even if DC demon-

strates under this section that a failure to file or failure to comply was not willful. See § 1.6038B-1(b) and (f) for the application of section 6038B.

(i) *Example 1.—Taxpayer failed to file a GRA due to accidental oversight.* (A) *Facts.* DC filed its tax return for the year of the FS Transfer, reporting no gain with respect to the exchange of the FS stock. DC, through its tax department, was aware of the requirement to file a GRA in order for DC to avoid recognizing gain with respect to the FS Transfer under section 367(a)(1), and had the experience and competency to properly prepare the GRA. DC had filed many GRAs over the years and had never failed to timely file a GRA. However, although DC prepared the GRA with respect to the FS Transfer, it was not filed with DC's tax return for the year of the FS Transfer due to an accidental oversight. During the preparation of the following year's tax return, DC discovered that the GRA was not filed. DC filed an amended return to file the GRA and complied with the procedures set forth under paragraph (p)(2) of this section promptly after it became aware of the failure.

(B) *Result.* Because DC failed to file a GRA with its timely filed tax return for the year of the FS Transfer, there is a failure to timely file the GRA as required by paragraph (d)(1) of this section. However, based on the facts of in paragraph (p)(3)(i)(A) of this section (the facts of this *Example 1*), including that the failure to timely file the GRA was an isolated and accidental oversight, the failure to timely file is not a willful failure to file. Accordingly, the timely filed requirement of paragraph (d)(1) of this section is considered to be satisfied, and DC is not required to recognize the gain realized on the FS Transfer under section 367(a)(1).

(ii) *Example 2.—Taxpayer's course of conduct is taken into account in determination.* (A) *Facts.* DC filed its tax return for the year of the FS Transfer, reporting no gain with respect to the exchange of the FS stock, but failed to file a GRA. DC, through its tax department, was aware of the requirement to file a GRA in order for DC to avoid recognizing gain with respect to the FS Transfer under section 367(a)(1). DC had not consistently and in a timely manner filed GRAs in the past, and also had an established history of failing to timely file other tax and information returns for which it was subject to penalties. In a year subsequent to Year 1, DC transferred stock of another foreign subsidiary with respect to which DC had a built-in gain (FS2) to FA in a transaction that qualified as both a reorganization under section 368(a)(1)(B) and an exchange described under section 351 (FS2 Transfer). DC was required to recognize gain on the FS2 Transfer under section 367(a)(1) unless DC timely filed a GRA as required by paragraph (d)(1) of this section and complied with the requirements of this section during the term of the GRA. DC reported no gain on the FS2 Transfer on its tax return, but failed to file a GRA. At the time of the FS2 Transfer, DC was already aware of its failure to file the GRA required for the prior FS Transfer, but had not implemented any safeguards to ensure that it would timely file GRAs for future transactions. DC filed an amended return to file the GRA for the FS2 Transfer and complied with the procedures set forth under paragraph (p)(2) of this section promptly after it became aware of the failure. DC asserts that its failure to timely file a GRA with respect to the FS2 Transfer was due to an isolated oversight similar to the one that occurred with respect to the FS Transfer. At issue is DC's failure to timely file a GRA for the FS2 Transfer.

(B) *Result.* Because DC failed to file a GRA with its timely filed tax return for the year of the FS2 Transfer, there is a failure to timely file the GRA as required by paragraph (d)(1) of this section. DC's course of conduct is taken into account in determining whether its failure to timely file a GRA for the FS2 Transfer was willful. Based on the facts of in paragraph (p)(3)(ii)(A) of this section (the facts of this *Example 2*), including DC's history of failing to file required tax and information returns in general and GRAs in particular, and its failure to implement safeguards to ensure that it would timely file GRAs, the failure to timely file a GRA with respect to the FS2 Transfer rises to the level of a willful failure to timely file. Accordingly, DC is ineligible for relief under paragraph (p) of this section, the GRA is not considered timely filed for purposes of paragraph (d)(1) of this section, and DC must recognize the full amount of the gain realized on the FS2 Transfer.

(iii) *Example 3.—GRA not completed in all material respects.* (A) *Facts.* DC timely filed its tax return for the year of the FS Transfer, reporting no gain with respect to the exchange of the FS stock. DC was aware of the requirement to file a GRA to avoid recognizing gain under section 367(a)(1), including the requirement to provide the basis and fair market value of the transferred stock. However, DC filed a purported GRA that did not contain the fair market value of the FS stock. Instead, the GRA was filed with the statement that the fair market value information was "available upon request." Other than the omission of the fair market value of the FS stock, the GRA contained all other information required by this section.

(B) *Result*. Because DC omitted the fair market value of the FS stock from the GRA, the GRA was not completed in all material respects. Accordingly, there is a failure to timely file the GRA. Furthermore, because DC knowingly omitted such information, DC's omission is a willful failure to timely file a GRA. Accordingly, DC is ineligible for relief under paragraph (p) of this section, the GRA is not considered timely filed for purposes of paragraph (d)(1) of this section, and DC must recognize the full amount of the gain realized on the FS Transfer. The same result would arise if DC had included the fair market value of the FS stock, but knowingly omitted its tax basis from the GRA.

(iv) *Example 4.—Taxpayer knew of GRA filing requirement, but intentionally chose not to file.* (A) *Facts.* When DC filed its tax return for the tax year of the FS Transfer, it was aware of the requirement to file a GRA to avoid recognizing gain under section 367(a)(1). However, because DC anticipated selling Business A in the following tax year, which was expected to produce a capital loss that could be carried back to fully offset the gain recognized on the FS Transfer, DC intentionally chose not to file a GRA. DC recognized the gain from the FS Transfer under section 367(a)(1) and reported the gain on its timely filed tax return. At the end of the following year, a large class action lawsuit was filed against Business A and, consequently, DC was unable to sell the business. As a result, DC did not realize the expected capital loss, and it was not able to offset the gain from the FS Transfer. DC now seeks to file a GRA for the FS Transfer.

(B) *Result*. Because DC failed to file a GRA with its timely filed tax return for the year of the FS Transfer, there is a failure to timely file the GRA as required by paragraph (d)(1) of this section. Furthermore, because DC intentionally chose not to file a GRA for the FS Transfer, its actions constitute a willful failure to timely file a GRA. Accordingly, DC is ineligible for relief under paragraph (p) of this section, the GRA is not considered timely filed for purposes of paragraph (d)(1) of this section, and DC must recognize the full amount of the gain realized on the FS Transfer in Year 1.

(q) *Examples.—*(1) *Presumed facts and references.*—For purposes of the examples in paragraph (q)(2) of this section, and except where otherwise indicated, the following is presumed.

(i) UST, USP, and DC are domestic corporations that each use a calendar taxable year.

(ii) USP wholly owns UST and is the common parent of the consolidated group of which UST is a member.

(iii) TFC, TFD, F1, and FA are foreign corporations.

(iv) UST wholly owns TFD.

(v) In a section 351 exchange, UST transfers all of the stock of TFD (TFD stock) to TFC in exchange solely for stock of TFC (the initial transfer).

(vi) Pursuant to §1.367(a)-3(b)(1)(ii) and this section, UST enters into a gain recognition agreement in connection with the initial transfer and makes the election described under paragraph (c)(2)(vi) of this section with respect to the gain recognition agreement.

(vii) As applicable, the section 1248 amount (within the meaning of §1.367(b)-2(c)) or all earnings and profits amount (within the meaning of §1.367(b)-2(d)) attributable to the stock of a foreign corporation is zero.

(viii) All transactions are respected under general principles of tax law, including the step transaction doctrine.

(ix) References to a U.S. transferor entering into a gain recognition agreement mean, where applicable, that the common parent of the consolidated group of which the U.S. transferor is a member has filed the gain recognition agreement on behalf of the U.S. transferor in accordance with paragraph (d)(3) of this section.

(x) Taxable years during the GRA term are referred to, for example, as year 1 and year 2.

(2) *Examples.*—The following examples illustrate the application of the rules of this section.

(i) *Example 1.—Basis adjustments from gain recognized under the gain recognition agreement.* (A) *Facts.* TFC wholly owns F1. In year 3, pursuant to a section 351 exchange, TFC transfers all of the TFD stock to F1 in exchange solely for voting stock of F1. UST enters into a new gain recognition agreement with respect to the initial transfer under paragraph (k)(3) of this section, and therefore the transfer by TFC of the TFD stock to F1 is not a triggering event. Under paragraph (c)(5)(i) of this section, the existing gain recognition agreement terminates without further effect. In year 4, in an exchange to which section 721 applies, UST contributes the TFC stock received in the initial transfer to PRS, a domestic partnership, in exchange for a partnership interest. UST enters into a new gain recognition agreement with respect to the initial transfer under paragraph (k)(1) of this section, and therefore the transfer by UST of the TFC stock to PRS is not a triggering event. Under paragraph (c)(5)(i) of this section, the new gain recognition agreement filed by UST in year 3 terminates

without further effect. In year 5, TFD disposes of substantially all of its assets in a transaction that constitutes a triggering event under paragraph (j)(2)(i) of this section. Under paragraph (c)(1)(i) of this section, UST recognizes the gain realized but not recognized on the initial transfer by reason of entering into the gain recognition agreement.

(B) *Result*. Under paragraph (c)(4) of this section, the basis of the PRS interest held by UST, the TFC stock held by PRS that was received from UST in year 4, the F1 stock held by TFC that was received in exchange for the TFD stock in year 3, and the TFD stock held by F1 that was received from TFC in year 3 is increased by the amount of gain recognized by UST (but not by the additional tax or interest paid as result of such gain) with respect to the initial transfer under the gain recognition agreement. However, the basis of the assets of TFD (including the assets disposed of in year 5) is not increased as a result of the gain recognized by UST.

(ii) *Example 2.—Impact of gain recognition event on computation of income.* (A) *Facts.* At the time of the initial transfer, the TFD stock has a $50x basis, a $100x fair market value, and a $30x section 1248 amount. The amount of gain subject to the gain recognition agreement is $50x. UST did not make an election under paragraph (c)(2)(vi) of this section with respect to the gain recognition agreement. In year 3, TFC disposes of the TFD stock received in the initial transfer in exchange for $120× cash.

(B) *Result*—(1) *Gain recognition without an election*. The disposition by TFC of the TFD stock in year 3 is a triggering event under paragraph (j)(1) of this section. As a result, under paragraph (c)(1)(i) of this section, UST must recognize and include in income $50x gain under the gain recognition agreement. Under paragraph (c)(1)(iii)(A) of this section, UST must report the $50x gain on an amended return filed for the taxable year of the initial transfer. Under paragraph (c)(1)(v) of this section, UST must pay applicable interest on any additional tax due with respect to the $50x gain recognized. Under section 1248(a), $30x of the gain recognized by UST under the gain recognition agreement is recharacterized as a dividend. Under paragraph (c)(4) of this section, as of the date of the initial transfer, the basis of the TFC stock received by UST in the initial transfer and the TFD stock received by TFC in the initial transfer, respectively, is increased by $50x. After taking into account the increase to the basis of the TFD stock, TFC recognizes $20x gain on the disposition of the TFD stock in year 3.

(2) *Gain recognition with an election*. If UST made an election under paragraph (c)(2)(vi) of this section with the gain recognition agreement filed for the initial transfer, the result would be the same as in paragraph (q)(2)(ii)(B)(1) of this section (paragraph (1) in the results in this *Example* 2), except that UST must include in income the $50x gain recognized under the gain recognition agreement on its tax return filed for year 3. Any additional tax due with respect to the $50x gain and applicable interest on the additional tax due must be included with such return. The amount, if any, of the $50x gain recognized by UST under the gain recognition agreement that is characterized as a dividend under section 1248(a) is determined in year 3.

(iii) *Example 3.—Transfer of stock of the transferee foreign corporation to a domestic corporation in a section 351 exchange.* (A) *Facts.* UST wholly owns DC. In year 3, pursuant to a section 351 exchange, UST transfers all of the TFC stock received in the initial transfer to DC in an exchange solely for voting stock of DC.

(B) *Result*. The year 3 transfer of the TFC stock by UST to DC constitutes a triggering event under paragraph (j)(4) of this section. However, the transfer shall not constitute a triggering event pursuant to paragraph (k)(1)(ii) of this section if DC enters into a new gain recognition agreement with respect to the initial transfer that designates DC as the U.S. transferor for purposes of this section. Pursuant to paragraphs (c)(4)(i) and (ii) of this section, if DC is required to recognize gain under the new gain recognition agreement, the basis of the stock of TFC and TFD would be increased by the amount of gain recognized. However, pursuant to paragraph (c)(4)(iii) of this section, no adjustment would be made to the basis of the DC voting stock received by UST in year 3 as a result of such gain recognition. Alternatively, if the conditions for the application of paragraph (k)(14) of this section are satisfied UST could instead enter into the new gain recognition agreement with respect to the initial transfer.

(iv) *Example 4.—Transfer of stock of the transferee foreign corporation in a triangular section 368(a)(1)(B) reorganization.* (A) *Facts.* DC wholly owns FA. In year 3, pursuant to a triangular reorganization described in section 368(a)(1)(B), UST transfers all of the TFC stock received in the initial transfer to FA in exchange solely for 20% of the outstanding voting stock of DC. At the time of the reorganization, the TFC stock has a basis in excess of fair market value.

(B) *Result*. (1) The transfer by UST of the TFC stock to FA is an indirect stock transfer under §1.367(a)-3(d)(1)(iii)(B). Accordingly, to preserve nonrecognition treatment, UST must enter into a separate gain recognition agreement under this section with respect to such transfer.

(2) With respect to the gain recognition agreement filed for the initial transfer of the TFD stock, the transfer by UST of the TFC stock to FA is a triggering event under paragraph (j)(4) of this section. However, the transfer shall not constitute a triggering event if the conditions of the exception provided by paragraph (k)(14) of this section are satisfied.

(*i*) The condition of paragraph (k)(14)(i) of this section is satisfied because the transfer qualifies as a nonrecognition transaction (assuming UST enters into a gain recognition agreement as described in paragraph (q)(2)(iv)(B)(*1*) of this section (paragraph (*1*) in the results in this *Example 4*).

(*ii*) The condition of paragraph (k)(14)(ii) of this section is satisfied because immediately after the transfer DC, a domestic corporation that is eligible to be a U.S. transferor, owns at least 5% (determined as provided in paragraph (k)(14)(ii) of this section) of the total voting power and total fair market value of the outstanding stock of FA. As a result, DC is treated as retaining an indirect interest in the TFD stock immediately following the transfer.

(*iii*) The condition of paragraph (k)(14)(iii) of this section is satisfied if DC enters into a new gain recognition agreement with respect to the initial transfer of the TFD stock that, based on the principles of paragraph (j) of this section, describes the subsequent dispositions or other events that would constitute triggering events for purposes of the new gain recognition agreement (other than the dispositions and other events described in paragraph (j) of this section). For example, a complete or partial disposition of the stock of FA would constitute a triggering event for purposes of the new gain recognition agreement.

(*v*) *Example 5.—Transfer of stock of the transferee foreign corporation to a domestic corporation pursuant to an asset reorganization.* (A) *Facts.* At the time of the initial transfer the TFD stock has a $50x basis and a $100x fair market value. Therefore, the amount of gain subject to the gain recognition agreement is $50x. In year 3, pursuant to an asset reorganization described in section 368(a)(1)(A), UST transfers its assets to DC in exchange solely for 20% of the outstanding stock of DC. UST distributes the stock of DC to USP pursuant to the plan of reorganization.

(B) *Result.* The transfer by UST of the TFC stock to DC constitutes a triggering event under paragraph (j)(4) of this section. However, pursuant to paragraph (k)(6)(i) of this section, if DC enters into a new gain recognition agreement with respect to the initial transfer that designates DC as the U.S. transferor, the transfer shall not constitute a triggering event.

(*vi*) *Example 6.—Transfer of stock of the transferee foreign corporation to a foreign corporation pursuant to an asset reorganization.* (A) *Facts.* The facts are the same as in *Example 5*, except the acquiring corporation in the asset reorganization is FA, and, at the time of the asset reorganization, the TFC stock transferred by UST to FA has a $50x basis and a $150x fair market value. All of the conditions under section 367(a)(5) and the regulations under that section are satisfied, and no adjustment is required to the basis of the FA stock received by USP in the transaction.

(B) *Result.* (1) The transfer by UST of the TFC stock to FA is described in section 361(a) and is therefore subject to section 367(a)(5). In general, UST cannot file a gain recognition agreement with respect to such transfer, and the transfer therefore is subject to the general rule of section 367(a)(1). However, if the conditions of §1.367(a)-3(e)(1)(i) through (iv) are satisfied, USP can enter into a gain recognition agreement with respect to the transfer to avoid the recognition of gain by UST on the transfer under section 367(a)(1). If the exception provided by paragraph (k)(14) of this section applies so that the transfer by UST of the TFC stock to FA is not a triggering event with respect to the gain recognition agreement filed for the initial transfer (discussed in paragraph (q)(2)(vi)(B)(2) of this section (paragraph (2) in the results in this *Example 6*), the amount of gain subject to the gain recognition agreement (if entered into) with respect to the transfer by UST of the TFC stock to FA in the asset reorganization is $100x.

(2) Under paragraph (j)(4) of this section, the transfer of the TFC stock by UST to FA is a triggering event with respect to the gain recognition agreement for the initial transfer. The exception provided by paragraph (k)(6)(i) of this section does not apply to such transfer because FA, the acquiring corporation in the asset reorganization, is foreign. However, the transfer shall not constitute a triggering event if the conditions of the exception provided by paragraph (k)(14) of this section are satisfied.

(*i*) The condition of paragraph (k)(14)(i) of this section is satisfied because the transfer of the TFC stock to FA qualifies as a nonrecognition transaction (assuming USP enters into a gain recognition agreement with respect to such transfer).

(*ii*) The condition of paragraph (k)(14)(ii) of this section is satisfied because immediately after the transfer USP, a domestic corporation that is eligible to be a U.S. transferor, owns at least 5% (determined as provided in paragraph (k)(14)(ii) of this section) of the total voting power and total fair market value of the outstanding stock of FA. As a result, USP is treated as retaining an indirect interest in the TFD stock immediately following the transfer.

(*iii*) The condition of paragraph (k)(14)(iii) of this section is satisfied if USP enters into a new gain recognition agreement with respect to the initial transfer of the TFD stock that, based on the principles of paragraph (j) of this section, describes the subsequent dispositions or other events that would constitute triggering events for purposes of the new gain recognition agreement, other than those already provided in paragraph (j) of this section. For example, a disposition of the stock of FA would constitute such a triggering event for purposes of the new gain recognition agreement.

(C) *Alternate facts.* Assume the same facts as in paragraph (q)(2)(vi)(A) of this section (the facts in this *Example 6*), including that paragraph (k)(14) of this section applies to the year 3 reorganization so that USP enters into a new gain recognition agreement with respect to the initial transfer of the TFD stock that occurred in year 1 (GRA 1), and that under §1.367(a)-3(e) USP enters into a separate gain recognition agreement with respect to the initial transfer of the TFC stock by UST to FA pursuant to the year 3 asset reorganization (GRA 2). Assume further that in year 4 TFC disposes of 10% of the TFD stock pursuant to a transaction that constitutes a triggering event with respect to GRA 1. The disposition of the TFD stock is not a triggering event with respect to GRA 2 because the TFD stock disposed of does not constitute substantially all the assets of TFC. Under paragraphs (j)(1) and (c)(1)(i) of this section, USP must recognize $5x gain (10% of $50x) under GRA 1. Under paragraph (c)(4)(i) and (ii) of this section, as of the date of the initial transfer (with respect to which GRA 1 was filed), the basis of the TFC stock and TFD stock, respectively, is increased by $5x. Under paragraph (c)(1)(i) of this section, the amount of gain subject to GRA 1 is reduced from $50x to $45x. Similarly, because the transferred stock for purposes of GRA 2 is the TFC stock, the amount of gain subject to GRA 2 is reduced from $100x to $95x to reflect the increase to the basis of the TFC stock.

(*vii*) *Example 7.—Transfer of transferred stock to a foreign corporation pursuant to an asset reorganization.* (A) *Facts.* UST wholly owns FA. In year 4, pursuant to a reorganization described in section 368(a)(1)(D), TFC transfers all of the TFD stock to FA in exchange solely for stock of FA. TFC distributes the FA stock to UST pursuant to the plan of reorganization.

(B) *Analysis.* In general, the year 4 transfer by TFC of the TFD stock to FA and the exchange by UST of the TFC stock for FA stock constitute triggering events under paragraphs (j)(1) and (4) of this section, respectively. However, under paragraph (k)(6)(ii) of this section, the transfers shall not constitute triggering events if UST enters into a new gain recognition agreement with respect to the initial transfer that designates FA as the transferee foreign corporation.

(*viii*) *Example 8.—Transfer of substantially all the assets of the transferred corporation pursuant to an asset reorganization.* (A) *Facts.* In year 4, pursuant to an asset reorganization described in section 368(a)(1)(C), TFD transfers all of its assets to FA in exchange solely for voting stock of FA. TFD distributes the FA voting stock to TFC pursuant to the plan of reorganization.

(B) *Analysis.* The year 4 transfer by TFD of all its assets to FA and the exchange by TFC of its TFD stock for FA voting stock pursuant to the reorganization constitute triggering events under paragraphs (j)(2) and (j)(1) of this section, respectively. However, under paragraph (k)(6)(iii) of this section, the transfers shall not constitute triggering events if UST enters into a new gain recognition agreement with respect to the initial transfer that designates FA as the transferred corporation. In addition, under paragraph (k)(6)(iii) of this section only the assets of TFD acquired by FA in the asset reorganization shall be treated as assets of the transferred corporation for purposes of the new gain recognition agreement.

(*ix*) *Example 9.—Complete liquidation of transferred corporation into transferee foreign corporation.* (A) *Facts.* UST does not make an election under paragraph (c)(2)(vi) of this section in connection with the gain recognition agreement entered into with respect to the initial transfer. In year 3, TFD distributes all of its assets to TFC pursuant to a complete liquidation to which sections 332 and 337 apply. Under paragraph (k)(8) of this section. UST enters into a new gain recognition agreement with respect to the initial transfer such that the liquidation is not a triggering event. Under paragraph (c)(5)(i) of this section, the new gain recognition agreement is subject to the conditions and requirements of this section to the same extent as the existing gain recognition agreement, except that the transferred stock is no longer subject to the gain recognition agreement because the transferred stock is cancelled by reason of the liquidation. In year 5

TFC disposes of substantially all of the assets received from TFD in the year 3 liquidation.

(B) *Result.* The year 5 disposition by TFC of substantially all of the assets received from TFD in the year 3 liquidation is a triggering event under paragraph (j)(2) of this section, and therefore UST must recognize the gain subject to the gain recognition agreement. UST must report the gain recognized on an amended return for the taxable year during which the initial transfer occurred. UST must also pay applicable interest on any additional tax due with respect to the gain recognized. Under paragraph (c)(4)(i) of this section, the basis of the TFC stock received by UST in the initial transfer is increased as of the date of the initial transfer by the amount of gain recognized under the gain recognition agreement. The basis of the assets of TFD, however, is not increased.

(x) *Example 10.—Transfer of transferred stock to foreign corporation in section 351 exchange, followed by a section 332 liquidation of the foreign corporation.* (A) *Facts.* In year 3, pursuant to a section 351 exchange, TFC transfers the TFD stock to F1, a newly formed corporation, in exchange solely for voting stock of F1. The transfer by TFC of the TFD stock to F1 is not a triggering event because UST complies with the conditions of paragraph (k)(3) of this section. In year 5, F1 distributes all of its assets to TFC in a complete liquidation to which sections 332 and 337 apply.

(B) *Result.* The distribution of the TFD stock by F1, and the exchange of F1 stock by TFC pursuant to the year 5 liquidation of F1 constitute triggering events under paragraphs (j)(1) and (k)(3)(i) of this section, respectively. However, if paragraph (k)(14) of this section applies, neither the distribution of the TFD stock by F1, nor the exchange by TFC of the F1 stock, shall constitute a triggering event.

(1) The condition of paragraph (k)(14)(i) of this section is satisfied because the distribution of the TFD stock, and the exchange of F1 stock, both qualify as nonrecognition transactions.

(2) The condition of paragraph (k)(14)(ii) of this section is satisfied because immediately after the distribution UST, a domestic corporation that is eligible to be a U.S. transferor, owns at least 5% (determined as provided in paragraph (k)(14)(ii) of this section) of the stock of TFC. As a result, UST is treated as retaining an indirect interest in the TFD stock following the complete liquidation of F1.

(3) The condition of paragraph (k)(14)(iii) of this section is satisfied if UST enters into a new gain recognition agreement. Because after the complete liquidation of F1, UST wholly owns TFC, which wholly owns TFD, as was the case immediately after the initial transfer, UST is not required to describe, with the new gain recognition agreement, other dispositions or events that would constitute triggering events based on the principles of paragraph (j) of this section, other than the dispositions or events described in paragraph (j) of this section.

(xi) *Example 11.—Disposition of stock of transferee foreign corporation pursuant to a divisive reorganization.* (A) *Facts.* In year 3, pursuant to a divisive reorganization described in section 368(a)(1)(D), UST transfers all of the TFC stock to DC, a newly-formed corporation, in exchange solely for stock of DC. UST then distributes all of the DC stock to USP in a transaction to which section 355 applies.

(B) *Result.* The transfer of the TFC stock by UST to DC constitutes a triggering event under paragraph (j)(4) of this section. However, under paragraph (k)(1)(iii) of this section, the transfer of the TFC stock shall not constitute a triggering event if DC enters into a new gain recognition agreement that designates DC as the U.S. transferor for purposes of this section.

(C) *Alternate facts.* The facts are the same as in paragraph (q)(2)(xi)(A) of this section (the facts in this *Example 11*), except that UST transfers only 90% of the TFC stock to DC. Paragraph (k)(1)(iii) of this section applies only with respect to the TFC stock transferred to DC. Thus, the conditions of paragraph (k)(1)(iii) of this section are satisfied if DC enters into a new gain recognition agreement with respect to the TFC stock received from UST. The amount of gain subject to the new gain recognition agreement entered into by DC equals 90% of the amount of gain subject to the gain recognition agreement entered into by UST with respect to the initial transfer. The amount of gain subject to the gain recognition agreement entered into by UST with respect to the initial transfer is reduced by the amount of gain subject to the new gain recognition agreement entered into by DC. The gain recognition agreement entered into by UST with respect to the initial transfer continues to apply to the remaining TFC stock held by UST.

(xii) *Example 12.—Disposition of transferred stock pursuant to a divisive reorganization.* (A) *Facts.* In year 3, pursuant to a divisive reorganization described in section 368(a)(1)(D), TFC transfers all of the TFD stock to F1, a newly formed corporation, in exchange solely for all of the outstanding stock of F1. TFC then distributes all of the F1 stock to UST in a transaction to which section 355 applies.

(B) *Result.* The transfer by TFC of the TFD stock to F1 constitutes a triggering event under paragraph (j)(1) of this section. However, if paragraph (k)(14) of this section applies, neither the transfer of the TFD stock by TFC to F1, nor the distribution of the F1 stock by TFC to UST, shall constitute triggering events.

(1) The condition of paragraph (k)(14)(i) of this section is satisfied because the dispositions of the TFD stock and F1 stock qualify as nonrecognition transactions.

(2) The condition of paragraph (k)(14)(ii) of this section is satisfied because immediately after the transfer UST, an eligible U.S. transferor, owns at least 5% (determined as provided in paragraph (k)(14)(ii) of this section) of the total voting power and the total fair market value of the outstanding stock of F1. As a result, UST is treated as retaining an indirect interest in the TFD stock following the dispositions.

(3) The condition of paragraph (k)(14)(iii) of this section is satisfied if UST enters into a new gain recognition agreement with respect to the initial transfer that describes the subsequent dispositions or other events that would constitute triggering events based on the principles of paragraph (j) of this section, other than those described in paragraph (j) of this section. For example, a complete or partial disposition of the F1 stock would constitute a triggering event for purposes of the new gain recognition agreement (subject to the exceptions provided by paragraph (k) of this section).

(xiii) *Example 13.—Receipt of boot by the transferee foreign corporation in a subsequent section 351 exchange.* (A) *Facts.* At the time of the initial transfer, the TFD stock has a $50x basis and $100x fair market value. The amount of gain subject to the gain recognition agreement is $50x. In year 3, TFC and X, an unrelated foreign corporation, form F1. TFC transfers the TFD stock to F1 in exchange for $35x cash and $65x stock of F1. At the time of the transfer, the TFD stock has a $50x basis and $100x fair market value. The F1 stock received by TFC represents 25% of the outstanding stock of F1. Without regard to the gain recognized under the gain recognition agreement and any adjustments to basis under paragraph (c)(4)(ii) of this section, under section 351(b) TFC would recognize $35x gain in connection with the transfer of the TFD stock to F1. UST complies with the conditions of paragraph (k)(3) of this section, and therefore the disposition by TFC of the TFD stock does not constitute a triggering event.

(B) *Result.* Under paragraph (m)(1) of this section, UST must recognize $35x gain under the gain recognition agreement as a result of the year 3 disposition by TFC of the TFD stock. Thus, the amount of gain subject to the new gain recognition agreement entered into by UST pursuant to paragraph (k)(3) of this section is $15x. Under paragraph (c)(4)(ii) of this section, as of the date of the initial transfer, the basis of the TFD stock held by TFC is increased by $35x, the amount of the gain recognized by UST under the gain recognition agreement. Under paragraph (c)(4)(i) of this section, the basis of the TFC stock received by UST in the initial transfer is also increased by $35x. After taking into account the increase to the basis of the TFD stock under paragraph (c)(4)(ii) of this section, TFC recognizes $15x gain under section 351(b) in connection with the year 3 transfer of the TFD stock to F1. Under section 362(a), the basis of the TFD stock in the hands of F1 is $100x.

(xiv) *Example 14.—Complete disposition of transferred stock pursuant to a section 304(a)(1) transaction.* (A) *Facts.* UST wholly owns FA. In year 3, in a transaction to which section 304(a)(1) applies, TFC transfers all of the TFD stock to FA in exchange for cash. Under section 304(a)(1), TFC and FA are treated as if TFC transferred the TFD stock to FA in a section 351 exchange in exchange solely for FA stock, and then FA redeemed the FA stock deemed issued in exchange for the cash. Under section 302(d), the redemption of the FA stock deemed issued by FA to TFC under section 304(a)(1) is treated as a distribution to which section 301 applies.

(B) *Result.* (1) In general, the deemed contribution by TFC of the TFD stock to FA in the section 351 exchange is a triggering event under paragraph (j)(1) of this section. However, under paragraph (k)(3) of this section the deemed contribution shall not be a triggering event if UST enters into a new gain recognition agreement with respect to the initial transfer in which it agrees to treat as a triggering event a complete or partial disposition of the FA stock deemed received by TFC.

(2) Under paragraph (n)(1) of this section, the redemption of the FA stock deemed received by TFC in exchange for the TFD stock shall not constitute a disposition if UST enters into a new gain recognition agreement with respect to the initial transfer that includes appropriate provisions to take into account such redemption. Therefore, under the new gain recognition agreement UST must agree to treat as a triggering event a complete or partial disposition of the stock of FA. Pursuant to paragraph (d)(2)(ii) of this section, UST is permitted to enter into a single new gain recognition agreement in year 3, but the gain recognition agreement must provide a

complete description of the section 304(a)(1) transaction including the deemed section 351 exchange and redemption of the FA stock.

(xv) *Example 15.—Reduction in amount of gain subject to gain recognition agreement, followed by triggering event.* (A) *Facts.* In year 3, UST disposes of 60% of the TFC stock received in the initial transfer in a transaction in which the conditions of paragraph (o)(1)(ii) of this section are satisfied. Thus, the amount of gain subject to the gain recognition agreement is reduced by 60%. In year 5, TFC disposes of 50% of the TFD stock in a transaction that constitutes a triggering event.

(B) *Result.* As a result of the year 5 disposition by TFC of 50% of the TFD stock, under paragraphs (j)(1) and (c)(1)(i) of this section, UST must recognize and include in income 50% of the gain subject to the gain recognition agreement (because of the year 3 disposition of TFC stock, the amount of gain subject to the gain recognition agreement equals 40% of the gain realized, but not recognized, on the initial transfer). UST must pay applicable interest on any additional tax due with respect to the gain recognized. The amount of gain subject to the gain recognition agreement is reduced by the amount of gain recognized by UST (the remaining gain equals 20% of the gain realized, but not recognized, by UST on the initial transfer).

(xvi) *Example 16.—Taxable sale of stock of transferee foreign corporation and election to reduce stock basis.* (A) *Facts.* UST wholly owns F1 and TFD. The F1 stock has a $90x basis and $90x fair market value, and the TFD stock has a $0x basis and $100x fair market value. UST also owns real property with a $10x basis and $10x fair market value. In year 1, pursuant to a section 351 exchange, UST transfers the real property, the TFD stock, and the F1 stock to TFC in exchange solely for 20 shares of TFC stock. UST enters into a gain recognition agreement with respect to the transfer of the TFD stock. The amount of the gain recognition agreement is $100x. UST takes the position that the basis of each share of TFC stock received in the exchange is $5.5x (a proportionate amount of the $110x aggregate basis of the transferred property). In year 3, UST disposes of all its TFC stock in a transaction in which all gain realized is recognized and included in taxable income.

(B) *Result.* The year 3 disposition of the TFC stock is a triggering event under paragraph (j)(4) of this section. The disposition does not terminate the gain recognition agreement pursuant to paragraph (o)(1)(i) of this section because the basis of each share of TFC stock received in exchange for the TFD stock in the initial transfer is $5.5×, which exceeds the $0× basis of the TFD stock at time of the initial transfer. However, under paragraph (o)(1)(iii) of this section, to satisfy the basis condition of paragraph (o)(1)(i) of this section, UST can reduce the basis of the 10 shares of the TFC stock received in exchange for the TFD stock to $0x. If UST reduces the basis of the 10 shares of TFC stock to $0x, under paragraph (o)(1)(i) of this section the disposition of the TFC stock shall not constitute a triggering event but instead shall terminate the gain recognition agreement without further effect.

(xvii) *Example 17.—Successive section 351 exchanges, section 301 distributions, and transactions involving partnerships.* (A) *Facts.* UST owns a 40 percent capital and profits interest in a foreign partnership (PRS). PRS wholly owns TFD and other assets with basis equal to fair market value. The TFD stock has a $50x basis and $200x fair market value. TFC wholly owns F1. On day 1 of year 1, in a section 351 exchange, UST transfers its PRS interest to TFC in exchange solely for stock of TFC (initial transfer). On that same day, in a section 351 exchange, TFC transfers the PRS interest received from UST to F1 in exchange solely for stock of F1. In year 3, PRS receives a $150x distribution from TFD to which section 301 applies. Under section 301(c), $25x of the distribution constitutes a dividend, $50x is applied against and reduces the basis of the TFD stock held by PRS, and the remaining $75x is treated as gain from the sale or exchange of property. With respect to the TFD stock deemed transferred by UST in the initial transfer, under section 301(c), $10x (40% of $25x) of the distribution constitutes a dividend, $20x (40% of $50x) is applied against and reduces the basis of TFD stock, and $30x (40% of $75x) is treated as gain from the sale or exchange of property. In year 5, pursuant to a distribution to which section 731 applies, PRS distributes all of the TFD stock to F1.

(B) *Result.* (1) *Successive section 351 transfers.* Under section 367(a)(4) and § 1.367(a)-1T(c)(3)(ii), the transfer of the PRS interest by UST to TFC is treated, for purposes of section 367(a), as a transfer by UST to TFC of its proportionate share of the TFD stock held by PRS (the initial transfer). The initial transfer by UST of the TFD stock to TFC is subject to the general rule of section 367(a)(1), unless UST enters into a gain recognition agreement with respect to such transfer pursuant to § 1.367(a)-3(b)(1)(ii) and this section. Under paragraph (c)(3)(viii) of this section, the gain recognition agreement must include a complete description of the transfer, including a description of the partners of PRS. Even if UST enters into a gain recognition agreement with respect to the initial transfer, under paragraph (j)(3)

of this section, the subsequent transfer by TFC of the PRS interest to F1 is a triggering event unless UST enters into a new gain recognition agreement with respect to the initial transfer under paragraph (k)(14) that provides that, in addition to the triggering events provided in paragraph (j) of this section, a complete or partial disposition of the F1 stock received by TFC in exchange for the PRS interest shall constitute a triggering event for purposes of the gain recognition agreement. The new gain recognition agreement must also provide that any other disposition that is inconsistent with the principles of paragraph (k), including an indirect disposition of the TFD stock or of substantially all of the assets of TFD, shall constitute a triggering event for purposes of the new gain recognition agreement. Under paragraph (d)(2)(ii) of this section, UST is permitted to enter into a single gain recognition agreement with respect to the initial transfer and the subsequent transfer by TFC of the PRS interest, but the agreement must include a complete description of the initial transfer and the subsequent transfer of the PRS interest.

(2) *Section 301 distribution from TFD to PRS.* Under paragraph (b)(1)(iii) of this section, the section 301 distribution received by PRS from TFD is not a disposition (and therefore does not affect the gain recognition agreement) to the extent it is described in section 301(c)(1) or (2). However, under paragraph (n)(2) of this section, to the extent the distribution is described in section 301(c)(3), UST must recognize gain ($30x) under the gain recognition agreement. For this purpose, the amount of the distribution that is described in section 301(c)(3) is determined before taking into account the increase to the basis of the TFD stock under paragraph (c)(4)(ii) of this section.

(3) *Distribution of TFD stock by PRS to F1.* The year 5 distribution of the TFD stock by PRS to F1 is a triggering event under paragraph (j)(1) of this section unless paragraph (k)(14) of this section applies.

(*i*) The condition of paragraph (k)(14)(i) of this section is satisfied because the distribution qualifies as a nonrecognition transaction.

(*ii*) The condition of paragraph (k)(14)(ii) of this section is satisfied because immediately after the distribution UST, a domestic corporation that is eligible to be a U.S. transferor, owns at least 5% (determined as provided in paragraph (k)(14)(ii) of this section) of the total voting power and total value of the outstanding stock of F1. As a result, UST is treated as retaining an indirect interest in the TFD stock following the distribution.

(*ii*) The condition of paragraph (k)(14)(iii) of this section is satisfied if UST enters into a new gain recognition agreement with respect to the initial transfer. The new gain recognition agreement need not describe additional dispositions or other events that would constitute triggering events because, pursuant to paragraph (c)(5) of this section, the dispositions or other events described in paragraph (j) of this section or in the existing gain recognition agreement apply to the new gain recognition agreement.

(xviii) *Example 18.—Complete liquidation of transferee foreign corporation.* (A) *Facts.* TFD has 10 shares of stock outstanding immediately before the initial transfer. On the date of the initial transfer, the TFD stock has a $0x basis and $90x fair market value. In year 2, in exchange for 1 share of TFD stock TFC transfers real estate to TFD with a $10x basis and $10x fair market value. In year 4, TFC distributes the 11 shares of TFD stock to UST in a complete liquidation to which sections 332 and 337 apply.

(B) *Result.* In determining whether the gain recognition agreement entered into by UST with respect to the initial transfer is terminated under paragraph (o)(5) of this section, or triggered under paragraphs (j)(1) and (j)(4) of this section, only the 10 shares of TFD stock transferred by UST in the initial transfer are considered. Thus, the 1 share of TFD stock received by TFC in exchange for the real estate in year 2 is not taken into account.

(xix) *Example 19.—Spin-off of transferred corporation.* (A) *Facts.* Before the initial transfer, the TFD stock has an $80x basis and a $100x fair market value, and the TFC stock has a $100x basis and $100x fair market value. In year 4, TFC distributes all of the TFD stock to UST in a transaction to which section 355 applies. At the time of the distribution, the TFD stock has a $200x fair market value, and the TFC stock (without regard to the value of the TFD stock held by TFC) has a $100x fair market value. At such time, the TFC stock has a $180x basis. As determined under section 358, immediately after the distribution, the TFC stock has a $60x basis, and the TFD stock has a $120x basis.

(B) *Result.* The distribution of the TFD stock by TFC in year 4 is a triggering event under paragraph (j)(1) of this section. The distribution does not terminate the gain recognition agreement under paragraph (o)(5) of this section because after the distribution, the basis of the TFD stock in the hands of UST ($120x) is greater than the basis of the TFD stock at the time of the initial transfer ($80x). However, if UST reduces the basis of the TFD stock to $80x (as provided under paragraph (o)(5)(iii) of this section) the gain recognition agreement will terminate without further effect. If UST does not elect to reduce the basis of the TFD stock, see paragraph (k)(14) of this section.

(xx) *Example 20.—Intercompany transaction followed by disposition to nonmember.* (A) *Facts.* At the time of the initial transfer, the TFD stock has a $50x basis and $100x fair market value. The amount of the gain recognition agreement is $50x. In year 3, UST distributes all of the TFC stock to USP in a transaction to which section 301 applies. At the time of the distribution, the TFC stock has a $50x basis and $90x fair market value. Under section 311(b), UST must recognize $40x gain (the intercompany item) on the distribution, but because the distribution is an intercompany transaction, under the provisions of § 1.1502-13, the $40x gain is not taken into account in year 3. In year 4, USP sells all of the TFC stock to X, an unrelated corporation. Under the provisions of § 1.1502-13, in year 4 UST takes into account the $40x intercompany item as a result of the sale of the TFC stock to X.

(B) *Result.* (1) The year 3 distribution of the TFC stock by UST to USP does not terminate the gain recognition agreement under paragraph (o)(1) of this section because UST does not include the $40x gain in taxable income during year 3. Under paragraph (j)(4) of this section, the year 3 distribution of the TFC stock by UST to USP is generally a triggering event; however, because the distribution is an intercompany transaction that creates an intercompany item, the distribution shall not constitute a triggering event if the conditions of paragraph (k)(12)(i) of this section are satisfied.

(i) The condition of paragraph (k)(12)(i)(A) of this section is satisfied because the aggregate basis of the TFC stock distributed ($50x) is not greater than the sum of the aggregate basis of the TFD stock at the time of the initial transfer ($50x).

(ii) The condition of paragraph (k)(12)(i)(B) of this section is satisfied if the next annual certification for the existing gain recognition agreement includes a complete description of the intercompany transaction and an explanation of how the basis condition of paragraph (k)(12)(i)(A) of this section is satisfied.

(2) Under paragraph (o)(6) of this section and the principles of paragraph (o)(1)(i) of this section, because the year 4 sale of the TFC stock to X requires UST to take into account the $40x gain (the intercompany item) from the year 3 distribution, the year 4 sale terminates the gain recognition agreement. If, alternatively, in year 4 USP had sold only 30% of the TFC stock, then under paragraph (o)(6) of this section and the principles of paragraph (o)(1)(ii) of this section the amount of gain subject to the gain recognition agreement would be reduced by 30%.

(C) *Alternate facts. Intercompany transaction followed by sale of transferee foreign corporation to member.* Assume the same facts as in paragraph (q)(2)(xx)(A) of this section (the facts in this *Example 20*), except that, instead of USP selling the TFC stock to X, in year 4 USP sells the TFC stock to USS in exchange for $90x cash. UST and USS are members of the USP consolidated group immediately after the sale. The results of the year 3 distribution of the TFC stock by UST to USP are the same as in paragraph (q)(2)(xx)(B) of this section (the results in this *Example 20*). In addition, under paragraph (k)(12)(ii) of this section, the year 4 sale by USP of the TFC stock to USS is not a triggering event, provided UST includes a complete description of the sale with the annual certification filed for the gain recognition agreement in year 4.

(D) *Alternate facts. Intercompany transaction followed by complete liquidation of transferee foreign corporation.* Assume the same facts as in paragraph (q)(2)(xx)(A) of this section (the facts in this *Example 20*), except that, instead of USP selling the TFC stock to X, in year 4 TFC distributes all of its assets to USP in a complete liquidation to which sections 332 and 337 apply. The result is the same as in paragraph (q)(2)(xx)(B) of this section (the facts in this *Example 20*) because, under the provisions of § 1.1502-13, in year 4 UST takes into account the $40x gain (the intercompany item) from the year 3 distribution.

(E) *Alternate facts. Intercompany transaction followed by triggering event.* Assume the same facts as in paragraph (q)(2)(xx)(A) of this section (the facts in this *Example 20*), except that instead of USP selling the TFC stock to X, in year 4 TFC disposes of all of the TFD stock in a transaction that constitutes a triggering event under paragraph (j)(1) of this section. Under paragraph (c)(1)(i) of this section UST must recognize $50x gain under the gain recognition agreement. Under paragraphs (c)(4)(i) and (ii) of this section, as of the date of the initial transfer the basis of the TFC stock and TFD stock, respectively, is increased by $50x.

(F) *Alternate facts. Intercompany transaction followed by section 351 transfer to member.* The facts are the same as in paragraph (q)(2)(xx)(A) of this section (the facts in this *Example 20*), except that, in year 3, in a section 351 exchange UST transfers all of the TFC stock to USS in exchange for $10x cash and $80x of stock of USS. USS is a member of the USP consolidated group immediately after the exchange. The transfer of the TFC stock by UST to USS is an intercom-

pany transaction. Under section 351(b), UST must generally recognize $10x gain (intercompany item) in connection with the transfer; however, under the provisions of § 1.1502-13, UST does not take the $10x gain into account in year 3. Under paragraph (k)(12) of this section, as result of the intercompany transaction creating an intercompany item ($10x gain), the existing gain recognition agreement ($50x gain) must be divided between UST and USS. UST shall remain subject to a gain recognition agreement of $10x (equal to the amount of the intercompany item). The amount of the gain recognition agreement entered into by USS under paragraph (k)(1) of this section is $40x (equal to the amount of the existing gain recognition agreement, reduced by the amount of the of the gain recognition agreement to which UST remains subject).

(xxi) *Example 21.—Transfer of transferred stock to United States person other than U.S. transferor.* (A) *Facts.* An individual (A) that is a United States citizen wholly owns TFD, TFC, and DC. A transfers the TFD stock to TFC in a section 351 exchange and enters into a gain recognition agreement with respect to such transfer. In year 5, pursuant to an asset reorganization, TFC transfers all of its assets to DC in exchange solely for DC stock. TFC distributes the DC stock to A pursuant to the plan of reorganization.

(B) *Result.* The transfer by TFC of the TFD stock to DC and the exchange by A of the TFC stock for DC stock pursuant to the asset reorganization are triggering events under paragraphs (j)(1) and (j)(4) of this section, respectively. The gain recognition agreement does not terminate under paragraph (o)(5) of this section because DC is neither the U.S. transferor, nor an individual that is a United States person, nor a member of the same consolidated group of which the U.S. transferor is a member. However, if paragraph (k)(14) of this section applies the exchanges shall not constitute triggering events.

(1) The condition of paragraph (k)(14)(i) of this section is satisfied because the transfer of the TFD stock to DC qualifies as a nonrecognition transaction.

(2) The condition of paragraph (k)(14)(ii) of this section is satisfied because immediately after the transfer DC, a domestic corporation that is eligible to be a U.S. transferor, retains a direct interest in the TFD stock following the transfer.

(3) The condition of paragraph (k)(14)(iii) of this section is satisfied if DC enters into a new gain recognition agreement with respect to the initial transfer. Under paragraph (k)(14)(iii)(B) of this section, DC is not required to describe any subsequent dispositions or other events that (based on the principles of paragraph (j) of this section) would constitute triggering events for purposes of the new gain recognition agreement, other than the dispositions or other events described in paragraph (j) of this section, because DC holds a direct interest in TFD after the asset reorganization.

(xxii) *Example 22.—Transfer of transferred stock to consolidated group member.* (A) *Facts.* UST wholly owns DC, a member of the USP consolidated group that includes UST. In year 5, pursuant to an asset reorganization described in section 368(a)(1)(A) TFC merges with and into DC. Immediately after the asset reorganization, DC wholly owns TFD, and the basis of the TFD stock is not greater than the aggregate basis of such stock at the time of the initial transfer.

(B) *Result.* The gain recognition agreement filed by UST with respect to the initial transfer terminates without further effect if the conditions of paragraph (o)(5) of this section are satisfied.

(1) The condition of paragraph (o)(5)(i) of this section is satisfied because the transfer of the TFD stock is a section 361 exchange.

(2) The condition of paragraph (o)(5)(ii) of this section is satisfied because DC is a member of the consolidated group that includes UST immediately after the section 361 exchange.

(3) The condition of paragraph (o)(5)(iii) of this section is satisfied because the aggregate basis of the TFD stock immediately after the section 361 exchange is not greater than the aggregate basis of the TFD stock at the time of the initial transfer (as adjusted for any gain recognized by UST on such transfer). If the basis condition of paragraph (o)(5)(iii) were not satisfied, under paragraph (o)(5)(iii) of this section, DC could reduce the basis of the TFD stock received in the reorganization. Alternatively, a new gain recognition agreement could be entered into if paragraph (k)(14) of this section applied to the disposition of the TFD stock pursuant to the section 361 exchange.

(C) *Alternate facts.* The facts are the same as in paragraph (q)(2)(xxii)(A) of this section (the facts in this *Example 22*), except that instead of TFC merging into DC, TFC merges into TFD in a reorganization described in section 368(a)(1)(A). The gain recognition agreement terminates without further effect if the conditions of paragraph (o)(5) of this section are satisfied.

(1) The condition of paragraph (o)(5)(i) of this section is satisfied because the TFD stock issued by TFD to TFC in the reorganization, which is treated as transferred stock under paragraph (b)(2)(iii) of this section, is distributed by TFC to UST pursuant to section 361(c).

(2) The condition of paragraph (o)(5)(ii) of this section is satisfied because UST is the U.S. transferor.

(3) The condition of paragraph (o)(5)(iii) of this section is satisfied if the aggregate basis of the TFD stock received by UST from TFC is not greater than the aggregate basis of the TFD stock at the time of the initial transfer (as adjusted for any gain recognized by UST on such transfer). If the basis condition of paragraph (o)(5)(iii) were not satisfied, under paragraph (o)(5)(iii) of this section, UST could reduce the basis of the TFD stock received in the reorganization.

(xxiii) *Example 23.—Split-off of transferred stock.* (A) *Facts.* X, a domestic corporation that is unrelated to USP and UST, wholly owns TFC. Pursuant to a reorganization described in section 368(a)(1)(B), UST transfers all of the TFD stock to TFC in exchange for 50% of the outstanding voting stock of TFC. UST enters into a gain recognition agreement with respect to such transfer. In year 4, in a split-off transaction to which section 355 applies, TFC distributes all of the TFD stock to X in exchange for all the TFC stock held by X.

(B) *Result.* Under paragraph (j)(1) of this section, the year 4 distribution of the TFD stock to X constitutes a triggering event. However, the distribution shall not constitute a triggering event if paragraph (k)(14) of this section applies. The gain recognition agreement does not terminate under paragraph (o)(5) of this section because X is not a recipient described in paragraph (o)(5)(ii) of this section.

(1) The condition of paragraph (k)(14)(i) of this section is satisfied because the distribution of the TFD stock qualifies as a nonrecognition transaction.

(2) The condition of paragraph (k)(14)(ii) of this section is satisfied because immediately after the distribution X, a domestic corporation that is eligible to be a U.S. transferor, retains a direct interest in the TFD stock.

(3) The condition of paragraph (k)(14)(iii) of this section is satisfied if X enters into a new gain recognition agreement with respect to the initial transfer. Under paragraph (k)(14)(iii)(B) of this section, X is not required to describe, with the new gain recognition agreement, any subsequent dispositions or other events that (based on the principles of paragraph (j) of this section) would constitute triggering events, other than the dispositions described in paragraph (j) of this section, because X directly owns TFD after the distribution.

(4) If X were a United States citizen, the gain recognition agreement would terminate if the condition of paragraph (o)(5)(iii) of this section were satisfied. Alternatively, the gain recognition agreement would continue for its remaining term if the conditions for the application of paragraph (k)(14) of this section were satisfied.

(C) *Alternate facts. Distribution to unrelated foreign corporation.* The facts are the same as in paragraph (q)(2)(xxiii)(A) of this section (the facts in this *Example 23*), except that X is a foreign corporation wholly owned by DC. DC is unrelated to UST. The results are the same as in paragraph (q)(2)(xxiii)(B) of this section (the results in this *Example 23*), except as follows.

(1) The condition of paragraph (k)(14)(ii) of this section is satisfied because immediately after the distribution DC, a domestic corporation that is eligible to be a U.S. transferor, owns at least 5% (determined as provided in paragraph (k)(14)(ii) of this section) of the total voting power and total value of the outstanding stock of X. As a result, DC is treated as retaining an indirect interest in the TFD stock immediately following the distribution.

(2) The condition of paragraph (k)(14)(iii) of this section is satisfied if DC enters into a new gain recognition agreement with respect to the initial transfer. Under paragraph (k)(14)(iii)(B) of this section, DC must, in addition to the dispositions described in paragraph (j) of this section, include as a triggering event a complete or partial disposition of the stock of X.

(D) *Alternate facts. Distribution to nonresident alien individual.* The facts are the same as in paragraph (q)(2)(xxiii)(A) of this section (the facts in this *Example 23*), except that X is a nonresident alien individual. Paragraph (k)(14) of this section does not apply to the distribution because the conditions of paragraph (k)(14)(ii) and (iii) of this section cannot be satisfied. Therefore, the distribution is a triggering event, and UST will recognize gain under the gain recognition agreement as required under paragraphs (c)(1)(i) and (v) of this section. The result would be the same if X were a foreign corporation and, immediately after the distribution, no United States person owned at least 5% (determined as provided in paragraph (k)(14)(ii) of this section) of the total voting power and value of the outstanding stock of X.

(xxiv) *Example 24.—Applicability of this section to gain recognition agreements filed before March 13, 2009.* (A) *Facts.* The facts are the same as in paragraph (q)(2)(vi)(A) of this section (the facts in *Example 6*), except that the initial transfer occurred on March 7, 2007, and the asset reorganization occurred on July 1, 2008.

(B) *Result.* Under paragraph (r)(1)(ii) of this section, the rules of §1.367(a)-8T (see 26 CFR part 1, revised April 1, 2007) apply to the transfers pursuant to the asset reorganization because the initial transfer occurred on March 7, 2007. As a result of the disposition of the TFC stock pursuant to the asset reorganization, under §1.367(a)-8T(d), USP is required to recognize the gain subject to the gain recognition agreement and pay applicable interest on any additional tax due with respect to such gain. Because the acquiring corporation in the asset reorganization is foreign, an exception under §1.367(a)-8T(e) is not available for the exchange of TFC stock by USP. However, pursuant to paragraph (r)(2)(i) of this section, because the exception provided by paragraph (k)(14) of this section is not included in §1.367(a)-8T, USP may apply paragraph (k)(14) of this section to such exchange (provided the conditions of paragraph (k)(14) of this section are satisfied), if the statute of limitations on assessments of tax for the 2007 tax year has not closed. If USP applies paragraph (k)(14) of this section to its exchange of the TFC stock pursuant to the asset reorganization, under paragraph (r)(2)(ii) of this section USP must include the new gain recognition agreement required under paragraph (k)(14)(iii) of this section with an amended Federal income tax return for its 2008 tax year that is filed August 10, 2009.

(xxv) *Example 25.—Applicability of this section to gain recognition agreements filed before March 13, 2009.* (A) *Facts.* The initial transfer occurs in 2004. In 2005, pursuant to a section 351 exchange, TFC transfers the TFD stock to F1 in exchange solely for F1 voting stock. UST does not file a new gain recognition agreement under §1.367(a)-8(g)(2) with respect to the exchange.

(B) *Result.* Under paragraph (r)(1)(ii) of this section, the rules of §1.367(a)-8 (see 26 CFR part 1, revised April 1, 2006) apply to the year 2005 disposition of the TFD stock because UST filed the gain recognition agreement after July 20, 1998, but before March 7, 2007. Under §1.367(a)-8(e) (see 26 CFR part 1, revised April 1, 2006), as a result of the disposition of the TFD stock by TFC, UST must recognize the amount of gain subject to the gain recognition agreement. Paragraph (r)(2)(i) of this section does not apply because the rule provided by paragraph (k)(3) of this section was included in §1.367(a)-8(g)(2) (see 26 CFR part 1, revised April 1, 2006). However, UST may request relief for reasonable cause under §1.367(a)-8(c)(2) (see 26 CFR part 1, revised April 1, 2006) to file a new gain recognition agreement with respect to the disposition of the TFD stock by TFC in 2005.

(r) *Applicability dates.—*(1) *General rule.—*(i) *Transfers occurring on or after March 13, 2009; relief for certain failures that are not willful.—*The rules of this section apply to gain recognition agreements filed with respect to transfers of stock or securities occurring on or after March 13, 2009. However, the rules of this section do not apply to gain recognition agreements filed with respect to any such transfer occurring on or after March 13, 2009, if such transfer was entered into pursuant to a written agreement that was (subject to customary conditions) binding before February 11, 2009, and at all times thereafter. Solely for purposes of this paragraph (r), a transfer described in the preceding sentence shall be deemed to be a transfer occurring before March 13, 2009 to which the rules of §1.367(a)-8 (see 26 CFR part 1, revised April 1, 2006) apply. See paragraph (r)(2)(iii) of this section for the ability to apply the rules of this section with respect to gain recognition agreements filed for taxable years ending before March 13, 2009. The eleventh sentence of paragraph (a) and paragraphs (b)(1)(iv), (b)(1)(vi), (b)(1)(xiii), (d)(1), (j)(8), and (p) of this section will apply to gain recognition agreement documents that are required to be filed on or after November 19, 2014, as well as to requests for relief submitted on or after November 19, 2014. Paragraph (k)(14)(ii) of this section applies to transfers occurring on or after October 1, 2019, and to transfers occurring before October 1, 2019, that result from an entity classification election made under §301.7701-3 of this chapter that is filed on or after October 1, 2019. For transfers occurring before October 1, 2019, other than transfers occurring before October 1, 2019, that result from an entity classification election made under §301.7701-3 of this chapter that is filed on or after October 1, 2019, a taxpayer may apply paragraph (k)(14)(ii) of this section to transfers occurring during the last taxable year of a transferee foreign corporation beginning before January 1, 2018, and each subsequent taxable year of the foreign corporation, provided that the taxpayer and United States persons that are related (within the meaning of section 267 or 707) to the taxpayer consistently apply such paragraph with respect to all foreign corporations. For transfers occurring before October 1, 2019, other than transfers occurring before October 1, 2019, that result from an entity classification election made under §301.7701-3 of this chapter that is filed on or after October 1, 2019, where the taxpayer does not apply paragraph (k)(14)(ii) of this section as described in the preceding sentence, see paragraph (k)(14)(ii) of this section as in effect and contained in 26 CFR part 1, as revised April 1, 2020.

(ii) *Transfers occurring before March 13, 2009.*—For matters covered in this section for periods before March 13, 2009 but on or after March 7, 2007, the corresponding rules of §1.367(a)-8T (see 26 CFR part 1, revised April 1, 2007) apply. For matters covered in this section for periods before March 7, 2007 but on or after July 20, 1998, the corresponding rules of §1.367(a)-8 (see 26 CFR part 1, revised April 1, 2006) apply. For matters covered in this section for periods before July 20, 1998, the corresponding rules of §1.367(a)-3T(g) (see 26 CFR part 1, revised April 1, 1998) and Notice 87-85 (1987-2 CB 395) apply. In addition, if a U.S. transferor entered into a gain recognition agreement for transfers before July 20, 1998, then the rules of §1.367(a)-3T(g) (see 26 CFR part 1, revised April 1, 1998) continue to apply in lieu of this section in the event of any direct or indirect nonrecognition transfer of the same property. See also, §1.367(a)-3(h).

(2) *Applicability to transfers occurring before March 13, 2009.*—(i) *General rule.*—Taxpayers may apply the rules of this regulation §1.367(a)-8 that were not included in §1.367(a)-8T (see 26 CFR part 1, revised April 1, 2007), to gain recognition agreements filed with respect to transfers of stock or securities for all open taxable years, if done consistently to all transfers. A U.S. transferor subject to section 877 and §1.367(a)-8T(d)(6) shall not apply the rules of this regulation to reach a contrary result. A taxpayer that failed to file a gain recognition agreement for a transfer, or to comply materially with any requirement of this section with respect to an existing gain recognition agreement, must obtain relief for reasonable cause for such failure under §1.367(a)-8T(e)(10) before applying the rules of this regulation §1.367(a)-8 that were not included in §1.367(a)-8T as permitted by this paragraph (r)(2). See paragraphs (q)(2)(xxiv) and (xxv) of this section for illustrations of the rule provided by this paragraph (r)(2)(i).

(ii) *Taxable years ending before March 13, 2009.*—Notwithstanding the requirements of §1.367(a)-8(d), any gain recognition agreement or other filing required by reason of electing to apply the rules of this regulation §1.367(a)-8 that were not included in §1.367(a)-8T, as permitted by this paragraph (r)(2), for a taxable year ending before Applicability to gain recognition agreements filed before March 13, 2009 shall be considered filed in accordance with the requirements of §1.367(a)-8(d), provided the gain recognition agreement or other filing is attached to an original or amended return for such taxable year. An amended return required to be filed by reason of electing to apply the rules of this regulation §1.367(a)-8 that were not included in §1.367(a)-8T, as permitted by this paragraph (r)(2), must be filed on or before August 10, 2009. A taxpayer that wishes to apply the rules of this regulation §1.367(a)-8 that were not included in §1.367(a)-8T, as permitted by this paragraph (r)(2), but that fails to meet the filing requirement described in the preceding sentence must request relief for reasonable cause under paragraph (p) of this section.

(iii) *Taxable years ending after effective date.*—A taxpayer that entered into a gain recognition agreement to which §1.367(a)-8T (see 26 CFR part 1, revised April 1, 2007) applies may apply the rules of this section in a tax year ending on or after Applicability to gain recognition agreements filed before March 13, 2009 by attaching the agreement, certification, or other information related to such gain recognition agreement that the rules of this section require in accordance with the rules of this section and with the time and manner rules provided in §1.367(a)-8(d).

(3) *Applicability to requests for relief submitted before November 19, 2014.*—The eleventh sentence of paragraph (a) and paragraphs (b)(1)(iv), (b)(1)(vi), (b)(1)(xiii), (d)(1), (j)(8), and (p) of this section will apply to requests for relief submitted before November 19, 2014 if—

(i) The statute of limitations on the assessment of tax has not expired for any year to which the request relates; and

(ii) The U.S. transferor resubmits the request under paragraph (p) of this section, notes on the request that the request is being submitted pursuant to this paragraph (r)(3), and acknowledges on the request that the last sentence of §1.6038B-1(g)(6) provides a special rule regarding the application of §1.6038B-1 to any transfer that is the subject of the request. [Reg. §1.367(a)-8.]

☐ [*T.D.* 8770, 6-18-98. *Amended by T.D.* 9243, 1-23-2006; *T.D.* 9311, 2-1-2007; *T.D.* 9446, 2-9-2009 (corrected 3-9-2009 and 3-26-2009); *T.D.* 9614, 3-18-2013, *T.D.* 9704, 11-18-2014 (corrected 1-2-2015), *T.D.* 9760, 3-18-2016, *T.D.* 9803, 12-15-2016 and *T.D.* 9908, 9-21-2020.]

[Reg. §1.367(a)-9T]

§1.367(a)-9T. Treatment of deemed section 351 exchanges pursuant to section 304(a)(1) (temporary).—(a) *Scope and general rule.*—This section applies to the extent that, pursuant to section 304(a)(1), a United States person is treated as transferring stock of a domestic or foreign corporation to a foreign corporation (foreign acquiring corporation) in exchange for stock of the foreign acquiring corporation in a transaction to which section 351(a) applies (deemed section 351 exchange). Except to the extent provided in paragraph (b) of this section, a transfer of stock by a United States person to a foreign acquiring corporation in a deemed section 351 exchange is not subject to section 367(a)(1).

(b) *Special rule.*—Notwithstanding paragraph (a) of this section, if the distribution received by the United States person in redemption of the stock of the foreign acquiring corporation deemed issued in the deemed section 351 exchange is applied against and reduces (in whole or in part), pursuant to section 301(c)(2), the basis of stock of the foreign acquiring corporation held by the United States person other than the stock deemed issued in the deemed section 351 exchange, the United States person shall recognize gain pursuant to this paragraph (b). The exceptions described in §1.367(a)-3(b)(1) and (c)(1) shall not apply to a transfer of stock described in paragraph (a) of this section. The amount of gain recognized by a United States person pursuant to this paragraph (b) shall equal the amount, if any, by which—

(1) The gain realized by the United States person with respect to the transferred stock in connection with the deemed section 351 exchange exceeds;

(2) The amount of the distribution received by the United States person in redemption of the stock of the foreign acquiring corporation deemed issued in the deemed section 351 exchange that is treated as a dividend under section 301(c)(1) and included in gross income by the United States person.

(c) *Ordering rule.*—For purposes of paragraph (b)(1) of this section, the amount of gain realized by the United States person in connection with the deemed section 351 exchange shall be determined without regard to the amount of gain recognized by the United States person under paragraph (b) of this section.

(d) *Allocation of recognized gain.*—Gain recognized by a United States person pursuant to paragraph (b) of this section shall be treated as recognized with respect to the stock transferred in the deemed section 351 exchange in proportion to the amount of gain realized by the United States person with respect to such stock. See §1.367(a)-1T(b)(4) for additional rules on the character, source, and adjustments relating to gain recognized under section 367(a).

(e) *Example.*—The following example illustrates the rules of this section:

Example. (i) *Facts.* (A) USP, a domestic corporation, wholly owns FC1 and FC2, each a foreign corporation. USP, FC1 and FC2 use a calendar taxable year. The FC1 stock has a $40x basis and $100x fair market value. The FC2 stock has a $100x basis and $100x fair market value. As of December 31, year 1, FC1 has zero earnings and profits, and FC2 has $20x earnings and profits. On December 31, year 1, in a transaction described in section 304(a)(1), USP sells the FC1 stock to FC2 for $100x cash.

(B) Because USP wholly owns FC1 before the transactions and is treated, under section 318, as indirectly owning 100% of the FC1 stock after the transfer, under section 304(a)(1), USP and FC2 are treated in the same manner as if USP contributed the FC1 stock to FC2 in a deemed section 351 exchange in exchange solely for $100x of FC2 stock, and then FC2 redeemed for $100x cash its stock deemed issued to USP. Because USP wholly owns FC1 before the sale and is treated as owning 100% of FC1 after the sale, section 302(a) does not apply to the redemption. Instead, under section 302(d), the redemption is treated as a distribution to which section 301 applies. Pursuant to section 304(b)(2), $20x of the distribution is treated as a dividend from FC2. With respect to the remaining $80x, USP takes the position that $40x is applied against and reduces the basis of the FC2 stock issued in the deemed section 351 exchange, and $40x is applied against and reduces the basis of the FC2 stock held by USP prior to (and after) the transaction.

(ii) *Analysis.* Under paragraph (b) of this section, USP must recognize gain of $40x on its transfer of the FC1 stock to FC2 in the deemed section 351 exchange (the amount by which the $60x gain realized by USP on the deemed section 351 exchange with respect to the F1 stock exceeds the $20x dividend inclusion). Pursuant to paragraph (b) of this section, the exception under §1.367(a)-3(b) is not available to the transfer of the FC1 stock by USP to FC2 in the deemed section 351 exchange. Thus, USP cannot avoid gain recognition under paragraph (b) of this section by entering into a gain recognition agreement with respect to its transfer of the FC1 stock to FC2 in the deemed section 351 exchange. Under paragraph (d) of this section, the $40x gain recognized is allocated among the shares of FC1 stock transferred to FC2 in the deemed section 351 exchange in proportion to the gain realized by USP on the transfer of such shares. Under paragraph (c) of this section, the application of paragraph (b) of this section is determined prior to taking into account the $40x increase to the basis of the FC1 stock transferred by USP. Under section 362, the basis of the FC1 stock in the hands of FC2 is increased by $40x, the amount of gain recognized by the USP on the transfer of the FC1 stock under paragraph (b) of this section. Under section 358, the basis of the FC2 stock received by USP in the deemed section 351 exchange is similarly increased by $40x. See §1.367(a)-1T(b)(4). The $40x increase to the basis of the FC2 stock is taken into account before determining the consequences of the redemption of such stock under section 304(a)(1).

(f) *Effective/applicability date.*—This section applies to transfers occurring on or after February 10, 2009. See §1.367(a)-3(a), as contained in 26 CFR part 1 revised as of April 1, 2008, for transfers occurring on or after February 21, 2006, and before February 10, 2009.

(g) *Expiration date.*—This section expires on or before February 10, 2012. [Temporary Reg. §1.367(a)-9T.]

☐ [*T.D.* 9444, 2-10-2009 (*corrected* 3-9-2009).]

[Reg. §1.367(b)-0]

☐ [T.D. 8862, 1-21-2000 *(corrected 11-3-2000). Amended by T.D. 8937, 1-10-2001; T.D. 9273, 8-7-2006; T.D. 9526, 5-17-2011 and T.D. 9614, 3-18-2013.*]

[Reg. §1.367(b)-1]

§1.367(b)-1. Other transfers.—(a) *Scope.*—The regulations promulgated under section 367(b) (the section 367(b) regulations) set forth rules regarding the proper inclusions and adjustments that must be made as a result of an exchange described in section 367(b) (a section 367(b) exchange). A section 367(b) exchange is any exchange described in section 332, 351, 354, 355, 356 or 361, with respect to which the status of a foreign corporation as a corporation is relevant for determining the extent to which income shall be recognized or for determining the effect of the transaction on earnings and profits, basis of stock or securities, basis of assets, or other relevant tax attributes. For rules coordinating the concurrent application of sections 367(a) and (b), see §1.367(a)-3(b)(2).

(b) *General rules.*—(1) *Rules.*—The following general rules apply under the section 367(b) regulations—

(i) A foreign corporation in a section 367(b) exchange is considered to be a corporation and, as a result, all of the related provisions (e.g., section 381) shall apply, except to the extent provided in the section 367(b) regulations; and

(ii) Nothing in the section 367(b) regulations shall permit—

(A) The nonrecognition of income that would otherwise be required to be recognized under another provision of the Internal Revenue Code or the regulations thereunder; or

(B) The recognition of a loss or deduction that would otherwise not be recognized under another provision of the Internal Revenue Code or the regulations thereunder.

(2) *Example.*—The following example illustrates the rules of this paragraph (b):

Example—(i) *Facts.* DC, a domestic corporation, owns 90 percent of P, a partnership. The remaining 10 percent of P is owned by a person unrelated to DC. P owns all of the outstanding stock of FC, a controlled foreign corporation. FC liquidates into P.

(ii) *Result.* FC's liquidation is not a transaction described in section 332. Nothing in the section 367(b) regulations, including § 1.367(b)-2(k), permits FC's liquidation to qualify as a liquidation described in section 332.

(c) *Notice required.*—(1) *In general.*—A notice under this paragraph (c) (section 367(b) notice) must be filed with regard to any person described in paragraph (c)(2) of this section. A section 367(b) notice must be filed in the time and manner described in paragraph (c)(3) of this section and must include the information described in paragraph (c)(4) of this section.

(2) *Persons subject to section 367(b) notice.*—The following persons are described in this paragraph (c)(2)—

(i) A shareholder described in § 1.367(b)-3(b)(1) that realizes income in a transaction described in § 1.367(b)-3(a);

(ii) A shareholder that makes the election described in § 1.367(b)-3(c)(3);

(iii) A shareholder described in § 1.367(b)-4(b)(1)(i)(A)(*1*) or (*2*) that realizes income in a transaction described in § 1.367(b)-4(a);

(iv) A shareholder that realizes income in a transaction described in § 1.367(b)-5(c) or 1.367(b)-5(d) and that is either—

(A) A section 1248 shareholder of the distributing or controlled corporation; or

(B) A foreign corporation with one or more shareholders that are described in paragraph (c)(2)(iv)(A) of this section; and

(v) A foreign surviving corporation described in § 1.367(b)-7(a).

(3) *Time and manner for filing notice.*—(i) *United States persons described in § 1.367(b)-1(c)(2).*—A United States person described in paragraph (c)(2) of this section must file a section 367(b) notice attached to a timely filed Federal tax return (including extensions) for the person's taxable year in which income is realized in the section 367(b) exchange. In the case of a shareholder that makes the election described in § 1.367(b)-3(c)(3), notification of such election must be sent to the foreign acquired corporation (or its successor in interest) on or before the date the section 367(b) notice is filed, so that appropriate corresponding adjustments can be made in accordance with the rules of § 1.367(b)-2(e).

(ii) *Foreign corporations described in § 1.367(b)-1(c)(2).*—Each United States person listed in this paragraph (c)(3)(ii) must file a section 367(b) notice with regard to a foreign corporation described in paragraph (c)(2) of this section. Such notice must be attached to a timely filed Federal tax return (including extensions) for the United States person's taxable year in which income is realized in the section 367(b) exchange and, if the United States person is required to file a Form 5471 (Information Return of U.S. Persons With Respect To Certain Foreign Corporations), the section 367(b) notice must be attached to the Form 5471. The following persons are listed in this paragraph (c)(3)(ii)—

(A) United States shareholders (as defined in § 1.367(b)-3(b)(2)) of foreign corporations described in paragraph (c)(2)(i) or (v) of this section; and

(B) Section 1248 shareholders of foreign corporations described in paragraph (c)(2)(iii) or (iv) of this section.

(4) *Information required.*—Except as provided in paragraph (c)(5) of this section, a section 367(b) notice shall include the following information—

(i) A statement that the exchange is a section 367(b) exchange;

(ii) A complete description of the exchange;

(iii) A description of any stock, securities or other consideration transferred or received in the exchange;

(iv) A statement that describes any amount (or amounts) required, under the section 367(b) regulations, to be taken into account as income or loss or as an adjustment (including an adjustment under § 1.367(b)-7 or 1.367(b)-9) to basis, earnings and profits, or other tax attributes as a result of the exchange;

(v) Any information that is or would be required to be furnished with a Federal income tax return pursuant to regulations

under section 332, 351, 354, 355, 356, 361, 368, or 381 (whether or not a Federal income tax return is required to be filed), if such information has not otherwise been provided by the person filing the section 367(b) notice;

(vi) Any information required to be furnished with respect to the exchange under sections 6038, 6038A, 6038B, 6038C or 6046, or the regulations under those sections, if such information has not otherwise been provided by the person filing the section 367(b) notice; and

(vii) If applicable, a statement that the shareholder is making the election described in § 1.367(b)-3(c)(3). This statement must include—

(A) A copy of the information the shareholder received from the foreign acquired corporation (or its successor in interest) establishing and substantiating the shareholder's all earnings and profits amount with respect to the shareholder's stock in the foreign acquired corporation; and

(B) A representation that the shareholder has notified the foreign acquired corporation (or its successor in interest) that the shareholder is making the election described in § 1.367(b)-3(c)(3).

(5) *Abbreviated notice provision for shareholders that make the election described in § 1.367(b)-3(c)(3).*—In the case of a foreign acquired corporation that has never had earnings and profits that would result in any shareholder having an all earnings and profits amount, a shareholder making the election described in § 1.367(b)-3(c)(3) may satisfy the information requirements of paragraph (c)(4) of this section by filing a section 367(b) notice that includes—

(i) A statement from the foreign acquired corporation (or its successor in interest) that the foreign acquired corporation has never had any earnings and profits that would result in any shareholder having an all earnings and profits amount; and

(ii) The information described in paragraphs (c)(4)(i) through (iii) of this section.

(6) *Supplemental published guidance.*—The section 367(b) notice requirements may be updated or amended by revenue procedure or other published guidance. [Reg. § 1.367(b)-1.]

☐ [*T.D. 8770*, 6-18-98. *Amended by T.D. 8862*, 1-21-2000 (*corrected* 11-3-2000); *T.D. 9243*, 1-23-2006 *and T.D. 9273*, 8-7-2006.]

[Reg. § 1.367(b)-2]

§ 1.367(b)-2. Definitions and special rules.—(a) *Controlled foreign corporation.*—The term *controlled foreign corporation* means a controlled foreign corporation as defined in section 957 (taking into account section 953(c)).

(b) *Section 1248 shareholder.*—The term *section 1248 shareholder* means any United States person that satisfies the ownership requirements of section 1248(a)(2) or (c)(2) with respect to a foreign corporation.

(c) *Section 1248 amount.*—(1) *Rule.*—The term *section 1248 amount* with respect to stock in a foreign corporation means the net positive earnings and profits (if any) that would have been attributable to such stock and includible in income as a dividend under section 1248 and the regulations thereunder if the stock were sold by the shareholder. In the case of a transaction in which the shareholder is a foreign corporation (foreign shareholder), the following additional rules shall apply—

(i) The foreign shareholder shall be deemed to be a United States person for purposes of this paragraph (c), except that the foreign shareholder shall not be considered a United States person for purposes of determining whether the stock owned by the foreign shareholder is stock of a controlled foreign corporation; and

(ii) The foreign shareholder's holding period in the stock of the foreign corporation shall be determined by reference to the period that the foreign shareholder's section 1248 shareholders held (directly or indirectly) an interest in the foreign corporation. This paragraph (c)(1)(ii) applies in addition to the section 1248 regulations' incorporation of section 1223 holding periods. See § 1.1248–8.

(2) *Examples.*—The following examples illustrate the rules of this paragraph (c):

Example 1—(i) *Facts.* DC, a domestic corporation, owns all of the outstanding stock of FC1, a controlled foreign corporation (CFC). FC1 owns all of the outstanding stock of FC2, a CFC. DC has always owned all of the stock of FC1, and FC1 has always owned all of the stock of FC2.

(ii) *Result.* Under this paragraph (c), DC's section 1248 amount with respect to its FC1 stock is computed by reference to all of FC1's and FC2's earnings and profits. See section 1248(c)(2). Because FC1's section 1248 shareholder (DC) always indirectly held all of the stock of FC2, FC1's section 1248 amount with respect to its FC2 stock is computed by reference to all of FC2's earnings and profits.

Example 2—(i) *Facts.* DC, a domestic corporation, owns 40 percent of the outstanding stock of FC1, a foreign corporation. The other 60 percent of FC1 stock is owned (directly and indirectly) by foreign persons that are unrelated to DC. FC1 owns all of the outstanding stock of FC2, a foreign corporation. On January 1, 2001, DC purchases the remaining 60 percent of FC1 stock.

(ii) *Result.* Under this paragraph (c), DC's section 1248 amount with respect to its FC1 stock is computed by reference to FC1's and FC2's earnings and profits that accumulated on or after January 1, 2001, the date FC1 and FC2 became controlled foreign corporations (CFCs). See section 1248(a). Because FC1 is not considered a United States person for purposes of determining whether FC2 is a CFC, FC1's section 1248 amount with respect to its FC2 stock is computed by reference to FC2's earnings and profits that accumulated on or after January 1, 2001, the date FC2 became an actual CFC.

Example 3—(i) *Facts.* FC1, a foreign corporation, owns all of the outstanding stock of FC2, a foreign corporation. DC is a domestic corporation that is unrelated to FC1, FC2, and their direct and indirect owners. On January 1, 2001, DC purchases all of the outstanding stock of FC1.

(ii) *Result.* Under this paragraph (c), DC's section 1248 amount with respect to its FC1 stock is computed by reference to FC1's and FC2's earnings and profits that accumulated on or after January 1, 2001, the first day DC held the stock of FC1. See section 1248(a). FC1's section 1248 amount with respect to its FC2 stock is computed by reference to FC2's earnings and profits that accumulated on or after January 1, 2001, the first day FC1's section 1248 shareholder (DC) indirectly held the stock of FC2.

(d) *All earnings and profits amount.*—(1) *General rule.*—The term *all earnings and profits amount* with respect to stock in a foreign corporation means the net positive earnings and profits (if any) determined as provided under paragraph (d)(2) of this section and attributable to such stock as provided under paragraph (d)(3) of this section. The all earnings and profits amount shall be determined without regard to the amount of gain that would be realized on a sale or exchange of the stock of the foreign corporation.

(2) *Rules for determining earnings and profits.*—(i) *Domestic rules generally applicable.*—For purposes of this paragraph (d), except as provided in sections 312(k)(4) and (n)(8), 964 and 986, the earnings and profits of a foreign corporation for any taxable year shall be determined according to principles substantially similar to those applicable to domestic corporations.

(ii) *Certain adjustments to earnings and profits.*—Notwithstanding paragraph (d)(2)(i) of this section, for purposes of this paragraph (d), the earnings and profits of a foreign corporation for any taxable year shall not include the amounts specified in section 1248(d). In the case of amounts specified in section 1248(d)(4), the preceding sentence requires that the earnings and profits for any taxable year be decreased by the net positive amount (if any) of earnings and profits attributable to activities described in section 1248(d)(4), and increased by the net reduction (if any) in earnings and profits attributable to activities described in section 1248(d)(4).

(iii) *Effect of section 332 liquidating distribution.*—The all earnings and profits amount with respect to stock of a corporation that distributes all of its property in a liquidation described in section 332 shall be determined without regard to the adjustments prescribed by section 312(a) and (b) resulting from the distribution of such property in liquidation, except that gain or loss realized by the corporation on the distribution shall be taken into account to the extent provided in section 312(f)(1). See § 1.367(b)-3(b)(3)(ii) *Example 3.*

(3) *Amount attributable to a block of stock.*—(i) *Application of section 1248 principles.*—(A) *In general.*—(1) *Rule.*—The all earnings and profits amount with respect to stock of a foreign corporation is determined according to the attribution principles of section 1248 and the regulations thereunder. The attribution principles of section 1248 shall apply without regard to the requirements of section 1248 that are not relevant to the determination of a shareholder's pro rata portion of earnings and profits. Thus, for example, the all earnings and profits amount is determined without regard to whether the foreign corporation was a controlled foreign corporation at any time during the five years preceding the section 367(b) exchange in question, without regard to whether the shareholder owned a 10 percent or greater interest in the stock, and without regard to whether the earnings and profits of the foreign corporation were accumulated in post-1962 taxable years or while the corporation was a controlled foreign corporation.

(2) *Example.*—The following example illustrates the rules of this paragraph (d)(3)(i)(A):

Example—(i) *Facts.* On January 1, 2001, DC, a domestic corporation, purchases 9 percent of the outstanding stock of FC, a

foreign corporation. On January 1, 2002, DC purchases an additional 1 percent of FC stock. On January 1, 2003, DC exchanges its stock in FC in a section 367(b) exchange in which DC is required to include the all earnings and profits amount in income. FC was not a controlled foreign corporation during the entire period DC held its FC stock.

(ii) *Result.* The all earnings and profits amount with respect to DC's stock in FC is computed by reference to 9 percent of FC's earnings and profits from January 1, 2001, through December 31, 2001, and by reference to 10 percent of FC's earnings and profits from January 1, 2002, through January 1, 2003.

(B) *Foreign shareholders.*—In the case of a transaction in which the exchanging shareholder is a foreign corporation (foreign shareholder), the following additional rules shall apply—

(1) The attribution principles of section 1248 shall apply without regard to whether the person directly owning the stock is a United States person; and

(2) The foreign shareholder's holding period in the stock of the foreign acquired corporation shall be determined by reference to the period that the foreign shareholder's United States shareholders (as defined in § 1.367(b)-3(b)(2)) held (directly or indirectly) an interest in the foreign acquired corporation. This paragraph (d)(3)(i)(B)(2) applies in addition to the section 1248 regulations' incorporation of section 1223 holding periods. See § 1.1248–8.

(ii) *Exclusion of lower-tier earnings.*—In applying the attribution principles of section 1248 and the regulations thereunder to determine the all earnings and profits amount with respect to stock of a foreign corporation, the earnings and profits of subsidiaries of the foreign corporation shall not be taken into account notwithstanding section 1248(c)(2).

(e) *Treatment of deemed dividends.*—(1) *In general.*—In certain circumstances these regulations provide that an exchanging shareholder shall include an amount in income as a deemed dividend. This paragraph provides rules for the treatment of the deemed dividend.

(2) *Consequences of dividend characterization.*—A deemed dividend described in paragraph (e)(1) of this section shall be treated as a dividend for purposes of the Internal Revenue Code. The deemed dividend shall be considered as paid out of the earnings and profits with respect to which the amount of the deemed dividend was determined. Thus, for example, a deemed dividend that is determined by reference to the all earnings and profits amount or the section 1248 amount will never be considered as paid out of (and therefore will never reduce) earnings and profits specified in section 1248(d), because such earnings and profits are excluded in computing the all earnings and profits amount (under paragraph (d)(2)(ii) of this section) and the section 1248 amount (under section 1248(d) and paragraph (c)(1) of this section). If the deemed dividend is determined by reference to the earnings and profits of a foreign corporation that is owned indirectly (i.e., through one or more tiers of intermediate owners) by the person that is required to include the deemed dividend in income, the deemed dividend shall be considered as having been paid by such corporation to such person through the intermediate owners, rather than directly to such person.

(3) *Ordering rules.*—In the case of an exchange of stock in which the exchanging shareholder is treated as receiving a deemed dividend from a foreign corporation, the following ordering rules concerning the timing, treatment, and effect of such a deemed dividend shall apply. See also paragraph (j)(2) of this section.

(i) For purposes of the section 367(b) regulations, the gain realized by an exchanging shareholder shall be determined before increasing (as provided in paragraph (e)(3)(ii) of this section) the basis in the stock of the foreign corporation by the amount of the deemed dividend.

(ii) Except as provided in paragraph (e)(3)(i) of this section, the deemed dividend shall be considered to be received immediately before the exchanging shareholder's receipt of consideration for its stock in the foreign corporation, and the shareholder's basis in the stock exchanged shall be increased by the amount of the deemed dividend. Such basis increase shall be taken into account before determining the gain otherwise recognized on the exchange (for example, under section 356), the basis that the exchanging shareholder takes in the property that it receives in the exchange (under section 358(a)(1)), and the basis that the transferee otherwise takes in the transferred stock (under section 362).

(iii) Except as provided in paragraph (e)(3)(i) of this section, the earnings and profits of the appropriate foreign corporation shall be reduced by the deemed dividend amount before determining the consequences of the recognition of gain in excess of the deemed dividend amount (for example, under section 356(a)(2) or sections 356(a)(1) and 1248).

(4) *Examples.*—The following examples illustrate the rules of this paragraph (e):

Example 1. DC, a domestic corporation, exchanges stock in FC, a foreign corporation, in a section 367(b) exchange in which DC includes the all earnings and profits amount in income as a deemed dividend. Under paragraph (e)(2) of this section, a deemed dividend is treated as a dividend for purposes of the Internal Revenue Code.

Example 2. DC, a domestic corporation, exchanges stock in FC1, a foreign corporation that is a controlled foreign corporation, in a transaction in which DC is required to include the section 1248 amount in income as a deemed dividend. A portion of the section 1248 amount is determined by reference to the earnings and profits of FC1 (the upper-tier portion of the section 1248 amount), and the remainder of the section 1248 amount is determined by reference to the earnings and profits of FC2, which is a wholly owned foreign subsidiary of FC1 (the lower-tier portion of the section 1248 amount). Under paragraph (e)(2) of this section, DC computes its deemed paid foreign tax credit as if the lower-tier portion of the section 1248 amount were distributed as a dividend by FC2 to FC1, and as if such portion and the upper-tier portion of the section 1248 amount were then distributed as a dividend by FC1 to DC.

Example 3. DC, a domestic corporation, exchanges stock in FC, a foreign corporation that is a controlled foreign corporation, in a transaction in which DC realizes gain of $100 (prior to the application of the section 367(b) regulations). In connection with the transaction, DC is required to include $40 in income as a deemed dividend under the section 367(b) regulations. In addition to receiving property permitted to be received under section 354 without the recognition of gain, DC also receives cash in the amount of $70. Under paragraph (e)(3) of this section, the $40 deemed dividend increases DC's basis in its FC stock before determining the gain to be recognized under section 356. Thus, in applying section 356, DC is considered to realize $60 of gain on the exchange, all of which is recognized under section 356(a)(1).

(f) *Deemed asset transfer and closing of taxable year in certain section 368(a)(1)(F) reorganizations.*—(1) *Scope.*—This paragraph applies to a reorganization described in section 368(a)(1)(F) in which the transferor corporation is a foreign corporation.

(2) *Deemed asset transfer.*—In a reorganization described in paragraph (f)(1) of this section, there is considered to exist—

(i) A transfer of assets by the foreign transferor corporation to the acquiring corporation in exchange for stock (or stock and securities) of the acquiring corporation and the assumption by the acquiring corporation of the foreign transferor corporation's liabilities;

(ii) A distribution of such stock (or stock and securities) by the foreign transferor corporation to its shareholders (or shareholders and security holders); and

(iii) An exchange by the foreign transferor corporation's shareholders (or shareholders and security holders) of their stock (or stock and securities) for stock (or stock and securities) of the acquiring corporation.

(3) *Other applicable rules.*—For purposes of this paragraph (f), it is immaterial that the applicable foreign or domestic law treats the acquiring corporation as a continuation of the foreign transferor corporation.

(4) *Closing of taxable year.*—In a reorganization described in paragraph (f)(1) of this section, the taxable year of the foreign transferor corporation shall end with the close of the date of the transfer and, except as otherwise required under the Internal Revenue Code (e.g. section 1502 and the regulations thereunder), the taxable year of the acquiring corporation shall end with the close of the date on which the transferor's taxable year would have ended but for the occurrence of the reorganization if—

(i) The acquiring corporation is a domestic corporation; or

(ii) The foreign transferor corporation has effectively connected earnings and profits (as defined in section 884(d)) or accumulated effectively connected earnings and profits (as defined in section 884(b)(2)(B)(ii)).

(g) *Stapled stock under section 269B.*—For rules addressing the deemed conversion of a foreign corporation to a domestic corporation under section 269B, see § 1.269B-1(c).

(h) *Section 953(d) domestication elections.*—(1) *Effect of election.*—A foreign corporation that elects under section 953(d) to be treated as a domestic corporation shall be treated for purposes of section 367(b) as transferring, as of the first day of the first taxable year for which the election is effective, all of its assets to a domestic corporation in a reorganization described in section 368(a)(1)(F). Notwithstanding paragraph (d) of this section, for purposes of determining the consequences of the reorganization under § 1.367(b)-3, the all earnings and profits amount shall not be considered to include earnings and

profits accumulated in taxable years beginning before January 1, 1988.

(2) *Post-election exchanges.*—For purposes of applying section 367(b) to post-election exchanges with respect to a corporation that has made a valid election under section 953(d) to be treated as a domestic corporation, such corporation shall be treated as a domestic corporation as to earnings and profits that were taken into account at the time of the section 953(d) election or which accrue after such election, and shall be treated as a foreign corporation as to earnings and profits accumulated in taxable years beginning before January 1, 1988. Thus, for example, if the section 953(d) corporation subsequently transfers its assets to a domestic corporation (other than another section 953(d) corporation) in a transaction described in section 381(a), the rules of § 1.367(b)-3 shall apply to such transaction to the extent of the section 953(d) corporation's earnings and profits accumulated in taxable years beginning before January 1, 1988.

(i) *Section 1504(d) elections.*—An election under section 1504(d), which permits certain foreign corporations to be treated as domestic corporations, is treated as a transfer of property to a domestic corporation and will generally constitute a reorganization described in section 368(a)(1)(F). However, if an election under section 1504(d) is made with respect to a foreign corporation from the first day of the foreign corporation's existence, then the foreign corporation shall be treated as a domestic corporation, and the section 367(b) regulations will not apply.

(j) *Sections 985 through 989.*—(1) *Change in functional currency of a qualified business unit.*—(i) *Rule.*—If, as a result of a section 367(b) exchange described in section 381(a), a qualified business unit (as defined in section 989(a)) (QBU) has a different functional currency determined under the rules of section 985(b) than it used prior to the transaction, then the QBU shall be deemed to have automatically changed its functional currency immediately prior to the transaction. A QBU that is deemed to change its functional currency pursuant to this paragraph (j) must make the adjustments described in § 1.985-5.

(ii) *Example.*—The following example illustrates the rule of this paragraph (j)(1):

Example—(i) *Facts.* DC, a domestic corporation, owns 100 percent of FC1, a foreign corporation. FC1 owns and operates a qualified business unit (QBU) (B1) in France, whose functional currency is the euro. FC2, an unrelated foreign corporation, owns and operates a QBU (B2) in France, whose functional currency is the dollar. FC2 acquires FC1's assets (including B1) in a reorganization described in section 368(a)(1)(C). As a part of the reorganization, B1 and B2 combine their operations into one QBU. Applying the rules of section 985(b), the functional currency of the combined operations of B1 and B2 is the euro.

(ii) *Result.* FC2's acquisition of FC1's assets is a section 367(b) exchange that is described in section 381(a). Because the functional currency of the combined operations of B1 and B2 after the exchange is the euro, B2 is deemed to have automatically changed its functional currency to the euro immediately prior to the section 367(b) exchange. B2 must make the adjustments described in § 1.985-5.

(2) *Previously taxed earnings and profits.*—(i) *Exchanging shareholder that is a United States person.*—If an exchanging shareholder that is a United States person is required to include in income either the all earnings and profits amount or the section 1248 amount under the provisions of § 1.367(b)-3 or 1.367(b)-4, then immediately prior to the exchange, and solely for the purpose of computing exchange gain or loss under section 986(c), the exchanging shareholder shall be treated as receiving a distribution of previously taxed earnings and profits from the appropriate foreign corporation that is attributable (under the principles of section 1248) to the exchanged stock. If an exchanging shareholder that is a United States person is a distributee in an exchange described in § 1.367(b)-5(c) or (d), then immediately prior to the exchange, and solely for the purpose of computing exchange gain or loss under section 986(c), the exchanging shareholder shall be treated as receiving a distribution of previously taxed earnings and profits from the appropriate foreign corporation to the extent such shareholder has a diminished interest in such previously taxed earnings and profits after the exchange. The exchange gain or loss recognized under this paragraph (j)(2)(i) will increase or decrease the exchanging shareholder's adjusted basis in the stock of the foreign corporation, including for purposes of computing gain or loss realized with respect to the stock on the transaction. The exchanging shareholder's dollar basis with respect to each account of previously taxed income shall be increased or decreased by the exchange gain or loss recognized.

(ii) *Exchanging shareholder that is a foreign corporation.*—If an exchanging shareholder that is a foreign corporation is required to include in income either the all earnings and profits amount or the section 1248 amount under the provisions of § 1.367(b)-3 or

1.367(b)-4, then, immediately prior to the exchange, the exchanging shareholder shall be treated as receiving a distribution of previously taxed earnings and profits from the appropriate foreign corporation that is attributable (under the principles of section 1248) to the exchanged stock. If an exchanging shareholder that is a foreign corporation is a distributee in an exchange described in §1.367(b)-5(c) or (d), then the exchanging shareholder shall be treated as receiving (immediately prior to the exchange) a distribution of previously taxed earnings and profits from the appropriate foreign corporation. Such distribution shall be measured by the extent to which the exchanging shareholder's direct or indirect United States shareholders (as defined in section 951(b)) have a diminished interest in such previously taxed earnings and profits after the exchange.

(3) *Other rules.*—See sections 985 through 989 for other currency rules that may apply in connection with a section 367(b) exchange.

(k) *Partnerships, trusts and estates.*—In applying the section 367(b) regulations, stock of a corporation that is owned by a foreign partnership, trust or estate shall be considered as owned proportionately by its partners, owners, or beneficiaries under the principles of §1.367(e)-1(b)(2). Stock owned by an entity that is disregarded as an entity separate from its owner under §301.7701-3 is owned directly by the owner of such entity. In applying §1.367(b)-5(b), the principles of §1.367(e)-1(b)(2) shall also apply to a domestic partnership, trust or estate.

(l) *Additional definitions.*—(1) *Foreign income taxes.*—The term *foreign income taxes* has the meaning set forth in §1.902-1(a)(7).

(2) *Post-1986 undistributed earnings.*—The term *post-1986 undistributed earnings* has the meaning set forth in §1.902-1(a)(9).

(3) *Post-1986 foreign income taxes.*—The term *post-1986 foreign income taxes* has the meaning set forth in §1.902-1(a)(8).

(4) *Pre-1987 accumulated profits.*—The term *pre-1987 accumulated profits* means the earnings and profits described in §1.902-1(a)(10)(i), computed in accordance with the rules of §1.902-1(a)(10)(ii).

(5) *Pre-1987 foreign income taxes.*—The term *pre-1987 foreign income taxes* has the meaning set forth in §1.902-1(a)(10)(iii).

(6) *Pre-1987 section 960 earnings and profits.*—The term *pre-1987 section 960 earnings and profits* means the earnings and profits of a foreign corporation accumulated in taxable years beginning before January 1, 1987, computed under §1.964-1(a) through (e), and translated into the functional currency (as determined under section 985) of the foreign corporation at the spot rate on the first day of the foreign corporation's first taxable year beginning after December 31, 1986. For further guidance, see Notice 88-70 (1988-2 C.B. 369, 370) (see also §601.601(d)(2) of this chapter). The term pre-1987 section 960 earnings and profits does not include earnings and profits that represent previously taxed earnings and profits described in section 959.

(7) *Pre-1987 section 960 foreign income taxes.*—The term *pre-1987 section 960 foreign income taxes* means the foreign income taxes related to pre-1987 section 960 earnings and profits, determined in accordance with the principles of §1.902-1(a)(10)(iii), except that the U.S. dollar amounts of pre-1987 section 960 foreign income taxes are determined by reference to the exchange rates in effect when the taxes were paid or accrued.

(8) *Earnings and profits.*—For purposes of §§1.367(b)-7 and 1.367(b)-9, the term *earnings and profits* means post-1986 undistributed earnings, pre-1987 accumulated profits, and pre-1987 section 960 earnings and profits.

(9) *Pooling corporation.*—The term *pooling corporation* means a foreign corporation with respect to which the requirements of section 902(c)(3)(B) have been met in the current taxable year or any prior taxable year.

(10) *Nonpooling corporation.*—The term *nonpooling corporation* means a foreign corporation that is not a pooling corporation.

(11) *Separate category.*—The term *separate category* has the meaning set forth in section 904(d)(1), and shall also include any other category of income to which section 904(a), (b), and (c) are applied separately under any other provision of the Internal Revenue Code (e.g., sections 56(g)(4)(C)(iii)(IV), 245(a)(10), 865(h), 901(j), and 904(h)(10) (or section 904(g)(10) for taxable years beginning on or before December 31, 2006).

(12) *Passive category.*—The term *passive category* means the separate category that includes income described in section 904(d)(1)(A).

(13) *General category.*—The term *general category* means the separate category that includes income described in section 904(d)(1)(B)

(or section 904(d)(1)(I) for taxable years beginning on or before December 31, 2006). [Reg. §1.367(b)-2.]

☐ [*T.D. 8397, 2-25-92. Amended by T.D. 8862, 1-21-2000 (corrected 11-3-2000); T.D. 9216, 7-28-2005; T.D. 9273, 8-7-2006; T.D. 9345, 7-27-2007, T.D. 9400, 5-23-2008 and T.D. 9959, 12-28-2021.*]

[Reg. §1.367(b)-3]

§1.367(b)-3. Repatriation of foreign corporate assets in certain nonrecognition transactions.—(a) *Scope.*—This section applies to an acquisition by a domestic corporation (the domestic acquiring corporation) of the assets of a foreign corporation (the foreign acquired corporation) in a liquidation described in section 332 or an asset acquisition described in section 368(a)(1).

(b) *Exchange of stock owned directly by a United States shareholder or by certain foreign corporate shareholders.*—(1) *Scope.*—This paragraph (b) applies in the case of an exchanging shareholder that is either—

(i) A United States shareholder of the foreign acquired corporation; or

(ii) A foreign corporation with respect to which there are one or more United States shareholders.

(2) *United States shareholder.*—For purposes of this section (and for purposes of the other section 367(b) regulation provisions that specifically refer to this paragraph (b)(2)), the term *United States shareholder* means any shareholder described in section 951(b) (without regard to whether the foreign corporation is a controlled foreign corporation), and also any shareholder described in section 953(c)(1)(A) (but only if the foreign corporation is a controlled foreign corporation as defined in section 953(c)(1)(B) subject to the rules of section 953(c)).

(3) *Income inclusion.*—(i) *Inclusion of all earnings and profits amount.*—An exchanging shareholder shall include in income as a deemed dividend the all earnings and profits amount with respect to its stock in the foreign acquired corporation. For the consequences of the deemed dividend, see §1.367(b)-2(e). Notwithstanding §1.367(b)-2(e), however, a deemed dividend from the foreign acquired corporation to an exchanging foreign corporate shareholder shall not qualify for the exception from foreign personal holding company income provided by section 954(c)(3)(A)(i), although it may qualify for the look-through treatment provided by section 904(d)(3) if the requirements of that section are met with respect to the deemed dividend.

(ii) *Examples.*—The following examples illustrate the rules of paragraph (b)(3)(i) of this section:

Example 1—(i) *Facts.* DC, a domestic corporation, owns all of the outstanding stock of FC, a foreign corporation. The stock of FC has a value of $100, and DC has a basis of $30 in such stock. The all earnings and profits amount attributable to the FC stock owned by DC is $20, of which $15 is described in section 1248(a) and the remaining $5 is not (for example, because it accumulated prior to 1963). FC has a basis of $50 in its assets. In a liquidation described in section 332, FC distributes all of its property to DC, and the FC stock held by DC is canceled.

(ii) *Result.* Under paragraph (b)(3)(i) of this section, DC must include $20 in income as a deemed dividend from FC. Under section 337(a) FC does not recognize gain or loss in the assets that it distributes to DC, and under section 334(b), DC takes a basis of $50 in such assets.

Example 2—(i) *Facts.* DC, a domestic corporation, owns all of the outstanding stock of FC, a foreign corporation. The stock of FC has a value of $100, and DC has a basis of $30 in such stock. The all earnings and profits amount attributable to the FC stock owned by DC is $75. FC has a basis of $50 in its assets. In a liquidation described in section 332, FC distributes all of its property to DC, and the FC stock held by DC is canceled.

(ii) *Result.* Under paragraph (b)(3)(i) of this section, DC must include $75 in income as a deemed dividend from FC. Under section 337(a) FC does not recognize gain or loss in the assets that it distributes to DC, and under section 334(b), DC takes a basis of $50 in such assets.

Example 3—(i) *Facts.* DC, a domestic corporation, owns 80 percent of the outstanding stock of FC, a foreign corporation. DC has owned its 80 percent interest in FC since FC was incorporated. The remaining 20 percent of the outstanding stock of FC is owned by a person unrelated to DC (the minority shareholder). The stock of FC owned by DC has a value of $80, and DC has a basis of $24 in such stock. The stock of FC owned by the minority shareholder has a value of $20, and the minority shareholder has a basis of $18 in such stock. FC's only asset is land having a value of $100, and FC has a basis of $50 in the land. Gain on the land would not generate earnings and profits qualifying under section 1248(d) for an exclusion from earnings and profits for purposes of section 1248. FC has earnings and profits of $20 (determined under the rules of §1.367(b)-2(d)(2)(i) and (ii)), $16 of which is attributable to the stock owned by DC under the rules of §1.367(b)-2(d)(3). FC subdivides the land and distributes to the minority shareholder land with a value of $20 and a basis of $10. As part of the same transaction, in a liquidation described in section 332, FC distributes the remainder of its land to DC, and the FC stock held by DC and the minority shareholder is canceled.

(ii) *Result*. Under section 336, FC must recognize the $10 of gain it realizes in the land it distributes to the minority shareholder, and under section 331 the minority shareholder recognizes its gain of $2 in the stock of FC. Such gain is included in income by the minority shareholder as a dividend to the extent provided in section 1248 if the minority shareholder is a United States person that is described in section 1248(a)(2). Under §1.367(b)-2(d)(2)(iii), the $10 of gain recognized by FC increases its earnings and profits for purposes of computing the all earnings and profits amount and, as a result, $8 of such increase (80 percent of $10) is considered to be attributable to the FC stock owned by DC under §1.367(b)-2(d)(3)(i)(A)(*1*). DC's all earnings and profits amount with respect to its stock in FC is $24 (the $16 of initial all earnings and profits amount with respect to the FC stock held by DC, plus the $8 addition to such amount that results from FC's recognition of gain on the distribution to the minority shareholder). Under paragraph (b)(3)(i) of this section, DC must include the $24 all earnings and profits amount in income as a deemed dividend from FC.

Example 4—(i) *Facts*. DC1, a domestic corporation, owns all of the outstanding stock of DC2, a domestic corporation. DC1 also owns all of the outstanding stock of FC, a foreign corporation. The stock of FC has a value of $100, and DC1 has a basis of $30 in such stock. The assets of FC have a value of $100. The all earnings and profits amount with respect to the FC stock owned by DC1 is $20. In a reorganization described in section 368(a)(1)(D), DC2 acquires all of the assets of FC solely in exchange for DC2 stock. FC distributes the DC2 stock to DC1, and the FC stock held by DC1 is canceled.

(ii) *Result*. DC1 must include $20 in income as a deemed dividend from FC under paragraph (b)(3)(i) of this section. Under section 361, FC does not recognize gain or loss in the assets that it transfers to DC2 or in the DC2 stock that it distributes to DC1, and under section 362(b) DC2 takes a basis in the assets that it acquires from FC equal to the basis that FC had therein. Under §1.367(b)-2(e)(3)(ii) and section 358(a)(1), DC1 takes a basis of $50 (its $30 basis in the stock of FC, plus the $20 that was treated as a deemed dividend to DC1) in the stock of DC2 that it receives in exchange for the stock of FC. Under §1.367(b)-2(e)(3)(iii) and section 312(a), the earnings and profits of FC are reduced by the $20 deemed dividend.

Example 5—(i) *Facts*. DC1, a domestic corporation, owns all of the outstanding stock of FC1, a foreign corporation. FC1 owns all of the outstanding stock of FC2, a foreign corporation. The all earnings and profits amount with respect to the FC2 stock owned by FC1 is $20. In a reorganization described in section 368(a)(1)(A), DC2, a domestic corporation unrelated to FC1 or FC2, acquires all of the assets and liabilities of FC2 pursuant to a State W merger. FC2 receives DC2 stock and distributes such stock to FC1. The FC2 stock held by FC1 is canceled, and FC2 ceases its separate legal existence.

(ii) *Result*. FC1 must include $20 in income as a deemed dividend from FC2 under paragraph (b)(3)(i) of this section. The deemed dividend is treated as a dividend for purposes of the Internal Revenue Code as provided in §1.367(b)-2(e)(2); however, under paragraph (b)(3)(i) of this section the deemed dividend cannot qualify for the exception from foreign personal holding company income provided by section 954(c)(3)(A)(i), even if the provisions of that section would otherwise have been met in the case of an actual dividend.

Example 6—(i) *Facts*. DC1, a domestic corporation, owns 99 percent of USP, a domestic partnership. The remaining 1 percent of USP is owned by a person unrelated to DC1. DC1 and USP each directly own 9 percent of the outstanding stock of FC, a foreign corporation that is not a controlled foreign corporation subject to the rule of section 953(c). In a reorganization described in section 368(a)(1)(C), DC2, a domestic corporation, acquires all of the assets and liabilities of FC in exchange for DC2 stock. FC distributes to its shareholders DC2 stock, and the FC stock held by its shareholders is canceled.

(ii) *Result*. (A) DC1 and USP are United States persons that are exchanging shareholders in a transaction described in paragraph (a) of this section. As a result, DC1 and USP are subject to the rules of paragraph (b) of this section if they qualify as United States shareholders as defined in paragraph (b)(2) of this section. Alternatively, if they do not qualify as United States shareholders as defined in paragraph (b)(2) of this section, DC1 and USP are subject to the rules of paragraph (c) of this section. Paragraph (b)(2) of this section defines the term United States shareholder to include any shareholder described in section 951(b) (without regard to whether the foreign corporation is a controlled foreign corporation). A share-

holder described in section 951(b) is a United States person that is considered to own, applying the rules of section 958(a) and 958(b), 10 percent or more of the total combined voting power of all classes of stock entitled to vote of a foreign corporation. Under section 958(b), the rules of section 318(a), as modified by section 958(b) and the regulations thereunder, apply so that, in general, stock owned directly or indirectly by a partnership is considered as owned proportionately by its partners, and stock owned directly or indirectly by a partner is considered as owned by the partnership. Thus, under section 958(b), DC1 is treated as owning its proportionate share of FC stock held by USP, and USP is treated as owning all of the FC stock held by DC1.

(B) Accordingly, for purposes of determining whether DC1 is a United States shareholder under paragraph (b)(2) of this section, DC1 is considered as owning 99 percent of the 9 percent of FC stock held by USP. Because DC1 also owns 9 percent of FC stock directly, DC1 is considered as owning more than 10 percent of FC stock. DC1 is thus a United States shareholder of FC under paragraph (b)(2) of this section and, as a result, is subject to the rules of paragraph (b) of this section. However, for purposes of determining DC1's all earnings and profits amount, DC1 is not treated as owning the FC stock held by USP. Under §1.367(b)-2(d)(3), DC1's all earnings and profits amount is determined by reference to the 9 percent of FC stock that it directly owns.

(C) For purposes of determining whether USP is a United States shareholder under paragraph (b)(2) of this section, USP is considered as owning the 9 percent of FC stock held by DC1. Because USP also owns 9 percent of FC stock directly, USP is considered as owning more than 10 percent of FC stock. USP is thus a United States shareholder of FC under paragraph (b)(2) of this section and, as a result, is subject to the rules of paragraph (b) of this section. However, for purposes of determining USP's all earnings and profits amount, USP is not treated as owning the FC shares held by DC1. Under §1.367(b)-2(d)(3), USP's all earnings and profits amount is determined by reference to the 9 percent of FC stock that it directly owns.

(iii) *Recognition of exchange gain or loss with respect to capital.*— [Reserved]

(4) *Reserved*.—For further guidance concerning section 367(b) exchanges occurring before February 24, 2001, see §1.367(b)-3T(b)(4).

(c) *Exchange of stock owned by a United States person that is not a United States shareholder.*—(1) *Scope.*—This paragraph (c) applies in the case of an exchanging shareholder that is a United States person not described in paragraph (b)(1)(i) of this section (i.e., a United States person that is not a United States shareholder of the foreign acquired corporation).

(2) *Requirement to recognize gain.*—An exchanging shareholder described in paragraph (c)(1) of this section shall recognize realized gain (but not loss) with respect to the stock of the foreign acquired corporation.

(3) *Election to include all earnings and profits amount.*—In lieu of the treatment prescribed by paragraph (c)(2) of this section, an exchanging shareholder described in paragraph (c)(1) of this section may instead elect to include in income as a deemed dividend the all earnings and profits amount with respect to its stock in the foreign acquired corporation. For the consequences of a deemed dividend, see §1.367(b)-2(e). Such election may be made only if—

(i) The foreign acquired corporation (or its successor in interest) has provided the exchanging shareholder information to substantiate the exchanging shareholder's all earnings and profits amount with respect to its stock in the foreign acquired corporation; and

(ii) The exchanging shareholder complies with the section 367(b) notice requirement described in §1.367(b)-1(c), including the specific rules contained therein concerning the time and manner for electing to apply the rules of this paragraph (c)(3).

(4) *De minimis exception.*—This paragraph (c) shall not apply in the case of an exchanging shareholder whose stock in the foreign acquired corporation has a fair market value of less than $50,000 on the date of the section 367(b) exchange.

(5) *Examples.*—The following examples illustrate the rules of this paragraph (c):

Example 1—(i) *Facts*. DC1, a domestic corporation, owns 5 percent of the outstanding stock of FC, a foreign corporation that is not a controlled foreign corporation subject to the rule of section 953(c). Persons unrelated to DC1 own the remaining 95 percent of the outstanding stock of FC. DC1 has owned its 5 percent interest in FC since FC was incorporated. DC1's stock in FC has a basis of $40,000 and a value of $100,000. The all earnings and profits amount with respect to DC1's stock in FC is $50,000. In a reorganization described in section 368(a)(1)(C), DC2, a domestic corporation, acquires all of the assets and liabilities of FC in exchange for DC2 stock. FC distributes DC2 stock to its shareholders, and the FC stock held by its shareholders is canceled.

(ii) *Alternate result 1.* If DC1 does not make the election described in paragraph (c)(3) of this section, then the general rule of paragraph (c)(2) of this section applies and DC1 must recognize its $60,000 gain in the FC stock. Under section 358(a)(1), DC1 has a $100,000 basis (its $40,000 basis in the FC stock, plus the $60,000 recognized gain) in the DC2 stock that it receives in exchange for its FC stock. Because DC1 is not a shareholder described in section 1248(a)(2), section 1248 does not apply to recharacterize any of DC1's gain as a dividend.

(iii) *Alternate result 2.* If DC1 makes a valid election under paragraph (c)(3) of this section, then DC1 must include in income as a deemed dividend the $50,000 all earnings and profits amount with respect to its FC stock. Under § 1.367(b)-2(e)(3) and section 358(a)(1), DC1 has a $90,000 basis (its $40,000 basis in the FC stock, plus the $50,000 that was treated as a deemed dividend to DC1) in the DC2 stock that it receives in exchange for its FC stock.

Example 2.—(i) Facts. The facts are the same as in *Example 1*, except that DC1's stock in FC has a fair market value of $48,000 on the date DC1 receives the DC2 stock.

(ii) *Result.* Because DC1's stock in FC has a fair market value of less than $50,000 on the date of the section 367(b) exchange, the de minimis exception of paragraph (c)(4) of this section applies. As a result, DC1 is not subject to the gain or income inclusion requirements of this paragraph (c).

(d) *Carryover of certain foreign taxes.—(1) Rule.*—Excess foreign taxes under section 904(c) allowable to the foreign acquired corporation under section 906 shall carry over to the domestic acquiring corporation and become allowable under section 901, subject to the limitations prescribed by the Internal Revenue Code (for example, sections 383, 904 and 907). The domestic acquiring corporation shall not succeed to any other foreign taxes paid or incurred by the foreign acquired corporation.

(2) *Example.*—The following example illustrates the rules of this paragraph (d):

Example—(i) Facts. DC, a domestic corporation owns 100 percent of the outstanding stock of FC, a foreign corporation. FC has net positive earnings and profits, none of which are attributable to DC's FC stock under § 1.367(b)-2(d)(3). FC has paid foreign taxes that are not eligible for credit under section 906. In a liquidation described in section 332, FC distributes all of its property to DC, and the FC stock held by DC is canceled.

(ii) *Result.* The liquidation of FC into DC is a section 367(b) exchange. Thus, DC is subject to the section 367(b) regulations, and must file a section 367(b) notice pursuant to § 1.367(b)-1(c). Pursuant to the provisions of paragraph (d)(1) of this section, the foreign taxes paid by FC do not carryover to DC because FC's foreign taxes are not eligible for credit under section 906.

(e) *Net operating loss and capital loss carryovers.*—A net operating loss or capital loss carryover of the foreign acquired corporation is described in section 381(c)(1) and (c)(3) and thus is eligible to carry over from the foreign acquired corporation to the domestic acquiring corporation only to the extent the underlying deductions or losses were allowable under chapter 1 of subtitle A of the Internal Revenue Code. Thus, only a net operating loss or capital loss carryover that is effectively connected with the conduct of a trade or business within the United States (or that is attributable to a permanent establishment, in the context of an applicable United States income tax treaty) is eligible to be carried over under section 381. For further guidance, see Rev. Rul. 72-421 (1972-2 C.B. 166) (see also § 601.601(d)(2) of this chapter).

(f) *Carryover of earnings and profits.—(1) General rule.*—Except to the extent otherwise specifically provided (see, e.g., Notice 89-79 (1989-2 C.B. 392) (see also § 601.601(d)(2) of this chapter)), earnings and profits of the foreign acquired corporation that are not included in income as a deemed dividend under the section 367(b) regulations (or deficit in earnings and profits) are eligible to carry over from the foreign acquired corporation to the domestic acquiring corporation under section 381(c)(2) only to the extent such earnings and profits (or deficit in earnings and profits) are effectively connected with the conduct of a trade or business within the United States (or are attributable to a permanent establishment in the United States, in the context of an applicable United States income tax treaty). All other earnings and profits (or deficit in earnings and profits) of the foreign acquired corporation shall not carry over to the domestic acquiring corporation and, as a result, shall be eliminated.

(2) *Previously taxed earnings and profits.*—[Reserved]

[Reg. § 1.367(b)-3.]

□ [*T.D.* 8862, 1-21-2000 (*corrected* 11-3-2000). *Amended by T.D.* 9243, 1-23-2006, T.D. 9273, 8-7-2006 *and T.D.* 9959, 12-28-2021.]

[Reg. § 1.367(b)-3T]

§ 1.367(b)-3T. Repatriation of foreign corporate assets in certain nonrecognition transactions (temporary).—(a) through (b)(3) [Reserved]For further guidance, see § 1.367(b)-3(a) through (b)(3).

(b)(4) *Election of taxable exchange treatment.—(i) Rules.—(A) In general.*—In lieu of the treatment prescribed by § 1.367(b)-3(b)(3)(i), an exchanging shareholder described in § 1.367(b)-3(b)(1) may instead elect to recognize the gain (but not loss) that it realizes in the exchange (taxable exchange election). To make a taxable exchange election, the following requirements must be satisfied—

(1) The exchanging shareholder (and its direct or indirect owners that would be affected by the election, in the case of an exchanging shareholder that is a foreign corporation) reports the exchange in a manner consistent therewith (see, e.g., sections 954(c)(1)(B)(i), 1001 and 1248);

(2) The notification requirements of paragraph (b)(4)(i)(C) of this section are satisfied; and

(3) The adjustments described in paragraph (b)(4)(i)(B) of this section are made when the following circumstances are present—

(i) The transaction is described in section 332 or is an asset acquisition described in section 368(a)(1), with regard to which one U.S. person owns (directly or indirectly) 100 percent of the foreign acquired corporation; and

(ii) The all earnings and profits amount described in § 1.367(b)-3(b)(3)(i) with respect to the exchange exceeds the gain recognized by the exchanging shareholder.

(B) *Attribute reduction.—(1) Reduction of NOL carryovers.*—The amount by which the all earnings and profits amount exceeds the gain recognized by the exchanging shareholder (the excess earnings and profits amount) shall be applied to reduce the net operating loss carryovers (if any) of the foreign acquired corporation to which the domestic acquiring corporation would otherwise succeed under section 381(a) and (c)(1). See also Rev. Rul. 72-421 (1972-2 C.B. 166) (see § 601.601(d)(2) of this chapter).

(2) *Reduction of capital loss carryovers.*—After the application of paragraph (b)(4)(i)(B)(1) of this section, any remaining excess earnings and profits amount shall be applied to reduce the capital loss carryovers (if any) of the foreign acquired corporation to which the domestic acquiring corporation would otherwise succeed under section 381(a) and (c)(3).

(3) *Reduction of basis.*—After the application of paragraph (b)(4)(i)(B)(2) of this section, any remaining excess earnings and profits amount shall be applied to reduce (but not below zero) the basis of the assets (other than dollar-denominated money) of the foreign acquired corporation that are acquired by the domestic acquiring corporation. Such remaining excess earnings and profits amount shall be applied to reduce the basis of such assets in the following order: first, tangible depreciable or depletable assets, according to their class lives (beginning with those assets with the shortest class life); second, other non-inventory tangible assets; third, intangible assets that are amortizable; and finally, the remaining assets of the foreign acquired corporation that are acquired by the domestic acquiring corporation. Within each of these categories, if the total basis of all assets in the category is greater than the excess earnings and profits amount to be applied against such basis, the taxpayer may choose to which specific assets in the category the basis reduction first applies.

(C) *Notification.*—The exchanging shareholder shall elect to apply the rules of this paragraph (b)(4)(i) by attaching a statement of its election to its section 367(b) notice. See § 1.367(b)-1(c) for the rules concerning filing a section 367(b) notice.

(D) *Example.*—The following example illustrates the rules of this paragraph (b)(4)(i):

Example—(i) Facts. DC, a domestic corporation, owns all of the outstanding stock of FC, a foreign corporation. The stock of FC has a value of $100, and DC has a basis of $80 in such stock. The assets of FC are one parcel of land with a value of $60 and a basis of $30, and tangible depreciable assets with a value of $40 and a basis of $80. FC has no net operating loss carryovers or capital loss carryovers. The all earnings and profits amount with respect to the FC stock owned by DC is $30, of which $19 is described in section 1248(a) and the remaining $11 is not (for example, because it was earned prior to 1963). In a liquidation described in section 332, FC distributes all of its property to DC, and the FC stock held by DC is canceled. Rather than including in income as a deemed dividend the all earnings and profits amount of $30 as provided in

§1.367(b)-3(b)(3)(i), DC instead elects taxable exchange treatment under paragraph (b)(4)(i)(A) of this section.

(ii) *Result.* DC recognizes the $20 of gain it realizes on its stock in FC. Of this $20 amount, $19 is included in income by DC as a dividend pursuant to section 1248(a). (For the source of the remaining $1 of gain recognized by DC, see section 865. For the treatment of the $1 for purposes of the foreign tax credit limitation, see generally section 904(d)(2)(A)(i).) Because the transaction is described in section 332 and because the all earnings and profits amount with respect to the FC stock held by DC ($30) exceeds by $10 the income recognized by DC ($20), the attribute reduction rules of paragraph (b)(4)(i)(B) of this section apply. Accordingly, the $10 excess earnings and profits amount is applied to reduce the basis of the tangible depreciable assets of FC, beginning with those assets with the shortest class lives. Under section 337(a) FC does not recognize gain or loss in the assets that it distributes to DC, and under section 334(b) (which is applied taking into account the basis reduction prescribed by paragraph (b)(4)(i)(A)(3) of this section) DC takes a basis of $30 in the land and $70 in the tangible depreciable assets that it receives from FC.

(ii) *Effective date.*—This paragraph (b)(4) applies for section 367(b) exchanges that occur between February 23, 2000 and February 23, 2001.

(c) and (d) [Reserved]For further guidance, see §1.367(b)-3(c) through (d). [Temporary Reg. §1.367(b)-3T.]

☐ [*T.D. 8863, 1-21-2000.*]

[Reg. §1.367(b)-4]

§1.367(b)-4. Acquisition of foreign corporate stock or assets by a foreign corporation in certain nonrecognition transactions.— (a) *Scope.*—This section applies to certain acquisitions by a foreign corporation of the stock or assets of a foreign corporation in an exchange described in section 351 or in a reorganization described in section 368(a)(1). Paragraph (b) of this section provides a rule regarding when an exchanging shareholder is required to include in income as a deemed dividend the section 1248 amount attributable to the stock that it exchanges. Paragraph (c) of this section provides a rule excluding deemed dividends from foreign personal holding company income. Paragraph (d) of this section provides rules for subsequent sales or exchanges. Paragraphs (e) and (f) of this section provide rules regarding certain exchanges following inversion transactions. Paragraph (g) of this section provides definitions and special rules, including special rules regarding triangular reorganizations and recapitalizations. Paragraph (h) of this section provides the applicability dates for certain paragraphs of this section. See also §1.367(a)-3(b)(2) for transactions subject to the concurrent application of sections 367(a) and (b) and §1.367(b)-2 for additional definitions that apply.

(b) *Income inclusion.*—If a foreign corporation (the transferee foreign corporation) acquires the stock of a foreign corporation in an exchange described in section 351 or the stock or assets of a foreign corporation in a reorganization described in section 368(a)(1) (in either case, the foreign acquired corporation), then an exchanging shareholder must, if its exchange is described in paragraph (b)(1)(i), (b)(2)(i), or (b)(3) of this section, include in income as a deemed dividend the section 1248 amount attributable to the stock that it exchanges.

(1) *Exchange that results in loss of status as section 1248 shareholder.*—(i) *General rule.*—Except as provided in paragraph (b)(1)(ii) of this section, an exchange is described in this paragraph (b)(1)(i) if—

(A) Immediately before the exchange, the exchanging shareholder is—

(1) A United States person that is a section 1248 shareholder with respect to the foreign acquired corporation; or

(2) A foreign corporation, and a United States person is a section 1248 shareholder with respect to such foreign corporation and with respect to the foreign acquired corporation;

(B) Either of the following conditions is satisfied—

(1) Immediately after the exchange, the stock received in *the exchange is not stock in a corporation* that is a controlled foreign corporation as to which the United States person described in paragraph (b)(1)(i)(A) of this section is a section 1248 shareholder; or

(2) Immediately after the exchange, the transferee foreign corporation or the foreign acquired corporation (in the case of the acquisition of the stock of a foreign acquired corporation) is not a controlled foreign corporation as to which the United States person described in paragraph (b)(1)(i)(A) of this section is a section 1248 shareholder; and

(C) The exchange is not a specified exchange to which paragraph (e)(1) of this section applies.

(ii) *Special rules.*—(A) *Receipt of foreign stock in an exchange to which §1.367(a)-7(c) applies.*—If an exchanging shareholder is a domestic corporation that transfers stock of a foreign acquired corporation in an exchange under section 361(a) or (b) (section 361 exchange) to which the exception to section 367(a)(5) in §1.367(a)-7(c) applies, and the exchanging shareholder receives stock in either the transferee foreign corporation or foreign controlling corporation (in the case of a triangular reorganization), such exchange will not be described in paragraph (b)(1)(i) of this section only if immediately after the exchanging shareholder's receipt of the foreign stock in the section 361 exchange, but prior to, and without taking into account, the exchanging shareholder's distribution of the foreign stock under section 361(c)(1), the foreign acquired corporation, transferee foreign corporation, and foreign controlling corporation (in the case of a triangular reorganization) are controlled foreign corporations as to which the exchanging shareholder is a section 1248 shareholder. See paragraph (b)(1)(iii) of this section, *Example 4*, for an illustration of this rule. If an exchange is not described in paragraph (b)(1)(i) of this section as a result of the application of this paragraph, see §§1.1248(f)-1(b)(3) and 1.1248(f)-2(c), as applicable. For adjustments to the basis of stock of the foreign surviving corporation in certain triangular reorganizations, see paragraph (b)(1)(ii)(B)(2)(i) of this section.

(B) *Special rules for certain triangular reorganizations.*—(1) *Receipt of domestic stock.*—In the case of a triangular reorganization in which the stock received in the exchange is stock of a domestic controlling corporation, such exchange is not described in paragraph (b)(1)(i) of this section if immediately after the exchange the following foreign corporations are controlled foreign corporations as to which the domestic controlling corporation is a section 1248 shareholder—

(i) The foreign acquired corporation and foreign surviving corporation, in the case of a section 354 exchange of the stock of the foreign acquired corporation pursuant to a triangular B reorganization.

(ii) The foreign surviving corporation, in the case of a section 354 or section 356 exchange of the stock of the foreign acquired corporation pursuant to a forward triangular merger, triangular C reorganization, reverse triangular merger, or triangular G reorganization. See paragraph (b)(1)(iii) of this section, *Example 3B* for an illustration of this rule.

(iii) The foreign acquired corporation and foreign surviving corporation, in the case of a section 361 exchange of the stock of the foreign acquired corporation by an exchanging shareholder that is a foreign corporation described in paragraph (b)(1)(i)(A)(2) of this section and that is a foreign acquired corporation the assets of which are acquired in a triangular reorganization described in paragraph (b)(1)(ii)(B)(1)(ii) of this section.

(iv) The foreign acquired corporation and foreign surviving corporation, in the case of a section 361 exchange of the stock of the foreign acquired corporation by an exchanging shareholder that is a domestic corporation described in paragraph (b)(1)(i)(A)(1) of this section and that is acquired in a triangular reorganization to which the exception to section 367(a)(5) in §1.367(a)-7(c) applies. See paragraph (b)(1)(iii) of this section, *Example 5* for an illustration of this rule.

(2) *Adjustments to basis of stock of foreign surviving corporation.*—(i) *Section 361 exchanges to which §1.367(a)-7(c) applies.*—If stock of the foreign acquired corporation is acquired by the foreign surviving corporation in a section 361 exchange by reason of triangular reorganization (other than a triangular B reorganization) to which the exception to section 367(a)(5) provided in §1.367(a)-7(c) applies, and if paragraph (b)(1)(i) of this section does not apply to the section 361 exchange by reason of (b)(1)(ii)(A) of this section (if the stock received is stock of a foreign controlling corporation) or by reason of (b)(1)(ii)(B)(1)(iv) of this section (if the stock received is stock of a domestic controlling corporation), then the controlling corporation (foreign or domestic) must apply the principles of §1.367(b)-13 to adjust the basis of the stock of the foreign surviving corporation so that the section 1248 amount in the stock of the foreign acquired corporation (determined when the foreign surviving corporation acquires such stock) is reflected in the stock of the foreign surviving corporation immediately after the exchange. See paragraph (b)(1)(iii) of this section, *Example 5*, for an illustration of this rule.

(ii) *Other exchanges.*—See §1.367(b)-13 for rules regarding the adjustment to the basis of the stock of the foreign surviving corporation in exchanges pursuant to triangular reorganizations that are not subject to paragraph (b)(1)(ii)(B)(2)(i) of this section.

(iii) *Examples.*—The following examples illustrate the rules of this paragraph (b)(1):

Example 1—(i) *Facts.* FC1 is a foreign corporation that is owned, directly and indirectly (applying the ownership rules of section 958), solely by foreign persons. DC is a domestic corporation that is unrelated to FC1. DC owns all of the outstanding stock of FC2, a foreign corporation. Thus, under §1.367(b)-2(a) and (b), DC is a section 1248 shareholder with respect to FC2, and FC2 is a controlled foreign corporation. Under §1.367(b)-2(c)(1), the section 1248 amount attributable to the stock of FC2 held by DC is $20. In a reorganization described in section 368(a)(1)(C), FC1 acquires all of the assets and assumes all of the liabilities of FC2 in exchange for FC1 voting stock. The FC1 voting stock received does not represent more than 50 percent of the voting power or value of FC1's stock. FC2 distributes the FC1 stock to DC, and the FC2 stock held by DC is canceled.

(ii) *Result.* FC1 is not a controlled foreign corporation immediately after the exchange. As a result, the exchange is described in paragraph (b)(1)(i) of this section. Under paragraph (b) of this section, DC must include in income, as a deemed dividend from FC2, the section 1248 amount ($20) attributable to the FC2 stock that DC exchanged.

Example 2—(i) *Facts.* The facts are the same as in *Example 1*, except that the voting stock of FC1, which is received by FC2 in exchange for its assets and distributed by FC2 to DC, represents more than 50 percent of the voting power of FC1's stock under the rules of section 957(a).

(ii) *Result.* Paragraph (b)(1)(i) of this section does not apply to require inclusion in income of the section 1248 amount, because FC1 is a controlled foreign corporation as to which DC is a section 1248 shareholder immediately after the exchange.

Example 3—(i) *Facts.* The facts are the same as in *Example 1*, except that FC2 receives and distributes voting stock of FP, a foreign corporation that is in control (within the meaning of section 368(c)) of FC1, instead of receiving and distributing voting stock of FC1.

(ii) *Result.* For purposes of section 367(a), the transfer is an indirect stock transfer subject to section 367(a). See §1.367(a)-3(d)(1)(iv). Accordingly, DC's exchange of FC2 stock for FP stock under section 354 will be taxable under section 367(a) (and section 1248 will be applicable) if DC fails to enter into a gain recognition agreement in accordance with §1.367(a)-8. Under §1.367(a)-3(b)(2), if DC enters into a gain recognition agreement, the exchange will be subject to the provisions of section 367(b) and the regulations thereunder, as well as section 367(a). If FP and FC1 are controlled foreign corporations as to which DC is a (direct or indirect) section 1248 shareholder immediately after the reorganization, then the section 367(b) result is the same as in *Example 2*—that is, paragraph (b)(1)(i) of this section does not apply to require inclusion in income of the section 1248 amount. Under these circumstances, the amount of the gain recognition agreement would equal the amount of the gain realized on the indirect stock transfer. If FP or FC1 is not a controlled foreign corporation as to which DC is a (direct or indirect) section 1248 shareholder immediately after the exchange, then the section 367(b) result is the same as in *Example 1*—that is, DC must include in income, as a deemed dividend from FC2, the section 1248 amount ($20) attributable to the FC2 stock that DC exchanged. Under these circumstances, the amount of the gain recognition agreement would equal the amount of the gain realized on the indirect stock transfer, less the $20 section 1248 amount inclusion.

Example 3A. (i) *Facts.* The facts are the same as in *Example 3*, except that FC1 merges into FC2 in a reorganization described in sections 368(a)(1)(A) and (a)(2)(E). Pursuant to the reorganization, DC exchanges its FC2 stock for stock of FP.

(ii) *Result.* The result is similar to the result in *Example 3*. The transfer is an indirect stock transfer subject to section 367(a). See §1.367(a)-3(d)(1)(ii). Accordingly, DC's exchange of FC2 stock for FP stock will be taxable under section 367(a) (and section 1248 will be applicable) if DC fails to enter into a gain recognition agreement. If DC enters into a gain recognition agreement, the exchange will be subject to the provisions of section 367(b) and the regulations thereunder, as well as section 367(a). If FP and FC2 are controlled foreign corporations as to which DC is a section 1248 shareholder immediately after the reorganization, then paragraph (b)(1)(i) of this section does not apply to require DC to include in income the section 1248 amount attributable to the FC2 stock that was exchanged and the amount of the gain recognition agreement is the amount of gain realized on the indirect stock transfer. If FP or FC2 is not a controlled foreign corporation as to which DC is a section 1248 shareholder immediately after the exchange, then DC must include in income as a deemed dividend from FC2 the section 1248 amount ($20) attributable to the FC2 stock that DC exchanged. Under these circumstances, the gain recognition agreement would be the amount of gain realized on the indirect transfer, less the $20 section 1248 amount inclusion.

Example 3B. (i) *Facts.* The facts are the same as *Example 3*, except that USP, a domestic corporation, owns the controlling interest (within the meaning of section 368(c)) in FC1 stock. In addition, FC2 merges into FC1 in a reorganization described in sections 368(a)(1)(A) and (a)(2)(D). Pursuant to the reorganization, DC exchanges its FC2 stock for USP stock.

(ii) *Result.* Because DC receives stock of a domestic corporation, USP, in the section 354 exchange, the transfer is not an indirect stock transfer subject to section 367(a). Accordingly, the exchange will be subject only to the provisions of section 367(b) and the regulations thereunder. Under paragraph (b)(1)(ii) of this section, because the stock received is stock of a domestic corporation (USP) and, immediately after the exchange, USP is a section 1248 shareholder of FC1 (the surviving corporation) and FC1 is a controlled foreign corporation, the exchange is not described in paragraph (b)(1)(i) of this section and DC is not required to include in income the section 1248 amount attributable to the FC2 stock that was exchanged. See §1.367(b)-13(c) for the basis and holding period rules applicable to this transaction, which cause USP's adjusted basis and holding period in the stock of FC1 after the transaction to reflect the basis and holding period that DC had in its FC2 stock.

Example 4. (i) *Facts.* DC1, a domestic corporation, owns all of the outstanding stock of DC2, a domestic corporation. DC2 owns various assets, including all of the outstanding stock of FC2, a foreign corporation. The stock of FC2 has a value of $100, and DC2 has a basis of $30 in the stock. The section 1248 earnings and profits attributable to the FC2 stock held by DC2 is $20. DC2 does not own any stock other than the FC2 stock. FC1 is a foreign corporation that is unrelated to DC1, DC2, and FC2. In a reorganization described in section 368(a)(1)(C), FC1 acquires all of the assets of DC2 in exchange for the assumption of DC2's liabilities and voting stock of FC1 that represents 20% of the outstanding voting stock of FC1. DC2 distributes the FC1 stock to DC1 under section 361(c)(1), and the DC2 stock held by DC1 is canceled. The exception to section 367(a)(5) provided in §1.367(a)-7(c) applies to the section 361 exchange. DC1 properly files a gain recognition agreement that satisfies the conditions of §§1.367(a)-T(e)(6) and 1.367(a)-8 to qualify for nonrecognition treatment under section 367(a) with respect to DC2's transfer of the FC2 stock to FC1. See §1.367(a)-3(e). FC1 is not a surrogate foreign corporation (within the meaning of section 7874) because DC1 does not hold at least 60% of the stock of FC1 by reason of holding stock of DC2.

(ii) *Result.* DC2, the exchanging shareholder, is a U.S. person and a section 1248 shareholder with respect to FC2, the foreign acquired corporation. Whether DC2 is required to include in income the section 1248 amount attributable to the FC2 stock under paragraph (b)(1)(i) of this section depends on whether, immediately after DC2's section 361 exchange of the FC2 stock for FC1 stock (and before the distribution of the FC1 stock to DC1 under section 361(c)(1)), FC1 and FC2 are controlled foreign corporations as to which DC2 is a section 1248 shareholder. See paragraph (b)(1)(ii)(A) of this section. If, immediately after the section 361 exchange (and before the distribution of the FC1 stock to DC1 under section 361(c)(1)), FC1 and FC2 are both controlled foreign corporations as to which DC2 is a section 1248 shareholder, then DC2 is not required to include in income the section 1248 amount attributable to the FC2 stock under paragraph (b)(1)(i) of this section because neither condition in paragraph (b)(1)(i)(B) of this section is satisfied. Alternatively, if immediately after the section 361 exchange (and before the distribution of the FC1 stock to DC1 under section 361(c)(1)) either FC1 or FC2 is not a controlled foreign corporation as to which DC2 is a section 1248 shareholder, then, pursuant to paragraph (b)(1)(i) of this section, DC2 must include in income the section 1248 amount attributable to the FC2 stock. For the treatment of DC2's transfer of assets other than the FC2 stock to FC1, see section 367(a)(1) and (a)(3) and the regulations under that section. Furthermore, because DC2's transfer of any other assets to FC1 is pursuant to a section 361 exchange, see section 367(a)(5) and §1.367(a)-7. If any of the assets transferred are intangible assets for purposes of section 367(d), see section 367(d). With respect to DC2's distribution of the FC1 stock to DC1 under section 361(c)(1), see section 1248(f)(1), and §§1.1248(f)-1 and 1.1248(f)-2.

Example 5. (i) *Facts.* DC1, a domestic corporation, wholly owns DC2, a domestic corporation. The DC2 stock has a $100x fair market value, and DC1 has a basis of $30x in the stock. DC2's only asset is all of the outstanding stock of FC2, a foreign corporation. The FC2 stock has a $100x fair market value, and DC2 has a basis of $30x in the stock. There are $20x of earnings and profits attributable to the FC2 stock for purposes of section 1248. USP, a domestic corporation unrelated to DC1, DC2, and FC2, wholly owns FC1, a foreign corporation. In a triangular reorganization described in section 368(a)(1)(C), DC2 transfers all the FC2 stock to FC1 in exchange solely for voting stock of USP, and distributes the USP stock to DC1 under section 361(c)(1). DC1 exchanges its DC2 stock for the USP stock under section 354. DC2's transfer of the FC2 stock to FC1 is described in section 361(a) and therefore, under section 367(a)(5) and §1.367(a)-7, is generally subject to section 367(a)(1). However, the exception to section 367(a)(5) provided in §1.367(a)-7(c) applies to the section 361 exchange. In addition, DC1 is not required to adjust the basis of its USP stock (determined under section 358) under section 367(a)(5) and §1.367(a)-7(c)(3). DC1 properly files a gain recognition agreement that satisfies the conditions of §§ 1.367(a)-3(e)(6) and 1.367(a)-8 to qualify for nonrecognition treatment under section 367(a) with respect to DC2's transfer of the FC2 stock to FC1. See § 1.367(a)-3(e).

(ii) *Result.* Immediately after the exchange, FC1 and FC2 are controlled foreign corporations as to which USP is a section 1248 shareholder because USP directly and indirectly owns all the FC1 stock and FC2 stock, respectively. Because DC2 receives stock of a domestic corporation (USP) in exchange for the FC2 stock and, immediately after the exchange, FC1 and FC2 are controlled foreign corporations as to which USP is a section 1248 shareholder, DC2's exchange of the FC2 stock for the USP stock is not described in paragraph (b)(1)(i) of this section. See paragraph (b)(1)(ii)(B)(*1*)(*iv*) of this section. Therefore, DC2 is not required to include in income the section 1248 amount in the FC2 stock. Under paragraph (b)(1)(ii)(B)(*2*)(*i*) of this section, USP must apply the principles of § 1.367(b)-13 to adjust the basis of its FC1 stock to preserve the section 1248 amount ($20x) in the FC2 stock. Under the principles of § 1.367(b)-13, each share of FC1 stock held by USP after the exchange must be divided into portions, one portion attributable to the FC1 stock owned before the exchange and one portion attributable to the FC2 stock received in the exchange. The $30x basis in the FC2 stock and the $20x earnings and profits attributable to the FC2 stock before the exchange are attributable to the divided portions of the FC1 stock to which the FC2 stock relates.

(2) *Receipt by exchanging shareholder of preferred or other stock in certain instances.*—(i) *Rule.*—An exchange is described in this paragraph (b)(2)(i) if—

(A) Immediately before the exchange, the foreign acquired corporation and the transferee foreign corporation are not members of the same affiliated group (within the meaning of section 1504(a), but without regard to the exceptions set forth in section 1504(b), and substituting the words "more than 50" in place of the words "at least 80" in sections 1504(a)(2)(A) and (B));

(B) Immediately after the exchange, a domestic corporation directly or indirectly owns 10 percent or more of the voting power or value of the transferee foreign corporation; and

(C) The exchanging shareholder receives preferred stock (other than preferred stock that is fully participating with respect to dividends, redemptions and corporate growth) in consideration for common stock or preferred stock that is fully participating with respect to dividends, redemptions and corporate growth, or, in the discretion of the Commissioner or the Commissioner's delegate (and without regard to whether the stock exchanged is common stock or preferred stock), receives stock that entitles it to participate (through dividends, redemption payments or otherwise) disproportionately in the earnings generated by particular assets of the foreign acquired corporation or transferee foreign corporation.

(ii) *Examples.*—The following examples illustrate the rules of this paragraph (b)(2):

Example 1—(i) *Facts.* FC1 is a foreign corporation. DC is a domestic corporation that is unrelated to FC1. DC owns all of the outstanding stock of FC2, a foreign corporation, and FC2 has no outstanding preferred stock. The value of FC2 is $100 and DC has a basis of $50 in the stock of FC2. Under § 1.367(b)-2(c)(1), the section 1248 amount attributable to the stock of FC2 held by DC is $20. In a reorganization described in section 368(a)(1)(B), FC1 acquires all of the stock of FC2 and, in exchange, DC receives FC1 voting preferred stock that constitutes 10 percent of the voting stock of FC1 for purposes of section 902(a). Immediately after the exchange, FC1 and FC2 are controlled foreign corporations and DC is a section 1248 shareholder of FC1 and FC2, so paragraph (b)(1)(i) of this section does not require inclusion in income of the section 1248 amount.

(ii) *Result.* Pursuant to § 1.367(a)-3(b)(2), the transfer is subject to both section 367(a) and section 367(b). Under § 1.367(a)-3(b)(1), DC will not be subject to tax under section 367(a)(1) if it enters into a gain recognition agreement in accordance with § 1.367(a)-8. Even though paragraph (b)(1)(i) of this section does not apply to require inclusion in income by DC of the section 1248 amount, DC must nevertheless include the $20 section 1248 amount in income as a deemed dividend from FC2 under paragraph (b)(2)(i) of this section. Thus, if DC enters into a gain recognition agreement, the amount is $30 (the $50 gain realized less the $20 recognized under section 367(b)). If DC fails to enter into a gain recognition agreement, it must include in income under section 367(a)(1) the $50 of gain realized ($20 of which is treated as a dividend under section 1248). Section 367(b) does not apply in such case.

Example 2—(i) *Facts.* The facts are the same as in *Example 1*, except that DC owns all of the outstanding stock of FC1 immediately before the transaction.

(ii) *Result.* Both section 367(a) and section 367(b) apply to the transfer. Paragraph (b)(2)(i) of this section does not apply to require inclusion of the section 1248 amount. Under paragraph (b)(2)(i)(A) of

this section, the transaction is outside the scope of paragraph (b)(2)(i) of this section because FC1 and FC2 are, immediately before the transaction, members of the same affiliated group (within the meaning of such paragraph). Thus, if DC enters into a gain recognition agreement in accordance with § 1.367(a)-8, the amount of such agreement is $50. As in *Example 1*, if DC fails to enter into a gain recognition agreement, it must include in income $50, $20 of which will be treated as a dividend under section 1248.

Example 3—(i) *Facts.* FC1 is a foreign corporation. DC is a domestic corporation that is unrelated to FC1. DC owns all of the outstanding stock of FC2, a foreign corporation. The section 1248 amount attributable to the stock of FC2 held by DC is $20. In a reorganization described in section 368(a)(1)(B), FC1 acquires all of the stock of FC2 in exchange for FC1 voting stock that constitutes 10 percent of the voting stock of FC1 for purposes of section 902(a). The FC1 voting stock received by DC in the exchange carries voting rights in FC1, but by agreement of the parties the shares entitle the holder to dividends, amounts to be paid on redemption, and amounts to be paid on liquidation, that are to be determined by reference to the earnings or value of FC2 as of the date of such event, and that are affected by the earnings or value of FC1 only if FC1 becomes insolvent or has insufficient capital surplus to pay dividends.

(ii) *Result.* Under § 1.367(a)-3(b)(1), DC will not be subject to tax under section 367(a)(1) if it enters into a gain recognition agreement with respect to the transfer of FC2 stock to FC1. Under § 1.367(a)-3(b)(2), the exchange will be subject to the provisions of section 367(b) and the regulations thereunder to the extent that it is not subject to tax under section 367(a)(1). Furthermore, even if DC would not otherwise be required to recognize income under this section, the Commissioner or the Commissioner's delegate may nevertheless require that DC include the $20 section 1248 amount in income as a deemed dividend from FC2 under paragraph (b)(2)(i) of this section.

(3) *Certain recapitalizations.*—An exchange pursuant to a recapitalization under section 368(a)(1)(E) shall be deemed to be an exchange described in this paragraph (b)(3) if the following conditions are satisfied—

(i) During the 24-month period immediately preceding or following the date of the recapitalization, the corporation that undergoes the recapitalization (or a predecessor of, or successor to, such corporation) also engages in a transaction that would be described in paragraph (b)(2)(i) of this section but for paragraph (b)(2)(i)(C) of this section, either as the foreign acquired corporation or the transferee foreign corporation; and

(ii) The exchange in the recapitalization is described in paragraph (b)(2)(i)(C) of this section.

(c) *Exclusion of deemed dividend from foreign personal holding company income.*—(1) *Rule.*—In the event the section 1248 amount is included in income as a deemed dividend by a foreign corporation under paragraph (b) of this section, such deemed dividend shall not be included as foreign personal holding company income under section 954(c).

(2) *Example.*—The following example illustrates the rule of this paragraph (c):

Example—(i) *Facts.* FC1 is a foreign corporation that is owned, directly and indirectly (applying the ownership rules of section 958), solely by foreign persons. DC is a domestic corporation that is unrelated to FC1. DC owns all of the outstanding stock of FC2, a foreign corporation. FC2 owns all of the outstanding stock of FC3, a foreign corporation. Under § 1.367(b)-2(c)(1), the section 1248 amount attributable to the stock of FC3 held by FC2 is $20. In a reorganization described in section 368(a)(1)(B), FC1 acquires from FC2 all of the stock of FC3 in exchange for FC1 voting stock. The FC1 voting stock received by FC2 does not represent more than 50 percent of the voting power or value of FC1's stock.

(ii) *Result.* FC1 is not a controlled foreign corporation immediately after the exchange. Under paragraph (b)(1) of this section, FC2 must include in income, as a deemed dividend from FC3, the section 1248 amount ($20) attributable to the FC3 stock that FC2 exchanged. The deemed dividend is treated as a dividend for purposes of the Internal Revenue Code as provided in § 1.367(b)-2(e)(2); however, under this paragraph (c) the deemed dividend is not foreign personal holding company income to FC2.

(d) *Rules for subsequent sales or exchanges.*—(1) *Rule.*—If an exchanging shareholder (as defined in § 1.1248-8(b)(1)(iv)) is not required to include in income as a deemed dividend the section 1248 amount under paragraph (b) or paragraph (e)(1) of this section (noninclusion exchange), then, for purposes of applying section 367(b) or 1248 to subsequent sales or exchanges, and subject to the limitation of § 1.367(b)-2(d)(3)(ii) (in the case of a transaction described in § 1.367(b)-3), the determination of the earnings and profits attributable to the stock an exchanging shareholder receives in the non-inclusion exchange is determined pursuant to the rules of section 1248 and the regulations under that section.

(2) *Example.*—The following example illustrates the rules of this section. For purposes of the example, assume that

(i) There is no immediate gain recognition pursuant to section 367(a)(1) and the regulations under that section (either through operation of the rules or because the appropriate parties have entered into a gain recognition agreement under §§ 1.367(a)-3(b) and 1.367(a)-8);

(ii) References to earnings and profits are to earnings and profits that would be includible in income as a dividend under section 1248 and the regulations under that section if stock to which the earnings and profits are attributable were sold or exchanged by its shareholder;

(iii) Each corporation has only a single class of stock outstanding and uses the calendar year as its taxable year; and

(iv) Each transaction is unrelated to all other transactions.

Example. Acquisition of the stock of a foreign corporation that controls a transferee foreign corporation in a reorganization described in section 368(a)(1)(C). (i) *Facts.* DC1, a domestic corporation, has owned all the stock of CFC1, a controlled foreign corporation, since its formation on January 1, year 1. CFC1 has owned all the stock of CFC2, a controlled foreign corporation, since its formation on January 1, year 1. FC, a foreign corporation that is not a controlled foreign corporation, has owned all of the stock of FC2, a foreign corporation, since its formation on January 1, year 2. On December 31, year 3, pursuant to a restructuring transaction that was a triangular reorganization described in section 368(a)(1)(C), CFC1 transfers all of its assets, including the CFC2 stock, to FC2 in exchange for 80% of the voting stock of FC. CFC1 transfers the voting stock of FC to DC1 and the CFC1 stock is cancelled. Pursuant to section 1223(1), DC1 is considered to have held the stock of FC since January 1, year 1. Under section 1223(2), FC2 is considered to have held the stock of CFC2 since January 1, year 1. On December 31, year 3, CFC1 has $100 of earnings and profits. From January 1, year 4, until December 31, year 5, FC (a controlled foreign corporation after the restructuring transaction) accumulates an additional $50 of earnings and profits. FC2, a controlled foreign corporation after the restructuring transaction, accumulates $100 of earnings and profits from January 1, year 4, until December 31, year 5. On December 31, year 5, FC is liquidated into DC1 in a transaction described in section 332.

(ii) *Result.* Generally, this paragraph (d) requires that DC1 include in income the earnings and profits attributable to its stock in FC as determined under § 1.1248-8. However, since the liquidation of FC into DC1 is a transaction described in § 1.367(b)-3, the earnings and profits attributable to the stock of FC are limited by § 1.367(b)-2(d) (3)(ii) to that portion of the earnings and profits accumulated by FC itself before or after the restructuring transaction, and do not include the earnings and profits of FC's subsidiaries accumulated before or after the restructuring transaction. Thus, DC1 will include $40 of earnings and profits in income (80% of the $50 of earnings and profits accumulated by FC after the restructuring transaction).

(e) *Income inclusion and gain recognition in certain exchanges following an inversion transaction.*—(1) *General rule.*—If a foreign corporation (the transferee foreign corporation) acquires stock of a foreign corporation in an exchange described in section 351 or stock or assets of a foreign corporation in a reorganization described in section 368(a)(1) (in either case, the foreign acquired corporation), then an exchanging shareholder must, if its exchange is a specified exchange and the exception in paragraph (e)(3) of this section does not apply—

(i) Include in income as a deemed dividend the section 1248 amount attributable to the stock that it exchanges; and

(ii) After taking into account the increase in basis provided in § 1.367(b)-2(e)(3)(ii) resulting from the deemed dividend (if any), recognize all realized gain with respect to the stock that would not otherwise be recognized.

(2) *Specified exchanges.*—An exchange is a specified exchange if—

(i) Immediately before the exchange, the foreign acquired corporation is an expatriated foreign subsidiary and the exchanging shareholder is either an expatriated entity described in paragraph (b)(1)(i)(A)(*1*) of this section or an expatriated foreign subsidiary described in paragraph (b)(1)(i)(A)(*2*) of this section;

(ii) The stock received in the exchange is stock of a foreign corporation; and

(iii) The exchange occurs during the applicable period.

(3) *De minimis exception.*—The exception in this paragraph (e)(3) applies if—

(i) Immediately after the exchange, the foreign acquired corporation (in the case of an acquisition of stock of the foreign acquired corporation) or the transferee foreign corporation (in the case of an

acquisition of assets of the foreign acquired corporation) is a controlled foreign corporation;

(ii) The post-exchange ownership percentage with respect to the foreign acquired corporation (in the case of an acquisition of stock of the foreign acquired corporation) or the transferee foreign corporation (in the case of an acquisition of assets of the foreign acquired corporation) is at least 90 percent of the pre-exchange ownership percentage with respect to the foreign acquired corporation; and

(iii) The post-exchange ownership percentage with respect to each lower-tier expatriated foreign subsidiary of the foreign acquired corporation is at least 90 percent of the pre-exchange ownership percentage with respect to the lower-tier expatriated foreign subsidiary.

(4) *Certain exceptions from foreign personal holding company not available.*—An income inclusion of a foreign corporation under paragraph (e)(1) of this section does not qualify for the exceptions from foreign personal holding company income provided by sections 954(c)(3)(A)(i) and 954(c)(6) (to the extent in effect).

(5) *Examples.*—The following examples illustrate the application of this paragraph (e). For purposes of all of the examples, unless otherwise indicated: FP, a foreign corporation, owns all of the stock of USP, a domestic corporation, and all 40 shares of stock of FS, a controlled foreign corporation for its taxable year beginning January 1, 2017, but not for prior taxable years, except as a result of a transaction described in the facts of an example. USP owns all 50 shares of stock of FT1, a controlled foreign corporation, which, in turn, owns all 50 shares of FT2, a controlled foreign corporation. FP acquired all of the stock of USP in an inversion transaction that was completed on July 1, 2016. Therefore, with respect to that inversion transaction, USP is an expatriated entity; FT1 and FT2 are expatriated foreign subsidiaries; and FP and FS are each a non-EFS foreign related person. All entities have a calendar year tax year for U.S. tax purposes. All shares of stock have a fair market value of $1x, and each corporation has a single class of stock outstanding.

Example 1. Specified exchange to which general rule applies—(i) *Facts.* During the applicable period, and pursuant to a reorganization described in section 368(a)(1)(B), FT1 transfers all 50 shares of FT2 stock to FS in exchange solely for 50 newly issued voting shares of FS. Immediately before the exchange, USP is a section 1248 shareholder with respect to FT1 and FT2. At the time of the exchange, the FT2 stock owned by FT1 has a fair market value of $50x and an adjusted basis of $5x, such that the FT2 stock has a built-in gain of $45x. In addition, the earnings and profits of FT2 attributable to FT1's stock in FT2 for purposes of section 1248 is $30x, taking into account the rules of § 1.367(b)-2(c)(1)(i) and (ii), and therefore the section 1248 amount with respect to the FT2 stock is $30x (the lesser of the $45x of built-in gain and the $30x of earnings and profits attributable to the stock).

(ii) *Analysis.* FT1's exchange is a specified exchange because the requirements set forth in paragraphs (e)(2)(i) through (iii) of this section are satisfied. The requirement set forth in paragraph (e)(2)(i) of this section is satisfied because, immediately before the exchange, FT2 (the foreign acquired corporation) is an expatriated foreign subsidiary and FT1 (the exchanging shareholder) is an expatriated foreign subsidiary that is described in paragraph (b)(1)(i)(A)(*2*) of this section. The requirement set forth in paragraph (e)(2)(ii) of this section is also satisfied because the stock received in the exchange (FS stock) is stock of a foreign corporation. The requirement set forth in paragraph (e)(2)(iii) of this section is satisfied because the exchange occurs during the applicable period. Accordingly, under paragraph (e)(1)(i) of this section, FT1 must include in income as a deemed dividend $30x, the section 1248 amount with respect to its FT2 stock. In addition, under paragraph (e)(1)(ii) of this section, FT1 must, after taking into account the increase in basis provided in § 1.367(b)-2(e)(3)(ii) resulting from the deemed dividend (which increases FT1's basis in its FT2 stock from $5x to $35x), recognize $15x ($50x amount realized less $35x basis), the realized gain with respect to the FT2 stock that would not otherwise be recognized.

Example 2. De minimis shift to non-EFS foreign related persons—(i) *Facts.* The facts are the same as in the introductory sentences of this paragraph (e)(5), except as follows. FT1 does not own any shares of FT2, and all 40 shares of FS are owned by DX, a domestic corporation wholly owned by individual A, and thus FS is not a non-EFS foreign related person. During the applicable period and pursuant to a reorganization described in section 368(a)(1)(D), FT1 transfers all of its assets to FS in exchange for 50 newly issued FS shares, FT1 distributes the 50 FS shares to USP in liquidation under section 361(c)(1), and USP exchanges its 50 shares of FT1 stock for the 50 FS shares under section 354. Further, immediately after the exchange, FS is a controlled foreign corporation.

(ii) *Analysis.* Although USP's exchange is a specified exchange, paragraph (e)(1) of this section does not apply to the exchange because, as described in paragraphs (ii)(A) through (C) of this *Example 2*, the requirements of paragraph (e)(3) of this section are satisfied.

(A) Because the assets, rather than the stock, of FT1 (the foreign acquired corporation) are acquired, the requirement set forth in paragraph (e)(3)(i) of this section is satisfied if FS (the transferee foreign corporation) is a controlled foreign corporation immediately after the exchange. As stated in the facts, FS is a controlled foreign corporation immediately after the exchange.

(B) The requirement set forth in paragraph (e)(3)(ii) of this section is satisfied if the post-exchange ownership percentage with respect to FS is at least 90% of the pre-exchange ownership percentage with respect to FT1. Because USP, a domestic corporation that is an expatriated entity, directly owns 50 shares of FT1 stock immediately before the exchange, none of those shares are treated as indirectly owned by FP (a non-EFS foreign related person) for purposes of calculating the pre-exchange ownership percentage with respect to FT1. See paragraph (g)(1) of this section. Thus, for purposes of calculating the pre-exchange ownership percentage with respect to FT1, FP is treated as directly or indirectly owning 0%, or 0 of 50 shares, of the stock of FT1. Accordingly, the pre-exchange ownership percentage with respect to FT1 is 100 (calculated as 100% less 0%, the percentage of FT1 stock that non-EFS foreign related persons are treated as directly or indirectly owning immediately before the exchange). Consequently, for the requirement set forth in paragraph (e)(3)(ii) of this section to be satisfied, the post-exchange ownership percentage with respect to FS must be at least 90. Because USP, a domestic corporation that is an expatriated entity, directly owns 50 shares of FS stock immediately after the exchange, none of those shares are treated as indirectly owned by FP (a non-EFS foreign related person) for purposes of calculating the post-exchange ownership percentage with respect to FS. See paragraph (g)(1) of this section. Thus, for purposes of calculating the post-exchange ownership percentage with respect to FS, FP is treated as directly or indirectly owning 0%, or 0 of 90 shares, of the stock of FS. As a result, the post-exchange ownership percentage with respect to FS is 100 (calculated as 100% less 0%, the percentage of FS stock that non-EFS foreign related persons are treated as directly or indirectly owning immediately after the exchange). Therefore, because the post-exchange ownership percentage with respect to FS (100) is at least 90, the requirement set forth in paragraph (e)(3)(ii) of this section is satisfied.

(C) Because there is not a lower-tier expatriated foreign subsidiary of FT1, the requirement set forth in paragraph (e)(3)(iii) of this section does not apply.

(f) *Gain recognition upon certain transfers of property described in section 351 following an inversion transaction.*—(1) *General rule.*—If, during the applicable period, an expatriated foreign subsidiary transfers specified property to a foreign corporation (the transferee foreign corporation) in an exchange described in section 351, then the expatriated foreign subsidiary must recognize all realized gain with respect to the specified property transferred that would not otherwise be recognized, unless the exception in paragraph (f)(2) of this section applies.

(2) *De minimis exception.*—The exception in this paragraph (f)(2) applies if—

(i) Immediately after the transfer, the transferee foreign corporation is a controlled foreign corporation; and

(ii) The post-exchange ownership percentage with respect to the transferee foreign corporation is at least 90 percent of the pre-exchange ownership percentage with respect to the expatriated foreign subsidiary.

(3) *Examples.*—The following examples illustrate the application of this paragraph (f). For purposes of all of the examples, unless otherwise indicated: FP, a foreign corporation, owns all of the stock of USP, a domestic corporation, and all 10 shares of stock of FS, a controlled foreign corporation for its taxable year beginning January 1, 2017, but not for prior taxable years, except as a result of a transaction described in the facts of an example. USP owns all 50 shares of stock of FT, a controlled foreign corporation. FT owns Asset A, which is specified property with a fair market value of $50x and an adjusted basis of $10x. FP acquired all of the stock of USP in an inversion transaction that was completed on or after September 22, 2014. Accordingly, with respect to that inversion transaction, USP is an expatriated entity, FT is an expatriated foreign subsidiary, and FP and FS are each a non-EFS foreign related person. All entities have a calendar year tax year for U.S. tax purposes. All shares of stock have a fair market value of $1x, and each corporation has a single class of stock outstanding.

Example 1. Transfer to which general rule applies—(i) *Facts.* In addition to the stock of USP and FS, FP owns Asset B, which has a fair market value of $40x. During the applicable period, and pursuant to an exchange described in section 351, FT transfers Asset A to FS in exchange for 50 newly issued shares of FS stock, and FP transfers Asset B to FS in exchange for 40 newly issued shares of FS stock.

(ii) *Analysis.* Paragraph (f)(1) of this section applies to the transfer by FT (an expatriated foreign subsidiary) of Asset A, which is specified property, to FS (the transferee foreign corporation). Thus, FT must recognize gain of $40x under paragraph (f)(1) of this section, which is the realized gain with respect to Asset A that would not otherwise be recognized ($50x amount realized less $10x basis). For rules regarding whether the FS stock held by FT is treated as United States property for purposes of section 956, see § 1.956-2(a)(4)(i).

Example 2. De minimis shift to non-EFS foreign related persons—(i) *Facts.* Individual, a United States person, owns Asset B, which has a fair market value of $40x. During the applicable period, and pursuant to an exchange described in section 351, FT transfers Asset A to FS in exchange for 50 newly issued shares of FS stock, and Individual transfers Asset B to FS in exchange for 40 newly issued shares of FS stock.

(ii) *Analysis.* Paragraph (f)(1) of this section does not apply to the transfer by FT (an expatriated foreign subsidiary) of Asset A, which is specified property, to FS (the transferee foreign corporation)) because the requirements set forth in paragraph (f)(2) of this section are satisfied. The requirement set forth in paragraph (f)(2)(i) of this section is satisfied because FS is a controlled foreign corporation immediately after the transfer. The requirement set forth in paragraph (f)(2)(ii) of this section is satisfied if the post-exchange ownership percentage with respect to FS is at least 90 percent of the pre-exchange ownership percentage with respect to FT. Because USP, a domestic corporation that is an expatriated entity, directly owns 50 shares of FT stock immediately before the transfer, none of those shares are treated as indirectly owned by FP (a non-EFS foreign related person) for purposes of calculating the pre-exchange ownership percentage with respect to FT. See paragraph (g)(1) of this section. Thus, for purposes of calculating the pre-exchange ownership percentage with respect to FT, FP is treated as directly or indirectly owning 0 percent, or 0 of 50 shares, of the stock of FT. Accordingly, the pre-exchange ownership percentage with respect to FT is 100 (calculated as 100 percent less 0 percent, the percentage of FT stock that non-EFS foreign related persons are treated as directly or indirectly owning immediately before the transfer). Consequently, for the requirement set forth in paragraph (f)(2)(ii) of this section to be satisfied, the post-exchange ownership percentage with respect to FS must be at least 90. Although FP directly owns 10 FS shares, none of the 50 FS shares that FP owns through USP (a domestic corporation that is an expatriated entity) are treated as indirectly owned by FP for purposes of calculating the post-exchange ownership percentage with respect to FS because USP directly owns them. See paragraph (g)(1) of this section. Thus for purposes of calculating the post-exchange ownership percentage with respect to FS, FP is treated as directly or indirectly owning 10 percent, or 10 of 100 shares, of the stock of FS. As a result, the post-exchange ownership percentage with respect to FS is 90 (calculated as 100 percent less 10 percent, the percentage of FS stock that non-EFS foreign related persons are treated as directly or indirectly owning immediately after the transfer). Therefore, because the post-exchange ownership percentage with respect to FS (90) is at least 90, the requirement set forth in paragraph (f)(2)(ii) of this section is satisfied.

(g) *Definitions and special rules.*—In addition to the definitions and special rules in §§ 1.367(b)-2 and 1.7874-12, the following definitions and special rules apply for purposes of this section.

(1) *Indirect ownership.*—To determine indirect ownership of the stock of a corporation for purposes of calculating a pre-exchange ownership percentage or post-exchange ownership percentage with respect to that corporation, the principles of section 958(a) apply without regard to whether an intermediate entity is foreign or domestic. For this purpose, stock of the corporation that is directly or indirectly (applying the principles of section 958(a) without regard to whether an intermediate entity is foreign or domestic) owned by a domestic corporation that is an expatriated entity is not treated as indirectly owned by a non-EFS foreign related person.

(2) A *lower-tier expatriated foreign subsidiary* means an expatriated foreign subsidiary whose stock is directly or indirectly owned (under the principles of section 958(a)) by an expatriated foreign subsidiary.

(3) *Pre-exchange ownership percentage* means, with respect to a corporation, 100 percent less the percentage of stock (by value) in the corporation that, immediately before an exchange, is owned, in the aggregate, directly or indirectly by non-EFS foreign related persons.

(4) *Post-exchange ownership percentage* means, with respect to a corporation, 100 percent less the percentage of stock (by value) in the corporation that, immediately after the exchange, is owned, in the aggregate, directly or indirectly by non-EFS foreign related persons.

(5) *Specified property* means any property other than stock of a lower-tier expatriated foreign subsidiary.

(6) *Recapitalizations.*—A foreign corporation that undergoes a reorganization described in section 368(a)(1)(E) is treated as both the foreign acquired corporation and the transferee foreign corporation.

(7) *Triangular reorganizations.*—(i) *Definition.*—A triangular reorganization means a reorganization described in §1.358-6(b)(2)(i) (forward triangular merger), (ii) (triangular C reorganization), (iii) (reverse triangular merger), (iv) (triangular B reorganization), and (v) (triangular G reorganization).

(ii) *Special rules.*—(A) *Triangular reorganizations other than a reverse triangular merger.*—In the case of a triangular reorganization other than a reverse triangular merger, the surviving corporation is the transferee foreign corporation that acquires the assets or stock of the foreign acquired corporation, and the reference to controlling corporation (foreign or domestic) is to the corporation that controls the surviving corporation.

(B) *Reverse triangular merger.*—In the case of a reverse triangular merger, the surviving corporation is the entity that survives the merger, and the controlling corporation (foreign or domestic) is the corporation that before the merger controls the merged corporation. In the case of a reverse triangular merger, this section applies only if stock of the foreign surviving corporation is exchanged for stock of a foreign corporation in control of the merging corporation; in such a case, the foreign surviving corporation is treated as a foreign acquired corporation.

(h) *Applicability date of certain paragraphs in this section.*—Except as otherwise provided in this paragraph (h), paragraphs (a), (b) introductory text, (b)(1)(i)(C), (d)(1), (e), (f), and (g) of this section apply to exchanges completed on or after September 22, 2014, but only if the inversion transaction was completed on or after September 22, 2014. Paragraph (e)(1)(ii) of this section applies to exchanges completed on or after November 19, 2015, but only if the inversion transaction was completed on or after September 22, 2014. The portion of paragraph (e)(2)(i) of this section that requires the exchanging shareholder to be an expatriated entity or an expatriated foreign subsidiary apply to exchanges completed on or after April 4, 2016, but only if the inversion transaction was completed on or after September 22, 2014. For inversion transactions completed on or after September 22, 2014, however, taxpayers may elect to apply the portion of paragraph (e)(2)(i) of this section that requires the exchanging shareholder to be an expatriated entity or an expatriated foreign subsidiary to exchanges completed on or after September 22, 2014, and before April 4, 2016. Paragraphs (f) and (g)(5) of this section apply to transfers completed on or after April 4, 2016, but only if the inversion transaction was completed or after September 22, 2014. See §1.367(b)-4, as contained in 26 CFR part 1 revised as of April 1, 2016, for exchanges completed before September 22, 2014. Paragraph (b)(2)(i)(B) of this section applies to exchanges completed in taxable years of exchanging shareholders ending on or after November 2, 2020, and to taxable years of exchanging shareholders ending before November 2, 2020, resulting from an entity classification election made under §301.7701-3 of this chapter that was effective on or before November 2, 2020, but was filed on or after November 2, 2020. [Reg. §1.367(b)-4.]

☐ [T.D. 8770, 6-18-98 *(corrected 3-31-99). Amended by T.D. 8862,* 1-21-2000 *(corrected 11-3-2000); T.D. 9243, 1-23-2006; T.D. 9250,* 2-17-2006; *T.D. 9311, 2-1-2007 T.D. 9345, 7-27-2007; T.D. 9446,* 2-9-2009; *T.D. 9444, 2-10-2009; T.D. 9614, 3-18-2013 T.D. 9760,* 3-18-2016; *T.D. 9761, 4-4-2016 (corrected 6-22-2016). T.D. 9834,* 7-11-2018 *and T.D. 9959, 12-28-2021 (corrected 7-26-2022).*]

[Reg. §1.367(b)-5]

§1.367(b)-5. Distributions of stock described in section 355.—(a) *In general.*—(1) *Scope.*—This section provides rules relating to a distribution described in section 355 (or so much of section 356 as relates to section 355) and to which section 367(b) applies. For purposes of this section, the terms *distributing corporation, controlled corporation,* and *distributee* have the same meaning as used in section 355 and the regulations thereunder.

(2) *Treatment of distributees as exchanging shareholders.*—For purposes of the section 367(b) regulations, all distributees in a transaction described in paragraph (b), (c), or (d) of this section shall be treated as exchanging shareholders that realize income in a section 367(b) exchange.

(b) *Distribution by a domestic corporation.*—(1) *General rule.*—In a distribution described in section 355, if the distributing corporation is a domestic corporation and the controlled corporation is a foreign corporation, the following general rules shall apply—

(i) If the distributee is a corporation, then the controlled corporation shall be considered to be a corporation; and

(ii) If the distributee is an individual, then, solely for purposes of determining the gain recognized by the distributing corporation, the controlled corporation shall not be considered to be a corporation, and the distributing corporation shall recognize any gain (but not loss) realized on the distribution.

(2) *Section 367(e) transactions.*—The rules of paragraph (b)(1) of this section shall not apply to a foreign distributee to the extent gain is recognized under section 367(e)(1) and the regulations thereunder.

(3) *Determining whether distributees are individuals.*—All distributees in a distribution described in paragraph (b)(1) of this section are presumed to be individuals. However, the shareholder identification principles of §1.367(e)-1(d) (including the reporting procedures in §1.367(e)-1(d)(2) and (3)) shall apply for purposes of rebutting this presumption.

(4) *Applicable cross-references.*—For rules with respect to a distributee that is a partnership, trust or estate, see §1.367(b)-2(k). For additional rules relating to a distribution of stock of a foreign corporation by a domestic corporation, see section 1248(f) and the regulations thereunder. For additional rules relating to a distribution described in section 355 by a domestic corporation to a foreign distributee, see section 367(e)(1) and the regulations thereunder.

(c) *Pro rata distribution by a controlled foreign corporation.*—(1) *Scope.*—This paragraph (c) applies to a distribution described in section 355 in which the distributing corporation is a controlled foreign corporation and in which the stock of the controlled corporation is distributed pro rata to each of the distributing corporation's shareholders.

(2) *Adjustment to basis in stock and income inclusion.*—If the distributee's postdistribution amount (as defined in paragraph (e)(2) of this section) with respect to the distributing or controlled corporation is less than the distributee's predistribution amount (as defined in paragraph (e)(1) of this section) with respect to such corporation, then the distributee's basis in such stock immediately after the distribution (determined under the normal principles of section 358) shall be reduced by the amount of the difference. However, the distributee's basis in such stock shall not be reduced below zero, and to the extent the foregoing reduction would have reduced basis below zero, the distributee shall instead include such amount in income as a deemed dividend from such corporation.

(3) *Interaction with §1.367(b)-2(e)(3)(ii).*—The basis increase provided in §1.367(b)-2(e)(3)(ii) shall not apply to a deemed dividend that is included in income pursuant to paragraph (c)(2) of this section.

(4) *Basis redistribution.*—If a distributee reduces the basis in the stock of the distributing or controlled corporation (or has an inclusion with respect to such stock) under paragraph (c)(2) of this section, the distributee shall increase its basis in the stock of the other corporation by the amount of the basis decrease (or deemed dividend inclusion) required by paragraph (c)(2) of this section. However, the distributee's basis in such stock shall not be increased above the fair market value of such stock and shall not be increased to the extent the increase diminishes the distributee's postdistribution amount with respect to such corporation.

(d) *Non-pro rata distribution by a controlled foreign corporation.*—(1) *Scope.*—This paragraph (d) applies to a distribution described in section 355 in which the distributing corporation is a controlled foreign corporation and in which the stock of the controlled corporation is not distributed pro rata to each of the distributing corporation's shareholders.

(2) *Treatment of certain shareholders as distributees.*—For purposes of the section 367(b) regulations, all persons owning stock of the distributing corporation immediately after a transaction described in paragraph (d)(1) of this section shall be treated as distributees of such stock. For other applicable rules, see paragraph (a)(2) of this section.

(3) *Inclusion of excess section 1248 amount by exchanging shareholder.*—If the distributee's postdistribution amount (as defined in paragraph (e)(2) of this section) with respect to the distributing or controlled corporation is less than the distributee's predistribution amount (as defined in paragraph (e)(1) of this section) with respect to such corporation, then the distributee shall include in income as a deemed dividend the amount of the difference. For purposes of this paragraph (d)(3), if a distributee owns no stock in the distributing or controlled corporation immediately after the distribution, the distributee's postdistribution amount with respect to such corporation shall be zero.

(4) *Interaction with §1.367(b)-2(e)(3)(ii).*—(i) *Limited application.*—The basis increase provided in §1.367(b)-2(e)(3)(ii) shall apply to a deemed dividend that is included in income pursuant to paragraph

(d)(3) of this section only to the extent that such basis increase does not increase the distributee's basis above the fair market value of such stock and does not diminish the distributee's postdistribution amount with respect to such corporation.

(ii) *Interaction with predistribution amount.*—For purposes of this paragraph (d), the distributee's predistribution amount (as defined in paragraph (e)(1) of this section) shall be determined without regard to any basis increase permitted under paragraph (d)(4)(i) of this section.

(e) *Definitions.*—(1) *Predistribution amount.*—For purposes of this section, the predistribution amount with respect to a distributing or controlled corporation is the distributee's section 1248 amount (as defined in § 1.367(b)-2(c)(1)) computed immediately before the distribution (and after any section 368(a)(1)(D) transfer connected with the section 355 distribution), but only to the extent that such amount is attributable to the distributing corporation and any corporations controlled by it immediately before the distribution (the distributing group) or the controlled corporation and any corporations controlled by it immediately before the distribution (the controlled group), as the case may be, under the principles of §§ 1.1248-1(d)(3), 1.1248-2 and 1.1248-3. However, the predistribution amount with respect to the distributing group shall be computed without taking into account the distributee's predistribution amount with respect to the controlled group.

(2) *Postdistribution amount.*—For purposes of this section, the postdistribution amount with respect to a distributing or controlled corporation is the distributee's section 1248 amount (as defined in § 1.367(b)-2(c)(1)) with respect to such stock, computed immediately after the distribution (but without regard to paragraph (c) or (d) of this section (whichever is applicable)). The postdistribution amount under this paragraph (e)(2) shall be computed before taking into account the effect (if any) of any inclusion under section 356(a) or (b).

(f) *Exclusion of deemed dividend from foreign personal holding company income.*—In the event an amount is included in income as a deemed dividend by a foreign corporation under paragraph (c) or (d) of this section (including amounts received as an intermediate owner under the rule of § 1.367(b)-2(e)(2)), such deemed dividend shall not be included as foreign personal holding company income under section 954(c).

(g) *Examples.*—The following examples illustrate the rules of this section:

Example 1—(i) *Facts.* USS, a domestic corporation, owns 40 percent of the outstanding stock of FD, a controlled foreign corporation (CFC). USS has owned the stock since FD was incorporated, and FD has always been a CFC. USS has a basis of $80 in its FD stock, which has a fair market value of $200. FD owns 100 percent of the outstanding stock of FC, a foreign corporation. FD has owned the stock since FC was incorporated. Neither FD nor FC own stock in any other corporation. FD has earnings and profits of $0 and a fair market value of $250 (not considering its ownership of FC). FC has earnings and profits of $300, none of which is described in section 1248(d), and a fair market value of $250. In a pro rata distribution described in section 355, FD distributes to USS stock in FC worth $100; thereafter, USS's FD stock is worth $100 as well.

(ii) *Result*—(A) FD's distribution is a transaction described in paragraph (c)(1) of this section. Under paragraph (c)(2) of this section, USS must compare its predistribution amounts with respect to FD and FC to its respective postdistribution amounts. Under paragraph (e)(1) of this section, USS's predistribution amount with respect to FD or FC is its section 1248 amount computed immediately before the distribution, but only to the extent such amount is attributable to FD or FC. Under § 1.367(b)-2(c)(1), USS's section 1248 amount computed immediately before the distribution is $120, all of which is attributable to FC. Thus, USS's predistribution amount with respect to FD is $0, and its predistribution amount with respect to FC is $120. These amounts are computed as follows: If USS had sold its FD stock immediately before the transaction, it would have recognized $120 of gain ($200 fair market value – $80 basis). All of the gain would have been treated as a dividend under section 1248, and all of the section 1248 amount would have been attributable to FC (based on USS's pro rata share of FC's earnings and profits (40 percent × $300)).

(B) Under paragraph (e)(2) of this section, USS's postdistribution amount with respect to FD or FC is its section 1248 amount with respect to such corporation, computed immediately after the distribution (but without regard to paragraph (c) of this section). Under § 1.367(b)-2(c)(1), USS's section 1248 amounts computed immediately after the distribution with respect to FD and FC are $0 and $60, respectively. These amounts, which are USS's postdistribution amounts, are computed as follows: Under the normal principles of section 358, USS allocates its $80 predistribution basis in FD between FD and FC according to the stock blocks' relative values, yielding a

$40 basis in each block. If USS sold its FD stock immediately after the distribution, none of the resulting gain would be treated as a dividend under section 1248. If USS sold its FC stock immediately after the distribution, it would have a $60 gain ($100 fair market value – $40 basis), all of which would be treated as a dividend under section 1248.

(C) The basis adjustment and income inclusion rules of paragraph (c)(2) of this section apply to the extent of any difference between USS's postdistribution and predistribution amounts. In the case of FD, there is no difference between the two amounts and, as a result, no adjustment or income inclusion is required. In the case of FC, USS's postdistribution amount is $60 less than its predistribution amount. Accordingly, under paragraph (c)(2) of this section, USS is required to reduce its basis in its FC stock from $40 to $0 and include $20 in income as a deemed dividend. Under § 1.367(b)-2(e)(2), the $20 deemed dividend is considered as having been paid by FC to FD, and by FD to USS, immediately prior to the distribution. Under paragraph (f) of this section, the deemed dividend is not included by FD as foreign personal holding company income under section 954(c). Under paragraph (c)(3) of this section, the basis increase provided in § 1.367(b)-2(e)(3)(ii) does not apply with regard to the $20 deemed dividend. Under the rules of paragraph (c)(4) of this section, USS increases its basis in FD by the amount by which it decreased its basis in FC, as well as by the amount of its deemed dividend inclusion ($40 + $40 + $20 = $100).

Example 2—(i) *Facts.* USS1 and USS2, domestic corporations, each own 50 percent of the outstanding stock of FD, a controlled foreign corporation (CFC). USS1 and USS2 have owned their FD stock since it was incorporated, and FD has always been a CFC. USS1 and USS2 each have a basis of $500 in their FD stock, and the fair market value of each block of FD stock is $750. FD owns 100 percent of the outstanding stock of FC, a foreign corporation. FD owned the stock since FC was incorporated. Neither FD nor FC own stock in any other corporation. FD has earnings and profits of $0 and a fair market value of $750 (not considering its ownership of FC). FC has earnings and profits of $500, none of which is described in section 1248(d), and a fair market value of $750. In a non-pro rata distribution described in section 355, FD distributes all of the stock of FC to USS2 in exchange for USS2's FD stock.

(ii) *Result*—(A) FD's distribution is a transaction described in paragraph (d)(1) of this section. Under paragraph (d)(2) of this section, USS1 is considered a distributee of FD stock. Under paragraph (d)(3) of this section, USS1 and USS2 must compare their predistribution amounts with respect to FD and FC stock to their respective postdistribution amounts. Under paragraph (e)(1) of this section, USS1's predistribution amount with respect to FD or FC is USS1's section 1248 amount computed immediately before the distribution, but only to the extent such amount is attributable to FD or FC. USS2's predistribution amount is determined in the same manner. Under § 1.367(b)-2(c)(1), USS1 and USS2 each have a section 1248 amount computed immediately before the distribution of $250, all of which is attributable to FC. Thus, USS1 and USS2 each have a predistribution amount with respect to FD of $0, and each have a predistribution amount with respect to FC of $250. These amounts are computed as follows: If either USS1 or USS2 had sold its FD stock immediately before the transaction, it would have recognized $250 of gain ($750 fair market value – $500 basis). All of the gain would have been treated as a dividend under section 1248, and all of the section 1248 amount would have been attributable to FC (based on USS1's and USS2's pro rata shares of FC's earnings and profits (50 percent × $500)).

(B) Under paragraph (d)(3) of this section, a distributee that owns no stock in the distributing or controlled corporation immediately after the distribution has a postdistribution amount with regard to that stock of zero. Accordingly, USS2 has a postdistribution amount of $0 with respect to FD and USS1 has a postdistribution amount of $0 with respect to FC. Under paragraph (e)(2) of this section, USS1's postdistribution amount with respect to FD is its section 1248 amount with respect to such corporation, computed immediately after the distribution (but without regard to paragraph (d) of this section). USS2's postdistribution amount with respect to FC is determined in the same manner. Under § 1.367(b)-2(c)(1), USS1's section 1248 amount computed immediately after the distribution with respect to FD is $0 and USS2's section 1248 amount computed immediately after the distribution with respect to FC is $250. These amounts, which are USS1's and USS2's postdistribution amounts, are computed as follows: After the non-pro rata distribution, USS1 owns all the stock of FD and USS2 owns all the stock of FC. If USS1 sold its FD stock immediately after the distribution, none of the resulting $250 gain ($750 fair market value – $500 basis) would be treated as a dividend under section 1248. If USS2 sold its FC stock immediately after the distribution, it would have a $250 gain ($750 fair market value – $500 basis), all of which would be treated as a dividend under section 1248.

(C) The income inclusion rule of paragraph (d)(3) of this section applies to the extent of any difference between USS1's and USS2's postdistribution and predistribution amounts. In the case of USS2, there is no difference between the two amounts with respect to either FD or FC and, as a result, no income inclusion is required. In the case of USS1, there is no difference between the two amounts with respect to its FD stock. However, USS1's postdistribution amount with respect to FC is $250 less than its predistribution amount. Accordingly, under paragraph (d)(3) of this section, USS1 is required to include $250 in income as a deemed dividend. Under § 1.367(b)-2(e)(2), the $250 deemed dividend is considered as having been paid by FC to FD, and by FD to USS1, immediately prior to the distribution. This deemed dividend increases USS1's basis in FD ($500 + $250 = $750). Under paragraph (f) of this section, the deemed dividend is not included by FD as foreign personal holding company income under section 954(c).

[Reg. § 1.367(b)-5.]

☐ [T.D. 8862, 1-21-2000 (corrected 11-3-2000).]

[Reg. § 1.367(b)-6]

§ 1.367(b)-6. Effective/applicability dates and coordination rules.—(a) *Effective/applicability dates.*—(1) *In general.*—(i) Except as otherwise provided in this paragraph (a)(1) and paragraph (a)(2) of this section, §§ 1.367(b)-1 through 1.367(b)-5, and this section, apply to section 367(b) exchanges that occur on or after February 23, 2000.

(ii) The rules of §§ 1.367(b)-3 and 1.367(b)-4, as they apply to reorganizations described in section 368(a)(1)(A) (including reorganizations described in section 368(a)(2)(D) or (a)(2)(E)) involving a foreign acquiring or foreign acquired corporation, apply only to transfers occurring on or after January 23, 2006.

(iii) Section 1.367(b)-1(c)(2)(v), (c)(3)(ii)(A), (c)(4)(iv), (c)(4)(v), § 1.367(b)-2(j)(1)(i) and (l), and § 1.367(b)-3(e) and (f), apply to section 367(b) exchanges that occur on or after November 6, 2006. For guidance with respect to § 1.367(b)-1(c)(3)(ii)(A), (c)(4)(iv), and (c)(4)(v) and § 1.367(b)-2(j)(1)(i) for exchanges that occur before November 6, 2006, see 26 CFR part 1 revised as of April 1, 2006.

(iv) Section 1.367(b)-4(b)(1)(i)(B)(2), § 1.367(b)-4(b)(1)(ii), § 1.367(b)-4(b)(1)(iii), *Example 4* and *Example 5* apply to section 367(b) exchanges that occur on or after April 18, 2013. For guidance with respect to § 1.367(b)-4(b)(1)(i)(B)(2), § 1.367(b)-4(b)(1)(ii) and § 1.367(b)-4(b)(1)(iii), *Example 4*, for exchanges that occur before April 18, 2013, see 26 CFR part 1 revised as of April 1, 2012.

(2) *Exception.*—A taxpayer may, however, elect to have §§ 1.367(b)-1 through 1.367(b)-5, and this section, apply to section 367(b) exchanges that occur (or occurred) before February 23, 2000, if the due date for the taxpayer's timely filed Federal tax return (including extensions) for the taxable year in which the section 367(b) exchange occurs (or occurred) is after February 23, 2000. The election under this paragraph (a)(2) will be valid only if—

(i) The electing taxpayer makes the election on a timely filed section 367(b) notice;

(ii) In the case of an exchanging shareholder that is a foreign corporation, the election is made on the section 367(b) notice that is filed by each of its shareholders listed in § 1.367(b)-1(c)(3)(ii); and

(iii) The electing taxpayer provides notice of the election to all corporations (or their successors in interest) whose earnings and profits are affected by the election on or before the date the section 367(b) notice is filed.

(b) *Certain recapitalizations described in § 1.367(b)-4(b)(3).*—In the case of a recapitalization described in § 1.367(b)-4(b)(3) that occurred prior to July 20, 1998, the exchanging shareholder shall include the section 1248 amount on its tax return for the taxable year that includes the exchange described in § 1.367(b)-4(b)(3)(i) (and not in the taxable year of the recapitalization), except that no inclusion is required if both the recapitalization and the exchange described in § 1.367(b)-4(b)(3)(i) occurred prior to July 20, 1998.

(c) *Use of reasonable method to comply with prior published guidance.*—(1) *Prior exchanges.*—The taxpayer may use a reasonable method to comply with the following prior published guidance to the extent such guidance relates to section 367(b): Notice 88-71 (1988-2 C.B. 374); Notice 89-30 (1989-1 C.B. 670); and Notice 89-79 (1989-2 C.B. 392) (see § 601.601(d)(2) of this chapter). This rule applies to section 367(b) exchanges that occur (or occurred) before February 23, 2000, or, if a taxpayer makes the election described in paragraph (a)(2) of this section, for section 367(b) exchanges that occur (or occurred) before the date described in paragraph (a)(2) of this section. This rule also applies to section 367(b) exchanges and distributions described in paragraph (d) of this section.

(2) *Future exchanges.*—Section 367(b) exchanges that occur on or after February 23, 2000, (or, if a taxpayer makes the election described in paragraph (a)(2) of this section, for section 367(b) ex-

changes that occur on or after the date described in paragraph (a)(2) of this section) are governed by the section 367(b) regulations and, as a result, paragraph (c)(1) of this section shall not apply.

(d) *Effect of removal of attribution rules.*—To the extent that the rules under §§ 7.367(b)-9 and 7.367(b)-10(h) of this chapter, as in effect prior to February 23, 2000 (see 26 CFR part 1 revised as of April 1, 1999), attributed earnings and profits to the stock of a foreign corporation in connection with an exchange described in section 351, 354, 355, or 356 before February 23, 2000, the foreign corporation shall continue to be subject to the rules of § 7.367(b)-12 of this chapter in the event of any subsequent exchanges and distributions with respect to such stock, notwithstanding the fact that such subsequent exchange or distribution occurs on or after the effective date described in paragraph (a) of this section. [Reg. § 1.367(b)-6.]

☐ [T.D. 8862, 1-21-2000. *Amended by* T.D. 9243, 1-23-2006 (*corrected* 5-15-2006); T.D. 9250, 2-17-2006; T.D. 9273, 8-7-2006 (*corrected* 3-17-2008); T.D. 9614, 3-18-2013 *and* T.D. 9834, 7-11-2018.]

[Reg. § 1.367(b)-7]

§ 1.367(b)-7. Carryover of earnings and profits and foreign income taxes in certain foreign-to-foreign nonrecognition transactions.—(a) *Scope.*—This section applies to an acquisition by a foreign corporation (foreign acquiring corporation) of the assets of another foreign corporation (foreign target corporation) in a transaction described in section 381 (foreign section 381 transaction). This section describes the manner and extent to which earnings and profits and foreign income taxes of the foreign acquiring corporation and the foreign target corporation carry over to the surviving foreign corporation (foreign surviving corporation) and the ordering of distributions by the foreign surviving corporation. See § 1.367(b)-9 for special rules governing reorganizations described in section 368(a)(1)(F) and foreign section 381 transactions involving foreign corporations that hold no property and have no tax attributes immediately before the transaction, other than a nominal amount of assets (and related tax attributes).

(b) *General rules.*—(1) *Non-previously taxed earnings and profits and related taxes.*—Earnings and profits and related foreign income taxes of the foreign acquiring corporation and the foreign target corporation (pre-transaction earnings and pre-transaction taxes, respectively) shall carry over to the foreign surviving corporation in the manner described in paragraphs (d), (e), and (f) of this section. Dividend distributions by the foreign surviving corporation (post-transaction distributions) shall be out of earnings and profits and shall reduce related foreign income taxes in the manner described in paragraph (c) of this section. See paragraph (g) of this section for rules applicable to taxable years of foreign corporations beginning on or after January 1, 2018, and taxable years of United States shareholders in which or with which such taxable years of foreign corporations end ("post-2017 taxable years").

(2) *Previously taxed earnings and profits.*—[Reserved]

(c) *Ordering rule for post-transaction distributions.*—Dividend distributions out of a foreign surviving corporation's earnings and profits shall be ordered in accordance with the rules of paragraph (c)(1) or (2) of this section, depending on whether the foreign surviving corporation is a pooling corporation or a nonpooling corporation.

(1) *If foreign surviving corporation is a pooling corporation.*—In the case of a foreign surviving corporation that is a pooling corporation, post-transaction distributions shall be first out of the post-1986 pool (as described in paragraph (d) of this section) and second out of the pre-pooling annual layers (as described in paragraph (e)(1) of this section) under an annual last-in, first-out (LIFO) method.

(2) *If foreign surviving corporation is a nonpooling corporation.*—In the case of a foreign surviving corporation that is a nonpooling corporation, post-transaction distributions shall be out of the pre-pooling annual layers (as described in paragraph (e)(2) of this section) under the LIFO method.

(d) *Post-1986 pool.*—If the foreign surviving corporation is a pooling corporation, then the post-1986 pool shall be determined under the rules of this paragraph (d).

(1) *In general.*—(i) *Qualifying earnings and taxes.*—The post-1986 pool shall consist of the post-1986 undistributed earnings and related post-1986 foreign income taxes of the foreign acquiring corporation and the foreign target corporation.

(ii) *Carryover rule.*—Subject to paragraph (d)(2) of this section, the amounts described in paragraph (d)(1)(i) of this section attributable to the foreign acquiring corporation and the foreign target corporation shall carry over to the foreign surviving corporation and shall be combined on a separate category-by-separate category basis.

(2) *Hovering deficit.*—(i) *In general.*—If immediately prior to the foreign section 381 transaction either the foreign acquiring corporation or the foreign target corporation has a deficit in one or more separate categories of post-1986 undistributed earnings or an aggregate deficit in pre-1987 accumulated profits, such deficit will be a hovering deficit of the foreign surviving corporation. The rules of this paragraph (d)(2) apply to hovering deficits in separate categories of post-1986 undistributed earnings. See paragraphs (e)(1)(iii) and (e)(2)(iii) of this section for rules that apply to hovering deficits in pre-1987 accumulated profits. If the foreign acquiring corporation and the foreign target corporation each have a post-1986 hovering deficit in the same separate category of post-1986 undistributed earnings, such deficits and their related post-1986 foreign income taxes shall be combined for purposes of applying this paragraph (d)(2). See also paragraphs (f)(1) and (4) of this section (describing other rules applicable to a deficit described in this paragraph (d)(2)).

(ii) *Offset rule.*—A hovering deficit in a separate category of post-1986 undistributed earnings shall offset only earnings and profits accumulated by the foreign surviving corporation after the foreign section 381 transaction (post-transaction earnings) in the same separate category of post-1986 undistributed earnings. For purposes of this rule, however, post-transaction earnings do not include post-1986 undistributed earnings in the same category that are earned after the foreign section 381 transaction, but are distributed or deemed distributed in the same year they are earned (that is, that do not become accumulated). The offset shall occur as of the first day of the foreign surviving corporation's first taxable year following the year in which the post-transaction earnings accumulated.

Foreign Corporation A

Separate Category	E&P	Foreign Taxes
General	300u	$60
Passive	100u	$40
	400u	$100

Foreign Corporation B

Separate Category	E&P	Foreign Taxes
General	300u	$70

(B) On January 1, 2007, foreign corporation B acquires the assets of foreign corporation A in a reorganization described in section 368(a)(1)(C). Immediately following the foreign section 381 transaction, foreign surviving corporation is a CFC.

Separate Category	E&P	Foreign Taxes
General	600u	$130
Passive	100u	$40
	700u	$170

(iii) *Post-transaction distribution.* (A) During 2007, foreign surviving corporation does not accumulate any earnings and profits or pay or accrue any foreign income taxes. On December 31, 2007, foreign surviving corporation distributes 350u to its shareholders. Under the

Separate Category	E&P	Foreign Taxes
General	300u	$65
Passive	50u	$20
	350u	$85

(B) The foreign income taxes deemed paid by qualifying shareholders of foreign surviving corporation upon the distribution are subject to generally applicable rules and limitations, such as those of sections 78, 902, and 904(d).

Separate Category	E&P	Foreign Taxes
General	300u	$65
Passive	50u	$20
	350u	$85

Example 2. (i) *Facts.* (A) On December 31, 2006, foreign corporations A and B have the following post-1986 undistributed earnings and post-1986 foreign income taxes:

Foreign Corporation A

Separate Category	E&P	Foreign Taxes
General	200u	$30
Passive	(100u)	$10
	100u	$40

Foreign Corporation B

Separate Category	E&P	Foreign Taxes
General	300u	$60
Passive	100u	$30
	400u	$90

(B) On January 1, 2007, foreign corporation B acquires the assets of foreign corporation A in a reorganization described in section

(iii) *Related taxes.*—Post-1986 foreign income taxes that are related to a hovering deficit in a separate category of post-1986 undistributed earnings shall only be added to the foreign surviving corporation's post-1986 foreign income taxes in that separate category on a pro rata basis as the hovering deficit is absorbed. Pro rata means in the same proportion as the portion of the hovering deficit that offsets post-transaction earnings in the separate category under paragraph (d)(2)(ii) of this section bears to the total amount of the hovering deficit.

(3) *Examples.*—The following examples illustrate the rules of this paragraph (d). The examples assume the following facts: foreign corporations A and B are controlled foreign corporations (CFCs) that were incorporated after December 31, 1986, have always been pooling corporations, and have always had calendar taxable years. None of the shareholders of foreign corporations A and B are required to include any amount in income under § 1.367(b)-4 as a result of the foreign section 381 transaction. Foreign corporations A and B (and all of their respective qualified business units as defined in section 989) maintain a "u" functional currency. Finally, unless otherwise stated, any post-1986 undistributed earnings in the passive category resulted from a look-through dividend that was paid by a lower-tier CFC out of earnings accumulated when the CFC was a noncontrolled section 902 corporation and that qualified for the subpart F same-country exception under section 954(c)(3)(A). The examples are as follows:

Example 1. (i) *Facts.* (A) On December 31, 2006, foreign corporations A and B have the following post-1986 undistributed earnings and post-1986 foreign income taxes:

(ii) *Result.* Under the rules described in paragraph (d)(1) of this section, foreign surviving corporation has the following post-1986 undistributed earnings and post-1986 foreign income taxes:

rules described in § 1.902-1(d)(1) and paragraph (c)(1) of this section, the distribution is out of, and reduces, post-1986 undistributed earnings and post-1986 foreign income taxes in the separate categories on a pro rata basis, as follows:

(C) Immediately after the distribution, foreign surviving corporation has the following post-1986 undistributed earnings and post-1986 foreign income taxes:

368(a)(1)(C). Immediately following the foreign section 381 transaction, foreign surviving corporation is a CFC.

(ii) *Result.* Under the rules described in paragraphs (d)(1) and (2) of this section, foreign surviving corporation has the following post-1986 undistributed earnings and post-1986 foreign income taxes:

	Earnings & Profits:		Foreign Taxes:	
Separate Category	Positive E&P	Hovering Deficit	Foreign Taxes Available	Foreign Taxes Associated with Hovering Deficit
General	500u		$ 90	
Passive	100u	(100u)	$ 30	$10
	600u	(100u)	$120	$10

(iii) *Post-transaction distribution.* (A) During 2007, foreign surviving corporation does not accumulate any earnings and profits or pay or accrue any foreign income taxes. On December 31, 2007, foreign surviving corporation distributes 300u to its shareholders. Under the rules described in §1.902-1(d)(1) and paragraph (c)(1) of this section, the distribution is out of, and reduces, post-1986 undistributed earnings and post-1986 foreign income taxes on a pro rata basis as follows:

Separate Category	E&P	Foreign Taxes
General	250u	$45
Passive	50u	$15
	300u	$60

(B) The foreign income taxes deemed paid by qualifying shareholders of foreign surviving corporation upon the distribution are subject to generally applicable rules and limitations, such as those of sections 78, 902, and 904(d).

(C) Immediately after the distribution, foreign surviving corporation has the following post-1986 undistributed earnings and post-1986 foreign income taxes:

	Earnings & Profits:		Foreign Taxes:	
Separate Category	Positive E&P	Hovering Deficit	Foreign Taxes Available	Foreign Taxes Associated with Hovering Deficit
General	250u		$45	
Passive	50u	(100u)	$15	$10
	300u	(100u)	$60	$10

(iv) *Post-transaction earnings*—(A) In its taxable year ending on December 31, 2008, foreign surviving corporation accumulates earnings and profits and pays related foreign income taxes as follows:

Separate Category	E&P	Foreign Taxes
General	100u	$20
Passive	50u	$10
	150u	$40

(B) None of foreign surviving corporation's earnings and profits for its 2008 taxable year qualifies as subpart F income as defined in section 952(a). Under the rules described in paragraphs (d)(2)(ii) and (iii) of this section, the hovering deficit in the passive category will offset the post-transaction earnings in that category and a proportionate amount of the foreign taxes related to the hovering deficit will be added to the post-1986 foreign income taxes pool. Because the post-transaction earnings in the passive category are half of the amount of the hovering deficit, half of the related taxes are added to the post-1986 foreign income taxes pool. Accordingly, foreign surviving corporation has the following post-1986 undistributed earnings and post-1986 foreign income taxes on January 1, 2009:

	Earnings & Profits:		Foreign Taxes:	
Separate Category	Positive E&P	Hovering Deficit	Foreign Taxes Available	Foreign Taxes Associated with Hovering Deficit
General	350u		$65	
Passive	50u	(50u)	$30	$5
	400u	(50u)	$95	$5

Example 3. (i) *Facts.* The facts are the same as *Example 2*, except that the 50u of earnings in the passive category accrued by foreign surviving corporation during 2008 is subpart F income, all of which is included in income under section 951(a) by United States shareholders (as defined in section 951(b)). This example assumes that none of the United States shareholders are able to reduce their subpart F income inclusion with a qualified deficit under section 952(c)(1)(B).

(ii) *Result.* (A) Under the rule described in paragraph (f)(1) of this section, the (100u) hovering deficit in the passive category does not reduce foreign surviving corporation's current passive earnings and profits for purposes of determining subpart F income or associated deemed paid credits. Thus, foreign surviving corporation's United States shareholders include their pro rata shares of 50u in taxable income for the year and are eligible for a deemed paid foreign tax credit under section 960, computed by reference to their pro rata shares of $12.50 (50u subpart F inclusion / (50u + 50u post-1986 undistributed earnings in the passive category = 100u) = 50%, × $25 post-1986 foreign income taxes in the passive category = $12.50). The United States shareholders will also include their pro rata shares of the deemed-paid taxes of $12.50 in taxable income for the year as a deemed dividend pursuant to section 78.

(B) Immediately after the subpart F inclusion and section 960 deemed paid taxes (and taking into account the taxable year 2008 earnings and profits and related taxes in the general category), foreign surviving corporation has the following post-1986 undistributed earnings and post-1986 foreign income taxes:

Separate Category	Earnings & Profits:		Foreign Taxes:	
	Positive E&P	Hovering Deficit	Foreign Taxes Available	Foreign Taxes Associated with Hovering Deficit
General	350u		$65.00	
Passive	50u	(100u)	$12.50	$10
	400u	(100u)	$77.50	$10

(C) The 50u included as subpart F income constitutes previously taxed earnings and profits under section 959.

Foreign Corporation A
Separate Category

	E&P	Foreign Taxes
General	50u	$10

Foreign Corporation B
Separate Category

	E&P	Foreign Taxes
General	(100u)	$20

(B) On January 1, 2007, foreign corporation B acquires the assets of foreign corporation A in a reorganization described in section 368(a)(1)(C). Immediately following the foreign section 381 transaction, foreign surviving corporation is a CFC.

Example 4. (i) *Facts.* (A) On December 31, 2006, foreign corporations A and B have the following post-1986 undistributed earnings and post-1986 foreign income taxes:

(ii) *Result.* Under the rules described in paragraphs (d)(1) and (2) of this section, foreign surviving corporation has the following post-1986 undistributed earnings and post-1986 foreign income taxes:

Separate Category	Earnings & Profits:		Foreign Taxes:	
	Positive E&P	Hovering Deficit	Foreign Taxes Available	Foreign Taxes Associated with Hovering Deficit
General	50u	(100u)	$10	$20

(iii) *Post-transaction earnings and distribution.* (A) In its taxable year ending on December 31, 2007, foreign surviving corporation earns 100u in the general category and pays related foreign income taxes of $24. On December 31, 2007, foreign surviving corporation distributes 75u to its shareholders.

(B) *Result.* For purposes of determining the dividend amount under section 316 and the foreign income taxes deemed paid with respect to that dividend under section 902, under paragraph (d)(2)(ii) of this section the hovering deficit does not offset the post-transaction current year earnings. Accordingly, the full 75u will be a dividend under section 316. The deemed paid taxes on that dividend are $17

(75u distribution / (100u current earnings + 50u accumulated earnings) = 50%, × ($10 accumulated foreign taxes + $24 current year foreign taxes) = $17). The 25u of undistributed earnings and profits in 2007 will be offset by (25u) of the hovering deficit for purposes of determining the opening balance of the post-1986 undistributed earnings pool in 2008. Because the amount of earnings offset by the hovering deficit is 25% of the amount of the hovering deficit, under paragraph (d)(2)(iii) of this section $5 (25% of $20) of the related taxes are added to the post-1986 foreign income taxes pool at the beginning of the next taxable year. Accordingly, foreign surviving corporation has the following post-1986 undistributed earnings and post-1986 foreign income taxes on January 1, 2008:

Separate Category	Earnings & Profits:		Foreign Taxes:	
	Positive E&P	Hovering Deficit	Foreign Taxes Available	Foreign Taxes Associated with Hovering Deficit
General	50u	(75u)	$22	$15

(e) *Pre-pooling annual layers.*—(1) *If foreign surviving corporation is a pooling corporation.*—If the foreign surviving corporation is a pooling corporation, the pre-pooling annual layers shall be determined under the rules of this paragraph (e)(1).

(i) *Qualifying earnings and taxes.*—The pre-pooling annual layers shall consist of the pre-1987 accumulated profits and the pre-1987 foreign income taxes of the foreign acquiring corporation and the foreign target corporation.

(ii) *Carryover rule.*—Subject to paragraph (e)(1)(iii) of this section, the amounts described in paragraph (e)(1)(i) of this section shall carry over to the foreign surviving corporation but shall not be combined. If the foreign acquiring corporation and the foreign target corporation have pre-1987 accumulated profits in the same year and a distribution is made therefrom, the rules of §1.902-1(b)(2)(ii) and (b)(3) shall apply separately to reduce pre-1987 accumulated profits and pre-1987 foreign income taxes of the foreign acquiring corporation and the foreign target corporation on a pro rata basis. For further guidance, see Rev. Rul. 68-351 (1968-2 C.B. 307); Rev. Rul. 70-373 (1970-2 C.B. 152) (see also §601.601(d)(2) of this chapter); see also paragraph (f)(2) of this section (governing the reconciliation of taxable years).

(iii) *Deficit.*—(A) *In general.*—The rules of this paragraph (e)(1)(iii) apply when, immediately prior to the foreign section 381 transaction, the foreign acquiring corporation or the foreign target corporation (or both) has a deficit in earnings and profits for one or more of the years that comprise its pre-1987 accumulated profits (see also paragraphs (f)(1) and (4) of this section, describing other rules applicable to a deficit described in this paragraph (e)(1)(iii)).

(B) *Aggregate positive pre-1987 accumulated profits.*—If the foreign acquiring corporation or the foreign target corporation (or both) has an aggregate positive (or zero) amount of pre-1987 accumulated profits, but a deficit in earnings and profits for one or more years, then the rules otherwise applicable to such deficits shall apply separately to the pre-1987 accumulated profits and related pre-1987 foreign income taxes of such corporation. A deficit in pre-1987 accumulated profits for one or more years is applied to reduce pre-1987 accumulated profits on a LIFO basis. Any remaining deficit shall be applied to reduce pre-1987 accumulated profits in succeeding years. See Rev. Rul. 74-550 (1974-2 C.B. 209) (see also §601.601(d)(2) of this chapter); *Champion Int'l Corp. v. Commissioner,* 81 T.C. 424 (1983), acq. in result, 1987-2 C.B. 1; Rev. Rul. 87-72 (1987-2 C.B. 170) (see also §601.601(d)(2) of this chapter). As a result, no amount in excess of the aggregate positive amount of pre-1987 accumulated profits shall be distributed from the pre-transaction earnings of the foreign acquiring corporation or the foreign target corporation.

(C) *Aggregate deficit in pre-1987 accumulated profits.*—If the foreign acquiring corporation or the foreign target corporation (or both) has an aggregate deficit in pre-1987 accumulated profits, a hovering deficit as defined under paragraph (d)(2)(i) of this section, then the rules under §1.902-2(b) shall apply to such hovering deficit (and related pre-1987 foreign income taxes) immediately prior to the transaction, except that the aggregate hovering deficit that is carried forward into the foreign surviving corporation's post-1986 pool shall offset only post-transaction earnings accumulated by the foreign surviving corporation in the same separate category of post-1986 undistributed earnings to which the relevant portion of the hovering deficit is attributable. Post-transaction earnings do not include earnings and profits that are earned after the foreign section 381 transaction but distributed or deemed distributed in the same year they are earned.

(D) *Deficit and positive separate categories within annual layers.*—For purposes of applying the rules of paragraphs (e)(1)(iii)(B) and (C) of this section, if within a single pre-pooling annual layer, the foreign acquiring corporation or the foreign target corporation (or both) has a deficit in pre-1987 accumulated profits in a separate category and positive pre-1987 accumulated profits in another separate category, the deficit shall first be used to offset the positive pre-1987 accumulated profits in the other separate category in the same pre-pooling annual layer. Any remaining deficit shall be carried forward or back to other years according to the rules of paragraph (e)(1)(iii)(B) or (C) of this section as applicable.

(iv) *Pre-1987 section 960 earnings and profits and foreign income taxes.*—The pre-1987 section 960 earnings and profits and pre-1987 section 960 foreign income taxes of the foreign acquiring corporation and the foreign target corporation shall carry over to the foreign surviving corporation but shall not be combined. The rules otherwise applicable to such amounts shall apply separately to the pre-1987 section 960 earnings and profits and pre-1987 section 960 foreign income taxes of the foreign acquiring corporation and the foreign

Foreign Corporation A	E&P	Foreign Taxes
Post-1986 pool	1,000u	$350
2004	400u	160u
2003	100u	5u
	1,500u	

Foreign Corporation B	E&P	Foreign Taxes
2006	100u	20u
2005	150u	30u
2004	0u	50u
2003	50u	5u
	300u	105u

(B) On January 1, 2007, foreign corporation B acquires the assets of foreign corporation A in a reorganization described in section 368(a)(1)(C). Immediately following the foreign section 381 transaction, foreign surviving corporation is a CFC.

	E&P	Foreign Taxes
Post-1986 pool	1,000u	$350
2006	100u	20u
2005	150u	30u
Two Side-by-Side Layers of 2004 E&P:		
2004 layer #1 (from Corp A)	400u	160u
2004 layer #2 (from Corp B)	0u	50u
Two Side-by-Side Layers of 2003 E&P:		
2003 layer #1 (from Corp A)	100u	5u
2003 layer #2 (from Corp B)	50u	5u
	1,800u	

(iii) *Post-transaction distribution.* (A) During 2007, foreign surviving corporation does not accumulate any earnings and profits or pay or accrue any foreign income taxes. On December 31, 2007, foreign surviving corporation distributes 1,725u to its shareholders.

	E&P	Foreign Taxes
Post-1986 pool	1,000u	$350
2006	100u	20u
2005	150u	30u
Two Side-by-Side Layers of 2004 E&P:		
2004 layer #1	400u	160u
2004 layer #2	0u	0u
Two Side-by-Side Layers of 2003 E&P:		
2003 layer #1	50u	2.5u
(100u in layer / 150u aggregate 2003 earnings = 66.67% × 75u distribution)		
2003 layer #2	25u	2.5u
(50u in layer / 150u aggregate 2003 earnings = 33.33% × 75u distribution)		
	1,725u	

(B) The foreign income taxes deemed paid by qualifying shareholders of foreign surviving corporation upon the distribution are subject to generally applicable rules and limitations, such as those of sections 78, 902, and 904(d).

	E&P	Foreign Taxes
2004 layer #2	0u	50u
Two Side-by-Side Layers of 2003 E&P:		
2003 layer #1	50u	2.5u
2003 layer #2	25u	2.5u
	75u	55u

target corporation on a pro rata basis. For further guidance, see Notice 88-70 (1988-2 C.B. 369) (see also §601.601(d)(2) of this chapter).

(v) *Examples.*—The following examples illustrate the rules of this paragraph (e)(1). The examples assume the following facts: foreign corporation A was incorporated in 2003 and was a nonpooling corporation through December 31, 2004. Foreign corporation A became a CFC on January 1, 2005 and, as a result, began to maintain a pool of post-1986 undistributed earnings on that date. Foreign corporation B was incorporated in 2003 and has always been owned by foreign shareholders (and thus never has met the requirements of section 902(c)(3)(B)). Both foreign corporation A and foreign corporation B have always had calendar taxable years. Foreign corporations A and B (and all of their respective qualified business units as defined in section 989) maintain a "u" functional currency. Finally, unless otherwise stated, all earnings and profits of foreign corporations A and B are in the general category. The examples are as follows:

Example 1. (i) *Facts.* (A) On December 31, 2006, foreign corporations A and B have the following earnings and profits and foreign income taxes:

(ii) *Result.* Under the rules described in paragraphs (e)(1)(i) and (ii) of this section, foreign surviving corporation has the following earnings and profits and foreign income taxes:

Under the rules of paragraph (c)(1) of this section, the distribution is first out of the post-1986 pool, and then out of the pre-pooling annual layers under the LIFO method, as follows:

(C) Immediately after the distribution, foreign surviving corporation has the following earnings and profits and foreign income taxes:

(iv) *Post-transaction earnings.* For the taxable year ending on December 31, 2008, foreign surviving corporation has 500u of current earnings and profits in the general category, none of which qualify as subpart F income under section 952(a), and pays $70 in foreign income taxes. As of the close of the 2008 taxable year, foreign surviving corporation has the following earnings and profits and foreign income taxes:

	E&P	Foreign Taxes
Post-1986 pool	500u	$70
2004	0u	50u
Two Side-by-Side Layers of 2003 E&P:		
2003 layer #1	50u	2.5u
2003 layer #2	25u	2.5u
	575u	

Example 2. (i) *Facts.* (A) On December 31, 2006, foreign corporations A and B have the following earnings and profits and foreign income taxes:

Foreign Corporation A	E&P	Foreign Taxes
Post-1986 pool	1,000u	$350
2004	100u	20u
2003	(50u)	5u
	1,050u	

Foreign Corporation B	E&P	Foreign Taxes
2006	100u	20u
2005	(50u)	5u
2004	0u	50u
2003	100u	10u
	150u	85u

(B) On January 1, 2007, foreign corporation B acquires the assets of foreign corporation A in a reorganization described in section 368(a)(1)(C). Immediately following the foreign section 381 transaction, foreign surviving corporation is a CFC.

(ii) *Result.* Because foreign corporations A and B have aggregate positive amounts of pre-1987 accumulated profits with a deficit in one or more years, the rules of paragraph (e)(1)(iii)(B) of this section apply. Accordingly, after the foreign section 381 transaction, foreign surviving corporation has the following earnings and profits and foreign income taxes:

	Earnings & Profits:		Foreign Taxes:	
	Positive E&P	Deficit E&P	Foreign Taxes Available	Foreign Taxes Associated with Deficit E&P
Post-1986 pool	1,000u		$350	
2006	100u		20u	
2005		(50u)		5u
Two Side-by-Side Layers of 2004 E&P:				
2004 layer #1 (from Corp A)	100u		20u	
2004 layer #2 (from Corp B)	0u		50u	
Two Side-by-Side Layers of 2003 E&P:				
2003 layer #1 (from Corp A)		(50u)		5u
2003 layer #2 (from Corp B)	100u		10u	
	1,300u	(100u)		10u

(iii) *Post-transaction distribution.* (A) During 2007, foreign surviving corporation does not accumulate any earnings and profits or pay or accrue any foreign income taxes. On December 31, 2007, foreign surviving corporation distributes 1,175u to its shareholders.

Under the rules described in paragraphs (c)(1) and (e)(1)(iii)(B) of this section, the distribution is first out of the post-1986 pool, and then out of the pre-pooling annual layers, as follows:

Distribution	E&P	Foreign Taxes
Post-1986 pool	1,000u	$350
2006	100u	20u
2005	0u	0u
Two Side-by-Side Layers of 2004 E&P:		
2004 layer #1	50u	20u
2004 layer #2	0u	0u
Two Side-by-Side Layers of 2003 E&P:		
2003 layer #1	0u	0u
2003 layer #2	25u	5u
	1,175u	

(B) Under paragraph (e)(1)(iii)(B) of this section, the rules otherwise applicable when a foreign corporation has an aggregate positive (or zero) amount of pre-1987 accumulated profits, but a deficit in one or more years, apply separately to the pre-1987 accumulated profits and related foreign income taxes of foreign corporation A and foreign corporation B. As a result, distributions out of the pre-pooling annual layers of foreign corporation A and foreign corporation B cannot exceed the aggregate positive amount of pre-1987 accumulated profits of each corporation. Accordingly, only 50u can be distributed from foreign corporation A's pre-pooling annual layers and is out of its 2004 layer #1 (after rolling forward the (50u) deficit in 2003 layer #1 to reduce earnings in 2004 layer #1 to 50u (100u - 50u)). Under the principles of §1.902-1(b)(3), the full 20u of taxes related to 2004 layer #1 is reduced or deemed paid ($20 ×

(50/50)). 100u is distributed from foreign corporation B's 2006 annual layer. Foreign corporation B's (50u) deficit in 2005 is then rolled back to offset its 2003 annual layer to reduce earnings in that layer to 50u, 25u of which is distributed. Thus, after the distribution, 25u remains in 2003 layer # 2 along with 5u of foreign income taxes (10u × (25u / 50u)).

(C) The foreign income taxes deemed paid by qualifying shareholders of foreign surviving corporation upon the distribution are subject to generally applicable rules and limitations, such as those of sections 78, 902, and 904(d).

(D) Immediately after the distribution, foreign surviving corporation has the following earnings and profits and foreign income taxes:

	E&P	Foreign Taxes
2005	0u	5u
2004 layer #2	0u	50u
Two Side-by-Side Layers of 2003 E&P:		
2003 layer #1	0u	5u
2003 layer #2	25u	5u
	25u	65u

(E) Under paragraph (e)(1)(iii)(B) of this section, the 5u, 50u, and 5u of pre-1987 foreign income taxes related to foreign surviving corporation's 2005 layer, 2004 layer #2, and 2003 layer #1, respectively, remain in those layers. These foreign income taxes generally will not be reduced or deemed paid unless a foreign tax refund restores a positive balance to the associated earnings pursuant to section 905(c), and thus will be trapped. See § 1.902-2(b)(2).

Example 3. (i) *Facts.* (A) On December 31, 2006, foreign corporations A and B have the following earnings and profits and foreign income taxes:

Foreign Corporation A

	E&P	Foreign Taxes
Post-1986 pool	1,000u	$350
2004	150u	20u
2003	100u	5u
	1,250u	

Foreign Corporation B

	E&P	Foreign Taxes
2006	100u	20u
2005	(250u)	5u
2004	0u	50u
2003	100u	10u
	(50u)	85u

(B) On January 1, 2007, foreign corporation B acquires the assets of foreign corporation A in a reorganization described in section 368(a)(1)(C). Immediately following the foreign section 381 transaction, foreign surviving corporation is a CFC.

(ii) *Result.* (A) Because foreign corporation B has an aggregate hovering deficit in pre-1987 accumulated profits, the rules of paragraph (e)(1)(iii)(C) of this section apply. Accordingly, § 1.902-2(b) graph (e)(1)(iii)(C) of this section apply. Accordingly, § 1.902-2(b)

applies immediately prior to the foreign section 381 transaction, except that the hovering deficit is carried forward into the foreign surviving corporation's post-1986 undistributed earnings pool and will offset only post-transaction earnings accumulated by foreign surviving corporation in the general category. Accordingly, after the foreign section 381 transaction, foreign surviving corporation has the following earnings and profits and foreign income taxes:

	Earnings & Profits:		Foreign Taxes:	
	Positive E&P	Hovering Deficit	Foreign Taxes Available	Foreign Taxes Associated with Hovering Deficit
Post-1986 pool	1,000u	(50u)	$350	$0
2006	0u		20u	
2005	0u		5u	
Two Side-by-Side Layers of 2004 E&P:				
2004 layer #1 (from Corp A)	150u		20u	
2004 layer #2 (from Corp B)	0u		50u	
Two Side-by-Side Layers of 2003 E&P:				
2003 layer #1 (from Corp A)	100u		5u	
2003 layer #2 (from Corp B)	0u		10u	
	1,250u	(50u)		$0

(B) Under paragraph (e)(1)(iii)(C) of this section, the 20u, 5u, 50u, and 10u of pre-1987 foreign income taxes associated with foreign corporation B's pre-1987 accumulated profits for 2006, 2005, 2004 layer #2, and 2003 layer #2, respectively, remain in those layers. These foreign income taxes generally will not be reduced or deemed paid unless a foreign tax refund restores a positive balance to the associated earnings pursuant to section 905(c), and thus will be trapped. See § 1.902-2(b)(2).

(2) *If foreign surviving corporation is a nonpooling corporation.*—If the foreign surviving corporation is a nonpooling corporation, then the pre-pooling annual layers shall be determined under the rules of this paragraph (e)(2).

(i) *Qualifying earnings and taxes.*—The pre-pooling annual layers shall consist of the pre-1987 accumulated profits and the pre-1987 foreign income taxes of the foreign acquiring corporation and the foreign target corporation. If the foreign acquiring corporation or the foreign target corporation (or both) has post-1986 undistributed earnings or a deficit in post-1986 undistributed earnings, then those earnings or deficits and any related post-1986 foreign income taxes shall be recharacterized as pre-1987 accumulated profits or deficits and pre-1987 foreign income taxes of the foreign acquiring corporation or the foreign target corporation accumulated immediately prior to the foreign section 381 transaction.

(ii) *Carryover rule.*—Subject to paragraph (e)(2)(iii) of this section, the amounts described in paragraph (e)(2)(i) of this section shall carry over to the foreign surviving corporation but shall not be combined. If the foreign acquiring corporation and the foreign target corporation have pre-1987 accumulated profits in the same year and a distribution is made therefrom, the principles of § 1.902-1(b)(2)(ii) and (3) shall apply separately to reduce pre-1987 accumulated profits

and pre-1987 foreign income taxes of the foreign acquiring corporation and the foreign target corporation on a pro rata basis. For further guidance, see Rev. Rul. 68-351 (1968-2 C.B. 307); Rev. Rul. 70-373 (1970-2 C.B. 152) (see also § 601.601(d)(2) of this chapter); see also paragraph (f)(2) of this section (governing the reconciliation of taxable years).

(iii) *Deficits.*—(A) *In general.*—The rules of this paragraph (e)(2)(iii) apply when, immediately prior to the foreign section 381 transaction (and after application of the last sentence of paragraph (e)(2)(i) of this section), the foreign acquiring corporation or the foreign target corporation (or both) has a deficit in one or more years that comprise its pre-1987 accumulated profits. See also paragraphs (f)(1) and (4) of this section (describing other rules applicable to a deficit described in this paragraph (e)(2)(iii)).

(B) *Aggregate positive pre-1987 accumulated profits.*—If the foreign acquiring corporation or the foreign target corporation (or both) has an aggregate positive (or zero) amount of pre-1987 accumulated profits, but a deficit in pre-1987 accumulated profits in one or more years, then the rules otherwise applicable to such deficits shall apply separately to the pre-1987 accumulated profits and related foreign income taxes of such corporation. A deficit in pre-1987 accumulated profits for one or more years is applied to reduce pre-1987 accumulated profits on a LIFO basis. Any remaining deficit shall be applied to reduce pre-1987 accumulated profits in succeeding years. See Rev. Rul. 74-550 (1974-2 C.B. 209) (see also § 601.601(d)(2) of this chapter); *Champion Int'l Corp. v. Commissioner,* 81 T.C. 424 (1983), acq. in result, 1987-2 C.B. 1; Rev. Rul. 87-72 (1987-2 C.B. 170) (see also § 601.601(d)(2) of this chapter). As a result, no amount in excess of the aggregate positive amount of pre-1987 accumulated profits shall be distributed from the pre-transaction earnings of the foreign acquiring corporation or the foreign target corporation.

(C) *Aggregate deficit in pre-1987 accumulated profits.*—If the foreign acquiring corporation or the foreign target corporation (or both) has an aggregate deficit in pre-1987 accumulated profits, a hovering deficit as defined under paragraph (d)(2)(i) of this section, then the rules otherwise applicable to such hovering deficits shall apply separately to the pre-transaction earnings and profits and related taxes of the relevant corporation. See, e.g., sections 316(a) and 381(c)(2)(B). Thus, any hovering deficit shall offset only post-transaction earnings accumulated by the foreign surviving corporation in the same separate category of earnings and profits to which the relevant portion of the hovering deficit is attributable. Post-transaction earnings do not include earnings and profits that are earned after the foreign section 381 transaction but distributed or deemed distributed in the same year they are earned. Following the principles of § 1.902-2(b), if there is an aggregate deficit in pre-1987 accumulated profits, any related pre-1987 foreign income taxes generally will not be reduced or deemed paid unless a foreign tax refund restores a positive balance to the associated earnings pursuant to section 905(c), and creates a pre-transaction aggregate positive balance for pre-1987 accumulated profits.

(D) *Deficit and positive separate categories within annual layers.*—For purposes of applying the rules of paragraphs (e)(2)(iii)(B) and (C) of this section, if within a single pre-pooling annual layer, the foreign acquiring corporation or the foreign target corporation (or both) has a deficit in pre-1987 accumulated profits in a separate category and positive pre-1987 accumulated profits in another separate category, the deficit shall first be used to offset the positive pre-1987 accumulated profits in the other separate category in the same pre-pooling annual layer. Any remaining deficit shall be carried forward or back to other years according to the rules of paragraph (e)(2)(iii)(B) or (C) as applicable.

Foreign Corporation A

	E&P	Foreign Taxes
2006	500u	350u
2005	400u	300u
2004	400u	160u
2003	100u	5u
	1,400u	815u

Foreign Corporation B

	E&P	Foreign Taxes
2006	100u	20u
2005	300u	60u
2004	0u	50u
2003	50u	5u
	450u	135u

(B) On January 1, 2007, foreign corporation B acquires the assets of foreign corporation A in a reorganization described in section 368(a)(1)(C). Immediately following the foreign section 381 transaction, foreign surviving corporation is a nonpooling corporation that does not meet the requirements of section 902(c)(3)(B).

	E&P	Foreign Taxes
Two Side-by-Side Layers of 2006 E&P:		
2006 layer #1 (from Corp A)	500u	350u
2006 layer #2 (from Corp B)	100u	20u
Two Side-by-Side Layers of 2005 E&P:		
2005 layer #1 (from Corp A)	400u	300u
2005 layer #2 (from Corp B)	300u	60u
Two Side-by-Side Layers of 2004 E&P:		
2004 layer #1 (from Corp A)	400u	160u
2004 layer #2 (from Corp B)	0u	50u
Two Side-by-Side Layers of 2003 E&P:		
2003 layer #1 (from Corp A)	100u	5u
2003 layer #2 (from Corp B)	50u	5u
	1,850u	950u

(iii) *Post-transaction distribution.* (A) During 2007, foreign surviving corporation does not accumulate any earnings and profits or pay or accrue any foreign income taxes. On December 31, 2007,

	E&P	Foreign Taxes
Two Side-by-Side Layers of 2006 E&P:		
2006 layer #1 (from Corp A)	500u	350u
2006 layer #2 (from Corp B)	100u	20u
	600u	370u

(B) Foreign surviving corporation's foreign income tax accounts are reduced to reflect the distribution of earnings and profits notwithstanding that no shareholders are eligible to claim deemed paid foreign income taxes under section 902. See § 1.902-1(a)(10)(iii).

	E&P	Foreign Taxes
Two Side-by-Side Layers of 2005 E&P:		
2005 layer #1 (from Corp A)	400u	300u
2005 layer #2 (from Corp B)	300u	60u

(iv) *Pre-1987 section 960 earnings and profits and foreign income taxes.*—The pre-1987 section 960 earnings and profits and pre-1987 section 960 foreign income taxes of the foreign acquiring corporation and the foreign target corporation shall carry over to the foreign surviving corporation but shall not be combined. The rules otherwise applicable to such amounts shall apply separately to the pre-1987 section 960 earnings and profits and pre-1987 section 960 foreign income taxes of the foreign acquiring corporation and the foreign target corporation on a pro rata basis. For further guidance, see Notice 88-70 (1988-2 C.B. 369) (see also § 601.601(d)(2) of this chapter).

(v) *Examples.*—The following examples illustrate the rules of this paragraph (e)(2). The examples assume the following facts: both foreign corporation A and foreign corporation B have always had calendar taxable years. Foreign corporations A and B (and all of their respective qualified business units as defined in section 989) maintain a "u" functional currency, and 1u = US$1 at all times. Finally, unless otherwise stated, all earnings and profits of foreign corporations A and B are in the general category. The examples are as follows:

Example 1. (i) *Facts.* (A) Foreign corporations A and B both were incorporated in 2003. Nine percent of the voting stock of foreign corporation A is owned by domestic corporate shareholder C. Nine percent of the voting stock of foreign corporation B is owned by domestic corporate shareholder D. Shareholders C and D are unrelated. The remaining 91% of the voting stock of each foreign corporation is owned by unrelated foreign shareholders. Thus, neither corporation meets the requirements of section 902(c)(3)(B). On December 31, 2006, foreign corporations A and B have the following earnings and profits and foreign income taxes:

(ii) *Result.* Under the rules described in paragraphs (e)(2)(i) and (ii) of this section, foreign surviving corporation has the following earnings and profits and foreign income taxes:

foreign surviving corporation distributes 600u to its shareholders. Under the rules of paragraph (c)(3) of this section, the distribution is out of pre-pooling annual layers under the LIFO method as follows:

(C) Immediately after the distribution, foreign surviving corporation has the following earnings and profits and foreign income taxes:

	E&P	Foreign Taxes
Two Side-by-Side Layers of 2004 E&P:		
2004 layer #1 (from Corp A)	400u	160u
2004 layer #2 (from Corp B)	0u	50u
Two Side-by-Side Layers of 2003 E&P:		
2003 layer #1 (from Corp A)	100u	5u
2003 layer #2 (from Corp B)	50u	5u
	1,250u	580u

Example 2. (i) *Facts.* (A) The facts are the same as in *Example 1* (i)(A), except that foreign corporation A met the requirements of section 902(c)(3)(B) on January 1, 2005, when U.S. corporate shareholder C acquired an additional 1% of voting stock for a total ownership interest of 10%; foreign corporation A thereby became a pooling corporation. On December 31, 2006, foreign corporations A and B have the following earnings and profits and foreign income taxes:

Foreign Corporation A

	E&P	Foreign Taxes
Post-1986 pool	900u	$650
2004	400u	160u
2003	100u	5u
	1,400u	

Foreign Corporation B

	E&P	Foreign Taxes
2006	100u	20u
2005	300u	60u
2004	0u	50u
2003	50u	5u
	450u	135u

(B) On January 1, 2007, foreign corporation B acquires the assets of foreign corporation A in a reorganization described in section 368(a)(1)(C). Immediately following the foreign section 381 transaction, foreign surviving corporation is a nonpooling corporation that does not meet the requirements of section 902(c)(3)(B).

(ii) *Result.* Under the rules described in paragraphs (e)(2)(i) and (ii) of this section, foreign surviving corporation has the following earnings and profits and foreign income taxes:

	E&P	Foreign Taxes
Two Side-by-Side Layers of 2006 E&P:		
2006 layer #1 (from Corp A's pool)	900u	$650
2006 layer #2 (from Corp B's layer)	100u	20u
2005 (from Corp B)	300u	60u
Two Side-by-Side Layers of 2004 E&P:		
2004 layer #1 (from Corp A)	400u	160u
2004 layer #2 (from Corp B)	0u	50u
Two Side-by-Side Layers of 2003 E&P:		
2003 layer #1 (from Corp A)	100u	5u
2003 layer #2 (from Corp B)	50u	5u
	1,850u	

(iii) *Subsequent ownership change.* On July 1, 2010, USS (a domestic corporation) acquires 100% of the stock of foreign surviving corporation. Under the rules of paragraph (f)(3) of this section, foreign surviving corporation begins to pool its earnings and profits under section 902(c)(3) as of January 1, 2010. Foreign surviving corporation's earnings and profits and foreign income taxes accrued before January 1, 2010 retain their character as pre-1987 accumulated profits and pre-1987 foreign income taxes.

Example 3. (i) *Facts.* (A) The facts are the same as in *Example 2* (i)(A), except that on December 31, 2006, foreign corporations A and B have the following earnings and profits and foreign income taxes:

Foreign Corporation A

	E&P	Foreign Taxes
Post-1986 pool	1,000u	$500
2004	(200u)	10u
2003	400u	5u
	1,200u	

Foreign Corporation B

	E&P	Foreign Taxes
2006	300u	20u
2005	(100u)	60u
2004	0u	50u
2003	50u	5u
	250u	135u

(B) On January 1, 2007, foreign corporation B acquires the assets of foreign corporation A in a reorganization described in section 368(a)(1)(C). Immediately following the foreign section 381 transaction, foreign surviving corporation is a nonpooling corporation that does not meet the requirements of section 902(c)(3)(B).

(ii) *Result.* Because foreign corporations A and B have aggregate positive amounts of pre-1987 accumulated profits with a deficit in one or more years, the rules of paragraph (e)(2)(iii)(B) of this section apply. Accordingly, after the foreign section 381 transaction, foreign surviving corporation has the following earnings and profits and foreign income taxes:

	Earnings & Profits:		Foreign Taxes:	
	Positive E&P	Deficit E&P	Foreign Taxes Available	Foreign Taxes Associated with Deficit E&P
Two Side-by-Side Layers of 2006 E&P:				
2006 layer #1 (from Corp A's pool)	1,000u		$500	
2006 layer #2 (from Corp B's layer)	300u		20u	
2005 (from Corp B)		(100u)		60u
Two Side-by-Side Layers of 2004 E&P:				
2004 layer #1 (from Corp A)		(200u)		10u
2004 layer #2 (from Corp B)	0u		50u	
Two Side-by-Side Layers of 2003 E&P:				

	Earnings & Profits:		Foreign Taxes:	
	Positive E&P	Deficit E&P	Foreign Taxes Available	Foreign Taxes Associated with Deficit E&P
2003 layer #1 (from Corp A)	400u		5u	
2003 layer #2 (from Corp B)	50u		5u	
	1,750u	(300u)		70u

(iii) *Post-transaction distribution.* (A) During 2007, foreign surviving corporation does not accumulate any earnings and profits or pay or accrue any foreign income taxes. On December 31, 2007, foreign surviving corporation distributes 1,300u to its shareholders.

	E&P	Foreign Taxes
Two Side-by-Side Layers of 2006 E&P:		
2006 layer #1	1,000u	$500
2006 layer #2	250u	20u
2003 E&P:		
2003 layer #1	50u	1.25u (25% of 5u taxes)
	1,300u	

Under the rules described in paragraphs (c)(3) and (e)(2)(iii)(B) of this section, the distribution is out of the pre-pooling annual layers, as follows:

(B) Under paragraph (e)(2)(iii)(B) of this section, the rules otherwise applicable when a foreign corporation has an aggregate positive (or zero) amount of pre-1987 accumulated profits, but a deficit in one or more years, apply separately to the pre-1987 accumulated profits and related pre-1987 foreign income taxes of foreign corporation A and foreign corporation B. As a result, distributions out of the pre-pooling annual layers of foreign corporation A and foreign corporation B cannot exceed the aggregate positive amount of pre-1987 accumulated profits of each corporation. Accordingly, only 1,200u and 250u can be distributed out of foreign corporation A's and foreign corporation B's pre-pooling annual layers, respectively. Thus, 1,000u of the distribution is out of foreign corporation A's 2006 layer #1 and 250u is out of foreign corporation B's 2006 layer #2. (after rolling forward (50u) of the deficit in 2005 layer to reduce earnings in 2006 layer #1 to 250u (300u - 50u)) Under the principles of

§ 1.902-1(b)(3), all of the taxes in each of those respective layers are reduced. The remaining 50u is distributed from foreign corporation A's 2003 layer #1 (after rolling back the (200u) deficit in 2004 layer #1 to reduce earnings in 2003 layer #1 to 200u (400u - 200u)). Thus, after the distribution, 150u remains in the 2003 layer #1 along with 3.75u of foreign income taxes (5u × (150u ÷ 200u)).

(C) Foreign surviving corporation's foreign income tax accounts are reduced to reflect the distribution of earnings and profits notwithstanding that no shareholders are eligible to claim a credit for deemed paid foreign income taxes under section 902. See § 1.902-1(a)(10)(iii).

(D) Immediately after the distribution, foreign surviving corporation has the following earnings and profits and foreign income taxes:

	E&P	Foreign Taxes
2005	0u	60u
Two Side-by-Side Layers of 2004 E&P:		
2004 layer #1	0u	10u
2004 layer #2	0u	50u
Two Side-by-Side Layers of 2003 E&P:		
2003 layer #1	150u	3.75u
2003 layer #2	0u	5u
	150u	128.75u

(E) Under paragraph (e)(2)(iii)(B) of this section, the 60u, 10u, 50u, and 5u of foreign income taxes related to foreign surviving corporation's 2005 layer, 2004 layer #1, 2004 layer #2, and 2003 layer #2, respectively, remain in those layers. These foreign income taxes generally will not be reduced or deemed paid unless a foreign tax

refund restores a positive balance to the associated earnings pursuant to section 905(c), and thus will be trapped. See § 1.902-2(b)(2).

Example 4. (i) *Facts.* (A) The facts are the same as in *Example 2* (i)(A), except that on December 31, 2006, foreign corporations A and B have the following earnings and profits and foreign income taxes:

Foreign Corporation A	E&P	Foreign Taxes
Post-1986 pool	(1,000u)	$20
2004	(200u)	10u
2003	400u	5u
	(800u)	

Foreign Corporation B	E&P	Foreign Taxes
2006	100u	20u
2005	300u	60u
2004	0u	50u
2003	50u	5u
	450u	135u

(B) On January 1, 2007, foreign corporation A acquires the assets of foreign corporation B in a reorganization described in section 368(a)(1)(C). Immediately following the foreign section 381 transaction, foreign surviving corporation is a nonpooling corporation.

(ii) *Result.* (A) Under paragraph (e)(2)(i) of this section, foreign corporation A's post-1986 pool is recharacterized as a 2006 layer of pre-1987 accumulated profits. Because after the foreign section 381 transaction foreign corporation A has an aggregate deficit in pre-1987

accumulated profits, the rules of paragraph (e)(2)(iii)(C) of this section apply and the rules otherwise applicable apply separately to the pre-1987 accumulated profits that carry over to foreign surviving corporation from foreign corporation A. The (800u) aggregate deficit in foreign corporation A's pre-1987 accumulated profits is a hovering deficit that will offset only post-transaction earnings accumulated by foreign surviving corporation in the general category. Accordingly, after the foreign section 381 transaction, foreign surviving corporation has the following earnings and profits and foreign income taxes:

	Earnings & Profits:		Foreign Taxes:	
	Positive E&P	Deficit E&P	Foreign Taxes Available	Foreign Taxes Associated with Deficit E&P
Hovering deficit from Corp A's annual layers		(800u)		0
Two Side-by-Side Layers of 2006 E&P:				
2006 layer #1 (from Corp A's pool)		0u		$20
2006 layer #2 (from Corp B's layer)	100u		20u	

	Earnings & Profits:		Foreign Taxes:	
	Positive E&P	Deficit E&P	Foreign Taxes Available	Foreign Taxes Associated with Deficit E&P
2005 (from Corp B)	300u		60u	
Two Side-by-Side Layers of 2004 E&P:				
2004 layer #1 (from Corp A)		0u		10u
2004 layer #2 (from Corp B)	0u		50u	
Two Side-by-Side Layers of 2003 E&P:				
2003 layer #1 (from Corp A)	0u		5u	
2003 layer #2 (from Corp B)	50u		5u	
	450u	(800u)	140u	

(B) Under paragraph (e)(2)(iii)(C) of this section, the $20, 10u, and 5u of pre-1987 foreign income taxes associated with foreign corporation A's pre-1987 accumulated profits for 2006 layer #1, 2004 layer #1, and 2003 layer #1, respectively, remain in those layers. These foreign income taxes generally will not be reduced or deemed paid unless a foreign tax refund restores a positive balance to the associated earnings pursuant to section 905(c), and thus will be trapped. See § 1.902-2(b)(2).

(iii) *Post-transaction distribution.* (A) During 2007, foreign surviving corporation does not accumulate any earnings and profits or pay or accrue any foreign income taxes. On December 31, 2007, foreign surviving corporation distributes 200u to its shareholders. Under the rules described in paragraph (e)(2)(iii)(C) of this section, no distribution can be made out of the pre-1987 accumulated profits of foreign corporation A (and the (800u) aggregate hovering deficit will offset only post-transaction earnings accumulated by foreign surviving corporation). Thus, the distribution is out of prepooling annual layers as follows:

	E&P	Foreign Taxes Paid
2006 layer #2	100u	20u
2005	100u	20u
	200u	40u

(B) Foreign surviving corporation's foreign income tax accounts are reduced to reflect the distribution of earnings and profits notwithstanding that no shareholders are eligible to claim deemed paid foreign income taxes under section 902. See § 1.902-1(a)(10)(iii).

(C) Immediately after the distribution, foreign surviving corporation has the following earnings and profits and foreign income taxes:

	Earnings & Profits:		Foreign Taxes:	
	Positive E&P	Deficit E&P	Foreign Taxes Available	Foreign Taxes Associated with Deficit E&P
Hovering deficit From Corp A's annual layers		(800u)		0
Two Side-by-Side Layers of 2006 E&P:				
2006 layer #1 (from Corp A's pool)		0u		$20
2006 layer #2 (from Corp B's layer)	0u		0u	
2005 (from Corp B)	200u		40u	
Two Side-by-Side Layers of 2004 E&P:				
2004 layer #1 (from Corp A)		0u		10u
2004 layer #2 (from Corp B)	0u		50u	
Two Side-by-Side Layers of 2003 E&P:				
2003 layer #1 (from Corp A)	0u		5u	
2003 layer #2 (from Corp B)	50u		5u	
	250u	(800u)	140u	

(f) *Special rules.*—(1) *Treatment of deficit.*—(i) *General rule.*—Any deficit described in paragraph (d)(2), (e)(1)(iii), or (e)(2)(iii) of this section shall not be taken into account in determining current or accumulated earnings and profits of a foreign surviving corporation other than to offset post-transaction accumulated earnings, as defined in paragraph (d)(2)(ii) of this section, including for purposes of calculating—

(A) The earnings and profits limitation of section 952(c)(1)(A); and

(B) the amount of the foreign surviving corporation's subpart F income as defined in section 952(a).

(ii) *Exceptions.*—The rule in paragraph (i) shall not apply for purposes of calculating an earnings and profits limitation under section 952(c)(1)(B) or (C).

(iii) *Examples.*—The following examples illustrate the principles of this paragraph (f)(1). The examples assume the following facts: foreign corporation A, incorporated in 2002, is and always has been a wholly owned subsidiary of USP, a domestic corporation.

Foreign Corporation A
Separate Category

	E&P	Foreign Taxes
General	(100u)	$25

Foreign Corporation
B Separate Category

	E&P	Foreign Taxes
General	0u	$10

(B) On January 1, 2008, foreign corporation B elects under § 301.7701-3(c) of this chapter to be disregarded as an entity separate from foreign corporation A. Accordingly, foreign corporation B is deemed to have distributed all its property to foreign corporation A in a liquidation described in section 332.

Foreign corporation B, incorporated in 2004, is and always has been a wholly owned subsidiary of foreign corporation A. Both foreign corporation A and foreign corporation B are organized under the laws of foreign country X and have always had a calendar taxable year. Foreign corporations A and B (and all of their respective qualified business units as defined in section 989) maintain a "u" functional currency. Unless otherwise stated, any earnings and profits or deficit in earnings and profits of foreign corporation A and B in the general category are attributable to subpart F income derived from foreign base company sales income. Foreign corporation C is a wholly owned subsidiary of USP2 and was organized in 2004 under the laws of foreign country Y. Foreign corporation C (and all of its qualified business units as defined in section 989) maintains a "u" functional currency. Earnings and profits of foreign corporation C in the general category are not attributable to subpart F income. The examples are as follows:

Example 1. (i) *Facts.* (A) On December 31, 2007, foreign corporations A and B have the following post-1986 undistributed earnings and post-1986 foreign income taxes:

(ii) *Result.* Under the rules described in paragraphs (d)(1) and (2) of this section, foreign surviving corporation A has the following post-1986 undistributed earnings and post-1986 foreign income taxes:

		Earnings & Profits:		Foreign Taxes:	
Separate Category	Positive E&P	Hovering Deficit		Foreign Taxes Available	Foreign Taxes Associated with Hovering Deficit
General	0u	(100u)		$10	$25

(iii) *Post-transaction earnings and subpart F limitations.* (A) In its taxable year ending on December 31, 2008, foreign surviving corporation A earns 300u of subpart F general category income with respect to which it pays $50 in foreign income taxes. The hovering deficit of (100u) meets the requirements under section 952(c)(1)(B) and therefore is taken into account as a qualified deficit that may be used by USP to offset a portion of its income inclusion related to foreign surviving corporation A's subpart F income of 300u in the 2008 taxable year. Accordingly, USP includes 200u in taxable income for the year and is eligible for a deemed paid foreign tax credit under section 960 of $40 (200u subpart F inclusion / 300 post-1986 undistributed earnings in the general category = 66.67%, × $60 foreign income taxes in the general category = $40). USP will also include the deemed paid foreign taxes of $40 in taxable income for the year as a

deemed dividend pursuant to section 78. The 100u offset under section 952(c)(1)(B) does not result in a reduction of the hovering deficit for purposes of section 316 or section 902.

(B) Foreign surviving corporation A's 100u of subpart F income not included in income by USP will accumulate and be added to its post-1986 undistributed earnings as of the beginning of 2009. This 100u of post-transaction earnings will be offset by the (100u) hovering deficit. Because the amount of earnings offset by the hovering deficit is 100% of the total amount of the hovering deficit, all $25 of the related taxes are added to the post-1986 foreign income taxes pool as well. Accordingly, foreign surviving corporation A has the following post-1986 undistributed earnings and post-1986 foreign income taxes on January 1, 2009:

	Earnings & Profits:	
	Positive E&P	Hovering Deficit
Separate Category		
General	0u	(0u)

(C) The 200u included as subpart F income constitutes previously taxed earnings under section 959.

Example 2. (i) *Facts.* (A) On July 1, 2007, foreign corporation B elects under § 301.7701-3(c) of this chapter to be disregarded as an entity separate from foreign corporation A. Accordingly, foreign corporation B is deemed to have distributed all of its property to foreign corporation A in a liquidation described in section 332.

(B) Neither foreign corporation A nor B has any post-1986 undistributed earnings or post-1986 foreign income taxes as of the beginning of the 2007 taxable year. For its short taxable year ending on June 30, 2007, foreign corporation B has the following post-1986 undistributed earnings and post-1986 foreign income taxes:

Foreign Corporation B Separate Category	E&P	Foreign Taxes
General	(200u)	$30

(C) For the 2007 taxable year, foreign surviving corporation A earns a total of 200u of subpart F foreign based company sales income in the general category with respect to which it pays $40 in foreign income taxes.

(ii) *Result.* (A) Under paragraph (d)(2) of this section, foreign corporation B's (200u) deficit carries over to foreign surviving corporation A as a hovering deficit. Nevertheless, because it is a deficit of a qualified chain member for a taxable year ending within the 2007 taxable year of foreign surviving corporation A, the (200u) deficit meets the requirements under section 952(c)(1)(C) and therefore may still be taken into account for purposes of limiting foreign surviving corporation A's subpart F income. Accordingly, foreign surviving corporation A's 200u of subpart F income for the 2007 taxable year is fully offset by the (200u) deficit of foreign corporation B, and USP will have no subpart F income inclusion for the 2007 taxable year. The offset under section 952(c)(1)(C) does not result in a reduction of the hovering deficit for purposes of section 316 or section 902. The hovering deficit may not also be taken into account under section 952(c)(1)(B).

(B) Because USP has no subpart F income inclusion, foreign surviving corporation A's subpart F earnings of 200u will accumulate and be added to its post-1986 undistributed earnings as of the beginning of 2008. Under the rules of paragraph (f)(5) of this section, a pro rata amount, in this case 50% or 100u, will be deemed to have been accumulated prior to the foreign section 381 transaction and the other 50%, or 100u, will be deemed to have been accumulated after the foreign section 381 transaction. The 100u of post-transaction earnings will be offset by (100u) of the hovering deficit for purposes of determining the opening balance of the post-1986 undistributed earnings pool in 2008. Because the amount of earnings offset by the hovering deficit is 50% of the total amount of the hovering deficit, $15 (50% of $30) of the related taxes are added to the post-1986 foreign income taxes pool as well. The 100u of pre-transaction earnings remain in the post-1986 undistributed earnings pool. Accordingly, foreign surviving corporation A has the following post-1986 undistributed earnings and post-1986 foreign income taxes on January 1, 2008:

		Earnings & Profits:		Foreign Taxes:	
Separate Category	Positive E&P	Hovering Deficit		Foreign Taxes Available	Foreign Taxes Associated with Hovering Deficit
General	100u	(100u)		$55	$15

Example 3. (i) *Facts.* (A) On January 1, 2007, foreign corporation B and foreign corporation C have the following post-1986 undistributed earnings and post-1986 foreign income taxes:

Foreign Corporation B Separate Category	E&P	Foreign Taxes
General	(100u)	$0

Foreign Corporation C Separate Category	E&P	Foreign Taxes
General	0u	$10

(B) On July 1, 2007, foreign corporation B acquires the assets of foreign corporation C in a reorganization described in section 368(a)(1)(C). Immediately following the foreign section 381 transaction, foreign surviving corporation B is a CFC.

(C) During the 2007 taxable year foreign surviving corporation B has a current deficit of (400u) and $60 of related foreign income taxes. During its short taxable year ending on June 30, 2007, foreign

corporation C has no additional earnings and pays or accrues no foreign income taxes.

(ii) *Result.* (A) Under the rules of paragraph (f)(5) of this section, a pro rata amount, in this case 50% or (200u), of foreign surviving corporation B's (400u) current year deficit for the 2007 taxable year will be deemed to have been accumulated prior to the foreign section 381 transaction and be treated as a hovering deficit.

Reg. § 1.367(b)-7(f)(1)(iii)

The other 50%, or (200u) of the deficit will be deemed to have been accumulated after the foreign section 381 transaction. The related foreign income taxes of $60 will also be allocated on a similar 50/50 basis.

Separate Category	Positive E&P (200u)
General	(200u)

(iii) *Subpart F income limitations.* Even though (200u) of the current year deficit is treated as a hovering deficit, the full (400u) current year deficit in 2007 of foreign surviving corporation B meets the requirements under section 952(c)(1)(C) and therefore is available as a limitation on subpart F income, to the extent foreign corporation A, which wholly owns foreign surviving corporation B, earns any subpart F income in the 2007 taxable year. Any such offset under section 952(c)(1)(C) will have no effect on the earnings and profits and foreign income tax accounts above of foreign surviving corporation B for purposes of sections 316 and 902. Moreover, to the extent the hovering deficit reduces subpart F income under section 952(c)(1)(C), it may not also be taken into account under section 952(c)(1)(B).

(2) *Reconciling taxable years.*—If a foreign acquiring corporation and a foreign target corporation had taxable years ending on different dates, then the pro rata distribution rules of paragraphs (e)(1)(ii) and (e)(2)(ii) of this section shall apply with respect to the taxable years that end within the same calendar year.

(3) *Post-transaction change of status.*—If a foreign surviving corporation that is subject to the rules of paragraph (c)(2) of this section subsequently becomes a pooling corporation (by reason, for example, of a reorganization, liquidation, or change of ownership), then post-1986 undistributed earnings and post-1986 foreign income taxes that were recharacterized as pre-1987 accumulated profits and pre-1987 foreign income taxes, respectively, under paragraph (e)(2)(i)

Foreign Corporation A
Post-1986 Pool Separate Category:

	E&P	Foreign Taxes
Passive	400u	$160
General	(300u)	$ 25
	100u	$185

Foreign Corporation B

	E&P	Foreign Taxes
2006	(300u)	50u
2005	100u	25u
	(200u)	75u

(B) On January 1, 2007, foreign corporation B acquires the assets of foreign corporation A in a reorganization described in section 368(a)(1)(C). Immediately following the foreign section 381 transaction, foreign surviving corporation is a CFC.

(iii) *Post-transaction earnings.* (A) In the taxable year ending on December 31, 2007, foreign surviving corporation accumulates earnings and profits and pays related foreign income taxes as follows:

Post-1986 Pool Separate Category

	E&P	Foreign Taxes
Passive	150u	$ 40
General	400u	$ 60
	550u	$100

(B) None of the earnings and profits qualify as subpart F income as defined in section 952(a). Under paragraph (f)(4)(i) of this section, the rules of paragraph (d)(2) of this section apply before the rules of paragraph (e)(1)(iii) of this section. Accordingly, post-transaction earnings in a separate category are first offset by a hovering deficit in the same separate category in the post-1986 pool. Thus,

(B) Under the rules described in paragraphs (d)(1) and (2) of this section, foreign surviving corporation B has the following post-1986 undistributed earnings and post-1986 foreign income taxes as of January 1, 2008:

	Earnings & Profits:		Foreign Taxes:	
Separate Category	Positive E&P	Hovering Deficit	Foreign Taxes Available	Foreign Taxes Associated with Hovering Deficit
General	(200u)	(300u)	$40	$30

of this section retain their characterization as a pre-pooling annual layer.

(4) *Ordering rule for multiple hovering deficits.*—(i) *Rule.*—A foreign surviving corporation shall apply the deficit rules of paragraphs (d)(2), (e)(1)(iii), and (e)(2)(iii) of this section in that order if more than one of such rules applies to the foreign surviving corporation.

(ii) *Example.*—The following example illustrates the principles of this paragraph (f)(4). The example assumes the following facts: foreign corporation A has been a pooling corporation since its incorporation on January 1, 1998. Foreign corporation B has been a nonpooling corporation since its incorporation on January 1, 2000. Foreign corporations A and B have always had calendar taxable years. Foreign corporations A and B (and all of their respective qualified business units as defined in section 989) maintain a "u" functional currency. All earnings and profits of foreign corporation B are in the general category. Finally, unless otherwise stated, any earnings and profits in the passive category resulted from a look-through dividend that was paid by a lower-tier CFC out of earnings accumulated when the CFC was a noncontrolled section 902 corporation and that qualified for the subpart F same-country exception under section 954(c)(3)(A). The example is as follows:

Example—(i) *Facts.* (A) On December 31, 2006, foreign corporations A and B have the following earnings and profits and foreign income taxes:

(ii) *Result.* Under the rules described in paragraphs (d)(1), (d)(2), (e)(1)(i), (e)(1)(ii), and (e)(1)(iii) of this section, foreign surviving corporation has the following earnings and profits and foreign income taxes:

	Earnings & Profits:		Foreign Taxes:	
Post-1986 Pool Separate Category	Positive E&P	Hovering Deficit	Foreign Taxes Available	Foreign Taxes Associated with Hovering Deficit
Passive	400u		$160	
General		(300u)		$25
Carryforward pre-pooling deficit from Corp B		(200u)		0
2006 (from Corp B)	0u		50u	
2005 (from Corp B)	0u		25u	
	400u	(500u)		$25

foreign surviving corporation's (300u) deficit in the general category offsets 300u of post-transaction earnings in the general category. After application of paragraph (d)(2) of this section, the (200u) deficit in the general category carried forward from foreign corporation B's pre-pooling aggregate deficit offsets the remaining 100u of post-transaction earnings in the general category. Accordingly, foreign surviving corporation has the following earnings and profits and foreign income taxes at the end of 2007:

Post-1986 Pool Separate Category	Positive E&P	Hovering Deficit	Foreign Taxes Available	Foreign Taxes Associated with Hovering Deficit
	Earnings & Profits:		Foreign Taxes:	
Passive	550u		$200	
General			$85	
Carryforward pre-pooling deficit from Corp B		(100u)		$0
2006 (from Corp B)	0u		50u	
2005 (from Corp B)	0u		25u	
	550u	(100u)		$0

(C) Under paragraph (d)(2)(iii) of this section, all of the $25 of post-1986 foreign income taxes related to the (300u) hovering deficit in the general category is added to the foreign surviving corporation's post-1986 foreign income taxes of $60 in that category (because post-transaction earnings in the general category have exceeded the deficit in that category). Under paragraph (e)(1)(iii)(C) of this section, the 50u and 25u of foreign income taxes associated with foreign corporation B's pre-1987 accumulated profits for 2006 and 2005 remain in those layers. These foreign income taxes generally will not be reduced or deemed paid unless a foreign tax refund restores a positive balance to the associated earnings pursuant to section 905(c), and thus will be trapped. See § 1.902-2(b)(2).

(5) *Pro rata rule for earnings and deficits during transaction year.*—(i) For purposes of offsetting post-transaction earnings of a foreign surviving corporation under the rules described in paragraphs (d)(2), (e)(1)(iii), and (e)(2)(iii) of this section, the earnings and profits, and any related foreign income taxes, in each separate category for the taxable year of the foreign surviving corporation in which the transaction occurs shall be deemed to have been accumulated after such transaction in an amount which bears the same ratio to the undistributed earnings and profits of the foreign surviving corporation for such taxable year (computed without regard to any earnings and profits carried over) as the number of days in the taxable year after the date of transaction bears to the total number of days in the taxable year. See, e.g., § 1.381(c)(2)-1(a)(7) *Example 2* (illustrating application of this rule with respect to domestic corporations).

(ii) For purposes of determining the amount of pre-transaction deficits described in paragraphs (d)(2), (e)(1)(iii), and (e)(2)(iii) of this section, of a foreign surviving corporation that has a deficit in earnings and profits in any separate category for its taxable year in which the transaction occurs, unless the actual accumulated earnings and profits, or deficit, as of such date can be shown, such pre-transaction deficit, and any related foreign income taxes, shall be deemed to have accumulated in a manner similar to that described in paragraph (f)(5)(i) of this section. See, e.g., § 1.381(c)(2)-1(a)(7) *Example 4* (illustrating application of this rule with respect to domestic corporations).

(g) *Post-2017 taxable years.*—As a result of the repeal of section 902 effective for taxable years of foreign corporations beginning on or after January 1, 2018, all foreign target corporations, foreign acquiring corporations, and foreign surviving corporations are treated as nonpooling corporations in post-2017 taxable years. Any amounts remaining in post-1986 undistributed earnings and post-1986 foreign income taxes of any such corporation in any separate category as of the end of the foreign corporation's last taxable year beginning before January 1, 2018, are treated as earnings and taxes in a single pre-pooling annual layer in the foreign corporation's post-2017 taxable years for purposes of this section. Foreign income taxes that are related to non-previously taxed earnings of a foreign acquiring corporation and a foreign target corporation that were accumulated in taxable years before the current taxable year of the foreign corporation, or in a foreign target's taxable year that ends on the date of the

section 381 transaction, are not treated as current year taxes (as defined in § 1.960-1(b)(4)) of a foreign surviving corporation in any post-2017 taxable year. In addition, foreign income taxes that are related to a hovering deficit are not treated as current year taxes of the foreign surviving corporation in any post-2017 taxable year, regardless of whether the hovering deficit is absorbed.

(h) *Applicability dates.*—Except as otherwise provided in this paragraph (h), this section applies to transactions in section 381 transactions that occur on or after November 6, 2006. Paragraph (g) of this section applies to taxable years of foreign corporations ending on or after November 2, 2020, and to taxable years of United States shareholders in which or with which such taxable years of foreign corporations end. [Reg. § 1.367(b)-7.]

☐ [*T.D.* 9273, 8-7-2006 (*corrected* 12-6-2006). *Amended by T.D.* 9959, 12-28-2021.]

[Reg. § 1.367(b)-8]

§1.367(b)-8. Allocation of earnings and profits and foreign income taxes in certain foreign corporate separation.—[Reserved]

☐ [*T.D.* 9273, 8-7-2006.]

[Reg. § 1.367(b)-9]

§1.367(b)-9. Special rule for F reorganizations and similar transactions.—(a) *Scope.*—This section applies to a foreign section 381 transaction (as defined in § 1.367(b)-7(a)) either—

(1) That is described in section 368(a)(1)(F); or

(2) That involves—

(i) At least one foreign corporation that holds no property and has no tax attributes immediately before the transaction, other than a nominal amount of assets (and related tax attributes) to facilitate its organization or preserve its existence as a corporation; and

(ii) No more than one foreign corporation that holds more than a nominal amount of property or has more than a nominal amount of tax attributes immediately before the transaction.

(b) *Hovering deficit rules inapplicable.*—If a transaction is described in paragraph (a) of this section, a foreign surviving corporation shall succeed to earnings and profits, deficits in earnings and profits, and foreign income taxes without regard to the hovering deficit rules of § 1.367(b)-7(d)(2), (e)(1)(iii), and (e)(2)(iii).

(c) *Foreign divisive transactions.*—[Reserved]

(d) *Examples.*—The following examples illustrate the principles of this section:

Example 1. (i) *Facts.* (A) Foreign corporation A is and always has been a wholly owned subsidiary of USP, a domestic corporation. Foreign corporation A was incorporated in 1995, and has always had a calendar taxable year. Foreign corporation A (and all of its respective qualified business units as defined in section 989) maintains a "u" functional currency. On December 31, 2006, foreign corporation A has the following post-1986 undistributed earnings and post-1986 foreign income taxes:

Separate Category	E&P	Foreign Taxes
Passive	(1,000u)	$5
General	200u	$200
	(800u)	$205

(B) On January 1, 2007, foreign corporation A moves its place of incorporation from Country 1 to Country 2 in a reorganization described in section 368(a)(1)(F).

(ii) *Result.* Under § 1.367(b)-7(d), as modified by paragraph (b) of this section, the pre-transaction deficit of foreign corporation A will not hover. Accordingly, foreign surviving corporation has the following post-1986 undistributed earnings and post-1986 foreign income taxes immediately after the foreign section 381 transaction:

Separate Category	E&P	Foreign Taxes
Passive	(1,000u)	$5
General	200u	$200
	(800u)	$205

Reg. § 1.367(b)-9(d)

Example 2. (i) *Facts.* (A) Foreign corporations B, C and D are and always have been wholly owned subsidiaries of USP, a domestic corporation. Foreign corporation B was incorporated in 2000 and foreign corporations C and D were incorporated in 2001. Foreign corporation B does not own any significant property and has no earnings and profits or foreign income taxes accounts. Both foreign corporations C and D have always had a calendar taxable year. Foreign corporations C and D (and all of their respective qualified business units as defined in section 989) maintain a "u" functional currency. On December 31, 2006, foreign corporations C and D have the following post-1986 undistributed earnings and post-1986 foreign income taxes:

Foreign corporation C

Separate Category	E&P	Foreign Taxes
Passive	(900u)	$ 50
General	(200u)	$100
	(1100u)	$150

Foreign corporation D

Separate Category	E&P	Foreign Taxes
Passive	1200u	$400
General	400u	$100
	1600u	$500

(B) On January 1, 2007, USP foreign corporations C and D merge into foreign corporation B in a reorganization described in section 368(a)(1)(A).

(ii) *Result.* Although the merger is a foreign section 381 transaction involving a foreign corporation with no property or tax attributes, paragraph (b) of this section does not apply because more than one foreign corporation with significant tax attributes is involved in the foreign section 381 transaction. Accordingly, under §1.367(b)-7(d), foreign surviving corporation B has the following post-1986 undistributed earnings and post-1986 foreign income taxes immediately after the foreign section 381 transaction:

	Earnings & Profits:		Foreign Taxes:	
Separate Category	Positive E&P	Hovering Deficit	Foreign Taxes Available	Foreign Taxes Associated with Hovering Deficit
General	1200u	(900u)	$400	$ 50
Passive	400u	(200u)	$100	$100
	1600u	(1100u)	$500	$150

(e) *Effective date.*—This section shall apply to section 367(b) transactions that occur on or after November 6, 2006. [Reg. §1.367(b)-9.]

☐ *[T.D. 9273, 8-7-2006.]*

[Reg. §1.367(b)-10]

§1.367(b)-10. Acquisition of parent stock or securities for property in triangular reorganizations.—(a) *In general.*—(1) *Scope.*—Except as provided in paragraphs (a)(2)(i) through (iii) of this section, this section applies to a triangular reorganization if P or S (or both) is a foreign corporation and, in connection with the reorganization, S acquires in exchange for property all or a portion of the P stock or P securities (P acquisition) that are used to acquire the stock, securities or property of T in the triangular reorganization. This section applies to a triangular reorganization regardless of whether P controls (within the meaning of section 368(c)) S at the time of the P acquisition.

(2) *Exceptions.*—This section shall not apply if —

(i) P and S are foreign corporations and neither P nor S is a controlled foreign corporation (within the meaning of §1.367(b)-2(a)) immediately before or immediately after the triangular reorganization;

(ii) S is a domestic corporation, P's stock in S is not a United States real property interest (within the meaning of section 897(c)), and P would not be subject to U.S. tax on a dividend (as determined under section 301(c)(1)) from S under either section 881 (for example, by reason of an applicable treaty) or section 882; or

(iii) In an exchange under section 354 or 356, one or more U.S. persons exchange stock or securities of T and the amount of gain in the T stock or securities recognized by such U.S. persons under section 367(a)(1) is equal to or greater than the sum of the amount of the deemed distribution that would be treated by P as a dividend under section 301(c)(1) and the amount of such deemed distribution that would be treated by P as gain from the sale or exchange of property under section 301(c)(3) if this section would otherwise apply to the triangular reorganization. See §1.367(a)-3(a)(2)(iv) (providing a similar rule that excludes certain transactions from the application of section 367(a)(1)).

(3) *Definitions.*—For purposes of this section, the following definitions apply:

(i) The terms *P, S,* and *T* have the meanings set forth in §1.358-6(b)(1)(i), (ii), and (iii), respectively.

(ii) The term *property* has the meaning set forth in section 317(a), except that the term property also includes —

(A) A liability assumed by S to acquire the P stock or securities; and

(B) S stock (or any rights to acquire S stock) to the extent such S stock (or rights to acquire S stock) is used by S to acquire P stock or securities from a person other than P.

(iii) The term *security* means an instrument that constitutes a security for purposes of section 354 or 356.

(iv) The term *triangular reorganization* has the meaning set forth in §1.358-6(b)(2).

(b) *General rules.*—(1) *Deemed distribution.*—If this section applies, adjustments shall be made that have the effect of a distribution of property (with no built-in gain or loss) from S to P under section 301 (deemed distribution). The amount of the deemed distribution shall equal the sum of the amount of money transferred by S, the amount of any liabilities that are assumed by S and constitute property, and the fair market value of other property transferred by S in the P acquisition in exchange for the P stock or P securities described in paragraph (i) or (ii), respectively, of this paragraph (b)(1)—

(i) P stock received by T shareholders or securityholders in an exchange to which section 354 or 356 applies.

(ii) P securities received by T shareholders or securityholders to the extent such securities are "other property" (within the meaning of section 356(d)).

(2) *Deemed contribution.*—If this section applies, adjustments shall be made that have the effect of a contribution of property (with no built-in gain or loss) by P to S in an amount equal to the amount of the deemed distribution from S to P under paragraph (b)(1) of this section (deemed contribution).

(3) *Timing of deemed distribution and deemed contribution.*—If P controls (within the meaning of section 368(c)) S at the time of the P acquisition, the adjustments described in paragraphs (b)(1) and (2) of this section shall be made as if the deemed distribution and deemed contribution, respectively, are separate transactions occurring immediately before the P acquisition. If P does not control (within the meaning of section 368(c)) S at the time of the P acquisition, the adjustments described in paragraphs (b)(1) and (2) of this section shall be made as if the deemed distribution and deemed contribution, respectively, are separate transactions occurring immediately after P acquires control of S, but prior to the triangular reorganization.

(4) *Application of other provisions.*—Nothing in this section shall prevent the application of other provisions of the Internal Revenue Code from applying to the P acquisition. For example, section 304

may apply to the P acquisition. Furthermore, section 1001 or 267 may apply to S's transfer of property to acquire P stock or securities from P or a person other than P. In addition, generally applicable provisions that apply to triangular reorganizations, such as §1.358-6 and §1.1032-2, shall apply to the triangular reorganization in a manner consistent with S acquiring the P stock or securities in exchange for property from P or a person other than P, as the case may be.

(5) *Example.*—The rules of this paragraph (b) are illustrated by the following example:

(i) *Facts.* P, a publicly traded domestic corporation, owns all of the outstanding stock of FS, a foreign corporation, and all of the outstanding stock of US1, a domestic corporation that is a member of the P consolidated group. US1 owns all of the outstanding stock of FT, a foreign corporation, the fair market value of which is $100x. US1's basis in the FT stock is $100x, such that there is a no built-in gain or loss in the FT stock. FS has earnings and profits in excess of $100x. FS purchases $100x of P stock from the public on the open market in exchange for $100x of cash. Pursuant to foreign law, FT merges with and into FS in a triangular reorganization that qualifies under section 368(a)(1)(A) by reason of section 368(a)(2)(D). In an exchange to which section 354 applies, US1 exchanges all the outstanding stock of FT for the $100x of P stock purchased by FS on the open market.

(ii) *Analysis.* The triangular reorganization is described in paragraph (a)(1) of this section. P is a domestic corporation and FS is a foreign corporation. In connection with FS purchasing the $100x of P stock in exchange for property (cash), FS uses the P stock to acquire the FT property in a triangular reorganization, and US1 receives the P stock in an exchange to which section 354 applies. Furthermore, none of the exceptions of paragraphs (a)(2)(i) through (iii) of this section apply. Therefore, pursuant to paragraph (b)(1) of this section, adjustments are made that have the effect of a deemed distribution of property (with no built-in gain or loss) in the amount of $100x from FS to P under section 301. Pursuant to paragraph (b)(2) of this section, adjustments are made that have the effect of a deemed contribution of property (with no built-in gain or loss) in the amount of $100x by P to FS. Pursuant to paragraph (b)(3) of this section, the adjustments described in paragraphs (b)(1) and (2) of this section are made as if the deemed distribution and deemed contribution, respectively, are separate transactions occurring immediately before FS's purchase of the P stock on the open market. Generally applicable provisions apply to FS's purchase of the P stock on the open market (see, for example, section 304) and in determining certain tax consequences to P and FS as a result of the triangular reorganization (see, for example, §1.358-6(d) and §1.1032-2(c)).

(c) *Collateral adjustments.*—This paragraph (c) provides additional rules that apply by reason of the deemed distribution and deemed contribution described in paragraphs (b)(1) and (b)(2), respectively, of this section.

(1) *Deemed distribution.*—A deemed distribution described in paragraph (b)(1) of this section shall be treated as occurring for all purposes of the Internal Revenue Code. Thus, for example, the ordering rules of section 301(c) apply to characterize the deemed distribution to P as a dividend from the earnings and profits of S, return of stock basis, or gain from the sale or exchange of property, as the case may be. Furthermore, section 959 may apply to the deemed distribution if S is a foreign corporation, and sections 881, 882, 897, 1442, or 1445 may apply to the deemed distribution if S is a domestic corporation. Appropriate corresponding adjustments shall be made to S's earnings and profits consistent with the principles of section 312.

(2) *Deemed contribution.*—A deemed contribution described in paragraph (b)(2) of this section shall be treated as occurring for all purposes of the Internal Revenue Code. Thus, for example, appropriate adjustments shall be made to P's basis in the S stock.

(d) *Anti-abuse rule.*—Appropriate adjustments shall be made pursuant to this section if, in connection with a triangular reorganization, a transaction is engaged in with a view to avoid the purpose of this section. For example, if S is created, organized, or funded to avoid the application of this section with respect to the earnings and profits of a corporation related (within the meaning of section 267(b)) to P or S, the earnings and profits of S will be deemed to include the earnings and profits of such related corporation for purposes of determining the consequences of the adjustments provided in this section, and appropriate corresponding adjustments will be made to account for the application of this section to the earnings and profits of such related corporation.

(e) *Applicability dates.*—This section applies to triangular reorganizations occurring on or after May 17, 2011. For triangular reorganizations that occur prior to May 17, 2011, see §1.367(b)-14T as contained in 26 CFR part 1 revised as of April 1, 2011. Paragraph (c)(1) of this section applies to deemed distributions that occur in taxable years ending on or after November 2, 2020. [Reg. §1.367(b)-10.]

☐ [*T.D. 9526, 5-17-2011. Amended by T.D. 9959, 12-28-2021.*]

[Reg. §1.367(b)-12]

§1.367(b)-12. Subsequent treatment of amounts attributed or included in income.—(a) *In general.*—This section applies to distributions with respect to, or a disposition of, stock—

(1) To which, in connection with an exchange occurring before February 23, 2000, an amount has been attributed pursuant to §7.367(b)-9 or 7.367(b)-10 of this chapter (as in effect prior to February 23, 2000, see 26 CFR part 1 revised as of April 1, 1999); or

(2) In respect of which, before February 23, 2000, an amount has been included in income or added to earnings and profits pursuant to §7.367(b)-7 or 7.367(b)-10 of this chapter (as in effect prior to February 23, 2000, see 26 CFR part 1 revised as of April 1, 1999).

(b) *Applicable rules.*—See §7.367(b)-12(b) through (e) of this chapter (as in effect prior to January 11, 2001, see 26 CFR part 1 revised as of April 1, 2000) for purposes of applying paragraph (a) of this section.

(c) *Effective date.*—This section applies to distributions or dispositions that occur on or after January 11, 2001. [Reg. §1.367(b)-12.]

☐ [*T.D. 8937, 1-10-2001.*]

[Reg. §1.367(b)-13]

§1.367(b)-13. Special rules for determining basis and holding period.—(a) *Scope and definitions.*—(1) *Scope.*—This section provides special basis and holding period rules to determine the basis and holding period of stock of certain foreign surviving corporations held by a controlling corporation whose stock is issued in an exchange under section 354 or 356 in a triangular reorganization. This section applies to transactions that are subject to section 367(b) as well as section 367(a), including transactions concurrently subject to sections 367(a) and (b).

(2) *Definitions.*—For purposes of this section, the following definitions apply:

(i) A block of stock has the meaning provided in §1.1248-2(b).

(ii) The terms *P*, *S*, and *T* have the meanings set forth in §1.358-6(b)(1)(i), (ii), and (iii), respectively.

(iii) A triangular reorganization is a reorganization described in §1.358-6(b)(2)(i), (ii), (iii), or (v) (a forward triangular merger, triangular C reorganization, reverse triangular merger, or triangular G reorganization, respectively).

(b) *Determination of basis for exchanges of foreign stock or securities under section 354 or 356.*—For rules determining the basis of stock or securities in a foreign corporation received in a section 354 or 356 exchange, see §1.358-2.

(c) *Determination of basis and holding period for triangular reorganizations.*—(1) *Application.*—In the case of a triangular reorganization described in paragraph (a)(2)(ii) of this section, this paragraph (c) applies, if—

(i)(A) Immediately before the transaction, either P is a section 1248 shareholder with respect to S, or P is a foreign corporation and a United States person is a section 1248 shareholder with respect to both P and S; and

(B) In the case of a reverse triangular merger, P's exchange of S stock is not described in §1.367(b)-3(a) and (b) or in §1.367(b)-4(b)(1)(i), (2)(i), or (3); or

(ii)(A) Immediately before the transaction, a shareholder of T is a section 1248 shareholder with respect to T, or a shareholder of T is a foreign corporation and a United States person is a section 1248 shareholder with respect to both such foreign corporation and T; and

(B) With respect to at least one of the exchanging shareholders described in paragraph (c)(1)(ii)(A) of this section, the exchange of T stock is not described in §1.367(b)-3(a) and (b) or in §1.367(b)-4(b)(1)(i), (2)(i), or (3).

(2) *Basis and holding period rules.*—In the case of a triangular reorganization described in paragraph (c)(1) of this section, each share of stock of the surviving corporation (S or T) held by P must be divided into portions attributable to the S stock and the T stock immediately before the exchange. See paragraph (e) of this section *Examples 1* through *4* for illustrations of this rule.

(i) *Portions attributable to S stock.*—(A) In the case of a forward triangular merger, a triangular C reorganization, or a triangular G reorganization, the basis and holding period of the portion of each share of surviving corporation stock attributable to the S stock is the basis and holding period of such share of stock immediately before the exchange.

(B) In the case of a reverse triangular merger, the basis and holding period of the portion of each share of surviving corporation stock attributable to the S stock is the basis and the holding period immediately before the exchange of a proportionate amount of the S stock to which the portion relates. If P is a shareholder described in paragraph (c)(1)(i)(A) of this section with respect to S, and P exchanges two or more blocks of S stock pursuant to the transaction, then each share of the surviving corporation (T) attributable to the S stock must be further divided into separate portions to account for the separate blocks of stock in S.

(C) If the value of S stock immediately before the triangular reorganization is less than one percent of the value of the surviving corporation stock immediately after the triangular reorganization, then P may determine its basis in the surviving corporation stock by applying the rules of paragraph (c)(2)(ii) of this section to determine the basis and holding period of the surviving corporation stock attributable to the T stock, and then increasing the basis of each share of surviving corporation stock by the proportionate amount of P's aggregate basis in the S stock immediately before the exchange (without dividing the stock of the surviving corporation into separate portions attributable to the S stock).

(ii) *Portions attributable to T stock.*—(A) If any exchanging shareholder of T stock is described in paragraph (c)(1)(ii) of this section, the basis and holding period of the portion of each share of stock in the surviving corporation attributable to the T stock is the basis and holding period immediately before the exchange of a proportionate amount of the T stock to which such portion relates. If any exchanging shareholder of T stock is described in paragraph (c)(1)(ii) of this section, and such shareholder exchanges two or more blocks of T stock pursuant to the transaction, then each share of surviving corporation stock attributable to the T stock must be further divided into separate portions to account for the separate blocks of T stock.

(B) If no exchanging shareholder of T stock is described in paragraph (c)(1)(ii) of this section, the rules of § 1.358-6 apply to determine the basis of the portion of each share of the surviving corporation attributable to T immediately before the exchange.

(d) *Special rules applicable to divided shares of stock.*—(1) *In general.*—(i) Shares of stock in different blocks are aggregated into one divided portion for basis purposes, if such shares immediately before the exchange are owned by one or more shareholders that are—

(A) Not section 1248 shareholders with respect to the corporation; or

(B) Foreign corporate shareholders, provided that no United States persons are section 1248 shareholders with respect to both such foreign corporate shareholders and the corporation.

(ii) For purposes of determining the amount of gain realized on the sale or exchange of stock that has a divided portion pursuant to paragraph (c) of this section, any amount realized on such sale or exchange will be allocated to each divided portion of the stock based on the relative fair market value of the stock to which the portion is attributable at the time the portions were created. See paragraph (e) *Example 5* of this section.

(iii) Shares of stock will no longer be required to be divided if section 1248 or section 964(e) would not apply to a disposition or exchange of such stock.

(2) *Pre-exchange earnings and profits.*—All earnings and profits (or deficits) accumulated by a foreign corporation before the reorganization and attributable to a share (or block) of stock for purposes of section 1248 are attributable to the divided portion of stock with the basis and holding period of that share (or block). See § 1.367(b)-4(d).

(3) *Post-exchange earnings and profits.*—Any earnings and profits (or deficits) accumulated by the surviving corporation subsequent to the reorganization are attributed to each divided share of stock pursuant to section 1248 and the regulations thereunder. The amount of earnings and profits (or deficits) attributable to a divided share of stock is further attributed to the divided portions of such share of stock based on the relative fair market value of each divided portion of stock. See paragraph (e) *Example 5* of this section.

(e) *Examples.*—The rules of this section are illustrated by the following examples:

Example 1. Blocks of stock exchanged in a triangular reorganization—(i) *Facts.* (A) US1, a domestic corporation, owns all the stock of F1, a foreign corporation. F1 owns all the stock of FT, a foreign corporation, with 100 shares of stock outstanding. Each share of FT stock is valued at $10x. Because F1 *acquired the stock of FT at two different dates, F1 owns two blocks of FT stock for purposes of section 1248.* The first block consists of 60 shares. The shares in the first block have a basis of $300x ($5x per share), a holding period of 10 years, and $240x ($4x per share) of earnings and profits attributable to the shares

for purposes of section 1248. The second block consists of 40 shares. The shares in the second block have a basis of $600x ($15x per share), a holding period of 2 years, and $80x ($2x per share) of earnings and profits attributable to the shares for purposes of section 1248.

(B) US2, a domestic corporation, owns all of the stock of FP, a foreign corporation, which owns all of the stock of FS, a foreign corporation. FP owns two blocks of FS stock. Each block consists of 10 shares with a value of $200x ($20x per share). The shares in the first block have a basis of $50x ($5x per share), a holding period of 10 years, and $50x ($5x per share) of earnings and profits attributable to such shares for purposes of section 1248. The shares in the second block had a basis of $100x ($10x per share), a holding period of 5 years, and $20x ($2x per share) of earnings and profits attributable to such shares for purposes of section 1248.

(C) FT merges into FS, with FS surviving, and F1 receives 50 shares of FP stock with a value of $1,000x in exchange for its FT stock. The merger of FT into FS qualifies as forward triangular merger, and immediately after the exchange US1 is a section 1248 shareholder with respect to F1, the exchanging shareholder, FP and FS, all of which are controlled foreign corporations.

(ii) *Basis and holding period determination.* (1) US1 is a section 1248 shareholder of F1, the exchanging shareholder, and FT (both of which are controlled foreign corporations) immediately before the transaction. Moreover, F1 is not required to include amounts in income under § 1.367(b)-3(b) or 1.367(b)-4(b) as described in paragraph (c)(1)(ii)(B) of this section. Accordingly, the basis and holding period of the FS stock held by FP immediately after the triangular reorganization is determined pursuant to paragraph (c) of this section.

(2) Pursuant to paragraph (c) of this section, each share of FS stock is divided into portions attributable to the basis and holding period of the FS stock held by FP immediately before the exchange (the FS portion) and the FT stock held by F1 immediately before the exchange (the FT portion). The basis and holding period of the FS portion is the basis and holding period of the FS stock held by FP immediately before the exchange. Thus, each share of FS stock in the first block has a portion with a basis of $5x, a value of $20x, a holding period of 10 years, and $5x of earnings and profits attributable to such portion for purposes of section 1248. Each share of FS stock in the second block has a portion with a basis of $10x, a value of $20x, a holding period of 5 years, and $2x of earnings and profits attributable to such portion for purposes of section 1248.

(3) Because the exchanging shareholder of FT stock (F1) has a section 1248 shareholder (US1), the holding period and basis of the FT portion is the holding period and the proportionate amount of the basis of the FT stock immediately before the exchange to which such portion relates. Further, because F1 exchanged two blocks of FT stock, the FT portion must be divided into two separate portions attributable to the two blocks of FT stock. Thus, each share of FS stock will have a second portion with a basis of $15x ($300x basis / 20 shares), a value of $30x ($600x value / 20 shares), a holding period of 10 years, and $12x of earnings and profits ($240x / 20 shares) attributable to such portion for purposes of section 1248. Each share of FS stock will have a third portion with a basis of $30x ($600x basis / 20 shares), a value of $20x ($400x value / 20 shares), a holding period of 2 years, and $4x of earnings and profits ($80x / 20 shares) attributable to such portion for purposes of section 1248.

(iii) *Subsequent disposition—first block.* Assume, immediately after the transaction, FP disposes of a share of FS stock from the first block. When FP disposes of any share of its FS stock, it is treated as disposing of each divided portion of such share. With respect to the first portion (attributable to the FS stock), FP recognizes a gain of $15x ($20x value - $5x basis), $5x of which is treated as a dividend under section 1248. With respect to the second portion (attributable to the first block of FT stock), FP recognizes a gain of $15x ($30x value - $15x basis), $12x of which is treated as a dividend under section 1248. With respect to the third portion (attributable to the second block of FT stock), FP recognizes a capital loss of $10x ($20x value - $30x basis).

(iv) *Subsequent disposition—second block.* Assume further, immediately after the transaction, FP also disposes of a share of stock from the second block of FS stock. With respect to the first portion (attributable to the FS stock), FP recognizes a gain of $10x ($20x value - $10x basis), $2x of which is treated as a dividend under section 1248. With respect to the second portion (attributable to the first block of FT stock), FP recognizes a gain of $15x ($30x value - $15x basis), $12x of which is treated as a dividend under section 1248. With respect to the third portion (attributable to the second block of FT stock), FP recognizes a capital loss of $10x ($20x value - $30x basis).

Example 2. (i) *Facts.* The facts are the same as in *Example 1*, except that FS merges into FT with FT surviving in a reverse triangular merger. Pursuant to the merger, F1 receives FP stock with a value of $1,000x in exchange for its FT stock, and FP receives 10 shares of FS stock with a value of $1,000x in exchange for its FS stock. Immediately after the exchange, US1 is a section 1248 shareholder with respect to F1, the exchanging shareholder, FP, and FT, all of which are controlled foreign corporations.

(ii) *Basis and holding period determination*—(A) The basis and holding period of the stock of the surviving corporation held by FP are the same as in *Example 1*, except that each share of the surviving corporation (FT, instead of FS) will be divided into four portions instead of three portions. Because FP exchanges two blocks of FS stock, the FS portion must be divided into two separate portions attributable to the two blocks of FS stock. Because F1 exchanges two blocks of FT stock, the FT portion must be divided into two separate portions attributable to the two blocks of FT stock.

(B) Thus, each share of the surviving corporation (FT) will have a first portion (attributable to the first block of FS stock) with a basis of $5x ($50x / 10 shares), a value of $20x ($200x / 10 shares), a holding period of 10 years, and $5x of earnings and profits ($50x / 10 shares) attributable to such portion for purposes of section 1248. Each share of FT stock will have a second portion (attributable to the second block of FS stock) with a basis of $10x ($100x / 10 shares), a value of $20x ($200x / 10 shares), a holding period of 5 years, and $2x of earnings and profits ($20x / 10 shares) attributable to such portion for purposes of section 1248. Moreover, each share of FT stock will have a third portion (attributable to the first block of FT stock) with a basis of $30x ($300x basis / 10 shares), a value of $60x ($600x value / 10 shares), a holding period of 10 years, and $24x of earnings and profits ($240x / 10 shares) attributable to such portion for purposes of section 1248. Lastly, each share of FT stock will have a fourth portion (attributable to the second block of FT stock) with a basis of $60x ($600x basis / 10 shares), a value of $40x ($400x value / 10 shares), a holding period of 2 years, and $8x of earnings and profits ($80x / 10 shares) attributable to such portion for purposes of section 1248.

Example 3. (i) *Facts.* USP, a domestic corporation, owns all the stock of FS, a foreign corporation with 10 shares of stock outstanding. Each share of FS stock has a value of $10x, a basis of $5x, a holding period of 10 years, and $7x of earnings and profits attributable to such share for purposes of section 1248. FP, a foreign corporation, owns the stock of FT, another foreign corporation. FP and FT do not have any section 1248 shareholders. FT has assets with a value of $100x, a basis of $50x, and no liabilities. The FT stock held by FP has a value of $100x and a basis of $75x. FT merges into FS with FS surviving in a forward triangular merger. Pursuant to the reorganization, FP receives USP stock with a value of $100x in exchange for its FT stock.

(ii) *Basis and holding period determination*—(A) Because USP is a section 1248 shareholder of FS immediately before the transaction, the basis and holding period of the FS stock held by USP immediately after the triangular reorganization is determined pursuant to paragraph (c) of this section.

(B) Pursuant to paragraph (c) of this section, each share of FS stock is divided into portions attributable to the basis and holding period of the FS stock held by USP immediately before the exchange (the FS portion) and the FT portion immediately before the exchange. Because FT does not have a section 1248 shareholder immediately before the transaction, the rules of §1.358-6 apply to determine the basis of the FT portion of each share of FS stock. Those rules determine the basis of FS stock held by USP by reference to the basis of FT's net assets. The basis and holding period of the FS portion is the basis and holding period of the FS stock held by USP immediately before the exchange. Thus, each share of FS stock has a portion with a basis of $5x, a value of $10x, a holding period of 10 years, and $7x of earnings and profits attributable to such portion for section 1248 purposes. The basis of the FT portion is the basis of the FT assets to which such portion relates. Thus, each share of FS stock has a second portion with a basis of $5x ($50x basis in FT's assets / 10 shares) and a value of $10x ($100x value of FT's assets / 10 shares). All of FS's earnings and profits prior to the transaction ($70x) is attributed solely to the FS portion in each share of FS stock. As a result of each share of stock being divided into portions, the basis of the FS stock is not averaged with the basis of the FT assets to increase the section 1248 amount with respect to the stock of the surviving corporation (FS).

Example 4. (i) *Facts.* US, a domestic corporation, owns all of the stock of FT, a foreign corporation. The FT stock held by US constitutes a single block of stock with a value of $1,000x, a basis of $600x, and holding period of 5 years. USP, a domestic corporation, forms FS, a foreign corporation, pursuant to the plan of reorganization and capitalizes it with $10x of cash. FS merges into FT with FT surviving in a reverse triangular merger and a reorganization described in section 368(a)(1)(B). Pursuant to the reorganization, US receives USP stock with a value of $1,000x in exchange for its FT stock, and USP receives 10 shares of FT stock with a value of $1,010x in exchange for its FS stock.

(ii) *Basis and holding period determination.* (A) US and USP are section 1248 shareholders of FT and FS, respectively, immediately before the transaction. Neither US nor USP is required to include amounts in income under §1.367(b)-3(b) or 1.367(b)-4(b) as described

in paragraph (c)(1)(i)(B) or (c)(1)(ii)(B) of this section. The basis and holding period of the FT stock held by USP is determined pursuant to paragraph (c) of this section.

(B) Pursuant to paragraph (c) of this section, because the exchanging shareholder of FT stock (US) is a section 1248 shareholder of FT, each share of the surviving corporation (FT) has a proportionate amount of the basis and holding period of the FT stock immediately before the exchange to which such share relates. Thus, the portion of each share of FT stock attributable to the FT stock has a basis of $60x ($600x basis / 10 shares), a value of $100x ($1,000x value / 10 shares), and a holding period of 5 years. Because the value of FS stock immediately before the triangular reorganization ($10x) is less than one percent of the value of the surviving corporation (FT) immediately after the triangular reorganization ($1,010x), USP may determine its basis in the stock of the surviving corporation (FT) attributable to its FS stock basis held prior to the reorganization by increasing the basis of each share of FT stock by the proportionate amount of USP's aggregate basis in the FS stock immediately before the exchange (without dividing each share of FT stock into separate portions to account for FS and FT). If USP so elects, USP's basis in each share of FT stock is increased by $1x ($10x basis in FS stock / 10 shares). As a result, each share of FT stock has a basis of $61x, a value of $101x, and a holding period of 5 years.

Example 5. (i) *Facts.* US, a domestic corporation, owns all the stock of F1, a foreign corporation, which owns all the stock of FT, a foreign corporation. The FT stock held by F1 constitutes one block of stock with a basis of $170x, a value of $200x, a holding period of 5 years, and $10x of earnings and profits attributable to such stock for purposes of section 1248. FP, a foreign corporation, owns all the stock of FS, a foreign corporation. FS has 10 shares of stock outstanding. No United States person is a section 1248 shareholder with respect to FP or FS. The FS stock held by FP has a value of $100x and a basis of $50x ($5x per share). FT merges into FS with FS surviving in a forward triangular merger. Pursuant to the merger, F1 receives FP stock with a value of $200x for its FT stock in an exchange that qualifies for non-recognition under section 354. US is a section 1248 shareholder with respect to F1, the exchanging shareholder, FP, and FS (all of which are controlled foreign corporations) immediately after the exchange.

(ii) *Basis and holding period determination.* (A) Because US is a section 1248 shareholder of F1, the exchanging shareholder, and FT immediately before the transaction, and US is a section 1248 shareholder of F1, FP, and FS immediately after the transactions, F1 is not required to include amounts in income under §§1.367(b)-3(b) and 1.367(b)-4(b) as described in paragraph (c)(1)(ii)(B) of this section. Thus, the basis and holding period of the FS stock held by FP immediately after the triangular reorganization is determined pursuant to paragraph (c) of this section.

(B) Pursuant to paragraph (c) of this section, each share of FS stock is divided into portions attributable to the basis and holding period of the FS stock held by FP immediately before the exchange (the FS portion) and the FT stock held by F1 immediately before the exchange (the FT portion). The basis and holding period of the FS portion is the basis and holding period of the FS stock held by FP immediately before the exchange. Thus, each share of FS stock has a portion with a basis of $5x and a value of $10x. Because the exchanging shareholder of FT stock (F1) has a section 1248 shareholder of both F1 and FT, the basis and holding period of the FT portion is the proportionate amount of the basis and the holding period of the FT stock immediately before the exchange to which such portion relates. Thus, each share of FS stock will have a second portion with a basis of $17x ($170x basis / 10 shares), a value of $20x ($200x value / 10 shares), a holding period of 5 years, and $1x of earnings and profits ($10x earnings and profits / 10 shares) attributable to such portion for purposes of section 1248.

(iii) *Subsequent disposition.* (A) Several years after the merger, FP disposes of all of its FS stock in a transaction governed by section 964(e). At the time of the disposition, FS stock has decreased in value to $210x (a post-merger reduction in value of $90x), and FS has incurred a post-merger deficit in earnings and profits of $30x.

(B) Pursuant to paragraph (d)(1)(ii) of this section, for purposes of determining the amount of gain realized on the sale or exchange of stock that has a divided portion, any amount realized on such sale or exchange is allocated to each divided portion of the stock based on the relative fair market value of the stock to which the portion is attributable at the time the portions were created. Immediately before the merger, the value of the FS stock in relation to the value of both the FS stock and the FT stock was one-third ($100x / ($100x plus $200x)). Likewise, immediately before the merger, the value of the FT stock in relation to the value of both the FT stock and the FS stock was two-thirds ($200x / $100x plus $200x). Accordingly, one-third of the $210x amount realized is allocated to the FS portion of each share and two-thirds to the FT portion of each share. Thus, the amount realized allocated to the FS portion of each share is $7x (one-third of $210x divided by 10 shares). The amount realized allocated to the FT portion of each share is $14x (two-thirds of $210x divided by 10 shares).

(C) Pursuant to paragraph (d)(3) of this section, any earnings and profits (or deficits) accumulated by the surviving corporation subsequent to the reorganization are attributed to the divided portions of shares of stock based on the relative fair market value of each divided portion of stock. Accordingly, one-third of the post-merger earnings and profits deficit of $30x is allocated to the FS portion of each share and two-thirds to the FT portion of each share. Thus, the deficit in earnings and profits allocated to the FS portion of each share is $1x (one-third of $30x divided by 10 shares). The deficit in earnings and profits allocated to the FT portion of each share is $2x (two-thirds of $30x divided by 10 shares).

»»→ *Caution: The Treasury Department has identified Reg. §1.367(d)-1, as added by T.D. 9803, as a significant tax regulation that imposes an undue financial burden on U.S. taxpayers and/or adds undue complexity to the federal tax laws, pursuant to Executive Order 13789 (issued April 21, 2017) (Notice 2017-38, I.R.B. 2017-30). In a subsequent report, issued October 4, 2017, Treasury recommended planned actions that would reduce the burden of these regulations.*

[Reg. §1.367(d)-1]

§1.367(d)-1. Transfers of intangible property to foreign corporations.—(a) [Reserved]. For further guidance, see §1.367(d)-1T(a).

(b) *Property subject to section 367(d).*—Section 367(d) and the rules of this section apply to the transfer of intangible property, as defined in §1.367(a)-1(d)(5), by a U.S. person to a foreign corporation in an exchange described in section 351 or 361. See section 367(a) and the regulations thereunder for the rules that apply to the transfer of any property other than intangible property.

(c)(1) through (2) [Reserved]. For further guidance, see §1.367(d)-1T(c)(1) and (2).

(3) *Useful life.*—(i) *In general.*—For purposes of determining the period of inclusions for deemed payments under §1.367(d)-1T(c)(1), the useful life of intangible property is the entire period during which exploitation of the intangible property is reasonably anticipated to affect the determination of taxable income, as of the time of transfer. Exploitation of intangible property includes any direct or indirect use or transfer of the intangible property, including use without further development, use in the further development of the intangible property itself (and any exploitation of the further developed intangible property), and use in the development of other intangible property (and any exploitation of the other developed intangible property).

(ii) *Procedure to limit inclusions to 20 years.*—In cases where the useful life of the transferred property is indefinite or is reasonably anticipated to exceed twenty years, taxpayers may, in lieu of including amounts during the entire useful life of the intangible property, choose in the year of transfer to increase annual inclusions during the 20-year period beginning with the first year in which the U.S transferor takes into account income pursuant to section 367(d), to reflect amounts that, but for this paragraph (c)(3)(ii), would have been required to be included following the end of the 20-year period. See §1.6038B-1(d)(1)(iv) for guidance on reporting this choice of method. If the taxpayer applies this method during the 20-year period, no adjustments will be made for taxable years beginning after the conclusion of the 20-year period. However, for purposes of determining whether amounts included during the 20-year period are commensurate with the income attributable to the transferred intangible property, the Commissioner may take into account information with respect to taxable years after that period, such as the income attributable to the transferred property during those later years. The application of this paragraph (c)(3)(ii) must be reflected in a statement (titled "Application of 20-Year Inclusion Period to Section 367(d) Transfers") attached to a timely filed original federal income tax return (including extensions) for the year of the transfer. An increase to the deemed payment rate made pursuant to this paragraph (c)(3)(ii) will be irrevocable, and a failure to timely file the statement under this paragraph (c)(3)(ii) may not be remedied.

$$\text{Loss recapture income} \times$$

(ii) For purposes of the formula in paragraph (g)(3)(i) of this section, the "loss recapture income" is the total amount required to be recognized by the U.S. transferor pursuant to section 904(f)(3) or §1.367(a)-6. The "gain from intangible property" is the total amount of gain realized by the U.S. transferor pursuant to section 904(f)(3) and §1.367(a)-6 upon the transfer of items of property that are subject to section 367(d). "Gain from intangible property" does not include gain realized with respect to intangible property by reason of an election under paragraph (g)(2) of this section. The "gain from all branch assets" is the total amount of gain realized by the transferor upon the transfer of items of property of the branch for which gain is realized.

(D) When FP disposes of its FS stock, FP is treated as disposing of each divided portion of a share of stock. With respect to the FS portion of each share of stock, FP recognizes a gain of $2x ($7x value - $5x basis), which is not recharacterized as a dividend because a deficit in earnings and profits of $1x is attributable to such portion for purposes of section 1248. With respect to the FT portion of each share of stock, FP recognizes a loss of $3x ($14x value -$17x basis).

(f) *Effective date.*—This section applies to exchanges occurring on or after January 23, 2006. [Reg. §1.367(b)-13.]

☐ [*T.D. 9243, 1-23-2006. Amended by T.D. 9400, 5-23-2008 and T.D. 9446, 2-9-2009.*]

(iii) *Example.* Property subject to section 367(d) is transferred from USP, a domestic corporation, to FA, a foreign corporation wholly owned by USP. The useful life of the transferred property, inclusive of derivative works, at the time of transfer is indefinite but is reasonably anticipated to exceed 20 years. In the first five years following the transfer, sales related to the property are expected to be $100x, $130x, $160x, $180x and $187.2x, respectively. Thereafter, for the remainder of the property's useful life, sales are expected to grow by four percent annually. In the first five years following the transfer, operating profits attributable to the property are expected to be $5x, $8x, $11x, $12.5x, and $13x, respectively. Thereafter, for the remainder of the property's useful life, operating profits are expected to grow by four percent annually. It is determined that the appropriate discount rate for sales and operating profits is 10 percent. The present value of operating profits through the property's indefinite useful life is $185x. The present value of sales through the property's indefinite useful life is $2698x. Accordingly, the sales based royalty rate during the property's useful life is 6.8 percent ($185x/$2698x). The taxpayer may choose to take income inclusions into account over a 20-year period. The present value of sales through the 20-year period is $1787x. Accordingly, the sales based royalty rate under the 20-year option is increased to 10.3 percent ($185x/$1787x).

(c)(4) through (g)(2) (introductory text) [Reserved]. For further guidance, see §1.367(d)-1T(c)(4) through (g)(2) (introductory text).

(g)(2)(i) The intangible property transferred constitutes an operating intangible, as defined in §1.367(a)-1(d)(6).

(g)(2)(ii) through (iii)(D) [Reserved]. For further guidance, see §1.367(d)-1T(g)(2)(ii) through (iii)(D).

(E) The transferred intangible property will be used in the active conduct of a trade or business outside of the United States within the meaning of §1.367(a)-2 and will not be used in connection with the manufacture or sale of products in or for use or consumption in the United States.

(g)(2)(iii) undesignated concluding paragraph [Reserved]. For further guidance, see §1.367(d)-1T(g)(2)(iii) undesignated concluding paragraph.

(3) *Intangible property transferred from branch with previously deducted losses.*—(i) If income is required to be recognized under section 904(f)(3) and the regulations thereunder or under §1.367(a)-6 upon the transfer of intangible property of a foreign branch that had previously deducted losses, then the income recognized under those sections with respect to that property is credited against amounts that would otherwise be required to be recognized with respect to that same property under paragraphs (c) through (f) of this section in either the current or future taxable years. The amount recognized under section 904(f)(3) or §1.367(a)-6 with respect to the transferred intangible property is determined in accordance with the following formula:

$$\frac{\text{gain from intangible property}}{\text{gain from all branch assets}}$$

(g)(4) through (i) [Reserved]. For further guidance, see §1.367(d)-1T(g)(4) through (i).

(j) *Effective/applicability dates.*—This section applies to transfers occurring on or after September 14, 2015, and to transfers occurring before September 14, 2015, resulting from entity classification elections made under §301.7701-3 that are filed on or after September 14, 2015. For transfers occurring before this section is applicable, see §1.367(d)-1T as contained in 26 CFR part 1 revised as of April 1, 2016. [Reg. §1.367(d)-1.]

☐ [*T.D. 9803, 12-15-2016.*]

>>> *Caution: The Treasury Department has identified Temporary Reg. §1.367(d)-1T, as amended by T.D. 9803, as a significant tax regulation that imposes an undue financial burden on U.S. taxpayers and/or adds undue complexity to the federal tax laws, pursuant to Executive Order 13789 (issued April 21, 2017) (Notice 2017-38, I.R.B. 2017-30). In a subsequent report, issued October 4, 2017, Treasury recommended planned actions that would reduce the burden of these regulations.*

[Reg. §1.367(d)-1T]

§1.367(d)-1T. Transfers of intangible property to foreign corporations (temporary).—(a) *Purpose and scope.*—This section provides rules under section 367(d) concerning transfers of intangible property by U.S. persons to foreign corporations pursuant to section 351 or 361. Paragraph (b) of this section specifies the transfers that are subject to section 367(d) and the rules of this section, while paragraph (c) provides rules concerning the consequences of such a transfer. In general, the U.S. transferor will be treated as receiving annual payments contingent on productivity or use of the transferred property, over the useful life of the property (regardless of whether such payments are in fact made by the transferee). Paragraphs (d), (e), and (f) of this section provide rules for cases in which there is a later direct or indirect disposition of the intangible property transferred. In general, deemed annual license payments will continue if a transfer is made to a related person, while gain must be recognized immediately if the transfer is to an unrelated person. Paragraph (g) of this section provides several special rules, including a rule allowing appropriate adjustments where deemed payments under section 367(d) are not in fact received by the U.S. transferor of the intangible property, and a rule providing for a limited election to treat certain transfers of intangible property as sales at fair market value (in lieu of applying the general useful life-contingent payment rule). In addition, paragraph (g) of this section provides rules coordinating the application of section 367(d) with other relevant Code sections. Paragraph (h) of this section defines the term "related person" for purposes of this section. Finally, paragraph (i) of this section provides the effective date of this section. For rules concerning transfers of intangible property pursuant to section 332, see §1.367(a)-5T(e). For purposes of determining whether a U.S. person has made a transfer of intangible property that is subject to the rules of section 367(d), the rules of §1.367(a)-1T(c) shall apply.

(b) [Reserved].

(c) *Deemed payments upon transfer of intangible property to foreign corporation.*—(1) *In general.*—If a U.S. person transfers intangible property that is subject to section 367(d) and the rules of this section to a foreign corporation in an exchange described in section 351 or 361, then such person shall be treated as having transferred that property in exchange for annual payments contingent on the productivity or use of the property. Such person shall, over the useful life of the property, annually include in gross income an amount that represents an appropriate arms-length charge for the use of the property. The appropriate charge shall be determined in accordance with the provisions of section 482 and regulations thereunder. See §1.482-2(d). The amount of the deemed payment thus calculated shall be reduced by any royalty or other periodic payment made or accrued by the transferee to an unrelated person during that taxable year for the right to use the intangible property. Amounts so included in the transferor's income shall be treated as ordinary income from sources within the United States. For purposes of computing estimated tax payments, deemed payments under this paragraph (c) shall be treated as received by the transferor on the last day of its taxable year.

(2) *Required adjustments.*—The following adjustments shall be made with respect to a U.S. person's recognition of a deemed payment for the use of intangible property under this paragraph (c):

(i) For purposes of chapter 1 of the Code, the earnings and profits of the transferee foreign corporation shall be reduced by the amount of such deemed payment; and

(ii) For purposes of subpart F of part III of subchapter N of the Code, the transferee foreign corporation may treat such deemed payment as an expense (whether or not that amount is actually paid), properly allocated and apportioned to gross income subject to subpart F, in accordance with the provisions of §§1.954-1(c) and 1.861-8. No other special adjustments to earnings and profits, basis, or gross income shall be permitted by reason of the recognition of a deemed payment under this paragraph (c). However, see paragraph (g)(1) of this section for rules permitting the establishment of an account receivable with respect to deemed payments not actually received by the U.S. person.

(3) [Reserved].

(4) *Blocked income.*—No deemed payment included in a taxpayer's income under paragraph (c)(1) of this section shall be treated as deferrable income for purposes of applying rules relating to blocked foreign income. See Revenue Ruling 74-351, 1974-2 C.B. 144.

(d) *Subsequent transfer of stock of transferee foreign corporation to unrelated person.*—(1) *Treatment as sale of intangible property.*—If a U.S.

person transfers intangible property that is subject to section 367(d) and the rules of this section to a foreign corporation in an exchange described in section 351 or 361, and within the useful life of the intangible property that U.S. transferor subsequently disposes of the stock of the transferee foreign corporation to a person that is not a related person (within the meaning of paragraph (h) of this section), then the U.S. transferor shall be treated as having simultaneously sold the intangible property to the person acquiring the stock of the transferee foreign corporation. The U.S. transferor shall be required to recognize gain (but not loss) from sources within the United States in an amount equal to the difference between the fair market value of the transferred intangible property on the date of the subsequent disposition and the U.S. transferor's former adjusted basis in that property (determined as of the original transfer). If the U.S. transferor's disposition of the stock of the transferee foreign corporation is subject to U.S. tax other than by reason of this paragraph (d), then the amount of gain otherwise required to be recognized with respect to the stock of the transferee foreign corporation shall be reduced by the amount of gain recognized with respect to the intangible property pursuant to this paragraph (d).

(2) *Required adjustments.*—If a U.S. person disposes of the stock of a transferee foreign corporation, and under paragraph (d)(1) of this section is treated as having simultaneously sold intangible property, then, for purposes of computing basis and earnings and profits, the person acquiring the stock of the transferee foreign corporation shall be deemed to have purchased that property at fair market value and to have immediately thereafter contributed it to the transferee foreign corporation in a transaction not covered by section 367(d). Therefore, for purposes of chapter 1 of the Code—

(i) The transferee foreign corporation's basis in the intangible property will be equal to its fair market value (as calculated for purposes of determining the gain required to be recognized by the U.S. transferor);

(ii) The acquiring person's basis in the stock of the transferee foreign corporation shall be determined as if no portion of the consideration given by the acquiring person for the stock is attributable to the intangible property; and

(iii) The earnings and profits of the transferee foreign corporation will not be affected by the transfer of its stock or the deemed transfer to it of the intangible property.

(e) *Subsequent transfer of stock of transferee foreign corporation to related person.*—(1) *Transfer to related U.S. person treated as disposition of intangible property.*—If a U.S. person transfers intangible property that is subject to section 367(d) and the rules of this section to a foreign corporation in an exchange described in section 351 or 361 and, within the useful life of the transferred intangible property, that U.S. transferor subsequently transfers the stock of the transferee foreign corporation to U.S. persons that are related to the transferor within the meaning of paragraph (h) of this section, then the following rules shall apply:

(i) Each such related U.S. person shall be treated as having received (with the stock of the transferee foreign corporation) a right to receive a proportionate share of the contingent annual payments that would otherwise be deemed to be received by the U.S. transferor under paragraph (c) of this section.

(ii) Each such related U.S. person shall, over the useful life of the property, annually include in gross income a proportionate share of the amount that would have been included in the income of the U.S. transferor pursuant to paragraph (c) of this section. Such amounts shall be treated as ordinary income from sources within the United States.

(iii) The amount of income required to be recognized by the U.S. transferor pursuant to the rule of paragraph (d)(1) of this section shall be reduced to the amount determined in accordance with the following formula:

$$(d)(1) \text{ amount} \times (100\% - (e) \text{ percentage}).$$

For purposes of the above formula, the "(d)(1) amount" is the income that would otherwise be required to be recognized by the transferor corporation pursuant to paragraph (d)(1) of this section, and the "(e) percentage" is the percentage of the transferor corporation's total deemed rights to receive contingent annual payments under paragraph (c) of this section that is deemed to be transferred to related U.S. persons under the rules of this paragraph (e).

(iv) The rules of paragraphs (d) and (e) of this section shall be reapplied in the case of any later transfer of the stock of the transferee foreign corporation by a related U.S. person that received such stock in a transfer that was subject to the rules of this paragraph (e). For purposes of reapplying the rules of paragraphs (d) and (e), each such related U.S. person shall be treated as a U.S. transferor of intangible property to the transferee foreign corporation (to the extent of the interest attributed to such person pursuant to subdivision (i) of this paragraph (e)(1)).

(2) *Required adjustments.*—If a U.S. person transfers stock of a transferee foreign corporation to a U.S. related person in a transaction that is subject to the rules of paragraph (e)(1) of this section, the following adjustments shall be made:

(i) For purposes of chapter 1 of the Code, the earnings and profits of the transferee foreign corporation shall be reduced by the amount of any payment deemed to be received by a related U.S. person under paragraph (e)(1)(ii) of this section;

(ii) For purposes of subpart F of part III of subchapter N of the Code, the transferee foreign corporation may allocate and apportion such deemed payments (whether or not such payments are actually made) to gross income subject to subpart F to the extent appropriate under the provisions of §§ 1.954-1(c) and 1.861-8;

(iii) For purposes of reapplying the rules of paragraphs (d) and (e) of this section, if the related U.S. person is deemed to have received a right to contingent annual payments for the use of intangible property, then the U.S. related person shall be deemed to have held a proportionate share of the property with a basis equal to a proportionate share of the U.S. transferor's adjusted basis plus the gain, if any, recognized by the U.S. transferor on the earlier transfer of the stock to the U.S. related person, and then to have transferred that proportionate share of the property to the foreign corporation in a transfer subject to section 367(d); and

(iv) If the U.S. transferor is itself required to recognize gain upon the transfer by reason of the operation of paragraphs (d)(1) and (e)(1)(iii) of this section (because stock of the transferee foreign corporation is also transferred to unrelated persons), then those unrelated persons shall be deemed to have purchased a proportionate share of the transferred intangible property at fair market value and immediately contributed that property to the transferee foreign corporation, consistent with the general rule of paragraph (d)(2) of this section concerning transfers of stock to unrelated persons. Therefore, for purposes of chapter 1 of the Code—

(A) Each unrelated person's basis in the stock of the transferee foreign corporation shall be increased to the extent of the gain recognized by the U.S. transferor upon the deemed purchase of intangible property by that person; and

(B) The transferee foreign corporation will receive an increase in its basis in the transferred intangible property equal to the fair market value of that portion of the intangible property deemed to be contributed to the transferee foreign corporation by unrelated persons (as calculated for purposes of determining the gain required to be recognized by the U.S. transferor).

(3) *Transfer to related foreign person not treated as disposition of intangible property.*—If a U.S. person transfers intangible property that is subject to section 367(d) and the rules of this section to a foreign corporation in an exchange described in section 351 or 361, and within the useful life of the transferred intangible property that U.S. transferor subsequently transfers any of the stock of the transferee foreign corporation to one or more foreign persons that are related to the transferor within the meaning of paragraph (h) of this section, then the U.S. transferor shall continue to include in its income the deemed payments described in paragraph (c) of this section in the same manner as if the subsequent transfer of stock had not occurred. The rule of this paragraph (e)(3) shall not apply with respect to the subsequent transfer by the U.S. person of any of the remaining stock to any related U.S. person or unrelated person.

(4) *Proportionate share.*—For purposes of this paragraph (e), any "proportionate share" shall be determined by reference to the fair market value (at the time of the original transfer) of the stock of the transferee foreign corporation that was transferred by the U.S. transferor and the fair market value of all of the stock of the transferee foreign corporation originally received by the U.S. transferor.

(f) *Subsequent disposition of transferred intangible property by transferee foreign corporation.*—(1) *In general.*—If a U.S. person transfers intangible property that is subject to section 367(d) and the rules of this section to a foreign corporation in an exchange described in section 351 or 361, and within the useful life of the intangible property that transferee foreign corporation subsequently disposes of the intangible property to an unrelated person, then—

(i) The U.S. transferor of the intangible property (or any person treated as such pursuant to paragraph (e)(1) of this section) shall be required to *recognize gain from U.S. sources (but not loss)* in an amount equal to the difference between the fair market value of the transferred intangible property on the date of the subsequent disposition and the U.S. transferor's former adjusted basis in that property (determined as of the original transfer); and

(ii) the U.S. transferor shall be required to recognize a deemed payment under paragraph (c) of this section for that part of its taxable year that the intangible property was held by the transferee foreign corporation and thereafter shall not be required to recognize any further deemed payments under paragraph (c) or (e)(1) of this section with respect to the transferred intangible property disposed of by the transferee foreign corporation.

(2) *Required adjustments.*—If a U.S. transferor is required to recognize gain under paragraph (f)(1) of this section, then—

(i) For purposes of chapter 1 of the Code, the earnings and profits of the transferee foreign corporation shall be reduced by the amount of gain required to be recognized; and

(ii) The U.S. transferor's recognition of gain will permit the establishment of an account receivable from the transferee foreign corporation, in accordance with paragraph (g)(1) of this section.

(3) *Subsequent transfer of intangible property to related person.*—The requirement that a U.S. person recognize gain under paragraph (c) or (e) of this section shall not be affected by the transferee foreign corporation's subsequent disposition of the transferred intangible property to a related person. For purposes of any required adjustments, and of any accounts receivable created under paragraph (g)(1) of this section, the related person that receives the intangible property shall be treated as the transferee foreign corporation.

(g) *Special rules.*—(1) *Establishment of accounts receivable.*—(i) *In general.*—If a U.S. person is required to recognize income under the provisions of paragraph (c), (e), or (f) of this section, and the amount deemed to be received is not actually paid by the transferee foreign corporation, then the U.S. person may establish an account receivable from the transferee foreign corporation equal to the amount deemed paid that was not actually paid. A separate account receivable must be established for each taxable year in which payments deemed to be received are not actually made. Payments received from the transferee foreign corporation must be designated as payments upon a particular account and must be deducted from that account. Accounts receivable under this paragraph (g)(1) may be established and paid without further U.S. income tax consequences to the U.S. transferor or the transferee foreign corporation. No interest shall be paid or accrued on an account receivable created under this paragraph (g)(1), nor shall any bad debt deduction be allowed under section 166 with respect to any failure to receive payment on an account.

(ii) *Unpaid receivable treated as contribution to capital.*—If any portion of an account receivable established under this paragraph (g)(1) remains unpaid as of the last day of the third taxable year following the taxable year to which the account relates, then—

(A) Such portion shall be deemed to have been paid on that date; and

(B) The U.S. person shall be deemed to have contributed an equivalent amount to the capital of the foreign corporation, and the U.S. person's basis in the stock of the foreign corporation shall, therefore, be increased by that amount.

(2) *Election to treat transfer as sale.*—A U.S. person that transfers intangible property to a foreign corporation in a transaction subject to section 367(d) may elect to recognize income in accordance with the rules of this paragraph (g)(2), if—

(i) [Reserved].

(ii) The transfer of the intangible property is either legally required by the government of the country in which the transferee corporation is organized as a condition of doing business in that country, or compelled by a genuine threat of immediate expropriation by the foreign government; or

(iii)(A) The U.S. person transferred the intangible property to the foreign corporation within three months of the organization of that corporation and as part of the original plan of capitalization of that corporation;

(B) Immediately after the transfer, the U.S. person owns at least 40 percent but not more than 60 percent of the total voting power and total value of the stock of the transferee foreign corporation;

(C) Immediately after the transfer, at least 40 percent of the total voting power and total value of the stock of the transferee foreign corporation is owned by foreign persons unrelated to the U.S. person;

(D) Intangible property constitutes at least 50 percent of the fair market value of the property transferred to the foreign corporation by the U.S. transferor; and

(E) [Reserved].

A person that makes the election under this paragraph (g)(2) shall not be subject to the provisions of paragraphs (c) through (f) of this section. Such person shall instead recognize in the year of the transfer ordinary income from sources within the United States in an amount equal to the difference between the fair market value of the intangible property transferred and its adjusted basis. A U.S. person shall make an election under this paragraph (g)(2) by notifying the Internal Revenue Service of the election in accordance with the requirements of section 6038B and regulations thereunder, and subsequently including the appropriate amounts in gross income in a timely filed tax return for the year of the transfer.

(3) [Reserved].

(4) *Coordination with section 482.*—(i) *In general.*—Section 367(d) and the rules of this section shall not apply in the case of an actual sale or license of intangible property by a U.S. person to a foreign corporation. If an adjustment under section 482 is required with respect to an actual sale or license of intangible property, then section 367(d) and the rules of this section shall not apply with respect to the required adjustment. If a U.S. person transfers intangible property to a related foreign corporation without consideration, or in exchange for stock or securities of the transferee in a transaction described in section 351 or 361, no sale or license subject to adjustment under section 482 will be deemed to have occurred. Instead, the U.S. person shall be treated as having made a transfer of the intangible property that is subject to section 367(d).

(ii) *Sham licenses and sales.*—For purposes of paragraph (g)(4)(i) of this section, a purported sale or license of intangible property may be disregarded, and treated as a transfer subject to section 367(d) and the rules of this section, if—

(A) The purported sale or license is made to a foreign corporation in which the transferor holds (or is acquiring) an interest; and

(B) The terms of the purported sale or license differ so greatly from the economic substance of the transaction or the terms that would obtain between unrelated persons that the purported sale or license is a sham.

The terms of a purported sale or license, for purposes of applying the rule of this paragraph (g)(4)(ii), shall be determined by reference not only to the nominal terms of the agreement but also to the actual practice of the parties under that agreement. A sale or license of intangible property shall not be disregarded under this paragraph (g)(4)(ii) solely because other property of an integrated business is simultaneously transferred to the foreign corporation by the U.S. transferor in a transaction described in section 367(a)(1) or any statutory or regulatory exception to section 367(a)(1).

(5) *Determination of fair market value.*—For purposes of determining the gain required to be recognized immediately under paragraph (d), (f) or (g)(2) or this section, the fair market value of transferred property shall be the single payment arm's-length price that would be paid for the property by an unrelated purchaser determined in accordance with the principles of section 482 and regulations thereunder. The allocation of a portion of the purchase price to intangible property agreed to by the parties to the transaction shall not necessarily be controlling for this purpose.

(6) *Anti-abuse rule.*—If a U.S. person—

(i) Transfers intangible property to a domestic corporation with a principal purpose of avoiding the effect of section 367(d) and the rules of this section; and

(ii) Thereafter transfers the stock of that domestic corporation to a related foreign corporation,

then solely for purposes of section 367(d) that U.S. person shall be treated as having transferred the intangible property directly to the foreign corporation. A U.S. person shall be presumed to have transferred intangible property for a principal purpose of avoiding the effect of section 367(d) if the property is transferred to the domestic corporation less than two years prior to the transfer of the stock of that domestic corporation to a foreign corporation. The presumption created by the previous sentence may be rebutted by clear evidence that the subsequent transfer of the stock of the domestic transferee corporation was not contemplated at the time the intangible property was transferred to that corporation and that avoidance of section 367(d) and the rules of this section was not a principal purpose of the transaction. A transfer may have more than one principal purpose.

(h) *Related person.*—For purposes of this section, persons are considered to be related if—

(1) They are partners or partnerships described in section 707(b)(1) of the Code; or

(2) They are related within the meaning of section 267(b), (c), and (f) of the Code, except that—

(i) "10 percent or more" shall be substituted for "more than 50 percent" each place it appears; and

(ii) Section 1563 shall apply (for purposes of section 267(f)), without regard to section 1563(b)(2).

(i) *Effective date.*—Except as specifically provided to the contrary elsewhere in this section, this section applies to transfers occurring after December 31, 1984. [Temporary Reg. § 1.367(d)-1T.]

☐ [T.D. 8087, 5-15-86. *Amended by T.D. 8770, 6-18-98 and T.D. 9803,* 12-15-2016.]

[Reg. §1.367(e)-0]

§1.367(e)-0. Outline of §§1.367(e)-1 and 1.367(e)-2.—This section lists captioned paragraphs contained in §§1.367(e)-1 and 1.367(e)-2 as follows:

(A) Conditions for nonrecognition.

(B) Exceptions when the liquidating corporation is a U.S. real property holding corporation.

(C) Anti-abuse rule.

(D) Required statement.

(3) Other consequences.

(i) Distributee basis in property.

(ii) Reporting under section 6038B.

(iii) Other rules.

(c) Distribution by a foreign corporation.

(1) General rule—gain and loss not recognized.

(2) Exceptions.

(i) Property used in a U.S. trade or business.

(A) General rule.

(B) Ten-year active U.S. business exception.

(C) Required statement.

(D) Operating rules.

(ii) Property formerly used in a U.S. trade or business.

(3) Other consequences.

(i) Distributee basis in property.

(ii) Other rules.

(d) Anti-abuse rule.

(e) Effective date.

[Reg. § 1.367(e)-0.]

☐ [*T.D. 8834, 8-6-99.*]

[Reg. § 1.367(e)-1]

§ 1.367(e)-1. Distributions described in section 367(e)(1).— (a) *Purpose and scope.*—This section provides rules for recognition (and nonrecognition) of gain by a domestic corporation (distributing corporation) on a distribution of stock or securities of a corporation (controlled corporation) to foreign persons that is described in section 355. Paragraph (b) of this section contains the general rule that gain is recognized on the distribution to the extent stock or securities of controlled are distributed to foreign persons. Paragraph (c) of this section provides an exception to the gain recognition rule for distributions of stock or securities of a domestic corporation. Paragraph (d) of this section contains rules for determining whether distributees of stock or securities in a section 355 distribution are qualified U.S. persons. Paragraph (e) of this section provides cross-references. Finally, paragraph (f) of this section specifies the effective date of this section.

(b) *Gain recognition.*—(1) *General rule.*—If a domestic corporation makes a distribution of stock or securities of a corporation that qualifies for nonrecognition under section 355 to a person who is not a qualified U.S. person, then, except as provided in paragraph (c) of this section, the distributing corporation shall recognize gain (but not loss) on the distribution under section 367(e)(1). A distributing corporation shall not recognize gain under this section with respect to a section 355 distribution to a qualified U.S. person. For purposes of this section, a qualified U.S. person is—

(A) A citizen or resident of the United States; or

(B) A domestic corporation.

(2) *Stock owned through partnerships, disregarded entities, trusts, and estates.*—For purposes of this section, distributing corporation stock or securities owned by or for a partnership (whether foreign or domestic) are owned proportionately by its partners. A partner's proportionate share of the stock or securities of the distributing corporation shall be equal to the partner's distributive share of the gain that would have been recognized had the partnership sold the stock or securities (at a taxable gain) immediately before the distribution. The partner's distributive share of gain shall be determined under the rules and principles of sections 701 through 761 and the regulations thereunder. For purposes of this section, stock or securities owned by or for an entity that is disregarded as an entity separate from its owner (disregarded entity) under § 301.7701-3 of this chapter are owned directly by the owner of such disregarded entity. For purposes of this section, stock or securities owned by or for a trust or estate (whether foreign or domestic) are owned proportionately by the persons who would be treated as owning such stock or securities under section 318(a)(2)(A) and (B). In applying section 318(a)(2)(B)(i), if a trust includes interests that are not actuarially ascertainable, all such interests shall be considered to be owned by foreign persons. In a case where an interest holder in a partnership, a disregarded entity, trust, or estate that (directly or indirectly) owns stock of the distributing corporation is itself a partnership, disregarded entity, trust, or estate, the rules of this paragraph (b)(2) apply to such interest holder.

(3) *Gain computation.*—Gain recognized under paragraph (b)(1) of this section shall be equal to the excess of the fair market value of the stock or securities distributed to persons who are not qualified

U.S. persons (determined as of the time of the distribution) over the distributing corporation's adjusted basis in the stock or securities distributed to such distributees. For purposes of the preceding sentence, the distributing corporation's adjusted basis in each unit of each class of stock or securities distributed to a distributee shall be equal to the distributing corporation's total adjusted basis in all of the units of the respective class of stock or securities owned immediately before the distribution, divided by the total number of units of the class of stock or securities owned immediately before the distribution.

(4) *Treatment of distributee.*—If the distribution otherwise qualifies for nonrecognition under section 355, each distributee shall be considered to have received stock or securities in a distribution qualifying for nonrecognition under section 355, even though the distributing corporation may recognize gain on the distribution under this section. Thus, the distributee shall not be considered to have received a distribution described in section 301 or a distribution in an exchange described in section 302(b) upon the receipt of the stock or securities of the controlled corporation, and the domestic distributing corporation shall have no withholding responsibilities under section 1441. Except where section 897(e)(1) and the regulations thereunder cause gain to be recognized by the distributee, the basis of the distributed domestic or foreign corporation stock in the hands of the foreign distributee shall be the basis of the distributed stock determined under section 358 without any increase for any gain recognized by the domestic corporation on the distribution.

(c) *Nonrecognition of gain.*—A domestic distributing corporation shall not recognize gain under paragraph (b)(1) of this section on the distribution of stock or securities of a domestic corporation.

(d) *Determining whether distributees are qualified U.S. persons.*—(1) *General rule—presumption of foreign status.*—Except as provided in paragraphs (d)(2) and (3) of this section, all distributions of stock or securities in a distribution described in section 355 in which the distributing corporation is domestic and the controlled corporation is foreign are presumed to be to persons who are not qualified U.S. persons, as defined in paragraph (b)(1) of this section.

(2) *Non-publicly traded distributing corporations.*—If the class of stock or securities of the distributing corporation (in respect to which stock or securities of the controlled corporation are distributed) is not regularly traded on a qualified exchange or other market (as defined in paragraph (d)(4) of this section), then the distributing corporation may only rebut the presumption contained in paragraph (d)(1) of this section by identifying the qualified U.S. persons to which controlled corporation stock or securities were distributed and by certifying the amount of stock or securities that were distributed to the qualified U.S. persons.

(3) *Publicly traded distributing corporations.*—If the class of stock or securities of the distributing corporation (in respect to which stock or securities of the controlled corporation are distributed) is regularly traded on a qualified exchange or other market (as defined in paragraph (d)(4) of this section), then the distributing corporation may only rebut the presumption contained in paragraph (d)(1) of this section as described in this paragraph (d)(3).

(i) *Five percent shareholders.*—A publicly traded distributing corporation may only rebut the presumption contained in paragraph (d)(1) of this section with respect to distributees that are five percent shareholders of the class of stock or securities of the distributing corporation (in respect to which stock or securities of the controlled corporation are distributed) by identifying the qualified U.S. persons to which controlled corporation stock or securities were distributed and by certifying the amount of stock or securities that were distributed to the qualified U.S. persons. A five percent shareholder is a distributee who is required under U.S. securities laws to file with the Securities and Exchange Commission (SEC) a Schedule 13D or 13G under 17 CFR 240.13d-1 or 17 CFR 240.13d-2, and provide a copy of same to the distributing corporation under 17 CFR 240.13d-7.

(ii) *Other distributees.*—A distributing corporation that has made a distribution described in paragraph (d)(3) of this section may rebut the presumption contained in paragraph (d)(1) of this section with respect to distributees that are not five percent shareholders (as defined in this paragraph (d)(3)) by relying on and providing a reasonable analysis of shareholder records and other relevant information that demonstrates a number of distributees that are qualified U.S. persons. Taxpayers may rely on such analysis, unless it is subsequently determined that there are actually fewer distributees who are qualified U.S. persons than were demonstrated in the analysis.

(4) *Qualified exchange or other market.*—For purposes of paragraph (d) of this section, the term qualified exchange or other market means, for any taxable year—

(i) A national securities exchange which is registered with the SEC or the national market system established pursuant to section 11A of the Securities Exchange Act of 1934 (15 U.S.C. 78f); or

(ii) A foreign securities exchange that is regulated or supervised by a governmental authority of the country in which the market is located and which has the following characteristics—

(A) The exchange has trading volume, listing, financial disclosure, and other requirements designed to prevent fraudulent and manipulative acts and practices, to remove impediments to and perfect the mechanism of a free and open market, and to protect investors; and the laws of the country in which the exchange is located and the rules of the exchange ensure that such requirements are actually enforced; and

»»→ *Caution: The Treasury Department has identified Reg. §1.367(e)-2, as amended by T.D. 9803, as a significant tax regulation that imposes an undue financial burden on U.S. taxpayers and/or adds undue complexity to the federal tax laws, pursuant to Executive Order 13789 (issued April 21, 2017) (Notice 2017-38, I.R.B. 2017-30). In a subsequent report, issued October 4, 2017, Treasury recommended planned actions that would reduce the burden of these regulations.*

[Reg. §1.367(e)-2]

§1.367(e)-2. Distributions described in section 367(e)(2).—(a) *Purpose and scope.*—(1) *In general.*—This section provides rules requiring gain and loss recognition by a corporation on its distribution of property to a foreign corporation in a complete liquidation described in section 332. Paragraph (b)(1) of this section contains the general rule that gain and loss are recognized when a domestic corporation makes a distribution of property in complete liquidation under section 332 to a foreign corporation that meets the stock ownership requirements of section 332(b) with respect to stock in the domestic corporation. Paragraph (b)(2) of this section provides the only exceptions to the gain and loss recognition rule of paragraph (b)(1) of this section. Paragraph (b)(3) of this section refers to other consequences of distributions described in paragraphs (b)(1) and (2) of this section. Paragraph (c)(1) of this section contains the general rule that gain and loss are not recognized when a foreign corporation makes a distribution of property in complete liquidation under section 332 to a foreign corporation that meets the stock ownership requirements of section 332(b) with respect to stock in the foreign liquidating corporation. Paragraph (c)(2) of this section provides the only exceptions to the nonrecognition rule of paragraph (c)(1) of this section. Paragraph (c)(3) of this section refers to other consequences of distributions described in paragraphs (c)(1) and (2) of this section. Paragraph (d) of this section contains an anti-abuse rule. Paragraph (e) of this section provides rules regarding failures to file statements or other documents required under this section or failures to comply with the requirements of this section. Paragraph (f) of this section provides relief for certain failures to file or comply. Finally, paragraph (g) of this section specifies the effective/applicability dates for the rules of this section. The rules of this section are issued pursuant to the authority conferred by section 367(e)(2).

(2) *Nonapplicability of section 367(a).*—Section 367(a) shall not apply to a complete liquidation described in section 332 by a domestic liquidating corporation into a foreign corporation that meets the stock ownership requirements of section 332(b).

(b) *Distribution by a domestic corporation.*—(1) *General rule.*—(i) *Recognition of gain and loss.*—If a domestic corporation (domestic liquidating corporation) makes a distribution of property in complete liquidation under section 332 to a foreign corporation (foreign distributee corporation) that meets the stock ownership requirements of section 332(b) with respect to stock in the domestic liquidating corporation, then—

(A) Section 337(a) and (b)(1) will not apply; and

(B) The domestic liquidating corporation will recognize gain or loss on the distribution of property to the foreign distributee corporation, except as provided in paragraph (b)(2) of this section.

(ii) *Operating rules.*—(A) *General rule.*—Except as provided in paragraphs (b)(1)(ii)(B) and (C) of this section, the rules contained in section 336 will apply to the gain and loss recognized pursuant to this section.

(B) *Overall loss limitation.*—(1) *Overall loss limitation rule.*—Loss in excess of gain from the distribution shall not be recognized. If realized losses exceed recognized losses, the losses shall be recognized on a pro rata basis with respect to the realized loss attributable to each distributed loss asset in the category of assets (i.e., capital or ordinary) to which the realized but unrecognized loss relates. For additional limitations on the recognition of losses, see, e.g., section 1211.

(2) *Example.*—The following example illustrates the overall loss limitation rule, the pro rata loss allocation method, and the general capital loss limitation rule in section 1211(a):

(B) The rules of the exchange ensure active trading of listed stocks.

(e) *Cross-references.*—For additional rules relating to the distribution of the stock of a foreign corporation by a domestic corporation, see §§1.367(a)-3(e), 1.367(a)-7, 1.367(b)-5, and 1.1248(f)-1 through 1.1248(f)-3. See the regulations under section 6038B for reporting requirements for distributions under this section.

(f) *Effective/applicability date.*—This section shall be applicable to distributions occurring in taxable years ending after August 8, 1999. [Reg. §1.367(e)-1.]

☐ [T.D. 8834, 8-6-99 (*corrected* 3-2-2000). *Amended by T.D.* 9614, 3-18-2013 *and T.D.* 9760, 3-18-2016.]

Example. F, a foreign corporation, owns all stock of US1, a domestic corporation. US1 owns the following capital assets: Asset A, which has a fair market value of $100 and an adjusted basis of $40; Asset B, which has a fair market value of $60 and an adjusted basis of $80; and, Asset C, which has a fair market value of $40 and an adjusted basis of $100. US1 also owns the following business assets that will generate ordinary income (or loss) upon disposition: Asset D, which has a fair market value of $100 and an adjusted basis of $40; Asset E, which has a fair market value of $60 and an adjusted basis of $100; and, Asset F, which has a fair market value of $40 and an adjusted basis of $80. US1 liquidates into F and distributes all assets to F in liquidation. None of the assets qualify for nonrecognition under paragraph (b)(2) of this section. US1's total realized capital loss is $80, but it may only recognize $60 of that loss. See section 1211(a). US1's total realized ordinary loss is $80, but it may only recognize $60 of that loss. See paragraph (b)(1)(ii)(B)(1) of this section. US1 will allocate $15 (60 × .25) of the recognized capital loss to Asset B and will allocate the remaining $45 (60 × .75) of recognized capital loss to Asset C. See paragraph (b)(1)(ii)(B)(1) of this section. US1 will allocate $30 (60 × .50) of the recognized ordinary loss to Asset E and will allocate the remaining $30 (60 × .50) to Asset F. See paragraph (b)(1)(ii)(B)(1) of this section.

(C) *Special rules for built-in gains and losses attributable to property received in liquidations and reorganizations.*—Built-in losses attributable to property received in a transaction described in sections 332 or 361 (during the two-year period ending on the date of the distribution in liquidation covered by this section) shall not offset gain from property not received in the same transaction. Built-in gains attributable to property received in a transaction described in sections 332 or 361 (during the two-year period ending on the date of the distribution in liquidation covered by this section) shall not be offset by a loss from property not received in the same transaction. Built-in gain or loss is that amount of gain or loss on property that existed at the time the domestic liquidating corporation acquired such property. See sections 336(d) and 382 for additional limitations on the recognition of losses.

(iii) *Distribution of partnership interest.*—(A) *General rule.*—If a domestic corporation distributes a partnership interest (whether foreign or domestic) in a distribution described in paragraph (b)(1)(i) of this section, then for purposes of applying this section the domestic liquidating corporation shall be treated as having distributed a proportionate share of partnership property. Accordingly, the applicability of the recognition rules of paragraphs (b)(1)(i) and (ii) of this section, and of any exception to recognition provided in this section shall be determined with reference to the partnership property, rather than to the partnership interest itself. Where the partnership property includes an interest in a lower-tier partnership, the applicability of any exception with respect to the interest in the lower-tier partnership shall be determined with reference to the lower-tier partnership property. In the case of multiple tiers of partnerships, the applicability of an exception shall be determined with reference to the property of each partnership, applying the rule contained in the preceding sentence. A domestic liquidating corporation's proportionate share of partnership property shall be determined under the rules and principles of sections 701 through 761 and the regulations thereunder.

(B) *Gain or loss calculation.*—[Reserved]

(C) *Basis adjustments.*—The foreign distributee corporation's basis in the distributed partnership interest shall be equal to the domestic liquidating corporation's basis in such partnership interest immediately prior to the distribution, increased by the amount of gain and reduced by the amount of loss recognized by the domestic liquidating corporation on the distribution of the partnership interest. Solely for purposes of sections 743 and 754, the foreign distributee corporation shall be treated as having purchased the partnership interest for an amount equal to the foreign corporation's adjusted basis therein.

(D) *Publicly traded partnerships.*—The distribution by a domestic liquidating corporation of an interest in a publicly traded partnership that is treated as a corporation for U.S. income tax purposes under section 7704(a) shall not be subject to the rules of paragraphs (b)(1)(iii)(A) and (B) of this section. Instead, the distribution of such an interest shall be treated in the same manner as a distribution of stock. Thus, a transfer of an interest in a publicly traded partnership that is treated as a U.S. corporation for U.S. income tax purposes shall be treated in the same manner as stock in a domestic corporation, and a transfer of an interest in a publicly traded partnership that is treated as a foreign corporation for U.S. income tax purposes shall be treated in the same manner as stock in a foreign corporation.

(2) *Exceptions.*—(i) *Distribution of property used in a U.S. trade or business.*—(A) *Conditions for nonrecognition.*—A domestic liquidating corporation shall not recognize gain or loss under paragraph (b)(1) of this section on its distribution of property (including inventory) used by the domestic liquidating corporation in the conduct of a trade or business within United States, if—

(1) The foreign distributee corporation, immediately thereafter and for the ten-year period beginning on the date of distribution of such property, uses the property in the conduct of a trade or business within the United States;

(2) The domestic liquidating corporation attaches the statement described in paragraph (b)(2)(i)(C) of this section to its timely filed U.S. income tax returns for the taxable years that include the distributions in liquidation; and

(3) The foreign distributee corporation attaches a copy of the property description contained in paragraph (b)(2)(i)(C)(2) of this section to its timely filed U.S. income tax return for the tax year that includes the date of distribution.

(B) *Qualifying property.*—Property is used by the foreign distributee corporation in the conduct of a trade or business in the United States within the meaning of this paragraph (b)(2)(i) only if all income from the use of the property and all income or gain from the sale or exchange of the property would be subject to taxation under section 882(a) as effectively connected income. Also, stock held by a dealer as inventory or for sale in the ordinary course of its trade or business shall be treated as inventory and not as stock in the hands of both the domestic liquidating corporation and the distributee foreign corporation. Notwithstanding the foregoing, the exception provided in this paragraph (b)(2)(i) shall not apply to intangibles described in section 936(h)(3)(B).

(C) *Required statement.*—The statement required by paragraph (b)(2)(i)(A) of this section shall be entitled "Required Statement under §1.367(e)-2(b)(2)(i)" and shall be prepared by the domestic liquidating corporation and signed under penalties of perjury by an authorized officer of the domestic liquidating corporation and by an authorized officer of the foreign distributee corporation. The statement shall contain the following items:

(1) *Declaration and certification.*—A declaration that the distribution to the foreign distributee corporation is one to which the rules of this paragraph (b)(2)(i) apply and a certification that the domestic liquidating corporation and the foreign distributee corporation agree to comply with all the conditions and requirements of this section, including, as provided in paragraph (e)(4)(ii)(B) of this section, to treat a failure to comply (as described in paragraph (e)(4)(i) of this section) as extending the period of limitations on assessment of tax for the taxable year in which gain is required to be reported.

(2) *Property description.*—A description of all property distributed by the domestic liquidating corporation (irrespective of whether the property qualifies for nonrecognition). Such description shall be entitled "Master Property Description" and shall identify the property that continues to be used by the foreign distributee corporation in the conduct of a trade or business within the United States, including the location, adjusted basis, estimated fair market value, a summary of the method (including appraisals if any) used for determining such value, and the date of distribution of such items of property. The description shall also identify the property excepted from gain recognition under paragraphs (b)(2)(ii) and (iii) of this section.

(3) *Distributee identification.*—An identification of the foreign distributee corporation, including its name and address, taxpayer identification number, residence, and place of incorporation.

(4) *Treaty benefits waiver.*—With respect to property entitled to nonrecognition pursuant to this paragraph (b)(2)(i), a declaration by the foreign distributee corporation that it irrevocably waives any right under any treaty (whether or not currently in force at the time of the liquidation) to sell or exchange any item of such property without U.S. income taxation or at a reduced rate of taxation, or to derive income from the use of any item of such property without U.S. income taxation or at a reduced rate of taxation.

(5) *Statute of limitations extension.*—An agreement by the domestic liquidating corporation and the foreign distributee corporation to extend the statute of limitations on assessments and collections (under section 6501) with respect to the domestic liquidating corporation on the distribution of each item of property until three years after the date on which all such items of property have ceased to be used in a trade or business within the United States, but in no event shall the extension be for a period longer than 13 years from the filing of the original U.S. income tax return for the taxable year of the last distribution of any such item of property. The agreement to extend the statute of limitation shall be executed on a Form 8838, "Consent to Extend the Time to Assess Tax Under Section 367—Gain Recognition Agreement."

(D) *Failure to file statement.*—If a domestic liquidating corporation that would otherwise qualify for nonrecognition on the distribution of property under this paragraph (b)(2)(i) fails to file the statement described in paragraph (b)(2)(i)(C) of this section or files a statement that does not comply with the requirements of paragraph (b)(2)(i)(C) of this section, the Commissioner may treat the domestic liquidating corporation as if it had claimed nonrecognition under this paragraph (b)(2)(i) and met all the requirements of paragraph (b)(2)(i)(C) of this section, if such treatment is necessary to prevent the domestic liquidating corporation or the foreign distributee corporation from otherwise deriving a tax benefit by such failure.

(E) *Operating rules.*—By the domestic liquidating corporation's claiming nonrecognition under this paragraph (b)(2)(i) and filing a statement described in paragraph (b)(2)(i)(C) of this section, the domestic liquidating corporation and the foreign distributee corporation agree to be subject to the rules of this paragraph (b)(2)(i)(E).

(1) *Gain or loss recognition by the foreign distributee corporation.*—(i) *Taxable dispositions.*—If, within the ten-year period from the date of a distribution of qualifying property, the foreign distributee corporation disposes of any qualifying property in a transaction subject to tax under section 882(a), then the foreign distributee corporation shall recognize such gain (or loss) and properly report it on a timely filed U.S. income tax return. If the foreign distributee corporation recognizes gain (or loss) under this paragraph (b)(2)(i)(E)(1)(i) and properly reports such gain (or loss) on its U.S. income tax return, then the domestic liquidating corporation shall not recognize gain attributable to such property under paragraph (b)(2)(i)(E)(2) of this section.

(ii) *Other triggering events.*—If, within the ten-year period from the date of distribution, any qualifying property ceases to be used by the foreign distributee corporation in the conduct of a trade or business in the United States (other than by reason of a taxable disposition described in paragraph (b)(2)(i)(E)(1)(i) of this section, a nontriggering event described in paragraph (b)(2)(i)(E)(4) of this section, or a nontriggering transfer described in paragraph (b)(2)(i)(E)(5) of this section), then the foreign distributee corporation shall recognize gain (but not loss) attributable to such property and properly report it on a timely filed U.S. income tax return. If the foreign distributee corporation properly reports gain under this paragraph (or if such qualified property is not gain property on the date that it ceases to be used in the foreign distributee corporation's U.S. trade or business), then the domestic liquidating corporation shall not recognize gain attributable to such property under paragraph (b)(2)(i)(E)(2) of this section. The gain recognized under this paragraph (b)(2)(i)(E)(1)(ii) shall be an amount equal to the fair market value of the property on the date it ceases to be used in the foreign distributee corporation's U.S. trade or business less the foreign distributee corporation's adjusted basis in such property.

(2) *Gain recognition by the domestic liquidating corporation.*—(i) *General rule.*—If, within the ten-year period from the date of distribution, any qualifying property described in paragraph (b)(2)(i)(B) of this section ceases to be used by the foreign distributee corporation (or a qualifying transferee described in paragraph (b)(2)(i)(E)(5) of this section) in the conduct of a trade or business in the United States for any reason (including but not limited to the sale or exchange of such property or the removal of the property from conduct of the trade or business), then, except to the extent gain (or loss) is recognized under paragraph (b)(1)(i)(E)(1) of this section, the domestic liquidating corporation shall recognize the gain (but not loss) realized but not recognized upon the initial distribution of such item of property. The domestic liquidating corporation shall recognize gain pursuant to this paragraph (b)(2)(i)(E)(2)(i) on the amended

U.S. income tax return described in paragraph (b)(2)(i)(E)(2)(ii) of this section.

(ii) *Amended return.*—If gain recognition is required pursuant to paragraph (b)(2)(i)(E)(2)(i) of this section, the foreign distributee corporation shall file an amended U.S. income tax return on behalf of the domestic liquidating corporation for the year of the distribution of such item of property. On the amended return, the domestic liquidating corporation may use any losses (or credits) existing in the year of the distribution to offset the gain recognized pursuant to paragraph (b)(2)(i)(E)(2)(i) of this section (or the tax thereon), provided that the losses (or credits) were otherwise available in the year distribution and were not used in another year. The amended return shall be filed no later than the due date (including extensions) for the return of the foreign distributee corporation for the taxable year in which the property ceases to be used by the foreign distributee corporation in the conduct of a trade or business in the United States.

(iii) *Interest.*—If the domestic liquidating corporation owes additional tax pursuant to paragraph (b)(2)(i)(E)(2)(i) of this section for the year of liquidation, then interest must be paid on that amount at the rates determined under section 6621. The interest due will be calculated from the due date of the domestic liquidating corporation's U.S. income tax return for the year of the distribution to the date on which the additional tax for that year is paid.

(iv) *Joint and several liability.*—The foreign distributee corporation shall be jointly and severally liable for any tax owed by the domestic liquidating corporation as a result of the application of this section, and shall succeed to the domestic liquidating corporation's agreement to extend the statute of limitations on assessments and collections under section 6501.

(3) *Schedule for property no longer used in a U.S. trade or business.*—If qualifying property (other than inventory) ceases to be used by the foreign distributee corporation in the conduct of a U.S. trade or business in the ten-year period beginning on the date of distribution of such property from the domestic liquidating corporation to the foreign distributee corporation, then the foreign distributee corporation shall list on a separate schedule (attached to its timely filed U.S. income tax return for the year of cessation) all such qualifying property. For purposes of this paragraph (b)(2)(i)(E)(3), property ceases to be used in a U.S. trade or business whenever such property is sold, exchanged, or otherwise removed from the U.S. trade or business, irrespective of whether the domestic liquidating corporation filed an amended return under paragraph (b)(2)(i)(E)(2) of this section, and irrespective of whether the property ceases to be used in the foreign distributee corporation's U.S. trade or business by virtue of a nontriggering event described in paragraph (b)(2)(i)(E)(4) of this section or a nontriggering transfer described in paragraph (b)(2)(i)(E)(5) of this section.

(4) *Nontriggering events.*—(i) *Conversions, certain exchanges, and abandonment.*—Gain (or loss) under this paragraph (b)(2)(i)(E) shall not be triggered if qualifying property described in paragraph (b)(2)(i)(B) of this section is involuntarily converted into, or exchanged for, similar qualifying property used in the conduct of a trade or business in the United States, to the extent such conversion or exchange qualifies for nonrecognition under sections 1033 or 1031. Also, the abandonment or disposal of worthless or obsolete property shall not trigger gain (or loss) under this paragraph (b)(2)(i)(E).

(ii) *Amendment to Master Property Description.*—If the foreign distributee corporation acquires replacement property by virtue of a conversion or exchange of the qualifying property under this paragraph (b)(2)(i)(E)(4), then the foreign distributee corporation shall attach to its timely filed U.S. income tax return for the year of the acquisition such replacement property a schedule entitled "Amendment to Master Property Description Required by §1.367(e)-2(b)(2)(i)" that lists the replacement property and the property being replaced.

(5) *Nontriggering transfers to qualified transferees.*—Gain (or loss) under this paragraph (b)(2)(i)(E) will not be triggered if qualifying property described in paragraph (b)(2)(i)(B) of this section is transferred to another person (qualified transferee) in a transaction qualifying for nonrecognition under the Internal Revenue Code (other than transactions described in paragraphs (b)(2)(i)(E)(4)(i) and (c)(1) of this section), if—

(i) The qualified transferee (and all other subsequent qualified transferees), immediately thereafter and for the ten-year period beginning on the date of the initial distribution of such qualifying property from the domestic liquidating corporation to the foreign distributee corporation, uses the property in the conduct of a trade or business in the United States;

(ii) The foreign distributee corporation (or its successor in interest) prepares and attaches to its timely filed U.S. income tax return for the year of transfer a statement entitled "Required Statement under §1.367(e)-2(b)(2)(i)(E)(5) for Property Transferred to a Qualified Transferee" that is signed under penalties of perjury by an authorized officer of the foreign distributee corporation and by a person similarly authorized by the qualified transferee;

(iii) The statement described in paragraph (b)(2)(i)(E)(5)(ii) of this section shall contain a description of all qualifying property transferred by the foreign distributee corporation (or qualified transferee) to the qualified transferee (or subsequent qualified transferee);

(iv) The statement described in paragraph (b)(2)(i)(E)(5)(ii) of this section shall also contain an identification of the qualified transferee (or subsequent qualified transferee), including its name and address, taxpayer identification number, residence, and place of incorporation (if applicable);

(v) The statement described in paragraph (b)(2)(i)(E)(5)(ii) of this section shall also contain a declaration by the qualifying transferee (or subsequent qualifying transferee) that it irrevocably waives any right under any treaty (whether or not currently in force at the time of the liquidation) to sell or exchange any item of such property without U.S. income taxation or at a reduced rate of taxation, or to derive income from the use of any item of such qualifying property without U.S. income taxation or at a reduced rate of taxation; and

(vi) A declaration that the transfer to the qualifying transferee (or subsequent qualifying transferee) is one to which the rules of this paragraph (b)(2)(i)(E)(5) apply and a certification that the foreign distributee corporation (or its successor in interest) and the qualifying transferee (or subsequent qualifying transferee) agree to all of the terms and conditions set forth in paragraph (b)(2)(i)(E)(1) of this section, replacing "foreign distributee corporation" with "qualifying transferee" and replacing references to "section 882(a)" with "section 871(b)" (as the case may be).

(ii) *Distribution of certain U.S. real property interests.*—A domestic liquidating corporation shall not recognize gain (or loss) under paragraph (b)(1) of this section on the distribution of a U.S. real property interest (other than stock in a former U.S. real property holding corporation that is treated as a U.S. real property interest for five years under section 897(c)(1)(A)(ii)). If property distributed by the domestic liquidating corporation is a U.S. real property interest that qualifies for nonrecognition under this paragraph (b)(2)(ii) in addition to nonrecognition provided by paragraph (b)(2)(i) of this section, then the domestic liquidating corporation shall secure nonrecognition pursuant to this paragraph (b)(2)(ii) and not pursuant to the provisions of paragraph (b)(2)(i) of this section.

(iii) *Distribution of stock of domestic subsidiary corporations.*—(A) *Conditions for nonrecognition.*—A domestic liquidating corporation shall not recognize gain or loss under paragraph (b)(1) of this section on a distribution of stock of an 80 percent domestic subsidiary corporation, if the domestic liquidating corporation attaches a statement described in paragraph (b)(2)(iii)(D) of this section to its timely filed U.S. income tax return for the year of the distribution of such stock. For purposes of this paragraph (b)(2)(iii), a corporation is an 80 percent domestic subsidiary corporation, if—

(1) The subsidiary corporation is a domestic corporation (but not a foreign corporation that has made an election under section 897(i) to be treated as a U.S. corporation for purposes of section 897);

(2) The domestic liquidating corporation owns (directly and without regard to paragraph (b)(1)(iii) of this section) at least 80 percent of the total voting power of the stock of such corporation; and

(3) The domestic liquidating corporation owns (directly and without regard to paragraph (b)(1)(iii) of this section) at least 80 percent of the total value of all stock of such corporation.

(B) *Exceptions when the liquidating corporation is a U.S. real property holding corporation.*—If the domestic liquidating corporation is a U.S. real property holding corporation (as defined in section 897(c)(2)) at the time of liquidation (or is a former U.S. real property holding corporation the stock of which is treated as a U.S. real property interest for five years under section 897(c)(1)(A)(ii)), then the exception in paragraph (b)(2)(iii)(A) of this section shall apply only to the distribution of stock of an 80 percent domestic subsidiary corporation that is a U.S. real property holding corporation (as defined in section 897(c)(2)) at the time of the liquidation and immediately thereafter.

(C) *Anti-abuse rule.*—(1) The exception in paragraph (b)(2)(iii)(A) of this section shall not apply, if a principal purpose of the distribution of the 80 percent domestic subsidiary corporation's stock is the avoidance of U.S. tax that would have been imposed on the domestic liquidating corporation's disposition of such stock (directly or indirectly) to an unrelated party. A distribution may have a principal purpose of tax avoidance even though the tax avoidance purpose is outweighed by other purposes when taken together.

(2) For purposes of paragraph (b)(2)(iii)(C)(1) of this section, a distribution of stock of the 80 percent domestic subsidiary corporation will be deemed to have been made pursuant to a plan, one of the principal purposes of which was the avoidance of U.S. tax, if the foreign distributee corporation disposes of (whether in a recognition or nonrecognition transaction) any such stock within two years of such distribution. The rule in this paragraph (b)(2)(iii)(C)(2) will not apply if the foreign distributee corporation can demonstrate to the satisfaction of the Commissioner that the avoidance of U.S. tax was not a principal purpose of the liquidation.

(D) *Required statement.*—The statement required by paragraph (b)(2)(iii)(A) of this section shall be entitled "Required Statement under § 1.367(e)-2(b)(2)(iii) for Stock of 80 Percent Domestic Subsidiary Corporations" and shall be prepared by the domestic liquidating corporation and shall be signed under penalties of perjury by an authorized officer of the domestic liquidating corporation and by an authorized officer of the foreign distributee corporation. The required statement shall contain a certification that states that if the foreign distributee corporation disposes of any stock subject to paragraph (b)(2)(iii)(A) of this section in a transaction described in paragraph (b)(2)(iii)(C) of this section, then the domestic liquidating corporation shall recognize all realized gain attributable to the distributed stock at the time of distribution, and the domestic liquidating corporation (or the foreign distributee corporation on behalf of the domestic liquidating corporation) shall file a U.S. income tax return (or amended U.S. income tax return, as the case may be) for the year of distribution reporting the gain attributable to such stock. The required statement shall also state that the domestic liquidating corporation agrees, as provided in paragraph (e)(4)(ii)(B) of this section, to treat a failure to comply (as described in paragraph (e)(4)(i) of this section) as extending the period of limitations on assessment of tax for the taxable year in which gain is required to be reported.

(3) *Other consequences.*—(i) *Distributee basis in property.*—The foreign distributee corporation's basis in property subject to this paragraph (b) shall be the same as the domestic liquidating corporation's basis in such property immediately before the liquidation, increased by any gain, or reduced by any loss recognized by the domestic liquidating corporation on such property pursuant to paragraph (b)(1) of this section.

(ii) *Reporting under section 6038B.*—Section 6038B and the regulations thereunder apply to a domestic liquidating corporation's transfer of property to a foreign distributee corporation under section 367(e)(2).

(iii) *Other rules.*—For other rules that may apply, see sections 381, 897, 1248, and § 1.482-1(f)(2)(i)(C).

(c) *Distribution by a foreign corporation.*—(1) *General rule—gain and loss not recognized.*—If a foreign corporation (foreign liquidating) makes a distribution of property in complete liquidation under section 332 to a foreign corporation (foreign distributee) that meets the stock ownership requirements of section 332(b) with respect to stock in the foreign liquidating corporation, then, except as provided in paragraph (c)(2) of this section, section 337(a) and (b)(1) shall apply and the foreign liquidating corporation shall not recognize gain (or loss) on the distribution under section 367(e)(2). If a foreign liquidating corporation distributes a partnership interest (whether foreign or domestic), then such corporation shall be treated as having distributed a proportionate share of partnership property in accordance with the principles of paragraph (b)(1)(iii) of this section.

(2) *Exceptions.*—(i) *Property used in a U.S. trade or business.*—(A) *General rule.*—A foreign liquidating corporation (including a corporation that has made an effective election under section 897(i)) that makes a distribution described in paragraph (c)(1) of this section shall recognize gain (or loss in accordance with principles contained in paragraph (b)(1)(ii) of this section) on the distribution of qualified property, as described in paragraph (b)(2)(i)(B) of this section (other than U.S. real property interests), that is used by the foreign liquidating corporation in the conduct of a trade or business within the United States at the time of distribution.

(B) *Ten-year active U.S. business exception.*—A foreign liquidating corporation shall not recognize gain under paragraph (c)(2)(i)(A) of this section, if—

(1) The foreign distributee corporation, immediately thereafter and for the ten-year period beginning on the date of the distribution of such property, uses the property in the conduct of a trade or business in the United States;

(2) The foreign distributee corporation is not entitled to benefits under a comprehensive income tax treaty (this requirement shall apply only if the foreign liquidating corporation (or predecessor corporation) was not entitled to benefits under a comprehensive income tax treaty); and

(3) The foreign liquidating corporation and foreign distributee corporation attach the statement described in paragraph (c)(2)(i)(C) of this section to their timely filed U.S. income tax returns for their taxable years that include the distribution.

(C) *Required statement.*—The statement required by paragraph (c)(2)(i)(B)(3) of this section shall be entitled "Required Statement under § 1.367(e)-2(c)(2)(i)," shall be prepared by foreign liquidating corporation, shall be signed under penalties of perjury by an authorized officer of the foreign liquidating corporation and by an authorized officer of the foreign distributee corporation, and shall be identical to the statement described in paragraph (b)(2)(i)(C) of this section, except that "§ 1.367(e)-2(c)(2)(i)(B)" shall be substituted for references to "§ 1.367(e)-2(b)(2)(i)" and "foreign liquidating corporation" shall be substituted for "domestic liquidating corporation" each time it appears. References in the rules of paragraph (b)(2)(i)(C) of this section to various rules in paragraph (b) of this section shall be applied as if such references were to this paragraph (c). However, the statement described in this paragraph (c)(2)(i)(C) shall be modified as follows:

(1) The foreign distributee corporation shall not be required to waive its income tax treaty benefits as required by § 1.367(e)-2(b)(2)(i)(C)(4), unless—

(i) The foreign liquidating corporation was required to waive its treaty benefits under paragraph (b)(2)(i)(C)(4) of this section in connection with the distribution of such property in a prior liquidation distribution subject to the provisions of this section; or

(ii) The foreign distributee corporation is entitled benefits under a treaty to which the foreign liquidating corporation was not entitled.

(2) If the foreign distributee is required to waive treaty benefits because of paragraph (c)(2)(i)(C)(1)(ii) of this section, then the foreign distributee shall only be required to waive benefits that were not available to the foreign liquidating corporation (or a predecessor corporation) prior to liquidation.

(3) The property description described in paragraph (b)(2)(i)(C)(2) of this section shall include only the qualified U.S. trade or business property described in paragraph (c)(2)(i) of this section.

(D) *Operating rules.*—By the foreign liquidating corporation's claiming nonrecognition under paragraph (c)(2)(i)(B) of this section and filing a statement described in paragraph (c)(2)(i)(C) of this section, the foreign liquidating corporation and the foreign distributee corporation agree to be subject to the rules of paragraph (c)(2)(i) of this section, as well as the rules of paragraphs (b)(2)(i)(D) and (E) of this section. In applying the rules of paragraphs (b)(2)(i)(D) and (E) of this section, "foreign liquidating corporation" shall be used instead of "domestic liquidating corporation" each time it appears. References in the rules of paragraphs (b)(2)(i)(D) and (E) of this section to various rules in paragraph (b) of this section shall be applied as if such references were to this paragraph (c).

(ii) *Property formerly used in a United States trade or business.*—A foreign liquidating corporation that makes a distribution described in paragraph (c)(1) of this section shall recognize gain (but not loss) on the distribution of property (other than U.S. real property interests) that had ceased to be used by the foreign liquidating corporation in the conduct of a U.S. trade or business within the ten-year period ending on the date of distribution and that would have been subject to section 864(c)(7) had it been disposed. Section 864(c)(7) shall govern the treatment of any gain recognized on the distribution of assets described in this paragraph as income effectively connected with the conduct of a trade or business within the United States.

(3) *Other consequences.*—(i) *Distributee basis in property.*—The foreign distributee corporation's basis in property subject to this paragraph (c) shall be the same as the foreign liquidating corporation's basis in such property immediately before the liquidation, increased by any gain, or reduced by any loss recognized by the foreign liquidating corporation on such property, pursuant to paragraph (c)(2) of this section.

(ii) *Other rules.*—For other rules that may apply, see sections 367(b) and 381.

(d) *Anti-abuse rule.*—The Commissioner may require a domestic liquidating corporation to recognize gain on a distribution in liquidation described in paragraph (b) of this section (or treat the liquidating corporation as if it had recognized loss on a distribution in liquidation), if a principal purpose of the liquidation is the avoidance of U.S. tax (including, but not limited to, the distribution of a liquidating corporation's earnings and profits with a principal purpose of avoiding U.S. tax). A liquidation may have a principal purpose of tax avoidance even though the tax avoidance purpose is outweighed by other purposes when taken together.

(e) *Failures to file or failures to comply.*—(1) *Scope.*—This paragraph (e) provides rules regarding a failure to file an initial liquidation document with respect to one or more liquidating distributions by a domestic liquidating corporation that, absent such failure, would qualify for nonrecognition treatment under paragraph (b)(2)(i) or (iii) of this section, or with respect to one or more liquidating distributions by a foreign liquidating corporation that, absent such failure, would qualify for nonrecognition treatment under paragraph (c)(2)(i)(B) of this section (failure to file). This paragraph (e) also provides rules regarding failures to comply in all material respects with the terms of this section with respect to one or more liquidating distributions for which nonrecognition treatment was initially claimed under paragraph (b)(2)(i), (b)(2)(iii), or (c)(2)(i)(B) of this section, as applicable (failure to comply).

(2) *Definitions.*—The following definitions apply for purposes of this section.

(i) An *initial liquidation document* means any statement, schedule, or form required to be filed under this section in order for the domestic liquidating corporation or foreign liquidating corporation, as applicable, to initially qualify to claim nonrecognition treatment with respect to one or more liquidating distributions described in this section, including—

(A) The statement and attachments described in paragraph (b)(2)(i)(C) of this section;

(B) The statement described in paragraph (b)(2)(iii)(D) of this section; and

(C) The statement and attachments described in paragraph (c)(2)(i)(C) of this section.

(ii) A *subsequent liquidation document* means any statement, schedule, or form (other than an initial liquidation document) required to be filed under this section in order for the domestic liquidating corporation or foreign liquidating corporation, as applicable, to continue to qualify for nonrecognition treatment with respect to one or more liquidating distributions described in this section, including—

(A) The schedule described in paragraph (b)(2)(i)(E)(*3*) of this section;

(B) The schedule described in paragraph (b)(2)(i)(E)(*4*)(*ii*) of this section; and

(C) The statement and attachments described in paragraph (b)(2)(i)(E)(*5*) of this section.

(iii) A *timely filed U.S. income tax return* means a Federal income tax return filed on or before the last date prescribed for filing (taking into account any extensions of time therefor) such return.

(3) *Failure to file.*—(i) *General rule.*—For purposes of this section and except as provided in paragraph (b)(2)(i)(D) or (f) of this section, there is a failure to file an initial liquidation document if—

(A) An initial liquidation document is not filed with the timely filed U.S. income tax return specified under this section, or

(B) An initial liquidation document is not completed in all material respects.

(ii) *Consequences of a failure to file.*—If there is a failure to file an initial liquidation document, then nonrecognition treatment under paragraph (b)(2)(i), (b)(2)(iii), or (c)(2)(i)(B) of this section (as appropriate) will not apply.

(4) *Failure to comply.*—(i) *General rule.*—For purposes of this section and except as provided in paragraph (b)(2)(i)(D) or (f) of this section, a failure to comply includes –

(A) A failure to report gain, or pay any additional tax or interest due, in accordance with the requirements under this section; and

(B) A failure to file a subsequent liquidation document, as determined by applying paragraph (e)(3)(i) of this section, but replacing the term "initial liquidation document" with the term "subsequent liquidation document."

(ii) *Consequences of a failure to comply.*—If there is a failure to comply in any material respect with the terms of paragraph (b)(2)(i), (b)(2)(iii), or (c)(2)(i) of this section, as applicable, then—

(A) Any gain (but not loss) that was not previously recognized by the domestic liquidating corporation or foreign liquidating corporation, as applicable, under paragraph (b)(2)(i), (b)(2)(iii), or (c)(2)(i)(B) of this section must be recognized; and

(B) The period of limitations on assessment of tax for the taxable year in which gain is required to be reported will be extended until the close of the third full taxable year ending after the date on which the domestic liquidating corporation, foreign distributee corporation, or foreign liquidating corporation, as applicable, furnishes to the Director of Field Operations, Cross Border Activities Practice Area of Large Business & International (or any successor to the roles and responsibilities of such position, as appropriate) (Director) the information that should have been provided under this section.

(f) *Relief for certain failures to file or failures to comply that are not willful.*—(1) *In general.*—This paragraph (f) provides relief if there is a failure to file an initial liquidation document as described in paragraph (e)(3)(i) of this section (failure to file), or a failure to comply in any material respect with the terms of this section as described in paragraph (e)(4)(i) of this section (failure to comply). A failure to file or a failure to comply will be deemed not to have occurred for purposes of paragraph (e)(3)(ii) or (e)(4)(ii) of this section if the taxpayer demonstrates that the failure was not willful using the procedure set forth in this paragraph (f). For this purpose, willful is to be interpreted consistent with the meaning of that term in the context of other civil penalties, which would include a failure due to gross negligence, reckless disregard, or willful neglect. Whether a failure to file or failure to comply was willful will be determined by the Director (as described in paragraph (e)(4)(ii)(B) of this section) based on all the facts and circumstances. The taxpayer must submit a request for relief and an explanation as provided in paragraph (f)(2)(i) of this section. Although a taxpayer whose failure to file or failure to comply is determined not to be willful will not be subject to gain or loss recognition under this section, the taxpayer will be subject to a penalty under section 6038B if the taxpayer fails to satisfy the reporting requirements, if any, under that section and does not demonstrate that the failure was due to reasonable cause and not willful neglect. See § 1.6038B-1(e)(4) and (f). The determination of whether the failure to file or failure to comply was willful under this section has no effect on any request for relief made under § 1.6038B-1(f).

(2) *Procedures for establishing that a failure to file or failure to comply was not willful.*—(i) *Time and manner of submission.*—A taxpayer's statement that a failure to file or failure to comply was not willful will be considered only if, promptly after the taxpayer becomes aware of the failure, an amended return is filed for the taxable year to which the failure relates that includes the information that should have been included with the original return for such taxable year or that otherwise complies with the rules of this section, and that includes a written statement explaining the reasons for the failure. In the case of a liquidating distribution described in paragraph (b)(2)(iii) of this section, the taxpayer must file, with the amended return, a Form 8838 extending the period of limitations on assessment of tax with respect to the gain realized but not recognized with respect to the liquidating distribution to the close of the third full taxable year ending after the date on which the required information is provided to the Director. In the case of a liquidating distribution described in paragraph (b)(2)(i) or (c)(2)(i)(B) of this section, the taxpayer must file, with the amended return, a Form 8838 extending the period of limitations on the assessment of tax with respect to the gain realized but not recognized with respect to the liquidating distribution to the later of: the date provided in paragraph (b)(2)(i)(C)(5), taking into account paragraph (c)(2)(i)(C) and (D), as applicable (date one); or, the close of the third full taxable year ending after the date on which the required information is provided to the Director (date two). However, the taxpayer is not required to file a Form 8838 with the amended return if both date one is later than date two and a Form 8838 was previously filed extending the period of limitations on assessment of tax with respect to the gain realized but not recognized with respect to the liquidating distribution to date one. If a Form 8838 is not required to be filed pursuant to the previous sentence, a copy of the previously filed Form 8838 must be filed with the amended return. The amended return and either a Form 8838 or a copy of the previously filed Form 8838, as the case may be, must be filed with the Internal Revenue Service at the location where the taxpayer filed its original return. The taxpayer may submit a request for relief from the penalty under section 6038B as part of the same submission. See § 1.6038B-1(f).

(ii) *Notice requirement.*—In addition to the requirements of paragraph (f)(2)(i) of this section, the taxpayer must comply with the notice requirements of this paragraph (f)(2)(ii). If any taxable year of the taxpayer is under examination when the amended return is filed, a copy of the amended return and any information required to be included with such return must be delivered to the Internal Revenue Service personnel conducting the examination. If no taxable year of the taxpayer is under examination when the amended return is filed, a copy of the amended return and any information required to be included with such return must be delivered to the Director.

(3) For illustrations of the application of the willfulness standard of this paragraph (f), see the examples in § 1.367(a)-8(p)(3).

(g) *Effective/applicability dates.*—Except as otherwise provided, this section applies to distributions occurring on or after September 7, 1999 or, if the taxpayer so elects, to distributions in taxable years ending after August 8, 1999. The ninth, tenth, and eleventh sentences of paragraph (a) of this section, and paragraphs (b)(1)(i), (b)(2)(i)(A)(2), (b)(2)(i)(A)(3), (b)(2)(i)(E)(3), (b)(2)(i)(E)(4)(ii), (b)(2)(i)(E)(5)(ii), (b)(2)(iii)(A), (c)(2)(i)(B)(3), (e), and (f) of this section will apply to liquidation documents that are required to be filed on or after November 19, 2014, as well as to requests for relief submitted on or after November 19, 2014. [Reg. § 1.367(e)-2.]

☐ [*T.D.* 8834, 8-6-99 (*corrected* 3-2-2000), *Amended by T.D.* 9066, 7-1-2003, *T.D.* 9704 11-18-2014 (*corrected* 1-2-2015) *and T.D.* 9803, 12-15-2016.]

[Reg. § 1.368-1]

§ 1.368-1. Purpose and scope of exception of reorganization exchanges.—(a) *Reorganizations.*—As used in the regulations under parts I, II, and III (section 301 and following), subchapter C of the Code, the terms "reorganization" and "party to a reorganization" mean only a reorganization or a party to a reorganization as defined in subsections (a) and (b) of section 368. In determining whether a transaction qualifies as a reorganization under section 368(a), the transaction must be evaluated under relevant provisions of law, including the step transaction doctrine. But see §§ 1.368-2(f) and (k) and 1.338-3(d). The preceding two sentences apply to transactions occurring after January 28, 1998, except that they do not apply to any transaction occurring pursuant to a written agreement which is binding on January 28, 1998, and at all times thereafter. With respect to insolvency reorganizations, see part IV of subchapter C, chapter 1 of the Code.

(b) *Purpose.*—Under the general rule, upon the exchange of property, gain or loss must be accounted for if the new property differs in a material particular, either in kind or in extent, from the old property. The purpose of the reorganization provisions of the Code is to except from the general rule certain specifically described exchanges incident to such readjustments of corporate structures made in one of the particular ways specified in the Code, as are required by business exigencies and which effect only a readjustment of continuing interest in property under modified corporate forms. Requisite to a reorganization under the Internal Revenue Code are a continuity of the business enterprise through the issuing corporation under the modified corporate form as described in paragraph (d) of this section, and (except as provided in section 368(a)(1)(D)) a continuity of interest as described in paragraph (e) of this section. (For rules regarding the continuity of interest requirement under section 355, see § 1.355-2(c).) For purposes of this section, the term *issuing corporation* means the acquiring corporation (as that term is used in section 368(a)), except that, in determining whether a reorganization qualifies as a triangular reorganization (as defined in § 1.358-6(b)(2)), the issuing corporation means the corporation in control of the acquiring corporation. The preceding three sentences apply to transactions occurring after January 28, 1998, except that they do not apply to any transaction occurring pursuant to a written agreement which is binding on January 28, 1998, and at all times thereafter. The continuity of business enterprise requirement is described in paragraph (d) of this section. Notwithstanding the requirements of this paragraph (b), for transactions occurring on or after February 25, 2005, a continuity of the business enterprise and a continuity of interest are not required for the transaction to qualify as a reorganization under section 368(a)(1)(E) or (F). The Code recognizes as a reorganization the amalgamation (occurring in a specified way) of two corporate enterprises under a single corporate structure if there exists among the holders of the stock and securities of either of the old corporations the requisite continuity of interest in the new corporation, but there is not a reorganization if the holders of the stock and securities of the old corporation are merely the holders of short-term notes in the new corporation. In order to exclude transactions not intended to be included, the specifications of the reorganization provisions of the law are precise. Both the terms of the specifications and their underlying assumptions and purposes must be satisfied in order to entitle the taxpayer to the benefit of the exception from the general rule. Accordingly, under the Code, a short-term purchase money note is not a security of a party to a reorganization, an ordinary dividend is to be treated as an ordinary dividend, and a sale is nevertheless to be treated as a sale even though the mechanics of a reorganization have been set up.

(c) *Scope.*—The nonrecognition of gain or loss is prescribed for two specifically described types of exchanges, viz.: The exchange that is provided for in section 354(a)(1) in which stock or securities in a corporation, a party to a reorganization, are, in pursuance of a plan of reorganization, exchanged for the stock or securities in a corporation, a party to the same reorganization; and the exchange that is provided for in section 361(a) in which a corporation, a party to a reorganiza-

tion, exchanges property, in pursuance of a plan of reorganization, for stock or securities in another corporation, a party to the same reorganization. Section 368(a)(1) limits the definition of the term "reorganization" to six kinds of transactions and excludes all others. From its context, the term "a party to a reorganization" can only mean a party to a transaction specifically defined as a reorganization by section 368(a). Certain rules respecting boot received in either of the two types of exchanges provided for in section 354(a)(1) and section 361(a) are prescribed in sections 356, 357, and 361(b). A special rule respecting a transfer of property with a liability in excess of its basis is prescribed in section 357(c). Under section 367 a limitation is placed on all these provisions by providing that except under specified conditions foreign corporations shall not be deemed within their scope. The provisions of the Code referred to in this paragraph are inapplicable unless there is a plan of reorganization. A plan of reorganization must contemplate the bona fide execution of one of the transactions specifically described as a reorganization in section 368(a) and for the bona fide consummation of each of the requisite acts under which nonrecognition of gain is claimed. Such transaction and such acts must be an ordinary and necessary incident of the conduct of the enterprise and must provide for a continuation of the enterprise. A scheme, which involves an abrupt departure from normal reorganization procedure in connection with a transaction on which the imposition of tax is imminent, such as a mere device that puts on the form of a corporate reorganization as a disguise for concealing its real character, and the object and accomplishment of which is the consummation of a preconceived plan having no business or corporate purpose, is not a plan of reorganization.

(d) *Continuity of business enterprise.*—(1) *General rule.*—Continuity of business enterprise (COBE) requires that the issuing corporation (P), as defined in paragraph (b) of this section, either continue the target corporation's (T's) historic business or use a significant portion of T's historic business assets in a business. The preceding sentence applies to transactions occurring after January 28, 1998, except that it does not apply to any transaction occurring pursuant to a written agreement which is binding on January 28, 1998, and at all times thereafter. The application of this general rule to certain transactions, such as mergers of holding companies, will depend on all facts and circumstances. The policy underlying this general rule, which is to ensure that reorganizations are limited to readjustments of continuing interests in property under modified corporate form, provides the guidance necessary to make these facts and circumstances determinations.

(2) *Business continuity.*—(i) The continuity of business enterprise requirement is satisfied if P continues T's historic business. The fact P is in the same line of business as T tends to establish the requisite continuity, but is not alone sufficient.

(ii) If T has more than one line of business, continuity of business enterprise requires only that P continue a significant line of business.

(iii) In general, a corporation's historic business is the business it has conducted most recently. However, a corporation's historic business is not one the corporation enters into as part of a plan of reorganization.

(iv) All facts and circumstances are considered in determining the time when the plan comes into existence and in determining whether a line of business is "significant".

(3) *Asset continuity.*—(i) The continuity of business enterprise requirement is satisfied if P uses a significant portion of T's historic business assets in a business.

(ii) A corporation's historic business assets are the assets used in its historic business. Business assets may include stock and securities and intangible operating assets such as good will, patents, and trademarks, whether or not they have a tax basis.

(iii) In general, the determination of the portion of a corporation's assets considered "significant" is based on the relative importance of the assets to operation of the business. However, all other facts and circumstances, such as the net fair market value of those assets, will be considered.

(4) *Acquired assets or stock held by members of the qualified group or partnerships.*—The following rules apply in determining whether the COBE requirement of paragraph (d)(1) of this section is satisfied:

(i) *Businesses and assets of members of a qualified group.*—The issuing corporation is treated as holding all of the businesses and assets of all of the members of the qualified group, as defined in paragraph (d)(4)(ii) of this section.

(ii) *Qualified group.*—A qualified group is one or more chains of corporations connected through stock ownership with the issuing corporation, but only if the issuing corporation owns directly stock meeting the requirements of section 368(c) in at least one other corporation, and stock meeting the requirements of section 368(c) in each of the corporations (except the issuing corporation) is owned directly (or indirectly as provided in paragraph (d)(4)(iii)(D) of this section) by one or more of the other corporations.

(iii) *Partnerships.*—(A) *Partnership assets.*—Each partner of a partnership will be treated as owning the T business assets used in a business of the partnership in accordance with that partner's interest in the partnership.

(B) *Partnership businesses.*—The issuing corporation will be treated as conducting a business of a partnership if—

(1) Members of the qualified group, in the aggregate, own an interest in the partnership representing a significant interest in that partnership business; or

(2) One or more members of the qualified group have active and substantial management functions as a partner with respect to that partnership business.

(C) *Conduct of the historic T business in a partnership.*—If a significant historic T business is conducted in a partnership, the fact that P is treated as conducting such T business under paragraph (d)(4)(iii)(B) of this section tends to establish the requisite continuity, but is not alone sufficient.

(D) *Stock attributed from certain partnerships.*—Solely for purposes of paragraph (d)(4)(ii) of this section, if members of the qualified group own interests in a partnership meeting requirements equivalent to section 368(c) (a section 368(c) controlled partnership), any stock owned by the section 368(c) controlled partnership shall be treated as owned by members of the qualified group. Solely for purposes of determining whether a lower-tier partnership is a section 368(c) controlled partnership, any interest in a lower-tier partnership that is owned by a section 368(c) controlled partnership shall be treated as owned by members of the qualified group.

(iv) *Effective/applicability dates.*—Paragraphs (d)(4)(i) and (d)(4)(iii) (other than paragraph (d)(4)(iii)(D)) of this section apply to transactions occurring after January 28, 1998, except that they do not apply to any transaction occurring pursuant to a written agreement which is binding on January 28, 1998, and at all times thereafter. Paragraphs (d)(4)(ii) and (d)(4)(iii)(D) of this section apply to transactions occurring on or after October 25, 2007, except that they do not apply to any transaction occurring pursuant to a written agreement which is binding before October 25, 2007, and at all times after that.

(5) *Examples.*—The following examples illustrate this paragraph (d). All the corporations have only one class of stock outstanding. The preceding sentence and paragraph (d)(5) *Example 6* and *Example 8* through *Example 13* apply to transactions occurring after January 28, 1998, except that they do not apply to any transaction occurring pursuant to a written agreement which is binding on January 28, 1998, and at all times thereafter. Paragraph (d)(5) *Example 7, Example 14,* and *Example 15* apply to transactions occurring on or after October 25, 2007, except that they do not apply to any transaction occurring pursuant to a written agreement which is binding before October 25, 2007, and at all times after that. The examples read as follows:

Example 1. T conducts three lines of business: manufacture of synthetic resins, manufacture of chemicals for the textile industry, and distribution of chemicals. The three lines of business are approximately equal in value. On July 1, 1981, T sells the synthetic resin and chemical distribution businesses to a third party for cash and marketable securities. On December 31, 1981, T transfers all of its assets to P solely for P voting stock. P continues the chemical manufacturing business without interruption. The continuity of business enterprise requirement is met. Continuity of business enterprise requires only that P continue one of T' s three significant lines of business.

Example 2. P manufactures computers and T manufactures components for computers. T sells all of its output to P. On January 1, 1981, P decides to buy imported components only. On March 1, 1981, T merges into P. P continues buying imported components but retains T' s equipment as a backup source of supply. The use of the equipment as a backup source of supply constitutes use of a significant portion of T' s historic business assets, thus establishing continuity of business enterprise. P is not required to continue T' s business.

Example 3. T is a manufacturer of boys' and men's trousers. On January 1, 1978, as part of a plan of reorganization, T sold all of its assets to a third party for cash and purchased a highly diversified portfolio of stocks and bonds. As part of the plan T operates an investment business until July 1, 1981. On that date, the plan of reorganization culminates in a transfer by T of all its assets to P, a regulated investment company, solely in exchange for P voting stock. The continuity of business enterprise requirement is not met. T' s investment activity is not its historic business, and the stocks and bonds are not T' s historic business assets.

Example 4. T manufactures children's toys and P distributes steel and allied products. On January 1, 1981, T sells all of its assets to a third party for $100,000 cash and $900,000 in notes. On March 1, 1981, T merges into P. Continuity of business enterprise is lacking. The use of the sales proceeds in P' s business is not sufficient.

Example 5. T manufactures farm machinery and P operates a lumber mill. T merges into P. P disposes of T' s assets immediately after the merger as part of the plan of reorganization. P does not continue T' s farm machinery manufacturing business. Continuity of business enterprise is lacking.

Example 6. Use of a significant portion of T's historic business assets by the qualified group. (i) *Facts.* T operates an auto parts distributorship. P owns 80 percent of the stock of a holding company (HC). HC owns 80 percent of the stock of ten subsidiaries, S-1 through S-10. S-1 through S-10 each separately operate a full service gas station. Pursuant to a plan of reorganization, T merges into P and the T shareholders receive solely P stock. As part of the plan of reorganization, P transfers T's assets to HC, which in turn transfers some of the T assets to each of the ten subsidiaries. No one subsidiary receives a significant portion of T's historic business assets. Each of the subsidiaries will use the T assets in the operation of its full service gas station. No P subsidiary will be an auto parts distributor.

(ii) *Continuity of business enterprise.* Under paragraph (d)(4)(i) of this section, P is treated as conducting the ten gas station businesses of S-1 through S-10 and as holding the historic T assets used in those businesses. P is treated as holding all the assets and conducting the businesses of all of the members of the qualified group, which includes S-1 through S-10 (paragraphs (d)(4)(i) and (ii) of this section). No member of the qualified group continues T's historic distributorship business. However, subsidiaries S-1 through S-10 continue to use the historic T assets in a business. Even though no one corporation of the qualified group is using a significant portion of T's historic business assets in a business, the COBE requirement of paragraph (d)(1) of this section is satisfied because, in the aggregate, the qualified group is using a significant portion of T's historic business assets in a business.

Example 7. Transfers of acquired stock to members of the qualified group - continuity of business enterprise satisfied. (i) *Facts.* The facts are the same as *Example 6,* except that, instead of P acquiring the assets of T, HC acquires all of the outstanding stock of T in exchange solely for stock of P. In addition, as part of the plan of reorganization, HC transfers 10 percent of the stock of T to each of subsidiaries S-1 through S-10. T will continue to operate an auto parts distributorship. Without regard to whether the transaction satisfies the COBE requirement, the transaction qualifies as a triangular B reorganization (as defined in § 1.358-6(b)(2)(iv)).

(ii) *Continuity of business enterprise.* Under paragraph (d)(4)(i) of this section, P is treated as holding the assets and conducting the business of T because T is a member of the qualified group (as defined in paragraph (d)(4)(ii) of this section). The COBE requirement of paragraph (d)(1) of this section is satisfied.

Example 8. Continuation of the historic T business in a Partnership satisfies continuity of business enterprise. (i) *Facts.* T manufactures ski boots. P owns all of the stock of S-1. S-1 owns all of the stock of S-2, and S-2 owns all of the stock of S-3. T merges into P and the T shareholders receive consideration consisting of P stock and cash. The T ski boot business is to be continued and expanded. In anticipation of this expansion, P transfers all of the T assets to S-1, S-1 transfers all of the T assets to S-2, and S-2 transfers all of the T assets to S-3. S-3 and X (an unrelated party) form a new partnership (PRS). As part of the plan of reorganization, S-3 transfers all the T assets to PRS, and S-3, in its capacity as a partner, performs active and substantial management functions for the PRS ski boot business, including making significant business decisions and regularly participating in the overall supervision, direction, and control of the employees of the ski boot business. S-3 receives a 20 percent interest in PRS. X transfers cash in exchange for an 80 percent interest in PRS.

(ii) *Continuity of business enterprise.* Under paragraph (d)(4)(iii)(B)(2) of this section, P is treated as conducting T's historic business because S-3 performs active and substantial management functions for the ski boot business in S-3's capacity as a partner. P is treated as holding all the assets and conducting the businesses of all of the members of the qualified group, which includes S-3 (paragraphs (d)(4)(i) and (ii) of this section). The COBE requirement of paragraph (d)(1) of this section is satisfied.

Example 9. Continuation of the historic T business in a partnership does not satisfy continuity of business enterprise. (i) *Facts.* The facts are the same as *Example 8,* except that S-3 transfers the historic T business to PRS in exchange for a 1 percent interest in PRS.

(ii) *Continuity of business enterprise.* Under paragraph (d)(4)(iii)(B)(2) of this section, P is treated as conducting T's historic business because S-3 performs active and substantial management functions for the ski boot business in S-3's capacity as a partner. The fact that a significant historic T business is conducted in PRS, and P is treated as conducting such T business under (d)(4)(iii)(B) tends to establish the requisite continuity, but is not alone sufficient (paragraph (d)(4)(iii)(C) of this section). The COBE requirement of paragraph (d)(1) of this section is not satisfied.

Example 10. Continuation of the T historic business in a partnership satisfies continuity of business enterprise. (i) *Facts.* The facts are the same as *Example 8,* except that S-3 transfers the historic T business to PRS in exchange for a 33 1/3 percent interest in PRS, and no member of P's qualified group performs active and substantial management functions for the ski boot business operated in PRS.

(ii) *Continuity of business enterprise.* Under paragraph (d)(4)(iii)(B)(1) of this section, P is treated as conducting T's historic business because S-3 owns an interest in the partnership representing a significant interest in that partnership business. P is treated as holding all the assets and conducting the businesses of all of the members of the qualified group, which includes S-3 (paragraphs (d)(4)(i) and (ii) of this section). The COBE requirement of paragraph (d)(1) of this section is satisfied.

Example 11. Use of T's historic business assets in a partnership business. (i) *Facts.* T is a fabric distributor. P owns all of the stock of S-1. T merges into P and the T shareholders receive solely P stock. S-1 and X (an unrelated party) own interests in a partnership (PRS). As part of the plan of reorganization, P transfers all of the T assets to S-1, and S-1 transfers all the T assets to PRS, increasing S-1's percentage interest in PRS from 5 to 33 1/3 percent. After the transfer, X owns the remaining 66 2/3 percent interest in PRS. Almost all of the T assets consist of T's large inventory of fabric, which PRS uses to manufacture sportswear. All of the T assets are used in the sportswear business. No member of P's qualified group performs active and substantial management functions for the sportswear business operated in PRS.

(ii) *Continuity of business enterprise.* Under paragraph (d)(4)(iii)(A) of this section, S-1 is treated as owning 33 1/3 percent of the T assets used in the PRS sportswear manufacturing business. Under paragraph (d)(4)(iii)(B)(1) of this section, P is treated as conducting the sportswear manufacturing business because S-1 owns an interest in the partnership representing a significant interest in that partnership business. P is treated as holding all the assets and conducting the businesses of all of the members of the qualified group, which includes S-1 (paragraphs (d)(4)(i) and (ii) of this section). The COBE requirement of paragraph (d)(1) of this section is satisfied.

Example 12. Aggregation of partnership interests among members of the qualified group: use of T's historic business assets in a partnership business. (i) *Facts.* The facts are the same as *Example 11,* except that S-1 transfers all the T assets to PRS, and P and X each transfer cash to PRS in exchange for partnership interests. After the transfers, P owns 11 percent, S-1 owns 22 1/3 percent, and X owns 66 2/3 percent of PRS.

(ii) *Continuity of business enterprise.* Under paragraph (d)(4)(iii)(B)(1) of this section, P is treated as conducting the sportswear manufacturing business because members of the qualified group, in the aggregate, own an interest in the partnership representing a significant interest in that business. P is treated as owning 11 percent of the assets directly, and S-1 is treated as owning 22 1/3 percent of the assets, used in the PRS sportswear business (paragraph (d)(4)(iii)(A) of this section). P is treated as holding all the assets of all of the members of the qualified group, which includes S-1, and thus in the aggregate, P is treated as owning 33 1/3 of the T assets (paragraph (d)(4)(i) and (ii) of this section). The COBE requirement of paragraph (d)(1) of this section is satisfied because P is treated as using a significant portion of T's historic business assets in its sportswear manufacturing business.

Example 13. Tiered partnerships: use of T's historic business assets in a partnership business. (i) *Facts.* T owns and manages a commercial office building in state Z. Pursuant to a plan of reorganization, T merges into P, solely in exchange for P stock, which is distributed to the T shareholders. P transfers all of the T assets to a partnership, PRS-1, which owns and operates television stations nationwide. After the transfer, P owns a 50 percent interest in PRS-1. P does not have active and substantial management functions as a partner with respect to the PRS-1 business. X, not a member of P's qualified group, owns the remaining 50 percent interest in PRS-1. PRS-1, in an effort to expand its state Z television operation, enters into a joint venture with U, an unrelated party. As part of the plan of reorganization, PRS-1 transfers all the T assets and its state Z television station to PRS-2, in exchange for a 75 percent partnership interest. U contributes cash to PRS-2 in exchange for a 25 percent partnership interest and oversees the management of the state Z television operation. PRS-1 does not actively and substantially manage PRS-2's business. PRS-2's state Z operations are moved into the acquired T office building. All of the assets that P acquired from T are used in PRS-2's business.

(ii) *Continuity of business enterprise.* Under paragraph (d)(4)(iii)(A) of this section, PRS-1 is treated as owning 75 percent of

the T assets used in PRS-2's business. P, in turn, is treated as owning 50 percent of PRS-1's interest the T assets. Thus, P is treated as owning 37 1/2 percent (50 percent×75 percent) of the T assets used in the PRS-2 business. Under paragraph (d)(4)(iii)(B)(1) of this section, P is treated as conducting PRS-2's business, the operation of the state Z television station, and under paragraph (d)(4)(iii)(A) of this section, P is treated as using 37 1/2 percent of the historic T business assets in that business. The COBE requirement of paragraph (d)(1) of this section is satisfied because P is treated as using a significant portion of T's television business assets in its television business.

Example 14. Transfer of acquired stock to a partnership - continuity of business enterprise satisfied. (i) *Facts.* Pursuant to a plan of reorganization, the T shareholders transfer all of their T stock to a subsidiary of P, S-1, solely in exchange for P stock. In addition, as part of the plan of reorganization, S-1 transfers the T stock to its subsidiary, S-2, and S-2 transfers the T stock to its subsidiary, S-3. S-2 and S-3 form a new partnership, PRS. Immediately thereafter, S-3 transfers all of the T stock to PRS in exchange for an 80 percent interest in PRS, and S-2 transfers cash to PRS in exchange for a 20 percent interest in PRS.

(ii) *Continuity of business enterprise.* Members of the qualified group, in the aggregate, own all of the interests in PRS. Because these interests in PRS meet requirements equivalent to section 368(c), under paragraph (d)(4)(iii)(D) of this section, the T stock owned by PRS is treated as owned by members of the qualified group. P is treated as holding all of the businesses and assets of T because T is a member of the qualified group (as defined in paragraph (d)(4)(ii) of this section). The COBE requirement of paragraph (d)(1) of this section is satisfied because P is treated as continuing T's business.

Example 15. Transfer of acquired stock to a partnership - continuity of business enterprise not satisfied. (i) *Facts.* The facts are the same as in *Example 14,* except that S-3 and U, an unrelated corporation, form a new partnership, PRS, and, immediately thereafter, S-3 transfers all of the T stock to PRS in exchange for a 50 percent interest in PRS, and U transfers cash to PRS in exchange for a 50 percent interest in PRS.

(ii) *Continuity of business enterprise.* Members of the qualified group, in the aggregate, own 50 percent of the interests in PRS. Because these interests in PRS do not meet requirements equivalent to section 368(c), the T stock owned by PRS is not treated as owned by members of the qualified group under paragraph (d)(4)(iii)(D) of this section. P is not treated as holding all of the businesses and assets of T because T has ceased to be a member of the qualified group (as defined in paragraph (d)(4)(ii) of this section). The COBE requirement of paragraph (d)(1) of this section is not satisfied because P is not treated as continuing T's business or using T's historic business assets in a business.

(e) *Continuity of interest.*—(1) *General rule.*—(i) The purpose of the continuity of interest requirement is to prevent transactions that resemble sales from qualifying for nonrecognition of gain or loss available to corporate reorganizations. Continuity of interest requires that in substance a substantial part of the value of the proprietary interests in the target corporation be preserved in the reorganization. A proprietary interest in the target corporation is preserved if, in a potential reorganization, it is exchanged for a proprietary interest in the issuing corporation (as defined in paragraph (b) of this section), it is exchanged by the acquiring corporation for a direct interest in the target corporation enterprise, or it otherwise continues as a proprietary interest in the target corporation. However, a proprietary interest in the target corporation is not preserved if, in connection with the potential reorganization, it is acquired by the issuing corporation for consideration other than stock of the issuing corporation, or stock of the issuing corporation furnished in exchange for a proprietary interest in the target corporation in the potential reorganization is redeemed. All facts and circumstances must be considered in determining whether, in substance, a proprietary interest in the target corporation is preserved. See paragraph (e)(6) of this section for rules related to when a creditor's claim against a target corporation is a proprietary interest in the corporation. For purposes of the continuity of interest requirement, a mere disposition of stock of the target corporation prior to a potential reorganization to persons not related (as defined in paragraph (e)(4) of this section determined without regard to paragraph (e)(4)(i)(A) of this section) to the target corporation or to persons not related (as defined in paragraph (e)(4) of this section) to the issuing corporation is disregarded and a mere disposition of stock of the issuing corporation received in a potential reorganization to persons not related (as defined in paragraph (e)(4) of this section) to the issuing corporation is disregarded.

(ii) For purposes of paragraph (e)(1)(i) of this section, a proprietary interest in the target corporation (other than one held by the acquiring corporation) is not preserved to the extent that consideration received prior to a potential reorganization, either in a redemption of the target corporation stock or in a distribution with respect to the target corporation stock, is treated as other property or money received in the exchange for purposes of section 356, or would be so treated if the target shareholder also had received stock of the issuing corporation in exchange for stock owned by the shareholder in the target corporation. A proprietary interest in the target corporation is not preserved to the extent that creditors (or former creditors) of the target corporation that own a proprietary interest in the corporation under paragraph (e)(6) of this section (or would be so treated if they had received the consideration in the potential reorganization) receive payment for the claim prior to the potential reorganization and such payment would be treated as other property or money received in the exchange for purposes of section 356 had it been a distribution with respect to stock.

(2) *Measuring continuity of interest.*—(i) *In general.*—In determining whether a proprietary interest in the target corporation is preserved, the consideration to be exchanged for the proprietary interests in the target corporation pursuant to a contract to effect the potential reorganization shall be valued on the last business day before the first date such contract is a binding contract (the pre-signing date), if such contract provides for fixed consideration. If a portion of the consideration provided for in such a contract consists of other property identified by value, then this specified value of such other property is used for purposes of determining the extent to which a proprietary interest in the target corporation is preserved. If the contract does not provide for fixed consideration, this paragraph (e)(2)(i) is not applicable.

(ii) *Binding contract.*—(A) *In general.*—A binding contract is an instrument enforceable under applicable law against the parties to the instrument. The presence of a condition outside the control of the parties (including, for example, regulatory agency approval) shall not prevent an instrument from being a binding contract. Further, the fact that insubstantial terms remain to be negotiated by the parties to the contract, or that customary conditions remain to be satisfied, shall not prevent an instrument from being a binding contract.

(B) *Modifications.*—(1) *In general.*—If a term of a binding contract that relates to the amount or type of the consideration the target shareholders will receive in a potential reorganization is modified before the closing date of the potential reorganization, and the contract as modified is a binding contract, the date of the modification shall be treated as the first date there is a binding contract.

(2) *Modification of a transaction that preserves continuity of interest.*—Notwithstanding paragraph (e)(2)(ii)(B)(1) of this section, a modification of a term that relates to the amount or type of consideration the target shareholders will receive in a transaction that would have resulted in the preservation of a substantial part of the value of the target corporation shareholders' proprietary interests in the target corporation if there had been no modification will not be treated as a modification if—

(i) The modification has the sole effect of providing for the issuance of additional shares of issuing corporation stock to the target corporation shareholders;

(ii) The modification has the sole effect of decreasing the amount of money or other property to be delivered to the target corporation shareholders; or

(iii) The modification has the effect of decreasing the amount of money or other property to be delivered to the target corporation shareholders and providing for the issuance of additional shares of issuing corporation stock to the target corporation shareholders.

(3) *Modification of a transaction that does not preserve continuity of interest.*—Notwithstanding paragraph (e)(2)(ii)(B)(1) of this section, a modification of a term that relates to the amount or type of consideration the target shareholders will receive in a transaction that would not have resulted in the preservation of a substantial part of the value of the target corporation shareholders' proprietary interests in the target corporation if there had been no modification will not be treated as a modification if—

(i) The modification has the sole effect of providing for the issuance of fewer shares of issuing corporation stock to the target corporation shareholders;

(ii) The modification has the sole effect of increasing the amount of money or other property to be delivered to the target corporation shareholders; or

(iii) The modification has the effect of increasing the amount of money or other property to be delivered to the target corporation shareholders and providing for the issuance of fewer shares of issuing corporation stock to the target corporation shareholders.

(C) *Tender offers.*—For purposes of this paragraph (e)(2), a tender offer that is subject to section 14(d) of the Securities and Exchange Act of 1934 [15 U.S.C. 78n(d)(1)] and Regulation 14D (17 CFR 240.14d-1 through 240.14d-101) and is not pursuant to a binding contract, is treated as a binding contract made on the date of its announcement, notwithstanding that it may be modified by the offeror or that it is not enforceable against the offerees. If a modification (not pursuant to a binding contract) of such a tender offer is subject to the provisions of Regulation 14d-6(c) (17 CFR 240.14d-6(c)) and relates to the amount or type of the consideration received in the tender offer, then the date of the modification shall be treated as the first date there is a binding contract.

(iii) *Fixed consideration.*—(A) *In general.*—A contract provides for fixed consideration if it provides the number of shares of each class of stock of the issuing corporation, the amount of money, and the other property (identified either by value or by specific description), if any, to be exchanged for all the proprietary interests in the target corporation, or to be exchanged for each proprietary interest in the target corporation. A shareholder's election to receive a number of shares of stock of the issuing corporation, money, or other property (or some combination of stock of the issuing corporation, money, or other property) in exchange for all of the shareholder's proprietary interests in the target corporation, or each of the shareholder's proprietary interests in the target corporation, will not prevent a contract from satisfying the definition of fixed consideration provided for in this paragraph (e)(2)(iii)(A).

(B) *Shareholder elections.*—A contract that provides a target corporation shareholder with an election to receive a number of shares of stock of the issuing corporation, money, or other property (or some combination of stock of the issuing corporation, money, or other property) in exchange for all of the shareholder's proprietary interests in the target corporation, or each of the shareholder's proprietary interests in the target corporation, provides for fixed consideration if the determination of the number of shares of issuing corporation stock to be provided to the target corporation shareholder is determined using the value of the issuing corporation stock on the last business day before the first date there is a binding contract. This is the case even though the shareholder election may preclude a determination, prior to the closing date, of the number of shares of each class of the issuing corporation, the amount of money, and the other property (or the combination of shares, money, and other property) to be exchanged for each proprietary interest in the target corporation.

(C) *Contingent adjustments to the consideration.*—(1) *In general.*—Except as provided in paragraph (e)(2)(iii)(C)(2) of this section, a contract that provides for contingent adjustments to the consideration will be treated as providing for fixed consideration if it would satisfy the requirements of paragraph (e)(2)(iii)(A) of this section without the contingent adjustment provision.

(2) *Exceptions.*—A contract will not be treated as providing for fixed consideration if the contract provides for contingent adjustments to the consideration that prevent (to any extent) the target corporation shareholders from being subject to the economic benefits and burdens of ownership of the issuing corporation stock after the last business day before the first date the contract is a binding contract. For example, a contract will not be treated as providing for fixed consideration if the contract provides for contingent adjustments to the consideration in the event that the value of the stock of the issuing corporation, the value of the assets of the issuing corporation, or the value of any surrogate for either the value of the stock of the issuing corporation or the assets of the issuing corporation increases or decreases after the last business day before the first date there is a binding contract. Similarly, a contract will not be treated as providing for fixed consideration if the contract provides for contingent adjustments to the number of shares of the issuing corporation stock to be provided to the target corporation shareholders computed using any value of the issuing corporation shares after the last business day before the first date there is a binding contract.

(D) *Escrows.*—Placing part of the consideration to be exchanged for proprietary interests in the target corporation in escrow to secure target's performance of customary pre-closing covenants or customary target representations and warranties will not prevent a contract from being treated as providing for fixed consideration.

(E) *Anti-dilution clauses.*—The presence of a customary anti-dilution clause will not prevent a contract from being treated as providing for fixed consideration. However, the absence of such a clause will prevent a contract from being treated as providing for fixed consideration if the issuing corporation alters its capital structure between the first date there is an otherwise binding contract to effect the transaction and the effective date of the transaction in a manner that materially alters the economic arrangement of the parties to the binding contract. If the number of shares of the issuing corporation to be issued to the target corporation shareholders is altered pursuant to a customary anti-dilution clause, the value of the shares determined under paragraph (e)(2)(i) of this section must be adjusted accordingly.

Reg. §1.368-1(e)(2)(iii)(E)

(F) *Dissenters' rights.*—The possibility that some shareholders may exercise dissenters' rights and receive consideration other than that provided for in the binding contract will not prevent the contract from being treated as providing for fixed consideration.

(G) *Fractional shares.*—The fact that money may be paid in lieu of issuing fractional shares will not prevent a contract from being treated as providing for fixed consideration.

(iv) *New issuances.*—For purposes of applying paragraph (e)(2)(i) of this section, any class of stock, securities, or indebtedness that the issuing corporation issues to the target corporation shareholders pursuant to the potential reorganization and that does not exist before the first date there is a binding contract to effect the potential reorganization is deemed to have been issued on the last business day before the first date there is a binding contract to effect the potential reorganization.

(v) *Examples.*—For purposes of the examples in this paragraph (e)(2)(v), P is the issuing corporation, T is the target corporation, S is a wholly owned subsidiary of P, all corporations have only one class of stock outstanding, A is an individual, no transactions other than those described occur, and the transactions are not otherwise subject to recharacterization. The following examples illustrate the application of this paragraph (e)(2):

Example 1. Application of signing date rule. On January 3 of year 1, P and T sign a binding contract pursuant to which T will be merged with and into P on June 1 of year 1. Pursuant to the contract, the T shareholders will receive 40 P shares and $60 of cash in exchange for all of the outstanding stock of T. Twenty of the P shares, however, will be placed in escrow to secure customary target representations and warranties. The P stock is listed on an established market. On January 2 of year 1, the value of the P stock is $1 per share. On June 1 of year 1, T merges with and into P pursuant to the terms of the contract. On that date, the value of the P stock is $.25 per share. None of the stock placed in escrow is returned to P. Because the contract provides for the number of shares of P and the amount of money to be exchanged for all of the proprietary interests in T, under this paragraph (e)(2), there is a binding contract providing for fixed consideration as of January 3 of year 1. Therefore, whether the transaction satisfies the continuity of interest requirement is determined by reference to the value of the P stock on the pre-signing date. Because, for continuity of interest purposes, the T stock is exchanged for $40 of P stock and $60 of cash, the transaction preserves a substantial part of the value of the proprietary interest in T. Therefore, the transaction satisfies the continuity of interest requirement.

Example 2. Treatment of forfeited escrowed stock. (i) Escrowed stock. The facts are the same as in *Example 1* except that T's breach of a representation results in the escrowed consideration being returned to P. Because the contract provides for the number of shares of P and the amount of money to be exchanged for all of the proprietary interests in T, under this paragraph (e)(2), there is a binding contract providing for fixed consideration as of January 3 of year 1. Therefore, whether the transaction satisfies the continuity of interest requirement is determined by reference to the value of the P stock on the pre-signing date. Pursuant to paragraph (e)(1)(i) of this section, for continuity of interest purposes, the T stock is exchanged for $20 of P stock and $60 of cash, and the transaction does not preserve a substantial part of the value of the proprietary interest in T. Therefore, the transaction does not satisfy the continuity of interest requirement.

(ii) *Escrowed stock and cash.* The facts are the same as in paragraph (i) of this *Example 2* except that the consideration placed in escrow consists solely of eight of the P shares and $12 of the cash. Because the contract provides for the number of shares of P and the amount of money to be exchanged for all of the proprietary interests in T, under this paragraph (e)(2), there is a binding contract providing for fixed consideration as of January 3 of year 1. Therefore, whether the transaction satisfies the continuity of interest requirement is determined by reference to the value of the P stock on the pre-signing date. Pursuant to paragraph (e)(1)(i) of this section, for continuity of interest purposes, the T stock is exchanged for $32 of P stock and $48 of cash, and the transaction preserves a substantial part of the value of the proprietary interest in T. Therefore, the transaction satisfies the continuity of interest requirement.

Example 3. Redemption of stock received pursuant to binding contract. The facts are the same as in *Example 1* except that A owns 50 percent of the outstanding stock of T immediately prior to the merger and receives 10 P shares and $30 in the merger and an additional 10 P shares upon the release of the stock placed in escrow. In connection with the merger, A and S agree that, immediately after the merger, S will purchase any P shares that A acquires in the merger for $1 per share. Shortly after the merger, S purchases A's P shares for $20. Because the contract provides for the number of shares of P and the amount of money to be exchanged for all of the proprietary interests

in T, under this paragraph (e)(2), there is a binding contract providing for fixed consideration as of January 3 of year 1. Therefore, whether the transaction satisfies the continuity of interest requirement is determined by reference to the value of the P stock on the pre-signing date. In addition, S is a person related to P under paragraph (e)(4)(i)(A) of this section. Accordingly, A is treated as exchanging his T shares for $50 of cash. Because, for continuity of interest purposes, the T stock is exchanged for $20 of P stock and $80 of cash, the transaction does not preserve a substantial part of the value of the proprietary interest in T. Therefore, the transaction does not satisfy the continuity of interest requirement.

Example 4. Modification of binding contract—continuity not preserved. The facts are the same as in *Example 1* except that on April 1 of year 1, the parties modify their contract. Pursuant to the modified contract, which is a binding contract, the T shareholders will receive 50 P shares (an additional 10 shares) and $75 of cash (an additional $15 of cash) in exchange for all of the outstanding T stock. On March 31 of year 1, the value of the P stock is $.50 per share. Under this paragraph (e)(2), although there was a binding contract providing for fixed consideration as of January 3 of year 1, terms of that contract relating to the consideration to be provided to the target shareholders were modified on April 1 of year 1. The execution of the transaction without modification would have resulted in the preservation of a substantial part of the value of the target corporation shareholders' proprietary interests in the target corporation if there had been no modification. However, because the modified contract provides for additional P stock and cash to be exchanged for all the proprietary interests in T, the exception in paragraph (e)(2)(ii)(B)(2) of this section does not apply to preserve the original signing date. Therefore, whether the transaction satisfies the continuity of interest requirement is determined by reference to the value of the P stock on March 31 of year 1. Because, for continuity of interest purposes, the T stock is exchanged for $25 of P stock and $75 of cash, the transaction does not preserve a substantial part of the value of the proprietary interest in T. Therefore, the transaction does not satisfy the continuity of interest requirement.

Example 5. Modification of binding contract disregarded—continuity preserved. The facts are the same as in *Example 4* except that, pursuant to the modified contract, which is a binding contract, the T shareholders will receive 60 P shares (an additional 20 shares as compared to the original contract) and $60 of cash in exchange for all of the outstanding T stock. In addition, on March 31 of year 1, the value of the P stock is $.40 per share. Under this paragraph (e)(2), although there was a binding contract providing for fixed consideration as of January 3 of year 1, terms of that contract relating to the consideration to be provided to the target shareholders were modified on April 1 of year 1. Nonetheless, the modification has the sole effect of providing for the issuance of additional P shares to the T shareholders. In addition, the execution of the terms of the contract without regard to the modification would have resulted in the preservation of a substantial part of the value of the T shareholders' proprietary interest in T because, for continuity of interest purposes, the T stock would have been exchanged for $40 of P stock and $60 of cash. Pursuant to paragraph (e)(2)(ii)(B)(2) of this section, the modification is not treated as a modification for purposes of paragraph (e)(2)(ii)(B)(1) of this section. Accordingly, whether the transaction satisfies the continuity of interest requirement is determined by reference to the value of the P stock on the pre-signing date. Because, for continuity of interest purposes, the T stock is exchanged for $60 of P stock and $60 of cash, the transaction preserves a substantial part of the value of the proprietary interest in T. Therefore the transaction satisfies the continuity of interest requirement.

Example 6. New issuance. The facts are the same as in *Example 1*, except that, instead of cash, the T shareholders will receive a new class of P securities that will be publicly traded. In the aggregate, the securities will have a stated principal amount of $60 and bear interest at the average LIBOR (London Interbank Offered Rates) during the 10 days prior to the potential reorganization. If the T shareholders had been issued the P securities on January 2 of year 1, the P securities would have had a value of $60 (determined by reference to the value of comparable publicly traded securities). Whether the transaction satisfies the continuity of interest requirement is determined by reference to the value of the P stock and the P securities to be issued to the T shareholders on January 2 of year 1. Under paragraph (e)(2)(iv) of this section, for purposes of valuing the new P securities, they will be treated as having been issued on the pre-signing date. Because, for continuity of interest purposes, the T stock is exchanged for $40 of P stock and $60 of other property, the transaction preserves a substantial part of the value of the proprietary interest in T. Therefore, the transaction satisfies the continuity of interest requirement.

Example 7. Fixed consideration—continuity not preserved. On January 3 of year 1, P and T sign a binding contract pursuant to which T will be merged with and into P on June 1 of year 1. Pursuant to the contract, 60 shares of the T stock will be exchanged for $80 of cash and 40 shares of the T stock will be exchanged for 20 shares of P stock. On January 2 of year 1, the value of the P stock is $1 per share. On June 1 of year 1, T merges with and into P pursuant to the terms of the contract. This contract provides for fixed consideration and therefore whether the transaction satisfies the continuity of interest requirement is determined by reference to the value of the P stock on the pre-signing date. However, applying the signing date rule, the P stock represents only 20 percent of the value of the total consideration to be received by the T shareholders. Accordingly, based on the economic realities of the exchange, the transaction does not preserve a substantial part of the value of the proprietary interest in T. Therefore, the transaction does not satisfy the continuity of interest requirement.

Example 8. Anti-dilution clause. (i) *Absence of anti-dilution clause.* On January 3 of year 1, P and T sign a binding contract pursuant to which T will be merged with and into P on June 1 of year 1. Pursuant to the contract, the T shareholders will receive 40 P shares and $60 of cash in exchange for all of the outstanding stock of T. The contract does not contain a customary anti-dilution provision. The P stock is listed on an established market. On January 2 of year 1, the value of the P stock is $1 per share. On April 10 of year 1, P issues its stock to effect a stock split; each shareholder of P receives an additional share of P for each P share that it holds. On April 11 of year 1, the value of the P stock is $.50 per share. Because P altered its capital structure between January 3 and June 1 of year 1 in a manner that materially alters the economic arrangement of the parties, under paragraph (e)(2)(iii)(E) of this section, the contract is not treated as a binding contract that provides for fixed consideration. Accordingly, whether the transaction satisfies the continuity of interest requirement cannot be determined by reference to the value of the P stock on January 2 of year 1.

(ii) *Adjustment for anti-dilution clause.* The facts are the same as in paragraph (i) of this *Example 8* except that the contract contains a customary anti-dilution provision, and the T shareholders receive 80 P shares and $60 of cash in exchange for all of the outstanding stock of T. Under paragraph (e)(2)(iii)(E) of this section, the contract is treated as a binding contract that provides for fixed consideration as of January 3 of year 1. Therefore, whether the transaction satisfies the continuity of interest requirement is generally determined by reference to the value of the P stock on January 2 of year 1. However, under paragraph (e)(2)(iii)(E) of this section, the value of the P stock on the pre-signing date must be adjusted to take the stock split into account. For continuity of interest purposes, the T stock is exchanged for $40 of P stock (($1/2) × 80) and $60 of cash. Therefore, the transaction satisfies the continuity of interest requirement.

Example 9. Shareholder election. On January 3 of year 1, P and T sign a binding contract pursuant to which T will be merged with and into P on June 1 of year 1. On January 2 of year 1, the value of the P stock and the T stock is $1 per share. Pursuant to the contract, at the shareholders' election, each share of T's 100 shares will be exchanged for cash of $1, or alternatively, P stock. The contract provides that the determination of the number of shares of P stock to be exchanged for a share of T stock is made using the value of the P stock on the last business day before the first date there is a binding contract (that is, $1 per share). The contract further provides that, in the aggregate, 40 shares of P stock and $60 will be delivered, and contains a proration mechanism in the event that either item of consideration is oversubscribed. On the closing date, the value of the P stock is $.20 per share, and all target shareholders elect to receive cash. Pursuant to the proration provision, each target share is exchanged for $.60 of cash and $.08 of P stock. Pursuant to paragraph (e)(2)(iii)(A) of this section, the contract provides for fixed consideration because it provides for the number of shares of P stock and the amount of money to be exchanged for all the proprietary interests in the target corporation. Furthermore, pursuant to paragraph (e)(2)(iii)(B) of this section, the contract provides for fixed consideration because the number of shares of issuing corporation stock to be provided to the target corporation shareholders is determined using the presigning date value of P stock. Accordingly, whether the transaction satisfies the continuity of interest requirement is determined by reference to the value of the P stock on January 2 of year 1. Because, for continuity purposes, the T stock is exchanged for $40 of P stock and $60 of cash, the transaction preserves a substantial part of the value of the proprietary interest in T. Therefore, the transaction satisfies the continuity of interest requirement.

Example 10. Contingent adjustment based on the value of the issuing corporation stock—continuity not preserved. On January 3 of year 1, P and T sign a binding contract pursuant to which T will be merged with and into P on June 1 of year 1. On January 2 of year 1, the value of the P stock is $1 per share. Pursuant to the contract, if the value of the P stock does not decrease after January 2 of year 1, the T shareholders will receive 40 P shares and $60 of cash in exchange for all of the outstanding stock of T. Furthermore, the contract provides that the T shareholders will receive $.16 of additional P shares and $.24 for every $.01 decrease in the value of one share of P stock after

January 2 of year 1. On June 1 of year 1, T merges with and into P pursuant to the terms of the contract. On that date, the value of the P stock is $.40 per share. Pursuant to the terms of the contract, the consideration is adjusted so that the T shareholders receive 24 more P shares ((60 × $.16)/$.40) and $14.40 more cash (60 × $.24) than they would absent an adjustment. Accordingly, at closing the T shareholders receive 64 P shares and $74.40 of cash. Because the contract provides that additional P shares and cash will be delivered to the T shareholders if the value of the stock of P decreases after January 2 of year 1, under paragraph (e)(2)(iii)(C) 2) of this section, the contract is not treated as providing for fixed consideration, and therefore whether the transaction satisfies the continuity of interest requirement cannot be determined by reference to the value of the P stock on January 2 of year 1. For continuity of interest purposes, the T stock is exchanged for $25.60 of P stock (64 × $.40) and $74.40 of cash and the transaction does not preserve a substantial part of the value of the proprietary interest in T. Therefore, the transaction does not satisfy the continuity of interest requirement.

Example 11. Contingent adjustment to boot based on the value of the target corporation stock—continuity not preserved. On January 3 of year 1, P and T sign a binding contract pursuant to which T will be merged with and into P on June 1 of year 1. On January 2 of year 1, T has 100 shares outstanding, and each T share is worth $1. On January 2 of year 1, each P share is worth $1. Pursuant to the contract, if the value of the T stock does not increase after January 3 of year 1, the T shareholders will receive 40 P shares and $60 of cash in exchange for all of the outstanding stock of T. Furthermore, the contract provides that the T shareholders will receive $1 of additional cash for every $.01 increase in the value of one share of T stock after January 3 of year 1. On June 1 of year 1, the value of the T stock is $1.40 per share and the value of the P stock is $.75 per share. Pursuant to the terms of the contract, the consideration is adjusted so that the T shareholders receive $40 more cash (40 × $1) than they would absent an adjustment. Accordingly, at closing the T shareholders receive 40 P shares and $100 of cash. Because the contract provides the number of shares of P stock and the amount of money to be exchanged for all the proprietary interests in T, and the contingent adjustment to the cash consideration is not based on changes in the value of the P stock, P assets, or any surrogate thereof, after January 2 of year 1, there is a binding contract providing for fixed consideration as of January 3 of year 1. Therefore, whether the transaction satisfies the continuity of interest requirement is determined by reference to the value of the P stock on January 2 of year 1. For continuity of interest purposes, the T stock is exchanged for $40 of P stock (40 × $1) and $100 of cash. Therefore, the transaction does not satisfy the continuity of interest requirement.

Example 12. Contingent adjustment to stock based on the value of the target corporation stock—continuity preserved. On January 3 of year 1, P and T sign a binding contract pursuant to which T will be merged with and into P on June 1 of year 1. On that date T has 100 shares outstanding, and each T share is worth $1. On January 2 of year 1, each P share is worth $1. Pursuant to the contract, if the value of the T stock does not decrease after January 3 of year 1, the T shareholders will receive 40 P shares and $60 of cash in exchange for all of the outstanding stock of T. Furthermore, the contract provides that the T shareholders will receive $.40 less P stock and $.60 less cash for every $.01 decrease in the value of one share of T stock after January 3 of year 1. The contract also provides that the number of P shares by which the consideration will be reduced as a result of this adjustment will be determined based on the value of the P stock on January 2 of year 1. On June 1 of year 1, T merges with and into P pursuant to the terms of the contract. On that date, the value of the T stock is $.70 per share and the value of the P stock is $.75 per share. Pursuant to the terms of the contract, the consideration is adjusted so that the T shareholders receive 12 fewer P shares ((30 × $.40)/$1) and $18 less cash (30 × $.60) than they would absent an adjustment. Accordingly, at closing the T shareholders receive 28 P shares and $42 of cash. Because the contract provides for the number of shares of P stock and the amount of money to be exchanged for all of the proprietary interests in T, the contract does not provide for contingent adjustments to the consideration based on a change in value of the P stock, P assets, or any surrogate thereof, after January 2 of year 1, and the adjustment to the number of P shares the T shareholders receive is determined based on the value of the P shares on January 2 of year 1, there is a binding contract providing for fixed consideration as of January 3 of year 1. Therefore, whether the transaction satisfies the continuity of interest requirement is determined by reference to the value of the P stock on January 2 of year 1. For continuity of interest purposes, the T stock is exchanged for $28 of P stock (28 × $1) and $42 of cash. Accordingly, the transaction satisfies the continuity of interest requirement.

(3) *Related person acquisitions.*—A proprietary interest in the target corporation is not preserved if, in connection with a potential reorganization, a person related (as defined in paragraph (e)(4) of this

section) to the issuing corporation acquires, for consideration other than stock of the issuing corporation, either a proprietary interest in the target corporation or stock of the issuing corporation that was furnished in exchange for a proprietary interest in the target corporation. The preceding sentence does not apply to the extent those persons who were the direct or indirect owners of the target corporation prior to the potential reorganization maintain a direct or indirect proprietary interest in the issuing corporation.

(4) *Definition of related person.*—(i) *In general.*—For purposes of this paragraph (e), two corporations are related persons if either—

(A) The corporations are members of the same affiliated group as defined in section 1504 (determined without regard to section 1504(b)); or

(B) A purchase of the stock of one corporation by another corporation would be treated as a distribution in redemption of the stock of the first corporation under section 304(a)(2) (determined without regard to § 1.1502-80(b)). 50%

(ii) *Special rules.*—The following rules apply solely for purposes of this paragraph (e)(4):

(A) A corporation will be treated as related to another corporation if such relationship exists immediately before or immediately after the acquisition of the stock involved.

(B) A corporation, other than the target corporation or a person related (as defined in paragraph (e)(4) of this section determined without regard to paragraph (e)(4)(i)(A) of this section) to the target corporation, will be treated as related to the issuing corporation if the relationship is created in connection with the potential reorganization.

(5) *Acquisitions by partnerships.*—For purposes of this paragraph (e), each partner of a partnership will be treated as owning or acquiring any stock owned or acquired, as the case may be, by the partnership in accordance with that partner's interest in the partnership. If a partner is treated as acquiring any stock by reason of the application of this paragraph (e)(5), the partner is also treated as having furnished its share of any consideration furnished by the partnership to acquire the stock in accordance with that partner's interest in the partnership.

(6) *Creditors' claims as proprietary interests.*—(i) *In general.*—A creditor's claim against a target corporation may be a proprietary interest in the target corporation if the target corporation is in a title 11 or similar case (as defined in section 368(a)(3)) or the amount of the target corporation's liabilities exceeds the fair market value of its assets immediately prior to the potential reorganization. In such cases, if any creditor receives a proprietary interest in the issuing corporation in exchange for its claim, every claim of that class of creditors and every claim of all equal and junior classes of creditors (in addition to the claims of shareholders) is a proprietary interest in the target corporation immediately prior to the potential reorganization to the extent provided in paragraph (e)(6)(ii) of this section.

(ii) *Value of proprietary interest.*—(A) *Claims of most senior class of creditor receiving stock.*—A claim of the most senior class of creditors receiving a proprietary interest in the issuing corporation and a claim of any equal class of creditors will be treated as a proprietary interest in accordance with the rules of this paragraph (e)(6)(ii). For a claim of the most senior class of creditors receiving a proprietary interest in the issuing corporation and a claim of any equal class of creditors, the value of the proprietary interest in the target corporation represented by the claim is determined by multiplying the fair market value of the claim by a fraction, the numerator of which is the fair market value of the proprietary interests in the issuing corporation that are received in the aggregate in exchange for the claims of those classes of creditors, and the denominator of which is the sum of the amount of money and the fair market value of all other consideration (including the proprietary interests in the issuing corporation) received in the aggregate in exchange for such claims. If only one class (or one set of equal classes) of creditors receives stock, such class (or set of equal classes) is treated as the most senior class of creditors receiving stock. When only one class (or one set of equal classes) of creditors receives issuing corporation stock in exchange for a creditor's proprietary interest in the target corporation, such stock will be counted for measuring continuity of interest provided that the stock issued by the issuing corporation is not de minimis in relation to the total consideration received by the insolvent target corporation, its shareholders, and its creditors.

(B) *Claims of junior classes of creditor receiving stock.*—The value of a proprietary interest in the target corporation held by a creditor whose claim is junior to the claims of other classes of target claims which are receiving proprietary interests in the issuing corporation is the fair market value of the junior creditor's claim.

(iii) *Bifurcated claims.*—If a creditor's claim is bifurcated into a secured claim and an unsecured claim pursuant to an order in a title 11 or similar case (as defined in section 368(a)(3)) or pursuant to an agreement between the creditor and the debtor, the bifurcation of the claim and the allocation of consideration to each of the resulting claims will be respected in applying the rules of this paragraph (e)(6).

(iv) *Effect of treating creditors as proprietors.*—The treatment of a creditor's claim as a proprietary interest in the target corporation shall not preclude treating shares of the target corporation as proprietary interests in the target corporation.

(7) *Successors and predecessors.*—For purposes of this paragraph (e), any reference to the issuing corporation or the target corporation includes a reference to any successor or predecessor of such corporation, except that the target corporation is not treated as a predecessor of the issuing corporation and the issuing corporation is not treated as a successor of the target corporation.

(8) *Examples.*—For purposes of the examples in this paragraph (e)(7), P is the issuing corporation, T is the target corporation, S is a wholly owned subsidiary of P, all corporations have only one class of stock outstanding, A and B are individuals, PRS is a partnership, all reorganization requirements other than the continuity of interest requirement are satisfied, and the transaction is not otherwise subject to recharacterization. The following examples illustrate the application of this paragraph (e):

Example 1. Sale of stock to third party. (i) *Sale of issuing corporation stock after merger.* A owns all of the stock of T. T merges into P. In the merger, A receives P stock having a fair market value of $50x and cash of $50x. Immediately after the merger, and pursuant to a preexisting binding contract, A sells all of the P stock received by A in the merger to B. Assume that there are no facts and circumstances indicating that the cash used by B to purchase A's P stock was in substance exchanged by P for T stock. Under paragraphs (e)(1) and (3) of this section, the sale to B is disregarded because B is not a person related to P within the meaning of paragraph (e)(4) of this section. Thus, the transaction satisfies the continuity of interest requirement because 50 percent of A's T stock was exchanged for P stock, preserving a substantial part of the value of the proprietary interest in T.

(ii) *Sale of target corporation stock before merger.* The facts are the same as paragraph (i) of this *Example 1*, except that B buys A's T stock prior to the merger of T into P and then exchanges the T stock for P stock having a fair market value of $50x and cash of $50x. The sale by A is disregarded. The continuity of interest requirement is satisfied because B's T stock was exchanged for P stock, preserving a substantial part of the value of the proprietary interest in T.

Example 2. Relationship created in connection with potential reorganization. Corporation X owns 60 percent of the stock of P and 30 percent of the stock of T. X owns the remaining 70 percent of the stock of T. X buys A's T stock for cash in a transaction which is not a qualified stock purchase within the meaning of section 338. T then merges into P. In the merger, X exchanges all of its T stock for additional stock of P. As a result of the issuance of the additional stock to X in the merger, X's ownership interest in P increases from 60 to 80 percent of the stock of P. X is not a person related to P under paragraph (e)(4)(i)(B) of this section, because a purchase of stock of P by X would not be treated as a distribution in redemption of the stock of P under section 304(a)(2). However, X is a person related to P under paragraphs (e)(4)(i)(A) and (ii)(B) of this section, because X becomes affiliated with P in the merger. The continuity of interest requirement is not satisfied, because X acquired a proprietary interest in T for consideration other than P stock, and a substantial part of the value of the proprietary interest in T is not preserved. See paragraph (e)(3) of this section.

Example 3. Participation by issuing corporation in post-merger sale. A owns 80 percent of the T stock and none of the P stock, which is widely held. T merges into P. In the merger, A receives P stock. In addition, A obtains rights pursuant to an arrangement with P to have P register the P stock under the Securities Act of 1933, as amended. P registers A's stock, and A sells the stock shortly after the merger. No person who purchased the P stock from A is a person related to P within the meaning of paragraph (e)(4) of this section. Under paragraphs (e)(1) and (3) of this section, the sale of the P stock by A is disregarded because no person who purchased the P stock from A is a person related to P within the meaning of paragraph (e)(4) of this section. The transaction satisfies the continuity of interest requirement because A's T stock was exchanged for P stock, preserving a substantial part of the value of the proprietary interest in T.

Example 4. Redemptions and purchases by issuing corporation or related persons. (i) *Redemption by issuing corporation.* A owns 100 percent of the stock of T and none of the stock of P. T merges into S. In the merger, A receives P stock. In connection with the merger, P redeems all of the P stock received by A in the merger for cash. The continuity of interest requirement is not satisfied, because, in connection with the merger, P redeemed the stock exchanged for a proprietary interest in T, and a substantial part of the value of the proprietary interest in T is not preserved. See paragraph (e)(1) of this section.

(ii) *Purchase of target corporation stock by issuing corporation.* The facts are the same as paragraph (i) of this *Example 4*, except that, instead of P redeeming its stock, prior to and in connection with the merger of T into S, P purchases 90 percent of the T stock from A for cash. The continuity of interest requirement is not satisfied, because in connection with the merger, P acquired a proprietary interest in T for consideration other than P stock, and a substantial part of the value of the proprietary interest in T is not preserved. See paragraph (e)(1) of this section. However, see §1.338-3(d) (which may change the result in this case by providing that, by virtue of section 338, continuity of interest is satisfied for certain parties after a qualified stock purchase).

(iii) *Purchase of issuing corporation stock by person related to issuing corporation.* The facts are the same as paragraph (i) of this *Example 4*, except that, instead of P redeeming its stock, S buys all of the P stock received by A in the merger for cash. S is a person related to P under paragraphs (e)(4)(i)(A) and (B) of this section. The continuity of interest requirement is not satisfied, because S acquired P stock issued in the merger, and a substantial part of the value of the proprietary interest in T is not preserved. See paragraph (e)(3) of this section.

Example 5. Redemption in substance by issuing corporation. A owns 100 percent of the stock of T and none of the stock of P. T merges into P. In the merger, A receives P stock. In connection with the merger, B buys all of the P stock received by A in a merger for cash. Shortly thereafter, in connection with the merger, P redeems the stock held by B for cash. Based on all the facts and circumstances, P in substance has exchanged solely cash for T stock in the merger. The continuity of interest requirement is not satisfied, because in substance P redeemed the stock exchanged for a proprietary interest in T, and a substantial part of the value of the proprietary interest in T is not preserved. See paragraph (e)(1) of this section.

Example 6. Purchase of issuing corporation stock through partnership. A owns 100 percent of the stock of T and none of the stock of P. S is an 85 percent partner in PRS. The other 15 percent of PRS is owned by unrelated persons. T merges into P. In the merger, A receives P stock. In connection with the merger, PRS purchases all of the P stock received by A in the merger for cash. Under paragraph (e)(5) of this section, S, as an 85 percent partner of PRS, is treated as having acquired 85 percent of the P stock exchanged for A's T stock in the merger, and as having furnished 85 percent of the cash paid by PRS to acquire the P stock. S is a person related to P under paragraphs (e)(4)(i)(A) and (B) of this section. The continuity of interest requirement is not satisfied, because S is treated as acquiring 85 percent of the P stock issued in the merger, and a substantial part of the value of the proprietary interest in T is not preserved. See paragraph (e)(3) of this section.

Example 7. Exchange by acquiring corporation for direct interest. A owns 30 percent of the stock of T. P owns 70 percent of the stock of T, which was not acquired by P in connection with the acquisition of T's assets. T merges into P. A receives cash in the merger. The continuity of interest requirement is satisfied, because P's 70 percent proprietary interest in T is exchanged by P for a direct interest in the assets of the target corporation enterprise.

Example 8. Maintenance of direct or indirect interest in issuing corporation. X, a corporation, owns all of the stock of each of corporations P and Z. Z owns all of the stock of T. T merges into P. Z receives P stock in the merger. Immediately thereafter and in connection with the merger, Z distributes the P stock received in the merger to X. X is a person related to P under paragraph (e)(4)(i)(A) of this section. The continuity of interest requirement is satisfied, because X was an indirect owner of T prior to the merger who maintains a direct or indirect proprietary interest in P, preserving a substantial part of the value of the proprietary interest in T. See paragraph (e)(3) of this section.

Example 9. Preacquisition redemption by target corporation. T has two shareholders, A and B. P expresses an interest in acquiring the stock of T. A does not wish to own P stock. T redeems A's shares in T *in exchange for cash.* No funds have been or will be provided by P for this purpose. P subsequently acquires all the outstanding stock of T from B solely in exchange for voting stock of P. The cash received by A in the prereorganization redemption is not treated as other property or money under section 356, and would not be so treated even if A had received some stock of P in exchange for his T stock. The prereorganization redemption by T does not affect continuity of interest, because B's proprietary interest in T is unaffected, and the value of the proprietary interest in T is preserved.

Example 10. Creditors treated as owning a proprietary interest. (i) *More than one class of creditor receives issuing corporation stock.* T has assets with a fair market value of $150x and liabilities of $200x. T has

two classes of creditors: two senior creditors with claims of $25x each; and one junior creditor with a claim of $150x. T transfers all of its assets to P in exchange for $95x in cash and shares of P stock with a fair market value of $55x. Each T senior creditor receives $20x in cash and P stock with a fair market value of $5x in exchange for his claim. The T junior creditor receives $55x in cash and P stock with a fair market value of $45x in exchange for his claim. The T shareholders receive no consideration in exchange for their T stock. Under paragraph (e)(6) of this section, because the amount of T's liabilities exceeds the fair market value of its assets immediately prior to the potential reorganization, the claims of the creditors of T may be proprietary interests in T. Because the senior creditors receive proprietary interests in P in the transaction in exchange for their claims, their claims and the claim of the junior creditor and the T stock are treated as proprietary interests in T immediately prior to the transaction. Under paragraph (e)(6)(ii)(A) of this section, the value of the proprietary interest of each of the senior creditors' claims is $5x (the fair market value of the senior creditor's claim, $25x, multiplied by a fraction, the numerator of which is $10x, the fair market value of the proprietary interests in the issuing corporation, P, received in the aggregate in exchange for the claims of all the creditors in the senior class, and the denominator of which is $50x, the sum of the amount of money and the fair market value of all other consideration (including the proprietary interests in P) received in the aggregate in exchange for such claims). Accordingly, $5x of the stock that each of the senior creditors receives is counted in measuring continuity of interest. Under paragraph (e)(6)(ii)(B) of this section, the value of the junior creditor's proprietary interest in T immediately prior to the transaction is $100x, the value of his claim. Thus, the value of the creditors' proprietary interests in total is $110x and the creditors received $55x worth of P stock in total in exchange for their proprietary interests. Therefore, P acquired 50 percent of the value of the proprietary interests in T in exchange for P stock. Because a substantial part of the value of the proprietary interests in T is preserved, the continuity of interest requirement is satisfied.

(ii) *One class of creditor receives issuing corporation stock and cash in disproportionate amounts.* T has assets with a fair market value of $80x and liabilities of $200x. T has one class of creditor with two creditors, A and B, each having a claim of $100x. T transfers all of its assets to P for $60x in cash and shares of P stock with a fair market value of $20x. A receives $40x in cash in exchange for its claim. B receives $20x in cash and P stock with a fair market value of $20x in exchange for its claim. The T shareholders receive no consideration in exchange for their T stock. The P stock is not de minimis in relation to the total consideration received. Under paragraph (e)(6) of this section, because the amount of T's liabilities exceeds the fair market value of its assets immediately prior to the potential reorganization, the claims of the creditors of T may be proprietary interests in T. Because the creditors of T received proprietary interests in P in the transaction in exchange for their claims, their claims and the T stock are treated as proprietary interests in T immediately prior to the transaction. Under paragraph (e)(6)(ii)(A) of this section, the value of the proprietary interest of each of the senior creditors is $10x (the fair market value of a senior creditor's claim, $40x, multiplied by a fraction, the numerator of which is $20x, the fair market value of the proprietary interests in the issuing corporation, P, received in the aggregate in exchange for the claims of all the creditors in the class, and the denominator of which is $80x, the sum of the amount of money and the fair market value of all other consideration (including the proprietary interests in P) received in the aggregate in exchange for such claims). Accordingly, $10x of the cash that was received by A and $10x of the P stock that was received by B are counted in measuring continuity of interest. Thus, the value of the creditors' proprietary interests in total is $20x and the creditors received $10x worth of P stock in total in exchange for their proprietary interests. Therefore, P acquired 50 percent of the value of the proprietary interests in T in exchange for P stock. Because a substantial part of the value of the proprietary interests in T is preserved, the continuity of interest requirement is satisfied.

(9) *Effective/applicability dates.*—(i) *In general.*—Paragraphs (e)(1) and (e)(3) through (e)(7) of this section apply to transactions occurring after January 28, 1998, except that they do not apply to any transaction occurring pursuant to a written agreement which is binding on January 28, 1998, and at all times thereafter. Paragraph (e)(1)(ii) of this section, however, applies to transactions occurring after August 30, 2000, unless the transaction occurs pursuant to a written agreement that is (subject to customary conditions) binding on that date and at all times thereafter. Taxpayers who entered into a binding agreement on or after January 28, 1998, and before August 30, 2000, may request a private letter ruling permitting them to apply the final regulations to their transaction. A private letter ruling will not be issued unless the taxpayer establishes to the satisfaction of the IRS that there is not a significant risk of different parties to the transaction taking inconsistent positions, for Federal tax purposes,

with respect to the applicability of the final regulations to the transaction. The sixth sentence of paragraph (e)(1)(i) of this section, the last sentence of paragraph (e)(1)(ii) of this section, paragraph (e)(3) of this section, paragraph (e)(6) of this section, and *Example 10* of paragraph (e)(8) of this section apply to transactions occurring after December 12, 2008.

(ii) *COI measurement date.*—Paragraph (e)(2) of this section applies to transactions occurring pursuant to binding contracts entered into after December 19, 2011. For transactions entered into after March 19, 2010, and occurring pursuant to binding contracts entered into on or before December 19, 2011, the parties to the transaction may elect to apply the provisions of §1.368-1T as contained in 26 CFR, Part 1, §§1.301-1.400, revised as of April 1, 2009. However, the target corporation, the issuing corporation, the controlling corporation of the acquiring corporation if stock thereof is provided as consideration in the transaction, and any direct or indirect transferee of transferred basis property from any of the foregoing, may not elect to apply the provisions of §1.368-1T as contained in 26 CFR, Part 1, §§1.301-1.400, revised as of April 1, 2009, unless all such taxpayers elect to apply such provisions. This election requirement will be satisfied if none of the specified parties adopts inconsistent treatment. For transactions entered into on or before March 19, 2010, see §1.368-1T as contained in 26 CFR, Part 1, §§1.301-1.400, revised as of April 1, 2009. [Reg. §1.368-1]

☐ [*T.D. 6152*, 12-2-55. *Amended by T.D. 7745*, 12-29-80; *T.D. 8760*, 1-23-98; *T.D. 8783*, 9-22-98; *T.D. 8858*, 1-5-2000; *T.D. 8898*, 8-30-2000; *T.D. 8940*, 2-12-2001; *T.D. 9182*, 2-24-2005; *T.D. 9225*, 9-15-2005; *T.D. 9316*, 3-19-2007; *T.D. 9361*, 10-24-2007; *T.D. 9434*, 12-11-2008 (*corrected* 12-23-2008) *and T.D. 9565*, 12-16-2011.]

[Reg. §1.368-2]

§1.368-2. Definition of terms.—(a) The application of the term "reorganization" is to be strictly limited to the specific transactions set forth in section 368(a). The term does not embrace the mere purchase by one corporation of the properties of another corporation. The preceding sentence applies to transactions occurring after January 28, 1998, except that it does not apply to any transaction occurring pursuant to a written agreement which is binding on January 28, 1998, and at all times thereafter. If the properties are transferred for cash and deferred payment obligations of the transferee evidenced by short-term notes, the transaction is a sale and not an exchange in which gain or loss is not recognized.

(b)(1)(i) *Definitions.*—For purposes of this paragraph (b)(1), the following terms shall have the following meanings:

(A) *Disregarded entity.*—A disregarded entity is a business entity (as defined in §301.7701-2(a) of this chapter) that is disregarded as an entity separate from its owner for Federal income tax purposes. Examples of disregarded entities include a domestic single member limited liability company that does not elect to be classified as a corporation for Federal income tax purposes, a corporation (as defined in §301.7701-2(b) of this chapter) that is a qualified REIT subsidiary (within the meaning of section 856(i)(2)), and a corporation that is a qualified subchapter S subsidiary (within the meaning of section 1361(b)(3)(B)).

(B) *Combining entity.*—A combining entity is a business entity that is a corporation (as defined in §301.7701-2(b) of this chapter) that is not a disregarded entity.

(C) *Combining unit.*—A combining unit is composed solely of a combining entity and all disregarded entities, if any, the assets of which are treated as owned by such combining entity for Federal income tax purposes.

(ii) *Statutory merger or consolidation generally.*—For purposes of section 368(a)(1)(A), a statutory merger or consolidation is a transaction effected pursuant to the statute or statutes necessary to effect the merger or consolidation, in which transaction, as a result of the operation of such statute or statutes, the following events occur simultaneously at the effective time of the transaction—

(A) All of the assets (other than those distributed in the transaction) and liabilities (except to the extent such liabilities are satisfied or discharged in the transaction or are nonrecourse liabilities to which assets distributed in the transaction are subject) of each member of one or more combining units (each a transferor unit) become the assets and liabilities of one or more members of one other combining unit (the transferee unit); and

(B) The combining entity of each transferor unit ceases its *separate legal existence for all purposes; provided, however, that this* requirement will be satisfied even if, under applicable law, after the effective time of the transaction, the combining entity of the transferor unit (or its officers, directors, or agents) may act or be acted against, or a member of the transferee unit (or its officers, directors,

or agents) may act or be acted against in the name of the combining entity of the transferor unit, provided that such actions relate to assets or obligations of the combining entity of the transferor unit that arose, or relate to activities engaged in by such entity, prior to the effective time of the transaction, and such actions are not inconsistent with the requirements of paragraph (b)(1)(ii)(A) of this section.

(iii) *Examples.*—The following examples illustrate the rules of paragraph (b)(1) of this section. In each of the examples, except as otherwise provided, each of R, V, Y, and Z is a C corporation. X is a domestic limited liability company. Except as otherwise provided, X is wholly owned by Y and is disregarded as an entity separate from Y for Federal income tax purposes. The examples are as follows:

Example 1. Divisive transaction pursuant to a merger statute. (i) *Facts.* Under State W law, Z transfers some of its assets and liabilities to Y, retains the remainder of its assets and liabilities, and remains in existence for Federal income tax purposes following the transaction. The transaction qualifies as a merger under State W corporate law.

(ii) *Analysis.* The transaction does not satisfy the requirements of paragraph (b)(1)(ii)(A) of this section because all of the assets and liabilities of Z, the combining entity of the transferor unit, do not become the assets and liabilities of Y, the combining entity and sole member of the transferee unit. In addition, the transaction does not satisfy the requirements of paragraph (b)(1)(ii)(B) of this section because the separate legal existence of Z does not cease for all purposes. Accordingly, the transaction does not qualify as a statutory merger or consolidation under section 368(a)(1)(A).

Example 2. Merger of a target corporation into a disregarded entity in exchange for stock of the owner. (i) *Facts.* Under State W law, Z merges into X. Pursuant to such law, the following events occur simultaneously at the effective time of the transaction: all of the assets and liabilities of Z become the assets and liabilities of X and Z's separate legal existence ceases for all purposes. In the merger, the Z shareholders exchange their stock of Z for stock of Y.

(ii) *Analysis.* The transaction satisfies the requirements of paragraph (b)(1)(ii) of this section because the transaction is effected pursuant to State W law and the following events occur simultaneously at the effective time of the transaction: all of the assets and liabilities of Z, the combining entity and sole member of the transferor unit, become the assets and liabilities of one or more members of the transferee unit that is comprised of Y, the combining entity of the transferee unit, and X, a disregarded entity the assets of which Y is treated as owning for Federal income tax purposes, and Z ceases its separate legal existence for all purposes. Accordingly, the transaction qualifies as a statutory merger or consolidation for purposes of section 368(a)(1)(A).

Example 3. Merger of a target S corporation that owns a QSub into a disregarded entity. (i) *Facts.* The facts are the same as in *Example 2*, except that Z is an S corporation and owns all of the stock of U, a QSub.

(ii) *Analysis.* The deemed formation by Z of U pursuant to §1.1361-5(b)(1) (as a consequence of the termination of U's QSub election) is disregarded for Federal income tax purposes. The transaction is treated as a transfer of the assets of U to X, followed by X's transfer of these assets to U in exchange for stock of U. See §1.1361-5(b)(3) *Example 9.* The transaction will, therefore, satisfy the requirements of paragraph (b)(1)(ii) of this section because the transaction is effected pursuant to State W law and the following events occur simultaneously at the effective time of the transaction: all of the assets and liabilities of Z and U, the sole members of the transferor unit, become the assets and liabilities of one or more members of the transferee unit that is comprised of Y, the combining entity of the transferee unit, and X, a disregarded entity the assets of which Y is treated as owning for Federal income tax purposes, and Z ceases its separate legal existence for all purposes. Moreover, the deemed transfer of the assets of U in exchange for U stock does not cause the transaction to fail to qualify as a statutory merger or consolidation. See §368(a)(2)(C). Accordingly, the transaction qualifies as a statutory merger or consolidation for purposes of section 368(a)(1)(A).

Example 4. Triangular merger of a target corporation into a disregarded entity. (i) *Facts.* The facts are the same as in *Example 2*, except that V owns 100 percent of the outstanding stock of Y and, in the merger of Z into X, the Z shareholders exchange their stock of Z for stock of V. In the transaction, Z transfers substantially all of its properties to X.

(ii) *Analysis.* The transaction is not prevented from qualifying as a statutory merger or consolidation under section 368(a)(1)(A), provided the requirements of section 368(a)(2)(D) are satisfied. Because the assets of X are treated for Federal income tax purposes as the assets of Y, Y will be treated as acquiring substantially all of the properties of Z in the merger for purposes of determining whether the merger satisfies the requirements of section 368(a)(2)(D). As a result, the Z shareholders that receive stock of V will be treated as receiving stock of a corporation that is in control of Y, the combining entity of the transferee unit that is the acquiring corporation for purposes of section 368(a)(2)(D). Accordingly, the merger will satisfy the requirements of section 368(a)(2)(D).

Example 5. Merger of a target corporation into a disregarded entity owned by a partnership. (i) *Facts.* The facts are the same as in *Example 2*, except that Y is organized as a partnership under the laws of State W and is classified as a partnership for Federal income tax purposes.

(ii) *Analysis.* The transaction does not satisfy the requirements of paragraph (b)(1)(ii)(A) of this section. All of the assets and liabilities of Z, the combining entity and sole member of the transferor unit, do not become the assets and liabilities of one or more members of a transferee unit because neither X nor Y qualifies as a combining entity. Accordingly, the transaction cannot qualify as a statutory merger or consolidation for purposes of section 368(a)(1)(A).

Example 6. Merger of a disregarded entity into a corporation. (i) *Facts.* Under State W law, X merges into Z. Pursuant to such law, the following events occur simultaneously at the effective time of the transaction: all of the assets and liabilities of X (but not the assets and liabilities of Y other than those of X) become the assets and liabilities of Z and X's separate legal existence ceases for all purposes.

(ii) *Analysis.* The transaction does not satisfy the requirements of paragraph (b)(1)(ii)(A) of this section because all of the assets and liabilities of a transferor unit do not become the assets and liabilities of one or more members of the transferee unit. The transaction also does not satisfy the requirements of paragraph (b)(1)(ii)(B) of this section because X does not qualify as a combining entity. Accordingly, the transaction cannot qualify as a statutory merger or consolidation for purposes of section 368(a)(1)(A).

Example 7. Merger of a corporation into a disregarded entity in exchange for interests in the disregarded entity. (i) *Facts.* Under State W law, Z merges into X. Pursuant to such law, the following events occur simultaneously at the effective time of the transaction: all of the assets and liabilities of Z become the assets and liabilities of X and Z's separate legal existence ceases for all purposes. In the merger of Z into X, the Z shareholders exchange their stock of Z for interests in X so that, immediately after the merger, X is not disregarded as an entity separate from Y for Federal income tax purposes. Following the merger, pursuant to § 301.7701-3(b)(1)(i) of this chapter, X is classified as a partnership for Federal income tax purposes.

(ii) *Analysis.* The transaction does not satisfy the requirements of paragraph (b)(1)(ii)(A) of this section because immediately after the merger X is not disregarded as an entity separate from Y and, consequently, all of the assets and liabilities of Z, the combining entity of the transferor unit, do not become the assets and liabilities of one or more members of a transferee unit. Accordingly, the transaction cannot qualify as a statutory merger or consolidation for purposes of section 368(a)(1)(A).

Example 8. Merger transaction preceded by distribution. (i) *Facts.* Z operates two unrelated businesses, Business P and Business Q, each of which represents 50 percent of the value of the assets of Z. Y desires to acquire and continue operating Business P, but does not want to acquire Business Q. Pursuant to a single plan, Z sells Business Q for cash to parties unrelated to Z and Y in a taxable transaction, and then distributes the proceeds of the sale pro rata to its shareholders. Then, pursuant to State W law, Z merges into Y. Pursuant to such law, the following events occur simultaneously at the effective time of the transaction: all of the assets and liabilities of Z related to Business P become the assets and liabilities of Y and Z's separate legal existence ceases for all purposes. In the merger, the Z shareholders exchange their Z stock for Y stock.

(ii) *Analysis.* The transaction satisfies the requirements of paragraph (b)(1)(ii) of this section because the transaction is effected pursuant to State W law and the following events occur simultaneously at the effective time of the transaction: all of the assets and liabilities of Z, the combining entity and sole member of the transferor unit, become the assets and liabilities of Y, the combining entity and sole member of the transferee unit, and Z ceases its separate legal existence for all purposes. Accordingly, the transaction qualifies as a statutory merger or consolidation for purposes of section 368(a)(1)(A).

Example 9. State law conversion of target corporation into a limited liability company. (i) *Facts.* Y acquires the stock of V from the V shareholders in exchange for consideration that consists of 50 percent voting stock of Y and 50 percent cash. Immediately after the stock acquisition, V files the necessary documents to convert from a corporation to a limited liability company under State W law. Y's acquisition of the stock of V and the conversion of V to a limited liability company are steps in a single integrated acquisition by Y of the assets of V.

(ii) *Analysis.* The acquisition by Y of the assets of V does not satisfy the requirements of paragraph (b)(1)(ii)(B) of this section because V, the combining entity of the transferor unit, does not cease its separate legal existence. Although V is an entity disregarded from its owner for Federal income tax purposes, it continues to exist as a

juridical entity after the conversion. Accordingly, Y's acquisition of the assets of V does not qualify as a statutory merger or consolidation for purposes of section 368(a)(1)(A).

Example 10. Dissolution of target corporation. (i) *Facts.* Y acquires the stock of Z from the Z shareholders in exchange for consideration that consists of 50 percent voting stock of Y and 50 percent cash. Immediately after the stock acquisition, Z files a certificate of dissolution pursuant to State W law and commences winding up its activities. Under State W dissolution law, ownership and title to Z's assets does not automatically vest in Y upon dissolution. Instead, Z transfers assets to its creditors in satisfaction of its liabilities and transfers its remaining assets to Y in the liquidation stage of the dissolution. Y's acquisition of the stock of Z and the dissolution of Z are steps in a single integrated acquisition by Y of the assets of Z.

(ii) *Analysis.* The acquisition by Y of the assets of Z does not satisfy the requirements of paragraph (b)(1)(ii) of this section because Y does not acquire all of the assets of Z as a result of Z filing the certificate of dissolution or simultaneously with Z ceasing its separate legal existence. Instead, Y acquires the assets of Z by reason of Z's transfer of its assets to Y. Accordingly, Y's acquisition of the assets of Z does not qualify as a statutory merger or consolidation for purposes of section 368(a)(1)(A).

Example 11. Merger of corporate partner into a partnership. (i) *Facts.* Y owns an interest in X, an entity classified as a partnership for Federal income tax purposes, that represents a 60 percent capital and profits interest in X. Z owns an interest in X that represents a 40 percent capital and profits interest. Under State W law, Z merges into X. Pursuant to such law, the following events occur simultaneously at the effective time of the transaction: all of the assets and liabilities of Z become the assets and liabilities of X and Z ceases its separate legal existence for all purposes. In the merger, the Z shareholders exchange their stock of Z for stock of Y. As a result of the merger, X becomes an entity that is disregarded as an entity separate from Y for Federal income tax purposes.

(ii) *Analysis.* The transaction satisfies the requirements of paragraph (b)(1)(ii) of this section because the transaction is effected pursuant to State W law and the following events occur simultaneously at the effective time of the transaction: all of the assets and liabilities of Z, the combining entity and sole member of the transferor unit, become the assets and liabilities of one or more members of the transferee unit that is comprised of Y, the combining entity of the transferee unit, and X, a disregarded entity the assets of which Y is treated as owning for Federal income tax purposes immediately after the transaction, and Z ceases its separate legal existence for all purposes. Accordingly, the transaction qualifies as a statutory merger or consolidation for purposes of section 368(a)(1)(A).

Example 12. State law consolidation. (i) *Facts.* Under State W law, Z and V consolidate. Pursuant to such law, the following events occur simultaneously at the effective time of the transaction: all of the assets and liabilities of Z and V become the assets and liabilities of Y, an entity that is created in the transaction, and the existence of Z and V continues in Y. In the consolidation, the Z shareholders and the V shareholders exchange their stock of Z and V, respectively, for stock of Y.

(ii) *Analysis.* With respect to each of Z and V, the transaction satisfies the requirements of paragraph (b)(1)(ii) of this section because the transaction is effected pursuant to State W law and the following events occur simultaneously at the effective time of the transaction: all of the assets and liabilities of Z and V, respectively, each of which is the combining entity of a transferor unit, become the assets and liabilities of Y, the combining entity and sole member of the transferee unit, and Z and V each ceases its separate legal existence for all purposes. Accordingly, the transaction qualifies as the statutory merger or consolidation of each of Z and V into Y for purposes of section 368(a)(1)(A).

Example 13. Transaction effected pursuant to foreign statutes. (i) *Facts.* Z and Y are entities organized under the laws of Country Q and classified as corporations for Federal income tax purposes. Z and Y combine. Pursuant to statutes of Country Q the following events occur simultaneously: all of the assets and liabilities of Z become the assets and liabilities of Y and Z's separate legal existence ceases for all purposes.

(ii) *Analysis.* The transaction satisfies the requirements of paragraph (b)(1)(ii) of this section because the transaction is effected pursuant to statutes of Country Q and the following events occur simultaneously at the effective time of the transaction: all of the assets and liabilities of Z, the combining entity of the transferor unit, become the assets and liabilities of Y, the combining entity and sole member of the transferee unit, and Z ceases its separate legal existence for all purposes. Accordingly, the transaction qualifies as a statutory merger or consolidation for purposes of section 368(a)(1)(A).

Example 14. Foreign law amalgamation using parent stock. (i) *Facts.* Z and V are entities organized under the laws of Country Q and classified as corporations for Federal income tax purposes. Z and V amalgamate. Pursuant to statutes of Country Q, the following events occur simultaneously: all the assets and liabilities of Z and V become the assets and liabilities of R, an entity that is created in the transaction and that is wholly owned by Y immediately after the transaction, and Z's and V's separate legal existences cease for all purposes. In the transaction, the Z and V shareholders exchange their Z and V stock, respectively, for stock of Y.

(ii) *Analysis.* With respect to each of Z and V, the transaction satisfies the requirements of paragraph (b)(1)(ii) of this section because the transaction is effected pursuant to Country Q law and the following events occur simultaneously at the effective time of the transaction: all of the assets and liabilities of Z and V, respectively, each of which is the combining entity of a transferor unit, become the assets and liabilities of R, the combining entity and sole member of the transferee unit, with regard to each of the above transfers, and Z and V each ceases its separate legal existence for all purposes. Because Y is in control of R immediately after the transaction, the Z shareholders and the V shareholders will be treated as receiving stock of a corporation that is in control of R, the combining entity of the transferee unit that is the acquiring corporation for purposes of section 368(a)(2)(D). Accordingly, the transaction qualifies as the statutory merger or consolidation of each of Z and V into R, a corporation controlled by Y, and is a reorganization under section 368(a)(1)(A) by reason of section 368(a)(2)(D).

(v) *Effective date.*—(A) *In general.*—This paragraph (b)(1) applies to transactions occurring on or after January 23, 2006. For rules regarding statutory mergers or consolidation occurring before January 23, 2006, see §1.368-2T as contained in 26 CFR part 1, revised April 1, 2005, and §1.368-2(b)(1) as in effect before January 24, 2003 (see 26 CFR part 1, revised April 1, 2002).

(B) *Transitional rule.*—A taxpayer may elect to apply the provisions of §1.368-2T(b) as contained in 26 CFR part 1, revised April 1, 2005 (the temporary regulations), instead of the provisions of this paragraph (b), to a transaction that occurs on or after January 23, 2006, pursuant to a written agreement which is (subject to customary conditions) binding on January 22, 2006, and at all times thereafter, or pursuant to a tender offer announced prior to January 23, 2006. However, the combining entity of the transferor unit, the combining entity of the transferee unit, any controlling corporation of the combining entity of the transferee unit if stock thereof is provided as consideration in the transaction, and any direct or indirect transferee of transferred basis property from any of the foregoing, may not elect to apply the provisions of the temporary regulations unless all such taxpayers elect to apply the provisions of the temporary regulations.

(2) In order for the transaction to qualify under section 368(a)(1)(A) by reason of the application of section 368(a)(2)(D), one corporation (the acquiring corporation) must acquire substantially all of the properties of another corporation (the acquired corporation) partly or entirely in exchange for stock of a corporation which is in control of the acquiring corporation (the controlling corporation), provided that (i) the transaction would have qualified under section 368(a)(1)(A) if the merger had been into the controlling corporation, and (ii) no stock of the acquiring corporation is used in the transaction. The foregoing test of whether the transaction would have qualified under section 368(a)(1)(A) if the merger had been into the controlling corporation means that the general requirements of a reorganization under section 368(a)(1)(A) (such as a business purpose, continuity of business enterprise, and continuity of interest) must be met in addition to the special requirements of section 368(a)(2)(D). Under this test, it is not relevant whether the merger into the controlling corporation could have been effected pursuant to State or Federal corporation law. The term "substantially all" has the same meaning as it has in section 368(a)(1)(C). Although no stock of the acquiring corporation can be used in the transaction, there is no prohibition (other than the continuity of interest requirement) against using other property, such as cash or securities, of either the acquiring corporation or the parent or both. In addition, the controlling corporation may assume liabilities of the acquired corporation without disqualifying the transaction under section 368(a)(2)(D), and for purposes of section 357(a) the controlling corporation is considered a party to the exchange. For example, if the controlling corporation agrees to substitute its stock for stock of the acquired corporation under an outstanding employee stock option agreement, this assumption of liability will not prevent the transaction from qualifying as a reorganization under section 368(a)(2)(D) and the assumption of liability is not treated as money or other property for purposes of section 361(b). Section 368(a)(2)(D) applies whether or not the controlling corporation (or the acquiring corporation) is formed immediately before the merger, in anticipation of the merger, or after preliminary steps have been taken to merge directly into the controlling corporation. Section 368(a)(2)(D) applies only to statutory mergers occurring after October 22, 1968.

(3) For regulations under section 368(a)(2)(E), see paragraph (j) of this section.

(c) In order to qualify as a "reorganization" under section 368(a)(1)(B), the acquisition by the acquiring corporation of stock of another corporation must be in exchange solely for all or a part of the voting stock of the acquiring corporation (or, in the case of transactions occurring after December 31, 1963, solely for all or a part of the voting stock of a corporation which is in control of the acquiring corporation), and the acquiring corporation must be in control of the other corporation immediately after the transaction. If, for example, corporation X in one transaction exchanges nonvoting preferred stock or bonds in addition to all or a part of its voting stock in the acquisition of stock of corporation Y, the transaction is not a reorganization under section 368(a)(1)(B). Nor is a transaction a reorganization described in section 368(a)(1)(B) if stock is acquired in exchange for voting stock both of the acquiring corporation and of a corporation which is in control of the acquiring corporation. The acquisition of the stock of another corporation by the acquiring corporation solely for its voting stock (or solely for voting stock of a corporation which is in control of the acquiring corporation) is permitted tax free even though the acquiring corporation already owns some of the stock of the other corporation. Such an acquisition is permitted tax free in a single transaction or in a series of transactions taking place over a relatively short period of time such as 12 months. For example, corporation A purchased 30 percent of the common stock of corporation W (the only class of stock outstanding) for cash in 1939. On March 1, 1955, corporation A offers to exchange its own voting stock for all the stock of corporation W tendered within 6 months from the date of the offer. Within the 6 months' period corporation A acquires an additional 60 percent of stock of corporation W solely for its own voting stock, so that it owns 90 percent of the stock of corporation W. No gain or loss is recognized with respect to the exchanges of stock of corporation A for stock of corporation W. For this purpose, it is immaterial whether such exchanges occurred before corporation A acquired control (80 percent) of corporation W or after such control was acquired. If corporation A had acquired 80 percent of the stock of corporation W for cash in 1939, it could likewise acquire some or all of the remainder of such stock solely in exchange for its own voting stock without recognition of gain or loss.

(d) In order to qualify as a reorganization under section 368(a)(1)(C), the transaction must be one described in subparagraph (1) or (2) of this paragraph:

(1) One corporation must acquire substantially all the properties of another corporation solely in exchange for all or a part of its own voting stock, or solely in exchange for all or a part of the voting stock of a corporation which is in control of the acquiring corporation. For example, Corporation P owns all the stock of Corporation A. All the properties of Corporation W are transferred to Corporation A either solely in exchange for voting stock of Corporation P or solely in exchange for less than 80 percent of the voting stock of Corporation A. Either of such transactions constitutes a reorganization under section 368(a)(1)(C). However, if the properties of Corporation W are acquired in exchange for voting stock of both Corporation P and Corporation A, the transaction will not constitute a reorganization under section 368(a)(1)(C). In determining whether the exchange meets the requirement of "solely for voting stock", the assumption by the acquiring corporation of liabilities of the transferor corporation, or the fact that property acquired from the transferor corporation is subject to a liability, shall be disregarded. Though such an assumption does not prevent an exchange from being solely for voting stock for the purposes of the definition of a reorganization contained in section 368(a)(1)(C), it may in some cases, however, so alter the character of the transaction as to place the transaction outside the purposes and assumptions of the reorganization provisions. Section 368(a)(1)(C) does not prevent consideration of the effect of an assumption of liabilities on the general character of the transaction but merely provides that the requirement that the exchange be solely for voting stock is satisfied if the only additional consideration is an assumption of liabilities.

(2) One corporation—

(i) Must acquire substantially all of the properties of another corporation in such manner that the acquisition would qualify under (1) above, but for the fact that the acquiring corporation exchanges money, or other property in addition to such voting stock, and

(ii) Must acquire solely for voting stock (either of the acquiring corporation or of a corporation which is in control of the acquiring corporation) properties of the other corporation having a fair market value which is at least 80 percent of the fair market value of all the properties of the other corporation.

(3) For the purposes of subparagraph (2)(ii) only, a liability assumed or to which the properties are subject is considered money paid for the properties. For example, Corporation A has properties with a fair market value of $100,000 and liabilities of $10,000. In exchange for these properties, Corporation Y transfers its own voting

stock, assumes the $10,000 liabilities, and pays $8,000 in cash. The transaction is a reorganization even though a part of the properties of Corporation A is acquired for cash. On the other hand, if the properties of Corporation A worth $100,000, were subject to $50,000 in liabilities, an acquisition of all the properties, subject to the liabilities, for any consideration other than solely voting stock would not qualify as a reorganization under this section since the liabilities alone are in excess of 20 percent of the fair market value of the properties. If the transaction would qualify under either subparagraph (1) or (2) of this paragraph and also under section 368(a)(1)(D), such transaction shall not be treated as a reorganization under section 368(a)(1)(C).

(4)(i) For purposes of paragraphs (d)(1) and (2)(ii) of this section, prior ownership of stock of the target corporation by an acquiring corporation will not by itself prevent the solely for voting stock requirement of such paragraphs from being satisfied. In a transaction in which the acquiring corporation has prior ownership of stock of the target corporation, the requirement of paragraph (d)(2)(ii) of this section is satisfied only if the sum of the money or other property that is distributed in pursuance of the plan of reorganization to the shareholders of the target corporation other than the acquiring corporation and to the creditors of the target corporation pursuant to section 361(b)(3), and all of the liabilities of the target corporation assumed by the acquiring corporation (including liabilities to which the properties of the target corporation are subject), does not exceed 20 percent of the value of all of the properties of the target corporation. If, in connection with a potential acquisition by an acquiring corporation of substantially all of a target corporation's properties, the acquiring corporation acquires the target corporation's stock for consideration other than the acquiring corporation's own voting stock (or voting stock of a corporation in control of the acquiring corporation if such stock is used in the acquisition of the target corporation's properties), whether from a shareholder of the target corporation or the target corporation itself, such consideration is treated, for purposes of paragraphs (d)(1) and (2) of this section, as money or other property exchanged by the acquiring corporation for the target corporation's properties. Accordingly, the transaction will not qualify under section 368(a)(1)(C) unless, treating such consideration as money or other property, the requirements of section 368(a)(2)(B) and paragraph (d)(2)(ii) of this section are met. The determination of whether there has been an acquisition in connection with a potential reorganization under section 368(a)(1)(C) of a target corporation's stock for consideration other than an acquiring corporation's own voting stock (or voting stock of a corporation in control of the acquiring corporation if such stock is used in the acquisition of the target corporation's properties) will be made on the basis of all of the facts and circumstances.

(ii) The following examples illustrate the principles of this paragraph (d)(4):

Example 1. Corporation P (P) holds 60 percent of the Corporation T (T) stock that P purchased several years ago in an unrelated transaction. T has 100 shares of stock outstanding. The other 40 percent of the T stock is owned by Corporation X (X), an unrelated corporation. T has properties with a fair market value of $110 and liabilities of $10. T transfers all of its properties to P. In exchange, P assumes the $10 of liabilities, and transfers to T $30 of P voting stock and $10 of cash. T distributes the P voting stock and $10 of cash to X and liquidates. The transaction satisfies the solely for voting stock requirement of paragraph (d)(2)(ii) of this section because the sum of $10 of cash paid to X and the assumption by P of $10 of liabilities does not exceed 20% of the value of the properties of T.

Example 2. The facts are the same as in *Example 1* except that P purchased the 60 shares of T for $60 in cash in connection with the acquisition of T's assets. The transaction does not satisfy the solely for voting stock requirement of paragraph (d)(2)(ii) of this section because P is treated as having acquired all of the T assets for consideration consisting of $70 of cash, $10 of liability assumption and $30 of P voting stock, and the sum of $70 of cash and the assumption by P of $10 of liabilities exceeds 20% of the value of the properties of T.

(iii) This paragraph (d)(4) applies to transactions occurring after December 31, 1999, unless the transaction occurs pursuant to a written agreement that is (subject to customary conditions) binding on that date and at all times thereafter.

(e) A "recapitalization", and therefore a reorganization, takes place if, for example:

(1) A corporation with $200,000 par value of bonds outstanding, instead of paying them off in cash, discharges them by issuing preferred shares to the bondholders;

(2) There is surrendered to a corporation for cancellation 25 percent of its preferred stock in exchange for no par value common stock;

(3) A corporation issues preferred stock, previously authorized but unissued, for outstanding common stock;

(4) An exchange is made of a corporation's outstanding preferred stock, having certain priorities with reference to the amount and time of payment of dividends and the distribution of the corporate assets upon liquidation, for a new issue of such corporation's common stock having no such rights;

(5) An exchange is made of an amount of a corporation's outstanding preferred stock with dividends in arrears for other stock of the corporation. However, if pursuant to such an exchange there is an increase in the proportionate interest of the preferred shareholders in the assets or earnings and profits of the corporation, then under § 1.305-7(c)(2), an amount equal to the lesser of (i) the amount by which the fair market value or liquidation preference, whichever is greater, of the stock received in the exchange (determined immediately following the recapitalization) exceeds the issue price of the preferred stock surrendered, or (ii) the amount of the dividends in arrears, shall be treated under section 305(c) as a deemed distribution to which sections 305(b)(4) and 301 apply.

(f) The term "a party to a reorganization" includes a corporation resulting from a reorganization, and both corporations in a transaction qualifying as a reorganization where one corporation acquires stock or properties of another corporation. If a transaction otherwise qualifies as a reorganization, a corporation remains a party to the reorganization even though stock or assets acquired in the reorganization are transferred in a transaction described in paragraph (k) of this section. If a transaction otherwise qualifies as a reorganization, a corporation shall not cease to be a party to the reorganization solely by reason of the fact that part or all of the assets acquired in the reorganization are transferred to a partnership in which the transferor is a partner if the continuity of business enterprise requirement is satisfied. See § 1.368-1(d). The preceding three sentences apply to transactions occurring after January 28, 1998, except that they do not apply to any transaction occurring pursuant to a written agreement which is binding on January 28, 1998, and at all times thereafter. A corporation controlling an acquiring corporation is a party to the reorganization when the stock of such controlling corporation is used in the acquisition of properties. Both corporations are parties to the reorganization if, under statutory authority, Corporation A is merged into Corporation B. All three of the corporations are parties to the reorganization if, pursuant to statutory authority, Corporation C and Corporation D are consolidated into Corporation E. Both corporations are parties to the reorganization if Corporation F transfers substantially all its assets to Corporation G in exchange for all or a part of the voting stock of Corporation G. All three corporations are parties to the reorganization if Corporation H transfers substantially all its assets to Corporation K in exchange for all or part of the voting stock of Corporation L, which is in control of Corporation K. Both corporations are parties to the reorganization if Corporation M transfers all or a part of its assets to Corporation N in exchange for all or a part of the stock and securities of Corporation N, but only if (1) immediately after such transfer, Corporation M, or one or more of its shareholders (including persons who were shareholders immediately before such transfer), or any combination thereof, is in control of Corporation N, and (2) in pursuance of the plan, the stock and securities of Corporation N are transferred or distributed by Corporation M in a transaction in which gain or loss is not recognized under section 354 or 355, or is recognized only to the extent provided in section 356. Both Corporation O and Corporation P, but not Corporation S, are parties to the reorganization if Corporation O acquires stock of Corporation P from Corporation S in exchange solely for a part of the voting stock of Corporation O, if (1) the stock of Corporation P does not constitute substantially all of the assets of Corporation S, (2) Corporation S is not in control of Corporation O immediately after the acquisition, and (3) Corporation O is in control of Corporation P immediately after the acquisition. If a transaction otherwise qualifies as a reorganization under section 368(a)(1)(B) or as a reverse triangular merger (as defined in § 1.358-6(b)(2)(iii)), the target corporation (in the case of a transaction that otherwise qualifies as a reorganization under section 368(a)(1)(B)) or the surviving corporation (in the case of a transaction that otherwise qualifies as a reverse triangular merger) remains a party to the reorganization even though its stock or assets are transferred in a transaction described in paragraph (k) of this section. If a transaction otherwise qualifies as a forward triangular merger (as defined in § 1.358-6(b)(2)(i)), a triangular B reorganization (as defined in § 1.358-6(b)(2)(iv)), a triangular C reorganization (as defined in § 1.358-6(b)(2)(ii)), or a reorganization under section 368(a)(1)(G) by reason of section 368(a)(2)(D), the acquiring corporation remains a party to the reorganization even though its stock is transferred in a transaction described in paragraph (k) of this section. The two preceding sentences apply to transactions occurring on or after October 25, 2007, except that they do not apply to any transaction occurring pursuant to a written agreement which is binding before October 25, 2007, and at all times after that.

(g) The term "plan of reorganization" has reference to a consummated transaction specifically defined as a reorganization under section 368(a). The term is not to be construed as broadening the definition of "reorganization" as set forth in section 368(a), but is to be taken as limiting the nonrecognition of gain or loss to such exchanges or distributions as are directly a part of the transaction specifically described as a reorganization in section 368(a). Moreover, the transaction, or series of transactions, embraced in a plan of reorganization must not only come within the specific language of section 368(a), but the readjustments involved in the exchanges or distributions effected in the consummation thereof must be undertaken for reasons germane to the continuance of the business of a corporation a party to the reorganization. Section 368(a) contemplates genuine corporate reorganizations which are designed to effect a readjustment of continuing interests under modified corporate forms.

(h) As used in section 368, as well as in other provisions of the Internal Revenue Code, if the context so requires, the conjunction "or" denotes both the conjunctive and the disjunctive, and the singular includes the plural. For example, the provisions of the statute are complied with if "stock and securities" are received in exchange as well as if "stock or securities" are received.

(i) [Reserved]

(j)(1) This paragraph (j) prescribes rules relating to the application of section 368(a)(2)(E).

(2) Section 368(a)(2)(E) does not apply to a consolidation.

(3) A transaction otherwise qualifying under section 368(a)(1)(A) is not disqualified by reason of the fact that stock of a corporation (the controlling corporation) which before the merger was in control of the merged corporation is used in the transaction, if the conditions of section 368(a)(2)(E) are satisfied. Those conditions are as follows:

(i) In the transaction, shareholders of the surviving corporation must surrender stock in exchange for voting stock of the controlling corporation. Further, the stock so surrendered must constitute control of the surviving corporation. Control is defined in section 368(c). The amount of stock constituting control is measured immediately before the transaction. For purposes of this subdivision (i), stock in the surviving corporation which is surrendered in the transaction (by any shareholder except the controlling corporation) in exchange for consideration furnished by the surviving corporation (and not by the controlling corporation or the merged corporation) is considered not to be outstanding immediately before the transaction. For effect on "substantially all" test of consideration furnished by the surviving corporation, see paragraph (j)(3)(iii) of this section.

(ii) Except as provided in paragraph (k) of this section, the controlling corporation must control the surviving corporation immediately after the transaction.

(iii) After the transaction, the surviving corporation must hold substantially all of its own properties and substantially all of the properties of the merged corporation (other than stock of the controlling corporation distributed in the transaction). The surviving corporation may transfer such properties as provided in paragraph (k) of this section. The term "substantially all" has the same meaning as in section 368(a)(1)(C). The "substantially all" test applies separately to the merged corporation and to the surviving corporation. In applying the "substantially all" test to the surviving corporation, consideration furnished in the transaction by the surviving corporation in exchange for its stock is property of the surviving corporation which it does not hold after the transaction. In applying the "substantially all" test to the merged corporation, assets transferred from the controlling corporation to the merged corporation in pursuance of the plan of reorganization are not taken into account. Thus, for example, money transferred from the controlling corporation to the merged corporation to be used for the following purposes is not taken into account for purposes of the "substantially all" test:

(A) To pay additional consideration to shareholders of the surviving corporation;

(B) To pay dissenting shareholders of the surviving corporation;

(C) To pay creditors of the surviving corporation;

(D) To pay reorganization expenses; or

(E) To enable the merged corporation to satisfy state minimum capitalization requirements (where the money is returned to the controlling corporation as part of the transaction).

(iv) Paragraph (j)(3)(ii) and the first two sentences of paragraph (j)(3)(iii) of this section apply to transactions occurring on or after October 25, 2007, except that they do not apply to any transaction occurring pursuant to a written agreement which is binding before October 25, 2007, and at all times thereafter. The remainder of paragraph (j)(3)(iii) of this section applies to transactions occurring after January 28, 1998, except that it does not apply to any transaction occurring pursuant to a written agreement which is binding on *January 28, 1998, and at all times after that.*

(4) The controlling corporation may assume liabilities of the surviving corporation without disqualifying the transaction under section 368(a)(2)(E). An assumption of liabilities of the surviving corporation by the controlling corporation is a contribution to capital

by the controlling corporation to the surviving corporation. If, in pursuance of the plan of reorganization, securities of the surviving corporation are exchanged for securities of the controlling corporation, or for other securities of the surviving corporation, see sections 354 and 356.

(5) In applying section 368(a)(2)(E), it makes no difference if the merged corporation is an existing corporation, or is formed immediately before the merger, in anticipation of the merger, or after preliminary steps have been taken to otherwise acquire control of the surviving corporation.

(6) The following examples illustrate the application of this paragraph (j). In each of the examples, Corporation P owns all of the stock of Corporation S and, except as otherwise stated, Corporation T has outstanding 1,000 shares of common stock and no shares of any other class. In each of the examples, it is also assumed that the transaction qualifies under section 368(a)(1)(A) if the conditions of section 368(a)(2)(E) are satisfied.

Example 1. P owns no T stock. On January 1, 1981, S merges into T. In the merger, T's shareholders surrender 950 shares of common stock in exchange for P voting stock. The holders of the other 50 shares (who dissent from the merger) are paid in cash with funds supplied by P. After the transaction, T holds all of its own assets and all of S's assets. Based on these facts, the transaction qualifies under section 368(a)(1)(A) by reason of the application of section 368(a)(2)(E). In the transaction, former shareholders of T surrender, in exchange for P voting stock, an amount of T stock (950/1,000 shares or 95 percent) which constitutes control of T.

Example 2. The facts are the same as in example (1) except that holders of 100 shares in corporation T, who dissented from the merger, are paid in cash with funds supplied by T (and not by P or S) and, in the merger, T's remaining shareholders surrender 720 shares of common stock in exchange for P voting stock and 180 shares of common stock for cash supplied by P. The requirements of section 368(a)(2)(E)(ii) are satisfied since, in the transaction, former shareholders of T surrender, in exchange for P voting stock, an amount of T stock (720/900 shares or 80 percent) which constitutes control of T. The T stock surrendered in exchange for consideration furnished by T is not considered outstanding for purposes of determining whether the amount of T stock surrendered by T shareholders for P stock constitutes control of T.

Example 3. T has outstanding 1,000 shares of common stock, 100 shares of nonvoting preferred stock, and no shares of any other class. On January 1, 1981, S merges into T. Prior to the merger, as part of the transaction, T distributes its own cash in redemption of the 100 shares of preferred stock. In the transaction, T's remaining shareholders surrender their 1,000 shares of common stock in exchange for P voting stock. The requirements of section 368(a)(2)(E)(ii) are satisfied since, in the transaction, former shareholders of T surrender, in exchange for P voting stock, an amount of T stock (1,000/1,000 shares or 100 percent) which constitutes control of T. The preferred stock surrendered in exchange for consideration furnished by T is not considered outstanding for purposes of determining whether the amount of T stock surrendered by T shareholders for P stock constitutes control of T. However, the consideration furnished by T for its stock is property of T which does not hold after the transaction for purposes of the substantially all test in paragraph (j)(3)(iii) of this section.

Example 4. On January 1, 1971, P purchased 201 shares of T's stock. On January 1, 1981, S merges into T. In the merger, T's shareholders (other than P) surrender 799 shares of T stock in exchange for P voting stock. Based on these facts, in the transaction, former shareholders of T do not surrender, in exchange for P voting stock, an amount of T stock which constitutes control of T (799/1,000 shares being less than 80 percent). Therefore, the transaction does not qualify under section 368(a)(1)(A). However, if S is a transitory corporation, formed solely for purposes of effectuating the transaction, the transaction may qualify as a reorganization described in section 368(a)(1)(B) provided all of the applicable requirements are satisfied.

Example 5. On January 1, 1971, P purchased 200 shares of T's stock. On January 1, 1981, S merges into T. Prior to the merger, as part of the transaction, T distributes its own cash in redemption of 1 share of T stock from a T shareholder other than P. In the merger, T's remaining shareholders (other than P) surrender 799 shares of T stock in exchange for P voting stock. Based on these facts, in the transaction, former shareholders of T do not surrender, in exchange for P voting stock, an amount of T stock which constitutes control of T (799/999 shares being less than 80 percent). Therefore, the transaction does not qualify under section 368(a)(1)(A). However, if S is a transitory corporation, formed for purposes of effectuating the transaction, the transaction may qualify as a reorganization described in section 368(a)(1)(B) provided all of the applicable requirements are satisfied.

Example 6. The stock of S has a value of $25,000. The stock of T has a value of $75,000. On January 1, 1984, S merges into T. In the merger, T's shareholders surrender all of their T stock in exchange for P voting stock. After the transaction, T holds all of its own assets and all of S's assets. Based on these facts, the transaction qualifies under section 368(a)(1)(A) by reason of the application of section 368(a)(2)(E). In the transaction, former shareholders of T surrender, in exchange for P voting stock, an amount of T stock (1,000/1,000 shares or 100 percent) which constitutes control of T. The stock of T received by P in exchange for P's prior interest in S is not taken into account for purposes of section 368(a)(2)(E)(ii) since the amount of T stock constituting control of T is measured before the transaction.

Example 7. The stock of T has a value of $75,000. On January 1, 1984, S merges into T. In the merger, T's shareholders surrender all of their T stock in exchange for P voting stock. As part of the transaction, P contributes $25,000 to T in exchange for new shares of T stock. None of the cash received by T is distributed or otherwise paid out to former T shareholders. After the transaction, T holds all of its own assets and all of S's assets. Based on these facts, the transaction qualifies under section 368(a)(1)(A) by reason of the application of section 368(a)(2)(E). In the transaction, former shareholders of T surrender, in exchange for P voting stock, an amount of T stock (1,000/1,000 shares or 100 percent) which constitutes control of T. The T stock received by P in exchange for its contribution to T is not taken into account for purposes of section 368(a)(2)(E)(ii) since the amount of T stock constituting control of T is measured before the transaction.

Example 8. The facts are the same as in example (7) except that, as part of the transaction, corporation R, instead of P, contributes $25,000 to T in exchange for T stock. Based on these facts, the transaction does not qualify under section 368(a)(1)(A) by reason of section 368(a)(2)(E) since P does not control T immediately after the transaction.

Example 9. T stock has a value of $75,000. P owns 500 shares (1/2) of that stock with a value of $37,500. The stock of S has a value of $125,000. On January 1, 1984, S merges into T. In the merger, T's shareholders (other than P) surrender their T stock in exchange for P voting stock. Based on these facts, in the transaction, former shareholders of T do not surrender, in exchange for P voting stock, an amount of T stock which constitutes control of T (500/1,000 shares being less than 80 percent). Therefore, the transaction does not qualify under section 368(a)(1)(A). The stock of T received by P in exchange for P's prior interest in S does not contribute to satisfaction of the requirement of section 368(a)(2)(E)(ii).

(k) *Certain transfers of assets or stock in reorganizations.*—(1) *General rule.*—A transaction otherwise qualifying as a reorganization under section 368(a) shall not be disqualified or recharacterized as a result of one or more subsequent transfers (or successive transfers) of assets or stock, provided that the requirements of §1.368-1(d) are satisfied and the transfer(s) are described in either paragraph (k)(1)(i) or (k)(1)(ii) of this section. However, this paragraph (k) shall not apply to a transfer to the former shareholders of the acquired corporation (other than a former shareholder that is also the acquiring corporation) or the surviving corporation, as the case may be, to the extent it constitutes the receipt of consideration for a proprietary interest in the acquired corporation or the surviving corporation, as the case may be. Similarly, this paragraph (k) shall not apply to a transfer by the former shareholders of the acquired corporation (other than a former shareholder that is also the acquiring corporation) or the surviving corporation, as the case may be, of consideration initially received in the potential reorganization to the issuing corporation or a person related to the issuing corporation (see definition of "related person" in §1.368-1(e)).

(i) *Distributions.*—One or more distributions to shareholders (including distribution(s) that involve the assumption of liabilities) are described in this paragraph (k)(1)(i) if—

(A) The property distributed consists of—

(1) Assets of the acquired corporation, the acquiring corporation, or the surviving corporation, as the case may be, or an interest in an entity received in exchange for such assets in a transfer described in paragraph (k)(1)(ii) of this section;

(2) Stock of the acquired corporation provided that such distribution(s) of stock do not cause the acquired corporation to cease to be a member of the qualified group (as defined in §1.368-1(d)(4)(ii)); or

(3) A combination thereof; and

(B) The aggregate of such distributions does not consist of—

(1) An amount of assets of the acquired corporation, the acquiring corporation (disregarding assets held prior to the potential reorganization), or the surviving corporation (disregarding assets of the merged corporation), as the case may be, that would result in a liquidation of such corporation for Federal income tax purposes; or

(2) All of the stock of the acquired corporation that was acquired in the transaction.

(ii) *Transfers Other Than Distributions.*—One or more other transfers are described in this paragraph (k)(1)(ii) if—

(A) The transfer(s) do not consist of one or more distributions to shareholders;

(B) The property transferred consists of—

(1) Part or all of the assets of the acquired corporation, the acquiring corporation, or the surviving corporation, as the case may be;

(2) Part or all of the stock of the acquired corporation, the acquiring corporation, or the surviving corporation, as the case may be, provided that such transfer(s) of stock do not cause such corporation to cease to be a member of the qualified group (as defined in §1.368-1(d)(4)(ii)); or

(3) A combination thereof; and

(C) The acquired corporation, the acquiring corporation, or the surviving corporation, as the case may be, does not terminate its corporate existence for Federal income tax purposes in connection with the transfer(s).

(2) *Examples.*—The following examples illustrate the application of this paragraph (k). Except as otherwise noted, P is the issuing corporation, and T is an unrelated target corporation. All corporations have only one class of stock outstanding. T operates a bakery that supplies delectable pastries and cookies to local retail stores. The acquiring corporate group produces a variety of baked goods for nationwide distribution. Except as otherwise noted, P owns all of the stock of S-1 and 80 percent of the stock of S-4, S-1 owns 80 percent of the stock of S-2 and 50 percent of the stock of S-5, S-2 owns 80 percent of the stock of S-3, and S-4 owns the remaining 50 percent of the stock of S-5. The examples are as follows:

Example 1. Transfers of acquired assets to members of the qualified group after a reorganization under section 368(a)(1)(C). (i) *Facts.* Pursuant to a plan of reorganization, T transfers all of its assets to S-1 solely in exchange for P stock, which T distributes to its shareholders, and S-1's assumption of T's liabilities. In addition, pursuant to the plan, S-1 transfers all of the T assets to S-2, and S-2 transfers all of the T assets to S-3.

(ii) *Analysis.* Under this paragraph (k), the transaction, which otherwise qualifies as a reorganization under section 368(a)(1)(C), is not disqualified by the successive transfers of all of the T assets to S-2 and from S-2 to S-3 because the transfers are not one or more distributions to shareholders, the transfers consist of part or all of the assets of the acquiring corporation, the acquiring corporation does not terminate its corporate existence for Federal income tax purposes in connection with the transfers, and the transaction satisfies the requirements of §1.368-1(d).

Example 2. Distribution of acquired assets to a member of the qualified group after a reorganization under section 368(a)(1)(C). (i) *Facts.* Pursuant to a plan of reorganization, T transfers all of its assets to S-1 solely in exchange for P stock, which T distributes to its shareholders, and S-1's assumption of T's liabilities. In addition, pursuant to the plan, S-1 distributes half of the T assets to P, and P assumes half of the T liabilities.

(ii) *Analysis.* Under this paragraph (k), the transaction, which otherwise qualifies as a reorganization under section 368(a)(1)(C), is not disqualified by the distribution of half of the T assets from S-1 to P, or P's assumption of half of the T liabilities from S-1, because the distribution consists of assets of the acquiring corporation, the distribution does not consist of an amount of S-1's assets that would result in a liquidation of S-1 for Federal income tax purposes (disregarding S-1's assets held prior to the acquisition of T), and the transaction satisfies the requirements of §1.368-1(d).

Example 3. Indirect distribution of acquired assets to a member of the qualified group after a reorganization under section 368(a)(1)(C). (i) *Facts.* The facts are the same as in Example 2, except that, instead of S-1 distributing half of the T assets to P and having P assume half of the T liabilities, S-1 contributes half of the T assets to newly formed S-6, S-6 assumes half of the T liabilities, and S-1 distributes all of the S-6 stock to P.

(ii) *Analysis.* Under this paragraph (k), the transaction, which otherwise qualifies as a reorganization under section 368(a)(1)(C), is not disqualified by the transfer of half of the T assets to S-6 and the distribution of the S-6 stock to P because the transfer of half of the T assets to S-6 is described in paragraph (k)(1)(ii) of this section, the distribution of the S-6 stock to P is an indirect distribution of assets of the acquiring corporation, the distribution does not consist of an amount of S-1's assets that would result in a liquidation of S-1 for Federal income tax purposes (disregarding S-1's assets held prior to the acquisition of T), and the transaction satisfies the requirements of §1.368-1(d).

Example 4. Distribution of acquired stock to a controlled partnership after a reorganization under section 368(a)(1)(B). (i) *Facts.* P owns 80 percent of the stock of S-1, and an 80-percent interest in PRS, a partnership. S-4 owns the remaining 20-percent interest in PRS. PRS owns the remaining 20 percent of the stock of S-1. Pursuant to a plan of reorganization, the T shareholders transfer all of their T stock to S-1 solely in exchange for P stock. In addition, pursuant to the plan, S-1 distributes 90 percent of the T stock to PRS in redemption of 5 percent of the stock of S-1 owned by PRS.

(ii) *Analysis.* Under this paragraph (k), the transaction, which otherwise qualifies as a reorganization under section 368(a)(1)(B), is not disqualified by the distribution of 90 percent of the T stock from S-1 to PRS because the distribution consists of less than all of the stock of the acquired corporation that was acquired in the transaction, the distribution does not cause T to cease to be a member of the qualified group (as defined in § 1.368-1(d)(4)(ii)), and the transaction satisfies the requirements of § 1.368-1(d).

Example 5. Transfer of acquired stock to a non-controlled partnership. (i) *Facts.* Pursuant to a plan, the T shareholders transfer all of their T stock to S-1 solely in exchange for P stock. In addition, as part of the plan, T distributes half of its assets to S-1, S-1 assumes half of the T liabilities, and S-1 transfers the T stock to S-2. S-2 and U, an unrelated corporation, form a new partnership, PRS. Immediately thereafter, S-2 transfers all of the T stock to PRS in exchange for a 50 percent interest in PRS, and U transfers cash to PRS in exchange for a 50 percent interest in PRS.

(ii) *Analysis.* Under this paragraph (k), the transaction, which otherwise qualifies as a reorganization under section 368(a)(1)(B), is not disqualified by the distribution of half of the T assets from T to S-1, or S-1's assumption of half of the T liabilities from T, because the distribution consists of assets of the acquired corporation, the distribution does not consist of an amount of T's assets that would result in a liquidation of T for Federal income tax purposes, and the transaction satisfies the requirements of § 1.368-1(d). Further, this paragraph (k) describes the transfer of the acquired stock from S-1 to S-2, but does not describe the transfer of the acquired stock from S-2 to PRS because such transfer causes T to cease to be a member of the qualified group (as defined in § 1.368-1(d)(4)(ii)). Therefore, the characterization of this transaction must be determined under the relevant provisions of law, including the step transaction doctrine. See § 1.368-1(a). The transaction fails to meet the control requirement of a reorganization described in section 368(a)(1)(B) because immediately after the acquisition of the T stock, the acquiring corporation does not have control of T.

Example 6. Transfers of acquired assets to members of the qualified group after a reorganization under section 368(a)(1)(D). (i) *Facts.* P owns all of the stock of T. Pursuant to a plan of reorganization, T transfers all of its assets to S-1 solely in exchange for S-1 stock, which T distributes to P, and S-1's assumption of T's liabilities. In addition, pursuant to the plan, S-1 transfers all of the T assets to S-2, and S-2 transfers all of the T assets to S-3.

(ii) *Analysis.* Under this paragraph (k), the transaction, which otherwise qualifies as a reorganization under section 368(a)(1)(D), is not disqualified by the successive transfers of all the T assets from S-1 to S-2 and from S-2 to S-3 because the transfers are not one or more distributions to shareholders, the transfers consist of part or all of the assets of the acquiring corporation, the acquiring corporation does not terminate its corporate existence for Federal income tax purposes in connection with the transfers, and the transaction satisfies the requirements of § 1.368-1(d).

Example 7. Transfer of stock of the acquiring corporation to a member of the qualified group after a reorganization under section 368(a)(1)(A) by reason of section 368(a)(2)(D). (i) *Facts.* Pursuant to a plan of reorganization, S-1 acquires all of the T assets in the merger of T into S-1. In the merger, the T shareholders receive solely P stock. Also, pursuant to the plan, P transfers all of the S-1 stock to S-4.

(ii) *Analysis.* Under this paragraph (k), the transaction, which otherwise qualifies as a reorganization under section 368(a)(1)(A) by reason of section 368(a)(2)(D), is not disqualified by the transfer of all of the S-1 stock to S-4 because the transfer is not a distribution to shareholders, the transfer consists of part or all of the stock of the acquiring corporation, the transfer does not cause S-1 to cease to be a member of the qualified group (as defined in § 1.368-1(d)(4)(ii)), the acquiring corporation does not terminate its corporate existence for Federal income tax purposes in connection with the transfer, and the transaction satisfies the requirements of § 1.368-1(d).

Example 8. Transfer of acquired assets to a partnership after a reorganization under section 368(a)(1)(A) by reason of section 368(a)(2)(D). (i) *Facts.* Pursuant to a plan of reorganization, S-1 acquires all of the T assets in the merger of T into S-1. In the merger, the T shareholders receive solely P stock. In addition, pursuant to the plan, S-1 transfers all of the T assets to PRS, a partnership in which S-1 owns a 33 1/3-percent interest. PRS continues T's historic business. S-1 does not perform active and substantial management functions as a partner with respect to PRS' business.

(ii) *Analysis.* Under this paragraph (k), the transaction, which otherwise qualifies as a reorganization under section 368(a)(1)(A) by reason of section 368(a)(2)(D), is not disqualified by the transfer of T

assets from S-1 to PRS because the transfer is not a distribution to shareholders, the transfer consists of part or all of the assets of the acquiring corporation, the acquiring corporation does not terminate its corporate existence for Federal income tax purposes in connection with the transfers, and the transaction satisfies the requirements of § 1.368-1(d).

Example 9. Sale of acquired assets to a member of the qualified group after a reorganization under section 368(a)(1)(C). (i) *Facts.* Pursuant to a plan of reorganization, T transfers all of its assets to S-1 in exchange for P stock, which T distributes to its shareholders, and S-1's assumption of T's liabilities. In addition, pursuant to the plan, S-1 sells all of the T assets to S-5 for cash equal to the fair market value of those assets.

(ii) *Analysis.* Under this paragraph (k), the transaction, which otherwise qualifies as a reorganization under section 368(a)(1)(C), is not disqualified by the sale of all of the T assets from S-1 to S-5 because the transfer is not a distribution to shareholders, the transfer consists of part or all of the assets of the acquiring corporation, the acquiring corporation does not terminate its corporate existence for Federal income tax purposes in connection with the transfer, and the transaction satisfies the requirements of § 1.368-1(d).

(3) *Effective/applicability dates.*—This paragraph (k) applies to transactions occurring on or after May 9, 2008, except that it does not apply to any transaction occurring pursuant to a written agreement which is binding before May 9, 2008, and at all times after that.

(l) *Certain transactions treated as reorganizations described in section 368(a)(1)(D).*—(1) *General rule.*—In order to qualify as a reorganization under section 368(a)(1)(D), a corporation (transferor corporation) must transfer all or part of its assets to another corporation (transferee corporation) and immediately after the transfer the transferor corporation, or one or more of its shareholders (including persons who were shareholders immediately before the transfer), or any combination thereof, must be in control of the transferee corporation; but only if, in pursuance of the plan, stock or securities of the transferee are distributed in a transaction which qualifies under section 354, 355, or 356.

(2) *Distribution requirement.*—(i) *In general.*—For purposes of paragraph (l)(1) of this section, a transaction otherwise described in section 368(a)(1)(D) will be treated as satisfying the requirements of sections 368(a)(1)(D) and 354(b)(1)(B) notwithstanding that there is no actual issuance of stock and/or securities of the transferee corporation if the same person or persons own, directly or indirectly, all of the stock of the transferor and transferee corporations in identical proportions. In cases where no consideration is received or the value of the consideration received in the transaction is less than the fair market value of the transferor corporation's assets, the transferee corporation will be treated as issuing stock with a value equal to the excess of the fair market value of the transferor corporation's assets over the value of the consideration actually received in the transaction. In cases where the value of the consideration received in the transaction is equal to the fair market value of the transferor corporation's assets, the transferee corporation will be deemed to issue a nominal share of stock to the transferor corporation in addition to the actual consideration exchanged for the transferor corporation's assets. The nominal share of stock in the transferee corporation will then be deemed distributed by the transferor corporation to the shareholders of the transferor corporation, as part of the exchange for the stock of such shareholders. Where appropriate, the nominal share will be further transferred through chains of ownership to the extent necessary to reflect the actual ownership of the transferor and transferee corporations. Similar treatment to that of the preceding two sentences shall apply where the transferee corporation is treated as issuing stock with a value equal to the excess of the fair market value of the transferor corporation's assets over the value of the consideration actually received in the transaction.

(ii) *Attribution.*—For purposes of paragraph (l)(2)(i) of this section, ownership of stock will be determined by applying the principles of section 318(a)(2) without regard to the 50 percent limitation in section 318(a)(2)(C). In addition, an individual and all members of his family described in section 318(a)(1) shall be treated as one individual.

(iii) *De minimis variations in ownership and certain stock not taken into account.*—For purposes of paragraph (l)(2)(i) of this section, the same person or persons will be treated as owning, directly or indirectly, all of the stock of the transferor and transferee corporations in identical proportions notwithstanding the fact that there is a de minimis variation in shareholder identity or proportionality of ownership. Additionally, for purposes of paragraph (l)(2)(i) of this section, stock described in section 1504(a)(4) is not taken into account.

(iv) *Exception.*—Paragraph (l)(2) of this section does not apply to a transaction otherwise described in § 1.358-6(b)(2).

(3) *Examples.*—The following examples illustrate the principles of paragraph (l) of this section. For purposes of these examples, each of A, B, C, and D is an individual, T is the acquired corporation, S is the acquiring corporation, P is the parent corporation, and each of S1, S2, S3, and S4 is a direct or indirect subsidiary of P. Further, all of the requirements of section 368(a)(1)(D) other than the requirement that stock or securities be distributed in a transaction to which section 354 or 356 applies are satisfied. The examples are as follows:

Example 1. A owns all the stock of T and S: The T stock has a fair market value of $100x. T sells all of its assets to S in exchange for $100x of cash and immediately liquidates. Because there is complete shareholder identity and proportionality of ownership in T and S, under paragraph (l)(2)(i) of this section, the requirements of sections 368(a)(1)(D) and 354(b)(1)(B) are treated as satisfied notwithstanding the fact that no S stock is issued. Pursuant to paragraph (l)(2)(i) of this section, S will be deemed to issue a nominal share of S stock to T in addition to the $100x of cash actually exchanged for the T assets, and T will be deemed to distribute all such consideration to A. The transaction qualifies as a reorganization described in section 368(a)(1)(D).

Example 2. The facts are the same as in *Example 1* except that C, A's son, owns all of the stock of S. Under paragraph (l)(2)(ii) of this section, A and C are treated as one individual. Accordingly, there is complete shareholder identity and proportionality of ownership in T and S. Therefore, under paragraph (l)(2)(i) of this section, the requirements of sections 368(a)(1)(D) and 354(b)(1)(B) are treated as satisfied notwithstanding the fact that no S stock is issued. Pursuant to paragraph (l)(2)(i) of this section, S will be deemed to issue a nominal share of S stock to T in addition to the $100x of cash actually exchanged for the T assets, and T will be deemed to distribute all such consideration to A. A will be deemed to transfer the nominal share of S stock to C. The transaction qualifies as a reorganization described in section 368(a)(1)(D).

Example 3. P owns all of the stock of S1 and S2. S1 owns all of the stock of S3, which owns all of the stock of T. S2 owns all of the stock of S4, which owns all of the stock of S. The T stock has a fair market value of $70x. T sells all of its assets to S in exchange for $70x of cash and immediately liquidates. Under paragraph (l)(2)(ii) of this section, there is indirect, complete shareholder identity and proportionality of ownership in T and S. Accordingly, the requirements of sections 368(a)(1)(D) and 354(b)(1)(B) are treated as satisfied notwithstanding the fact that no S stock is issued. Pursuant to paragraph (l)(2)(i) of this section, S will be deemed to issue a nominal share of S stock to T in addition to the $70x of cash actually exchanged for the T assets, and T will be deemed to distribute all such consideration to S3. S3 will be deemed to distribute the nominal share of S stock to S1, which, in turn, will be deemed to distribute the nominal share of S stock to P. P will be deemed to transfer the nominal share of S stock to S2, which, in turn, will be deemed to transfer such share of S stock to S4. The transaction qualifies as a reorganization described in section 368(a)(1)(D).

Example 4. A, B, and C own 34%, 33%, and 33%, respectively, of the stock of T. The T stock has a fair market value of $100x. A, B, and C each own 33% of the stock of S. D owns the remaining 1% of the stock of S. T sells all of its assets to S in exchange for $100x of cash and immediately liquidates. For purposes of determining whether the distribution requirement of sections 368(a)(1)(D) and 354(b)(1)(B) is met, under paragraph (l)(2)(iii) of this section, D's ownership of a de minimis amount of stock of S is disregarded and the transaction is treated as if there is complete shareholder identity and proportionality of ownership in T and S. Because there is complete shareholder identity and proportionality of ownership in T and S, under paragraph (l)(2)(i) of this section, the requirements of sections 368(a)(1)(D) and 354(b)(1)(B) are treated as satisfied notwithstanding the fact that no S stock is issued. Pursuant to paragraph (l)(2)(i) of this section, S will be deemed to issue a nominal share of S stock to T in addition to the $100x of cash actually exchanged for the T assets, T will be deemed to distribute all such consideration to A, B, and C, and the nominal S stock will be deemed transferred among the S shareholders to the extent necessary to reflect their actual ownership of S. The transaction qualifies as a reorganization described in section 368(a)(1)(D).

Example 5. The facts are the same as in *Example 4* except that A, B, and C own 34%, 33%, and 33%, respectively, of the common stock of T and S. D owns preferred stock in S described in section 1504(a)(4). For purposes of determining whether the distribution requirement of sections 368(a)(1)(D) and 354(b)(1)(B) is met, under paragraph (l)(2)(iii) of this section, D's ownership of S stock described in section 1504(a)(4) is ignored and the transaction is treated as if there is complete shareholder identity and proportionality of ownership in T and S. Because there is complete shareholder identity and proportionality of ownership in T and S, under paragraph (l)(2)(i) of this section, the requirements of sections 368(a)(1)(D) and 354(b)(1)(B) are treated as satisfied notwithstanding the fact that no S stock is issued. Pursuant to paragraph (l)(2)(i) of this section, S will be deemed to

issue a nominal share of S stock to T in addition to the $100x of cash actually exchanged for the T assets, and T will be deemed to distribute all such consideration to A, B, and C. The transaction qualifies as a reorganization described in section 368(a)(1)(D).

Example 6. A and B each own 50% of the stock of T. The T stock has a fair market value of $100x. B and C own 90% and 10%, respectively, of the stock of S. T sells all of its assets to S in exchange for $100x of cash and immediately liquidates. Because complete shareholder identity and proportionality of ownership in T and S does not exist, paragraph (l)(2)(i) of this section does not apply. The requirements of sections 368(a)(1)(D) and 354(b)(1)(B) are not satisfied, and the transaction does not qualify as a reorganization described in section 368(a)(1)(D).

(4) *Effective/applicability date.*—(i) *In general.*—This section applies to transactions occurring on or after December 18, 2009. For rules regarding transactions occurring before December 18, 2009, see section 1.368-2T(l) as contained in 26 CFR part 1.

(ii) *Transitional rule.*—A taxpayer may apply the provisions of these regulations to transactions occurring before December 18, 2009. However, the transferor corporation, the transferee corporation, any direct or indirect transferee of transferred basis property from either of the foregoing, and any shareholder of the transferor or transferee corporation may not apply the provisions of these regulations unless all such taxpayers apply the provisions of the regulations.

(m) *Qualification as a reorganization under section 368(a)(1)(F).*—(1) *Mere change.*—To qualify as a reorganization under section 368(a)(1)(F), a transaction must result in a mere change in identity, form, or place of organization of one corporation, however effected (a mere change). A mere change can consist of a transaction that involves an actual or deemed transfer of property from one corporation (a transferor corporation) to one other corporation (a resulting corporation). Such a transaction is a mere change and qualifies as a reorganization under section 368(a)(1)(F) only if all the requirements set forth in paragraphs (m)(1)(i) through (vi) of this section are satisfied. For purposes of this paragraph (m), a transaction or a series of related transactions that can be tested against the requirements set forth in paragraphs (m)(1)(i) through (vi) of this section (a potential F reorganization) begins when the transferor corporation begins transferring (or is deemed to begin transferring) its assets, directly or indirectly, to the resulting corporation, and it ends when the transferor corporation has distributed (or is deemed to have distributed) to its shareholders the consideration it receives (or is deemed to receive) from the resulting corporation and has completely liquidated for federal income tax purposes. For purposes of this paragraph (m), deemed transfers include, for example, those provided in §301.7701-3(g)(1)(iv) of this chapter (when an entity disregarded as separate from its owner elects under paragraph §301.7701-3(c)(1)(i) of this chapter to be classified as an association, the owner of the entity is deemed to transfer all of the assets and liabilities of the entity to the association in exchange for stock of the association). Deemed transfers also include those resulting from the application of step transaction principles. For example, step transaction principles may disregard a transitory holding of property by an individual after a liquidation of the transferor corporation and before a subsequent transfer of the transferor corporation's property to the resulting corporation. Step transaction principles may also treat a contribution of all the stock of the transferor corporation to the resulting corporation, followed by a liquidation (or deemed liquidation) of the transferor corporation, as a deemed transfer of the transferor corporation's property to the resulting corporation, followed by a distribution of stock of the resulting corporation in complete liquidation of the transferor corporation.

(i) *Resulting corporation stock distributed in exchange for transferor corporation stock.*—Immediately after the potential F reorganization, all the stock of the resulting corporation, including any stock of the resulting corporation issued before the potential F reorganization, must have been distributed (or deemed distributed) in exchange for stock of the transferor corporation in the potential F reorganization. However, for purposes of this paragraph (m)(1)(i) and paragraph (m)(1)(ii) of this section, a de minimis amount of stock issued by the resulting corporation other than in respect of stock of the transferor corporation to facilitate the organization of the resulting corporation or maintain its legal existence is disregarded.

(ii) *Identity of stock ownership.*—The same person or persons must own all of the stock of the transferor corporation, determined immediately before the potential F reorganization, and of the resulting corporation, determined immediately after the potential F reorganization, in identical proportions. However, this requirement is not violated if one or more holders of stock in the transferor corporation exchange stock in the transferor corporation for stock of equivalent value in the resulting corporation, but having different terms from those of the stock in the transferor corporation, or receive a distribution of money or other property from either the transferor corporation or the resulting corporation, whether or not in exchange for stock in the transferor corporation or the resulting corporation.

(iii) *Prior assets or attributes of resulting corporation.*—The resulting corporation may not hold any property or have any tax attributes (including those specified in section 381(c)) immediately before the potential F reorganization. However, this requirement is not violated if the resulting corporation holds or has held a de minimis amount of assets to facilitate its organization or maintain its legal existence, and has tax attributes related to holding those assets, or holds the proceeds of borrowings undertaken in connection with the potential F reorganization.

(iv) *Liquidation of transferor corporation.*—The transferor corporation must completely liquidate, for federal income tax purposes, in the potential F reorganization. However, the transferor corporation is not required to dissolve under applicable law and may retain a de minimis amount of assets for the sole purpose of preserving its legal existence.

(v) *Resulting corporation is the only acquiring corporation.*—Immediately after the potential F reorganization, no corporation other than the resulting corporation may hold property that was held by the transferor corporation immediately before the potential F reorganization, if such other corporation would, as a result, succeed to and take into account the items of the transferor corporation described in section 381(c).

(vi) *Transferor corporation is the only acquired corporation.*—Immediately after the potential F reorganization, the resulting corporation may not hold property acquired from a corporation other than the transferor corporation if the resulting corporation would, as a result, succeed to and take into account the items of such other corporation described in section 381(c).

(2) *Non-application of continuity of interest and continuity of business enterprise requirements.*—A continuity of the business enterprise and a continuity of interest are not required for a potential F reorganization to qualify as a reorganization under section 368(a)(1)(F). *See* § 1.368-1(b).

(3) *Related transactions.*—(i) *Series of transactions.*—A potential F reorganization consisting of a series of related transactions that together result in a mere change of one corporation may qualify as a reorganization under section 368(a)(1)(F), whether or not certain steps in the series, viewed in isolation, could be subject to other Code provisions, such as sections 304(a), 331, 332, or 351. However, *see* paragraph (k) of this section for transactions that qualify as reorganizations under section 368(a) and will not be recharacterized as a mere change as a result of one or more subsequent transfers of assets or stock.

(ii) *Mere change within a larger transaction.*—A potential F reorganization that qualifies as a reorganization under section 368(a)(1)(F) may occur before, within, or after other transactions that effect more than a mere change, even if the resulting corporation has only transitory existence. Related events that precede or follow the potential F reorganization generally will not cause that potential F reorganization to fail to qualify as a reorganization under section 368(a)(1)(F). Qualification of a potential F reorganization as a reorganization under section 368(a)(1)(F) will not alter the character of other transactions for federal income tax purposes, and step transaction principles may be applied to other transactions without regard to whether certain steps qualify as a reorganization or part of a reorganization under section 368(a)(1)(F).

(iii) *Distributions treated as separate transactions.*—As provided in paragraph (m)(1)(ii) of this section, a potential F reorganization may qualify as a mere change even though a holder of stock in the transferor corporation receives a distribution of money or other property from either the transferor corporation or the resulting corporation. If a shareholder receives money or other property (including in exchange for its shares) from the transferor corporation or the resulting corporation in a potential F reorganization that qualifies as a reorganization under section 368(a)(1)(F), then the receipt of money or other property (including any exchanged for shares) is treated as an unrelated, separate transaction from the reorganization, whether or not connected in a formal sense. See § 1.301-1(j).

(iv) *Transactions also qualifying under other provisions of section 368(a)(1).*—In certain cases, a potential F reorganization would (but for this paragraph (m)(3)(iv)) qualify both as a reorganization under section 368(a)(1)(F) and as a reorganization or part of a reorganization under another provision of section 368(a)(1). The following rules determine which of these overlapping qualifications applies.

(A) If the potential F reorganization or a step thereof qualifies as a reorganization or part of a reorganization under another

provision of section 368(a)(1), and if a corporation in control (within the meaning of section 368(c)) of the resulting corporation is a party to such other reorganization (within the meaning of section 368(b)), the potential F reorganization will not qualify as a reorganization under section 368(a)(1)(F).

(B) Except as provided in paragraph (m)(3)(iv)(A) of this section, if, but for this paragraph (m)(3)(iv)(B), the potential F reorganization would qualify as a reorganization under both section 368(a)(1)(F) and one or more of sections 368(a)(1)(A), 368(a)(1)(C), or 368(a)(1)(D), then for all federal income tax purposes the potential F reorganization will qualify as a reorganization only under section 368(a)(1)(F).

(4) *Examples.*—The following examples illustrate the application of this paragraph (m). Unless the facts otherwise indicate, A, B, and C are domestic individuals; P, S, T, X, Y, and Z (and similar designations) are domestic corporations; each transaction is entered into for a valid business purpose; all persons and transactions are unrelated; and all other relevant facts are set forth in the examples.

Example 1. Cash contribution and redemption – no mere change. C owns all of the stock of X, a State A corporation. The net value of X's assets and liabilities is $1,000,000. Y, a State B corporation, seeks to acquire the assets of X for cash. To effect the acquisition, Y and X enter into an agreement under which Y will contribute $1,000,000 to Z, a newly formed corporation of which Y is the sole shareholder, in exchange for Z stock and X will merge into Z. In the merger, C surrenders all of the X stock and receives the $1,000,000 Y contributed to Z. C receives no Z stock in the transaction. After the merger, Y holds all of the Z stock, and Z holds all of the assets and liabilities previously held by X. Z stock is not distributed to the shareholders of X in exchange for their stock in X as required by paragraph (m)(1)(i) of this section, and the transaction results in a change in the ownership of X that does not result from an exchange or distribution described in paragraph (m)(1)(ii) of this section. Therefore, the merger of X into Z is not a mere change of X and does not qualify as a reorganization under section 368(a)(1)(F).

Example 2. Cash redemption – mere change. A owns 75%, and B owns 25%, of the stock of X, a State A corporation. The management of X determines that it would be in the best interest of X to reorganize under the laws of State B. Accordingly, X forms Y, a State B corporation, and X and Y enter into an agreement under which X will merge into Y. A does not wish to own stock in Y. In the merger, A surrenders A's X stock and receives cash, and B surrenders all of B's X stock and receives all the stock of Y. The change in ownership caused by A's surrender of X stock results from a distribution and exchange described in paragraph (m)(1)(ii) of this section. Therefore, the merger of X into Y is a mere change of X and qualifies as a reorganization under section 368(a)(1)(F). Under paragraph (m)(3)(iii) of this section, A's surrender of X stock for cash is treated as a transaction, separate from the reorganization, to which section 302(a) applies.

Example 3. Pre-transaction de minimis stock issuance – mere change – other provisions of section 368(a)(1). P owns all of the stock of S, a Country A corporation. The management of P determines that it would be in the best interest of S to change its place of incorporation to Country B. Under Country B law, a corporation must have at least two shareholders to enjoy limited liability. P is advised by its Country B advisors that the new corporation should issue 1% of its stock to a shareholder that is not P's nominee to assure satisfaction of the two-shareholder requirement. As part of an integrated plan, C, an officer of S, organizes Y, a Country B corporation with 1,000 shares of common stock authorized, and contributes cash to Y in exchange for ten of the common shares. S then merges into Y under the laws of Country A and Country B. Pursuant to the plan of merger, P surrenders its shares of S stock and receives 990 shares of Y common stock. The ten shares of Y stock issued to C not in respect of the S stock are de minimis and are used to facilitate the organization of Y within the meaning of paragraph (m)(1)(i) of this section. Therefore, the issuance of this stock to a new shareholder does not prevent the merger of S into Y from qualifying as a mere change of S. Accordingly, the merger is a reorganization under section 368(a)(1)(F). Without regard to the merger's qualification under section 368(a)(1)(F), the merger would also qualify as a reorganization under both section 368(a)(1)(A) and section 368(a)(1)(D). Under paragraph (m)(3)(iv)(B) of this section, if a potential F reorganization qualifies as a reorganization under section 368(a)(1)(F), and would also qualify under one or more of sections 368(a)(1)(A) or 368(a)(1)(D), the potential F reorganization qualifies only as a reorganization under 368(a)(1)(F), and neither section 368(a)(1)(A) nor section 368(a)(1)(D) will apply.

Example 4. Pre-transaction assets, attributes – no mere change. A owns all of the stock of P, and P owns all of the stock of S, which is engaged in a manufacturing business. P has owned the stock of S for many years. P owns no assets other than the stock of S. A decides to eliminate the holding company structure by merging P into S. Because it operates a manufacturing business, the potential resulting corporation, S, holds property and has tax attributes immediately before the potential F reorganization. Therefore, under paragraph (m)(1)(iii) of this section, the merger of P into S is not a mere change of P and does not qualify as a reorganization under section 368(a)(1)(F). The same result would occur under paragraph (m)(1)(iii) of this section if, instead of P merging into S, S merged into P, because P, the potential resulting corporation, holds property (the stock of S) and has tax attributes immediately before the potential F reorganization.

Example 5. Series of related transactions – mere change. P owns all of the stock of S1, a State A corporation. The management of P determines that it would be in the best interest of S1 to change its place of incorporation to State B. Accordingly, under an integrated plan, P forms S2, a new State B corporation; P contributes the S1 stock to S2; and S1 merges into S2 under the laws of State A and State B. Under paragraph (m)(3)(i) of this section, a series of transactions that together result in a mere change of one corporation may qualify as a reorganization under section 368(a)(1)(F). The contribution of S1 stock to S2 and the merger of S1 into S2 together constitute a mere change of S1. Therefore, the potential F reorganization qualifies as a reorganization under section 368(a)(1)(F). Without regard to its qualification under section 368(a)(1)(F), the potential F reorganization would also qualify as a reorganization under both section 368(a)(1)(A) and section 368(a)(1)(D). Under paragraph (m)(3)(iv)(B) of this section, if a potential F reorganization qualifies as a reorganization under section 368(a)(1)(F) and would also qualify under one or more of sections 368(a)(1)(A) or 368(a)(1)(D), it qualifies only as a reorganization under 368(a)(1)(F), and neither section 368(a)(1)(A) nor section 368(a)(1)(D) will apply. The result would be the same with respect to qualification under section 368(a)(1)(F) if, instead of merging into S2, S1 completely liquidates or is deemed to liquidate by reason of a conversion an entity disregarded as separate from its owner under §301.7701-3 of this chapter.

Example 6. Post-transaction stock sale – mere change. P owns all of the stock of S, a State A corporation. The management of P determines that it would be in the best interest of S1 to change its place of incorporation to State B. Accordingly, P forms S2, a new State B corporation. S1 then merges into S2 under the laws of State A and State B. Immediately thereafter, and as part of the same plan, P sells all of its stock in S2 to an unrelated party. Without regard to P's sale of S2 stock, the merger of S1 into S2 is a potential F reorganization that qualifies as a mere change of S1 within the meaning of paragraph (m)(1) of this section. Under paragraph (m)(3)(ii) of this section, related events that occur before or after a potential F reorganization that qualifies as a mere change generally do not cause that potential F reorganization to fail to qualify as a reorganization under section 368(a)(1)(F). Therefore, P's sale of the S2 stock is disregarded in determining whether the merger of S1 into S2 is a mere change of S1. Accordingly, the merger of S1 into S2 qualifies as a reorganization under section 368(a)(1)(F). The result would be the same if, instead of the S2 stock being sold by P, S2 merges into a previously unrelated corporation and terminates its separate existence.

Example 7. Post-transaction redemption – mere change. A owns all of the stock of T. P owns all of the stock of S. Each of T, P, and S is a State A corporation engaged in a manufacturing business. The following transactions occur pursuant to a single plan. First, T merges into S with A receiving solely stock in P. Second, P changes its state of incorporation to State B by merging into newly incorporated New P under the laws of State A and State B. Third, New P redeems all the New P stock issued to A in respect of A's P stock (initially issued to A in respect of A's T stock) for cash. Without regard to the other steps, the merger of P into New P is a potential F reorganization that qualifies as a reorganization under section 368(a)(1)(F). Under paragraph (m)(3)(ii) of this section, related events that occur before or after a potential F reorganization that qualifies as a mere change generally do not prevent that potential F reorganization from qualifying as a reorganization under section 368(a)(1)(F). Therefore, the merger of P into New P qualifies as a reorganization under section 368(a)(1)(F). Under paragraph (m)(3)(ii) of this section, the qualification of the merger of P into New P as a reorganization under section 368(a)(1)(F) does not alter the tax treatment of the merger of T into S. Because the P shares received by A in respect of the T shares (exchanged for New P shares in the mere change of P into New P) are redeemed for cash pursuant to the plan, the merger of T into S does not satisfy the continuity of interest requirement of §1.368-1(e) and therefore does not qualify as a reorganization under section 368(a).

Example 8. Series of related transactions – mere change. P owns all of the stock of S, a State A corporation. The management of P determines that it would be in the best interest of S to change its form from a State A corporation to a State A limited partnership but to continue to be treated as a corporation for federal tax purposes. Accordingly, P contributes 1% of the S stock to newly formed LLC, a limited liability company, in exchange for all of the membership interests in LLC. P is the sole member of LLC. Under §301.7701-3 of

this chapter, LLC is disregarded as an entity separate from its owner, P. Then, under a State A statute, S converts to a State A limited partnership. In the conversion, P's interest as a 99% shareholder of S is converted into a 99% limited partner interest, and LLC's interest as a 1% shareholder of S is converted into a 1% general partner interest. S also elects, under §301.7701-3(c) of this chapter, to be classified as a corporation for federal income tax purposes, effective on the same day as the conversion. Under paragraph (m)(3)(i) of this section, the conversion of S from a State A corporation to a State A limited partnership, together with the election to treat S as a corporation for federal tax purposes, results in a mere change of S and qualifies as a reorganization under section 368(a)(1)(F).

Example 9. Other acquiring corporation – no mere change. P owns 80%, and A owns 20%, of the stock of S. A and the management of P determine that it would be in the best interest of S to completely liquidate while A continues to operate part of the business of S in corporate form. Accordingly, S distributes 80% of its assets to P and 20% of its assets to A; S dissolves; and A contributes the assets it receives from S to newly incorporated New S in exchange for all of the stock of New S. S's distribution of 80% of its property to P as part of the complete liquidation of S meets the requirements of section 332. Thus, section 381(a)(1) applies to P's acquisition of 80% of the property held by S immediately before the transaction. Under paragraph (m)(1)(v) of this section, the potential F reorganization in which 20% of the property held by S immediately before the transaction is transferred to New S cannot be a mere change of S, because section 381(a) applies to P's acquisition of property held by S immediately before the potential F reorganization. Accordingly, sections 331 and 336 apply to A's acquisition of property from S and S's distribution of property to A, and section 351 applies to A's contribution of that property to New S.

Example 10. Other acquiring corporation – no mere change. P owns all of the stock of S1. The management of P determines that it would be in the best interest of S1 to merge S1 into P. Accordingly, pursuant to a state merger statute, S1 merges into P. Immediately afterward and as part of the same plan, P contributes 50% of the former assets of S1 to newly incorporated S2 in exchange for all of the stock of S2. The transaction does not qualify as a complete liquidation of S1 under section 332 (because of the reincorporation of some of S1's assets) but does qualify as a reorganization under section 368(a)(1)(A) by reason of section 368(a)(2)(C) and paragraph (k) of this section. Under paragraph (m)(1)(v) of this section, the potential F reorganization in which some of the former assets of S1 are transferred (in form) first to P, and then to S2, is not a mere change of S1, because section 381(a) applies to P's acquisition of property held by S1 immediately before the potential F reorganization. Furthermore, under paragraph (m)(3)(iv)(A) of this section, P, the corporation in control of S2 within the meaning of section 368(c), is a party to the reorganization within the meaning of section 368(b). Thus, the indirect transfer of property from S1 to S2 does not qualify under section 368(a)(1)(F).

Example 11. Other acquiring corporation – mere change. P owns all of the stock of S1. S1's only asset is all of the equity interest in LLC2, a domestic limited liability company. Under §301.7701-3 of this chapter, LLC2 is disregarded as an entity separate from its owner, S1. Pursuant to an integrated plan to undergo a reorganization under 368(a)(1)(F), S1 and LLC2 undergo the following two state law conversions. First, under state law LLC2 converts into S2, a corporation. Second, under state law S1 converts into LLC1, a domestic limited liability company. Under §301.7701-3 of this chapter, LLC1 is disregarded as an entity separate from its owner, P. As a result of the two conversions, S1 is deemed to transfer its assets to S2 in exchange for all of the stock in S2 and then distribute the S2 stock to P in complete liquidation of S1. The two conversions, viewed as a potential F reorganization, constitute a mere change of S1, and that potential F reorganization qualifies as a reorganization under section 368(a)(1)(F). The result would be the same if, instead of converting into S2 pursuant to state law, LLC2 elected under §301.7701-3(c) to change its classification for federal tax purposes and be treated as an association taxable as a corporation, provided the effective date of the election (and its resulting deemed transactions) occurs before the conversion of S1.

Example 12. Other acquiring corporation – no mere change. The facts are the same facts as in *Example 11*, except that S1 converts into LLC1 prior to the conversion of LLC2 into S2. As a result of these conversions, S1 is deemed to distribute all of its assets to P in exchange for all of P's S1 stock, and P is deemed to transfer all of those assets to S2 in exchange for all of the stock in S2. The transaction does not qualify as a complete liquidation of S1 under section 332 (because of the reincorporation of S1's assets), but does qualify as a reorganization under section 368(a)(1)(C) by reason of section 368(a)(2)(C) and paragraph (k) of this section. Under paragraph (m)(1)(v) of this section, the potential F reorganization in which the former assets of S1 are deemed transferred, first by S1 to P, and then by P to S2, is not a mere change of S1 because section 381(a) applies to P's acquisition of property held by S1 immediately before the potential F reorganization. Furthermore, the corporation in control of S2, within the meaning of section 368(c), is a party to the reorganization within the meaning of section 368(b). Thus, the indirect transfer of property from S1 to S2 does not qualify under section 368(a)(1)(F).

Example 13. *Series of related transactions – no mere change.* X owns all of the stock of T. P acquires all of the stock of T in exchange for consideration consisting of $50 cash and P voting stock with $50 value. No election is made under section 338. Immediately thereafter and as part of the same plan, P forms S as a wholly-owned subsidiary, and T is merged into S. Viewed in isolation as a potential F reorganization, the merger of T into S appears to constitute a mere change of T. However, the acquisition of the T stock by P and the merger of T into S, viewed together, qualify as a reorganization under section 368(a)(1)(A) by reason of section 368(a)(2)(D). The step transaction doctrine is applied treat the transaction as a statutory merger of T into S in exchange for $50 cash and $50 of P's voting stock (and S's assumption of T's liabilities), P's momentary ownership of T stock is disregarded. Under paragraph (m)(3)(iv)(A) of this section, P, the corporation in control of S, is a party to the reorganization within the meaning of section 368(b). Thus, the transfer of property from T to S does not qualify under section 368(a)(1)(F).

Example 14. *Multiple transferor corporations – no mere change.* P owns all the stock of S1 and S2. The management of P determines it would be in the best interest of S1 and S2 to operate as a single corporation. P forms S3 and, under applicable corporate law, S1 and S2 simultaneously merge into S3. Immediately after the merger, P owns all the stock of S3. Each of the mergers can be tested as a potential F reorganization. However, immediately after the simultaneous mergers. the resulting corporation, S3, holds property acquired from a corporation other than the transferor corporation, and section 381(a) would apply to the acquisition of such property. Therefore, under paragraph (m)(1)(vi) of this section, neither potential F reorganization is a mere change, and neither merger into S3 qualifies as a reorganization under section 386(a)(1)(F). The result would be different if the mergers were not simultaneous. If S1 completed its merger into S3 before S2 began its merger into S3, the merger of S1 into S3 would qualify as a reorganization under section 368(a)(1)(F), but the merger of S2 into S3 would not so qualify (although it would qualify as a reorganization under sections 368(a)(1)(A) and 368(a)(1)(D)).

(5) *Effective/Applicability Date.*—This paragraph (m) applies to transactions occurring on or after September 21, 2015. [Reg. § 1.368-2.]

☐ [*T.D. 6152, 12-2-55. Amended by T.D. 7281, 7-11-73; T.D. 7422, 6-25-76; T.D. 8059, 10-21-85; T.D. 8760, 1-23-98; T.D. 8885, 5-18-2000; T.D. 9038, 1-23-2003; T.D. 9242, 1-23-2006; T.D. 9259, 4-24-2006; T.D. 9303, 12-18-2006; T.D. 9361, 10-24-2007; T.D. 9396, 5-8-2008, T.D. 9475, 12-17-2009 (corrected 1-19-2010), T.D. 9739, 9-18-2015 (corrected 12-7-2015) and T.D. 9954, 9-21-2021.]*

[Reg. § 1.368-3]

§ 1.368-3. Records to be kept and information to be filed with returns.—(a) *Parties to the reorganization.*—The plan of reorganization must be adopted by each of the corporations that are parties thereto. Each such corporation must include a statement entitled, "STATEMENT PURSUANT TO § 1.368-3(a) BY [INSERT NAME AND EMPLOYER IDENTIFICATION NUMBER (IF ANY) OF TAXPAYER], A CORPORATION A PARTY TO A REORGANIZATION," on or with its return for the taxable year of the exchange. If any such corporation is a controlled foreign corporation (within the meaning of section 957), each United States shareholder (within the meaning of section 951(b)) with respect thereto must include this statement on or with its return. However, it is not necessary for any taxpayer to include more than one such statement on or with the same return for the same reorganization. The statement must include—

(1) The names and employer identification numbers (if any) of all such parties;

(2) The date of the reorganization;

(3) The value and basis of the assets, stock or securities of the target corporation transferred in the transaction, determined immediately before the transfer and aggregated as follows—

(i) Importation property transferred in a loss importation transaction, as defined in § 1.362-3(c)(2) and (3), respectively;

(ii) Loss duplication property as defined in § 1.362-4(g)(1);

(iii) Property with respect to which any gain or loss was recognized on the transfer (without regard to whether such property is also identified in paragraph (a)(3)(i) or (ii) of this section);

(iv) Property not described in paragraph (a)(3)(i), (ii), or (iii) of this section; and

(4) The date and control number of any private letter ruling(s) issued by the Internal Revenue Service in connection with this reorganization.

(b) *Significant holders.* Every significant holder, other than a corporation a party to the reorganization, must include a statement

entitled, "STATEMENT PURSUANT TO § 1.368-3(b) BY [INSERT NAME AND TAXPAYER IDENTIFICATION NUMBER (IF ANY) OF TAXPAYER], A SIGNIFICANT HOLDER," on or with such holder's return for the taxable year of the exchange. If a significant holder is a controlled foreign corporation (within the meaning of section 957), each United States shareholder (within the meaning of section 951(b)) with respect thereto must include this statement on or with its return. The statement must include—

(1) The names and employer identification numbers (if any) of all of the parties to the reorganization;

(2) The date of the reorganization; and

(3) The value and basis of all the stock or securities of the target corporation held by the significant holder that is transferred in the transaction and such holder's basis in that stock or securities, determined immediately before the transfer and aggregated as follows—

(i) Stock and securities with respect to which an election is made under section 362(e)(2)(C); and

(ii) Stock and securities not described in paragraph (b)(3)(i) of this section.

(c) *Definitions.*—For purposes of this section:

(1) Significant holder means—

(i) A holder of stock of the target corporation that receives stock or securities in an exchange described in section 354 (or so much of section 356 as relates to section 354) if, immediately before the exchange, such holder—

(A) Owned at least five percent (by vote or value) of the total outstanding stock of the target corporation if the stock owned by such holder is publicly traded; or

(B) Owned at least one percent (by vote or value) of the total outstanding stock of the target corporation if the stock owned by such holder is not publicly traded; or

(ii) A holder of securities of the target corporation that receives stock or securities in an exchange described in section 354 (or so much of section 356 as relates to section 354) if, immediately before the exchange, such holder owned securities in such target corporation with a basis of $1,000,000 or more.

(2) Publicly traded stock means stock that is listed on—

(i) A national securities exchange registered under section 6 of the Securities Exchange Act of 1934 (15 U.S.C. 78f); or

(ii) An interdealer quotation system sponsored by a national securities association registered under section 15A of the Securities Exchange Act of 1934 (15 U.S.C. 78o-3).

(d) *Substantiation information.*—Under § 1.6001-1(e), taxpayers are required to retain their permanent records and make such records available to any authorized Internal Revenue Service officers and employees. In connection with the reorganization described in this section, these records should specifically include information regarding the amount, basis, and fair market value of all transferred property, and relevant facts regarding any liabilities assumed or extinguished as part of such reorganization.

(e) *Effective/applicability date.*—This section applies to any taxable year beginning on or after May 30, 2006. However, taxpayers may apply this section to any original Federal income tax return (including any amended return filed on or before the due date (including extensions) of such original return) timely filed on or after May 30, 2006. For taxable years beginning before May 30, 2006, see § 1.368-3 as contained in 26 CFR part 1 in effect on April 1, 2006. Paragraphs (a)(3) and (b)(3) of this section apply with respect to reorganizations occurring on or after March 28, 2016, and also with respect to reorganizations occurring before such date as a result of an entity classification election under § 301.7701-3 of this chapter filed on or after March 28, 2016, unless such reorganization is pursuant to a binding agreement that was in effect prior to March 28, 2016 and at all times thereafter. [Reg. § 1.368–3.]

☐ [*T.D. 9329, 6-13-2007. Amended by T.D. 9759, 3-25-2016.*]

[Reg. § 1.381(a)-1]

§ 1.381(a)-1. General rule relating to carryovers in certain corporate acquisitions.—(a) *Allowance of carryovers.*—Section 381 provides that a corporation which acquires the assets of another corporation in certain liquidations and reorganizations shall succeed to, and take into account, as of the close of the date of distribution or transfer, the items described in section 381(c) of the distributor or transferor corporation. These items shall be taken into account by the acquiring corporation subject to the conditions and limitations specified in sections 381, 382(b) and 383 and the regulations thereunder.

(b) *Determination of transactions and items to which section 381 applies.*—(1) *Qualified transactions.*—Except to the extent provided in section 381(c)(20), relating to the carryover of unused pension trust deductions in certain liquidations, the items described in section 381(c) are required by section 381 to be carried over to the acquiring corporation (as defined in subparagraph (2) of this paragraph) only in the following liquidations and reorganizations:

(i) The complete liquidation of a subsidiary corporation upon which no gain or loss is recognized in accordance with the provisions of section 332;

(ii) A statutory merger or consolidation qualifying under section 368(a)(1)(A) to which section 361 applies;

(iii) A reorganization qualifying under section 368(a)(1)(C);

(iv) A reorganization qualifying under section 368(a)(1)(D) if the requirements of section 354(b)(1)(A) and (B) are satisfied; and

(v) A mere change in identify, form, or place of organization qualifying under section 368(a)(1)(F).

(2) *Acquiring corporation defined.*—(i) Only a single corporation may be an acquiring corporation for purposes of section 381 and the regulations thereunder. The corporation which acquires the assets of its subsidiary corporation in a complete liquidation to which section 381(a)(1) applies is the acquiring corporation for purposes of section 381. In a transaction to which section 381(a)(2) applies, the acquiring corporation is the corporation that, pursuant to the plan of reorganization, directly acquires the assets transferred by the transferor corporation, even if that corporation ultimately retains none of the assets so transferred.

(ii) The application of this subparagraph may be illustrated by the following examples:

Example (1). Y Corporation, a wholly-owned subsidiary of X Corporation, directly acquired all the assets of Z Corporation solely in exchange for voting stock of X Corporation in a transaction qualifying under section 368(a)(1)(C). Y Corporation is the acquiring corporation for purposes of section 381.

Example (2). X Corporation acquired all the assets of Z Corporation solely in exchange for voting stock of X Corporation in a transaction qualifying under section 368(a)(1)(C). Thereafter, pursuant to the plan of reorganization X Corporation transferred all the assets so acquired to Y Corporation, its wholly-owned subsidiary (see section 368(a)(2)(C)). X Corporation is the acquiring corporation for purposes of section 381.

Example (3). X Corporation acquired all the assets of Z Corporation solely in exchange for the voting stock of X Corporation in a transaction qualifying under section 368(a)(1)(C). Thereafter, pursuant to the plan of reorganization X Corporation transferred one-half of the assets so acquired to Y Corporation, its wholly-owned subsidiary, and retained the other half of such assets. X Corporation is the acquiring corporation for purposes of section 381.

Example (4). X Corporation acquired all the assets of Z Corporation solely in exchange for voting stock of X Corporation in a transaction qualifying under section 368(a)(1)(C). Thereafter, pursuant to the plan of reorganization X Corporation transferred one-half of the assets so acquired to Y Corporation, its wholly-owned subsidiary, and the other half of such assets to M Corporation, another wholly-owned subsidiary of X Corporation. X Corporation is the acquiring corporation for purposes of section 381.

(3) *Transactions and items not covered by section 381.*—Section 381 does not apply to partial liquidations, divisive reorganizations, or other transactions not described in subparagraph (1) of this paragraph. Moreover, section 381 does not apply to the carryover of an item or tax attribute not specified in subsection (c) thereof. In a case where section 381 does not apply to a transaction, item, or tax attribute by reason of either of the preceding sentences, no inference is to be drawn from the provisions of section 381 as to whether any item or tax attribute shall be taken into account by the successor corporation.

(c) *Foreign corporations.*—For additional rules involving foreign corporations, see § § 1.367(b)-7 through 1.367(b)-9.

(d) *Internal Revenue Code of 1939.*—Any reference in the regulations under section 381 to any provision of the Internal Revenue Code of 1954 shall, where appropriate, be deemed also to refer to the corresponding provision of the Internal Revenue Code of 1939.

(e) *Effective/applicability date.*—The rules of paragraph (b)(1)(i) of this section apply to corporate reorganizations and tax-free liquidations described in section 381(a) that occur on or after August 31, 2011. The last sentence of paragraph (b)(2)(i) of this section and *Example 2* of paragraph (b)(2)(ii) of this section apply to transactions occurring on or after November 10, 2014. [Reg. § 1.381(a)-1.]

☐ *[T.D. 6480, 7-12-60. Amended by T.D. 7343, 1-8-75; T.D. 9273, 8-7-2006; T.D. 9534, 7-29-2011 and T.D. 9700, 11-7-2014.]*

[Reg. § 1.381(b)-1]

§1.381(b)-1. Operating rules applicable to carryovers in certain corporate acquisitions.—(a) *Closing of taxable year.*—(1) *In general.*—Except in the case of certain reorganizations qualifying under section

368(a)(1)(F), the taxable year of the distributor or transferor corporation shall end with the close of the date of distribution or transfer. With regard to the closing of the taxable year of the transferor corporation in certain reorganizations under section 368(a)(1)(F) involving a foreign corporation after December 31, 1986, see § § 1.367(a)-1(e) and 1.367(b)-2(f).

(2) *Reorganizations under section 368(a)(1)(F).*—In the case of a reorganization qualifying under section 368(a)(1)(F) (whether or not such reorganization also qualifies under any other provision of section 368(a)(1)), the acquiring corporation shall be treated (for purposes of section 381) just as the transferor corporation would have been treated if there had been no reorganization. Thus, the taxable year of the transferor corporation shall not end on the date of transfer merely because of the transfer; a net operating loss of the acquiring corporation for any taxable year ending after the date of transfer shall be carried back in accordance with section 172(b) in computing the taxable income of the transferor corporation for a taxable year ending before the date of transfer; and the tax attributes of the transferor corporation enumerated in section 381(c) shall be taken into account by the acquiring corporation as if there had been no reorganization.

(b) *Date of distribution or transfer.*—(1) The date of distribution or transfer shall be that day on which are distributed or transferred all those properties of the distributor or transferor corporation which are to be distributed or transferred pursuant to a liquidation or reorganization described in paragraph (b)(1) of § 1.381(a)-1. If the distribution or transfer of all such properties is not made on one day, then, except as provided in subparagraph (2) of this paragraph, the date of distribution or transfer shall be that day on which the distribution or transfer of all such properties is completed.

(2) If the distributor or transferor and acquiring corporations file the statements described in subparagraph (3) of this paragraph, the date of distribution or transfer shall be that day as of which (i) substantially all of the properties to be distributed or transferred have been distributed or transferred, and (ii) the distributor or transferor corporation has ceased all operations (other than liquidating activities). Such day also shall be the date of distribution or transfer if the completion of the distribution or transfer is unreasonably postponed beyond the date as of which substantially all the properties to be distributed or transferred have been distributed or transferred and the distributor or transferor corporation has ceased all operations other than liquidating activities. A corporation shall be considered to have distributed or transferred substantially all of its properties to be distributed or transferred even though it retains money or other property in a reasonable amount to pay outstanding debts or preserve the corporation's legal existence. A corporation shall be considered to have ceased all operations, other than liquidating activities, when it ceases to be a going concern and its activities are merely for the purpose of winding up its affairs, paying its debts, and distributing any remaining balance of its money or other properties to its shareholders.

(3) *Election.*—(i) *Content of statements.*—The statements referred to in paragraph (b)(2) of this section must be entitled, "ELECTION OF DATE OF DISTRIBUTION OR TRANSFER PURSUANT TO § 1.381(b)-1(b)(2)," and must include: [INSERT NAME AND EMPLOYER IDENTIFICATION NUMBER (IF ANY) OF DISTRIBUTOR OR TRANSFEROR CORPORATION] AND [INSERT NAME AND EMPLOYER IDENTIFICATION NUMBER (IF ANY) OF ACQUIRING CORPORATION] ELECT TO DETERMINE THE DATE OF DISTRIBUTION OR TRANSFER UNDER § 1.381(b)-1(b)(2). SUCH DATE IS [INSERT DATE (mm/dd/yyyy)].

(ii) *Filing of statements.*—One statement must be included on or with the timely filed Federal income tax return of the distributor or transferor corporation for its taxable year ending with the date of distribution or transfer. An identical statement must be included on or with the timely filed Federal income tax return of the acquiring corporation for its first taxable year ending after that date. If the distributor or transferor corporation, or the acquiring corporation, is a controlled foreign corporation (within the meaning of section 957), each United States shareholder (within the meaning of section 951(b)) with respect thereto must include this statement on or with its return.

(4) If—

(i) The last day of the acquiring corporation's taxable year is a Saturday, Sunday, or legal holiday, and

(ii) The day specified in subparagraph (1) and (2) of this paragraph as the date of distribution or transfer is the last business day before such Saturday, Sunday, or holiday,

then the last day of the acquiring corporation's taxable year shall be the date of distribution or transfer for purposes of section 381(b) and this section. For purposes of this subparagraph, the term "business day" means a day which is not a Saturday, Sunday, or legal holiday, and also means a Saturday, Sunday, or legal holiday if the date of distribution or transfer determined under subparagraph (1) or (2) of this paragraph is such Saturday, Sunday, or holiday.

(c) *Return of distributor or transferor corporation.*—The distributor or transferor corporation shall file an income tax return for the taxable year ending with the date of distribution or transfer described in paragraph (b) of this section. If the distributor or transferor corporation remains in existence after such date of distribution or transfer, it shall file an income tax return for the taxable year beginning on the day following the date of distribution or transfer and ending with the date on which the distributor or transferor corporation's taxable year would have ended if there had been no distribution or transfer.

(d) *Carryback of net operating losses.*—For provisions relating to the carryback of net operating losses of the acquiring corporation, see paragraph (b) of § 1.381(c)(1)-1.

(e) *Effective/applicability date.*—Paragraph (b)(3) of this section applies to any taxable year beginning on or after May 30, 2006. However, taxpayers may apply paragraph (b)(3) of this section to any original Federal income tax return (including any amended return filed on or before the due date (including extensions) of such original return) timely filed on or after May 30, 2006. For taxable years beginning before May 30, 2006, see § 1.381(b)-1 as contained in 26 CFR part 1 in effect on April 1, 2006. [Reg. § 1.381(b)-1.]

☐ [T.D. 6480, 7-12-60. *Amended by T.D. 8280,* 1-12-90; *T.D. 8862,* 1-21-2000; *T.D. 9264,* 5-26-2006, *T.D. 9329,* 6-13-2007 *and T.D. 9739,* 9-18-2015.]

[Reg. § 1.381(c)(1)-1]

§ 1.381(c)(1)-1. Net operating loss carryovers in certain corporate acquisitions.—(a) *Carryover requirement.*—(1) Section 381(c)(1) requires the acquiring corporation to succeed to, and take into account, the net operating loss carryovers of the distributor or transferor corporation. To determine the amount of these carryovers as of the close of the date of distribution or transfer, and to integrate them with any carryovers and carrybacks of the acquiring corporation for purposes of determining the taxable income of the acquiring corporation for taxable years ending after the date of distribution or transfer, it is necessary to apply the provisions of section 172 in accordance with the conditions and limitations of section 381(c)(1) and this section. See also section 382(b) and the regulations thereunder.

(2) The net operating loss carryovers and carrybacks of the acquiring corporation determined as of the close of the date of distribution or transfer shall be computed without reference to any net operating loss of a distributor or transferor corporation. The net operating loss carryovers of a distributor or transferor corporation as of the close of the date of distribution or transfer shall be determined without reference to any net operating loss of the acquiring corporation.

(3) For purposes of the tax imposed under section 56, the acquiring corporation succeeding to and taking into account any net operating loss carryovers of the distributor or transferor corporation shall also succeed to and take into account along with such net operating loss carryforward any deferred tax liability under section 56(b) and the regulations thereunder attributable to such net operating loss carryover.

(b) *Carryback of net operating losses.*—A net operating loss of the acquiring corporation for any taxable year ending after the date of distribution or transfer shall not be carried back in computing the taxable income of a distributor or transferor corporation. However, a net operating loss of the acquiring corporation for any such taxable year shall be carried back in accordance with section 172(b) in computing the taxable income of the acquiring corporation for a taxable year ending on or before the date of distribution or transfer. If a distributor or transferor corporation remains in existence after the date of distribution or transfer, a net operating loss sustained by it for any taxable year beginning after such date shall be carried back in accordance with section 172(b) in computing the taxable income of such corporation for a taxable year ending on or before that date, but may not be carried back or over in computing the taxable income of the acquiring corporation. This paragraph may be illustrated by the following examples:

Example (1). On December 31, 1954, X Corporation merged into Y Corporation in a statutory merger to which section 361 applies, and the charter of Y Corporation continued after the merger. Y Corporation sustained a net operating loss for the calendar year 1955. Y Corporation's net operating loss for 1955 may not be carried back in computing the taxable income of X Corporation but shall be carried back in computing the taxable income of Y Corporation.

Example (2). On December 31, 1954, X Corporation and Y Corporation transferred all their assets to Z Corporation in a statutory consolidation to which section 361 applies. Z Corporation sustained a net operating loss for the calendar year 1955. Z Corporation's net operat-

ing loss for 1955 may not be carried back in computing the taxable income of X Corporation or Y Corporation.

Example (3). On December 31, 1954, X Corporation ceased all operations (other than liquidating activities) and transferred substantially all its properties to Y Corporation in a reorganization qualifying under section 368(a)(1)(C). Such properties comprised all of X Corporation's properties which were to be transferred pursuant to the reorganization. In the process of liquidating its assets and winding up its affairs, X Corporation sustained a net operating loss for its taxable year beginning on January 1, 1955. This net operating loss of X Corporation shall be carried back in computing the taxable income of that corporation but may not be carried back or over in computing the taxable income of Y Corporation.

(c) *First taxable year to which carryovers apply.*—(1) The net operating loss carryovers available to the distributor or transferor corporation as of the close of the date of distribution or transfer shall first be carried to the first taxable year of the acquiring corporation ending after that date. This rule applies irrespective of whether the date of distribution or transfer is on the last day, or any other day, of the acquiring corporation's taxable year. Thus, such net operating loss carryovers shall first be used by the acquiring corporation with respect to the computation of its net operating loss deduction under section 172(a), and its taxable income determined under the provisions of section 172(b)(2), for such first taxable year. However, see paragraph (f) of this section.

(2) The net operating loss carryovers available to the distributor or transferor corporation as of the close of the date of distribution or transfer shall be carried to the acquiring corporation without diminution by reason of the fact that the acquiring corporation does not acquire 100 percent of the assets of the distributor or transferor corporation. Thus, if a parent corporation owning 80 percent of all classes of stock of its subsidiary corporation were to acquire its share of the assets of the subsidiary corporation upon a complete liquidation described in paragraph (b)(1)(i) of § 1.381(a)-1, then, subject to the conditions and limitations of this section, 100 percent of the net operating loss carryovers available to the subsidiary corporation as of the close of the date of distribution would be carried over to the parent corporation.

(d) *Limitation on net operating loss deduction for first taxable year ending after date of distribution or transfer.*—(1) That part of the acquiring corporation's net operating loss deduction, determined in accordance with sections 172(a) and 381(c)(1), for its first taxable year ending after the date of distribution or transfer which is attributable to the net operating loss carryovers of the distributor or transferor corporation, is limited by section 381(c)(1)(B) and this paragraph to an amount equal to the acquiring corporation's postacquisition part year taxable income. Such postacquisition part year taxable income is the amount which bears the same ratio to the acquiring corporation's taxable income for the first taxable year ending after the date of distribution or transfer (determined under section 63 without regard to any net operating loss deduction but taking into account other items to which the acquiring corporation succeeds under section 381) as the number of days in such first taxable year which follow the date of distribution or transfer bears to the total number of days in such taxable year. Thus, if the date of distribution or transfer is the last day of the acquiring corporation's taxable year, the net operating loss carryovers of the distributor or transferor are allowed in full in computing under section 172(a) the net operating loss deduction of the acquiring corporation for its first taxable year ending after that date. In such instance, the number of days in the first taxable year which follow the date of distribution or transfer is the total number of days in such taxable year.

(2) The limitation provided by section 381(c)(1)(B) applies solely for the purpose of computing the net operating loss deduction of the acquiring corporation under section 172(a) for the acquiring corporation's first taxable year ending after the date of distribution or transfer. The limitation does not apply for purposes of determining the portion of any net operating loss (whether of the distributor, transferor, or acquiring corporation) which may be carried to any taxable year of the acquiring corporation following its first taxable year ending after the date of distribution or transfer since such determination is made pursuant to section 172(b) and section 381(c)(1)(C). See paragraphs (e) and (f) of this section.

(3) The limitation provided by section 381(c)(1)(B) shall be applied to the aggregate of the allowable net operating loss carryovers of the distributor or transferor corporation without reference to the taxable years in which the net operating losses were sustained by such corporation. If the acquiring corporation has acquired the assets of two or more distributor or transferor corporations on the same date of distribution or transfer, then the limitation provided by section 381(c)(1)(B) shall be applied to the aggregate of the net operating loss carryovers from all such distributor or transferor corporations.

(4) If the acquiring corporation succeeds to the net operating loss carryovers of two or more distributor or transferor corporations on two or more different dates of distribution or transfer within one taxable year of the acquiring corporation, the limitation to be applied under section 381(c)(1)(B) to the aggregate of such carryovers shall be governed by the rules prescribed in paragraph (b) of § 1.381(c)(1)-2.

(5) *Illustrations.*—The application of this paragraph may be illustrated by the following examples:

Taxable Year		
1956	($35,000)	($5,000)
Ending 12/16/57	(30,000)	xxx
1957	xxx	36,500

(ii) The aggregate of the net operating loss carryovers of X Corporation carried under section 381(c)(1)(A) to Y Corporation's taxable year ending December 31, 1957, is $65,000; but pursuant to section 381(c)(1)(B), only $1,500 of such aggregate amount ($36,500 × 15/365) may be used in computing the net operating loss deduction of Y Corporation for such taxable year under section 172(a). This limitation applies even though Y Corporation's own net operating loss carryover to such year is only $5,000 with the result that Y Corporation has taxable income under section 63 of $30,000 for its taxable year ending December 31, 1957, that is, $36,500 less the sum of $5,000 and $1,500.

(iii) For rules determining the portion of any given loss of X Corporation or Y Corporation which may be carried to a taxable year

Taxable Year		
1954	($5,000)	xxx
1955	(15,000)	xxx
1956	(10,000)	$20,000
1957	xxx	40,000

(ii) The aggregate of the net operating loss carryovers of X Corporation carried under section 381(c)(1)(A) to Y Corporation's taxable year 1957 is $30,000, and the full amount of such carryovers is allowed in such taxable year to Y Corporation as a deduction under section 172(a), since such amount does not exceed the limitation ($40,000 × 365/365) for such taxable year under section 381(c)(1)(B).

Example (3). (i) X Corporation, Y Corporation, and Z Corporation were organized on January 1, 1954, and each corporation makes its

Taxable Year	X Corporation (Transferor)	Y Corporation (Transferor)	Z Corporation (Acquirer)
1954	($5,000)	($3,000)	($40,000)
1955	(4,000)	(2,000)	10,000
Ending 9/30/56	(1,000)	(9,000)	xxx
1956	xxx	xxx	73,200

(ii) The aggregate of the net operating loss carryovers of X Corporation and Y Corporation carried under section 381(c)(1)(A) to Z Corporation's taxable year 1956 is $24,000; but, pursuant to section 381(c)(1)(B), only $18,400 of such aggregate amount ($73,200 × 92/366) may be used in computing the net operating loss deduction of Z Corporation for such taxable year under section 172(a). For this purpose, Z Corporation may not use the total of the aggregate carryovers ($10,000) from X Corporation plus the aggregate carryovers ($14,000) from Y Corporation, even though each such aggregate of carryovers is separately less than the limitation ($18,400) applicable under section 381(c)(1)(B) and this section.

(iii) For rules determining the portion of any given loss of X Corporation, Y Corporation, or Z Corporation which may be carried to a taxable year of Z Corporation following its taxable year ending December 31, 1956, see sections 172(b)(2) and 381(c)(1)(C) and paragraph (f) of this section.

(e) *Computation of carryovers and carrybacks; general rule.*—(1) *Sequence for applying losses and computation of taxable income.*—The portion of any net operating loss which is carried back or carried over to any taxable year is the excess, if any, of the amount of the loss over the sum of the taxable income for each of the prior taxable years to which the loss may be carried under sections 172(b)(1) and 381. In determining the taxable income for each such prior taxable year for this purpose, the various net operating loss carryovers and carrybacks to such prior taxable year are considered to be applied in reduction of the taxable income in the order of the taxable years in which the net operating losses are sustained, beginning with the loss for the earliest taxable year. The application of this rule to the taxable income of the acquiring corporation for any taxable year ending after the date of distribution or transfer involves the use of carryovers of the distributor or transferor corporation, and of carryovers and carrybacks of the acquiring corporation. In such instance, the sequence for the use of loss years remains the same, and the requirement is to begin with the net operating loss of the earliest taxable year, whether or not it is a loss of the distributor, transferor, or acquiring corporation. The taxable income of the acquiring corporation for any taxable

Example (1). (i) X Corporation and Y Corporation were organized on January 1, 1956, and make their returns on the calendar year basis. On December 16, 1957, X Corporation transferred all its assets to Y Corporation in a statutory merger to which section 361 applies. The net operating losses and taxable income (computed without the net operating loss deduction) of the two corporations are as follows, the assumption being made that none of the modifications specified in section 172(b)(2)(A) apply to any taxable year:

of Y Corporation following its taxable year ending December 31, 1957, see sections 172(b)(2) and 381(c)(1)(C) and paragraph (f) of this section.

Example (2). (i) X Corporation was organized on January 1, 1954, and Y Corporation was organized on January 1, 1956. Each corporation makes its return on the basis of the calendar year. On December 31, 1956, X Corporation transferred all its assets to Y Corporation in a statutory merger to which section 361 applies. The net operating losses and the taxable income (computed without any net operating loss deduction) of the two corporations are as follows, the assumption being made that none of the modifications specified in section 172(b)(2)(A) apply to any taxable year:

return on the basis of the calendar year. On September 30, 1956, X Corporation and Y Corporation transferred all their assets to Z Corporation in a statutory merger to which section 361 applies. The net operating losses and the taxable income (computed without any net operating loss deduction) of the three corporations are as follows, the assumption being made that none of the modifications specified in section 172(b)(2)(A) apply to any taxable year:

year ending after the date of distribution or transfer shall be determined in the manner prescribed by section 172(b)(2), except that, if the date of distribution or transfer is on a day other than the last day of a taxable year of the acquiring corporation, the taxable income of such corporation for the taxable year which includes such date shall be computed in the special manner prescribed by section 381(c)(1)(C) and paragraph (f) of this section.

(2) *Loss year of transferor or distributor considered prior taxable year.*—Section 381(c)(1)(C) provides that, for the purpose of determining the net operating loss carryovers under section 172(b)(2), a net operating loss for a loss year of a distributor or transferor corporation which ends on or before the last day of a loss year of the acquiring corporation shall be considered to be a net operating loss for a year prior to such loss year of the acquiring corporation. In a case where the acquiring corporation has acquired the assets of two or more distributor or transferor corporations on the same date of distribution or transfer, the loss years of the distributor or transferor corporations shall be taken into account in the order in which such loss years terminate; if any one of the loss years of a distributor or transferor corporation ends on the same day as the loss year of another distributor or transferor corporation, either loss year may be taken into account before the other.

(3) *Years to which losses may be carried.*—The taxable years to which a net operating loss shall be carried back or carried over are prescribed by section 172(b)(1). Since the taxable year of the distributor or transferor corporation ends with the close of the date of distribution or transfer, such taxable year and the first taxable year of the acquiring corporation which ends after that date shall be considered two separate taxable years to which a net operating loss of the distributor or transferor corporation for any taxable year ending before that date may be carried over. This rule applies even though the taxable year of the distributor or transferor corporation which ends on the date of distribution or transfer is a period of less than twelve months. However, for the purpose of determining under section 172(b)(1) the taxable years to which a net operating loss of the

acquiring corporation is carried over or carried back, the first taxable year of the acquiring corporation which ends after the date of distribution or transfer shall be treated as only one taxable year even though such taxable year is considered under section 381(c)(1)(C) and paragraph (f)(2) of this section as two taxable years. The application of this subparagraph may be illustrated by the following example:

Example. X Corporation was organized on January 1, 1954, and thereafter it sustained net operating losses in its calendar years 1954,

Loss Year	
X 1954	X 1955, X 1956, X 6/30/57, Y 1957, Y 1958.
X 1955	X 1954, X 1956, X 6/30/57, Y 1957, Y 1958, Y 1959.
Y 1955	Y 1956, Y 1957, Y 1958, Y 1959, Y 1960.
X 1956	X 1954, X 1955, X 6/30/57, Y 1957, Y 1958, Y 1959, Y 1960.
Y 1956	Y 1955, Y 1957, Y 1958, Y 1959, Y 1960, Y 1961.
X 6-30-57	X 1955, X 1956, Y 1957, Y 1958, Y 1959, Y 1960, Y 1961.
Y 1958	Y 1955, Y 1956, Y 1957, Y 1959, Y 1960, Y 1961, Y 1962, Y 1963.

(4) *Computation of carryovers in a case where the date of distribution or transfer occurs on last day of acquiring corporation's taxable year.*—The computation of the net operating loss carryovers from the distributor or transferor corporation and from the acquiring corporation in a case where the date of distribution or transfer occurs on the last day of a taxable year of the acquiring corporation may be illustrated by the following example:

1955, and 1956. On June 30, 1957, X Corporation transferred all its assets to Y Corporation, which was organized on January 1, 1955, in a statutory merger to which section 361 applies. In its taxable year ending June 30, 1957, X Corporation sustained a net operating loss. Y Corporation sustained net operating losses in its calendar years 1955, 1956, and 1958, but had taxable income for the year 1957. The years to which these losses of X Corporation and Y Corporation shall be carried, and the sequence in which carried, are as follows:

Example. X Corporation and Y Corporation were organized on January 1, 1955, and each corporation makes its return on the basis of the calendar year. On December 31, 1956, X Corporation transferred all its assets to Y Corporation in a statutory merger to which section 361 applies. The net operating losses and the taxable income (computed without any net operating loss deduction) of the two corporations are as follows, the assumption being made that none of the modifications specified in section 172(b)(2)(A) apply to any taxable year:

Taxable Year	X Corporation (Transferor)	Y Corporation (Acquirer)
1955	($2,000)	($11,000)
1956	(3,000)	10,000
1957	xxx	(15,000)

The sequence in which the losses of X Corporation and Y Corporation are applied, and the computation of the carryovers to Y Corporation's calendar year 1958, may be illustrated as follows:

(i) *X Corporation's 1955 loss.* The carryover to 1958 is $2,000, computed as follows:

Net operating loss		$2,000
Less:		
X's 1956 taxable income	$0	
Y's 1957 taxable income	0	0
Carryover		2,000

(ii) *Y Corporation's 1955 loss.* The carryover to 1958 is $1,000, computed as follows:

Net operating loss		$11,000
Less:		
Y's 1956 taxable income	$10,000	
Y's 1957 taxable income	0	10,000
Carryover		1,000

(iii) *X Corporation's 1956 loss.* The carryover to 1958 is $3,000, computed as follows:

Net operating loss		$3,000
Less:		
X's 1955 taxable income	$0	
Y's 1957 taxable income	0	0
Carryover		3,000

(iv) *Y Corporation's 1957 loss.* The carryover to 1958 is $15,000, computed as follows:

Net operating loss			$15,000
Less:			
Y's 1955 taxable income		$0	
Y's 1956 taxable income before net operating loss deduction	$10,000		
Minus Y's 1956 net operating loss deduction (i.e., Y's 1955 carryover)	11,000	$0	0
Carryover			15,000

(v) *Summary of carryovers to 1958.* The aggregate of the net operating loss carryovers to 1958 is $21,000, computed as follows:

X's 1955 loss	$2,000
Y's 1955 loss	1,000
X's 1956 loss	3,000
Total	21,000

(f) *Computation of carryovers and carrybacks when date of distribution or transfer is not on last day of acquiring corporation's taxable year.*— (1) *General rule.*—Pursuant to the provisions of section 381(c)(1)(C), the taxable income of the acquiring corporation for its taxable year which is a prior taxable year for purposes of section 172(b)(2) and paragraph (e) of this section shall be determined in the manner prescribed in this paragraph, if the date of distribution or transfer occurs within, but not on the last day of, such taxable year.

(2) *Taxable year considered as two taxable years.*—Such taxable year of the acquiring corporation shall be considered as though it were two taxable years, but only for the limited purpose of applying section 172(b)(2). The first of such two taxable years shall be referred to in this section as the preacquisition part year; the second, as the

postacquisition part year. For purposes of section 172(b)(2), a net operating loss of the acquiring corporation shall be carried to the preacquisition part year and then to the postacquisition part year, whereas a net operating loss of a distributor or transferor corporation shall be carried to the postacquisition part year and then to the acquiring corporation's subsequent taxable years. In determining under section 172(b)(2) and this paragraph the portion of any net operating loss of a distributor or transferor corporation which is carried to any taxable year of the acquiring corporation ending after the postacquisition part year, the taxable income (as determined under this paragraph) of the postacquisition part year shall be taken into account but the taxable income of the preacquisition part year (as so determined) shall not be taken into account. Though considered as two separate taxable years for purposes of section 172(b)(2), the preacquisition part year and the postacquisition part year are treated as one taxable year in determining the years to which a net operating loss is carried under section 172(b)(1). See paragraph (e)(3) of this section.

(3) *Preacquisition part year.*—The preacquisition part year shall begin with the beginning of such taxable year of the acquiring corporation and shall end with the close of the date of distribution or transfer.

(4) *Postacquisition part year.*—The postacquisition part year shall begin with the day following the date of distribution or transfer and shall end with the close of such taxable year of the acquiring corporation.

(5) *Division of taxable income.*—The taxable income for such taxable year (computed with the modifications specified in section 172(b)(2)(A) but without any net operating loss deduction) of the acquiring corporation shall be divided between the preacquisition part year and the postacquisition part year in proportion to the number of days in each. Thus, if in a statutory merger to which section 361 applies Y Corporation acquires the assets of X Corporation on June 30, 1960, and Y Corporation has taxable income (computed in the manner so prescribed) of $36,600 for its calendar year 1960, then the preacquisition part year taxable income would be $18,200 ($36,600 × 182/366) and the postacquisition part year taxable income would be $18,400 ($36,000 × 184/366).

(6) *Net operating loss deduction.*—After obtaining the taxable income of the preacquisition part year and of the postacquisition part year in the manner described in subparagraph (5) of this paragraph, it is necessary to compute the net operating loss deduction for each

such part year. This deduction shall be determined in the manner prescribed by section 172(b)(2)(B) but subject to the provisions of this subparagraph. The net operating loss deduction for the preacquisition part year shall, for purposes of section 172(b)(2) only, be determined in the same manner as that prescribed by section 172(b)(2)(B) but shall be computed without taking into account any net operating loss of the distributor or transferor corporation. Therefore, only net operating loss carryovers and carrybacks of the acquiring corporation to the preacquisition part year shall be taken into account in computing the net operating loss deduction for such part year. The net operating loss deduction for the postacquisition part year shall, for purposes of section 172(b)(2) only, be determined in the same manner as that prescribed by section 172(b)(2)(B) and shall be computed by taking into account all the net operating loss carryovers available to the distributor or transferor corporation as of the close of the date of distribution or transfer, as well as the net operating loss carryovers and carrybacks of the acquiring corporation to the postacquisition part year. The sequence in which the net operating losses of the two corporations shall be applied for purposes of this subparagraph shall be determined in the manner prescribed in paragraph (e) of this section.

(7) *Limitation on taxable income.*—In no case shall the taxable income of the preacquisition part year or the postacquisition part year, as computed under this paragraph, be considered to be less than zero.

(8) *Cross reference.*—If the acquiring corporation succeeds to the net operating loss carryovers of two or more distributor or transferor corporations on two or more dates of distribution or transfer during the same taxable year of the acquiring corporation, the determination of the taxable income of the acquiring corporation for such year pursuant to section 381(c)(1)(C) shall be governed by the rules prescribed in paragraph (c) of § 1.381(c)(1)-2.

(9) *Illustration.*—The application of this paragraph may be illustrated by the following example:

Example—(i) *Facts.* X Corporation was organized on January 1, 1955, and Y Corporation was organized on January 1, 1954. Each corporation makes its return on the basis of the calendar year. On June 30, 1956, X Corporation transferred all its assets to Y Corporation in a statutory merger to which section 361 applies. The net operating losses and the taxable income (computed without any net operating loss deduction) of the two corporations are as follows, the assumption being made that none of the modifications specified in section 172(b)(2)(A) apply to any taxable year:

Taxable Year	X Corporation (Transferor)	Y Corporation (Acquirer)
1954	xxx	($5,000)
1955	($65,000)	(20,000)
Ending 6-30-56	1,000	xxx
1956	xxx	36,600

(ii) *Y Corporation's 1954 loss.* The carryover to 1957 is $0, computed as follows:

Net operating loss		$5,000
Less:		
Y's 1955 taxable income		0
Carryover to Y's preacquisition part year		5,000
Less:		
Y's preacquisition part year taxable income computed under subparagraph (5) of this paragraph ($36,600 × 182/366)	$18,200	
Minus Y's net operating loss deduction for preacquisition part year	xxx	18,200
Carryover to Y's postacquisition part year and also to Y 1957		0

(iii) *X Corporation's 1955 loss.* The carryover to 1957 is $45,600, computed as follows:

Net operating loss		$65,000
Less:		
X's 6/30/56 year taxable income		1,000
Carryover to Y's postacquisition part year		64,000
Less:		
Y's postacquisition part year taxable income computed under subparagraph (5) of this paragraph ($36,600 × 184/366)	$18,400	
Minus Y's net operating loss deduction for postacquisition part year (i.e., Y's 1954 carryover of $0 to such part year)	0	18,400
Carryover to Y 1957		45,600

(iv) *Y Corporation's 1955 loss.* The carryover to 1957 is $6,800, computed as follows:

Net operating loss		$20,000
Less:		
Y's 1954 taxable income		0
Carryover to Y's preacquisition part year		20,000

Less:

Y's preacquisition part year taxable income computed under subparagraph (5) of this paragraph	$18,200	
Minus Y's net operating loss deduction for preacquisition part year (i.e., Y's 1954 carryover to such part year)	$5,000	$13,200
Carryover to Y's postacquisition part year		6,800

Less:

Y's postacquisition part year taxable income computed under subparagraph (5) of this paragraph	$18,400	
Minus Y's net operating loss deduction for postacquisition part year (i.e., Y's 1954 carryover of $0, and X's 1955 carryover of $64,000, to such part year)	64,000	0
Carryover to Y 1957		6,800

(v) *Summary of carryovers to 1957.* The aggregate of the net operating loss carryovers to 1957 is $52,400, determined as follows:

Y's 1954 loss	$0
X's 1955 loss	45,600
Y's 1955 loss	6,800
Total	52,400

(g) *Successive acquiring corporations.*—An acquiring corporation which, in a distribution or transfer to which section 381(a) applies, acquires the assets of a distributor or transferor corporation which previously acquired the assets of another corporation in a transaction to which section 381(a) applies, shall succeed to and take into account, subject to the conditions and limitations of sections 172 and 381, the net operating loss carryovers available to the first acquiring corporation under sections 172 and 381.

(h) *Illustration.*—The application of this section may be further illustrated by the following example:

Example—(1) *Facts.* X Corporation was organized on January 1, 1954, and Y Corporation was organized on January 1, 1955. Each corporation makes its return on the basis of the calendar year. On August 31, 1957, X Corporation transferred all its assets to Y Corporation in a statutory merger to which section 361 applies. The net operating losses and the taxable income of the two corporations for the taxable years involved are set forth in the tabulation below. The taxable income so shown is computed without the modifications required by section 172(b)(2)(A) and without the benefit of any net operating loss deduction. In its calendar year 1957, Y Corporation had a deduction of $365 which is disallowed by section 172(b)(2)(A).

Taxable year	X Corporation (Transferor)	Y Corporation (Acquirer)
1954	($7,000)	xxx
1955	(10,000)	($10,000)
1956	(25,000)	(15,000)
Ending 8-31-57	1,000	xxx
1957	xxx	54,750
1958	xxx	(5,000)
1959	xxx	50,000

(2) *Computation of carryovers and carrybacks.* The sequence in which the losses of X Corporation and Y Corporation are applied and the computation of the carryovers to Y Corporation's calendar year 1959 may be illustrated as follows:

(i) *X Corporation's 1954 loss.* The carryover to 1958, which is the last year to which this loss may be carried, is $0, computed as follows:

Net operating loss		$7,000
Less:		
X's 1955 taxable income	$0	
X's 1956 taxable income	0	0
Carryover to X's 8/31/57-year		7,000
Less:		
X's 8/31/57-year taxable income		1,000
Carryover to Y's postacquisition part year		6,000
Less:		
Y's postacquisition part year taxable income computed under paragraph (f)(5) of this section (($54,750 + $365) × 122/365)	$18,422	
Minus Y's net operating loss deduction for postacquisition part year	xxx	$18,422
Carryover to Y 1958		0

(ii) *X Corporation's 1955 loss.* The carryover to 1959 is $0, computed as follows:

Net operating loss		$10,000
Less:		
X's 1954 taxable income	$0	
X's 1956 taxable income	0	0
Carryover to X's 8/31/57-year		10,000
Less:		
X's 8/31/57-year taxable income before net operating loss deduction	$1,000	
Minus X's net operating loss deduction for 8/31/57-year (i.e., X's 1954 carryover)	7,000	0
Carryover to Y's postacquisition part year		10,000
Less:		
Y's postacquisition part year taxable income computed under paragraph (f)(5) of this section	$18,422	
Minus Y's net operating loss deduction for postacquisition part year (i.e., X's 1954 carryover to such part year)	6,000	$12,422
Carryover to Y 1958 and Y 1959		0

(iii) *Y Corporation's 1955 loss.* The carryover to 1959 is $0, computed as follows:

Net operating loss		$10,000
Less:		
Y's 1956 taxable income	0	
Y's preacquisition part year taxable income		
Carryover to Y's preacquisition part year		10,000
Less:		

Y's preacquisition part year taxable income computed under paragraph (f)(5) of this section (($54,750 + $365) × 243/365)	$36,693	
Minus Y's net operating loss deduction for preacquisition part year	xxx	36,693
Carryover to Y's post acquisition part year to Y 1958, and to Y 1959		0

(iv) *X Corporation's 1956 loss.* The carryover to 1959 is $22,578, computed as follows:

Net operating loss			$25,000
Less:			
X's 1954 taxable income	$0		
X's 1955 taxable income	0		
X's 8/31/57-year taxable income before net operating loss deduction	$1,000		
Minus X's net operating loss deduction for 8/31/57-year (i.e., X's 1954 carryover of $7,000 and X's 1955 carryover of $10,000)	17,000	$0	$0
Carryover to Y's postacquisition part year			$25,000
Less:			
Y's postacquisition part year taxable income computed under paragraph (f)(5) of this section	$18,422		
Minus Y's net operating loss deduction for postacquisition part year (i.e., X's 1954 carryover of $6,000, X's 1955 carryover of $10,00 0 and Y's 1955 carryover of $0, to such part year)	16,000		2,422
Carryover to Y 1958			22,578
Less:			
Y's 1958 taxable income			$0
Carryover to Y 1959			22,578

(v) *Y Corporation's 1956 loss.* The carryover to 1959 is $0, computed as follows:

Net operating loss		$15,000
Less:		
Y's 1955 taxable income		$0
Carryover to Y's preacquisition part year		15,000
Less:		
Y's preacquisition part year taxable income computed under paragraph (f)(5) of this section	$36,693	
Minus Y's net operating loss deduction for preacquisition part year (i.e., Y's 1955 carryover to such part year)	10,000	$26,693
Carryover to Y's postacquisition part year, to Y 1958, and to Y 1959		0

(vi) *Y Corporation's 1958 loss.* The carryover to 1959 is $0, computed as follows:

Net operating loss		$5,000
Less:		
Y's 1955 taxable income[1]	$0	
Y's 1956 taxable income	0	0
Carryback to Y's preacquisition part year		5,000
Less:		
Y's preacquisition part year taxable income computed under paragraph (f)(5) of this section . . .	$36,693	
Minus Y's net operating loss deduction for preacquisition part year (i.e., Y's 1955 carryover of $10,000, and Y's 1956 carryover of $1 5,000, to such part year)	25,000	$11,693
Carryback to Y's postacquisition part year and carryover to Y 1959		0

[1] Three-year carryback in case of loss years ending after December 31, 1957.

(vii) *Summary of carryovers to 1959.* The aggregate of the net operating loss carryovers to 1959 is $22,578, computed as follows:

X's 1955 loss		$0
Y's 1955 loss		0
X's 1956 loss		22,578
Y's 1956 loss		0
Y's 1958 loss		0
Total		22,578

(3) *Net operating loss deduction for 1957.* (i) The net operating loss deduction available to Y Corporation under section 172(a) for the calendar year 1957, determined in accordance with paragraph (d) of this section, is $48,300, computed as follows:

Aggregate of the net operating loss carryovers available to the transferor corporation as of the close of August 31, 1957, but limited by paragraph (d) of this section to $18,300 (Y's 1957 taxable income of $54,750, computed without any net operating loss deduction, multiplied by 122/365).

Carryover of X's 1954 loss	$6,000	
Carryover of X's 1955 loss	10,000	
Carryover of X's 1956 loss	25,000	
	41,000	
Aggregate of carryovers, limited as above		$18,300
Carryover of Y's 1955 loss		10,000
Carryover of Y's 1956 loss		15,000
Carryback of Y's 1958 loss		5,000
Net operating loss deduction		48,300

(ii) The taxable income under section 63 for 1957 is $6,450, computed as follows:

Taxable income determined without any net operating loss deduction		$54,750
Less:		

Net operating loss deduction for 1957, as determined under subdivision (i) of this subparagraph	$48,300
Taxable income under section 63	6,450

(4) *Net operating loss deduction for 1959.* The taxable income under section 63 for 1959 is $27,422, computed as follows:

Taxable income determined without any net operating loss deduction	$50,000
Less:	
Net operating loss deduction for 1959 (i.e., the aggregate carryovers determined under subparagraph (2)(vii) of this paragraph)	22,578
Taxable income under section 63	$27,422

(5) *Years to which losses may be carried.* The taxable years to which the losses of X Corporation and Y Corporation may be carried, and the sequence in which carried, are as follows:

Loss Year	Carried to
X 1954	X 1955, X 1956, X 8/31/57, Y 1957, Y 1958.
X 1955	X 1954, X 1956, X 8/31/57, Y 1957, Y 1958, Y 1959.
Y 1955	Y 1956, Y 1957, Y 1958, Y 1959, Y 1960.
X 1956	X 1954, X 1955, X 8/31/57, Y 1957, Y 1958, Y 1959, Y 1960.
Y 1956	Y 1955, Y 1957, Y 1958, Y 1959, Y 1960, Y 1961.
Y 1958	Y 1955, Y 1956, Y 1957, Y 1959, Y 1960, Y 1961, Y 1962, Y 1963.

[Reg. § 1.381(c)(1)-1.]

☐ [T.D. 6480, 7-12-60. Amended by T.D. 7564, 9-11-78.]

[Reg. § 1.381(c)(1)-2]

§1.381(c)(1)-2. Net operating loss carryovers; two or more dates of distribution or transfer in the taxable year.—(a) *In general.*—If the acquiring corporation succeeds to the net operating loss carryovers of two or more distributor or transferor corporations on two or more dates of distribution or transfer within one taxable year of the acquiring corporation, the limitation to be applied under section 381(c)(1)(B) to the aggregate of the net operating loss carryovers to that taxable year from all of the distributor or transferor corporations shall be determined by applying the rules prescribed in paragraph (b) of this section, and the taxable income of the acquiring corporation for that taxable year under sections 381(c)(1)(C) and 172(b)(2) shall be determined by applying the rules prescribed in paragraph (c) of this section. For purposes of this section, the term "postacquisition income" means postacquisition part year taxable income determined under paragraph (d)(1) of § 1.381(c)(1)-1 by treating the first date of distribution or transfer as though it were the only date of distribution or transfer during the taxable year of the acquiring corporation.

(b) *Determination of limitation under section 381(c)(1)(B).*—(1) *In general.*—If the acquiring corporation succeeds to the net operating loss carryovers of two or more distributor or transferor corporations on two or more dates of distribution or transfer during the same taxable year of the acquiring corporation, and if the amount of the net operating loss carryovers acquired on the first date of distribution or transfer equals or exceeds the postacquisition income, then the limitation under section 381(c)(1)(B) shall be an amount equal to such postacquisition income. If the amount of the net operating loss carryovers acquired on the first date of distribution or transfer is less than such postacquisition income, then the limitation under section 381(c)(1)(B) shall be determined as provided in subparagraphs (2) through (5) of this paragraph.

(2) *Allocation of postacquisition income among partial postacquisition years.*—That part of the taxable year of the acquiring corporation

Corporation	Carryovers
Y	$1,000
Z	50,000
	$51,000

(ii) The limitation provided by section 381(c)(1)(B) equals the postacquisition income of $36,400 reduced by $32,400, the excess of the income for the first partial year ($33,400) over the net operating loss carryovers acquired on the first date of transfer ($1,000). Accordingly, the limitation is $4,000 ($36,400 minus $32,400). Therefore, although X Corporation acquired carryovers aggregating $51,000 during 1955, it can utilize only $4,000 of such carryovers in computing its net operating loss deduction for 1955.

(4) *Three dates of distribution or transfer.*—If the acquiring corporation succeeds to the net operating loss carryovers of three distributor or transferor corporations on three dates of distribution or transfer during the same taxable year of the acquiring corporation, and if the amount of the net operating loss carryovers acquired on the first date equals or exceeds the income for the first and second partial postacquisition years, the limitation provided by section 381(c)(1)(B) shall be the amount of the postacquisition income. If the amount of the carryovers acquired on the first date equals or exceeds the income for the first partial postacquisition year but does not

beginning on the day following the first date of distribution or transfer and ending with the close of the taxable year of the acquiring corporation shall be divided into the same number of partial postacquisition years as the number of dates of distribution or transfer on which the acquiring corporation succeeds to net operating loss carryovers during its taxable year. The first partial postacquisition year shall begin with the day following the first date of distribution or transfer and shall end with the close of the second date of distribution or transfer. The second and succeeding partial postacquisition years shall begin with the day following the close of the preceding such partial year and shall end with the close of the succeeding date of distribution or transfer, or, if there is no such succeeding date, then with the close of the taxable year of the acquiring corporation. The postacquisition income of the acquiring corporation shall be allocated among the partial postacquisition years in proportion to the number of days in each such partial year.

(3) *Two dates of distribution or transfer.*—If the acquiring corporation succeeds to the net operating loss carryovers of two distributor or transferor corporations on two dates of distribution or transfer during the same taxable year of the acquiring corporation, and if the amount of the net operating loss carryovers acquired on the first date equals or exceeds the income for the first partial postacquisition year, the limitation provided by section 381(c)(1)(B) shall be the amount of the postacquisition income. If the income for the first partial postacquisition year exceeds the net operating loss carryovers acquired on the first date of distribution or transfer, the limitation provided by section 381(c)(1)(B) shall be the amount of the postacquisition income reduced by the amount of such excess. The application of this subparagraph may be illustrated by the following example:

Example. (i) X Corporation has taxable income (computed without any net operating loss deduction) of $36,500 for its calendar year 1955. During 1955, X Corporation acquires the assets of Y and Z Corporations in statutory mergers to each of which section 361 applies, the dates of transfer being January 1 and December 1, respectively. The net operating loss carryovers of each transferor corporation and the income for each partial postacquisition year are:

	Income for Partial Years		Reduction
$33,400	($36,500 × 334/365)		$32,400
3,000	($36,500 × 30/365)		0
$36,400			$32,400

equal or exceed the income for the first and second partial postacquisition years, the limitation shall be the amount of the postacquisition income reduced by the excess of the income for the first and second partial postacquisition years over the amount of carryovers acquired on the first and second dates of distribution or transfer. If the income for the first partial postacquisition year exceeds the carryovers acquired on the first date, the limitation shall be the postacquisition income reduced by the sum of the amount of such excess plus the amount, if any, by which the income for the second partial postacquisition year exceeds the carryovers acquired on the second date. This subparagraph may be illustrated by the following examples:

Example (1). (i) X Corporation has taxable income (computed without any net operating loss deduction) of $36,500 for its calendar year 1955. During 1955, X Corporation acquires the assets of M, N, and Z Corporations in statutory mergers to each of which section 361 applies, the dates of transfer being January 1, January 31, and December 1, respectively. The net operating loss carryovers of each transferor corporation and the income for each partial postacquisition year are:

Corporation		Carryovers		Income for Partial Years		Reduction
M	. . . .	$4,000	$3,000	($36,500 × 30/365)		
N	. . . .	6,000	30,400	($36,500 × 304/365)		$23,400
Z	. . . .	50,000	3,000	($36,500 × 30/365)		0
		$60,000	$36,400			$23,400

(ii) Since the carryovers of $4,000 acquired on the first date of transfer exceed the income for the first partial year ($3,000), the limitation provided by section 381(c)(1)(B) is the amount of the postacquisition income ($36,400) reduced by the excess of the income for the first and second partial years ($33,400) over the carryovers acquired on the first and second dates of transfer ($10,000). Therefore, the limitation is $13,000 ($36,400 less $23,400).

Corporation		Carryovers		Income for Partial Years		Reduction
M	. . . .	$1,000	$3,000	($36,500 × 30/365)		$2,000
N	. . . .	6,000	30,400	($36,500 × 304/365)		$24,400
Z	. . . .	50,000	3,000	($36,500 × 30/365)		0
		$57,000	$36,400			$26,400

(ii) Since the income for the first partial year ($3,000) exceeds the $1,000 of carryovers acquired on the first date by $2,000, the limitation provided by section 381(c)(1)(B) is the postacquisition income of $36,400 reduced by such excess and also reduced by the excess of the income for the second partial year ($30,400) over the carryovers

Corporation		Carryovers		Income for Partial Years		Reduction
M	. . . .	$1,000	$3,000	($36,500 × 30/365)		$2,000
N	. . . .	75,000	30,400	($36,500 × 304/365)		0
Z	. . . .	50,000	3,000	($36,500 × 30/365)		0
		$126,000	$36,400			$2,000

(ii) Since the income for the first partial year ($3,000) exceeds the $1,000 of carryovers acquired on the first date by $2,000, the limitation provided by section 381(c)(1)(B) is the postacquisition income of $36,400 reduced by $2,000, or $34,400. No further reduction is made since the income for the second partial year ($30,400) does not exceed the carryovers of $75,000 acquired on the second date of transfer.

(5) *Four or more dates of distribution or transfer.*—If the acquiring corporation succeeds to the net operating loss carryovers of four or more distributor or transferor corporations on four or more dates of distribution or transfer during the same taxable year of the acquiring corporation, the limitation provided by section 381(c)(1)(B) shall be

Corporation		Carryovers		Income for Partial Years		Reduction
M	. . . .	$1,000	$3,000	($36,500 × 30/365)		$2,000
N	. . . .	4,000	3,100	($36,500 × 31/365)	}	
O	. . . .	1,000	3,000	($36,500 × 30/365)	}	1,100
Y	. . . .	10,000	24,300	($36,500 × 243/365)		14,300
Z	. . . .	20,000	3,000	($36,500 × 30/365)		0
		$36,000	$36,400			$17,400

(ii) The limitation provided by section 381(c)(1)(B) equals the postacquisition income of $36,400 reduced by the sum of the (a) $2,000 excess of the income for the first partial year ($3,000) over the carryovers acquired from M Corporation ($1,000), (b) the $1,100 excess of the income for the second and third partial years ($6,100) over the carryovers acquired from N and O Corporations ($5,000), and (c) the $14,300 excess of the income for the fourth partial year ($24,300) over the carryovers acquired from Y Corporation ($10,000). Accordingly, the limitation is $19,000 ($36,400 minus $17,400). Therefore, although X's Corporation acquired carryovers aggregating $36,000 during 1955, it can utilize only $19,000 of such carryovers in computing its net operating loss deduction for 1955.

(c) *Determination of taxable income of acquiring corporation under section 381(c)(1)(C).*—(1) *In general.*—If the acquiring corporation succeeds to the net operating loss carryovers of two or more distributor or transferor corporations on two or more dates of distribution or transfer within one taxable year of the acquiring corporation, then pursuant to section 381(c)(1)(C) the taxable income of the acquiring corporation for its taxable year which is a prior taxable year for purposes of section 172(b)(2) and paragraph (e) of § 1.381(c)(1)-1 shall be determined as provided in this paragraph.

(2) *Division of taxable income.*—The taxable income of the acquiring corporation (computed with the modifications specified in section 172(b)(2)(A) but without any net operating loss deduction) shall be allocated proportionally on a daily basis among a preacquisition part year (determined under paragraph (f)(3) of § 1.381(c)(1)-1 by treating the first date of distribution or transfer as though it were the only date of distribution or transfer during the taxable year of the acquiring corporation) and two or more partial postacquisition years (determined as provided in paragraph (b)(2) of this section). The preacquisition part year and each partial postacquisition year shall be

Example (2). (i) Assume the same facts as in example (1) except that the amount of the net operating loss carryovers acquired from M Corporation is $1,000. The net operating loss carryovers of each transferor corporation and the income for each partial postacquisition year are:

acquired on the second date of transfer ($6,000). Therefore, the limitation is $10,000 ($36,400 less the sum of $2,000 and $24,400).

Example (3). (i) Assume the same facts as in example (2) except that the carryovers acquired from N Corporation are $75,000. The net operating loss carryovers of each transferor corporation and the income for each partial postacquisition year are:

determined consistently with the methods prescribed in subparagraphs (3) and (4) of this paragraph. The application of this subparagraph may be illustrated by the following example:

Example. (i) X Corporation has taxable income (computed without any net operating loss deduction) of $36,500 for its calendar year 1955. During 1955, X Corporation acquired the assets of M, N, O, Y, and Z Corporations in statutory mergers to each of which section 361 applied, the dates of transfer being, respectively, January 1, January 31, March 3, April 2, and December 1. The net operating loss carryovers of each transferor corporation and the income for each partial postacquisition year are:

considered a separate taxable year, but only for the limited purpose of applying sections 172(b)(2) and 381(c)(1)(C).

(3) *Net operating loss deduction.*—The net operating loss deduction of the preacquisition part year and the partial postacquisition years shall be determined consistently with the manner described in paragraph (f)(6) of § 1.381(c)(1)-1 but by taking into account, in the case of any partial postacquisition year, only the net operating loss carryovers and carrybacks of the acquiring corporation and those net operating loss carryovers from a distributor or transferor corporation which become available to the acquiring corporation as of the close of those dates of distribution or transfer which occur before the beginning of that specific partial postacquisition year. The sequence in which the net operating losses of the distributor or transferor and acquiring corporations shall be applied for this purpose shall be determined in the manner described in paragraph (e) of § 1.381(c)(1)-1. Subject to the preceding sentence, the net operating loss carryovers to any specific partial postacquisition year, whether from a distributor, transferor, or acquiring corporation, shall be taken into account in the order of the taxable years in which the net operating losses arose, beginning with the loss for the earliest taxable year.

(4) *Illustration.*—The application of this paragraph may be illustrated by the following example:

Example—(i) *Facts.* X Corporation, which was organized on January 1, 1957, sustained a net operating loss of $20,000 for its calendar year 1957 and had taxable income (computed without any net operating loss deduction) of $36,500 for its calendar year 1958. During 1958, X Corporation acquired the assets of Y and Z Corporations in statutory mergers to each of which section 361 applied, the dates of transfer being June 30 and September 30, respectively. None of the modifications specified in section 172(b)(2)(A) apply to any of the corporations for any taxable year. The taxable income (computed without any net operating loss deduction) and net operating losses of Y and Z Corporations (which were organized on January 1, 1957, and January 1, 1954, respectively) are set forth below:

Taxable Year	Acquiring Corporation X	Transferor Corporation Y	Transferor Corporation Z
1954	xxx	xxx	($30,000)
1955	xxx	xxx	1,000
1956	xxx	xxx	1,000
1957	($20,000)	($25,000)	1,000
Ending 6-30-58	xxx	1,000	xxx
Ending 9-30-58	xxx	xxx	1,000
1958	36,500	xxx	xxx

The sequence in which the losses of the acquiring corporation and the transferor corporations are applied and the computation of the carryovers to X Corporation's calendar year 1959 are illustrated in the following subdivisions of this example.

Year	
Preacquisition part year	
Partial No. 1	
Partial No. 2	

(iii) *Z Corporation's 1954 loss.* The carryover to 1959 is $0, computed as follows:

Net operating loss		$30,000
Less:		
Z's 1955, 1956, 1957, and 9/30/58-year income		4,000
Net operating loss carryover to Partial No. 2 year		26,000
Less:		
Partial No. 2 year taxable income		9,200
		16,800

The balance of $16,800 is not carried over to 1959 since X Corporation's taxable year 1958 is the last of the five years to which Z's 1954 loss may be carried under section 172(b)(1).

(ii) *Computation of taxable income.* X Corporation's taxable income, determined in the manner described in subparagraph (2) of this paragraph, for the preacquisition part year and for the partial postacquisition years is as follows:

Taxable Income	Computation
$18,100	$36,500 × 181/365
9,200	$36,500 × 92/365
9,200	$36,500 × 92/365

(iv) *Y Corporation's 1957 loss.* The carryover to 1959 is $14,800, computed as follows:

Net operating loss		$25,000
Less:		
Y's 6/30/58-year income		1,000
Net operating loss carryover to Partial No. 1 year		24,000
Less:		
Partial No. 1 year taxable income		9,200
Carryover to Partial No. 2 year		14,800
Less:		
X's Partial No. 2 year taxable income	$9,200	
Minus X's net operating loss deduction for Partial No. 2 year (i.e., Z's 1954 carryover of $26,000 to such partial year)	26,000	$0
Carryover to 1959		14,800

(v) *X Corporation's 1957 loss.* The carryover to 1959 is $1,900, computed as follows:

Net operating loss		$20,000
Less:		
X's preacquisition part year taxable income		18,100
Carryover to Partial No. 1 year		1,900
Less:		
Partial No. 1 year taxable income	$9,200	
Minus X's net operating loss deduction for Partial No. 1 year (i.e., Y's 1957 carryover of $24,000 to such partial year)	24,000	0
Carryover to Partial No. 2 year		$1,900
Less:		
Partial No. 2 year taxable income	$9,200	
Minus X's net operating loss deduction for Partial No. 2 year (i.e., Z's 1954 carryover of $26,000, and Y's 1957 carryover of $14,800, to such partial year)	40,800	$0
Carryover to 1959		1,900

(vi) *Summary of carryovers to 1959.* The aggregate of the net operating loss carryovers to 1959 is $16,700, computed as follows:

Z's 1954 loss	xxx
Y's 1957 loss	$14,800
X's 1957 loss	1,900
Total	16,700

[Reg. § 1.381(c)(1)-2.]

☐ [*T.D.* 6480, 7-12-60. *Amended by T.D.* 7564, 9-11-78.]

[Reg. § 1.381(c)(2)-1]

§1.381(c)(2)-1. Earnings and profits.—(a) *In general.*.—(1) Section 381(c)(2) requires the acquiring corporation in a transaction to which section 381(a) applies to succeed to, and take into account, the earnings and profits, or deficit in earnings and profits, of the distributor or transferor corporation as of the close of the date of distribution or transfer. In determining the amount of such earnings and profits, or deficit, to be carried over, and the manner in which they are to be used by the acquiring corporation after such date, the provisions of section 381(c)(2) and this section shall apply. For purposes of section 381(c)(2) and this section, if the distributor or transferor corporation accumulates earnings and profits, or incurs a deficit in earnings and

profits, after the date of distribution or transfer and before the completion of the reorganization or liquidation, such earnings and profits, or deficit, shall be deemed to have been accumulated or incurred as of the close of the date of distribution or transfer.

(2) If the distributor or transferor corporation has accumulated earnings and profits as of the close of the date of distribution or transfer, such earnings and profits shall (except as hereinafter provided in this section) be deemed to be received by, and to become a part of the accumulated earnings and profits of, the acquiring corporation as of such time. Similarly, if the distributor or transferor corporation has a deficit in accumulated earnings and profits as of the close of the date of distribution or transfer, such deficit shall (except as hereinafter provided in this section) be deemed to be incurred by the acquiring corporation as of such time. In no event, however, shall the accumulated earnings and profits, or deficit, of the

distributor or transferor corporation be taken into account in determining earnings and profits of the acquiring corporation for the taxable year during which occurs the date of distribution or transfer.

(3) Any part of the accumulated earnings and profits, or deficit in accumulated earnings and profits, of the distributor or transferor corporation which consists of earnings and profits, or deficits, accumulated before March 1, 1913, shall be deemed to become earnings and profits, or deficits, of the acquiring corporation accumulated before March 1, 1913, and any part of the accumulated earnings and profits of the distributor or transferor corporation which consists of increase in value of property accrued before March 1, 1913, shall be deemed to become earnings and profits of the acquiring corporation consisting of increase in value of property accrued before March 1, 1913.

(4) If the acquiring corporation and each distributor or transferor corporation has accumulated earnings and profits as of the close of the date of distribution or transfer, or if each of such corporations has a deficit in accumulated earnings and profits as of such time, then the accumulated earnings and profits (or deficit) of each such corporation shall be consolidated as of the close of the date of distribution or transfer in the accumulated earnings and profits account of the acquiring corporation. See subparagraph (6) of this paragraph for determination of the accumulated earnings and profits (or deficit) of the acquiring corporation as of the close of the date of distribution or transfer.

(5) If (i) one or more corporations a party to a distribution or transfer has accumulated earnings and profits as of the close of the date of distribution or transfer, and (ii) one or more of such corporations has a deficit in accumulated earnings and profits as of such time, the total of any such deficits shall be used only to offset earnings and profits accumulated, or deemed to have been accumulated under subparagraph (6) of this paragraph, by the acquiring corporation after the date of distribution or transfer. In such instance, the acquiring corporation will be considered as maintaining two separate earnings and profits accounts after the date of distribution or transfer. The first such account shall contain the total of the accumulated earnings and profits as of the close of the date of distribution or transfer of each corporation which has accumulated earnings and profits as of such time, and the second such account shall contain the total of the deficits in accumulated earnings and profits of each corporation which has a deficit as of such time. The total deficit in the second account may not be used to reduce the accumulated earnings and profits in the first account (although such

earnings and profits may be offset by deficits incurred, or deemed to have been incurred, after the date of distribution or transfer) but shall be used only to offset earnings and profits accumulated, or deemed to have been accumulated under subparagraph (6) of this paragraph, by the acquiring corporation after the date of distribution or transfer.

(6) In any case in which it is necessary to compute the accumulated earnings and profits, or the deficit in accumulated earnings and profits, of the acquiring corporation as of the close of the date of distribution or transfer and such date is a day other than the last day of a taxable year of the acquiring corporation—

(i) If the acquiring corporation has earnings and profits for its taxable year during which occurs the date of distribution or transfer, such earnings and profits (a) shall be deemed to have accumulated as of the close of such date in an amount which bears the same ratio to the undistributed earnings and profits of such corporation for such year as the number of days in the taxable year preceding the date following the date of distribution or transfer bears to the total number of days in the taxable year, and (b) shall be deemed to have accumulated after the date of distribution or transfer in an amount which bears the same ratio to the undistributed earnings and profits of such corporation for such year as the number of days in the taxable year following such date bears to the total number of days in such taxable year. For purposes of the preceding sentence, the undistributed earnings and profits of the acquiring corporation for such taxable year shall be the earnings and profits for such taxable year reduced by any distributions made therefrom during such taxable year.

(ii) If the acquiring corporation has an operating deficit for its taxable year during which occurs the date of distribution or transfer, then, unless the actual accumulated earnings and profits, or deficit, as of such date can be shown, such operating deficit shall be deemed to have accumulated in a manner similar to that described in subdivision (i) of this subparagraph.

(7) This paragraph may be illustrated by the following examples, in which it is assumed that none of the accumulated earnings and profits, or deficits, consist of earnings and profits or deficits accumulated, or increase in value of property accrued, before March 1, 1913.

Example (1). (i) M and N Corporations make their returns on the basis of the calendar year. On June 30, 1959, M Corporation transfers all its assets to N Corporation in a statutory merger to which section 361 applies. The books of the two corporations reveal the following information:

Description	M Corporation (transferor)	N Corporation (acquirer)
Accumulated earnings and profits at close of calendar year 1958	$100,000	$150,000
Earnings and profits of taxable year ending June 30, 1959	$15,000	
Earnings and profits of calendar year 1959		$36,500
Distributions during calendar year 1959	0	0

(ii) As of the close of June 30, 1959, N acquires from M accumulated earnings and profits of $115,000. Since M and N each has accumulated earnings and profits as of the close of the date of transfer, M's accumulated earnings and profits are added to N's accumulated earnings and profits as of such time. However, no part of M's accumulated earnings and profits is taken into account in determining N's earnings and profits for the calendar year 1959.

Therefore, N's earnings and profits for the calendar year 1959 are $36,500.

Example (2). (i) X and Y Corporations make their returns on the basis of the calendar year. On June 30, 1959, X Corporation transfers all its assets to Y Corporation in a statutory merger to which section 361 applies. The books of the two corporations reveal the following information:

Description	X Corporation (transferor)	Y Corporation (acquirer)
Accumulated earnings and profits at close of calendar year 1958	$20,000	$100,000
Deficit in earnings and profits for taxable year ending June 30, 1959	(80,000)	
Earnings and profits of calendar year 1959		36,500
Distributions during calendar year 1959	0	0

(ii) As of the close of June 30, 1959, Y acquires from X a deficit in accumulated earnings and profits in the amount of $60,000. This deficit may be used only to reduce those earnings and profits of Y which are accumulated, or deemed to have accumulated, after June 30, 1959. Accordingly, as of December 31, 1959, the accumulated earnings and profits of Y amount to $118,100; at such time Y also has a separate deficit in accumulated earnings and profits in the amount of $41,600. These amounts are determined as follows:

Accumulated earnings and profits of Y as of the close of 1958	$100,000
Add:	
Portion of undistributed earnings and profits of Y for 1959 deemed to have accumulated as of close of June 30, 1959 ($36,500 × 181/365)	18,100
Accumulated earnings and profits of Y as of close of June 30, 1959, and also as of Dec. 31, 1959	$118,100
Portion of undistributed earnings and profits of Y for 1959 deemed to have accumulated after June 30, 1959 ($36,500 × 184/365)	$18,400
Less:	
Deficit in accumulated earnings and profits acquired by Y from X Corporation as of close of June 30, 1959	(60,000)
Separate deficit in accumulated earnings and profits of Y as of Dec. 31, 1959	($41,600)

Example (3). Assume the same facts as in example (2), except that on September 15, 1959, Y Corporation makes a cash distribution of $96,500. The entire distribution is a dividend: $36,500 from earnings and profits for the taxable year 1959 and $60,000 from earnings and profits accumulated as of December 31, 1958. Accordingly, as of December 31, 1959, Y has accumulated earnings and profits of $40,000, and also has a separate deficit in accumulated earnings and profits of $60,000. These amounts are determined as follows:

Earnings and profits of Y for calendar year 1959	$36,500
Accumulated earnings and profits of Y as of close of 1958	100,000
Total	136,500
Less:	
Distributions during 1959	96,500
Accumulated earnings and profits of Y as of Dec. 31, 1959	40,000
Deficit in accumulated earnings and profits acquired from X as of close of June 30, 1959	($60,000)
Less:	
Portion of Y's undistributed earnings and profits for 1959 deemed to have accumulated after June 30, 1959	0
Separate deficit in accumulated earnings and profits of Y as of Dec. 31, 1959	(60,000)

Example (4). (i) M and N Corporations make their returns on the basis of the calendar year. On June 30, 1959, M Corporation transfers all its assets to N Corporation in a statutory merger to which section 361 applies. The books of the two corporations reveal the following information:

Description	M Corporation (transferor)	N Corporation (acquirer)
Accumulated earnings and profits at close of calendar year 1958	$100,000	$50,000
Earnings and profits for taxable year ending June 30, 1959	10,000	. . .
Deficit in earnings and profits for calendar year 1959	. . .	(146,000)
Distributions during calendar year 1959	0	0

(ii) Assuming that N has not shown its actual accumulated earnings and profits, or deficit, as of the close of June 30, 1959, N has a deficit in accumulated earnings and profits at such time which amounts to $22,400, determined as follows:

Accumulated earnings and profits of N as of close of 1958	$50,000
Less:	
Portion of deficit in earnings and profits of N for 1959 deemed to have accumulated as of close of June 30, 1959 ($146,000 × 181/365)	(72,400)
Deficit in accumulated earnings and profits of N as of close of June 30, 1959, and also as of Dec. 31, 1959	(22,400)

As of the close of June 30, 1959, N acquires from M accumulated earnings and profits in the amount of $110,000, no part of which may be offset by N's own deficit of $22,400; however, such earnings and profits may be offset by deficits incurred, or deemed incurred, by N after June 30, 1959. Thus, as of December 31, 1959, N has the above-mentioned deficit of $22,400; at such time N also has accumulated earnings and profits in the amount of $36,400, determined as follows:

Accumulated earnings and profits acquired from M as of close of June 30, 1959	$110,000
Less:	
Portion of deficit in earnings and profits of N for 1959 deemed to have accumulated after June 30, 1959 ($146,000 × 184/365)	(73,600)
Accumulated earnings and profits of N as of Dec. 31, 1959	$36,400

Example (5). Assume the same facts as in example (4), except that on September 9, 1959, N Corporation makes a cash distribution of $100,000. The amount of $82,000 is a dividend from accumulated earnings and profits, computed as follows:

Accumulated earnings and profits acquired from M as of close of June 30, 1959	$110,000
Less:	
Deficit in earnings and profits of N for 1959 deemed to have accumulated from June 30 through Sept. 8, 1959 ($146,000 × 70/365) .	(28,000)
Accumulated earnings and profits as of close of Sept. 8, 1959	82,000

As of December 31, 1959, N Corporation has a deficit in accumulated earnings and profits of $68,000, computed as follows:

Deficit in accumulated earnings and profits of N as of close of June 30, 1959	($22,400)
Add:	
Portion of N's deficit in earnings and profits for 1959 deemed to have accumulated after Sept. 8, 1959 ($146,000 × 114/365)	(45,600)
Deficit in accumulated earnings and profits of N as of Dec. 31, 1959	(68,000)

Example (6). (i) X, Y, and Z Corporations make their returns on the basis of the calendar year. On June 30, 1959, X Corporation and Y Corporation transfer all their assets to Z Corporation in a statutory merger to which section 361 applies. The books of the three corporations reveal the following information:

Description	X Corporation (transferor)	Y Corporation (transferor)	Z Corporation (acquirer)
Accumulated earnings and profits (or deficit) at close of calendar year 1958	$35,000	($25,000)	($20,000)
Earnings and profits (or deficit) for taxable year ended June 30, 1959 . . .	5,000	(5,000)	. . .
Earnings and profits for calendar year 1959	. . .	. . .	36,500
Distributions during 1959	0	0	0

(ii) As of the close of June 30, 1959, Z acquires from Y a deficit in accumulated earnings and profits of $30,000. As of such time, Z's own deficit in accumulated earnings and profits amounts to $1,900, determined as follows:

Deficit in accumulated earnings and profits of Z as of close of 1958	($20,000)
Less:	
Portion of undistributed earnings of profits of Z for 1959 deemed to have accumulated as of close of June 30, 1959 ($36,500 × 181/365)	18,100
Deficit in accumulated earnings and profits of Z as of close of June 30, 1959	(1,900)

The total deficit of $31,900 may be used only to offset earnings and profits of Z accumulated, or deemed to have accumulated, after June 30, 1959; such deficit may not be used to reduce the accumulated earnings and profits of $40,000 acquired from X as of the close of June 30, 1959. Thus, as of December 31, 1959, the accumulated earnings and profits of Z amount to $40,000; at such time Z Corporation also has a separate deficit in accumulated earnings and profits in the amount of $13,500, determined as follows:

Deficit in accumulated earnings and profits as of close of June 30, 1959	($31,900)
Less:	
Portion of undistributed earnings and profits of Z for 1959 deemed to have accumulated after June 30, 1959 ($36,500 × 184/365) . . .	18,400
Separate deficit in accumulated earnings and profits as of Dec. 31, 1959	(13,500)

Example (7). X and Y Corporations make their returns on the basis of the calendar year. On December 31, 1954, X transfers all its assets to Y in a statutory merger to which section 361 applies. The books of the two corporations reveal the following information:

Description	X Corporation (transferor)	Y Corporation (acquirer)
Accumulated earnings and profits (or deficit) at close of calendar year 1954	($50,000)	$210,000
Earnings and profits (or deficit) for calendar years:		
1955		5,000
1956		(20,000)
1957		70,000
1958		60,000
1959		55,000
Cash distributions on		
September 1, 1957		80,000
September 1, 1958		40,000
September 1, 1959		30,000

The balances in the accumulated earnings and profits account and the separate deficit account of Y Corporation at the close of the taxable year involved are as follows:

Year	Deficit acquired from X Corporation	Accumulated earnings and profits of Y Corporation
1954	($50,000)	$210,000
1955	(45,000)	210,000
1956	(45,000)	190,000
1957	(45,000)	180,000
1958	(25,000)	180,000
1959	None	180,000

(b) *Successive acquisitions.*—(1) If, as of the date of distribution or transfer, either the acquiring corporation, or the distributor or transferor corporation, or both, is considered under paragraph (a) of this section to be maintaining separate earnings and profits accounts as the result of a prior transaction or transactions to which section 381(a) applied, the accumulated earnings and profits, or deficit in accumulated earnings and profits, of each such corporation shall be combined with the appropriate earnings and profits account of the other such corporation. For example, if, as of the date of transfer, the acquiring corporation and the transferor corporation are each maintaining separate accounts, one containing accumulated earnings and profits and the other containing a deficit in accumulated earnings and profits, the amounts in the two accumulated earnings and profits accounts shall be combined into one account, and the amounts in the two deficit accounts shall be combined into a second account, and the amount in one combined account may not be used to offset the amount in the other combined account.

(2) This paragraph may be illustrated by the following examples, in which it is assumed that none of the accumulated earnings and profits, or deficits, consist of earnings and profits or deficits accumulated, or increase in value of property accrued, before March 1, 1913.

Example (1). (i) X, Y, and Z Corporations make their returns on the basis of the calendar year. On June 30, 1958, X Corporation transfers all its assets to Z Corporation in a statutory merger to which section 361 applies, and on August 31, 1958, Y Corporation transfers all its assets to Z Corporation in another statutory merger to which section 361 applies. The books of the three corporations reveal the following information:

Description	X Corporation (transferor)	Y Corporation (transferor)	Z Corporation (acquirer)
Accumulated earnings and profits (deficit) at close of calendar year 1957	($40,000)	$10,000	$60,000
Deficit in earnings and profits for taxable year ending June 30, 1958	(5,000)		
Earnings and profits for taxable year ending Aug. 31, 1958		2,000	
Earnings and profits of calendar year 1958			36,500
Distributions during calendar year 1958	0	0	0

(ii) As of the close of June 30, 1958, Z acquires from X a deficit in accumulated earnings and profits in the amount of $45,000, which deficit may be used only to reduce those earnings and profits of Z which are accumulated, or deemed to have been accumulated, after June 30, 1958. As of the close of August 31, 1958, Z acquires from Y earnings and profits of $12,000, no portion of which may be reduced by the deficit acquired by Z from X. Accordingly, as of December 31, 1958, Z has accumulated earnings and profits of $90,100, and also has a separate deficit in accumulated earnings and profits of $26,600. These amounts are determined as follows:

Accumulated earnings and profits of Z as of Dec. 31, 1957	$60,000
Add:	
Portion of undistributed earnings and profits of Z for 1958 deemed to have accumulated as of close of June 30, 1958 ($36,500 × 181/365)	18,100
Accumulated earnings and profits of Z as of June 30, 1958	78,100
Add:	
Accumulated earnings and profits acquired by Z from Y as of close of Aug. 31, 1958	12,000
Accumulated earnings and profits of Z as of close of Aug. 31, 1958, and also as of Dec. 31, 1958	90,100
Deficit in accumulated earnings and profits acquired by Z from X as of close of June 30, 1958	(45,000)
Less:	
Portion of undistributed earnings and profits of Z for 1958 deemed to have accumulated from June 30 through Aug. 31, 1958 ($36,500 × 62/365)	6,200
Separate deficit in accumulated earnings and profits of Z as of Aug. 31, 1958	(38,800)
Less:	
Portion of undistributed earnings and profits of Z for 1958 deemed to have accumulated after Aug. 31, 1958 ($36,500 × 122/365)	12,200
Separate deficit in accumulated earnings and profits of Z as of Dec. 31, 1958	(26,600)

Example (2). (i) Assume the same facts as in example (1), plus the additional fact that on June 30, 1959, Z Corporation transfers all its assets to M Corporation (which makes its return on the basis of the calendar year) in a statutory merger to which section 361 applies, and that as of such time M Corporation is considered to be maintaining separate earnings and profits accounts as the result of a previous transaction to which section 381(a) applied. The books of the two corporations reveal the following information:

Description	Z Corporation (transferor)	M Corporation (acquirer)
Accumulated earnings and profits as of Dec. 31, 1958	$90,100	$50,000
Separate deficit in accumulated earnings and profits as of Dec. 31, 1958	(26,600)	(30,000)
Earnings and profits for taxable year ending June 30, 1959	5,000	
Earnings and profits of calendar year 1959		36,500
Distributions during 1959	0	0

Reg. §1.381(c)(2)-1(b)(2)

(ii) As of June 30, 1959, M acquires from Z accumulated earnings and profits of $90,100, which amount is combined with M's own accumulated earnings and profits of $50,000; M also acquires from Z a deficit in accumulated earnings and profits of $21,600 ($26,600 minus $5,000), which amount is combined with M's own deficit of $11,900. The total deficit of $33,500 may be used only to reduce

earnings and profits of M which are accumulated, or deemed to have accumulated, after June 30, 1959. Accordingly, as of December 31, 1959, M has accumulated earnings and profits of $140,100, and also has a separate deficit in accumulated earnings and profits in the amount of $15,100. These amounts are determined as follows:

Deficit of M as of Dec. 31, 1958	($30,000)
Less:	
Portion of M's undistributed earnings and profits for 1959 deemed to have accumulated as of close of June 30, 1959 ($36,500 × 181/365)	18,100
Deficit of M as of June 30, 1959	(11,900)
Plus:	
Deficit of Z as of June 30, 1959	(21,600)
Combined deficit of M as of close of June 30, 1959	(33,500)
Less:	
Portion of M's undistributed earnings and profits for 1959 deemed to have accumulated after June 30, 1959 ($36,500 × 184/365)	18,400
Separate deficit of M as of Dec. 31, 1959	(15,100)
Accumulated earnings and profits of M as of Dec. 31, 1958, and also as of June 30, 1959	$50,000
Accumulated earnings and profits of Z as of Dec. 31, 1958, and also as of June 30, 1959	90,100
Combined accumulated earnings and profits of M as of close of June 30, 1959, and also as of Dec. 31, 1959	140,100

(c) *Distribution of earnings and profits pursuant to reorganization or liquidation.*—(1) If, in a reorganization to which section 381(a)(2) applies, the transferor corporation pursuant to the plan of reorganization distributes to its stockholders property consisting not only of property permitted by section 354 to be received without recognition of gain, but also of other property or money, then the accumulated earnings and profits of the transferor corporation as of the close of the date of transfer shall be computed by taking into account the amount of earnings and profits properly applicable to the distribution, regardless of whether such distribution occurs before or after the close of the date of transfer.

(2) If, in a distribution to which section 381(a)(1) (relating to certain liquidations of subsidiaries) applies, the acquiring corporation receives less than 100 percent of the assets distributed by the distributor corporation, then the accumulated earnings and profits of the distributor corporation as of the close of the date of distribution shall be computed by taking into account the amount of earnings and profits properly applicable to the distributions to minority stockholders, regardless of whether such distributions occur before or after the close of the date of distribution. [Reg. §1.381(c)(2)-1.]

☐ [*T.D.* 6586, 12-27-61. *Amended by T.D.* 6692, 12-2-63 *and T.D.* 9700 11-7-2014.]

[Reg. §1.381(c)(3)-1]

§1.381(c)(3)-1. Capital loss carryovers.—(a) *Carryover requirement.*—(1) Section 381(c)(3) requires the acquiring corporation in a transaction to which section 381(a) applies to succeed to, and take into account, the capital loss carryovers of the distributor or transferor corporation. To determine the amount of these carryovers as of the close of the date of distribution or transfer, and to integrate them with the capital loss carryovers of the acquiring corporation for purposes of determining the taxable income of the acquiring corporation for taxable years ending after the date of distribution or transfer, it is necessary to apply the provisions of section 1212 in accordance with the conditions and limitations of section 381(c)(3) and this section.

(2) The capital loss carryovers of the acquiring corporation as of the close of the date of distribution or transfer shall be determined without reference to any capital gains or capital losses of the distributor or transferor corporation. The capital loss carryovers of a distributor or transferor corporation as of the close of the date of distribution or transfer shall be determined without reference to any capital gains or capital losses of the acquiring corporation.

(3) This section contains rules applicable to capital loss carryovers determined without reference to the amendment of section 1212(a) made by section 7 of the Act of September 2, 1964 (Public Law 88-571, 78 Stat. 860) in respect of foreign expropriation capital losses. If the distributor, transferor, or acquiring corporation sustains a net capital loss in a taxable year ending after December 31, 1958, any portion of which is attributable to a foreign expropriation capital loss, such portion shall be carried over to each of the ten succeeding taxable years consistently with the rules prescribed in this section and paragraph (a)(2) of §1.1212-1.

(b) *First taxable year to which carryovers apply.*—(1) The capital loss carryovers available to the distributor or transferor corporation as of the close of the date of distribution or transfer shall first be carried to the first taxable year of the acquiring corporation ending after that

date. This rule applies irrespective of whether the date of distribution or transfer is on the last day, or any other day, of the acquiring corporation's taxable year.

(2) The capital loss carryovers available to the distributor or transferor corporation as of the close of the date of distribution or transfer shall be carried to the acquiring corporation without diminution by reason of the fact that the acquiring corporation does not acquire 100 percent of the assets of the distributor or transferor corporation.

(c) *Limitation on capital loss carryovers for first taxable year ending after date of distribution or transfer.*—(1) Any capital loss carryover of a distributor or transferor corporation which is available to the acquiring corporation as of the close of the date of distribution or transfer shall be a short-term capital loss of the acquiring corporation in each of the taxable years to which the net capital loss giving rise to such carryover may be carried to the extent provided in section 1212 and this section. However, in the first taxable year of the acquiring corporation ending after the date of distribution or transfer, the total capital loss carryovers of the distributor or transferor corporation which may be treated in that year as short-term capital losses of the acquiring corporation is limited by section 381(c)(3)(B) to an amount which bears the same ratio to the acquiring corporation's capital gain net income (net capital gain for taxable years beginning before January 1, 1977) for such first taxable year (determined without regard to any capital loss carryovers) as the number of days in such first taxable year which follow the date of distribution or transfer bears to the total number of days in such taxable year. Thus, if the date of distribution or transfer is the last day of the acquiring corporation's taxable year, there is no limitation under section 381(c)(3)(B) on the amount of such carryovers which may be treated as short-term capital losses of the acquiring corporation for its first taxable year ending after that date.

(2) The limitation provided by section 381(c)(3)(B) shall be applied to the aggregate of the capital loss carryovers of the distributor or transferor corporation without reference to the taxable years in which the net capital losses giving rise to the carryovers were sustained. If the acquiring corporation has acquired the assets of two or more distributor or transferor corporations on the same date of distribution or transfer, then the limitation provided by section 381(c)(3)(B) shall be applied to the aggregate of the capital loss carryovers from all of such distributor or transferor corporations.

(3) If the acquiring corporation succeeds to the capital loss carryovers of two or more distributor or transferor corporations on two or more dates of distribution or transfer during the same taxable year of the acquiring corporation, the limitation to be applied under section 381(c)(3)(B) to the aggregate of such carryovers shall be determined consistently with the rules prescribed in paragraph (b) of §1.381(c)(1)-2.

(4) The application of this paragraph may be illustrated by the following example:

Example. (i) X and Y Corporations are organized on January 1, 1954, and make their returns on the basis of the calendar year. On July 4, 1957, X Corporation transfers all its assets to Y Corporation in a statutory merger to which section 361 applies. The net capital losses and the net capital gains (capital gain net income for taxable years beginning after December 31, 1976) (computed without regard to any capital loss carryovers) of the two corporations are as follows:

Taxable year:	X Corporation (transferor)	Y Corporation (acquirer)
1954	($5,000)	0
1955	(10,000)	$5,000
1956	(25,000)	(7,000)
Ending 7-4-57	(8,000)	. . . .
1957		36,500

(ii) The capital loss carryovers of X Corporation which are available to Y Corporation as of the close of July 4, 1957, amount to $48,000 in the aggregate; but only $18,000 ($36,500 × 180/365) of such amount may be treated as short-term capital losses of Y Corporation for 1957.

(d) *Computation of carryovers; general rule.*—(1) *Sequence for applying losses and determination of capital gain net income.*—Section 1212 provides that a net capital loss sustained in any taxable year (hereinafter referred to as the "loss year") shall be carried over to each of the five succeeding taxable years and treated in each of such succeeding years as a short-term capital loss to the extent not allowed as a deduction against any capital gain net income (net capital gain for taxable years beginning before January 1, 1977) of any taxable years intervening between the loss year and the taxable year to which such loss is carried. For this purpose, the capital gain net income (net capital gain for taxable years beginning before January 1, 1977) of any intervening taxable year is determined without regard to the net capital loss for the loss year or for any taxable year thereafter, and the various capital loss carryovers from taxable years preceding the loss year to any such intervening taxable year are considered to be applied in reduction of the capital gain net income (net capital gain for taxable years beginning before January 1, 1977) for such year in the order of the taxable years in which the losses were sustained, beginning with the loss for the earliest preceding taxable year. The application of these rules to the capital gain net income (net capital gain for taxable years beginning before January 1, 1977) of the acquiring corporation for any taxable year ending after the date of distribution or transfer involves the use of carryovers of the distributor or transferor corporation and of the acquiring corporation. In determining the order in which the capital loss carryovers of the distributor or transferor and acquiring corporations from taxable years ending on or before the date of distribution or transfer are considered to be applied in reduction of the capital gain net income (net capital gain for taxable years beginning before January 1, 1977) of the acquiring corporation for any intervening taxable year ending after such date, the following rules shall apply:

(i) Each taxable year of the distributor or transferor and acquiring corporations which, with respect to the first taxable year of the acquiring corporation ending after the date of distribution or transfer, constitutes a first preceding taxable year, shall be treated as if each such year ended on the same day, whether or not such taxable years actually end on the same day. In like manner, each taxable year of the distributor or transferor and acquiring corporations which, with respect to such first taxable year of the acquiring corporation ending after the date of distribution or transfer, constitutes a second preceding taxable year, shall be treated as if each such year ended on the same day (whether or not such taxable years actually end on the same day), and a similar rule shall be applied with respect to those

taxable years of the distributor or transferor and acquiring corporations which constitute third, fourth, and fifth preceding taxable years;

(ii) If in the same preceding taxable year both the distributor or transferor and acquiring corporations incurred a net capital loss which is a carryover to an intervening taxable year of the acquiring corporation ending after the date of distribution or transfer, then in applying such losses in reduction of the capital gain net income (net capital gain for taxable years beginning before January 1, 1977) for such an intervening year, either such loss may be taken into account before the other; and

(iii) The rules of subdivisions (i) and (ii) of this subparagraph shall apply regardless of the number of distributor or transferor corporations the assets of which are acquired by the acquiring corporation on the same date of distribution or transfer.

(2) *Cross reference.*—If the date of distribution or transfer is a day other than the last day of a taxable year of the acquiring corporation, then in determining the capital gain net income (net capital gain for taxable years beginning before January 1, 1977) of the acquiring corporation for its first taxable year ending after the date of distribution or transfer, section 1212 and this paragraph shall be applied in the special manner set forth in paragraph (e) of this section.

(3) *Years to which losses may be carried.*—The taxable years to which a net capital loss shall be carried are prescribed by section 1212. Since the taxable year of a distributor or transferor corporation ends with the close of the date of distribution or transfer, such taxable year and the first taxable year of the acquiring corporation which ends after that date are considered two separate taxable years to which a net capital loss of the distributor or transferor corporation for any taxable year ending before that date shall be carried. This rule applies even though the taxable year of the distributor or transferor corporation which ends on the date of distribution or transfer is a period of less than twelve months. However, the distribution or transfer has no effect in determining under section 1212 the taxable years to which a net capital loss of the acquiring corporation is carried. For this purpose, the first taxable year of the acquiring corporation which ends after the date of distribution or transfer constitutes only one taxable year even though such taxable year is considered under paragraph (e) of this section as two taxable years for certain purposes. The application of this subparagraph may be illustrated by the following example:

Example. R and S Corporations are organized on January 1, 1954, and both corporations make their returns on the basis of the calendar year. R Corporation has net capital losses for its years 1954, 1955, and 1957, and S Corporation has net capital losses for its years 1954 and 1956. On June 30, 1958, R Corporation transfers all its assets to S Corporation in a statutory merger to which section 361 applies. The taxable years to which these losses of R and S Corporations may be carried are as follows:

Loss year	Carried to
R 1954	R 1955, R 1956, R 1957, R 6/30/58, S 1958.
S 1954	S 1955, S 1956, S 1957, S 1958, S 1959.
R 1955	R 1956, R 1957, R 6/30/58, S 1958, S 1959.
S 1956	S 1957, S 1958, S 1959, S 1960, S 1961.
R 1957	R 6/30/58, S 1958, S 1959, S 1960, S 1961.

(4) *Computation of carryovers in case where date of distribution or transfer occurs on last day of acquiring corporation's taxable year.*—The computation of the capital loss carryovers from the distributor or transferor corporation and from the acquiring corporation in a case where the date of distribution or transfer occurs on the last day of a taxable year of the acquiring corporation may be illustrated by the following example:

Example. X and Y Corporations are organized on January 1, 1955, and make their returns on the basis of the calendar year. On December 31, 1956, X Corporation transfers all its assets to Y Corporation in a statutory merger to which section 361 applies. The net capital losses and the net capital gains (capital gain net income for taxable years beginning after December 31, 1976) (computed without regard to any capital loss carryovers) of the two corporations are as follows:

Taxable year:	X Corporation (transferor)	Y Corporation (acquirer)
1955	($20,000)	($2,000)
1956	(10,000)	(8,000)
1957		25,000
1958		10,000

The sequence in which the net capital losses of X and Y Corporations are applied, and the computation of the capital loss carryovers to Y Corporation's taxable year 1959, may be illustrated as follows. (For purposes of this example, the carryover from a preceding taxable year of the transferor corporation will be applied before the carry-

over from the same preceding taxable year of the acquiring corporation):

(i) *X Corporation's 1955 loss.* The carryover to 1959 is $0, computed as follows:

Net capital loss		$20,000
Less:		
Y's 1957 net capital gain (capital gain net income for taxable years beginning after December 31, 1976) (computed without regard to any capital loss carryovers)		25,000
Carryover to Y 1958 and Y 1959		$0

(ii) *Y Corporation's 1955 loss.* The carryover to 1959 is $0, computed as follows:

Net capital loss		$2,000
Less:		
Y's 1957 net capital gain (capital gain net income for taxable years beginning after December 31, 1976) (computed without regard to any capital loss carryovers)	$25,000	
Minus capital loss carryovers to Y 1957 (i.e., carryover of $20,000 from X 1955)	20,000	5,000
Carryover to Y 1958 and Y 1959		$0

(iii) *X Corporation's 1956 loss.* The carryover to 1959 is $0, computed as follows:

Net capital loss		$10,000
Less:		
Y's 1957 net capital gain (capital gain net income for taxable years beginning after December 31, 1976) (computed without regard to any capital loss carryovers)	$25,000	
Minus capital loss carryovers to Y 1957 (i.e., carryovers of $20,000 from X 1955 and $2,000 from Y 1955)		
. . . .	22,000	3,000
Carryover to Y 1958		$7,000
Less:		
Y's 1958 net capital gain (capital gain net income for taxable years beginning after December 31, 1976) (computed without regard to any capital loss carryovers)	$10,000	
Minus capital loss carryovers to Y 1958	0	10,000
Carryover to Y 1959		$0

(iv) *Y Corporation's 1956 loss.* The carryover to 1959 is $5,000, computed as follows:

Net capital loss		$8,000
Less:		
Y's 1957 net capital gain (capital gain net income for taxable years beginning after December 31, 1976) (computed without regard to any capital loss carryovers)	$25,000	
Minus capital loss carryovers to Y 1957 (i.e., carryovers of $20,000 from X 1955, $2,000 from Y 1955, and $10,000 from X 1956)	32,000	0
Carryover to Y 1958		$8,000
Less:		
Y's 1958 net capital gain (capital gain net income for taxable years beginning after December 31, 1976) (computed without regard to any capital loss carryovers)	$10,000	
Minus capital loss carryovers to Y 1958 (i.e., carryover of $7,000 from X 1956)	7,000	$3,000
Carryover to Y 1959		$5,000

(e) *Computation of carryovers when date of distribution or transfer is not on last day of acquiring corporation's taxable year.*—(1) *General rule.*—If, in determining under paragraph (d) of this section the portion of a net capital loss for any taxable year which is carried over to a succeeding taxable year, an intervening taxable year is a taxable year of the acquiring corporation which includes, but does not end on, the date of distribution or transfer, the capital gain net income (net capital gain for taxable years beginning before January 1, 1977) of such intervening year shall be determined by applying section 1212 in the special manner provided by this paragraph.

(2) *Taxable year considered as two taxable years.*—Such intervening taxable year of the acquiring corporation shall be considered as though it were two taxable years, but only for the limited purpose of computing capital loss carryovers to subsequent taxable years. The first of such two taxable years shall be referred to in this paragraph as the preacquisition part year; the second, as the postacquisition part year. Though considered as two separate taxable years for purposes of this paragraph, the preacquisition part year and the postacquisition part year are treated as one taxable year in determining the years to which a net capital loss is carried under section 1212. See paragraph (d)(3) of this section.

(3) *Preacquisition part year.*—The preacquisition part year shall begin with the beginning of such taxable year of the acquiring corporation and shall end with the close of the date of distribution or transfer.

(4) *Postacquisition part year.*—The postacquisition part year shall begin with the day following the date of distribution or transfer and shall end with the close of such taxable year of the acquiring corporation.

(5) *Division of capital gain net income.*—The capital gain net income (net capital gain for taxable years beginning before January 1, 1977) for such intervening taxable year (computed without regard to any capital loss carryovers) of the acquiring corporation shall be divided between the preacquisition part year and the postacquisition

part year in proportion to the number of days in each. Thus, if in a statutory merger to which section 361 applies Y Corporation acquires the assets of X Corporation on June 30, 1956, and Y Corporation has capital gain net income (net capital gain for taxable years beginning before January 1, 1977, computed in the manner so prescribed) of $36,600 for its calendar year 1956, then the preacquisition part year capital gain net income (net capital gain for taxable years beginning before January 1, 1977) would be $18,200 ($36,600 × 182/366) and the postacquisition part year capital gain net income (net capital gain for taxable years beginning before January 1, 1977) would be $18,400 ($36,600 × 184/366).

(6) *Application of capital loss carryovers.*—After obtaining the capital gain net income (net capital gain for taxable years beginning before January 1, 1977) of the preacquisition part year and postacquisition part year in the manner described in subparagraph (5) of this paragraph, it is necessary to determine the capital loss carryovers which are taken into account with respect to each such part year. The carryovers to be taken into account and the sequence in which such carryovers are applied, shall be determined in accordance with paragraph (d)(1) of this section but subject to the provisions of this subparagraph. With respect to the preacquisition part year, no capital loss carryovers of the distributor or transferor corporation shall be taken into account; that is, only capital loss carryovers of the acquiring corporation shall be taken into account. With respect to the postacquisition part year, capital loss carryovers of both the distributor or transferor corporation and the acquiring corporation shall be taken into account.

(7) *Cross reference.*—If any intervening taxable year is a taxable year of the acquiring corporation during which the acquiring corporation succeeds to the capital loss carryovers of two or more distributor or transferor corporations on two or more dates of distribution or transfer, the capital gain net income (net capital gain for taxable years beginning before January 1, 1977) of the acquiring corporation for such intervening taxable year shall be determined consistently with the rules prescribed in paragraph (c) of §1.381(c)(1)-2 except that the sequence in which the capital loss carryovers of the distributor or

transferor and acquiring corporations shall be applied shall be determined under paragraph (d)(1) of this section.

(8) *Illustration.*—The application of this paragraph may be illustrated as follows:

Example. X Corporation is organized on April 1, 1959, and makes its return on the basis of the fiscal year ending March 31. Y Corporation is organized on January 1, 1959, and makes its return on the basis of the calendar year. On June 30, 1961, X Corporation transfers all its assets to Y Corporation in a statutory merger to which section 361 applies. The net capital losses and the net capital gains (capital gain net income for taxable years beginning after December 31, 1976) (computed without regard to any capital loss carryovers) of the two corporations are as follows:

Taxable year	X Corporation (transferor)	Y Corporation (acquirer)
1959		($24,000)
Ending 3-31-60	($19,000)	
1960		(6,000)
Ending 3-31-61	(5,000)	
Ending 6-30-61	0	
1961		36,500
1962		12,000

The following table shows those taxable years of the transferor and acquiring corporations which, with respect to Y Corporation's calendar year 1961, are first, second, and third preceding taxable years:

	X Corporation	Y Corporation
First preceding year	Ending 6-30-61	1960
Second preceding year	Ending 3-31-61	1959
Third preceding year	Ending 3-31-60	.....

The sequence in which the net capital losses of X and Y Corporation are applied, and the computation of the capital loss carryovers to Y Corporation's calendar year 1963, may be illustrated as follows. (For purposes of this example, the carryover from a preceding taxable year of the acquiring corporation will be applied before the carryover from the same preceding taxable year of the transferor corporation):

(i) *X Corporation's 3/31/60 loss.* The carryover to 1963 is $0, computed as follows:

Net capital loss		$19,000
Less:		
Y's postacquisition part year net capital gain (capital gain net income for taxable years beginning after December 31, 1976) computed under subparagraph (5) of ths paragraph ($36,500 × 184/365)		18,400
Carryover to Y 1962		$600
Less:		
Y's 1962 net capital gain (capital gain net income for taxable years beginning after December 31, 1976) (computed without regard to any capital loss carryovers)		12,000
Carryover to Y 1963		$0

(ii) *Y Corporation's 1959 loss.* The carryover to 1963 is $0, computed as follows:

Net capital loss		$24,000
Less:		
Y's preacquisition part year net capital gain (capital gain net income for taxable years beginning after December 31, 1976) computed under subparagraph (5) of this paragraph ($36,500 × 181/365)		18,100
Carryover to Y's postacquisition part year		$5,900
Less:		
Y's postacquisition part year net capital gain (capital gain net income for taxable years beginning after December 31, 1976) computed under subparagraph (5) of this paragraph	$18,400	
Minus capital loss carryovers to postacquisition part year (i.e., carryover of $19,000 from X 3/31/60)	19,000	0
Carryover to Y 1962		$5,900
Less:		
Y's 1962 net capital gain (capital gain net income for taxable years beginning after December 31, 1976) (computed without regard to any capital loss carryovers)	$12,000	
Minus capital loss carryovers to Y 1962 (i.,e., carryover of $600 from X 3/31/60)	600	11,400
Carryover to Y 1963		$0

(iii) *X Corporation's 3/31/61 loss.* The carryover to 1963 is $0, computed as follows:

Net capital loss		$5,000
Less:		
Y's postacquisition part year net capital gain (capital gain net income for taxable years beginning after December 31, 1976) computed under subparagraph (5) of this paragraph	$18,400	
Minus capital loss carryovers to postacquisition part year (i.e., carryovers of $19,000 from X 3/31/60 and $5,900 from Y 1959)	24,900	0
Carryover to Y 1962		$5,000
Less:		
Y's 1962 net capital gain (capital gain net income for taxable years beginning after December 31, 1976) (computed without regard to any capital loss carryovers)	$12,000	
Minus capital loss carryovers to Y 1962 (i.e., carryovers of $600 from X 3/31/60 and $5,900 from Y 1959)	6,500	$5,500
Carryover to Y 1963		$0

(iv) *Y Corporation's 1960 loss.* The carryover to 1963 is $5,500, computed as follows:

Net capital loss		$6,000
Less:		
Y's preacquisition part year net capital gain (capital gain net income for taxable years beginning after December 31, 1976) computed under subparagraph (5) of this paragraph	$18,100	
Minus capital loss carryovers to preacquisition part year (i.e., carryover of $24,000 from Y 1959)	24,000	0
Carryover to Y's postacquisition part year		$6,000

Less:			
Y's postacquisition part year net capital gain (capital gain net income for taxable years beginning after December 31, 1976) computed under subparagraph (5) of this paragraph	$18,400		
Minus capital loss carryovers to postacquisition part year (i.e., carryovers of $19,000 from X 3/31/60, $5,900 from Y 1959, and $5,000 from X 3/31/61)	29,900		$0
Carryover to Y 1962			$6,000
Less:			
Y's 1962 net capial gain (capital gain net income for taxable years beginning after December 31, 1976) (computed without regard to any capital loss carryovers)	$12,000		
Minus capital loss carryovers to Y 1962 (i.e., carryovers of $600 from X 3/31/60, $5,900 from Y 1959, and $5,000 from X 3/31/61)	11,500		500
Carryover to Y 1963			$5,500

(f) *Successive acquiring corporations.*—An acquiring corporation which, in a transaction to which section 381(a) applies, acquires the assets of a distributor or transferor corporation which previously acquired the assets of another corporation in a transaction to which section 381(a) applies, shall succeed to and take into account, subject to the conditions and limitations of section 1212 and 381, the capital loss carryovers available to the first acquiring corporation under sections 1212 and 381. [Reg. § 1.381(c)(3)-1.]

☐ [*T.D.* 6552, 3-7-61. *Amended by T.D.* 6867, 12-6-65 *and by T.D.* 7728, 10-31-80.]

[Reg. § 1.381(c)(4)-1]

§ 1.381(c)(4)-1. Method of accounting.—(a) *Introduction.*—(1) *Purpose.*—This section provides guidance regarding the method of accounting or combination of methods (other than inventory and depreciation methods) an acquiring corporation must use following a distribution or transfer to which sections 381(a) and 381(c)(4) apply and how to implement any associated change in method of accounting. See § 1.381(c)(5)-1 for guidance regarding the inventory method an acquiring corporation must use following a distribution or transfer to which sections 381(a) and 381(c)(5) apply. See § 1.381(c)(6)-1 for guidance regarding the depreciation method an acquiring corporation must use following a distribution or transfer to which sections 381(a) and 381(c)(6) apply.

(2) *Carryover method requirement for separate and distinct trades or businesses.*—In a transaction to which section 381(a) applies, if an acquiring corporation continues to operate a trade or business of the parties to the section 381(a) transaction as a separate and distinct trade or business after the date of distribution or transfer, the acquiring corporation must use a carryover method as defined in paragraph (b)(5) of this section for each continuing trade or business, unless either the carryover method is impermissible and must be changed under paragraph (a)(4) of this section or the acquiring corporation changes the carryover method in accordance with paragraph (a)(5) of this section. The carryover method requirement applies to the overall method of accounting (for example, an accrual method of accounting) and any special method of accounting (for example, the percentage of completion method of accounting described in section 460) as defined in paragraph (b)(2) of this section used by each trade or business after the date of distribution or transfer. The acquiring corporation need not secure the Commissioner's consent to continue a carryover method.

(3) *Principal method requirement for trades or businesses not operated as separate and distinct trades or businesses.*—In a transaction to which section 381(a) applies, if an acquiring corporation does not operate the trades or businesses of the parties to the section 381(a) transaction as separate and distinct trades or businesses after the date of distribution or transfer, the acquiring corporation must use a principal method determined under paragraph (c) of this section, unless either the principal method is impermissible and must be changed under paragraph (a)(4) of this section or the acquiring corporation changes the principal method in accordance with paragraph (a)(5) of this section. The principal method requirement applies to the overall method of accounting (for example, the cash receipts and disbursements method of accounting) and any special method of accounting (for example, the installment method under section 453) as defined in paragraph (b)(2) of this section used by each integrated trade or business after the date of distribution or transfer. The acquiring corporation must change to a principal method in accordance with paragraph (d)(1) of this section for each integrated trade or business and need not secure the Commissioner's consent to use a principal method.

(4) *Carryover method or principal method not a permissible method.*—If a carryover method or principal method is not a permissible method of accounting, the acquiring corporation must secure the Commissioner's consent to change to a permissible method of accounting as provided in paragraph (d)(2) of this section. If the acquiring corporation must use a single method of accounting for a particular item after the date of distribution or transfer regardless of

the number of separate and distinct trades or businesses operated on that date, the acquiring corporation must use the principal method for that item as determined under paragraph (c) of this section, unless either the principal method is impermissible and must be changed under this paragraph (a)(4) or the acquiring corporation changes the principal method in accordance with paragraph (a)(5) of this section.

(5) *Voluntary change.*—Any party to a section 381(a) transaction may request permission under section 446(e) to change a method of accounting for the taxable year in which the transaction occurs or is expected to occur. For trades or businesses that will not operate as separate and distinct trades or businesses after the date of distribution or transfer, a change in method of accounting for the taxable year that includes that date will be granted only if the requested method is the method that the acquiring corporation must use after the date of distribution or transfer. The time and manner of obtaining the Commissioner's consent to change to a different method of accounting is described in paragraph (d)(2) of this section.

(6) *Examples.*—The following examples illustrate the rules of this paragraph (a). Unless otherwise noted, the carryover method is a permissible method of accounting.

Example (1). Carryover method for separate and distinct trades or businesses after the date of distribution or transfer—(i) *Facts.* X Corporation operates an employment agency that uses the overall cash receipts and disbursements method of accounting. T Corporation operates an educational institution that uses an overall accrual method of accounting. X Corporation acquires the assets of T Corporation in a transaction to which section 381(a) applies. After the date of distribution or transfer, X Corporation operates the employment agency as a trade or business that is separate and distinct from the educational institution.

(ii) *Conclusion.* Because after the date of distribution or transfer X Corporation operates the employment agency as a separate and distinct trade or business, under paragraph (a)(2) of this section X Corporation must use the carryover method for each continuing trade or business, unless either the carryover method is impermissible and must be changed under paragraph (a)(4) of this section or X Corporation changes the carryover method in accordance with paragraph (a)(5) of this section. As defined in paragraph (b)(5) of this section, the carryover method for the employment agency is the cash receipts and disbursements method of accounting and the carryover method for the educational institution is the accrual method of accounting used by T Corporation immediately prior to the date of distribution or transfer. There is no change in method of accounting, and X Corporation need not secure the Commissioner's consent to use either carryover method.

Example (2). Carryover method for a special method of accounting—(i) *Facts.* X Corporation provides personal grooming consulting and T Corporation provides weight management consulting. Both X Corporation and T Corporation use the same overall accrual method of accounting. X Corporation has elected to use the recurring item exception under § 1.461-5. T Corporation does not use the recurring item exception. X Corporation acquires the assets of T Corporation in a transaction to which section 381(a) applies. After the date of distribution or transfer, X Corporation operates the personal grooming consulting business as a trade or business that is separate and distinct from the weight management consulting business.

(ii) *Conclusion.* Because after the date of distribution or transfer, X Corporation operates the personal grooming consulting business as a separate and distinct trade or business, under paragraph (a)(2) of this section X Corporation must use a carryover method for each continuing trade or business, unless either the carryover method is impermissible and must be changed under paragraph (a)(4) of this section or X Corporation changes the carryover method in accordance with paragraph (a)(5) of this section. As defined in paragraph (b)(5) of this section, the carryover method for the overall method of accounting for each trade or business is the accrual method used immediately prior to the date of distribution or transfer. The carryover method for the special method of accounting for the personal grooming consulting business is the recurring item exception under

Corporate Organizations and Reorganizations
See p. 20,601 for regulations not amended to reflect law changes

31,989

§1.461-5 while the carryover method for the weight management consulting business is not to use the recurring item exception under §1.461-5. There is no change in method of accounting, and X Corporation need not secure the Commissioner's consent to use the carryover methods of accounting.

Example (3). Carryover method for a special method of accounting not permissible—(i) *Facts.* X Corporation is an engineering firm that uses the overall cash receipts and disbursements method of accounting and has elected under section 171 to amortize bond premium with respect to its taxable bonds acquired at a premium. T Corporation is a manufacturer that uses an overall accrual method of accounting and has not made a section 171 election to amortize bond premium with respect to its taxable bonds acquired at a premium. X Corporation acquires the assets of T Corporation in a transaction to which section 381(a) applies. After the date of distribution or transfer, X Corporation operates the engineering firm as a trade or business that is separate and distinct from the manufacturing business.

(ii) *Conclusion.* Because after the date of distribution or transfer X Corporation operates the engineering firm as a separate and distinct trade or business, under paragraph (a)(2) of this section X Corporation must use a carryover method for each continuing trade or business, unless either the carryover method is impermissible and must be changed under paragraph (a)(4) of this section or X Corporation changes the carryover method in accordance with paragraph (a)(5) of this section. As defined in paragraph (b)(5) of this section, the carryover method for the overall method of accounting for the engineering firm is the cash receipts and disbursements method used by X Corporation immediately prior to the date of distribution or transfer, and the carryover method for the overall method of accounting for the manufacturing business is the accrual method used by T Corporation immediately prior to the date of distribution or transfer. There is no change in method of accounting, and X Corporation need not secure the Commissioner's consent to use either carryover method. Notwithstanding that after the date of distribution or transfer X Corporation has two separate and distinct trades or businesses, X Corporation is permitted only one method of accounting for amortizable bond premium under section 171. Because after the date of distribution or transfer X Corporation must use a single method of accounting for bond premium for all trades or businesses, X Corporation must use the principal method for that item as determined under paragraph (c) of this section, unless either the principal method is impermissible and must be changed under paragraph (a)(4) of this section or X Corporation changes that method in accordance with paragraph (a)(5) of this section. X Corporation must change to the principal method in accordance with paragraph (d)(1) of this section. If amortizing bond premium is not the principal method, X Corporation may make an election to amortize bond premium to the extent permitted by section 171. See paragraph (e)(2) of this section for rules on making elections.

(b) *Definitions.*—For purposes of this section—

(1) *Method of accounting.*—A method of accounting has the same meaning as provided in section 446 and any applicable Income Tax Regulations.

(2) *Special method of accounting.*—A special method of accounting is a method expressly permitted or required by the Internal Revenue Code, Income Tax Regulations, or administrative guidance published in the Internal Revenue Bulletin that deviates from the normal application of the cash receipts and disbursements method or an accrual method of accounting. The installment method under section 453, the mark-to-market method under section 475, the amortization of bond premium under section 171, the percentage of completion method under section 460, the recurring item exception of §1.461-5, and the income deferral method under section 455 are examples of special methods of accounting. See §1.446-1(c)(1)(iii).

(3) *Adoption of a method of accounting.*—Adoption of a method of accounting has the same meaning as provided in §1.446-1(e)(1).

(4) *Change in method of accounting.*—A change in method of accounting has the same meaning as provided in §1.446-1(e)(2).

(5) *Carryover method.*—A carryover method for the overall method of accounting is the *overall method of accounting* that each party to a section 381(a) transaction uses for each separate and distinct trade or business immediately prior to the date of distribution or transfer. The carryover method for a *special method of accounting* for an item is the special method of accounting for that item that each party to a section 381(a) transaction uses for each separate and distinct trade or business immediately prior to the date of distribution or transfer.

(6) *Principal method.*—A principal method is an overall or special method of accounting that is determined under paragraph (c) of this section.

(7) *Permissible method of accounting.*—A permissible method of accounting is a method of accounting that is proper or permitted under the Internal Revenue Code or any applicable Income Tax Regulations.

(8) *Acquiring corporation.*—An acquiring corporation has the same meaning as provided in §1.381(a)-1(b)(2).

(9) *Distributor corporation.*—A distributor corporation means the corporation, foreign or domestic, that distributes its assets to another corporation described in section 332(b) in a distribution to which section 332 (relating to liquidations of subsidiaries) applies.

(10) *Transferor corporation.*—A transferor corporation means the corporation, foreign or domestic, that transfers its assets to another corporation in a transfer to which section 361 (relating to nonrecognition of gain or loss to corporations) applies, but only if—

(i) The transfer is in connection with a reorganization described in section 368(a)(1)(A), (a)(1)(C), or (a)(1)(F), or

(ii) The transfer is in connection with a reorganization described in section 368(a)(1)(D) or (a)(1)(G), provided the requirements of section 354(b) are met.

(11) *Parties to the section 381(a) transaction.*—Parties to the section 381(a) transaction means the acquiring corporation and the distributor or transferor corporation that participate in a transaction to which section 381(a) applies.

(12) *Date of distribution or transfer.*—The date of distribution or transfer has the same meaning as provided in section 381(b)(2) and §1.381(b)-1(b).

(13) *Separate and distinct trades or businesses.*—Separate and distinct trades or businesses has the same meaning as provided in §1.446-1(d).

(14) *Gross receipts.*—Gross receipts means all the receipts, including amounts that are excludible from gross income, that must be taken into account under the method of accounting used in a representative period (determined without regard to this section) for federal income tax purposes. For example, gross receipts includes income from investments, amounts received for services, rents, total sales (net of returns and allowances), and both taxable and tax-exempt interest. See paragraph (e)(5) of this section for rules on determining the representative period.

(15) *Audit protection.*—Audit protection means, for purposes of paragraph (d)(1) of this section, that the IRS will not require an acquiring corporation that is required to change a method of accounting under paragraph (a)(3) of this section to change that method for a taxable year ending prior to the taxable year that includes the date of distribution or transfer.

(16) *Section 481(a) adjustment.*—The section 481(a) adjustment means an adjustment that must be taken into account as required under section 481(a) to prevent amounts from being duplicated or omitted when the taxable income of an acquiring corporation is computed under a method of accounting different from the method used to compute taxable income for the preceding taxable year.

(17) *Cut-off basis.*—A cut-off basis means a manner in which a change in method of accounting is made without a section 481(a) adjustment and under which only the items arising after the beginning of the year of change (or, in the case of a change made under paragraph (d)(1) of this section, after the date of distribution or transfer) are accounted for under the new method of accounting.

(18) *Adjustment period.*—The adjustment period means the number of taxable years for taking into account the section 481(a) adjustment required as a result of a change in method of accounting.

(19) *Component trade or business.*—A component trade or business is a trade or business of a party to the section 381(a) transaction that will be combined and integrated with a trade or business of the other party to the section 381 transaction. See paragraph (e)(4)(ii) of this section for the determination of whether a trade or business is operated as a separate and distinct trade or business after the date of distribution or transfer.

(c) *Principal method.*—(1) *In general.*—For each integrated trade or business, the principal method is generally the method of accounting used by the component trade or business of the acquiring corporation immediately prior to the date of distribution or transfer. If, however, the component trade or business of the distributor or transferor corporation is larger than the component trade or business of the acquiring corporation on the date of distribution or transfer, the principal method is the method used by the component trade or business of the distributor or transferor corporation immediately prior to that date. If the larger component trade or business does not have a special method of accounting for a particular item immediately prior to the date of distribution or transfer, the principal method for that item is the method of accounting used by the component trade or business that does have a special method of accounting for that item. See paragraph (e)(9) of this section for special rules concerning methods of accounting that are elected on a project-by-project, job-by-job, or other similar basis. For each integrated trade or business, the component trade or business of the distributor or transferor corporation is larger than the component trade or business of the acquiring corporation on the date of distribution or transfer if—

(i) The aggregate of the adjusted bases of the assets held by each component trade or business of the distributor or transferor corporation (determined under section 1011 and any applicable Income Tax Regulations) exceeds the aggregate of the adjusted bases of the assets of each component trade or business of the acquiring corporation immediately prior to the date of distribution or transfer, and

(ii) The aggregate of the gross receipts for a representative period of each component trade or business of the distributor or transferor corporation exceeds the aggregate of the gross receipts for the same period of each component trade or business of the acquiring corporation. See paragraph (e)(5) of this section for rules on determining the representative period.

(2) *Multiple component trades or businesses with different principal methods.*—If a party to the section 381(a) transaction has multiple component trades or businesses and more than one principal overall method of accounting or more than one principal special method of accounting for an item, then the acquiring corporation may choose which of the principal methods of accounting used by such component trades or businesses will be the principal methods of the integrated trade or business. The acquiring corporation must choose a principal method that is a permissible method of accounting. In general, a change to a principal method in a transaction to which section 381(a) and paragraph (a)(3) of this section applies is made under paragraph (d)(1) of this section.

(3) *Examples.*—The following examples illustrate the rules of this paragraph (c). Unless otherwise noted, the principal method is a permissible method of accounting.

Example (1). *Principal method is the method used by the acquiring corporation*— (i) *Facts.* X Corporation and T Corporation each operate an employment agency. X Corporation uses the overall cash receipts and disbursements method of accounting, and T Corporation uses an overall accrual method of accounting. X Corporation acquires the assets of T Corporation in a transaction to which section 381(a) applies. The adjusted bases of the assets in X Corporation's employment agency immediately prior to the date of distribution or transfer exceed the adjusted bases of the assets in T Corporation's employment agency, and the gross receipts in X Corporation's employment agency for the representative period exceed the gross receipts of T Corporation's employment agency for the period. After the date of distribution or transfer, X Corporation's employment agency will not be operated as a trade or business that is separate and distinct from T Corporation's employment agency.

(ii) *Conclusion.* Because after the date of distribution or transfer X Corporation will not operate its employment agency as a separate and distinct trade or business, X Corporation must use a principal method under paragraph (a)(3) of this section, unless either the principal method is impermissible and must be changed under paragraph (a)(4) of this section or X Corporation changes the principal method in accordance with paragraph (a)(5) of this section. Because on the date of distribution or transfer T Corporation's employment agency is not larger than X Corporation's employment agency, the principal method for the overall method of accounting is the cash receipts and disbursements method used by X Corporation's employment agency. X Corporation need not secure the Commissioner's consent to use this method of accounting. However, in accordance with paragraph (d)(1) of this section, X Corporation must change the method of accounting for the employment agency acquired from T Corporation to the cash receipts and disbursements method.

Example (2). *Principal method is the method used by the acquiring corporation*— (i) *Facts.* The facts are the same as in *Example* (1), except that the gross receipts of T Corporation's employment agency for the representative period exceed the gross receipts of X Corporation's employment agency for the period.

(ii) *Conclusion.* The result is the same as in *Example* (1). Although the gross receipts of T Corporation's employment agency exceed the gross receipts of X Corporation's employment agency, T Corporation's employment agency is not larger than X Corporation's employment agency because the adjusted bases of the assets of T Corporation's employment agency do not exceed the adjusted bases of the assets of X Corporation's employment agency. Thus, the principal method for the overall method of accounting is the cash

receipts and disbursements method of accounting used by X Corporation's employment agency immediately prior to the date of distribution or transfer. X Corporation need not secure the Commissioner's consent to use this method of accounting. However, in accordance with paragraph (d)(1) of this section, X Corporation must change the method of accounting for the employment agency business acquired from T Corporation to the cash receipts and disbursements method.

Example (3). *Principal method is the method used by the distributor or transferor corporation*—(i) *Facts.* The facts are the same as in *Example* (2), except that the adjusted bases of the assets held by T Corporation's employment agency immediately prior to the date of distribution or transfer exceed the adjusted bases of the assets held by X Corporation's employment agency.

(ii) *Conclusion.* The principal method for the overall method of accounting is the accrual method of accounting used by T Corporation's employment agency immediately prior to the date of distribution or transfer because on the date of distribution or transfer T Corporation's employment agency is larger than X Corporation's employment agency. The adjusted bases of the assets of T Corporation's employment agency exceed the adjusted bases of the assets of X Corporation's employment agency, and the gross receipts of T Corporation's employment agency exceed the gross receipts of X Corporation's employment agency. X Corporation need not secure the Commissioner's consent to use this method of accounting. However, in accordance with paragraph (d)(1) of this section, X Corporation must change the method of accounting for the employment agency business it operated prior to the date of distribution or transfer to the accrual method of accounting used by T Corporation's employment agency immediately prior to the date of distribution or transfer.

Example (4). *Impermissible principal method*—(i) *Facts.* The facts are the same as in *Example* (1), except that X Corporation is prohibited under section 448 from using the cash receipts and disbursements method of accounting after the date of distribution or transfer.

(ii) *Conclusion.* Because section 448 prohibits X Corporation from using the cash receipts and disbursements method of accounting, X Corporation is not permitted to use the principal method for the overall method of accounting as determined in *Example* (1). Because after the date of distribution or transfer that method is not a permissible method, under paragraph (a)(4) of this section X Corporation must secure the Commissioner's consent to change to a permissible method in accordance with the procedures set forth in paragraph (d)(2) of this section.

Example (5). *Voluntary change not allowable*—(i) *Facts.* The facts are the same as in *Example* (4), except that T Corporation wants to discontinue using the overall accrual method of accounting for its employment agency and change to the cash receipts and disbursements method for the taxable year in which the section 381(a) transaction occurs or is expected to occur.

(ii) *Conclusion.* Under paragraph (a)(5) of this section, the Commissioner will grant a request to change a method of accounting for the taxable year that includes the date of distribution or transfer only if the requested method is the method that the acquiring corporation must use after the date of distribution or transfer. The Commissioner will not consent to a request by T Corporation to change to the cash receipts and disbursements method for the taxable year in which the section 381(a) transaction occurs or is expected to occur because X Corporation cannot use the cash receipts and disbursements method after the date of distribution or transfer.

Example (6). *Principal methods are the acquiring corporation's methods*—(i) *Facts.* X Corporation and T Corporation each publishes magazines. X Corporation acquires the assets of T Corporation in a transaction to which section 381(a) applies. Both X Corporation and T Corporation use an overall accrual method of accounting. X Corporation has elected to defer income from its subscription sales under section 455. T Corporation has not elected to defer income from its subscription sales under section 455 and instead has recognized the income from these sales in accordance with section 451. The adjusted bases of the assets in X Corporation's publication business immediately prior to the date of distribution or transfer exceed the adjusted bases of the assets in T Corporation's publication business, and the gross receipts in X Corporation's publication business for the representative period exceed the gross receipts in T Corporation's publication business for the representative period. After the date of distribution or transfer, X Corporation will not operate its publication business as a trade or business that is separate and distinct from T Corporation's publication business.

(ii) *Conclusion.* Because after the date of distribution or transfer X Corporation will not operate its publication business as a separate and distinct trade or business, X Corporation must use the principal method under paragraph (a)(3) of this section, unless either the principal method is impermissible and must be changed under paragraph (a)(4) of this section or X Corporation changes the principal method in accordance with paragraph (a)(5) of this section. The adjusted bases of the assets in T Corporation's publication business do not exceed the adjusted bases of the assets in X Corporation's publication business, and the gross receipts in T Corporation's publication business do not exceed the gross receipts in X Corporation's publication business. Because on the date of distribution or transfer T Corporation's publication business is not larger than X Corporation's publication business, the principal method for the overall method of accounting is the accrual method used by X Corporation's publication business immediately prior to the date of distribution or transfer. The principal method for subscription sales is the section 455 deferral method used by X Corporation immediately prior to the date of distribution or transfer. X Corporation need not secure the Commissioner's consent to use the principal method for either the overall method of accounting or the special method of accounting. However, in accordance with paragraph (d)(1) of this section, X Corporation must change both the overall method of accounting and the special method of accounting for the publication business acquired from T Corporation to the accrual method and the section 455 deferral method used by X Corporation immediately prior to the date of distribution or transfer.

Example (7). Principal methods are the acquiring corporation's methods—(i) *Facts.* The facts are the same as in *Example (6)*, except that the adjusted bases of the assets in T Corporation's publication business immediately prior to the date of distribution or transfer exceed the adjusted bases of the assets in X Corporation's business.

(ii) *Conclusion.* The result is the same as in *Example (6)*. Because on the date of distribution or transfer T Corporation's publication business is not larger than X Corporation's publication business, the principal method for the overall method of accounting is the accrual method used by X Corporation's publication business immediately prior to the date of distribution or transfer. The principal method for subscription sales is the section 455 deferral method used by X Corporation immediately prior to the date of distribution or transfer. X Corporation need not secure the Commissioner's consent to use the principal method for either the overall method of accounting or the special method of accounting. However, in accordance with paragraph (d)(1) of this section, X Corporation must change both the overall method of accounting and the special method of accounting for the publication business acquired from T Corporation to the accrual method and the section 455 deferral method used by X Corporation immediately prior to the date of distribution or transfer.

Example (8). Principal method determination when larger component trade or business does not have a special method of accounting—(i) *Facts.* X Corporation and T Corporation both install ice skating rinks. Both X Corporation and T Corporation use an overall accrual method of accounting for their respective businesses. X Corporation completes its installation contracts within the contracting year and uses an accrual method of accounting to recognize the revenue from its installation contracts. T Corporation's installation contracts are subject to section 460, and T Corporation recognizes the revenue from such contracts under the percentage-of-completion method. X Corporation acquires the assets of T Corporation in a transaction to which section 381(a) applies. The adjusted bases of the assets in X Corporation's installation business immediately prior to the date of distribution or transfer exceed the adjusted bases of the assets in T Corporation's installation business, and the gross receipts in X Corporation's installation business for the representative period exceed the gross receipts in T Corporation's installation business for the representative period. After the date of distribution or transfer, X Corporation will not operate its installation business as a trade or business that is separate and distinct from T Corporation's installation business.

(ii) *Conclusion.* Because after the date of distribution or transfer X Corporation will not operate its installation business as a separate and distinct trade or business, X Corporation must use a principal method under paragraph (a)(3) of this section, unless either the principal method is impermissible and must be changed under paragraph (a)(4) of this section or X Corporation changes the principal method in accordance with paragraph (a)(5) of this section. The adjusted bases of the assets in T Corporation's installation business do not exceed the adjusted bases of the assets in X Corporation's installation business, and the gross receipts in T Corporation's installation business do not exceed the gross receipts in X Corporation's installation business. Because on the date of distribution or transfer T Corporation's installation business is not larger than X Corporation's installation business, the principal method for the overall method of accounting is the accrual method used by X Corporation's installation business immediately prior to the date of distribution or transfer. X Corporation need not secure the Commissioner's consent to use the principal method for the overall method of accounting. However, in accordance with paragraph (d)(1) of this section, X Corporation must change the overall method of accounting for the installation business acquired from T Corporation to the accrual method used by X Corporation. Under paragraph (c) of this section,

the principal method for T Corporation's long-term contracts is the percentage-of-completion method used by T Corporation immediately prior to the date of distribution or transfer because X Corporation's installation business does not have a method of accounting for long-term contracts. There is no change in method of accounting, and X Corporation need not secure the Commissioner's consent to use T Corporation's percentage-of-completion method.

Example (9). Principal method determination with a combined trade or business and a separate and distinct trade or business—(i) *Facts.* X Corporation operates a tennis academy as a trade or business that is separate and distinct from its trade or business of operating a golf academy. X Corporation uses the overall cash receipts and disbursements method of accounting for the tennis academy and an overall accrual method of accounting for the golf academy. T Corporation operates a tennis academy and uses an accrual method of accounting for the overall method. X Corporation acquires the assets of T Corporation in a transaction to which section 381(a) applies. After the date of distribution or transfer, X Corporation will not operate its tennis academy as a trade or business that is separate and distinct from T Corporation's tennis academy. X Corporation will continue to operate its golf academy as a trade or business that is separate and distinct from the operation of the tennis academy. The adjusted bases of the assets in T Corporation's tennis academy exceed the adjusted bases of the assets in X Corporation's tennis academy immediately prior to the date of distribution or transfer. The gross receipts of T Corporation's tennis academy for the representative period exceed the gross receipts of X Corporation's tennis academy for that period.

(ii) *Conclusion.* Because after the date of distribution or transfer X Corporation will not operate its tennis academy as a separate and distinct trade or business, X Corporation must use a principal method under paragraph (a)(3) of this section, unless either the principal method is impermissible and must be changed under paragraph (a)(4) of this section or X Corporation changes the principal method in accordance with paragraph (a)(5) of this section. Because on the date of distribution or transfer the tennis academy operated by T Corporation is larger than the tennis academy operated by X Corporation, the principal method for the overall method of accounting for the combined tennis academy business is the accrual method used by T Corporation's tennis academy immediately prior to the date of distribution or transfer. X Corporation need not secure the Commissioner's consent to use the principal method for the overall method of accounting. However, in accordance with paragraph (d)(1) of this section, X Corporation must change the method of accounting for its tennis academy to the accrual method. Because X Corporation will operate the golf academy as a separate trade or business, under paragraph (a)(2) of this section X Corporation must continue to use the accrual method that it used immediately prior to the date of distribution or transfer as the carryover method for the golf academy. There is no change in method of accounting, and X Corporation need not secure the Commissioner's consent to use the carryover method.

Example (10). Principal method determination with multiple component trades or businesses—(i) *Facts.* The facts are the same as in *Example (9)*, except that after the date of distribution or transfer X Corporation will not operate its golf academy as a trade or business that is separate and distinct from the tennis academy. In addition, X Corporation's component trades or businesses are larger than T Corporation's component trade or business: (1) the adjusted bases of the assets of X Corporation's tennis academy and golf academy businesses, in the aggregate, exceed the adjusted bases of the assets held by T Corporation's tennis academy; and (2) the gross receipts for the representative period of X Corporation's tennis academy and golf academy businesses, in the aggregate, exceed the gross receipts in T Corporation's tennis academy.

(ii) *Conclusion.* Because on the date of distribution or transfer T Corporation's tennis academy is not larger than X Corporation's combined tennis academy and golf academy, the principal method for the overall method of accounting is the method of accounting used by the component trades or businesses of X Corporation that will be combined with T Corporation's component trade or business on that date. Because on the date of distribution or transfer X Corporation operates two component trades or businesses with different overall methods of accounting that will be integrated after the date of distribution or transfer, X Corporation may choose under paragraph (c)(2) of this section which overall method (and any special method of accounting) used by its component trades or businesses will be the principal method. X Corporation may choose to use either the accrual method used by the golf academy or the cash receipts and disbursements method used by its tennis academy as the principal method after the date of distribution or transfer, if either method is a permissible method. In accordance with paragraph (d)(1) of this section, X Corporation must change T Corporation's overall method of accounting to the principal method. Under paragraph (a)(3) of this section, X Corporation also must change either its golf academy business or its tennis academy business, depending on which principal method X Corporation selects, to the principal method.

(d) *Procedures for changing a method of accounting.*—(1) *Change made to principal method under paragraph (a)(3) of this section.*—(i) *Section 481(a) adjustment.*—(A) *In general.*—An acquiring corporation that changes its method of accounting or the distributor or transferor corporation's method of accounting under paragraph (a)(3) of this section does not need to secure the Commissioner's consent to use the principal method. To the extent the use of a principal method constitutes a change in method of accounting, the change in method is treated as a change initiated by the acquiring corporation for purposes of section 481(a)(2). Any change to a principal method, whether the change relates to a trade or business of the acquiring corporation or a trade or business of the distributor or transferor corporation, must be reflected on the acquiring corporation's federal income tax return for the taxable year that includes the date of distribution or transfer. The amount of the section 481(a) adjustment and the adjustment period, if any, necessary to implement a change to the principal method are determined under § 1.446-1(e) and the applicable administrative procedures that govern voluntary changes in methods of accounting under section 446(e). If the Internal Revenue Code, the Income Tax Regulations, or administrative procedures require that a method of accounting be implemented on a cut-off basis, the acquiring corporation must implement the change on a cut-off basis as of the date of distribution or transfer on its federal income tax return for the taxable year that includes the date of distribution or transfer. If the Internal Revenue Code, the Income Tax Regulations, or administrative procedures require a section 481(a) adjustment, the acquiring corporation must determine the section 481(a) adjustment and include the appropriate amount of the section 481(a) adjustment on its federal income tax return for the taxable year that includes the date of distribution or transfer and subsequent taxable year(s), as necessary. This adjustment is determined by the acquiring corporation as of the beginning of the day that is immediately after the date of distribution or transfer.

(B) *Example.*—The following example illustrates the rules of this paragraph (d)(1)(i):

Example. X Corporation uses the overall cash receipts and disbursements method of accounting, and T Corporation uses an overall accrual method of accounting. X Corporation acquires the assets of T Corporation in a transaction to which section 381(a) applies. X Corporation determines that under the rules of paragraph (c)(1) of this section X Corporation must change the method of accounting for the business acquired from T Corporation to the cash receipts and disbursements method. X Corporation will determine the section 481(a) adjustment pertaining to the change to the cash receipts and disbursements method by consolidating the adjustments (whether the amounts thereof represent increases or decreases in items of income or deductions) arising with respect to balances in the various accounts, such as accounts receivable, as of the beginning of the day that immediately follows the day on which X Corporation acquires the assets of T Corporation. X Corporation will reflect this adjustment, or an appropriate part thereof, on its federal income tax return for the taxable year that includes the date of distribution or transfer.

(ii) *Audit protection.* Notwithstanding any other provision in any other Income Tax Regulation or administrative procedure, no audit protection is provided for any change in method of accounting under paragraph (d)(1) of this section.

(iii) *Other terms and conditions.* Except as otherwise provided in this section, other terms and conditions provided in § 1.446-1(e) and the applicable administrative procedures for voluntary changes in method of accounting under section 446(e) apply to a change in method of accounting under this section. Thus, for example, if the administrative procedures for a particular change in method of accounting have a term and condition that provides for the acceleration of the section 481(a) adjustment period, this term and condition applies to a change made under this paragraph (d)(1). However, any scope limitation in the applicable administrative procedures will not apply for purposes of making a change under this paragraph (d)(1). For example, if the administrative procedures provide as a limitation that an identical change in method of accounting is barred for a period of years, this limitation will not bar a change to the principal method made under this section.

(2) *Change made to a method of accounting under paragraph (a)(4) or (a)(5) of this section.*—(i) *In general.*—A party to a section 381(a) transaction that changes a method of accounting under either paragraph (a)(4) or paragraph (a)(5) of this section must follow the provisions of § 1.446-1(e) and the applicable administrative procedures, including scope limitations, for voluntary changes in method of accounting under section 446(e), except as provided in paragraphs (d)(2)(ii) and (d)(2)(iii) of this section. An application on Form 3115,

"Application for Change in Accounting Method," filed with the IRS to change a method of accounting under this paragraph (d)(2) should be labeled "Filed under section 381(c)(4)" at the top.

(ii) *Final year limitation.*—Any scope limitation relating to the final year of a trade or business will not apply to a taxpayer that changes its method of accounting in the final year of a trade or business that is terminated as the result of a section 381(a) transaction.

(iii) *Time to file.*—Under the authority of § 1.446-1(e)(3)(ii), for a change in method of accounting requiring advance consent, the application for a change in method of accounting (for example, Form 3115) must be filed with the IRS on or before the later of—

(A) The due date for filing a Form 3115 as specified in § 1.446-1(e), for example, the last day of the taxable year in which the distribution or transfer occurred, or

(B) The earlier of—

(1) The day that is 180 days after the date of distribution or transfer, or

(2) The day on which the acquiring corporation files its federal income tax return for the taxable year in which the distribution or transfer occurred.

(e) *Rules and procedures.*—(1) *No method of accounting.*—If a party to a section 381(a) transaction is not using a method of accounting, does not have a method of accounting for a particular item, or came into existence as a result of the transaction, the party will not be treated as having a method of accounting different from that used by another party to the section 381(a) transaction.

(2) *Elections and adoptions allowed.*—If an election does not require the Commissioner's consent, an acquiring corporation or a distributor or transferor corporation is not precluded from making any election that is otherwise permissible for the taxable year that includes the date of distribution or transfer. For purposes of this section, a corporation shall be deemed as having made any election as of the first day of the taxable year that includes the date of distribution or transfer. Similarly, where adoption is permissible, an acquiring corporation or a distributor or transferor corporation may adopt any permissible method of accounting for the taxable year that includes the date of distribution or transfer.

(3) *Elections continue after section 381(a) transaction.*—(i) *General rule.*—An acquiring corporation is not required to renew any election not otherwise requiring renewal and previously made by it or by a distributor or transferor corporation for a carryover method or a principal method if the acquiring corporation uses the method after the section 381(a) transaction. If the acquiring corporation uses a method after the date of distribution or transfer, an election made by the acquiring corporation or by a distributor or transferor corporation for that method that was in effect on the date of distribution or transfer continues after the section 381(a) transaction as though the distribution or transfer had not occurred.

(ii) *Example.*—The following example illustrates the rules of this paragraph (e)(3):

Example. The acquiring corporation, X Corporation, previously elected to amortize bond premium under section 171. X Corporation acquires the assets of T Corporation in a transaction to which section 381(a) applies. X Corporation determines under the rules of paragraph (c)(1) of this section that X Corporation's method of amortizing bond premium is the principal method. After the date of distribution or transfer, X Corporation is not required to renew its bond premium amortization election and is bound by it. Additionally, X Corporation would not be required to renew its election to amortize bond premium if the method were the carryover method under paragraph (a)(2) of this section.

(4) *Appropriate times for certain determinations.*—(i) *Determining the method of accounting.*—The method of accounting used by a party to a section 381(a) transaction on the date of distribution or transfer is the method of accounting used by that party as of the end of the day that is immediately prior to the date of distribution or transfer.

(ii) *Determining whether there are separate and distinct trades or businesses after the date of distribution or transfer.*—Whether an acquiring corporation will operate the trades or businesses of the parties to a section 381(a) transaction as separate and distinct trades or businesses after the date of distribution or transfer will be determined as of the date of distribution or transfer based upon the facts and circumstances. Intent to combine books and records of the trades or businesses may be demonstrated by contemporaneous records and documents or by other objective evidence that reflects the acquiring corporation's ultimate plan of operation, even though the actual combination of the books and records may extend beyond the end of the taxable year that includes the date of distribution or transfer.

(5) *Representative period for aggregating gross receipts.*—The representative period for measuring gross receipts is generally the 12 consecutive months preceding the date of distribution or transfer. If a component trade or business was not in existence for the 12 consecutive months preceding the date of distribution or transfer, then all component trades or businesses of each integrated trade or business will compare their gross receipts for the period that such trade or business was in existence. For example, if the acquiring corporation's component trade or business was formed in August and the date of distribution or transfer occurred in December of the same year, the gross receipts for those five months will be compared with the gross receipts of the other component trades or businesses for the same period.

(6) *Establishing a method of accounting.*—A method of accounting used by the distributor or transferor corporation immediately prior to the date of distribution or transfer that continues to be used by the acquiring corporation after the date of distribution or transfer is an established method of accounting for purposes of section 446(e), whether or not such method is proper or is permitted under the Internal Revenue Code or any applicable Income Tax Regulations.

(7) *Other applicable provisions.*—This section does not preempt any other provision of the Internal Revenue Code or the Income Tax Regulations that is applicable to the acquiring corporation's circumstances. For example, income, deductions, credits, allowances, and exclusions may be allocated among the parties to a section 381(a) transaction and other taxpayers under sections 269 and 482, if appropriate. Similarly, transfers of contracts accounted for using a long-term contract method of accounting are governed by the rules provided in §1.460-4(k). Further, if other paragraphs of section 381(c) apply for purposes of determining the methods of accounting to be used following the date of distribution or transfer, section 381(c)(4) and this §1.381(c)(4)-1 will not apply to the tax treatment of the items. For example, this section does not apply to inventories that an acquiring corporation obtains in a transaction to which section 381(a) applies. Instead, the rules of section 381(c)(5) govern the inventory method to be used by the acquiring corporation after the distribution or transfer. Similarly, if the acquiring corporation assumes an obligation of the distributor or transferor corporation that gives rise to a liability after the date of distribution or transfer and to which §1.381(c)(16)-1 applies, the deductibility of the item is determined under this section only after the rules of section 381(c)(16) are applied.

(8) *Character of items of income and deduction.*—After the date of distribution or transfer, items of income and deduction have the same character in the hands of the acquiring corporation as they would have had in the hands of the distributor or transferor corporation if no distribution or transfer had occurred.

(9) *Method of accounting selected by project or job.*—If other sections of the Internal Revenue Code, Income Tax Regulations, or other administrative guidance permit an acquiring corporation to elect a method of accounting on a project-by-project, job-by-job, or other similar basis, then for purposes of this section the method elected with respect to each project or job is the established method only for that project or job. For example, the election under section 460 to classify a contract to perform both manufacturing and construction activities as a long-term construction contract if at least 95 percent of the estimated total allocable contract costs are reasonably allocated to the construction activities is made on a contract-by-contract basis. Accordingly, the method of accounting previously elected for a project or job generally continues after the date of distribution or transfer. However, if the trades or businesses of the parties to a section 381(a) transaction are not operated as separate and distinct trades or businesses after the date of distribution or transfer, and two or more of the parties to the section 381(a) transaction previously worked on the same project or job and used different methods of accounting for the project or job immediately before the distribution or transfer, then the acquiring corporation must determine the principal method for that project or job under paragraph (c) of this section and make changes, if necessary, to the principal method in accordance with paragraph (d)(1) of this section.

(10) *Impermissible method of accounting.*—This section does not limit the Commissioner's ability under section 446(b) to determine whether a taxpayer's method of accounting is an impermissible method or otherwise fails to clearly reflect income. For example, an acquiring corporation may not use the method of accounting determined under paragraph (a)(2) of this section if the method fails to clearly reflect the acquiring corporation's income within the meaning of section 446(b).

(f) *Effective/applicability date.*—This section applies to corporate reorganizations and tax-free liquidations described in section 381(a) that occur on or after August 31, 2011. [Reg. §1.381(c)(4)-1.]

☐ [*T.D. 6750, 8-4-64. Amended by T.D. 8071, 1-16-86, T.D. 8995, 5-14-2002, T.D. 9534, 7-29-2011 and T.D. 9870, 7-11-2019.*]

[Reg. §1.381(c)(5)-1]

§1.381(c)(5)-1. Inventories.—(a) *introduction.*—(1) *Purpose.*—This section provides guidance regarding the inventory method an acquiring corporation must use following a distribution or transfer to which sections 381(a) and 381(c)(5) apply and how to implement any associated change in method of accounting. See §1.381(c)(4)-1 for guidance regarding the method of accounting or combination of methods (other than inventory and depreciation methods) an acquiring corporation must use following a distribution or transfer to which sections 381(a) and 381(c)(4) apply. See §1.381(c)(6)-1 for guidance regarding the depreciation method an acquiring corporation must use following a distribution or transfer to which sections 381(a) and 381(c)(6) apply.

(2) *Carryover method requirement for separate and distinct trades or businesses.*—In a transaction to which section 381(a) applies, if an acquiring corporation continues to operate a trade or business of the parties to the section 381(a) transaction as a separate and distinct trade or business after the date of distribution or transfer, the acquiring corporation must use a carryover method as defined in paragraph (b)(4) of this section for each continuing trade or business, unless either the carryover method is impermissible and must be changed under paragraph (a)(4) of this section or the acquiring corporation changes the carryover method in accordance with paragraph (a)(5) of this section. The acquiring corporation need not secure the Commissioner's consent to continue a carryover method.

(3) *Principal method requirement for trades or businesses not operated as separate and distinct trades or businesses.*—In a transaction to which section 381(a) applies, if an acquiring corporation does not operate the trades or businesses of the parties to the section 381(a) transaction as separate and distinct trades or businesses after the date of distribution or transfer, the acquiring corporation must use a principal method determined under paragraph (c) of this section, unless either the principal method is impermissible and must be changed under paragraph (a)(4) of this section or the acquiring corporation changes the principal method in accordance with paragraph (a)(5) of this section. The acquiring corporation must change to a principal method in accordance with paragraph (d)(1) of this section for each integrated trade or business and need not secure the Commissioner's consent to use a principal method.

(4) *Carryover method or principal method not a permissible method.*—If a carryover method or principal method is not a permissible inventory method, the acquiring corporation must secure the Commissioner's consent to change to a permissible inventory method as provided in paragraph (d)(2) of this section. If the acquiring corporation must use a single inventory method for a particular type of goods after the date of distribution or transfer regardless of the number of separate and distinct trades or businesses operated on that date, the acquiring corporation must use the principal method for that type of goods as determined under paragraph (c) of this section, unless either the principal method is impermissible and must be changed under this paragraph (a)(4) or the acquiring corporation changes the principal method in accordance with paragraph (a)(5) of this section.

(5) *Voluntary change.*—Any party to a section 381(a) transaction may request permission under section 446(e) to change an inventory method for the taxable year in which the transaction occurs or is expected to occur. For trades or businesses that will not operate as separate and distinct trades or businesses after the date of distribution or transfer, a change in method of accounting for the taxable year that includes that date will be granted only if the requested inventory method is the method that the acquiring corporation must use after the date of distribution or transfer. The time and manner of obtaining the Commissioner's consent to change to a different inventory method is described in paragraph (d)(2) of this section.

(6) *Examples.*—The following examples illustrate the rules of this paragraph (a). Unless otherwise noted, the carryover method is a permissible inventory method.

(i) *Example (1).*—*Carryover method for separate and distinct trades or businesses after the date of distribution or transfer*—(A) *Facts.* X Corporation manufactures radios and television sets. X Corporation uses the first-in, first-out (FIFO) method of inventory identification, the cost method of valuing its inventories, and capitalizes inventory costs in accordance with section 263A. T Corporation manufactures washing machines and dryers. T Corporation uses the last-in, first-out (LIFO) method of inventory identification, the cost method of valuing its inventories, and capitalizes inventory costs under section 263A using methods other than those used by X Corporation. X Corporation acquires the inventory of T Corporation in a transaction to which section 381(a) applies. After the date of distribution or transfer, X Corporation operates its radio and television manufacturing business as a trade or business that is separate and distinct from its washing machines and dryers manufacturing business.

(B) *Conclusion.* Because after the date of distribution or transfer X Corporation operates its manufacturing businesses as separate and distinct trades or businesses, under paragraph (a)(2) of this section X Corporation must use the carryover methods for each continuing trade or business, unless either the carryover methods are impermissible and must be changed under paragraph (a)(4) of this section or X Corporation changes the carryover methods in accordance with paragraph (a)(5) of this section. As defined in paragraph (b)(4) of this section, the carryover methods for the radios and television sets manufacturing business are the FIFO method, the cost basis of valuation, and X Corporation's methods of accounting for section 263A costs immediately prior to the date of distribution or transfer. The carryover methods for the washing machines and dryers manufacturing business are the LIFO method, the cost basis of valuation, and T Corporation's methods of accounting for section 263A costs immediately prior to the date of distribution or transfer. There is no change in method of accounting, and X Corporation need not secure the Commissioner's consent to use any carryover method.

(ii) *Example (2).—Carryover method not permissible—(A) Facts.* X Corporation manufactures food and beverages and uses the FIFO method of inventory identification, the cost method of valuing its inventories, and capitalizes costs in accordance with section 263A. T Corporation sells sporting equipment. T Corporation uses the FIFO method of inventory identification and the cost method of valuing its inventories. T Corporation does not capitalize costs under section 263A because it meets the small business taxpayer exception under section 263A. X Corporation acquires the inventory of T Corporation in a transaction to which section 381(a) applies. After the date of distribution or transfer, X Corporation operates the food and beverages business as a trade or business that is separate and distinct from the sporting equipment business, and X Corporation does not qualify for the small business taxpayer exception under section 263A for its sporting equipment business.

(B) *Conclusion.* Because after the date of distribution or transfer X Corporation operates the food and beverages business as a separate and distinct trade or business, under paragraph (a)(2) of this section X Corporation must use the carryover methods for each continuing trade or business, unless either the carryover methods are impermissible and must be changed under paragraph (a)(4) of this section or X Corporation changes the carryover methods in accordance with paragraph (a)(5) of this section. As defined in paragraph (b)(4) of this section, the carryover methods for the food and beverages business are the FIFO method, the cost basis of valuation, and X Corporation's methods of capitalizing costs under section 263A immediately prior to the date of distribution or transfer. The carryover methods for the sporting equipment business are the FIFO method and the cost basis of valuation. There is no change in method of accounting, and X Corporation need not secure the Commissioner's consent to use any carryover method. However, because X Corporation does not qualify for the small business taxpayer exception under section 263A for its sporting equipment business, X Corporation's method of not capitalizing additional section 263A costs is an impermissible carryover method under paragraph (a)(4) of this section. X Corporation must secure the Commissioner's consent to change to a permissible method of capitalizing costs under section 263A for the sporting equipment business as provided in paragraph (d)(2) of this section.

(b) *Definitions.*—For purposes of this section—

(1) *Inventory method.*—An inventory method is a method of accounting used to account for merchandise on hand (including finished goods, work in process, and raw materials) at the beginning of a year for purposes of computing taxable income for that year. The term includes not only the method for identifying inventory, for example, the FIFO inventory method or the LIFO inventory method, but also all other methods necessary to account for merchandise.

(2) *Adoption of a method of accounting.*—Adoption of a method of accounting has the same meaning as provided in § 1.446-1(e)(1).

(3) *Change in method of accounting.*—A change in method of accounting has the same meaning as provided in § 1.446-1(e)(2).

(4) *Carryover method.*—A carryover method is an inventory method that each party to a section 381(a) transaction uses for each separate and distinct trade or business immediately prior to the date of distribution or transfer.

(5) *Principal method.*—A principal method is an inventory method that is determined under paragraph (c) of this section.

(6) *Permissible method of accounting.*—A permissible method of accounting is a method of accounting that is proper or permitted under the Internal Revenue Code or any applicable Income Tax Regulations.

(7) *Acquiring corporation.*—An acquiring corporation has the same meaning as provided in § 1.381(a)-1(b)(2).

(8) *Distributor corporation.*—A distributor corporation means the corporation, foreign or domestic, that distributes its assets to another corporation described in section 332(b) in a distribution to which section 332 (relating to liquidations of subsidiaries) applies.

(9) *Transferor corporation.*—A transferor corporation means the corporation, foreign or domestic, that transfers its assets to another corporation in a transfer to which section 361 (relating to nonrecognition of gain or loss to corporations) applies, but only if—

(i) The transfer is in connection with a reorganization described in section 368(a)(1)(A), (a)(1)(C), or (a)(1)(F), or

(ii) The transfer is in connection with a reorganization described in section 368(a)(1)(D) or (a)(1)(G), provided the requirements of section 354(b) are met.

(10) *Parties to the section 381(a) transaction.*—Parties to the section 381(a) transaction means the acquiring corporation and the distributor or transferor corporation that participate in a transaction to which section 381(a) applies.

(11) *Date of distribution or transfer.*—The date of distribution or transfer has the same meaning as provided in section 381(b)(2) and § 1.381(b)-1(b).

(12) *Separate and distinct trades or businesses.*—Separate and distinct trades or businesses has the same meaning as provided in § 1.446-1(d).

(13) *Audit protection.*—Audit protection means, for purposes of paragraph (d)(1) of this section, that the IRS will not require an acquiring corporation that is required to change a method of accounting under paragraph (a)(3) of this section to change that method for a taxable year ending prior to the taxable year that includes the date of distribution or transfer.

(14) *Section 481(a) adjustment.*—The section 481(a) adjustment means an adjustment that must be taken into account as required under section 481(a) to prevent amounts from being duplicated or omitted when the taxable income of an acquiring corporation is computed under a method of accounting different from the method used to compute taxable income for the preceding taxable year.

(15) *Cut-off basis.*—A cut-off basis means a manner in which a change in method of accounting is made without a section 481(a) adjustment and under which only the items arising after the beginning of the year of change (or, in the case of a change made under paragraph (d)(1) of this section, after the date of distribution or transfer) are accounted for under the new method of accounting. When it implements the change on a cut-off basis, a taxpayer using the LIFO inventory method to identify its inventory goods that makes a change in method of accounting within the LIFO inventory method from one LIFO method or sub-method to another LIFO method or sub-method uses the new LIFO inventory method to determine its current-year cost and base-year cost of ending inventories for the year of change, but does not recompute the cost of beginning inventories for the year of change using the new LIFO inventory method.

(16) *Adjustment period.*—The adjustment period means the number of taxable years for taking into account the section 481(a) adjustment required as a result of a change in method of accounting.

(17) *Component trade or business.*—A component trade or business is a trade or business of a party to the section 381(a) transaction that will be combined and integrated with a trade or business of the other party to the section 381 transaction. See paragraph (e)(7)(ii) of this section for the determination of whether a trade or business is operated as a separate and distinct trade or business after the date of distribution or transfer.

(c) *Principal method.*—(1) *In general.*—For each integrated trade or business, the principal method for a particular type of goods is generally the inventory method used by the component trade or business of the acquiring corporation immediately prior to the date of distribution or transfer for that type of goods. If, however, on the date of distribution or transfer the component trade or business of the distributor or transferor corporation holds more inventory of a type of goods than the component trade or business of the acquiring corporation, the principal method for such goods is the inventory method used by the component trade or business of the distributor or transferor corporation immediately prior to that date. For each integrated trade or business, the component trade or business of the distributor or transferor corporation holds more inventory if, for a particular type of goods, the aggregate of the fair market value of goods held by each component trade or business of the distributor or transferor corporation exceeds the aggregate of the fair market value of the goods held by each component trade or business of the acquiring corporation immediately prior to the date of distribution or transfer. Alternatively, as a simplifying convention, the acquiring corporation may elect to apply the preceding sentence to the aggregate fair market value of the entire inventories, held by each component trade or business of the acquiring corporation and each component trade or business of the distributor or transferor corporation, that will be integrated after the date of distribution or transfer. If the component trade or business with the larger aggregate fair market value of the entire inventories does not have an inventory method for a particular type of goods immediately prior to the date of distribution or transfer, the principal method for that type of goods is the inventory method used by the component trade or business that does have an inventory method for that type of goods.

(2) *Multiple component trades or businesses with different principal methods.*—If a party to the section 381(a) transaction has multiple component trades or businesses and more than one principal inventory method for a particular type of goods, then the acquiring corporation may choose which of the inventory methods used by such component trades or businesses will be the principal method of the integrated trade or business. The acquiring corporation must choose a principal method that is a permissible method of accounting. In general, a change to a principal method in a transaction to which section 381(a) and paragraph (a)(3) of this section apply is made under paragraph (d)(1) of this section.

(3) *Examples.*—The following examples illustrate the rules of this paragraph (c). Unless otherwise noted, the principal method is a permissible inventory method.

Example (1). Principal methods are the methods used by the acquiring corporation—(i) *Facts.* X Corporation and T Corporation each manufacture tennis equipment. X Corporation's manufacturing business uses the FIFO method of inventory identification, the cost method of valuing inventories, and allocates indirect costs to the property produced using the burden rate method provided in § 1.263A-1(f)(3)(i). T Corporation's manufacturing business uses the LIFO method of inventory identification, the cost method of valuing its inventories, and allocates indirect costs to the property it produces using the standard cost method provided in § 1.263A-1(f)(3)(ii). X Corporation acquires the inventory of T Corporation in a transaction to which section 381(a) applies. The fair market value of each particular type of goods held by X Corporation's manufacturing business immediately prior to the date of distribution or transfer exceeds the fair market value of each particular type of goods held by T Corporation's manufacturing business on that date. After the date of distribution or transfer, X Corporation will not operate its manufacturing business as a trade or business that is separate and distinct from T Corporation's manufacturing business.

(ii) *Conclusion.* Because after the date of distribution or transfer X Corporation will not operate its manufacturing business as a separate and distinct trade or business, X Corporation must use the principal methods under paragraph (a)(3) of this section, unless either the principal methods are impermissible and must be changed under paragraph (a)(4) of this section or X Corporation changes the principal methods in accordance with paragraph (a)(5) of this section. The fair market value of each particular type of goods held by T Corporation's manufacturing business immediately prior to the date of distribution or transfer does not exceed the fair market value of each particular type of goods held by X Corporation's manufacturing business on that date. Because on the date of distribution or transfer T Corporation's manufacturing business does not hold more inventory than X Corporation's manufacturing business, the principal methods are the FIFO method of inventory identification, the cost method of valuation, and X Corporation's method of allocating indirect costs under section 263A using the burden rate method. X Corporation need not secure the Commissioner's consent to use these methods. However, in accordance with paragraph (d)(1) of this section, X Corporation must change the inventory methods for the manufacturing business acquired from T Corporation to the principal methods.

Example (2). Principal methods are the methods used by the acquiring corporation—(i) *Facts.* The facts are the same as in *Example* (1), except that the fair market value of each particular type of goods held by X Corporation's manufacturing business immediately prior to the date of distribution or transfer is identical to the fair market value of each particular type of goods held by T Corporation's manufacturing business on that date.

(ii) *Conclusion.* The result is the same as in *Example* (1). The principal methods are the FIFO method of inventory identification,

the cost method of valuation, and X Corporation's method of allocating indirect costs under section 263A using the burden rate method. X Corporation need not secure the Commissioner's consent to use the principal methods. However, in accordance with paragraph (d)(1) of this section, X Corporation must change the inventory methods for the manufacturing business acquired from T Corporation to the principal methods.

Example (3). Principal methods are the methods used by the distributor or transferor corporation—(i) *Facts.* The facts are the same as in *Example* (1), except that the fair market value of each particular type of goods held by T Corporation's manufacturing business immediately prior to the date of distribution or transfer exceeds the fair market value of each particular type of goods held by X Corporation's manufacturing business on that date.

(ii) *Conclusion.* Because after the date of distribution or transfer X Corporation will not operate its manufacturing business as a separate and distinct trade or business, X Corporation must use the principal methods under paragraph (a)(3) of this section, unless either the principal methods are impermissible and must be changed under paragraph (a)(4) of this section or X Corporation changes the principal methods in accordance with paragraph (a)(5) of this section. The fair market value of each particular type of goods held by T Corporation's manufacturing business immediately prior to the date of distribution or transfer exceeds the fair market value of each particular type of goods held by X Corporation's manufacturing business on that date. Because on the date of distribution or transfer T Corporation's manufacturing business holds more inventory than X Corporation's manufacturing business, the principal methods are the LIFO method of inventory identification, the cost method of valuation, and T Corporation's method of allocating indirect costs under section 263A using the standard cost method. X Corporation need not secure the Commissioner's consent to use the principal methods. However, in accordance with paragraph (d)(1) of this section, X Corporation must change the inventory methods for the manufacturing business operated by X Corporation prior to the date of distribution or transfer to the principal methods.

Example (4). Voluntary change allowable—(i) *Facts.* The facts are the same as in *Example* (1), except that T Corporation wants to discontinue using the LIFO method for its manufacturing business and change to the FIFO method for the taxable year in which the section 381(a) transaction occurs or is expected to occur.

(ii) *Conclusion.* Under paragraph (a)(5) of this section, the Commissioner will grant a request to change a method of accounting for the taxable year that includes the date of distribution or transfer only if the requested method is the method that the acquiring corporation must use after the date of distribution or transfer. The Commissioner will consent to a request by T Corporation to change to the FIFO method for the taxable year in which the section 381(a) transaction occurs or is expected to occur because X Corporation will use this method after the date of distribution or transfer.

Example (5). Principal method determination when larger component trade or business does not have a method of accounting for a particular type of goods—(i) *Facts.* The facts are the same as in *Example* (1), except that T Corporation's manufacturing business has a particular type of goods that is not held by X Corporation's manufacturing business.

(ii) *Conclusion.* The result is similar to *Example* (1). In general, the principal methods are the FIFO method of inventory identification, the cost method of valuation, and X Corporation's method of allocating indirect costs to the property produced using the burden rate method. X Corporation need not secure the Commissioner's consent to use the principal methods. However, in accordance with paragraph (d)(1) of this section, X Corporation must change the inventory methods for the manufacturing business acquired from T Corporation to the principal methods. Under paragraph (c) of this section, the principal methods for the particular type of goods held only by T Corporation's manufacturing business are the LIFO method of inventory identification, the cost method of valuation, and T Corporation's method of allocating indirect costs to the property it produces using the standard cost method. X Corporation must determine whether the principal methods for the type of goods previously held by T Corporation are permissible given that such methods are different than the principal methods that must be used by X for all other goods. If X Corporation's use of the standard cost method would be impermissible after the date of distribution or transfer, X Corporation must change to a permissible method under section 263A for those goods in accordance with paragraph (a)(4) of this section.

Example (6). Inventory convention elected—(i) *Facts.* X Corporation manufactures planes and T Corporation manufactures planes and communications satellites. X Corporation's manufacturing business uses the FIFO method of inventory identification and values its inventories at cost or market, whichever is lower, while T Corporation's manufacturing business uses the LIFO method of inventory identification and values its inventories at cost. X Corporation's manufacturing business and T Corporation's manufacturing business use the same methods to capitalize costs under section 263A. X Corporation acquires the inventory of T Corporation in a transaction to which section 381(a) applies. In lieu of determining the fair market value of each particular type of goods held on the date of distribution or transfer, X Corporation elects to value the entire inventories of its manufacturing business and the entire inventories of T Corporation's manufacturing business in accordance with paragraph (c)(1) of this section. The fair market value of the inventory held by T Corporation's manufacturing business immediately prior to the date of distribution or transfer does not exceed the fair market value of the inventory held by X Corporation's manufacturing business on that date. After the date of distribution or transfer, X Corporation will not operate its manufacturing business as a trade or business that is separate and distinct from T Corporation's manufacturing business.

(ii) *Conclusion.* Because after the date of distribution or transfer X Corporation will not operate its manufacturing business as a separate and distinct trade or business, X Corporation must use the principal methods under paragraph (a)(3) of this section, unless either the principal methods are impermissible and must be changed under paragraph (a)(4) of this section or X Corporation changes the principal methods in accordance with paragraph (a)(5) of this section. The fair market value of the entire inventory held by T Corporation's manufacturing business immediately prior to the date of distribution or transfer does not exceed the fair market value of the entire inventory of X Corporation's manufacturing business on that date. Because on the date of distribution or transfer T Corporation's manufacturing business does not hold more inventory than X Corporation's manufacturing business, the principal methods are the FIFO method, the cost or market, whichever is lower, method of valuation, and X Corporation's method of capitalizing costs under section 263A on the date of distribution or transfer. X Corporation need not secure the Commissioner's consent to use the principal methods. However, in accordance with paragraph (d)(1) of this section, X Corporation must change the inventory methods for the manufacturing business acquired from T Corporation to the principal methods.

Example (7). *Principal method determination with a combined trade or business and a separate and distinct trade or business*—(i) *Facts.* X Corporation manufactures tennis equipment in a trade or business that is separate and distinct from its trade or business of manufacturing golf equipment. X Corporation uses the FIFO method of inventory identification for its tennis equipment and the LIFO method of inventory identification for its golf equipment. X Corporation values the goods in both inventories at cost and allocates indirect costs to the property produced using the burden rate method provided in §1.263A-1(f)(3)(i). T Corporation manufactures tennis equipment. T Corporation's manufacturing business uses the FIFO method of inventory identification, values inventories at cost, and allocates indirect costs to the property it produces using the standard cost method provided in §1.263A-1(f)(3)(ii). X Corporation acquires the inventory of T Corporation in a transaction to which section 381(a) applies. Immediately prior to the date of distribution or transfer, the fair market value of T Corporation's inventories in the tennis equipment manufacturing business exceeds the fair market value of the inventories held by X Corporation's tennis equipment manufacturing business. After the date of distribution or transfer, X Corporation will not operate its tennis equipment manufacturing business as a trade or business that is separate and distinct from T Corporation's tennis equipment manufacturing business, but X Corporation will operate its golf equipment manufacturing business as a trade or business that is separate and distinct from the tennis equipment manufacturing business.

(ii) *Conclusion.* Because after the date of distribution or transfer X Corporation will not operate its tennis equipment manufacturing business as a separate and distinct trade or business, X Corporation must use the principal methods under paragraph (a)(3) of this section, unless either the principal methods are impermissible and must be changed under paragraph (a)(4) of this section or X Corporation changes the principal methods in accordance with paragraph (a)(5) of this section. Under paragraph (c)(1) of this section, X Corporation elects to compare the fair market values of the entire inventories of the component trades or businesses on the date of distribution or transfer to determine whether T Corporation holds more inventory than X Corporation. The fair market value of the inventory held by T Corporation's tennis equipment manufacturing business exceeds the fair market value of the tennis equipment held by X Corporation's tennis equipment manufacturing business. Because on the date of distribution or transfer T Corporation's tennis equipment manufacturing business holds more inventory than X Corporation's tennis equipment manufacturing business, the principal methods for the combined tennis equipment business are the FIFO method of inventory identification, the cost basis of valuation, and T Corporation's methods of allocating indirect costs under section 263A using the standard cost method provided in §1.263A-1(f)(3)(ii). X Corporation need not secure the Commissioner's consent to use the principal

methods. However, in accordance with paragraph (d)(1) of this section, X Corporation must change the methods of accounting for its tennis equipment manufacturing business to the principal methods. Under paragraph (a)(2) of this section, because X Corporation will operate the golf equipment manufacturing business as a separate trade or business, for the inventories held by the golf equipment manufacturing business X Corporation must continue to use the LIFO method of inventory identification, use the cost basis of valuation, and allocate indirect costs under section 263A using the burden rate method provided in §1.263A-1(f)(3)(i). There are no changes in method of accounting for the golf manufacturing business, and X Corporation need not secure the Commissioner's consent to use these carryover methods.

Example (8). *Principal method determination with multiple component trades or businesses*—(i) *Facts.* The facts are the same as in *Example* (7), except that after the date of distribution or transfer X Corporation will not operate the golf equipment manufacturing business as a trade or business that is separate and distinct from the tennis equipment manufacturing business. In addition, the fair market value of the inventories of X Corporation's tennis equipment manufacturing business and golf equipment manufacturing business, in the aggregate, exceed the fair market value of the inventories of T Corporation's tennis equipment manufacturing business.

(ii) *Conclusion.* Because on the date of distribution or transfer T Corporation's tennis equipment manufacturing business does not hold more inventory than X Corporation's tennis equipment manufacturing business and golf equipment manufacturing business, in the aggregate, the principal method for identifying inventory is the method used by X Corporation's component trade or business on the date of distribution or transfer. However, because on the date of distribution or transfer X Corporation operates two separate and distinct trades or businesses with different inventory identification methods that will be combined after the date of distribution or transfer, X Corporation may choose under paragraph (c)(2) of this section which method used by its component trades or businesses will be the principal method. After the date of distribution or transfer, X Corporation may use either the FIFO method of inventory identification used by the tennis equipment manufacturing business or the LIFO method of inventory identification used by the golf equipment manufacturing business as the principal method of identification, if either method is a permissible method. For the integrated trade or business, X Corporation will use the cost method of valuation and allocate indirect costs under section 263A using the burden rate method provided in §1.263A-1(f)(3)(i). In accordance with paragraph (d)(1) of this section, X Corporation must change the inventory methods of T Corporation's manufacturing business to the principal methods. Under paragraph (a)(3) of this section, X Corporation also must change either its golf equipment manufacturing business or its tennis equipment manufacturing business, depending on which principal method X Corporation selects, to the principal method.

(d) *Procedures for changing a method of accounting.*—(1) *Change made to principal method under paragraph (a)(3) of this section.*—(i) *Section 481(a) adjustment.*—(A) *In general.*—An acquiring corporation that changes its method of accounting or the distributor or transferor corporation's method of accounting under paragraph (a)(3) of this section does not need to secure the Commissioner's consent to use a principal method. To the extent the use of a principal method constitutes a change in method of accounting, the change in method is treated as a change initiated by the acquiring corporation for purposes of section 481(a)(2). Any change to a principal method, whether the change relates to a trade or business of the acquiring corporation or a trade or business of the distributor or transferor corporation, must be reflected on the acquiring corporation's federal income tax return for the taxable year that includes the date of distribution or transfer. The amount of the section 481(a) adjustment and the adjustment period, if any, necessary to implement a change to the principal method are determined under §1.446-1(e) and the applicable administrative procedures that govern voluntary changes in methods of accounting under section 446(e). If the Internal Revenue Code, the Income Tax Regulations, or administrative procedures require that a method of accounting be implemented on a cut-off basis, the acquiring corporation must implement the change, on a cut-off basis as of the date of distribution or transfer, on its federal income tax return for the taxable year that includes the date of distribution or transfer. If the Internal Revenue Code, the Income Tax Regulations, or administrative procedures require a section 481(a) adjustment, the acquiring corporation must determine the section 481(a) adjustment and include the appropriate amount of the section 481(a) adjustment on its federal income tax return for the taxable year that includes the date of distribution or transfer and subsequent taxable year(s), as necessary. This adjustment is determined by the acquiring corporation as of the beginning of the day that is immediately after the date of distribution or transfer.

(B) *Example.*—The following example illustrates the rules of this paragraph (d)(1)(i):

Example. X Corporation uses the FIFO method of inventory identification, and T Corporation uses the LIFO method of inventory identification. X Corporation acquires the inventory of T Corporation in a transaction to which section 381(a) applies. X Corporation determines that under the rules of paragraph (c)(1) of this section, X Corporation must change the inventory method for the business acquired from T Corporation to the FIFO method. X Corporation will determine the section 481(a) adjustment pertaining to the change to the FIFO method (whether the amounts thereof represent increases or decreases in income) as of the beginning of the day that immediately follows the day on which X Corporation acquires the inventory of T Corporation. X Corporation will reflect this adjustment, or an appropriate part thereof, on its federal income tax return for the taxable year that includes the date of distribution or transfer.

(ii) *Audit protection.*—Notwithstanding any other provision in any other Income Tax Regulation or administrative procedure, no audit protection is provided for any change in method of accounting under paragraph (d)(1) of this section.

(iii) *Other terms and conditions.*—Except as otherwise provided in this section, other terms and conditions provided in §1.446-1(e) and the applicable administrative procedures for voluntary changes in method of accounting under section 446(e) apply to a change in method of accounting under this section. Thus, for example, if the administrative procedures for a particular change in method of accounting have a term and condition that provides for the acceleration of the section 481(a) adjustment period, this term and condition applies to a change made under this paragraph (d)(1). However, any scope limitation in the applicable administrative procedures will not apply for purposes of making a change under this paragraph (d)(1). For example, if the administrative procedures provide as a limitation that an identical change in method of accounting is barred for a period of years, this limitation will not bar a change to the principal method made under this section.

(2) *Change made to a method of accounting under paragraph (a)(4) or (a)(5) of this section.*—(i) *In general.*—A party to a section 381(a) transaction that changes a method of accounting under either paragraph (a)(4) or paragraph (a)(5) of this section must follow the provisions of §1.446-(1)(e) and the applicable administrative procedures, including scope limitations, for voluntary changes in method of accounting under section 446(e), except as provided in paragraphs (d)(2)(ii) and (d)(2)(iii) of this section. An application on Form 3115, "Application for Change in Accounting Method," filed with the IRS to change a method of accounting under this paragraph (d)(2) should be labeled "Filed under section 381(c)(5)" at the top.

(ii) *Final year limitation.*—Any scope limitation relating to the final year of a trade or business will not apply to a taxpayer that changes its method of accounting in the final year of a trade or business that is terminated as the result of a section 381(a) transaction.

(iii) *Time to file.*—Under the authority of §1.446-1(e)(3)(ii), for a change in method of accounting requiring advance consent, the application for a change in method of accounting (for example, Form 3115), must be filed with the IRS on or before the later of—

(A) The due date for filing a Form 3115 as specified in §1.446-1(e), for example, the last day of the taxable year in which the distribution or transfer occurred, or

(B) The earlier of—

(1) The day that is 180 days after the date of distribution or transfer, or

(2) The day on which the acquiring corporation files its federal income tax return for the taxable year in which the distribution or transfer occurred.

(e) *Rules and procedures.*—(1) *Inventory method selected for a particular type of goods.*—If other sections of the Internal Revenue Code or Income Tax Regulations allow a taxpayer to elect an inventory method for a particular type of goods, the method elected with respect to those goods is the established inventory method only for those goods. For example, an election to use the LIFO inventory method to identify specified goods in inventory, such as certain products in finished goods, is the inventory method only for those products.

(2) *No method of accounting.*—If a party to a section 381(a) transaction is not using an inventory method, does not have an inventory method for a particular type of goods, or came into existence as a result of the transaction, the party will not be treated as having an inventory method different from that used by another party to the section 381(a) transaction.

(3) *Elections and adoptions allowed.*—If an election does not require the Commissioner's consent, an acquiring corporation or a distributor or transferor corporation is not precluded from making any election that is otherwise permissible for the taxable year that includes the date of distribution or transfer. For example, an acquiring corporation may elect to identify its inventory using the LIFO inventory method in the year of the distribution or transfer. For purposes of this section, a corporation shall be deemed as having made any election as of the first day of the taxable year that includes the date of distribution or transfer. Similarly, where adoption is permissible, an acquiring corporation or a distributor or transferor corporation may adopt any permissible method of accounting for the taxable year that includes the date of distribution or transfer.

(4) *Elections continue after section 381(a) transaction.*—(i) *General rule.*—An acquiring corporation is not required to renew any election not requiring renewal and previously made by it or by a distributor or transferor corporation for a carryover method or a principal method if the acquiring corporation uses the method after the section 381(a) transaction. If the acquiring corporation uses a method after the date of distribution or transfer, an election made by the acquiring corporation or by a distributor or transferor corporation for that method that was in effect on the date of distribution or transfer continues after the section 381(a) transaction as though the distribution or transfer had not occurred.

(ii) *Example.*—The following example illustrates the rules of paragraph (e)(4):

Example. Since its incorporation in 1982, X Corporation elected to use the LIFO inventory method under section 472 to identify its inventory of tennis balls. Since its incorporation in 2002, T Corporation elected to use the FIFO inventory method to identify its inventory of tennis balls. X Corporation acquires the assets of T Corporation in a transaction to which section 381(a) applies. Immediately prior to the date of distribution or transfer, the fair market value of X Corporation's inventory in its tennis balls exceeds the fair market value of the tennis balls inventory held by T Corporation. After the date of distribution or transfer, X Corporation will not operate its business as a trade or business that is separate and distinct from T Corporation's business. Because on the date of distribution or transfer T Corporation does not hold more inventory than X Corporation, the principal method for identifying inventory is the method used by X Corporation on the date of distribution or transfer. After the date of distribution or transfer, X Corporation need not renew its election to identify inventory using the LIFO inventory method, and X Corporation is bound by the election.

(5) *Adopting the LIFO inventory method.*—A party to a section 381(a) transaction will be deemed to be using the LIFO inventory method for a particular type of goods on the date of distribution or transfer if that party elects under section 472 to adopt that inventory method with respect to those goods for its taxable year within which the date of distribution or transfer occurs. See section 472 for the requirements to adopt the LIFO inventory method.

(6) *Inventory layers treatment.*—(i) *Adjustments required after a section 381(a) transaction.*—An acquiring corporation that determines the principal method of taking an inventory after a section 381(a) transaction under paragraphs (a)(3) and (c) of this section after the date of distribution or transfer may need to integrate inventories and make appropriate adjustments as provided in paragraphs (e)(6)(ii) and (e)(6)(iii) of this section.

(ii) *LIFO inventory method used after the section 381(a) transaction.*—(A) *LIFO inventory method used by the acquiring corporation and the distributor or transferor corporation.*—(1) *Principal method is the dollar-value LIFO method.*—If, under paragraphs (a)(3) and (c) of this section, the acquiring corporation changes its inventory method or the inventory method of the distributor or transferor corporation from the specific goods LIFO method of pricing inventories to the dollar-value LIFO method of pricing inventories (dollar-value LIFO method) for a particular type of goods, the inventory accounted for under the specific goods method shall be placed on the dollar-value method as provided in §1.472-8(f), and then the inventory shall be integrated with the inventory previously accounted for under the dollar-value LIFO method. If pools of each corporation are permitted or required to be combined, the pools must be combined as provided in §1.472-8(g)(2). For purposes of combining pools, all base year inventories or layers of increment that occur in taxable years including the same December 31 shall be combined. A base year inventory or layer of increment occurring in any short taxable year of a distributor or transferor corporation shall be merged with and considered a layer of increment of its immediately preceding taxable year.

(2) *Principal method is the specific goods LIFO method.*—If, under paragraphs (a)(3) and (c) of this section, the acquiring corporation changes its inventory method or the inventory method of the

distributor or transferor corporation from the dollar-value LIFO method of pricing inventories to the specific goods LIFO method of pricing inventories, the acquiring corporation shall treat the inventory being changed to the specific goods LIFO method as having the same acquisition dates and costs as such inventory had under the dollar-value LIFO method.

(B) *Change from the FIFO inventory method to either the specific goods LIFO method or the dollar-value LIFO method.*—If, under paragraphs (a)(3) and (c) of this section, the acquiring corporation changes its inventory method or the inventory method of the distributor or transferor corporation from the FIFO inventory method to either the specific goods LIFO method or the dollar-value method of pricing LIFO inventories, the inventory accounted for under the FIFO inventory method shall be treated by the acquiring corporation as having been acquired at their average unit cost in a single transaction on the date of the distribution or transfer. Thus, if an inventory of a particular type of goods is combined in an existing dollar-value pool, the goods shall be treated as if they were purchased by the acquiring corporation at the average unit cost on the date of the distribution or transfer with respect to such pool. Alternatively, if the goods are not combined in an existing pool, the goods will be treated as if they were purchased by the acquiring corporation at the average unit cost on the date of the distribution or transfer with respect to a new pool, with the base-year being the year of the section 381(a) transaction. Adjustments resulting from a restoration to cost of any write-down to market value of the inventories shall be taken into account by the acquiring corporation ratably in each of the three taxable years beginning with the taxable year that includes the date of the distribution or transfer. See section 472(d).

(iii) *FIFO inventory method used after the section 381(a) transaction.*—(A) *FIFO inventory method used by the acquiring corporation and the distributor or transferor corporation.*—If, under paragraphs (a)(3) and (c) of this section, the FIFO inventory method is the principal method and the component trades or businesses of both the acquiring corporation and the distributor or transferor corporation use the FIFO method immediately prior to the distribution or transfer, the acquiring corporation must treat the inventory that must change to the principal method as having the same acquisition dates and costs as such inventory had immediately prior to the date of distribution or transfer. However, if the principal method of valuing inventories is the cost or market, whichever is lower, method, the acquiring corporation must treat the inventories that must change to the principal method as having been acquired at cost or market, whichever is lower.

(B) *Change from either the specific goods LIFO method or the dollar-value LIFO method to the FIFO inventory method.*—If, under paragraphs (a)(3) and (c) of this section, the acquiring corporation changes its inventory method or the inventory method of the distributor or transferor corporation from either the specific goods LIFO method or the dollar-value LIFO method to the FIFO inventory method, the acquiring corporation must treat the inventory accounted for under the LIFO method as having the same acquisition dates and costs that the inventory would have had if the FIFO inventory method had been used on the date of distribution or transfer. However, if the principal method of valuing inventories is the cost or market, whichever is lower, method, the acquiring corporation must treat the inventories accounted for under the LIFO method as having been acquired at cost or market, whichever is lower.

(7) *Appropriate times for certain determinations.*—(i) *Determining the inventory method.*—The inventory method used by a party to a section 381(a) transaction on the date of distribution or transfer is the method used by that party as of the end of the day that is immediately prior to the date of distribution or transfer.

(ii) *Determining whether there are separate and distinct trades or businesses after the date of distribution or transfer.*—Whether an acquiring corporation will operate the trades or businesses of the parties to a section 381(a) transaction as separate and distinct trades or businesses after the date of distribution or transfer will be determined as of the date of distribution or transfer based upon the facts and circumstances. Intent to combine books and records of the trades or businesses may be demonstrated by contemporaneous records and documents or by other objective evidence that reflects the acquiring corporation's ultimate plan of operation, even though the actual combination of the books and records may extend beyond the end of the taxable year that includes the date of distribution or transfer.

(8) *Establishing an inventory method.*—An inventory method used by the distributor or transferor corporation immediately prior to the date of distribution or transfer that continues to be used by the acquiring corporation after the date of distribution or transfer is an established method of accounting for purposes of section 446(e),

whether or not such method is proper or is permitted under the Internal Revenue Code or any applicable Income Tax Regulations.

(9) *Other applicable provisions.*—This section does not preempt any other provision of the Internal Revenue Code or the Income Tax Regulations that is applicable to the acquiring corporation's circumstances. Section 381(c)(5) and this § 1.381(c)(5)-1 determine only the inventory method to be used after a section 381(a) transaction. If other paragraphs of section 381(c) apply for purposes of determining the methods of accounting to be used following the date of distribution or transfer, section 381(c)(5) and this § 1.381(c)(5)-1 will not apply to the tax treatment of the items. Specifically, section 381(c)(5) and this § 1.381(c)(5)-1 do not apply to assets other than inventory that an acquiring corporation obtains in a transaction to which section 381(a) applies.

(10) *Use of the cash receipts and disbursements method of accounting.*—If immediately prior to the date of distribution or transfer, an acquiring corporation or a distributor or transferor corporation uses the cash receipts and disbursements method of accounting within the meaning of section 446(c)(1) and § 1.446-1(c)(1)(i), or is not required to use an inventory method for its goods, section 381(c)(5) and § 1.381(c)(5)-1 do not apply. Instead, section 381(c)(4) and § 1.381(c)(4)-1 must be applied to determine the methods of accounting that continue after the transaction.

(11) *Character of items of income and deduction.*—After the date of distribution or transfer, items of income and deduction have the same character in the hands of the acquiring corporation as they would have had in the hands of the distributor or transferor corporation if no distribution or transfer had occurred.

(12) *Impermissible inventory method.*—This section does not limit the Commissioner's ability under section 446(b) to determine whether a taxpayer's inventory method is an impermissible method or otherwise fails to clearly reflect income. For example, an acquiring corporation may not use the method of accounting determined under paragraph (a)(2) of this section if the method fails to clearly reflect the acquiring corporation's income within the meaning of section 446(b).

(f) *Effective/applicability date.*—This section applies to corporate reorganizations and tax-free liquidations described in section 381(a) that occur on or after August 31, 2011. The designations of paragraphs (a)(6)(ii)(A) and (B) of this section and removal of the term "small reseller" and replacement with the term "small business taxpayer" apply to taxable years beginning on or after January 5, 2021. [Reg. § 1.381(c)(5)-1.]

☐ [*T.D. 7344, 1-14-75. Amended by T.D. 9534, 7-29-2011 (corrected 8-29-2011) and T.D. 9942, 12-31-2020.*]

[**Reg. § 1.381(c)(6)-1**]

§ 1.381(c)(6)-1. Depreciation method.—(a) *Carryover requirement.*—(1) *Distributions in taxable years ending before July 25, 1969.*—(i) Section 381(c)(6) provides that if, in a transaction in a taxable year which ends before July 25, 1969, to which section 381(a) applies, an acquiring corporation acquires depreciable property from a distributor or transferor corporation which computes its allowance for the depreciation of the property under section 167(b)(2), (3), or (4), the acquiring corporation shall compute its depreciation allowance by the same method used by the distributor or transferor corporation with respect to such property. Thus, if the distributor or transferor corporation used the sum of the years-digits method under section 167(b)(3) with respect to an asset distributed or transferred to an acquiring corporation, the acquiring corporation will be required to use the sum of the years-digits method with respect to such asset acquired. The computation of the depreciation allowance with respect to the property acquired shall be made under the provisions of section 167 and the regulations thereunder.

(ii) The rules provided in section 381(c)(6) and subdivision (i) of this subparagraph will apply only with respect to that part or all of the basis of the property in the hands of the acquiring corporation immediately after the date of distribution or transfer as does not exceed the basis of the property in the hands of the distributor or transferor corporation on the date of the distribution or transfer. For this purpose, the basis of the property in the hands of the distributor or transferor corporation shall be the adjusted basis provided in section 1011 for the purpose of determining gain on the sale or other disposition of such property. For provisions defining the date of distribution or transfer see § 1.381-1(b).

(2) *Distributions in taxable years ending after July 24, 1969.*—(i) Section 381(c)(6) provides that if, in a transaction in a taxable year ending after July 24, 1969, to which section 381(a) applies, an acquiring corporation acquires depreciable property from a distributor or transferor corporation which computes its allowances for the depre-

ciation of the property under subsection (b), (j) or (k) of section 167, the acquiring corporation shall compute its depreciation allowance by the same method used by the distributor or transferor corporation with respect to such property. Thus, if the distributor or transferor corporation used the straight line method under section 167(b)(1) with respect to an asset distributed or transferred to an acquiring corporation, the acquiring corporation will be required to use the straight line method with respect to such asset. Similarly, if the distributor or transferor corporation elected to compute depreciation under section 167(k) with respect to property attributable to rehabilitation expenditures, and such property is transferred to an acquiring corporation, the acquiring corporation will be required to compute depreciation under section 167(k) with respect to the property acquired. The computation of the depreciation allowance with respect to the property acquired shall be made under the provisions of section 167 and the regulations thereunder.

(ii) The rules provided in section 381(c)(6) and subdivision (i) of this subparagraph shall apply only with respect to that part or all of the basis of the property in the hands of the acquiring corporation immediately after the date of distribution or transfer as does not exceed the basis of the property in the hands of the distributor or transferor corporation on the date of the distribution or transfer. For this purpose, the basis of the property in the hands of the distributor or transferor corporation shall be the adjusted basis provided in section 1011 for the purpose of determining gain on the sale or other disposition of such property. For provisions defining the date of distribution or transfer see § 1.381(b)-1(b).

(b) *Portion in excess of distributor or transferor corporation's basis.*— (1) *General rule.*—With respect to that part of the basis of the depreciable property (other than certain section 1250 property described in subparagraph (2) of this paragraph) which in the hands of the acquiring corporation exceeds the adjusted basis to the distributor or transferor corporation, the acquiring corporation may use any reasonable method of computing depreciation, other than the methods provided in section 167(b)(2), (3), or (4). See paragraph (b) of § 1.167(b)-0 for methods which are acceptable under section 167(a) with respect to such property. See also sections 334(b)(1) and 362(b) for the determination of basis of property in the hands of the acquiring corporation in connection with a transaction to which section 381(a) applies.

(2) *Section 1250 property.*—With respect to that part of the basis of section 1250 property acquired after July 24, 1969, which in the hands of the acquiring corporation exceeds the adjusted basis to the distributor or transferor corporation, the acquiring corporation shall be subject to the limitations contained in section 167(j)(4) (relating to used section 1250 property) or 167(j)(5) (relating to used residential rental property). Thus, for example, if section 1250 property which is not residential rental property is acquired in a section 381(a) transaction after July 24, 1969, the straight line method of depreciation (or other method allowable under section 167(j)(4)(B)) is the only acceptable method with respect to that portion of the basis of the property which, in the hands of the acquiring corporation, exceeds the adjusted basis to the transferor or distributor corporation.

(c) *Records required.*—Records shall be maintained in sufficient detail to identify any depreciable property to which this section applies, and to establish the basis thereof.

(d) *Agreement under section 167(d).*—To the extent not inconsistent with paragraph (b) of this section, an acquiring corporation shall be treated as the distributor or transferor corporation in the case of an agreement between the distributor or transferor corporation and the district director under section 167(d) and § 1.167(d)-1 with respect to property to which section 381(c)(6) and this section apply. Thus, in the case where the basis of an asset in the hands of an acquiring corporation exceeds the basis of such asset in the hands of the distributor or transferor corporation, such an agreement will not have the effect of permitting the acquiring corporation to compute its depreciation allowance with respect to such excess basis under the methods provided in section 167(b)(2), (3), or (4). However, the provisions of the agreement will continue to apply with respect to the useful life of the asset.

(e) *Change of method of depreciation.*—Although the acquiring corporation is required to use the method of computing depreciation used by the distributor or transferor with respect to depreciable property to which this section applies, such acquiring corporation may use another method with respect to such property if consent of the Commissioner is obtained in accordance with paragraph (e) of § 1.446-1. Further, subject to the provisions of paragraph (b) of § 1.167(e)-1 the acquiring corporation may change from the declining balance method described in section 167(b)(2) to the straight line method without consent of the Commissioner.

(f) *Successive transactions to which section 381(a) applies.*—The provisions of this section shall apply in the case of successive transactions to which section 381(a) applies. Thus, for example, if X Corporation, a transferor corporation, used the sum of the years-digits method under section 167(b)(3) with respect to an asset transferred to Y Corporation, an acquiring corporation, in a transaction to which section 381(a) applies, and subsequently Y Corporation, using the same method, transfers such asset to Z Corporation in a transaction to which section 381(a) also applies, then Z Corporation shall be required to use the sum of the years-digits method with respect to such asset.

(g) *Illustration.*—The application of this section may be illustrated by the following example:

Example. M and N Corporations compute their taxable incomes on the basis of the calendar year. On December 31, 1959, M Corporation transfers all of its assets to N Corporation in a transaction to which section 381(a) applies. Included among these assets is an item of depreciable property which on that date has an adjusted basis (for determining gain) of $800,000 after M Corporation takes into account for 1959 its allowance for depreciation under section 167(b)(2). The basis attributable to the asset under section 362(b) is determined to be $900,000 in the hands of N Corporation. Under the provisions of section 381(c)(6) and paragraph (a) of this section. N Corporation is required to compute its allowance for the depreciation of the asset under section 167(b)(2) for 1960 and subsequent years but only in respect of $800,000 of its basis. N Corporation may use any reasonable method other than the methods provided in section 167(b)(2), (3), or (4) in computing its depreciation allowance of the remaining $100,000. [Reg. § 1.381(c)(6)-1.]

☐ [*T.D. 6559, 4-6-61. Amended by T.D. 7166, 3-10-72.*]

[Reg. § 1.381(c)(8)-1]

§ 1.381(c)(8)-1. Installment method.—(a) *Carryover requirement.*— (1) Section 381(c)(8) provides that if, in a transaction to which section 381(a) applies, an acquiring corporation acquires installment obligations, the income from which the distributor or transferor corporation has elected under section 453 and the regulations thereunder to report on the installment method, then the acquiring corporation shall be treated as the distributor or transferor corporation would have been treated under section 453 had it not transferred the installment obligations. Thus, if the distributor or transferor corporation had properly elected to return income from the sale or other disposition of property giving rise to the obligations on the installment method, then the acquiring corporation shall be required to return the income from all such installment obligations in the same manner and to the same extent as the distributor or transferor corporation, unless consent of the Commissioner to use another method is obtained in accordance with paragraph (e) of § 1.446-1. Amounts received by the acquiring corporation on or after the date of distribution or transfer with respect to an installment sale made by the distributor or transferor corporation will not be taken into account in applying the limitation under section 453(b)(2) with respect to the amount of payments received in the year of sale or other disposition.

(2) Section 381(c)(8) and this section have no application to sales or other dispositions of property made by the acquiring corporation on or after the date of distribution or transfer. For provisions defining the date of distribution or transfer, see § 1.381(b)-1(b). See section 381(c)(4) and the regulations thereunder for rules relating to the proper method or combination of methods of accounting to be used by the acquiring corporation.

(b) *Basis of obligations.*—The basis in the hands of an acquiring corporation of installment obligations described in section 381(c)(8) and paragraph (a) of this section shall be the same as in the hands of the distributor or transferor corporation.

(c) *Repossession of property sold in prior years.*—If the acquiring corporation repossesses property, previously sold by the distributor or transferor corporation, by reason of default by the purchaser in payment of the acquired installment obligations, then the acquiring corporation shall be treated as though it were the vendor corporation for purposes of determining, under section 453 and the regulations thereunder, the gain, loss, income or deduction with respect to the property repossessed. [Reg. § 1.381(c)(8)-1.]

☐ [*T.D. 6559, 4-6-61.*]

[Reg. § 1.381(c)(9)-1]

§ 1.381(c)(9)-1. Amortization of bond discount or premium.— (a) *Carryover requirement.*—If, in a transaction to which section 381(a) applies, the acquiring corporation assumes liability for the payment of bonds of a distributor or transferor corporation which were issued at a discount or premium, then under the provisions of section 381(c)(9) the acquiring corporation is to be treated as the distributor or transferor corporation after the date of distribution or transfer for purposes of determining the amount of amortization allowable, or includible, with respect to such discount or premium in computing taxable income. Thus, if subsequent to February 28, 1913, a distributor or transferor corporation issues bonds at a premium and the liability for them is assumed by the acquiring corporation in a transaction to which section 381(a) applies, then the net amount of the premium is income which should be prorated or amortized over the life of the bonds, including the period during which the acquiring corporation is liable upon the obligations assumed. On the other hand, if a distributor or transferor corporation issues bonds at a discount and the liability for them is assumed by the acquiring corporation in a transaction to which section 381(a) applies, then the net amount of the discount is deductible in computing taxable income but should be prorated or amortized over the life of the bonds, including the period during which the acquiring corporation is liable upon the obligations assumed.

(b) *Expense incurred upon issuance of bonds.*—If, in a transaction to which section 381(a) applies, the acquiring corporation assumes liability for bonds of a distributor or transferor corporation which were issued at a discount or premium, the acquiring corporation shall be treated as the distributor or transferor corporation after the date of distribution or transfer with respect to the expense incurred upon the issuance of such bonds.

(c) *Purchase of bonds.*—If, in a transaction to which section 381(a) applies, the acquiring corporation assumes liability for bonds of a distributor or transferor corporation which were issued at a discount or premium and if the acquiring corporation subsequently purchases such bonds, then the acquiring corporation shall be treated as the distributor or transferor corporation for the purpose of determining the amount of any income or deduction resulting from the purchase. See paragraph (c) of § 1.61-12. For rules relating to the exchange or substitution of bonds issued by the acquiring corporation for bonds of a distributor or transferor corporation, see paragraph (d) of this section.

(d) *Exchange of new for old bonds.*—Notwithstanding any other provision of this section, if—

(1) In a transaction to which section 381(a) applies, bonds of the acquiring corporation are exchanged or substituted for bonds of a distributor or transferor corporation which were issued at a discount or premium, or

(2) Bonds of the acquiring corporation are exchanged or substituted for bonds of a distributor or transferor corporation which were issued at a discount or premium and in respect of which the acquiring corporation has assumed liability in a transaction to which section 381(a) applies,

then, with respect to any unamortized discount, premium, or expense of issuance attributable to such bonds of the distributor or transferor corporation, the acquiring corporation shall be treated as the distributor or transferor corporation.

(e) *Bonds of a distributor or transferor corporation.*—For purposes of applying section 381(c)(9), the term "bonds of a distributor or transferor corporation" includes not only bonds issued by the distributor or transferor corporation but also bonds for which the distributor or transferor corporation has assumed liability. Thus, if the distributor or transferor corporation has assumed liability for bonds in a transaction in which any unamortized discount or premium attributable to such bonds carried over to such corporation, then the acquiring corporation assuming liability for the bonds shall be treated as the distributor or transferor corporation after the date of distribution or transfer for purposes of determining the amount of amortization allowable, or includible, with respect to such discount or premium. On the other hand, if the distributor or transferor corporation has assumed liability for bonds in a transaction in which any unamortized discount or premium attributable to such bonds did not carry over to such corporation, then there can be no carryover to the acquiring corporation under this section. [Reg. § 1.381(c)(9)-1.]

☐ [*T.D.* 6532, 1-18-61.]

[Reg. § 1.381(c)(10)-1]

§ 1.381(c)(10)-1. Deferred exploration and development expenditures.—(a) *Carryover requirement.*—(1) If for any taxable year a distributor or transferor corporation has elected under section 615 or section 616 (or corresponding provisions of prior law) to defer and deduct on a ratable basis any exploration or development expenditures made in connection with any ore, mineral, mine, or other natural deposit transferred to the acquiring corporation in a transaction described in section 381(a), then under the provisions of section 381(c)(10) the acquiring corporation shall be entitled to deduct such expenditures on a ratable basis in the same manner, and to the same extent, as they would have been deductible by the distributor or transferor corporation in the absence of the distribution or transfer.

For this purpose, the acquiring corporation shall be treated as though it were the distributor or transferor corporation. The principles set forth in paragraph (e) of § 1.615-3 and paragraph (f) of § 1.616-2 are applicable in computing the amount of the deduction allowable to the acquiring corporation in respect of expenditures deferred by a distributor or transferor corporation.

Example. X and Y Corporations are both organized on January 1, 1955, and both corporations compute their taxable income on the basis of the calendar year. During 1955, X Corporation purchases a mineral property which it begins to develop in 1956. During 1956, X Corporation incurs development expenditures of $500,000 in respect of such property which it elects to defer under section 616(b). On December 31, 1956, Y Corporation acquires all of the assets of X Corporation in a reorganization to which section 381(a) applies, no gain being recognized to X Corporation on the transfer. In 1957, Y Corporation sells 150,000 units of produced ore benefited by the development expenditures incurred and deferred by X Corporation, and the number of units remaining as of the end of 1957, plus the number of units sold during that year, is estimated to be 1,000,000. In addition to its deduction for depletion, Y Corporation is, in 1957, entitled to a deduction under sections 616(b) and 381(c)(10) of $75,000 of the development expenditures previously deferred by X Corporation, that is $500,000 × 150,000/1,000,000.

(2) If a distributor or transferor corporation has elected under section 615 or section 616 (or corresponding provisions of prior law) to defer exploration or development expenditures in respect of a mine or other natural deposit which it subsequently disposes of except for a retained economic interest therein, such as the right to royalty income or in-ore payments, and such retained economic interest is transferred to the acquiring corporation in a transaction to which section 381(a) applies, then the acquiring corporation shall be entitled to deduct such deferred expenditures attributable to the economic interest retained on a ratable basis to the same extent they would have been deductible by the distributor or transferor corporation in the absence of the distribution or transfer. See paragraph (c) of § 1.615-3 and paragraph (c) of § 1.616-2.

(3) For purposes of this section, the terms "exploration expenditures" and "development expenditures" shall have the same meaning as that ascribed to them in the regulations under sections 615 and 616 of the Internal Revenue Code of 1954, or under sections 23(cc) and 23(ff) of the Internal Revenue Code of 1939, whichever applies. See, for example, paragraph (a) of § 1.615-1 and paragraph (a) of § 1.616-1.

(b) *Effect and identification of election previously made.*—(1) The election made by a distributor or transferor corporation under the provisions of section 615 or section 616 (or corresponding provisions of prior law) to defer exploration or development expenditures in respect of any taxable year may not be revoked by the acquiring corporation for any reason whatsoever.

(2) When filing its return for the first taxable year for which it deducts exploration or development expenditures which were deferred under section 615 or section 616 (or corresponding provisions of prior law) by a distributor or transferor corporation, the acquiring corporation shall attach thereto a statement properly identifying the taxable year for which the election to defer was made by the distributor or transferor corporation, the name of the corporation which made the election, and the district director with whom the election was filed.

(3) It is unnecessary for an acquiring corporation to renew an election to defer exploration or development expenditures which was made by a distributor or transferor corporation.

(c) *Successive transactions to which section 381(a) applies.*—If, by virtue of section 381(c)(10), the acquiring corporation is entitled to deduct exploration or development expenditures deferred by a distributor or transferor corporation, then such acquiring corporation shall be deemed to have made the election to defer such expenditures for purposes of applying section 381(c)(10) to any subsequent transaction in which such acquiring corporation is a distributor or transferor corporation.

(d) *Carryover of limitation requirements.*—(1) If a distributor or transferor corporation transfers any mineral property to the acquiring corporation in a transaction described in section 381(a) and the acquiring corporation pays or incurs exploration expenditures in a taxable year ending after the date of the distribution or transfer, then in applying the 4-year or $400,000 limitations described in section 615(c) and paragraphs (a) and (b) of § 1.615-4, whichever is applicable, the acquiring corporation shall be deemed to have been allowed any deduction which, for any taxable year ending on or before the date of distribution or transfer, was allowed to the distributor or transferor corporation under section 615(a), or under section 23(ff)(1) of the Internal Revenue Code of 1939, or to have made any election which, for any such preceding year, was made by the distributor or transferor corporation under section 615(b), or under section 23(ff)(2) of the Internal Revenue Code of 1939. Thus, in such instance, the acquiring corporation shall take into account the years in which the distributor or transferor corporation exercised the election to deduct or defer exploration expenditures and any amounts so deducted or deferred. For this purpose, it is immaterial whether the deduction has been allowed to, or the election has been made by, the distributor or transferor corporation with respect to the specific mineral property transferred by that corporation to the acquiring corporation.

(2) Generally, for purposes of applying the 4-year limitation described in paragraph (a) of §1.615-4, if there are two or more distributor or transferor corporations that transfer any mineral property to the acquiring corporation, each taxable year of any such corporation ending on or before the date of distribution or transfer in which exploration expenditures were deducted or deferred shall be treated as a separate taxable year regardless of the fact that the taxable years of two or more such corporations normally end on the same date. However, if the date of distribution or transfer is the same with respect to more than one distributor or transferor corporation, then the taxable years of such corporations ending on the same date of distribution or transfer shall be considered as one taxable year for purposes of applying the 4-year limitation even though more than one such corporation deducted or deferred exploration expenditures for such taxable years.

(3) For purposes of applying the $400,000 limitation described in paragraph (b) of §1.615-4, if there are two or more distributor or transferor corporations that transfer any mineral property to the acquiring corporation, any exploration expenditures which were deducted or treated as deferred expenses by such corporations for taxable years ending after December 31, 1950, shall be taken into account by the acquiring corporation.

(4) If a distributor or transferor corporation that transfers any mineral property to the acquiring corporation was required to take into account any taxable years or amounts of its transferor, as provided by paragraph (e) of §1.615-4, for purposes of either the 4-year limitation described in paragraph (a) of §1.615-4 or the $400,000 limitation described in paragraph (b) of §1.615-4, then the acquiring corporation shall also take these taxable years and amounts into account in applying the same limitations.

(5) The provisions of this paragraph may be illustrated by the following examples:

Example (1). M and N Corporations were organized on January 1, 1956, and each corporation computes its taxable income on the basis of the calendar year. For each of its taxable years 1956 and 1957, M Corporation expended $60,000 for exploration expenditures and exercised the option to deduct such amounts under section 615(a). N Corporation made no exploration expenditures during its taxable years 1956 and 1957. On December 31, 1957, M Corporation transferred all of its assets to N Corporation in a transaction to which section 381(a) applies, no gain being recognized to the transferor corporation on the transfer. N Corporation made exploration expenditures of $100,000, $120,000, $110,000, and $100,000 for the years 1958, 1959, 1960, and 1961, respectively, which expenditures it desired to deduct under section 615(a) to the extent allowable. On the basis of these facts, N Corporation may deduct up to $100,000 for each of the years 1958 and 1959. No deduction or deferral is allowable for 1960 since the benefits of section 615(c) were previously availed of for 4 taxable years. However, N Corporation may deduct $80,000 for 1961 (the 4-year limitation not applying to such year) but, if such deduction is made, N Corporation will not be allowed any further deductions or deferrals since the $400,000 limitation of paragraph (b) of §1.615-4 will have been reached.

Example (2). R and S Corporations were organized on January 1, 1955, and each corporation computes its income on the basis of the calendar year. For the 1955 taxable year neither corporation made any exploration expenditures under section 615(a). On June 30, 1956, R Corporation transferred all its assets to S Corporation in a transaction to which section 381(a) applies, no gain being recognized to the transferor corporation on the transfer. During its short taxable year ending June 30, 1956, R Corporation made exploration expenditures of $60,000 which it elected to deduct under section 615. For its taxable year ending December 31, 1956, S Corporation may deduct or defer exploration expenditures up to $100,000 since this is a separate election for purposes of utilizing section 615 and is not affected by the $60,000 previously deducted by R Corporation. Assuming S Corporation exercises an election under section 615 for its taxable year ending December 31, 1956, S Corporation may elect to apply the benefits of section 615 to exploration expenditures for two more taxable years. However, for taxable years beginning after July 6, 1960 (the 4-year limitation not applying), S Corporation is entitled under section 615 to deduct or defer exploration expenditures made in such years to the extent that the combined deductions and deferrals by R and S Corporations in prior years did not exceed $400,000.

Example (3). O and P Corporations were organized on January 1, 1955, and each corporation computes its taxable income on the basis

of the calendar year. For their taxable years 1955, 1956, and 1957, each corporation deducted exploration expenditures made in such years under section 615(a). On June 30, 1958, O Corporation transferred all its assets to P Corporation in a transaction to which section 381(a) applies, no gain being recognized to the transferor corporation on the transfer. If, during its short taxable year ending June 30, 1958, O Corporation made additional exploration expenditures, it may deduct or defer such expenditures (up to $100,000) under section 615 since O Corporation has utilized section 615 in only three previous taxable years. For its taxable years ending after June 30, 1958, and beginning before July 7, 1960, P Corporation may not deduct or defer exploration expenditures under section 615, since the benefits of that section were utilized by O and P Corporations for 4 taxable years. However, for taxable years beginning after July 6, 1960 (the 4-year limitation not applying), P is entitled under section 615 to deduct or defer exploration expenditures made in such years to the extent that the combined deductions and deferrals by O and P Corporations in prior years do not exceed $400,000. See paragraph (b) of §1.615-4.

Example (4). X, Y, and Z Corporations were organized on January 1, 1955, and each corporation computes its taxable income on the basis of the calendar year. For their taxable years ending December 31, 1955, X and Y Corporations each deferred $100,000 for exploration expenditures made in such taxable years under section 615(b). Z Corporation made no exploration expenditures during its taxable year ending December 31, 1955. On March 31, 1956, X and Y Corporations transferred all their assets to Z Corporation in a transaction to which section 381(a) applies, no gain being recognized to the transferor corporations on the transfer. X and Y Corporations each made exploration expenditures of $75,000 during their short taxable years ending March 31, 1956, which they deducted under section 615(a). For purposes of taxable years beginning before July 7, 1960, Z Corporation must take into account the taxable years in which X and Y Corporations deducted or deferred exploration expenditures. In so doing, each taxable year in which exploration expenditures were deducted or deferred must be taken into account except that the taxable years of X and Y Corporations ending on March 31, 1956, shall be considered as one taxable year. Therefore Z Corporation may deduct or defer exploration expenditures in accordance with section 615 for any one taxable year ending after March 31, 1956, and beginning before July 7, 1960. However, for taxable years beginning after July 6, 1960 (the 4-year limitation not applying), Z Corporation must take into account for purposes of the $400,000 limitation all of the $350,000 of exploration expenditures deducted or deferred by X, Y, and Z Corporations during taxable years ending after December 31, 1950. Therefore, Z Corporation, assuming it has not deducted or deferred any exploration expenditures, is entitled under section 615 to deduct or defer in taxable years beginning after July 6, 1960, up to $50,000 for exploration expenditures made in such years.

Example (5). For purposes of this example, assume that each taxpayer computes taxable income on the basis of the calendar year. Taxpayer A, an individual who has deducted exploration expenditures of $75,000 under section 23(ff) of the Internal Revenue Code of 1939 for each of his taxable years 1952 and 1953, transferred a mineral property to K Corporation on January 1, 1954, in a transaction in which the basis of the mineral property in the hands of K Corporation is determined under section 362(a). For its taxable year 1954 and pursuant to section 615(a), K Corporation deducted exploration expenditures of $100,000 which it made in such year. K Corporation had made no exploration expenditures in any preceding taxable year. On December 31, 1954, K Corporation transferred all its assets to L Corporation in a reorganization to which section 381(a) applies, no gain being recognized to the transferor corporation on the transfer. Assuming that L Corporation has not deducted or deferred exploration expenditures in any preceding taxable year, L Corporation may deduct or defer exploration expenditures (up to $100,000) in accordance with section 615 for any one taxable year ending after December 31, 1954, and beginning before July 7, 1960, in view of the 4-year limitation. However, if L Corporation does not deduct or defer exploration expenditures in that period, then for taxable years beginning after July 6, 1960 (the 4-year limitation not applying), L Corporation is entitled to deduct or defer up to $150,000 (but not to exceed $100,000 per year) for exploration expenditures made in such years. See paragraph (b) of §1.615-4. [Reg. §1.381(c)(10)-1.]

☐ [T.D. 6552, 3-7-61. *Amended by* T.D. 6685, 10-23-63.]

[Reg. §1.381(c)(11)-1]

§1.381(c)(11)-1. Contributions to pension plans, employees' annuity plans, and stock bonus and profit-sharing plans.— (a) *Carryover requirement.*—Section 381(c)(11) provides that, for purposes of determining amounts deductible under section 404 for any taxable year, the acquiring corporation shall be considered after the date of distribution or transfer to be the distributor or transferor corporation in respect of any pension, annuity, stock bonus, or profit-sharing plan.

(b) *Nature of carryover.*—(1) Primarily, section 381(c)(11) and this section apply to the amount of any unused deductions or excess contribution carryovers which, in the absence of the transaction causing section 381 to apply, would have been available to the distributor or transferor corporation under section 404. Thus, for example, this section applies to unused deductions under a profit-sharing or stock bonus trust which, in accordance with the second sentence of section 404(a)(3)(A), would have been available in succeeding taxable years to the transferor corporation if the transfer of assets to the acquiring corporation had not occurred.

(2) Section 381(c)(11) also permits or requires the acquiring corporation to be treated as though it were the distributor or transferor corporation for the purpose of satisfying any conditions which would have been required of the distributor or transferor corporation in the absence of the distribution or transfer, so that it may be determined whether the distributor or transferor corporation, or the acquiring corporation, is entitled to take a deduction under section 404 in respect of a trust or plan established by the distributor or transferor corporation. Thus, for example, in a case when the taxable year of the transferor corporation ends on the date of transfer pursuant to section 381(b)(1), that corporation is entitled, pursuant to the provisions of section 404(a)(6) and paragraph (c) of §1.404(a)-1, to a deduction in such taxable year for a payment to a qualified trust of that corporation made by the acquiring corporation after the close of such taxable year but within the time specified in section 404(a)(6). In further illustration, if the transferor corporation were to establish a qualified plan, and if the plan were maintained as a qualified plan by the acquiring corporation, than any contributions paid under the plan by the acquiring corporation (other than those which are deductible by the transferor corporation by reason of section 404(a)(6)) would be deductible under section 404 by the acquiring corporation even though the plan were exclusively for the benefit of former employees of the transferor corporation. Also, for example, if the transferor corporation were to adopt an annuity plan during its taxable year ending on the date of transfer, the acquiring corporation would be entitled, subject to the provisions of section 401(b), to amend the plan so as to make it retroactively satisfy the requirements of section 401(a)(3), (4), (5), and (6) for the period beginning with the date on which the plan was put into effect.

(c) *Taxable year of deduction.*—The first taxable year of the acquiring corporation in which any amount shall be allowed as a deduction to that corporation by reason of section 381(c)(11) and this section shall be its first taxable year ending after the date of distribution or transfer.

(d) *Requirements for deductions.*—(1) In order for any amount paid by the acquiring corporation (other than amounts deductible under section 404(a)(5)) to be deductible by the acquiring corporation by reason of this section in respect of a trust or nontrusteed annuity plan which is established by a distributor or transferor corporation and maintained by the acquiring corporation, the contributions must be paid (or deemed to have been paid under section 404(a)(6)) by the acquiring corporation in a taxable year of that corporation which ends with or within a year of the trust for which it is exempt under section 501(a), or, in the case of a nontrusteed annuity plan, for which it meets the requirements of section 404(a)(2). See, however, section 404(a)(4) and §1.404(a)-11 for rules relating to deductions for contributions to foreign-situs trusts. The trust or plan which is established by the distributor or transferor corporation and maintained by the acquiring corporation may separately satisfy the requirements of section 401(a) or section 404(a)(2) or may, together with other trusts or plans of the acquiring corporation, constitute a single plan which qualifies under section 401(a) or meets the requirements of section 404(a)(2).

(2) Excess contributions paid under a qualified trust or plan established by the transferor or distributor corporation may be carried over and, subject to the applicable limitations, deducted by the acquiring corporation in a taxable year ending after the date of distribution or transfer regardless of whether the trust is exempt, or the plan meets the requirements of section 404(a)(2), during such taxable year. There are, however, special rules for computing the limitations on the amount of excess contributions which are deductible in a taxable year ending after the trust or plan has terminated (see paragraph (a) of §1.404(a)-13). For this purpose, the pension, annuity, stock bonus, or profit-sharing plan of the distributor or transferor corporation under which the excess contributions were made shall be considered continued (and not terminated) by the acquiring corporation if, after the date of distribution or transfer, the acquiring corporation continues the plan as a separate and distinct plan of its own which continues to qualify under section 401(a), or to meet the requirements of section 404(a)(2), or consolidates or replaces that plan with a comparable plan. See subparagraph (4) of this paragraph for rules relating to what constitutes a "comparable" plan.

(3) In order for any amount paid by the acquiring corporation to be deductible by the acquiring corporation as an unused deduction carried over from a qualified profit-sharing or stock bonus trust established by a distributor or transferor corporation, the acquiring corporation must continue such trust established by the distributor or transferor corporation as a separate and distinct trust of its own which continues to qualify under section 401(a), or must consolidate or replace that trust with a comparable trust. In addition, the amount paid by the acquiring corporation will be deductible as an unused deduction carried over from the transferor or distributor corporation only if it is paid into the profit-sharing or stock bonus trust established by the transferor or distributor corporation, or the comparable trust, in a taxable year of the acquiring corporation which ends with or within a year of such trust (or such comparable trust) for which it meets the requirements of section 401(a) and is exempt under section 501(a). See subparagraph (4) of this paragraph for rules relating to what constitutes a "comparable" trust.

(4) For purposes of subparagraphs (2) and (3) of this paragraph, a plan under which deductions are determined pursuant to paragraph (1) or (2) of section 404(a) shall be considered comparable to another plan under which deductions are determined pursuant to either of those paragraphs, and a plan under which deductions are determined pursuant to paragraph (3) of section 404(a) shall be considered comparable to another plan under which deductions are determined pursuant to such paragraph (3). Thus, a profit-sharing plan (which qualifies under section 401(a)) established by the transferor or distributor corporation shall, for purposes of subparagraphs (2) and (3) of this paragraph, be considered terminated if, after the date of distribution or transfer, the acquiring corporation transfers the funds accumulated under the profit-sharing plan into a pension plan covering the same employees. In such a case, excess contributions paid under the profit-sharing plan by the distributor or transferor corporation may be carried over and deducted by the acquiring corporation in a taxable year ending after the date of distribution or transfer subject to the limitations in section 404(a)(3)(A). On the other hand, unused deductions attributable to the profit-sharing plan may not be carried over and used by the acquiring corporation as a basis for deducting amounts contributed by it to the pension plan.

(e) *Effect of consolidation or replacement of plan on prior contributions.*—If a pension, annuity, stock bonus, or profit-sharing plan which was established by a distributor or transferor corporation is terminated after the date of distribution or transfer because of consolidation or replacement with a comparable plan of the acquiring corporation, then the contributions paid to or under its plan by the distributor or transferor corporation on or before the date of distribution or transfer shall not be disallowed under section 404 merely because of the termination of the plan which was established by that corporation, provided that the termination does not cause the plan to fail to qualify under section 401(a).

(f) *Amounts deductible under section 404.*—Section 381(c)(11) and this section apply only to amounts which are otherwise deductible under section 404 and the regulations thereunder. See §§1.404(a) through 1.404(d)-1. Thus, to be deductible by reason of this section, contributions paid by the acquiring corporation must be expenses which otherwise satisfy the conditions of section 162 (relating to trade or business expenses). No deduction shall be allowed by reason of section 381(c)(11) and this section for a contribution which is allowable under section 162 but is not allowable under section 404. Thus, the acquiring corporation shall not be allowed a deduction by reason of this section in respect of a plan established by a distributor or transferor corporation if the contribution would not otherwise be deductible under section 404 by reason of section 404(c) and §1.404(c)-1. On the other hand, any unused deductions or excess contributions of a distributor or transferor corporation which are carried over from 1939 Code years shall be deductible by the acquiring corporation if the requirements of this section, section 404(d), and §1.404(d)-1 are satisfied.

(g) *Cost of past service credits.*—In computing the cost of past service credits under a plan with respect to employees of the distributor or transferor corporation, the acquiring corporation may include the cost of credits for periods during which the employees were in the service of the distributor or transferor corporation.

(h) *Separate carryovers required.*—The excess contributions which are available to a distributor or transferor corporation under the provisions of section 404(a)(1)(D) and section 404(a)(3)(A) at the close of the date of distribution or transfer and are carried over to the acquiring corporation under this section shall be kept separate and distinct from each other and from any excess contributions which are available to the distributor or transferor corporation at that time under the provisions of section 404(a)(7) and are carried over to the acquiring corporation under this section. If there are excess contributions carried over to the acquiring corporation from more than one transferor or distributor corporation, the excess contributions of each transferor or distributor corporation shall be kept separate and distinct from those of the other transferor or distributor corporations and, with respect to each such transferor or distributor corporation shall be kept separate and distinct as provided in the preceding sentence. See, however, paragraph (i) of this section for rules for applying the provisions of section 404(a)(3)(A) when the acquiring corporation maintains two or more profit-sharing or stock bonus trusts, one or more of which was established by a distributor or transferor corporation. The requirements in this paragraph shall apply with respect to any excess contributions which are carried over to the acquiring corporation from a distributor or transferor corporation under the provisions of section 404(d) and this section.

(i) *Limitations applicable to profit-sharing or stock bonus trusts.*—When contributions are paid by the acquiring corporation after the date of distribution or transfer to two or more profit-sharing or stock bonus trusts, and one or more of such trusts was established by a distributor or transferor corporation, such trusts shall be considered as a single trust in applying the provisions of section 404(a)(3)(A) under this section. Accordingly, in determining its secondary limitation, and its excess contributions carryover, under section 404(a)(3)(A) in any taxable year ending after the date of distributions or transfer, the acquiring corporation shall take into account its primary limitations, and the deductions allowed or allowable to it, for all prior years under the limitations provided in those sections, and also the primary limitations of, and deductions allowed or allowable to, the distributor or transferor corporation or corporations for all prior years under the limitations provided in those sections.

(j) *Successive carryovers.*—The provisions of section 381(c)(11) and this section shall apply to an acquiring corporation which, in a distribution or transfer to which section 381(a) applies, acquires the assets of a distributor or transferor corporation which has previously acquired the assets of another corporation in a transaction to which section 381(a) applies, even though, in computing an unused deductions or excess contributions carryover to the second acquiring corporation, it is necessary to take into account contributions paid by, and limitations applicable to, the first distributor or transferor corporation.

(k) *Information to be furnished by acquiring corporation.*—The acquiring corporation shall furnish such information with respect to a plan established by a distributor or transferor corporation as will, consistently with the principles of section 404, establish that the provisions of such section and this section apply. For purposes of this section, the district director may require any other information that he considers necessary to determine deductions allowable under section 404 and this section or qualification under section 401. Any unused deductions or excess contributions carried over from a distributor or transferor corporation pursuant to this section shall be properly identified with the corporation which would have been permitted to use those deductions or contributions in the absence of the transaction causing section 381 to apply.

(l) *Illustration.*—The application of this section may be illustrated by the following example:

Example. In 1955, X Corporation, which makes its return on the basis of the calendar year, paid $400,000 to completely fund past service credits under a qualified pension plan and deducted 10 percent ($40,000) of that cost in each of the taxable years 1955, 1956, and 1957. The pension plan established by X Corporation had an anniversary date of January 1. On December 31, 1957, on which date the undeducted part of the cost amounted to $280,000, X Corporation transferred all its assets to Y Corporation in a statutory merger to which section 361 applies. Y Corporation which also makes its return on the basis of the calendar year, had a qualified pension plan and trust which also had an anniversary date of January 1. Since Y Corporation had many more employees than X Corporation on the date of transfer, it covered the former employees of X Corporation under its own plan. Y Corporation is entitled to deductions under section 404(a)(1)(D) and this section in 1958 and succeeding taxable years, in order of time, with respect to the undeducted balance of $280,000, to the extent of the difference between the amount paid and deductible by that corporation in each such taxable year and the maximum amount deductible by that corporation for such taxable year in accordance with the applicable limitations of section 404(a)(1). In computing the maximum amount deductible by Y Corporation for 1958 and 1959 under section 404(a)(1)(C), that corporation may include $40,000 for each year, the amount that X Corporation could have included for each of those years in computing the maximum amount that would have been deductible by X

Corporation under section 404(a)(1)(C) if the merger had not occurred. Thus, assuming that Y Corporation's appropriate limitation so computed under section 404(a)(1)(C) is $1,000,000 (including the $40,000 carried over from X Corporation under this section) for each of those taxable years, and that Y Corporation contributed $925,000 to its trust in 1958 and $975,000 in 1959, then Y Corporation is entitled under section 404(a)(1)(D) and this section to deduct in 1958 $75,000, and in 1959 $25,000, of the amount ($280,000) carried over from X Corporation. The undeducted balance of such amount ($180,000) available to Y Corporation on December 31, 1959, would be deductible by that corporation in succeeding taxable years in accordance with section 404(a)(1)(D) and this section. [Reg. § 1.381(c)(11)-1.]

☐ [*T.D.* 6556, 3-21-61. *Amended by T.D.* 7168, 3-8-72 *and T.D.* 9849, 3-11-2019.]

[Reg. § 1.381(c)(12)-1]

§ 1.381(c)(12)-1. Recovery of bad debts, prior taxes, or delinquency amounts.—(a) *Carryover requirement.*—(1) If, as a result of a distribution or transfer to which section 381(a) applies, the acquiring corporation is entitled to the recovery of a bad debt, prior tax, or delinquency amount on account of which a deduction or credit was allowed to a distributor or transferor corporation for a prior taxable year, and such debt, tax, or amount is recovered by the acquiring corporation after the date of distribution or transfer, then under the provisions of section 381(c)(12) the acquiring corporation is required to include in its gross income for the taxable year of recovery the same amount of income attributable to the recovery as the distributor or transferor corporation would have been required to include under section 111 and the regulations thereunder had the distribution or transfer not occurred.

(2) The rule prescribed by paragraph (a)(1) of this section and by section 381(c)(12) with respect to bad debts, prior taxes, and delinquency amounts applies equally with respect to the recovery by the acquiring corporation of all other losses, expenditures, and accruals made the basis of deductions from the gross income of a distributor or transferor corporation for prior taxable years, including war losses referred to in section 127 of the Internal Revenue Code of 1939, but not including deductions with respect to depreciation, depletion, amortization, or amortizable bond premiums. An item which is not a "section 111 item" for purposes of the regulations under section 111 is not subject to the provisions of section 381(c)(12). The provisions of section 111(c) shall be applied with respect to a recovery by the acquiring corporation in the same manner as they would have been applied by the distributor or transferor corporation.

(b) *Amount of recovery exclusion allowable for year of recovery.*—For the year of any recovery by the acquiring corporation, the amount of the recovery exclusion for the original taxable year shall be determined in accordance with paragraph (b) of § 1.111-1. For the purpose of this paragraph and section 381(c)(12), the recovery exclusion for any year with respect to section 111 items of the acquiring corporation shall be kept separate from the recovery exclusion for any year with respect to section 111 items of each distributor or transferor corporation. The recovery by the acquiring corporation of any section 111 item of such corporation after the date of the distribution or transfer shall be considered separately from recoveries by the acquiring corporation of any such item which was deducted or credited by a distributor or transferor corporation. Any recovery by the acquiring corporation of a section 111 item shall be excluded from the gross income of the acquiring corporation to the extent of the recovery exclusion (1) determined for the original year for which that item was deducted or credited by the specific corporation which claimed the deduction or credit and (2) reduced by the excludable recoveries (whether made by the acquiring corporation, or by the distributor or transferor corporation) in intervening years with respect to the recovery exclusion of such corporation for such original year. There shall be taken into account the effect of net operating loss carryovers and carrybacks or capital loss carryovers.

(c) *Illustration of carryover of recovery exclusion.*—(1) *Facts.*—(i) The application of section 381(c)(12) may be illustrated by the following example. M and N Corporations are both organized on January 1, 1957, and both corporations compute their taxable income on the basis of the calendar year. On December 31, 1959, M Corporation transfers all its assets to N Corporation in a reorganization to which section 381(a) applies.

(ii) The section 111 items of the two corporations for the following taxable years are as follows, identification of such items being made by an appropriate letter:

Taxable year of deduction or credit	M Corporation (transferor)	N Corporation (acquirer)
1957	$500(g)	$200(h)
1958	300(i)	400(j)
1959	600(k)	100(m)

(iii) The recovery exclusions in respect of such taxable years, computed in accordance with §1.111-1(b)(2), are assumed to be as follows:

Taxable year	M Corporation (transferor)	N Corporation (acquirer)
1957	$400	$150
1958	200	300
1959	500	75

(iv) The recoveries of the above-mentioned section 111 items by the two corporations are as follows:

Taxable year of recovery	M Corporation (transferor)	N Corporation (acquirer)
1958	$25(g)	$50(h)
1959	50(g)	20(h)
	30(i)	15(j)
1960		350(g)
		225(i)
		550(k)
		100(h)
		350(j)
		85(m)

(2)   *M Corporation's 1958 recovery.*

Total recovery of section 111 items for 1957		$25
Less: Recovery exclusion for 1957		400
Amount included in gross income of M Corporation for 1958		$0

(3)   *M Corporation's 1959 recoveries.*

(i)	Total recovery of section 111 items for 1957		50
	Less: Recovery exclusion for 1957	$400	
	Minus excludable recovery	25	375
	Amount included in gross income of M Corporation for 1959		$0

(4)   *N Corporation's 1958 recovery.*

(ii)	Total recovery of section 111 items for 1958		30
	Less: Recovery exclusion for 1958		200
	Amount included in gross income of M corporation for 1959		$0
	Total recovery of section 111 items for 1957		50
	Less: Recovery exclusion for 1957		150
	Amount included in gross income of N Corporation for 1958		$0

(5)   *N Corporation's 1959 recoveries.*

(i)	Total recovery of section 111 items for 1957		20
	Minus excludable recovery in 1958	50	100
	Amount included in gross income of N Corporation for 1959		$0
(ii)	Total recovery of section 111 items for 1958		15
	Less: Recovery exclusion for 1958		300
	Amount included in gross income of N Corporation for 1959		$0

(6)   *N Corporation's 1960 recoveries.*

(i)	Total recovery of section 111 items of M Corporation for 1957			$350
	Less: Recovery exclusion of M Corporation for 1957		$400	
	Minus: Excludable recovery in 1959		$50	
	Excludable recovery in 1958	25	75	325
	Amount included in gross income of N Corporation for 1960			$25
(ii)	Total recovery of section 111 items of M corporation for 1958			225
	Less: Recovery exclusion of M Corporation for 1958		$200	
	Minus excludable recovery in 1959		30	170
	Amount included in gross income of N Corporation for 1960			$55
(iii)	Total recovery of section 111 items of M Corporation for 1959			550
	Less: Recovery exclusion of M Corporation for 1959			500
	Amount included in gross income of N Corporation for 1960			$50
(iv)	Total recovery of section 111 items of N Corporation for 1957			100
	Less: Recovery exclusion of N Corporation for 1957		$150	
	Minus: Excludable recovery in 1959	$20		
	Excludable recovery in 1958	50	70	80
	Amount included in gross income of N Corporation for 1960			$20
(v)	Total recovery of section 111 items of N Corporation for 1958			$350
	Less: Recovery exclusion of N Corporation for 1958			$300
	Minus excludable recovery in 1959	15	285	
	Amount included in gross income of N Corporation for 1960			$65
(vi)	Total recovery of section 111 items of N Corporation for 1959			85
	Less: Recovery exclusion of N Corporation for 1959			75
	Amount included in gross income of N Corporation for 1960			$10

(7)   *Summary of recoveries included in gross income of N Corporation for 1960.*

     (i) Recovery of M Corporation items for:

1957		$25
1958		55

1959	50	130
(ii) Recovery of N Corporation items for:		
1957	$20	
1958	65	
1959	10	$95
Total amount included in gross income	$225	

[Reg. § 1.381(c)(12)-1.]

☐ [T.D. 6559, 4-6-61.]

[Reg. § 1.381(c)(13)-1]

§ 1.381(c)(13)-1. Involuntary conversions.—(a) *Carryover requirement.*—(1) *General rule.*—Section 381(c)(13) requires that after the date of distribution or transfer the acquiring corporation, in a transaction to which section 381(a) applies, shall be treated as the distributor or transferor corporation for purposes of applying section 1033, relating to involuntary conversions. This rule shall apply even though the property similar or related in service or use to the property converted, or the stock of a corporation owning such similar property, is purchased by the acquiring corporation after the date of distribution or transfer and is not received from the distributor or transferor corporation in the transaction to which section 381(a) applies. Accordingly, if any factor essential to the application of section 1033 occurs on or before the date of distribution or transfer and any other such factor also occurs after that date, then, in accordance with section 381(c)(13) and this section, the provisions of section 1033 shall apply to the acquiring corporation in the same manner that they would have applied to the distributor or transferor corporation in the absence of the distribution or transfer. For purposes of this section, the terms "involuntary conversion" and "disposition of the converted property" shall have the meaning ascribed to them by the regulations under section 1033.

(2) *Application to other transactions.*—The provisions of this section shall apply to any transaction which, under provisions of the Internal Revenue Code of 1954, is treated as though it were an involuntary conversion within the meaning of section 1033. See, for example, section 1071, relating to gain from a sale or exchange to effectuate the policies of the Federal Communications Commission; and sections 1332(b)(3) and 1333(3), relating to war loss recoveries.

(b) *Conversion into similar property.*—Section 1033(a)(1) provides that no gain shall be recognized if property is involuntarily converted only into property which is similar or related in service or use to the property so converted. If there is a disposition of property of a distributor or transferor corporation and, subsequent to the date of distribution or transfer, property similar or related in service or use to the property disposed of is received by the acquiring corporation as compensation for the property so disposed of, then no gain shall be recognized to the acquiring corporation, provided that no gain would have been recognized under section 1033(a)(1) if the similar property had been received directly by the distributor or transferor corporation.

Example. Property of S Corporation with an adjusted basis of $100 is condemned by the local government. Shortly after the property is so condemned, S Corporation liquidates and distributes its assets to P Corporation in a distribution to which section 381(a) applies. Subsequent to the date of distribution, P Corporation receives from the government (in settlement of the condemnation proceedings) property with a market value of $500 which is similar or related in service or use to the property so condemned. No gain is recognized to either corporation upon P Corporation's receipt of the similar property, and the property so received has a basis of $100 in the hands of P Corporation on the date of its acquisition.

(c) *Conversion into money or dissimilar property when disposition occurs after December 31, 1950.*—(1) *General rule.*—Section 1033(a)(3) and § 1.1033(a)-2 provide rules for involuntary conversions of property into money or dissimilar property where the disposition of the converted property occurs after December 31, 1950. In such a case, the gain on the conversion, if any, shall be recognized, at the election of the taxpayer, only to the extent that the amount realized on the conversion exceeds the cost of other property purchased by the taxpayer which is similar or related in service or use to the property so converted, or exceeds the cost of stock purchased by the taxpayer in the acquisition of control of a corporation owning such other property, provided (i) the taxpayer purchases such other property or stock for the purpose of replacing the property so converted and (ii) the purchase occurs during the period of time specified in section 1033(a)(3)(B). The provisions of this paragraph shall apply to involuntary conversions where the disposition of the property occurs after December 31, 1950, and where the election to have section 1033(a)(3) apply to the treatment of the gain upon the conversion is contingent upon activities of both the distributor or transferor corporation and the acquiring corporation. For purposes of section 381(c)(13), the period of time specified in section 1033(a)(3)(B) shall be determined by taking into account taxable years of, and extensions of time

granted to, both the distributor or transferor corporation and the acquiring corporation.

(2) *Replacement period.*—The period during which the purchase of similar property or stock must be made in order to prevent the recognition of gain on the involuntary conversion terminates two years (or, in the case of a disposition occurring before December 31, 1969, one year) after the close of the first taxable year in which any part of the gain upon the conversion is realized, or at the close of such later date as may be designated pursuant to an application of the taxpayer. See paragraph (c)(3) of § 1.1033(a)-2. Therefore, if, in a case to which this subparagraph applies, the first taxable year in which gain is realized is the taxable year of the distributor or transferor corporation ending with the close of the date of distribution or transfer, the acquiring corporation will have a maximum of only two years (or, in the case of a disposition occurring before December 31, 1969, one year) after that date in which to purchase the similar property or stock, unless an extension of time has been granted upon application by the distributor, transferor, or acquiring corporation within the time prescribed. See paragraph (a) of § 1.381(b)-1 as to the termination of the taxable year of the distributor or transferor corporation. See paragraph (c)(3) of § 1.1033(a)-2 as to applications to extend the period within which to replace the converted property. In addition to the information otherwise required under paragraph (c)(3) of § 1.1033(a)-2, the application shall contain sufficient detail in connection with the distribution or transfer to establish that section 381(c)(13) applies to the involuntary conversion involved.

(3) *Examples.*—The application of this paragraph may be illustrated by the following examples:

Example (1). A and B Corporations compute their taxable income on the basis of the calendar year, and both corporations use the cash method of accounting. During 1970 property of A Corporation is destroyed by fire, and in January 1971, A corporation receives $15,000 from an insurance company as compensation for its loss of property. The adjusted basis of the property on the date of destruction is $10,000; as a consequence, A Corporation realizes a gain of $5,000 on the involuntary conversion. On June 30, 1971, B Corporation acquires all of the assets of A Corporation in a reorganization to which section 381(a) applies. In accordance with paragraph (c)(2) of § 1.1033(a)-2, A Corporation reports in its return for the short taxable year ending June 30, 1971, all the details in connection with the involuntary conversion but does not include the realized gain in gross income, thereby electing to have the gain recognized only to the extent provided in section 1033(a)(3). On June 15, 1973, B Corporation purchases for $20,000 property which is similar or related in service or use of the property previously destroyed. In its return for 1973, B Corporation reports all of the details in connection with its replacement of the property, as required by paragraph (c)(2) of § 1.1033(a)-2. As a result of this replacement by B Corporation, none of the gain realized by A Corporation is recognized. The replacement property which is purchased by B Corporation has a basis to that corporation of $15,000 on the date of its purchase, that is, the cost of such property ($20,000) decreased by the amount of gain not recognized to A Corporation on the involuntary conversion ($5,000).

Example (2). Assume the same facts as in example (1), except that B Corporation does not purchase similar property on or before June 30, 1973, and does not apply on or before that date (in accordance with paragraph (c)(3) of § 1.1033(a)-2) for an extension of time in which to make a replacement. In such event, the gain realized by A Corporation is recognized to that corporation for its taxable year ending June 30, 1971. A Corporation's tax liability for such taxable year must be recomputed in accordance with paragraph (c)(2) of § 1.1033(a)-2 in order to reflect this additional income.

Example (3). Assume the same facts as in example (1), except that the property of A Corporation is destroyed in 1968, A Corporation receives the $15,000 from an insurance company in January 1969, B Corporation acquires all of the assets of A Corporation on June 30, 1969, and A Corporation's return is filed for the short taxable year ending June 30, 1969. B Corporation would have to purchase property which is similar or related in service or use to the property previously destroyed by June 30, 1970, in order to take advantage of the provisions of section 1033.

Example (4). M and N Corporations compute their taxable income on the basis of the calendar year, and both corporations use the cash method of accounting. During 1970, property of M Corporation is destroyed by fire. The adjusted basis of the property on the date of destruction is $10,000. The property is insured against loss by fire, but the insurance claim is not satisfied on or before June 30, 1971, the date on which N Corporation acquires all of the assets (including the insurance claim) of M Corporation in a reorganization to which section 381(a) applies. On September 1, 1972, N Corporation receives $15,000 from the insurance company as compensation for the fire loss suffered by M Corporation. Upon receipt of the insurance proceeds, N Corporation realizes a gain of $5,000 upon the involuntary conversion; however, in its return for 1972, N Corporation elects under the provisions of paragraph (c)(2) of §1.1033(a)-2 to have the gain recognized only to the extent provided by section 1033(a)(3). On December 30, 1974, N Corporation purchases for $20,000 property which is similar or related in service or use to the property previously destroyed in the hands of M Corporation. As a result of this replacement by N Corporation, none of the gain realized by N Corporation in 1972 is recognized. The replacement property which is purchased by N Corporation has a basis to that corporation of $15,000 on the date of its purchase, that is, the cost of such property ($20,000) decreased by the amount of gain not recognized to N Corporation on the involuntary conversion ($5,000).

Example (5). R and S Corporations compute their taxable income on the basis of the calendar year, and both corporations use the cash method of accounting. During 1970 property of R Corporation is destroyed by fire. The adjusted basis of the property on the date of destruction is $10,000. In anticipation of taking the benefit of section 1033(a)(3), R Corporation purchases for $20,000 on June 1, 1971, property which is similar or related in service or use to the destroyed property. In its return for 1971, R Corporation reports all of the details in connection with the replacement of the property, as required by paragraph (c)(2) of §1.1033(a)-2. The property destroyed in 1970 is insured against loss by fire, but the insurance claim is not satisfied on or before March 1, 1972, the date on which S Corporation acquires all of the assets (including the insurance claim) of R Corporation in a reorganization to which section 381(a) applies. On October 1, 1972, S Corporation receives $12,000 from the insurance company as compensation for the fire loss suffered by R Corporation. Upon receipt of the insurance proceeds, S Corporation realizes a gain of $2,000 upon the involuntary conversion; however, in its return for 1972, S Corporation elects under the provisions of paragraph (c)(2) of §1.1033(a)-2 to have the gain recognized only to the extent provided by section 1033(a)(3). As a result of the replacement by R Corporation, none of the gain realized by S Corporation in 1972 is recognized. Assuming there are no adjustments for depreciation, the replacement property has a basis on October 1, 1972, of $18,000, that is, the cost of such property ($20,000) decreased by the amount of gain not recognized to S Corporation on the involuntary conversion ($2,000).

(d) *Conversion into money when disposition occurs before January 1, 1951.*—Section 1033(a)(2) provides that, if property is disposed of in an involuntary conversion before January 1, 1951, and money is received as compensation for the conversion, no gain shall be recognized if such money is forthwith expended in the acquisition of other property similar or related in service or use to the property so converted, or in the acquisition of control of a corporation owning such other property, or in the establishment of a replacement fund. That section also provides that, if any part of the money is not so expended, the gain, if any, shall be recognized to the extent of the money which is not so expended. For example, if, pursuant to section 381(c)(13) and section 1033(a)(2), property of a distributor or transferor corporation is disposed of before January 1, 1951, in an involuntary conversion, and the proceeds from the conversion are received by the acquiring corporation so that the gain on the conversion is realized by that corporation, the acquiring corporation may avoid recognition of the gain if it complies with the provisions of section 1033(a)(2) for nonrecognition of gain. Thus, the acquiring corporation must forthwith expend the proceeds in the acquisition of similar property or stock, or in the establishment of a replacement fund, in order to avoid recognition of the gain, if the disposition occurred before January 1, 1951. See the provisions of §1.1033(a)-3 and §1.1033(a)-4 relating to involuntary conversions and replacement funds when disposition of the converted property occurred before January 1, 1951.

(e) *Successive acquiring corporations.*—An acquiring corporation which, in a transaction to which section 381(a) applies, acquires the assets of a corporation which previously acquired the assets of another corporation in a transaction to which section 381(a) applies, shall be treated as such other corporation for purposes of applying sections 381(c)(13) and 1033 (relating to involuntary conversions). Thus, for example, if any factor essential to the application of section 1033 occurs on or before the date of distribution or transfer in one transaction to which section 381(a) applies, and any other such factor occurs after the date of distribution or transfer in a subsequent transaction to which section 381(a) applies, then the acquiring corporation in such *subsequent transaction shall be treated as the first* distributor or transferor corporation subject to the rules and limitations of this section for purposes of sections 381(c)(13) and 1033. [Reg. §1.381(c)(13)-1.]

☐ [*T.D. 6552, 3-7-61. Amended by T.D. 7075, 11-23-70.*]

[Reg. §1.381(c)(14)-1]

§1.381(c)(14)-1. Dividend carryover to personal holding company.—(a) *Carryover requirement.*—Section 381(c)(14) provides that an acquiring corporation shall succeed to and take into account the dividend carryover (described in section 564) of a distributor or transferor corporation in computing its dividends paid deduction under section 561 for taxable years ending after the date of distribution or transfer for which the acquiring corporation is a personal holding company under section 542. To determine the amount of such dividend carryover and to integrate it with the dividend carryover of the acquiring corporation in computing the dividends paid deduction for taxable years ending after the date of distribution or transfer, it is necessary to apply the provisions of section 564 and §1.564-1 in accordance with this section.

(b) *Manner of computing dividend carryover.*—(1) *Preceding taxable years.*—If the acquiring corporation is a personal holding company under section 542 for its first taxable year ending after the date of distribution or transfer, the taxable year of the distributor or transferor corporation ending with such date is a first preceding taxable year for purposes of section 564, and the taxable year of the distributor or transferor corporation immediately preceding such first preceding year is a second preceding taxable year for purposes of section 564. If the acquiring corporation is a personal holding company for its second taxable year ending after the date of distribution or transfer, the taxable year of the distributor or transferor corporation ending with such date is a second preceding taxable year for purposes of section 564.

(2) *Determination of dividends paid deduction and taxable income.*—The dividends paid deduction of any distributor or transferor corporation (determined under section 561 but without regard to any dividend carryover) and the taxable income of any such corporation (adjusted as provided in section 545(b)) for any taxable year ending on or before the date of distribution or transfer shall be determined without reference to any dividends paid deduction, or taxable income, of the acquiring corporation or any other distributor or transferor corporation; in like manner, the dividends paid deduction and the taxable income of the acquiring corporation for any such taxable year shall be determined without reference to any dividends paid deduction, or taxable income, of a distributor or transferor corporation.

(3) *Computation of dividend carryover.*—(i) For the purpose of determining the dividend carryover to the first taxable year of the acquiring corporation ending after the date of distribution or transfer, the amount of the dividend carryover from the distributor or transferor corporation shall be determined under section 564 without reference to the dividends paid deduction or taxable income of the acquiring corporation or any other corporation. If two or more transactions to which section 381(a) applies have the same date of distribution or transfer, or if a particular taxable year of the acquiring corporation is the first taxable year ending after the dates of distribution or transfer of two or more such transactions occurring on different dates, the amount of the dividend carryover from each distributor or transferor corporation shall be determined separately as provided in the preceding sentence. Except as provided in subdivision (iii) of this subparagraph, the aggregate of the dividend carryovers from each distributor or transferor corporation and the dividend carryover of the acquiring corporation (computed without regard to this section) shall constitute the dividend carryover under section 561(a)(3) of the acquiring corporation for its first taxable year ending after the date (or dates) of distribution or transfer.

(ii) For the purpose of determining the dividend carryover to the second taxable year of the acquiring corporation ending after the date (or dates) of distribution or transfer, the excess, if any, of the dividends paid deduction (determined under section 561 without regard to any dividend carryover) over the taxable income (adjusted as provided in section 545(b)) for the taxable year of each distributor or transferor corporation and the acquiring corporation referred to as a second preceding taxable year shall be determined separately without reference to the dividends paid deduction or taxable income of any other of such corporations. The excesses thus determined shall be aggregated and such aggregate shall be—

(a) Increased by the excess of the dividends paid deduction (determined without regard to any dividend carryover) over the taxable income (adjusted as provided in section 545(b)), or

(b) Reduced by the excess of the taxable income (adjusted as provided in section 545(b)) over the dividends paid deduction (determined without regard to any dividend carryover),
for the first preceding taxable year of the acquiring corporation. Except as provided in subdivision (iii) of this subparagraph, the amount thus determined shall constitute the dividend carryover under section 561(a)(3) of the acquiring corporation for its second taxable year ending after the date (or dates) of distribution or transfer.

(iii) If a particular taxable year of the acquiring corporation is its first taxable year ending after the date (or dates) of distribution or transfer of one or more transactions to which section 381(a) applies, and if the same taxable year of the acquiring corporation is also its second taxable year ending after the date (or dates) of distribution or transfer of one or more other transactions to which section 381(a) applies, then, for the purpose of determining the dividend carryover to such taxable year of the acquiring corporation, the rules contained in both subdivisions (i) and (ii) of this subparagraph shall be applied. Insofar as such taxable year constitutes the first taxable year ending after the date (or dates) of distribution or transfer of any transaction, the amount of the dividend carryover from any distributor or transferor corporation involved in such transaction shall be determined separately as provided in subdivision (i) of this subparagraph. Insofar as such taxable year constitutes the second taxable year ending after the date (or dates) of distribution or transfer of any transaction, the amount of the dividend carryover from any distributor or transferor corporation involved in the transaction and the acquiring corporation shall be determined as provided in subdivision (ii) of this subparagraph. The aggregate of the dividend carryovers thus determined shall constitute the dividend carryover under section 561(a)(3) of the acquiring corporation for such taxable year. See example (4) in paragraph (c) of this section.

	M Corporation	N Corporation
Second preceding taxable year:		
Dividends paid deduction	$25,000	$12,000
Taxable income	15,000	13,000
Excess dividends paid deduction	$10,000	$0
First preceding taxable year:		
Dividends paid deduction	$23,000	$20,000
Taxable income	21,000	10,000
Excess dividends paid deduction	2,000	10,000
Separate dividend carryovers	$12,000	$10,000

The aggregate dividend carryover of $22,000 is the sum of $12,000 (the separate dividend carryover from M Corporation) and $10,000 (the separate dividend carryover from N Corporation's own preceding taxable years).

(iii) *Dividend carryover to N Corporation's taxable year ending December 31, 1961.* With respect to N Corporation's taxable year ending December 31, 1961, the first preceding taxable year is N Corpora-

	M Corporation	N Corporation
Second preceding taxable year:		
Dividends paid deduction	$23,000	$20,000
Taxable income	21,000	10,000
Separate excess of dividends paid deduction over taxable income	$2,000	$10,000

The aggregate excess of dividends paid deduction over taxable income for the second preceding taxable year is $12,000, the sum of $2,000 (separate excess from M Corporation) and $10,000 (separate

(c) *Illustrations.*—The rules set forth in paragraphs (a) and (b) of this section may be illustrated by the following examples:

Example (1). (i) *Facts.* N Corporation acquired on June 30, 1960, all the assets of M Corporation in a reorganization to which section 381(a) applies. Both corporations compute taxable income on the basis of the calendar year. N Corporation is a personal holding company for its taxable years ending December 31, 1960, and December 31, 1961.

(ii) *Dividend carryover to N Corporation's taxable year ending December 31, 1960.* With respect to N Corporation's taxable year ending December 31, 1960, the taxable years referred to as first preceding taxable years and second preceding taxable years are—

(a) M Corporation's taxable years ending June 30, 1960, and December 31, 1959, respectively; and

(b) N Corporation's taxable years ending December 31, 1959, and December 31, 1958, respectively.

The dividend carryover to N Corporation's taxable year ending December 31, 1960, is $22,000 computed as follows, assuming the dividends paid deduction before dividend carryovers, and the taxable income after section 545(b) adjustments, to be as stated in the computation:

tion's taxable year ending December 31, 1960; and the taxable years referred to as second preceding taxable years are M Corporation's taxable year ending June 30, 1960, and N Corporation's taxable year ending December 31, 1959. The dividend carryover to N Corporation's taxable year ending December 31, 1961, is $17,000 computed as follows, assuming the dividends paid deduction before dividend carryovers, and the taxable income after section 545(b) adjustments, to be as stated in the computation:

excess from N Corporation). Such aggregate excess is increased by the excess dividends paid deduction, or is reduced by the excess of taxable income, for the first preceding taxable year as follows:

Aggregate excess of dividends paid deduction for second preceding taxable year		$12,000
Dividends paid deduction of N Corporation for first preceding taxable year	$50,000	
Taxable income of N Corporation for first preceding taxable year	45,000	
		5,000
Dividend carryover to N Corporation's taxable year ending December 31, 1961		$17,000

Example (2). (i) *Facts.* X Corporation is organized on May 1, 1956, and computes its taxable income on the basis of the fiscal year ending April 30. Y Corporation and Z Corporation are both organized on January 1, 1955, and both compute their taxable income on the basis of the calendar year. On July 31, 1957, X Corporation and Y Corporation transfer all their assets to Z Corporation in a statutory merger to which section 381(a) applies. For its taxable years ending December 31, 1957, and December 31, 1958, Z Corporation is a personal holding company.

(ii) *Dividend carryover to Z Corporation's taxable year ending December 31, 1957.* With respect to Z Corporation's taxable year ending December 31, 1957, the taxable years referred to as first preceding taxable years and second preceding taxable years are—

(a) X Corporation's taxable years ending July 31, 1957, and April 30, 1957, respectively;

(b) Y Corporation's taxable years ending July 31, 1957, and December 31, 1956, respectively; and

(c) Z Corporation's taxable years ending December 31, 1956, and December 31, 1955, respectively.

The dividend carryover to Z Corporation's taxable year ending December 31, 1957, is $40,000 computed as follows, assuming the dividends paid deduction before dividend carryovers, and the taxable income after section 545(b) adjustments, to be as stated in the computation:

	X Corporation		Y Corporation		Z Corporation	
Second preceding taxable year:						
Dividends paid deduction	$56,000		$19,000		$6,000	
Taxable income	24,000		17,000		5,000	
Excess		$32,000		$2,000		$1,000
First preceding taxable year:						
Dividends paid deduction	$9,000		$4,000		$10,000	
Taxable income	7,000		8,000		5,000	
Excess		$2,000		$(4,000)		$5,000
Separate dividend carryovers		$34,000		$0		$6,000

The aggregate dividend carryover of $40,000 is the sum of $34,000 (the separate dividend carryover from X Corporation) and $6,000 (the separate dividend carryover from Z Corporation's own preceding taxable years).

Reg. § 1.381(c)(14)-1(c)

(iii) *Dividend carryover to Z Corporation's taxable year ending December 31, 1958.* With respect to Z Corporation's taxable year ending December 31, 1958, the first preceding taxable year is Z Corporation's taxable year ending December 31, 1957; and the taxable years referred to as second preceding taxable years are X Corporation's taxable year ending July 31, 1957, Y Corporation's taxable year

ending July 31, 1957, and Z Corporation's taxable year ending December 31, 1956. The dividend carryover to Z Corporation's taxable year ending December 31, 1958, is $1,000 computed as follows, assuming the dividends paid deduction before dividend carryovers, and the taxable income after section 545(b) adjustments, to be as stated in the computation:

	X Corporation	Y Corporation	Z Corporation
Second preceding taxable year:			
Dividends paid deduction	$9,000	$4,000	$10,000
Taxable income	7,000	8,000	5,000
Separate excess of dividends paid deduction over taxable income	$2,000	$0	$5,000

The aggregate excess of dividends paid deduction over taxable income for the second preceding taxable year is $7,000, the sum of $2,000 (separate excess from X Corporation) and $5,000 (separate

excess from Z Corporation). Such aggregate excess is increased by the excess dividends paid deduction, or is reduced by the excess of taxable income, for the first preceding taxable year as follows:

Aggregate excess of dividends paid deduction for second preceding taxable year	$7,000
Dividends paid deduction of Z Corporation for first preceding taxable year ... $102,000	
Taxable income of Z Corporation for first preceding taxable year ... $108,000	
	$(6,000)
Dividend carryover to Z Corporation's taxable year ending December 31, 1958	$1,000

Example (3). Assume the facts stated in example (2), except that Y Corporation transferred all its assets to Z Corporation on May 31, 1957. Assume also that the facts for Y Corporation's taxable year ending May 31, 1957, are otherwise the same as those stated for its taxable year in example (2) ending July 31, 1957. In such case, the dividend carryovers to Z Corporation's taxable years ending on December 31, 1957, and December 31, 1958, are the same as in example (2) notwithstanding the fact that the transfers from X Corporation and Y Corporation occurred on the different dates.

Example (4). (i) *Facts.* T Corporation acquired on June 30, 1960, all the assets of U Corporation in a statutory merger to which section 381(a) applies, and in a like transaction acquired on June 30, 1961, all the assets of V Corporation. Such corporations all compute taxable income on the basis of the calendar year. T Corporation is a personal holding company for its taxable years 1960 and 1961.

(ii) *Dividend carryover to T Corporation's taxable year 1960.* With respect to T Corporation's taxable year ending December 31, 1960, the taxable years referred to as first preceding taxable years and second preceding taxable years are—

(*a*) U Corporation's taxable years ending June 30, 1960, and December 31, 1959, respectively; and

(*b*) T Corporation's taxable years ending December 31, 1959, and December 31, 1958, respectively.

The dividend carryover to T Corporation's taxable year ending December 31, 1960, is $7,000 computed as follows, assuming the dividends paid deduction before dividend carryovers, and the taxable income after section 545(b) adjustments, to be as stated in the computation:

	U Corporation		T Corporation	
Second preceding taxable year:				
Dividends paid deduction	$16,000		$10,000	
Taxable income	12,000		13,000	
Excess		$4,000		$0
First preceding taxable year:				
Dividends paid deduction	7,000		17,000	
Taxable income	5,000		16,000	
Excess		2,000		1,000
Separate dividend carryovers		6,000		1,000

The aggregate dividend carryover of $7,000 is the sum of $6,000 (the separate dividend carryover from U Corporation) and $1,000 (the separate dividend carryover from T Corporation's own first preceding taxable year).

(iii) *Dividend carryover to T Corporation's taxable year 1961.* Inasmuch as T Corporation's taxable year 1961 is the second taxable year ending after the date of distribution or transfer from U Corporation, paragraph (b)(3)(ii) of this section governs the determination of the dividend carryover from taxable years of T Corporation and U Corporation. On the other hand, inasmuch as T Corporation's taxable year 1961 is the first taxable year ending after the date of distribution or transfer from V Corporation, paragraph (b)(3)(i) governs the deter-

mination of the dividend carryover from taxable years of V Corporation.

(*a*) *Application of paragraph (b)(3)(ii) of this section.* With respect to T Corporation's taxable year 1961, the first preceding taxable year is T Corporation's taxable year ending December 31, 1960; and the taxable years referred to as second preceding taxable years are T Corporation's taxable year ending December 31, 1959, and U Corporation's taxable year ending June 30, 1960. The dividend carryover from taxable years of T Corporation and U Corporation is $1,500 computed as follows, assuming the dividends paid deduction before dividend carryovers, and the taxable income after section 545(b) adjustments, to be as stated in the computation:

	U Corporation		T Corporation	
Second preceding taxable year:				
Dividends paid deduction	$7,000		$17,000	
Taxable income	5,000		16,000	
Separate excess of dividends paid deduction over taxable income		2,000		1,000

The aggregate excess of dividends paid deduction over taxable income for the second preceding taxable year is $3,000, the sum of $2,000 (separate excess from U Corporation) and $1,000 (separate

excess from T Corporation). Such aggregate is increased by the excess dividends paid deduction, or is reduced by the excess of taxable income, for the first preceding taxable year as follows:

		T Corporation
Aggregate excess of dividends paid deduction for second preceding taxable year		$3,000
First preceding taxable year:		
Dividends paid deduction of T Corporation	$21,000	
Taxable income of T Corporation	22,500	
Excess taxable income		(1,500)
Separate dividend carryover (without regard to V Corporation)		1,500

(*b*) *Application of paragraph (b)(3)(i) of this section.* With respect to T Corporation's taxable year 1961, V Corporation's taxable year ending June 30, 1961, is a first preceding taxable year, and its taxable year

ending December 31, 1960, is a second preceding taxable year. The separate dividend carryover from V Corporation is $8,000 computed as follows, assuming the dividends paid deduction before dividend carryovers, and the taxable income after section 545(b) adjustments, to be as stated in the computation:

		V Corporation
Second preceding taxable year:		
Dividends paid deduction	$11,000	
Taxable income	6,000	
Excess		$5,000
First preceding taxable year:		
Dividends paid deduction	$9,000	
Taxable income	6,000	
Excess		3,000
Separate dividend carryover from V Corporation		$8,000

(c) *Dividend carryover.* The dividend carryover to T Corporation's taxable year 1961 is $9,500, the sum of $8,000 (the separate dividend carryover from V Corporation) and $1,500 (the aggregate dividend carryover from T Corporation and U Corporation).

(d) *Successive carryovers.*—The provisions of this section shall apply for the purpose of determining a dividend carryover to an acquiring corporation which, in a distribution or transfer to which section 381(a) applies, acquires the assets of a distributor or transferor corporation which has previously acquired the assets of another corporation in a transaction to which section 381(a) applies; even though, in computing the dividend carryover to such second acquiring corporation, it is necessary to take into account the deduction for dividends paid, and the adjusted taxable income, of the first distributor or transferor corporation.

(e) *Acquiring corporation not receiving all the assets.*—The dividend carryover acquired from a distributor or transferor corporation by an acquiring corporation in a transaction to which section 381(a) applies is not reduced by reason of the fact that the acquiring corporation does not acquire 100 percent of the assets of the distributor or transferor corporation.

(f) *Dividends paid after the close of taxable year.*—A transaction to which section 381(a) applies does not prevent the application of section 563(b) to a dividend paid by a distributor or transferor corporation after the close of its taxable year ending with the date of distribution or transfer but on or before the 15th day of the third month following the close of such taxable year. However, dividends paid by the acquiring corporation may not be taken into account under section 563(b) for the purpose of determining the dividends paid deduction of the distributor or transferor corporation for its taxable year ending with the date of distribution or transfer. [Reg. §1.381(c)(14)-1.]

☐ [*T.D. 6532, 1-18-61.*]

[Reg. §1.381(c)(15)-1]

§1.381(c)(15)-1. Indebtedness of certain personal holding companies.—(a) *Qualified indebtedness.*—(1) *Carryover requirement.*—If, in a transaction to which section 381(a) applies, the acquiring corporation assumes liability for any indebtedness which was qualified indebtedness (as defined in section 545(c) and §1.545-3) in the hands of the distributor or transferor corporation immediately before the assumption of such indebtedness, then, under section 381(c)(15), in computing its undistributed personal holding company income for any taxable year beginning after December 31, 1963, and ending after the date of distribution or transfer, the acquiring corporation shall be considered the distributor or transferor corporation for purposes of computing the deduction under section 545(c) and §1.545-3. Such deduction shall be allowed to the acquiring corporation in accordance with section 545(c) and §1.545-3.

(2) *Successive transactions to which section 381(a) applies.*—If in a transaction to which section 381(a) applies, an acquiring corporation assumes liability for qualified indebtedness, such acquiring corporation shall be deemed to have incurred such qualified indebtedness for the purpose of applying section 381(c)(15) to any subsequent transaction in which such acquiring corporation is the distributor or transferor corporation.

(b) *Pre-1934 indebtedness.*—(1) *Carryover requirement.*—If, in a transaction to which section 381(a) applies, the acquiring corporation assumes liability for any indebtedness incurred, or assumed, before January 1, 1934, by a distributor or transferor corporation, then under section 381(c)(15) the acquiring corporation shall be allowed, in com-

puting its undistributed personal holding company income for any taxable year ending after the date of distribution or transfer, a deduction under section 545(b)(7) for amounts used or irrevocably set aside to pay or to retire such indebtedness. Such deduction shall be allowed to the acquiring corporation in accordance with section 545(b)(7) and paragraph (g) of §1.545-2 as though the indebtedness had been incurred, or assumed, by the acquiring corporation before January 1, 1934.

(2) *Successive transactions to which section 381(a) applies.*—If, in a transaction to which section 381(a) applies, an acquiring corporation assumes liability for indebtedness described in subparagraph (1) of this paragraph, such acquiring corporation shall be deemed to have incurred the indebtedness before January 1, 1934, for the purpose of applying section 381(c)(15) to any subsequent transaction in which such acquiring corporation is the distributor or transferor corporation.

(c) *Special rule.*—For purposes of this section, if, in a transaction otherwise described in this section, an acquiring corporation acquires real estate—(1) of which the distributor or transferor corporation is the legal or equitable owner immediately before the acquisition, and (2) which is subject to indebtedness that, with respect to the distributor or transferor corporation, is indebtedness described in this section immediately before the acquisition, then the acquiring corporation will be treated as having assumed such indebtedness, provided it shows to the satisfaction of the Commissioner that under all the facts and circumstances it bears the burden of discharging such indebtedness. [Reg. §1.381(c)(15)-1.]

☐ [*T.D. 6532, 1-18-61. Amended by T.D. 6949, 4-8-68.*]

[Reg. §1.381(c)(16)-1]

§1.381(c)(16)-1. Obligations of distributor or transferor corporation.—(a) *Deduction allowed to acquiring corporation.*—(1) If, in a transaction to which section 381(a) applies, the acquiring corporation assumes an obligation of a distributor or transferor corporation which gives rise to a liability after the date of distribution or transfer and if the distributor or transferor corporation would be entitled to deduct such liability in computing taxable income were it paid or accrued after that date by such corporation, then, under the provisions of section 381(c)(16) and this section, the acquiring corporation shall be entitled to deduct such liability as if it were the distributor or transferor corporation. However, in the case of a transaction to which section 381(a)(2) applies, section 381(c)(16) shall not apply to an obligation which is reflected in the amount of consideration, that is, the stock, securities, or other property, transferred by the acquiring corporation to a transferor corporation or its shareholders in exchange for the property of that transferor corporation. An obligation which is so reflected in the amount of consideration will be treated as an item or tax attribute not specified in section 381(c)(16). Such an obligation is subject to section 381(c)(4). See subparagraph (2) of this paragraph. Any deduction allowed under section 381(c)(16) to the acquiring corporation shall be taken by that corporation in the taxable year ending after the date of distribution or transfer in which the liability is paid or accrued by that corporation, as the case may be.

(2) In order to determine whether, in the case of obligations of a distributor or transferor corporation assumed by an acquiring corporation, section 381(c)(16) and this section, or section 381(c)(4) and the regulations thereunder, apply, the following rules shall govern:

(i) If the obligation gave rise to a liability before the date of distribution or transfer, see section 381(c)(4) and the regulations thereunder.

(ii) If the obligation gives rise to a liability after the date of distribution or transfer, and the obligation was not reflected in the amount of consideration transferred by the acquiring corporation to the distributor or transferor corporation or its shareholders in exchange for the property of the distributor or transferor corporation, then section 381(c)(16) and this section shall apply.

(iii) In the case of a transaction to which section 381(a)(1) applies, if the obligation gives rise to a liability after the date of a distribution, and the obligation was reflected in the amount of consideration transferred by the acquiring corporation to the distributor corporation or its shareholders in exchange for the property of the distributor corporation, then section 381(c)(16) and this section shall apply.

(iv) In the case of a transaction to which section 381(a)(2) applies, if the obligation gives rise to a liability after the date of a transfer, and the obligation was reflected in the amount of consideration transferred by the acquiring corporation to the transferor corporation or its shareholders in exchange for the property of the transferor corporation, then see section 381(c)(4) and the regulations thereunder.

(3) The rules of this section apply to obligations assumed by agreement of the parties as well as by operation of law.

(4) For purposes of this section, an obligation of a distributor or transferor corporation gives rise to a liability when the liability would be accruable by a taxpayer using the accrual method of accounting notwithstanding the fact that the distributor or transferor corporation is not using the accrual method of accounting. See paragraph (a)(2) of § 1.461-1.

(5) In the case of a transaction to which section 381(a)(2) applies, the determination as to whether or not an obligation was reflected in the amount of consideration transferred by the acquiring corporation to the transferor corporation or its shareholders in exchange for the property of the transferor corporation shall be made on the basis of all the facts of each particular transfer. Where, on the date of distribution or transfer, the parties were aware of the existence of a specific obligation and reduced the amount of consideration to be transferred by the acquiring corporation by a specific amount because of the existence of such obligation, then such obligation shall be considered to have been reflected in the amount of consideration transferred. In the absence of such facts, it shall be presumed that the obligation was not reflected in the amount of consideration transferred.

(b) *Distribution or transfer occurring under the Internal Revenue Code of 1939.*—Subject to the provisions of section 381(c)(16) and this section, a corporation which would have been an acquiring corporation (under the provisions of paragraph (b) of § 1.381(a)-1) in a transaction to which section 381(a) applies if the date of distribution or transfer had occurred on or after the effective date of the provisions of subchapter C, chapter 1 of the Internal Revenue Code of 1954, applicable to a liquidation or reorganization, as the case may be, shall be entitled to take a deduction for amounts paid or accrued in any taxable year beginning after December 31, 1953, in respect of any obligation which it has assumed from a corporation which would have been a distributor or transferor corporation in such transaction. However, this paragraph shall have no application to a situation described in paragraph (a)(2)(iv) of this section.

(c) *Examples.*—The application of the foregoing rules may be illustrated by the following examples:

Example (1). X Corporation and Y Corporation compute their taxable income on the basis of the calendar year, and both corporations use an accrual method of accounting. On December 31, 1954, Y Corporation acquires the assets of X Corporation in a transfer to which section 381(a)(2) applies. By reason of State law, Y Corporation assumes responsibility for all of the obligations for which X Corporation is then, or may become, liable. The parties have no knowledge of any specific obligations of X Corporation which are not yet fixed and ascertainable, but it is agreed to reduce the amount of consideration that Y Corporation is to transfer in exchange for the assets of X Corporation by $5,000 to reflect any unforeseen contingent liabilities of X Corporation for which Y Corporation might subsequently become liable. After the date of the transfer, a claim for damages on account of the alleged negligence of an alleged agent of X Corporation is filed. After commencement of legal action by the claimant and in order to eliminate the possibility of injury to its business, Y Corporation settles the claim in 1955 by paying the claimant the amount of $3,000. Assuming that such sum would have been deductible under section 162 if paid by X Corporation, Y Corporation is entitled to deduct such sum in accordance with the provisions of section 381(c)(16) and this section in computing its taxable income for 1955, since the claim gave rise to a liability after the date of transfer, *the parties were not aware of a specific obligation,* and the specific obligation was not reflected in the consideration transferred by Y Corporation in exchange for the assets of X Corporation.

Example (2). Assume the same facts as in example (1), except that the claim for damages was filed prior to the transfer of X Corpora-

tion's assets to Y Corporation, but the parties considered the chances for recovery by the claimant so remote that no specific amount other than the $5,000 reduction in consideration for all contingent liabilities as a whole is reflected in the consideration transferred by Y Corporation in exchange for the assets of X Corporation. Assuming that such sum would have been deductible under section 162 if paid by X Corporation, the $3,000 paid by Y Corporation in 1955 is deductible in accordance with the provisions of section 381(c)(16) and this section in 1955.

Example (3). Assume the same facts as in example (1), except that the parties consider the chances of recovery by the claimant of sufficient probability that Y Corporation reduces the amount of consideration it transfers in exchange for the assets of X Corporation by $1,000 in addition to the $5,000 reduction for all other contingent liabilities. The $3,000 paid by Y Corporation in 1955 is not deductible under section 381(c)(16) and this section, since the specific obligation was reflected in the consideration transferred by Y Corporation in exchange for the assets of X Corporation. The deductibility of the payment is accordingly governed by the provisions of section 381(c)(4) and the regulations thereunder. Similarly, if in this case Y Corporation had transferred $10,000 less in consideration for the assets of X Corporation because of this particular claim, Y Corporation would not be entitled to any deduction for the $3,000 paid in 1955 under section 381(c)(16) and this section, and the deductibility of the payment would be governed by the provisions of section 381(c)(4) and the regulations thereunder. If the date of transfer of X Corporation's assets had occurred prior to the effective date of subchapter C, chapter 1 of the Internal Revenue Code of 1954, applicable to a reorganization, no deduction would be allowed to Y corporation under that section. [Reg. § 1.381(c)(16)-1.]

☐ [*T.D.* 6750, 8-4-64.]

[Reg. § 1.381(c)(17)-1]

§ 1.381(c)(17)-1. Deficiency dividend of personal holding company.—(a) *Carryover requirement.*—If a determination (as defined in section 547(c)) establishes that a distributor or transferor corporation in a transaction to which section 381(a) applies is liable for personal holding company tax imposed by section 541 (or by a corresponding provision of prior income tax law) for any taxable year ending on or before the date of distribution or transfer, then in computing such tax the deduction described in section 547 shall be allowed pursuant to section 381(c)(17) to such corporation for the amount of deficiency dividends paid by the acquiring corporation with respect to the distributor or transferor corporation. Except as otherwise provided in this section, the provisions of section 547 and the regulations thereunder apply with respect to a deficiency dividend deduction allowable pursuant to section 381(c)(17).

(b) *Deficiency dividends paid by the acquiring corporation with respect to the distributor or transferor corporation.*—A deficiency dividend paid by the acquiring corporation with respect to the distributor or transferor corporation is a distribution that would satisfy the definition of a deficiency dividend under section 547(d)(1) if paid by the distributor or transferor corporation to its own shareholders except that it shall be paid by the acquiring corporation to its own shareholders and shall be paid after the date of distribution or transfer and on, or within 90 days after, the date of the determination but before the acquiring corporation files claim under paragraph (c) of this section.

(c) *Claim for deduction.*—A claim for a deduction under this section shall be made by the acquiring corporation on Form 976, and shall be filed within 120 days after the date of the determination. The form shall contain, or be accompanied by, the information required under paragraph (b)(2) of § 1.547-2 in sufficient detail to properly identify the facts with the distributor or transferor corporation and the acquiring corporation. The statement required with respect to the shareholders on the date of payment of the deficiency dividend shall relate to the shareholders of the acquiring corporation, and the required certified copy of the resolution authorizing the payment of the dividend shall be that of the board of directors, or other authority, of the acquiring corporation. Necessary changes may be made in Form 976 in order to carry out the provisions of this paragraph. The claim shall be filed with the district director for the internal revenue district in which the return of the distributor or transferor corporation to which such claim relates was filed.

(d) *Effect on dividends paid deduction.*—A deficiency dividend paid by the acquiring corporation, which is allowable as a deduction to a distributor or transferor corporation pursuant to section 381(c)(17), shall not become a part of the dividends paid deduction of the acquiring corporation under section 561 for any taxable year.

(e) *Successive transactions to which section 381(a) applies.*—The provisions of this section shall apply in the case of successive transactions to which section 381(a) applies. Thus, if X Corporation transfers its assets to Y Corporation in a transaction to which section 381(a) applies and if Y Corporation transfers its assets to Z Corporation in a subsequent transaction to which section 381(a) applies, then, subject to the provisions of this section, X Corporation may take a deficiency dividend deduction for the amount of deficiency dividends paid by Z Corporation with respect to X Corporation.

(f) *Example.*—The provisions of this section may be illustrated by the following example:

Example. M Corporation, a personal holding company, computes its taxable income on the basis of the calendar year. On December 31, 1956, N Corporation acquires the assets of M Corporation in a transaction to which section 381(a) applies. On July 31, 1958, a determination (as defined in section 547(c)) establishes that M Corporation is liable for the taxable year 1955 for personal holding company tax in the amount of $35,500 based on undistributed personal holding company income of $42,000 for such taxable year. N Corporation complies with the provisions of this section and on September 30, 1958, distributes $42,000 to its shareholders as deficiency dividends with respect to M Corporation's taxable year 1955. The distribution of $42,000 by N Corporation is a taxable dividend under section 316(b)(2) regardless of whether N Corporation is a personal holding company for the taxable year 1958 or whether it had any current or accumulated earnings and profits. See example (3) in paragraph (e) of §1.316-1. Because N Corporation has paid deficiency dividends of $42,000 in accordance with this section, M Corporation is entitled to a deficiency dividend deduction of $42,000 for the taxable year 1955 and is thus relieved of its liability for personal holding company tax of $35,500 for such taxable year. To prevent duplication of deductions, the amount distributed by N Corporation in 1958 does not become a part of N Corporation's dividends paid deduction under section 561 for any taxable year. [Reg. §1.381(c)(17)-1.]

☐ [T.D. 6532, 1-16-61. *Amended by* T.D. 7604, 3-28-79 *and by* T.D. 7767, 2-3-81.]

[Reg. §1.381(c)(18)-1]

§1.381(c)(18)-1. Depletion on extraction of ores or minerals from the waste or residue of prior mining.—(a) *Carryover requirement.*—Section 381(c)(18) provides that the acquiring corporation in a transaction described in section 381(a) shall be considered as though it were the distributor or transferor corporation after the date of distribution or transfer for the purpose of determining the applicability of section 613(c)(3) (relating to extraction of ores or minerals from the ground). Thus, an acquiring corporation which has acquired the waste or residue of prior mining from a distributor or transferor corporation in a transaction described in section 381(a) shall be entitled, after the date of distribution or transfer, to an allowance for depletion under section 611 in respect of ores or minerals extracted from such waste or residue if the distributor or transferor corporation would have been entitled to such an allowance for depletion in the absence of the distribution or transfer. See paragraph (f) of §1.613-4 to determine whether a distributor or transferor corporation is entitled to an allowance for depletion with respect to the waste or residue of prior mining.

(b) *Application of section 614 to waste or residue of prior mining.*—If, in a transaction described in section 381(a), the acquiring corporation acquires waste or residue of prior mining from a distributor or transferor corporation, then the acquiring corporation shall be considered as though it were the distributor or transferor corporation for the purpose of applying section 614 and the regulations thereunder to the waste or residue so acquired. Thus, if the distributor or transferor corporation was required under paragraph (c) of §1.614-1 to treat the waste or residue as part of the mineral deposit from which it was extracted and if the acquiring corporation acquires both the waste or residue and the mineral deposit from which it was extracted in a transaction described in section 381(a), then such waste or residue shall be treated as a part of such mineral deposit in the hands of the acquiring corporation. On the other hand, if the waste or residue was required to be treated as a separate mineral deposit in the hands of the distributor or transferor corporation, such waste or residue shall be treated as a separate mineral deposit in the hands of the acquiring corporation. [Reg. §1.381(c)(18)-1.]

☐ [T.D. 6552, 3-7-61. *Amended by* T.D. 7170, 3-10-72.]

[Reg. §1.381(c)(19)-1]

§1.381(c)(19)-1. Charitable contributions carryovers in certain acquisitions.—(a) *Carryover requirement.*—Section 381(c)(19) provides that, in computing taxable income for its taxable years which begin after the date of distribution or transfer to which section 381(a) applies, the acquiring corporation shall take into account any charitable contributions made by a distributor or transferor corporation during the taxable year ending on the date of distribution or transfer, and in certain immediately preceding taxable years, which are in excess of the maximum amount deductible for those taxable years under section 170(b)(2) in the following manner:

(1) If the taxable year of the distributor or transferor corporation ending on the date of distribution or transfer begins before January 1, 1962, the acquiring corporation shall, in computing taxable income for its first 2 taxable years which begin after the date of such distribution or transfer, take into account the excess contributions made by the distributor or transferor corporation in the taxable year ending on the date of distribution or transfer and in the immediately preceding taxable year;

(2) If the taxable year of the distributor or transferor corporation ending on the date of distribution or transfer begins after December 31, 1961, the acquiring corporation shall, in computing taxable income for certain taxable years which begin after the date of distribution or transfer, take into account the excess contributions made by the distributor or transferor corporation in the taxable year ending on such date of distribution or transfer and in any of the 4 taxable years immediately preceding such taxable year but excluding any taxable year beginning before January 1, 1962 (see paragraph (c)(3) of this section). Notwithstanding the preceding sentence, if the taxable year of the distributor or transferor corporation ending on the date of distribution or transfer begins after December 31, 1961, and before January 1, 1963, the acquiring corporation shall, in computing taxable income for its first taxable year which begins after the date of distribution or transfer, also take into account the excess contributions made by the distributor or transferor corporation in the taxable year immediately preceding the taxable year of the distributor or transferor corporation ending on the date of distribution or transfer (see paragraph (c)(2) of this section).

To determine the amount of excess contributions made by a distributor or transferor corporation and to integrate them with contributions made by the acquiring corporation for the purpose of determining the charitable contributions deductible by the acquiring corporation for its taxable years beginning immediately after the date of distribution or transfer, it is necessary to apply the provisions of section 170(b)(2) and §1.170-3 (or, if applicable, section 170(b)(2) and (d)(2) and §1.170A-11) in accordance with the conditions and limitations of section 381(c)(19) and this section. For taxable years beginning before January 1, 1970, see §1.170 for provisions of section 170(b)(2) as referred to in this section. For taxable years beginning after December 31, 1969, see §1.170A for provisions of section 170(b)(2) or (d)(2) as referred to in this section. For special rules for applying section 170(d)(2) with respect to contributions paid, or treated as paid, in taxable years beginning before January 1, 1970, see paragraph (d) of §1.170A-11.

(b) *Manner of computing excess charitable contribution carryovers.*—(1) The amount of any charitable contribution made by a distributor or transferor corporation in any taxable year ending on or before the date of distribution or transfer, or made by the acquiring corporation in any taxable year before its taxable year beginning after the date of distribution or transfer, in excess of the amount allowable as a deduction to such corporation for such taxable year under section 170(b)(2) shall be determined by taking into account the taxable income of, and the contributions made by, that corporation only.

(2) An acquiring corporation which, in a distribution or transfer to which section 381(a) applies, acquires the assets of a distributor or transferor corporation which previously acquired the assets of another corporation in a transaction to which section 381(a) applies, shall succeed to and take into account, subject to the conditions and limitations of sections 170 and 381, the charitable contribution carryovers available to the first acquiring corporation under sections 170 and 381, including those derived by such first acquiring corporation from its distributor or transferor corporation.

(3) The excess charitable contributions made by a distributor or transferor corporation in its taxable year ending on the date of distribution or transfer and in certain immediately preceding taxable years (see paragraph (c) of this section) which are not deductible by the distributor or transferor corporation because of the 5-percent limitation of section 170(b)(2) shall be available to the acquiring corporation without diminution by reason of the fact that the acquiring corporation does not acquire 100 percent of the assets of the distributor or transferor corporation. Thus, if a parent corporation owning 80 percent of all classes of stock of its subsidiary corporation were to acquire its share of the assets of the subsidiary corporation upon a complete liquidation described in paragraph (b)(1)(i) of §1.381(a)-1, then, subject to the conditions and limitations of this section, 100 percent of the excess contributions made by the subsidiary corporation would be available to the acquiring corporations.

(c) *Taxable years to which carryovers apply and amount deductible.*—
(1) *Taxable years beginning before January 1, 1962.*—If the taxable year of the distributor or transferor corporation ending on the date of distribution or transfer begins before January 1, 1962:

(i) The excess charitable contributions made by a distributor or transferor corporation in its taxable year immediately preceding that ending on the date of distribution or transfer, to the extent not deductible by it because of the limitations of section 170(b)(2) in its taxable year ending on that date, shall be deductible by the acquiring corporation to the extent prescribed by section 170(b)(2) in its first taxable year beginning after the date of distribution or transfer. Any portion of such excess which is not deductible under this section by the acquiring corporation in such first taxable year shall not be deducted by that corporation in any other taxable year.

(ii) The excess charitable contributions made by a distributor or transferor corporation in its taxable year ending on the date of distribution or transfer shall first be deductible by the acquiring corporation to the extent prescribed by section 170(b)(2) and this section in its first taxable year beginning after that date and then, to the extent prescribed by section 170(b)(2) and this section, in its second taxable year beginning after that date. Any portion of such excess which is not deductible under this section by the acquiring corporation in such first and second taxable years shall not be deducted by that corporation in any other taxable year.

(2) *Taxable years beginning in 1962.*—If the taxable year of the distributor or transferor corporation ending on the date of distribution or transfer begins after December 31, 1961, and before January 1, 1963:

(i) The excess charitable contributions made by a distributor or transferor corporation in its taxable year immediately preceding that ending on the date of distribution or transfer, to the extent not deductible by it because of the limitations of section 170(b)(2) in its taxable year ending on that date, shall be deductible by the acquiring corporation to the extent prescribed by section 170(b)(2) in its first taxable year beginning after the date of distribution or transfer. Any portion of such excess which is not deductible under this section by the acquiring corporation in such first year shall not be deducted by that corporation in any other taxable year.

(ii) The excess charitable contributions made by a distributor or transferor corporation in its taxable year ending on the date of distribution or transfer and beginning after December 31, 1961, and before January 1, 1963, shall first be deductible by the acquiring corporation to the extent prescribed by section 170(b)(2) and this section in its first taxable year beginning after that date and then, to the extent prescribed by section 170(b)(2) and this section, in its second, third, fourth, and fifth taxable year,' in order of time, beginning after that date. Any portion of such excess which is not deductible under this section by the acquiring corporation in such 5 taxable years shall not be deducted by that corporation in any other taxable year.

(3) *Taxable years beginning after December 31, 1962.*—(i) If the taxable year of the distributor or transferor corporation ending on the date of distribution or transfer begins after December 31, 1962, the excess charitable contributions made by a distributor or transferor corporation in its taxable year ending on the date of distribution or transfer and in each of its 4 immediately preceding taxable years (excluding any taxable year beginning before January 1, 1962), to the extent not deductible by it because of the limitations of section 170(b)(2) in its taxable year ending on the date of distribution or transfer or its prior taxable years, shall be deductible by the acquiring corporation to the extent prescribed by section 170(b)(2) (or, if applicable, section 170(d)(2)) and subdivision (ii) of this subparagraph, in its taxable years which begin after the date of distribution or transfer. However, any portion of the excess charitable contributions made by a distributor or transferor corporation in a particular taxable year, to which this subparagraph is applicable, which is not deductible under this section within the 5 taxable years immediately following the taxable year in which the contribution was paid by the distributor or transferor corporation shall not be deductible by the acquiring corporation in any other taxable year.

(ii) For purposes of determining the 5 taxable years in which the excess contributions may be deducted, all taxable years of the distributor or transferor corporation subsequent to the taxable year in which the excess contribution was made, including the taxable year ending on the date of distribution or transfer, shall be treated as taxable years of the acquiring corporation.

(iii) The provisions of this subparagraph may be illustrated by the following example:

Example. X Corporation and Y Corporation both compute taxable income on the calendar year basis. X Corporation has excess charitable contributions for 1962 and 1964. On December 31, 1966, X

Corporation distributes all its assets to Y Corporation in a complete liquidation to which section 381(a) applies. The excess 1962 charitable contributions of X Corporation (to the extent not deductible by X because of the limitations of section 170(b)(2) in its taxable years 1963 through 1966) may be deducted by Y Corporation only in 1967. Y Corporation's taxable year 1967 is the fifth taxable year succeeding the taxable year 1962 (the year in which the excess contributions were made), and the portion of such excess contributions which is not deductible in the 5 taxable years immediately succeeding 1962 (1963 through 1967) is not deductible by Y Corporation in any other taxable year. Any excess charitable contributions for 1964 to which Y Corporation may be entitled must be deducted by Y Corporation (if deductible at all) in 1967, 1968, and 1969 since such years are the third, fourth, and fifth taxable years succeeding the taxable year 1964 (the year in which the excess contributions were paid).

(4) *General rules.*—No excess charitable contributions made by a distributor or transferor corporation shall be deductible by the acquiring corporation in its taxable year which includes the date of distribution or transfer. In addition, an excess charitable contribution made by a distributor or transferor corporation in a taxable year prior to the taxable year of the transfer is only deductible by the distributor or transferor corporation, subject to the limitations of section 170(b)(2) (or, if applicable, section 170(d)(2)), in its subsequent taxable years which begin on or before the date of distribution or transfer, and by the acquiring corporation in its taxable year or years beginning after the date of distribution or transfer.

(d) *Rules governing amounts deductible by acquiring corporations.*—(1) In applying the provisions of section 170(b)(2) (or, if applicable, section 170 (d)(2)) for the purpose of determining the amount of excess charitable contributions which are deductible by the acquiring corporation in its taxable years beginning after the date of distribution or transfer, all taxable years of the distributor or transferor and acquiring corporations which, with respect to a particular taxable year beginning after the date of distribution or transfer, constitute the same numbered preceding taxable year shall together be considered as one taxable year even though the taxable years involved may not end on the same date. Thus, for example, all taxable years of the distributor or transferor and acquiring corporations which, with respect to the first taxable year of the acquiring corporation beginning after the date of distribution or transfer, constitute the second preceding taxable year shall together be considered as one taxable year even though the taxable years involved may not end on the same date. Any excess charitable contributions carried over from preceding taxable years which are considered as one taxable year shall be taken into account by the acquiring corporation as one amount, without regard to the extent to which the contributions were made by a distributor or transferor corporation or the acquiring corporation.

(2) For purposes of this paragraph, each taxable year of the distributor or transferor corporation beginning on or before the date of distribution or transfer shall be treated as a preceding taxable year with reference to the acquiring corporation's taxable years beginning after such date. For example, the taxable year of a distributor or transferor corporation which ends on the date of distribution or transfer shall be considered a first preceding taxable year with reference to the acquiring corporation's first taxable year beginning after that date, a second preceding taxable year with reference to the acquiring corporation's second taxable year beginning after that date, and so forth with respect to succeeding taxable years of the acquiring corporation. Also for example, the taxable year of a distributor or transferor corporation which immediately precedes its taxable year ending on the date of distribution or transfer shall be considered a second preceding taxable year with reference to the acquiring corporation's first taxable year beginning after that date.

(e) *Illustration.*—The application of this section may be illustrated by the following example:

Example. (i) X Corporation is organized on April 1, 1956, and computes its taxable income on the basis of the fiscal year ending March 31. Y Corporation is organized on July 1, 1955, and computes its taxable income on the basis of the fiscal year ending June 30. Z Corporation is organized on January 1, 1956, and computes its taxable income on the basis of the calendar year. On June 30, 1957, X Corporation distributes all its assets to Y Corporation in a complete liquidation to which section 381(a) applies. On November 30, 1957, Y Corporation transfers all its assets to Z Corporation in a statutory merger to which section 381(a) applies.

(ii) The 5-percent limitation (computed in the manner prescribed by section 170(b)(2)), the charitable contributions actually paid, and the excess contributions with respect to each such corporation during the taxable years involved are as follows:

Name of corporation Taxable year ending	X 3-31-57	X 6-30-57	
5-percent limitation	$20,000	$9,000	
Current contributions	32,000	15,000	
(Excess contributions)	(12,000)	(6,000)	

Name of corporation Taxable year ending	Y 6-30-56	Y 6-30-57	Y 11-30-57
5-percent limitation	$15,000	$10,000	$18,000
Current contributions	29,000	0	17,000
(Excess contributions)	(14,000)		
Balance of 5-percent limitation		$10,000	$1,000

Name of corporation Taxable year ending	Z 12-31-56	Z 12-31-57	Z 12-31-58
5-percent limitation	$10,000	$30,000	$58,000
Current contributions	40,000	28,000	2,000
(Excess contributions)	(30,000)		
Balance of 5-percent limitation		$2,000	$56,000

(iii) X Corporation was in existence for two taxable years, in each of which it made charitable contributions in excess of the maximum amount deductible for those years under section 170(b)(2). The excess contributions made in the year ending March 31, 1957, of $12,000, are deductible by X Corporation in its short taxable year ending June 30, 1957, and then by Y Corporation in its short taxable year ending November 30, 1957, in each instance in the manner and to the extent prescribed by section 170(b)(2) and this section. The excess contributions made by X Corporation in the year ending June 30, 1957, of $6,000, are deductible by Y Corporation in its short taxable year ending November 30, 1957, and then by Z Corporation in its taxable year 1958, in each instance in the manner and to the extent prescribed by section 170(b)(2) and this section.

(iv) Y Corporation was in existence for three taxable years. In the year ended June 30, 1956, its contributions in excess of the amount deductible for that year under section 170(b)(2) amounted to $14,000. Such excess is deductible by Y Corporation in its taxable year ending June 30, 1957, and, together with X Corporation's excess contributions of $18,000, in its short taxable year ending November 30, 1957, in each instance in the manner and to the extent prescribed by section 170(b)(2) and this section. Accordingly, since Y Corporation made no contributions in its taxable year ending June 30, 1957, its deduction for that year on account of excess contributions carried over is $10,000, an amount equal to the 5-percent limitation of section 170(b)(2). The deduction is attributable to excess contributions made by Y Corporation in the taxable year ended June 30, 1956; thus, the excess of those contributions over $10,000, namely, $4,000, is deductible by Y Corporation in its short taxable year ending November 30, 1957, in the manner and to the extent prescribed by section 170(b)(2) and this section. With respect to the short taxable year ending November 30, 1957, the excess contributions of the second preceding year are X Corporation's excess contributions of $12,000 made in the year ending March 31, 1957, and Y Corporation's excess contributions of $4,000 made in the year ending June 30, 1956, which were not deductible by Y Corporation in the taxable year ending June 30, 1957, because of the 5-percent limitation prescribed by section 170(b)(2), an aggregate of $16,000. Inasmuch as Y Corporation's limitation for the short taxable year ended November 30, 1957, exceeds the contributions made in that year by $1,000, the excess contributions of the second preceding taxable year are deductible in the taxable year ending November 30, 1957, to the extent of $1,000 and the remainder ($15,000) is not deductible by any corporation in any taxable year. The excess contributions of the first preceding taxable year, namely, X Corporation's excess contributions made in the short taxable year ending June 30, 1957, are deductible by Z Corporation in its taxable year 1958, in the manner and to the extent prescribed by section 170(b)(2) and this section.

(v) Z Corporation has been in existence for 3 taxable years. The contributions made in 1956 in excess of the amount deductible for that year under section 170(b)(2) amounted to $30,000. Such excess is deductible by Z Corporation in its taxable year 1957 and, together with X Corporation's excess contributions of $6,000 (derived through Y Corporation) made in the taxable year ending June 30, 1957, in the taxable year 1958, in each instance in the manner and to the extent prescribed by section 170(b)(2) and this section. Thus, $2,000 of the $30,000 excess contributions made in the year 1956 are deducted in 1957 and the remainder ($28,000) together with X Corporation's excess contributions of $6,000 made in the short taxable year ending June 30, 1957, are deducted in 1958 since the aggregate of such amounts plus the contributions actually made in that year does not exceed the 5-percent limitation prescribed by section 170(b)(2). [Reg. §1.381(c)(19)-1.]

☐ [*T.D.* 6552, 3-7-61. *Amended by T.D.* 6900, 11-16-66 *and by T.D.* 7207, 10-3-72.]

[Reg. §1.381(c)(20)-1]

§1.381(c)(20)-1. Carryforward of disallowed business interest.—
(a) *Carryover requirement.*—Section 381(c)(20) provides that the acquiring corporation in a transaction described in section 381(a) will succeed to and take into account the carryover of disallowed business interest described in section 163(j)(2) to taxable years ending after the date of distribution or transfer.

(b) *Carryover of disallowed business interest described in section 163(j)(2).*—For purposes of section 381(c)(20) and this section, the term *carryover of disallowed business interest described in section 163(j)(2)* means the disallowed business interest expense carryforward (as defined in §1.163(j)-1(b)(11)), including any disallowed disqualified interest (as defined in §1.163(j)-1(b)(12)), and including the distributor or transferor corporation's disallowed business interest expense from the taxable year that ends on the date of distribution or transfer. For the application of section 382 to disallowed business interest expense described in section 163(j)(2), see the regulations in this part under section 382 of the Code, including but not limited to §1.382-2.

(c) *Limitation on use of disallowed business interest expense carryforwards in the acquiring corporation's first taxable year ending after the date of distribution or transfer.*—(1) *In general.*—In determining the extent to which the acquiring corporation may use disallowed business interest expense carryforwards in its first taxable year ending after the date of distribution or transfer, the principles of §§1.381(c)(1)-1 and 1.381(c)(1)-2 apply with appropriate adjustments, including but not limited to the adjustments described in paragraphs (c)(2) and (3) of this section.

(2) *One date of distribution or transfer within the acquiring corporation's taxable year.*—If the acquiring corporation succeeds to the disallowed business interest expense carryforwards of one or more distributor or transferor corporations on a single date of distribution or transfer within one taxable year of the acquiring corporation, then, for the acquiring corporation's first taxable year ending after the date of distribution or transfer, that part of the acquiring corporation's business interest expense deduction (if any) that is attributable to the disallowed business interest expense carryforwards of the distributor or transferor corporation is limited under this paragraph (c) to an amount equal to the post-acquisition portion of the acquiring corporation's section 163(j) limitation, as defined in paragraph (c)(4) of this section.

(3) *Two or more dates of distribution or transfer in the taxable year.*—If the acquiring corporation succeeds to the disallowed business interest expense carryforwards of two or more distributor or transferor corporations on two or more dates of distribution or transfer within one taxable year of the acquiring corporation, the limitation to be applied under this paragraph (c) is determined by applying the principles of §1.381(c)(1)-2(b) to the post-acquisition portion of the acquiring corporation's section 163(j) limitation, as defined in paragraph (c)(4) of this section.

(4) *Definition.*—For purposes of this paragraph (c), the term *post-acquisition portion of the acquiring corporation's section 163(j) limitation* means the amount that bears the same ratio to the acquiring corporation's section 163(j) limitation (within the meaning of §1.163(j)-1(b)(31)) (or, if the acquiring corporation is a member of a consolidated group, the consolidated group's section 163(j) limitation) for the first taxable year ending after the date of distribution or transfer (taking into account items to which the acquiring corporation succeeds under section 381, other than disallowed business interest expense carryforwards) as the number of days in that year

after the date of distribution or transfer bears to the total number of days in that year.

(5) *Examples.*—For purposes of this paragraph (c)(5), unless otherwise stated, X, Y, and Z are taxable domestic C corporations that were incorporated on January 1, 2021 and that file their tax returns on a calendar-year basis; none of X, Y, or Z is a member of a consolidated group; the small business exemption in §1.163(j)-2(d) does not apply; interest expense is deductible except to the extent of the potential application of section 163(j); and the facts set forth the only corporate activity. The principles of this paragraph (c) are illustrated by the following examples.

(i) *Example 1: Transfer before last day of acquiring corporation's taxable year.*—(A) *Facts.* On October 31, 2022, X transferred all of its assets to Y in a statutory merger to which section 361 applies. For the 2021 taxable year, X had $400x of disallowed business interest expense, and Y had $0 of disallowed business interest expense. For the taxable year ending October 31, 2022, X had an additional $350x of disallowed business interest expense (X did not deduct any of its 2021 carryforwards in its 2022 taxable year). For the taxable year ending December 31, 2022, Y had business interest expense of $100x, business interest income of $200x, and ATI of $1,000x. Y's section 163(j) limitation for the 2022 taxable year was $500x ($200x + (30 percent x $1,000x) = $500x).

(B) *Analysis.* Pursuant to §1.163(j)-5(b)(2), Y deducts its $100x of current-year business interest expense (as defined in §1.163(j)-1(b)(9)) before any disallowed business interest expense carryforwards (including X's carryforwards) from a prior taxable year are deducted. The aggregate disallowed business interest expense of X carried forward under section 381(c)(20) to Y's taxable year ending December 31, 2022, is $750x. However, pursuant to paragraph (c)(2) of this section, for Y's first taxable year ending after the date of distribution or transfer, the maximum amount of X's disallowed business interest expense carryforwards that Y can deduct is equal to the post-acquisition portion of Y's section 163(j) limitation. Pursuant to paragraph (c)(4) of this section, the post-acquisition portion of Y's section 163(j) limitation means Y's section 163(j) limitation times the ratio of the number of days in the taxable year after the date of distribution or transfer to the total number of days in that year. Therefore, only $84x of the aggregate amount ($500x x (61/365) = $84x) may be deducted by Y in that year, and the remaining $666x ($750x - $84x = $666x) is carried forward to the succeeding taxable year.

(C) *Transfer on last day of acquiring corporation's taxable year.* The facts are the same as in *Example 1* in paragraph (c)(5)(i)(A) of this section, except that X's transfer of its assets to Y occurred on December 31, 2022. For the taxable year ending December 31, 2022, X had an additional $350x of disallowed business interest expense (X did not deduct any of its 2021 carryforwards in its 2022 taxable year). For the taxable year ending December 31, 2023, Y had business interest expense of $100x, business interest income of $200x, and ATI of $1,000x. Y's section 163(j) limitation for the 2023 taxable year was $500x ($200x + (30 percent x $1,000x) = $500x). The aggregate disallowed business interest expense of X carried under section 381(c)(20) to Y's taxable year ending December 31, 2023, is $750x. Paragraph (c)(2) of this section does not limit the amount of X's disallowed business interest expense carryforwards that may be deducted by Y in the 2023 taxable year. Since the amount of Y's section 163(j) limit for the 2023 taxable year was $500x, Y may deduct the full amount ($100x) of its own business interest expense for the 2023 taxable year, along with $400x of X's disallowed business interest expense carryforwards.

(ii) *Example 2: Multiple transferors on same date.*—(A) *Facts.* On October 31, 2022, X and Y transferred all of their assets to Z in statutory mergers to which section 361 applies. For the 2021 taxable year, X had $300x of disallowed business interest expense, Y had $200x, and Z had $0. For the taxable year ending October 31, 2022, each of X and Y had an additional $125x of disallowed business interest expense (neither X nor Y deducted any of its 2021 carryforwards in 2022). For the taxable year ending December 31, 2022, Z had business interest expense of $100x, business interest income of $200x, and ATI of $1,000x. Z's section 163(j) limitation for the 2022 taxable year was $500x ($200x + (30 percent x $1,000x) = $500x).

(B) *Analysis.* The aggregate disallowed business interest expense of X and Y carried under section 381(c)(20) to Z's taxable year ending December 31, 2022, is $750x. However, pursuant to paragraph (c)(2) of this section, only $84x of the aggregate amount ($500x x (61/365) = $84x) may be deducted by Z in that year. Moreover, under paragraph (b)(2) of this section, this amount only may be deducted by Z in that year after Z has deducted its $100x of current-year business interest expense (as defined in §1.163(j)-1(b)(9)).

(d) *Applicability date.*—This section applies to taxable years beginning on or after November 13, 2020. However, taxpayers and their

related parties, within the meaning of sections 267(b) and 707(b)(1), may choose to apply the rules of this section to a taxable year beginning after December 31, 2017, so long as the taxpayers and their related parties consistently apply the rules of the section 163(j) regulations (as defined in §1.163(j)-1(b)(37)), and, if applicable, §§1.263A-9, 1.263A-15, 1.382-1, 1.382-2, 1.382-5, 1.382-6, 1.382-7, 1.383-0, 1.383-1, 1.469-9, 1.469-11, 1.704-1, 1.882-5, 1.1362-3, 1.1368-1, 1.1377-1, 1.1502-13, 1.1502-21, 1.1502-36, 1.1502-79, 1.1502-91 through 1.1502-99 (to the extent they effectuate the rules of §§1.382-2, 1.382-5, 1.382-6, and 1.383-1), and 1.1504-4, to that taxable year. [Reg. §1.381(c)(20)-1.]

☐ [*T.D.* 9905, 9-3-2020.]

[Reg. §1.381(c)(22)-1]

§1.381(c)(22)-1. Successor life insurance company.—(a) *Carryover requirement.*—If in a taxable year beginning after December 31, 1957, a distributor or transferor corporation which is an insurance company is acquired by a corporation which is an insurance company in a transaction to which section 381(a) applies, section 381(c)(22) provides that the acquiring corporation shall take into account the appropriate items which the distributor or transferor corporation was required to take into account for purposes of part I, subchapter L, chapter 1 of the Internal Revenue Code. Furthermore, except as otherwise provided by this section, the acquiring corporation shall take into account the items described in paragraphs (2) through (21), other than paragraphs (14), (15), and (17), of section 381(c) and the regulations thereunder. For example, the acquiring corporation shall take into account the reserves described in section 810(c) distributed or transferred to it as of the close of the date of distribution or transfer by the distributor or transferor corporation in accordance with the provisions of section 381(c)(4) and the regulations thereunder. For provisions defining the date of distribution or transfer, see paragraph (b) of §1.381(b)-1.

(b) *Items required to be taken into account by acquiring corporation.*—If a transaction meets the requirements of paragraph (a) of this section, the acquiring corporation shall, except as otherwise provided, take into account as of the close of the date of distribution or transfer the following items of the distributor or transferor corporation:

(1) The operations loss carryovers (as determined under section 812), subject to conditions and limitations consistent with the conditions and limitations prescribed in section 381(c)(1) and the regulations thereunder. For example, a loss from operations for a loss year of a distributor or transferor corporation which ends on or before the last day of a loss year of the acquiring corporation shall be considered to be a loss from operations for a year prior to such loss year of the acquiring corporation. All references in section 381(c)(1) and the regulations thereunder to section 172 shall be construed as referring to the appropriate corresponding provisions of section 812. Thus, a reference to section 172(b) shall be construed as referring to section 812(b) and (d). In determining the span of years for which a loss from operations may be carried, the number of taxable years for which the distributor or transferor corporation was authorized to do business as an insurance company shall be taken into account. For purposes of this determination, the taxable year of the distributor or transferor corporation which ends on the date of distribution or transfer shall be taken into account even though such taxable year is a period of less than 12 months.

(2)(i) The investment yield and the beginning of the year asset balance for the distributor or transferor corporation's taxable year ending with the close of the date of distribution or transfer. Such items shall be integrated with the investment yield and beginning of the year asset balance of the acquiring corporation for its first taxable year ending after such date of distribution or transfer for purposes of determining the current earnings rate of the acquiring corporation for such taxable year. Furthermore, for purposes of determining the average earnings rate of the acquiring corporation, the investment yield and mean of the assets of the distributor or transferor corporation for its 4 taxable years immediately preceding its taxable year which closes with the date of distribution or transfer shall be integrated with the investment yield and mean of the assets of the acquiring corporation for such corresponding taxable years.

(ii) The provisions of this subparagraph may be illustrated by the following examples:

Example (1). X qualified as a life insurance company in 1949. Y qualified as a life insurance company in 1951. On June 30, 1961, at which time both X and Y were life insurance companies (as defined in section 801(a)), X transferred all its assets to Y in a statutory merger to which section 361 applies. For its taxable year ending on June 30, 1961, X had investment yield of $15 and assets at the beginning of such taxable year of $450. For purposes of determining its current earnings rate for its taxable year ending on December 31, 1961, Y had investment yield of $45 (including the $15 of investment yield of X), assets at the beginning of such taxable year of $1,250 (including the $450 of X's assets at the beginning of its taxable year 1961), and assets at the end of such taxable year of $1,750 (after the application of section 806(a)). Under the provisions of subdivision (i) of this subparagraph, the current earnings rate of Y for the taxable year 1961 would be 3 percent, determined by dividing the investment yield of Y, $45, by the mean of the assets of Y, $1,500 ($1,250 + $1,750 ÷ 2). In order to determine its average earnings rate and adjusted reserves rate for the taxable year 1961, Y would make up the following schedule:

| Taxable Year | Investment Yield | | | Mean of Assets | | | Current Earnings Rate of Y |
	Col. 1X	Col. 2Y	Col. 3 (Col. 1 + Col. 2) Integrated Investment Yield	Col. 4X	Col. 5Y	Col. 6 (Col. 4 + Col. 5) Integrated means of assets	Col. 7 (Col. 3 + Col. 6)
1960	$16	$26	$42	$400	$800	$1,200	
1959	16	24	40	500	750	1,250	3.5
1958	17	22	39	650	650	1,300	3.2
1957	19	21	40	700	500	1,200	3.0
							3.3

For the taxable year 1961, Y would have an average earnings rate of 3.2 percent, computed by taking into account the current earnings rates for the taxable year 1961 and each of the 4 taxable years immediately preceding such taxable year. The adjusted reserves rate for such taxable year would be 3 percent since the current earnings rate of 3 percent for 1961 is lower than the average earnings rate of 3.2 percent.

Example (2). The facts are the same as in example (1), except that the taxable year in issue is 1962, and the current earnings rate of Y for such taxable year was 3.8 percent. For the taxable year 1962, Y would have an average earnings rate of 3.3 percent, computed by taking into account only the current earnings rates for the taxable year 1962 and each of the 4 taxable years immediately preceding such taxable year. The adjusted reserves rate for such taxable year would be 3.3 percent since the average earnings rate of 3.3 percent is lower than the 1962 current earnings rate of 3.8 percent.

(3) To the extent there are any amounts accrued for discounts in the nature of interest which have not been included as interest paid under section 805(e)(3), the acquiring corporation shall be treated as the distributor or transferor corporation for purposes of including such amounts as interest paid.

(4) Any adjustment required by section 806(b) with respect to an item described in section 810(c) shall be made by the acquiring corporation in its first taxable year which begins after the date of distribution or transfer.

(5) The amount of the deduction provided by section 809(d)(6), as limited by section 809(f), for all taxable years of the distributor or transferor corporation which end on and before the date of distribution or transfer (irrespective of whether or not the distributor or transferor corporation claimed this deduction for such taxable years) for the purpose of determining the limitation under section 809(d)(6).

(6) [Reserved].

(7)(i) The dollar balances in the shareholders surplus account, policyholders surplus account, and other accounts provided, however, that the acquiring corporation is a stock life insurance company. The dollar balance in the policyholders surplus account shall reflect the amount (if any) treated as a subtraction from such account by reason of the application of the limitation provided under section 815(d)(4) immediately prior to the close of the date of distribution or transfer. To the extent that any amount must be added to the shareholders surplus account as a result of the application of the limitation provided under section 815(d)(4), the acquiring corporation shall be treated as the distributor or transferor corporation as of its first taxable year which begins after the date of distribution or transfer. However, any amounts attributable to money or other property not permitted to be received without the recognition of gain (i.e., boot) distributed to a person other than the acquiring corporation under section 381(a) shall be treated as a distribution under section 815.

(ii) Notwithstanding paragraph (b)(7)(i) of this section, if the distributor or transferor corporation distributes or transfers less than 50 percent of its insurance business to the acquiring corporation, then the acquiring corporation shall succeed to a ratable portion of the dollar balances in the distributor's or transferor's shareholders surplus account, policyholders surplus account, and other accounts. The percentage of the accounts to which the acquiring corporation succeeds is determined by the ratio of the distributor's or transferor's insurance reserves for the contracts transferred to the acquiring corporation, as maintained under section 816(b), to the distributor's or transferor's reserves for all of its contracts maintained under section 816(b) immediately before the earlier of the distribution or transfer or the adoption of the plan of liquidation or reorganization. For transactions in which the distributor liquidates pursuant to an election under section 338(h)(10), see §1.338-11(f) for the treatment of its remaining policyholders surplus account. For all other transactions subject to this paragraph, the distributor or transferor must take into account as income its remaining policyholders surplus account to the extent the fair market value of its assets (net of liabilities) distributed

or transferred to the acquiring corporation or to the transferor's shareholders pursuant to the plan of liquidation or reorganization exceeds the distributor's or transferor's remaining shareholders surplus account.

(iii) If, pursuant to a plan in existence at the time of the liquidation or reorganization, the acquiring corporation transfers any insurance or annuity contract it received in the liquidation or reorganization to another person, then, for purposes of paragraph (b)(7)(ii) of this section, that contract shall be deemed to have been transferred by the transferor to that other person after the adoption of the plan of liquidation or reorganization. If the transferor is an old target within the meaning of §1.338(h)(10)-1(d)(2), any transfer by the acquiring corporation to the purchasing corporation (as defined in §1.338-2(c)(11)) or to any person related to the purchasing corporation within the meaning of section 197(f)(9)(C) within two years of the transfer described in section 381(a) will be presumed to have been pursuant to a plan in existence at the time of the liquidation or reorganization.

(iv) If the acquiring corporation is a mutual life insurance company, the dollar balances in the shareholders surplus account, policyholders surplus account, and other accounts shall not be taken into account by such acquiring corporation and the distributor or transferor corporation shall be subject to the provisions of section 815(d)(2)(A) as of the close of the date of distribution or transfer.

(v) The provisions of this paragraph (b)(7) are illustrated by the following examples:

Example 1. P buys the stock of insurance company target, T, from S for $16, and P and S make a section 338(h)(10) election for T. T transfers no insurance contracts to S, or any related party, in connection with the transaction. Further, assume that T had $10 in its policyholders surplus account and no balance in its shareholders surplus account or other accounts. Immediately before the deemed asset sale, old T is required to include as ordinary income the $10 in the policyholders surplus account.

Example 2. Assume the same facts as in *Example 1*, except that T holds a block of life insurance contracts P does not wish to acquire, and, immediately before the sale of T stock, S causes T to distribute the unwanted block of insurance contracts to S. Further, assume that S is an insurance company, that the distribution of contracts is one of series of distributions in complete cancellation or redemption of all of its stock (the others occurring under §1.338(h)(10)-1(d)(4)(i)) that qualifies as a complete liquidation under section 332, and that old T's tax reserves with respect to the distributed contracts represent one-tenth of old T's tax reserves with respect to all of its life insurance contracts. Because T transfers less than 50 percent of its life insurance business to S in a transaction to which section 381(a) applies, S succeeds to a ratable portion of old T's policyholders surplus account ($1), and old T includes as ordinary income the remaining $9 of that account.

Example 3. Assume the same facts as in *Example 2*, except that 14 months after the deemed asset sale, S and X, a person related to new T under section 197(f)(9)(C), engage in an indemnity reinsurance transaction involving the contracts transferred to S from old T. Because X is related to the purchasing corporation (P) under section 197(f)(9)(C), and X receives contracts from the acquiring corporation (S) that S acquired from old T within two years of the transfer from old T to S, the contracts are presumed to have been transferred pursuant to a plan in existence at the time of old T's liquidation. If S cannot establish otherwise, old T is treated as having distributed the remainder of its policyholders surplus account. In that case, in the taxable year of the indemnity reinsurance transaction, S takes into account as ordinary income the portion of the old T's accounts ($1) that old T or S has not previously taken into account as income.

(8) To the extent that any amount must be added to the shareholders surplus account as a result of an election made under section 815(d)(1) by the distributor or transferor corporation, the acquiring corporation shall be treated as the distributor or transferor corpora-

tion as of its first taxable year which begins after the date of distribution or transfer.

(9) The amount of the life insurance reserves at the end of 1958, but only for the purpose of applying the limitation provided under section 815(d)(4)(B).

(10) To the extent there are amounts subject to the provisions of section 817(d), the acquiring corporation shall be treated as the distributor or transferor corporation.

(11) To the extent there are any installments of tax imposed by section 818(e)(3)(A) remaining to be paid, the acquiring corporation shall be treated as the distributor or transferor corporation for the purpose of paying such installments.

(12) The capital loss carryovers, subject to conditions and limitations consistent with the conditions and limitations prescribed in section 381(c)(3) and the regulations thereunder, except that any net capital loss of the distributor or transferor corporation for a taxable year beginning before January 1, 1959, shall not be taken into account. See section 817(c).

(13)(i) The transferor's unamortized policy acquisition expenses or positive or negative capitalization requirements on its specified insurance contracts.

(ii) Notwithstanding paragraph (b)(13)(i) of this section, if the distributor or transferor corporation transfers less than 50 percent of its insurance business to the acquiring corporation, then the acquiring corporation shall succeed to a ratable portion of the transferor's unamortized policy acquisition expenses or positive or negative capitalization requirements on its specified insurance contracts. The percentage of such acquisition expenses or positive or negative capitalization requirements to which the acquiring corporation succeeds is determined by the ratio of the distributor's or transferor's insurance reserves for the contracts transferred to the acquiring corporation, as maintained under section 816(b), to the distributor's or transferor's reserves for all of its contracts maintained under section 816(b) immediately before the earlier of the distribution or transfer or the adoption of the plan of liquidation or reorganization. For amounts of the distributor's or transferor's unamortized policy acquisition expenses or positive or negative capitalization requirements on its specified insurance contracts to which the acquirer does not succeed under this paragraph, and, for transactions in which the transferor liquidates pursuant to an election under section 338(h)(10), see § 1.338-11(f) for the treatment of its capitalized amounts under section 848.

(iii) If, pursuant to a plan in existence at the time of the liquidation or reorganization, the acquiring corporation transfers any insurance or annuity contract it received in the liquidation or reorganization to another person, then, for purposes of paragraph (b)(13)(ii) of this section, that contract shall be deemed to have been transferred by the transferor to that other person after the adoption of the plan of liquidation or reorganization. If the transferor is an old target within the meaning of § 1.338(h)(10)-1(d)(2), any transfer by the acquiring corporation to the purchasing corporation (as defined in § 1.338-2(c)(11)) or to any person related to the purchasing corporation within the meaning of section 197(f)(9)(C) within two years of the transfer described in section 381(a) will be presumed to have been pursuant to a plan in existence at the time of the liquidation or reorganization.

(14) The special loss discount account, provided, however, that the acquiring corporation will succeed to the special loss discount account only to the extent that it is attributable to the portion of the transferor's insurance business acquired by the acquiring corporation in the section 381 transaction.

(c) *Effective dates.*—(1) *In general.*—This section applies to the acquisition of assets of an insurance company by another insurance company in a transaction to which section 381 applies for taxable years beginning after December 31, 1957.

(2) *Special rules for section 381 transactions.*—Paragraphs (a), (b)(7), (b)(13), and (b)(14) of this section apply to the acquisition of assets of an insurance company by another insurance company in a transaction to which section 381 applies on or after April 10, 2006.

(3) *Joint retroactive election.*—The distributor or transferor and the acquiring corporation may jointly make an irrevocable election to apply paragraphs (a), (b)(7), (b)(13), and (b)(14) of this section to a transaction to which section 381 applies occurring before April 10, 2006 the taxable year that includes the acquisition and all subsequent affected taxable years of both the distributor or transferor and the acquiring corporation are years for which an assessment of deficiency or a refund for overpayment is not prevented by any law or rule of law.

(4) *Time and manner of making the joint election.*—The distributor or transferor and the acquiring corporation may make an election described in paragraph (c)(2) of this section by each attaching a statement to its original or amended income tax return for the taxable

year that includes the acquisition of assets in a transaction to which section 381 applies. The statement must be entitled "Election to retroactively apply the rules of section 1.381(c)(22)-1 to a transaction completed before April 10, 2006" and must include the following information—

(i) The name and EIN of the distributor or transferor and the acquiring corporation; and

(ii) The following declaration (or a substantially similar declaration): The distributor or transferor and the acquiring corporation have each amended its income tax returns for the taxable year that includes the acquisition of assets in a transaction to which section 381 applies and for all affected subsequent years to reflect the rules in paragraphs (a), (b)(7), (b)(13), and (b)(14) of section 1.381(c)(22)-1. [Reg. § 1.381(c)(22)-1.]

☐ [*T.D.* 6625, 12-18-62. *Amended by T.D.* 9257, 4-7-2006, *T.D.* 9377, 1-22-2008 *and T.D.* 9911, 10-9-2020.]

[Reg. § 1.381(c)(23)-1]

§ 1.381(c)(23)-1. Investment credit carryovers in certain corporate acquisitions.—(a) *Carryover requirement.*—(1) Section 381(c)(23) requires the acquiring corporation in a transaction to which section 381 applies to succeed to and take into account under such regulations as may be prescribed by the Secretary or his delegate, the investment credit carryovers of the distributor or transferor corporation. To determine the amount of these carryovers as of the close of the date of distribution or transfer, and to integrate them with any carryovers and carrybacks of the acquiring corporation for purposes of determining the amount of credit allowed by section 38 to the acquiring corporation for taxable years ending after the date of distribution or transfer, it is necessary to apply the provisions of sections 46, 47, and 48 in accordance with the conditions and limitations of this section.

(2) The investment credit carryovers and carrybacks of the acquiring corporation determined as of the close of the date of distribution or transfer shall be computed without reference to any unused credit of a distributor or transferor corporation. The investment credit carryovers of a distributor or transferor corporation as of the close of the date of distribution or transfer shall be determined without reference to any unused credit of the acquiring corporation.

(b) *Carryback of unused credits.*—An unused credit of the acquiring corporation for any taxable year ending after the date of distribution or transfer shall not be carried back in computing the credit allowed by section 38 to a distributor or transferor corporation. However, an unused credit of the acquiring corporation for any such taxable year shall be carried back in accordance with section 46(b)(1) in computing the credit allowed to the acquiring corporation for a taxable year ending on or before the date of distribution or transfer. If a distributor or transferor corporation remains in existence after the date of distribution or transfer, an unused credit sustained by it for any taxable year beginning after such date shall be carried back in accordance with section 46(b)(1) in computing the credit allowed by section 38 to such corporation for a taxable year ending on or before that date, but may not be carried back or over in computing the credit allowed by section 38 to the acquiring corporation.

(c) *Computation of carryovers and carrybacks.*—(1) Subject to the modifications set forth in this paragraph, the provisions of § 1.46-2 shall apply in computing carryovers and carrybacks of unused credits to taxable years of the acquiring corporation.

(2)(i) The investment credit carryovers available to the distributor or transferor corporation as of the close of the date of distribution or transfer shall first be carried to the first taxable year of the acquiring corporation ending after that date. This rule applies whether the date of distribution or transfer is on the last day, or any other day, of the acquiring corporation's taxable year.

(ii) The investment credit carryovers available to the distributor or transferor corporation as of the close of the date of distribution or transfer shall be carried to the acquiring corporation without diminution by reason of the fact that the acquiring corporation does not acquire 100 percent of the assets of the distributor or transferor corporation.

(3) An unused credit of a distributor or transferor corporation for a taxable year which ends on or before the last day of a taxable year of the acquiring corporation shall be considered to be an unused credit for a year prior to such taxable year of the acquiring corporation. If the acquiring corporation has acquired the assets of two or more distributor or transferor corporations on the same date of distribution or transfer, the unused credit years of the distributor or transferor corporations shall be taken into account in the order in which such years terminate. If any one of the unused credit years of a distributor or transferor corporation ends on the same day as the unused credit year of another distributor or transferor corporation, either unused credit year may be taken into account before the other.

(4) The extent to which an investment credit carryover of a distributor or transferor corporation or of an acquiring corporation

from an unused credit year ending before January 1, 1971, may be taken into account by the acquiring corporation for a taxable year beginning after December 31, 1970, shall be determined without regard to the credit earned by the acquiring corporation for such year. Thus, in such a case, the amount of unused credit from such unused credit years which may be taken into account in a taxable year of the acquiring corporation beginning after December 31, 1970, shall be determined solely with reference to the limitation based on amount of tax for such taxable year (without reduction for the credit earned for such year).

(d) *Computation of carryovers when date of distribution or transfer occurs on last day of acquiring corporation's taxable year.*—The computa-

X Corporation's taxable year		Credit earned
1971	. . . .	$10,000
1972	. . . .	5,000

Y's credit earned and its limitation based on amount of tax for its taxable years 1971 through 1973 are as follows:

Y Corporation's taxable year		Credit earned
1971	. . . .	$6,000
1972	. . . .	5,000
1973	. . . .	3,000

The sequence for the allowance of unused credits of X Corporation and Y Corporation, and the computation of the carryovers to Y Corporation's calendar year 1974, may be illustrated as follows:

Unused credit	$5,000
Excess of X's 1972 limitation based on tax over credit earned	0
Carryover to Y's year 1973	$5,000
Excess of Y's 1973 limitation based on tax over credit earned	$7,000
Carryover to Y's year 1974	0

(2) *Y Corporation's 1971 unused credit.* The carryover to Y 1974 is $0, computed as follows:

Unused credit	$1,000
Excess of Y's 1972 limitation based on tax over credit earned	0
Carryover to Y's year 1973	$1,000
Excess of Y's 1973 limitation based on tax over credit earned $7,000	
Less: X's $5,000 carryover from 1971 . . . . $5,000	
	$2,000
Carryover to Y's year 1974	0

(3) *X Corporation's 1972 unused credit.* The carryover to Y 1974 is $1,000, computed as follows:

Unused credit	$2,000
Excess of Y's 1973 limitation based on tax over credit earned $7,000	
Less: X's $5,000 carryover from 1971 and Y's $1,000 carryover from 1971 . . . . $6,000	
	$1,000
Carryover to Y's year 1974	$1,000

(4) *Y Corporation's 1972 unused credit.* The carryover to Y 1974 is $2,000, computed as follows:

Unused credit	$2,000
Excess of Y's 1973 limitation based on tax over credit earned $7,000	
Less: X's $5,000 carryover from 1971, Y's $1,000 carryover from 1971 and X's $1,000 carryover from 1972 . . . . $7,000	
	$0
Carryover to Y's year 1974	$2,000

(5) The aggregate of the investment credit carryovers to Y's year 1974 is $3,000, computed as follows:

X's 1972 unused credit	$1,000
Y's 1972 unused credit	$2,000
Total	$3,000

(e) *Computation of carryovers when date of distribution or transfer is not on last day of acquiring corporation's taxable year.*—(1) If the date of distribution or transfer occurs on any day other than the last day of a taxable year of the acquiring corporation, the amount which may be added to the amount allowable as a credit by section 38 for the first taxable year of the acquiring corporation ending after the date of distribution or transfer (hereinafter called the "year of acquisition") shall be determined in the following manner. The year of acquisition shall be considered as though it were two taxable years. The first of such two taxable years shall be referred to in this paragraph as the preacquisition part year and shall begin with the beginning of the year of acquisition and end with the close of the date of distribution or transfer. The second of such two taxable years shall be referred to in this paragraph as the postacquisition part year and shall begin with the day following the date of distribution or transfer and shall end with the close of the year of acquisition.

tion of the investment credit carryovers from the distributor or transferor corporation and from the acquiring corporation in a case where the date of distribution or transfer occurs on the last day of a taxable year of the acquiring corporation may be illustrated by the following example:

Example. X Corporation and Y Corporation were organized on January 1, 1971, and each corporation files its return on the calendar year basis. On December 31, 1972, X transfers all its assets to Y in a statutory merger to which section 361 applies. X's credit earned and its limitation based on amount of tax for its taxable years 1971 and 1972 are as follows:

	Limitation based on amount of tax
	$5,000
	3,000

	Limitation based on amount of tax
	$5,000
	3,000
	10,000

(1) *X Corporation's 1971 unused credit.* The carryover to Y 1974 is $0, computed as follows:

(2) The excess limitation for the year of acquisition (*i.e.*, the excess of the limitation based on the amount of tax for such year over the amount of credit earned for such year) shall be divided between the preacquisition part year and the postacquisition part year in proportion to the number of days in each. Thus, if in a statutory merger to which section 361 applies Y Corporation, a calendar year taxpayer, acquires the assets of X Corporation on June 30, 1975, and Y Corporation has an excess limitation of $36,500 for its calendar year 1975, then the excess limitation for the preacquisition part year would be $18,100 ($36,500 × 181/365) and the excess limitation for the postacquisition part year would be $18,400 ($36,500 × 184/365).

(3) An unused credit of the acquiring corporation shall be carried to and applied against the excess limitation for the preacquisition part year and then carried to and applied against the excess limitation for the postacquisition part year, whereas an unused credit

of the distributor or transferor corporation shall not be carried to the preacquisition part year but shall only be carried to and applied against the excess limitation for the postacquisition part year. For special rule relating to carryovers from taxable years ending before January 1, 1971, to taxable years beginning after December 31, 1970, see subparagraph (6) of this paragraph.

(4) Though considered as two separate taxable years for purposes of this paragraph, the preacquisition part year and the postacquisition part year are treated as one taxable year in determining the years to which an unused credit is carried under section 46(b)(1).

X Corporation's taxable year	Credit earned	Limitation based on amount of tax
1971	$11,000	$5,000
Ending 5-1-72	$3,000	$6,000

Y's credit earned and its limitation based on amount of tax for its taxable years 1971 and 1972 are as follows:

Y Corporation's taxable year	Credit earned	Limitation based on amount of tax
1971	$7,000	$3,000
1972	$3,000	$9,000

The sequence for the allowance of unused credits of X Corporation and Y Corporation, and the computation of carryovers to Y Corporation's calendar year 1973, may be illustrated as follows:

Unused credit $6,000
   Excess of X's 5-1-72 limitation based on tax over credit earned $3,000
Carryover to Y's postacquisition part year 1972 .... $3,000
   Excess limitation for Y's postacquisition part year ($6,000 × 244/366) ... $4,000
Carryover to Y's year 1973 0

(ii) *Y Corporation's 1971 unused credit.* The carryover to Y 1973 is $1,000, computed as follows:

Unused credit $4,000
   Excess limitation for Y's preacquisition part year ($6,000 × 122/366) ... $2,000
Carryover to Y's postacquisition part year $2,000
   Excess limitation for Y's postacquisition part year ($6,000 × 244/366) ... $4,000
   Less: X's $3,000 carryover from 1971 .... $3,000
                                      $1,000
Carryover to Y's year 1973 .... $1,000

(iii) The aggregate of the investment credit carryovers to Y's year 1973 is $1,000, computed as follows:

X's 1971 unused credit $0
Y's 1971 unused credit $1,000
Total $1,000

(6) If the year of acquisition is a taxable year beginning after December 31, 1970, and if there is an unused credit of the distributor or transferor corporation or of the acquiring corporation arising in an unused credit year ending before January 1, 1971, which may be carried to such year of acquisition (see paragraph (c)(4) of this section), then in applying subparagraphs (1), (2), and (3) of this paragraph, in lieu of dividing the excess limitation for the year of acquisition between the preacquisition and postacquisition part years, only the limitation based on the amount of tax for such year (*i.e.*, without reduction for the credit earned) shall be divided between the preacquisition and postacquisition part years. If there is also an unused credit arising in an unused credit year ending after December 31, 1970, which may be carried to the year of acquisition, then for the purpose of determining the amount of such unused credit which may be taken into account for such year of acquisition, the credit earned for the year of acquisition shall first be applied

(5) The preceding subparagraphs may be illustrated by the following example:

Example. X Corporation and Y Corporation were organized on January 1, 1971, and each corporation files its return on the calendar year basis. On May 1, 1972, X transfers all its assets to Y in a statutory merger to which section 361 applies. X's credit earned and its limitation based on amount of tax for its taxable years 1971 and ending May 1, 1972, are as follows:

(i) *X Corporation's 1971 unused credit.* The carryover to Y 1973 is $0, computed as follows:

against the limitation based on amount of tax for the preacquisition part year (reduced by any investment credit carryovers to such part year from unused credit years ending before January 1, 1971) and the excess, if any, shall then be applied against the limitation based on amount of tax for the postacquisition part year (also reduced by any investment credit carryovers to such part year from unused credit years ending before January 1, 1971).

(7) Subparagraph (6) may be illustrated by the following example:

Example. X Corporation and Y Corporation were organized on January 1, 1970, and each corporation files its return on the calendar year basis. On May 1, 1972, X transfers all its assets to Y in a statutory merger to which section 361 applies. X's credit earned and its limitation based on amount of tax for its taxable years 1970, 1971, and ending May 1, 1972, are as follows:

X Corporation's taxable year	Credit earned	Limitation based on amount of tax
1970	$300	$0
1971	$100	$0
Ending 5-1-72	$200	$0

Y's credit earned and its limitation based on amount of tax for its taxable years 1970 through 1972 are as follows:

Y Corporation's taxable year	Credit earned	Limitation based on amount of tax
1970	$100	$0
1971	$200	$0
1972	$300	$900

The sequence for the allowance of unused credits of X Corporation and Y Corporation, and the computation of carryovers to Y Corporation's calendar year 1973, may be illustrated as follows:

Unused credit $300
    X Corporation's 1971 limitation based on tax $0
    X Corporation's 5-1-72 limitation based on tax $0
                                $0
Carryover to Y's postacquisition part year 1972 .... $300
    Limitation based on tax for Y's post-acquisition part year 1972 ($900 × 244/366) $600
Carryover to Y's year 1973 .... $0

(ii) *Y Corporation's 1970 unused credit.* The carryover to Y 1973 is $0, computed as follows:

Unused credit $100
    Y Corporation's 1971 limitation based on tax $0
Carryover to Y's preacquisition part year 1972 .... $100
    Limitation based on tax for Y's preacquisition part year 1972 ($900 × 122/366) $300
Carryover to Y's postacquisition part year 1972 .... $0

(iii) *Y Corporation's credit earned for 1972.* The carryover to Y 1973 is $0, computed as follows:

Credit earned $300
    Limitation based on tax for preacquisition part year 1972 ($900 × 122/366) $300
    Less: Y's $100 carryover from 1970 .... $100
                                $200
Carryover to Y's postacquisition part year 1972 .... $100
    Limitation based on tax for postacquistion part year 1972 ($900 × 244/366) $600
    Less: X's $300 carryover from 1970 .... $300
                                $300
Carryover to Y's year 1973 .... $0

(iv) *X Corporation's 1971 unused credit.* The carryover to Y 1973 is $0, computed as follows:

Unused credit $100
    Excess of X's 1972 limitation based on tax over credit earned $0
Carryover to Y's postacquisition part year 1972 .... $100
    Limitation based on tax for postacquisition part year 1972 ($900 × 244/366) $600
    Less: X's $300 carryover from 1970 .... $300
    Y's 1972 credit earned for postacquisition part year $100
                                $400
                                $200
Carryover to Y's year 1973 .... $0

(v) *Y Corporation's 1971 unused credit.* The carryover to Y 1973 is $100, computed as follows:

Unused credit $200
    Limitation based on tax for preacquisition part year 1972 ($900 × 122/366) $300
    Less: Y's $100 carryover from 1970 .... $100
    Y's 1972 credit earned for preacquisition part year 1972 .... $200
                                $300
                                $0
Carryover to Y's postacquisition part year $200
    Limitation based on tax for postacquisition part year 1972 ($900 × 244/366) $600
    Less: X's $300 carryover from 1970 .... $300
    Y's 1972 credit earned for postacquisition part year 1972 .... $100
    X's $100 carryover from 1971 .... $100
                                $500
                                $100
Carryover to Y's year 1973 .... $100

(vi) *X Corporation's 5-1-72 unused credit.* The carryover to Y 1973 is $200, computed as follows:

Unused credit $200
    Limitation based on tax for postacquisition part year 1972 ($900 × 244/366) $600
    Less: X's $300 carryover from 1970 .... $300
    Y's 1972 credit earned for postacquisition part year 1972 .... $100
    X's $100 carryover from 1971, and Y's $100 carryover from 1971 .... $200
                                $600
                                $0
Carryover to Y's year 1973 .... $200

(vii) The aggregate of the investment credit carryovers to Y 1973 is $300, computed as follows:

Y's 1971 unused credit $100
X's 1972 unused credit $200
    Total $300

(8) If the year of acquisition is a taxable year to which the limitation provided in § 1.46-2(b)(2) (relating to 20-percent limitation on carryovers and carrybacks to certain taxable years) applies, then for purposes of applying such limitation the preacquisition part year and the postacquisition part year shall each be considered a fractional part of a year, but, if the date of distribution or transfer is not on the last day of a month, the entire month in which the date of distribution or transfer occurs shall be considered as included in the preacquisition part year and no portion thereof shall be considered as included in the postacquisition part year.

(9) If the acquiring corporation succeeds to the investment credit carryovers of two or more distributor or transferor corporations on two or more dates of distribution or transfer during the same taxable year of the acquiring corporation, the manner in which the unused credits of the distributor or transferor corporations shall be applied shall be determined consistently with the rules prescribed in paragraph (c) of § 1.381(c)(1)-2.

(f) *Successive acquiring corporations.*—An acquiring corporation which, in a distribution or transfer to which section 381(a) applies, acquires the assets of a distributor or transferor corporation which previously acquired the assets of another corporation in a transaction to which section 381(a) applies, shall succeed to and take into account, subject to the conditions and limitations of § 1.46-2 and this section, the investment credit carryovers available to the first acquiring corporation under § 1.46-2 and this section.

(g) *Recomputation of credit allowed by section 38 on certain property of acquiring corporation.*—If section 38 property acquired by an acquiring corporation in a transaction to which section 381(a) applies is disposed of, or otherwise ceases to be section 38 property (or becomes public utility property) with respect to the acquiring corporation, before the close of the estimated useful life which was taken into account in computing the distributor or transferor corporation's qualified investment, see paragraph (e) of § 1.47-3.

(h) *Electing small business corporation.*—An unused credit of a distributor or transferor corporation arising in an unused credit year for which such corporation is not an electing small business corporation (as defined in section 1371(b)) may not be carried over in a transaction to which section 381 applies to a taxable year of the acquiring corporation for which such corporation is an electing small business corporation and may not be added to the amount allowable as a credit under section 38 to the shareholders of the acquiring corporation for such taxable year. However, in such a case, a taxable year for which the acquiring corporation is an electing small business corporation shall be counted as a taxable year for purposes of determining the taxable years to which such unused credit may be carried.

(i) [Reserved]

(j) *Carryover of operating capacity for qualified intercity bus.*—For rules for determining an acquiring corporation's qualified investment for the energy credit for a qualified intercity bus, see § 1.48-9(q)(11). [Reg. § 1.381(c)(23)-1.]

☐ [*T.D.* 7289, 11-5-73. *Amended by T.D.* 7982, 10-5-84.]

[Reg. § 1.381(c)(24)-1]

§ 1.381(c)(24)-1. Work incentive program credit carryovers in certain corporate acquisitions.—The computation of carryovers and carrybacks of unused WIN credits in a transaction to which section 381 applies shall be made under the principles of § 1.381(c)(23)-1 (relating to the computation of carryovers and carrybacks of unused investment credits), except that provisions of paragraph (c)(4) and paragraph (e)(6), (7), and (8) of such section shall not apply. [Reg. § 1.381(c)(24)-1.]

☐ [*T.D.* 7289, 11-5-73.]

[Reg. § 1.381(c)(25)-1]

§ 1.381(c)(25)-1. Deficiency dividend of a qualified investment entity.—(a) *Carryover requirement.*—If a distributor or transferor corporation in a transaction to which section 381(a) applies—

(1) Was a qualified investment entity (within the meaning of section 860(b)) for any taxable year ending on or before the date of distribution or transfer, and

(2) A determination (as defined in section 860(e)) establishes that the transferor or transferee corporation is liable for the tax imposed by section 11(a), 56(a), 852(b), 857(b)(1), 857(b)(3)(A), or 1201(a) for such taxable year, then in determining the liability for such tax the deduction described in section 860 shall be allowed pursuant to section 381(c)(25) to such corporation for the amount of deficiency dividends paid by the acquiring corporation with respect to the distributor or transferor corporation. Except as otherwise provided in this section, the provisions of section 860 and the regulations thereunder apply with respect to a deficiency dividend deduction allowable pursuant to section 381(c)(25).

(b) *Deficiency dividends paid by the acquiring corporation with respect to the distributor or transferor corporation.*—A deficiency dividend paid by the acquiring corporation with respect to the distributor or trans-

feror corporation must be a distribution that would satisfy the definition of a deficiency dividend under section 860(f) if paid by the distributor or transferor corporation to its own shareholders. The distribution, however, shall be paid by the acquiring corporation to its own shareholders. The distribution also shall be paid after the date of distribution or transfer and on, or within 90 days after, the date of the determination but before the acquiring corporation files a claim under paragraph (c) of this section.

(c) *Claim for deduction.*—A claim for deduction under this section shall be made by the acquiring corporation on Form 976 and shall be filed within 120 days after the date of the determination. The form shall contain, or be accompanied by, the information required under § 1.860-2(b)(2) in sufficient detail to properly identify the facts with respect to the distributor or transferor corporation and the acquiring corporation. The required certified copy of the resolution authorizing the payment of the dividend shall be that of the trustees, board of directors, or other authority, of the acquiring corporation. Necessary changes may be made in Form 976 in order to carry out the provisions of this paragraph. The claim shall be filed with the district director, or director of the internal revenue service center, with whom the return of the distributor or transferor corporation to which the claim relates was filed.

(d) *Effect on dividends paid deduction.*—A deficiency dividend paid by the acquiring corporation that is allowable as a deduction to a distributor or transferor corporation pursuant to section 381(c)(25) shall not become a part of the dividends paid deduction of the acquiring corporation under section 561 for any taxable year.

(e) *Successive transactions to which section 381(a) applies.*—The provisions of this section shall apply in the case of successive transactions to which section 381(a) applies. Thus, if X corporation transfers its assets to Y corporation in a transaction to which section 381(a) applies and if Y corporation transfers its assets to Z corporation in a subsequent transaction to which section 381(a) applies, then, subject to the provisions of this section, X corporation may take a deficiency dividend deduction for the amount of deficiency dividends paid by Z corporation with respect to X corporation. [Reg. § 1.381(c)(25)-1.]

☐ [*T.D.* 7767, 2-3-81. *Amended by T.D.* 7936, 1-17-84.]

[Reg. § 1.381(c)(26)-1]

§ 1.381(c)(26)-1. Credit for employment of certain new employees.—(a) *Carryovers and carrybacks.*—For taxable years beginning before January 1, 1984, the computation of carryovers and carrybacks of unused targeted jobs credit (new jobs credit in the case of wages paid before 1979) under section 44B (as in effect prior to enactment of the Tax Reform Act of 1984) in a transaction to which section 381(a) applies shall be made under the principles of § 1.381(c)(23)-1 (relating to the computation of carryovers and carrybacks of unused investment credit), except that the provisions of paragraph (c)(4) and paragraph (e)(6), (7) and (8) of such section shall not apply.

(b) *Other items.*—See § 1.51-1(h) for a rule that applies to certain transfers of a trade or business in which a member of a targeted group is employed. [Reg. § 1.381(c)(26)-1.]

☐ [*T.D.* 7921, 11-18-83. *Amended by T.D.* 8062, 11-5-85.]

[Reg. § 1.381(d)-1]

§ 1.381(d)-1. Operations loss carryovers of life insurance companies.—For the application of part V, subchapter C, chapter 1 of the Code to operations loss carryovers of life insurance companies, see section 812(f) and § 1.812-7 and section 381(c)(22) and § 1.381(c)(22)-1. [Reg. § 1.381(d)-1.]

☐ [*T.D.* 6625, 12-18-62.]

[Reg. § 1.382-1]

§ 1.382-1. Table of contents.—This section lists the captions that appear in the regulations for §§ 1.382-2 through 1.382-12.

§ 1.382-2. General rules for ownership change.

(a) Certain definitions for purposes of sections 382 and 383 and the regulations thereunder.

  (1) Loss corporation.

    (i) In general.

    (ii) Distributor or transferor loss corporation in a transaction under section 381.

    (iii) Separate accounting required for losses and credits of an acquiring corporation and a distributor or transferor loss corporation.

    (iv) End of separate accounting for losses and credits of distributor or transferor corporation.

    (v) Application to other successor corporations.

    (vi) Any section 382 disallowed business interest carryforward.

  (2) Pre-change loss.

  (3) Stock.

    (i) In general.

    (ii) Convertible stock.

(4) Testing date.
  (i) In general.
  (ii) Exceptions.
(5) Successor corporation.
(6) Predecessor corporation.
(7) Section 382 disallowed business interest carryforward.
(8) Testing period.
(b) Effective dates.
  (1) In general. [Reserved]
  (2) Rules provided in paragraph (a)(3)(ii) of this section.
    (i) In general.
    (ii) Certain convertible preferred stock.
  (3) Rules provided in paragraphs (a)(1)(i)(A), (a)(1)(ii), (iv), and (v), (a)(2)(iv) through (vi), (a)(3)(i), and (a)(4) through (8) of this section.

§ 1.382-3. Definitions and rules relating to a 5-percent shareholder.

(a) Definitions.
  (1) Entity.
    (i) In general.
    (ii) Examples.
    (iii) Effective date.
      (A) In general.
      (B) Special rule.
      (C) Example.
  (2) [Reserved].
(b) through (i) [Reserved]
(j) Modification of the segregation rules of § 1.382-2T(j)(2)(iii) in the case of certain issuances of stock.
  (1) Introduction.
  (2) Small issuance exception.
    (i) In general.
    (ii) Small issuance defined.
    (iii) Small issuance limitation.
      (A) In general.
      (B) Class of stock defined.
      (C) Adjustments for stock splits and similar transactions.
      (D) Exception.
    (iv) Short taxable years.
  (3) Other issuances of stock for cash.
    (i) In general.
    (ii) Solely for cash.
      (A) In general.
      (B) Related issuances.
    (iii) Coordination with paragraph (j)(2) of this section.
  (4) Limitation on exempted stock.
  (5) Proportionate acquisition of exempted stock.
    (i) In general.
    (ii) Actual knowledge of greater overlapping ownership.
  (6) Exception for equity structure shifts.
  (7) Transitory ownership by underwriter disregarded.
  (8) Certain related issuances.
  (9) Application to options.
  (10) Issuance of stock pursuant to the exercise of certain options.
  (11) Application to first tier and higher tier entities.
  (12) Certain non-stock ownership interests.
  (13) Examples.
  (14) Effective date.
    (i) In general.
    (ii) Effective date for paragraph (j)(10) of this section.
    (iii) Election to apply this paragraph (j) retroactively.
      (A) Election.
      (B) Amended returns.
      (C) Revised information statements.
(k) Special rules for certain regulated investment companies.
  (1) In general.
  (2) Effective date.
    (i) General rule.
    (ii) Election to apply prospectively.

§ 1.382-4. Constructive ownership of stock.

(a) In general. [Reserved]
(b) Attribution from corporations, partnerships, estates and trusts.

  (1) [Reserved].
  (2) Limitation.
(c) Attribution to corporations, partnerships, estates and trusts. [Reserved]
(d) Treatment of options as exercised.
  (1) General rule.
  (2) Options treated as exercised.
    (i) Issuance or transfer.
    (ii) Subsequent testing dates.
  (3) The ownership test.
  (4) The control test.
    (i) In general.
    (ii) Operating rules.
      (A) Person and related persons.
      (B) Indirect ownership interest.
  (5) The income test.
  (6) Application of the ownership, control, and income tests.
    (i) In general.
    (ii) Application of ownership test.
    (iii) Application of control test.
    (iv) Application of income test.
  (7) Safe Harbors.
    (i) Contracts to acquire stock.
    (ii) Escrow, pledge, or other security agreements.
    (iii) Compensatory options.
    (iv) Options exercisable only upon death, disability, mental incompetency or retirement.
    (v) Rights of first refusal.
    (vi) Options designated in the Internal Revenue Bulletin.
  (8) Additional rules.
    (i) Contracts to acquire stock.
    (ii) Indirect transfer of an option.
    (iii) Options related to interests in non-corporate entities.
    (iv) Puts.
  (9) Definition of option.
    (i) In general.
    (ii) Convertible stock.
    (iii) Series of options.
    (iv) General principles of tax law.
  (10) Subsequent treatment of options treated as exercised on a change date.
    (i) In general.
    (ii) Alternative look-back rule for options exercised within 3 years after change date.
  (11) Transfers not subject to deemed exercise.
  (12) Certain rules regarding non-stock interests as stock.
(e) Stock transferred under certain agreements. [Reserved]
(f) Family attribution. [Reserved]
(g) Definitions.
(h) Effective date.
  (1) In general. [Reserved]
  (2) Option attribution rules.
    (i) General rule.
    (ii) Special rule for control test.
    (iii) Convertible stock issued prior to July 20, 1988.
      (A) In general.
      (B) Exceptions.
        (1) Nonvoting convertible preferred stock.
        (2) Other convertible stock.
    (iv) Convertible stock issued on or after July 20, 1988, and before November 5, 1992.
    (v) Certain options in existence immediately before and after an ownership change.
    (vi) Election to apply § 1.382-2T(h)(4).
      (A) In general.
      (B) Additional consequences of election.
      (C) Time and manner of making the election.
      (D) Amended returns.
  (3) Special rule for options subject to attribution under § 1.382-2T(h)(4).

§ 1.382-5. Section 382 limitation.

(a) Scope.
(b) Computation of value.

☐ [T.D. 8149, 8-5-87. *Amended by T.D. 8264, 9-19-89 and T.D. 8352, 6-26-91. Redesignated and amended by T.D. 8440, 10-2-92. Amended by T.D. 8490, 10-1-93; T.D. 8529, 3-17-94; T.D. 8530, 3-17-94; T.D. 8531, 3-17-94; T.D. 8546, 6-21-94; T.D. 8679, 6-26-96; T.D. 8825, 6-25-99; T.D. 9063, 6-26-2003; T.D. 9264, 5-26-2006; T.D. 9269, 6-23-2006; T.D. 9329, 6-13-2007, T.D. 9487, 6-11-2010, T.D. 9763, 4-25-2016, T.D. 9811, 1-18-2017 and T.D. 9905, 9-3-2020.*]

[Reg. § 1.382-1T]

§ 1.382-1T. Table of contents (temporary).—This section lists the captions that appear in the regulations for § 1.382-2T.

1.382-2T Definition of ownership change under section 382, as amended by the Tax Reform Act of 1986 (temporary).

(B) Right to receive or obligation to issue a fixed dollar amount of value of stock upon maturity of certain debt.

(C) Right or obligation to redeem stock of the loss corporation.

(D) Options exercisable only upon death, disability or mental incompetency.

(E) Right to receive or obligation to issue stock as interest or dividends.

(F) Options outstanding following an ownership change.

    (1) In general.

    (2) Example.

(G) Right to acquire loss corporation stock pursuant to a default under loan agreement.

(H) Agreement to acquire or sell stock owned by certain shareholders upon retirement.

(I) [Reserved]

(J) Title 11 or similar case.

(K)-(Y) [Reserved]

  (xi) Certain transfers of options disregarded.

  (xii) Exercise of an option that has not been treated as stock.

  (xiii) Effective date.

(5) Stock transferred under certain agreements.

(6) Family attribution.

(i) [Reserved]

(j) *Aggregation and segregation rules.*

(1) Aggregation of public shareholders and public owners into public groups.

  (i) Public group.

  (ii) Treatment of public group that is a 5-percent shareholder.

  (iii) Presumption of no cross-ownership.

  (iv) Identification of the public groups treated as 5-percent shareholders.

    (A) Analysis of highest tier entities.

    (B) Analysis of other higher tier entities and first tier entities.

    (C) Aggregation of the public shareholders.

  (v) Appropriate adjustments.

  (vi) Examples.

(2) Segregation rules applicable to transactions involving the loss corporation.

  (i) In general.

  (ii) Direct public group.

  (iii) Transactions to which segregation rules apply.

    (A) In general.

    (B) Certain equity structure shifts and transactions to which section 1032 applies.

      (1) In general.

      (2) Examples.

    (C) Redemption-type transactions.

      (1) In general.

      (2) Examples.

    (D) Acquisition of loss corporation stock as the result of the ownership of a right to acquire stock.

      (1) In general.

      (2) Example.

    (E) Transactions identified in the Internal Revenue Bulletin.

    (F) Issuance of rights to acquire loss corporation stock.

      (1) In general.

      (2) Example.

  (iv) Combination of de minimis public groups.

    (A) In general.

    (B) Example.

  (v) Multiple transactions.

    (A) In general.

    (B) Example.

  (vi) Acquisitions made by either a 5-percent shareholder or the loss corporation following application of the segregation rules.

(3) Segregation rules applicable to transactions involving first tier entities or higher tier entities.

  (i) Dispositions.

  (ii) Example.

  (iii) Other transactions affecting direct public groups of a first tier entity or higher tier entity.

  (iv) Examples.

  (v) *Acquisitions made by a 5-percent shareholder,* a higher tier entity, or a first tier entity following application of the segregation rules.

(k) *Operating rules.*

  (1) Presumptions regarding stock ownership.

  (i) Stock subject to regulation by the Securities and Exchange Commission. 12

  (ii) Statements under penalties of perjury.

(2) Actual knowledge regarding stock ownership.

(3) Duty to inquire as to actual stock ownership in the loss corporation.

(4) Ownership interests structured to avoid the section 382 limitation.

(5) Example.

(6) First tier entity or higher tier entity that is a foreign corporation or entity. [Reserved]

(l) *Changes in percentage ownership which are attributable to fluctuations in value.* [Reserved]

(m) *Effective date.*

(1) In general.

(2) Plan of reorganization.

(3) Earliest commencement of the testing period.

(4) Transitional rules.

  (i) Rules provided in paragraph (j) of this section for testing dates before September 4, 1987.

  (ii) Example.

  (iii) Rules provided in paragraph (j) of this section for testing dates on or after September 4, 1987.

  (iv) Rules provided in paragraphs (f)(18)(ii) and (iii) of this section.

  (v) Rules provided in paragraph (a)(2)(ii) of this section.

  (vi) Rules provided in paragraph (h)(4) of this section.

  (vii) Rules provided in paragraph (a)(2)(i) of this section.

(5) Bankruptcy proceedings.

  (i) In general.

  (ii) Example.

(6) Transactions of domestic building and loan associations.

(7) Transactions not subject to section 382.

  (i) Application of old section 382.

  (ii) Effect on testing period.

  (iii) Termination of old section 382. [Reserved]

(8) Options issued or transferred before January 1, 1987.

  (i) Options issued before May 6, 1986.

  (ii) Options issued on or after May 6, 1986 and before September 18, 1986.

  (iii) Options issued on or after September 18, 1986 and before January 1, 1987.

(9) Examples.

[Temporary Reg. § 1.382-1T.]

☐ [*T.D.* 9487, 6-11-2010 (*corrected* 7-27-2010).]

[Reg. § 1.382-2]

§ 1.382-2. General rules for ownership change.—(a) *Certain definitions for purposes of sections 382 and 383 and the regulations thereunder.*—The following definitions apply for purposes of sections 382 and 383 and the regulations thereunder.

(1) *Loss corporation.*—(i) *In general.*—The term "loss corporation" means a corporation which—

  (A) Is entitled to use a net operating loss carryforward, a capital loss carryover, a carryover of excess foreign taxes under section 904(c), a carryforward of a general business credit under section 39, a carryover of a minimum tax credit under section 53, or a section 382 disallowed business interest carryforward described in paragraph (a)(7) of this section;

  (B) for the taxable year that includes a testing date, as defined in paragraph (a)(4) of this section or § 1.382-2T(a)(2)(i), whichever is applicable (determined for purposes of this paragraph (a)(1) without regard to whether the corporation is a loss corporation), has a net operating loss, a net capital loss, excess foreign taxes under section 904(c), unused general business credits under section 38, or an unused minimum tax credit under section 53; or

  (C) has a net unrealized built-in loss (determined for purposes of this paragraph (a)(1) by treating the date on which such determination is made as the change date). See section 382(h)(3) for the definition of net unrealized built-in loss. See section 383 and § 1.383-1 for rules relating to a loss corporation that has an ownership change and has capital losses, excess foreign taxes, general business credits or minimum tax credits. Any predecessor or successor to a loss corporation described in this paragraph (a)(1) is also a loss corporation.

  (ii) *Distributor or transferor loss corporation in a transaction under section 381.*—Notwithstanding that a loss corporation ceases to exist under state law, if its disallowed business interest expense carryforwards, net operating loss carryforwards, excess foreign taxes, or other items described in section 381(c) are succeeded to and taken into account by an acquiring corporation in a transaction described in section 381(a), such loss corporation will be treated as continuing in existence until—

(A) Any pre-change losses (excluding pre-change credits described in § 1.383-1(c)(3)), determined as if the date of such transaction were the change date, are fully utilized or expire under section 163(j), 172, or 1212;

(B) any net unrealized built-in losses, determined as if the date of such transaction were the change date, may no longer be treated as pre-change losses; and

(C) any pre-change credits (described in § 1.383-1(c)(3)), determined as if the date of such transaction were the change date, are fully utilized or expire under sections 39, 53, or 904(c).

Following a transaction described in the preceding sentence, the stock of the acquiring corporation shall be treated as the stock of the loss corporation for purposes of determining whether an ownership change occurs with respect to the pre-change losses and net unrealized built-in losses that may be treated as pre-change losses of the distributor or transferor corporation.

(iii) *Separate accounting required for losses and credits of an acquiring corporation and a distributor or transferor loss corporation.*—Except as provided in paragraph (a)(1)(iv) of this section, pre-change losses (determined as if the testing date were the change date and treating the amount of any net unrealized built-in loss as a pre-change loss), that are succeeded to and taken into account by an acquiring corporation in a transaction to which section 381(a) applies must be accounted for separately from losses and credits of the acquiring corporation for purposes of applying this section. See Example (2) of § 1.382-2T(e)(2)(iv).

(iv) *End of separate accounting for losses and credits of distributor or transferor loss corporation.*—The separate tracking of owner shifts of the stock of an acquiring corporation required by paragraph (a)(1)(iii) of this section with respect to the net operating loss carryovers and other attributes described in paragraph (a)(1)(ii) of this section ends when a fold-in event occurs. A fold-in event is either an ownership change of the distributor or transferor corporation in connection with, or after, the transaction to which section 381(a) applies, or a period of 5 consecutive years following the section 381(a) transaction during which the distributor or transferor corporation has not had an ownership change. Starting on the day after the earlier of the change date (but not earlier than the day of the section 381(a) transaction) or the last day of the 5 consecutive year period, the losses and other attributes of the distributor or transferor corporation are treated as losses and attributes of the acquiring corporation for purposes of determining whether an ownership change occurs with respect to such losses. Also, for purposes of determining the beginning of the acquiring corporation's testing period, such losses are considered to arise either in a taxable year that begins not earlier than the later of the day following the change date or the day of the section 381(a) transaction, or in a taxable year that begins 3 years before the end of the 5 consecutive year period. Pre-change losses of a distributor or transferor corporation that are subject to a limitation under section 382 continue to be subject to the limitation notwithstanding the occurrence of a fold-in event. Any ownership change that occurs in connection with, or subsequent to, the section 381 transaction may result in an additional, lesser limitation with respect to such pre-change losses.

(v) *Application to other successor corporations.*—This paragraph (a)(1) also applies, as the context may require, to successor corporations other than successors in section 381(a) transactions. For example, if a corporation receives assets from the loss corporation that have basis in excess of value, the recipient corporation's basis for the assets is determined, directly or indirectly, in whole or in part, by reference to the loss corporation's basis, and the amount by which basis exceeds value is material, the recipient corporation is a successor corporation subject to this paragraph (a)(1).

(2) *Pre-change loss.*—The term pre-change loss means—

(i) any net operating loss carryforward of the old loss corporation to the taxable year ending on the change date or in which the change date occurs;

(ii) any net operating loss of the old loss corporation for the taxable year in which the ownership change occurs to the extent such loss is allocable to the period in such year on or before the change date;

(iii) any recognized built-in loss for any recognition period taxable year (within the meaning of section 382(h));

(iv) any pre-change capital losses described in § 1.383-1(c)(2)(i) and (ii);

(v) any pre-change credits described in § 1.383-1T(c)(3); and

(vi) Any section 382 disallowed business interest carryforward.

(3) *Stock.*—(i) *In general.*—Except as provided in this paragraph (a)(3)(i) and § 1.382-2T(f)(18)(ii) and (iii), the term "stock" means stock other than stock described in section 1504(a)(4). Notwithstanding the preceding sentence, stock that is not described in section 1504(a)(4) solely because it is entitled to vote as a result of dividend arrearages shall be treated as so described and thus shall not be considered stock. Stock described in section 1504(a)(4), however, is not excluded for purposes of determining the value of the loss corporation under section 382(e). The determination of the percentage of stock of any corporation owned by any person shall be made on the basis of the relative fair market value of the stock owned by such person to the total fair market value of the outstanding stock of the corporation. Solely for purposes of determining the percentage of stock owned by a person, each share of all the outstanding shares of stock that have the same material terms is treated as having the same value. Thus, for example, a control premium or blockage discount is disregarded in determining the percentage of stock owned by any person.

(ii) *Convertible stock.*—The term "stock" includes any convertible stock. For rules regarding the treatment of certain convertible stock as an option, see § 1.382-4(d)(9)(i).

(4) *Testing date.*—(i) *In general.*—Except as provided in paragraph (a)(4)(ii) of this section, a loss corporation is required to determine whether an ownership change has occurred immediately after any owner shift, or issuance or transfer (including an issuance or transfer described in § 1.382-4(d)(8)(i) or (ii)) of an option with respect to stock of the loss corporation that is treated as exercised under § 1.382-4(d)(2). Each date on which a loss corporation is required to make a determination of whether an ownership change has occurred is referred to as a testing date. All computations of increases in percentage ownership are to be made as of the close of the testing date and any transactions described in this paragraph (a)(4) that occur on that date are treated as occurring simultaneously at the close of the testing date. See § 1.382-2T(e)(1) for the definition of owner shift. The term *option*, as used in this paragraph (a)(4), includes interests that are treated as options under § 1.382-4(d)(9).

(ii) *Exceptions.*—A loss corporation is not required to determine whether an ownership change has occurred immediately after—

(A) Any transfer of stock, or an option with respect to stock, of the loss corporation in any of the circumstances described in section 382(l)(3)(B) (death, gift, divorce, etc.); or

(B) The transfer of an option described in § 1.382-4(d)(11)(i) or (ii) (relating to transfers between persons who are not 5-percent shareholders or between members of certain public groups).

(5) *Successor corporation.*—A successor corporation is a distributee or transferee corporation that succeeds to and takes into account items described in section 381(c) from a corporation as the result of an acquisition of assets described in section 381(a). A successor corporation also includes, as the context may require, a corporation which receives an asset or assets from another corporation if the corporation's basis for the asset(s) is determined, directly or indirectly, in whole or in part, by reference to the other corporation's basis and the amount by which basis differs from value is, in the aggregate, material.

(6) *Predecessor corporation.*—A predecessor corporation is a distributor or transferor corporation that distributes or transfers its assets to an acquiring corporation in a transaction described in section 381(a). A predecessor corporation also includes, as the context may require, a corporation which transfers an asset or assets to another corporation if the transferee's basis for the asset(s) is determined, directly or indirectly, in whole or in part, by reference to the corporation's basis and the amount by which basis differs from value is, in the aggregate, material. The previous sentence of this paragraph (a)(6) applies to any testing date occurring on or after January 1, 1997.

(7) *Section 382 disallowed business interest carryforward.*—The term *section 382 disallowed business interest carryforward* includes the following items:

(i) The loss corporation's disallowed business interest expense carryforwards (as defined in § 1.163(j)-1(b)(11)), including disallowed disqualified interest (as defined in § 1.163(j)-1(b)(12)), as of the date of the ownership change.

(ii) The loss corporation's current-year business interest expense (as defined in § 1.163(j)-1(b)(9)) in the change year (as defined in § 1.382-6(g)(1)) that is allocable to the pre-change period (as defined in § 1.382-6(g)(2)) under § 1.382-6(a) or (b) and that becomes disallowed business interest expense (as defined in § 1.163(j)-1(b)(10)).

Reg. § 1.382-2(a)(7)(ii)

(8) *Testing period.*—Notwithstanding the temporal limitations provided in §1.382-2T(d)(3)(i), the testing period for a loss corporation can begin as early as the first day of the first taxable year from which there is a section 382 disallowed business interest carryforward to the first taxable year ending after the testing date.

(b) *Effective dates.*—(1) *In general*

[Reserved]

(2) *Rules provided in paragraph (a)(3)(ii) of this section.*—(i) *In general.*—Except as provided in paragraph (b)(2)(ii) of this section, the rules provided in paragraph (a)(3)(ii) of this section apply with respect to any convertible stock.

(ii) *Certain convertible preferred stock.*—Convertible stock that, when issued, would be described in section 1504(a)(4) by disregarding subparagraph (D) thereof and by ignoring the potential participation in corporate growth that the conversion feature may offer is treated as stock described in that section (and thus is not treated as stock for the purpose of determining whether an ownership change occurs, but is taken into account for the purpose of determining the value of the loss corporation immediately before an ownership change; see sections 382(e)(1) and 382(k)(6)(A)) if—

(A) The stock was issued on or after July 20, 1988, and prior to November 5, 1992; or

(B) The stock was issued prior to July 20, 1988, and the loss corporation makes the election described in Notice 88-67, 1988-1 C.B. 555, (see §601.601(d)(2)(ii)(*b*) of this chapter for availability of Cumulative Bulletins (C.B.)) on or before the earlier of the date prescribed in the Notice or December 7, 1992.

(3) *Rules provided in paragraphs (a)(1)(i)(A), (a)(1)(ii), (iv), and (v), (a)(2)(iv) through (vi), (a)(3)(i), and (a)(4) through (8) of this section.*—The rules provided in paragraphs (a)(1)(i)(A), (a)(1)(ii), (iv), and (v), (a)(2)(iv) through (vi), (a)(3)(i), and (a)(4) through (8) of this section apply to testing dates occurring on or after November 13, 2020. For loss corporations that have testing dates occurring before November 13, 2020, see §1.382-2 as contained in 26 CFR part 1, revised April 1, 2019. However, taxpayers and their related parties, within the meaning of sections 267(b) and 707(b)(1), may choose to apply the rules of this section to testing dates occurring during a taxable year beginning after December 31, 2017, and before November 13, 2020, so long as the taxpayers and their related parties consistently apply the rules of this section, the section 163(j) regulations (as defined in §1.163(j)-1(b)(37)), §§1.382-1, 1.382-5, 1.382-6, 1.382-7, 1.383-0, 1.383-1, and, if applicable, §§1.263A-9, 1.263A-15, 1.381(c)(20)-1, 1.469-9, 1.469-11, 1.704-1, 1.882-5, 1.1362-3, 1.1368-1, 1.1377-1, 1.1502-13, 1.1502-21, 1.1502-36, 1.1502-79, 1.1502-91 through 1.1502-99 (to the extent they effectuate the rules of §§1.382-2, 1.382-5, 1.382-6, and 1.383-1), and 1.1504-4, to that taxable year. [Reg. §1.382-2.]

☐ [T.D. 8352, 6-26-91. *Amended by* T.D. 8405, 3-27-92, T.D. 8440, 10-2-92; T.D. 8531, 3-17-94; T.D. 8679, 6-26-96, T.D. 8825, 6-25-99 *and* T.D. 9905, 9-3-2020.]

[Reg. §1.382-2T]

§1.382-2T. Definition of ownership change under section 382, as amended by the Tax Reform Act of 1986 (temporary).—(a) *Ownership change.*—(1) *In general.*—A corporation is a new loss corporation and thus subject to limitation under section 382 only if an ownership change has occurred with respect to such corporation. An ownership change occurs with respect to a corporation if it is a loss corporation on a testing date and, immediately after the close of the testing date, the percentage of stock of the corporation owned by one or more 5-percent shareholders has increased by more than 50 percentage points over the lowest percentage of stock of such corporation owned by such shareholders at any time during the testing period. See (a)(2)(i) of this section for the definition of testing date. See paragraph (d) of this section for the definition of testing period. See paragraphs §1.382-2(a)(1) and paragraph (f)(3) of this section for the respective definitions of loss corporation and new loss corporation. See paragraph (g) of this section for the definition of 5-percent shareholder. See section 383 and §1.383-1 for rules relating to loss corporations that have an ownership change and have capital loss carryovers, excess foreign taxes carried over under section 904(c), carryovers of general business credits under section 39, or unused minimum tax credits under section 53.

(2) *Events requiring a determination of whether an ownership change has occurred.*—(i) *Testing dates prior to November 5, 1992.*—Except as otherwise provided in this paragraph (a)(2)(i), a loss corporation is required to determine whether an ownership change has occurred immediately after any owner shift, any equity structure shift, or any transaction in which an option with respect to stock of the loss corporation is—

(A) Transferred to (or by) a 5-percent shareholder (or a person who would be 5-percent shareholder if the option were treated as exercised), or

(B) Issued by the loss corporation, a first tier entity, or a higher tier entity that owns five percent or more of the loss corporation (determined without regard to the application of paragraph (h)(2)(i)(A) of this section). Notwithstanding the preceding sentence, any transfer of stock of the loss corporation (or an option with respect to such stock) in any of the circumstances described in section 382(l)(3)(B), or any equity structure shift that is not also an owner shift, is not an event that requires the loss corporation to make a determination of whether an ownership change has occurred. For purposes of this section, each date on which a loss corporation is required to make a determination of whether an ownership change has occurred is referred to as a testing date, all computations of increases in percentage ownership are to be made as of the close of the testing date, and any transactions described in this paragraph (a)(2)(i) that occur on that date are treated as occurring simultaneously at the close of the testing date. See paragraphs (e)(1) and (2) of this section for the respective definitions of owner shift and equity structure shift. See paragraphs (f)(9) and (14) of this section for the respective definitions of first tier entity and higher tier entity. See paragraph (m)(4)(vii) of this section for special rules regarding the effective date of the provisions of this paragraph (a)(2)(i).

(ii) [Reserved]. For further guidance, see §1.382-11(a).

(iii) *Records to be maintained by loss corporation.*—A loss corporation shall keep such records as are necessary to determine (A) the identity of its 5-percent shareholders, (B) the percentage of its stock owned by each such 5-percent shareholder, and (C) whether the section 382 limitation is applicable. Such records shall be retained so long as they may be material in the administration of any internal revenue law.

(b) *Nomenclature and assumptions.*—For purposes of the examples in this section—

(1) L is a loss corporation, and, if there is more than one loss corporation, they are designated as L_1, L_2, L_3, etc.

(2) P is a corporation that is not a loss corporation, and, if there is more than one such corporation, they are designated as P_1, P_2, P_3, etc.

(3) HC is a corporation whose assets consist solely of the stock of other corporations.

(4) E is an entity other than a corporation (e.g., a partnership), and, if there is more than one such entity, they are designated as E_1, E_2, E_3, etc.

(5) Unless otherwise stated—

(i) A, B, C, D, AA, BB, CC, and DD are unrelated individuals who own interests in corporations or other entities only to the extent expressly stated,

(ii) all corporations have one class of stock outstanding and each share of stock has the same fair market value as each other share,

(iii) the capital structure of the loss corporation and its business do not change over time, and

(iv) the rules of paragraphs (k)(2) and (4) of this section are not applicable.

(6) Public L represents a group of unrelated individuals and entities that own direct (and not indirect) stock ownership interests in loss corporation L, each of whom owns less than five percent of the stock of the loss corporation, and, if there is more than one loss corporation, such groups are designated as Public L_1, Public L_2, Public L_3, etc.

(7) Public P represents a group of unrelated individuals and entities that own direct (and not indirect) stock ownership interests in corporation P, each of whom owns less than five percent of the stock of the corporation, and, if there is more than one corporation, such groups are designated as Public P_1, Public P_2, Public P_3, etc.

(8) Public E represents a group of unrelated individuals and entities that own direct (and not indirect) ownership interests in entity E, each of whom owns less than five percent of the entity, and, if there is more than one entity, such groups are designated as Public E_1, Public E_2, Public E_3, etc.

(c) *Computing the amount of increases in percentage ownership.*—(1) *In general.*—In order to determine whether an ownership change has occurred on a testing date, the loss corporation must identify each 5-percent shareholder whose percentage of stock ownership in the loss corporation immediately after the close of the testing date has increased, compared to such shareholder's lowest percentage of stock ownership in such corporation at any time during the testing period. The amount of the increase in the percentage of stock ownership in the loss corporation of each 5-percent shareholder must be computed separately by comparing the percentage ownership of each such 5-percent shareholder immediately after the close of the testing date to such shareholder's lowest percentage ownership at any time during the testing period. Each such increase in the percentage ownership of a 5-percent shareholder is then added together with any other such increases of other 5-percent shareholders to determine whether an ownership change has occurred. Because only those 5-percent shareholders whose percentages of stock ownership have increased are taken into account, a 5-percent shareholder is disregarded if his percentage of stock ownership, immediately after the close of the testing date, has decreased (or has remained the same), compared to his lowest percentage ownership interest on any previous date during the testing period.

(2) *Example.*—(i) A and B each own 40 percent of the outstanding L stock. The remaining 20 percent of the L stock is owned by 100 unrelated individuals, none of whom own as much as five percent of L stock ("Public L"). C negotiates with A and B to purchase all their stock in L.

(ii) The acquisitions from both A and B are completed on September 13, 1990. C's acquisition of 80 percent of L stock results in an ownership change because C's percentage ownership has increased by 80 percentage points as of the testing date, compared to his lowest percentage ownership in L at any time during the testing period (0 percent).

(3) *Related and unrelated increases in percentage stock ownership.*— The determination whether an ownership change has occurred is made without regard to whether the changes in stock ownership of the loss corporation (by one or more 5-percent shareholders) result from related or unrelated events.

(4) *Example.*—(i) L has outstanding 200 shares of common stock. A, B and C respectively own 100, 50 and 50 shares of the L stock. On January 2, 1988, A sells 60 shares of L stock to B. Thus, B's percentage ownership interest in L increases by 30 percentage points, from 50 shares to 110 shares. On January 1, 1989, A purchases C's entire interest in L. Thus, A's percentage ownership interest in L increases by 25 percentage points, compared to his lowest percentage ownership interest in L, from 40 shares immediately following the January 2, 1988 sale to B to 90 shares. Even though A's ownership interest in L as of January 1, 1989 has decreased, compared to his 50 percent ownership interest at the beginning of the testing period, A is a 5-percent shareholder who must be taken into account for purposes of the computation required under paragraph (c)(1) of this section because his interest in L on that testing date (45 percent) has increased, compared to his lowest percentage ownership interest in L at any time during the testing period (20 percent following the sale to B).

(ii) Accordingly, although A and B jointly have increased their aggregate total ownership interest in L between January 2, 1988 and January 1, 1989 by only 25 percentage points (*i.e.*, the total ownership interest in L held by A and B at all times is not less than a 75 percent interest), the total of their separate increases in the percentage stock ownership of L, compared to their respective lowest percentage ownership interests at any time during the testing period, is 55 percentage points. Thus, an ownership change occurs as a result of A's acquisition of L stock on January 1, 1989.

(d) *Testing period.*—(1) *In general.*—Except as otherwise provided in this paragraph (d) and paragraph (m) of this section, the testing period for any testing date is the three-year period ending on the testing date. See paragraph (a)(2)(i) of this section for the definition of testing date.

(2) *Effect of a prior ownership change.*—Following an ownership change, the testing period for determining whether a subsequent ownership change has occurred shall begin no earlier than the first day following the change date of the most recent ownership change. See paragraph (f)(19) of this section for the definition of change date.

(3) *Commencement of the testing period.*—(i) *In general.*—Except as otherwise provided in paragraph (d)(3)(ii) of this section, the testing period for any loss corporation shall not begin before the earlier of the first day of either—

(A) the first taxable year from which there is a loss or excess credit carryforward to the first taxable year ending after the testing date, or

(B) the taxable year in which the testing date occurs.

(ii) *Exception for corporations with net unrealized built-in loss.*— Paragraph (d)(3)(i) of this section shall not apply if the corporation has a net unrealized built-in loss (determined after application of section 382(h)(3)(B)) on the testing date, unless the loss corporation establishes the taxable year in which the net unrealized built-in loss first accrued. In that event, the testing period shall not begin before the earlier of—

(A) the first day of the taxable year in which the net unrealized built-in loss first accrued, or

(B) the day described in paragraph (d)(3)(i) of this section. See section 382(h) for the definition of net unrealized built-in loss.

(4) *Disregarding testing dates.*—Any testing date that occurs before the beginning of the testing period shall be disregarded for purposes of this section.

(5) *Example.*—(i) A owns all 100 outstanding shares of L stock. A sells 40 shares to B on January 1, 1988. C purchases 20 shares of L stock from A on July 1, 1991. In determining if an ownership change occurs on the July 1, 1991 testing date, B's acquisition of L stock is disregarded because it occurred before the testing period that ends on such testing date. Thus, B's ownership interest in L does not increase during the testing period, and no ownership change results from C's acquisition.

(ii) The facts are the same as in (i), except that throughout the period during which B negotiated his stock purchase transaction with A, B knew that C intended to attempt to acquire a significant stock interest in L. Also, B and C have been partners in a number of significant business ventures. The result is the same as in (i).

(e) *Owner shift and equity structure shift.*—(1) *Owner shift.*— (i) *Defined.*—For purposes of this section, an owner shift is any change in the ownership of the stock of a loss corporation that affects the percentage of such stock owned by any 5-percent shareholder. See paragraph (g) of this section for the definition of a 5-percent shareholder. An owner shift includes, but is not limited to, the following transactions:

(A) a purchase or disposition of loss corporation stock by a 5-percent shareholder,

(B) a section 351 exchange that affects the percentage of stock owned by a 5-percent shareholder,

(C) a redemption or a recapitalization that affects the percentage of stock owned by a 5-percent shareholder,

(D) an issuance of loss corporation stock that affects the percentage of stock owned by a 5-percent shareholder, and

(E) an equity structure shift that affects the percentage of stock owned by a 5-percent shareholder.

(ii) *Transactions between persons who are not 5-percent shareholders disregarded.*—Transfers of loss corporation stock between persons who are not 5-percent shareholders of such corporation (and between members of separate public groups resulting from the application of the segregation rules of paragraphs (j)(2) and (3)(iii) of this section) are not owner shifts and thus are not taken into account. See paragraph (h)(4)(xi) of this section for a similar rule applicable to transfers of options.

(iii) *Examples.*—*Example (1).* A has owned all 1000 shares of outstanding L stock for more than three years. On June 15, 1988, A sells 300 of his L shares to B. This transaction is an owner shift. No other 5-percent shareholder has increased his percentage ownership of L stock during the testing period. Thus, the owner shift resulting from B's acquisition does not result in an ownership change, because B has increased his stock ownership in L by only 30 percentage points.

Example (2). The facts are the same as in Example (1). In addition, on June 15, 1989, L issues 100 shares to each of C, D and AA. The stock issuance is an owner shift. The transaction, however, does not result in an ownership change, because B, C, D and AA (the 5-percent shareholders whose stock ownership has increased as of the testing date, compared to any other time during the testing period) have increased their percentage of stock ownership in L by a total of only 46.2 percentage points during the testing period (by 23.1 percentage points [300 shares/1300 shares] for B, and 7.7 percentage points [100 shares/1300 shares] for each of C, D and AA).

Example (3). All 1000 shares of L stock are owned by a group of 100 unrelated individuals, none of whom own as much as five percent of L stock ("Public L"). Several of the members of Public L sell their L stock, amounting to a 30 percent ownership interest in L, to B on June 15, 1988. The sale of stock to B is an owner shift. Between June 16, 1988 and June 15, 1989, each of the remaining individuals in Public L sells his stock to another person who is not a 5-percent shareholder. Under paragraph (e)(1)(ii) of this section, trading activity among the members of Public L is disregarded and does not result in an owner shift. On June 15, 1989, L issues 100 shares to each of C, D and AA. The only sale transactions by members of Public L that are taken into account in determining whether an ownership change occurs on June 15, 1989 are the sales to B on June 15, 1988. Because B, C, D and AA together have increased their percentage ownership of L stock as a result of B's purchase and the stock issuance by an amount not in excess of 50 percentage points during the testing period ending on June 15, 1988, an ownership change does not occur on that date.

Example (4). The facts are the same as in Example (2). In addition, on December 15, 1989, L redeems 200 of the L shares from

A. The redemption is an owner shift that results in an ownership change, because B, C, D and AA are 5-percent shareholders whose percentage ownership of L increase by a total of 54.6 percentage points during the testing period (by 27.3 percentage points [300 shares/1100 shares] for B and 9.1 percentage points [100 shares/1100 shares]for each of C, D and AA).

Example (5). L is owned entirely by 10,000 unrelated shareholders, none of whom owns as much as five percent of the stock of L ("Public L"). Accordingly, Public L is L's only 5-percent shareholder. See paragraph (j)(1) of this section. There are one million shares of common stock outstanding. On December 1, 1988, L issues two million new shares of its common stock to members of the public, none of whom owned any L stock prior to the issuance. Following the public offering, no shareholder of L owns, directly or indirectly, five percent or more of L stock. Under paragraph (j)(2) of this section, however, all of the newly issued stock is treated as acquired by a 5-percent shareholder ("Public NL") that is unrelated to Public L. Therefore, the public offering constitutes an owner shift that results in an ownership change because Public NL's percentage of stock ownership in L increased by 66²/₃ percentage points (two million shares acquired in the public offering/three million shares outstanding following the offering) over its lowest percentage ownership during the testing period (0 percent prior to the offering).

Example (6). The facts are the same as in Example (5), except that L issues only 500,000 new shares of L stock on December 1, 1988, and Public NL's percentage ownership interest in L increases by only 33¹/₃ percentage points (500,000 shares acquired in the public offering/1.5 million shares outstanding following the offering). During the two years following December 2, 1988, 14 percent of the stock outstanding on that date is sold over a public stock exchange. On December 3, 1990, A purchases five percent of L stock (75,000 shares) over a public stock exchange. The purchase of five percent of L stock by A is an owner shift and is presumed to have been made proportionately from Public L and Public NL under paragraph (j)(2)(vi) of this section. Under paragraph (e)(1)(ii) of this section, transfers of L stock in transactions not involving A (*i.e.,* in transactions among or between members of separate public groups resulting from the application of paragraphs (j)(2) and (3) of this section) are not taken into account, and do not constitute owner shifts. (Transfers between members of Public NL and Public L, which are treated as separate 5-percent shareholders solely by virtue of paragraph (j)(2) of this section, are disregarded even if L has actual knowledge of any such transfers.) A and Public NL, the only 5-percent shareholders whose interests in L have increased during the testing period, have increased their respective stock ownership by only 36²/₃ percentage points—five percentage points for A [75,000 shares/1.5 million shares outstanding]and 31²/₃ percentage points for Public NL [((500,000 shares issued in the public offering) – (5 percent × 500,000 shares presumed to have been acquired by A))/1.5 million shares outstanding]. Accordingly, there is no ownership change with respect to L notwithstanding that, taking into account the public trading, a change of more than 50 percentage points in the ultimate beneficial ownership of L stock occurred during the three-year period ending on the December 3, 1990 testing date.

Example (7). The facts are the same as in Example 6, except that five percent of the L stock has always been owned by P which, in turn, has always been owned by Public P. On December 6, 1990, P sells all of its L stock over a public stock exchange. Although the trading of P stock among persons that are not 5-percent shareholders (without regard to the segregation rules of paragraph (j) of this section) are disregarded under paragraph (e)(1)(ii) of this section, the disposition of the L stock by P is not disregarded because the L stock is transferred in a transaction that is subject to paragraph (j)(3)(i) of this section.

(2) *Equity structure shift.*—(i) *Tax-free reorganizations.*—An equity structure shift is any reorganization within the meaning of section 368 with respect to which the loss corporation is a party to the reorganization, except that such term does not include a reorganization described in—

(A) Section 368(a)(1)(D) or (G) unless the requirements of section 354(b)(1) are met, or

(B) Section 368(a)(1)(F).

(ii) *Transactions designated under section 382(g)(3)(B) treated as equity structure shifts.*—[Reserved].

(iii) *Overlap of owner shift and equity structure shift.*—Any equity structure shift that affects the percentage of loss corporation stock owned by a 5-percent shareholder also constitutes an owner shift. See paragraph (e)(1)(i)(E) of this section.

(iv) *Examples.*—*Example (1).* A owns all of the stock of L and B owns all of the stock of P. On October 13, 1988, L merges into P in a reorganization described in section 368(a)(1)(A). As a result of the merger, A and B own 25 and 75 percent, respectively, of the stock of

P. The merger is an equity structure shift (and, because it affects the percentage of L stock owned by 5-shareholders, it also constitutes an owner shift). On the October 13, 1988 testing date, B is a 5-percent shareholder whose stock ownership in the loss corporation following the merger has increased by 75 percentage points over his lowest percentage of stock ownership in L at any time during the testing period (0 percent prior to the merger). Accordingly, an ownership change occurs as a result of the merger. P is thus a new loss corporation and L's pre-change losses are subject to limitation under section 382.

Example (2)—(i) A owns 100 percent of L₁ stock and B owns 100 percent of L₂ stock. On January 1, 1988, L₁ merges into L₂ in a reorganization described in section 368(a)(1)(A). Immediately after the merger, A and B own 40 percent and 60 percent, respectively, of the L₂ stock. There is an equity structure shift (as well as an owner shift) with respect to both L₁ and L₂ on January 1, 1988.

(ii) Because the percentage of L₂ stock owned by B immediately after the merger (60 percent) increases by more than 50 percentage points over the lowest percentage of the stock of L₁ owned by B during the testing period (0 percent prior to the merger), there is an ownership change with respect to L₁. L₂ is a new loss corporation and thus, under §1.382-2(a)(1)(iii) of this section, the pre-change losses of L₁ must be accounted for separately by L₂ from the losses of L₂ (immediately before the ownership change) and are subject to limitation under section 382. See §1.382-2(a)(1)(iv) of this section for rules that end separate accounting for L₁'s pre-change losses on any testing date occurring on or after January 29, 1991.

(iii) L₂ is a new loss corporation because it is a successor corporation to L. There is no ownership change with respect to L₂, however, because A's stock ownership in L₂ increased by only 40 percentage points (to 40 percent) over the amount owned by A prior to the merger (0 percent). Therefore, the pre-change losses of L₂ are not limited under section 382 as a result of the merger.

Example (3). The result in Example (2) would be the same if L₁ had survived the merger (*i.e.,* L₂ merged into L₁) with A and B owning 40 and 60 percent, respectively, of L₁ stock. L₁'s pre-change losses would be accounted for separately and limited under section 382 and the pre-change losses of L₂ would be accounted for separately under §1.382-2(a)(1)(iii) of this section; but would not be limited under section 382. See §1.382-2(a)(1)(ii) for the treatment of L₂ following the transaction.

Example (4). The facts are the same as Example (2), except, instead of acquiring L₁ in a merger, L₂ acquires all of the L₁ stock from A on January 1, 1988, solely in exchange for stock representing a 40 percent interest in L₂, in a reorganization described in section 368(a)(1)(B). The acquisition of stock by L₂ is an equity structure shift (as well as an owner shift) with respect to L₁ that results in an ownership change with respect to L₁ because the percentage of L₁ stock owned by B immediately after the reorganization (60 percent, by virtue of B's ownership of L₂, through the operation of the constructive ownership rules of paragraph (h) of this section) increases by more than 50 percentage points over the lowest percentage of L₁ stock owned by B at any time during the testing period (0 percent prior to the reorganization). The acquisition also results in an equity structure shift and an owner shift with respect to L₂, but L₂ incurs no ownership change, because A's stock ownership in L₂ increased by only 40 percentage points over the percentage of L₂ stock owned by A prior to the reorganization (0 percent).

(f) *Definitions.*—For purposes of this section—

(1) *Loss corporation.*—See section 382 and §1.382-2(a)(1) for the definition of a loss corporation.

(2) *Old loss corporation.*—The term "old loss corporation" means any corporation with respect to which there is an ownership change and that was a loss corporation immediately before the ownership change.

(3) *New loss corporation.*—The term "new loss corporation" means a corporation with respect to which there is an ownership change if, immediately after such change, it is a loss corporation. A successor corporation to the corporation described in the preceding sentence also is a new loss corporation.

(4) *Successor corporation.*—See §1.382-2(a)(5) for the definition of successor corporation.

(5) *Predecessor corporation.*—See §1.382-2(a)(6) for the definitions of predecessor corporation.

(6) *Shift.*—As the context may require, a shift means an equity structure shift, an owner shift or both.

(7) *Entity.*—See §1.382-3(a)(1) for the definition of an entity.

(8) *Direct ownership interest.*—A direct ownership interest means the interest a person owns in an entity, including a loss corporation,

without regard to the constructive ownership rules of paragraph (h) of this section.

(9) *First tier entity.*—A first tier entity is an entity that, at any time during the testing period, owns a five percent or more direct ownership interest in the loss corporation.

(10) *5-percent owner.*—A 5-percent owner is any individual that, at any time during the testing period, owns a five percent or more direct ownership interest in a first tier entity or a higher tier entity. See paragraph (g) of this section for rules to determine whether, as a result of the constructive ownership rules of paragraph (h) of this section, a 5-percent owner is a 5-percent shareholder.

(11) *Public shareholder.*—A public shareholder is any individual, entity, or other person with a direct ownership interest in a loss corporation of less than five percent at all times during the testing period.

(12) *Public owner.*—A public owner is any individual, entity, or other person that, at all times during the testing period, owns less than a five percent direct ownership interest in a first tier entity or any higher tier entity.

(13) *Public group.*—A public group is a group of individuals, entities, or other persons each of whom owns, directly or constructively, less than five percent of the loss corporation. See paragraphs (g) and (j) of this section for the rules applicable to identify public groups and to determine whether a public group is a 5-percent shareholder.

(14) *Higher tier entity.*—A higher tier entity is any entity that, at any time during the testing period, owns a five percent or more direct ownership interest in a first tier entity or in any higher tier entity.

(15) *Indirect ownership interest.*—An indirect ownership interest is an interest a person owns in an entity determined solely as a result of the application of the constructive ownership rules of paragraph (h) of this section and without regard to any direct ownership interest (or other beneficial ownership interest) in the entity.

(16) *Highest tier entity.*—A highest tier entity is a first tier entity or a higher tier entity that is not owned, in whole or in part, at any time during the testing period by a higher tier entity.

(17) *Next lower tier entity.*—The next lower tier entity with respect to a first tier entity is the loss corporation. The next lower tier entity with respect to a higher tier entity is any first tier entity or other higher tier entity in which the higher tier entity owns, at any time during the testing period, a five percent or more direct ownership interest.

(18) *Stock.*—(i) *In general.*—For further guidance, see §1.382-2(a)(3)(i).

(ii) *Treating stock as not stock.*—Any ownership interest that otherwise would be treated as stock under paragraph (f)(18)(i) of this section shall not be treated as stock if—

(A) As of the time of its issuance or transfer to (or by) a 5-percent shareholder, the likely participation of such interest in future corporate growth is disproportionately small when compared to the value of such stock as a proportion of the total value of the outstanding stock of the corporation,

(B) Treating the interest as not constituting stock would result in an ownership change, and

(C) The amount of the pre-change loss (determined as if the testing date were the change date and treating the amount of any net unrealized built-in loss as a pre-change loss) is more than twice the amount determined by multiplying (1) the value of the loss corporation (as determined under section 382(e)) on the testing date, by (2) the long-term tax exempt rate (as defined in section 382(f)) for the calendar month in which the testing date occurs. Stock that is not treated as stock under this paragraph (f)(18)(ii), however, is taken into account for purposes of determining the value of the loss corporation under section 382(e).

(iii) *Treating interests not constituting stock as stock.*—Any ownership interest that would not be treated as stock under paragraph (f)(18)(i) of this section (other than an option that is subject to paragraph (h)(4) of this section) shall be treated as constituting stock if—

(A) As of the time of its issuance or transfer to (or by) a 5-percent shareholder (or a person who would be a 5-percent shareholder if the interest not constituting stock were treated as stock), such interest offers a potential significant participation in the growth of the corporation,

(B) Treating the interest as constituting stock would result in an ownership change, and

(C) The amount of the pre-change losses (determined as if the testing date were the change date and treating the amount of any net unrealized built-in loss as a pre-change loss) is more than twice the amount determined by multiplying (1) the value of the loss corporation (as determined under section 382(e)) on the testing date, by (2) the long-term tax exempt rate (as defined in section 382(f)) for the calendar month in which the testing date occurs. An ownership interest that is treated as stock under this paragraph (f)(18)(iii) is taken into account for purposes of determining the value of the loss corporation under section 382(e).

See §1.382-4(d)(12) for rules that apply with respect to options and this paragraph (f)(18)(iii).

(iv) *Stock of the loss corporation.*—The stock of the loss corporation means stock of such corporation within the meaning of this paragraph (f)(18) and, as the context may require, includes any indirect ownership interest in the loss corporation.

(19) *Change date.*—The change date means the date on which a shift (or any other transaction described in paragraph (a)(2)(i) of this section) that is the last component of an ownership change occurs.

(20) *Year.*—A year, or any multiple thereof, means a 365-day period (or a 366-day period in the case of a leap year), or any multiple thereof, unless the year is specifically identified as a taxable year.

(21) *Old section 382.*—Old section 382 means section 382, as in effect prior to the effective date of section 382 in the Tax Reform Act of 1986 (the "Act"), but taking into account section 621(f)(2) of the Act.

(22) *Pre-change loss.*—See section 382 and §1.382-2(a)(2) for the definition of pre-change loss.

(23) *Unrelated.*—Any two persons are unrelated if the constructive ownership rules of paragraph (h) of this section do not apply to treat either person as owning stock that is owned, directly or constructively, by the other person.

(24) *Percentage ownership interest.*—A person's percentage ownership interest in—

(i) a corporation shall be determined under the rules of this section that are applicable to the determination of a shareholder's percentage stock ownership interest in a loss corporation (see paragraphs (f)(18)(i) through (iii) of this section),

(ii) a partnership shall be equal to the relative fair market value of such person's partnership interest to the total fair market value of all outstanding partnership interests, determined without regard to any limited and preferred partnership interest that is described in paragraph (h)(2)(ii)(C) of this section,

(iii) a trust shall be determined in accordance with the principles of section 318(a)(2)(B) for determining the constructive ownership of stock,

(iv) an estate shall be determined in accordance with the principles of section 318(a)(2)(A) for determining the constructive ownership of stock, and

(v) all other entities shall be determined by reference to the person's relative economic interest in the entity, taking into account all of the relevant facts and circumstances.

(g) *5-percent shareholder.*—(1) *In general.*—Subject to the rules of paragraphs (k)(2) and (4) of this section, the term "5-percent shareholder" means—

(i) an individual that owns, at any time during the testing period, (A) a direct ownership interest in the stock of the loss corporation of five percent or more or (B) an indirect ownership interest in the stock of the loss corporation of five percent or more by virtue of an ownership interest in any one first tier entity or higher tier entity,

(ii) a public group, of either a first tier entity or a higher tier entity, identified as a 5-percent shareholder under paragraphs (j)(1)(iv)(A) or (B) of this section,

(iii) a public group of the loss corporation identified as a 5-percent shareholder under paragraph (j)(1)(iv)(C) of this section, and

(iv) a public group, of the loss corporation, a first tier entity or a higher tier entity, identified as a 5-percent shareholder under paragraphs (j)(2) or (3) of this section. An individual owning five percent or more of the stock of the loss corporation at any time during the testing period is a 5-percent shareholder notwithstanding that the individual may own less than five percent of the stock of the loss corporation on the testing date. See paragraph (g)(5)(i)(B) of this section for rules permitting a loss corporation to make an adjustment in cases described in the preceding sentence.

(2) *Determination of whether a person is a 5-percent shareholder.*— Except as provided in paragraphs (k)(2) and (4) of this section, a person shall be treated as constructively owning stock of the loss corporation pursuant to paragraph (h)(2) of this section only if the loss corporation stock is attributed to such person in the person's capacity as a higher tier entity or a 5-percent owner of the first tier entity or higher tier entity from which such stock is attributed. See paragraph (k)(3) of this section for rules explaining the extent of the obligation of the loss corporation to determine the identity of its 5-percent shareholders. Nothing in this paragraph (g)(2), however, shall limit the attribution of loss corporation stock under section 318(a)(2) and paragraph (h) of this section to a public owner.

(3) *Determination of the percentage stock ownership interest of a 5-percent shareholder.*—Subject to the rules of paragraphs (k)(2) and (4) of this section, in determining a 5-percent shareholder's percentage ownership interest in the loss corporation, the shareholder's direct

ownership interest, if any, and each indirect ownership interest that he may have in the loss corporation in his capacity as a 5-percent owner of any one first tier entity or higher tier entity, if any, are required to be added together and taken into account with respect to such shareholder only to the extent that each such direct or indirect ownership interest constitutes five percent or more of the stock of the loss corporation.

(4) *Examples.*—*Example (1)*—(i) Twenty percent of L stock is owned by A, 10 percent is owned by P_1, 20 percent is owned by E, a joint venture, and the remaining 50 percent of L stock is owned by Public L. P_1 is owned 15 percent by B and 85 percent by Public P_1. E is owned 30 percent by P_2 and 70 percent by P_3, which, in turn, are owned by Public P_2 and Public P_3, respectively.

(ii) The ownership structure of L is illustrated by the following chart:

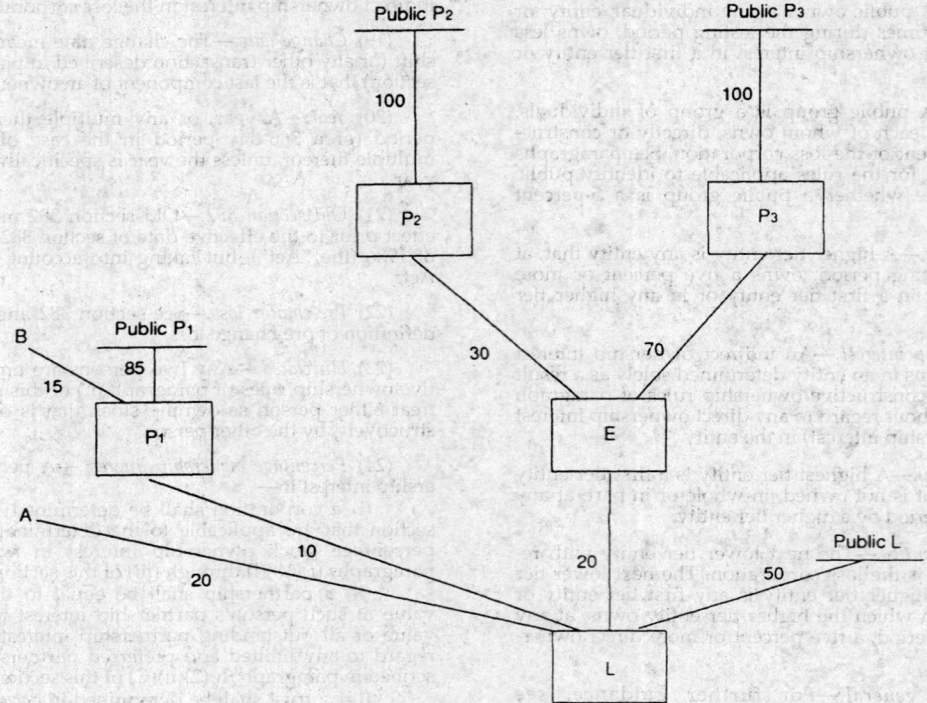

(iii) P_1 and E, each of which has a direct ownership interest in L of five percent or more, are first tier entities. The shareholders with direct ownership interests in L who individually own less than five percent of L are public shareholders (Public L). B, who has a direct ownership interest of five percent or more in P_1, is a 5-percent owner of P_1. P_2 and P_3, each of which has a direct ownership interest in a first tier entity (E) of five percent or more, are higher tier entities with respect to L and, because neither entity is owned at any time during the testing period by a higher tier entity, they also are highest tier entities. The shareholders of P_2 and P_3 (Public P_2 and Public P_3, respectively) are public owners of such entities, because none of those shareholders own five percent or more of either entity at any time during the testing period.

(iv) A, who has a 20 percent direct ownership interest in L, is a 5-percent shareholder of L. Because, by application of the construc-

tive ownership rules of paragraph (h) of this section, B owns only 1.5 percent of L stock in his capacity as a 5-percent owner of P_1 (15 percent ownership of $P_1 \times$ 10 percent ownership of L), B is not a 5-percent shareholder of L, even though he is a 5-percent owner of P_1. Under the rules of paragraph (j) of this section, therefore, B is treated as a member of Public P_1. See Example (3) of paragraph (j)(1)(vi) of this section for a determination of which public owners and public shareholders constitute public groups that are treated as 5-percent shareholders of L.

Example (2)—(i) The facts are the same as in Example (1), except that P_3 is owned 60 percent by C, 30 percent by P_4, and 10 percent by Public P_3. The stock of P_4 is owned by a group of persons (Public P_4), none of whom own five percent or more of the stock of P_4.

(ii) The ownership structure of L is illustrated by the following chart:

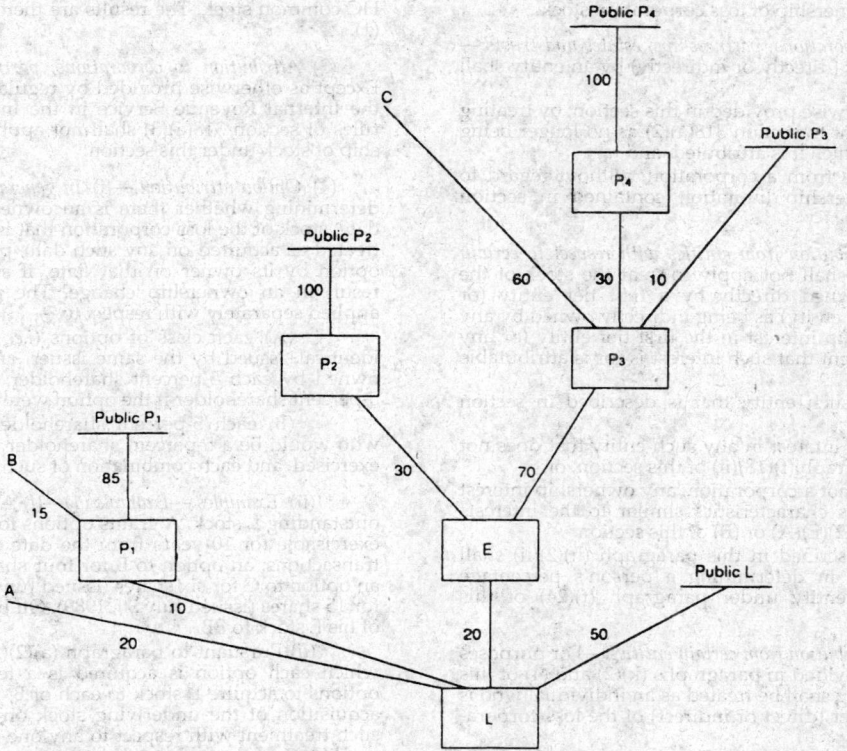

(iii) The defined terms are the same as in Example (1), except that P_3 is a higher tier entity, not a highest tier entity, because five percent or more of P_3 is, in turn, owned by another entity (P_4). P_4, which owns five percent or more of a higher tier entity (P_3), also is a higher tier entity and, because it is not owned at any time during any testing period by any entity that is also a higher tier entity, P_4 is a highest tier entity. All of the shareholders of P_4, none of which own a direct ownership interest of five percent or more in P_4, are public owners of P_4.

(iv) C is a 5-percent owner of P_3 and, under the constructive ownership rules of paragraph (h) of this section, C indirectly owns 8.4 percent of L ([60 percent ownership of P_3] × [70 percent ownership of E] × [20 percent ownership of L]), in his capacity as a 5-percent owner of P_3. B is a 5-percent owner of P_1 and, under the constructive ownership rules of paragraph (h) of this section, B owns 1.5 percent of L ([15 percent ownership of P_1]× [10 percent ownership of L]) in his capacity as a 5-percent owner of P_1. Therefore, C is a 5-percent shareholder of L, but B is not a 5-percent shareholder of L, even though he is a 5-percent owner of P_1. See Example (4) of paragraph (j)(1)(vi) of this section for a determination of which public owners and public shareholders constitute public groups that are treated as separate 5-percent shareholders of L.

Example (3)—(i) L is owned 30 percent by A and 70 percent by P. A owns six percent of P stock and the balance (94 percent) is owned equally by 500 unrelated shareholders ("Public P").

(ii) A is a 5-percent shareholder because he directly owns 30 percent of L. Even though A is a 5-percent owner of P, A's 4.2 percent indirect ownership interest in L (six percent ownership interest in P × P's 70 percent ownership of L) is generally not taken into account in determining A's ownership interest, because such indirect ownership interest is less than five percent. Instead, A's 4.2 percent indirect interest is treated under paragraph (j)(1)(iv) of this section as owned by Public P. If, however, L has actual knowledge of A's less-than-five-percent indirect ownership interest in L and is thus subject to paragraph (k)(2) of this section, or paragraph (k)(4) of this section otherwise applies, L must take A's total 34.2 percent ownership interest into account in determining A's percentage ownership in L.

Example (4). The facts are the same as in Example (3), except that A owns ten percent of P's stock. Because A's indirect ownership interest in L in his capacity as a 5-percent owner of P is five percent or more, both A's 30 percent direct ownership interest in L and his seven percent indirect ownership interest in L (10 percent ownership interest in P × P's 70 percent ownership of L) are taken into account in determining his ownership interest in L, without regard to L's actual knowledge or whether paragraph (k)(4) of this section applies.

Example (5). See § 1.382-3(a)(1)(i.) for additional examples with respect to the definition of an entity.

(5) *Stock ownership presumptions in connection with certain acquisitions and dispositions of loss corporatior. stock.*—(i) *In general.*—For purposes of this section—

(A) if an individual owns less than five percent of the stock of a loss corporation during the testing period (excluding the testing date) and acquires an amount of stock stock so that the individual becomes a 5-percent shareholder on the testing date, the loss corporation may treat any interest in the loss corporation owned by such individual prior to that acquisition as owned by a public group during the period of such individual's ownership of that interest and as not owned by the 5-percent shareholder during the same period, and

(B) if a 5-percent shareholder's percentage ownership interest in the loss corporation is reduced to less than five percent, the loss corporation may presume that the remaining stock owned by such 5-percent shareholder immediately after such reduction is the stock owned by such shareholder for each subsequent testing date having a testing period that includes the date on which the reduction occurred as long as such shareholder continues to own less than five percent of the stock of the loss corporation. In that event, such ownership interest shall be treated as owned by a separate public group for purposes of the rules of paragraph (j)(2)(vi) of this section.

(ii) *Example.*—L has 100,000 shares of stock outstanding. All of the L stock is owned equally by 40 unrelated, individual shareholders, including A (who owns 2.5 percent of L stock). Because no person owns as much as five percent of L stock, Public L is the only 5-percent shareholder of L. See paragraph (j)(1) of this section. A purchases 5,000 shares of L stock over a public stock exchange on June 8, 1989. The purchase is an owner shift. When added to his ownership interest before that date (the testing date), A owns 7,500 shares of L stock (7.5 percent). Under paragraph (g)(5)(i)(A) of this section, L may treat A and Public L as having owned 0 percent and 100 percent, respectively, at all times prior to June 8, 1989 (rather than having owned 2.5 percent by A and 97.5 percent by Public L, even if L has actual knowledge of A's less than five percent ownership interest). The increase in A's stock ownership of L as of June 8, 1989 thus would be 7.5 percentage points, rather than 5.0 percentage points, for purposes of determining whether an ownership change occurs on that testing date and any subsequent testing date.

(h) *Constructive ownership of stock.*—(1) *In general.*—Subject to certain modifications set forth in this section and section 382(l)(3), the constructive ownership rules of section 318(a) generally apply for purposes of determining ownership of loss corporation stock.

(2) *Attribution from corporations, partnerships, estates and trusts.*—(i) *In general.*—Stock owned (directly or indirectly) by an entity shall be attributed to its owners—

(A) except as otherwise provided in this section, by treating the stock attributed pursuant to section 318(a)(2) as no longer being owned by the entity from which it is attributed, and

(B) if attribution is from a corporation, without regard to the 50 percent stock ownership limitation contained in section 318(a)(2)(C).

(ii) *Limitation on attribution from entities with respect to certain interests.*—Section 318(a)(2) shall not apply to treat the stock of the loss corporation that is owned directly by a first tier entity (or indirectly by any higher tier entity) as being indirectly owned by any person that has an ownership interest in the first tier entity (or any higher tier entity) to the extent that such interest is (or is attributable to)—

(A) stock of any such entity that is described in section 1504(a)(4),

(B) any ownership interest in any such entity that does not constitute stock under paragraph (f)(18)(ii) of this section, or

(C) if the entity is not a corporation, any ownership interest in any such entity that has characteristics similar to the interests described in paragraphs (h)(2)(ii)(A) or (B) of this section.
The ownership interests described in this paragraph (h)(2)(ii) shall not be taken into account in determining a person's percentage ownership interest in an entity under paragraph (f)(24) of this section.

(iii) *Limitation on attribution from certain entities.*—For purposes of this section, except as provided in paragraphs (k)(2) and (4) of this section, each of the following shall be treated as an individual who is unrelated to any other owner (direct or indirect) of the loss corporation—

(A) any entity other than a higher tier entity that owns five percent or more of the loss corporation stock (determined without regard to paragraph (h)(2)(i)(A) of this section) on a testing date, a first tier entity or the loss corporation,

(B) a qualified trust described in section 401(a),

(C) any State, any possession of the United States, the District of Columbia, the United States (or any agency or instrumentality thereof), any foreign government, or any political subdivision of any of the foregoing, and

(D) any other person designated by the Internal Revenue Service in the Internal Revenue Bulletin.

Stock of a loss corporation that is owned by any such person shall thus not be attributed to any other person for purposes of this section. See paragraph (g)(2) of this section limiting attribution from a first tier entity or a higher tier entity to any person that is not a 5-percent owner or a higher tier entity.

(iv) *Examples.*—*Example (1).* All the stock of L is owned by A. B and C respectively own 70 and 30 percent of the outstanding P stock. P acquires 60 percent of the outstanding L stock from A on July 1, 1988 (a testing date). After the acquisition, P is a first tier entity and a highest tier entity of L. B and C are each 5-percent owners of P and also are 5-percent shareholders of L having a 42 percent and 18 percent stock ownership interest in L, respectively, through the operation of the constructive ownership rules of paragraph (h) of this section. Because B and C together have increased their ownership in L by more than 50 percentage points during the testing period ending on the testing date (60 percent on the testing date and 0 percent prior thereto), an ownership change occurs with respect to L on July 1, 1988.

Example (2). The facts are the same as in Example (1), except that B and C are not shareholders in a corporation, but instead are partners in a general partnership, E. B and C respectively own 70 percent and 30 percent of E. E acquires 60 percent of the L stock on July 1, 1988. The results are the same as in Example (1).

Example (3). The facts are the same as in Example (1), except that the acquisition is accomplished in a transaction that qualifies under section 351(a). In that transaction, HC is formed through (i) a contribution of money by P in exchange for 60 shares of HC common stock and (ii) a contribution of all the outstanding shares of L stock plus cash by A in exchange for 40 shares of HC common stock and 30 shares of HC preferred stock that is described in section 1504(a)(4). The respective values of each share of HC stock, common and preferred, are equal. The stock of L is attributed to A through his interest in HC common stock, but not through his interest in HC preferred stock (see paragraph (h)(2)(ii)(A) of this section). Thus, A is treated as owning indirectly only 40 percent of L. B and C are 5-percent shareholders of L having indirect ownership interests in L

of 42 percent and 18 percent, respectively, through their ownership of HC common stock. The results are therefore the same as in Example (1).

(3) *Attribution to corporations, partnerships, estates and trusts.*—Except as otherwise provided by regulation under section 382 or by the Internal Revenue Service in the Internal Revenue Bulletin, the rules of section 318(a)(3) shall not apply in determining the ownership of stock under this section.

(4) *Option attribution.*—(i) *In general.*—Solely for the purpose of determining whether there is an ownership change on any testing date, stock of the loss corporation that is subject to an option shall be treated as acquired on any such date, pursuant to an exercise of the option by its owner on that date, if such deemed exercise would result in an ownership change. The preceding sentence shall be applied separately with respect to—

(A) each class of options (*i.e.,* options with terms that are identical, issued by the same issuer, and issued on the same date) owned by each 5-percent shareholder (or person who would be a 5-percent shareholder if the option were treated as exercised), and

(B) each 5-percent shareholder, each owner of an option who would be a 5-percent shareholder if the option were treated as exercised, and each combination of such persons.

(ii) *Examples.*—*Example (1)*—(i) A owns all of the 100 shares of outstanding L stock. A grants options for the purchase of his L stock, exercisable for 10 years from the date of issuance, in the following transactions: an option to B for four shares (issued January 1, 1988), an option to C for six shares (issued June 1, 1989), and an option to D for 15 shares (issued July 30, 1989). On July 30, 1990, A sells 41 shares of his L stock to BB.

(ii) Pursuant to paragraph (a)(2)(i) of this section, the date on which each option is acquired is a testing date. The issuance of options to acquire L stock to each of B, C, and D is not treated as an acquisition of the underlying stock on any such testing date since such treatment with respect to any one of the option owners (or any combination thereof) would not have resulted in an ownership change on any of those testing dates.

(iii) The date on which BB acquires 41 shares also is a testing date. BB's acquisition of 41 percent of the L stock, taken together with the shift in ownership that would result if the options held by B, C and D were exercised, would result in an ownership change, because the stock owned or treated as owned by Public L (a group including only B, the sole shareholder who owns less than five percent of L stock), C, D and BB would have increased by 66 percentage points (four, six, 15, and 41 percentage points, respectively) during the testing period. Subject to paragraph (h)(4)(ix) of this section, the options are treated as exercised and an ownership change occurs on July 30, 1990, pursuant to paragraph (h)(4)(i) of this section. Accordingly, no new testing period can begin before July 31, 1990. Under paragraph (h)(4)(x)(F) of this section, the option attribution rules of paragraph (h)(4)(i) of this section shall not be applicable with respect to any of the options owned by B, C, and D immediately before the ownership change until such time, if any, that such options are transferred to (or by) a 5-percent shareholder (or a person who would be a 5-percent shareholder if such option were exercised). In addition, the subsequent exercise of any of those options by A, B, or C (the persons owning such options immediately before the ownership change) is disregarded. See paragraph (h)(4)(vi) of this section. Also see paragraph (h)(4)(viii) of this section for the treatment of options that lapse or are forfeited.

(iv) The facts are the same as in (i), except that the sale of A's 41 shares of L stock to BB occurs on July 30, 1995. Because the options are treated as exercised and the related stock is treated as acquired on the July 30, 1995 testing date, the results are the same as described in (iii).

Example (2)—(i) A owns all of the outstanding 100 shares of the stock of L. On July 22, 1988, the value of A's stock in L is $500 and the following agreements are entered into: (i) A sells 40 shares of his L stock to B for $200, (ii) in exchange for $10, A grants B an option to acquire the balance of his L stock for $305 at any time before July 22, 1992, and (iii) L grants A an option to acquire 100 shares of L stock at a price of $600 exercisable until such time as B's option is no longer outstanding.

(ii) If the stock subject to the options owned by both A and B were treated as acquired on the July 22, 1988 testing date, B would have increased his ownership interest in L by only 50 percentage points to 50 percent ([40 shares purchased + 60 shares acquired pursuant to the option]/200 outstanding shares of L stock, including 100 shares deemed outstanding pursuant to the option issued to A by L) as compared with 0 percent prior to July 22, 1988. In determining whether the options with respect to the stock of L would, if exercised, result in an ownership change, paragraph (h)(4)(i)(B) of this section requires that such options be treated as exercised separately with respect to each 5-percent shareholder, each person who would be a 5-percent shareholder if the option were treated as exercised or each combination of such persons. Therefore, by treating the option owned by A as not having been exercised and the option owned by B as having been exercised, B's interest in L increases by 100 percentage points during the testing period. An ownership change with respect to L therefore results from the transactions occurring on July 22, 1988.

(iii) *Contingencies.*—Except as provided in paragraph (h)(4)(x)(D) of this section, the extent to which an option is contingent or otherwise not currently exercisable shall be disregarded for purposes of this section.

(iv) *Series of options.*—For purposes of this section, an option to acquire an option with respect to the stock of the loss corporation, and each one of a series of such options, shall be considered as an option to acquire such stock.

(v) *Interests that are similar to options.*—For purposes of this section, (A) an interest that is similar to an option includes, but is not limited to, a warrant, a convertible debt instrument, an instrument other than debt that is convertible into stock, a put, a stock interest subject to risk of forfeiture, and a contract to acquire or sell stock, and (B) any such interest shall be treated as an option.

(vi) *Actual exercise of options.*—(A) *In general.*—The actual exercise of any option in existence immediately before and after an ownership change, whether or not the option was treated as exercised in connection with the ownership change under paragraph (h)(4)(i) of this section, shall be disregarded for purposes of this section, but only if the option is exercised by the 5-percent shareholder (or person who would have been a 5-percent shareholder if the options owned by such person had been exercised immediately before the ownership change) who owned the option immediately before and after such ownership change.

(B) *Actual exercise within 120 days of deemed exercise.*—If the actual exercise of an option occurs on or before the end of the period which is 120 days after the date on which the option is treated as exercised under paragraph (h)(4)(i) of this section, the loss corporation may elect to treat paragraphs (h)(4)(i) and (vi)(A) of this section as not applying to such option and take into account only the acquisition of loss corporation stock resulting from the actual exercise of the option. An election under this paragraph (h)(4)(vi)(B) shall have no effect on the determination of whether an ownership change occurs, but shall apply only for the purpose of determining the date on which the change date occurs. An election under this paragraph (h)(4)(vi)(B) shall be made in the statement described in §1.382-11(a).

(vii) *Effect of deemed exercise of options on the outstanding stock of the loss corporation.*—(A) *Right or obligation to issue stock.*—Solely for purposes of determining whether an ownership change has occurred under paragraph (h)(4)(i) of this section, the deemed exercise of an option with respect to unissued stock (or treasury stock) of a corporation shall result in a corresponding increase in the amount of its total outstanding stock.

(B) *Right or obligation to acquire outstanding stock by the loss corporation.*—Solely for purposes of determining whether an ownership change has occurred under paragraph (h)(4)(i) of this section, the deemed exercise of a right to transfer outstanding stock to the issuing corporation (or a right of the issuing corporation to acquire its stock) shall result in a corresponding decrease in the amount of its total outstanding stock.

(C) *Effect on value of old loss corporation.*—The deemed exercise of an option with respect to unissued stock (or treasury stock) under paragraph (h)(4)(i) of this section shall have no effect on the determination of the value of the old loss corporation and the computation of the section 382 limitation. See section 382(l)(1)(B) disregarding capital contributions made during the two-year period preceding the change date for purposes of computing the section 382 limitation.

(viii) *Options that lapse or are forfeited.*—If an option that is treated as exercised under paragraph (h)(4)(i) of this section lapses unexercised or the owner of such option irrevocably forfeits his right to acquire stock pursuant to the option, the option shall be treated for purposes of this section as if it never had been issued. In that case, the loss corporation may file an amended return for prior years (subject to any applicable statute of limitations) if the section 382 limitation was thus inapplicable. If paragraph (h)(4)(i) of this section applied to an option (or options) with respect to a taxable year for which an income tax return has not been filed by the date that the option (or options) lapses or is irrevocably forfeited, the loss corporation may treat paragraph (h)(4)(i) of this section as inapplicable to such option (or options).

(ix) *Option rule inapplicable if pre-change losses are de minimis.*—Paragraph (h)(4)(i) of this section shall not apply to treat the stock of the loss corporation as acquired by the owner of an option if, on a testing date, the amount of pre-change losses (determined as if the testing date were a change date and treating the amount of any net unrealized built-in loss as a pre-change loss) is less than twice the amount determined by multiplying (A) the value of the loss corporation (as determined under section 382(e)) on the testing date, by (B) the long-term tax exempt rate (as defined in section 382(f)) for the calendar month in which the testing date occurs.

(x) *Options not subject to attribution.*—Paragraph (h)(4)(i) of this section shall not apply to—

(A) *Long-held options with respect to actively traded stock.*—Any option with respect to stock of the loss corporation which stock is actively traded on an established securities market (within the meaning of section 1273(b)) for which market quotations are readily available, if such option has been continuously owned by the same 5-percent shareholder (or a person who would be a 5-percent shareholder if such option were exercised) for at least three years, but only until the earlier of such time as—

(1) the option is transferred by or to a 5-percent shareholder (or a person who would be a 5-percent shareholder if such option were exercised), or

(2) the fair market value of the stock that is subject to the option exceeds the exercise price for such stock on the testing date. For purposes of this paragraph (h)(4)(x)(A), options with respect to the stock of a loss corporation that are assumed (or substituted) in a reorganization and converted into options with respect to the stock of another party to the reorganization shall not be treated as transferred, provided that there are no changes in the terms of the options, other than that the stock that may be acquired pursuant to the option is that of another party to the reorganization and that the amount of stock subject to the option is adjusted only to reflect the exchange ratio for the exchange of stock of the loss corporation in the reorganization.

(B) *Right to receive or obligation to issue a fixed dollar amount of value of stock upon maturity of certain debt.*—Any right to receive or obligation to issue stock pursuant to the terms of a debt instrument that, in economic terms, is equivalent to nonconvertible debt because the right to receive stock of the issuer of a fixed dollar amount is based upon the fair market value for such stock determined at or about the date the stock is transferred pursuant to such right or obligation (*i.e.*, the amount of the stock transferred pursuant to the option is equal to a fixed dollar amount, divided by the value of each share of such stock at or about the date of the stock transfer). This paragraph (h)(4)(x)(B) shall not apply if the method for determining the fair market value of the stock of the issuer is intended to or, in fact, provides the owner of the debt instrument with a participation in any appreciation of any stock of the issuer.

(C) *Right or obligation to redeem stock of the loss corporation.*—Any right or obligation of the loss corporation to redeem any of its stock at the time such stock is issued, but only to the extent such stock is issued to persons who are not 5-percent shareholders immediately before the issuance.

(D) *Options exercisable only upon death, disability or mental incompetency.*—Any option entered into between owners of the same entity (or an owner and the entity in which the owner has a direct ownership interest) with respect to such owner's ownership interest in the entity that is exercisable only upon the death, complete disability or mental incompetency of such owner.

(E) *Right to receive or obligation to issue stock as interest or dividends.*—Any right to receive or obligation to issue stock of a corporation in payment of interest or dividends by the issuing corporation. (For an example illustrating this exception, see paragraph (j)(2)(iv)(B) of this section.)

(F) *Options outstanding following an ownership change.*—(1) *In general.*—Any option in existence immediately before and after an ownership change, whether or not the option was treated as exercised in connection with the ownership change under paragraph (h)(4)(i) of this section, but only so long as the option continues to be owned by the 5-percent shareholder (or person who was treated as a 5-percent shareholder) who owned the option immediately before and after such ownership change.

(2) *Example.*—(i) A, B, C and D own all of the outstanding stock of L. A owns 70 shares of L stock and each of B, C and D own 10 shares of L stock. On July 12, 1988, L issues warrants to each of its shareholders entitling them to acquire an additional 8.5 shares of L stock for each share of stock owned.

(ii) If B, C and D, but not A, each exercise their respective rights to acquire an additional 85 shares of L stock (10 shares × 8.5 shares that may be acquired for each share owned) on July 12, 1988, their combined ownership interest in L on that date would exceed 80 percent (255 shares deemed to be acquired + 30 shares actually owned/355 shares outstanding (actual and deemed)). B, C and D thus would increase their ownership interest in L by 50.3 percentage points during the testing period, causing an ownership change, because, under paragraph (h)(4)(i)(B) of this section, the options are treated as exercised if the exercise would cause an ownership change.

(iii) Following the ownership change, paragraph (h)(4)(i) of this section applies to prevent A's right to acquire 595 shares of L stock (70 shares × 8.5 shares that may be acquired for each share owned) or the rights held by B, C, or D, to be treated as exercised on any subsequent testing date, except to the extent that those rights are transferred. To the extent any of those options are transferred following the ownership change, paragraph (h)(4)(i) of this section will apply to any such options on the date of the transfer and on any subsequent testing date.

(G) Right to acquire loss corporation stock pursuant to a default under a loan agreement.—Any right to acquire stock of a corporation by a bank (as that term is defined in section 581), an insurance company (as that term is defined in §1.801-3(a)), or a trust qualified under section 401(a) solely as the result of a default under a loan agreement entered into in the ordinary course of the trade or business of such bank, life insurance company or qualified trust.

(H) Agreement to acquire or sell stock owned by certain shareholders upon retirement.—Any option entered into between noncorporate owners of the same entity (or a noncorporate owner and the entity in which the owner has a direct ownership interest) with respect to such owner's ownership interest in the entity, but only if each of such owners actively participate in the management of the entity's trade or business, the option is issued at a time that the loss corporation is not a loss corporation and the option is exercisable solely upon the retirement of such owner. An option with terms described in both this paragraph (h)(4)(x)(H) and in paragraph (h)(4)(x)(D) of this section shall also not be subject to paragraph (h)(4)(i) of this section.

(I) [Reserved]

(J) Title 11 or similar case.—See §1.382-9(o) which excepts certain options created by or under a plan of reorganization in a title 11 or similar case from the operation of paragraph (h)(4)(i) of this section.

(K)—(Y) [Reserved]

(xi) Certain transfers of options disregarded.—Transfers of options between persons who are not 5-percent shareholders (and between members of separate public groups resulting from the application of the segregation rules of paragraphs (j)(2) and (3)(iii) of this section) are not taken into account. Transfers of options in any of the circumstances described in section 382(l)(3)(B) are also disregarded and the transferee shall be treated as having owned the option for the period that it was owned by the transferor.

(xii) Exercise of an option that has not been treated as stock.—The acquisition of stock pursuant to the actual exercise of an option (other than an option described in paragraph (h)(4)(vi)(A) of this section) shall not be disregarded.

(xiii) Effective date.—See paragraph (m)(4)(vi) of this section for special rules regarding the effective date of the provisions of this paragraph (h)(4).

(5) Stock transferred under certain agreements.—Notwithstanding paragraph (h)(4) of this section, no shift results solely because under section 1058(a)—

(i) a shareholder transfers stock of a corporation pursuant to an agreement that meets the requirements of section 1058(b), or

(ii) a person having rights under such an agreement exchanges those rights for stock identical to the stock transferred pursuant to the agreement.

(6) Family attribution.—For purposes of this section—

(i) paragraphs (1) and (5)(B) of section 318(a) shall not apply,

(ii) an individual and all members of his family described in section 318(a)(1) shall be treated as one individual,

(iii) subject to paragraph (k)(2) of this section, paragraph (h)(6)(ii) of this section shall not apply to members of a family who, without regard to that paragraph (h)(6)(ii), would not be 5-percent shareholders, and

(iv) if under paragraph (h)(6)(ii) of this section, an individual may be treated as a member of more than one family, and each

family that is treated as one individual is a 5-percent shareholder (or would be treated as a 5-percent shareholder if such individual were treated as a member of such family), then such individual shall be treated only as a member of the family that results in the smallest increase in the total percentage stock ownership of the 5-percent shareholders on the testing date and shall not be treated as the member of any other family.

(i) [Reserved].

(j) Aggregation and segregation rules.—For purposes of this section, except as provided in paragraphs (k)(2) and (4) of this section—

(1) Aggregation of public shareholders and public owners into public groups.—(i) *Public group.*—Under this paragraph (j), a loss corporation or other entity can be treated as owned, in whole or in part, by one or more public groups. A public group can include public shareholders, public owners, and 5-percent owners who are not 5-percent shareholders of the loss corporation.

(ii) *Treatment of a public group that is a 5-percent shareholder.*—Each public group that is treated as a 5-percent shareholder under paragraphs (g)(1)(ii), (iii) or (iv) of this section shall be treated as one individual. See paragraph (j)(2)(iv) for a rule combining certain de minimis public groups.

(iii) *Presumption of no cross-ownership.*—The public owners, 5-percent owners who are not 5-percent shareholders and public shareholders in any public group, subject to paragraphs (j)(2)(iii), (k)(2) and (k)(4) of this section, are presumed not to be members of any other public group. It also is presumed that each such person is unrelated to all other shareholders (direct and indirect) of the loss corporation. See paragraph (h)(6)(iii) of this section. The members of a public group that exists by virtue of its direct ownership interest in an entity are presumed not to be members (and not to be related to a member) of any other public group that exists at any time by virtue of its direct ownership interest in any other entity. To the extent that the presumptions adopted in this paragraph (j)(1)(iii) are not applicable because the loss corporation has actual knowledge of facts to the contrary and is thus subject to paragraph (k)(2) of this section, public shareholders, public owners and 5-percent owners who are not 5-percent shareholders may be aggregated into additional public groups.

(iv) *Identification of the public groups treated as 5-percent shareholders.*—(A) *Analysis of highest tier entities.*—The loss corporation must identify first tier entities and higher tier entities in order to identify any highest tier entities that must be identified under paragraph (k)(3) of this section. The loss corporation must then identify any 5-percent owners of each such highest tier entity who indirectly own, at any time during the testing period, five percent or more of the loss corporation through the ownership interest in such highest tier entity. Under paragraph (g)(1)(i)(B) of this section, any such 5-percent owner is a 5-percent shareholder. See paragraph (k)(3) of this section for rules explaining the extent of the obligation of the loss corporation to determine the identity of its shareholders. Each person who has an ownership interest in any highest tier entity and who is not treated as a 5-percent shareholder (*i.e.*, persons who are public owners or 5-percent owners who are not 5-percent shareholders) is a member of the public group of that highest tier entity. A public group, so identified, that indirectly owns five percent or more of the loss corporation on the testing date is treated under paragraph (g)(1)(ii) of this section as a 5-percent shareholder. If the public group so identified owns less than five percent of the loss corporation on the testing date, such public group is treated as part of the public group of the next lower tier entity.

(B) *Analysis of other higher tier entities and first tier entities.*—The analysis and aggregation of public groups described in paragraph (j)(1)(iv)(A) of this section is repeated for any next lower tier entity and successively for any next lower tier entity of any entity described in this paragraph (j)(1)(iv)(B) until applied to each first tier entity.

(C) *Aggregation of the public shareholders.*—The public shareholders are aggregated and, under paragraph (g)(1)(iii) of this section, are treated as a public group that is a 5-percent shareholder without regard to whether such group, at any time during the testing period, owns five percent or more of the loss corporation. For this purpose, if the public group of any first tier entity indirectly owns less than five percent of the loss corporation on the testing date, and is thus not treated as a 5-percent shareholder, but is treated as part of the public group of the loss corporation under paragraph (j)(1)(iv)(A) or (B) of this section, the ownership interest of that group is included in the public group of the loss corporation referred to in the preceding sentence.

(v) *Appropriate adjustments.*—A loss corporation may apply the principles of paragraph (g)(5) of this section with respect to—

(A) any public group that is treated as a 5-percent shareholder on the testing date if such public group, at any time during the testing period, was treated as part of the public group of the next lower tier entity, or

(B) any public group that is treated as part of the public group of a next lower tier entity if such public group, at any time during the testing period, was part of the public group of a higher tier entity that was treated as a 5-percent shareholder and had a direct or indirect ownership interest in such next lower tier entity.

(vi) *Examples.—Example (1)—(i)* All of the stock of L is owned by 1,000 shareholders, none of whom own as much as five percent of L stock ("Public L"). All of the stock of P is owned by 150,000 shareholders, none of whom own as much as five percent of P stock ("Public P"). Between July 12, 1988 and August 13, 1988, P purchases all of the L stock through a series of transactions on a public stock exchange. P's percentage of direct stock ownership in L increases from 4.9 percent to five percent on July 15, 1988, and from 50 percent to 51 percent on July 30, 1988.

(ii) Before July 15, 1988, P is a public shareholder of L. On and after July 15, 1988, P is a first tier entity (and a highest tier entity) of L. Accordingly, under the rules of paragraph (j)(1) of this section, Public P, on and after July 15, 1988, is treated as a public group that is a 5-percent shareholder. Each acquisition by P on and after such date affects the percentage of L stock that is owned by Public P and thus constitutes an owner shift.

(iii) Immediately after the transaction on July 30, 1988, P owns 51 percent of L stock. Under paragraph (j)(1)(iv)(A) of this section, Public P thus owns 51 percent of L. Under paragraph (j)(1)(iv)(C) of this section, Public L, the public group that includes the public shareholders of L, is treated as a 5-percent shareholder that owns 49 percent of L. Under paragraph (j)(1)(iii) of this section, Public L and Public P are presumed not to have any common members and it is also presumed that no member of either public group is related to any other member of either of the two public groups.

(iv) Assuming that the presumption provided in paragraph (j)(1)(iii) of this section (*i.e.*, that no person owns stock in both P and L) is not rebutted to any extent, Public P is treated as a 5-percent shareholder whose stock ownership in L, as of the July 30, 1988 testing date, has increased by 51 percentage points over its lowest percentage of stock ownership in L at any time during the testing period (0 percent prior to July 12, 1988). Accordingly, an ownership change with respect to L occurs as a result of P's acquisition on July 30, 1988. L is thus a new loss corporation and its pre-change losses are subject to limitation under section 382.

Example (2)—(i) All of the stock of P is owned by 1,000 unrelated shareholders, none of whom owns as much as five percent of P stock. L_1 is a wholly owned subsidiary of P. On January 2, 1988, P distributes all of the L_1 stock pro rata to its shareholders.

(ii) Prior to the stock distribution, the public owners of P are members of a public group ("Public P") that is treated as a 5-percent shareholder owning 100 percent of the stock of L_1. See paragraph (j)(1)(iv)(A) of this section. Following the stock distribution to the P shareholders, L_1 is owned by 1,000 public shareholders that are members of a public group ("Public L_1") that is treated as a 5-percent shareholder owning 100 percent of the stock of L_1. See paragraph (j)(1)(iv)(C) of this section.

(iii) Public P and Public L_1 are treated as unrelated, individual 5-percent shareholders under paragraph (j)(1)(iii) of this section. Although the members of one public group are presumed not to be members of any other public group under paragraph (j)(1)(iii) of this section, L_1 has actual knowledge that all of its public shareholders immediately following the distribution (Public L_1) received L_1 stock pro rata in respect of the outstanding P stock and thus were also members of Public P. Applying paragraph (k)(2) of this section, the loss corporation may take into account the identity of ownership interests between Public L_1 and Public P to establish that Public L_1 did not increase its percentage ownership in L_1. Accordingly, the transaction would not constitute an owner shift.

Example (3)—(i) The facts are the same as in Example (1) of paragraph (g)(4) of this section. Thus, 20 percent of L stock is owned by A, 10 percent is owned by P_1, 20 percent is owned by E, a joint venture, and the remaining 50 percent of L stock is owned by Public L. P_1 is owned 15 percent by B and 85 percent by Public P_1. E is owned 30 percent by P_2 and 70 percent by P_3, which are owned by Public P_2 and Public P_3, respectively. See Example (1)(ii) of paragraph (g)(4) of this section for a chart illustrating this ownership structure.

(ii) The public owners of P_2 and P_3 (Public P_2 and Public P_3, respectively), are public groups that are treated as 5-percent shareholders of L, because each such public group indirectly owns five percent or more of L stock (six percent by Public P_2 [(30 percent ownership of E) × (20 percent ownership of L)] and 14 percent by Public P_3 [(70 percent ownership of E) × (20 percent ownership of L)]. The public owners of P_1 ("Public P_1"), who indirectly own 8.5 percent of L stock [(85 percent ownership of P_1) × (10 percent ownership of L)] and B, who indirectly owns 1.5 percent of L and is thus included in Public P_1 under paragraph (j)(1)(iv)(A) of this section, are members of a public group that is treated as a 5-percent shareholder of L that owns ten percent of L stock. Finally, the public group of L ("Public L") is a 5-percent shareholder that owns 50 percent of L. Accordingly, A, Public L, Public P_1 (including B), Public P_2, and Public P_3 are the only 5-percent shareholders of L.

Example (4)—(i) The facts are the same as Example (3) above, except that P_3 is owned 60 percent by C, 30 percent by P_4 and 10 percent by Public P_3. The stock of P_4 is publicly traded and is owned by Public P_4. The facts are thus the same as in Example (2) in paragraph (g)(4) of this section. See Example (2)(ii) of paragraph (g)(4) of this section for a chart illustrating this ownership structure.

(ii) The public owners of P_4 (a highest tier entity) are members of a public group that indirectly owns 4.2 percent of L ([30 percent ownership of P_3]× [70 percent ownership of E] × [20 percent ownership of L]). For purposes of identifying public groups that are 5-percent shareholders, L is not required to identify P_4 as a highest tier entity under paragraph (k)(3) of this section because P_4 does not own five percent or more of L stock. Moreover, under paragraph (h)(2)(iii) of this section, P_4 generally is treated as an individual from which there is no attribution of loss corporation stock. The public group of P_3 (including P_4) indirectly owns 5.6 percent of L ([40 percent of P_3] × [70 percent ownership of E] × [20 percent of L]), and is thus a 5-percent shareholder of L. The public groups of P_2 and P_1 (both Public P_1 and B), respectively, also own five percent or more of L stock and are thus 5-percent shareholders of L. In addition, the public group of L is a 5-percent shareholder regardless of whether it owns five percent of L stock. Accordingly, A, Public L, Public P_3 (including P_4), Public P_2, and Public P_1 (including B), are the only 5-percent shareholders of L.

Example (5)—(i) On September 4, 1987, L is owned 14 percent by each of A and B, 30 percent by each of P_1 and P_2, four percent by each of C and P_3, and two percent by each of D and AA. P_1 is owned 30 percent by each of A, B, and P_4 and 10 percent by D. P_2 is owned 70 percent by A, 10 percent by each of B and D, six percent by DD and four percent by C. AA owns 100 percent of the stock of P_3. P_4 is owned 60 percent by C and 20 percent by each of BB and CC.

(ii) The ownership structure of L is illustrated by the following chart:

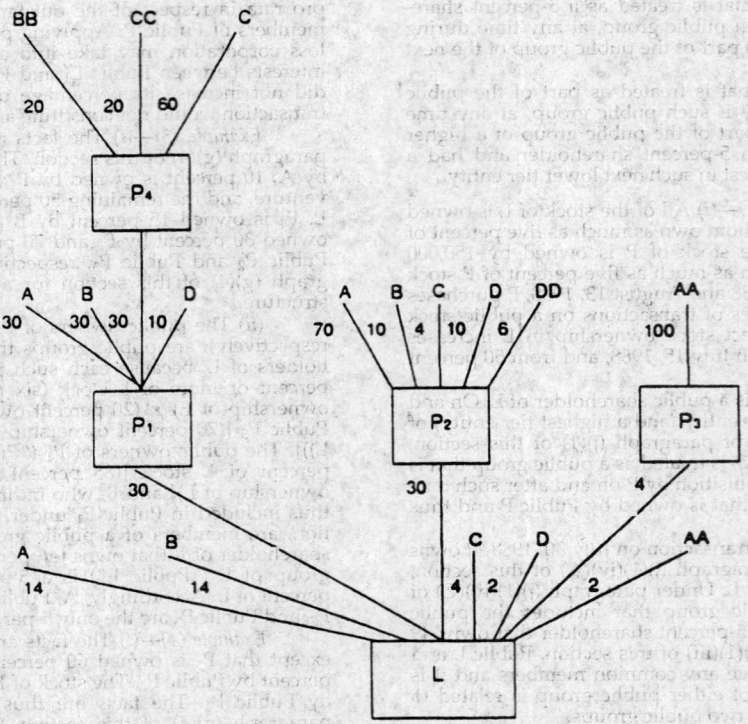

(iii) In order to identify L's 5-percent shareholders and their respective ownership interests in L on September 4, 1987, the rules of paragraph (j)(1) of this section apply to identify the public groups that are treated as separate 5-percent shareholders. Analysis begins with any highest tier entity, such as P_4. Each of P_4's shareholders is a 5-percent owner of P_4. C owns 5.4 percent of L in his capacity as a 5-percent owner of P_4 and therefore is a 5-percent shareholder. Notwithstanding that C actually owns, directly and by attribution, 10.6 percent of L (four percent directly, 5.4 percent indirectly through P_4, and 1.2 percent through P_2), C's ownership interest in L as a 5-percent shareholder is presumed to include only the 5.4 percent indirect ownership through P_4. (Under paragraphs (g) and (k)(2) of this section, however, L must account for C's direct and indirect ownership interests in determining whether an ownership change occurs on any testing date if it has actual knowledge of such ownership on or before the date that its income tax return is filed for the taxable year that includes the testing date.) Although BB and CC are each 5-percent owners of P_4, they are not 5-percent shareholders and therefore are members of the public group of P_4. Because the public group of P_4 indirectly owns only 3.6 percent of L, it is treated under paragraph (j)(1)(iv)(A) of this section as part of the public group of the next lower tier entity, P_1.

(iv) With respect to P_1, a first tier entity, each of its shareholders are 5-percent owners. Because A and B each indirectly own nine percent of L as 5-percent owners of P_1 and A indirectly owns 21 percent of L as a 5-percent owner of P_2, they are each 5-percent shareholders without regard to their direct ownership interests in L. A's ownership interest in L as a 5-percent shareholder is 44 percent (14 percent directly, nine percent in his capacity as a 5-percent owner of P_1, and 21 percent in his capacity as a 5-percent owner of P_2). B's ownership interest in L as a 5-percent shareholder is 23 percent (14 percent directly and nine percent in his capacity as a 5-percent owner of P_1). B's ownership interest as a 5-percent shareholder does not include the three percent interest he owns indirectly through P_2. (Under paragraph (g) and (k)(2) of this section, however, L must account for B's direct and indirect ownership interests, including his three percent interest through P_2, in determining whether an ownership change occurs on any testing date if L has actual knowledge of such ownership on or before the date that its income tax return is filed for the taxable year that includes the testing date.) D is a 5-percent owner of P_1. Although D owns eight percent of L (two percent directly, three percent indirectly through P_1, and three percent indirectly through P_2), he is not a 5-percent shareholder because he does not own five percent or more of L stock either directly or in his capacity as a 5-percent owner of either P_1 or P_2. (Under paragraphs (g) and (k)(2) of this section, however, L must account for D's direct and indirect ownership interests in determining whether an ownership change occurs on any testing date to the extent L has actual knowledge of such ownership amounting to five percent or

more of L stock before the date that its income tax return is filed for the taxable year that includes the testing date.) The public group of P_1 (comprised of the public group of P_4 and D's direct ownership interest in P_1) has a 6.6 percent interest in L and is therefore treated as a separate 5-percent shareholder.

(v) With respect to highest tier entity P_2, D is a 5-percent owner who is not a 5-percent shareholder for the reason described in the preceding subdivision. DD is a 5-percent owner of P_2, who is not a 5-percent shareholder, because DD indirectly owns only 1.8 percent of L. Assuming that L does not have actual knowledge of B's and C's direct ownership interest in P_2, those interests are accounted for in computing the ownership interest of the public group of P_2. Therefore, each of P_2's shareholders, except A who is a 5-percent shareholder in his capacity as a 5-percent owner of P_2, are treated as members of the public group of P_2 that owns nine percent of L and is thus treated as separate 5-percent shareholder.

(vi) Because the direct ownership interest of P_3 is less than five percent, it is a public shareholder. Therefore, assuming that L does not have actual knowledge of C's, D's or AA's direct and/or indirect ownership interests in L, the public group of L is a separate 5-percent shareholder owning 12 percent of L (comprised of the direct ownership interests of C, D, AA and P_3).

(2) *Segregation rules applicable to transactions involving the loss corporation.*—(i) *In general.*—For purposes of this section, if—

(A) a transaction is described in paragraph (j)(2)(iii) of this section, and

(B) the loss corporation has one or more direct public groups immediately before and after the transaction,
the stock owned by such direct public group or groups is subject to the segregation rules described in paragraph (j)(2)(iii) of this section for purposes of determining whether an ownership change has occurred on the date of the transaction (and on any subsequent testing date with a testing period that includes the date of such transaction). See paragraph (j)(3) of this section for the application of the rules of this paragraph (j)(2) to transactions involving first tier entities or higher tier entities.

(ii) *Direct public group.*—For purposes of this section, a direct public group is any public group of the loss corporation described in paragraph (j)(1)(iv)(C) of this section or any public group of the loss corporation resulting from the application of paragraphs (j)(2)(iii) or (j)(3)(i) of this section.

(iii) *Transactions to which segregation rules apply.*—(A) *In general.*—The segregation rules of this paragraph (j)(2)(iii) apply to any transaction described in paragraphs (j)(2)(iii)(B), (C), (D), (E), or (F) of this section in the manner specified. The presumptions adopted by this paragraph (j)(2)(iii) shall not apply only if, and to the extent that, the loss corporation either has actual knowledge of facts to the contrary regarding its stock ownership and is thus subject to paragraph (k)(2) of this section, or is subject to paragraph (k)(4) of this section. Any direct public group that is required to be identified as a result of a transaction described in paragraph (j)(2)(iii) of this section shall be treated as a 5-percent shareholder under paragraph (g)(1)(iv) of this section without regard to whether such group, at any time during the testing period, owns five percent or more of the loss corporation stock. To the extent that the presumptions are rebutted, the public shareholders, public owners and 5-percent owners who are not 5-percent shareholders may be aggregated into additional public groups. For an exception applicable to certain regulated investment companies, see § 1.382-3(k)(1).

(B) *Certain equity structure shifts and transactions to which section 1032 applies.*—(*1*) *In general.*—In the case of—

(*i*) a transaction that is an equity structure shift that also is described in section 381(a)(2) and in which the loss corporation is a party to the reorganization, or

(*ii*) a transfer of the stock of the loss corporation (including treasury stock) by the loss corporation in any other transaction to which section 1032 applies,

each direct public group that exists immediately after such transaction shall be segregated so that each direct public group that existed immediately before the transaction is treated separately from the direct public group that acquires stock of the loss corporation in the transaction. The direct public group that acquires stock of the loss corporation in the transaction is presumed not to include any members of any direct public group that existed immediately before the transaction. For purposes of this paragraph (j)(2)(iii)(B), a person is treated as acquiring stock of the loss corporation in a reorganization as the result of the person's ownership interest in another corporation that succeeds to the loss corporation's pre-change losses (determined as if the testing date were the change date and treating the amount of any net unrealized built-in loss as a pre-change loss) in a transaction to which section 381(a)(2) applies. In determining whether a transaction is described in section 1032 for purposes of this paragraph (j)(2)(iii)(B), the transfer by the loss corporation of any interest not constituting stock that is treated as stock under paragraph (f)(18)(iii) of this section shall be treated as the transfer of stock. See § 1.382-3(j) for exceptions to the segregation rules of this paragraph (j)(2)(iii)(B)(*1*).

(*2*) *Examples.*—*Example (1)*—(*i*) P₁ owns 60 percent of the stock of L. The remaining L stock (40 percent) is owned by Public L. A owns 40 percent of the P₁ stock. The remaining P₁ stock (60 percent) is owned by Public P₁. P₂ is a publicly traded corporation owned by shareholders who each own less than five percent of P₂ stock (Public P₂).

(*ii*) On May 22, 1988, L merges into P₂ in a transaction described in section 368(a)(1)(A), with the shareholders of L receiving an amount of P₂ stock equal to 70 percent of the value of P₂ immediately after the reorganization.

(*iii*) Immediately before the merger, L's 5-percent shareholders were Public L (40 percent), Public P₁ (36 percent), and A (24 percent). Although the shareholders of P₂ (immediately before the merger) do not acquire any stock in the merger, they are treated as acquiring a direct ownership interest in the loss corporation in the reorganization because P₂ succeeds to the pre-change losses of L in a transaction to which section 381(a)(2) applies. As a result of the merger, which constitutes a transaction described in (j)(2)(iii)(B)(*1*) of this section, L's direct public group, Public L, must be segregated from the direct public group that would otherwise exist after the transaction (Public L and Public P₂). Public L, the direct public group that exists before the merger, has a continuing 28 percent interest in the loss corporation [70 percent of P₂ shares received in the merger × 40 percent of shares of L owned prior to the merger] that must be segregated from the interests acquired by Public P₂.

(*iv*) In addition, Public P₁, which owns five percent or more of the stock of P₂ through P₁'s ownership interest in P₂, also is segregated from any other public group (*i.e.*, both Public L and Public P₂) under paragraph (j)(1) of this section. Therefore, under paragraphs (j)(1) and (2) of this section, Public P₂ (excluding the members of Public L and Public P₁ immediately before the merger) is treated as a separate public group and 5-percent shareholder.

(*v*) The only 5-percent shareholders whose interest in the loss corporation, P₂, has increased during the testing period is Public P₂. Its interest has increased by 30 percentage points. Accordingly, no ownership change results from the merger. For purposes of measuring the shift in ownership of P₂ on any subsequent testing date with a testing period that includes May 22, 1988 (the date on which L merged into P₂), Public P₂ will continue to be treated as a direct public group, separate from Public L (the members of which own P₂ stock as a result of the merger) and Public P₁.

Example (2)—(*i*) P and L are each owned by 21 equal shareholders. Each of 14 of the shareholders of P and L are owners of

both corporations ("common owners"). L has actual knowledge of this cross ownership. Therefore, as a group, these persons own 66²/₃ percent of each of P and L. P stock has a value of $600 and L stock has a value of $400.

(*ii*) P merges into L under section 368(a)(1)(A) on June 10, 1988. Ordinarily, the direct public group of L that exists immediately before the transaction would be segregated from the direct public group that acquires stock in the merger (the public group of P immediately before the merger). In view of the common ownership of P and L, however, a third group may be created under paragraph (j)(2)(iii)(A) of this section so that L's owners following the merger would be: the common owners (66²/₃ percent), Public L, less the common owners, (13¹/₃ percent), and Public P, less the common owners (20 percent). Accordingly, the only 5-percent shareholder increasing its ownership interest in L, Public P, would increase its ownership interest by 20 percentage points and no ownership change occurs as a result of the merger.

Example (3)—(*i*) L is entirely owned by Public L. L commences and completes a public offering of common stock on January 22, 1988, with the result that its outstanding stock increases from 100,000 shares to 300,000 shares. No person owns as much as five percent of L stock following the public offering.

(*ii*) The public offering of L stock is a transaction to which section 1032 applies. Immediately before the public offering, L's only 5-percent shareholder was Public L, a direct public group. Therefore, Public L (as in existence immediately before the transaction) must be segregated from the direct public group that would otherwise exist immediately after the transaction. Under paragraph (j)(2)(iii)(B)(*1*) of this section, the acquisition of 200,000 shares of L stock in the public offering must be treated as acquired by a direct public group ("New Public L") that is separate from Public L. Each such public group is treated as an individual that is a separate 5-percent shareholder. See paragraphs (g)(1)(iv) and (j)(1)(ii) of this section.

(*iii*) As a result of the public offering, L has two 5-percent shareholders, Public L and New Public L, which own 33¹/₃ percent and 66²/₃ percent of the stock of L, respectively. Because the members of New Public L are presumed not to be members of Public L (and not to be related to any such members), the ownership interest of New Public L immediately prior to the offering of stock was 0 percent.

(*iv*) New Public L is a 5-percent shareholder that has increased its ownership interest in L by more than 50 percentage points during the testing period (by 66²/₃ percentage points). Thus, there is an ownership change with respect to L. For purposes of subsequent transactions, Public L and New Public L will not be segregated into two public groups because a new testing period commences on the day following the change date, January 23, 1988 (*i.e.*, any subsequent testing date will not have a testing period that includes the date of the public offering).

Example (4). The facts are the same as in Example (3), but L establishes that 60,000 shares of the newly issued L stock were acquired by its shareholders of record on the date of the stock issuance (*i.e.*, members of Public L, referred to as Acquiring Public L) by persons owning 27 percent of the L stock immediately before the stock issuance. Accordingly, L has actual knowledge that New Public L acquired no more than 140,000 shares of L stock in the public offering. Under paragraphs (j)(2)(iii) and (k)(2) of this section, New Public L may be treated as having increased its ownership interest in L by 46²/₃ percentage points (140,000 shares acquired in the offering/300,000 shares outstanding). L also has actual knowledge that the members of Public L owning 27 percent of L stock immediately before the stock issuance (27,000 shares/100,000 shares outstanding) own 29 percent of L stock immediately after such issuance ([27,000 shares + 60,000 shares acquired in the offering]/300,000 shares outstanding). Assuming that L chooses to take its actual knowledge into account for purposes of determining whether an ownership change occurred on January 22, 1988, Public L is segregated into two direct public groups immediately before the stock issuance so that the two percentage point increase in the ownership interest in L by Acquiring Public L is taken into account. The total increased ownership interest in L by New Public L and Acquiring Public L on the testing date over their lowest ownership interest during the testing period is 48²/₃ percent. Thus, no ownership change occurs with respect to L.

Example (5)—(*i*) L is owned entirely by 10,000 unrelated individuals, none of whom own as much as five percent of L stock ("Public L"). P is owned entirely by 1,500 unrelated individuals, none of whom own as much as five percent of P stock ("Public P"). On December 22, 1988, L acquires all of the P stock from Public P in exchange for L stock representing 25 percent of the value of L, in a transaction described in section 368(a)(1)(B).

(*ii*) Under paragraph (j)(2)(iii)(B)(*1*) of this section, Public L, the direct public group that owns L stock immediately before and after the transaction to which section 1032 applies, is treated separately from Public P, the direct public group that acquires L stock in the transaction. Because Public P's percentage ownership interest in L increases to only 25 percent (as compared with 0 percent before the acquisition), no ownership change occurs. For purposes of determining whether an ownership change occurs on any testing date with a testing period that includes December 22, 1988, Public L and Public P will continue to be treated as separate 5-percent shareholders.

(iii) See Example (4) in paragraph (j)(3)(iv) of this section for the application of paragraph (j)(2)(iii)(B) of this section to a reorganization under section 368(a)(1)(B) in which the loss corporation is acquired.

(C) *Redemption-type transactions.*—*(1) In general.*—In the case of a transaction in which the loss corporation acquires its stock in exchange for property, each direct public group that exists immediately before the transaction shall be segregated at that time (and thereafter) so that the stock that is acquired in the transaction is treated as owned by a separate public group from each public group that owns the stock that is not acquired. For purposes of the preceding sentence, the term property shall include stock described in section 1504(a)(4) and stock described paragraph (f)(18)(ii) of this section. Each direct public group that owned the stock that is acquired in the transaction is presumed not to own any such stock immediately after the transaction.

(2) Examples.—*Example (1).* L is entirely owned by Public L. There are 500,000 shares of L stock outstanding. On July 12, 1988, L acquires 150,000 shares of its stock for cash. Because L's acquisition is a redemption, Public L is segregated into two different public groups immediately before the transaction (and thereafter) so that the redeemed interests ("Public RL") are treated as part of a public group that is separate from the ownership interests that are not redeemed ("Public CL"). Therefore, as a result of the redemption, Public CL's interest in L increases by 30 percentage points (from 70 percent (350,000/500,000) to 100 percent) on the July 12, 1988 testing date. Because the resulting increase is not more than 50 percentage points, no ownership change occurs. For purposes of determining whether an ownership change occurs on any subsequent testing date having a testing period that includes such redemption, Public CL is treated as a 5-percent shareholder whose percentage ownership interest in L increased by 30 percentage points as a result of the redemption.

Example (2). L is entirely owned by Public L. There are 250,000 shares of L common stock outstanding. On April 22, 1988, L acquires 100,000 shares of its outstanding common stock in exchange for 100,000 shares of preferred stock described in section 1504(a)(4). (The transaction thus constitutes a recapitalization within the meaning of section 368(a)(1)(E).) As a result of the recapitalization, which is a transaction described in paragraph (j)(2)(iii)(C) of this section, Public L is segregated into two different public groups immediately before the transaction (and thereafter) so that the stock acquired by L is treated as owned by a public group ("Public RL") that is separate from the public group that owns the stock that is not so acquired ("Public CL"). Therefore, as a result of the transaction, Public CL's interest in L increases by 40 percentage points (from 60 percent to 100 percent). Because the resulting increase is not more than 50 percentage points, no ownership change occurs. For purposes of determining whether an ownership change occurs on any subsequent testing date with a testing period that includes the date of the recapitalization, Public CL is treated as a separate 5-percent shareholder whose percentage ownership interest increased by 40 percentage points as a result of the redemption type transaction.

(D) *Acquisition of loss corporation stock as the result of the ownership of a right to acquire stock.*—*(1) In general.*—In the case of a deemed acquisition of stock of the loss corporation as the result of the ownership of a right issued by the loss corporation to acquire such stock (see paragraph (h)(4) of this section), each direct public group that exists immediately after such acquisition shall be segregated so that each direct public group that existed immediately before the transaction is treated separately from the direct public group that is deemed to acquire stock of the loss corporation as a result of the ownership of the right to acquire such stock. The direct public group that is treated as acquiring stock of the loss corporation in the transaction is presumed not to include any members of any direct public group that existed immediately before the transaction. In applying the rules of paragraph (h)(4) of this section, the segregation rules of this paragraph (j)(2)(iii)(D) shall apply before making the determination required under that paragraph (h)(4) of this section. See § 1.382-3(j)(9) for rules relating to this paragraph (j)(2)(iii)(D).

(2) Example.—*(i)* L has 700,000 shares of common stock outstanding. Public L owns all of the outstanding L common stock. On May 20, 1988, L issues a class of debentures to the public that, in the aggregate, may be converted into 300,000 shares of L common stock. On September 7, 1988, P₁ acquires 210,000 shares of L common

stock over a public stock exchange. None of the L debentures have been converted as of that date.

(ii) By virtue of L's issuance of convertible debentures, May 20, 1988 is a testing date. See paragraph (a)(2)(i) of this section. Immediately before the issuance of the convertible debentures, L's only 5-percent shareholder was Public L, a direct public group. Therefore, under paragraph (j)(2)(iii)(D) of this section, Public L must be segregated from the direct public group that would otherwise exist immediately after the transaction for the purpose of applying paragraph (h)(4) of this section, so that any acquisition of L stock through the conversion of L's debentures is treated as made by a public group other than Public L ("New Public L"). Assuming the largest increase in the total percentage stock ownership of New Public L on the testing date (see paragraph (h)(4) of this section), New Public L would have increased its ownership interest in L by 30 percentage points. Therefore, the stock of L would not be treated as acquired pursuant to a deemed conversion of the L debentures on May 20, 1988, under paragraph (h)(4) of this section, because the conversion would not cause an ownership change.

(iii) P₁'s acquisition of L common stock results in second testing date. For the purpose of applying paragraph (h)(4) of this section, Public L must again be segregated from the direct public group that would otherwise result from conversion of the debentures, so that a deemed acquisition of L stock through the conversion of L's debentures on September 7, 1988 is treated as made by a public group other than Public L ("New Public L"). As on the previous testing date, New Public L would have increased its ownership interest in L by 30 percentage points if it were treated as having acquired L common stock pursuant to the conversion of the L debentures. The increase in New Public L's ownership, taken together with P₁'s 21 percentage point ownership increase in L during the testing period [210,000 shares deemed converted/(700,000 (actual) + 300,000 (deemed) shares outstanding)], results in an ownership change.

(E) *Transactions identified in the Internal Revenue Bulletin.*— Any transaction that is designated by the Internal Revenue Service in the Internal Revenue Bulletin shall be subject to rules, as provided in such bulletin, similar to the rules described in this paragraph (j)(2)(iii).

(F) *Issuance of rights to acquire loss corporation stock.*—*(1) In general.*—In the case of any transaction that is described in paragraphs (j)(2)(iii)(B), (D) or (E) of this section in which the loss corporation issues rights to acquire its stock to the members of more than one public group, those rights shall be presumed to be exercised pro rata by each such public group as those rights are actually exercised. See § 1.382-3(j)(10) for an exception to the application of the rule of this paragraph (j)(2)(iii)(F)(*1*) to stock issued on the exercise of a transferable option.

(2) Example.—*(i)* L, which has six million shares outstanding, is owned entirely by Public L and P is owned entirely by Public P. On November 30, 1988, P merges into L in a transaction qualifying under section 368(a)(1)(A) with Public P receiving four million shares of L stock as a result of the reorganization. Under paragraph (j)(2)(iii)(B) of this section, Public L and Public P continue to be treated as separate public groups following the merger. Pursuant to the plan of reorganization, L also issues an amount of warrants in L stock pro rata to Public L and Public P that, if exercised, would result in the issuance of an additional two million shares of L stock. On November 30, 1989, when only one-half of the outstanding warrants have been exercised, A acquires all of the unexercised warrants.

(ii) Without regard to the warrants distributed in reorganization, Public P's ownership interest in L increases by 40 percentage points on November 30, 1988, relative to its lowest ownership interest in L at any time during the testing period (0 percent prior to the merger). For purposes of determining whether an ownership change occurs on November 30, 1988, the segregation rules of paragraphs (j)(2)(iii)(B) and (D) of this section does not require that a third direct public group be separately identified and treated as acquiring the warrants, because L has actual knowledge that Public L and Public P acquired the distributed warrants in proportion to their respective ownership interests in L stock. Because the largest increase in the ownership of L on the testing date results from treating only Public P as exercising the distributed warrants, in which event, its ownership interest would increase by 44.4 percentage points ([four million shares acquired in the merger + 800,000 shares deemed acquired]/10.8 million (actual and deemed) shares outstanding), the issuance of the warrants by L does not cause an ownership change on November 30, 1988.

(iii) Under paragraph (j)(2)(iii)(F)(1) of this section, each actual exercise of warrants to acquire one million shares of L stock between November 30, 1988 and November 30, 1989 is treated as made pro rata by Public L and Public P (600,000 shares to Public L and 400,000 shares to Public P). Accordingly, as a result of the actual exercises of warrants during that period the ownership interests of

the only 5-percent shareholders, Public L and Public P, are proportionately increased.

(iv) A's acquisition of the all of the outstanding warrants on November 30, 1989 requires the determination whether there has been an ownership change with respect to L, because A would be a 5-percent shareholder under paragraph (g)(1)(i) of this section owning $8^1/_3$ percent of the L stock if the acquired warrants were exercised (one million shares deemed acquired/12 million (actual and deemed) shares outstanding). See paragraph (a)(2)(i) of this section. Under paragraph (h)(4)(i) of this section, A is not treated as having exercised those warrants, because an ownership change would not result. (Public P's $36^2/_3$ percentage point increase [(four million shares acquired in the merger + 400,000 shares deemed acquired)/12 million (actual and deemed) shares outstanding] and A's $8^1/_3$ percentage point increase is not greater than 50 percentage points).

(iv) Combination of de minimis public groups.—(A) *In general.*— Notwithstanding paragraph (j)(2)(iii)(A) of this section, any public group first identified during a taxable year, as a result of any transaction described in paragraphs (j)(2)(iii)(B), (D), (E) or (F) of this section, that owns less than five percent of loss corporation stock may be combined, at the option of the loss corporation, with any other such groups also first identified as a result of any such transaction that occurs during such taxable year.

(B) Example.—(i) L is widely held with no person owning as much as five percent of the L stock at any time ("Public L"). L's taxable year ends on December 31. On January 1, 1989, L issues a class of debt maturing on December 31, 2019 ("Class A Debentures") with respect to which it will semi-annually issue L stock in discharge of its interest obligation. In addition, L issues an amount of L stock to the public in two separate transactions during 1989. As a percentage of the L stock outstanding at the close of L's taxable year on December 31, 1989, L issued .45 percent of its stock on each of two dates in payment of interest with respect to the Class A Debentures, 4.5 percent of its stock in the first stock offering and six percent of its stock in the second stock offering. During 1990, L did not issue stock other than in payment of interest with respect to the Class A Debentures. As a percentage of L stock outstanding on December 31, 1990, L issued .41 percent of its stock on each of two dates during 1990 with respect to its outstanding debt.

(ii) Under paragraph (h)(4)(x)(E) of this section, L's obligation to issue stock in satisfaction of the interest with respect to the Class A Debentures until December 31, 2019, is not subject to paragraph (h)(4)(i) of this section and thus is taken into account only as such stock is issued.

(iii) The application of the segregation rules of paragraphs (j)(2)(iii)(B) and (iv) of this section require the identification of at least two additional, separate direct public groups during 1989. First, the persons who acquire six percent of L stock in a public offering to which section 1032 applies must be treated as a separate 5-percent shareholder ("Public 1L"). See paragraph (j)(2)(iii)(B) of this section. Even though this group was first identified in 1989, it may not be combined with other public groups also first identified in 1989 because it owns five percent or more of L stock. Second, although each of the three other issuances of L stock during the year ordinarily result in the identification of an additional, separate direct public group, each such direct public group may be combined with the two other such groups into a single public group ("Public 2L"). As of the end of 1989, Public 2L would own a total of 5.4 percent of the stock of L.

(iv) The application of the segregation rules of paragraph (j)(2)(iii)(B) and (iv) of this section require the identification of at least one additional, direct public group during 1990. Because each additional, direct public group first identified in 1990 acquires less than five percent of L stock, they may be combined into a single public group ("Public 3L") owning .82 percent of the stock of L. Public 3L is treated as a five percent shareholder even though it owns less than five percent of the stock of L. See paragraph (j)(2)(iv)(A) of this section.

(v) Multiple transactions.—(A) *In general.*—If a transaction (or any part thereof) is described by more than one subdivision of paragraph (j)(2)(iii) of this section, each such subdivision shall apply to the transaction (or each part of the transaction) in the manner that results in the largest increase in the percentage stock ownership by the 5-percent shareholders.

(B) Example.—(i) All of the common stock of L is owned by 1,000 unrelated persons, none of whom owns as much as five percent of the L stock ("Public CL"). L has outstanding a class of preferred stock described in section 1504(a)(4) that is owned in equal amounts by 500 unrelated persons ("Public PL").

(ii) On September 4, 1988, L rearranges its capital structure by redeeming 70 percent of the common stock owned by 700 of

the shareholders in exchange for cash. In addition, all of the preferred stock is exchanged for a new class of common stock (nonvoting) representing 40 percent of the value of L.

(iii) With respect to the part of the transaction that is treated as a redemption under paragraph (j)(2)(iii)(C) of this section (the exchange of common stock for cash), Public CL is segregated into two different public groups immediately before the transaction (and thereafter) so that the owners of the redeemed stock ("Public RCL") are treated as part of a public group that is separate from the public group comprised of the owners of the stock that is not redeemed ("Public CCL"). As a result of the redemption, Public CCL's percentage ownership interest in L thus increases by 30 percentage points from 30 percent to 60 percent (taking into account all transactions occurring on the testing date, because the change in ownership is measured under paragraph (a)(1)(i) of this section by reference to each 5-percent shareholder's ownership interest immediately after the testing date). In addition, the exchange of preferred stock for nonvoting common stock is a transaction to which section 1032 applies. Under paragraph (j)(2)(v) of this section, the part of the transaction to which section 1032 applies is also subject to the segregation rules in the manner specified in paragraph (j)(2)(iii)(B) of this section. Accordingly, Public PL, the direct public group that acquires L nonvoting common stock in exchange for L preferred stock, must be treated as a separate public group from the other direct public groups, Public CCL and Public RCL. As a separate public group, Public PL's percentage stock ownership in L increases by 40 points (as compared to 0 percent prior to the transaction).

(iv) In summary, Public CCL increases its percentage ownership in L by 30 percentage points and Public PL increases its percentage ownership by 40 percentage points. Consequently, an ownership change occurs with respect to L on September 4, 1988.

(vi) Acquisitions made by either a 5-percent shareholder or the loss corporation following application of the segregation rules.—Unless a different proportion is established by either the loss corporation or the Internal Revenue Service, the acquisition of loss corporation stock by either a 5-percent shareholder or the loss corporation on any date on which more than one public group of the loss corporation exists by virtue of the application of the rules of this paragraph (j)(2) shall be treated as being made proportionately from each public group existing immediately before such acquisition. See paragraph (g)(5)(i)(B) of this section for the application of this paragraph to the ownership interest of a 5-percent shareholder that owns less than five percent of the stock of the loss corporation on the testing date.

(3) Segregation rules applicable to transactions involving first tier entities or higher tier entities.—(i) *Dispositions.*—If a loss corporation is owned, in whole or in part, by a public group (or groups), the rules of paragraphs (j)(2)(iii)(B) and (iv) of this section shall apply to any transaction in which a first tier entity or an individual that owns a direct ownership interest in the loss corporation of five percent or more transfers a direct ownership interest in the loss corporation to public shareholders. Therefore, each direct public group that exists immediately after such a disposition shall be segregated so that the ownership interests of each public group that existed immediately before the transaction are treated separately from the public group that acquires stock of the loss corporation as a result of the disposition by the individual or first tier entity. The principles of this paragraph (j)(3)(i) shall also apply to transactions in which an ownership interest in a higher tier entity that owns five percent or more of the loss corporation (determined without regard to the application of paragraph (h)(2)(i)(A) of this section) or a first tier entity is transferred to a public owner or 5-percent owner who is not a 5-percent shareholder.

(ii) Example.—(A) L is owned equally by Public L, P and E. Public L consists of 150 equal, unrelated shareholders. P is owned by Public P, a group consisting of 1,500 equal, unrelated shareholders. E is a partnership and none of its partners are 5-percent owners. On October 22, 1988, E sells its entire interest in L over a public stock exchange. No individual or entity acquires as much as five percent of L's stock as the result of E's disposition of the L stock.

(B) The disposition of the L stock by E is a transaction that causes the segregation of L's direct public group that exists immediately before the transaction (Public L) from the direct public group that acquires L stock in the transaction (Public EL). As a result, L has three 5-percent shareholders, Public L, Public P (through the application of paragraph (j)(1) of this section) and Public EL, each of which owns $33^1/_3$ percent of L stock. Therefore, Public EL is a 5-percent shareholder that has increased its ownership interest in L by $33^1/_3$ percentage points during the testing period. For purposes of subsequent transactions, Public L and Public EL will continue to be treated as separate direct public groups until any subsequent testing date that does not have a testing period that includes E's disposition of L stock.

(iii) *Other transactions affecting direct public groups of a first tier entity or higher tier entity.*—The rules of paragraphs (j)(2)(i), (iii), (iv) and (v) of this section shall apply to transactions described in such paragraphs that involve either a higher tier entity that owns five percent or more of the loss corporation (determined without regard to the application of paragraph (h)(2)(i)(A) of this section) or a first tier entity. In applying those rules for purposes of this paragraph (j)(3)(iii), each direct public group of a first tier entity or a higher tier entity is any public group of any such entity identified in paragraph (j)(1)(iv)(A) or (B) of this section or resulting from the application of this paragraph (j)(3)(iii). The principles of paragraph (j)(2)(iii)(C) of this section also shall apply to any transaction that has the effect of a redemption-type transaction (e.g., an acquisition by the loss corporation of stock in a first tier entity).

(iv) *Examples.—Example (1).* The facts are the same as in Example (1) of paragraph (j)(2)(iii)(B)(2) of this section, except that Public L and P_1 own 40 percent and 60 percent, respectively, of the stock of HC which, in turn, owns 100 percent of L and HC merges into P_2. Under paragraph (j)(3)(iii) of this section, the rules of paragraph (j)(2)(iii)(B) of this section apply to segregate HC's direct public group (Public L) immediately before the merger from the direct public group (Public P_2) that acquires loss corporation stock in the merger. The consequences of the merger of HC into P_2 are thus the same as in Example (1) of paragraph (j)(2)(iii)(B)(2) of this section.

Example (2)—(i) Twenty-five individual shareholders each own four percent of L ("Public L"). Public L is therefore the only 5-percent shareholder of L. Each of the shareholders of L contribute their L stock to a newly formed corporation, HC. In exchange for their contribution of L stock, HC issues 100 percent of each of its two classes of common stock (voting and nonvoting).

(ii) The formation of HC, a first tier entity of L, is a transaction to which section 1032 applies. Under paragraph (j)(3)(iii) of this section, the rules of paragraphs (j)(1)(iii) and (j)(2)(iii)(B) of this section are applied to this transaction with the result that the shareholders of HC, immediately after the issuance of HC stock, are presumed not to include any persons that previously had a direct or indirect ownership interest in L. The presumption underlying those rules, however, is rebutted by establishing that all of the HC stock outstanding immediately after the transaction was issued solely in exchange for L stock. Thus, public HC (immediately after the transaction) and Public L (immediately before the transaction) would be treated owned by the same direct public group.

Example (3)—(i) All of the stock of L is owned by unrelated shareholders, none of whom owns as much as five percent of L stock. P also is owned by unrelated shareholders, none of whom owns as much as five percent of P stock. On November 22, 1988, P incorporates P_1 with a contribution of P stock. Immediately thereafter, P_1 acquires all of the properties of L in exchange for its P stock in a forward triangular merger qualifying under sections 368(a)(1)(A) and (a)(2)(D). The P stock transferred by P_1 equals 45 percent of the total outstanding P stock.

(ii) Immediately before the merger of L into P_1, P's only 5-percent shareholder was Public P, a direct public group of P. The rules of paragraph (j)(2)(iii)(B) of this section thus apply to the transaction under paragraph (j)(3)(i) of this section since P, a first tier entity, is a party to the reorganization described in such paragraph. Although Public P does not acquire any stock in the merger, it is treated as acquiring stock in the loss corporation, P_1, because such corporation succeeds to the pre-change losses of L in a transaction to which 381(a) applies. As a result of the merger, Public P, the direct public group of P that exists immediately before the merger, must be segregated from the direct public groups acquiring P stock in the reorganization. Public P is, therefore, treated as acquiring 55 percent of the outstanding stock of the loss corporation, P_1, in the transaction. The transaction, therefore, results in an ownership change for P_1.

Example (4)—(i) L is owned 20 percent by A and 80 percent by 1,000 unrelated individuals and entities, none of whom owns as much as five percent of L stock ("Public L"). P is owned 10 percent by B, 40 percent by E, and 50 percent by 5,000 unrelated individuals, none of whom owns as much as five percent of P stock ("Public P"). E is owned 30 percent by C and 70 percent by 30 unrelated individuals, none of whom owns as much as five percent of E ("Public E").

(ii) On October 31, 1987, P acquires all of the L stock from A and Public L in exchange for P stock representing 20 percent of the value of P (determined immediately after the acquisition) in a transaction described in section 368(a)(1)(B). After the acquisition, P is owned eight percent by B, 32 percent by E, four percent by A, and 56 percent by 6,000 unrelated individuals, none of whom owns as much as five percent of P. Because L is wholly owned by P immediately after the acquisition, L, under paragraph (j)(1) of this section, is treated as owned as follows: eight percent by B, 9.6 percent by C (through C's ownership interest in E, a highest tier entity, and E's ownership interest in P, a first tier entity), 22.4 percent by Public E (through its ownership interest in E and E's ownership interest in P), four percent by A, and 56 percent by the shareholders who each own less than five percent of L through their ownership interest in P.

(iii) Under paragraph (j)(3)(iii) of this section, the rules of paragraph (j)(2)(iii)(B) of this section apply to the reorganization since the transaction involved a first tier entity of L. Thus, the direct public group of P that exists immediately after the transaction must be segregated into two public groups—the direct public group of P that existed immediately before the acquisition (Public P) is treated separately from the direct public group consisting of the persons who acquire P stock in the transaction (Public L). Accordingly, immediately after the reorganization, Public P and Public L own 40 percent and 16 percent of L, respectively. See paragraph (h) of this section. (Under paragraph (g)(5)(ii)(B) of this section, L may treat the four percent of L stock owned by A immediately after the reorganization as the amount of L stock owned by A for each subsequent testing date having a testing period that includes the reorganization.)

(iv) In summary, after applying the rules of paragraphs (j)(1) and (3) of this section, L is treated as owned as follows:

5-percent shareholder	*Percentage ownership interest*
A	4.0 percent
B	8.0 percent
C	9.6 percent
Public E	22.4 percent
Public P	40.0 percent
Public L	16.0 percent

(v) The reorganization results in an ownership change, because B, C, Public E and Public P, all of whom are 5-percent shareholders, together have increased their percentage ownership in L by 80 percentage points as compared to their lowest percentage ownership in L at any time during the testing period (0 percent prior to the acquisition).

(v) *Acquisitions made by a 5-percent shareholder, a higher tier entity, or a first tier entity following application of the segregation rules.*—The rules of paragraph (j)(2)(vi) of this section shall apply to the acquisition of an ownership interest in a first tier entity (or higher tier entity) if more than one direct public group of any such entity are segregated under the rules of this paragraph (j)(3). Accordingly, an acquisition by such an entity or a 5-percent shareholder of any ownership interest in such an entity shall be treated as made proportionately from the direct public groups resulting from the application of this paragraph (j)(3).

(k) *Operating rules.*—(1) *Presumptions regarding stock ownership.*—Subject to paragraphs (k)(2) and (4) of this section, for purposes of applying paragraphs (f), (g), (h), and (j)(1) of this section—

(i) *Stock subject to regulation by the Securities and Exchange Commission.*—With respect to loss corporation stock that is described in Rule 13d-1(d) of Regulation 13D-G (or any rule or regulation to generally the same effect), promulgated by the Securities and Ex-

change Commission under the Securities and Exchange Act of 1934 ("registered stock"), a loss corporation may rely on the existence and absence of filings of Schedules 13D and 13G (or any similar schedules) as of any date to identify all of the corporation's shareholders who have a direct ownership interest of five percent or more (both individuals and first tier entities) on such date. A loss corporation may similarly rely on the existence and absence of such filings as of any date with respect to registered stock of any first tier entity or any higher tier entity to identify the 5-percent owners of any such entities on such date who indirectly own five percent or more of the loss corporation stock, and are thus 5-percent shareholders, and to identify any higher tier entities of such entities.

(ii) *Statements under penalties of perjury.*—A loss corporation may rely on a statement, signed under penalties of perjury, by an officer, director, partner, trustee, executor or similar responsible person, on behalf of a first tier entity or a higher tier entity to establish the extent, if any, to which the ownership interests of any 5-percent owners or higher tier entities with respect to such entities have changed during a testing period. A loss corporation may not rely on such a statement (A) that it knows to be false or (B) that is made by either a first tier entity or higher tier entity that owns 50 percent or more of the stock of the loss corporation. For purposes of the preceding sentence, any first tier entities and higher tier entities that are known by the loss corporation to be members of the same controlled group (within the meaning of section 267(f)) shall be treated as one corporation.

(2) *Actual knowledge regarding stock ownership.*—For purposes of this section (other than paragraphs (g)(5) and (j)(1)(v) of this section), to the extent that the loss corporation has actual knowledge of stock ownership on any testing date (or acquires such knowledge before the date that the income tax return is filed for the taxable year in which the testing date occurs) by—

(i) an individual who would be a 5-percent shareholder, but for the application of paragraphs (h)(2)(iii), (h)(6)(iii) or (g)(2) of this section, or

(ii) a 5-percent shareholder that would be taken into account, but for paragraphs (h)(2)(iii), (h)(6)(iii) or (g)(3) of this section,

the loss corporation must take such stock ownership into account for purposes of determining whether an ownership change has occurred on that testing date. If a loss corporation acquires such knowledge after such income tax return is filed, the loss corporation may take such ownership into account for purposes of determining whether an ownership change occurred on that testing date and, if appropriate, file an amended income tax return (subject to any applicable statute of limitations). To the extent the loss corporation has actual knowledge on or after any testing date regarding the ownership interest in the loss corporation by members of one public group (described in paragraphs (g)(1)(ii), (iii) or (iv) of this section) and the ownership interest of those members in the loss corporation as members in another such public group, the loss corporation may take such ownership into account for purposes of determining whether an ownership change occurred on that testing date.

(3) *Duty to inquire as to actual stock ownership in the loss corporation.*—For purposes of this section, the loss corporation is required to determine the stock ownership on each testing date (and, except as otherwise provided in this section, the changes in the stock ownership during the testing period) of—

(i) any individual shareholder who has a direct ownership interest of five percent or more in the loss corporation,

(ii) any first tier entity,

(iii) any higher tier entity that has an indirect ownership interest of five percent or more in the loss corporation (determined without regard to paragraph (h)(2)(i)(A) of this section), and

(iv) any 5-percent owner who indirectly owns five percent or more of the stock of the loss corporation in his capacity as a 5-percent owner in any one first tier entity or higher tier entity.

The loss corporation does not have any obligation to inquire or to determine facts relating to the stock ownership of any shareholders other than those described in the preceding sentence. In addition, the loss corporation does not have any obligation to inquire or to determine if the actual facts relating to the stock ownership of any shareholder are consistent with the ownership interests of the loss corporation as determined by applying the presumptions and other rules of paragraphs (g), (h), (j) or (k)(1) of this section.

(4) *Ownership interest structured to avoid the section 382 limitation.*—For purposes of this section, if the ownership interests in a loss corporation are structured by a person with a direct or indirect ownership interest in the loss corporation to avoid treating a person as a 5-percent shareholder (or to permit the loss corporation to rely on the presumption provided in paragraph (g)(5)(i)(B) of this section) for a principal purpose of circumventing the section 382 limitation, then—

(i) paragraph (h)(2)(iii) of this section shall not apply with respect to the ownership interests so structured and the constructive ownership rules of paragraph (h)(2)(i) of this section shall thus apply to attribute stock from any entity without regard to the amount of stock it owns in the loss corporation or any other corporation,

(ii) paragraphs (g)(2) and (3) of this section shall be modified with respect to the ownership interests so structured so that the ownership interest of a person includes all of an individual's direct and indirect ownership in the loss corporation, without regard to whether each such interest represents five percent or more of the stock of the loss corporation, and

(iii) paragraph (g)(5)(i)(B) of this section shall not apply with respect to the ownership interests so structured so that the ownership interest of a person takes into account his actual ownership interest in the loss corporation.

This paragraph (k)(4) shall apply, however, only if application would result in an ownership change.

(5) *Example.*—L is owned by 25 individuals who each own four percent of the outstanding L stock. A purchases 40 percent of L stock from such shareholders on August 13, 1988. Thereafter, B plans to acquire 15 percent of the L stock. B is advised concerning the potential application of section 382 to L. On February 1, 1989, B acquires a 15 percent interest in L pursuant to a program in which each of four

corporations, P_1 through P_4, each of which is wholly-owned by B, acquire a 3.75 percent interest in L. A principal purpose of acquiring the L stock through four corporations is to avoid treating B as owning any ownership interest in L amounting to as much as five percent, and thus to circumvent the section 382 limitation by avoiding an ownership change. Under paragraph (k)(4) of this section, the limitation on the constructive ownership rules of paragraph (h)(2)(iii) of this section are disregarded and B is treated as a 5-percent shareholder owning 15 percent of the stock of L by virtue of his ownership interests in P_1 through P_4, notwithstanding paragraph (g)(2) of this section. Accordingly, an ownership change occurs with respect to L.

(6) *First tier entity or higher tier entity that is a foreign corporation or entity.*—[Reserved.]

(l) *Changes in percentage ownership which are attributable to fluctuations in value.*—[Reserved.]

(m) *Effective Date.*—(1) *In general.*—Except as provided in this paragraph (m), section 382 shall apply to any ownership change that occurs immediately after an owner shift or an equity structure shift that occurs after December 31, 1986, or any other event occurring after such date that requires the determination of whether an ownership change has occurred under paragraph (a)(2)(i) of this section. In the case of an equity structure shift (including an equity structure shift that also constitutes an owner shift), any equity structure shift completed pursuant to a plan of reorganization adopted before January 1, 1987, shall be treated as occurring on the date such plan was adopted. Therefore, section 382 shall apply to any ownership change occurring immediately after—

(i) an owner shift (excluding an owner shift that also constitutes an equity structure shift) that occurs on or after January 1, 1987,

(ii) an equity structure shift that occurs after December 31, 1986, if it is completed pursuant to a plan of reorganization adopted on or after January 1, 1987, or

(iii) any transfer or issuance of an option, or other interest that is similar to an option, that occurs on or after January 1, 1987 and that is taken into account under paragraph (a)(2)(i) of this section.

With respect to equity structure shifts completed pursuant to plans adopted before January 1, 1987, section 382 shall be inapplicable only if the equity structure shift that is treated as occurring on the date the plan of reorganization for such shift was adopted (or other event occurring after the adoption of such plan) results in an ownership change before January 1, 1987. In that event, a new testing period for the loss corporation shall begin on the day after such ownership change.

(2) *Plan of reorganization.*—For purposes of paragraph (m)(1) of this section, a plan of reorganization shall be treated as adopted on the earlier of—

(i) the first date that the boards of directors of all the parties to the reorganization have adopted the plan or have recommended adoption to their shareholders, or

(ii) the date the shareholders approve such reorganization.

If there is an ownership change with respect to a subsidiary as the result of a reorganization of the parent, the treatment of the subsidiary under this paragraph (m)(2) shall be governed by the classification of the parent-level transaction. For purposes of the preceding sentence, a corporation shall be treated as a subsidiary of another corporation only if the other corporation owns stock in that corporation meeting the requirements of section 1504(a)(2).

(3) *Earliest commencement of the testing period.*—For purposes of determining if an ownership change has occurred at any time after May 5, 1986, the testing period shall begin no earlier than May 6, 1986. Under paragraph (d)(4) of this section, therefore, shifts in the ownership of stock of the loss corporation prior to May 6, 1986 are disregarded.

(4) *Transitional rules.*—(i) *Rules provided in paragraph (j) of this section for testing dates before September 4, 1987.*—For purposes of determining whether an ownership change occurs for any testing date before September 4, 1987—

(A) The rules of paragraph (j)(1) of this section shall apply only to stock of the loss corporation acquired after May 5, 1986, by any first tier entity or higher tier entity and shall not apply to any stock acquired by such an entity on or before that date,

(B) The rules of paragraph (j)(2) of this section shall apply only to equity structure shifts in which more than one corporation is a party to the reorganization and shall not apply to any other transactions, and

(C) The rules of paragraph (j)(3) of this section shall apply only to—

(1) dispositions of stock acquired by an individual, a first tier entity or higher tier entity after May 5, 1986 (and shall not apply to dispositions of stock acquired on or before such date), and

(2) equity structure shifts in which more than one corporation is a party to the reorganization (and shall not apply to any other transactions).

For any testing date before September 4, 1987, however, the loss corporation is permitted to apply all of the rules of paragraph (j) of this section. A loss corporation that applies the rules of paragraph (j) of this section under the preceding sentence must apply all of the rules of such paragraph in determining whether any ownership change occurs on any testing dates after May 5, 1986.

(ii) Example.—*(i)* L is owned entirely by 10,000 unrelated individuals, none of whom owns as much as five percent of the stock of L ("Public L"). P is owned entirely by 1,000 unrelated individuals, none of whom owns as much as five percent of the stock of P ("Public P").

(ii) Between March 1, 1987 and June 1, 1987, P acquires 45 percent of L stock in a series of transactions. On June 15, 1987, L redeems 20 percent of the L stock from Public L.

(iii) Under paragraph (m)(4)(i)(A) of this section, the rules of paragraph (j)(1) of this section apply to the acquisitions made by P, because they occurred after May 5, 1986. Accordingly, following those acquisitions, the stock of L is owned 45 percent by Public P and 55 percent by Public L. Because the increase in the percentage ownership by Public P as a result of P's stock purchases is not more than 50 percent, no ownership change occurs as the result of P's purchases.

(iv) On or after September 4, 1987, the rules of paragraph (j)(2)(iii)(C) of this section apply to treat any L stock that is redeemed as owned by a public group that is separate from the public group owning the stock that is not redeemed. (Under paragraph (j)(2)(iii)(C) of this section, the continuing shareholders of Public L, who owned 35 percent of the stock of L before the redemption ([55 percent − 20 percent]/100 percent) increase their ownership interest in L by 8.8 percentage points as a result of such redemption (43.8 percent − 35 percent)). Those rules, however, do not apply to the June 15, 1987 redemption because it occurs before the date that paragraph (j)(2)(iii) of this section generally is effective. (Until September 4, 1987, paragraph (j)(2)(iii) of this section generally is effective only for equity structure shifts in which more than one corporation is a party to the reorganization.) Solely because of the application of paragraph (j)(1) of this section to P's acquisitions of L stock, Public P's ownership interest in L as a result of the redemption has increased from 45 percentage points to 56.2 percentage points which, compared to its lowest percentage ownership interest at any time during the testing period (0 percent prior to March 1, 1987), is a more than 50 percentage point increase thus causing an ownership change with respect to L on June 15, 1987.

(iii) Rules provided in paragraph (j) of this section for testing dates on or after September 4, 1987.—For purposes of determining whether an ownership change occurs for any testing date on or after September 4, 1987, the rules of paragraphs (j)(2) and (3) of this section shall not apply to identify any public group resulting from—

(A) any transaction described in such paragraphs (j)(2) and (3), unless that transaction is also described in paragraphs (m)(4)(i)(B) or (C) of this section, or

(B) any disposition of stock acquired on or before May 5, 1986,

but only if such disposition or other transaction occurs before September 4, 1987. Thus, for example, the rules of paragraph (j)(2)(iii)(D) of this section shall apply only to rights to acquire stock of the loss corporation issued on or after such date.

(iv) Rules provided in paragraphs (f)(18)(ii) and (iii) of this section.—For purposes of determining whether an ownership change occurs for any testing date, the rules of paragraphs (f)(18)(ii) and (iii) of this section apply only to stock (or any other ownership interest) that is—

(A) issued on or after September 4, 1987, or

(B) transferred to (or by) a person who is a 5-percent shareholder (or would be a 5-percent shareholder if paragraph (f)(18)(iii) of this section were applicable) on or after September 4, 1987.

(v) Rules provided in paragraph (a)(2)(ii) of this section.—The information statement required under paragraph (a)(2)(ii) of this section is not required to be filed with respect to any taxable year for which the due date (including extensions) of the income tax return of the loss corporation is on or before October 5, 1987.

(vi) Rules provided in paragraph (h)(4) of this section.—The rules provided in paragraph (h)(4) of this section do not apply on any testing date on or after November 5, 1992. The rule provided in paragraph (h)(4)(viii) of this section applies to the lapse or forfeiture of any option treated as exercised under paragraph (h)(4)(i) of this section. If an option is treated as exercised under paragraph (h)(4)(i) of this section, and the option is actually exercised on a day that is within 120 days after the date on which the option is treated as exercised, the rule provided in paragraph (h)(4)(vi)(B) of this section

applies (even if the actual exercise of the option occurs on a date on which the rules of paragraph (h)(4) of this section would not otherwise apply). Thus, in such a case, the loss corporation may elect to treat paragraphs (h)(4)(i) and (vi)(A) of this section as not applying to the option and take into account only the acquisition of loss corporation stock resulting from the actual exercise of the option.

(vii) Rules provided in paragraph (a)(2)(i) of this section.—The rules provided in paragraph (a)(2)(i) of this section apply to determine whether dates prior to November 5, 1992, are testing dates. For rules regarding the determination of whether dates on or after November 5, 1992, are testing dates, see § 1.382-2(a)(4).

(5) Bankruptcy proceedings.—*(i) In general.*—In the case of a reorganization described in section 368(a)(1)(G) or an exchange of debt for stock in a title 11 or similar case (within the meaning of section 368(a)(3)), section 382 shall not apply to any ownership change resulting from such a reorganization or proceeding if a petition in such case was filed with the court before August 14, 1986. Accordingly, any shift in ownership in the loss corporation arising out of such reorganization or proceeding shall not be taken into account for purposes of determining whether an ownership change occurs on any testing date that occurs after December 31, 1986.

(ii) Example.—*(i)* L filed a petition in bankruptcy on September 29, 1985. As a result of a title 11 bankruptcy reorganization of L that is confirmed by a court on February 2, 1988, there is a shift in the ownership of L so that JK increased her interest in L by 24 percentage points relative to her lowest ownership interest in L during the testing period. JK is the only 5-percent shareholder of L following the reorganization whose interest in L increased as a result of the transaction. On December 25, 1988, GK purchases 42 percent of the outstanding stock of L from shareholders other than JK.

(ii) There is no ownership change on December 25, 1988 because the 24 percentage point increase in JK's ownership interest in L is not taken into account under paragraph (m)(6)(i) of this section.

(iii) The facts are the same as in *(i)*, except that the acquisitions by JK and GK occurred on August 5, 1986 and September 26, 1986, respectively. Because paragraph (m)(6)(i) of this section is only applicable with respect to the determination of whether an ownership change has occurred on any testing date that occurs after December 31, 1986, there is an ownership change as a result of GK's acquisition on September 26, 1986. Accordingly, section 382 is inapplicable to such ownership change under paragraph (m)(1) of this section because it occurred prior to January 1, 1987. Under paragraph (d)(2) of this section, the testing period for determining whether an ownership change occurs on any subsequent testing date shall commence no earlier than September 27, 1986.

(6) Transactions of domestic building and loan associations.—The rules of paragraph (j)(2)(iii)(B) of this section (and the application of those rules by virtue of paragraph (j)(3) of this section) shall not apply to a public offering of stock by a domestic building and loan association described in section 591 (or any corporation that owns stock in the association meeting the requirements of section 1504(a)(2)) prior to January 1, 1989. In the case of any transaction described in the preceding sentence, any transitory ownership of stock by any entity that is an underwriter shall be disregarded so that the rules of paragraph (j)(1) of this section shall not apply to treat such stock as owned by the owners of the underwriter and thus the rules of paragraph (j)(3)(i) of this section shall not apply to the disposition of such stock by the underwriter. For purposes of this paragraph (m)(7)—

(i) ownership shall be considered transitory only with respect to an underwriter acquiring stock in a firm commitment underwriting to the extent the stock is disposed of pursuant to the offer (but in no event later than sixty (60) days after the initial offering) and,

(ii) to the extent a transaction may be described both by paragraph (j)(2)(iii)(B) of this section and any other provision of paragraphs (j)(2)(iii) or (3) of this section, paragraph (j)(2)(v)(A) of this section shall not apply and the transaction shall be treated as described solely by paragraph (j)(2)(iii)(B) of this section.

(7) Transactions not subject to section 382.—*(i) Application of old section 382.*—Old section 382 shall not apply to a loss corporation on or after the date on which an ownership change occurs, but only if such ownership change results in the application of the section 382 limitation (as defined in section 382(b)) with respect to the loss corporation.

(ii) Effect on testing period.—The application of old section 382 to a transaction is disregarded for purposes of paragraph (d)(2) of this section unless the transaction that results in such application is the last component of an ownership change after May 5, 1986 that is not subject to section 382 under the effective date rules of this paragraph (m) (*e.g.*, an ownership change occurring as the result of

an individual's purchase of more than 50 percent of L stock on any date on or before December 31, 1986).

(iii) *Termination of old section 382.*—[Reserved].

(8) *Options issued or transferred before January 1, 1987.*—(i) *Options issued before May 6, 1986.*—An option issued before May 6, 1986, is subject to the rules of paragraph (h)(4) of this section only if it is transferred by (or to) a 5-percent shareholder (or a person who would be a 5-percent shareholder if the option were treated as exercised) on or after such date. In all other cases, such an option shall not be subject to paragraph (h)(4)(i) of this section, but shall be subject to paragraph (h)(4)(xii) of this section. Thus, for example, a warrant to acquire stock of the loss corporation issued before May 6, 1986 shall be not be subject to paragraph (h)(4) of this section unless the warrant is transferred by (or to) a 5-percent shareholder. The exercise of such a warrant, however, would be taken into account as required by this paragraph (m)(8)(i) and paragraph (h)(4)(xii) of this section.

(ii) *Options issued on or after May 6, 1986 and before September 18, 1986.*—An option issued or transferred on or after May 6, 1986, and before September 18, 1986, is subject to the rules of paragraph (h)(4) of this section.

(iii) *Options issued on or after September 18, 1986 and before January 1, 1987.*—An option issued or transferred on or after September 18, 1986, and before January 1, 1987, is subject to the rules of paragraph (h)(4) of this section, except that the option shall be treated for purposes of this section as if it never had been issued in the event that either—

(A) the option lapses unexercised or is irrevocably forfeited by the holder thereof, or

(B) on the date the option was issued, there was no significant likelihood that such option would be exercised within the five-year period from the date of such issuance and a purpose for the issuance of the option was to cause an ownership change prior to January 1, 1987.

(9) *Examples.*—The rules of this paragraph (m) may be illustrated by the following examples.

Example (1)—(i) A owns all 100 outstanding shares of L stock. A sells 11 shares to B on January 1, 1986. The January 1, 1986 testing date is disregarded under paragraph (m)(3) of this section. A sells another 40 shares to B on January 1, 1988. B's second stock purchase is an owner shift that does not result in an ownership change. B's percentage ownership interest on the testing date (51 percent) is only 40 percentage points greater than the lowest percentage of L stock owned by B at any time during the testing period (11 percent on and after May 6, 1986).

(ii) The facts are the same as in (i). In addition A sells 20 shares of his L stock to C on July 1, 1990. C's stock purchase is an owner shift. Because B and C together have increased their respective ownership interests in L by 40 and 20 percentage points relative to their lowest percentage stock ownership interests in L at any time during the testing period, C's purchase causes an ownership change. The testing period for any subsequent ownership change begins on the first day following C's acquisition, July 2, 1990.

Example (2)—(i) C has owned 100 percent of L since March 22, 1980. On October 13, 1986, P merges into L. As a result of the merger, 40 percent of L stock is acquired by A, the sole shareholder of P. The merger of P into L is both an equity structure shift and an owner shift. The transaction, however, is not an ownership change with respect to L, because A's percentage ownership interest has increased by only 40 percentage points. On August 22, 1987, B purchases 15 percent of the L stock from C. B's purchase constitutes an owner shift resulting in an ownership change that is subject to section 382 because the aggregate increases in percentage ownership by B and C (respectively 40 percent and 15 percent) is more than 50 percentage points.

(ii) The facts are the same as in (i), except that the plan of reorganization is adopted on October 13, 1986, and the merger is completed on July 22, 1987. The result is the same as in (i).

(iii) The facts are the same as in (ii), except that the reorganization is completed on August 22, 1987, and B's purchase of the L stock occurs one month earlier, on July 22, 1987. Assume that after the reorganization on August 22, 1987, A and B own 40 percent and 15 percent, respectively, of L stock. Although the merger occurred pursuant to a plan of reorganization adopted before 1987, L is subject to section 382 following the equity structure shift, because the merger would not have caused an ownership change if it had been completed in 1986 after the commencement of the L's testing period.

(iv) The facts are the same as in (ii), except that B's purchase occurs on June 7, 1986. Assume that immediately after the reorganization on August 22, 1987, A and B own 40 percent and 15 percent, respectively, of L stock. Since the reorganization pursuant to a plan

adopted before 1987, taken together with the other shifts in the ownership of L's stock between May 5, 1986, and December 31, 1986, would have caused an ownership charge, section 382 does not apply as a result of the merger. Since an ownership change occurs as a result of the merger, L's testing period for purposes of any subsequent ownership change begins on October 14, 1986.

(v) The facts are the same as in (iv), except that B makes an additional purchase from C of one percent of L's stock on February 14, 1987. The result is the same as in (iv). B's additional purchase, however, is taken into account for the purpose of determining whether there is a second ownership change with respect to L. [Temporary Reg. §1.382-2T.]

☐ [T.D. 8149, 8-5-87. *Amended by* T.D. 8264, 9-19-89; T.D. 8277, 12-22-89; T.D. 8352, 6-26-91; T.D. 8405, 3-27-92; T.D. 8407, 4-8-92; T.D. 8428, 8-21-92; T.D. 8440, 10-2-92; T.D. 8490, 10-1-93 T.D. 8531, 3-17-94; T.D. 8679, 6-26-96; T.D. 8825, 6-25-99; T.D. 9264, 5-26-2006 *and* T.D. 9329, 6-13-2007.]

[Reg. §1.382-3]

§1.382-3. Definitions and rules relating to a 5-percent shareholder.—(a) *Definitions.*—(1) *Entity.*—(i) *In general.*—An entity is any corporation, estate, trust, association, company, partnership or similar organization. An entity includes a group of persons who have a formal or informal understanding among themselves to make a coordinated acquisition of stock. A principal element in determining if such an understanding exists is whether the investment decision of each member of a group is based upon the investment decision of one or more other members. However, the participation by creditors in formulating a plan for an insolvency workout or a reorganization in a title 11 or similar case (whether as members of a creditors' committee or otherwise) and the receipt of stock by creditors in satisfaction of indebtedness pursuant to the workout or reorganization do not cause the creditors to be considered an entity.

(ii) *Examples.*—The following examples illustrate the provisions of paragraph (a)(1)(i) of this section.

Example 1. (i) L corporation has 1,000 shares of common stock outstanding. For the three-year period ending on October 1, 1992, L's stock was owned by unrelated individuals, none of whom owned five percent or more of L. A group of 20 individuals who previously owned no stock (the "Group") agree among themselves to acquire more than 5 percent of L's stock. The Group is not a corporation, trust, association, partnership or company. On October 1, 1992, pursuant to their understanding, the members of the Group purchase 600 shares of L common stock from the old shareholders of L (a total of 60 percent of L stock), with each member purchasing 30 shares.

(ii) Before the members of the Group acquired L's stock on October 1, 1992, no individual or entity owned, directly or indirectly, five percent or more of the stock of L. As a result, all shareholders were aggregated into a public group and L was considered to be owned by a single 5-percent shareholder ("Public L") in accordance with section 1.382-2T(g)(1) and (j)(1).

(iii) Under paragraph (a)(1)(i) of this section, the members of the Group have a formal or informal understanding among themselves to make a coordinated acquisition of stock and, therefore, the Group is an entity. Thus, the acquisition of more than five percent of the stock of L on October 1, 1992, by members of the Group is not disregarded under section 1.382-2T(e)(1)(ii). Because no member of the Group owns, directly or indirectly, five percent or more of the stock of L, sections 1.382-2T(g)(1) and (j)(1) require that the members of the Group be aggregated into a separate public group, which will be presumed to consist of persons unrelated to the members of Public L. Because there is a shift of more than fifty percentage points in the ownership of L stock during the three-year testing period ending on October 1, 1992, an ownership change occurs on October 1, 1992, as a result of the Group's purchase of the 600 shares.

Example 2. (i) Prior to October 1, 1992, L's 1,000 shares of outstanding stock were owned by unrelated individuals, none of whom owned five percent or more of the stock of L. L's management is concerned that L may become subject to a takeover bid. In separate meetings, L's management meets with potential investors who own no stock and are friendly to management to convince them to acquire L's stock based on an understanding that L will assemble a group that in the aggregate will acquire more than 50 percent of L's stock. On October 1, 1992, 15 of these investors each purchase 4 percent of L's stock.

(ii) Under paragraph (a)(1)(i) of this section, the 15 investors (the "Group") are treated as an entity because the members of the Group purchase L stock pursuant to a formal or informal understanding among themselves to make a coordinated acquisition of stock. Sections 1.382-2T(g)(1) and (j)(1) require that on October 1, 1992, the Group be aggregated into a separate public group, which has increased its ownership of L stock by 60 percentage points over its lowest level of ownership in the three-year period ending on

October 1, 1992. Accordingly, an ownership change occurs on that date.

Example 3. (i) Prior to October 1, 1992, L's 1,000 shares of outstanding stock were owned by unrelated individuals, none of whom owned five percent or more of the stock of L. On October 1, 1992, an investment advisor advises its clients that it believes L's stock is undervalued and recommends that they acquire L stock. Acting on the investment advisor's recommendation, 20 unrelated individuals purchase 6 percent of L's stock in aggregate, with each individual purchasing less than 5 percent. Each client's decision was not based upon the investment decisions made by one or more other clients.

(ii) Because there is no formal or informal understanding among the clients to make a coordinated acquisition of L stock, their purchase of stock is not made by an entity under paragraph (a)(1)(i) of this section. As a result, they remain part of the public group which owns L stock, and no owner shift results upon their purchase of L stock under section 1.382-2T(e)(1)(ii).

(iii) The result in this example would be the same under paragraph (a)(3)(i) of this section if the only additional fact was that the investment advisor is also the underwriter (without regard to whether it is a firm commitment or best efforts underwriting) for a primary or secondary offering of L stock.

(iv) Assume that the facts are the same except that, instead of an investment advisor recommending that clients purchase L stock, the trustee of several trusts qualified under section 401(a) sponsored by unrelated corporations causes each trust to purchase the L stock. In this case, the result is the same, so long as the investment decision made on behalf of each trust was not based on the investment decision made on behalf of one or more of the other trusts.

(iii) *Effective date.*—(A) *In general.*—The second, third and fourth sentences of paragraph (a)(1)(i) of this section and Examples 1, 2 and 3 of paragraph (a)(1)(ii) of this section apply to testing dates (determined by applying such sentence and examples) on or after November 20, 1990, but with respect to any group of persons that pursuant to a formal or informal understanding among themselves makes a coordinated acquisition of stock before November 20, 1990, only if the group increases or decreases its ownership of stock of the loss corporation relative to its percentage ownership interest at the close of November 19, 1990, by five percentage points or more on or after November 20, 1990.

(B) *Special rule.*—If pursuant to a formal or informal understanding among themselves a group consisting only of regulated investment companies under section 851, qualified trusts under section 401, common trust funds under section 584, or trusts or estates that are clients of a trust department of a bank under section 581, make a coordinated acquisition of stock before November 20, 1990, the second, third and fourth sentences of paragraph (a)(1)(i) of this section and *Examples 1, 2,* and *3* of paragraph (a)(1)(ii) of this section apply for testing dates (determined by applying such sentences and examples) on or after November 20, 1990, only if the group increases its ownership of stock of the loss corporation relative to its percentage ownership interest at the close of November 19, 1990, by five percentage points or more on or after November 20, 1990.

(C) *Example.*—The following example illustrates the provisions of paragraph (a)(1)(iii) of this section.

Example. Prior to November 1, 1990, L, a loss corporation, is owned entirely by 1,000 unrelated individuals, none of whom owns as much as 5 percent of the stock of L ("Public L"). On November 1, 1990, 15 individuals (the "Group") each acquired 3 percent, or 45 percent, in total, of L stock pursuant to an understanding among themselves to make a coordinated acquisition of stock. The Group is not a corporation, trust, association, partnership or company. On March 1, 1992, six members of the Group each purchased an additional one percent of L stock, or 6 percent, in total, pursuant to the understanding. Accordingly, the Group increased its ownership in L stock by 51 percentage points during the three-year testing period ending on March 1, 1992. As a result, an ownership change of L occurs on March 1, 1992.

(2) [Reserved].

(b) through (i) [Reserved].

(j) *Modification of the segregation rules of §1.382-2T(j)(2)(iii) and (3).*—(1) *Introduction.*—This paragraph (j) exempts, in whole or in part, certain transfers of stock from the segregation rules of §1.382-2T(j)(2)(iii) and (3). Terms and nomenclature used in this paragraph (j), and not otherwise defined herein, have the same meanings as in section 382 and the regulations issued under section 382.

(2) *Small issuance exception.*—(i) *In general.*—Section 1.382-2T(j)(2)(iii)(B) does not apply to a small issuance (as defined in paragraph (j)(2)(ii) of this section), except to the extent that the total

amount of stock issued in that issuance and all other small issuances previously made in the same taxable year (determined in each case on issuance) exceeds the small issuance limitation. This paragraph (j)(2) does not apply to an issuance of stock that, by itself, exceeds the small issuance limitation.

(ii) *Small issuance defined.*—Small issuance means an issuance (other than an issuance described in paragraph (j)(6) of this section) by the loss corporation of an amount of stock not exceeding the small issuance limitation. For purposes of this paragraph (j)(2)(ii), all stock issued in the issuance is taken into account, including stock owned immediately after the issuance by a 5-percent shareholder that is not a direct public group.

(iii) *Small issuance limitation.*—(A) *In general.*—For each taxable year, the loss corporation may, at its option, apply this paragraph (j)(2)—

(1) On a corporation-wide basis, in which case the small issuance limitation is 10 percent of the total value of the loss corporation's stock outstanding at the beginning of the taxable year (excluding the value of stock described in section 1504(a)(4)); or

(2) On a class-by-class basis, in which case the small issuance limitation is 10 percent of the number of shares of the class outstanding at the beginning of the taxable year.

(B) *Class of stock defined.*—For purposes of this paragraph (j)(2)(iii), a class of stock includes all stock with the same material terms.

(C) *Adjustments for stock splits and similar transactions.*—Appropriate adjustments to the number of shares of a class outstanding at the beginning of a taxable year must be made to take into account any stock split, reverse stock split, stock dividend to which section 305(a) applies, recapitalization, or similar transaction occurring during the taxable year.

(D) *Exception.*—The loss corporation may not apply this paragraph (j)(2)(iii) on a class-by-class basis if, during the taxable year, more than one class of stock is issued in a single issuance (or in two or more issuances that are treated as a single issuance under paragraph (j)(8)(ii) of this section).

(iv) *Short taxable years.*—In the case of a taxable year that is less than 365 days, the small issuance limitation is reduced by multiplying it by a fraction, the numerator of which is the number of days in the taxable year, and the denominator of which is 365.

(3) *Other issuances of stock for cash.*—(i) *In general.*—If the loss corporation issues stock solely for cash, §1.382-2T(j)(2)(iii)(B) does not apply to such stock in an amount equal (as a percentage of the total stock issued) to one-half of the aggregate percentage ownership interest of direct public groups immediately before the issuance.

(ii) *Solely for cash.*—(A) *In general.*—A share of stock is not issued solely for cash if—

(1) The acquiror, as a condition of acquiring that share for cash, is required to purchase other stock for consideration other than cash; or

(2) The share is acquired upon the exercise of an option that was not issued solely for cash or was not distributed with respect to stock.

(B) *Related issuances.*—Paragraph (j)(8)(i) of this section (relating to the treatment of one or more issuances as a single issuance) does not apply in determining whether stock is issued solely for cash.

(iii) *Coordination with paragraph (j)(2) of this section.*—This paragraph (j)(3) does not apply to a small issuance exempted in whole from §1.382-2T(j)(2)(iii)(B) under paragraph (j)(2) of this section. In the case of a small issuance exempted in part from §1.382-2T(j)(2)(iii)(B) under paragraph (j)(2) of this section, this paragraph (j)(3) applies only to the portion of the issuance not so exempted, and that portion is treated as a separate issuance for purposes of this paragraph (j)(3).

(4) *Limitation on exempted stock.*—The total amount of stock that is exempted from the application of §1.382-2T(j)(2)(iii)(B) under paragraphs (j)(2) and (j)(3) of this section cannot exceed the total amount of stock issued in the issuance less the amount of that stock owned by a 5-percent shareholder (other than a direct public group) immediately after the issuance. Except to the extent that the loss corporation has actual knowledge to the contrary, any increase in the amount of the loss corporation's stock owned by a 5-percent shareholder on the day of the issuance is considered to be attributable to an acquisition of stock in the issuance.

(5) *Proportionate acquisition of exempted stock.*—(i) *In general.*—Each direct public group that exists immediately before an issuance to which paragraph (j)(2) or (j)(3) of this section applies is treated as

acquiring its proportionate share of the amount of stock exempted from the application of §1.382-2T(j)(2)(iii)(B) under paragraph (j)(2) or (j)(3) of this section.

(ii) *Actual knowledge of greater overlapping ownership.*—Under the last sentence of §1.382-2T(k)(2), the loss corporation may treat direct public groups existing immediately before an issuance to which paragraph (j)(2) or (j)(3) of this section applies as acquiring in the aggregate more stock than the amount determined under paragraph (j)(5)(i) of this section, but only if the loss corporation actually knows that the aggregate amount acquired by those groups in the issuance exceeds the amount so determined.

(6) *Exception for equity structure shifts.*—This paragraph (j) does not apply to any issuance of stock in an equity structure shift, except that paragraph (j)(2) of this section applies (if its requirements are met) to the issuance of stock in a recapitalization under section 368(a)(1)(E).

(7) *Transitory ownership by underwriter disregarded.*—For purposes of §1.382-2T(g)(1) and (j), and this paragraph (j), the transitory ownership of stock by an underwriter of the issuance is disregarded.

(8) *Certain related issuances.*—For purposes of this paragraph (j), two or more issuances (including issuances of stock by first tier or higher tier entities) are treated as a single issuance if—

(i) The issuances occur at approximately the same time pursuant to the same plan or arrangement; or

(ii) A principal purpose of issuing the stock in separate issuances rather than in a single issuance is to minimize or avoid an owner shift under the rules of this paragraph (j).

(9) *Application to options.*—The principles of this paragraph (j) apply for purposes of applying §1.382-2T(j)(2)(iii)(D) (relating to the deemed acquisition of stock as a result of the ownership of an option).

(10) *Issuance of stock pursuant to the exercise of certain options.*—If stock is issued on the exercise of a transferable option issued by the loss corporation, §1.382-2T(j)(2)(iii)(F) does not apply and, in applying the last sentence of §1.382-2T(k)(2), the loss corporation must take into account any transfers of the option (including transfers described in §1.382-2T(h)(4)(xi)). Therefore, even if transferable options are distributed pro rata to members of existing public groups, the actual knowledge exception of §1.382-2T(k)(2) applies only to the extent that the loss corporation actually knows that the persons acquiring stock on exercise of the options are members of a pre-existing public group. Moreover, if transferable options are issued to more than one public group, §1.382-2T(j)(2)(iii)(F) does not apply to treat the options as exercised pro rata by each such public group as the options are actually exercised.

(11) *Application to first tier and higher tier entities.*—(i) *In general.*—The principles of paragraphs (j)(1) through (10) and paragraph (j)(12) apply to issuances of stock by a first tier entity or a higher tier entity that owns 5 percent or more of the loss corporation's stock (determined without regard to §1.382-2T(h)(2)(1)(A)).

(ii) *Small issuance limitation.*—In applying paragraph (j)(2) of this section to any issuance of stock by a first tier or higher tier entity, the small issuance limitations of paragraph (j)(2)(iii)(A) and (B) of this section are computed by reference to the stock value and the stock classes of the issuing corporation.

(12) *Certain non-stock ownership interests.*—As the context may require, a non-stock ownership interest in an entity other than a corporation is treated as stock for purposes of this paragraph (j).

(13) *Secondary transfer exception.*—The segregation rules of §1.382-2T(j)(3)(i) will not apply to the transfer of a direct ownership interest in the loss corporation by a first tier entity or an individual that owns five percent or more of the loss corporation to public shareholders. Instead, each public group existing at the time of the transfer will be treated under §1.382-2T(j)(3)(i) as acquiring its proportionate share of the stock exempted from the application of *§1.382-2T(j)(3)(i).* The segregation rules also will not apply if an ownership interest in an entity that owns five percent or more of the loss corporation (determined without regard to the application of §1.382-2T(h)(2)(i)(A)) is transferred to a public owner or a 5-percent owner who is not a 5-percent shareholder of the loss corporation. Instead, provided that the transferor is either a 5-percent owner that is a 5-percent shareholder of the loss corporation or a higher tier entity owning five percent or more of the loss corporation (determined without regard to the application of section 1.382-2T(h)(2)(i)(A)), each public group of the entity existing at the time of the transfer is treated under §1.382-2T(j)(3)(i) as acquiring its proportionate share of the transferred ownership interest. With re-

gard to a transferor that is neither a 5-percent shareholder of the loss corporation nor a higher tier entity owning five percent or more of the loss corporation (determined without regard to the application of §1.382-2T(h)(2)(i)(A)), see generally §1.382-2T(e)(1)(ii) (disregarding these transactions if the transferee is not a 5-percent shareholder).

(14) *Small redemption exception.*—(i) *In general.*—Section 1.382-2T(j)(2)(iii)(C) does not apply to a small redemption (as defined in paragraph (j)(14)(ii) of this section), except to the extent that the total amount of stock redeemed in that redemption and all other small redemptions previously made in the same taxable year (determined in each case on redemption) exceeds the small redemption limitation. This paragraph (j)(14) does not apply to a redemption of stock that, by itself, exceeds the small redemption limitation.

(ii) *Small redemption defined.*—Small redemption means a redemption of public shareholders by the loss corporation of an amount of stock not exceeding the small redemption limitation.

(iii) *Small redemption limitation.*—(A) *In general.*—For each taxable year, the loss corporation may, at its option, apply this paragraph (j)(14)—

(1) On a corporation-wide basis, in which case the small redemption limitation is 10 percent of the total value of the loss corporation's stock outstanding at the beginning of the taxable year (excluding the value of stock described in section 1504(a)(4)); or

(2) On a class-by-class basis, in which case the small redemption limitation is 10 percent of the number of shares of the class redeemed that are outstanding at the beginning of the taxable year.

(B) *Class of stock defined.*—For purposes of this paragraph (j)(14)(iii), a class of stock includes all stock with the same material terms.

(C) *Adjustments for stock splits and similar transactions.*—Appropriate adjustments to the number of shares of a class outstanding at the beginning of a taxable year must be made to take into account any stock split, reverse stock split, stock dividend to which section 305(a) applies, recapitalization, or similar transaction occurring during the taxable year.

(D) *Exception.*—The loss corporation may not apply this paragraph (j)(14)(iii) on a class-by-class basis if, during the taxable year, more than one class of stock is redeemed in a single redemption (or in two or more redemptions that are treated as a single redemption under paragraph (j)(14)(v) of this section).

(E) *Short taxable years.*—In the case of a taxable year that is less than 365 days, the small redemption limitation is reduced by multiplying it by a fraction, the numerator of which is the number of days in the taxable year, and the denominator of which is 365.

(iv) *Proportionate redemption of exempted stock.*—(A) *In general.*—Each direct public group that exists immediately before a redemption to which this paragraph (j)(14) applies is treated as having been redeemed of its proportionate share of the amount of stock exempted from the application of §1.382-2T(j)(2)(iii)(C) under this paragraph (j)(14).

(B) *Actual knowledge of greater redemption.*—Under the last sentence of §1.382-2T(k)(2), the loss corporation may treat direct public groups existing immediately before a redemption to which this paragraph (j)(14) applies as having been redeemed of more stock than the amount determined under paragraph (j)(14)(iv)(A) of this section, but only if the loss corporation actually knows that the amount redeemed from those groups in the redemption exceeds the amount so determined.

(v) *Certain related redemptions.*—For purposes of this paragraph (j)(14), two or more redemptions (including redemptions of stock by first tier or higher tier entities) are treated as a single redemption if—

(A) The redemptions occur at approximately the same time pursuant to the same plan or arrangement; or

(B) A principal purpose of redeeming the stock in separate redemptions rather than in a single redemption is to minimize or avoid an owner shift under the rules of this paragraph (j)(14).

(vi) *Certain non-stock ownership interests.*—As the context may require, a non-stock ownership interest in an entity other than a corporation is treated as stock for purposes of this paragraph (j)(14).

(vii) *Application to first tier and higher tier entities.*—(A) *In general.*—The principles of this paragraph (j)(14) apply to redemptions of stock by a first tier entity or a higher tier entity that owns 5 percent of the loss corporation stock (determined without regard to §1.382-2T(h)(2)(i)(A)).

(B) *Small redemption limitation.*—In applying this paragraph (j)(14) to any redemption of stock by a first tier or a higher tier entity, the small redemption limitations of paragraph (j)(14)(iii)(A) of this section are computed by reference to the stock value and the stock classes of the redeeming corporation.

(15) *Exception for first tier and higher tier entities.*—(i) *In general.*—The segregation rules of §1.382-2T(j)(3)(iii) will not apply to a transaction involving stock in a first tier or a higher tier entity if, after taking into account the results of such transaction and all other transactions occurring on that date, the first tier or higher tier entity owns 10 percent or less (by value) of all the outstanding stock (without regard to §1.382-2(a)(3)) of the loss corporation.

(ii) *Anti-avoidance rule.*—The rules of paragraph (j)(15)(i) of this section do not apply to a transaction involving an ownership interest in a first tier or higher tier entity if the loss corporation, directly or through one or more persons, has participated in planning or structuring the transaction with a view to avoiding the application of the segregation rules. For this purpose, a transaction includes any event that would result in segregation under §1.382-2T(j)(3)(iii), absent the application of this paragraph (j)(15), and any event (for example, the formation of a holding company) occurring as part of the same plan that includes the event that would result in segregation (without the application of this paragraph (j)(15)). Other anti-avoidance rules continue to be applicable. See, for example, §§1.382-2T(k)(4) and 1.382-3(a)(1).

(iii) *Special rules.*—If application of paragraph (j)(15)(i) of this section results in the combination of public groups, then—

(A) The amount of increase in the percentage of stock ownership of the continuing public group will be the sum of its increase and a proportionate amount of any increase by any public group that is combined with the continuing public group (the former public group); and

(B) The continuing public group's lowest percentage ownership will be the sum of its lowest percentage ownership and a proportionate amount of the former public group's lowest percentage ownership.

(iv) *Ownership of the loss corporation.*—In making the determination under paragraph (j)(15)(i) of this section—

(A) The rules of §1.382-2T(h)(2) will not apply;

(B) The entity will be treated as owning the loss corporation stock that it actually owns, and any other loss corporation stock if that other stock would be attributed to the entity under section 318(a) (without regard to paragraph (4) thereof) unless an option is treated as exercised under §1.382-4(d)); and

(C) The operating rules of paragraph (j)(15)(v) of this section will apply.

(v) *Operating rules.*—Subject to the principles of §1.382-2T(k)(4), a loss corporation may establish the ownership limitation of paragraph (j)(15)(i) of this section through either—

(A) Actual knowledge; or

(B) Absent actual knowledge to the contrary, the presumptions regarding stock ownership in §1.382-2T(k)(1).

(16) *Examples.*—The provisions of this paragraph (j) are illustrated by the following examples:

Example 1. (i) L corporation is a calendar year taxpayer. On January 1, 1994, L has 1,000 shares of a single class of common stock outstanding, all of which are owned by a single direct public group (Public L). On February 1, 1994, L issues to employees as compensation 60 new common shares of the same class. On May 1, 1994, L issues 50 new common shares of the same class solely for cash. Following each issuance, L's stock is owned entirely by public shareholders. No other changes in the ownership of L's stock occur prior to May 1, 1994. L chooses to determine its small issuance limitation for 1994 on a class-by-class basis under paragraph (j)(2)(iii)(A)(2) of this section.

(ii) The February issuance is a small issuance because the number of shares issued (60) does not exceed 100, the small issuance limitation (10 percent of the number of common shares outstanding on January 1, 1994). Under paragraph (j)(2) of this section, the segregation rules of §1.382-2T(j)(2)(iii)(B) do not apply to the February issuance. Under paragraph (j)(5) of this section, Public L is treated as acquiring all 60 shares issued.

(iii) The May issuance is a small issuance because the number of shares issued (50) does not exceed 100, the small issuance limitation *(10 percent of the number of common shares outstanding on January 1, 1994).* However, under paragraph (j)(2) of this section, only 40 of the 50 shares issued are exempted from the segregation rules of §1.382-2T(j)(2)(iii)(B) because the total number of shares of common stock issued in the February and May issuances exceeds 100, the

small issuance limitation, by 10. Because the May issuance is solely for cash, paragraph (j)(3) of this section exempts 5 of the 10 remaining shares from the segregation rules of §1.382-2T(j)(2)(iii)(B) (10 shares multiplied by 50 percent, one-half of Public L's 100 percent ownership interest immediately before the May issuance—1,060 shares/1,060 shares). Accordingly, under paragraph (j)(5) of this section, Public L is treated as acquiring 45 shares in the May issuance. Section 1.382-2T(j)(2)(iii)(B) applies to the remaining 5 shares issued, which are treated as acquired by a direct public group separate from Public L. Each such public group is treated as an individual who is a separate 5-percent shareholder. See §1.382-2T(g)(1)(iv) and (j)(1)(ii).

(iv) Assume that L actually knows that at least 10 shares of the May issuance are acquired by members of Public L. The result is the same. See paragraph (j)(5)(ii) of this section.

(v) Assume instead that L actually knows that all 50 shares of the May issuance are acquired by members of Public L. Under paragraph (j)(5)(ii) of this section, L may treat Public L as acquiring 50 shares in the May issuance.

Example 2. (i) L corporation is a calendar year taxpayer. On January 1, 1995, L has 1,000 shares of Class A common stock outstanding, the aggregate value of which is $1,000. Five hundred shares are owned by one direct public group (Public 1), and 500 shares are owned by another direct public group (Public 2). On August 1, 1995, L issues 200 shares of Class B common stock for $200 cash. A, an individual, acquires 120 Class B shares in the transaction. The remaining 80 Class B shares are acquired by public shareholders. No other changes in ownership of L's stock occur prior to August 1, 1995.

(ii) The August issuance is not a small issuance. The total value of the Class B stock issued ($200) exceeds $100, the small issuance limitation as calculated under paragraph (j)(2)(iii)(A)(1) of this section (10 percent of the value of L's stock on January 1, 1995). The total number of Class B shares issued (200) exceeds 0, the small issuance limitation as calculated under paragraph (j)(2)(iii)(A)(2) of this section (10 percent of the number of Class B shares outstanding on January 1, 1995). Accordingly, paragraph (j)(2) of this section does not apply to the August issuance.

(iii) Paragraph (j)(3) of this section, as limited by paragraph (j)(4) of this section, exempts 80 Class B shares from the segregation rule of §1.382-2T(j)(2)(iii)(B). Paragraph (j)(3) of this section, without regard to paragraph (j)(4) of this section, would exempt 100 Class B shares: the product of the 200 Class B shares issued and 50 percent (one-half of the combined 100 percent pre-issuance ownership interest of Public 1 and Public 2). Paragraph (j)(4), however, limits the total number of Class B shares that may be excluded to 80 Class B shares: the difference between the 200 shares issued and the 120 shares acquired by A. Under paragraph (j)(5) of this section, Public 1 and Public 2 are treated as acquiring the 80 exempted Class B shares. Because Public 1 and Public 2 each owned 500 Class A shares prior to the issuance, Public 1 and Public 2 are considered to acquire 40 Class B shares each.

Example 3. (i) L has 1,000 shares of a single class of common stock outstanding, all of which are owned by a direct public group (Public L). At the same time pursuant to the same plan, L issues 500 shares of its stock to its creditors in exchange for its outstanding debt and 500 shares of its stock to the public for cash. Assume that the separate issuances of stock for debt and stock for cash do not have a principal purpose of minimizing or avoiding an owner shift. L has no individual 5-percent shareholders immediately after the issuances.

(ii) The 500 shares of stock issued by L to its former creditors were not issued solely for cash. Therefore, paragraph (j)(3) of this section does not apply to those 500 shares, which are treated as owned by a public group separate from Public L. See §1.382-2T(j)(2)(iii)(B)(1)(ii).

(iii) Paragraph (j)(3) of this section applies to the 500 shares of stock issued by L to the public because that stock was issued solely for cash. Because the two issuances occur at the same time pursuant to the same plan, they are generally treated as a single issuance for purposes of this paragraph (j). See paragraph (j)(8)(i) of this section. The treatment of the two issuances as a single issuance does not apply, however, for the purpose of determining whether the stock issued to the public was issued solely for cash. See paragraph (j)(3)(ii)(B) of this section.

(iv) Paragraph (j)(3) of this section applies to exempt 250 of the 500 shares issued solely for cash from the segregation rules of §1.382-2T(j)(2)(iii)(B) (the product of the 500 shares issued for cash and 50 percent (one-half of the 100 percent pre-issuance ownership interest of Public L)). The creditors that receive stock in exchange for their debt would not be treated as acquiring any of the 250 exempted shares even if their exchange of debt for stock occurs prior to the cash issuance. Paragraph (j)(5)(i) of this section allocates exempted shares among the direct public groups that exist immediately before an issuance. Because the issuance for cash and the issuance for debt are generally treated as a single issuance, the public group comprised of the former creditors of L was not a public group that existed immediately before the issuance.

(v) Three public groups owning L stock exist immediately after the two issuances. Public L owns 1,250 shares—the 1,000 shares it owned prior to the issuances plus the 250 shares it is treated as acquiring in the cash issuance. A separate group comprised of the former creditors of L owns the 500 shares issued for debt. A third public group owns the 250 shares that are not treated as acquired by Public L in the cash issuance.

Example 4. (i) L has 1,000 shares of a single class of common stock outstanding, all of which are owned by a direct public group (Public L). L issues 1,000 shares pursuant to an offer under which 500 shares must be acquired in exchange for debt and the remainder may be acquired for cash. Under the terms of the offer, only persons that acquire stock for debt are eligible to acquire stock for cash. L has no 5-percent shareholders other than direct public groups immediately after the issuance.

(ii) As a condition of acquiring shares for cash, the creditors are required to purchase stock for debt. Therefore, paragraph (j)(3) of this section does not apply to any part of the issuance because it is not an issuance of stock solely for cash. The segregation rules of § 1.382-2T(j)(2)(iii)(B) apply to treat all 1,000 shares as acquired by a new public group separate from Public L.

Example 5. Secondary transfer exception to segregation rules - no new public group. (i) *Facts.* L is owned 60 percent by one public group (Public L₁) and 40 percent by another public group (Public L₂). On July 1, 2014, individual A acquires 10 percent of L's stock over a public stock exchange. On December 31, 2014, A sells all of his L stock over a public stock exchange. No individual or entity acquires as much as five percent of L's stock as a result of A's disposition of his L stock. On January 3, 2015, individual B acquires 10 percent of L's stock over a public stock exchange. On June 30, 2015, B sells all of her L stock over a public stock exchange. No individual or entity acquires as much as five percent of L's stock as a result of B's disposition of her L stock.

(ii) *Analysis.* The dispositions of the L stock by A and B are not transactions that cause the segregation of L's direct public groups that exist immediately before the transaction (Public L₁ and Public L₂). When A and B sell their shares to public shareholders over the public stock exchange, the shares are treated as being reacquired by Public L₁ and Public L₂. As a result, Public L₁'s ownership interest is treated as increasing from 54 percent to 60 percent during the testing period, and Public L₂'s ownership interest is treated as increasing from 36 percent to 40 percent during the testing period.

Example 6. Secondary transfer exception - first tier entity. (i) *Facts.* L has a single class of common stock outstanding that is owned 60 percent by a direct public group (Public L) and 40 percent by P. P is owned 20 percent by individual A and 80 percent by a direct public group (Public P). On October 6, 2014, A sells 50 percent of his interest in P to B, an individual who is, and remains, a member of Public P.

(ii) *Analysis.* P is an entity that owns five percent or more of L. A is a 5-percent owner of P that is a 5-percent shareholder of L. Because A's sale of the P stock is to a member of Public P, the disposition of the P stock by A is not a transaction that causes the segregation of P's direct public group that exists immediately before the transaction (Public P). See paragraph (j)(13) of this section. When A sells his shares to B, the shares are treated as being acquired by Public P. As a result, Public P's ownership interest in L is treated as increasing from 32 percent to 36 percent during the testing period.

Example 7. Small redemption exception. (i) *Facts.* L is a calendar year taxpayer. On January 1, 2014, L has 1,060 shares of a single class of common stock outstanding, all of which are owned by a single direct public group (Public L). On July 1, 2014, L acquires 60 shares of its stock for cash. On December 31, 2014, in an unrelated redemption, L acquires 90 more shares of its stock for cash. Following each redemption, L's stock is owned entirely by public shareholders. No other changes in the ownership of L's stock occur prior to December 31, 2014.

(ii) *Analysis - (A) July redemption.* The July redemption is a small redemption because the number of shares redeemed (60) does not exceed 106, the small redemption limitation (10 percent of the number of common shares outstanding on January 1, 2014). Under paragraph (j)(14) of this section, the segregation rules of § 1.382-2T(j)(2)(iii)(C) do not apply to the July redemption. Under paragraph (j)(14)(iv) of this section, Public L is treated as having all 60 shares redeemed.

(B) *December redemption.* The December redemption is a small redemption because the number of shares redeemed (90) does not exceed 106, the small redemption limitation (10 percent of the number of common shares outstanding on January 1, 2014). However, under paragraph (j)(14)(i) of this section, only 46 of the 90 shares redeemed are exempted from the segregation rules of § 1.382-2T(j)(2)(iii)(C) because the total number of shares of common

stock redeemed in the July and December redemptions exceeds 106, the small redemption limitation, by 44. Accordingly, under paragraph (j)(14)(iv) of this section, Public L is treated as having 46 shares redeemed in the December redemption. Section 1.382-2T(j)(2)(iii)(C) applies to the remaining 44 shares redeemed. Accordingly, Public L is segregated into two different public groups immediately before the transaction (and thereafter) so that the redeemed interests (Public RL) are treated as part of a public group that is separate from the ownership interests that are not redeemed (Public CL). Therefore, as a result of the December redemption, Public CL's interest in L increases by 4.4 percentage points (from 95.6 percent (956/1,000) to 100 percent (910/910)) on the December 31, 2014 testing date. For purposes of determining whether an ownership change occurs on any subsequent testing date having a testing period that includes the December redemption, Public CL is treated as a 5-percent shareholder whose percentage ownership interests in L increased by 4.4 percentage points as a result of such redemption.

Example 8. Segregation rules inapplicable - proportionate amount. (i) *Facts.* P₁ is a corporation that owns 8 percent of the stock of L. The remaining L stock (92 percent) is owned by Public L. P₁ is entirely owned by Public P₁. P₂ is a corporation owned 90 percent by individual A and 10 percent by a public group (Public P₂). On May 22, 2014, P₁ merges into P₂ with the shareholders of P₁ receiving an amount of P₂ stock equal to 25 percent of the value of P₂ immediately after the reorganization. L was owned 92 percent by Public L and 8 percent by P₁ throughout the testing period ending on the date of the merger.

(ii) *Analysis.* Assuming L can establish that P₂ owns 10 percent or less (by value) of L on May 22, 2014 pursuant to the operating rules of paragraph (j)(15)(v) of this section, the segregation rules of § 1.382-2T(j)(3)(iii) will not apply to segregate P₁'s direct public group (Public P₁) immediately before the merger from P₂'s direct public group (Public P₂). Thus, following the merger, P₂ is owned 67.5 percent (90 percent × 75 percent) by A and 32.5 percent (25 percent + (10 percent × 75 percent)) by Public P₂. Pursuant to paragraph (j)(15)(iii)(B) of this section, Public P₂'s lowest percentage of ownership is the sum of its lowest percentage of ownership (zero) and a proportionate amount of former Public P₁'s lowest ownership percentage of L of 2.6 percent (32.5 percent × 8 percent). P₂ will be treated as having one public group whose ownership interest in L was 2.6 percent before the merger and remains 2.6 percent after the merger. Because Public P₂ owns less than 5 percent of L, Public P₂ is treated as part of Public L. See § 1.382-2T(j)(1)(iv). Thus, pursuant to paragraph (j)(15)(iii)(B) of this section, Public L's lowest ownership percentage of L during the testing period is 94.6 percent.

Example 9. Segregation rules inapplicable - prior increase in ownership by former public group during testing period. (i) *Facts.* The facts are the same as *Example 8*, except that P₁ acquired its 8 percent interest in L during the testing period that includes the merger.

(ii) *Analysis.* Pursuant to the rules of paragraph (j)(15)(iii)(A) of this section, the amount of increase in the percentage of stock ownership by Public P₂ is the sum of its increase (zero) and a proportionate amount of the increase by former Public P₁ of 2.6 percent (32.5 percent × 8 percent). Pursuant to paragraph (j)(15)(iii)(B) of this section, Public P₂'s lowest percentage of ownership is zero, because both former Public P₁ and Public P₂ owned no L stock at the beginning of the testing period. Accordingly, Public P₂, the continuing public group, is treated as having increased its ownership interest by 2.6 percent. Because Public P₂ is treated as part of Public L, Public L is treated as increasing its ownership interest by 2.6 percent.

Example 10. Ownership limitation based upon fair market value. (i) *Facts.* L has one class of common stock and one class of preferred stock outstanding. The preferred stock is stock within the meaning of § 1.382-2(a)(3). Before December 23, 2014, a direct public group (Public L) owns all of the common stock of L. On December 23, 2014, P purchases all of the preferred stock of L and a portion of the common stock of L. On the date of purchase, the value of the L common stock held by P was greater than 5 percent of the value of L, and the total value of L common and L preferred stock held by P was less than 10 percent of the value of all stock of L. P has one class of common stock outstanding, all of which is owned by a direct public group (Public P). On October 7, 2015, P redeems 30 percent of its single outstanding class of common stock. On the redemption date of the P stock, due to a decline in the relative value of the common stock of L, the preferred stock of L owned by P represents 40 percent of the value of all the outstanding stock of L. No ownership change of L occurs between December 23, 2014, and October 7, 2015.

(ii) *Analysis.* The rules of paragraph (j)(15) of this section do not apply to the redemption because P owns more than 10 percent of L (by value) on that date.

Example 11. Ownership limitation - fair market value includes preferred stock. The facts are the same as in *Example 10*, except that the preferred stock is not stock within the meaning of § 1.382-2(a)(3). Although the preferred stock is not stock for the purpose of determining owner shifts, the value of that stock is taken into account in computing the 10-percent limitation of paragraph (j)(15)(i) of this section. Therefore, the results are the same as in *Example 10.*

Example 12. Ownership limitation - application of attribution rules. (i) *Facts.* Individual A owns all the outstanding stock of X. A also owns preferred stock in Y that is not stock within the meaning § 1.382-2(a)(3), which represents 50 percent of the value of Y. All the Y common stock is owned by public owners. Each of X and Y own 6 percent of the single class of L stock outstanding. On October 6, 2014, Y redeems 15 percent of its common stock.

(ii) *Analysis.* In determining satisfaction of the ownership limitation of paragraph (j)(15)(i) of this section, the attribution rules of section 318(a) apply. Pursuant to section 318(a)(2), A is treated as owning the L stock owned by X. Pursuant to section 318(a)(3), Y is treated as owning the L stock that A indirectly owns. Because Y's ownership of L exceeds the 10 percent ownership limitation of paragraph (j)(15)(i) of this section, the rules of paragraph (j)(15) of this section do not apply.

Example 13. Anti-avoidance rule. (i) *Facts.* P_1 is a corporation that owns 10 percent of the stock of L. P_1 is owned entirely by a direct public group (Public P). L has had owner shifts of 45 percentage points in its current testing period. P_1 is planning to merge into P_2, a corporation which has a public group. Advisers to L, upon learning of the proposed merger, asked the management of P_1 for details of the proposed merger, including the stock ownership of P_1 after P_1 merges into P_2. After finding out that information, L or L's advisers did not request any changes in the planned transaction.

(ii) *Analysis.* The anti-avoidance rule of paragraph (j)(15)(ii) of this section does not apply because L did not participate in planning or structuring the transaction. Pursuant to paragraph (j)(15)(i) of this section, § 1.382-2T(j)(3)(iii) does not apply to cause the segregation of P_1's public group from P_2's public group.

(17) *Effective/applicability date.*—This paragraph (j) generally applies to issuances or deemed issuances of stock in taxable years beginning on or after November 4, 1992. However, paragraphs (j)(11)(ii) and (j)(13) through (15) of this section and *Examples 5* through *13* of paragraph (j)(16) of this section apply to testing dates occurring on or after October 22, 2013, other than with respect to the sale of a Program Instrument by the Treasury Department. For purposes of this paragraph (j)(17), a Program Instrument is an instrument issued pursuant to a Program, as defined in Internal Revenue Service Notice 2010-2 (2010-2 IRB 251 (December 16, 2009)) (see § 601.601(a)(2)(ii)(*b*) of this chapter), or a Covered Instrument, as defined in that Notice. Taxpayers may apply paragraphs (j)(11)(ii) and (j)(13) through (15) of this section and *Examples 5* through *13* of paragraph (j)(16) of this section in their entirety (other than with respect to a sale of a Program Instrument by the Treasury Department) to all testing dates that are included in a testing period beginning before and ending on or after October 22, 2013. However, the provisions described in the preceding sentence may not be applied to any date on or before the date of any ownership change that occurred before October 22, 2013, under the regulations in effect before October 22, 2013, and they may not be applied as described in the preceding sentence if such application would result in an ownership change occurring on a date before October 22, 2013, that did not occur under the regulations in effect before October 22, 2013. See § 1.382-3(j)(14)(ii) and (iii), as contained in 26 CFR part 1 revised as of April 1, 1994 for the application of paragraph (j)(10) of this section to stock issued on the exercise of certain options exercised on or after November 4, 1992, and for an election to apply paragraphs (j)(1) through (12) of this section retroactively to certain issuances and deemed issuances of stock occurring in taxable years prior to November 4, 1992.

(k) *Special rules for certain regulated investment companies.*—(1) *In general.*—The segregation rules of § 1.382-2T(j)(2) do not apply to the issuance (as described in § 1.382-2T(j)(2)(iii)(B)(1)(*ii*)) or the redemption (as described in § 1.382-2T(j)(2)(iii)(C)) of any redeemable security, as defined in 15 U.S.C. section 80a-2(a)(32), by a regulated investment company in the ordinary course of business.

(2) *Effective date.*—(i) *General rule.*—Paragraph (k)(1) of this section applies to testing dates after December 31, 1986. A corporation may file an amended return for taxable years ending before August 21, 1992 (subject to any applicable statute of limitations) to take into account paragraph (k)(1) of this section only if corresponding adjustments are made in amended returns for all affected taxable years ending after December 31, 1986 (subject to any applicable statute of limitations).

(ii) *Election to apply prospectively.*—A corporation may elect to apply paragraph (k)(1) of this section only to testing dates on or after October 29, 1991. The election must be made on the first return which is filed after October 20, 1992 by stating on such return, "THIS IS AN ELECTION TO APPLY § 1.382-3(k)(1) ONLY TO TESTING DATES ON OR AFTER OCTOBER 29, 1991." [Reg. § 1.382-3.]

□ [*T.D. 8428, 8-21-92. Redesignated and amended by T.D. 8440, 10-2-92. Amended by T.D. 8490, 10-1-93; T.D. 9638, 10-21-2013, T.D. 9685, 7-30-2014 and T.D. 9721, 6-4-2015.*]

[Reg. § 1.382-4]

§ 1.382-4. Constructive ownership of stock.—(a) *In general.*—[Reserved]

(b) *Attribution from corporations, partnerships, estates and trusts.*—(1) [Reserved].

(2) *Limitation.*—Section 1.382-2T(h)(2)(i)(A) applies solely for purposes of determining whether a loss corporation has an ownership change.

(c) *Attribution to corporations, partnerships, estates and trusts.*—[Reserved]

(d) *Treatment of options as exercised.*—(1) *General rule.*—Except as provided in paragraph (d)(2) of this section, an option is not treated as exercised under section 382(l)(3)(A).

(2) *Options treated as exercised.*—(i) *Issuance or transfer.*—For purposes of determining whether an ownership change occurs, an option is treated as exercised on the date of its issuance or transfer if, on that date, the option satisfies—

    (A) The *ownership test* of paragraph (d)(3) of this section,

    (B) The *control test* of paragraph (d)(4) of this section, or

    (C) The *income test* of paragraph (d)(5) of this section.

    (ii) *Subsequent testing dates.*—Except as provided in paragraph (d)(10) of this section, an option that is treated as exercised on the date of its issuance or transfer is treated as exercised on any subsequent testing date (as defined in § 1.382-2(a)(4)) for purposes of determining whether an ownership change occurs.

(3) *The ownership test.*—An option satisfies the ownership test if a principal purpose of the issuance, transfer, or structuring of the option (alone or in combination with other arrangements) is to avoid or ameliorate the impact of an ownership change of the loss corporation by providing the holder of the option, prior to its exercise or transfer, with a substantial portion of the attributes of ownership of the underlying stock.

(4) *The control test.*—(i) *In general.*—An option satisfies the control test if—

    (A) A principal purpose of the issuance, transfer, or structuring of the option (alone or in combination with other arrangements) is to avoid or ameliorate the impact of an ownership change of the loss corporation, and

    (B) The holder of the option and any persons related to the option holder have, in the aggregate, a direct and indirect ownership interest in the loss corporation of more than 50 percent (determined as if the increase in such persons' percentage ownership interest that would result from the exercise of the option in question and any other options to acquire stock held by such persons, and any other intended increases in such persons' percentage ownership interest, actually occurred on the date the option is issued or transferred).

    (ii) *Operating rules.*—(A) *Person and related persons.*—For purposes of this paragraph (d)(4)—

      (1) The term *person* includes an individual or entity, but not a public group, as defined in § 1.382-2T(f)(13), and

      (2) Persons are related if they bear a relationship specified in section 267(b) or 707(b) or if they have a formal or informal understanding among themselves to make a coordinated acquisition of stock, within the meaning of § 1.382-3(a)(1)(i).

    (B) *Indirect ownership interest.*—The indirect ownership interest that the holder of the option and any persons related to the holder have in the loss corporation is determined by applying the constructive ownership rules of § 1.382-2T(h), other than § 1.382-2T(h)(2)(i)(A) (which treats stock attributed pursuant to section 318(a)(2) as no longer being owned by the entity from which it is attributed) and § 1.382-2T(h)(4) (which treats options as exercised in certain circumstances). If, however, the application of such constructive ownership rules without regard to § 1.382-2T(h)(2)(i)(A) would result in the same stock of the loss corporation being owned by two or more such persons, appropriate adjustments must be made so that such stock is not counted more than once in computing the aggregate ownership interests of such persons.

(5) *The income test.*—An option satisfies the income test if a principal purpose of the issuance, transfer, or structuring of the option (alone or in combination with other arrangements) is to avoid or ameliorate the impact of an ownership change of the loss corporation by facilitating the creation of income (including accelerating

income or deferring deductions) or value (including unrealized built-in gains) prior to the exercise or transfer of the option.

(6) *Application of the ownership, control, and income tests.*—(i) *In general.*—Whether an option satisfies the ownership, control, or income test depends on all the relevant facts and circumstances. Among the factors that are relevant in applying all three tests are any business purposes for the issuance, transfer, or structure of the option, the likelihood of exercise of the option (taking into account, for example, any contingencies to its exercise), transactions related to the issuance or transfer of the option, and the consequences of treating the option as exercised. An option is not treated as exercised under any of the three tests, however, if a principal purpose of its issuance, transfer, or structuring is to avoid an ownership change by having it treated as exercised. Paragraphs (d)(6)(ii), (iii) and (iv) of this section describe additional examples of factors that are relevant in applying each test. The weight given to any factor depends on all the facts and circumstances. The presence or absence of any factor described in this paragraph (d)(6) does not create a presumption.

(ii) *Application of ownership test.*—Among the additional factors that are taken into account in applying the ownership test are the relationship, at the time of issuance or transfer of the option, between the exercise price of the option and the value of the underlying stock, whether the option provides its holder or a related person with the right to participate in the management of the loss corporation or with other rights that ordinarily would be afforded to owners of the underlying stock, and the existence of reciprocal options (e.g., a call option held by the prospective purchaser and a corresponding put option held by the prospective seller). The ability of the holder of an option with a fixed exercise price to share in future appreciation of the underlying stock is also a relevant factor, but is not sufficient, by itself, for the option to satisfy the ownership test. Conversely, the fact that the holder of such an option does not bear the risk of loss due to declines in value of the underlying stock does not preclude the option from satisfying the ownership test.

(iii) *Application of control test.*—Among the additional factors that are taken into account in applying the control test are the economic interests in the loss corporation of the option holder or related persons and the influence of those persons over the management of the loss corporation (in either case, through the option or a related arrangement, or through rights in stock).

(iv) *Application of income test.*—Among the additional factors that are taken into account in applying the income test are whether, in connection with the issuance or transfer of the option, the loss corporation engages in income acceleration transactions or the holder of the option or a related person purchases stock (including section 1504(a)(4) stock) from, or makes a capital contribution or loan to, the loss corporation that can reasonably be expected to avoid or ameliorate the impact of an ownership change. Examples of income acceleration transactions are those outside the ordinary course of the loss corporation's business that accelerate income or gain into the period prior to the exercise of the option (or defer deductions to the period after the exercise of the option). A stock purchase, capital contribution, or loan is more probative toward an option satisfying the income test the larger the amount received by the loss corporation in the transaction or related transactions. A stock purchase, capital contribution, or loan is generally not taken into account in applying the income test if it is made to enable the loss corporation to continue basic operations of its business (e.g., to meet the monthly payroll or fund other operating expenses of the loss corporation).

(7) *Safe harbors.*—Except as provided in paragraph (d)(7)(i) of this section, an option described in this paragraph (d)(7) is not treated as exercised pursuant to the ownership, control, or income test. The failure of an option to be described in this paragraph (d)(7) does not affect the determination of whether the option satisfies the ownership, income, or control test. The following options are described in this paragraph (d)(7):

(i) *Contracts to acquire stock.*—A stock purchase agreement or a similar arrangement, the terms of which are commercially reasonable, in which the parties' obligations to complete the transaction are subject only to reasonable closing conditions, and which is closed on a change date within one year after it is entered into. An option is not exempt from the income test of paragraph (d)(5) of this section solely by reason of its description in this paragraph (d)(7)(i).

(ii) *Escrow, pledge, or other security agreements.*—An option that is part of a security arrangement in a typical lending transaction (including a purchase money loan), if the arrangement is subject to customary commercial conditions. For this purpose, a security arrangement includes, for example, an agreement for holding stock in escrow or under a pledge or other security agreement, or an option to acquire stock contingent upon a default under a loan.

(iii) *Compensatory options.*—An option to acquire stock in a corporation with customary terms and conditions provided to an employee, director, or independent contractor in connection with the performance of services for the corporation or a related person (and that is not excessive by reference to the services performed) and which—

(A) Is nontransferable within the meaning of §1.83-3(d); and

(B) Does not have a readily ascertainable fair market value as defined in §1.83-7(b) on the date the option is issued.

(iv) *Options exercisable only upon death, disability, mental incompetency, or retirement.*—An option entered into between stockholders of a corporation (or a stockholder and the corporation) with respect to stock of either stockholder, that is exercisable only upon the death, disability, mental incompetency of the stockholder, or, in the case of stock acquired in connection with the performance of services for the corporation or a related person (and that is not excessive by reference to the services performed), the stockholder's retirement.

(v) *Rights of first refusal.*—A bona fide right of first refusal with customary terms, entered into between stockholders of a corporation (or between the corporation and a stockholder), and regarding the corporation's stock.

(vi) *Options designated in the Internal Revenue Bulletin.*—An option designated by the Internal Revenue Service in the Internal Revenue Bulletin as being exempt from one or more of the ownership, control, or income tests. See §601.601(d)(2)(ii) of this chapter (relating to the Internal Revenue Bulletin).

(8) *Additional rules.*—(i) *Contracts to acquire stock.*—For purposes of this paragraph (d), a contract is considered to be issued or transferred on the date it is entered into or assigned, respectively.

(ii) *Indirect transfer of an option.*—If an entity is formed or availed of for a principal purpose of facilitating an indirect transfer of an option by issuing or transferring interests in the entity, an issuance or transfer of an interest in the entity will be treated as a transfer of the option for purposes of applying the ownership, control, and income tests of paragraphs (d)(3) through (5) of this section.

(iii) *Options related to interests in non-corporate entities.*—The rules of this paragraph (d) apply, with appropriate adjustments, to options to acquire or transfer interests in non-corporate entities.

(iv) *Puts.*—In applying the rules of this section to puts, appropriate adjustments must be made to take into account that the put provides its holder with a right to transfer, instead of acquire, stock.

(9) *Definition of option.*—(i) *In general.*—Any contingent purchase, warrant, convertible debt, put, stock subject to a risk of forfeiture, contract to acquire stock, or similar interest is treated as an option for purposes of this paragraph (d), regardless of whether it is contingent or otherwise not currently exercisable.

(ii) *Convertible stock.*—Convertible stock is treated as an option for purposes of this paragraph (d) in addition to being treated as stock under §1.382-2(a)(3)(ii)) only if the terms of the conversion feature permit or require consideration other than the stock being converted.

(iii) *Series of options.*—For purposes of this paragraph (d), an option to acquire an option with respect to the stock of the loss corporation, and each one of a series of such options, is treated as an option to acquire such stock.

(iv) *General principles of tax law.*—This paragraph (d) does not affect the determination under general principles of tax law (such as substance over form) of whether an instrument is an option or stock.

(10) *Subsequent treatment of options treated as exercised on a change date.*—(i) *In general.*—The following rules apply to options that are treated as exercised under paragraph (d)(2) of this section on a change date:

(A) The option is not treated as exercised under paragraph (d)(2) of this section on any testing date after the change date and prior to a transfer of the option that would itself (i.e., without regard to the purposes for the issuance or any prior transfers of the option) cause the option to satisfy the ownership test of paragraph (d)(3) of this section, the control test of paragraph (d)(4) of this section, or the income test of paragraph (d)(5) of this section; and

(B) The exercise of the option, if by the person who owned the option immediately after the ownership change (or by a transferee of the option who acquired the option, directly or indirectly, from that person in one or more transfers described in paragraph (d)(11) of this section), does not contribute to another ownership change on any testing date on or after the date of exercise.

Reg. §1.382-4(d)(10)(i)(B)

(ii) *Alternative look-back rule for options exercised within 3 years after change date.*—If a loss corporation, on its return, as originally filed, for a taxable year that includes a change date, properly treats an option as exercised under paragraph (d)(2) of this section on the change date, and the option is actually exercised within three years after the change date, the loss corporation may treat the rules of paragraph (d)(10)(i) of this section as inapplicable to the option and instead treat the option as having been exercised on the change date for the purpose of determining whether an ownership change occurs on any and all testing dates after the change date (filing such amended returns as may be necessary for taxable years ending after the change date and before the date of exercise of the option). A transfer after the change date of an option to which this paragraph (d)(10)(ii) applies is treated as a transfer of the stock subject to the option. The exercise of an option to which this paragraph (d)(10)(ii) applies is not taken into account for the purpose of determining whether an ownership change occurs on or after the date of exercise.

(11) *Transfers not subject to deemed exercise.*—Paragraph (d)(2) of this section does not apply to the transfer of an option (including a transfer described in paragraph (d)(8)(i) or (ii) of this section), if—

(i) Neither the transferor nor the transferee is a 5-percent shareholder and neither person would be a 5-percent shareholder if all options held by that person to acquire stock were treated as exercised;

(ii) The transfer is between members of separate public groups resulting from the application of the segregation rules of § 1.382-2T(j)(2) and (3)(iii); or

(iii) The transfer occurs in any of the circumstances described in section 382(l)(3)(B) (relating to stock acquired by reason of death, gift, divorce, separation, etc.).

(12) *Certain rules regarding non-stock interests as stock.*—Section 1.382-2T(f)(18)(iii) does not apply to treat an option (whether or not treated as exercised under this paragraph (d)) as stock.

(e) *Stock transferred under certain agreements.*—[Reserved]

(f) *Family attribution.*—[Reserved]

(g) *Definitions.*—The terms and nomenclature used in this section, and not otherwise defined herein, have the same meaning as in section 382 and the regulations thereunder.

(h) *Effective date.*—(1) *In general.*—[Reserved]

(2) *Option attribution rules.*—(i) *General rule.*—The rules of paragraph (d) of this section apply, instead of the rules of § 1.382-2T(h)(4), on any testing date on or after November 5, 1992. See paragraph (h)(2)(vi) of this section for an election relating to the effective date.

(ii) *Special rule for control test.*—An option issued on or before March 17, 1994, or an option issued within 60 days after that date pursuant to a plan existing before that date, is not treated as exercised under the control test provided in paragraph (d)(4) of this section on any testing date prior to a transfer of the option after March 17, 1994, that would itself cause the option to satisfy the control test.

(iii) *Convertible stock issued prior to July 20, 1988.*—(A) *In general.*—Except as provided in paragraph (h)(2)(iii)(B) of this section, convertible stock issued prior to July 20, 1988, is not treated as an option subject to the rules of § 1.382-2T(h)(4) or paragraph (d)(2) of this section.

(B) *Exceptions.*—(1) *Nonvoting convertible preferred stock.*—Convertible stock issued prior to July 20, 1988, is treated as an option subject to the rules of § 1.382-2T(h)(4) or paragraph (d)(2) of this section if—

(i) The stock, when issued, would be described in section 1504(a)(4) by disregarding subparagraph (D) thereof and by ignoring the potential participation in corporate growth that the conversion feature may offer; and

(ii) The loss corporation makes the election described in Notice 88-67, 1988-1 C.B. 555 (see § 601.601(d)(2)(ii)(b) of this chapter for availability of Cumulative Bulletins (C.B.)), on or before the earlier of the date prescribed in Notice 88-67 or December 7, 1992.

(2) *Other convertible stock.*—Convertible stock issued prior to July 20, 1988, is treated as an option subject to the rules of § 1.382-2T(h)(4) or paragraph (d)(2) of this section if—

(i) The terms of the conversion feature permit or require the tender of consideration other than the stock being converted; and

(ii) The loss corporation makes the election described in Notice 88-67 on or before the date prescribed in the Notice.

(iv) *Convertible stock issued on or after July 20, 1988, and before November 5, 1992.*—Convertible stock issued on or after July 20, 1988, and before November 5, 1992, is treated as an option subject to the rules of § 1.382-2T(h)(4) or paragraph (d) of this section only if—

(A) The stock, when issued, would be described in section 1504(a)(4) by disregarding subparagraph (D) thereof and by ignoring the potential participation in corporate growth that the conversion feature may offer; or

(B) The terms of the conversion feature permit or require the tender of consideration other than the stock being converted.

(v) *Certain options in existence immediately before and after an ownership change.*—If an option existed immediately before and after an ownership change occurring on a testing date to which § 1.382-2T(h)(4) applies—

(A) The option is not treated as exercised under paragraph (d)(2) of this section on any testing date after the change date and prior to a transfer of the option that would itself cause the option to satisfy the ownership test of paragraph (d)(3) of this section, the control test of paragraph (d)(4) of this section, or the income test of paragraph (d)(5) of this section; and

(B) Except as provided in § 1.382-2T(m)(4)(vi) (which relates to the effective date of the rules provided in § 1.382-2T(h)(4) and includes a special rule related to options that are actually exercised within 120 days after they are treated as exercised under that section), the actual exercise of the option, if by the person who owned the option immediately after the ownership change (or by a transferee of the option who acquired the option, directly or indirectly, from that person in one or more transfers described in paragraph (d)(11) of this section), will not contribute to an ownership change on any testing date on or after the date of exercise.

(vi) *Election to apply § 1.382-2T(h)(4).*—(A) *In general.*—If a loss corporation makes an election under this paragraph (h)(2)(vi), §§ 1.382-2T(a)(2)(i) and (h)(4) (relating to testing dates and option attribution) apply (instead of the definition of testing date in § 1.382-2(a)(4) and paragraph (d) of this section) for the purpose of determining whether an ownership change occurs—

(1) On any testing date on or before May 17, 1994; or

(2) In the case of a loss corporation that is under the jurisdiction of a court in a title 11 or similar case filed on or before May 17, 1994, subject to § 1.382-9(o)(1), on any testing date at or before the time the plan of reorganization becomes effective.

(B) *Additional consequences of election.*—If a loss corporation makes an election under this paragraph (h)(2)(vi)—

(1) In determining whether any convertible preferred stock issued by the loss corporation during the period that the election is in effect is treated as stock or as an option, the convertible preferred stock is treated as if it were issued on November 4, 1992, and

(2) The special effective date for the control test provided in paragraph (h)(2)(ii) of this section does not apply to any option with respect to stock of the loss corporation.

(C) *Time and manner of making the election.*—The election described in paragraph (h)(2)(vi)(A) of this section is made by attaching a statement to the loss corporation's income tax return for the first taxable year ending after November 4, 1992, in which a testing date (within the meaning of § 1.382-2T(a)(2)(i)) occurs, or if such return is filed on or before May 17, 1994, with its first return filed after May 17, 1994. However, a loss corporation that is under the jurisdiction of a court in a title 11 or similar case filed on or before May 17, 1994, may make the election described in paragraph (h)(2)(vi)(A) by attaching a statement to its tax return for its first taxable year ending after that date. The statement must say "THIS IS AN ELECTION UNDER § 1.382-4(h)(2)(vi) TO APPLY § 1.382-2T(h)(4) ON OR AFTER NOVEMBER 5, 1992." Any amended returns required by paragraph (h)(2)(vi)(D) of this section must accompany the return with which the election is made. An election under paragraph (h)(2)(vi)(A) of this section is irrevocable.

(D) *Amended returns.*—If an election under this paragraph (h)(2)(vi) affects the amount of taxable income or loss for a prior taxable year, the loss corporation (or the common parent of any consolidated group of which the loss corporation was a member for the year) must file an amended return for the year that reflects the effect of the election.

(3) *Special rule for options subject to attribution under § 1.382-2T(h)(4).*—Section § 1.382-2T(h)(4)(i) does not apply to any option designated by the Internal Revenue Service in the Internal Revenue Bulletin as being excepted from the operation of § 1.382-2T(h)(4)(i). [Reg. § 1.382-4.]

☐ [T.D. 8440, 10-2-92. *Amended by T.D. 8531, 3-17-94 and T.D. 8825,* 6-25-99.]

[Reg. §1.382-5]

§1.382-5. Section 382 limitation.—(a) *Scope.*—Following an ownership change, the section 382 limitation for any post-change year is an amount equal to the value of the loss corporation multiplied by the long-term tax-exempt rate that applies with respect to the ownership change, and adjusted as required by section 382 and the regulations thereunder. See, for example, section 382(b)(2) (relating to the carryforward of unused section 382 limitation), section 382(b)(3)(B) (relating to the section 382 limitation for the post-change year that includes the change date), section 382(m)(2) (relating to short taxable years), and section 382(h) (relating to recognized built-in gains and section 338 gains).

(b) *Computation of value.*—[Reserved]

(c) *Short taxable year.*—The section 382 limitation for any post-change year that is less than 365 days is the amount that bears the same ratio to the section 382 limitation determined under section 382(b)(1) as the number of days in the post-change year bears to 365. The section 382 limitation, as so determined, is adjusted as required by section 382 and the regulations thereunder. This paragraph (c) does not apply to a 52-53 week taxable year that is less than 365 days unless a return is required under section 443 (relating to short periods) for such year.

(d) *Successive ownership changes and absorption of a section 382 limitation.*—(1) *In general.*—If a loss corporation has two (or more) ownership changes, any losses or section 382 disallowed business interest carryforwards ((within the meaning of §1.382-2(a)(7)) attributable to the period preceding the earlier ownership change are treated as pre-change losses with respect to both ownership changes. Thus, the later ownership change may result in a lesser (but never in a greater) section 382 limitation with respect to such pre-change losses. In any case, the amount of taxable income for any post-change year that can be offset by pre-change losses may not exceed the section 382 limitation for such ownership change, reduced by the amount of taxable income offset by pre-change losses subject to any earlier ownership change(s).

(2) *Recognized built-in gains and losses.*—[Reserved]

(3) *Effective date.*—This paragraph (d) applies to taxable years of a loss corporation beginning on or after January 1, 1997.

(e) *Controlled groups.*—See §1.382-8 for rules for determining the value of a loss corporation that is a member of a controlled group.

(f) *Effective date.*—Except as otherwise provided, this section applies to a loss corporation that has an ownership change to which section 382(a), as amended by the Tax Reform Act of 1986, applies. Paragraph (d)(1) of this section applies with respect to an ownership change occurring on or after November 13, 2020. For loss corporations that have undergone an ownership change before or after November 13, 2020, see §1.382-5 as contained in 26 CFR part 1, revised April 1, 2019. However, taxpayers and their related parties, within the meaning of sections 267(b) and 707(b)(1), may choose to apply the rules of this section to testing dates occurring during a taxable year beginning after December 31, 2017, so long as the taxpayers and their related parties consistently apply the rules of this section, the section 163(j) regulations (as defined in §1.163(j)-1(b)(37)), §§1.382-1, 1.382-2, 1.382-6, 1.382-7, 1.383-0, 1.383-1, and, if applicable, §§1.263A-9, 1.263A-15, 1.381(c)(20)-1, 1.469-9, 1.469-11, 1.704-1, 1.882-5, 1.1362-3, 1.1368-1, 1.1377-1, 1.1502-13, 1.1502-21, 1.1502-36, 1.1502-79, 1.1502-91 through 1.1502-99 (to the extent they effectuate the rules of §§1.382-2, 1.382-5, 1.382-6, and 1.383-1), and 1.1504-4, to that taxable year. [Reg. §1.382-5.]

☐ [*T.D. 8679, 6-26-96. Redesignated and amended by T.D. 8825, 6-25-99. Amended by T.D. 9905, 9-3-2020.*]

[Reg. §1.382-6]

§1.382-6. Allocation of income and loss to periods before and after the change date for purposes of section 382.—(a) *General rule.*—(1) *In general.*—Except as provided in paragraphs (b) and (d) of this section, a loss corporation must allocate its net operating loss or *taxable income (see section 382(k)(4))*, and its net capital loss (see section 1222(10)) or modified capital gain net income (as defined in paragraph (g)(4) of this section), for the change year between the pre-change period and the post-change period by ratably allocating an equal portion to each day in the year.

(2) *Allocation of business interest expense.*—(i) *Scope.*—Except as provided in paragraph (b)(4) of this section, this paragraph (a)(2) applies if a loss corporation has business interest expense (as defined in §1.163(j)-1(b)(3)) in the change year. The rules of this paragraph (a)(2) apply to determine the amount of current-year business interest expense (as defined in §1.163(j)-1(b)(9)) that is deducted in the

change year. These rules also apply to determine the amount of any current-year business interest expense that is characterized as disallowed business interest expense (as defined in §1.163(j)-1(b)(10)) allocable to the pre-change period and the post-change period, and to allocate disallowed business interest expense carryforwards (as defined in §1.163(j)-1(b)(11)) to the change year for deduction in the pre-change period and the post-change period.

(ii) *Deductibility of business interest expense.*—The rules of this paragraph (a)(2)(ii) apply in the following order.

(A) First, the loss corporation calculates its section 163(j) limitation (as defined in §1.163(j)-1(b)(36)) for the change year.

(B) Second, the loss corporation calculates its deductible current-year BIE and deducts this amount in determining its taxable income or net operating loss for the change year. For purposes of this paragraph (a)(2)(ii), the term *deductible current-year BIE* means the loss corporation's current-year business interest expense (including its floor plan financing interest expense, as defined in §1.163(j)-1(b)(19)), to the extent of its section 163(j) limitation.

(C) Third, if the loss corporation has disallowed business interest expense paid or accrued (without regard to section 163(j)) in the change year that is carried forward to post-change years, it allocates an equal portion of that disallowed business interest expense to each day in the change year. Any amount of disallowed business interest expense that is allocated to the pre-change period pursuant to this paragraph (a)(2)(ii)(C) is carried forward subject to section 382(d)(3). Any amount of disallowed business interest expense that is allocated to the post-change period pursuant to this paragraph (a)(2)(ii)(C) is carried forward and is not subject to section 382(d)(3).

(D) Fourth, if the loss corporation has excess section 163(j) limitation, then the loss corporation calculates its deductible disallowed business interest expense carryforward and allocates an equal portion to each day in the change year. For purposes of this paragraph (a)(2)(ii), the term *excess section 163(j) limitation* means the excess, if any, of the loss corporation's section 163(j) limitation over its deductible current-year BIE, and the term *deductible disallowed business interest expense carryforward* means the loss corporation's disallowed business interest expense carryforward to the extent of its excess section 163(j) limitation.

(E) Fifth, the loss corporation deducts its deductible disallowed business interest expense carryforward that was allocated to the pre-change period under paragraph (a)(2)(ii)(D) of this section. Subject to the application of sections 382(b)(3)(B) and 382(d)(3), the loss corporation deducts its deductible disallowed business interest expense carryforward that was allocated to the post-change period under paragraph (a)(2)(ii)(D) of this section. Any amount of disallowed business interest expense carryforward that is not deducted pursuant to this paragraph (a)(2)(ii)(E) is carried forward subject to section 382(d)(3).

(b) *Closing-of-the-books election.*—(1) *In general.*—Subject to paragraphs (b)(3)(ii), (b)(4), and (d) of this section, a loss corporation may elect to allocate its net operating loss or taxable income and its net capital loss or modified capital gain net income for the change year between the pre-change period and the post-change period as if the loss corporation's books were closed on the change date. An election under this paragraph (b)(1) does not terminate the loss corporation's taxable year as of the change date (e.g., the change year is a single tax year for purposes of section 172).

(2) *Making the closing-of-the-books election.*—(i) *Time and manner.*—A loss corporation makes the closing-of-the-books election by including the following statement on the information statement required by §1.382-11(a) for the change year: "THE CLOSING-OF-THE-BOOKS ELECTION UNDER §1.382-6(b) IS HEREBY MADE WITH RESPECT TO THE OWNERSHIP CHANGE OCCURRING ON [INSERT DATE]." The election must be made on or before the due date (including extensions) of the loss corporation's income tax return for the change year.

(ii) *Election irrevocable.*—An election under this paragraph (b) is irrevocable.

(3) *Special rules relating to consolidated and controlled groups.*—(i) *Consolidated groups.*—If an election under this paragraph (b) is made with respect to an ownership change occurring in a consolidated return year, all allocations under this section with respect to that ownership change must be consistent with the election.

(ii) *Controlled groups.*—If paragraph (b)(3)(i) of this section does not apply, and if, as part of the same plan or arrangement, two or more members of a controlled group (as defined in section 1563(a), determined by substituting "50 percent" for "80 percent" each place that it appears, and without regard to section 1563(a)(4)), have ownership changes and continue to be members of the controlled group (or become members of the same other controlled group), a closing-of-the-books election applies only if the election is made by all members having the ownership changes.

(4) *Allocation of business interest expense.*—(i) *Scope.*—This paragraph (b)(4) applies if a loss corporation makes a closing-of-the-books election pursuant to paragraph (b) of this section and has business interest expense in the change year. The rules of this paragraph (b)(4) apply to determine the amount of deductible current-year business interest expense that is allocable to the pre-change period and the post-change period for purposes of the allocations referred to in paragraph (b)(1) of this section. These rules also apply to determine the amount of any current-year business interest expense that is characterized as disallowed business interest expense allocable to the pre-change period and the post-change period, and to allocate disallowed business interest expense carryforwards to the change year between the pre-change period and the post-change period for deduction.

(ii) *Deductibility of business interest expense.*—The rules of this paragraph (b)(4)(ii) apply in the order provided.

(A) The loss corporation calculates its ATI limit, which is the product of its ATI (as defined in § 1.163(j)-1(b)(1)) for the change year and 30 percent. For purposes of this paragraph (b)(4)(ii), the terms *pre-change ATI limit* and *post-change ATI limit* mean the amount of ATI limit allocated to the pre-change period or the post-change period, respectively, computed by allocating an equal portion of the ATI limit to each day in the change year.

(B) Pursuant to paragraph (b)(1) of this section, the loss corporation allocates its current-year business interest expense (including its floor plan financing interest expense) and its business interest income (as defined in § 1.163(j)-1(b)(4)) to the pre-change and post-change periods as if the loss corporation's books were closed on the change date. For purposes of this paragraph (b)(4)(ii), the terms *pre-change BIE* and *post-change BIE* mean the amount of the loss corporation's current-year business interest expense that is allocated to the pre-change period or the post-change period, respectively, under this paragraph (b)(4)(ii)(B).

(C) The loss corporation deducts its pre-change BIE to the extent of its pre-change section 163(j) limit, and the loss corporation deducts its post-change BIE to the extent of its post-change section 163(j) limit. For purposes of this paragraph (b)(4)(ii), the term *pre-change section 163(j) limit* means the sum of the pre-change ATI and the amount of business interest income and floor plan financing interest expense allocated to the pre-change period; the term *post-change section 163(j) limit* means the sum of the post-change ATI limit and the amount of business interest income and floor plan financing interest expense allocated to the post-change period.

(D) If any pre-change BIE or post-change BIE has not been deducted under paragraph (b)(4)(ii)(C) of this section, the loss corporation deducts either any pre-change BIE that has not been deducted to the extent of its surplus post-change section 163(j) limit or any post-change BIE that has not been deducted to the extent of its surplus pre-change section 163(j) limit. For purposes of this paragraph (b)(4)(ii), the term *surplus pre-change section 163(j) limit* means the amount by which the pre-change section 163(j) limit exceeds the amount of pre-change BIE deducted pursuant to paragraph (b)(4)(ii)(C) of this section; the term *surplus post-change section 163(j) limit* means the amount by which the post-change section 163(j) limit exceeds the amount of post-change BIE deducted pursuant to paragraph (b)(4)(ii)(C) of this section.

(E) If the loss corporation has any excess pre-change section 163(j) limit or excess post-change section 163(j) limit, the loss corporation allocates its disallowed business interest expense carryforward, if any, ratably between the pre-change and post-change periods based upon the relative amounts of excess pre-change section 163(j) limit and excess post-change section 163(j) limit. For purposes of this paragraph (b)(4)(ii), the term *excess pre-change section 163(j) limit* means the amount by which the surplus pre-change section 163(j) limit exceeds the amount of post-change BIE deducted pursuant to paragraph (b)(4)(ii)(D) of this section; the term *excess post-change section 163(j) limit* means the amount by which the surplus post-change section 163(j) limit exceeds the amount of pre-change BIE deducted pursuant to paragraph (b)(4)(ii)(D) of this section.

(F) The loss corporation deducts its disallowed business interest expense carryforward that was allocated to the pre-change period under paragraph (b)(4)(ii)(E) of this section to the extent of its excess pre-change section 163(j) limit. Subject to the application of sections 382(b)(3)(B) and 382(d)(3), the loss corporation deducts its disallowed business interest expense carryforward that was allocated to the post-change period under paragraph (b)(4)(ii)(E) of this section to the extent of its excess post-change section 163(j) limit. Any amount of disallowed business interest expense carryforward that is not deducted pursuant to this paragraph (b)(4)(ii)(F) is subject to section 382(d)(3) irrespective of the period to which it was allocated pursuant to paragraph (b)(4)(ii)(E) of this section.

(iii) *Example 1.*—(A) *Facts.* X is a calendar-year domestic C corporation that is not a member of a consolidated group. As of January 1, 2021, X has no disallowed business interest expense carryforwards. On October 19, 2021, X experiences an ownership change under section 382(g). For calendar year 2021, X's ATI is $500. For the period beginning on January 1, 2021 and ending on October 19, 2021, X pays or accrues $250 of current-year business interest expense that is deductible but for the potential application of section 163(j), including $50 of floor plan financing interest expense, and X has $60 of business interest income. For the period beginning on October 20, 2021 and ending on December 31, 2021, X pays or accrues $100 of current-year business interest expense that is deductible but for the potential application of section 163(j), including $40 of floor plan financing interest expense, and X has $70 of business interest income. X makes a closing-of-the-books election pursuant to paragraph (b) of this section.

(B) *Analysis*—(1) *Calculation and allocation of ATI limit.* For purposes of allocating its net operating loss or taxable income for the change year between the pre-change period and the post-change period under § 1.382-6, X applies paragraph (b)(4) of this section to allocate items related to section 163(j). X's ATI for calendar year 2021 is $500x. Therefore, pursuant to paragraph (b)(4)(ii)(A) of this section, X's ATI limit is $150 ($500 x 30 percent). Additionally, pursuant to paragraph (b)(4)(ii)(A) of this section, X's pre-change ATI limit is $120 ($150 x (292 days / 365 days)), and X's post-change ATI limit is $30 ($150 x (73 days / 365 days)).

(2) *Determination of pre-change BIE and post-change BIE.* Pursuant to paragraph (b)(4)(ii)(B) of this section, X's pre-change BIE and post-change BIE are $250 and $100, respectively.

(3) *Determination of pre-change section 163(j) limit and post-change section 163(j) limit.* Pursuant to paragraph (b)(4)(ii)(C) of this section, X's pre-change section 163(j) limit is $230 ($120 (X's pre-change ATI limit) + $60 (X's business interest income allocated to the pre-change period) + $50 (X's floor plan financing interest expense allocated to the pre-change period)). Additionally, pursuant to paragraph (b)(4)(ii)(C) of this section, X's post-change section 163(j) limit is $140 ($30 (X's post-change ATI limit) + $70 (X's business interest income allocated to the post-change period) + $40 (X's floor plan financing interest expense allocated to the post-change period)).

(4) *Initial deduction of BIE.* Pursuant to paragraph (b)(4)(ii)(C) of this section, X deducts $230 (its pre-change section 163(j) limit) of its $250 pre-change BIE and all $100 (less than its $140 post-change section 163(j) limit) of its post-change BIE.

(5) *Deduction of BIE due to surplus post-change section 163(j) limit.* After applying paragraph (b)(4)(ii)(C) of this section, X has $20 of pre-change BIE that has not been deducted ($250 - $230) and a surplus post-change section 163(j) limit of $40 ($140 - $100). As a result, pursuant to paragraph (b)(4)(ii)(D) of this section, X deducts its remaining $20 of pre-change BIE. (If, after applying paragraph (b)(4)(ii)(C) of this section, X instead had $20 of post-change BIE that had not yet been deducted and a $40 surplus pre-change section 163(j) limit, then X would deduct its remaining $20 of post-change BIE pursuant to paragraph (b)(4)(ii)(D) of this section.)

(iv) *Example 2—Potential deduction of disallowed business interest expense carryforwards.*—The facts are the same as in paragraph (b)(4)(iii)(A) of this section, except that, as of January 1, 2021, X has $90 of disallowed business interest expense carryforwards and $150 (rather than $250) of pre-change BIE. X's pre-change section 163(j) limit and post-change section 163(j) limit are the same as in paragraph (b)(4)(iii)(B)(3) of this section. Pursuant to paragraph (b)(4)(ii)(C) of this section, X deducts all $150 of its pre-change BIE and all $100 of its post-change BIE. X has no remaining pre-change BIE or post-change BIE to deduct under paragraph (b)(4)(ii)(D) of this section. Paragraph (b)(4)(ii)(E) of this section applies because X has $80 of excess pre-change section 163(j) limit ($230 - $150) and $40 of excess post-change section 163(j) limit ($140 - $100). Under paragraph (b)(4)(ii)(E) of this section, X allocates $60 of its disallowed business interest expense carryforwards to the pre-change period ($90 x ($80 / ($80 + $40))) and $30 of its disallowed business interest expense carryforwards to the post-change period ($90 x ($40 / ($80 + $40))). As provided in paragraph (b)(4)(ii)(F) of this section, X deducts all $60 of its disallowed business interest expense carryforwards that are allocated to the pre-change period; subject to the application of section 382, X deducts all $30 of its disallowed business interest expense carryforwards that are allocated to the post-change period.

(c) *Operating rules for determining net operating loss, taxable income, net capital loss, modified capital gain net income, and special allocations.*—For purposes of this section, for the change year—

(1) *In general.*—(i) Net operating loss or taxable income is determined without regard to gains or losses on the sale or exchange of capital assets; and

(ii) Net operating loss or taxable income and net capital loss or modified capital gain net income are determined without regard to the section 382 limitation and do not include the following items, which are allocated entirely to the post-change period—

(A) Any income, gain, loss, or deduction to which section 382(h)(5)(A) applies; and

(B) Any income or gain recognized on the disposition of assets transferred to the loss corporation during the post-change period for a principal purpose of ameliorating the section 382 limitation.

(2) *Adjustment to net operating loss.*—(i) *Determination of remaining capital gain.*—The amount of modified capital gain net income (defined in paragraph (g)(4) of this section) allocated to each period is offset by capital losses to which section 382(h)(5)(A) applies and capital loss carryovers, subject to the section 382 limitation (in the case of modified capital gain net income allocated to the post-change period).

(ii) *Reduction of net operating loss by remaining capital gain.*—The amount of net operating loss allocated to each period is reduced (but not below zero) without regard to the section 382 limitation, first by the modified capital gain net income remaining in the same period, and then by the modified capital gain net income remaining in the other period.

(d) *Coordination with rules relating to the allocation of income under § 1.1502-76(b).*—If § 1.1502-76 applies (relating to the taxable year of members of a consolidated group), an allocation of items under paragraph (a) or (b) of this section is determined after applying § 1.1502-76. Thus, if a short taxable year under § 1.1502-76 is a change year for which an allocation under this section is to be made, the allocation under this section applies only to the items allocated to that short taxable year under § 1.1502-76.

(e) *Allocation of certain credits.*—The principles of this section apply for purposes of allocating, under section 383, excess foreign taxes under section 904(c), current year business credits under section 38, and the minimum tax credit under section 53. The loss corporation must use the same method of allocation (ratable allocation or closing-of-the-books) for purposes of sections 382 and 383.

(f) *Examples.*—The rules of this section are illustrated by the following examples:

Example 1. (i) Assume that the loss corporation, L, a calendar year taxpayer with a May 26, 1995, change date, determines a section 382 limitation under section 382(b)(1) of $100,000. Thus, for the change year, its section 382 limitation is $100,000 × (219/365) = $60,000. L makes the closing-of-the-books election under paragraph (b) of this section.

(ii) Assume that L has a $150,000 capital loss carryover (from its 1994 taxable year) and a $300,000 net operating loss carryover (from its 1994 taxable year) to the change year. L recognizes, in the pre-change period, $200,000 of ordinary loss, and, in the post-change period, $150,000 of capital gain and $100,000 of ordinary income. Assume that section 382(h) does not apply to the capital gain or the ordinary income.

(iii) L has a $100,000 net operating loss for the change year ($200,000 pre-change loss less $100,000 post-change income), as determined under paragraph (c)(1)(i) of this section. Because L has no current year capital losses, L's $150,000 capital gain recognized in the post-change period is its modified capital gain net income for the change year (as defined at paragraph (g)(4) of this section). L allocates $100,000 of net operating loss to the pre-change period and $150,000 of modified capital gain net income to the post-change period.

(iv) Under paragraph (c)(2)(i) of this section, L uses its capital loss carryover to offset its modified capital gain net income allocated to the post-change period, subject to its section 382 limitation. L's section 382 limitation is $60,000, so L uses $60,000 of its capital loss carryover to offset $60,000 of its $150,000 modified capital gain net income. L has absorbed its entire section 382 limitation for the change year and has $90,000 of modified capital gain net income remaining in the post-change period.

(v) Under paragraph (c)(2)(ii) of this section, L offsets its $100,000 net operating loss allocated to the pre-change period by the $90,000 of modified capital gain net income remaining in the post-change period, without regard to the section 382 limitation, thereby reducing its pre-change net operating loss to $10,000.

(vi) From its 1994 taxable year, L will carry over $90,000 of capital loss and $300,000 of net operating loss to its 1996 taxable year. From its 1995 taxable year, L will carry over $10,000 of net operating loss subject to the section 382 limitation to its 1996 taxable year.

Example 2. (i) Assume the facts of *Example 1,* except that L does not make the closing-of-the-books election under paragraph (b) of this section.

(ii) L ratably allocates its $100,000 net operating loss and its $150,000 of modified capital gain net income for the change year. $40,000 of net operating loss ($100,000 × (146/365)) and $60,000 of modified capital gain net income ($150,000 × (146/365)) are allocated to the pre-change period. $60,000 of net operating loss ($100,000 × (219/365)) and $90,000 of modified capital gain net income ($150,000 × (219/365)) are allocated to the post-change period.

(iii) Under paragraph (c)(2)(i) of this section, L uses its capital loss carryovers to offset modified capital gain net income. The capital loss carryovers offset the $60,000 modified capital gain net income allocated to the pre-change period without limitation. Subject to the section 382 limitation, the remaining $90,000 of capital loss carryovers offset the modified capital gain net income allocated to the post-change period. Accordingly, L uses $60,000 of its capital loss carryovers to offset $60,000 of its $90,000 modified capital gain net income allocated to the post-change period. L has absorbed its entire section 382 limitation for the change year.

(iv) Under paragraph (c)(2)(ii) of this section, L's $60,000 net operating loss allocated to the post-change period is offset by its remaining $30,000 of post-change modified capital gain net income, reducing its post-change net operating loss to $30,000.

(v) From its 1994 taxable year, L will carry over $30,000 of capital loss and $300,000 of net operating loss to its 1996 taxable year. From its 1995 taxable year, L will carry over $70,000 of net operating loss ($40,000 pre-change + $30,000 post-change) to its 1996 taxable year. The $40,000 pre-change portion of that carryover is subject to the section 382 limitation.

(g) *Definitions and nomenclature.*—The terms and nomenclature used in this section and not otherwise defined herein have the same meanings as in sections 382 and 383 and the regulations thereunder. For purposes of this section:

(1) *Change year.*—A loss corporation's taxable year that includes the change date is its *change year.*

(2) *Pre-change period.*—The *pre-change period* is the portion of the change year ending on the close of the change date.

(3) *Post-change period.*—The *post-change period* is the portion of the change year beginning with the day after the change date.

(4) *Modified capital gain net income.*—A loss corporation's *modified capital gain net income* is the excess of the gains from sales or exchanges of capital assets over the losses from such sales or exchanges for the change year, determined by excluding any short-term capital losses under section 1212.

(h) *Applicability date.*—(1) *In general.*—This section applies to ownership changes occurring on or after June 22, 1994.

(2) *Ownership changes.*—Paragraphs (a) and (b)(1) and (4) of this section apply with respect to an ownership change occurring during a taxable year beginning on or after November 13, 2020. For ownership changes occurring during a taxable year beginning before November 13, 2020, see § 1.382-6 as contained in 26 CFR part 1, revised April 1, 2019. However, taxpayers and their related parties, within the meaning of sections 267(b) and 707(b)(1), may choose to apply the rules of this section to testing dates occurring during a taxable year beginning after December 31, 2017, so long as the taxpayers and their related parties consistently apply the rules of this section, the section 163(j) regulations (as defined in § 1.163(j)-1(b)(37)), § § 1.382-1, 1.382-2, 1.382-5, 1.383-0, and 1.383-1, and, if applicable, § § 1.263A-9, 1.263A-15, 1.381(c)(20)-1, 1.469-9, 1.469-11, 1.704-1, 1.882-5, 1.1362-3, 1.1368-1, 1.1377-1, 1.1502-13, 1.1502-21, 1.1502-36, 1.1502-79, 1.1502-91 through 1.1502-99 (to the extent they effectuate the rules of § § 1.382-2, 1.382-5, 1.382-6, 1.382-7, and 1.383-1), and 1.1504-4, to taxable years beginning after December 31, 2017. [Reg. § 1.382-6.]

☐ [T.D. 8440, 10-2-92. *Amended by T.D.* 8546, 6-21-94; *T.D.* 9264, 5-26-2006, *T.D.* 9329, 6-13-2007 *and T.D.* 9905, 9-3-2020.]

[Reg. § 1.382-7]

§ 1.382-7. Built-in gains and losses.—(a) *Treatment of prepaid income.*—For purposes of section 382(h), prepaid income is not recognized built-in gain. The term *prepaid income* means any amount received prior to the change date that is attributable to performance occurring on or after the change date. Examples to which this paragraph (a) will apply include, but are not limited to, income received prior to the change date that is deferred under section 455 or Rev. Proc. 2004-34 (2004-1 CB 991 (June 1, 2004)) (or any successor revenue procedure) (see § 601.601(d)(2)(ii)(b)).

(b) *Effective/applicability dates.*—This section applies to loss corporations that have undergone an ownership change on or after June 11, 2010. For loss corporations that have undergone an ownership change before June 11, 2010, see § 1.382-7T as contained in 26 CFR part 1, revised April 1, 2009. [Reg. § 1.382-7.]

(c) [Reserved]

(d) *Effective/applicability dates.*—This paragraph (d) contains special rules regarding the identification of recognized built-in losses.

(1)-(4) [Reserved]

(5) *Section 382 disallowed business interest carryforwards.*—Section 382 disallowed business interest carryforwards are not treated as recognized built-in losses.

(e)-(f) [Reserved]

(g) *Applicability dates.*—(1)-(3) [Reserved]

(4) *Paragraph (d)(5) of this section.*—Paragraph (d)(5) of this section applies with respect to an ownership change occurring on or after November 13, 2020. For loss corporations that have undergone an ownership change before or after November 13, 2020, see §1.382-7 as contained in 26 CFR part 1, revised April 1, 2019. However, taxpayers and their related parties, within the meaning of sections 267(b) and 707(b)(1), may choose to apply the rules of paragraph (d)(5) of this section to testing dates occurring during a taxable year beginning after December 31, 2017. [Reg. §1.382-7.]

☐ [T.D. 9487, 6-11-2010. *Amended by* T.D. 9870, 7-11-2019 *and* T.D. 9905, 9-3-2020.]

[Reg. §1.382-8]

§1.382-8. Controlled groups.—(a) *Introduction.*—This section provides rules to adjust the value of a loss corporation that is a member of a controlled group of corporations on a change date so that the same value is not included more than once in computing the limitations under section 382 for the loss corporations that are members of the controlled group. In general, the adjustment is made under paragraph (c) of this section by reducing the value of the loss corporation by the value of the stock of each component member of the controlled group that the loss corporation owns immediately after the ownership change. The loss corporation's value may, however, be increased under paragraph (c) of this section by any amount of value that the other member elects to restore to the loss corporation.

(b) *Controlled group loss and controlled group with respect to a controlled group loss.*—(1) *In general.*—A controlled group loss is a pre-change loss (or a net unrealized built-in loss) of a loss corporation that is attributable to a taxable year of the corporation with respect to which the corporation is a component member of a controlled group (as defined by paragraphs (e)(2) and (3) of this section). The controlled group with respect to each controlled group loss is composed of the loss corporation and each other corporation that is a component member of a controlled group that includes the loss corporation both—

(i) With respect to the taxable year to which the controlled group loss is attributable; and

(ii) On the date the loss corporation has an ownership change.

(2) *Presumption regarding net unrealized built-in loss.*—For purposes of determining whether a net unrealized built-in loss of a loss corporation is attributable to a taxable year (the determination year) with respect to which the corporation is a component member of a controlled group, the built-in loss in a prior change date asset is deemed to be attributable to a period ending before the determination year. A prior change date asset is any asset held by the loss corporation at all times during the period beginning on the change date of its most recent ownership change after 1986 (the first change date), and ending on the first day of the determination year. The built-in loss in a prior change date asset is the amount by which the adjusted basis of the asset on the first change date exceeds the fair market value of the asset on that date. The principles of this paragraph (b)(2) also apply to items described in section 382(h)(6)(B).

(c) *Computation of value.*—For purposes of computing the limitation under section 382 with respect to each controlled group loss, the value of the stock of each component member of the controlled group with respect to that loss is determined immediately before the ownership change, and is adjusted by applying the following rules:

(1) *Reduction in value.*—The value of the stock of each component member is reduced by the value (immediately before the ownership change and without regard to any restoration of value or other adjustment under this section) of the stock of any other component member directly owned by the component member immediately after the ownership change.

(2) *Restoration of value.*—After the value of the stock of each component member is reduced pursuant to paragraph (c)(1) of this section, the value of the stock of each component member is increased by the amount of value, if any, restored to the component

member by another component member (the electing member) pursuant to this paragraph (c)(2). The electing member may elect (or may be deemed to elect under paragraph (h)(2)(i) of this section in the case of a foreign component member) to restore value to another component member in an amount that does not exceed the lesser of—

(i) The sum of—

(A) The value, determined immediately before the ownership change, of the electing member's stock (after adjustment under paragraph (c)(1) of this section and before any restoration of value under this paragraph (c)(2)); plus

(B) Any amount of value restored to the electing member by another component member under this paragraph (c)(2); or

(ii) The value, determined immediately before any ownership change, of the electing member's stock (without regard to any adjustment under this section) that is directly owned by the other component member immediately after the ownership change.

(3) *Reduction in value by the amount restored.*—The value of the stock of the electing member is reduced by any amount of value that the electing member elects to restore under paragraph (c)(2) of this section to another component member.

(4) *Appropriate adjustments.*—Appropriate additional adjustments consistent with paragraphs (c)(1), (2), and (3) of this section must be made to prevent any duplication of value. Thus, for example, adjustments must be made to reflect—

(i) Any indirect ownership interest in another component member;

(ii) Any cross ownership of stock by component members of the controlled group with respect to the controlled group loss; and

(iii) Any value used to determine a limitation under section 382 with respect to controlled group losses from the same period.

(5) *Certain reductions in the value of members of a controlled group.*—A loss corporation that has an ownership change is required to make adjustments consistent with this paragraph (c) with respect to its stock if the stock of another corporation in which it had a direct or indirect ownership interest was disposed of before the ownership change, and;

(i) Both corporations were component members of a controlled group—

(A) With respect to a taxable year to which a controlled group loss of the loss corporation is attributable; and

(B) At any time during the 2 year period before the ownership change; and

(ii) Both corporations are component members of a controlled group at any time during the 2 year period following the ownership change.

(d) *No double reduction.*—To the extent consistent with the purposes of this section, section 382 and this section shall not be applied to duplicate a reduction in the value of a loss corporation. Thus, for example, if the value of a loss corporation is reduced under section 382(l)(1) to reflect a capital contribution of stock of a component member, it is not again reduced by such amount under paragraph (c)(1) of this section. If this paragraph (d) applies to prevent a reduction in value from being duplicated, the application of the other rules of this section, such as those relating to the restoration of value, is correspondingly limited in a manner consistent with the principles of this section.

(e) *Definitions and nomenclature.*—(1) *Definitions in section 382 and the regulations thereunder.*—Except as otherwise provided, the definitions and nomenclature contained in section 382 and the regulations thereunder apply to this section.

(2) *Controlled group.*—Controlled group has the same meaning as in section 1563(a), determined by substituting "50 percent" for "80 percent" each place that it appears, and without regard to section 1563(a)(4).

(3) *Component member.*—Component member has the same meaning as in section 1563(b), determined by substituting "December 31 (or the change date, if earlier)" for "December 31" each place it appears, and without regard to section 1563(b)(2), (b)(3)(C), and (b)(4).

(4) *Foreign component member.*—(i) *In general.*—Except as provided in paragraph (e)(4)(ii) of this section, foreign component member means a component member that is a foreign corporation.

(ii) *Exception.*—A foreign component member shall not include a foreign corporation that has items treated as connected with the conduct of a trade or business in the United States that it takes into account in determining its value pursuant to section 382(e)(3).

(5) *Predecessor and successor corporation.*—As the context may require, a reference to a corporation, or component member includes a reference to a predecessor or successor corporation.

(f) *Coordination between consolidated groups and controlled groups.*—Some or all of the component members of a controlled group may also be members of a consolidated group, and a controlled group loss may be subject to a consolidated section 382 limitation or subgroup section 382 limitation determined under §1.1502-93. Except as otherwise provided in this paragraph(f) and §§1.1502-91 through 1.1502-99, §1.1502-93 applies instead of this section when both sections, by their terms, are otherwise applicable. This section is applicable and may require an adjustment to value if a member of a consolidated group, a loss group, or loss subgroup (as those terms are defined in §§1.1502-1(h) and 1.1502-91) is also a component member of a controlled group with respect to a controlled group loss. Solely for purposes of applying this section, a consolidated group, loss group, or loss subgroup is treated as a single corporation. Thus to determine the limitation with respect to any portion of the pre-change consolidated attributes or pre-change subgroup attributes of the loss group or loss subgroup that is a controlled group loss, the consolidated section 382 limitation or subgroup section 382 limitation is computed by treating the loss group or the loss subgroup as a single corporation, and adjusting value in accordance with paragraph (c) of this section. See paragraph (g) *Example 4* of this section.

(g) *Examples.*—For purposes of the examples in this section, unless otherwise stated, the nomenclature and assumptions of the examples in §1.382-2T(b) apply, all corporations file separate income tax returns on a calendar year basis, the only 5-percent shareholder of a corporation is a public group, and the facts set forth the only owner shifts with respect to the corporations during the testing period.

Example 1. Controlled group with respect to a controlled group loss. (a) Public L owns all of the L stock, L and Public L1 own 30 percent and 70 percent, respectively, of the L1 stock, and L1 owns all of the corporation T stock. L1 has a net operating loss arising in Year 1 that is carried over to Year 4. L has a net operating loss arising in Year 2 that is carried over to Year 4. On August 1, Year 3, L acquires 30 percent of the stock of L1, thereby increasing its percentage ownership interest in L1 to 60 percent. On December 1, Year 3, L1 purchases all of the stock of corporation S from Public S. On November 1, Year 4, P acquires all of the L stock. The acquisition by P of all of the L stock on November 1, Year 4, causes ownership changes of both L and L1 under the rules of §1.382-2T. The following is a graphic illustration of these facts.

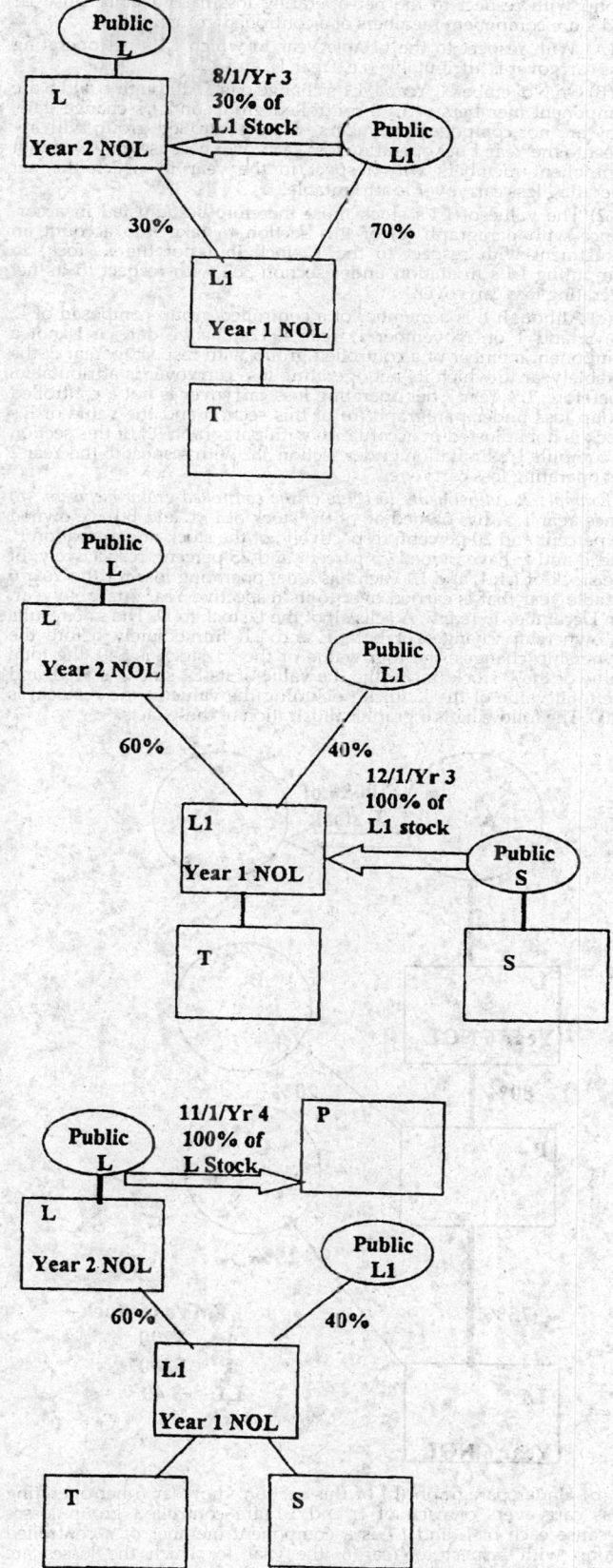

(b)(1) Under paragraph (b) of this section, the Year 1 net operating loss carryover of L1 is a controlled group loss because L1 is a component member of a controlled group with respect to Year 1, the year to which the loss is attributable L1 and T compose a controlled group with respect to the net operating loss carryover because L1 and T are component members of a controlled group both—

(A) With respect to the taxable year to which L1's net operating loss carryover is attributable (i.e., Year 1); and

(B) On November 1, Year 4, L1's change date. Although L and S are component members of L1's controlled group on L1's change date, they are not component members of the controlled group with respect to the Year 1 net operating loss carryover because they were not component members with respect to the year to which the net operating loss carryover is attributable.

(2) The value of L1's stock must therefore be adjusted in accordance with paragraph (c) of this section to take into account an adjustment with respect to the T stock (but not the S stock) in computing L1's limitation under section 382 with respect to its net operating loss carryover.

(c) Although L is a member of a controlled group composed of L, L1, S, and T on November 1, Year 4, L's change date, it is not a component member of a controlled group with respect to Year 2, the taxable year to which its net operating loss carryover is attributable. Therefore, L's Year 2 net operating loss carryover is not a controlled group loss under paragraph (b) of this section and the value of L's stock is not adjusted in accordance with paragraph (c) of this section to compute L's limitation under section 382 with respect to the Year 2 net operating loss carryover.

Example 2. Adjustments to value of the controlled group members. (a) Since Year 1, A has owned all of the stock of L, L and B have owned 80 percent and 20 percent, respectively, of the stock of corporation P, and P and C have owned 75 percent and 25 percent, respectively, of the stock of L1. L and L1 each has a net operating loss for the Year 6 taxable year that is carried over to its respective Year 7 taxable year. On December 1, Year 7, A sells all of the L stock to D. The sale results in ownership changes of both L and L1. Immediately before the ownership changes, the total value of the L1 stock is $40, the total value of the P stock (including the value of its L1 stock) is $100, and the total value of the L stock (including the value of the P stock) is $200. The following is a graphic illustration of these facts.

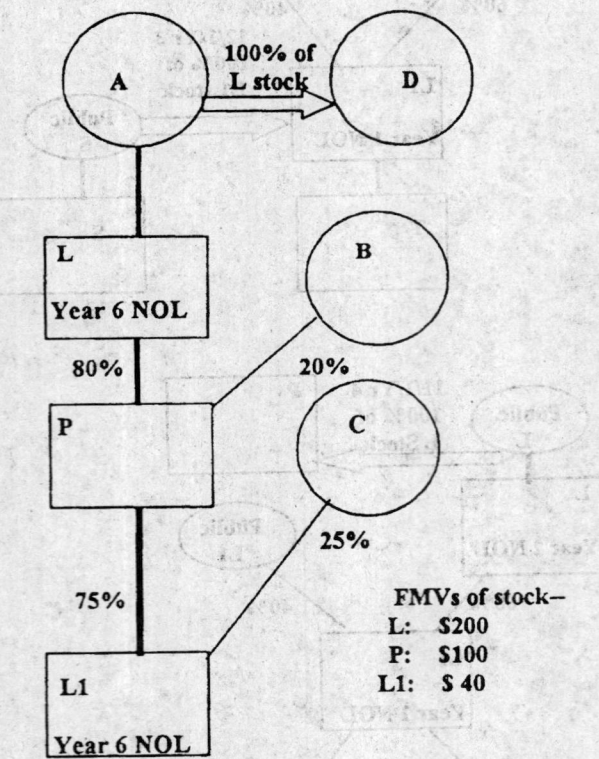

(b) Under paragraph (b) of this section, the Year 6 net operating loss carryovers of each of L and L1 are controlled group losses because each of L and L1 is a component member of a controlled group with respect to Year 6, the year to which the losses are attributable. L, P, and L1 compose controlled groups with respect to both Year 6 net operating loss carryovers because L, P, and L1 are component members of a controlled group both—

(1) With respect to the taxable years to which the net operating loss carryovers are attributable (i.e., Year 6); and

(2) On December 1, Year 7, the change date.

(c) The value of the stock of L1 for purposes of determining its limitation under section 382 with respect to its net operating loss carryover from Year 6 is $40. L1 does not elect to restore any value to P under paragraph (c)(2) of this section.

(d) The value of the stock of P ($100) is reduced under paragraph (c)(1) of this section by the value of the stock of L1 that it directly owns, $30 (75% × $40). Following the adjustment, the value of the stock of P is $70. P elects to restore this entire $70 of value to L.

(e) The value of the stock of L, $200, is reduced under paragraph (c)(1) of this section by the value of the stock of P it directly owns, i.e., $80 (80% × $100), and increased under paragraph (c)(2) of this section by the amount P elects to restore to L, i.e., $70. Thus, the value of the L stock for purposes of determining L's limitation under section 382 with respect to its net operating loss carryover from Year 6 is $190 ($200 – $80 + $70).

Example 3. Limitation on restoration of value. (a) The facts are the same as in *Example 2*, except that L1 elects to restore $20 to P. For purposes of determining L1's limitation under section 382 with respect to the Year 6 net operating loss carryover, the value of the stock of L1 is $20 ($40 – $20) because the value of its stock is reduced under paragraph (c)(3) of this section by the $20 of value it elects to restore to P.

(b) The value of the stock of P ($100) is reduced under paragraph (c)(1) of this section by the value of the L1 stock it directly owns ($30), and is increased under paragraph (c)(2) of this section by the value that L1 elects to restore to P ($20). Thus, the value of the P stock is $90 ($100 – $30 + $20).

(c)(1) P elects to restore to L the maximum value permitted under this section. The value of the stock of L, $200, is reduced under paragraph (c)(1) of this section by the value of the P stock it directly owns ($80), and is increased by the value that P elects to restore to L. P may elect to restore to L the lesser of—

(A) The sum of the value of its stock immediately after adjustment under paragraph (c)(1) of this section (i.e., $70) plus the value restored to it by L1 (i.e., $20) (a total of $90); or

(B) The value of the P stock (without regard to the adjustment required by paragraph (c)(1) and (2) of this section) that is directly owned by L immediately before the ownership change (i.e., $80).

(2) Thus, $80 is the maximum amount that P may elect to restore to L. Following the restoration of value by P, the value of the L stock for purposes of determining L's limitation under section 382 is $200 ($200 –$80 + $80).

Example 4. Coordination with consolidated return regulations. (a) P and its wholly owned subsidiary L file a consolidated return. L owns 79 percent of the outstanding stock of L1. P acquired the stock of L in Year 1 and L acquired the stock of L1 in Year 2. The P consolidated group has a consolidated net operating loss arising in the Year 6 consolidated return year that is carried over to Year 8. L1 has a net operating loss arising in its Year 6 taxable year that is also carried over to Year 8. On January 1, Year 8, the P consolidated group has an ownership change under §1.1502-92(b)(1)(i) and L1 has an ownership change under §1.382-2T.

(b)(1) Under paragraph (b) of this section, the Year 6 net operating loss carryover of the P group is a controlled group loss because P, L, and L1 are component members of a controlled group with respect to Year 6, the year to which the loss is attributable. P, L, and L1 compose a controlled group with respect to the Year 6 net operating loss carryover of the P loss group because they are component members of a controlled group both—

(A) With respect to the taxable years to which the net operating loss carryover is attributable (i.e., Year 6); and

(B) On January 1, Year 8, the P group's change date.

(2) Because P and L compose a loss group (within the meaning of §1.1502-91(c)) with respect to its Year 6 net operating loss carryover, the P loss group must compute a consolidated section 382 limitation with respect to its Year 6 net operating loss carryover as a result of the ownership change.

(c) In computing the consolidated section 382 limitation under §1.1502-93 with respect to the Year 6 net operating loss carryover, the value of the P stock immediately before the ownership change is reduced under paragraphs (c)(1) and (f) of this section by the value immediately before the ownership change of the L1 stock directly owned by L immediately after the ownership change. L1 may, however, elect to restore such value to the P consolidated group to the extent permitted under paragraph (c)(2) of this section.

Example 5. Appropriate adjustments for indirect ownership interest. (a) Individual A owns all of the stock of L, L owns an 80 percent interest in the capital and profits of partnership PS, and PS owns 75 percent of the stock of L1. Both L and L1 have net operating losses for the Year 1 taxable year that are carried over to their respective Year 2 taxable years. On December 19, Year 2, A sells all of the L stock to an unrelated individual. The sale results in an ownership change of L and L1.

(b) Under paragraph (b) of this section, the Year 1 net operating loss carryovers of each of L and L1 are controlled group losses because each of L and L1 is a component member of a controlled group with respect to Year 1, the year to which the losses are attributable. L and L1 compose controlled groups with respect to each corporation's net operating loss carryovers because L and L1 are component members of a controlled group both—

(1) With respect to the taxable years to which the net operating loss carryovers are attributable (i.e., Year 1); and

(2) On December 19, Year 2, the change date.

(c) L has an indirect ownership interest in L1 which, under paragraph (c)(4) of this section, must be taken into account in applying this section. As a result, the value of the L stock for purposes of determining its limitation under section 382 with respect to the Year 1 net operating loss carryover must be reduced by the value of L's indirect ownership interest in the L1 stock (60 percent) that it owns through PS immediately before the ownership change, and is increased by the amount (if any) that L1 elects to restore to L under paragraph (c)(2) of this section. The value of L1 is reduced under paragraph (c)(3) of this section to the extent that L1 elects to restore value to L.

(h) *Time and manner of filing election to restore.*—(1) Statements required—

(i) *Filing by loss corporation.*—The election to restore value described in paragraph (c)(2) of this section must be in the form set forth in this paragraph (h)(1)(i). It must be filed by the loss corporation by including a statement on or with its income tax return for the taxable year in which the ownership change occurs (or with an amended return for that year filed on or before the due date (including extensions) of the income tax return of any component member with respect to the taxable year in which the ownership change occurs). The common parent of a consolidated group must make the election on behalf of the group. The election is made in the form of a statement entitled, "STATEMENT PURSUANT TO § 1.382-8(h)(1) TO ELECT TO RESTORE ALL OR PART OF THE VALUE OF [INSERT NAME AND EMPLOYER IDENTIFICATION NUMBER (IF ANY) OF THE ELECTING MEMBER] TO [INSERT NAME AND EMPLOYER IDENTIFICATION NUMBER (IF ANY) OF THE CORPORATION TO WHICH VALUE IS RESTORED]." The statement must include the amount of the value being restored and must also indicate that an agreement signed and dated by both parties, as described in paragraph (h)(1)(iii) of this section, has been entered into. Each such party must retain either the original or a copy of this agreement as part of its records. See § 1.6001-1(e).

(ii) *Filing by electing member.*—An electing member must include a statement identical to the one described in paragraph (h)(1)(i) of this section on or with its income tax return (or with an amended return for that year filed on or before the due date (including extensions) of the income tax return of any component member with respect to the taxable year which includes the change date in connection with which the election described in paragraph (c)(2) of this section is made. If the electing member is a controlled foreign corporation (within the meaning of section 957), each United States shareholder (within the meaning of section 951(b)) with respect thereto must include this statement on or with its return. It is not necessary for the electing member (or the United States shareholder, as the case may be) to include this statement on or with its return if the loss corporation includes an identical statement on or with the same return for the same election.

(iii) *Agreement.*—Both the electing member and the corporation to which value is restored must sign and date an agreement. The agreement must—

(A) Identify the change date for the loss corporation in connection with which the election is made;

(B) State the value of the electing member's stock (without regard to any adjustment under paragraph (c) of this section) immediately before the ownership change;

(C) State the amount of any reduction required under paragraph (c)(1) of this section with respect to stock of the electing member that is owned directly or indirectly by the corporation to which value is restored;

(D) State the amount of value that the electing member elects to restore to the corporation; and

(E) State whether the value of either component member's stock was adjusted pursuant to paragraph (c)(4) of this section.

(2) *Special rule for foreign component members.*—(i) *Deemed election to restore full value.*—Unless the election described in paragraph (h)(2)(ii) of this section is made for a foreign component member, each foreign component member of the controlled group is deemed to have elected to restore to each other component member the

maximum value allowable under paragraph (c)(2) of this section, taking into account the limitations of this section.

(ii) *Election not to restore full value.*—(A) A loss corporation may elect to reduce the amount of value restored from a foreign component member (the electing foreign component member) to another component member under paragraph (h)(2)(i) of this section in the form set forth in this paragraph (h)(2)(ii). It must be filed by the loss corporation by including a statement on or with its income tax return for the taxable year in which the ownership change occurs (or with an amended return for that year filed on or before the due date (including extensions) of the income tax return of any component member with respect to the taxable year in which the ownership change occurs). The common parent of a consolidated group must make the election on behalf of the group. The election is made in the form of a statement entitled, "STATEMENT PURSUANT TO § 1.382-8(h)(2)(ii) TO ELECT NOT TO RESTORE FULL VALUE OF [INSERT NAME AND EMPLOYER IDENTIFICATION NUMBER (IF ANY) OF ELECTING FOREIGN COMPONENT MEMBER] TO [INSERT NAME AND EMPLOYER IDENTIFICATION NUMBER (IF ANY) OF THE CORPORATION TO WHICH SUCH VALUE IS NOT TO BE RESTORED]." The statement must include the amount of the value not being restored and must also indicate that an agreement signed and dated by both parties, as described in paragraph (h)(2)(iii) of this section, has been entered into. Each such party must retain either the original or a copy of the agreement as part of its records. See § 1.6001-1(e).

(B) An electing foreign component member must include a statement identical to the one described in paragraph (h)(2)(ii)(A) of this section on or with its income tax return (or with an amended return for that year filed on or before the due date (including extensions) of the income tax return of any component member with respect to the taxable year in which the ownership change occurs) (if any) for the taxable year which includes the change date in connection with which the election described in paragraph (h)(2)(ii)(A) of this section is made. If the electing foreign component member is a controlled foreign corporation (within the meaning of section 957), each United States shareholder (within the meaning of section 951(b)) with respect thereto must include this statement on or with its return. It is not necessary for the electing foreign component member (or United States shareholder, as the case may be) to include this statement on or with its return if the loss corporation includes an identical statement on or with the same return for the same election.

(iii) *Agreement.*—Both the electing foreign component member and the corporation to which full value is not restored must sign and date an agreement. The agreement must—

(A) Identify the change date for the loss corporation in connection with which the election is made;

(B) State the value of the electing foreign component member's stock (without regard to any adjustment under paragraph (c) of this section) immediately before the ownership change;

(C) State the amount of any reduction required under paragraph (c)(1) of this section with respect to stock of the electing foreign component member that is owned directly or indirectly by the corporation to which value is not restored;

(D) State the amount of value that the electing foreign component member elects not to restore to the corporation; and

(E) State whether the value of either component member's stock was adjusted pursuant to paragraph (c)(4) of this section.

(3) *Revocation of election.*—An election (other than the deemed election described in paragraph (h)(2)(i) of this section) made under this section is revocable only with the consent of the Commissioner.

(i) *References to former temporary regulations.*—As the context requires, a reference in this section to § 1.382-8 includes a reference to § 1.382-8T in effect prior to June 25, 1999, as contained in 26 CFR part I revised as of April 1, 1999, a reference to §§ 1.1502-91, 1.1502-92, 1.1502-93, and §§ 1.1502-91 through 1.1502-99 includes a references to §§ 1.1502-91A, 1.1502-92A, 1.1502-93A and §§ 1.1502-91A through 1.1502-99A.

(j) *Effective date.*—(1) *In general.*—This section applies to a loss corporation that has an ownership change with respect to a controlled group loss on or after January 1, 1997.

(2) *Transition rule.*—(i) *In general.*—The members of a controlled group on January 1, 1997, that have had an ownership change with respect to a controlled group loss before January 1, 1997, must determine the limitations under section 382 for any post-change year with respect to controlled group losses by using a reasonable method to preclude the value of stock of a component member that was owned directly or indirectly by another member immediately after an ownership change from being taken into account more than once in determining the limitations under section 382 with respect to controlled group losses. If such a reasonable method was not used for

Reg. § 1.382-8(j)(2)(i)

a post-change year, subject to the exception in paragraph (j)(3) of this section, the members of the controlled group described in the preceding sentence must reduce their limitations under section 382 for post-change years for which the income tax return is filed after January 1, 1997, to recapture, as quickly as possible, any limitation that members took into account in excess of the amount that would be allowable under this section.

(ii) *Special transition rule for controlled groups that had ownership changes before January 29, 1991.*—For purposes of this section, in the case of an ownership change occurring before January 29, 1991, the controlled group with respect to a controlled group loss does not include a corporation that is not a component member of the controlled group on January 29, 1991. Thus, in the case of an ownership change occurring before January 29, 1991, paragraph (c) of this section does not require that a loss corporation that is a component member of a controlled group to disregard the value of stock of another corporation directly owned immediately after the ownership change in determining the value of its own stock unless the other corporation is a component member of the controlled group on January 29, 1991.

(3) *Amended returns.*—A taxpayer that has had an ownership change before January 1, 1997, may file an amended return for any taxable year to modify the amount of a limitation under section 382 with respect to a controlled group loss only if—

(i) The modification complies with the rules contained in this section for computing a limitation under section 382;

(ii) Any other component member of the controlled group with respect to the controlled group loss who elects to restore value and whose taxable income is affected by the election to restore value also files amended returns that comply with such rules; and

(iii) Corresponding adjustments are made in amended returns for all taxable years ending after December 31, 1986.

(4) *Effective/applicability date.*—Paragraphs (c)(2), (e)(4) and (h) of this section apply to any taxable year beginning on or after May 30, 2006. However, taxpayers may apply paragraphs (c)(2), (e)(4) and (h) of this section to any original Federal income tax return (including any amended return filed on or before the due date (including extensions) of such original return) timely filed on or after May 30, 2006. For taxable years beginning before May 30, 2006, see § 1.382-8 as contained in 26 CFR part 1 in effect on April 1, 2006. [Reg. § 1.382-8.]

☐ [T.D. 8679, 6-26-96. *Redesignated and amended by T.D. 8825,* 6-25-99. *Amended by T.D. 9264, 5-26-2006 and T.D. 9329, 6-13-2007.*]

[Reg. § 1.382-9]

§ 1.382-9. Special rules under section 382 for corporations under the jurisdiction of a court in a title 11 or similar case.— (a) *Introduction.*—Either section 382(l)(5) or section 382(l)(6) may apply to an ownership change which occurs in a title 11 or similar case (as defined in section 368(a)(3)(A)) if the transaction resulting in the ownership change is ordered by the court or is pursuant to a plan approved by the court. Terms and nomenclature used in this section, and not otherwise defined herein (including the nomenclature and assumptions in § 1.382-2T(b) relating to the examples) have the same respective meanings as in section 382 and the regulations thereunder.

(b) *Application of section 382(l)(5).*—Section 382(a) does not apply to any ownership change if—

(1) The old loss corporation is (immediately before the ownership change) under the jurisdiction of the court in a title 11 or similar case; and

(2) The pre-change shareholders and qualified creditors of the old loss corporation (determined immediately before the ownership change) own (after the ownership change and as a result of being pre-change shareholders or qualified creditors immediately before the ownership change) stock of the new loss corporation (or stock of a controlling corporation if also in bankruptcy) that meets the requirements of section 1504(a)(2) (determined by substituting "50 percent" for "80 percent" each place it appears).

(c) [Reserved]

(d) *Rules for determining whether stock of the loss corporation is owned as a result of being a qualified creditor.*—(1) *Qualified creditor.*—A qualified creditor is the beneficial owner, immediately before the ownership change, of qualified indebtedness of the loss corporation. A qualified creditor owns stock of the new loss corporation (or a controlling corporation) as a result of being a qualified creditor only to the extent that the qualified creditor receives stock in full or partial satisfaction of qualified indebtedness (including interest accrued on such indebtedness) in a transaction that is ordered by the court or is pursuant to a plan approved by the court in a title 11 or similar case. For purposes of this paragraph (d)(1), ownership of stock after the

ownership change is determined without applying the attribution rules generally applicable under section 382(l)(3)(A) or § 1.382-2T(h).

(2) *General rules for determining whether indebtedness is qualified indebtedness.*—(i) *Definition.*—Indebtedness of the loss corporation is qualified indebtedness if it—

(A) Has been owned by the same beneficial owner since the date that is 18 months before the date of the filing of the title 11 or similar case; or

(B) Arose in the ordinary course of the trade or business of the loss corporation and has been owned at all times by the same beneficial owner.

(ii) *Determination of beneficial ownership.*—For purposes of paragraph (d)(2)(i) of this section, beneficial ownership of indebtedness is determined without applying attribution rules.

(iii) *Duty of inquiry.*—The loss corporation must determine that indebtedness that the loss corporation treats as qualified indebtedness, other than indebtedness to which paragraph (d)(3)(i) of this section applies, has been owned for the requisite period by the beneficial owner who owns the indebtedness immediately before the ownership change. The loss corporation may rely on a statement, signed under penalties of perjury, by a beneficial owner regarding the amount of indebtedness the beneficial owner owns and the length of time that the beneficial owner has owned the indebtedness.

(iv) *Ordinary course indebtedness.*—For purposes of this paragraph (d)(2), indebtedness arises in the ordinary course of the loss corporation's trade or business only if the indebtedness is incurred by the loss corporation in connection with the normal, usual, or customary conduct of business, determined without regard to whether the indebtedness funds ordinary or capital expenditures of the loss corporation. For example, indebtedness (other than indebtedness acquired for a principal purpose of being exchanged for stock) arises in the ordinary course of the loss corporation's trade or business if it is trade debt; a tax liability; a liability arising from a past or present employment relationship, a past or present business relationship with a supplier, customer, or competitor of the loss corporation, a tort, a breach of warranty, or a breach of statutory duty; or indebtedness incurred to pay an expense deductible under section 162 or included in the cost of goods sold. A claim that arises upon the rejection of a burdensome contract or lease pursuant to the title 11 or similar case is treated as arising in the ordinary course of the loss corporation's trade or business if the contract or lease so arose.

(3) *Treatment of certain indebtedness as continuously owned by the same owner.*—(i) *In general.*—For purposes of paragraph (d)(2) of this section, a loss corporation may treat indebtedness as always having been owned by the beneficial owner of the indebtedness immediately before the ownership change if the beneficial owner is not, immediately after the ownership change, either a 5-percent shareholder or an entity through which a 5-percent shareholder owns an indirect ownership interest in the loss corporation (a *5-percent entity*). This paragraph (d)(3)(i) does not apply to indebtedness beneficially owned by a person whose participation in formulating a plan of reorganization makes evident to the loss corporation (whether or not the loss corporation had previous knowledge) that the person has not owned the indebtedness for the requisite period.

(ii) *Operating rules.*—For purposes of paragraph (d)(3)(i) of this section:

(A) If a loss corporation has actual knowledge of a coordinated acquisition of its indebtedness by a group of persons, through a formal or informal understanding among themselves, for a principal purpose of exchanging the indebtedness for stock, the indebtedness (and any stock received in exchange therefor) is treated as owned by an entity. A principal element in determining if an understanding exists among members of a group is whether the investment decision of each member is based upon the investment decision of one or more other members.

(B) If the loss corporation has actual knowledge regarding stock ownership described in § 1.382-2T(k)(2), the loss corporation must take that ownership into account in determining which beneficial owners of indebtedness are, immediately after the ownership change, 5-percent shareholders or 5-percent entities. The loss corporation is not required to take into account an ownership interest described in § 1.382-2T(k)(4) unless the loss corporation has actual knowledge of the ownership interest.

(C) The term *5-percent shareholder* includes any person who is a 5-percent shareholder of the loss corporation within the meaning of § 1.382-2T(g), without regard to the option attribution rules of section 382(l)(3)(A) or § 1.382-4(d) (or, if applicable, § 1.382-2T(h)(4)).

(D) Paragraph (d)(3)(i) of this section does not apply to indebtedness if the loss corporation has actual knowledge immediately after the ownership change that the exercise of an option to acquire or dispose of stock of the loss corporation would cause the beneficial owner of the indebtedness immediately before the ownership change to be, after the ownership change, either a 5-percent shareholder or a 5-percent entity. An interest that is treated as an option under §1.382-4(d)(9) (or §1.382-2T(h)(4)(v) if applicable) is treated as an option for purposes of this paragraph (d)(3)(ii)(D).

(iii) *Indebtedness owned by beneficial owner who becomes a 5-percent shareholder or 5-percent entity.*—If the beneficial owner of indebtedness immediately before the ownership change is a 5-percent shareholder or 5-percent entity immediately after the ownership

A	
B	
C	
P1	
P2	
P3	
P4	
P5	

(2) P2 is owned by Public P2. B owns 10 percent of the stock of P1 and L has no actual knowledge of this ownership. L has actual knowledge that D owns P3, P4 and P5. In addition, L has actual knowledge, immediately after the ownership change, that C owns an option to acquire newly-issued stock of L that, if exercised, would increase C's percentage ownership of L stock from 2.5 percent to 8 percent. An ownership change of L occurs on the date the plan becomes effective.

(B) Under paragraph (d)(3)(i) of this section, L may treat the indebtedness owned by A and P1 immediately before the ownership change as always having been owned by A and P1. Neither A nor P1 is a 5-percent shareholder immediately after the ownership change. Further, because P1 owns less than 5 percent of the L stock (and L has no actual knowledge of B's ownership interest in P1), P1 is treated as an individual, and the L stock owned by P1 is not attributed to any other person, including B. See §1.382-2T(h)(2)(iii). Therefore, P1 is not a 5-percent entity.

(C) Paragraph (d)(3)(i) of this section does not apply to the indebtedness owned by B, C, P2, P3, P4, or P5. B is a 5-percent shareholder immediately after the ownership change. L has actual knowledge immediately after the ownership change that the exercise of C's option would cause C to be a 5-percent shareholder immediately after the ownership change. (L does not take into account the effect of the exercise of the option, however, in determining the percentage stock ownership of any person other than C because the deemed exercise would not cause any other person to be a 5-percent shareholder or a 5-percent entity after the ownership change.) P2 is a 5-percent entity, because Public P2, a 5-percent shareholder, owns an indirect ownership interest in L through P2. P3, P4, and P5 are 5-percent entities because D, a 5-percent shareholder, owns an indirect ownership interest in L through P3, P4, and P5. Because L has actual knowledge that D would be a 5-percent shareholder but for the application of §1.382-2T(h)(2)(iii), that section does not apply to P3, P4, or P5. See §1.382-2T(k)(2). Thus, under §1.382-2T(h)(2)(i), the L stock owned by P3, P4, and P5 is attributed to D, and D is a 5-percent shareholder. Because paragraph (d)(3)(i) of this section does not apply to the indebtedness owned by B, C, P2, P3, P4, and P5, L may treat as qualified indebtedness only indebtedness that it determines had been owned by such persons for the requisite period. See paragraph (d)(2)(iii) of this section.

(4) *Special rule if indebtedness is a large portion of creditor's assets.*—(i) *In general.*—Indebtedness is not qualified indebtedness if—

(A) The beneficial owner of the indebtedness is a corporation or other entity that had an ownership change on any day during the applicable period;

(B) The indebtedness represents more than 25 percent of the fair market value of the total gross assets (excluding cash or cash equivalents) of the beneficial owner on its change date; and

(C) The beneficial owner is a 5-percent entity immediately after the ownership change of the loss corporation (determined by applying the rules of paragraph (d)(3) of this section).

(ii) *Applicable period.*—For purposes of paragraph (d)(4)(i) of this section, the term *applicable period* means the period beginning on the day 18 months before the filing of the title 11 or similar case (or the day on which the beneficial owner acquired the indebtedness, if later) and ending with the change date of the loss corporation.

(iii) *Determination of ownership change.*—For purposes of paragraph (d)(4)(i) of this section, the determination whether a beneficial owner of indebtedness has an ownership change is made under the principles of section 382 and the regulations thereunder, without regard to whether the beneficial owner is a loss corporation and beginning the testing period no earlier than the latest of the day three years before the change date, the day 18 months before the filing of

change, the general rules of paragraph (d)(2) of this section apply to determine whether the indebtedness has been owned for the requisite period by the beneficial owner.

(iv) *Example.*—The following example illustrates paragraph (d)(3) of this section.

(A)(1) L is a loss corporation in a title 11 case. The plan of reorganization of L approved by the bankruptcy court provides for the satisfaction of claims by the issuance of new L common stock to its creditors as follows:

A	2.0 percent
B	7.5 percent
C	2.5 percent
P1	3.0 percent
P2	10.0 percent
P3	4.9 percent
P4	4.9 percent
P5	4.9 percent

the title 11 or similar case, or the day on which the beneficial owner acquired the indebtedness.

(iv) *Reliance on statement.*—Paragraph (d)(4)(i) of this section does not apply to indebtedness if the loss corporation obtains a statement, signed under penalties of perjury, by the beneficial owner of the indebtedness that states that paragraph (d)(4)(i) of this section does not apply to the indebtedness.

(5) *Tacking of ownership periods.*—(i) *Transferee treated as owning indebtedness for period owned by transferor.*—To determine whether indebtedness transferred in a qualified transfer is qualified indebtedness, the transferee is treated as having owned the indebtedness for the period that it was owned by the transferor.

(ii) *Qualified transfer.*—For purposes of paragraph (d)(5)(i) of this section, a transfer of indebtedness is a qualified transfer if—

(A) The transfer is between parties who bear a relationship to each other described in section 267(b) or 707(b) (substituting *at least 80 percent* for *more than 50 percent* each place it appears in section 267(b) (and section 267(f)(1)) or 707(b));

(B) The transfer is a transfer of a loan within 90 days after its origination, pursuant to a customary syndication transaction;

(C) The transfer is a transfer of newly incurred indebtedness by an underwriter that owned the indebtedness for a transitory period pursuant to an underwriting;

(D) The transferee's basis in the indebtedness is determined under section 1014, 1015, or 1022 or with reference to the transferor's basis in the indebtedness;

(E) The transfer is in satisfaction of a right to receive a pecuniary bequest;

(F) The transfer is pursuant to any divorce or separation instrument (within the meaning of section 71(b)(2));

(G) The transfer is pursuant to a subrogation in which the transferee acquires a claim against the loss corporation by reason of a payment to the claimant pursuant to an insurance policy or a guarantee, letter of credit or similar security arrangement; or

(H) The transfer is a transfer of an account receivable in a customary commercial factoring transaction made within 30 days after the account arose to a transferee that regularly engages in such transactions.

(iii) *Exception.*—A transfer of indebtedness is not a qualified transfer for purposes of paragraph (d)(5)(i) of this section if the transferee acquired the indebtedness for a principal purpose of benefiting from the losses of the loss corporation by—

(A) Exchanging the indebtedness for stock of the loss corporation pursuant to the title 11 or similar case; or

(B) Selling the indebtedness at a profit that reflects the expectation that, by reason of section 382(l)(5), section 382(a) will not apply to any ownership change resulting from the title 11 or similar case.

(iv) *Debt-for-debt exchanges.*—If the loss corporation satisfies its indebtedness with new indebtedness, either through an exchange of new indebtedness for old indebtedness or a change in the terms of indebtedness that results in an exchange under section 1001—

(A) The owner of the new indebtedness is treated as having owned that indebtedness for the period that it owned the old indebtedness; and

(B) The new indebtedness is treated as having arisen in the ordinary course of the trade or business of the loss corporation if the old indebtedness so arose.

(6) *Effective/applicability date.*—(i) *In general.*—This paragraph (d) applies to ownership changes occurring on or after March 17, 1994.

The provisions of paragraph (d)(5)(ii)(D) of this section relating to section 1022 are effective on and after January 19, 2017.

(ii) *Elections and amended returns.*—(A) *Election to apply this paragraph (d) retroactively.*—A loss corporation may elect to apply this paragraph (d) to an ownership change occurring prior to March 17, 1994. This election must be made by the later of the due date (including any extensions of time) of the loss corporation's tax return for the taxable year which includes the change date or the date that the loss corporation files its first tax return after March 17, 1994. The election is made by attaching the following statement to the return: "THIS IS AN ELECTION TO APPLY § 1.382-9(d) RETROACTIVELY WITH RESPECT TO THE OWNERSHIP CHANGE ON [INSERT DATE OF OWNERSHIP CHANGE] THAT OCCURRED IN CONNECTION WITH THE TITLE 11 OR SIMILAR CASE FILED ON [INSERT DATE OF FILING]." This statement must be accompanied by the amended returns described in paragraph (d)(6)(ii)(C) of this section. An election under this paragraph (d)(6) is irrevocable.

(B) *Election to revoke section 382(l)(5)(H) election.*—A loss corporation may elect to revoke a prior election made under section 382(l)(5)(H) with respect to an ownership change occurring before March 17, 1994, by including the following statement with its election to apply § 1.382-9(d) retroactively: "THIS IS AN ELECTION TO REVOKE A PRIOR ELECTION MADE UNDER SECTION 382(l)(5)(H) WITH RESPECT TO THE OWNERSHIP CHANGE ON [INSERT DATE OF OWNERSHIP CHANGE] THAT OCCURRED IN CONNECTION WITH THE TITLE 11 OR SIMILAR CASE FILED ON [INSERT DATE OF FILING]."

(C) *Amended returns.*—If the retroactive application of this paragraph (d) affects the amount of taxable income or loss for a prior taxable year, then, except as precluded by the applicable statute of limitations, the loss corporation (or the common parent of any consolidated group of which the loss corporation was a member for the year) must file an amended return for the year that reflects the effects of the retroactive application of the rules of this paragraph (d). If the statute of limitations precludes the filing of an amended return for one or more such prior taxable years, the loss corporation (or the common parent) must make appropriate adjustments under the principles of section 382(l)(2)(A) in subsequent taxable years to reflect the difference between the losses and credits actually used in such prior taxable years and the amount that would have been used in those years applying the rules of this paragraph (d).

(e) *Option attribution for purposes of determining stock ownership under section 382(l)(5)(A)(ii).*—(1) *In general.*—Solely for purposes of determining whether the stock ownership requirements of section 382(l)(5)(A)(ii) are satisfied at the time of an ownership change, stock of the loss corporation (or of a controlling corporation if also in bankruptcy) that is subject to an option is treated as acquired at that time, pursuant to an exercise of the option by its owner, if such deemed exercise would cause the pre-change shareholders and qualified creditors of the loss corporation to own (after such ownership change and as a result of being pre-change shareholders or qualified creditors immediately before such change) less than an amount of such stock sufficient to satisfy the ownership requirements of section 382(l)(5)(A)(ii). An option that is owned as a result of being a pre-change shareholder or qualified creditor and that, if exercised, would result in the ownership of stock by a pre-change shareholder or qualified creditor is not treated as exercised under this paragraph (e). For purposes of this paragraph (e)(1), rules similar to those option attribution rules under § 1.382-2T(h)(4)(iii), (iv), (v), (vii), and (x)(A), (B) (except with respect to a debt instrument that was issued after the filing of the petition in the title 11 or similar case), (D), (E) (except with respect to a right to receive or obligation to issue stock as interest or dividends on a debt instrument or stock that was issued after the filing of the petition in the title 11 or similar case), (G), (H), and (Z), apply.

(2) *Special rules.*—(i) *Lapse or forfeiture of options deemed exercised.*—A loss corporation may apply rules similar to the rules of § 1.382-2T(h)(4)(viii) with respect to an option except to the extent any person owning the option at any time on or after the change date acquires additional stock or an option to acquire additional stock during the period of time on or after the ownership change and on or before the lapse or forfeiture of the option.

(ii) *Actual exercise of options not deemed exercised.*—In determining whether the ownership change pursuant to the plan of reorganization qualifies under section 382(l)(5), a loss corporation may take into account stock acquired pursuant to the actual exercise of an option issued pursuant to the plan of reorganization if that option was not deemed exercised under paragraph (e)(1) of this section. However, this paragraph (e)(2)(ii) applies only if the option is actually exercised within the 3 years of the ownership change by the

5-percent shareholder who, as a result of being a pre-change shareholder or qualified creditor, acquired the option under the plan.

(iii) *Amended returns.*—A loss corporation may file an amended return for a prior taxable year (subject to any applicable statute of limitations) if it determines that section 382(l)(5) applies to an ownership change as a result of the operation of paragraph (e)(2)(i) or (ii) of this section, but only if the loss corporation makes corresponding adjustments on amended returns for all affected taxable years (subject to any applicable statute of limitations).

(3) *Examples.*—In each of the examples in this paragraph (e)(3), assume that there is an ownership change of loss corporation L on the date the plan of reorganization is effective.

Example 1. L is a loss corporation in a title 11 case. The plan of reorganization of L approved by the bankruptcy court provides for the cancellation of all existing L stock, the issuance of 100 shares of new L common stock to qualified creditors, and the issuance of an option to a new investor to acquire, at any time during the next 3 years, 90 shares of new L common stock from L at its fair market value on the date the plan becomes effective. Under paragraph (e)(1) of this section, on the date the plan becomes effective, the option held by the new investor is deemed exercised if the exercise would cause the qualified creditors of L to own less than 50 percent of the total voting power or value of the L stock after the ownership change. Because the qualified creditors would receive at least 50 percent of the voting power and value of the new L common stock even if the option were deemed exercised, the stock ownership requirements of section 382(l)(5)(A)(ii) are satisfied.

Example 2. The facts are the same as in *Example 1*, except that L issues an option to the new investor to acquire 110 shares of new L common stock. This option is deemed exercised under paragraph (e)(1) of this section on the date the plan becomes effective, because, as a result of the deemed exercise, the qualified creditors would own only 100 of 210 shares of the new L common stock (approximately 48 percent) after the ownership change. Accordingly, the stock ownership requirements of section 382(l)(5)(A)(ii) are not satisfied and section 382(a) applies to the ownership change.

Example 3. (a) L is a loss corporation in a title 11 case. The plan of reorganization of L approved by the bankruptcy court provides for the cancellation of all existing L stock, the issuance of new L common stock and 5-year options to acquire L common stock as follows:

(i) To qualified creditors—100 shares of stock and options to acquire 50 shares;

(ii) To a new investor—options to acquire 110 shares.

(b) Under paragraph (e)(1) of this section, the option held by the new investor is deemed exercised on the date the plan becomes effective because the exercise would cause the qualified creditors of L to own less than 50 percent of the total voting power and value of the L stock after the ownership change (100 of 210 shares or approximately 48 percent). Accordingly, the stock ownership requirements of section 382(l)(5)(A)(ii) are not satisfied initially and section 382(a) applies to the ownership change.

(c) Assume, however, that the qualified creditors actually exercise enough options that were acquired pursuant to the plan of reorganization to purchase 30 additional shares during the 3 year period after the plan becomes effective. Under paragraph (e)(2)(ii) of this section, L may take into account the 30 shares purchased by the qualified creditors by the exercise of the options in determining whether the stock ownership requirements of section 382(l)(5)(A)(ii) were satisfied on the date the plan of reorganization became effective. If L takes such purchases into account, the qualified creditors of L are deemed to own as of the date of the ownership change more than 50 percent of the total voting power or value of the L stock after the ownership change (130 of 240 shares or approximately 54 percent), with the result that the stock ownership requirements of section 382(l)(5)(A)(ii) are satisfied and section 382(l)(5) applies to the ownership change as of the effective date of the plan.

(d) Assume instead that the qualified creditors acquire 30 additional shares by exercise of options more than 3 years after the plan becomes effective. Such exercise is not taken into account under paragraph (e)(2)(ii) of this section for purposes of determining whether the stock ownership requirements of section 382(l)(5)(A)(ii) are satisfied as of the effective date of the plan. Thus, the qualified creditors are deemed to own less than 50 percent of the total voting power and value of the L stock after the ownership change (100 of 210 shares) and section 382(l)(5) does not apply to the ownership change.

(e) Assume instead that, during the 3 year period after the plan becomes effective, the new investor exercises part of his option and purchases 105 shares of stock. The exercise causes a lapse of the rights to acquire the remaining 5 shares of stock. Also during that time, the qualified creditors exercise part of their options and acquire 6 additional shares of stock. Under paragraph (e)(2)(i) of this section, L may treat the lapse of that part of the new investor's option to acquire 5 shares of stock as if that part of the option had never been issued for purposes of determining whether the stock ownership requirements of section 382(l)(5)(A)(ii) are satisfied as of the effective date of the plan. Also, under paragraph (e)(2)(ii) of this section, L may take into account the 6 shares purchased by the qualified creditors by the exercise of the options in determining whether the stock ownership requirements of section 382(l)(5)(A)(ii) are satisfied as of the effective date of the plan. If L takes all of this information into account, the qualified creditors are deemed to own more than 50 percent of the total voting power or value of the L stock after the ownership change (106 of 211 shares or approximately 50.2 percent) and section 382(l)(5) applies to the ownership change as of the effective date of the plan.

(4) *Effective dates.*—(i) *In general.*—This paragraph (e) applies to ownership changes occurring on or after September 5, 1990.

(ii) *Special rule for interest or dividends.*—Rules similar to the rules of §1.382-2T(h)(4)(x)(E) (relating to option attribution for purposes of determining whether an ownership change occurs) apply to a right to receive or obligation to issue stock as interest or dividends on a debt instrument or stock that was issued after the filing of the petition in the title 11 or similar case for ownership changes occurring before April 8, 1992.

(f) through (h) [Reserved]

(i) *Election not to apply section 382(l)(5).*—Under section 382(l)(5)(H), a loss corporation may elect not to have the provisions of section 382(l)(5) apply to an ownership change in a title 11 or similar case. This election is irrevocable and must be made by the due date (including any extensions of time) of the loss corporation's tax return for the taxable year which includes the change date. The election is to be made by attaching the following statement to the tax return of the loss corporation for that taxable year: "THIS IS AN ELECTION UNDER §1.382-9(i) NOT TO APPLY THE PROVISIONS OF SECTION 382(l)(5) TO THE OWNERSHIP CHANGE OCCURRING PURSUANT TO A PLAN OF REORGANIZATION CONFIRMED BY THE COURT ON [INSERT CONFIRMATION DATE]."

(j) *Value of the loss corporation in an ownership change to which section 382(l)(6) applies.*—Section 382(l)(6) applies to any ownership change occurring pursuant to a plan of reorganization in a title 11 or similar case to which section 382(l)(5) does not apply. In such case, the value of the loss corporation under section 382(e) is equal to the lesser of—

(1) The value of the stock of the loss corporation immediately after the ownership change (determined under the rules of paragraph (k) of this section); or

(2) The value of the loss corporation's pre-change assets (determined under the rules of paragraph (l) of this section).

(k) *Rules for determining the value of the stock of the loss corporation.*— (1) *Certain ownership interests treated as stock.*—For purposes of paragraph (j)(1) of this section—

(i) Stock includes stock described in section 1504(a)(4) and any stock that is not treated as stock under §1.382-2T(f)(18)(ii) for purposes of determining whether a loss corporation has an ownership change; and

(ii) Stock does not include an ownership interest that is treated as stock under §1.382-2T(f)(18)(iii) for purposes of determining whether a loss corporation has an ownership change.

(2) *Coordination with section 382(e)(2).*—In the case of a redemption or other corporate contraction occurring after and in connection with the ownership change, the value of the stock of the loss corporation under paragraph (j)(1) of this section is reduced under section 382(e)(2).

(3) *Coordination with section 382(e)(3).*—If the loss corporation is a foreign corporation, in determining the value of the stock under paragraph (j)(1) of this section, only items treated as connected with the conduct of a trade or business in the United States are taken into account.

(4) *Coordination with section 382(l)(1).*—Section 382(l)(1) does not apply in determining the value of the stock of the loss corporation under paragraph (j)(1) of this section.

(5) *Coordination with section 382(l)(4).*—If, immediately after the ownership change, the loss corporation has substantial nonbusiness assets (as determined under section 382(l)(4)(B) taking into account only those assets the loss corporation held immediately before the ownership change), the value of the stock of the loss corporation under paragraph (j)(1) of this section is reduced by the excess of the value of such nonbusiness assets over those assets' share of the loss corporation's indebtedness (determined under section 382(l)(4)(D) taking into account the loss corporation's assets and liabilities immediately after the ownership change).

(6) *Special rule for stock not subject to the risk of corporate business operations.*—(i) *In general.*—The value of the stock of the loss corporation under paragraph (j)(1) of this section is reduced by the value of stock that is issued as part of a plan one of the principal purposes of which is to increase the section 382 limitation without subjecting the investment to the entrepreneurial risks of corporate business operations.

(ii) *Coordination of special rule and other rules affecting value.*—If the value of the loss corporation is modified under another rule affecting value, appropriate adjustments are to be made so that such modification is not duplicated under this paragraph (k)(6).

(7) *Limitation on value of stock.*—For purposes of paragraph (j)(1) of this section, the value of stock of the loss corporation issued in connection with the ownership change cannot exceed the cash and the value of any property (including indebtedness of the loss corporation) received by the loss corporation in consideration for the issuance of that stock.

(l) *Rules for determining the value of the loss corporation's pre-change assets.*—(1) *In general.*—Except as otherwise provided in this paragraph (l), the value of the loss corporation's pre-change assets is the value of its assets (determined without regard to liabilities) immediately before the ownership change.

(2) *Coordination with section 382(e)(2).*—Section 382(e)(2) does not apply in determining the value of the pre-change assets of the loss corporation under paragraph (j)(2) of this section.

(3) *Coordination with section 382(e)(3).*—If the loss corporation is a foreign corporation, in determining the value of the pre-change assets under paragraph (j)(2) of this section, only assets treated as connected with the conduct of a trade or business in the United States are taken into account.

(4) *Coordination with section 382(l)(1).*—For purposes of paragraph (j)(2) of this section, the value of the pre-change assets of the loss corporation is determined without regard to the amount of any capital contribution to which section 382(l)(1) applies. For purposes of applying this paragraph (l)(4), the receipt of cash or property by the loss corporation in exchange for the issuance of indebtedness is considered a capital contribution if it is part of a plan one of the principal purposes of which is to increase the value of the loss corporation under paragraph (j) of this section.

(5) *Coordination with section 382(l)(4).*—If, immediately after the ownership change, the loss corporation has substantial nonbusiness assets (as determined under section 382(l)(4)(B) taking into account only those assets the loss corporation held immediately before the ownership change), the value of the loss corporation's pre-change assets is reduced by the value of the nonbusiness assets.

(m) *Continuity of business requirement.*—(1) *Under section 382(l)(5).*—If section 382(l)(5) applies to an ownership change of a loss corporation, section 382(c) and the regulations thereunder do not apply with respect to the ownership change.

(2) *Under section 382(l)(6).*—If section 382(l)(6) applies to an ownership change of a loss corporation, section 382(c) and the regulations thereunder apply to the ownership change.

(n) *Ownership change in a title 11 or similar case succeeded by another ownership change within two years.*—(1) *Section 382(l)(5) applies to the first ownership change.*—If section 382(l)(5) applies to an ownership change and, within the two-year period immediately following such ownership change, a second ownership change occurs, section 382(l)(5) cannot apply to the second ownership change and the section 382(a) limitation with respect to the second ownership change is zero.

(2) *Section 382(l)(6) applies to the first ownership change.*—If the value of a loss corporation in an ownership change was determined under section 382(l)(6) and a second ownership change occurs within the two-year period immediately following the first ownership change, the value of the loss corporation under section 382(e) with respect to the second ownership change is not reduced under section 382(l)(1) for any increase in value of the loss corporation previously taken into account under section 382(l)(6) with respect to the first ownership change.

(o) *Treatment of certain options for ownership change purposes.*— (1) Neither §1.382-2T(h)(4)(i) nor §1.382-4(d) (relating to the treatment of options as exercised) applies to the following options to acquire stock of a loss corporation reorganized pursuant to a plan of reorganization that is confirmed in a title 11 or similar case (within the meaning of section 368(a)(3)(A)) but only until the time the plan becomes effective—

(i) Any option created by the solicitation or receipt of acceptances to the plan;

(ii) The option created by the confirmation of the plan; and

(iii) Any option created under the plan.

(2) This paragraph (o) generally applies to any testing date occurring on or after September 5, 1990. However, this paragraph (o) does not apply on any testing date occurring on or after April 8, 1992, if, in connection with the plan of reorganization, the loss corporation issues stock (including stock described in section 1504(a)(4)) or otherwise receives a capital contribution before the effective date of the plan for a principal purpose of using before the effective date losses and credits that would be subject to limitation under section 382(a) or would be eliminated under section 382(l)(5)(B) or (C) if this paragraph (o) did not apply on the testing date. A loss corporation may elect to apply this paragraph (o) to any testing date occurring before September 5, 1990, by filing a statement substantially similar to the following with its income tax return: "THIS IS AN ELECTION TO APPLY § 1.382-3(o) (OR § 1.382-9(o) AFTER REDESIGNATION) FOR TESTING DATES PRIOR TO SEPTEMBER 5, 1990, TO OPTIONS CREATED BY OR UNDER A PLAN OF REORGANIZATION CONFIRMED IN A TITLE 11 OR SIMILAR CASE." A loss corporation may elect to not apply this paragraph (o) to testing dates occurring on or after September 5, 1990, to April 8, 1992, by filing a statement substantially similar to the following with its income tax return: "THIS IS AN ELECTION TO NOT APPLY § 1.382-3(o) (OR § 1.389-2(o) AFTER REDESIGNATION) FOR TESTING DATES OCCURRING ON OR AFTER SEPTEMBER 5, 1990, TO APRIL 8, 1992, TO OPTIONS CREATED BY OR UNDER A PLAN OF REORGANIZATION CONFIRMED IN A TITLE 11 OR SIMILAR CASE." Either of these statements must be filed with an income tax return (including an amended return) of the loss corporation not later than the due date (including extensions) for filing the income tax return of the loss corporation for the taxable year including or ending with April 8, 1992.

(p) *Effective date for rules relating to section 382(l)(6).*—(1) *In general.*—Paragraphs (i), (j), (k), (l), (m)(2), and (n)(2) of this section apply to any ownership change occurring on or after March 17, 1994.

(2) *Ownership change to which section 382(l)(6) applies occurring before March 17, 1994.*—In the case of an ownership change occurring before March 17, 1994, the loss corporation may elect to apply the rules of paragraphs (j), (k), (l), (m)(2), and (n)(2) of § 1.382-9 in their entirety. The election must be made by the later of the due date (including any extensions of time) of the loss corporation's tax return for the taxable year which includes the change date or the date that the loss corporation files its first tax return after May 16, 1994. The election is made by attaching the following statement to the return: "THIS IS AN ELECTION TO APPLY § § 1.382-9(j), (k), (l), (m)(2), AND (n)(2) OF THE INCOME TAX REGULATIONS TO THE OWNERSHIP CHANGE OCCURRING PURSUANT TO A PLAN OF REORGANIZATION CONFIRMED BY THE COURT ON [INSERT CONFIRMATION DATE]." In connection with making this election, on the same return the loss corporation may also elect not to apply section 382(l)(5) to the ownership change under paragraph (i) of this section (if the loss corporation has not already done so pursuant to § 301.9100-7T(a) of this chapter). If, under the applicable statute of limitations, the loss corporation may file amended returns for the year of the ownership change and all subsequent years (an open year), an electing loss corporation must file an amended return for each prior affected year to reflect the elections. If, under the applicable statute of limitations, the loss corporation may not file an amended return for the year of the ownership change or any subsequent year (a closed year), an electing loss corporation must file an amended return for each affected open year to reflect the elections and the section 382 limitation resulting from the ownership change must be appropriately adjusted for the earliest open year (or years) to reflect the difference between the amount of pre-change losses actually used in closed years and the amount of pre-change losses that would have been used in such years applying the rules of paragraphs (j), (k), (l), (m)(2), (n)(2) of this section to the ownership change. [Reg. § 1.382-9.]

☐ [T.D. 8388, 12-31-91. *Amended by T.D. 8407, 4-8-92. Redesignated and amended by T.D. 8440, 10-2-92. Amended by T.D. 8529, 3-17-94; T.D. 8530, 3-17-94, T.D. 8531, 3-17-94 and T.D. 9811, 1-18-2017.]*

[Reg. § 1.382-10]

§ 1.382-10. Special rules for determining time and manner of acquisition of an interest in a loss corporation.—(a) *Distributions from qualified trusts.*—(1) *In general.*—For purposes of § 1.382-2T, if a qualified trust described in section 401(a) (qualified trust) distributes an ownership interest in an entity (as defined in § 1.382-3(a)(1)), then for testing dates on or after the date of the distribution, the distributed ownership interest is treated as having been acquired by the distributee on the date and in the manner acquired by the trust and not as having been acquired or disposed of by the trust. The distribution does not cause the day of the distribution to be a testing date.

(2) *Accounting for dispositions.*—(i) *General rule.*—For purposes of this paragraph (a), in order to determine which ownership interest in an entity is distributed from a qualified trust, a loss corporation must either specifically identify the ownership interests that are the subject of all dispositions by the qualified trust of ownership interests in an entity, or apply the first-in, first-out (FIFO) method to all such dispositions.

(ii) *Special rules.*—For purposes of this paragraph (a)(2):

(A) The FIFO method must be applied on a class-by-class basis; and

(B) The term *dispositions* includes distributions, sales, and other transfers.

(3) *Examples.*—The following examples illustrate the principles of this paragraph (a). For purposes of these examples, unless otherwise stated, the nomenclature and assumptions of the examples in § 1.382-2T(b) apply, all corporations file separate income tax returns on a calendar year basis, the only 5-percent shareholder of a loss corporation is a public group, and the facts set forth the only acquisitions of stock by any participants in a qualified plan and the only owner shifts with respect to the loss corporation during the testing period. The examples are as follows:

Example 1—(i) *Facts.* In 1994, E, a qualified trust established under Plan F, acquires 10 percent of L stock. A is a participant in Plan F. On January 1, 2002, A acquires 4 percent of L stock, and B, who is not a participant or a beneficiary of a participant in Plan F, acquires 5 percent of L stock. On January 1, 2004, E distributes 2 percent of L stock to A. On July 1, 2004, A acquires 1 percent of L stock.

(ii) *Analysis.* January 1, 2002, is a testing date because B's acquisition of 5 percent of L stock causes an increase in the percentage ownership of B, a 5-percent shareholder. As of the close of that testing date, A is treated as owning only 4 percent of L stock. Therefore, A is treated as a member of the public group of L. In addition, E is treated as owning 10 percent of L stock that it acquired in 1994.

(iii) As a result of the application of paragraph (a)(1) of this section to E's distribution of 2 percent of L stock to A on January 1, 2004, for testing dates on and after January 1, 2004, A is treated as having acquired that 2 percent interest in L in 1994, and E is treated as having acquired only 8 percent of L stock in 1994. Because there are no owner shifts on January 1, 2004, that date is not a testing date.

(iv) July 1, 2004, is a testing date because on that date A, a 5-percent shareholder, acquires 1 percent of L stock. As of the close of that testing date, A's percentage of ownership of L stock is 7 percent, and A's lowest percentage of ownership of L stock at any time within the testing period is 2 percent (deemed acquired in 1994), representing an increase of 5 percentage points. In addition, as of the close of July 1, 2004, B's percentage of ownership of L stock is 5 percent, and B's lowest percentage of ownership of L stock at any time within the testing period is 0 percent, representing an increase of 5 percentage points. Thus, on July 1, 2004, L must take into account an increase of 10 (5 + 5) percentage points in determining whether it has an ownership change.

Example 2—(i) *Facts.* E is a qualified trust established under Plan F. L, a publicly traded corporation, has 100x shares of stock outstanding. As of January 1, 2006, C owns 5x shares of L stock and is not a participant or beneficiary of a participant in Plan F. At all times prior to January 1, 2006, E owns no L stock. On January 1, 2006, E acquires 10x shares of L stock from members of the public group of L. On December 1, 2007, E distributes 5x shares of L stock to some of the participants in Plan F. No one participant acquires all 5x shares as a result of the distribution. On February 1, 2008, C purchases 1x shares of L stock from the public group of L.

(ii) *Analysis.* Because E's acquisition of 10x shares of L stock on January 1, 2006, is an owner shift, that date is a testing date. As of the close of that date, E's percentage of stock ownership in L has increased by 10 percentage points.

(iii) As a result of the application of paragraph (a)(1) of this section to E's distribution of 5x shares of L stock to some Plan F participants on December 1, 2007, for testing dates on and after December 1, 2007, those distributees are treated as having acquired those shares of stock on January 1, 2006, from members of the public group of L, and E is not treated as having acquired those shares on that date. E's distribution of the 5x shares is not an owner shift. Therefore, December 1, 2007, is not a testing date.

(iv) February 1, 2008, is a testing date because on that date an owner shift results from C's purchase of 1x shares of L stock. As of the close of that testing date, the distributees of 5x shares of L stock are treated as members of the public group of L having acquired 5x shares of L stock from other members of the public group of L on January 1, 2006. Because those acquisitions are not by 5-percent shareholders, L does not take them into account. In addition, as of the close of February 1, 2008, E's percentage of stock ownership in L is 5 percent, and E's lowest percentage of stock ownership in L at any time within the testing period is 0 percent, representing an increase of 5 percentage points. In addition, as of the close of February 1, 2008, C's percentage of stock ownership in L is 6 percent, and C's lowest percentage of stock ownership in L at any time within the testing period is 5 percent, representing an increase of 1 percentage point. Therefore, on February 1, 2008, L must take into account an increase of 6 (5 + 1) percentage points in determining whether it has an ownership change.

(4) *Effective dates.*—This section applies to all distributions after June 23, 2006. For distributions on or before June 23, 2006, see § 1.382-10T as contained in 26 CFR part 1, revised April 1, 2006.

(b) [Reserved]. [Reg. § 1.382-10.]

☐ [*T.D. 9269, 6-23-2006.*]

[Reg. § 1.382-11]

§ 1.382-11. Reporting requirements.—(a) *Information statement required.*—A loss corporation must include a statement entitled, "STATEMENT PURSUANT TO § 1.382-11(a) BY [INSERT NAME AND EMPLOYER IDENTIFICATION NUMBER OF TAXPAYER], A LOSS CORPORATION," on or with its income tax return for each taxable year that it is a loss corporation in which an owner shift, equity structure shift or other transaction described in § 1.382-2T(a)(2)(i) occurs. The statement must include the date(s) of any owner shifts, equity structure shifts, or other transactions described in § 1.382-2T(a)(2)(i), the date(s) on which any ownership change(s) occurred, and the amount of any attributes described in § 1.382-2(a)(1)(i) that caused the corporation to be a loss corporation. A loss corporation may also be required to include certain elections on this statement, including—

(1) An election made under § 1.382-2T(h)(4)(vi)(B) to disregard the deemed exercise of an option if the actual exercise of that option occurred within 120 days of the ownership change; and

(2) An election made under § 1.382-6(b)(2) to close the books of the loss corporation for purposes of allocating income and loss to periods before and after the change date for purposes of section 382.

(b) *Effective/applicability date.*—This section applies to any taxable year beginning on or after May 30, 2006. However, taxpayers may apply this section to any original Federal income tax return (including any amended return filed on or before the due date (including extensions) of such original return) timely filed on or after May 30, 2006. For taxable years beginning before May 30, 2006, see § 1.382-2T as contained in 26 CFR part 1 in effect on April 1, 2006. [Reg. § 1.382-11.]

☐ [*T.D. 9329, 6-13-2007.*]

[Reg. § 1.382-12]

§ 1.382-12. Determination of adjusted Federal long-term rate.—(a) *In general.*—The long-term tax-exempt rate for an ownership change is the highest of the adjusted Federal long-term rates in effect for any month in the 3-calendar-month period ending with the calendar month in which the change date occurs. For purposes of the previous sentence, the adjusted Federal long-term rate is the Federal long-term rate determined under section 1274(d) (without regard to paragraphs (2) and (3) thereof), adjusted for differences between rates on long-term taxable and tax-exempt obligations. The Secretary calculates the adjusted Federal long-term rate as provided in paragraph (b) of this section. The Internal Revenue Service publishes the long-term tax-exempt rate and the adjusted Federal long-term rate for each month in the Internal Revenue Bulletin (see § 601.601(d)(2)(ii) of this chapter).

(b) *Adjusted Federal long-term rate.*—The adjusted Federal long-term rate for a calendar month is the product of the Federal long-term rate determined under section 1274(d) for that month, based on annual compounding, multiplied by the adjustment factor described in paragraph (c) of this section.

(c) *Adjustment factor.*—The adjustment factor is a percentage equal to—

(1) The excess of 100 percent, over

(2) The product of—

(i) 59 percent, and

(ii) The sum of the maximum rate in effect under section 1 applicable to individuals and the maximum rate in effect under section 1411 applicable to individuals for the month to which the adjusted applicable Federal rate applies.

(d) *Effective/applicability date.*—The rules of this section apply to the determination of the long-term tax-exempt rate and the adjusted

Federal long-term rate beginning with the rates determined during August 2016 that apply during September 2016. [Reg. § 1.382-12.]

☐ [*T.D. 9763, 4-25-2016.*]

[Reg. § 1.383-0]

§ 1.383-0. Effective date.—(a) The regulations in this part under section 383 of the Code (other than the regulations described in paragraph (b) of this section) reflect the amendments made to sections 382 and 383 by the Tax Reform Act of 1986 and the amendments made to section 382 by Public Law No. 115-97 (2017). See § 1.383-1(j) for effective date rules.

(b) Sections 1.383-1A, 1.383-2A, and 1.383-3A do not reflect the amendments made to sections 382 and 383 by the Tax Reform Act of 1986. [Reg. § 1.383-0.]

☐ [*T.D. 8352, 6-26-91 and T.D. 9905, 9-3-2020.*]

[Reg. § 1.383-1]

§ 1.383-1. Special limitations on certain capital losses and excess credits.—(a) *Outline of topics.*—In order to facilitate the use of this section, this paragraph lists the paragraphs, subparagraphs and subdivisions contained in this section.

(a) Outline of topics.

(b) In general.

(c) Definitions.

(1) Coordination with definitions and nomenclature used in section 382.

(2) Pre-change capital loss.

(3) Pre-change credit.

(4) Pre-change loss.

(5) Regular tax liability.

(6) Section 383 credit limitation.

(i) Definition.

(ii) Example.

(d) Limitation on use of pre-change losses and pre-change credits.

(1) In general.

(i) In general.

(ii) Ordering rule for losses or credits from same taxable year.

(2) Ordering rules for utilization of pre-change losses and pre-change credits and for absorption of the section 382 limitation and the section 383 credit limitation.

(3) Coordination with other limitations.

(i) In general.

(ii) Examples.

(e) Carryforward of unused section 382 limitation.

(1) Computation of carryforward amount.

(2) Section 383 credit reduction amount.

(3) [Reserved]

(4) Special rules for determining the section 383 credit reduction amount.

(i) Ordering rules.

(ii) Special rule for credits under section 38(a).

(f) Examples.

(g) Coordination with section 382 and the regulations thereunder.

(h) Alternative minimum tax.

(i) [Reserved]

(j) Applicability date.

(1) In general.

(2) Interaction with section 163(j).

(b) *In general.*—Under section 383, if an ownership change occurs with respect to a loss corporation, the section 382 limitation and the section 383 credit limitation (as defined in paragraph (c)(6) of this section) for a post-change year shall apply to limit the amount of taxable income and regular tax liability, respectively, that can be offset by pre-change capital losses and pre-change credits of the new loss corporation. The section 383 credit limitation for a post-change year bears a direct relationship to the amount, if any, of the section 382 limitation that remains after taking into account the reduction in the loss corporation's taxable income during a post-change year as a result of its pre-change losses (as defined in paragraph (c)(4) of this section). In general, the section 383 credit limitation is an amount equal to the tax liability of the new loss corporation for the post-change year which is attributable to so much of the corporation's taxable income that would be reduced by allowing as a deduction its section 382 limitation remaining after accounting for the use of pre-change losses. As pre-change losses and pre-change credits of a corporation are used, they absorb the section 382 limitation and the section 383 credit limitation, respectively, in the manner prescribed by paragraph (d) of this section. See also section 382 and the regulations thereunder.

(c) *Definitions.*—(1) *Coordination with definitions and nomenclature used in section 382.*—Terms and nomenclature used in this section, and not otherwise defined herein, shall have the same respective meanings as in section 382 and the regulations thereunder, taking into account that the limitations of section 383 and this section apply to pre-change capital losses and pre-change credits.

(2) *Pre-change capital loss.*—The term "pre-change capital loss" means—

(i) Any capital loss carryover under section 1212 of the old loss corporation to the taxable year ending on the change date or in which the change date occurs,

(ii) Any net capital loss of the old loss corporation for the taxable year in which the ownership change occurs, to the extent such loss is allocable to the period in such year ending on or before the change date, and

(iii) If the old loss corporation has a net unrealized built-in loss, any recognized built-in loss for any recognition period taxable year (within the meaning of section 382(h)) that is a capital loss.

(3) *Pre-change credit.*—The term "pre-change credit" means—

(i) Any excess foreign taxes under section 904(c) of the old loss corporation—

(A) carried forward to the taxable year ending on the change date or in which the change date occurs, or

(B) carried forward from the taxable year that includes the change date, to the extent such credit is allocable to the period in such year ending on or before the change date,

(ii) Any credit under section 38 of the old loss corporation—

(A) carried forward to the taxable year ending on the change date or in which the change date occurs, or

(B) carried forward from a taxable year that includes the change date to the extent such credit is allocable to the period in such year ending on or before the change date, and

(iii) The available minimum tax credit of the old loss corporation under section 53 to the extent attributable to periods ending on or before the change date.

(4) *Pre-change loss.*—Solely for purposes of this section, the term "pre-change loss" means any pre-change loss described in §1.382-2(a)(2) other than pre-change credits described in parargraph (c)(3) of this section.

(5) *Regular tax liability.*—For purposes of this section, the term "regular tax liability" has the same meaning as provided in section 26(b).

(6) *Section 383 credit limitation.*—(i) *Definition.*—The "section 383 credit limitation" for a post-change year of a new loss corporation is an amount equal to the excess of—

(A) The new loss corporation's regular tax liability for the post-change year, over

(B) The new loss corporation's regular tax liability for the post-change year computed, for this purpose, by allowing as an additional deduction an amount equal to the section 382 limitation remaining after the application of paragraphs (d)(2)(i) through (v) of this section.

(ii) *Example.*—L, a new loss corporation, is a calendar-year taxpayer. L has an ownership change on December 31, 2021. For 2022, L has taxable income (prior to the use of any pre-change losses) of $100,000. In addition, L has a section 382 limitation of $25,000, a pre-change net operating loss carryover of $12,000, a pre-change general business credit carryforward under section 39 of $50,000, and no items described in §1.383-1(d)(2)(i) through (iv). L's section 383 credit limitation for 2022 is the excess of its regular tax liability computed after allowing a $12,000 net operating loss deduction (taxable income of $88,000; regular tax liability of $18,480), over its regular tax liability computed after allowing an additional deduction in the amount of L's section 382 limitation remaining after the application of paragraphs (d)(2)(i) through (v) of this section, or $13,000 (taxable income of $75,000; regular tax liability of $15,750). L's section 383 credit limitation is therefore $2,730 ($18,480 minus $15,750).

(d) *Limitation on use of pre-change losses and pre-change credits.*—(1) *In general.*—(i) *General rule.*—The amount of taxable income of a new loss corporation for any post-change year that may be offset by pre-change losses shall not exceed the amount of the section 382 limitation for the post-change year. The amount of the regular tax liability of a new loss corporation for any post-change year that may be offset by pre-change credits shall not exceed the amount of the section 383 credit limitation for the post-change year.

(ii) *Ordering rule for losses or credits from same taxable year.*—A loss corporation's taxable income is offset first by losses subject to a section 382 limitation, to the extent the section 382 limitation for that taxable year has not yet been absorbed, before being offset by losses of the same type from the same taxable year that are not subject to a section 382 limitation. For example, assume that Corporation X has an ownership change in Year 1 and carries over disallowed business interest expense as defined in §1.163(j)-1(b)(10), some of which constitutes a section 382 disallowed business interest carryforward, from Year 1 to Year 2. To the extent of its section 163(j) limitation, as defined in §1.163(j)-1(b)(36), and its remaining section 382 limitation, Corporation X offsets its Year 2 income with the section 382 disallowed business interest carryforward before using any of the disallowed business interest expense that is not a section 382 disallowed business interest carryforward. Similar principles apply to the use of tax credits.

(2) *Ordering rules for utilization of pre-change losses and pre-change credits and for absorption of the section 382 limitation and the section 383 credit limitation.*—Pre-change losses described in any subdivision of this paragraph (d)(2) can offset taxable income in a post-change year only to the extent that the section 382 limitation for that year has not been absorbed by pre-change losses described in any lower-numbered subdivisions. Pre-change credits described in any subdivision of this paragraph (d)(2) can offset regular tax liability in a post-change year only to the extent that the section 383 credit limitation for that year has not been absorbed by pre-change credits described in any lower numbered subdivisions. The section 382 limitation is absorbed by one dollar for each dollar of pre-change loss that is used to offset taxable income. The section 383 credit limitation is absorbed by one dollar for each dollar of pre-change credit that is used to offset regular tax liability. For each post-change year, the section 382 limitation and the section 383 credit limitation of a new loss corporation are absorbed by such corporation's pre-change losses and pre-change credits in the following order:

(i) Pre-change capital losses described in paragraph (c)(2)(iii) of this section that are recognized and are subject to the section 382 limitation in such post-change year;

(ii) Pre-change capital losses described in paragraphs (c)(2)(i) and (ii) of this section;

(iii) Pre-change losses that are described in §1.382-2(a)(2)(iii), other than losses that are pre-change capital losses, that are recognized and are subject to the section 382 limitation in such post-change year;

(iv)(A) With respect to an ownership change date occurring prior to November 13, 2020, but during the taxable year which includes November 13, 2020, the pre-change loss described in section 382(d)(3);

(B) With respect to an ownership change date occurring on or after November 13, 2020, section 382 disallowed business interest carryforwards (within the meaning of §1.382-2(a)(7));

(v) Pre-change losses not described in paragraphs (d)(2)(i) through (iv) of this section;

(vi) Pre-change credits described in paragraph (c)(3)(i) of this section (excess foreign taxes);

(vii) Pre-change credits described in paragraph (c)(3)(ii) of this section (business credits); and

(viii) Pre-change credits described in paragraph (c)(3)(iii) of this section (minimum tax credit).

(3) *Coordination with other limitations.*—(i) *In general.*—Paragraphs (d)(1) and (2) of this section shall be applied after the application of all other limitations contained in Subtitle A which are applicable to the use of a pre-change loss or pre-change credit in a post-change year. Thus, only otherwise currently allowable pre-change losses and pre-change credits will result in the absorption of the section 382 limitation and the section 383 credit limitation. The application of section 59A is not a limitation contained in subtitle A for purposes of this paragraph (d)(3)(i). Therefore, the treatment of pre-change losses and pre-change credits in the computation of the base erosion minimum tax amount will not affect whether such losses or credits result in absorption of the section 382 limitation and the section 383 credit limitation.

(ii) *Example.*—L, a calendar-year taxpayer, has an ownership change on December 31, 2021. For 2022, L has taxable income of $300,000 and a regular tax liability of $63,000. L has no pre-change losses, but it has a business credit carryforward from 2020 of $25,000. L has a section 382 limitation for 2022 of $50,000. L's section 383 credit limitation is $10,500, an amount equal to the excess of L's regular tax liability ($63,000) over its regular tax liability calculated by allowing an additional deduction of $50,000 ($52,500). Pursuant to the limitation contained in section 38(c), however, L is entitled to use only $9,500 (($63,000 - $25,000) x 25 percent) of its business credit carryforward in 2022. The unabsorbed portion of L's section 382 limitation, $1,000 (computed pursuant to paragraph (e) of this section), is carried forward under section 382(b)(2). The unused portion of L's business credit carryforward, $14,500, is carried forward to the extent provided in section 39.

(e) *Carryforward of unused section 382 limitation.*—(1) *Computation of carryforward amount.*—The section 382 limitation that can be carried forward under section 382(b)(2) is the excess, if any, of (i) the section 382 limitation for the post-change year remaining after the application of paragraphs (d)(2)(i) through (v) of this section, over (ii) the section 383 credit reduction amount for that post-change year.

(2) *Section 383 credit reduction amount.*—The section 383 credit reduction amount for s post-change year is equal to the amount of taxable income attributable to the portion of the new loss corporation's regular tax liability for the year that is offset by pre-change credits. Each dollar of regular tax liability that is offset by a dollar of pre-change credit is divided by the effective marginal rate at which that dollar of tax was imposed to determine the amount of taxable income that resulted in that particular dollar of regular tax liability. The sum of these "grossed-up" amounts for the taxable year is the section 383 credit reduction amount. In determining the effective marginal rate at which a dollar of tax was imposed, special rules regarding rates of tax (*e.g.*, section 15) or taxable income brackets (*e.g.*, section 1561), or both, shall be taken into account.

(3) [Reserved]

(4) *Special rules for determining the section 383 credit reduction amount.*—(i) *Ordering rules.*—For purposes of this paragraph (e), credits, including pre-change credits, are considered to offset regular tax liability in the order that such credits are applied under the ordering rules of part IV of subchapter A of chapter 1 and section 904. For example, for purposes of this paragraph (e), excess foreign taxes carried over under section 904(c) (whether or not a pre-change credit) are considered (under section 38(c)) to offset regular tax liability before the general business credit under section 38, and general business credit carryovers to the taxable year are considered (under section 39) to offset regular tax liability before general business credits arising in the taxable year.

(ii) *Special rule for credits under section 38(a).*—For purposes of applying this paragraph (e), credits under section 38(a) that, under section 38(c)(2), as applicable, taking into account amendments made by section 11813 of the Revenue Reconciliation Act of 1990, effec-

tively offset both regular tax liability and the tax imposed by section 55 (relating to minimum tax), are considered to offset regular tax liability.

(f) *Examples.*—The following examples illustrate the operation of paragraphs (b) through (e) of this section. For purposes of these examples, the term "modified tax liability" means the amount determined under paragraph (c)(6)(i)(B) of this section.

(1) *Example 1.*—(i) L, a calendar year taxpayer, has an ownership change on December 31, 1987. Before the application of carryovers, L, a new loss corporation, has $60,000 of capital gain, $100,000 of ordinary taxable income and a section 382 limitation of $100,000 for its first post-change year beginning after the change date. L's only carryovers are an $80,000 capital loss carryover and a $100,000 net operating loss carryover. Both carryovers are from taxable years ending before the change date and thus are pre-change losses.

(ii) L first uses $60,000 of its pre-change capital loss carryover to offset its capital gain. This reduces its section 382 limitation to $40,000 (i.e., $100,000 – $60,000). L's pre-charge net operating loss carryover can therefore be used only to the extent of $40,000. L's remaining $20,000 pre-change capital loss carryover and remaining $60,000 pre-change net operating loss carryover are carried to later years to the extent permitted under this section and sections 172, 382(1)(2) and 1212.

(2) *Example 2.*—(i) *Facts.* L, a calendar-year taxpayer, has an ownership change on December 31, 2021. For 2022, L has $750,000 of ordinary taxable income (before the application of carryovers) and a section 382 limitation of $1,500,000. L's only carryovers are from pre-2021 taxable years and consist of a $500,000 net operating loss (NOL) carryover, and a $200,000 foreign tax credit carryover (all of which may be used under the section 904 limitation). The NOL carryover is a pre-change loss, and the foreign tax credit carryover is a pre-change credit. L has no other pre-change losses or credits that can be used in 2022.

(ii) *Analysis.* The following computation illustrates the application of this section for 2022:

Table 1 to paragraph (f)(2)(ii)

1. Taxable income before carryovers	$750,000
2. Pre-change NOL carryover	$500,000
3. Section 382 limitation	$1,500,000
4. Amount of pre-change NOL carryover that can be used (least of line 1, 2, or 3)	$500,000
5. Taxable income (line 1 minus line 4)	$250,000
6. Section 382 limitation remaining (line 3 minus line 4)	$1,000,000
7. Pre-change credit carryover	$200,000
8. Regular tax liability (line 5 x section 11 rates)	$52,500
9. Modified tax liability (line 5 minus line 6 (but not less than zero) x section 11 rates)	$0
10. Section 383 credit limitation (line 8 minus line 9)	$52,500
11. Amount of pre-change credits that can be used in 2022 (lesser of line 7 or line 10)	$52,500
12. Amount of pre-change credits to be carried over to 2023 under section 904(c) (line 7 minus line 11)	$147,500
13. Section 383 credit reduction amount: $52,500/0.21	$250,000
14. Section 382 limitation to be carried to 2023 under section 382(b)(2) (line 6 minus line 13)	$750,000

(3) *Example 3.*—(i) *Facts.* L, a calendar-year taxpayer, has an ownership change on December 31, 2021. L has $80,000 of ordinary taxable income (before the application of carryovers) and a section 382 limitation of $25,000 for 2022, a post-change year. L's only carryover is from a pre-2021 taxable year and is a general business credit carryforward under section 39 in the amount of $10,000 (no

portion of which is attributable to the investment tax credit under section 46). The general business credit carryforward is a pre-change credit. L has no other credits which can be used in 2022.

(ii) *Analysis.* The following computation illustrates the application of this section:

Table 2 to paragraph (f)(3)(ii)

1. Taxable income before carryovers	$80,000
2. Section 382 limitation	$25,000
3. Pre-change credit carryover	$10,000
4. Regular tax liability (line 1 x section 11 rates)	$16,800
5. Modified tax liability ((line 1 minus line 2) x section 11 rates)	$11,550
6. Section 383 credit limitation (line 4 minus line 5)	$5,250
7. Amount of pre-change credits that can be used (lesser of line 3 or line 6)	$5,250
8. Amount of pre-change credits to be carried over to 2023 under sections 39 and 382(l)(2) (line 3 minus line 7)	$4,750
9. Regular tax payable (line 4 minus line 7)	$11,550
10. Section 383 credit reduction amount: $5,250/0.21	$25,000
11. Section 382 limitation to be carried to 2023 under section 382(b)(2) (line 2 minus line 10)	$0

32,066

Corporate Interests Treated as Stock or Indebtedness
See p. 20,601 for regulations not amended to reflect law changes

(g) *Coordination with section 382 and the regulations thereunder.*—The rules and principles of section 382 (including, for example, section 382(b)(3) and section 382(l)(2)) and the regulations thereunder shall also apply with respect to section 383 and this section. To the extent section 382(h)(6) applies to credits, the principles of this section apply to such credits. In applying the rules and principles of section 382 and the regulations thereunder, appropriate adjustments shall be made to take into account that section 383 and this section apply to pre-change capital losses and pre-change credits. For example, in applying §1.382-2T (f)(18)(ii)(C), (f)(18)(iii)(C) and (h)(4)(ix), any pre-change credits, as defined in paragraph (c)(3) of this section, must be converted to a deduction equivalent by dividing the amount of such credits by the maximum effective rate of tax provided for under section 11.

(h) *Alternative minimum tax.*—See §1.383-2T for the application of the limitations contained in sections 382 and 383 in computing the alternative minimum tax under section 55.

(i) [Reserved]

(j) *Applicability date.*—(1) *In general.*—Subject to any exception from the application of section 382 or the section 382 limitation with respect to a loss corporation, section 383 and this section apply to any loss corporation with respect to which an ownership change occurs after December 31, 1986. See §1.382-2T(m) for effective date rules relating to ownership changes. If section 383 was not taken into account or was applied other than in accordance with this section in a prior taxable year with respect to which section 383 applies, the taxpayer should, within the period of limitation, file an amended return and pay any additional tax due plus interest.

(2) *Interaction with section 163(j).*—Paragraphs (c)(6)(i)(B) and (c)(6)(ii), (d)(1), (d)(2)(iii) through (viii), (d)(3)(ii), (e)(1) through (3),

(f), and (g) of this section apply with respect to ownership changes occurring during a taxable year beginning on or after November 13, 2020. For loss corporations that have undergone an ownership change during a taxable year beginning before November 13, 2020, see §1.383-1 as contained in 26 CFR part 1, revised April 1, 2019. However, taxpayers and their related parties, within the meaning of sections 267(b) and 707(b)(1), may choose to apply the rules of this section to an ownership change occurring during a taxable year beginning after December 31, 2017, so long as the taxpayers and their related parties consistently apply either the rules of this section (except paragraph (d)(2)(iv)(B) of this section), the section 163(j) regulations (as defined in §1.163(j)-1(b)(37)), §§1.382-1, 1.382-2, 1.382-5, 1.382-6, 1.382-7, and 1.383-0, and, if applicable, §§1.263A-9, 1.263A-15, 1.381(c)(20)-1, 1.469-9, 1.469-11, 1.704-1, 1.882-5, 1.1362-3, 1.1368-1, 1.1377-1, 1.1502-13, 1.1502-21, 1.1502-36, 1.1502-79, 1.1502-91 through 1.1502-99 (to the extent they effectuate the rules of §§1.382-2, §1.382-5, 1.382-6, and 1.383-1), and 1.1504-4; or the rules of this section (except paragraph (d)(2)(iv)(A) of this section), the section 163(j) regulations (as defined in §1.163(j)-1(b)(37)) and §§1.382-1, §§1.382-2, 1.382-5, 1.382-6, and 1.383-0, and, if applicable, §§1.263A-9, 1.263A-15, 1.381(c)(20)-1, 1.469-9, 1.469-11, 1.704-1, 1.882-5, 1.1362-3, 1.1368-1, 1.1377-1, 1.1502-13, 1.1502-21, 1.1502-36, 1.1502-79, 1.1502-91 through 1.1502-99 (to the extent they effectuate the rules of §§1.382-2, 1.382-5, 1.382-6, 1.382-7, and 1.383-1), and 1.1504-4, to those ownership changes. [Reg. §1.383-1.]

☐ [*T.D. 8264, 9-19-89. Amended by T.D. 8352, 6-26-91, T.D. 9885, 12-2-2019 and T.D. 9905, 9-3-2020.*]

[Reg. §1.383-2]

§1.383-2. Limitations on certain capital losses and excess credits in computing alternative minimum tax.—[Reserved]

Treatment of Certain Corporate Interests as Stock or Indebtedness

⠀⠀➤ *Caution: The Treasury Department has identified Reg. §1.385-1, as added by T.D. 9790, as a significant tax regulation that imposes an undue financial burden on U.S. taxpayers and/or adds undue complexity to the federal tax laws, pursuant to Executive Order 13789 (issued April 21, 2017) (Notice 2017-38, I.R.B. 2017-30). In a subsequent report, issued October 4, 2017, Treasury recommended planned actions that would reduce the burden of these regulations.*

[Reg. §1.385-1]

§1.385-1. General provisions.—(a) *Overview of section 385 regulations.*—This section and §§1.385-3 through 1.385-4 (collectively, the section 385 regulations) provide rules under section 385 to determine the treatment of an interest in a corporation as stock or indebtedness (or as in part stock and in part indebtedness) in particular factual situations. Paragraph (b) of this section provides the general rule for determining the treatment of an interest based on provisions of the Internal Revenue Code and on common law, including the factors prescribed under common law. Paragraphs (c), (d), and (e) of this section provide definitions and rules of general application for purposes of the section 385 regulations. Section 1.385-3 sets forth additional factors that, when present, control the determination of whether an interest in a corporation that is held by a member of the corporation's expanded group is treated (in whole or in part) as stock or indebtedness.

(b) *General rule.*—Except as otherwise provided in the Internal Revenue Code and the regulations thereunder, including the section 385 regulations, whether an interest in a corporation is treated for purposes of the Internal Revenue Code as stock or indebtedness (or as in part stock and in part indebtedness) is determined based on common law, including the factors prescribed under such common law.

(c) *Definitions.*—The definitions in this paragraph (c) apply for purposes of the section 385 regulations. For additional definitions that apply for purposes of their respective sections, see §§1.385-3(g) and 1.385-4(e).

(1) *Controlled partnership.*—The term controlled partnership means, with respect to an expanded group, a partnership with respect to which at least 80 percent of the interests in partnership capital or profits are owned, directly or indirectly, by one or more members of the expanded group. For purposes of identifying a controlled partnership, indirect ownership of a partnership interest is determined by applying the principles of paragraph (c)(4)(iii) of this section. Such determination is separate from the determination of the status of a corporation as a member of an expanded group. An unincorporated organization described in §1.761-2 that elects to be excluded from all of subchapter K of chapter 1 of the Internal Revenue Code is not a controlled partnership.

(2) *Covered member.*—The term covered member means a member of an expanded group that is—

(i) A domestic corporation; and

(ii) [Reserved]

(3) *Disregarded entity.*—The term disregarded entity means a business entity (as defined in §301.7701-2(a) of this chapter) that is disregarded as an entity separate from its owner for federal income tax purposes under §§301.7701-1 through 301.7701-3 of this chapter.

(4) *Expanded group.*—(i) *In general.*—The term expanded group means one or more chains of corporations (other than S corporations) connected through stock ownership with a common parent corporation that is not an S corporation or a regulated investment company or a real estate investment trust subject to tax under subchapter M of chapter 1 of the Internal Revenue Code (a RIC or a REIT, respectively) (such common parent corporation, an expanded group parent), but only if—

(A) The expanded group parent owns directly or indirectly stock meeting the requirements of section 1504(a)(2) (modified by substituting "or" for "and" in section 1504(a)(2)(A)) in at least one of the other corporations; and

(B) Stock meeting the requirements of section 1504(a)(2) (modified by substituting "or" for "and" in section 1504(a)(2)(A)) in each of the other corporations (except the expanded group parent) is owned directly or indirectly by one or more of the other corporations.

(ii) *Definition of stock.*—For purposes of paragraph (c)(4)(i) of this section, the term stock has the same meaning as "stock" in section 1504 (without regard to §1.1504-4) and all shares of stock within a single class are considered to have the same value. Thus, control premiums and minority and blockage discounts within a single class are not taken into account.

(iii) *Indirect stock ownership.*—For purposes of paragraph (c)(4)(i) of this section, indirect stock ownership is determined by applying the constructive ownership rules of section 318(a) with the following modifications:

(A) Section 318(a)(1) and (a)(3) do not apply except as set forth in paragraph (c)(4)(v) of this section;

(B) Section 318(a)(2)(C) applies by substituting "5 percent" for "50 percent;" and

Corporate Interests Treated as Stock or Indebtedness
See p. 20,601 for regulations not amended to reflect law changes

32,067

(C) Section 318(a)(4) only applies to options (as defined in §1.1504-4(d)) that are reasonably certain to be exercised as described in §1.1504-4(g).

(iv) *Member of an expanded group or expanded group member.*— The expanded group parent and each of the other corporations described in paragraphs (c)(4)(i)(A) and (c)(4)(i)(B) of this section is a member of an expanded group (also referred to as an expanded group member). For purposes of the section 385 regulations, a corporation is a member of an expanded group if it is described in this paragraph (c)(4)(iv) immediately before the relevant time for determining membership (for example, immediately before the issuance of a debt instrument (as defined in §1.385-3(g)(4)) or immediately before a distribution or acquisition that may be subject to §1.385-3(b)(2) or (3)).

(v) *Brother-sister groups with non-corporate owners.*—[Reserved]

(vi) *Special rule for indirect ownership through options for certain members of consolidated groups.*—In the case of an option of which a member of a consolidated group, other than the common parent, is the issuing corporation (as defined in §1.1504-4(c)(1)), section 318(a)(4) only applies (for purposes of applying paragraph (c)(4)(iii)(C) of this section) to the option if the option is treated as stock or as exercised under §1.1504-4(b) for purposes of determining whether a corporation is a member of an affiliated group.

(vii) *Examples.*—The following examples illustrate the rules of this paragraph (c)(4). Except as otherwise stated, for purposes of the examples in this paragraph (c)(4)(vii), all persons described are corporations that have a single class of stock outstanding and file separate federal tax returns and are not an S corporation, a RIC, or a REIT. In addition, the stock of each publicly traded corporation is widely held such that no person directly or indirectly owns stock in the publicly traded corporation meeting the requirements of section 1504(a)(2) (as modified by this paragraph (c)(4)).

(A) *Example 1. Two different expanded group parents.* (1) *Facts.* P has two classes of common stock outstanding: Class A and Class B. X, a publicly traded corporation, directly owns all shares of P's Class A common stock, which is high-vote common stock representing 85% of the vote and 15% of the value of the stock of P. Y, a publicly traded corporation, directly owns all shares of P's Class B common stock, which is low-vote common stock representing 15% of the vote and 85% of the value of the stock of P. P directly owns 100% of the stock of S1.

(2) *Analysis.* X owns directly 85% of the vote of the stock of P, which is stock meeting the requirements of section 1504(a)(2) (as modified by paragraph (c)(4)(i)(A) of this section). Therefore, X is an expanded group parent described in paragraph (c)(4)(i) of this section with respect to P. Y owns 85% of the value of the stock of P, which is stock meeting the requirements of section 1504(a)(2) (as modified by paragraph (c)(4)(i)(A) of this section). Therefore, Y is also an expanded group parent described in paragraph (c)(4)(i) of this section with respect to P. P owns directly 100% of the voting power and value of the stock of S1, which is stock meeting the requirements of section 1504(a)(2) (as modified by paragraph (c)(4)(i)(B) of this section). Therefore, X, P, and S1 constitute an expanded group as defined in paragraph (c)(4)(i) of this section. Additionally, Y, P, and S1 constitute an expanded group as defined in paragraph (c)(4) of this section. X and Y are not members of the same expanded group under paragraph (c)(4) of this section because X does not directly or indirectly own any of the stock of Y and Y does not directly or indirectly own any of the stock of X, such that X and Y do not comprise a chain of corporations described in paragraph (c)(4)(i) of this section.

(B) *Example 2. Inclusion of a REIT within an expanded group.* (1) *Facts.* All of the stock of P is publicly traded. In addition to other assets representing 85% of the value of its total assets, P directly owns all of the stock of S1. S1 owns 99% of the stock of S2. The remaining 1% of the stock of S2 is owned by 100 unrelated individuals. In addition to other assets representing 85% of the value of its total assets, S2 owns all of the stock of S3. Both P and S2 are REITs.

(2) *Analysis.* P directly owns 100% of the stock of S1. However, under paragraph (c)(4)(i) of this section, P cannot be the expanded group parent because P is a REIT. Because no other corporation owns stock in P meeting the requirements described in paragraph (c)(4)(i) of this section, P is not an expanded group member. S1 directly owns 99% of the stock of S2, which is stock meeting the requirements of section 1504(a)(2) (as modified by paragraph (c)(4)(i)(A) of this section). Although S2 is a corporation that is a REIT, a REIT may be a member of an expanded group described under paragraph (c)(4)(i) of this section provided the corporation is not the expanded group parent. In this case, S1 is the expanded group parent. S2 directly owns 100% of the stock of S3, which is stock meeting the requirements of section 1504(a)(2) (as modified by para-

graph (c)(4)(i)(B) of this section). Therefore, S1, S2, and S3 constitute an expanded group as defined in paragraph (c)(4) of this section.

(C) *Example 3. Attribution of hook stock.* (1) *Facts.* P, a publicly traded corporation, directly owns 50% of the stock of S1. S1 directly owns 100% of the stock of S2. S2 directly owns the remaining 50% of the stock of S1.

(2) *Analysis.* (i) P directly owns 50% of the stock of S1. Under paragraph (c)(4)(iii) of this section (which applies section 318(a)(2) with modifications), P constructively owns 50% of the stock of S2 because P directly owns 50% of the stock of S1, which directly owns 100% of S2. Under section 318(a)(5)(A), stock constructively owned by P by reason of the application of section 318(a)(2) is, for purposes of section 318(a)(2), considered as actually owned by P.

(ii) S2 directly owns 50% of the stock of S1. Thus, under paragraph (c)(4)(iii) of this section, P is treated as constructively owning an additional 25% of the stock of S1. For purposes of determining the expanded group, P's ownership must be recalculated treating the additional 25% of S1 stock as actually owned. Under the second application of section 318(a)(2)(C) as modified by paragraph (c)(4)(iii) of this section, P constructively owns an additional 12.5% of the stock of S1 as follows: 25% (P's new attributed ownership of S1) x 100% (S1's ownership of S2) x 50% (S2's ownership of S1) = 12.5%. After two iterations, P's ownership in S1 is 87.5% (50% direct ownership + 25% first order constructive ownership + 12.5% second order constructive ownership) and thus S1 is a member of the expanded group that includes P and S2. Subsequent iterative calculations of P's ownership, treating constructive ownership as actual ownership, would demonstrate that P owns, directly and indirectly, 100% of the stock of S1. P, S1, and S2 therefore constitute an expanded group as defined in paragraph (c)(4) of this section and P is the expanded group parent.

(D) *Example 4. Attribution of hook stock when an intermediary has multiple owners.* (1) *Facts.* The facts are the same as in paragraph (c)(4)(vii)(C) (1) of this section (*Example 3*), except that P directly owns only 25% of the stock of S1. X, a corporation unrelated to P, also directly owns 25% of the stock of S1.

(2) *Analysis.* (i) P and X each directly owns 25% of the stock of S1. Under paragraph (c)(4)(iii) of this section, P and X each constructively owns 25% of the stock of S2 because P and X each directly owns 25% of the stock of S1, which directly owns 100% of the stock of S2. Under section 318(a)(5)(A), stock constructively owned by P or X by reason of the application of section 318(a)(2) is, for purposes of section 318(a)(2), considered as actually owned by P or X, respectively.

(ii) S2 directly owns 50% of the stock of S1. Thus, under paragraph (c)(4)(iii) of this section, P and X each is treated as constructively owning an additional 12.5% of the stock of S1. Under a second application of section 318(a)(2)(C) as modified by paragraph (c)(4)(iii) of this section, P and X each constructively owns an additional 6.25% of the stock of S1 as follows: 12.5% (each of P's and X's new attributed ownership of S1) x 100% (S1's ownership of S2) x 50% (S2's ownership of S1) = 6.25%. After two iterations, each of P's and X's ownership in S1 is 43.75% (25% direct ownership + 12.5% first order constructive ownership + 6.25% second order constructive ownership). Subsequent iterative calculations of each of P's and X's ownership, treating constructive ownership as actual ownership, would demonstrate that P and X each owns, directly and indirectly, 50% of the stock of S1.

(iii) S1 and S2 constitute an expanded group as defined under paragraph (c)(4)(i) of this section because S1 directly owns 100% of the stock of S2. S1 is the expanded group parent of the expanded group and neither P nor X are a member of the expanded group that includes S1 and S2.

(5) *Regarded owner.*—The term *regarded owner* means a person (which cannot be a disregarded entity) that is the single owner (within the meaning of §301.7701-2(c)(2)(i) of this chapter) of a disregarded entity.

(d) *Treatment of deemed exchanges.*—(1) *Debt instrument deemed to be exchanged for stock.*—(i) *In general.*—If a debt instrument (as defined in §1.385-3(g)(4)) is deemed to be exchanged under the section 385 regulations, in whole or in part, for stock, the holder is treated for all Federal tax purposes as having realized an amount equal to the holder's adjusted basis in that portion of the debt instrument as of the date of the deemed exchange (and as having basis in the stock deemed to be received equal to that amount), and, except as provided in paragraph (d)(1)(iv)(B) of this section, the issuer is treated for all Federal tax purposes as having retired that portion of the debt instrument for an amount equal to its adjusted issue price as of the date of the deemed exchange. In addition, neither party accounts for any accrued but unpaid qualified stated interest on the debt instrument or any foreign exchange gain or loss with respect to that accrued but unpaid qualified stated interest (if any) as of the deemed exchange. This paragraph (d)(1)(i) does not affect any rules in Title 26

Reg. §1.385-1(d)(1)(i)

of the United States Code that otherwise apply to the debt instrument prior to the date of the deemed exchange (for example, this paragraph (d)(1)(i) does not affect the issuer's deduction of accrued but unpaid qualified stated interest otherwise deductible prior to the date of the deemed exchange). Moreover, the stock issued in the deemed exchange is not treated as a payment of accrued but unpaid original issue discount or qualified stated interest on the debt instrument for Federal tax purposes.

(ii) *Section 988.*—Notwithstanding the first sentence of paragraph (d)(1)(i) of this section, the rules of § 1.988-2(b)(13) apply to require the holder and the issuer of a debt instrument that is deemed to be exchanged under the section 385 regulations, in whole or in part, for stock to recognize any exchange gain or loss, other than any exchange gain or loss with respect to accrued but unpaid qualified stated interest that is not taken into account under paragraph (d)(1)(i) of this section at the time of the deemed exchange. For purposes of this paragraph (d)(1)(ii), in applying § 1.988-2(b)(13) the exchange gain or loss under section 988 is treated as the total gain or loss on the exchange.

(iii) *Section 108(e)(8).*—For purposes of section 108(e)(8), if the issuer of a debt instrument is treated as having retired all or a portion of the debt instrument in exchange for stock under paragraph (d)(1)(i) of this section, the stock is treated as having a fair market value equal to the adjusted issue price of that portion of the debt instrument as of the date of the deemed exchange.

(iv) *Issuer of stock deemed exchanged for debt.*—For purposes of applying paragraph (d)(1)(i) of this section—

(A) A debt instrument that is issued by a disregarded entity is deemed to be exchanged for stock of the regarded owner under § 1.385-3(d)(4);

(B) A debt instrument that is issued by a partnership that becomes a deemed transferred receivable, in whole or in part, is deemed to be exchanged by the holder for deemed partner stock under § 1.385-3(f)(4) and the partnership is therefore not treated for any federal tax purpose as having retired any portion of the debt instrument; and

(C) A debt instrument that is issued in any situation not described in paragraph (d)(1)(iv)(A) or (B) of this section is deemed to be exchanged for stock of the issuer of the debt instrument.

(2) *Stock deemed to be exchanged for newly-issued debt instrument.*—(i) [Reserved].

(ii) *Debt instruments recharacterized under § 1.385-3.*—If a debt instrument treated as stock under § 1.385-3(b) is deemed to be exchanged under § 1.385-3(d)(2), in whole or in part, for a newly-issued debt instrument, the issue price of the newly-issued debt instrument is determined under either section 1273(b)(4) or 1274, as applicable.

(e) *Indebtedness in part.*—[Reserved]

(f) *Applicability date.*—This section applies to taxable years ending on or after January 19, 2017. [Reg. § 1.385-1.]

☐ [*T.D. 9790, 10-13-2016 (corrected 1-23-2017). Amended by T.D. 9880, 10-31-2019 and T.D. 9897, 5-13-2020.*]

⫸→ *Caution: The Treasury Department has identified Reg. § 1.385-3, as added by T.D. 9790, as a significant tax regulation that imposes an undue financial burden on U.S. taxpayers and/or adds undue complexity to the federal tax laws, pursuant to Executive Order 13789 (issued April 21, 2017) (Notice 2017-38, I.R.B. 2017-30). In a subsequent report, issued October 4, 2017, Treasury recommended planned actions that would reduce the burden of these regulations.*

[Reg. § 1.385-3]

§ 1.385-3. Certain distributions of debt instruments and similar transactions.—(a) *Scope.*—This section sets forth factors that control the determination of whether an interest is treated as stock or indebtedness. Specifically, this section addresses the issuance of a covered debt instrument to a related person as part of a transaction or series of transactions that does not result in new investment in the operations of the issuer. Paragraph (b) of this section sets forth rules for determining when these factors are present, such that a covered debt instrument is treated as stock under this section. Paragraph (c) of this section provides exceptions to the application of paragraph (b) of this section. Paragraph (d) of this section provides operating rules. Paragraph (e) of this section reserves on the affirmative use of this section. Paragraph (f) of this section provides rules for the aggregate treatment of controlled partnerships. Paragraph (g) of this section provides definitions. Paragraph (h) of this section provides examples illustrating the application of the rules of this section. Paragraph (j) of this section provides dates of applicability. For rules regarding the application of this section to members of a consolidated group, see generally § 1.385-4.

(b) *Covered debt instrument treated as stock.*—(1) *Effect of characterization as stock.*—Except as otherwise provided in paragraph (d)(7) of this section, to the extent a covered debt instrument is treated as stock under paragraphs (b)(2), (3), or (4) of this section, it is treated as stock for all federal tax purposes.

(2) *General rule.*—Except as otherwise provided in paragraphs (c) and (e) of this section, a covered debt instrument is treated as stock to the extent the covered debt instrument is issued by a covered member to a member of the covered member's expanded group in one or more of the following transactions:

(i) In a distribution;

(ii) In exchange for expanded group stock, other than in an exempt exchange; or

(iii) In exchange for property in an asset reorganization, but only to the extent that, pursuant to the plan of reorganization, a shareholder in the transferor corporation that is a member of the issuer's expanded group immediately before the reorganization receives the covered debt instrument with respect to its stock in the transferor corporation.

(3) *Funding rule.*—(i) *In general.*—Except as otherwise provided in paragraphs (c) and (e) of this section, a covered debt instrument that is not a qualified short-term debt instrument (as defined in paragraph (b)(3)(vii) of this section) is treated as stock to the extent that it is both issued by a covered member to a member of the covered member's expanded group in exchange for property and, pursuant to paragraph (b)(3)(iii) or (b)(3)(iv) of this section, treated as funding a distribution or acquisition described in one or more of paragraphs (b)(3)(i)(A) through (C) of this section. A covered member that makes a distribution or acquisition described in paragraphs (b)(3)(i)(A) through (C) is referred to as a "funded member," regardless of when it issues a covered debt instrument in exchange for property.

(A) A distribution of property by the funded member to a member of the funded member's expanded group, other than in an exempt distribution;

(B) An acquisition of expanded group stock, other than an exempt exchange, by the funded member from a member of the funded member's expanded group in exchange for property other than expanded group stock; or

(C) An acquisition of property by the funded member in an asset reorganization but only to the extent that, pursuant to the plan of reorganization, a shareholder in the transferor corporation that is a member of the funded member's expanded group immediately before the reorganization receives other property or money within the meaning of section 356 with respect to its stock in the transferor corporation.

(ii) *Transactions described in more than one paragraph.*—For purposes of this section, to the extent that a distribution or acquisition by a funded member is described in more than one of paragraphs (b)(3)(i)(A) through (C) of this section, the funded member is treated as making only a single distribution or acquisition described in paragraph (b)(3)(i) of this section. In the case of an asset reorganization, to the extent an acquisition by the transferee corporation is described in paragraph (b)(3)(i)(C) of this section, a distribution or acquisition by the transferor corporation is not also described in paragraph (b)(3)(i)(A) through (C) of this section. For purposes of this paragraph (b)(3)(ii), whether a distribution or acquisition is described in paragraphs (b)(3)(i)(A) through (C) of this section is determined without regard to paragraph (c) of this section.

(iii) *Per se funding rule.*—(A) *In general.*—A covered debt instrument is treated as funding a distribution or acquisition described in paragraphs (b)(3)(i)(A) through (C) of this section if the covered debt instrument is issued by a funded member during the period beginning 36 months before the date of the distribution or acquisition, and ending 36 months after the date of the distribution or acquisition (*per se period*).

(B) *Multiple interests.*—If, pursuant to paragraph (b)(3)(iii)(A) of this section, two or more covered debt instruments may be treated as stock by reason of this paragraph (b)(3), the covered debt instruments are tested under paragraph (b)(3)(iii)(A) of this section based on the order in which they are issued, with the earliest issued covered debt instrument tested first. See paragraph (h)(3) of this section, *Example 6*, for an illustration of this rule.

(C) *Multiple distributions or acquisitions.*—If, pursuant to paragraph (b)(3)(iii)(A) of this section, a covered debt instrument may be treated as funding more than one distribution or acquisition described in paragraphs (b)(3)(i)(A) through (C) of this section, the covered debt instrument is treated as funding one or more distributions or acquisitions based on the order in which the distributions or acquisitions occur, with the earliest distribution or acquisition treated as the first distribution or acquisition that is funded. See paragraph (h)(3) of this section, *Example 9*, for an illustration of this rule.

(D) *Transactions that straddle different expanded groups.*—(1) *In general.*—For purposes of paragraph (b)(3)(iii)(A) of this section, a covered debt instrument is not treated as issued by a funded member during the per se period with respect to a distribution or acquisition described in paragraphs (b)(3)(i)(A) through (C) of this section if all of the conditions described in paragraphs (b)(3)(iii)(D)(1)(*i*) through (*iii*) of this section are satisfied.

(*i*) The distribution or acquisition occurs prior to the issuance of the covered debt instrument by the funded member or, if the funded member is treated as making the distribution or acquisition of a predecessor or a successor, the predecessor or successor is not a member of the expanded group of which the funded member is a member on the date on which the distribution or the acquisition occurs.

(*ii*) The distribution or acquisition is made by the funded member when the funded member is a member of an expanded group that does not have an expanded group parent that is the funded member's expanded group parent when the covered debt instrument is issued. For purposes of the preceding sentence, a reference to an expanded group parent includes a reference to a predecessor or successor of the expanded group parent.

(*iii*) On the date of the issuance of the covered debt instrument, the recipient member (as defined in paragraph (b)(3)(iii)(D)(2) of this section) is neither a member nor a controlled partnership of an expanded group of which the funded member is a member.

(2) *Recipient member.*—For purposes of this paragraph (b)(3)(iii)(D), the term *recipient member* means, with respect to a distribution or acquisition by a funded member described in paragraphs (b)(3)(i)(A) through (C) of this section, the expanded group member that receives a distribution of property, property in exchange for expanded group stock, or other property or money within the meaning of section 356 with respect to its stock in the transferor corporation. For purposes of this paragraph (b)(3)(iii)(D), a reference to the recipient member includes a predecessor or successor of the recipient member or one or more other entities that, in the aggregate, acquire substantially all of the property of the recipient member.

(E) *Modifications of a covered debt instrument.*—(1) *In general.*—For purposes of paragraph (b)(3)(iii)(A) of this section, if a covered debt instrument is treated as exchanged for a modified covered debt instrument pursuant to § 1.1001-3(b), the modified covered debt instrument is treated as issued on the original issue date of the covered debt instrument.

(2) *Effect of certain modifications.*—Notwithstanding paragraph (b)(3)(iii)(E)(1) of this section, if a covered debt instrument is treated as exchanged for a modified covered debt instrument pursuant to § 1.1001-3(b) and the modification, or one of the modifications, that results in the deemed exchange includes the substitution of an obligor on the covered debt instrument, the addition or deletion of a co-obligor on the covered debt instrument, or the material deferral of scheduled payments due under the covered debt instrument, then the modified covered debt instrument is treated as issued on the date of the deemed exchange for purposes of paragraph (b)(3)(iii)(A) of this section.

(3) *Additional principal amount.*—For purposes of paragraph (b)(3)(iii)(A) of this section, if the principal amount of a covered debt instrument is increased, the portion of the covered debt instrument attributable to such increase is treated as issued on the date of such increase.

(iv) *Principal purpose rule.*—For purposes of this paragraph (b)(3), a covered debt instrument that is not issued by a funded member during the per se period with respect to a distribution or acquisition described in paragraphs (b)(3)(i)(A) through (C) of this section is treated as funding the distribution or acquisition to the extent that it is issued by a funded member with a principal purpose of funding a distribution or acquisition described in paragraphs (b)(3)(i)(A) through (C) of this section. Whether a covered debt instrument is issued with a principal purpose of funding a distribution or acquisition described in paragraphs (b)(3)(i)(A) through (C) of this section is determined based on all the facts and circumstances. A covered debt instrument may be treated as issued with a principal purpose of funding a distribution or acquisition described in paragraphs (b)(3)(i)(A) through (C) of this section regardless of whether it is issued before or after the distribution or acquisition.

(v) *Predecessors and successors.*—(A) *In general.*—Subject to the limitations in paragraph (b)(3)(v)(B) of this section, for purposes of this paragraph (b)(3), references to a funded member include references to any predecessor or successor of such member. See paragraph (h)(3) of this section, *Examples 9* and *10*, for illustrations of this rule.

(B) *Limitations to the application of the per se funding rule.*—For purposes of paragraph (b)(3)(iii)(A) of this section, a covered debt instrument issued by a funded member that satisfies the condition described in paragraph (b)(3)(iii)(A) with respect to a distribution or acquisition described in paragraphs (b)(3)(i)(A) through (C) of this section made by a predecessor or successor of the funded member is not treated as issued during the per se period with respect to the distribution or acquisition unless the conditions described in paragraphs (b)(3)(v)(B)(1) and (2) of this section are satisfied:

(1) The covered debt instrument is issued by the funded member during the period beginning 36 months before the date of the transaction in which the predecessor or successor becomes a predecessor or successor and ending 36 months after the date of the transaction.

(2) The distribution or acquisition is made by the predecessor or successor during the period beginning 36 months before the date of the transaction in which the predecessor or successor becomes a predecessor or successor of the funded member and ending 36 months after the date of the transaction.

(vi) *Treatment of funded transactions.*—When a covered debt instrument is treated as stock pursuant to paragraph (b)(3) of this section, the distribution or acquisition described in paragraphs (b)(3)(i)(A) through (C) of this section that is treated as funded by such covered debt instrument is not recharacterized as a result of the treatment of the covered debt instrument as stock.

(vii) *Qualified short-term debt instrument.*—The term qualified short-term debt instrument means a covered debt instrument that is described in paragraphs (b)(3)(vii)(A) though (D) of this section.

(A) *Short-term funding arrangement.*—A covered debt instrument is described in this paragraph (b)(3)(vii)(A) if the requirements of the specified current assets test described in paragraph (b)(3)(vii)(A)(1) of this section or the 270-day test described in paragraph (b)(3)(vii)(A)(2) of this section (the alternative tests) are satisfied, provided that an issuer may only claim the benefit of one of the alternative tests with respect to covered debt instruments issued by the issuer in the same taxable year.

(1) *Specified current assets test.*—(i) *In general.*—The requirements of this paragraph (b)(3)(vii)(A)(1) are satisfied with respect to a covered debt instrument if the requirement of paragraph (b)(3)(vii)(A)(1)(*ii*) of this section is satisfied, but only to the extent the requirement of paragraph (b)(3)(vii)(A)(1)(*iii*) of this section is satisfied.

(*ii*) *Maximum interest rate.*—The rate of interest charged with respect to the covered debt instrument does not exceed an arm's length interest rate, as determined under section 482 and §§ 1.482-1 through 1.482-9, that would be charged with respect to a comparable debt instrument of the issuer with a term that does not exceed the longer of 90 days and the issuer's normal operating cycle.

(*iii*) *Maximum outstanding balance.*—The amount owed by the issuer under covered debt instruments issued to members of the issuer's expanded group that satisfy the requirements of paragraph (b)(3)(vii)(A)(1)(*ii*), (b)(3)(vii)(A)(2) (if the covered debt instrument was issued in a prior taxable year), or (b)(3)(vii)(B) or (C) of this section immediately after the covered debt instrument is issued does not exceed the maximum of the amounts of specified current assets reasonably expected to be reflected, under applicable accounting principles, on the issuer's balance sheet as a result of transactions in the ordinary course of business during the subsequent 90–day period or the issuer's normal operating cycle, whichever is longer. For purposes of the preceding sentence, in the case of an issuer that is a qualified cash pool header, the amount owed by the issuer shall not take into account deposits described in paragraph (b)(3)(vii)(D) of this section. Additionally, the amount owed by any issuer shall be reduced by the amount of the issuer's deposits with a qualified cash pool header, but only to the extent of amounts borrowed from the same qualified cash pool header that satisfy the requirements of paragraph (b)(3)(vii)(A)(2) (if the covered debt instrument was issued in a prior taxable year) or (b)(3)(vii) A)(1)(*ii*) of this section.

(*iv*) *Specified current assets.*—For purposes of paragraph (b)(3)(vii)(A)(1)(*iii*) of this section, the term *specified current assets* means assets that are reasonably expected to be realized in cash or sold (including by being incorporated into inventory that is sold) during the normal operating cycle of the issuer, other than cash, cash

32,070

Corporate Interests Treated as Stock or Indebtedness
See p. 20,601 for regulations not amended to reflect law changes

equivalents, and assets that are reflected on the books and records of a qualified cash pool header.

(v) Normal operating cycle.—For purposes of paragraph (b)(3)(vii)(A)(*1*) of this section, the term *normal operating cycle* means the issuer's normal operating cycle as determined under applicable accounting principles, except that if the issuer has no single clearly defined normal operating cycle, then the normal operating cycle is determined based on a reasonable analysis of the length of the operating cycles of the multiple businesses and their sizes relative to the overall size of the issuer.

(vi) Applicable accounting principles.—For purposes of paragraph (b)(3)(vii)(A)(*1*) of this section, the term *applicable accounting principles* means the financial accounting principles generally accepted in the United States, or an international financial accounting standard, that is applicable to the issuer in preparing its financial statements, computed on a consistent basis.

(2) 270-day test.—*(i) In general.*—A covered debt instrument is described in this paragraph (b)(3)(vii)(A)(2) if the requirements of paragraphs (b)(3)(vii)(A)(2)(*ii*) through (*iv*) of this section are satisfied.

(ii) Maximum term and interest rate.—The covered debt instrument must have a term of 270 days or less or be an advance under a revolving credit agreement or similar arrangement and must bear a rate of interest that does not exceed an arm's length interest rate, as determined under section 482 and §§1.482-1 through 1.482-9, that would be charged with respect to a comparable debt instrument of the issuer with a term that does not exceed 270 days.

(iii) Lender-specific indebtedness limit.—The issuer is a net borrower from the lender for no more than 270 days during the taxable year of the issuer, and in the case of a covered debt instrument outstanding during consecutive tax years, the issuer is a net borrower from the lender for no more than 270 consecutive days, in both cases taking into account only covered debt instruments that satisfy the requirement of paragraph (b)(3)(vii)(A)(2)(*ii*) of this section other than covered debt instruments described in paragraph (b)(3)(vii)(B) or (C) of this section.

(iv) Overall indebtedness limit.—The issuer is a net borrower under all covered debt instruments issued to members of the issuer's expanded group that satisfy the requirements of paragraphs (b)(3)(vii)(A)(2)(*ii*) and (*iii*) of this section, other than covered debt instruments described in paragraph (b)(3)(vii)(B) or (C) of this section, for no more than 270 days during the taxable year of the issuer, determined without regard to the identity of the lender under such covered debt instruments.

(v) Inadvertent error.—An issuer's failure to satisfy the 270-day test will be disregarded if the failure is reasonable in light of all the facts and circumstances and the failure is promptly cured upon discovery. A failure to satisfy the 270-day test will be considered reasonable if the taxpayer maintains due diligence procedures to prevent such failures, as evidenced by having written policies and operational procedures in place to monitor compliance with the 270-day test and management-level employees of the expanded group having undertaken reasonable efforts to establish, follow, and enforce such policies and procedures.

(B) Ordinary course loans.—A covered debt instrument is described in this paragraph (b)(3)(vii)(B) if the covered debt instrument is issued as consideration for the acquisition of property other than money in the ordinary course of the issuer's trade or business, provided that the obligation is reasonably expected to be repaid within 120 days of issuance.

(C) Interest-free loans.—A covered debt instrument is described in this paragraph (b)(3)(vii)(C) if the instrument does not provide for stated interest or no interest is charged on the instrument, the instrument does not have original issue discount (as defined in section 1273 and §§1.1273-1 and 1.1273-2), interest is not imputed under section 483 or section 7872 and §§1.483-1 through 1.483-4 or §§1.7872-1 through 1.7872-16, respectively, and interest is not required to be charged under section 482 and §§1.482-1 through 1.482-9.

(D) Deposits with a qualified cash pool header.—*(1) In general.*—A covered debt instrument is described in this paragraph (b)(3)(vii)(D) if it is a demand deposit received by a qualified cash pool header described in paragraph (b)(3)(vii)(D)(2) of this section pursuant to a cash-management arrangement described in paragraph (b)(3)(vii)(D)(3) of this section. This paragraph (b)(3)(vii)(D) does not apply if a purpose for making the demand deposit is to facilitate the avoidance of the purposes of this section with respect to a qualified

business unit (as defined in section 989(a) and §1.989(a)-1) (QBU) that is not a qualified cash pool header.

(2) Qualified cash pool header.—The term *qualified cash pool header* means an expanded group member, controlled partnership, or QBU described in §1.989(a)-1(b)(2)(ii), that has as its principal purpose managing a cash-management arrangement for participating expanded group members, provided that the excess (if any) of funds on deposit with such expanded group member, controlled partnership, or QBU (header) over the outstanding balance of loans made by the header is maintained on the books and records of the header in the form of cash or cash equivalents, or invested through deposits with, or the acquisition of obligations or portfolio securities of, persons that do not have a relationship to the header (or, in the case of a header that is a QBU described in §1.989(a)-1(b)(2)(ii), its owner) described in section 267(b) or section 707(b).

(3) Cash-management arrangement.—The term *cash-management arrangement* means an arrangement the principal purpose of which is to manage cash for participating expanded group members. For purposes of the preceding sentence, managing cash means borrowing excess funds from participating expanded group members and lending funds to participating expanded group members, and may also include foreign exchange management, clearing payments, investing excess cash with an unrelated person, depositing excess cash with another qualified cash pool header, and settling intercompany accounts, for example through netting centers and pay-on-behalf-of programs.

(viii) Distributions or acquisitions occurring before April 5, 2016.—A distribution or acquisition that occurs before April 5, 2016, is not taken into account for purposes of applying this paragraph (b)(3).

(4) Anti-abuse rule.—If a member of an expanded group enters into a transaction with a principal purpose of avoiding the purposes of this section or §1.385-3, an interest issued or held by that member or another member of the member's expanded group may, depending on the relevant facts and circumstances, be treated as stock. Paragraphs (b)(4)(i) and (ii) of this section include a non-exhaustive list of transactions that could result in an interest being treated as stock under this paragraph (b)(4).

(i) Interests.—An interest is treated as stock if it is issued with a principal purpose of avoiding the purposes of this section or §1.385-3. Interests subject to this paragraph (b)(4)(i) may include:

(A) An interest that is not a covered debt instrument for purposes of this section (for example, a contract to which section 483 applies that is not otherwise a covered debt instrument or a non-periodic swap payment that is not otherwise a covered debt instrument).

(B) A covered debt instrument issued to a person that is not a member of the issuer's expanded group, if the covered debt instrument is later acquired by a member of the issuer's expanded group or such person later becomes a member of the issuer's expanded group.

(C) A covered debt instrument issued to an entity that is not taxable as a corporation for federal tax purposes.

(D) A covered debt instrument issued in connection with a reorganization or similar transaction.

(E) A covered debt instrument issued as part of a plan or a series of transactions to expand the applicability of the transition rules described in §1.385-3(j)(2) or §1.385-3(k)(2).

(ii) Other transactions.—A covered debt instrument is treated as stock if the funded member or any member of the expanded group engages in a transaction (including a distribution or acquisition) with a principal purpose of avoiding the purposes of this section or §1.385-3. Transactions subject to this paragraph (b)(4)(ii) may include:

(A) A member of the issuer's expanded group is substituted as a new obligor or added as a co-obligor on an existing covered debt instrument.

(B) A covered debt instrument is transferred in connection with a reorganization or similar transaction.

(C) A covered debt instrument funds a distribution or acquisition where the distribution or acquisition is made by a member other than the funded member and the funded member acquires the assets of the other member in a transaction that does not make the other member a predecessor to the funded member.

(D) Members of a consolidated group engage in transactions as part of a plan or a series of transactions through the use of the consolidated group rules set forth in §1.385-4, including through the use of the departing member rules.

(5) Coordination between general rule and funding rule.—For purposes of this section, a distribution or acquisition described in paragraph (b)(2) of this section is not also described in paragraph (b)(3)(i)

of this section. In the case of an asset reorganization, an acquisition described in paragraph (b)(2)(iii) of this section by the transferee corporation is not also a distribution or acquisition described in paragraph (b)(3)(i) of this section by the transferor corporation. For purposes of this paragraph (b)(5), whether a distribution or acquisition is described in paragraphs (b)(2)(i) through (iii) of this section is determined without regard to paragraph (c) of this section.

(6) *Non-duplication.*—Except as otherwise provided in paragraph (d)(2) of this section, to the extent a distribution or acquisition described in paragraphs (b)(3)(i)(A) through (C) of this section is treated as funded by a covered debt instrument under paragraph (b)(3) of this section, the distribution or acquisition is not treated as funded by another covered debt instrument and the covered debt instrument is not treated as funding another distribution or acquisition for purposes of paragraph (b)(3).

(c) *Exceptions.*—(1) *In general.*—This paragraph (c) provides exceptions for purposes of applying paragraphs (b)(2) and (b)(3) of this section to a covered member. These exceptions are applied in the following order: first, paragraph (c)(2) of this section; second, paragraph (c)(3) of this section; and, third, paragraph (c)(4) of this section. The exceptions under §1.385-3(c)(2) and (c)(3) apply to distributions and acquisitions that are otherwise described in paragraph (b)(2) or (b)(3)(i) of this section after applying paragraphs (b)(3)(ii) and (b)(5) of this section. Except as otherwise provided, the exceptions are applied by taking into account the aggregate treatment of controlled partnerships described in §1.385-3(f).

(2) *Exclusions for transactions otherwise described in paragraph (b)(2) or (b)(3)(i) of this section.*—(i) *Exclusion for certain acquisitions of subsidiary stock.*—(A) *In general.*—An acquisition of expanded group stock (including by issuance) is not treated as described in paragraph (b)(2)(ii) or (b)(3)(i)(B) of this section if, immediately after the acquisition, the covered member that acquires the expanded group stock (acquirer) controls the member of the expanded group from which the expanded group stock is acquired (seller), and the acquirer does not relinquish control of the seller pursuant to a plan that existed on the date of the acquisition, other than in a transaction in which the seller ceases to be a member of the expanded group of which the acquirer is a member. For purposes of the preceding sentence, an acquirer and seller do not cease to be members of the same expanded group by reason of a complete liquidation described in section 331.

(B) *Control.*—For purposes of this paragraph (c)(2)(i) and paragraph (c)(3)(ii)(E) of this section, control of a corporation means the direct or indirect ownership of more than 50 percent of the total combined voting power of all classes of stock of the corporation entitled to vote and more than 50 percent of the total value of the stock of the corporation. For purposes of the preceding sentence, indirect ownership is determined by applying the principles of section 958(a) without regard to whether an intermediate entity is foreign or domestic.

(C) *Rebuttable presumption.*—For purposes of paragraph (c)(2)(i)(A) of this section, the acquirer is presumed to have a plan to relinquish control of the seller on the date of the acquisition if the acquirer relinquishes control of the seller within the 36-month period following the date of the acquisition. The presumption created by the previous sentence may be rebutted by facts and circumstances clearly establishing that the loss of control was not contemplated on the date of the acquisition and that the avoidance of the purposes of this section or §1.385-3 was not a principal purpose for the subsequent loss of control.

(ii) *Exclusion for compensatory stock acquisitions.*—An acquisition of expanded group stock is not treated as described in paragraph (b)(2)(ii) or (b)(3)(i)(B) of this section if the expanded group stock is delivered to individuals that are employees, directors, or independent contractors in consideration for services rendered by such individuals to a member of the expanded group or a controlled partnership in which a member of the expanded group is an expanded group partner.

(iii) *Exclusion for distributions or acquisitions resulting from transfer pricing adjustments.*—A distribution or acquisition deemed to occur under §1.482-1(g) (including adjustments made pursuant to Revenue Procedure 99-32, 1999-2 C.B. 296) is not treated as described in paragraph (b)(3)(i)(A) or (B) of this section.

(iv) *Exclusion for acquisitions of expanded group stock by a dealer in securities.*—An acquisition of expanded group stock by a dealer in securities (within the meaning of section 475(c)(1)), or by an expanded group partner treated as acquiring expanded group stock pursuant to §1.385-3(f)(2) if the relevant controlled partnership is a dealer in securities, is not treated as described in paragraph (b)(2)(ii) or (b)(3)(i)(B) of this section to the extent the expanded group stock is

acquired in the ordinary course of the dealer's business of dealing in securities. The preceding sentence applies solely to the extent that—

(A) The dealer accounts for the stock as securities held primarily for sale to customers in the ordinary course of business;

(B) The dealer disposes of the stock within a period of time that is consistent with the holding of the stock for sale to customers in the ordinary course of business, taking into account the terms of the stock and the conditions and practices prevailing in the markets for similar stock during the period in which it is held; and

(C) The dealer does not sell or otherwise transfer the stock to a person in the same expanded group, other than in a sale to a dealer that in turn satisfies the requirements of paragraph (c)(2)(iv) of this section.

(v) *Exclusion for certain acquisitions of expanded group stock resulting from application of this section.*—The following deemed acquisitions are not treated as acquisitions of expanded group stock described in paragraph (b)(3)(i)(B) of this section, provided that they are not part of a plan or arrangement to prevent the application of paragraph (b)(3)(i) to a covered debt instrument:

(A) An acquisition of a covered debt instrument that is treated as stock by means of paragraph (b)(3) of this section.

(B) An acquisition of stock of a regarded owner that is deemed to be issued under §1.385-3(c)(4).

(C) An acquisition of deemed partner stock pursuant to a deemed transfer or a specified event described in §1.385-3(f)(4) or (5).

(3) *Reductions for transactions described in paragraph (b)(2) or (b)(3)(i) of this section.*—(i) *Reduction for expanded group earnings.*—(A) *In general.*—The aggregate amount of any distributions or acquisitions by a covered member described in paragraph (b)(2) or (b)(3)(i) of this section in a taxable year during the covered member's expanded group period is reduced by the covered member's expanded group earnings account (as defined in paragraph (c)(3)(i)(B) of this section) for the expanded group period as of the close of the taxable year. The reduction described in this paragraph (c)(3)(i)(A) applies to one or more distributions or acquisitions based on the order in which the distributions or acquisitions occur, regardless of whether any distribution or acquisition would be treated as funded by a covered debt instrument without regard to this paragraph (c)(3).

(B) *Expanded group earnings account.*—The term *expanded group earnings account* means, with respect to a covered member and an expanded group period (as defined in paragraph (c)(3)(i)(E) of this section) of the covered member, the excess, if any, of the covered member's expanded group earnings (as defined in paragraph (c)(3)(i)(C) of this section) for the expanded group period over the covered member's expanded group reductions (as defined in paragraph (c)(3)(i)(D) of this section) for the expanded group period.

(C) *Expanded group earnings.*—(1) *In general.*—The term expanded group earnings means, with respect to a covered member and an expanded group period of the covered member, the earnings and profits accumulated by the covered member during the expanded group period, computed as of the close of the taxable year of the covered member, without diminution by reason of any distributions or acquisitions by the covered member described in paragraphs (b)(2) and (b)(3)(i) of this section. Notwithstanding the preceding sentence, the expanded group earnings of a covered member do not include earnings and profits accumulated by the covered member in any taxable year ending before April 5, 2016.

(2) *Special rule for change in expanded group within a taxable year.*—For purposes of calculating a covered member's expanded group earnings for a taxable year that is not wholly included in an expanded group period, the covered member's expanded group earnings are ratably allocated among the portion of the taxable year included in the expanded group period and the portion of the taxable year not included in the expanded group period. For purposes of the preceding sentence, the expanded group period is determined by excluding the day on which the covered member becomes a member of an expanded group with the same expanded group parent and including the day on which the covered member ceases to be a member of an expanded group with the same expanded group parent.

(3) *Look-through rule for dividends.*—(i) *In general.*—For purposes of paragraph (c)(3)(i)(C)(1) of this section, a dividend from a member of the same expanded group (*distributing member*) is not taken into account for purposes of calculating a covered member's expanded group earnings, except to the extent the dividend is attributable to earnings and profits accumulated by the distributing member in a taxable year ending after April 4, 2016, during its expanded group period (*qualified earnings and profits*). For purposes of the preceding sentence, a dividend received from a member (*intermediate distributing member*) is not taken into account for purposes of calculating the qualified earnings and profits of a distributing member (or

32,072

Corporate Interests Treated as Stock or Indebtedness
See p. 20,601 for regulations not amended to reflect law changes

another intermediate distributing member), except to the extent the dividend is attributable to qualified earnings and profits of the intermediate distributing member. A dividend from distributing member or an intermediate distributing member is considered to be attributable to qualified earnings and profits to the extent thereof. If a controlled partnership receives a dividend from a distributing member and a portion of the dividend is allocated (including through one or more partnerships) to a covered member, then, for purposes of this paragraph (c)(3)(i)(C)(3), the covered member is treated as receiving the dividend from the distributing member.

(ii) *Dividend.*—For purposes of paragraph (c)(3)(i)(C)(3)(i) of this section, the term dividend has the meaning specified in section 316, including the portion of gain recognized under section 1248 that is treated as a dividend and deemed dividends under section 367(b) and the regulations thereunder. In addition, the term dividend includes inclusions with respect to stock (for example, inclusions under sections 951(a) and 1293).

(4) *Effect of interest deductions.*—For purposes of calculating the expanded group earnings of a covered member for a taxable year, expanded group earnings are calculated without regard to the application of this section during the taxable year to a covered debt instrument issued by the covered member that was not treated as stock under paragraph (b) of this section as of the close of the preceding taxable year, or, if the covered member is an expanded group partner in a controlled partnership that is the issuer of a debt instrument, without regard to the application of §1.385-3(f)(4)(i) during the taxable year with respect to the covered member's share of the debt instrument. To the extent that the application of this paragraph (c)(3)(i)(C)(4) reduces the expanded group earnings of the covered member for the taxable year, the expanded group earnings of the covered member are increased as of the beginning of the succeeding taxable year during the expanded group period.

(D) *Expanded group reductions.*—The term expanded group reductions means, with respect to a covered member and an expanded group period of the covered member, the amounts by which acquisitions or distributions described in paragraph (b)(2) or (b)(3)(i) of this section were reduced by reason of paragraph (c)(3)(i)(A) of this section during the portion of the expanded group period preceding the taxable year.

(E) *Expanded group period.*—(1) *In general.*—For purposes of this paragraph (c)(3)(i) and paragraph (c)(3)(ii) of this section, the term expanded group period means, with respect to a covered member, the period during which a covered member is a member of an expanded group with the same expanded group parent.

(2) *Mere change.*—For purposes of paragraph (c)(3)(i)(E)(1) of this section, an expanded group parent that is a resulting corporation (within the meaning of §1.368-2(m)(1)) in a reorganization described in section 368(a)(1)(F) is treated as the same expanded group parent as an expanded group parent that is a transferor corporation (within the meaning of §1.368-2(m)(1)) in the same reorganization, provided that either—

(i) The transferor corporation is not a covered member; or

(ii) Both the transferor corporation and the resulting corporation are covered members.

(F) *Special rules for certain corporate transactions.*—(1) *Reduction for expanded group earnings in an asset reorganization.*—For purposes of applying paragraph (c)(3)(i) of this section, a distribution or acquisition described in paragraph (b)(2) or (b)(3)(i) of this section that occurs pursuant to a reorganization described in section 381(a)(2) is reduced solely by the expanded group earnings account of the acquiring member after taking into account the adjustment to its expanded group earnings account provided in paragraph (c)(3)(i)(F)(2)(ii) of this section.

(2) *Effect of certain corporate transactions on the calculation of expanded group earnings account.*—(i) *In general.*—Section 381 and §1.312-10 are not taken into account for purposes of calculating a covered member's expanded group earnings account for an expanded group period. The expanded group earnings account that a covered member succeeds to under paragraphs (c)(3)(i)(F)(2)(ii) through (iv) of this section is attributed to the covered member's expanded group period as of the close of the date of the distribution or transfer.

(ii) *Section 381 transactions.*—If a covered member (*acquiring member*) acquires the assets of another covered member (*acquired member*) in a transaction described in section 381(a), and, immediately before the transaction, both corporations are members of the same expanded group, then the acquiring member succeeds to the expanded group earnings account of the acquired member, if

any, determined after application of paragraph (c)(3)(i) of this section with respect to the final taxable year of the acquired member.

(iii) *Section 1.312-10(a) transactions.*—If a covered member (*transferor member*) transfers property to another covered member (*transferee member*) in a transaction described in §1.312-10(a), the expanded group earnings account of the transferor member is allocated between the transferor member and the transferee member in the same proportion as the earnings and profits of the transferor member are allocated between the transferor member and the transferee member under §1.312-10(a).

(iv) *Section 1.312-10(b) transactions.*—If a covered member (*distributing member*) distributes the stock of another covered member (*controlled member*) in a transaction described in §1.312-10(b), the expanded group earnings account of the distributing member is decreased by the amount that the expanded group earnings account of the distributing member would have been decreased under paragraph (c)(3)(i)(F)(2)(iii) of this section if the distributing member had transferred the stock of the controlled member to a newly formed corporation in a transaction described in §1.312-10(a). If the amount of the decrease described in the preceding sentence exceeds the expanded group earnings account of the controlled member immediately before the transaction described in §1.312-10(b), then the expanded group earnings account of the controlled member after the transaction is equal to the amount of the decrease.

(G) *Overlapping expanded groups.*—A covered member that is a member of two expanded groups at the same time has a single expanded group earnings account with respect to a single expanded group period. In this case, the expanded group period is determined by reference to the shorter of the two periods during which the covered member is a member of an expanded group with the same expanded group parent.

(ii) *Reduction for qualified contributions.*—(A) *In general.*—The amount of a distribution or acquisition by a covered member described in paragraph (b)(2) or (b)(3)(i) of this section is reduced by the aggregate fair market value of the stock issued by the covered member in one or more qualified contributions (as defined in paragraph (c)(3)(ii)(B) of this section) during the qualified period (as defined in paragraph (c)(3)(ii)(C) of this section), but only to the extent the qualified contribution or qualified contributions have not reduced another distribution or acquisition. The reduction described in this paragraph (c)(3)(ii)(A) applies to one or more distributions or acquisitions based on the order in which the distributions or acquisitions occur, regardless of whether any distribution or acquisition would be treated as funded by a covered debt instrument without regard to this paragraph (c)(3).

(B) *Qualified contribution.*—The term *qualified contribution* means, with respect to a covered member, except as provided in paragraph (c)(3)(ii)(E) of this section, a contribution of property, other than excluded property (defined in paragraph (c)(3)(ii)(D) of this section), to the covered member by a member of the covered member's expanded group (or by a controlled partnership of the expanded group) in exchange for stock.

(C) *Qualified period.*—The term *qualified period* means, with respect to a covered member, a qualified contribution, and a distribution or acquisition described in paragraph (b)(2) or (b)(3)(i) of this section, the period beginning on the later of the beginning of the periods described in paragraphs (c)(3)(ii)(C)(1) and (2) of this section, and ending on the earlier of the ending of the periods described in paragraphs (c)(3)(ii)(C)(1) and (2) of this section or the date described in paragraph (c)(3)(ii)(C)(3) of this section.

(1) The period beginning 36 months before the date of the distribution or acquisition, and ending 36 months after the date of the distribution or acquisition.

(2) The covered member's expanded group period (as defined in paragraph (c)(3)(i)(E) of this section) that includes the distribution or acquisition.

(3) The last day of the first taxable year that a covered debt instrument issued by the covered member would, absent the application of this paragraph (c)(3)(ii) with respect to the distribution or acquisition, be treated, in whole or in part, as stock under paragraph (b) of this section or, in the case of a covered debt instrument issued by a controlled partnership in which the covered member is an expanded group partner, the covered debt instrument would be treated, in whole or in part, as a specified portion.

(D) *Excluded property.*—The term *excluded property* means—

(1) Expanded group stock;

(2) Property acquired by the covered member in an asset reorganization from a member of the expanded group of which the covered member is a member;

(3) A covered debt instrument of any member of the same expanded group, including a covered debt instrument issued by the covered member;

(4) Property acquired by the covered member in exchange for a covered debt instrument issued by the covered member that is recharacterized under paragraph (b)(3) of this section;

(5) A debt instrument issued by a controlled partnership of the expanded group of which the covered member is a member, including the portion of such a debt instrument that is a deemed transferred receivable or a retained receivable; and

(6) Any other property acquired by the covered member with a principal purpose to avoid the purposes of this section or §1.385-3, including a transaction involving an indirect transfer of property described in paragraphs (c)(3)(ii)(D)(*1*) through (5) of this section.

(E) *Excluded contributions.—(1) Upstream contributions from certain subsidiaries.—*For purposes of paragraph (c)(3)(ii)(B) of this section, a contribution of property from a corporation (*controlled member*) that the covered member controls, within the meaning of paragraph (c)(2)(i)(B) of this section, is not a qualified contribution.

*(2) Contributions to a predecessor or successor.—*For purposes of paragraph (c)(3)(ii)(B) of this section, a contribution of property to a covered member from a corporation of which the covered member is a predecessor or successor, or from a corporation controlled by that corporation within the meaning of paragraph (c)(2)(i)(B) of this section, is not a qualified contribution.

*(3) Contributions that do not increase fair market value.—*A contribution of property to a covered member that is not described in paragraph (c)(3)(ii)(E)(*1*) or (2) of this section is not a qualified contribution to the extent that the contribution does not increase the aggregate fair market value of the outstanding stock of the covered member immediately after the transaction and taking into account all related transactions, other than distributions and acquisitions described in paragraphs (b)(2) and (b)(3)(i) of this section.

*(4) Contributions that become excluded contributions after the date of the contribution.—*If a contribution of property described in paragraph (c)(3)(ii)(E)(*1*) or (2) of this section occurs before the covered member acquires control of the controlled member described in paragraph (c)(3)(ii)(E)(*1*) or before the transaction in which the corporation described in paragraph (c)(3)(ii)(E)(2) becomes a predecessor or successor to the covered member, the contribution of property ceases to be a qualified contribution on the date that the covered member acquires control of the controlled member or on the date of the transaction in which the corporation becomes a predecessor or successor to the covered member (*transaction date*). If the contribution of property occurs within 36 months before the transaction date, the covered member is treated as making a distribution described in paragraph (b)(3)(i)(A) of this section on the transaction date equal to the amount by which any distribution or acquisition described in paragraph (b)(2) or (b)(3)(i) of this section was reduced under paragraph (c)(3)(ii)(A) of this section because the contribution of property was treated as a qualified contribution.

(F) *Special rules for certain corporate transactions.—(1) Reduction for qualified contributions in an asset reorganization.—*For purposes of applying paragraph (c)(3)(ii)(A) of this section, a distribution or acquisition described in paragraph (b)(2) or (b)(3)(i) of this section that occurs pursuant to a reorganization described in section 381(a)(2) is reduced solely by the qualified contributions of the acquiring member after taking into account the adjustment to its qualified contributions provided in paragraph (c)(3)(ii)(F)(2) of this section.

*(2) Effect of certain corporate transactions on the calculation of qualified contributions.—(i) In general.—*This paragraph (c)(3)(ii)(F)(2) provides rules for allocating or reducing the qualified contributions of a covered member as a result of certain corporation transactions. For purposes of paragraph (c)(3)(ii)(C)(*1*) of this section, a qualified contribution that a covered member succeeds to under paragraphs (c)(3)(ii)(F)(2)(*ii*) and (*iii*) of this section is treated as made to the covered member on the date on which the qualified contribution was made to the covered member that received the qualified contribution. For purposes of paragraph (c)(3)(ii)(C)(2) of this section, a qualified contribution that a covered member succeeds to under paragraphs (c)(3)(ii)(F)(2)(*ii*) and (*iii*) of this section is attributed to the covered member's expanded group period as of the close of the date of the distribution or transfer. For purposes of paragraph (c)(3)(ii)(C)(3) of this section, a qualified contribution a covered member succeeds to under paragraphs (c)(3)(ii)(F)(2)(*ii*) and (*iii*) of this section is treated as made to the covered member as of the close of the date of the distribution or transfer.

*(ii) Section 381 transactions.—*If a covered member (acquiring member) acquires the assets of another covered member (acquired member) in a transaction described in section 381(a), and, immediately before the transaction, both corporations are members of the same expanded group, the acquiring member succeeds to the qualified contributions of the acquired member, if any, adjusted for the application of paragraph (c)(3)(ii)(E)(4) of this section.

*(iii) Section 1.312-10(a) transactions.—*If a covered member (transferor member) transfers property to another covered member (transferee member) in a transaction described in §1.312-10(a), each qualified contribution of the transferor member is allocated between the transferor member and the transferee member in the same proportion as the earnings and profits of the transferor member are allocated between the transferor member and the transferee member under §1.312-10(a).

*(iv) Section 1.312-10(b) transactions.—*If a covered member (distributing member) distributes the stock of another covered member (controlled member) in a transaction described in §1.312-10(b), each qualified contribution of the distributing member is decreased by the amount that each qualified contribution of the distributing member would have been decreased under paragraph (c)(3)(ii)(F)(2)(*iii*) of this section if the distributing member had transferred the stock of the controlled member to a newly formed corporation in a transaction described in §1.312-10(a). No amount of the qualified contributions of the distributing member is allocated to the controlled member.

*(iii) Predecessors and successors.—*For purposes of this paragraph (c)(3), references to a covered member do not include references to any corporation of which the covered member is a predecessor or successor. Accordingly, a distribution or acquisition by a covered member described in paragraphs (b)(3)(i)(A) through (C) is reduced solely by the expanded group earnings account of the covered member (taking into account the application of paragraph (c)(3)(i)(F)(2) of this section) and the qualified contributions of the covered member (taking into account the application of paragraph (c)(3)(ii)(F)(2) of this section), notwithstanding that the distribution or acquisition is treated as made by a funded member of which the covered member is a predecessor or successor.

*(iv) Ordering rule.—*The exceptions described in this paragraph (c)(3) are applied in the following order: first, paragraph (c)(3)(i) of this section; and, second, paragraph (c)(3)(ii) of this section.

*(4) Threshold exception.—*A covered debt instrument is not treated as stock under this section if, immediately after the covered debt instrument would be treated as stock under this section but for the application of this paragraph (c)(4), the aggregate adjusted issue price of covered debt instruments held by members of the issuer's expanded group that would be treated as stock under this section but for the application of this paragraph (c)(4) does not exceed $50 million. To the extent a debt instrument issued by a controlled partnership would be treated as a specified portion (as defined in paragraph (g)(23) of this section) but for the application of this paragraph (c)(4), the debt instrument is treated as a covered debt instrument described in the preceding sentence for purposes of this paragraph (c)(4). To the extent that, immediately after a covered debt instrument would be treated as stock under this section but for the application of this paragraph (c)(4), the aggregate adjusted issue price of covered debt instruments held by members of the issuer's expanded group that would be treated as stock under this section but for the application of this paragraph (c)(4) exceeds $50 million, only the amount of the covered debt instrument in excess of $50 million is treated as stock under this section. For purposes of this rule, any covered debt instrument that is not denominated in U.S. dollars is translated into U.S. dollars at the spot rate (as defined in §1.988-1(d)) on the date that the covered debt instrument is issued.

(d) *Operating rules.—(1) Timing.—*This paragraph (d)(1) provides rules for determining when a covered debt instrument is treated as stock under paragraph (b) of this section. For special rules regarding the treatment of a deemed exchange of a covered debt instrument that occurs pursuant to paragraphs (d)(1)(ii), (d)(1)(iii), or (d)(1)(iv) of this section, see §1.385-1(d).

(i) *General timing rule.—*Except as otherwise provided in this paragraph (d)(1), when paragraph (b) of this section applies to treat a covered debt instrument as stock, the covered debt instrument is treated as stock when the covered debt instrument is issued. When paragraph (b)(3) of this section applies to treat a covered debt instrument as stock when the covered debt instrument is issued, see also paragraph (b)(3)(vi) of this section.

(ii) *Exception when a covered debt instrument is treated as funding a distribution or acquisition that occurs after the issuance of the covered*

32,074

Corporate Interests Treated as Stock or Indebtedness
See p. 20,601 for regulations not amended to reflect law changes

debt instrument.—When paragraph (b)(3)(iii) of this section applies to treat a covered debt instrument as funding a distribution or acquisition described in paragraph (b)(3)(i)(A) through (C) of this section that occurs after the covered debt instrument is issued, the covered debt instrument is deemed to be exchanged for stock on the date that the distribution or acquisition occurs. See paragraph (h)(3) of this section, *Examples 4 and 9*, for an illustration of this rule.

(iii) *Exception for certain predecessor and successor transactions.*— To the extent that a covered debt instrument would not be treated as stock but for the fact that a funded member is treated as the predecessor or successor of another expanded group member under paragraph (b)(3)(v) of this section, the covered debt instrument is deemed to be exchanged for stock on the later of the date that the funded member completes the transaction causing it to become a predecessor or successor of the other expanded group member or the date that the covered debt instrument would be treated as stock under paragraph (d)(1)(i) or (ii) of this section.

(iv) *Exception when a covered debt instrument is re-tested under paragraph (d)(2) of this section.*—When paragraph (b)(3)(iii) of this section applies to treat a covered debt instrument as funding a distribution or acquisition described in paragraphs (b)(3)(i)(A) through (C) of this section as a result of a re-testing described in paragraph (d)(2)(ii) of this section that occurs in a taxable year subsequent to the taxable year in which the covered debt instrument is issued, the covered debt instrument is deemed to be exchanged for stock on the later of the date of the re-testing or the date that the covered debt instrument would be treated as stock under paragraph (d)(1)(i) or (ii) of this section. See paragraph (h)(3) of this section, *Example 7*, for an illustration of this rule.

(2) *Covered debt instrument treated as stock that leaves the expanded group.*—(i) *Events that cause a covered debt instrument to cease to be treated as stock.*—Subject to paragraph (b)(4) of this section, this paragraph (d)(2)(i) applies with respect to a covered debt instrument that is treated as stock under this section when the holder and issuer of a covered debt instrument cease to be members of the same expanded group, either because the covered debt instrument is transferred to a person that is not a member of the expanded group that includes the issuer or because the holder or the issuer ceases to be a member of the same expanded group, or in the case of a holder that is a controlled partnership, when the holder ceases to be a controlled partnership with respect to the expanded group of which the issuer is a member, either because the partnership ceases to be a controlled partnership or because the issuer ceases to be a member of the same expanded group with respect to which the holder is a controlled partnership. In such a case, the covered debt instrument ceases to be treated as stock under this section. For this purpose, immediately before the transaction that causes the holder and issuer of the covered debt instrument to cease to be members of the same expanded group, or, if the holder is a controlled partnership, that causes the holder to cease to be a controlled partnership with respect to the expanded group of which the issuer is a member, the issuer is deemed to issue a new covered debt instrument to the holder in exchange for the covered debt instrument that was treated as stock in a transaction that is disregarded for purposes of paragraphs (b)(2) and (b)(3) of this section.

(ii) *Re-testing of covered debt instruments and certain distributions and acquisitions.*—(A) *General rule.*—For purposes of paragraph (b)(3)(iii) of this section, when paragraph (d)(2)(i) of this section or §1.385-4(c)(2) causes a covered debt instrument that previously was treated as stock pursuant to paragraph (b)(3) of this section to cease to be treated as stock, all other covered debt instruments of the issuer that are not treated as stock on the date that the transaction occurs that causes paragraph (d)(2)(i) of this section to apply are re-tested to determine whether those other covered debt instruments are treated as funding the distribution or acquisition that previously was treated as funded by the covered debt instrument that ceases to be treated as stock pursuant to paragraph (d)(2)(i) of this section. In addition, a covered debt instrument that is issued after an application of paragraph (d)(2)(i) of this section and within the per se period may also be treated as funding that distribution or acquisition. See paragraph (h)(3) of this section, *Example 7*, for an illustration of this rule.

(B) *Re-testing upon a specified event with respect to a debt instrument issued by a controlled partnership.*—If, with respect to a covered member that is an expanded group partner and a debt instrument issued by the controlled partnership, there is reduction in the covered member's specified portion under §1.385-3(f)(5)(i) by reason of a specified event, the covered member must re-test its debt instruments as described in paragraph (d)(2)(ii)(A) of this section.

(3) *Inapplicability of section 385(c)(1).*—Section 385(c)(1) does not apply with respect to a covered debt instrument to the extent that it is treated as stock under this section.

(4) *Treatment of disregarded entities.*—This paragraph (d)(4) applies to the extent that a covered debt instrument issued by a disregarded entity, the regarded owner of which is a covered member, would, absent the application of this paragraph (d)(4), be treated as stock under this section. In this case, rather than the covered debt instrument being treated as stock to such extent (applicable portion), the covered member that is the regarded owner of the disregarded entity is deemed to issue its stock in the manner described in this paragraph (d)(4). If the applicable portion otherwise would have been treated as stock under paragraph (b)(2) of this section, then the covered member is deemed to issue its stock to the expanded group member to which the covered debt instrument was, in form, issued (or transferred) in the transaction described in paragraph (b)(2) of this section. If the applicable portion otherwise would have been treated as stock under paragraph (b)(3)(i) of this section, then the covered member is deemed to issue its stock to the holder of the covered debt instrument in exchange for a portion of the covered debt instrument equal to the applicable portion. In each case, the covered member that is the regarded owner of the disregarded entity is treated as the holder of the applicable portion of the debt instrument issued by the disregarded entity, and the actual holder is treated as the holder of the remaining portion of the covered debt instrument and the stock deemed to be issued by the regarded owner. Under Federal tax principles, the applicable portion of the debt instrument issued by the disregarded entity generally is disregarded. This paragraph (d)(4) must be applied in a manner that is consistent with the principles of paragraph (f)(4) of this section. Thus, for example, stock deemed issued is deemed to have the same terms as the covered debt instrument issued by the disregarded entity, other than the identity of the issuer, and payments on the stock are determined by reference to payments made on the covered debt instrument issued by the disregarded entity. See §1.385-4(b)(3) for additional rules that apply if the regarded owner of the disregarded entity is a member of a consolidated group. If the regarded owner of a disregarded entity is a controlled partnership, then paragraph (f) of this section applies as though the controlled partnership were the issuer in form of the debt instrument.

(5) *Payments with respect to partially recharacterized covered debt instruments.*—(i) *General rule.*—Except as otherwise provided in paragraph (d)(5)(ii) of this section, a payment with respect to an instrument that is partially recharacterized as stock is treated as made pro rata to the portion treated as stock and to the portion treated as indebtedness.

(ii) *Special rule for payments not required pursuant to the terms of the instrument..*—A payment with respect to an instrument that is partially recharacterized as stock and that is a payment that is not required to be made pursuant to the terms of the instrument (for example, a prepayment of principal) may be designated by the issuer and the holder as with respect to the portion treated as stock or to the portion treated as indebtedness, in whole or in part. In the absence of such designation, see paragraph (d)(5)(i) of this section.

(6) *Treatment of a general rule transaction to which an exception applies.*—To the extent a covered member would, absent the application of paragraph (c)(2) or (c)(3) of this section, be treated as making a distribution or acquisition described in paragraph (b)(2) of this section, then, solely for purposes of applying paragraph (b)(3) of this section, the covered member is treated as issuing the covered debt instrument issued in the distribution or acquisition to a member of the covered member's expanded group in exchange for property.

(7) *Treatment for purposes of section 1504(a).*—(i) *Debt instruments treated as stock.*—A covered debt instrument that is treated as stock under paragraph (b)(2), (3), or (4) of this section and that is not described in section 1504(a)(4) is not treated as stock for purposes of determining whether the issuer is a member of an affiliated group (within the meaning of section 1504(a)).

(ii) *Deemed partner stock and stock deemed issued by a regarded owner.*—If deemed partner stock or stock that is deemed issued by a regarded owner under §1.385-3(d)(4) is not described in section 1504(a)(4), then that stock is not treated as stock for purposes of determining whether the issuer of the stock is a member of an affiliated group (within the meaning of section 1504(a)).

(e) *No affirmative use.*—[Reserved]

(f) *Treatment of controlled partnerships.*—(1) *In general.*—For purposes of this section and §1.385-4, a controlled partnership is treated as an aggregate of its partners in the manner described in this paragraph (f). Paragraph (f)(2) of this section sets forth rules concerning the aggregate treatment when a controlled partnership acquires property from a member of the expanded group. Paragraph (f)(3) of this section sets forth rules concerning the aggregate treatment when a controlled partnership issues a debt instrument. Paragraph (f)(4) of this section deems a debt instrument issued by a controlled partnership to be held by an expanded group partner rather than the holder-in-form in certain cases. Paragraph (f)(5) of this section sets forth the rules concerning events that cause the deemed results described in paragraph (f)(4) of this section to cease. Paragraph (f)(6) of this section exempts certain issuances of a controlled partnership's debt to a partner and a partner's debt to a controlled partnership from the application of this section. For definitions applicable for this section, see paragraph (g) of this section. For examples illustrating the application of this section, see paragraph (h) of this section.

(2) *Acquisitions of property by a controlled partnership.*— (i) *Acquisitions of property when a member of the expanded group is a partner on the date of the acquisition.*—(A) *Aggregate treatment.*—Except as otherwise provided in paragraphs (f)(2)(i)(C) and (f)(6) of this section, if a controlled partnership, with respect to an expanded group, acquires property from a member of the expanded group (transferor member), then, for purposes of this section, a member of the expanded group that is an expanded group partner on the date of the acquisition is treated as acquiring its share (as determined under paragraph (f)(2)(i)(B) of this section) of the property. The expanded group partner is treated as acquiring its share of the property from the transferor member in the manner (for example, in a distribution, in an exchange for property, or in an issuance), and on the date on which, the property is actually acquired by the controlled partnership from the transferor member. Accordingly, this section applies to a member's acquisition of property described in this paragraph (f)(2)(i)(A) in the same manner as if the member actually acquired the property from the transferor member, unless explicitly provided otherwise.

(B) *Expanded group partner's share of property.*—For purposes of paragraph (f)(2)(i)(A) of this section, a partner's share of property acquired by a controlled partnership is determined in accordance with the partner's liquidation value percentage (as defined in paragraph (g)(17) of this section) with respect to the controlled partnership. The liquidation value percentage is determined on the date on which the controlled partnership acquires the property.

(C) *Exception if transferor member is an expanded group partner.*—If a transferor member is an expanded group partner in the controlled partnership, paragraph (f)(2)(i)(A) of this section does not apply to such partner.

(ii) *Acquisitions of expanded group stock when a member of the expanded group becomes a partner after the acquisition.*—(A) *Aggregate treatment.*—Except as otherwise provided in paragraph (f)(2)(ii)(C) of this section, if a controlled partnership, with respect to an expanded group, owns expanded group stock, and a member of the expanded group becomes an expanded group partner in the controlled partnership, then, for purposes of this section, the member is treated as acquiring its share (as determined under paragraph (f)(2)(ii)(B) of this section) of the expanded group stock owned by the controlled partnership. The member is treated as acquiring its share of the expanded group stock on the date on which the member becomes an expanded group partner. Furthermore, the member is treated as if it acquires its share of the expanded group stock from a member of the expanded group in exchange for property other than expanded group stock, regardless of the manner in which the partnership acquired the stock and in which the member acquires its partnership interest. Accordingly, this section applies to a member's acquisition of expanded group stock described in this paragraph (f)(2)(ii)(A) in the same manner as if the member actually acquired the stock from a member of the expanded group in exchange for property other than expanded group stock, unless explicitly provided otherwise.

(B) *Expanded group partner's share of expanded group stock.*— For purposes of paragraph (f)(2)(ii)(A) of this section, a partner's share of expanded group stock owned by a controlled partnership is determined in accordance with the partner's liquidation value percentage with respect to the controlled partnership. The liquidation value percentage is determined on the date on which a member of the expanded group becomes an expanded group partner in the controlled partnership.

(C) *Exception if an expanded group partner acquires its interest in a controlled partnership in exchange for expanded group stock.*—Paragraph (f)(2)(ii)(A) of this section does not apply to a member of an expanded group that acquires its interest in a controlled partnership either from another partner in exchange solely for expanded group stock or upon a partnership contribution to the controlled partnership comprised solely of expanded group stock.

(3) *Issuances of debt instruments by a controlled partnership to a member of an expanded group.*—(i) *Aggregate treatment.*—If a controlled partnership, with respect to an expanded group, issues a debt instrument to a member of the expanded group, then, for purposes of this

section, a covered member that is an expanded group partner is treated as the issuer with respect to its share (as determined under paragraph (f)(3)(ii) of this section) of the debt instrument issued by the controlled partnership. This section applies to the portion of the debt instrument treated as issued by the covered member as described in this paragraph (f)(3)(i) in the same manner as if the covered member actually issued the debt instrument to the holder-in-form, unless otherwise provided. See paragraph (f)(4) of this section, which deems a debt instrument issued by a controlled partnership to be held by an expanded group partner rather than the holder-in-form in certain cases.

(ii) *Expanded group partner's share of a debt instrument issued by a controlled partnership.*—(A) *General rule.*—An expanded group partner's share of a debt instrument issued by a controlled partnership is determined on each date on which the partner makes a distribution or acquisition described in paragraph (b)(2) or (b)(3)(i) of this section (testing date). An expanded group partner's share of a debt instrument issued by a controlled partnership to a member of the expanded group is determined in accordance with the partner's issuance percentage (as defined in paragraph (g)(16) of this section) on the testing date. A partner's share determined under this paragraph (f)(3)(ii)(A) is adjusted as described in paragraph (f)(3)(ii)(B) of this section.

(B) *Additional rules if there is a specified portion with respect to a debt instrument.*—(1) An expanded group partner's share (as determined under paragraph (f)(3)(ii)(A) of this section) of a debt instrument issued by a controlled partnership is reduced, but not below zero, by the sum of all of the specified portions (as defined in paragraph (g)(23) of this section), if any, with respect to the debt instrument that correspond to one or more deemed transferred receivables (as defined in paragraph (g)(8) of this section) that are deemed to be held by the partner.

(2) If the aggregate of all of the expanded group partners' shares (as determined under paragraph (f)(3)(ii)(A) of this section and reduced under paragraph (f)(3)(ii)(B)(1) of this section) of the debt instrument exceeds the adjusted issue price of the debt, reduced by the sum of all of the specified portions with respect to the debt instrument that correspond to one or more deemed transferred receivables that are deemed to be held by one or more expanded group partners (excess amount), then each expanded group partner's share (as determined under paragraph (f)(3)(ii)(A) of this section and reduced under paragraph (f)(3)(ii)(B)(1) of this section) of the debt instrument is reduced. The amount of an expanded group partner's reduction is the excess amount multiplied by a fraction, the numerator of which is the partner's share, and the denominator of which is the aggregate of all of the expanded group partners' shares.

(iii) *Qualified short-term debt instrument.*—The determination of whether a debt instrument is a qualified short-term debt instrument for purposes of paragraph (b)(3)(vii) of this section is made at the partnership-level without regard to paragraph (f)(3)(i) of this section.

(4) *Recharacterization when there is a specified portion with respect to a debt instrument issued by a controlled partnership.*—(i) *General rule.*— A specified portion, with respect to a debt instrument issued by a controlled partnership and an expanded group partner, is not treated as stock under paragraph (b)(2) or (b)(3)(i) of this section. Except as otherwise provided in paragraphs (f)(4)(ii) and (iii) of this section, the holder-in-form (as defined in paragraph (g)(15) of this section) of the debt instrument is deemed to transfer a portion of the debt instrument (a deemed transferred receivable, as defined in paragraph (g)(8) of this section) with a principal amount equal to the adjusted issue price of the specified portion to the expanded group partner in exchange for stock in the expanded group partner (deemed partner stock, as defined in paragraph (g)(6) of this section) with a fair market value equal to the principal amount of the deemed transferred receivable. Except as otherwise provided in paragraph (f)(4)(vi) of this section (concerning the treatment of a deemed transferred receivable for purposes of section 752) and paragraph (f)(5) of this section (concerning specified events subsequent to the deemed transfer), the deemed transfer described in this paragraph (f)(4)(i) is deemed to occur for all Federal tax purposes.

(ii) *Expanded group partner is the holder-in-form of a debt instrument.*—If the specified portion described in paragraph (f)(4)(i) of this section is with respect to an expanded group partner that is the holder-in-form of the debt instrument, then paragraph (f)(4)(i) of this section will not apply with respect to that specified portion except that only the first sentence of paragraph (f)(4)(i) of this section is applicable.

(iii) *Expanded group partner is a consolidated group member.*— This paragraph (f)(4)(iii) applies when one or more expanded group partners is a member of a consolidated group that files (or is required to file) a consolidated U.S. Federal income tax return. In this case,

32,076

Corporate Interests Treated as Stock or Indebtedness
See p. 20,601 for regulations not amended to reflect law changes

notwithstanding § 1.385-4(b)(1) (which generally treats members of a consolidated group as one corporation for purposes of this section), the holder-in-form of the debt instrument issued by the controlled partnership is deemed to transfer the deemed transferred receivable or receivables to the expanded group partner or partners that are members of a consolidated group that make, or are treated as making under paragraph (f)(2) of this section, the regarded distributions or acquisitions (within the meaning of § 1.385-4(e)(5)) described in paragraph (b)(2) or (b)(3)(i) of this section in exchange for deemed partner stock in such partner or partners. To the extent those regarded distributions or acquisitions are made by a member of the consolidated group that is not an expanded group partner (excess amount), the holder-in-form is deemed to transfer a portion of the deemed transferred receivable or receivables to each member of the consolidated group that is an expanded group partner in exchange for deemed partner stock in the expanded group partner. The portion is the excess amount multiplied by a fraction, the numerator of which is the portion of the consolidated group's share (as determined under paragraph (f)(3)(ii) of this section) of the debt instrument issued by the controlled partnership that would have been the expanded group partner's share if the partner was not a member of a consolidated group, and the denominator of which is the consolidated group's share of the debt instrument issued by the controlled partnership.

(iv) *Rules regarding deemed transferred receivables and deemed partner stock.*—(A) *Terms of deemed partner stock.*—Deemed partner stock has the same terms as the deemed transferred receivable with respect to the deemed transfer, other than the identity of the issuer.

(B) *Treatment of payments with respect to a debt instrument for which there is one or more deemed transferred receivables.*—When a payment is made with respect to a debt instrument issued by a controlled partnership for which there is one or more deemed transferred receivables, then, if the amount of the retained receivable (as defined in paragraph (g)(22) of this section) held by the holder-in-form is zero and a single deemed holder is deemed to hold all of the deemed transferred receivables, the entire payment is allocated to the deemed transferred receivables held by the single deemed holder. If the amount of the retained receivable held by the holder-in-form is greater than zero or there are multiple deemed holders of deemed transferred receivables, or both, the payment is apportioned among the retained receivable, if any, and each deemed transferred receivable in proportion to the principal amount of all the receivables. The portion of a payment allocated or apportioned to a retained receivable or a deemed transferred receivable reduces the principal amount of, or accrued interest with respect to, as applicable depending on the payment, the retained receivable or deemed transferred receivable. When a payment allocated or apportioned to a deemed transferred receivable reduces the principal amount of the receivable, the expanded group partner that is the deemed holder with respect to the deemed transferred receivable is deemed to redeem the same amount of deemed partner stock, and the specified portion with respect to the debt instrument is reduced by the same amount. When a payment allocated or apportioned to a deemed transferred receivable reduces accrued interest with respect to the receivable, the expanded group partner that is the deemed holder with respect to the deemed transferred receivable is deemed to make a matching distribution in the same amount with respect to the deemed partner stock. The controlled partnership is treated as the paying agent with respect to the deemed partner stock.

(v) *Holder-in-form transfers debt instrument in a transaction that is not a specified event.*—If the holder-in-form transfers the debt instrument (which is disregarded for Federal tax purposes) to a member of the expanded group or a controlled partnership (and therefore the transfer is not a specified event described in paragraph (f)(5)(iii)(F) of this section), then, for Federal tax purposes, the holder-in-form is deemed to transfer the retained receivable and the deemed partner stock to the transferee.

(vi) *Allocation of deemed transferred receivable under section 752.*—A partnership liability that is a debt instrument with respect to which there is one or more deemed transferred receivables is allocated for purposes of section 752 without regard to any deemed transfer.

(5) *Specified events affecting ownership following a deemed transfer.*—(i) *General rule.*—If a specified event (within the meaning of paragraph (f)(5)(iii) of this section) occurs with respect to a deemed transfer, then, immediately before the specified event, the expanded group partner that is both the issuer of the deemed partner stock and the deemed holder of the deemed transferred receivable is deemed to *distribute the deemed transferred receivable* (or portion thereof, as determined under paragraph (f)(5)(iv) of this section) to the holder-in-form in redemption of the deemed partner stock (or portion thereof, as determined under paragraph (f)(5)(iv) of this section) deemed to be held by the holder-in-form. The deemed distribution is

deemed to occur for all Federal tax purposes, except that the distribution is disregarded for purposes of paragraph (b) of this section. Except when the deemed transferred receivable (or portion thereof, as determined under paragraph (f)(5)(iv) of this section) is deemed to be retransferred under paragraph (f)(5)(ii) of this section, the principal amount of the retained receivable held by the holder-in-form is increased by the principal amount of the deemed transferred receivable, the deemed transferred receivable ceases to exist for Federal tax purposes, and the specified portion (or portion thereof) that corresponds to the deemed transferred receivable (or portion thereof) ceases to be treated as a specified portion for purposes of this section.

(ii) *New deemed transfer when a specified event involves a transferee that is a covered member that is an expanded group partner.*—If the specified event is described in paragraph (f)(5)(iii)(E) of this section, the holder-in-form of the debt instrument is deemed to retransfer the deemed transferred receivable (or portion thereof, as determined under paragraph (f)(5)(iv) of this section) that the holder-in-form is deemed to have received pursuant to paragraph (f)(5)(i) of this section, to the transferee expanded group partner in exchange for deemed partner stock issued by the transferee expanded group partner with a fair market value equal to the principal amount of the deemed transferred receivable (or portion thereof) that is retransferred. For purposes of this section, this deemed transfer is treated in the same manner as a deemed transfer described in paragraph (f)(4)(i) of this section.

(iii) *Specified events.*—A specified event, with respect to a deemed transfer, occurs when, immediately after the transaction and taking into account all related transactions:

(A) The controlled partnership that is the issuer of the debt instrument either ceases to be a controlled partnership or ceases to have an expanded group partner that is a covered member.

(B) The holder-in-form is a member of the expanded group immediately before the transaction, and the holder-in-form and the deemed holder cease to be members of the same expanded group for the reasons described in paragraph (d)(2) of this section.

(C) The holder-in-form is a controlled partnership immediately before the transaction, and the holder-in-form ceases to be a controlled partnership.

(D) The expanded group partner that is both the issuer of deemed partner stock and the deemed holder transfers (directly or indirectly through one or more partnerships) all or a portion of its interest in the controlled partnership to a person that neither is a covered member nor a controlled partnership with an expanded group partner that is a covered member. If there is a transfer of only a portion of the interest, see paragraph (f)(5)(iv) of this section.

(E) The expanded group partner that is both the issuer of deemed partner stock and the deemed holder transfers (directly or indirectly through one or more partnerships) all or a portion of its interest in the controlled partnership to a covered member or a controlled partnership with an expanded group partner that is a covered member. If there is a transfer of only a portion of the interest, see paragraph (f)(5)(iv) of this section.

(F) The holder-in-form transfers the debt instrument (which is disregarded for Federal tax purposes) to a person that is neither a member of the expanded group nor a controlled partnership. See paragraph (f)(4)(v) of this section if the holder-in-form transfers the debt instrument to a member of the expanded group or a controlled partnership.

(iv) *Specified event involving a transfer of only a portion of an interest in a controlled partnership.*—If, with respect to a specified event described in paragraph (f)(5)(iii)(D) or (E) of this section, an expanded group partner transfers only a portion of its interest in a controlled partnership, then, only a portion of the deemed transferred receivable that is deemed to be held by the expanded group partner is deemed to be distributed in redemption of an equal portion of the deemed partner stock. The portion of the deemed transferred receivable referred to in the preceding sentence is equal to the product of the entire principal amount of the deemed transferred receivable deemed to be held by the expanded group partner multiplied by a fraction, the numerator of which is the portion of the expanded group partner's capital account attributable to the interest that is transferred, and the denominator of which is the expanded group partner's capital account with respect to its entire interest, determined immediately before the specified event.

(6) *Issuance of a partnership's debt instrument to a partner and a partner's debt instrument to a partnership.*—If a controlled partnership, with respect to an expanded group, issues a debt instrument to an expanded group partner, or if a covered member that is an expanded group partner issues a covered debt instrument to a controlled partnership, and in each case, no partner deducts or receives an allocation of expense with respect to the debt instrument, then this section does not apply to the debt instrument.

(g) *Definitions.*—The definitions in this paragraph (g) apply for purposes of this section and §§ 1.385-3 and 1.385-4.

(1) *Asset reorganization.*—The term asset reorganization means a reorganization described in section 368(a)(1)(A), (C), (D), (F), or (G).

(2) *Consolidated group.*—The term consolidated group has the meaning specified in § 1.1502-1(h).

(3) *Covered debt instrument.*—(i) *In general.*—The term covered debt instrument means a debt instrument issued after April 4, 2016, that is not a qualified dealer debt instrument (as defined in paragraph (g)(3)(ii) of this section) or an excluded statutory or regulatory debt instrument (as defined in paragraph (g)(3)(iii) of this section), and that is issued by a covered member that is not an excepted regulated financial company (as defined in paragraph (g)(3)(iv) of this section) or a regulated insurance company (as defined in paragraph (g)(3)(v) of this section).

(ii) *Qualified dealer debt instrument.*—For purposes of this paragraph (g)(3), the term qualified dealer debt instrument means a debt instrument that is issued to or acquired by an expanded group member that is a dealer in securities (within the meaning of section 475(c)(1)) in the ordinary course of the dealer's business of dealing in securities. The preceding sentence applies solely to the extent that—

(A) The dealer accounts for the debt instruments as securities held primarily for sale to customers in the ordinary course of business;

(B) The dealer disposes of the debt instruments (or the debt instruments mature) within a period of time that is consistent with the holding of the debt instruments for sale to customers in the ordinary course of business, taking into account the terms of the debt instruments and the conditions and practices prevailing in the markets for similar debt instruments during the period in which it is held; and

(C) The dealer does not sell or otherwise transfer the debt instrument to a member of the dealer's expanded group unless that sale or transfer is to a dealer that satisfies the requirements of this paragraph (g)(3)(ii).

(iii) *Excluded statutory or regulatory debt instrument.*—For purposes of this paragraph (g)(3), the term excluded statutory or regulatory debt instrument means a debt instrument that is described in any of the following paragraphs:

(A) Production payments treated as a loan under section 636(a) or (b).

(B) A "regular interest" in a real estate mortgage investment conduit described in section 860G(a)(1).

(C) A debt instrument that is deemed to arise under § 1.482-1(g)(3) (including adjustments made pursuant to Revenue Procedure 99-32, 1999-2 C.B. 296).

(D) A stripped bond or coupon described in section 1286, unless such instrument was issued with a principal purpose of avoiding the purposes of this section or § 1.385-3.

(E) A lease treated as a loan under section 467.

(iv) *Excepted regulated financial company.*—For purposes of this paragraph (g)(3), the term excepted regulated financial company means a covered member that is a regulated financial company (as defined in paragraph (g)(3)(iv)(A) of this section) or a member of a regulated financial group (as defined in paragraph (g)(3)(iv)(B) of this section).

(A) *Regulated financial company.*—For purposes of paragraph (g)(3)(iv), the term regulated financial company means—

(1) A bank holding company, as defined in 12 U.S.C. 1841;

(2) A covered savings and loan holding company, as defined in 12 CFR 217.2;

(3) A national bank;

(4) A bank that is a member of the Federal Reserve System and is incorporated by special law of any State, or organized under the general laws of any State, or of the United States, including a Morris Plan bank, or other incorporated banking institution engaged in a similar business;

(5) An insured depository institution, as defined in 12 U.S.C. 1813(c)(2);

(6) A nonbank financial company subject to a determination under 12 U.S.C. 5323(a)(1) or (b)(1);

(7) A U.S. intermediate holding company formed by a foreign banking organization in compliance with 12 C.F.R. 252.153;

(8) An Edge Act corporation organized under section 25A of the Federal Reserve Act (12 U.S.C. 611-631);

(9) Corporations having an agreement or undertaking with the Board of Governors of the Federal Reserve System under section 25 of the Federal Reserve Act (12 U.S.C. 601-604a);

(10) A supervised securities holding company, as defined in 12 U.S.C. 1850a(a)(5);

(11) A broker or dealer that is registered with the Securities and Exchange Commission under 15 U.S.C. 78o(b);

(12) A futures commission merchant, as defined in 7 U.S.C. 1a(28);

(13) A swap dealer, as defined in 7 U.S.C. 1a(49);

(14) A security-based swap dealer, as defined in 15 U.S.C. 78c(a)(71);

(15) A Federal Home Loan Bank, as defined in 12 U.S.C. 1422(1)(A);

(16) A Farm Credit System Institution chartered and subject to the provisions of the Farm Credit Act of 1971 (12 U.S.C. 2001 et seq.); or

(17) A small business investment company, as defined in 15 U.S.C. 662(3).

(B) *Regulated financial group.*—(1) *General rule.*—For purposes of paragraph (g)(3)(iv) of this section, except as otherwise provided in paragraph (g)(3)(iv)(B)(2) of this section, the term regulated financial group means any expanded group of which a covered member that is a regulated financial company within the meaning of paragraphs (g)(3)(iv)(A)(1) through (10) of this section would be the expanded group parent if no person owned, directly or indirectly (as defined in § 1.385-1(c)(4)(iii)), the regulated financial company. A domestic eligible entity (within the meaning of § 301.7701-5(a) of this chapter) treated as a partnership or disregarded as an entity separate from its owner is, for purposes of this paragraph (g)(3)(iv)(B), also treated as a covered member.

(2) *Exception for certain non-financial entities.*—A corporation is not a member of a regulated financial group if it is held by a regulated financial company pursuant to 12 U.S.C. 1843(k)(1)(B), 12 U.S.C. 1843(k)(4)(H), or 12 U.S.C. 1843(o).

(v) *Regulated insurance company.*—For purposes of this paragraph (g)(3), the term regulated insurance company means a covered member that is—

(A) Subject to tax under subchapter L of chapter 1 of the Internal Revenue Code;

(B) Domiciled or organized under the laws of one of the 50 states or the District of Columbia (for purposes of paragraph (g)(3)(v) of this section, each being a "state");

(C) Licensed, authorized, or regulated by one or more states to sell insurance, reinsurance, or annuity contracts to persons other than related persons (within the meaning of section 954(d)(3)) in such states, but in no case will a corporation satisfy the requirements of this paragraph (g)(3)(v)(C) if a principal purpose for obtaining such license, authorization, or regulation was to qualify the issuer as a regulated insurance company; and

(D) Engaged in regular issuances of (or subject to ongoing liability with respect to) insurance, reinsurance, or annuity contracts with persons that are not related persons (within the meaning of section 954(d)(3)).

(4) *Debt instrument.*—The term debt instrument means an interest that would, but for the application of this section, be treated as a debt instrument as defined in section 1275(a) and § 1.1275-1(d).

(5) *Deemed holder.*—The term deemed holder means, with respect to a deemed transfer, the expanded group partner that is deemed to hold a deemed transferred receivable by reason of the deemed transfer.

(6) *Deemed partner stock.*—The term deemed partner stock means, with respect to a deemed transfer, the stock deemed issued by an expanded group partner as described in paragraphs (f)(4)(i) and (iii) and (f)(5)(ii) of this section. The amount of deemed partner stock is reduced as described in paragraphs (f)(4)(iv)(B) and (f)(5)(i) of this section.

(7) *Deemed transfer.*—The term deemed transfer means, with respect to a specified portion, the transfer described in paragraph (f)(4)(i) or (iii) or (f)(5)(ii) of this section.

(8) *Deemed transferred receivable.*—The term deemed transferred receivable means, with respect to a deemed transfer, the portion of the debt instrument described in paragraph (f)(4)(i) or (iii) or (f)(5)(ii) of this section. The deemed transferred receivable is reduced as described in paragraphs (f)(4)(iv)(B) and (f)(5)(i) of this section.

(9) *Distribution.*—The term distribution means any distribution made by a corporation with respect to its stock.

(10) *Exempt distribution.*—The term exempt distribution means either—

32,078

Corporate Interests Treated as Stock or Indebtedness
See p. 20,601 for regulations not amended to reflect law changes

(i) A distribution of stock that is permitted to be received without the recognition of gain or income under section 354(a)(1) or 355(a)(1), or, if section 356 applies, that is not treated as other property or money described in section 356; or

(ii) A distribution of property in a complete liquidation under section 336(a) or 337(a).

(11) *Exempt exchange.*—The term exempt exchange means an acquisition of expanded group stock in which either—

(i) In a case in which the transferor and transferee of the expanded group stock are parties to an asset reorganization, either—

(A) Section 361(a) or (b) applies to the transferor of the expanded group stock and the stock is not transferred by issuance; or

(B) Section 1032 or §1.1032-2 applies to the transferor of the expanded group stock and the stock is distributed by the transferee pursuant to the plan of reorganization;

(ii) The transferor of the expanded group stock is a shareholder that receives property in a complete liquidation to which section 331 or 332 applies; or

(iii) The transferor of the expanded group stock is an acquiring entity that is deemed to issue the stock in exchange for cash from an issuing corporation in a transaction described in §1.1032-3(b).

(12) *Expanded group partner.*—The term expanded group partner means, with respect to a controlled partnership of an expanded group, a member of the expanded group that is a partner (directly or indirectly through one or more partnerships).

(13) *Expanded group stock.*—The term expanded group stock means, with respect to a member of an expanded group, stock of a member of the same expanded group.

(14) *Funded member.*—The term funded member has the meaning provided in paragraph (b)(3)(i) of this section.

(15) *Holder-in-form.*—The term *holder-in-form* means, with respect to a debt instrument issued by a controlled partnership, the person that, absent the application of paragraph (f)(4) of this section, would be the holder of the debt instrument for Federal tax purposes. Therefore, the term holder-in-form does not include a deemed holder (as defined in paragraph (g)(5) of this section).

(16) *Issuance percentage.*—The term *issuance percentage* means, with respect to a controlled partnership and an expanded group partner, the ratio (expressed as a percentage) of the partner's reasonably anticipated distributive share of all the partnership's interest expense over a reasonable period, divided by all of the partnership's reasonably anticipated interest expense over that same period, taking into account any and all relevant facts and circumstances. The relevant facts and circumstances include, without limitation, the term of the debt instrument; whether the partnership anticipates issuing other debt instruments; and the partnership's anticipated section 704(b) income and expense, and the partners' respective anticipated allocation percentages, taking into account anticipated changes to those allocation percentages over time resulting, for example, from anticipated contributions, distributions, recapitalizations, or provisions in the controlled partnership agreement.

(17) *Liquidation value percentage.*—The term *liquidation value percentage* means, with respect to a controlled partnership and an expanded group partner, the ratio (expressed as a percentage) of the liquidation value of the expanded group partner's interest in the partnership divided by the aggregate liquidation value of all the partners' interests in the partnership. The liquidation value of an expanded group partner's interest in a controlled partnership is the amount of cash the partner would receive with respect to the interest if the partnership (and any partnership through which the partner indirectly owns an interest in the controlled partnership) sold all of its property for an amount of cash equal to the fair market value of the property (taking into account section 7701(g)), satisfied all of its liabilities (other than those described in §1.752-7), paid an unrelated third party to assume all of its §1.752-7 liabilities in a fully taxable transaction, and then the partnership (and any partnership through which the partner indirectly owns an interest in the controlled partnership) liquidated.

(18) *Member of a consolidated group.*—The term member of a consolidated group means a corporation described in §1.1502-1(b).

(19) *Per se period.*—The term per se period has the meaning provided in paragraph (b)(3)(iii)(A) of this section.

(20) *Predecessor.*—(i) *In general.*—Except as otherwise provided in paragraph (g)(20)(ii) of this section, the term predecessor means, with respect to a corporation—

(A) The distributor or transferor corporation in a transaction described in section 381(a) in which the corporation is the acquiring corporation; or

(B) The distributing corporation in a distribution or exchange to which section 355 (or so much of section 356 that relates to section 355) applies in which the corporation is a controlled corporation.

(ii) *Predecessor ceasing to be a member of the same expanded group as corporation.*—The term predecessor does not include the distributing corporation described in paragraph (g)(20)(i)(B) of this section from the date that the distributing corporation ceases to be a member of the expanded group of which the controlled corporation is a member.

(iii) *Multiple predecessors.*—A corporation may have more than one predecessor, including by reason of a predecessor of the corporation having a predecessor or successor. Accordingly, references to a corporation also include references to a predecessor or successor of a predecessor of the corporation.

(21) *Property.*—The term property has the meaning specified in section 317(a).

(22) *Retained receivable.*—The term *retained receivable* means, with respect to a debt instrument issued by a controlled partnership, the portion of the debt instrument that is not transferred by the holder-in-form pursuant to one or more deemed transfers. The retained receivable is adjusted for decreases described in paragraph (f)(4)(iv)(B) of this section and increases described in paragraph (f)(5)(i) of this section.

(23) *Specified portion.*—The term *specified portion* means, with respect to a debt instrument issued by a controlled partnership and a covered member that is an expanded group partner, the portion of the debt instrument that is treated under paragraph (f)(3)(i) of this section as issued on a testing date (within the meaning of paragraph (f)(3)(ii) of this section) by the covered member and that, absent the application of paragraph (f)(4)(i) of this section, would be treated as stock under paragraph (b)(2) or (b)(3)(i) of this section on the testing date. A specified portion is reduced as described in paragraphs (f)(4)(iv)(B) and (f)(5)(i) of this section.

(24) *Successor.*—(i) *In general.*—Except as otherwise provided in paragraph (g)(24)(iii) of this section, the term successor means, with respect to a corporation—

(A) The acquiring corporation in a transaction described in section 381(a) in which the corporation is the distributor or transferor corporation;

(B) A controlled corporation in a distribution or exchange to which section 355 (or so much of section 356 that relates to section 355) applies in which the corporation is the distributing corporation; or

(C) Subject to the rules in paragraph (g)(24)(ii) of this section, a seller in an acquisition described in paragraph (c)(2)(i)(A) of this section in which the corporation is the acquirer.

(ii) *Special rules for certain acquisitions of subsidiary stock.*—The following rules apply with respect to a successor described in paragraph (g)(24)(i)(C) of this section:

(A) The seller is a successor to the acquirer only to the extent of the value (adjusted as described in paragraph (g)(24)(ii)(C) of this section) of the expanded group stock acquired from the seller in exchange for property (other than expanded group stock) in the acquisition described in paragraph (c)(2)(i)(A) of this section.

(B) A distribution or acquisition by either the seller or a successor seller to or from either the acquirer, the seller, or a successor seller is not treated as described in paragraph (b)(3) of this section for purposes of applying paragraph (b)(3) of this section to a covered debt instrument of the acquirer. For purposes of the preceding sentence, the term successor seller means a member of the expanded group that receives property (other than expanded group stock) in a distribution or acquisition from the seller or another successor seller and is controlled by the acquirer as determined under the principles of paragraph (c)(2)(i) of this section. A successor seller is treated as a successor to the acquirer to the extent of the value of the property received in a distribution or acquisition described in the preceding sentence and, for purposes of applying this paragraph (g)(24)(ii)(B).

(C) To the extent that a covered debt instrument of the acquirer is treated as funding a distribution or acquisition by the seller or successor seller described in paragraphs (b)(3)(i)(A) through (C) of this section, or would be treated but for the exceptions described in paragraphs (c)(3)(i) and (ii) of this section, the value of the expanded group stock described in paragraph (g)(24)(ii)(A) of this section is reduced by an amount equal to the distribution or acquisition for purposes of any further application of paragraph (g)(24)(ii)(A) of this section with respect to the acquirer and seller.

(iii) *Successor ceasing to be a member of the same expanded group as corporation.*—The term successor does not include a controlled

Corporate Interests Treated as Stock or Indebtedness
See p. 20,601 for regulations not amended to reflect law changes

32,079

corporation described in paragraph (g)(24)(i)(B) of this section with respect to a distributing corporation or a seller described in paragraph (g)(24)(i)(C) of this section with respect to an acquirer from the date that the controlled corporation or the seller ceases to be a member of the expanded group of which the controlled corporation or acquirer, respectively, is a member.

(iv) *Multiple successors.*—A corporation may have more than one successor, including by reason of a successor of the corporation having a predecessor or successor. Accordingly, references to a corporation also include references to a predecessor or successor of a successor of the corporation.

(25) *Taxable year.*—The term taxable year refers to the taxable year of the issuer of the covered debt instrument.

(h) *Examples.*—(1) *Assumed facts.*—Except as otherwise stated, the following facts are assumed for purposes of the examples in paragraph (h)(3) of this section:

(i) FP is a foreign corporation that owns 100% of the stock of USS1, a covered member, 100% of the stock of USS2, a covered member, and 100% of the stock of FS, a foreign corporation;

(ii) USS1 owns 100% of the stock of DS, a covered member, and CFC, which is a controlled foreign corporation within the meaning of section 957;

(iii) At the beginning of Year 1, FP is the common parent of an expanded group comprised solely of FP, USS1, USS2, FS, DS, and CFC (the FP expanded group);

(iv) The FP expanded group has more than $50 million of covered debt instruments described in paragraph (c)(4) of this section at all times;

(v) No issuer of a covered debt instrument has a positive expanded group earnings account within the meaning of paragraph (c)(3)(i)(B) of this section or has received qualified contributions within the meaning of paragraph (c)(3)(ii) of this section;

(vi) All notes are covered debt instruments (as defined in paragraph (g)(3) of this section) and are not qualified short-term debt instruments (as defined in paragraph (b)(3)(vii) of this section);

(vii) Each entity has as its taxable year the calendar year;

(viii) PRS is a partnership for federal income tax purposes;

(ix) No corporation is a member of a consolidated group;

(x) No domestic corporation is a United States real property holding corporation within the meaning of section 897(c)(2);

(xi) Each note is issued with adequate stated interest (as defined in section 1274(c)(2)); and

(xii) Each transaction occurs after January 19, 2017.

(2) *No inference.*—Except as otherwise provided in this section, it is assumed for purposes of the examples in paragraph (h)(3) of this section that the form of each transaction is respected for federal tax purposes. No inference is intended, however, as to whether any particular note would be respected as indebtedness or as to whether the form of any particular transaction described in an example in paragraph (h)(3) of this section would be respected for federal tax purposes.

(3) *Examples.*—The following examples illustrate the rules of this section.

(i) *Example 1: Distribution of a covered debt instrument.*—(A) *Facts.* On Date A in Year 1, FS lends $100x to USS1 in exchange for USS1 Note A. On Date B in Year 2, USS1 issues USS1 Note B, which is has a value of $100x, to FP in a distribution.

(B) *Analysis.* USS1 Note B is a covered debt instrument that is issued by USS1 to FP, a member of the expanded group of which USS1 is a member, in a distribution. Accordingly, USS1 Note B is treated as stock under paragraph (b)(2)(i) of this section. Under paragraph (d)(1)(i) of this section, USS1 Note B is treated as stock when it is issued by USS1 to FP on Date B in Year 2. Accordingly, USS1 is treated as distributing USS1 stock to its shareholder FP in a distribution that is subject to section 305. Under paragraph (b)(5) of this section, because the distribution of USS1 Note B is described in paragraph (b)(2)(i) of this section, the distribution of USS1 Note B is not treated as a distribution of property described in paragraph (b)(3)(i)(A) of this section. Accordingly, USS1 Note A is not treated as funding the distribution of USS1 Note B for purposes of paragraph (b)(3)(i)(A) of this section.

(ii) *Example 2: Covered debt instrument issued for expanded group stock that is exchanged for stock in a corporation that is not a member of the same expanded group.*—(A) *Facts.* UST is a publicly traded domestic corporation. On Date A in Year 1, USS1 issues USS1 Note to FP in exchange for FP stock. Subsequently, on Date B of Year 1, USS1 transfers the FP stock to UST's shareholders, which are not members of the FP expanded group, in exchange for all of the stock of UST.

(B) *Analysis.* (1) Because USS1 and FP are both members of the FP expanded group, USS1 Note is treated as stock when it is issued by USS1 to FP in exchange for FP stock on Date A in Year 1 under paragraphs (b)(2)(ii) and (d)(1)(i) of this section. This result applies even though, pursuant to the same plan, USS1 transfers the FP stock to persons that are not members of the FP expanded group. The exchange of USS1 Note for FP stock is not an exempt exchange within the meaning of paragraph (g)(11) of this section.

(2) Because USS1 Note is treated as stock for federal tax purposes when it is issued by USS1, pursuant to section § 1.367(b)-10(a)(3)(ii) (defining property for purposes of § 1.367(b)-10) there is no potential application of § 1.367(b)-10(a) to USS1's acquisition of the FP stock.

(iii) *Example 3: Issuance of a note in exchange for expanded group stock.*—(A) *Facts.* On Date A in Year 1, USS1 issues USS1 Note to FP in exchange for 40% of the FS stock owned by FP.

(B) *Analysis.* (1) Because USS1 and FP are both members of the FP expanded group, USS1 Note is treated as stock when it is issued by USS1 to FP in exchange for FS stock on Date A in Year 1 under paragraphs (b)(2)(ii) and (d)(1)(i) of this section. The exchange of USS1 Note for FS stock is not an exempt exchange within the meaning of paragraph (g)(11) of this section.

(2) Because USS1 Note is treated as stock for federal tax purposes when it is issued by USS1, USS1 Note is not treated as property for purposes of section 304(a) because it is not property within the meaning specified in section 317(a). Therefore, USS1's acquisition of FS stock from FP in exchange for USS1 Note is not an acquisition described in section 304(a)(1).

(iv) *Example 4: Funding occurs in same taxable year as distribution.*—(A) *Facts.* On Date A in Year 1, FP lends $200x to DS in exchange for DS Note A. On Date B in Year 1, DS distributes $400x of cash to USS1 in a distribution.

(B) *Analysis.* Under paragraph (b)(3)(iii)(A) of this section, DS Note A is treated as funding the distribution by DS to USS1 because DS Note A is issued to a member of the FP expanded group during the per se period with respect to DS's distribution to USS1. Accordingly, under paragraphs (b)(3)(i)(A) and (d)(1)(ii) of this section, DS Note A is treated as stock on Date B in Year 1.

(v) *Example 5: Additional funding.*—(A) *Facts.* The facts are the same as in paragraph (h)(3)(iv)(A) of this section (*Example 4*), except that, in addition, on Date C in Year 2, FP lends an additional $300x to DS in exchange for DS Note B.

(B) *Analysis.* The analysis is the same as in paragraph (h)(3)(iv)(B) of this section (*Example 4*) with respect to DS Note A. DS Note B is also issued to a member of the FP expanded group during the per se period with respect to DS's distribution to USS1. Under paragraphs (b)(3)(iii)(A) and (b)(6) of this section, DS Note B is treated as funding only the remaining portion of DS's distribution to USS1, which is $200x. Accordingly, $200x of DS Note B is treated as stock under paragraph (b)(3)(i)(A) of this section. Under paragraph (d)(1)(i) of this section, $200x of DS Note B is treated as stock when it is issued by DS to FP on Date C in Year 2. The remaining $100x of DS Note B continues to be treated as indebtedness.

(vi) *Example 6. Funding involving multiple interests.*—(A) *Facts.* On Date A in Year 1, FP lends $300x to USS1 in exchange for USS1 Note A. On Date B in Year 2, USS1 distributes $300x of cash to FP. On Date C in Year 3, FP lends another $300x to USS1 in exchange for USS1 Note B.

(B) *Analysis.* (1) Under paragraph (b)(3)(iii)(B) of this section, USS1 Note A is tested under paragraph (b)(3) of this section before USS1 Note B is tested. USS1 Note A is issued during the per se period with respect to USS1's $300x distribution to FP and, therefore, is treated as funding the distribution under paragraph (b)(3)(iii)(A) of this section. Beginning on Date B in Year 2, USS1 Note A is treated as stock under paragraphs (b)(3)(i)(A) and (d)(1)(ii) of this section.

(2) Under paragraph (b)(3)(iii)(B) of this section, USS1 Note B is tested under paragraph (b)(3) of this section after USS1 Note A is tested. Because USS1 Note A is treated as funding the entire $300x distribution by USS1 to FP, USS1 Note B will continue to be treated as indebtedness. See paragraph (b)(6) of this section.

(vii) *Example 7. Re-testing.*—(A) *Facts.* The facts are the same as in paragraph (h)(3)(vi)(A) of this section (*Example 6*), except that on Date D in Year 4, FP sells USS1 Note A to Bank.

(B) *Analysis.* (1) Under paragraph (d)(2)(i) of this section, USS1 Note A ceases to be treated as stock when FP sells USS1 Note A to Bank on Date D in Year 4. Immediately before FP sells USS1 Note A to Bank, USS1 is deemed to issue a debt instrument to FP in exchange for USS1 Note A in a transaction that is disregarded for purposes of paragraphs (b)(2) and (b)(3) of this section.

(2) Under paragraph (d)(2)(ii) of this section, after USS1 Note A is deemed exchanged for a new debt instrument, USS1's other

32,080

Corporate Interests Treated as Stock or Indebtedness
See p. 20,601 for regulations not amended to reflect law changes

covered debt instruments that are not treated as stock as of Date D in Year 4 (USS1 Note B) are re-tested for purposes of paragraph (b)(3)(iii) of this section to determine whether the instruments are treated as funding the $300x distribution by USS1 to FP on Date B in Year 2. USS1 Note B was issued by USS1 to FP during the per se period. Accordingly, USS1 Note B is re-tested under paragraph (b)(3)(iii) of this section. Under paragraph (b)(3)(iii) of this section, USS1 Note B is treated as funding the distribution on Date C in Year 3 and, accordingly, is treated as stock under paragraph (b)(3)(i)(A) of this section. USS1 Note B is deemed to be exchanged for stock on Date D in Year 4, the re-testing date, under paragraph (d)(1)(iv) of this section. See § 1.385-1(d) for rules regarding the treatment of this deemed exchange.

(viii) *Example 8. Distribution of expanded group stock and covered debt instrument in a reorganization that qualifies under section 355.*—(A) *Facts.* On Date A in Year 1, FP lends $200x to USS2 in exchange for USS2 Note. In a transaction that is treated as independent from the transaction on Date A in Year 1, on Date B in Year 2, USS2 transfers a portion of its assets to DS2, a newly formed domestic corporation, in exchange for all of the stock of DS2 and DS2 Note. Immediately afterwards, USS2 distributes all of the DS2 stock and the DS2 Note to FP with respect to FP's USS2 stock in a transaction that qualifies under section 355. USS2's transfer of a portion of its assets to DS2 qualifies as a reorganization described in section 368(a)(1)(D). The DS2 stock has a value of $150x and DS2 Note has a value of $50x. The DS2 stock is not non-qualified preferred stock as defined in section 351(g)(2). Absent the application of this section, DS2 Note would be treated by FP as other property within the meaning of section 356.

(B) *Analysis.* (1) The contribution and distribution transaction is a reorganization described in section 368(a)(1)(D) involving a transfer of property by USS2 to DS2 in exchange for DS2 stock and DS2 Note. The transfer of property by USS2 to DS2 is a contribution of excluded property described in paragraph (c)(3)(ii)(D)(2) of this section and an excluded contribution described in paragraph (c)(3)(ii)(E)(2) of this section. Accordingly, USS2's contribution of property to DS2 is not a qualified contribution described in paragraph (c)(3)(ii)(B) of this section.

(2) DS2 Note is a covered debt instrument that is issued by DS2 to USS2, both members of the FP expanded group, in exchange for property of USS2 in an asset reorganization (as defined in paragraph (g)(1) of this section), and received by FP, another FP expanded group member immediately before the reorganization, as other property with respect to FP's USS2 stock. Accordingly, the transaction is described in paragraph (b)(2)(iii) of this section, and DS2 Note is treated as stock when it is issued by DS2 to USS2 on Date B in Year 2 pursuant to paragraphs (b)(2)(iii) and (d)(1)(i) of this section.

(3) Because the issuance of DS2 Note by DS2 in exchange for the property of USS2 in an asset reorganization is described in paragraph (b)(2)(iii) of this section, the distribution and acquisition of DS2 Note by USS2 is not treated as a distribution or acquisition described in paragraph (b)(3)(i) of this section. Accordingly, USS2 Note is not treated as funding the distribution of DS2 Note for purposes of paragraph (b)(3)(i) of this section.

(4) USS2's acquisition of DS2 stock is not an acquisition described in paragraph (b)(3)(i)(B) of this section because it is an exempt exchange (as defined in paragraph (g)(11) of this section). USS2's acquisition of DS2 stock is an exempt exchange because USS2 and DS2 are both parties to a reorganization that is an asset reorganization, section 1032 applies to DS2, the transferor of the expanded group stock, and the DS2 stock is distributed by USS2, the transferee of the expanded group stock, pursuant to the plan of reorganization.

(5) USS2's distribution of $150x of the DS2 stock is a distribution of stock that is permitted to be received by FP without recognition of gain under section 355(a)(1). Accordingly, USS2's distribution of the DS2 stock (other than the DS2 Note) to FP is an exempt distribution, and is not described in paragraph (b)(3)(i)(A) of this section.

(6) Because USS2 has not made a distribution or acquisition that is described in paragraph (b)(3)(i)(A), (B), or (C) of this section, USS2 Note is not treated as stock.

(ix) *Example 9. Funding a distribution by a successor to funded member.*—(A) *Facts.* The facts are the same as in *Example 8* of this paragraph (h)(3), except that on Date C in Year 3, DS2 distributes $200x of cash to FP and, subsequently, on Date D in Year 3, USS2 distributes $100x of cash to FP.

(B) *Analysis.* (1) USS2 is a predecessor of DS2 under paragraph (g)(20)(i)(B) of this section and DS2 is a successor to USS2 under paragraph (g)(24)(i)(B) of this section because USS2 is the distributing corporation and DS2 is the controlled corporation in a distribution to which section 355 applies. Accordingly, under paragraph (b)(3)(v) of this section, a distribution by DS2 is treated as a distribution by USS2. Under paragraphs (b)(3)(iii)(A) and (b)(3)(v)(B) of this

section, USS2 Note is treated as funding the distribution by DS2 to FP because USS2 Note was issued during the per se period with respect to DS2's $200x cash distribution, and because both the issuance of USS2 Note and the distribution by DS2 occur during the per se period with respect to the section 355 distribution. Accordingly, under paragraphs (b)(3)(i)(A) and (d)(1)(ii) of this section, USS2 Note is treated as stock beginning on Date C in Year 3. See § 1.385-1(d) for rules regarding the treatment of this deemed exchange.

(2) Because the entire amount of USS2 Note is treated as funding DS2's $200x distribution to FP, under paragraph (b)(3)(iii)(C) of this section, USS2 Note is not treated as funding the subsequent distribution by USS2 on Date D in Year 3.

(x) *Example 10. Asset reorganization; section 354 qualified property.*—(A) *Facts.* On Date A in Year 1, FS lends $100x to USS2 in exchange for USS2 Note. On Date B in Year 2, in a transaction that qualifies as a reorganization described in section 368(a)(1)(D), USS2 transfers all of its assets to USS1 in exchange for stock of USS1 and the assumption by USS1 of all of the liabilities of USS2, and USS2 distributes to FP, with respect to FP's USS2 stock, all of the USS1 stock that USS2 receives. FP does not recognize gain under section 354(a)(1).

(B) *Analysis.* (1) USS1 is a successor to USS2 under paragraph (g)(24)(i)(A) of this section. For purposes of paragraph (b)(3) of this section, USS2 and, under paragraph (b)(3)(v)(A) of this section, its successor, USS1, are funded members with respect to USS2 Note. Although USS1, a funded member, distributes property (USS1 stock) to its shareholder, FP, pursuant to the reorganization, the distribution of USS1 stock is not described in paragraph (b)(3)(i)(A) of this section because the stock is distributed in an exempt distribution (as defined in paragraph (g)(10) of this section). In addition, neither USS1's acquisition of the assets of USS2 nor USS2's acquisition of USS1 stock is described in paragraph (b)(3)(i)(C) of this section because FP does not receive other property within the meaning of section 356 with respect to its stock in USS2.

(2) USS2's acquisition of USS1 stock is not an acquisition described in paragraph (b)(3)(i)(B) of this section because it is an exempt exchange (as defined in paragraph (g)(11) of this section). USS2's acquisition of USS1 stock is an exempt exchange because USS1 and USS2 are both parties to an asset reorganization, section 1032 applies to USS1, the transferor of the USS1 stock, and the USS1 stock is distributed by USS2, the transferee, pursuant to the plan of reorganization. Furthermore, USS2's acquisition of its own stock from FS is not an acquisition described in paragraph (b)(3)(i)(B) of this section because USS2 acquires its stock in exchange for USS1 stock.

(3) Because neither USS1 nor USS2 has made a distribution or acquisition described in paragraph (b)(3)(i)(A), (B), or (C) of this section, USS2 Note is not treated as stock under paragraph (b)(3)(iii)(A) of this section.

(xi) *Example 11. Distribution of a covered debt instrument and issuance of a covered debt instrument with a principal purpose of avoiding the purposes of this section.*—(A) Facts. On Date A in Year 1, USS1 issues USS1 Note A, which has a value of $100x, to FP in a distribution. On Date B in Year 1, with a principal purpose of avoiding the purposes of this section, FP sells USS1 Note A to Bank for $100x of cash and lends $100x to USS1 in exchange for USS1 Note B.

(B) *Analysis.* USS1 Note A is a covered debt instrument that is issued by USS1 to FP, a member of USS1's expanded group, in a distribution. Accordingly, under paragraphs (b)(2)(i) and (d)(1)(i) of this section, USS1 Note A is treated as stock when it is issued by USS1 to FP on Date A in Year 1. Accordingly, USS1 is treated as distributing USS1 stock to FP. Because the distribution of USS1 Note A is described in paragraph (b)(2)(i) of this section, the distribution of USS1 Note A is not described in paragraph (b)(3)(i)(A) of this section under paragraph (b)(5) of this section. Under paragraph (d)(2)(i) of this section, USS1 Note A ceases to be treated as stock when FP sells USS1 Note A to Bank on Date B in Year 1. Immediately before FP sells USS1 Note A to Bank, USS1 is deemed to issue a debt instrument to FP in exchange for USS1 Note A in a transaction that is disregarded for purposes of paragraphs (b)(2) and (b)(3)(i) of this section. USS1 Note B is not treated as stock under paragraph (b)(3)(i)(A) of this section because the funded member, USS1, has not made a distribution of property. However, because the transactions occurring on Date B of Year 1 were undertaken with a principal purpose of avoiding the purposes of this section, USS1 Note B is treated as stock on Date B of Year 1 under paragraph (b)(4) of this section.

(xii) *Example 12: Distribution of a covered debt instrument to a controlled partnership.*—(A) *Facts.* CFC and FS are equal partners in PRS. PRS owns 100% of the stock in X Corp, a domestic corporation. On Date A in Year 1, X Corp issues X Note to PRS in a distribution.

(B) *Analysis.* (1) Under § 1.385-1(c)(4), in determining whether X Corp is a member of the FP expanded group that includes CFC and

FS, CFC and FS are each treated as owning 50% of the X Corp stock held by PRS. Accordingly, 100% of X Corp's stock is treated as owned by CFC and FS, and X Corp is a member of the FP expanded group.

(2) Together CFC and FS own 100% of the interests in PRS capital and profits, such that PRS is a controlled partnership under § 1.385-1(c)(1). CFC and FS are both expanded group partners on the date on which PRS acquired X Note. Therefore, pursuant to paragraph (f)(2)(i)(A) of this section, each of CFC and FS is treated as acquiring its share of X Note in the same manner (in this case, by a distribution of X Note), and on the date on which, PRS acquired X Note. Likewise, X Corp is treated as issuing to each of CFC and FS its share of X Note. Under paragraph (f)(2)(i)(B) of this section, each of CFC's and FS's share of X Note, respectively, is determined in accordance with its liquidation value percentage determined on Date A in Year 1, the date X Corp distributed X Note to PRS. On Date A in Year 1, pursuant to paragraph (g)(17) of this section, each of CFC's and FS's liquidation value percentages is 50%. Accordingly, on Date A in Year 1, under paragraph (f)(2)(i)(A) of this section, for purposes of this section, CFC and FS are each treated as acquiring 50% of X Note in a distribution.

(3) Under paragraphs (b)(2)(i) and (d)(1)(i) of this section, X Note is treated as stock on the date of issuance, which is Date A in Year 1. Under paragraph (f)(2)(i)(A) of this section, each of CFC and FS are treated as acquiring 50% of X Note in a distribution for purposes of this section. Therefore, X Corp is treated as distributing its stock to PRS in a distribution described in section 305.

(xiii) *Example 13: Loan to a controlled partnership; proportionate distributions by expanded group partners.*—(A) *Facts.* DS, USS2, and USP are partners in PRS. USP is a domestic corporation that is not a member of the FP expanded group. Each of DS and USS2 own 45% of the interests in PRS profits and capital, and USP owns 10% of the interests in PRS profits and capital. The PRS partnership agreement provides that all items of PRS income, gain, loss, deduction, and credit are allocated in accordance with the percentages in the preceding sentence. On Date A in Year 1, FP lends $200x to PRS in exchange for PRS Note with stated principal amount of $200x, which is payable at maturity. PRS Note also provides for annual payments of interest that are qualified stated interest. PRS uses all $200x in its business and does not distribute any money or other property to a partner. Subsequently, on Date B in Year 1, DS distributes $90x to USS1, USS2 distributes $90x to FP, and USP distributes $20x to its shareholder. Each of DS's and USS2's issuance percentage is 45% on Date B in Year 1, the date of the distributions and therefore a testing date under paragraph (f)(3)(ii)(A) of this section.

(B) *Analysis.* (1) DS and USS2 together own 90% of the interests in PRS profits and capital and therefore PRS is a controlled partnership under § 1.385-1(c)(1). Under § 1.385-1(c)(2), each of DS and USS2 is a covered member.

(2) Under paragraph (f)(3)(i) of this section, each of DS and USS2 is treated as issuing its share of PRS Note, and under paragraph (f)(3)(ii)(A) of this section, DS's and USS2's share is each $90x (45% of $200x). USP is not an expanded group partner and therefore has no issuance percentage and is not treated as issuing any portion of PRS Note.

(3) The $90x distributions made by DS to USS1 and by USS2 to FP are described in paragraph (b)(3)(i)(A) of this section. Under paragraph (b)(3)(iii)(A) of this section, the portions of PRS Note treated as issued by each of DS and USS2 are treated as funding the distributions made by DS and USS2 because the distributions occurred within the per se period with respect to PRS Note. Under paragraph (b)(3)(i) of this section, the portions of PRS Note treated as issued by each of DS and USS2 would, absent the application of paragraph (f)(4)(i) of this section, be treated as stock of DS and USS2 on Date B in Year 1, the date of the distributions. See paragraph (d)(1)(ii) of this section. Under paragraph (g)(23) of this section, each of the $90x portions is a specified portion.

(4) Under paragraph (f)(4)(i) of this section, the specified portions are not treated as stock under paragraph (b)(3)(i) of this section. Instead, FP is deemed to transfer a portion of PRS Note with a principal amount equal to $90x (the adjusted issue price of the specified portion with respect to DS) to DS in exchange for deemed partner stock in DS with a fair market value of $90x. Similarly, FP is deemed to transfer a portion of PRS Note with a principal amount equal to $90x (the adjusted issue price of the specified portion with respect to USS2) to USS2 in exchange for deemed partner stock in USS2 with a fair market value of $90x. The principal amount of the retained receivable held by FP is $20x ($200x – $90x – $90x).

(xiv) *Example 14: Loan to a controlled partnership; disproportionate distributions by expanded group partners.*—(A) *Facts.* The facts are the same as in paragraph (h)(3)(xiii)(A) of this section (*Example 13*), except that on Date B in Year 1, DS distributes $45x to USS1 and USS2 distributes $135x to FP.

(B) *Analysis.* (1) The analysis is the same as in paragraph (h)(3)(xiii)(B)(1) of this section (*Example 13*).

(2) The analysis is the same as in paragraph (h)(3)(xiii)(B)(2) of this section (*Example 13*).

(3) The $45x and $135x distributions made by DS to USS1 and by USS2 to FP, respectively, are described in paragraph (b)(3)(i)(A) of this section. Under paragraph (b)(3)(iii)(A) of this section, the portion of PRS Note treated as issued by DS is treated as funding the distribution made by DS because the distribution occurred within the per se period with respect to PRS Note, but under paragraph (b)(3)(i) of this section, only to the extent of DS's $45x distribution. USS2 is treated as issuing $90x of PRS Note, all of which is treated as funding $90x of USS2's $135x distribution under paragraph (b)(3)(iii)(A) of this section. Under paragraph (b)(3)(i) of this section, absent the application of paragraph (f)(4)(i) of this section, $45x of PRS Note would be treated as stock of DS and $90x of PRS Note would be treated as stock of USS2 on Date B in Year 1, the date of the distributions. See paragraph (d)(1)(ii) of this section. Under paragraph (g)(23) of this section, $45x of PRS Note is a specified portion with respect to DS and $90x of PRS Note is a specified portion with respect to USS2.

(4) Under paragraph (f)(4)(i) of this section, the specified portions are not treated as stock under paragraph (b)(3)(i) of this section. Instead, FP is deemed to transfer a portion of PRS Note with a principal amount equal to $45x (the adjusted issue price of the specified portion with respect to DS) to DS in exchange for stock of DS with a fair market value of $90x. Similarly, FP is deemed to transfer a portion of PRS Note with a principal amount equal to $90x (the adjusted issue price of the specified portion with respect to USS2) to USS2 in exchange for stock of USS2 with a fair market value of $90x. The principal amount of the retained receivable held by FP is $65x ($200x-$45x-$90x).

(xv) *Example 15: Loan to partnership; distribution in later year.*—(A) *Facts.* The facts are the same as in paragraph (h)(3)(xiii)(A) of this section (*Example 13*), except that USS2 does not distribute $90x to FP until Date C in Year 2, which is less than 36 months after Date A in Year 1. On Date C in Year 2, DS's, USS2's, and USP's issuance percentages under paragraph (g)(16) of this section are unchanged at 45%, 45%, and 10%, respectively.

(B) *Analysis.* (1) The analysis is the same as in paragraph (h)(3)(xiii)(B)(1) of this section (*Example 13*).

(2) The analysis is the same as in paragraph (h)(3)(xiii)(B)(2) of this section (*Example 13*).

(3) With respect to the distribution made by DS, the analysis is the same as in paragraph (h)(3)(xiii)(B)(3) of this section (*Example 13*).

(4) With respect to the deemed transfer to DS, the analysis is the same as in paragraph (h)(3)(xiii)(B)(4) of this section (*Example 13*). Accordingly, the amount of the retained receivable held by FP as of Date B in Year 1 is $110x ($200x-$90x).

(5) Under paragraph (f)(3)(ii)(A) of this section, USS2's share of PRS Note is determined on Date C in Year 2. On Date C in Year 2, DS's, USS2's, and USP's respective shares of PRS Note under paragraph (f)(3)(ii)(A) of this section are $90x, $90x, and $20x. However, because DS is treated as the issuer with respect to a $90x specified portion of PRS Note, DS's share of PRS Note is reduced by $90x to $0 under paragraph (f)(3)(ii)(B)(1) of this section. No reduction to either of USS2's or USP's share of PRS Note is required under paragraph (f)(3)(ii)(B)(2) of this section because the aggregate of DS's, USS2's, and USP's shares of PRS Note as reduced is $110x (DS has a $0 share, USS2 has a $90x share, and USP has a $20x share), which does not exceed $110x (the $200x adjusted issue price of PRS Note reduced by the $90x specified portion with respect to DS). Under paragraph (f)(3)(i) of this section, USS2 is treated as issuing its share of PRS Note.

(6) The $90x distribution made by USS2 to FP is described in paragraph (b)(3)(i)(A) of this section. Under paragraph (b)(3)(iii)(A) of this section, the portion of PRS Note treated as issued by USS2 is treated as funding the distribution made by USS2, because the distribution occurred within the per se period with respect to PRS Note. Accordingly, the portion of PRS Note treated as issued by USS2 would, absent the application of paragraph (f)(4)(i) of this section, be treated as stock of USS2 under paragraph (b)(3)(i) of this section on Date C in Year 2. See paragraph (d)(1)(ii) of this section. Under paragraph (g)(23) of this section, the $90x portion is a specified portion.

(7) Under paragraph (f)(4)(i) of this section, the specified portion of PRS Note treated as issued by USS2 is not treated as stock under paragraph (b)(3)(i) of this section. Instead, on Date C in Year 2, FP is deemed to transfer a portion of PRS Note with a principal amount equal to $90x (the adjusted issue price of the specified portion with respect to USS2) to USS2 in exchange for stock in USS2 with a fair market value of $90x. The principal amount of the retained receivable held by FP is reduced from $110x to $20x.

32,082

Corporate Interests Treated as Stock or Indebtedness
See p. 20,601 for regulations not amended to reflect law changes

(xvi) Example 16: Loan to a controlled partnership; partnership ceases to be a controlled partnership.—(A) *Facts.* The facts are the same as in paragraph (h)(3)(xiii)(A) of this section (*Example 13*), except that on Date C in Year 4, USS2 sells its entire interest in PRS to an unrelated person.

(B) *Analysis.* (1) On date C in Year 4, PRS ceases to be a controlled partnership with respect to the FP expanded group under §1.385-1(c)(1). This is the case because DS, the only remaining partner that is a member of the FP expanded group, only owns 45% of the total interest in PRS profits and capital. Because PRS ceases to be a controlled partnership, a specified event (within the meaning of paragraph (f)(5)(iii)(A) of this section) occurs with respect to the deemed transfers with respect to each of DS and USS2.

(2) Under paragraph (f)(5)(i) of this section, on Date C in Year 4, immediately before PRS ceases to be a controlled partnership, each of DS and USS2 is deemed to distribute its deemed transferred receivable to FP in redemption of FP's deemed partner stock in DS and USS2. The specified portion that corresponds to each of the deemed transferred receivables ceases to be treated as a specified portion. Furthermore, the deemed transferred receivables cease to exist, and the retained receivable held by FP increases from $20x to $200x.

(xvii) Example 17: Transfer of an interest in a partnership to a covered member.—(A) *Facts.* The facts are the same as in paragraph (h)(3)(xiii)(A) of this section (*Example 13*), except that on Date C in Year 4, USS2 sells its entire interest in PRS to USS1.

(B) *Analysis.* (1) After USS2 sells its interest in PRS to USS1, DS and USS1 together own 90% of the interests in PRS profits and capital and therefore PRS continues to be a controlled partnership under §1.385-1(c)(1). A specified event (within the meaning of paragraph (f)(5)(iii)(E) of this section) occurs as result of the sale only with respect to the deemed transfer with respect to USS2.

(2) Under paragraph (f)(5)(i) of this section, on Date C in Year 4, immediately before USS2 sells its entire interest in PRS to USS1, USS2 is deemed to distribute its deemed transferred receivable to FP in redemption of FP's deemed partner stock in USS2. Because the specified event is described in paragraph (f)(5)(iii)(E) of this section, under paragraph (f)(5)(ii) of this section, FP is deemed to retransfer the deemed transferred receivable deemed received from USS2 to USS1 in exchange for deemed partner stock in USS1 with a fair market value equal to the principal amount of the deemed transferred receivable that is retransferred to USS1.

(xviii) Example 18: Loan to partnership and all partners are members of a consolidated group.—(A) *Facts.* USS1 and DS are equal partners in PRS. USS1 and DS are members of a consolidated group, as defined in §1.1502-1(h). The PRS partnership agreement provides that all items of PRS income, gain, loss, deduction, and credit are allocated equally between USS1 and DS. On Date A in Year 1, FP lends $200x to PRS in exchange for PRS Note. PRS uses all $200x in its business and does not distribute any money or other property to any partner. On Date B in Year 1, DS distributes $200x to USS1, and USS1 distributes $200x to FP. If neither of USS1 or DS were a member of the consolidated group, each would have an issuance percentage under paragraph (g)(16) of this section, determined as of Date A in Year 1, of 50%.

(B) *Analysis.* (1) Pursuant to §1.385-4(b)(6), PRS is treated as a partnership for purposes of this section. Under §1.385-4(b)(1), DS and USS1 are treated as one corporation for purposes of this section, and thus a single covered member under §1.385-1(c)(2). For purposes of this section, the single covered member owns 100% of the PRS profits and capital and therefore PRS is a controlled partnership under §1.385-1(c)(1). Under paragraph (f)(3)(i) of this section, the single covered member is treated as issuing all $200x of PRS Note to FP, a member of the same expanded group as the single covered member. DS's distribution to USS1 is a disregarded distribution because it is a distribution between members of a consolidated group that is disregarded under the one-corporation rule described in §1.385-4(b)(1). However, under paragraph (b)(3)(iii)(A) of this section, PRS Note, treated as issued by the single covered member, is treated as funding the distribution by USS1 to FP, which is described in paragraph (b)(3)(i)(A) of this section and which is a regarded distribution. Accordingly, PRS Note, absent the application of paragraph (f)(4)(i) of this section, would be treated as stock under paragraph (b) of this section on Date B in Year 1. Thus, pursuant to paragraph (g)(23) of this section, the entire PRS Note is a specified portion.

(2) Under paragraphs (f)(4)(i) and (iii) of this section, the specified portion is not treated as stock and, instead, FP is deemed to transfer PRS Note with a principal amount equal to $200x to USS1 in exchange for stock of USS1 with a fair market value of $200x. Under paragraph (f)(4)(iii) of this section, FP is deemed to transfer PRS Note to USS1 because only USS1 made a regarded distribution described in paragraph (b)(3)(i) of this section.

(xix) Example 19: Loan to a disregarded entity.—(A) *Facts.* DS owns DRE, a disregarded entity within the meaning of §1.385-1(c)(3). On Date A in Year 1, FP lends $200x to DRE in exchange for DRE Note. Subsequently, on Date B in Year 1, DS distributes $100x of cash to USS1.

(B) *Analysis.* Under paragraph (b)(3)(iii)(A) of this section, $100x of DRE Note would be treated as funding the distribution by DS to USS1 because DRE Note is issued to a member of the FP expanded group during the per se period with respect to DS's distribution to USS1. Accordingly, under paragraphs (b)(3)(i)(A) and (d)(1)(ii) of this section, $100x of DRE Note would be treated as stock on Date B in Year 1. However, under paragraph (d)(4) of this section, DS, as the regarded owner, within the meaning of §1.385-1(c)(5), of DRE is deemed to issue its stock to FP in exchange for a portion of DRE Note equal to the $100x applicable portion (as defined in paragraph (d)(4) of this section). Thus, DS is treated as the holder of $100x of DRE Note, which is disregarded, and FP is treated as the holder of the remaining $100x of DRE Note. The $100x of stock deemed issued by DS to FP has the same terms as DRE Note, other than the issuer, and payments on the stock are determined by reference to payments on DRE Note.

(i) [*Reserved*]

(j) *Applicability date and transition rules.*—(1) *In general.*—Except as provided in paragraph (j)(2) or (3) or (k) of this section, this section applies to taxable years ending on or after January 19, 2017.

(2) *Transition rules.*—(i) *Transition rule for covered debt instruments that would be treated as stock in taxable years ending before January 19, 2017.* If paragraphs (b) and (d)(1) of this section, taking into account §§1.385-1, 1.385-3, and 1.385-4, would have treated a covered debt instrument as stock in a taxable year ending before January 19, 2017 but for the application of paragraph (j)(1) of this section, to the extent that the covered debt instrument is held by a member of the expanded group of which the issuer is a member immediately after January 19, 2017, then the covered debt instrument is deemed to be exchanged for stock immediately after January 19, 2017.

(ii) *Transition rule for certain covered debt instruments treated as stock in taxable years ending on or after January 19, 2017.* If paragraphs (b) and (d)(1) of this section, taking into account §§1.385-1, 1.385-3, and 1.385-4, would treat a covered debt instrument as stock on or before January 19, 2017 but in a taxable year ending on or after January 19, 2017, that covered debt instrument is not treated as stock during the 90-day period after January 19, 2017. Instead, to the extent that the covered debt instrument is held by a member of the expanded group of which the issuer is a member immediately after January 19, 2017, the covered debt instrument is deemed to be exchanged for stock immediately after January 19, 2017.

(iii) *Transition funding rule.*—When a covered debt instrument would be recharacterized as stock after April 4, 2016, and on or before January 19, 2017 (the *transition period*), but that covered debt instrument is not recharacterized as stock on such date due to the application of paragraph (j)(1), (j)(2)(i), or (j)(2)(ii) of this section, any payments made with respect to such covered debt instrument (other than stated interest), including pursuant to a refinancing, after the date that the covered debt instrument would have been recharacterized as stock and through the remaining portion of the transition period are treated as distributions for purposes of applying paragraph (b)(3) of this section for taxable years ending on or after January 19, 2017. In addition, to the extent that the holder and the issuer of the covered debt instrument cease to be members of the same expanded group during the transition period, the distribution or acquisition that would have caused the covered debt instrument to be treated as stock is available to be treated as funded by other covered debt instruments of the issuer for purposes of paragraph (b)(3) of this section (to the extent provided in paragraph (b)(3)(iii) of this section). The prior sentence is applied in a manner that is consistent with the rules set forth in paragraph (d)(2) of this section.

(iv) *Coordination between the general rule and funding rule.*—When a covered debt instrument would be recharacterized as stock pursuant to paragraph (b)(2) of this section after April 4, 2016, and on or before January 19, 2017, but that covered debt instrument is not recharacterized as stock on such date due to the application of paragraph (j)(1), (j)(2)(i), or (j)(2)(ii) of this section, the issuance of such covered debt instrument is not treated as a distribution or acquisition described in §1.385-3(b)(3)(i), but only to the extent that the covered debt instrument is held by a member of the expanded group of which the issuer is a member immediately after January 19, 2017.

(v) *Option to apply proposed regulations.*—In lieu of applying §§1.385-1, 1.385-3, and 1.385-4, taxpayers may apply the provisions matching §§1.385-1, 1.385-3, and 1.385-4 from the Internal Revenue Bulletin (IRB) 2016-17 (*https://www.irs.gov/pub/irs-irbs/irb16-17.pdf*) to

Corporate Interests Treated as Stock or Indebtedness
See p. 20,601 for regulations not amended to reflect law changes

32,083

all debt instruments issued by a particular issuer (and members of its expanded group that are covered members) after April 4, 2016, and before October 13, 2016, solely for purposes of determining whether a debt instrument is treated as stock, provided that those sections are consistently applied. [Reg. §1.385-3.]

(3) *Paragraph (f)(4)(iii) of this section.*—Paragraph (f)(4)(iii) of this section applies to taxable years for which the U.S. Federal income tax return is due, without extensions, after May 14, 2020. For taxable years ending on or after January 19, 2017, and for which the U.S. Federal income tax return is due, without extensions, on or before May 14, 2020, see §1.385-3T(f)(4)(iii), as contained in 26 CFR in part 1 in effect on April 1, 2019. In the case of a taxable year that ends after October 13, 2019, and on or before May 14, 2020, a taxpayer may choose to apply paragraph (f)(4)(iii) of this section to the portion of the taxable year that occurs after the expiration of §1.385-3T on October 13, 2019, provided that all members of the taxpayer's expanded group apply such paragraph.

(k) Additional transition rules.—See transition rules in §1.385-3T(k)(2) as contained in 26 CFR in part 1 in effect on April 1, 2019. [Reg. §1.385-3.]

☐ [T.D. 9790, 10-13-2016 (corrected 1-23-2017). Amended by T.D. 9880, 10-31-2019 and T.D. 9897, 5-13-2020.]

[Reg. §1.385-4]

§1.385-4. Treatment of consolidated groups.—(a) *Scope.*—This section provides rules for applying §1.385-3 to members of consolidated groups. Paragraph (b) of this section sets forth rules concerning the extent to which, solely for purposes of applying §1.385-3, members of a consolidated group that file (or that are required to file) a consolidated U.S. Federal income tax return are treated as one corporation. Paragraph (c) of this section sets forth rules concerning the treatment of a debt instrument that ceases to be, or becomes, a consolidated group debt instrument. Paragraph (d) of this section provides rules for applying the funding rule of §1.385-3(b)(3) to members that depart a consolidated group. For definitions applicable to this section, see paragraph (e) of this section and §§1.385-1(c) and 1.385-3(g). For examples illustrating the application of this section, see paragraph (f) of this section.

(b) *Treatment of consolidated groups.*—(1) *Members treated as one corporation.*—For purposes of this section and §1.385-3, and except as otherwise provided in this section and §1.385-3, all members of a consolidated group (as defined in §1.1502-1(h)) that file (or that are required to file) a consolidated U.S. Federal income tax return are treated as one corporation. Thus, for example, when a member of a consolidated group issues a covered debt instrument that is not a consolidated group debt instrument, the consolidated group generally is treated as the issuer of the covered debt instrument for purposes of this section and §1.385-3. Also, for example, when one member of a consolidated group issues a covered debt instrument that is not a consolidated group debt instrument and therefore is treated as issued by the consolidated group, and another member of the consolidated group makes a distribution or acquisition described in §1.385-3(b)(3)(i)(A) through (C) with an expanded group member that is not a member of the consolidated group, §1.385-3(b)(3)(i) may treat the covered debt instrument as funding the distribution or acquisition made by the consolidated group. In addition, except as otherwise provided in this section, acquisitions and distributions described in §1.385-3(b)(2) and (b)(3)(i) in which all parties to the transaction are members of the same consolidated group both before and after the transaction are disregarded for purposes of this section and §1.385-3.

(2) *One-corporation rule inapplicable to expanded group member determination.*—The one-corporation rule described in paragraph (b)(1) of this section does not apply in determining the members of an expanded group. Notwithstanding the previous sentence, an expanded group does not exist for purposes of this section and §1.385-3 if it consists only of members of a single consolidated group.

(3) *Application of §1.385-3 to debt instruments issued by members of a consolidated group.*—(i) *Debt instrument treated as stock of the issuing member of a consolidated group.*—If a covered debt instrument treated as issued by a consolidated group under the one-corporation rule described in paragraph (b)(1) of this section is treated as stock under §1.385-3, the covered debt instrument is treated as stock in the member of the consolidated group that would be the issuer of such debt instrument without regard to this section. But see §1.385-3(d)(7) (providing that a covered debt instrument that is treated as stock under §1.385-3(b)(2), (3), or (4) and that is not described in section 1504(a)(4) is not treated as stock for purposes of determining whether the issuer is a member of an affiliated group (within the meaning of section 1504(a)).

(ii) *Application of the covered debt instrument exclusions.*—For purposes of determining whether a debt instrument issued by a member of a consolidated group is a covered debt instrument, each test described in §1.385-3(g)(3) is applied on a separate member basis without regard to the one-corporation rule described in paragraph (b)(1) of this section.

(iii) *Qualified short-term debt instrument.*—The determination of whether a member of a consolidated group has issued a qualified short-term debt instrument for purposes of §1.385-3(b)(3)(vii) is made on a separate member basis without regard to the one-corporation rule described in paragraph (b)(1) of this section.

(4) *Application of the reductions of §1.385-3(c)(3) to members of a consolidated group.*—(i) *Application of the reduction for expanded group earnings.*—(A) *In general.*—A consolidated group maintains one expanded group earnings account with respect to an expanded group period, and only the earnings and profits, determined in accordance with §1.1502-33 (without regard to the application of §1.1502-33(b)(2), (e), and (f)), of the common parent (within the meaning of section 1504) of the consolidated group are considered in calculating the expanded group earnings for the expanded group period of the consolidated group. Accordingly, a regarded distribution or acquisition made by a member of a consolidated group is reduced to the extent of the expanded group earnings account of the consolidated group.

(B) *Effect of certain corporate transactions on the calculation of expanded group earnings.*—(1) *Consolidation.*—A consolidated group succeeds to the expanded group earnings account of a joining member under the principles of §1.385-3(c)(3)(i)(F)(2)(ii).

(2) *Deconsolidation.*—(i) *In general.*—Except as otherwise provided in paragraph (b)(4)(i)(B)(2)(ii) of this section, no amount of the expanded group earnings account of a consolidated group for an expanded group period, if any, is allocated to a departing member. Accordingly, immediately after leaving the consolidated group, the departing member has no expanded group earnings account with respect to its expanded group period.

(ii) *Allocation of expanded group earnings to a departing member in a distribution described in section 355.*—If a departing member leaves the consolidated group by reason of an exchange or distribution to which section 355 (or so much of section 356 that relates to section 355) applies, the expanded group earnings account of the consolidated group is allocated between the consolidated group and the departing member in proportion to the earnings and profits of the consolidated group and the earnings and profits of the departing member immediately after the transaction.

(ii) *Application of the reduction for qualified contributions.*—(A) *In general.*—For purposes of applying §1.385-3(c)(3)(ii)(A) to a consolidated group—

(1) A qualified contribution to any member of a consolidated group that remains a member of the consolidated group immediately after the qualified contribution from a person other than a member of the same consolidated group is treated as made to the one corporation described in paragraph (b)(1) of this section;

(2) A qualified contribution that causes a member of a consolidated group to become a departing member of that consolidated group is treated as made to the departing member and not to the consolidated group of which the departing member was a member immediately prior to the qualified contribution; and

(3) No contribution of property by a member of a consolidated group to any other member of the consolidated group is a qualified contribution.

(B) *Effect of certain corporate transactions on the calculation of qualified contributions.*—(1) *Consolidation.*—A consolidated group succeeds to the qualified contributions of a joining member under the principles of §1.385-3(c)(3)(ii)(F)(2)(i).

(2) *Deconsolidation.*—(i) *In general.*—Except as otherwise provided in paragraph (b)(4)(ii)(B)(2)(ii) of this section, no amount of the qualified contributions of a consolidated group for an expanded group period, if any, is allocated to a departing member. Accordingly, immediately after leaving the consolidated group, the departing member has no qualified contributions with respect to its expanded group period.

(ii) *Allocation of qualified contributions to a departing member in a distribution described in section 355.*—If a departing member leaves the consolidated group by reason of an exchange or distribution to which section 355 (or so much of section 356 that relates to section 355) applies, each qualified contribution of the consolidated group is allocated between the consolidated group and the departing member in proportion to the earnings and profits of the consolidated

32,084

Corporate Interests Treated as Stock or Indebtedness
See p. 20,601 for regulations not amended to reflect law changes

group and the earnings and profits of the departing member immediately after the transaction.

(5) *Order of operations.*—For purposes of this section and § 1.385-3, the consequences of a transaction involving one or more members of a consolidated group are determined as provided in paragraphs (b)(5)(i) and (ii) of this section.

(i) First, determine the characterization of the transaction under Federal tax law without regard to the one-corporation rule described in paragraph (b)(1) of this section.

(ii) Second, apply this section and § 1.385-3 to the transaction as characterized to determine whether to treat a debt instrument as stock, treating the consolidated group as one corporation under paragraph (b)(1) of this section, unless otherwise provided.

(6) *Partnership owned by a consolidated group.*—For purposes of this section and § 1.385-3, and notwithstanding the one-corporation rule described in paragraph (b)(1) of this section, a partnership that is wholly owned by members of a consolidated group is treated as a partnership. Thus, for example, if members of a consolidated group own all of the interests in a controlled partnership that issues a debt instrument to a member of the consolidated group, such debt instrument would be treated as a consolidated group debt instrument because, under § 1.385-3(f)(3)(i), for purposes of this section and § 1.385-3, a consolidated group member that is an expanded group partner is treated as the issuer with respect to its share of the debt instrument issued by the partnership.

(7) *Predecessor and successor.*—(i) *In general.*—Pursuant to paragraph (b)(5) of this section, the determination as to whether a member of an expanded group is a predecessor or successor of another member of the consolidated group is made without regard to paragraph (b)(1) of this section. For purposes of § 1.385-3(b)(3), if a consolidated group member is a predecessor or successor of a member of the same expanded group that is not a member of the same consolidated group, the consolidated group is treated as a predecessor or successor of the expanded group member (or the consolidated group of which that expanded group member is a member). Thus, for example, a departing member that departs a consolidated group in a distribution or exchange to which section 355 applies is a successor to the consolidated group and the consolidated group is a predecessor of the departing member.

(ii) *Joining members.*—For purposes of § 1.385-3(b)(3), the term *predecessor* also means, with respect to a consolidated group, a joining member and the term successor also means, with respect to a joining member, a consolidated group.

(c) *Consolidated group debt instruments.*—(1) *Debt instrument ceases to be a consolidated group debt instrument but continues to be issued and held by expanded group members.*—(i) *Consolidated group member leaves the consolidated group.*—For purposes of this section and § 1.385-3, when a debt instrument ceases to be a consolidated group debt instrument as a result of a transaction in which the member of the consolidated group that issued the instrument (the issuer) or the member of the consolidated group holding the instrument (the holder) ceases to be a member of the same consolidated group but both the issuer and the holder continue to be members of the same expanded group, the issuer is treated as issuing a new debt instrument to the holder in exchange for property immediately after the debt instrument ceases to be a consolidated group debt instrument. To the extent the newly-issued debt instrument is a covered debt instrument that is treated as stock under § 1.385-3(b)(3), the covered debt instrument is then immediately deemed to be exchanged for stock of the issuer. For rules regarding the treatment of the deemed exchange, see § 1.385-1(d). For examples illustrating the rule in this paragraph (c)(1)(i), see paragraphs (f)(3)(iv) and (v) of this section (*Examples 4 and 5*).

(ii) *Consolidated group debt instrument that is transferred outside of the consolidated group.*—For purposes of this section and § 1.385-3, when a member of a consolidated group that holds a consolidated group debt instrument transfers the debt instrument to an expanded group member that is not a member of the same consolidated group (transferee expanded group member), the debt instrument is treated as issued by the consolidated group to the transferee expanded group member immediately after the debt instrument ceases to be a consolidated group debt instrument. Thus, for example, for purposes of this section and § 1.385-3, the sale of a consolidated group debt instrument to a transferee expanded group member is treated as an issuance of the debt instrument by the consolidated group to the transferee expanded group member in exchange for property. To the extent the newly-issued debt instrument is a covered debt instrument that is treated as stock upon being transferred, the covered debt instrument is deemed to be exchanged for stock of the member of the consolidated group treated as the issuer of the debt instrument

(determined under paragraph (b)(3)(i) of this section) immediately after the covered debt instrument is transferred outside of the consolidated group. For rules regarding the treatment of the deemed exchange, see § 1.385-1(d). For examples illustrating the rule in this paragraph (c)(1)(ii), see paragraphs (f)(3)(ii) and (iii) of this section (*Examples 2 and 3*).

(iii) *Overlap transactions.*—If a debt instrument ceases to be a consolidated group debt instrument in a transaction to which both paragraphs (c)(1)(i) and (ii) of this section apply, then only the rules of paragraph (c)(1)(ii) of this section apply with respect to such debt instrument.

(iv) *Subgroup exception.*—A debt instrument is not treated as ceasing to be a consolidated group debt instrument for purposes of paragraphs (c)(1)(i) and (ii) of this section if both the issuer and the holder of the debt instrument are members of the same consolidated group immediately after the transaction described in paragraph (c)(1)(i) or (ii) of this section.

(2) *Covered debt instrument treated as stock becomes a consolidated group debt instrument.*—When a covered debt instrument that is treated as stock under § 1.385-3 becomes a consolidated group debt instrument, then immediately after the covered debt instrument becomes a consolidated group debt instrument, the issuer is deemed to issue a new covered debt instrument to the holder in exchange for the covered debt instrument that was treated as stock. In addition, in a manner consistent with § 1.385-3(d)(2)(ii)(A), when the covered debt instrument that previously was treated as stock becomes a consolidated group debt instrument, other covered debt instruments issued by the issuer of that instrument (including a consolidated group that includes the issuer) that are not treated as stock when the instrument becomes a consolidated group debt instrument are retested to determine whether those other covered debt instruments are treated as funding the regarded distribution or acquisition that previously was treated as funded by the instrument (unless such distribution or acquisition is disregarded under paragraph (b)(1) of this section). Further, also in a manner consistent with § 1.385-3(d)(2)(ii)(A), a covered debt instrument that is issued by the issuer (including a consolidated group that includes the issuer) after the application of this paragraph (c)(2) and within the per se period may also be treated as funding that regarded distribution or acquisition.

(3) *No interaction with the intercompany obligation rules of § 1.1502-13(g).*—The rules of this section do not affect the application of the rules of § 1.1502-13(g). Thus, any deemed satisfaction and reissuance of a debt instrument under § 1.1502-13(g) and any deemed issuance and deemed exchange of a debt instrument under this paragraph (c) that arise as part of the same transaction or series of transactions are not integrated. Rather, each deemed satisfaction and reissuance under the rules of § 1.1502-13(g), and each deemed issuance and exchange under the rules of this section, are respected as separate steps and treated as separate transactions.

(d) *Application of the funding rule of § 1.385-3(b)(3) to members departing a consolidated group.*—This paragraph (d) provides rules for applying the funding rule of § 1.385-3(b)(3) when a departing member ceases to be a member of a consolidated group, but only if the departing member and the consolidated group are members of the same expanded group immediately after the deconsolidation.

(1) *Continued application of the one-corporation rule.*—A disregarded distribution or acquisition by any member of the consolidated group continues to be disregarded when the departing member ceases to be a member of the consolidated group.

(2) *Continued recharacterization of a departing member's covered debt instrument as stock.*—A covered debt instrument of a departing member that is treated as stock of the departing member under § 1.385-3(b) continues to be treated as stock when the departing member ceases to be a member of the consolidated group.

(3) *Effect of issuances of covered debt instruments that are not consolidated group debt instruments on the departing member and the consolidated group.*—If a departing member has issued a covered debt instrument (determined without regard to the one-corporation rule described in paragraph (b)(1) of this section) that is not a consolidated group debt instrument and that is not treated as stock immediately before the departing member ceases to be a consolidated group member, then the departing member (and not the consolidated group) is treated as issuing the covered debt instrument on the date and in the manner the covered debt instrument was issued. If the departing member is not treated as the issuer of a covered debt instrument pursuant to the preceding sentence, then the consolidated group continues to be treated as issuing the covered debt instrument on the date and in the manner the covered debt instrument was issued.

(4) *Treatment of prior regarded distributions or acquisitions.*—This paragraph (d)(4) applies when a departing member ceases to be a consolidated group member in a transaction other than a distribution to which section 355 (or so much of section 356 as relates to section 355) applies, and the consolidated group has made a regarded distribution or acquisition. In this case, to the extent the distribution or acquisition has not caused a covered debt instrument of the consolidated group to be treated as stock under § 1.385-3(b) on or before the date the departing member leaves the consolidated group, then—

(i) If the departing member made the regarded distribution or acquisition (determined without regard to the one-corporation rule described in paragraph (b)(1) of this section), the departing member (and not the consolidated group) is treated as having made the regarded distribution or acquisition.

(ii) If the departing member did not make the regarded distribution or acquisition (determined without regard to the one-corporation rule described in paragraph (b)(1) of this section), then the consolidated group (and not the departing member) continues to be treated as having made the regarded distribution or acquisition.

(e) *Definitions.*—The definitions in this paragraph (e) apply for purposes of this section.

(1) *Consolidated group debt instrument.*—The term *consolidated group debt instrument* means a covered debt instrument issued by a member of a consolidated group and held by a member of the same consolidated group.

(2) *Departing member.*—The term *departing member* means a member of an expanded group that ceases to be a member of a consolidated group but continues to be a member of the same expanded group. In the case of multiple members leaving a consolidated group as a result of a single transaction that continue to be members of the same expanded group, if such members are treated as one corporation under paragraph (b)(1) of this section immediately after the transaction, that one corporation is a departing member with respect to the consolidated group.

(3) *Disregarded distribution or acquisition.*—The term *disregarded distribution or acquisition* means a distribution or acquisition described in § 1.385-3(b)(2) or (b)(3)(i) between members of a consolidated group that is disregarded under the one-corporation rule described in paragraph (b)(1) of this section.

(4) *Joining member.*—The term *joining member* means a member of an expanded group that becomes a member of a consolidated group and continues to be a member of the same expanded group. In the case of multiple members joining a consolidated group as a result of a single transaction that continue to be members of the same expanded group, if such members were treated as one corporation under paragraph (b)(1) of this section immediately before the transaction, that one corporation is a joining member with respect to the consolidated group.

(5) *Regarded distribution or acquisition.*—The term *regarded distribution or acquisition* means a distribution or acquisition described in § 1.385-3(b)(2) or (b)(3)(i) that is not disregarded under the one-corporation rule described in paragraph (b)(1) of this section.

(f) *Examples.*—(1) *Assumed facts.*—Except as otherwise stated, the following facts are assumed for purposes of the examples in paragraph (f)(3) of this section:

(i) FP is a foreign corporation that owns 100% of the stock of USS1, a covered member, and 100% of the stock of FS, a foreign corporation;

(ii) USS1 owns 100% of the stock of DS1 and DS3, both covered members;

(iii) DS1 owns 100% of the stock of DS2, a covered member;

(iv) FS owns 100% of the stock of UST, a covered member;

(v) At the beginning of Year 1, FP is the common parent of an expanded group comprised solely of FP, USS1, FS, DS1, DS2, DS3, and UST (the FP expanded group);

(vi) USS1, DS1, DS2, and DS3 are members of a consolidated group of which USS1 is the common parent (the USS1 consolidated group);

(vii) The FP expanded group has outstanding more than $50 million of debt instruments described in § 1.385-3(c)(4) at all times;

(viii) No issuer of a covered debt instrument has a positive expanded group earnings account, within the meaning of § 1.385-3(c)(3)(i)(B), or has received a qualified contribution, within the meaning of § 1.385-3(c)(3)(ii)(B);

(ix) All notes are covered debt instruments, within the meaning of § 1.385-3(g)(3), and are not qualified short-term debt instruments, within the meaning of § 1.385-3(b)(3)(vii);

(x) All notes between members of a consolidated group are intercompany obligations within the meaning of § 1.1502-13(g)(2)(ii);

(xi) Each entity has as its taxable year the calendar year;

(xii) No domestic corporation is a United States real property holding corporation within the meaning of section 897(c)(2);

(xiii) Each note is issued with adequate stated interest (as defined in section 1274(c)(2)); and

(xiv) Each transaction occurs after January 19, 2017.

(2) *No inference.*—Except as otherwise provided in this section, it is assumed for purposes of the examples in paragraph (f)(3) of this section that the form of each transaction is respected for Federal tax purposes. No inference is intended, however, as to whether any particular note would be respected as indebtedness or as to whether the form of any particular transaction described in an example in paragraph (f)(3) of this section would be respected for Federal tax purposes.

(3) *Examples.*—The following examples illustrate the rules of this section.

(i) *Example 1: Order of operations.*—(A) *Facts.* On Date A in Year 1, UST issues UST Note to USS1 in exchange for DS3 stock representing less than 20% of the value and voting power of DS3.

(B) *Analysis.* UST is acquiring the stock of DS3, the non-common parent member of a consolidated group. Pursuant to paragraph (b)(5)(i) of this section, the transaction is first analyzed without regard to the one-corporation rule described in paragraph (b)(1) of this section, and therefore UST is treated as issuing a covered debt instrument in exchange for expanded group stock. The exchange of UST Note for DS3 stock is not an exempt exchange within the meaning of § 1.385-3(g)(11) because UST and USS1 are not parties to an asset reorganization. Pursuant to paragraph (b)(5)(ii) of this section, § 1.385-3 (including § 1.385-3(b)(2)(ii)) is then applied to the transaction, thereby treating UST Note as stock for Federal tax purposes when it is issued by UST to USS1. The UST Note is not treated as property for purposes of section 304(a) because it is not property within the meaning specified in section 317(a). Therefore, UST's acquisition of DS3 stock from USS1 in exchange for UST Note is not an acquisition described in section 304(a)(1).

(ii) *Example 2: Distribution of consolidated group debt instrument.*—(A) *Facts.* On Date A in Year 1, DS1 issues DS1 Note to USS1 in a distribution. On Date B in Year 2, USS1 distributes DS1 Note to FP.

(B) *Analysis.* Under paragraph (b)(1) of this section, the USS1 consolidated group is treated as one corporation for purposes of § 1.385-3. Accordingly, when DS1 issues DS1 Note to USS1 in a distribution on Date A in Year 1, DS1 is not treated as issuing a debt instrument to another member of DS1's expanded group in a distribution for purposes of § 1.385-3(b)(2), and DS1 Note is not treated as stock under § 1.385-3. When USS1 distributes DS1 Note to FP, DS1 Note is deemed satisfied and reissued under § 1.1502-13(g)(3)(ii), immediately before DS1 Note ceases to be an intercompany obligation. Under paragraph (c)(1)(ii) of this section, when USS1 distributes DS1 Note to FP, the USS1 consolidated group is treated as issuing DS1 Note to FP in a distribution on Date B in Year 2. Accordingly, DS1 Note is treated as stock under § 1.385-3(b)(2)(i). Under paragraph (c)(1)(ii) of this section, DS1 Note is deemed to be exchanged for stock of the issuing member, DS1, immediately after DS1 Note is transferred outside of the USS1 consolidated group. Under paragraph (c)(3) of this section, the deemed satisfaction and reissuance under § 1.1502-13(g)(3)(ii) and the deemed issuance and exchange under paragraph (c)(1)(ii) of this section, are respected as separate steps and treated as separate transactions.

(iii) *Example 3: Sale of consolidated group debt instrument.*—(A) *Facts.* On Date A in Year 1, DS1 lends $200x of cash to USS1 in exchange for USS1 Note. On Date B in Year 2, USS1 distributes $200x of cash to FP. Subsequently, on Date C in Year 2, DS1 sells USS1 Note to FS for $200x.

(B) *Analysis.* Under paragraph (b)(1) of this section, the USS1 consolidated group is treated as one corporation for purposes of § 1.385-3. Accordingly, when USS1 issues USS1 Note to DS1 for property on Date A in Year 1, the USS1 consolidated group is not treated as a funded member, and when USS1 distributes $200x to FP on Date B in Year 2, that distribution is a transaction described in § 1.385-3(b)(3)(i)(A), but does not cause USS1 Note to be recharacterized under § 1.385-3(b)(3). When DS1 sells USS1 Note to FS, USS1 Note is deemed satisfied and reissued under § 1.1502-13(g)(3)(ii), immediately before USS1 Note ceases to be an intercompany obligation. Under paragraph (c)(1)(ii) of this section, when the USS1 Note is transferred to FS for $200x on Date C in Year 2, the USS1 consolidated group is treated as issuing USS1 Note to FS in exchange for $200x on that date. Because USS1 Note is issued by the USS1 consolidated group to FS within the per se period as defined in § 1.385-3(g)(19) with respect to the distribution by the USS1 consolidated group to FP, USS1 Note is treated as funding the distribution under

32,086

Corporate Interests Treated as Stock or Indebtedness
See p. 20,601 for regulations not amended to reflect law changes

§ 1.385-3(b)(3)(iii)(A) and, accordingly, is treated as stock under § 1.385-3(b)(3). Under § 1.385-3(d)(1)(i) and paragraph (c)(1)(ii) of this section, USS1 Note is deemed to be exchanged for stock of the issuing member, USS1, immediately after USS1 Note is transferred outside of the USS1 consolidated group. Under paragraph (c)(3) of this section, the deemed satisfaction and reissuance under § 1.1502-13(g)(3)(ii) and the deemed issuance and exchange under paragraph (c)(1)(ii) of this section are respected as separate steps and treated as separate transactions.

(iv) *Example 4: Treatment of consolidated group debt instrument and departing member's regarded distribution or acquisition when the issuer of the instrument leaves the consolidated group.*—(A) *Facts.* The facts are the same as provided in paragraph (f)(1) of this section, except that USS1 and FS own 90% and 10% of the stock of DS1, respectively. On Date A in Year 1, DS1 distributes $80x of cash and newly-issued DS1 Note, which has a value of $10x, to USS1. Also on Date A in Year 1, DS1 distributes $10x of cash to FS. On Date B in Year 2, FS purchases all of USS1's stock in DS1 (90% of the stock of DS1), resulting in DS1 ceasing to be a member of the USS1 consolidated group.

(B) *Analysis.* Under paragraph (b)(1) of this section, the USS1 consolidated group is treated as one corporation for purposes of § 1.385-3. Accordingly, DS1's distribution of $80x of cash to USS1 on Date A in Year 1 is a disregarded distribution or acquisition, and under paragraph (d)(1) of this section, continues to be a disregarded distribution or acquisition when DS1 ceases to be a member of the USS1 consolidated group. In addition, when DS1 issues DS1 Note to USS1 in a distribution on Date A in Year 1, DS1 is not treated as issuing a debt instrument to a member of DS1's expanded group in a distribution for purposes of § 1.385-3(b)(2)(i), and DS1 Note is not treated as stock under § 1.385-3(b)(2)(i). DS1's issuance of DS1 Note to USS1 is also a disregarded distribution or acquisition, and under paragraph (d)(1) of this section, continues to be a disregarded distribution or acquisition when DS1 ceases to be a member of the USS1 consolidated group. The distribution of $10x cash by DS1 to FS on Date A in Year 1 is a regarded distribution or acquisition. When FS purchases 90% of the stock of DS1's from USS1 on Date B in Year 2 and DS1 ceases to be a member of the USS1 consolidated group, DS1 Note is deemed satisfied and reissued under § 1.1502-13(g)(3)(ii), immediately before DS1 Note ceases to be an intercompany obligation. Under paragraph (c)(1)(i) of this section, for purposes of § 1.385-3, DS1 is treated as issuing a new debt instrument to USS1 in exchange for property immediately after DS1 Note ceases to be a consolidated group debt instrument. Under paragraph (d)(4)(i) of this section, the departing member, DS1 (and not the USS1 consolidated group) is treated as having distributed $10x to FS on Date A in Year 1 (a regarded distribution or acquisition) for purposes of applying § 1.385-3(b)(3) after DS1 ceases to be a member of the USS1 consolidated group. Because DS1 Note is reissued by DS1 to USS1 within the per se period (as defined in § 1.385-3(g)(19)) with respect to DS1's regarded distribution to FS, DS1 Note is treated as funding the distribution under § 1.385-3(b)(3)(iii)(A) and, accordingly, is treated as stock under § 1.385-3(b)(3). Under § 1.385-3(d)(1)(i) and paragraph (c)(1)(i) of this section, DS1 Note is immediately deemed to be exchanged for stock of DS1 on Date B in Year 2. Under paragraph (c)(3) of this section, the deemed satisfaction and reissuance under § 1.1502-13(g)(3)(ii) and the deemed issuance and exchange under paragraph (c)(1)(i) of this section are respected as separate steps and treated as separate transactions. Under § 1.385-3(d)(7)(i), after DS1 Note is treated as stock held by USS1, DS1 Note is not treated as stock for purposes of determining whether DS1 is a member of the USS1 consolidated group.

(v) *Example 5: Treatment of consolidated group debt instrument and consolidated group's regarded distribution or acquisition.*—(A) *Facts.*

On Date A in Year 1, DS1 issues DS1 Note to USS1. On Date B in Year 2, USS1 distributes $100x of cash to FP. On Date C in Year 3, USS1 sells all of its interest in DS1 to FS, resulting in DS1 ceasing to be a member of the USS1 consolidated group.

(B) *Analysis.* Under paragraph (b)(1) of this section, the USS1 consolidated group is treated as one corporation for purposes of § 1.385-3. Accordingly, when DS1 issues DS1 Note to USS1 in a distribution on Date A in Year 1, DS1 is not treated as issuing a debt instrument to a member of DS1's expanded group in a distribution for purposes of § 1.385-3(b)(2)(i), and DS1 Note is not treated as stock under § 1.385-3(b)(2)(i). DS1's issuance of DS1 Note to USS1 is also a disregarded distribution or acquisition, and under paragraph (d)(1) of this section, continues to be a disregarded distribution or acquisition when DS1 ceases to be a member of the USS1 consolidated group. The distribution of $100x cash by DS1 to USS1 on Date B in Year 2 is a regarded distribution or acquisition. When FS purchases all of the stock of DS1 from USS1 on Date C in Year 3 and DS1 ceases to be a member of the USS1 consolidated group, DS1 Note is deemed satisfied and reissued under § 1.1502-13(g)(3)(ii), immediately before DS1 Note ceases to be an intercompany obligation. Under paragraph (c)(1)(i) of this section, for purposes of § 1.385-3, DS1 is treated as issuing a new debt instrument to USS1 in exchange for property immediately after DS1 Note ceases to be a consolidated group debt instrument. Under paragraph (d)(4)(ii) of this section, the USS1 consolidated group (and not DS1) is treated as having distributed $100x to FP on Date B in Year 2 (a regarded distribution or acquisition) for purposes of applying § 1.385-3(b)(3) after DS1 ceases to be a member of the USS1 consolidated group. Because DS1 has not engaged in a regarded distribution or acquisition that would have been treated as funded by the reissued DS1 Note, the reissued DS1 Note is not treated as stock.

(vi) *Example 6: Treatment of departing member's issuance of a covered debt instrument.*—(A) *Facts.* On Date A in Year 1, FS lends $100x of cash to DS1 in exchange for DS1 Note. On Date B in Year 2, USS1 distributes $30x of cash to FP. On Date C in Year 2, USS1 sells all of its DS1 stock to FP, resulting in DS1 ceasing to be a member of the USS1 consolidated group.

(B) *Analysis.* Under paragraph (b)(1) of this section, the USS1 consolidated group is treated as one corporation for purposes of § 1.385-3. Accordingly, on Date A in Year 1, the USS1 consolidated group is treated as issuing DS1 Note to FS, and on Date B in Year 2, the USS1 consolidated group is treated as distributing $30x of cash to FP. Because DS1 Note is issued by the USS1 consolidated group to FS within the per se period as defined in § 1.385-3(g)(19) with respect to the distribution by the USS1 consolidated group of $30x cash to FP, $30x of DS1 Note is treated as funding the distribution under § 1.385-3(b)(3)(iii)(A), and, accordingly, is treated as stock on Date B in Year 2 under § 1.385-3(b)(3) and § 1.385-3(d)(1)(ii). Under paragraph (d)(3) of this section, DS1 (and not the USS1 consolidated group) is treated as the issuer of the remaining portion of DS1 Note for purposes of applying § 1.385-3(b)(3) after DS1 ceases to be a member of the USS1 consolidated group.

(g) *Applicability date.*—This section applies to taxable years for which the U.S. Federal income tax return is due, without extensions, after May 14, 2020. For taxable years ending on or after January 19, 2017, and for which the U.S. Federal income tax return is due, without extensions, on or before May 14, 2020, see § 1.385-4T, as contained in 26 CFR in part 1 in effect on April 1, 2019. In the case of a taxable year that ends after October 13, 2019, and on or before May 14, 2020, a taxpayer may choose to apply this section to the portion of the taxable year that occurs after the expiration of § 1.385-4T on October 13, 2019, provided that all members of the taxpayer's expanded group apply this section in its entirety. [Reg. § 1.385-4.]

☐ [T.D. 9897, 5-13-2020.]

[The next page is 33,301.]

DEFERRED COMPENSATION, ETC.

Pension, Profit-Sharing, Stock Bonus Plans, Etc.

See p. 20,601 for regulations not amended to reflect law changes

[Reg. § 1.401-0]

§ 1.401-0. Scope and definitions.—(a) *In general.*—Sections 1.401 through 1.401-14 (inclusive) reflect the provisions of section 401 prior to amendment by the Employee Retirement Income Security Act of 1974. The sections following § 1.401-14 and preceding § 1.402(a) (hereafter referred to in this section as the "Post-ERISA Regulations") reflect the provisions of section 401 after amendment by such Act.

(b) *Definitions.*—For purposes of the Post-ERISA regulations—

(1) *Qualified plan.*—The term "qualified plan" means a plan which satisfies the requirements of section 401(a).

(2) *Qualified trust.*—The term "qualified trust" means a trust which satisfies the requirements of section 401(a). [Reg. § 1.401-0.]

☐ [T.D. 7501, 8-22-77.]

[Reg. § 1.401-1]

§ 1.401-1. Qualified pension, profit-sharing, and stock bonus plans.—(a) *Introduction.*—(1) Sections 401 through 405 relate to pension, profit-sharing, stock bonus, and annuity plans, compensation paid under a deferred-payment plan, and bond purchase plans. Section 401(a) prescribes the requirements which must be met for qualification of a trust forming part of a pension, profit-sharing, or stock bonus plan.

(2) A qualified pension, profit-sharing, or stock bonus plan is a definite written program and arrangement which is communicated to the employees and which is established and maintained by an employer—

(i) In the case of a pension plan, to provide for the livelihood of the employees or their beneficiaries after the retirement of such employees through the payment of benefits determined without regard to profits (see paragraph (b)(1)(i) of this section);

(ii) In the case of a profit-sharing plan, to enable employees or their beneficiaries to participate in the profits of the employer's trade or business, or in the profits of an affiliated employer who is entitled to deduct his contributions to the plan under section 404(a)(3)(B), pursuant to a definite formula for allocating the contributions and for distributing the funds accumulated under the plan (see paragraph (b)(1)(ii) of this section); and

(iii) In the case of a stock bonus plan, to provide employees or their beneficiaries benefits similar to those of profit-sharing plans, except that such benefits are distributable in stock of the employer, and that the contributions by the employer are not necessarily dependent upon profits. If the employer's contributions are dependent upon profits, the plan may enable employees or their beneficiaries to participate not only in the profits of the employer, but also in the profits of an affiliated employer who is entitled to deduct his contributions to the plan under section 404(a)(3)(B) (see paragraph (b)(1)(iii) of this section).

(3) In order for a trust forming part of a pension, profit-sharing, or stock bonus plan to constitute a qualified trust under section 401(a), the following tests must be met:

(i) It must be created or organized in the United States, as defined in section 7701(a)(9), and it must be maintained at all times as a domestic trust in the United States;

(ii) It must be part of a pension, profit-sharing, or stock bonus plan established by an employer for the exclusive benefit of his employees or their beneficiaries (see paragraph (b)(2) through (5) of this section);

(iii) It must be formed or availed of for the purpose of distributing to the employees or their beneficiaries the corpus and income of the fund accumulated by the trust in accordance with the plan, and, in the case of a plan which covers (as defined in paragraph (a)(2) of § 1.401.10) any self-employed individual, the time and method of such distribution must satisfy the requirements of section 401(a)(9) with respect to each employee covered by the plan;

(iv) It must be impossible under the trust instrument at any time before the satisfaction of all liabilities with respect to employees and their beneficiaries under the trust, for any part of the corpus or income to be used for, or diverted to, purposes other than for the exclusive benefit of the employees or their beneficiaries (see § 1.401-2);

(v) It must be part of a plan which benefits prescribed percentages of the employees, or which benefits such employees as qualify under a classification set up by the employer and found by the Commissioner not to be discriminatory in favor of certain specified classes of employees (see § 1.401-3);

(vi) It must be part of a plan under which contributions or benefits do not discriminate in favor of certain specified classes of employees (see §§ 1.401-1(a)(4)-0 through 1.401-(a)(4)-13);

(vii) It must be part of a plan which provides the nonforfeitable rights described in section 401(a)(7) (see § 1.401-6);

(viii) If the trust forms part of a pension plan, the plan must provide that forfeitures must not be applied to increase the benefits any employee would receive under such plan (see § 1.401-7);

(ix) It must, if the plan benefits any self-employed individual who is an owner-employee, satisfy the additional requirements for qualification contained in section 401(a)(10) and (d).

(4) For taxable years beginning after December 31, 1962, self-employed individuals may be included in qualified plans. See generally § 1.401-10.

(b) *General rules.*—(1)(i) A pension plan within the meaning of section 401(a) is a plan established and maintained by an employer primarily to provide systematically for the payment of definitely determinable benefits to his employees over a period of years, usually for life, after retirement. Retirement benefits generally are measured by, and based on, such factors as years of service and compensation received by the employees. The determination of the amount of retirement benefits and the contributions to provide such benefits are not dependent upon profits. Benefits are not definitely determinable if funds arising from forfeitures on termination of service, or other reason, may be used to provide increased benefits for the remaining participants (see § 1.401-7, relating to the treatment of forfeitures under a qualified pension plan). A plan designed to provide benefits for employees or their beneficiaries to be paid upon retirement or over a period of years after retirement will, for the purposes of section 401(a), be considered a pension plan if the employer contributions under the plan can be determined actuarially on the basis of definitely determinable benefits, or, as in the case of money purchase pension plans, such contributions are fixed without being geared to profits. A pension plan may provide for the payment of a pension due to disability and may also provide for the payment of incidental death benefits through insurance or otherwise. However, a plan is not a pension plan if it provides for the payment of benefits not customarily included in a pension plan such as layoff benefits or benefits for sickness, accident, hospitalization, or medical expenses (except medical benefits described in section 401(h) as defined in paragraph (a) of § 1.401-14).

(ii) A profit-sharing plan is a plan established and maintained by an employer to provide for the participation in his profits by his employees or their beneficiaries. The plan must provide a definite predetermined formula for allocating the contributions made to the plan among the participants and for distributing the funds accumulated under the plan after a fixed number of years, the attainment of a stated age, or upon the prior occurrence of some event such as layoff, illness, disability, retirement, death, or severance of employment. A formula for allocating the contributions among the participants is definite if, for example, it provides for an allocation in proportion to the basic compensation of each participant. A plan (whether or not it contains a definite predetermined formula for determining the profits to be shared with the employees) does not qualify under section 401(a) if the contributions to the plan are made at such times or in such amounts that the plan in operation discriminates in favor of officers, shareholders, persons whose principal duties consist in supervising the work of other employees, or highly compensated employees. For the rules with respect to discrimination, see §§ 1.401-3 and 1.401-1(a)(4)-0 through 1.401-1(a)(4)-13. A profit-sharing plan within the meaning of section 401 is primarily a plan of deferred compensation, but the amounts allocated to the account of a participant may be used to provide for him or his family incidental life or accident or health insurance. See §§ 1.72-15, 1.72-16, and 1.402(a)-1(e) for rules regarding the tax treatment of incidental life or accident or health insurance.

(iii) A stock bonus plan is a plan established and maintained by an employer to provide benefits similar to those of a profit-sharing plan, except that the contributions by the employer are not necessarily dependent upon profits and the benefits are distributable in stock of the employer company. For the purpose of allocating and distributing the stock of the employer which is to be shared among his employees or their beneficiaries, such a plan is subject to the same requirements as a profit-sharing plan.

(iv) As to inclusion of full-time life insurance salesmen within the class of persons considered to be employees, see section 7701(a)(20).

(2) The term "plan" implies a permanent as distinguished from a temporary program. Thus, although the employer may reserve the right to change or terminate the plan, and to discontinue contributions thereunder, the abandonment of the plan for any reason other than business necessity within a few years after it has taken effect will be evidence that the plan from its inception was not a bona fide program for the exclusive benefit of employees in general. Especially will this be true if, for example, a pension plan is abandoned soon after pensions have been fully funded for persons in favor of whom discrimination is prohibited under section 401(a). The permanency of the plan will be indicated by all of the surrounding facts and circumstances, including the likelihood of the employer's ability to continue contributions as provided under the plan. In the case of a profit-sharing plan, other than a profit-sharing plan which covers employees and owner-employees (see section 401(d)(2)(B)), it is not necessary that the employer contribute every year or that he contribute the same amount or contribute in accordance with the same ratio every year. However, merely making a single or occasional contribution out of profits for employees does not establish a plan of profit-sharing. To be a profit-sharing plan, there must be recurring and substantial contributions out of profits for the employees. In the event a plan is abandoned, the employer should promptly notify the district director, stating the circumstances which led to the discontinuance of the plan.

(3) If the plan is so designed as to amount to a subterfuge for the distribution of profits to shareholders, it will not qualify as a plan for the exclusive benefit of employees even though other employees who are not shareholders are also included under the plan. The plan must benefit the employees in general although it need not provide benefits for all of the employees. Among the employees to be benefited may be persons who are officers and shareholders. However, a plan is not for the exclusive benefit of employees in general if, by any device whatever, it discriminates either in eligibility requirements, contributions, or benefits in favor of employees who are officers, shareholders, persons whose principal duties consist in supervising the work of other employees, or the highly compensated employees. See section 401(a)(3), (4), and (5). Similarly, a stock bonus or profit-sharing plan is not a plan for the exclusive benefit of employees in general if the funds therein may be used to relieve the employer from contributing to a pension plan operating concurrently and covering the same employees. All of the surrounding and attendant circumstances and the details of the plan will be indicative of whether it is a bona fide stock bonus, pension, or profit-sharing plan for the exclusive benefit of employees in general. The law is concerned not only with the form of a plan but also with its effects in operation. For example, section 401(a)(5) specifies certain provisions which of themselves are not discriminatory. However, this does not mean that a plan containing these provisions may not be discriminatory in actual operation.

(4) A plan is for the exclusive benefit of employees or their beneficiaries even though it may cover former employees as well as present employees and employees who are temporarily on leave, as, for example, in the Armed Forces of the United States. A plan covering only former employees may qualify under section 401(a) if it complies with the provisions of section 401(a)(3)(B), with respect to coverage, and section 401(a)(4), with respect to contributions and benefits, as applied to all of the former employees. The term "beneficiaries" of an employee within the meaning of section 401 includes the estate of the employee, dependents of the employee, persons who are the natural objects of the employee's bounty, and any persons designated by the employee to share in the benefits of the plan after the death of the employee.

(5)(i) No specific limitations are provided in section 401(a) with respect to investments which may be made by the trustees of a trust qualifying under section 401(a). Generally, the contributions may be used by the trustees to purchase any investments permitted by the trust agreement to the extent allowed by local law. However, such a trust will be subject to tax under section 511 with respect to any "unrelated business taxable income" (as defined in section 512) realized by it from its investments.

(ii) Where the trust funds are invested in stock or securities of, or loaned to, the employer or other person described in section 503(b), full disclosure must be made of the reasons for such arrangement and the conditions under which such investments are made in order that a determination may be made whether the trust serves any purpose other than constituting part of a plan for the exclusive benefit of employees. The trustee shall report any of such investments on the return which under section 6033 it is required to file and shall with respect to any such investment furnish the information required by such return. See § 1.6033-1.

(c) *Portions of years.*—A qualified status must be maintained throughout the entire taxable year of the trust in order for the trust to obtain any exemption for such year. But see section 401(a)(6) and § 1.401-3.

(d) *Plan of several employers.*—A trust forming part of a plan of several employers for their employees will be qualified if all the requirements are otherwise satisfied.

(e) *Determination of exemptions and returns.*—(1) An employees' trust may request a determination letter as to its qualification under section 401 and exemption under section 501. For the procedure for obtaining such a determination letter see paragraph (1) of § 601.201 of this chapter (Statement of Procedural Rules).

(2) A trust which qualifies under section 401(a) and which is exempt under section 501(a) must file a return in accordance with section 6033 and the regulations thereunder. See §§ 1.6033-1 and 1.6033-2(a)(3). In case such a trust realizes any unrelated business taxable income, as defined in section 512, such trust is also required to file a return with respect to such income. See paragraph (e) of § 1.6012-2 and paragraph (a)(5) of § 1.6012-3 for requirements with respect to such returns. For information required to be furnished periodically by an employer with respect to the qualification of a plan, see §§ 1.404(a)–2, and 1.6033–2(a)(2)(ii)(I). [Reg. § 1.401-1.]

☐ [T.D. 6203, 9-24-56. *Amended by* T.D. 6301, 7-8-58; T.D. 6675, 9-16-63, T.D. 6722, 4-13-64, T.D. 7168, 3-8-72, T.D. 7428, 8-13-76, T.D. 9665, 5-9-2014, T.D. 9849, 3-11-2019 *and* T.D. 9898, 5-26-2020.]

[Reg. § 1.401-2]

§ 1.401-2. Impossibility of diversion under the trust instrument.—(a) *In general.*—(1) Under section 401(a)(2) a trust is not qualified unless under the trust instrument it is impossible (in the taxable year and at any time thereafter before the satisfaction of all liabilities to employees or their beneficiaries covered by the trust) for any part of the trust corpus or income to be used for, or diverted to, purposes other than for the exclusive benefit of such employees or their beneficiaries. This section does not apply to funds of the trust which are allocated to provide medical benefits described in section 401(h) as defined in paragraph (a) of § 1.401-14. For the rules prohibiting diversion of such funds and the requirement of reversion to the employer after satisfaction of all liabilities under the medical benefits account, see paragraphs (c)(4) and (5) of § 1.401-14. For rules permitting reversion to the employer of amounts held in a section 415 suspense account, see § 1.401(a)-2(b).

(2) As used in section 401(a)(2), the phrase "if under the trust instrument it is impossible" means that the trust instrument must definitely and affirmatively make it impossible for the nonexempt diversion or use to occur, whether by operation or natural termination of the trust, by power of revocation or amendment, by the happening of a contingency, by collateral arrangement, or by any other means. Although it is not essential that the employer relinquish all power to modify or terminate the rights of certain employees covered by the trust, it must be impossible for the trust funds to be used or diverted for purposes other than for the exclusive benefit of his employees or their beneficiaries.

(3) As used in section 401(a)(2), the phrase "purposes other than for the exclusive benefit of his employees or their beneficiaries" includes all objects or aims not solely designed for the proper satisfaction of all liabilities to employees or their beneficiaries covered by the trust.

(b) *Meaning of "liabilities".*—(1) The intent and purpose in section 401(a)(2) of the phrase "prior to the satisfaction of all liabilities with respect to employees and their beneficiaries under the trust" is to permit the employer to reserve the right to recover at the termination of the trust, and only at such termination, any balance remaining in the trust which is due to erroneous actuarial computations during the previous life of the trust. A balance due to an "erroneous actuarial computation" is the surplus arising because actual requirements differ from the expected requirements even though the latter were based upon previous actuarial valuations of liabilities or determinations of costs of providing pension benefits under the plan and were made by a person competent to make such determinations in accordance with reasonable assumptions as to mortality, interest, etc., and correct procedures relating to the method of funding. For example, a trust has accumulated assets of $1,000,000 at the time of liquidation, determined by acceptable actuarial procedures using reasonable assumptions as to interest, mortality, etc., as being necessary to provide the benefits in accordance with the provisions of the plan. Upon such liquidation it is found that $950,000 will satisfy all of the liabilities under the plan. The surplus of $50,000 arises, therefore, because of the difference between the amounts actuarially determined and the amounts actually required to satisfy the liabilities. This $50,000, therefore, is the amount which may be returned to the employer as the result of an erroneous actuarial computation. If, however, the surplus of $50,000 had been accumulated as a result of a change in the benefit provisions or in the eligibility requirements of the plan, the $50,000 could not revert to the employer because such surplus would not be the result of an erroneous actuarial computation.

(2) The term "liabilities" as used in section 401(a)(2) includes both fixed and contingent obligations to employees. For example, if 1,000 employees are covered by a trust forming part of a pension plan, 300 of whom have satisfied all the requirements for a monthly pension, while the remaining 700 employees have not yet completed the required period of service, contingent obligations to such 700 employees have nevertheless arisen which constitute "liabilities" within the meaning of that term. It must be impossible for the employer (or other nonemployee) to recover any amounts other than such amounts as remain in the trust because of "erroneous actuarial computations" after the satisfaction of all fixed and contingent obligations. Furthermore, the trust instrument must contain a definite affirmative provision to this effect, irrespective of whether the obligations to employees have their source in the trust instrument itself, in the plan of which the trust forms a part, or in some collateral instrument or arrangement forming a part of such plan, and regardless of whether such obligations are, technically speaking, liabilities of the employer, of the trust, or of some other person forming a part of the plan or connected with it. [Reg. § 1.401-2.]

☐ [*T.D. 6203, 9-24-56. Amended by T.D. 6722, 4-13-64 and T.D. 7748, 12-30-80.*]

[Reg. § 1.401-3]

§ 1.401-3. Requirements as to coverage.—
***

(e)(1) Section 401(a)(5) contains a provision to the effect that a classification shall not be considered discriminatory within the meaning of section 401(a)(3)(B) merely because all employees whose entire annual remuneration constitutes "wages" under section 3121(a)(1) (for purposes of the Federal Insurance Contributions Act, chapter 21 of the Code) are excluded from the plan. A reference to section 3121(a)(1) for years after 1954 shall be deemed a reference to section 1426(a)(1) of the Internal Revenue Code of 1939 for years before 1955. This provision, in conjunction with section 401(a)(3)(B), is intended to permit the qualification of plans which supplement the old-age, survivors, and disability insurance benefits under the Social Security Act (42 U.S.C. ch. 7). Thus, a classification which excludes all employees whose entire remuneration constitutes "wages" under section 3121(a)(1), will not be considered discriminatory merely because of such exclusion. Similarly, a plan which includes all employees will not be considered discriminatory solely because the contributions or benefits based on that part of their remuneration which is excluded from wages under section 3121(a)(1) differ from the contributions or benefits based on that part of their remuneration which is not so excluded. However, in making his determination with respect to discrimination in classification under section 401(a)(3)(B), the Commissioner will consider whether the total benefits resulting to each employee under the plan and under the Social Security Act, or under the Social Security Act only, establish an integrated and correlated retirement system satisfying the tests of section 401(a). If, therefore, a classification of employees under a plan results in relatively or proportionately greater benefits for employees earning above any specified salary amount or rate than for those below any such salary amount or rate, it may be found to be discriminatory within the meaning of section 401(a)(3)(B). If, however, the relative or proportionate differences in benefits which result from such classification are approximately offset by the old-age, survivors, and disability insurance benefits which are provided by the Social Security Act and which are not attributable to employee contributions under the Federal Insurance Contributions Act, the plan will be considered to be properly integrated with the Social Security Act and will, therefore, not be considered discriminatory.

(2)(i) For purposes of determining whether a plan is properly integrated with the Social Security Act, the amount of old-age, survivors, and disability insurance benefits which may be considered as attributable to employer contributions under the Federal Insurance Contributions Act is computed on the basis of the following:

(a) The rate at which the maximum monthly old-age insurance benefit is provided under the Social Security Act is considered to be the average of (1) the rate at which the maximum benefit currently payable under the Act (i.e., in 1971) is provided to an employee retiring at age 65, and (2) the rate at which the maximum benefit ultimately payable under the Act (i.e., in 2010) is provided to *an employee retiring at age 65. The resulting figure is 43 percent* of the average monthly wage on which such benefit is computed.

(b) The total old-age, survivors, and disability insurance benefits with respect to an employee is considered to be 162 percent of the employee's old-age insurance benefits. The resulting figure is 70 percent of the average monthly wage on which it is computed.

(c) In view of the fact that social security benefits are funded through equal contributions by the employer and employee, 50 percent of such benefits is considered attributable to employer contributions. The resulting figure is 35 percent of the average monthly wage on which the benefit is computed.

Under these assumptions, the maximum old-age, survivors, and disability insurance benefits which may be attributed to employer contributions under the Federal Insurance Contributions Act is an amount equal to 35 percent of the earnings on which they are computed. These computations take into account all amendments to the Social Security Act through the Social Security Amendments of 1971 (85 Stat. 6). It is recognized, however, that subsequent amendments to this Act may increase the percentages described in (a) or (b) of this subdivision (i), or both. If this occurs, the method used in this subparagraph for determining the integration formula may result in a figure under (c) of this subdivision (i) which is greater than 35 percent and a plan could be amended to adopt such greater figure in its benefit formula. In order to minimize future plan amendments of this nature, an employer may anticipate future changes in the Social Security Act by immediately utilizing such a higher figure, but not in excess of 37½ percent, in developing its benefit formula.

(ii) Under the rules provided in this subparagraph, a classification of employees under a noncontributory pension or annuity plan which limits coverage to employees whose compensation exceeds the applicable integration level under the plan will not be considered discriminatory within the meaning of section 401(a)(3)(B), where:

(a) The integration level applicable to an employee is his covered compensation, or is (1) in the case of an active employee, a stated dollar amount uniformly applicable to all active employees which is not greater than the covered compensation of any active employee, and (2) in the case of a retired employee, an amount which is not greater than his covered compensation. (For rules relating to determination of an employee's covered compensation, see subdivision (iv) of this subparagraph.)

(b) The rate at which normal annual retirement benefits are provided for any employee with respect to his average annual compensation in excess of the plan's integration level applicable to him does not exceed 37½ percent.

(c) Average annual compensation is defined to mean the average annual compensation over the highest 5 consecutive years.

(d) There are no benefits payable in case of death before retirement.

(e) The normal form of retirement benefits is a straight life annuity, and if there are optional forms, the benefit payments under each optional form are actuarially equivalent to benefit payments under the normal form.

(f) In the case of any employee who reaches normal retirement age before completion of 15 years of service with the employer, the rate at which normal annual retirement benefits are provided for him with respect to his average annual compensation in excess of the plan's integration level applicable to him does not exceed 2½ percent for each year of service.

(g) Normal retirement age is not lower than age 65.

(h) Benefits payable in case of retirement or any other severance of employment before normal retirement age cannot exceed the actuarial equivalent of the maximum normal retirement benefits, which might be provided in accordance with (a) through (g) of this subdivision (ii), multiplied by a fraction, the numerator of which is the actual number of years of service of the employee at retirement or severance, and the denominator of which is the total number of years of service he would have had if he had remained in service until normal retirement age. A special disabled life mortality table shall not be used in determining the actuarial equivalent in the case of severance due to disability.

(iii)(a) If a plan was properly integrated with old-age and survivors insurance benefits on July 5, 1968 (hereinafter referred to as an "existing plan"), then, notwithstanding the fact that such plan does not satisfy the requirements of subdivision (ii) of this subparagraph, it will continue to be considered properly integrated with such benefits until January 1, 1972. Such plan will be considered properly integrated after December 31, 1971, so long as the benefits provided under the plan for each employee equal the sum of—

(1) The benefits to which he would be entitled under a plan which, on July 5, 1968, would have been considered properly integrated with old-age and survivors insurance benefits, and under which benefits are provided at the same (or a lesser) rate with respect to the same portion of compensation with respect to which benefits are provided under the existing plan, multiplied by the percentage of his total service with the employer performed before a specified date not later than January 1, 1972; and

(2) The benefits to which he would be entitled under a plan satisfying the requirements of subdivision (ii) of this subparagraph, multiplied by the percentage of his total service with the employer performed on and after such specified date.

(b) A plan which, on July 5, 1968, was properly integrated with old-age and survivors insurance benefits will not be considered not to be properly integrated with such benefits thereafter merely because such plan provides a minimum benefit for each employee (other than an employee who owns, directly or indirectly, stock possessing more than 10 percent of the total combined voting power or value of all classes of stock of the employer corporation) equal to the benefit to which he would be entitled under the plan as in effect on July 5, 1968, if he continued to earn annually until retirement the same amount of compensation as he earned in 1967.

(c) If a plan was properly integrated with old-age and survivors insurance benefits on May 17, 1971, notwithstanding the fact that such plan does not satisfy the requirements of subdivision (ii) of this subparagraph, it will continue to be considered properly integrated with such benefits until January 1, 1972.

(iv) For purposes of this subparagraph, an employee's covered compensation is the amount of compensation with respect to which old-age insurance benefits would be provided for him under the Social Security Act (as in effect at any uniformly applicable date occurring before the employee's separation from the service) if for each year until he attains age 65 his annual compensation is at least equal to the maximum amount of earnings subject to tax in each such year under the Federal Insurance Contributions Act. A plan may provide that an employee's covered compensation is the amount determined under the preceding sentence rounded to the nearest whole multiple of a stated dollar amount which does not exceed $600.

(v) In the case of an integrated plan providing benefits different from those described in subdivision (ii) or (iii) (whichever is applicable) of this subparagraph, or providing benefits related to years of service, or providing benefits purchasable by stated employer contributions, or under the terms of which the employees contribute, or providing a combination of any of the foregoing variations, the plan will be considered to be properly integrated only if, as determined by the Commissioner, the benefits provided thereunder by employer contributions cannot exceed in value the benefits described in subdivision (ii) or (iii) (whichever is applicable) of this subparagraph. Similar principles will govern in determining whether a plan is properly integrated if participation therein is limited to employees earning in excess of amounts other than those specified in subdivision (iv) of this subparagraph, or if it bases benefits or contributions on compensation in excess of such amounts, or if it provides for an offset of benefits otherwise payable under the plan on account of old-age, survivors, and disability insurance benefits. Similar principles will govern in determining whether a profit-sharing or stock bonus plan is properly integrated with the Social Security Act.

(3) A plan supplementing the Social Security Act and excluding all employees whose entire annual remuneration constitutes "wages" under section 3121(a)(1) will not, however, be deemed discriminatory merely because, for administrative convenience, it provides a reasonable minimum benefit not to exceed $20 a month.

(4) Similar considerations, to the extent applicable in any case, will govern classifications under a plan supplementing the benefits provided by other Federal or State laws. See section 401(a)(5).

(5) If a plan provides contributions or benefits for a self-employed individual, the rules relating to the integration of such a plan with the contributions or benefits under the Social Security Act are set forth in paragraph (c) of §1.401-11 and paragraph (h) of §1.401-12 of the Treasury Regulations in effect on April 1, 2017.

(6) This paragraph (e) does not apply to plan years beginning on or after January 1, 1989. * * * [Reg. §1.401-3.]

☐ [T.D. 6203, 9-24-56. *Amended by* T.D. 6447, 1-21-60, T.D. 6675, 9-16-63, T.D. 6982, 11-12-68, T.D. 7134, 7-21-71, T.D. 8359, 9-12-91 *and* T.D. 9849, 3-11-2019.]

[Reg. §1.401-4]

§1.401-4. [Reserved].

☐ [T.D. 6203, 9-24-56. *Amended by* T.D. 6675, 9-16-63; T.D. 7934, 1-9-84; T.D. 8360, 9-12-91 *and* T.D. 8485, 8-30-93. *Removed and reserved by* T.D. 9849, 3-11-2019.]

[Reg. §1.401-5]

§1.401-5. [Reserved].

☐ [T.D. 6500, 11-26-60. *Amended by* T.D. 7436, 9-28-76. *Removed and reserved by* T.D. 9849, 3-11-2019.]

[Reg. §1.401-6]

§1.401-6. Termination of a qualified plan.—(a) *General rules.*—(1) In order for a pension, profitsharing, or stock bonus trust to satisfy the requirements of section 401, the plan of which such trust forms a part must expressly provide that, upon the termination of the plan or upon the complete discontinuance of contributions under the plan, the rights of each employee to benefits accrued to the date of such termination or discontinuance, to the extent then funded, or the rights of each employee to the amounts credited to his account at

such time, are nonforfeitable. As to what constitutes nonforfeitable rights of an employee, see paragraph (a)(2) of §1.402(b)-1.

(2)(i) A qualified plan must also provide for the allocation of any previously unallocated funds to the employees covered by the plan upon the termination of the plan or the complete discontinuance of contributions under the plan. Such provision may be incorporated in the plan at its inception or by an amendment made prior to the termination of the plan or the discontinuance of contributions thereunder.

(ii) Any provision for the allocation of unallocated funds is acceptable if it specifies the method to be used and does not conflict with the provisions of section 401(a)(4) and the regulations thereunder. The allocation of unallocated funds may be in cash or in the form of other benefits provided under the plan. However, the allocation of the funds contributed by the employer among the employees need not necessarily benefit all the employees covered by the plan. For example, an allocation may be satisfactory if priority is given to benefits for employees over the age of 50 at the time of the termination of the plan, or those who then have at least 10 years of service, if there is no possibility of discrimination in favor of employees who are officers, shareholders, employees whose principal duties consist in supervising the work of other employees, or highly compensated employees.

(iii) Subdivisions (i) and (ii) of this subparagraph do not require the allocation of amounts to the account of any employee if such amounts are not required to be used to satisfy the liabilities with respect to employees and their beneficiaries under the plan (see section 401(a)(2)).

(b) *Termination defined.*—(1) Whether a plan is terminated is generally a question to be determined with regard to all the facts and circumstances in a particular case. For example, a plan is terminated when, in connection with the winding up of the employer's trade or business, the employer begins to discharge his employees. However, a plan is not terminated, for example, merely because an employer consolidates or replaces that plan with a comparable plan. Similarly, a plan is not terminated merely because the employer sells or otherwise disposes of his trade or business if the acquiring employer continues the plan as a separate and distinct plan of its own, or consolidates or replaces that plan with a comparable plan. See paragraph (d)(4) of §1.381(c)(11)-1 for the definition of comparable plan. In addition, the Commissioner may determine that other plans are comparable for purposes of this section.

(2) For purposes of this section, the term *termination* includes both a partial termination and a complete termination of a plan. Whether or not a partial termination of a qualified plan occurs when a group of employees who have been covered by the plan are subsequently excluded from such coverage either by reason of an amendment to the plan, or by reason of being discharged by the employer, will be determined on the basis of all the facts and circumstances. Similarly, whether or not a partial termination occurs when benefits or employer contributions are reduced, or the eligibility or vesting requirements under the plan are made less liberal, will be determined on the basis of all the facts and circumstances. However, if a partial termination of a qualified plan occurs, the provisions of section 401(a)(7) and this section apply only to the part of the plan that is terminated.

(c) *Complete discontinuance defined.*—(1) For purposes of this section, a complete discontinuance of contributions under the plan is contrasted with a suspension of contributions under the plan, which is merely a temporary cessation of contributions by the employer. A complete discontinuance of contributions may occur although some amounts are contributed by the employer under the plan if such amounts are not substantial enough to reflect the intent on the part of the employer to continue to maintain the plan. The determination of whether a complete discontinuance of contributions under the plan has occurred will be made with regard to all the facts and circumstances in the particular case, and without regard to the amount of any contributions made under the plan by employees.

(2) In the case of a pension plan, a suspension of contributions will not constitute a discontinuance if—

(i) The benefits to be paid or made available under the plan are not affected at any time by the suspension, and

(ii) The unfunded past service cost at any time (which includes the unfunded prior normal cost and unfunded interest on any unfunded cost) does not exceed the unfunded past service cost as of the date of establishment of the plan, plus any additional past service or supplemental costs added by amendment.

(3) In any case in which a suspension of a profitsharing plan is considered a discontinuance, the discontinuance becomes effective not later than the last day of the taxable year of the employer following the last taxable year of such employer for which a substantial contribution was made under the profitsharing plan.

(d) *Contributions or benefits which remain forfeitable.*—The provisions of this section do not apply to amounts which are reallocated to prevent the discrimination prohibited by section 401(a)(4).

(e) *Effective date.*—This section shall apply to taxable years of a qualified plan commencing after September 30, 1963. In the case of the termination or complete discontinuance (as defined in this section) of any qualified plan during any such taxable year, the rights accorded to each employee covered under the plan must conform to the requirements of this section. However, a plan which is qualified on September 30, 1963, will not be disqualified merely because it does not expressly include the provisions prescribed by this section. [Reg. § 1.401-6.]

☐ [*T.D. 6675, 9-16-63. Amended by T.D. 9849, 3-11-2019.*]

[Reg. § 1.401-7]

§ 1.401-7. Forfeitures under a qualified pension plan.— (a) *General rules.*—In the case of a trust forming a part of a qualified pension plan, the plan must expressly provide that forfeitures arising from severance of employment, death, or for any other reason, must not be applied to increase the benefits any employee would otherwise receive under the plan at any time prior to the termination of the plan or the complete discontinuance of employer contributions thereunder. The amounts so forfeited must be used as soon as possible to reduce the employer's contributions under the plan. However, a qualified pension plan may anticipate the effect of forfeitures in determining the costs under the plan. Furthermore, a qualified plan will not be disqualified merely because a determination of the amount of forfeitures under the plan is made only once during each taxable year of the employer.

(b) *Examples.*—The rules of paragraph (a) of this section may be illustrated by the following examples:

Example (1). The B Company Pension Trust forms a part of a pension plan which is funded by individual level annual premium annuity contracts. The plan requires ten years of service prior to obtaining a vested right to benefits under the plan. One of the company's employees resigns his position after two years of service. The insurance company paid to the trustees the cash surrender value of the contract—$750. The B Company must reduce its next contribution to the pension trust by this amount.

Example (2). The C Corporation's trusteed pension plan has been in existence for 20 years. It is funded by individual contracts issued by an insurance company, and the premiums thereunder are paid annually. Under such plan, the annual premium accrued for the year 1966 is due and is paid on January 2, 1966, and on July 1 of the same year the plan is terminated due to the liquidation of the employer. Some forfeitures were incurred and collected by the trustee with respect to those participants whose employment terminated between January 2 and July 1. The plan provides that the amount of such forfeitures is to be applied to provide additional annuity benefits for the remaining employees covered by the plan. The pension plan of the C Corporation satisfies the provisions of section 401(a)(8). Although forfeitures are used to increase benefits in this case, this use of forfeitures is permissible since no further contributions will be made under the plan.

(c) *Effective date.*—This section applies to taxable years of a qualified plan commencing after September 30, 1963. However, a plan which is qualified on September 30, 1963, will not be disqualified merely because it does not expressly include the provisions prescribed by this section. [Reg. § 1.401-7.]

☐ [*T.D. 6675, 9-16-63.*]

[Reg. § 1.401-8]

§ 1.401-8. [Reserved].

☐ [*T.D. 6675, 9-16-63. Amended by T.D. 7565, 9-15-78. Redesignated and amended by T.D. 7748, 1-7-81. Removed and reserved by T.D. 9849, 3-11-2019.*]

[Reg. § 1.401-9]

§ 1.401-9. Face-amount certificates—nontransferable annuity contracts.—(a) *Face-amount certificates treated as annuity contracts.*— Section 401(g) provides that a face-amount certificate (as defined in section 2(a)(15) of the Investment Company Act of 1940 (15 U.S.C. sec. 80a-2)) which is not transferable within the meaning of paragraph (b)(3) of this section shall be treated as an annuity contract for purposes of sections 401 through 404 for any taxable year of a plan subject to such sections beginning after December 31, 1962. Accordingly, there may be established for any such taxable year a qualified plan under which such face-amount certificates are purchased for the participating employees without the creation of a trust or custodial account. However, for such a plan to qualify, the plan must satisfy all

the requirements applicable to a qualified annuity plan (see section 403(a) and the regulations thereunder).

(b) *Nontransferability of face-amount certificates and annuity contracts.*—(1)(i) Section 401(g) provides that, in order for any face-amount certificate, or any other contract issued after December 31, 1962, to be subject to any provision under sections 401 through 404 which is applicable to annuity contracts, as compared to other forms of investment, such certificate or contract must be nontransferable at any time when it is held by any person other than the trustee of a trust described in section 401(a) and exempt under section 501(a). Thus, for example, in order for a group or individual retirement income contract to be treated as an annuity contract, if such contract is not held by the trustee of an exempt employees' trust, it must satisfy the requirements of this section. Furthermore, a face-amount certificate or an annuity contract will be subject to the tax treatment under section 403(b) only if it satisfies the requirements of section 401(g) and this section. Any certificate or contract in order to satisfy the provisions of this section must expressly contain the provisions that are necessary to make such certificate or contract not transferable within the meaning of this paragraph.

(ii) In the case of any group contract purchased by an employer under a plan to which sections 401 through 404 apply, the restriction on transferability required by section 401(g) and this section applies to the interest of the employee participants under such group contract but not to the interest of the employee under such contract.

(2) If a trust described in section 401(a) which is exempt from tax under section 501(a) distributes any annuity, endowment, retirement income, or life insurance contract, then the rules relating to the taxability of the distributee of any such contract are set forth in paragraph (a)(2) of § 1.402(a)-1.

(3) A face-amount certificate or an annuity contract is transferable if the owner can transfer any portion of his interest in the certificate or contract to any person other than the issuer thereof. Accordingly, such a certificate or contract is transferable if the owner can sell, assign, discount, or pledge as collateral for a loan or as security for the performance of an obligation or for any other purpose his interest in the certificate or contract to any person other than the issuer thereof. On the other hand, for purposes of section 401(g), a face-amount certificate or annuity contract is not considered to be transferable merely because such certificate or contract, or the plan of which it is a part, contains a provision permitting the employee to designate a beneficiary to receive the proceeds of the certificate or contract in the event of his death, or contains a provision permitting the employee to elect to receive a joint and survivor annuity, or contains other similar provisions.

(4) A material modification in the terms of an annuity contract constitutes the issuance of a new contract regardless of the manner in which it is made.

(c) *Examples.*—The rules of this section may be illustrated by the following examples:

Example (1). The P Employees' Annuity Plan is a nontrusteed plan which is funded by individual annuity contracts issued by the Y Insurance Company. Each annuity contract issued by such company after December 31, 1962, provides, on its face, that it is "NOT TRANSFERABLE." The terms of each such contract further provide that, "This contract may not be sold, assigned, discounted, or pledged as collateral for a loan or as security for the performance of an obligation or for any other purpose, to any person other than this company." The annuity contracts of the P Employees' Annuity Plan satisfy the requirements of section 401(g) and this section.

Example (2). The R Company Pension Trust forms a part of a pension plan which is funded by individual level premium annuity contracts. Such contracts are purchased by the trustee of the R Company Pension Trust from the Y Insurance Company. The trustee of the R Company Pension Trust is the legal owner of each such contract at all times prior to the distribution of such contract to a qualifying annuitant. The trustee purchases such a contract on January 3, 1963, in the name of an employee who qualifies on that date for coverage under the plan. At the time such contract is purchased, and while the contract is held by the trustee of the R Company Pension Trust, the contract does not contain any restrictions with respect to its transferability. The annuity contract purchased by the trustee of the R Company Pension Trust satisfies the requirements of section 401(g) and this section while it is held by the trustee.

Example (3). A is the trustee of the X Corporation's Employees' Pension Trust. The trust forms a part of a pension plan which is funded by individual level premium annuity contracts. The trustee is the legal owner of such contracts, but the employees covered under the plan obtain beneficial interests in such contracts after ten years of service with the X Corporation. On January 15, 1980, A distributes to D an annuity contract issued to A in D's name on June 25, 1959, and distributes to E an annuity contract issued to A in E's name on

September 30, 1963. The contract issued to D need not be nontransferable, but the contract issued to E must be nontransferable in order to satisfy the requirements of section 401(g) and this section.

Example (4). The corpus of the Y Corporation's Employees' Pension Plan consists of individual insurance contracts in the names of the covered employees and an auxiliary fund which is used to convert such policies to annuity contracts at the time a beneficiary of such trust retires. F retires on June 15, 1963, and the trustee converts the individual insurance contract on F's life to a life annuity which is distributed to him. The life annuity issued on F's life must be nontransferable in order to satisfy the requirements of section 401(g) and this section. [Reg. §1.401-9.]

☐ [T.D. 6675, 9-16-63.]

[Reg. §1.401-10]

§1.401-10. Definitions relating to plans covering self-employed individuals.—(a) *In general.*—(1) Certain self-employed individuals may be covered by a qualified pension, annuity, or profit-sharing plan for taxable years beginning after December 31, 1962. This section contains definitions relating to plans covering self-employed individuals.

(2) A self-employed individual is covered under a qualified plan during the period beginning with the date a contribution is first made by, or for, him under the qualified plan and ending when there are no longer funds under the plan which can be used to provide him or his beneficiaries with benefits.

(b) *Treatment of a self-employed individual as an employee.*—(1) For purposes of section 401, a self-employed individual who receives earned income from an employer during a taxable year of such employer beginning after December 31, 1962, shall be considered an employee of such employer for such taxable year. Moreover, such an individual will be considered an employee for a taxable year if he would otherwise be treated as an employee but for the fact that the employer did not have net profits for that taxable year. Accordingly, the employer may cover such an individual under a qualified plan during years of the plan beginning with or within a taxable year of the employer after December 31, 1962.

(2) If a self-employed individual is engaged in more than one trade or business, each such trade or business shall be considered a separate employer for purposes of applying the provisions of sections 401 through 404 to such individual. Thus, if a qualified plan is established for one trade or business but not the others, the individual will be considered an employee only if he received earned income with respect to such trade or business and only the amount of such earned income derived from that trade or business shall be taken into account for purposes of the qualified plan.

(3)(i) The term "employee", for purposes of section 401, does not include a self-employed individual when the term "common-law" employee is used or when the context otherwise requires that the term "employee" does not include a self-employed individual. The term "common-law" employee also includes an individual who is treated as an employee for purposes of section 401 by reason of the provisions of section 7701(a)(20), relating to the treatment of certain full-time life insurance salesmen as employees. Furthermore, an individual who is a common-law employee is not a self-employed individual with respect to income attributable to such employment, even though such income constitutes net earnings from self-employment as defined in section 1402(a). Thus, for example, a minister who is a common-law employee is not a self-employed individual with respect to income attributable to such employment, even though such income constitutes net earnings from self-employment as defined in section 1402(a).

(ii) An individual may be treated as an employee within the meaning of section 401(c)(1) of one employer even though such individual is also a common-law employee of another employer. For example, an attorney who is a common-law employee of a corporation and who, in the evenings maintains an office in which he practices law as a self-employed individual is an employee within the meaning of section 401(c)(1) with respect to the law practice. This example would not be altered by the fact that the corporation maintained a qualified plan under which the attorney is benefited as a common-law employee.

(4) For the purpose of determining whether an employee within the meaning of section 401(c)(1) satisfies the requirements for eligibility under a qualified plan established by an employer, such an employer may take into account past services rendered by such an employee both as a self-employed individual and as a common-law employee if past services rendered by other employees, including *common-law employees,* are similarly taken into account. However, an employer cannot take into account only past services rendered by employees within the meaning of section 401(c)(1) if past services rendered to such employer by individuals who are, or were, common-law employees are not taken into account. Past service as de-

scribed in this subparagraph may be taken into account for the purpose of determining whether an individual who is, or was, an employee within the meaning of section 401(c)(1) satisfies the requirements for eligibility even if such service was rendered prior to January 1, 1963. On the other hand, past service cannot be taken into account for purposes of determining the contributions which may be made on such an individual's behalf under a qualified plan.

(c) *Definition of earned income.*—(1) *General rule.*—For purposes of section 401 and the regulations thereunder, "earned income" means, in general, net earnings from self-employment (as defined in section 1402(a)) to the extent such net earnings constitute compensation for personal services actually rendered within the meaning of section 911(b).

(2) *Net earnings from self-employment.*—(i). The computation of the net earnings from self-employment shall be made in accordance with the provisions of section 1402(a) and the regulations thereunder, with the modifications and exceptions described in subdivisions (ii) through (iv) of this subparagraph. Thus, an individual may have net earnings from self-employment, as defined in section 1402(a), even though such individual does not have self-employment income, as defined in section 1402(b), and, therefore, is not subject to the tax on self-employment income imposed by section 1401.

(ii) Items which are not included in gross income for purposes of chapter 1 of the Code and the deductions properly attributable to such items must be excluded from the computation of net earnings from self-employment even though the provisions of section 1402(a) specifically require the inclusion of such items. For example, if an individual is a resident of Puerto Rico, so much of his net earnings from self-employment as are excluded from gross income under section 933 must not be taken into account in computing his net earnings from self-employment which are earned income for purposes of section 401.

(iii) In computing net earnings from self-employment for the purpose of determining earned income, a self-employed individual may disregard only deductions for contributions made on his own behalf under a qualified plan. However, such computation must take into account the deduction allowed by section 404 or 405 for contributions under a qualified plan on behalf of the common-law employees of the trade or business.

(iv) For purposes of determining whether an individual has net earnings from self-employment and, thus, whether he is an employee within the meaning of section 401(c)(1), the exceptions in section 1402(c)(4) and (5) shall not apply. Thus, certain ministers, certain members of religious orders, doctors of medicine, and Christian Science practitioners are treated for purposes of section 401 as being engaged in a trade or business from which net earnings from self-employment are derived. In addition, the exceptions in section 1402(c)(2) shall not apply in the case of any individual who is treated as an employee under section 3121(d)(3)(A), (C), or (D). Therefore, such individuals are treated, for purposes of section 401, as being engaged in a trade or business from which net earnings from self-employment may be derived.

(3) *Compensation for personal services actually rendered.*—(i) For purposes of section 401, the term "earned income" includes only that portion of an individual's net earnings from self-employment which constitutes earned income as defined in section 911(b) and the regulations thereunder. Thus, such term includes only professional fees and other amounts received as compensation for personal services actually rendered by the individual. There is excluded from "earned income" the amount of any item of income, and any deduction properly attributable to such item, if such amount is not received as compensation for personal services actually rendered. Therefore, an individual who renders no personal services has no "earned income" even though such an individual may have net earnings from self-employment from a trade or business.

(ii) If a self-employed individual is engaged in a trade or business in which capital is a material income-producing factor, then, under section 911(b), his earned income is only that portion of the net profits from the trade or business which constitutes a reasonable allowance as compensation for personal services actually rendered. However, such individual's earned income cannot exceed 30 percent of the net profits of such trade or business. The net profits of the trade or business is [sic]not necessarily the same as the net earnings from self-employment derived from such trade or business.

(4) *Minimum earned income when both personal services and capital are material income-producing factors.*—(i) If a self-employed individual renders personal services on a full-time, or substantially full-time, basis to only one trade or business, and if with respect to such trade or business capital is a material income-producing factor, then the amount of such individual's earned income from the trade or business is considered to be not less than so much of his share in the net profits of such trade or business as does not exceed $2,500.

(ii) If a self-employed individual renders substantial personal services to more than one trade or business, and if with respect to all such trades or businesses such self-employed individual actually renders personal services on a full-time, or substantially full-time, basis, then the earned income of the self-employed individual from trades or businesses for which he renders substantial personal services and in which both personal services and capital are material income-producing factors is considered to be not less than—

(A) So much of such individual's share of the net profits from all trades or businesses in which he renders substantial personal services as does not exceed $2,500, reduced by

(B) Such individual's share of the net profits of any trade or business in which only personal services is a material income-producing factor.

However, in no event shall the share of the net profits of any trade or business in which capital is a material income-producing factor be reduced below the amount which would, without regard to the provisions of this subdivision, be treated as the earned income derived from such trade or business under section 911(b). In making the computation required by this subdivision, any trade or business with respect to which the individual renders substantial personal services shall be taken into account irrespective of whether a qualified plan has been established by such trade or business.

(iii) If the provisions of subdivision (ii) of this subparagraph apply in determining the earned income of a self-employed individual, and such individual is engaged in two or more trades or businesses in which capital and personal services are material income-producing factors, then the total amount treated as the earned income shall be allocated to each such trade or business for which he performs substantial personal services in the same proportion as his share of net profits from each such trade or business bears to his share of the total net profits from all such trades or businesses. Thus, in such case, the amount of earned income attributable to any such trade or business is computed by multiplying the total earned income as determined under subdivision (ii) of this subparagraph by the individual's net profits from such trade or business and dividing that product by the individual's total net profits from all such trades or businesses.

(iv) For purposes of this subparagraph, the determination of whether an individual renders personal services on a full-time, or substantially full-time, basis is to be made with regard to the aggregate of the trades and businesses with respect to which the employee renders substantial personal services as a common-law employee or as a self-employed individual. However, for all other purposes in applying the rules of this subparagraph, a trade or business with respect to which an individual is a common-law employee shall be disregarded.

(d) *Definition of owner-employee.*—For purposes of section 401 and the regulations thereunder, the term "owner-employee" means a proprietor of a proprietorship, or, in the case of a partnership, a partner who owns either more than 10 percent of the capital interest, or more than 10 percent of the profits interest, of the partnership. Thus, an individual who owns only 2 percent of the profits interest but 11 percent of the capital interest of a partnership is an owner-employee. A partner's interest in the profits and the capital of the partnership shall be determined by the partnership agreement. In the absence of any provision regarding the sharing of profits, the interest in profits of the partners will be determined in the same manner as their distributive shares of partnership taxable income. However, a guaranteed payment (as described in section 707(c)) is not considered a distributive share of partnership income for such purpose. See section 704(b), relating to the determination of the distributive share by the income or loss ratio, and the regulations thereunder. In the absence of a provision in the partnership agreement, a partner's capital interest in a partnership shall be determined on the basis of his interest in the assets of the partnership which would be distributable to such partner upon his withdrawal from the partnership, or upon liquidation of the partnership, whichever is the greater.

(e) *Definition of employer.*—(1) For purposes of section 401, a sole proprietor is considered to be his own employer, and the partnership is considered to be the employer of each of the partners. Thus, an individual partner is not an employer who may establish a qualified plan with respect to his services to the partnership.

(2) Regardless of the provision of local law, a partnership is deemed, for purposes of section 401, to be continuing until such time as it is terminated within the meaning of section 708, relating to the continuation of a partnership. [Reg. § 1.401-10.]

☐ [*T.D.* 6675, 9-16-63. *Amended by T.D.* 9849, 3-11-2019.]

[Reg. §1.401-11]

§1.401-11. [Reserved].

☐ [*T.D.* 6675, 9-16-63. *Amended by T.D.* 6982, 11-12-68. *Removed and reserved by T.D.* 9849, 3-11-2019.]

[Reg. §1.401-12]

§1.401-12. [Reserved].

☐ [*T.D.* 6675, 9-16-63. *Amended by T.D.* 6982, 11-12-68; *T.D.* 6985, 12-26-68; *T.D.* 7428, 8-13-76; *T.D.* 7611, 4-19-79 *and T.D.* 8635, 12-19-95. *Removed and reserved by T.D.* 9849, 3-11-2019.]

[Reg. §1.401-13]

§1.401-13. [Reserved].

☐ [*T.D.* 6676, 9-17-63. *Amended by T.D.* 7636, 8-10-79. *Removed and reserved by T.D.* 9849, 3-11-2019.]

[Reg. §1.401-14]

§1.401-14. Inclusion of medical benefits for retired employees in qualified pension or annuity plans.—(a) *Introduction.*—Under section 401(h) a qualified pension or annuity plan may make provision for the payment of sickness, accident, hospitalization, and medical expenses for retired employees, their spouses, and their dependents. The term "medical benefits described in section 401(h)" is used in this section to describe such payments.

(b) *In general.*—(1) *Coverage.*—Under section 401(h), a qualified pension or annuity plan may provide for the payment of medical benefits described in section 401(h) only for retired employees, their spouses, or their dependents. To be "retired" for purposes of eligibility to receive medical benefits described in section 401(h), an employee must be eligible to receive retirement benefits provided under the pension plan, or else be retired by an employer providing such medical benefits by reason of permanent disability. For purposes of the preceding sentence, an employee is not considered to be eligible to receive retirement benefits provided under the plan if he is still employed by the employer and a separation from employment is a condition to receiving the retirement benefits.

(2) *Discrimination.*—A plan which provides medical benefits described in section 401(h) must not discriminate in favor of officers, shareholders, supervisory employees, or highly compensated employees with respect to coverage and with respect to the contributions or benefits under the plan. The determination of whether such a plan so discriminates is made with reference to the retirement portion of the plan as well as the portion providing the medical benefits described in section 401(h). Thus, for example, a plan will not be qualified under section 401 if it discriminates in favor of employees who are officers or shareholders with respect to either portion of the plan.

(3) *Funding medical benefits.*—Contributions to provide the medical benefits described in section 401(h) may be made either on a contributory or noncontributory basis, without regard to whether the contributions to fund the retirement benefits are made on a similar basis. Thus, for example, the contributions to fund the medical benefits described in section 401(h) may be provided for entirely out of employer contributions even though the retirement benefits under the plan are determined on the basis of both employer and employee contributions.

(4) *Definitions.*—For purposes of section 401(h) and this section:

(i) The term "dependent" shall have the same meaning as that assigned to it by section 152, and

(ii) The term "medical expense" means expenses for medical care as defined in section 213(e)(1).

(c) *Requirements.*—The requirements which must be met for a qualified pension or annuity plan to provide medical benefits described in section 401(h) are set forth in subparagraphs (1) through (5) of this paragraph.

(1) *Benefits.*—(i) The plan must specify the medical benefits described in section 401(h) which will be available and must contain provisions for determining the amount which will be paid. Such benefits, when added to any life insurance protection provided for under the plan, must be subordinate to the retirement benefits provided by such plan. For purposes of this section, life insurance protection includes any benefit paid under the plan on behalf of an employee-participant as a result of the employee-participant's death to the extent such payment exceeds the amount of the reserve to provide the retirement benefits for the employee-participant existing at his death. The medical benefits described in section 401(h) are considered subordinate to the retirement benefits if at all times the aggregate of contributions (made after the date on which the plan

first includes such medical benefits) to provide such medical benefits and any life insurance protection does not exceed 25 percent of the aggregate contributions (made after such date) other than contributions to fund past service credits.

(ii) The meaning of the term "subordinate" may be illustrated by the following example:

Example. The X Corporation amends its qualified pension plan to provide medical benefits described in section 401(h) effective for the taxable year 1964. The total contributions under the plan (excluding those for past service credits) for the taxable year 1964 are $125,000, allocated as follows: $100,000 for retirement benefits, $10,000 for life insurance protection, and $15,000 for medical benefits described in section 401(h). The medical benefits described in section 401(h) are considered subordinate to the retirement benefits since the portion of the contributions allocated to the medical benefits described in section 401(h) ($15,000) and to life insurance protection after such medical benefits were included in the plan ($10,000), or $25,000, does not exceed 25 percent of $125,000. For the taxable year 1965, the X Corporation contributes $140,000 (exclusive of contributions for past service credits) allocated as follows: $100,000 for retirement benefits, $10,000 for life insurance protection, and $30,000 for medical benefits described in section 401(h). The medical benefits described in section 401(h) are considered subordinate to the retirement benefits since the aggregate contributions allocated to the medical benefits described in section 401(h) ($45,000) and to life insurance protection after such medical benefits were included in the plan ($20,000) or $65,000 does not exceed 25 percent of $265,000, the aggregate of the contributions made in 1964 and 1965.

(2) *Separate accounts.*—Where medical benefits described in section 401(h) are provided for under a qualified pension or annuity plan, a separate account must be maintained with respect to contributions to fund such benefits. The separation required by this section is for recordkeeping purposes only. Consequently, the funds in the medical benefits account need not be separately invested. They may be invested with funds set aside for retirement purposes without identification of which investment properties are allocable to each account. However, where the investment properties are not allocated to each account, the earnings on such properties must be allocated to each account in a reasonable manner.

(3) *Reasonable and ascertainable.*—Section 401(h) further requires that amounts contributed fo fund medical benefits therein described must be reasonable and ascertainable. For the rules relating to the deduction of such contributions, see paragraph (f) of §1.404(a)-3. The employer must, at the time he makes a contribution, designate that portion of such contribution allocable to the funding of medical benefits.

(4) *Impossibility of diversion prior to satisfaction of all liabilities.*— Section 401(h) further requires that it must be impossible, at any time prior to the satisfaction of all liabilities under the plan to provide for the payment of medical benefits described in section 401(h), for any part of the corpus or income of the medical benefits account to be (within the taxable year or thereafter) used for, or diverted to, any purpose other than the providing of such benefits. Consequently, a plan which, for example, under its terms, permits funds in the medical benefits account to be used for any retirement benefit provided under the plan does not satisfy the requirements of section 401(h) and will not qualify under section 401(a). However, the payment of any necessary or appropriate expenses attributable to the administration of the medical benefits account does not affect the qualification of the plan.

(5) *Reversion upon satisfaction of all liabilities.*—The plan must provide that any amounts which are contributed to fund medical benefits described in section 401(h) and which remain in the medical benefits account upon the satisfaction of all liabilities arising out of the operation of the medical benefits portion of the plan are to be returned to the employer.

(6) *Forfeitures.*—The plan must expressly provide that in the event an individual's interest in the medical benefits account is forfeited prior to termination of the plan an amount equal to the amount of the forfeiture must be applied as soon as possible to reduce employer contributions to fund the medical benefits described in section 401(h).

(d) *Effective date.*—This section applies to taxable years of a qualified pension or annuity plan beginning after October 23, 1962. [Reg. §1.401-14.]

☐ [T.D. 6722, 4-13-64.]

[Reg. §1.401(a)-1]

§1.401(a)-1. Post-ERISA qualified plans and qualified trusts; in general.—(a) *Introduction.*—(1) *In general.*—This section and the fol-

lowing regulation sections under section 401 reflect the provisions of section 401 after amendment by the Employee Retirement Income Security Act of 1974 (Pub. L. 93-406) ("ERISA").

(2) [Reserved]

(b) *Requirements for pension plans.*—(1) *Definitely determinable benefits.*—(i) In order for a pension plan to be a qualified plan under section 401(a), the plan must be established and maintained by an employer primarily to provide systematically for the payment of definitely determinable benefits to its employees over a period of years, usually for life, after retirement or attainment of normal retirement age (subject to paragraph (b)(2) of this section). A plan does not fail to satisfy this paragraph (b)(1)(i) merely because the plan provides, in accordance with section 401(a)(36), that a distribution may be made from the plan to an employee who has attained age 62 and who is not separated from employment at the time of such distribution.

(ii) Section 1.401-1(b)(1)(i), a pre-ERISA regulation, provides rules applicable to this requirement, and that regulation is applicable except as otherwise provided.

(iii) The use of the type of plan provision described in §1.415(a)-1(d)(1) which automatically freezes or reduces the rate of benefit accrual or the annual addition to insure that the limitations of section 415 will not be exceeded, will not be considered to violate the requirements of this subparagraph provided that the operation of such provision precludes discretion by the employer.

(2) *Normal retirement age.*—(i) *General rule.*—The normal retirement age under a plan must be an age that is not earlier than the earliest age that is reasonably representative of the typical retirement age for the industry in which the covered workforce is employed.

(ii) *Age 62 safe harbor.*—A normal retirement age under a plan that is age 62 or later is deemed to be not earlier than the earliest age that is reasonably representative of the typical retirement age for the industry in which the covered workforce is employed.

(iii) *Age 55 to age 62.*—In the case of a normal retirement age that is not earlier than age 55 and is earlier than age 62, whether the age is not earlier than the earliest age that is reasonably representative of the typical retirement age for the industry in which covered workforce is employed is based on all of the relevant facts and circumstances.

(iv) *Under age 55.*—A normal retirement age that is lower than age 55 is presumed to be earlier than the earliest age that is reasonably representative of the typical retirement age for the industry in which the covered workforce is employed, unless the Commissioner determines that under the facts and circumstances the normal retirement age is not earlier than the earliest age that is reasonably representative of the typical retirement age for the industry in which the covered workforce is employed.

(v) *Age 50 safe harbor for qualified public safety employees.*—A normal retirement age under a plan that is age 50 or later is deemed to be not earlier than the earliest age that is reasonably representative of the typical retirement age for the industry in which the covered workforce is employed if substantially all of the participants in the plan are qualified public safety employees (within the meaning of section 72(t)(10)(B)).

(3) *Benefit distribution prior to retirement.*—For purposes of paragraph (b)(1)(i) of this section, retirement does not include a mere reduction in the number of hours that an employee works. Accordingly, benefits may not be distributed prior to normal retirement age solely due to a reduction in the number of hours that an employee works.

(4) *Effective date.*—Except as otherwise provided in this paragraph (b)(4), paragraphs (b)(2) and (3) of this section are effective May 22, 2007. In the case of a governmental plan (as defined in section 414(d)), paragraphs (b)(2) and (3) of this section are effective for plan years beginning on or after January 1, 2009. In the case of a plan maintained pursuant to one or more collective bargaining agreements that have been ratified and are in effect on May 22, 2007, paragraphs (b)(2) and (3) of this section do not apply before the first plan year that begins after the last of such agreements terminate determined without regard to any extension thereof (or, if earlier, May 24, 2010. See §1.411(d)-4, A-12, for a special transition rule in the case of a plan amendment that increases a plan's normal retirement age pursuant to paragraph (b)(2) of this section. [Reg. §1.401(a)-1.]

☐ [T.D. 7748, 12-30-80. *Amended by T.D. 9319, 4-4-2007 and T.D. 9325, 5-21-2007.*]

[Reg. §1.401(a)-2]

§1.401(a)-2. Impossibility of diversion under qualified plan or trust.—(a) *General rule.*—Section 401(a)(2) requires that in order for a trust to be qualified, it must be impossible under the trust instrument (in the taxable year and at any time thereafter before the satisfaction of all liabilities to employees or their beneficiaries covered by the trust) for any part of the trust corpus or income to be used for, or diverted to, purposes other than for the exclusive benefit of those employees or their beneficiaries. Section 1.401-2, a pre-ERISA regulation, provides rules under section 401(a)(2) and that regulation is applicable except as otherwise provided.

(b) *Section 415 suspense account.*—Notwithstanding paragraph (a) of this section, a plan, or trust forming part of a plan, may provide for the reversion to the employer, upon termination of the plan, of amounts contributed to the plan that exceed the limitations imposed under section 415(c), to the extent set forth in rules prescribed by the Commissioner in revenue rulings, notices, or other guidance published in the Internal Revenue Bulletin (see §601.601(d)(2) of this chapter). [Reg. §1.401(a)-2.]

☐ [*T.D. 7748, 12-30-80. Amended by T.D. 9319, 4-4-2007.*]

[Reg. §1.401(a)-4]

§1.401(a)-4. Optional forms of benefit (before 1994).—

Q-1: How does section 401(a)(4) apply to optional forms of benefits?

A-1: (a) *In general*—(1) *Scope.* The nondiscrimination requirements of section 401(a)(4) apply to the amount of contributions or benefits, optional forms of benefit, and other benefits, rights and features (e.g., actuarial assumptions, methods of benefit calculation, loans, social security supplements, and disability benefits) under a plan. This section addresses the application of section 401(a)(4) only to optional forms of benefit under a plan. Generally, the determination of whether an optional form is nondiscriminatory under section 401(a)(4) is made by reference to the availability of such optional form, and not by reference to the utilization or actual receipt of such optional form. See Q&A-2 of this section. Even though an optional form of benefit under a plan may be nondiscriminatory under section 401(a)(4) and this §1.401(a)-4 because the availability of such optional form does not impermissibly favor employees in the highly compensated group, such plan may fail to satisfy section 401(a)(4) with respect to the amount of contributions or benefits or with respect to other benefits, rights and features if, for example, the method of calculation or the amount or value of benefits payable under such optional form impermissibly favors the highly compensated group. See §1.411(d)-4, Q&A-1 for the definition of "optional form of benefit."

(2) *Nondiscrimination requirements.* Each optional form of benefit provided under a plan is subject to the nondiscrimination requirement of section 401(a)(4) and thus the availability of each optional form of benefit must not discriminate in favor of the employees described in section 401(a)(4) in whose favor discrimination is prohibited (the "highly compensated group"). See paragraph (b) of this Q&A-1 for a description of the employees included in such group. This is true without regard to whether a particular optional form of benefit is the actuarial equivalent of any other optional form of benefit under the plan. Thus, for example, a plan may not condition, or otherwise limit, the availability of a single sum distribution of an employee's benefit in a manner that impermissibly favors the highly compensated group.

(b) *Highly compensated group.* For plan years commencing prior to the applicable effective date for the amendment made to section 401(a)(4) by section 1114 of the Tax Reform Act of 1986 (TRA '86), the highly compensated group consists of those employees who are officers, shareholders, or highly compensated. For plan years beginning on or after the applicable effective date of the amendments to section 401(a)(4) made by TRA '86, the highly compensated group consists of those employees who are highly compensated within the meaning of section 414(q). The amendment to section 401(a)(4) made by section 1114 of TRA '86 is, generally effective for plan years commencing after December 31, 1988. See section 1114(a) of TRA '86.

Q-2: How is it determined whether an optional form of benefit satisfies the nondiscrimination requirements of section 401(a)(4)?

A-2: (a) *Nondiscrimination requirement*—(1) *In general.* An optional form of benefit under a plan is nondiscriminatory under section 401(a)(4) only if the requirements of paragraphs (a)(2) and (a)(3) of this Q&A-2 are satisfied with respect to such optional form. The determination of whether an optional form of benefit satisfies these requirements is made by reference to the availability of the optional form, and not by reference to the utilization or actual receipt of such optional form. Thus, an optional form of benefit that satisfies the requirements of paragraphs (a)(2) and (a)(3) of this Q&A-2 is nondiscriminatory under section 401(a)(4) even though the highly compensated group disproportionately utilizes such optional form. However, the composition of the group of employees who actually receive benefits in an optional form may be relevant in determining

whether such optional form satisfies the requirement of paragraph (a)(3) of this Q&A-2 with respect to effective availability.

(2) *Current availability*—(i) *Plan years prior to TRA '86 effective date.* Except as provided in paragraph (a)(2)(iii) of this Q&A-2, for plan years prior to the effective date of the amendments made to section 410(b) by section 1112(a) of TRA '86, the requirement of this paragraph (a)(2) is satisfied only if the group of employees to whom the optional form is currently available satisfies either the seventy percent test of section 410(b)(1)(A) or the nondiscriminatory classification test of section 410(b)(1)(B).

(ii) *Plan years commencing on or after TRA '86 effective date.* Except as provided in paragraph (a)(2)(iii) of this Q&A-2, for plan years commencing on or after the effective date on which the amendments made to section 410(b) by section 1112(a) of TRA '86 first apply to a plan, the requirement of this paragraph (a)(2) is satisfied only if the group of employees to whom the optional form is currently available satisfies either the percentage test set forth in section 410(b)(1)(A), the ratio test set forth in section 410(b)(1)(B), or the nondiscriminatory classification test set forth in section 410(b)(2)(A)(i). The employer need not satisfy the average benefit percentage test in section 410(b)(2)(A)(ii) in order for the optional form to be currently available to a nondiscriminatory group of employees.

(iii) *Special rule for certain governmental or church plans.* Plans described in section 410(c) will be treated as satisfying the current availability test of this paragraph (a)(2) if the group of employees with respect to whom the optional form is currently available satisfies the requirements of section 401(a)(3) as in effect on September 1, 1974.

(iv) *Effective date for TRA '86 amendments to section 410(b).* The amendments to section 410(b) made by section 1112(a) of TRA '86 are generally effective for plan years commencing after December 31, 1988. See section 1112(e)(1) of TRA '86.

(v) *Elimination of optional forms*— A) *In general.* Notwithstanding paragraphs (a)(2)(i) and (a)(2)(ii) of this Q&A-2, in the case of an optional form of benefit that has been eliminated under a plan with respect to specified employees for benefits accrued after the later of the eliminating amendment's adoption date or effective date, the determination of whether such optional form satisfies this paragraph (a)(2) with respect to such employees is to be made immediately prior to the elimination. Accordingly, if, as of the later of the adoption date or effective date of an amendment eliminating an optional form with respect to future benefit accruals, the current availability of such optional form immediately prior to such amendment satisfies this paragraph (a)(2), then the optional form will be treated as satisfying this paragraph (a)(2) for all subsequent years.

(B) *Example.* A profit-sharing plan that provides for a single sum distribution available to all employees on termination of employment is amended January 1, 1990, to eliminate such single sum optional form of benefit with respect to benefits accrued after January 1, 1991. As of January 1, 1991, the single sum optional form of benefit is available to a group of employees that satisfies the percentage test of section 410(b)(1)(A). As of January 1, 1995, all nonhighly compensated employees who were entitled to the single sum optional form of benefit have terminated from employment with the employer and taken a distribution of their benefits. The only remaining employees who have a right to take a portion of their benefits in the form of a single sum distribution on termination of employment are highly compensated employees. Because the availability of the single sum optional form of benefit satisfied the current availability test as of January 1, 1991, the availability of such optional form of benefit is deemed to continue to satisfy the current availability test of this paragraph (a)(2).

(3) *Effective availability*—(i) *In general.* The requirement of this paragraph (a)(3) is satisfied only if, based on the facts and circumstances, the group of employees to whom the optional form is effectively available does not substantially favor the highly compensated group. This is the case even if the optional form is, or has been, currently available to a group of employees that satisfies the applicable requirements in paragraph (a)(2)(i) or (ii) of this Q&A-2.

(ii) *Examples.* The provisions of paragraph (a)(3)(i) of this Q&A-2 can be illustrated by the following examples:

Example 1. Employer X maintains a defined benefit plan that covers both of the 2 highly compensated employees of the employer and 8 of the twelve nonhighly compensated employees of the employer. Plan X provides for a normal retirement benefit payable as an annuity and based on a normal retirement age of 65, and an early retirement benefit payable upon termination in the form of an annuity to employees who terminate from service with the employer on or after age 55 with 30 or more years of service. Each of the 2 employees of employer X who are in the highly compensated group currently meet the age and service requirement, or will have 30 years of service by the time they reach age 55. All but 2 of the 8 nonhighly compensated employees of employer X who are covered by the plan were hired on or after age 35 and thus, cannot qualify for the early retirement benefit provision. Even though the group of employees to whom the early retirement benefit is currently available does not impermissibly favor the highly compensated group by reason of disregarding age and service, these facts and circumstances indicate that the effective availability of the early retirement benefit in plan X substantially favors the highly compensated group.

Example 2. Assume the same facts as in *Example 1* except that the early retirement benefit is added by a plan amendment first adopted, announced and effective December 1, 1991, and is available only to employees who terminate from employment with the employer prior to December 15, 1991. Further assume that all employees were hired prior to attaining age 25, and that the group of employees who have, or will have attained age 55 with 30 years of service, by December 15, 1991, satisfies the ratio test of section 410(b)(1)(B). Finally, assume that the only employees who terminate from employment with the employer during the two week period in which the early retirement benefit is available are employees in the highly compensated group. These facts and circumstances indicate that the effective availability of the early retirement benefit substantially favors the highly compensated group. This is the case even though the limitation of the early retirement benefit to a specified period satisfies section 411(d)(6).

Example 3. Employer Y amends plan Y on June 30, 1990, to provide for a single sum distribution for employees who terminate from employment with the employer after June 30, 1990, and prior to January 1, 1991. The availability of this single sum distribution is conditioned on the employee having a particular disability at the time of termination of employment. The only employee of the employer who meets this disability requirement at the time of the amendment and thereafter through December 31, 1990, is a highly compensated employee. Generally, a disability condition with respect to the availability of a single sum distribution may be disregarded in determining whether the current availability of such optional form of benefit is discriminatory. However, these facts and circumstances indicate that the effective availability of the optional form of benefit substantially favors the highly compensated group.

Example 4. Employer Z maintains a money purchase pension plan that covers all employees of the employer. The plan provides for distribution in the form of a joint and survivor annuity, a life annuity, or equal installments over 10 years. During the 1992 calendar year the employer winds up his business. In December of 1992, only two employees remain in the employment of the employer, both of whom are highly compensated. Employer Z then amends the plan to provide for a single sum distribution to employees who terminate from employment on or after the date of the amendment. Both highly compensated employees terminate from employment on December 31, 1992, taking a single sum distribution of their benefits. These facts and circumstances indicate that the effective availability of the single sum optional form of benefit substantially favors the highly compensated group.

(b) *Application of tests*—(1) *Current availability*—(i) *In general.* Except as otherwise provided in this paragraph (b), in determining whether an optional form of benefit that is subject to specified eligibility conditions is currently available to an employee for purposes of paragraph (a) of this Q&A-2, the determination of current availability generally is to be based on the current facts and circumstances with respect to the employee (e.g., the employee's current compensation or the employee's current net worth). Thus, for example, the fact that an employee may, in the future, satisfy an eligibility condition generally does not cause an optional form of benefit to be treated as currently available to such employee.

(ii) *Exceptions for age, service, employment termination and certain other conditions*—(A) *Age and service conditions.* For purposes of applying paragraph (a)(2) of this Q&A-2, except as provided in paragraph (b)(1)(ii)(B) of this Q&A-2, a service condition, or both are to be disregarded. For example, an employer that maintains a plan that provides for an early retirement benefit payable as an annuity for employees in division A, subject to a requirement that the employee has attained his or her 55th birthday and has at least twenty years of service with the employer, is to disregard the age and service conditions in determining the group of employees to whom the early retirement annuity benefit is currently available. Thus, the early retirement annuity benefit is treated as currently available to all employees of division A, without regard to their ages or years of service and without regard to whether they could potentially meet the age and service conditions prior to attaining the plan's normal retirement age.

(B) *Exception for certain age and service conditions.* Age and service conditions that must be satisfied within a specified period of time may not be disregarded pursuant to paragraph (b)(1)(ii)(A) of this Q&A-2. However, in determining the current availability of an optional form of benefit subject to such an age condition, service condition, or both, an employer may project the age and service of

employees to the last date on which the optional form of benefit subject to the age condition or service condition (or both) is available under the plan. An employer's ability to project age and service to the last date on which the optional form of benefit is available under the plan is not cut off by a plan termination occurring prior to that date. Thus, for example, assume that an employer maintaining a plan that permits employees terminating from employment on or after age 55 between June 1, 1991 to May 31, 1992, to elect a single sum distribution, decides to terminate the plan on December 31, 1991. In determining the group of employees to whom the single sum optional form of benefit is currently available, this employer may project employees' ages through May 31, 1992.

(C) *Certain other conditions disregarded.* Conditions on the availability of optional forms of benefit requiring termination of employment, death, satisfaction of a specified health condition (or failure to meet such condition), disability, hardship, marital status, default on a plan loan secured by a participant's account balance, or execution of a covenant not to compete may be disregarded in determining the group of employees to whom an optional form of benefit is currently available.

(2) *Employees taken into account.* For purposes of applying paragraph (a) of this Q&A-2, the tests are to be applied on the basis of the employer's nonexcludable employees (whether or not they are participants in the plan) in the same manner as such tests would be applied in determining whether the plan providing the optional form of benefit satisfies the tests under section 410(b).

(3) *Definition of "plan".* For purposes of applying paragraph (a) of this Q&A-2, the term "plan" has the meaning that such term has for purposes of determining whether the amount of contributions or benefits and whether other benefits, rights, and features are nondiscriminatory under section 401(a)(4).

(4) *Restructuring optional forms of benefit*—(i) *In general.* For purposes of applying paragraph (a) of this Q&A-2, the availability of two or more optional forms of benefit under a plan may be tested by restructuring such benefits into two or more restructured optional forms of benefit and testing the availability of such restructured optional forms of benefit. If two or more optional forms of benefit under a plan contain both common and distinct components, such optional forms of benefit may be restructured as a single optional form of benefit comprising the common component, and one or more optional forms of benefit comprising each distinct component. Components of optional forms of benefit may be treated as common only if they are identical with respect to all characteristics taken into account under Q&A-1(b) of § 1.411(d)-4. The availability of each restructured optional form of benefit must satisfy the applicable nondiscrimination requirements of paragraph (a) of this Q&A-2.

(ii) *Example.* A profit-sharing plan covering all the employees of an employer provides a single sum distribution option upon termination from employment for all employees earning less than $50,000 and a single sum distribution option upon termination from employment after the attainment of age 55 for all employees earning $50,000 or more. These distribution options are identical in all other respects. For purposes of applying section 401(a)(4), such optional forms of benefit may be restructured into two different optional forms of benefit: (A) a single sum distribution option upon termination from employment after the attainment of age 55 for all employees (i.e., the common component), and (B) a single sum distribution option upon termination from employment before the attainment of age 55 for all employees earning less than $50,000. The availability of each of these restructured optional forms of benefit must satisfy section 401(a)(4).

(c) *Commissioner may provide additional tests.* The Commissioner may provide such additional factors, tests, and safe harbors as are necessary or appropriate for purposes of determining whether the availability of an optional form of benefit is discriminatory under section 401(a)(4). In addition, the Commissioner may provide that additional eligibility conditions not related directly or indirectly to compensation or wealth may be disregarded under paragraph (b)(1)(ii)(C) of this Q&A-2 in determining the current availability of an optional form of benefit. The Commissioner may provide such additional guidance only through the publication of revenue rulings, notices or other documents of general applicability.

Q-3: May a plan condition the availability of an optional form of benefit on employer discretion?

A-3: No. Even if the availability of an optional form of benefit that is conditioned on employer discretion satisfies the nondiscrimination requirements of section 401(a)(4), the plan providing the optional form of benefit will fail to satisfy certain other requirements of section 401(a), including, in applicable circumstances, the definitely determinable requirement of section 401(a) and the requirements of section 401(a)(25) and section 411(d)(6). See § 1.411(d)-4.

Q-4: Will a plan provision violate section 401(a)(4) merely because it requires that an employee who terminates from service with the employer receive a single sum distribution in the event that the present value of the employee's benefit is not more than $3,500, as permitted by sections 411(a)(11) and 417(e)?

A-4: No. A plan will not be treated as discriminatory under section 401(a)(4) merely because the plan mandates a single sum distribution when the present value of an employee's benefit is not more than $3,500, as permitted by sections 411(a)(11) and 417(e). This is an exception to the general principles of this section. (No similar provision exists excepting such single sum distributions from the limits on employer discretion under section 411(d)(6). See § 1.411(d)-4 Q&A-4.)

Q-5: If the availability of an optional form of benefit discriminates, or may reasonably be expected to discriminate, in favor of the highly compensated group, what acceptable alternatives exist for amending the plan without violating section 411(d)(6)?

A-5: (a) *Transitional rules*—(1) *In general.* The following rules apply for purposes of making necessary amendments to existing plans (as defined in Q&A-6 of this section) under which the availability of an optional form of benefit violates the nondiscrimination requirements of section 401(a)(4) or may reasonably be expected to violate such requirements. These transitional rules are provided under the authority of section 411(d)(6), which allows the elimination of certain optional forms of benefit if permitted by regulations, and section 7805(b).

(2) *Nondiscrimination*—(i) *In general.* The determination of whether the availability of an optional form of benefit violates section 401(a)(4) is to be made in accordance with Q&A-2 of this section. In addition, the availability of a particular optional form of benefit may reasonably be expected to violate the nondiscrimination requirements of section 401(a)(4) if, under the applicable facts and circumstances, there is a significant possibility that the current availability of such optional form of benefit will impermissibly favor the highly compensated group. This determination must be made on the basis of the seventy percent test of section 410(b)(1)(A) or the nondiscriminatory classification test of section 410(b)(1)(B) as such tests existed prior to the effective date of the amendments made to section 410(b) by section 1112(a) of TRA '86. Thus, a condition may not reasonably be expected to discriminate for purposes of these rules merely because it results in a significant possibility that discrimination will result because of the amendments made to section 410(b) by section 1112(a) of TRA '86. In addition, the availability of an optional form of benefit may not reasonably be expected to discriminate merely because of an age or service condition that may be disregarded in determining the current availability of such optional form of benefit under paragraph (b)(1)(ii)(A) of Q&A-2 of this section. Similarly, the availability of an optional form of benefit may not reasonably be expected to discriminate merely because of an age or service condition that, after permitted projection, does not cause such optional form to fail to satisfy the requirement of this paragraph (a)(2).

(ii) *Examples.* The provisions of paragraph (a)(2)(i) of this Q&A-5 can be illustrated by the following examples:

Example (1). A plan provides that a single sum distribution option is available only to (A) employees earning $50,000 or more in the final year of employment, (B) employees who furnish evidence that they have a net worth above a certain specified amount, and (C) employees who present a letter from an accountant or attorney declaring that it is in the employee's best interest to receive a single sum distribution. Whether the availability of such optional form of benefit discriminates depends on whether it meets the requirements of Q&A-2 of this § 1.401(a)-4. However, each of the specified conditions limiting the availability of the optional form of benefit may reasonably be expected to discriminate in favor of the highly compensated group in operation because of the likelihood of a significant positive correlation between the ability to meet any of the specified conditions and membership in the highly compensated group.

Example (2). A plan limits the availability of a single sum distribution option to employees employed in one particular division of the employer's company. All the employees of the company are participants in the plan. During the 1988 plan year, the division employs individuals who represent a nondiscriminatory classification of that company's employees (under section 410(b)(1)(B) prior to the effective date of the amendments made to section 410(b) by section 1112(a) of TRA '86) and is unlikely to cease employing such a nondiscriminatory classification in the future. The availability of a single sum distribution under this plan does not result in discrimination during the 1988 plan year and may not reasonably be expected to do so.

(b) *Transitional alternatives.* If the availability of an optional form of benefit under an existing plan is discriminatory under section 401(a)(4), the plan must be amended either to eliminate the optional form of benefit or to make the availability of the optional form of benefit nondiscriminatory. For example, the availability of an optional form of benefit may be made nondiscriminatory by making such benefit available to sufficient additional employees who are not in the highly compensated group or by imposing nondiscriminatory objective criteria on its availability such that the group of employees

to whom the benefit is available is nondiscriminatory. See Q&A-6 of § 1.411(d)-4 for requirements with respect to such objective criteria. If, under an existing plan, the availability of an optional form of benefit may reasonably be expected to discriminate, the plan may be amended in the same manner permitted where the availability of an optional form of benefit is discriminatory. See paragraph (d) of this Q&A-5 for rules limiting the period during which the availability of optional forms of benefit may be eliminated or reduced under this paragraph.

(c) *Compliance and amendment date provisions*—(1) *Operational compliance requirement.* On or before the applicable effective date for the plan (see Q&A-6 of this section), the plan sponsor must select one of the alternatives permitted under paragraph (b) of this Q&A-5 with respect to each affected optional form of benefit and the plan must be operated in accordance with this selection. This is an operational requirement and does not require a plan amendment prior to the period set forth in paragraph (c)(2) of this Q&A-5. There is no special reporting requirement under the Code or this section with respect to this selection.

(2) *Deferred amendment date.* If paragraph (c)(1) of this Q&A-5 is satisfied, a plan amendment conforming the plan to the particular alternative selected under paragraph (b) of this Q&A-5 must be adopted within the time period permitted for amending plans in order to meet the requirements of section 410(b) as amended by TRA '86. Such conforming amendment must be consistent with the sponsor's selection as reflected by plan practice during the period from the effective date to the date the amendment is adopted. Thus, for example, if an existing calendar year noncollectively bargained defined benefit plan has a single sum distribution form subject to a discriminatory condition, that was available as of January 30, 1986 (subject to such condition), and such employer makes one or more single sum distributions available on or after the first day of the first plan year commencing on or after January 1, 1989, and before the plan amendment, then such employer may not adopt a plan amendment eliminating the single sum distribution form. Instead, such employer must adopt an amendment making the distribution form available to a nondiscriminatory group of employees while retaining the availability of such distribution form with respect to the group of employees to whom the benefit is already available. Similarly, any objective criteria that are adopted as part of such amendment must be consistent with the plan practice for the applicable period prior to the amendment. A conforming amendment under this paragraph (c)(2) must be made with respect to each optional form of benefit for which such amendment is required and must be retroactive to the applicable effective date.

(d) *Limitation on transitional alternatives.* The transitional alternatives permitting the elimination or reduction of optional forms of benefit will not violate section 411(d)(6) during the period prior to the applicable effective date for the plan (see Q&A-6 of this section). After the applicable effective date, any amendment (other than one described in paragraph (c)(2) of this Q&A-5) that eliminates or reduces an optional form of benefit or imposes new objective criteria restricting the availability of such optional form of benefit will fail to qualify for the exception to section 411(d)(6) provided in this Q&A-5. This is the case without regard to whether the availability of the optional form of benefit is discriminatory or may reasonably be expected to be discriminatory.

Q-6: For what period are the rules of this section effective?

A-6: (a) *General effective date*—(1) *In general.* Except as otherwise provided in this section, the provisions of this section are effective January 30, 1986 and do not apply to plan years beginning on or after January 1, 1994. For rules applicable to plan years beginning on or after January 1, 1994, see § § 1.401(a)(4)-1 through 1.401(a)(4)-13.

(2) *Plans of tax-exempt organizations.* In the case of plans maintained by organizations exempt from income taxation under section 501(a), including plans subject to section 403(b)(12)(A)(i) (nonelective plans), except as otherwise provided in this section, the provisions of this section are effective January 30, 1986, and do not apply to plan years beginning on or after January 1, 1996. For rules applicable to plan years beginning on or after January 1, 1996, see § § 1.401(a)(4)-1 through 1.401(a)(4)-13.

(b) *New plans*—(1) *In general.* Unless otherwise provided in paragraph (b)(2) of this Q&A-6, plans that are either adopted or made effective on or after January 30, 1986, are "new plans". With respect to such new plans, this section is effective January 30, 1986. This effective date is applicable to such plans whether or not they are collectively bargained.

(2) *Exception with respect to certain new plans.* Plans that are new plans as defined in paragraph (b)(1) of this Q&A-6, under which the availability of an optional form of benefit is discriminatory or may reasonably be expected to be discriminatory, and that receive a favorable determination letter that covered such plan provisions with respect to an application submitted prior to July 11, 1988, will be treated as existing plans with respect to such optional form of benefit

for purposes of the transitional rules of this section. Thus, such plans are eligible for the compliance and amendment alternatives set forth in the transitional rule in Q&A-5 of this section.

(c) *Existing plans*—(1) *In general.* Plans that are both adopted and in effect prior to January 30, 1986, are "existing plans". In addition, new plans described in paragraph (b)(2) of this Q&A-6 are treated as existing plans with respect to certain optional forms of benefit. Subject to the limitations in paragraph (d) of this Q&A-6, the effective dates set forth in paragraphs (c)(2) and (c)(3) of this Q&A-6 apply to these existing plans for purposes of this section.

(2) *Existing noncollectively bargained plans.* With respect to existing noncollectively bargained plans, this section is effective for the first day of the first plan year commencing on or after January 1, 1989.

(3) *Existing collectively bargained plans.* With respect to existing collectively bargained plans, this section is effective for the later of the first day of the first plan year commencing on or after January 1, 1989, or the first day of the first plan year that the requirements of section 410(b) as amended by TRA `86 apply to such plan.

(d) *Delayed effective dates not applicable to new optional forms of benefit or conditions*—(1) *In general.* The delayed effective dates in paragraph (c)(2) and (3) of this Q&A-6 for existing plans are applicable with respect to an optional form of benefit only if both the optional form of benefit and any applicable condition either causing the availability of such optional form of benefit to be discriminatory or making it reasonable to expect that the availability of such optional form will be discriminatory were both adopted and in effect prior to January 30, 1986. If the preceding sentence is not satisfied with respect to an optional form of benefit, this section is effective with respect to such optional form of benefit as if the plan were a new plan.

(2) *Exception for certain amendments covered by a favorable determination letter.* If a condition causing the availability of an optional form of benefit to be discriminatory, or to be reasonably expected to discriminate, was adopted or made effective on or after January 30, 1986, and a favorable determination letter that covered such plan provision is or was received with respect to an application submitted before July 11, 1988, the effective date of this section with respect to such provision is the applicable effective date determined under the rules with respect to existing plans, as though such provision had been adopted and in effect prior to January 30, 1986.

(e) *Transitional rule effective date.* The transitional rule provided in Q&A-5 of this section is effective January 30, 1986. [Reg. § 1.401(a)-4.]

□ [T.D. 8212, 7-8-88. *Amended by T.D. 8360, 9-12-91 and T.D. 8485, 8-30-93.*]

[Reg. § 1.401(a)(2)-1]

§ 1.401(a)(2)-1. Refund of mistaken employer contributions and withdrawal liability payments to multiemployer plans.—(a) *Introduction.*—(1) *In general.*—Section 401(a)(2) provides that a contribution or payment of withdrawal liability made to a multiemployer plan due to a mistake of fact or mistake of law can be returned to the employer under certain conditions. This section specifies the conditions under which an employer's contribution or payment may be returned.

(2) *Effective dates.*—This section applies to refunds made after July 22, 2002.

(b) *Conditions for return of contribution.*—(1) *In general.*—In the case of a contribution or a withdrawal liability payment to a multiemployer plan which was made because of a mistake of fact or a mistake of law, the plan will not violate section 401(a)(2) merely because the contribution or payment is returned within six months after the date on which the plan administrator determines that the contribution or payment was the result of a mistake of fact or law. The contribution or payment is considered as returned within the required period if the employer establishes a right to a refund of the amount mistakenly contributed or paid by filing a claim with the plan administrator within six months after the date on which the plan administrator determines that a mistake did occur. For purposes of this section, plan administrator is defined in section 414(g) and the regulations thereunder.

(2) *Applicable conditions.*—(i) *In general.*—The employer making the contribution or withdrawal liability payment to a multiemployer plan must demonstrate that an excessive contribution or overpayment has been made due to a mistake of fact or law. A mistake of fact or law relating to plan qualification under section 401 or to trust exemption under section 501 is not considered to be a mistake of fact or law which entitles an employer to a refund under this section. For purposes of this section, a multiemployer plan is defined in section 414(f) and the regulations thereunder.

(ii) *Amount to be returned.*—(A) *General rule.*—The amount to be returned to the employer is the excess of the amount contributed or paid over the amount that would have been contributed or paid

had no mistake been made. This amount is the excess contribution or overpayment. Except as provided in paragraph (b)(2)(ii)(B) of this section, interest or earnings attributable to an excess contribution shall not be returned to the employer, and any losses attributable to an excess contribution must reduce the amount returned to the employer. For purposes of the previous sentence, the application of plan-wide investment experience to the excess contribution would be an acceptable method of calculating losses. A refund of a mistaken contribution must in no event reduce a participant's account balance in a defined contribution plan to an amount less than that amount which would properly have been in that participant's account had no mistake occurred. Thus, to the extent that the refund of an excess contribution would reduce a participant's account balance in a defined contribution plan to an amount less than the amount which would properly be in the participant's account had no mistake occurred, the return of the excess contribution would be prohibited by this section.

(B) *Overpayment of withdrawal liability.*—In the case of an overpayment of withdrawal liability established by the plan sponsor under section 4219(c)(2) of ERISA, the plan will not fail to satisfy section 401(a)(2) if, in accordance with Pension Benefit Guaranty Corporation regulations regarding the overpayments of withdrawal liability (29 CFR 4219.31(d)), the overpayment, with interest, is returned to the employer.

(c) *Amount refunded includible in employer's income.*—In general, the amount of the excess contribution or overpayment must be included in gross income by the employer if the excess contribution or overpayment resulted in a tax benefit in a prior year. Any interest credited or paid on the refund of mistaken withdrawal liability payments must also be included in gross income by the employer.

(d) *Application of section 412.*—An amount returned under paragraph (b)(2)(ii) of this section is charged to the funding standard account under section 412 in the year in which the amount is returned. [Reg. § 1.401(a)(2)-1.]

□ [T.D. 9005, 7-19-2002.]

[Reg. § 1.401(a)(4)-0]

§ 1.401(a)(4)-0. Table of contents.—This section contains a listing of the major headings of § § 1.401(a)(4)-1 through 1.401(a)(4)-13.

(c) General test for nondiscrimination in amount of contributions.
 (1) General rule.
 (2) Determination of allocation rates.
 (3) Satisfaction of section 410(b) by a rate group.
 (4) Examples.

§1.401(a)(4)-3. *Nondiscrimination in amount of employer-provided benefits under a defined benefit plan.*
 (a) Introduction.
  (1) Overview.
  (2) Alternative methods of satisfying nondiscriminatory amount requirement.
 (b) Safe harbors.
  (1) In general.
  (2) Uniformity requirements.
  (3) Safe harbor for unit credit plans.
  (4) Safe harbor for plans using fractional accrual rule.
  (5) Safe harbor for insurance contract plans.
  (6) Use of safe harbors not precluded by certain plan provisions.
 (c) General test for nondiscrimination in amount of benefits.
  (1) General rule.
  (2) Satisfaction of section 410(b) by a rate group.
  (3) Certain violations disregarded.
  (4) Examples.
 (d) Determination of accrual rates.
  (1) Definitions.
  (2) Rules of application.
  (3) Optional rules.
  (4) Examples.
 (e) Compensation rules.
  (1) In general.
  (2) Average annual compensation.
  (3) Examples.
 (f) Special rules.
  (1) In general.
  (2) Certain qualified disability benefits.
  (3) Accruals after normal retirement age.
  (4) Early retirement window benefits.
  (5) Unpredictable contingent event benefits.
  (6) Determination of benefits on other than plan-year basis.
  (7) Adjustments for certain plan distributions.
  (8) Adjustment for certain QPSA charges.
  (9) Disregard of certain offsets.
  (10) Special rule for multiemployer plans.

§1.401(a)(4)-4. *Nondiscriminatory availability of benefits, rights, and features.*
 (a) Introduction.
 (b) Current availability.
  (1) General rule.
  (2) Determination of current availability.
  (3) Benefits, rights, and features that are eliminated prospectively.
 (c) Effective availability.
  (1) General rule.
  (2) Examples.
 (d) Special rules.
  (1) Mergers and acquisitions.
  (2) Frozen participants.
  (3) Early retirement window benefits.
  (4) Permissive aggregation of certain benefits, rights, or features.
  (5) Certain spousal benefits.
  (6) Special ESOP rules.
  (7) Special testing rule for unpredictable contingent event benefits.
 (e) Definitions.
  (1) Optional form of benefit.
  (2) Ancillary benefit.
  (3) Other right or feature.

§1.401(a)(4)-5. *Plan amendments and plan terminations.*
 (a) Introduction.
  (1) Overview.
  (2) Facts-and-circumstances determination.
  (3) Safe harbor for certain grants of benefits for past periods.
  (4) Examples.
 (b) Pre-termination restrictions.
  (1) Required provisions in defined benefit plans.

  (2) Restriction of benefits upon plan termination.
  (3) Restrictions on distributions.
  (4) Operational restrictions on certain money purchase pension plans.

§1.401(a)(4)-6. *Contributory defined benefit plans.*
 (a) Introduction.
 (b) Determination of employer-provided benefit.
  (1) General rule.
  (2) Composition-of-work-force method.
  (3) Minimum-benefit method.
  (4) Grandfather rules for plans in existence on May 14, 1990.
  (5) Government-plan method.
  (6) Cessation of employee contributions.
 (c) Rules applicable in determining whether employee-provided benefits are nondiscriminatory in amount.
  (1) In general.
  (2) Same rate of contributions.
  (3) Total-benefits method.
  (4) Grandfather rule for plans in existence on May 14, 1990.

§1.401(a)(4)-7. *Imputation of permitted disparity.*
 (a) Introduction.
 (b) Adjusting allocation rates.
  (1) In general.
  (2) Employees whose plan year compensation does not exceed taxable wage base.
  (3) Employees whose plan year compensation exceeds taxable wage base.
  (4) Definitions.
  (5) Example.
 (c) Adjusting accrual rates.
  (1) In general.
  (2) Employees whose average annual compensation does not exceed covered compensation.
  (3) Employees whose average annual compensation exceeds covered compensation.
  (4) Definitions.
  (5) Employees with negative unadjusted accrual rates.
  (6) Example.
 (d) Rules of general application.
  (1) Eligible plans.
  (2) Exceptions from consistency requirements.
  (3) Overall permitted disparity.

§1.401(a)(4)-8. *Cross-testing.*
 (a) Introduction.
 (b) Nondiscrimination in amount of benefits provided under a defined contribution plan.
  (1) General rule and gateway.
  (2) Determination of equivalent accrual rates.
  (3) Safe-harbor testing method for target benefit plans.
 (c) Nondiscrimination in amount of contributions under a defined benefit plan.
  (1) General rule.
  (2) Determination of equivalent allocation rates.
  (3) Safe-harbor testing method for cash balance plans.
 (d) Safe-harbor testing method for defined benefit plans that are part of a floor-offset arrangement.
  (1) General rule.
  (2) Application of safe-harbor testing method to qualified offset arrangements.

§1.401(a)(4)-9. *Plan aggregation and restructuring.*
 (a) Introduction.
 (b) Application of nondiscrimination requirements to DB/DC plans.
  (1) General rule.
  (2) Special rules for demonstrating nondiscrimination in amount of contributions or benefits.
  (3) Optional rules for demonstrating nondiscrimination in availability of certain benefits, rights, and features.
 (c) Plan restructuring.
  (1) General rule.
  (2) Identification of component plans.
  (3) Satisfaction of section 401(a)(4) by a component plan.
  (4) Satisfaction of section 410(b) by a component plan.
  (5) Effect of restructuring under other sections.
  (6) Examples.

§1.401(a)(4)-10. *Testing of former employees.*
 (a) Introduction.

(b) Nondiscrimination in amount of contributions or benefits.
  (1) General rule.
  (2) Permitted disparity.
  (3) Examples.
(c) Nondiscrimination in availability of benefits, rights, or features.

§ 1.401(a)(4)-11. *Additional rules.*
  (a) Introduction.
  (b) Rollovers, transfers, and buybacks.
    (1) Rollovers and elective transfers.
    (2) Other transfers. [Reserved]
    (3) Employee buybacks.
  (c) Vesting.
    (1) General rule.
    (2) Deemed equivalence of statutory vesting schedules.
    (3) Safe harbor for vesting schedules.
    (4) Examples.
  (d) Service-crediting rules.
    (1) Overview.
    (2) Manner of crediting service.
    (3) Service-crediting period.
  (e) Family aggregation rules. [Reserved]
  (f) Governmental plans. [Reserved]
  (g) Corrective amendments.
    (1) In general.
    (2) Scope of corrective amendments.
    (3) Conditions for corrective amendments.
    (4) Corrective amendments must have substance.
    (5) Effect under other statutory requirements.
    (6) Examples.

§ 1.401(a)(4)-12. *Definitions.*

§ 1.401(a)(4)-13. *Effective dates and fresh-start rules.*
  (a) General effective dates.
    (1) In general.
    (2) Plans of tax-exempt organizations.
    (3) Compliance during transition period.
  (b) Effective date for governmental plans.
  (c) Fresh-start rules for defined benefit plans.
    (1) Introduction.
    (2) General rule.
    (3) Definition of frozen.
    (4) Fresh-start formulas.
    (5) Rules of application.
    (6) Examples.
  (d) Compensation adjustments to frozen accrued benefits.
    (1) Introduction.
    (2) In general.
    (3) Plan requirements.
    (4) Meaningful coverage as of fresh-start date.
    (5) Meaningful ongoing coverage.
    (6) Meaningful current benefit accruals.
    (7) Minimum benefit adjustment.
    (8) Adjusted accrued benefit.
    (9) Examples.
  (e) Determination of initial theoretical reserve for target benefit plans.
    (1) General rule.
    (2) Example.
  (f) Special fresh-start rules for cash balance plans.
    (1) In general.
    (2) Alternative formula.
    (3) Limitations on formulas.
[Reg. § 1.401(a)(4)-0.]

☐ [*T.D. 8360, 9-12-91. Amended by T.D. 8485, 8-30-93 and T.D. 8954,* 6-28-2001.]

[Reg. § 1.401(a)(4)-1]

§ 1.401(a)(4)-1. Nondiscrimination requirements of section 401(a)(4).—(a) *In general.*—Section 401(a)(4) provides that a plan is a qualified plan only if the contributions or the benefits provided under the plan do not discriminate in favor of HCEs. Whether a plan satisfies this requirement depends on the form of the plan and on its *effect in operation. In making this determination,* intent is irrelevant. This section sets forth the exclusive rules for determining whether a plan satisfies section 401(a)(4). A plan that complies in form and operation with the rules in this section therefore satisfies section 401(a)(4).

(b) *Requirements a plan must satisfy.*—(1) *In general.*—In order to satisfy section 401(a)(4), a plan must satisfy each of the requirements of this paragraph (b).

(2) *Nondiscriminatory amount of contributions or benefits.*—(i) *General rule.*—Either the contributions or the benefits provided under the plan must be nondiscriminatory in amount. It need not be shown that both the contributions and the benefits provided are nondiscriminatory in amount, but only that either the contributions alone or the benefits alone are nondiscriminatory in amount.

(ii) *Defined contribution plans.*—(A) *General rule.*—A defined contribution plan satisfies this paragraph (b)(2) if the contributions allocated under the plan (including forfeitures) are nondiscriminatory in amount under § 1.401(a)(4)-2. Alternatively, a defined contribution plan (other than an ESOP) satisfies this paragraph (b)(2) if the equivalent benefits provided under the plan are nondiscriminatory in amount under § 1.401(a)(4)-8(b). Section 1.401(a)(4)-8(b) includes a safe-harbor testing method for contributions provided under a target benefit plan.

(B) *Section 401(k) plans and section 401(m) plans.*—A section 401(k) plan is deemed to satisfy this paragraph (b)(2) because § 1.410(b)-9 defines a section 401(k) plan as a plan consisting of elective contributions under a qualified cash or deferred arrangement (i.e., one that satisfies section 401(k)(3), the nondiscriminatory amount requirement applicable to qualified cash or deferred arrangements). A section 401(m) plan satisfies this paragraph (b)(2) only if the plan satisfies §§ 1.401(m)-1(b) and 1.401(m)-2. Contributions under a nonqualified cash or deferred arrangement, elective contributions described in § 1.401(k)-2(a)(5)(i) that fail to satisfy the allocation and compensation requirements of § 1.401(k)-2(a)(4)(i), matching contributions that fail to satisfy § 1.401(m)-2(a)(4)(iii), and qualified nonelective contributions treated as elective or matching contributions for certain purposes under §§ 1.401(k)-2(a)(6) and 1.401(m)-2(a)(6), respectively, are not subject to the special rule in this paragraph (b)(2)(ii)(B), because they are not treated as part of a seciton 401(k) plan or section 401(m) plan as those terms are defined in § 1.410(b)-9. The contributions described in the preceding sentence must satisfy paragraph (b)(2)(ii)(A) of this section.

(iii) *Defined benefit plans.*—A defined benefit plan satisfies this paragraph (b)(2) if the benefits provided under the plan are nondiscriminatory in amount under § 1.401(a)(4)-3. Alternatively, a defined benefit plan satisfies this paragraph (b)(2) if the equivalent allocations provided under the plan are nondiscriminatory in amount under § 1.401(a)(4)-8(c). Section 1.401(a)(4)-8(b) includes a safe-harbor testing method for benefits provided under a cash balance plan. In addition, § 1.401(a)(4)-8(d) provides a safe-harbor testing method for benefits provided under a defined benefit plan that is part of a floor-offset arrangement.

(3) *Nondiscriminatory availability of benefits, rights, and features.*—All benefits, rights, and features provided under the plan must be made available in the plan in a nondiscriminatory manner. Rules for determining whether this requirement is satisfied are set forth in § 1.401(a)(4)-4.

(4) *Nondiscriminatory effect of plan amendments and terminations.*—The timing of plan amendments must not have the effect of discriminating significantly in favor of HCEs. Rules for determining whether this requirement is satisfied are set forth in § 1.401(a)(4)-5(a). Section 1.401(a)(4)-5(b) provides additional requirements regarding plan terminations.

(c) *Application of requirements.*—(1) *In general.*—The requirements of paragraph (b) of this section must be applied in accordance with the rules set forth in this paragraph (c).

(2) *Interpretation.*—The provisions of §§ 1.401(a)(4)-1 through 1.401(a)(4)-13 must be interpreted in a reasonable manner consistent with the purpose of preventing discrimination in favor of HCEs.

(3) *Plan-year basis of testing.*—The requirements of paragraph (b) of this section are generally applied on the basis of the plan year and on the basis of the terms of the plan in effect during the plan year. Thus, unless otherwise provided, the compensation, contributions, benefit accruals, and other items used to apply these requirements must be determined with respect to the plan year being tested. However, § 1.401(a)(4)-11(g) provides rules allowing for corrective amendments made after the close of the plan year to be taken into account in satisfying certain requirements under paragraph (b) of this section.

(4) *Application of section 410(b) rules.*—(i) *Relationship between sections 401(a)(4) and 410(b).*—To be a qualified plan, a plan must satisfy both sections 410(b) and 401(a)(4). Section 410(b) requires that a plan benefit a nondiscriminatory group of employees, and section

401(a)(4) requires that the contributions or benefits provided to employees benefiting under the plan not discriminate in favor of HCEs. Consistent with this requirement, the definition of a plan subject to testing under section 401(a)(4) is the same as the definition of a plan subject to testing under section 410(b), i.e., the plan determined after applying the mandatory disaggregation rules of §1.410(b)-7(c) and the permissive aggregation rules of §1.410(b)-7(d). In addition, whichever testing option is used for the plan year under §1.410(b)-8(a) (e.g., quarterly testing) must also be used for purposes of determining whether the plan satisfies section 401(a)(4) for the plan year.

(ii) *Special rules for certain aggregated plans.*—Special rules are set forth in §1.401(a)(4)-9(b) for applying the nondiscriminatory amount and availability requirements of paragraphs (b)(2) and (b)(3) of this section to a plan that includes one or more defined benefit plans and one or more defined contribution plans that have been permissively aggregated under §1.410(b)-7(d).

(iii) *Restructuring.*—In certain circumstances, a plan may be restructured on the basis of employee groups and treated as comprising two or more plans, each of which is treated as a separate plan that must independently satisfy sections 401(a)(4) and 410(b). Rules relating to restructuring plans for purposes of applying the requirements of paragraph (b) of this section are set forth in §1.401(a)(4)-9(c).

(iv) *References to section 410(b).*—Except as otherwise specifically provided, references to satisfying section 410(b) in §§1.401(a)(4)-1 through 1.401(a)(4)-13 mean satisfying §1.410(b)-2 (taking into account any special rules available in satisfying that section, other than the permissive aggregation rules of §1.410(b)-7(d)). In the case of a plan described in section 410(c)(1) that has not made the election described in section 410(d) and is not subject to section 403(b)(12)(A)(i), references in §§1.401(a)(4)-1 through 1.401(a)(4)-13 to satisfying section 410(b) mean satisfying section 410(c)(2).

(5) *Collectively-bargained plans.*—The requirements of paragraph (b) of this section are treated as satisfied by a collectively-bargained plan that automatically satisfies section 410(b) under §1.410(b)-2(b)(7).

(6) *Former employees.*—In applying the nondiscriminatory amount and availability requirements of paragraphs (b)(2) and (b)(3) of this section, former employees are tested separately from active employees, unless otherwise provided. Rules for applying paragraphs (b)(2) and (b)(3) of this section to former employees are set forth in §1.401(a)(4)-10.

(7) *Employee-provided contributions and benefits.*—In applying the nondiscriminatory amount requirement of paragraph (b)(2) of this section, employee-provided contributions and benefits are tested separately from employer-provided contributions and benefits, unless otherwise provided. Rules for determining the amount of employer-provided benefits under a defined benefit plan that include employee contributions not allocated to separate accounts are set forth in §1.401(a)(4)-6(b), and rules for applying paragraph (b)(2) of this section to employee contributions under such a plan are set forth in §1.401(a)(4)-6(c). See paragraph (b)(2)(ii)(B) of this section for rules applicable to employee contributions allocated to separate accounts.

(8) *Allocation of earnings.*—Notwithstanding any other provision in §§1.401(a)(4)-1 through 1.401(a)(4)-13, a defined contribution plan does not satisfy paragraph (b)(2) of this section if the manner in which income, expenses, gains, or losses are allocated to accounts under the plan discriminates in favor of HCEs or former HCEs.

(9) *Rollovers, transfers, and buybacks.*—In applying the requirements of paragraph (b) of this section, rollover (including direct rollover) contributions described in section 402(c), 402(e)(6), 403(a)(4), 403(a)(5), or 408(d)(3), elective transfers described in §1.411(d)-4, Q&A-3(b), transfers of assets and liabilities described in section 414(l), and employee buybacks are treated in accordance with the rules set forth in §1.401(a)(4)-11(b).

(10) *Vesting.*—A plan does not satisfy the nondiscriminatory amount requirement of paragraph (b)(2) of this section unless it satisfies §1.401(a)(4)-11(c) with respect to the manner in which employees vest in their accrued benefits.

(11) *Crediting service.*—A plan does not satisfy paragraphs (b)(2) and (b)(3) of this section unless it satisfies §1.401(a)(4)-11(d) with respect to the manner in which employees' service is credited under the plan. Service other than actual service with the employer may not be taken into account in determining whether the plan satisfies paragraphs (b)(2) and (b)(3) of this section except as provided in §1.401(a)(4)-11(d).

(12) *Governmental plans.*—The rules of this section apply to a governmental plan within the meaning of section 414(d), except as provided in §§1.401(a)(4)-11(f) and 1.401(a)(4)-13(b).

(13) *Employee stock ownership plans.*—[Reserved]

(14) *Section 401(h) benefits.*—In applying the requirements of paragraph (b) of this section, the portion of a plan providing benefits described in section 401(h) is tested separately from the portion of the same plan providing retirement benefits, and thus is not required to satisfy this section. Rules applicable to section 401(h) benefits are set forth in §1.401-14(b)(2).

(15) *Definitions.*—In applying the requirements of this section, the definitions in §1.401(a)(4)-12 govern.

(16) *Effective dates and fresh-start rules.*—In applying the requirements of this section, the effective dates set forth in §1.401(a)(4)-13 govern. Section 1.401(a)(4)-13 also provides certain transition and fresh-start rules that apply for purposes of this section.

(d) *Additional guidance.*—The Commissioner may, in revenue rulings, notices, and other guidance, published in the Internal Revenue Bulletin, provide any additional guidance that may be necessary or appropriate in applying the nondiscrimination requirements of section 401(a)(4), including additional safe harbors and alternative methods and procedures for satisfying those requirements. See §601.601(d)(2)(ii)(b) of this chapter. [Reg. §1.401(a)(4)-1.]

☐ [T.D. 8360, 9-12-91. Amended by T.D. 8485, 8-30-93 and T.D. 9169, 12-28-2004.]

[Reg. §1.401(a)(4)-2]

§1.401(a)(4)-2. Nondiscrimination in amount of contributions under a defined contribution plan.—(a) *Introduction.*—(1) *Overview.*—This section provides rules for determining whether the employer contributions allocated under a defined contribution plan are nondiscriminatory in amount as required by §1.401(a)(4)-1(b)(2)(ii)(A). Certain defined contribution plans that provide uniform allocations are permitted to satisfy this requirement by meeting one of the safe harbors in paragraph (b) of this section. Plans that do not provide uniform allocations may satisfy this requirement by satisfying the general test in paragraph (c) of this section. See §1.401(a)(4)-1(b)(2)(ii)(B) for the exclusive tests applicable to section 401(k) plans and section 401(m) plans.

(2) *Alternative methods of satisfying nondiscriminatory amount requirement.*—A defined contribution plan is permitted to satisfy paragraph (b)(2) or (c) of this section on a restructured basis pursuant to §1.401(a)(4)-9(c). Alternatively, a defined contribution plan (other than an ESOP) is permitted to satisfy the nondiscriminatory amount requirement of §1.401(a)(4)-1(b)(2)(ii)(A) on the basis of equivalent benefits pursuant to §1.401(a)(4)-8(b).

(b) *Safe harbors.*—(1) *In general.*—The employer contributions allocated under a defined contribution plan are nondiscriminatory in amount for a plan year if the plan satisfies either of the safe harbors in paragraph (b)(2) or (b)(3) of this section. Paragraph (b)(4) of this section provides exceptions for certain plan provisions that do not cause a plan to fail to satisfy this paragraph (b).

(2) *Safe harbor for plans with uniform allocation formula.*—(i) *General rule.*—A defined contribution plan satisfies the safe harbor in this paragraph (b)(2) for a plan year if the plan allocates all amounts taken into account under paragraph (c)(2)(ii) of this section for the plan year under an allocation formula that allocates to each employee the same percentage of plan year compensation, the same dollar amount, or the same dollar amount for each uniform unit of service (not to exceed one week) performed by the employee during the plan year.

(ii) *Permitted disparity.*—If a plan satisfies section 401(l) in form, differences in employees' allocations under the plan attributable to uniform disparities permitted under §1.401(l)-2 (including differences in disparities that are deemed uniform under §1.401(l)-2(c)(2)) do not cause the plan to fail to satisfy this paragraph (b)(2).

(3) *Safe harbor for plans with uniform points allocation formula.*—(i) *General rule.*—A defined contribution plan (other than an ESOP) satisfies the safe harbor in this paragraph (b)(3) for a plan year if it satisfies both of the following requirements:

(A) The plan must allocate amounts under a uniform points allocation formula. A uniform points allocation formula defines each employee's allocation for the plan year as the product of the total of all amounts taken into account under paragraph (c)(2)(ii) of this section and a fraction, the numerator of which is the employee's points for the plan year and the denominator of which is the sum of the points of all employees in the plan for the plan year. For this purpose, an employee's points for a plan year equal the sum of the employee's points for age, service, and units of plan year compensation for the plan year. Under a uniform points allocation formula, each employee must receive the same number of points for each year of age, the same number of points for each year of service, and the same number of points for each unit of plan year compensation. (See §1.401(a)(4)-11(d)(3) regarding service that may be taken into account as years of service.) A uniform points allocation formula need not grant points for both age and service, but it must grant points for at least one of them. If the allocation formula grants points for years of service, the plan is permitted to limit the number of years of service taken into account to a single maximum number of years of service. A uniform points allocation formula need not grant points for units of plan year compensation, but if it does, the unit used must be a single dollar amount for all employees that does not exceed $200.

(B) For the plan year, the average of the allocation rates for the HCEs in the plan must not exceed the average of the allocation rates for the NHCEs in the plan. For this purpose, allocation rates are

Employee	Years of Service	Plan Year Compensation
H1	20	$150,000
H2	10	$150,000
H3	30	$100,000
H4	3	$100,000
N1	10	$40,000
N2	5	$35,000
N3	3	$30,000
N4	1	$25,000
Total	—	—

(b) Under these facts, for the 1994 plan year, Plan A allocates amounts under a uniform points allocation formula within the meaning of paragraph (b)(3)(i)(A) of this section.

(c) For the 1994 plan year, the average allocation rate for the HCEs (HI through H4) is 11.3 percent, and the average allocation rate for NHCEs (N1 through N4) is 11.3 percent. Because the average of the allocation rates for the HCEs does not exceed the average of the allocation rates for the NHCEs, Plan A satisfies paragraph (b)(3)(i)(B) of this section and, thus, the safe harbor in this paragraph (b)(3) for the 1994 plan year.

(4) *Use of safe harbors not precluded by certain plan provisions.*—(i) *In general.*—A plan does not fail to satisfy this paragraph (b) merely because the plan contains one or more of the provisions described in this paragraph (b)(4). Unless otherwise provided, any such provision must apply uniformly to all employees.

(ii) *Entry dates.*—The plan provides one or more entry dates during the plan year as permitted by section 410(a)(4).

(iii) *Certain conditions on allocations.*—The plan provides that an employee's allocation for the plan year is conditioned on either the employee's employment on the last day of the plan year or the employee's completion of a minimum number of hours of service during the plan year (not to exceed 1,000), or both. Such a provision may include an exception from this condition for all employees whose employment terminates during the plan year or only for those employees whose employment terminates during the plan year on account of one or more of the following circumstances: retirement, disability, death, or military service.

(iv) *Certain limits on allocations.*—The plan limits allocations otherwise provided under the allocation formula to a maximum dollar amount or a maximum percentage of plan year compensation, limits the dollar amount of plan year compensation taken into account in determining the amount of allocations, or applies the restrictions of section 409(n) or the limits of section 415.

(v) *Lower allocations for HCEs.*—The allocations provided to one or more HCEs under the plan are less than the allocations that would otherwise be provided to those employees if the plan satisfied this paragraph (b) (without regard to this paragraph (b)(4)(v)).

(vi) *Multiple formulas.*—(A) *General rule.*—The plan provides that an employee's allocation under the plan is the greater of the allocations determined under two or more formulas, or is the sum of the allocations determined under two or more formulas. This paragraph (b)(4)(vi) does not apply to a plan unless each of the formulas under the plan satisfies the requirements of paragraph (b)(4)(vi)(B) through (D) of this section.

(B) *Sole formulas.*—The formulas must be the only formulas under the plan.

determined in accordance with paragraph (c)(2) of this section, without imputing permitted disparity and without grouping allocation rates under paragraphs (c)(2)(iv) and (v) of this section, respectively.

(ii) *Example.*—The following example illustrates the safe harbor in this paragraph (b)(3):

Example. (a) Plan A has a single allocation formula that applies to all employees, under which each employee's allocation for the plan year equals the product of the total of all amounts taken into account for all employees for the plan year under paragraph (c)(2)(ii) of this section and a fraction, the numerator of which is the employee's points for the plan year and the denominator of which is the sum of the points of all employees for the plan year. Plan A grants each employee 10 points for each year of service (including pre-participation service and imputed service credited under Plan A that satisfies §1.401(a)(4)-1 1(d)(3)) and one point for each $100 of plan year compensation. For the 1994 plan year, the total allocations are $71,200, and the total points for all employees are 7,120. Each employee's allocation for the 1994 plan year is set forth in the table below.

Points	Amount of Allocation	Allocation Rate
1,700	$17,000	11.3%
1,600	$16,000	10.7%
1,300	$13,000	13.0%
1,030	$10,300	10.3%
500	$5,000	12.5%
400	$4,000	11.4%
330	$3,300	11.0%
260	$2,600	10.4%
7,120	$71,200	—

(C) *Separate testing.*—Each of the formulas must separately satisfy this paragraph (b). A formula that is available solely to some or all NHCEs is deemed to satisfy this paragraph (b)(4)(vi)(C).

(D) *Availability.*—(1) *General rule.*—All of the formulas must be available on the same terms to all employees.

(2) *Formulas for NHCEs.*—A formula does not fail to be available on the same terms to all employees merely because the formula is not available to any HCEs, but is available to some or all NHCEs on the same terms as all of the other formulas in the plan.

(3) *Top-heavy formulas.*—In the case of a plan that provides the greater of the allocations under two or more formulas, one of which is a top-heavy formula, the top-heavy formula does not fail to be available on the same terms to all employees merely because it is available solely to all non-key employees on the same terms as all the other formulas under the plan. Furthermore, the top-heavy formula does not fail to be available on the same terms as the other formulas under the plan merely because it is conditioned on the plan's being top-heavy within the meaning of section 416(g). Finally, the top-heavy formula does not fail to be available on the same terms as the other formulas under the plan merely because it is available to all employees described in §1.416-1, Q&A M-10 (i.e., all non-key employees who have not separated from service as of the last day of the plan year). The preceding sentence does not apply, however, unless the plan would satisfy section 410(b) if all employees who are benefiting under the plan solely as a result of receiving allocations under the top-heavy formula were treated as not currently benefiting under the plan. For purposes of this paragraph (b)(4)(vi)(D)(3), a top-heavy formula is a formula that provides the minimum benefit described in section 416(c)(2) (taking into account, if applicable, the modification in section 416(h)(2)(A)(ii)(II)).

(E) *Provisions may be applied more than once.*—The provisions of this paragraph (b)(4)(vi) may be applied more than once. For example, a plan satisfies this paragraph (b) if an employee's allocation under the plan is the greater of the allocations under two or more formulas, and one or more of those formulas is the sum of the allocations under two or more other formulas, provided that each of the formulas under the plan satisfies the requirements of paragraph (b)(4)(vi)(B) through (D) of this section.

(F) *Examples.*—The following examples illustrate the rules in this paragraph (b)(4)(vi):

Example 1. Under Plan A, each employee's allocation equals the sum of the allocations determined under two formulas. The first formula provides an allocation of five percent of plan year compensation. The second formula provides an allocation of $100. Plan A satisfies this paragraph (b)(4)(vi).

Example 2. Under Plan B, each employee's allocation equals the greater of the allocations determined under two formulas. The first formula provides an allocation of seven percent of plan year

Reg. §1.401(a)(4)-2(b)(3)(i)(B)

compensation and is available to all employees who complete at least 1,000 hours of service during the plan year and who have not separated from service as of the last day of the plan year. The second formula is a top-heavy formula that provides an allocation of three percent of plan year compensation and that is available to all employees described in §1.416-1, Q&A M-10. Plan B does not satisfy the general rule in paragraph (b)(4)(vi)(D)(1) of this section because the two formulas are not available on the same terms to all employees (i.e., an employee is required to complete 1,000 hours of service during the plan year to receive an allocation under the first formula, but not under the second formula). Nonetheless, because the second formula is a top-heavy formula, the special availability rules for top-heavy formulas in paragraph (b)(4)(vi)(D)(3) of this section apply. Thus, the second formula does not fail to be available on the same terms as the first formula merely because the second formula is available to all employees described in §1.416-1, Q&A M-10, as long as the plan would satisfy section 410(b) if all employees who are benefiting under the plan solely as a result of receiving allocations under the top-heavy formula were treated as not currently benefiting under the plan. This is true even if the plan conditions the availability of the second formula on the plan's being top-heavy for the plan year.

Example 3. The facts are the same as in *Example 2*, except that the first formula is available to all employees who have not separated from service as of the last day of the plan year, regardless of whether they complete at least 1,000 hours of service during the plan year. Plan B still does not satisfy the general rule in paragraph (b)(4)(vi)(D)(1) of this section because the two formulas are not available on the same terms to all employees (i.e., the second formula is only available to all non-key employees). Nonetheless, because the second formula is a top-heavy formula, the special availability rules for top-heavy formulas in paragraph (b)(4)(vi)(D)(3) of this section apply. Thus, the second formula does not fail to be available on the same terms as the first formula merely because the second formula is available solely to all non-key employees.

(c) *General test for nondiscrimination in amount of contributions.*— (1) *General rule.*—The employer contributions allocated under a defined contribution plan are nondiscriminatory in amount for a plan year if each rate group under the plan satisfies section 410(b). For purposes of this paragraph (c), a rate group exists under a plan for each HCE and consists of the HCE and all other employees in the plan (both HCEs and NHCEs) who have an allocation rate greater than or equal to the HCE's allocation rate. Thus, an employee is in the rate group for each HCE who has an allocation rate less than or equal to the employee's allocation rate.

(2) *Determination of allocation rates.*—(i) *General rule.*—The allocation rate for an employee for a plan year equals the sum of the allocations to the employee's account for the plan year, expressed either as a percentage of plan year compensation or as a dollar amount.

(ii) *Allocations taken into account.*—The amounts taken into account in determining allocation rates for a plan year include all employer contributions and forfeitures that are allocated or treated as allocated to the account of an employee under the plan for the plan year, other than amounts described in paragraph (c)(2)(iii) of this section. For this purpose, employer contributions include annual additions described in §1.415(c)-1(b)(4) (regarding amounts arising from certain transactions between the plan and the employer). In the case of a defined contribution plan subject to section 412, an employer contribution is taken into account in the plan year for which it is required to be contributed and allocated to employees' accounts under the plan, even if all or part of the required contribution is not actually made.

(iii) *Allocations not taken into account.*—Allocations of income, expenses, gains, and losses attributable to the balance in an employee's account are not taken into account in determining allocation rates.

(iv) *Imputation of permitted disparity.*—The disparity permitted under section 401(l) may be imputed in accordance with the rules of §1.401(a)(4)-7.

(v) *Grouping of allocation rates.*—(A) *General rule.*—An employer may treat all employees who have allocation rates within a specified range above and below a midpoint rate chosen by the employer as having an allocation rate equal to the midpoint rate within that range. Allocation rates within a given range may not be grouped under this paragraph (c)(2)(v) if the allocation rates of HCEs within the range generally are significantly higher than the allocation rates of NHCEs in the range. The specified ranges within which all employees are treated as having the same allocation rate may not overlap and may be no larger than provided in paragraph (c)(2)(v)(B) of this section. Allocation rates of employees that are not within any

of these specified ranges are determined without regard to this paragraph (c)(2)(v).

(B) *Size of specified ranges.*—The lowest and highest allocation rates in the range must be within five percent (not five percentage points) of the midpoint rate. If allocation rates are determined as a percentage of plan year compensation, the lowest and highest allocation rates need not be within five percent of the midpoint rate, if they are no more than one quarter of a percentage point above or below the midpoint rate.

(vi) *Consistency requirement.*—Allocation rates must be determined in a consistent manner for all employees for the plan year.

(3) *Satisfaction of section 410(b) by a rate group.*—(i) *General rule.*— For purposes of determining whether a rate group satisfies section 410(b), the rate group is treated as if it were a separate plan that benefits only the employees included in the rate group for the plan year. Thus, for example, under §1.401(a)(4)-1(c)(4)(iv), the ratio percentage of the rate group is determined taking into account all nonexcludable employees regardless of whether they benefit under the plan. Paragraph (c)(3)(ii) and (iii) of this section provide additional special rules for determining whether a rate group satisfies section 410(b).

(ii) *Application of nondiscriminatory classification test.*—A rate group satisfies the nondiscriminatory classification test of §1.410(b)-4 (including the reasonable classification requirement of §1.410(b)-4(b)) if and only if the ratio percentage of the rate group is greater than or equal to the lesser of—

(A) The midpoint between the safe and the unsafe harbor percentages applicable to the plan; and

(B) The ratio percentage of the plan.

(iii) *Application of average benefit percentage test.*—A rate group satisfies the average benefit percentage test of §1.410(b)-5 if the plan of which it is a part satisfies §1.410(b)-5 (without regard to §1.410(b)-5(f)). In the case of a plan that relies on §1.410(b)-5(f) to satisfy the average benefit percentage test, each rate group under the plan satisfies the average benefit percentage test (if applicable) only if the rate group separately satisfies §1.410(b)-5(f).

(4) *Examples.*—The following examples illustrate the general test in this paragraph (c):

Example 1. Employer X maintains two defined contribution plans, Plan A and Plan B, that are aggregated and treated as a single plan for purposes of sections 410(b) and 401(a)(4) pursuant to §1.410(b)-7(d). For the 1994 plan year, Employee M has plan year compensation of $10,000 and receives an allocation of $200 under Plan A and an allocation of $800 under Plan B. Employee M's allocation rate under the aggregated plan for the 1994 plan year is 10 percent (i.e., $1,000 divided by $10,000).

Example 2. The employees in Plan C have the following allocation rates (expressed as a percentage of plan year compensation): 2.75 percent, 2.80 percent, 2.85 percent, 3.25 percent, 6.65 percent, 7.33 percent, 7.34 percent, and 7.35 percent. Because the first four rates are within a range of no more than one quarter of a percentage point above and below 3.0 percent (a midpoint rate chosen by the employer), under paragraph (c)(2)(v) of this section the employer may treat the employees who have those rates as having an allocation rate of 3.0 percent (provided that the allocation rates of HCEs within the range generally are not significantly higher than the allocation rates of NHCEs within the range). Because the last four rates are within a range of no more than five percent above and below 7.0 percent (a midpoint rate chosen by the employer), the employer may treat the employees who have those rates as having an allocation rate of 7.0 percent (provided that the allocation rates of HCEs within the range generally are not significantly higher than the allocation rates of NHCEs within the range).

Example 3. (a) Employer Y has only six nonexcludable employees, all of whom benefit under Plan D. The HCEs are H1 and H2, and the NHCEs are N1 through N4. For the 1994 plan year, H1 and N1 through N4 have an allocation rate of 5.0 percent of plan year compensation. For the same plan year, H2 has an allocation rate of 7.5 percent of plan year compensation.

(b) There are two rate groups under Plan D. Rate group 1 consists of H1 and all those employees who have an allocation rate greater than or equal to H1's allocation rate (5.0 percent). Thus, rate group 1 consists of H1, H2, and N1 through N4. Rate group 2 consists only of H2 because no other employee has an allocation rate greater than or equal to H2's allocation rate (7.5 percent).

(c) The ratio percentage for rate group 2 is zero percent—i.e., zero percent (the percentage of all nonhighly compensated nonexcludable employees who are in the rate group) divided by 50 percent (the percentage of all highly compensated nonexcludable employees who are in the rate group). Therefore rate group 2 does not satisfy the ratio percentage test under §1.410(b)-2(b)(2). Rate group 2 also does not satisfy the nondiscriminatory classification test of §1.410(b)-4 (as modified by paragraph (c)(3) of this section). Rate group 2 therefore does not satisfy section 410(b) and, as a result, Plan D does not satisfy the general test in paragraph (c)(1) of this section. This is true regardless of whether rate group 1 satisfies §1.410(b)-2(b)(2).

Example 4. (a) The facts are the same as in *Example 3*, except that N4 has an allocation rate of 8.0 percent.

(b) There are two rate groups in Plan D. Rate group 1 consists of H1 and all those employees who have an allocation rate greater than or equal to H1's allocation rate (5.0 percent). Thus, rate group 1 consists of H1, H2, and N1 through N4. Rate group 2 consists of H2, and all those employees who have an allocation rate greater than or equal to H2's allocation rate (7.5 percent). Thus, rate group 2 consists of H2 and N4.

(c) Rate group 1 satisfies the ratio percentage test under §1.410(b)-2(b)(2) because the ratio percentage of the rate group is 100 percent—i.e., 100 percent (the percentage of all nonhighly compensated nonexcludable employees who are in the rate group) divided by 100 percent (the percentage of all highly compensated nonexcludable employees who are in the rate group).

(d) Rate group 2 does not satisfy the ratio percentage test of §1.410(b)-2(b)(2) because the ratio percentage of the rate group is 50 percent—i.e., 25 percent (the percentage of all nonhighly compensated nonexcludable employees who are in the rate group) divided by 50 percent (the percentage of all highly compensated nonexcludable employees who are in the rate group).

(e) However, rate group 2 does satisfy the nondiscriminatory classification test of §1.410(b)-4 because the ratio percentage of the rate group (50 percent) is greater than the safe harbor percentage applicable to the plan under §1.410(b)-4(c)(4) (45.5 percent).

(f) Under paragraph (c)(3)(iii) of this section, rate group 2 satisfies the average benefit percentage test, if Plan D satisfies the average benefit percentage test. (The requirement that Plan D satisfy the average benefit percentage test applies even though Plan D satisfies the ratio percentage test and would ordinarily not need to run the average benefit percentage test.) If Plan D satisfies the average benefit percentage test, then rate group 2 satisfies section 410(b) and thus, Plan D satisfies the general test in paragraph (c)(1) of this section, because each rate group under the plan satisfies section 410(b).

Example 5. (a) Plan E satisfies section 410(b) by satisfying the nondiscriminatory classification test of §1.410(b)-4 and the average benefit percentage test of §1.410(b)-5 (without regard to §1.410(b)-5(f)). See §1.410(b)-2(b)(3). Plan E uses the facts-and-circumstances requirements of §1.410(b)-4(c)(3) to satisfy the nondiscriminatory classification test of §1.410(b)-4. The safe and unsafe harbor percentages applicable to the plan under §1.410(b)-4(c)(4) are 29 and 20 percent, respectively. Plan E has a ratio percentage of 22 percent.

(b) Rate group 1 under Plan E has a ratio percentage of 23 percent. Under paragraph (c)(3)(ii) of this section, the rate group satisfies the nondiscriminatory classification requirement of §1.410(b)-4, because the ratio percentage of the rate group (23 percent) is greater than the lesser of—

(1) The ratio percentage for the plan as a whole (22 percent); and

(2) The midpoint between the safe and unsafe harbor percentages (24.5 percent).

(c) Under paragraph (c)(3)(iii) of this section, the rate group satisfies section 410(b) because the plan satisfies the average benefit percentage test of §1.410(b)-5. *§1.401(a)(4)-3 Nondiscrimination in amount of employer-provided benefits under a defined benefit plan.* [Reg. §1.401(a)(4)-2.]

☐ [*T.D. 8360, 9-12-91. Amended by T.D. 8485, 8-30-93 and T.D. 9319, 4-4-2007.*]

[Reg. §1.401(a)(4)-3]

§1.401(a)(4)-3. Nondiscrimination in amount of benefits under a defined benefit plan.—(a) *Introduction.*—(1) *Overview.*—This section provides rules for determining whether the employer-provided benefits under a defined benefit plan are nondiscriminatory in amount as required by §1.401(a)(4)-1(b)(2)(iii). Certain defined benefit plans that provide uniform benefits are permitted to satisfy this requirement by meeting one of the safe harbors in paragraph (b) of this section. Plans that do not provide uniform benefits may satisfy this requirement by satisfying the general test in paragraph (c) of this section. Paragraph (d) of this section provides rules for determining the individual benefit accrual rates needed for the general test. Paragraph (e) of this section provides rules for determining compensation for purposes of applying the requirements of this section. Paragraph (f) of this section provides additional rules that apply generally for purposes of both the safe harbors in paragraph (b) of this section and the general test in paragraph (c) of this section. See §1.401(a)(4)-6 for rules for determining the amount of employer-provided benefits

under a contributory DB plan, and for determining whether the employee-provided benefits under such a plan are nondiscriminatory in amount.

(2) *Alternative methods of satisfying nondiscriminatory amount requirement.*—A defined benefit plan is permitted to satisfy paragraph (b) or (c) of this section on a restructured basis pursuant to §1.401(a)(4)-9(c). Alternatively, a defined benefit plan is permitted to satisfy the nondiscriminatory amount requirement of §1.401(a)(4)-1(b)(2)(iii) on the basis of equivalent allocations pursuant to §1.401(a)(4)-8(c). In addition, a defined benefit plan that is part of a floor-offset arrangement is permitted to satisfy this section pursuant to §1.401(a)(4)-8(d).

(b) *Safe harbors.*—(1) *In general.*—The employer-provided benefits under a defined benefit plan are nondiscriminatory in amount for a plan year if the plan satisfies each of the uniformity requirements of paragraph (b)(2) of this section and any one of the safe harbors in paragraphs (b)(3) (unit credit plans), (b)(4) (fractional accrual plans), and (b)(5) (insurance contract plans) of this section. Paragraph (b)(6) of this section provides exceptions for certain plan provisions that do not cause a plan to fail to satisfy this paragraph (b). Paragraph (f) of this section provides additional rules that apply in determining whether a plan satisfies this paragraph (b).

(2) *Uniformity requirements.*—(i) *Uniform normal retirement benefit.*—The same benefit formula must apply to all employees. The benefit formula must provide all employees with an annual benefit payable in the same form commencing at the same uniform normal retirement age. The annual benefit must be the same percentage of average annual compensation or the same dollar amount for all employees who will have the same number of years of service at normal retirement age. (See §1.401(a)(4)-11(d)(3) regarding service that may be taken into account as years of service.) The annual benefit must equal the employee's accrued benefit at normal retirement age (within the meaning of section 411(a)(7)(A)(i)) and must be the normal retirement benefit under the plan (within the meaning of section 411(a)(9)).

(ii) *Uniform post-normal retirement benefit.*—With respect to an employee with a given number of years of service at any age after normal retirement age, the annual benefit commencing at that employee's age must be the same percentage of average annual compensation or the same dollar amount that would be payable commencing at normal retirement age to an employee who had that same number of years of service at normal retirement age.

(iii) *Uniform subsidies.*—Each subsidized optional form of benefit available under the plan must be currently available (within the meaning of §1.401(a)(4)-4(b)(2)) to substantially all employees. Whether an optional form of benefit is considered subsidized for this purpose may be determined using any reasonable actuarial assumptions.

(iv) *No employee contributions.*—The plan must not be a contributory DB plan.

(v) *Period of accrual.*—Each employee's benefit must be accrued over the same years of service that are taken into account in applying the benefit formula under the plan to that employee. For this purpose, any year in which the employee benefits under the plan (within the meaning of §1.410(b)-3(a)) is included as a year of service in which a benefit accrues. Thus, for example, a plan does not satisfy the safe harbor in paragraph (b)(4) of this section unless the plan uses the same years of service to determine both the normal retirement benefit under the plan's benefit formula and the fraction by which an employee's fractional rule benefit is multiplied to derive the employee's accrued benefit as of any plan year.

(vi) *Examples.*—The following examples illustrate the rules in this paragraph (b)(2):

Example 1. Plan A provides a normal retirement benefit equal to two percent of average annual compensation times each year of service commencing at age 65 for all employees. Plan A provides that employees of Division S receive their benefit in the form of a straight life annuity and that employees of Division T receive their benefit in the form of a life annuity with an automatic cost-of-living increase. Plan A does not provide a uniform normal retirement benefit within the meaning of paragraph (b)(2)(i) of this section because the annual benefit is not payable in the same form to all employees.

Example 2. Plan B provides a normal retirement benefit equal to 1.5 percent of average annual compensation times each year of service at normal retirement age for all employees. The normal retirement age under the plan is the earlier of age 65 or the age at which the employee completes 10 years of service, but in no event earlier than age 62. Plan B does not provide a uniform normal retirement benefit within the meaning of paragraph (b)(2)(i) of this section because the same uniform normal retirement age does not apply to all employees.

Example 3. Plan C is an accumulation plan under which the benefit for each year of service equals one percent of plan year compensation payable in the same form to all employees commencing at the same uniform normal retirement age. Under paragraph (e)(2) of this section, an accumulation plan may substitute plan year compensation for average annual compensation. Plan C provides a uniform normal retirement benefit within the meaning of paragraph (b)(2)(i) of this section, because all employees with the same number of years of service at normal retirement age will receive an annual benefit that is treated as the same percentage of average annual compensation.

Example 4. The facts are the same as in *Example 3*, except that the benefit for each year of service equals one percent of plan year compensation increased by reference to the increase in the cost of living from the year of service to normal retirement age. Plan C does not provide a uniform normal retirement benefit, because the annual benefit defined by the benefit formula can vary for employees with the same number of years of service at normal retirement age, depending on the age at which those years of service were credited to the employee under the plan.

Example 5. Plan D provides a normal retirement benefit of 50 percent of average annual compensation at normal retirement age (age 65) for employees with 30 years of service at normal retirement age. Plan D provides that, in the case of an employee with less than 30 years of service at normal retirement age, the normal retirement benefit is reduced on a pro rata basis for each year of service less than 30. However, if an employee with less than 30 years of service at normal retirement age continues to work past normal retirement age, Plan D provides that the additional years of service worked past normal retirement age are taken into account for purposes of the 30 years of service requirement. Thus, an employee who has 26 years of service at age 65 but who does not retire until age 69 with 30 years of service will receive a benefit of 50 percent of average annual compensation. Plan D provides uniform post-normal retirement benefits within the meaning of paragraph (b)(2)(ii) of this section.

Example 6. (a) Plan E is amended on February 14, 1994, to provide an early retirement window benefit that consists of an unreduced early retirement benefit to employees who terminate employment after attainment of age 55 with 10 years of service and between June 1, 1994, and November 30, 1994. The early retirement window benefit is a single subsidized optional form of benefit. Paragraph (b)(2)(iii) of this section requires that the subsidized optional form of benefit be currently available (within the meaning of § 1.401(a)(4)-4(b)(2)) to substantially all employees. Section 1.401(a)(4)-4(b)(2)(ii)(A)(2) provides that age and service requirements are not disregarded in determining the current availability of an optional form of benefit if those requirements must be satisfied within a specified period of time. The early retirement window benefit is not currently available to an employee unless the employee will satisfy the eligibility requirements for the early retirement window benefit by the close of the early retirement window benefit period. Plan E will fail to satisfy paragraph (b)(2)(iii) of this section unless substantially all of the employees satisfy the eligibility requirements for the early retirement window benefit by November 30, 1994. However, see § 1.401(a)(4)-9(c)(6), *Example 2* for an example of how a plan with an early retirement window benefit may be restructured into two component plans, each of which satisfies the safe harbors of this paragraph (b).

(b) A similar analysis would apply if, instead of an unreduced early retirement benefit, the early retirement window benefit consisted of a special schedule of early retirement factors, defined by starting with the plan's usual schedule and then treating each employee eligible for the early retirement window benefit as being five years older than the employee actually is, but not older than the employee's normal retirement age.

Example 7. Plan F generally provides a normal retirement benefit of 1.5 percent of an employee's average annual compensation multiplied by the employee's years of service with the employer. For *employees transferred outside of the group of employees covered by* the plan, the plan's benefit formula takes into account only years of service prior to the transfer, but determines average annual compensation taking into account section 414(s) compensation both before and after the transfer. Plan F does not satisfy the requirements of paragraph (b)(2)(v) of this section with respect to transferred employees, because their benefits are accrued over years of service (i.e., after transfer) that are not taken into account in applying the plan's benefit formula to them. However, see *Example 2* of paragraph (b)(6)(x)(B) of this section for an example of how a plan that continues to take transferred employees' section 414(s) compensation into account after their transfer may still satisfy this paragraph (b).

(3) *Safe harbor for unit credit plans.*—(i) *General rule.*—A plan satisfies the safe harbor in this paragraph (b)(3) for a plan year if it satisfies both of the following requirements:

(A) The plan must satisfy the $133^{1}/_{3}$ percent accrual rule of section 411(b)(1)(B).

(B) Each employee's accrued benefit under the plan as of any plan year must be determined by applying the plan's benefit formula to the employee's years of service and (if applicable) average annual compensation, both determined as of that plan year.

(ii) *Example.*—The following example illustrates the rules in this paragraph (b)(3):

Example. Plan A provides that the accrued benefit of each employee as of any plan year equals the employee's average annual compensation times a percentage that depends on the employee's years of service determined as of that plan year. The percentage is two percent for each of the first 10 years of service, plus 1.5 percent for each of the next 10 years of service, plus two percent for all additional years of service. Plan A satisfies this paragraph (b)(3).

(4) *Safe harbor for plans using fractional accrual rule.*—(i) *General rule.*—A plan satisfies the safe harbor in this paragraph (b)(4) for a plan year if it satisfies each of the following requirements:

(A) The plan must satisfy the fractional accrual rule of section 411(b)(1)(C).

(B) Each employee's accrued benefit under the plan as of any plan year before the employee reaches normal retirement age must be determined by multiplying the employee's fractional rule benefit (within the meaning of § 1.411(b)-1(b)(3)(ii)(A)) by a fraction, the numerator of which is the employee's years of service determined as of the plan year, and the denominator of which is the employee's projected years of service as of normal retirement age.

(C) The plan must satisfy one of the following requirements:

(1) Under the plan, it must be impossible for any employee to accrue in a plan year a portion of the normal retirement benefit described in paragraph (b)(2)(i) of this section that is more than one third larger than the portion of the same benefit accrued in that or any other plan year by any other employee, when each portion of the benefit is expressed as a percentage of each employee's average annual compensation or as a dollar amount. In making this determination, actual and potential employees in the plan with any amount of service at normal retirement must be taken into account (other than employees with more than 33 years of service at normal retirement age). In addition, in the case of a plan that satisfies section 401(l) in form, an employee is treated as accruing benefits at a rate equal to the excess benefit percentage in the case of a defined benefit excess plan or at a rate equal to the gross benefit percentage in the case of an offset plan.

(2) The normal retirement benefit under the plan must be a flat benefit that requires a minimum of 25 years of service at normal retirement age for an employee to receive the unreduced flat benefit, determined without regard to section 415. For this purpose, a flat benefit is a benefit that is the same percentage of average annual compensation or the same dollar amount for all employees who have a minimum number of years of service at normal retirement age (e.g., 50 percent of average annual compensation), with a pro rata reduction in the flat benefit for employees who have less than the minimum number of years of service at normal retirement age. An employee is permitted to accrue the maximum benefit permitted under section 415 over a period of less than 25 years, provided that the flat benefit under the plan, determined without regard to section 415, can accrue over no less than 25 years.

(3) The plan must satisfy the requirements of paragraph (b)(4)(i)(C)(2) of this section (other than the requirement that the minimum number of years of service for receiving the unreduced flat benefit is at least 25 years), and, for the plan year, the average of the normal accrual rates for all nonhighly compensated nonexcludable employees must be at least 70 percent of the average of the normal accrual rates for all highly compensated nonexcludable employees. The averages in the preceding sentence are determined taking into account all nonexcludable employees (regardless of whether they benefit under the plan). In addition, contributions and benefits under other plans of the employer are disregarded. For purposes of this paragraph (h)(4)(i)(C)(3), normal accrual rates are determined under paragraph (d) of this section.

(ii) *Examples.*—The following examples illustrate the rules in this paragraph (b)(4). In each example, it is assumed that the plan has never permitted employee contributions.

Example 1. Plan A provides a normal retirement benefit equal to 1.6 percent of average annual compensation times each year of service up to 25. Plan A further provides that an employee's accrued benefit as of any plan year equals the employee's fractional rule benefit multiplied by a fraction, the numerator of which is the employee's years of service as of the plan year, and the denominator of which is the employee's projected years of service as of normal retirement age. The greatest benefit that an employee could accrue in any plan year is 1.6 percent of average annual compensation (this is the case for an employee with 25 or fewer years of projected service at normal retirement age). Among potential employees with 33 or fewer years of projected service at normal retirement age, the lowest benefit that an employee could accrue in any plan year is 1.212 percent of average annual compensation (this is the case for an employee with 33 years of projected service at normal retirement age). Plan A satisfies paragraph (b)(4)(i)(C)(1) of this section because 1.6 percent is not more than one third larger than 1.212 percent.

Example 2. Plan B provides a normal retirement benefit equal to 1.0 percent of average annual compensation up to the integration level, and 1.6 percent of average annual compensation above the integration level, times each year of service up to 35. Plan B further provides that an employee's accrued benefit as of any plan year equals the employee's fractional rule benefit multiplied by a fraction, the numerator of which is the employee's years of service as of the plan year and the denominator of which is the employee's projected years of service as of normal retirement age. For purposes of satisfying the one third larger rule in paragraph (b)(4)(i)(C)(1) of this section, because Plan B satisfies section 401(1) in form, all employees with less than 35 projected years of service are assumed to accrue benefits at the rate of 1.6 percent of average annual compensation (the excess benefit percentage under the plan). Plan B satisfies paragraph (b)(4)(i)(C) of this section because all employees with 33 or fewer years of projected service at normal retirement age accrue in each plan year a benefit of 1.6 percent of average annual compensation.

Example 3. Plan C provides a normal retirement benefit equal to four percent of average annual compensation times each year of service up to 10 and one percent of average annual compensation times each year of service in excess of 10 and not in excess of 30. Plan C further provides that an employee's accrued benefit as of any plan year equals the employee's fractional rule benefit multiplied by a fraction, the numerator of which is the employee's years of service as of the plan year, and the denominator of which is the employee's projected years of service as of normal retirement age. The greatest benefit that an employee could accrue in any plan year is four percent of average annual compensation (this is the case for an employee with 10 or fewer years of projected service at normal retirement age). Among employees with 33 or fewer years of projected service at normal retirement age, the lowest benefit that an employee could accrue in a plan year is 1.82 percent of average annual compensation (this is the case of an employee with 33 years of projected service at normal retirement age). Plan C fails to satisfy this paragraph (b)(4) because four percent is more than one third larger than 1.82 percent. See also § 1.401(a)(4)-9(c)(6), *Example 3.*

Example 4. Plan D provides a normal retirement benefit of 100 percent of average annual compensation, reduced by four percentage points for each year of service below 25 the employee has at normal retirement age. Plan D further provides that an employee's accrued benefit as of any plan year is equal to the employee's fractional rule benefit multiplied by a fraction, the numerator of which is the employee's years of service as of the plan year, and the denominator of which is the employee's projected years of service at normal retirement age. In the case of an employee who has five years of service as of the current plan year, and who is projected to have 10 years of service at normal retirement age, the employee's fractional rule benefit would be 40 percent of average annual compensation, and the employee's accrued benefit as of the current plan year would be 20 percent of average annual compensation (the fractional rule benefit multiplied by a fraction of five years over 10 years). Plan D satisfies this paragraph (b)(4).

Example 5. The facts are the same as in *Example 4,* except that the normal retirement benefit is 125 percent of average annual compensation, reduced by five percentage points for each year of service below 25 that the employee has at normal retirement age. Plan D satisfies this paragraph (b)(4), even though an employee may accrue the maximum benefit allowed under section 415 (i.e., 100 percent of the participant's average compensation for the high three years of service) in less than 25 years.

Example 6. The facts are the same as in *Example 1,* except that the plan determines each employee's accrued benefit by multiplying the employee's projected normal retirement benefit (rather than the fractional rule benefit) by the fraction described in *Example 1.* In determining an employee's projected normal retirement benefit, the plan defines each employee's average annual compensation as the average annual compensation the employee would have at normal retirement age if the employee's annual section 414(s) compensation in future plan years equaled the employee's plan year compensation for the prior plan year. Under these facts, Plan A does not satisfy paragraph (b)(4)(i)(B) of this section because the employee's accrued benefit is determined on the basis of a projected normal retirement

benefit that is not the same as the employee's fractional rule benefit determined in accordance with § 1.411(b)-1(b)(3)(ii)(A).

Example 7. Plan E provides a normal retirement benefit of 50 percent of average annual compensation, with a pro rata reduction for employees with less than 30 years of service at normal retirement age. Plan E further provides that an employee's accrued benefit as of any plan year is equal to the employee's fractional rule benefit multiplied by a fraction, the numerator of which is the employee's years of service as of the plan year, and the denominator of which is the employee's projected years of service at normal retirement age. For purposes of determining this fraction, the plan limits the years of service taken into account for an employee to the number of years the employee has participated in the plan. However, all years of service (including years of service before the employee commenced participation in the plan) are taken into account in determining an employee's normal retirement benefit under the plan's benefit formula. Plan E fails to satisfy this paragraph (b)(4) because the years of service over which benefits accrue differ from the years of service used in applying the benefit formula under the plan. See paragraph (b)(2)(v) of this section.

Example 8. (a) Plan F provides a normal retirement benefit equal to 2.0 percent of average annual compensation, plus 0.65 percent of average annual compensation above covered compensation, for each year of service up to 25. Plan F further provides that an employee's accrued benefit as of any plan year equals the sum of—

(1) The employee's fractional rule benefit (determined as if the normal retirement benefit under the plan equaled 2.0 percent of average annual compensation for each year of service up to 25) multiplied by a fraction, the numerator of which is the employee's years of service as of the plan year and the denominator of which is the employee's projected years of service as of normal retirement age; plus

(2) 0.65 percent of the employee's average annual compensation above covered compensation multiplied by the employee's years of service (up to 25) as of the current plan year.

(b) Although Plan F satisfies the fractional accrual rule of section 411(b)(1)(C), the plan fails to satisfy this paragraph (b)(4) because the plan does not determine employees' accrued benefits in accordance with paragraph (b)(4)(i)(B) of this section.

(5) *Safe harbor for insurance contract plans.*—A plan satisfies the safe harbor in this paragraph (b)(5) if it satisfies each of the following requirements:

(i) The plan must satisfy the accrual rule of section 411(b)(1)(F).

(ii) The plan must be an insurance contract plan within the meaning of section 412(i).

(iii) The benefit formula under the plan must be one that would satisfy the requirements of paragraph (b)(4) of this section if the stated normal retirement benefit under the formula accrued ratably over each employee's period of plan participation through normal retirement age in accordance with paragraph (b)(4)(i)(B) of this section. Thus, the benefit formula may not recognize years of service before an employee commenced participation in the plan because, otherwise, the definition of years of service for determining the normal retirement benefit would differ from the definition of years of service for determining the accrued benefit under paragraph (b)(4)(i)(B) of this section. See paragraph (b)(4)(ii), *Example 7,* of this section. Notwithstanding the foregoing, an insurance contract plan adopted and in effect on September 19, 1991, may continue to recognize years of service prior to an employee's participation in the plan for an employee who is a participant in the plan on that date to the extent provided by the benefit formula in the plan on such date.

(iv) The scheduled premium payments under an individual or group insurance contract used to fund an employee's normal retirement benefit must be level annual payments to normal retirement age. Thus, payments may not be scheduled to cease before normal retirement age.

(v) The premium payments for an employee who continues benefiting after normal retirement age must be equal to the amount necessary to fund additional benefits that accrue under the plan's benefit formula for the plan year.

(vi) Experience gains, dividends, forfeitures, and similar items must be used solely to reduce future premiums.

(vii) All benefits must be funded through contracts of the same series. Among other requirements, contracts of the same series must have cash values based on the same terms (including interest and mortality assumptions) and the same conversion rights. A plan does not fail to satisfy this requirement, however, if any change in the contract series or insurer applies on the same terms to all employees. But see § 1.401(a)(4)-5(a)(4), *Example 12* (change in insurer considered a plan amendment subject to § 1.401(a)(4)-5(a)).

(viii) If permitted disparity is taken into account, the normal retirement benefit stated under the plan's benefit formula must satisfy § 1.401(l)-3. For this purpose, the 0.75-percent factor in the maximum excess or offset allowance in § 1.401(l)-3(b)(2)(i) or (b)(3)(i), respectively, adjusted in accordance with § 1.401(l)-3(d)(9) and (e), is reduced by multiplying the factor by 0.80.

(6) *Use of safe harbors not precluded by certain plan provisions.*—(i) *In general.*—A plan does not fail to satisfy this paragraph (b) merely because the plan contains one or more of the provisions described in this paragraph (b)(6). Unless otherwise provided, any such provision must apply uniformly to all employees.

(ii) *Section 401(l) permitted disparity.*—The plan takes permitted disparity into account in a manner that satisfies section 401(l) in form. Thus, differences in employees' benefits under the plan attributable to uniform disparities permitted under § 1.401(l)-3 (including differences in disparities that are deemed uniform under § 1.401(l)-3(c)(2)) do not cause a plan to fail to satisfy this paragraph (b).

(iii) *Different entry dates.*—The plan provides one or more entry dates during the plan year as permitted by section 410(a)(4).

(iv) *Certain conditions on accruals.*—The plan provides that an employee's accrual for the plan year is less than a full accrual (including a zero accrual) because of a plan provision permitted by the year-of-participation rules of section 411(b)(4).

(v) *Certain limits on accruals.*—The plan limits benefits otherwise provided under the benefit formula or accrual method to a maximum dollar amount or to a maximum percentage of average annual compensation (e.g., by limiting service taken into account in the benefit formula) or in accordance with section 401(a)(5)(D), applies the limits of section 415, or limits the dollar amount of compensation taken into account in determining benefits.

(vi) *Dollar accrual per uniform unit of service.*—The plan determines accruals based on the same dollar amount for each uniform unit of service (not to exceed one week) performed by each employee with the same number of years of service under the plan during the plan year. The preceding sentence applies solely for purposes of the unit credit safe harbor in paragraph (b)(3) of this section.

(vii) *Prior benefits accrued under a different formula.*—The plan determines benefits for years of service after a fresh-start date for all employees under a benefit formula and accrual method that differ from the benefit formula and accrual method previously used to determine benefit accruals for employees in a fresh-start group for years of service before the fresh-start date. This paragraph (b)(6)(vii) applies solely to plans that satisfy § 1.401(a)(4)-13(c) with respect to the fresh start.

(viii) *Employee contributions.*—The plan is a contributory DB plan that would satisfy the requirements of paragraph (b) of this section if the plan's benefit formula provided benefits at employees' employer-provided benefit rates determined under § 1.401(a)(4)-6(b). This paragraph (b)(6)(viii) does not apply to a plan tested under paragraph (b)(4) or (b)(5) of this section unless the plan satisfies one of the methods in § 1.401(a)(4)-6(b)(4)through (b)(6). A minimum benefit added to the plan solely to satisfy § 1.401(a)(4)-6(b)(3) is not taken into account in determining whether this paragraph (b)(6)(viii) is satisfied.

(ix) *Certain subsidized optional forms.*—The plan provides a subsidized optional form of benefit that is available to fewer than substantially all employees because the optional form of benefit has been eliminated prospectively as provided in § 1.401(a)(4)-4(b)(3).

(x) *Lower benefits for HCEs.*—(A) *General rule.*—The benefits (including any subsidized optional form of benefit) provided to one or more HCEs under the plan are inherently less valuable to those HCEs (determined by applying the principles of § 1.401(a)(4)-4(d)(4)) than the benefits that would otherwise be provided to those HCEs if the plan satisfied this paragraph (b) (determined without regard to this paragraph (b)(6)(x)). These inherently less valuable benefits are deemed to satisfy this paragraph (b).

(B) *Examples.*—The following examples illustrate the rules in this paragraph (b)(6)(x):

Example 1. Plan A would satisfy this paragraph (b) (determined without regard to this paragraph (b)(6)(x)), except for the fact that it fails to satisfy the requirement of paragraph (b)(2)(iii) of this section (i.e., a subsidized optional form must be available to substantially all employees on similar terms). Each subsidized optional form in the plan is available to all the NHCEs on similar terms, but one of the subsidized optional forms of benefit is not available to any of the HCEs. Plan A satisfies this paragraph (b), because Plan A is a safe harbor plan with respect to the NHCEs and provides inherently less valuable benefits to the HCEs.

Example 2. (a) Plan B would satisfy this paragraph (b) (determined without regard to this paragraph (b)(6)(x)), except for the fact that some employees are not being credited with years of service under the plan, but are continuing to accrue benefits as a result of compensation increases. These are employees who have been transferred from the employer that sponsors Plan B to another member of the controlled group whose employees are not covered by Plan B. For these employees, Plan B fails to satisfy the requirement of paragraph (b)(2)(v) of this section (i.e., each employee's benefit must accrue over the same years of service used in applying the benefit formula).

(b) Plan B is restructured into two component plans under the provisions of § 1.401(a)(4)-9(c). One component plan (Component Plan B1) consists of all NHCEs who are not being credited with years of service under the plan's benefit formula but are continuing to accrue benefits as a result of compensation increases, and the other component plan (Component Plan B2) consists of the balance of the employees.

(c) Component Plan B1 satisfies this section and section 410(b), because it benefits only NHCEs.

(d) Component Plan B2 is treated as satisfying this paragraph (b), because Plan B would satisfy this paragraph (b) (determined without regard to this paragraph (b)(6)(x)) with respect to the employees in Component Plan B2 but for the fact that it provides inherently less valuable benefits to some HCEs in that component plan (i.e., the employees who are credited only with compensation increases rather than both years of service and compensation increases).

(e) Under § 1.401(a)(4)-9(c), if Component Plan B2 satisfies section 410(b), then Plan B satisfies this section.

(xi) *Multiple formulas.*—(A) *General rule.*—The plan provides that an employee's benefit under the plan is the greater of the benefits determined under two or more formulas, or is the sum of the benefits determined under two or more formulas. This paragraph (b)(6)(xi) does not apply to a plan unless each of the formulas under the plan satisfies the requirements of paragraph (b)(6)(xi)(B) through (D) of this section.

(B) *Sole formulas.*—The formulas must be the only formulas under the plan.

(C) *Separate testing.*—Each of the formulas must separately satisfy the uniformity requirements of paragraph (b)(2) of this section and also separately satisfy one of the safe harbors in paragraphs (b)(3) through (b)(5) of this section. A formula that is available solely to some or all NHCEs is deemed to satisfy this paragraph (b)(6)(xi)(C).

(D) *Availability.*—(1) *General rule.*—All of the formulas must be available on the same terms to all employees.

(2) *Formulas for NHCEs.*—A formula does not fail to be available on the same terms to all employees merely because the formula is not available to any HCEs, but is available to some or all NHCEs on the same terms as all of the other formulas in the plan.

(3) *Top-heavy formulas.*—Rules parallel to those in § 1.401(a)(4)-2(b)(4)(vi)(D)(3) apply in the case of a plan that provides the greater of the benefits under two or more formulas, one of which is a top-heavy formula. For purposes of this paragraph (b)(6)(xi)(D)(3), a top-heavy formula is a formula that provides a benefit equal to the minimum benefit described in section 416(c)(1) (taking into account, if applicable, the modification in section 416(h)(2)(A)(ii)(I)).

(E) *Provisions may be applied more than once.*—The provisions of this paragraph (b)(6)(xi) may be applied more than once. See § 1.401(a)(4)-2(b)(4)(vi)(E) for an example of the application of these provisions more than once.

(F) *Examples.*—The following examples illustrate the rules in this paragraph (b)(6)(xi):

Example 1. Under Plan A, each employee's benefit equals the sum of the benefits determined under two formulas. The first formula provides one percent of average annual compensation per year of service. The second formula provides $10 per year of service. Plan A is eligible to apply the rules in this paragraph (b)(6)(xi).

Example 2. Under Plan B, each employee's benefit equals the greater of the benefits determined under two formulas. The first formula provides $15 per year of service and is available to all employees who complete at least 500 hours of service during the plan year. The second formula provides 1.5 percent of average annual compensation per year of service and is available to all employees who complete at least 1,000 hours of service during the plan year. Plan B does not satisfy this paragraph (b)(6)(xi) because the two formulas are not available on the same terms to all employees.

Reg. § 1.401(a)(4)-3(b)(6)(xi)(F)

Example 3. Under Plan C, each employee's benefit equals the greater of the benefits determined under two formulas. The first formula provides $15 per year of service and is available to all employees who complete at least 1,000 hours of service during the plan year. The second formula provides the minimum benefit described in section 416(c)(1) and is available to all non-key employees who complete at least 1,000 hours of service during the plan year. Plan C does not satisfy the general rule in paragraph (b)(6)(xi)(D)(1) of this section because the two formulas are not available on the same terms to all employees (i.e., the second formula is only available to all non-key employees). Nonetheless, because the second formula is a top-heavy formula, the special availability rules for top-heavy formulas in paragraph (b)(6)(xi)(D)(3) of this section apply. Thus, the second formula does not fail to be available on the same terms as the first formula merely because the second formula is available solely to all non-key employees on the same terms. This is true even if the plan conditions the availability of the second formula on the plan's being top-heavy for the plan year.

Example 4. Under Plan D, each employee's benefit equals the greater of the benefits determined under two formulas. The first formula is available to all employees and provides a benefit equal to 1.5 percent of average annual compensation per year of service. The second formula is only available to NHCEs and provides a benefit equal to two percent of average annual compensation per year of service, minus two percent of the primary insurance amount per year of service. The amount of the offset is not limited to the maximum permitted offset under §1.401(l)-3(b). Under paragraph (b)(6)(xi)(D)(2) of this section, both formulas are treated as available to all employees on the same terms. Furthermore, even though the second formula does not satisfy any of the safe harbors in this paragraph (b), the formula is deemed to satisfy the separate testing requirement under paragraph (b)(6)(xi)(C) of this section, because the formula is available solely to some or all NHCEs.

Example 5. Plan E is a unit credit plan that provides a benefit of one percent of average annual compensation per year of service to all employees. In 1994, the plan is amended to provide a benefit of two percent of average annual compensation per year of service after 1993, while continuing to provide a benefit of one percent of average annual compensation per year of service for all years of service before 1994. Thus, the plan's amended benefit formula provides a benefit equal to the sum of the benefits determined under two benefit formulas: one percent of average annual compensation per year of service, plus one percent of average annual compensation per year of service after 1993. Plan E satisfies this paragraph (b)(6)(xi).

Example 6. The facts are the same as in *Example 5*, except that the plan amendment in 1994 decreases the benefit to 0.75 percent of average annual compensation per year of service after 1993, while retaining the one-percent formula for all years of service before 1994. Thus, the plan's amended benefit formula provides a benefit equal to the sum of the benefits determined under two benefit formulas: 0.75 percent of average annual compensation per year of service, plus 0.25 percent of average annual compensation per year of service before 1994. Under these facts, the second formula does not separately satisfy any of the safe harbors in this paragraph (b) because the years of service over which each employee's benefit accrues under the second formula (i.e., all years of service) are not the same years of service that are taken into account in applying the benefit formula under the plan to that employee (i.e., years of service before 1994). See paragraph (b)(2)(v) of this section. But see paragraph (b)(6)(vii) of this section and §1.401(a)(4)-13, which provide rules under which Plan E, as amended, may be able to satisfy this paragraph (b).

Example 7. Plan F provides a benefit to all employees of one percent of average annual compensation per year of service. Employee M was hired as the president of the employer in December 1994 and was not a HCE under section 414(q) during the 1994 calendar plan year. In 1994, Plan F is amended to provide a benefit that is the greater of the benefit determined under the pre-existing formula in the plan and a new formula that is available solely to some NHCEs (including Employee M). The new formula does not satisfy the uniformity requirements of paragraph (b)(2) of this section, because it provides a different benefit for some NHCEs than for other NHCEs. As a result of this change, Employee M receives a higher accrual in 1994 than the NHCEs who are not eligible for the new formula. In 1995, when Employee M first becomes a HCE, the second formula no longer applies to Employee M. It would be inconsistent with the purpose of preventing discrimination in favor of HCEs for Plan F to use the special rule for a formula that is available solely to some or all NHCEs to satisfy the separate testing requirement of paragraph (b)(6)(xi)(C) of this section for the 1994 calendar plan year. See §1.401(a)(4)-1(c)(2).

(c) *General test for nondiscrimination in amount of benefits.*—(1) *General rule.*—The employer-provided benefits under a defined benefit plan are nondiscriminatory in amount for a plan year if each rate group under the plan satisfies section 410(b). For purposes of this

paragraph (c)(1), a rate group exists under a plan for each HCE and consists of the HCE and all other employees (both HCEs and NHCEs) who have a normal accrual rate greater than or equal to the HCE's normal accrual rate, and who also have a most valuable accrual rate greater than or equal to the HCE's most valuable accrual rate. Thus, an employee is in the rate group for each HCE who has a normal accrual rate less than or equal to the employee's normal accrual rate, and who also has a most valuable accrual rate less than or equal to the employee's most valuable accrual rate.

(2) *Satisfaction of section 410(b) by a rate group.*—For purposes of determining whether a rate group satisfies section 410(b), the same rules apply as in §1.401(a)(4)-2(c)(3). See paragraph (c)(4) of this section and §1.401(a)(4)-2(c)(4), *Example 3* through *Example 5*, for examples of this rule.

(3) *Certain violations disregarded.*—A plan is deemed to satisfy paragraph (c)(1) of this section if the plan would satisfy that paragraph by treating as not benefiting no more than five percent of the HCEs in the plan, and the Commissioner determines that, on the basis of all of the relevant facts and circumstances, the plan does not discriminate with respect to the amount of employer-provided benefits. For this purpose, five percent of the number of HCEs may be determined by rounding to the nearest whole number (e.g., 1.4 rounds to 1 and 1.5 rounds to 2). Among the relevant factors that the Commissioner may consider in making this determination are—

(i) The extent to which the plan has failed the test in paragraph (c)(1) of this section;

(ii) The extent to which the failure is for reasons other than the design of the plan;

(iii) Whether the HCEs causing the failure are five-percent owners or are among the highest paid nonexcludable employees;

(iv) Whether the failure is attributable to an event that is not expected to recur (e.g., a plant closing); and

(v) The extent to which the failure is attributable to benefits accrued under a prior benefit structure or to benefits accrued when a participant was not a HCE.

(4) *Examples.*—The following examples illustrate the rules in this paragraph (c):

Example 1. (a) Employer X has 1100 nonexcludable employees, N1 through N1000, who are NHCEs, and H1 through H100, who are HCEs. Employer X maintains Plan A, a defined benefit plan that benefits all of these nonexcludable employees. The normal and most valuable accrual rates (determined as a percentage of average annual compensation) for the employees in Plan A for the 1994 plan year are listed in the following table.

Employee	Normal Accrual Rate	Most Valuable Accrual Rate
N1 through N100	1.0	1.4
N101 through N500	1.5	3.0
N501 through N750	2.0	2.65
N751 through N1000	2.3	2.8
H1 through H50	1.5	2.0
H51 through H100	2.0	2.65

(b) There are 100 rate groups in Plan A because there are 100 HCEs in Plan A.

(c) Rate group 1 consists of H1 and all those employees who have a normal accrual rate greater than or equal to H1's normal accrual rate (1.5 percent) and who also have a most valuable accrual rate greater than or equal to H1's most valuable accrual rate (2.0 percent). Thus, rate group 1 consists of H1 through H100 and N101 through N1000.

(d) Rate group 1 satisfies the ratio percentage test of §1.410(b)-2(b)(2) because the ratio percentage of the rate group is 90 percent, i.e., 90 percent (the percentage of all non-highly compensated nonexcludable employees who are in the rate group) divided by 100 percent (the percentage of all highly compensated nonexcludable employees who are in the rate group).

(e) Because H1 through H50 have the same normal accrual rates and the same most valuable accrual rates, the rate group with respect to each of them is identical. Thus, because rate group 1 satisfies section 410(b), rate groups 2 through 50 also satisfy section 410(b).

(f) Rate group 51 consists of H51 and all those employees who have a normal accrual rate greater than or equal to H51's normal accrual rate (2.0 percent) and who also have a most valuable accrual rate greater than or equal to H51's most valuable accrual rate (2.65 percent). Thus, rate group 51 consists of H51 through H100 and N501 through N1000. (Even though N101 through N500 have a most valuable accrual rate (3.0 percent) greater than H51's most valuable accrual rate (2.65 percent), they are not included in this rate group because their normal accrual rate (1.5 percent) is less than H51's normal accrual rate (2.0 percent).)

(g) Rate group 51 satisfies the ratio percentage test of §1.410(b)-2(b)(2) because the ratio percentage of the rate group is 100 percent, i.e., 50 percent (the percentage of all non-highly compensated nonexcludable employees who are in the rate group) divided by 50 percent (the percentage of all highly compensated nonexcludable employees who are in the rate group).

(h) Because H51 through H100 have the same normal accrual rates and the same most valuable accrual rates, the rate group with respect to each of them is identical. Thus, because rate group 51 satisfies section 410(b), rate groups 52 through 100 also satisfy section 410(b).

(i) The employer-provided benefits under Plan A are nondiscriminatory in amount because each rate group under the plan satisfies section 410(b).

Example 2. The facts are the same as in *Example 1,* except that H96 has a most valuable accrual rate of 3.5. Each of the rate groups is the same as in *Example 1,* except that rate group 96 consists solely of H96 because no other employee has a most valuable accrual rate greater than 3.5. Because the plan would satisfy the test in paragraph (c)(1) of this section by treating H96 (who constitutes less than five percent of the HCEs in the plan) as not benefiting, the Commissioner may determine under paragraph (c)(3) of this section that, on the basis of all of the relevant facts and circumstances, the plan does not discriminate with respect to the amount of benefits.

(d) *Determination of accrual rates.*—(1) *Definitions.*—(i) *Normal accrual rate.*—The normal accrual rate for an employee for a plan year is the increase in the employee's accrued benefit (within the meaning of section 411(a)(7)(A)(i)) during the measurement period, divided by the employee's testing service during the measurement period, and expressed either as a dollar amount or as a percentage of the employee's average annual compensation.

(ii) *Most valuable accrual rate.*—The most valuable accrual rate for an employee for a plan year is the increase in the employee's most valuable optional form of payment of the accrued benefit during the measurement period, divided by the employee's testing service during the measurement period, and expressed either as a dollar amount or as a percentage of the employee's average annual compensation. The employee's most valuable optional form of payment of the accrued benefit is determined by calculating for the employee the normalized QJSA associated with the accrued benefit that is potentially payable in the current or any future plan year at any age under the plan and selecting the largest (per year of testing service). If the plan provides a QSUPP, the most valuable accrual rate also takes into account the QSUPP payable in conjunction with the QJSA at each age under the plan. Thus, the most valuable accrual rate reflects the value of all benefits accrued or treated as accrued under section 411(d)(6) that are payable in any form and at any time under the plan, including early retirement benefits, retirement-type subsidies, early retirement window benefits, and QSUPPs. In addition, the most valuable accrual rate must take into account any such benefits that are available during a plan year, even if the benefits cease to be available before the end of the current or any future plan year.

(iii) *Measurement period.*—The measurement period can be—
(A) The current plan year;
(B) The current plan year and all prior years; or
(C) The current plan year and all prior and future years.

(iv) *Testing service.*—(A) *General rule.*—Testing service means an employee's years of service as defined in the plan for purposes of applying the benefit formula under the plan, subject to the requirements of paragraph (d)(1)(iv)(B) of this section. Alternatively, testing service means service determined for all employees in a reasonable manner that satisfies the requirements of paragraph (d)(1)(iv)(B) of this section. For example, the number of plan years that an employee has benefited under the plan within the meaning of §1.410(b)-3(a) is an acceptable definition of testing service because it determines service in a reasonable manner and satisfies paragraph (d)(1)(iv)(B) of this section. See also §1.401(a)(4)11(d)(3) (additional limits on service that may be taken into account as testing service).

(B) *Requirements for testing service.*—(1) Employees not credited with years of service under the benefit formula. An employee must be credited with testing service for any year in which the employee benefits under the plan (within the meaning of §1.410(b)-3(a)), unless that year is part of a period of service that may not be taken into account under §1.401(a)(4)-11(d)(3). (This rule applies even if the employee does not receive service credit under the benefit formula for that year (e.g., because of a service cap in the benefit formula or because of a transfer out of the group of employees covered by the plan).

(2) *Current year testing service.*—In the case of a measurement period that is the current plan year, testing service for the plan year equals one (1).

(2) *Rules of application.*—(i) *Consistency requirement.*—Both normal and most valuable accrual rates must be determined in a consistent manner for all employees for the plan year. Thus, for example, the same measurement periods must be used, and the rules of this paragraph (d)(2) and any available options described in paragraph (d)(3) of this section must be applied consistently. If plan benefits are not expressed as straight life annuities beginning at employees' testing ages, they must be normalized.

(ii) *Determining plan benefits, service and compensation.*—(A) *In general.*—Potential plan benefits, testing service, and average annual compensation must be determined in a reasonable manner, reflecting actual or projected service and compensation only through the end of the measurement period. The determination of potential plan benefits is not reasonable if it incorporates an assumption that, in future years, an employee's compensation will increase or the employee will terminate employment before the employee's testing age (other than the assumptions under paragraph (d)(1)(ii) of this section that the employee's service will end in connection with the payment of each potential QJSA in future years).

(B) *Section 415 limits.*—For purposes of determining accrual rates under this paragraph (d), plan benefits are generally determined without regard to whether those benefits are permitted to be paid under section 415. However, plan provisions implementing any of the limits of section 415 may be taken into account in applying this paragraph (d) if the plan does not provide for benefit increases resulting from section 415(d)(1) adjustments for former employees who were employees in a plan year in which such plan provisions were taken into account in applying this paragraph (d). If the limits of section 415 are taken into account under this paragraph (d)(2)(ii)(B) as of the end of the measurement period, they must also be taken into account as of the beginning of the measurement period. If the limits of section 415 are not taken into account in testing the plan for the current plan year, but were taken into account in testing the plan for the preceding plan year, any resulting increase in the accrued benefits taken into account in testing the plan is treated as an increase in accrued benefits during the current plan year.

(iii) *Requirements for measurement period that includes future years.*—(A) *Discriminatory pattern of accruals.*—A measurement period that includes future years (as described in paragraph (d)(1)(iii)(C) of this section) may not be used if the pattern of accruals under the plan discriminates in favor of HCEs (i.e., if projected benefits for HCEs are relatively front-loaded when compared to the degree of frontloading or backloading for NHCEs). This determination is made based on all of the relevant facts and circumstances.

(B) *Future-period limitation.*—Future years beginning after an employee's attainment of the employee's testing age (or after the employee's assumed termination in the case of most valuable accrual rates) may not be included in the measurement period.

(3) *Optional rules.*—(i) *Imputation of permitted disparity.*—The disparity permitted under section 401(l) may be imputed in accordance with the rules of §1.401(a)(4)-7.

(ii) *Grouping of accrual rates.*—(A) *General rule.*—An employer may treat all employees who have accrual rates within a specified range above and below a midpoint rate chosen by the employer as having an accrual rate equal to the midpoint rate within that range. Accrual rates within a given range may not be grouped under this paragraph (d)(3)(ii) if the accrual rates of HCEs within the range generally are significantly higher than the accrual rates of NHCEs in the range. The specified ranges within which all employees are treated as having the same accrual rate may not overlap and may be no larger than provided in paragraph (d)(3)(ii)(B) of this section. Accrual rates of employees that are not within any of these specified ranges are determined without regard to this paragraph (d)(3)(ii).

(B) *Size of specified ranges.*—In the case of normal accrual rates, the lowest and highest accrual rates in the range must be within five percent (not five percentage points) of the midpoint rate. In the case of most valuable accrual rates, the lowest and highest accrual rates in the range must be within 15 percent (not 15 percentage points) of the midpoint rate. If accrual rates are determined as a percentage of average annual compensation, the lowest and highest accrual rates need not be within five percent (or 15 percent) of the midpoint rate, if they are no more than one twentieth of a percentage point above or below the midpoint rate.

(iii) *Fresh-start alternative.*—(A) *General rule.*—Notwithstanding the definition of measurement period provided in paragraph (d)(1)(iii) of this section, a measurement period for a fresh-start group is permitted to be limited to the period beginning after the fresh-start date with respect to that group if the plan makes a fresh start that satisfies §1.401(a)(4)-13(c) (without regard to §1.401(a)(4)-13(c)(2)(i) and (ii)). If the measurement period is so limited or the measurement period is the plan year (whether or not so limited), any compensation adjustments during the measurement period to the frozen accrued benefit as of the fresh-start date that are permitted under the rules of §1.401(a)(4)-13(d) may be disregarded in determining the increase in accrued benefits during the measurement period, but only if—

(1) The plan makes a fresh start as of the fresh-start date that satisfies §1.401(a)(4)-13(c) (without regard to §1.401(a)(4)-13(c)(2)(ii)) in conjunction with a bona fide amendment to the benefit formula or accrual method under the plan; and

(2) The amendment provides for adjustments to employees' frozen accrued benefits as of the fresh-start date in accordance with the rules of §1.401(a)(4)-13(d).

(B) *Application of consistency requirements.*—Limiting the application of the fresh-start alternative in this paragraph (d)(3)(iii) to a fresh-start group that consists of fewer than all employees does not violate the consistency requirement of paragraph (d)(2)(i) of this section.

(iv) *Floor on most valuable accrual rate.*—In lieu of determining an employee's most valuable accrual rate in accordance with the definition in paragraph (d)(1)(ii) of this section, an employer may determine an employee's most valuable accrual rate for the current plan year as the employee's highest most valuable accrual rate determined for any prior plan year. This option may be used only if the employee's normal accrual rate has not changed significantly from the normal accrual rate for the relevant prior plan year, and there have been no plan amendments in the interim period since that prior plan year that affect the determination of most valuable accrual rate.

(4) *Examples.*—The following examples illustrate the rules in this paragraph (d):

Example 1. The employees in Plan A have the following normal accrual rates (expressed as percentage of average annual compensation): 0.8 percent, 0.83 percent, 0.9 percent, 1.9 percent, 2.0 percent, and 2.1 percent. Because the first three rates are within a range of no more than one twentieth of a percentage point above or below 0.85 percent (a midpoint rate chosen by the employer), the employer may treat the employees who have those rates as having an accrual rate of 0.85 percent (provided that the accrual rates of HCEs within the range are not significantly higher than the accrual rates for NHCEs within the range). Because the last three rates are within a range of no more than five percent above or below 2.0 percent (a midpoint rate chosen by the employer), the employer may treat the employees who have those rates as having an accrual rate of 2.0 percent (provided that the accrual rates of HCEs within the range are not significantly higher than the accrual rates for NHCEs within the range).

Example 2. Employer X maintains a plan under which headquarters employees accrue a benefit of 1.25 percent of average compensation for the first 10 years of service and 0.75 percent of average compensation for subsequent years of service, while all other employees accrue a benefit of one percent of compensation for all years of service. Assume that the group of headquarters employees does not satisfy section 410(b). Under these facts, the pattern of accruals under the plan discriminates in favor of HCEs, and, therefore, under paragraph (d)(2)(iii)(A) of this section, the measurement period for determining accrual rates under the plan may not include future service.

(e) *Compensation rules.*—(1) *In general.*—This paragraph (e) provides rules for determining average annual compensation. Safe harbor plans that satisfy paragraph (b) of this section must determine benefits either as a dollar amount unrelated to employees' compensation or as a percentage of each employee's average annual compensation. In contrast, plans that must satisfy the general test of paragraph (c) of this section are not required under this section to determine benefits under any particular definition of compensation or in any particular manner, but the accrual rates used in testing these plans must be expressed either as a dollar amount or determined as a percentage of each employee's average annual compensation.

(2) *Average annual compensation.*—(i) *General rule.*—An employee's average annual compensation is the average of the employee's annual section 414(s) compensation determined over the averaging period in the employee's compensation history during which the average of the employee's annual section 414(s) compensation is the highest. For this purpose, an averaging period must consist of three or more consecutive 12-month periods, but need not be longer than the employee's period of employment. An employee's compensation history may begin at any time, but must be continuous, be no shorter than the averaging period, and end in the current plan year.

(ii) *Certain permitted modifications to average annual compensation.*—(A) *Use of plan year compensation.*—If the measurement period for determination of accrual rates is the current plan year, or the plan is an accumulation plan that satisfies paragraph (b) of this section, then plan year compensation may be substituted for average annual compensation.

(B) *Drop-out years.*—Any of the following types of 12-month periods in an employee's compensation history may be disregarded in determining the employee's average annual compensation (including for purposes of the requirement to average section 414(s) compensation over consecutive 12-month periods), but only if the plan disregards the employee's compensation for those periods in determining benefits—

(1) The 12-month period in which the employee terminates employment;

(2) All 12-month periods in which the employee performs no services; or

(3) All 12-month periods in which the employee performs services for less than a specified number of hours or specified period of time in the 12-month period. The specified number of hours or specified period of time may be selected by the employer, but may not exceed three quarters of the time that an employee in the same job category working on a full-time basis would perform services during that 12-month period.

(C) *Drop-out months within 12-month periods.*—If a plan determines an employee's average annual compensation using 12-month periods that do not end on a fixed date (e.g., average annual compensation as of a date is defined as the average of the employee's section 414(s) compensation for the 60 consecutive months within the compensation history in which the average is highest), then, for purposes of determining a 12-month period, any of the following type of months may be disregarded (including for purposes of the requirement to average section 414(s) compensation over consecutive 12-month periods), but only if the plan disregards the employee's compensation for those months in determining benefits—

(1) The month in which the employee terminates employment;

(2) All months in which the employee performs no services; or

(3) All months in which the employee performs services for less than a specified number of hours or specified period of time in the month. The specified number of hours or specified period of time may be selected by the employer, but may not exceed three quarters of the time that an employee in the same job category working on a full-time basis would perform services during that month.

(D) *Employees working less than full-time.*—In the case of an employee who normally works less than full-time, the rules in paragraphs (e)(2)(ii)(B)(3) and (e)(2)(ii)(C)(3) of this section may be applied in relation to that employee's normal work schedule (instead of a full-time employee's work schedule) by prorating the specified number of hours or specified period of time, based on the employee's normal work schedule as a fraction of a full-time schedule.

(E) *Exception from consecutive-periods requirement for certain plans.*—The requirement that the periods taken into account under paragraph (e)(2)(i) of this section be consecutive does not apply in the case of a plan that is not a section 401(l) plan, provided that it does not take permitted disparity into account under §1.401(a)(4)-7. This paragraph (e)(2)(ii)(E) applies only if the plan does not take into account whether 12-month periods of compensation are consecutive in determining average compensation for purposes of calculating benefits.

(iii) *Consistency requirements.*—Average annual compensation must be determined in a consistent manner for all employees.

(3) *Examples.*—The following examples illustrate the rules in this paragraph (e):

Example 1. Plan A is a defined benefit plan. Plan A determines benefits on the basis of the average of each employee's annual compensation for the five consecutive plan years (or the employee's period of employment, if shorter) during the employee's compensation history in which the average of the employee's annual compensation is the highest. The compensation history used for this purpose is the last 10 plan years, plus the current plan year. In determining compensation for each plan year in the compensation history, Plan A defines compensation using a single definition that satisfies section 414(s) as a safe harbor definition under §1.414(s)-1(c). Plan A determines benefits on the basis of average annual compensation.

Example 2. Plan B is a defined benefit plan. Plan B determines benefits on the basis of the average of each employee's compensation for the five consecutive 12-month periods (or the employee's period of employment, if shorter) during the employee's compensation history in which the average of the employee's annual compensation is the highest. The compensation history used for this purpose is the 10 consecutive 12-month periods ending on the employee's termination date. In determining the average, Plan B disregards all months in which the employee performs services for less than 100 hours (60 percent of a full-time work schedule of 173 hours). In the case of an employee whose normal work schedule is less than a full-time schedule, Plan B disregards all months in which that employee performs services for less than 60 percent of the employee's normal work schedule. Plan B defines compensation for each 12-month period using a single definition that satisfies §1.414(s)-1. Plan B determines benefits on the basis of average annual compensation.

Example 3. (a) The facts are the same as in *Example 1*, except that, for plan years prior to 1996, the compensation for a plan year was determined under a rate of pay definition of compensation that satisfies section 414(s), while, for plan years after 1995, the compensation for a plan year is determined using a definition that satisfies section 414(s) as a safe harbor definition under §1.414(s)-1(c).

(b) The underlying definition of compensation for each plan year in the employee's compensation history is section 414(s) compensation, because for each plan year the definition satisfies the requirements for section 414(s) compensation under §1.401(a)(4)-12. Therefore, Plan A determines benefits on the basis of average annual compensation, even though the underlying definition used to measure the amount of compensation for each plan year in an employee's compensation history is not the same for all plan years.

Example 4. The facts are the same as in *Example 1*, except that Plan A determines benefits on the basis of the average of the employee's annual section 414(s) compensation for the five consecutive 12-month periods ending on June 30 during the employee's compensation history in which the average is highest. An employee's compensation history begins when the employee commences participation in the plan and ends in the current plan year. In the case of an employee with less than five consecutive years of plan participation as of June 30, the compensation history is extended prior to the employee's commencement of participation to include the five consecutive 12-month periods ending on June 30 of the current plan year (or the employee's total period of employment, if shorter). Plan A determines benefits on the basis of average annual compensation.

Example 5. The facts are the same as in *Example 4*, except that Plan A determines benefits on the basis of the average of each employee's compensation for the employee's entire compensation history. Plan A determines benefits on the basis of average annual compensation.

(f) *Special rules.*—(1) *In general.*—The special rules in this paragraph (f) apply for purposes of applying the provisions of this section to a defined benefit plan. Any special rule provided in this paragraph (f) that is optional must, if used, apply uniformly to all employees.

(2) *Certain qualified disability benefits.*—In general, qualified disability benefits (within the meaning of section 411(a)(9)) are not taken into account under this section. However, a qualified disability benefit that results from the crediting of compensation or service for a period of disability in the same manner as actual compensation or service is credited under a plan's benefit formula is permitted to be taken into account under this section as an accrued benefit upon the employee's return to service with the employer following the period of disability, provided that the qualified disability benefit is then treated in the same manner as an accrued benefit for all purposes under the plan.

(3) *Accruals after normal retirement age.*—(i) *General rule.*—An employee's accruals for any plan year after the plan year in which the employee attains normal retirement age are taken into account for purposes of this section. However, any plan provision that provides for increases in an employee's accrued benefit solely because the employee has delayed commencing benefits beyond the normal retirement age applicable to the employee under the plan may be disregarded, but only if—

(A) The same uniform normal retirement age applies to all employees; and

(B) The percentage factor used to increase the employee's accrued benefit is no greater than the largest percentage factor that could be applied to increase actuarially the employee's accrued benefit using any standard mortality table and any standard interest rate.

(ii) *Examples.*—The following examples illustrate the rules of this paragraph (f)(3). In each example, it is assumed that the plan satisfies the requirements of paragraph (f)(3)(i)(A) and (B) of this section.

Example 1. Plan A provides a benefit of two percent of average annual compensation per year of service for all employees. In addi-

tion, Plan A provides an actuarial increase in an employee's accrued benefit of six percent for each year that an employee defers commencement of benefits beyond normal retirement age. For employees who continue in service beyond normal retirement age, the employee's two-percent accrual for the current plan year is offset by the six-percent actuarial increase, as permitted under section 411(b)(1)(H)(iii)(II). For purposes of this section, the actuarial increase (and hence the offset) may be disregarded, and thus all employees may be treated as if they were accruing at the rate of two percent of average annual compensation per year.

Example 2. The facts are the same as in *Example 1*, except that the employee's two-percent accrual for the current plan year is not offset by the six-percent actuarial increase. The employer may disregard the actuarial increase and thus may treat all employees as if they were accruing at the rate of two percent of average annual compensation per year.

(4) *Early retirement window benefits.*—(i) *General rule.*—In applying the requirements of this section, all early retirement benefits, retirement-type subsidies, QSUPPs, and other optional forms of benefit under a plan, and changes in the plan's benefit formula, are taken into account regardless of whether they are permanent features of the plan or are offered only to employees whose employment terminates within a limited period of time. Additional rules and examples relevant to the testing of early retirement window benefits are found in *Example 6* of paragraph (b)(2)(vi) of this section; paragraph (b)(2)(ii)(A)(2), *Example 2* of paragraph (c)(2), paragraph (d)(3), and *Example 3* of paragraph (e)(1)(iii) of §1.401(a)(4)-4; paragraph (c)(4)(i) and *Example 2* of paragraph (c)(6) of §1.401(a)(4)-9; and the definition of benefit formula in §1.401(a)(4)-12.

(ii) *Special rules.*—(A) *Year in which early retirement window benefit taken into account.*—Notwithstanding paragraph (f)(4)(i) of this section, an early retirement window benefit is disregarded for purposes of determining whether a plan satisfies this section with respect to an employee for all plan years other than the first plan year in which the benefit is currently available (within the meaning of §1.401(a)(4)-4(b)(2)) to the employee. For purposes of this paragraph (f)(4)(ii)(A), in determining which plan years the benefit is currently available, an early retirement window benefit that consists of a temporary change in the plan's benefit formula is treated as an optional form of benefit.

(B) *Treatment of early retirement window benefit that consists of temporary change in benefit formula.*—An early retirement window benefit is disregarded for purposes of determining an employee's normal accrual rate, even if the early retirement window benefit consists of a temporary change in a plan's benefit formula. However, if an early retirement window benefit consists of a temporary change in a plan's benefit formula, the plan does not satisfy paragraph (b) of this section during the period for which the change is effective unless the plan satisfies paragraph (b) of this section both reflecting the temporary change in the benefit formula and disregarding that change.

(C) *Effect of early retirement window benefit on most valuable accrual rate.*—In determining an employee's most valuable optional form of payment of the accrued benefit (which is used in determining the employee's most valuable accrual rate under paragraphs (d)(1)(ii) and (f)(4)(i) of this section), an early retirement window benefit that is currently available to the employee (within the meaning of paragraph (f)(4)(ii)(A) of this section) and that is not disregarded for a plan year under paragraph (f)(4)(ii)(A) of this section is taken into account in that plan year with respect to the employee's accrued benefit as of the earliest of the employee's date of termination, the close of the early retirement window, or the last day of that plan year.

(D) *Effect of early retirement window benefit on average benefit percentage test.*—Notwithstanding paragraph (c)(2) of this section, a rate group under a plan that provides an early retirement window benefit is deemed to satisfy the average benefit percentage test of §1.410(b)-5 if—

(1) All rate groups under the plan would satisfy the ratio percentage test of §1.410(b)-2(b)(2) if the early retirement window benefit were disregarded; and

(2) The group of employees to whom the early retirement window benefit is currently available (within the meaning of paragraph (f)(4)(ii)(A) of this section) satisfies section 410(b) without regard to the average benefit percentage test of §1.410(b)-5.

(iii) *Early retirement window benefit defined.*—For purposes of this paragraph (f)(4), an early retirement window benefit is an early retirement benefit, retirement-type subsidy, QSUPP, or other optional form of benefit under a plan that is available, or a change in the plan's benefit formula that is applicable, only to employees who terminate employment within a limited period specified by the plan (not to exceed one year) under circumstances specified by the plan. A benefit does not fail to be described in the preceding sentence merely because the plan contains provisions under which certain employees may receive the benefit even though, for bona fide business reasons, they terminate employment within a reasonable period after the end of the limited period. An amendment to an early retirement window benefit that merely extends the periods in the preceding sentences is not treated as a separate early retirement window benefit, provided that the periods, as extended, satisfy the preceding sentences. However, any other amendment to an early retirement window benefit creates a separate early retirement window benefit.

(iv) *Examples.*—The following examples illustrate the rules of this paragraph (f)(4):

Example 1. (a) Plan A provides a benefit of one percent of average annual compensation per year of service and satisfies the requirements of paragraph (b)(2) of this section. Thus, the plan provides the same benefit to all employees with the same years of service under the Plan. Plan A is amended to treat all employees with ten or more years of service who terminate employment after attainment of age 55 and between March 1, 1999, and January 31, 2000, as if they had an additional five years of service under the benefit formula. However, in order to ensure the orderly implementation of the early retirement window, the plan amendment provides that designated employees in the human resources department who would otherwise be eligible for the early retirement window benefit are eligible to be treated as having the additional five years of service only if they terminate between January 1, 2000, and April 30, 2000.

(b) The additional benefits provided under this amendment are tested as benefits provided to employees rather than former employees. The effect of this amendment is temporarily to change the benefit formula for employees who are eligible for the early retirement window benefit because the amendment changes (albeit temporarily) the amount of the benefit payable to those employees at normal retirement age. See the definition of benefit formula in §1.401(a)(4)-12. Assume that the additional years of service credited to employees eligible for the window benefit do not represent past service (within the meaning of §1.401(a)(4)-11(d)(3)(i)(B)) or pre-participation or imputed service (within the meaning of §1.401(a)(4)-11(d)(3)(ii)(A) or (B), respectively) and thus may not be taken into account as years of service. See §1.401(a)(4)-11(d)(3)(i)(A) (regarding years of service that may not be taken into account under §1.401(a)(4)-1(b)(2)). Thus, the window-eligible employees are entitled to a larger benefit (as a percentage of average annual compensation) than other employees with the same number of years of service, and the plan does not satisfy the uniform normal retirement benefit requirement of paragraph (b)(2)(i) of this section.

(c) Plan A is restructured under the provisions of §1.401(a)(4)-9(c) into two component plans: Component Plan A1, consisting of all employees who are not eligible for the early retirement window benefit and all of their accruals and benefits, rights, and features under the plan, and Component Plan A2, consisting of all employees who are eligible for the early retirement window benefit (including the designated employees in the human resource department) and all of their accruals and benefits, rights, and features under the plan.

(d) Component Plan A1 still satisfies paragraph (b) of this section, because there has been no change for the employees in that component plan. Similarly, Component Plan A2 satisfies paragraph (b) of this section disregarding the change in the benefit formula.

(e) Because the early retirement window benefit consists of a temporary change in the benefit formula, paragraph (f)(4)(ii)(B) of this section requires that the plan satisfy the requirements of paragraph (b) of this section reflecting the change in order to remain a safe harbor plan. After reflecting the change, Component Plan A2 still provides the same benefit (albeit higher than under the regular benefit formula) to all employees with the same years of service that may be taken into account in testing the plan, and thus the benefit formula (as temporarily amended) satisfies the requirements of paragraphs (b)(2)(i) and (ii) of this section.

(f) Since Component Plan A2 also satisfies all of the other requirements of paragraph (b)(2) of this section and the safe harbor of paragraph (b)(3) of this section reflecting the change in the benefit formula, Component Plan A2 satisfies this paragraph (b) both reflecting and disregarding the change in the benefit formula. Thus, Component Plan A2 satisfies paragraph (b) of this section.

Example 2. The facts are the same as in *Example 1*, except that Plan A's benefit formula used the maximum amount of permitted disparity under section 401(l) prior to the amendment. The analysis is the same as in paragraphs (a) through the first sentence of paragraph (e) of *Example 1*. In order to satisfy the requirements of paragraph (b)(2) of this section, a plan that uses permitted disparity must satisfy the requirements of section 401(l) after reflecting the change in the benefit formula. Because, as stated in *Example 1*, the additional five years of service may not be taken into account for purposes of

satisfying paragraph (b) of this section, the disparity that results from crediting that service exceeds the maximum permitted disparity under section 401(l). Thus, Component Plan A2 does not satisfy the requirements of paragraph (b) of this section.

Example 3. The facts are the same as in *Example 1*, except that Plan A is tested under the general test in paragraph (c) of this section. The early retirement window benefit is disregarded for purposes of determining the normal accrual rates, but is taken into account in 1999 for purposes of determining the most valuable accrual rates, of employees who were eligible for the early retirement window benefit (regardless of whether they elected to receive it). As stated in *Example 1*, the additional five years of service do not represent past service, pre-participation service, or imputed service, and thus under §1.401(a)(4)-11(d)(3)(i)(A) may not be taken into account as testing service.

(5) *Unpredictable contingent event benefits.*—(i) *General rule.*—In general, an unpredictable contingent event benefit (within the meaning of section 412(l)(7)(B)(ii)) is not taken into account under this section until the occurrence of the contingent event. Thus, the special rule in §1.401(a)(4)-4(d)(7) (treating the contingent event as having occurred) does not apply for purposes of this section. In the case of an unpredictable contingent event that is expected to result in the termination from employment of certain employees within a period of time consistent with the rules for defining an early retirement window benefit in paragraph (f)(4)(iii) of this section, the unpredictable contingent event benefit available to those employees is permitted to be treated as an early retirement window benefit, thus permitting the rules of paragraph (f)(4) of this section to be applied to it.

(ii) *Example.*—The following example illustrates the rules of this paragraph (f)(5):

Example. (a) Employer X operates various manufacturing plants and maintains Plan A, a defined benefit plan that covers all of its nonexcludable employees. Plan A provides an early retirement benefit under which employees who retire after age 55 but before normal retirement age and who have at least 10 years of service receive a benefit equal to their normal retirement benefit reduced by four percent per year for each year prior to normal retirement age. Plan A also provides a plant-closing benefit under which employees who satisfy the conditions for receiving the early retirement benefit and who work at a plant where operations have ceased and whose employment has been terminated will receive an unreduced normal retirement benefit. The plant-closing benefit is an unpredictable contingent event benefit.

(b) During the 1997 plan year, Employer X had no plant closings. Therefore, the plant-closing benefit is not taken into account for the 1997 plan year in determining accrual rates or in applying the safe harbors in paragraph (b) of this section.

(c) During the 1998 plan year, Employer X begins to close one plant. Employees M through Z, who are employees at the plant that is closing, are expected to terminate employment with Employer X during the plan year and will satisfy the conditions for the plant-closing benefit. Therefore, in testing Plan A under this section for the 1998 plan year, the availability of the plant-closing benefit to Employees M through Z must be taken into account in determining their accrual rates or in determining whether the plan satisfies one of the safe harbors under paragraph (b) of this section.

(d) Because the employees eligible for the unpredictable contingent event benefit are expected to terminate employment with Employer X during a period consistent with the rules for defining an early retirement window benefit, in testing Plan A under this section for the 1998 plan year, the special rules in paragraph (f)(4)(ii) of this section may be applied. Thus, for example, normal accrual rates may be determined without reference to the unpredictable contingent event benefit.

(e) Despite the closing of the plant, Employee Q remains an employee into the 1999 plan year. Under paragraph (f)(4)(ii)(A) of this section, the availability of the plant-closing benefit to Employee Q may be disregarded in the 1999 plan year.

(6) *Determination of benefits on other than plan-year basis.*—For purposes of this section, accruals are generally determined based on the plan year. Nevertheless, an employer may determine accruals on the basis of any period ending within the plan year as long as the period is at least 12 months in duration. For example, accruals for all employees may be determined based on accrual computation periods ending within the plan year.

(7) *Adjustments for certain plan distributions.*—For purposes of this section, an employee's accrued benefit includes the actuarial equivalent of prior distributions of accrued benefits from the plan to the employee if the years of service taken into account in determining the accrued benefits that were distributed continue to be taken into account under the plan for purposes of determining the em-

ployee's current accrued benefit. For purposes of this paragraph (f)(7), actuarial equivalence must be determined in a uniform manner for all employees using reasonable actuarial assumptions. A standard interest rate and a standard mortality table are among the assumptions considered reasonable for this purpose. Thus, for example, if an employee has commenced receipt of benefits in accordance with the minimum distribution requirements of section 401(a)(9), and the plan reduces the employee's accrued benefit to take into account the amount of the distributions, the employee's accrued benefit for purposes of this section is restored to the value it would have had if the distributions had not occurred.

(8) *Adjustment for certain QPSA charges.*—For purposes of this section, an employee's accrued benefit includes the cost of a qualified preretirement survivor annuity (QPSA) that reduces the employee's accrued benefit otherwise determined under the plan, as permitted under §1.401(a)-20, Q&A-21. Thus, an employee's accrued benefit for purposes of this section is determined as if the cost of the QPSA had not been charged against the accrued benefit. This paragraph (f)(8) applies only if the QPSA charges apply uniformly to all employees.

(9) *Disregard of certain offsets.*—(i) *General rule.*—For purposes of this section, an employee's accrued benefit under a plan includes that portion of the benefit that is offset under an offset provision described in §1.401(a)(4)-11(d)(3)(i)(D). The rule in the preceding sentence applies only to the extent that the benefit by which the benefit under the plan being tested is offset is attributable to periods for which the plan being tested credits pre-participation service (within the meaning of §1.401(a)(4)-11(d)(3)(ii)(A)) that satisfies §1.401(a)(4)-11(d)(3)(iii) or past service (within the meaning of §1.401(a)(4)-11(d)(3)(i)(B)), and only if—

(A) The benefit under the plan being tested is offset by either—

(1) Benefits under a qualified defined benefit plan or defined contribution plan (whether or not terminated); or

(2) Benefits under a foreign plan that are reasonably expected to be paid; and,

(B) If any portion of the benefit that is offset is nonforfeitable (within the meaning of section 411), that portion is offset by a benefit (or portion of a benefit) that is also nonforfeitable (or vested, in the case of a foreign plan).

(ii) *Examples.*—The following examples illustrate the rules in this paragraph (f)(9):

Example 1. (a) Employer X maintains two qualified defined benefit plans, Plan A and Plan B. Plan B provides that, whenever an employee transfers to Plan B from Plan A, the service that was credited under Plan A is credited in determining benefits under Plan B. The Plan A service credited under Plan B is pre-participation service that satisfies §1.401(a)(4)-11(d)(3)(iii). Plan B offsets the benefits determined under Plan B by the employee's vested benefits under Plan A. Plan A does not credit additional benefit service or accrual service after employees transfer to Plan B.

(b) The Plan B provision providing for an offset of benefits under Plan A satisfies §1.401(a)(4)-11(d)(3)(i)(D). This is because the provision applies to similarly-situated employees and the benefits under Plan A that are offset against the Plan B benefits are attributable to pre-participation service taken into account under Plan B.

(c) This paragraph (f)(9) applies in determining the benefits that are taken into account under this section for employees in Plan B who are transferred from Plan A. This is because the offset provision is described in §1.401(a)(4)-11(d)(3)(i)(D), the benefits under the other plan by which the benefits under the plan being tested are offset are attributable solely to pre-participation service that satisfies §1.401(a)(4)-11(d)(3)(iii), and the benefits are offset solely by vested benefits under another qualified plan. Thus, for example, the accrual rates of employees in Plan B are determined as if there were no offset, i.e., by adding back the benefits that are offset to the net benefits under Plan B.

(d) The result would be the same even if Plan A continued to recognize compensation paid after the transfer in the determination of benefits under Plan A. However, if Plan A continued to credit benefit or accrual service after the transfer, then, to the extent that Plan B's offset of benefits under Plan A increased as a result, the additional benefits offset under Plan B would not be added back in determining the benefits under Plan B that are taken into account under this section.

Example 2. The facts are the same as in *Example 1*, except that Plan A is not a plan described in paragraph (f)(9)(i)(A) of this section. None of the benefits under Plan B that are offset by benefits under Plan A may be added back in determining the benefits under Plan B that are taken into account under this section. Thus, benefits under Plan B are tested on a net basis.

(10) *Special rule for multiemployer plans.*—For purposes of this section, if a multiemployer plan increases benefits for service prior to

a specific date subject to a plan provision requiring employees to complete a specified amount of service (not to exceed five years) after that date, then benefits are permitted to be determined disregarding the service condition, provided that the condition is applicable to all employees in the multiemployer plan (including collectively bargained employees). [Reg. §1.401(a)(4)-3.]

☐ [*T.D. 8360, 9-12-91. Amended by T.D. 8485, 8-30-93.*]

[Reg. §1.401(a)(4)-4]

§1.401(a)(4)-4. Nondiscriminatory availability of benefits, rights and features.—(a) *Introduction.*—This section provides rules for determining whether the benefits, rights, and features provided under a plan (i.e., all optional forms of benefit, ancillary benefits, and other rights and features available to any employee under the plan) are made available in a nondiscriminatory manner. Benefits, rights, and features provided under a plan are made available to employees in a nondiscriminatory manner only if each benefit, right, or feature satisfies the current availability requirement of paragraph (b) of this section and the effective availability requirement of paragraph (c) of this section. Paragraph (d) of this section provides special rules for applying these requirements. Paragraph (e) of this section defines optional form of benefit, ancillary benefit, and other right or feature.

(b) *Current availability.*—(1) *General rule.*—The current availability requirement of this paragraph (b) is satisfied if the group of employees to whom a benefit, right, or feature is currently available during the plan year satisfies section 410(b) (without regard to the average benefit percentage test of §1.410(b)-5). In determining whether the group of employees satisfies section 410(b), an employee is treated as benefiting only if the benefit, right, or feature is currently available to the employee.

(2) *Determination of current availability.*—(i) *General rule.*—Whether a benefit, right, or feature that is subject to specified eligibility conditions is currently available to an employee generally is determined based on the current facts and circumstances with respect to the employee (e.g., current compensation, accrued benefit, position, or net worth).

(ii) *Certain conditions disregarded.*—(A) *Certain age and service conditions.*—(1) *General rule.*—Notwithstanding paragraph (b)(2)(i) of this section, any specified age or service condition with respect to an optional form of benefit or a social security supplement is disregarded in determining whether the optional form of benefit or the social security supplement is currently available to an employee. Thus, for example, an optional form of benefit that is available to all employees who terminate employment on or after age 55 with at least 10 years of service is treated as currently available to an employee, without regard to the employee's current age or years of service, and without regard to whether the employee could potentially meet the age and service conditions prior to attaining the plan's normal retirement age.

(2) *Time-limited age or service conditions not disregarded.*—Notwithstanding paragraph (b)(2)(i)(A)(1) of this section, an age or service condition is not disregarded in determining the current availability of an optional form of benefit or social security supplement if the condition must be satisfied within a limited period of time. However, in determining the current availability of an optional form of benefit or a social security supplement subject to such an age or service condition, the age and service of employees may be projected to the last date by which the age condition or service condition must be satisfied in order to be eligible for the optional form of benefit or social security supplement under the plan. Thus, for example, an optional form of benefit that is available only to employees who terminate employment between July 1, 1995, and December 31, 1995, after attainment of age 55 with at least 10 years of service is treated as currently available to an employee only if the employee could satisfy those age and service conditions by December 31, 1995.

(B) *Certain other conditions.*—Specified conditions on the availability of a benefit, right, or feature requiring a specified percentage of the employee's accrued benefit to be nonforfeitable, termination of employment, death, satisfaction of a specified health condition (or failure to meet such condition), disability, hardship, family status, default on a plan loan secured by a participant's account balance, execution of a covenant not to compete, application for benefits or similar ministerial or mechanical acts, election of a benefit form, execution of a waiver of rights under the Age Discrimination in Employment Act or other federal or state law, or absence from service, are disregarded in determining the employees to whom the benefit, right, or feature is currently available. In addition, if a multiemployer plan includes a reasonable condition that limits eligibility for an ancillary benefit, or other right or feature, to those employees who have recent service under the plan (e.g., a condition on a death benefit that requires an employee to have a minimum number of hours credited during the last two years) and the condition applies to all employees in the multiemployer plan (including the collectively bargained employees) to whom the ancillary benefit, or other right or feature, is otherwise currently available, then the condition is disregarded in determining the employees to whom the ancillary benefit, or other right or feature, is currently available.

(C) *Certain conditions relating to mandatory cash-outs.*—In the case of a plan that provides for mandatory cash-outs of all terminated employees who have a vested accrued benefit with an actuarial present value less than or equal to a specified dollar amount (not to exceed the cash-out limit in effect under § 1.411(a)-11(c)(3)(ii)) as permitted by sections 411(a)(11) and 417(e), the implicit condition on any benefit, right, or feature (other than the mandatory cash-out) that requires the employee to have a vested accrued benefit with an actuarial present value in excess of the specified dollar amount is disregarded in determining the employees to whom the benefit, right, or feature is currently available.

(D) *Other dollar limits.*—A condition that the amount of an employee's vested accrued benefit or the actuarial present value of that benefit be less than or equal to a specified dollar amount is disregarded in determining the employees to whom the benefit, right, or feature is currently available.

(E) *Certain conditions on plan loans.*—In the case of an employee's right to a loan from the plan, the condition that an employee must have an account balance sufficient to be eligible to receive a minimum loan amount specified in the plan (not to exceed $1,000) is disregarded in determining the employees to whom the right is currently available.

(3) *Benefits, rights, and features that are eliminated prospectively.*—(i) *Special testing rule.*—Notwithstanding paragraph (b)(1) of this section, a benefit, right, or feature that is eliminated with respect to benefits accrued after the later of the eliminating amendment's adoption or effective date (the elimination date), but is retained with respect to benefits accrued as of the elimination date, and that satisfies this paragraph (b) as of the elimination date, is treated as satisfying this paragraph (b) for all subsequent periods. This rule does not apply if the terms of the benefit, right, or feature (including the employees to whom it is available) are changed after the elimination date.

(ii) *Elimination of a benefit, right, or feature.*—(A) *General rule.*—For purposes of this paragraph (b)(3), a benefit, right, or feature provided to an employee is eliminated with respect to benefits accrued after the elimination date if the amount or value of the benefit, right, or feature depends solely on the amount of the employee's accrued benefit (within the meaning of section 411(a)(7)) as of the elimination date, including subsequent income, expenses, gains, and losses with respect to that benefit in the case of a defined contribution plan.

(B) *Special rule for benefits, rights, and features that are not section 411(d)(6)-protected benefits.*—Notwithstanding paragraph (b)(3)(ii)(A) of this section, in the case of a benefit, right, or feature under a defined contribution plan that is not a section 411(d)(6)-protected benefit (within the meaning of § 1.411(d)-4, Q&A-1), e.g., the availability of plan loans, for purposes of this paragraph (b)(3)(ii) each employee's accrued benefit as of the elimination date may be treated, on a uniform basis, as consisting exclusively of the dollar amount of the employee's account balance as of the elimination date.

(C) *Special rule for benefits, rights, and features that depend on adjusted accrued benefits.*—For purposes of this paragraph (b)(3), a benefit, right, or feature provided to an employee under a plan that has made a fresh start does not fail to be eliminated as of an elimination date that is the fresh-start date merely because it depends solely on the amount of the employee's adjusted accrued benefit (within the meaning of § 1.401(a)(4)-13(d)(8)).

(c) *Effective availability.*—(1) *General rule.*—Based on all of the relevant facts and circumstances, the group of employees to whom a benefit, right, or feature is effectively available must not substantially favor HCEs.

(2) *Examples.*—The following examples illustrate the rules of this paragraph (c):

Example 1. Employer X maintains Plan A, a defined benefit plan that covers both of its highly compensated nonexcludable employees and nine of its 12 nonhighly compensated nonexcludable employees. Plan A provides for a normal retirement benefit payable as an annuity and based on a normal retirement age of 65, and an early retirement benefit payable upon termination in the form of an annuity to employees who terminate from service with the employer on or after age 55 with 30 or more years of service. Both HCEs of Employer X currently meet the age and service requirement, or will have 30 years

of service by the time they reach age 55. All but two of the nine NHCEs of Employer X who are covered by Plan A were hired on or after age 35 and, thus, cannot qualify for the early retirement benefit. Even though the group of employees to whom the early retirement benefit is currently available satisfies the ratio percentage test of § 1.410(b)-2(b)(2) when age and service are disregarded pursuant to paragraph (b)(2)(ii)(A) of this section, absent other facts, the group of employees to whom the early retirement benefit is effectively available substantially favors HCEs.

Example 2. Employer Y maintains Plan B, a defined benefit plan that provides for a normal retirement benefit payable as an annuity and based on a normal retirement age of 65. By a plan amendment first adopted and effective December 1, 1998, Employer Y amends Plan B to provide an early retirement benefit that is available only to employees who terminate employment by December 15, 1998, and who are at least age 55 with 30 or more years of service. Assume that all employees were hired prior to attaining age 25 and that the group of employees who have, or will have, attained age 55 with 30 years of service by December 15, 1998, satisfies the ratio percentage test of § 1.410(b)-2(b)(2). Assume, further, that the employer takes no steps to inform all eligible employees of the early retirement option on a timely basis and that the only employees who terminate from employment with the employer during the two-week period in which the early retirement benefit is available are HCEs. Under these facts, the group of employees to whom this early retirement window benefit is effectively available substantially favors HCEs.

Example 3. Employer Z amends Plan C on June 30, 1999, to provide for a single sum optional form of benefit for employees who terminate from employment with Employer Z after June 30, 1999, and before January 1, 2000. The availability of this single sum optional form of benefit is conditioned on the employee's having a particular disability at the time of termination of employment. The only employee of the employer who meets this disability requirement at the time of the amendment and thereafter through December 31, 1999, is a HCE. Under paragraph (b)(2)(ii)(B) of this section, the disability condition is disregarded in determining the current availability of the single sum optional form of benefit. Nevertheless, under these facts, the group of employees to whom the single sum optional form of benefit is effectively available substantially favors HCEs.

(d) *Special rules.*—(1) *Mergers and acquisitions.*—(i) *Special testing rule.*—A benefit, right, or feature available under a plan solely to an acquired group of employees is treated as satisfying paragraphs (b) and (c) of this section during the period that each of the following requirements is satisfied:

(A) The benefit, right, or feature must satisfy paragraphs (b) and (c) of this section (determined without regard to the special rule in section 410(b)(6)(C)) on the date that is selected by the employer as the latest date by which an employee must be hired or transferred into the acquired trade or business for an employee to be included in the acquired group of employees. This determination is made with reference to the plan of the current employer and its nonexcludable employees.

(B) The benefit, right, or feature must be available under the plan of the current employer after the transaction on the same terms as it was available under the plan of the prior employer before the transaction. This requirement is not violated merely because of a change made to the benefit, right, or feature that is permitted by section 411(d)(6), provided that—

(1) The change is a replacement of the benefit, right, or feature with another benefit, right, or feature that is available to the same employees as the original benefit, right, or feature, and the original benefit, right, or feature is of inherently equal or greater value (within the meaning of paragraph (d)(4)(i)(A) of this section) than the benefit, right, or feature that replaces it; or

(2) The change is made before January 12, 1993.

(ii) *Scope of special testing rule.*—This paragraph (d)(1) applies only to benefits, rights, and features with respect to benefits accruing under the plan of the current employer, and not to benefits, rights, and features with respect to benefits accrued under the plan of the prior employer (unless, pursuant to the transaction, the plan of the prior employer becomes the plan of the current employer, or the assets and liabilities with respect to the acquired group of employees under the plan of the prior employer are transferred to the plan of the current employer in a plan merger, consolidation, or other transfer described in section 414(l)).

(iii) *Example.*—The following example illustrates the rules of this paragraph (d)(1):

Example. Employer X maintains Plan A, a defined benefit plan with a single sum optional form of benefit for all employees. Employer Y acquires Employer X and merges Plan A into Plan B, a defined benefit plan maintained by Employer Y that does not otherwise provide a single sum optional form of benefit. Employer Y continues to provide the single sum optional form of benefit under Plan B on the same terms as it was offered under Plan A to all employees who were acquired in the transaction with Employer X (and to no other employees). The optional form of benefit satisfies paragraphs (b) and (c) of this section immediately following the transaction (determined without taking into account section 410(b)(6)(C)) when tested with reference to Plan B and Employer Y's nonexcludable employees. Under these facts, Plan B is treated as satisfying this section with respect to the single sum optional form of benefit for the plan year of the transaction and all subsequent plan years.

(2) *Frozen participants.*—A plan must satisfy the nondiscriminatory availability requirement of this section not only with respect to benefits, rights, and features provided to employees who are currently benefiting under the plan, but also separately with respect to benefits, rights, and features provided to nonexcludable employees with accrued benefits who are not currently benefiting under the plan (frozen participants). Thus, each benefit, right, and feature available to any frozen participant under the plan is separately subject to the requirements of this section. A plan satisfies paragraphs (b) and (c) of this section with respect to a benefit, right, or feature available to any frozen participant under the plan only if one or more of the following requirements is satisfied:

(i) The benefit, right, or feature must be one that would satisfy paragraphs (b) and (c) of this section if it were not available to any employee currently benefiting under the plan.

(ii) The benefit, right, or feature must be one that would satisfy paragraphs (b) and (c) of this section if all frozen participants were treated as employees currently benefiting under the plan.

(iii) No change in the availability of the benefit, right, or feature may have been made that is first effective in the current plan year with respect to a frozen participant.

(iv) Any change in the availability of the benefit, right, or feature that is first effective in the current plan year with respect to a frozen participant must be made in a nondiscriminatory manner. Thus, any expansion in the availability of the benefit, right, or feature to any highly compensated frozen participant must be applied on a consistent basis to all nonhighly compensated frozen participants. Similarly, any contraction in the availability of the benefit, right, or feature that affects any nonhighly compensated frozen participant must be applied on a consistent basis to all highly compensated frozen participants.

(3) *Early retirement window benefits.*—If a benefit, right, or feature meets the definition of an early retirement window benefit in §1.401(a)(4)-3(f)(4)(iii) (or would meet that definition if the definition applied to all benefits, rights, and features), the benefit, right, or feature is disregarded for purposes of applying this section with respect to an employee for all plan years other than the first plan year in which the benefit is currently available to the employee.

(4) *Permissive aggregation of certain benefits, rights, or features.*— (i) *General rule.*—An optional form of benefit, ancillary benefit, or other right or feature may be aggregated with another optional form of benefit, ancillary benefit, or other right or feature, respectively, and the two may be treated as a single optional form of benefit, ancillary benefit, or other right or feature, if both of the following requirements are satisfied:

(A) One of the two optional forms of benefit, ancillary benefit, or other rights or features must in all cases be of inherently equal or greater value than the other. For this purpose, one benefit, right, or feature is of inherently equal or greater value than another benefit, right, or feature only if, at any time and under any conditions, it is impossible for any employee to receive a smaller amount or a less valuable right under the first benefit, right, or feature than under the second benefit, right, or feature.

(B) The optional form of benefit, ancillary benefit, or other right or feature of inherently equal or greater value must separately satisfy paragraphs (b) and (c) of this section (without regard to this paragraph (d)(4)).

(ii) *Aggregation may be applied more than once.*—The aggregation rule in this paragraph (d)(4) may be applied more than once. Thus, for example, an optional form of benefit may be aggregated with another optional form of benefit that itself constitutes two separate optional forms of benefit that are aggregated and treated as a single optional form of benefit under this paragraph (d)(4).

(iii) *Examples.*—The following examples illustrate the rules in this paragraph (d)(4):

Example 1. Plan A is a defined benefit plan that provides a single sum optional form of benefit to all employees. The single sum optional form of benefit is available on the same terms to all employees, except that, for employees in Division S, a five-percent discount factor is applied and, for employees of Division T, a seven-percent

discount factor is applied. Under paragraph (e)(1) of this section, the single sum optional form of benefit constitutes two separate optional forms of benefit. Assume that the single sum optional form of benefit available to employees of Division S separately satisfies paragraphs (b) and (c) of this section without taking into account this paragraph (d)(4). Because a lower discount factor is applied in determining the single sum optional form of benefit available to employees of Division S than is applied in determining the single sum optional form of benefit available to employees of Division T, the first single sum optional form of benefit is of inherently greater value than the second single sum optional form of benefit. Under these facts, these two single sum optional forms of benefit may be aggregated and treated as a single optional form of benefit for purposes of this section.

Example 2. The facts are the same as in *Example 1*, except that, in order to receive the single sum optional form of benefit, employees of Division S (but not employees of Division T) must have completed at least 20 years of service. The single sum optional form of benefit available to employees of Division S is not of inherently equal or greater value than the single sum optional form of benefit available to employees of Division T, because an employee of Division S who terminates employment with less than 20 years of service would receive a smaller single sum amount (i.e., zero) than a similarly-situated employee of Division T who terminates employment with less than 20 years of service. Under these facts, the two single sum optional forms of benefit may not be aggregated and treated as a single optional form of benefit for purposes of this section.

(5) *Certain spousal benefits.*—In the case of a plan that includes two or more plans that have been permissively aggregated under §1.410(b)-7(d), the aggregated plan satisfies this section with respect to the availability of any nonsubsidized qualified joint and survivor annuities, qualified preretirement survivor annuities, or spousal death benefits described in section 401(a)(11), if each plan that is part of the aggregated plan satisfies section 401(a)(11). Whether a benefit is considered subsidized for this purpose may be determined using any reasonable actuarial assumptions. For purposes of this paragraph (d)(5), a qualified joint and survivor annuity, qualified preretirement survivor annuity, or spousal death benefit is deemed to be nonsubsidized if it is provided under a defined contribution plan.

(6) *Special ESOP rules.*—An ESOP does not fail to satisfy paragraphs (b) and (c) of this section merely because it makes an investment diversification right or feature or a distribution option available solely to all qualified participants (within the meaning of section 401(a)(28)(B)(iii)), or merely because the restrictions of section 409(n) apply to certain individuals.

(7) *Special testing rule for unpredictable contingent event benefits.*— A benefit, right, or feature that is contingent on the occurrence of an unpredictable contingent event (within the meaning of section 412(l)(7)(B)(ii)) is tested under this section as if the event had occurred. Thus, the current availability of a benefit that becomes an optional form of benefit upon the occurrence of an unpredictable contingent event is tested by deeming the event to have occurred and by disregarding age and service conditions on the eligibility for that benefit to the extent permitted for optional forms of benefit under paragraph (b)(2) of this section.

(e) *Definitions.*—(1) *Optional form of benefit.*—(i) *General rule.*—The term optional form of benefit means a distribution alternative (including the normal form of benefit) that is available under a plan with respect to benefits described in section 411(d)(6)(A) or a distribution alternative that is an early retirement benefit or retirement-type subsidy described in section 411(d)(6)(B)(i), including a QSUPP. Except as provided in paragraph (e)(1)(ii) of this section, different optional forms of benefit exist if a distribution alternative is not payable on substantially the same terms as another distribution alternative. The relevant terms include all terms affecting the value of the optional form, such as the method of benefit calculation and the actuarial assumptions used to determine the amount distributed. Thus, for example, different optional forms of benefit may result from differences in terms relating to the payment schedule, timing, commencement, medium of distribution (e.g., in cash or in kind), election rights, differences in eligibility requirements, or the portion of the benefit to which the distribution alternative applies.

(ii) *Exceptions.*—(A) *Differences in benefit formula or accrual method.*—A distribution alternative available under a defined benefit plan does not fail to be a single optional form of benefit merely because the benefit formulas, accrual methods, or other factors (including service-computation methods and definitions of compensation) underlying, or the manner in which employees vest in, the accrued benefit that is paid in the form of the distribution alternative are different for different employees to whom the distribution alternative is available. Notwithstanding the foregoing, differences in the normal retirement ages of employees or in the form in which the accrued benefit of employees is payable at normal retirement age under a plan are taken into account in determining whether a distribution alternative constitutes one or more optional forms of benefit.

(B) *Differences in allocation formula.*—A distribution alternative available under a defined contribution plan does not fail to be a single optional form of benefit merely because the allocation formula or other factors (including service-computation methods, definitions of compensation, and the manner in which amounts described in §1.401(a)(4)-2(c)(2)(iii) are allocated) underlying, or the manner in which employees vest in, the accrued benefit that is paid in the form of the distribution alternative are different for different employees to whom the distribution alternative is available.

(C) *Distributions subject to section 417(e).*—A distribution alternative available under a defined benefit plan does not fail to be a single optional form of benefit merely because, in determining the amount of a distribution, the plan applies a lower interest rate to determine the distribution for employees with a vested accrued benefit having an actuarial present value not in excess of $25,000, as required by section 417(e)(3) and §1.417(e)-1.

(D) *Differences attributable to uniform normal retirement age.*— A distribution alternative available under a defined benefit plan does not fail to be a single optional form of benefit, to the extent that the differences are attributable to differences in normal retirement dates among employees, provided that the differences do not prevent the employees from having the same uniform normal retirement age under the definition of uniform normal retirement age in §1.401(a)(4)-12.

(iii) *Examples.*—The following examples illustrate the rules in this paragraph (e)(1):

Example 1. Plan A is a defined benefit plan that benefits all employees of Divisions S and T. The plan offers a qualified joint and 50-percent survivor annuity at normal retirement age, calculated by multiplying an employee's single life annuity payment by a factor. For an employee of Division S whose benefit commences at age 65, the plan provides a factor of 0.90, but for a similarly-situated employee of Division T the plan provides a factor of 0.85. The qualified joint and survivor annuity is not available to employees of Divisions S and T on substantially the same terms, and thus it constitutes two separate optional forms of benefit.

Example 2. Plan B is a defined benefit plan that benefits all employees of Divisions U and V. The plan offers a single sum distribution alternative available on the same terms and determined using the same actuarial assumptions, to all employees. However, different benefit formulas apply to employees of each division. Under the exception provided in paragraph (e)(1)(ii)(A) of this section, the single sum optional form of benefit available to employees of Division U is not a separate optional form of benefit from the single sum optional form of benefit available to employees of Division V.

Example 3. Defined benefit Plan C provides an early retirement benefit based on a schedule of early retirement factors that is a single optional form of benefit. Plan C is amended to provide an early retirement window benefit that consists of a temporary change in the plan's benefit formula (e.g., the addition of five years of service to an employee's actual service under the benefit formula) applicable in determining the benefits for certain employees who terminate employment within a limited period of time. Under the exception provided in paragraph (e)(1)(ii)(A) of this section, the early retirement optional form of benefit available to window-eligible employees is not a separate optional form of benefit from the early retirement optional form of benefit available to the other employees.

(2) *Ancillary benefit.*—The term ancillary benefit means social security supplements (other than QSUPPs), disability benefits not in excess of a qualified disability benefit described in section 411(a)(9), ancillary life insurance and health insurance benefits, death benefits under a defined contribution plan, preretirement death benefits under a defined benefit plan, shut-down benefits not protected under section 411(d)(6), and other similar benefits. Different ancillary benefits exist if an ancillary benefit is not available on substantially the same terms as another ancillary benefit. Principles similar to those in paragraph (e)(1)(ii) of this section apply in making this determination.

(3) *Other right or feature.*—(i) *General rule.*—The term other right or feature generally means any right or feature applicable to employees under the plan. Different rights or features exist if a right or feature is not available on substantially the same terms as another right or feature.

(ii) *Exceptions to definition of other right or feature.*—Notwithstanding paragraph (e)(3)(i) of this section, a right or feature is not considered an other right or feature if it—

(A) Is an optional form of benefit or an ancillary benefit under the plan;

(B) Is one of the terms that are taken into account in determining whether separate optional forms of benefit or ancillary benefits exist, or that would be taken into account but for paragraph (e)(1)(ii) of this section (e.g., benefit formulas or the manner in which benefits vest); or

(C) Cannot reasonably be expected to be of meaningful value to an employee (e.g., administrative details).

(iii) *Examples.*—Other rights and features include, but are not limited to—

(A) Plan loan provisions (other than those relating to a distribution of an employee's accrued benefit upon default under a loan);

(B) The right to direct investments;

(C) The right to a particular form of investment, including, for example, a particular class or type of employer securities (taking into account, in determining whether different forms of investment exist, any differences in conversion, dividend, voting, liquidation preference, or other rights conferred under the security);

(D) The right to make each rate of elective contributions described in §1.401(k)-6 (determining the rate based on the plan's definition of the compensation out of which the elective contributions are made (regardless of whether that definition satisfies section 414(s)), but also treating different rates as existing if they are based on definitions of compensation or other requirements or formulas that are not substantially the same);

(E) The right to make after-tax employee contributions to a defined benefit plan that are not allocated to separate accounts;

(F) The right to make each rate of after-tax employee contributions described in §1.401(m)-1(a)(3) (determining the rate based on the plan's definition of the compensation out of which the after-tax employee contributions are made (regardless of whether that definition satisfies section 414(s)), but also treating different rates as existing if they are based on definitions of compensation or other requirements or formulas that are not substantially the same);

(G) The right to each rate of allocation of matching contributions described in §1.401(m)-1(a)(2) (determining the rate using the amount of matching, elective, and after-tax employee contributions determined after any corrections under §§1.401(k)-2(b)(1)(i), 1.401(m)-2(b)(1)(i), but also treating different rates as existing if they are based on definitions of compensation or other requirements or formulas that are not substantially the same);

(H) The right to purchase additional retirement or ancillary benefits under the plan; and

(I) The right to make rollover contributions and transfers to and from the plan. [Reg. §1.401(a)(4)-4.]

☐ [*T.D.* 8360, 9-12-91. *Amended by T.D.* 8485, 8-30-93; *T.D.* 8794, 12-18-98; *T.D.* 8891, 7-18-2000 *and T.D.* 9169, 12-28-2004.]

[Reg. §1.401(a)(4)-5]

§1.401(a)(4)-5. Plan amendments and plan terminations.— (a) *Introduction.*—(1) *Overview.*—This paragraph (a) provides rules for determining whether the timing of a plan amendment or series of amendments has the effect of discriminating significantly in favor of HCEs or former HCEs. For purposes of this section, a plan amendment includes, for example, the establishment or termination of the plan, and any change in the benefits, rights, or features, benefit formulas, or allocation formulas under the plan. Paragraph (b) of this section sets forth additional requirements that must be satisfied in the case of a plan termination.

(2) *Facts-and-circumstances determination.*—Whether the timing of a plan amendment or series of plan amendments has the effect of discriminating significantly in favor of HCEs or former HCEs is determined at the time the plan amendment first becomes effective for purposes of section 401(a), based on all of the relevant facts and circumstances. These include, for example, the relative numbers of current and former HCEs and NHCEs affected by the plan amendment, the relative length of service of current and former HCEs and NHCEs, the length of time the plan or plan provision being amended has been in effect, and the turnover of employees prior to the plan amendment. In addition, the relevant facts and circumstances include the relative accrued benefits of current and former HCEs and NHCEs before and after the plan amendment and any additional benefits provided to current and former HCEs and NHCEs under other plans (including plans of other employers, if relevant). In the case of a plan amendment that provides additional benefits based on an employee's service prior to the amendment, the relevant facts and circumstances also include the benefits that employees and former employees who do not benefit under the amendment would have received had the plan, as amended, been in effect throughout the period on which the additional benefits are based.

(3) *Safe harbor for certain grants of benefits for past periods.*—The timing of a plan amendment that credits (or increases benefits attributable to) years of service for a period in the past is deemed not to have the effect of discriminating significantly in favor of HCEs or former HCEs if the period for which the service credit (or benefit increase) is granted does not exceed the five years immediately preceding the year in which the amendment first becomes effective, the service credit (or benefit increase) is granted on a reasonably uniform basis to all employees, benefits attributable to the period are determined by applying the current plan formula, and the service credited is service (including pre-participation or imputed service) with the employer or a previous employer that may be taken into account under § 1.401(a)(4)-11(d)(3) (without regard to § 1.401(a)(4)-11(d)(3)(i)(B)). However, this safe harbor is not available if the plan amendment granting the service credit (or increasing benefits) is part of a pattern of amendments that has the effect of discriminating significantly in favor of HCEs or former HCEs.

(4) *Examples.*—The following examples illustrate the rules in this paragraph (a):

Example 1. Plan A is a defined benefit plan that covered both HCEs and NHCEs for most of its existence. The employer decides to wind up its business. In the process of ceasing operations, but at a time when the plan covers only HCEs, Plan A is amended to increase benefits and thereafter is terminated. The timing of this plan amendment has the effect of discriminating significantly in favor of HCEs.

Example 2. Plan B is a defined benefit plan that provides a social security supplement that is not a QSUPP. After substantially all of the HCEs of the employer have benefited from the supplement, but before a substantial number of NHCEs have become eligible for the supplement, Plan B is amended to reduce significantly the amount of the supplement. The timing of this plan amendment has the effect of discriminating significantly in favor of HCEs.

Example 3. Plan C is a defined benefit plan that contains an ancillary life insurance benefit available to all employees. The plan is amended to eliminate this benefit at a time when life insurance payments have been made only to beneficiaries of HCEs. Because all employees received the benefit of life insurance coverage before Plan C was amended, the timing of this plan amendment does not have the effect of discriminating significantly in favor of HCEs or former HCEs.

Example 4. Plan D provides for a benefit of one percent of average annual compensation per year of service. Ten years after Plan D is adopted, it is amended to provide a benefit of two percent of average annual compensation per year of service, including years of service prior to the amendment. The amendment is effective only for employees currently employed at the time of the amendment. The ratio of HCEs to former HCEs is significantly higher than the ratio of NHCEs to former NHCEs. In the absence of any additional factors, the timing of this plan amendment has the effect of discriminating significantly in favor of HCEs.

Example 5. The facts are the same as in *Example 4*, except that, in addition, the years of prior service are equivalent between HCEs and NHCEs who are current employees, and the group of current employees with prior service would satisfy the nondiscriminatory classification test of § 1.410(b)-4 in the current and all prior plan years for which past service credit is granted. The timing of this plan amendment does not have the effect of discriminating significantly in favor of HCEs or former HCEs.

Example 6. Employer V maintains Plan E, an accumulation plan. In 1994, Employer V amends Plan E to provide that the compensation used to determine an employee's benefit for all preceding plan years shall not be less than the employee's average annual compensation as of the close of the 1994 plan year. The years of service and percentage increases in compensation for HCEs are reasonably comparable to those of NHCEs. In addition, the ratio of HCEs to former HCEs is reasonably comparable to the ratio of NHCEs to former NHCEs. The timing of this plan amendment does not have the effect of discriminating significantly in favor of HCEs or former HCEs.

Example 7. Employer W currently has six nonexcludable employees, two of whom, H1 and H2, are HCEs, and the remaining four of whom, N1 through N4, are NHCEs. The ratio of HCEs to former HCEs is significantly higher than the ratio of NHCEs to former NHCEs. Employer W establishes Plan F, a defined benefit plan providing a benefit of one percent of average annual compensation per year of service, including years of service prior to the establishment of the plan. H1 and H2 each have 15 years of prior service, N1 has nine years of past service, N2 has five years, N3 has three years, and N4 has one year. The timing of this plan establishment has the effect of discriminating significantly in favor of HCEs.

Example 8. Assume the same facts as in *Example 7*, except that N1 through N4 were hired in the current year, and Employer W never employed any NHCEs prior to the current year. Thus, no NHCEs would have received additional benefits had Plan F been in existence during the preceding 15 years. The timing of this plan establishment

does not have the effect of discriminating significantly in favor of HCEs or former HCEs.

Example 9. The facts are the same as in *Example 7*, except that Plan F limits the grant of past service credit to five years, and the grant of past service otherwise satisfies the safe harbor in paragraph (a)(3) of this section. The timing of this plan establishment is deemed not to have the effect of discriminating significantly in favor of HCEs or former HCEs.

Example 10. The facts are the same as in *Example 9*, except that, five years after the establishment of Plan F, Employer W amends the plan to provide a benefit equal to two percent of average annual compensation per year of service, taking into account all years of service since the establishment of the plan. The ratio of HCEs to former HCEs who terminated employment during the five-year period since the establishment of the plan is significantly higher than the ratio of NHCEs to former NHCEs who terminated employment during the five-year period since the establishment of the plan. Although the amendment described in this example might separately satisfy the safe harbor in paragraph (a)(3) of this section, the safe harbor is not available with respect to the amendment because, under these facts, the amendment is part of a pattern of amendments that has the effect of discriminating significantly in favor of HCEs.

Example 11. Employer Y maintains Plan G, a defined benefit plan, covering all its employees. In 1995, Employer Y acquires Division S from Employer Z. Some of the employees of Division S had been covered under a defined benefit plan maintained by Employer Z. Soon after the acquisition, Employer Y amends Plan G to cover all employees of Division S and to credit those who were in Division S's defined benefit plan with years of service for years of employment with Employer Z. Because the timing of the plan amendment was determined by the timing of the transaction, the timing of this plan amendment does not have the effect of discriminating significantly in favor of HCEs or former HCEs. See also § 1.401(a)(4)-11(d)(3) for other rules regarding the crediting of pre-participation service.

Example 12. Plan H is an insurance contract plan within the meaning of section 412(i). For all plan years before 1999, Plan H purchases insurance contracts from Insurance Company J. In 1999, Plan H shifts future purchases of insurance contracts to Insurance Company K. The shift in insurance companies is a plan amendment subject to this paragraph (a).

(b) *Pre-termination restrictions.*—(1) *Required provisions in defined benefit plans.*—A defined benefit plan has the effect of discriminating significantly in favor of HCEs or former HCEs unless it incorporates provisions restricting benefits and distributions as described in paragraph (b)(2) and (3) of this section at the time the plan is established or, if later, as of the first plan year to which § § 1.401(a)(4)-1 through 1.401(a)(4)-13 apply to the plan under § 1.401(a)(4)-13(a) or (b). This paragraph (b) does not apply if the Commissioner determines that such provisions are not necessary to prevent the prohibited discrimination that may occur in the event of an early termination of the plan. The restrictions in this paragraph (b) apply to a plan within the meaning of § 1.410(b)-7(b) (i.e., a section 414(1) plan). Any plan containing a provision described in this paragraph (b) satisfies section 411(d)(2) and does not fail to satisfy section 411(a) or (d)(3) merely because of the provision.

(2) *Restriction of benefits upon plan termination.*—A plan must provide that, in the event of plan termination, the benefit of any HCE (and any former HCE) is limited to a benefit that is nondiscriminatory under section 401(a)(4).

(3) *Restrictions on distributions.*—(i) *General rule.*—A plan must provide that, in any year, the payment of benefits to or on behalf of a restricted employee shall not exceed an amount equal to the payments that would be made to or on behalf of the restricted employee in that year under—

(A) A straight life annuity that is the actuarial equivalent of the accrued benefit and other benefits to which the restricted employee is entitled under the plan (other than a social security supplement); and

(B) A social security supplement, if any, that the restricted employee is entitled to receive.

(ii) *Restricted employee defined.*—For purposes of this paragraph (b), the term restricted employee generally means any HCE or former HCE. However, an HCE or former HCE need not be treated as a restricted employee in the current year if the HCE or former HCE is not one of the 25 (or a larger number chosen by the employer) nonexcludable employees and former employees of the employer with the largest amount of compensation in the current or any prior year. Plan provisions defining or altering this group can be amended at any time without violating section 411(d)(6).

(iii) *Benefit defined.*—For purposes of this paragraph (b), the term benefit includes, among other benefits, loans in excess of the amounts set forth in section 72(p)(2)(A), any periodic income, any withdrawal values payable to a living employee or former employee, and any death benefits not provided for by insurance on the employee's or former employee's life.

(iv) *Nonapplicability in certain cases.*—The restrictions in this paragraph (b)(3) do not apply, however, if any one of the following requirements is satisfied:

(A) After taking into account payment to or on behalf of the restricted employee of all benefits payable to or on behalf of that restricted employee under the plan, the value of plan assets must equal or exceed 110 percent of the value of current liabilities, as defined in section 412(1)(7).

(B) The value of the benefits payable to or on behalf of the restricted employee must be less than one percent of the value of current liabilities before distribution.

(C) The value of the benefits payable to or on behalf of the restricted employee must not exceed the amount described in section 411(a)(11)(A) (restrictions on certain mandatory distributions).

(v) *Determination of current liabilities.*—For purposes of this paragraph (b), any reasonable and consistent method may be used for determining the value of current liabilities and the value of plan assets.

(4) *Operational restrictions on certain money purchase pension plans.*—A money purchase pension plan that has an accumulated funding deficiency, within the meaning of section 412(a), or an unamortized funding waiver, within the meaning of section 412(d), must comply in operation with the restrictions on benefits and distributions as described in paragraphs (b)(2) and (b)(3) of this section. Such a plan does not fail to satisfy section 411(d)(6) merely because of restrictions imposed by the requirements of this paragraph (b)(4). [Reg. §1.401(a)(4)-5.]

□ [*T.D. 8360, 9-12-91. Amended by T.D. 8485, 8-30-93.*]

[Reg. §1.401(a)(4)-6]

§1.401(a)(4)-6. Contributory defined benefit plans.— (a) *Introduction.*—This section provides rules necessary for determining whether a contributory DB plan satisfies the nondiscriminatory amount requirement of §1.401(a)(4)-1(b)(2). Paragraph (b) of this section provides rules for determining the amount of benefits derived from employer contributions (employer-provided benefits) under a contributory DB plan for purposes of determining whether the plan satisfies §1.401(a)(4)-1(b)(2) with respect to such amounts. Paragraph (c) of this section provides the exclusive rules for determining whether a contributory DB plan satisfies §1.401(a)(4)-1(b)(2) with respect to the amount of benefits derived from employee contributions not allocated to separate accounts (employee-provided benefits). See §1.401(a)(4)-1(b)(2)(ii)(B) for the exclusive tests applicable to employee contributions allocated to separate accounts under a section 401(m) plan.

(b) *Determination of employer-provided benefit.*—(1) *General rule.*— An employee's employer-provided benefit under a contributory DB plan for purposes of section 401(a)(4) equals the difference between the employee's total benefit and the employee's employee-provided benefit under the plan. The rules of section 411(c) generally must be used to determine the employee's employer-provided benefit for this purpose. However, paragraphs (b)(2) through (b)(6) of this section provide alternative methods for determining the employee's employer-provided benefit.

(2) *Composition-of-workforce method.*—(i) *General rule.*—A contributory DB plan that satisfies paragraph (b)(2)(ii)(A) and (B) of this section may determine employees' employer-provided benefit rates under the rules of paragraph (b)(2)(iii) of this section.

(ii) *Eligibility requirements.*—(A) *Uniform rate of employee contributions.*—A contributory DB plan satisfies this paragraph (b)(2)(ii)(A) if all employees make employee contributions at the same rate, expressed as a percentage of plan year compensation (the employee contribution rate). A plan does not fail to satisfy this paragraph (b)(2)(ii)(A) merely because it eliminates employee contributions for all employees with plan year compensation below a specified contribution breakpoint that is either a stated dollar amount or a stated percentage of covered compensation (within the meaning of §1.401(1)-1(c)(7)); or merely because all employees make employee contributions at the same rate (expressed as a percentage of plan year compensation) with respect to plan year compensation up to the contribution breakpoint (base employee contribution rate) and at a higher rate (expressed as a percentage of plan year compensation) that is the same for all employees with respect to plan year compensation above the contribution breakpoint (excess employee contribution rate). A plan described in paragraph (c)(4)(i) of this section that

satisfies paragraph (c)(4)(iii) of this section is deemed to satisfy this paragraph.

(B) *Demographic requirements.*—(1) *In general.*—A contributory DB plan satisfies this paragraph (b)(2)(ii)(B) if it satisfies either of the demographic tests in paragraph (b)(2)(ii)(B)(2) or in (3) of this section.

(2) *Minimum percentage test.*—This test is satisfied only if more than 40 percent of the NHCEs in the plan have attained ages at least equal to the plan's target age, and more than 20 percent of the NHCEs in the plan have attained ages at least equal to the average attained age of the HCEs in the plan. For this purpose, a plan's target age is the lower of age 50 or the average attained age of the HCEs in the plan minus X years, where X equals 20 minus the product of five times the employee contribution rate under the plan. In no case, however, may X years be fewer than zero (0) years. Thus, for example, if the average attained age of the HCEs in the plan is 53 and the employee contribution rate is two percent of plan year compensation, the plan's target age is 43 years (i.e., 53 – (20 – (5 × 2))).

(3) *Ratio test.*—This test is satisfied only if the percentage of all nonhighly compensated nonexcludable employees, who are in the plan and who have attained ages at least equal to the average attained age of the HCEs in the plan, is at least 70 percent of the percentage of all highly compensated nonexcludable employees, who are in the plan and who have attained ages at least equal to the average attained age of the HCEs in the plan. Attained ages must be determined as of the beginning of the plan year. In lieu of determining the actual distribution of the attained ages of the HCEs, an employer may assume that 50 percent of all HCEs have attained ages at least equal to the average attained age of the HCEs.

(iii) *Determination of employer-provided benefit.*—(A) *Safe harbor plans other than section 401(l) plans.*—For purposes of applying the exception to the safe harbor in §1.401(a)(4)-3(b)(6)(viii) with respect to employer-provided benefits under a plan other than a section 401(l) plan, the employee's entire accrued benefit is treated as employer-provided.

(B) *Section 401(l).*—(1) *General rule.*—For purposes of applying the exception to the safe harbor in §1.401(a)(4)-3(b)(6)(viii) with respect to employer-provided benefits under a section 401(l) plan, an employee's base benefit percentage and excess benefit percentage are reduced, or an employee's gross benefit percentage is reduced, by subtracting the product of the employee contribution rate and the factor determined under paragraph (b)(2)(iv) of this section from the respective percentages for the plan year. For this purpose, the employee contribution rate is the highest rate of employee contributions applicable to any potential level of plan year compensation for that plan year under the plan.

(2) *Excess plans with varying contribution rates.*—In the case of a defined benefit excess plan described in the second sentence of paragraph (b)(2)(ii)(A) of this section, solely for purposes of reducing an employee's base benefit percentage as required under paragraph (b)(2)(iii)(B)(1) of this section, it may be assumed that the employee's employee contribution rate equals the weighted average of the base employee contribution rate and the excess employee contribution rate. In determining this weighted average, the weight of the base employee contribution rate is equal to a fraction, the numerator of which is the lesser of the integration level and the contribution breakpoint and the denominator of which is the integration level. The weight of the excess employee contribution rate is equal to the difference between one and the weight of the base employee contribution rate.

(3) *Offset plans with varying contribution rates.*—In the case of an offset plan described in the second sentence of paragraph (b)(2)(ii)(A) of this section, an equivalent adjustment to the alternative method in paragraph (b)(2)(iii)(B)(2) of this section may be made to the offset percentage.

(C) *Employer-provided benefits under the general test.*—For purposes of applying the general test of §1.401(a)(4)-3(c) with respect to employer-provided benefits, an employee's normal and most valuable accrual rates otherwise determined under §1.401(a)(4)-3(d) (without applying any of the options under §1.401(a)(4)-3(d)(3) other than the fresh-start alternative of §1.401(a)(4)-3(d)(3)(iii)) are each reduced by subtracting the product of the employee's contributions (expressed as a percentage of plan year compensation) and the factor determined under paragraph (b)(2)(iv) of this section from the respective accrual rates. A plan may then apply the optional rules in §1.401(a)(4)-3(d)(3)(i) and (ii) to this resulting accrual rate.

(D) *Additional limitation.*—A plan may not use the composition-of-workforce method provided in this paragraph (b)(2) to determine an employee's base benefit percentage, excess benefit percentage, gross benefit percentage, offset percentage, or accrual rates unless employee contributions have been made at the same rate (or rates) throughout the period after the fresh-start date or throughout the measurement period used to determine accrual rates.

(iv) *Determination of plan factor.*—The factor for a plan is determined under the following table based on the average entry age of the employees in the plan and on whether the plan determines benefits based on average compensation. For this purpose, average entry age equals the average attained age of all employees in the plan, minus the average years of participation of all employees in the plan. A plan is treated as determining benefits based on average compensation if it determines benefits based on compensation averaged over a specified period not exceeding five consecutive years (or the employee's entire period of employment with the employer, if shorter).

TABLE OF FACTORS

| Average Entry Age | Factors | |
	Average Compensation Benefit Formula	Other Formulas
Less than 30	0.5	0.75
30 to 40	0.4	0.6
Over 40	0.2	0.3

(v) *Examples.*—The following examples illustrate the rules of this paragraph (b)(2):

Example 1. Plan A is a contributory DB plan that is a defined benefit excess plan providing a benefit equal to 2.0 percent of employees' average annual compensation at or below covered compensation, plus 2.5 percent of average annual compensation above covered compensation, times years of service up to 35. Under the plan, average annual compensation is determined using a five-consecutive-year period for purposes of §1.401(a)(4)-3(e)(2). The plan requires employee contributions at a rate of four percent of plan year compensation for all employees. Assume that the plan satisfies the demographic requirements of paragraph (b)(2)(ii)(B) of this section. Under these facts, the plan satisfies the eligibility requirements of paragraph (b)(2)(ii) of this section. Assume, further, that the average attained age for all employees in the plan is 55, and that the average years of participation of all employees in the plan is 10. The average entry age for the plan is therefore 45, and, accordingly, the appropriate factor under the table is 0.2. Thus, in applying the safe harbor requirements of §1.401(a)(4)-3(b) to this plan for the plan year (including the requirements of §1.401(1)-3), the employee's base benefit percentage and excess benefit percentage are each reduced by 0.8 percent (4 percent × 0.2) and equal 1.2 percent and 1.7 percent, respectively.

Example 2. The facts are the same as in *Example 1*, except that the employee contribution rate is two percent of plan year compensation up to the covered compensation level, and four percent for plan year compensation at or above that contribution breakpoint. The employer elects to apply the alternative method in paragraph (b)(2)(iii)(B)(2) of this section to determine the reduction in the base benefit percentage. Because the contribution breakpoint is equal to the integration level, the weight of the employee contribution rate below the contribution breakpoint is 100 percent, and the weight of the employee contribution rate above the contribution breakpoint is zero. Thus, the weighted average of employee contribution rates is two percent. Under the alternative method in paragraph (b)(2)(iii)(B)(2) of this section, the reduction in the employee's base benefit percentage is 0.4. In applying the safe harbor requirements of §1.401(a)(4)-3(b) to this plan (including the requirements of §1.401(1)-3), the employee's base benefit percentage is 1.6 percent, and the employee's excess benefit percentage is 1.7.

Example 3. The facts are the same as in *Example 1*, except that the employee contribution rate is two percent of plan year compensation up to 50 percent of the covered compensation level, and four percent for plan year compensation at or above that contribution breakpoint. Because the contribution breakpoint is equal to 50 percent of the integration level, the weight of the employee contribution rate below the contribution breakpoint is 50 percent, and the weight of the employee contribution rate above the contribution breakpoint is 50 percent. Thus, the weighted average of employee contribution rates is three percent. Under the alternative method in paragraph (b)(2)(iii)(B)(2) of this section, the reduction in the employee's base benefit percentage is 0.6. In applying the safe harbor requirements of §1.401(a)(4)-3(b) to this plan (including the requirements of §1.401(1)-3), the employee's base benefit percentage is 1.4 percent, and the employee's excess benefit percentage is 1.7.

Example 4. The facts are the same as in *Example 1*, except that the plan is tested using the general test in §1.401(a)(4)-3(c). Assume

Employee M benefits under Plan A and has a normal accrual rate for the plan year (calculated with respect to Employee M's total accrued benefit) of 2.2 percent of average annual compensation. In applying the general test in §1.401(a)(4)-3(c) with respect to employer-provided benefits, this rate is reduced by 0.8 to yield a normal accrual rate of 1.4 percent. This rate may then be adjusted using either of the optional rules in §1.401(a)(4)-3(d)(3)(i) or (ii).

(3) *Minimum-benefit method.*—(i) *Application of uniform factors.*—A contributory DB plan that satisfies the uniform rate requirement of paragraph (b)(2)(ii)(A) of this section and the minimum benefit requirement of paragraph (b)(3)(ii) of this section may apply the adjustments provided in paragraph (b)(2)(iii) of this section as if the average entry age of employees in the plan were within the range of 30 to 40, without regard to the actual demographics of the employees in the plan.

(ii) *Minimum benefit requirement.*—This requirement is satisfied if the plan provides that, in plan years beginning on or after the effective date of these regulations, as set forth in §1.401(a)(4)-13(a) and (b), each employee will accrue a benefit that equals or exceeds the sum of—

(A) The accrued benefit derived from employee contributions made for plan years beginning on or after the effective date of these regulations, determined in accordance with section 411(c); and

(B) Fifty percent of the total benefit accrued in plan years beginning on or after the effective date of these regulations, as determined under the plan benefit formula without regard to that portion of the formula designed to satisfy the minimum benefit requirement of this paragraph (b)(3)(ii).

(iii) *Example.*—The following example illustrates the minimum-benefit method of this paragraph (b)(3):

Example. Plan A is contributory DB plan. For the plan year beginning in 1994, Employee M participates in Plan A and accrues a benefit under the terms of the plan (without regard to the minimum benefit requirement of paragraph (b)(3)(ii) of this section) of $3,000. The portion of Employee M's benefit accrual for the plan year beginning in 1994 derived from employee contributions is $2,000, determined by applying the rules of section 411(c) to such contributions. The requirement of paragraph (b)(3)(ii) of this section is not satisfied for the plan year beginning in 1994 unless the plan provides that Employee M's benefit accrual for the plan year beginning in 1994 is equal to $3,500 ($2,000 + (50 percent × $3,000)).

(4) *Grandfather rule for plans in existence on May 14, 1990.*—A contributory DB plan that satisfies paragraph (c)(4) of this section may determine an employee's employer-provided benefit by subtracting from the employee's total benefit the employee-provided benefits determined using any reasonable method set forth in the plan, provided that it is the same method used in determining whether the plan satisfies paragraph (c)(4)(ii)(D) of this section.

(5) *Government-plan method.*—A contributory DB plan that is established and maintained for its employees by the government of any state or political subdivision or by any agency or instrumentality thereof may treat an employee's total benefit as entirely employer-provided.

(6) *Cessation of employee contributions.*—If a contributory DB plan provides that no employee contributions may be made to the plan after the last day of the first plan year beginning on or after the effective date of these regulations, as set forth in §1.401(a)(4)-13(a) and (b), the plan may treat an employee's total benefit as entirely employer-provided.

(c) *Rules applicable in determining whether employee-provided benefits are nondiscriminatory in amount.*—(1) *In general.*—A contributory DB plan satisfies §1.401(a)(4)-1(b) with respect to the amount of employee-provided benefits for a plan year only if the plan satisfies the requirements of paragraph (c)(2), (c)(3), or (c)(4) of this section for the plan year. This requirement applies regardless of the method used to determine the amount of employer-provided benefits under paragraph (b) of this section.

(2) *Same rate of contributions.*—This requirement is satisfied for a plan year if the employee contribution rate (within the meaning of paragraph (b)(2)(ii)(A) of this section) is the same for all employees for the plan year.

(3) *Total-benefits method.*—This requirement is satisfied for a plan year if—

(i) The total benefits (i.e., the sum of employer-provided and employee-provided benefits) under the plan would satisfy §1.401(a)(4)-3 if all benefits were treated as employer-provided benefits; and

(ii) The plan's contribution requirements satisfy paragraph (b)(2)(ii)(A) of this section.

(4) *Grandfather rules for plans in existence on May 14, 1990.*—(i) *In general.*—This requirement is satisfied for a plan year if the plan contained provisions as of May 14, 1990, that meet the requirements of paragraph (c)(4)(ii) or (c)(4)(iii) of this section.

(ii) *Graded contribution rates.*—The plan's provisions meet the requirements of this paragraph (c)(4)(ii) if all the following requirements are met:

(A) The provisions require employee contributions at a greater rate (expressed as a percentage of compensation) at higher levels of compensation than at lower levels of compensation.

(B) The required rate of employee contributions is not increased after May 14, 1990, although the level of compensation at which employee contributions are required may be increased or decreased.

(C) All employees are permitted to make employee contributions under the plan at a uniform rate with respect to all compensation, beginning no later than the last day of the first plan year to which these regulations apply, as set forth in §1.401(a)(4)-13(a) and (b).

(D) The benefits provided on account of employee contributions at lower levels of compensation are comparable to those provided on account of employee contributions at higher levels of compensation.

(iii) *Prior year compensation.*—The plan's provisions meet the requirements of this paragraph (c)(4)(iii) if they are part of a plan maintained by more than one employer that requires employee contributions and the rate of required employee contributions, expressed as a percentage of compensation for the last calendar year ending before the beginning of the plan year, is the same for all employees. [Reg. §1.401(a)(4)-6.]

□ [*T.D. 8360, 9-12-91. Amended by T.D. 8485, 8-30-93.*]

[Reg. §1.401(a)(4)-7]

§1.401(a)(4)-7. Imputation of permitted disparity.—(a) *Introduction.*—In determining whether a plan satisfies section 401(a)(4) with respect to the amount of contributions or benefits, section 401(a)(5)(C) allows the disparities permitted under section 401(l) to be taken into account. For purposes of satisfying the safe harbors of §§1.401(a)(4)-2(b)(2) and 1.401(a)(4)-3(b), permitted disparity may be taken into account only by satisfying section 401(l) in form in accordance with §1.401(l)-2 or 1.401(l)-3, respectively. For

purposes of the general tests of §§1.401(a)(4)-2(c) and 1.401(a)(4)-3(c), permitted disparity may be taken into account only in accordance with the rules of this section. In general, this section allows permitted disparity to be arithmetically imputed with respect to employer-provided contributions or benefits by determining an adjusted allocation or accrual rate that appropriately accounts for the permitted disparity with respect to each employee. Paragraph (b) of this section provides rules for imputing permitted disparity with respect to employer-provided contributions by adjusting each employee's unadjusted allocation rate. Paragraph (c) of this section provides rules for imputing permitted disparity with respect to employer-provided benefits by adjusting each employee's unadjusted accrual rate. Paragraph (d) of this section provides rules of general application.

(b) *Adjusting allocation rates.*—(1) *In general.*—The rules in this paragraph (b) produce an adjusted allocation rate for each employee by determining the excess contribution percentage under the hypothetical formula that would yield the allocation actually received by the employee, if the plan took into account the full disparity permitted under section 401(l)(2) and used the taxable wage base as the integration level. This adjusted allocation rate is used to determine whether the amount of contributions under the plan satisfies the general test of §1.401(a)(4)-2(c) and to apply the average benefit percentage test on the basis of contributions under §1.410(b)-5(d). Paragraphs (b)(2) and (b)(3) of this section apply to employees whose plan year compensation does not exceed and does exceed, respectively, the taxable wage base, and paragraph (b)(4) of this section provides definitions.

(2) *Employees whose plan year compensation does not exceed taxable wage base.*—If an employee's plan year compensation does not exceed the taxable wage base, the employee's adjusted allocation rate is the lesser of the A rate and the B rate determined under the formulas below, where the permitted disparity rate and the unadjusted allocation rate are determined under paragraph (b)(4)(ii) and (iv) of this section, respectively.

A Rate = 2 × unadjusted allocation rate
B Rate = unadjusted allocation rate + permitted disparity rate

(3) *Employees whose plan year compensation exceeds taxable wage base.*—If an employee's plan year compensation exceeds the taxable wage base, the employee's adjusted allocation rate is the lesser of the C rate and the D rate determined under the formulas below, where allocations and the permitted disparity rate are determined under paragraph (b)(4)(i) and (ii) of this section, respectively.

$$C \text{ Rate} = \frac{\text{allocations}}{\text{plan year compensation} - \tfrac{1}{2} \text{ taxable wage base}}$$

$$D \text{ Rate} = \frac{\text{allocations} + (\text{permitted disparity rate} \times \text{taxable wage base})}{\text{plan year compensation}}$$

(4) *Definitions.*—In applying this paragraph (b), the following definitions govern—

(i) *Allocations.*—Allocations means the amount determined by multiplying the employee's plan year compensation by the employee's unadjusted allocation rate.

(ii) *Permitted disparity rate.*—(A) *General rule.*—Permitted disparity rate means the rate in effect as of the beginning of the plan year under section 401(l)(2)(A)(ii) (e.g., 5.7 percent for plan years beginning in 1990).

(B) *Cumulative permitted disparity limit.*—Notwithstanding paragraph (b)(4)(ii)(A) of this section, the permitted disparity rate is zero for an employee who has benefited under a defined benefit plan taken into account under §1.401(l)-5(a)(3) for a plan year that begins on or after one year from the first day of the first plan year to which these regulations apply, as set forth in §1.401(a)(4)-13(a) and (b), if imputing permitted disparity would result in a cumulative disparity fraction for the employee, as defined in §1.401(l)-5(c)(2), that exceeds 35. See §1.401(l)-5(c)(1) for special rules for determining whether an employee has benefited under a defined benefit plan for this purpose.

(iii) *Taxable wage base.*—Taxable wage base means the taxable wage base, as defined in §1.401(l)-1(c)(32), in effect as of the beginning of the plan year.

(iv) *Unadjusted allocation rate.*—Unadjusted allocation rate means the employee's allocation rate determined under §1.401(a)(4)-2(c)(2)(i) for the plan year (expressed as a percentage of plan year compensation), without imputing permitted disparity under this section.

(5) *Example.*—The following example illustrates the rules in this paragraph (b):

Example. (a) Employees M and N participate in a defined contribution plan maintained by Employer X. Employee M has plan year compensation of $30,000 in the 1990 plan year and has an unadjusted allocation rate of five percent. Employee N has plan year compensation of $100,000 in the 1990 plan year and has an unadjusted allocation rate of eight percent. The taxable wage base in 1990 is $51,300.

(b) Because Employee M's plan year compensation does not exceed the taxable wage base, Employee M's A rate is 10 percent (2 x 5 percent), and Employee M's B rate is 10.7 percent (5 percent + 5.7 percent). Thus, Employee M's adjusted allocation rate is 10 percent, the lesser of the A rate and the B rate.

(c) Employee N's allocations are $8,000 (8 percent x $100,000). Because Employee N's plan year compensation exceeds the taxable wage base, Employee N's C rate is 10.76 percent ($8,000 divided by ($100,000 − (1/2 × $51,300))), and Employee N's D rate is 10.92 percent (($8,000 + (5.7 percent × $51,300)) divided by $100,000). Thus, Employee N's adjusted allocation rate is 10.76 percent, the lesser of the C rate and the D rate.

(c) *Adjusting accrual rates.*—(1) *In general.*—The rules in this paragraph (c) produce an adjusted accrual rate for each employee by determining the excess benefit percentage under the hypothetical plan formula that would yield the employer-provided accrual actually received by the employee, if the plan took into account the full permitted disparity under section 401(l)(3)(A) in each of the first 35 years of an employee's testing service under the plan and used the employee's covered compensation as the integration level. This adjusted accrual rate is used to determine whether the amount of employer-provided benefits under the plan satisfies the alternative safe harbor for flat benefit plans under §1.401(a)(4)-3(b)(4)(i)(C)(3) or the general test of § 1.401(a)(4)-3(c), and to apply the average benefit percentage test on the basis of benefits under § 1.410(b)-5. Paragraphs (c)(2) and (c)(3) of this section apply to employees whose average annual compensation does not exceed and does exceed, respectively, covered compensation, and paragraph (c)(4) of this section provides definitions. Paragraph (c)(5) of this section provides a special rule for employees with negative unadjusted accrual rates.

(2) *Employees whose average annual compensation does not exceed covered compensation.*—If an employee's average annual compensation does not exceed the employee's covered compensation, the employee's adjusted accrual rate is the lesser of the A rate and the B rate determined under the formulas below, where the permitted

$$\text{C Rate} = \frac{\text{employer-provided accrual}}{\text{average annual compensation} - {}^{1}\!/_{2} \text{ covered compensation}}$$

$$\text{D Rate} = \frac{\text{employer-provided accrual} + (\text{permitted disparity factor} \times \text{covered compensation})}{\text{average annual compensation}}$$

(4) *Definitions.*—For purposes of this paragraph (c), the following definitions apply.

(i) *Covered compensation.*—Covered compensation means covered compensation as defined in § 1.401(l)-1(c)(7). Notwithstanding § 1.401(l)-1(c)(7)(iii), an employee's covered compensation must be automatically adjusted each plan year for purposes of applying this paragraph (c).

(ii) *Employer-provided accrual.*—Employer-provided accrual means the amount determined by multiplying the employee's average annual compensation by the employee's unadjusted accrual rate.

(iii) *Permitted disparity factor.*—(A) *General rule.*—Permitted disparity factor for an employee means the sum of the employee's annual permitted disparity factors determined under paragraph (c)(4)(iii)(B) of this section for each of the years in the measurement period used for determining the employee's accrual rate in § 1.401(a)(4)-3(d)(1), divided by the employee's testing service during that measurement period.

(B) *Annual permitted disparity factor.*—(1) *Definition.*—An employee's annual permitted disparity factor is generally 0.75 percent adjusted, pursuant to § 1.401(l)-3(e), using as the age at which benefits commence the lesser of age 65 or the employee's testing age. No adjustments are made in the annual permitted disparity factor unless an employee's testing age is different from the employee's social security retirement age. An annual permitted disparity factor that is less than the annual permitted disparity factor described in the first sentence of this paragraph (c)(4)(iii)(B)(1) may be used if it is a uniform percentage of that factor (e.g., 50 percent of the annual permitted disparity factor) or a fixed percentage (e.g., 0.65 percent) for all employees.

(2) *Annual permitted disparity factor after 35 years.*—For purposes of determining the sum described in paragraph (c)(4)(iii)(A) of this section, the annual permitted disparity factor for each of the employee's first 35 years of testing service is the amount described in paragraph (c)(4)(iii)(B)(1) of this section, and the annual permitted disparity factor in any subsequent year equals zero. This rule applies regardless of whether the end of the measurement period extends beyond an employee's first 35 years of testing service. Thus, for example, if the measurement period is the current plan year and the employee completed 35 years of testing service prior to the beginning of the current plan year, under this paragraph (c)(4)(iii)(B)(2) the annual permitted disparity factor in the current plan year (and hence the sum of the annual permitted disparity factors for each year in the measurement period) is zero.

(3) *Cumulative permitted disparity limit.*—The 35 years used in paragraph (c)(4)(iii)(B)(2) of this section must be reduced by the employee's cumulative disparity fraction, as defined in § 1.401(l)-5(c)(2), but determined solely with respect to the employee's total years of service under all plans taken into account under § 1.401(l)-5(a)(3) during the measurement period, other than the plan being tested.

(iv) *Social security retirement age.*—Social security retirement age means social security retirement age as defined in section 415(b)(8).

(v) *Unadjusted accrual rate.*—Unadjusted accrual rate means the normal or most valuable accrual rate, whichever is being determined for the employee under § 1.401(a)(4)-3(d), expressed as a per-

disparity factor and the unadjusted accrual rate are determined under paragraph (c)(4)(iii) and (v) of this section, respectively.

A Rate = 2 × unadjusted accrual rate

B Rate = unadjusted accrual rate + permitted disparity factor

(3) *Employees whose average annual compensation exceeds covered compensation.*—If an employee's average annual compensation exceeds the employee's covered compensation, the employee's adjusted accrual rate is the lesser of the C rate and D rate determined under the formulas below, where the employer-provided accrual and the permitted disparity factor are determined under paragraph (c)(4)(ii) and (iii) of this section, respectively.

centage of average annual compensation, without imputing permitted disparity under this section.

(5) *Employees with negative unadjusted accrual rates.*—Notwithstanding the formulas in paragraph (c)(2) and (c)(3) of this section, if an employee's unadjusted accrual rate is less than zero, the employee's adjusted accrual rate is deemed to be the employee's unadjusted accrual rate.

(6) *Example.*—The following example illustrates the rules in this paragraph (c):

Example. (a) Employees M and N participate in a defined benefit plan that uses a normal retirement age of 65. The plan is being tested for the plan year under § 1.401(a)(4)-3(c), using unadjusted accrual rates determined using a plan year measurement period under § 1.401(a)(4)-3(d)(1)(iii)(A). Employee M has an unadjusted normal accrual rate of 1.48 percent, average annual compensation of $21,000, and an employer-provided accrual of $311 (1.48 percent x $21,000). Employee N has an unadjusted normal accrual rate of 1.7 percent, average annual compensation of $106,000, and an employer-provided accrual of $1,802 (1.7 percent x $106,000). The covered compensation of both Employees M and N is $25,000, and social security retirement age for both employees is 65. Neither employee has testing service of more than 35 years and neither has ever participated in another plan.

(b) Because Employee M's average annual compensation does not exceed covered compensation, Employee M's A rate is 2.96 percent (2.0 x 1.48 percent), and Employee M's B rate is 2.23 percent (1.48 percent + 0.75 percent). Thus, Employee M's adjusted accrual rate is 2.23 percent, the lesser of the A rate and the B rate.

(c) Because Employee N's average annual compensation exceeds covered compensation, Employee N's C rate is 1.93 percent ($1,802/($106,000 − (0.5 × $25,000))), and Employee N's D rate is 1.88 percent (($1,802 + (0.75 percent × $25,000))/$106,000). Thus, Employee N's adjusted accrual rate is 1.88 percent, the lesser of the C rate and the D rate.

(d) *Rules of general application.*—(1) *Eligible plans.*—The rules in this section may be used only for those plans to which the permitted disparity rules of section 401(l) are available. See § 1.401(l)-1(a)(3).

(2) *Exceptions from consistency requirements.*—A plan does not fail to satisfy the consistency requirements of § 1.401(a)(4)-2(c)(2)(vi) or § 1.401(a)(4)-3(d)(2)(i) merely because the plan does not impute disparity for some employees to the extent required to comply with paragraph (d)(3) of this section, or because the plan does not impute disparity for any employees (including self-employed individuals within the meaning of section 401(c)(1)) who are not covered by any of the taxes under section 3111(a), section 3221, or section 1401.

(3) *Overall permitted disparity.*—The annual overall permitted disparity limits of § 1.401(l)-5(b) apply to the employer-provided contributions and benefits for an employee under all plans taken into account under § 1.401(l)-5(a)(3). Thus, if an employee who benefits under the plan for the current plan year also benefits under a section 401(l) plan for the plan year ending with or within the current plan year, permitted disparity may not be imputed for that employee for the plan year. See § 1.401(l)-5(b)(9), *Example 4.* Similarly, if an employee who benefits under the plan for the current plan year also benefits under another plan of the employer for the plan year ending with or within the current plan year, disparity may be imputed for that employee under only one of the plans. [Reg. § 1.401(a)(4)-7.]

☐ [T.D. 8360, 9-12-91. *Amended by* T.D. 8485, 8-30-93.]

[Reg. §1.401(a)(4)-8]

§1.401(a)(4)-8. Cross-testing.—(a) *Introduction.*—This section provides rules for testing defined benefit plans on the basis of equivalent employer-provided contributions and defined contribution plans on the basis of equivalent employer-provided benefits under §1.401(a)(4)-1(b)(2). Paragraphs (b)(1) and (c)(1) of this section provide general tests for nondiscrimination based on individual equivalent accrual or allocation rates determined under paragraphs (b)(2) and (c)(2) of this section, respectively. Paragraphs (b)(3), (c)(3), and (d) of this section provide additional safe-harbor testing methods for target benefit plans, cash balance plans, and defined benefit plans that are part of floor-offset arrangements, respectively, that generally may be satisfied on a design basis.

(b) *Nondiscrimination in amount of benefits provided under a defined contribution plan.*—(1) *General rule and gateway.*—(i) *General rule.*—Equivalent benefits under a defined contribution plan (other than an ESOP) are nondiscriminatory in amount for a plan year if—

(A) The plan would satisfy §1.401(a)(4)-2(c)(1) for the plan year if an equivalent accrual rate, as determined under paragraph (b)(2) of this section, were substituted for each employee's allocation rate in the determination of rate groups; and

(B) For plan years beginning on or after January 1, 2002, the plan satisfies one of the following conditions—

(1) The plan has broadly available allocation rates (within the meaning of paragraph (b)(1)(iii) of this section) for the plan year;

(2) The plan has age-based allocation rates that are based on either a gradual age or service schedule (within the meaning of paragraph (b)(1)(iv) of this section) or a uniform target benefit allocation (within the meaning of paragraph (b)(1)(v) of this section) for the plan year; or

(3) The plan satisfies the minimum allocation gateway of paragraph (b)(1)(vi) of this section for the plan year.

(ii) *Allocations after testing age.*—A plan does not fail to satisfy paragraph (b)(1)(i)(A) of this section merely because allocations are made at the same rate for employees who are older than their testing age (determined without regard to the current-age rule in paragraph (4) of the definition of *testing age* in §1.401(a)(4)-12) as they are made for employees who are at that age.

(iii) *Broadly available allocation rates.*—(A) *In general.*—A plan has broadly available allocation rates for the plan year if each allocation rate under the plan is currently available during the plan year (within the meaning of §1.401(a)(4)4(b)(2)), to a group of employees that satisfies section 410(b) (without regard to the average benefit percentage test of §1.410(b)-5). For this purpose, if two allocation rates could be permissively aggregated under §1.401(a)(4)-4(d)(4), assuming the allocation rates were treated as benefits, rights or features, they may be aggregated and treated as a single allocation rate. In addition, the disregard of age and service conditions described in §1.401(a)(4)4(b)(2)(ii)(A) does not apply for purposes of this paragraph (b)(1)(iii)(A).

(B) *Certain transition allocations.*—In determining whether a plan has broadly available allocation rates for the plan year within the meaning of paragraph (b)(1)(iii)(A) of this section, an employee's allocation may be disregarded to the extent that the allocation is a transition allocation for the plan year. In order for an allocation to be a transition allocation, the allocation must comply with the requirements of paragraph (b)(1)(iii)(C) of this section and must be either—

(1) A defined benefit replacement allocation within the meaning of paragraph (b)(1)(iii)(D) of this section; or

(2) A pre-existing replacement allocation or pre-existing merger and acquisition allocation, within the meaning of paragraph (b)(1)(iii)(E) of this section.

(C) *Plan provisions relating to transition allocations.*—(1) *In general.*—Plan provisions providing for transition allocations for the plan year must specify both the group of employees who are eligible for the transition allocations and the amount of the transition allocations.

(2) *Limited plan amendments.*—Allocations are not transition allocations within the meaning of paragraph (b)(1)(iii)(B) of this section for the plan year if the plan provisions relating to the allocations are amended after the date those plan provisions are both adopted and effective. The preceding sentence in this paragraph (b)(1)(iii)(C)(2) does not apply to amendment that reduces transition allocations to HCEs, makes de minimis changes in the calculation of the transition allocations (such as a change in the definition of compensation to include section 132(f) elective reductions), or adds or removes a provision permitted under paragraph (b)(1)(iii)(C)(3) of this section.

(3) *Certain permitted plan provisions.*—An allocation does not fail to be a transition allocation within the meaning of paragraph (b)(1)(iii)(B) of this section merely because the plan provides that each employee who is eligible for a transition allocation receives the greater of such allocation and the allocation for which the employee would otherwise be eligible under the plan. In a plan that contains such a provision, for purposes of determining whether the plan has broadly available allocation rates within the meaning of paragraph (b)(1)(iii)(A) of this section, the allocation for which an employee would otherwise be eligible is considered currently available to the employee, even if the employee's transition allocation is greater.

(D) *Defined benefit replacement allocation.*—An allocation is a defined benefit replacement allocation for the plan year if it is provided in accordance with guidance prescribed by the Commissioner published in the Internal Revenue Bulletin (see §601.601 (d)(2)(ii)(b) of this chapter) and satisfies the following conditions—

(1) The allocations are provided to a group of employees who formerly benefitted under an established nondiscriminatory defined benefit plan of the employer or of a prior employer that provided age-based equivalent allocation rates;

(2) The allocations for each employee in the group were reasonably calculated, in a consistent manner, to replace the retirement benefits that the employee would have been provided under the defined benefit plan if the employee had continued to benefit under the defined benefit plan;

(3) Except as provided in paragraph (b)(1)(iii)(C) of this section, no employee who receives the allocation receives any other allocations under the plan for the plan year; and

(4) The composition of the group of employees who receive the allocations is nondiscriminatory.

(E) *Pre-existing transition allocation's.*—(1) *Pre-existing replacement allocations.*—An allocation is a pre-existing replacement allocation for the plan year if the allocation satisfies the following conditions—

(i) The allocations are provided pursuant to a plan provision adopted before June 29, 2001;

(ii) The allocations are provided to employees who formerly benefitted under a defined benefit plan of the employer; and

(iii) The allocations for each employee in the group are reasonably calculated, in a consistent manner, to replace some or all of the retirement benefits that the employee would have received under the defined benefit plan and any other plan or arrangement of the employer if the employee had continued to benefit under such defined benefit plan and such other plan or arrangement.

(2) *Pre-existing merger and acquisition allocations.*—An allocation is a pre-existing merger and acquisition allocation for the plan year if the allocation satisfies the following conditions—

(i) The allocations are provided solely to employees of a trade or business that has been acquired by the employer in a stock or asset acquisition, merger, or other similar transaction occurring prior to August 28, 2001 involving a change in the employer of the employees of the trade or business;

(ii) The allocations are provided only to employees who were employed by the acquired trade or business before a specified date that is no later than two years after the transaction (or January 1, 2002, if earlier);

(iii) The allocations are provided pursuant a plan provision adopted no later than the specified date; and

(iv) The allocations for each employee in the group are reasonably calculated, in a consistent manner, to replace some or all of the retirement benefits that the employee would have received under any plan of the employer if the new employer had continued to provide the retirement benefits that the prior employer was providing for employees of the trade or business.

(F) *Successor employers.*—An employer that accepts a transfer of assets (within the meaning of section 414(l)) from the plan of a prior employer may continue to treat any transition allocations provided under that plan as transition allocations under paragraph (b)(1)(iii)(B) of this section, provided that the successor employer continues to satisfy the applicable requirements set forth in paragraphs (b)(1)(iii)(C) through (E) of this section for the plan year.

(iv) *Gradual age or service schedule.*—(A) *In general.*—A plan has a gradual age or service schedule for the plan year if the allocation formula for all employees under the plan provides for a single schedule of allocation rates under which—

(1) The schedule defines a series of bands based solely on age, years of service, or the number of points representing the sum of age and years of service (age and service points), under which the same allocation rate applies to all employees whose age, years of service, or age and service points are within each band; and

(2) The allocation rates under the schedule increase smoothly at regular intervals, within the meaning of paragraphs (b)(1)(iv)(B) and (C) of this section.

(B) *Smoothly increasing schedule of allocation rates.*—A schedule of allocation rates increases smoothly if the allocation rate for each band within the schedule is greater than the allocation rate for the immediately preceding band (i.e., the band with the next lower number of years of age, years of service, or age and service points) but by no more than 5 percentage points. However, a schedule of allocation rates will not be treated as increasing smoothly if the ratio of the allocation rate for any band to the rate for the immediately preceding band is more than 2.0 or if it exceeds the ratio of allocation rates between the two immediately preceding bands.

(C) *Regular intervals.*—A schedule of allocation rates has regular intervals of age, years of service or age and service points, if each band, other than the band associated with the highest age, years of service, or age and service points, is the same length. For this purpose, if the schedule is based on age, the first band is deemed to be of the same length as the other bands if it ends at or before age 25. If the first age band ends after age 25, then, in determining whether the length of the first band is the same as the length of other bands, the starting age for the first age band is permitted to be treated as age 25 or any age earlier than 25. For a schedule of allocation rates based on age and service points, the rules of the preceding two sentences are applied by substituting 25 age and service points for age 25. For a schedule of allocation rates based on service, the starting service for the first service band is permitted to be treated as one year of service or any lesser amount of service.

(D) *Minimum allocation rates permitted.*—A schedule of allocation rates under a plan does not fail to increase smoothly at regular intervals, within the meaning of paragraphs (b)(1)(iv)(B) and (C) of this section, merely because a minimum uniform allocation rate is provided for all employees or the minimum benefit described in section 416(c)(2) is provided for all non-key employees (either because the plan is top heavy or without regard to whether the plan is top heavy) if the schedule satisfies one of the following conditions—

(1) The allocation rates under the plan that are greater than the minimum allocation rate can be included in a hypothetical schedule of allocation rates that increases smoothly at regular intervals, within the meaning of paragraphs (b)(1)(iv)(B) and (C) of this section, where the hypothetical schedule has a lowest allocation rate no lower than 1% of plan year compensation; or

(2) For a plan using a schedule of allocation rates based on age, for each age band in the schedule that provides an allocation rate greater than the minimum allocation rate, there could be an employee in that age band with an equivalent accrual rate that is less than or equal to the equivalent accrual rate that would apply to an employee whose age is the highest age for which the allocation rate equals the minimum allocation rate.

(v) *Uniform target benefit allocations.*—A plan has allocation rates that are based on a uniform target benefit allocation for the plan year if the plan fails to satisfy the requirements for the safe harbor testing method in paragraph (b)(3) of this section merely because the determination of the allocations under the plan differs from the allocations determined under that safe harbor testing method for any of the following reasons—

(A) The interest rate used for determining the actuarial present value of the stated plan benefit and the theoretical reserve is lower than a standard interest rate;

(B) The stated benefit is calculated assuming compensation increases at a specified rate; or

(C) The plan computes the current year contribution using the actual account balance instead of the theoretical reserve.

(vi) *Minimum allocation gateway.*—(A) *General rule.*—A plan satisfies the minimum allocation gateway of this paragraph (b)(1)(vi) if each NHCE has an allocation rate that is at least one third of the allocation rate of the HCE with the highest allocation rate.

(B) *Deemed satisfaction.*—A plan is deemed to satisfy the minimum allocation gateway of this paragraph (b)(1)(vi) if each NHCE receives an allocation of at least 5% of the NHCE's compensation within the meaning of section 415(c)(3), measured over a period of time permitted under the definition of plan year compensation.

(vii) *Determination of allocation rate.*—For purposes of paragraph (b)(1)(i)(B) of this section, allocations and allocation rates are determined under §1.401(a)(4)-2(c)(2), but without taking into account the imputation of permitted disparity under §1.401(a)(4)-7. However, in determining whether the plan has broadly available allocation rates as provided in paragraph (b)(1)(iii) of this section, differences in allocation rates attributable solely to the use of permitted disparity described in §1.401(1)-2 are disregarded.

(viii) *Examples.*—The following examples illustrate the rules in this paragraph (b)(1):

Example 1. (i) Plan M, a defined contribution plan without a minimum service requirement, provides an allocation formula under which allocations are provided to all employees according to the following schedule:

Completed Years of Service	Allocation Rate	Ratio of Allocation Rate for Band to Allocation Rate for Immediately Preceding Band
0-5	3.0%	not applicable
6-10	4.5%	1.50
11-15	6.5%	1.44
16-20	8.5%	1.31
21-25	10.0%	1.18
26 or more	11.5%	1.15

(ii) Plan M provides that allocation rates for all employees are determined using a single schedule based solely on service, as described in paragraph (b)(1)(iv)(A)(*1*) of this section. Therefore, if the allocation rates under the schedule increase smoothly at regular intervals as described in paragraph (b)(1)(iv)(A)(*2*) of this section, then the plan has a gradual age or service schedule described in paragraph (b)(1)(iv) of this section.

(iii) The schedule of allocation rates under Plan M does not increase by more than 5 percentage points between adjacent bands and the ratio of the allocation rate for any band to the allocation rate for the immediately preceding band is never more than 2.0 and does not increase. Therefore, the allocation rates increase smoothly as described in paragraph (b)(1)(iv)(B) of this section. In addition, the bands (other than the highest band) are all 5 years long, so the increases occur at regular intervals as described in paragraph (b)(1)(iv)(C) of this section. Thus, the allocation rates under the plan's schedule increase smoothly at regular intervals as described in paragraph (b)(1)(iv)(A)(*2*) of this section. Accordingly, the plan has a gradual age or service schedule described in paragraph (b)(1)(iv) of this section.

(iv) Under paragraph (b)(1)(i) of this section, Plan M satisfies the nondiscrimination in amount requirement of §1.401(a)(4)-1 (b)(2) on the basis of benefits if it satisfies paragraph (b)(1)(i)(A) of this section, regardless of whether it satisfies the minimum allocation gateway of paragraph (b)(1)(vi) of this section.

Example 2. (i) The facts are the same as in *Example 1*, except that the 4.5% allocation rate applies for all employees with 10 years of service or less.

(ii) Plan M provides that allocation rates for all employees are determined using a single schedule based solely on service, as described in paragraph (b)(1)(iv)(A)(*1*) of this section. Therefore, if the allocation rates under the schedule increase smoothly at regular intervals as described in paragraph (b)(1)(iv)(A)(*2*) of this section, then the plan has a gradual age or service schedule described in paragraph (b)(1)(iv) of this section.

(iii) The bands (other than the highest band) in the schedule are not all the same length, since the first band is 10 years long while other bands are 5 years long. Thus, the schedule does not have regular intervals as described in paragraph (b)(1)(iv)(C) of this section. However, under paragraph (b)(1)(iv)(D) of this section, the schedule of allocation rates does not fail to increase smoothly at regular intervals merely because the minimum allocation rate of 4.5% results in a first band that is longer than the other bands, if either of the conditions of paragraph (b)(1)(iv)(D)(*1*) or (*2*) of this section is satisfied.

(iv) In this case, the schedule of allocation rates satisfies the condition in paragraph (b)(1)(iv)(D)(*1*) of this section because the allocation rates under the plan that are greater than the 4.5% minimum allocation rate can be included in the following hypothetical schedule of allocation rates that increases smoothly at regular intervals and has a lowest allocation rate of at least 1% of plan year compensation:

Completed Years of Service	Allocation Rate	Ratio of Allocation Rate for Band to Allocation Rate for Immediately Preceding Band
0-5	2.5%	not applicable
6-10	4.5%	1.80
11-15	6.5%	1.44
16-20	8.5%	1.31
21-25	10.0%	1.18
26 or more	11.5%	1.15

(v) Accordingly, the plan has a gradual age or service schedule described in paragraph (b)(1)(iv) of this section. Under paragraph (b)(1)(i) of this section, Plan M satisfies the nondiscrimination in amount requirement of §1.401(a)(4)-1(b)(2) on the basis of benefits if it satisfies paragraph (b)(1)(i)(A) of this section, regardless of whether it satisfies the minimum allocation gateway of paragraph (b)(1)(vi) of this section.

Example 3. (i) Plan N, a defined contribution plan, provides an allocation formula under which allocations are provided to all employees according to the following schedule:

Age	Allocation rate	Ratio of Allocation Rate for Band to Allocation Rate for Immediately Preceding Band
under 25	3.0%	not applicable
25-34	6.0%	2.00
35-44	9.0%	1.50
45-54	12.0%	1.33
55-64	16.0%	1.33
65 or older	21.0%	1.31

(ii) Plan N provides that allocation rates for all employees are determined using a single schedule based solely on age, as described in paragraph (b)(1)(iv)(A)(1) of this section. Therefore, if the allocation rates under the schedule increase smoothly at regular intervals as described in paragraph (b)(1)(iv)(A)(2) of this section, then the plan has a gradual age or service schedule described in paragraph (b)(1)(iv) of this section.

(iii) The schedule of allocation rates under Plan N does not increase by more than 5 percentage points between adjacent bands and the ratio of the allocation rate for any band to the allocation rate for the immediately preceding band is never more than 2.0 and does not increase. Therefore, the allocation rates increase smoothly as described in paragraph (b)(1)(iv)(B) of this section. In addition, the bands (other than the highest band and the first band, which is deemed to be the same length as the other bands because it ends prior to age 25) are all 5 years long, so the increases occur at regular intervals as described in paragraph (b)(1)(iv)(C) of this section. Thus, the allocation rates under the plan's schedule increase smoothly at regular intervals as described in paragraph (b)(1)(iv)(A)(2) of this section. Accordingly, the plan has a gradual age or service schedule described in paragraph (b)(1)(iv) of this section.

(iv) Under paragraph (b)(1)(i) of this section, Plan N satisfies the nondiscrimination in amount requirement of §1.401(a)(4)-1(b)(2) on the basis of benefits if it satisfies paragraph (b)(1)(i)(A) of this section, regardless of whether it satisfies the minimum allocation gateway of paragraph (b)(1)(vi) of this section.

Example 4. (i) Plan O, a defined contribution plan, provides an allocation formula under which allocations are provided to all employees according to the following schedule:

Age	Allocation rate	Ratio of Allocation Rate for Band to Allocation Rate for Immediately Preceding Band
under 40	3 %	not applicable
40-44	6 %	2.00
45-49	9 %	1.50
50-54	12%	1.33
55-59	16%	1.33
60-64	20%	1.25
65 or older	25%	1.25

(ii) Plan O provides that allocation rates for all employees are determined using a single schedule based solely on age, as described in paragraph (b)(1)(iv)(A)(1) of this section. Therefore, if the allocation rates under the schedule increase smoothly at regular intervals as described in paragraph (b)(1)(iv)(A)(2) of this section, then the plan has a gradual age or service schedule described in paragraph (b)(1)(iv) of this section.

(iii) The bands (other than the highest band) in the schedule are not all the same length, since the first band is treated as 15 years long while other bands are 5 years long. Thus, the schedule does not have regular intervals as described in paragraph (b)(1)(iv)(C) of this section. However, under paragraph (b)(1)(iv)(D) of this section, the schedule of allocation rates does not fail to increase smoothly at regular intervals merely because the minimum allocation rate of 3% results in a first band that is longer than the other bands, if either of the conditions of paragraph (b)(1)(iv)(D)(1) or (2) of this section is satisfied.

(iv) In this case, in order to define a hypothetical schedule that could include the allocation rates in the actual schedule of allocation rates, each of the bands below age 40 would have to be 5 years long (or be treated as 5 years long). Accordingly, the hypothetical schedule would have to provide for a band for employees under age 30, a band for employees in the range 30-34 and a band for employees age 35-39.

(v) The ratio of the allocation rate for the age 40-44 band to the next lower band is 2.0. Accordingly, in order for the applicable allocations rates under this hypothetical schedule to increase smoothly, the ratio of the allocation rate for each band in the hypothetical schedule below age 40 to the allocation rate for the immediately preceding band would have to be 2.0. Thus, the allocation rate for the hypothetical band applicable for employees under age 30 would be .75%, the allocation rate for the hypothetical band for employees in the range 30-34 would be 1.5% and the allocation rate for employees in the range 35-39 would be 3%.

(vi) Because the lowest allocation rate under any possible hypothetical schedule is less than 1% of plan year compensation, Plan O will be treated as satisfying the requirements of paragraphs (b)(1)(iv)(B) and (C) of this section only if the schedule of allocation rates satisfies the steepness condition described in paragraph (b)(1)(iv)(D)(2) of this section. In this case, the steepness condition is not satisfied because the equivalent accrual rate for an employee age 39 is 2.81%, but there is no hypothetical employee in the band for

Mw

ages 40-44 with an equal or lower equivalent accrual rate (since the lowest equivalent accrual rate for hypothetical employees within this band is 3.74% at age 44).

(vii) Since the schedule of allocation rates under the plan does not increase smoothly at regular intervals, Plan O's schedule of allocation rates is not a gradual age or service schedule. Further, Plan O does not provide uniform target benefit allocations. Therefore, under paragraph (b)(1)(i) of this section, Plan O cannot satisfy the nondiscrimination in amount requirement of § 1.401 (a)(4)-1(b)(2) for the plan year on the basis of benefits unless either Plan O provides for broadly available allocation rates for the plan year as described in paragraph (b)(1)(iii) of this section (i.e., the allocation rate at each age is provided to a group of employees that satisfies section 410(b) without regard to the average benefit percentage test), or Plan O satisfies the minimum allocation gateway of paragraph (b)(1)(vi) of this section for the plan year.

Example 5. (i) Plan P is a profit-sharing plan maintained by Employer A that covers all of Employer A's employees, consisting of two HCEs, X and Y, and 7 NHCEs. Employee X's compensation is $170,000 and Employee Y's compensation is $150,000. The allocation for Employees X and Y is $30,000 each, resulting in an allocation rate of 17.65% for Employee X and 20% for Employee Y. Under Plan P, each NHCE receives an allocation of 5% of compensation within the meaning of section 415(c)(3), measured over a period of time permitted under the definition of plan year compensation.

(ii) Because the allocation rate for X is not currently available to any NHCE, Plan P does not have broadly available allocation rates within the meaning of paragraph (b)(1)(iii) of this section. Furthermore, Plan P does not provide for age based-allocation rates within the meaning of paragraph (b)(1)(iv) or (v) of this section. Thus, under paragraph (b)(1)(i) of this section, Plan P can satisfy the nondiscrimination in amount requirement of § 1.401(a)(4)-1(b)(2) for the plan year on the basis of benefits only if Plan P satisfies the minimum allocation gateway of paragraph (b)(1)(vi) of this section for the plan year.

(iii) The highest allocation rate for any HCE under Plan P is 20%. Accordingly, Plan P would satisfy the minimum allocation gateway of paragraph (b)(1)(vi) of this section if all NHCEs have an allocation rate of at least 6.67%, or if all NHCEs receive an allocation of at least 5% of compensation within the meaning of section 415(c)(3) (measured over a period of time permitted under the definition of plan year compensation).

(iv) Under Plan P, each NHCE receives an allocation of 5% of compensation within the meaning of section 415(c)(3) (measured over a period of time permitted under the definition of plan year compensation). Accordingly, Plan P satisfies the minimum allocation gateway of paragraph (b)(1)(vi) of this section.

(v) Under paragraph (b)(1)(i) of this section, Plan P satisfies the nondiscrimination in amount requirement of § 1.401(a)(4)-1(b)(2) on the basis of benefits if it satisfies paragraph (b)(1)(i)(A) of this section.

(2) *Determination of equivalent accrual rates.*—(i) *Basic definition.*—An employee's equivalent accrual rate for a plan year is the annual benefit that is the result of normalizing the increase in the employee's account balance during the measurement period, divided by the number of years in which the employee benefited under the plan during the measurement period, and expressed either as a dollar amount or as a percentage of the employee's average annual compensation. A measurement period that includes future years may not be used for this purpose.

(ii) *Rules of application.*—(A) *Determination of account balance.*—The increase in the account balance during the measurement period taken into account under paragraph (b)(2)(i) of this section does not include income, expenses, gains, or losses allocated during the measurement period that are attributable to the account balance as of the beginning of the measurement period, but does include any additional amounts that would have been included in the increase in the account balance but for the fact that they were previously distributed (including a reasonable adjustment for interest). In the case of a measurement period that is the current plan year, an employer may also elect to disregard the income, expenses, gains, and losses allocated during the current plan year that are attributable to the increase in account balance since the beginning of the year, and thus, determine the increase in account balance during the plan year taking into account only the allocations described in § 1.401(a)(4)-2(c)(2)(ii). In addition, an employer may disregard distributions made to a NHCE as well as distributions made to any employee in plan years beginning before a selected date no later than January 1, 1986.

(B) *Normalization.*—The account balances determined under paragraph (b)(2)(ii)(A) of this section are normalized by treating them as single-sum benefits that are immediately and unconditionally payable to the employee. A standard interest rate, and a straight life annuity factor that is based on the same or a different standard interest rate and on a standard mortality table, must be used in normalizing these benefits. In addition, no mortality may be assumed prior to the employee's testing age.

(iii) *Options.*—Any of the optional rules in § 1.401(a)(4)-3(d)(3) (e.g., imputation of permitted disparity) may be applied in determining an employee's equivalent accrual rate by substituting the employee's equivalent accrual rate (determined without regard to the option) for the employee's normal accrual rate (i.e., not most valuable accrual rate) in that section where appropriate. For this purpose, however, the last sentence of the fresh-start alternative in § 1.401(a)(4)-3(d)(3)(iii)(A) (dealing with compensation adjustments to the frozen accrued benefit) is not applicable. No other options are available in determining an employee's equivalent accrual rate except those (e.g., selection of alternative measurement periods) specifically provided in this paragraph (b)(2). Thus, for example, none of the optional special rules in § 1.401(a)(4)-3(f) (e.g., determination of benefits on other than a plan year basis under § 1.401(a)(4)-3(f)(6)) is available.

(iv) *Consistency rule.*—Equivalent accrual rates must be determined in a consistent manner for all employees for the plan year. Thus, for example, the same measurement periods and standard interest rates must be used, and any available options must be applied consistently if at all.

(3) *Safe-harbor testing method for target benefit plans.*—(i) *General rule.*—A target benefit plan is a money purchase pension plan under which contributions to an employee's account are determined by reference to the amounts necessary to fund the employee's stated benefit under the plan. Whether a target benefit plan satisfies section 401(a)(4) with respect to an equivalent amount of benefits is generally determined under paragraphs (b)(1) and (b)(2) of this section. A target benefit plan is deemed to satisfy section 401(a)(4) with respect to an equivalent amount of benefits, however, if each of the following requirements is satisfied:

(A) *Stated benefit formula.*—Each employee's stated benefit must be determined as the straight life annuity commencing at the employee's normal retirement age under a formula that would satisfy the requirements of § 1.401(a)(4)-3(b)(4)(i)(C)(1) or (2), and that would satisfy each of the uniformity requirements in § 1.401(a)(4)-3(b)(2) (taking into account the relevant exceptions provided in § 1.401(a)(4)-3(b)(6)), if the plan were a defined benefit plan with the same benefit formula. In determining whether these requirements are satisfied, the rules of § 1.401(a)(4)-3(f) do not apply, and, in addition, except as provided in paragraph (b)(3)(vii) of this section, an employee's stated benefit at normal retirement age under the stated benefit formula is deemed to accrue ratably over the period ending with the plan year in which the employee is projected to reach normal retirement age and beginning with the latest of: the first plan year in which the employee benefited under the plan, the first plan year taken into account in the stated benefit formula, and any plan year immediately following a plan year in which the plan did not satisfy this paragraph (b)(3). Thus, except as provided in paragraph (b)(3)(vii) of this section, under § 1.401(a)(4)-3(b)(2)(v) an employee's stated benefit may not take into account service in years prior to the first plan year that the employee benefited under the plan, and an employee's stated benefit may not take into account service in plan years prior to the current plan year unless the plan satisfied this paragraph (b)(3) in all of those prior plan years.

(B) *Employer and employee contributions.*—Employer contributions with respect to each employee must be based exclusively on the employee's stated benefit using the method provided in paragraph (b)(3)(iv) of this section, and forfeitures and any other amounts under the plan taken into account under § 1.401(a)(4)-2(c)(2)(ii) (other than employer contributions) are used exclusively to reduce employer contributions. Employee contributions (if any) may not be used to fund the stated benefit.

(C) *Permitted disparity.*—If permitted disparity is taken into account, the stated benefit formula must satisfy § 1.401(l)-3. For this purpose, the 0.75-percent factor in the maximum excess or offset allowance in § 1.401(l)-3(b)(2)(i) or (c)(3)(i), respectively, as adjusted in accordance with § 1.401(l)-3(d)(9) (and, if the employee's normal retirement age is not the employee's social security retirement age, § 1.401(l)-3(e)), is further reduced by multiplying the factor by 0.80.

(ii) *Changes in stated benefit formula.*—A plan does not fail to satisfy paragraph (b)(3)(i) of this section merely because the plan determines each employee's stated benefit in the current plan year under a stated benefit formula that differs from the stated benefit formula used to determine the employee's stated benefit in prior plan years.

(iii) *Stated benefits after normal retirement age.*—A target benefit plan may limit increases in the stated benefit after normal retirement age consistent with the requirements applicable to defined benefit plans under section 411(b)(1)(H) (without regard to section 411(b)(1)(H)(iii)), provided that the limitation applies on the same terms to all employees. Thus, post-normal retirement benefits required under §1.401(a)(4)-3(b)(2)(ii) must be provided under the stated benefit formula, subject to any uniformly applicable service cap under the formula.

(iv) *Method for determining required employer contributions.*—(A) *General rule.*—An employer's required contribution to the account of an employee for a plan year is determined based on the employee's stated benefit and the amount of the employee's theoretical reserve as of the date the employer's required contribution is determined for the plan year (the determination date). Paragraph (b)(3)(iv)(B) of this section provides rules for determining an employee's theoretical reserve. Paragraph (b)(3)(iv)(C) and (D) of this section provides rules for determining an employer's required contributions.

(B) *Theoretical reserve.*—(1) *Initial theoretical reserve.*—An employee's theoretical reserve as of the determination date for the first plan year in which the employee benefits under the plan, the first plan year taken into account under the stated benefit formula (if that is the current plan year), or the first plan year immediately following any plan year in which the plan did not satisfy this paragraph (b)(3), is zero.

(2) *Theoretical reserve in subsequent plan years.* An employee's theoretical reserve as of the determination date for a plan year (other than a plan year described in paragraph (b)(3)(iv)(B)(1) of this section) is the employee's theoretical reserve as of the determination date for the prior plan year, plus the employer's required contribution for the prior plan year (as limited by section 415, but without regard to the additional contributions described in paragraph (b)(3)(v) of this section) both increased by interest from the determination date for the prior plan year through the determination date for the current plan year, but not beyond the determination date for the plan year that includes the employee's normal retirement date. (Thus, an employee's theoretical reserve as of the determination date for a plan year does not include the amount of the employer's required contribution for the plan year.) The interest rate for determining employer contributions that was in effect on the determination date in the prior plan year must be applied to determine the required interest adjustment for this period. For plan years beginning after the effective date applicable to the plan under §1.401(a)(4)-13(a) or (b), a standard interest rate must be used, and may not be changed except on the determination date for a plan year.

(C) *Required contributions for employees under normal retirement age.*—The required employer contributions with respect to an employee whose attained age is less than the employee's normal retirement age must be determined for each plan year as follows:

(1) Determine the employee's fractional rule benefit (within the meaning of §1.411(b)-1(b)(3)(ii)(A)) under the plan's stated benefit formula as if the plan were a defined benefit plan with the same benefit formula.

(2) Determine the actuarial present value of the fractional rule benefit determined in paragraph (b)(3)(iv)(C)(1) of this section as of the determination date for the current plan year, using a standard interest rate and a standard mortality table that are set forth in the plan and that are the same for all employees, and assuming no mortality before the employee's normal retirement age.

(3) Determine the excess, if any, of the amount determined in paragraph (b)(3)(iv)(C)(2) of this section over the employee's theoretical reserve for the current plan year determined under paragraph (b)(3)(iv)(B) of this section.

(4) Determine the required employer contribution for the current plan year by amortizing on a level annual basis, using the same interest rate used for paragraph (b)(3)(iv)(C)(2) of this section, the result in paragraph (b)(3)(iv)(C)(3) of this section over the period beginning with the determination date for the current plan year and ending with the determination date for the plan year in which the employee is projected to reach normal retirement age.

(D) *Required contributions for employees over normal retirement age.*—The required employer contributions with respect to an employee whose attained age equals or exceeds the employee's normal retirement age is the excess, if any, of the actuarial present value, as of the determination date for the current plan year, of the employee's stated benefit for the current plan year (determined using an immediate straight life annuity factor based on a standard interest rate and a standard mortality table, for an employee whose attained age equals the employee's normal retirement age) over the employee's theoretical reserve as of the determination date.

(v) *Effect of section 415 and 416 requirements.*—A target benefit plan does not fail to satisfy this paragraph (b)(3) merely because required contributions under the plan are limited by section 415 in a

plan year. Similarly, a target benefit plan does not fail to satisfy this paragraph (b)(3) merely because additional contributions are made consistent with the requirements of section 416(c)(2) (regardless of whether the plan is top-heavy).

(vi) *Certain conditions on allocations.*—A target benefit plan does not fail to satisfy this paragraph (b)(3) merely because required contributions under the plan are subject to the conditions on allocations permitted under §1.401(a)(4)-2(b)(4)(iii).

(vii) *Special rules for target benefit plans qualified under prior law.*—(A) *Service taken into account prior to satisfaction of this paragraph.*—For purposes of determining whether the stated benefit formula satisfies paragraph (b)(3)(i)(A) of this section (e.g., whether the period over which an employee's stated benefit is deemed to accrue is the same as the period taken into account under the stated benefit formula as required by paragraph (b)(3)(i)(A) of this section), a target benefit plan that was adopted and in effect on September 19, 1991, is deemed to have satisfied this paragraph (b)(3), and an employee is treated as benefiting under the plan, in any year prior to the effective date applicable to the plan under §1.401(a)(4)-13(a) or (b) that was taken into account in the stated benefit formula under the plan on September 19, 1991, if the plan satisfied the applicable nondiscrimination requirements for target benefit plans for that prior year.

(B) *Initial theoretical reserve.*—Notwithstanding paragraph (b)(3)(iv)(B)(1) of this section, a target benefit plan under which the stated benefit formula takes into account service for an employee for plan years prior to the first plan year in which the plan satisfied this paragraph (b)(3), as permitted under paragraph (b)(3)(vii)(A) of this section, must determine an initial theoretical reserve for the employee as of the determination date for the last plan year beginning before such plan year under the rules of §1.401(a)(4)-13(e).

(C) *Satisfaction of prior law.*—In determining whether a plan satisfied the applicable nondiscrimination requirements for target benefit plans for any period prior to the effective date applicable to the plan under §1.401(a)(4)-13(a) or (b), no amendments after September 19, 1991, other than amendments necessary to satisfy section 401(l), are taken into account.

(viii) *Examples.*—The following examples illustrate the rules in this paragraph (b)(3):

Example 1. (a) Employer X maintains a target benefit plan with a calendar plan year that bases contributions on a stated benefit equal to 40 percent of each employee's average annual compensation, reduced pro rata for years of participation less than 25, payable annually as a straight life annuity commencing at normal retirement age. The UP-84 mortality table and an interest rate of 7.5 percent are used to calculate the contributions necessary to fund the stated benefit. Required contributions are determined on the last day of each plan year. The normal retirement age under the plan is 65. Employee M is 39 years old in 1994, has participated in the plan for six years, and has average annual compensation equal to $60,000 for the 1994 plan year. Assume that Employee M's theoretical reserve as of the last day of the 1993 plan year is $13,909, determined under §1.401(a)(4)-13(e), and that required employer contributions for 1993 were determined using an interest rate of six percent.

(b) Under these facts, Employer X's 1994 required contribution to fund Employee M's stated benefit is $1,318, calculated as follows:

(1) Employee M's fractional rule benefit is $24,000 (40 percent of Employee M's average annual compensation of $60,000).

(2) The actuarial present value of Employee M's fractional rule benefit as of the last day of the 1994 plan year is $30,960 (Employee M's fractional rule benefit of $24,000 multiplied by 1.290, the actuarial present value factor for an annual straight life annuity commencing at age 65 applicable to a 39-year-old employee, determined using the stated interest rate of 7.5 percent and the UP-84 mortality table, and assuming no mortality before normal retirement age).

(3) The actuarial present value of Employee M's fractional rule benefit ($30,960) is reduced by Employee M's theoretical reserve as of the last day of the 1994 plan year. The theoretical reserve on that day is $14,744—the $13,909 theoretical reserve as of the last day of the 1993 plan year, increased by interest for one year at the rate of six percent. Because the required contribution for the 1993 plan year is taken into account under §1.401(a)(4)-13(e)(2) in determining the theoretical reserve as of the last day of the 1993 plan year, it is not added to the theoretical reserve again in this paragraph (b)(3) of this *Example 1.* The resulting difference is $16,216 ($30,960 – $14,744).

(4) The $16,216 excess of the actuarial present value of Employee M's fractional rule benefit over Employee M's theoretical reserve is multiplied by 0.0813, the amortization factor applicable to a 39-year-old employee determined using the stated interest rate of 7.5 percent. The product of $1,318 is the amount of the required employer contribution for Employee M for the 1994 plan year.

Example 2. (a) The facts are the same as in *Example 1*, except that as of January 1, 1995, the plan's stated benefit formula is amended to provide for a stated benefit equal to 45 percent of average annual compensation, reduced pro rata for years of participation less than 25, payable annually as a straight life annuity commencing at normal retirement age. For the 1995 plan year, Employee M's average annual compensation continues to be $60,000. The mortality table used for the calculation of the employer's required contributions remains the same as in the prior plan year, but the plan's stated interest rate is changed to 8.0 percent effective as of December 31, 1995.

(b) Under these facts, Employer X's required contribution for Employee M is $1,290, calculated as follows:

(1) Employee M's fractional rule benefit is $27,000 (45 percent of $60,000).

(2) The actuarial present value of Employee M's fractional rule benefit as of the last day of the 1995 plan year is $32,319 ($27,000 multiplied by 1.197, the actuarial present value factor for an annuity commencing at age 65 applicable to a 40-year-old employee, determined using the stated interest rate of 8.0 percent and the UP-84 mortality table, and assuming no mortality before normal retirement age).

(3) The actuarial present value of Employee M's fractional rule benefit ($32,319) is reduced by Employee M's theoretical reserve as of the last day of the 1995 plan year. The theoretical reserve as of that day is $17,267—the $14,744 theoretical reserve as of the last day of the 1994 plan year plus the $1,318 required contribution for the 1994 plan year, both increased by interest for one year at the rate of 7.5 percent. The resulting difference is $15,052 ($32,319 – $17,267).

(4) The result in paragraph (b)(3) of this *Example 2* is multiplied by 0.0857, the amortization factor applicable to a 40-year-old employee determined using the stated interest rate of 8.0 percent. The product, $1,290, is the amount of the required employer contribution for Employee M for the 1995 plan year.

(c) *Nondiscrimination in amount of contributions under a defined benefit plan.*—(1) *General rule.*—Equivalent allocations under a defined benefit plan are nondiscriminatory in amount for a plan year if the plan would satisfy § 1.401(a)(4)-3(c)(1) (taking into account § 1.401(a)(4)-3(c)(3)) for the plan year if an equivalent normal and most valuable allocation rate, as determined under paragraph (c)(2) of this section, were substituted for each employee's normal and most valuable accrual rate, respectively, in the determination of rate groups.

(2) *Determination of equivalent allocation rates.*—(i) *Basic definitions.*—An employee's equivalent normal and most valuable allocation rates for a plan year are, respectively, the actuarial present value of the increase over the plan year in the benefit that would be taken into account in determining the employee's normal and most valuable accrual rates for the plan year, expressed either as a dollar amount or as a percentage of the employee's plan year compensation. In the case of a contributory DB plan, the rules in § 1.401(a)(4)-6(b)(1), (b)(5), or (b)(6) must be used to determine the amount of each employee's employer-provided benefit that would be taken into account for this purpose.

(ii) *Rules for determining actuarial present value.*—The actuarial present value of the increase in an employee's benefit must be determined using a standard interest rate and a standard mortality table, and no mortality may be assumed prior to the employee's testing age.

(iii) *Options.*—The optional rules in § 1.401(a)(4)-2(c)(2)(iv) (imputation of permitted disparity) and (v) (grouping of rates) may be applied to determine an employee's equivalent normal and most valuable allocation rates by substituting those rates (determined without regard to the option) for the employee's allocation rate in that section where appropriate. In addition, the limitations under section 415 may be taken into account under § 1.401(a)(4)-3(d)(2)(ii)(B), and qualified disability benefits may be taken into account as accrued benefits under § 1.401(a)(4)-3(f)(2), in determining the increase in an employee's accrued benefit during a plan year for purposes of paragraph (c)(2)(i) of this section, if those rules would otherwise be available. No other options are available in determining an employee's equivalent normal and most valuable allocations rate except those (e.g., selection of alternative standard interest rates) specifically provided in this paragraph (c)(2). Thus, while all of the mandatory rules in § 1.401(a)(4)-3(d) and (f) for determining the amount of benefits used to determine an employee's normal and most valuable accrual rates (e.g., the treatment of early retirement window benefits in § 1.401(a)(4)-3(f)(4)) are applicable in determining an employee's equivalent normal and most valuable allocation rates, none of the optional rules under § 1.401(a)(4)-3 is available (except the options relating to the section 415 limits and qualified disability benefits noted above).

(iv) *Consistency rule.*—Equivalent allocation rates must be determined in a consistent manner for all employees for the plan year. Thus, for example, the same standard interest rates must be used, and any available options must be applied consistently if at all.

(3) *Safe harbor testing method for cash balance plans.*—(i) *General rule.*—A cash balance plan is a defined benefit plan that defines benefits for each employee by reference to the employee's hypothetical account. An employee's hypothetical account is determined by reference to hypothetical allocations and interest adjustments that are analogous to actual allocations of contributions and earnings to an employee's account under a defined contribution plan. Because a cash balance plan is a defined benefit plan, whether it satisfies section 401(a)(4) with respect to the equivalent amount of contributions is generally determined under paragraphs (c)(1) and (c)(2) of this section. However, a cash balance plan that satisfies each of the requirements in paragraphs (c)(3)(ii) through (xi) of this section is deemed to satisfy section 401(a)(4) with respect to an equivalent amount of contributions.

(ii) *Plan requirements in general.*—The plan must be an accumulation plan. The benefit formula under the plan must provide for hypothetical allocations for each employee in the plan that satisfy paragraph (c)(3)(iii) of this section, and interest adjustments to these hypothetical allocations that satisfy paragraph (c)(3)(iv) of this section. The benefit formula under the plan must provide that these hypothetical allocations and interest adjustments are accumulated as a hypothetical account for each employee, determined in accordance with paragraph (c)(3)(v) of this section. The plan must provide that an employee's accrued benefit under the plan as of any date is an annuity that is the actuarial equivalent of the employee's projected hypothetical account as of normal retirement age, determined in accordance with paragraph (c)(3)(vi) of this section. In addition, the plan must satisfy paragraphs (c)(3)(vii) through (xi) of this section (to the extent applicable) regarding optional forms of benefit, past service credits, post-normal retirement age benefits, certain uniformity requirements, and changes in the plan's benefit formula, respectively.

(iii) *Hypothetical allocations.*—(A) *In general.*—The hypothetical allocations provided under the plan's benefit formula must satisfy either paragraph (c)(3)(iii)(B) or (C) of this section. Paragraph (c)(3)(iii)(B) of this section provides a design-based safe harbor that does not require the annual comparison of hypothetical allocations under the plan. Paragraph (c)(3)(iii)(C) of this section requires the annual comparison of hypothetical allocations.

(B) *Uniform hypothetical allocation formula.*—To satisfy this paragraph (c)(3)(iii)(B), the plan's benefit formula must provide for hypothetical allocations for all employees in the plan for all plan years of amounts that would satisfy § 1.401(a)(4)-2(b)(3) for each such plan year if the hypothetical allocations were the only allocations under a defined contribution plan for the employees for those plan years. Thus, the plan's benefit formula must provide for hypothetical allocations for all employees in the plan for all plan years that are the same percentage of plan year compensation or the same dollar amount. In determining whether the hypothetical allocations satisfy § 1.401(a)(4)-2(b)(3), the only provisions of § 1.401(a)(4)-2(b)(5) that apply are § 1.401(a)(4)-2(b)(5)(ii) (section 401(l) permitted disparity), (iii) (entry dates), (vi) (certain limits on allocations), and (vii) (dollar allocation per uniform unit of service). Thus, for example, the plan's benefit formula may take permitted disparity into account in a manner allowed under § 1.401(l)-2 for defined contribution plans.

(C) *Modified general test.*—To satisfy this paragraph (c)(3)(iii)(C), the plan's benefit formula must provide for hypothetical allocations for all employees in the plan for the plan year that would satisfy the general test in § 1.401(a)(4)-2(c) for the plan year, if the hypothetical allocations were the only allocations for the employees taken into account under § 1.401(a)(4)-2(c)(2)(ii) under a defined contribution plan for the plan year. In determining whether the hypothetical allocations satisfy § 1.401(a)(4)-2(c), the provisions of § 1.401(a)(4)-2(c)(2)(iii) through (v) apply. Thus, for example, permitted disparity may be imputed under § 1.401(a)(4)-2(c)(2)(iv) in accordance with the rules of § 1.401(a)(4)-7(b) applicable to defined contribution plans.

(iv) *Interest adjustments to hypothetical allocations.*—(A) *General rule.*—The plan benefit formula must provide that the dollar amount of the hypothetical allocation for each employee for a plan year is automatically adjusted using an interest rate that satisfies paragraph (c)(3)(iv)(B) of this section, compounded no less frequently than annually, for the period that begins with a date in the plan year and that ends at normal retirement age. This requirement is not satisfied if any portion of the interest adjustments to a hypothetical allocation are contingent on the employee's satisfaction of any requirement. Thus, for example, the interest adjustments to a hypothetical allocation must be provided through normal retirement age, even though

Reg. § 1.401(a)(4)-8(c)(3)(iv)(A)

the employee terminates employment or commences benefits before that age.

(B) *Requirements with respect to interest rates.*—The interest rate must be a single interest rate specified in the plan that is the same for all employees in the plan for all plan years. The interest rate must be either a standard interest rate or a variable interest rate. If the interest rate is a variable interest rate, it must satisfy paragraph (c)(3)(iv)(C) of this section.

(C) *Variable interest rates.*—(1) *General rule.*—The plan must specify the variable interest rate, the method for determining the current value of the variable interest rate, and the period (not to exceed 1 year) for which the current value of the variable interest rate applies. Permissible variable interest rates are listed in paragraph (c)(3)(iv)(C)(2) of this section. Permissible methods for determining the current value of the variable interest rate are provided in paragraph (c)(3)(iv)(C)(3) of this section.

(2) *Permissible variable interest rates.*—The variable interest rate specified in the plan must be one of the following—
(i) The rate on 3-month Treasury Bills,
(ii) The rate on 6-month Treasury Bills,
(iii) The rate on 1-year Treasury Bills,
(iv) The yield on 1-year Treasury Constant Maturities,
(v) The yield on 2-year Treasury Constant Maturities,
(vi) The yield on 5-year Treasury Constant Maturities,
(vii) The yield on 10-year Treasury Constant Maturities,
(viii) The yield on 30-year Treasury Constant Maturities, or

(ix) The single interest rate such that, as of a single age specified in the plan, the actuarial present value of a deferred straight life annuity of an amount commencing at the normal retirement age under the plan, calculated using that interest rate and a standard mortality table but assuming no mortality before normal retirement age, is equal to the actuarial present value, as of the single age specified in the plan, of the same annuity calculated using the section 417(e) rates applicable to distributions in excess of $25,000 (determined under § 1.417(e)-1(d)), and the same mortality assumptions.

(3) *Current value of variable interest rate.*—The current value of the variable interest rate that applies for a period must be either the value of the variable interest rate determined as of a specified date in the period or the immediately preceding period, or the average of the values of the variable interest rate as of two or more specified dates during the current period or the immediately preceding period. The value as of a date of the rate on a Treasury Bill is the average auction rate for the week or month in which the date falls, as reported in the Federal Reserve Bulletin. The value as of a date of the yield on a Treasury Constant Maturity is the average yield for the week, month, or year in which the date falls, as reported in the Federal Reserve Bulletin. (The Federal Reserve Bulletin is published by the Board of Governors of the Federal Reserve System and is available from Publication Services, Mail Stop 138, Board of Governors of the Federal Reserve System, Washington, D.C. 20551.) The plan may limit the current value of the variable interest rate to a maximum (not less than the highest standard interest rate), or a minimum (not more than the lowest standard interest rate), or both.

(v) *Hypothetical account.*—(A) *Current value of hypothetical account.*—As of any date, the current value of an employee's hypothetical account must equal the sum of all hypothetical allocations and the respective interest adjustments to each such hypothetical allocation provided through that date for the employee under the plan's benefit formula (without regard to any interest adjustments provided under the plan's benefit formula for periods after that date).

(B) *Value of hypothetical account as of normal retirement age.*—Under paragraph (c)(3)(vi) of this section, the value of an employee's hypothetical account must be determined as of normal retirement age in order to determine the employee's accrued benefit as of any date at or before normal retirement age. As of any date at or before normal retirement age, the value of an employee's hypothetical account as of normal retirement age must equal the sum of each hypothetical allocation provided through that date for the employee under the plan's benefit formula, plus the interest adjustments provided through normal retirement age on each of those hypothetical allocations for the employee under the plan's benefit formula (without regard to any hypothetical allocations that might be provided after that date under the plan's benefit formula). If the interest rate specified in the plan is a variable interest rate, the plan must specify that the determination in the preceding sentence is made by assuming that the current value of the variable interest rate for all future periods is either the current value of the variable interest rate for the current period or the average of the current values of the variable interest rate for the current period and one or more periods immedi-

ately preceding the current period (not to exceed 5 years in the aggregate).

(vi) *Determination of accrued benefit.*—(A) *Definition of accrued benefit.*—The plan must provide that at any date at or before normal retirement age the accrued benefit (within the meaning of section 411(a)(7)(A)(i)) of each employee in the plan is an annuity commencing at normal retirement age that is the actuarial equivalent of the employee's hypothetical account as of normal retirement age (as determined under paragraph (c)(3)(v)(B) of this section). The separate benefit that each employee accrues for a plan year is an annuity that is the actuarial equivalent of the employee's hypothetical allocation for that plan year, including the automatic adjustments for interest through normal retirement age required under paragraph (c)(3)(iv) of this section.

(B) *Normal form of benefit.*—The annuity specified in paragraph (c)(3)(vi)(A) of this section must provide an annual benefit payable in the same form at the same uniform normal retirement age for all employees in the plan. The annual benefit must be the normal retirement benefit under the plan (within the meaning of section 411(a)(9)) under the plan.

(C) *Determination of actuarial equivalence.*—For purposes of this paragraph (c)(3)(vi) and paragraph (c)(3)(ix) of this section, actuarial equivalence must be determined using a standard mortality table and either a standard interest rate or the interest rate specified in the plan for making interest adjustments to hypothetical allocations. If the interest rate used is the interest rate specified in the plan, and that rate is a variable interest rate, the assumed value of the variable interest rate for all future periods must be the same value that would be assumed for purposes of paragraph (c)(3)(v)(B) of this section. The same actuarial assumptions must be used for all employees in the plan.

(D) *Effect of section 415 and 416 requirements.*—A plan does not fail to satisfy this paragraph (c)(3)(vi) merely because the accrued benefits under the plan are limited by section 415, or merely because the accrued benefits under the plan are the greater of the accrued benefits otherwise determined under the plan and the minimum benefit described in section 416(c)(1) (regardless of whether the plan is top-heavy).

(vii) *Optional forms of benefit.*—(A) *In general.*—The plan must satisfy the uniform subsidies requirement of § 1.401(a)(4)-3(b)(2)(iv) with respect to all subsidized optional forms of benefit.

(B) *Limitation on subsidies.*—Unless hypothetical allocations are determined under a uniform hypothetical allocation formula that satisfies paragraph (c)(3)(iii)(B) of this section, the actuarial present value of any QJSA provided under the plan must not be greater than the single sum distribution to the employee that would satisfy paragraph (c)(3)(vii)(C) of this section assuming that it was distributed to the employee on the date of commencement of the QJSA.

(C) *Distributions subject to section 417(e).*—Except as otherwise required under section 415(b), if the plan provides for a distribution alternative that is subject to the interest rate restrictions under section 417(e), the actuarial present value of the benefit paid to an employee under the distribution alternative must equal the nonforfeitable percentage (determined under the plan's vesting schedule) of the greater of the following two amounts—
(1) The current value of the employee's hypothetical account as of the date the distribution commences, calculated in accordance with paragraph (c)(3)(v)(A) of this section.
(2) The actuarial present value (calculated in accordance with § 1.417(e)-1(d)) of the employee's accrued benefit.

(D) *Determination of actuarial present value.*—For purposes of this paragraph (c)(3)(vii), actuarial present value must be determined using a reasonable interest rate and mortality table. A standard interest rate and a standard mortality table are considered reasonable for this purpose.

(viii) *Past service credit.*—The benefit formula under the plan may not provide for hypothetical allocations in the current plan year that are attributable to years of service before the current plan year, unless each of the following requirements is satisfied—
(A) The years of past service credit are granted on a uniform basis to all current employees in the plan.
(B) Hypothetical allocations for the current plan year are determined under a uniform hypothetical allocation formula that satisfies paragraph (c)(3)(iii)(B) of this section.
(C) The hypothetical allocations attributable to the years of past service would have satisfied the uniform hypothetical allocation formula requirement of paragraph (c)(3)(iii)(B) of this section, and the interest adjustments to those hypothetical allocations would have satisfied paragraph (c)(3)(iv)(A) of this section, if the plan provision

granting past service had been in effect for the entire period for which years of past service are granted to any employee. In order to satisfy this requirement, the hypothetical allocation attributable to a year of past service must be adjusted for interest in accordance with paragraph (c)(3)(iv) of this section for the period (including the retroactive period) beginning with the year of past service to which the hypothetical allocation is attributable and ending at normal retirement age. If the interest rate specified in the plan is a variable interest rate, the interest adjustments for the period prior to the current plan year either must be based on the current value of the variable interest rate for the period in which the grant of past service first becomes effective or must be reconstructed based on the then current value of the variable interest rate that would have applied during each prior period.

(ix) *Employees beyond normal retirement age.*—In the case of an employee who commences receipt of benefits after normal retirement age, the plan must provide that interest adjustments continue to be made to an employee's hypothetical account until the employee's benefit commencement date. In the case of an employee described in the previous sentence, the employee's accrued benefit is defined as an annuity that is the actuarial equivalent of the employee's hypothetical account determined in accordance with paragraph (c)(3)(v)(A) of this section as of the date of benefit commencement.

(x) *Additional uniformity requirements.*—In addition to any uniformity requirements provided elsewhere in this paragraph (c)(3), the plan must satisfy the uniformity requirements in § 1.401(a)(4)-3(b)(2)(v) (uniform vesting and service requirements) and (vi) (no employee contributions). A plan does not fail to satisfy the uniformity requirements of this paragraph (c)(3)(x) or any other uniformity requirement provided in this paragraph (c)(3) merely because the plan contains one or more of the provisions described in § 1.401(a)(4)-3(b)(8)(iv) (prior vesting schedules), (v) (certain conditions on accruals), or (xi) (multiple definitions of service).

(xi) *Changes in benefit formula, allocation formula, or interest rates.*—A plan does not fail to satisfy this paragraph (c)(3) merely because the plan is amended to change the benefit formula, hypothetical allocation formula, or the interest rate used to adjust hypothetical allocations for plan years after a fresh-start date, provided that the accrued benefits for plan years beginning after the fresh-start date are determined in accordance with § 1.401(a)(4)-13(c), as modified by § 1.401(a)(4)-13(f).

(d) *Safe-harbor testing method for defined benefit plans that are part of a floor-offset arrangement.*—(1) *General rule.*—A defined benefit plan that is part of a floor-offset arrangement is deemed to satisfy the nondiscriminatory amount requirement of § 1.401(a)(4)-1(b)(2) if all of the following requirements are satisfied:

(i) Under the floor-offset arrangement, the accrued benefit (as defined in section 411(a)(7)(A)(i)) that would otherwise be provided to an employee under the defined benefit plan must be reduced solely by the actuarial equivalent of all or part of the employee's account balance attributable to employer contributions under a defined contribution plan maintained by the same employer (plus the actuarial equivalent of all or part of any prior distributions from that portion of the account balance). If any portion of the benefit that is being offset is nonforfeitable, that portion may be offset only by a benefit (or portion of a benefit) that is also nonforfeitable. In determining the actuarial equivalent of amounts provided under the defined contribution plan, an interest rate no higher than the highest standard interest rate must be used, and no mortality may be assumed in determining the actuarial equivalent of any prior distributions from the defined contribution plan or for periods prior to the benefit commencement date under the defined benefit plan.

(ii) The defined benefit plan may not be a contributory DB plan (unless it satisfies § 1.401(a)(4)-6(b)(6)), and benefits under the defined benefit plan may not be reduced by any portion of the employee's account balance under the defined contribution plan (or prior distributions from that account) that are attributable to employee contributions.

(iii) The defined benefit plan and the defined contribution plan must benefit the same employees.

(iv) The offset under the defined benefit plan must be applied to all employees on the same terms.

(v) All employees must have available to them under the defined contribution plan the same investment options and the same options with respect to the timing of preretirement distributions.

(vi) The defined benefit plan must satisfy the uniformity requirements of § 1.401(a)(4)-3(b)(2) and the unit credit safe harbor in § 1.401(a)(4)-3(b)(3) without taking into account the offset described in paragraph (d)(1)(i) of this section (i.e., on a gross-benefit basis), and the defined contribution plan must satisfy any of the tests in § 1.401(a)(4)-2(b) or (c). Alternatively, the defined benefit plan must satisfy any of the tests in § 1.401(a)(4)-3(b) or (c) without taking into account the offset described in paragraph (d)(1)(i) of this section, and the defined contribution plan must satisfy the uniform allocation safe harbor in § 1.401(a)(4)-2(b)(2).

(vii) The defined contribution plan may not be a section 401(k) plan or a section 401(m) plan.

(2) *Application of safe-harbor testing method to qualified offset arrangements.*—A defined benefit plan that is part of a qualified offset arrangement as defined in section 1115(f)(5) of the Tax Reform Act of 1986, Pub. L. No. 99-514, is deemed to satisfy the requirements of paragraph (d)(1)(vi) and (vii) of this section, if the only defined contribution plans included in the qualified offset arrangement are section 401(k) plans, section 401(m) plans, or both, and the defined benefit plan would satisfy the requirements of paragraph (d)(1)(vi) of this section assuming the elective contributions for each employee under the defined contribution plan were the same (either as a dollar amount or as a percentage of compensation) for all plan years since the establishment of the plan. [Reg. § 1.401(a)(4)-8.]

□ [T.D. 8360, 9-12-91. *Amended by T.D. 8485, 8-30-93 and T.D. 8954, 6-28-2001.*]

[Reg. § 1.401(a)(4)-9]

§ 1.401(a)(4)-9. Plan aggregation and restructuring.—(a) *Introduction.*—Two or more plans that are permissively aggregated and treated as a single plan under §§ 1.410(b)-7(d) must also be treated as a single plan for purposes of section 401(a)(4). See § 1.401(a)(4)-12 (definition of plan). An aggregated plan is generally tested under the same rules applicable to single plans. Paragraph (b) of this section, however, provides special rules for determining whether a plan that consists of one or more defined contribution plans and one or more defined benefit plans (a DB/DC plan) satisfies section 401(a)(4) with respect to the amount of employer-provided benefits and the availability of benefits, rights, and features. Paragraph (c) of this section provides rules allowing a plan to be treated as consisting of separate component plans and allowing the component plans to be tested separately under section 401(a)(4).

(b) *Application of nondiscrimination requirements to DB/DC plans.*—(1) *General rule.*—Except as provided in paragraph (b)(2) of this section, whether a DB/DC plan satisfies section 401(a)(4) is determined using the same rules applicable to a single plan. In addition, paragraph (b)(3) of this section provides an optional rule for demonstrating nondiscrimination in availability of benefits, rights, and features provided under a DB/DC plan.

(2) *Special rules for demonstrating nondiscrimination in amount of contributions or benefits.*—(i) *Application of general tests.*—A DB/DC plan satisfies section 401(a)(4) with respect to the amount of contributions or benefits for a plan year if it would satisfy § 1.401(a)(4)-3(c)(1) (without regard to the special rule in § 1.401(a)(4)-3(c)(3)) for the plan year if an employee's aggregate normal and most valuable allocation rates, as determined under paragraph (b)(2)(ii)(A) of this section, or an employee's aggregate normal and most valuable accrual rates, as determined under paragraph (b)(2)(ii)(B) of this section, were substituted for each employee's normal and most valuable accrual rates, respectively, in the determination of rate groups.

(ii) *Determination of aggregate rates.*—(A) *Aggregate allocation rates.*—An employee's aggregate normal and most valuable allocation rates are determined by treating all defined contribution plans that are part of the DB/DC plan as a single plan, and all defined benefit plans that are part of the DB/DC plan as a separate single plan; and determining an allocation rate and equivalent normal and most valuable allocation rates for the employee under each plan under §§ 1.401(a)(4)-2(c)(2) and 1.401(a)(4)-8(c)(2), respectively. The employee's aggregate normal allocation rate is the sum of the employee's allocation rate and equivalent normal allocation rate determined in this manner, and the employee's aggregate most valuable allocation rate is the sum of the employee's allocation rate and equivalent most valuable allocation rate determined in this manner.

(B) *Aggregate accrual rates.*—An employee's aggregate normal and most valuable accrual rates are determined by treating all defined contribution plans that are part of the DB/DC plan as a single plan, and all defined benefit plans that are part of the DB/DC plan as a separate single plan; and determining an equivalent accrual rate and normal and most valuable accrual rates for the employee under each plan under §§ 1.401(a)(4)-8(b)(2) and 1.401(a)(4)-3(d), respectively. The employee's aggregate normal accrual rate is the sum of the employee's equivalent accrual rate and the normal accrual rate determined in this manner, and the employee's aggregate most valuable accrual rate is the sum of the employee's equivalent accrual rate and most valuable accrual rate determined in this manner.

(iii) *Options applied on an aggregate basis.*—The optional rules in § 1.401(a)(4)-2(c)(2)(iv) (imputation of permitted disparity) and (v) (grouping of rates) may not be used to determine an employee's allocation or equivalent allocation rate, but may be applied to determine an employee's aggregate normal and most valuable allocation rates by substituting those rates (determined without regard to the option) for the employee's allocation rate in that section where appropriate. The optional rules in §1.401(a)(4)-3(d)(3) (e.g., imputation of permitted disparity) may not be used to determine an employee's accrual or equivalent accrual rate, but may be applied to determine an employee's aggregate normal and most valuable accrual rate by substituting those rates (determined without regard to the option) for the employee's normal and most valuable accrual rates, respectively, in that section where appropriate.

(iv) *Consistency rule.*—(A) *General rule.*—Aggregate normal and most valuable allocation rates and aggregate normal and most valuable accrual rates must be determined in a consistent manner for all employees for the plan year. Thus, for example, the same measurement periods and interest rates must be used, and any available options must be applied consistently, if at all, for the entire DB/DC plan. Consequently, options that are not permitted to be used under §1.401(a)(4)-8 in cross-testing a defined contribution plan or a defined benefit plan (such as measurement periods that include future periods, non-standard interest rates, the option to disregard compensation adjustments described in §1.401(a)(4)-13(d), or the option to disregard plan provisions providing for actuarial increases after normal retirement age under §1.401(a)(4)-3(f)(3)) may not be used in testing a DB/DC plan on either a benefits or contributions basis, because their use would inevitably result in inconsistent determinations under the defined contribution and defined benefit portions of the plan.

(B) *Exception for section 415 alternative.*—A DB/DC plan does not fail to satisfy the consistency rule in paragraph (b)(2)(iv)(A) of this section merely because the limitations under section 415 are not taken into account, or may not be taken into account, under §1.401(a)(4)-33(d)(2)(ii)(B) in determining employees' accrual or equivalent allocation rates under the defined benefit portion of the plan, even though those limitations are applied in determining employees' allocation and equivalent accrual rates under the defined contribution portion of the plan.

(v) *Eligibility for testing on a benefits basis.*—(A) *General rule.*—For plan years beginning on or after January 1, 2002, unless, for the plan year, a DB/DC plan is primarily defined benefit in character (within the meaning of paragraph (b)(2)(v)(B) of this section) or consists of broadly available separate plans (within the meaning of paragraph (b)(2)(v)(C) of this section), the DB/DC plan must satisfy the minimum aggregate allocation gateway of paragraph (b)(2)(v)(D) of this section for the plan year in order to be permitted to demonstrate satisfaction of the nondiscrimination in amount requirement of §1.401(a)(4)-1(b)(2) on the basis of benefits.

(B) *Primarily defined benefit in character.*—A DB/DC plan is primarily defined benefit in character if, for more than 50% of the NHCEs benefitting under the plan, the normal accrual rate for the NHCE attributable to benefits provided under defined benefit plans that are part of the DB/DC plan exceeds the equivalent accrual rate for the NHCE attributable to contributions under defined contribution plans that are part of the DB/DC plan.

(C) *Broadly available separate plans.*—A DB/DC plan consists of broadly available separate plans if the defined contribution plan and the defined benefit plan that are part of the DB/DC plan each would satisfy the requirements of section 410(b) and the nondiscrimination in amount requirement of §1.401(a)(4)-1(b)(2) if each plan were tested separately and assuming that the average benefit percentage test of §1.410(b)-5 were satisfied. For this purpose, all defined contribution plans that are part of the DB/DC plan are treated as a single defined contribution plan and all defined benefit plans that are part of the DB/DC plan are treated as a single defined benefit plan. In addition, if permitted disparity is used for an em-

ployee for purposes of satisfying the separate testing requirement of this paragraph (b)(2)(v)(C) for plans of one type, it may not be used in satisfying the separate testing requirement for plans of the other type for the employee.

(D) *Minimum aggregate allocation gateway.*—(1) *General rule.*—A DB/DC plan satisfies the minimum aggregate allocation gateway if each NHCE has an aggregate normal allocation rate that is at least one third of the aggregate normal allocation rate of the HCE with the highest such rate (HCE rate), or, if less, 5% of the NHCE's compensation, provided that the HCE rate does not exceed 25% of compensation. If the HCE rate exceeds 25% of compensation, then the aggregate normal allocation rate for each NHCE must be at least 5% increased by one percentage point for each 5-percentage-point increment (or portion thereof) by which the HCE rate exceeds 25% (e.g., the NHCE minimum is 6% for an HCE rate that exceeds 25% but not 30%, and 7% for an HCE rate that exceeds 30% but not 35%).

(2) *Deemed satisfaction.*—A plan is deemed to satisfy the minimum aggregate allocation gateway of this paragraph (b)(2)(v)(D) if the aggregate normal allocation rate for each NHCE is at least 7 1/2% of the NHCE's compensation within the meaning of section 415(c)(3), measured over a period of time permitted under the definition of plan year compensation.

(3) *Averaging of equivalent allocation rates for NHCEs.*—For purposes of this paragraph (b)(2)(v)(D), a plan is permitted to treat each NHCE who benefits under the defined benefit plan as having an equivalent normal allocation rate equal to the average of the equivalent normal allocation rates under the defined benefit plan for all NHCEs benefitting under that plan.

(E) *Determination of rates.*—For purposes of this paragraph (b)(2)(v), the normal accrual rate and the equivalent normal allocation rate attributable to defined benefit plans, the equivalent accrual rate attributable to defined contribution plans, and the aggregate normal allocation rate are determined under paragraph (b)(2)(ii) of this section, but without taking into account the imputation of permitted disparity under §1.401(a)(4)-7, except as otherwise permitted under paragraph (b)(2)(v)(C) of this section.

(F) *Examples.*—The following examples illustrate the application of this paragraph (b)(2)(v):

Example 1. (i) Employer A maintains Plan M, a defined benefit plan, and Plan N, a defined contribution plan. All HCEs of Employer A are covered by Plan M (at a 1% accrual rate), but are not covered by Plan N. All NHCEs of Employer A are covered by Plan N (at a 3% allocation rate), but are not covered by Plan M. Because Plan M does not satisfy section 410(b) standing alone, Plans M and N are aggregated for purposes of satisfying sections 410(b) and 401(a)(4).

(ii) Because none of the NHCEs participate in the defined benefit plan, the aggregated DB/DC plan is not primarily defined benefit in character within the meaning of paragraph (b)(2)(v)(B) of this section nor does it consist of broadly available separate plans within the meaning of paragraph (b)(2)(v)(C) of this section. Accordingly, the aggregated Plan M and Plan N must satisfy the minimum aggregate allocation gateway of paragraph (b)(2)(v)(D) of this section in order to be permitted to demonstrate satisfaction of the nondiscrimination in amount requirement of §1.401(a)(4)-1(b)(2) on the basis of benefits.

Example 2. (i) Employer B maintains Plan O, a defined benefit plan, and Plan P, a defined contribution plan. All of the six employees of Employer B are covered under both Plan O and Plan P. Under Plan O, all employees have a uniform normal accrual rate of 1% of compensation. Under Plan P, Employees A and B, who are HCEs, receive an allocation rate of 15%, and participants C, D, E and F, who are NHCEs, receive an allocation rate of 3%. Employer B aggregates Plans O and P for purposes of satisfying sections 410(b) and 401(a)(4). The equivalent normal allocation and normal accrual rates under Plans O and P are as follows:

Employee	Equivalent Normal Allocation Rates for the 1% Accrual under Plan O (defined benefit plan)	Equivalent Normal Accrual Rates for the 15%/3% Allocations under Plan P (defined contribution plan)
HCE A (age 55)	3.93%	3.82%
HCE B (age 50)	2.61%	5.74%
C (age 60)	5.91%	.51%
D (age 45)	1.74%	1.73%
E (age 35)	.77%	3.90%
F (age 25)	.34%	8.82%

(ii) Although all of the NHCEs benefit under Plan O (the defined benefit plan), the aggregated DB/DC plan is not primarily

defined benefit in character because the normal accrual rate attributable to defined benefit plans (which is 1% for each of the NHCEs) is

Reg. §1.401(a)(4)-9(b)(2)(iv)(A)

greater than the equivalent accrual rate under defined contribution plans only for Employee C. In addition, because the 15% allocation rate is available only to HCEs, the defined contribution plan cannot satisfy the requirements of §1.401(a)(4)-2 and does not have broadly available allocation rates within the meaning of §1.401(a)(4)-8(b)(1)(iii). Further, the defined contribution plan does not satisfy the minimum allocation gateway of §1.401(a)(4)-8(b)(1)(vi) (3% is less than 1/3 of the 15% HCE rate). Therefore, the defined contribution plan within the DB/DC plan cannot separately satisfy §1.401(a)(4)-1(b)(2) and does not constitute a broadly available separate plan within the meaning of paragraph (b)(2)(v)(C) of this section. Accordingly, the aggregated plans are permitted to demonstrate satisfaction of the nondiscrimination in amounts requirement of §1.401(a)(4)-1(b)(2) on the basis of benefits only if the aggregated plans satisfy the minimum aggregate allocation gateway of paragraph (b)(2)(v)(D) of this section.

(iii) Employee A has an aggregate normal allocation rate of 18.93% under the aggregated plans (3.93% from Plan O plus 15% from Plan P), which is the highest aggregate normal allocation rate for any HCE under the plans. Employee F has an aggregate normal allocation rate of 3.34% under the aggregated plans (.34% from Plan O plus 3% from Plan P) which is less than the 5% aggregate normal allocation rate that Employee F would be required to have to satisfy the minimum aggregate allocation gateway of paragraph (b)(2)(v)(D) of this section.

(iv) However, for purposes of satisfying the minimum aggregate allocation gateway of paragraph (b)(2)(v)(D) of this section, Employer B is permitted to treat each NHCE who benefits under Plan O (the defined benefit plan) as having an equivalent allocation rate equal to the average of the equivalent allocation rates under Plan O for all NHCEs benefitting under that plan. The average of the equivalent allocation rates for all of the NHCEs under Plan O is 2.19% (the sum of 5.91%, 1.74%, .77%, and .34%, divided by 4). Accordingly, Employer B is permitted to treat all of the NHCEs as having an equivalent allocation rate attributable to Plan O equal to 2.19%. Thus, all of the NHCEs can be treated as having an aggregate normal allocation rate of 5.19% for this purpose (3% from the defined contribution plan and 2.19% from the defined benefit plan) and the aggregated DB/DC plan satisfies the minimum aggregate allocation gateway of paragraph (b)(2)(v)(D) of this section.

(3) *Optional rules for demonstrating nondiscrimination in availability of certain benefits, rights, and features.*—(i) *Current availability.*—A DB/DC plan is deemed to satisfy §1.401(a)(4)-4(b)(1) with respect to the current availability of a benefit, right, or feature other than a single sum benefit, loan, ancillary benefit, or benefit commencement date (including the availability of in-service withdrawals), that is provided under only one type of plan (defined benefit or defined contribution) included in the DB/DC plan, if the benefit, right, or feature is currently available to all NHCEs in all plans of the same type as the plan under which it is provided.

(ii) *Effective availability.*—The fact that it may be difficult or impossible to provide a benefit, right, or feature described in paragraph (b)(3)(i) of this section under a plan of a different type than the plan or plans under which it is provided is one of the factors taken into account in determining whether the plan satisfies the effective availability requirement of §1.401(a)(4)-4(c)(1).

(c) *Plan restructuring.*—(1) *General rule.*—A plan may be treated, in accordance with this paragraph (c), as consisting of two or more component plans for purposes of determining whether the plan satisfies section 401(a)(4). If each of the component plans of a plan satisfies all of the requirements of sections 401(a)(4) and 410(b) as if it were a separate plan, then the plan is treated as satisfying section 401(a)(4).

(2) *Identification of component plans.*—A plan may be restructured into component plans, each consisting of all the allocations, accruals, and other benefits, rights, and features provided to a selected group of employees. The employer may select the group of employees used for this purpose in any manner, and the composition of the groups may be changed from plan year to plan year. Every employee must be included in one and only one component plan under the same plan for a plan year.

(3) *Satisfaction of section 401(a)(4) by a component plan.*—(i) *General rule.*—The rules applicable in determining whether a component plan satisfies section 401(a)(4) are the same as those applicable to a plan. Thus, for this purpose, any reference to a plan in section 401(a)(4) and the regulations thereunder (other than this paragraph (c)) is interpreted as a reference to a component plan. As is true for a plan, whether a component plan satisfies the uniformity and other requirements applicable to safe harbor plans under §§1.401(a)(4)-2(b) and 1.401(a)(4)-3(b) is determined on a design basis. Thus, for example, plan provisions are not disregarded merely

because they do not currently apply to employees in the component plan if they will apply to those employees as a result of the mere passage of time.

(ii) *Restructuring not available for certain testing purposes.*—The safe harbor in §1.401(a)(4)-2(b)(3) for plans with uniform points allocation formulas is not available in testing (and thus cannot be satisfied by) contributions under a component plan. Similarly, component plans cannot be used for purposes of determining whether a plan provides broadly available allocation rates (as defined in §1.401(a)(4)-8(b)(1)(iii)), determining whether a plan has a gradual age or service schedule (as defined in §1.401(a)(4)-8(b)(1)(iv)), determining whether a plan has allocation rates that are based on a uniform target benefit allocation (as defined in §1.401(a)(4)-8(b)(1)(v)), or determining whether a plan is primarily defined benefit in character or consists of broadly available separate plans (as defined in paragraphs (b)(2)(v)(B) and (C) of this section). In addition, the minimum allocation gateway of §1.401(a)(4)-8(b)(1)(vi) and the minimum aggregate allocation gateway of paragraph (b)(2)(v)(D) of this section cannot be satisfied on the basis of component plans. See §§1.401(k)-1(b)(4)(iv)(B) and 1.401(m)-1(b)(4)(iv)(B) for rules regarding the inapplicability of restructuring to section 401(k) plans and section 401(m) plans.

(4) *Satisfaction of section 410(b) by a component plan.*—(i) *General rule.*—The rules applicable in determining whether a component plan satisfies section 410(b) are generally the same as those applicable to a plan. However, a component plan is deemed to satisfy the average benefit percentage test of §1.410(b)-5 if the plan of which it is a part satisfies §1.410(b)-5 (without regard to §1.410(b)-5(f)). In the case of a component plan that is part of a plan that relies on §1.410(b)-5(f) to satisfy the average benefit percentage test, the component plan is deemed to satisfy the average benefit percentage test only if the component plan separately satisfies §1.410(b)-5(f). In addition, all component plans of a plan are deemed to satisfy the average benefit percentage test if the plan makes an early retirement window benefit (within the meaning of §1.401(a)(4)-3(f)(4)(iii)) currently available (within the meaning of §1.401(a)(4)-3(f)(4)(ii)(A)) to a group of employees that satisfies section 410(b) (without regard to the average benefit percentage test), and if it would not be necessary for the plan or any rate group or component plan of the plan to satisfy that test in order for the plan to satisfy sections 401(a)(4) and 410(b) in the absence of the early retirement window benefit.

(ii) *Relationship to satisfaction of section 410(b) by the plan.*—Satisfaction of section 410(b) by a component plan is relevant solely for purposes of determining whether the plan of which it is a part satisfies section 401(a)(4), and not for purposes of determining whether the plan satisfies section 410(b) itself. The plan must still independently satisfy section 410(b) in order to be a qualified plan. Similarly, satisfaction of section 410(b) by a plan is relevant solely for purposes of determining whether the plan, and not the component plan, satisfies section 410(b). Thus, for example, a component plan that does not satisfy the ratio percentage test of §1.410(b)-2(b)(2) must still satisfy the average benefit test of §1.410(b)-2(b)(3), even though the plan of which it is a part satisfies the ratio percentage test.

(5) *Effect of restructuring under other sections.*—The restructuring rules provided in this paragraph (c) apply solely for purposes of sections 401(a)(4) and 401(l), and those portions of sections 410(b), 414(s), and any other provisions that are specifically applicable in determining whether the requirements of section 401(a)(4) are satisfied. Thus, for example, a component plan is not treated as a separate plan under section 401(a)(26).

(6) *Examples.*—The following examples illustrate the rules in this paragraph (c):

Example 1. Employer X maintains a defined benefit plan. The plan provides a normal retirement benefit equal to 1.0 percent of average annual compensation times years of service to employees at Plant S, and 1.5 percent of average annual compensation times years of service to employees at Plant T Under paragraph (c)(2) of this section, the plan may be treated as consisting of two component defined benefit plans, one providing retirement benefits equal to 1.0 percent of average annual compensation times years of service to the employees at Plant S, and another providing benefits equal to 1.5 percent of average annual compensation times years of service to employees at Plant T. If each component plan satisfies sections 401(a)(4) and 410(b) as if it were a separate plan under the rules of this paragraph (c), then the entire plan satisfies section 401(a)(4).

Example 2. (a) Employer Y maintains Plan A, a defined benefit plan, for its Employees M, N, O, P, Q, and R. Plan A provides benefits under a uniform formula that satisfies the requirements of §1.401(a)(4)-3(b)(2) and (b)(3) before it is amended on February 14, 1994. The amendment provides an early retirement window benefit that is a subsidized optional form of benefit under

§ 1.401(a)(4)-3(b)(2)(iii) and that is available on the same terms to all employees who satisfy the eligibility requirements for the window. The early retirement window benefit is available only to employees who retire between June 1, 1994, and November 30, 1994.

(b) Assume that Employees M, N, and O will be eligible to receive the window benefit by the end of the window period and Employees P, Q, and R will not. Because substantially all employees will not satisfy the eligibility requirements for the early retirement window benefit by the close of the early retirement window benefit period, Plan A fails to satisfy the uniform subsidies requirement of § 1.401(a)(4)-3(b)(2)(iii). See § 1.401(a)(4)-3(b)(2)(vi), *Example 6.*

(c) Under paragraph (c)(2) of this section, Employees M, N, O, P, Q, and R may be grouped into two component plans, one consisting of Employees M, N, and O and all their accruals and other benefits, rights, and features under the plan (including the early retirement window benefit), and another consisting of Employees P, Q, and R, and all their accruals and other benefits, rights, and features under the plan. Each of the component plans identified in this manner satisfies the uniform subsidies requirement of § 1.401(a)(4)-3(b)(2)(iii), and thus satisfies § 1.401(a)(4)-3(b). The entire plan satisfies section 401(a)(4) under the rules of this paragraph (c), if each of these component plans also satisfies section 410(b) as if it were a separate plan (including, if applicable, the reasonable classification requirement of § 1.410(b)-4(b), and taking into account the special rule of paragraph (c)(4)(i) of this section that forgives the average benefit percentage test in certain situations in which the average benefit percentage test would be required solely as a result of the early retirement window benefit).

Example 3. (a) Employer Z maintains Plan B, a defined benefit plan with a benefit formula that provides two percent of average annual compensation for each year of service up to 20 to each employee. Assume that Plan B would satisfy the fractional accrual rule safe harbor in § 1.401(a)(4)-3(b)(4), except that some employees accrue a portion of their normal retirement benefit in the current plan year that is more than one third larger than the portion of the same benefit accrued by other employees for the current plan year, and the plan therefore fails to satisfy the one-third-larger-requirement of § 1.401(a)(4)-3(b)(4)(i)(C)(*1*).

(b) Employer Z restructures Plan B into two plans, one covering employees with 30 years or less of service at normal retirement age, and the other covering all other employees. Each component plan would separately satisfy the one-third-larger requirement of § 1.401(a)(4)-3(b)(4)(i)(C)(*1*) if the only employees taken into account were those employees included in the component plan in the current plan year. Under paragraph (c)(3)(i) of this section and § 1.401(a)(4)-3(b)(4)(i)(C)(*1*), however, the component plans do not satisfy the one-third-larger requirement because the safe harbor determination is made taking into account the effect of the plan benefit formula on any potential employee in the component plan (other than employees with more than 33 years of service at normal retirement age), and not just those employees included in the component plan in the current plan year. [Reg. § 1.401(a)(4)-9.]

☐ [*T.D. 8360, 9-12-91. Amended by T.D. 8485, 8-30-93; T.D. 8954, 6-28-2001 and T.D. 9169, 12-28-2004.*]

[Reg. § 1.401(a)(4)-10]

§ 1.401(a)(4)-10. Testing of former employees.—(a) *Introduction.*— This section provides rules for determining whether a plan satisfies the nondiscriminatory amount and nondiscriminatory availability requirements of § 1.401(a)(4)-1(b)(2) and (3), respectively, with respect to former employees. Generally, this section is relevant only in the case of benefits provided through an amendment to the plan effective in the current plan year. See the definitions of employee and former employee in § 1.401(a)(4)-12.

(b) *Nondiscrimination in amount of contributions or benefits.*— (1) *General rule.*—A plan satisfies § 1.401(a)(4)-1(b)(2) with respect to the amount of contributions or benefits provided to former employees if, under all of the relevant facts and circumstances, the amount of contributions or benefits provided to former employees does not discriminate significantly in favor of former HCEs. For this purpose, contributions or benefits provided to former employees includes all contributions or benefits provided to former employees or, at the employer's option, only those contributions or benefits arising out of the amendment providing the contributions or benefits. A plan under which no former employee currently benefits (within the meaning of § 1.410(b)-3(b)) is deemed to satisfy this paragraph (b).

(2) *Permitted disparity.*—Section 401(l) and § 1.401(a)(4)-7 generally apply to benefits provided to former employees in the same manner as those provisions apply to employees. Thus, for example, for purposes of determining a former employee's cumulative permitted disparity limit, the sum of the former employee's total annual disparity fractions (within the meaning of § 1.401(l)-5) as an employee continues to be taken into account. However, the permitted

disparity rate applicable to a former employee is determined under § 1.401(l)-3(e) as of the age the former employee commenced receipt of benefits, not as of the date the employee receives the accrual for the current plan year.

(3) *Examples.*—The following examples illustrate the rules in this paragraph (b):

Example 1. Employer X maintains a section 401(l) plan, Plan A, that uses maximum permitted disparity. Plan A is amended to increase the benefits of all former employees in pay status. The percentage increase for each former employee is reasonably comparable to the adjustment in social security benefits under section 215(i)(2)(A) of the Social Security Act since the former employee commenced receipt of benefits. Plan A does not fail to satisfy this paragraph (b) merely because of the amendment.

Example 2. The facts are the same as in *Example 1,* except that the amendment provides an across-the-board 20 percent increase in benefits for all former employees in pay status. The cost of living has increased at an average rate of three percent in the two years preceding the amendment, and some HCEs have retired and become former HCEs during that period. Because this amendment increases the disparity in the plan formula beyond the maximum permitted disparity adjusted for any reasonable approximation of the increase in the cost of living since the HCEs retired, Plan A discriminates significantly in favor of former HCEs, and thus does not satisfy this paragraph (b).

Example 3. The facts are the same as in *Example 1,* except that Plan A is only amended to increase the benefits of former employees in pay status who terminated employment with Employer X after attaining early retirement age. The determination of whether the amendment causes Plan A to fail to satisfy this paragraph (b) must take into account the relative numbers of former HCEs and former NHCEs who have terminated employment with Employer X after attaining early retirement age.

(c) *Nondiscrimination in availability of benefits, rights, or features.*—A plan satisfies section 401(a)(4) with respect to the availability of benefits, rights, and features provided to former employees if any change in the availability of any benefit, right, or feature to any former employee is applied in a manner that, under all of the relevant facts and circumstances, does not discriminate significantly in favor of former HCEs. For purposes of demonstrating that a plan satisfies section 401(a)(4) with respect to the availability of loans provided to former employees, an employer may treat former employees who are parties in interest within the meaning of section 3(14) of the Employee Retirement Income Security Act of 1974 as employees. [Reg. § 1.401(a)(4)-10.]

☐ [*T.D. 8360, 9-12-91. Amended by T.D. 8485, 8-30-93.*]

[Reg. § 1.401(a)(4)-11]

§ 1.401(a)(4)-11. Additional rules.—(a) *Introduction.*—This section provides additional rules for determining whether a plan satisfies section 401(a)(4). Paragraph (b) of this section provides rules for the treatment of the portion of an employee's accrued benefit or account balance that is attributable to rollovers, transfers between plans, and employee buybacks. Paragraph (c) of this section provides rules regarding vesting. Paragraph (d) of this section provides rules regarding service crediting. Paragraph (e) of this section, regarding family aggregation, and paragraph (f) of this section, regarding governmental plans, are reserved. Paragraph (g) of this section provides rules regarding the extent to which corrective amendments may be made for purposes of section 401(a).

(b) *Rollovers, transfers, and buybacks.*—(1) *Rollovers and elective transfers.*—The portion of an employee's accrued benefit or account balance under a plan that is attributable to rollover (including direct rollover) contributions to the plan that are described in section 402(c), 402(e)(6), 403(a)(4), 403(a)(5), or 408(d)(3), or elective transfers to the plan that are described in § 1.411(d)-4, Q&A-3(b), is not taken into account in determining whether the plan satisfies the nondiscriminatory amount requirement of § 1.401(a)(4)-1(b)(2).

(2) *Other transfers.*—[Reserved]

(3) *Employee buybacks.*—(i) *Rehired employee buyback of previous service.*—An employee's repayment to a plan of a prior distribution from the plan (including reasonable interest from the time of the distribution) that results in the restoration of the employee's accrued benefit under the plan (or the service associated with that accrued benefit) that would otherwise be disregarded in determining the employee's accrued benefit in accordance with section 411 on account of the distribution is not treated as an employee contribution for purposes of § § 1.401(a)(4)-1 through 1.401(a)(4)-13.

(ii) *Make-up of missed employee contributions.*—If a contributory DB plan gives all employees who did not make employee contributions for a prior period the right to make the missed contributions at a later date (including reasonable interest from the time of the missed contributions) and, once the contributions have been made, determines benefits under the plan by treating the employee contributions (excluding the interest) as if they were actually made during that prior period, then those contributions must satisfy § 1.401(a)(4)-6(c) as if they were employee contributions actually made during that prior period. Thus, for example, § 1.401(a)(4)-6(c)(2) is not satisfied for the current plan year if the employee contribution rate (within the meaning of § 1.401(a)(4)-6(b)(2)(ii)(A) but determined without regard to the interest) for the employees making up missed contributions is different than the employee contribution rate applicable to other employees during the prior period. The rule in this paragraph (b)(3)(ii) may be extended to employees who did not make employee contributions for a period of service that is or would otherwise have been credited under the plan and that preceded their participation in the plan.

(c) *Vesting.*—(1) *General rule.*—A plan satisfies this paragraph (c) if the manner in which employees vest in their accrued benefits under the plan does not discriminate in favor of HCEs. Whether the manner in which employees vest in their accrued benefits under a plan discriminates in favor of HCEs is determined under this paragraph (c) based on all of the relevant facts and circumstances, taking into account any relevant provisions of sections 401(a)(5)(E), 411(a)(10), 411(d)(1), 411(d)(2), 411(d)(3), 411(e), and 420(c)(2), and taking into account any plan provisions that affect the nonforfeitability of employees' accrued benefits (e.g., plan provisions regarding suspension of benefits permitted under section 411(a)(3)(B)), other than the method of crediting years of service for purposes of applying the vesting schedule provided in the plan.

(2) *Deemed equivalence of statutory vesting schedules.*—For purposes of this paragraph (c), the manner in which employees vest in their accrued benefits under the vesting schedules in section 411(a)(2)(A) and (B) are treated as equivalent to one another, and the manner in which employees vest in their accrued benefits under the vesting schedules in section 416(b)(1)(A) and (B) are treated as equivalent to one another.

(3) *Safe harbor for vesting schedules.*—The manner in which employees vest in their accrued benefits under a plan is deemed not to discriminate in favor of HCEs if each combination of plan provisions that affect the nonforfeitability of any employee's accrued benefit would satisfy the nondiscriminatory availability requirements of § 1.401(a)(4)-4 if that combination were another right or feature.

(4) *Examples.*—The following examples illustrate the rules in this paragraph (c):

Example 1. Plan A provides the six-year graded vesting schedule described in section 416(b)(1)(B). In 1996, Plan A is amended to provide the five-year vesting schedule described in section 411(a)(2)(A). To comply with section 411(a)(10)(B), the plan amendment also provides that all employees with at least three years of service may elect to retain the prior vesting schedule. The manner in which employees vest in their accrued benefits under Plan A does not discriminate in favor of HCEs merely because the prior vesting schedule continues to apply to the accrued benefits of electing employees, even if, at the time of the election or in future years, the prior vesting schedule applies only to a group of employees that does not satisfy section 410(b).

Example 2. The facts are the same as in *Example 1*, except that, for administrative convenience in complying with section 411(a)(10)(B), the plan amendment automatically provides all employees employed on the date of the amendment with the higher of the nonforfeitable percentages determined under either schedule. The manner in which employees vest in their accrued benefits under Plan A does not discriminate in favor of HCEs merely because, for administrative convenience in complying with section 411(a)(10), the amendment exceeds the requirements of section 411(a)(10). The result would be the same if the plan amendment automatically provided the higher of the nonforfeitable percentages only to those employees with at least three years of service.

Example 3. (a) Employer Y maintains Plan B covering all of its employees. On January 1, 1996, Employer Y sells Division M to Employer Z, and all of the employees in Division M become employees of Employer Z. Employer Y obtains a determination letter that the resulting cessation of participation by these employees in Plan B constitutes a partial termination. Therefore, in order to satisfy section 411(d)(3), Plan B fully vests the accrued benefit of each of the employees of Division M whose participation in Plan B ceased as a result of the sale on January 1, 1996.

(b) The manner in which employees vest in their accrued benefits under Plan B does not discriminate in favor of HCEs merely because, in order to satisfy section 411(d)(3), the accrued benefits of all employees affected by the partial termination become fully vested.

This is true even if the affected group of employees does not satisfy section 410(b).

Example 4. (a) The facts are the same as in *Example 3*, except that Employer Y does not obtain a determination letter that the sale of Division M to Employer Z will cause a partial termination. Instead, based on its reasonable belief that the sale will cause a partial termination, and in order to ensure that Plan B will satisfy section 411(d)(3), Employer Y amends Plan B to vest fully the accrued benefit on January 1, 1996 of each of the employees it reasonably believes to be an affected employee.

(b) The manner in which employees vest in their accrued benefits under Plan B does not discriminate in favor of HCEs merely because, based on Employer Y's reasonable belief that the sale will cause a partial termination, Plan B is amended to vest fully the accrued benefits of each of the employees it reasonably believes to be an affected employee.

(d) *Service-crediting rules.*—(1) *Overview.*—(i) *In general.*—A defined benefit plan or a defined contribution plan does not satisfy this paragraph (d) with respect to the manner in which service is credited under the plan unless the plan satisfies paragraph (d)(2) of this section. Paragraph (d)(3) of this section provides rules for determining whether service other than actual service with the employer may be taken into account in determining whether a defined benefit plan or a defined contribution plan satisfies § 1.401(a)(4)-1(b)(2) or (b)(3). (However, for purposes of cross-testing a defined contribution plan, only years in which the employee benefited under the plan may be taken into account in determining equivalent accrual rates. See § 1.401(a)(4)-8(b)(2)(i).) The rules of this paragraph (d) apply separately to service credited under a plan for each different purpose under the plan, including, but not limited to: application of the benefit formula (benefit service), application of the accrual method (accrual service), application of the vesting schedule (vesting service), entitlement to benefits, rights, and features (entitlement service), application of the requirements for eligibility to participate in the plan (eligibility service).

(ii) *Special rule for pre-effective date service.*—A plan is deemed to satisfy this paragraph (d) with respect to service credited for periods prior to the effective date applicable to the plan under § 1.401(a)(4)-13(a) or (b) under a plan provision adopted and in effect as of February 11, 1993 (and any such service may be taken into account for purposes of satisfying § 1.401(a)(4)-1(b)(2) or (b)(3)), if the plan satisfied the applicable nondiscrimination requirements with respect to the service that were in effect for all relevant periods prior to the applicable effective date.

(2) *Manner of crediting service.*—(i) *General rule.*—A plan satisfies this paragraph (d)(2) if, on the basis of all of the relevant facts and circumstances, the manner in which employees' service is credited for all purposes under the plan does not discriminate in favor of HCEs.

(ii) *Equivalent service-crediting methods.*—For purposes of this paragraph (d)(2), a service-crediting method used for a specified purpose that is based on hours of service, as provided in 29 CFR 2530.200b-2, and a service-crediting method used for the same purpose that is based on one of the equivalencies set forth in 29 CFR 2530.200b-3, are treated as equivalent if the service-crediting methods are otherwise the same.

(iii) *Safe harbor for service-crediting.*—The manner in which service is credited under a plan for a specified purpose is deemed to satisfy this paragraph (d)(2) if each combination of service-crediting provisions applied for that purpose would satisfy the nondiscriminatory availability requirements of § 1.401(a)(4)-4 if that combination were an other right or feature.

(iv) *Examples.*—The following examples illustrate the rules in this paragraph (d)(2):

Example 1. (a) Plan A covers both salaried employees and hourly employees. All of the HCEs in Plan A are salaried employees. For administrative convenience, salaried employees in Plan A (none of whom are part-time) have their years of service calculated in accordance with the elapsed time provisions in § 1.410(a)-7. Hourly employees in Plan A (most of whom are scheduled to work 2,000 hours in a year) have their hours of service calculated in accordance with 29 CFR 2530.200b-2 and are credited with a year of service for each plan year in which they complete 1,000 hours of service.

(b) Plan A does not fail to satisfy this paragraph (d)(2) merely because different service-crediting provisions are applied to salaried and hourly employees for administrative convenience. The service-crediting provisions for hourly employees in Plan A are reasonably comparable to the service-crediting provisions for salaried employees. This is because the amount of service credited to hourly employees who complete fewer than 1,000 hours of service before termination of employment (i.e., quit, retirement, discharge, or death) during the plan year (and are treated less favorably than the salaried employees with the same period of employment during the plan year) is balanced by the amount of service credited to hourly employees who complete more than 1,000 hours of service before termination of employment during the plan year (who are treated more favorably than the salaried employees with the same period of employment during the plan year).

Example 2. (a) The facts are the same as in *Example 1*, except Plan A requires hourly employees to complete 2,000 hours of service in order to be credited with a full year of service, with a pro rata reduction for hourly employees who complete fewer than 2,000 hours of service.

(b) Plan A does not fail to satisfy this paragraph (d)(2) merely because different service-crediting provisions are applied to salaried and hourly employees for administrative convenience. The service-crediting provisions for hourly employees in Plan A are reasonably comparable to the service-crediting provisions for salaried employees. This is because the amount of service credited to hourly employees whose employment terminates (i.e., quit, retire, are discharged, or die) during the plan year is reasonably comparable to the amount of service credited to salaried employees whose employment is terminated during the plan year with the same period of employment during the plan year.

(3) *Service-crediting period.*—(i) *Limitation on service taken into account.*—(A) *General rule.*—Except as otherwise provided in this paragraph (d)(3), service for periods in which an employee does not perform services as an employee of the employer or in which the employee did not participate in the plan may not be taken into account in determining whether the plan satisfies § 1.401(a)(4)-1(b)(2) and (b)(3). In addition, in determining whether a plan satisfies § 1.401(a)(4)-1(b)(2) and (b)(3), no more than one year of service may be taken into account with respect to any 12-consecutive-month period (with adjustments for shorter periods, if appropriate) unless the additional service is required to be credited under section 410 or 411, whichever is applicable.

(B) *Past service.*—Notwithstanding paragraph (d)(3)(i)(A) of this section, service for periods in which an employee performed services as an employee of the employer and did not participate in a plan, but in which the employee would have participated in the plan but for the fact that the plan (or the plan amendment extending coverage to the employee) was not in existence during that period, may be taken into account in determining whether the plan satisfies § 1.401(a)(4)-1(b)(2) and (b)(3). This is because service for such periods generally would have been credited for the employee but for the timing of the plan establishment or amendment, and the timing of the plan establishment or amendment must satisfy § 1.401(a)(4)-5(a).

(C) *Pre-participation and imputed service.*—Notwithstanding paragraph (d)(3)(i)(A) of this section, to the extent that a plan treats pre-participation service and imputed service as actual service with the employer, such service may be taken into account in determining whether the plan satisfies § 1.401(a)(4)-1(b)(2) and (b)(3) if the service satisfies each of the requirements in paragraph (d)(3)(iii) of this section taking into account, in the case of imputed service, the additional rules in paragraph (d)(3)(iv) of this section.

(D) *Additional limitations on service-crediting in the case of certain offsets.*—Notwithstanding paragraphs (d)(3)(i)(B) and (C) of this section, if a plan credits benefit service or accrual service under paragraph (d)(3)(i)(B) or (C) of this section for a period before an employee becomes a participant in the plan, but offsets the benefits determined under the plan by benefits under another plan (whether or not qualified or terminated) that are attributable to the same period for which that service is credited, then that service may not be taken into account for purposes of determining whether the first plan satisfies § 1.401(a)(4)-1(b)(2) or (b)(3) unless the offset provision applies on the same basis to all similarly-situated employees (within the meaning of paragraph (d)(3)(iii)(A) of this section).

(ii) *Definitions.*—(A) *Pre-participation service.*—For purposes of this section, pre-participation service includes all years of service credited under a plan for years of service with the employer or a prior employer for periods before the employee commenced or recommenced participation in the plan (other than past service described in paragraph (d)(3)(i)(B) of this section).

(B) *Imputed service.*—For purposes of this section, imputed service includes any service credited for periods after an employee has commenced participation in a plan while the employee is not performing services as an employee for the employer (including a period in which the employee performs services for another employer, e.g., a joint venture), or while the employee has a reduced work schedule and would not otherwise be credited with service at the level being credited under the general terms of the plan.

(iii) *Requirements for pre-participation and imputed service.*—(A) *Provision applied to all similarly-situated employees.*—(1) *General rule.*—A plan provision crediting pre-participation service or imputed service to any HCE must apply on the same terms to all similarly-situated NHCEs. Whether two employees are similarly situated for this purpose must be determined based on reasonable business criteria, generally taking into account only the circumstances resulting in the employees being covered under the plan or being granted imputed service and on the situation of the employees (e.g., the plan in which the employees benefit or the employer by which they are employed) during the period for which the pre-participation service or imputed service is credited. For example, employees who enter a plan as a result of a particular merger and who participated in the same plan of a prior employer are generally similarly situated. As another example, employees who are transferred to different joint ventures or different spun-off divisions are generally not similarly situated.

(2) *Examples.*—The following examples illustrate the rules in this paragraph (d)(3)(iii)(A):

Example 1. Employer X maintains defined benefit Plans A and B and defined contribution Plan C. Plan A covers all employees who work at the headquarters of Employer X. Plan B covers some employees in Division M of Employer X, and Plan C covers the other employees of Division M. Plans B and C have not been aggregated for purposes of satisfying section 401(a)(4) or 410(b) for the period for which service is being credited. Plan A provides that, whenever an employee covered by Plan B transfers from Division M to the headquarters, the employee's service credited under Plan B is credited under Plan A, and the employee's benefit under Plan A is offset by the employee's benefit under Plan B. However, Plan A provides for no similar recognition of service or offset for employees covered by Plan C who transfer from Division M to the headquarters. Plan A does not fail to satisfy this paragraph (d)(3)(iii)(A) merely because it credits service for employees transferring from Plan B but not from Plan C, because it is reasonable to treat employees participating in different plans that have not been aggregated as not being similarly situated.

Example 2. The facts are the same as in *Example 1*, except that Employer X acquires two trades or businesses from different employers. Employees of the acquired trades or businesses become employees of Division M and become covered by Plan B. In addition, Plan B is amended to credit service with one of the trades or businesses but not the other. Plan B does not fail to satisfy this paragraph (d)(3)(iii)(A) merely because it credits service for one acquired trade or business but not another, because it is reasonable to treat employees of one acquired trade or business as not similarly situated to employees of another acquired trade or business.

(B) *Legitimate business reason.*—(1) *General rule.*—There must be a legitimate business reason, based on all of the relevant facts and circumstances, for a plan to credit imputed service or for a plan to credit pre-participation service for a period of service with another employer.

(2) *Relevant facts and circumstances when crediting service with another employer.*—The following are examples of relevant facts and circumstances for determining whether a legitimate business reason exists for a plan to credit pre-participation or imputed service for a period of service with another employer as service with the employer: whether one employer has a significant ownership, control, or similar interest in, or relationship with, the other employer (though not enough to cause the two employers to be treated as a single employer under section 414); whether the two employers share interrelated business operations; whether the employers maintain the same multiple-employer plan; whether the employers share similar attributes, such as operation in the same industry or the same geographic area; and whether the employees are an acquired group of employees or the employees became employed by the other employer in a transaction between the two employers that was a stock or asset acquisition, merger, or other similar transaction involving a change in the employer of the employees of a trade or business. Other factors may also be relevant for this purpose, such as the plan's treatment of service with other employers with which the employer has a similar relationship and the type of service being credited (e.g., vesting service as compared to benefit service or accrual service). A legitimate business reason is deemed to exist for a plan to credit military service as service with the employer.

(3) *Examples.*—The following examples illustrate the rules in this paragraph (d)(3)(iii)(B):

Example 1. Twenty unrelated employers jointly sponsor a multiple-employer plan that covers all employees of the employers. From time to time, employees transfer employment among the employers. There is a legitimate business reason for a disaggregated portion of the plan that benefits the employees of one of the employers to treat service with any of the other employers as service with the employer.

Example 2. Employer X owns 20 percent of the outstanding stock of Employer Y. From time to time, employees transfer from Employer X to Employer Y at the request of Employer X. Employer X maintains defined benefit Plan A. Plan A provides that years of service include an employee's years of service with Employer Y. There is a legitimate business reason for Plan A to credit service with Employer Y because Employer X, through its 20-percent ownership interest, benefits from the service that the transferred employees provide to Employer Y.

Example 3. Employer Z manufactures widgets and belongs to the National Widget Manufacturers' Association. From time to time, Employer Z hires employees from other widget manufacturers. Employer Z maintains a defined benefit plan, Plan B, which credits pre-participation service for periods of service with all other members of the Association located in the western half of the United States as service with Employer Z. There is a legitimate business reason for Plan B to treat service with other members of the Association as service with Employer Z.

(C) *No significant discrimination.*—(1) *General rule.*—Based on all of the relevant facts and circumstances, a plan provision crediting pre-participation or imputed service must not by design or in operation discriminate significantly in favor of HCEs.

(2) *Relevant facts and circumstances.*—The following are examples of relevant facts and circumstances for determining whether a plan provision crediting pre-participation service or imputed service discriminates significantly in favor of HCEs: whether the service credit does not duplicate benefits but merely makes an employee whole (i.e., prevents the employee from being disadvantaged with respect to benefits by a change in job or employer or provides the employee with benefits comparable to those of other employees); the degree of business ties between the current employer and the prior employer, such as the degree of ownership interest or other affiliation; the degree of excess coverage under section 410(b) of NHCEs for the plan crediting the service, taking into account employees who are credited with pre-participation service; whether the other employer maintains a qualified plan for its employees; the existence of reciprocal service credit under other plans of the employer or the prior employer; the circumstances underlying the employee's transfer into the group of employees covered by the plan; the type of service being credited; and the relative number of employees other than five-percent owners or the most highly-paid HCEs of the employer (determined without regard to the one officer rule of section 414(q)(5)(B)) who are being credited with pre-participation service or imputed service. The relative number referred to in the last factor is determined taking into account all employees who have been over time, or are reasonably expected to be in the future, credited with such service.

(3) *Examples.*—The following examples illustrate the rules in this paragraph (d)(3)(iii)(C). It is assumed that facts not described in an example do not, in the aggregate, suggest that the relevant plan provision either does or does not discriminate significantly in favor of HCEs.

Example 1. (a) Employer U maintains defined benefit Plans A and B. Plan A covers all employees who work at the headquarters of Employer U. Plan B covers all employees of Division M of Employer U. Plan A provides that, whenever an employee transfers from Division M to the headquarters, the employee's service credited under Plan B is credited under Plan A, and the employee's benefit under Plan A is offset by the employee's benefit under Plan B. Employees, including a meaningful number of NHCEs, are periodically transferred from Division M to the headquarters of Employer U for bona fide business reasons.

(b) The Plan A provision crediting service under Plan B does not discriminate significantly in favor of HCEs. The provision is designed only to prevent employees from being disadvantaged by being transferred from Division M to the headquarters, and a meaningful number of NHCEs can be expected to benefit from it.

Example 2. (a) The facts are the same as in *Example 1,* except that the only employees transferred from Division M to the headquarters of Employer U are HCEs (but not the most highly-paid HCEs of Employer U).

(b) Employer U determines that Plan A would have satisfied sections 401(a)(4) and 410(b) for the period for which the transferred employees are being credited with pre-participation service had the employees participated in Plan A during that period. This determination is based on test results under sections 401(a)(4) and 410(b) for the current year, taking into account significant demographic changes over this period.

(c) The Plan A provision crediting service under Plan B does not significantly discriminate in favor of HCEs in the current

year. This conclusion is based on the fact that the circumstances underlying the transfers indicate that they were made for bona fide business reasons, that Plan A would have satisfied sections 401(a)(4) and 410(b) had the transferred employees participated in Plan A during the period for which the pre-participation service is credited, and that the transferred employees are not the most highly-paid HCEs of Employer U.

Example 3. (a) The facts are the same as in *Example 1,* except that the only employee who is transferred from Division M to the headquarters of Employer U is Employee P, who is among the most highly-paid HCEs of Employer U. Plan A provides an unreduced early retirement benefit at age 55 for employees with 20 years of service, but Plan B's early retirement benefits are not subsidized. Employee P is transferred to the headquarters with 20 years of service credited under Plan B and shortly before attainment of age 55. Employee P is expected to retire upon reaching age 55.

(b) The Plan A provision crediting service under Plan B discriminates significantly in favor of HCEs in the year of the transfer. This is because the circumstances underlying this transfer (i.e., its occurrence shortly before Employee P's expected retirement and the fact that the transfer significantly increased Employee P's early retirement benefits) indicate that Employee P was transferred to the headquarters primarily to obtain the higher pension benefits provided under Plan A.

(c) Because of this conclusion, the pre-participation service credited to Employee P cannot be taken into account in determining whether Plan A satisfies § 1.401(a)(4)-1(b)(2) and (b)(3). Thus, if Plan A credits the service, it cannot be a safe harbor plan because the benefit formula will take into account service that may not be taken into account under this paragraph (d)(3). In addition, Employee P's accrual rates under the general test in § 1.401(a)(4)-3(c) are likely to be higher than those of other employees because, while the pre-participation service may be used to determine Employee P's benefits under Plan A, the service must be disregarded in determining Employee P's testing service. Also, if Employee P's pre-participation service is used in determining Employee P's entitlement to a benefit, right, or feature under Plan A, the fact that the service must be disregarded in determining Employee P's entitlement service for purposes of § 1.401(a)(4)-4 may cause the benefit, right, or feature to be treated as a separate benefit, right, or feature that is currently available only to Employee P.

Example 4. (a) Employer V manufactures widgets and belongs to the National Widget Manufacturers' Association. Each member of the Association maintains a defined benefit plan that credits pre-participation service for periods of service with other members and offsets benefits under the plan by benefits under the plans of the other members. Employer V maintains defined benefit Plan C. Employer V periodically hires employees from other widget manufacturers who are not among its most highly-paid HCEs. In 1997, however, the only employee hired by Employer V from another member of the Association is Employee Q, who is among Employer V's most highly-paid HCEs. Employee Q receives pre-participation service credit in accordance with the terms of Plan C. Some of the plans maintained by other members of the Association credited pre-participation service to NHCEs for the same period for which the pre-participation service is credited to Employee Q.

(b) The provision of Plan C crediting pre-participation service with other members of the Association does not discriminate significantly in 1997, despite the fact that the only employee who received pre-participation service credit under the provision in that year was among the most highly-paid HCEs of Employer V. This conclusion is based on the relative number of employees other than Employer V's most highly-paid HCEs who have been credited in the past, or are reasonably expected to be credited in the future, with pre-participation service for periods of service with other members of the Association, and the fact that other employees who are NHCEs are being credited with pre-participation service under a reciprocal agreement.

Example 5. Employer W owns 79 percent of the outstanding stock of Employer X. From time to time, employees transfer from Employer W to Employer X at the request of Employer W. All of the employees who have ever been transferred are HCEs. Employer W maintains a defined benefit plan, Plan D, which credits employees transferred to Employer X with imputed benefit and accrual service while employed by Employer X. Employer X maintains no qualified plan. Plan D would fail either section 401(a)(4) or section 410(b) in the current plan year if the individuals employed by Employer X were treated as employed by Employer W. In addition, Plan D would fail either section 401(a)(4) or section 410(b) in the current plan year if the portion of Plan D covering the transferred employees were treated as maintained by Employer X. The Plan D provision crediting imputed benefit and accrual service to employees transferred to Employer X significantly discriminates in favor of HCEs in the current plan year.

Example 6. The facts are the same as in *Example 5* except that Plan D credits the individuals who transfer to Employer X only with imputed vesting and entitlement service. The Plan D provision crediting imputed vesting and entitlement service to individuals transferred to Employer X does not significantly discriminate in favor of HCEs in the current plan year, because there is less potential for discrimination when the only types of service being imputed are vesting and entitlement service.

(iv) *Additional rules for imputed service.*—(A) *Legitimate business reasons for crediting imputed service.*—(1) *General rule.*—A legitimate business reason does not exist for a plan to impute service after an individual has permanently ceased to perform services as an employee (within the meaning of §1.410(b)-9) for the employer maintaining the plan, i.e., is not expected to resume performing services as an employee for the employer. The preceding sentence does not apply in the case of an individual who is not performing services for the employer because of disability or is performing services for another employer under an arrangement (such as a transfer of the employee to another employer) that provides some ongoing business benefit to the original employer. The first sentence in this paragraph (d)(3)(iv)(A)(1) also does not apply in the case of vesting and entitlement service if the employee is performing services for another employer that is being treated under the plan as actual service with the original employer.

(2) *Certain presumptions applicable.*—Whether an individual has permanently ceased to perform services as an employee for an employer is determined taking into account all of the relevant facts and circumstances. There is a rebuttable presumption for a period of up to two years that an individual who has ceased to perform services as an employee for an employer is nonetheless expected to resume performing services as an employee for the employer, if the employer continues to treat the individual as an employee for significant purposes unrelated to the plan. After two years, there is a rebuttable presumption that an individual who has ceased to perform services as an employee for the employer is not expected to resume performing services as an employee for the employer. The fact that an individual is absent to perform jury duty or military service automatically rebuts the latter presumption. Other evidence, such as the employer's layoff policy, the terms of an employment contract, or specific leave to pursue a degree requiring more than two years of study, may also rebut this presumption.

(3) *Imputed service for part-time employees.*—Rules similar to the rules in paragraph (d)(3)(iv)(A)(1) and (2) of this section apply in the case of an employee whose work hours are temporarily reduced and who therefore would normally be credited with service at a reduced rate, but who continues to be credited with service at the same rate as before the reduction (e.g., an employee who continues to be credited with service as if the employee were a full-time employee during a temporary change from a full-time to a part-time work schedule).

(B) *Additional factors for determining whether a provision crediting imputed service discriminates significantly.*—In addition to the factors described in paragraph (d)(3)(iii)(C)(2) of this section, relevant facts and circumstances for determining whether a plan provision crediting imputed service during a leave of absence or a period of reduced services discriminates significantly include any employer policies or practices that restrict the ability of employees to take leaves of absence or work temporarily on a part-time basis, respectively.

(v) *Satisfaction of other service-crediting rules.*—A plan does not fail to satisfy this paragraph (d)(3) merely because it credits service to the extent necessary to satisfy the service-crediting rules in section 410(a), 411(a), 413, or 414(a), §1.410(a)-7 (elapsed-time method of service-crediting) or 29 CFR 2530.200b-2 (regarding hours of service to be credited), whichever is applicable, or 29 CFR §2530.204-2(d) (regarding double proration of service and compensation).

(e) *Family aggregation rules.*—[Reserved]

(f) *Governmental plans.*—[Reserved]

(g) *Corrective amendments.*—(1) *In general.*—A corrective amendment that satisfies the rules of this paragraph (g) is taken into account for purposes of satisfying certain section 401(a) requirements for a plan year, by treating the corrective amendment as if it were adopted and effective as of the first day of the plan year. These rules apply in addition to the rules of section 401(b). Paragraph (g)(2) of this section describes the scope of the corrective amendments that are permitted to be made. Paragraph (g)(3) of this section specifies the conditions under which a corrective amendment may be made. Paragraph (g)(4) of this section provides a rule prohibiting a corrective amendment from being taken into account to the extent that it does not have substance. Paragraph (g)(5) of this section discusses the

effect of the corrective amendments permitted under this paragraph (g) under provisions other than section 401(a).

(2) *Scope of corrective amendments.*—For purposes of satisfying the minimum coverage requirements of section 410(b), the nondiscriminatory amount requirement of §1.401(a)(4)1(b)(2), or the nondiscriminatory plan amendment requirement of §1.401(a)(4)-1(b)(4), a corrective amendment may retroactively increase accruals or allocations for employees who benefited under the plan during the plan year being corrected, or may grant accruals or allocations to individuals who did not benefit under the plan during the plan year being corrected. In addition, for purposes of satisfying the nondiscriminatory current availability requirement of §1.401(a)(4)-4(b) for benefits, rights, or features, a corrective amendment may make a benefit, right, or feature available to employees to whom it was previously not available. A corrective amendment may not, however, correct for a failure to incorporate the pretermination restrictions of §1.401(a)(4)-5(b).

(3) *Conditions for corrective amendments.*—(i) *In general.*—A corrective amendment is not taken into account prior to its adoption under this paragraph (g) unless it satisfies each of the requirements of paragraph (g)(3)(ii) through (vii) of this section, whichever are applicable. Thus, for example, if any of the applicable requirements are not satisfied, any additional accruals arising from an amendment adopted after the end of a plan year are not given retroactive effect and, thus, are tested in the plan year in which the amendment is adopted.

(ii) *Benefits not reduced.*—Except as permitted under paragraph (g)(3)(vi)(C)(2) of this section, the corrective amendment may not result in a reduction of an employee's benefits (including any benefit, right, or feature), determined based on the terms of the plan in effect immediately before the amendment.

(iii) *Amendment effective for all purposes.*—For purposes of determining an employee's rights and benefits under the plan, the corrective amendment must generally be effective as if the amendment had been made on the first day of the plan year being corrected. Thus, if the corrective amendment is made after the close of the plan year being corrected, an employee's allocations or accrual, along with the associated benefits, rights, and features, must be increased to the level at which they would have been had the amendment been in effect for the entire preceding plan year. Accordingly, such increases are taken into account for testing purposes as if the increases had actually occurred in the prior plan year. However, to the extent that an amendment makes a benefit, right, or feature available to a group of employees, the amendment does not fail to satisfy this paragraph (g)(3)(iii) merely because it is not effective prior to the date of adoption and, therefore, the benefit, right, or feature is not made currently available to those employees before that date.

(iv) *Time when amendment must be adopted and put into effect.*—(A) *General rule.*—Any corrective amendment intended to apply to the preceding plan year must be adopted and implemented on or before the 15th day of the 10th month after the close of the plan year in order to be taken into account for the preceding plan year.

(B) *Determination letter requested by employer or plan administrator.*—If, on or before the end of the period set forth in paragraph (g)(3)(iv)(A) of this section, the employer or plan administrator files a request pursuant to §601.201(o) of this chapter (Statement of Procedural Rules) for a determination letter on the amendment, the initial or continuing qualification of the plan, or the trust that is part of the plan, the period set forth in paragraph (g)(3)(iv)(A) of this section is extended in the same manner as provided for an extension of the remedial amendment period under §1.401(b)-1(d)(3).

(v) *Corrective amendment for coverage or amounts testing.*—(A) *Retroactive benefits must be provided to nondiscriminatory group.*—Except as provided in paragraph (g)(3)(v)(B) of this section, if the corrective amendment is adopted after the close of the plan year, the additional allocations or accruals for the preceding plan year resulting from the corrective amendment must separately satisfy section 401(a)(4) for the preceding plan year and must benefit a group of employees that separately satisfies section 410(b) (determined by applying the same rules as are applied in determining whether a component plan separately satisfies section 410(b) under §1.401(a)(4)-9(c)(4)). Thus, for example, in applying the rules of this paragraph (g)(3)(v), an employer may not aggregate the additional accruals or allocations for the preceding plan year resulting from the corrective amendment with the other accruals or allocations already provided under the terms of the plan as in effect during the preceding plan year without regard to the corrective amendment.

(B) *Corrective amendment to conform to safe harbor.*—The requirements of paragraph (g)(3)(v)(A) of this section need not be met if the corrective amendment is for purposes of conforming the plan to one of the safe harbors in §1.401(a)(4)-2(b) or §1.401(a)(4)-3(b) (including for purposes of applying the requirements of those safe harbors under the optional testing methods in §1.401(a)(4)-8(b)(3) or (c)(3)), or ensuring that the plan continues to meet one of those safe harbors.

(vi) *Conditions for corrective amendment of the availability of benefits, rights, and features.*—A corrective amendment may not be taken into account under this paragraph (g) for purposes of satisfying §1.401(a)(4)-4(b) for a given plan year unless—

(A) The corrective amendment is not part of a pattern of amendments being used to correct repeated failures with respect to a particular benefit, right, or feature;

(B) The relevant provisions of the plan immediately after the corrective amendment with respect to the benefit, right, or feature (including a corrective amendment eliminating the benefit, right, or feature) remain in effect until the end of the first plan year beginning after the date of the amendment; and

(C) The corrective amendment either—

(1) Expands the group of employees to whom the benefit, right, or feature is currently available so that for each plan year in which the corrective amendment is taken into account in determining whether the plan satisfies §1.401(a)(4)-4(b), the group of employees to whom the benefit, right, or feature is currently available, after taking into account the amendment, satisfies the nondiscriminatory classification requirement of §1.410(b)-4 (and thus the current availability requirement of §1.401(a)(4)-4(b)) with a ratio percentage greater than or equal to the lesser of—

(i) The safe harbor percentage applicable to the plan; and

(ii) The ratio percentage of the plan; or

(2) Eliminates the benefit, right, or feature (to the extent permitted under section 411(d)(6)) on or before the last day of the plan year for which the corrective amendment is taken into account.

(vii) *Special rules for section 401(k) plans and section 401(m) plans.*—(A) *Minimum coverage requirements.*—In the case of a section 401(k) plan, a corrective amendment may only be taken into account for purposes of satisfying §1.410(b)-3(a)(2)(i) under this paragraph (g) for a given plan year to the extent that the corrective amendment grants qualified nonelective contributions within the meaning of §1.401(k)-6 (QNECs) to nonhighly compensated nonexcludable employees who were not eligible employees within the meaning of §1.401(k)-6 for the given plan year, and the amount of the QNECs granted to each nonhighly compensated nonexcludable employee equals the product of the nonhighly compensated nonexcludable employee's plan year compensation and the actual deferral percentage (within the meaning of section 401(k)(3)(B)) for the given plan year for the group of NHCEs who are eligible employees. Similarly, in the case of a section 401(m) plan, a corrective amendment may only be taken into account for purposes of satisfying §1.410(b)-3(a)(2)(i) under this paragraph (g) for a given plan year to the extent that the corrective amendment grants qualified nonelective contributions (QNECs) to nonhighly compensated nonexcludable employees who were not eligible employees within the meaning of §1.401(m)-5 for the given plan year, and the amount of the QNECs granted to each nonhighly compensated nonexcludable employee equals the product of the nonhighly compensated nonexcludable employee's plan year compensation and the actual contribution percentage (within the meaning of section 401(m)(3)) for the given plan year for the group of NHCEs who are eligible employees.

(B) *Correction of rate of match.*—In the case of a section 401(m) plan, allocations for a given plan year granted under a corrective amendment to NHCEs who made contributions for the plan year eligible for a matching contribution may be treated as matching contributions. These allocations treated as matching contributions may be taken into account for purposes of satisfying the current availability requirement of §1.401(a)(4)-4(b) with respect to the right to a rate of match, but may not be taken into account for satisfying other amounts testing.

(4) *Corrective amendments must have substance.*—A corrective amendment is not taken into account in determining whether a plan satisfies section 401(a)(4) or 410(b) to the extent the amendment affects nonvested employees whose employment with the employer terminated on or before the close of the preceding year, and who therefore would not have received any economic benefit from the amendment if it had been made in the prior year. Similarly, in determining whether the requirements of paragraph (g)(3)(vi)(C)(1) of this section are satisfied, a corrective amendment making a benefit, right, or feature available to employees is not taken into account to the extent the benefit, right, or feature is not currently available to any of those employees immediately after the amendment. However, a plan will not fail to satisfy the requirements of paragraph (g)(3)(vi)(C)(1) of this section by operation of the provisions in this

paragraph (g)(4) if the benefit, right, or feature is made available to all employees in the plan as of the date of the amendment.

(5) *Effect under other statutory requirements.*—A corrective amendment under this paragraph (g) is treated as if it were adopted and effective as of the first day of the plan year only for the specific purposes described in this paragraph (g). Thus, for example, the corrective amendment is taken into account not only for purposes of sections 401(a)(4) and 410(b), but also for purposes of determining whether the plan satisfies sections 401(l). By contrast, the amendment is not given retroactive effect for purposes of section 404 (deductions for employer contributions) or section 412 (minimum funding standards), unless otherwise provided for in rules applicable to those sections.

(6) *Examples.*—The following examples illustrate the rules in this paragraph (g):

Example 1. Employer U maintains a calendar year defined benefit plan that in 1994 is tested using the safe harbor for flat benefit plans in §1.401(a)(4)-3(b)(4). In 1996, Employer U is concerned that the plan will not satisfy the demographic requirement in §1.401(a)(4)-3(b)(4)(i)(C)(3) for the 1995 plan year because the average of the normal accrual rates for all NHCEs is less than 70 percent of the average of the normal accrual rates for all HCEs. Provided the corrective amendment would otherwise satisfy this paragraph (g), Employer U may make a corrective amendment to the plan to increase the number of NHCEs so that the amended plan satisfies the safe harbor for the 1995 plan year. The corrective amendment need not satisfy paragraph (g)(3)(v)(A) of this section because Employer U is retroactively amending the plan to conform to a safe harbor in §1.401(a)(4)-3(b). See paragraph (g)(3)(v)(B) of this section.

Example 2. (a) Employer V maintains a calendar year defined contribution plan covering all the employees in Division M and Division N. Under the plan, only employees in Division M have the right to direct the investments in their account. For plan years prior to 1996, the plan met the current availability requirement of §1.401(a)(4)-4(b) because the employees in Division M were a group of employees that satisfied the nondiscriminatory classification test of §1.410(b)-4. Because of attrition in the employee population in Division M in 1996, the group of employees to whom the right to direct investments is available during that plan year no longer meets the nondiscriminatory classification test of §1.410(b)-4. Thus, the right to direct investments under the plan does not meet the current availability requirement of §1.401(a)(4)-4(b) during the 1996 plan year.

(b) Employer V may amend the plan in 1997 (but on or before October 15) to make the right to direct investments available from the date of the corrective amendment to a larger group of employees and the corrective amendment may be taken into account for purposes of satisfying the current availability requirement of §1.401(a)(4)-4(b) for 1996 if the amendment satisfies this paragraph (g). Thus, for example, the group of employees to whom the right to direct investments is currently available, after taking into account the corrective amendment, must satisfy the nondiscriminatory classification test of §1.410(b)-4 for 1996 using a safe harbor percentage (or if lower, the ratio percentage of the plan for 1996). In addition, the corrective amendment making the right to direct investments available to a larger group of employees must remain in effect though the end of the 1998 plan year.

(c) In order for Employer V to take the corrective amendment into account for purposes of satisfying the current availability requirement of §1.401(a)(4)-4(b) for the portion of the 1997 plan year before the amendment, the group of employees to whom the right to direct investments is currently available, taking into account the amendment, must satisfy the nondiscriminatory classification test of §1.410(b)-4 for 1997 using a safe harbor percentage (or if lower, the ratio percentage of the plan for 1997).

(d) Alternatively, if Employer V adopts the corrective amendment before the end of the 1996 plan year, the corrective amendment need only remain in force through the end of the 1997 plan year, or the corrective amendment may eliminate the right to direct investments (provided that the elimination remains in effect through the end of the 1997 plan year).

Example 3. The facts are the same as in *Example 2.* In 1997, Employer V makes a corrective amendment to extend the plan to employees of Division O as well as Divisions M and N. Assume that the corrective amendment satisfies paragraph (g)(3)(v)(A) of this section, and thus, may be taken into account for purposes of satisfying the nondiscriminatory amounts requirement of §1.401(a)(4)-1(b)(2) or the minimum coverage requirements of section 410(b). However, the employees in Division O will not be taken into account in determining whether the right to direct investments meets the current availability requirements of §1.401(a)(4)-4(b) unless the corrective amendment meets the requirements of paragraph (g)(3)(vi) of this section. Thus, for example, the group of employees to whom the right to direct investments is made available as a result of the expansion of coverage, after taking into account the corrective amendment, must satisfy the nondiscriminatory clarification test of §1.410(b)-4 for 1996 using a safe harbor percentage (or if lower, the ratio percentage of the plan for 1996). In addition, the amendment making the right to direct investments available to a larger group of employees must remain in effect though the end of the 1998 plan year.

Example 4. Employer W maintains a defined benefit plan that covers all employees and that offsets an employee's benefit by the employee's projected primary insurance amount. The plan is not eligible to use the safe harbors under §1.401(a)(4)-3(b) because the plan does not satisfy section 401(l). Under the plan, the accrual rates for all HCEs (determined under the general test of §1.401(a)(4)-3(c) for 1998 are less than 1.5 percent of average annual compensation, and the accrual rates for all NHCEs (determined under the general test of §1.401(a)(4)-3(c)) for 1998 are two percent of average annual compensation. If Employer W adopts a corrective amendment adopted in 1999 that retroactively increases HCEs' benefits under the plan so that their accrual rates equal those of the NHCEs, the corrective amendment may not be taken into account in testing the 1998 plan year (i.e., the accruals that result from the corrective amendment are treated as 1999 accruals), because the accruals for the 1998 plan year resulting from the corrective amendment would not separately satisfy sections 410(b) and 401(a)(4). This is the case even if, after taking the amendment into account, the plan would satisfy sections 410(b) and 401(a)(4) for the 1998 plan year.

Example 5. Employer X maintains two plans—Plan A and Plan B. Plan A satisfies the ratio percentage test of §1.410(b)-2(b)(2), but Plan B does not. Thus, in order to satisfy section 410(b), Plan B must satisfy the average benefits test of §1.410(b)-2(b)(3). The average benefit percentage of Plan B is 60 percent. Employer X may take into account a corrective amendment that increases the accruals under either Plan A or Plan B so that the average benefit percentage meets the 70 percent requirement of the average benefits test, if the amendment satisfies paragraph (g)(3)(v) of this section.

Example 6. Employer Y maintains Plan C, which does not satisfy section 401(a)(4) in a plan year. Under the terms of paragraph (g)(2) of this section, Employer Y amends Plan C to increase the benefits of certain employees retroactively. In designing the amendment, Employer Y identifies those employees who have terminated without vested benefits during the period after the end of the prior plan year and before the adoption date of the amendment, and the amendment provides increases in benefits primarily to those employees. It would be inconsistent with the purpose of preventing discrimination in favor of HCEs for Plan C to treat the amendment as retroactively effective under this paragraph (g). See §1.401(a)(4)-1(c)(2).

Example 7. Employer Z maintains both a section 401(k) plan and a section 401(m) plan that provides matching contributions at a rate of 50 percent with respect to elective contributions under the section 401(k) plan. In plan year 1995, the section 401(k) plan fails to satisfy the actual deferral percentage test of section 401(k)(3). In order to satisfy section 401(k)(3), Employer Z makes corrective distributions to HCEs H1 through H10 of their excess contributions as provided under §1.401(k)-2(b). The matching contributions that H1 through H10 had received on account of their excess contributions are not forfeited, however. Thus, the effective rate of matching contributions provided to H1 through H10 is increased as a result of the corrective distributions. See §1.401(a)(4)-4(e)(3)(iii)(G). Since no NHCE in the section 401(m) plan is provided with an equivalent rate of matching contributions, the rate of matching contributions provided to H1 through H10 does not satisfy the nondiscriminatory availability requirement of §1.401(a)(4)-4 in plan year 1995. Employer Z makes a corrective amendment by October 15, 1996, that grants allocations to NHCEs who made contributions for the 1995 plan year eligible for a matching contribution. Employer Z may treat the allocations granted under the corrective amendment to those NHCEs as matching contributions for the 1995 plan year and, as a result, take them into account in determining whether the availability of the rate of matching contributions provided to H1 through H10 satisfies the current availability requirement of §1.401(a)(4)-4(b) for the 1995 plan year. [Reg. §1.401(a)(4)-11.]

☐ [*T.D. 8360, 9-12-91. Amended by T.D. 8485, 8-30-93 and T.D. 9169, 12-28-2004.*]

[Reg. §1.401(a)(4)-12]

§1.401(a)(4)-12. Definitions.—Unless otherwise provided, the definitions in this section govern in applying the provisions of §§1.401(a)(4)-1 through 1.401(a)(4)-13.

Accumulation plan. Accumulation plan means a defined benefit plan under which the benefit of every employee for each plan year is separately determined, using plan year compensation (if benefits are determined as a percentage of compensation rather as than a dollar

amount) separately calculated for the plan year, and each employee's total accrued benefit as of the end of a plan year is the sum of the separately determined benefit for that plan year and the total accrued benefit as of the end of the preceding plan year.

Acquired group of employees. Acquired group of employees means employees of a prior employer who become employed by the employer in a transaction between the employer and the prior employer that is a stock or asset acquisition, merger, or other similar transaction involving a change in the employer of the employees of a trade or business, plus employees hired by or transferred into the acquired trade or business on or before a date selected by the employer that is within the transition period defined in section 410(b)(6)(C)(ii). In addition, in the case of a transaction prior to the effective date of these regulations, the date by which employees must be hired by or transferred into the acquired trade or business in order to be included in the acquired group of employees may be any date prior to February 11, 1993, without regard to whether it is later than the end of the transition period defined in section 410(b)(6)(C)(ii).

Actuarial equivalent. An amount or benefit is the actuarial equivalent of, or is actuarially equivalent to, another amount or benefit at a given time if the actuarial present value of the two amounts or benefits (calculated using the same actuarial assumptions) at that time is the same.

Actuarial present value. Actuarial present value means the value as of a specified date of an amount or series of amounts due thereafter, where each amount is—

(1) Multiplied by the probability that the condition or conditions on which payment of the amount is contingent will be satisfied; and

(2) Discounted according to an assumed rate of interest to reflect the time value of money.

Ancillary benefit. Ancillary benefit is defined in §1.401(a)(4)-4(e)(2).

Average annual compensation. Average annual compensation is defined in §1.401(a)(4)-3(e)(2).

Base benefit percentage. Base benefit percentage is defined in §1.401(l)-1(c)(3).

Benefit formula. Benefit formula means the formula a defined benefit plan applies to determine the accrued benefit (within the meaning of section 411(a)(7)(A)(i)) in the form of an annual benefit commencing at normal retirement age of an employee who continues in service until normal retirement age. Thus, for example, the benefit formula does not include the accrual method the plan applies (in conjunction with the benefit formula) to determine the accrued benefit of an employee who terminates employment before normal retirement age. For purposes of this definition, a change in plan provisions that applies only to certain employees who terminate within a limited period of time (e.g., an early retirement window benefit) is treated as a change in the plan's benefit formula for the employees to whom the change is potentially applicable during the period that the change is potentially applicable to them. The preceding sentence applies only to the extent that the change in plan provisions would result in a change in the benefit formula if it were permanent and applied without regard to when the employees' employment was terminated.

Benefit, right, or feature. Benefit, right, or feature means an optional form of benefit, an ancillary benefit, or an other right or feature within the meaning of §1.401(a)(4)-4(e).

Contributory DB plan. Contributory DB plan means a defined benefit plan that includes employee contributions not allocated to separate accounts.

Defined benefit excess plan. Defined benefit excess plan is defined in §1.401(l)-1(c)(16)(i).

Defined benefit plan. Defined benefit plan is defined in §1.410(b)-9.

Defined contribution plan. Defined contribution plan is defined in §1.410(b)-9.

Determination date. Determination date is defined in §1.401(a)(4)-8(b)(3)(iv)(A).

Employee. With respect to a plan for a given plan year, employee means an employee (within the meaning of §1.410(b)-9) who benefits as an employee under the plan for the plan year (within the meaning of §1.410(b)-3).

Employer. Employer is defined in §1.410(b)-9.

ESOP. ESOP is defined in §1.410(b)-9.

Excess benefit percentage. Excess benefit percentage is defined in §1.401(l)-1(c)(14).

Former employee. With respect to a plan for a given plan year, former employee means a former employee (within the meaning of §1.410(b)-9).

Former HCE. Former HCE means a highly compensated former employee as defined in §1.410(b)-9.

Former NHCE. Former NHCE means a former employee who is not a former HCE.

Fresh-start date. Fresh-start date is defined in §1.401(a)(4)-13(c)(5)(iii).

Fresh-start group. Fresh-start group is defined in §1.401(a)(4)-13(c)(5)(ii).

Gross benefit percentage. Gross benefit percentage is defined in §1.401(l)-1(c)(18).

HCE. HCE means a highly compensated employee as defined in §1.410(b)-9 who benefits under the plan for the plan year (within the meaning of §1.410(b)-3).

Integration level. Integration level is defined in §1.401(l)-1(c)(20).

Measurement period. Measurement period is defined in §1.401(a)(4)-3(d)(1)(iii).

Multiemployer plan. Multiemployer plan is defined in §1.410(b)-9.

NHCE. NHCE means an employee who is not a HCE.

Nonexcludable employee. Nonexcludable employee means an employee within the meaning of §1.410(b)-9, other than an excludable employee with respect to the plan as determined under §1.410(b)-6. A nonexcludable employee may be either a highly or nonhighly compensated nonexcludable employee, depending on the nonexcludable employee's status under section 414(q).

Normalize. With respect to a benefit payable to an employee in a particular form, normalize means to convert the benefit to an actuarially equivalent straight life annuity commencing at the employee's testing age. The actuarial assumptions used in normalizing a benefit must be reasonable and must be applied on a gender-neutral basis. A standard interest rate and a standard mortality table are among the assumptions considered reasonable for this purpose.

Offset plan. Offset plan is defined in §1.401(l)-1(c)(24).

Optional form of benefit. Optional form of benefit is defined in §1.401(a)(4)-4(e)(1).

Other right or feature. Other right or feature is defined in §1.401(a)(4)-4(e)(3).

Plan. Plan means a plan within the meaning of §1.410(b)-7(a) and (b), after application of the mandatory disaggregation rules of §1.410(b)-7(c) and the permissive aggregation rules of §1.410(b)-7(d).

Plan year. Plan year is defined in §1.410(b)-9.

Plan year compensation—(1) *In general.* Plan year compensation means section 414(s) compensation for the plan year determined by measuring section 414(s) compensation during one of the periods described in paragraphs (2) through (4) of this definition. Whichever period is selected must be applied uniformly to determine the plan year compensation of every employee.

(2) *Plan year.* This period consists of the plan year.

(3) *Twelve-month period ending in the plan year.* This period consists of a specified 12-month period ending with or within the plan year, such as the calendar year or the period for determining benefit accruals described in §1.401(a)(4)-3(f)(6).

(4) *Period of plan participation during the plan year.* This period consists of the portion of the plan year during which the employee is a participant in the plan. This period may be used to determine plan year compensation for the plan year in which participation begins, the plan year in which participation ends, or both. This period may be used to determine plan year compensation when substituted for average annual compensation in §1.401(a)(4)-3(e)(2)(ii)(A) only if the plan year is also the period for determining benefit accruals under the plan rather than another period as permitted under §1.401(a)(4)-3(f)(6). Further, selection of this period must be made on a reasonably consistent basis from plan year to plan year in a manner that does not discriminate in favor of HCEs.

(5) *Special rule for new employees.* Notwithstanding the uniformity requirement of paragraph (1) of this definition, if employees' plan year compensation for a plan year is determined based on a 12-month period ending within the plan year under paragraph (3) of this definition, then the plan year compensation of any employees whose date of hire was less than 12 months before the end of that 12-month period must be determined uniformly based either on the plan year or on the employees' periods of participation during the plan year, as provided in paragraphs (2) and (4), respectively, of this definition.

QJSA. QJSA means a qualified joint and survivor annuity as defined in section 417(b).

QSUPP—(1) *In general.* QSUPP or qualified social security supplement means a social security supplement that meets each of the requirements in paragraphs (2) through (6) of this definition.

(2) *Accrual*—(i) *General rule.* The amount of the social security supplement payable at any age for which the employee is eligible for the social security supplement must be equal to the lesser of—

(A) The employee's old-age insurance benefit, unreduced on account of age, under title II of the Social Security Act; and

(B) The accrued social security supplement, determined under one of the methods in paragraph (2)(ii) through (iv) of this definition.

(ii) *Section 401(l) plans.* In the case of a section 401(l) plan that is a defined benefit excess plan, each employee's accrued social security supplement equals the employee's average annual compensation up to the integration level, multiplied by the disparity provided by the plan for the employee's years of service used in determining the employee's accrued benefit under the plan. In the case of a section 401(l) plan that is an offset plan, each employee's accrued social security supplement equals the dollar amount of the offset accrued for the employee under the plan.

(iii) *PIA offset plan.* In the case of a PIA offset plan, each employee's accrued social security supplement equals the dollar amount of the offset accrued for the employee under the plan. For this purpose, a PIA offset plan is a plan that reduces an employee's benefit by an offset based on a stated percentage of the employee's primary insurance amount under the Social Security Act.

(iv) *Other plans.* In the case of any other plan, each employee's social security supplement accrues ratably over the period beginning with the later of the employee's commencement of participation in the plan or the effective date of the social security supplement and ending with the earliest age at which the social security supplement is payable to the employee. The effective date of the social security supplement is the later of the effective date of the amendment adding the social security supplement or the effective date of the amendment modifying an existing social security supplement to comply with the requirements of this definition. If, by the end of the first plan year to which these regulations apply, as set forth in §1.401(a)(4)-13(a) and (b), an amendment is made to a social security supplement in existence on September 19, 1991, the employer may treat the accrued portion of the social security supplement, as determined under the plan without regard to amendments made after September 19, 1991, as included in the employee's accrued social security supplement, provided that the remainder of the social security supplement is accrued under the otherwise-applicable method.

(3) *Vesting.* The plan must provide that an employee's right to the accrued social security supplement becomes nonforfeitable within the meaning of section 411 as if it were an early retirement benefit.

(4) *Eligibility.* The plan must impose the same eligibility conditions on receipt of the social security supplement as on receipt of the early retirement benefit in conjunction with which the social security supplement is payable. Furthermore, if the service required for an employee to become eligible for the social security supplement exceeds 15 years, then the ratio percentage of the group of employees who actually satisfy the eligibility conditions on receipt of the QSUPP in the current plan year must equal or exceed the unsafe harbor percentage applicable to the plan under §1.410(b)-4(c)(4)(ii).

(5) *QJSA.* At each age, the most valuable QSUPP commencing at that age must be payable in conjunction with the QJSA commencing at that age. In addition, the plan must provide that, in the case of a social security supplement payable in conjunction with a QJSA, the social security supplement will be paid after the employee's death on the same terms as the QJSA, but in no event for a period longer than the period for which the social security supplement would have been paid to the employee had the employee not died. For example, if the QJSA is in the form of a joint annuity with a 50-percent survivor's benefit, the social security supplement must provide a 50-percent survivor's benefit. When section 417(c) requires the determination of a QJSA for purposes of determining a qualified pre-retirement survivor's annuity as defined in section 417(c) (QPSA), the social security supplement payable in conjunction with that QJSA must be paid in conjunction with the QPSA.

(6) *Protection.* The plan must specifically provide that the social security supplement is treated as an early retirement benefit that is protected under section 411(d)(6) (other than for purposes of sections 401(a)(11) and 417). Thus, the accrued social security supplement must continue to be payable notwithstanding subsequent amendment of the plan (including the plan's termination), and an employee may meet the eligibility requirements for the social security supplement after plan termination.

Qualified plan. Qualified plan means a plan that satisfies section 401(a). For this purpose, a qualified plan includes an annuity plan described in section 403(a).

Rate group. Rate group is defined in §1.401(a)(4)-2(c)(1) or is defined in §1.401(a)(4)-3(c)(1).

Ratio percentage. Ratio percentage is defined in §1.410(b)-9.

Section 401(a)(17) employee. Section 401(a)(17) employee is defined in §1.401(a)(17)-1(e)(2)(ii).

Section 401(k) plan. Section 401(k) plan is defined in §1.410(b)-9.

Section 401(l) plan. Section 401(l) plan is defined in §1.410(b)-9.

Section 401(m) plan. Section 401(m) plan is defined in §1.410(b)-9.

Section 414(s) compensation—(1) *General rule.* When used with reference to compensation for a plan year, 12-month period, or other specified period, section 414(s) compensation means compensation measured using an underlying definition that satisfies section 414(s) for the applicable plan year. Whether an underlying definition of compensation satisfies section 414(s) is determined on a year-by-year basis, based on the provisions of section 414(s) in effect for the applicable plan year and, if relevant, the employer's HCEs and NHCEs for that plan year. See §1.414(s)-1(i) for transition rules for plan years beginning before the effective date applicable to the plan under §1.401(a)(4)-13(a) or (b). For a plan year or 12-month period beginning before January 1, 1988, any underlying definition of compensation may be used to measure the amount of employees' compensation for purposes of this definition, provided that the definition was nondiscriminatory based on the facts and circumstances in existence for that plan year or for the plan year in which that 12-month period ends.

(2) *Determination period for section 414(s) nondiscrimination requirement*—(i) *General rule.* If an underlying definition of compensation must satisfy the nondiscrimination requirement in §1.414(s)-1(d)(3) in order to satisfy section 414(s) for a plan year, any one of the following determination periods may be used to satisfy the nondiscrimination requirement—

(A) The plan year;

(B) The calendar year ending in the plan year; or

(C) The 12-month period ending in the plan year that is used to determine the underlying definition of compensation.

(ii) *Exception for partial plan year compensation.* Notwithstanding the general rule in paragraph (2)(i) of this definition, if the period for measuring the underlying compensation is the portion of the plan year during which each employee is a participant in the plan (as provided in paragraph (4) of the definition of plan year compensation in this section), that period must be used as the determination period.

(3) *Plans using permitted disparity.* In the case of a section 401(l) plan or a plan that imputes permitted disparity in accordance with §1.401(a)(4)-7, an underlying definition of compensation is not section 414(s) compensation if the definition results in significant under-inclusion of compensation for employees.

(4) *Double proration of service and compensation.* If a defined benefit plan prorates benefit accruals as permitted under section 411(b)(4)(B) by crediting less than full years of participation, then compensation for a plan year, 12-month period, or other specified period that is used to determine the amount of an employee's benefits under the plan will not fail to be section 414(s) compensation, merely because the amount of compensation for that period is adjusted to reflect the equivalent of full-time compensation to the extent necessary to satisfy the requirements of 29 CFR 2530.204-2(d) (regarding double proration of service and compensation). This adjustment is disregarded in determining whether the underlying definition of compensation used satisfies the requirements of section 414(s). Thus, for example, if the underlying definition of compensation is an alternative definition that must satisfy the nondiscrimination requirement of §1.414(s)-1(d)(3), in determining whether that requirement is satisfied with regard to the underlying definition, the compensation included for any employee is determined without any adjustment to reflect the equivalent of full-time compensation required by 29 CFR 2530.204-2(d).

Social security supplement. Social security supplement is defined in §1.411(a)-7(c)(4)(ii).

Standard interest rate. Standard interest rate means an interest rate that is neither less than 7.5 percent nor greater than 8.5 percent, compounded annually. The Commissioner may, in revenue rulings, notices, and other guidance of general applicability, change the definition of standard interest rate.

Standard mortality table. Standard mortality table means one of the following tables: the UP-1984 Mortality Table (Unisex); the 1983 Group Annuity Mortality Table (1983 GAM) (Female); the 1983 Group Annuity Mortality Table (1983 GAM) (Male); the 1983 Individual Annuity Mortality Table (1983 IAM) (Female); the 1983 Individual Annuity Mortality Table (1983 IAM) (Male); the 1971 Group Annuity Mortality Table (1971 GAM) (Female); the 1971 Group Annuity Mortality Table (1971 GAM) (Male); the 1971 Individual Annuity Mortality Table (1971 IAM) (Female); or the 1971 Individual Annuity Mortality Table (1971 IAM) (Male). These standard mortality tables are available from the Society of Actuaries, 475 N. Martingale Road, Suite 800, Schaumb[u]rg, Illinois 60173. The Commissioner may, in revenue rulings, notices, and other guidance of general applicability, change the definition of standard mortality table. See §601.601(d)(2)(ii)(*b*) of this Chapter. The applicable mortality table under section 417(e)(3)(A)(ii)(l) is also a standard mortality table.

Straight life annuity. Straight life annuity means an annuity payable in equal installments for the life of the employee that terminates upon the employee's death.

Testing age. With respect to an employee, testing age means the age determined for the employee under the following rules:

(1) If the plan provides the same uniform normal retirement age for all employees, the employee's testing age is the employee's normal retirement age under the plan.

(2) If a plan provides different uniform normal retirement ages for different employees or different groups of employees, the employee's testing age is the employee's latest normal retirement age under any uniform normal retirement age under the plan, regardless of whether that particular uniform normal retirement age actually applies to the employee under the plan.

(3) If the plan does not provide a uniform normal retirement age, the employee's testing age is 65.

(4) If an employee is beyond the testing age otherwise determined for the employee under paragraphs (1) through (3) of this definition, the employee's testing age is the employee's current age. The rule in the preceding sentence does not apply in the case of a defined benefit plan that fails to satisfy the requirements of §1.401(a)(4)-3(f)(3)(i) (permitting certain increases in benefits that commence after normal retirement age to be disregarded).

Testing service. Testing service is defined in §1.401(a)(4)-3(d)(1)(iv).

Uniform normal retirement age—(1) *General rule.* Uniform normal retirement age means a single normal retirement age under the plan that does not exceed the maximum age in paragraph (2) of this definition and that is the same for all of the employees in a given group. A group of employees does not fail to have a uniform normal retirement age merely because the plan contains provisions described in paragraphs (3) and (4) of this definition.

(2) *Maximum age.* The maximum age is generally 65. However, if all employees have the same social security retirement age (within the meaning of section 415(b)(8)), the maximum age is the employees' social security retirement age. Thus, for example, a component plan has a uniform normal retirement age of 67 if it defines normal retirement age as social security retirement age and all employees in the component plan have a social security retirement age of 67.

(3) *Stated anniversary date*—(i) *General rule.* A group of employees does not fail to have a uniform normal retirement age merely because the plan provides that the normal retirement age of all employees in the group is the later of a stated age (not exceeding the maximum age in paragraph (2) of this definition) or a stated anniversary no later than the fifth anniversary of the time each employee commenced participation in the plan. For employees who commenced participation in the plan before the first plan year beginning on or after January 1, 1988, the stated anniversary date may be later than the anniversary described in the preceding sentence if it is no later than the earlier of the tenth anniversary of the date the employee commenced participation in the plan (or such earlier anniversary selected by the employer, if less than 10) or the fifth anniversary of the first day of the first plan year beginning on or after January 1, 1988.

(ii) *Use of service other than anniversary of commencement of participation.* In lieu of using a stated anniversary date as permitted under paragraph (3)(i) of this definition, a plan may use a stated number of years of service measured on another basis, provided that the determination is made on a basis that satisfies section 411(a)(8) and that the stated number of years of service does not exceed the number of anniversaries permitted under paragraph (3)(i) of this definition. For example, a uniform normal retirement age could be based on the earlier of the fifth anniversary of the commencement of participation and the completion of five years of vesting service.

(4) *Conversion of normal retirement age to normal retirement date.* A group of employees does not fail to have a uniform normal retirement age merely because a defined benefit plan provides for the commencement of normal retirement benefits on different retirement dates for different employees if each employee's normal retirement date is determined on a reasonable basis with reference to an otherwise uniform normal retirement age and the difference between the normal retirement date and the uniform normal retirement age cannot exceed six months for any employee. Thus, for example, benefits under a plan do not fail to commence at a uniform normal retirement age of age 62 for purposes of §1.401(a)(4)-3(b)(2)(i), merely because the plan's normal retirement date is defined as the last day of the plan year nearest attainment of age 62.

Year of service. Year of service means a year of service as defined in the plan for a specific purpose, including the method of crediting service for that purpose under the plan. [Reg. §1.401(a)(4)-12.]

☐ [*T.D. 8360, 9-12-91. Amended by T.D. 8485, 8-30-93 and T.D. 8954, 6-28-2001.*]

[Reg. §1.401(a)(4)-13]

§1.401(a)(4)-13. Effective dates and fresh-start rules.—(a) *General effective dates.*—(1) *In general.*—Except as otherwise provided in this section, §§1.401(a)(4)-1 through 1.401(a)(4)-13 apply to plan years beginning on or after January 1, 1994.

(2) *Plans of tax-exempt organizations.*—In the case of plans maintained by organizations exempt from income taxation under section 501(a), including plans subject to section 403(b)(12)(A)(i) (nonelective plans), §§1.401(a)(4)-1 through 1.401(a)(4)-13 apply to plan years beginning on or after January 1, 1996.

(3) *Compliance during transition period.*—For plan years beginning before the effective date of these regulations, as set forth in paragraph (a)(1) and (2) of this section, and on or after the first day of the

first plan year to which the amendments made to section 410(b) by section 1112(a) of the Tax Reform Act of 1986 (TRA '86) apply, a plan must be operated in accordance with a reasonable, good faith interpretation of section 401(a)(4), taking into account pre-existing guidance and the amendments made by TRA '86 to related provisions of the Code (including, for example, sections 401(l), 401(a)(17), and 410(b)). Whether a plan is operated in accordance with a reasonable, good faith interpretation of section 401(a)(4) will generally be determined on the basis of all the relevant facts and circumstances, including the extent to which an employer has resolved unclear issues in its favor. A plan will be deemed to be operated in accordance with a reasonable, good faith interpretation of section 401(a)(4) if it is operated in accordance with the terms of §§ 1.401(a)(4)-1 through 1.401(a)(4)-13.

(b) *Effective date for governmental plans.*—In the case of governmental plans described in section 414(d), including plans subject to section 403(b)(12)(A)(i) (nonelective plans), §§ 1.401(a)(4)-1 through 1.401(a)(4)-13 apply to plan years beginning on or after the later of January 1, 1996, or 90 days after the opening of the first legislative session beginning on or after January 1, 1996, of the governing body with authority to amend the plan, if that body does not meet continuously. Such plans are deemed to satisfy section 401(a)(4) for plan years before that effective date. For purposes of this paragraph (b), the governing body with authority to amend the plan is the legislature, board, commission, council, or other governing body with authority to amend the plan.

(c) *Fresh-start rules for defined benefit plans.*—(1) *Introduction.*—This paragraph (c) provides rules that must be satisfied in order to use the fresh-start testing options for defined benefit plans in § 1.401(a)(4)-3(b)(6)(vii) and (d)(3)(iii), relating to the safe harbors and the general test, respectively. Those fresh-start options are designed to allow a plan to be tested without regard to benefits accrued before a selected fresh-start date. To the extent provided in paragraph (d) of this section, those options also may be used to disregard certain increases in benefits attributable to compensation increases after a fresh-start date. Although this paragraph (c) generally requires a plan to be amended to freeze employees' accrued benefits as of a fresh-start date and to provide any additional accrued benefits after the fresh-start date solely in accordance with certain specified formulas, certain of these requirements do not apply to a plan that is tested under the general test of § 1.401(a)(4)-3(c). See § 1.401(a)(4)-3(b)(6)(vii) and (d)(3)(iii).

(2) *General rule.*—A defined benefit plan satisfies this paragraph (c) if—

(i) Accrued benefits of employees in the fresh-start group are frozen as of the fresh-start date in accordance with paragraph (c)(3) of this section;

(ii) Accrued benefits after the fresh-start date for employees in the fresh-start group are determined under one of the fresh-start formulas in paragraph (c)(4) of this section; and

(iii) Paragraph (c)(5) of this section is satisfied.

(3) *Definition of frozen.*—(i) *General rule.*—An employee's accrued benefit under a plan is frozen as of the fresh-start date if it is determined as if the employee terminated employment with the employer as of the fresh-start date (or the date the employee actually terminated employment with the employer, if earlier), and without regard to any amendment to the plan adopted after that date, other than amendments recognized as effective as of or before that date under section 401(b) or § 1.401(a)(4)-11(g). The assumption that an employee has terminated employment applies solely for purposes of this paragraph (c)(3). Thus, for example, the fresh start has no effect on the service taken into account for purposes of determining vesting and eligibility for benefits, rights, and features under the plan.

(ii) *Permitted compensation adjustments.*—An employee's accrued benefit under a plan that satisfies paragraph (d) of this section does not fail to be frozen as of the fresh-start date merely because the plan makes the adjustments described in paragraph (d)(7) and (8) of this section with regard to the fresh-start date. In addition, if the frozen accrued benefit of an employee under the plan includes top-heavy minimum benefits, an employee's accrued benefit under a plan does not fail to be frozen as of the fresh-start date merely because the plan increases the frozen accrued benefit of each employee in the fresh-start group solely to the extent necessary to comply with the average compensation requirement of section 416(c)(1)(D)(i).

(iii) *Permitted changes in optional forms.*—An employee's accrued benefit under a plan does not fail to be frozen as of the fresh-start date merely because the plan provides a new optional form of benefit with respect to the frozen accrued benefit, if—

(A) The optional form is provided with respect to each employee's entire accrued benefit (i.e., accrued both before and after the fresh-start date);

(B) The plan provided meaningful coverage as of the fresh-start date, as described in paragraph (d)(4) of this section; and

(C) The plan provides meaningful current benefit accruals as described in paragraph (d)(6) of this section.

(iv) *Floor-offset plans.*—In the case of a plan that was a floor-offset plan described in § 1.401(a)(4)-8(d) prior to the fresh-start date, an employee's accrued benefit as of the fresh-start date does not fail to be frozen merely because the actuarial equivalent of the account balance in the defined contribution plan that is offset against the defined benefit plan varies as a result of investment return that is different from the assumed interest rate used to determine the actuarial equivalent of the account balance.

(4) *Fresh-start formulas.*—(i) *Formula without wear-away.*—An employee's accrued benefit under the plan is equal to the sum of—

(A) The employee's frozen accrued benefit; and

(B) The employee's accrued benefit determined under the formula applicable to benefit accruals in the current plan year (current formula) as applied to the employee's years of service after the fresh-start date.

(ii) *Formula with wear-away.*—An employee's accrued benefit under the plan is equal to the greater of—

(A) The employee's frozen accrued benefit; or

(B) The employee's accrued benefit determined under the current formula as applied to the employee's total years of service (before and after the fresh-start date) taken into account under the current formula.

(iii) *Formula with extended wear-away.*—An employee's accrued benefit under the plan is equal to the greater of—

(A) The amount determined under paragraph (c)(4)(i) of this section; or

(B) The amount determined under paragraph (c)(4)(ii)(B) of this section.

(5) *Rules of application.*—(i) *Consistency requirement.*—This paragraph (c)(5) is not satisfied unless the fresh-start rules in this paragraph (c) (and paragraph (d) of this section, if applicable) are applied consistently to all employees in the fresh-start group. Thus, for example, the same fresh-start date and fresh-start formula (within the meaning of paragraph (c)(4) of this section) must apply to all employees in the fresh-start group. Similarly, if a plan makes a fresh start for all employees with accrued benefits on the fresh-start date and, for a later plan year, is aggregated for purposes of section 401(a)(4) with another plan that did not make the same fresh start, the aggregated plan must make a new fresh start in order to use the fresh-start rules for that later plan year or any subsequent plan year.

(ii) *Definition of fresh-start group.*—Generally, the fresh-start group with respect to a fresh start consists of all employees who have accrued benefits as of the fresh-start date and have at least one hour of service with the employer after that date. However, a fresh-start group with respect to a fresh start may consist exclusively of all employees who have accrued benefits as of the fresh-start date, have at least one hour of service with the employer after that date, and are—

(A) Section 401(a)(17) employees;

(B) Members of an acquired group of employees (provided the fresh-start date is the date determined under paragraph (c)(5)(iii)(B) of this section); or

(C) Employees with a frozen accrued benefit that is attributable to assets and liabilities transferred to the plan as of a fresh-start date in connection with the transfer (provided the fresh-start date is the date determined under paragraph (c)(5)(iii)(C) of this section) and for whom the current formula is different from the formula used to determine the frozen accrued benefit.

(iii) *Definition of fresh-start date.*—Generally, the fresh-start date is the last day of a plan year. However, a plan may use a fresh-start date other than the last day of the plan year if—

(A) The plan satisfied the safe harbor rules of § 1.401(a)(4)-3(b) for the period from the beginning of the plan year through the fresh-start date;

(B) The fresh-start group is an acquired group of employees, and the fresh-start date is the latest date of hire or transfer into an acquired trade or business selected by the employer for any employees to be included in the acquired group of employees; or

(C) The fresh-start group is the group of employees with a frozen accrued benefit that is attributable to assets and liabilities transferred to the plan and the fresh-start date is the date as of which the employees begin accruing benefits under the plan.

(6) *Examples.*—The following examples illustrate the rules in this paragraph (c):

Example 1. (a) Employer X maintains a defined benefit plan with a calendar plan year. The plan formula provides an employee with a normal retirement benefit at age 65 of one percent of average annual compensation up to covered compensation multiplied by the employee's years of service for Employer X, plus 1.5 percent of average annual compensation in excess of covered compensation, multiplied by the employee's years of service for Employer X up to 40.

(b) For plan years beginning after 1994, Employer X amends the plan formula to provide a normal retirement benefit of 0.75 percent of average annual compensation up to covered compensation multiplied by the employee's total years of service for Employer X up to 35, plus 1.4 percent of average annual compensation in excess of covered compensation multiplied by the employee's years of service for Employer X up to 35. For plan years after 1994, each employee's accrued benefit is determined under the fresh-start formula in paragraph (c)(4)(iii) of this section (formula with extended wear-away), using December 31, 1994, as the fresh-start date.

(c) As of December 31, 1994, Employee M has 10 years of service for Employer X, has average annual compensation of $38,000, and has covered compensation of $30,000. Employee M's accrued benefit as of December 31, 1994, is therefore $4,200 ((1 percent × $30,000 × 10 years) + (1.5 percent × $8,000 × 10 years)). As of December 31, 1995, Employee M has 11 years of service for Employer X, has average annual compensation of $40,000 (determined by taking into account compensation before and after the fresh-start date), and has covered compensation of $32,000. Employee M's accrued benefit as of December 31, 1995, is $4,552, the greater of—

(1) $4,552, the sum of Employee M's accrued benefit frozen as of December 31, 1994, ($4,200) and the amended formula applied to Employee M's years of service after 1994 ((0.75 percent × $32,000 × 1 year) + (1.4 percent × $8,000 × 1 year), or $352); or

(2) $3,872, the amended formula applied to Employee M's total years of service ((0.75 percent × $32,000 × 11 years) + (1.4 percent × $8,000 × 11 years)).

Example 2. (a) Employer Y maintains a defined benefit plan, Plan A, that has a calendar plan year. For the 1995 plan year, Plan A satisfies the requirements for a safe harbor plan in § 1.401(a)(4)-3(b). Employer Y selects a date in 1995 for all the employees, freezes the employees' accrued benefits as of that date under the rules of paragraph (c)(3) of this section, and, in accordance with the rules of this paragraph (c), amends Plan A to determine benefits for all employees after that date using the formula with wear-away described in paragraph (c)(4)(ii) of this section. The new benefit formula would satisfy the requirements for a safe harbor plan in § 1.401(a)(4)-3(b) if all accrued benefits were determined under it.

(b) Because Plan A satisfied the requirements for a safe harbor plan for the period from the beginning of the plan year through the selected date, paragraph (c)(5)(iii)(A) of this section permits the selected date to be a fresh-start date, even if it is not the last day of the plan year. Thus, Plan A satisfies the requirements in this paragraph (c) for a fresh start as of the fresh-start date.

(c) Under § 1.401(a)(4)-3(b)(6)(vii), a plan does not fail to satisfy the requirements of § 1.401(a)(4)-3(b), merely because of benefits accrued under a different formula prior to a fresh-start date. Thus, Plan A still satisfies the safe harbor requirements of § 1.401(a)(4)-3(b) after the amendment to the benefit formula. Because Plan A satisfied the requirements for a safe harbor plan for the period from the beginning of the plan year, taking the amendment into account, Employer Y may select any date within the plan year (which may be the same date as the first fresh-start date) and apply the fresh-start rules in this paragraph (c) a second time as of that date.

(d) *Compensation adjustments to frozen accrued benefits.*—(1) *Introduction.*—In addition to the fresh-start rules in paragraph (c) of this section, this paragraph (d) sets forth requirements that must be satisfied in order for a plan to disregard increases in benefits accrued as of a fresh-start date that are attributable to increases in employees' compensation after the fresh-start date.

(2) *In general.*—In the case of a defined benefit plan that is tested under the safe harbors in § 1.401(a)(4)-3(b) or § 1.401(a)(4)-8(c)(3), an employee's adjusted accrued benefit (determined under the rules in paragraph (d)(8) of this section) may be substituted for the employee's frozen accrued benefit in applying the formulas in paragraph (c)(4) of this section (or paragraph (f)(2) of this section, if applicable) if paragraphs (d)(3) through (d)(7) of this section are satisfied. Thus, for example, in determining whether such a plan satisfies § 1.401(a)(4)-3(b), any compensation adjustments to the employee's frozen accrued benefit described in paragraph (d)(8) of this section are disregarded. Similarly, in the case of a defined benefit plan tested under the general test in § 1.401(a)(4)-3(c), the compensation adjustments described in paragraph (d)(8) of this section may be disregarded under the rules of § 1.401(a)(4)-3(d)(3)(iii) if paragraphs

(d)(3) through (d)(7) of this section are satisfied. Of course, any increases in accrued benefits exceeding these adjustments must be taken into account under the general test, and a plan providing such excess increases generally will fail to satisfy the safe harbor requirements of § 1.401(a)(4)-3(b). Where paragraphs (d)(3) through (d)(7) of this section are satisfied with respect to a plan as of the fresh-start date, but one or more of those paragraphs fail to be satisfied for a later plan year, further compensation adjustments described in paragraph (d)(8) of this section may not be disregarded in testing the plan under § 1.401(a)(4)-3.

(3) *Plan requirements.*—(i) *Pre-fresh-start date.*—As of the fresh-start date, the plan must have contained a benefit formula under which benefits of each employee in the fresh-start group that are accrued as of the fresh-start date and are attributable to service before the fresh-start date would be affected by the employee's compensation after the fresh-start date. A plan satisfies this requirement, for example, if it based benefits on an employee's highest average pay over a fixed period of years or on an employee's average pay over the employee's entire career with the employer. A plan does not satisfy this paragraph (d)(3)(i) if the Commissioner determines, based on all of the relevant facts and circumstances, that the plan provision described in the first sentence of this paragraph (d)(3) was added primarily in order to provide additional benefits to HCEs that are disregarded under the special testing rules described in this paragraph (d).

(ii) *Post-fresh-start date.*—The plan by its terms must provide that the accrued benefits of each employee in the fresh-start group after the fresh-start date be at least equal to the employee's adjusted accrued benefit (i.e., the frozen accrued benefit as of the fresh-start date, adjusted as provided under paragraph (d)(7) of this section, plus the compensation adjustments described in paragraph (d)(8) of this section).

(4) *Meaningful coverage as of fresh-start date.*—The plan must have provided meaningful coverage as of the fresh-start date. A plan provided meaningful coverage as of the fresh-start date if the group of employees with accrued benefits under the plan as of the fresh-start date satisfied the minimum coverage requirements of section 410(b) as in effect on that date (determined without regard to section 410(b)(6)(C)). In order to satisfy the requirement in the preceding sentence, an employer may amend the plan to grant past service credit under the formula in effect as of the fresh-start date to NHCEs, if the amount of past service granted them is reasonably comparable, on average, to the amount of past service HCEs have under the plan. Any benefit increase that results from the grant of past service credit to an NHCE under this paragraph (d)(4) is included in the employee's frozen accrued benefit.

(5) *Meaningful ongoing coverage.*—(i) *General rule.*—The fresh-start group must have satisfied the minimum coverage requirements of section 410(b) for all plan years from the first plan year beginning after the fresh-start date through the current plan year. Thus, if a fresh-start group fails to satisfy the minimum coverage requirements of section 410(b) for any plan year, this paragraph (d)(5) is not satisfied for that plan year or any subsequent plan year; however, such a failure is not taken into account in determining whether this paragraph (d)(5) is satisfied for any previous plan year.

(ii) *Alternative rules.*—Notwithstanding paragraph (d)(5)(i) of this section, a fresh-start group is deemed to satisfy this paragraph (d)(5) for all plan years following the fresh-start date if any one of the following requirements is satisfied:

(A) *Section 410(b) coverage for first five years.*—The fresh-start group must have satisfied the minimum coverage requirements of section 410(b) for the first five plan years beginning after the fresh-start date.

(B) *Ratio percentage coverage as of fresh-start date.*—The fresh-start group must have satisfied the ratio percentage test of § 1.410(b)-2(b)(2) as of the fresh-start date.

(C) *Fresh start for acquired group of employees.*—The fresh-start group must consist of an acquired group of employees that satisfied the minimum coverage requirements of section 410(b) (determined without regard to section 410(b)(6)(C)) as of the fresh-start date.

(D) *Fresh start before applicable effective date.*—The fresh-start date with respect to the fresh-start group must have been on or before the effective date applicable to the plan under paragraph (a) or (b) of this section.

(6) *Meaningful current benefit accruals.*—The benefit formula and accrual method under the plan that apply to the fresh-start group in the aggregate must provide benefit accruals in the current plan year

(other than increases in benefits accrued as of the fresh-start date) at a rate that is meaningful in comparison to the rate at which benefits accrued for the fresh-start group in plan years beginning before the fresh-start date. Whether this requirement is satisfied with respect to a fresh-start group that does not include all employees in the plan with an hour of service after the fresh-start date may be determined taking into account the rate at which benefits are provided to other employees in the plan.

(7) *Minimum benefit adjustment.*—(i) *In general.*—In the case of a section 401(l) plan or a plan that imputes disparity under § 1.401(a)(4)-7, the plan must make the minimum benefit adjustment described in paragraph (d)(7)(ii) or (iii) of this section.

(ii) *Excess or offset plans.*—In the case of a plan that is a defined benefit excess plan as of the fresh-start date, each employee's frozen accrued benefit is adjusted so that the base benefit percentage is not less than 50 percent of the excess benefit percentage. In the case of a plan that is a PIA offset plan (as defined in paragraph (2)(iii) of the definition of QSUPP in § 1.401(a)(4)-12) as of the fresh-start date, each employee's offset as applied to determine the frozen accrued benefit is adjusted so that it does not exceed 50 percent of the benefit determined without applying the offset.

(iii) *Other plans.*—In the case of a plan that is not described in paragraph (d)(7)(ii) of this section, each employee's frozen accrued benefit is adjusted in a manner that is economically equivalent to the adjustment required under that paragraph, taking into account the plan's benefit formula, accrual rate, and relevant employee factors, such as period of service.

(8) *Adjusted accrued benefit.*—(i) *General rule.*—The term adjusted accrued benefit means an employee's frozen accrued benefit that is adjusted as provided in paragraph (d)(7) of this section and then multiplied by a fraction (not less than one), the numerator of which is the employee's compensation for the current plan year and the denominator of which is the employee's compensation as of the fresh-start date determined under the same definition. For purposes of this adjustment, the compensation definition must be either the same compensation definition and formula used to determine the frozen accrued benefit or average annual compensation (determined without regard to § 1.401(a)(4)-3(e)(2)(ii)(A) (use of plan year compensation)).

(ii) *Alternative formula for pre-effective-date fresh starts.*—In the case of a fresh-start date before the effective date that applies to the plan under paragraph (a) or (b) of this section, the adjusted accrued benefit may be determined by multiplying the frozen accrued benefit by a fraction (not less than one) determined under this paragraph (d)(8)(ii). The numerator of the fraction is the employee's average annual compensation for the current plan year. The denominator of the fraction is the employee's reconstructed average annual compensation as of the fresh-start date. An employee's reconstructed average annual compensation is determined by—

(A) Selecting a single plan year beginning after the fresh-start date but beginning not later than the last day of the first plan year to which these regulations apply under paragraph (a) or (b) of this section;

(B) Determining the employee's average annual compensation for the selected plan year under the same method used to determine the employee's average annual compensation for the current plan year under this paragraph (d)(8)(ii); and

(C) Multiplying the employee's average annual compensation for the selected plan year by a fraction, the numerator of which is the employee's compensation as of the fresh-start date determined under the same compensation definition and formula used to determine the employee's frozen accrued benefit and the denominator of which is the employee's compensation for the selected plan year determined under the compensation definition and formula used to determine the employee's frozen accrued benefit.

(iii) *Effect of section 401(a)(17).*—In determining the numerators and the denominators of the fractions described in this paragraph (d)(8), the annual compensation limit under section 401(a)(17) generally applies. See, however, § 1.401(a)(17)-1(e)(4) for special rules applicable to section 401(a)(17) employees.

(iv) *Option to make less than the full permitted adjustment.*—A plan may limit the increase in an employee's frozen accrued benefit for the current and all future years to a percentage (not more than 100 percent) of the increase otherwise provided under this paragraph (d)(8). Furthermore, the plan may, at any time, terminate all future adjustments permitted under this paragraph (d).

(v) *Alternative determination of adjusted accrued benefit.*—In lieu of applying the fractions in paragraph (d)(8)(i) or (ii) of this section, a plan may determine an employee's adjusted accrued benefit by sub-stituting the employee's compensation for the current plan year (determined under the same compensation formula and underlying definition of compensation used to determine the employee's frozen accrued benefit) in the benefit formula used to determine the frozen accrued benefit. For this purpose, insignificant changes in the underlying definition of compensation to reflect current compensation practices will not be treated as a change in the definition of compensation. A plan may apply the alternative in this paragraph (d)(8)(v) only if it is reasonable to expect as of the fresh-start date that, over time, the use of this method instead of the general rule of paragraph (d)(8)(i) will not discriminate significantly in favor of HCEs.

(9) *Examples.*—The following examples illustrate the rules of this paragraph (d).

Example 1. (a) Employer X maintains a defined benefit plan that is an excess plan with a calendar plan year. For plan years before 1989, the plan is integrated with benefits provided under the Social Security Act, providing each employee with a normal retirement benefit equal to one percent of the employee's average annual compensation in excess of the employee's covered compensation, multiplied by the employee's years of service for Employer X. The benefit formula thus provides no benefit with respect to average annual compensation up to covered compensation.

(b) As of December 31, 1988, Employee M has 10 years of service for Employer X and has covered compensation of $25,000 and average annual compensation of $20,000. Employee M's average annual compensation has never exceeded $20,000. Therefore, as of December 31, 1988, Employee M's accrued benefit under the plan is zero.

(c) Effective with the 1989 plan year, the plan is amended to provide each employee with a normal retirement benefit of 0.6 percent of average annual compensation up to covered compensation plus 1.2 percent of average annual compensation in excess of covered compensation, multiplied by the employee's years of service up to 35. The plan also provides that, for plan years after 1988, each employee's accrued benefit is determined under the formula in paragraph (c)(4)(i) of this section (formula without wear-away) and, in applying the fresh-start formula, each employee's frozen accrued benefit under paragraph (c)(4)(i) of this section will be adjusted under this paragraph (d), using the same compensation definition and formula used to determine the frozen accrued benefit under paragraph (d)(8)(i) of this section.

(d) The plan uses the permitted disparity of section 401(l) and thus must also make the minimum benefit adjustment under paragraph (d)(7) of this section. Because the excess benefit percentage under the plan for years before 1989 was one percent, the plan must provide a base benefit percentage for those years of at least 0.5 percent. After the minimum benefit adjustment, Employee M's accrued benefit as of December 31, 1988, is $1,000 (0.5 percent × $20,000 × 10 years).

(e) As of December 31, 1992, Employee M has 14 years of service and has covered compensation of $30,000 and average annual compensation of $35,000. Employee M's adjusted accrued benefit as of December 31, 1992, is $1,750 ($1,000 × $35,000/$20,000), and Employee M's accrued benefit as of December 31, 1992, is $2,710 (the sum of $1,750 plus $960 ((0.6 percent × $30,000 × 4 years) plus (1.2 percent × $5,000 × 4 years))).

Example 2. (a) The facts are the same as in *Example 1*, except that in determining adjusted accrued benefits, the plan specifies the alternative method of paragraph (d)(8)(v) of this section. This method may be used because it is reasonable to expect as of the fresh-start date that, over time, the use of this method instead of the general rule of paragraph (d)(8)(i) will not discriminate significantly in favor of HCEs.

(b) As of December 31, 1992, Employee M's adjusted accrued benefit is $2,000 (10 years of service prior to the fresh-start date × (0.5 percent of $30,000 + 1.0 percent of the excess of $35,000 over $30,000)).

(c) Alternatively, Employer X may choose to use the method of paragraph (d)(8)(v) of this section but freezes the covered compensation level at the dollar level in place as of the fresh-start date. In such case, Employee M's adjusted accrued benefit as of December 31, 1992, would have been $2,250 (10 years of service prior to the fresh-start date × (0.5 percent of $25,000 + 1.0 percent of the excess of $35,000 over $25,000)). This method may be used because it is reasonable to expect as of the fresh-start date that, over time, the use of this method instead of the general rule of paragraph (d)(8)(i) will not discriminate significantly in favor of HCEs.

Example 3. (a) The facts are the same as in *Example 1*, except that for plan years before 1989, the plan provided a minimum benefit to certain employees equal to $120 per year of service. Employee M is entitled to the minimum benefit, and thus, Employee M's frozen accrued benefit as of December 31, 1988 was $1,200 (the greater of 10 years of service × $120 and $1,000, Employee M's benefit under the underlying formula, after the minimum benefit adjustment of paragraph (d)(7) of this section).

(b) Employer X's plan specifies instead the alternative method of adjusting accrued benefits described in paragraph (d)(8)(v) of this section. (The fact that a minimum benefit applying to certain employees is not adjusted under the alternative method of paragraph (d)(8)(v) of this section, but would be adjusted under the general rule of paragraph (d)(8)(i) of this section does not change the conclusion in *Example 2*, that the plan may apply the alternative method.)

(e) *Determination of initial theoretical reserve for target benefit plans.*—(1) *General rule.*—In the case of a target benefit plan the stated benefit formula under which takes into account service for years in which the plan did not satisfy §1.401(a)(4)-8(b)(3), as permitted under §1.401(a)(4)-8(b)(3)(vii), the theoretical reserve as of the determination date for the last plan year beginning before the first day of the first plan year in which the plan satisfies §1.401(a)(4)-8(b)(3) of an employee who was a participant in the plan on that determination date, is determined as follows:

(i) Determine the actuarial present value, as of that determination date, of the stated benefit that the employee is projected to have at the employee's normal retirement age, using the actuarial assumptions, the provisions of the plan, and the employee's compensation as of that determination date. For an employee whose attained age equals or exceeds the employee's normal retirement age, determine the actuarial present value of the employee's stated benefit at the employee's current age, but using an immediate straight life annuity factor for an employee whose attained age equals the employee's normal retirement age.

(ii) Calculate the actuarial present value of future required employer contributions (without regard to limitations under section 415 or additional contributions described in §1.401(a)(4)-8(b)(3)(v)) as of that determination date (i.e., the actuarial present value of the level contributions due for each plan year through the end of the plan year in which the employee attains normal retirement age). This calculation is made assuming that the required contribution in each future year will be equal to the required contribution for the plan year that includes that determination date, and applying the interest rate that was used in determining that required contribution.

(iii) Determine the excess, if any, of the amount determined in paragraph (e)(1)(i) of this section over the amount determined in paragraph (e)(1)(ii) of this section. This excess is the employee's theoretical reserve on that determination date.

(2) *Example.*—The following example illustrates the determination of an employee's theoretical reserve.

Example. (a) A target benefit plan was adopted and in effect before September 19, 1991, and satisfied the requirements of Rev. Rul. 76-464, 1976-2 C.B. 115, with respect to all years credited under the stated benefit formula through 1993. The plan provides a stated benefit equal to 40 percent of compensation, payable annually as a straight life annuity beginning at normal retirement age. Normal retirement age under the plan is 65. The stated interest rate under the plan is six percent. The determination date for required contributions under the plan is the last day of the plan year. Employee M is 38 years old on the determination date for the 1993 plan year, has participated in the plan for five years, and has compensation equal to $60,000 in 1993. The amount of employer contribution to Employee M's account for 1993 was $2,468.

(b) Under these facts, Employee M's theoretical reserve is equal to $13,909, calculated as follows:

(1) The actuarial present value of Employee M's stated benefit is calculated using the actuarial assumptions, provisions of the plan and Employee M's compensation as of the determination date for the 1993 plan year. This amount is equal to $46,512, Employee M's stated benefit of $24,000 ($60,000 multiplied by 40 percent), multiplied by 1.938, the actuarial present value factor applicable to a participant who is 38 years old using a stated interest rate of six percent.

(2) The actuarial present value of future employer contributions is calculated assuming that the required contribution in each future year will be equal to the required contribution for the 1993 plan year and assuming the same interest rate as was used in determining that contribution. This amount is equal to $32,603, which is equal to the amount of the level annual employer contribution ($2,468) multiplied by a factor of 13.2105 (the temporary annuity factor for a period of 27 years, assuming the six percent interest rate that was used to determine the required employer contribution).

(3) Employee M's theoretical reserve is $13,909, the excess of the amount determined in paragraph (b)(1) of this *Example* over the amount determined in paragraph (b)(2) of this *Example.*

(f) *Special fresh-start rules for cash balance plans.*—(1) *In general.*—In order to satisfy the optional testing method of §1.401(a)(4)-8(c)(3) after a fresh-start date, a cash balance plan must apply the rules of paragraph (c) of this section as modified under this paragraph (f). Paragraph (f)(2) of this section provides an alternative formula that may be used in addition to the formulas in paragraphs (c)(2) through

(c)(4) of this section. Paragraph (f)(3) of this section sets forth certain limitations on use of the formulas in paragraph (c) or (f)(2) of this section.

(2) *Alternative formula.*—(i) *In general.*—An employee's accrued benefit under the plan is equal to the greater of—

(A) The employee's frozen accrued benefit, or

(B) The employee's accrued benefit determined under the plan's benefit formula applicable to benefit accruals in the current plan year as applied to years of service after the fresh-start date, modified in accordance with paragraph (f)(2)(ii) of this section.

(ii) *Addition of opening hypothetical account.*—As of the first day after the fresh-start date, the plan must credit each employee's hypothetical account with an amount equal to the employee's opening hypothetical account (determined under paragraph (f)(2)(iii) of this section), adjusted for interest for the period that begins on the first day after the fresh-start date and that ends at normal retirement age. The interest adjustment in the preceding sentence must be made using the same interest rate applied to the hypothetical allocation for the first plan year beginning after the fresh-start date.

(iii) *Determination of opening hypothetical account.*—(A) *General rule.*—An employee's opening hypothetical account equals the actuarial present value of the employee's frozen accrued benefit as of the fresh-start date. For this purpose, if the plan provides for a single sum distribution as of the fresh-start date, the actuarial present value of the employee's frozen accrued benefit as of the fresh-start date equals the amount of a single sum distribution payable under the plan on that date, assuming that the employee terminated employment on the fresh-start date, the employee's accrued benefit was 100-percent vested, and the employee satisfied all eligibility requirements under the plan for the single sum distribution. If the plan does not offer a single sum distribution as of the fresh-start date, the actuarial present value of the employee's frozen accrued benefit as of the fresh-start date must be determined using a standard mortality table and the applicable section 417(e) rates, as defined in §1.417(e)-1(d).

(B) *Alternative opening hypothetical account.*—Alternatively, the employee's opening hypothetical account is the greater of the opening hypothetical account determined under paragraph (f)(2)(ii)(A) of this section and the employee's hypothetical account as of the fresh-start date determined in accordance with §1.401(a)(4)-8(c)(3)(v)(A) calculated under the plan's benefit formula applicable to benefit accruals in the current plan year as applied to the employee's total years of service through the fresh-start date in a manner that satisfies the past service credit rules of §1.401(a)(4)-8(c)(3)(viii).

(3) *Limitations on formulas.*—(i) *Past service restriction.*—If the plan does not satisfy the uniform hypothetical allocation formula requirement of §1.401(a)(4)-8(c)(3)(iii)(B) as of the fresh-start date, under §1.401(a)(4)-8(c)(3)(viii) the plan may not provide for past service credits, and thus may not use the formula in paragraph (c)(3) of this section (formula with wear-away), the formula in paragraph (c)(4) of this section (formula with extended wear-away), or the alternative determination of the opening hypothetical account in paragraph (f)(2)(iii)(B) of this section.

(ii) *Change in interest rate.*—If the interest rate used to adjust employees' hypothetical allocations under §1.401(a)(4)-8(c)(3)(iv) for the plan year is different from the interest rate used for this purpose in the immediately preceding plan year, the plan must use the formula in paragraph (c)(2) of this section (formula without wear-away).

(iii) *Meaningful benefit requirement.*—A plan is permitted to use the formula provided in paragraph (f)(2) of this section only if the plan satisfies paragraphs (d)(3) through (d)(5) of this section (regarding coverage as of fresh-start date, current benefit accruals, and minimum benefit adjustment, respectively). [Reg. §1.401(a)(4)-13.]

☐ [*T.D. 8360, 9-12-91. Amended by T.D. 8485, 8-30-93.*]

[Reg. §1.401(a)(5)-1]

§1.401(a)(5)-1. Special rules relating to nondiscrimination requirements.—(a) *In general.*—Section 401(a)(5) sets out certain provisions that will not of themselves be discriminatory within the meaning of section 410(b)(2)(A)(i) or section 401(a)(4). The exceptions specified in section 401(a)(5) are not an exclusive enumeration, but are merely a recital of provisions frequently encountered that will not of themselves constitute prohibited discrimination in contributions or benefits. See section 401(a)(4) and the regulations thereunder for the basic nondiscrimination rules. See §1.410(b)-4 for the rule of section 410(b)(2)(A)(i) (relating to the nondiscriminatory classification test that is part of the minimum coverage requirements) referred to in section 401(a)(5)(A). See paragraphs (b) through (f) of this section for special rules used in applying the section 401(a)(4) nondiscrimination requirements under the remaining provisions of section 401(a)(5).

(b) *Salaried or clerical employees.*—A plan does not fail to satisfy the nondiscrimination requirements of section 401(a)(4) merely because contributions or benefits provided under the plan are limited to salaried or clerical employees.

(c) *Uniform relationship to compensation.*—A plan does not fail to satisfy the nondiscrimination requirements of section 401(a)(4) merely because the contributions or benefits of, or on behalf of, the employees under the plan bear a uniform relationship to the compensation (within the meaning of section 414(s)) of those employees.

(d) *Certain disparity permitted.*—Under section 401(a)(5)(C), a plan does not discriminate in favor of highly compensated employees (as defined in section 414(q)), within the meaning of section 401(a)(4), in the amount of employer-provided contributions or benefits solely because—

(1) In the case of a defined contribution plan, employer contributions allocated to the accounts of employees favor highly compensated employees in a manner permitted by section 401(l) (relating to permitted disparity in plan contributions and benefits), and

(2) In the case of a defined benefit plan, employer-provided benefits favor highly compensated employees in a manner permitted by section 401(l) (relating to permitted disparity in plan contributions and benefits).

See §§ 1.401(l)-1 through 1.401(l)-6 for rules under which a plan may satisfy section 401(l) for purposes of the safe harbors of §§ 1.401(a)(4)-2(b)(3) and 1.401(a)(4)-3(b).

(e) *Defined benefit plans integrated with social security.*—(1) *In general.*—Under section 401(a)(5)(D), a defined benefit plan does not discriminate in favor of highly compensated employees (as defined in section 414(q)) with respect to the amount of employer-provided contributions or benefits solely because the plan provides that, with respect to each employee, the employer-provided accrued retirement benefit under the plan is limited to the excess (if any) of—

(i) The employee's final pay from the employer, over

(ii) The employer-provided retirement benefit created under the Social Security Act and attributable to service by the employee for the employer.

(2) *Final pay.*—For purposes of paragraph (e)(1)(i) of this section, an employee's final pay from the employer as of a plan year is the employee's compensation (as defined in section 414(q)(7)) for the year (ending with or within the 5-plan-year period ending with the plan year in which the employee terminates from employment with the employer) in which the employee receives the highest compensation from the employer. Notwithstanding the preceding sentence, final pay for each employee under the plan may be determined with reference to the 5-plan-year period ending with the plan year before the plan year in which the employee terminates from employment with the employer. In determining an employee's final pay, the plan may specify any 12-month period (ending with or within the applicable 5-plan-year period) as a year provided the specified 12-month period is uniformly and consistently applied with respect to all employees. In determining an employee's final pay, compensation for any year in excess of the applicable limit under section 401(a)(17) for the year may not be taken into account.

(3) *Rules for determining amount of employer-provided social security retirement benefit.*—For purposes of paragraph (e)(l)(ii) of this section, the following rules apply.

(i) The employer-provided retirement benefit on which any reduction or offset in the employee's accrued retirement benefit is based is limited solely to the employer-provided primary insurance amount payable under section 215 of the Social Security Act attributable to service by the employee for the employer.

(ii) The employer-provided primary insurance amount attributable to service by the employee for the employer is determined by multiplying the employer-provided portion of the employee's projected primary insurance amount by a fraction (not exceeding 1), the numerator of which is the employee's number of complete years of covered service for the employer under the Social Security Act, and the denominator of which is 35.

(4) *Projected primary insurance amount.*—(i) As of a plan year, an employee's projected primary insurance amount is the primary insurance amount, determined as of the close of the plan year (the "determination date"), payable to the employee upon attainment of the employee's social security retirement age (as determined under section 415(b)(8)), assuming the employee's annual compensation from the employer that is treated as wages for purposes of the Social Security Act remains the same from the plan year until the employee's attainment of social security retirement age. With respect to service by the employee for the employer before the determination

date, the actual compensation paid to the employee by the employer during all periods of service of the employee for the employer covered by the Social Security Act must be used in determining an employee's projected primary insurance amount. With respect to years before the employee's commencement of service for the employer, in determining the employee's projected primary insurance amount, it may be assumed that the employee received compensation in an amount computed by using a six-percent salary scale projected backwards from the determination date to the employee's 21st birthday. However, if the employee provides the employer with satisfactory evidence of the employee's actual past compensation for the prior years treated as wages under the Social Security Act at the time the compensation was earned and the actual past compensation results in a smaller projected primary insurance amount, the plan must use the actual past compensation. The plan administrator must give clear written notice to each employee of the employee's right to supply actual compensation history and of the financial consequences of failing to supply the history. The notice must be given each time the summary plan description is provided to the employee and must also be given upon the employee's separation from service. The notice must also state that the employee can obtain the actual compensation history from the Social Security Administration. In determining the employee's projected primary insurance amount, the employer may not take into account any compensation from any other employer while the employee is employed by the employer.

(ii) As of a plan year, the employer-provided portion of the employee's projected primary insurance amount under the Social Security Act is 50 percent of the employee's projected primary insurance amount (as determined under paragraph (e)(4)(i) of this section).

(5) *Employer-provided accrued retirement benefit.*—For purposes of this section, the employee's employer-provided accrued retirement benefit as of a plan year is the employee's accrued retirement benefit under the plan (determined on an actual basis and not on a projected basis) attributable to employer contributions under the plan. With respect to plans that provide for employee contributions, see section 411(c) for rules relating to the allocation of accrued benefits between employer contributions and employee contributions.

(6) *Additional rules.*—(i) As of a plan year, paragraph (e)(1) of this section does not apply to the extent that its application would result in a decrease in an employee's accrued benefit. See sections 411(b)(1)(G) and 411(d)(6).

(ii) Section 401(a)(5)(D) and this paragraph (e) do not apply to a plan maintained by an employer, determined for purposes of the Federal Insurance Contributions Act or the Railroad Retirement Tax Act, as applicable, that does not pay any wages within the meaning of section 3121(a) or compensation within the meaning of section 3231(e). For this purpose, a plan maintained for a self-employed individual within the meaning of section 401(c)(1), who is also subject to the tax under section 1401, is deemed to be a plan maintained by an employer that pays wages within the meaning of section 3121(a).

(iii) If a plan provides for the payment of an employee's accrued retirement benefit (whether or not subsidized) commencing before an employee's social security retirement age, the projected employer-provided primary insurance amount attributable to service by the employee for the employer (as determined under paragraphs (e)(3) and (e)(4) of this section) that may be applied as an offset to limit the employee's accrued retirement benefit must be reduced in accordance with § 1.401(l)-3(e)(1). The reduction is made by multiplying the employee's projected employer-provided primary insurance amount by a fraction, the numerator of which is the appropriate factor under § 1.401(l)-3(e)(1), and the denominator of which is 0.75 percent.

(iv) The Commissioner may, in revenue rulings, notices or other documents of general applicability, prescribe additional rules that may be necessary or appropriate to carry out the purposes of this section, including rules relating to the determination of an employee's projected primary insurance amount attributable to the employee's service for former employers and rules applying section 401(a)(5)(D) with respect to an employer that pays wages within the meaning of section 3121(a) or compensation within the meaning of section 3231(e) for some years and not for other years.

(7) *Examples.*—The following examples illustrate this paragraph (e).

Example 1. Employer Z maintains a noncontributory defined benefit plan that uses the calendar year as its plan year. The plan provides a normal retirement benefit commencing at age 65, equal to $500 a year, multiplied by the employee's years of service for Z, limited to the excess of the amount of the employee's final pay from Z (as determined in accordance with paragraph (e)(2) of this section) over the employee's employer-provided primary insurance amount attributable to the employee's service for Z. If an employee's social security retirement age is greater than 65, the plan provides for reduction of the employee's employer-provided primary insurance amount in accordance with paragraph (e)(6)(iii) of this section. The plan provides no limitation on the number of years of service taken into account in determining benefits under the plan. Employee A retires on July 6, 1995, at A's social security retirement age of 65 with 35 years of service for Z. The plan uses the plan year as the 12-month period for determining an employee's year of final highest pay from the employer. A's compensation for A's final 5 plan years is as follows:

1995 plan year	=	$10,500
1994 plan year	=	$20,000
1993 plan year	=	$18,000
1992 plan year	=	$17,000
1991 plan year	=	$16,500

A's annual primary insurance amount under social security, determined as of A's social security retirement age, is $9,000, of which $4,500 is the employer-provided portion attributable to A's service for Z ($9,000 × 50 percent × 35/35). Under the plan's benefit formula (disregarding the final pay limitation), A would be entitled to receive a normal retirement benefit of $17,500 ($500 × 35 years). However, under the plan, A's otherwise determined normal retirement benefit of $17,500 is limited to the excess of the amount of A's final pay from Z over A's employer-provided primary insurance amount under social security attributable to A's service for Z. Accordingly, A's normal retirement benefit is determined to be $15,500 ($20,000 (A's final pay from Z) less $4,500 (A's employer-provided primary insurance amount attributable to A's service for Z)) rather than $17,500. The final pay limitation in Z's plan satisfies section 401(a)(5)(D) and this paragraph (e). Accordingly, the plan maintained by Z does not discriminate in favor of highly compensated employees within the meaning of section 401(a)(4) merely because of the final pay limitation contained in the plan.

Example 2. Assume the same facts as in *Example 1*, except that A has 32 years of service for Z when A retires at A's social security retirement age. Under the plan's benefit formula (disregarding the final pay limitation), A would be entitled to receive an annual normal retirement benefit of $16,000 ($500 × 32 years). However, the plan provides that A's normal retirement benefit of $16,000 will be limited to $15,500 ($20,000 (the amount of A's final pay from Z) less $4,500 (1/2 of A's primary insurance amount under the Social Security Act)). The final pay limitation does not satisfy this paragraph (e). The portion of A's employer-provided primary insurance amount under the Social Security Act attributable to A's service for Z is 32/35 × $4,500, or $4,114. Therefore, to satisfy this paragraph (e), the final pay provision in Z's plan may not limit A's otherwise determined normal retirement benefit of $16,000 to less than $15,886 ($20,000 (the amount of X's final pay) minus $4,114 (the portion of A's employer-provided primary insurance amount attributable to A's service for Z)).

Example (3). (a) Employer X maintains a noncontributory defined benefit plan that uses the calendar year as its plan year. The formula for determining benefits under the plan provides a normal retirement benefit at age 65 equal to 90 percent of an employee's final average compensation, with the benefit reduced by 1/30th for each year of the employee's service less than 30 and limited to the employee's final pay (as determined in accordance with paragraph (e)(2) of this section) less the employee's employer-provided primary insurance amount under social security attributable to the employee's service for X. The plan determines an employee's employer-provided projected primary insurance amount under social security attributable to the employee's service for X in accordance with paragraph (e)(3) of this section and applies the reductions applicable under paragraph (e)(6)(iii) of this section if benefits commence before social security retirement age. The plan determines an employee's accrued benefit under the fractional accrual method of section 411(b)(1)(C).

(b) Employee A commences participation in the plan on January 1, 1990, when A is 35 years of age. A's social security retirement age is age 67. As of the close of the 2014 plan year, A's final average compensation from X is $15,000; A's final pay from X is $15,400, and A's projected employer-provided annual primary insurance amount under social security attributable to A's service for X is $4,000 (after the reduction applicable under paragraph (e)(6) of this section). Under the plan formula, A's accrued benefit as of the close of the 2014 plan year is $11,250 (90 percent × $15,000 × 25/30). As of the close of the 2014 plan year, the plan's final pay limitation does not affect A's benefit because A's benefit under the plan as of the close of the plan year and before application of the final pay limitation ($11,250) does not exceed A's final pay of $15,400 from X, determined as of the close of the plan year, less A's employer-provided projected primary insurance amount under social security attributable to A's service for X ($4,000).

(c) Assume that, as of the close of the 2015 plan year, A's final average compensation from X is $14,500 and A's final pay from X is $15,400. Assume also that as of the close of the 2015 plan year, A's employer-provided primary insurance amount attributable to A's service for X is $4,200 (after the reduction applicable under paragraph (e)(6)(iii) of this section). Accordingly, A's benefit as of the close of the 2015 plan year and before application of the final pay limitation is $11,310 (90 percent × $14,500 × 26/30). Under the plan's final pay limitation, A's benefit of $11,310 would be limited to $11,200, the amount of A's final pay from X ($15,400), less A's employer-provided projected primary insurance amount under social security attributable to A's service for X ($4,200). However, the plan's final pay limitation may not be applied to limit A's accrued benefit for the 2015 plan year to an amount below $11,250, which was A's accrued benefit under the plan as of the close of the prior plan year. The foregoing is further illustrated in the following table for the plan years presented above and for additional years of service performed by A for X.

TABLE

1 Years of service	2 Final average compensation	3 Benefit under plan formula (Column 2 × 0.9 × years of service/30)	4 Final pay	5 Employer-provided projected primary insurance amount under social security attributable to service for employer	6 Benefit if final pay reduction is applied in full (Column 4 − Column 5)	7 Benefit to which A is entitled (smaller of Column 6 or Column 3, but not less than Column 7 for prior year)
25	$15,000	$11,250	$15,400	$4,000	$11,400	$11,250
26	$14,500	$11,310	$15,400	$4,200	$11,200	$11,250
27	$15,500	$12,555	$15,800	$4,400	$11,400	$11,400
28	$15,500	$13,020	$16,000	$4,500	$11,500	$11,500
29	$15,000	$13,050	$16,000	$4,800	$11,200	$11,500
30	$14,500	$13,050	$16,000	$5,000	$11,000	$11,500

(f) *Certain benefits not taken into account.*—In determining whether a plan satisfies section 401(a)(4) and this section, other benefits created under state or federal law (e.g., worker's compensation benefits or black lung benefits) may not be taken into account.

(g) *More than one plan treated as single plan.*—[Reserved]

(h) *Effective date.*—(1) *In general.*—Except as provided in paragraph (h)(2) of this section, this section is effective for plan years beginning on or after January 1, 1994.

(2) *Plans of tax-exempt organizations.*—In the case of plans maintained by organizations exempt from income taxation under section 501(a), including plans subject to section 403(b)(12)(A)(i) (nonelective plans), this section is effective for plan years beginning on or after January 1, 1996.

(3) *Compliance during transition period.*—For plan years beginning before the effective date of these regulations, as set forth in paragraphs (h)(1) and (h)(2) of this section, and on or after the first day of the first plan year to which the amendments made to section 401(a)(5) by section 1111(b) of the Tax Reform Act of 1986 (TRA '86) apply, a plan must be operated in accordance with a reasonable, good faith interpretation of section 401(a)(5), taking into account pre-existing guidance and the amendments made by TRA '86 to related provisions of the Code. Whether a plan is operated in accordance with a reasonable, good faith interpretation of section 401(a)(5) will generally be determined based on all of the relevant facts and circumstances, including the extent to which an employer has resolved unclear issues in its favor. A plan will be deemed to be operated in accordance with a reasonable, good faith interpretation of section

401(a)(5) if it is operated in accordance with the terms of this section. [Reg. §1.401(a)(5)-1.]

☐ [*T.D. 8359, 9-12-91. Amended by T.D. 8486, 8-31-93.*]

[Reg. §1.401(a)(9)-0]

§1.401(a)(9)-0. Required minimum distributions; table of contents.—This table of contents lists the regulations relating to required minimum distributions under section 401(a)(9) of the Internal Revenue Code as follows:

[Reg. §1.401(a)(9)-0.]

☐ [*T.D. 8987, 4-16-2002. Amended by T.D. 9130, 6-14-2004.*]

[Reg. §1.401(a)(9)-1]

§1.401(a)(9)-1. Minimum distribution requirement in general.—

Q-1. What plans are subject to the minimum distribution requirement under section 401(a)(9), this section, and §§1.401(a)(9)-2 through 1.401(a)(9)-9?

A-1. Under section 401(a)(9), all stock bonus, pension, and profit-sharing plans qualified under section 401(a) and annuity contracts described in section 403(a) are subject to required minimum distribution rules. See this section and §§1.401(a)(9)-2 through 1.401(a)(9)-9 for the distribution rules applicable to these plans. Under section 403(b)(10), annuity contracts or custodial accounts described in section 403(b) are subject to required minimum distribution rules. See §1.403(b)-6(e) for the distribution rules applicable to these annuity contracts or custodial accounts. Under section 408(a)(6) and 408(b)(3), individual retirement plans (including, for some purposes, Roth IRAs under section 408A) are subject to required minimum distribution rules. See §1.408-8 for the distribution rules applicable to individual retirement plans and see §1.408A-6 for the distribution rules applicable to Roth IRAs under section 408A. Under section 457(d)(2), certain deferred compensation plans for employees of tax exempt organizations or state and local government employees are subject to required minimum distribution rules.

Q-2. Which employee account balances and benefits held under qualified trusts and plans are subject to the distribution rules of section 401(a)(9), this section, and §§1.401(a)(9)-2 through 1.401(a)(9)-9?

A-2. (a) *In general.* The distribution rules of section 401(a)(9) apply to all account balances and benefits in existence on or after January 1, 1985. This section and §§1.401(a)(9)-2 through 1.401(a)(9)-9 apply for purposes of determining required minimum distributions for calendar years beginning on or after January 1, 2003.

(b) *Beneficiaries.* (1) The distribution rules of this section and §§1.401(a)(9)-2 through 1.401(a)(9)-9 apply to account balances and benefits held for the benefit of a beneficiary for calendar years beginning on or after January 1, 2003, even if the employee died prior to January 1, 2003. Thus, in the case of an employee who died prior to January 1, 2003, the designated beneficiary must be redetermined in accordance with the provisions of §1.401(a)(9)-4 and the applicable distribution period (determined under §1.401(a)(9)-5 or 1.401(a)(9)-6, whichever is applicable) must be reconstructed for purposes of determining the amount required to be distributed for calendar years beginning on or after January 1, 2003.

(2) A designated beneficiary that is receiving payments under the 5-year rule of section 401(a)(9)(B)(ii), either by affirmative election or default provisions, may, if the plan so provides, switch to using the life expectancy rule of section 401(a)(9)(B)(iii) provided any amounts that would have been required to be distributed under the life expectancy rule of section 401(a)(9)(B)(iii) for all distribution calendar years before 2004 are distributed by the earlier of December 31, 2003 or the end of the 5-year period determined under A-2 of §1.401(a)(9)-3.

(c) *Trust documentation.* If a trust fails to meet the rule of A-5 of §1.401(a)(9)-4 (permitting the beneficiaries of the trust, and not the trust itself, to be treated as the employee's designated beneficiaries) solely because the trust documentation was not provided to the plan administrator by October 31 of the calendar year following the calendar year in which the employee died, and such documentation is provided to the plan administrator by October 31, 2003, the benefi-ciaries of the trust will be treated as designated beneficiaries of the employee under the plan for purposes of determining the distribution period under section 401(a)(9).

(d) *Special rule for governmental plans.* Notwithstanding anything to the contrary in this A-2, a governmental plan (within the meaning of section 414(d)), or an eligible governmental plan described in §1.457-2(f), is treated as having complied with section 401(a)(9) for all years to which section 401(a)(9) applies to the plan if the plan complies with a reasonable and good faith interpretation of section 401(a)(9).

Q-3. What specific provisions must a plan contain in order to satisfy section 401(a)(9)?

A-3. (a) *Required provisions.* In order to satisfy section 401(a)(9), the plan must include the provisions described in this paragraph reflecting section 401(a)(9). First, the plan must generally set forth the statutory rules of section 401(a)(9), including the incidental death benefit requirement in section 401(a)(9)(G). Second, the plan must provide that distributions will be made in accordance with this section and §§1.401(a)(9)-2 through 1.401(a)(9)-9. The plan document must also provide that the provisions reflecting section 401(a)(9) override any distribution options in the plan inconsistent with section 401(a)(9). The plan also must include any other provisions reflecting section 401(a)(9) that are prescribed by the Commissioner in revenue rulings, notices, and other guidance published in the Internal Revenue Bulletin. See §601.601(d)(2)(ii)(b) of this chapter.

(b) *Optional provisions.* The plan may also include written provisions regarding any optional provisions governing plan distributions that do not conflict with section 401(a)(9) and the regulations thereunder.

(c) *Absence of optional provisions.* Plan distributions commencing after an employee's death will be required to be made under the default provision set forth in §1.401(a)(9)-3 for distributions unless the plan document contains optional provisions that override such default provisions. Thus, if distributions have not commenced to the employee at the time of the employee's death, distributions after the death of an employee are to be made automatically in accordance with the default provisions in A-4(a) of §1.401(a)(9)-3 unless the plan either specifies in accordance with A-4(b) of §1.401(a)(9)-3 the method under which distributions will be made or provides for elections by the employee (or beneficiary) in accordance with A-4(c) of §1.401(a)(9)-3 and such elections are made by the employee or beneficiary. [Reg. §1.401(a)(9)-1.]

☐ [*T.D. 8987, 4-16-2002. Amended by T.D. 9130, 6-14-2004; T.D. 9340, 7-23-2007 and T.D. 9459, 9-4-2009.*]

[Reg. §1.401(a)(9)-2]

§1.401(a)(9)-2. Distributions commencing during an employee's lifetime.—

Q-1. In the case of distributions commencing during an employee's lifetime, how must the employee's entire interest be distributed in order to satisfy section 401(a)(9)(A)?

A-1. (a) In order to satisfy section 401(a)(9)(A), the entire interest of each employee must be distributed to such employee not later than the required beginning date, or must be distributed, beginning not later than the required beginning date, over the life of the employee or joint lives of the employee and a designated beneficiary or over a period not extending beyond the life expectancy of the employee or the joint life and last survivor expectancy of the employee and the designated beneficiary.

(b) Section 401(a)(9)(G) provides that lifetime distributions must satisfy the incidental death benefit requirements.

(c) The amount required to be distributed for each calendar year in order to satisfy section 401(a)(9)(A) and (G) generally depends on whether a distribution is in the form of distributions under a defined contribution plan or annuity payments under a defined benefit plan or under an annuity contract. For the method of determining the required minimum distribution in accordance with section 401(a)(9)(A) and (G) from an individual account under a defined contribution plan, see §1.401(a)(9)-5. For the method of determining the required minimum distribution in accordance with section 401(a)(9)(A) and (G) in the case of annuity payments from a defined benefit plan or an annuity contract, see §1.401(a)(9)-6.

Q-2. For purposes of section 401(a)(9)(C), what does the term *required beginning date* mean?

A-2. (a) Except as provided in paragraph (b) of this A-2 with respect to a 5-percent owner, as defined in paragraph (c) of this A-2, the term *required beginning date* means April 1 of the calendar year following the later of the calendar year in which the employee attains age $70^{1}/_{2}$ or the calendar year in which the employee retires from employment with the employer maintaining the plan.

(b) In the case of an employee who is a 5-percent owner, the term *required beginning date* means April 1 of the calendar year following the calendar year in which the employee attains age $70^{1}/_{2}$.

(c) For purposes of section 401(a)(9), a 5-percent owner is an employee who is a 5-percent owner (as defined in section 416) with respect to the plan year ending in the calendar year in which the employee attains age 70½.

(d) Paragraph (b) of this A-2 does not apply in the case of a governmental plan (within the meaning of section 414(d)) or a church plan. For purposes of this paragraph, the term *church plan* means a plan maintained by a church for church employees, and the term *church* means any church (as defined in section 3121(w)(3)(A)) or qualified church-controlled organization (as defined in section 3121(w)(3)(B)).

(e) A plan is permitted to provide that the required beginning date for purposes of section 401(a)(9) for all employees is April 1 of the calendar year following the calendar year in which an employee attains age 70½ regardless of whether the employee is a 5-percent owner.

Q-3. When does an employee attain age 70½?

A-3. An employee attains age 70½ as of the date six calendar months after the 70th anniversary of the employee's birth. For example, if an employee's date of birth was June 30, 1933, the 70th anniversary of such employee's birth is June 30, 2003. Such employee attains age 70½ on December 30, 2003. Consequently, if the employee is a 5-percent owner or retired, such employee's required beginning date is April 1, 2004. However, if the employee's date of birth was July 1, 1933, the 70th anniversary of such employee's birth would be July 1, 2003. Such employee would then attain age 70½ on January 1, 2004 and such employee's required beginning date would be April 1, 2005.

Q-4. Must distributions made before the employee's required beginning date satisfy section 401(a)(9)?

A-4. Lifetime distributions made before the employee's required beginning date for calendar years before the employee's first distribution calendar year, as defined in A-1(b) of § 1.401(a)(9)-5, need not be made in accordance with section 401(a)(9). However, if distributions commence before the employee's required beginning date under a particular distribution option, such as in the form of an annuity, the distribution option fails to satisfy section 401(a)(9) at the time distributions commence if, under terms of the particular distribution option, distributions to be made for the employee's first distribution calendar year or any subsequent distribution calendar year will fail to satisfy section 401(a)(9).

Q-5. If distributions have begun to an employee during the employee's lifetime (in accordance with section 401(a)(9)(A)(ii), how must distributions be made after an employee's death?

A-5. Section 401(a)(9)(B)(i) provides that if the distribution of the employee's interest has begun in accordance with section 401(a)(9)(A)(ii) and the employee dies before his entire interest has been distributed to him, the remaining portion of such interest must be distributed at least as rapidly as under the distribution method being used under section 401(a)(9)(A)(ii) as of the date of his death. The amount required to be distributed for each distribution calendar year following the calendar year of death generally depends on whether a distribution is in the form of distributions from an individual account under a defined contribution plan or annuity payments under a defined benefit plan. For the method of determining the required minimum distribution in accordance with section 401(a)(9)(B)(i) from an individual account, see § 1.401(a)(9)-5. In the case of annuity payments from a defined benefit plan or an annuity contract, see § 1.401(a)(9)-6.

Q-6. For purposes of section 401(a)(9)(B), when are distributions considered to have begun to the employee in accordance with section 401(a)(9)(A)(ii)?

A-6. (a) *General rule.* Except as otherwise provided in A-10 of § 1.401(a)(9)-6, distributions are not treated as having begun to the employee in accordance with section 401(a)(9)(A)(ii) until the employee's required beginning date, without regard to whether payments have been made before that date. Thus, section 401(a)(9)(B)(i) only applies if an employee dies on or after the employee's required beginning date. For example, if employee A retires in 2003, the calendar year A attains age 65½, and begins receiving installment distributions from a profit-sharing plan over a period not exceeding the joint life and last survivor expectancy of A and A's spouse, benefits are not treated as having begun in accordance with section 401(a)(9)(A)(ii) until April 1, 2009 (the April 1 following the calendar year in which A attains age 70½). Consequently, if A dies before April 1, 2009 (A's required beginning date), distributions after A's death must be made in accordance with section 401(a)(9)(B)(ii) or (iii) and (iv) and § 1.401(a)(9)-3, and not section 401(a)(9)(B)(i). This is the case without regard to whether the plan has distributed the minimum distribution for the first distribution calendar year (as defined in A-1(b) of § 1.401(a)(9)-5) before A's death.

(b) If a plan provides, in accordance with A-2(e) of this section, that the required beginning date for purposes of section 401(a)(9) for all employees is April 1 of the calendar year following the calendar year

in which an employee attains age 70½, an employee who dies on or after the required beginning date determined under the plan terms is treated as dying after the employee's distributions have begun for purposes of this A-6 even though the employee dies before the April 1 following the calendar year in which the employee retires. [Reg. § 1.401(a)(9)-2.]

☐ [*T.D. 8987, 4-16-2002. Amended by T.D. 9130, 6-14-2004.*]

[Reg. § 1.401(a)(9)-3]

§ 1.401(a)(9)-3. Death before required beginning date.—

Q-1. If an employee dies before the employee's required beginning date, how must the employee's entire interest be distributed in order to satisfy section 401(a)(9)?

A-1. (a) Except as otherwise provided in A-10 of § 1.401(a)(9)-6, if an employee dies before the employee's required beginning date (and, thus, before distributions are treated as having begun in accordance with section 401(a)(9)(A)(ii)), distribution of the employee's entire interest must be made in accordance with one of the methods described in section 401(a)(9)(B)(ii) or (iii) and (iv). One method (the 5-year rule in section 401(a)(9)(B)(ii)) requires that the entire interest of the employee be distributed within 5 years of the employee's death regardless of who or what entity receives the distribution. Another method (the life expectancy rule in section 401(a)(9)(B)(iii) and (iv)) requires that any portion of an employee's interest payable to (or for the benefit of) a designated beneficiary be distributed, commencing within one year of the employee's death, over the life of such beneficiary (or over a period not extending beyond the life expectancy of such beneficiary). Section 401(a)(9)(B)(iv) provides special rules where the designated beneficiary is the surviving spouse of the employee, including a special commencement date for distributions under section 401(a)(9)(B)(iii) to the surviving spouse.

(b) See A-4 of this section for the rules for determining which of the methods described in paragraph (a) of this A-1 applies. See A-3 of this section to determine when distributions under the exception to the 5-year rule in section 401(a)(9)(B)(iii) and (iv) must commence. See A-2 of this section to determine when the 5-year period in section 401(a)(9)(B)(ii) ends. For distributions using the life expectancy rule in section 401(a)(9)(B)(iii) and (iv), see § 1.401(a)(9)-4 in order to determine the designated beneficiary under section 401(a)(9)(B)(iii) and (iv), see § 1.401(a)(9)-5 for the rules for determining the required minimum distribution under a defined contribution plan, and see § 1.401(a)(9)-6 for required minimum distributions under defined benefit plans.

Q-2. By when must the employee's entire interest be distributed in order to satisfy the 5-year rule in section 401(a)(9)(B)(ii)?

A-2. In order to satisfy the 5-year rule in section 401(a)(9)(B)(ii), the employee's entire interest must be distributed by the end of the calendar year which contains the fifth anniversary of the date of the employee's death. For example, if an employee dies on January 1, 2003, the entire interest must be distributed by the end of 2008, in order to satisfy the 5-year rule in section 401(a)(9)(B)(ii).

Q-3. When are distributions required to commence in order to satisfy the life expectancy rule in section 401(a)(9)(B)(iii) and (iv)?

A-3. (a) *Nonspouse beneficiary.* In order to satisfy the life expectancy rule in section 401(a)(9)(B)(iii), if the designated beneficiary is not the employee's surviving spouse, distributions must commence on or before the end of the calendar year immediately following the calendar year in which the employee died. This rule also applies to the distribution of the entire remaining benefit if another individual is a designated beneficiary in addition to the employee's surviving spouse. See A-2 and A-3 of § 1.401(a)(9)-8, however, if the employee's benefit is divided into separate accounts.

(b) *Spousal beneficiary.* In order to satisfy the rule in section 401(a)(9)(B)(iii) and (iv), if the sole designated beneficiary is the employee's surviving spouse, distributions must commence on or before the later of—

(1) The end of the calendar year immediately following the calendar year in which the employee died; and

(2) The end of the calendar year in which the employee would have attained age 70½.

Q-4. How is it determined whether the 5-year rule in section 401(a)(9)(B)(ii) or the life expectancy rule in section 401(a)(9)(B)(iii) and (iv) applies to a distribution?

A-4. (a) *No plan provision.* If a plan does not adopt an optional provision described in paragraph (b) or (c) of this A-4 specifying the method of distribution after the death of an employee, distribution must be made as follows:

(1) If the employee has a designated beneficiary, as determined under § 1.401(a)(9)-4, distributions are to be made in accordance with the life expectancy rule in section 401(a)(9)(B)(iii) and (iv).

(2) If the employee has no designated beneficiary, distributions are to be made in accordance with the 5-year rule in section 401(a)(9)(B)(ii).

(b) *Optional plan provisions.* A plan may adopt a provision specifying either that the 5-year rule in section 401(a)(9)(B)(ii) will apply to certain distributions after the death of an employee even if the employee has a designated beneficiary or that distribution in every case will be made in accordance with the 5-year rule in section 401(a)(9)(B)(ii). Further, a plan need not have the same method of distribution for the benefits of all employees in order to satisfy section 401(a)(9).

(c) *Elections.* A plan may adopt a provision that permits employees (or beneficiaries) to elect on an individual basis whether the 5-year rule in section 401(a)(9)(B)(ii) or the life expectancy rule in section 401(a)(9)(B)(iii) and (iv) applies to distributions after the death of an employee who has a designated beneficiary. Such an election must be made no later than the earlier of the end of the calendar year in which distribution would be required to commence in order to satisfy the requirements for the life expectancy rule in section 401(a)(9)(B)(iii) and (iv) (see A-3 of this section for the determination of such calendar year) or the end of the calendar year which contains the fifth anniversary of the date of death of the employee. As of the last date the election may be made, the election must be irrevocable with respect to the beneficiary (and all subsequent beneficiaries) and must apply to all subsequent calendar years. If a plan provides for the election, the plan may also specify the method of distribution that applies if neither the employee nor the beneficiary makes the election. If neither the employee nor the beneficiary elects a method and the plan does not specify which method applies, distribution must be made in accordance with paragraph (a) of this A-4.

Q-5. If the employee's surviving spouse is the employee's sole designated beneficiary and such spouse dies after the employee, but before distributions have begun to the surviving spouse under section 401(a)(9)(B)(iii) and (iv), how is the employee's interest to be distributed?

A-5. Pursuant to section 401(a)(9)(B)(iv)(II), if the surviving spouse is the employee's sole designated beneficiary and dies after the employee, but before distributions to such spouse have begun under section 401(a)(9)(B)(iii) and (iv), the 5-year rule in section 401(a)(9)(B)(ii) and the life expectancy rule in section 401(a)(9)(B)(iii) are to be applied as if the surviving spouse were the employee. In applying this rule, the date of death of the surviving spouse shall be substituted for the date of death of the employee. However, in such case, the rules in section 401(a)(9)(B)(iv) are not available to the surviving spouse of the deceased employee's surviving spouse.

Q-6. For purposes of section 401(a)(9)(B)(iv)(II), when are distributions considered to have begun to the surviving spouse?

A-6. Distributions are considered to have begun to the surviving spouse of an employee, for purposes of section 401(a)(9)(B)(iv)(II), on the date, determined in accordance with A-3 of this section, on which distributions are required to commence to the surviving spouse, even though payments have actually been made before that date. See A-11 of § 1.401(a)(9)-6 for a special rule for annuities. [Reg. § 1.401(a)(9)-3.]

☐ [*T.D. 8987, 4-16-2002. Amended by T.D. 9130, 6-14-2004.*]

[Reg. § 1.401(a)(9)-4]

§ 1.401(a)(9)-4. Determination of the designated beneficiary.—

Q-1. Who is a designated beneficiary under section 401(a)(9)(E)?

A-1. A designated beneficiary is an individual who is designated as a beneficiary under the plan. An individual may be designated as a beneficiary under the plan either by the terms of the plan or, if the plan so provides, by an affirmative election by the employee (or the employee's surviving spouse) specifying the beneficiary. A beneficiary designated as such under the plan is an individual who is entitled to a portion of an employee's benefit, contingent on the employee's death or another specified event. For example, if a distribution is in the form of a joint and survivor annuity over the life of the employee and another individual, the plan does not satisfy section 401(a)(9) unless such other individual is a designated beneficiary under the plan. A designated beneficiary need not be specified by name in the plan or by the employee to the plan in order to be a designated beneficiary so long as the individual who is to be the beneficiary is identifiable under the plan. The members of a class of beneficiaries capable of expansion or contraction will be treated as being identifiable if it is possible, to identify the class member with the shortest life expectancy. The fact that an employee's interest under the plan passes to a certain individual under a will or otherwise under applicable state law does not make that individual a designated beneficiary unless the individual is designated as a beneficiary under the plan. See A-6 of § 1.401(a)(9)-8 for rules which apply to qualified domestic relation orders.

Q-2. Must an employee (or the employee's spouse) make an affirmative election specifying a beneficiary for a person to be a designated beneficiary under section 401(a)(9)(E)?

A-2. No, a designated beneficiary is an individual who is designated as a beneficiary under the plan whether or not the designation

under the plan was made by the employee. The choice of beneficiary is subject to the requirements of sections 401(a)(11), 414(p), and 417.

Q-3. May a person other than an individual be considered to be a designated beneficiary for purposes of section 401(a)(9)?

A-3. No, only individuals may be designated beneficiaries for purposes of section 401(a)(9). A person that is not an individual, such as the employee's estate, may not be a designated beneficiary. If a person other than an individual is designated as a beneficiary of an employee's benefit, the employee will be treated as having no designated beneficiary for purposes of section 401(a)(9), even if there are also individuals designated as beneficiaries. However, see A-5 of this section for special rules that apply to trusts and A-2 and A-3 of § 1.401(a)(9)-8 for rules that apply to separate accounts.

Q-4. When is the designated beneficiary determined?

A-4. (a) *General rule.* In order to be a designated beneficiary, an individual must be a beneficiary as of the date of death. Except as provided in paragraph (b) and § 1.401(a)(9)-6, the employee's designated beneficiary will be determined based on the beneficiaries designated as of the date of death who remain beneficiaries as of September 30 of the calendar year following the calendar year of the employee's death. Consequently, except as provided in § 1.401(a)(9)-6, any person who was a beneficiary as of the date of the employee's death, but is not a beneficiary as of that September 30 (e.g., because the person receives the entire benefit to which the person is entitled before that September 30), is not taken into account in determining the employee's designated beneficiary for purposes of determining the distribution period for required minimum distributions after the employee's death. Accordingly, if a person disclaims entitlement to the employee's benefit, pursuant to a disclaimer that satisfies section 2518 by that September 30 thereby allowing other beneficiaries to receive the benefit in lieu of that person, the disclaiming person is not taken into account in determining the employee's designated beneficiary.

(b) *Surviving spouse.* As provided in A-5 of § 1.401(a)(9)-3, if the employee's spouse is the sole designated beneficiary as of September 30 of the calendar year following the calendar year of the employee's death, and the surviving spouse dies after the employee and before the date on which distributions have begun to the surviving spouse under section 401(a)(9)(B)(iii) and (iv), the rule in section 401(a)(9)(B)(iv)(II) will apply. Thus, for example, the relevant designated beneficiary for determining the distribution period after the death of the surviving spouse is the designated beneficiary of the surviving spouse. Similarly, such designated beneficiary will be determined based on the beneficiaries designated as of the date of the surviving spouse's death and who remain beneficiaries as of September 30 of the calendar year following the calendar year of the surviving spouse's death. Further, if, as of that September 30, there is no designated beneficiary under the plan with respect to that surviving spouse, distribution must be made in accordance with the 5-year rule in section 401(a)(9)(B)(ii) and A-2 of § 1.401(a)(9)-3.

(c) *Deceased beneficiary.* For purposes of this A-4, an individual who is a beneficiary as of the date of the employee's death and dies prior to September 30 of the calendar year following the calendar year of the employee's death without disclaiming continues to be treated as a beneficiary as of the September 30 of the calendar year following the calendar year of the employee's death in determining the employee's designated beneficiary for purposes of determining the distribution period for required minimum distributions after the employee's death, without regard to the identity of the successor beneficiary who is entitled to distributions as the beneficiary of the deceased beneficiary. The same rule applies in the case of distributions to which A-5 of § 1.401(a)(9)-3 applies so that, if an individual is designated as a beneficiary of an employee's surviving spouse as of the spouse's date of death and dies prior to September 30 of the year following the year of the surviving spouse's death, that individual will continue to be treated as a designated beneficiary.

Q-5. If a trust is named as a beneficiary of an employee, will the beneficiaries of the trust with respect to the trust's interest in the employee's benefit be treated as having been designated as beneficiaries of the employee under the plan for purposes of determining the distribution period under section 401(a)(9)?

A-5. (a) If the requirements of paragraph (b) of this A-5 are met with respect to a trust that is named as the beneficiary of an employee under the plan, the beneficiaries of the trust (and not the trust itself) will be treated as having been designated as beneficiaries of the employee under the plan for purposes of determining the distribution period under section 401(a)(9).

(b) The requirements of this paragraph (b) are met if, during any period during which required minimum distributions are being determined by treating the beneficiaries of the trust as designated beneficiaries of the employee, the following requirements are met—

(1) The trust is a valid trust under state law, or would be but for the fact that there is no corpus.

(2) The trust is irrevocable or will, by its terms, become irrevocable upon the death of the employee.

(3) The beneficiaries of the trust who are beneficiaries with respect to the trust's interest in the employee's benefit are identifiable within the meaning of A-1 of this section from the trust instrument.

(4) The documentation described in A-6 of this section has been provided to the plan administrator.

(c) In the case of payments to a trust having more than one beneficiary, see A-7 of § 1.401(a)(9)-5 for the rules for determining the designated beneficiary whose life expectancy will be used to determine the distribution period and A-3 of this section for the rules that apply if a person other than an individual is designated as a beneficiary of an employee's benefit. However, the separate account rules under A-2 of § 1.401(a)(9)-8 are not available to beneficiaries of a trust with respect to the trust's interest in the employee's benefit.

(d) If the beneficiary of the trust named as beneficiary of the employee's interest is another trust, the beneficiaries of the other trust will be treated as being designated as beneficiaries of the first trust, and thus, having been designated by the employee under the plan for purposes of determining the distribution period under section 401(a)(9)(A)(ii), provided that the requirements of paragraph (b) of this A-5 are satisfied with respect to such other trust in addition to the trust named as beneficiary.

Q-6. If a trust is named as a beneficiary of an employee, what documentation must be provided to the plan administrator?

A-6. (a) *Required minimum distributions before death.* If an employee designates a trust as the beneficiary of his or her entire benefit and the employee's spouse is the sole beneficiary of the trust, in order to satisfy the documentation requirements of this A-6 so that the spouse can be treated as the sole designated beneficiary of the employee's benefits (if the other requirements of paragraph (b) of A-5 of this section are satisfied), the employee must either—

(1) Provide to the plan administrator a copy of the trust instrument and agree that if the trust instrument is amended at any time in the future, the employee will, within a reasonable time, provide to the plan administrator a copy of each such amendment; or

(2) Provide to the plan administrator a list of all of the beneficiaries of the trust (including contingent and remaindermen beneficiaries with a description of the conditions on their entitlement sufficient to establish that the spouse is the sole beneficiary) for purposes of section 401(a)(9); certify that, to the best of the employee's knowledge, this list is correct and complete and that the requirements of paragraph (b)(1), (2), and (3) of A-5 of this section are satisfied; agree that, if the trust instrument is amended at any time in the future, the employee will, within a reasonable time, provide to the plan administrator corrected certifications to the extent that the amendment changes any information previously certified; and agree to provide a copy of the trust instrument to the plan administrator upon demand.

(b) *Required minimum distributions after death.* In order to satisfy the documentation requirement of this A-6 for required minimum distributions after the death of the employee (or spouse in a case to which A-5 of § 1.401(a)(9)-3 applies), by October 31 of the calendar year immediately following the calendar year in which the employee died, the trustee of the trust must either—

(1) Provide the plan administrator with a final list of all beneficiaries of the trust (including contingent and remaindermen beneficiaries with a description of the conditions on their entitlement) as of September 30 of the calendar year following the calendar year of the employee's death; certify that, to the best of the trustee's knowledge, this list is correct and complete and that the requirements of paragraph (b)(1), (2), and (3) of A-5 of this section are satisfied; and agree to provide a copy of the trust instrument to the plan administrator upon demand; or

(2) Provide the plan administrator with a copy of the actual trust document for the trust that is named as a beneficiary of the employee under the plan as of the employee's date of death.

(c) *Relief for discrepancy between trust instrument and employee certifications or earlier trust instruments.* (1) If required minimum distributions are determined based on the information provided to the plan administrator in certifications or trust instruments described in paragraph (a) or (b) of this A-6, a plan will not fail to satisfy section 401(a)(9) merely because the actual terms of the trust instrument are inconsistent with the information in those certifications or trust instruments previously provided to the plan administrator, but only if the plan administrator reasonably relied on the information provided and the required minimum distributions for calendar years after the calendar year in which the discrepancy is discovered are determined based on the actual terms of the trust instrument.

(2) For purposes of determining the amount of the excise tax under section 4974, the required minimum distribution is determined for any year based on the actual terms of the trust in effect during the year. [Reg. § 1.401(a)(9)-4.]

□ [*T.D. 8987, 4-16-2002. Amended by T.D. 9130, 6-14-2004.*]

Reg. § 1.401(a)(9)-5

[Reg. § 1.401(a)(9)-5]

§ 1.401(a)(9)-5. Required minimum distributions from defined contribution plans.—

Q-1. If an employee's benefit is in the form of an individual account under a defined contribution plan, what is the amount required to be distributed for each calendar year?

A-1. (a) *General rule.* If an employee's accrued benefit is in the form of an individual account under a defined contribution plan, the minimum amount required to be distributed for each distribution calendar year, as defined in paragraph (b) of this A-1, is equal to the quotient obtained by dividing the account (determined under A-3 of this section) by the applicable distribution period (determined under A-4 or A-5 of this section, whichever is applicable). However, the required minimum distribution amount will never exceed the entire account balance on the date of the distribution. See A-8 of this section for rules that apply if a portion of the employee's account is not vested. Further, the minimum distribution required to be distributed on or before an employee's required beginning date is always determined under section 401(a)(9)(A)(ii) and this A-1 and not section 401(a)(9)(A)(i).

(b) *Distribution calendar year.* A calendar year for which a minimum distribution is required is a distribution calendar year. If an employee's required beginning date is April 1 of the calendar year following the calendar year in which the employee attains age $70^1/_2$, the employee's first distribution calendar year is the year the employee attains age $70^1/_2$. If an employee's required beginning date is April 1 of the calendar year following the calendar year in which the employee retires, the employee's first distribution calendar year is the calendar year in which the employee retires. In the case of distributions to be made in accordance with the life expectancy rule in § 1.401(a)(9)-3 and in section 401(a)(9)(B)(iii) and (iv), the first distribution calendar year is the calendar year containing the date described in A-3(a) or A-3(b) of § 1.401(a)(9)-3, whichever is applicable.

(c) *Time for distributions.* The distribution required to be made on or before the employee's required beginning date shall be treated as the distribution required for the employee's first distribution calendar year (as defined in paragraph (b) of this A-1). The required minimum distribution for other distribution calendar years, including the required minimum distribution for the distribution calendar year in which the employee's required beginning date occurs, must be made on or before the end of that distribution calendar year.

(d) *Minimum distribution incidental benefit requirement.* If distributions of an employee's account balance under a defined contribution plan are made in accordance with this section, the minimum distribution incidental benefit requirement of section 401(a)(9)(G) is satisfied. Further, with respect to the retirement benefits provided by that account balance, to the extent the incidental benefit requirement of § 1.401-1(b)(1)(i) requires a distribution, that requirement is deemed to be satisfied if distributions satisfy the minimum distribution incidental benefit requirement of section 401(a)(9)(G) and this section.

(e) *Annuity contracts.* Instead of satisfying this A-1, the minimum distribution requirement may be satisfied by the purchase of an annuity contract from an insurance company in accordance with A-4 of § 1.401(a)(9)-6 with the employee's entire individual account. If such an annuity is purchased after distributions are required to commence (the required beginning date, in the case of distributions commencing before death, or the date determined under A-3 of § 1.401(a)(9)-3, in the case of distributions commencing after death), payments under the annuity contract purchased will satisfy section 401(a)(9) for distribution calendar years after the calendar year of the purchase if payments under the annuity contract are made in accordance with § 1.401(a)(9)-6. In such a case, payments under the annuity contract will be treated as distributions from the individual account for purposes of determining if the individual account satisfies section 401(a)(9) for the calendar year of the purchase. An employee may also purchase an annuity contract with a portion of the employee's account under the rules of A-2(a)(3) of § 1.401(a)(9)-8.

Q-2. If an employee's benefit is in the form of an individual account and, in any calendar year, the amount distributed exceeds the minimum required, will credit be given in subsequent calendar years for such excess distribution?

A-2. If, for any distribution calendar year, the amount distributed exceeds the minimum required, no credit will be given in subsequent calendar years for such excess distribution.

Q-3. What is the amount of the account of an employee used for determining the employee's required minimum distribution in the case of an individual account?

A-3. (a) In the case of an individual account, the benefit used in determining the required minimum distribution for a distribution calendar year is the account balance as of the last valuation date in the calendar year immediately preceding that distribution calendar year (valuation calendar year) adjusted in accordance with paragraphs (b), (c), and (d) of this A-3.

(b) The account balance is increased by the amount of any contributions or forfeitures allocated to the account balance as of dates in the valuation calendar year after the valuation date. For this purpose, contributions that are allocated to the account balance as of dates in the valuation calendar year after the valuation date, but that are not actually made during the valuation calendar year, are permitted to be excluded.

(c) The account balance is decreased by distributions made in the valuation calendar year after the valuation date.

(d) The account balance does not include the value of any qualifying longevity annuity contract (QLAC), defined in A-17 of §1.401(a)(9)-6, that is held under the plan. This paragraph (d) applies only to contracts purchased on or after July 2, 2014.

(e) If an amount is distributed from a plan and rolled over to another plan (receiving plan), A-2 of §1.401(a)(9)-7 provides additional rules for determining the benefit and required minimum distribution under the receiving plan. If an amount is transferred from one plan (transferor plan) to another plan (transferee plan) in a transfer to which section 414(l) applies, A-3 and A-4 of §1.401(a)(9)-7 provide additional rules for determining the amount of the required minimum distribution and the benefit under both the transferor and transferee plans.

Q-4. For required minimum distributions during an employee's lifetime, what is the applicable distribution period?

A-4. (a) *General rule.* Except as provided in paragraph (b) of this A-4, the applicable distribution period for required minimum distributions for distribution calendar years up to and including the distribution calendar year that includes the employee's date of death is determined using the Uniform Lifetime Table in §1.401(a)(9)-9(c) for the employee's age as of the employee's birthday in the relevant distribution calendar year. If an employee dies on or after the required beginning date, the distribution period applicable for calculating the amount that must be distributed during the distribution calendar year that includes the employee's death is determined as if the employee had lived throughout that year. Thus, a minimum required distribution, determined as if the employee had lived throughout that year, is required for the year of the employee's death and that amount must be distributed to a beneficiary to the extent it has not already been distributed to the employee.

(b) *Spouse is sole beneficiary*—(1) *General rule.* Except as otherwise provided in paragraph (b)(2) of this A-4, if the sole designated beneficiary of an employee is the employee's surviving spouse, for required minimum distributions during the employee's lifetime, the applicable distribution period is the longer of the distribution period determined in accordance with paragraph (a) of this A-4 or the joint life expectancy of the employee and spouse using the employee's and spouse's attained ages as of the employee's and the spouse's birthdays in the distribution calendar year. The spouse is sole designated beneficiary for purposes of determining the applicable distribution period for a distribution calendar year during the employee's lifetime only if the spouse is the sole beneficiary of the employee's entire interest at all times during the distribution calendar year.

(2) *Change in marital status.* If the employee and the employee's spouse are married on January 1 of a distribution calendar year, but do not remain married throughout that year (i.e., the employee or the employee's spouse die or they become divorced during that year), the employee will not fail to have a spouse as the employee's sole beneficiary for that year merely because they are not married throughout that year. If an employee's spouse predeceases the employee, the spouse will not fail to be the employee's sole beneficiary for the distribution calendar year that includes the date of the spouse's death solely because, for the period remaining in that year after the spouse's death, someone other than the spouse is named as beneficiary. However, the change in beneficiary due to the death or divorce of the spouse will be effective for purposes of determining the applicable distribution period under section 401(a)(9) in the distribution calendar year following the distribution calendar year that includes the date of the spouse's death or divorce.

Q-5. For required minimum distributions after an employee's death, what is the applicable distribution period?

A-5. (a) *Death on or after the employee's required beginning date.* If an employee dies after distribution has begun as determined under A-6 of §1.401(a)(9)-2 (generally on or after the employee's required beginning date), in order to satisfy section 401(a)(9)(B)(i), the applicable distribution period for distribution calendar years after the distribution calendar year containing the employee's date of death is either—

(1) If the employee has a designated beneficiary as of the date determined under A-4 of §1.401(a)(9)-4, the longer of—

(i) The remaining life expectancy of the employee's designated beneficiary determined in accordance with paragraph (c)(1) or (2) of this A-5; and

(ii) The remaining life expectancy of the employee determined in accordance with paragraph (c)(3) of this A-5; or

(2) If the employee does not have a designated beneficiary as of the date determined under A-4 of §1.401(a)(9)-4, the remaining life expectancy of the employee determined in accordance with paragraph (c)(3) of this A-5.

(b) *Death before an employee's required beginning date.* If an employee dies before distribution has begun, as determined under A-5 of §1.401(a)(9)-2 (generally before the employee's required beginning date), in order to satisfy section 401(a)(9)(B)(iii) or (iv) and the life expectancy rule described in A-1 of §1.401(a)(9)-3, the applicable distribution period for distribution calendar years after the distribution calendar year containing the employee's date of death is determined in accordance with paragraph (c) of this A-5. See A-4 of §1.401(a)(9)-3 to determine when the 5-year rule of in section 401(a)(9)(B)(ii) applies (e.g., there is no designated beneficiary or the 5-year rule is elected or specified by plan provision).

(c) *Life expectancy*—(1) *Nonspouse designated beneficiary.* Except as otherwise provided in paragraph (c)(2), the applicable distribution period measured by the beneficiary's remaining life expectancy is determined using the beneficiary's age as of the beneficiary's birthday in the calendar year immediately following the calendar year of the employee's death. In subsequent calendar years, the applicable distribution period is reduced by one for each calendar year that has elapsed after the calendar year immediately following the calendar year of the employee's death.

(2) *Spouse designated beneficiary.* If the surviving spouse of the employee is the employee's sole beneficiary, the applicable distribution period is measured by the surviving spouse's life expectancy using the surviving spouse's birthday for each distribution calendar year after the calendar year of the employee's death up through the calendar year of the spouse's death. For calendar years after the calendar year of the spouse's death, the applicable distribution period is the life expectancy of the spouse using the age of the spouse as of the spouse's birthday in the calendar year of the spouse's death, reduced by one for each calendar year that has elapsed after the calendar year of the spouse's death.

(3) *No designated beneficiary.* If the employee does not have a designated beneficiary, the applicable distribution period measured by the employee's remaining life expectancy is the life expectancy of the employee using the age of the employee as of the employee's birthday in the calendar year of the employee's death. In subsequent calendar years the applicable distribution period is reduced by one for each calendar year that has elapsed after the calendar year of the employee's death.

Q-6. What life expectancies must be used for purposes of determining required minimum distributions under section 401(a)(9)?

A-6. Life expectancies for purposes of determining required minimum distributions under section 401(a)(9) must be computed using the Single Life Table in §1.401(a)(9)-9(b) and the Joint and Last Survivor Table in §1.401(a)(9)-9(d).

Q-7. If an employee has more than one designated beneficiary, which designated beneficiary's life expectancy will be used to determine the applicable distribution period?

A-7. (a) *General rule*—(1) Except as otherwise provided in paragraph (c) of this A-7, if more than one individual is designated as a beneficiary with respect to an employee as of the applicable date for determining the designated beneficiary under A-4 of §1.401(a)(9)-4, the designated beneficiary with the shortest life expectancy will be the designated beneficiary for purposes of determining the applicable distribution period.

(2) See A-3 of §1.401(a)(9)-4 for rules that apply if a person other than an individual is designated as a beneficiary and see A-2 and A-3 of §1.401(a)(9)-8 for special rules that apply if an employee's benefit under a plan is divided into separate accounts and the beneficiaries with respect to a separate account differ from the beneficiaries of another separate account.

(b) *Contingent beneficiary.* Except as provided in paragraph (c)(1) of this A-7, if a beneficiary's entitlement to an employee's benefit after the employee's death is a contingent right, such contingent beneficiary is nevertheless considered to be a beneficiary for purposes of determining whether a person other than an individual is designated as a beneficiary (resulting in the employee being treated as having no designated beneficiary under the rules of A-3 of §1.401(a)(9)-4) and which designated beneficiary has the shortest life expectancy under paragraph (a) of this A-7.

(c) *Successor beneficiary*—(1) A person will not be considered a beneficiary for purposes of determining who is the beneficiary with the shortest life expectancy under paragraph (a) of this A-7, or whether a person who is not an individual is a beneficiary, merely because the person could become the successor to the interest of one of the employee's beneficiaries after that beneficiary's death. However, the preceding sentence does not apply to a person who has any right (including a contingent right) to an employee's benefit beyond being a mere potential successor to the interest of one of the employee's beneficiaries upon that beneficiary's death. Thus, for example, if the first beneficiary has a right to all income with respect to an employee's individual account during that beneficiary's life and a second beneficiary has a right to the principal but only after the death of the first income beneficiary (any portion of the principal distributed during the life of the first income beneficiary to be held in trust until that first beneficiary's death), both beneficiaries must be taken into account in determining the beneficiary with the shortest life expectancy and whether only individuals are beneficiaries.

(2) If the individual beneficiary whose life expectancy is being used to calculate the distribution period dies after September 30 of the calendar year following the calendar year of the employee's death, such beneficiary's remaining life expectancy will be used to determine the distribution period without regard to the life expectancy of the subsequent beneficiary.

(3) This paragraph (c) is illustrated by the following examples:

Example 1. (i) Employer M maintains a defined contribution plan, Plan X. Employee A, an employee of M, died in 2005 at the age of 55, survived by spouse, B, who was 50 years old. Prior to A's death, M had established an account balance for A in Plan X. A's account balance is invested only in productive assets. A named a testamentary trust (Trust P) established under A's will as the beneficiary of all amounts payable from A's account in Plan X after A's death. A copy of the Trust P and a list of the trust beneficiaries were provided to the plan administrator of Plan X by October 31 of the calendar year following the calendar year of A's death. As of the date of A's death, the Trust P was irrevocable and was a valid trust under the laws of the state of A's domicile. A's account balance in Plan X was includible in A's gross estate under §2039.

(ii) Under the terms of Trust P, all trust income is payable annually to B, and no one has the power to appoint Trust P principal to any person other than B. A's children, who are all younger than B, are the sole remainder beneficiaries of the Trust P. No other person has a beneficial interest in Trust P. Under the terms of the Trust P, B has the power, exercisable annually, to compel the trustee to withdraw from A's account balance in Plan X an amount equal to the income earned on the assets held in A's account in Plan X during the calendar year and to distribute that amount through Trust P to B. Plan X contains no prohibition on withdrawal from A's account of amounts in excess of the annual required minimum distributions under section 401(a)(9). In accordance with the terms of Plan X, the trustee of Trust P elects, in order to satisfy section 401(a)(9), to receive annual required minimum distributions using the life expectancy rule in section 401(a)(9)(B)(iii) for distributions over a distribution period equal to B's life expectancy. If B exercises the withdrawal power, the trustee must withdraw from A's account under Plan X the greater of the amount of income earned in the account during the calendar year or the required minimum distribution. However, under the terms of Trust P, and applicable state law, only the portion of the Plan X distribution received by the trustee equal to the income earned by A's account in Plan X is required to be distributed to B (along with any other trust income.)

(iii) Because some amounts distributed from A's account in Plan X to Trust P may be accumulated in Trust P during B's lifetime for the benefit of A's children, as remaindermen beneficiaries of Trust P, even though access to those amounts are delayed until after B's death, A's children are beneficiaries of A's account in Plan X in addition to B and B is not the sole designated beneficiary of A's account. Thus the designated beneficiary used to determine the distribution period from A's account in Plan X is the beneficiary with the shortest life expectancy. B's life expectancy is the shortest of all the potential beneficiaries of the testamentary trust's interest in A's account in Plan X (including remainder beneficiaries). Thus, the distribution period for purposes of section 401(a)(9)(B)(iii) is B's life expectancy. Because B is not the sole designated beneficiary of the testamentary trust's interest in A's account in Plan X, the special rule in 401(a)(9)(B)(iv) is not available and the annual required minimum distributions from the account to Trust M must begin no later than the end of the calendar year immediately following the calendar year of A's death.

Example 2. (i) The facts are the same as *Example 1* except that the testamentary trust instrument provides that all amounts distributed from A's account in Plan X to the trustee while B is alive will be paid directly to B upon receipt by the trustee of Trust P.

(ii) In this case, B is the sole designated beneficiary of A's account in Plan X for purposes of determining the designated beneficiary under section 401(a)(9)(B)(iii) and (iv). No amounts distributed from A's account in Plan X to Trust P are accumulated in Trust P during B's lifetime for the benefit of any other beneficiary. Therefore, the residuary beneficiaries of Trust P are mere potential successors to B's interest in Plan X. Because B is the sole beneficiary of the testamentary trust's interest in A's account in Plan X, the annual required minimum distributions from A's account to Trust P must begin no later than the end of the calendar year in which A would have

attained age 70½, rather than the calendar year immediately following the calendar year of A's death.

Q-8. If a portion of an employee's individual account is not vested as of the employee's required beginning date, how is the determination of the required minimum distribution affected?

A-8. If the employee's benefit is in the form of an individual account, the benefit used to determine the required minimum distribution for any distribution calendar year will be determined in accordance with A-1 of this section without regard to whether or not all of the employee's benefit is vested. If any portion of the employee's benefit is not vested, distributions will be treated as being paid from the vested portion of the benefit first. If, as of the end of a distribution calendar year (or as of the employee's required beginning date, in the case of the employee's first distribution calendar year), the total amount of the employee's vested benefit is less than the required minimum distribution for the calendar year, only the vested portion, if any, of the employee's benefit is required to be distributed by the end of the calendar year (or, if applicable, by the employee's required beginning date). However, the required minimum distribution for the subsequent distribution calendar year must be increased by the sum of amounts not distributed in prior calendar years because the employee's vested benefit was less than the required minimum distribution.

Q-9. Which amounts distributed from an individual account are taken into account in determining whether section 401(a)(9) is satisfied and which amounts are not taken into account in determining whether section 401(a)(9) is satisfied?

A-9. (a) *General rule.* Except as provided in paragraph (b), all amounts distributed from an individual account are distributions that are taken into account in determining whether section 401(a)(9) is satisfied, regardless of whether the amount is includible in income. Thus, for example, amounts that are excluded from income as recovery of investment in the contract under section 72 are taken into account for purposes of determining whether section 401(a)(9) is satisfied for a distribution calendar year. Similarly, amounts excluded from income as net unrealized appreciation on employer securities also are amounts distributed for purposes of determining if section 401(a)(9) is satisfied.

(b) *Exceptions.* The following amounts are not taken into account in determining whether the required minimum amount has been distributed for a calendar year:

(1) Elective deferrals (as defined in section 402(g)(3)) and employee contributions that, pursuant to rules prescribed by the Commissioner in revenue rulings, notices, or other guidance published in the Internal Revenue Bulletin (see §601.601(d)(2) of this chapter), are returned to the employee (together with the income allocable thereto) in order to comply with the section 415 limitations.

(2) Corrective distributions of excess deferrals as described in §1.402(g)-1(e)(3), together with the income allocable to these distributions.

(3) Corrective distributions of excess contributions under a qualified cash or deferred arrangement under section 401(k)(8) and excess aggregate contributions under section 401(m)(6), together with the income allocable to these distributions.

(4) Loans that are treated as deemed distributions pursuant to section 72(p).

(5) Dividends described in section 404(k) that are paid on employer securities. (Amounts paid to the plan that, pursuant to section 404(k)(2)(A)(iii)(II), are included in the account balance and subsequently distributed from the account lose their character as dividends.)

(6) The costs of life insurance coverage (P.S. 58 costs).

(7) Similar items designated by the Commissioner in revenue rulings, notices, and other guidance published in the Internal Revenue Bulletin. See §601.601(d)(2)(ii)(b) of this chapter. [Reg. §1.401(a)(9)-5.]

☐ [T.D. 8987, 4-16-2002. *Amended by* T.D. 9130, 6-14-2004; T.D. 9319, 4-4-2007 T.D. 9673, 7-1-2014 *and* T.D. 9930, 11-5-2020.]

[Reg. §1.401(a)(9)-6]

§1.401(a)(9)-6. Required minimum distributions for defined benefit plans and annuity contracts.—

Q-1. How must distributions under a defined benefit plan be paid in order to satisfy section 401(a)(9)?

A-1. (a) *General rules.* In order to satisfy section 401(a)(9), except as otherwise provided in this section, distributions of the employee's entire interest under a defined benefit plan must be paid in the form of periodic annuity payments for the employee's life (or the joint lives of the employee and beneficiary) or over a period certain that does not exceed the maximum length of the period certain determined in accordance with A-3 of this section. The interval between payments for the annuity must be uniform over the entire distribution period and must not exceed one year. Once payments have commenced over a period, the period may only be changed in accordance with A-13 of this section. Life (or joint and survivor) annuity payments must satisfy the minimum distribution incidental benefit requirements of A-2 of this section. Except as otherwise provided in this section (such as permitted increases described in A-14 of this section), all payments (whether paid over an employee's life, joint lives, or a period certain) also must be nonincreasing.

(b) *Life annuity with period certain.* The annuity may be a life annuity (or joint and survivor annuity) with a period certain if the life (or lives, if applicable) and period certain each meet the requirements of paragraph (a) of this A-1. For purposes of this section, if distributions are permitted to be made over the lives of the employee and the designated beneficiary, references to a life annuity include a joint and survivor annuity.

(c) *Annuity commencement.* (1) Annuity payments must commence on or before the employee's required beginning date (within the meaning of A-2 of §1.401(a)(9)-2). The first payment, which must be made on or before the employee's required beginning date, must be the payment which is required for one payment interval. The second payment need not be made until the end of the next payment interval even if that payment interval ends in the next calendar year. Similarly, in the case of distributions commencing after death in accordance with section 401(a)(9)(B)(iii) and (iv), the first payment, which must be made on or before the date determined under A-3(a) or (b) (whichever is applicable) of §1.401(a)(9)-3, must be the payment which is required for one payment interval. Payment intervals are the periods for which payments are received, e.g., bimonthly, monthly, semi-annually, or annually. All benefit accruals as of the last day of the first distribution calendar year must be included in the calculation of the amount of annuity payments for payment intervals ending on or after the employee's required beginning date.

(2) This paragraph (c) is illustrated by the following example:

Example. A defined benefit plan (Plan X) provides monthly annuity payments of $500 for the life of unmarried participants with a 10-year period certain. An unmarried, retired participant (A) in Plan X attains age 70¹/₂ in 2005. In order to meet the requirements of this paragraph, the first monthly payment of $500 must be made on behalf of A on or before April 1, 2006, and the payments must continue to be made in monthly payments of $500 thereafter for the life and 10-year period certain.

(d) *Single sum distributions.* In the case of a single sum distribution of an employee's entire accrued benefit during a distribution calendar year, the amount that is the required minimum distribution for the distribution calendar year (and thus not eligible for rollover under section 402(c)) is determined using either the rule in paragraph (d)(1) or the rule in paragraph (d)(2) of this A-1.

(1) The portion of the single sum distribution that is a required minimum distribution is determined by treating the single sum distribution as a distribution from an individual account plan and treating the amount of the single sum distribution as the employee's account balance as of the end of the relevant valuation calendar year. If the single sum distribution is being made in the calendar year containing the required beginning date and the required minimum distribution for the employee's first distribution calendar year has not been distributed, the portion of the single sum distribution that represents the required minimum distribution for the employee's first and second distribution calendar years is not eligible for rollover.

(2) The portion of the single sum distribution that is a required minimum distribution is permitted to be determined by expressing the employee's benefit as an annuity that would satisfy this section with an annuity starting date as of the first day of the distribution calendar year for which the required minimum distribution is being determined, and treating one year of annuity payments as the required minimum distribution for that year, and not eligible for rollover. If the single sum distribution is being made in the calendar year containing the required beginning date and the required minimum distribution for the employee's first distribution calendar year has not been made, the benefit must be expressed as an annuity with an annuity starting date as of the first day of the first distribution calendar year and the payments for the first two distribution calendar years would be treated as required minimum distributions, and not eligible for rollover.

(e) *Death benefits.* The rule in paragraph (a) of this A-1, prohibiting increasing payments under an annuity applies to payments made upon the death of an employee. However, for purposes of this section, an ancillary death benefit described in this paragraph (e) may be disregarded in applying that rule. Such an ancillary death benefit is excluded in determining an employee's entire interest and the rules prohibiting increasing payments do not apply to such an ancillary death benefit. A death benefit with respect to an employee's benefit is an ancillary death benefit for purposes of this A-1 if—

(1) It is not paid as part of the employee's accrued benefit or under any optional form of the employee's benefit; and

(2) The death benefit, together with any other potential payments with respect to the employee's benefit that may be provided to a survivor, satisfy the incidental benefit requirement of §1.401-1(b)(1)(i).

(f) *Additional guidance.* Additional guidance regarding how distributions under a defined benefit plan must be paid in order to satisfy section 401(a)(9) may be issued by the Commissioner in revenue rulings, notices, or other guidance published in the Internal Revenue Bulletin. See §601.601(d)(2)(ii)(b) of this chapter.

Q-2. How must distributions in the form of a life (or joint and survivor) annuity be made in order to satisfy the minimum distribution incidental benefit (MDIB) requirement of section 401(a)(9)(G) and the distribution component of the incidental benefit requirement of §1.401-1(b)(1)(i)?

A-2. (a) *Life annuity for employee.* If the employee's benefit is paid in the form of a life annuity for the life of the employee satisfying section 401(a)(9) without regard to the MDIB requirement, the MDIB requirement of section 401(a)(9)(G) will be satisfied.

(b) *Joint and survivor annuity, spouse beneficiary.* If the employee's sole beneficiary, as of the annuity starting date for annuity payments, is the employee's spouse and the distributions satisfy section 401(a)(9) without regard to the MDIB requirement, the distributions to the employee will be deemed to satisfy the MDIB requirement of section 401(a)(9)(G). For example, if an employee's benefit is being distributed in the form of a joint and survivor annuity for the lives of the employee and the employee's spouse and the spouse is the sole beneficiary of the employee, the amount of the periodic payment payable to the spouse would not violate the MDIB requirement if it was 100 percent of the annuity payment payable to the employee, regardless of the difference in the ages between the employee and the employee's spouse.

(c) *Joint and survivor annuity, nonspouse beneficiary*—(1) *Explanation of rule.* If distributions commence under a distribution option that is in the form of a joint and survivor annuity for the joint lives of the employee and a beneficiary other than the employee's spouse, the minimum distribution incidental benefit requirement will not be satisfied as of the date distributions commence unless under the distribution option, the annuity payments to be made on and after the employee's required beginning date will satisfy the conditions of this paragraph (c). The periodic annuity payment payable to the survivor must not at any time on and after the employee's required beginning date exceed the applicable percentage of the annuity payment payable to the employee using the table in paragraph (c)(2) of this A-2. The applicable percentage is based on the adjusted employee/beneficiary age difference. The adjusted employee/beneficiary age difference is determined by first calculating the excess of the age of the employee over the age of the beneficiary based on their ages on their birthdays in a calendar year. Then, if the employee is younger than age 70, the age difference determined in the previous sentence is reduced by the number of years that the employee is younger than age 70 on the employee's birthday in the calendar year that contains the annuity starting date. In the case of an annuity that provides for increasing payments, the requirement of this paragraph (c) will not be violated merely because benefit payments to the beneficiary increase, provided the increase is determined in the same manner for the employee and the beneficiary.

(2) *Table.*

Adjusted employee/beneficiary age difference	Applicable percentage
10 years or less	100%
11	96%
12	93%
13	90%
14	87%
15	84%
16	82%
17	79%
18	77%
19	75%
20	73%
21	72%
22	70%
23	68%
24	67%
25	66%
26	64%
27	63%
28	62%
29	61%

Adjusted employee/ beneficiary age difference	Applicable percentage
30	60%
31	59%
32	59%
33	58%
34	57%
35	56%
36	56%
37	55%
38	55%
39	54%
40	54%
41	53%
42	53%
43	53%
44 and greater	52%

(3) *Example.* This paragraph (c) is illustrated by the following example:

Example. Distributions commence on January 1, 2003 to an employee (Z), born March 1, 1937, after retirement at age 65. Z's daughter (Y), born February 5, 1967, is Z's beneficiary. The distributions are in the form of a joint and survivor annuity for the lives of Z and Y with payments of $500 a month to Z and upon Z's death of $500 a month to Y, i.e., the projected monthly payment to Y is 100 percent of the monthly amount payable to Z. Accordingly, under A-10 of this section, compliance with the rules of this section is determined as of the annuity starting date. The adjusted employee/beneficiary age difference is calculated by taking the excess of the employee's age over the beneficiary's age and subtracting the number of years the employee is younger than age 70. In this case, Z is 30 years older than Y and is commencing benefit 4 years before attaining age 70 so the adjusted employee/beneficiary age difference is 26 years. Under the table in paragraph (c)(2) of this A-2, the applicable percentage for a 26-year adjusted employee/beneficiary age difference is 64 percent. As of January 1, 2003 (the annuity starting date) the plan does not satisfy the MDIB requirement because, as of such date, the distribution option provides that, as of Z's required beginning date, the monthly payment to Y upon Z's death will exceed 66 percent of Z's monthly payment.

(d) *Period certain and annuity features.* If a distribution form includes a period certain, the amount of the annuity payments payable to the beneficiary need not be reduced during the period certain, but in the case of a joint and survivor annuity with a period certain, the amount of the annuity payments payable to the beneficiary must satisfy paragraph (c) of this A-2 after the expiration of the period certain.

(e) *Deemed satisfaction of incidental benefit rule.* Except in the case of distributions with respect to an employee's benefit that include an ancillary death benefit described in paragraph A-1(e) of this section, to the extent the incidental benefit requirement of § 1.401-1(b)(1)(i) requires a distribution, that requirement is deemed to be satisfied if distributions satisfy the minimum distribution incidental benefit requirement of this A-2. If the employee's benefits include an ancillary death benefit described in paragraph A-1(e) of this section, the benefits (including the ancillary death benefit) must be distributed in accordance with the incidental benefit requirement described in § 1.401-1(b)(1)(i) and the benefits (excluding the ancillary death benefit) must also satisfy the minimum distribution incidental benefit requirement of this A-2.

Q-3. How long is a period certain under a defined benefit plan permitted to extend?

A-3. (a) *Distributions commencing during the employee's life.* The period certain for any annuity distributions commencing during the life of the employee with an annuity starting date on or after the employee's required beginning date generally is not permitted to exceed the applicable distribution period for the employee (determined in accordance with the Uniform Lifetime Table in § 1.401(a)(9)-9(c) for the calendar year that contains the annuity starting date. See A-10 of this section for the rule for annuity payments with an annuity starting date before the required beginning date. However, if the employee's sole beneficiary is the employee's spouse, the period certain is permitted to be as long as the joint life and last survivor expectancy of the employee and the employee's spouse, if longer than the applicable distribution period for the employee, provided the period certain is not provided in conjunction with a life annuity under A-1(b) of this section.

(b) *Distributions commencing after the employee's death.* (1) If annuity distributions commence after the death of the employee under the life expectancy rule (under section 401(a)(9)(B)(iii) or (iv)), the period certain for any distributions commencing after death cannot exceed the applicable distribution period determined under A-5(b) of § 1.401(a)(9)-5 for the distribution calendar year that contains the annuity starting date.

(2) If the annuity starting date is in a calendar year before the first distribution calendar year, the period certain may not exceed the life expectancy of the designated beneficiary using the beneficiary's age in the year that contains the annuity starting date.

Q-4. Will a plan fail to satisfy section 401(a)(9) merely because distributions are made from an annuity contract which is purchased from an insurance company?

A-4. A plan will not fail to satisfy section 401(a)(9) merely because distributions are made from an annuity contract which is purchased with the employee's benefit by the plan from an insurance company, as long as the payments satisfy the requirements of this section. If the annuity contract is purchased after the required beginning date, the first payment interval must begin on or before the purchase date and the payment required for one payment interval must be made no later than the end of such payment interval. If the payments actually made under the annuity contract do not meet the requirements of section 401(a)(9), the plan fails to satisfy section 401(a)(9). See also A-14 of this section permitting certain increases under annuity contracts.

Q-5. In the case of annuity distributions under a defined benefit plan, how must additional benefits that accrue after the employee's first distribution calendar year be distributed in order to satisfy section 401(a)(9)?

A-5. (a) In the case of annuity distributions under a defined benefit plan, if any additional benefits accrue in a calendar year after the employee's first distribution calendar year, distribution of the amount that accrues in the calendar year must commence in accordance with A-1 of this section beginning with the first payment interval ending in the calendar year immediately following the calendar year in which such amount accrues.

(b) A plan will not fail to satisfy section 401(a)(9) merely because there is an administrative delay in the commencement of the distribution of the additional benefits accrued in a calendar year, provided that the actual payment of such amount commences as soon as practicable. However, payment must commence no later than the end of the first calendar year following the calendar year in which the additional benefit accrues, and the total amount paid during such first calendar year must be no less than the total amount that was required to be paid during that year under A-5(a) of this section.

Q-6. If a portion of an employee's benefit is not vested as of December 31 of a distribution calendar year, how is the determination of the required minimum distribution affected?

A-6. In the case of annuity distributions from a defined benefit plan, if any portion of the employee's benefit is not vested as of December 31 of a distribution calendar year, the portion that is not vested as of such date will be treated as not having accrued for purposes of determining the required minimum distribution for that distribution calendar year. When an additional portion of the employee's benefit becomes vested, such portion will be treated as an additional accrual. See A-5 of this section for the rules for distributing benefits which accrue under a defined benefit plan after the employee's first distribution calendar year.

Q-7. If an employee (other than a 5-percent owner) retires after the calendar year in which the employee attains age 70¹/₂, for what period must the employee's accrued benefit under a defined benefit plan be actuarially increased?

A-7. (a) *Actuarial increase starting date.* If an employee (other than a 5-percent owner) retires after the calendar year in which the employee attains age 70¹/₂, in order to satisfy section 401(a)(9)(C)(iii), the employee's accrued benefit under a defined benefit plan must be actuarially increased to take into account any period after age 70¹/₂ in which the employee was not receiving any benefits under the plan. The actuarial increase required to satisfy section 401(a)(9)(C)(iii) must be provided for the period starting on the April 1 following the calendar year in which the employee attains age 70¹/₂, or January 1, 1997, if later.

(b) *Actuarial increase ending date.* The period for which the actuarial increase must be provided ends on the date on which benefits commence after retirement in an amount sufficient to satisfy section 401(a)(9).

(c) *Nonapplication to plan providing same required beginning date for all employees.* If, as permitted under A-2(e) of § 1.401(a)(9)-2, a plan provides that the required beginning date for purposes of section 401(a)(9) for all employees is April 1 of the calendar year following the calendar year in which the employee attains age 70¹/₂ (regardless of whether the employee is a 5-percent owner) and the plan makes distributions in an amount sufficient to satisfy section 401(a)(9) using that required beginning date, no actuarial increase is required under section 401(a)(9)(C)(iii).

(d) *Nonapplication to governmental and church plans.* The actuarial increase required under this A-7 does not apply to a governmental plan (within the meaning of section 414(d)) or a church plan. For purposes of this paragraph, the term *church plan* means a plan maintained by a church for church employees, and the term *church* means any church (as defined in section 3121(w)(3)(A)) or qualified church-controlled organization (as defined in section 3121(w)(3)(B)).

Q-8. What amount of actuarial increase is required under section 401(a)(9)(C)(iii)?

A-8. In order to satisfy section 401(a)(9)(C)(iii), the retirement benefits payable with respect to an employee as of the end of the period for actuarial increases (described in A-7 of this section) must be no less than: the actuarial equivalent of the employee's retirement benefits that would have been payable as of the date the actuarial increase must commence under paragraph (a) of A-7 of this section if benefits had commenced on that date; plus the actuarial equivalent of any additional benefits accrued after that date; reduced by the actuarial equivalent of any distributions made with respect to the employee's retirement benefits after that date. Actuarial equivalence is determined using the plan's assumptions for determining actuarial equivalence for purposes of satisfying section 411.

Q-9. How does the actuarial increase required under section 401(a)(9)(C)(iii) relate to the actuarial increase required under section 411?

A-9. In order for any of an employee's accrued benefit to be nonforfeitable as required under section 411, a defined benefit plan must make an actuarial adjustment to an accrued benefit, the payment of which is deferred past normal retirement age. The only exception to this rule is that generally no actuarial adjustment is required to reflect the period during which a benefit is suspended as permitted under section 203(a)(3)(B) of the Employee Retirement Income Security Act of 1974 (ERISA) (88 Stat. 829). The actuarial increase required under section 401(a)(9)(C)(iii) for the period described in A-7 of this section is generally the same as, and not in addition to, the actuarial increase required for the same period under section 411 to reflect any delay in the payment of retirement benefits after normal retirement age. However, unlike the actuarial increase required under section 411, the actuarial increase required under section 401(a)(9)(C)(iii) must be provided even during any period during which an employee's benefit has been suspended in accordance with ERISA section 203(a)(3)(B).

Q-10. What rule applies if distributions commence to an employee on a date before the employee's required beginning date over a period permitted under section 401(a)(9)(A)(ii) and the distribution form is an annuity under which distributions are made in accordance with the provisions of A-1 of this section?

A-10. (a) *General rule.* If distributions commence to an employee on a date before the employee's required beginning date over a period permitted under section 401(a)(9)(A)(ii) and the distribution form is an annuity under which distributions are made in accordance with the provisions of A-1 of this section, the annuity starting date will be treated as the required beginning date for purposes of applying the rules of this section and §1.401(a)(9)-2. Thus, for example, the designated beneficiary distributions will be determined as of the annuity starting date. Similarly, if the employee dies after the annuity starting date but before the required beginning date determined under A-2 of §1.401(a)(9)-2, after the employee's death, the remaining portion of the employee's interest must continue to be distributed in accordance with this section over the remaining period over which distributions commenced. The rules in §1.401(a)(9)-3 and section 401(a)(9)(B)(ii) or (iii) and (iv) do not apply.

(b) *Period certain.* If, as of the employee's birthday in the year that contains the annuity starting date, the age of the employee is under 70, the following rule applies in applying the rule in paragraph (a) of A-3 of this section. The applicable distribution period for the employee is the distribution period for age 70, determined in accordance with the Uniform Lifetime Table in §1.401(a)(9)-9(c), plus the excess of 70 over the age of the employee as of the employee's birthday in the year that contains the annuity starting date.

(c) *Adjustment to employee/beneficiary age difference.* See A-2(c)(1) of this section for the determination of the adjusted employee/beneficiary age difference in the case of an employee whose age on the annuity starting date is less than 70.

Q-11. What rule applies if distributions commence to the surviving spouse of an employee over a period permitted under section 401(a)(9)(B)(iii)(II) before the date on which distributions are required to commence and the distribution form is an annuity under which distributions are made as of the date distributions commence in accordance with the provisions of A-1 of this section.

A-11. If distributions commence to the surviving spouse of an employee over a period permitted under section 401(a)(9)(B)(iii)(II) before the date on which distributions are required to commence and the distribution form is an annuity under which distributions are made as of the date distributions commence in accordance with the provisions of A-1 of this section, distributions will be considered to have begun on the actual commencement date for purposes of section 401(a)(9)(B)(iv)(II). Consequently, in such case, A-5 of §1.401(a)(9)-3 and section 401(a)(9)(B)(ii) and (iii) will not apply upon the death of the surviving spouse as though the surviving

spouse were the employee. Instead, the annuity distributions must continue to be made, in accordance with the provisions of A-1 of this section, over the remaining period over which distributions commenced.

Q-12. In the case of an annuity contract under an individual account plan that has not yet been annuitized, how is section 401(a)(9) satisfied with respect to the employee's or beneficiary's entire interest under the annuity contract for the period prior to the date annuity payments so commence?

A-12. (a) *General rule.* Prior to the date that an annuity contract under an individual account plan is annuitized, the interest of an employee or beneficiary under that contract is treated as an individual account for purposes of section 401(a)(9). Thus, the required minimum distribution for any year with respect to that interest is determined under §1.401(a)(9)-5 rather than this section. See A-1(e) of §1.401(a)(9)-5 for rules relating to the satisfaction of section 401(a)(9) in the year that annuity payments commence, A-3(d) of §1.401(a)(9)-5 for rules relating to qualifying longevity annuity contracts (QLACs), defined in A-17 of this section, and A-2(a)(3) of §1.401(a)(9)-8 for rules relating to the purchase of an annuity contract with a portion of an employee's account balance.

(b) *Entire interest.* For purposes of applying the rules in §1.401(a)(9)-5, the entire interest under the annuity contract as of December 31 of the relevant valuation calendar year is treated as the account balance for the valuation calendar year described in A-3 of §1.401(a)(9)-5. The entire interest under an annuity contract is the dollar amount credited to the employee or beneficiary under the contract plus the actuarial present value of any additional benefits (such as survivor benefits in excess of the dollar amount credited to the employee or beneficiary) that will be provided under the contract. However, paragraph (c) of this A-12 describes certain additional benefits that may be disregarded in determining the employee's entire interest under the annuity contract. The actuarial present value of any additional benefits described under this A-12 is to be determined using reasonable actuarial assumptions, including reasonable assumptions as to future distributions, and without regard to an individual's health.

(c) *Exclusions.* (1) The actuarial present value of any additional benefits provided under an annuity contract described in paragraph (b) of this A-12 may be disregarded if the sum of the dollar amount credited to the employee or beneficiary under the contract and the actuarial present value of the additional benefits is no more than 120 percent of the dollar amount credited to the employee or beneficiary under the contract and the contract provides only for the following additional benefits:

(i) Additional benefits that, in the case of a distribution, are reduced by an amount sufficient to ensure that the ratio of such sum to the dollar amount credited does not increase as a result of the distribution, and

(ii) An additional benefit that is the right to receive a final payment upon death that does not exceed the excess of the premiums paid less the amount of prior distributions.

(2) If the only additional benefit provided under the contract is the additional benefit described in paragraph (c)(1)(ii) of this A-12, the additional benefit may be disregarded regardless of its value in relation to the dollar amount credited to the employee or beneficiary under the contract.

(3) The Commissioner in revenue rulings, notices, or other guidance published in the Internal Revenue Bulletin (see §601.601(d)(2) of this chapter) may provide additional guidance on additional benefits that may be disregarded.

(d) *Examples.* The following examples, which use a 5 percent interest rate and the Mortality Table provided in Rev. Rul. 2001-62 (2001-2 C.B. 632), illustrate the application of the rules in this A-12:

Example 1. (i) G is the owner of a variable annuity contract (Contract S) under an individual account plan which has not been annuitized. Contract S provides a death benefit until the end of the calendar year in which the owner attains the age of 84 equal to the greater of the current Contract S notional account value (dollar amount credited to G under the contract) and the largest notional account value at any previous policy anniversary reduced proportionally for subsequent partial distributions (High Water Mark). Contract S provides a death benefit in calendar years after the calendar year in which the owner attains age 84 equal to the current notional account value. Contract S provides that assets within the contract may be invested in a Fixed Account at a guaranteed rate of 2 percent. Contract S provides no other additional benefits.

(ii) At the end of 2008, when G has an attained age of 78 and 9 months the notional account value of Contract S (after the distribution for 2008 of 4.93% of the notional account value as of December 31, 2007) is $550,000, and the High Water Mark, before adjustment for any withdrawals from Contract S in 2008 is $1,000,000. Thus, Contract S will provide additional benefits (i.e. the death benefits in excess of the notional account value) through 2014, the year S turns

84. The actuarial present value of these additional benefits at the end of 2008 is determined to be $84,300 (15 percent of the notional account value). In making this determination, the following assumptions are made: on the average, deaths occur mid-year; the investment return on his notional account value is 2 percent per annum; and minimum required distributions (determined without regard to additional benefits under the Contract S) are made at the end of each year. The following table summarizes the actuarial methodology used in determining the actuarial present value of the additional benefit.

Year	Death Benefit During Year	End-of-Year Notional Account Before Withdrawal	Average Notional Account	Withdrawal at End of Year	End-of-Year Notional Account After Withdrawal
2008	$1,000,000				$550,000
2009	$950,739 [1]	$561,000 [2]	$555,500 [3]	$28,205 [4]	$532,795
2010	$901,983	$543,451	$538,123	$28,492	$514,959
2011	$853,749	$525,258	$520,109	$28,769	$496,490
2012	$806,053	$506,419	$501,454	$29,034	$477,385
2013	$758,916	$486,933	$482,159	$29,287	$457,645
2014	$712,356	$466,798	$462,222	$29,525	$437,273

Year	Survivorship to Start of Year	Interest Discount to End of 2008	Mortality Rate During Year	Discounted Additional Benefits Within Year
2008				
2009	1.00000	.97590	.04426 [5]	$17,070
2010	.95574	.92943 [6]	.04946	$15,987 [7]
2011	.90847 [8]	.88517	.05519	$14,807
2012	.85833	.84302	.06146	$13,546
2013	.80558	.80288	.06788	$12,150
2014	.75090	.76464	.07477	$10,739
				$84,300

[1] $1,000,000 death benefit reduced 4.93 percent for withdrawal during 2008.
[2] Notional account value at end of prior year (after distribution) increased by 2 percent return for year.
[3] Average of $550,000 notional account value at end of prior year (after distribution) and $561,000 notional account value at end of current year (before distribution).
[4] December 31, 2008 notional account (before distribution) divided by uniform lifetime table age 79 factor of 19.5.
[5] One-quarter age 78 rate plus three-quarters age 79 rate.
[6] Five percent discounted 18 months (1.05^(-1.5)).
[7] Blended age 79/age 80 mortality rate (.04946) multiplied by the $363,860 excess of death benefit over the average notional account value (901,983 less 538,123) multiplied by .95574 probability of survivorship to the start of 2010 multiplied by 18 month interest discount of .92943.
[8] Survivorship to start of preceding year (.95574) multiplied by probability of survivorship during prior year (1 – .04946).

(iii) Because Contract S provides that, in the case of a distribution, the value of the additional death benefit (which is the only additional benefit available under the contract) is reduced by an amount that is at least proportional to the reduction in the notional account value and, at age 78 and 9 months, the sum of the notional account value (dollar amount credited to the employee under the contract) and the actuarial present value of the additional death benefit is no more than 120 percent of the notional account value, the exclusion under paragraph (c)(2) of this A-12 is applicable for 2009. Therefore, for purposes of applying the rules in § 1.401(a)(9)-5, the entire interest under Contract S may be determined as the notional account value (i.e. without regard to the additional death benefit).

Example 2. (i) The facts are the same as in *Example 1* except that the notional account value is $450,000 at the end of 2008. In this instance, the actuarial present value of the death benefit in excess of the notional account value in 2008 is determined to be $108,669 (24 percent of the notional account value). The following table summarizes the actuarial methodology used in determining the actuarial present value of the additional benefit.

Year	Death Benefit During Year	End-of-Year Notional Account Before Withdrawal	Average Notional Account	Withdrawal at End of Year	End-of-Year Notional Account After Withdrawal
2008	$1,000,000				$450,000
2009	$950,739	$459,000	$454,500	$23,077	$435,923
2010	$901,983	$444,642	$440,282	$23,311	$421,330
2011	$853,749	$429,757	$425,543	$23,538	$406,219
2012	$806,053	$414,343	$410,281	$23,755	$390,588
2013	$758,916	$398,399	$394,494	$23,962	$374,437
2014	$712,356	$381,926	$378,181	$24,157	$357,768

Year	Survivorship to Start of Year	Interest Discount to End of 2008	Mortality Rate During Year	Discounted Additional Benefits Within Year
2008				
2009	1.00000	.97590	.04426	$21,432
2010	.95574	.92943	.04946	$20,286
2011	.90847	.88517	.05519	$19,004
2012	.85833	.84302	.06146	$17,601
2013	.80558	.80288	.06788	$15,999
2014	.75090	.76464	.07477	$14,347
				$108,669

(ii) Because the sum of the notional account balance and the actuarial present value of the additional death benefit is more than 120 percent of the notional account value, the exclusion under paragraph (b)(1) of this A-12 does not apply for 2009. Therefore, for purposes of applying the rules in § 1.401(a)(9)-5, the entire interest under Contract S must include the actuarial present value of the *additional death benefit.*

Q-13: When can an annuity payment period be changed?

A-13. (a) *In general.* An annuity payment period may be changed in accordance with the provisions set forth in paragraph (b) of this A-13

or in association with an annuity payment increase described in A-14 of this section.

(b) *Reannuitization.* If, in a stream of annuity payments that otherwise satisfies section 401(a)(9), the annuity payment period is changed and the annuity payments are modified in association with that change, this modification will not cause the distributions to fail to satisfy section 401(a)(9) provided the conditions set forth in paragraph (c) of this A-13 are satisfied, and either—

(1) The modification occurs at the time that the employee retires or in connection with a plan termination;

(2) The annuity payments prior to modification are annuity payments paid over a period certain without life contingencies; or

(3) The annuity payments after modification are paid under a qualified joint and survivor annuity over the joint lives of the employee and a designated beneficiary, the employee's spouse is the sole designated beneficiary, and the modification occurs in connection with the employee becoming married to such spouse.

(c) *Conditions.* In order to modify a stream of annuity payments in accordance with paragraph (b) of this A-13, the following conditions must be satisfied—

(1) The future payments under the modified stream satisfy section 401(a)(9) and this section (determined by treating the date of the change as a new annuity starting date and the actuarial present value of the remaining payments prior to modification as the entire interest of the participant);

(2) For purposes of sections 415 and 417, the modification is treated as a new annuity starting date;

(3) After taking into account the modification, the annuity stream satisfies section 415 (determined at the original annuity starting date, using the interest rates and mortality tables applicable to such date); and

(4) The end point of the period certain, if any, for any modified payment period is not later than the end point available under section 401(a)(9) to the employee at the original annuity starting date.

(d) *Examples.* For the following examples in this A-13, assume that the Applicable Interest Rate throughout the period from 2005 through 2008 is 5 percent and throughout 2009 is 4 percent, the Applicable Mortality Table throughout the period from 2005 to 2009 is the table provided in Rev. Rul. 2001-62 (2001-C.B. 632) and the section 415 limit in 2005 at age 70 for a straight life annuity is $255,344:

Example 1. (i) A participant (D), who has 10 years of participation in a frozen defined benefit plan (Plan W), attains age 70$^1/_2$ in 2005. D is not retired and elects to receive distributions from Plan W in the form of a straight life (i.e. level payment) annuity with annual payments of $240,000 per year beginning in 2005 at a date when D has an attained age of 70. Plan W offers non-retired employees in pay status the opportunity to modify their annuity payments due to an associated change in the payment period at retirement. Plan W treats the date of the change in payment period as a new annuity starting date for the purposes of sections 415 and 417. Thus, for example, the plan provides a new qualified and joint survivor annuity election and obtains spousal consent.

(ii) Plan W determines modifications of annuity payment amounts at retirement such that the present value of future new annuity payment amounts (taking into account the new associated payment period) is actuarially equivalent to the present value of future pre-modification annuity payments (taking into account the pre-modification annuity payment period). Actuarial equivalency for this purpose is determined using the Applicable Interest Rate and the Applicable Mortality Table as of the date of modification.

(iii) D retires in 2009 at the age of 74 and, after receiving four annual payments of $240,000, elects to receive his remaining distributions from Plan W in the form of an immediate final lump sum payment (calculated at 4 percent interest) of $2,399,809.

(iv) Because payment of retirement benefits in the form of an immediate final lump sum payment satisfies (in terms of form) section 401(a)(9), the condition under paragraph (c)(1) of this A-13 is met.

(v) Because Plan W treats a modification of an annuity payment stream at retirement as a new annuity starting date for purposes of sections 415 and 417, the condition under paragraph (c)(2) of this A-13 is met.

(vi) After taking into account the modification, the annuity stream determined as of the original annuity starting date consists of annual payments beginning at age 70 of $240,000, $240,000, $240,000, $240,000, and $2,399,809. This benefit stream is actuarially equivalent to a straight life annuity at age 70 of $250,182, an amount less than the section 415 limit determined at the original annuity starting date, using the interest and mortality rates applicable to such date. Thus, the condition under paragraph (c)(3) of this A-13 is met.

(vii) Thus, because a stream of annuity payments in the form of a straight life annuity satisfies section 401(a)(9), and because each of the conditions under paragraph (c) of this A-13 are satisfied, the modification of annuity payments to D described in this example meets the requirements of this A-13.

Example 2. The facts are the same as in *Example 1* except that the straight life annuity payments are paid at a rate of $250,000 per year and after D retires the lump sum payment at age 75 is $2,499,801. Thus, after taking into account the modification, the annuity stream determined as of the original annuity starting date consists of annual payments beginning at age 70 of $250,000, $250,000, $250,000, $250,000, and $2,499,801. This benefit stream is actuarially equivalent to a straight life annuity at age 70 of $260,606, an amount greater than the section 415 limit determined at the original annuity starting date, using the interest and mortality rates applicable to such date. Thus, the lump sum payment to D fails to satisfy the condition under paragraph (c)(3) of this A-13. Therefore, the lump sum payment to D fails to meet the requirements of this A-13 and thus fails to satisfy the requirements of section 401(a)(9).

Example 3. (i) A participant (E), who has 10 years of participation in a frozen defined benefit plan (Plan X), attains age 70$^1/_2$ and retires in 2005 at a date when his attained age is 70. E was born in 1935. E elects to receive annual distributions from Plan X in the form of a 27 year period certain annuity (i.e., a 27 year annuity payment period without a life contingency) paid at a rate of $37,000 per year beginning in 2005 with future payments increasing at a rate of 4 percent per year (i.e., the 2006 payment will be $38,480, the 2007 payment will be $40,019 and so on). Plan X offers participants in pay status whose annuity payments are in the form of a term-certain annuity the opportunity to modify their payment period at any time and treats such modifications as a new annuity starting date for the purposes of sections 415 and 417. Thus, for example, the plan provides a new qualified and joint survivor annuity election and obtains spousal consent

(ii) Plan X determines modifications of annuity payment amounts such that the present value of future new annuity payment amounts (taking into account the new associated payment period) is actuarially equivalent to the present value of future premodification annuity payments (taking into account the pre-modification annuity payment period). Actuarial equivalency for this purpose is determined using 5 percent and the Applicable Mortality Table as of the date of modification.

(iii) In 2008, E, after receiving annual payments of $37,000, $38,480, and $40,019, elects to receive his remaining distributions from Plan W in the form of a straight life annuity paid with annual payments of $92,133 per year.

(iv) Because payment of retirement benefits in the form of a straight life annuity satisfies (in terms of form) section 401(a)(9), the condition under paragraph (c)(1) of this A-13 is met.

(v) Because Plan X treats a modification of an annuity payment stream at retirement as a new annuity starting date for purposes of sections 415 and 417, the condition under paragraph (c)(2) of this A-13 is met.

(vi) After taking into account the modification, the annuity stream determined as of the original annuity starting date consists of annual payments beginning at age 70 of $37,000, $38,480, $40,019, and a straight life annuity beginning at age 73 of $92,133. This benefit stream is equivalent to a straight life annuity at age 70 of $82,539, an amount less than the section 415 limit determined at the original annuity starting date, using the interest and mortality rates applicable to such date. Thus, the condition under paragraph (c)(3) of this A-13 is met.

(vii) Thus, because a stream of annuity payments in the form of a straight life annuity satisfies section 401(a)(9), and because each of the conditions under paragraph (c) of this A-13 are satisfied, the modification of annuity payments to E described in this example meets the requirements of this A-13.

Q-14. Are annuity payments permitted to increase?

A-14. (a) *General rules.* Except as otherwise provided in this section, all annuity payments (whether paid over an employee's life, joint lives, or a period certain) must be nonincreasing or increase only in accordance with one or more of the following—

(1) With an annual percentage increase that does not exceed the percentage increase in an eligible cost-of-living index as defined in paragraph (b) of this A-14 for a 12-month period ending in the year during which the increase occurs or the prior year;

(2) With a percentage increase that occurs at specified times (e.g., at specified ages) and does not exceed the cumulative total of annual percentage increases in an eligible cost-of-living index as defined in paragraph (b) of this A-14 since the annuity starting date, or if later, the date of the most recent percentage increase. However, in cases providing such a cumulative increase, an actuarial increase may not be provided to reflect the fact that increases were not provided in the interim years;

(3) To the extent of the reduction in the amount of the employee's payments to provide for a survivor benefit, but only if there is no longer a survivor benefit because the beneficiary whose life was being used to determine the period described in section 401(a)(9)(A)(ii) over which payments were being made dies or is no longer the employee's beneficiary pursuant to a qualified domestic relations order within the meaning of section 414(p);

(4) To pay increased benefits that result from a plan amendment;

(5) To allow a beneficiary to convert the survivor portion of a joint and survivor annuity into a single sum distribution upon the employee's death; or

(6) To the extent increases are permitted in accordance with paragraph (c) or (d) of this A-14.

(b)(1) For purposes of this A-14, an eligible cost-of-living index means an index described in paragraphs (b)(2), (b)(3), or (b)(4) of this A-14.

(2) A consumer price index that is based on prices of all items (or all items excluding food and energy) and issued by the Bureau of Labor Statistics, including an index for a specific population (such as urban consumers or urban wage earners and clerical workers) and an index for a geographic area or areas (such as a given metropolitan area or state).

(3) A percentage adjustment based on a cost-of-living index described in paragraph (b)(2) of this A-14, or a fixed percentage if less. In any year when the cost-of-living index is lower than the fixed percentage, the fixed percentage may be treated as an increase in an eligible cost-of-living index, provided it does not exceed the sum of:

(i) the cost-of-living index for that year, and

(ii) the accumulated excess of the annual cost-of-living index from each prior year over the fixed annual percentage used in that year (reduced by any amount previously utilized under this paragraph (b)(3)(ii)).

(4) A percentage adjustment based on the increase in compensation for the position held by the employee at the time of retirement, and provided under either the terms of a governmental plan within the meaning of section 414(d) or under the terms of a nongovernmental plan as in effect on April 17, 2002.

(c) *Additional permitted increases for annuity payments under annuity contracts purchased from insurance companies.* In the case of annuity payments paid from an annuity contract purchased from an insurance company, if the total future expected payments (determined in accordance with paragraph (e)(3) of this A-14) exceed the total value being annuitized (within the meaning of paragraph (e)(1) of this A-14), the payments under the annuity will not fail to satisfy the nonincreasing payment requirement in A-1(a) of this section merely because the payments are increased in accordance with one or more of the following—

(1) By a constant percentage, applied not less frequently than annually;

(2) To provide a final payment upon the death of the employee that does not exceed the excess of the total value being annuitized (within the meaning of paragraph (e)(1) of this A-14) over the total of payments before the death of the employee;

(3) As a result of dividend payments or other payments that result from actuarial gains (within the meaning of paragraph (e)(2) of this A-14), but only if actuarial gain is measured no less frequently than annually and the resulting dividend payments or other payments are either paid no later than the year following the year for which actuarial experience is measured or paid in the same form as the payment of the annuity over the remaining period of the annuity (beginning no later than the year following the year for which the actuarial experience is measured); and

(4) an acceleration of payments under the annuity (within the meaning of paragraph (e)(4) of this A-14).

(d) *Additional permitted increases for annuity payments from a qualified trust.* In the case of annuity payments paid under a defined benefit plan qualified under section 401(a) (other than annuity payments under an annuity contract purchased from an insurance company that satisfy paragraph (c) of this section), the payments under the annuity will not fail to satisfy the nonincreasing payment requirement in A-1(a) of this section merely because the payments are increased in accordance with one of the following—

(1) By a constant percentage, applied not less frequently than annually, at a rate that is less than 5 percent per year;

(2) To provide a final payment upon the death of the employee that does not exceed the excess of the actuarial present value of the employee's accrued benefit (within the meaning of section 411(a)(7)) calculated as the annuity starting date using the applicable interest rate and the applicable mortality table under section 417(e) (or, if greater, the total amount of employee contributions) over the total of payments before the death of the employee; or

(3) As a result of dividend payments or other payments that result from actuarial gains (within the meaning of paragraph (e)(2) of this A-14), but only if—

(i) Actuarial gain is measured no less frequently than annually;

(ii) The resulting dividend payments or other payments are either paid no later than the year following the year for which the actuarial experience is measured or paid in the same form as the payment of the annuity over the remaining period of the annuity (beginning no later than the year following the year for which the actuarial experience is measured);

(iii) The actuarial gain taken into account is limited to actuarial gain from investment experience;

(iv) The assumed interest used to calculate such actuarial gains is not less than 3 percent; and

(v) The payments are not increasing by a constant percentage as described in paragraph (d)(1) of this A-14.

(e) *Definitions.* For purposes of this A-14, the following definitions apply—

(1) Total value being annuitized means—

(i) In the case of annuity payments under a section 403(a) annuity plan or under a deferred annuity purchased by a section 401(a) trust, the value of the employee's entire interest (within the meaning of A-12 of this section) being annuitized (valued as of the date annuity payments commence);

(ii) In the case of annuity payments under an immediate annuity contract purchased by a trust for a defined benefit plan qualified under section 401(a), the amount of the premium used to purchase the contract; and

(iii) In the case of a defined contribution plan, the value of the employee's account balance used to purchase an immediate annuity under the contract.

(2) Actuarial gain means the difference between an amount determined using the actuarial assumptions (i.e., investment return, mortality, expense, and other similar assumptions) used to calculate the initial payments before adjustment for any increases and the amount determined under the actual experience with respect to those factors. Actuarial gain also includes differences between the amount determined using actuarial assumptions when an annuity was purchased or commenced and such amount determined using actuarial assumptions used in calculating payments at the time the actuarial gain is determined.

(3) Total future expected payments means the total future payments expected to be made under the annuity contract as of the date of the determination, calculated using the Single Life Table in §1.401(a)(9)-9(b) (or, if applicable, the Joint and Last Survivor Table in §1.401(a)(9)-9(d)) for annuitants who are still alive, without regard to any increases in annuity payments after the date of determination, and taking into account any remaining period certain.

(4) Acceleration of payments means a shortening of the payment period with respect to an annuity or a full or partial commutation of the future annuity payments. An increase in the payment amount will be treated as an acceleration of payments in the annuity only if the total future expected payments under the annuity (including the amount of any payment made as a result of the acceleration) is decreased as a result of the change in payment period.

(f) *Examples.* Paragraph (c) of this A-14 is illustrated by the following examples:

Example 1. Variable annuity. A retired participant (Z1) in defined contribution plan X attains age 70 on March 5, 2005, and thus, attains age 70^1/$_2$ in 2005. Z1 elects to purchase annuity Contract Y1 from Insurance Company W in 2005. Contract Y1 is a single life annuity contract with a 10-year period certain. Contract Y1 provides for an initial annual payment calculated with an assumed interest rate (AIR) of 3 percent. Subsequent payments are determined by multiplying the prior year's payment by a fraction the numerator of which is 1 plus the actual return on the separate account assets underlying Contract Y1 since the preceding payment and the denominator of which is 1 plus the AIR during that period. The value of Z1's account balance in Plan X at the time of purchase is $105,000, and the purchase price of Contract Y1 is $105,000. Contract Y1 provides Z1 with an initial payment of $7,200 at the time of purchase in 2005. The total future expected payments to Z1 under Contract Y1 are $122,400, calculated as the initial payment of $7,200 multiplied by the age 70 life expectancy of 17 provided in the Single Life Table in §1.401(a)(9)-9(b). Because the total future expected payments on the purchase date exceed the total value used to purchase Contract Y1 and payments may only increase as a result of actuarial gain, with such increases, beginning no later than the next year, paid in the same form as the payment of the annuity over the remaining period of the annuity, distributions received by Z1 from Contract Y1 meet the requirements under paragraph (c)(3) of this A-14.

Example 2. Participating annuity. A retired participant (Z2) in defined contribution plan X attains age 70 on May 1, 2005, and thus, attains age 70^1/$_2$ in 2005. Z2 elects to purchase annuity Contract Y2 from Insurance Company W in 2005. Contract Y2 is a participating single life annuity contract with a 10-year period certain. Contract Y2 provides for level annual payments with dividends paid in a lump sum in the year after the year for which the actuarial experience is measured or paid out levelly beginning in the year after the year for which the actuarial gain is measured over the remaining lifetime and period certain, i.e., the period certain ends at the same time as the original period certain. Dividends are determined annually by the Board of Directors of Company W based upon a comparison of actual actuarial experience to expected actuarial experience in the past year. The value of Z2's account balance in Plan X at the time of purchase is $265,000, and the purchase price of Contract Y2 is $265,000. Contract Y2 provides Z2 with an initial payment of $16,000 in 2005. The total future expected payments to Z2 under Contract Y2 are calculated as the annual initial payment of $16,000 multiplied by the age 70 life expectancy of 17 provided in the Single Life Table in §1.401(a)(9)-9(b) for a total of $272,000. Because the total future expected payments on the purchase date exceeds the total value used to purchase Contract Y2 and payments may only increase as a result of actuarial gain, with such increases, beginning no later than the next year, paid in the same form as the payment of the annuity over the remaining period of the annuity, distributions received by Z2 from Contract Y2 meet the requirements under paragraph (c)(3) of this A-14.

Example 3. Participating annuity with dividend accumulation. The facts are the same as in *Example 2* except that the annuity provides a dividend accumulation option under which Z2 may defer receipt of the dividends to a time selected by Z2. Because the dividend accumulation option permits dividends to be paid later than the end of the year following the year for which the actuarial experience is measured or as a stream of payments that only increase as a result of actuarial gain, with such increases beginning no later than the next year, paid in the same form as the payment of the annuity over the remaining period of the annuity in *Example 2*, the dividend accumulation option does not meet the requirements of paragraph (c)(3) of this A-14. Neither does the dividend accumulation option fit within any of the other increases described in paragraph (c) of this A-14. Accordingly, the dividend accumulation option causes the contract, and consequently any distributions from the contract, to fail to meet the requirements of this A-14 and thus fail to satisfy the requirements of section 401(a)(9).

Example 4. Participating annuity with dividends used to purchase additional death benefits. The facts are the same as in *Example 2* except that the annuity provides an option under which actuarial gain under the contract is used to provide additional death benefit protection for Z2. Because this option permits payments as a result of actuarial gain to be paid later than the end of the year following the year for which the actuarial experience is measured or as a stream of payments that only increase as a result of actuarial gain, with such increases beginning no later than the next year, paid in the same form as the payment of the annuity over the remaining period of the annuity in *Example 2*, the option does not meet the requirements of paragraph (c)(3) of this A-14. Neither does the option fit within any of the other increases described in paragraph (c) of this A-14. Accordingly, the addition of the option causes the contract, and consequently any distributions from the contract, to fail to meet the requirements of this A-14 and thus fail to satisfy the requirements of section 401(a)(9).

Example 5. Annuity with a fixed percentage increase. A retired participant (Z3) in defined contribution plan X attains age 70^1/$_2$ in 2005. Z3 elects to purchase annuity contract Y3 from Insurance Company W. Contract Y3 is a single life annuity contract with a 20-year period certain (which does not exceed the maximum period certain permitted under A-3(a) of this section) with fixed annual payments increasing 3 percent each year. The value of Z3's account balance in Plan X at the time of purchase is $110,000, and the purchase price of Contract Y3 is $110,000. Contract Y3 provides Z3 with an initial payment of $6,000 at the time of purchase in 2005. The total future expected payments to Z3 under Contract Y3 are $120,000, calculated as the initial annual payment of $6,000 multiplied by the period certain of 20 years. Because the total future expected payments on the purchase date exceed the total value used to purchase Contract Y3 and payments only increase as a constant percentage applied not less frequently than annually, distributions received by Z3 from Contract Y3 meet the requirements under paragraph (c)(1) of this A-14.

Example 6. Annuity with excessive increases. The facts are the same as in *Example 5* except that the initial payment is $5,400 and the annual rate of increase is 4 percent. In this example, the total future expected payments are $108,000, calculated as the initial payment of $5,400 multiplied by the period certain of 20 years. Because the total future expected payments are less than the total value of $110,000 used to purchase Contract Y3, distributions received by Z3 do not meet the requirements under paragraph (c) of this A-14 and thus fail to meet the requirements of section 401(a)(9).

Example 7. Annuity with full commutation feature. (i) A retired participant (Z4) in defined contribution Plan X attains age 78 in 2005. Z4 elects to purchase Contract Y4 from Insurance Company W. Contract Y4 provides for a single life annuity with a 10 year period certain (which does not exceed the maximum period certain permitted under A-3(a) of this section) with annual payments. Contract Y4 provides that Z4 may cancel Contract Y4 at any time before Z4 attains age 84, and receive, on his next payment due date, a final payment in an amount determined by multiplying the initial payment amount by a factor obtained from Table M of Contract Y4 using the Y4's age as of Y4's birthday in the calendar year of the final payment. The value of Z4's account balance in Plan X at the time of purchase is $450,000, and the purchase price of Contract Y4 is $450,000. Contract Y4 provides Z4 with an initial payment in 2005 of $40,000. The factors in Table M are as follows:

Age at Final Payment	Factor
79	10.5
80	10.0
81	9.5
82	9.0
83	8.5
84	8.0

(ii) The total future expected payments to Z4 under Contract Y4 are $456,000, calculated as the initial payment of $40,000 multiplied by the age 78 life expectancy of 11.4 provided in the Single Life Table in §1.401(a)(9)-9(b). Because the total future expected payments on the purchase date exceed the total value being annuitized (i.e., the $450,000 used to purchase Contract Y4), the permitted increases set forth in paragraph (c) of this A-14 are available. Furthermore, because the factors in Table M are less than the life expectancy of each of the ages in the Single Life Table provided in §1.401(a)(9)-9(b), the final payment is always less than the total future expected payments. Thus, the final payment is an acceleration of payments within the meaning of paragraph (c)(4) of this A-14.

(iii) As an illustration of the above, if Participant Z4 were to elect to cancel Contract Y4 on the day before he was to attain age 84, his contractual final payment would be $320,000. This amount is determined as $40,000 (the annual payment amount due under Contract Y4) multiplied by 8.0 (the factor in Table M for the next payment due date, age 84). The total future expected payments under Contract Y4 at age 84 before the final payment is $324,000, calculated as the initial payment amount multiplied by 8.1, the age 84 life expectancy provided in the Single Life Table in §1.401(a)(9)-9(b). Because $320,000 (the total future expected payments under the annuity contract, including the amount of the final payment) is less than $324,000 (the total future expected payments under the annuity contract, determined before the election), the final payment is an acceleration of payments within the meaning of paragraph (c)(4) of this A-14.

Example 8. Annuity with partial commutation feature. (i) The facts are the same as in *Example 7* except that the annuity provides Z4 may request, at any time before Z4 attains age 84, an ad hoc payment on his next payment due date with future payments reduced by an amount equal to the ad hoc payment divided by the factor obtained from Table M (from *Example 7*) corresponding to Z4's age at the time of the ad hoc payment. Because, at each age, the factors in Table M are less than the corresponding life expectancies in the Single Life Table in §1.401(a)(9)-9(b), total future expected payments under Contract Y4 will decrease after an ad hoc payment. Thus, ad hoc distributions received by Z4 from Contract Y4 will satisfy the requirements under paragraph (c)(4) of this A-4.

(ii) As an illustration of paragraph (c)(i) of this *Example 8*, if Z4 were to request, on the day before he was to attain age 84, an ad hoc payment of $100,000 on his next payment due date, his recalculated annual payment amount would be reduced to $27,500. This amount is determined as $40,000 (the amount of Z4's next annual payment) reduced by $12,500 (his $100,000 ad hoc payment divided by the Table M factor at age 84 of 8.0). Thus, Z4's total future expected payments after the ad hoc payment (and including the ad hoc payment) are equal to $322,750 ($100,000 plus $27,500 multiplied by the Single Life Table value of 8.1). Note that this $322,750 amount is less than the amount of Z4's total future expected payments before the ad hoc payment ($324,000, determined as $40,000 multiplied by 8.1), and the requirements under paragraph (c)(4) of this A-4 are satisfied.

Example 9. Annuity with excessive increases. (i) A retired participant (Z5) in defined contribution plan X attains age 70^1/$_2$ in 2005. Z5 elects to purchase annuity Contract Y5 from Insurance Company W in 2005 with a premium of $1,000,000. Contract Y5 is a single life annuity contract with a 20-year period certain. Contract Y5 provides for an initial payment of $200,000, a second payment one year from the time of purchase of $40,000, and 18 succeeding annual payments each increasing at a constant percentage rate of 4.5 percent from the preceding payment.

(ii) Contract Y5 fails to meet the requirements of section 401(a)(9) because the total future expected payments without regard to any increases in the annuity payment, calculated as $200,000 in year one and $40,000 in each of years two through twenty, is only $960,000 (i.e., an amount that does not exceed the total value used to purchase the annuity).

Q-15: Are there special rules applicable to payments made under a defined benefit plan or annuity contract to a surviving child?

A-15: Yes, pursuant to section 401(a)(9)(F), payments under a defined benefit plan or annuity contract that are made to an employee's child until such child reaches the age of majority (or dies, if earlier) may be treated, for purposes of section 401(a)(9), as if such payments were made to the surviving spouse to the extent they become payable to the surviving spouse upon cessation of the payments to the child. For purposes of the preceding sentence, a child may be treated as having not reached the age of majority if the child has not completed a specified course of education and is under the age of 26. In addition, a child who is disabled within the meaning of section

Reg. §1.401(a)(9)-6

72(m)(7) when the child reaches the age of majority may be treated as having not reached the age of majority so long as the child continues to be disabled. Thus, when payments described in this paragraph A-15 become payable to the surviving spouse because the child attains the age of majority, recovers from a disabling illness, dies, or completes a specified course of education, there is not an increase in benefits under A-1 of this section. Likewise, the age of child receiving such payments is not taken into consideration for purposes of the minimum incidental benefit requirement of A-2 of this section.

Q-16: What are the rules for determining required minimum distributions for defined benefit plans and annuity contracts for calendar years 2003, 2004, and 2005?

A-16: A distribution from a defined benefit plan or annuity contract for calendar years 2003, 2004, and 2005 will not fail to satisfy section 401(a)(9) merely because the payments do not satisfy A-1 through A-15 of this section, provided the payments satisfy section 401(a)(9) based on a reasonable and good faith interpretation of the provisions of section 401(a)(9).

Q-17. What is a qualifying longevity annuity contract?

A-17. (a) *Definition of qualifying longevity annuity contract.* A qualifying longevity annuity contract (QLAC) is an annuity contract that is purchased from an insurance company for an employee and that, in accordance with the rules of application of paragraph (d) of this A-17, satisfies each of the following requirements—

(1) Premiums for the contract satisfy the requirements of paragraph (b) of this A-17;

(2) The contract provides that distributions under the contract must commence not later than a specified annuity starting date that is no later than the first day of the month next following the 85th anniversary of the employee's birth;

(3) The contract provides that, after distributions under the contract commence, those distributions must satisfy the requirements of this section (other than the requirement in A-1(c) of this section that annuity payments commence on or before the required beginning date);

(4) The contract does not make available any commutation benefit, cash surrender right, or other similar feature;

(5) No benefits are provided under the contract after the death of the employee other than the benefits described in paragraph (c) of this A-17;

(6) When the contract is issued, the contract (or a rider or endorsement with respect to that contract) states that the contract is intended to be a QLAC; and

(7) The contract is not a variable contract under section 817, an indexed contract, or a similar contract, except to the extent provided by the Commissioner in revenue rulings, notices, or other guidance published in the Internal Revenue Bulletin and made available by the Superintendent of Documents, U.S. Government Printing Office, Washington, DC 20402 and on the IRS Web site at http://www.irs.gov.

(b) *Limitations on premiums*—(1) *In general.* The premiums paid with respect to the contract on a date satisfy the requirements of this paragraph (b) if they do not exceed the lesser of the dollar limitation in paragraph (b)(2) of this A-17 or the percentage limitation in paragraph (b)(3) of this A-17.

(2) *Dollar limitation.* The dollar limitation is an amount equal to the excess of—

(i) $125,000 (as adjusted under paragraph (d)(2) of this A-17), over

(ii) The sum of—

(A) The premiums paid before that date with respect to the contract, and

(B) The premiums paid on or before that date with respect to any other contract that is intended to be a QLAC and that is purchased for the employee under the plan, or any other plan, annuity, or account described in section 401(a), 403(a), 403(b), or 408 or eligible governmental plan under section 457(b).

(3) *Percentage limitation.* The percentage limitation is an amount equal to the excess of—

(i) 25 percent of the employee's account balance under the plan (including the value of any QLAC held under the plan for the employee) as of that date, determined in accordance with paragraph (d)(1)(iii) of this A-17, over

(ii) The sum of—

(A) The premiums paid before that date with respect to the contract, and

(B) The premiums paid on or before that date with respect to any other contract that is intended to be a QLAC and that is held or was purchased for the employee under the plan.

(c) *Payments after death of the employee*—(1) *Surviving spouse is sole beneficiary*—(i) *Death on or after annuity starting date.* If the employee dies on or after the annuity starting date for the contract and the employee's surviving spouse is the sole beneficiary under the contract then, except as provided in paragraph (c)(4) of this A-17, the

only benefit permitted to be paid after the employee's death is a life annuity payable to the surviving spouse where the periodic annuity payment is not in excess of 100 percent of the periodic annuity payment that is payable to the employee.

(ii) *Death before annuity starting date*—(A) *Amount of annuity.* If the employee dies before the annuity starting date and the employee's surviving spouse is the sole beneficiary under the contract then, except as provided in paragraph (c)(4) of this A-17, the only benefit permitted to be paid after the employee's death is a life annuity payable to the surviving spouse where the periodic annuity payment is not in excess of 100 percent of the periodic annuity payment that would have been payable to the employee as of the date that benefits to the surviving spouse commence. However, the annuity is permitted to exceed 100 percent of the periodic annuity payment that would have been payable to the employee to the extent necessary to satisfy the requirement to provide a qualified preretirement survivor annuity (as defined under section 417(c)(2) or ERISA section 205(e)(2)) pursuant to section 401(a)(11)(A)(ii) or ERISA section 205(a)(2).

(B) *Commencement date for annuity.* Any life annuity payable to the surviving spouse under paragraph (c)(1)(ii)(A) of this A-17 must commence no later than the date on which the annuity payable to the employee would have commenced under the contract if the employee had not died.

(2) *Surviving spouse is not sole beneficiary*—(i) *Death on or after annuity starting date.* If the employee dies on or after the annuity starting date for the contract and the employee's surviving spouse is not the sole beneficiary under the contract then, except as provided in paragraph (c)(4) of this A-17, the only benefit permitted to be paid after the employee's death is a life annuity payable to the designated beneficiary where the periodic annuity payment is not in excess of the applicable percentage (determined under paragraph (c)(2)(iii) of this A-17) of the periodic annuity payment that is payable to the employee.

(ii) *Death before annuity starting date*—(A) *Amount of annuity.* If the employee dies before the annuity starting date and the employee's surviving spouse is not the sole beneficiary under the contract then, except as provided in paragraph (c)(4) of this A-17, the only benefit permitted to be paid after the employee's death is a life annuity payable to the designated beneficiary where the periodic annuity payment is not in excess of the applicable percentage (determined under paragraph (c)(2)(iii) of this A-17) of the periodic annuity payment that would have been payable to the employee as of the date that benefits to the designated beneficiary commence under this paragraph (c)(2)(ii).

(B) *Commencement date for annuity.* In any case in which the employee dies before the annuity starting date, any life annuity payable to a designated beneficiary under this paragraph (c)(2)(ii) must commence by the last day of the calendar year immediately following the calendar year of the employee's death.

(iii) *Applicable percentage*—(A) *Contracts without pre-annuity starting date death benefits.* If, as described in paragraph (c)(2)(iv) of this A-17, the contract does not provide for a pre-annuity starting date non-spousal death benefit, the applicable percentage is the percentage described in the table in A-2(c) of this section.

(B) *Contracts with set beneficiary designation.* If the contract provides for a set non-spousal beneficiary designation as described in paragraph (c)(2)(v) (and is not a contract described in paragraph (c)(2)(iv)) of this A-17, the applicable percentage is the percentage described in the table set forth in paragraph (c)(2)(iii)(D) of this A-17. A contract is still considered to provide for a set beneficiary designation even if the surviving spouse becomes the sole beneficiary before the annuity starting date. In such a case, the requirements of paragraph (c)(1) of this A-17 apply and not the requirements of this paragraph (c)(2).

(C) *Contracts providing for return of premium.* If the contract provides for a return of premium as described in paragraph (c)(4) of this A-17, the applicable percentage is 0.

(D) *Applicable percentage table.* The applicable percentage is based on the adjusted employee/beneficiary age difference, determined in the same manner as in A-2(c) of this section.

Adjusted employee/beneficiary age difference	Applicable percentage
2 years or less	100%
3	88%
4	78%
5	70%
6	63%
7	57%
8	52%
9	48%
10	44%
11	41%
12	38%
13	36%

Adjusted employee/beneficiary age difference	Applicable percentage
14	34%
15	32%
16	30%
17	28%
18	27%
19	26%
20	25%
21	24%
22	23%
23	22%
24	21%
25 and greater	20%

(iv) *No pre-annuity starting date non-spousal death benefit.* A contract is described in this paragraph (c)(2)(iv) if the contract provides that no benefit is permitted to be paid to a beneficiary other than the employee's surviving spouse after the employee's death—

(A) In any case in which the employee dies before the annuity starting date under the contract; and

(B) In any case in which the employee selects an annuity starting date that is earlier than the specified annuity starting date under the contract and the employee dies less than 90 days after making that election.

(v) *Contracts permitting set non-spousal beneficiary designation.* A contract is described in this paragraph (c)(2)(v) if the contract provides that if the beneficiary under the contract is not the employee's surviving spouse, benefits are payable to the beneficiary only if the beneficiary was irrevocably designated on or before the later of the date of purchase or the employee's required beginning date.

(3) *Calculation of early annuity payments.* For purposes of paragraphs (c)(1)(ii) and (c)(2)(ii) of this A-17, to the extent the contract does not provide an option for the employee to select an annuity starting date that is earlier than the date on which the annuity payable to the employee would have commenced under the contract if the employee had not died, the contract must provide a way to determine the periodic annuity payment that would have been payable if the employee were to have an option to accelerate the payments and the payments had commenced to the employee immediately prior to the date that benefit payments to the surviving spouse or designated beneficiary commence.

(4) *Return of premiums*—(i) *In general.* In lieu of a life annuity payable to a designated beneficiary under paragraph (c)(1) or (2) of this A-17, a QLAC is permitted to provide for a benefit to be paid to a beneficiary after the death of the employee in an amount equal to excess of—

(A) The premium payments made with respect to the QLAC over

(B) The payments already made under the QLAC.

(ii) *Payments after death of surviving spouse.* If a QLAC is providing a life annuity to a surviving spouse (or will provide a life annuity to a surviving spouse) under paragraph (c)(1) of this A-17, it is also permitted to provide for a benefit paid to a beneficiary after the death of both the employee and the spouse in an amount equal to the excess of—

(A) The premium payments made with respect to the QLAC over

(B) The payments already made under the QLAC.

(iii) *Other rules*—(A) *Timing of return of premium payment following death of employee.* A return of premium payment under this paragraph (c)(4) must be paid no later than the end of the calendar year following the calendar year in which the employee dies. If the employee's death is after the required beginning date, the return of premium payment is treated as a required minimum distribution for the year in which it is paid and is not eligible for rollover.

(B) *Timing of return of premium payment following death of surviving spouse receiving life annuity.* If the return of premium payment is paid after the death of a surviving spouse who is receiving a life annuity (or after the death of a surviving spouse who has not yet commenced receiving a life annuity after the death of the employee), the return of premium payment under this paragraph (c)(4) must be made no later than the end of the calendar year following the calendar year in which the surviving spouse dies. If the surviving spouse's death is after the required beginning date for the surviving spouse, then the return of premium payment is treated as a required minimum distribution for the year in which it is paid and is not eligible for rollover.

(5) *Multiple beneficiaries.* If an employee has more than one designated beneficiary under a QLAC, the rules in A-2(a) of § 1.401(a)(9)-8 apply for purposes of paragraphs (c)(1) and (c)(2) of this A-17.

(d) *Rules of application*—(1) *Rules relating to premiums*—(i) *Reliance on representations.* For purposes of the limitation on premiums described in paragraphs (b)(2) and (3) of this A-17, unless the plan administrator has actual knowledge to the contrary, the plan administrator may rely on an employee's representation (made in writing or such other form as may be prescribed by the Commissioner) of the

amount of the premiums described in paragraphs (b)(2)(ii)(B) and (b)(3)(ii)(B) of this A-17, but only with respect to premiums that are not paid under a plan, annuity, or contract that is maintained by the employer or an entity that is treated as a single employer with the employer under section 414(b), (c), (m), or (o).

(ii) *Consequences of excess premiums*—(A) *General Rule.* If an annuity contract fails to be a QLAC solely because a premium for the contract exceeds the limits under paragraph (b) of this A-17, then the contract is not a QLAC beginning on the date that premium payment is made unless the excess premium is returned to the non-QLAC portion of the employee's account in accordance with paragraph (d)(1)(ii)(B) of this A-17. If the contract fails to be a QLAC, then the value of the contract may not be disregarded under A-3(d) of § 1.401(a)(9)-5 as of the date on which the contract ceases to be a QLAC.

(B) *Correction in year following year of excess.* If the excess premium is returned (either in cash or in the form of a contract that is not intended to be a QLAC) to the non-QLAC portion of the employee's account by the end of the calendar year following the calendar year in which the excess premium was originally paid, then the contract will not be treated as exceeding the limits under paragraph (b) of this A-17 at any time, and the value of the contract will not be included in the employee's account balance under A-3(d) of § 1.401(a)(9)-5. If the excess premium (including the fair market value of an annuity contract that is not intended to be a QLAC, if applicable) is returned to the non-QLAC portion of the employee's account after the last valuation date for the calendar year in which the excess premium was originally paid, then the employee's account balance for that calendar year must be increased to reflect that excess premium in the same manner as an employee's account balance is increased under A-2 of § 1.401(a)(9)-7 to reflect a rollover received after the last valuation date.

(C) *Return of excess premium not a commutation benefit.* If the excess premium is returned to the non-QLAC portion of the employee's account as described in paragraph (d)(1)(ii)(B) of this A-17, it will not be treated as a violation of the requirement in paragraph (a)(4) of this A-17 that the contract not provide a commutation benefit.

(iii) *Application of 25-percent limit.* For purposes of the 25-percent limit under paragraph (b)(3) of this A-17, an employee's account balance on the date on which premiums for a contract are paid is the account balance as of the last valuation date preceding the date of the premium payment, adjusted as follows. The account balance is increased for contributions allocated to the account during the period that begins after the valuation date and ends before the date the premium is paid and decreased for distributions made from the account during that period.

(2) *Dollar and age limitations subject to adjustments*—(i) *Dollar limitation.* In the case of calendar years beginning on or after January 1, 2015, the $125,000 amount under paragraph (b)(2)(i) of this A-17 will be adjusted at the same time and in the same manner as the limits are adjusted under section 415(d), except that the base period shall be the calendar quarter beginning July 1, 2013, and any increase under this paragraph (d)(2)(i) that is not a multiple of $10,000 will be rounded to the next lowest multiple of $10,000.

(ii) *Age limitation.* The maximum age set forth in paragraph (a)(2) of this A-17 may be adjusted to reflect changes in mortality, with any such adjusted age to be prescribed by the Commissioner in revenue rulings, notices, or other guidance published in the Internal Revenue Bulletin and made available by the Superintendent of Documents, U.S. Government Printing Office, Washington, DC 20402 and on the IRS Web site at http://www.irs.gov.

(iii) *Prospective application of adjustments.* If a contract fails to be a QLAC because it does not satisfy the dollar limitation in paragraph (b)(2) of this A-17 or the age limitation in paragraph (a)(2) of this A-17, any subsequent adjustment that is made pursuant to paragraph (d)(2)(i) or paragraph (d)(2)(ii) of this A-17 will not cause the contract to become a QLAC.

(3) *Determination of whether contract is intended to be a QLAC*—(i) *Structural deficiency.* If a contract fails to be a QLAC at any time for a reason other than an excess premium described in paragraph (d)(1)(ii) of this A-17, then as of the date of purchase the contract will not be treated as a QLAC (for purposes of A-3(d) of § 1.401(a)(9)-5) or as a contract that is intended to be a QLAC (for purposes of paragraph (b) of this A-17).

(ii) *Roth IRAs.* A contract that is purchased under a Roth IRA is not treated as a contract that is intended to be a QLAC for purposes of applying the dollar and percentage limitation rules in paragraphs (b)(2)(ii)(B) and (b)(3)(ii)(B) of this A-17. See A-14(d) of § 1.408A-6. If a QLAC is purchased or held under a plan, annuity, account, or traditional IRA, and that contract is later rolled over or converted to a Roth IRA, the contract is not treated as a contract that is intended to be a QLAC after the date of the rollover or conversion. Thus, premiums paid with respect to the contract will not be taken into account under paragraph (b)(2)(ii)(B) or paragraph (b)(3)(ii)(B) of this A-17 after the date of the rollover or conversion.

Reg. § 1.401(a)(9)-6

(4) *Certain contracts not treated as similar contracts*—(i) *Participating annuity contract.* An annuity contract is not treated as a contract described in paragraph (a)(7) of this A-17 merely because it provides for the payment of dividends described in A-14(c)(3) of §1.401(a)(9)-6.

(ii) *Contracts with cost-of-living adjustments.* An annuity contract is not treated as a contract described in paragraph (a)(7) of this A-17 merely because it provides for a cost-of-living adjustment as described in A-14(b) of §1.401(a)(9)-6.

(5) *Group annuity contract certificates.* The requirement under paragraph (a)(6) of this A-17 that the contract state that it is intended to be a QLAC when issued is satisfied if a certificate is issued under a group annuity contract and the certificate, when issued, states that the employee's interest under the group annuity contract is intended to be a QLAC.

(e) *Effective/applicability date*—(1) *General applicability date.* This A-17 and §1.403(b)-6(e)(9) apply to contracts purchased on or after July 2, 2014. If on or after July 2, 2014, an existing contract is exchanged for a contract that satisfies the requirements of this A-17, the new contract will be treated as purchased on the date of the exchange and the fair market value of the contract that is exchanged for a QLAC will be treated as a premium paid with respect to the QLAC.

(2) *Delayed applicability date for requirement that contract state that it is intended to be QLAC.* An annuity contract purchased before January 1, 2016, will not fail to be a QLAC merely because the contract does not satisfy the requirement of paragraph (a)(6) of this A-17, provided that—

(i) When the contract (or a certificate under a group annuity contract) is issued, the employee is notified that the annuity contract is intended to be a QLAC; and

(ii) The contract is amended (or a rider, endorsement or amendment to the certificate is issued) no later than December 31, 2016, to state that the annuity contract is intended to be a QLAC. [Reg. §1.401(a)(9)-6.]

☐ *[T.D. 9130, 6-14-2004 (corrected 11-22-2004). Amended by T.D. 9459, 9-4-2009 T.D. 9673, 7-1-2014 (corrected 8-5-2014) and T.D. 9930, 11-5-2020.]*

[Reg. §1.401(a)(9)-7]

§1.401(a)(9)-7. Rollovers and transfers.—
Q-1. If an amount is distributed by one plan (distributing plan) and is rolled over to another plan, is the required minimum distribution under the distributing plan affected by the rollover?

A-1. No, if an amount is distributed by one plan and is rolled over to another plan, the amount distributed is still treated as a distribution by the distributing plan for purposes of section 401(a)(9), notwithstanding the rollover. See A-1 of §1.402(c)-2 for the definition of a rollover and A-7 of §1.402(c)-2 for rules for determining the portion of any distribution that is not eligible for rollover because it is a required minimum distribution.

Q-2. If an amount is distributed by one plan (distributing plan) and is rolled over to another plan (receiving plan), how are the benefit and the required minimum distribution under the receiving plan affected?

A-2. If an amount is distributed by one plan (distributing plan) and is rolled over to another plan (receiving plan), the benefit of the employee under the receiving plan is increased by the amount rolled over for purposes of determining the required minimum distribution for the calendar year immediately following the calendar year in which the amount rolled over is distributed. If the amount rolled over is received after the last valuation date in the calendar year under the receiving plan, the benefit of the employee as of such valuation date, adjusted in accordance with A-3 of §1.401(a)(9)-5, will be increased by the rollover amount valued as of the date of receipt. In addition, if the amount rolled over is received in a different calendar year from the calendar year in which it is distributed, the amount rolled over is deemed to have been received by the receiving plan in the calendar year in which it was distributed.

Q-3. In the case of a transfer of an amount of an employee's benefit from one plan (transferor plan) to another plan (transferee plan), are there any special rules for satisfying section 401(a)(9) or determining the employee's benefit under the transferor plan?

A-3. (a) In the case of a transfer of an amount of an employee's benefit from one plan (transferor plan) to another (transferee plan), the transfer is not treated as a distribution by the transferor plan for purposes of section 401(a)(9). Instead, the benefit of the employee under the transferor plan is decreased by the amount transferred. However, if any portion of an employee's benefit is transferred in a distribution calendar year with respect to that employee, in order to *satisfy section 401(a)(9), the transferor plan must determine the* amount of the required minimum distribution with respect to that employee for the calendar year of the transfer using the employee's benefit under the transferor plan before the transfer. Additionally, if any portion of an employee's benefit is transferred in the employee's

second distribution calendar year but on or before the employee's required beginning date, in order to satisfy section 401(a)(9), the transferor plan must determine the amount of the minimum distribution requirement for the employee's first distribution calendar year based on the employee's benefit under the transferor plan before the transfer. The transferor plan may satisfy the minimum distribution requirement for the calendar year of the transfer (and the prior year if applicable) by segregating the amount which must be distributed from the employee's benefit and not transferring that amount. Such amount may be retained by the transferor plan and must be distributed on or before the date required under section 401(a)(9).

(b) For purposes of determining any required minimum distribution for the calendar year immediately following the calendar year in which the transfer occurs, in the case of a transfer after the last valuation date for the calendar year of the transfer under the transferor plan, the benefit of the employee as of such valuation date, adjusted in accordance with A-3 of §1.401(a)(9)-5, will be decreased by the amount transferred, valued as of the date of the transfer.

Q-4. If an amount of an employee's benefit is transferred from one plan (transferor plan) to another plan (transferee plan), how are the benefit and the required minimum distribution under the transferee plan affected?

A-4. In the case of a transfer from one plan (transferor plan) to another (transferee plan), the benefit of the employee under the transferee plan is increased by the amount transferred in the same manner as if it were a plan receiving a rollover contribution under A-2 of this section.

Q-5. How is a spinoff, merger or consolidation (as defined in §1.414(l)-1) treated for purposes of determining an employee's benefit and required minimum distribution under section 401(a)(9)?

A-5. For purposes of determining an employee's benefit and required minimum distribution under section 401(a)(9), a spinoff, a merger, or a consolidation (as defined in §1.414(l)-1) will be treated as a transfer of the benefits of the employees involved. Consequently, the benefit and required minimum distribution of each employee involved under the transferor and transferee plans will be determined in accordance with A-3 and A-4 of this section. [Reg. §1.401(a)(9)-7.]

☐ *[T.D. 8987, 4-16-2002.]*

[Reg. §1.401(a)(9)-8]

§1.401(a)(9)-8. Special rules.—
Q-1. What distribution rules apply if an employee is a participant in more than one plan?

A-1. If an employee is a participant in more than one plan, the plans in which the employee participates are not permitted to be aggregated for purposes of testing whether the distribution requirements of section 401(a)(9) are met. The distribution of the benefit of the employee under each plan must separately meet the requirements of section 401(a)(9). For this purpose, a plan described in section 414(k) is treated as two separate plans, a defined contribution plan to the extent benefits are based on an individual account and a defined benefit plan with respect to the remaining benefits.

Q-2. If an employee's benefit under a defined contribution plan is divided into separate accounts (or under a defined benefit plan is divided into segregated shares), do the distribution rules in section 401(a)(9) and these regulations apply separately to each separate account?

A-2. (a) *Defined contribution plan.* (1) Except as otherwise provided in this A-2, if an employee's benefit under a defined contribution plan is divided into separate accounts under the plan, the separate accounts will be aggregated for purposes of satisfying the rules in section 401(a)(9). Thus, except as otherwise provided in this A-2, all separate accounts, including a separate account for employee contributions under section 72(d)(2), will be aggregated for purposes of section 401(a)(9).

(2) If the employee's benefit in a defined contribution plan is divided into separate accounts and the beneficiaries with respect to one separate account differ from the beneficiaries with respect to the other separate accounts of the employee under the plan, for years subsequent to the calendar year containing the date as of which the separate accounts were established, or date of death if later, such separate account under the plan is not aggregated with the other separate accounts under the plan in order to determine whether the distributions from such separate account under the plan satisfy section 401(a)(9). Instead, the rules in section 401(a)(9) separately apply to such separate account under the plan. However, the applicable distribution period for each such separate account is determined disregarding the other beneficiaries of the employee's benefit only if the separate account is established on a date no later than the last day of the year following the calendar year of the employee's death. For example, if, in the case of a distribution described in section 401(a)(9)(B)(iii) and (iv), the only beneficiary of a separate account under the plan established on a date no later than the end of the year

following the calendar year of the employee's death is the employee's surviving spouse, and beneficiaries other than the surviving spouse are designated with respect to the other separate accounts with respect to the employee, distribution of the spouse's separate account under the plan need not commence until the date determined under the first sentence in A-3(b) of §1.401(a)(9)-3, even if distribution of the other separate accounts under the plan must commence at an earlier date. Similarly, in the case of a distribution after the death of an employee to which section 401(a)(9)(B)(i) does not apply, distribution from a separate account of an employee established on a date no later than the end of the year following the year of the employee's death may be made over a beneficiary's life expectancy in accordance with section 401(a)(9)(B)(iii) and (iv) even though distributions from other separate accounts under the plan with different beneficiaries are being made in accordance with the 5-year rule in section 401(a)(9)(B)(ii).

(3) A portion of an employee's account balance under a defined contribution plan is permitted to be used to purchase an annuity contract while another portion stays in the account. In that case, the remaining account under the plan must be distributed in accordance with §1.401(a)(9)-5 in order to satisfy section 401(a)(9) and the annuity payments under the annuity contract must satisfy §1.401(a)(9)-6 in order to satisfy section 401(a)(9).

(b) *Defined benefit plan.* The rules of paragraph (a)(2) and (3) of this A-2 also apply to benefits under a defined benefit plan where the benefits under the plan are separated into separate identifiable components which are separately distributed.

Q-3. What are separate accounts for purposes of section 401(a)(9)?

A-3. For purposes of section 401(a)(9), separate accounts in an employee's account are separate portions of an employee's benefit reflecting the separate interests of the employee's beneficiaries under the plan as of the date of the employee's death for which separate accounting is maintained. The separate accounting must allocate all post-death investment gains and losses, contributions, and forfeitures, for the period prior to the establishment of the separate accounts on a pro rata basis in a reasonable and consistent manner among the separate accounts. However, once the separate accounts are actually established, the separate accounting can provide for separate investments for each separate account under which gains and losses from the investment of the account are only allocated to that account, or investment gain or losses can continue to be allocated among the separate accounts on a pro rata basis. A separate accounting must allocate any post-death distribution to the separate account of the beneficiary receiving that distribution.

Q-4. If a distribution is required to be made to an employee by section 401(a)(9)(A) or is required to be made to a surviving spouse under section 401(a)(9)(B), must the distribution be made even if the employee, or spouse where applicable, fails to consent to a distribution while a benefit is immediately distributable?

A-4. Yes, section 411(a)(11) and section 417(e) (see §§1.411(a)(11)-1(c)(2) and 1.417(e)-1(c) require employee and spousal consent to certain distributions of plan benefits while such benefits are immediately distributable. If an employee's normal retirement age is later than the employee's required beginning date and, therefore, benefits are still immediately distributable, the plan must, nevertheless, distribute plan benefits to the employee (or where applicable, to the spouse) in a manner that satisfies the requirements of section 401(a)(9). Section 401(a)(9) must be satisfied even though the employee (or spouse, where applicable) fails to consent to the distribution. In such a case, the plan may distribute in the form of a qualified joint and survivor annuity (QJSA) or in the form of a qualified preretirement survivor annuity (QPSA), as applicable, and the consent requirements of sections 411(a)(11) and 417(e) are deemed to be satisfied if the plan has made reasonable efforts to obtain consent from the employee (or spouse if applicable) and if the distribution otherwise meets the requirements of section 417. If, because of section 401(a)(11)(B), the plan is not required to distribute in the form of a QJSA to a employee or a QPSA to a surviving spouse, the plan may distribute the required minimum distribution amount to satisfy section 401(a)(9) and the consent requirements of sections 411(a)(11) and 417(e) are deemed to be satisfied if the plan has made reasonable efforts to obtain consent from the employee (or spouse if applicable) and if the distribution otherwise meets the requirements of section 417.

Q-5. Who is an employee's spouse or surviving spouse for purposes of section 401(a)(9)?

A-5. Except as otherwise provided in A-6(a) of this section (in the case of distributions of a portion of an employee's benefit payable to a former spouse of an employee pursuant to a qualified domestic relations order), for purposes of section 401(a)(9), an individual is a spouse or surviving spouse of an employee if such individual is treated as the employee's spouse under applicable state law. In the case of distributions after the death of an employee, for purposes of

determining whether, under the life expectancy rule in section 401(a)(9)(B)(iii) and (iv), the provisions of section 401(a)(9)(B)(iv) apply, the spouse of the employee is determined as of the date of death of the employee.

Q-6. In order to satisfy section 401(a)(9), are there any special rules which apply to the distribution of all or a portion of an employee's benefit payable to an alternate payee pursuant to a qualified domestic relations order as defined in section 414(p) (QDRO)?

A-6. (a) A former spouse to whom all or a portion of the employee's benefit is payable pursuant to a QDRO will be treated as a spouse (including a surviving spouse) of the employee for purposes of section 401(a)(9), including the minimum distribution incidental benefit requirement, regardless of whether the QDRO specifically provides that the former spouse is treated as the spouse for purposes of sections 401(a)(11) and 417.

(b)(1) If a QDRO provides that an employee's benefit is to be divided and a portion is to be allocated to an alternate payee, such portion will be treated as a separate account (or segregated share) which separately must satisfy the requirements of section 401(a)(9) and may not be aggregated with other separate accounts (or segregated shares) of the employee for purposes of satisfying section 401(a)(9). Except as otherwise provided in paragraph (b)(2) of this A-6, distribution of such separate account allocated to an alternate payee pursuant to a QDRO must be made in accordance with section 401(a)(9). For example in general, distribution of such account will satisfy section 401(a)(9)(A) if required minimum distributions from such account during the employee's lifetime begin not later than the employee's required beginning date and the required minimum distribution is determined in accordance with §1.401(a)(9)-5 for each distribution calendar year (using an applicable distribution period determined under A-4 of §1.401(a)(9)-5 for the employee in the distribution calendar year either using the Uniform Lifetime Table in §1.401(a)(9)-9(c) or using the joint life expectancy of the employee and a spousal alternate payee in the distribution calendar year if the spousal alternate payee is more than 10 years younger than the employee). The determination of whether distribution from such account after the death of the employee to the alternate payee will be made in accordance with section 401(a)(9)(B)(i) or section 401(a)(9)(B)(ii) or (iii) and (iv) will depend on whether distributions have begun as determined under A-6 of §1.401(a)(9)-2 (which provides, in general, that distributions are not treated as having begun until the employee's required beginning date even though payments may actually have begun before that date). For example, if the alternate payee dies before the employee and distribution of the separate account allocated to the alternate payee pursuant to the QDRO is to be made to the alternate payee's beneficiary, such beneficiary may be treated as a designated beneficiary for purposes of determining the minimum distribution required from such account after the death of the employee if the beneficiary of the alternate payee is an individual and if such beneficiary is a beneficiary under the plan or specified to or in the plan. Specification in or pursuant to the QDRO is treated as specification to the plan.

(2) Distribution of the separate account allocated to an alternate payee pursuant to a QDRO will satisfy the requirements of section 401(a)(9)(A)(ii) if such account is to be distributed, beginning not later than the employee's required beginning date, over the life of the alternate payee (or over a period not extending beyond the life expectancy of the alternate payee). Also, if the plan permits the employee to elect whether distribution upon the death of the employee will be made in accordance with the 5-year rule in section 401(a)(9)(B)(ii) or the life expectancy rule in section 401(a)(9)(B)(iii) and (iv) pursuant to A-4(c) of §1.401(a)(9)-3, such election is to be made only by the alternate payee for purposes of distributing the separate account allocated to the alternate payee pursuant to the QDRO. If the alternate payee dies after distribution of the separate account allocated to the alternate payee pursuant to a QDRO has begun (determined under A-6 of §1.401(a)(9)-2) but before the employee dies, distribution of the remaining portion of that portion of the benefit allocated to the alternate payee must be made in accordance with the rules in §1.401(a)(9)-5 or 1.401(a)(9)-6 for distributions during the life of the employee. Only after the death of the employee is the amount of the required minimum distribution determined in accordance with the rules of section 401(a)(9)(B).

(c) If a QDRO does not provide that an employee's benefit is to be divided but provides that a portion of an employee's benefit (otherwise payable to the employee) is to be paid to an alternate payee, such portion will not be treated as a separate account (or segregated share) of the employee. Instead, such portion will be aggregated with any amount distributed to the employee and will be treated as having been distributed to the employee for purposes of determining whether section 401(a)(9) has been satisfied with respect to that employee.

Q-7. Will a plan fail to satisfy section 401(a)(9) merely because it fails to distribute an amount otherwise required to be distributed by section 401(a)(9) during the period in which the issue of whether a domestic relations order is a QDRO is being determined?

A-7. A plan will not fail to satisfy section 401(a)(9) merely because it fails to distribute an amount otherwise required to be distributed by section 401(a)(9) during the period in which the issue of whether a domestic relations order is a QDRO is being determined pursuant to section 414(p)(7), provided that the period does not extend beyond the 18-month period described in section 414(p)(7)(E). To the extent that a distribution otherwise required under section 401(a)(9) is not made during this period, any segregated amounts, as defined in section 414(p)(7)(A), will be treated as though the amounts are not vested during the period and any distributions with respect to such amounts must be made under the relevant rules for nonvested benefits described in either A-8 of §1.401(a)(9)-5 or A-6 of §1.401(a)(9)-6, as applicable.

Q-8. Will a plan fail to satisfy section 401(a)(9) where an individual's distribution from the plan is less than the amount otherwise required to satisfy section 401(a)(9) because distributions were being paid under an annuity contract issued by a life insurance company in state insurer delinquency proceedings and have been reduced or suspended by reasons of such state proceedings?

A-8. A plan will not fail to satisfy section 401(a)(9) merely because an individual's distribution from the plan is less than the amount otherwise required to satisfy section 401(a)(9) because distributions were being paid under an annuity contract issued by a life insurance company in state insurer delinquency proceedings and have been reduced or suspended by reasons of such state proceedings. To the extent that a distribution otherwise required under section 401(a)(9) is not made during the state insurer delinquency proceedings, this amount and any additional amount accrued during this period will be treated as though such amounts are not vested during the period and any distributions with respect to such amounts must be made under the relevant rules for nonvested benefits described in either A-8 of §1.401(a)(9)-5 or A-6 of §1.401(a)(9)-6, as applicable.

Q-9. Will a plan fail to qualify as a pension plan within the meaning of section 401(a) solely because the plan permits distributions to commence to an employee on or after April 1 of the calendar year following the calendar year in which the employee attains age 70½ even though the employee has not retired or attained the normal retirement age under the plan as of the date on which such distributions commence?

A-9. No, a plan will not fail to qualify as a pension plan within the meaning of section 401(a) solely because the plan permits distributions to commence to an employee on or after April 1 of the calendar year following the calendar year in which the employee attains age 70½ even though the employee has not retired or attained the normal retirement age under the plan as of the date on which such distributions commence. This rule applies without regard to whether the employee is a 5-percent owner with respect to the plan year ending in the calendar year in which distributions commence.

Q-10. Is the distribution of an annuity contract a distribution for purposes of section 401(a)(9)?

A-10. No, the distribution of an annuity contract is not a distribution for purposes of section 401(a)(9).

Q-11. Will a payment by a plan after the death of an employee fail to be treated as a distribution for purposes of section 401(a)(9) solely because it is made to an estate or a trust?

A-11. A payment by a plan after the death of an employee will not fail to be treated as a distribution for purposes of section 401(a)(9) solely because it is made to an estate or a trust. As a result, the estate or trust which receives a payment from a plan after the death of an employee need not distribute the amount of such payment to the beneficiaries of the estate or trust in accordance with section 401(a)(9)(B). Pursuant to A-3 of §1.401(a)(9)-4, an estate may not be a designated beneficiary. Thus, pursuant to A-4 of §1.401(a)(9)-3, distribution to the estate must satisfy the 5-year rule in section 401(a)(9)(B)(iii) if the distribution to the employee had not begun (as defined in A-6 of §1.401(a)(9)-2) as of the employee's date of death. However, see A-5 and A-6 of §1.401(a)(9)-4 for provisions under which beneficiaries of a trust with respect to the trust's interest in an employee's benefit are treated as having been designated as beneficiaries of the employee under the plan.

Q-12. Will a plan fail to satisfy section 411(d)(6) if the plan is amended to eliminate the availability of an optional form of benefit to the extent that the optional form does not satisfy section 401(a)(9)?

A-12. No, pursuant to section 411(d)(6)(B), a plan will not fail to satisfy section 411(d)(6) merely because the plan is amended to eliminate the availability of an optional form of benefit to the extent that the optional form does not satisfy section 401(a)(9). (See also A-3 of §1.401(a)(9)-1, which requires a plan to provide that, notwithstanding any other plan provision, it will not distribute benefits under any option that does not satisfy section 401(a)(9).)

Q-13. Is a plan disqualified merely because it pays benefits under a designation made before January 1, 1984, in accordance with section 242(b)(2) of the Tax Equity and Fiscal Responsibility Act (TEFRA)?

A-13. No, even though the distribution requirements added by TEFRA were retroactively repealed by the Tax Reform Act of 1984 (TRA of 1984), the transitional election rule in section 242(b) of TEFRA was preserved. Satisfaction of the spousal consent requirements of section 417(a) and (e) (added by the Retirement Equity Act of 1984) will not be considered a revocation of the pre-1984 designation. However, sections 401(a)(11) and 417 must be satisfied with respect to any distribution subject to those sections. The election provided in section 242(b) of TEFRA is hereafter referred to as a section 242(b)(2) election.

Q-14. If an amount is transferred from one plan (transferor plan) to another plan (transferee plan), may the transferee plan distribute the amount transferred in accordance with a section 242(b)(2) election made under either the transferor plan or under the transferee plan?

A-14. (a) If an amount is transferred from one plan (transferor plan) to another plan (transferee plan), the amount transferred may be distributed in accordance with a section 242(b)(2) election made under the transferor plan if the employee did not elect to have the amount transferred and if the amount transferred is separately accounted for by the transferee plan. However, only the benefit attributable to the amount transferred, plus earnings thereon, may be distributed in accordance with the section 242(b)(2) election made under the transferor plan. If the employee elected to have the amount transferred, the transfer will be treated as a distribution and rollover of the amount transferred for purposes of this section.

(b) In the case in which an amount is transferred from one plan to another plan, the amount transferred may not be distributed in accordance with a section 242(b)(2) election made under the transferee plan. If a section 242(b)(2) election was made under the transferee plan, the amount transferred must be separately accounted for. If the amount transferred is not separately accounted for under the transferee plan, the section 242(b)(2) election under the transferee plan is revoked and section 401(a)(9) will apply to subsequent distributions by the transferee plan.

(c) A merger, spinoff, or consolidation, as defined in §1.414(l)-1(b), will be treated as a transfer for purposes of the section 242(b)(2) election.

Q-15. If an amount is distributed by one plan (distributing plan) and rolled over into another plan (receiving plan), may the receiving plan distribute the amount rolled over in accordance with a section 242(b)(2) election made under either the distributing plan or the receiving plan?

A-15. No, if an amount is distributed by one plan (distributing plan) and rolled over into another plan (receiving plan), the receiving plan must distribute the amount rolled over in accordance with section 401(a)(9) whether or not the employee made a section 242(b)(2) election under the distributing plan. Further, if the amount rolled over was not distributed in accordance with the election, the election under the distributing plan is revoked and section 401(a)(9) will apply to all subsequent distributions by the distributing plan. Finally, if the employee made a section 242(b)(2) election under the receiving plan and such election is still in effect, the amount rolled over must be separately accounted for under the receiving plan and distributed in accordance with section 401(a)(9). If amounts rolled over are not separately accounted for, any section 242(b)(2) election under the receiving plan is revoked and section 401(a)(9) will apply to subsequent distributions by the receiving plan.

Q-16. May a section 242(b)(2) election be revoked after the date by which distributions are required to commence in order to satisfy section 401(a)(9) and this section of the regulations?

A-16. Yes, a section 242(b)(2) election may be revoked after the date by which distributions are required to commence in order to satisfy section 401(a)(9) and this section of the regulations. However, if the section 242(b)(2) election is revoked after the date by which distributions are required to commence in order to satisfy section 401(a)(9) and this section of the regulations and the total amount of the distributions which would have been required to be made prior to the date of the revocation in order to satisfy section 401(a)(9), but for the section 242(b)(2) election, have not been made, the plan must distribute by the end of the calendar year following the calendar year in which the revocation occurs the total amount not yet distributed which was required to have been distributed to satisfy the requirements of section 401(a)(9) and continue distributions in accordance with such requirements. [Reg. §1.401(a)(9)-8.]

☐ [*T.D. 8987, 4-16-2002. Amended by T.D. 9130, 6-14-2004 and T.D. 9930, 11-5-2020.*]

[Reg. §1.401(a)(9)-9]

§1.401(a)(9)-9. Life expectancy and distribution period tables.—
(a) *In general.*—This section specifies the life expectancy and applicable distribution period tables that apply for purposes of determining

required minimum distributions under section 401(a)(9). Paragraphs (b), (c), and (d) of this section set forth these tables. Paragraph (e) of this section provides the mortality rates that are used to develop these tables. Paragraph (f) of this section provides applicability date rules.

(b) *Single Life Table.*—The following table, referred to as the Single Life Table, sets forth the life expectancy of an individual at each age.

Table 1 to Paragraph (b)

Age	Life expectancy
0	84.6
1	83.7
2	82.8
3	81.8
4	80.8
5	79.8
6	78.8
7	77.9
8	76.9
9	75.9
10	74.9
11	73.9
12	72.9
13	71.9
14	70.9
15	69.9
16	69.0
17	68.0
18	67.0
19	66.0
20	65.0
21	64.1
22	63.1
23	62.1
24	61.1
25	60.2
26	59.2
27	58.2
28	57.3
29	56.3
30	55.3
31	54.4
32	53.4
33	52.5
34	51.5
35	50.5
36	49.6
37	48.6
38	47.7
39	46.7
40	45.7
41	44.8
42	43.8
43	42.9
44	41.9
45	41.0
46	40.0
47	39.0
48	38.1
49	37.1
50	36.2
51	35.3
52	34.3
53	33.4

Age	Life expectancy
54	32.5
55	31.6
56	30.6
57	29.8
58	28.9
59	28.0
60	27.1
61	26.2
62	25.4
63	24.5
64	23.7
65	22.9
66	22.0
67	21.2
68	20.4
69	19.6
70	18.8
71	18.0
72	17.2
73	16.4
74	15.6
75	14.8
76	14.1
77	13.3
78	12.6
79	11.9
80	11.2
81	10.5
82	9.9
83	9.3
84	8.7
85	8.1
86	7.6
87	7.1
88	6.6
89	6.1
90	5.7
91	5.3
92	4.9
93	4.6
94	4.3
95	4.0
96	3.7
97	3.4
98	3.2
99	3.0
100	2.8
101	2.6
102	2.5
103	2.3
104	2.2
105	2.1
106	2.1
107	2.1
108	2.0
109	2.0
110	2.0
111	2.0
112	2.0
113	1.9

Age	Life expectancy
114	1.9
115	1.8
116	1.8
117	1.6
118	1.4
119	1.1
120 +	1.0

(c) *Uniform Lifetime Table.*—The following table, referred to as the Uniform Lifetime Table, sets forth the distribution period that applies for lifetime distributions to an employee in situations in which the employee's surviving spouse is not the sole designated beneficiary. This table is also used if the employee's surviving spouse is the sole designated beneficiary but is not more than 10 years younger than the employee.

Table 2 to Paragraph (c)

Age of employee	Distribution period
72	27.4
73	26.5
74	25.5
75	24.6
76	23.7
77	22.9
78	22.0
79	21.1
80	20.2
81	19.4
82	18.5
83	17.7
84	16.8
85	16.0
86	15.2
87	14.4
88	13.7
89	12.9

Age of employee	Distribution period
90	12.2
91	11.5
92	10.8
93	10.1
94	9.5
95	8.9
96	8.4
97	7.8
98	7.3
99	6.8
100	6.4
101	6.0
102	5.6
103	5.2
104	4.9
105	4.6
106	4.3
107	4.1
108	3.9
109	3.7
110	3.5
111	3.4
112	3.3
113	3.1
114	3.0
115	2.9
116	2.8
117	2.7
118	2.5
119	2.3
120 +	2.0

(d) *Joint and Last Survivor Table.*—The following table, referred to as the Joint and Last Survivor Table, is used for determining the joint and last survivor life expectancy of two individuals.

Table 3 to Paragraph (d)

Ages	0	1	2	3	4	5	6	7	8
0	91.9	91.4	91.0	90.5	90.1	89.7	89.4	89.0	88.7
1	91.4	90.9	90.4	90.0	89.5	89.1	88.8	88.4	88.1
2	91.0	90.4	89.9	89.4	89.0	88.5	88.1	87.8	87.4
3	90.5	90.0	89.4	88.9	88.4	88.0	87.6	87.1	86.8
4	90.1	89.5	89.0	88.4	87.9	87.4	87.0	86.6	86.2
5	89.7	89.1	88.6	88.0	87.4	86.9	86.5	86.0	85.6
6	89.4	88.8	88.1	87.6	87.0	86.5	85.9	85.5	85.0
7	89.0	88.4	87.8	87.1	86.6	86.0	85.5	84.9	84.5
8	88.7	88.1	87.4	86.8	86.2	85.6	85.0	84.5	83.9
9	88.4	87.8	87.1	86.4	85.8	85.2	84.6	84.0	83.5
10	88.2	87.5	86.8	86.1	85.4	84.8	84.2	83.6	83.0
11	87.9	87.2	86.5	85.8	85.1	84.4	83.8	83.2	82.6
12	87.7	87.0	86.2	85.5	84.8	84.1	83.4	82.8	82.2
13	87.5	86.7	86.0	85.2	84.5	83.8	83.1	82.4	81.8
14	87.3	86.5	85.7	85.0	84.2	83.5	82.8	82.1	81.4
15	87.1	86.3	85.5	84.7	84.0	83.2	82.5	81.8	81.1
16	86.9	86.1	85.3	84.5	83.7	83.0	82.2	81.5	80.8
17	86.8	86.0	85.1	84.3	83.5	82.7	82.0	81.2	80.5
18	86.6	85.8	85.0	84.1	83.3	82.5	81.7	81.0	80.2
19	86.5	85.7	84.8	84.0	83.1	82.3	81.5	80.7	80.0
20	86.4	85.5	84.7	83.8	83.0	82.2	81.3	80.5	79.8
21	86.2	85.4	84.5	83.7	82.8	82.0	81.2	80.3	79.5
22	86.1	85.3	84.4	83.5	82.7	81.8	81.0	80.2	79.3
23	86.0	85.2	84.3	83.4	82.5	81.7	80.8	80.0	79.2

Ages	0	1	2	3	4	5	6	7	8
24	85.9	85.1	84.2	83.3	82.4	81.6	80.7	79.8	79.0
25	85.9	85.0	84.1	83.2	82.3	81.4	80.6	79.7	78.8
26	85.8	84.9	84.0	83.1	82.2	81.3	80.4	79.6	78.7
27	85.7	84.8	83.9	83.0	82.1	81.2	80.3	79.4	78.6
28	85.6	84.7	83.8	82.9	82.0	81.1	80.2	79.3	78.4
29	85.6	84.7	83.8	82.8	81.9	81.0	80.1	79.2	78.3
30	85.5	84.6	83.7	82.8	81.8	80.9	80.0	79.1	78.2
31	85.4	84.6	83.6	82.7	81.8	80.9	79.9	79.0	78.1
32	85.4	84.5	83.6	82.6	81.7	80.8	79.9	78.9	78.0
33	85.3	84.5	83.5	82.6	81.6	80.7	79.8	78.9	77.9
34	85.3	84.4	83.5	82.5	81.6	80.7	79.7	78.8	77.9
35	85.3	84.4	83.4	82.5	81.5	80.6	79.7	78.7	77.8
36	85.2	84.3	83.4	82.4	81.5	80.5	79.6	78.7	77.7
37	85.2	84.3	83.3	82.4	81.4	80.5	79.5	78.6	77.7
38	85.2	84.3	83.3	82.3	81.4	80.4	79.5	78.6	77.6
39	85.1	84.2	83.3	82.3	81.4	80.4	79.5	78.5	77.6
40	85.1	84.2	83.2	82.3	81.3	80.4	79.4	78.5	77.5
41	85.1	84.2	83.2	82.2	81.3	80.3	79.4	78.4	77.5
42	85.0	84.1	83.2	82.2	81.3	80.3	79.3	78.4	77.4
43	85.0	84.1	83.1	82.2	81.2	80.3	79.3	78.3	77.4
44	85.0	84.1	83.1	82.2	81.2	80.2	79.3	78.3	77.3
45	85.0	84.1	83.1	82.1	81.2	80.2	79.2	78.3	77.3
46	84.9	84.0	83.1	82.1	81.1	80.2	79.2	78.2	77.3
47	84.9	84.0	83.1	82.1	81.1	80.2	79.2	78.2	77.3
48	84.9	84.0	83.0	82.1	81.1	80.1	79.2	78.2	77.2
49	84.9	84.0	83.0	82.1	81.1	80.1	79.1	78.2	77.2
50	84.9	84.0	83.0	82.0	81.1	80.1	79.1	78.1	77.2
51	84.8	84.0	83.0	82.0	81.0	80.1	79.1	78.1	77.2
52	84.8	83.9	83.0	82.0	81.0	80.1	79.1	78.1	77.1
53	84.8	83.9	83.0	82.0	81.0	80.0	79.1	78.1	77.1
54	84.8	83.9	82.9	82.0	81.0	80.0	79.0	78.1	77.1
55	84.8	83.9	82.9	82.0	81.0	80.0	79.0	78.1	77.1
56	84.8	83.9	82.9	81.9	81.0	80.0	79.0	78.0	77.1
57	84.8	83.9	82.9	81.9	81.0	80.0	79.0	78.0	77.0
58	84.8	83.9	82.9	81.9	80.9	80.0	79.0	78.0	77.0
59	84.7	83.9	82.9	81.9	80.9	80.0	79.0	78.0	77.0
60	84.7	83.8	82.9	81.9	80.9	79.9	79.0	78.0	77.0
61	84.7	83.8	82.9	81.9	80.9	79.9	79.0	78.0	77.0
62	84.7	83.8	82.9	81.9	80.9	79.9	78.9	78.0	77.0
63	84.7	83.8	82.9	81.9	80.9	79.9	78.9	78.0	77.0
64	84.7	83.8	82.8	81.9	80.9	79.9	78.9	77.9	77.0
65	84.7	83.8	82.8	81.9	80.9	79.9	78.9	77.9	77.0
66	84.7	83.8	82.8	81.9	80.9	79.9	78.9	77.9	76.9
67	84.7	83.8	82.8	81.9	80.9	79.9	78.9	77.9	76.9
68	84.7	83.8	82.8	81.8	80.9	79.9	78.9	77.9	76.9
69	84.7	83.8	82.8	81.8	80.9	79.9	78.9	77.9	76.9
70	84.7	83.8	82.8	81.8	80.9	79.9	78.9	77.9	76.9
71	84.7	83.8	82.8	81.8	80.9	79.9	78.9	77.9	76.9
72	84.7	83.8	82.8	81.8	80.9	79.9	78.9	77.9	76.9
73	84.6	83.8	82.8	81.8	80.8	79.9	78.9	77.9	76.9
74	84.6	83.8	82.8	81.8	80.8	79.9	78.9	77.9	76.9
75	84.6	83.8	82.8	81.8	80.8	79.9	78.9	77.9	76.9
76	84.6	83.8	82.8	81.8	80.8	79.9	78.9	77.9	76.9
77	84.6	83.8	82.8	81.8	80.8	79.8	78.9	77.9	76.9
78	84.6	83.8	82.8	81.8	80.8	79.8	78.9	77.9	76.9
79	84.6	83.8	82.8	81.8	80.8	79.8	78.9	77.9	76.9
80	84.6	83.8	82.8	81.8	80.8	79.8	78.9	77.9	76.9
81	84.6	83.8	82.8	81.8	80.8	79.8	78.9	77.9	76.9
82	84.6	83.8	82.8	81.8	80.8	79.8	78.9	77.9	76.9
83	84.6	83.7	82.8	81.8	80.8	79.8	78.9	77.9	76.9
84	84.6	83.7	82.8	81.8	80.8	79.8	78.9	77.9	76.9

Reg. §1.401(a)(9)-9(d)

Pension, Profit-Sharing, Stock Bonus Plans, Etc.
See p. 20,601 for regulations not amended to reflect law changes

Ages	0	1	2	3	4	5	6	7	8
85	84.6	83.7	82.8	81.8	80.8	79.8	78.8	77.9	76.9
86	84.6	83.7	82.8	81.8	80.8	79.8	78.8	77.9	76.9
87	84.6	83.7	82.8	81.8	80.8	79.8	78.8	77.9	76.9
88	84.6	83.7	82.8	81.8	80.8	79.8	78.8	77.9	76.9
89	84.6	83.7	82.8	81.8	80.8	79.8	78.8	77.9	76.9
90	84.6	83.7	82.8	81.8	80.8	79.8	78.8	77.9	76.9
91	84.6	83.7	82.8	81.8	80.8	79.8	78.8	77.9	76.9
92	84.6	83.7	82.8	81.8	80.8	79.8	78.8	77.9	76.9
93	84.6	83.7	82.8	81.8	80.8	79.8	78.8	77.9	76.9
94	84.6	83.7	82.8	81.8	80.8	79.8	78.8	77.9	76.9
95	84.6	83.7	82.8	81.8	80.8	79.8	78.8	77.9	76.9
96	84.6	83.7	82.8	81.8	80.8	79.8	78.8	77.9	76.9
97	84.6	83.7	82.8	81.8	80.8	79.8	78.8	77.9	76.9
98	84.6	83.7	82.8	81.8	80.8	79.8	78.8	77.9	76.9
99	84.6	83.7	82.8	81.8	80.8	79.8	78.8	77.9	76.9
100	84.6	83.7	82.8	81.8	80.8	79.8	78.8	77.9	76.9
101	84.6	83.7	82.8	81.8	80.8	79.8	78.8	77.9	76.9
102	84.6	83.7	82.8	81.8	80.8	79.8	78.8	77.9	76.9
103	84.6	83.7	82.8	81.8	80.8	79.8	78.8	77.9	76.9
104	84.6	83.7	82.8	81.8	80.8	79.8	78.8	77.9	76.9
105	84.6	83.7	82.8	81.8	80.8	79.8	78.8	77.9	76.9
106	84.6	83.7	82.8	81.8	80.8	79.8	78.8	77.9	76.9
107	84.6	83.7	82.8	81.8	80.8	79.8	78.8	77.9	76.9
108	84.6	83.7	82.8	81.8	80.8	79.8	78.8	77.9	76.9
109	84.6	83.7	82.8	81.8	80.8	79.8	78.8	77.9	76.9
110	84.6	83.7	82.8	81.8	80.8	79.8	78.8	77.9	76.9
111	84.6	83.7	82.8	81.8	80.8	79.8	78.8	77.9	76.9
112	84.6	83.7	82.8	81.8	80.8	79.8	78.8	77.9	76.9
113	84.6	83.7	82.8	81.8	80.8	79.8	78.8	77.9	76.9
114	84.6	83.7	82.8	81.8	80.8	79.8	78.8	77.9	76.9
115	84.6	83.7	82.8	81.8	80.8	79.8	78.8	77.9	76.9
116	84.6	83.7	82.8	81.8	80.8	79.8	78.8	77.9	76.9
117	84.6	83.7	82.8	81.8	80.8	79.8	78.8	77.9	76.9
118	84.6	83.7	82.8	81.8	80.8	79.8	78.8	77.9	76.9
119	84.6	83.7	82.8	81.8	80.8	79.8	78.8	77.9	76.9
120+	84.6	83.7	82.8	81.8	80.8	79.8	78.8	77.9	76.9

Ages	9	10	11	12	13	14	15	16	17
0	88.4	88.2	87.9	87.7	87.5	87.3	87.1	86.9	86.8
1	87.8	87.5	87.2	87.0	86.7	86.5	86.3	86.1	86.0
2	87.1	86.8	86.5	86.2	86.0	85.7	85.5	85.3	85.1
3	86.4	86.1	85.8	85.5	85.2	85.0	84.7	84.5	84.3
4	85.8	85.4	85.1	84.8	84.5	84.2	84.0	83.7	83.5
5	85.2	84.8	84.4	84.1	83.8	83.5	83.2	83.0	82.7
6	84.6	84.2	83.8	83.4	83.1	82.8	82.5	82.2	82.0
7	84.0	83.6	83.2	82.8	82.4	82.1	81.8	81.5	81.2
8	83.5	83.0	82.6	82.2	81.8	81.4	81.1	80.8	80.5
9	82.9	82.5	82.0	81.6	81.2	80.8	80.4	80.1	79.8
10	82.5	81.9	81.5	81.0	80.6	80.2	79.8	79.4	79.1
11	82.0	81.5	80.9	80.5	80.0	79.6	79.2	78.8	78.4
12	81.6	81.0	80.5	79.9	79.5	79.0	78.6	78.2	77.8
13	81.2	80.6	80.0	79.5	79.0	78.5	78.0	77.6	77.2
14	80.8	80.2	79.6	79.0	78.5	78.0	77.5	77.0	76.6
15	80.4	79.8	79.2	78.6	78.0	77.5	77.0	76.5	76.0
16	80.1	79.4	78.8	78.2	77.6	77.0	76.5	76.0	75.5
17	79.8	79.1	78.4	77.8	77.2	76.6	76.0	75.5	75.0
18	79.5	78.8	78.1	77.4	76.8	76.2	75.6	75.0	74.5
19	79.2	78.5	77.8	77.1	76.4	75.8	75.2	74.6	74.0
20	79.0	78.2	77.5	76.8	76.1	75.4	74.8	74.2	73.6
21	78.8	78.0	77.2	76.5	75.8	75.1	74.4	73.8	73.2

Reg. §1.401(a)(9)-9(d)

Ages	9	10	11	12	13	14	15	16	17
22	78.5	77.8	77.0	76.2	75.5	74.8	74.1	73.4	72.8
23	78.3	77.5	76.8	76.0	75.2	74.5	73.8	73.1	72.5
24	78.2	77.3	76.5	75.8	75.0	74.2	73.5	72.8	72.1
25	78.0	77.2	76.4	75.6	74.8	74.0	73.3	72.5	71.8
26	77.8	77.0	76.2	75.4	74.6	73.8	73.0	72.3	71.5
27	77.7	76.8	76.0	75.2	74.4	73.6	72.8	72.0	71.3
28	77.6	76.7	75.8	75.0	74.2	73.4	72.6	71.8	71.0
29	77.4	76.6	75.7	74.9	74.0	73.2	72.4	71.6	70.8
30	77.3	76.4	75.6	74.7	73.9	73.0	72.2	71.4	70.6
31	77.2	76.3	75.5	74.6	73.7	72.9	72.0	71.2	70.4
32	77.1	76.2	75.3	74.5	73.6	72.7	71.9	71.0	70.2
33	77.0	76.1	75.2	74.3	73.5	72.6	71.7	70.9	70.0
34	77.0	76.0	75.1	74.2	73.3	72.5	71.6	70.7	69.9
35	76.9	76.0	75.0	74.1	73.2	72.4	71.5	70.6	69.7
36	76.8	75.9	75.0	74.0	73.1	72.2	71.4	70.5	69.6
37	76.7	75.8	74.9	74.0	73.1	72.1	71.3	70.4	69.5
38	76.7	75.7	74.8	73.9	73.0	72.1	71.2	70.3	69.4
39	76.6	75.7	74.7	73.8	72.9	72.0	71.1	70.2	69.3
40	76.6	75.6	74.7	73.7	72.8	71.9	71.0	70.1	69.2
41	76.5	75.6	74.6	73.7	72.8	71.8	70.9	70.0	69.1
42	76.5	75.5	74.6	73.6	72.7	71.8	70.8	69.9	69.0
43	76.4	75.5	74.5	73.6	72.6	71.7	70.8	69.8	68.9
44	76.4	75.4	74.5	73.5	72.6	71.6	70.7	69.8	68.8
45	76.4	75.4	74.4	73.5	72.5	71.6	70.6	69.7	68.8
46	76.3	75.4	74.4	73.4	72.5	71.5	70.6	69.7	68.7
47	76.3	75.3	74.4	73.4	72.4	71.5	70.5	69.6	68.7
48	76.3	75.3	74.3	73.4	72.4	71.5	70.5	69.6	68.6
49	76.2	75.3	74.3	73.3	72.4	71.4	70.5	69.5	68.6
50	76.2	75.2	74.3	73.3	72.3	71.4	70.4	69.5	68.5
51	76.2	75.2	74.2	73.3	72.3	71.3	70.4	69.4	68.5
52	76.2	75.2	74.2	73.2	72.3	71.3	70.4	69.4	68.4
53	76.1	75.2	74.2	73.2	72.3	71.3	70.3	69.4	68.4
54	76.1	75.1	74.2	73.2	72.2	71.3	70.3	69.3	68.4
55	76.1	75.1	74.2	73.2	72.2	71.2	70.3	69.3	68.3
56	76.1	75.1	74.1	73.2	72.2	71.2	70.2	69.3	68.3
57	76.1	75.1	74.1	73.1	72.2	71.2	70.2	69.3	68.3
58	76.1	75.1	74.1	73.1	72.1	71.2	70.2	69.2	68.3
59	76.0	75.1	74.1	73.1	72.1	71.2	70.2	69.2	68.2
60	76.0	75.0	74.1	73.1	72.1	71.1	70.2	69.2	68.2
61	76.0	75.0	74.1	73.1	72.1	71.1	70.1	69.2	68.2
62	76.0	75.0	74.0	73.1	72.1	71.1	70.1	69.2	68.2
63	76.0	75.0	74.0	73.0	72.1	71.1	70.1	69.1	68.2
64	76.0	75.0	74.0	73.0	72.1	71.1	70.1	69.1	68.2
65	76.0	75.0	74.0	73.0	72.0	71.1	70.1	69.1	68.1
66	76.0	75.0	74.0	73.0	72.0	71.1	70.1	69.1	68.1
67	76.0	75.0	74.0	73.0	72.0	71.0	70.1	69.1	68.1
68	75.9	75.0	74.0	73.0	72.0	71.0	70.1	69.1	68.1
69	75.9	75.0	74.0	73.0	72.0	71.0	70.0	69.1	68.1
70	75.9	74.9	74.0	73.0	72.0	71.0	70.0	69.1	68.1
71	75.9	74.9	74.0	73.0	72.0	71.0	70.0	69.0	68.1
72	75.9	74.9	73.9	73.0	72.0	71.0	70.0	69.0	68.1
73	75.9	74.9	73.9	73.0	72.0	71.0	70.0	69.0	68.1
74	75.9	74.9	73.9	73.0	72.0	71.0	70.0	69.0	68.0
75	75.9	74.9	73.9	72.9	72.0	71.0	70.0	69.0	68.0
76	75.9	74.9	73.9	72.9	72.0	71.0	70.0	69.0	68.0
77	75.9	74.9	73.9	72.9	72.0	71.0	70.0	69.0	68.0
78	75.9	74.9	73.9	72.9	71.9	71.0	70.0	69.0	68.0
79	75.9	74.9	73.9	72.9	71.9	71.0	70.0	69.0	68.0
80	75.9	74.9	73.9	72.9	71.9	71.0	70.0	69.0	68.0
81	75.9	74.9	73.9	72.9	71.9	71.0	70.0	69.0	68.0
82	75.9	74.9	73.9	72.9	71.9	70.9	70.0	69.0	68.0

Ages	9	10	11	12	13	14	15	16	17
83	75.9	74.9	73.9	72.9	71.9	70.9	70.0	69.0	68.0
84	75.9	74.9	73.9	72.9	71.9	70.9	70.0	69.0	68.0
85	75.9	74.9	73.9	72.9	71.9	70.9	70.0	69.0	68.0
86	75.9	74.9	73.9	72.9	71.9	70.9	70.0	69.0	68.0
87	75.9	74.9	73.9	72.9	71.9	70.9	70.0	69.0	68.0
88	75.9	74.9	73.9	72.9	71.9	70.9	69.9	69.0	68.0
89	75.9	74.9	73.9	72.9	71.9	70.9	69.9	69.0	68.0
90	75.9	74.9	73.9	72.9	71.9	70.9	69.9	69.0	68.0
91	75.9	74.9	73.9	72.9	71.9	70.9	69.9	69.0	68.0
92	75.9	74.9	73.9	72.9	71.9	70.9	69.9	69.0	68.0
93	75.9	74.9	73.9	72.9	71.9	70.9	69.9	69.0	68.0
94	75.9	74.9	73.9	72.9	71.9	70.9	69.9	69.0	68.0
95	75.9	74.9	73.9	72.9	71.9	70.9	69.9	69.0	68.0
96	75.9	74.9	73.9	72.9	71.9	70.9	69.9	69.0	68.0
97	75.9	74.9	73.9	72.9	71.9	70.9	69.9	69.0	68.0
98	75.9	74.9	73.9	72.9	71.9	70.9	69.9	69.0	68.0
99	75.9	74.9	73.9	72.9	71.9	70.9	69.9	69.0	68.0
100	75.9	74.9	73.9	72.9	71.9	70.9	69.9	69.0	68.0
101	75.9	74.9	73.9	72.9	71.9	70.9	69.9	69.0	68.0
102	75.9	74.9	73.9	72.9	71.9	70.9	69.9	69.0	68.0
103	75.9	74.9	73.9	72.9	71.9	70.9	69.9	69.0	68.0
104	75.9	74.9	73.9	72.9	71.9	70.9	69.9	69.0	68.0
105	75.9	74.9	73.9	72.9	71.9	70.9	69.9	69.0	68.0
106	75.9	74.9	73.9	72.9	71.9	70.9	69.9	69.0	68.0
107	75.9	74.9	73.9	72.9	71.9	70.9	69.9	69.0	68.0
108	75.9	74.9	73.9	72.9	71.9	70.9	69.9	69.0	68.0
109	75.9	74.9	73.9	72.9	71.9	70.9	69.9	69.0	68.0
110	75.9	74.9	73.9	72.9	71.9	70.9	69.9	69.0	68.0
111	75.9	74.9	73.9	72.9	71.9	70.9	69.9	69.0	68.0
112	75.9	74.9	73.9	72.9	71.9	70.9	69.9	69.0	68.0
113	75.9	74.9	73.9	72.9	71.9	70.9	69.9	69.0	68.0
114	75.9	74.9	73.9	72.9	71.9	70.9	69.9	69.0	68.0
115	75.9	74.9	73.9	72.9	71.9	70.9	69.9	69.0	68.0
116	75.9	74.9	73.9	72.9	71.9	70.9	69.9	69.0	68.0
117	75.9	74.9	73.9	72.9	71.9	70.9	69.9	69.0	68.0
118	75.9	74.9	73.9	72.9	71.9	70.9	69.9	69.0	68.0
119	75.9	74.9	73.9	72.9	71.9	70.9	69.9	69.0	68.0
120+	75.9	74.9	73.9	72.9	71.9	70.9	69.9	69.0	68.0

Ages	18	19	20	21	22	23	24	25	26
0	86.6	86.5	86.4	86.2	86.1	86.0	85.9	85.9	85.8
1	85.8	85.7	85.5	85.4	85.3	85.2	85.1	85.0	84.9
2	85.0	84.8	84.7	84.5	84.4	84.3	84.2	84.1	84.0
3	84.1	84.0	83.8	83.7	83.5	83.4	83.3	83.2	83.1
4	83.3	83.1	83.0	82.8	82.7	82.5	82.4	82.3	82.2
5	82.5	82.3	82.2	82.0	81.8	81.7	81.6	81.4	81.3
6	81.7	81.5	81.3	81.2	81.0	80.8	80.7	80.6	80.4
7	81.0	80.7	80.5	80.3	80.2	80.0	79.8	79.7	79.6
8	80.2	80.0	79.8	79.5	79.3	79.2	79.0	78.8	78.7
9	79.5	79.2	79.0	78.8	78.5	78.3	78.2	78.0	77.8
10	78.8	78.5	78.2	78.0	77.8	77.5	77.3	77.2	77.0
11	78.1	77.8	77.5	77.2	77.0	76.8	76.5	76.4	76.2
12	77.4	77.1	76.8	76.5	76.2	76.0	75.8	75.6	75.4
13	76.8	76.4	76.1	75.8	75.5	75.2	75.0	74.8	74.6
14	76.2	75.8	75.4	75.1	74.8	74.5	74.2	74.0	73.8
15	75.6	75.2	74.8	74.4	74.1	73.8	73.5	73.3	73.0
16	75.0	74.6	74.2	73.8	73.4	73.1	72.8	72.5	72.3
17	74.5	74.0	73.6	73.2	72.8	72.5	72.1	71.8	71.5
18	74.0	73.5	73.0	72.6	72.2	71.8	71.5	71.1	70.8
19	73.5	73.0	72.5	72.0	71.6	71.2	70.8	70.5	70.1

Ages	18	19	20	21	22	23	24	25	26
20	73.0	72.5	72.0	71.5	71.0	70.6	70.2	69.8	69.5
21	72.6	72.0	71.5	71.0	70.5	70.0	69.6	69.2	68.8
22	72.2	71.6	71.0	70.5	70.0	69.5	69.0	68.6	68.2
23	71.8	71.2	70.6	70.0	69.5	69.0	68.5	68.0	67.6
24	71.5	70.8	70.2	69.6	69.0	68.5	68.0	67.5	67.1
25	71.1	70.5	69.8	69.2	68.6	68.0	67.5	67.0	66.5
26	70.8	70.1	69.5	68.8	68.2	67.6	67.1	66.5	66.0
27	70.5	69.8	69.1	68.5	67.8	67.2	66.6	66.1	65.5
28	70.3	69.5	68.8	68.1	67.5	66.8	66.2	65.6	65.1
29	70.0	69.3	68.5	67.8	67.1	66.5	65.8	65.2	64.6
30	69.8	69.0	68.3	67.5	66.8	66.2	65.5	64.9	64.2
31	69.6	68.8	68.0	67.3	66.6	65.8	65.2	64.5	63.9
32	69.4	68.6	67.8	67.0	66.3	65.6	64.9	64.2	63.5
33	69.2	68.4	67.6	66.8	66.0	65.3	64.6	63.9	63.2
34	69.0	68.2	67.4	66.6	65.8	65.1	64.3	63.6	62.9
35	68.9	68.0	67.2	66.4	65.6	64.8	64.1	63.3	62.6
36	68.7	67.9	67.1	66.2	65.4	64.6	63.8	63.1	62.3
37	68.6	67.7	66.9	66.1	65.2	64.4	63.6	62.8	62.1
38	68.5	67.6	66.8	65.9	65.1	64.2	63.4	62.6	61.9
39	68.4	67.5	66.6	65.8	64.9	64.1	63.3	62.4	61.6
40	68.3	67.4	66.5	65.6	64.8	63.9	63.1	62.3	61.5
41	68.2	67.3	66.4	65.5	64.6	63.8	62.9	62.1	61.3
42	68.1	67.2	66.3	65.4	64.5	63.6	62.8	61.9	61.1
43	68.0	67.1	66.2	65.3	64.4	63.5	62.7	61.8	61.0
44	67.9	67.0	66.1	65.2	64.3	63.4	62.5	61.7	60.8
45	67.9	66.9	66.0	65.1	64.2	63.3	62.4	61.5	60.7
46	67.8	66.9	65.9	65.0	64.1	63.2	62.3	61.4	60.6
47	67.7	66.8	65.9	65.0	64.0	63.1	62.2	61.3	60.5
48	67.7	66.7	65.8	64.9	64.0	63.0	62.1	61.2	60.3
49	67.6	66.7	65.7	64.8	63.9	63.0	62.1	61.2	60.3
50	67.6	66.6	65.7	64.8	63.8	62.9	62.0	61.1	60.2
51	67.5	66.6	65.6	64.7	63.8	62.8	61.9	61.0	60.1
52	67.5	66.5	65.6	64.7	63.7	62.8	61.9	60.9	60.0
53	67.4	66.5	65.5	64.6	63.7	62.7	61.8	60.9	59.9
54	67.4	66.5	65.5	64.6	63.6	62.7	61.7	60.8	59.9
55	67.4	66.4	65.5	64.5	63.6	62.6	61.7	60.8	59.8
56	67.4	66.4	65.4	64.5	63.5	62.6	61.6	60.7	59.8
57	67.3	66.4	65.4	64.5	63.5	62.5	61.6	60.7	59.7
58	67.3	66.3	65.4	64.4	63.5	62.5	61.6	60.6	59.7
59	67.3	66.3	65.4	64.4	63.4	62.5	61.5	60.6	59.6
60	67.3	66.3	65.3	64.4	63.4	62.4	61.5	60.5	59.6
61	67.2	66.3	65.3	64.3	63.4	62.4	61.5	60.5	59.6
62	67.2	66.2	65.3	64.3	63.4	62.4	61.4	60.5	59.5
63	67.2	66.2	65.3	64.3	63.3	62.4	61.4	60.5	59.5
64	67.2	66.2	65.2	64.3	63.3	62.3	61.4	60.4	59.5
65	67.2	66.2	65.2	64.3	63.3	62.3	61.4	60.4	59.5
66	67.2	66.2	65.2	64.2	63.3	62.3	61.3	60.4	59.4
67	67.1	66.2	65.2	64.2	63.3	62.3	61.3	60.4	59.4
68	67.1	66.2	65.2	64.2	63.2	62.3	61.3	60.3	59.4
69	67.1	66.1	65.2	64.2	63.2	62.3	61.3	60.3	59.4
70	67.1	66.1	65.2	64.2	63.2	62.2	61.3	60.3	59.4
71	67.1	66.1	65.1	64.2	63.2	62.2	61.3	60.3	59.3
72	67.1	66.1	65.1	64.2	63.2	62.2	61.3	60.3	59.3
73	67.1	66.1	65.1	64.2	63.2	62.2	61.2	60.3	59.3
74	67.1	66.1	65.1	64.1	63.2	62.2	61.2	60.3	59.3
75	67.1	66.1	65.1	64.1	63.2	62.2	61.2	60.3	59.3
76	67.1	66.1	65.1	64.1	63.2	62.2	61.2	60.2	59.3
77	67.0	66.1	65.1	64.1	63.1	62.2	61.2	60.2	59.3
78	67.0	66.1	65.1	64.1	63.1	62.2	61.2	60.2	59.3
79	67.0	66.1	65.1	64.1	63.1	62.2	61.2	60.2	59.3
80	67.0	66.1	65.1	64.1	63.1	62.1	61.2	60.2	59.2

Reg. §1.401(a)(9)-9(d)

Ages	18	19	20	21	22	23	24	25	26
81	67.0	66.0	65.1	64.1	63.1	62.1	61.2	60.2	59.2
82	67.0	66.0	65.1	64.1	63.1	62.1	61.2	60.2	59.2
83	67.0	66.0	65.1	64.1	63.1	62.1	61.2	60.2	59.2
84	67.0	66.0	65.1	64.1	63.1	62.1	61.2	60.2	59.2
85	67.0	66.0	65.1	64.1	63.1	62.1	61.2	60.2	59.2
86	67.0	66.0	65.1	64.1	63.1	62.1	61.1	60.2	59.2
87	67.0	66.0	65.0	64.1	63.1	62.1	61.1	60.2	59.2
88	67.0	66.0	65.0	64.1	63.1	62.1	61.1	60.2	59.2
89	67.0	66.0	65.0	64.1	63.1	62.1	61.1	60.2	59.2
90	67.0	66.0	65.0	64.1	63.1	62.1	61.1	60.2	59.2
91	67.0	66.0	65.0	64.1	63.1	62.1	61.1	60.2	59.2
92	67.0	66.0	65.0	64.1	63.1	62.1	61.1	60.2	59.2
93	67.0	66.0	65.0	64.1	63.1	62.1	61.1	60.2	59.2
94	67.0	66.0	65.0	64.1	63.1	62.1	61.1	60.2	59.2
95	67.0	66.0	65.0	64.1	63.1	62.1	61.1	60.2	59.2
96	67.0	66.0	65.0	64.1	63.1	62.1	61.1	60.2	59.2
97	67.0	66.0	65.0	64.1	63.1	62.1	61.1	60.2	59.2
98	67.0	66.0	65.0	64.1	63.1	62.1	61.1	60.2	59.2
99	67.0	66.0	65.0	64.1	63.1	62.1	61.1	60.2	59.2
100	67.0	66.0	65.0	64.1	63.1	62.1	61.1	60.2	59.2
101	67.0	66.0	65.0	64.1	63.1	62.1	61.1	60.2	59.2
102	67.0	66.0	65.0	64.1	63.1	62.1	61.1	60.2	59.2
103	67.0	66.0	65.0	64.1	63.1	62.1	61.1	60.2	59.2
104	67.0	66.0	65.0	64.1	63.1	62.1	61.1	60.2	59.2
105	67.0	66.0	65.0	64.1	63.1	62.1	61.1	60.2	59.2
106	67.0	66.0	65.0	64.1	63.1	62.1	61.1	60.2	59.2
107	67.0	66.0	65.0	64.1	63.1	62.1	61.1	60.2	59.2
108	67.0	66.0	65.0	64.1	63.1	62.1	61.1	60.2	59.2
109	67.0	66.0	65.0	64.1	63.1	62.1	61.1	60.2	59.2
110	67.0	66.0	65.0	64.1	63.1	62.1	61.1	60.2	59.2
111	67.0	66.0	65.0	64.1	63.1	62.1	61.1	60.2	59.2
112	67.0	66.0	65.0	64.1	63.1	62.1	61.1	60.2	59.2
113	67.0	66.0	65.0	64.1	63.1	62.1	61.1	60.2	59.2
114	67.0	66.0	65.0	64.1	63.1	62.1	61.1	60.2	59.2
115	67.0	66.0	65.0	64.1	63.1	62.1	61.1	60.2	59.2
116	67.0	66.0	65.0	64.1	63.1	62.1	61.1	60.2	59.2
117	67.0	66.0	65.0	64.1	63.1	62.1	61.1	60.2	59.2
118	67.0	66.0	65.0	64.1	63.1	62.1	61.1	60.2	59.2
119	67.0	66.0	65.0	64.1	63.1	62.1	61.1	60.2	59.2
120+	67.0	66.0	65.0	64.1	63.1	62.1	61.1	60.2	59.2

Ages	27	28	29	30	31	32	33	34	35
0	85.7	85.6	85.6	85.5	85.4	85.4	85.3	85.3	85.3
1	84.8	84.7	84.7	84.6	84.6	84.5	84.5	84.4	84.4
2	83.9	83.8	83.8	83.7	83.6	83.6	83.5	83.5	83.4
3	83.0	82.9	82.8	82.8	82.7	82.6	82.6	82.5	82.5
4	82.1	82.0	81.9	81.8	81.8	81.7	81.6	81.6	81.5
5	81.2	81.1	81.0	80.9	80.9	80.8	80.7	80.7	80.6
6	80.3	80.2	80.1	80.0	79.9	79.9	79.8	79.7	79.7
7	79.4	79.3	79.2	79.1	79.0	78.9	78.9	78.8	78.7
8	78.6	78.4	78.3	78.2	78.1	78.0	77.9	77.9	77.8
9	77.7	77.6	77.4	77.3	77.2	77.1	77.0	77.0	76.9
10	76.8	76.7	76.6	76.4	76.3	76.2	76.1	76.0	76.0
11	76.0	75.8	75.7	75.6	75.5	75.3	75.2	75.1	75.0
12	75.2	75.0	74.9	74.7	74.6	74.5	74.3	74.2	74.1
13	74.4	74.2	74.0	73.9	73.7	73.6	73.5	73.3	73.2
14	73.6	73.4	73.2	73.0	72.9	72.7	72.6	72.5	72.4
15	72.8	72.6	72.4	72.2	72.0	71.9	71.7	71.6	71.5
16	72.0	71.8	71.6	71.4	71.2	71.0	70.9	70.7	70.6
17	71.3	71.0	70.8	70.6	70.4	70.2	70.0	69.9	69.7

Ages	27	28	29	30	31	32	33	34	35
18	70.5	70.3	70.0	69.8	69.6	69.4	69.2	69.0	68.9
19	69.8	69.5	69.3	69.0	68.8	68.6	68.4	68.2	68.0
20	69.1	68.8	68.5	68.3	68.0	67.8	67.6	67.4	67.2
21	68.5	68.1	67.8	67.5	67.3	67.0	66.8	66.6	66.4
22	67.8	67.5	67.1	66.8	66.6	66.3	66.0	65.8	65.6
23	67.2	66.8	66.5	66.2	65.8	65.6	65.3	65.1	64.8
24	66.6	66.2	65.8	65.5	65.2	64.9	64.6	64.3	64.1
25	66.1	65.6	65.2	64.9	64.5	64.2	63.9	63.6	63.3
26	65.5	65.1	64.6	64.2	63.9	63.5	63.2	62.9	62.6
27	65.0	64.5	64.1	63.7	63.2	62.9	62.5	62.2	61.9
28	64.5	64.0	63.5	63.1	62.7	62.3	61.9	61.5	61.2
29	64.1	63.5	63.0	62.6	62.1	61.7	61.3	60.9	60.5
30	63.7	63.1	62.6	62.0	61.6	61.1	60.7	60.3	59.9
31	63.2	62.7	62.1	61.6	61.1	60.6	60.1	59.7	59.3
32	62.9	62.3	61.7	61.1	60.6	60.1	59.6	59.1	58.7
33	62.5	61.9	61.3	60.7	60.1	59.6	59.1	58.6	58.1
34	62.2	61.5	60.9	60.3	59.7	59.1	58.6	58.1	57.6
35	61.9	61.2	60.5	59.9	59.3	58.7	58.1	57.6	57.1
36	61.6	60.9	60.2	59.5	58.9	58.3	57.7	57.2	56.6
37	61.3	60.6	59.9	59.2	58.6	57.9	57.3	56.7	56.2
38	61.1	60.3	59.6	58.9	58.2	57.6	56.9	56.3	55.7
39	60.9	60.1	59.4	58.6	57.9	57.2	56.6	55.9	55.3
40	60.7	59.9	59.1	58.4	57.6	56.9	56.3	55.6	55.0
41	60.5	59.7	58.9	58.1	57.4	56.7	56.0	55.3	54.6
42	60.3	59.5	58.7	57.9	57.1	56.4	55.7	55.0	54.3
43	60.1	59.3	58.5	57.7	56.9	56.2	55.4	54.7	54.0
44	60.0	59.1	58.3	57.5	56.7	55.9	55.2	54.4	53.7
45	59.8	59.0	58.1	57.3	56.5	55.7	54.9	54.2	53.4
46	59.7	58.8	58.0	57.2	56.3	55.5	54.7	54.0	53.2
47	59.6	58.7	57.9	57.0	56.2	55.4	54.5	53.7	53.0
48	59.5	58.6	57.7	56.9	56.0	55.2	54.4	53.6	52.8
49	59.4	58.5	57.6	56.7	55.9	55.0	54.2	53.4	52.6
50	59.3	58.4	57.5	56.6	55.8	54.9	54.1	53.2	52.4
51	59.2	58.3	57.4	56.5	55.6	54.8	53.9	53.1	52.2
52	59.1	58.2	57.3	56.4	55.5	54.7	53.8	52.9	52.1
53	59.0	58.1	57.2	56.3	55.4	54.6	53.7	52.8	52.0
54	59.0	58.0	57.1	56.2	55.3	54.5	53.6	52.7	51.8
55	58.9	58.0	57.1	56.2	55.3	54.4	53.5	52.6	51.7
56	58.8	57.9	57.0	56.1	55.2	54.3	53.4	52.5	51.6
57	58.8	57.9	56.9	56.0	55.1	54.2	53.3	52.4	51.5
58	58.7	57.8	56.9	56.0	55.0	54.1	53.2	52.3	51.4
59	58.7	57.8	56.8	55.9	55.0	54.1	53.2	52.2	51.3
60	58.7	57.7	56.8	55.9	54.9	54.0	53.1	52.2	51.3
61	58.6	57.7	56.7	55.8	54.9	54.0	53.0	52.1	51.2
62	58.6	57.6	56.7	55.8	54.8	53.9	53.0	52.1	51.1
63	58.6	57.6	56.7	55.7	54.8	53.9	52.9	52.0	51.1
64	58.5	57.6	56.6	55.7	54.8	53.8	52.9	52.0	51.0
65	58.5	57.5	56.6	55.7	54.7	53.8	52.8	51.9	51.0
66	58.5	57.5	56.6	55.6	54.7	53.7	52.8	51.9	50.9
67	58.5	57.5	56.5	55.6	54.7	53.7	52.8	51.8	50.9
68	58.4	57.5	56.5	55.6	54.6	53.7	52.7	51.8	50.9
69	58.4	57.5	56.5	55.6	54.6	53.7	52.7	51.8	50.8
70	58.4	57.4	56.5	55.5	54.6	53.6	52.7	51.7	50.8
71	58.4	57.4	56.5	55.5	54.6	53.6	52.7	51.7	50.8
72	58.4	57.4	56.5	55.5	54.5	53.6	52.6	51.7	50.8
73	58.4	57.4	56.4	55.5	54.5	53.6	52.6	51.7	50.7
74	58.3	57.4	56.4	55.5	54.5	53.6	52.6	51.7	50.7
75	58.3	57.4	56.4	55.5	54.5	53.5	52.6	51.6	50.7
76	58.3	57.4	56.4	55.4	54.5	53.5	52.6	51.6	50.7
77	58.3	57.3	56.4	55.4	54.5	53.5	52.6	51.6	50.7
78	58.3	57.3	56.4	55.4	54.5	53.5	52.6	51.6	50.6

Reg. §1.401(a)(9)-9(d)

Ages	27	28	29	30	31	32	33	34	35
79	58.3	57.3	56.4	55.4	54.5	53.5	52.5	51.6	50.6
80	58.3	57.3	56.4	55.4	54.4	53.5	52.5	51.6	50.6
81	58.3	57.3	56.4	55.4	54.4	53.5	52.5	51.6	50.6
82	58.3	57.3	56.3	55.4	54.4	53.5	52.5	51.6	50.6
83	58.3	57.3	56.3	55.4	54.4	53.5	52.5	51.6	50.6
84	58.3	57.3	56.3	55.4	54.4	53.5	52.5	51.5	50.6
85	58.3	57.3	56.3	55.4	54.4	53.5	52.5	51.5	50.6
86	58.2	57.3	56.3	55.4	54.4	53.5	52.5	51.5	50.6
87	58.2	57.3	56.3	55.4	54.4	53.4	52.5	51.5	50.6
88	58.2	57.3	56.3	55.4	54.4	53.4	52.5	51.5	50.6
89	58.2	57.3	56.3	55.4	54.4	53.4	52.5	51.5	50.6
90	58.2	57.3	56.3	55.4	54.4	53.4	52.5	51.5	50.6
91	58.2	57.3	56.3	55.3	54.4	53.4	52.5	51.5	50.6
92	58.2	57.3	56.3	55.3	54.4	53.4	52.5	51.5	50.6
93	58.2	57.3	56.3	55.3	54.4	53.4	52.5	51.5	50.6
94	58.2	57.3	56.3	55.3	54.4	53.4	52.5	51.5	50.6
95	58.2	57.3	56.3	55.3	54.4	53.4	52.5	51.5	50.6
96	58.2	57.3	56.3	55.3	54.4	53.4	52.5	51.5	50.6
97	58.2	57.3	56.3	55.3	54.4	53.4	52.5	51.5	50.6
98	58.2	57.3	56.3	55.3	54.4	53.4	52.5	51.5	50.6
99	58.2	57.3	56.3	55.3	54.4	53.4	52.5	51.5	50.6
100	58.2	57.3	56.3	55.3	54.4	53.4	52.5	51.5	50.6
101	58.2	57.3	56.3	55.3	54.4	53.4	52.5	51.5	50.6
102	58.2	57.3	56.3	55.3	54.4	53.4	52.5	51.5	50.6
103	58.2	57.3	56.3	55.3	54.4	53.4	52.5	51.5	50.5
104	58.2	57.3	56.3	55.3	54.4	53.4	52.5	51.5	50.5
105	58.2	57.3	56.3	55.3	54.4	53.4	52.5	51.5	50.5
106	58.2	57.3	56.3	55.3	54.4	53.4	52.5	51.5	50.5
107	58.2	57.3	56.3	55.3	54.4	53.4	52.5	51.5	50.5
108	58.2	57.3	56.3	55.3	54.4	53.4	52.5	51.5	50.5
109	58.2	57.3	56.3	55.3	54.4	53.4	52.5	51.5	50.5
110	58.2	57.3	56.3	55.3	54.4	53.4	52.5	51.5	50.5
111	58.2	57.3	56.3	55.3	54.4	53.4	52.5	51.5	50.5
112	58.2	57.3	56.3	55.3	54.4	53.4	52.5	51.5	50.5
113	58.2	57.3	56.3	55.3	54.4	53.4	52.5	51.5	50.5
114	58.2	57.3	56.3	55.3	54.4	53.4	52.5	51.5	50.5
115	58.2	57.3	56.3	55.3	54.4	53.4	52.5	51.5	50.5
116	58.2	57.3	56.3	55.3	54.4	53.4	52.5	51.5	50.5
117	58.2	57.3	56.3	55.3	54.4	53.4	52.5	51.5	50.5
118	58.2	57.3	56.3	55.3	54.4	53.4	52.5	51.5	50.5
119	58.2	57.3	56.3	55.3	54.4	53.4	52.5	51.5	50.5
120+	58.2	57.3	56.3	55.3	54.4	53.4	52.5	51.5	50.5

Ages	36	37	38	39	40	41	42	43	44
0	85.2	85.2	85.2	85.1	85.1	85.1	85.0	85.0	85.0
1	84.3	84.3	84.3	84.2	84.2	84.2	84.1	84.1	84.1
2	83.4	83.3	83.3	83.3	83.2	83.2	83.2	83.1	83.1
3	82.4	82.4	82.3	82.3	82.3	82.2	82.2	82.2	82.2
4	81.5	81.4	81.4	81.4	81.3	81.3	81.3	81.2	81.2
5	80.5	80.5	80.4	80.4	80.4	80.3	80.3	80.3	80.2
6	79.6	79.5	79.5	79.5	79.4	79.4	79.3	79.3	79.3
7	78.7	78.6	78.6	78.5	78.5	78.4	78.4	78.3	78.3
8	77.7	77.7	77.6	77.6	77.5	77.5	77.4	77.4	77.3
9	76.8	76.7	76.7	76.6	76.6	76.5	76.5	76.4	76.4
10	75.9	75.8	75.7	75.7	75.6	75.6	75.5	75.5	75.4
11	75.0	74.9	74.8	74.7	74.7	74.6	74.6	74.5	74.5
12	74.0	74.0	73.9	73.8	73.7	73.7	73.6	73.6	73.5
13	73.1	73.1	73.0	72.9	72.8	72.8	72.7	72.6	72.6
14	72.2	72.1	72.1	72.0	71.9	71.8	71.8	71.7	71.6
15	71.4	71.3	71.2	71.1	71.0	70.9	70.8	70.8	70.7

Reg. §1.401(a)(9)-9(d)

Ages	36	37	38	39	40	41	42	43	44
16	70.5	70.4	70.3	70.2	70.1	70.0	69.9	69.8	69.8
17	69.6	69.5	69.4	69.3	69.2	69.1	69.0	68.9	68.8
18	68.7	68.6	68.5	68.4	68.3	68.2	68.1	68.0	67.9
19	67.9	67.7	67.6	67.5	67.4	67.3	67.2	67.1	67.0
20	67.1	66.9	66.8	66.6	66.5	66.4	66.3	66.2	66.1
21	66.2	66.1	65.9	65.8	65.6	65.5	65.4	65.3	65.2
22	65.4	65.2	65.1	64.9	64.8	64.6	64.5	64.4	64.3
23	64.6	64.4	64.2	64.1	63.9	63.8	63.6	63.5	63.4
24	63.8	63.6	63.4	63.3	63.1	62.9	62.8	62.7	62.5
25	63.1	62.8	62.6	62.4	62.3	62.1	61.9	61.8	61.7
26	62.3	62.1	61.9	61.6	61.5	61.3	61.1	61.0	60.8
27	61.6	61.3	61.1	60.9	60.7	60.5	60.3	60.1	60.0
28	60.9	60.6	60.3	60.1	59.9	59.7	59.5	59.3	59.1
29	60.2	59.9	59.6	59.4	59.1	58.9	58.7	58.5	58.3
30	59.5	59.2	58.9	58.6	58.4	58.1	57.9	57.7	57.5
31	58.9	58.6	58.2	57.9	57.6	57.4	57.1	56.9	56.7
32	58.3	57.9	57.6	57.2	56.9	56.7	56.4	56.2	55.9
33	57.7	57.3	56.9	56.6	56.3	56.0	55.7	55.4	55.2
34	57.2	56.7	56.3	55.9	55.6	55.3	55.0	54.7	54.4
35	56.6	56.2	55.7	55.3	55.0	54.6	54.3	54.0	53.7
36	56.1	55.6	55.2	54.7	54.3	54.0	53.6	53.3	53.0
37	55.6	55.1	54.6	54.2	53.8	53.4	53.0	52.6	52.3
38	55.2	54.6	54.1	53.6	53.2	52.8	52.4	52.0	51.6
39	54.7	54.2	53.6	53.1	52.7	52.2	51.8	51.4	51.0
40	54.3	53.8	53.2	52.7	52.2	51.7	51.2	50.8	50.4
41	54.0	53.4	52.8	52.2	51.7	51.2	50.7	50.2	49.8
42	53.6	53.0	52.4	51.8	51.2	50.7	50.2	49.7	49.2
43	53.3	52.6	52.0	51.4	50.8	50.2	49.7	49.2	48.7
44	53.0	52.3	51.6	51.0	50.4	49.8	49.2	48.7	48.2
45	52.7	52.0	51.3	50.7	50.0	49.4	48.8	48.3	47.7
46	52.4	51.7	51.0	50.3	49.7	49.0	48.4	47.8	47.3
47	52.2	51.5	50.7	50.0	49.3	48.7	48.0	47.4	46.8
48	52.0	51.2	50.5	49.7	49.0	48.4	47.7	47.1	46.4
49	51.8	51.0	50.2	49.5	48.8	48.1	47.4	46.7	46.1
50	51.6	50.8	50.0	49.2	48.5	47.8	47.1	46.4	45.7
51	51.4	50.6	49.8	49.0	48.3	47.5	46.8	46.1	45.4
52	51.3	50.4	49.6	48.8	48.0	47.3	46.5	45.8	45.1
53	51.1	50.3	49.5	48.6	47.8	47.1	46.3	45.6	44.8
54	51.0	50.1	49.3	48.5	47.7	46.9	46.1	45.3	44.6
55	50.9	50.0	49.1	48.3	47.5	46.7	45.9	45.1	44.3
56	50.7	49.9	49.0	48.2	47.3	46.5	45.7	44.9	44.1
57	50.6	49.8	48.9	48.0	47.2	46.3	45.5	44.7	43.9
58	50.5	49.7	48.8	47.9	47.1	46.2	45.4	44.5	43.7
59	50.5	49.6	48.7	47.8	46.9	46.1	45.2	44.4	43.6
60	50.4	49.5	48.6	47.7	46.8	46.0	45.1	44.3	43.4
61	50.3	49.4	48.5	47.6	46.7	45.8	45.0	44.1	43.3
62	50.2	49.3	48.4	47.5	46.6	45.7	44.9	44.0	43.1
63	50.2	49.3	48.3	47.4	46.5	45.7	44.8	43.9	43.0
64	50.1	49.2	48.3	47.4	46.5	45.6	44.7	43.8	42.9
65	50.1	49.1	48.2	47.3	46.4	45.5	44.6	43.7	42.8
66	50.0	49.1	48.2	47.2	46.3	45.4	44.5	43.6	42.7
67	50.0	49.0	48.1	47.2	46.3	45.4	44.4	43.5	42.6
68	49.9	49.0	48.1	47.1	46.2	45.3	44.4	43.5	42.6
69	49.9	49.0	48.0	47.1	46.2	45.2	44.3	43.4	42.5
70	49.9	48.9	48.0	47.0	46.1	45.2	44.3	43.3	42.4
71	49.8	48.9	47.9	47.0	46.1	45.1	44.2	43.3	42.4
72	49.8	48.9	47.9	47.0	46.0	45.1	44.2	43.2	42.3
73	49.8	48.8	47.9	46.9	46.0	45.1	44.1	43.2	42.3
74	49.8	48.8	47.9	46.9	46.0	45.0	44.1	43.2	42.2
75	49.7	48.8	47.8	46.9	45.9	45.0	44.1	43.1	42.2
76	49.7	48.8	47.8	46.9	45.9	45.0	44.0	43.1	42.2

Reg. §1.401(a)(9)-9(d)

Ages	36	37	38	39	40	41	42	43	44
77	49.7	48.8	47.8	46.9	45.9	45.0	44.0	43.1	42.1
78	49.7	48.7	47.8	46.8	45.9	44.9	44.0	43.0	42.1
79	49.7	48.7	47.8	46.8	45.9	44.9	44.0	43.0	42.1
80	49.7	48.7	47.8	46.8	45.9	44.9	43.9	43.0	42.1
81	49.7	48.7	47.7	46.8	45.8	44.9	43.9	43.0	42.0
82	49.7	48.7	47.7	46.8	45.8	44.9	43.9	43.0	42.0
83	49.6	48.7	47.7	46.8	45.8	44.9	43.9	43.0	42.0
84	49.6	48.7	47.7	46.8	45.8	44.9	43.9	42.9	42.0
85	49.6	48.7	47.7	46.8	45.8	44.8	43.9	42.9	42.0
86	49.6	48.7	47.7	46.7	45.8	44.8	43.9	42.9	42.0
87	49.6	48.7	47.7	46.7	45.8	44.8	43.9	42.9	42.0
88	49.6	48.7	47.7	46.7	45.8	44.8	43.9	42.9	42.0
89	49.6	48.7	47.7	46.7	45.8	44.8	43.9	42.9	41.9
90	49.6	48.6	47.7	46.7	45.8	44.8	43.9	42.9	41.9
91	49.6	48.6	47.7	46.7	45.8	44.8	43.9	42.9	41.9
92	49.6	48.6	47.7	46.7	45.8	44.8	43.8	42.9	41.9
93	49.6	48.6	47.7	46.7	45.8	44.8	43.8	42.9	41.9
94	49.6	48.6	47.7	46.7	45.8	44.8	43.8	42.9	41.9
95	49.6	48.6	47.7	46.7	45.8	44.8	43.8	42.9	41.9
96	49.6	48.6	47.7	46.7	45.8	44.8	43.8	42.9	41.9
97	49.6	48.6	47.7	46.7	45.8	44.8	43.8	42.9	41.9
98	49.6	48.6	47.7	46.7	45.8	44.8	43.8	42.9	41.9
99	49.6	48.6	47.7	46.7	45.8	44.8	43.8	42.9	41.9
100	49.6	48.6	47.7	46.7	45.8	44.8	43.8	42.9	41.9
101	49.6	48.6	47.7	46.7	45.8	44.8	43.8	42.9	41.9
102	49.6	48.6	47.7	46.7	45.8	44.8	43.8	42.9	41.9
103	49.6	48.6	47.7	46.7	45.8	44.8	43.8	42.9	41.9
104	49.6	48.6	47.7	46.7	45.8	44.8	43.8	42.9	41.9
105	49.6	48.6	47.7	46.7	45.7	44.8	43.8	42.9	41.9
106	49.6	48.6	47.7	46.7	45.7	44.8	43.8	42.9	41.9
107	49.6	48.6	47.7	46.7	45.7	44.8	43.8	42.9	41.9
108	49.6	48.6	47.7	46.7	45.7	44.8	43.8	42.9	41.9
109	49.6	48.6	47.7	46.7	45.7	44.8	43.8	42.9	41.9
110	49.6	48.6	47.7	46.7	45.7	44.8	43.8	42.9	41.9
111	49.6	48.6	47.7	46.7	45.7	44.8	43.8	42.9	41.9
112	49.6	48.6	47.7	46.7	45.7	44.8	43.8	42.9	41.9
113	49.6	48.6	47.7	46.7	45.7	44.8	43.8	42.9	41.9
114	49.6	48.6	47.7	46.7	45.7	44.8	43.8	42.9	41.9
115	49.6	48.6	47.7	46.7	45.7	44.8	43.8	42.9	41.9
116	49.6	48.6	47.7	46.7	45.7	44.8	43.8	42.9	41.9
117	49.6	48.6	47.7	46.7	45.7	44.8	43.8	42.9	41.9
118	49.6	48.6	47.7	46.7	45.7	44.8	43.8	42.9	41.9
119	49.6	48.6	47.7	46.7	45.7	44.8	43.8	42.9	41.9
120+	49.6	48.6	47.7	46.7	45.7	44.8	43.8	42.9	41.9

Ages	45	46	47	48	49	50	51	52	53
0	85.0	84.9	84.9	84.9	84.9	84.9	84.8	84.8	84.8
1	84.1	84.0	84.0	84.0	84.0	84.0	84.0	83.9	83.9
2	83.1	83.1	83.1	83.0	83.0	83.0	83.0	83.0	83.0
3	82.1	82.1	82.1	82.1	82.1	82.0	82.0	82.0	82.0
4	81.2	81.1	81.1	81.1	81.1	81.1	81.0	81.0	81.0
5	80.2	80.2	80.2	80.1	80.1	80.1	80.1	80.1	80.0
6	79.2	79.2	79.2	79.2	79.1	79.1	79.1	79.1	79.1
7	78.3	78.2	78.2	78.2	78.2	78.1	78.1	78.1	78.1
8	77.3	77.3	77.3	77.2	77.2	77.2	77.2	77.1	77.1
9	76.4	76.3	76.3	76.3	76.2	76.2	76.2	76.2	76.1
10	75.4	75.4	75.3	75.3	75.3	75.2	75.2	75.2	75.2
11	74.4	74.4	74.4	74.3	74.3	74.3	74.2	74.2	74.2
12	73.5	73.4	73.4	73.4	73.3	73.3	73.3	73.2	73.2
13	72.5	72.5	72.4	72.4	72.4	72.3	72.3	72.3	72.3

Reg. §1.401(a)(9)-9(d)

Ages	45	46	47	48	49	50	51	52	53
14	71.6	71.5	71.5	71.5	71.4	71.4	71.3	71.3	71.3
15	70.6	70.6	70.5	70.5	70.5	70.4	70.4	70.4	70.3
16	69.7	69.7	69.6	69.6	69.5	69.5	69.4	69.4	69.4
17	68.8	68.7	68.7	68.6	68.6	68.5	68.5	68.4	68.4
18	67.9	67.8	67.7	67.7	67.6	67.6	67.5	67.5	67.4
19	66.9	66.9	66.8	66.7	66.7	66.6	66.6	66.5	66.5
20	66.0	65.9	65.9	65.8	65.7	65.7	65.6	65.6	65.5
21	65.1	65.0	65.0	64.9	64.8	64.8	64.7	64.7	64.6
22	64.2	64.1	64.0	64.0	63.9	63.8	63.8	63.7	63.7
23	63.3	63.2	63.1	63.0	63.0	62.9	62.8	62.8	62.7
24	62.4	62.3	62.2	62.1	62.1	62.0	61.9	61.9	61.8
25	61.5	61.4	61.3	61.2	61.2	61.1	61.0	60.9	60.9
26	60.7	60.6	60.5	60.3	60.3	60.2	60.1	60.0	59.9
27	59.8	59.7	59.6	59.5	59.4	59.3	59.2	59.1	59.0
28	59.0	58.8	58.7	58.6	58.5	58.4	58.3	58.2	58.1
29	58.1	58.0	57.9	57.7	57.6	57.5	57.4	57.3	57.2
30	57.3	57.2	57.0	56.9	56.7	56.6	56.5	56.4	56.3
31	56.5	56.3	56.2	56.0	55.9	55.8	55.6	55.5	55.4
32	55.7	55.5	55.4	55.2	55.0	54.9	54.8	54.7	54.6
33	54.9	54.7	54.5	54.4	54.2	54.1	53.9	53.8	53.7
34	54.2	54.0	53.7	53.6	53.4	53.2	53.1	52.9	52.8
35	53.4	53.2	53.0	52.8	52.6	52.4	52.2	52.1	52.0
36	52.7	52.4	52.2	52.0	51.8	51.6	51.4	51.3	51.1
37	52.0	51.7	51.5	51.2	51.0	50.8	50.6	50.4	50.3
38	51.3	51.0	50.7	50.5	50.2	50.0	49.8	49.6	49.5
39	50.7	50.3	50.0	49.7	49.5	49.2	49.0	48.8	48.6
40	50.0	49.7	49.3	49.0	48.8	48.5	48.3	48.0	47.8
41	49.4	49.0	48.7	48.4	48.1	47.8	47.5	47.3	47.1
42	48.8	48.4	48.0	47.7	47.4	47.1	46.8	46.5	46.3
43	48.3	47.8	47.4	47.1	46.7	46.4	46.1	45.8	45.6
44	47.7	47.3	46.8	46.4	46.1	45.7	45.4	45.1	44.8
45	47.2	46.7	46.3	45.9	45.5	45.1	44.7	44.4	44.1
46	46.7	46.2	45.7	45.3	44.9	44.5	44.1	43.8	43.4
47	46.3	45.7	45.2	44.8	44.3	43.9	43.5	43.1	42.8
48	45.9	45.3	44.8	44.3	43.8	43.3	42.9	42.5	42.1
49	45.5	44.9	44.3	43.8	43.3	42.8	42.3	41.9	41.5
50	45.1	44.5	43.9	43.3	42.8	42.3	41.8	41.4	40.9
51	44.7	44.1	43.5	42.9	42.3	41.8	41.3	40.8	40.4
52	44.4	43.8	43.1	42.5	41.9	41.4	40.8	40.3	39.9
53	44.1	43.4	42.8	42.1	41.5	40.9	40.4	39.9	39.4
54	43.8	43.1	42.5	41.8	41.2	40.6	40.0	39.4	38.9
55	43.6	42.9	42.2	41.5	40.8	40.2	39.6	39.0	38.4
56	43.4	42.6	41.9	41.2	40.5	39.8	39.2	38.6	38.0
57	43.1	42.4	41.6	40.9	40.2	39.5	38.9	38.2	37.6
58	42.9	42.2	41.4	40.7	39.9	39.2	38.6	37.9	37.3
59	42.8	42.0	41.2	40.4	39.7	39.0	38.3	37.6	36.9
60	42.6	41.8	41.0	40.2	39.5	38.7	38.0	37.3	36.6
61	42.4	41.6	40.8	40.0	39.2	38.5	37.7	37.0	36.3
62	42.3	41.5	40.6	39.8	39.0	38.3	37.5	36.8	36.1
63	42.2	41.3	40.5	39.7	38.9	38.1	37.3	36.6	35.8
64	42.1	41.2	40.4	39.5	38.7	37.9	37.1	36.3	35.6
65	41.9	41.1	40.2	39.4	38.6	37.7	36.9	36.2	35.4
66	41.8	41.0	40.1	39.3	38.4	37.6	36.8	36.0	35.2
67	41.8	40.9	40.0	39.1	38.3	37.5	36.6	35.8	35.0
68	41.7	40.8	39.9	39.0	38.2	37.3	36.5	35.7	34.9
69	41.6	40.7	39.8	38.9	38.1	37.2	36.4	35.5	34.7
70	41.5	40.6	39.7	38.8	38.0	37.1	36.2	35.4	34.6
71	41.5	40.6	39.7	38.8	37.9	37.0	36.1	35.3	34.5
72	41.4	40.5	39.6	38.7	37.8	36.9	36.0	35.2	34.3
73	41.4	40.4	39.5	38.6	37.7	36.8	36.0	35.1	34.2
74	41.3	40.4	39.5	38.6	37.7	36.8	35.9	35.0	34.1

Reg. §1.401(a)(9)-9(d)

Pension, Profit-Sharing, Stock Bonus Plans, Etc.
See p. 20,601 for regulations not amended to reflect law changes

Ages	45	46	47	48	49	50	51	52	53
75	41.3	40.3	39.4	38.5	37.6	36.7	35.8	34.9	34.1
76	41.2	40.3	39.4	38.5	37.5	36.6	35.7	34.9	34.0
77	41.2	40.3	39.3	38.4	37.5	36.6	35.7	34.8	33.9
78	41.2	40.2	39.3	38.4	37.5	36.5	35.6	34.7	33.9
79	41.1	40.2	39.3	38.3	37.4	36.5	35.6	34.7	33.8
80	41.1	40.2	39.2	38.3	37.4	36.5	35.5	34.6	33.7
81	41.1	40.1	39.2	38.3	37.3	36.4	35.5	34.6	33.7
82	41.1	40.1	39.2	38.3	37.3	36.4	35.5	34.6	33.7
83	41.1	40.1	39.2	38.2	37.3	36.4	35.4	34.5	33.6
84	41.0	40.1	39.2	38.2	37.3	36.3	35.4	34.5	33.6
85	41.0	40.1	39.1	38.2	37.3	36.3	35.4	34.5	33.6
86	41.0	40.1	39.1	38.2	37.2	36.3	35.4	34.5	33.5
87	41.0	40.1	39.1	38.2	37.2	36.3	35.4	34.4	33.5
88	41.0	40.0	39.1	38.2	37.2	36.3	35.3	34.4	33.5
89	41.0	40.0	39.1	38.1	37.2	36.3	35.3	34.4	33.5
90	41.0	40.0	39.1	38.1	37.2	36.3	35.3	34.4	33.5
91	41.0	40.0	39.1	38.1	37.2	36.2	35.3	34.4	33.5
92	41.0	40.0	39.1	38.1	37.2	36.2	35.3	34.4	33.5
93	41.0	40.0	39.1	38.1	37.2	36.2	35.3	34.4	33.4
94	41.0	40.0	39.1	38.1	37.2	36.2	35.3	34.4	33.4
95	41.0	40.0	39.1	38.1	37.2	36.2	35.3	34.4	33.4
96	41.0	40.0	39.1	38.1	37.2	36.2	35.3	34.3	33.4
97	41.0	40.0	39.1	38.1	37.2	36.2	35.3	34.3	33.4
98	41.0	40.0	39.1	38.1	37.2	36.2	35.3	34.3	33.4
99	41.0	40.0	39.1	38.1	37.2	36.2	35.3	34.3	33.4
100	41.0	40.0	39.0	38.1	37.1	36.2	35.3	34.3	33.4
101	41.0	40.0	39.0	38.1	37.1	36.2	35.3	34.3	33.4
102	41.0	40.0	39.0	38.1	37.1	36.2	35.3	34.3	33.4
103	41.0	40.0	39.0	38.1	37.1	36.2	35.3	34.3	33.4
104	41.0	40.0	39.0	38.1	37.1	36.2	35.3	34.3	33.4
105	41.0	40.0	39.0	38.1	37.1	36.2	35.3	34.3	33.4
106	41.0	40.0	39.0	38.1	37.1	36.2	35.3	34.3	33.4
107	41.0	40.0	39.0	38.1	37.1	36.2	35.3	34.3	33.4
108	41.0	40.0	39.0	38.1	37.1	36.2	35.3	34.3	33.4
109	41.0	40.0	39.0	38.1	37.1	36.2	35.3	34.3	33.4
110	41.0	40.0	39.0	38.1	37.1	36.2	35.3	34.3	33.4
111	41.0	40.0	39.0	38.1	37.1	36.2	35.3	34.3	33.4
112	41.0	40.0	39.0	38.1	37.1	36.2	35.3	34.3	33.4
113	41.0	40.0	39.0	38.1	37.1	36.2	35.3	34.3	33.4
114	41.0	40.0	39.0	38.1	37.1	36.2	35.3	34.3	33.4
115	41.0	40.0	39.0	38.1	37.1	36.2	35.3	34.3	33.4
116	41.0	40.0	39.0	38.1	37.1	36.2	35.3	34.3	33.4
117	41.0	40.0	39.0	38.1	37.1	36.2	35.3	34.3	33.4
118	41.0	40.0	39.0	38.1	37.1	36.2	35.3	34.3	33.4
119	41.0	40.0	39.0	38.1	37.1	36.2	35.3	34.3	33.4
120+	41.0	40.0	39.0	38.1	37.1	36.2	35.3	34.3	33.4

Ages	54	55	56	57	58	59	60	61	62
0	84.8	84.8	84.8	84.8	84.8	84.7	84.7	84.7	84.7
1	83.9	83.9	83.9	83.9	83.9	83.9	83.8	83.8	83.8
2	82.9	82.9	82.9	82.9	82.9	82.9	82.9	82.9	82.9
3	82.0	82.0	81.9	81.9	81.9	81.9	81.9	81.9	81.9
4	81.0	81.0	81.0	81.0	80.9	80.9	80.9	80.9	80.9
5	80.0	80.0	80.0	80.0	80.0	80.0	79.9	79.9	79.9
6	79.0	79.0	79.0	79.0	79.0	79.0	79.0	79.0	78.9
7	78.1	78.1	78.0	78.0	78.0	78.0	78.0	78.0	78.0
8	77.1	77.1	77.1	77.0	77.0	77.0	77.0	77.0	77.0
9	76.1	76.1	76.1	76.1	76.1	76.0	76.0	76.0	76.0
10	75.1	75.1	75.1	75.1	75.1	75.1	75.0	75.0	75.0
11	74.2	74.2	74.1	74.1	74.1	74.1	74.1	74.1	74.0

Reg. §1.401(a)(9)-9(d)

Ages	54	55	56	57	58	59	60	61	62
12	73.2	73.2	73.2	73.1	73.1	73.1	73.1	73.1	73.1
13	72.2	72.2	72.2	72.2	72.1	72.1	72.1	72.1	72.1
14	71.3	71.2	71.2	71.2	71.2	71.2	71.1	71.1	71.1
15	70.3	70.3	70.2	70.2	70.2	70.2	70.2	70.1	70.1
16	69.3	69.3	69.3	69.3	69.2	69.2	69.2	69.2	69.2
17	68.4	68.3	68.3	68.3	68.3	68.2	68.2	68.2	68.2
18	67.4	67.4	67.4	67.3	67.3	67.3	67.3	67.2	67.2
19	66.5	66.4	66.4	66.4	66.3	66.3	66.3	66.3	66.2
20	65.5	65.5	65.4	65.4	65.4	65.4	65.3	65.3	65.3
21	64.6	64.5	64.5	64.5	64.4	64.4	64.4	64.3	64.3
22	63.6	63.6	63.5	63.5	63.5	63.4	63.4	63.4	63.4
23	62.7	62.6	62.6	62.5	62.5	62.5	62.4	62.4	62.4
24	61.7	61.7	61.6	61.6	61.6	61.5	61.5	61.5	61.4
25	60.8	60.8	60.7	60.7	60.6	60.6	60.5	60.5	60.5
26	59.9	59.8	59.8	59.7	59.7	59.6	59.6	59.6	59.5
27	59.0	58.9	58.8	58.8	58.7	58.7	58.7	58.6	58.6
28	58.0	58.0	57.9	57.9	57.8	57.8	57.7	57.7	57.6
29	57.1	57.1	57.0	56.9	56.9	56.8	56.8	56.7	56.7
30	56.2	56.2	56.1	56.0	56.0	55.9	55.9	55.8	55.8
31	55.3	55.3	55.2	55.1	55.0	55.0	54.9	54.9	54.8
32	54.5	54.4	54.3	54.2	54.1	54.1	54.0	54.0	53.9
33	53.6	53.5	53.4	53.3	53.2	53.2	53.1	53.0	53.0
34	52.7	52.6	52.5	52.4	52.3	52.2	52.2	52.1	52.1
35	51.8	51.7	51.6	51.5	51.4	51.3	51.3	51.2	51.1
36	51.0	50.9	50.7	50.6	50.5	50.5	50.4	50.3	50.2
37	50.1	50.0	49.9	49.8	49.7	49.6	49.5	49.4	49.3
38	49.3	49.1	49.0	48.9	48.8	48.7	48.6	48.5	48.4
39	48.5	48.3	48.2	48.0	47.9	47.8	47.7	47.6	47.5
40	47.7	47.5	47.3	47.2	47.1	46.9	46.8	46.7	46.6
41	46.9	46.7	46.5	46.3	46.2	46.1	46.0	45.8	45.7
42	46.1	45.9	45.7	45.5	45.4	45.2	45.1	45.0	44.9
43	45.3	45.1	44.9	44.7	44.5	44.4	44.3	44.1	44.0
44	44.6	44.3	44.1	43.9	43.7	43.6	43.4	43.3	43.1
45	43.8	43.6	43.4	43.1	42.9	42.8	42.6	42.4	42.3
46	43.1	42.9	42.6	42.4	42.2	42.0	41.8	41.6	41.5
47	42.5	42.2	41.9	41.6	41.4	41.2	41.0	40.8	40.6
48	41.8	41.5	41.2	40.9	40.7	40.4	40.2	40.0	39.8
49	41.2	40.8	40.5	40.2	39.9	39.7	39.5	39.2	39.0
50	40.6	40.2	39.8	39.5	39.2	39.0	38.7	38.5	38.3
51	40.0	39.6	39.2	38.9	38.6	38.3	38.0	37.7	37.5
52	39.4	39.0	38.6	38.2	37.9	37.6	37.3	37.0	36.8
53	38.9	38.4	38.0	37.6	37.3	36.9	36.6	36.3	36.1
54	38.4	37.9	37.5	37.1	36.7	36.3	36.0	35.7	35.4
55	37.9	37.4	36.9	36.5	36.1	35.7	35.3	35.0	34.7
56	37.5	36.9	36.5	36.0	35.5	35.1	34.8	34.4	34.1
57	37.1	36.5	36.0	35.5	35.0	34.6	34.2	33.8	33.4
58	36.7	36.1	35.5	35.0	34.5	34.1	33.6	33.2	32.8
59	36.3	35.7	35.1	34.6	34.1	33.6	33.1	32.7	32.3
60	36.0	35.3	34.8	34.2	33.6	33.1	32.6	32.2	31.7
61	35.7	35.0	34.4	33.8	33.2	32.7	32.2	31.7	31.2
62	35.4	34.7	34.1	33.4	32.8	32.3	31.7	31.2	30.8
63	35.1	34.4	33.8	33.1	32.5	31.9	31.3	30.8	30.3
64	34.9	34.2	33.5	32.8	32.2	31.5	31.0	30.4	29.9
65	34.6	33.9	33.2	32.5	31.9	31.2	30.6	30.0	29.5
66	34.4	33.7	33.0	32.3	31.6	30.9	30.3	29.7	29.1
67	34.2	33.5	32.7	32.0	31.3	30.6	30.0	29.4	28.7
68	34.1	33.3	32.5	31.8	31.1	30.4	29.7	29.1	28.4
69	33.9	33.1	32.3	31.6	30.9	30.1	29.4	28.8	28.1
70	33.8	33.0	32.2	31.4	30.7	29.9	29.2	28.5	27.9
71	33.6	32.8	32.0	31.2	30.5	29.7	29.0	28.3	27.6
72	33.5	32.7	31.9	31.1	30.3	29.5	28.8	28.1	27.4

Reg. §1.401(a)(9)-9(d)

Ages	54	55	56	57	58	59	60	61	62
73	33.4	32.6	31.7	30.9	30.1	29.4	28.6	27.9	27.2
74	33.3	32.4	31.6	30.8	30.0	29.2	28.4	27.7	27.0
75	33.2	32.4	31.5	30.7	29.9	29.1	28.3	27.5	26.8
76	33.1	32.3	31.4	30.6	29.8	29.0	28.2	27.4	26.6
77	33.0	32.2	31.3	30.5	29.7	28.8	28.0	27.3	26.5
78	33.0	32.1	31.2	30.4	29.6	28.7	27.9	27.1	26.4
79	32.9	32.0	31.2	30.3	29.5	28.7	27.8	27.0	26.2
80	32.9	32.0	31.1	30.3	29.4	28.6	27.8	26.9	26.1
81	32.8	31.9	31.1	30.2	29.3	28.5	27.7	26.9	26.0
82	32.8	31.9	31.0	30.1	29.3	28.4	27.6	26.8	26.0
83	32.7	31.8	31.0	30.1	29.2	28.4	27.5	26.7	25.9
84	32.7	31.8	30.9	30.0	29.2	28.3	27.5	26.7	25.8
85	32.7	31.8	30.9	30.0	29.1	28.3	27.4	26.6	25.8
86	32.6	31.7	30.9	30.0	29.1	28.2	27.4	26.6	25.7
87	32.6	31.7	30.8	29.9	29.1	28.2	27.4	26.5	25.7
88	32.6	31.7	30.8	29.9	29.0	28.2	27.3	26.5	25.6
89	32.6	31.7	30.8	29.9	29.0	28.2	27.3	26.4	25.6
90	32.6	31.7	30.8	29.9	29.0	28.1	27.3	26.4	25.6
91	32.5	31.6	30.7	29.9	29.0	28.1	27.3	26.4	25.6
92	32.5	31.6	30.7	29.8	29.0	28.1	27.2	26.4	25.5
93	32.5	31.6	30.7	29.8	29.0	28.1	27.2	26.4	25.5
94	32.5	31.6	30.7	29.8	28.9	28.1	27.2	26.3	25.5
95	32.5	31.6	30.7	29.8	28.9	28.1	27.2	26.3	25.5
96	32.5	31.6	30.7	29.8	28.9	28.0	27.2	26.3	25.5
97	32.5	31.6	30.7	29.8	28.9	28.0	27.2	26.3	25.5
98	32.5	31.6	30.7	29.8	28.9	28.0	27.2	26.3	25.5
99	32.5	31.6	30.7	29.8	28.9	28.0	27.1	26.3	25.4
100	32.5	31.6	30.7	29.8	28.9	28.0	27.1	26.3	25.4
101	32.5	31.6	30.7	29.8	28.9	28.0	27.1	26.3	25.4
102	32.5	31.6	30.7	29.8	28.9	28.0	27.1	26.3	25.4
103	32.5	31.6	30.7	29.8	28.9	28.0	27.1	26.3	25.4
104	32.5	31.6	30.7	29.8	28.9	28.0	27.1	26.3	25.4
105	32.5	31.6	30.7	29.8	28.9	28.0	27.1	26.3	25.4
106	32.5	31.6	30.7	29.8	28.9	28.0	27.1	26.3	25.4
107	32.5	31.6	30.7	29.8	28.9	28.0	27.1	26.3	25.4
108	32.5	31.6	30.7	29.8	28.9	28.0	27.1	26.3	25.4
109	32.5	31.6	30.7	29.8	28.9	28.0	27.1	26.3	25.4
110	32.5	31.6	30.7	29.8	28.9	28.0	27.1	26.3	25.4
111	32.5	31.6	30.7	29.8	28.9	28.0	27.1	26.3	25.4
112	32.5	31.6	30.7	29.8	28.9	28.0	27.1	26.3	25.4
113	32.5	31.6	30.7	29.8	28.9	28.0	27.1	26.3	25.4
114	32.5	31.6	30.7	29.8	28.9	28.0	27.1	26.3	25.4
115	32.5	31.6	30.7	29.8	28.9	28.0	27.1	26.3	25.4
116	32.5	31.6	30.7	29.8	28.9	28.0	27.1	26.3	25.4
117	32.5	31.6	30.7	29.8	28.9	28.0	27.1	26.3	25.4
118	32.5	31.6	30.7	29.8	28.9	28.0	27.1	26.3	25.4
119	32.5	31.6	30.7	29.8	28.9	28.0	27.1	26.2	25.4
120+	32.5	31.6	30.6	29.8	28.9	28.0	27.1	26.2	25.4

Ages	63	64	65	66	67	68	69	70	71
0	84.7	84.7	84.7	84.7	84.7	84.7	84.7	84.7	84.7
1	83.8	83.8	83.8	83.8	83.8	83.8	83.8	83.8	83.8
2	82.9	82.8	82.8	82.8	82.8	82.8	82.8	82.8	82.8
3	81.9	81.9	81.9	81.9	81.9	81.8	81.8	81.8	81.8
4	80.9	80.9	80.9	80.9	80.9	80.9	80.9	80.9	80.9
5	79.9	79.9	79.9	79.9	79.9	79.9	79.9	79.9	79.9
6	78.9	78.9	78.9	78.9	78.9	78.9	78.9	78.9	78.9
7	78.0	77.9	77.9	77.9	77.9	77.9	77.9	77.9	77.9
8	77.0	77.0	77.0	76.9	76.9	76.9	76.9	76.9	76.9
9	76.0	76.0	76.0	76.0	76.0	75.9	75.9	75.9	75.9

Reg. §1.401(a)(9)-9(d)

Ages	63	64	65	66	67	68	69	70	71
10	75.0	75.0	75.0	75.0	75.0	75.0	75.0	74.9	74.9
11	74.0	74.0	74.0	74.0	74.0	74.0	74.0	74.0	74.0
12	73.0	73.0	73.0	73.0	73.0	73.0	73.0	73.0	73.0
13	72.1	72.1	72.0	72.0	72.0	72.0	72.0	72.0	72.0
14	71.1	71.1	71.1	71.1	71.0	71.0	71.0	71.0	71.0
15	70.1	70.1	70.1	70.1	70.1	70.1	70.0	70.0	70.0
16	69.1	69.1	69.1	69.1	69.1	69.1	69.1	69.1	69.0
17	68.2	68.2	68.1	68.1	68.1	68.1	68.1	68.1	68.1
18	67.2	67.2	67.2	67.2	67.1	67.1	67.1	67.1	67.1
19	66.2	66.2	66.2	66.2	66.2	66.2	66.1	66.1	66.1
20	65.3	65.2	65.2	65.2	65.2	65.2	65.2	65.2	65.1
21	64.3	64.3	64.3	64.2	64.2	64.2	64.2	64.2	64.2
22	63.3	63.3	63.3	63.3	63.3	63.2	63.2	63.2	63.2
23	62.4	62.3	62.3	62.3	62.3	62.3	62.3	62.2	62.2
24	61.4	61.4	61.4	61.3	61.3	61.3	61.3	61.3	61.3
25	60.5	60.4	60.4	60.4	60.4	60.3	60.3	60.3	60.3
26	59.5	59.5	59.5	59.4	59.4	59.4	59.4	59.4	59.3
27	58.6	58.5	58.5	58.5	58.5	58.4	58.4	58.4	58.4
28	57.6	57.6	57.5	57.5	57.5	57.5	57.5	57.4	57.4
29	56.7	56.6	56.6	56.6	56.5	56.5	56.5	56.5	56.5
30	55.7	55.7	55.7	55.6	55.6	55.6	55.6	55.5	55.5
31	54.8	54.8	54.7	54.7	54.7	54.6	54.6	54.6	54.6
32	53.9	53.8	53.8	53.7	53.7	53.7	53.7	53.6	53.6
33	52.9	52.9	52.8	52.8	52.8	52.7	52.7	52.7	52.7
34	52.0	52.0	51.9	51.9	51.8	51.8	51.8	51.7	51.7
35	51.1	51.0	51.0	50.9	50.9	50.9	50.8	50.8	50.8
36	50.2	50.1	50.1	50.0	50.0	49.9	49.9	49.9	49.8
37	49.3	49.2	49.1	49.1	49.0	49.0	49.0	48.9	48.9
38	48.3	48.3	48.2	48.2	48.1	48.1	48.0	48.0	47.9
39	47.4	47.4	47.3	47.2	47.2	47.1	47.1	47.0	47.0
40	46.5	46.5	46.4	46.3	46.3	46.2	46.2	46.1	46.1
41	45.7	45.6	45.5	45.4	45.4	45.3	45.2	45.2	45.1
42	44.8	44.7	44.6	44.5	44.4	44.4	44.3	44.3	44.2
43	43.9	43.8	43.7	43.6	43.5	43.5	43.4	43.3	43.3
44	43.0	42.9	42.8	42.7	42.6	42.6	42.5	42.4	42.4
45	42.2	42.1	41.9	41.8	41.8	41.7	41.6	41.5	41.5
46	41.3	41.2	41.1	41.0	40.9	40.8	40.7	40.6	40.6
47	40.5	40.4	40.2	40.1	40.0	39.9	39.8	39.7	39.7
48	39.7	39.5	39.4	39.3	39.1	39.0	38.9	38.8	38.8
49	38.9	38.7	38.6	38.4	38.3	38.2	38.1	38.0	37.9
50	38.1	37.9	37.7	37.6	37.5	37.3	37.2	37.1	37.0
51	37.3	37.1	36.9	36.8	36.6	36.5	36.4	36.2	36.1
52	36.6	36.3	36.2	36.0	35.8	35.7	35.5	35.4	35.3
53	35.8	35.6	35.4	35.2	35.0	34.9	34.7	34.6	34.5
54	35.1	34.9	34.6	34.4	34.2	34.1	33.9	33.8	33.6
55	34.4	34.2	33.9	33.7	33.5	33.3	33.1	33.0	32.8
56	33.8	33.5	33.2	33.0	32.7	32.5	32.3	32.2	32.0
57	33.1	32.8	32.5	32.3	32.0	31.8	31.6	31.4	31.2
58	32.5	32.2	31.9	31.6	31.3	31.1	30.9	30.7	30.5
59	31.9	31.5	31.2	30.9	30.6	30.4	30.1	29.9	29.7
60	31.3	31.0	30.6	30.3	30.0	29.7	29.4	29.2	29.0
61	30.8	30.4	30.0	29.7	29.4	29.1	28.8	28.5	28.3
62	30.3	29.9	29.5	29.1	28.7	28.4	28.1	27.9	27.6
63	29.8	29.4	28.9	28.5	28.2	27.8	27.5	27.2	26.9
64	29.4	28.9	28.4	28.0	27.6	27.2	26.9	26.6	26.3
65	28.9	28.4	28.0	27.5	27.1	26.7	26.3	26.0	25.7
66	28.5	28.0	27.5	27.0	26.6	26.2	25.8	25.4	25.1
67	28.2	27.6	27.1	26.6	26.1	25.7	25.3	24.9	24.5
68	27.8	27.2	26.7	26.2	25.7	25.2	24.8	24.3	24.0
69	27.5	26.9	26.3	25.8	25.3	24.8	24.3	23.9	23.4
70	27.2	26.6	26.0	25.4	24.9	24.3	23.9	23.4	22.9

Reg. §1.401(a)(9)-9(d)

Ages	63	64	65	66	67	68	69	70	71
71	26.9	26.3	25.7	25.1	24.5	24.0	23.4	22.9	22.5
72	26.7	26.0	25.4	24.8	24.2	23.6	23.1	22.5	22.0
73	26.5	25.8	25.1	24.5	23.9	23.3	22.7	22.2	21.6
74	26.2	25.5	24.9	24.2	23.6	23.0	22.4	21.8	21.3
75	26.1	25.3	24.6	24.0	23.3	22.7	22.1	21.5	20.9
76	25.9	25.2	24.4	23.7	23.1	22.4	21.8	21.2	20.6
77	25.7	25.0	24.3	23.5	22.9	22.2	21.5	20.9	20.3
78	25.6	24.8	24.1	23.4	22.7	22.0	21.3	20.6	20.0
79	25.5	24.7	23.9	23.2	22.5	21.8	21.1	20.4	19.8
80	25.3	24.6	23.8	23.1	22.3	21.6	20.9	20.2	19.6
81	25.2	24.5	23.7	22.9	22.2	21.5	20.7	20.0	19.4
82	25.2	24.4	23.6	22.8	22.1	21.3	20.6	19.9	19.2
83	25.1	24.3	23.5	22.7	22.0	21.2	20.5	19.7	19.0
84	25.0	24.2	23.4	22.6	21.9	21.1	20.4	19.6	18.9
85	25.0	24.1	23.3	22.6	21.8	21.0	20.3	19.5	18.8
86	24.9	24.1	23.3	22.5	21.7	20.9	20.2	19.4	18.7
87	24.9	24.0	23.2	22.4	21.6	20.9	20.1	19.3	18.6
88	24.8	24.0	23.2	22.4	21.6	20.8	20.0	19.2	18.5
89	24.8	24.0	23.1	22.3	21.5	20.7	20.0	19.2	18.4
90	24.7	23.9	23.1	22.3	21.5	20.7	19.9	19.1	18.4
91	24.7	23.9	23.1	22.3	21.5	20.7	19.9	19.1	18.3
92	24.7	23.9	23.0	22.2	21.4	20.6	19.8	19.0	18.3
93	24.7	23.8	23.0	22.2	21.4	20.6	19.8	19.0	18.2
94	24.7	23.8	23.0	22.2	21.4	20.6	19.8	19.0	18.2
95	24.6	23.8	23.0	22.2	21.4	20.6	19.7	18.9	18.2
96	24.6	23.8	23.0	22.2	21.3	20.5	19.7	18.9	18.1
97	24.6	23.8	23.0	22.1	21.3	20.5	19.7	18.9	18.1
98	24.6	23.8	22.9	22.1	21.3	20.5	19.7	18.9	18.1
99	24.6	23.8	22.9	22.1	21.3	20.5	19.7	18.9	18.1
100	24.6	23.8	22.9	22.1	21.3	20.5	19.7	18.9	18.1
101	24.6	23.8	22.9	22.1	21.3	20.5	19.7	18.9	18.1
102	24.6	23.7	22.9	22.1	21.3	20.5	19.7	18.8	18.0
103	24.6	23.7	22.9	22.1	21.3	20.5	19.6	18.8	18.0
104	24.6	23.7	22.9	22.1	21.3	20.5	19.6	18.8	18.0
105	24.6	23.7	22.9	22.1	21.3	20.5	19.6	18.8	18.0
106	24.6	23.7	22.9	22.1	21.3	20.5	19.6	18.8	18.0
107	24.6	23.7	22.9	22.1	21.3	20.5	19.6	18.8	18.0
108	24.6	23.7	22.9	22.1	21.3	20.5	19.6	18.8	18.0
109	24.6	23.7	22.9	22.1	21.3	20.4	19.6	18.8	18.0
110	24.6	23.7	22.9	22.1	21.3	20.4	19.6	18.8	18.0
111	24.6	23.7	22.9	22.1	21.3	20.4	19.6	18.8	18.0
112	24.6	23.7	22.9	22.1	21.3	20.4	19.6	18.8	18.0
113	24.6	23.7	22.9	22.1	21.3	20.4	19.6	18.8	18.0
114	24.6	23.7	22.9	22.1	21.3	20.4	19.6	18.8	18.0
115	24.6	23.7	22.9	22.1	21.3	20.4	19.6	18.8	18.0
116	24.6	23.7	22.9	22.1	21.3	20.4	19.6	18.8	18.0
117	24.6	23.7	22.9	22.1	21.2	20.4	19.6	18.8	18.0
118	24.5	23.7	22.9	22.1	21.2	20.4	19.6	18.8	18.0
119	24.5	23.7	22.9	22.1	21.2	20.4	19.6	18.8	18.0
120+	24.5	23.7	22.9	22.0	21.2	20.4	19.6	18.8	18.0

Ages	72	73	74	75	76	77	78	79	80
0	84.7	84.6	84.6	84.6	84.6	84.6	84.6	84.6	84.6
1	83.8	83.8	83.8	83.8	83.8	83.8	83.8	83.8	83.8
2	82.8	82.8	82.8	82.8	82.8	82.8	82.8	82.8	82.8
3	81.8	81.8	81.8	81.8	81.8	81.8	81.8	81.8	81.8
4	80.9	80.8	80.8	80.8	80.8	80.8	80.8	80.8	80.8
5	79.9	79.9	79.9	79.9	79.9	79.8	79.8	79.8	79.8
6	78.9	78.9	78.9	78.9	78.9	78.9	78.9	78.9	78.9
7	77.9	77.9	77.9	77.9	77.9	77.9	77.9	77.9	77.9

Ages	72	73	74	75	76	77	78	79	80
8	76.9	76.9	76.9	76.9	76.9	76.9	76.9	76.9	76.9
9	75.9	75.9	75.9	75.9	75.9	75.9	75.9	75.9	75.9
10	74.9	74.9	74.9	74.9	74.9	74.9	74.9	74.9	74.9
11	73.9	73.9	73.9	73.9	73.9	73.9	73.9	73.9	73.9
12	73.0	73.0	73.0	72.9	72.9	72.9	72.9	72.9	72.9
13	72.0	72.0	72.0	72.0	72.0	72.0	71.9	71.9	71.9
14	71.0	71.0	71.0	71.0	71.0	71.0	71.0	71.0	71.0
15	70.0	70.0	70.0	70.0	70.0	70.0	70.0	70.0	70.0
16	69.0	69.0	69.0	69.0	69.0	69.0	69.0	69.0	69.0
17	68.1	68.1	68.0	68.0	68.0	68.0	68.0	68.0	68.0
18	67.1	67.1	67.1	67.1	67.1	67.0	67.0	67.0	67.0
19	66.1	66.1	66.1	66.1	66.1	66.1	66.1	66.1	66.1
20	65.1	65.1	65.1	65.1	65.1	65.1	65.1	65.1	65.1
21	64.2	64.2	64.1	64.1	64.1	64.1	64.1	64.1	64.1
22	63.2	63.2	63.2	63.2	63.2	63.1	63.1	63.1	63.1
23	62.2	62.2	62.2	62.2	62.2	62.2	62.2	62.2	62.1
24	61.3	61.2	61.2	61.2	61.2	61.2	61.2	61.2	61.2
25	60.3	60.3	60.3	60.3	60.2	60.2	60.2	60.2	60.2
26	59.3	59.3	59.3	59.3	59.3	59.3	59.3	59.3	59.2
27	58.4	58.4	58.3	58.3	58.3	58.3	58.3	58.3	58.3
28	57.4	57.4	57.4	57.4	57.4	57.3	57.3	57.3	57.3
29	56.5	56.4	56.4	56.4	56.4	56.4	56.4	56.4	56.4
30	55.5	55.5	55.5	55.5	55.4	55.4	55.4	55.4	55.4
31	54.5	54.5	54.5	54.5	54.5	54.5	54.5	54.5	54.4
32	53.6	53.6	53.6	53.5	53.5	53.5	53.5	53.5	53.5
33	52.6	52.6	52.6	52.6	52.6	52.6	52.6	52.5	52.5
34	51.7	51.7	51.7	51.6	51.6	51.6	51.6	51.6	51.6
35	50.8	50.7	50.7	50.7	50.7	50.7	50.6	50.6	50.6
36	49.8	49.8	49.8	49.7	49.7	49.7	49.7	49.7	49.7
37	48.9	48.8	48.8	48.8	48.8	48.8	48.7	48.7	48.7
38	47.9	47.9	47.9	47.8	47.8	47.8	47.8	47.8	47.8
39	47.0	46.9	46.9	46.9	46.9	46.9	46.8	46.8	46.8
40	46.0	46.0	46.0	45.9	45.9	45.9	45.9	45.9	45.9
41	45.1	45.1	45.0	45.0	45.0	45.0	44.9	44.9	44.9
42	44.2	44.1	44.1	44.1	44.0	44.0	44.0	44.0	43.9
43	43.2	43.2	43.2	43.1	43.1	43.1	43.0	43.0	43.0
44	42.3	42.3	42.2	42.2	42.2	42.1	42.1	42.1	42.1
45	41.4	41.4	41.3	41.3	41.2	41.2	41.2	41.1	41.1
46	40.5	40.4	40.4	40.3	40.3	40.3	40.2	40.2	40.2
47	39.6	39.5	39.5	39.4	39.4	39.3	39.3	39.3	39.2
48	38.7	38.6	38.6	38.5	38.5	38.4	38.4	38.3	38.3
49	37.8	37.7	37.7	37.6	37.5	37.5	37.5	37.4	37.4
50	36.9	36.8	36.8	36.7	36.6	36.6	36.5	36.5	36.5
51	36.0	36.0	35.9	35.8	35.7	35.7	35.5	35.6	35.5
52	35.2	35.1	35.0	34.9	34.9	34.8	34.7	34.7	34.6
53	34.3	34.2	34.1	34.1	34.0	33.9	33.9	33.8	33.7
54	33.5	33.4	33.3	33.2	33.1	33.0	33.0	32.9	32.9
55	32.7	32.6	32.4	32.4	32.3	32.2	32.1	32.0	32.0
56	31.9	31.7	31.6	31.5	31.4	31.3	31.2	31.2	31.1
57	31.1	30.9	30.8	30.7	30.6	30.5	30.4	30.3	30.3
58	30.3	30.1	30.0	29.9	29.8	29.7	29.6	29.5	29.4
59	29.5	29.4	29.2	29.1	29.0	28.8	28.7	28.7	28.6
60	28.8	28.6	28.4	28.3	28.2	28.0	27.9	27.8	27.8
61	28.1	27.9	27.7	27.5	27.4	27.3	27.1	27.0	26.9
62	27.4	27.2	27.0	26.8	26.6	26.5	26.4	26.2	26.1
63	26.7	26.5	26.2	26.1	25.9	25.7	25.6	25.5	25.3
64	26.0	25.8	25.5	25.3	25.2	25.0	24.8	24.7	24.6
65	25.4	25.1	24.9	24.6	24.4	24.3	24.1	23.9	23.8
66	24.8	24.5	24.2	24.0	23.7	23.5	23.4	23.2	23.1
67	24.2	23.9	23.6	23.3	23.1	22.9	22.7	22.5	22.3
68	23.6	23.3	23.0	22.7	22.4	22.2	22.0	21.8	21.6

Reg. §1.401(a)(9)-9(d)

Ages	72	73	74	75	76	77	78	79	80
69	23.1	22.7	22.4	22.1	21.8	21.5	21.3	21.1	20.9
70	22.5	22.2	21.8	21.5	21.2	20.9	20.6	20.4	20.2
71	22.0	21.6	21.3	20.9	20.6	20.3	20.0	19.8	19.6
72	21.6	21.1	20.7	20.4	20.0	19.7	19.4	19.2	18.9
73	21.1	20.7	20.3	19.9	19.5	19.1	18.8	18.6	18.3
74	20.7	20.3	19.8	19.4	19.0	18.6	18.3	18.0	17.7
75	20.4	19.9	19.4	18.9	18.5	18.1	17.8	17.4	17.1
76	20.0	19.5	19.0	18.5	18.1	17.7	17.3	16.9	16.6
77	19.7	19.1	18.6	18.1	17.7	17.2	16.8	16.4	16.1
78	19.4	18.8	18.3	17.8	17.3	16.8	16.4	16.0	15.6
79	19.2	18.6	18.0	17.4	16.9	16.4	16.0	15.6	15.2
80	18.9	18.3	17.7	17.1	16.6	16.1	15.6	15.2	14.7
81	18.7	18.1	17.4	16.9	16.3	15.8	15.3	14.8	14.4
82	18.5	17.9	17.2	16.6	16.0	15.5	15.0	14.5	14.0
83	18.3	17.7	17.0	16.4	15.8	15.2	14.7	14.2	13.7
84	18.2	17.5	16.8	16.2	15.6	15.0	14.4	13.9	13.4
85	18.1	17.4	16.7	16.0	15.4	14.8	14.2	13.6	13.1
86	17.9	17.2	16.5	15.9	15.2	14.6	14.0	13.4	12.9
87	17.8	17.1	16.4	15.7	15.1	14.4	13.8	13.2	12.7
88	17.7	17.0	16.3	15.6	14.9	14.3	13.7	13.1	12.5
89	17.7	16.9	16.2	15.5	14.8	14.2	13.5	12.9	12.3
90	17.6	16.9	16.1	15.4	14.7	14.1	13.4	12.8	12.2
91	17.5	16.8	16.1	15.3	14.6	14.0	13.3	12.7	12.1
92	17.5	16.7	16.0	15.3	14.6	13.9	13.2	12.6	11.9
93	17.4	16.7	15.9	15.2	14.5	13.8	13.1	12.5	11.9
94	17.4	16.6	15.9	15.2	14.4	13.7	13.1	12.4	11.8
95	17.4	16.6	15.9	15.1	14.4	13.7	13.0	12.3	11.7
96	17.4	16.6	15.8	15.1	14.3	13.6	12.9	12.3	11.6
97	17.3	16.6	15.8	15.0	14.3	13.6	12.9	12.2	11.6
98	17.3	16.5	15.8	15.0	14.3	13.6	12.9	12.2	11.5
99	17.3	16.5	15.7	15.0	14.3	13.5	12.8	12.2	11.5
100	17.3	16.5	15.7	15.0	14.2	13.5	12.8	12.1	11.5
101	17.3	16.5	15.7	15.0	14.2	13.5	12.8	12.1	11.4
102	17.3	16.5	15.7	14.9	14.2	13.5	12.8	12.1	11.4
103	17.3	16.5	15.7	14.9	14.2	13.5	12.8	12.1	11.4
104	17.2	16.5	15.7	14.9	14.2	13.5	12.7	12.0	11.4
105	17.2	16.5	15.7	14.9	14.2	13.4	12.7	12.0	11.4
106	17.2	16.5	15.7	14.9	14.2	13.4	12.7	12.0	11.4
107	17.2	16.5	15.7	14.9	14.2	13.4	12.7	12.0	11.4
108	17.2	16.5	15.7	14.9	14.2	13.4	12.7	12.0	11.4
109	17.2	16.4	15.7	14.9	14.2	13.4	12.7	12.0	11.3
110	17.2	16.4	15.7	14.9	14.2	13.4	12.7	12.0	11.3
111	17.2	16.4	15.7	14.9	14.2	13.4	12.7	12.0	11.3
112	17.2	16.4	15.7	14.9	14.2	13.4	12.7	12.0	11.3
113	17.2	16.4	15.7	14.9	14.2	13.4	12.7	12.0	11.3
114	17.2	16.4	15.7	14.9	14.1	13.4	12.7	12.0	11.3
115	17.2	16.4	15.7	14.9	14.1	13.4	12.7	12.0	11.3
116	17.2	16.4	15.6	14.9	14.1	13.4	12.7	12.0	11.3
117	17.2	16.4	15.6	14.9	14.1	13.4	12.7	12.0	11.3
118	17.2	16.4	15.6	14.9	14.1	13.4	12.6	11.9	11.3
119	17.2	16.4	15.6	14.8	14.1	13.4	12.6	11.9	11.2
120+	17.2	16.4	15.6	14.8	14.1	13.3	12.6	11.9	11.2

Ages	81	82	83	84	85	86	87	88	89
0	84.6	84.6	84.6	84.6	84.6	84.6	84.6	84.6	84.6
1	83.8	83.8	83.7	83.7	83.7	83.7	83.7	83.7	83.7
2	82.8	82.8	82.8	82.8	82.8	82.8	82.8	82.8	82.8
3	81.8	81.8	81.8	81.8	81.8	81.8	81.8	81.8	81.8
4	80.8	80.8	80.8	80.8	80.8	80.8	80.8	80.8	80.8
5	79.8	79.8	79.8	79.8	79.8	79.8	79.8	79.8	79.8

Reg. §1.401(a)(9)-9(d)

Ages	81	82	83	84	85	86	87	88	89
6	78.9	78.9	78.9	78.9	78.8	78.8	78.8	78.8	78.8
7	77.9	77.9	77.9	77.9	77.9	77.9	77.9	77.9	77.9
8	76.9	76.9	76.9	76.9	76.9	76.9	76.9	76.9	76.9
9	75.9	75.9	75.9	75.9	75.9	75.9	75.9	75.9	75.9
10	74.9	74.9	74.9	74.9	74.9	74.9	74.9	74.9	74.9
11	73.9	73.9	73.9	73.9	73.9	73.9	73.9	73.9	73.9
12	72.9	72.9	72.9	72.9	72.9	72.9	72.9	72.9	72.9
13	71.9	71.9	71.9	71.9	71.9	71.9	71.9	71.9	71.9
14	71.0	70.9	70.9	70.9	70.9	70.9	70.9	70.9	70.9
15	70.0	70.0	70.0	70.0	70.0	70.0	70.0	69.9	69.9
16	69.0	69.0	69.0	69.0	69.0	69.0	69.0	69.0	69.0
17	68.0	68.0	68.0	68.0	68.0	68.0	68.0	68.0	68.0
18	67.0	67.0	67.0	67.0	67.0	67.0	67.0	67.0	67.0
19	66.0	66.0	66.0	66.0	66.0	66.0	66.0	66.0	66.0
20	65.1	65.1	65.1	65.1	65.1	65.1	65.0	65.0	65.0
21	64.1	64.1	64.1	64.1	64.1	64.1	64.1	64.1	64.1
22	63.1	63.1	63.1	63.1	63.1	63.1	63.1	63.1	63.1
23	62.1	62.1	62.1	62.1	62.1	62.1	62.1	62.1	62.1
24	61.2	61.2	61.2	61.2	61.2	61.1	61.1	61.1	61.1
25	60.2	60.2	60.2	60.2	60.2	60.2	60.2	60.2	60.2
26	59.2	59.2	59.2	59.2	59.2	59.2	59.2	59.2	59.2
27	58.3	58.3	58.3	58.3	58.3	58.2	58.2	58.2	58.2
28	57.3	57.3	57.3	57.3	57.3	57.3	57.3	57.3	57.3
29	56.4	56.3	56.3	56.3	56.3	56.3	56.3	56.3	56.3
30	55.4	55.4	55.4	55.4	55.4	55.4	55.4	55.4	55.4
31	54.4	54.4	54.4	54.4	54.4	54.4	54.4	54.4	54.4
32	53.5	53.5	53.5	53.5	53.5	53.5	53.4	53.4	53.4
33	52.5	52.5	52.5	52.5	52.5	52.5	52.5	52.5	52.5
34	51.6	51.6	51.6	51.5	51.5	51.5	51.5	51.5	51.5
35	50.6	50.6	50.6	50.6	50.6	50.6	50.6	50.6	50.6
36	49.7	49.7	49.6	49.6	49.6	49.6	49.6	49.6	49.6
37	48.7	48.7	48.7	48.7	48.7	48.7	48.7	48.7	48.7
38	47.7	47.7	47.7	47.7	47.7	47.7	47.7	47.7	47.7
39	46.8	46.8	46.8	46.8	46.8	46.7	46.7	46.7	46.7
40	45.8	45.8	45.8	45.8	45.8	45.8	45.8	45.8	45.8
41	44.9	44.9	44.9	44.9	44.8	44.8	44.8	44.8	44.8
42	43.9	43.9	43.9	43.9	43.9	43.9	43.9	43.9	43.9
43	43.0	43.0	43.0	42.9	42.9	42.9	42.9	42.9	42.9
44	42.0	42.0	42.0	42.0	42.0	42.0	42.0	42.0	41.9
45	41.1	41.1	41.1	41.0	41.0	41.0	41.0	41.0	41.0
46	40.1	40.1	40.1	40.1	40.1	40.1	40.1	40.0	40.0
47	39.2	39.2	39.2	39.2	39.1	39.1	39.1	39.1	39.1
48	38.3	38.3	38.2	38.2	38.2	38.2	38.2	38.2	38.1
49	37.3	37.3	37.3	37.3	37.3	37.2	37.2	37.2	37.2
50	36.4	36.4	36.4	36.3	36.3	36.3	36.3	36.3	36.3
51	35.5	35.5	35.4	35.4	35.4	35.4	35.4	35.3	35.3
52	34.6	34.6	34.5	34.5	34.5	34.5	34.4	34.4	34.4
53	33.7	33.7	33.6	33.6	33.6	33.5	33.5	33.5	33.5
54	32.8	32.8	32.7	32.7	32.7	32.6	32.6	32.6	32.6
55	31.9	31.9	31.8	31.8	31.8	31.7	31.7	31.7	31.7
56	31.1	31.0	31.0	30.9	30.9	30.9	30.8	30.8	30.8
57	30.2	30.1	30.1	30.0	30.0	30.0	29.9	29.9	29.9
58	29.3	29.3	29.2	29.2	29.1	29.1	29.1	29.0	29.0
59	28.5	28.4	28.4	28.3	28.3	28.2	28.2	28.2	28.2
60	27.7	27.6	27.5	27.5	27.4	27.4	27.4	27.3	27.3
61	26.9	26.8	26.7	26.7	26.6	26.6	26.5	26.5	26.4
62	26.0	26.0	25.9	25.8	25.8	25.7	25.7	25.6	25.6
63	25.2	25.2	25.1	25.0	25.0	24.9	24.9	24.8	24.8
64	24.5	24.4	24.3	24.2	24.1	24.1	24.0	24.0	24.0
65	23.7	23.6	23.5	23.4	23.3	23.3	23.2	23.2	23.1
66	22.9	22.8	22.7	22.6	22.6	22.5	22.4	22.4	22.3

Reg. §1.401(a)(9)-9(d)

Ages	81	82	83	84	85	86	87	88	89
67	22.2	22.1	22.0	21.9	21.8	21.7	21.6	21.6	21.5
68	21.5	21.3	21.2	21.1	21.0	20.9	20.9	20.8	20.7
69	20.7	20.6	20.5	20.4	20.3	20.2	20.1	20.0	20.0
70	20.0	19.9	19.7	19.6	19.5	19.4	19.3	19.2	19.2
71	19.4	19.2	19.0	18.9	18.8	18.7	18.6	18.5	18.4
72	18.7	18.5	18.3	18.2	18.1	17.9	17.8	17.7	17.7
73	18.1	17.9	17.7	17.5	17.4	17.2	17.1	17.0	16.9
74	17.4	17.2	17.0	16.8	16.7	16.5	16.4	16.3	16.2
75	16.9	16.6	16.4	16.2	16.0	15.9	15.7	15.6	15.5
76	16.3	16.0	15.8	15.6	15.4	15.2	15.1	14.9	14.8
77	15.8	15.5	15.2	15.0	14.8	14.6	14.4	14.3	14.2
78	15.3	15.0	14.7	14.4	14.2	14.0	13.8	13.7	13.5
79	14.8	14.5	14.2	13.9	13.6	13.4	13.2	13.1	12.9
80	14.4	14.0	13.7	13.4	13.1	12.9	12.7	12.5	12.3
81	14.0	13.6	13.2	12.9	12.6	12.4	12.2	12.0	11.8
82	13.6	13.2	12.8	12.5	12.2	11.9	11.7	11.5	11.3
83	13.2	12.8	12.4	12.1	11.8	11.5	11.2	11.0	10.8
84	12.9	12.5	12.1	11.7	11.4	11.1	10.8	10.5	10.3
85	12.6	12.2	11.8	11.4	11.0	10.7	10.4	10.1	9.9
86	12.4	11.9	11.5	11.1	10.7	10.4	10.0	9.8	9.5
87	12.2	11.7	11.2	10.8	10.4	10.0	9.7	9.4	9.1
88	12.0	11.5	11.0	10.5	10.1	9.8	9.4	9.1	8.8
89	11.8	11.3	10.8	10.3	9.9	9.5	9.1	8.8	8.5
90	11.6	11.1	10.6	10.1	9.7	9.3	8.9	8.6	8.3
91	11.5	10.9	10.4	9.9	9.5	9.1	8.7	8.3	8.0
92	11.4	10.8	10.3	9.8	9.3	8.9	8.5	8.1	7.8
93	11.3	10.7	10.1	9.6	9.2	8.7	8.3	7.9	7.6
94	11.2	10.6	10.0	9.5	9.0	8.6	8.2	7.8	7.4
95	11.1	10.5	9.9	9.4	8.9	8.5	8.0	7.6	7.3
96	11.0	10.4	9.9	9.3	8.8	8.4	7.9	7.5	7.1
97	11.0	10.4	9.8	9.2	8.7	8.3	7.8	7.4	7.0
98	10.9	10.3	9.7	9.2	8.7	8.2	7.7	7.3	6.9
99	10.9	10.2	9.7	9.1	8.6	8.1	7.6	7.2	6.8
100	10.8	10.2	9.6	9.1	8.5	8.0	7.6	7.2	6.8
101	10.8	10.2	9.6	9.0	8.5	8.0	7.5	7.1	6.7
102	10.8	10.1	9.6	9.0	8.5	8.0	7.5	7.0	6.6
103	10.7	10.1	9.5	9.0	8.4	7.9	7.4	7.0	6.6
104	10.7	10.1	9.5	8.9	8.4	7.9	7.4	7.0	6.6
105	10.7	10.1	9.5	8.9	8.4	7.9	7.4	6.9	6.5
106	10.7	10.1	9.5	8.9	8.4	7.9	7.4	6.9	6.5
107	10.7	10.1	9.5	8.9	8.4	7.9	7.4	6.9	6.5
108	10.7	10.1	9.5	8.9	8.4	7.8	7.4	6.9	6.5
109	10.7	10.1	9.5	8.9	8.4	7.8	7.4	6.9	6.5
110	10.7	10.1	9.5	8.9	8.3	7.8	7.4	6.9	6.5
111	10.7	10.1	9.5	8.9	8.3	7.8	7.3	6.9	6.5
112	10.7	10.1	9.5	8.9	8.3	7.8	7.3	6.9	6.5
113	10.7	10.0	9.4	8.9	8.3	7.8	7.3	6.9	6.4
114	10.7	10.0	9.4	8.9	8.3	7.8	7.3	6.9	6.4
115	10.7	10.0	9.4	8.8	8.3	7.8	7.3	6.8	6.4
116	10.6	10.0	9.4	8.8	8.3	7.7	7.3	6.8	6.4
117	10.6	10.0	9.4	8.8	8.2	7.7	7.2	6.8	6.3
118	10.6	10.0	9.3	8.8	8.2	7.7	7.2	6.7	6.3
119	10.6	9.9	9.3	8.7	8.2	7.6	7.1	6.6	6.2
120+	10.5	9.9	9.3	8.7	8.1	7.6	7.1	6.6	6.1

Ages	90	91	92	93	94	95	96	97	98
0	84.6	84.6	84.6	84.6	84.6	84.6	84.6	84.6	84.6
1	83.7	83.7	83.7	83.7	83.7	83.7	83.7	83.7	83.7
2	82.8	82.8	82.8	82.8	82.8	82.8	82.8	82.8	82.8
3	81.8	81.8	81.8	81.8	81.8	81.8	81.8	81.8	81.8

Ages	90	91	92	93	94	95	96	97	98
4	80.8	80.8	80.8	80.8	80.8	80.8	80.8	80.8	80.8
5	79.8	79.8	79.8	79.8	79.8	79.8	79.8	79.8	79.8
6	78.8	78.8	78.8	78.8	78.8	78.8	78.8	78.8	78.8
7	77.9	77.9	77.9	77.9	77.9	77.9	77.9	77.9	77.9
8	76.9	76.9	76.9	76.9	76.9	76.9	76.9	76.9	76.9
9	75.9	75.9	75.9	75.9	75.9	75.9	75.9	75.9	75.9
10	74.9	74.9	74.9	74.9	74.9	74.9	74.9	74.9	74.9
11	73.9	73.9	73.9	73.9	73.9	73.9	73.9	73.9	73.9
12	72.9	72.9	72.9	72.9	72.9	72.9	72.9	72.9	72.9
13	71.9	71.9	71.9	71.9	71.9	71.9	71.9	71.9	71.9
14	70.9	70.9	70.9	70.9	70.9	70.9	70.9	70.9	70.9
15	69.9	69.9	69.9	69.9	69.9	69.9	69.9	69.9	69.9
16	69.0	69.0	69.0	69.0	69.0	69.0	69.0	69.0	69.0
17	68.0	68.0	68.0	68.0	68.0	68.0	68.0	68.0	68.0
18	67.0	67.0	67.0	67.0	67.0	67.0	67.0	67.0	67.0
19	66.0	66.0	66.0	66.0	66.0	66.0	66.0	66.0	66.0
20	65.0	65.0	65.0	65.0	65.0	65.0	65.0	65.0	65.0
21	64.1	64.1	64.1	64.1	64.1	64.1	64.1	64.1	64.1
22	63.1	63.1	63.1	63.1	63.1	63.1	63.1	63.1	63.1
23	62.1	62.1	62.1	62.1	62.1	62.1	62.1	62.1	62.1
24	61.1	61.1	61.1	61.1	61.1	61.1	61.1	61.1	61.1
25	60.2	60.2	60.2	60.2	60.2	60.2	60.2	60.2	60.2
26	59.2	59.2	59.2	59.2	59.2	59.2	59.2	59.2	59.2
27	58.2	58.2	58.2	58.2	58.2	58.2	58.2	58.2	58.2
28	57.3	57.3	57.3	57.3	57.3	57.3	57.3	57.3	57.3
29	56.3	56.3	56.3	56.3	56.3	56.3	56.3	56.3	56.3
30	55.4	55.3	55.3	55.3	55.3	55.3	55.3	55.3	55.3
31	54.4	54.4	54.4	54.4	54.4	54.4	54.4	54.4	54.4
32	53.4	53.4	53.4	53.4	53.4	53.4	53.4	53.4	53.4
33	52.5	52.5	52.5	52.5	52.5	52.5	52.5	52.5	52.5
34	51.5	51.5	51.5	51.5	51.5	51.5	51.5	51.5	51.5
35	50.6	50.6	50.6	50.6	50.6	50.6	50.6	50.6	50.6
36	49.6	49.6	49.6	49.6	49.6	49.6	49.6	49.6	49.6
37	48.6	48.6	48.6	48.6	48.6	48.6	48.6	48.6	48.6
38	47.7	47.7	47.7	47.7	47.7	47.7	47.7	47.7	47.7
39	46.7	46.7	46.7	46.7	46.7	46.7	46.7	46.7	46.7
40	45.8	45.8	45.8	45.8	45.8	45.8	45.8	45.8	45.8
41	44.8	44.8	44.8	44.8	44.8	44.8	44.8	44.8	44.8
42	43.9	43.9	43.8	43.8	43.8	43.8	43.8	43.8	43.8
43	42.9	42.9	42.9	42.9	42.9	42.9	42.9	42.9	42.9
44	41.9	41.9	41.9	41.9	41.9	41.9	41.9	41.9	41.9
45	41.0	41.0	41.0	41.0	41.0	41.0	41.0	41.0	41.0
46	40.0	40.0	40.0	40.0	40.0	40.0	40.0	40.0	40.0
47	39.1	39.1	39.1	39.1	39.1	39.1	39.1	39.1	39.1
48	38.1	38.1	38.1	38.1	38.1	38.1	38.1	38.1	38.1
49	37.2	37.2	37.2	37.2	37.2	37.2	37.2	37.2	37.2
50	36.3	36.2	36.2	36.2	36.2	36.2	36.2	36.2	36.2
51	35.3	35.3	35.3	35.3	35.3	35.3	35.3	35.3	35.3
52	34.4	34.4	34.4	34.4	34.4	34.4	34.3	34.3	34.3
53	33.5	33.5	33.5	33.4	33.4	33.4	33.4	33.4	33.4
54	32.6	32.5	32.5	32.5	32.5	32.5	32.5	32.5	32.5
55	31.7	31.6	31.6	31.6	31.6	31.6	31.6	31.6	31.6
56	30.8	30.7	30.7	30.7	30.7	30.7	30.7	30.7	30.7
57	29.9	29.9	29.8	29.8	29.8	29.8	29.8	29.8	29.8
58	29.0	29.0	29.0	29.0	28.9	28.9	28.9	28.9	28.9
59	28.1	28.1	28.1	28.1	28.1	28.1	28.0	28.0	28.0
60	27.3	27.3	27.2	27.2	27.2	27.2	27.2	27.2	27.2
61	26.4	26.4	26.4	26.4	26.3	26.3	26.3	26.3	26.3
62	25.6	25.6	25.5	25.5	25.5	25.5	25.5	25.5	25.5
63	24.7	24.7	24.7	24.7	24.7	24.6	24.6	24.6	24.6
64	23.9	23.9	23.9	23.8	23.8	23.8	23.8	23.8	23.8

Reg. §1.401(a)(9)-9(d)

Ages	90	91	92	93	94	95	96	97	98
65	23.1	23.1	23.0	23.0	23.0	23.0	23.0	23.0	22.9
66	22.3	22.3	22.2	22.2	22.2	22.2	22.2	22.1	22.1
67	21.5	21.5	21.4	21.4	21.4	21.4	21.3	21.3	21.3
68	20.7	20.7	20.6	20.6	20.6	20.6	20.5	20.5	20.5
69	19.9	19.9	19.8	19.8	19.8	19.7	19.7	19.7	19.7
70	19.1	19.1	19.0	19.0	19.0	18.9	18.9	18.9	18.9
71	18.4	18.3	18.3	18.2	18.2	18.2	18.1	18.1	18.1
72	17.6	17.5	17.5	17.4	17.4	17.4	17.4	17.3	17.3
73	16.9	16.8	16.7	16.7	16.6	16.6	16.6	16.6	16.5
74	16.1	16.1	16.0	15.9	15.9	15.9	15.8	15.8	15.8
75	15.4	15.3	15.3	15.2	15.2	15.1	15.1	15.0	15.0
76	14.7	14.6	14.6	14.5	14.4	14.4	14.3	14.3	14.3
77	14.1	14.0	13.9	13.8	13.7	13.7	13.6	13.6	13.6
78	13.4	13.3	13.2	13.1	13.1	13.0	12.9	12.9	12.9
79	12.8	12.7	12.6	12.5	12.4	12.3	12.3	12.2	12.2
80	12.2	12.1	11.9	11.9	11.8	11.7	11.6	11.6	11.5
81	11.6	11.5	11.4	11.3	11.2	11.1	11.0	11.0	10.9
82	11.1	10.9	10.8	10.7	10.6	10.5	10.4	10.4	10.3
83	10.6	10.4	10.3	10.1	10.0	9.9	9.9	9.8	9.7
84	10.1	9.9	9.8	9.6	9.5	9.4	9.3	9.2	9.2
85	9.7	9.5	9.3	9.2	9.0	8.9	8.8	8.7	8.7
86	9.3	9.1	8.9	8.7	8.6	8.5	8.4	8.3	8.2
87	8.9	8.7	8.5	8.3	8.2	8.0	7.9	7.8	7.7
88	8.6	8.3	8.1	7.9	7.8	7.6	7.5	7.4	7.3
89	8.3	8.0	7.8	7.6	7.4	7.3	7.1	7.0	6.9
90	8.0	7.7	7.5	7.3	7.1	6.9	6.8	6.7	6.6
91	7.7	7.5	7.2	7.0	6.8	6.6	6.5	6.4	6.2
92	7.5	7.2	7.0	6.7	6.5	6.4	6.2	6.1	5.9
93	7.3	7.0	6.7	6.5	6.3	6.1	5.9	5.8	5.7
94	7.1	6.8	6.5	6.3	6.1	5.9	5.7	5.5	5.4
95	6.9	6.6	6.4	6.1	5.9	5.7	5.5	5.3	5.2
96	6.8	6.5	6.2	5.9	5.7	5.5	5.3	5.1	5.0
97	6.7	6.4	6.1	5.8	5.5	5.3	5.1	4.9	4.8
98	6.6	6.2	5.9	5.7	5.4	5.2	5.0	4.8	4.6
99	6.5	6.1	5.8	5.5	5.3	5.0	4.8	4.6	4.5
100	6.4	6.0	5.7	5.4	5.2	4.9	4.7	4.5	4.3
101	6.3	6.0	5.6	5.3	5.1	4.8	4.6	4.4	4.2
102	6.3	5.9	5.6	5.3	5.0	4.7	4.5	4.3	4.1
103	6.2	5.9	5.5	5.2	4.9	4.7	4.5	4.2	4.1
104	6.2	5.8	5.5	5.2	4.9	4.6	4.4	4.2	4.0
105	6.1	5.8	5.4	5.1	4.9	4.6	4.4	4.1	4.0
106	6.1	5.8	5.4	5.1	4.8	4.6	4.3	4.1	3.9
107	6.1	5.8	5.4	5.1	4.8	4.6	4.3	4.1	3.9
108	6.1	5.7	5.4	5.1	4.8	4.5	4.3	4.1	3.9
109	6.1	5.7	5.4	5.1	4.8	4.5	4.3	4.1	3.9
110	6.1	5.7	5.4	5.1	4.8	4.5	4.3	4.1	3.9
111	6.1	5.7	5.4	5.1	4.8	4.5	4.3	4.1	3.9
112	6.1	5.7	5.4	5.1	4.8	4.5	4.3	4.0	3.8
113	6.1	5.7	5.3	5.0	4.7	4.5	4.2	4.0	3.8
114	6.0	5.7	5.3	5.0	4.7	4.4	4.2	4.0	3.8
115	6.0	5.6	5.3	5.0	4.7	4.4	4.2	4.0	3.8
116	6.0	5.6	5.2	4.9	4.6	4.4	4.1	3.9	3.7
117	5.9	5.5	5.2	4.9	4.6	4.3	4.0	3.8	3.6
118	5.8	5.5	5.1	4.8	4.5	4.2	3.9	3.7	3.5
119	5.8	5.4	5.0	4.7	4.4	4.1	3.8	3.6	3.3
120+	5.7	5.3	4.9	4.6	4.3	4.0	3.7	3.4	3.2

Ages	99	100	101	102	103	104	105	106	107
0	84.6	84.6	84.6	84.6	84.6	84.6	84.6	84.6	84.6
1	83.7	83.7	83.7	83.7	83.7	83.7	83.7	83.7	83.7

Reg. §1.401(a)(9)-9(d)

Ages	99	100	101	102	103	104	105	106	107
2	82.8	82.8	82.8	82.8	82.8	82.8	82.8	82.8	82.8
3	81.8	81.8	81.8	81.8	81.8	81.8	81.8	81.8	81.8
4	80.8	80.8	80.8	80.8	80.8	80.8	80.8	80.8	80.8
5	79.8	79.8	79.8	79.8	79.8	79.8	79.8	79.8	79.8
6	78.8	78.8	78.8	78.8	78.8	78.8	78.8	78.8	78.8
7	77.9	77.9	77.9	77.9	77.9	77.9	77.9	77.9	77.9
8	76.9	76.9	76.9	76.9	76.9	76.9	76.9	76.9	76.9
9	75.9	75.9	75.9	75.9	75.9	75.9	75.9	75.9	75.9
10	74.9	74.9	74.9	74.9	74.9	74.9	74.9	74.9	74.9
11	73.9	73.9	73.9	73.9	73.9	73.9	73.9	73.9	73.9
12	72.9	72.9	72.9	72.9	72.9	72.9	72.9	72.9	72.9
13	71.9	71.9	71.9	71.9	71.9	71.9	71.9	71.9	71.9
14	70.9	70.9	70.9	70.9	70.9	70.9	70.9	70.9	70.9
15	69.9	69.9	69.9	69.9	69.9	69.9	69.9	69.9	69.9
16	69.0	69.0	69.0	69.0	69.0	69.0	69.0	69.0	69.0
17	68.0	68.0	68.0	68.0	68.0	68.0	68.0	68.0	68.0
18	67.0	67.0	67.0	67.0	67.0	67.0	67.0	67.0	67.0
19	66.0	66.0	66.0	66.0	66.0	66.0	66.0	66.0	66.0
20	65.0	65.0	65.0	65.0	65.0	65.0	65.0	65.0	65.0
21	64.1	64.1	64.1	64.1	64.1	64.1	64.1	64.1	64.1
22	63.1	63.1	63.1	63.1	63.1	63.1	63.1	63.1	63.1
23	62.1	62.1	62.1	62.1	62.1	62.1	62.1	62.1	62.1
24	61.1	61.1	61.1	61.1	61.1	61.1	61.1	61.1	61.1
25	60.2	60.2	60.2	60.2	60.2	60.2	60.2	60.2	60.2
26	59.2	59.2	59.2	59.2	59.2	59.2	59.2	59.2	59.2
27	58.2	58.2	58.2	58.2	58.2	58.2	58.2	58.2	58.2
28	57.3	57.3	57.3	57.3	57.3	57.3	57.3	57.3	57.3
29	56.3	56.3	56.3	56.3	56.3	56.3	56.3	56.3	56.3
30	55.3	55.3	55.3	55.3	55.3	55.3	55.3	55.3	55.3
31	54.4	54.4	54.4	54.4	54.4	54.4	54.4	54.4	54.4
32	53.4	53.4	53.4	53.4	53.4	53.4	53.4	53.4	53.4
33	52.5	52.5	52.5	52.5	52.5	52.5	52.5	52.5	52.5
34	51.5	51.5	51.5	51.5	51.5	51.5	51.5	51.5	51.5
35	50.6	50.6	50.6	50.6	50.5	50.5	50.5	50.5	50.5
36	49.6	49.6	49.6	49.6	49.6	49.6	49.6	49.6	49.6
37	48.6	48.6	48.6	48.6	48.6	48.6	48.6	48.6	48.6
38	47.7	47.7	47.7	47.7	47.7	47.7	47.7	47.7	47.7
39	46.7	46.7	46.7	46.7	46.7	46.7	46.7	46.7	46.7
40	45.8	45.8	45.8	45.8	45.8	45.8	45.7	45.7	45.7
41	44.8	44.8	44.8	44.8	44.8	44.8	44.8	44.8	44.8
42	43.8	43.8	43.8	43.8	43.8	43.8	43.8	43.8	43.8
43	42.9	42.9	42.9	42.9	42.9	42.9	42.9	42.9	42.9
44	41.9	41.9	41.9	41.9	41.9	41.9	41.9	41.9	41.9
45	41.0	41.0	41.0	41.0	41.0	41.0	41.0	41.0	41.0
46	40.0	40.0	40.0	40.0	40.0	40.0	40.0	40.0	40.0
47	39.1	39.0	39.0	39.0	39.0	39.0	39.0	39.0	39.0
48	38.1	38.1	38.1	38.1	38.1	38.1	38.1	38.1	38.1
49	37.2	37.1	37.1	37.1	37.1	37.1	37.1	37.1	37.1
50	36.2	36.2	36.2	36.2	36.2	36.2	36.2	36.2	36.2
51	35.3	35.3	35.3	35.3	35.3	35.3	35.3	35.3	35.3
52	34.3	34.3	34.3	34.3	34.3	34.3	34.3	34.3	34.3
53	33.4	33.4	33.4	33.4	33.4	33.4	33.4	33.4	33.4
54	32.5	32.5	32.5	32.5	32.5	32.5	32.5	32.5	32.5
55	31.6	31.6	31.6	31.6	31.6	31.6	31.6	31.6	31.6
56	30.7	30.7	30.7	30.7	30.7	30.7	30.7	30.7	30.7
57	29.8	29.8	29.8	29.8	29.8	29.8	29.8	29.8	29.8
58	28.9	28.9	28.9	28.9	28.9	28.9	28.9	28.9	28.9
59	28.0	28.0	28.0	28.0	28.0	28.0	28.0	28.0	28.0
60	27.2	27.1	27.1	27.1	27.1	27.1	27.1	27.1	27.1
61	26.3	26.3	26.3	26.3	26.3	26.3	26.3	26.3	26.3
62	25.4	25.4	25.4	25.4	25.4	25.4	25.4	25.4	25.4

Reg. §1.401(a)(9)-9(d)

Ages	99	100	101	102	103	104	105	106	107
63	24.6	24.6	24.6	24.6	24.6	24.6	24.6	24.6	24.6
64	23.8	23.8	23.8	23.7	23.7	23.7	23.7	23.7	23.7
65	22.9	22.9	22.9	22.9	22.9	22.9	22.9	22.9	22.9
66	22.1	22.1	22.1	22.1	22.1	22.1	22.1	22.1	22.1
67	21.3	21.3	21.3	21.3	21.3	21.3	21.3	21.3	21.3
68	20.5	20.5	20.5	20.5	20.5	20.5	20.5	20.5	20.5
69	19.7	19.7	19.7	19.7	19.6	19.6	19.6	19.6	19.6
70	18.9	18.9	18.9	18.8	18.8	18.8	18.8	18.8	18.8
71	18.1	18.1	18.1	18.0	18.0	18.0	18.0	18.0	18.0
72	17.3	17.3	17.3	17.3	17.3	17.2	17.2	17.2	17.2
73	16.5	16.5	16.5	16.5	16.5	16.5	16.5	16.5	16.5
74	15.7	15.7	15.7	15.7	15.7	15.7	15.7	15.7	15.7
75	15.0	15.0	15.0	14.9	14.9	14.9	14.9	14.9	14.9
76	14.3	14.2	14.2	14.2	14.2	14.2	14.2	14.2	14.2
77	13.5	13.5	13.5	13.5	13.5	13.5	13.4	13.4	13.4
78	12.8	12.8	12.8	12.8	12.8	12.7	12.7	12.7	12.7
79	12.2	12.1	12.1	12.1	12.1	12.0	12.0	12.0	12.0
80	11.5	11.5	11.4	11.4	11.4	11.4	11.4	11.4	11.4
81	10.9	10.8	10.8	10.8	10.7	10.7	10.7	10.7	10.7
82	10.2	10.2	10.2	10.1	10.1	10.1	10.1	10.1	10.1
83	9.7	9.6	9.6	9.6	9.5	9.5	9.5	9.5	9.5
84	9.1	9.1	9.0	9.0	9.0	8.9	8.9	8.9	8.9
85	8.6	8.5	8.5	8.5	8.4	8.4	8.4	8.4	8.4
86	8.1	8.0	8.0	8.0	7.9	7.9	7.9	7.9	7.9
87	7.6	7.6	7.5	7.5	7.4	7.4	7.4	7.4	7.4
88	7.2	7.2	7.1	7.0	7.0	7.0	6.9	6.9	6.9
89	6.8	6.8	6.7	6.6	6.6	6.6	6.5	6.5	6.5
90	6.5	6.4	6.3	6.3	6.2	6.2	6.1	6.1	6.1
91	6.1	6.0	6.0	5.9	5.9	5.8	5.8	5.8	5.8
92	5.8	5.7	5.6	5.6	5.5	5.5	5.4	5.4	5.4
93	5.5	5.4	5.3	5.3	5.2	5.2	5.1	5.1	5.1
94	5.3	5.2	5.1	5.0	4.9	4.9	4.9	4.8	4.8
95	5.0	4.9	4.8	4.7	4.7	4.6	4.6	4.6	4.6
96	4.8	4.7	4.6	4.5	4.5	4.4	4.4	4.3	4.3
97	4.6	4.5	4.4	4.3	4.2	4.2	4.1	4.1	4.1
98	4.5	4.3	4.2	4.1	4.1	4.0	4.0	3.9	3.9
99	4.3	4.2	4.1	4.0	3.9	3.8	3.8	3.8	3.7
100	4.2	4.1	3.9	3.8	3.7	3.7	3.6	3.6	3.6
101	4.1	3.9	3.8	3.7	3.6	3.5	3.5	3.5	3.4
102	4.0	3.8	3.7	3.6	3.5	3.4	3.4	3.3	3.3
103	3.9	3.7	3.6	3.5	3.4	3.3	3.3	3.2	3.2
104	3.8	3.7	3.5	3.4	3.3	3.3	3.2	3.2	3.2
105	3.8	3.6	3.5	3.4	3.3	3.2	3.1	3.1	3.1
106	3.8	3.6	3.5	3.3	3.2	3.2	3.1	3.1	3.1
107	3.7	3.6	3.4	3.3	3.2	3.2	3.1	3.1	3.0
108	3.7	3.6	3.4	3.3	3.2	3.1	3.1	3.0	3.0
109	3.7	3.6	3.4	3.3	3.2	3.1	3.1	3.0	3.0
110	3.7	3.5	3.4	3.3	3.2	3.1	3.1	3.0	3.0
111	3.7	3.5	3.4	3.3	3.2	3.1	3.0	3.0	3.0
112	3.7	3.5	3.4	3.3	3.2	3.1	3.0	3.0	3.0
113	3.6	3.5	3.4	3.2	3.1	3.1	3.0	3.0	2.9
114	3.6	3.5	3.3	3.2	3.1	3.0	3.0	2.9	2.9
115	3.6	3.4	3.3	3.2	3.1	3.0	2.9	2.9	2.9
116	3.5	3.3	3.2	3.1	3.0	2.9	2.8	2.8	2.8
117	3.4	3.3	3.1	3.0	2.9	2.8	2.7	2.7	2.7
118	3.3	3.1	3.0	2.8	2.7	2.6	2.6	2.5	2.5
119	3.1	2.9	2.8	2.6	2.5	2.4	2.4	2.3	2.3
120+	3.0	2.8	2.6	2.5	2.3	2.2	2.1	2.1	2.1

Reg. §1.401(a)(9)-9(d)

Ages	108	109	110	111	112	113	114	115	116
0	84.6	84.6	84.6	84.6	84.6	84.6	84.6	84.6	84.6
1	83.7	83.7	83.7	83.7	83.7	83.7	83.7	83.7	83.7
2	82.8	82.8	82.8	82.8	82.8	82.8	82.8	82.8	82.8
3	81.8	81.8	81.8	81.8	81.8	81.8	81.8	81.8	81.8
4	80.8	80.8	80.8	80.8	80.8	80.8	80.8	80.8	80.8
5	79.8	79.8	79.8	79.8	79.8	79.8	79.8	79.8	79.8
6	78.8	78.8	78.8	78.8	78.8	78.8	78.8	78.8	78.8
7	77.9	77.9	77.9	77.9	77.9	77.9	77.9	77.9	77.9
8	76.9	76.9	76.9	76.9	76.9	76.9	76.9	76.9	76.9
9	75.9	75.9	75.9	75.9	75.9	75.9	75.9	75.9	75.9
10	74.9	74.9	74.9	74.9	74.9	74.9	74.9	74.9	74.9
11	73.9	73.9	73.9	73.9	73.9	73.9	73.9	73.9	73.9
12	72.9	72.9	72.9	72.9	72.9	72.9	72.9	72.9	72.9
13	71.9	71.9	71.9	71.9	71.9	71.9	71.9	71.9	71.9
14	70.9	70.9	70.9	70.9	70.9	70.9	70.9	70.9	70.9
15	69.9	69.9	69.9	69.9	69.9	69.9	69.9	69.9	69.9
16	69.0	69.0	69.0	69.0	69.0	69.0	69.0	69.0	69.0
17	68.0	68.0	68.0	68.0	68.0	68.0	68.0	68.0	68.0
18	67.0	67.0	67.0	67.0	67.0	67.0	67.0	67.0	67.0
19	66.0	66.0	66.0	66.0	66.0	66.0	66.0	66.0	66.0
20	65.0	65.0	65.0	65.0	65.0	65.0	65.0	65.0	65.0
21	64.1	64.1	64.1	64.1	64.1	64.1	64.1	64.1	64.1
22	63.1	63.1	63.1	63.1	63.1	63.1	63.1	63.1	63.1
23	62.1	62.1	62.1	62.1	62.1	62.1	62.1	62.1	62.1
24	61.1	61.1	61.1	61.1	61.1	61.1	61.1	61.1	61.1
25	60.2	60.2	60.2	60.2	60.2	60.2	60.2	60.2	60.2
26	59.2	59.2	59.2	59.2	59.2	59.2	59.2	59.2	59.2
27	58.2	58.2	58.2	58.2	58.2	58.2	58.2	58.2	58.2
28	57.3	57.3	57.3	57.3	57.3	57.3	57.3	57.3	57.3
29	56.3	56.3	56.3	56.3	56.3	56.3	56.3	56.3	56.3
30	55.3	55.3	55.3	55.3	55.3	55.3	55.3	55.3	55.3
31	54.4	54.4	54.4	54.4	54.4	54.4	54.4	54.4	54.4
32	53.4	53.4	53.4	53.4	53.4	53.4	53.4	53.4	53.4
33	52.5	52.5	52.5	52.5	52.5	52.5	52.5	52.5	52.5
34	51.5	51.5	51.5	51.5	51.5	51.5	51.5	51.5	51.5
35	50.5	50.5	50.5	50.5	50.5	50.5	50.5	50.5	50.5
36	49.6	49.6	49.6	49.6	49.6	49.6	49.6	49.6	49.6
37	48.6	48.6	48.6	48.6	48.6	48.6	48.6	48.6	48.6
38	47.7	47.7	47.7	47.7	47.7	47.7	47.7	47.7	47.7
39	46.7	46.7	46.7	46.7	46.7	46.7	46.7	46.7	46.7
40	45.7	45.7	45.7	45.7	45.7	45.7	45.7	45.7	45.7
41	44.8	44.8	44.8	44.8	44.8	44.8	44.8	44.8	44.8
42	43.8	43.8	43.8	43.8	43.8	43.8	43.8	43.8	43.8
43	42.9	42.9	42.9	42.9	42.9	42.9	42.9	42.9	42.9
44	41.9	41.9	41.9	41.9	41.9	41.9	41.9	41.9	41.9
45	41.0	41.0	41.0	41.0	41.0	41.0	41.0	41.0	41.0
46	40.0	40.0	40.0	40.0	40.0	40.0	40.0	40.0	40.0
47	39.0	39.0	39.0	39.0	39.0	39.0	39.0	39.0	39.0
48	38.1	38.1	38.1	38.1	38.1	38.1	38.1	38.1	38.1
49	37.1	37.1	37.1	37.1	37.1	37.1	37.1	37.1	37.1
50	36.2	36.2	36.2	36.2	36.2	36.2	36.2	36.2	36.2
51	35.3	35.3	35.3	35.3	35.3	35.3	35.3	35.3	35.3
52	34.3	34.3	34.3	34.3	34.3	34.3	34.3	34.3	34.3
53	33.4	33.4	33.4	33.4	33.4	33.4	33.4	33.4	33.4
54	32.5	32.5	32.5	32.5	32.5	32.5	32.5	32.5	32.5
55	31.6	31.6	31.6	31.6	31.6	31.6	31.6	31.6	31.6
56	30.7	30.7	30.7	30.7	30.7	30.7	30.7	30.7	30.7
57	29.8	29.8	29.8	29.8	29.8	29.8	29.8	29.8	29.8
58	28.9	28.9	28.9	28.9	28.9	28.9	28.9	28.9	28.9
59	28.0	28.0	28.0	28.0	28.0	28.0	28.0	28.0	28.0

Reg. §1.401(a)(9)-9(d)

Ages	108	109	110	111	112	113	114	115	116
60	27.1	27.1	27.1	27.1	27.1	27.1	27.1	27.1	27.1
61	26.3	26.3	26.3	26.3	26.3	26.3	26.3	26.3	26.3
62	25.4	25.4	25.4	25.4	25.4	25.4	25.4	25.4	25.4
63	24.6	24.6	24.6	24.6	24.6	24.6	24.6	24.6	24.6
64	23.7	23.7	23.7	23.7	23.7	23.7	23.7	23.7	23.7
65	22.9	22.9	22.9	22.9	22.9	22.9	22.9	22.9	22.9
66	22.1	22.1	22.1	22.1	22.1	22.1	22.1	22.1	22.1
67	21.3	21.3	21.3	21.3	21.3	21.3	21.3	21.3	21.3
68	20.5	20.4	20.4	20.4	20.4	20.4	20.4	20.4	20.4
69	19.6	19.6	19.6	19.6	19.6	19.6	19.6	19.6	19.6
70	18.8	18.8	18.8	18.8	18.8	18.8	18.8	18.8	18.8
71	18.0	18.0	18.0	18.0	18.0	18.0	18.0	18.0	18.0
72	17.2	17.2	17.2	17.2	17.2	17.2	17.2	17.2	17.2
73	16.5	16.4	16.4	16.4	16.4	16.4	16.4	16.4	16.4
74	15.7	15.7	15.7	15.7	15.7	15.7	15.7	15.7	15.6
75	14.9	14.9	14.9	14.9	14.9	14.9	14.9	14.9	14.9
76	14.2	14.2	14.2	14.2	14.2	14.2	14.1	14.1	14.1
77	13.4	13.4	13.4	13.4	13.4	13.4	13.4	13.4	13.4
78	12.7	12.7	12.7	12.7	12.7	12.7	12.7	12.7	12.7
79	12.0	12.0	12.0	12.0	12.0	12.0	12.0	12.0	12.0
80	11.4	11.3	11.3	11.3	11.3	11.3	11.3	11.3	11.3
81	10.7	10.7	10.7	10.7	10.7	10.7	10.7	10.7	10.6
82	10.1	10.1	10.1	10.1	10.1	10.0	10.0	10.0	10.0
83	9.5	9.5	9.5	9.5	9.5	9.4	9.4	9.4	9.4
84	8.9	8.9	8.9	8.9	8.9	8.9	8.9	8.8	8.8
85	8.4	8.4	8.3	8.3	8.3	8.3	8.3	8.3	8.3
86	7.8	7.8	7.8	7.8	7.8	7.8	7.8	7.8	7.7
87	7.4	7.4	7.4	7.3	7.3	7.3	7.3	7.3	7.3
88	6.9	6.9	6.9	6.9	6.9	6.9	6.9	6.8	6.8
89	6.5	6.5	6.5	6.5	6.5	6.4	6.4	6.4	6.4
90	6.1	6.1	6.1	6.1	6.1	6.1	6.0	6.0	6.0
91	5.7	5.7	5.7	5.7	5.7	5.7	5.7	5.6	5.6
92	5.4	5.4	5.4	5.4	5.4	5.3	5.3	5.3	5.2
93	5.1	5.1	5.1	5.1	5.1	5.0	5.0	5.0	4.9
94	4.8	4.8	4.8	4.8	4.8	4.7	4.7	4.7	4.6
95	4.5	4.5	4.5	4.5	4.5	4.5	4.4	4.4	4.4
96	4.3	4.3	4.3	4.3	4.3	4.2	4.2	4.2	4.1
97	4.1	4.1	4.1	4.1	4.0	4.0	4.0	4.0	3.9
98	3.9	3.9	3.9	3.9	3.8	3.8	3.8	3.8	3.7
99	3.7	3.7	3.7	3.7	3.7	3.6	3.6	3.6	3.5
100	3.6	3.6	3.5	3.5	3.5	3.5	3.5	3.4	3.3
101	3.4	3.4	3.4	3.4	3.4	3.4	3.3	3.3	3.2
102	3.3	3.3	3.3	3.3	3.3	3.2	3.2	3.2	3.1
103	3.2	3.2	3.2	3.2	3.2	3.1	3.1	3.1	3.0
104	3.1	3.1	3.1	3.1	3.1	3.1	3.0	3.0	2.9
105	3.1	3.1	3.1	3.0	3.0	3.0	3.0	2.9	2.8
106	3.0	3.0	3.0	3.0	3.0	3.0	2.9	2.9	2.8
107	3.0	3.0	3.0	3.0	3.0	2.9	2.9	2.9	2.8
108	3.0	3.0	3.0	3.0	2.9	2.9	2.9	2.8	2.8
109	3.0	3.0	3.0	3.0	2.9	2.9	2.9	2.8	2.8
110	3.0	3.0	3.0	2.9	2.9	2.9	2.9	2.8	2.7
111	3.0	3.0	2.9	2.9	2.9	2.9	2.8	2.8	2.7
112	2.9	2.9	2.9	2.9	2.9	2.9	2.8	2.8	2.7
113	2.9	2.9	2.9	2.9	2.9	2.8	2.8	2.8	2.7
114	2.9	2.9	2.9	2.8	2.8	2.8	2.8	2.7	2.6
115	2.8	2.8	2.8	2.8	2.8	2.8	2.7	2.7	2.6
116	2.8	2.8	2.7	2.7	2.7	2.7	2.6	2.6	2.5
117	2.7	2.6	2.6	2.6	2.6	2.6	2.5	2.5	2.4
118	2.5	2.5	2.5	2.4	2.4	2.4	2.4	2.3	2.2
119	2.3	2.3	2.2	2.2	2.2	2.2	2.1	2.1	2.0
120+	2.0	2.0	2.0	2.0	2.0	1.9	1.9	1.8	1.8

Reg. §1.401(a)(9)-9(d)

Ages	117	118	119	120+
0	84.6	84.6	84.6	84.6
1	83.7	83.7	83.7	83.7
2	82.8	82.8	82.8	82.8
3	81.8	81.8	81.8	81.8
4	80.8	80.8	80.8	80.8
5	79.8	79.8	79.8	79.8
6	78.8	78.8	78.8	78.8
7	77.9	77.9	77.9	77.9
8	76.9	76.9	76.9	76.9
9	75.9	75.9	75.9	75.9
10	74.9	74.9	74.9	74.9
11	73.9	73.9	73.9	73.9
12	72.9	72.9	72.9	72.9
13	71.9	71.9	71.9	71.9
14	70.9	70.9	70.9	70.9
15	69.9	69.9	69.9	69.9
16	69.0	69.0	69.0	69.0
17	68.0	68.0	68.0	68.0
18	67.0	67.0	67.0	67.0
19	66.0	66.0	66.0	66.0
20	65.0	65.0	65.0	65.0
21	64.1	64.1	64.1	64.1
22	63.1	63.1	63.1	63.1
23	62.1	62.1	62.1	62.1
24	61.1	61.1	61.1	61.1
25	60.2	60.2	60.2	60.2
26	59.2	59.2	59.2	59.2
27	58.2	58.2	58.2	58.2
28	57.3	57.3	57.3	57.3
29	56.3	56.3	56.3	56.3
30	55.3	55.3	55.3	55.3
31	54.4	54.4	54.4	54.4
32	53.4	53.4	53.4	53.4
33	52.5	52.5	52.5	52.5
34	51.5	51.5	51.5	51.5
35	50.5	50.5	50.5	50.5
36	49.6	49.6	49.6	49.6
37	48.6	48.6	48.6	48.6
38	47.7	47.7	47.7	47.7
39	46.7	46.7	46.7	46.7
40	45.7	45.7	45.7	45.7
41	44.8	44.8	44.8	44.8
42	43.8	43.8	43.8	43.8
43	42.9	42.9	42.9	42.9
44	41.9	41.9	41.9	41.9
45	41.0	41.0	41.0	41.0
46	40.0	40.0	40.0	40.0
47	39.0	39.0	39.0	39.0
48	38.1	38.1	38.1	38.1
49	37.1	37.1	37.1	37.1
50	36.2	36.2	36.2	36.2
51	35.3	35.3	35.3	35.3
52	34.3	34.3	34.3	34.3
53	33.4	33.4	33.4	33.4
54	32.5	32.5	32.5	32.5
55	31.6	31.6	31.6	31.6
56	30.7	30.7	30.7	30.6
57	29.8	29.8	29.8	29.8
58	28.9	28.9	28.9	28.9
59	28.0	28.0	28.0	28.0

Ages	117	118	119	120+
60	27.1	27.1	27.1	27.1
61	26.3	26.3	26.2	26.2
62	25.4	25.4	25.4	25.4
63	24.6	24.5	24.5	24.5
64	23.7	23.7	23.7	23.7
65	22.9	22.9	22.9	22.9
66	22.1	22.1	22.1	22.0
67	21.2	21.2	21.2	21.2
68	20.4	20.4	20.4	20.4
69	19.6	19.6	19.6	19.6
70	18.8	18.8	18.8	18.8
71	18.0	18.0	18.0	18.0
72	17.2	17.2	17.2	17.2
73	16.4	16.4	16.4	16.4
74	15.6	15.6	15.6	15.6
75	14.9	14.9	14.8	14.8
76	14.1	14.1	14.1	14.1
77	13.4	13.4	13.4	13.3
78	12.7	12.6	12.6	12.6
79	12.0	11.9	11.9	11.9
80	11.3	11.3	11.2	11.2
81	10.6	10.6	10.6	10.5
82	10.0	10.0	9.9	9.9
83	9.4	9.3	9.3	9.3
84	8.8	8.8	8.7	8.7
85	8.2	8.2	8.2	8.1
86	7.7	7.7	7.6	7.6
87	7.2	7.2	7.1	7.1
88	6.8	6.7	6.6	6.6
89	6.3	6.3	6.2	6.1
90	5.9	5.8	5.8	5.7
91	5.5	5.5	5.4	5.3
92	5.2	5.1	5.0	4.9
93	4.9	4.8	4.7	4.6
94	4.6	4.5	4.4	4.3
95	4.3	4.2	4.1	4.0
96	4.0	3.9	3.8	3.7
97	3.8	3.7	3.6	3.4
98	3.6	3.5	3.3	3.2
99	3.4	3.3	3.1	3.0
100	3.3	3.1	2.9	2.8
101	3.1	3.0	2.8	2.6
102	3.0	2.8	2.6	2.5
103	2.9	2.7	2.5	2.3
104	2.8	2.6	2.4	2.2
105	2.7	2.6	2.4	2.1
106	2.7	2.5	2.3	2.1
107	2.7	2.5	2.3	2.1
108	2.7	2.5	2.3	2.0
109	2.6	2.5	2.3	2.0
110	2.6	2.5	2.2	2.0
111	2.6	2.4	2.2	2.0
112	2.6	2.4	2.2	2.0
113	2.6	2.4	2.2	1.9
114	2.5	2.4	2.1	1.9
115	2.5	2.3	2.1	1.8
116	2.4	2.2	2.0	1.8
117	2.3	2.1	1.9	1.6
118	2.1	1.9	1.7	1.4
119	1.9	1.7	1.3	1.1
120+	1.6	1.4	1.1	1.0

Reg. §1.401(a)(9)-9(d)

(e) *Mortality rates.*—The following are the mortality rates used to calculate the tables set forth in paragraphs (b), (c), and (d) of this section.

Table 4 to Paragraph (e)

Age	Probability of Death
0	0.001762
1	0.000441
2	0.000292
3	0.000232
4	0.000177
5	0.000161
6	0.000153
7	0.000145
8	0.000132
9	0.000127
10	0.000128
11	0.000135
12	0.000146
13	0.000164
14	0.000192
15	0.000223
16	0.000253
17	0.000276
18	0.000293
19	0.000304
20	0.000313
21	0.000343
22	0.000377
23	0.000421
24	0.000466
25	0.000520
26	0.000581
27	0.000630
28	0.000677
29	0.000720
30	0.000763
31	0.000799
32	0.000824
33	0.000833
34	0.000830
35	0.000823
36	0.000819
37	0.000824
38	0.000836
39	0.000853
40	0.000879
41	0.000909
42	0.000945
43	0.000980
44	0.001019
45	0.001065
46	0.001132
47	0.001225
48	0.001345
49	0.001485
50	0.001656
51	0.001874
52	0.002121
53	0.002397
54	0.002701
55	0.003032
56	0.003390

Age	Probability of Death
57	0.003774
58	0.004181
59	0.004613
60	0.005071
61	0.005554
62	0.006071
63	0.006624
64	0.007225
65	0.007884
66	0.008238
67	0.008659
68	0.009163
69	0.009767
70	0.010491
71	0.011358
72	0.012385
73	0.013598
74	0.015014
75	0.016670
76	0.018587
77	0.020815
78	0.023391
79	0.026387
80	0.029850
81	0.033883
82	0.038544
83	0.043880
84	0.049956
85	0.056799
86	0.064436
87	0.072882
88	0.082137
89	0.092172
90	0.102919
91	0.114344
92	0.126605
93	0.139936
94	0.154844
95	0.171902
96	0.187210
97	0.204659
98	0.222921
99	0.241884
100	0.261476
101	0.281536
102	0.301847
103	0.322371
104	0.342940
105	0.361261
106	0.372886
107	0.381098
108	0.383358
109	0.385709
110	0.388092
111	0.390353
112	0.392822
113	0.395188
114	0.397567
115	0.400000
116	0.400000
117	0.400000

Age	Probability of Death
118	0.400000
119	0.400000
120	0.400000

(f) *Applicability dates.*—(1) *In general.*—The life expectancy tables and Uniform Lifetime Table set forth in this section apply for distribution calendar years beginning on or after January 1, 2022. For life expectancy tables and the Uniform Lifetime Table applicable for earlier distribution calendar years, see § 1.401(a)(9)-9, as set forth in 26 CFR part 1 revised as of April 1, 2020 (formerly applicable § 1.401(a)(9)-9).

(2) *Application to life expectancies that may not be recalculated.*—(i) *Redetermination of initial life expectancy using current tables.*—If an employee died before January 1, 2022, and, under the rules of § 1.401(a)(9)-5, the distribution period that applies for a calendar year following the calendar year of the employee's death is equal to a single life expectancy calculated as of the calendar year of the employee's death (or, if applicable, the following calendar year), reduced by 1 for each subsequent year, then that life expectancy is reset as provided in paragraph (f)(2)(ii) of this section. Similarly, if an employee's sole beneficiary is the employee's surviving spouse, and the spouse dies before January 1, 2022, then the spouse's life expectancy for the calendar year of the spouse's death (which is used to determine the applicable distribution period for later years) is reset as provided in paragraph (f)(2)(ii) of this section.

(ii) *Determination of applicable distribution period.*—(A) *Distribution period based on new life expectancy.*—With respect to a life expectancy described in paragraph (f)(2)(i) of this section, the distribution period that applies for a distribution calendar year beginning on or after January 1, 2022, is determined by using the Single Life Table in paragraph (b) of this section to determine the initial life expectancy for the age of the relevant individual in the relevant calendar year and then reducing the resulting distribution period by 1 for each subsequent year. However, see section 401(a)(9)(H)(ii) and (iii) for rules limiting the availability of a life expectancy distribution period.

(B) *Example of redetermination.*—Assume that an employee died at age 80 in 2019 and the employee's designated beneficiary (who was not the employee's spouse) was age 75 in the year of the employee's death. For 2020, the distribution period that would have applied for the beneficiary was 12.7 years (the period applicable for a 76-year-old under the Single Life Table in formerly applicable § 1.401(a)(9)-9), and for 2021, it would have been 11.7 years (the original distribution period, reduced by 1 year). For 2022, if the designated beneficiary is still alive, then the applicable distribution period would be 12.1 years (the 14.1-year life expectancy for a 76-year-old under the Single Life Table in paragraph (b) of this section, reduced by 2 years). However, see section 401(a)(9)(H)(iii) for rules regarding how to apply the required distribution rules to defined contribution plans if the eligible designated beneficiary dies prior to distribution of the employee's entire interest. [Reg. § 1.401(a)(9)-9.]

☐ [*T.D. 8987, 4-16-2002. Amended by T.D. 9930, 11-5-2020.*]

[Reg. § 1.401(a)-11]

§ 1.401(a)-11. Qualified joint and survivor annuities.—(a) *General rule.*—(1) *Required provisions.*—A trust, to which section 411 (relating to minimum vesting standards) applies without regard to section 411(e)(2), which is a part of a plan providing for the payment of benefits in any form of a life annuity (as defined in paragraph (b)(1) of this section), shall not constitute a qualified trust under section 401(a)(1) and this section unless such plan provides that:

(i) Unless the election provided in paragraph (c)(1) of this section has been made, life annuity benefits will be paid in a form having the effect of a qualified joint and survivor annuity (as defined in paragraph (b)(2) of this section) with respect to any participant who—

(A) Begins to receive payments under such plan on or after the date the normal retirement age is attained, or

(B) Dies (on or after the date the normal retirement age is attained) while in active service of the employer maintaining the plan, or

(C) In the case of a plan which provides for the payment of benefits before the normal retirement age, begins to receive payments under such plan on or after the date the qualified early retirement age (as defined in paragraph (b)(4) of this section) is attained, or

(D) Separates from service on or after the date the normal retirement age (or the qualified early retirement age) is attained and after satisfaction of eligibility requirements for the payment of bene-

fits under the plan (except for any plan requirement that there be filed a claim for benefits) and thereafter dies before beginning to receive such benefits;

(ii) Any participant may elect, as provided in paragraph (c)(1) of this section, not to receive life annuity benefits in the form of a qualified joint and survivor annuity; and

(iii) If the plan provides for the payment of benefits before the normal retirement age, any participant may elect, as provided in paragraph (c)(2) of this section, that life annuity benefits be payable as an early survivor annuity (as defined in paragraph (b)(3) of this section) upon his death in the event that he—

(A) Attains the qualified early retirement age (as defined in paragraph (b)(4) of this section), and

(B) Dies on or before the day normal retirement age is attained while employed by an employer maintaining the plan.

(2) *Certain cash-outs.*—A plan will not fail to satisfy the requirements of section 401(a)(11) and this section merely because it provides that if the present value of the entire nonforfeitable benefit derived from employer contributions of a participant at the time of this separation from service does not exceed $1,750 (or such smaller amount as the plan may specify), such benefit will be paid to him in a lump sum.

(3) *Illustrations.*—The provisions of subparagraph (1) of this paragraph may be illustrated by the following examples:

Example (1). The X Corporation Defined Contribution Plan was established in 1960. As in effect on January 1, 1974, the plan provided that, upon the participant's retirement, the participant may elect to receive the balance of his account in the form of (1) a single-sum cash payment, (2) a single-sum distribution consisting of X Corporation stock, (3) five equal annual cash payments, (4) a life annuity, or (5) a combination of options (1) through (4). The plan also provided that, if a participant did not elect another form of distribution, the balance of his account would be distributed to him in the form of a single-sum cash payment upon his retirement. Assume that section 401(a)(11) and this section became applicable to the plan as of its plan year beginning January 1, 1976, with respect to persons who were active participants in the plan as of such date (see paragraph (f) of this section). If X Corporation Defined Contribution Plan continues to allow the life annuity payment option after December 31, 1975, it must be amended to provide that if a participant elects a life annuity option the life annuity benefit will be paid in a form having the effect of a qualified joint and survivor annuity, except to the extent that the participant elects another form of benefit payment. However, the plan can continue to provide that, if no election is made, the balance will be paid as a single-sum cash payment. If the trust is not so amended, it will fail to qualify under section 401(a).

Example (2). The Y Corporation Retirement Plan provides that plan benefits are payable only in the form of a life annuity and also provides that a participant may retire before the normal retirement age of 65 and receive a benefit if he has completed 30 years of service. Under this plan, an employee who begins employment at the age of 18 will be eligible to receive retirement benefits at the age of 48 if he then has 30 years of service. This plan must allow a participant to elect in the time and manner prescribed in paragraph (c)(2) of this section an early survivor annuity (defined in paragraph (b)(3) of this section) to be payable on the death of the participant if death occurs while the participant is in active service for the employer maintaining the plan and on or after the date of participant reaches the qualified early retirement age of 55 (the later of the date the participant reaches the earliest retirement age (age 48) or 10 years before normal retirement age (age 55)) but before the day after the day the participant reaches normal retirement age (age 65).

Example (3). Assume the same facts as in Example (2). A, B, and C began employment with Y Corporation when they each attained age 18. A retires and begins to receive benefit payments at age 48 after completing 30 years of service. The plan is not required to pay a qualified joint and survivor annuity to A and his spouse at any time. B does not elect an early survivor annuity at age 55, but retires at age 57 after completing 39 years of service. Unless B makes an election under subparagraph (1)(ii) of this paragraph, the plan is required to pay a qualified joint and survivor annuity to B and his spouse. C makes no elections described in subparagraph (1) of this paragraph, and dies while in active service at age 66 after completing 48 years of service. The plan is required to pay a qualified survivor annuity to C's spouse.

(b) *Definitions.*—As used in this section—

(1) *Life annuity.*—(i) The term "life annuity" means an annuity that provides retirement payments and requires the survival of the participant or his spouse as one of the conditions for any payment or possible payment under the annuity. For example, annuities that make payments for 10 years or until death, whichever occurs first or whichever occurs last, are life annuities.

(ii) However, the term "life annuity" does not include an annuity, or that portion of an annuity, that provides those benefits which, under section 411(a)(9), would not be taken into account in the determination of the normal retirement benefit or early retirement benefit. For example, "social security supplements" described in the third sentence of section 411(a)(9) are not considered to be life annuities for the purposes of this section, whether or not early retirement benefit is provided under the plan.

(2) *Qualified joint and survivor annuity.*—The term "qualified joint and survivor annuity" means an annuity for the life of the participant with a survivor annuity for the life of his spouse which is neither (i) less than one-half of, nor (ii) greater than, the amount of the annuity payable during the joint lives of the participant and his spouse. For purposes of the preceding sentence, amounts described in §1.401(a)-11(b)(1)(ii) may be disregarded. A qualified joint and survivor annuity must be at least the actuarial equivalent of the normal form of life annuity or, if greater, of any optional form of life annuity offered under the plan. Equivalence may be determined, on the basis of consistently applied reasonable actuarial factors, for each participant or for all participants or reasonable groupings of participants, if such determination does not result in discrimination in favor of employees who are officers, shareholders, or highly compensated. An annuity is not a qualified joint and survivor annuity if payments to the spouse of a deceased participant are terminated, or reduced, because of such spouse's remarriage.

(3) *Early survivor annuity.*—The term "early survivor annuity" means an annuity for the life of the participant's spouse the payments under which must not be less than the payments which would have been made to the spouse under the joint and survivor annuity if the participant had made the election described in paragraph (c)(2) of this section immediately prior to his retirement and if his retirement had occurred on the day before his death and within the period during which an election can be made under such paragraph (c)(2). For example, if a participant would be entitled to a single life annuity of $100 per month or a reduced amount under a qualified joint and survivor annuity of $80 per month, his spouse is entitled to a payment of at least $40 per month. However, the payments may be reduced to reflect the number of months of coverage under the survivor annuity pursuant to paragraph (e) of this section.

(4) *Qualified early retirement age.*—The term "qualified early retirement age" means the latest of—

(i) The earliest date, under the plan, on which the participant could elect (without regard to any requirement that approval of early retirement be obtained) to receive retirement benefits (other than disability benefits),

(ii) The first day of the 120th month beginning before the participant reaches normal retirement age, or

(iii) The date on which the participant begins participation.

(5) *Normal retirement age.*—The term "normal retirement age" has the meaning set forth in section 411(a)(8).

(6) *Annuity starting date.*—The term "annuity starting date" means the first day of the first period with respect to which an amount is received as a life annuity, whether by reason of retirement or by reason of disability.

(7) *Day.*—The term "day" means a calendar day.

(c) *Elections.*—(1) *Election not to take joint and survivor annuity form.*—(i) *In general.*—(A) A plan shall not be treated as satisfying the requirements of this section unless it provides that each participant may elect, during the election period described in subdivision (ii) of this subparagraph, not to receive a qualified joint and survivor annuity. However, if a plan provides that a qualified joint and survivor annuity is the only form of benefit payable under the plan with respect to a married participant, no election need be provided.

(B) The election shall be in writing and clearly indicate that the participant is electing to receive all or, if permitted by the plan, part of his benefits under the plan in a form other than that of a qualified joint and survivor annuity. A plan will not fail to meet the requirements of this section merely because the plan requires the participant to obtain the written approval of his spouse in order for the participant to make this election or if the plan provides that such approval is not required.

(ii) *Election period.*—(A) For purposes of the election described in paragraph (c)(1)(i) of this section, the plan shall provide an election period which shall include a period of at least 90 days following the furnishing of all of the applicable information required by subparagraph (3)(i) of this paragraph and ending prior to commencement of benefits. In no event may the election period end earlier than the 90th day before the commencement of benefits. Thus, for example, the commencement of benefits may be delayed until the end of such election period because the amount of payments to be made to a participant cannot be ascertained before the end of such period; see §1.401(a)-14(d).

If a participant makes a request for additional information as provided in subparagraph (3)(iii) of this paragraph on or before the last day of the election period, the election period shall be extended to the extent necessary to include at least the 90 calendar days immediately following the day the requested additional information is personally delivered or mailed to the participant. Notwithstanding the immediately preceding sentence, a plan may provide in cases in which the participant has been furnished by mail or personal delivery all of the applicable information required by subparagraph (3)(i) of this paragraph, that a request for such additional information must be made on or before a date which is not less than 60 days from the date of such mailing or delivery; and if the plan does so provide, the election period shall be extended to the extent necessary to include at least the 60 calendar days following the day the requested additional information is personally delivered or mailed to the participant.

(B) In the case of a participant in a plan to which this subparagraph applies who separated from service after section 401(a)(11) and this section became applicable to such plan with respect to such participant, and to whom an election required by this subparagraph has not been previously made available (and will not become available in normal course), the plan must provide an election to receive the balance of his benefits (properly adjusted, if applicable, for payments received, prior to the exercise of such election, in the form of a qualified joint and survivor annuity) in a form other than that of a qualified joint and survivor annuity. The provisions of paragraph (c)(1)(ii)(A) shall apply except that in no event shall the election period end before the 90th day after the date on which notice of the availability of such election and the applicable information required by subparagraph (3)(i) of this paragraph is given directly to the participant. If such notice and information is given by mail, it shall be treated as given on the date of mailing. If such participant has died, such election shall be made available to such participant's personal representative.

(2) *Election of early survivor annuity.*—(i) *In general.*—(A) A plan described in paragraph (a)(1)(iii) of this section shall not be treated as satisfying the requirements of this section unless it provides that each participant may elect, during the period described in subdivision (ii) of this subparagraph, an early survivor annuity as described in paragraph (a)(1)(iii) of this section. Breaks in service after the participant has attained the qualified early retirement age neither invalidate a previous election or revocation nor prevent an election from being made or revoked during the election period.

(B) The election shall be in writing and clearly indicate that the participant is electing the early survivor annuity form.

(C) A plan is not required to provide an election under this subparagraph if—

(1) The plan provides that an early survivor annuity is the only form of benefit payable under the plan with respect to a married participant who dies while employed by an employer maintaining the plan,

(2) In the case of a defined contribution plan, the plan provides a survivor benefit at least equal in value to the vested portion of the participant's account balance, if the participant dies while in active service with an employer maintaining the plan, or

(3) In the case of a defined benefit plan, the plan provides a survivor benefit at least equal in value to the present value of the vested portion of the participant's normal form of the accrued benefit payable at normal retirement age (determined immediately prior to death), if the participant dies while in active service with an employer maintaining the plan. Any present values must be determined in accordance with either the actuarial assumptions or factors specified in the plan, or a variable standard independent of employer discretion for converting optional benefits specified in the plan.

(ii) *Election period.*—(A) For purposes of the election described in paragraph (c)(2)(i) of this section the plan shall provide an election period which, except as provided in the following sentence, shall begin not later than the later of either the 90th day before a participant attains the qualified early retirement age or the date on which his participation begins, and shall end on the date the participant terminates his employment. If such a plan contains a provision that any election made under this subparagraph does not become effective or ceases to be effective if the participant dies within a certain period beginning on the date of such election, the election period prescribed in this subdivision (ii) shall begin not later than the later of (1) a date which is 90 days plus such certain period before the participant attains the qualified early retirement age or (2) the date on which his participation begins. For example, if a plan provides that an election made under this paragraph does not become effective if the participant dies less than 2 years after the date of such election, the period for making an election under this paragraph must begin not later than the later of (1) 2 years and 90 days before the participant attains the qualified early retirement age, or (2) the date on which his participation begins. However, the election period for an individual who was an active participant on the date this section became effective with regard to the plan need not begin earlier than such effective date.

(B) In the case of a participant in a plan to which this subparagraph applies who dies after section 401(a)(11) and this section became applicable to such plan with respect to such participant and to whom an election required by this subparagraph has not been previously made available, the plan must give the participant's surviving spouse or, if dead, such spouse's personal representative the option of electing an early survivor annuity. The plan may reduce the surviving spouse's annuity to take into account any benefits already received. The period for making such election shall not end before the 90th day after the date on which written notice of the availability of such election and applicable information required by subparagraph (3)(i) of this paragraph is given directly to such surviving spouse or personal representative. If such notice and information is given by mail, it shall be treated as given on the date of mailing.

(3) *Information to be provided by plan.*—For rules regarding the information required to be provided with respect to the election to waive a QJSA or a QPSA, see § 1.417(a)(3)-1.

(4) *Election is revocable.*—A plan to which this section applies must provide that any election made under this paragraph may be revoked in writing during the specified election period, and that after such election has been revoked, another election under this paragraph may be made during the specified election period.

(5) *Election by surviving spouse.*—A plan will not fail to meet the requirements of section 401(a)(11) and this section merely because it provides that the spouse of a deceased participant may elect to have benefits paid in a form other than a survivor annuity. If the plan provides that such a spouse may make such an election, the plan administrator must furnish to this spouse, within a reasonable amount of time after a written request has been made by this spouse, a written explanation in non-technical language of the survivor annuity and any other form of payment which may be selected. This explanation must state the financial effect (in terms of dollars) of each form of payment. A plan need not respond to more than one such request.

(d) *Permissible additional plan provisions.*—(1) *In general.*—A plan will not fail to meet the requirements of section 401(a)(11) and this section merely because it contains one or more of the provisions described in paragraph (d)(2) through (5) of this section.

(2) *Claim for benefits.*—A plan may provide that as a condition precedent to the payment of benefits, a participant must express in writing to the plan administrator the form in which he prefers benefits to be paid and provide all the information reasonably necessary for the payment of such benefits. However, if a participant files a claim for benefits with the plan administrator and provides the plan administrator with all the information necessary for the payment of benefits but does not indicate a preference as to the form for the payment of benefits, benefits must be paid in the form of a qualified joint and survivor annuity if the participant has attained the qualified early retirement age unless such participant has made an effective election not to receive benefits in such form. For rules relating to provisions in a plan to the effect that a claim for benefits must be filed before the payment of benefits will commence, see § 1.401(a)-14.

(3) *Marriage requirements.*—A plan may provide that a joint and survivor annuity will be paid only if—

(i) The participant and his spouse have been married to each other throughout a period (not exceeding one year) ending on the annuity starting date.

(ii) The spouse of the participant is not entitled to receive a survivor annuity (whether or not the election described in paragraph (c)(2) of this section has been made) unless the participant and his spouse have been married to each other throughout a period (not exceeding one year) ending on the date of such participant's death.

(iii) The same spouse must satisfy the requirements of subdivisions (i) and (ii) of this subparagraph.

(iv) The participant must notify the plan administrator (as defined by section 414(g)) of his marital status within any reasonable time period specified in the plan.

(4) *Effect of participant's death on an election or revocation of an election under paragraph (c).*—A plan may provide that any election described in paragraph (c) of this section or any revocation of any such election does not become effective or ceases to be effective if the participant dies within a period, not in excess of 2 years, beginning on the date of such election or revocation. However, a plan contain-

ing a provision described in the preceding sentence shall not satisfy the requirements of this section unless it also provides that any such election or any revocation of any such election will be given effect in any case in which—

(i) The participant dies from accidental causes,

(ii) A failure to give effect to the election or revocation would deprive the participant's survivor of a survivor annuity, and

(iii) Such election or revocation is made before such accident occurred.

(5) *Benefit option approval by third party.*—(i) A plan may provide that an optional form of benefit elected by a participant is subject to the approval of an administrative committee or similar third party. However, the administrative committee cannot deny a participant any of the benefits required by section 401(a)(11). For example, if a plan offers a life annuity option, the committee may deny the participant a qualified joint and survivor annuity only by denying the participant access to all life annuity options without knowledge of whether the participant wishes to receive a qualified joint and survivor annuity. Alternatively, if the committee knows which form of life annuity the participant has chosen before the committee makes its decision, the committee cannot withhold its consent for payment of a qualified joint and survivor annuity even though it denies all other life annuity options. This subparagraph (5) only applies before the effective date of the amendment made to section 411(d)(6) by section 301 of the Retirement Equity Act of 1984. See section 411(d)(6) and the regulations thereunder for rules limiting employer discretion.

(ii) The provisions of this subparagraph may be illustrated by the following example:

Example. In 1980 plan M provides that the automatic form of benefit is a single sum distribution. The plan also permits, subject to approval by the administrative committee, the election of several optional forms of life annuity. On the election form that is reviewed by the administrative committee the participant indicates whether any life annuity option is preferred, without indicating the particular life annuity chosen. Thus, the committee approves or disapproves the election without knowledge of whether a qualified joint and survivor annuity will be elected. The administrative committee approval provision in Plan M does not cause the plan to fail to satisfy this section. On the other hand, if the form indicates which form of life annuity is preferred, committee disapproval of any election of the qualified joint and survivor annuity would cause the plan to fail to satisfy this section.

(e) *Costs of providing qualified joint and survivor annuity form or early survivor annuity form.*—A plan may take into account in any equitable manner consistent with generally accepted actuarial principles applied on a consistent basis any increased costs resulting from providing qualified joint and survivor annuity and early survivor annuity benefits. A plan may give a participant the option of paying premiums only if it provides another option under which an out-of-pocket expense by the participant is not required.

(f) *Application and effective date.*—Section 401(a)(11) and this section shall apply to a plan only with respect to plan years beginning after December 31, 1975, and shall apply only if—

(1) The participant's annuity starting date did not fall within a plan year beginning before January 1, 1976, and

(2) The participant was an active participant in the plan on or after the first day of the first plan year beginning after December 31, 1975.

For purposes of this paragraph, the term "active participant" means a participant for whom benefits are being accrued under the plan on his behalf (in the case of a defined benefit plan), the employer is obligated to contribute to or under the plan on his behalf (in the case of a defined contribution plan other than a profit-sharing plan), or the employer either is obligated to contribute to or under the plan on his behalf or would have been obligated to contribute to or under the plan on his behalf if any contribution were made to or under the plan (in the case of a profit-sharing plan).

If benefits under a plan are provided by the distribution to the participants of individual annuity contracts, the annuity starting date will be considered for purposes of this paragraph to fall within a plan year beginning before January 1, 1976, with respect to any such individual contract that was distributed to the participant during a plan year beginning before January 1, 1976, if no premiums are paid with respect to such contract during a plan year beginning after December 31, 1975. In the case of individual annuity contracts that are distributed to participants before January 1, 1978, and which contain an option to provide a qualified joint and survivor annuity, the requirements of this section will be considered to have been satisfied if, not later than January 1, 1978, holders of individual annuity contracts who are participants described in the first sentence of this paragraph are given an opportunity to have such contracts amended, so as to provide for a qualified joint and survivor annuity in the absence of a contrary election, within a period of not less than one year from the date such opportunity was offered. In no event, however, shall the preceding sentence apply with respect to benefits attributable to premiums paid after December 31, 1977.

(g) *Effect of REA 1984.*—(1) *In general.*—The Retirement Equity Act of 1984 (REA 1984) significantly changed the qualified joint and survivor annuity rules generally effective for plan years beginning after December 31, 1984. The new survivor annuity rules are primarily in sections 401(a)(11) and 417 as revised by REA 1984 and §§ 1.401(a)-20 and 1.417(e)-1.

(2) *Regulations after REA 1984.*—(i) REA and the regulations thereunder to the extent inconsistent with pre-REA 1984 section 401(a)(11) and this section are controlling for years to which REA 1984 applies. See *e.g.*, paragraphs (a)(1) and (2) of this section, relating to required provisions and certain cash-outs, respectively, and (e), relating to costs of providing annuities, for rules that are inconsistent with REA 1984 and, therefore, are not applicable to REA 1984 years.

(ii) To the extent that the pre-REA 1984 law either is the same as or consistent with REA 1984 and the new regulations hereunder, the rules in this section shall continue to apply for years to which REA 1984 applies. (See, *e.g.*, paragraph (c) (relating to how information is furnished participants and spouses) and paragraph (b) (defining a life annuity) for some of the rules that apply to REA 1984 years.) The rules in this section shall not apply for such year to the extent that they are inconsistent with REA 1984 and the regulations thereunder.

(iii) The Commissioner may provide additional guidance as to the continuing effect of the various rules in this section for years to which REA 1984 applies. [Reg. § 1.401(a)-11.]

☐ [*T.D. 7458, 1-4-77. Amended by T.D. 7510, 10-3-77; T.D. 8219, 8-19-88 and T.D. 9099, 12-16-2003.*]

[Reg. § 1.401(a)-12]

§ 1.401(a)-12. Mergers and consolidations of plans and transfers of plan assets.—A trust will not be qualified under section 401 unless the plan of which the trust is a part provides that in the case of any merger or consolidation with, or transfer of assets or liabilities to, another plan after September 2, 1974, each participant in the plan would receive a minimum benefit if the plan terminated immediately after the merger, consolidation, or transfer. This benefit must be equal to or greater than the benefit the participant would have been entitled to receive immediately before the merger, consolidation, or transfer if the plan in which he was a participant had then terminated. This section applies to a multiemployer plan only to the extent determined by the Pension Benefit Guaranty Corporation. For additional rules concerning mergers or consolidations of plans and transfers of plan assets, see section 414(l) and § 1.414(l)-1. [Reg. § 1.401(a)-12.]

☐ [*T.D. 7638, 8-16-79.*]

[Reg. § 1.401(a)-13]

§ 1.401(a)-13. Assignment or alienation of benefits.—(a) *Scope of the regulations.*—This section applies only to plans to which section 411 applies without regard to section 411(e)(2). Thus, for example, it does not apply to a governmental plan, within the meaning of section 414(d), a church plan, within the meaning of section 414(e), for which there has not been made the election under section 410(a) to have the participation, vesting, funding, etc., requirements apply; or a plan which at no time after September 2, 1974, provided for employer contributions.

(b) *No assignment or alienation.*—(1) *General rule.*—Under section 401(a)(13), a trust will not be qualified unless the plan of which the trust is a part provides that benefits provided under the plan may not be anticipated, assigned (either at law or in equity), alienated or subject to attachment, garnishment, levy, execution or other legal or equitable process.

(2) *Federal tax levies and judgments.*—A plan provision satisfying the requirements of subparagraph (1) of this paragraph shall not preclude the following:

(i) The enforcement of a Federal tax levy made pursuant to section 6331.

(ii) The collection by the United States on a judgment resulting from an unpaid tax assessment.

(c) *Definition of assignment and alienation.*—(1) *In general.*—For purposes of this section, the terms "assignment" and "alienation" include—

(i) Any arrangement providing for the payment to the employer of plan benefits which otherwise would be due the participant under the plan, and

(ii) Any direct or indirect arrangement (whether revocable or irrevocable) whereby a party acquires from a participant or beneficiary a right or interest enforceable against the plan in, or to, all or any part of a plan benefit payment which is, or may become, payable to the participant or beneficiary.

(2) *Specific arrangements not considered an assignment or alienation.*—The terms "assignment" and "alienation" do not include, and paragraph (e) of this section does not apply to, the following arrangements:

(i) Any arrangement for the recovery of amounts described in section 4045(b) of the Employee Retirement Income Security Act of 1974, 88 Stat. 1027 (relating to the recapture of certain payments),

(ii) Any arrangement for the withholding of Federal, State or local tax from plan benefit payments,

(iii) Any arrangement for the recovery by the plan of overpayments of benefits previously made to a participant,

(iv) Any arrangement for the transfer of benefit rights from the plan to another plan, or

(v) Any arrangement for the direct deposit of benefit payments to an account in a bank, savings and loan association or credit union, provided such arrangement is not part of an arrangement constituting an assignment or alienation. Thus, for example, such an arrangement could provide for the direct deposit of a participant's benefit payments to a bank account held by the participant and the participant's spouse as joint tenants.

(d) *Exceptions to general rule prohibiting assignments or alienations.*—(1) *Certain voluntary and revocable assignments or alienations.*—Notwithstanding paragraph (b)(1) of this section, a plan may provide that once a participant or beneficiary begins receiving benefits under the plan, the participant or beneficiary may assign or alienate the right to future benefit payments provided that the provision is limited to assignments or alienations which—

(i) Are voluntary and revocable;

(ii) Do not in the aggregate exceed 10 percent of any benefit payment; and

(iii) Are neither for the purpose, nor have the effect, of defraying plan administration costs.

For purposes of this subparagraph, an attachment, garnishment, levy, execution or other legal or equitable process is not considered a voluntary assignment or alienation.

(2) *Benefits assigned or alienated as security for loans.*—(i) Notwithstanding paragraph (b)(1) of this section, a plan may provide for loans from the plan to a participant or a beneficiary to be secured (by whatever means) by the participant's accrued nonforfeitable benefit provided that the following conditions are met.

(ii) The plan provision providing for the loans must be limited to loans from the plan. A plan may not provide for the use of benefits accrued or to be accrued under the plan as security for a loan from a party other than the plan, regardless of whether these benefits are nonforfeitable within the meaning of section 411 and the regulations thereunder.

(iii) The loan, if made to a participant or beneficiary who is a disqualified person (within the meaning of section 4975(e)(2)), must be exempt from the tax imposed by section 4975 (relating to the tax imposed on prohibited transactions) by reason of section 4975(d)(1). If the loan is made to a participant or beneficiary who is not a disqualified person, the loan must be one which would be exempt from the tax imposed by section 4975 by reason of section 4975(d)(1) if the loan were made to a disqualified person.

(e) *Special rule for certain arrangements.*—(1) *In general.*—For purposes of this section and notwithstanding paragraph (c)(1) of this section, an arrangement whereby a participant or beneficiary directs the plan to pay all, or any portion, of a plan benefit payment to a third party (which includes the participant's employer) will not constitute an "assignment or alienation" if—

(i) It is revocable at any time by the participant or beneficiary; and

(ii) The third party files a written acknowledgement with the plan administrator pursuant to subparagraph (2) of this paragraph.

(2) *Acknowledgement requirement for third party arrangements.*—In accordance with paragraph (e)(1)(ii) of this section, the third party is required to file a written acknowledgement with the plan administrator. This acknowledgement must state that the third party has no enforceable right in, or to, any plan benefit payment or portion thereof (except to the extent of payments actually received pursuant to the terms of the arrangement). A blanket written acknowledgement for all participants and beneficiaries who are covered under the arrangement with the third party is sufficient. The written acknowledgement must be filed with the plan administrator no later than the later of—

(i) 18 August 1978; or

(ii) 90 days after the arrangement is entered into.

(f) *Effective date.*—Section 401(a)(13) is applicable as of January 1, 1976, and the plan provision required by this section must be effective as of that date. However, regardless of when the provision is adopted, it will not affect—

(1) Attachments, garnishments, levies or other legal or equitable process permitted under the plan that are made before January 1, 1976;

(2) Assignments permitted under the plan that are irrevocable on December 31, 1975, including assignments made before January 1, 1976, as security for loans to a participant or beneficiary from a party other than the plan; and

(3) Renewals or extensions of loans described in subparagraph (2) of this paragraph, if—

(i) The principal amount of the obligation outstanding on December 31, 1975 (or, if less, the principal amount outstanding on the date of renewal or extension), is not increased;

(ii) The loan, as renewed or extended, does not bear a rate of interest in excess of the rate prevailing for similar loans at the time of the renewal or extension; and

(iii) With respect to loans that are renewed or extended to bear a variable interest rate, the formula for determining the applicable rate is consistent with the formula or formulae prevailing for similar loans at the time of the renewal or extension.

For purposes of subparagraphs (2) and (3) of this paragraph, a loan from a party other than the plan made after December 31, 1975, will be treated as a new loan. This is so even if the lender's security interest for the loan arises from an assignment of the participant's accrued nonforfeitable benefit made before that date.

(g) *Special rules for qualified domestic relations orders.*—(1) *Definition.*—The term "qualified domestic relations order" (QDRO) has the meaning set forth in section 414(p). For purposes of the Internal Revenue Code, a QDRO also includes any domestic relations order described in section 303(d) of the Retirement Equity Act of 1984.

(2) *Plan amendments.*—A plan will not fail to satisfy the qualification requirements of section 401(a) or 403(a) merely because it does not include provisions with regard to a QDRO.

(3) *Waiver of distribution requirements.*—A plan shall not be treated as failing to satisfy the requirements of sections 401(a) and (k) and 409(d) solely because of a payment to an alternate payee pursuant to a QDRO. This is the case even if the plan provides for payments pursuant to a QDRO to an alternate payee prior to the time it may make payments to a participant. Thus, for example, a pension plan may pay an alternate payee even though the participant may not receive a distribution because he continues to be employed by the employer.

(4) *Coordination with section 417.*—(i) *Former spouse.*—(A) *In general.*—Under section 414(p)(5), a QDRO may provide that a former spouse shall be treated as the current spouse of a participant for all or some purposes under sections 401(a)(11) and 417.

(B) *Consent.*—(1) To the extent a former spouse is treated as the current spouse of the participant by reason of a QDRO, any current spouse shall not be treated as the current spouse. For example, assume H is divorced from W, but a QDRO provides that H shall be treated as W's current spouse with respect to all of W's benefits under a plan. H will be treated as the surviving spouse under the QPSA and QJSA unless W obtains H's consent to waive the QPSA or QJSA or both. The fact that W married S after W's divorce from H is disregarded. If, however, the QDRO had provided that H shall be treated as W's current spouse only with respect to benefits that accrued prior to the divorce, then H's consent would be needed by W to waive the QPSA or QJSA with respect to benefits accrued before the divorce. S's consent would be required with respect to the remainder of the benefits.

(2) In the preceding examples, if the QDRO ordered that a portion of W's benefit (either through separate accounts or a percentage of the benefit) must be distributed to H rather than ordering that H be treated as W's spouse, the survivor annuity requirements of sections 401(a)(11) and 417 would not apply to the part of W's benefit awarded H. Instead, the terms of the QDRO would determine how H's portion of W's accrued benefit is paid. W is required to obtain S's consent if W elects to waive either the QJSA or QPSA with respect to the remaining portion of W's benefit.

(C) *Amount of the QPSA or QJSA.*—(1) Where, because of a QDRO, more than one individual is to be treated as the surviving spouse, a plan may provide that the total amount to be paid in the form of a QPSA or survivor portion of a QJSA may not exceed the amount that would be paid if there were only one surviving spouse. The QPSA or survivor portion of the QJSA, as the case may be, payable to each surviving spouse must be paid as an annuity based on the life of each such spouse.

(2) Where the QDRO splits the participant's accrued benefit between the participant and a former spouse (either through separate accounts or percentage of the benefit), the surviving spouse of the participant is entitled to a QPSA or QJSA based on the participant's accrued benefit as of the date of death or the annuity starting date, less the separate account or percentage that is payable to the former spouse. The calculation is made as if the separate account or percentage had been distributed to the participant prior to the relevant date.

(ii) *Current spouse.*—Under section 414(p)(5), even if the applicable election periods (*i.e.*, the first day of the year in which the participant attains age 35 and 90 days before the annuity starting date) have not begun, a QDRO may provide that a current spouse shall not be treated as the current spouse of the participant for all or some purposes under sections 401(a)(11) and 417. A QDRO may provide that the current spouse waives all future rights to a QPSA or QJSA.

(iii) *Effects on benefits.*—(A) A plan is not required to provide additional vesting or benefits because of a QDRO.

(B) If an alternative payee is treated pursuant to a QDRO as having an interest in the plan benefit, including a separate account or percentage of the participant's account, then the QDRO can not provide the alternate payee with a greater right to designate a beneficiary for the alternate payee's benefit amount than the participant's right. The QJSA or QPSA provisions of section 417 do not apply to the spouse of an alternate payee.

(C) If the former spouse who is treated as a current spouse dies prior to the participant's annuity starting date, then any actual current spouse of the participant is treated as the current spouse, except as otherwise provided in a QDRO.

(iv) *Section 415 requirements.*—Even though a participant's benefits are awarded to an alternate payee pursuant to a QDRO, the benefits are benefits of the participant for purposes of applying the limitations of section 415 to the participant's benefits. [Reg. §1.401(a)-13.]

☐ [*T.D. 7534, 2-17-78. Amended by T.D. 8219, 8-19-88.*]

[Reg. §1.401(a)-14]

§1.401(a)-14. Commencement of benefits under qualified trusts.—(a) *In general.*—Under section 401(a)(14), a trust to which section 411 applies (without regard to section 411(e)(2)) is not qualified under section 401 unless the plan of which such trust is a part provides that the payment of benefits under the plan to the participant will begin not later than the 60th day after the close of the plan year in which the latest of the following events occurs:

(1) The attainment by the participant of age 65, or, if earlier, the normal retirement age specified under the plan,

(2) The 10th anniversary of the date on which the participant commenced participation in the plan,

(3) The termination of the participant's service with the employer, or

(4) The date specified in an election made pursuant to paragraph (b) of this section.
Notwithstanding the preceding sentence, a plan may require that a participant file a claim for benefits before payment of benefits will commence.

(b) *Election of later date.*—(1) *General rule.*—A plan may permit a participant to elect that the payment to him of any benefit under a plan will commence at a date later than the dates specified under paragraphs (a)(1), (2), and (3) of this section.

(2) *Manner of election.*—A plan permitting an election under this paragraph shall require that such election must be made by submitting to the plan administrator a written statement, signed by the participant, which describes the benefit and the date on which the payment of such benefit shall commence.

(3) *Restriction.*—An election may not be made pursuant to a plan provision permitted by this paragraph if the exercise of such election will cause benefits payable under the plan with respect to the participant in the event of his death to be more than "incidental" within the meaning of paragraph (b)(1)(i) of §1.401-1.

(c) *Special early retirement rule.*—(1) *Separation prior to early retirement age.*—A trust forming part of a plan which provides for the payment of an early retirement benefit is not qualified under section 401 unless, upon satisfaction of the age requirement for such early retirement benefit, a participant who:

(i) Satisfied the service requirements for such early retirement benefit, but

(ii) Separated from service (with any nonforfeitable right to an accrued benefit) before satisfying such age requirement,
is entitled to receive not less than the reduced normal retirement benefit described in paragraph (c)(2) of this section. A plan may establish reasonable conditions for payments of early retirement benefits (including, for example, a requirement that a claim for benefits be made) if the conditions are equally applicable to participants who separate from service when eligible for an early retirement benefit and participants who separate from service earlier.

(2) *Reduced normal retirement benefit.*—For purposes of this section, the reduced normal retirement benefit is the benefit to which the participant would have been entitled under the plan at normal retirement age, reduced in accordance with reasonable actuarial assumptions.

(3) *Separation prior to effective date of this section.*—The provisions of this paragraph shall not apply in the case of a plan participant who separates from service before attainment of early retirement age and prior to the effective date of this section set forth in paragraph (e) of this section.

(4) *Illustration.*—The provisions of this paragraph may be illustrated by the following example:
Example: The X Corporation Defined Benefit Plan provides that a normal retirement benefit will be payable to a participant upon attainment of age 65. The plan also provides that an actuarially reduced retirement benefit will be payable upon application, to any participant who has completed 10 years of service with the X Corporation and attained age 60. When he is 55 years of age and has completed 10 years of service with X Corporation, A, a participant in the plan, leaves the service of X Corporation and does not return. The plan will not be qualified under section 401 unless, upon attainment of age 60 and application for benefits, A is entitled to receive a reduced normal retirement benefit described in subparagraph (2) of this paragraph.

(d) *Retroactive payment rule.*—If the amount of the payment required to commence on the date determined under this section cannot be ascertained by such date, or if it is not possible to make such payment on such date because the plan administrator has been unable to locate the participant after making reasonable efforts to do so, a payment retroactive to such date may be made no later than 60 days after the earliest date on which the amount of such payment can be ascertained under the plan or the date on which the participant is located (whichever is applicable).

(e) *Effective date.*—This section shall apply to a plan for those plan years to which section 411 of the Code applies without regard to section 411(e)(2). [Reg. § 1.401(a)-14.]

☐ [T.D. 7436, 9-23-76.]

[Reg. § 1.401(a)-15]

§1.401(a)-15. Requirement that plan benefits are not decreased on account of certain social security increases.—(a) *In general.*—Under section 401(a)(15), a trust which is part of a plan to which section 411 applies (without regard to section 411(e)(2)) is not qualified under section 401 unless, under the plan of which such trust is a part:

(1) *Benefit being received by participant or beneficiary.*—A benefit (including a death or disability benefit) being received under the plan by a participant or beneficiary (other than a participant to whom subparagraph (2)(ii) of this paragraph applies, or a beneficiary of such a participant) is not decreased by reason of any post-separation social security benefit increase effective after the later of—

(i) September 2, 1974, or

(ii) The date of first receipt of any retirement benefit, death benefit, or disability benefit under the plan by the participant or by a beneficiary of the participant (whichever receipt occurs first).

(2) *Benefit to which participant separated from service has nonforfeitable right.*—In the case of a benefit to which a participant has a nonforfeitable right under such plan—

(i) If such participant is separated from service and does not subsequently return to service and resume participation in the plan, such benefit is not decreased by reason of any post-separation social security benefit increase effective after the later of September 2, 1974, or separation from service, or

(ii) If such participant is separated from service and subsequently returns to service and resumes participation in the plan, such benefit is not decreased by reason of any post-separation social security benefit increase effective after September 2, 1974, which occurs during separation from service and which would decrease such benefit to a level below the level of benefits to which he would have been entitled had he not returned to service after his separation.

(b) *Post-separation social security benefit increase.*—For purposes of this section, the term "post-separation social security benefit increase" means, with respect to a participant or a beneficiary of the participant, an increase in a benefit level or wage base under title II of the Social Security Act (whether such increase is a result of an amendment of such title II or is a result of the application of the provisions of such title II) occurring after the earlier of such participant's separation from service or commencement of benefits under the plan.

(c) *Illustrations.*—The provisions of paragraphs (a) and (b) of this section may be illustrated by the following examples:
Example (1). A plan to which section 401(a)(15) applies provides an annual benefit at the normal retirement age, 65, in the form of a stated benefit formula amount less a specified percentage of the primary insurance amount payable under title II of the Social Security Act. The plan provides no early retirement benefits. In the case of a participant who separates from service before age 65 with a nonforfeitable right to a benefit under the plan, the plan defines the primary insurance amount as the amount which the participant is entitled to receive under title II of the Social Security Act at age 65, multiplied by the ratio of the number of years of service with the employer to the number of years of service the participant would have had if he had worked for the employer until age 65. The plan does not satisfy the requirements of section 401(a)(15), because social security increases that occur after a participant's separation from service will reduce the benefit the participant will receive under the plan.

Example (2). A plan to which section 401(a)(15) applies provides an annual benefit at the normal retirement age, 65, in the form of a stated benefit formula amount less a specified percentage of the primary insurance amount payable under title II of the Social Security Act. The plan provides no early retirement benefits. In the case of a participant who separates from service before age 65 with a nonforfeitable right to a benefit under the plan, the plan defines the primary insurance amount as the amount which the participant is entitled to receive under title II of the Social Security Act at age 65 based upon the assumption that he will continue to receive until reaching age 65 compensation which would be treated as wages for purposes of the Social Security Act at the same rate as he received such compensation at the time he separated from service, but determined without regard to any post-separation social security benefit increase, multiplied by the ratio of the number of years of service with the employer to the number of years of service the participant would have had if he had worked for the employer until age 65. The plan satisfies the requirements of section 401(a)(15), because social security increases that occur after a participant's separation from service will not reduce the benefit the participant will receive under the plan.

(d) *Other Federal or State laws.*—To the extent applicable, the rules discussed in this section will govern classifications under a plan supplementing the benefits provided by other Federal or State laws, such as the Railroad Retirement Act of 1937. See section 206(b) of the Employee Retirement Income Security Act of 1974 (Public Law 93-406, 88 Stat. 864).

(e) *Effect on prior law.*—Nothing in this section shall be construed as amending or modifying the rules applicable to post-separation social security increases prior to September 2, 1974. See paragraph (e) of § 1.401-3.

(f) *Effective date.*—Section 401(a)(15) and this section shall apply to a plan only with respect to plan years to which section 411 (relating to minimum vesting standards) is applicable to the plan without regard to section 411(e)(2). [Reg. § 1.401(a)-15.]

☐ [T.D. 7434, 9-27-76.]

[Reg. § 1.401(a)-16]

§1.401(a)-16. Limitations on benefits and contributions under qualified plans.—A trust will not be a qualified trust and a plan will not be a qualified plan if the plan provides for benefits or contributions which exceed the limitations of section 415. Section 415 and the regulations thereunder provide rules concerning these limitations on benefits and contributions. [Reg. § 1 401(a)-16.]

☐ [T.D. 7748, 12-30-80.]

[Reg. § 1.401(a)(17)-1]

§1.401(a)(17)-1. Limitation on annual compensation.—(a) *Compensation limit requirement.*—(1) *In general.*—In order to be a qualified plan, a plan must satisfy section 401(a)(17). Section 401(a)(17) provides an annual compensation limit for each employee under a qualified plan. This limit applies to a qualified plan in two ways. First, a plan may not base allocations, in the case of a defined contribution plan, or benefit accruals, in the case of a defined benefit plan, on compensation in excess of the annual compensation limit. Second, the amount of an employee's annual compensation that may be taken into account in applying certain specified nondiscrimination rules under the Internal Revenue Code is subject to the annual compensation limit. These two limitations are set forth in paragraphs (b) and (c) of this section, respectively. Paragraph (d) of this section provides the effective dates of section 401(a)(17), the amendments made by section 13212 of the Omnibus Budget Reconciliation Act of 1993 (OBRA '93), and this section. Paragraph (e) of this section provides rules for determining post-effective-date accrued benefits under the fresh-start rules.

(2) *Annual compensation limit for plan years beginning before January 1, 1994.*—For purposes of this section, for plan years beginning prior to the OBRA '93 effective date, annual compensation limit means $200,000, adjusted as provided by the Commissioner. The amount of the annual compensation limit is adjusted at the same time and in the same manner as under section 415(d). The base period for the annual adjustment is the calendar quarter ending December 31, 1988, and the first adjustment is effective on January 1, 1990. Any increase in the annual compensation limit is effective as of January 1 of a calendar year and applies to any plan year beginning in that calendar year. In any plan year beginning prior to the OBRA '93 effective date, if compensation for any plan year beginning prior to the statutory effective date is used for determining allocations or benefit accruals, or when applying any nondiscrimination rule, then the annual compensation limit for the first plan year beginning on or after the statutory effective date (generally $200,000) must be applied to compensation for that prior plan year.

(3) *Annual compensation limit for plan years beginning on or after January 1, 1994.*—(i) *In general.*—For purposes of this section, for plan years beginning on or after the OBRA '93 effective date, annual compensation limit means $150,000, adjusted as provided by the Commissioner. The adjusted dollar amount of the annual compensation limit is determined by adjusting the $150,000 amount for changes in the cost of living as provided in paragraph (a)(3)(ii) of this section and rounding this adjusted dollar amount as provided in paragraph (a)(3)(iii) of this section. Any increase in the annual compensation limit is effective as of January 1 of a calendar year and applies to any plan year beginning in that calendar year. For example, if a plan has a plan year beginning July 1, 1994, and ending June 30, 1995, the annual compensation limit in effect on January 1, 1994 ($150,000), applies to the plan for the entire plan year.

(ii) *Cost of living adjustment.*—The $150,000 amount is adjusted for changes in the cost of living by the Commissioner at the same time and in the same manner as under section 415(d). The base period for the annual adjustment is the calendar quarter ending December 31, 1993.

(iii) *Rounding of adjusted compensation limit.*—After the $150,000, adjusted in accordance with paragraph (a)(3)(ii) of this section, exceeds the annual compensation limit for the prior calendar year by $10,000 or more, the annual compensation limit will be increased by the amount of such excess, rounded down to the next lowest multiple of $10,000.

(4) *Additional guidance.*—The Commissioner may, in revenue rulings and procedures, notices, and other guidance, published in the Internal Revenue Bulletin (see § 601.601(d)(2)(ii)(*b*) of this chapter), provide any additional guidance that may be necessary or appropriate concerning the annual limits on compensation under section 401(a)(17).

(b) *Plan limit on compensation.*—(1) *General rule.*—A plan does not satisfy section 401(a)(17) unless it provides that the compensation taken into account for any employee in determining plan allocations or benefit accruals for any plan year is limited to the annual compensation limit. For purposes of this rule, allocations and benefit accruals under a plan include all benefits provided under the plan, including ancillary benefits.

(2) *Plan-year-by-plan-year requirement.*—For purposes of this paragraph (b), the limit in effect for the current plan year applies only to the compensation for that year that is taken into account in determining plan allocations or benefit accruals for the year. The compensation for any prior plan year taken into account in determining an employee's allocations or benefit accruals for the current plan year is subject to the applicable annual compensation limit in effect for that prior year. Thus, increases in the annual compensation limit apply only to compensation taken into account for the plan year in which the increase is effective. In addition, if compensation for any plan year beginning prior to the OBRA '93 effective date is used for determining allocations or benefit accruals in a plan year beginning on or after the OBRA '93 effective date, then the annual compensation limit for that prior year is the annual compensation limit in effect for the first plan year beginning on or after the OBRA '93 effective date (generally $150,000).

(3) *Application of limit to a plan year.*—(i) *In general.*—For purposes of applying this paragraph (b), the annual compensation limit is applied to the compensation for the plan year on which allocations or benefit accruals are based.

(ii) *Compensation for the plan year.*—If a plan determines compensation used in determining allocations or benefit accruals for a plan year based on compensation for the plan year, then the annual compensation limit that applies to the compensation for the plan year is the limit in effect for the calendar year in which the plan year begins. Alternatively, if a plan determines compensation used in determining allocations or benefit accruals for the plan year on the basis of compensation for a 12-consecutive-month period, or periods, ending no later than the last day of the plan year, then the annual compensation limit applies to compensation for each of those periods based on the annual compensation limit in effect for the respective calendar year in which each 12-month period begins.

(iii) *Compensation for a period of less than 12-months.*—(A) *Proration required.*—If compensation for a period of less than 12 months is used for a plan year, then the otherwise applicable annual compensation limit is reduced in the same proportion as the reduction in the 12-month period. For example, if a defined benefit plan provides that the accrual for each month in a plan year is separately determined based on the compensation for that month and the plan year accrual is the sum of the accruals for all months, then the annual compensation limit for each month is 1/12th of the annual compensation limit for the plan year. In addition, if the period for determining compensation used in calculating an employee's allocation or accrual for a plan year is a short plan year (i.e., shorter than 12 months), the annual compensation limit is an amount equal to the otherwise applicable annual compensation limit multiplied by a fraction, the numerator of which is the number of months in the short plan year, and the denominator of which is 12.

(B) *No proration required for participation for less than a full plan year.*—Notwithstanding paragraph (b)(3)(iii)(A) of this section, a plan is not treated as using compensation for less than 12 months for a plan year merely because the plan formula provides that the allocation or accrual for each employee is based on compensation for the portion of the plan year during which the employee is a participant in the plan. In addition, no proration is required merely because an employee is covered under a plan for less than a full plan year, provided that allocations or benefit accruals are otherwise determined using compensation for a period of at least 12 months. Finally, notwithstanding paragraph (b)(3)(iii)(A) of this section, no proration is required merely because the amount of elective contributions (within the meaning of § 1.401(k)-6), matching contributions (within the meaning of § 1.401(m)-5), or employee contributions (within the meaning of § 1.401(m)-5) that is contributed for each pay period during a plan year is determined separately using compensation for that pay period.

(4) *Limits on multiple employer and multiemployer plans.*—For purposes of this paragraph (b), in the case of a plan described in section 413(c) or 414(f) (a plan maintained by more than one employer), the annual compensation limit applies separately with respect to the compensation of an employee from each employer maintaining the plan instead of applying to the employee's total compensation from all employers maintaining the plan.

(5) *Family aggregation.*—[Reserved]

(6) *Examples.*—The following examples illustrate the rules in this paragraph (b).

Example 1. Plan X is a defined benefit plan with a calendar year plan year and bases benefits on the average of an employee's high 3 consecutive years' compensation. The OBRA '93 effective date for Plan X is January 1, 1994. Employee A's high 3 consecutive years' compensation prior to the application of the annual compensation limits is $160,000 (1994), $155,000 (1993), and $135,000 (1992). To satisfy this paragraph (b), Plan X cannot base plan benefits for Employee A in 1994 on compensation in excess of $145,000 (the average of $150,000 (A's 1994 compensation capped by the annual compensation limit), $150,000 (A's 1993 compensation capped by the $150,000 annual compensation limit applicable to all years before 1994), and $135,000 (A's 1992 compensation capped by the $150,000 annual compensation limit applicable to all years before 1994)). For purposes of determining the 1994 accrual, each year (1994, 1993, and 1992), not the average of the 3 years, is subject to the 1994 annual compensation limit of $150,000.

Example 2. Assume the same facts as *Example 1*, except that Employee A's high 3 consecutive years' compensation prior to the application of the limits is $185,000 (1997), $175,000 (1996), and $165,000 (1995). Assume that the annual compensation limit is first adjusted to $160,000 for plan years beginning on or after January 1, 1997. Plan X cannot base plan benefits for Employee A in 1997 on compensation in excess of $153,333 (the average of $160,000 (A's 1997 compensation capped by the 1997 limit), $150,000, (A's 1996 compensation capped by the 1996 limit), and $150,000 (A's 1995 compensation capped by the 1995 limit)).

Example 3. Plan Y is a defined benefit plan that bases benefits on an employee's high consecutive 36 months of compensation ending within the plan year. Employee B's high 36 months are the period September 1995 to August 1998, in which Employee B earned $50,000 in each month. Assume that the annual compensation limit is first adjusted to $160,000 for plan years beginning on or after January 1, 1997. The annual compensation limit is $150,000, $150,000, and $160,000 in 1995, 1996, and 1997, respectively. To satisfy this paragraph (b), Plan Y cannot base Employe[e] B's plan benefits for the 1998 plan year on compensation in excess of $153,333. This amount is determined by applying the applicable annual compensation limit to compensation for each of the three 12-consecutive-month periods. The September 1995 to August 1996 period is capped by the annual compensation limit of $150,000 for 1995; the September 1996 to August 1997 period is capped by the annual compensation limit of $150,000 for 1996; and the September 1997 to August 1998 period is capped by the annual compensation limit of $160,000 for 1997. The average of these capped amounts is the annual compensation limit applicable in determining benefits for the 1998 year.

Example 4. (a) Employer P is a partnership. Employer P maintains Plan Z, a profit-sharing plan that provides for an annual allocation of employer contributions of 15 percent of plan year compensation for employees other than self-employed individuals, and 13.0435 percent of plan year compensation for self-employed individuals. The plan year of Plan Z is the calendar year. The OBRA '93 effective date for Plan Z is January 1, 1994. In order to satisfy section 401(a)(17), as amended by OBRA '93, the plan provides that, beginning with the 1994 plan year, the plan year compensation used in determining the allocation of employer contributions for each employee may not exceed the annual limit in effect for the plan year under OBRA '93. Plan Z defines compensation for self-employed individuals (employees within the meaning of section 401(c)(1)) as the self-employed individual's net profit from self-employment attributable to Employer P minus the amount of the self-employed individual's deduction under section 164(f) for one-half of self-employment taxes. Plan Z defines compensation for all other employees as wages within the meaning of section 3401(a). Employee C and Employee D are partners of Employer P and thus are self-employed individuals. Neither Employee C nor Employee D owns an interest in any other business or is a common-law employee in any business. For the 1994 calendar year, Employee C has net profit from self-employment of $80,000, and Employee D has net profit from self-employment of $175,000. The deduction for Employee C under section 164(f) for one-half of self-employment taxes is $4,828. The deduction for Employee D under section 164(f) for one-half of self-employment taxes is $6,101.

(b) The plan year compensation under the plan formula for Employee C is $75,172 ($80,000 minus $4,828). The allocation of employer contributions under the plan allocation formula for 1994 for Employee C is $9,805 ($75,172 (Employee C's plan year compensation for 1994) multiplied by 13.0435%). The plan year compensation under the plan formula before application of the annual limit under section 401(a)(17) for Employee D is $168,899 ($175,000 minus $6101). After application of the annual limit, the plan year compensation for the 1994 plan year for Employee D is $150,000 (the annual limit for 1994). Therefore, the allocation of employer contributions under the plan allocation formula for 1994 for Employee D is $19,565 ($150,000 (Employee D's plan year compensation after application of the annual limit for 1994) multiplied by 13.0435%).

Example 5. The facts are the same as in *Example 4*, except that Plan Z provides that plan year compensation for self-employed individuals is defined as earned income within the meaning of section 401(c)(2) attributable to Employer P. In addition, Plan Z provides for an annual allocation of employer contributions of 15 percent of plan year compensation for all employees in the plan, including self-employed individuals, such as Employees C and D. The net profit from self-employment for Employee C and the net profit from self-employment for Employee D are the same as provided in *Example 4*. However, the earned income of Employee C determined in accordance with section 401(c)(2) is $65,367 ($80,000 minus $4,828 minus $9,805). The earned income of Employee D determined in accordance with section 401(c)(2) is $146,869 ($175,000 minus $6,101 minus $22,030). Therefore, the allocation of employer contributions under the plan allocation formula for 1994 for Employee C is $9,805 ($65,367 (Employee C's plan year compensation for 1994) multiplied by 15%). Employee D's earned income for 1994 does not exceed the 1994 annual limit of $150,000. Therefore, the allocation of employer contributions under the plan allocation formula for 1994 for Employee D is $22,030 ($146,869 (Employee D's plan year compensation for 1994) multiplied by 15%).

(c) *Limit on compensation for nondiscrimination rules.*—(1) *General rule.*—The annual compensation limit applies for purposes of applying the nondiscrimination rules under sections 401(a)(4), 401(a)(5), 401(l), 401(k)(3), 401(m)(2), 403(b)(12), 404(a)(2) and 410(b)(2). The annual compensation limit also applies in determining whether an alternative method of determining compensation impermissibly discriminates under section 414(s)(3). Thus, for example, the annual compensation limit applies when determining a self-employed individual's total earned income that is used to determine the equivalent alternative compensation amount under § 1.414(s)-1(g)(1). This paragraph (c) provides rules for applying the annual compensation limit for these purposes. For purposes of this paragraph (c), compensation means the compensation used in applying the applicable nondiscrimination rule.

(2) *Plan-year-by-plan-year requirement.*—For purposes of this paragraph (c), when applying an applicable nondiscrimination rule for a plan year, the compensation for each plan year taken into account is limited to the applicable annual compensation limit in effect for that year, and an employee's compensation for that plan year in excess of the limit is disregarded. Thus, if the nondiscrimination provision is applied on the basis of compensation determined over a period of more than one year (for example, average annual compensation), the annual compensation limit in effect for each of the plan years that is taken into account in determining the average applies to the respective plan year's compensation. In addition, if compensation for any plan year beginning prior to the OBRA '93 effective date is used when applying any nondiscrimination rule in a plan year beginning on or after the OBRA '93 effective date, then the annual compensation limit for that prior year is the annual compensation limit for the first plan year beginning on or after the OBRA '93 effective date (generally $150,000).

(3) *Plan-by-plan limit.*—For purposes of this paragraph (c), the annual compensation limit applies separately to each plan (or group of plans treated as a single plan) of an employer for purposes of the applicable nondiscrimination requirement. For this purpose, the plans included in the testing group taken into account in determining whether the average benefit percentage test of § 1.410(b)-5 is satisfied are generally treated as a single plan.

(4) *Application of limit to a plan year.*—The rules provided in paragraph (b)(3) of this section regarding the application of the limit to a plan year apply for purposes of this paragraph (c).

(5) *Limits on multiple employer and multiemployer plans.*—The rule provided in paragraph (b)(4) of this section regarding the application of the limit to multiple employer and multiemployer plans applies for purposes of this paragraph (c).

(d) *Effective date.*—(1) *Statutory effective date.*—(i) *General rule.*—Except as otherwise provided in this paragraph (d), section 401(a)(17) applies to a plan as of the first plan year beginning on or after January 1, 1989. For purposes of this section, statutory effective date generally means the first day of the first plan year that section 401(a)(17) is applicable to a plan. In the case of governmental plans, statutory effective date means the first day of the first plan year for which the plan is not deemed to satisfy section 401(a)(17) by reason of paragraph (d)(4) of this section.

(ii) *Exception for collectively bargained plans.*—In the case of a plan maintained pursuant to one or more collective bargaining agreements between employee representatives and one or more employers ratified before March 1, 1986, section 401(a)(17) applies to allocations and benefit accruals for plan years beginning on or after the earlier of—

(A) January 1, 1991; or

(B) The later of January 1, 1989, or the date on which the last of the collective bargaining agreements terminates (determined without regard to any extension or renegotiation of any agreement occurring after February 28, 1986).

For purposes of this paragraph (d)(1)(ii), the rules of § 1.410(b)-10(a)(2) apply for purposes of determining whether a plan is maintained pursuant to one or more collective bargaining agreements, and any extension or renegotiation of a collective bargaining agreement, which extension or renegotiation is ratified after February 28, 1986, is to be disregarded in determining the date on which the agreement terminates.

(2) *OBRA '93 effective date.*—(i) *In general.*—For purposes of this section, OBRA '93 effective date means the first day of the first plan year beginning on or after January 1, 1994, except as provided in this paragraph (d)(2).

(ii) *Exception for collectively bargained plans.*—(A) *In general.*—In the case of a plan maintained pursuant to one or more collective bargaining agreements between employee representatives and 1 or more employers ratified before August 10, 1993, OBRA '93 effective date means the first day of the first plan year beginning on or after the earlier of—

(1) The latest of—

(i) January 1, 1994;

(ii) The date on which the last of such collective bargaining agreements terminates (without regard to any extension, amendment, or, modification of such agreements on or after August 10, 1993); or

(iii) In the case of a plan maintained pursuant to collective bargaining under the Railway Labor Act, the date of execution of an extension or replacement of the last of such collective bargaining agreements in effect on August 10, 1993; or

(2) January 1, 1997.

(B) *Determination of whether plan is collectively bargained.*— For purposes of this paragraph (d)(2)(ii), the rules of § 1.410(b)-10(a)(2) apply for purposes of determining whether a plan is maintained pursuant to one or more collective bargaining agreements, except that August 10, 1993, is substituted for March 1, 1986, as the date before which the collective bargaining agreements must be ratified.

(3) *Regulatory effective date.*—This § 1.401(a)(17)-1 applies to plan years beginning on or after the OBRA '93 effective date. However, in the case of a plan maintained by an organization that is exempt from income taxation under section 501(a), including plans subject to section 403(b)(12)(A)(i) (nonelective plans), this § 1.401(a)(17)-1 applies to plan years beginning on or after January 1, 1996. For plan years beginning before the effective date of these regulations and on or after the statutory effective date, a plan must be operated in accordance with a reasonable, good faith interpretation of section 401(a)(17), taking into account, if applicable, the OBRA '93 reduction to the annual compensation limit under section 401(a)(17).

(4) *Special rules for governmental plans.*—(i) *Deemed satisfaction by governmental plans.*—In the case of governmental plans described in section 414(d), including plans subject to section 403(b)(12)(A)(i) (nonelective plans), section 401(a)(17) is considered satisfied for plan years beginning before the later of January 1, 1996, or 90 days after the opening of the first legislative session beginning on or after January 1, 1996, of the governing body with authority to amend the plan, if that body does not meet continuously. For purposes of this paragraph (d)(4), the term governing body with authority to amend the plan means the legislature, board, commission, council, or other governing body with authority to amend the plan.

(ii) *Transition rule for governmental plans.*—(A) *In general.*—In the case of an eligible participant in a governmental plan (within the meaning of section 414(d)), the annual compensation limit under this section shall not apply to the extent that the application of the limitation would reduce the amount of compensation that is allowed to be taken into account under the plan below the amount that was allowed to be taken into account under the plan as in effect on July 1, 1993. Thus, for example, if a plan as in effect on July 1, 1993, determined benefits without any reference to a limit on compensation, then the annual compensation limit in effect under this section will not apply to any eligible participant in any future year.

(B) *Eligible participant.*—For purposes of this paragraph (d)(4)(ii), an eligible participant is an individual who first became a participant in the plan prior to the first day of the first plan year beginning after the earlier of—

(1) The last day of the plan year by which a plan amendment to reflect the amendments made by section 13212 of OBRA '93 is both adopted and effective; or

(2) December 31, 1995.

(C) *Plan must be amended to incorporate limits.*—This paragraph (d)(4)(ii) shall not apply to any eligible participant in a plan unless the plan is amended so that the plan incorporates by reference the annual compensation limit under section 401(a)(17), effective with respect to noneligible participants for plan years beginning after December 31, 1995 (or earlier, if the plan amendment so provides).

(5) *Benefits earned prior to effective date.*—(i) *In general.*—Allocations under a defined contribution plan or benefits accrued under a defined benefit plan for plan years beginning before the statutory effective date are not subject to the annual compensation limit. Allocations under a defined contribution plan or benefits accrued under a defined benefit plan for plan years beginning on or after the statutory effective date, but before the OBRA '93 effective date, are subject to the annual compensation limit under paragraph (a)(2) of this section. However these allocations or accruals are not subject to the OBRA '93 reduction to the annual compensation limit described in paragraph (a)(3) of this section.

(ii) *Allocation for a plan year.*—The allocations for a plan year include amounts described in § 1.401(a)(4)-2(c)(ii) or § 1.401(m)-1(a)(3) plus the earnings, expenses, gains, and losses attributable to those amounts.

(iii) *Benefits accrued for years before the effective date.*—The benefits accrued for plan years prior to a specified date by any employee are the employee's benefits accrued under the plan, determined as if those benefits had been frozen (as defined in § 1.401(a)(4)-13(c)(3)(i)) as of the day immediately preceding such specified date. Thus, for example, benefits accrued for those plan years generally do not include any benefits accrued under an amendment increasing prior benefits that is adopted after the date on which the employee's benefits under the plan must be treated as frozen.

(e) *Determination of post-effective-date accrued benefits.*—(1) *In general.*—The plan formula that is used to determine the amount of allocations or benefit accruals for plan years beginning on or after the dates described in paragraph (d)(1) or (2) must comply with section 401(a)(17) as in effect on such date. This paragraph (e) provides rules for applying section 401(a)(17) in the case of section 401(a)(17) employees who accrue additional benefits under a defined benefit plan in a plan year beginning on or after the relevant effective date. Paragraph (e)(2) of this section contains definitions used in applying these rules. Paragraphs (e)(3) and (e)(4) of this section explain the application of the fresh-start rules in § 1.401(a)(4)-13 to the determination of the accrued benefits of section 401(a)(17) employees.

(2) *Definitions.*—For purposes of this paragraph (e), the following definitions apply:

(i) *Section 401(a)(17) employee.*—An employee is a section 401(a)(17) employee as of a date, on or after the statutory effective date, if the employee's current accrued benefit as of that date is based on compensation for a year prior to the statutory effective date that exceeded the annual compensation limit for the first plan year beginning on or after the statutory effective date. In addition, an employee is a section 401(a)(17) employee as of a date, on or after the OBRA '93 effective date, if the employee's current accrued benefit as of that date is based on compensation for a year prior to the OBRA '93 effective date that exceeded the annual compensation limit for the first plan year beginning on or after the OBRA '93 effective date. For this purpose, a current accrued benefit is not treated as based on compensation that exceeded the relevant annual compensation limit, if a plan makes a fresh start using the formula with wear-away described in § 1.401(a)(4)-13(c)(4)(ii), and the employee's accrued benefit determined under § 1.401(a)(4)-13(c)(4)(ii)(B), taking into account the annual compensation limit, exceeds the employee's frozen accrued benefit (or, if applicable, the employee's adjusted accrued benefit) as of the fresh-start date.

(ii) *Section 401(a)(17) fresh-start date.*—Section 401(a)(17) fresh-start date means a fresh-start date as defined in § 1.401(a)(4)-12 not earlier than the last day of the last plan year beginning before the statutory effective date, and not later than the last day of the last plan year beginning before the effective date of these regulations.

(iii) *OBRA '93 fresh-start date.*—OBRA '93 fresh-start date means a fresh-start date as defined in § 1.401(a)(4)-12 not earlier than the last day of the last plan year beginning before the OBRA '93 effective date, and not later than the last day of the last plan year beginning before the effective date of these regulations.

(iv) *Section 401(a)(17) frozen accrued benefit.*—Section 401(a)(17) frozen accrued benefit means the accrued benefit for any section 401(a)(17) employee frozen (as defined in § 1.401(a)(4)-13(c)(3)(i)) as of the last day of the last plan year beginning before the statutory effective date.

(v) *OBRA '93 frozen accrued benefit.*—OBRA '93 frozen accrued benefit means the accrued benefit for any section 401(a)(17) employee frozen (as defined in § 1.401(a)(4)-13(c)(3)(i)) as of the OBRA '93 fresh-start date.

(3) *Application of fresh-start rules.*—(i) *General rule.*—In order to satisfy section 401(a)(17), a defined benefit plan must determine the accrued benefit of each section 401(a)(17) employee by applying the fresh-start rules in § 1.401(a)(4)-13(c). The fresh-start rules must be applied using a section 401(a)(17) fresh-start date and using the plan benefit formula, after amendment to comply with section 401(a)(17) and this section, as the formula applicable to benefit accruals in the current plan year. In addition, the fresh-start rules must be applied to determine the accrued benefit of each section 401(a)(17) employee using an OBRA '93 fresh-start date and using the plan benefit formula, after amendment to comply with the reduction in the section 401(a)(17) annual compensation limit described in paragraph (a)(3) of this section, as the formula applicable to benefit accruals in the current plan year.

(ii) *Consistency rules in §1.401(a)(4)-13(c) and (d).*—(A) *General rule.*—In applying the fresh-start rules of §1.401(a)(4)-13(c) and (d), the group of section 401(a)(17) employees is a fresh-start group. See §1.401(a)(4)-13(c)(5)(ii)(A). Thus, the consistency rules of those sections govern, unless otherwise provided. For example, if the plan is using a fresh-start date applicable to all employees and is not adjusting frozen accrued benefits under §1.401(a)(4)-13(d) for employees who are not section 401(a)(17) employees, then the frozen accrued benefits for section 401(a)(17) employees may not be adjusted under §1.401(a)(4)-13(d) or this paragraph (e).

(B) *Determination of adjusted accrued benefit.*—If the fresh-start rules of §1.401(a)(4)-13(c) and (d) are applied to determine the benefits of all employees after a fresh-start date, the plan will not fail to satisfy the consistency requirement of §1.401(a)(4)-13(c)(5)(i) merely because the plan makes the adjustment described in §1.401(a)(4)-13(d) to the frozen accrued benefits of employees who are not section 401(a)(17) employees, but does not make the adjustment to the frozen accrued benefits of section 401(a)(17) employees. In addition, the plan does not fail to satisfy the consistency requirement of §1.401(a)(4)-13(c)(5)(i) merely because the plan makes the adjustment described in §1.401(a)(4)-13(d) for section 401(a)(17) employees on the basis of the compensation formula that was used to determine the frozen accrued benefit (as required under paragraph (e)(4)(iii) of this section) but makes the adjustment for employees who are not section 401(a)(17) employees on the basis of any other method provided in §1.401(a)(4)-13(d)(8).

(4) *Permitted adjustments to frozen accrued benefit of section 401(a)(17) employees.*—(i) *General rule.*—Except as otherwise provided in paragraphs (e)(4)(ii) and (iii) of this section, the rules in §1.401(a)(4)-13(c)(3) (permitting certain adjustments to frozen accrued benefits) apply to section 401(a)(17) frozen accrued benefits or OBRA '93 frozen accrued benefits.

(ii) *Optional forms of benefit.*—After either the section 401(a)(17) fresh-start date or the OBRA '93 fresh-start date, a plan may be amended either to provide a new optional form of benefit or to make an optional form of benefit available with respect to the section 401(a)(17) frozen accrued benefit or the OBRA '93 frozen accrued benefit, provided that the optional form of benefit is not subsidized. Whether an optional form is subsidized may be determined using any reasonable actuarial assumptions.

(iii) *Adjusting section 401(a)(17) accrued benefits.*—(A) *In general.*—If the plan adjusts accrued benefits for employees under the rules of §1.401(a)(4)-13(d) as of a fresh-start date, the adjusted accrued benefit (within the meaning of section §1.401(a)(4)-13(d)) for each section 401(a)(17) employee must be determined after the fresh-start date by reference to the plan's compensation formula that was actually used to determine the frozen accrued benefit as of the fresh-start date. For this purpose, the plan's compensation formula incorporates the plan's underlying compensation definition and compensation averaging period. In making the adjustment, the denominator of the adjustment fraction described in §1.401(a)(4)-13(d)(8)(i) is the employee's compensation as of the fresh-start date using the plan's compensation formula as of that date and, in the case of an OBRA '93 fresh-start date, reflecting the annual compensation limits that applied as of the fresh-start date. The numerator of the adjustment fraction is the employee's updated compensation (i.e., compensation for the current plan year within the meaning of §1.401(a)(4)-13(d)(8)), determined after applying the annual compensation limits to each year's compensation that is used in the plan's compensation formula as of the fresh-start date. Similarly, in applying the alternative rule in §1.401(a)(4)-13(d)(8)(v), the updated compensation that is substituted must be determined after applying the annual compensation limits to each year's compensation that is used in the plan's compensation formula. Thus, no adjustment will be permitted unless the updated compensation (determined after applying the annual compensation limit) exceeds the compensation that was used to determine the employee's frozen accrued benefit.

(B) *Multiple fresh starts.*—If a plan makes more than one fresh start with respect to a section 401(a)(17) employee, the employee's frozen accrued benefit as of the latest fresh-start date will either be determined by applying the current benefit formula to the employee's total years of service as of that fresh-start date or will consist of the sum of the employee's frozen accrued benefit (or adjusted accrued benefit (as defined in §1.401(a)(4)-13(d)(8)(i))) as of the previous fresh-start date plus additional frozen accruals since the previous fresh start. If the frozen accrued benefit consists of such a sum, in making the adjustments described in paragraph (e)(4)(iii)(A) of this section, separate adjustments must be made to that previously frozen accrued benefit (or adjusted accrued benefit) and the additional frozen accruals to the extent that the frozen accrued benefit and the additional accruals have been determined using different compensation formulas or different compensation limits (i.e., the

section 401(a)(17) limit before and after the reduction in limit described in paragraph (a)(3) of this section). In this case, if the plan is applying the adjustment fraction of §1.401(a)(4)-13(d)(8)(i), the denominator of the separate adjustment fraction for adjusting each portion of the frozen accrued benefit must reflect the actual compensation formula, and, if applicable, compensation limit, originally used for determining that portion. For example, the frozen accrued benefit of a section 401(a)(17) employee as of the OBRA '93 fresh-start date may be based on the sum of the section 401(a)(17) frozen accrued benefit (determined without any annual compensation limit) plus benefit accruals in the years between the statutory effective date and the OBRA '93 effective date (based on compensation that was subject to the annual compensation limits for those years). In this example, in adjusting the section 401(a)(17) frozen accrued benefit, the denominator of the adjustment fraction does not reflect any annual compensation limit. Similarly, in adjusting the frozen accruals for years between the statutory effective date and the OBRA '93 effective date, the denominator of the adjustment fraction reflects the level of the annual compensation limit in effect for those years.

(5) *Examples.*—The following examples illustrate the rules in this paragraph (e).

Example 1. (a) Employer X maintains Plan Y, a calendar year defined benefit plan providing an annual benefit for each year of service equal to 2 percent of compensation averaged over an employee's high 3 consecutive calendar years' compensation. Section 401(a)(17) applies to Plan Y in 1989. As of the close of the last plan year beginning before January 1, 1989 (i.e., the 1988 plan year), Employee A, with 5 years of service, had accrued a benefit of $25,000 which equals 10 percent (2 percent multiplied by 5 years of service) of average compensation of $250,000. Employer X decides to comply with the provisions of this section for plan years before the effective date of this section. Employer X decides to make the amendment effective for plan years beginning on or after January 1, 1989, and uses December 31, 1988 as the section 401(a)(17) fresh-start date. Plan Y, as amended, provides that, in determining an employee's benefit, compensation taken into account is limited in accordance with the provisions of this section to the annual compensation limit under section 401(a)(17), and that, for section 401(a)(17) employees, the employee's accrued benefit is the greater of—

(i) The employee's benefit under the plan's benefit formula (after the plan formula is amended to comply with section 401(a)(17)) as applied to the employee's total years of service; and

(ii) The employee's accrued benefit as of December 31, 1988, determined as though the employee terminated employment on that date without regard to any plan amendments after that date.

Employer X decides not to amend Plan Y to provide for the adjustments permitted under §1.401(a)(4)-13(d) to the accrued benefit of section 401(a)(17) employees as of December 31, 1988.

(b) Under Plan Y, Employee A's accrued benefit at the end of 1989 is $25,000, which is the greater of Employee A's accrued benefit as of the last day of the 1988 plan year ($25,000), and $24,000, which is Employee A's benefit based on the plan's benefit formula applied to Employee A's total years of service ($200,000 multiplied by (2 percent multiplied by 6 years of service)). The formula of Plan Y applicable to section 401(a)(17) employees for calculating their accrued benefits for years after the section 401(a)(17) fresh-start date is the formula in §1.401(a)-13(c)(4)(ii) (formula with wear-away). The fresh-start formula is applied using a benefit formula for the 1989 plan year that satisfies section 401(a)(17) and this section, and the December 31, 1988 fresh-start date used for the plan is a section 401(a)(17) fresh-start date within the meaning of paragraph (e)(2)(ii) of this section. Thus, Plan Y, as amended, satisfies paragraph (e)(3)(i) of this section for plan years commencing prior to the OBRA '93 effective date.

Example 2. Assume the same facts as in *Example 1*, except that the plan formula provides that effective January 1, 1989, for section 401(a)(17) employees, an employee's benefit will equal the sum of the employee's accrued benefit as of December 31, 1988 (determined as though the employee terminated employment on that date and without regard to any amendments after that date), and 2 percent of compensation averaged over an employee's high 3 consecutive years' compensation times years of service taking into account only years of service after December 31, 1988. Thus, under Plan Y's formula, Employee A's accrued benefit as of December 31, 1989 is $29,000, which is equal to the sum of $25,000 (Employee A's accrued benefit as of December 31, 1988) plus $4,000 ($200,000 multiplied by (2 percent multiplied by 1 year of service)). The formula of Plan Y applicable to section 401(a)(17) employees for calculating their accrued benefits for years after the section 401(a)(17) fresh-start date is the formula in §1.401(a)-13(c)(4)(i) (formula without wear-away). The fresh-start formula is applied using a benefit formula for the 1989 plan year that satisfies section 401(a)(17) and this section, and the December 31, 1988 fresh-start date used for the plan is a section 401(a)(17) fresh-start date within the meaning of paragraph (e)(2)(ii) of this section. Thus, Plan Y, as amended, satisfies paragraph (e)(3)(i) of this section for plan years commencing prior to the OBRA '93 effective date.

Example 3. (a) Assume the same facts as in *Example 1,* except that the plan formula provides that effective January 1, 1989, an employee's benefit equals the greater of the plan formulas in *Example 1* and *Example 2.* The formula of Plan Y applicable to section 401(a)(17) employees for calculating their accrued benefits for years after the section 401(a)(17) fresh-start date is the formula in § 1.401(a)-13(c)(4)(iii) (formula with extended wear-away). The fresh-start formula is applied using a benefit formula for the 1989 plan year that satisfies section 401(a)(17) and this section, and the December 31, 1988 fresh-start date used for the plan is a section 401(a)(17) fresh-start date within the meaning of paragraph (e)(2)(ii) of this section. Thus, Plan Y, as amended, satisfies paragraph (e)(3)(i) of this section for plan years commencing prior to the OBRA '93 effective date.

(b) Assume that for each of the years 1991-93 Employee A's annual compensation under the plan compensation formula, disregarding the amendment to comply with section 401(a)(17) is $300,000. The annual compensation limit is adjusted to $222,220, $228,860, and $235,840 for plan years beginning January 1, 1991, 1992, and 1993, respectively. Because Employer X has decided to amend Plan Y to comply with the provisions of this section effective for plan years beginning on or after January 1, 1989, and has used December 31, 1988 as the section 401(a)(17) fresh-start date, the compensation that may be taken into account for plan benefits in 1993 cannot exceed $228,973 (the average of $222,220, $228,860, and $235,840). Therefore, as of December 31, 1993, the benefit determined under the fresh-start formula with wear-away would be $45,795 ($228,973 multiplied by (2 percent multiplied by 10 years of service)). The benefit determined under the fresh-start formula without wear-away would be $47,897, which is equal to $25,000 (Employee A's section 401(a)(17) frozen accrued benefit) plus $22,897 ($228,973 multiplied by (2 percent multiplied by 5 years of service)). Because Employee A's accrued benefit is being determined using the fresh-start formula with extended wear-away, Employee A's accrued benefit as of December 31, 1993, is equal to $47,897, the greater of the two amounts.

Example 4. (a) Assume the same facts as in *Example 3,* except that Plan Y satisfies § 1.401(a)(4)-13(d)(3) through (d)(7) and that the amendment to Plan Y effective for plan years beginning after December 31, 1988, also provided for adjustments to the section 401(a)(17) frozen accrued benefit in accordance with § 1.401(a)(4)-13(d) using the fraction described in § 1.401(a)(4)-13(d)(8)(i).

(b) As of December 31, 1993, the numerator of Employee A's compensation fraction is $228,973 (the average of Employee A's annual compensation for 1991, 1992, and 1993, as limited by the respective annual limit for each of those years). The denominator of Employee A's compensation fraction determined in accordance with paragraph (e)(4)(iii) of this section is $250,000 (the average of Employee A's high 3 consecutive calendar year compensation as of December 31, 1988, determined without regard to section 401(a)(17)). Therefore, Employee A's compensation fraction is $228,973/$250,000. Because the compensation adjustment fraction is less than 1, Employee A's section 401(a)(17) frozen accrued benefit is not adjusted. Therefore, Employee A's accrued benefit as December 31, 1993, would still be $47,897, which is equal to $25,000 (Employee A's section 401(a)(17) frozen accrued benefit) plus $22,897 ($228,973 multiplied by (2 percent multiplied by 5 years of service)).

Example 5. (a) Assume the same facts as in *Example 3,* except that as of January 1, 1994, Plan Y is amended to provide that benefits will be determined based on compensation of $150,000 (the limit in effect under section 401(a)(17) for plan years beginning on or after the OBRA '93 effective date) and that for section 401(a)(17) employees, each employee's accrued benefit will be determined under § 1.401(a)(4)-13(c)(4)(i) (formula without wear-away) using December 31, 1993 as the OBRA '93 fresh-start date.

(b) Assume that for each of the years 1996-98 Employee A's annual compensation under the plan compensation definition, disregarding the amendment to comply with section 401(a)(17), is $400,000. Assume that the annual compensation limit is first adjusted to $160,000 for plan years beginning on or after January 1, 1997, and is not adjusted for the plan year beginning on or after January 1, 1998. The compensation that may be taken into account for the 1998 plan year cannot exceed $156,667 (the average of $150,000 for 1996, $160,000 for 1997, and $160,000 for 1998).

(c) Therefore, at the end of December 31, 1998, Employee A's accrued benefit is $63,564, which is equal to $47,897 (Employee A's OBRA '93 frozen accrued benefit) plus $15,667 ($156,667 multiplied by (2 percent multiplied by 5 years of service)).

Example 6. (a) Assume the same facts as in *Example 5,* except that, for the fresh-start group (in this case the section 401(a)(17) employees), the amendments to Plan Y provide for adjustments to the section 401(a)(17) frozen accrued benefit and the OBRA '93 frozen

accrued benefit in accordance with § 1.401(a)(4)-13(d) using the fraction described in § 1.401(a)(4)-13(d)(8)(i).

(b) Employee A's frozen accrued benefit as of December 31, 1993, is adjusted as of December 31, 1998, as follows:

(1) Employee A's frozen accrued benefit as of December 31, 1993, is the sum of Employee A's section 401(a)(17) frozen accrued benefit ($25,000) and Employee A's frozen accruals for the years 1989-93 ($22,897).

(2) The numerator of Employee A's adjustment fraction is $156,667 (the average of $150,000, $160,000, and $160,000). The denominator of Employee A's adjustment fraction with respect to Employee A's section 401(a)(17) frozen accrued benefit is $250,000, and the denominator of Employee A's adjustment fraction with respect to the rest of Employee A's frozen accrued benefit is $228,973 (the average of Employee A's annual compensation for 1991, 1992, and 1993, as limited by the respective annual limit for each of those years).

(3) Employee A's section 401(a)(17) frozen accrued benefit as adjusted through December 31, 1998, remains $25,000. The compensation adjustment fraction determined in accordance with paragraph (e)(4)(iii) of this section is less than one ($156,667 divided by $250,000).

(4) Employee A's frozen accruals for the years 1989-93, as adjusted through December 31, 1998, remain $22,897 because the adjustment fraction is less than one ($156,667 divided by $228,973).

(5) Employee A's adjusted accrued benefit as of December 31, 1998, equals $47,897 (the sum of the $25,000 and $22,897 amounts from paragraphs (b)(3) and (b)(4), respectively, of this *Example*).

(c) Employee A's section 401(a)(17) frozen accrued benefit will not be adjusted for compensation increases until the numerator of the fraction used to adjust that frozen accrued benefit exceeds the denominator of $250,000 used in determining those accruals.

Similarly, the portion of Employee A's OBRA '93 frozen accrued benefit attributable to the frozen accruals for the years 1989-1993 will not be adjusted for compensation increases until the numerator of the fraction used to adjust those frozen accruals exceeds the denominator of $228,973 used in determining those accruals. [Reg. § 1.401(a)(17)-1.]

☐ [T.D. 8362, 9-12-91. *Amended by* T.D. 8547, 6-23-94 *and* T.D. 9169, 12-28-2004.]

[Reg. § 1.401(a)-19]

§ 1.401(a)-19. Nonforfeitability in case of certain withdrawals.— (a) *Application of section.*—Section 401(a)(19) and this section apply to a plan to which section 411(a) applies. (See section 411(e) and § 1.411(a)-2 for applicability of section 411.)

(b) *Prohibited forfeitures.*—(1) *General rule.*—A plan to which this section applies is not a qualified plan (and a trust forming a part of such plan is not a qualified trust) if, under such plan, any part of a participant's accrued benefit derived from employer contributions is forfeitable solely because a benefit derived from the participant's contributions under the plan is voluntarily withdrawn by him after he has become a 50 percent vested participant.

(2) *50 percent vested participant.*—For purposes of subparagraph (1) of this paragraph, a participant is a 50 percent vested participant when he has a nonforfeitable right (within the meaning of section 411 and the regulations thereunder) to at least 50 percent of his accrued benefit derived from employer contributions. Whether or not a participant is 50 percent vested shall be determined by the ratio of the participant's total nonforfeitable employer-derived accrued benefit under the plan to his total employer-derived accrued benefit under the plan.

(3) *Certain forfeitures.*—Subparagraph (1) of this paragraph does not apply in the case of a forfeiture permitted by section 411(a)(3)(D)(iii) and § 1.411(a)-7(d)(3) (relating to forfeitures of certain benefits accrued before September 2, 1974).

(c) *Supersession.*—Section 11.401(a)-(19) of the Temporary Income Tax Regulations under the Employee Retirement Income Security Act of 1974 is superseded by this section. [Reg. § 1.401(a)-19.]

☐ [T.D. 7501, 8-22-77.]

[Reg. § 1.401(a)-20]

§ 1.401(a)-20. Requirements of qualified joint and survivor annuity and qualified preretirement survivor annuity.—
Q-1: What are the survivor annuity requirements added to the Code by the Retirement Equity Act of 1984 (REA 1984)?
A-1: REA 1984 replaced section 401(a)(11) with a new section 401(a)(11) and added section 417. Plans to which new section 401(a)(11) applies must comply with the requirements of sections 401(a)(11) and 417 in order to remain qualified under sections 401(a) or 403(a). In general, these plans must provide both a qualified joint

and survivor annuity (QJSA) and a qualified preretirement survivor annuity (QPSA) to remain qualified. These survivor annuity requirements are applicable to any benefit payable under a plan, including a benefit payable to a participant under a contract purchased by the plan and paid by a third party.

Q-2: Must annuity contracts purchased and distributed to a participant or spouse by a plan subject to the survivor annuity requirements of sections 401(a)(11) and 417 satisfy the requirements of those sections?

A-2: Yes. Rights and benefits under section 401(a)(11) or 417 may not be eliminated or reduced because the plan uses annuity contracts to provide benefits merely because (a) such a contract is held by a participant or spouse instead of a plan trustee, or (b) such contracts are distributed upon plan termination. Thus, the requirements of sections 401(a)(11) and 417 apply to payments under the annuity contracts, not to the distributions of the contracts.

Q-3: What plans are subject to the survivor annuity requirements of section 401(a)(11)?

A-3: (a) Section 401(a)(11) applies to any defined benefit plan and to any defined contribution plan that is subject to the minimum funding standards of section 412. This section also applies to any participant under any other defined contribution plan unless all of the following conditions are satisfied—

(1) The plan provides that the participant's nonforfeitable accrued benefit is payable in full, upon the participant's death, to the participant's surviving spouse (unless the participant elects, with spousal consent that satisfies the requirements of section 417(a)(2), that such benefit be provided instead to a designated beneficiary);

(2) The participant does not elect the payment of benefits in the form of a life annuity; and

(3) With respect to the participant, the plan is not a transferee or an offset plan. (See Q&A 5 of this section.)

(b) A defined contribution plan not subject to the minimum funding standards of section 412 will not be treated as satisfying the requirement of paragraph (a)(1) unless both of the following conditions are satisfied—

(1) The benefit is available to the surviving spouse within a reasonable time after the participant's death. For this purpose, availability within the 90-day period following the date of death is deemed to be reasonable and the reasonableness of longer periods shall be determined based on the particular facts and circumstances. A time period longer than 90 days, however, is deemed unreasonable if it is less favorable to the surviving spouse than any time period under the plan that is applicable to other distributions. Thus, for example, the availability of a benefit to the surviving spouse would be unreasonable if the distribution was required to be made by the close of the plan year including the participant's death while distributions to employees who separate from service were required to be made within 90 days of separation.

(2) The benefit payable to the surviving spouse is adjusted for gains or losses occurring after the participant's death in accordance with plan rules governing the adjustment of account balances for other plan distributions. Thus, for example, the plan may not provide for distributions of an account balance to a surviving spouse determined as of the last day of the quarter in which the participant's death occurred with no adjustments of an account balance for gains or losses after death if the plan provides for such adjustments for a participant who separates from service within a quarter.

(c) For purposes of determining the extent to which section 401(a)(11) applies to benefits under an employee stock ownership plan (as defined in section 4975(e)(7)), the portion of a participant's accrued benefit that is subject to section 409(h) is to be treated as though such benefit were provided under a defined contribution plan not subject to section 412.

(d) The requirements set forth in section 401(a)(11) apply to other employee benefit plans that are covered by applicable provisions under Title I of the Employee Retirement Income Security Act of 1974. For purposes of applying the regulations under sections 401(a)(11) and 417, plans subject to ERISA section 205 are treated as if they were described in section 401(a). For example, to the extent that section 205 covers section 403(b) contracts and custodial accounts, they are treated as section 401(a) plans. Individual retirement plans (IRAs), including IRAs to which contributions are made under simplified employee pensions described in section 408(k) and IRAs that are treated as plans subject to Title I, are not subject to these requirements.

Q-4: What rules apply to a participant who elects a life annuity option under a defined contribution plan not subject to section 412?

A-4: If a participant elects at any time (irrespective of the applicable election period defined in section 417(a)(6)) a life annuity option under a defined contribution plan not subject to section 412, the survivor annuity requirements of sections 401(a)(11) and 417 will always thereafter apply to all of the participant's benefits under such plan unless there is a separate accounting of the account balance

subject to the election. A plan may allow a participant to elect an annuity option prior to the applicable election period described in section 417(a)(6). If a participant elects an annuity option, the plan must satisfy the applicable written explanation, consent, election, and withdrawal rules of section 417, including waiver of the QJSA within 90 days of the annuity starting date. If a participant selecting such an option dies, the surviving spouse must be able to receive the QPSA benefit described in section 417(c)(2) which is a life annuity, the actuarial equivalent of which is not less than 50 percent of the nonforfeitable account balance (adjusted for loans as described in Q&A 24(d) of this section). The remaining account balance may be paid to a designated nonspouse beneficiary.

Q-5: How do sections 401(a)(11) and 417 apply to transferee plans which are defined contribution plans not subject to section 412?

A-5: (a) *Transferee plans.* Although the survivor annuity requirements of sections 401(a)(11) and 417 generally do not apply to defined contribution plans not subject to section 412, such plans are subject to the survivor annuity requirements to the extent that they are transferee plans with respect to any participant. A defined contribution plan is a transferee plan with respect to any participant if the plan is a direct or indirect transferee of such participant's benefits held on or after January 1, 1985, by:

(1) A defined benefit plan,

(2) A defined contribution plan subject to section 412, or

(3) A defined contribution plan that is subject to the survivor annuity requirements of sections 401(a)(11) and 417 with respect to that participant.

If through a merger, spinoff, or other transaction having the effect of a transfer, benefits subject to the survivor annuity requirements of sections 401(a)(11) and 417 are held under a plan that is not otherwise subject to such requirements, such benefits will be subject to the survivor annuity requirements even though they are held under such plan. Even if a plan satisfies the survivor annuity requirements, other rules apply to these transactions. See, *e.g.,* section 411(d)(6) and the regulations thereunder. A transfer made before January 1, 1985, and any rollover contribution made at any time, are not transactions that subject the transferee plan to the survivor annuity requirements with respect to a participant. If a plan is a transferee plan with respect to a participant, the survivor annuity requirements do not apply with respect to other plan participants solely because of the transfer. Any plan that would not otherwise be subject to the survivor annuity requirements of sections 401(a)(11) and 417 whose benefits are used to offset benefits in a plan subject to such requirements is subject to the survivor annuity requirements with respect to those participants whose benefits are offset. Thus, if a stock bonus or profit-sharing plan offsets benefits under a defined benefit plan, such a plan is subject to the survivor annuity requirements.

(b) *Benefits covered.* The survivor annuity requirements apply to all accrued benefits held for a participant with respect to whom the plan is a transferee plan unless there is an acceptable separate accounting between the transferred benefits and all other benefits under the plan. A separate accounting is not acceptable unless gains, losses, withdrawals, contributions, forfeitures, and other credits or charges are allocated on a reasonable and consistent basis between the accrued benefits subject to the survivor annuity requirements and other benefits. If there is an acceptable separate accounting between transferred benefits and any other benefits under the plan, only the transferred benefits are subject to the survivor annuity requirements.

Q-6: Is a frozen or terminated plan required to satisfy the survivor annuity requirements of sections 401(a)(11) and 417?

A-6: In general, benefits provided under a plan that is subject to the survivor annuity requirements of sections 401(a)(11) and 417 must be provided in accordance with those requirements even if the plan is frozen or terminated. However, any plan that has a termination date prior to September 17, 1985, and that distributed all remaining assets as soon as administratively feasible after the termination date, is not subject to the survivor annuity requirements. The date of termination is determined under section 411(d)(3) and § 1.411(d)-2(c).

Q-7: If the Pension Benefit Guaranty Corporation (PBGC) is administering a plan, are benefits payable in the form of a QPSA or QJSA?

A-7: Yes, the PBGC will pay benefits in such forms.

Q-8: How do the survivor annuity requirements of sections 401(a)(11) and 417 apply to participants?

A-8: (a) If a participant dies before the annuity starting date with vested benefits attributable to employer or employee contributions (or both), benefits must be paid to the surviving spouse in the form of a QPSA. If a participant survives until the annuity starting date with vested benefits attributable to employer or employee contributions (or both), benefits must be provided to the participant in the form of a QJSA.

(b) A participant may waive the QPSA or the QJSA (or both) if the applicable notice, election, and spousal consent requirements of section 417 are satisfied.

(c) Benefits are not required to be paid in the form of a QPSA or QJSA if at the time of death or distribution the participant was vested only in employee contributions and such death occurred, or distribution commenced, before October 22, 1986.

(d) *Certain mandatory distributions.* A distribution may occur without satisfying the spousal consent requirements of section 417(a) and (e) if the present value of the nonforfeitable benefit does not exceed the cash-out limit in effect under §1.411(a)-11(c)(3)(ii). See §1.417(e)-1.

Q-9: May separate portions of a participant's accrued benefit be subject to QPSA and QJSA requirements at any particular point in time?

A-9: (a) *Dual QPSA and QJSA rights.* One portion of a participant's benefit may be subject to the QPSA and another portion to the QJSA requirements at the same time. For example, in order for a money purchase pension plan to distribute any portion of a married participant's benefit to the participant, the plan must distribute such portion in the form of a QJSA (unless the plan satisfies the applicable consent requirements of section 417(a) and (e) with respect to such portion of the participant's benefit). This rule applies even if the distribution is merely an in-service distribution attributable to voluntary employee contributions and regardless of whether the participant has attained the normal retirement age under the plan. The QJSA requirements apply to such a distribution because the annuity starting date has occurred with respect to this portion of the participant's benefit. In the event of a participant's death following the commencement of a distribution in the form of a QJSA, the remaining payments must be made to the surviving spouse under the QJSA. In addition, the plan must satisfy the QPSA requirements with respect to any portion of the participant's benefits for which the annuity starting date had not yet occurred.

(b) *Example.* Assume that participant A has a $100,000 account balance in a money purchase pension plan. A makes an in-service withdrawal of $20,000 attributable to voluntary employee contributions. The QJSA requirements apply to A's withdrawal of the $20,000. Accordingly, unless the QJSA form is properly waived such amount must be distributed in the form of a QJSA. A's remaining account balance ($80,000) remains subject to the QPSA requirements because the annuity starting date has not occurred with respect to the $80,000. (If A survives until the annuity starting date, the $80,000 would be subject to the QJSA requirements.) If A died on the day following the annuity starting date for the withdrawal, A's spouse would be entitled to a QPSA with a value equal to at least $40,000 with respect to the $80,000 account balance, in addition to any survivor benefit without respect to the $20,000. If the $20,000 payment to A had been the first payment of an annuity purchased with the entire $100,000 account balance rather than an in-service distribution, then the QJSA requirements would apply to the entire account balance at the time of the annuity starting date. In such event, the plan would have no obligation to provide A's spouse with a QPSA benefit upon A's death. Of course, A's spouse would receive the QJSA benefit (if the QJSA had not been waived) based on the full $100,000.

Q-10: What is the relevance of the annuity starting date with respect to the survivor benefit requirements?

A-10: (a) *Relevance.* The annuity starting date is relevant to whether benefits are payable as either a QJSA or QPSA, or other selected optional form of benefit. If a participant is alive on the annuity starting date, the benefits must be payable as a QJSA. If the participant is not alive on the annuity starting date, the surviving spouse must receive a QPSA. The annuity starting date is also used to determine when a spouse may consent to and a participant may waive a QJSA. A waiver is only effective if it is made 90 days before the annuity starting date. Thus, a deferred annuity cannot be selected and a QJSA waived until 90 days before payments commence under the deferred annuity. In some cases, the annuity starting date will have occurred with respect to a portion of the participant's accrued benefit and will not have occurred with respect to the remaining portion. (See Q&A-9.)

(b) *Annuity starting date*—(1) *General rule.* For purposes of sections 401(a)(11), 411(a)(11) and 417, the annuity starting date is the first day of the first period for which an amount is paid as an annuity or any other form.

(2) *Annuity payments.* The annuity starting date is the first date for which an amount is paid, not the actual date of payment. Thus, if participant A is to receive annuity payments as of the first day of the first month after retirement but does not receive any payments until three months later, the annuity starting date is the first day of the first month. For example, if an annuity is to commence on January 1, January 1 is the annuity starting date even though the payment for January is not actually made until a later date. In the case of a deferred annuity, the annuity starting date is the date for which the annuity payments are to commence, not the date that the deferred annuity is elected or the date the deferred annuity contract is distributed.

(3) *Administrative delay.* A payment shall not be considered to occur after the annuity starting date merely because actual payment is reasonably delayed for calculation of the benefit amount if all payments are actually made.

(4) *Forfeitures on death.* Prior to the annuity starting date, section 411(a)(3)(A) allows a plan to provide for a forfeiture of a participant's benefit, except in the case of a QPSA or a spousal benefit described in section 401(a)(11)(B)(iii)(I). Once the annuity starting date has occurred, even if actual payment has not yet been made, a plan must pay the benefit in the distribution form elected.

(5) *Surviving spouses, alternate payees, etc.* The definition of "annuity starting date" for surviving spouses, other beneficiaries and alternate payees under section 414(p) is the same as it is for participants.

(c) *Disability auxiliary benefit*—(1) *General rule.* The annuity starting date for a disability benefit is the first day of the first period for which the benefit becomes payable unless the disability benefit is an auxiliary benefit. The payment of any auxiliary disability benefits is disregarded in determining the annuity starting date. A disability benefit is an auxiliary benefit if upon attainment of early or normal retirement age, a participant receives a benefit that satisfies the accrual and vesting rules of section 411 without taking into account the disability benefit payments up to that date.

(2) *Example.* (i) Assume that participant A at age 45 is entitled to a vested accrued benefit of $100 per month commencing at age 65 in the form of a joint and survivor annuity under Plan X. If prior to age 65 A receives a disability benefit under Plan X and the payment of such benefit does not reduce the amount of A's retirement benefit of $100 per moth commencing at age 65, any disability benefit payments made to A between ages 45 and 65 are auxiliary benefits. Thus, A's annuity starting date does not occur until A attains age 65. A's surviving spouse B would be entitled to receive a QPSA if A died before age 65. B would be entitled to receive the survivor portion of a QJSA (unless waived) if A died after age 65. The QPSA payable to B upon A's death prior to age 65 would be computed by reference to the QJSA that would have been payable to A and B had A survived to age 65.

(ii) If in the above example A's benefit payable at age 65 is reduced to $99 per month because a disability benefit is provided to A prior to age 65, the disability benefit would not be an auxiliary benefit. The benefit of $99 per month payable to A at age 65 would not, without taking into account the disability benefit payments to A prior to age 65, satisfy the minimum vesting and accrual rules of section 411. Accordingly, the first day of the first period for which the disability payments are to be made to A would constitute A's annuity starting date, and any benefit paid to A would be required to be paid in the form of a QJSA (unless waived by A with the consent of B).

(d) *Other rules*—(1) *Suspension of benefits.* If benefit payments are suspended after the annuity starting date pursuant to a suspension of benefits described in section 411(a)(3)(B) after an employee separates from service, the recommencement of benefit payments after the suspension is not treated as a new annuity starting date unless the plan provides otherwise. In such case, the plan administrator is not required to provide new notices nor to obtain new waivers for the recommenced distributions if the form of distribution is the same as the form that was appropriately selected prior to the suspension. If benefits are suspended for an employee who continues in service without a separation and who never receives payments, the commencement of payments after the period of suspension is treated as the annuity starting date unless the plan provides otherwise.

(2) *Additional accruals.* In the case of an annuity starting date that occurs on or after normal retirement age, such date applies to any additional accruals after the annuity starting date, unless the plan provides otherwise. For example, if a participant who continues to accrue benefits elects to have benefits paid in an optional form at normal retirement age, the additional accruals must be paid in the optional form selected unless the plan provides otherwise. In the case of an annuity starting date that occurs prior to normal retirement age, such date does not apply to any additional accruals after such date.

Q-11: Do the survivor annuity requirements apply to benefits derived from both employer and employee contributions?

A-11: Yes. The survivor annuity benefit requirements apply to benefits derived from both employer and employee contributions. Benefits are not required to be paid in the form of a QPSA or QJSA if the participant was vested only in employee contributions at the time of death or distribution and such death or distribution occurred before October 22, 1986. All benefits provided under a plan, including benefits attributable to rollover contributions, are subject to the survivor annuity requirements.

Q-12: To what benefits do the survivor annuity requirements of sections 401(a)(11) and 417 apply?

A-12: (a) *Defined benefit plans.* Under a defined benefit plan, sections 401(a)(11) and 417 apply only to benefits in which a participant was vested immediately prior to death. They do not apply to benefits to which a participant's beneficiary becomes entitled by reason of death or to the proceeds of a life insurance contract to the extent such proceeds exceed the present value of the participant's nonforfeitable benefits that existed immediately prior to death.

(b) *Defined contribution plans.* Sections 401(a)(11) and 417 apply to all nonforfeitable benefits which are payable under a defined contribution plan, whether nonforfeitable before or upon death, including the proceeds of insurance contracts.

Q-13: Does the rule of section 411(a)(3)(A) which permits forfeitures on account of death apply to a QPSA or the spousal benefit described in section 401(a)(11)(B)(iii)?

A-13: No. Section 411(a)(3)(A) permits forfeiture on account of death prior to the time all the events fixing payment occur. However, this provision does not operate to deprive a surviving spouse of a QPSA or the spousal benefit described in section 401(a)(11)(B)(iii). Therefore, sections 401(a)(11) and 417 apply to benefits that were nonforfeitable immediately prior to death (determined without regard to section 411(a)(3)(A)). Thus, in the case of the death of a married participant in a defined contribution plan not subject to section 412 which provides that, upon a participant's death, the entire nonforfeitable accrued benefit is payable to the participant's spouse, the nonforfeitable benefit is determined without regard to the provisions of section 411(a)(3)(A).

Q-14: Do sections 411(a)(11), 401(a)(11) and 417 apply to accumulated deductible employee contributions, as defined in section 72(o)(5)(B) (Accumulated DECs)?

A-14: (a) *Employee consent, section 411.* The requirements of section 411(a)(11) apply to Accumulated DECs. Thus, Accumulated DECs may not be distributed without participant consent unless the applicable exemptions apply.

(b) *Survivor requirements.* Accumulated DECs are treated as though held under a separate defined contribution plan that is not subject to section 412. Thus, section 401(a)(11) applies to Accumulated DECs only as provided in section 401(a)(11)(B)(iii). All Accumulated DECs are treated in this manner, including Accumulated DECs that are the only benefit held under a plan and Accumulated DECs that are part of a defined benefit or a defined contribution plan.

(c) *Effective date.* Sections 401(a)(11) and 411(a)(11) shall not apply to distributions of Accumulated DECs until the first plan year beginning after December 31, 1988.

Q-15: How do the survivor annuity requirements of sections 401(a)(11) and 417 apply to a defined benefit plan that includes an accrued benefit based upon a contribution to a separate account or mandatory employee contributions?

A-15: (a) *414(k) plans.* In the case of a section 414(k) plan that includes both a defined benefit plan and a separate account, the rules of sections 401(a)(11) and 417 apply separately to the defined benefit portion and the separate account portion of the plan. The separate account portion is subject to the survivor annuity requirements of sections 401(a)(11) and 417 and the special QPSA rules in section 417(c)(2).

(b) *Employee contributions*—(1) *Voluntary.* In the case of voluntary employee contributions to a defined benefit plan, the plan must maintain a separate account with respect to the voluntary employee contributions. This separate account is subject to the survivor annuity requirements of sections 401(a)(11) and 417 and the special QPSA rules in section 417(c)(2).

(2) *Mandatory.* In the case of a defined benefit plan providing for mandatory employee contributions, the entire accrued benefit is subject to the survivor annuity requirements of sections 401(a)(11) and 417 as a defined benefit plan.

(c) *Accumulated DECs.* See Q&A 14 of this section for the rule applicable to accumulated deductible employee contributions.

Q-16: Can a plan provide a benefit form more valuable than the QJSA and if a plan offers more than one annuity option satisfying the requirements of a QJSA, is spousal consent required when the participant chooses among the various forms?

A-16: In the case of an unmarried participant, the QJSA may be less valuable than other optional forms of benefit payable under the plan. In the case of a married participant, the QJSA must be at least as valuable as any other optional form of benefit payable under the plan at the same time. Thus, if a plan has two joint and survivor annuities that would satisfy the requirements for a QJSA, but one has a greater actuarial value than the other, the more valuable joint and survivor annuity is the QJSA. If there are two or more actuarially equivalent joint and survivor annuities that satisfy the requirements for a QJSA, the plan must designate which one is the QJSA and, therefore, the automatic form of benefit payment. A plan, however, may allow a participant to elect out of such a QJSA, without spousal consent, in favor of another actuarially equivalent joint and survivor annuity that satisfies the QJSA conditions. Such an election is not subject to the requirement that it be made within the 90-day period before the annuity starting date. For example, if a plan designates a joint and 100% survivor annuity as the QJSA and also offers an actuarially equivalent joint and 50% survivor annuity that would satisfy the

requirements of a QJSA, the participant may elect the joint and 50% survivor annuity without spousal consent. The participant, however, does need spousal consent to elect a joint and survivor annuity that was not actuarially equivalent to the automatic QJSA. A plan does not fail to satisfy the requirements of this Q&A-16 merely because the amount payable under an optional form of benefit that is subject to the minimum present value requirement of section 417(e)(3) is calculated using the applicable interest rate (and, for periods when required, the applicable mortality table) under section 417(e)(3).

Q-17: When must distributions to a participant under a QJSA commence?

A-17: (a) *QJSA benefits upon earliest retirement.* A plan must permit a participant to receive a distribution in the form of a QJSA when the participant attains the earliest retirement age under the plan. Written consent of the participant is required. However, the consent of the participant's spouse is not required. Any payment not in the form of a QJSA is subject to spousal consent. For example, if the participant separates from service under a plan that allows for distributions on separation from service or if a plan allows for in-service distributions, the participant may receive a QJSA without spousal consent in such events. Payments in any other form, including a single sum, would require waiver of the QJSA by the participant's spouse.

(b) *Earliest retirement age.* (1) This paragraph (b) defines the term "earliest retirement age" for purposes of sections 401(a)(11), 411(a)(11) and 417.

(2) In the case of a plan that provides for voluntary distributions that commence upon the participant's separation from service, earliest retirement age is the earliest age at which a participant could separate from service and receive a distribution. Death of a participant is treated as a separation from service.

(3) In the case of a plan that provides for in-service distributions, earliest retirement age is the earliest age at which such distributions may be made.

(4) In the case of a plan not described in subparagraph (2) or (3) of this paragraph, the rule below applies. Earliest retirement age is the early retirement age determined under the plan, or if no early retirement age, the normal retirement age determined under the plan. If the participant dies or separates from service before such age, then only the participant's actual years of service at the time of the participant's separation from service or death are taken into account. Thus, in the case of a plan under which benefits are not payable until the attainment of age 65, or upon attainment of age 55 and completion of 10 years of service, the earliest retirement age of a participant who died or separated from service with 8 years of service is when the participant would have attained age 65 (if the participant had survived). On the other hand, if a participant died or separated from service after 10 years of service, the earliest retirement age is when the participant would have attained age 55 (if the participant had survived).

Q-18: What is a qualified preretirement survivor annuity (QPSA) in a defined benefit plan?

A-18: A QPSA is an immediate annuity for the life of the surviving spouse of a participant. Each payment under a QPSA under a defined benefit plan is not to be less than the payment that would have been made to the survivor under the QJSA payable under the plan if (a) in the case of a participant who dies after attaining the earliest retirement age under the plan, the participant had retired with a QJSA on the day before the participant's death, and (b) in the case of a participant who dies on or before the participant's earliest retirement age under the plan, the participant had separated from service at the earlier of the actual time of separation or death, survived until the earliest retirement age, retired at that time with a QJSA, and died on the day thereafter. If the participant elects before the annuity starting date a form of joint and survivor annuity that satisfies the requirements for a QJSA and dies before the annuity starting date, the elected form is treated as the QJSA and the QPSA must be based on such form.

Q-19: What rules apply in determining the amount and forfeitability of a QPSA?

A-19: The QPSA is calculated as of the earliest retirement age if the participant dies before such time, or at death if the participant dies after the earliest retirement age. The plan must make reasonable actuarial adjustments to reflect a payment earlier or later than the earliest retirement age. A defined benefit plan may provide that the QPSA is forfeited if the spouse does not survive until the date prescribed under the plan for commencement of the QPSA (*i.e.*, the earliest retirement age). Similarly, if the spouse survives past the participant's earliest retirement age (or other earlier QPSA distribution date under the plan) and elects after the death of the participant to defer the commencement of the QPSA to a later date, a defined benefit plan may provide for a forfeiture of the QPSA benefit if the spouse does not survive until the deferred commencement date. The account balance in a defined contribution plan may not be forfeited even though the spouse does not survive until the time the account balance is used to purchase the QPSA. See Q&A-17 of this section for the meaning of earliest retirement age.

Q-20: What preretirement survivor annuity benefits must a defined contribution plan subject to the survivor annuity requirements of sections 401(a)(11) and 417 provide?

A-20: A defined contribution plan that is subject to the survivor annuity requirements of sections 401(a)(11) and 417 must provide a preretirement survivor annuity with a value which is not less than 50 percent of the nonforfeitable account balance of the participant as of the date of the participant's death. If a contributory defined contribution plan has a forfeiture provision permitted by section 411(a)(3)(A), not more than a proportional percent of the account balance attributable to contributions that may not be forfeited at death (for example, employee and section 401(k) contributions) may be used to satisfy the QPSA benefit. Thus, for example, if the QPSA benefit is to be provided from 50 percent of the account balance, not more than 50 percent of the nonforfeitable contributions may be used for the QPSA.

Q-21: May a defined benefit plan charge the participant for the cost of the QPSA benefit?

A-21: Prior to the later of the time the plan allows the participant to waive the QPSA or provides notice of the ability to waive the QPSA, a defined benefit plan may not charge the participant for the cost of the QPSA by reducing the participant's plan benefits or by any other method. The preceding sentence does not apply to any charges prior to the first plan year beginning after December 31, 1988. Once the participant is given the opportunity to waive the QPSA or the notice of the QPSA if later, the plan may charge the participant for the cost of the QPSA. A charge for the QPSA that reasonably reflects the cost of providing the QPSA will not fail to satisfy section 411 even if it reduces the accrued benefit.

Q-22: When must distributions to a surviving spouse under a QPSA commence?

A-22: (a) In the case of a defined benefit plan, the plan must permit the surviving spouse to direct the commencement of payments under QPSA no later than the month in which the participant would have attained the earliest retirement age. However, a plan may permit the commencement of payments at an earlier date.

(b) In the case of a defined contribution plan, the plan must permit the surviving spouse to direct the commencement of payments under the QPSA within a reasonable time after the participant's death.

Q-23: Must a defined benefit plan obtain the consent of a participant and the participant's spouse to commence payments in the form of a QJSA in order to avoid violating section 415 or 411(b)?

A-23: No. A defined benefit plan may commence distributions in the form of a QJSA without the consent of the participant and spouse, even if consent would otherwise be required (see §1.417(e)-1(b)), to the extent necessary to avoid a violation of section 415 or 411(b). For example, assume a plan has a normal retirement age of 55. A is a married participant, age 55, and has accrued a $75,000 joint and 100 percent survivor annuity that satisfies section 415. If an actuarial increase would be required under section 411 because of deferred commencement and the increase would cause the benefit to exceed the applicable limit under section 415, the plan may commence payment of a QJSA at age 55 without the participant's election or consent and without the spouse's consent.

Q-24: What are the rules under sections 401(a)(11) and 417 applicable to plan loans?

A-24: (a) *Consent rules.* (1) A plan does not satisfy the survivor annuity requirements of sections 401(a)(11) and 417 unless the plan provides that, at the time the participant's accrued benefit is used as security for a loan, spousal consent to such use is obtained. Consent is required even if the accrued benefit is not the primary security for the loan. No spousal consent is necessary if, at the time the loan is secured, no consent would be required for a distribution under section 417(a)(2)(B). Spousal consent is not required if the plan or the participant is not subject to section 401(a)(11) at the time the accrued benefit is used as security, or if the total accrued benefit subject to the security is not in excess of the cash-out limit in effect under §1.411(a)-11(c)(3)(ii). The spousal consent must be obtained no earlier than the beginning of the 90-day period that ends on the date on which the loan is to be so secured. The consent is subject to the requirements of section 417(a)(2). Therefore, the consent must be in writing, must acknowledge the effect of the loan and must be witnessed by a plan representative or a notary public.

(2) Participant consent is deemed obtained at the time the participant agrees to use his accrued benefit as security for a loan for purposes of satisfying the requirements for participant consent under sections 401(a)(11), 411(a)(11) and 417.

(b) *Change in status.* If spousal consent is obtained or is not required under paragraph (a) of this Q&A 24 at the time the benefits are used as security, spousal consent is not required at the time of any setoff of the loan against the accrued benefit resulting from a default, even if the participant is married to a different spouse at the time of the

setoff. Similarly, in the case of a participant who secured a loan while unmarried, no consent is required at the time of a setoff of the loan against the accrued benefit even if the participant is married at the time of the setoff.

(c) *Renegotiation.* For purposes of obtaining any required spousal consent, any renegotiation, extension, renewal, or other revision of a loan shall be treated as a new loan made on the date of the renegotiation, extension, renewal, or other revision.

(d) *Effect on benefits.* For purposes of determining the amount of a QPSA or QJSA, the accrued benefit of a participant shall be reduced by any security interest held by the plan by reason of a loan outstanding to the participant at the time of death or payment, if the security interest is treated as payment in satisfaction of the loan under the plan. A plan may offset any loan outstanding at the participant's death which is secured by the participant's account balance against the spousal benefit required to be paid under section 401(a)(11)(B)(iii).

(e) *Effective date.* Loans made prior to August 19, 1985, are deemed to satisfy the consent requirements of paragraph (a) of this Q&A 24.

Q-25: How do the survivor annuity requirements of sections 401(a)(11) and 417 apply with respect to participants who are not married or to surviving spouses and participants who have a change in marital status?

A-25: (a) *Unmarried participant rule.* Plans subject to the survivor annuity requirements of sections 401(a)(11) and 417 must satisfy those requirements applicable to QJSAs with respect to participants who are not married. A QJSA for a participant who is not married is an annuity for the life of the participant. Thus, an unmarried participant must be provided the written explanation described in section 417(a)(3)(A) and a single life annuity unless another form of benefit is elected by the participant. An unmarried participant is deemed to have waived the QPSA requirements. This deemed waiver is null and void if the participant later marries.

(b) *Marital status change.*—(1) *Remarriage.* If a participant is married on the date of death, payments to a surviving spouse under a QPSA or QJSA must continue even if the surviving spouse remarries.

(2) *One-year rule.* (i) A plan is not required to treat a participant as married unless the participant and the participant's spouse have been married throughout the one-year period ending on the earlier of (A) the participant's annuity starting date or (B) the date of the participant's death. Nevertheless, for purposes of the preceding sentence, a participant and the participant's spouse must be treated as married throughout the one-year period ending on the participant's annuity starting date even though they are married to each other for less than one year before the annuity starting date if they remain married to each other for at least one year. See section 417(d)(2). If a plan adopts the one-year rule provided in section 417(d), the plan must treat the participant and spouse who are married on the annuity starting date as married and must provide benefits which are to commence on the annuity starting date in the form of a QJSA unless the participant (with spousal consent) elects another form of benefit. The plan is not required to provide the participant with a new or retroactive election or the spouse with a new consent when the one-year period is satisfied. If the participant and the spouse do not remain married for at least one year, the plan may treat the participant as having not been married on the annuity starting date. In such event, the plan may provide that the spouse loses any survivor benefit right; further, no retroactive correction of the amount paid the participant is required.

(ii) *Example.* Plan X provides that participants who are married on the annuity starting date for less than one year are treated as unmarried participants. Plan X provides benefits in the form of a QJSA or an optional single sum distribution. Participant A was married 6 months prior to the annuity starting date. Plan X must treat A as married and must commence payments to A in the form of a QJSA unless another form of benefit is elected by A with spousal consent. If a QJSA is paid and A is divorced from his spouse S, within the first year of the marriage, S will no longer have any survivor rights under the annuity (unless a QDRO provides otherwise). If A continues to be married to S, and A dies within the one-year period, Plan X may treat A as unmarried and forfeit the QJSA benefit payable to S.

(3) *Divorce.* If a participant divorces his spouse prior to the annuity starting date, any elections made while the participant was married to his former spouse remain valid, unless otherwise provided in a QDRO, or unless the participant changes them or is remarried. If a participant dies after the annuity starting date, the spouse to whom the participant was married on the annuity starting date is entitled to the QJSA protection under the plan. The spouse is entitled to this protection (unless waived and consented to by such spouse) even if the participant and spouse are not married on the date of the participant's death, except as provided in a QDRO.

Q-26: In the case of a defined contribution plan not subject to section 412, does the requirement that a participant's nonforfeitable accrued benefit be payable in full to a surviving spouse apply to a spouse who has been married to the participant for less than one year?

A-26: A plan may provide that a spouse who has not been married to a participant throughout the one-year period ending on the earlier of (a) the participant's annuity starting date or (b) the date of the participant's death is not treated as a surviving spouse and is not required to receive the participant's account balance. The special exception described in section 417(d)(2) and Q&A 25 of this section does not apply.

Q-27: Are there circumstances when spousal consent to a participant's election to waive the QJSA or the QPSA is not required?

A-27: Yes. If it is established to the satisfaction of a plan representative that there is no spouse or that the spouse cannot be located, spousal consent to waive the QJSA or the QPSA is not required. If the spouse is legally incompetent to give consent, the spouse's legal guardian, even if the guardian is the participant, may give consent. Also, if the participant is legally separated or the participant has been abandoned (within the meaning of local law) and the participant has a court order to such effect, spousal consent is not required unless a QDRO provides otherwise. Similar rules apply to a plan subject to the requirements of section 401(a)(11)(B)(iii)(I).

Q-28: Does consent contained in an antenuptial agreement or similar contract entered into prior to marriage satisfy the consent requirements of sections 401(a)(11) and 417?

A-28: No. An agreement entered into prior to marriage does not satisfy the applicable consent requirements, even if the agreement is executed within the applicable election period.

Q-29: If a participant's spouse consents under section 417(a)(2)(A) to the participant's waiver of a survivor annuity form of benefit, is a subsequent spouse of the same participant bound by the consent?

A-29: No. A consent under section 417(a)(2)(A) by one spouse is binding only with respect to the consenting spouse. See Q&A-24 of this section for an exception in the case of plan benefits securing plan loans.

Q-30: Does the spousal consent requirement of section 417(a)(2)(A) require that a spouse's consent be revocable?

A-30: No. A plan may preclude a spouse from revoking consent once it has been given. Alternatively, a plan may also permit a spouse to revoke a consent after it has been given, and thereby to render ineffective the participant's prior election not to receive a QPSA or QJSA. A participant must always be allowed to change his election during the applicable election period. Spousal consent is required in such cases to the extent provided in Q&A 31, except that spousal consent is never required for a QPSA or QJSA.

Q-31: What rules govern a participant's waiver of a QPSA or QJSA under section 417(a)(2)?

A-31: (a) *Specific beneficiary.* Both the participant's waivers of a QPSA and QJSA and the spouse's consents thereto must state the specific nonspouse beneficiary (including any class of beneficiaries or any contingent beneficiaries) who will receive the benefit. Thus, for example, if spouse B consents to participant A's election to waive a QPSA, and to have any benefits payable upon A's death before the annuity starting date paid to A's children, A may not subsequently change beneficiaries without the consent of B (except if the change is back to a QPSA). If the designated beneficiary is a trust, A's spouse need only consent to the designation of the trust and need not consent to the designation of trust beneficiaries or any changes of trust beneficiaries.

(b) *Optional form of benefit.*—(1) *QJSA.* Both the participant's waiver of a QJSA (and any required spouse's consent thereto) must specify the particular optional form of benefit. The participant who has waived a QJSA with the spouse's consent in favor of another form of benefit may not subsequently change the optional form of benefit without obtaining the spouse's consent (except back to a QJSA). Of course, the participant may change the form of benefit if the plan so provides after the spouse's death or a divorce (other than as provided in a QDRO). A participant's waiver of a QJSA (and any required spouse's consent thereto) made prior to the first plan year beginning after December 31, 1986, is not required to specify the optional form of benefit.

(2) *QPSA.* A participant's waiver of a QPSA and the spouse's consent thereto are not required to specify the optional form of any *preretirement benefit.* Thus, a participant who waives the QPSA with spousal consent may subsequently change the form of the preretirement benefit, but not the nonspouse beneficiary, without obtaining the spouse's consent.

(3) *Change in form.* After the participant's death, a beneficiary may change the optional form of survivor benefit as permitted by the plan.

(c) *General consent.* In lieu of satisfying paragraphs (a) and (b) of this Q&A 31, a plan may permit a spouse to execute a general consent that satisfies the requirements of this paragraph (c). A general consent permits the participant to waive a QPSA or QJSA, and change the designated beneficiary or the optional form of benefit

payment without any requirement of further consent by such spouse. No general consent is valid unless the general consent acknowledges that the spouse has the right to limit consent to a specific beneficiary and a specific optional form of benefit, where applicable, and that the spouse voluntarily elects to relinquish both of such rights. Notwithstanding the previous sentence, a spouse may execute a general consent that is limited to certain beneficiaries or forms of benefit payment. In such case, paragraphs (a) and (b) of this Q&A 31 shall apply to the extent that the limited general consent is not applicable and this paragraph (c) shall apply to the extent that the limited general consent is applicable. A general consent, including a limited general consent, is not effective unless it is made during the applicable election period. A general consent executed prior to October 22, 1986 does not have to satisfy the specificity requirements of this Q&A 31.

Q-32: What rules govern a participant's waiver of the spousal benefit under section 401(a)(11)(B)?

A-32: (a) *Application.* In the case of a defined contribution plan that is not subject to the survivor annuity requirements of sections 401(a)(11) and 417, a participant may waive the spousal benefit of section 401(a)(11)(B)(iii) if the conditions of paragraph (b) are satisfied. In general, a spousal benefit is the nonforfeitable account balance on the participant's date of death.

(b) *Conditions.* In general, the same conditions, other than the age 35 requirement, that apply to the participant's waiver of a QPSA and the spouse's consent thereto apply to the participant's waiver of the spousal benefit and the spouse's consent thereto. See Q&A-31. Thus, the participant's waiver of the spousal benefit must state the specific nonspouse beneficiary who will receive such benefit. The waiver is not required to specify the optional form of benefit. The participant may change the optional form of benefit, but not the nonspouse beneficiary, without obtaining the spouse's consent.

Q-33: When, and in what manner, may a participant waive a spousal benefit or a QPSA?

A-33: (a) *Plans not subject to section 401(a)(11).* A participant in a plan that is not subject to the survivor annuity requirements of section 401(a)(11) (because of subparagraph (B)(iii) thereof) may waive the spousal benefit at any time, provided that no such waiver shall be effective unless the spouse has consented to the waiver. The spouse may consent to a waiver of the spousal benefit at any time, even prior to the participant attaining age 35. No spousal consent is required for a payment to the participant or the use of the accrued benefit as security for a plan loan to the participant.

(b) *Plans subject to section 401(a)(11).* A participant in a plan subject to the survivor annuity requirements of section 401(a)(11) generally may waive the QPSA benefit (with spousal consent) only on or after the first day of the plan year in which the participant attains age 35. However, a plan may provide for an earlier waiver (with spousal consent), provided that a written explanation of the QPSA is given to the participant and such waiver becomes invalid upon the beginning of the plan year in which the participant's 35th birthday occurs. If there is no new waiver after such date, the participant's spouse must receive the QPSA benefit upon the participant's death.

Q-34: Must the written explanations required by section 417(a)(3) be provided to nonvested participants?

A-34: Such written explanations must be provided to nonvested participants who are employed by an employer maintaining the plan. Thus, they are not required to be provided to those nonvested participants who are no longer employed by such an employer.

Q-35: When must a plan provide the written explanation, required by section 417(a)(3)(B), of the QPSA to a participant?

A-35: (a) *General rule.* A plan must provide the written explanation of the QPSA to a participant within the applicable period. Except as provided in paragraph (b), the applicable period means, with respect to a participant, whichever of the following periods ends last:

(1) The period beginning with the first day of the plan year in which the participant attains age 32 and ending with the close of the plan year preceding the plan year in which the participant attains age 35.

(2) A reasonable period ending after the individual becomes a participant.

(3) A reasonable period ending after the QPSA is no longer fully subsidized.

(4) A reasonable period ending after section 401(a)(11) first applies to the participant. Section 401(a)(11) would first apply when a benefit is transferred from a plan not subject to the survivor annuity requirements of section 401(a)(11) to a plan subject to such section or at the time of an election of an annuity under a defined contribution plan described in section 401(a)(11)(B)(iii).

(b) *Pre-35 separations.* In the case of a participant who separates from service before attaining age 35, the applicable period means the period beginning one year before the separation from service and ending one year after such separation. If such a participant returns to service, the plan must also comply with paragraph (a).

(c) *Reasonable period*. For purposes of applying paragraph (a), a reasonable period ending after the enumerated events described in paragraphs (a)(2), (3) and (4) is the end of the one-year period beginning with the date the applicable event occurs. The applicable period for such events begins one year prior to the occurrence of the enumerated events.

(d) *Transition rule*. In the case of an individual who was a participant in the plan on August 23, 1984, and, as of that date had attained age 34, the plan will satisfy the requirement of section 417(a)(3)(B) if it provided the explanation not later than December 31, 1985.

Q-36: How do plans satisfy the requirements of providing participants explanations of QPSAs and QJSAs?

A-36. For rules regarding the explanation of QPSAs and QJSAs required under section 417(a)(3), see §1.417(a)(3)-1. However, the rules of §1.401(a)-20, Q&A-36, as it appeared in 26 CFR Part 1 revised April 1, 2003, apply to the explanation of a QJSA under section 417(a)(3) for an annuity starting date prior to February 1, 2006.

Q-37: What are the consequences of fully subsidizing the cost of either a QJSA or a QPSA in accordance with section 417(a)(5)?

A-37: If a plan fully subsidizes a QJSA or QPSA in accordance with section 417(a)(5) and does not allow a participant to waive such QJSA or QPSA or to select a nonspouse beneficiary, the plan is not required to provide the written explanation required by section 417(a)(3). However, if the plan offers an election to waive the benefit or designate a beneficiary, it must satisfy the election, consent, and notice requirements of section 417(a)(1), (2), and (3), with respect to such subsidized QJSA or QPSA, in accordance with section 417(a)(5).

Q-38: What is a fully subsidized benefit?

A-38: (a) *QJSA*—(1) *General rule*. A fully subsidized QJSA is one under which no increase in cost to, or decrease in actual amounts received by, the participant may result from the participant's failure to elect another form of benefit.

(2) *Examples*.

Example (1). If a plan provides a joint and survivor annuity and a single sum option, the plan does not fully subsidize the joint and survivor annuity, regardless of the actuarial value of the joint and survivor annuity because, in the event of the participant's early death, the participant would have received less under the annuity than he would have received under the single sum option.

Example (2). If a plan provides for a life annuity of $100 per month and a joint and 100% survivor benefit of $99 per month, the plan does not fully subsidize the joint and survivor benefit.

(b) *QPSA*. A QPSA is fully subsidized if the amount of the participant's benefit is not reduced because of the QPSA coverage and if no charge to the participant under the plan is made for the coverage. Thus, a QPSA is fully subsidized in a defined contribution plan.

Q-39: When do the survivor annuity requirements of sections 401(a)(11) and 417 apply to plans?

A-39: Sections 401(a)(11) and 417 generally apply to plan years beginning after December 31, 1984. Sections 302 and 303 of REA 1984 provide specific effective dates and transitional rules under which the QJSA or QPSA (or pre-REA 1984 section 401(a)(11)) requirements may be applicable to particular plans or with respect to benefits provided to (as amended by REA 1984) particular participants. In general, the section 401(a)(11) (as amended by REA 1984) survivor annuity requirements do not apply with respect to a participant who does not have at least one hour of service or one hour of paid leave under the plan after August 22, 1984.

Q-40: Are there special effective dates for plans maintained pursuant to collective bargaining agreements?

A-40: Yes. Section 302(b) of REA 1984 as amended by section 1898(g) of the Tax Reform Act of 1986 provides a special deferred effective date for such plans. Whether a plan is described in section 302(b) of REA 1984 is determined under the principles applied under section 1017(c) of the Employee Retirement Income Security Act of 1974. See H.R. Rep. No. 1280, 93d Cong., 2d Sess. 266 (1974). In addition, a plan will not be treated as maintained under a collective bargaining agreement unless the employee representatives satisfy section 7701(a)(46) of the Internal Revenue Code after March 31, 1984. See §301.7701-17T for other requirements for a plan to be considered to be collectively bargained. Nothing in section 302(b) of REA 1984 denies a participant or spouse the rights set forth in sections 303(c)(2), 303(c)(3), 303(e)(1), and 303(e)(2) of REA 1984.

Q-41: What is one hour of service or paid leave under the plan for purposes of the transition rules in section 303 of REA 1984?

A-41: One hour of service or paid leave under the plan is one hour of service or paid leave recognized or required to be recognized under the plan for any purpose, *e.g.*, participation, vesting percentage, or benefit accrual purposes. For plans that do not compute hours of service, one hour of service or paid leave means any service or paid leave recognized or required to be recognized under the plan for any purpose.

Q-42: Must a plan be amended to provide for the QPSA required by section 303(c)(2) of REA 1984, or for the survivor annuities required by section 303(e) of REA 1984?

A-42: A plan will not fail to satisfy the qualification requirements of section 401(a) or 403(a) merely because it is not amended to provide the QPSA required by section 303(c)(2) or the survivor annuities required by section 303(e). The plan must, however, satisfy those requirements in operation.

Q-43: Is a participant's election, or a spouse's consent to an election, with respect to a QPSA, made before August 23, 1984, valid?

A-43: No.

Q-44: Is spousal consent required for certain survivor annuity elections made by the participant after December 31, 1984, and before the first plan year to which new sections 401(a)(11) and 417 apply?

A-44: Yes. Section 303(c)(3) of REA 1984 provides that any election not to take a QJSA made after December 31, 1984, and before the date sections 401(a)(11) and 417 apply to the plan by a participant who has 1 hour of service or leave under the plan after August 23, 1984, is not effective unless the spousal consent requirements of section 417 are met with respect to such election. Unless the participant's annuity starting date occurred before January 1, 1985, the spousal consent required by section 417(a)(2) and (e) must be obtained even though the participant elected the benefit prior to January 1, 1985. The plan is not required to be amended to comply with section 303(c)(3) of REA 1984, but the plan must satisfy this requirement in operation.

Q-45: Are there special rules for certain participants who separated from service prior to August 23, 1984?

A-45: Yes. Section 303(e) of REA 1984 provides special rules for certain participants who separated from service before August 23, 1984. Section 303(e)(1), which applies only to plans subject to section 401(a)(11) of the Code (as in effect on August 22, 1984), provides that participants whose annuity starting date did not occur before August 24, 1984, and who had one hour of service on or after September 2, 1974, but not in a plan year beginning after December 31, 1975, may elect to receive the benefits required to be provided under section 401(a)(11) of the Code (as in effect on August 22, 1984). Section 303(e)(2) provides that certain participants who had one hour of service in a plan year beginning on or after January 1, 1976, but not after August 22, 1984, may elect QPSA coverage under new sections 401(a)(11) and 417 in plans subject to these provisions. Section 303(e)(4)(A) requires plans or plan administrators to notify those participants of the provisions of section 303(e).

Q-46: When must a plan provide the notice required by section 303(e)(4)(A) of REA 1984?

A-46: The notice required by section 303(e)(4)(A) must be provided no later than the earlier of:

(a) The date the first summary annual report provided after September 17, 1985 is distributed to participants; or

(b) September 30, 1985.

A plan will not fail to satisfy the preceding sentence if the plan provides a fully subsidized QPSA with respect to any participant described in section 303(e) who dies on or after July 19, 1985 and before the notice is received. If the plan ceases to fully subsidize the QPSA, the cessation must not be effective until the notice is given. For this purpose, an annuity payable to a nonspouse beneficiary elected by the participant, in lieu of a spouse, shall satisfy the QPSA requirement, so long as the survivor benefit is fully subsidized. The notice required by this paragraph must be in writing and sent to the participant's last known address.

Q-47: Is there another time when plans must provide notice of the right, described in section 303(e)(1) of REA '84, to elect a pre-REA 1984 qualified joint and survivor annuity?

A-47: Yes. Notice of this right must also be provided to a participant at the time the participant applies for benefit payments. [Reg. §1.401(a)-20.]

☐ [*T.D.* 8219, 8-19-88. *Amended by T.D.* 8794, 12-18-98; *T.D.* 8891, 7-18-2000; *T.D.* 9099, 12-16-2003 *and T.D.* 9256, 3-23-2006.]

[Reg. §1.401(a)-21]

§1.401(a)-21. Rules relating to the use of an electronic medium to provide applicable notices and to make participant elections.— (a) *Introduction*.—(1) *In general*.—(i) *Permission to use an electronic medium*.—This section provides rules relating to the use of an electronic medium to provide applicable notices and to make participant elections as defined in paragraph (e)(1) and (6) of this section with respect to retirement plans, employee benefit arrangements, and individual retirement plans described in paragraph (a)(2) of this section. The rules in this section reflect the provisions of the Electronic Signatures in Global and National Commerce Act, Public Law 106-229 (114 Stat. 464 (2000) (E-SIGN)).

(ii) *Notices and elections required to be in writing or in written form*.—(A) *In general*.—The rules of this section must be satisfied in order to use an electronic medium to provide an applicable notice or to make a participant election if the notice or election is required to be in writing or in written form under the Internal Revenue Code, Department of Treasury regulations, or other guidance issued by the Commissioner.

(B) *Rules relating to applicable notices.*—An applicable notice that is provided using an electronic medium is treated as being provided in writing or in written form if and only if the requirements of paragraph (a)(5) of this section are satisfied and either the consumer consent requirements of paragraph (b) of this section or the requirements for exemption from the consumer consent requirements under paragraph (c) of this section are satisfied. For example, in order to provide a section 402(f) notice electronically, a qualified plan must satisfy either the consumer consent requirements of paragraph (b) of this section or the requirements for exemption under paragraph (c) of this section. If a plan fails to satisfy either of these requirements, the plan must provide the section 402(f) notice using a written paper document in order to satisfy the requirements of section 402(f).

(C) *Rules relating to participant elections.*—A participant election that is made using an electronic medium is treated as being provided in writing or in written form if and only if the requirements of paragraphs (a)(5) and (d) of this section are satisfied.

(iii) *Safe harbor method for applicable notices and participant elections that are not required to be in writing or written form.*—For an applicable notice or a participant election that is not required to be in writing or in written form, the rules of this section provide a safe harbor method for using an electronic medium to provide the applicable notice or to make the participant election.

(2) *Application of rules.*—(i) *Notices, elections, or consents under retirement plans.*—The rules of this section apply to any applicable notice or any participant election relating to the following retirement plans: a qualified retirement plan under section 401(a) or 403(a); a section 403(b) plan; a simplified employee pension (SEP) under section 408(k); a simple retirement plan under section 408(p); or an eligible governmental plan under section 457(b).

(ii) *Notices, elections, or consents under other employee benefit arrangements.*—The rules of this section also apply to any applicable notice or any participant election relating to the following employee benefit arrangements: an accident and health plan or arrangement under sections 104(a)(3) and 105; a cafeteria plan under section 125; an educational assistance program under section 127; a qualified transportation fringe program under section 132; an Archer MSA under section 220; or a health savings account under section 223.

(iii) *Notices, elections, or consents under individual retirement plans.*—The rules of this section also apply to any applicable notice or any participant election relating to individual retirement plans, including a Roth IRA under section 408A; or a deemed IRA under a qualified employer plan described in section 408(q).

(3) *Limitation on application of rules.*—(i) *In general.*—The rules of this section do not apply to any notice, election, consent, disclosure, or obligation required under the provisions of title I or IV of the Employee Retirement Income Security Act of 1974, as amended (ERISA), over which the Department of Labor or the Pension Benefit Guaranty Corporation has interpretative and enforcement authority. For example, the rules in 29 CFR 2520.104b-1 of the Department of Labor Regulations apply with respect to an employee benefit plan providing disclosure documents, such as a summary plan description or a summary annual report. The rules in this section also do not apply to Internal Revenue Code section 411(a)(3)(B) (relating to suspension of benefits), Internal Revenue Code section 4980B(f)(6) (relating to an individual's COBRA rights), or any other Internal Revenue Code provision over which Department of Labor or the Pension Benefit Guaranty Corporation has similar interpretative authority.

(ii) *Recordkeeping and other requirements.*—The rules in this section only apply with respect to applicable notices and participant elections relating to an individual's rights under a retirement plan, an employee benefit arrangement, or an individual retirement plan. Thus, the rules in this section do not alter the otherwise applicable requirements under the Internal Revenue Code, such as the requirements relating to tax reporting, tax records, or substantiation of expenses. See section 6001 for rules relating to the maintenance of records, statements, and special returns. See also section 101(e) of E-SIGN, which provides that if an electronic record of an applicable notice or a participant election is not maintained in a form that is capable of being retained and accurately reproduced for later reference, then the legal effect, validity, or enforceability of such electronic record may be denied.

(4) *General requirements related to applicable notices and participant elections.*—The rules of this section supplement the general require-

ments related to each applicable notice and participant election. Thus, in addition to satisfying the rules for timing and content, the rules in this section must be satisfied.

(5) *Requirements related to the design of an electronic system used to deliver applicable notices and to make participant elections.*—(i) *The electronic system must take into account the content of a notice.*—With respect to the content of an applicable notice, the electronic system must be reasonably designed to provide the information in the notice to a recipient in a manner that is no less understandable to the recipient than a written paper document.

(ii) *Identification of the significance of information in the notice.*—The electronic system must be designed to alert the recipient, at the time an applicable notice is provided, to the significance of information in the notice (including identification of the subject matter of the notice), and provide any instructions needed to access the notice, in a manner that is readily understandable.

(b) *Consumer consent requirements*—(1) *Requirements.*—With respect to an applicable notice, the consumer consent requirements of this paragraph (b) are satisfied if —

(i) The requirements in paragraphs (b)(2) through (4) of this section are satisfied; and

(ii) In accordance with section 101(c)(6) of E-SIGN, the applicable notice is not provided through the use of oral communication or a recording of an oral communication.

(2) *Consent.*—(i) *In general.*—The recipient must affirmatively consent to the delivery of the applicable notice using an electronic medium. This consent must be either—

(A) Made electronically in a manner that reasonably demonstrates that the recipient can access the applicable notice in the electronic medium in the form that will be used to provide the notice; or

(B) Made using a written paper document (or using another form not described in paragraph (b)(2)(i)(A) of this section), but only if the recipient confirms the consent electronically in a manner that reasonably demonstrates that the recipient can access the applicable notice in the electronic medium in the form that will be used to provide the notice.

(ii) *Withdrawal of consumer consent.*—The consent to receive electronic delivery requirement of this paragraph (b)(2) is not satisfied if the recipient withdraws his or her consent before the applicable notice is delivered.

(3) *Required disclosure statement.*—The recipient, prior to consenting under paragraph (b)(2)(i) of this section, must be provided with a clear and conspicuous statement containing the disclosures described in paragraphs (b)(3)(i) through (v) of this section:

(i) *Right to receive paper document.*—(A) *In general.*—The statement informs the recipient of any right to have the applicable notice be provided using a written paper document or other nonelectronic form.

(B) *Post-consent request for paper copy.*—The statement informs the recipient how, after having provided consent to receive the applicable notice electronically, the recipient may, upon request, obtain a paper copy of the applicable notice and whether any fee will be charged for such copy.

(ii) *Right to withdraw consumer consent.*—The statement informs the recipient of the right to withdraw consent to receive electronic delivery of an applicable notice on a prospective basis at any time and explains the procedures for withdrawing that consent and any conditions, consequences, or fees in the event of the withdrawal.

(iii) *Scope of the consumer consent.*—The statement informs the recipient whether the consent to receive electronic delivery of an applicable notice applies only to the particular transaction that gave rise to the applicable notice or to other identified transactions that may be provided or made available during the course of the parties' relationship. For example, the statement may provide that a recipient's consent to receive electronic delivery will apply to all future applicable notices of the recipient relating to the employee benefit arrangement until the recipient is no longer a participant in the employee benefit arrangement (or withdraws the consent).

(iv) *Description of the contact procedures.*—The statement describes the procedures to update information needed to contact the recipient electronically.

(v) *Hardware or software requirements.*—The statement describes the hardware and software requirements needed to access and retain the applicable notice.

(4) *Post-consent change in hardware or software requirements.*—If, after a recipient provides consent to receive electronic delivery, there is a change in the hardware or software requirements needed to access or retain the applicable notice and such change creates a material risk that the recipient will not be able to access or retain the applicable notice in electronic format—

(i) The recipient must receive a statement of—

(A) The revised hardware or software requirements for access to and retention of the applicable notice; and

(B) The right to withdraw consent to receive electronic delivery without the imposition of any fees for the withdrawal and without the imposition of any condition or consequence that was not previously disclosed in paragraph (b)(3) of this section; and

(ii) The recipient must reaffirm consent to receive electronic delivery in accordance with the requirements of paragraph (b)(2) of this section.

(c) *Exemption from consumer consent requirements.*—(1) *In general.*—This paragraph (c) is satisfied if the conditions in paragraphs (c)(2) and (3) of this section are satisfied. This paragraph (c) constitutes an exemption from the consumer consent requirements of section 101(c) of E-SIGN pursuant to the authority granted in section 104(d)(1) of E-SIGN.

(2) *Effective ability to access.*—For purposes of this paragraph (c), the electronic medium used to provide an applicable notice must be a medium that the recipient has the effective ability to access.

(3) *Free paper copy of applicable notice.*—At the time the applicable notice is provided, the recipient must be advised that he or she may request and receive the applicable notice in writing on paper at no charge, and, upon request, that applicable notice must be provided to the recipient at no charge.

(d) *Special rules for participant elections.*—(1) *In general.*—This paragraph (d) is satisfied if the conditions described in the following paragraphs (d)(2) through (6) are satisfied:

(2) *Effective ability to access.*—The electronic medium under an electronic system used to make a participant election must be a medium that the person who is eligible to make the election is effectively able to access. If the appropriate individual is not effectively able to access the electronic medium for making the participant election, the participant election will not be treated as made available to that individual. Thus, for example, the participant election will not be treated as made available to that individual for purposes of the rules under section 401(a)(4).

(3) *Authentication.*—The electronic system used in making participant elections is reasonably designed to preclude any person other than the appropriate individual from making the election. Whether this condition is satisfied is based on facts and circumstances, including whether the participant election has the potential for a conflict of interest between the individuals involved in the election. See Examples 3, 4, and 5 of paragraph (f) of this section for illustrations of electronic systems that satisfy the authentication requirement of this paragraph (d)(3).

(4) *Opportunity to review.*—The electronic system used in making participant elections provides the person making the participant election with a reasonable opportunity to review, confirm, modify, or rescind the terms of the election before the election becomes effective.

(5) *Confirmation of action.*—The person making the participant election receives, within a reasonable time, a confirmation of the effect of the election under the terms of the plan or arrangement through either a written paper document or an electronic medium under a system that satisfies the requirements of either paragraph (b) or (c) of this section (as if the confirmation were an applicable notice).

(6) *Participant elections, including spousal consents, that are required to be witnessed by a plan representative or a notary public.*—(i) *In general.*—In the case of a participant election which is required to be witnessed by a plan representative or a notary public (such as a spousal consent under section 417), the signature of the individual making the participant election is witnessed in the physical presence of a plan representative or a notary public.

(ii) *Electronic notarization permitted.*—If the requirements of paragraph (d)(6)(i) of this section are satisfied, an electronic notarization acknowledging a signature (in accordance with section 101(g) of E-SIGN and State law applicable to notary publics) will not be denied legal effect if the signature of the individual is witnessed in the physical presence of a notary public.

(iii) *Delegation to Commissioner.*—In guidance published in the Internal Revenue Bulletin, the Commissioner may provide that the use of procedures under an electronic system is deemed to satisfy the

physical presence requirement under paragraph (d)(6)(i) of this section, but only if those procedures with respect to the electronic system provide the same safeguards for participant elections as are provided through the physical presence requirement. See § 601.601(d)(2)(ii)(b) of this chapter.

(e) *Definitions.*—The definitions in this paragraph (e) apply for purposes of this section.

(1) *Applicable notice.*—The term *applicable notice* includes any notice, report, statement, or other document required to be provided to a recipient under a retirement plan, employee benefit arrangement, or individual retirement plan as described in paragraph (a)(2) of this section.

(2) *Electronic.*—The term *electronic* means technology having electrical, digital, magnetic, wireless, optical, electromagnetic, voice-recording systems, or similar capabilities.

(3) *Electronic medium.*—The term *electronic medium* means an electronic method of communication (e.g., Web site, electronic mail, telephonic system, magnetic disk, and CD-ROM).

(4) *Electronic record.*—The term *electronic record* means an applicable notice or a participant election that is created, generated, sent, communicated, received, or stored by electronic media.

(5) *Electronic system.*—The term *electronic system* means a system designed for creating, generating, sending, receiving, storing, retrieving, displaying, or processing information that makes use of any electronic medium.

(6) *Participant election.*—The term *participant election* includes any consent, election, request, agreement, or similar communication made by or from a participant, beneficiary, alternate payee, or an individual entitled to benefits under a retirement plan, employee benefit arrangement, or individual retirement plan as described in paragraph (a)(2) of this section.

(7) *Recipient.*—The term *recipient* means a plan participant, beneficiary, employee, alternate payee, or any other person to whom an applicable notice is to be provided.

(f) *Examples.*—The following examples illustrate the rules of this section. *Examples 1, 2, 3,* and *6* assume that the requirements of paragraph (a)(4) and (5) of this section are satisfied.

Example 1. (i) *Facts involving using the consumer consent requirements to deliver a section 402(f) notice via e-mail.* Plan A, a qualified plan, permits participants to request benefit distributions from the plan on Plan A's Internet Web site. Under Plan A's system for such transactions, a participant must enter his or her account number, personal identification number (PIN), and his or her e-mail address to which the notice is to be sent. The participant's PIN and account number must match the information in Plan A's records in order for the transaction to proceed. Participant H requests a distribution from Plan A on Plan A's Web site, and, at the time of the request for distribution, a disclosure statement appears on the computer screen that explains that Participant H can consent to receive the section 402(f) notice electronically. The disclosure statement provides information relating to the consent, including how to receive a paper copy of the notice, how to withdraw consent, the hardware and software requirements, and the procedures for accessing the section 402(f) notice, which is in a file format from a specific spreadsheet program. After reviewing the disclosure statement, which satisfies the requirements of paragraph (b)(3) of this section, Participant H consents to receive the section 402(f) notice via e-mail by selecting the consent button at the end of the disclosure statement. As a part of the consent procedure, an e-mail is sent to Participant H's e-mail address in order to demonstrate that Participant H can access the spreadsheet program. In the e-mail, Participant H is prompted to answer a question from the spreadsheet program, which is in an attachment to the e-mail. Once Participant H correctly answers the question, the section 402(f) notice is then delivered to Participant H via e-mail.

(ii) *Conclusion.* In this *Example 1,* Plan A's delivery of the section 402(f) notice to Participant H satisfies the requirements of paragraph (b) of this section.

Example 2. (i) *Facts*—(A) *Facts involving using the alternative method to deliver a section 411(a)(11) notice via e-mail.* Plan B, a qualified plan, permits participants to request benefit distributions from the plan on Plan B's Internet Web site. Under Plan B's system for such transactions, a participant must enter his or her account number and personal identification number (PIN), and his or her e-mail address to which the notice is to be sent. The participant's PIN and account number must match the information in Plan B's records in order for the transaction to proceed. After Participant K, a single employee, requests a distribution from Plan B on Plan B's Internet Web site, the plan administrator provides Participant K with a section 411(a)(11) notice in an attachment to an e-mail. Plan B sends the e-mail with a request for a computer generated notification that the message was received and opened. The e-mail instructs Participant K to read the attachment for important information regarding the request for a distribution. In addition, the e-mail also states that Participant K may request the section 411(a)(11) notice on a written paper document and that, if Participant K requests the notice on a written paper document, it will be provided at no charge. Plan B receives notification indicating that the e-mail was received and opened by Participant K.

(B) *Facts involving making a participant's consent to a distribution.* In order to consent to a distribution, Plan B requires a participant to enter the participant's account number and PIN in order to preclude any person other than the participant from making the election. After the authentication process, Participant K completes a distribution request form on the Web site. After completing the request form, the Web site provides a summary of the information entered on the form and gives Participant K an opportunity to review or modify the distribution request form before the transaction is completed. Within a reasonable period of time after Participant K consents to the distribution, the plan administrator, by e-mail, sends confirmation of the terms (including the form) of the distribution to Participant K and advises Participant K that, upon request, the confirmation may be provided to Participant K on a written paper document at no charge. Plan B retains an electronic copy of the consent to the distribution in a form that is capable of being retained and accurately reproduced for later reference by Participant K.

(ii) *Conclusion.* In this *Example 2*, Plan B's delivery of the section 411(a)(11) notice and the electronic system used to make Participant K's consent to a distribution satisfy the requirements of paragraphs (a), (c), and (d) of this section.

Example 3. (i) *Facts involving the transmission of a spousal consent via electronic notarization.* Plan C, a qualified money purchase pension plan, permits a married participant to request a plan loan through the Plan C's Internet Web site with the notarized consent of the spouse. Under Plan C's system for requesting a plan loan, a participant must enter his or her account number, personal identification number (PIN), and his or her e-mail address. The information entered by the participant must match the information in Plan C's records in order for the transaction to proceed. Participant M, a married participant, is effectively able to access the Web site available to apply for a plan loan. In order to apply for a loan, Plan C requires a participant to enter the participant's account number and PIN in order to preclude any person other than the participant from making the election. Participant M completes the loan application on Plan C's Web site. Within a reasonable period of time after submitting the plan loan application, the plan administrator, by e-mail, sends Participant M the loan application, including all attachments setting forth the terms of the loan agreement and all other required information. In the e-mail, Plan C also notifies Participant M that, upon request, the loan application may be provided to Participant M on a written paper document at no charge. Plan C then instructs Participant M that, in order for the loan application to proceed, Participant M must submit to the plan administrator a notarized spousal consent form. Participant M and M's spouse go to a notary public and the notary witnesses Participant M's spouse signing the spousal consent for the loan agreement on an electronic signature capture pad with adequate security. After witnessing M's spouse signing the spousal consent, the notary public sends an e-mail with an electronic acknowledgement that is attached to or logically associated with the signature of M's spouse to the plan administrator. The electronic acknowledgement is in accordance with section 101(g) of E-SIGN and the relevant State law applicable to notary publics. After the plan receives the e-mail, Plan C sends an e-mail to Participant M, giving M a reasonable period to review and confirm the completed loan application and to determine whether the loan application should be modified or rescinded. In addition, the e-mail to Participant M also provides that M may request the completed loan application on a written paper document and that, if M requests the written paper document, it will be provided at no charge. Plan C retains an electronic copy of the loan agreement, including the spousal consent, in a form that is capable of being retained and accurately reproduced for later reference by all parties.

(ii) *Conclusion.* In this *Example 3*, the transmission of the plan loan agreement satisfies the requirements of paragraphs (a), (c), and (d) of this section. By requiring that the spouse sign the spousal consent on an electronic signature capture pad in the physical presence of a notary public, the electronic system satisfies the requirement that the system be reasonably designed to preclude any person other than the appropriate individual from making the election. Thus, the electronic notarization of spousal consent satisfies the requirements of paragraphs (a) and (d) of this section.

Example 4. (i) *Facts*—(A) *Facts involving using the alternative method of compliance to deliver a section 411(a)(11) notice via an automated telephone system.* A qualified profit-sharing plan (Plan D) permits participants to request distributions through an automated telephone

system. Under Plan D's system for such transactions, a participant must enter his or her account number and personal identification number (PIN); this information must match the information in Plan D's records in order for the transaction to proceed. Plan D provides only the following distribution options: single-sum payment; and annual installments over 5, 10, or 20 years. Participant N, a single participant, requests a distribution from Plan D by following the applicable instructions on the automated telephone system. After Participant N has requested the distribution, the automated telephone system recites the section 411(a)(11) notice over the phone. The automated telephone system also advises Participant N that, upon request, the notice may be provided on a written paper document and that, if Participant N so requests, the notice will be provided on a written paper document at no charge.

(B) *Facts involving making a participant's consent to a distribution via an automated telephone system.* In order to consent to a distribution, Plan D requires a participant to enter the participant's account number and PIN in order to preclude any person other than the participant from making the election. Participant N requests a distribution by entering information on the automated telephone system. After completing the request, the automated telephone system provides an oral summary of the information entered and gives Participant N an opportunity to review or modify the distribution request before the transaction is completed. Plan D's automated telephone system confirms the distribution request to Participant N and advises Participant N that, upon request, a confirmation may be provided on a written paper document at no charge. Plan D retains an electronic copy of the consent to the distribution in a form that is capable of being retained and accurately reproduced for later reference by Participant N.

(ii) *Conclusion.* In this *Example 4*, because Plan D has relatively few and simple distribution options, the provision of the section 411(a)(11) notice through the automated telephone system is no less understandable to the participant than a written paper notice for purposes of paragraph (a)(5)(i) of this section. In addition, the automated telephone procedures of Plan D satisfy the applicable requirements of paragraphs (a), (c), and (d) of this section.

Example 5. (i) *Facts.* Same facts as *Example 4* of this paragraph (f), except that, pursuant to Plan D's system for processing such transactions, a participant who so requests is transferred to a customer service representative whose conversation with the participant is recorded. The customer service representative provides the section 411(a)(11) notice from a prepared text and processes the participant's distribution in accordance with the predetermined instructions from the plan administrator.

(ii) *Conclusion.* As in *Example 4* of this paragraph (f), because Plan D has relatively few and simple distribution options, the provision of the section 411(a)(11) notice through the automated telephone system is no less understandable to the participant than a written paper notice for purposes of paragraph (a)(4) of this section. Further, in this *Example 5*, the customer service telephone procedures of Plan D satisfy the requirements of paragraphs (a), (c), and (d) of this section.

Example 6. (i) *Facts.* Plan E, a qualified plan, permits participants to request distributions by e-mail on the employer's e-mail system. Under this system, a participant must enter his or her account number, personal identification number (PIN), and e-mail address. This information must match that in Plan E's records in order for the transaction to proceed. If a participant requests a distribution by e-mail, the plan administrator provides the participant with a section 411(a)(11) notice by e-mail. The plan administrator also advises the participant by e-mail that he or she may request the section 411(a)(11) notice on a written paper document and that, if the participant requests the notice on a written paper document, it will be provided at no charge. Participant Q requests a distribution and receives the section 411(a)(11) notice from the plan administrator by reply e-mail. However, before Participant Q elects a distribution, Q terminates employment. Following termination of employment, Participant Q no longer has access to the employer's e-mail system.

(ii) *Conclusion.* In this *Example 6*, Plan E does not satisfy the participant election requirements under paragraph (d) of this section because Participant Q is not effectively able to access the electronic medium used to make the participant election. Plan E must provide Participant Q with the opportunity to make the participant election through a written paper document or another system that Participant Q is effectively able to access, such as the automated telephone systems described in *Example 4* and *Example 5* of this paragraph (f).

(g) *Effective date.*—The rules provided in this section apply to applicable notices provided, and to participant elections made, on or after January 1, 2007. However, a retirement plan, an employee benefit arrangement, or an individual retirement plan that provides an applicable notice or makes a participant election that complies with the requirements set forth in these regulations on or after October 1, 2000, and before January 1, 2007, will not be treated as failing to provide an applicable notice or to make a participant election merely because the notice or election was not in writing or written form. [Reg. § 1.401(a)-21.]

☐ [*T.D. 9294, 10-19-2006.*]

[Reg. § 1.401(a)(26)-0]

§ 1.401(a)(26)-0. Table of contents.—This section contains a listing of the headings of §§ 1.401(a)(26)-1 through 1.401(a)(26)-9.

[Reg. § 1.401(a)(26)-0.]

☐ [*T.D. 8375, 12-2-91.*]

[Reg. § 1.401(a)(26)-1]

§ 1.401(a)(26)-1. Minimum participation requirements.—(a) *General rule.*—A plan is a qualified plan for a plan year only if the plan satisfies section 401(a)(26) for the plan year. A plan that satisfies any of the exceptions described in paragraph (b) of this section passes section 401(a)(26) automatically for the plan year. A plan that does not satisfy one of the exceptions in paragraph (b) of this must satisfy § 1.401(a)(26)-2(a). In addition, a defined benefit plan must satisfy § 1.401(a)(26)-3 with respect to its prior benefit structure. Finally, a defined benefit plan that benefits former employees (for example, a defined benefit plan that is amended to provide an ad hoc cost-of-living adjustment to former employees) must separately satisfy § 1.401(a)(26)-4 with respect to its former employees.

(b) *Exceptions to section 401(a)(26).*—(1) *Plans that do not benefit any highly compensated employees.*—A plan, other than a frozen defined benefit plan as defined in § 1.401(a)(26)-2(b), satisfies section 401(a)(26) for a plan year if the plan is not a top-heavy plan under section 416 and the plan meets the following requirements:

(i) The plan benefits no highly compensated employee or highly compensated former employee of the employer; and

(ii) The plan is not aggregated with any other plan of the employer to enable the other plan to satisfy section 401(a)(4) or 410(b). The plan may, however, be aggregated with the employer's other plans for purposes of the average benefit percentage test in section 410(b)(2)(A)(ii).

(2) *Multiemployer plans.*—(i) *In general.*—The portion of a multiemployer plan that benefits only employees included in a unit of employees covered by a collective bargaining agreement may be treated as a separate plan that satisfies section 401(a)(26) for a plan year.

(ii) *Multiemployer plans covering noncollectively bargained employees.*—(A) *In general.*—The rule provided in paragraph (b)(2)(i) does not apply to the portion of a multiemployer plan that benefits employees who are not included in any collective bargaining unit covered by a collective bargaining agreement. Thus, the portion of the plan benefiting these employees must separately satisfy section 401(a)(26).

(B) *Special testing rule.*—A multiemployer plan that benefits employees who are not included in any collective bargaining unit covered by a collective bargaining agreement satisfies section 401(a)(26) if the plan benefits 50 employees. For purposes of this special testing rule, employees who are included in a unit of employees covered by a collective bargaining agreement may be included in determining whether the plan benefits 50 employees.

(3) *Certain underfunded defined benefit plans.*—(i) *In general.*—A defined benefit plan is deemed to satisfy section 401(a)(26) for a plan year if all of the conditions of paragraphs (b)(3)(ii) through (b)(3)(iv) of this section are satisfied with respect to the plan for the plan year.

(ii) *Eligible plans.*—This condition is satisfied for a plan year only if the plan is subject to Title IV of the Employee Retirement Income Security Act of 1974 (ERISA) for the plan year or, if the plan is not a Title IV plan under ERISA, it is not a top-heavy plan within the meaning of section 416. This condition does not apply for plan years beginning before January 1, 1992.

(iii) *Actuarial certification.*—This condition is satisfied for a plan year only if the employer's timely filed actuarial report, as required by section 6059, evidences that the plan does not have sufficient assets to satisfy all liabilities under the plan (determined in accordance with section 401(a)(2)).

(iv) *Cessation of all benefit accruals.*—This condition is satisfied for a plan year only if, for the plan year, no employee or former employee is benefiting within the meaning of § 1.401(a)(26)-5(a) or (b). For this purpose, an employee is not treated as benefiting solely by reason of being a non-key employee receiving minimum benefit accruals required by section 416.

(4) *Section 401(k) plan maintained by employers that include certain governmental or tax-exempt entities.*—Section 401(k)(4)(B) prevents certain State and local governments and tax-exempt organizations from maintaining a qualified cash or deferred arrangement. A plan (or portion of a plan) that is either a section 401(k) plan or a section 401(m) plan that is provided under the same general arrangement as a section 401(k) plan may be treated as a separate plan that satisfies section 401(a)(26) for a plan year if the following requirements are satisfied:

(i) The section 401(k) plan is maintained by an employer who has employees precluded from being eligible employees under the arrangement by reason of section 401(k)(4)(B), and

(ii) More than 95 percent of the employees of the employer who are not precluded from being eligible employees under a section 401(k) plan by reason of section 401(k)(4)(B) benefit under the section 401(k) plan.

(5) *Certain acquisitions or dispositions.*—(i) *General rule.*—Rules similar to the rules prescribed under section 410(b)(6)(C) apply under section 401(a)(26). Pursuant to these rules, the requirements of section 401(a)(26) are treated as satisfied for certain plans of an employer involved in an acquisition or disposition (transaction) for the transition period. The transition period begins on the date of the transaction and ends on the last day of the first plan year beginning after the date of the transaction.

(ii) *Special rule for transactions that occur in the plan year prior to the first plan year to which section 401(a)(26) applies.*—Where there has been a transaction described in section 410(b)(6)(C) in the plan year prior to the first plan year in which section 401(a)(26) applies to a plan, the plan satisfies section 401(a)(26) for the transition period if the plan benefited 50 employees or 40 percent of the employees of the employer immediately prior to the transaction.

(iii) *Definition of "acquisition" and "disposition".*—For purposes of this paragraph (b)(5), the terms "acquisition" and "disposition" refer to an asset or stock acquisition, merger, or other similar transaction involving a change in employer of the employees of a trade or business.

(c) *Additional rules.*—The Commissioner may, in revenue rulings, notices, and other guidance of general applicability, provide any additional rules that may be necessary or appropriate in applying the minimum participation requirements of section 401(a)(26). [Reg. § 1.401(a)(26)-1.]

☐ [*T.D. 8375, 12-2-91. Amended by T.D. 8487, 8-31-93.*]

[Reg. § 1.401(a)(26)-2]

§ 1.401(a)(26)-2. Minimum participation rule.—(a) *General rule.*—A plan satisfies this paragraph (a) for a plan year only if the plan benefits at least the lesser of—

(1) 50 employees of the employer, or

(2) 40 percent of the employees of the employer.

(b) *Frozen plans.*—A plan under which no employee or former employee benefits (within the meaning of § 1.401(a)(26)-5(a) or (b)), is a frozen plan for purposes of this section and satisfies paragraph (a) of this section automatically. Thus, a frozen defined contribution plan satisfies section 401(a)(26) automatically and a frozen defined benefit plan satisfies section 401(a)(26) for a plan year by satisfying the prior benefit structure requirements in § 1.401(a)(26)-3. For purposes of the rule in this paragraph (b), a defined benefit plan that provides only the minimum benefits for non-key employees required by section 416 is a frozen defined benefit plan.

(c) *Plan.*—"Plan" means a plan within the meaning of § 1.410(b)-7(a) and (b), after the application of the mandatory disaggregation rules of paragraph (d)(1) of this section and, if applicable, the permissive disaggregation rules of paragraph (d)(2) of this section.

(d) *Disaggregation of certain plans.*—(1) *Mandatory disaggregation.*—(i) *ESOPs and non-ESOPs.*—The portion of a plan that is an ESOP and the portion of the plan that is not an ESOP are treated as separate plans for purposes of section 401(a)(26), except as otherwise permitted under § 54.4975-11(e) of this Chapter.

(ii) *Plans maintained by more than one employer.*—(A) *Multiple employer plans.*—If a plan benefits employees of more than one employer and those employees are not included in a unit of employees covered by one or more collective bargaining agreements, the plan is a multiple employer plan. A multiple employer plan is treated as separate plans, each of which is maintained by a separate employer and must separately satisfy section 401(a)(26) by reference only to that employer's employees.

(B) *Multiemployer plans.*—The portion of a multiemployer plan that benefits employees who are included in one or more units of employees covered by one or more collective bargaining agreements and the portion of that plan that benefits employees who are not included in a unit of employees covered pursuant to any collective bargaining agreement are treated as separate plans. The portion of a multiemployer plan that benefits employees who are not included in a unit of employees covered by a collective bargaining agreement is a multiple employer plan as described in paragraph (d)(1)(ii)(A) of this section. This paragraph (d)(1)(ii)(B) does not apply to the extent that the special testing rule in § 1.401(a)(26)-1(b)(1)(ii) applies. Also, this paragraph (d)(1)(B)(2) does not apply for purposes of prior benefit structure testing under § 1.401(a)(26)-3.

(iii) *Defined benefit plans with other arrangements.*—(A) *In general.*—A defined benefit plan is treated as comprising separate plans if, under the facts and circumstances, there is an arrangement (either under or outside the plan) that has the effect of providing any employee with a greater interest in a portion of the assets of a plan in a way that has the effect of creating separate accounts. Separate plans are not created, however, merely because a partnership agreement provides for allocation among partners, in proportion to their partnership interests, of either the cost of funding the plan or surplus assets upon plan termination.

(B) *Examples.*—The following examples illustrate certain situations in which other arrangements relating to a defined benefit plan are or are not treated as creating separate plans:

Example 1. Employer A maintains a defined benefit plan under which each highly compensated employee can direct the investment of the portion of the plan's assets that represents the accumulated contributions with respect to that employee's plan benefits. In addition, by agreement outside the plan, if the product of the employee's investment direction exceeds the value needed to fund that employee's benefits, Employer A agrees to make a special payment to the participant. In this case, each separate portion of the pool of assets over which an employee has investment authority is a separate plan for the employee.

Example 2. Employer B is a partnership that maintains a defined benefit plan. The partnership agreement provides that, upon termination of the plan, a special allocation of any excess plan assets after reversion is made to the partnership on the basis of partnership share. This arrangement does not create separate plans with respect to the partners.

(iv) *Plans benefiting employees of qualified separate lines of business.*—If an employer is treated as operating qualified separate lines of business for purposes of section 401(a)(26) in accordance with §1.414(r)-1(b), the portion of a plan that benefits employees of one qualified separate line of business is treated as a separate plan from the portions of the same plan that benefit employees of the other qualified separate lines of business of the employer. See §§1.414(r)-1(c)(3) and 1.414(r)-9 (separate application of section 401(a)(26) to the employees of a qualified separate line of business). The rule in this paragraph (d)(6) does not apply to a plan that is tested under the special rule for employer-wide plans in §1.414(r)-1(c)(3)(ii) for a plan year.

(2) *Permissive disaggregation.*—(i) *Plans benefiting collectively bargained employees.*—For purposes of section 401(a)(26), an employer may treat the portion of a plan that benefits employees who are included in a unit of employees covered by a collective bargaining agreement as a plan separate from the portion of a plan that benefits employees who are not included in such a collective bargaining unit. This paragraph (d)(2)(i) applies separately to each collective bargaining agreement. Thus, for example, the portion of a plan that benefits employees included in a unit of employees covered by one collective bargaining agreement may be treated as a plan that is separate from the portion of the plan that benefits employees included in a unit of employees covered by another collective bargaining agreement.

(ii) *Plans benefiting otherwise excludable employees.*—If an employer applies section 401(a)(26) separately to the portion of a plan that benefits only employees who satisfy age and service conditions under the plan that are lower than the greatest minimum age and service conditions permissible under section 410(a), the plan is treated as comprising separate plans, one benefiting the employees who have not satisfied the lower minimum age and service but not the greatest minimum age and service conditions permitted under section 410(a) and one benefiting employees who have satisfied the greatest minimum age and service conditions permitted under section 410(a). See §1.401(a)(26)-6(b)(1)(ii) for rules concerning testing of otherwise excludable employees. [Reg. §1.401(a)(26)-2.]

☐ [*T.D.* 8375, 12-2-91.]

[Reg. §1.401(a)(26)-3]

§1.401(a)(26)-3. Rules applicable to a defined benefit plan's prior benefit structure.—(a) *General rule.*—A defined benefit plan that does not meet one of the exceptions in §1.401(a)(26)-1(b) must satisfy paragraph (c) of this section with respect to its prior benefit structure. Defined contribution plans are not subject to this section.

(b) *Prior benefit structure.*—Each defined benefit plan has only one prior benefit structure, and all accrued benefits under the plan as of the beginning of a plan year (including benefits rolled over or transferred to the plan) are included in the prior benefit structure for the year.

(c) *Testing a prior benefit structure.*—(1) *General rule.*—A plan's prior benefit structure satisfies this paragraph if the plan provides meaningful benefits to a group of employees that includes the lesser of 50 employees or 40 percent of the employer's employees. Thus, a plan satisfies the requirements of this paragraph (c) if at least 50 employees or 40 percent of the employer's employees currently accrue meaningful benefits under the plan. Alternatively, a plan satisfies this paragraph if at least 50 employees and former employ-

ees or 40 percent of the employer's employees and former employees have meaningful accrued benefits under the plan.

(2) *Meaningful benefits.*—Whether a plan is providing meaningful benefits, or whether individuals have meaningful accrued benefits under a plan, is determined on the basis of all the facts and circumstances. The relevant factors in making this determination include, but are not limited to, the following: the level of current benefit accruals; the comparative rate of accruals under the current benefit formula compared to prior rates of accrual under the plan; the projected accrued benefits under the current benefit formula compared to accrued benefits as of the close of the immediately preceding plan year; the length of time the current benefit formula has been in effect; the number of employees with accrued benefits under the plan; and the length of time the plan has been in effect. A rule for determining whether an offset plan provides meaningful benefits is provided in §1.401(a)(26)-5(a)(2). A plan does not satisfy this paragraph (c) if it exists primarily to preserve accrued benefits for a small group of employees and thereby functions more as an individual plan for the small group of employees or for the employer.

(d) *Multiemployer plan rule.*—A multiemployer plan is deemed to satisfy the prior benefit structure rule in paragraph (c)(1) of this section for a plan year if the multiemployer plan provides meaningful benefits to at least 50 employees for a plan year, or 50 employees have meaningful accrued benefits under the plan. For purposes of this paragraph, all employees benefiting under the multiemployer plan may be considered, whether or not these employees are included in a unit of employees covered pursuant to any collective bargaining agreement. [Reg. §1.401(a)(26)-3.]

☐ [*T.D.* 8375, 12-2-91.]

[Reg. §1.401(a)(26)-4]

§1.401(a)(26)-4. Testing former employees.—(a) *Scope.*—This section applies to any defined benefit plan that benefits former employees in a plan year within the meaning of §1.401(a)(26)-5(b) and does not meet one of the exceptions in §1.401(a)(26)-1(b).

(b) *Minimum participation rule for former employees.*—Except as set forth in paragraph (c) of this section, a plan that is subject to this section must benefit at least the lesser of:

(1) 50 former employees of the employer, or

(2) 40 percent of the former employees of the employer.

(c) *Special rule.*—A plan satisfies the minimum participation rule in paragraph (b) of this section if the plan benefits at least five former employees, and if either:

(1) More than 95 percent of all former employees with vested accrued benefits under the plan benefit under the plan for the plan year, or

(2) At least 60 percent of the former employees who benefit under the plan for the plan year are nonhighly compensated former employees.

(d) *Excludable former employees.*—(1) *General rule.*—Whether a former employee is an excludable former employee for purposes of this section is determined under §1.401(a)(26)-6(c).

(2) *Exception.*—Solely for purposes of paragraph (c) of this section, the rule in §1.401(a)(26)-6(c)(4) (regarding vested accrued benefits eligible for mandatory distribution) does not apply to any former employee having a vested accrued benefit. Thus, a former employee who has a vested accrued benefit is not an excludable former employee merely because that vested accrued benefit does not exceed the cash-out limit in effect under §1.411(a)-11(c)(3)(ii). [Reg. §1.401(a)(26)-4.]

☐ [*T.D.* 8375, 12-2-91. *Amended by T.D.* 8794, 12-18-98 *and T.D.* 8891, 7-18-2000.]

[Reg. §1.401(a)(26)-5]

§1.401(a)(26)-5. Employees who benefit under a plan.—(a) *Employees benefiting under a plan.*—(1) *In general.*—Except as provided in paragraph (a)(2) of this section, an employee is treated as benefiting under a plan for a plan year if and only if, for that plan year, the employee would be treated as benefiting under the provisions of §1.410(b)-3(a), without regard to §1.410(b)-3(a)(iv).

(2) *Sequential or concurrent benefit offset arrangements.*—(i) *In general.*—An employee is treated as accruing a benefit under a plan that includes an offset or reduction of benefits that satisfies either paragraph (a)(2)(ii) or (a)(2)(iii) of this section if either the employee accrues a benefit under the plan for the year, or the employee would have accrued a benefit if the offset or reduction portion of the benefit formula were disregarded. In addition, an employee is treated as accruing a meaningful benefit for purposes of prior benefit structure testing under §1.401(a)(26)-3 if the employee would have accrued a

meaningful benefit if the offset or reduction portion of the benefit formula were disregarded.

(ii) *Offset by sequential or grandfathered benefits.*—An offset or reduction of benefits under a defined benefit plan satisfies this paragraph (a)(2) if the benefit formula provides that an employee will not accrue additional benefits under the current portion of the benefit formula until the employee has accrued, under such portion, a benefit in excess of such employee's benefit under one or more formulas in effect for prior years that are based wholly on prior years of service. The prior benefit may have accrued under the same or a separate plan, may be provided under the same or a separate plan and may relate to service with the same or previous employers. Benefits will not fail to be treated as based wholly on prior years if they are based, directly or indirectly, on compensation earned after such prior years (including compensation earned in the current year), if they are adjusted to reflect increases in the section 415 limitations, or if they are increased to provide an ad hoc cost of living adjustment designed to adjust, in whole or in part, for inflation. Furthermore, benefits do not fail to be treated as based wholly on prior years merely because the benefits (e.g., early retirement benefits) are subject to an age or years-of-service condition and, in applying the condition or conditions, the current and prior years are taken into account.

(iii) *Concurrent benefit offset arrangements.*—(A) *General rule.*— An offset or reduction of benefits under a defined benefit plan satisfies the requirements of this paragraph (a)(2)(iii) if the benefit formula provides a benefit that is offset or reduced by contributions or benefits under another plan that is maintained by the same employer and the following additional requirements are met:

(1) The contributions or benefits under a plan that are used to offset or reduce the benefits under the positive portion of the formula being tested accrued under such other plan;

(2) The employees who benefit under the formula being tested also benefit under the other plan on a reasonable and uniform basis; and

(3) The contributions or benefits under the plan that are used to offset or reduce the benefits under the formula being tested are not used to offset or reduce that employee's benefits under any other plan or any other formula.

(B) *Special rules for certain section 414(n) employer-recipients.*— The same employer requirement in the concurrent benefit offset rule in paragraph (a)(2)(iii)(A) of this section is waived for certain section 414(n) employer-recipients. Under this exception, an employer-recipient (within the meaning of sections 414(n) and (o)) may treat contributions or benefits under a plan maintained by a leasing organization as contributions or benefits accrued under the recipient organization plan provided the following requirements are met: the employer-recipient maintains a plan covering leased employees (which employees are treated as employees of the employer-recipient within the meaning of sections 414(n)(2) and 414(o)(2)); the leased employees are also covered under a plan maintained by the leasing organization; and contributions or benefits under the plan maintained by the employer-recipient are offset or reduced by the contributions or benefits under the leasing organization plan that are attributable to service with the recipient organization. Also, for purposes of the benefiting condition requirement in paragraph (a)(2)(iii)(A)(2) of this section, the employees of the employer-recipient who are not leased from the leasing organization are not required to benefit under the plan of the leasing organization.

(b) *Former employees benefiting under a plan.*—A former employee is treated as benefiting for a plan year if and only if the former employee would be treated as benefiting under the rules in §1.410(b)-3(b). [Reg. §1.401(a)(26)-5.]

☐ [T.D. 8375, 12-2-91.]

[Reg. §1.401(a)(26)-6]

§1.401(a)(26)-6. Excludable employees.—(a) *In general.*—For purposes of applying section 401(a)(26) with respect to either employees, former employees, or both employees and former employees, as applicable, all employees other than excludable employees described in paragraph (b) of this section, all former employees other than excludable former employees described in paragraph (c) of this section, or both, as the case may be, must be taken into account. Except as specifically provided otherwise in this section, the rules of this section are applied by reference only to the particular plan and must be applied on a uniform and consistent basis.

(b) *Excludable employees.*—An employee is an excludable employee if the employee is covered by one or more of the following exclusions:

(1) *Minimum age and service exclusions.*—(i) *In general.*—If a plan applies minimum age and service eligibility conditions permissible under section 410(a)(1) and excludes all employees who do not meet those conditions from benefiting under the plan, then all employees who fail to satisfy those conditions may be treated as excludable employees with respect to that plan. An employee is treated as meeting the age and service requirements on the date any employee with the same age and service would be eligible to commence participation in the plan, as provided in section 410(b)(4)(C).

(ii) *Plans benefiting otherwise excludable employees.*—An employer may treat a plan benefiting otherwise excludable employees as two separate plans, one for the otherwise excludable employees and one for the other employees benefiting under the plan. The effect of this rule is that employees who would be excludable under paragraph (b)(1) of this section (applied without regard to section 410(a)(1)(B)), but for the fact that the plan does not apply the greatest permissible minimum age and service conditions, may be treated as excludable employees with respect to the plan. This treatment is only available if each of the following conditions is satisfied:

(A) The plan under which the otherwise excludable employees benefit also benefits employees who are not otherwise excludable.

(B) The plan under which the otherwise excludable employees benefit satisfies section 401(a)(26), both by reference only to otherwise excludable employees and by reference only to employees who are not otherwise excludable.

(C) The contributions or benefits provided to the otherwise excludable employees (expressed as percentages of compensation) are not greater than the contributions or benefits provided to the employees who are not otherwise excludable under the plan.

(D) No highly compensated employee is included in the group of otherwise excludable employees for more than one plan year.

(iii) *Examples.*—The following examples illustrate some of the minimum-age-and-service exclusion requirements:

Example 1. Employer X maintains a defined contribution plan, Plan X, under which employees who have not completed 1 year of service are not eligible to participate. Employer X has six employees. Two of the employees participate in Plan X. The other four employees have not completed 1 year of service and are therefore not eligible to participate in Plan X. The four employees who have not completed 1 year of service are excludable employees and may be disregarded for purposes of applying the minimum participation test. Therefore, Plan X satisfies section 401(a)(26) because both of the two employees who must be considered are participants in Plan X.

Example 2. Employer Y has 100 employees and maintains two plans, Plan 1 and Plan 2. Plan 1 provides that employees who have not completed 1 year of service are not eligible to participate. Plan 2 has no minimum age or service requirement. Twenty of Y's employees do not meet the minimum service requirement under Plan 1. Each plan satisfies the ratio test under section 410(b)(1)(B). In testing Plan 1 to determine whether it satisfies section 401(a)(26), the 20 employees not meeting the minimum age and service requirement under Plan 1 are treated as excludable employees. In testing Plan 2 to determine whether it satisfies section 401(a)(26), no employees are treated as excludable employees because Plan 2 does not have a minimum age or service requirement.

(2) *Certain air pilots.*—An employee who is excluded from consideration under section 410(b)(3)(B) (relating to certain air pilots) may be treated as an excludable employee.

(3) *Certain nonresident aliens.*—(i) *In general.*—An employee who is excluded from consideration under section 410(b)(3)(C) (relating to certain nonresident aliens) may be treated as an excludable employee.

(ii) *Special treaty rule.*—In addition, an employee who is a nonresident alien (within the meaning of section 7701(b)(1)(B)) and who does receive earned income (within the meaning of section 911(d)(2)) from the employer that constitutes income from sources within the United States (within the meaning of section 861(a)(3)) is permitted to be excluded, if all of the employee's earned income from the employer from sources within the United States is exempt from United States income tax under an applicable income tax convention. This paragraph (b)(3)(ii) applies only if all employees described in the preceding sentence are so excluded.

(4) *Employees covered pursuant to a collective bargaining agreement.*—When testing a plan benefiting only noncollectively bargained employees, an employee who is excluded from consideration under section 410(b)(3)(A) (exclusion for employees included in a unit of employees covered by a collective bargaining agreement) may be treated as an excludable employee. This rule may be applied separately to each collective bargaining agreement. See

§1.401(a)(26)-8 for the definitions of the terms "collective bargaining agreement", "collectively bargained employee," and "covered pursuant to a collective bargaining agreement".

(5) *Employees not covered pursuant to a collective bargaining agreement.*—When testing a plan that benefits only employees who are included in a group of employees who are covered pursuant to a collective bargaining agreement, an employee who is not included in the group of employees who are covered by the collective bargaining agreement may be treated as an excludable employee.

(6) *Examples.*—The following examples illustrate the excludable employee rules that relate to employees covered pursuant to collective bargaining agreements. For purposes of these examples assume that no other exclusion rules are applicable.

Example 1. Employer W has 70 collectively bargained employees and 30 non-collectively bargained employees. Employer W maintains Plan W, which benefits only the 30 non-collectively bargained employees. The 70 collectively bargained employees may be treated as excludable employees and thus may be disregarded in applying section 401(a)(26) to Plan W.

Example 2. Assume the same facts as *Example 1*, except that the Commissioner has determined that the employee representative is not a bona fide employee representative under section 7701(a)(46) and thus there are no "collectively bargained employees." In this case, all employees of W must be considered in determining whether section 401(a)(26) is met.

Example 3. Employer X has 30 collectively bargained employees and 70 non-collectively bargained employees. Employer X maintains Plan X, which benefits only the 30 collectively bargained employees. Employer X may treat the non-collectively bargained employees as excludable employees and disregard them in applying section 401(a)(26) to the collectively bargained plan.

Example 4. Assume the same facts as *Example 3*, except that the Commissioner has determined that the employee representative is not a bona fide employee representative under section 7701(a)(46) and thus there is no recognized collective bargaining agreement. In this case, Employer X may not treat the non-collectively bargained employees of X as excludable employees.

Example 5. Assume the same facts as *Example 3*, except that 3 percent of the 30 collectively bargained employees are professionals. In this case, Employer X may not treat the non-collectively bargained employees of X as excludable employees.

Example 6. Employer Y has 100 collectively bargained employees. Thirty of Y's employees are represented by Collective Bargaining Unit 1 and covered under Plan 1. Seventy of Y's employees are represented by Collective Bargaining Unit 2 and covered under Plan 2. For purposes of testing Plan 1, the employees of Collective Bargaining Unit 2 may be treated as excludable employees. Similarly, for purposes of testing Plan 2, the employees of Collective Bargaining Unit 1 may be treated as excludable employees.

(7) *Certain terminating employees.*—(i) *In general.*—An employee may be treated as an excludable employee for a plan year with respect to a particular plan if—

(A) The employee does not benefit under the plan for the plan year,

(B) The employee is eligible to participate in the plan,

(C) The plan has a minimum period of service requirement or a requirement that an employee be employed on the last day of the plan year (last-day requirement) in order for an employee to accrue a benefit or receive an allocation for the plan year,

(D) The employee fails to accrue a benefit or receive an allocation under the plan solely because of the failure to satisfy the minimum period of service or last-day requirement,

(E) The employee terminates employment during the plan year with no more than 500 hours of service, and the employee is not an employee as of the last day of the plan year (for purposes of this paragraph (b)(7)(i)(E), a plan that uses the elapsed time method of determining years of service may use either 91 consecutive calendar days or 3 consecutive calendar months instead of 500 hours of service, provided it uses the same convention for all employees during a plan year), and

(F) If this paragraph (b)(7) is applied with respect to any employee with respect to a plan for a plan year, it is applied with respect to all employees with respect to the plan for the plan year.

(ii) *Hours of service.*—For purposes of this paragraph (b)(7), the term "hour of service" has the same meaning as set forth in 29 CFR §2530.200b-2 under the general method of crediting service for the *employee*. If one of the equivalencies set forth in 29 CFR §2530.200b-3 is used for crediting service under the plan, the 500-hour requirement must be adjusted accordingly.

(8) *Employees of qualified separate lines of business.*—If an employer is treated as operating qualified separate lines of business for pur-

poses of section 401(a)(26) in accordance with §1.414(r)-1(b), in testing a plan that benefits employees of one qualified separate line of business, the employees of the other qualified separate lines of business of the employer are treated as excludable employees. See §§1.414(r)-1(c)(3) and 1.414(r)-9 (separate application of section 401(a)(26) to the employees of a qualified separate line of business). The rule in this paragraph (b)(8) does not apply to a plan that is tested under the special rule for employer-wide plans in §1.414(r)-1(C)(3)(ii) for a plan year.

(c) *Former employees.*—(1) *In general.*—For purposes of applying section 401(a)(26) with respect to former employees, all former employees of the employer are taken into account, except that the employer may treat a former employee described in paragraphs (c)(2) through (c)(4) of this section as an excludable former employee. If any of the former employee exclusion rules under paragraphs (c)(2) through (c)(4) of this section is applied, it must be applied to all former employees for the plan year on a consistent basis.

(2) *Employees terminated before a specified date.*—The employer may treat a former employee as excludable if—

(i) The former employee became a former employee either prior to January 1, 1984, or prior to the tenth calendar year preceding the calendar year in which the current plan year begins, and

(ii) The former employee became a former employee in a calendar year that precedes the earliest calendar year in which any former employee who benefits under the plan in the current plan year became a former employee.

(3) *Previously excludable employees.*—The employer may treat a former employee as excludable if the former employee was an excludable employee (or would have been an excludable employee if these regulations had been in effect) under the rules of paragraphs (a) and (b) of this section during the plan year in which the former employee became a former employee. If the employer treats a former employee as excludable pursuant to this paragraph (c)(3), the former employee is not taken into account with respect to a plan even if the former employee is benefiting under the plan.

(4) *Vested accrued benefits eligible for mandatory distribution.*—A former employee may be treated as an excludable former employee if the present value of the former employee's vested accrued benefit does not exceed the cash-out limit in effect under §1.411(a)-11(c)(3)(ii). This determination is made in accordance with the rules of sections 411(a)(11) and 417(e).

(d) *Certain police or firefighters.*—An employer may apply section 401(a)(26) separately with respect to any classification of qualified public safety employees for whom a separate plan is maintained. Thus, for purposes of testing a separate plan covering a class of qualified public safety employees, all employees who are not in that classification are treated as excludable employees. Also, such employees need not be taken into account in determining whether or not any other plan satisfies section 401(a)(26). For purposes of this paragraph (d), "qualified public safety employee" means any employee of any police department or fire department organized and operated by a State or political subdivision if the employee provides police protection, firefighting services, or emergency medical services for any area within the jurisdiction of a State or political subdivision. [Reg. §1.401(a)(26)-6.]

☐ [*T.D. 8375, 12-2-91. Amended by T.D. 8794, 12-18-98 and T.D. 8891, 7-18-2000.*]

[Reg. §1.401(a)(26)-7]

§1.401(a)(26)-7. Testing methods.—(a) *Testing on each day of the plan year.*—A plan satisfies section 401(a)(26) for a plan year only if the plan satisfies section 401(a)(26) on each day of the plan year. An employee benefits on a day if the employee is a participant for such day and the employee benefits under the plan for the year under the rules in §1.401(a)(26)-5.

(b) *Simplified testing method.*—A plan is treated as satisfying the requirements of paragraph (a) of this section if it satisfies section 401(a)(26) on any single plan day during the plan year, but only if that day is reasonably representative of the employer's workforce and the plan's coverage. A plan does not have to be tested on the same day each plan year.

(c) *Retroactive correction.*—If a plan fails to satisfy section 401(a)(26) for a plan year, the plan may be retroactively amended during the same period and under the same conditions as provided for in §1.401(a)(4)-11(g)(3) through (g)(5) to satisfy section 401(a)(26). A plan merger that occurs by the end of the period provided in §1.401(a)(4)-11(g)(3)(iv) is treated solely for purposes of section 401(a)(26) as if it were effective as of the first day of the plan year. The rule of this paragraph (c) may be illustrated by the following example.

Example. Assume that an employer with 500 employees maintains two defined contribution plans. Plan A benefits 45 employees. Plan B benefits 50 employees. Immediately before the end of the period provided for in §1.401(a)(4)-11(g)(3)(iv), the employer expands coverage under Plan A to benefit 20 more employees retroactively for the plan year. Thus, Plan A satisfies paragraph (a) of this section for the plan year. Alternatively, before the end of the period provided for in §1.401(a)(4)-11(g)(3)(iv), or later if a later period is applicable under section 401(b), the employer could merge Plan A with Plan B to satisfy section 401(a)(26). [Reg. §1.401(a)(26)-7.]

☐ [T.D. 8375, 12-2-91.]

[Reg. §1.401(a)(26)-8]

§1.401(a)(26)-8. Definitions.—In applying this section and §§1.401(a)(26)-1 through 1.401(a)(26)-9 the definitions in this section govern unless otherwise provided.

Collective bargaining agreement. "Collective bargaining agreement" means an agreement that the Secretary of Labor finds to be a collective bargaining agreement between employee representatives and the employer that satisfies §301.7701-17T. Employees described in section 413(b)(8) who are employees of the union or the plan and are treated as employees of an employer are not employees covered pursuant to a collective bargaining agreement for purposes of section 401(a)(26) unless the employees are actually covered pursuant to such an agreement.

Collectively bargained employee. "Collectively bargained employee" means a collectively bargained employee within the meaning of §1.410(b)-6(d)(2).

Covered by a collective bargaining agreement. "Covered by a collective bargaining agreement" means covered by a collective bargaining agreement within the meaning of §1.410-6(d)(2)(iii).

Defined benefit plan. "Defined benefit plan" means a defined benefit plan within the meaning of §1.410(b)-9.

Defined contribution plan. "Defined contribution plan" means a defined contribution plan within the meaning of §1.410(b)-9.

Employee. "Employee" means an employee, within the meaning of §1.410(b)-9.

Employer. "Employer" means the employer within the meaning of §1.410(b)-9.

ESOP. "ESOP" means an employee stock ownership plan within the meaning of section 4975(e)(7) or a tax credit employee stock ownership plan within the meaning of section 409(a).

Former employee. "Former employee" means a former employee within the meaning of §1.410(b)-9.

Highly compensated employee. "Highly compensated employee" means an employee who is highly compensated within the meaning of section 414(q).

Highly compensated former employee. "Highly compensated former employee" means a former employee who is highly compensated within the meaning of section 414(q)(9).

Multiemployer plan. "Multiemployer plan" means a multiemployer plan within the meaning of section 414(f).

Noncollectively bargained employee. "Noncollectively bargained employee" means an employee who is not a collectively bargained employee.

Nonhighly compensated employee. "Nonhighly compensated employee" means an employee who is not a highly compensated employee.

Nonhighly compensated former employee. "Nonhighly compensated former employee" means a former employee who is not a highly compensated former employee.

Plan. "Plan" means plan as defined in §1.401(a)(26)-2(c).

Plan year. "Plan year" means the plan year of the plan as defined in the written plan document. In the absence of a specifically designated plan year, the plan year is deemed to be the calendar year.

Professional employee. "Professional employee" means a professional employee as defined in §1.410(b)-9.

Section 401(k) plan. "Section 401(k) plan" means a plan consisting of elective contributions described in §1.401(k)-1(g)(3) under a qualified cash or deferred arrangement described in §1.401(k)-1(a)(4)(i).

Section 401(m) plan. "Section 401(m) plan" means a plan consisting of employee contributions described in §1.401(m)-1(f)(6) or matching contributions described in §1.401(m)-1(f)(12), or both. [Reg. §1.401(a)(26)-8.]

☐ [T.D. 8375, 12-2-91.]

[Reg. §1.401(a)(26)-9]

§1.401(a)(26)-9. Effective dates and transition rules.—(a) *In general.*—Except as provided in paragraphs (b), (c), and (d) of this section, section 401(a)(26) and the regulations thereunder apply to plan years beginning on or after January 1, 1989.

(b) *Transition rules.*—(1) *Governmental plans and certain section 403(b) annuities.*—Section 401(a)(26) is treated as satisfied for plan years beginning before the later of January 1, 1996, or 90 days after the opening of the first legislative session beginning on or after January 1, 1996, of the governing body with authority to amend the plan, if that body does not meet continuously, in the case of governmental plans described in section 414(d), including plans subject to section 403(b)(12)(A)(i) (nonelective plans). For purposes of this paragraph (b)(1), the term "governing body with authority to amend the plan" means the legislature, board, commission, council, or other governing body with authority to amend the plan.

(2) *Early retirement "window-period" benefits.*—Early retirement benefits available under a plan only to employees who retire within a limited period of time, not to exceed one year, are treated as satisfying section 401(a)(26) if such benefits are provided under plan terms that were adopted and in effect on or before March 14, 1989.

(3) *Employees who do not benefit because of a minimum-period-of-service requirement or a last-day requirement.*—For the first plan year beginning after December 31, 1988, and before January 1, 1990, employees who are eligible to participate under the plan and who fail to accrue a benefit solely because of the failure to satisfy either a minimum-period-of-service requirement of 1000 hours of service or less or a last-day requirement may be treated as benefiting under the plan.

(4) *Certain plan terminations.*—(i) *In general.*—Except as provided in paragraph (b)(4)(ii) of this section, if a plan terminates after section 401(a)(26) becomes effective with respect to the plan (as determined under paragraph (a) of this section), the plan is not treated as a qualified plan upon termination unless it complies with section 401(a)(26) and the regulations thereunder (to the extent they are applicable) for all periods for which section 401(a)(26) is effective with respect to the plan.

(ii) *Exception.*—Notwithstanding paragraphs (a) and (b)(4)(i) of this section, a plan does not fail to be treated as a qualified plan upon termination merely because the plan fails to satisfy the requirements of section 401(a)(26) and the regulations thereunder if the plan is terminated with a termination date on or before December 31, 1989, and either of the following conditions is satisfied:

(A) In the case of a defined benefit plan, no highly compensated employee has an accrued benefit under the plan exceeding the lesser of either the benefit the employee had accrued as of the close of the last plan year beginning before January 1, 1989, or the benefit the employee would have accrued as of the close of the last plan year under the terms of the plan in effect and applicable with respect to the employee on December 13, 1988.

(B) In the case of a defined contribution plan, no highly compensated employee receives a contribution allocation for any plan year beginning after December 31, 1988. For this purpose, a contribution allocation with respect to an employee for a plan year beginning before January 1, 1989, may be treated as a contribution allocation for a plan year beginning after December 31, 1988, if the allocation for the prior year exceeds the allocation that the employee would have received for such year under the terms of the plan in effect and applicable with respect to the employee on December 13, 1988. An allocation of forfeitures to highly compensated employees with respect to contributions made for plan years beginning before January 1, 1988, does not cause a defined contribution plan to fail to satisfy the conditions of this paragraph (b)(4)(ii)(B).

(5) *ESOPs and non-ESOPs.*—Notwithstanding paragraph (a) of this section and §54.4975-11(a)(5) of this Chapter, an employer may treat the rule in §1.401(a)(26)-2(d)(1)(i), regarding mandatory disaggregation of ESOPs and non-ESOPs as not effective for plan years beginning before January 1, 1990.

(c) *Waiver of excise tax on reversions.*—(1) *In general.*—Pursuant to section 1112(e)(3) of the Tax Reform Act of 1986 (TRA '86), if certain conditions are satisfied, a waiver of the excise tax under section 4980 applies with respect to any employer reversion that occurs by reason of the termination or merger of a plan before the first year to which section 401(a)(26) applies to the plan. In general, the applicable conditions are that the plan must have been in existence on August 16, 1986; that if section 401(a)(26) was in effect for the plan year including August 16, 1986, the plan would have failed to satisfy the requirements of section 401(a)(26) and would have continued to fail the requirements at all times thereafter; that the plan satisfies the applicable conditions in paragraph (b)(4)(ii)(A) or (B) of this section; and that certain requirements regarding asset or liability transfers and mergers and spinoffs involving the plan after August 16, 1986, are satisfied.

(2) *Termination date.*—An employer reversion with respect to a plan is eligible for the section 4980 excise tax waiver only if the

employer reversion occurs by reason of the termination of the plan with a termination date prior to the first plan year for which section 401(a)(26) applies to the plan. Solely for purposes of this waiver, the employer reversion is treated as satisfying this paragraph (c)(2) even though the plan's termination date is during the first plan year for which section 401(a)(26) applies to the plan if the plan's termination date is on or before May 31, 1989. If the termination date occurs in the first plan year for which section 401(a)(26) applied to the plan and the employer receives a reversion that is eligible for the waiver of the section 4980 tax, the plan is subject to the interest rate restriction set forth in section 1112(e)(3)(B) of TRA '86 as amended.

(3) *Failure to satisfy section 401(a)(26).*—An employer reversion with respect to a plan is eligible for the excise tax waiver only if the plan was in existence on August 16, 1986, and, if section 401(a)(26) had applied to the plan for the plan year including such date, the plan would have failed to satisfy section 401(a)(26) for the plan year and continuously thereafter until the plan's termination or merger. For purposes of this paragraph (c)(3), a plan is treated as though it would have failed to satisfy section 401(a)(26) before such section actually applied to the plan only if the plan (as defined under section 414(l)), failed to benefit at least the lesser of 50 employees or 40 percent of the employer's employees. In general, this determination is to be made on the basis of only the applicable statutory provisions, without regard to the regulations under section 401(a)(26). Thus, for example, the prior benefit structure rules in § 1.401(a)(26)-3 do not apply in determining whether a plan would have failed to satisfy section 401(a)(26) for plan years beginning prior to the effective date of section 401(a)(26) with respect to the plan.

(d) *Special rule for collective bargaining agreements.*—In the case of a plan maintained pursuant to one or more collective bargaining agreements (as defined in § 1.401(a)(26)-8(a)) that were ratified before March 1, 1986, section 401(a)(26) and the regulations thereunder shall not apply to plan years beginning before the earlier of—

(1) January 1, 1991, or

(2) The later of—

(i) January 1, 1989, or

(ii) The date on which the last of such collective bargaining agreements terminates. For purposes of this paragraph (d), any extension or renegotiation of any collective bargaining agreement that is ratified after February 28, 1986, is disregarded in determining the date on which such collective bargaining agreement terminates. [Reg. § 1.401(a)(26)-9.]

☐ [*T.D.* 8375, 12-2-91. *Amended by T.D.* 8487, 8-31-93.]

[Reg. § 1.401(a)-30]

§ 1.401(a)-30. Limit on elective deferrals.—(a) *General Rule.*—A trust that is part of a plan under which elective deferrals may be made during a calendar year is not qualified under section 401(a) unless the plan provides that the elective deferrals on behalf of an individual under the plan and all other plans, contracts, or arrangements of the employer maintaining the plan may not exceed the applicable limit for the individual's taxable year beginning in the calendar year. A plan may incorporate the applicable limit by reference. In the case of a plan maintained by more than one employer to which section 413(b) or (c) applies, section 401(a)(30) and this section are applied as if each employer maintained a separate plan. See § 1.402(g)-1(e) for rules permitting the distribution of excess deferrals to prevent disqualification of a plan or trust for failure to comply in operation with section 401(a)(30).

(b) *Definitions.*—For purposes of this section:

(1) *Applicable limit.*—The term "applicable limit" has the meaning provided in § 1.402(g)-1(d).

(2) *Elective deferrals.*—The term "elective deferrals" has the meaning provided in § 1.402(g)-1(b).

(c) *Effective date.*—(1) *In general.*—Except as otherwise provided in this paragraph (c), this section is effective for plan years beginning after December 31, 1987.

(2) *Transition rule.*—For plan years beginning in 1988, a plan may rely on a reasonable interpretation of the law as in effect on December 31, 1987.

(3) *Deferrals under collective bargaining agreements.*—In the case of a plan maintained pursuant to one or more collective bargaining agreements between employee representatives and one or more employers ratified before March 1, 1986, this section does not apply to *contributions made pursuant to a collective bargaining agreement* for plan years beginning before the earlier of:

(i) The later of January 1, 1988, or the date on which the last collective bargaining agreement terminates (determined without regard to any extension thereof after February 28, 1986), or

(ii) January 1, 1989. [Reg. § 1.401(a)-30.]

☐ [*T.D.* 8357, 8-8-91.]

[Reg. § 1.401(a)(31)-1]

§ 1.401(a)(31)-1. Requirement to offer direct rollover of eligible rollover distributions; questions and answers.—The following questions and answers relate to the qualification requirement imposed by section 401(a)(31) of the Internal Revenue Code of 1986, pertaining to the direct rollover option for eligible rollover distributions from pension, profit-sharing, and stock bonus plans. Section 401(a)(31) was added by section 522(a) of the Unemployment Compensation Amendments of 1992, Public Law 102-318, 106 Stat. 290 (UCA). For additional UCA guidance under sections 402(c), 402(f), 403(b)(8) and (10), and 3405(c), see §§ 1.402(c)-2, 1.402(f)-1, and 1.403(b)-7(b), and § 31.3405(c)-1 of this chapter, respectively.

LIST OF QUESTIONS

Q-1: What are the direct rollover requirements under section 401(a)(31)?

Q-2: Does section 401(a)(31) require that a qualified plan permit a direct rollover to be made to a qualified trust that is not part of a defined contribution plan?

Q-3: What is a *direct rollover* that satisfies section 401(a)(31), and how is it accomplished?

Q-4: Is providing a distributee with a check for delivery to an eligible retirement plan a reasonable means of accomplishing a direct rollover?

Q-5: Is an eligible rollover distribution that is paid to an eligible retirement plan in a direct rollover currently includible in gross income or subject to 20-percent withholding?

Q-6: What procedures may a plan administrator prescribe for electing a direct rollover, and what information may the plan administrator require a distributee to provide when electing a direct rollover?

Q-7: May the plan administrator treat a distributee as having made an election under a default procedure where the distributee does not affirmatively elect to make or not make a direct rollover within a certain time period?

Q-8: May the plan administrator establish a deadline after which the distributee may not revoke an election to make or not make a direct rollover?

Q-9: Must the plan administrator permit a distributee to elect to have a portion of an eligible rollover distribution paid to an eligible retirement plan in a direct rollover and to have the remainder of that distribution paid to the distributee?

Q-10: Must the plan administrator allow a distributee to divide an eligible rollover distribution into two or more separate distributions to be paid in direct rollovers to two or more eligible retirement plans?

Q-11: Will a plan satisfy section 401(a)(31) if the plan administrator does not permit a distributee to elect a direct rollover if his or her eligible rollover distributions during a year are reasonably expected to total less than $200?

Q-12: Is a plan administrator permitted to treat a distributee's election to make or not make a direct rollover with respect to one payment in a series of periodic payments as applying to all subsequent payments in the series?

Q-13: Is the eligible retirement plan designated by a distributee to receive a direct rollover distribution required to accept the distribution?

Q-14: If a plan accepts an invalid rollover contribution, whether or not as a direct rollover, how will the contribution be treated for purposes of applying the qualification requirements of section 401(a) or 403(a) to the plan?

Q-15: For purposes of applying the plan qualification requirements of section 401(a), is an eligible rollover distribution that is paid to an eligible retirement plan in a direct rollover a distribution and rollover or is it a transfer of assets and liabilities?

Q-16: Must a direct rollover option be provided for an eligible rollover distribution that is in the form of a plan loan offset amount?

Q-17: Must a direct rollover option be provided for an eligible rollover distribution from a qualified plan distributed annuity contract?

Q-18: What assumptions may a plan administrator make regarding whether a benefit is an eligible rollover distribution?

Q-19: When must a qualified plan be amended to comply with section 401(a)(31)?

QUESTIONS AND ANSWERS

Q-1: What are the direct rollover requirements under section 401(a)(31)?

A-1: (a) *General rule.* To satisfy section 401(a)(31), added by UCA, a plan must provide that if the distributee of any eligible rollover distribution elects to have the distribution paid directly to an eligible retirement plan, and specifies the eligible retirement plan to which the distribution is to be paid, then the distribution will be paid to that eligible retirement plan in a direct rollover described in Q&A-3 of this section. Thus, the plan must give the distributee the option of having his or her distribution paid in a direct rollover to an eligible retirement plan specified by the distributee. For purposes of section 401(a)(31) and this section, eligible rollover distribution has the meaning set forth in section 402(c)(4) and §1.402(c)-2, Q&A-3 through Q&A-10 and Q&A-14, except as otherwise provided in Q&A-2 of this section, eligible retirement plan has the meaning set forth in section 402(c)(8)(B) and §1.402(c)-2, Q&A-2.

(b) *Related Internal Revenue Code provisions*—(1) *Mandatory withholding*. If a distributee of an eligible rollover distribution does not elect to have the eligible rollover distribution paid directly from the plan to an eligible retirement plan in a direct rollover under section 401(a)(31), the eligible rollover distribution is subject to 20-percent income tax withholding under section 3405(c). See §31.3405(c)-1 of this chapter for guidance concerning the withholding requirements applicable to eligible rollover distributions.

(2) *Notice requirement*. Section 402(f) requires the plan administrator of a qualified plan to provide, within a reasonable period of time before making an eligible rollover distribution, a written explanation to the distributee of the distributee's right to elect a direct rollover and the withholding consequences of not making that election. The explanation also is required to provide certain other relevant information relating to the taxation of distributions. See §1.402(f)-1 for guidance concerning the written explanation required under section 402(f).

(3) *Section 403(b) annuities*. Section 403(b)(10) provides that requirements similar to those imposed by section 401(a)(31) apply to annuities described in section 403(b). See §1.403(b)-7(b) for guidance concerning the direct rollover requirements for distributions from annuities described in section 403(b).

(c) *Effective date*—(1) *Statutory effective date*. Section 401(a)(31) applies to eligible rollover distributions made on or after January 1, 1993.

(2) *Regulatory effective date*. This section applies to eligible rollover distributions made on or after October 19, 1995. For eligible rollover distributions made on or after January 1, 1993 and before October 19, 1995, §1.401(a)(31)-1T (as it appeared in the April 1, 1995 edition of 26 CFR part 1), applies. However, for any distribution made on or after January 1, 1993 but before October 19, 1995, a plan may satisfy section 401(a)(31) by substituting any or all provisions of this section for the corresponding provisions of §1.401(a)(31)-1T, if any.

Q-2: Does section 401(a)(31) require that a qualified plan permit a direct rollover to be made to a qualified trust that is not part of a defined contribution plan?

A-2: No. Section 401(a)(31)(D) limits the types of qualified trusts that are treated as eligible retirement plans to defined contribution plans that accept eligible rollover distributions. Therefore, although a plan is permitted, at a participant's election, to make a direct rollover to any type of eligible retirement plan, as defined in section 402(c)(8)(B) (including a defined benefit plan), a plan will not fail to satisfy section 401(a)(31) solely because the plan will not permit a direct rollover to a qualified trust that is part of a defined benefit plan. In contrast, if a distributee elects a direct rollover of an eligible rollover distribution to an annuity plan described in section 403(a), that distribution must be paid to the annuity plan, even if the recipient annuity plan is a defined benefit plan.

Q-3: What is a *direct rollover* that satisfies section 401(a)(31), and how is it accomplished?

A-3: A direct rollover that satisfies section 401(a)(31) is an eligible rollover distribution that is paid directly to an eligible retirement plan for the benefit of the distributee. A direct rollover may be accomplished by any reasonable means of direct payment to an eligible retirement plan. Reasonable means of direct payment include, for example, a wire transfer or the mailing of a check to the eligible retirement plan. If payment is made by check, the check must be negotiable only by the trustee of the eligible retirement plan. If the payment is made by wire transfer, the wire transfer must be directed only to the trustee of the eligible retirement plan. In the case of an eligible retirement plan that does not have a trustee (such as a custodial individual retirement account or an individual retirement annuity), the custodian of the plan or issuer of the contract under the plan, as appropriate, should be substituted for the trustee for purposes of this Q&A-3, and Q&A-4 of this section.

Q-4: Is providing a distributee with a check for delivery to an eligible retirement plan a reasonable means of accomplishing a direct rollover?

A-4: Providing the distributee with a check and instructing the distributee to deliver the check to the eligible retirement plan is a reasonable means of direct payment, provided that the check is made payable as follows: [Name of the trustee] as trustee of [name of the eligible retirement plan]. For example, if the name of the eligible retirement plan is "Individual Retirement Account of John Q. Smith," and the name of the trustee is "ABC Bank," the payee line of a check

would read "ABC Bank as trustee of Individual Retirement Account of John Q. Smith." Unless the name of the distributee is included in the name of the eligible retirement plan, the check also must indicate that it is for the benefit of the distributee. If the eligible retirement plan is not an individual retirement account or an individual retirement annuity, the payee line of the check need not identify the trustee by name. For example, the payee line of a check for the benefit of distributee Jane Doe might read, "Trustee of XYZ Corporation Savings Plan FBO Jane Doe."

Q-5: Is an eligible rollover distribution that is paid to an eligible retirement plan in a direct rollover currently includible in gross income or subject to 20-percent withholding?

A-5: No. An eligible rollover distribution that is paid to an eligible retirement plan in a direct rollover is not currently includible in the distributee's gross income under section 402(c) and is exempt from the 20-percent withholding imposed under section 3405(c)(2). However, when any portion of the eligible rollover distribution is subsequently distributed from the eligible retirement plan, that portion will be includible in gross income to the extent required under section 402, 403, or 408.

Q-6: What procedures may a plan administrator prescribe for electing a direct rollover, and what information may the plan administrator require a distributee to provide when electing a direct rollover?

A-6: (a) *Permissible procedures*. Except as otherwise provided in paragraph (b) of this Q&A-6, the plan administrator may prescribe any procedure for a distributee to elect a direct rollover under section 401(a)(31), provided that the procedure is reasonable. The procedure may include any reasonable requirement for information or documentation from the distributee in addition to the items of adequate information specified in §31.3405(c)-1(b), Q&A-7 of this chapter. For example, it would be reasonable for the plan administrator to require that the distributee provide a statement from the designated recipient plan that the plan will accept the direct rollover for the benefit of the distributee and that the recipient plan is, or is intended to be, an individual retirement account, an individual retirement annuity, a qualified annuity plan described in section 403(a), or a qualified trust described in section 401(a), as applicable. In the case of a designated recipient plan that is a qualified trust, it also would be reasonable for the plan administrator to require a statement that the qualified trust is not excepted from the definition of an eligible retirement plan by section 401(a)(31)(D) (i.e., is not a defined benefit plan).

(b) *Impermissible procedures*. A plan will fail to satisfy section 401(a)(31) if the plan administrator prescribes any unreasonable procedure, or requires information or documentation, that effectively eliminates or substantially impairs the distributee's ability to elect a direct rollover. For example, it would effectively eliminate or substantially impair the distributee's ability to elect a direct rollover if the recipient plan required the distributee to obtain an opinion of counsel stating that the eligible retirement plan receiving the rollover is a qualified plan or individual retirement account. Similarly, it would effectively eliminate or substantially impair the distributee's ability to elect a direct rollover if the distributing plan required a letter from the recipient eligible retirement plan stating that, upon request by the distributing plan, the recipient plan will automatically return any direct rollover amount that the distributing plan advises the recipient plan was paid incorrectly. It would also effectively eliminate or substantially impair the distributee's ability to elect a direct rollover if the distributing plan required, as a condition for making a direct rollover, a letter from the recipient eligible retirement plan indemnifying the distributing plan for any liability arising from the distribution.

Q-7: May the plan administrator treat a distributee as having made an election under a default procedure where the distributee does not affirmatively elect to make or not make a direct rollover within a certain time period?

A-7: Yes, the plan administrator may establish a default procedure whereby any distributee who fails to make an affirmative election is treated as having either made or not made a direct rollover election. However, the plan administrator may not make a distribution under any default procedure unless the distributee has received an explanation of the default procedure and an explanation of the direct rollover option as required under section 402(f) and §1.402(f)-1, Q&A-1 and unless the timing requirements described in §1.402(f)-1, Q&A-2 and Q&A-3 have been satisfied with respect to the explanations of both the default procedure and the direct rollover option.

Q-8: May the plan administrator establish a deadline after which the distributee may not revoke an election to make or not make a direct rollover?

A-8: Yes, but the plan administrator is not permitted to prescribe any deadline or time period with respect to revocation of a direct rollover election that is more restrictive for the distributee than that which otherwise applies under the plan to revocation of the form of distribution elected by the distributee.

Reg. §1.401(a)(31)-1

Q-9: Must the plan administrator permit a distributee to elect to have a portion of an eligible rollover distribution paid to an eligible retirement plan in a direct rollover and to have the remainder of that distribution paid to the distributee?

A-9: Yes, the plan administrator must permit a distributee to elect to have a portion of an eligible rollover distribution paid to an eligible retirement plan in a direct rollover and to have the remainder paid to the distributee. However, the plan administrator is permitted to require that, if the distributee elects to have only a portion of an eligible rollover distribution paid to an eligible retirement plan in a direct rollover, that portion be equal to at least a specified minimum amount, provided the specified minimum amount is less than or equal to $500 or any greater amount as prescribed by the Commissioner in revenue rulings, notices, and other guidance published in the Internal Revenue Bulletin. See §601.601(d)(2)(ii)(b) of this chapter. If the entire amount of the eligible rollover distribution is less than or equal to the specified minimum amount, the plan administrator need not allow the distributee to divide the distribution.

Q-10: Must the plan administrator allow a distributee to divide an eligible rollover distribution into two or more separate distributions to be paid in direct rollovers to two or more eligible retirement plans?

A-10: No. The plan administrator is not required (but is permitted) to allow the distributee to divide an eligible rollover distribution into separate distributions to be paid to two or more eligible retirement plans in direct rollovers. Thus, the plan administrator may require that the distributee select a single eligible retirement plan to which the eligible rollover distribution (or portion thereof) will be distributed in a direct rollover.

Q-11: Will a plan satisfy section 401(a)(31) if the plan administrator does not permit a distributee to elect a direct rollover if his or her eligible rollover distributions during a year are reasonably expected to total less than $200?

A-11: Yes. A plan will satisfy section 401(a)(31) even though the plan administrator does not permit any distributee to elect a direct rollover with respect to eligible rollover distributions during a year that are reasonably expected to total less than $200 or any lower minimum amount specified by the plan administrator. The rules described in §31.3405(c)-1, Q&A-14 of this chapter (relating to whether withholding under section 3405(c) is required for an eligible rollover distribution that is less than $200) also apply for purposes of determining whether a direct rollover election under section 401(a)(31) must be provided for an eligible rollover distribution that is less than $200 or the lower specified amount.

Q-12: Is a plan administrator permitted to treat a distributee's election to make or not make a direct rollover with respect to one payment in a series of periodic payments as applying to all subsequent payments in the series?

A-12: (a) Yes. A plan administrator is permitted to treat a distributee's election to make or not make a direct rollover with respect to one payment in a series of periodic payments as applying to all subsequent payments in the series, provided that:

(1) The employee is permitted at any time to change, with respect to subsequent payments, a previous election to make or not make a direct rollover; and

(2) The written explanation provided under section 402(f) explains that the election to make or not make a direct rollover will apply to all future payments unless the employee subsequently changes the election.

(b) See §1.402(f)-1, Q&A-3 for further guidance concerning the rules for providing section 402(f) notices when eligible rollover distributions are made in a series of periodic payments.

Q-13: Is the eligible retirement plan designated by a distributee to receive a direct rollover distribution required to accept the distribution?

A-13: No. Although section 401(a)(31) requires qualified plans to provide distributees the option to make a direct rollover of their eligible rollover distributions to an eligible retirement plan, it imposes no requirement that any eligible retirement plan accept rollovers. Thus, a plan can refuse to accept rollovers. Alternatively, a plan can limit the circumstances under which it will accept rollovers. For example, a plan can limit the types of plans from which it will accept a rollover or limit the types of assets it will accept in a rollover (such as accepting only cash or its equivalent).

Q-14. If a plan accepts an invalid rollover contribution, whether or not as a direct rollover, how will the contribution be treated for purposes of applying the qualification requirements of section 401(a) or 403(a) to the plan?

A-14. (a) *Acceptance of invalid rollover contribution*. If a plan accepts an invalid rollover contribution, the contribution will be treated, for *purposes of applying the qualification requirements of section 401(a) or 403(a)* to the receiving plan, as if it were a valid rollover contribution, if the following two conditions are satisfied. First, when accepting the amount from the employee as a rollover contribution, the plan administrator of the receiving plan reasonably concludes that

the contribution is a valid rollover contribution. While evidence that the distributing plan is the subject of a determination letter from the Commissioner indicating that the distributing plan is qualified would be useful to the receiving plan administrator in reasonably concluding that the contribution is a valid rollover contribution, it is not necessary for the distributing plan to have such a determination letter in order for the receiving plan administrator to reach that conclusion. Second, if the plan administrator of the receiving plan later determines that the contribution was an invalid rollover contribution, the amount of the invalid rollover contribution, plus any earnings attributable thereto, is distributed to the employee within a reasonable time after such determination.

(b) *Definitions*. For purposes of this Q&A-14:

(1) An *invalid rollover contribution* is an amount that is accepted by a plan as a rollover within the meaning of §1.402(c)-2, Q&A-1 (or as a rollover contribution within the meaning of section 408(d)(3)(A)(ii)) but that is not an eligible rollover distribution from a qualified plan (or an amount described in section 408(d)(3)(A)(ii)) or that does not satisfy the other requirements of section 401(a)(31), 402(c), or 408(d)(3) for treatment as a rollover or a rollover contribution.

(2) A *valid rollover contribution* is a contribution that is accepted by a plan as a rollover within the meaning of §1.402(c)-2, Q&A-1 or as a rollover contribution within the meaning of section 408(d)(3) and that satisfies the requirements of section 401(a)(31), 402(c), or 408(d)(3) for treatment as a rollover or a rollover contribution.

(c) *Examples*. The provisions of paragraph (a) of this Q&A-14 are illustrated by the following examples:

Example 1. (i) Employer X maintains for its employees Plan M, a profit sharing plan qualified under section 401(a). Plan M provides that any employee of Employer X may make a rollover contribution to Plan M. Employee A is an employee of Employer X, will not have attained age $70^1/2$ by the end of the year, and has a vested account balance in Plan O (a plan maintained by Employee A's prior employer). Employee A elects a single sum distribution from Plan O and elects that it be paid to Plan M in a direct rollover.

(ii) Employee A provides the plan administrator of Plan M with a letter from the plan administrator of Plan O stating that Plan O has received a determination letter from the Commissioner indicating that Plan O is qualified.

(iii) Based upon such a letter, absent facts to the contrary, a plan administrator may reasonably conclude that Plan O is qualified and that the amount paid as a direct rollover is an eligible rollover distribution.

Example 2. (i) The facts are the same as *Example 1*, except that, instead of the letter provided in paragraph (ii) of *Example 1*, Employee A provides the plan administrator of Plan M with a letter from the plan administrator of Plan O representing that Plan O satisfies the requirements of section 401(a) (or representing that Plan O is intended to satisfy the requirements of section 401(a) and that the administrator of Plan O is not aware of any Plan O provision or operation that would result in the disqualification of Plan O).

(ii) Based upon such a letter, absent facts to the contrary, a plan administrator may reasonably conclude that Plan O is qualified and that the amount paid as a direct rollover is an eligible rollover distribution.

Example 3. (i) Same facts as *Example 1*, except that Employee A elects to receive the distribution from Plan O and wishes to make a rollover contribution described in section 402 rather than a direct rollover.

(ii) When making the rollover contribution, Employee A certifies that, to the best of Employee A's knowledge, Employee A is entitled to the distribution as an employee and not as a beneficiary, the distribution from Plan O to be contributed to Plan M is not one of a series of periodic payments, the distribution from Plan O was received by Employee A not more than 60 days before the date of the rollover contribution, and the entire amount of the rollover contribution would be includible in gross income if it were not being rolled over.

(iii) As support for these certifications, Employee A provides the plan administrator of Plan M with two statements from Plan O. The first is a letter from the plan administrator of Plan O, as described in *Example 1*, stating that Plan O has received a determination letter from the Commissioner indicating that Plan O is qualified. The second is the distribution statement that accompanied the distribution check. The distribution statement indicates that the distribution is being made by Plan O to Employee A, indicates the gross amount of the distribution, and indicates the amount withheld as Federal income tax. The amount withheld as Federal income tax is 20 percent of the gross amount of the distribution. Employee A contributes to Plan M an amount not greater than the gross amount of the distribution stated in the letter from Plan O and the contribution is made within 60 days of the date of the distribution statement from Plan O.

(iv) Based on the certifications and documentation provided by Employee A, absent facts to the contrary, a plan administrator may reasonably conclude that Plan O is qualified and that the distribution otherwise satisfies the requirements of section 402(c) for treatment as a rollover contribution.

Example 4. (i) The facts are the same as in *Example 3*, except that, rather than contributing the distribution from Plan O to Plan M, Employee A contributes the distribution from Plan O to IRA P, an individual retirement account described in section 408(a). After the contribution of the distribution from Plan O to IRA P, but before the year in which Employee A attains age 70¹/₂;, Employee A requests a distribution from IRA P and decides to contribute it to Plan M as a rollover contribution. To make the rollover contribution, Employee A endorses the check received from IRA P as payable to Plan M.

(ii) In addition to providing the certifications described in *Example 3* with respect to the distribution from Plan O, Employee A certifies that, to the best of Employee A's knowledge, the contribution to IRA P was not made more than 60 days after the date Employee A received the distribution from Plan O, no amount other than the distribution from Plan O has been contributed to IRA P, and the distribution from IRA P was received not more than 60 days earlier than the rollover contribution to Plan M.

(iii) As support for these certifications, in addition to the two statements from Plan O described in *Example 3*, Employee A provides copies of statements from IRA P. The statements indicate that the account is identified as an IRA, the account was established within 60 days of the date of the letter from Plan O informing Employee A that an amount had been distributed, and the opening balance in the IRA does not exceed the amount of the distribution described in the letter from Plan O. There is no indication in the statements that any additional contributions have been made to IRA P since the account was opened. The date on the check from IRA P is less than 60 days before the date that Employee A makes the contribution to Plan M.

(iv) Based on the certifications and documentation provided by Employee A, absent facts to the contrary, a plan administrator may reasonably conclude that Plan O is qualified and that the contribution by Employee A is a rollover contribution described in section 408(d)(3)(A)(ii) that satisfies the other requirements of section 408(d)(3) for treatment as a rollover contribution.

Q-15: For purposes of applying the plan qualification requirements of section 401(a), is an eligible rollover distribution that is paid to an eligible retirement plan in a direct rollover a distribution and rollover or is it a transfer of assets and liabilities?

A-15: For purposes of applying the plan qualification requirements of section 401(a), a direct rollover is a distribution and rollover of the eligible rollover distribution and not a transfer of assets and liabilities. For example, if the consent requirements under section 411(a)(11) or sections 401(a)(11) and 417(a)(2) apply to the distribution, they must be satisfied before the eligible rollover distribution may be distributed in a direct rollover. Similarly, the direct rollover is not a transfer of assets and liabilities that must satisfy the requirements of section 414(l). Finally, a direct rollover is not a transfer of benefits for purposes of applying the requirements under section 411(d)(6), as described in §1.411(d)-4, Q&A-3. Therefore, for example, the eligible retirement plan is not required to provide, with respect to amounts paid to it in a direct rollover, the same optional forms of benefits that were provided under the plan that made the direct rollover. The direct rollover requirements of section 401(a)(31) do not affect the ability of a qualified plan to make an elective or nonelective transfer of assets and liabilities to another qualified plan in accordance with applicable law (such as section 414(l)).

Q-16: Must a direct rollover option be provided for an eligible rollover distribution that is in the form of a plan loan offset amount?

A-16: A plan will not fail to satisfy section 401(a)(31) merely because the plan does not permit a distributee to elect a direct rollover of an eligible rollover distribution in the form of a plan loan

offset amount. Section 1.402(c)-2(b), Q&A-9 defines a plan loan offset amount, in general, as a distribution that occurs when, under the terms governing a plan loan, the participant's accrued benefit is reduced (offset) in order to repay the loan. A plan administrator is permitted to allow a direct rollover of a participant note for a plan loan to a qualified trust described in section 401(a) or a qualified annuity plan described in section 403(a). See §1.402(c)-2, Q&A-9 for examples illustrating the rules for plan loan offset amounts that are set forth in this Q&A-16. See §31.3405(c)-1, Q&A-11 of this chapter for guidance concerning special withholding rules that apply to a distribution in the form of a plan loan offset amount.

Q-17: Must a direct rollover option be provided for an eligible rollover distribution from a qualified plan distributed annuity contract?

A-17: Yes. If any amount to be distributed under a qualified plan distributed annuity contract is an eligible rollover distribution (in accordance with §1.402(c)-2), Q&A-10 the annuity contract must satisfy section 401(a)(31) in the same manner as a qualified plan under section 401(a). Section 1.402(c)-2, Q&A-10 defines a qualified plan distributed annuity contract as an annuity contract purchased for a participant, and distributed to the participant, by a qualified plan. In the case of a qualified plan distributed annuity contract, the payor under the contract is treated as the plan administrator. See §31.3405(c)-1, Q&A-13 of this chapter concerning the application of mandatory 20-percent withholding requirements to distributions from a qualified plan distributed annuity contract.

Q-18: What assumptions may a plan administrator make regarding whether a benefit is an eligible rollover distribution?

A-18: (a) *General rule.* For purposes of section 401(a)(31), a plan administrator may make the assumptions described in paragraphs (b) and (c) of this Q&A-18 in determining the amount of a distribution that is an eligible rollover distribution for which a direct rollover option must be provided. Section 31.3405(c)-1, Q&A-10 of this chapter provides assumptions for purposes of complying with section 3405(c). See §1.402(c)-2, Q&A-15 concerning the effect of these assumptions for purposes of section 402(c).

(b) *$5,000 death benefit.* A plan administrator is permitted to assume that a distribution from the plan that qualifies for the $5,000 death benefit exclusion under section 101(b) is the only death benefit being paid with respect to a deceased employee that qualifies for that exclusion. Thus, to the extent that such a distribution would be excludible from gross income based on this assumption, the plan administrator is permitted to assume that it is not an eligible rollover distribution.

(c) *Determination of designated beneficiary.* For the purpose of determining the amount of the minimum distribution required to satisfy section 401(a)(9)(A) for any calendar year, the plan administrator is permitted to assume that there is no designated beneficiary.

Q-19: When must a qualified plan be amended to comply with section 401(a)(31)?

A-19: Even though section 401(a)(31) applies to distributions from qualified plans made after on or after January 1, 1993, a qualified plan is not required to be amended before the last day by which amendments must be made to comply with the Tax Reform Act of 1986 and related provisions, as permitted in other administrative guidance of general applicability, provided that:

(a) In the interim period between January 1, 1993, and the date on which the plan is amended, the plan is operated in accordance with the requirements of section 401(a)(31); and

(b) The amendment applies retroactively to January 1, 1993.

[Reg. §1.401(a)(31)-1.]

☐ [*T.D.* 8619, 9-15-95. *Amended by T.D.* 8880, 4-20-2000 *and T.D.* 9340, 7-23-2007.]

⟫⟫→ *Caution: Reg. §1.401(a)(35)-1, below, is generally applicable for plan years beginning on or after January 1, 2011. However, for plan years beginning before January 1, 2011, a plan is generally permitted to rely on Notice 2006-107, Proposed Reg. §1.401(a)(35)-1 or this final regulation.*

[Reg. §1.401(a)(35)-1]

§1.401(a)(35)-1. Diversification Requirements for Certain Defined Contribution Plans.—(a) *General rule.*—(1) *Diversification requirements.*—Section 401(a)(35) imposes diversification requirements on applicable defined contribution plans. A trust that is part of an applicable defined contribution plan is not a qualified trust under section 401(a) unless the plan—

(i) Satisfies the diversification election requirements for elective deferrals and employee contributions set forth in paragraph (b) of this section;

(ii) Satisfies the diversification election requirements for employer nonelective contributions set forth in paragraph (c) of this section;

(iii) Satisfies the investment option requirement set forth in paragraph (d) of this section; and

(iv) Does not apply any restrictions or conditions on investments in employer securities that violate the requirements of paragraph (e) of this section.

(2) *Definitions, effective dates, and transition rules.*—The definitions of applicable defined contribution plan, employer security, parent corporation, and publicly traded are set forth in paragraph (f) of this section. Applicability dates and transition rules are set forth in paragraph (g) of this section.

(b) *Diversification requirements for elective deferrals and employee contributions invested in employer securities.*—(1) *General rule.*—With respect to any individual described in paragraph (b)(2) of this section, if any portion of the individual's account under an applicable defined contribution plan attributable to elective deferrals (as described in section 402(g)(3)(A)), employee contributions, or rollover contributions is invested in employer securities, then the plan satisfies the requirements of this paragraph (b) if the individual may elect to

⫸→ Caution: *Reg. §1.401(a)(35)-1, below, is generally applicable for plan years beginning on or after January 1, 2011. However, for plan years beginning before January 1, 2011, a plan is generally permitted to rely on Notice 2006-107, Proposed Reg. §1.401(a)(35)-1 or this final regulation.*

divest those employer securities and reinvest an equivalent amount in other investment options. The plan may limit the time for divestment and reinvestment to periodic, reasonable opportunities occurring no less frequently than quarterly.

(2) *Applicable individual with respect to elective deferrals and employee contributions.*—An individual is described in this paragraph (b)(2) if the individual is—

(i) A participant;

(ii) An alternate payee who has an account under the plan; or

(iii) A beneficiary of a deceased participant.

(c) *Diversification requirements for employer nonelective contributions invested in employer securities.*—(1) *General rule.*—With respect to any individual described in paragraph (c)(2) of this section, if a portion of the individual's account under an applicable defined contribution plan attributable to employer nonelective contributions is invested in employer securities, then the plan satisfies the requirements of this paragraph (c) if the individual may elect to divest those employer securities and reinvest an equivalent amount in other investment options. The plan may limit the time for divestment and reinvestment to periodic, reasonable opportunities occurring no less frequently than quarterly.

(2) *Applicable individual with respect to employer nonelective contributions.*—An individual is described in this paragraph (c)(2) if the individual is—

(i) A participant who has completed at least three years of service;

(ii) An alternate payee who has an account under the plan with respect to a participant who has completed at least three years of service; or

(iii) A beneficiary of a deceased participant.

(3) *Completion of three years of service.*—For purposes of paragraph (c)(2) of this section, a participant completes three years of service on the last day of the vesting computation period provided for under the plan that constitutes the completion of the third year of service under section 411(a)(5). However, for a plan that uses the elapsed time method of crediting service for vesting purposes (or a plan that provides for immediate vesting without using a vesting computation period or the elapsed time method of determining vesting), a participant completes three years of service on the day immediately preceding the third anniversary of the participant's date of hire.

(d) *Investment options.*—An applicable defined contribution plan must offer not less than three investment options, other than employer securities, to which an individual who has the right to divest under paragraph (b)(1) or (c)(1) of this section may direct the proceeds from the divestment of employer securities. Each of the three investment options must be diversified and have materially different risk and return characteristics. For this purpose, investment options that constitute a broad range of investment alternatives within the meaning of Department of Labor Regulation section 2550.404c-1(b)(3) are treated as being diversified and having materially different risk and return characteristics.

(e) *Restrictions or conditions on investments in employer securities.*—(1) *Impermissible restrictions or conditions.*—(i) *General rule.*—Except as provided in paragraph (e)(2) of this section, an applicable defined contribution plan violates the requirements of this paragraph (e) if the plan imposes restrictions or conditions with respect to the investment of employer securities that are not imposed on the investment of other assets of the plan. A restriction or condition with respect to employer securities means—

(A) A restriction on an individual's right to divest an investment in employer securities that is not imposed on an investment that is not employer securities; or

(B) A benefit that is conditioned on investment in employer securities.

(ii) *Indirect restrictions or conditions.*—(A) Except as provided in paragraph (e)(3) of this section, a plan violates the requirements of this paragraph (e) if the plan imposes a restriction or condition described in paragraph (e)(1)(i)(A) or (B) of this section either directly or indirectly.

(B) A plan imposes an indirect restriction on an individual's right to divest an investment in employer securities if, for example, the plan provides that a participant who divests his or her account balance with respect to the investment in employer securities is not permitted for a period of time thereafter to reinvest in employer securities.

(C) A plan does not impose an indirect restriction or condition merely because there are tax consequences that result from an individual's divestment of an investment in employer securities. Thus, the loss of the special treatment for net unrealized appreciation provided under section 402(e)(4) with respect to employer securities is disregarded. Similarly, a plan does not impose an impermissible restriction or condition merely because it provides that an individual may not reinvest divested amounts in the same employer securities account but is permitted to invest such divested amounts in another employer securities account where the only relevant difference between the separate accounts is the section 402(e)(4) cost (or other basis) of the trust in the shares held in each account. (See § 1.402(a)-1(b) for rules regarding section 402(e)(4).)

(2) *Permitted restrictions or conditions.*—(i) *In general.*—An applicable defined contribution plan does not violate the requirements of this paragraph (e) merely because it imposes a restriction or a condition set forth in paragraph (e)(2)(ii) or (e)(2)(iii) of this section.

(ii) *Securities laws.*—A plan is permitted to impose a restriction or condition on the divestiture of employer securities that is either required in order to ensure compliance with applicable securities laws or is reasonably designed to ensure compliance with applicable securities laws. For example, it is permissible for a plan to limit divestiture rights for participants who are subject to section 16(b) of the Securities Exchange Act of 1934 (15 U.S.C. 78f) to a reasonable period (such as 3 to 12 days) following publication of the employer's quarterly earnings statements because it is reasonably designed to ensure compliance with Rule 10b-5 of the Securities and Exchange Commission.

(iii) *Deferred application of the diversification requirements.*—(A) *Becoming an applicable defined contribution plan.*—An applicable defined contribution plan is permitted to restrict the application of the diversification requirements of section 401(a)(35) and this section for up to 90 days after the plan becomes an applicable defined contribution plan (for example, a plan becoming an applicable defined contribution plan because the employer securities held under the plan become publicly traded).

(B) *Loss of exception for indirect investments.*—In the case where an investment fund described in paragraph (f)(3)(ii)(A) of this section no longer meets the requirement in paragraph (f)(3)(ii)(B) of this section that the investment must be independent of the employer (including the situation where the fund no longer meets the percentage limitation rule in paragraph (f)(3)(ii)(C) of this section), the plan does not fail to satisfy the diversification requirements of section 401(a)(35) and this section merely because it does not offer those rights with respect to that investment fund for up to 90 days after the investment fund ceases to meet those requirements.

(3) *Permitted indirect restrictions or conditions.*—(i) *In general.*—An applicable defined contribution plan does not violate the requirements of this paragraph (e) merely because it imposes an indirect restriction or condition set forth in this paragraph (e)(3).

(ii) *Limitation on investment in employer securities.*—A plan is permitted to limit the extent to which an individual's account balance can be invested in employer securities, provided the limitation applies without regard to a prior exercise of rights to divest employer securities. For example, a plan does not impose a restriction that violates this paragraph (e) merely because the plan prohibits a participant from investing additional amounts in employer securities if more than 10 percent of that participant's account balance is invested in employer securities.

(iii) *Trading frequency.*—A plan is permitted to impose reasonable restrictions on the timing and number of investment elections that an individual can make to invest in employer securities, provided that the restrictions are designed to limit short-term trading in the employer securities. For example, a plan could provide that a participant may not elect to invest in employer securities if the employee has elected to divest employer securities within a short period of time, such as seven days, prior to the election to invest in employer securities.

(iv) *Fees.*—The plan has not provided an indirect benefit that is conditioned on investment in employer securities merely because the plan imposes fees on other investment options that are not imposed on the investment in employer securities. In addition, the plan has not provided a restriction on the right to divest an investment in employer securities merely because the plan imposes a reasonable fee for the divestment of employer securities.

(v) *Stable value or similar fund.*—A plan is permitted to allow transfers to be made into or out of a stable value or similar fund more

>>>→ *Caution: Reg. §1.401(a)(35)-1, below, is generally applicable for plan years beginning on or after January 1, 2011. However, for plan years beginning before January 1, 2011, a plan is generally permitted to rely on Notice 2006-107, Proposed Reg. §1.401(a)(35)-1 or this final regulation.*

frequently than a fund invested in employer securities for purposes of paragraph (e)(1)(ii) of this section. Thus, a plan that includes a broad range of investment alternatives as described in paragraph (d) of this section, including a stable value or similar fund, does not impose an impermissible restriction under paragraph (e)(1)(ii) of this section merely because it permits transfers into or out of that fund more frequently than other funds under the plan, provided that the plan would otherwise satisfy this paragraph (e) (taking into account any restrictions or conditions imposed with respect to the other investment options under the plan). For purposes of this section, a stable value fund or similar fund means an investment product or fund designed to preserve or guarantee principal and provide a reasonable rate of return, while providing liquidity for benefit distributions or transfers to other investment alternatives (such as a product or fund described in Department of Labor Regulation § 2550.404c-5(e)(4)(iv)(A) or (v)(A)).

(vi) *Transfers out of a qualified default investment alternative (QDIA).*—A plan is permitted to provide for transfers out of a QDIA within the meaning of Department of Labor Regulation section 2550.404c-5(e) more frequently than a fund invested in employer securities.

(vii) *Frozen funds.*—(A) *General rule.*—A plan is permitted to prohibit any further investment in employer securities. Thus, a plan is not treated as imposing an indirect restriction merely because it provides that an employee that divests an investment in employer securities is not permitted to reinvest in employer securities, but only if the plan does not permit additional contributions or other investments to be invested in employer securities. For this purpose, a plan does not provide for further investment in employer securities merely because dividends paid on employer securities under the plan are reinvested in employer securities.

(B) *Transitional relief for certain leveraged employee stock ownership plans (ESOPs).*—An employer stock fund does not fail to be a frozen fund under this paragraph (e)(3)(vii) merely because of the allocation of employer securities that are released as matching contributions from the plan's suspense account that holds employer securities acquired with an exempt loan under section 4975(d)(3). This paragraph (e)(3)(vii)(B) only applies to employer securities that were acquired in a plan year beginning before January 1, 2007, with the proceeds of an exempt loan within the meaning of section 4975(d)(3) which is not refinanced after the end of the last plan year beginning before January 1, 2007.

(4) *Delegation of authority to Commissioner.*—The Commissioner may provide for additional permitted restrictions or conditions or permitted indirect restrictions or conditions in revenue rulings, notices, or other guidance published in the Internal Revenue Bulletin.

(f) *Definitions.*—(1) *Application of definitions.*—This paragraph (f) contains definitions that are applicable for purposes of this section.

(2) *Applicable defined contribution plan.*—(i) *General rule.*—Except as provided in this paragraph (f)(2), an applicable defined contribution plan means any defined contribution plan which holds employer securities that are publicly traded. See paragraph (f)(2)(iv) of this section for a special rule that treats certain plans that hold employer securities that are not publicly traded as applicable defined contribution plans and paragraph (f)(3)(ii) of this section for a special rule that treats certain plans as not holding publicly traded employer securities for purposes of this section.

(ii) *Exception for certain ESOPs.*—An employee stock ownership plan (ESOP), as defined in section 4975(e)(7), is not an applicable defined contribution plan if the plan is a separate plan for purposes of section 414(l) with respect to any other defined benefit plan or defined contribution plan maintained by the same employer or employers and holds no contributions (or earnings thereunder) that are (or were ever) subject to section 401(k) or 401(m). Thus, an ESOP is an applicable defined contribution plan if the ESOP is a portion of a larger plan (whether or not that larger plan includes contributions that are subject to section 401(k) or 401(m)). For purposes of this paragraph (f)(2)(ii), a plan is not considered to hold amounts ever subject to section 401(k) or 401(m) merely because the plan holds amounts attributable to rollover amounts in a separate account that were previously subject to section 401(k) or 401(m).

(iii) *Exception for one-participant plans.*—A one-participant plan, as defined in section 401(a)(35)(E)(iv), is not an applicable defined contribution plan.

(iv) *Certain defined contribution plans treated as holding publicly traded employer securities.*—(A) *General rule.*—A defined contribution plan holding employer securities that are not publicly traded is treated as an applicable defined contribution plan if any employer maintaining the plan or any member of a controlled group of corporations that includes such employer has issued a class of stock which is publicly traded. For purposes of this paragraph (f)(2)(iv), a controlled group of corporations has the meaning given such term by section 1563(a), except that "50 percent" is substituted for "80 percent" each place it appears.

(B) *Exception for certain plans.*—Paragraph (f)(2)(iv)(A) of this section does not apply to a plan if—

(1) No employer maintaining the plan (or a parent corporation with respect to such employer) has issued stock that is publicly traded; and

(2) No employer maintaining the plan (or parent corporation with respect to such employer) has issued any special class of stock which grants to the holder or issuer particular rights, or bears particular risks for the holder or issuer, with respect to any employer maintaining the plan (or any member of a controlled group of corporations that includes such employer) which has issued any stock that is publicly traded.

(3) *Employer security.*—(i) *General rule.*—Employer security has the meaning given such term by section 407(d)(1) of the Employee Retirement Income Security Act of 1974, as amended (ERISA).

(ii) *Certain defined contribution plans or investment funds not treated as holding employer securities.*—(A) *Exception for certain indirect investments.*—Subject to paragraphs (f)(3)(ii)(B) and (C) of this section, a plan (and an investment option described in paragraph (d) of this section) is not treated as holding employer securities for purposes of this section to the extent the employer securities are held indirectly as part of a broader fund that is—

(1) A regulated investment company described in section 851(a);

(2) A common or collective trust fund or pooled investment fund maintained by a bank or trust company supervised by a State or a Federal agency;

(3) A pooled investment fund of an insurance company that is qualified to do business in a State;

(4) An investment fund managed by an investment manager within the meaning of section 3(38) of ERISA for a multiemployer plan; or

(5) Any other investment fund designated by the Commissioner in revenue rulings, notices, or other guidance published in the Internal Revenue Bulletin.

(B) *Investment must be independent.*—The exception set forth in paragraph (f)(3)(ii)(A) of this section applies only if the investment in the employer securities is held in a fund under which—

(1) There are stated investment objectives of the fund; and

(2) The investment is independent of the employer (or employers) and any affiliate thereof.

(C) *Percentage limitation rule.*—For purposes of paragraph (f)(3)(ii)(B)(2) of this section, an investment in employer securities in a fund is not considered to be independent of the employer (or employers) and any affiliate thereof if the aggregate value of the employer securities held in the fund is in excess of 10 percent of the total value of all of the fund's investments for the plan year. The determination of whether the value of employer securities exceeds 10 percent of the total value of the fund's investments for the plan year is made as of the end of the preceding plan year. The determination can be based on the information in the latest disclosure of the fund's portfolio holdings that was filed with the Securities and Exchange Commission (SEC) in that preceding plan year.

(4) *Parent corporation.*—Parent corporation has the meaning given such term by section 424(e).

(5) *Publicly traded.*—(i) *In general.*—A security is publicly traded if it is readily tradable on an established securities market.

(ii) *Readily tradable on an established securities market.*—For purposes of this paragraph (f)(5), except as provided by the Commissioner in revenue rulings, notices, or other guidance published in the Internal Revenue Bulletin, a security is readily tradable on an established securities market if—

(A) The security is traded on a national securities exchange that is registered under section 6 of the Securities Exchange Act of 1934 (15 U.S.C. 78f); or

(B) The security is traded on a foreign national securities exchange that is officially recognized, sanctioned, or supervised by a

>>> *Caution: Reg. §1.401(a)(35)-1, below, is generally applicable for plan years beginning on or after January 1, 2011. However, for plan years beginning before January 1, 2011, a plan is generally permitted to rely on Notice 2006-107, Proposed Reg. §1.401(a)(35)-1 or this final regulation.*

governmental authority and the security is deemed by the SEC as having a "ready market" under SEC Rule 15c3-1 (17 CFR 240.15c3-1).

(g) *Applicability date and transition rules.*—(1) *Statutory effective date.*—(i) *General rule.*—Except as otherwise provided in this paragraph (g) and section 901(c)(3)(A) and (B) of the Pension Protection Act of 2006, Public Law 109-280 (120 Stat. 780 (2006)) (PPA '06), section 401(a)(35) is effective for plan years beginning after December 31, 2006.

(ii) *Collectively bargained plans.*—(A) *Delayed statutory effective date.*—In the case of a plan maintained pursuant to one or more collective bargaining agreements between employee representatives and one or more employers ratified on or before August 17, 2006, section 401(a)(35) is effective for plan years beginning after the earlier of—

(1) The later of—
(i) December 31, 2007; or
(ii) The date on which the last such collective bargaining agreement terminates (determined without regard to any extension thereof); or
(2) December 31, 2008.

Plan year to which paragraph (c) of this section applies:
1st 33
2nd 66
3rd and following 100

(B) *Special rule.*—For a plan for which the special effective date under section 901(c)(3) of PPA '06 applies, the applicable percentage under this paragraph (g)(3)(ii) is determined without regard to the delayed effective date in section 901(c)(3)(A) and (B) of PPA '06.

(iii) *Nonapplication for participants age 55 with three years of service.*—Paragraph (g)(3)(i) of this section does not apply to an individual who is a participant who attained age 55 and had completed at least three years of service (as defined in paragraph (c)(3) of this section) before the first day of the first plan year beginning after December 31, 2005.

(iv) *Separate application by class of securities.*—This paragraph (g)(3) applies separately with respect to each class of securities. [Reg. §1.401(a)(35)-1.]

☐ [*T.D.* 9484, 5-18-2010.]

[Reg. §1.401(a)-50]

§1.401(a)-50. Puerto Rican trusts; election to be treated as a domestic trust.—(a) *In general.*—Section 401(a) requires, among other things, that a trust forming part of a pension, profit-sharing, or stock bonus plan must be created or organized in the United States to be a qualified trust. Section 1022(i)(2) of the Employee Retirement Income Security Act of 1974 (ERISA) (88 Stat. 942) provides that trusts under certain pension, etc., plans created or organized in Puerto Rico whose administrators have made the election referred to in section 1022(i)(2) are to be treated as trusts created or organized in the United States for purposes of section 401(a). Thus, if a plan otherwise satisfies the qualification requirements of section 401(a), any trust forming part of the plan for which an election is made will be treated as a qualified trust under that section.

(B) *Treatment of plans with both collectively bargained and non-collectively bargained employees.*—If a collective bargaining agreement applies to some, but not all, of the plan participants, the definition of whether the plan is considered a collectively bargained plan for purposes of this paragraph (g)(1)(ii) is made in the same manner as the definition of whether a plan is collectively bargained under section 436(f)(3).

(2) *Regulatory effective/applicability date.*—This section is effective and applicable for plan years beginning on or after January 1, 2011.

(3) *Statutory transition rules.*—(i) *General rule.*—Pursuant to section 401(a)(35)(H), in the case of the portion of an account to which paragraph (c) of this section applies and that consists of employer securities acquired in a plan year beginning before January 1, 2007, the requirements of paragraph (c) of this section only apply to the applicable percentage of such securities.

(ii) *Applicable percentage.*—(A) *Phase-in percentage.*—For purposes of this paragraph (g)(3), the applicable percentage is determined as follows—

The applicable percentage is:

(b) *Manner and effect of election.*—A plan administrator may make an election under ERISA section 1022(i)(2) by filing a statement making the election, along with a copy of the plan, with the Director's Representative of the Internal Revenue Service in Puerto Rico. The statement making the election must indicate that it is being made under ERISA section 1022(i)(2). The statement may also be filed in conjunction with a written request for a determination letter. If the election is made with a written request for a determination letter, the election may be conditioned upon issuance of a favorable determination letter and will be irrevocable upon issuance of such letter. Otherwise, once made, an election is irrevocable. It is generally effective for plan years beginning after the date it has been made. However, an election made before March 3, 1983, may, at the option of the plan administrator at the time he or she makes the election, be considered to have been made on any date between September 2, 1974, and the actual date of the election. The election will then be effective for plan years beginning on or after the date chosen by the plan administrator.

(c) *Annuities, custodial accounts, etc.*—See section 401(f) for rules relating to the treatment of certain annuities, custodial accounts or other contracts, as trusts for purposes of section 401(a).

(d) *Source of plan distributions to participants and beneficiaries residing outside the United States.*—Except as provided under section 871(f) (relating to amounts received as an annuity by nonresident aliens), the amount of a distribution from an electing plan that is to be treated as income from sources within the United States is determined as described below. The portion of the distribution considered to be a return of employer contributions is to be treated as income from sources within the United States in an amount equal to the portion of the distribution considered to be a return of employer contributions multiplied by the following fraction:

Days of performance of labor or services within the United States for the employer.

Total days of performance of labor or services for the employer.

The days of performance of labor or services within the United States shall not include the time period for which the employee's compensation is deemed not to be income from sources within the United States under subtitle A of the Code. Thus, for example, if an employee's compensation was not deemed to be income from sources within the United States under section 861(a)(3), then the time the employee was present in the United States while such compensation was earned would not be included in determining the days of performance of labor or services within the United States in the numerator of the above fraction. In addition, days of performance of labor or services for the employer in both the numerator and denominator of the above fraction are limited to days of plan participation by the employee and any service used for determining an employee's accrued benefit under the plan. The remaining portion of the distribution, that is, any amount other than the portion of the distribution considered to be a return of employer contributions, is not to be treated as income from sources within the United States. For example, if a distribution consists of amounts representing employer contributions, employee contributions, and earnings on employer

and employee contributions, no part of the portion of the distribution attributable to employee contributions, or earnings on employer and employee contributions, will be treated as income from sources within the United States. [Reg. §1.401(a)-50.]

☐ [*T.D.* 7859, 12-1-82.]

[Reg. §1.401(b)-1]

§1.401(b)-1. Certain retroactive changes in plan.—(a) *General rule.*—Under section 401(b) a stock bonus, pension, profit-sharing, annuity, or bond purchase plan which does not satisfy the requirements of section 401(a) on any day solely as a result of a disqualifying provision (as defined in paragraph (b) of this section) shall be considered to have satisfied such requirements on such date if, on or before the last day of the remedial amendment period (as determined under paragraphs (d), (e) and (f) of this section) with respect to such disqualifying provision, all provisions of the plan which are necessary to satisfy all requirements of sections 401(a), 403(a), or 405(a) are in effect and have been made effective for all purposes for the whole of such period. Under some facts and circumstances, it may not be possible to amend a plan retroactively so that all provisions of the plan which are necessary to satisfy the requirements of section 401(a) are in fact made effective for the whole remedial amendment period. If it is not possible, the requirements of this section will not be satisfied even if the employer adopts a retroactive plan amendment which, in form, appears to satisfy such requirements. Section 401(b) does not permit a plan to be made retroactively effective, for qualification purposes, for a taxable year prior to the taxable year of the employer in which the plan was adopted by such employer.

(b) *Disqualifying provisions.*—For purposes of this section, with respect to a plan described in paragraph (a) of this section, the term "disqualifying provision" means:

(1) A provision of a new plan, the absence of a provision from a new plan, or an amendment to an existing plan, which causes such plan to fail to satisfy the requirements of the Code applicable to qualification of such plan as of the date such plan or amendment is first made effective.

(2) A plan provision which results in the failure of the plan to satisfy the qualification requirements of the Code by reason of a change in such requirements—

(i) Effected by the Employee Retirement Income Security Act of 1974 (Pub. L. 93-406, 88 Stat. 829), hereafter referred to as "ERISA", or the Tax Equity and Fiscal Responsibility Act of 1982 (Pub. L. 97-248, 96 Stat. 324), hereafter referred to as "TEFRA," or

(ii) Effective before the first day of the first plan year beginning after December 31, 1989 and that is effected by the Tax Reform Act of 1986 (Pub. L. 99-514, 100 Stat. 2085, 2489), hereafter referred to as "TRA '86," the Omnibus Budget Reconciliation Act of 1986, (Pub. L. 99-509, 100 Stat. 1874), hereafter referred as a "OBRA '86," or the Omnibus Budget Reconciliation Act of 1987 (Pub. L. 100-203, 101 Stat. 1330), hereafter referred to as "OBRA 87". For purposes of this paragraph (b)(2)(ii), a disqualifying provision includes any plan provision that is integral to a qualification requirement changed by TRA '86, OBRA '86, or OBRA '87 or any requirement treated by the Commissioner, directly or indirectly, as if section 1140 of TRA '86 applied to it, but only to the extent such provision is effective before the first day of the first plan year beginning after December 31, 1989. With respect to disqualifying provisions described in this paragraph (b)(2)(ii) effective before the first day of the first plan year which begins after December 31, 1988, there must be compliance with the conditions of section 1140 of TRA '86 (other than the requirement that the plan amendment be made on or before the last day of the first plan year beginning after December 31, 1988), including operation in accordance with the plan provision as of its effective date with respect to the plan.

(3) A plan provision designated by the Commissioner, at the Commissioner's discretion, as a disqualifying provision that either—

(i) Results in the failure of the plan to satisfy the qualification requirements of the Internal Revenue Code by reason of a change in those requirements; or

(ii) Is integral to a qualification requirement of the Internal Revenue Code that has been changed.

(c) *Special rules applicable to disqualifying provisions.*—(1) *Absence of plan provision.*—For purposes of paragraphs (b)(2) and (3) of this section, a disqualifying provision includes the absence from a plan of a provision required by, or, if applicable, integral to the applicable change to the qualification requirements of the Internal Revenue Code, if the plan was in effect on the date the change became effective with respect to the plan.

(2) *Method of designating disqualifying provisions.*—The Commissioner may designate a plan provision as a disqualifying provision pursuant to paragraph (b)(3) of this section only in revenue rulings, notices, and other guidance published in the Internal Revenue Bulletin. See § 601.601(d)(2) of this chapter.

(3) *Authority to impose limitations.*—In the case of a provision that has been designated as a disqualifying provision by the Commissioner pursuant to paragraph (b)(3) of this section, the Commissioner may impose limits and provide additional rules regarding the amendments that may be made with respect to that disqualifying provision during the remedial amendment period. The Commissioner may provide guidance in revenue rulings, notices, and other *guidance published in the Internal Revenue Bulletin. See* § 601.601(d)(2) of this chapter.

(d) *Remedial amendment period.*—(1) The remedial amendment period with respect to a disqualifying provision begins:

(i) In the case of a provision of, or absence of a provision from, a new plan, described in paragraph (b)(1) of this section, the date the plan is put into effect,

(ii) In the case of an amendment to an existing plan, described in paragraph (b)(1) of this section, the date the plan amendment is adopted or put into effect (whichever is earlier),

(iii) In the case of a disqualifying provision described in paragraph (b)(2) of this section, the date on which the change effected by ERISA, TEFRA, TRA '86, OBRA '86, OBRA '87, or a qualification requirement that is treated, directly or indirectly, as subject to the conditions of section 1140 of TRA '86, described in paragraph (b)(2) of this section, became effective with respect to such plan or, in the case of a provision, described in paragraph (b)(2)(ii) of this section, that is integral to such qualification requirement, the first day on which the plan was operated in accordance with such provision, or

(iv) In the case of a disqualifying provision described in paragraph (b)(3)(i) of this section, the date on which the change effected by an amendment to the Internal Revenue Code became effective with respect to the plan; or

(v) In the case of a disqualifying provision described in paragraph (b)(3)(ii) of this section, the first day on which the plan was operated in accordance with such provision, as amended, unless another time is specified by the Commissioner in revenue rulings, notices, and other guidance published in the Internal Revenue Bulletin. See § 601.601(d)(2) of this chapter.

(2) Unless further extended as provided by paragraph (e) of this section, the remedial amendment period ends with the latest of:

(i) In the case of a plan maintained by one employer, the time prescribed by law, including extensions, for filing the income tax return (or partnership return of income) of the employer for the employer's taxable year in which falls the latest of:

(A) The date on which the remedial amendment period begins,

(B) The date on which a plan amendment described in paragraph (b)(1) of this section is adopted, or

(C) The date on which a plan amendment described in paragraph (b)(1) of this section is made effective,

(ii) In the case of a plan maintained by one employer, the last day of the plan year within which falls the latest of:

(A) The date on which the remedial amendment period begins,

(B) The date on which a plan amendment described in paragraph (b)(1) of this section is adopted, or

(C) The date on which a plan amendment described in paragraph (b)(1) of this section is made effective,

(iii) In the case of a plan maintained by more than one employer, the last day of the tenth month following the last day of the plan year in which falls the latest of:

(A) The date on which the remedial amendment period begins,

(B) The date on which a plan amendment described in paragraph (b)(1) of this section is adopted, or

(C) The date on which a plan amendment described in paragraph (b)(1) of this section is made effective, or

(iv) December 31, 1976, but only in the case of a plan to which section 411 (relating to minimum vesting standards) applies without regard to section 411(e)(2), and only in the case of a remedial amendment period which began on or after September 2, 1974.

(3) For purposes of paragraphs (d)(2)(i), (d)(2)(ii) and (d)(2)(iii) of this section, for any disqualifying provision described in paragraph (b)(2)(ii) of this section, the remedial amendment period shall be deemed to have begun with the first day of the first plan year which begins after December 31, 1988.

(4) For purposes of this paragraph (d)(2) of this section, a master or prototype plan shall not be considered to be a plan maintained by more than one employer, and whether or not a plan is maintained by more than one employer shall be determined without regard to section 414(b) and (c) except that if a plan is maintained solely by an affiliated group of corporations (within the meaning of section 1504) which files a consolidated income tax return pursuant to section 1501 for a taxable year within which falls the latest of the dates described in paragraph (d)(2)(i) of this section, such plan shall be deemed to be maintained by one employer.

(e) *Extensions of remedial amendment period.*—(1) *Opinion letter request by sponsoring organization of master or prototype plan.*—In the case of an employer who has adopted a master or prototype plan, a remedial amendment period that began on or after September 2, 1974, shall not end prior to the later of:

(i) June 30, 1977, or

(ii) The last day of the month that is six months after the month in which:

(A) The opinion letter with respect to the request of the sponsoring organization is issued by the Internal Revenue Service,

(B) Such request is withdrawn, or

(C) Such request is otherwise disposed of by the Internal Revenue Service. The rules contained in this subparagraph apply only if the sponsoring organization of such master or prototype plan has, after September 2, 1974, and on or before December 31, 1976, filed a request for an opinion letter with respect to the initial or continuing qualification of the plan (or a trust which is part of the plan). The provisions of this paragraph (e)(1) apply to a master or prototype plan adopted to replace another plan even though the remedial amendment period applicable to the replaced plan has expired at the time of adoption of the replacement plan.

(2) *Notification letter request by law firm sponsor of district-approved plan.*—In the case of an employer who has adopted a pattern plan, a remedial amendment period that began on or after September 2, 1974, shall not end prior to the later of:

(i) June 30, 1977, or

(ii) The last day of the month that is six months after the month in which:

(A) The notification letter with respect to the request of the sponsoring law firm is issued by the Internal Revenue Service,

(B) Such request is withdrawn, or

(C) Such request is otherwise disposed of by the Internal Revenue Service. The rules contained in this subparagraph shall apply only if the sponsoring law firm of such pattern plan has, on or before December 31, 1976, filed a request for a notification letter with the Internal Revenue Service with respect to the initial or continuing qualification of the plan (or a trust which is part of the plan). The provisions of this paragraph (e)(2) apply to a pattern plan adopted to replace another plan even though the remedial amendment period applicable to the replaced plan has expired at the time of the adoption of the replacement plan.

(3) *Determination letter request by employer or plan administrator.*—If on or before the end of a remedial amendment period determined without regard to this paragraph (e), or in a case to which paragraph (e)(1) or (2) of this section applies, on or before the 90th day following the later of the dates described in paragraph (e)(1) or (2) of this section, the employer or plan administrator files a request pursuant to § 601.201(s) of this chapter (Statement of Procedural Rules) for a determination letter with respect to the initial or continuing qualification of the plan, or a trust which is part of such plan, such remedial amendment period shall be extended until the expiration of 91 days after:

(i) The date on which notice of the final determination with respect to such request for a determination letter is issued by the Internal Revenue Service, such request is withdrawn, or such request is otherwise finally disposed of by the Internal Revenue Service, or

(ii) If a petition is timely filed with the United States Tax Court for a declaratory judgment under section 7476 with respect to the final determination (or the failure of the Internal Revenue Service to make a final determination) in response to such request, the date on which the decision of the United States Tax Court in such proceeding becomes final.

(4) *Transitional rule.*—In the case of a request for a determination letter described in and filed within the time prescribed in paragraph (e)(3) of this section with respect to which a final determination is issued by the Internal Revenue Service on or before September 28, 1976 the remedial amendment period described in paragraph (d) of this section shall not end prior to the expiration of 150 days beginning on the date of such final determination by the Internal Revenue Service.

(5) *Disqualifying provision prior to September 2, 1974.*—If the remedial amendment period with respect to a disqualifying provision described in paragraph (b)(1) of this section began prior to September 2, 1974, and the provisions of paragraphs (e)(5)(i), (ii) and (iii) of this section are satisfied, the remedial amendment period described in paragraph (d) shall not end prior to December 31, 1976. This subparagraph shall apply only if—

(i) A request pursuant to § 601.201 of this chapter for a determination letter with respect to the initial or continuing qualification of the plan (or a trust which is part of the plan) was filed not later than the later of:

(A) The time prescribed by law, including extensions, for filing the income tax return (or partnership return of income) of the employer for the employer's taxable year in which falls the date on which the remedial amendment period began, or

(B) The date 6 months after the close of such taxable year,

(ii) The employer, either:

(A) While such request for a determination letter is or was under consideration by the Internal Revenue Service or,

(B) Promptly after the date on which notice of the final determination with respect to such request for a determination letter is issued by the Internal Revenue Service, such request is withdrawn, or such request is otherwise finally disposed of by the Internal Revenue Service, adopts or adopted either a plan amendment retroactive to the date on which the remedial amendment period began, or a prospective plan amendment, and

(iii) The amendment described in paragraph (e)(5)(ii) of this section would have resulted in the plan's satisfying the requirements of section 401(a) of the Code from the beginning of the remedial amendment period to the date such amendment was made if this section had been in effect during such period, and in the case of a prospective amendment, if such amendment had been made retroactive to such beginning date.

(f) *Discretionary extensions.*—At his discretion, the Commissioner may extend the remedial amendment period or may allow a particular plan to be amended after the expiration of its remedial amendment period and any applicable extension of such period. In determining whether such an extension will be granted, the Commissioner shall consider, among other factors, whether substantial hardship to the employer would result if such an extension were not granted, whether such an extension is in the best interest of plan participants, and whether the granting of the extension is adverse to the interests of the Government. The mere absence of final regulations with respect to issues covered under the Special Reliance Procedure announced by the Internal Revenue Service in Technical Information Release 1416 on November 5, 1975, and as extended by Internal Revenue Service News Release IR-1616 on May 14, 1976, shall not be deemed to satisfy the criteria of this paragraph. With regard to a particular plan, a request for extension of time pursuant to this paragraph shall be submitted prior to the expiration of the remedial amendment period determined without regard to this paragraph, or within such time thereafter as the Internal Revenue Service may consider reasonable under the circumstances. The request should be submitted to the appropriate District Director, determined under § 601.201(s)(3)(xii) of this chapter (Statement of Procedural Rules). This subparagraph applies to disqualifying provisions that were adopted or became effective prior to September 2, 1974, as well as disqualifying provisions adopted or made effective on or after September 2, 1974. [Reg. § 1.401(b)-1.]

□ [*T.D. 7437, 9-23-76. Amended by T.D. 7896, 5-26-83; T.D. 7997, 12-28-84; T.D. 8217, 8-5-88; T.D. 8727, 7-31-97 and T.D. 8871, 2-3-2000.*]

[Reg. § 1.401(f)-1]

§ 1.401(f)-1. Certain custodial accounts and annuity contracts.— (a) *Treatment of a custodial account or an annuity contract as a qualified trust.*—Beginning on January 1, 1974, a custodial account or an annuity contract may be used, in lieu of a trust, under any qualified pension, profit-sharing, or stock bonus plan if the requirements of paragraph (b) of this section are met. A custodial account or an annuity contract may be used under such a plan, whether the plan covers common-law employees, self-employed individuals who are treated as employees by reason of section 401(c), or both. The use of a custodial account or annuity contract as part of a plan does not preclude the use of a trust or another custodial account or another annuity contract as part of the same plan. A plan under which a custodial account or an annuity contract is used may be considered in connection with other plans of the employer in determining whether the requirements of section 401 are satisfied.

(b) *Rules applicable to custodial accounts and annuity contracts.*— (1) Beginning on January 1, 1974, a custodial account or an annuity contract is treated as a qualified trust under section 401 if the following requirements are met:

(i) The custodial account or annuity contract would, except for that fact that it is not a trust, constitute a qualified trust under section 401; and

(ii) In the case of a custodial account, the custodian either is a bank or is another person who demonstrates, to the satisfaction of the Commissioner, that the manner in which he will hold the assets will be consistent with the requirements of section 401. This demonstration must be made in the same manner as the demonstration required by § 1.408-2(e).

(2) If a custodial account would, except for the fact that it is not a trust, constitute a qualified trust under section 401, it must, for example, be created pursuant to a written agreement which constitutes a valid contract under local law. In addition, the terms of the contract must make it impossible, prior to the satisfaction of all liabilities with respect to the employees and their beneficiaries covered by the plan, for any part of the funds of the custodial account to be used for, or diverted to, purposes other than for the exclusive benefit of the employees or their beneficiaries as provided for in the plan (see paragraph (a) of § 1.401-2).

(3) An annuity contract would, except for the fact that it is not a trust, constitute a qualified trust under section 401 if it is purchased by an employer for an employee under a plan which meets the requirements of section 404(a)(2) and the regulations thereunder, except that the plan may be either a pension or a profit-sharing plan.

(c) *Effect of this section.*—(1)(i) Any custodial account or annuity contract which satisfies the requirements of paragraph (b) of this section is treated as a qualified trust for all purposes of the Internal Revenue Code of 1954. Such a custodial account or annuity contract is treated as a separate legal person which is exempt from the income tax under section 501(a). In addition, the person holding the assets of such account or holding such contract is treated as the trustee thereof. Accordingly, such person is required to file the returns described in sections 6033 and 6047 and to supply any other information which the trustee of a qualified trust is required to furnish.

(ii) Any procedure which has the effect of merely substituting one custodian for another shall not be considered as terminating or interrupting the legal existence of a custodial account which otherwise satisfies the requirements of paragraph (b) of this section.

(2)(i) The beneficiary of a custodial account which satisfies the requirements of paragraph (b) of this section is taxed in accordance with section 402. In determining whether the funds of a custodial account are distributed or made available to an employee or his beneficiary, the rules which under section 402(a) are applicable to trusts will also apply to the custodial account as though it were a separate legal person and not an agent of the employee.

(ii) If a custodial account which has qualified under section 401 fails to qualify under such section for any taxable year, such custodial account will not thereafter be treated as a separate legal person, and the funds in such account shall be treated as made available within the meaning of section 402(a)(1) to the employees for whom they are held.

(3) The beneficiary of an annuity contract which satisfies the requirements of paragraph (b) of this section is taxed as if he were the beneficiary of an annuity contract described in section 403(a).

(d) *Definitions.*—For purposes of this section—
(1) The term "bank" means a bank as defined in section 408(n).
(2) The term "annuity" means an annuity as defined in section 401(g).
Thus, any contract or certificate issued after December 31, 1962, which is transferable is not treated as a qualified trust under this section.

(e) *Other contracts.*—For purposes of this section, other than the nontransferability restriction of paragraph (d)(2), a contract issued by an insurance company qualified to do business in a state shall be treated as an annuity contract. For purposes of the preceding sentence, the contract does not include a life, health or accident, property, casualty or liability insurance contract. For purposes of this paragraph, a contract which is issued by an insurance company will not be considered a life insurance contract merely because the contract provides incidental life insurance protection. The provisions of this paragraph are effective for taxable years beginning after December 31, 1975.

(f) *Cross reference.*—For the requirement that the assets of an employee benefit plan be placed in trust, and exceptions thereto, see section 403 of the Employee Retirement Income Security Act of 1974, 29 U.S.C. 1103, and the regulations prescribed thereunder by the Secretary of Labor. [Reg. § 1.401(f)-1.]

☐ [*T.D. 7565, 9-14-78. Amended by T.D. 7748, 12-30-80, T.D. 8635, 12-19-95 and T.D. 9849, 3-11-2019.*]

[Reg. § 1.401(k)-0]

§ 1.401(k)-0. Table of contents.—This section contains first a list of section headings and then a list of the paragraphs in each section in §§ 1.401(k)-1 through 1.401(k)-6.

(4) Rules applicable to distributions upon plan termination.
    (i) No alternative defined contribution plan.
    (ii) Lump sum requirement for certain distributions.
(5) Rules applicable to all distributions.
    (i) Exclusive distribution rules.
    (ii) Deemed distributions.
    (iii) ESOP dividend distributions.
    (iv) Limitations apply after transfer.
(6) Examples.
(e) Additional requirements for qualified cash or deferred arrangements.
(1) Qualified plan requirement.
(2) Election requirements.
    (i) Cash must be available.
    (ii) Frequency of elections.
(3) Separate accounting requirement.
    (i) General rule.
    (ii) Satisfaction of separate accounting requirement.
(4) Limitations on cash or deferred arrangements of state and local governments.
    (i) General rule.
    (ii) Rural cooperative plans and Indian tribal governments.
    (iii) Adoption after May 6, 1986.
    (iv) Adoption before May 7, 1986.
(5) One-year eligibility requirement.
(6) Other benefits not contingent upon elective contributions.
    (i) General rule.
    (ii) Definition of other benefits.
    (iii) Effect of certain statutory limits.
    (iv) Nonqualified deferred compensation.
    (v) Plan loans and distributions.
    (vi) Examples.
(7) Plan provision requirement.
(f) Special rules for designated Roth contributions.
(1) In general.
(2) Inclusion treatment.
(3) Separate accounting required.
(4) Designated Roth contributions must satisfy rules applicable to elective contributions.
    (i) In general.
    (ii) Special rules for direct rollovers.
(5) Rules regarding designated Roth contribution elections.
    (i) Frequency of elections.
    (ii) Default elections.
(6) Effective date.
(g) Effective dates.
(1) General rule.
(2) Early implementation permitted.
(3) Collectively bargained plans.
(4) Applicability of prior regulations.
§ 1.401(k)-2 ADP test.
(a) Actual deferral percentage (ADP) test.
(1) In general.
    (i) ADP test formula.
    (ii) HCEs as sole eligible employees.
    (iii) Special rule for early participation.
(2) Determination of ADP.
    (i) General rule.
    (ii) Determination of applicable year under current year and prior year testing method.
(3) Determination of ADR.
    (i) General rule.
    (ii) ADR of HCEs eligible under more than one arrangement.
      (A) General rule.
      (B) Plans not permitted to be aggregated.
    (iii) Examples.
(4) Elective contributions taken into account under the ADP test.
    (i) General rule.
    (ii) Elective contributions for partners and self-employed individuals.
    (iii) Elective contributions for HCEs.
(5) Elective contributions not taken into account under the ADP test.
    (i) General rule.
    (ii) Elective contributions for NHCEs.
    (iii) Elective contributions treated as catch-up contributions.
    (iv) Elective contributions used to satisfy the ACP test.
    (v) Additional elective contributions pursuant to section 414(u).

    (vi) Default elective contributions pursuant to section 414(w).
(6) Qualified nonelective contributions and qualified matching contributions that may be taken into account under the ADP test.
    (i) Timing of allocation.
    (ii) Requirement that amount satisfy section 401(a)(4).
    (iii) Aggregation must be permitted.
    (iv) Disporportionate contributions not taken into account.
      (A) General rule.
      (B) Definition of representative contribution rate.
      (C) Definition of applicable contribution rate.
      (D) Special rule for prevailing wage contributions.
    (v) Qualified matching contributions.
    (vi) Contributions only used once.
(7) Examples.
(b) Correction of excess contributions.
(1) Permissible correction methods.
    (i) In general.
      (A) Qualified nonelective contributions or qualified matching contributions.
      (B) Excess contributions distributed.
      (C) Excess contributions recharacterized.
    (ii) Combination of correction methods.
    (iii) Exclusive means of correction.
(2) Corrections through distribution.
    (i) General rule.
    (ii) Calculation of total amount to be distributed.
      (A) Calculate the dollar amount of excess contributions for each HCE.
      (B) Determination of the total amount of excess contributions.
      (C) Satisfaction of ADP.
    (iii) Apportionment of total amount of excess contributions among the HCEs.
      (A) Calculate the dollar amount of excess contributions for each HCE.
      (B) Limit on amount apportioned to any individual.
      (C) Apportionment to additional HCEs.
    (iv) Income allocable to excess contributions.
      (A) General rule.
      (B) Method of allocating income.
      (C) Alternative method of allocating plan year income.
      (D) Plan years before 2008.
      (E) Alternative method for allocating plan year and gap period income.
    (v) Distribution.
    (vi) Tax treatment of corrective distributions.
      (A) Corrective distributions for plan years beginning on or after January 1, 2008.
      (B) Corrective distributions for plan years beginning before January 1, 2008.
      (C) Corrective distributions attributable to designated Roth contributions.
    (vii) Other rules.
      (A) No employee or spousal consent required.
      (B) Treatment of corrective distributions as elective contributions.
      (C) No reduction of required minimum distribution.
      (D) Partial distributions.
    (viii) Examples.
(3) Recharacterization of excess contributions.
    (i) General rule.
    (ii) Treatment of recharacterized excess contributions.
    (iii) Additional rules.
      (A) Time of recharacterization.
      (B) Employee contributions must be permitted under plan.
      (C) Treatment of recharacterized excess contributions.
(4) Rules applicable to all corrections.
    (i) Coordination with distribution of excess deferrals.
      (A) Treatment of excess deferrals that reduce excess contributions.
      (B) Treatment of excess contributions that reduce excess deferrals.
    (ii) Forfeiture of match on distributed excess contributions.
    (iii) Permitted forfeiture of QMAC.
    (iv) No requirement for recalculation.
    (v) Treatment of excess contributions that are catch-up contributions.
(5) Failure to timely correct.
    (i) Failure to correct within 2½ months after end of plan year.

(ii) Failure to correct within 12 months after end of plan year.

(iii) Special rule for eligible automatic contribution arrangements.

(c) Additional rules for prior year testing method.

(1) Rules for change in testing method.

(i) General rule.

(ii) Situations permitting a change to the prior year testing method.

(2) Calculation of ADP under the prior year testing method for the first plan year.

(i) Plans that are not successor plans.

(ii) First plan year defined.

(iii) Successor plans.

(3) Plans using different testing methods for the ADP and ACP test.

(4) Rules for plan coverage changes.

(i) In general.

(ii) Optional rule for minor plan coverage changes.

(iii) Definitions.

(A) Plan coverage change.

(B) Prior year subgroup.

(C) Weighted average of the ADPs for the prior year subgroups.

(iv) Examples.

§1.401(k)-3 Safe harbor requirements.

(a) ADP test safe harbor.

(1) Section 401(k)(12) safe harbor.

(2) Section 401(k)(13) safe harbor.

(3) Requirements applicable to safe harbor contributions.

(b) Safe harbor nonelective contribution requirement.

(1) General rule.

(2) Safe harbor compensation defined.

(c) Safe harbor matching contribution requirement.

(1) In general.

(2) Basic matching formula.

(3) Enhanced matching formula.

(4) Limitation on HCE matching contributions.

(5) Use of safe harbor match not precluded by certain plan provisions.

(i) Safe harbor matching contributions on employee contributions.

(ii) Periodic matching contributions.

(6) Permissible restrictions on elective contributions by NHCEs.

(i) General rule.

(ii) Restrictions on election periods.

(iii) Restrictions on amount of elective contributions.

(iv) Restrictions on types of compensation that may be deferred.

(v) Restrictions due to limitations under the Internal Revenue Code.

(7) Examples.

(d) Notice requirement.

(1) General rule.

(2) Content requirement.

(i) General rule.

(ii) Minimum content requirement.

(iii) References to SPD.

(3) Timing requirement.

(i) General rule.

(ii) Deemed satisfaction of timing requirement.

(e) Plan year requirement.

(1) General rule.

(2) Initial plan year.

(3) Change of plan year.

(4) Final plan year.

(f) Plan amendments adopting safe harbor nonelective contributions.

(1) General rule.

(2) Contingent notice provided.

(3) Follow-up notice requirement.

(g) Permissible reduction or suspension of safe harbor contributions.

(1) General rule.

(i) Matching contributions.

(ii) Nonelective contributions.

(2) Supplemental notice.

(h) Additional rules.

(1) Contributions taken into account.

(2) Use of safe harbor nonelective contributions to satisfy other nondiscrimination tests.

(3) Early participation rules.

(4) Satisfying safe harbor contribution requirement under another defined contribution plan.

(5) Contributions used only once.

(i) [Reserved].

(j) Qualified automatic contribution arrangement.

(1) Automatic contribution requirement.

(i) In general.

(ii) Automatic contribution arrangement.

(iii) Exception to automatic enrollment for certain current employees.

(2) Qualified percentage.

(i) In general.

(ii) Minimum percentage requirements.

(A) Initial-period requirement.

(B) Second-year requirement.

(C) Third-year requirement.

(D) Later years requirement.

(iii) Exception to uniform percentage requirement.

(iv) Treatment of periods without default contributions.

(k) Modifications to contribution requirements and notice requirements for automatic contribution safe harbor.

(1) In general.

(2) Lower matching requirement.

(3) Modified nonforfeiture requirement.

(4) Additional notice requirements.

(i) In general.

(ii) Additional information.

(iii) Timing requirements.

§1.401(k)-4 SIMPLE 401(k) plan requirements.

(a) General rule.

(b) Eligible employer.

(1) General rule.

(2) Special rule.

(c) Exclusive plan.

(1) General rule.

(2) Special rule.

(d) Election and notice.

(1) General rule.

(2) Employee elections.

(i) Initial plan year of participation.

(ii) Subsequent plan years.

(iii) Election to terminate.

(3) Employee notices.

(e) Contributions.

(1) General rule.

(2) Elective contributions.

(3) Matching contributions.

(4) Nonelective contributions.

(5) SIMPLE compensation.

(f) Vesting.

(g) Plan year.

(h) Other rules.

§1.401(k)-5 Special rules for mergers, acquisitions and similar events. [Reserved]

§1.401(k)-6 Definitions.

[Reg. §1.401(k)-0.]

□ [T.D. 8217, 8-5-88. Amended by T.D. 8357, 8-8-91; T.D. 8376, 12-2-91; T.D. 8581, 12-22-94; T.D. 9169, 12-28-2004; T.D. 9237, 12-30-2005; T.D. 9324, 4-27-2007; T.D. 9447, 2-23-2009, T.D. 9641, 11-14-2013 and T.D. 9875, 9-19-2019.]

[Reg. §1.401(k)-1]

§1.401(k)-1. Certain cash or deferred arrangements.—(a) *General rules.*—(1) *Certain plans permitted to include cash or deferred arrangements.*—A plan, other than a profit-sharing, stock bonus, pre-ERISA money purchase pension, or rural cooperative plan, does not satisfy the requirements of section 401(a) if the plan includes a cash or deferred arrangement. A profit-sharing, stock bonus, pre-ERISA money purchase pension, or rural cooperative plan does not fail to satisfy the requirements of section 401(a) merely because the plan includes a cash or deferred arrangement. A cash or deferred arrangement is part of a plan for purposes of this section if any contributions to the plan, or accruals or other benefits under the plan, are made or provided pursuant to the cash or deferred arrangement.

(2) *Rules applicable to cash or deferred arrangements generally.*— (i) *Definition of cash or deferred arrangement.*—Except as provided in paragraphs (a)(2)(ii) and (iii) of this section, a cash or deferred

arrangement is an arrangement under which an eligible employee may make a cash or deferred election with respect to contributions to, or accruals or other benefits under, a plan that is intended to satisfy the requirements of section 401(a) (including a contract that is intended to satisfy the requirements of section 403(a)).

(ii) *Treatment of after-tax employee contributions.*—A cash or deferred arrangement does not include an arrangement under which amounts contributed under a plan at an employee's election are designated or treated at the time of contribution as after-tax employee contributions (e.g., by treating the contributions as taxable income subject to applicable withholding requirements). See also section 414(h)(1). A designated Roth contribution, however, is not treated as an after-tax contribution for purposes of this section, § 1.401(k)-2 through § 1.401(k)-6 and § 1.401(m)-1 through § 1.401(m)-5. A contribution can be an after-tax employee contribution under the rule of this paragraph (a)(2)(ii) even if the employee's election to make after-tax employee contributions is made before the amounts subject to the election are currently available to the employee.

(iii) *Treatment of ESOP dividend election.*—A cash or deferred arrangement does not include an arrangement under an ESOP under which dividends are either distributed or invested pursuant to an election made by participants or their beneficiaries in accordance with section 404(k)(2)(A)(iii).

(iv) *Treatment of elective contributions as plan assets.*—The extent to which elective contributions constitute plan assets for purposes of the prohibited transaction provisions of section 4975 and Title I of the Employee Retirement Income Security Act of 1974 (88 Stat. 829), Public Law 93-406, is determined in accordance with regulations and rulings issued by the Department of Labor. See 29 CFR 2510.3-102.

(3) *Rules applicable to cash or deferred elections generally.*—(i) *Definition of cash or deferred election.*—A cash or deferred election is any direct or indirect election (or modification of an earlier election) by an employee to have the employer either—

(A) Provide an amount to the employee in the form of cash (or some other taxable benefit) that is not currently available; or

(B) Contribute an amount to a trust, or provide an accrual or other benefit, under a plan deferring the receipt of compensation.

(ii) *Automatic enrollment.*—For purposes of determining whether an election is a cash or deferred election, it is irrelevant whether the default that applies in the absence of an affirmative election is described in paragraph (a)(3)(i)(A) of this section (i.e., the employee receives an amount in cash or some other taxable benefit) or in paragraph (a)(3)(i)(B) of this section (i.e., the employer contributes an amount to a trust or provides an accrual or other benefit under a plan deferring the receipt of compensation).

(iii) *Rules related to timing.*—(A) *Requirement that amounts not be currently available.*—A cash or deferred election can only be made with respect to an amount that is not currently available to the employee on the date of the election. Further, a cash or deferred election can only be made with respect to amounts that would (but for the cash or deferred election) become currently available after the later of the date on which the employer adopts the cash or deferred arrangement or the date on which the arrangement first becomes effective.

(B) *Contribution may not precede election.*—A contribution is made pursuant to a cash or deferred election only if the contribution is made after the election is made.

(C) *Contribution may not precede services.*—(1) *General rule.*—Contributions are made pursuant to a cash or deferred election only if the contributions are made after the employee's performance of service with respect to which the contributions are made (or when the cash or other taxable benefit would be currently available, if earlier).

(2) *Exception for bona fide administrative considerations.*—The timing of contributions will not be treated as failing to satisfy the requirements of this paragraph (a)(3)(iii)(C) merely because contributions for a pay period are occasionally made before the services with respect to that pay period are performed, provided the contributions are made early in order to accommodate bona fide administrative considerations (for example, the temporary absence of the bookkeeper with responsibility to transmit contributions to the plan) and are not paid early with a principal purpose of accelerating deductions.

(iv) *Current availability defined.*—Cash or another taxable benefit is currently available to the employee if it has been paid to the employee or if the employee is able currently to receive the cash or

other taxable benefit at the employee's discretion. An amount is not currently available to an employee if there is a significant limitation or restriction on the employee's right to receive the amount currently. Similarly, an amount is not currently available as of a date if the employee may under no circumstances receive the amount before a particular time in the future. The determination of whether an amount is currently available to an employee does not depend on whether it has been constructively received by the employee for purposes of section 451.

(v) *Certain one-time elections not treated as cash or deferred elections.*—A cash or deferred election does not include a one-time irrevocable election made no later than the employee's first becoming eligible under the plan or any other plan or arrangement of the employer that is described in section 219(g)(5)(A) (whether or not such other plan or arrangement has terminated), to have contributions equal to a specified amount or percentage of the employee's compensation (including no amount of compensation) made by the employer on the employee's behalf to the plan and a specified amount or percentage of the employee's compensation (including no amount of compensation) divided among all other plans or arrangements of the employer (including plans or arrangements not yet established) for the duration of the employee's employment with the employer, or in the case of a defined benefit plan to receive accruals or other benefits (including no benefits) under such plans. Thus, for example, employer contributions made pursuant to a one-time irrevocable election described in this paragraph are not treated as having been made pursuant to a cash or deferred election and are not includible in an employee's gross income by reason of § 1.402(a)-1(d). In the case of an irrevocable election made on or before December 23, 1994—

(A) The election does not fail to be treated as a one-time irrevocable election under this paragraph (a)(3)(v) merely because an employee was previously eligible under another plan of the employer (whether or not such other plan has terminated); and

(B) In the case of a plan in which partners may participate, the election does not fail to be treated as a one-time irrevocable election under this paragraph (a)(3)(v) merely because the election was made after commencement of employment or after the employee's first becoming eligible under any plan of the employer, provided that the election was made before the first day of the first plan year beginning after December 31, 1988, or, if later, March 31, 1989.

(vi) *Tax treatment of employees.*—An amount generally is includible in an employee's gross income for the taxable year in which the employee actually or constructively receives the amount. But for section 402(e)(3), an employee is treated as having received an amount that is contributed to an exempt trust or plan described in section 401(a) or 403(a) pursuant to the employee's cash or deferred election. This is the case even if the election to defer is made before the year in which the amount is earned, or before the amount is currently available. See § 1.402(a)-1(d).

(vii) *Examples.*—The following examples illustrate the application of this paragraph (a)(3):

Example 1. (i) An employer maintains a profit-sharing plan under which each eligible employee has an election to defer an annual bonus payable on January 30 each year. The bonus equals 10% of compensation during the previous calendar year. Deferred amounts are not treated as after-tax employee contributions. The bonus is currently available on January 30.

(ii) An election made prior to January 30 to defer all or part of the bonus is a cash or deferred election, and the bonus deferral arrangement is a cash or deferred arrangement.

Example 2. (i) An employer maintains a profit-sharing plan which provides for discretionary profit sharing contributions and under which each eligible employee may elect to reduce his compensation by up to 10% and to have the employer contribute such amount to the plan. The employer pays each employee every two weeks for services during the immediately preceding two weeks. The employee's election to defer compensation for a payroll period must be made prior to the date the amount would otherwise be paid. The employer contributes to the plan the amount of compensation that each employee elected to defer, at the time it would otherwise be paid to the employee, and does not treat the contribution as an after-tax employee contribution.

(ii) The election is a cash or deferred election and the contributions are elective contributions.

Example 3. (i) The facts are the same as in *Example 2*, except that the employer makes a $10,000 contribution on January 31 of the plan year that is in addition to the contributions that satisfy the employer's obligation to make contributions with respect to cash or deferred elections for prior payroll periods. Employee A makes an election on February 15 to defer $2,000 from compensation that is not currently available and the employer reduces the employee's compensation to reflect the election.

(ii) None of the additional $10,000 contributed January 31 is a contribution made pursuant to Employee A's cash or deferred election, because the contribution was made before the election was made. Accordingly, the employer must make an additional contribution of $2,000 in order to satisfy its obligation to contribute an amount to the plan pursuant to Employee A's election. The $10,000 contribution may be allocated under the plan terms providing for discretionary profit sharing contributions.

Example 4. (i) The facts are the same as in *Example 3*, except that Employee A had an outstanding election to defer $500 from each payroll period's compensation. The $10,000 additional payment that is contributed early is not made early in order to accommodate bona fide administrative considerations.

(ii) None of the additional $10,000 contributed January 31 is a contribution made pursuant to Employee A's cash or deferred election for future payroll periods, because the contribution was made before the earlier of Employee A's performance of services to which the contribution is attributable or when the compensation would be currently available. Furthermore, the exception for early contributions in paragraph (a)(3)(iii)(C)(2) of this section does not apply. Accordingly, the employer must make an additional contribution of $500 per payroll period in order to satisfy its obligation to contribute an amount to the plan pursuant to Employee A's election. The $10,000 contribution may be allocated under the plan terms providing for discretionary profit sharing contributions.

Example 5. (i) Employer B establishes a money purchase pension plan in 1986. This is the first qualified plan established by Employer B. All salaried employees are eligible to participate under the plan. Hourly-paid employees are not eligible to participate under the plan. In 2000, Employer B establishes a profit-sharing plan under which all employees (both salaried and hourly) are eligible. Employer B permits all employees on the effective date of the profit-sharing plan to make a one-time irrevocable election to have Employer B contribute 5% of compensation on their behalf to the plan and make no other contribution to any other plan of Employer B (including plans not yet established) for the duration of the employee's employment with Employer B, and have their salaries reduced by 5%.

(ii) The election provided under the profit-sharing plan is not a one-time irrevocable election within the meaning of paragraph (a)(3)(v) of this section with respect to the salaried employees of Employer B who, before becoming eligible to participate under the profit-sharing plan, became eligible to participate under the money purchase pension plan. The election under the profit-sharing plan is a one-time irrevocable election within the meaning of paragraph (a)(3)(v) of this section with respect to the hourly employees, because they were not previously eligible to participate under another plan of the employer.

(4) *Rules applicable to qualified cash or deferred arrangements.*—(i) *Definition of qualified cash or deferred arrangement.*—A qualified cash or deferred arrangement is a cash or deferred arrangement that satisfies the requirements of paragraphs (b), (c), (d), and (e) of this section.

(ii) *Treatment of elective contributions as employer contributions.*—Except as otherwise provided in § 1.401(k)-2(b)(3), elective contributions under a qualified cash or deferred arrangement (including designated Roth contributions) are treated as employer contributions. Thus, for example, elective contributions under such an arrangement are treated as employer contributions for purposes of sections 401(a), 401(k), 402, 404, 409, 411, 412, 415, 416, and 417.

(iii) *Tax treatment of employees.*—Except as provided in section 402(g), 402A (effective for taxable years beginning after December 31, 2005), or § 1.401(k)-2(b)(3), elective contributions under a qualified cash or deferred arrangement are neither includible in an employee's gross income at the time the cash would have been includible in the employee's gross income (but for the cash or deferred election), nor at the time the elective contributions are contributed to the plan. See § 1.402(a)-1(d)(2)(i).

(iv) *Application of nondiscrimination requirements to plan that includes a qualified cash or deferred arrangement.*—(A) *Exclusive means of amounts testing.*—Elective contributions (including elective contributions that are designated Roth contributions) under a qualified cash or deferred arrangement satisfy the requirements of section 401(a)(4) with respect to amounts if and only if the amount of elective contributions satisfies the nondiscrimination test of section 401(k) under paragraph (b)(1) of this section. See § 1.401(a)(4)-1(b)(2)(ii)(B).

(B) *Testing benefits, rights and features.*—A plan that includes a qualified cash or deferred arrangement must satisfy the requirements of section 401(a)(4) with respect to benefits, rights and features

in addition to the requirements regarding amounts described in paragraph (a)(4)(iv)(A) of this section. For example, the right to make each level of elective contributions under a cash or deferred arrangement and the right to make designated Roth contributions are rights or features subject to the requirements of section 401(a)(4). See § 1.401(a)(4)-4(e)(3)(i) and (iii)(D). Thus, for example, if all employees are eligible to make a stated level of elective contributions under a cash or deferred arrangement, but that level of contributions can only be made from compensation in excess of a stated amount, such as the Social Security taxable wage base, the arrangement will generally favor HCEs with respect to the availability of elective contributions and thus will generally not satisfy the requirements of section 401(a)(4).

(C) *Minimum coverage requirement.*—A qualified cash or deferred arrangement is treated as a separate plan that must satisfy the requirements of section 410(b). See § 1.410(b)-7(c)(1) for special rules. The determination of whether a cash or deferred arrangement satisfies the requirements of section 410(b) must be made without regard to the modifications to the disaggregation rules set forth in paragraph (b)(4)(v) of this section. See also § 1.401(a)(4)-11(g)(3)(vii)(A), relating to corrective amendments that may be made to satisfy the minimum coverage requirements of section 410(b).

(5) *Rules applicable to nonqualified cash or deferred arrangements.*—(i) *Definition of nonqualified cash or deferred arrangement.*—A nonqualified cash or deferred arrangement is a cash or deferred arrangement that fails to satisfy one or more of the requirements in paragraph (b), (c), (d) or (e) of this section.

(ii) *Treatment of elective contributions as nonelective contributions.*—Except as specifically provided otherwise, elective contributions under a nonqualified cash or deferred arrangement are treated as nonelective employer contributions. Thus, for example, the elective contributions under such an arrangement are treated as nonelective employer contributions for purposes of sections 401(a) (including section 401(a)(4)) and 401(k), 404, 409, 411, 412, 415, 416, and 417 and are not subject to the requirements of section 401(m).

(iii) *Tax treatment of employees.*—Elective contributions under a nonqualified cash or deferred arrangement are includible in an employee's gross income at the time the cash or other taxable amount that the employee would have received (but for the cash or deferred election) would have been includible in the employee's gross income. See § 1.402(a)-1(d)(1).

(iv) *Qualification of plan that includes a nonqualified cash or deferred arrangement.*—(A) *In general.*—A profit-sharing, stock bonus, pre-ERISA money purchase pension, or rural cooperative plan does not fail to satisfy the requirements of section 401(a) merely because the plan includes a nonqualified cash or deferred arrangement. In determining whether the plan satisfies the requirements of section 401(a)(4), the nondiscrimination tests of sections 401(k), paragraph (b)(1) of this section, section 401(m)(2) and § 1.401(m)-1(b) may not be used. See § § 1.401(a)(4)-1(b)(2)(ii)(B) and 1.410(b)-9 (definition of section 401(k) plan).

(B) *Application of section 401(a)(4) to certain plans.*—The amount of employer contributions under a nonqualified cash or deferred arrangement is treated as satisfying section 401(a)(4) if the arrangement is part of a collectively bargained plan that automatically satisfies the requirements of section 410(b). See § § 1.401(a)(4)-1(c)(5) and 1.410(b)-2(b)(7). Additionally, the requirements of sections 401(a)(4) and 410(b) do not apply to a governmental plan (within the meaning of section 414(d)) maintained by a State or local government or political subdivision thereof (or agency or instrumentality thereof). See sections 401(a)(5) and 410(c)(1)(A).

(v) *Example.*—The following example illustrates the application of this paragraph (a)(5):

Example. (i) For the 2006 plan year, Employer A maintains a collectively bargained plan that includes a cash or deferred arrangement. Employer contributions under the cash or deferred arrangement do not satisfy the nondiscrimination test of section 401(k) and paragraph (b) of this section.

(ii) The arrangement is a nonqualified cash or deferred arrangement. The employer contributions under the cash or deferred arrangement are considered to be nondiscriminatory under section 401(a)(4), and the elective contributions are generally treated as employer contributions under paragraph (a)(5)(ii) of this section. Under paragraph (a)(5)(iii) of this section and under § 1.402(a)-1(d)(1), however, the elective contributions are includible in each employee's gross income.

(6) *Rules applicable to cash or deferred arrangements of self-employed individuals.*—(i) *Application of general rules.*—Generally, a partnership or sole proprietorship is permitted to maintain a cash or deferred

arrangement, and individual partners or owners are permitted to make cash or deferred elections with respect to compensation attributable to services rendered to the entity, under the same rules that apply to other cash or deferred arrangements. For example, any contributions made on behalf of an individual partner or owner pursuant to a cash or deferred arrangement of a partnership or sole proprietorship are elective contributions unless they are designated or treated as after-tax employee contributions. In the case of a partnership, a cash or deferred arrangement includes any arrangement that directly or indirectly permits individual partners to vary the amount of contributions made on their behalf. Consistent with § 1.402(a)-1(d), the elective contributions under such an arrangement are includible in income and are not deductible under section 404(a) unless the arrangement is a qualified cash or deferred arrangement (i.e., the requirements of section 401(k) and this section are satisfied). Also, even if the arrangement is a qualified cash or deferred arrangement, the elective contributions are includible in gross income and are not deductible under section 404(a) to the extent they exceed the applicable limit under section 402(g). See also § 1.401(a)-30.

(ii) *Treatment of matching contributions made on behalf of self-employed individuals.*—Under section 402(g)(8), matching contributions made on behalf of a self-employed individual are not treated as elective contributions made pursuant to a cash or deferred election, without regard to whether such matching contributions indirectly permit individual partners to vary the amount of contributions made on their behalf.

(iii) *Timing of self-employed individual's cash or deferred election.*—For purposes of paragraph (a)(3)(iv) of this section, a partner's compensation is deemed currently available on the last day of the partnership taxable year and a sole proprietor's compensation is deemed currently available on the last day of the individual's taxable year. Accordingly, a self-employed individual may not make a cash or deferred election with respect to compensation for a partnership or sole proprietorship taxable year after the last day of that year. See § 1.401(k)-2(a)(4)(ii) for the rules regarding when these contributions are treated as allocated.

(iv) *Special rule for certain payments to self-employed individuals.*—For purposes of sections 401(k) and 401(m), the earned income of a self-employed individual for a taxable year constitutes payment for services during that year. Thus, for example, if a partnership provides for cash advance payments during the taxable year to be made to a partner based on the value of the partner's services prior to the date of payment (and which do not exceed a reasonable estimate of the partner's earned income for the taxable year), a contribution of a portion of these payments to a profit sharing plan in accordance with an election to defer the portion of the advance payments does not fail to be made pursuant to a cash or deferred election within the meaning of paragraph (a)(3)(iii) of this section merely because the contribution is made before the amount of the partner's earned income is finally determined and reported. However, see § 1.401(k)-2(a)(4)(ii) for rules on when earned income is treated as received.

(b) *Coverage and nondiscrimination requirements.*—(1) *In general.*—A cash or deferred arrangement satisfies this paragraph (b) for a plan year only if—

(i) The group of eligible employees under the cash or deferred arrangement (including any employees taken into account for purposes of section 410(b) pursuant to § 1.401(a)(4)-11(g)(3)(vii)(A)) satisfies the requirements of section 410(b) (including the average benefit percentage test, if applicable); and

(ii) The cash or deferred arrangement satisfies—

(A) The ADP test of section 401(k)(3) described in § 1.401(k)-2;

(B) The ADP safe harbor provisions of section 401(k)(12) described in § 1.401(k)-3; or

(C) The ADP safe harbor provisions of section 401(k)(13) described in § 1.401(k)-3; or

(D) The SIMPLE 401(k) provisions of section 401(k)(11) described in § 1.401(k)- 4.

(2) *Automatic satisfaction by certain plans.*—Notwithstanding paragraph (b)(1) of this section, a governmental plan (within the meaning of section 414(d)) maintained by a State or local government or political subdivision thereof (or agency or instrumentality thereof) shall be treated as meeting the requirements of this paragraph (b).

(3) *Anti-abuse provisions.*—This section and § § 1.401(k)-2 through 1.401(k)-6 are designed to provide simple, practical rules that accommodate legitimate plan changes. At the same time, the rules are intended to be applied by employers in a manner that does not make use of changes in plan testing procedures or other plan provisions to inflate inappropriately the ADP for NHCEs (which is used as a benchmark for testing the ADP for HCEs) or to otherwise manipulate

the nondiscrimination testing requirements of this paragraph (b). Further, this paragraph (b) is part of the overall requirement that benefits or contributions not discriminate in favor of HCEs. Therefore, a plan will not be treated as satisfying the requirements of this paragraph (b) if there are repeated changes to plan testing procedures or plan provisions that have the effect of distorting the ADP so as to increase significantly the permitted ADP for HCEs, or otherwise manipulate the nondiscrimination rules of this paragraph, if a principal purpose of the changes was to achieve such a result.

(4) *Aggregation and restructuring.*—(i) *In general.*—This paragraph (b)(4) contains the exclusive rules for aggregating and disaggregating plans and cash or deferred arrangements for purposes of this section, and § § 1.401(k)-2 through 1.401(k)-6.

(ii) *Aggregation of cash or deferred arrangements within a plan.*—Except as otherwise specifically provided in this paragraph (b)(4), all cash or deferred arrangements included in a plan are treated as a single cash or deferred arrangement and a plan must apply a single test under paragraph (b)(1)(ii) of this section with respect to all such arrangements within the plan. Thus, for example, if two groups of employees are eligible for separate cash or deferred arrangements under the same plan, all contributions under both cash or deferred arrangements must be treated as made under a single cash or deferred arrangement subject to a single test, even if they have significantly different features, such as different limits on elective contributions.

(iii) *Aggregation of plans.*—(A) *In general.*—For purposes of this section and § § 1.401(k)-2 through 1.401(k)-6, the term *plan* means a plan within the meaning of § 1.410(b)-7(a) and (b), after application of the mandatory disaggregation rules of § 1.410(b)-7(c), and the permissive aggregation rules of § 1.410(b)-7(d), as modified by paragraph (b)(4)(v) of this section. Thus, for example, two plans (within the meaning of § 1.410(b)-7(b)) that are treated as a single plan pursuant to the permissive aggregation rules of § 1.410(b)-7(d) are treated as a single plan for purposes of sections 401(k) and (m).

(B) *Plans with inconsistent ADP testing methods.*—Pursuant to paragraph (b)(4)(ii) of this section, a single testing method must apply with respect to all cash or deferred arrangements under a plan. Thus, in applying the permissive aggregation rules of § 1.410(b)-7(d), an employer may not aggregate plans (within the meaning of § 1.410(b)-7(b)) that apply inconsistent testing methods. For example, a plan (within the meaning of § 1.410(b)-7(b)) that applies the current year testing method may not be aggregated with another plan that applies the prior year testing method. Similarly, an employer may not aggregate a plan (within the meaning of § 1.410(b)-7(b)) using the ADP safe harbor provisions of section 401(k)(12) and another plan that is using the ADP test of section 401(k)(3).

(iv) *Disaggregation of plans and separate testing.*—(A) *In general.*—If a cash or deferred arrangement is included in a plan (within the meaning of § 1.410(b)-7(b)) that is mandatorily disaggregated under the rules of section 410(b) (as modified by this paragraph (b)(4)), the cash or deferred arrangement must be disaggregated in a consistent manner. For example, in the case of an employer that is treated as operating qualified separate lines of business under section 414(r), if the eligible employees under a cash or deferred arrangement are in more than one qualified separate line of business, only those employees within each qualified separate line of business may be taken into account in determining whether each disaggregated portion of the plan complies with the requirements of section 401(k), unless the employer is applying the special rule for employer-wide plans in § 1.414(r)-1(c)(2)(ii) with respect to the plan. Similarly, if a cash or deferred arrangement under which employees are permitted to participate before they have completed the minimum age and service requirements of section 410(a)(1) applies section 410(b)(4)(B) for determining whether the plan complies with section 410(b)(1), then the arrangement must be treated as two separate arrangements, one comprising all eligible employees who have met the age and service requirements of section 410(a)(1) and one comprising all eligible employees who have not met the age and service requirements under section 410(a)(1), unless the plan is using the rule in § 1.401(k)-2(a)(1)(iii)(A).

(B) *Restructuring prohibited.*—Restructuring under § 1.401(a)(4)-9(c) may not be used to demonstrate compliance with the requirements of section 401(k). See § 1.401(a)(4)-9(c)(3)(ii).

(v) *Modifications to section 410(b) rules.*—(A) *Certain disaggregation rules not applicable.*—The mandatory disaggregation rules relating to section 401(k) plans and section 401(m) plans set forth in § 1.410(b)-7(c)(1) and ESOP and non-ESOP portions of a plan set forth in § 1.410(b)-7(c)(2) shall not apply for purposes of this section and § § 1.401(k)-2 through 1.401(k)-6. Accordingly, notwithstanding § 1.410(b)-7(d)(2), an ESOP and a non-ESOP which are different plans (within the meaning of section 414(l), as described in §1.410(b)-7(b)) are permitted to be aggregated for these purposes.

(B) *Permissive aggregation of collective bargaining units.*—Notwithstanding the general rule under section 410(b) and §1.410(b)-7(c) that a plan that benefits employees who are included in a unit of employees covered by a collective bargaining agreement and employees who are not included in the collective bargaining unit is treated as comprising separate plans, an employer can treat two or more separate collective bargaining units as a single collective bargaining unit for purposes of this section and §§1.401(k)-2 through 1.401(k)-6, provided that the combinations of units are determined on a basis that is reasonable and reasonably consistent from year to year. Thus, for example, if a plan benefits employees in three categories (e.g., employees included in collective bargaining unit A, employees included in collective bargaining unit B, and employees who are not included in any collective bargaining unit), the plan can be treated as comprising three separate plans, each of which benefits only one category of employees. However, if collective bargaining units A and B are treated as a single collective bargaining unit, the plan will be treated as comprising only two separate plans, one benefiting all employees who are included in a collective bargaining unit and another benefiting all other employees. Similarly, if a plan benefits only employees who are included in collective bargaining unit A and employees who are included in collective bargaining unit B, the plan can be treated as comprising two separate plans. However, if collective bargaining units A and B are treated as a single collective bargaining unit, the plan will be treated as a single plan. An employee is treated as included in a unit of employees covered by a collective bargaining agreement if and only if the employee is a collectively bargained employee within the meaning of §1.410(b)-6(d)(2).

(C) *Multiemployer plans.*—Notwithstanding §1.410(b)-7(c)(4)(ii)(C), the portion of the plan that is maintained pursuant to a collective bargaining agreement (within the meaning of §1.413-1(a)(2)) is treated as a single plan maintained by a single employer that employs all the employees benefiting under the same benefit computation formula and covered pursuant to that collective bargaining agreement. The rules of paragraph (b)(4)(v)(B) of this section (including the permissive aggregation of collective bargaining units) apply to the resulting deemed single plan in the same manner as they would to a single employer plan, except that the plan administrator is substituted for the employer where appropriate and that appropriate fiduciary obligations are taken into account. The noncollectively bargained portion of the plan is treated as maintained by one or more employers, depending on whether the noncollectively bargaining unit employees who benefit under the plan are employed by one or more employers.

(vi) *Examples.*—The following examples illustrate the application of this paragraph (b)(4):

Example 1. (i) Employer A maintains Plan V, a profit-sharing plan that includes a cash or deferred arrangement in which all of the employees of Employer A are eligible to participate. For purposes of applying section 410(b), Employer A is treated as operating qualified separate lines of business under section 414(r) in accordance with §1.414(r)-1(b). However, Employer A applies the special rule for employer-wide plans in §1.414(r)-1(c)(2)(ii) to the portion of its profit-sharing plan that consists of elective contributions under the cash or deferred arrangement (and to no other plans or portions of plans).

(ii) Under these facts, the requirements of this section and §§1.401(k)-2 through 1.401(k)-6 must be applied on an employer-wide rather than a qualified separate line of business basis.

Example 2. (i) Employer B maintains Plan W, a profit-sharing plan that includes a cash or deferred arrangement in which all of the employees of Employer B are eligible to participate. For purposes of applying section 410(b), the plan treats the cash or deferred arrangement as two separate plans, one for the employees who have completed the minimum age and service eligibility conditions under section 410(a)(1) and the other for employees who have not completed the conditions. The plan provides that it will satisfy the section 401(k) safe harbor requirement of §1.401(k)-3 with respect to the employees who have met the minimum age and service conditions and that it will meet the ADP test requirements of §1.401(k)-2 with respect to the employees who have not met the minimum age and service conditions.

(ii) Under these facts, the cash or deferred arrangement must be disaggregated on a consistent basis with the disaggregation of Plan W. Thus, the requirements of §1.401(k)-2 must be applied by comparing the ADP for eligible HCEs who have not completed the minimum age and service conditions with the ADP for eligible NHCEs for the applicable year who have not completed the minimum age and service conditions.

Example 3. (i) Employer C maintains Plan X, a stock-bonus plan including an ESOP. The plan also includes a cash or deferred arrangement for participants in the ESOP and non-ESOP portions of the plan.

(ii) Pursuant to paragraph (b)(4)(v)(A) of this section the ESOP and non-ESOP portions of the stock-bonus plan are a single cash or deferred arrangement for purposes of this section and §§1.401(k)-2 through 1.401(k)-6. However, as provided in paragraph (a)(4)(iv)(C) of this section, the ESOP and non-ESOP portions of the plan are still treated as separate plans for purposes of satisfying the requirements of section 410(b).

(c) *Nonforfeitability requirements.*—(1) *General rule.*—A cash or deferred arrangement satisfies this paragraph (c) only if the amount attributable to an employee's elective contributions are immediately nonforfeitable, within the meaning of paragraph (c)(2) of this section, are disregarded for purposes of applying section 411(a)(2) to other contributions or benefits, and the contributions remain nonforfeitable even if the employee makes no additional elective contributions under a cash or deferred arrangement.

(2) *Definition of immediately nonforfeitable.*—An amount is immediately nonforfeitable if it is immediately nonforfeitable within the meaning of section 411, and would be nonforfeitable under the plan regardless of the age and service of the employee or whether the employee is employed on a specific date. An amount that is subject to forfeitures or suspensions permitted by section 411(a)(3) does not satisfy the requirements of this paragraph (c).

(3) *Example.*—The following example illustrates the application of this paragraph (c):

Example. (i) Employees B and C are covered by Employer Y's stock bonus plan, which includes a cash or deferred arrangement. All employees participating in the plan have a nonforfeitable right to a percentage of their account balance derived from all contributions (including elective contributions) as shown in the following table:

Years of service	Nonforfeitable percentage
Less than 1	0%
1	20%
2	40%
3	60%
4	80%
5 or more	100%

(ii) The cash or deferred arrangement does not satisfy paragraph (c) of this section because elective contributions are not immediately nonforfeitable. Thus, the cash or deferred arrangement is a nonqualified cash or deferred arrangement.

(d) *Distribution limitation.*—(1) *General rule.*—A cash or deferred arrangement satisfies this paragraph (d) only if amounts attributable to elective contributions may not be distributed before one of the following events, and any distributions so permitted also satisfy the additional requirements of paragraphs (d)(2) through (5) of this section (to the extent applicable)—

(i) The employee's death, disability, or severance from employment;

(ii) In the case of a profit-sharing, stock bonus or rural cooperative plan—

(A) The employee's attainment of age 59½; or

(B) In accordance with section 401(k)(14), the employee's hardship;

(iii) In accordance with section 401(k)(10), the termination of the plan; or

(iv) In the case of a qualified reservist distribution defined in section 72(t)(2)(G)(iii), the date the reservist was ordered or called to active duty.

(2) *Rules applicable to distributions upon severance from employment.*—An employee has a severance from employment when the employee ceases to be an employee of the employer maintaining the plan. An employee does not have a severance from employment if, in connection with a change of employment, the employee's new employer maintains such plan with respect to the employee. For example, a new employer maintains a plan with respect to an employee by continuing or assuming sponsorship of the plan or by accepting a transfer of plan assets and liabilities (within the meaning of section 414(l)) with respect to the employee.

(3) *Rules applicable to hardship distributions.*—(i) *Distribution must be on account of hardship.*—A distribution is treated as made after an employee's hardship for purposes of paragraph (d)(1)(ii) of this section if and only if it is made on account of the hardship. For purposes of this rule, a distribution is made on account of hardship

only if the distribution both is made on account of an immediate and heavy financial need of the employee and is necessary to satisfy the financial need. The determination of the existence of an immediate and heavy financial need and of the amount necessary to meet the need must be made in accordance with nondiscriminatory and objective standards set forth in the plan.

(ii) *Immediate and heavy financial need.*—(A) *In general.*— Whether an employee has an immediate and heavy financial need is to be determined based on all the relevant facts and circumstances. Generally, for example, the need to pay the funeral expenses of a family member would constitute an immediate and heavy financial need. A distribution made to an employee for the purchase of a boat or television would generally not constitute a distribution made on account of an immediate and heavy financial need. A financial need may be immediate and heavy even if it was reasonably foreseeable or voluntarily incurred by the employee.

(B) *Deemed immediate and heavy financial need.*—A distribution is deemed to be made on account of an immediate and heavy financial need of the employee if the distribution is for—

(1) Expenses for (or necessary to obtain) medical care that would be deductible under section 213(d), determined without regard to the limitations in section 213(a) (relating to the applicable percentage of adjusted gross income and the recipients of the medical care) provided that, if the recipient of the medical care is not listed in section 213(a), the recipient is a primary beneficiary under the plan;

(2) Costs directly related to the purchase of a principal residence for the employee (excluding mortgage payments);

(3) Payment of tuition, related educational fees, and room and board expenses, for up to the next 12 months of post-secondary education for the employee, for the employee's spouse, child or dependent (as defined in section 152 without regard to section 152(b)(1), (b)(2) and (d)(1)(B)), or for a primary beneficiary under the plan;

(4) Payments necessary to prevent the eviction of the employee from the employee's principal residence or foreclosure on the mortgage on that residence;

(5) Payments for burial or funeral expenses for the employee's deceased parent, spouse, child or dependent (as defined in section 152 without regard to section 152(d)(1)(B)), or for a deceased primary beneficiary under the plan;

(6) Expenses for the repair of damage to the employee's principal residence that would qualify for the casualty deduction under section 165 (determined without regard to section 165(h)(5) and whether the loss exceeds 10% of adjusted gross income); or

(7) Expenses and losses (including loss of income) incurred by the employee on account of a disaster declared by the Federal Emergency Management Agency (FEMA) under the Robert T. Stafford Disaster Relief and Emergency Assistance Act, Pub. L. 100-707, provided that the employee's principal residence or principal place of employment at the time of the disaster was located in an area designated by FEMA for individual assistance with respect to the disaster.

(C) *Primary beneficiary under the plan.*—For purposes of paragraph (d)(3)(ii)(B) of this section, a "primary beneficiary under the plan" is an individual who is named as a beneficiary under the plan and has an unconditional right, upon the death of the employee, to all or a portion of the employee's account balance under the plan.

(iii) *Distribution necessary to satisfy financial need.*— (A) *Distribution may not exceed amount of need.*—A distribution is treated as necessary to satisfy an immediate and heavy financial need of an employee only to the extent the amount of the distribution is not in excess of the amount required to satisfy the financial need (including any amounts necessary to pay any federal, state, or local income taxes or penalties reasonably anticipated to result from the distribution).

(B) *No alternative means reasonably available.*—A distribution is not treated as necessary to satisfy an immediate and heavy financial need of an employee unless each of the following requirements is satisfied—

(1) The employee has obtained all other currently available distributions (including distributions of ESOP dividends under section 404(k), but not hardship distributions) under the plan and all other plans of deferred compensation, whether qualified or nonqualified, maintained by the employer;

(2) The employee has provided to the plan administrator a representation in writing (including by using an electronic medium as defined in § 1.401(a)-21(e)(3)), or in such other form as may be prescribed by the Commissioner, that he or she has insufficient cash or other liquid assets reasonably available to satisfy the need; and

(3) The plan administrator does not have actual knowledge that is contrary to the representation.

(C) *Additional conditions.*—A plan generally may provide for additional conditions, such as those described in 26 CFR 1.401(k)-1(d)(3)(iv)(B) and (C) (revised as of April 1, 2019), to demonstrate that a distribution is necessary to satisfy an immediate and heavy financial need of an employee. For example, a plan may provide that, before a hardship distribution may be made, an employee must obtain all nontaxable loans (determined at the time a loan is made) available under the plan and all other plans maintained by the employer. However, a plan may not provide for a suspension of an employee's elective contributions or employee contributions under any plan described in section 401(a) or 403(a), any section 403(b) plan, or any eligible governmental plan described in § 1.457-2(f) as a condition of obtaining a hardship distribution.

(iv) *Commissioner may expand standards.*—The Commissioner may prescribe additional guidance of general applicability, published in the Internal Revenue Bulletin (see § 601.601(d)(2) of this chapter), expanding the list of distributions deemed to be made on account of immediate and heavy financial needs and setting forth additional methods to demonstrate that a distribution is necessary to satisfy an immediate and heavy financial need.

(v) *Applicability date.*—(A) *General rule.*—Except as otherwise provided in this paragraph (d)(3)(v), the rules in this paragraph (d)(3) apply to distributions made on or after January 1, 2020. For distributions made before January 1, 2020, the rules in 26 CFR 1.401(k)-1(d)(3) (revised as of April 1, 2019) apply.

(B) *Options for earlier application.*—The rules in this paragraph (d)(3) may be applied to distributions made in plan years beginning after December 31, 2018, and the last sentence of paragraph (d)(3)(iii)(C) of this section (prohibiting the suspension of contributions as a condition of obtaining a hardship distribution) may be applied as of the first day of the first plan year beginning after December 31, 2018, even if the distribution was made in the prior plan year. Thus, for example, a calendar-year plan that provides for hardship distributions under the rules in 26 CFR 1.401(k)-1(d)(3)(iv)(E) (revised as of April 1, 2019) may be amended to provide that an employee who receives a hardship distribution in the second half of the 2018 plan year will be prohibited from making contributions only until January 1, 2019 (or may continue to provide that contributions will be suspended for the originally scheduled 6 months). In addition, paragraph (d)(3)(ii)(B) of this section (listing distributions deemed to be made on account of an immediate and heavy financial need) may be applied to distributions made on or after a date that is as early as January 1, 2018.

(C) *Certain rules optional in 2019.*—If, in accordance with paragraph (d)(3)(v)(B) of this section, the rules in this paragraph (d)(3) are applied to distributions made before January 1, 2020, then the rules in paragraphs (d)(3)(iii)(B)(2) and (3) of this section (relating to an employee representation) and the last sentence of paragraph (d)(3)(iii)(C) of this section (prohibiting the suspension of contributions as a condition of obtaining a hardship distribution) may be disregarded with respect to such distributions.

(4) *Rules applicable to distributions upon plan termination.*—(i) *No alternative defined contribution plan.*—A distribution may not be made under paragraph (d)(1)(iii) of this section if the employer establishes or maintains an alternative defined contribution plan. For purposes of the preceding sentence, the definition of the term "employer" contained in § 1.401(k)-6 is applied as of the date of plan termination, and a plan is an alternative defined contribution plan only if it is a defined contribution plan that exists at any time during the period beginning on the date of plan termination and ending 12 months after distribution of all assets from the terminated plan. However, if at all times during the 24-month period beginning 12 months before the date of plan termination, fewer than 2% of the employees who were eligible under the defined contribution plan that includes the cash or deferred arrangement as of the date of plan termination are eligible under the other defined contribution plan, the other plan is not an alternative defined contribution plan. In addition, a defined contribution plan is not treated as an alternative defined contribution plan if it is an employee stock ownership plan as defined in section 4975(e)(7) or 409(a), a simplified employee pension as defined in section 408(k), a SIMPLE IRA plan as defined in section 408(p), a plan or contract that satisfies the requirements of section 403(b), or a plan that is described in section 457(b) or (f).

(ii) *Lump sum requirement for certain distributions.*—A distribution may be made under paragraph (d)(1)(iii) of this section only if it is a lump sum distribution. The term lump sum distribution has the meaning provided in section 402(e)(4)(D) (without regard to section 402(e)(4)(D)(i)(I), (II), (III) and (IV)). In addition, a lump sum distribution includes a distribution of an annuity contract from a trust that is part of a plan described in section 401(a) and which is exempt from tax under section 501(a) or an annuity plan described in 403(a).

(5) *Rules applicable to all distributions.*—(i) *Exclusive distribution rules.*—Amounts attributable to elective contributions may not be distributed on account of any event not described in this paragraph (d), such as completion of a stated period of plan participation or the lapse of a fixed number of years. For example, if excess deferrals (and income) for an employee's taxable year are not distributed within the time prescribed in § 1.402(g)-1(e)(2) or (3), the amounts may be distributed only on account of an event described in this paragraph (d). Pursuant to section 401(k)(8), the prohibition on distributions set forth in this section does not apply to a distribution of excess contributions under § 1.401(k)-2(b).

(ii) *Deemed distributions.*—The cost of life insurance (determined under section 72) is not treated as a distribution for purposes of section 401(k)(2) and this paragraph (d). The making of a loan is not treated as a distribution, even if the loan is secured by the employee's accrued benefit attributable to elective contributions or is includible in the employee's income under section 72(p). However, the reduction, by reason of default on a loan, of an employee's accrued benefit derived from elective contributions is treated as a distribution.

(iii) *ESOP dividend distributions.*—A plan does not fail to satisfy the requirements of this paragraph (d) merely by reason of a dividend distribution described in section 404(k)(2).

(iv) *Limitations apply after transfer.*—The limitations of this paragraph (d) generally continue to apply to amounts attributable to elective contributions (including QNECs and qualified matching contributions taken into account for the ADP test under § 1.401(k)-2(a)(6)) that are transferred to another qualified plan of the same or another employer. Thus, the transferee plan will generally fail to satisfy the requirements of section 401(a) and this section if transferred amounts may be distributed before the times specified in this paragraph (d). In addition, a cash or deferred arrangement fails to satisfy the limitations of this paragraph (d) if it transfers amounts to a plan that does not provide that the transferred amounts may not be distributed before the times specified in this paragraph (d). The transferor plan does not fail to comply with the preceding sentence if it reasonably concludes that the transferee plan provides that the transferred amounts may not be distributed before the times specified in this paragraph (d). What constitutes a basis for a reasonable conclusion is determined under standards comparable to those under the rules related to acceptance of rollover distributions. See § 1.401(a)(31)-1, A-14. The limitations of this paragraph (d) cease to apply after the transfer, however, if the amounts could have been distributed at the time of the transfer (other than on account of hardship), and the transfer is an elective transfer described in § 1.411(d)-4, Q&A-3(b)(1). The limitations of this paragraph (d) also do not apply to amounts that have been paid in a direct rollover to the plan after being distributed by another plan.

(6) *Examples.*—The following examples illustrate the application of this paragraph (d):

(i) *Example 1.* Employer M maintains Plan V, a profit-sharing plan that includes a cash or deferred arrangement. Elective contributions under the arrangement may be withdrawn for any reason after two years following the end of the plan year in which the contributions were made. Because the plan permits distributions of elective contributions before the occurrence of one of the events specified in section 401(k)(2)(B) and this paragraph (d), the cash or deferred arrangement is a nonqualified cash or deferred arrangement and the elective contributions are currently includible in income under section 402.

(ii) *Example 2.* (A) Employer N maintains Plan W, a profit-sharing plan that includes a cash or deferred arrangement. Plan W provides for distributions upon a participant's severance from employment, death or disability. All employees of Employer N and its wholly owned subsidiary, Employer O, are eligible to participate in Plan W. Employer N agrees to sell all issued and outstanding shares of Employer O to an unrelated entity, Employer T, effective on December 31, 2006. Following the transaction, Employer O will be a wholly owned subsidiary of Employer T. Additionally, individuals who are employed by Employer O on the effective date of the sale continue to be employed by Employer O following the sale. Following the transaction, all employees of Employer O will cease to participate in Plan W and will become eligible to participate in the cash or deferred arrangement maintained by Employer T, Plan X. No assets will be transferred from Plan W to Plan X, except in the case of a direct rollover within the meaning of section 401(a)(31).

(B) Employer O ceases to be a member of Employer N's controlled group as a result of the sale. Therefore, employees of Employer O who participated in Plan W will have a severance from employment and are eligible to receive a distribution from Plan W.

(iii) *Example 3.* Employer R maintains a pre-ERISA money purchase pension plan that includes a cash or deferred arrangement

that is not a rural cooperative plan. Elective contributions under the arrangement may be distributed to an employee on account of hardship. Under paragraph (d)(1) of this section, hardship is a permissible distribution event only in a profit-sharing, stock bonus or rural cooperative plan. Since elective contributions under the arrangement may be distributed before a permissible distribution event occurs, the cash or deferred arrangement does not satisfy this paragraph (d), and is not a qualified cash or deferred arrangement. Moreover, the plan is not a qualified plan because a money purchase pension plan may not provide for payment of benefits upon hardship. See § 1.401-1(b)(1)(i).

(e) *Additional requirements for qualified cash or deferred arrangements.*—(1) *Qualified plan requirement.*—A cash or deferred arrangement satisfies this paragraph (e) only if the plan of which it is a part is a profit-sharing, stock bonus, pre-ERISA money purchase or rural cooperative plan that otherwise satisfies the requirements of section 401(a) (taking into account the cash or deferred arrangement). A plan that includes a cash or deferred arrangement may provide for other contributions, including employer contributions (other than elective contributions), employee contributions, or both. However, except as expressly permitted under section 401(m), 410(b)(2)(A)(ii) or 416(c)(2)(A), elective contributions and matching contributions taken into account under § 1.401(k)-2(a) may not be taken into account for purposes of determining whether any other contributions under any plan (including the plan to which the contributions are made) satisfy the requirements of section 401(a).

(2) *Election requirements.*—(i) *Cash must be available.*—A cash or deferred arrangement satisfies this paragraph (e) only if the arrangement provides that the amount that each eligible employee may defer as an elective contribution is available to the employee in cash. Thus, for example, if an eligible employee is provided the option to receive a taxable benefit (other than cash) or to have the employer contribute on the employee's behalf to a profit-sharing plan an amount equal to the value of the taxable benefit, the arrangement is not a qualified cash or deferred arrangement. Similarly, if an employee has the option to receive a specified amount in cash or to have the employer contribute an amount in excess of the specified cash amount to a profit-sharing plan on the employee's behalf, any contribution made by the employer on the employee's behalf in excess of the specified cash amount is not treated as made pursuant to a qualified cash or deferred arrangement, but would be treated as a matching contribution. This cash availability requirement applies even if the cash or deferred arrangement is part of a cafeteria plan within the meaning of section 125.

(ii) *Frequency of elections.*—A cash or deferred arrangement satisfies this paragraph (e) only if the arrangement provides an employee with an effective opportunity to make (or change) a cash or deferred election at least once during each plan year. Whether an employee has an effective opportunity is determined based on all the relevant facts and circumstances, including the adequacy of notice of the availability of the election, the period of time during which an election may be made, and any other conditions on elections.

(3) *Separate accounting requirement.*—(i) *General rule.*—A cash or deferred arrangement satisfies this paragraph (e) only if the portion of an employee's benefit subject to the requirements of paragraphs (c) and (d) of this section is determined by an acceptable separate accounting between that portion and any other benefits. Separate accounting is not acceptable unless contributions and withdrawals are attributed to the separate accounts and gains, losses, and other credits or charges are separately allocated on a reasonable and consistent basis to the accounts subject to the requirements of paragraphs (c) and (d) of this section and to other accounts. Subject to section 401(a)(4), forfeitures are not required to be allocated to the accounts in which benefits are subject to paragraphs (c) and (d) of this section. The separate accounting requirement of this paragraph (e)(3)(i) applies at the time the elective contribution is contributed to the plan and continues to apply until the contribution is distributed under the plan.

(ii) *Satisfaction of separate accounting requirement.*—The requirements of paragraph (e)(3)(i) of this section are treated as satisfied if all amounts held under a plan that includes a qualified cash or deferred arrangement (and, if applicable, under another plan to which QNECs and QMACs are made) are subject to the requirements of paragraphs (c) and (d) of this section.

(4) *Limitations on cash or deferred arrangements of state and local governments.*—(i) *General rule.*—A cash or deferred arrangement does not satisfy the requirements of this paragraph (e) if the arrangement is adopted after May 6, 1986, by a State or local government or political subdivision thereof, or any agency or instrumentality thereof (a governmental unit). For purposes of this paragraph (e)(4), an employer that has made a legally binding commitment to adopt a

cash or deferred arrangement is treated as having adopted the arrangement on that date.

(ii) *Rural cooperative plans and Indian tribal governments.*—This paragraph (e)(4) does not apply to a rural cooperative plan or to a plan of an employer which is an Indian tribal government (as defined in section 7701(a)(40)), a subdivision of an Indian tribal government (determined in accordance with section 7871(d)), an agency or instrumentality of an Indian tribal government or subdivision thereof, or a corporation chartered under Federal, State or tribal law which is owned in whole or in part by any of the entities in this paragraph (e)(4)(ii).

(iii) *Adoption after May 6, 1986.*—A cash or deferred arrangement is treated as adopted after May 6, 1986, with respect to all employees of any employer that adopts the arrangement after such date.

(iv) *Adoption before May 7, 1986.*—If a governmental unit adopted a cash or deferred arrangement before May 7, 1986, then any cash or deferred arrangement adopted by the unit at any time is treated as adopted before that date. If an employer adopted an arrangement prior to such date, all employees of the employer may participate in the arrangement.

(5) *One-year eligibility requirement.*—A cash or deferred arrangement satisfies this paragraph (e) only if no employee is required to complete a period of service with the employer maintaining the plan extending beyond the period permitted under section 410(a)(1) (determined without regard to section 410(a)(1)(B)(i)) to be eligible to make a cash or deferred election under the arrangement.

(6) *Other benefits not contingent upon elective contributions.*—(i) *General rule.*—A cash or deferred arrangement satisfies this paragraph (e) only if no other benefit is conditioned (directly or indirectly) upon the employee's electing to make or not to make elective contributions under the arrangement. The preceding sentence does not apply to —

(A) Any matching contribution (as defined in § 1.401(m)-1(a)(2)) made by reason of such an election;

(B) Any benefit, right or feature (such as a plan loan) that requires, or results in, an amount to be withheld from an employee's pay (e.g. to pay for the benefit or to repay the loan), to the extent the cash or deferred arrangement restricts elective contributions to amounts available after such withholding from the employee's pay (after deduction of all applicable income and employment taxes);

(C) Any reduction in the employer's top-heavy contributions under section 416(c)(2) because of matching contributions that resulted from the elective contributions; or

(D) Any benefit that is provided at the employee's election under a plan described in section 125(d) in lieu of an elective contribution under a qualified cash or deferred arrangement.

(ii) *Definition of other benefits.*—For purposes of this paragraph (e)(6), other benefits include, but are not limited to, benefits under a defined benefit plan; nonelective contributions under a defined contribution plan; the availability, cost, or amount of health benefits; vacations or vacation pay; life insurance; dental plans; legal services plans; loans (including plan loans); financial planning services; subsidized retirement benefits; stock options; property subject to section 83; and dependent care assistance. Also, increases in salary, bonuses or other cash remuneration (other than the amount that would be contributed under the cash or deferred election) are benefits for purposes of this paragraph (e)(6). The ability to make after-tax employee contributions is a benefit, but that benefit is not contingent upon an employee's electing to make or not make elective contributions under the arrangement merely because the amount of elective contributions reduces dollar-for-dollar the amount of after-tax employee contributions that may be made. Additionally, benefits under any other plan or arrangement (whether or not qualified) are not contingent upon an employee's electing to make or not to make elective contributions under a cash or deferred arrangement merely because the elective contributions are or are not taken into account as compensation under the other plan or arrangement for purposes of determining benefits.

(iii) *Effect of certain statutory limits.*—Any benefit under an excess benefit plan described in section 3(36) of the Employee Retirement Income Security Act of 1974 (88 Stat. 829), Public Law 93-406, that is dependent on the employee's electing to make or not to make elective contributions is not treated as contingent. Deferred compensation under a nonqualified plan of deferred compensation that is dependent on an employee's having made the maximum elective deferrals under section 402(g) or the maximum elective contributions permitted under the terms of the plan also is not treated as contingent.

(iv) *Nonqualified deferred compensation.*—Except as otherwise provided in paragraph (e)(6)(iii) of this section, participation in a nonqualified deferred compensation plan is treated as contingent for purposes of this paragraph (e)(6) to the extent that an employee may receive additional deferred compensation under the nonqualified plan to the extent the employee makes or does not make elective contributions.

(v) *Plan loans and distributions.*—A loan or distribution of elective contributions is not a benefit conditioned on an employee's electing to make or not make elective contributions under the arrangement merely because the amount of the loan or distribution is based on the amount of the employee's account balance.

(vi) *Examples.*—The following examples illustrate the application of this paragraph (e)(6):

Example 1. Employer T maintains a cash or deferred arrangement for all of its employees. Employer T also maintains a nonqualified deferred compensation plan for two highly paid executives, Employees R and C. Under the terms of the nonqualified deferred compensation plan, R and C are eligible to participate only if they do not make elective contributions under the cash or deferred arrangement. Participation in the nonqualified plan is a contingent benefit for purposes of this paragraph (e)(6), because R's and C's participation is conditioned on their electing not to make elective contributions under the cash or deferred arrangement.

Example 2. Employer T maintains a cash or deferred arrangement for all its employees. Employer T also maintains a nonqualified deferred compensation plan for two highly paid executives, Employees R and C. Under the terms of the arrangements, Employees R and C may defer a maximum of 10% of their compensation, and may allocate their deferral between the cash or deferred arrangement and the nonqualified deferred compensation plan in any way they choose (subject to the overall 10% maximum). Because the maximum deferral available under the nonqualified deferred compensation plan depends on the elective deferrals made under the cash or deferred arrangement, the right to participate in the nonqualified plan is a contingent benefit for purposes of this paragraph (e)(6).

(7) *Plan provision requirement.*—A plan that includes a cash or deferred arrangement satisfies this paragraph (e) only if it provides that the nondiscrimination requirements of section 401(k) will be met. Thus, the plan must provide for satisfaction of one of the specific alternatives described in paragraph (b)(1)(ii) of this section and, if with respect to that alternative there are optional choices, which of the optional choices will apply. For example, a plan that uses the ADP test of section 401(k)(3), as described in paragraph (b)(1)(ii)(A) of this section, must specify whether it is using the current year testing method or prior year testing method. Additionally, a plan that uses the prior year testing method must specify whether the ADP for eligible NHCEs for the first plan year is 3% or the ADP for the eligible NHCEs for the first plan year. Similarly, a plan that uses the safe harbor method of section 401(k)(12), as described in paragraph (b)(1)(ii)(B) of this section, must specify whether the safe harbor contribution will be the nonelective safe harbor contribution or the matching safe harbor contribution and is not permitted to provide that ADP testing will be used if the requirements for the safe harbor are not satisfied. In addition, a plan that uses the safe harbor method of section 401(k)(13), as described in paragraph (b)(1)(ii)(C) of this section, must specify the default percentages that apply for the plan year and whether the safe harbor contribution will be the nonelective safe harbor contribution or the matching safe harbor contribution, and is not permitted to provide that ADP testing will be used if the requirements for the safe harbor are not satisfied. For purposes of this paragraph (e)(7), a plan may incorporate by reference the provisions of section 401(k)(3) and § 1.401(k)-2 if that is the nondiscrimination test being applied. The Commissioner may, in guidance of general applicability, published in the Internal Revenue Bulletin (see § 601.601(d)(2) of this chapter), specify the options that will apply under the plan if the nondiscrimination test is incorporated by reference in accordance with the preceding sentence.

(8) *Section 415 compensation required.*—With respect to compensation that is paid (or would have been paid but for a cash or deferred election) in plan years beginning on or after July 1, 2007, a cash or deferred arrangement satisfies this paragraph (e) only if cash or deferred elections can only be made with respect to amounts that are compensation within the meaning of section 415(c)(3) and § 1.415(c)-2. Thus, for example, the arrangement is not a qualified cash or deferred arrangement if an eligible employee who is not in qualified military service (as that term is defined in section 414(u)) and who is not permanently and totally disabled (as defined in section 22(e)(3)) can make a cash or deferred election with respect to an amount paid after severance from employment, unless the amount is paid by the later of 2 1/2 months after severance from

employment or the end of the year that includes the date of severance from employment and is described in §1.415(c)-2(e)(3)(ii) or (iii).

(f) *Special rules for designated Roth contributions.*—(1) *In general.*—The term *designated Roth contribution* means an elective contribution under a qualified cash or deferred arrangement that, to the extent permitted under the plan, is—

(i) Designated irrevocably by the employee at the time of the cash or deferred election as a designated Roth contribution that is being made in lieu of all or a portion of the pre-tax elective contributions the employee is otherwise eligible to make under the plan;

(ii) Treated by the employer as not excludible from the employee's gross income (in accordance with paragraph (f)(2) of this section);

(iii) Maintained by the plan in a separate account (in accordance with paragraph (f)(3) of this section).

(2) *Inclusion treatment.*—An elective contribution is generally treated as not excludible from gross income if it is treated as includible in gross income by the employer (e.g., by treating the contribution as wages subject to applicable income tax withholding). However, in the case of a self-employed individual, an elective contribution is treated as not excludible from gross income only if the individual does not claim a deduction for such amount. If an elective contribution would not have been includible in gross income if the amount had been paid directly to the employee (rather than being subject to a cash or deferral election), the elective contribution is nevertheless permitted to be a designated Roth contribution, provided the employee is entitled to treat the amount as an investment in the contract pursuant to section 72(f)(2).

(3) *Separate accounting required.*—Under the separate accounting requirement of this paragraph (f)(3), contributions and withdrawals of designated Roth contributions must be credited and debited to a designated Roth account maintained for the employee and the plan must maintain a record of the employee's investment in the contract (that is, designated Roth contributions that have not been distributed) with respect to the employee's designated Roth account. In addition, gains, losses, and other credits or charges must be separately allocated on a reasonable and consistent basis to the designated Roth account and other accounts under the plan. However, forfeitures may not be allocated to the designated Roth account and no contributions other than designated Roth contributions and rollover contributions described in section 402A(c)(3)(B) may be allocated to such account. The separate accounting requirement applies at the time the designated Roth contribution is contributed to the plan and must continue to apply until the designated Roth account is completely distributed. See A-13 of §1.402A-1 for additional requirements for separate accounting.

(4) *Designated Roth contributions must satisfy rules applicable to elective contributions.*—(i) *In general.*—A designated Roth contribution must satisfy the requirements applicable to elective contributions made under a qualified cash or deferred arrangement. Thus, for example, a designated Roth contribution must satisfy the requirements of paragraphs (c) and (d) of this section and is treated as an employer contribution for purposes of sections 401(a), 401(k), 402, 404, 409, 411, 412, 415, 416 and 417. In addition, the designated Roth contributions are treated as elective contributions for purposes of the ADP test. Similarly, the designated Roth account under the plan is subject to the rules of section 401(a)(9)(A) and (B) in the same manner as an account that contains pre-tax elective contributions.

(ii) *Special rules for direct rollovers.*—A direct rollover from a designated Roth account under a qualified cash or deferred arrangement may only be made to another designated Roth account under an applicable retirement plan described in section 402A(e)(1) or to a Roth IRA described in section 408A, and only to the extent the rollover is permitted under the rules of section 402(c). Moreover, a participant's designated Roth account and the participant's other accounts under a plan are treated as accounts held under two separate plans (within the meaning of section 414(l)) for purposes of applying the automatic rollover rules for mandatory distributions under section 401(a)(31)(B)(i)(I) and the special rules in A-9 through A-11 of §1.401(a)(31)-1.

(5) *Rules regarding designated Roth contribution elections.*—(i) *Frequency of elections.*—The rules under paragraph (e)(2)(ii) of this section regarding frequency of elections apply in the same manner to both pre-tax elective contributions and designated Roth contributions. Thus, an employee must have an effective opportunity to make (or change) an election to make designated Roth contributions at least once during each plan year.

(ii) *Default elections.*—(A) In the case of a plan that provides for both pre-tax elective contributions and designated Roth contributions and in which, under paragraph (a)(3)(ii) of this section, the

default in the absence of an affirmative election is to make a contribution under the cash or deferred arrangement, the plan terms must provide the extent to which the default contributions are pre-tax elective contributions and the extent to which the default contributions are designated Roth contributions.

(B) If the default contributions under the plan are designated Roth contributions, then an employee who has not made an affirmative election is deemed to have irrevocably designated the contributions (in accordance with section 402A(c)(1)(B)) as designated Roth contributions.

(6) *Effective date.*—Section 402A and the provisions of this section 1.401(k)-1(f) apply to taxable years beginning after December 31, 2005.

(g) *Effective dates.*—(1) *General rule.*—Except as otherwise provided in this paragraph (g), this section and §§1.401(k)-2 through 1.401(k)-6 apply to plan years that begin on or after January 1, 2006.

(2) *Early implementation permitted.*—A plan is permitted to apply the rules of this section and §§1.401(k)-2 through 1.401(k)-6 to any plan year that ends after December 29, 2004, provided the plan applies all the rules of this section and §§1.401(k)-2 through 1.401(k)-6 and all the rules of §§1.401(m)-1 through 1.401(m)-5, to the extent applicable, for that plan year and all subsequent plan years.

(3) *Collectively bargained plans.*—In the case of a plan maintained pursuant to one or more collective bargaining agreements between employee representatives and one or more employers in effect on the date described in paragraph (g)(1) of this section, the provisions of this section and §§1.401(k)-2 through 1.401(k)-6 apply to the later of the first plan year beginning after the termination of the last such agreement or the first plan year described in paragraph (g)(1) of this section.

(4) *Applicability of prior regulations.*—For any plan year before a plan applies this section and §§1.401(k)-2 through 1.401(k)-6 (either the first plan year beginning on or after January 1, 2006, or such earlier year, as provided in paragraph (g)(2) of this section), §1.401(k)-1 (as it appeared in the April 1, 2004 edition of 26 CFR part 1) applies to the plan to the extent that section, as it so appears, reflects the statutory provisions of section 401(k) as in effect for the relevant year.

(5) *Applicability date for definitions of qualified matching contributions (QMACs) and qualified nonelective contributions (QNECs).*—The revisions to the second sentence in the definitions of QMACs and QNECs in §1.401(k)-6 apply to plan years ending on or after July 20, 2018. [Reg. §1.401(k)-1.]

☐ [T.D. 8217, 8-5-88. Amended by T.D. 8357, 8-8-91; T.D. 8376, 12-2-91; T.D. 8581, 12-22-94; T.D. 9169, 12-28-2004; T.D. 9237, 12-30-2005; T.D. 9319, 4-4-2007; T.D. 9324, 4-27-2007; T.D. 9447, 2-23-2009, T.D. 9835, 7-19-2018 and T.D. 9875, 9-19-2019.]

[Reg. §1.401(k)-2]

§1.401(k)-2. ADP test.—(a) *Actual deferral percentage (ADP) test.*—(1) *In general.*—(i) *ADP test formula.*—A cash or deferred arrangement satisfies the ADP test for a plan year only if—

(A) The ADP for the eligible HCEs for the plan year is not more than the ADP for the eligible NHCEs for the applicable year multiplied by 1.25; or

(B) The excess of the ADP for the eligible HCEs for the plan year over the ADP for the eligible NHCEs for the applicable year is not more than 2 percentage points, and the ADP for the eligible HCEs for the plan year is not more than the ADP for the eligible NHCEs for the applicable year multiplied by 2.

(ii) *HCEs as sole eligible employees.*—If, for the applicable year for determining the ADP of the NHCEs for a plan year, there are no eligible NHCEs (i.e, all of the eligible employees under the cash or deferred arrangement for the applicable year are HCEs), the arrangement is deemed to satisfy the ADP test for the plan year.

(iii) *Special rule for early participation.*—If a cash or deferred arrangement provides that employees are eligible to participate before they have completed the minimum age and service requirements of section 410(a)(1)(A), and if the plan applies section 410(b)(4)(B) in determining whether the cash or deferred arrangement meets the requirements of section 410(b)(1), then in determining whether the arrangement meets the requirements under paragraph (a)(1) of this section, either—

(A) Pursuant to section 401(k)(3)(F), the ADP test is performed under the plan (determined without regard to disaggregation under §1.410(b)-7(c)(3)), using the ADP for all eligible HCEs for the plan year and the ADP of eligible NHCEs for the applicable year, disregarding all NHCEs who have not met the minimum age and service requirements of section 410(a)(1)(A); or

(B) Pursuant to §1.401(k)-1(b)(4), the plan is disaggregated into separate plans and the ADP test is performed separately for all eligible employees who have completed the minimum age and service requirements of section 410(a)(1)(A) and for all eligible employees who have not completed the minimum age and service requirements of section 410(a)(1)(A).

(2) *Determination of ADP.*—(i) *General rule.*—The ADP for a group of eligible employees (either eligible HCEs or eligible NHCEs) for a plan year or applicable year is the average of the ADRs of the eligible employees in that group for that year. The ADP for a group of eligible employees is calculated to the nearest hundredth of a percentage point.

(ii) *Determination of applicable year under current year and prior year testing method.*—The ADP test is applied using the prior year testing method or the current year testing method. Under the prior year testing method, the applicable year for determining the ADP for the eligible NHCEs is the plan year immediately preceding the plan year for which the ADP test is being performed. Under the prior year testing method, the ADP for the eligible NHCEs is determined using the ADRs for the eligible employees who were NHCEs in that preceding plan year, regardless of whether those NHCEs are eligible employees or NHCEs in the plan year for which the ADP test is being calculated. Under the current year testing method, the applicable year for determining the ADP for the eligible NHCEs is the same plan year as the plan year for which the ADP test is being performed. Under either method, the ADP for eligible HCEs is the average of the ADRs of the eligible HCEs for the plan year for which the ADP test is being performed. See paragraph (c) of this section for additional rules for the prior year testing method.

(3) *Determination of ADR.*—(i) *General rule.*—The ADR of an eligible employee for a plan year or applicable year is the sum of the employee's elective contributions taken into account with respect to such employee for the year, determined under the rules of paragraphs (a)(4) and (5) of this section, and the qualified nonelective contributions and qualified matching contributions taken into account with respect to such employee under paragraph (a)(6) of this section for the year, divided by the employee's compensation taken into account for the year. The ADR is calculated to the nearest hundredth of a percentage point. If no elective contributions, qualified nonelective contributions, or qualified matching contributions are taken into account under this section with respect to an eligible employee for the year, the ADR of the employee is zero.

(ii) *ADR of HCEs eligible under more than one arrangement.*—(A) *General rule.*—Pursuant to section 401(k)(3)(A), the ADR of an HCE who is an eligible employee in more than one cash or deferred arrangement of the same employer is calculated by treating all contributions with respect to such HCE under any such arrangement as being made under the cash or deferred arrangement being tested. Thus, the ADR for such an HCE is calculated by accumulating all contributions under any cash or deferred arrangement (other than a cash or deferred arrangement described in paragraph (a)(3)(ii)(B) of this section) that would be taken into account under this section for the plan year, if the cash or deferred arrangement under which the contribution was made applied this section and had the same plan year. For example, in the case of a plan with a 12-month plan year, the ADR for the plan year of that plan for an HCE who participates in multiple cash or deferred arrangements of the same employer is the sum of all contributions during such 12-month period that would be taken into account with respect to the HCE under all such arrangements in which the HCE is an eligible employee, divided by the HCE's compensation for that 12-month period (determined using the compensation definition for the plan being tested), without regard to the plan year of the other plans and whether those plans are satisfying this section or §1.401(k)-3.

(B) *Plans not permitted to be aggregated.*—Cash or deferred arrangements under plans that are not permitted to be aggregated under §1.401(k)-1(b)(4) (determined without regard to the prohibition on aggregating plans with inconsistent testing methods set forth in §1.401(k)-1(b)(4)(iii)(B) and the prohibition on aggregating plans with different plan years set forth in §1.410(b)-7(d)(5)) are not aggregated under this paragraph (a)(3)(ii).

(iii) *Examples.*—The following examples illustrate the application of this paragraph (a)(3):

Example 1. (i) Employee A, an HCE with compensation of $120,000, is eligible to make elective contributions under Plan S and Plan T, two profit-sharing plans maintained by Employer H with calendar year plan years, each of which includes a cash or deferred arrangement. During the current plan year, Employee A makes elective contributions of $6,000 to Plan S and $4,000 to Plan T.

(ii) Under each plan, the ADR for Employee A is determined by dividing Employee A's total elective contributions under both arrangements by Employee A's compensation taken into account under the plan for the year. Therefore, Employee A's ADR under each plan is 8.33% ($10,000/$120,000).

Example 2. (i) The facts are the same as in *Example 1*, except that Plan T defines compensation (for deferral and testing purposes) to exclude all bonuses paid to an employee. Plan S defines compensation (for deferral and testing purposes) to include bonuses paid to an employee. During the current year, Employee A's compensation included a $10,000 bonus. Therefore, Employee A's compensation under Plan T is $110,000 and Employee A's compensation under Plan S is $120,000.

(ii) Employee A's ADR under Plan T is 9.09% ($10,000/$110,000) and under Plan S, Employee A's ADR is 8.33% ($10,000/$120,000).

Example 3. (i) Employer J sponsors two profit-sharing plans, Plan U and Plan V, each of which includes a cash or deferred arrangement. Plan U's plan year begins on July 1 and ends on June 30. Plan V has a calendar year plan year. Compensation under both plans is limited to the participant's compensation during the period of participation. Employee B is an HCE who participates in both plans. Employee B's monthly compensation and elective contributions to each plan for the 2005 and 2006 calendar years are as follows:

Calendar year	Monthly Compensation	Monthly Elective Contribution to Plan U	Monthly Elective Contribution to Plan V
2005	$10,000	$500	$400
2006	$11,500	$700	$550

(ii) Under Plan U, Employee B's ADR for the plan year ended June 30, 2006, is equal to Employee B's total elective contributions under Plan U and Plan V for the plan year ending June 30, 2006, divided by Employee B's compensation for that period. Therefore, Employee B's ADR under Plan U for the plan year ending June 30, 2006, is (($900 × 6) + ($1,250 × 6)) / (($10,000 × 6) + ($11,500 × 6)), or 10%.

(iii) Under Plan V, Employee B's ADR for the plan year ended December 31, 2005, is equal to total elective contributions under Plan U and V for the plan year ending December 31, 2005, divided by Employee B's compensation for that period. Therefore, Employee B's ADR under Plan V for the plan year ending December 31, 2005, is ($10,800/$120,000), or 9%.

Example 4. (i) The facts are the same as *Example 3*, except that Employee B first becomes eligible to participate in Plan U on January 1, 2006.

(ii) Under Plan U, Employee B's ADR for the plan year ended June 30, 2006, is equal to Employee B's total elective contributions under Plan U and V for the plan year ending June 30, 2006, divided by Employee B's compensation for that period. Therefore, Employee B's ADR under Plan U for the plan year ending June 30, 2006, is (($400 × 6) + ($1,250 × 6)) / (($10,000 × 6) + ($11,500 × 6)), or 7.67%.

(4) *Elective contributions taken into account under the ADP test.*—(i) *General rule.*—An elective contribution is taken into account in determining the ADR for an eligible employee for a plan year or applicable year only if each of the following requirements is satisfied—

(A) The elective contribution is allocated to the eligible employee's account under the plan as of a date within that year. For purposes of this rule, an elective contribution is considered allocated as of a date within a year only if—

(1) The allocation is not contingent on the employee's participation in the plan or performance of services on any date subsequent to that date; and

(2) The elective contribution is actually paid to the trust no later than the end of the 12-month period immediately following the year to which the contribution relates.

(B) The elective contribution relates to compensation that either—

(1) Would have been received by the employee in the year but for the employee's election to defer under the arrangement; or

(2) Is attributable to services performed by the employee in the year and, but for the employee's election to defer, would have been received by the employee within 2½ months after the close of

the year, but only if the plan provides for elective contributions that relate to compensation that would have been received after the close of a year to be allocated to such prior year rather than the year in which the compensation would have been received.

(ii) *Elective contributions for partners and self-employed individuals.*—For purposes of this paragraph (a)(4), a partner's distributive share of partnership income is treated as received on the last day of the partnership taxable year and a sole proprietor's compensation is treated as received on the last day of the individual's taxable year. Thus, an elective contribution made on behalf of a partner or sole proprietor is treated as allocated to the partner's account for the plan year that includes the last day of the partnership taxable year, provided the requirements of paragraph (a)(4)(i) of this section are met.

(iii) *Elective contributions for HCEs.*—Elective contributions of an HCE must include any excess deferrals, as described in §1.402(g)-1(a), even if those excess deferrals are distributed, pursuant to §1.402(g)-1(e).

(5) *Elective contributions not taken into account under the ADP test.*—(i) *General rule.*—Elective contributions that do not satisfy the requirements of paragraph (a)(4)(i) of this section may not be taken into account in determining the ADR of an eligible employee for the plan year or applicable year with respect to which the contributions were made, or for any other plan year. Instead, the amount of the elective contributions must satisfy the requirements of section 401(a)(4) (without regard to the ADP test) for the plan year for which they are allocated under the plan as if they were nonelective contributions and were the only nonelective contributions for that year. See §§1.401(a)(4)-1(b)(2)(ii)(B) and 1.410(b)-7(c)(1).

(ii) *Elective contributions for NHCEs.*—Elective contributions of an NHCE shall not include any excess deferrals, as described in §1.402(g)-1(a), to the extent the excess deferrals are prohibited under section 401(a)(30). However, to the extent that the excess deferrals are not prohibited under section 401(a)(30), they are included in elective contributions even if distributed pursuant to §1.402(g)-1(e).

(iii) *Elective contributions treated as catch-up contributions.*—Elective contributions that are treated as catch-up contributions under section 414(v) because they exceed a statutory limit or employer-provided limit (within the meaning of §1.414(v)-1(b)(1)) are not taken into account under paragraph (a)(4) of this section for the plan year for which the contributions were made, or for any other plan year.

(iv) *Elective contributions used to satisfy the ACP test.*—Except to the extent necessary to demonstrate satisfaction of the requirement of §1.401(m)-2(a)(6)(ii), elective contributions taken into account for the ACP test under §1.401(m)-2(a)(6) are not taken into account under paragraph (a)(4) of this section.

(v) *Additional elective contributions pursuant to section 414(u).*—Additional elective contributions made pursuant to section 414(u) by reason of an eligible employee's qualified military service are not taken into account under paragraph (a)(4) of this section for the plan year for which the contributions are made, or for any other plan year.

(vi) *Default elective contributions pursuant to section 414(w).*—Default elective contributions made under an eligible automatic contribution arrangement (within the meaning of §1.414(w)-1(b)) that are distributed pursuant to §1.414(w)-1(c) for plan years beginning on or after January 1, 2008, are not taken into account under paragraph (a)(4) of this section for the plan year for which the contributions are made, or for any other plan year.

(6) *Qualified nonelective contributions and qualified matching contributions that may be taken into account under the ADP test.*—Qualified nonelective contributions and qualified matching contributions may be taken into account in determining the ADR for an eligible employee for a plan year or applicable year but only to the extent the contributions satisfy the following requirements—

(i) *Timing of allocation.*—The qualified nonelective contribution or qualified matching contribution is allocated to the employee's account as of a date within that year within the meaning of paragraph (a)(4)(i)(A) of this section. Consequently, under the prior year testing method, in order to be taken into account in calculating the ADP for the eligible NHCEs for the applicable year, a qualified nonelective contribution or qualified matching contribution must be contributed no later than the end of the 12-month period immediately following the applicable year even though the applicable year is different than the plan year being tested.

(ii) *Requirement that amount satisfy section 401(a)(4).*—The amount of nonelective contributions, including those qualified nonelective contributions taken into account under this paragraph

(a)(6) and those qualified nonelective contributions taken into account for the ACP test of section 401(m)(2) under §1.401(m)-2(a)(6), satisfies the requirements of section 401(a)(4). See §1.401(a)(4)-1(b)(2). The amount of nonelective contributions, excluding those qualified nonelective contributions taken into account under this paragraph (a)(6) and those qualified nonelective contributions taken into account for the ACP test of section 401(m)(2) under §1.401(m)-2(a)(6), satisfies the requirements of section 401(a)(4). See §1.401(a)(4)-1(b)(2). In the case of an employer that is applying the special rule for employer-wide plans in §1.414(r)-1(c)(2)(ii) with respect to the cash or deferred arrangement, the determination of whether the qualified nonelective contributions satisfy the requirements of this paragraph (a)(6)(ii) must be made on an employer-wide basis regardless of whether the plans to which the qualified nonelective contributions are made are satisfying the requirements of section 410(b) on an employer-wide basis. Conversely, in the case of an employer that is treated as operating qualified separate lines of business, and does not apply the special rule for employer-wide plans in §1.414(r)-1(c)(2)(ii) with respect to the cash or deferred arrangement, then the determination of whether the qualified nonelective contributions satisfy the requirements of this paragraph (a)(6)(ii) is not permitted to be made on an employer-wide basis regardless of whether the plans to which the qualified nonelective contributions are made are satisfying the requirements of section 410(b) on that basis.

(iii) *Aggregation must be permitted.*—The plan that contains the cash or deferred arrangement and the plan or plans to which the qualified nonelective contributions or qualified matching contributions are made, are plans that would be permitted to be aggregated under §1.401(k)-1(b)(4). If the plan year of the plan that contains the cash or deferred arrangement is changed to satisfy the requirement under §1.410(b)-7(d)(5) that aggregated plans have the same plan year, qualified nonelective contributions and qualified matching contributions may be taken into account in the resulting short plan year only if such qualified nonelective contributions and qualified matching contributions could have been taken into account under an ADP test for a plan with the same short plan year.

(iv) *Disproportionate contributions not taken into account.*—(A) *General rule.*—Qualified nonelective contributions cannot be taken into account for a plan year for an NHCE to the extent such contributions exceed the product of that NHCE's compensation and the greater of 5% or two times the plan's representative contribution rate. Any qualified nonelective contribution taken into account under an ACP test under §1.401(m)-2(a)(6) (including the determination of the representative contribution rate for purposes of §1.401(m)-2(a)(6)(v)(B)), is not permitted to be taken into account for purposes of this paragraph (a)(6) (including the determination of the representative contribution rate under paragraph (a)(6)(iv)(B) of this section).

(B) *Definition of representative contribution rate.*—For purposes of this paragraph (a)(6)(iv), the plan's representative contribution rate is the lowest applicable contribution rate of any eligible NHCE among a group of eligible NHCEs that consists of half of all eligible NHCEs for the plan year (or, if greater, the lowest applicable contribution rate of any eligible NHCE in the group of all eligible NHCEs for the plan year and who is employed by the employer on the last day of the plan year).

(C) *Definition of applicable contribution rate.*—For purposes of this paragraph (a)(6)(iv), the applicable contribution rate for an eligible NHCE is the sum of the qualified matching contributions taken into account under this paragraph (a)(6) for the eligible NHCE for the plan year and the qualified nonelective contributions made for the eligible NHCE for the plan year, divided by the eligible NHCE's compensation for the same period.

(D) *Special rule for prevailing wage contributions.*—Notwithstanding paragraph (a)(6)(iv)(A) of this section, qualified nonelective contributions that are made in connection with an employer's obligation to pay prevailing wages under the Davis-Bacon Act (46 Stat. 1494), Public Law 71-798, Service Contract Act of 1965 (79 Stat. 1965), Public Law 89-286, or similar legislation can be taken into account for a plan year for an NHCE to the extent such contributions do not exceed 10 percent of that NHCE's compensation.

(v) *Qualified matching contributions.*—Qualified matching contributions satisfy this paragraph (a)(6) only to the extent that such qualified matching contributions are matching contributions that are not precluded from being taken into account under the ACP test for the plan year under the rules of §1.401(m)-2(a)(5)(ii).

(vi) *Contributions only used once.*—Qualified nonelective contributions and qualified matching contributions cannot be taken into account under this paragraph (a)(6) to the extent such contributions are taken into account for purposes of satisfying any other ADP test, any ACP test, or the requirements of §1.401(k)-3, 1.401(m)-3 or 1.401(k)-4. Thus, for example, matching contributions that are made pursuant to §1.401(k)-3(c) cannot be taken into account under the ADP test. Similarly, if a plan switches from the current year testing method to the prior year testing method pursuant to §1.401(k)-2(c), qualified nonelective contributions that are taken into account under the current year testing method for a year may not be taken into account under the prior year testing method for the next year.

(7) *Examples.*—The following examples illustrate the application of this paragraph (a):

Example 1. (i) Employer X has three employees, A, B, and C. Employer X sponsors a profit-sharing plan (Plan Z) that includes a cash or deferred arrangement. Each year, Employer X determines a bonus attributable to the prior year. Under the cash or deferred arrangement, each eligible employee may elect to receive none, all or any part of the bonus in cash. X contributes the remainder to Plan Z. The portion of the bonus paid in cash, if any, is paid 2 months after the end of the plan year and thus is included in compensation for the following plan year. Employee A is an HCE, while Employees B and C are NHCEs. The plan uses the current year testing method and defines compensation to include elective contributions and bonuses paid during each plan year. In February of 2005, Employer X determined that no bonuses will be paid for 2004. In February of 2006, Employer X provided a bonus for each employee equal to 10% of regular compensation for 2005. For the 2005 plan year, A, B, and C have the following compensation and make the following elections:

Employee	Compensation	Elective Contribution
A	$100,000	$4,340
B	60,000	2,860
C	45,000	1,250

(ii) For each employee, the ratio of elective contributions to the employee's compensation for the plan year is:

Employee	Ratio of Elective Contribution to Compensation	ADR
A	$4,340/$100,000	4.34%
B	2,860/60,000	4.77
C	1,250/45,000	2.78

(iii) The ADP for the HCEs (Employee A) is 4.34%. The ADP for the NHCEs is 3.78% ((4.77% + 2.78%)/2). Because 4.34% is less than 4.73% (3.78% multiplied by 1.25), the plan satisfies the ADP test under paragraph (a)(1)(i) of this section.

Example 2. (i) The facts are the same as in *Example 1*, except that elective contributions are made pursuant to a salary reduction agreement throughout the plan year, and no bonuses are paid. As provided by section 414(s)(2), Employer X includes elective contributions in compensation. During the year, B and C defer the same amount as in *Example 1*, but A defers $5,770. Thus, the compensation and elective contributions for A, B, and C are:

Employee	Compensation	Elective Contributions	ADR
A	$100,000	$5,770	5.77%
B	60,000	2,860	4.77
C	45,000	1,250	2.78

(ii) The ADP for the HCEs (Employee A) is 5.77 %. The ADP for the NHCEs is 3.78% ((4.77% + 2.78%)/2). Because 5.77% exceeds 4.73% (3.78% × 1.25), the plan does not satisfy the ADP test under paragraph (a)(1)(i) of this section. However, because the ADP for the HCEs does not exceed the ADP for the NHCEs by more than 2 percentage points and the ADP for the HCEs does not exceed the ADP for the NHCEs multiplied by 2 (3.78% × 2 = 7.56%), the plan satisfies the ADP test under paragraph (a)(1)(ii) of this section.

Example 3. (i) Employees D through L are eligible employees in Plan T, a profit-sharing plan that contains a cash or deferred arrangement. The plan is a calendar year plan that uses the prior year testing method. Plan T provides that elective contributions are included in compensation (as provided under section 414(s)(2)). Each eligible employee may elect to defer up to 6% of compensation under the cash or deferred arrangement. Employees D and E are HCEs. The compensation, elective contributions, and ADRs of Employees D and E for the 2006 plan year are shown below:

Employee	Compensation for 2006 Plan Year	Elective Contributions for 2006 Plan Year	ADR for 2006 Plan Year
D	$100,000	$10,000	10%
E	$95,000	$4,750	5%

(ii) During the 2005 plan year, Employees F through L were eligible NHCEs. The compensation, elective contributions and ADRs of Employees F through L for the 2005 plan year are shown in the following table:

Employee	Compensation for 2005 Plan Year	Elective Contributions for 2005 Plan Year	ADR for 2005 Plan Year
F	$60,000	$3,600	6%
G	$40,000	$1,600	4%
H	$30,000	$1,200	4%
I	$20,000	$600	3%
J	$20,000	$600	3%
K	$10,000	$300	3%
L	$5,000	$150	3%

(iii) The ADP for 2006 for the HCEs is 7.5%. Because Plan T is using the prior year testing method, the applicable year for determining the NHCE ADP is the prior plan year (i.e., 2005). The NHCE ADP is determined using the ADRs for NHCEs eligible during the prior plan year (without regard to whether they are eligible under the plan during the plan year). The ADP for the NHCEs is 3.71% (the sum of the individual ADRs, 26%, divided by 7 employees). Because 7.5% exceeds 4.64% (3.71% × 1.25), Plan T does not satisfy the ADP test under paragraph (a)(1)(i) of this section. In addition, because the ADP for the HCEs exceeds the ADP for the NHCEs by more than 2 percentage points, Plan T does not satisfy the ADP test under para-

graph (a)(1)(ii) of this section. Therefore, the cash or deferred arrangement fails to be a qualified cash or deferred arrangement unless the ADP failure is corrected under paragraph (b) of this section.

Example 4. (i) Plan U is a calendar year profit-sharing plan that contains a cash or deferred arrangement and uses the current year testing method. Plan U provides that elective contributions are included in compensation (as provided under section 414(s)(2)). The following amounts are contributed under Plan U for the 2006 plan year: QNECs equal to 2% of each employee's compensation; Contributions equal to 6% of each employee's compensation that are not immediately vested under the terms of the plan; 3% of each employee's compensation that the employee may elect to receive as cash or to defer under the plan. Both types of nonelective contributions are made for the HCEs (employees M and N) and the NHCEs (employees O through S) for the plan year and are contributed after the end of the plan year and before the end of the following plan year. In addition, neither type of nonelective contributions is used for any other ADP or ACP test.

(ii) For the 2006 plan year, the compensation, elective contributions, and actual deferral ratios of employees M through S are shown in the following table:

Employee	Compensation	Elective Contributions	Actual Deferral Ratio
M	$100,000	$3,000	3%
N	$100,000	$2,000	2%
O	$ 60,000	$1,800	3%
P	$40,000	0	0
Q	$30,000	0	0
R	$ 5,000	0	0
S	$20,000	0	0

(iii) The elective contributions alone do not satisfy the ADP test of section 401(k)(3) and paragraph (a)(1) of this section because the ADP for the HCEs, consisting of employees M and N, is 2.5% and the ADP for the NHCEs is 0.6%.

(iv) The 2% QNECs satisfies the timing requirement of paragraph (a)(6)(i) of this section because it is paid within 12-month after the plan year for which allocated. All nonelective contributions also satisfy the requirements relating to section 401(a)(4) set forth in paragraph (a)(6)(ii) of this section (because all employees receive an 8% nonelective contribution and the nonelective contributions excluding the QNECs is 6% for all employees). In addition, the QNECs are not disproportionate under paragraph (a)(6)(iv) of this section because no QNEC for an NHCE exceeds the product of the plan's applicable contribution rate (2%) and that NHCE's compensation.

(v) Because the rules of paragraph (a)(6) of this section are satisfied, the 2% QNECs may be taken into account in applying the ADP test of section 401(k)(3) and paragraph (a)(1) of this section. The 6% nonelective contributions, however, may not be taken into account because they are not QNECs.

(vi) If the 2% QNECs are taken into account, the ADP for the HCEs is 4.5%, and the actual deferral percentage for the NHCEs is 2.6%. Because 4.5% is not more than two percentage points greater than 2.6 percent, and not more than two times 2.6, the cash or deferred arrangement satisfies the ADP test of section 401(k)(3) under paragraph (a)(1)(ii) of this section.

Example 5. (i) The facts are the same as *Example 4*, except the plan uses the prior year testing method. In addition, the NHCE ADP for the 2005 plan year (the prior plan year) is 0.8% and no QNECs are contributed for the 2005 plan year during 2005 or 2006.

(ii) In 2007, it is determined that the elective contributions alone do not satisfy the ADP test of section 401(k)(3) and paragraph (a)(1) of this section for 2006 because the 2006 ADP for the eligible HCEs, consisting of employees M and N, is 2.5% and the 2005 ADP for the eligible NHCEs is 0.8%. An additional QNEC of 2% of compensation is made for each eligible NHCE in 2007 and allocated for 2005.

(iii) The 2% QNECs that are made in 2007 and allocated for the 2005 plan year do not satisfy the timing requirement of paragraph (a)(6)(i) of this section for the applicable year for the 2005 plan year because they were not contributed before the last day of the 2006 plan year. Accordingly, the 2% QNECs do not satisfy the rules of paragraph (a)(6) of this section and may not be taken into account in applying the ADP test of section 401(k)(3) and paragraph (a)(1) of this section for the 2006 plan year. The cash or deferred arrangement fails to be a qualified cash or deferred arrangement unless the ADP failure is corrected under paragraph (b) of this section.

Example 6. (i) The facts are the same as *Example 4*, except that the ADP for the HCEs is 4.6% and there is no 6% nonelective contribution under the plan. The employer would like to take into account the 2% QNEC in determining the ADP for the NHCEs but not in determining the ADP for the HCEs.

(ii) The elective contributions alone fail the requirements of section 401(k) and paragraph (a)(1) of this section because the HCE ADP for the plan year (4.6%) exceeds 0.75% (0.6% × 1.25) and 1.2% (0.6% × 2).

(iii) The 2% QNECs may not be taken into account in determining the ADP of the NHCEs because they fail to satisfy the requirements relating to section 401(a)(4) set forth in paragraph (a)(6)(ii) of this section. This is because the amount of nonelective contributions, excluding those QNECs that would be taken into account under the ADP test, would be 2% of compensation for the HCEs and 0% for the NHCEs. Therefore, the cash or deferred arrangement fails to be a qualified cash or deferred arrangement unless the ADP failure is corrected under paragraph (b) of this section.

Example 7. (i) The facts are the same as *Example 6*, except that Employee R receives a QNEC in an amount of $500 and no QNECs are made on behalf of the other employees.

(ii) If the QNEC could be taken into account under paragraph (a)(6) of this section, the ADP for the NHCEs would be 2.6% and the plan would satisfy the ADP test. The QNEC is disproportionate under paragraph (a)(6)(iv) of this section, and cannot be taken into account under paragraph (a)(6) of this section, to the extent it exceeds the greater of 5% and two times the plan's representative contribution rate (0%), multiplied by Employee R's compensation. The plan's representative contribution rate is 0% because it is the lowest applicable contribution rate among a group of NHCEs that is at least half of all NHCEs, or all the NHCEs who are employed on the last day of the plan year. Therefore, the QNEC may be taken into account under the ADP test only to the extent it does not exceed 5% times Employee R's compensation (or $250) and the cash or deferred arrangement fails to satisfy the ADP test and must correct under paragraph (b) of this section.

Example 8. (i) The facts are the same as in *Example 4* except that the plan changes from the current year testing method to the prior year testing method for the following plan year (2007 plan year). The ADP for the HCEs for the 2007 plan year is 3.5%.

(ii) The 2% QNECs may not be taken into account in determining the ADP for the NHCEs for the applicable year (2006 plan year) in satisfying the ADP test for the 2007 plan year because they were taken into account in satisfying the ADP test for the 2006 plan year. Accordingly, the NHCE ADP for the applicable year is 0.6%. The elective contributions for the plan year fail the requirements of section 401(k) and paragraph (a)(1) of this section because the HCE ADP for the plan year (3.5%) exceeds the ADP limit of 1.2% (the greater of 0.75% (0.6% × 1.25) and 1.2% (0.6% × 2)), determined using the applicable year ADP for the NHCEs. Therefore, the cash or deferred arrangement fails to be a qualified cash or deferred arrangement unless the ADP failure is corrected under paragraph (b) of this section.

Example 9. (i)(A) Employer N maintains Plan X, a profit sharing plan that contains a cash or deferred arrangement and that uses the current year testing method. Plan X provides for employee contributions, elective contributions, and matching contributions. Matching contributions on behalf of NHCEs are qualified matching contributions (QMACs) and are contributed during the 2005 plan year. Matching contributions on behalf of HCEs are not QMACs, because they fail to satisfy the nonforfeitability requirement of § 1.401(k)-1(c). The elective contributions and matching contributions with respect to HCEs for the 2005 plan year are shown in the following table:

	Elective Contributions	Total Matching Contributions	Matching contributions that are not QMACs	QMACs
Highly compensated employees	15%	5%	5%	0%

(B) The elective contributions and matching contributions with respect to the NHCEs for the 2005 plan year are shown in the following table:

	Elective Contributions	Total Matching Contributions	Matching contributions that are not QMACs	QMACs
Nonhighly compensated employees	11%	4%	0%	4%

(ii) The plan fails to satisfy the ADP test of section 401(k)(3)(A) and paragraph (a)(1) of this section because the ADP for HCEs (15%) is more than 125% of the ADP for NHCEs (11%), and more than 2 percentage points greater than 11%. However, the plan provides that QMACs may be used to meet the requirements of section 401(k)(3)(A)(ii) provided that they are not used for any other ADP or ACP test. QMACs equal to 1% of compensation are taken into account for each NHCE in applying the ADP test. After this adjustment, the applicable ADP and ACP (taking into account the provisions of §1.401(m)-2(a)(5)(ii)) for the plan year are as follows:

	Actual Deferral Percentage	Actual Contribution Percentage
HCEs	15%	5%
Nonhighly compensated employees	12	3

(iii) The elective contributions and QMACs taken into account for purposes of the ADP test of section 401(k)(3) satisfy the requirements of section 401(k)(3)(A)(ii) under paragraph (a)(1)(ii) of this section because the ADP for HCEs (15%) is not more than the ADP for NHCEs multiplied by 1.25 (12% × 1.25 = 15%).

(b) *Correction of excess contributions.*—(1) *Permissible correction methods.*—(i) *In general.*—A cash or deferred arrangement does not fail to satisfy the requirements of section 401(k)(3) and paragraph (a)(1) of this section if the employer, in accordance with the terms of the plan that includes the cash or deferred arrangement, uses any of the following correction methods—

(A) *Qualified nonelective contributions or qualified matching contributions.*—The employer makes qualified nonelective contributions or qualified matching contributions that are taken into account under this section and, in combination with other amounts taken into account under paragraph (a) of this section, allow the cash or deferred arrangement to satisfy the requirements of paragraph (a)(1) of this section.

(B) *Excess contributions distributed.*—Excess contributions are distributed in accordance with paragraph (b)(2) of this section.

(C) *Excess contributions recharacterized.*—Excess contributions are recharacterized in accordance with paragraph (b)(3) of this section.

(ii) *Combination of correction methods.*—A plan may provide for the use of any of the correction methods described in paragraph (b)(1)(i) of this section, may limit elective contributions in a manner designed to prevent excess contributions from being made, or may use a combination of these methods, to avoid or correct excess contributions. A plan may permit an HCE to elect whether any excess contributions are to be recharacterized or distributed. Similarly, a plan may permit an HCE with elective contributions for a year that includes both pre-tax elective contributions and designated Roth contributions to elect whether the excess contributions are to be attributed to pre-tax elective contributions or designated Roth contributions. If the plan uses a combination of correction methods, any contribution made under paragraph (b)(1)(i)(A) of this section must be taken into account before application of the correction methods in paragraph (b)(1)(i)(B) or (C) of this section.

(iii) *Exclusive means of correction.*—A failure to satisfy the requirements of paragraph (a)(1) of this section may not be corrected using any method other than the ones described in paragraphs (b)(1)(i) and (ii) of this section. Thus, excess contributions for a plan year may not remain unallocated or be allocated to a suspense account for allocation to one or more employees in any future year. In addition, excess contributions may not be corrected using the retroactive correction rules of §1.401(a)(4)-11(g). See §1.401(a)(4)-11(g)(3)(vii) and (5).

(2) *Corrections through distribution.*—(i) *General rule.*—This paragraph (b)(2) contains the rules for correction of excess contributions through a distribution from the plan. Correction through a distribution generally involves a 4-step process. First, the plan must determine, in accordance with paragraph (b)(2)(ii) of this section, the total amount of excess contributions that must be distributed under the plan. Second, the plan must apportion the total amount of excess contributions among HCEs in accordance with paragraph (b)(2)(iii) of this section. Third, the plan must determine the income allocable to excess contributions in accordance with paragraph (b)(2)(iv) of this section. Finally, the plan must distribute the apportioned excess contributions and allocable income in accordance with paragraph (b)(2)(v) of this section. Paragraph (b)(2)(vi) of this section provides rules relating to the tax treatment of these distributions. Paragraph (b)(2)(vii) provides other rules relating to these distributions.

(ii) *Calculation of total amount to be distributed.*—The following procedures must be used to determine the total amount of the excess contributions to be distributed—

(A) *Calculate the dollar amount of excess contributions for each HCE.*—The amount of excess contributions attributable to a given HCE for a plan year is the amount (if any) by which the HCE's contributions taken into account under this section must be reduced for the HCE's ADR to equal the highest permitted ADR under the plan. To calculate the highest permitted ADR under a plan, the ADR of the HCE with the highest ADR is reduced by the amount required to cause that HCE's ADR to equal the ADR of the HCE with the next highest ADR. If a lesser reduction would enable the arrangement to satisfy the requirements of paragraph (b)(2)(ii)(C) of this section, only this lesser reduction is used in determining the highest permitted ADR.

(B) *Determination of the total amount of excess contributions.*—The process described in paragraph (b)(2)(ii)(A) of this section must be repeated until the arrangement would satisfy the requirements of paragraph (b)(2)(ii)(C) of this section. The sum of all reductions for all HCEs determined under paragraph (b)(2)(ii)(A) of this section is the total amount of excess contributions for the plan year.

(C) *Satisfaction of ADP.*—A cash or deferred arrangement satisfies this paragraph (b)(2)(ii)(C) if the arrangement would satisfy the requirements of paragraph (a)(1)(ii) of this section if the ADR for each HCE were determined after the reductions described in paragraph (b)(2)(ii)(A) of this section.

(iii) *Apportionment of total amount of excess contributions among the HCEs.*—The following procedures must be used in apportioning the total amount of excess contributions determined under paragraph (b)(2)(ii) of this section among the HCEs:

(A) *Calculate the dollar amount of excess contributions for each HCE.*—The contributions of the HCE with the highest dollar amount of contributions taken into account under this section are reduced by the amount required to cause that HCE's contributions to equal the dollar amount of the contributions taken into account under this section for the HCE with the next highest dollar amount of contributions taken account under this section. If a lesser apportionment to the HCE would enable the plan to apportion the total amount of excess contributions, only the lesser apportionment would apply.

(B) *Limit on amount apportioned to any individual.*—For purposes of this paragraph (b)(2)(iii), the amount of contributions taken into account under this section with respect to an HCE who is an eligible employee in more than one plan of an employer is determined by taking into account all contributions otherwise taken into account with respect to such HCE under any plan of the employer during the plan year of the plan being tested as being made under the plan being tested. However, the amount of excess contributions apportioned for a plan year with respect to any HCE must not exceed the amount of contributions actually contributed to the plan for the HCE for the plan year. Thus, in the case of an HCE who is an eligible employee in more than one plan of the same employer to which elective contributions are made and whose ADR is calculated in accordance with paragraph (a)(3)(ii) of this section, the amount required to be distributed under this paragraph (b)(2)(iii) shall not exceed the contributions actually contributed to the plan and taken into account under this section for the plan year.

(C) *Apportionment to additional HCEs.*—The procedure in paragraph (b)(2)(iii)(A) of this section must be repeated until the total amount of excess contributions determined under paragraph (b)(2)(ii) of this section has been apportioned.

(iv) *Income allocable to excess contributions.*—(A) *General rule.*—For plan years beginning on or after January 1, 2008, the income allocable to excess contributions is equal to the allocable gain or loss through the end of the plan year. See paragraph (b)(2)(iv)(D) of this section for rules that apply to plan years beginning before January 1, 2008.

(B) *Method of allocating income.*—A plan may use any reasonable method for computing the income allocable to excess contributions, provided that the method does not violate section 401(a)(4), is used consistently for all participants and for all corrective distributions under the plan for the plan year, and is used by the plan for allocating income to participant's accounts. See § 1.401(a)(4)-1(c)(8). A plan will not fail to use a reasonable method for computing the income allocable to excess contributions merely because the income allocable to excess contributions is determined on a date that is no more than 7 days before the distribution.

(C) *Alternative method of allocating plan year income.*—A plan may allocate income to excess contributions for the plan year by multiplying the income for the plan year allocable to the elective contributions and other amounts taken into account under this section (including contributions made for the plan year), by a fraction, the numerator of which is the excess contributions for the employee for the plan year, and the denominator of which is the sum of the—

(1) Account balance attributable to elective contributions and other contributions taken into account under this section as of the beginning of the plan year, and

(2) Any additional amount of such contributions made for the plan year.

(D) *Plan years before 2008.*—For plan years beginning before January 1, 2008, the income allocable to excess contributions is determined under § 1.401(k)-2(b)(2)(iv) (as it appeared in the April 1, 2007, edition of 26 CFR part 1).

(v) *Distribution.*—Within 12 months after the close of the plan year in which the excess contribution arose, the plan must distribute to each HCE the excess contributions apportioned to such HCE under paragraph (b)(2)(iii) of this section and the allocable income. Except as otherwise provided in this paragraph (b)(2)(v) and paragraph (b)(4)(i) of this section, a distribution of excess contributions must be in addition to any other distributions made during the year and must be designated as a corrective distribution by the employer. In the event of a complete termination of the plan during the plan year in which an excess contribution arose, the corrective distribution must be made as soon as administratively feasible after the date of termination of the plan, but in no event later than 12 months after the date of termination. If the entire account balance of an HCE is distributed prior to when the plan makes a distribution of excess contributions in accordance with this paragraph (b)(2), the distribution is deemed to have been a corrective distribution of excess contributions (and income) to the extent that a corrective distribution would otherwise have been required.

(vi) *Tax treatment of corrective distributions.*—(A) *Corrective distributions for plan years beginning on or after January 1, 2008.*—Except as provided in this paragraph (b)(2)(vi), for plan years beginning on or after January 1, 2008, a corrective distribution of excess contributions (and allocable income) is includible in the employee's gross income for the employee's taxable year in which distributed. In addition, the corrective distribution is not subject to the early distribution tax of section 72(t). See paragraph (b)(5) of this section for additional rules relating to the employer excise tax on amounts distributed more than 21/2 months (6 months in the case of certain plans that include an eligible automatic contribution arrangement within the meaning of section 414(w)) after the end of the plan year. See also § 1.402(c)-2, A-4 for restrictions on rolling over distributions that are excess contributions.

(B) *Corrective distributions for plan years beginning before January 1, 2008.*—The tax treatment of corrective distributions for plan years beginning before January 1, 2008, is determined under § 1.401(k)-2(b)(2)(vi) (as it appeared in the April 1, 2007, edition of 26 CFR Part 1). If the total amount of excess contributions, determined under this paragraph (b)(2), and excess aggregate contributions determined under § 1.401(m)-2(b)(2) distributed to a recipient under a plan for any plan year is less than $100 (excluding income), a corrective distribution of excess contributions (and income) is includible in the gross income of the recipient in the taxable year of the recipient in which the corrective distribution is made, except to the extent provided in paragraph (b)(2)(vi)(C) of this section.

(C) *Corrective distributions attributable to designated Roth contributions.*—Notwithstanding paragraphs (b)(2)(vi)(A) and (B) of this section, a distribution of excess contributions is not includible in gross income to the extent it represents a distribution of designated Roth contributions. However, the income allocable to a corrective distribution of excess contributions that are designated Roth contri-

butions is included in gross income in accordance with paragraph (b)(2)(vi)(A) or (B) of this section (i.e., in the same manner as income allocable to a corrective distribution of excess contributions that are pre-tax elective contributions).

(vii) *Other rules.*—(A) *No employee or spousal consent required.*—A corrective distribution of excess contributions (and income) may be made under the terms of the plan without regard to any notice or consent otherwise required under sections 411(a)(11) and 417.

(B) *Treatment of corrective distributions as elective contributions.*—Excess contributions are treated as employer contributions for purposes of sections 404 and 415 even if distributed from the plan.

(C) *No reduction of required minimum distribution.*—A distribution of excess contributions (and income) is not treated as a distribution for purposes of determining whether the plan satisfies the minimum distribution requirements of section 401(a)(9). See § 1.401(a)(9)-5, A-9(b).

(D) *Partial distributions.*—Any distribution of less than the entire amount of excess contributions (and allocable income) with respect to any HCE is treated as a pro rata distribution of excess contributions and allocable income.

(viii) *Examples.*—The following examples illustrate the application of this paragraph (b)(2). For purposes of these examples, none of the plans provide for catch-up contributions under section 414(v). The examples are as follows:

Example 1. (i) Plan P, a calendar year profit-sharing plan that includes a cash or deferred arrangement, provides for distribution of excess contributions to HCEs to the extent necessary to satisfy the ADP test. For the 2006 plan year, Employee A, an HCE, has elective contributions of $12,000 and $200,000 in compensation, for an ADR of 6%, and Employee B, a second HCE, has elective contributions of $8,960 and compensation of $128,000, for an ADR of 7%. The ADP for the NHCEs is 3% for the 2006 plan year. Under the ADP test, the ADP of the two HCEs under the plan may not exceed 5% (i.e., 2 percentage points more than the ADP of the NHCEs under the plan). The ADP for the 2 HCEs under the plan is 6.5%. Therefore, there must be a correction of excess contributions for the 2006 plan year.

(ii) The total amount of excess contributions for the HCEs is determined under paragraph (b)(2)(ii) of this section as follows: the elective contributions of Employee B (the HCE with the highest ADR) are reduced by $1,280 in order to reduce his ADR to 6% ($7,680/$128,000), which is the ADR of Employee A.

(iii) Because the ADP of the HCEs determined after the $1,280 reduction to Employee B still exceeds 5%, further reductions in elective contributions are necessary in order to reduce the ADP of the HCEs to 5%. The elective contributions of Employee A and Employee B are each reduced by 1% of compensation ($2,000 and $1,280 respectively). Because the ADP of the HCEs determined after the reductions equals 5%, the plan would satisfy the requirements of (a)(1)(ii) of this section.

(iv) The total amount of excess contributions ($4,560 = $1,280+$2,000+$1,280) is apportioned among the HCEs under paragraph (b)(2)(iii) of this section first to the HCE with the highest amount of elective contributions. Therefore, Employee A is apportioned $3,040 (the amount required to cause Employee A's elective contributions to equal the next highest dollar amount of elective contributions).

(v) Because the total amount of excess contributions has not been apportioned, further apportionment is necessary. The balance ($1,520) of the total amount of excess contributions is apportioned equally among Employee A and Employee B ($760 to each).

(vi) Therefore, the cash or deferred arrangement will satisfy the requirements of paragraph (a)(1) of this section if, by the end of the 12 month period following the end of the 2006 plan year, Employee A receives a corrective distribution of excess contributions equal to $3,800 ($3,040 + $760) and allocable income and Employee B receives a corrective distribution of $760 and allocable income.

Example 2. (i) The facts are the same as in *Example 1*, except Employee A's ADR is based on $3,000 of elective contributions to this plan and $9,000 of elective contributions to another plan of the employer.

(ii) The total amount of excess contributions ($4,560 = $1,280+$2,000+$1,280) is apportioned among the HCEs under paragraph (b)(2)(iii) of this section first to the HCE with the highest amount of elective contributions. The amount of elective contributions for Employee A is $12,000. Therefore, Employee A is apportioned $3,040 (the amount required to cause Employee A's elective contributions to equal the next highest dollar amount of elective contributions). However, pursuant to paragraph (b)(2)(iii)(B) of this section, no more than the amount actually contributed to the plan may be apportioned to an HCE. Accordingly, no more than $3,000 may be apportioned to Employee A. Therefore, the remaining $1,560 must be apportioned to Employee B.

(iii) The cash or deferred arrangement will satisfy the requirements of paragraph (a)(1) of this section if, by the end of the 12 month period following the end of the 2006 plan year, Employee A receives a corrective distribution of excess contributions equal to $3,000 (total amount of elective contributions actually contributed to the plan for Employee A) and allocable income and Employee B receives a corrective distribution of $1,560 and allocable income.

(3) *Recharacterization of excess contributions.*—(i) *General rule.*—Excess contributions are recharacterized in accordance with this paragraph (b)(3) only if the excess contributions that would have to be distributed under (b)(2) of this section if the plan was correcting through distribution of excess contributions are recharacterized as described in paragraph (b)(3)(ii) of this section, and all of the conditions set forth in paragraph (b)(3)(iii) of this section are satisfied.

(ii) *Treatment of recharacterized excess contributions.*—Recharacterized excess contributions are includible in the employee's gross income as if such amounts were distributed under paragraph (b)(2) of this section. The recharacterized excess contributions are treated as employee contributions for purposes of section 72, sections 401(a)(4), 401(m), §1.401(k)-1(d) and §1.401(k)-2. This requirement is not treated as satisfied unless the payor or plan administrator reports the recharacterized excess contributions as employee contributions to the Internal Revenue Service and the employee by timely providing such Federal tax forms and accompanying instructions and timely taking such other action as is prescribed by the Commissioner in revenue rulings, notices and other guidance published in the Internal Revenue Bulletin (see §601.601(d)(2) of this chapter) as well as the applicable Federal tax forms and accompanying instructions.

(iii) *Additional rules.*—(A) *Time of recharacterization.*—Excess contributions may not be recharacterized under this paragraph (b)(3) after 2½ months after the close of the plan year to which the recharacterization relates. Recharacterization is deemed to have occurred on the date on which the last of those HCEs with excess contributions to be recharacterized is notified in accordance with paragraph (b)(3)(ii) of this section.

(B) *Employee contributions must be permitted under plan.*—The amount of recharacterized excess contributions, in combination with the employee contributions actually made by the HCE, may not exceed the maximum amount of employee contributions (determined without regard to the ACP test of section 401(m)(2)) permitted under the provisions of the plan as in effect on the first day of the plan year.

(C) *Treatment of recharacterized excess contributions.*—Recharacterized excess contributions continue to be treated as employer contributions for all purposes under the Internal Revenue Code (other than those specified in paragraph (b)(3)(ii) of this section), including section 401(a) and sections 404, 409, 411, 412, 415, 416, and 417. Thus, for example, recharacterized excess contributions remain subject to the requirements of §1.401(k)-1(c); must be deducted under section 404; and are treated as employer contributions described in section 415(c)(2)(A).

(4) *Rules applicable to all corrections.*—(i) *Coordination with distribution of excess deferrals.*—(A) *Treatment of excess deferrals that reduce excess contributions.*—The amount of excess contributions (and allocable income) to be distributed under paragraph (b)(2) of this section or the amount of excess contributions recharacterized under paragraph (b)(3) of this section with respect to an employee for a plan year, is reduced by any amounts previously distributed to the employee from the plan to correct excess deferrals for the employee's taxable year ending with or within the plan year in accordance with section 402(g)(2).

(B) *Treatment of excess contributions that reduce excess deferrals.*—Under §1.402(g)-1(e), the amount required to be distributed to correct an excess deferral to an employee for a taxable year is reduced by any excess contributions (and allocable income) previously distributed or excess contributions recharacterized with respect to the employee for the plan year beginning with or within the taxable year. The amount of excess contributions includible in the gross income of the employee, and the amount of excess contributions reported by the payer or plan administrator as includible in the gross income of the employee, does not include the amount of any reduction under §1.402(g)-1(e)(6).

(ii) *Forfeiture of match on distributed excess contributions.*—A matching contribution is taken into account under section 401(a)(4) even if the match is with respect to an elective contribution that is distributed or recharacterized under this paragraph (b). This requires that, after correction of excess contributions, each level of matching contributions be currently and effectively available to a group of employees that satisfies section 410(b). See §1.401(a)(4)-4(e)(3)(iii)(G).

Thus, a plan that provides the same rate of matching contributions to all employees will not meet the requirements of section 401(a)(4) if elective contributions are distributed under this paragraph (b) to HCEs to the extent needed to meet the requirements of section 401(k)(3), while matching contributions attributable to those elective contributions remain allocated to the HCEs' accounts. Under section 411(a)(3)(G) and §1.411(a)-4(b)(7), a plan may forfeit matching contributions attributable to excess contributions, excess aggregate contributions or excess deferrals to avoid a violation of section 401(a)(4). See also §1.401(a)(4)-11(g)(3)(vii)(B) regarding the use of additional allocations to the accounts of NHCEs for the purpose of correcting a discriminatory rate of matching contributions.

(iii) *Permitted forfeiture of QMAC.*—Pursuant to section 401(k)(8)(E), a qualified matching contribution is not treated as forfeitable under §1.401(k)-1(c) merely because under the plan it is forfeited in accordance with paragraph (b)(4)(ii) of this section or §1.414(w)-1(d)(2).

(iv) *No requirement for recalculation.*—If excess contributions are distributed or recharacterized in accordance with paragraphs (b)(2) and (3) of this section, the cash or deferred arrangement is treated as meeting the nondiscrimination test of section 401(k)(3) regardless of whether the ADP for the HCEs, if recalculated after the distributions or recharacterizations, would satisfy section 401(k)(3).

(v) *Treatment of excess contributions that are catch-up contributions.*—A cash or deferred arrangement does not fail to meet the requirements of section 401(k)(3) and paragraph (a)(1) of this section merely because excess contributions that are catch-up contributions because they exceed the ADP limit, as described in §1.414(v)-1(b)(1)(iii), are not corrected in accordance with this paragraph (b).

(5) *Failure to timely correct.*—(i) *Failure to correct within 2½ months after end of plan year.*—If a plan does not correct excess contributions within 2½ months after the close of the plan year for which the excess contributions are made, the employer will be liable for a 10% excise tax on the amount of the excess contributions. See section 4979 and §54.4979-1 of this chapter. Qualified nonelective contributions and qualified matching contributions properly taken into account under paragraph (a)(6) of this section for a plan year may enable a plan to avoid having excess contributions, even if the contributions are made after the close of the 2½ month period.

(ii) *Failure to correct within 12 months after end of plan year.*—If excess contributions are not corrected within 12 months after the close of the plan year for which they were made, the cash or deferred arrangement will fail to satisfy the requirements of section 401(k)(3) for the plan year for which the excess contributions are made and all subsequent plan years during which the excess contributions remain in the trust.

(iii) *Special rule for eligible automatic contribution arrangements.*—In the case of excess contributions under a plan that includes an eligible automatic contribution arrangement within the meaning of section 414(w), 6 months is substituted for 21/2 months in paragraph (b)(5)(i) of this section. The additional time described in this paragraph (b)(5)(iii) applies to a distribution of excess contributions for a plan year beginning on or after January 1, 2010 only where all the eligible NHCEs and eligible HCEs are covered employees under the eligible automatic contribution arrangement (within the meaning of §1.414(w)-1(e)(3)) for the entire plan year (or for the portion of the plan year that the eligible NHCEs and eligible HCEs are eligible employees).

(c) *Additional rules for prior year testing method.*—(1) *Rules for change in testing method.*—(i) *General rule.*—A plan is permitted to change from the prior year testing method to the current year testing method for any plan year. A plan is permitted to change from the current year testing method to the prior year testing method only in situations described in paragraph (c)(1)(ii) of this section. For purposes of this paragraph (c)(1), a plan that uses the safe harbor method described in §1.401(k)-3 or a SIMPLE 401(k) plan is treated as using the current year testing method for that plan year.

(ii) *Situations permitting a change to the prior year testing method.*—The situations described in this paragraph (c)(1)(ii) are:

(A) The plan is not the result of the aggregation of two or more plans, and the current year testing method was used under the plan for each of the 5 plan years preceding the plan year of the change (or if lesser, the number of plan years the plan has been in existence, including years in which the plan was a portion of another plan).

(B) The plan is the result of the aggregation of two or more plans, and for each of the plans that are being aggregated (the aggregating plans), the current year testing method was used for each of the 5 plan years preceding the plan year of the change (or if lesser, the number of plan years since that aggregating plan has been in existence, including years in which the aggregating plan was a portion of another plan).

(C) A transaction described in section 410(b)(6)(C)(i) and §1.410(b)-2(f) occurs and—

(1) As a result of the transaction, the employer maintains both a plan using the prior year testing method and a plan using the current year testing method; and

(2) The change from the current year testing method to the prior year testing method occurs within the transition period described in section 410(b)(6)(C)(ii).

(2) *Calculation of ADP under the prior year testing method for the first plan year.*—(i) *Plans that are not successor plans.*—If, for the first plan year of any plan (other than a successor plan), the plan uses the prior year testing method, the plan is permitted to use either that first plan year as the applicable year for determining the ADP for eligible NHCEs, or use 3% as the ADP for eligible NHCEs, for applying the ADP test for that first plan year. A plan (other than a successor plan) that uses the prior year testing method but has elected for its first plan year to use that year as the applicable year is not treated as changing its testing method in the second plan year and is not subject to the limitations on double counting on QNECs under paragraph (a)(6)(vi) of this section for the second plan year.

(ii) *First plan year defined.*—For purposes of this paragraph (c)(2), the first plan year of any plan is the first year in which the plan provides for elective contributions. Thus, the rules of this paragraph (c)(2) do not apply to a plan (within the meaning of §1.410(b)-7(b)) for a plan year if for such plan year the plan is aggregated under §1.401(k)-1(b)(4) with any other plan that provided for elective contributions in the prior year.

(iii) *Successor plans.*—A plan is a successor plan if 50% or more of the eligible employees for the first plan year were eligible employees under a qualified cash or deferred arrangement maintained by the employer in the prior year. If a plan that is a successor plan uses the prior year testing method for its first plan year, the ADP for the group of NHCEs for the applicable year must be determined under paragraph (c)(4) of this section.

(3) *Plans using different testing methods for the ADP and ACP test.*—Except as otherwise provided in this paragraph (c)(3), a plan may use the current year testing method or prior year testing method for the ADP test for a plan year without regard to whether the current year testing method or prior year testing method is used for the ACP test for that year. For example, a plan may use the prior year testing method for the ADP test and the current year testing method for its ACP test for the plan year. However, plans that use different testing methods under this paragraph (c)(3) cannot use—

(i) The recharacterization method of paragraph (b)(3) of this section to correct excess contributions for a plan year;

(ii) The rules of §1.401(m)-2(a)(6)(ii) to take elective contributions into account under the ACP test (rather than the ADP test); or

(iii) The rules of paragraph (a)(6)(v) of this section to take qualified matching contributions into account under the ADP test (rather than the ACP test).

(4) *Rules for plan coverage changes.*—(i) *In general.*—A plan that uses the prior year testing method and experiences a plan coverage change during a plan year satisfies the requirements of this section for that year only if the plan provides that the ADP for the NHCEs for the plan year is the weighted average of the ADPs for the prior year subgroups.

(ii) *Optional rule for minor plan coverage changes.*—If a plan coverage change occurs and 90% or more of the total number of the NHCEs from all prior year subgroups are from a single prior year subgroup, then, in lieu of using the weighted averages described in paragraph (c)(4)(i) of this section, the plan may provide that the ADP for the group of eligible NHCEs for the prior year under the plan is the ADP of the NHCEs for the prior year of the plan under which that single prior year subgroup was eligible.

(iii) *Definitions.*—The following definitions apply for purposes of this paragraph (c)(4):

(A) *Plan coverage change.*—The term *plan coverage change* means a change in the group or groups of eligible employees under a plan on account of—

(1) The establishment or amendment of a plan;

(2) A plan merger or spinoff under section 414(l);

(3) A change in the way plans (within the meaning of §1.410(b)-7(b)) are combined or separated for purposes of §1.401(k)-1(b)(4) (e.g., permissively aggregating plans not previously

aggregated under §1.410(b)-7(d), or ceasing to permissively aggregate plans under §1.410(b)-7(d));

(4) A reclassification of a substantial group of employees that has the same effect as amending the plan (e.g., a transfer of a substantial group of employees from one division to another division); or

(5) A combination of any of paragraphs (c)(4)(iii)(A)(1) through (4) of this section.

(B) *Prior year subgroup.*—The term *prior year subgroup* means all NHCEs for the prior plan year who, in the prior year, were eligible employees under a specific plan maintained by the employer that included a qualified cash or deferred arrangement and who would have been eligible employees in the prior year under the plan being tested if the plan coverage change had first been effective as of the first day of the prior plan year instead of first being effective during the plan year. The determination of whether an NHCE is a member of a prior year subgroup is made without regard to whether the NHCE terminated employment during the prior year.

(C) *Weighted average of the ADPs for the prior year subgroups.*—The term *weighted average of the ADPs for the prior year subgroups* means the sum, for all prior year subgroups, of the adjusted ADPs for the plan year. The term *adjusted ADP with respect to a prior year subgroup* means the ADP for the prior plan year of the specific plan under which the members of the prior year subgroup were eligible employees on the first day of the prior plan year, multiplied by a fraction, the numerator of which is the number of NHCEs in the prior year subgroup and denominator of which is the total number of NHCEs in all prior year subgroups.

(iv) *Examples.*—The following examples illustrate the application of this paragraph (c)(4):

Example 1. (i) Employer B maintains two calendar year plans, Plan O and Plan P, each of which includes a cash or deferred arrangement. The plans were not permissively aggregated under §1.410(b)-7(d) for the 2005 plan year. Both plans use the prior year testing method. Plan O had 300 eligible employees who were NHCEs for the 2005 plan year, and their ADP for that year was 6%. Sixty of the eligible employees who were NHCEs for the 2005 plan year under Plan O, terminated their employment during that year. Plan P had 100 eligible employees who were NHCEs for 2005, and the ADP for those NHCEs for that plan was 4%. Plan O and Plan P are permissively aggregated under §1.410(b)-7(d) for the 2006 plan year.

(ii) The permissive aggregation of Plan O and Plan P for the 2006 plan year under §1.410(b)-7(d) is a plan coverage change that results in treating the plans as one plan (Plan OP) for purposes of §1.401(k)-1(b)(4). Therefore, the prior year ADP for the NHCEs under Plan OP for the 2006 plan year is the weighted average of the ADPs for the prior year subgroups: the Plan O prior year subgroup and the Plan P prior year subgroup.

(iii) The Plan O prior year subgroup consists of the 300 employees who, in the 2005 plan year, were eligible NHCEs under Plan O and who would have been eligible under Plan OP for the 2005 plan year if Plan O and Plan P had been permissively aggregated for that plan year. The Plan P prior year subgroup consists of the 100 employees who, in the 2005 plan year, were eligible NHCEs under Plan P and would have been eligible under Plan OP for the 2005 plan year if Plan O and Plan P had been permissively aggregated for that plan year.

(iv) The weighted average of the ADPs for the prior year subgroups is the sum of the adjusted ADP for the Plan O prior year subgroup and the adjusted ADP for the Plan P prior year subgroup. The adjusted ADP for the Plan O prior year subgroup is 4.5%, calculated as follows: 6% (the ADP for the NHCEs under Plan O for the 2005 plan year) × 300/400 (the number of NHCEs in the Plan O prior year subgroup divided by the total number of NHCEs in all prior year subgroups). The adjusted ADP for the Plan P prior year subgroup is 1%, calculated as follows: 4% (the ADP for the NHCEs under Plan P for the 2005 plan year) × 100/400 (the number of NHCEs in the Plan P prior year subgroup divided by the total number of NHCEs in all prior year subgroups). Thus, the prior year ADP for NHCEs under Plan OP for the 2006 plan year is 5.5% (the sum of adjusted ADPs for the prior year subgroups, 4.5% plus 1%).

(v) As provided in paragraph (c)(4)(iii)(B) of this section, the determination of whether an NHCE is a member of a prior year subgroup is made without regard to whether that NHCE terminated employment during the prior year. Thus, the prior ADP for the NHCEs under Plan OP for the 2006 plan year is unaffected by the termination of the 60 NHCEs covered by Plan O during the 2005 plan year.

Example 2. (i) The facts are the same as *Example 1*, except that the 60 employees who terminated employment during the 2005 plan are instead spun-off to another plan.

(ii) The permissive aggregation of Plan O and Plan P for the 2006 plan year under §1.410(b)-7(d) is a plan coverage change that results in treating the plans as one plan (Plan OP) for purposes of §1.401(k)-1(b)(4) and the spin-off of the 60 employees is a plan coverage change. Therefore, the prior year ADP for the NHCEs under Plan OP for the 2006 plan year is the weighted average of the ADPs for the prior year subgroups: the Plan O prior year subgroup and the Plan P prior year subgroup.

(iii) For purposes of determining the prior year subgroups, the employees who would have been eligible employees in the prior year under the plan being tested are determined as if both plan coverage changes had first been effective as of the first day of the prior plan year. The Plan O prior year subgroup consists of the 240 employees who, in the 2005 plan year, were eligible NHCEs under Plan O and would have been eligible under Plan OP for the 2005 plan year if the spin-off had occurred at the beginning of the 2005 plan year and Plan O and Plan P had been permissively aggregated under §1.410(b)-7(d) for that plan year. The Plan P prior year subgroup consists of the 100 employees who, in the 2005 plan year, were eligible NHCEs under Plan P and would have been eligible under Plan OP for the 2005 plan year if Plan O and Plan P had been permissively aggregated under §1.410(b)-7(d) for that plan year.

(iv) The weighted average of the ADPs for the prior year subgroups is the sum of the adjusted ADP with respect to the prior year subgroup consisting of eligible NHCEs from Plan O and the adjusted ADP with respect to the prior year subgroup consisting of eligible NHCEs from Plan P. The adjusted ADP for the prior year subgroup consisting of eligible NHCEs under Plan O is 4.23%, calculated as follows: 6% (the ADP for the NHCEs under Plan O for the 2005 plan year) × 240/340 (the number of NHCEs in that prior year subgroup divided by the total number of NHCEs in all prior year subgroups). The adjusted ADP for the prior year subgroup consisting of the eligible NHCEs from Plan P is 1.18%, calculated as follows: 4% (the ADP for the NHCEs under Plan P for the 2005 plan year) × 100/340 (the number of NHCEs in that prior year subgroup divided by the total number of NHCEs in all prior year subgroups). Thus, the prior year ADP for NHCEs under Plan OP for the 2006 plan year is 5.41% (the sum of adjusted ADPs for the prior year subgroups, 4.23% plus 1.18%).

Example 3. (i) The facts are the same as in *Example 1*, except that instead of Plan O and Plan P being permissively aggregated for the 2006 plan year, 200 of the employees eligible under Plan O were spun-off from Plan O and merged into Plan P.

(ii) The spin-off from Plan O and merger to Plan P for the 2006 plan year are plan coverage changes for Plan P. Therefore, the prior year ADP for the NHCEs under Plan P for the 2006 plan year is the weighted average of the ADPs for the prior year subgroups under Plan P. There are 2 subgroups under Plan P for the 2006 plan year. The Plan O prior year subgroup consists of the 200 employees who, in the 2005 plan year, were eligible NHCEs under Plan O and who would have been eligible under Plan P for the 2005 plan year if the spin-off and merger had occurred on the first day of the 2005 plan year. The Plan P prior year subgroup consists of the 100 employees who, in the 2005 plan year, were eligible NHCEs under Plan P for the 2005 plan year.

(iii) The weighted average of the ADPs for the prior year subgroups is the sum of the adjusted ADP for the Plan O prior year subgroup and the adjusted ADP for the Plan P prior year subgroup. The adjusted ADP for the Plan O prior year subgroup is 4.0%, calculated as follows: 6% (the ADP for the NHCEs under Plan O for the 2005 plan year) × 200/300 (the number of NHCEs in the Plan O prior year subgroup divided by the total number of NHCEs in all prior year subgroups). The adjusted ADP for the Plan P prior year subgroup is 1.33%, calculated as follows: 4% (the ADP for the NHCEs under Plan P for the 2005 plan year) × 100/300 (the number of NHCEs in the Plan P prior year subgroup divided by the total number of NHCEs in all prior year subgroups). Thus, the prior year ADP for NHCEs under Plan P for the 2006 plan year is 5.33% (the sum of adjusted ADPs for the 2 prior year subgroups, 4.0% plus 1.33%).

(iv) The spin-off from Plan O for the 2006 plan year is a plan coverage change for Plan O. Therefore, the prior year ADP for the NHCEs under Plan O for the 2006 plan year is the weighted average of the ADPs for the prior year subgroups under Plan O. In this case, there is only one prior year subgroup under Plan O, the employees who were NHCEs of Employer B for the 2005 plan year and who were eligible for the 2005 plan year under Plan O. Because there is only one prior year subgroup under Plan O, the weighted average of the ADPs for the prior year subgroup under Plan O is equal to the NHCE ADP for the prior year (2005 plan year) under Plan O, or 6%.

Example 4. (i) Employer C maintains a calendar year plan, Plan Q, which includes a cash or deferred arrangement that uses the prior year testing method. Plan Q covers employees of Division A and Division B. In 2005, Plan Q had 500 eligible employees who were

NHCEs, and the ADP for those NHCEs for 2005 was 2%. Effective January 1, 2006, Employer C amends the eligibility provisions under Plan Q to exclude employees of Division B effective January 1, 2006. In addition, effective on that same date, Employer C establishes a new calendar year plan, Plan R, which includes a cash or deferred arrangement that uses the prior year testing method. The only eligible employees under Plan R are the 100 employees of Division B who were eligible employees under Plan Q.

(ii) Plan R is a successor plan, within the meaning of paragraph (c)(2)(iii) of this section (because all of the employees were eligible employees under Plan Q in the prior year). Therefore, Plan R cannot use the first plan year rule set forth in paragraph (c)(2)(i) of this section.

(iii) The amendment to the eligibility provisions of Plan Q and the establishment of Plan R are plan coverage changes within the meaning of paragraph (c)(4)(iii)(A) of this section for Plan Q and Plan R. Accordingly, each plan must determine the NHCE ADP for the 2006 plan year under the rules set forth in paragraph (c)(4) of this section.

(iv) The prior year ADP for NHCEs under Plan Q is the weighted average of the ADPs for the prior year subgroups. Plan Q has only one prior year subgroup (because the only NHCEs who would have been eligible employees under Plan Q for the 2005 plan year if the amendment to the Plan Q eligibility provisions had occurred as of the first day of that plan year were eligible employees under Plan Q). Therefore, for purposes of the 2006 plan year under Plan Q, the ADP for NHCEs for the prior year is the weighted average of the ADPs for the prior year subgroups, or 2%, the same as if the plan amendment had not occurred.

(v) Similarly, Plan R has only one prior year subgroup (because the only NHCEs who would have been eligible employees under Plan R for the 2005 plan year if the plan were established as of the first day of that plan year were eligible employees under Plan Q). Therefore, for purposes of the 2006 testing year under Plan R, the ADP for NHCEs for the prior year is the weighted average of the ADPs for the prior year subgroups, or 2%, the same as that of Plan Q.

Example 5. (i) The facts are the same as in *Example 4*, except that the provisions of Plan R extend eligibility to 50 hourly employees who previously were not eligible employees under any qualified cash or deferred arrangement maintained by Employer C.

(ii) Plan R is a successor plan (because 100 of Plan R's 150 eligible employees were eligible employees under another qualified cash or deferred arrangement maintained by Employer C in the prior year). Therefore, Plan R cannot use the first plan year rule set forth in paragraph (c)(2)(i) of this section.

(iii) The establishment of Plan R is a plan coverage change that affects Plan R. Because the 50 hourly employees were not eligible employees under any qualified cash or deferred arrangement of Employer C for the prior plan year, they do not comprise a prior year subgroup. Accordingly, Plan R still has only one prior year subgroup. Therefore, for purposes of the 2006 testing year under Plan R, the ADP for NHCEs for the prior year is the weighted average of the ADPs for the prior year subgroups, or 2%, the same as that of Plan Q. [Reg. §1.401(k)-2.]

☐ [*T.D. 9169, 12-28-2004. Amended by T.D. 9237, 12-30-2005 and T.D. 9447, 2-23-2009.*]

[Reg. §1.401(k)-3]

§1.401(k)-3. Safe harbor requirements.—(a) *ADP test safe harbor.*—(1) *Section 401(k)(12) safe harbor.*—A cash or deferred arrangement satisfies the ADP safe harbor provision of section 401(k)(12) for a plan year if the arrangement satisfies the safe harbor contribution requirement of paragraph (b) or (c) of this section for the plan year, the notice requirement of paragraph (d) of this section, the plan year requirements of paragraph (e) of this section, and the additional rules of paragraphs (f), (g), and (h) of this section, as applicable.

(2) *Section 401(k)(13) safe harbor.*—For plan years beginning on or after January 1, 2008, a cash or deferred arrangement satisfies the ADP safe harbor provision of section 401(k)(13) for a plan year if the arrangement is described in paragraph (j) of this section and satisfies the safe harbor contribution requirement of paragraph (k) of this section for the plan year, the notice requirement of paragraph (d) of this section (modified to include the information set forth in paragraph (k)(4) of this section), the plan year requirements of paragraph (e) of this section, and the additional rules of paragraphs (f), (g), and (h) of this section, as applicable. A cash or deferred arrangement that satisfies the requirements of this paragraph (a)(2) is referred to as a qualified automatic contribution arrangement.

(3) *Requirements applicable to safe harbor contributions.*—Pursuant to section 401(k)(12)(E)(ii) and section 401(k)(13)(D)(iv), the safe harbor contribution requirement of paragraph (b), (c), or (k) of this section must be satisfied without regard to section 401(l). The contri-

butions made under paragraph (b) or (c) of this section (and the corresponding contributions under paragraph (k) of this section) are referred to as safe harbor nonelective contributions and safe harbor matching contributions.

(b) *Safe harbor nonelective contribution requirement.*—(1) *General rule.*—The safe harbor nonelective contribution requirement of this paragraph is satisfied if, under the terms of the plan, the employer is required to make a qualified nonelective contribution on behalf of each eligible NHCE equal to at least 3% of the employee's safe harbor compensation.

(2) *Safe harbor compensation defined.*—For purposes of this section, safe harbor compensation means compensation as defined in §1.401(k)-6 (which incorporates the definition of compensation in §1.414(s)-1); provided, however, that the rule in the last sentence of §1.414(s)-1(d)(2)(iii) (which generally permits a definition of compensation to exclude all compensation in excess of a specified dollar amount) does not apply in determining the safe harbor compensation of NHCEs. Thus, for example, the plan may limit the period used to determine safe harbor compensation to the eligible employee's period of participation.

(c) *Safe harbor matching contribution requirement.*—(1) *In general.*—The safe harbor matching contribution requirement of this paragraph (c) is satisfied if, under the plan, qualified matching contributions are made on behalf of each eligible NHCE in an amount determined under the basic matching formula of section 401(k)(12)(B)(i)(l), as described in paragraph (c)(2) of this section, or under an enhanced matching formula of section 401(k)(12)(B)(i)(ll), as described in paragraph (c)(3) of this section.

(2) *Basic matching formula.*—Under the basic matching formula, each eligible NHCE receives qualified matching contributions in an amount equal to the sum of—

(i) 100% of the amount of the employee's elective contributions that do not exceed 3% of the employee's safe harbor compensation; and

(ii) 50% of the amount of the employee's elective contributions that exceed 3% of the employee's safe harbor compensation but that do not exceed 5% of the employee's safe harbor compensation.

(3) *Enhanced matching formula.*—Under an enhanced matching formula, each eligible NHCE receives a matching contribution under a formula that, at any rate of elective contributions by the employee, provides an aggregate amount of qualified matching contributions at least equal to the aggregate amount of qualified matching contributions that would have been provided under the basic matching formula of paragraph (c)(2) of this section. In addition, under an enhanced matching formula, the ratio of matching contributions on behalf of an employee under the plan for a plan year to the employee's elective contributions may not increase as the amount of an employee's elective contributions increases.

(4) *Limitation on HCE matching contributions.*—The safe harbor matching contribution requirement of this paragraph (c) is not satisfied if the ratio of matching contributions made on account of an HCE's elective contributions under the cash or deferred arrangement for a plan year to those elective contributions is greater than the ratio of matching contributions to elective contributions that would apply with respect to any eligible NHCE with elective contributions at the same percentage of safe harbor compensation.

(5) *Use of safe harbor match not precluded by certain plan provisions.*—(i) *Safe harbor matching contributions on employee contributions.*—The safe harbor matching contribution requirement of this paragraph (c) will not fail to be satisfied merely because safe harbor matching contributions are made on both elective contributions and employee contributions if safe harbor matching contributions are made with respect to the sum of elective contributions and employee contributions on the same terms as safe harbor matching contributions are made with respect to elective contributions. Alternatively, the safe harbor matching contribution requirement of this paragraph (c) will not fail to be satisfied merely because safe harbor matching contributions are made on both elective contributions and employee contributions if safe harbor matching contributions on elective contributions are not affected by the amount of employee contributions.

(ii) *Periodic matching contributions.*—The safe harbor matching contribution requirement of this paragraph (c) will not fail to be satisfied merely because the plan provides that safe harbor matching contributions will be made separately with respect to each payroll period (or with respect to all payroll periods ending with or within each month or quarter of a plan year) taken into account under the plan for the plan year, provided that safe harbor matching contributions with respect to any elective contributions made during a plan year quarter are contributed to the plan by the last day of the immediately following plan year quarter.

(6) *Permissible restrictions on elective contributions by NHCEs.*—(i) *General rule.*—The safe harbor matching contribution requirement of this paragraph (c) is not satisfied if elective contributions by NHCEs are restricted, unless the restrictions are permitted by this paragraph (c)(6).

(ii) *Restrictions on election periods.*—A plan may limit the frequency and duration of periods in which eligible employees may make or change cash or deferred elections under a plan. However, an employee must have a reasonable opportunity (including a reasonable period after receipt of the notice described in paragraph (d) of this section) to make or change a cash or deferred election for the plan year. For purposes of this paragraph (c)(6)(ii), a 30-day period is deemed to be a reasonable period to make or change a cash or deferred election.

(iii) *Restrictions on amount of elective contributions.*—A plan is permitted to limit the amount of elective contributions that may be made by an eligible employee under a plan, provided that each NHCE who is an eligible employee is permitted (unless the employee is restricted under paragraph (c)(6)(v) of this section) to make elective contributions in an amount that is at least sufficient to receive the maximum amount of matching contributions available under the plan for the plan year, and the employee is permitted to elect any lesser amount of elective contributions. However, a plan may require eligible employees to make cash or deferred elections in whole percentages of compensation or whole dollar amounts.

(iv) *Restrictions on types of compensation that may be deferred.*—A plan may limit the types of compensation that may be deferred by an eligible employee under a plan, provided that each eligible NHCE is permitted to make elective contributions under a definition of compensation that would be a reasonable definition of compensation within the meaning of §1.414(s)-1(d)(2). Thus, the definition of compensation from which elective contributions may be made is not required to satisfy the nondiscrimination requirement of §1.414(s)-1(d)(3).

(v) *Restrictions due to limitations under the Internal Revenue Code.*—A plan may limit the amount of elective contributions made by an eligible employee under a plan—

(A) Because of the limitations of section 402(g) or 415;

(B) Due to a suspension under section 414(u)(12)(B)(ii); or

(C) Because, on account of a hardship distribution made before January 1, 2020, an employee's ability to make elective contributions has been suspended for 6 months.

(7) *Examples.*—The following examples illustrate the safe harbor contribution requirement of this paragraph (c):

Example 1. (i) Beginning January 1, 2006, Employer A maintains Plan L covering employees in Divisions D and E, each of which includes HCEs and NHCEs. Plan L contains a cash or deferred arrangement and provides qualified matching contributions equal to 100% of each eligible employee's elective contributions up to 3% of compensation and 50% of the next 2% of compensation. For purposes of the matching contribution formula, safe harbor compensation is defined as all compensation within the meaning of section 415(c)(3) (a definition that satisfies section 414(s)). Also, each employee is permitted to make elective contributions from all safe harbor compensation within the meaning of section 415(c)(3) and may change a cash or deferred election at any time. Plan L limits the amount of an employee's elective contributions for purposes of section 402(g) and section 415. All contributions under Plan L are nonforfeitable and are subject to the withdrawal restrictions of section 401(k)(2)(B). Plan L provides for no other contributions and Employer A maintains no other plans. Plan L is maintained on a calendar-year basis, and all contributions for a plan year are made within 12 months after the end of the plan year.

(ii) Based on these facts, matching contributions under Plan L are safe harbor matching contributions because they are qualified matching contributions equal to the basic matching formula. Accordingly, Plan L satisfies the safe harbor contribution requirement of this paragraph (c).

Example 2. (i) The facts are the same as in *Example 1*, except that instead of providing a basic matching contribution, Plan L provides a qualified matching contribution equal to 100% of each eligible employee's elective contributions up to 4% of safe harbor compensation.

(ii) Plan L's formula is an enhanced matching formula because each eligible NHCE receives safe harbor matching contributions at a rate that, at any rate of elective contributions, provides an aggregate amount of qualified matching contributions at least equal to the aggregate amount of qualified matching contributions that would have been received under the basic safe harbor matching formula, and the rate of matching contributions does not increase as the rate of an employee's elective contributions increases. Accordingly, Plan L satisfies the safe harbor contribution requirement of this paragraph (c).

Example 3. (i) The facts are the same as in *Example 2*, except that instead of permitting each employee to make elective contributions from all compensation within the meaning of section 415(c)(3), each employee's elective contributions under Plan L are limited to 15% of the employee's basic compensation. *Basic compensation* is defined under Plan L as compensation within the meaning of section 415(c)(3), but excluding overtime pay.

(ii) The definition of basic compensation under Plan L is a reasonable definition of compensation within the meaning of §1.414(s)-1(d)(2).

(iii) Plan L will not fail to satisfy the safe harbor contribution requirement of this paragraph (c) merely because Plan L limits the amount of elective contributions and the types of compensation that may be deferred by eligible employees, provided that each eligible NHCE may make elective contributions equal to at least 4% of the employee's safe harbor compensation.

Example 4. (i) The facts are the same as in *Example 1*, except that Plan L provides that only employees employed on the last day of the plan year will receive a safe harbor matching contribution.

(ii) Even if the plan that provides for employee contributions and matching contributions satisfies the minimum coverage requirements of section 410(b)(1) taking into account this last-day requirement, Plan L would not satisfy the safe harbor contribution requirement of this paragraph (c) because safe harbor matching contributions are not made on behalf of all eligible NHCEs who make elective contributions.

(iii) The result would be the same if, instead of providing safe harbor matching contributions, Plan L provides for a 3% safe harbor nonelective contribution that is restricted to eligible employees under the cash or deferred arrangement who are employed on the last day of the plan year.

Example 5. (i) The facts are the same as in *Example 1*, except that instead of providing qualified matching contributions under the basic matching formula to employees in both Divisions D and E, employees in Division E are provided qualified matching contributions under the basic matching formula, while safe harbor matching contributions continue to be provided to employees in Division D under the enhanced matching formula described in *Example 2*.

(ii) Even if Plan L satisfies §1.401(a)(4)-4 with respect to each rate of matching contributions available to employees under the plan, the plan would fail to satisfy the safe harbor contribution requirement of this paragraph (c) because the rate of matching contributions with respect to HCEs in Division D at a rate of elective contributions between 3% and 5% would be greater than that with respect to NHCEs in Division E at the same rate of elective contributions. For example, an HCE in Division D who would have a 4% rate of elective contributions would have a rate of matching contributions of 100% while an NHCE in Division E who would have the same rate of elective contributions would have a lower rate of matching contributions.

(d) *Notice requirement.*—(1) *General rule.*—The notice requirement of this paragraph (d) is satisfied for a plan year if each eligible employee is given notice of the employee's rights and obligations under the plan and the notice satisfies the content requirement of paragraph (d)(2) of this section and the timing requirement of paragraph (d)(3) of this section. The notice must be in writing or in such other form as may be approved by the Commissioner. See §1.401(a)-21 of this chapter for rules permitting the use of electronic media to provide applicable notices to recipients with respect to retirement plans.

(2) *Content requirement.*—(i) *General rule.*—The content requirement of this paragraph (d)(2) is satisfied if the notice is—

(A) Sufficiently accurate and comprehensive to inform the employee of the employee's rights and obligations under the plan; and

(B) Written in a manner calculated to be understood by the average employee eligible to participate in the plan.

(ii) *Minimum content requirement.*—Subject to the requirements of paragraph (d)(2)(iii) of this section, a notice is not considered sufficiently accurate and comprehensive unless the notice accurately describes—

(A) The safe harbor matching contribution or safe harbor nonelective contribution formula used under the plan (including a *description of the levels of safe harbor matching contributions*, if any, available under the plan);

(B) Any other contributions under the plan or matching contributions to another plan on account of elective contributions or employee contributions under the plan (including the potential for

discretionary matching contributions) and the conditions under which such contributions are made;

(C) The plan to which safe harbor contributions will be made (if different than the plan containing the cash or deferred arrangement);

(D) The type and amount of compensation that may be deferred under the plan;

(E) How to make cash or deferred elections, including any administrative requirements that apply to such elections;

(F) The periods available under the plan for making cash or deferred elections;

(G) Withdrawal and vesting provisions applicable to contributions under the plan; and

(H) Information that makes it easy to obtain additional information about the plan (including an additional copy of the summary plan description) such as telephone numbers, addresses and, if applicable, electronic addresses, of individuals or offices from whom employees can obtain such plan information.

(iii) *References to SPD.*—A plan will not fail to satisfy the content requirements of this paragraph (d)(2) merely because, in the case of information described in paragraph (d)(2)(ii)(B) of this section (relating to any other contributions under the plan), paragraph (d)(2)(ii)(C) of this section (relating to the plan to which safe harbor contributions will be made) or paragraph (d)(2)(ii)(D) of this section (relating to the type and amount of compensation that may be deferred under the plan), the notice cross-references the relevant portions of a summary plan description that provides the same information that would be provided in accordance with such paragraphs and that has been provided (or is concurrently provided) to employees.

(3) *Timing requirement.*—(i) *General rule.*—The timing requirement of this paragraph (d)(3) is satisfied if the notice is provided within a reasonable period before the beginning of the plan year (or, in the year an employee becomes eligible, within a reasonable period before the employee becomes eligible). The determination of whether a notice satisfies the timing requirement of this paragraph (d)(3) is based on all of the relevant facts and circumstances.

(ii) *Deemed satisfaction of timing requirement.*—The timing requirement of this paragraph (d)(3) is deemed to be satisfied if at least 30 days (and no more than 90 days) before the beginning of each plan year, the notice is given to each eligible employee for the plan year. In the case of an employee who does not receive the notice within the period described in the previous sentence because the employee becomes eligible after the 90th day before the beginning of the plan year, the timing requirement is deemed to be satisfied if the notice is provided no more than 90 days before the employee becomes eligible (and no later than the date the employee becomes eligible). Thus, for example, the preceding sentence would apply in the case of any employee eligible for the first plan year under a newly established plan that provides for elective contributions, or would apply in the case of the first plan year in which an employee becomes eligible under an existing plan that provides for elective contributions. If it is not practicable for the notice to be provided on or before the date specified in the plan that an employee becomes eligible, the notice will nonetheless be treated as provided timely if it is provided as soon as practicable after that date and the employee is permitted to elect to defer from all types of compensation that may be deferred under the plan earned beginning on the date the employee becomes eligible.

(e) *Plan year requirement.*—(1) *General rule.*—Except as provided in this paragraph (e) or in paragraph (f) of this section, a plan will fail to satisfy the requirements of sections 401(k)(12), 401(k)(13), and this section unless plan provisions that satisfy the rules of this section are adopted before the first day of the plan year and remain in effect for an entire 12-month plan year. In addition, except as provided in paragraph (g) of this section or in guidance of general applicability published in the Internal Revenue Bulletin (see §601.601(d)(2)(ii)(*b*) of this chapter), a plan which includes provisions that satisfy the rules of this section will not satisfy the requirements of §1.401(k)-1(b) if it is amended to change such provisions for that plan year. Moreover, if, as described under paragraph (h)(4) of this section, safe harbor matching or nonelective contributions will be made to another plan for a plan year, provisions under that other plan specifying that the safe harbor contributions will be made and providing that the contributions will be QNECs or QMACs must also be adopted before the first day of that plan year.

(2) *Initial plan year.*—A newly established plan (other than a successor plan within the meaning of §1.401(k)-2(c)(2)(iii)) will not be treated as violating the requirements of this paragraph (e) merely because the plan year is less than 12 months, provided that the plan year is at least 3 months long (or, in the case of a newly established

employer that establishes the plan as soon as administratively feasible after the employer comes into existence, a shorter period). Similarly, a cash or deferred arrangement will not fail to satisfy the requirement of this paragraph (e) if it is added to an existing profit sharing, stock bonus, or pre-ERISA money purchase pension plan for the first time during that year provided that—

(i) The plan is not a successor plan; and

(ii) The cash or deferred arrangement is made effective no later than 3 months prior to the end of the plan year.

(3) *Change of plan year.*—A plan that has a short plan year as a result of changing its plan year will not fail to satisfy the requirements of paragraph (e)(1) of this section merely because the plan year has less than 12 months, provided that—

(i) The plan satisfied the requirements of this section for the immediately preceding plan year; and

(ii) The plan satisfies the requirements of this section (determined without regard to paragraph (g) of this section) for the immediately following plan year (or for the immediately following 12 months if the immediately following plan year is less than 12 months).

(4) *Final plan year.*—A plan that terminates during a plan year will not fail to satisfy the requirements of paragraph (e)(1) of this section merely because the final plan year is less than 12 months, provided that the plan satisfies the requirement of this section through the date of termination and either—

(i) The plan would satisfy the requirements of paragraph (g) of this section, treating the termination of the plan as a reduction or suspension of safe harbor contributions, other than the requirements of paragraph (g)(1)(i)(A) or (g)(1)(ii)(A) of this section (relating to the employer's financial condition and information included in the initial notice for the plan year) and paragraph (g)(1)(i)(D) or (g)(1)(ii)(D) of this section (requiring that employees have a reasonable opportunity to change their cash or deferred elections and, if applicable, employee contribution elections); or

(ii) The plan termination is in connection with a transaction described in section 410(b)(6)(C) or the employer incurs a substantial business hardship comparable to a substantial business hardship described in section 412(c).

(f) *Plan amendments adopting safe harbor nonelective contributions.*—(1) *General rule.*—Notwithstanding paragraph (e)(1) of this section, a plan that provides for the use of the current year testing method may be amended after the first day of the plan year and no later than 30 days before the last day of the plan year to adopt the safe harbor method of this section, effective as of the first day of the plan year, using nonelective contributions under paragraph (b) of this section, but only if the plan provides the contingent and follow-up notices described in this section. A plan amendment made pursuant to this paragraph (f)(1) for a plan year may provide for the use of the safe harbor method described in this section solely for that plan year and a plan sponsor is not limited in the number of years for which it is permitted to adopt an amendment providing for the safe harbor method of this section using nonelective contributions under paragraph (b) of this section and this paragraph (f).

(2) *Contingent notice provided.*—A plan satisfies the requirement to provide the contingent notice under this paragraph (f)(2) if it provides a notice that would satisfy the requirements of paragraph (d) of this section, except that, in lieu of setting forth the safe harbor contributions used under the plan as set forth in paragraph (d)(2)(ii)(A) of this section, the notice specifies that the plan may be amended during the plan year to include the safe harbor nonelective contribution and that, if the plan is amended, a follow-up notice will be provided.

(3) *Follow-up notice requirement.*—A plan satisfies the requirement to provide a follow-up notice under this paragraph (f)(3) if, no later than 30 days before the last day of the plan year, each eligible employee is given a notice that states that the safe harbor nonelective contributions will be made for the plan year. The notice must be in writing or in such other form as may be prescribed by the Commissioner and is permitted to be combined with a contingent notice provided under paragraph (f)(2) of this section for the next plan year.

(g) *Permissible reduction or suspension of safe harbor contributions.*—(1) *General rule.*—(i) *Matching contributions.*—A plan that provides for safe harbor matching contributions intended to satisfy the requirements of paragraph (c) of this section for a plan year will not fail to satisfy the requirements of section 401(k)(3) merely because the plan is amended during the plan year to reduce or suspend safe harbor matching contributions on future elective contributions (and, if applicable, employee contributions) provided that—

(A) In the case of plan years beginning on or after January 1, 2015, the employer either—

(1) Is operating at an economic loss as described in section 412(c)(2)(A) for the plan year; or

(2) Includes in the notice described in paragraph (d) of this section a statement that the plan may be amended during the plan year to reduce or suspend safe harbor matching contributions and that the reduction or suspension will not apply until at least 30 days after all eligible employees are provided notice of the reduction or suspension;

(B) All eligible employees are provided a supplemental notice that satisfies the requirements of paragraph (g)(2) of this section;

(C) The reduction or suspension of safe harbor matching contributions is effective no earlier than the later of the date the amendment is adopted or 30 days after eligible employees are provided the supplemental notice described in paragraph (g)(2) of this section;

(D) Eligible employees are given a reasonable opportunity (including a reasonable period after receipt of the supplemental notice) prior to the reduction or suspension of safe harbor matching contributions to change their cash or deferred elections and, if applicable, their employee contribution elections;

(E) The plan is amended to provide that the ADP test will be satisfied for the entire plan year in which the reduction or suspension occurs using the current year testing method described in § 1.401(k)-2(a)(2)(ii); and

(F) The plan satisfies the requirements of this section (other than this paragraph (g)) with respect to amounts deferred through the effective date of the amendment.

(ii) *Nonelective contributions.*—For amendments adopted after May 18, 2009, a plan that provides for safe harbor nonelective contributions intended to satisfy the requirements of paragraph (b) of this section for the plan year will not fail to satisfy the requirements of section 401(k)(3) merely because the plan is amended during the plan year to reduce or suspend safe harbor nonelective contributions provided that—

(A) The employer either—

(1) Is operating at an economic loss, as described in section 412(c)(2)(A) for the plan year; or

(2) Includes in the notice described in paragraph (d) of this section a statement that the plan may be amended during the plan year to reduce or suspend safe harbor nonelective contributions and that the reduction or suspension will not apply until at least 30 days after all eligible employees are provided notice of the reduction or suspension;

(B) All eligible employees are provided a supplemental notice that satisfies the requirements of paragraph (g)(2) of this section;

(C) The reduction or suspension of safe harbor nonelective contributions is effective no earlier than the later of the date the amendment is adopted or 30 days after eligible employees are provided the supplemental notice described in paragraph (g)(2) of this section;

(D) Eligible employees are given a reasonable opportunity (including a reasonable period after receipt of the supplemental notice) prior to the reduction or suspension of nonelective contributions to change their cash or deferred elections and, if applicable, their employee contribution elections;

(E) The plan is amended to provide that the ADP test will be satisfied for the entire plan year in which the reduction or suspension occurs using the current year testing method described in § 1.401(k)-2(a)(2)(ii); and

(F) The plan satisfies the requirements of this section (other than this paragraph (g)) with respect to safe harbor compensation paid through the effective date of the amendment.

(2) *Supplemental notice.*—The supplemental notice requirement of this paragraph (g)(2) is satisfied if each eligible employee is given a notice (in writing or such other form as prescribed by the Commissioner) that explains—

(i) The consequences of the amendment that reduces or suspends future safe harbor contributions;

(ii) The procedures for changing their cash or deferred elections and, if applicable, their employee contribution elections; and

(iii) The effective date of the amendment.

(h) *Additional rules.*—(1) *Contributions taken into account.*—A contribution is taken into account for purposes of this section for a plan year if and only if the contribution would be taken into account for such plan year under the rules of § 1.401(k)-2(a) or 1.401(m)-2(a). Thus, for example, a safe harbor matching contribution must be made within 12 months of the end of the plan year. Similarly, an elective contribution that would be taken into account for a plan year under § 1.401(k)-2(a)(4)(i)(B)(2) must be taken into account for such plan year for purposes of this section, even if the compensation would have been received after the close of the plan year.

(2) *Use of safe harbor nonelective contributions to satisfy other non-discrimination tests.*—A safe harbor nonelective contribution used to satisfy the nonelective contribution requirement under paragraph (b) of this section may also be taken into account for purposes of determining whether a plan satisfies section 401(a)(4). Thus, these contributions are not subject to the limitations on qualified nonelective contributions under §1.401(k)-2(a)(6)(ii), but are subject to the rules generally applicable to nonelective contributions under section 401(a)(4). See §1.401(a)(4)-1(b)(2)(ii). However, pursuant to section 401(k)(12)(E)(ii) and section 401(k)(13)(D)(iv), to the extent they are needed to satisfy the safe harbor contribution requirement of paragraph (b) of this section, safe harbor nonelective contributions may not be taken into account under any plan for purposes of section 401(l) (including the imputation of permitted disparity under §1.401(a)(4)-7).

(3) *Early participation rules.*—Section 401(k)(3)(F) and §1.401(k)-2(a)(1)(iii)(A), which provide an alternative nondiscrimination rule for certain plans that provide for early participation, do not apply for purposes of section 401(k)(12), section 401(k)(13), and this section. Thus, a plan is not treated as satisfying this section with respect to the eligible employees who have not completed the minimum age and service requirements of section 410(a)(1)(A) unless the plan satisfies the requirements of this section with respect to such eligible employees. However, a plan is permitted to apply the rules of section 410(b)(4)(B) to treat the plan as two separate plans for purposes of section 410(b) and apply the safe harbor requirements of this section to one plan and apply the requirements of §1.401(k)-2 to the other plan. See §1.401(k)-1(b)(4)(vi), *Example 2.*

(4) *Satisfying safe harbor contribution requirement under another defined contribution plan.*—Safe harbor matching or nonelective contributions may be made to the plan that contains the cash or deferred arrangement or to another defined contribution plan that satisfies section 401(a) or 403(a). If safe harbor contributions are made to another defined contribution plan, the safe harbor plan must specify the plan to which the safe harbor contributions are made and the contribution requirement of paragraph (b) or (c) of this section must be satisfied in the other defined contribution plan in the same manner as if the contributions were made to the plan that contains the cash or deferred arrangement. Consequently, the plan to which the contributions are made must have the same plan year as the plan containing the cash and deferred arrangement and each employee eligible under the plan containing the cash or deferred arrangement must be eligible under the same conditions under the other defined contribution plan. The plan to which the safe harbor contributions are made need not be a plan that can be aggregated with the plan that contains the cash or deferred arrangement.

(5) *Contributions used only once.*—Safe harbor matching or nonelective contributions cannot be used to satisfy the requirements of this section with respect to more than one plan.

(i) [Reserved].

(j) *Qualified automatic contribution arrangement.*—(1) *Automatic contribution requirement.*—(i) *In general.*—A cash or deferred arrangement is described in this paragraph (j) if it is an automatic contribution arrangement described in paragraph (j)(1)(ii) of this section where the default election under that arrangement is a contribution equal to the qualified percentage described in paragraph (j)(2) of this section multiplied by the eligible employee's compensation from which elective contributions are permitted to be made under the cash or deferred arrangement. For plan years beginning on or after January 1, 2010, the compensation used for this purpose must be safe harbor compensation as defined under paragraph (b)(2) of this section.

(ii) *Automatic contribution arrangement.*—An automatic contribution arrangement is a cash or deferred arrangement within the meaning of §1.401(k)-1(a)(2) that provides that, in the absence of an eligible employee's affirmative election, a default election applies under which the employee is treated as having made an election to have a specified contribution made on his or her behalf under the plan. The default election begins to apply with respect to an eligible employee no earlier than a reasonable period of time after receipt of the notice describing the automatic contribution arrangement. The default election ceases to apply with respect to an eligible employee for periods of time with respect to which the employee has an affirmative election that is currently in effect to—

(A) Have elective contributions made in a different amount on his or her behalf (in a specified amount or percentage of compensation); or

(B) Not have any elective contributions made on his or her behalf.

(iii) *Exception to automatic enrollment for certain current employees.*—An automatic contribution arrangement will not fail to be a qualified automatic contribution arrangement merely because the default election provided under paragraph (j)(1)(i) of this section is not applied to an employee who was an eligible employee under the cash or deferred arrangement (or a predecessor arrangement) immediately prior to the effective date of the qualified automatic contribution arrangement and on that effective date had an affirmative election in effect (that remains in effect) to—

(A) Have elective contributions made on his or her behalf (in a specified amount or percentage of compensation); or

(B) Not have elective contributions made on his or her behalf.

(2) *Qualified percentage.*—(i) *In general.*—A percentage is a qualified percentage only if it—

(A) Is uniform for all employees (except to the extent provided in paragraph (j)(2)(iii) of this section);

(B) Does not exceed 10 percent; and

(C) Satisfies the minimum percentage requirements of paragraph (j)(2)(ii) of this section.

(ii) *Minimum percentage requirements.*—(A) *Initial-period requirement.*—The minimum percentage requirement of this paragraph (j)(2)(ii)(A) is satisfied only if the percentage that applies for the initial period is at least 3 percent. For this purpose, the initial period begins when the employee first has contributions made pursuant to a default election under an arrangement that is intended to be a qualified automatic contribution arrangement for a plan year and ends on the last day of the following plan year.

(B) *Second-year requirement.*—The minimum percentage requirement of this paragraph (j)(2)(ii)(B) is satisfied only if the percentage that applies for the plan year immediately following the last day described in paragraph (j)(2)(ii)(A) of this section is at least 4 percent.

(C) *Third-year requirement.*—The minimum percentage requirement of this paragraph (j)(2)(ii)(C) is satisfied only if the percentage that applies for the plan year immediately following the plan year described in paragraph (j)(2)(ii)(B) of this section is at least 5 percent.

(D) *Later years requirement.*—A percentage satisfies the minimum percentage requirement of this paragraph (j)(2)(ii)(D) only if the percentage that applies for all plan years following the plan year described in paragraph (j)(2)(ii)(C) of this section is at least 6 percent.

(iii) *Exception to uniform percentage requirement.*—A plan does not fail to satisfy the uniform percentage requirement of paragraph (j)(2)(i)(A) of this section merely because—

(A) The percentage varies based on the number of years (or portions of years) since the beginning of the initial period for an eligible employee;

(B) The rate of elective contributions under a cash or deferred election that is in effect for an employee immediately prior to the effective date of the default percentage under the qualified automatic contribution arrangement is not reduced;

(C) The rate of elective contributions is limited so as not to exceed the limits of sections 401(a)(17), 402(g) (determined with or without catch-up contributions described in section 402(g)(1)(C) or 402(g)(7)), and 415; or

(D) The default election provided under paragraph (j)(1)(i) of this section is not applied during the period an employee is not permitted to make elective contributions in order for the plan to satisfy the requirements of §1.401(k)-3(c)(6)(v)(B).

(iv) *Treatment of periods without default contributions.*—The minimum percentages described in paragraph (j)(2)(ii) of this section are based on the date the initial period begins, regardless of whether the employee is eligible to make elective contributions under the plan after that date. However, for purposes of determining the date the initial period described in paragraph (j)(2)(ii)(A) of this section begins, a plan is permitted to treat an employee who for an entire plan year did not have contributions made pursuant to a default election under the qualified automatic contribution arrangement as if the employee had not had such contributions made for any prior plan year as well.

(k) *Modifications to contribution requirements and notice requirements for automatic contribution safe harbor.*—(1) *In general.*—A cash or deferred arrangement satisfies the contribution requirements of this paragraph (k) only if it satisfies the contribution requirements of either paragraph (b) or (c) of this section, as modified by the rules of paragraphs (k)(2) and (k)(3) of this section. In addition, a cash or deferred arrangement satisfies the notice requirement of section 401(k)(13)(E) only if the notice satisfies the additional requirements of paragraph (k)(4) of this section.

(2) *Lower matching requirement.*—In applying the requirement of paragraph (c) of this section in the case of a cash or deferred arrangement, the basic matching formula is modified so that each eligible NHCE must receive the sum of—

(i) 100 percent of the employee's elective contributions that do not exceed 1 percent of the employee's safe harbor compensation; and

(ii) 50 percent of the employee's elective contributions that exceed 1 percent of the employee's safe harbor compensation but that do not exceed 6 percent of the employee's safe harbor compensation.

(3) *Modified nonforfeiture requirement.*—A cash or deferred arrangement described in paragraph (j) of this section will not fail to satisfy the requirements of paragraph (b) or (c) of this section, as applicable, merely because the safe harbor contributions are not qualified nonelective contributions or qualified matching contributions provided that—

(i) The contributions are subject to the withdrawal restrictions that apply to QNECs and QMACs, as set forth in § 1.401(k)-1(d); and

(ii) Any employee who has completed 2 years of service (within the meaning of section 411(a)) has a nonforfeitable right to the account balance attributable to the safe harbor contributions.

(4) *Additional notice requirements.*—(i) *In general.*—A notice satisfies the requirements of this paragraph (k)(4) only if it includes the additional information described in paragraph (k)(4)(ii) of this section and satisfies the timing requirements of paragraph (k)(4)(iii) of this section.

(ii) *Additional information.*—A notice satisfies the additional information requirement of this paragraph (k)(4)(ii) only if it explains—

(A) The level of elective contributions which will be made on the employee's behalf if the employee does not make an affirmative election;

(B) The employee's right under the arrangement to elect not to have elective contributions made on the employee's behalf (or to elect to have such contributions made in a different amount or percentage of compensation); and

(C) How contributions under the arrangement will be invested (including, in the case of an arrangement under which the employee may elect among 2 or more investment options, how contributions will be invested in the absence of an investment election by the employee).

(iii) *Timing requirements.*—A notice satisfies the timing requirements of this paragraph (k)(4)(iii) only if it is provided sufficiently early so that the employee has a reasonable period of time after receipt of the notice to make the elections described under paragraph (k)(4)(ii)(B) and (C) of this section. However, the requirement in the preceding sentence that an employee have a reasonable period of time after receipt of the notice to make an alternative election does not permit a plan to make the default election effective any later than the earlier of—

(A) The pay date for the second payroll period that begins after the date the notice is provided; and

(B) The first pay date that occurs at least 30 days after the notice is provided. [Reg. § 1.401(k)-3.]

☐ [*T.D. 9169, 12-28-2004. Amended by T.D. 9294, 10-19-2006; T.D. 9447, 2-23-2009, T.D. 9641, 11-14-2013 and T.D. 9875, 9-19-2019.*]

[Reg. §1.401(k)-4]

§1.401(k)-4. SIMPLE 401(k) plan requirements.—(a) *General rule.*—A cash or deferred arrangement satisfies the SIMPLE 401(k) plan provision of section 401(k)(11) for a plan year if the arrangement satisfies the requirements of paragraphs (b) through (i)[(h)] of this section for that year. A plan that contains a cash or deferred arrangement that satisfies this section is referred to as a SIMPLE 401(k) plan. Pursuant to section 401(k)(11), a SIMPLE 401(k) plan is treated as satisfying the ADP test of section 401(k)(3)(A)(ii) for that year.

(b) *Eligible employer.*—(1) *General rule.*—A SIMPLE 401(k) plan must be established by an eligible employer. Eligible employer for purposes of this section means, with respect to any plan year, an employer that had no more than 100 employees who each received at least $5,000 of SIMPLE compensation, as defined in paragraph (e)(5) of this section, from the employer for the prior calendar year.

(2) *Special rule.*—An eligible employer that establishes a SIMPLE 401(k) plan for a plan year and that fails to be an eligible employer for any subsequent plan year, is treated as an eligible employer for the 2 plan years following the last plan year the employer was an eligible employer. If the failure is due to any acquisition, disposition, or similar transaction involving an eligible employer, the preceding sentence applies only if the provisions of section 410(b)(6)(C)(i) are satisfied.

(c) *Exclusive plan.*—(1) *General rule.*—The SIMPLE 401(k) plan must be the exclusive plan for each SIMPLE 401(k) plan participant for the plan year. This requirement is satisfied if there are no contributions made, or benefits accrued, for services during the plan year on behalf of any SIMPLE 401(k) plan participant under any other qualified plan maintained by the employer. Other qualified plan for purposes of this section means any plan, contract, pension, or trust described in section 219(g)(5)(A) or (E).

(2) *Special rule.*—A SIMPLE 401(k) plan will not be treated as failing the requirements of this paragraph (c) merely because any SIMPLE 401(k) plan participant receives an allocation of forfeitures under another plan of the employer.

(d) *Election and notice.*—(1) *General rule.*—An eligible employer establishing or maintaining a SIMPLE 401(k) plan must satisfy the election and notice requirements in paragraphs (d)(2) and (3) of this section.

(2) *Employee elections.*—(i) *Initial plan year of participation.*—For the plan year in which an employee first becomes eligible under the SIMPLE 401(k) plan, the employee must be permitted to make a cash or deferred election under the plan during a 60-day period that includes either the day the employee becomes eligible or the day before.

(ii) *Subsequent plan years.*—For each subsequent plan year, each eligible employee must be permitted to make or modify his cash or deferred election during the 60-day period immediately preceding such plan year.

(iii) *Election to terminate.*—An eligible employee must be permitted to terminate his cash or deferred election at any time. If an employee does terminate his cash or deferred election, the plan is permitted to provide that such employee cannot have elective contributions made under the plan for the remainder of the plan year.

(3) *Employee notices.*—The employer must notify each eligible employee within a reasonable time prior to each 60-day election period, or on the day the election period starts, that he or she can make a cash or deferred election, or modify a prior election, if applicable, during that period. The notice must state whether the eligible employer will make the matching contributions described in paragraph (e)(3) of this section or the nonelective contributions described in paragraph (e)(4) of this section.

(e) *Contributions.*—(1) *General rule.*—A SIMPLE 401(k) plan satisfies the contribution requirements of this paragraph (e) for a plan year only if no contributions may be made to the SIMPLE 401(k) plan during such year, other than contributions described in this paragraph (e) and rollover contributions described in §1.402(c)-2, Q&A-1(a).

(2) *Elective contributions.*—Subject to the limitations on annual additions under section 415, each eligible employee must be permitted to make an election to have up to $10,000 of elective contributions made on the employee's behalf under the SIMPLE 401(k) plan for a plan year. The $10,000 limit is increased beginning in 2006 in the same manner as the $160,000 amount is adjusted under section 415(d), except that pursuant to section 408(p)(2)(E)(ii) the base period shall be the calendar quarter beginning July 1, 2004 and any increase which is not a multiple of $500 is rounded to the next lower multiple of $500.

(3) *Matching contributions.*—Each plan year, the eligible employer must contribute a matching contribution to the account of each eligible employee on whose behalf elective contributions were made for the plan year. The amount of the matching contribution must equal the lesser of the eligible employee's elective contributions for the plan year or 3% of the eligible employee's SIMPLE compensation for the entire plan year.

(4) *Nonelective contributions.*—For any plan year, in lieu of contributing matching contributions described in paragraph (e)(3) of this section, an eligible employer may, in accordance with plan terms, contribute a nonelective contribution to the account of each eligible employee in an amount equal to 2% of the eligible employee's SIMPLE compensation for the entire plan year. The eligible employer may limit the nonelective contributions to those eligible employees who received at least $5,000 of SIMPLE compensation from the employer for the entire plan year.

(5) *SIMPLE compensation.*—Except as otherwise provided, the term *SIMPLE compensation* for purposes of this section means the sum of wages, tips, and other compensation from the eligible employer subject to federal income tax withholding (as described in section 6051(a)(3)) and the employee's elective contributions made under any other plan, and if applicable, elective deferrals under a section 408(p) SIMPLE IRA plan, a section 408(k)(6) SARSEP, or a

plan or contract that satisfies the requirements of section 403(b), and compensation deferred under a section 457 plan, required to be reported by the employer on Form W-2 (as described in section 6051(a)(8)). For selfemployed individuals, SIMPLE compensation means net earnings from selfemployment determined under section 1402(a) prior to subtracting any contributions made under the SIMPLE 401(k) plan on behalf of the individual.

(f) *Vesting.*—All benefits attributable to contributions described in paragraph (e) of this section must be nonforfeitable at all times.

(g) *Plan year.*—The plan year of a SIMPLE 401(k) plan must be the whole calendar year. Thus, in general, a SIMPLE 401(k) plan can be established only on January 1 and can be terminated only on December 31. However, in the case of an employer that did not previously maintain a SIMPLE 401(k) plan, the establishment date can be as late as October 1 (or later in the case of an employer that comes into existence after October 1 and establishes the SIMPLE 401(k) plan as soon as administratively feasible after the employer comes into existence).

(h) *Other rules.*—A SIMPLE 401(k) plan is not treated as a top-heavy plan under section 416. See section 416(g)(4)(G). [Reg. § 1.401(k)-4.]

☐ [*T.D. 9169, 12-28-2004.*]

[Reg. § 1.401(k)-5]

§ 1.401(k)-5. Special rules for mergers, acquisitions and similar events.—[*Reserved*].

☐ [*T.D. 9169, 12-28-2004.*]

[Reg. § 1.401(k)-6]

§ 1.401(k)-6. *Definitions.*.—Unless otherwise provided, the definitions of this section govern for purposes of section 401(k) and the regulations thereunder.

Actual contribution percentage (ACP) test. Actual contribution percentage test or *ACP test* means the test described in § 1.401(m)-2(a)(1).

Actual deferral percentage (ADP). Actual deferral percentage or *ADP* means the ADP of the group of eligible employees as defined in § 1.401(k)-2(a)(2).

Actual deferral percentage (ADP) test. Actual deferral percentage test or *ADP test* means the test described in § 1.401(k)-2(a)(1).

Actual deferral ratio (ADR). Actual deferral ratio or *ADR* means the ADR of an eligible employee as defined in § 1.401(k)-2(a)(3).

Cash or deferred arrangement. Cash or deferred arrangement is defined in § 1.401(k)-1(a)(2).

Cash or deferred election. Cash or deferred election is defined in § 1.401(k)-1(a)(3).

Compensation. Compensation means compensation as defined in section 414(s) and § 1.414(s)-1. The period used to determine an employee's compensation for a plan year must be either the plan year or the calendar year ending within the plan year. Whichever period is selected must be applied uniformly to determine the compensation of every eligible employee under the plan for that plan year. A plan may, however, limit the period taken into account under either method to that portion of the plan year or calendar year in which the employee was an eligible employee, provided that this limit is applied uniformly to all eligible employees under the plan for the plan year. In the case of an HCE whose ADR is determined under § 1.401(k)-2(a)(3)(ii), period of participation includes periods under another plan for which elective contributions are aggregated under § 1.401(k)-2(a)(3)(ii). See also section 401(a)(17) and § 1.401(a)(17)-1(c)(1).

Current year testing method. Current year testing method means the testing method described in § 1.401(k)-2(a)(2)(ii) or 1.401(m)-2(a)(2)(ii) under which the applicable year is the current plan year.

Designated Roth account. Designated Roth account means a separate account maintained by a plan to which only designated Roth contributions (including income, expenses, gains and losses attributable thereto) are made.

Designated Roth contributions. Designated Roth contributions means designated Roth contributions as defined in § 1.401(k)-1(f)(1).

Elective contributions. Elective contributions means employer contributions made to a plan pursuant to a cash or deferred election under a cash or deferred arrangement (whether or not the arrangement is a qualified cash or deferred arrangement under § 1.401(k)-1(a)(4)).

Eligible employee—(1) *General rule. Eligible employee* means an employee who is directly or indirectly eligible to make a cash or deferred election under the plan for all or a portion of the plan year. For example, if an employee must perform purely ministerial or mechanical acts (e.g., formal application for participation or consent to payroll withholding) in order to be eligible to make a cash or deferred election for a plan year, the employee is an eligible employee

for the plan year without regard to whether the employee performs the acts.

(2) *Conditions on eligibility.* An employee who is unable to make a cash or deferred election because the employee has not contributed to another plan is also an eligible employee. By contrast, if an employee must perform additional service (e.g., satisfy a minimum period of service requirement) in order to be eligible to make a cash or deferred election for a plan year, the employee is not an eligible employee for the plan year unless the service is actually performed. See § 1.401(k)-1(e)(5), however, for certain limits on the use of minimum service requirements. Finally, an employee does not fail to be treated as an eligible employee merely because the employee may receive no additional annual additions because of section 415(c)(1).

(3) *Certain one-time elections.* An employee is not an eligible employee merely because the employee, no later than the employee's first becoming eligible to make a cash or deferred election under any plan or arrangement of the employer (described in section 219(g)(5)(A)), is given the one-time opportunity to elect, and the employee does in fact elect, not to be eligible to make a cash or deferred election under the plan or any other plan or arrangement maintained by the employer (including plans not yet established) for the duration of the employee's employment with the employer. This rule applies in addition to the rules in § 1.401(k)-1(a)(3)(v) relating to the definition of a cash or deferred election. In no event is an election made after December 23, 1994, treated as a one-time irrevocable election under this paragraph if the election is made by an employee who previously became eligible under another plan or arrangement (whether or not terminated) of the employer.

Eligible HCE. Eligible HCE means an eligible employee who is an HCE.

Eligible NHCE. Eligible NHCE means an eligible employee who is not an HCE.

Employee. Employee means an employee within the meaning of § 1.410(b)-9.

Employee stock ownership plan (ESOP). Employee stock ownership plan or *ESOP* means the portion of a plan that is an ESOP within the meaning of § 1.410(b)-7(c)(2).

Employer. Employer means an employer within the meaning of § 1.410(b)-9.

Excess contributions. Excess contributions means, with respect to a plan year, the amount of total excess contributions apportioned to an HCE under § 1.401(k)-2(b)(2)(iii).

Excess deferrals. Excess deferrals means excess deferrals as defined in § 1.402(g)-1(e)(3).

Highly compensated employee (HCE). Highly compensated employee or *HCE* has the meaning provided in section 414(q).

Matching contributions. Matching contributions means matching contributions as defined in § 1.401(m)-1(a)(2).

Nonelective contributions. Nonelective contributions means employer contributions (other than matching contributions) with respect to which the employee may not elect to have the contributions paid to the employee in cash or other benefits instead of being contributed to the plan.

Non-employee stock ownership plan (non-ESOP). Non-employee stock ownership plan or *non-ESOP* means the portion of a plan that is not an ESOP within the meaning of § 1.410(b)-7(c)(2).

Non-highly compensated employee (NHCE). Non-highly compensated employee or *NHCE* means an employee who is not an HCE.

Plan. Plan is defined in § 1.401(k)-1(b)(4).

Pre-ERISA money purchase pension plan. (1) *Pre-ERISA money purchase pension plan* is a pension plan—

(i) That is a defined contribution plan (as defined in section 414(i));

(ii) That was in existence on June 27, 1974, and as in effect on that date, included a salary reduction agreement; and

(iii) Under which neither the employee contributions nor the employer contributions, including elective contributions, may exceed the levels (as a percentage of compensation) provided for by the contribution formula in effect on June 27, 1974.

(2) A plan was in existence on June 27, 1974, if it was a written plan adopted on or before that date, even if no funds had yet been paid to the trust associated with the plan.

Pre-tax elective contributions. Pre-tax elective contributions means elective contributions under a qualified cash or deferred arrangement that are not designated Roth contributions.

Prior year testing method. Prior year testing method means the testing method under which the applicable year is the prior plan year, as described in § 1.401(k)-2(a)(2)(ii) or 1.401(m)-2(a)(2)(ii).

Qualified matching contributions (QMACs). Qualified matching contributions or *QMACs* means matching contributions that satisfy the requirements of § 1.401(k)-1(c) and (d) as though the contributions were elective contributions, without regard to whether the contributions are actually taken into account under the ADP test under § 1.401(k)-2(a)(6) or the ACP test under § 1.401(m)-2(a)(6). Thus, the matching contributions must satisfy the nonforfeitability requirements of § 1.401(k)-1(c) and be subject to the distribution limitations of § 1.401(k)-1(d) when they are allocated to participants' accounts. See also § 1.401(k)-2(b)(4)(iii) for a rule providing that a matching contribution does not fail to qualify as a QMAC solely because it is forfeitable under section 411(a)(3)(G) as a result of being a matching contribution with respect to an excess deferral, excess contribution, or excess aggregate contribution, or it is forfeitable under § 1.414(w)-1(d)(2).

Qualified nonelective contributions (QNECs). Qualified nonelective contributions or QNECs means employer contributions, other than elective contributions or matching contributions, that satisfy the requirements of § 1.401(k)-1(c) and (d) as though the contributions were elective contributions, without regard to whether the contributions are actually taken into account under the ADP test under § 1.401(k)-2(a)(6) or the ACP test under § 1.401(m)-2(a)(6). Thus, the nonelective contributions must satisfy the nonforfeitability requirements of § 1.401(k)-1(c) and be subject to the distribution limitations of § 1.401(k)-1(d) when they are allocated to participants' accounts.

Rural cooperative plans. Rural cooperative plan means a plan described in section 401(k)(7).

[Reg. § 1.401(k)-6.]

☐ [*T.D.* 9169, 12-28-2004. *Amended by T.D.* 9237, 12-30-2005; *T.D.* 9447, 2-23-2009, *T.D.* 9835, 7-19-2018 *and T.D.* 9875, 9-19-2019.]

[Reg. § 1.401(l)-0]

§ 1.401(l)-0. Table of contents.—This section contains a listing of the headings of § § 1.401(l)-1 through 1.401(l)-6.

(ii) Attained age requirement.
(iii) Nondiscrimination requirement.
   (A) Minimum percentage test.
   (B) Ratio test.
   (C) High dollar amount test.
   (D) Individual disparity reductions.
(9) Reduction in the 0.75-percent factor if integration or offset level exceeds covered compensation.
   (i) In general.
   (ii) Uniform percentage of covered compensation.
   (iii) Single dollar amount.
     (A) Plan-wide reduction.
     (B) Individual reductions.
   (iv) Reductions.
     (A) Table.
     (B) Interpolation.
(10) Examples.
(e) Adjustments to the 0.75-percent factor for benefits commencing at ages other than social security retirement age.
   (1) In general.
   (2) Adjustments.
     (i) Benefits commencing on or after age 55 and before social security retirement age.
     (ii) Benefits commencing after social security retirement age and on or before age 70.
     (iii) Benefits commencing before age 55.
     (iv) Benefits commencing after age 70.
   (3) Tables.
   (4) Benefit commencement date.
     (i) In general.
     (ii) Qualified social security supplement.
   (5) Examples.
(f) Benefits, rights, and features.
   (1) Defined benefit excess plan.
   (2) Offset plan.
   (3) Examples.
(g) No reductions in 0.75-percent factor for ancillary benefits.
(h) Benefits attributable to employee contributions not taken into account.
(i) Multiple integration levels. [Reserved]
(j) Additional rules.

§ 1.401(l)-4. Special rules for railroad plans.
(a) In general.
(b) Defined contribution plans.
   (1) In general.
   (2) Single integration level method.
     (i) In general.
     (ii) Definitions.
   (3) Two integration level method.
     (i) In general.
     (ii) Total disparity requirement.
     (iii) Intermediate disparity requirement.
     (iv) Definitions.
(c) Defined benefit excess plans.
   (1) In general.
   (2) Single integration level method.
     (i) In general.
     (ii) Definitions.
   (3) Two integration level method.
     (i) In general.
     (ii) Employee with lower covered compensation.
     (iii) Employee with lower railroad retirement covered compensation.
     (iv) Definitions.
(d) Offset plans.
   (1) In general.
   (2) Maximum tier 2 and supplementary annuity offset allowance.
(e) Additional rules.
   (1) Definitions.
   (2) Adjustments to 0.75-percent factor.
   (3) Adjustments to 0.56-percent factor.
   (4) Overall permitted disparity.

§ 1.401(l)-5. Overall permitted disparity limits.
(a) Introduction.
   (1) In general.
   (2) Plan requirements.
   (3) Plans taken into account.
(b) Annual overall permitted disparity limit.

(1) In general.
(2) Total annual disparity fraction.
(3) Annual defined contribution plan disparity fraction.
(4) Annual defined benefit excess plan disparity fraction.
(5) Annual offset plan disparity fraction.
   (i) In general.
   (ii) PIA offset plans.
(6) Annual imputed disparity fraction.
(7) Annual nondisparate fraction.
(8) Determination of fraction.
   (i) General rule.
   (ii) Multiple formulas.
   (iii) Offset arrangements.
     (A) In general.
     (B) Defined benefit plans.
     (C) Defined contribution plans.
   (iv) Applicable percentages.
   (v) Fractional accrual plans.
(9) Examples.
(c) Cumulative permitted disparity limit.
   (1) In general.
     (i) Employees who benefit under defined benefit plans.
     (ii) Employees who do not benefit under defined benefit plans.
     (iii) Certain plan years disregarded.
     (iv) Determination of type of plan.
     (v) Applicable plan years.
     (vi) Transition rule for defined contribution plans.
   (2) Cumulative disparity fraction.
   (3) Determination of total annual disparity fractions for prior years.
   (4) Special rules for greater of formulas and offset arrangements.
     (i) Greater of formulas.
       (A) In general.
       (B) Separate satisfaction by formulas.
       (C) Single plan.
     (ii) Offset arrangements.
       (A) In general.
       (B) Separate satisfaction by plans.
       (C) No other plan.
   (5) Examples.
(d) Additional rules.

§ 1.401(l)-6. Effective dates and transition rules.
(a) Statutory effective date.
   (1) In general.
   (2) Collectively bargained plans.
(b) Regulatory effective date.
   (1) In general.
   (2) Plans of tax-exempt organizations.
   (3) Defined contribution plans.
   (4) Defined benefit plans.
(c) Compliance during transition period.
[Reg. § 1.401(l)-0.]

   ☐ [*T.D.* 8359, 9-12-91. *Amended by T.D.* 8486, 8-31-93.]

[Reg. § 1.401(l)-1]

§ 1.401(l)-1. Permitted disparity in employer-provided contributions or benefits.—(a) *Permitted disparity.*—(1) *In general.*—Section 401(a)(4) provides that a plan is a qualified plan only if the amount of contributions or benefits provided under the plan does not discriminate in favor of highly compensated employees. See § 1.401(a)(4)-1(b)(2). Section 401(a)(5)(C) provides that a plan does not discriminate in favor of highly compensated employees merely because of disparities in employer-provided contributions or benefits provided to, or on behalf of, employees under the plan that are permitted under section 401(l). Thus, if a plan satisfies section 401(l), permitted disparities in employer-provided contributions or benefits under a plan are disregarded, by reason of section 401(a)(5)(C), in determining whether the plan satisfies any of the safe harbors under §§ 1.401(a)(4)-2(b)(2) and 1.401(a)(4)-3(b). However, even if disparities in employer-provided contributions or benefits under a plan are permitted under section 401 (l) and thus do not cause the plan to fail to satisfy § 1.401(a)(4)-1(b)(2), the plan may still fail to satisfy section 401(a)(4) for other reasons. Similarly, even if disparities in employer-provided contributions or benefits under a plan are not permitted under section 401(l) and thus may not be disregarded under section 401(a)(5)(C) by reason of section 401(l), the plan may still be found to be nondiscriminatory under the tests of section 401(a)(4), including the rules for imputing permitted disparity under § 1.401(a)(4)-7.

(2) *Overview.*—Rules relating to disparities in employer-provided contributions under a defined contribution plan are provided in § 1.401(l)-2. For rules relating to disparities in employer-provided benefits under a defined benefit plan, see § 1.401(l)-3. For rules relating to the application of section 401(l) to a plan maintained by a railroad employer, see § 1.401(l)-4. For rules relating to the overall permitted disparity limits, see § 1.401(l)-5. For rules relating to the effective date of section 401(l), see § 1.401(l)-6.

(3) *Exclusive rules.*—The rules provided in §§ 1.401(l)-1 through 1.401(l)-6 are the exclusive means for a plan to satisfy sections 401(l) and 401(a)(5)(C). Accordingly, a plan that provides disparities in employer-provided contributions or benefits that are not permitted under §§ 1.401(l)-1 through 1.401(l)-6 does not satisfy section 401(l) or 401(a)(5)(C).

(4) *Exceptions.*—Sections 401(a)(5)(C) and 401(l) are not available in the following arrangements—

(i) A plan maintained by an employer, determined for purposes of the Federal Insurance Contributions Act or the Railroad Retirement Tax Act, as applicable, that does not pay any wages within the meaning of section 3121(a) or compensation within the meaning of section 3231(e). For this purpose, a plan maintained for a self-employed individual within the meaning of section 401(c)(1), who is also subject to the tax under section 1401, is deemed to be a plan maintained by an employer that pays wages within the meaning of section 3121(a).

(ii) A plan, or the portion of a plan, that is an employee stock ownership plan described in section 4975(e)(7) (an ESOP) or a tax credit employee stock ownership plan described in section 409(a) (a TRASOP), except as provided in § 54.4975-11(a)(7)(ii) of this chapter, which contains a limited exception to this rule for certain ESOPs in existence on November 1, 1977.

(iii) With respect to elective contributions as defined in § 1.401(k)-6 under a qualified cash or deferred arrangement as defined in § 1.401(k)-1(a)(4)(i) or with respect to employee or matching contributions defined in § 1.401(m)-1(a)(3) or (a)(2), respectively.

(iv) With respect to contributions to a simplified employee pension made under a salary reduction arrangement described in section 408(k)(6) (a SARSEP).

(5) *Additional rules.*—The Commissioner may, in revenue rulings, notices, or other documents of general applicability, prescribe additional rules that may be necessary or appropriate to carry out the purposes of section 401(l), including rules applying section 401(l) with respect to an employer that pays wages within the meaning of section 3121(a) or compensation within the meaning of section 3231(e) for some years and not other years.

(b) *Relationship to other requirements.*—Unless explicitly provided otherwise, section 401(l) does not provide an exception to any other requirement under section 401(a). Thus, for example, even if the plan complies with section 401(l), the plan may not provide a benefit lower than the minimum benefit required under section 416. Moreover, a plan may not adjust benefits in any manner that results in a decrease in any employee's accrued benefit in violation of section 411(d)(6) and section 411(b)(1)(G). However, a plan does not fail to satisfy section 401(l) merely because, in order to ensure compliance with section 411, an employee's accrued benefit under the plan is defined as the greater of the employee's previously accrued benefit and the benefit determined under a strict application of the plan's benefit formula and accrual method. See section 401(a)(15) for additional rules relating to circumstances under which plan benefits may not be decreased because of increases in social security benefits.

(c) *Definitions.*—In applying §§ 1.401(l)-1 through 1.401(l)-6, the definitions in this paragraph (c) govern unless otherwise provided.

(1) *Accumulation plan.*—"Accumulation plan" means an accumulation plan within the meaning of § 1.401(a)(4)-12.

(2) *Average annual compensation.*—Average annual compensation means average annual compensation within the meaning of § 1.401(a)(4)-3(e)(2).

(3) *Base benefit percentage.*—"Base benefit percentage" means the rate at which employer-provided benefits are determined under a defined benefit excess plan with respect to an employee's average annual compensation at or below the integration level (expressed as a percentage of such average annual compensation).

(4) *Base contribution percentage.*—"Base contribution percentage" means the rate at which employer contributions are allocated to the account of an employee under a defined contribution excess plan with respect to the employee's plan year compensation at or below the integration level (expressed as a percentage of such plan year compensation).

(5) *Benefit formula.*—"Benefit formula" means benefit formula within the meaning of § 1.401(a)(4)-12.

(6) *Benefit, right, or feature.*—*Benefit, right, or feature* means a benefit, right, or feature within the meaning of § 1.401(a)(4)-12.

(7) *Covered compensation.*—(i) *In general.*—"Covered compensation" for an employee means the average (without indexing) of the taxable wage bases in effect for each calendar year during the 35-year period ending with the last day of the calendar year in which the employee attains (or will attain) social security retirement age. A 35-year period is used for all individuals regardless of the year of birth of the individual. In determining an employee's covered compensation for a plan year, the taxable wage base for all calendar years beginning after the first day of the plan year is assumed to be the same as the taxable wage base in effect as of the beginning of the plan year. An employee's covered compensation for a plan year beginning after the 35-year period applicable under this paragraph (c)(7)(i) is the employee's covered compensation for the plan year during which the 35-year period ends. An employee's covered compensation for a plan year beginning before the 35-year period applicable under this paragraph (c)(7)(i) is the taxable wage base in effect as of the beginning of the plan year.

(ii) *Special rules.*—(A) *Rounded table.*—For purposes of determining the amount of an employee's covered compensation under paragraph (c)(7)(i) of this section, a plan may use tables, provided by the Commissioner, that are developed by rounding the actual amounts of covered compensation for different years of birth.

(B) *Proposed regulation definition.*—For plan years beginning before January 1, 1995, in lieu of the definition of covered compensation contained in paragraph (c)(7)(i) of this section, a plan may define covered compensation as the average (without indexing) of the taxable wage bases in effect for each calendar year during the 35-year period ending with the last day of the calendar year preceding the calendar year in which the employee attains (or will attain) social security retirement age.

(iii) *Period for using covered compensation amount.*—A plan must generally provide that an employee's covered compensation is automatically adjusted for each plan year. However, a plan may use an amount of covered compensation for employees equal to each employee's covered compensation (as defined in paragraph (c)(7)(i) or (c)(7)(ii) of this section) for a plan year earlier than the current plan year, provided the earlier plan year is the same for all employees and is not earlier than the later of—

(A) the plan year that begins 5 years before the current plan year, and

(B) the plan year beginning in 1989.
In the case of an accumulation plan, the benefit accrued for an employee in prior years is not affected by changes in the employee's covered compensation that occur in later years.

(8) *Defined benefit plan.*—"Defined benefit plan" means a defined benefit plan within the meaning of § 1.410(b)-9.

(9) *Defined contribution plan.*—*Defined contribution plan* means a defined contribution plan within the meaning of § 1.410(b)-9. In addition, for purposes of §§ 1.401(l)-1 through 1.401(l)-6, a defined contribution plan includes a simplified employee pension as defined in section 408(k) (SEP), other than a SEP (or portion or a SEP) that is a salary reduction arrangement described in section 408(k)(6) (SARSEP).

(10) *Disparity.*—"Disparity" means—
(i) In the case of a defined contribution excess plan, the amount by which the excess contribution percentage exceeds the base contribution percentage,
(ii) In the case of a defined benefit excess plan, the amount by which the excess benefit percentage exceeds the base benefit percentage, and
(iii) In the case of an offset plan, the offset percentage.

(11) *Employee.*—"Employee" means employee within the meaning of § 1.401(a)(4)-12.

(12) *Employer.*—"Employer" means the employer within the meaning of § 1.410(b)-9.

(13) *Employer contributions.*—"Employer contributions" means all amounts taken into account with respect to an employee under a plan under § 1.401(a)(4)-2(c)(2)(ii).

(14) *Excess benefit percentage.*—"Excess benefit percentage" means the rate at which employer-provided benefits are determined under a defined benefit excess plan with respect to an employee's average annual compensation above the integration level (expressed as a percentage of such average annual compensation).

(15) *Excess contribution percentage.*—"Excess contribution percentage" means the rate at which employer contributions are allocated to the account of an employee under a defined contribution excess plan with respect to the employee's plan year compensation above the integration level (expressed as a percentage of such plan year compensation).

(16) *Excess plan.*—(i) *Defined benefit excess plan.*—"Defined benefit excess plan" means a defined benefit plan under which the rate at which employer-provided benefits are determined with respect to average annual compensation above the integration level under the plan (expressed as a percentage of such average annual compensation) is greater than the rate at which employer-provided benefits are determined with respect to average annual compensation at or below the integration level (expressed as a percentage of such average annual compensation).

(ii) *Defined contribution excess plan.*—"Defined contribution excess plan" means a defined contribution plan under which the rate at which employer contributions are allocated to the account of an employee with respect to plan year compensation above the integration level (expressed as a percentage of such plan year compensation) is greater than the rate at which employer contributions are allocated to the account of an employee with respect to plan year compensation at or below the integration level (expressed as a percentage of such plan year compensation).

(17) *Final average compensation.*—(i) *In general.*—Final average compensation for an employee means the average of the employee's annual section 414(s) compensation for the 3-consecutive-year period ending with or within the plan year or for the employee's period of employment if shorter. The year in which an employee terminates employment may be disregarded in determining final average compensation. The definition of final average compensation used in the plan must be applied consistently with respect to all employees. For example, if the plan provides that the year in which the employee terminates employment is disregarded in determining final average compensation, the year must be disregarded for all employees who terminate employment in that year. The plan may specify any 3-consecutive-year period ending in the plan year, provided the period is determined consistently for all employees. See § 1.401(a)(4)-11(d)(3)(iii) and § 1.414(s)-1(f) for rules permitting service and compensation with another employer to be taken into account for purposes of nondiscrimination testing, including satisfying section 401(l).

(ii) *Limitations.*—In determining an employee's final average compensation under this paragraph (c)(17), annual section 414(s) compensation for any year in excess of the taxable wage base in effect at the beginning of that year must not be taken into account. A plan may provide that each employee's final average compensation for a plan year is limited to the employee's average annual compensation for the plan year.

(iii) *Determination of section 414(s) compensation.*—A plan must use the same definition of section 414(s) compensation to determine final average compensation as the plan uses to determine average annual compensation (or plan year compensation in the case of an accumulation plan).

(18) *Gross benefit percentage.*—"Gross benefit percentage" means the rate at which employer-provided benefits are determined under an offset plan (before application of the offset) with respect to an employee's average annual compensation (expressed as a percentage of average annual compensation).

(19) *Highly compensated employee.*—Highly compensated employee means HCE within the meaning of § 1.401(a)(4)-12.

(20) *Integration level.*—"Integration level" means the dollar amount specified in an excess plan at or below which the rate of employer-provided contributions or benefits (expressed in each case as a percentage of an employee's plan year compensation or average annual compensation up to the specified dollar amount) under the plan is less than the rate of employer-provided contributions or benefits (expressed in each case as a percentage of the employee's plan year compensation or average annual compensation above the specified dollar amount) under the plan above such dollar amount.

(21) *Nonexcludable employee.*—Nonexcludable employee means nonexcludable employee within the meaning of § 1.410(a)(4)-12.

(22) *Nonhighly compensated employee.*—Nonhighly compensated employee means NHCE within the meaning of § 1.401(a)(4)-12.

(23) *Offset level.*—"Offset level" means the dollar limit specified in the plan on the amount of each employee's final average compensation taken into account in determining the offset under an offset plan.

(24) *Offset percentage.*—"Offset percentage" means the rate at which an employee's employer-provided benefit is reduced or offset under an offset plan (expressed as a percentage of the employee's final average compensation up to the offset level).

(25) *Offset plan.*—"Offset plan" means a defined benefit plan that is not a defined benefit excess plan and that provides that each employee's employer-provided benefit is reduced or offset by a specified percentage of the employee's final average compensation up to the offset level under the plan.

(26) *PIA.*—PIA or *primary insurance amount* means the old-age insurance benefit under section 202 of the Social Security Act (42 U.S.C. 402) payable to each employee at a single age that is not earlier than age 62 and not later than age 65. PIA must be determined under the Social Security Act as in effect at the time the employee's offset is determined. Thus, it is determined without assuming any future increases in compensation, any future increases in the taxable wage base, any changes in the formulas used under the Social Security Act to determine PIA (for example, changes in the breakpoints), or any future increases in the consumer price index. However, it may be assumed that the employee will continue to receive compensation at the same rate as that received at the time the offset is being determined, until reaching the single age described in the first sentence of this paragraph (c)(26). PIA must be determined in a consistent manner for all employees and in accordance with revenue rulings or other guidance provided by the Commissioner.

(27) *Plan.*—"Plan" means a plan within the meaning of § 1.401(a)(4)-12 or a component plan treated as a plan under § 1.401(a)(4)-9(c).

(28) *Plan year compensation.*—"Plan year compensation" means plan year compensation within the meaning of § 1.401(a)(4)-12.

(29) *Qualified plan.*—"Qualified plan" means a qualified plan within the meaning of § 1.401(a)(4)-12.

(30) *Section 401(l) plan.*—"Section 401(l) plan" means a section 401(l) plan within the meaning of § 1.401(a)(4)-12.

(31) *Section 414(s) compensation.*—"Section 414(s) compensation" means section 414(s) compensation within the meaning of § 1.401(a)(4)-12.

(32) *Social security retirement age.*—"Social security retirement age" for an employee means the social security retirement age of the employee as determined under section 415(b)(8).

(33) *Straight life annuity.*—"Straight life annuity" means a straight life annuity within the meaning of § 1.401(a)(4)-12.

(34) *Taxable wage base.*—"Taxable wage base" means the contribution and benefit base under section 230 of the Social Security Act (42 U.S.C. § 430).

(35) *Year of service.*—Year of service means a year of service as defined in the plan for purposes of the benefit formula and the accrual method under the plan, unless the context clearly indicates otherwise. See § 1.401(a)(4)-11(d)(3) for rules on years of service that may be taken into account for purposes of nondiscrimination testing, including satisfying section 401(l). [Reg. § 1.401(l)-1.]

☐ [*T.D. 8359, 9-12-91. Amended by T.D. 8486, 8-31-93 and T.D. 9169,* 12-28-2004.]

[Reg. § 1.401(l)-2]

§ 1.401(l)-2. Permitted disparity for defined contribution plans.—(a) *Requirements.*—(1) *In general.*—Disparity in the rates of employer contributions allocated to employees' accounts under a defined contribution plan is permitted under section 401(l) and this section for a plan year only if the plan satisfies paragraphs (a)(2) through (a)(5) of this section. A plan that otherwise satisfies this paragraph (a) will not be considered to fail section 401(l) merely because it contains one or more provisions described in § 1.401(a)(4)-2(b)(4). See § 1.401(a)(4)-8(b)(3)(i)(C) for special rules applicable to target benefit plans.

(2) *Excess plan requirement.*—The plan must be a defined contribution excess plan.

(3) *Maximum disparity.*—The disparity for all employees under the plan must not exceed the maximum permitted disparity prescribed in paragraph (b) of this section.

(4) *Uniform disparity.*—The disparity for all employees under the plan must be uniform within the meaning of paragraph (c) of this section.

(5) *Integration level.*—The integration level specified in the plan must satisfy paragraph (d) of this section.

(b) *Maximum permitted disparity.*—(1) *In general.*—The disparity provided for the plan year must not exceed the maximum excess allowance as defined in paragraph (b)(2) of this section. In addition, the plan must satisfy the overall permitted disparity limits of § 1.401(l)-5.

(2) *Maximum excess allowance.*—The maximum excess allowance for a plan year is the lesser of—

(i) The base contribution percentage, or

(ii) The greater of—

(A) 5.7 percent, reduced as required under paragraph (d) of this section, or

(B) The percentage rate of tax under section 3111(a), in effect as of the beginning of the plan year, that is attributable to the old age insurance portion of the Old Age, Survivors and Disability Insurance provisions of the Social Security Act, reduced as required under paragraph (d) of this section. For a year in which the percentage rate of tax described in this paragraph (b)(2)(ii)(B) exceeds 5.7 percent, the Commissioner will publish the rate of such tax and a revised table under paragraph (d)(4) of this section.

(c) *Uniform disparity.*—(1) *In general.*—The disparity provided under a plan is uniform only if the plan uses the same base contribution percentage and the same excess contribution percentage for all employees in the plan.

(2) *Deemed uniformity.*—(i) *In general.*—The disparity under a plan does not fail to be uniform for purposes of this paragraph (c) merely because the plan contains one or more of the provisions described in paragraphs (c)(2)(ii) and (iii) of this section.

(ii) *Overall permitted disparity.*—The plan provides that, in the case of each employee who has reached the cumulative permitted disparity limit applicable to the employee under § 1.401(l)-5(c), employer contributions are allocated to the account of the employee with respect to the employee's total plan year compensation at the excess contribution percentage.

(iii) *Non-FICA employees.*—The plan provides that, in the case of each employee under the plan with respect to whom none of the taxes under section 3111(a), section 3221, or section 1401 is required to be paid, employer contributions are allocated to the account of the employee with respect to the employee's total plan year compensation at the excess contribution percentage.

(d) *Integration level.*—(1) *In general.*—The integration level under the plan must satisfy paragraph (d)(2), (d)(3), or (d)(4) of this section, as modified by paragraph (d)(5) of this section in the case of a short plan year. If a reduction applies to the disparity factor under this paragraph (d), the reduced factor is used for all purposes in determining whether the permitted disparity rules for defined contribution plans are satisfied.

(2) *Taxable wage base.*—The requirement of this paragraph (d)(2) is satisfied only if the integration level under the plan for each employee is the taxable wage base in effect as of the beginning of the plan year.

(3) *Single dollar amount.*—The requirement of this paragraph (d)(3) is satisfied only if the integration level under the plan for all employees is a single dollar amount (either specified in the plan or determined under a formula specified in the plan) that does not exceed the greater of $10,000 or 20 percent of the taxable wage base in effect as of the beginning of the plan year.

(4) *Intermediate amount.*—The requirement of this paragraph (d)(4) is satisfied only if—

(i) The integration level under the plan for all employees is a single dollar amount (either specified in the plan or determined under a formula specified in the plan) that is greater than the highest amount determined under paragraph (d)(3) of this section and less than the taxable wage base, and

(ii) the plan adjusts the factor determined under paragraph (b)(2)(ii) of this section in accordance with the table below.

TABLE

If the integration level is more than	But not more than	The 5.7 percent factor in the maximum excess allowance is reduced to—
Greater of $10,000 or 20% of taxable wage base	80% of taxable wage base	4.3%
80% of taxable wage	Amount less than taxable wage base	5.4%

(5) *Prorated integration level for short plan year.*—If a plan uses paragraph (2) or (4) of the definition of plan year compensation under § 1.401(a)(4)-12 (i.e., section 414(s) compensation for the plan year or the period of plan participation) and has a plan year that comprises fewer than 12 months, the integration level under the plan for each employee must be an amount equal to the otherwise applicable integration level described in paragraph (d)(2), (d)(3), or (d)(4) of this section, multiplied by a fraction, the numerator of which is the number of months in the plan year, and the denominator of which is 12. No adjustment to the maximum excess allowance is required as a result of the application of this paragraph (d)(5), other than any adjustment already required under paragraph (d)(4) of this section.

(e) *Examples.*—The following examples illustrate this section. In each example, 5.7 percent exceeds the percentage rate of tax described in paragraph (b)(2)(ii)(B) of this section.

Example 1. Employer X maintains a profit-sharing plan with the calendar year as its plan year. For the 1989 plan year, the plan provides that the account of each employee who has plan year compensation in excess of the taxable wage base in effect at the beginning of the plan year will receive an allocation for the plan year of 5.7 percent of plan year compensation in excess of the taxable wage base. The plan provides that no allocation will be made to the account of any employee for the plan year with respect to plan year compensation not in excess of the taxable wage base. The maximum excess allowance is exceeded for the 1989 plan year because the excess contribution percentage (5.7 percent) for the plan year exceeds the base contribution percentage (0 percent) for the plan year by more than the lesser of the base contribution percentage (0 percent) or the percentage determined under paragraph (b)(2)(ii) of this section (5.7 percent) for the plan year.

Example 2. Employer Y maintains a money purchase pension plan with the calendar year as its plan year. For the 1990 plan year, the plan provides that the account of each employee will receive an allocation of 5 percent of the employee's plan year compensation up to the taxable wage base in effect at the beginning of the plan year plus an allocation of 10 percent of the employee's plan year compensation in excess of the taxable wage base. The maximum excess allowance is not exceeded for the plan year because the excess contribution percentage (10 percent) for the plan year does not exceed the base contribution percentage (5 percent) for the plan year by more than the lesser of the base contribution percentage (5 percent) or the percentage determined under paragraph (b)(2)(ii) of this section (5.7 percent) for the plan year.

Example 3. Assume the same facts as in *Example 2*, except that the plan provides that, with respect to plan year compensation in excess of the taxable wage base, the account of each employee will receive an allocation for the plan year of 12 percent of such compensation. The maximum excess allowance is exceeded for the plan year because the excess contribution percentage (12 percent) for the plan year exceeds the base contribution percentage (5 percent) for the plan year by more than the lesser of the base contribution percentage (5 percent) or the percentage determined under paragraph (b)(2)(ii) of this section (5.7 percent) for the plan year.

Example 4. Employer Z maintains a money purchase pension plan with a plan year beginning July 1 and ending June 30. The taxable wage base for the 1990 calendar year is $51,300 and the taxable wage base for the 1991 calendar year is $53,400. For the plan year beginning July 1, 1990, and ending June 30, 1991, the plan provides that the account of each employee will receive an allocation of 4 percent of the employee's plan year compensation up to $53,400 plus an allocation of 6 percent of the employee's plan year compensation in excess of $53,400. Although the excess contribution percentage (6 percent) for the plan year does not exceed the base contribution percentage (4 percent) for the plan year by more than the lesser of the base contribution percentage (4 percent) or the percentage determined under paragraph (b)(2)(ii) of this section (5.7 percent), the plan does not satisfy paragraph (a)(5) of this section because the integration level of $53,400 exceeds the maximum permitted integration level of $51,300 (the taxable wage base in effect as of the beginning of the plan year).

Example 5. Assume the same facts as in *Example 4*, except that for the plan year beginning July 1, 1990, and ending June 30, 1991, the plan provides that the account of each employee will receive an allocation of 5 percent of the employee's plan year compensation up to $30,000 plus an allocation of 9 percent of the employee's plan year compensation in excess of $30,000. The integration level of $30,000 is 58 percent of the taxable wage base of $51,300 for the 1990 calendar year. The maximum excess allowance is not exceeded for the plan year because the excess contribution percentage (9 percent) for the plan year does not exceed the base contribution percentage (5 percent) for the plan year by more than the lesser of the base contribution percentage (5 percent) or the percentage determined under paragraphs (b)(2)(ii) and (d) of this section (4.3 percent) for the plan year. [Reg. § 1.401(l)-2.]

☐ [T.D. 8359, 9-12-91. Amended by T.D. 8486, 8-31-93.]

[Reg. § 1.401(l)-3]

§ 1.401(l)-3. Permitted disparity for defined benefit plans.— (a) *Requirements.*—(1) *In general.*—Disparity in the rates of employer-provided benefits under a defined benefit plan is permitted under section 401(l) and this section for a plan year only if the plan satisfies paragraphs (a)(2) through (a)(6) of this section. A plan that otherwise satisfies this paragraph (a) will not be considered to fail section 401(l) merely because it contains one or more provisions described in § 1.401(a)(4)-3(b)(6) (such as multiple formulas). Section 401(a)(5)(D) and § 1.401(a)(5)-1(d) provide other rules under which benefits provided under a defined benefit plan (including defined benefit excess and offset plans) may be limited. See § 1.401(a)(4)-3(b)(5)(viii) for special rules under which an insurance contract plan may satisfy § 1.401(a)(4)-1(b)(2) and section 401(l). See § 1.401(a)(4)-8(c)(3)(iii)(B) for special rules applicable to cash balance plans.

(2) *Excess or offset plan requirement.*—The plan must be a defined benefit excess plan or an offset plan.

(3) *Maximum disparity.*—The disparity for all employees under the plan must not exceed the maximum permitted disparity prescribed in paragraph (b) of this section.

(4) *Uniform disparity.*—The disparity for all employees under the plan must be uniform within the meaning of paragraph (c) of this section.

(5) *Integration or offset level.*—The integration or offset level specified in the plan must satisfy paragraph (d) of this section.

(6) *Benefits, rights, and features.*—The benefits, rights, and features provided under the plan must satisfy paragraph (f) of this section.

(b) *Maximum permitted disparity.*—(1) *In general.*—In the case of a defined benefit excess plan, the disparity provided for the plan year may not exceed the maximum excess allowance as defined in paragraph (b)(2) of this section. In the case of an offset plan, the disparity provided for the plan year may not exceed the maximum offset allowance as defined in paragraph (b)(3) of this section. In addition, either type of plan must satisfy the overall permitted disparity limits of § 1.401(l)-5.

(2) *Maximum excess allowance.*—The maximum excess allowance for a plan year is the lesser of—

(i) 0.75 percent, reduced as required under paragraphs (d) and (e) of this section, or

(ii) The base benefit percentage for the plan year.

(3) *Maximum offset allowance.*—The maximum offset allowance for a plan year is the lesser of—

(i) 0.75 percent, reduced as required under paragraphs (d) and (e) of this section, or

(ii) One-half of the gross benefit percentage, multiplied by a fraction (not to exceed one), the numerator of which is the employee's average annual compensation, and the denominator of which is the employee's final average compensation up to the offset level.

(4) *Rules of application.*—(i) *Disparity provided for the plan year.*—Disparity provided for the plan year generally means the disparity provided under the plan's benefit formula for the employee's year of service with respect to the plan year. However, if a plan determines each employee's accrued benefit under the fractional accrual method of section 411(b)(1)(C), disparity provided under the plan also means the disparity in the benefit accrued for the employee for the plan year. Thus, a plan using the fractional accrual method must satisfy this paragraph (b) with respect to the plan's benefit formula and with respect to the benefits accrued for the plan year.

(ii) *Reductions in disparity rate.*—Any reductions in the 0.75-percent factor required under paragraphs (d) and (e) of this section are cumulative.

(iii) *Normal and optional forms of benefit.*—(A) *In general.*—A plan satisfies the maximum permitted disparity requirement of this paragraph (b) only if the plan satisfies this paragraph (b) with respect to each optional form of benefit (including the normal form of benefit) provided under the plan.

(B) *Level annuity forms.*—In the case of an optional form of benefit payable as a level annuity over a period of not less than the life of the employee, the optional form must satisfy the maximum permitted disparity requirement of this paragraph (b). Thus, for example, if the form of a defined benefit plan's normal retirement benefit is an annuity for life with a 10-year certain feature and the plan permits employees to elect an optional form of benefit in the form of a straight life annuity, the plan must satisfy the maximum disparity requirement of this paragraph (b) with respect to each of the optional forms of benefit. An annuity that decreases only after the death of the employee, or that decreases only after the death of either the employee or the joint annuitant, is considered a level annuity for purposes of this paragraph (b).

(C) *Other forms.*—In the case of an optional form of benefit that is not described in paragraph (b)(4)(iii)(B) of this section, the optional form must satisfy the maximum permitted disparity requirement of this paragraph (b), when the respective portions of the optional form are normalized under the rules of § 1.401(a)(4)-12 to a straight life annuity commencing at the same time as the optional form of benefit, regardless of whether the straight life annuity form is actually provided under the plan. In the case of a defined benefit excess plan, the respective portions are the portion of the optional form attributable to average annual compensation up to the integration level (the "base portion") and the portion of the optional form attributable to average annual compensation in excess of the integration level (the "excess portion"). In the case of an offset plan, the respective portions are the optional form determined without regard to the offset (the "gross amount") and the offset applied to the gross amount to determine the optional form (the "offset amount").

(D) *Post-retirement cost-of-living adjustments.*—(1) *In general.*—A benefit does not fail to be a level annuity described in paragraph (b)(4)(iii)(B) of this section merely because it provides an automatic post-retirement cost-of-living adjustment that satisfies paragraph (b)(4)(iii)(D)(2) of this section. Thus, increases in the employee's annuity pursuant to such a cost-of-living adjustment do not cause the disparity provided under the optional form of benefit to exceed the maximum disparity permitted under this paragraph (b). For rules on ad hoc post-retirement cost-of-living adjustments, see § 1.401(a)(4)-10(b).

(2) *Requirements.*—A cost-of-living adjustment satisfies this paragraph (b)(4)(iii)(D)(2) if—

(i) It is included in the accrued benefit of all employees, and

(ii) It increases, on a uniform and consistent basis, the benefits of all former employees who are no younger than age 62, at a rate no greater than adjustments to social security benefits under section 215(i)(2)(A) of the Social Security Act that have occurred since the later of the employee's attainment of age 62 or commencement of benefits.

(E) *Section 417(e) exception.*—A plan will not fail to satisfy this paragraph (b) merely because the disparity in a benefit that is subject to the interest rate restrictions of sections 401(a)(11) and 417(e) exceeds the maximum disparity that would otherwise be allowed under this paragraph (b) if the increase in disparity is required to satisfy § 1.417(e)-1(d). In applying the exception in this paragraph (b)(4)(iii)(E), for purposes of determining what is required under § 1.417(e)-1(d), a plan may use the rate described in § 1.417(e)-1(d)(2)(i) for all employees, without regard to whether the present value of an employee's vested benefit exceeds $25,000.

(5) *Examples.*—The following examples illustrate this paragraph (b). Unless otherwise provided, the following facts apply. The plan is noncontributory and is the only plan ever maintained by the employer. The plan uses a normal retirement age of 65 and contains no provision that would require a reduction in the 0.75-percent factor under paragraph (b)(2) or (b)(3) of this section. In the case of a defined benefit excess plan, the plan uses each employee's covered compensation as the integration level; in the case of an offset plan, the plan uses each employee's covered compensation as the offset level and provides that an employee's final average compensation is limited to the employee's average annual compensation. Each example discusses the benefit formula applicable to an employee who has a social security retirement age of 65.

Example 1. Plan N is a defined benefit excess plan that provides a normal retirement benefit of 0.5 percent of average annual compensation in excess of the integration level, for each year of service. The plan provides no benefits with respect to average annual compensation up to the integration level. The disparity provided under the plan exceeds the maximum excess allowance because the excess benefit percentage (0.5 percent) exceeds the base benefit percentage (0 percent) by more than the base benefit percentage (0 percent).

Example 2. Plan O is an offset plan that provides a normal retirement benefit equal to 2 percent of average annual compensation, minus 0.75 percent of final average compensation up to the offset level, for each year of service up to 35. The disparity provided under the plan satisfies this paragraph (b) because the offset percentage (0.75 percent) does not exceed the maximum offset allowance equal to the lesser of 0.75 percent or one-half of the gross benefit percentage (1 percent).

Example 3. Plan P is a defined benefit excess plan that provides a normal retirement benefit of 0.5 percent of average annual compensation up to the integration level, plus 1.25 percent of average annual compensation in excess of the integration level, for each year of up to 35. The disparity provided under the plan exceeds the maximum excess allowance because the excess benefit percentage (1.25 percent) exceeds the base benefit percentage (0.5 percent) by more than the base benefit percentage (0.5 percent).

Example 4. Plan Q is an offset plan that provides a normal retirement benefit of 1 percent of average annual compensation, minus 0.75 percent of final average compensation up to the offset level, for each year of service up to 35. The disparity under the plan exceeds the maximum offset allowance because the offset percentage exceeds one-half of the gross benefit percentage (0.5 percent).

Example 5. (a) Plan R is an offset plan that provides a normal retirement benefit of 1 percent of average annual compensation, minus 0.5 percent of final average compensation up to the offset level, for each year of service up to 35. The plan determines an employee's average annual compensation using an averaging period comprising five consecutive 12-month periods and taking into account the employee's compensation for the ten consecutive 12-month periods ending with the plan year. The plan does not provide that an employee's final average compensation is limited to the employee's average annual compensation.

(b) Employee A has average annual compensation of $20,000, final average compensation of $25,000, and covered compensation of $32,000. The maximum offset allowance applicable to Employee A for the plan year under paragraph (b)(3) of this section is one-half of the gross benefit percentage multiplied by the ratio, not to exceed one, of Employee A's average annual compensation to Employee A's final average compensation up to the offset level. Thus, the maximum offset allowance is 0.4 percent ($1/2 \times$ 1 percent $\times$ $20,000/$25,000). With respect to Employee A, the benefit formula provides an offset that exceeds the maximum offset allowance. The plan must therefore reduce Employee A's offset percentage to 0.4 percent. (Under paragraph (c)(2)(viii) of this section, Employee A's adjusted disparity rate is deemed uniform.)

(c) Alternatively, under §1.401(l)-1(c)(17)(ii) (the definition of final average compensation), the plan could specify that an employee's final average compensation is limited to the amount of the employee's average annual compensation. Thus, the ratio of average annual compensation to final average compensation would always be equal to at least one, and the maximum offset allowance under the plan would be one-half of the gross benefit percentage.

Example 6. Plan S is a defined benefit excess plan that provides a base benefit percentage of 1 percent of average annual compensation up to the integration level for each year of service. The plan also provides, for each of the first 10 years of service, an excess benefit percentage of 1.85 percent of average annual compensation in excess of the integration level. For each year of service after 10, the plan provides an excess benefit percentage of 1.65 percent of the employee's average annual compensation in excess of the integration level. The disparity provided under the plan exceeds the maximum excess allowance because the excess benefit percentage for each of the first ten years of service (1.85 percent) exceeds the base benefit percentage (1 percent) by more than 0.75 percent.

Example 7. The facts are the same as in *Example 6,* except that the plan provides an excess benefit percentage of 1.65 percent of average annual compensation in excess of the integration level for each of the first 10 years of service and an excess benefit percentage of 1.85 percent of average annual compensation in excess of the integration level for each year of service after 10. The disparity provided under the plan exceeds the maximum excess allowance because the excess benefit percentage for each year of service after 10 (1.85 percent) exceeds the base benefit percentage (1 percent) by more than 0.75 percent.

Example 8. Plan T is a defined benefit excess plan that provides a normal retirement benefit of 1.0 percent of average annual compensation up to the integration level, plus 1.7 percent of average annual compensation in excess of the integration level, for each year of service up to 35, payable in the form of a joint and survivor annuity. The plan also allows an employee to receive the retirement benefit in the form of an actuarially equivalent straight life annuity. The actuarially equivalent straight life annuity equals 1.09 percent of average annual compensation up to the integration level, plus 1.85 percent of average annual compensation in excess of the integration level, for

each year of service up to 35. The disparity provided under the plan with respect to the straight life annuity form of benefit (0.76 percent) exceeds the maximum excess allowance because the excess benefit percentage (1.85 percent) exceeds the base benefit percentage (1.09 percent) by more than 0.75 percent.

Example 9. Plan U is a defined benefit excess plan that provides a normal retirement benefit of 1.0 percent of average annual compensation up to the integration level, plus 1.7 percent of average annual compensation in excess of the integration level, for each year of service up to 35, payable in the form of a straight life annuity. Plan U provides a single sum optional form of benefit at normal retirement age equal to 100 times the monthly annuity payable at that age. Thus, if an employee elects the single sum optional form of benefit, the base portion of the single sum benefit is 8.33 percent (100 times 1.0 percent/12) of average annual compensation up to the integration level per year of service, and the excess portion of the single sum benefit is 14.17 percent (100 times 1.7 percent/12) of average annual compensation in excess of the integration level per year of service. Each respective portion of the single sum option is normalized to a straight life annuity commencing at normal retirement age, using 8-percent interest and the UP-84 mortality table. After normalization, the base portion of the benefit is 1.02 percent of average annual compensation up to the integration level, and the excess portion of the benefit is 1.73 percent of average annual compensation in excess of the integration level. The single sum optional form of benefit satisfies this paragraph (b) because the disparity provided in the optional form of benefit does not exceed the maximum excess allowance.

(c) *Uniform disparity.*—(1) *In general.*—The disparity provided under a defined benefit excess plan is uniform only if the plan uses the same base benefit percentage and the same excess benefit percentage for all employees with the same number of years of service. The disparity provided under an offset plan is uniform only if the plan uses the same gross benefit percentage and the same offset percentage for all employees with the same number of years of service. The disparity provided under a plan that determines each employee's accrued benefit under the fractional accrual method of section 411(b)(1)(C) is uniform only if the plan satisfies one of the deemed uniformity rules of paragraph (c)(2)(ii) or (iii) of this section.

(2) *Deemed uniformity.*—(i) *In general.*—The disparity provided under a plan does not fail to be uniform for purposes of this paragraph (c) merely because the plan contains one or more of the provisions described in paragraphs (c)(2)(ii) through (ix) of this section.

(ii) *Use of fractional accrual and disparity for 35 years.*—The plan contains a benefit formula as described in paragraphs (c)(2)(ii)(A) and (B) of this section, and the plan determines each employee's accrued benefit under the method described in §1.401(a)(4)-3(b)(4)(i)(B), i.e., by multiplying the employee's fractional rule benefit (within the meaning of §1.411(b)-1(b)(3)(ii)(A)) by a fraction, the numerator of which is the employee's years of service determined as of the plan year, and the denominator of which is the employee's projected years of service as of normal retirement age.

(A) For each year of service at least up to 35, the benefit formula provides the same base benefit percentage and the same excess benefit percentage for all employees in the case of a defined benefit excess plan or the same gross benefit percentage and the same offset percentage for all employees in the case of an offset plan.

(B) For each additional year of service, the benefit formula provides a uniform percentage of all average annual compensation that is no greater than the excess benefit percentage or the gross benefit percentage under paragraph (c)(2)(ii)(A) of this section, whichever is applicable.

(iii) *Use of fractional accrual and disparity for fewer than 35 years.*—The plan contains a benefit formula as described in paragraphs (c)(2)(iii)(A) through (C) of this section, and the plan determines each employee's accrued benefit under the method described in §1.401(a)(4)-3(b)(4)(i)(B).

(A) For each year in the employee's initial period of service comprising fewer than 35 years, the benefit formula provides the same base benefit percentage and the same excess benefit percentage for all employees in the case of a defined benefit excess plan or the same gross benefit percentage and the same offset percentage for all employees in the case of an offset plan.

(B) For each year of service after the initial period and at least up to 35, the benefit formula provides a uniform percentage of all average annual compensation, that is equal to the excess benefit percentage or the gross benefit percentage under paragraph (c)(2)(iii)(A) of this section.

(C) For each year of service after the period described in paragraph (c)(2)(iii)(B) of this section, the benefit formula provides a uniform percentage of all average annual compensation that is no greater than the excess benefit percentage or the gross benefit percentage under paragraph (c)(2)(iii)(A) of this section.

(iv) *Different social security retirement ages.*—The benefit formula uses the same excess benefit percentage or the same gross benefit percentage for all employees with the same number of years of service and, for employees with social security retirement ages later than age 65, adjusts the 0.75-percent factor in the maximum excess or offset allowance as required under paragraph (e)(1) of this section, by increasing the base benefit percentage in the case of a defined benefit excess plan, or reducing the offset percentage in the case of an offset plan.

(v) *Reduction for integration level.*—The plan uses an integration level or offset level greater than each employee's covered compensation and makes individual reductions in the 0.75-percent factor, as permitted under paragraph (d)(9)(iii)(B) of this section, by increasing the base benefit percentage in the case of a defined benefit excess plan or reducing the offset percentage in the case of an offset plan.

(vi) *Overall permitted disparity.*—(A) *In general.*—The benefit formula provides that, with respect to each employee's years of service after reaching the cumulative permitted disparity limit applicable to the employee under §1.401(l)-5(c), employer-provided benefits are determined with respect to the employee's total average annual compensation at a rate equal to the nondisparate percentage. For purposes of this paragraph (c)(2)(vi), the nondisparate percentage is generally the excess benefit percentage or gross benefit percentage otherwise applicable under the benefit formula to an employee with the same number of years of service.

(B) *Unit credit plans.*—In the case of a unit credit plan described in §1.401(a)(4)-3(b)(3), if the 411(b)(1)(B) limit percentage is less than the nondisparate percentage, the 411(b)(1)(B) limit percentage must be substituted for the nondisparate percentage. For this purpose, the 411(b)(1)(B) limit percentage is 133⅓ percent of the smallest base benefit, or 133⅓ percent of the smallest difference between the gross benefit percentage and the offset percentage, whichever is applicable, where the smallest base benefit percentage or difference is determined by reference to the benefit formula as applied to employees with no more years of service than the employee.

(C) *Fractional accrual plans.*—In the case of a fractional accrual plan described in §1.401(a)(4)-3(b)(4), the benefit formula must provide for the nondisparate percentage with respect to years of service after the employee would reach the cumulative permitted disparity limit applicable to the employee under §1.401(l)-5(c) as modified by this paragraph (c)(2)(vi)(C). Solely for purposes of this paragraph (c)(2)(vi)(C), the employee's annual disparity fractions (and thus the year in which the employee would reach the cumulative permitted disparity limit) are determined using the disparity provided under the benefit formula (rather than the special rule for fractional accrual plans in §1.401(l)-5(b)(8)(v)).

(vii) *Non-FICA employees.*—The plan provides that, in the case of each employee under the plan with respect to whom none of the taxes under section 3111(a), section 3221, or section 1401 is required to be paid, employer-provided benefits are determined with respect to the employee's total average annual compensation at the excess benefit percentage or gross benefit percentage applicable to an employee with the same number of years of service.

(viii) *Average annual compensation adjustment for offset plan.*—In the case of each employee whose final average compensation exceeds the employee's average annual compensation, the plan adjusts the offset percentage as required under paragraph (b)(3)(ii) of this section in order to satisfy the maximum offset allowance.

(ix) *PIA offsets.*—In the case of an offset plan, the plan provides that the offset applied to each employee's benefit is the lesser of a specified percentage of the employee's PIA and an offset that otherwise satisfies the requirements of this section (the "section 401(l) overlay"). The specified percentage of PIA must be the same for all employees with the same number of years of service. In the case of a plan that determines each employee's accrued benefit under the fractional accrual method of section 411(b)(1)(C), the specified percentage of PIA is deemed to be the same for all employees with the same number of years of service if the plan satisfies either of the deemed uniformity rules in paragraph (c)(2)(ii) or (iii) of this section, substituting "offset, expressed as a percentage of PIA, per year of service" for the term "offset percentage" (in addition to satisfying either of those rules with respect to the section 401(l) overlay).

(3) *Examples.*—The following examples illustrate this paragraph (c). Unless otherwise provided, the following facts apply. The plan is noncontributory and is the only plan ever maintained by the employer. The plan uses a normal retirement age of 65 and contains no

provision that would require a reduction in the 0.75-percent factor under paragraph (b)(2) or (b)(3) of this section. In the case of a defined benefit excess plan, the plan uses each employee's covered compensation as the integration level; in the case of an offset plan, the plan uses each employee's covered compensation as the offset level and provides that an employee's final average compensation is limited to the employee's average annual compensation. Each example discusses the benefit formula applicable to an employee who has a social security retirement age of 65.

Example 1. Plan M is a defined benefit excess plan that satisfies the 133⅓ percent accrual rule of section 411(b)(1)(B). The plan provides a normal retirement benefit of 1.0 percent of average annual compensation up to the integration level, plus 1.65 percent of average annual compensation in excess of the integration level, for each year of service up to 25. The plan also provides a benefit of 1.0 percent of all average annual compensation for each year of service in excess of 25. The disparity provided under the plan is uniform because the plan uses the same base and excess benefit percentages for all employees with the same number of years of service. If the plan formula were the same except that it used a different excess benefit percentage for some of the years of service between one and 25, the disparity under the plan would continue to be uniform.

Example 2. Plan O is a defined benefit excess plan that provides a normal retirement benefit of 50 percent of average annual compensation up to the integration level and 68.75 percent of average annual compensation in excess of the integration level, multiplied by a fraction, the numerator of which is the employee's service, up to 25 years, and the denominator of which is 25. The plan determines an employee's accrued benefit as described in §1.401(a)(4)-3(b)(4)(i)(B). The benefit formula thus provides a base benefit percentage of 2 percent (50 percent × 1/25) and an excess benefit percentage of 2.75 percent (68.75 percent × 1/25) for each of an employee's first 25 years of service and no benefit for years of service after 25. The disparity provided under the plan is not uniform within the meaning of this paragraph (c) because the benefit formula does not satisfy either of the uniform disparity rules for fractional accrual plans under paragraphs (c)(2)(ii) and (iii) of this section.

Example 3. Plan P is an offset plan that provides a normal retirement benefit of 2 percent of average annual compensation for each year of service up to 35, minus 0.75 percent of final average compensation up to the offset level for each year of service up to 25. The plan determines an employee's accrued benefit under the method described in §1.401(a)(4)-3(b)(4)(i)(B). Because the formula under the plan provides the same gross benefit percentage and offset percentage for 25 years of service (fewer than 35) and, for years of service after 25 and up to 35, provides a benefit at a uniform rate (equal to the gross benefit percentage) of all average annual compensation, and the plan accrues the benefit ratably, the disparity under the plan is deemed to be uniform under paragraph (c)(2)(iii) of this section.

Example 4. Plan Q is an offset plan that benefits employees with social security retirement ages of 65, 66, and 67. For each year of service up to 35, the plan provides a normal retirement benefit equal to 2 percent of average annual compensation, minus an offset based on the employee's final average compensation up to the offset level. For employees with a social security retirement age of 65, the offset percentage is 0.75 percent; for employees with a social security retirement age of 66, the offset percentage is 0.70 percent; and for employees with a social security retirement age of 67, the offset percentage is 0.65 percent. The disparity under the plan is deemed to be uniform under paragraph (c)(2)(iv) of this section because the plan uses the same gross benefit percentage for all employees and reduces the offset percentage for employees with social security retirement ages of 66 and 67 to comply with the adjustments in the 0.75-percent factor in the maximum excess or offset allowance required under paragraph (e)(1) of this section. (Because Plan Q effectively provides unreduced benefits prior to the social security retirement age for employees with social security retirement ages of 66 and 67, the 0.75-percent factor in the maximum offset allowance must be reduced to 0.70 percent and 0.65 percent respectively.) Alternatively, Plan Q could satisfy this paragraph (c) if it provided a uniform offset percentage of 0.65 percent for all employees because 0.65 percent is the maximum offset allowance under the plan for an employee with a social security retirement age of 67.

Example 5. Plan R is an offset plan that provides a normal retirement benefit of 2 percent of average annual compensation, minus an offset determined as a percentage of total final average compensation, for each year of service up to 35. For an employee whose final average compensation does not exceed the employee's covered compensation, the offset percentage is 0.75 percent. For an employee whose final average compensation exceeds the employee's covered compensation, the plan reduces the offset percentage, as required by paragraph (d) of this section. The reduced offset percentage is determined by comparing the employee's final average compensation to the employee's covered compensation as permitted under paragraph (d)(9)(iii)(B) of this section. The disparity provided under the plan is deemed uniform under paragraph (c)(2)(v) of this section because the plan uses the same gross benefit percentage for all employees and makes individual reductions in the 0.75-percent factor, as permitted under paragraph (d)(9)(iii)(B) of this section, by reducing the offset percentage in the case of an employee whose final average compensation exceeds covered compensation.

(d) *Requirements for integration or offset level.*—(1) *In general.*—The integration level under a defined benefit excess plan or the offset level under an offset plan must satisfy paragraphs (d)(2), (d)(3), (d)(4), (d)(5) or (d)(6) of this section, as modified by paragraph (d)(7) of this section in the case of a short plan year. Paragraph (d)(8) of this section contains demographic tests that apply to certain defined benefit plans. Paragraph (d)(9) of this section explains certain reductions required in the 0.75-percent factor under paragraph (b)(2) or (b)(3) of this section. Paragraph (d)(10) of this section contains examples. If a reduction applies to the 0.75-percent factor under this paragraph (d), the reduced factor is used for all purposes in determining whether the permitted disparity rules for defined benefit plans are satisfied.

(2) *Covered compensation.*—The requirement of this paragraph (d)(2) is satisfied only if the integration or offset level under the plan for each employee is the employee's covered compensation.

(3) *Uniform percentage of covered compensation.*—The requirement of this paragraph (d)(3) is satisfied only if—

(i) The integration or offset level under the plan for each employee is a uniform percentage (greater than 100 percent) of each employee's covered compensation,

(ii) In the case of a defined benefit excess plan, the integration level does not exceed the taxable wage base in effect for the plan year, and, in the case of an offset plan, the offset level does not exceed the employee's final average compensation, and

(iii) The plan adjusts the 0.75-percent factor in the maximum excess or offset allowance in accordance with paragraph (d)(9) of this section.

(4) *Single dollar amount.*—The requirement of this paragraph (d)(4) is satisfied only if the integration or offset level under the plan for all employees is a single dollar amount (either specified in the plan or determined under a formula specified in the plan) that does not exceed the greater of $10,000 or one-half of the covered compensation of an individual who attains social security retirement age in the calendar year in which the plan year begins. In the case of a calendar year in which no individual could attain social security retirement age, for example, the year 2003, this rule is applied using covered compensation of an individual attaining social security retirement age in the preceding calendar year.

(5) *Intermediate amount.*—The requirement of this paragraph (d)(5) is satisfied only if—

(i) The integration or offset level under the plan for all employees is a single dollar amount (either specified in the plan or determined under a formula specified in the plan) that is greater than the highest amount determined under paragraph (d)(4) of this section,

(ii) In the case of a defined benefit excess plan, the single dollar amount does not exceed the taxable wage base in effect for the plan year, and, in the case of an offset plan, the single dollar amount does not exceed the employee's final average compensation,

(iii) The plan satisfies the demographic requirements of paragraph (d)(8) of this section, and

(iv) The plan adjusts the 0.75-percent factor in the maximum excess or offset allowance in accordance with paragraph (d)(9) of this section.

For purposes of this paragraph (d)(5), an offset level of each employee's final average compensation is considered a single dollar amount determined under a formula specified in the plan.

(6) *Intermediate amount safe harbor.*—The requirement of this paragraph (d)(6) is satisfied only if—

(i) The integration or offset level under the plan for all employees is a single dollar amount described in paragraph (d)(5) of this section, and

(ii) The 0.75-percent factor in the maximum excess or offset allowance under paragraph (b)(2) or (b)(3) of this section is reduced to the lesser of the adjusted factor determined under paragraph (d)(9) of this section or 80 percent of the otherwise applicable factor under paragraph (b)(2) or (b)(3) of this section, determined without regard to paragraph (d)(9) of this section.

(7) *Prorated integration level for short plan year.*—If an accumulation plan uses paragraph (2) or (4) of the definition of plan year compensation under §1.401(a)(4)-12 (i.e., section 414(s) compensation

for the plan year or the period of plan participation) and has a plan year that comprises fewer than 12 months, the integration or offset level under the plan for each employee must be an amount equal to the otherwise applicable integration or offset level described in paragraph (d)(2), (d)(3), (d)(4), (d)(5), or (d)(6) of this section, multiplied by a fraction, the numerator of which is the number of months in the plan year and the denominator of which is 12. No adjustment to the maximum excess or offset allowance is required as a result of the application of this paragraph (d)(7), other than any adjustment already required under paragraph (d)(6) or (d)(9) of this section.

(8) *Demographic requirements.*—(i) *In general.*—A plan that satisfies the demographic requirements of paragraphs (d)(8)(ii) and (iii) of this section may use an integration level described in paragraph (d)(5) of this section.

(ii) *Attained age requirement.*—The requirement of this paragraph (d)(8)(ii) is satisfied only if the average attained age of the nonhighly compensated employees in the plan is not greater than the greater of—

(A) Age 50, or

(B) 5 plus the average attained age of the highly compensated employees in the plan.

For purposes of this paragraph (d)(3)(ii), attained ages are determined as of the beginning of the plan year.

(iii) *Nondiscrimination requirement.*—The requirement of this paragraph (d)(8)(iii) is satisfied only if at least one of the following tests in paragraphs (d)(8)(iii)(A) through (D) of this section is satisfied.

(A) *Minimum percentage test.*—This test is satisfied only if more than 50 percent of the nonhighly compensated employees in the plan have average annual compensation at least equal to 120 percent of the integration or offset level.

(B) *Ratio test.*—This test is satisfied only if the percentage of nonhighly compensated nonexcludable employees, who are in the plan and who have average annual compensation at least equal to 120 percent of the integration or offset level, is at least 70 percent of the percentage of highly compensated nonexcludable employees who are employees in the plan.

(C) *High dollar amount test.*—This test is satisfied only if the integration or offset level exceeds 150 percent of the covered compensation of an individual who attains social security retirement age in the calendar year in which the plan year begins. In the case of a calendar year in which no individual could attain social security retirement age, for example, the year 2003, this rule is applied using covered compensation of an individual attaining social security retirement age in the preceding calendar year.

(D) *Individual disparity reductions.*—This test is satisfied only if the plan is an offset plan that uses an offset level of each employee's final average compensation and makes individual disparity reductions as permitted under paragraph (d)(9)(iii)(B) of this section.

(9) *Reduction in the 0.75-percent factor if integration or offset level exceeds covered compensation.*—(i) *In general.*—If the integration or offset level specified under the plan is each employee's covered compensation as of the plan year, no reduction in the 0.75-percent factor in the maximum excess or offset allowance is required for the plan year under this paragraph (d)(9). If a plan specifies an integration or offset level that exceeds an employee's covered compensation, the 0.75-percent factor in the maximum excess or offset allowance must be reduced as required in paragraph (d)(9)(ii) or (iii) of this section. Paragraph (d)(9)(iv) of this section contains a table of the applicable reductions.

(ii) *Uniform percentage of covered compensation.*—If a plan specifies an integration or offset level that is a uniform percentage (in excess of 100 percent) of each employee's covered compensation, the 0.75-percent factor in the maximum excess or offset allowance must be reduced in accordance with the table in paragraph (d)(9)(iv) of this section. Thus, for example, if a plan specifies an integration or offset level of 120 percent of each employee's covered compensation, the 0.75-percent factor in the maximum excess or offset allowance must be reduced to 0.69 percent in accordance with the table because the specified integration or offset level is more than covered compensation but not more than 125 percent of covered compensation.

(iii) *Single dollar amount.*—If a plan specifies an integration or offset level of a single dollar amount as permitted under paragraph (d)(5) of this section (for example, $30,000), the applicable reduction in the maximum excess or offset allowance must be determined under paragraph (d)(9)(iii)(A) or (E) of this section, as specified under the plan.

(A) *Plan-wide reduction.*—The applicable reduction in the maximum excess or offset allowance under the table in paragraph (d)(9)(iv) of this section may be determined by comparing the single dollar amount specified in the plan to the covered compensation of an individual attaining social security retirement age in the calendar year in which the plan year begins. Thus, for example, if a plan specifies a single integration or offset level of $30,000 that is uniformly applicable to all employees for a plan year and the covered compensation of an individual attaining social security retirement age in the calendar year in which the plan year begins is $20,000, the 0.75-percent factor in the maximum excess or offset allowance must be reduced to 0.60 percent for all employees in accordance with the table in paragraph (d)(9)(iv) of this section because the specified integration or offset level of $30,000 is more than 125 percent of $20,000 but not more than 150 percent of $20,000. In the case of a calendar year in which no individual could attain social security retirement age (for example, 2003), the comparison is made with covered compensation of an individual who attained social security retirement age in the preceding calendar year. If an offset plan uses an offset level of each employee's final average compensation, the reduction under this paragraph (d)(9)(iii)(A) is determined by comparing the highest possible amount of final average compensation to the covered compensation of an individual attaining social security retirement age in the calendar year in which the plan year begins.

(B) *Individual reductions.*—The applicable reduction in the maximum excess or offset allowance under the table in paragraph (d)(9)(iv) of this section may be determined by comparing the single dollar amount specified in the plan to the covered compensation of each employee under the plan. Thus, for example, if a plan specifies a single integration or offset level of $30,000 that is uniformly applicable to all employees for a plan year, the 0.75-percent factor in the maximum excess or offset allowance must be reduced to 0.60 percent for an employee with covered compensation of $20,000, but need not be reduced for an employee whose covered compensation is $30,000 or greater.

(iv) *Reductions.*—(A) *Table.*—

TABLE

If the integration or offset level is	the permitted disparity factor is
100 percent of covered compensation	0.75 percent
125 percent of covered compensation	0.69 percent
150 percent of covered compensation	0.60 percent
175 percent of covered compensation	0.53 percent
200 percent of covered compensation	0.47 percent
The taxable wage base or final average compensation	0.42 percent

(B) *Interpolation.*—If the integration or offset level used under a plan is between the percentages of covered compensation in the table, the permitted disparity factor applicable to the plan can be determined either by straight-line interpolation between the permitted disparity factors in the table or by rounding the integration or offset level up to the next highest percentage of covered compensation in the table.

(10) *Examples.*—The following examples illustrate this paragraph (d). Unless otherwise provided, the following facts apply. The plan is noncontributory and is the only plan ever maintained by the employer. The plan uses a normal retirement age of 65 and contains no provision that would require a reduction in the 0.75-percent factor under paragraph (b)(2) or (b)(3) of this section. In the case of an offset plan, the plan provides that an employee's final average compensation is limited to the employee's average annual compensation. Each example discusses the benefit formula applicable to an employee who has a social security retirement age of 65.

Example 1. (a) Plan M is a defined benefit excess plan that uses the calendar year as its plan year. For the 1989 plan year, the plan uses an integration level of $20,000, which is 118 percent of the 1989 covered compensation of $16,968 for an individual reaching social security retirement age in 1989. The plan may use that integration level without satisfying paragraph (d)(8) of this section, provided the adjustment to the 0.75-percent factor required under paragraph (d)(6) of this section is made. That adjustment is the lesser of the factor determined under paragraph (d)(9) of this section or 80 percent of the factor otherwise applicable under paragraph (b)(2) or (b)(3) of this section.

(b) The plan determines the factor under paragraph (d)(9) of this section by comparing the integration level to the covered compensation of an individual attaining social security retirement age in the calendar year in which the plan year begins and by rounding the integration level up to 125 percent of that covered compensation amount. The 0.75-percent factor is therefore replaced by 0.69 percent pursuant to the table in paragraph (d)(9) of this section. The 0.69-percent factor is 92 percent of the 0.75-percent factor. Because the lesser of 80 percent and 92 percent is 80 percent, the 0.75-percent factor is reduced to 0.6-percent (80 percent of 0.75 percent) under paragraph (d)(6) of this section. The 0.6-percent factor applies to benefits commencing at age 65 for an employee with a social security retirement age of 65. In determining normal retirement benefits for employees with social security requirement ages of 66 or 67, the applicable factors for benefits commencing at age 65 are, respectively, 0.56 percent (80 percent of 0.7 percent) and 0.52 percent (80 percent of 0.65 percent).

(c) The plan could also determine the factor under paragraph (d)(9) of this section by comparing the integration level to the covered compensation of each employee under the plan, or by straight line interpolation between the disparity factors contained in the table in paragraph (d)(9) of this section, or both. (Of course, if the plan satisfied paragraph (d)(8) of this section, the plan could use the factor determined under paragraph (d)(9) of this section.)

Example 2. (a) Plan N, an accumulation plan, is a defined benefit excess plan that, for each year of service up to 35 accrues a normal retirement benefit of 1 percent of plan year compensation up to the taxable wage base, plus 1.75 percent of plan year compensation above the taxable wage base, for each year of service up to 35. An employee's total retirement benefit is the sum of the accruals for all years. The plan satisfies paragraph (d)(8) of this section.

(b) Because the plan uses the taxable wage base (an amount above covered compensation) as the integration level, it must reduce the 0.75-percent factor in the maximum excess allowance as required under paragraphs (d)(5) and (d)(9) of this section. The reduced factor, if determined on a plan-wide basis under paragraph (d)(9)(iii)(A) of this section, is 0.42 percent. The plan must therefore reduce the disparity in the plan so that it does not exceed 0.42 percent.

Example 3. (a) For the 1990 plan year, Plan O provides a normal retirement benefit of 2 percent of average annual compensation, minus a percentage of final average compensation up to $48,000, for each year of service up to 35. The plan satisfies paragraph (d)(8) of this section. As permitted under paragraph (d)(9) of this section, the plan provides that each employee's offset percentage is determined by comparing $48,000 to the employee's covered compensation and by rounding the result up to the next highest percentage of covered compensation.

(b) Employee A has a social security retirement age of 66 and covered compensation of $40,000. Because the plan provides for commencement of Employee A's benefit at age 65, the 0.75-percent factor in the maximum offset allowance is reduced to 0.7 percent under paragraph (e)(1) of this section (the "paragraph (e) factor"). In addition, because $48,000 is rounded up to 125 percent of Employee A's covered compensation, the 0.75-percent factor in the maximum offset allowance is reduced to 0.69 percent under paragraph (d)(9) of this section (the "paragraph (d) factor"). The reductions are cumulative under paragraph (b)(3)(ii) of this section.

(c) The cumulative reductions can be made by multiplying the paragraph (e) factor by the ratio of the paragraph (d) factor to 0.75 percent or by multiplying the paragraph (d) factor by the ratio of the paragraph (e) factor to 0.75 percent. The disparity factor for Employee A is therefore 0.64 percent ((0.7 percent × 0.69 percent ÷ 0.75 percent) or (0.69 percent × 0.7 percent ÷ 0.75 percent)).

Example 4. Plan P is an offset plan that uses the calendar year as the plan year and uses an offset level of each employee's final average compensation. Assume that the taxable wage bases for 1990-1992 are the following:

1990—$51,300
1991—$53,400
1992—$58,000

Employee B's final average compensation, determined as of the close of the 1992 plan year, is the average of Employee B's annual compensation for the period 1990-1992. Employee B's annual compensation for each year is the following:

1990—$47,000
1991—$59,000
1992—$65,000

For purposes of determining the offset applied to Employee B's employer-provided benefit under the plan, Employee B's final average compensation as of the close of the 1992 plan year is $52,800 ($47,000 + $53,400 + $58,000) ÷ 3). This is because annual compensation in excess of the taxable wage base in effect at the beginning of the year may not be taken into account in determining an employee's final average compensation or in determining the employee's offset. If the plan determines the offset applied to Employee B's benefit by reference to compensation in excess of $52,800, the plan fails to satisfy this paragraph (d).

(e) *Adjustments to the 0.75-percent factor for benefits commencing at ages other than social security retirement age.*—(1) *In general.*—The 0.75-percent factor in the maximum excess allowance and in the maximum offset allowance applies to a benefit commencing at an employee's social security retirement age. Except as provided in paragraph (g) of this section, if a benefit payable to an employee under a defined benefit excess plan or a defined benefit offset plan commences at an age before the employee's social security retirement age (including a benefit payable at the normal retirement age under the plan), the 0.75-percent factor in the maximum excess allowance or in the maximum offset allowance, respectively, is reduced in accordance with paragraph (e)(2)(i) of this section. If a benefit payable to an employee under a defined benefit excess plan or a defined benefit offset plan commences at an age after the employee's social security retirement age, the 0.75-percent factor in the maximum excess allowance or in the maximum offset allowance, respectively, may be increased in accordance with paragraph (e)(2)(ii) of this section. Paragraph (e)(4) of this section provides rules on the age at which a benefit commences. See paragraph (f) of this section for the requirements applicable to optional forms of benefit.

(2) *Adjustments.*—(i) *Benefits commencing on or after age 55 and before social security retirement age.*—If benefits commence before an employee's social security retirement age, the 0.75-percent factor in the maximum excess allowance and in the maximum offset allowance must be reduced for such early commencement of benefits in accordance with the tables set forth in paragraph (e)(3)of this section.

(ii) *Benefits commencing after social security retirement age and on or before age 70.*—If benefits commence after an employee's social security retirement age, the 0.75-percent factor in the maximum excess allowance and in the maximum offset allowance may be increased for such delayed commencement of benefits in accordance with the tables set forth in paragraph (e)(3) of this section.

(iii) *Benefits commencing before age 55.*—If benefits commence before the employee attains age 55, the 0.75-percent factor in the maximum excess allowance and in the maximum offset allowance is further reduced (on a monthly basis to reflect the month in which benefits commence) to a factor that is the actuarial equivalent of the 0.75-percent factor, as adjusted under the tables in paragraph (e)(3) of this section, applicable to a benefit commencing in the month in which the employee attains age 55. In determining actuarial equivalence for this purpose, a reasonable interest rate must be used. In addition, a reasonable mortality table must be used to determine the actuarial present value, as defined in §1.401(a)(4)-12, of the benefits commencing at age 55 and at the earlier commencement age, and a reasonable mortality table may be used to determine the actuarial present value at the earlier commencement age of the benefits commencing at age 55. A standard interest rate and a standard mortality table, as defined in §1.401(a)(4)-12, are considered reasonable.

(iv) *Benefits commencing after age 70.*—If benefits commence after the employee attains age 70, the 0.75-percent factor in the maximum excess allowance and in the maximum offset allowance may be further increased (on a monthly basis to reflect the month in which benefits commence) to a factor that is the actuarial equivalent of the 0.75-percent factor (as adjusted in accordance with this paragraph (e)) applicable to a benefit commencing in the month in which the employee attains age 70. In determining actuarial equivalence for this purpose, a reasonable interest rate must be used. In addition, a reasonable mortality table must be used to determine the actuarial present value, as defined in §1.401(a)(4)-12, of the benefits commencing at age 70 and at the later commencement age, and a reasonable mortality table may be used to determine the value at the later commencement age of the benefits commencing at age 70. A standard interest rate and a standard mortality table, as defined in §1.401(a)(4)-12, are considered reasonable.

(3) *Tables.*—Tables I, II, and III provide the adjustments in the 0.75-percent factor in the maximum excess allowance and in the maximum offset allowance applicable to benefits commencing on or after age 55 and on or before age 70 to an employee who has a social security retirement age of 65, 66 or 67. Table IV is a simplified table for a plan that uses a single disparity factor of 0.65 percent for all employees at age 65. The factors in the following tables are applicable to benefits that commence in the month the employee attains the specified age. Accordingly, if benefits commence in a month other than the month in which the employee attains the specified age, appropriate adjustments in the 0.75-percent factor in the maximum excess allowance and the maximum offset allowance must be made. For this purpose, adjustments may be based on straight-line interpolation from the factors in the tables or in accordance with the methods of adjustment specified in paragraphs (e)(2)(iii) and (iv) of this section.

TABLE I
Social security retirement age 67

Age at which benefits commence	Annual factor in maximum excess allowance and maximum offset allowance (percent)
70	1.002
69	0.908
68	0.825
67	0.750
66	0.700
65	0.650
64	0.600
63	0.550
62	0.500
61	0.475
60	0.450
59	0.425
58	0.400
57	0.375
56	0.344
55	0.316

TABLE II
Social security retirement age 66

Age at which benefits commence	Annual factor in maximum excess allowance and maximum offset allowance (percent)
70	1.101
69	0.998
68	0.907
67	0.824
66	0.750
65	0.700
64	0.650
63	0.600
62	0.550
61	0.500
60	0.475
59	0.450

Age at which benefits commence	Annual factor in maximum excess allowance and maximum offset allowance (percent)
58	0.425
57	0.400
56	0.375
55	0.344

TABLE III
Social security retirement age 65

Age at which benefits commence	Annual factor in maximum excess allowance and maximum offset allowance (percent)
70	1.209
69	0.096
68	0.996
67	0.905
66	0.824
65	0.750
64	0.700
63	0.650
62	0.600
61	0.550
60	0.500
59	0.475
58	0.450
57	0.425
56	0.400
55	0.375

TABLE IV
Simplified table

Age at which benefits commence	Annual factor in maximum excess allowance and maximum offset allowance (percent)
70	1.048
69	0.950
68	0.863
67	0.784
66	0.714
65	0.650
64	0.607
63	0.563
62	0.520
61	0.477
60	0.433
59	0.412
58	0.390
57	0.368
56	0.347
55	0.325

(4) *Benefit commencement date.*—(i) *In general.*—Except as provided in paragraph (e)(4)(ii) of this section, a benefit commences for purposes of this paragraph (e) on the first day of the period for which the benefit is paid under the plan.

(ii) *Qualified social security supplement.*—If a plan uses a qualified social security supplement, as defined in §1.401(a)(4)-12, to provide an aggregate benefit at retirement before social security retirement age that is a uniform percentage of average annual compensation, benefits will be considered to commence on the first day of the period for which the qualified social security supplement is no longer payable. In order for this paragraph (e)(4)(ii) to apply, the uniform percentage must be equal to the excess benefit percentage in the case of an excess plan or the gross benefit percentage in the case of an offset plan.

(5) *Examples.*—The following examples illustrate this paragraph (e). Unless otherwise provided, the following facts apply. The plan is noncontributory and is the only plan ever maintained by the employer. The plan uses a normal retirement age of 65 and contains no provision that would require a reduction in the 0.75-percent factor under paragraph (b)(2) or (b)(3) of this section. In the case of a defined benefit excess plan, the plan uses each employee's covered compensation as the integration level; in the case of an offset plan, the plan uses each employee's covered compensation as the offset level and provides that an employee's final average compensation is limited to the employee's average annual compensation. Each example discusses the benefit formula applicable to an employee who has a social security retirement age of 65.

Example 1. Plan M is a defined benefit excess plan that, for an employee with a social security retirement age of 65, provides a normal retirement benefit of 1.25 percent of average annual compensation up to the integration level, plus 2.0 percent of average annual compensation in excess of the integration level, for each year of service up to 35. For an employee with at least 20 years of service, the plan provides a benefit commencing at age 55 that is equal to the benefit payable at age 65. For that employee, the disparity provided under the plan at age 55 is 0.75 percent (2 percent – 1.25 percent). Because this disparity exceeds the 0.375 percent factor provided in the table for a benefit payable at age 55 to an employee with a social security retirement age of 65, the plan fails to satisfy paragraphs (b) and (e) of this section with respect to the early retirement benefit.

Example 2. Assume the same facts as in *Example 1*, except that the base benefit percentage under the plan is 1.75 percent. Thus, the disparity provided under the plan at age 55 is 0.25 percent (2 percent – 1.75 percent). Because the disparity does not exceed the 0.375 percent factor provided in the table for a benefit payable at age 55 to an employee with a social security retirement age of 65, the plan does not fail to satisfy paragraphs (b) and (e) of this section with respect to the early retirement benefit.

Example 3. Plan N is an offset plan that, for an employee with a social security retirement age of 65, provides a normal retirement benefit of 1.75 percent of average annual compensation, minus 0.75 percent of final average compensation up to the offset level, for each year of service up to 35. For an employee with at least 20 years of service, the plan provides a benefit commencing at age 55 that is equal to the benefit payable at age 65. For that employee, the disparity provided under the plan at age 55 is 0.75 percent. Because this disparity exceeds the 0.375-percent factor provided in the table for an offset applied to a benefit payable at age 55 to an employee with a social security retirement age of 65, the plan fails to satisfy paragraphs (b) and (e) of this section with respect to the early retirement benefit. The plan would not fail to satisfy paragraphs (b) and (e) of this section with respect to the early retirement benefit if the applicable factor for determining the offset applied to the benefit were reduced to 0.375 percent.

Example 4. Plan O is a defined benefit excess plan that, for an employee with a social security retirement age of 65, provides a normal retirement benefit of 1.25 percent of average annual compensation up to the integration level, plus 2.0 percent of average annual compensation in excess of the integration 1, for each year of service up to 35. The plan provides benefits commencing before normal retirement age with the following reductions:

Age	Percentage of normal retirement benefit
64	90%
63	85%
62	80%

Under the plan, a benefit payable at age 64 is equal to 90 percent of the normal retirement benefit payable at age 65. Thus, the excess benefit percentage under the plan is 1.8 percent, the base benefit percentage under the plan is 1.125 percent, and the disparity provided under the plan at age 64 is 0.675 percent. Similarly, a benefit payable at age 63 is equal to 85 percent of the normal retirement benefit payable at age 65. Thus, the excess benefit percentage under the plan is 1.7 percent, the base benefit percentage under the plan is 1.0625 percent, and the disparity provided under the plan at age 63 is 0.6375 percent. Finally, a benefit payable at age 62 is equal to 80 percent of the normal retirement benefit payable at age 65. Thus, the excess benefit percentage under the plan is 1.6 percent, the base benefit percentage under the plan is 1.0 percent, and the disparity provided under the plan at age 62 is 0.6 percent. Because the disparities provided under the plan at each early commencement age do not exceed the factors provided in the applicable table in paragraph (e)(3) of this section, the plan does not fail to satisfy paragraphs (b) and (e) of this section with respect to the early retirement benefits.

Example 5. Plan P is a defined benefit excess plan that provides a normal retirement benefit of 0.75 percent of average annual compensation up to the integration level, plus 1.5 percent of average annual compensation in excess of the integration level, for each year of service up to 35. The plan does not provide any benefits, other than normal retirement benefits, commencing before an employee's social security retirement age. Employee A, born in 1947, has a social security retirement age of 66. Because the plan provides for the distribution of normal retirement benefits before Employee A's social security retirement age, the 0.75-percent factor in the maximum excess allowance applicable to Employee A must be reduced to 0.70 percent in accordance with this paragraph (e). Accordingly, the disparity provided to A under the plan exceeds the maximum excess allowance because the excess benefit percentage (1.5 percent) exceeds the base benefit percentage (0.75 percent) by more than the maximum excess allowance of 0.70 percent, as reduced in accordance with this paragraph (e).

Example 6. Assume the same facts as in *Example 5*, except that the plan also provides an early retirement benefit, commencing at age 62, to an employee who satisfies the conditions for early retirement specified in the plan. The early retirement benefit is based upon the employee's accrued benefit at early retirement age and equals the amount that would have been paid commencing at the employee's normal retirement age based upon the employee's average annual compensation, covered compensation and years of service at the date of the employee's early retirement. Employee B, who has a social security retirement age of 65, meets the conditions for early retirement under the plan and retires at age 62 with 30 years of service. At the time of early retirement, Employee B has average annual compensation of $20,000 and covered compensation of $16,000. Under the plan's benefit formula, Employee B has accrued a normal retirement benefit, commencing at age 65, of $5,400 ((22.5 percent × $16,000) + (45 percent × $4,000)) based on Employee B's average annual compensation, covered compensation and years of service at early retirement. Accordingly, under the plan's early retirement provisions, Employee B is entitled to receive, commencing at early retirement, a benefit of $5,400. Because the early retirement benefit is a benefit commencing at age 62 (before Employee B's social security retirement age), the 0.75-percent factor in the maximum excess allowance must be reduced to 0.60 percent in accordance with this paragraph (e). Accordingly, the disparity provided to Employee B under the plan at early retirement exceeds the maximum excess allowance.

Example 7. (a) Plan Q is a defined benefit excess plan that provides a normal retirement benefit of 1.35 percent of average annual compensation up to the integration level, plus 2 percent of average annual compensation in excess of the integration level, for each year of service up to 35. The plan provides that an employee with 10 years of service at age 55 may receive an unreduced retirement benefit. The plan also provides that employee with a supplemental benefit of 0.65 percent of average annual compensation up to the integration level for each year of service up to 35, payable from early retirement until age 65. The supplemental benefit is a qualified social security supplement under §1.401(a)(4)-12. The effect of the supplement is to provide an employee with a uniform benefit of 2 percent of average annual compensation from early retirement until age 65, when the supplement is no longer payable. Therefore, for purposes of this paragraph (e), the employee's benefit will be considered to commence at age 65.

(b) Assume that Plan Q is instead an offset plan that provides a normal retirement benefit of 2 percent of average annual compensation, minus 0.65 percent of final average compensation up to the offset level, for each year of service up to 35. The plan provides the same early retirement benefit on the same conditions, except that the supplement is 0.65 percent of an employee's final average compensation up to the offset level. An employee at age 55 thus receives a uniform benefit of 2 percent of average annual compensation until age 65, when the supplement is no longer payable. Therefore, for purposes of this paragraph (e), the employee's benefit will be considered to commence at age 65.

(f) *Benefits, rights, and features.*—(1) *Defined benefit excess plan.*—In the case of a defined benefit excess plan, each benefit, right, or feature provided under the plan with respect to employer-provided benefits attributable to average annual compensation above the integration level (an "excess benefit, right, or feature") must also be provided on the same terms with respect to employer-provided benefits attributable to average annual compensation up to the integration level (a "base benefit, right, or feature"). Alternatively, an excess benefit, right, or feature may be provided on different terms than the base benefit, right, or feature, if the terms used to determine the base benefit, right, or feature produce a benefit, right, or feature of inherently equal or greater value than the benefit, right, or feature that would be produced under the terms used to determine the excess benefit right, or feature.

(2) *Offset plan.*—In the case of an offset plan, each benefit, right, or feature provided under the plan with respect to employer-provided benefits before application of the offset (a "gross benefit, right, or feature") must be provided on the same terms as those used to determine the offset applied to the gross benefit, right, or feature. Alternatively, a gross benefit, right, or feature may be provided on different terms from those used to determine the offset applied to the gross benefit, right, or feature, if the terms used to determine the gross benefit, right, or feature produce a benefit, right, or feature of inherently equal or greater value than the benefit, right, or feature that would be produced under the terms used to determine the offset applied to the gross benefit, right, or feature. In addition, if benefits commence before an employee's normal retirement age, the gross benefit percentage under the plan must be reduced by a number of percentage points that is not less than the number of percentage points by which the offset percentage must be reduced from normal retirement age to the age at which benefits commence, under the rules of paragraph (e) of this section.

(3) *Examples.*—The following examples illustrate this paragraph (f). Unless otherwise provided, the following facts apply. The plan is noncontributory and is the only plan ever maintained by the employer. The plan uses a normal retirement age of 65 and contains no provision that would require a reduction in the 0.75-percent factor under paragraph (b)(2) or (b)(3) of this section. In the case of a defined benefit excess plan, the plan uses each employee's covered compensation as the integration level; in the case of an offset plan, the plan uses each employee's covered compensation as the offset level and provides that an employee's final average compensation is limited to the employee's average annual compensation. Each example discusses the benefit formula applicable to an employee who has a social security retirement age of 65. All optional forms of benefit under each plan are provided on the same terms.

Example 1. Plan M is a defined benefit excess plan that provides a normal retirement benefit of 1 percent of average annual compensation up to the integration level, plus 1.65 percent of average annual compensation above the integration level, for each year of service up to 35. The plan provides an early retirement benefit for any employee who terminates employment at or after age 55 with 10 or more years of service. In determining an employee's early retirement, the 1.65 percent excess benefit percentage is reduced in accordance with the table in paragraph (e)(3) of this section for a plan that uses a single disparity factor of 0.65 percent for all employees at age 65. However, a larger reduction factor is applied to determine the base benefit percentage at early retirement. The plan violates this paragraph (f) because the excess early retirement benefit is not provided on the same terms as the base early retirement benefit, nor do the terms used to determine the base early retirement benefit produce an early retirement benefit of inherently equal or greater value than the early retirement benefit that would be produced under the terms used to determine the excess benefit, right, or feature.

Example 2. The facts are the same as in *Example 1* except that the plan determines the early retirement benefit by applying the same reduction factors under paragraph (e)(3) of this section to the base and excess benefit percentages. Furthermore, if an employee terminates employment at or after age 55 with 30 or more years of service, the plan provides that the base benefit percentage of 1 percent is not reduced. Although the excess early retirement benefit is provided on different terms than the base early retirement benefit, the plan satisfies this paragraph (f) because the terms used to determine the base early retirement benefit produce an early retirement of inherently equal or greater value than the early retirement benefit that would be produced under the terms used to determine the excess benefit, right, or feature.

Example 3. Plan N is an offset plan that provides a normal retirement benefit of 2 percent of average annual compensation, minus 0.65 percent of final average compensation up to the offset level, for each year of service up to 35. In determining the qualified joint and survivor ("QJSA") form of the normal retirement benefit, the plan applies a factor of 80 percent to the gross benefit percentage and a factor of 100 percent to the offset percentage. Thus, the QJSA form is 1.6 percent of average annual compensation, minus 0.65 percent of final average compensation up to the offset level, for each year of service up to 35. The plan violates this paragraph (f) because the gross QJSA form is not provided on the same terms as the terms used to determine the offset applied to the QJSA, nor does it produce a QJSA benefit that is of inherently equal or greater value than the QJSA benefit that would be produced under the terms used to determine the offset under the plan.

Example 4. Plan O is a defined benefit excess plan that provides a normal retirement benefit of 1 percent of average annual compensation up to the integration level, plus 1.65 percent of average annual compensation above the integration level, for each year of service up to 35. The plan also provides a single sum optional form of benefit determined by applying a single interest rate and mortality assumption to the entire normal retirement benefit. The plan satisfies this paragraph (f) because the excess optional form is provided on the same terms as the base optional form. The plan would also satisfy this paragraph (f) if it used a lower interest rate to determine the base optional form than used to determine the excess optional form because the lower interest rate would produce an optional form of inherently equal or greater value than the optional form produced by using the same interest rate.

Example 5. Plan R is a defined benefit excess plan that provides a normal retirement benefit of 1 percent of average annual compensation up to the integration level, plus 1.65 percent of average annual compensation above the integration level, for each year of service up to 35. If an employee continues to work after normal retirement age, the plan provides that the employee receives credit for additional years of service up to the service limit of 35. The plan also provides that the disparity provided under the plan will increase as permitted under paragraph (e) of this section for benefits commencing after social security retirement age. However, the plan does not provide an increase in the base benefit percentage to reflect the fact that the employee has delayed commencement of benefits past normal retirement age. Thus, for example, for an employee at age 68, the plan provides a benefit of 1 percent of average annual compensation up to the integration level, plus 1.86 percent of average annual compensation above the integration level, for each year of service up to 35. The plan violates this paragraph (f) because the excess benefit provided for an employee after normal retirement age is not provided on the same terms as the base benefit, nor do the terms used to determine the base benefit produce a benefit of inherently equal or greater value than the benefit that would be produced under the terms used to determine the excess benefit.

Example 6. Plan Q is an offset plan that provides a normal retirement benefit of 2 percent of average annual compensation, minus 0.65 percent of final average compensation up to the offset level, for each year of service up to 35. In accordance with paragraph (e) of this section, the plan reduces the offset percentage under the plan for early retirement and provides a benefit at age 55 of 2 percent of average annual compensation, minus 0.325 percent of final average compensation up to the offset level, for each year of service up to 35. However, the early retirement benefit does not meet this paragraph (f) because an employee's gross benefit percentage is not reduced for early retirement.

Example 7. The facts are the same as in *Example 6* except that the plan reduces the gross benefit percentage for early retirement at age 55 to 1.675 percent. Because the gross benefit percentage is reduced by 0.325 percent (from 2.0 percent to 1.675 percent), the same percentage point reduction made in the offset percentage (from 0.65 percent to 0.325 percent), the early retirement benefit meets this paragraph (f).

(g) *No reductions in 0.75-percent factor for ancillary benefits.*—For purposes of applying the maximum excess allowance or the maximum offset allowance under paragraph (b)(2) or (3) of this section, no reduction is made to the 0.75-percent factor merely because the plan provides disparity in qualified disability benefits (within the meaning of section 411(a)(9)) or preretirement death benefits and the relevant benefits are payable before an employee's social security retirement age.

(h) *Benefits attributable to employee contributions not taken into account.*—Benefits attributable to employee contributions to a defined benefit plan are not taken into account in determining whether the disparity provided under a defined benefit excess plan or an offset plan exceeds the maximum permitted disparity described in paragraph (b) of this section. See §1.401(a)(4)-6(b) for methods of determining the employer-provided benefit under a plan that includes employee contributions not allocated to separate accounts (i.e., a contributory DB plan), including §1.401(a)(4)-6(b)(2)(iii)(B) for adjustments to the base and excess benefit percentages of the gross benefit percentage under a section 401(l) plan. If, after adjustment, the employee's base benefit percentage or gross benefit percentage (whichever is applicable) is less than zero, such percentage is deemed to be zero for purposes of the maximum excess allowance or maximum offset allowance under paragraph (b)(2) or (3) of this section.

(i) *Multiple integration levels.*—[Reserved].

(j) *Additional rules.*—The Commissioner may, in revenue rulings, notices or other documents of general applicability, prescribe additional rules as may be necessary or appropriate to carry out the purposes of this section, including updated tables under paragraphs (d) and (e) of this section providing for reductions in the 0.75-percent factor in the maximum excess allowance and in the maximum offset allowance and rules in paragraph (h)of this section for determining the portion of an employee's benefit attributable to employee contributions. [Reg. §1.401(l)-3.]

☐ [*T.D. 8359, 9-12-91. Amended by T.D. 8486, 8-31-93.*]

[Reg. §1.401(l)-4]

§1.401(l)-4. Special rules for railroad plans.—(a) *In general.*—Section 401(*l*)(6) provides that, in the case of a plan maintained by a railroad employer that covers employees who are entitled to benefits under the Railroad Retirement Act of 1974, in determining whether such a plan satisfies section 401(*l*) rules similar to the rules under section 401(*l*) apply and such rules take into account the employer-derived portion of tier 2 and supplemental annuity benefits provided under the railroad retirement system. In general, for purposes of determining whether a defined contribution plan or a defined benefit plan maintained by a railroad employer and covering employees described in the preceding sentence, satisfies section 401(*l*), the employer-derived portion of an employee's tier 2 benefits and supplementary annuity benefits under the Railroad Retirement Act of 1974 are treated as though such benefits were provided by the railroad employer under a qualified plan. Paragraph (b) of this section contains rules for defined contribution plans. Paragraph (c) of this section contains rules for defined benefit excess plans. Paragraph (d) of this section contains rules for offset plans. Paragraph (e) of this section contains definitions and additional rules of application.

(b) *Defined contribution plans.*—(1) *In general.*—A defined contribution plan maintained by a railroad employer satisfies section 401(l) and §1.401(l)-2 for a plan year only if the plan satisfies paragraph (b)(2) or (b)(3) of this section for the plan year.

(2) *Single integration level method.*—(i) *In general.*—A plan satisfies this paragraph (b)(2) if—

(A) The plan specifies a single integration level for all employees that does not exceed the railroad retirement taxable wage base in effect as of the beginning of the plan year,

(B) The plan uses the same base contribution percentage and the same excess contribution percentage for all employees, and

(C) The excess contribution percentage does not exceed the sum of 11.4 percentage points and the base contribution percentage.

(ii) *Definitions.*—The following definitions govern for purposes of this paragraph (b)(2).

(A) "Base contribution percentage" means the rate at which employer contributions are allocated to the account of an employee under the plan with respect to the employee's plan year compensation at or below the railroad retirement taxable wage base (expressed as a percentage of such plan year compensation).

(B) "Excess contribution percentage" means the rate at which employer contributions are allocated to the account of an employee under the plan with respect to the employee's plan year compensation above the railroad retirement taxable wage base (expressed as a percentage of such plan year compensation).

(3) *Two integration level method.*—(i) *In general.*—A plan satisfies this paragraph (b)(3) if—

(A) The plan specifies two integration levels for all employees, equal to the railroad retirement taxable wage base in effect as of the beginning of the plan year and the taxable wage base in effect as of the beginning of the plan year, and

(B) The plan satisfies paragraphs (b)(3)(ii) and (iii) of this section.

(ii) *Total disparity requirement.*—A plan satisfies this paragraph (b)(3)(ii) if—

(A) The plan uses the same base contribution percentage and the same excess contribution percentage for all employees, and

(B) The excess contribution percentage does not exceed the sum of 11.4 percentage points and the base contribution percentage.

(iii) *Intermediate disparity requirement.*—A plan satisfies this paragraph (b)(3)(iii) if—

(A) The plan uses the same base contribution percentage and the same intermediate contribution percentage for all employees, and

(B) The intermediate contribution percentage does not exceed the sum of 5.7 percentage points and the base contribution percentage.

(iv) *Definitions.*—The following definitions govern for purposes of this paragraph (b)(3).

(A) "Base contribution percentage" means the rate at which employer contributions are allocated to the account of an employee under the plan with respect to the employee's plan year compensation at or below the railroad retirement taxable wage base (expressed as a percentage of such plan year compensation).

(B) "Intermediate contribution percentage" means the rate at which employer contributions are allocated to the account of an employee under the plan with respect to the employee's plan year compensation between the railroad retirement taxable wage base and the taxable wage base (expressed as a percentage of such plan year compensation).

(C) "Excess contribution percentage" means the rate at which employer contributions are allocated to the account of an employee under the plan with respect to the employee's plan year compensation above the taxable wage base (expressed as a percentage of such plan year compensation).

(c) *Defined benefit excess plans.*—(1) *In general.*—A defined benefit excess plan maintained by a railroad employer satisfies section 401(l) and §1.401(l)-3 for a plan year only if the plan satisfies paragraph (c)(2) or (c)(3) of this section for the plan year.

(2) *Single integration level method.*—(i) *In general.*—A plan satisfies this paragraph (c)(2) if—

(A) The plan specifies a single integration level for all employees that does not exceed railroad retirement covered compensation,

(B) The plan uses the same base benefit percentage and the same excess benefit percentage for all employees, and

(C) The excess benefit percentage does not exceed the lesser of—

(1) Two times the sum of 0.56 percent and the base benefit percentage, or

(2) 0.56 percent plus the base benefit percentage plus 0.75 percent.

(ii) *Definitions.*—The following definitions govern for purposes of this paragraph (c)(2).

(A) "Base benefit percentage" means the rate at which employer-provided benefits are determined under the plan with respect to an employee's average annual compensation at or below the employee's railroad retirement covered compensation (expressed as a percentage of such average annual compensation).

(B) "Excess benefit percentage" means the rate at which employer-provided benefits are determined under the plan with respect to an employee's average annual compensation above the employee's railroad retirement covered compensation (expressed as a percentage of such average annual compensation).

(3) *Two integration level method.*—(i) *In general.*—A plan satisfies this paragraph (c)(3) for a plan year if—

(A) The plan specifies two integration levels for all employees, equal to each employee's railroad retirement covered compensation and each employee's covered compensation, and

(B) The plan satisfies paragraphs (c)(3)(ii) and (iii) of this section.

(ii) *Employee with lower covered compensation.*—A plan satisfies this paragraph (c)(3)(ii) if, with respect to each employee whose lower integration level is the employee's covered compensation—

(A) The plan uses the same base benefit percentage and the same intermediate benefit percentage for all employees,

(B) The intermediate benefit percentage does not exceed the base benefit percentage by more than the lesser of 0.75 percent or the base benefit percentage,

(C) The plan uses the same intermediate benefit percentage and the same excess benefit percentage for all employees, and

(D) The excess benefit percentage does not exceed the intermediate benefit percentage by more than 0.56 percent.

(iii) *Employee with lower railroad retirement covered compensation.*—A plan satisfies this paragraph (c)(3)(iii) if, with respect to each employee whose lower integration level is the employee's railroad retirement covered compensation—

(A) The plan uses the same base benefit percentage and the same excess benefit percentage for all employees,

(B) The excess benefit percentage does not exceed the lesser of—

(1) Two times the sum of 0.56 percent and the base benefit percentage, or

(2) The sum of 0.56 percent plus the base benefit percentage plus 0.75 percent,

(C) The plan uses the same the base benefit percentage and the same intermediate benefit percentage for all employees, and

(D) The intermediate benefit percentage does not exceed the sum of 0.56 percent plus the base benefit percentage.

(iv) *Definitions.*—The following definitions govern for purposes of this paragraph (c)(3).

(A) "Base benefit percentage" means the rate at which employer-provided benefits are determined under the plan with respect to an employee's average annual compensation at or below the lower integration level specified in the plan (expressed as a percentage of such average annual compensation).

(B) "Intermediate benefit percentage" means the rate at which employer-provided benefits are determined under the plan with respect to an employee's average annual compensation between the lower and higher integration levels specified in the plan (expressed as a percentage of such average annual compensation).

(C) "Excess benefit percentage" means the rate at which employer-provided benefits are determined under the plan with respect to an employee's average annual compensation above the higher integration level specified in the plan (expressed as a percentage of such average annual compensation).

(d) *Offset plans.*—(1) *In general.*—An offset plan maintained by a railroad employer satisfies section 401(l) and §1.401(l)-3 for a plan year only if—

(i) The plan satisfies §1.401(l)-3 for the plan year without regard to the offset for the employer-derived portion of tier 2 and supplementary annuity benefits provided under the railroad retirement system, and

(ii) The offset for the employer-derived portion of tier 2 and supplementary annuity benefits provided under the railroad retirement system does not exceed the maximum tier 2 and supplementary annuity offset allowance.

(2) *Maximum tier 2 and supplementary annuity offset allowance.*—For purposes of paragraph (d)(1) of this section, the maximum tier 2 and supplementary annuity offset allowance for a plan year is equal to 0.56 percent of the employee's railroad retirement covered compensation for the plan year.

(e) *Additional rules.*—(1) *Definitions.*—The following definitions govern for purposes of this section.

(i) "Railroad retirement taxable wage base" means the applicable base, as determined under section 3231(e)(2)(B)(ii), for purposes of the tax under section 3221(b) (the tier 2 tax).

(ii) "Railroad retirement covered compensation" for an employee means 12 multiplied by the average of the 60 highest monthly railroad retirement taxable wage bases in effect for the employee's period of employment. The monthly railroad retirement taxable wage base is determined by dividing the railroad retirement taxable wage base for the calendar year in which the month occurs by 12. An employee's railroad retirement covered compensation for the plan year is determined as of the beginning of the plan year. A plan must provide that an employee's railroad retirement covered compensation is automatically adjusted for each plan year. See §1.401(l)-1(b) for rules relating to prohibited decreases in an employee's accrued benefit within the meaning of section 411(d)(6) or section 411(b)(1)(G).

(2) *Adjustments to 0.75-percent factor.*—The 0.75-percent factor in the maximum excess allowance and in the maximum offset allowance is subject to the reductions prescribed in §1.401(l)-3(d) and (e),

except that in the case of an employee with at least 30 years of service with a railroad employer, the following tables are substituted for Tables I through III contained in §1.401(l)-3(e)(3).

TABLE I
Social security retirement age 67

Age at which benefits commence	Annual factor in maximum excess allowance and maximum offset allowance (percent)
66	0.750
65	0.750
64	0.750
63	0.750
62	0.750
61	0.525
60	0.525
59	0.508
58	0.490
57	0.472
56	0.433
55	0.398

TABLE II
Social security retirement age 66

Age at which benefits commence	Annual factor in maximum excess allowance and maximum offset allowance (percent)
65	0.750
64	0.750
63	0.750
62	0.750
61	0.563
60	0.563
59	0.544
58	0.525
57	0.506
56	0.488
55	0.447

TABLE III
Social security retirement age 65

Age at which benefits commence	Annual factor in maximum excess allowance and maximum offset allowance (percent)
64	0.750
63	0.750
62	0.750
61	0.600
60	0.600
59	0.580
58	0.560
57	0.540
56	0.520
55	0.500

(3) *Adjustments to 0.56-percent factor.*—The 0.56-percent factor for defined benefit excess plans and offset plans under paragraphs (c) and (d) of this section respectively is subject to the reductions prescribed in §1.401(l)-3(d) and (e), except that, for purposes of applying this paragraph (e)(3)—

(i) "Railroad retirement covered compensation" is substituted for "covered compensation" in §1.401(l)-3(d),

(ii) The reductions under §1.401(l)-3(d) are made by multiplying the 0.56-percent factor by the ratio of the applicable factor from the table in §1.401(l)-(3)(d)(9)(iv)(A) to 0.75, and

(iii) The following tables are substituted for Tables I through III set forth in §1.401(l)-3(e)(3).

(A) Tables Applicable to 0.56% Factor for Employees Covered by Tier 2 of Railroad Retirement With 30 or More Years of Railroad Service

TABLE I
Social security retirement age 67

Age at which benefits commence	Annual factor in maximum excess allowance and maximum offset allowance (percent)
66	0.560
65	0.560
64	0.560
63	0.560
62	0.560
61	0.560
60	0.560
59	0.541
58	0.523
57	0.504
56	0.462
55	0.425

TABLE II
Social security retirement age 66

Age at which benefits commence	Annual factor in maximum excess allowance and maximum offset allowance (percent)
65	0.560
64	0.560
63	0.560
62	0.560
61	0.560
60	0.560
59	0.541
58	0.523
57	0.504
56	0.485
55	0.445

TABLE III
Social security retirement age 65

Age at which benefits commence	Annual factor in maximum excess allowance and maximum offset allowance (percent)
64	0.560
63	0.560
62	0.560
61	0.560
60	0.560
59	0.541
58	0.523
57	0.504
56	0.485
55	0.467

(B) Tables Applicable to 0.56% Factor for Employees Covered by Tier 2 of Railroad Retirement With Less than 30 Years of Railroad Service
TABLE I
Social security retirement age 67

Age at which benefits commence	Annual factor in maximum excess allowance and maximum offset allowance (percent)
66	0.523
65	0.485
64	0.448
63	0.420
62	0.392
61	0.379
60	0.366
59	0.353
58	0.340
57	0.327
56	0.300
55	0.275

TABLE II
Social security retirement age 66

Age at which benefits commence	Annual factor in maximum excess allowance and maximum offset allowance (percent)
65	0.523
64	0.485
63	0.448
62	0.420
61	0.392
60	0.378
59	0.364
58	0.350
57	0.336
56	0.322
55	0.295

TABLE III
Social security retirement age 65

Age at which benefits commence	Annual factor in maximum excess allowance and maximum offset allowance (percent)
64	0.523
63	0.485
62	0.448
61	0.418
60	0.388
59	0.373
58	0.358
57	0.343
56	0.329
55	0.314

(4) *Overall permitted disparity.*—The overall permitted disparity rules of §1.401(l)-5 apply to employees who benefit under a plan maintained by a railroad employer. [Reg. §1.401(l)-4.]

☐ [*T.D.* 8359, 9-12-91.]

[Reg. §1.401(l)-5]

§1.401(l)-5. Overall permitted disparity limits.— (a) *Introduction.*—(1) *In general.*—The maximum excess allowance and maximum offset allowance limit the disparity that can be provided under a plan for a plan year. The overall permitted disparity rules apply to limit the disparity provided for a plan year if an employee benefits under more than one plan maintained by the employer (the "annual overall permitted disparity limit") and to limit the disparity provided for an employee's total years of service, either in a single plan or in more than one plan of the employer (the "cumulative overall permitted disparity limit"). The overall permitted disparity rules take into account the disparity provided under a section 401(l) plan and the permitted disparity imputed under a plan that satisfies section 401(a)(4) by relying on §1.401(a)(4)-7. A plan that is not a section 401(l) plan is generally deemed to impute permitted disparity under §1.401(a)(4)-7 unless established otherwise. Paragraph (b) of this section provides rules on the annual overall permitted disparity limit. Paragraph (c) of this section provides rules on the cumulative overall permitted disparity limit.

(2) *Plan requirements.*—In order to satisfy section 401(l), a plan must provide that the overall permitted disparity limits may not be exceeded and must specify how employer-provided contributions or benefits under the plan are adjusted, if necessary, to satisfy the overall permitted disparity limits. Any adjustments made to satisfy the overall permitted disparity limits must be made in a uniform manner for all employees.

(3) *Plans taken into account.*—For purposes of this section, all plans of the employer are taken into account. In addition, all plans of any other employer are taken into account for all periods of service with the other employer for which the employee receives credit for purposes of benefit accrual under any plan of the current employer.

(b) *Annual overall permitted disparity limit.*—(1) *In general.*—If, in the plan year, an employee benefits under more than one plan, the annual overall permitted disparity limit is satisfied only if the employee's total annual disparity fraction, as defined in paragraph (b)(2) of this section, does not exceed one. Paragraphs (b)(3) through (b)(8) of this section explain the determination of an employee's annual disparity fractions. Paragraph (b)(9) of this section provides examples.

(2) *Total annual disparity fraction.*—An employee's total annual disparity fraction is the sum of the employee's annual disparity fractions, as defined in paragraphs (b)(3) through (b)(7) of this section. An employee's total annual disparity fraction is determined as of the end of the current plan year, based on the employee's annual disparity fractions under all plans with plan years ending in the current plan year.

(3) *Annual defined contribution plan disparity fraction.*—For a plan year, the annual defined contribution plan disparity fraction for an employee benefiting under a defined contribution plan that is a section 401(l) plan is a fraction—

(i) The numerator of which is the disparity provided under the plan for the plan year, and

(ii) The denominator of which is the maximum excess allowance under §1.401(l)-2(b)(2) for the plan year.

(4) *Annual defined benefit excess plan disparity fraction.*—For a plan year, the annual defined benefit excess plan disparity fraction for an employee benefiting under a defined benefit excess plan that is a section 401(l) plan is a fraction—

(i) The numerator of which is the disparity provided under the plan for the plan year, and

(ii) The denominator of which is the maximum excess allowance under §1.401(l)-3(b)(2) for the plan year.

(5) *Annual offset plan disparity fraction.*—(i) *In general.*—For a plan year, the annual offset plan disparity fraction for an employee benefiting under an offset plan that is a section 401(l) plan is a fraction—

(A) The numerator of which is the disparity provided under the plan for the plan year, and

(B) The denominator of which is the maximum offset allowance under §1.401(l)-3(b)(3) for the plan year.

(ii) *PIA offset plans.*—In the case of an offset plan that applies an offset of a specified percentage of the employee's PIA, as permitted under §1.401(l)-3(c)(2)(ix), the numerator of the annual offset

plan disparity fraction is the offset percentage used in the section 401(l) overlay under the plan.

(6) *Annual imputed disparity fraction.*—For a plan year, the annual imputed disparity fraction for an employee benefiting under a plan that imputes permitted disparity with respect to the employee under §1.401(a)(4)-7 is one.

(7) *Annual nondisparate fraction.*—For a plan year, the annual nondisparate fraction for an employee benefiting under a plan that neither is a section 401(l) plan nor imputes permitted disparity under §1.401(a)(4)-7 is zero.

(8) *Determination of fraction.*—(i) *General rule.*—A separate annual disparity fraction is generally determined for each plan under which the employee benefits. Thus, for example, if two plans are aggregated and treated as a single plan for purposes of section 401(a)(4), a single annual disparity fraction applies to the aggregated plan.

(ii) *Multiple formulas.*—If a plan provides an allocation or benefit equal to the sum of two or more formulas, each formula is considered a separate plan for purposes of this section. If a plan provides an allocation or benefit equal to the greater of two or more formulas, an annual disparity fraction is calculated for the employee under each formula and the largest of the fractions is the employee's annual disparity fraction under the plan.

(iii) *Offset arrangements.*—(A) *In general.*—If an employee benefits under two plans taken in account under paragraph (a)(3) of this section as described in paragraph (b)(8)(iii)(B) or (C) of this section, the employee's annual disparity fraction under both plans is the larger of the annual disparity fractions calculated separately under each plan.

(B) *Defined benefit plans.*—The employee's employer-provided accrued benefit under a defined benefit plan is offset by the employee's total employer-provided accrued benefit under another defined benefit plan or by the actuarial equivalent (as defined in §1.401(a)(4)-12) of the employee's total account balance under a defined contribution plan that is attributable to employer contributions.

(C) *Defined contribution plans.*—The amount allocated to the employee's account under a defined contribution plan is offset by the total amount allocated to the employee's account under another defined contribution plan.

(iv) *Applicable percentages.*—The disparity provided under a plan is determined on the base and excess percentages under an excess plan and the offset percentage under an offset plan, regardless of whether the employee's plan year or average annual compensation exceeds the integration or offset level under the plan.

(v) *Fractional accrual plans.*—If a section 401(l) plan determines each employee's accrued benefit under the fractional accrual method of section 411(b)(1)(C), the numerator of an employee's annual disparity fraction is based on the disparity provided in the benefit accrued for the employee for the plan year.

(9) *Examples.*—The following examples illustrate this paragraph (b). Except as otherwise provided, each plan is a section 401(l) plan.

Example 1. (a) Employee A benefits for the plan year under a defined contribution excess plan, Plan X, and a defined benefit excess plan, Plan Y, of the employer. Plan X and Y have the same plan year. Employee A benefits under no other plan of the employer for the plan year of any other plan ending in the plan year of Plans X and Y. Plan X provides a base contribution percentage of 5 percent and an excess contribution percentage of 7 percent, thus providing Employee A with disparity of 2 percent for the plan year. The maximum excess allowance for the plan year under Plan X is 5 percent. Plan Y provides a base benefit percentage of 1 percent and an excess benefit percentage of 1.35 percent, thus providing Employee A with disparity of 0.35 percent for the plan year. The maximum excess allowance for the plan year under Plan Y is 0.75 percent.

(b) Employee A's annual defined contribution plan disparity fraction under Plan X for the plan year is 0.4 (2 percent divided by 5 percent). Employee A's annual defined benefit excess plan disparity fraction under Plan Y for the plan year is 0.47 (0.35 percent divided by 0.75 percent). Employee A's total annual disparity fraction is the sum of 0.4 and 0.47 or 0.87. Because Employee A's total annual disparity fraction does not exceed one, the plans satisfy the annual overall permitted disparity limit with respect to Employee A for the plan year.

Example 2. (a) The facts are the same as in *Example 1*, except that Plan Y is a defined contribution plan, rather than a defined benefit plan. Plan X and Plan Y cover the same employees and are identical in their terms except for the base and excess contribution percentages provided under the plans. Plan Y provides a base contribution percentage of 3 percent and an excess contribution percentage of 6 percent, thus providing Employee A with disparity of 3 percent for the plan year. The maximum excess allowance for the plan year under Plan Y is 3 percent.

(b) Employee A's annual defined contribution plan disparity fraction under Plan X for the plan year is 0.4 (2 percent divided by 5 percent). Employee A's annual defined contribution plan disparity fraction under Plan Y for the plan year is 1 (3 percent divided by 3 percent). Because Employee A's total annual disparity fraction (the sum of 0.4 and 1 or 1.4) exceeds one, the plans do not satisfy the annual overall permitted disparity requirements with respect to Employee A for the plan year.

(c) Plan X and Plan Y are aggregated for purposes of section 401(a)(4) and form a single section 401(l) plan. Under the plan, the base contribution percentage is 8 percent (5 percent plus 3 percent), and the excess contribution percentage is 13 percent (7 percent plus 6 percent). A single annual defined contribution plan disparity fraction is determined for Employee A for the plan year, the numerator of which is the disparity of 5 percent provided under the plan (13 percent minus 8 percent), and the denominator of which is 5.7 percent, the maximum excess allowance that applies to the plan. Because Employee A's only annual disparity fraction of 0.88 (5 percent divided by 5.7 percent) does not exceed one, Employee A's total annual disparity fraction also does not exceed one. The plan thus satisfies the annual overall permitted disparity limit with respect to Employee A for the plan year.

Example 3. Assume the same facts as in *Example 2,* except that Plan X and Plan Y use different integration levels. Therefore, when Plan X and Plan Y are aggregated to form a single plan for purposes of section 401(a)(4), the single plan does not satisfy section 401(l). In applying the general test of §1.401(a)(4)-2(c), the plan imputes disparity under §1.401(a)(4)-7. Employee A's only annual disparity fraction is the annual imputed disparity fraction of one. Employee A's total annual disparity fraction is also one, and the plan satisfies the annual overall permitted disparity limit with respect to Employee A for the plan year.

Example 4. (a) Employee B participates in two plans: Plan M, which is a section 401(l) plan, and Plan N, which is subject to the general test under §1.401(a)(4)-3(c). Plan M provides that the disparity provided an employee for the plan year will be reduced to the extent necessary to satisfy the annual overall permitted disparity limits. The employer wishes to impute permitted disparity under §1.401(a)(4)-7 in order for Plan N to satisfy section 401(a)(4). Employee B's imputed disparity fraction under Plan N is therefore one, and Plan M provides no disparity for Employee B for the plan year. As a result, Plan M provides disparity that is neither uniform nor deemed uniform under §1.401(l)-3(c); Plan M therefore does not satisfy section 401(l).

(b) Assume instead that Plan M provides that the annual overall permitted disparity limits must be satisfied without reducing the disparity provided for an employee under Plan M, thus requiring a reduction in the employee's annual disparity fraction under another plan. In that case, the disparity provided under Plan M would be uniform for the plan year and Plan M would continue to satisfy section 401(l). However, imputation of permitted disparity with respect to Employee B would not be allowed under Plan N.

(c) *Cumulative permitted disparity limit.*—(1) *In general.*—(i) *Employees who benefit under defined benefit plans.*—In the case of an employee who has benefited under one or more defined benefit plans for a plan year described in paragraph (c)(1)(v) of this section, the cumulative permitted disparity limit is satisfied if the employee's cumulative disparity fraction, as defined in paragraph (c)(2) of this section, does not exceed 35.

(ii) *Employees who do not benefit under defined benefit plans.*—In the case of an employee who has not benefited under a defined benefit plan for any plan year described in paragraph (c)(1)(v) of this section, the cumulative permitted disparity limit is satisfied.

(iii) *Certain plan years disregarded.*—For purposes of this paragraph (c), an employee is not treated as benefiting under a defined benefit plan for a plan year described in paragraph (c)(1)(v) of this section if the employer can establish that for that plan year the defined benefit plan was not a section 401(l) plan and did not impute permitted disparity under §1.401(a)(4)-7.

(iv) *Determination of type of plan.*—For purposes of this paragraph (c), a target benefit plan that relies on the special rule of §1.401(a)(4)-8(b)(3) to satisfy section 401(a)(4) and a DB/DC plan within the meaning of §1.401(a)(4)-9(a) are treated as defined benefit plans. Similarly, a cash balance plan that relies on the special rule of §1.401(a)(4)-8(c)(3) to satisfy section 401(a)(4) is treated as a defined contribution plan.

(v) *Applicable plan years.*—In applying paragraphs (c)(1)(i), (ii), and (iii) of this section, for purposes of determining whether an employee benefits under a defined benefit plan, the applicable plan years are all plan years that begin on or after the regulatory effective date, as set forth in §1.401(l)-6(b), or, in the case of governmental plans, as set forth in §1.401(a)(4)-13(b).

(vi) *Transition rule for defined contribution plans.*—A defined contribution plan is deemed to satisfy the cumulative permitted disparity limit for the first plan year to which these regulations apply, as set forth in §1.401(l)-6(b), or, in the case of governmental plans, as set forth in §1.401(a)(4)-13(b).

(2) *Cumulative disparity fraction.*—An employee's cumulative disparity fraction is the sum of the employee's total annual disparity fractions, as defined in paragraph (b)(2) of this section, attributable to the employee's total years of service under all plans.

(3) *Determination of total annual disparity fractions for prior years.*—For each of the employee's years of service credited as of the end of the last plan year beginning before January 1, 1989, not to exceed 35, under all plans as of that time that are taken into account under paragraph (a)(3) of this section (whether or not terminated), the employee's total annual disparity fraction is one. Therefore, if, before the first plan year beginning on or after January 1, 1989, an employee never participated in or benefited under any plan taken into account under paragraph (a)(3) of this section, the employee's total annual disparity fractions are determined without regard to this paragraph (c)(3). An employer may apply the rule in this paragraph (c)(3) with respect to all employees, using a year (including the current year) that is chosen by the employer and is later than 1989. Thus, for example, in lieu of calculating annual disparity fractions for all plan years, the employer may assume that the full disparity limit has been used in each prior plan year for which an employee has been credited with a year of service.

(4) *Special rules for greater of formulas and offset arrangements.*—(i) *Greater of formulas.*—(A) *In general.*—A defined benefit plan that is a section 401(l) plan and that provides a benefit equal to the greater of the benefits determined under two or more formulas is deemed to satisfy the cumulative permitted disparity limit with respect to an employee if each of the requirements in paragraphs (c)(4)(i)(B) and (C) of this section is satisfied. For this purpose, a plan that uses a fresh-start formula that determines the accrued benefit as the greater of two amounts under §1.401(a)(4)-13(c)(4)(ii) or (iii) provides a benefit equal to the greater of the benefits determined under two or more formulas.

(B) *Separate satisfaction by formulas.*—Each formula under the plan would satisfy the cumulative permitted disparity limit if it were the only formula under the plan. In the case of a current formula that applies to the employee's total years of service (as, for example, under §1.401(a)(4)-13(c)(4)(ii)(B) or (iii)(B)), for purposes of determining whether that formula would satisfy the cumulative permitted disparity limit if it were the only formula under the plan, the special rule for prior years under paragraph (c)(3) of this section may be disregarded.

(C) *Single plan.*—The employee has never benefited under another plan taken into account under paragraph (a)(3) of this section that is a section 401(l) plan or that satisfies section 401(a)(4) by relying on §1.401(a)(4)-7. For this purpose, if the benefit under the plan is offset in an offset arrangement described in paragraph (b)(8)(iii)(B) of this section, the other plan is disregarded. In addition, a plan does not fail the requirements of this paragraph (c)(4)(i)(C) merely because the employee benefits under another defined benefit plan, provided that—

(1) With respect to each benefit formula under the plan, no years of service taken into account under that benefit formula are taken into account under a benefit formula of the other plan; and

(2) Paragraph (c)(4)(i)(B) of this section would be satisfied if the plans were treated as a single plan that provided a benefit equal to the greater of the benefits provided under two or more formulas. For this purpose, a formula consists of the sum of a formula for the years of service taken into account under one plan and a formula for the years of service taken into account under the other plan. Thus, each possible combination of the formulas under the plans must satisfy paragraph (c)(4)(i)(B) of this section.

(ii) *Offset arrangements.*—(A) *In general.*—If a defined benefit plan is a section 401(l) plan and the benefit under the plan (the gross benefit plan) is offset by the benefit under another plan (the offsetting plan) in an offset arrangement described in paragraph (b)(8)(iii)(B) of this section, the gross benefit plan is deemed to satisfy the cumulative permitted disparity limit with respect to an employee if each of the requirements in paragraphs (c)(4)(ii)(B) and (C) of this section is satisfied.

(B) *Separate satisfaction by plans.*—This requirement is satisfied if the gross benefit plan would satisfy the cumulative disparity limit if no offset applied, and the offsetting plan satisfies the cumulative permitted disparity limit, not taking into account the gross benefit plan.

(C) *No other plan.*—Except for the plans in the offset arrangement, the employee has never benefited under another plan taken into account under paragraph (a)(3) of this section that is a section 401(l) plan or that satisfies section 401(a)(4) by relying on §1.401(a)(4)-7. An offset arrangement does not fail the requirements of this paragraph (c)(4)(ii)(C) merely because the employee benefits under another defined benefit plan, provided no years of service taken into account under a benefit formula of any plan in the offset arrangement are also taken into account under a benefit formula of the other plan.

(5) *Examples.*—The following examples illustrate this paragraph (c). In each example the plan is noncontributory and, unless provided otherwise, is the only plan ever maintained by the employer. Each plan uses a normal retirement age of 65 and contains no provision that would require a reduction in the 0.75-percent factor under §1.401(l)-3(b)(2) or (3). Each example discusses the benefit formula applicable to an employee who has a social security retirement age of 65.

Example 1. Plan M is a defined benefit excess plan that provides a normal retirement benefit of 1 percent of average annual compensation up to covered compensation, plus 1.75 percent of average annual compensation above covered compensation, for each year of service without limit. The disparity provided under the plan for the plan year is 0.75 percent, the excess benefit percentage of 1.75 percent minus the base benefit percentage of 1 percent. The maximum excess allowance for the plan year is 0.75 percent. Thus, each employee's annual defined benefit excess plan disparity fraction under the plan for each plan year is one. Because the plan contains no limit on the years of service taken into account under the plan, the sum of the total annual disparity fractions for a potential employee with more than 35 years of service will exceed 35. In addition, the plan does not provide that the overall permitted disparity limits may not be exceeded as required by paragraph (a)(2) of this section. The plan therefore does not satisfy the cumulative permitted disparity limit of this paragraph (c).

Example 2. Plan N is an offset plan that provides a normal retirement benefit of 2 percent of average annual compensation, minus 0.75 percent of final average compensation up to the lesser of covered compensation and average annual compensation, for each year of service up to 35. The disparity provided under the plan for the plan year is 0.75 percent, the offset percentage. The maximum offset allowance for the plan year is 0.75 percent. Thus, each employee's annual offset plan disparity fraction under the plan for each plan year is one. Because the plan limits the years of service taken into account under the plan to 35, the sum of the total annual disparity fractions for an employee cannot exceed 35. The plan therefore satisfies the cumulative permitted disparity limit of this paragraph (c).

Example 3. Plan O is a defined benefit excess plan that provides a normal retirement benefit of 0.75 percent of average annual compensation up to covered compensation, plus 1.25 percent of average annual compensation above covered compensation, for each year of service up to 45. The disparity provided under the plan for the plan year is 0.5 percent, the excess benefit percentage of 1.25 percent minus the base benefit percentage of 0.75 percent. The maximum excess allowance for the plan year is 0.75 percent. Thus, each employee's annual defined benefit excess plan disparity fraction under the plan for each plan year is 0.67 (0.5 percent divided by 0.75 percent). Because the plan limits the years of service taken into account under the plan to 45, the sum of the total annual disparity fractions for an employee cannot exceed 30 (0.67 x 45). The plan therefore satisfies the cumulative permitted disparity limit of this paragraph (c).

Example 4. (a) Plan P is a defined contribution excess plan. Plan P provides a base contribution percentage of 6 percent and an excess contribution percentage of 11.7 percent, thus providing disparity of 5.7 percent for the plan year. Because the maximum excess allowance for each plan year under Plan P is 5.7 percent, each employee's annual defined contribution plan disparity fraction under Plan P for each plan year is one. Plan Q is a defined benefit excess plan maintained by the same employer. Plan Q provides a base benefit percentage of 1 percent and an excess benefit percentage of 1.75 percent for each year of service up to 35, thus providing disparity of 0.75 percent for the plan year. Because the maximum excess allowance for each plan year under Plan Q is 0.75 percent, each employee's annual defined benefit excess plan disparity fraction under Plan Q for each plan year is one.

(b) Employee A benefits under Plan P for the 1980 through the 1994 plan years. The sum of Employee A's total annual disparity fractions under Plan P is 15. (Under paragraph (c)(3)(i) of this section, Employee A's annual disparity fraction for each year of service as of the end of the 1988 plan year is one.) As of the 1995 plan year, Employee A no longer benefits under Plan P and begins to benefit under Plan Q for the first time. In order to satisfy the cumulative permitted disparity limit of this paragraph (c), Plan Q must provide that no disparity will be provided if the sum of an employee's total annual disparity fractions reaches 35, taking into account the employee's annual defined contribution plan disparity fractions under Plan P as well as the employee's annual defined benefit excess plan disparity fractions under Plan Q. Thus, after Employee A has benefited under Plan Q for 20 years, Plan Q may not provide any disparity in additional benefits accrued for Employee A.

Example 5. (a) Plan O is a noncontributory defined benefit excess plan. Plan O provides an employee whose social security retirement age is 65 with the greater of the benefits determined under two formulas. The first formula provides a benefit of 1 percent of average annual compensation up to covered compensation, plus 1.75 percent of average annual compensation above covered compensation, for each year of service up to 35. The second formula provides a benefit of 1 percent of average annual compensation up to covered compensation, plus 1.6 percent of average annual compensation above covered compensation, for each year of service up to 40.

(b) Under paragraph (b)(4) of this section, an employee's annual defined benefit excess plan fraction for each of the 35 years under the first formula is 0.75/0.75 or one, and an employee's annual defined benefit excess plan fraction for each of the 40 years under the second formula is 0.6/0.75 or 0.8. Under paragraph (b)(8)(ii) of this section, an employee's annual defined benefit excess plan fraction (and total annual disparity fraction because the employee benefits only under Plan O) for the plan year is the larger fraction under the two formulas or one. Therefore, after 35 years, the employee has a cumulative disparity fraction of 35. The disparity provided under the second formula for years of service after 35 thus exceeds the cumulative permitted disparity limit unless the plan qualifies for the special rule in paragraph (c)(4)(i) of this section.

(c) Assume the condition in paragraph (c)(4)(i)(C) of this section is satisfied because no employee has benefited under another plan taken into account under paragraph (a)(3) of this section. In addition, the largest cumulative disparity fraction possible under the first formula is 35 times one or 35, and the largest cumulative disparity fraction possible under the second formula is 40 times 0.8 or 32. Thus, the requirement of paragraph (c)(4)(i)(B) of this section is also satisfied because each formula would satisfy the cumulative permitted disparity limit if it were the only formula under the plan. Under paragraph (c)(4)(i) of this section, the plan is deemed to satisfy the cumulative permitted disparity limit with respect to an employee whose social security retirement age is 65.

(d) *Additional rules.*—The Commissioner may prescribe additional rules under this section as the Commissioner considers appropriate. Additional rules may include (without being limited to) rules for computing the fractions described in this section with respect to terminated plans, rules for applying the overall permitted disparity limits to employees who benefit under plans maintained by railroad employers, and rules for determining which plans do not satisfy section 401(l) if the overall permitted disparity limits are exceeded. [Reg. §1.401(l)-5.]

☐ [*T.D. 8359, 9-12-91. Amended by T.D. 8486, 8-31-93.*]

[Reg. §1.401(l)-6]

§1.401(l)-6. Effective dates and transitional rules.—(a) *Statutory effective date.*—(1) *In general.*—Except as otherwise provided in paragraph (a)(2) of this section, section 401(a)(5)(C) is effective for plan years beginning on or after January 1, 1989, and section 401(l) is effective with respect to plan years, and benefits attributable to plan years, beginning on or after January 1, 1989. The preceding sentence is applicable to a plan without regard to whether the plan was in existence as of a particular date.

(2) *Collectively bargained plans.*—(i) In the case of a plan maintained pursuant to 1 or more collective bargaining agreements between employee representatives and 1 or more employers ratified before March 1, 1986, sections 401(a)(5) and 401(l) are applicable for plan years beginning on or after the later of—

(A) January 1, 1989; or

(B) The date on which the last of such collective bargaining agreements terminates (determined without regard to any extension of any such agreement occurring on or after March 1, 1986). However, notwithstanding the preceding sentence, sections 401(a)(5) and 401(l) apply to plans described in this paragraph (a)(2) no later than the first plan year beginning after January 1, 1991.

(ii) For purposes of paragraph (a)(2)(i)(B) of this section, a change made after October 22, 1986, in the terms or conditions of a collectively bargained plan, pursuant to a collective bargaining agreement ratified before March 1, 1986, is not treated as a change in the terms and conditions of the plan.

(iii) In the case of a collectively bargained plan described in paragraph (a)(2)(i) of this section, if the date in paragraph (a)(2)(i)(B) of this section precedes November 15, 1988, then the date in this paragraph (a)(2) is replaced with the date on which the last of any collective bargaining agreements in effect on November 15, 1988, terminates, provided that the plan complies during this period with a reasonable good faith interpretation of section 401(l).

(iv) Whether a plan is maintained pursuant to a collective bargaining agreement is determined under the principles applied under section 1017(c) of the Employee Retirement Income Security Act of 1974. See H.R. Rep. No. 1280, 93d Cong., 2d Sess. 266 (1974). In addition, a plan is not treated as maintained under a collective bargaining agreement unless the employee representatives satisfy section 7701(a)(46) of the Internal Revenue Code after March 31, 1984. See §301.7701-17T of this chapter for other requirements for a plan to be considered to be collectively bargained.

(b) *Regulatory effective date.*—(1) *In general.*—Except as otherwise provided in paragraph (b)(2) of this section, §§1.401(l)-1 through 1.401(l)-6 apply to plan years beginning on or after January 1, 1994.

(2) *Plans of tax-exempt organizations.*—In the case of plans maintained by an organization exempt from income taxation under section 501(a), including plans subject to section 403(b)(12)(A)(i) (nonelective plans), §§1.401(l)-1 through 1.401(l)-6 apply to plan years beginning on or after January 1, 1996.

(3) *Defined contribution plans.*—A defined contribution plan satisfies section 401(l) with respect to a plan year beginning on or after the effective date of these regulations, as set forth in paragraphs (b)(1) and (b)(2) of this section, if it satisfies the applicable requirements of §§1.401(l)-1 through 1.401(l)-5 for the plan year.

(4) *Defined benefit plans.*—A defined benefit excess plan or offset plan satisfies section 401(l) with respect to all plan years, and benefits attributable to all plan years, beginning on or after the effective date of these regulations, as set forth in paragraphs (b)(1) and (b)(2) of this section, by satisfying the applicable requirements of §§1.401(l)-1 through 1.401(l)-5 and the requirements of §1.401(a)(4)-13(c) (and §1.401(a)(4)-13(d), if applicable), using a fresh-start date that is on or after December 31, 1988, and before the effective date of these regulations. A defined benefit excess plan or offset plan that does not satisfy section 401(l) with respect to all plan years beginning on or after the effective date of these regulations may, under the rules of §1.401(a)(4)-13(c) (and §1.401(a)(4)-13(d), if applicable), satisfy section 401(l) for plan years beginning after a fresh-start date by satisfying the applicable requirements of §§1.401(l)-1 through 1.401(l)-5 after the fresh-start date.

(c) *Compliance during transition period.*—For plan years beginning on or after January 1, 1989, and before the effective date of these regulations, as set forth in paragraph (b) of this section, a plan must be operated in accordance with a reasonable, good faith interpretation of section 401(l). Whether a plan is operated in accordance with a reasonable, good faith interpretation of section 401(l) will generally be determined based on all of the relevant facts and circumstances, including the extent to which an employer has resolved unclear issues in its favor. A plan will be deemed to be operated in accordance with a reasonable, good faith interpretation of section 401(*l*) if it is operated in accordance with the terms of §§1.401(l)-1 through 1.401(l)-5. [Reg. §1.401(l)-6.]

☐ [*T.D. 8359, 9-12-91 Amended by T.D. 8486, 8-31-93.*]

[Reg. §1.401(m)-0]

§1.401(m)-0. Table of contents.—This section contains first a list of section headings and then a list of the paragraphs in each section in §§1.401(m)-1 through 1.401(m)-5.

(A) General rule.
(B) Definition of representative contribution rate.
(C) Definition of applicable contribution rate.
(D) Special rule for prevailing wage contributions.
(vi) Contribution only used once.
(7) Examples.
(b) Correction of excess aggregate contributions.
(1) Permissible correction methods.
(i) In general.
(A) Additional contributions.
(B) Excess aggregate contributions distributed or forfeited.
(ii) Combination of correction methods.
(iii) Exclusive means of correction.
(2) Correction through distribution.
(i) General rule.
(ii) Calculation of total amount to be distributed.
(A) Calculate the dollar amount of excess aggregate contributions for each HCE.
(B) Determination of the total amount of excess aggregate contributions.
(C) Satisfaction of ACP.
(iii) Apportionment of total amount of excess aggregate contributions among the HCEs.
(A) Calculate the dollar amount of excess aggregate contributions for each HCE.
(B) Limit on amount apportioned to any HCE.
(C) Apportionment to additional HCEs.
(iv) Income allocable to excess aggregate contributions.
(A) General rule.
(B) Method of allocating income.
(C) Alternative method of allocating income for the plan year.
(D) Plan years before 2008.
(E) Allocable income for recharacterized elective contributions.
(v) Distribution and forfeiture.
(vi) Tax treatment of corrective distributions.
(A) Corrective distributions for plan years beginning on or after January 1, 2008.
(B) Corrective distributions for plan years beginning before January 1, 2008.
(C) Corrective distributions attributable to designated Roth contributions.
(3) Other rules.
(i) No employee or spousal consent required.
(ii) Treatment of corrective distributions and forfeited contributions as employer contributions.
(iii) No reduction of required minimum distribution.
(iv) Partial correction.
(v) Matching contributions on excess contributions, excess deferrals and excess aggregate contributions.
(A) Corrective distributions not permitted.
(B) Coordination with section 401(a)(4).
(vi) No requirement for recalculation.
(4) Failure to timely correct.
(i) Failure to correct within 2^1/$_2$ months after end of plan year.
(ii) Failure to correct within 12 months after end of plan year.
(iii) Special rule for eligible automatic contribution arrangements.
(5) Examples.
(c) Additional rules for prior year testing method.
(1) Rules for change in testing method.
(2) Calculation of ACP under the prior year testing method for the first plan year.
(i) Plans that are not successor plans.
(ii) First plan year defined.
(iii) Plans that are successor plans.
(3) Plans using different testing methods for the ACP and ADP test.
(4) Rules for plan coverage change.
(i) In general.
(ii) Optional rule for minor plan coverage changes.
(iii) Definitions.
(A) Plan coverage change.
(B) Prior year subgroup.
(C) Weighted average of the ACPs for the prior year subgroups.
(iv) Examples.
§ 1.401(m)-3 Safe harbor requirements.
(a) ACP test safe harbor.

(1) Section 401(m)(11) safe harbor.
(2) Section 401(m)(12) safe harbor.
(3) Requirements applicable to safe harbor contributions.
(b) Safe harbor nonelective contribution requirement.
(c) Safe harbor matching contribution requirement.
(d) Limitation on contributions.
(1) General rule.
(2) Matching rate must not increase.
(3) Limit on matching contributions.
(4) Limitation on rate of match.
(5) HCEs participating in multiple plans.
(6) Permissible restrictions on elective deferrals by NHCEs.
(i) General rule.
(ii) Restrictions on election periods.
(iii) Restrictions on amount of contributions.
(iv) Restrictions on types of compensation that may be deferred.
(v) Restrictions due to limitations under the Internal Revenue Code.
(e) Notice requirement.
(f) Plan year requirement.
(1) General rule.
(2) Initial plan year.
(3) Change of plan year.
(4) Final plan year.
(g) Plan amendments adopting nonelective safe harbor contributions.
(h) Permissible reduction or suspension of safe harbor contributions.
(1) General rule.
(i) Matching contributions.
(ii) Nonelective contributions.
(2) Supplemental notice.
(i) Reserved.
(j) Other rules.
(1) Contributions taken into account.
(2) Use of safe harbor nonelective contributions to satisfy other nondiscrimination tests.
(3) Early participation rules.
(4) Satisfying safe harbor contribution requirement under another defined contribution plan.
(5) Contributions used only once.
(6) Plan must satisfy ACP with respect to employee contributions.
§ 1.401(m)-4 Special rules for mergers, acquisitions and similar events. [Reserved].
§ 1.401(m)-5 Definitions.
[Reg. § 1.401(m)-0.]

☐ [T.D. 8357, 8-8-91. Amended by T.D. 8376, 12-2-91; T.D. 8581, 12-22-94; T.D. 9169, 12-28-2004; T.D. 9237, 12-30-2005; T.D. 9447, 2-23-2009 and T.D. 9641, 11-14-2013.]

[Reg. § 1.401(m)-1]

§ 1.401(m)-1. Employee contributions and matching contributions.—(a) General nondiscrimination rules.—(1) Nondiscriminatory amount of contributions.—(i) Exclusive means of amounts testing.—A defined contribution plan does not satisfy section 401(a) for a plan year unless the amount of employee contributions and matching contributions to the plan for the plan year satisfies section 401(a)(4). The amount of employee contributions and matching contributions under a plan satisfies the requirements of section 401(a)(4) with respect to amounts if and only if the amount of employee contributions and matching contributions satisfies the nondiscrimination test of section 401(m) under paragraph (b) of this section and the plan satisfies the additional requirements of paragraph (c) of this section. See § 1.401(a)(4)-1(b)(2)(ii)(B).

(ii) Testing benefits, rights and features.—A plan that provides for employee contributions or matching contributions must satisfy the requirements of section 401(a)(4) relating to benefits, rights and features in addition to the requirement regarding amounts described in paragraph (a)(1)(i) of this section. For example, the right to make each level of employee contributions and the right to each level of matching contributions under the plan are benefits, rights or features subject to the requirements of section 401(a)(4). See § 1.401(a)(4)-4(e)(3)(i) and (iii)(F) through (G).

(2) Matching contributions.—(i) In general.—For purposes of section 401(m), this section and §§ 1.401(m)-2 through 1.401(m)-5, matching contributions are—

(A) Any employer contribution (including a contribution made at the employer's discretion) to a defined contribution plan on account of an employee contribution to a plan maintained by the employer;

(B) Any employer contribution (including a contribution made at the employer's discretion) to a defined contribution plan on account of an elective deferral; and

(C) Any forfeiture allocated on the basis of employee contributions, matching contributions, or elective deferrals.

(ii) *Employer contributions made on account of an employee contribution or elective deferral.*—Whether an employer contribution is made on account of an employee contribution or an elective deferral is determined on the basis of all the relevant facts and circumstances, including the relationship between the employer contribution and employee actions outside the plan. An employer contribution made to a defined contribution plan on account of contributions made by an employee under an employer-sponsored savings arrangement that are not held in a plan that is intended to be a qualified plan or other arrangement described in § 1.402(g)-1(b) is not a matching contribution.

(iii) *Employer contributions not on account of an employee contribution or elective deferral.*—(A) *General rule.*—Employer contributions are not matching contributions made on account of elective deferrals if they are contributed before the cash or deferred election is made or before the employees' performance of services with respect to which the elective deferrals are made (or when the cash that is subject to the cash or deferred elections would be currently available, if earlier). In addition, an employer contribution is not a matching contribution made on account of an employee contribution if it is contributed before the employee contribution.

(B) *Exceptions for forfeitures and released ESOP shares.*—The rule of paragraph (a)(3)(iii)(A) of this section does not apply to a forfeiture that is allocated as a matching contribution. In addition, an allocation of shares from an ESOP loan suspense account described in § 54.4975-11(c) and (d) of this chapter will not fail to be treated as a matching contribution solely because the employer contribution that resulted in the release and allocation of those shares from the suspense account is made before the employees' performance of services with respect to which the elective deferrals are made (or when the cash that is subject to the cash or deferred elections would be currently available, if earlier) provided that—

(1) The contribution is for a required payment that is due under the loan terms; and

(2) The contribution is not made early with a principal purpose of accelerating deductions.

(C) *Exception for bona fide administrative considerations.*—The timing of contributions will not be treated as failing to satisfy the requirements of this paragraph (a)(3)(iii) merely because contributions are occasionally made before the employees' performance of services with respect to which the elective deferrals are made (or when the cash that is subject to the cash or deferred elections would be currently available, if earlier) in order to accommodate bona fide administrative considerations and are not paid early with a principal purpose of accelerating deductions.

(3) *Employee contributions.*—(i) *In general.*—For purposes of section 401(m), this section and §§ 1.401(m)-2 through 1.401(m)-5, employee contributions are contributions to a plan that are designated or treated at the time of contribution as after-tax employee contributions (e.g., by treating the contributions as taxable income subject to applicable withholding requirements) and are allocated to an individual account for each eligible employee to which attributable earnings and losses are allocated. See § 1.401(k)-1(a)(2)(ii). The term *employee contributions* includes—

(A) Employee contributions to the defined contribution portion of a plan described in section 414(k);

(B) Employee contributions applied to the purchase of whole life insurance protection or survivor benefit protection under a defined contribution plan;

(C) Amounts attributable to excess contributions within the meaning of section 401(k)(8)(B) that are recharacterized as employee contributions under § 1.401(k)-2(b)(3); and

(D) *Employee contributions to a plan or contract that satisfies the requirements of section 403(b).*

(ii) *Certain contributions not treated as employee contributions.*—The term employee contributions does not include designated Roth contributions, repayment of loans, rollover contributions, repayment of distributions described in section 411(a)(7)(C), or employee contributions that are transferred to the plan from another plan.

(iii) *Qualified cost-of-living arrangements.*—Employee contributions to a qualified cost-of-living arrangement described in section 415(k)(2)(B) are treated as employee contributions to a defined contri-

bution plan, without regard to the requirement that the employee contributions be allocated to an individual account to which attributable earnings and losses are allocated.

(b) *Nondiscrimination requirements for amount of contributions.*—(1) *Matching contributions and employee contributions.*—The matching contributions and employee contributions under a plan satisfy this paragraph (b) for a plan year only if the plan satisfies—

(i) The ACP test of section 401(m)(2) described in § 1.401(m)-2;

(ii) The ACP safe harbor provisions of section 401(m)(11) described in § 1.401(m)-3; or

(iii) The ACP safe harbor provisions of section 401(m)(12) described in § 1.401(m)-3; or

(iv) The SIMPLE 401(k) provisions of sections 401(k)(11) and 401(m)(10) described in § 1.401(k)-4.

(2) *Automatic satisfaction by certain plans.*—Notwithstanding paragraph (b)(1) of this section, the requirements of this section are treated as satisfied with respect to employee contributions and matching contributions under a collectively bargained plan (or the portion of a plan) that automatically satisfies section 410(b). See §§ 1.401(a)(4)-1(c)(5) and 1.410(b)-2(b)(7). Additionally, the requirements of sections 401(a)(4) and 410(b) do not apply to a governmental plan (within the meaning of section 414(d)) maintained by a State or local government or political subdivision thereof (or agency or instrumentality thereof) and, accordingly such plans are not required to comply with this section. See sections 401(a)(5)(G), 403(b)(12)(C) and 410(c)(1)(A).

(3) *Anti-abuse provisions.*—Sections 1.401(m)-1 through 1.401(m)-5 are designed to provide simple, practical rules that accommodate legitimate plan changes. At the same time, the rules are intended to be applied by employers in a manner that does not make use of changes in plan testing procedures or other plan provisions to inflate inappropriately the ACP for NHCEs (which is used as a benchmark for testing the ACP for HCEs) or to otherwise manipulate the nondiscrimination testing requirements of this paragraph (b). Further, this paragraph (b) is part of the overall requirement that benefits or contributions do not discriminate in favor of HCEs. Therefore, a plan will not be treated as satisfying the requirements of this paragraph (b) if there are repeated changes to plan testing procedures or plan provisions that have the effect of distorting the ACP so as to increase significantly the permitted ACP for HCEs, or otherwise manipulate the nondiscrimination rules of this paragraph, if a principal purpose of the changes was to achieve such a result.

(4) *Aggregation and restructuring.*—(i) *In general.*—This paragraph (b)(4) contains the exclusive rules for aggregating and disaggregating plans that provide for employee contributions and matching contributions for purposes of this section and §§ 1.401(m)-2 through 1.401(m)-5.

(ii) *Aggregation of employee contributions and matching contributions within a plan.*—Except as otherwise specifically provided in this paragraph (b)(4) and § 1.401(m)-3(j)(6), a plan must be subject to a single test under paragraph (b)(1) of this section with respect to all employee contributions and matching contributions and all eligible employees under the plan. Thus, for example, if two groups of employees are eligible for matching contributions under a plan, all employee contributions and matching contributions under the plan must be subject to a single test, even if they have significantly different features, such as different rates of match.

(iii) *Aggregation of plans.*—(A) *In general.*—The term *plan* means a plan within the meaning of § 1.410(b)-7(a) and (b), after application of the mandatory disaggregation rules of § 1.410(b)-7(c), and the permissive aggregation rules of § 1.410(b)-7(d), as modified by paragraph (b)(4)(v) of this section. Thus, for example, two plans (within the meaning of § 1.410(b)-7(b)) that are treated as a single plan pursuant to the permissive aggregation rules of § 1.410(b)-7(d) are treated as a single plan for purposes of sections 401(k) and 401(m).

(B) *Arrangements with inconsistent ACP testing methods.*—Pursuant to paragraph (b)(4)(ii) of this section, a single testing method must apply with respect to all employee contributions and matching contributions and all eligible employees under a plan. Thus, in applying the permissive aggregation rules of § 1.410(b)-7(d), an employer may not aggregate plans (within the meaning of § 1.410(b)-7(b)) that apply inconsistent testing methods. For example, a plan (within the meaning of § 1.410(b)-7) that applies the current year testing method may not be aggregated with another plan that applies the prior year testing method. Similarly, an employer may not aggregate a plan (within the meaning of § 1.410(b)-7) that is using the ACP safe harbor provisions of section 401(m)(11) or 401(m)(12) and another plan that is using the ACP test of section 401(m)(2).

(iv) *Disaggregation of plans and separate testing.*—(A) *In general.*—If employee contributions or matching contributions are included in a plan (within the meaning of §1.410(b)-7(b)) that is mandatorily disaggregated under the rules of section 410(b) (as modified by this paragraph (b)(4)), the matching contributions and employee contributions under that plan must be disaggregated in a consistent manner. For example, in the case of an employer that is treated as operating qualified separate lines of business under section 414(r), if the eligible employees under a plan which provides for employee contributions or matching contributions are in more than one qualified separate line of business, only those employees within each qualified separate line of business may be taken into account in determining whether each disaggregated portion of the plan complies with the requirements of section 401(m), unless the employer is applying the special rule for employer-wide plans in §1.414(r)-1(c)(2)(ii) with respect to the plan. Similarly, if a plan that provides for employee contributions or matching contributions under which employees are permitted to participate before they have completed the minimum age and service requirements of section 410(a)(1) applies section 410(b)(4)(B) for determining whether the plan complies with section 410(b)(1), then the plan must be treated as two separate plans, one comprising all eligible employees who have met the minimum age and service requirements of section 410(a)(1) and one comprising all eligible employees who have not met the minimum age and service requirements of section 410(a)(1), unless the plan is using the rule in §1.401(m)-2(a)(1)(iii)(A).

(B) *Restructuring prohibited.*—Restructuring under §1.401(a)(4)-9(c) may not be used to demonstrate compliance with the requirements of section 401(m). See §1.401(a)(4)-9(c)(3)(ii).

(v) *Certain disaggregation rules not applicable.*—The mandatory disaggregation rules relating to section 401(k) plans and section 401(m) plans set forth in §1.410(b)-7(c)(1) and to ESOP and non-ESOP portions of a plan set forth in §1.410(b)-7(c)(2) shall not apply for purposes of this section and §§1.401(m)-2 through 1.401(m)-5. Accordingly, notwithstanding §1.410(b)-7(d)(2), an ESOP and a non-ESOP which are different plans (within the meaning of section 414(l), as described in §1.410(b)-7(b)) are permitted to be aggregated for these purposes.

(c) *Additional requirements.*—(1) *Separate testing for employee contributions and matching contributions.*—Under §1.410(b)-7(c)(1), the group of employees who are eligible to make employee contributions or eligible to receive matching contributions must satisfy the requirements of section 410(b) as if those employees were covered under a separate plan. The determination of whether the separate plan satisfies the requirements of section 410(b) must be made without regard to the modifications to the disaggregation rules set forth in paragraph (b)(4)(v) of this section. In addition, except as expressly permitted under section 401(k), 410(b)(2)(A)(ii), or 416(c)(2)(A), employee contributions, matching contributions and elective contributions taken into account under §1.401(m)-2(a)(6) may not be taken into account for purposes of determining whether any other contributions under any plan (including the plan to which the employee contributions or matching contributions are made) satisfy the requirements of section 401(a). See also §1.401(a)(4)-11(g)(3)(vii) for special rules relating to corrections of violations of the minimum coverage requirements or discriminatory rates of matching contributions.

(2) *Plan provision requirement.*—A plan that provides for employee contributions or matching contributions satisfies this section only if it provides that the nondiscrimination requirements of section 401(m) will be met. Thus, the plan must provide for satisfaction of one of the specific alternatives described in paragraph (b)(1) of this section and, if with respect to that alternative there are optional choices, which of the optional choices will apply. For example, a plan that uses the ACP test of section 401(m)(2), as described in paragraph (b)(1)(i) of this section, must specify whether it is using the current year testing method or prior year testing method. Additionally, a plan that uses the prior year testing method must specify whether the ACP for eligible NHCEs for the first plan year is 3% or the ACP for the eligible NHCEs for the first plan year. Similarly, a plan that uses the safe harbor method of section 401(m)(11) or 401(m)(12), as described in paragraphs (b)(1)(ii) and (b)(1)(iii) of this section, must specify the default percentages that apply for the plan year and whether the safe harbor contribution will be the nonelective safe harbor contribution or the matching safe harbor contribution, and is not permitted to provide that ACP testing will be used if the requirements for the safe harbor are not satisfied. For purposes of this paragraph (c)(2), a plan may incorporate by reference the provisions of section 401(m)(2) and §1.401(m)-2 if that is the nondiscrimination test being applied. The Commissioner may, in guidance of general applicability, published in the Internal Revenue Bulletin (see §601.601(d)(2) of this chapter), specify the options that will apply

under the plan if the nondiscrimination test is incorporated by reference in accordance with the preceding sentence.

(d) *Effective date.*—(1) *General rule.*—Except as otherwise provided in this paragraph (d), this section and §§1.401(m)-2 through 1.401(m)-5 apply to plan years that begin on or after January 1, 2006.

(2) *Early implementation permitted.*—A plan is permitted to apply the rules of this section and §§1.401(m)-2 through 1.401(m)-5 to any plan year that ends after December 29, 2004, provided the plan applies all the rules of this section and §§1.401(m)-2 through 1.401(m)-5 and all the rules of §§1.401(k)-1 through 1.401(k)-6, to the extent applicable, for that plan year and all subsequent plan years.

(3) *Applicability of prior regulations.*—For any plan year, before a plan applies this section and §§1.401(m)-2 through 1.401(m)-5 (either the first plan year beginning on or after January 1, 2006 or such earlier year, as provided in paragraph (d)(2) of this section), §1.401(m)-1 and §1.401(m)-2 (as they appeared in the April 1, 2004 edition of 26 CFR part 1) apply to the plan to the extent those sections, as they so appear, reflect the statutory provisions of section 401(m) as in effect for the relevant year.

(4) *Effective date for definitions of qualified matching contributions (QMACs) and qualified nonelective contributions (QNECs).*—The revisions to the definitions of QMACs and QNECs in §1.401(m)-5 apply to plan years ending on or after July 20, 2018. [Reg. §1.401(m)-1.]

☐ [T.D. 8357, 8-8-91. *Amended by* T.D. 8376, 12-2-9; T.D. 8581, 12-22-94; T.D. 9169, 12-28-2004; T.D. 9447, 2-23-2009 and T.D. 9835, 7-19-2018.]

[Reg. §1.401(m)-2]

§1.401(m)-2. ACP test.—(a) *Actual contribution percentage (ACP) test.*—(1) *In general.*—(i) *ACP test formula.*—A plan satisfies the ACP test for a plan year only if—

(A) The ACP for the eligible HCEs for the plan year is not more than the ACP for the eligible NHCEs for the applicable year multiplied by 1.25; or

(B) The excess of the ACP for the eligible HCEs for the plan year over the ACP for the eligible NHCEs for the applicable year is not more than 2 percentage points, and the ACP for the eligible HCEs for the plan year is not more than the ACP for the eligible NHCEs for the applicable year multiplied by 2.

(ii) *HCEs as sole eligible employees.*—If, for the applicable year there are no eligible NHCEs (i.e., all of the eligible employees under the plan for the applicable year are HCEs), the plan is deemed to satisfy the ACP test.

(iii) *Special rule for early participation.*—If a plan providing for employee contributions or matching contributions provides that employees are eligible to participate before they have completed the minimum age and service requirements of section 410(a)(1)(A), and if the plan applies section 410(b)(4)(B) in determining whether the plan meets the requirements of section 410(b)(1), then in determining whether the plan meets the requirements under paragraph (a)(1) of this section either—

(A) Pursuant to section 401(m)(5)(C), the ACP test is performed under the plan (determined without regard to disaggregation under §1.410(b)-7(c)(3)), using the ACP for all eligible HCEs for the plan year and the ACP of eligible NHCEs for the applicable year, disregarding all NHCEs who have not met the minimum age and service requirements of section 410(a)(1)(A); or

(B) Pursuant to §1.401(m)-1(b)(4), the plan is disaggregated into separate plans and the ACP test is performed separately for all eligible employees who have completed the minimum age and service requirements of section 410(a)(1)(A) and for all eligible employees who have not completed the minimum age and service requirements of section 410(a)(1)(A).

(2) *Determination of ACP.*—(i) *General rule.*—The ACP for a group of eligible employees (either eligible HCEs or eligible NHCEs) for a plan year or applicable year is the average of the ACRs of eligible employees in the group for that year. The ACP for a group of eligible employees is calculated to the nearest hundredth of a percentage point.

(ii) *Determination of applicable year under current year and prior year testing method.*—The ACP test is applied using the prior year testing method or the current year testing method. Under the prior year testing method, the applicable year for determining the ACP for the eligible NHCEs is the plan year immediately preceding the plan year for which the ACP test is being calculated. Under the prior year testing method, the ACP for the eligible NHCEs is determined using the ACRs for the eligible employees who were NHCEs in that preceding plan year, regardless of whether those NHCEs are eligible employees or NHCEs in the plan year for which the ACP test is being performed. Under the current year testing method, the applicable year for determining the ACP for eligible NHCEs is the same plan year as the plan year for which the ACP test is being calculated. Under either method, the ACP for the eligible HCEs is determined using the ACRs of eligible employees who are HCEs for the plan year for which the ACP test is being performed. See paragraph (c) of this section for additional rules for the prior year testing method.

(3) *Determination of ACR.*—(i) *General rule.*—The ACR of an eligible employee for the plan year or applicable year is the sum of the employee contributions and matching contributions taken into account with respect to such employee (determined under the rules of paragraphs (a)(4) and (5) of this section), and the qualified nonelective and elective contributions taken into account under paragraph (a)(6) of this section for the year, divided by the employee's compensation taken into account for the year. The ACR is calculated to the nearest hundredth of a percentage point. If no employee contributions, matching contributions, elective contributions, or qualified nonelective contributions are taken into account under this section with respect to an eligible employee for the year, the ACR of the employee is zero.

(ii) *ACR of HCEs eligible under more than one plan.*—(A) *General rule.*—Pursuant to section 401(m)(2)(B), the ACR of an HCE who is an eligible employee in more than one plan of an employer to which matching contributions or employee contributions are made is calculated by treating all contributions with respect to such HCE under any such plan as being made under the plan being tested. Thus, the ACR for such an HCE is calculated by accumulating all matching contributions and employee contributions under any plan (other than a plan described in paragraph (a)(3)(ii)(B) of this section) that would be taken into account under this section for the plan year, if the plan under which the contribution was made applied this section and had the same plan year. For example, in the case of a plan with a 12-month plan year, the ACR for the plan year of that plan for an HCE who participates in multiple plans of the same employer that provide for matching contributions or employee contributions is the sum of all such contributions during such 12-month period that would be taken into account with respect to the HCE under all plans in which the HCE is an eligible employee, divided by the HCE's compensation for that 12-month period (determined using the compensation definition for the plan being tested), without regard to the plan year of the other plans and whether those plans are satisfying this section or § 1.401(m)-3.

(B) *Plans not permitted to be aggregated.*—Contributions under plans that are not permitted to be aggregated under § 1.401(m)-1(b)(4) (determined without regard to the prohibition on aggregating plans with inconsistent testing methods set forth in § 1.401(m)-1(b)(4)(iii)(B) and the prohibition on aggregating plans with different plan years set forth in § 1.410(b)-7(d)(5)) are not aggregated under this paragraph (a)(3)(ii).

(iii) *Example.*—The following example illustrates the application of paragraph (a)(3)(ii) of this section. See also § 1.401(k)-2(a)(3)(iii) for additional examples of the application of the parallel rule under section 401(k)(3)(A). The example is as follows:

Example. Employee A, an HCE with compensation of $120,000, is eligible to make employee contributions under Plan S and Plan T, two calendar-year profit-sharing plans of Employer H. Plan S and Plan T use the same definition of compensation. Plan S provides a match equal to 50% of each employee's contributions and Plan T has no match. During the current plan year, Employee A elects to contribute $4,000 in employee contributions to Plan T and $4,000 in employee contributions to Plan S. There are no other contributions made on behalf of Employee A. Each plan must calculate Employee A's ACR by dividing the total employee contributions by Employee A and matching contributions under both plans by $120,000. Therefore, Employee A's ACR under each plan is 8.33% ($4,000+ $4,000+ $2,000/$120,000).

(4) *Employee contributions and matching contributions taken into account under the ACP test.*—(i) *Employee contributions.*—An employee contribution is taken into account in determining the ACR for an eligible employee for the plan year or applicable year in which the contribution is made. For purposes of the preceding sentence, an amount withheld from an employee's pay (or a payment by the employee to an agent of the plan) is treated as contributed at the time of such withholding (or payment) if the funds paid are transmitted to the trust within a reasonable period after the withholding (or payment).

(ii) *Recharacterized elective contributions.*—Excess contributions recharacterized in accordance with § 1.401(k)-2(b)(3) are taken into account as employee contributions for the plan year that includes the time at which the excess contribution is includible in the gross income of the employee under § 1.401(k)-2(b)(3)(ii).

(iii) *Matching contributions.*—A matching contribution is taken into account in determining the ACR for an eligible employee for a plan year or applicable year only if each of the following requirements is satisfied—

(A) The matching contribution is allocated to the employee's account under the terms of the plan as of a date within that year;

(B) The matching contribution is made on account of (or the matching contribution is allocated on the basis of) the employee's elective deferrals or employee contributions for that year; and

(C) The matching contribution is actually paid to the trust no later than the end of the 12-month period immediately following the year that contains that date.

(5) *Employee contributions and matching contributions not taken into account under the ACP test.*—(i) *General rule.*—Matching contributions that do not satisfy the requirements of paragraph (a)(4)(iii) of this section may not be taken into account in the ACP test for the plan year with respect to which the contributions were made, or for any other plan year. Instead, the amount of the matching contributions must satisfy the requirements of section 401(a)(4) (without regard to the ACP test) for the plan year for which they are allocated under the plan as if they were nonelective contributions and were the only nonelective contributions for that year. See §§ 1.401(a)(4)-1(b)(2)(ii)(B) and 1.410(b)-7(c)(1).

(ii) *Disproportionate matching contributions.*—(A) *Matching contributions in excess of 100%.*—A matching contribution with respect to an elective deferral for an NHCE is not taken into account under the ACP test to the extent it exceeds the greatest of:

(1) 5% of compensation;

(2) the employee's elective deferrals for a year; and

(3) the product of 2 times the plan's representative matching rate and the employee's elective deferrals for a year.

(B) *Representative matching rate.*—For purposes of this paragraph (a)(5)(ii), the plan's representative matching rate is the lowest matching rate for any eligible NHCE among a group of NHCEs that consists of half of all eligible NHCEs in the plan for the plan year who make elective deferrals for the plan year (or, if greater, the lowest matching rate for all eligible NHCEs in the plan who are employed by the employer on the last day of the plan year and who make elective deferrals for the plan year).

(C) *Definition of matching rate.*—For purposes of this paragraph (a)(5)(ii), the matching rate for an employee generally is the matching contributions made for such employee divided by the employee's elective deferrals for the year. If the matching rate is not the same for all levels of elective deferrals for an employee, the employee's matching rate is determined assuming that an employee's elective deferrals are equal to 6 percent of compensation.

(D) *Application to matching contributions that match employee contributions.*—If a plan provides a match with respect to the sum of the employee's employee contributions and elective deferrals, that sum is substituted for the amount of the employee's elective deferrals in paragraphs (a)(5)(ii)(A) and (C) of this section and employees who make either employee contributions or elective deferrals are taken into account under paragraph (a)(5)(ii)(B) of this section. Similarly, if a plan provides a match with respect to the employee's employee contributions, but not elective deferrals, the employee's employee contributions are substituted for the amount of the employee's elective deferrals in paragraphs (a)(5)(ii)(A) and (C) of this section and employees who make employee contributions are taken into account under paragraph (a)(5)(ii)(B) of this section.

(iii) *Qualified matching contributions used to satisfy the ADP test.*—Qualified matching contributions that are taken into account for the ADP test of section 401(k)(3) under § 1.401(k)-2(a)(6) are not taken into account in determining an eligible employee's ACR.

(iv) *Matching contributions taken into account under safe harbor provisions.*—A plan that satisfies the ACP safe harbor requirements of section 401(m)(11) or 401(m)(12) for a plan year but nonetheless must satisfy the requirements of this section because it provides for employee contributions for such plan year is permitted to apply this section disregarding all matching contributions with respect to all eligible employees. In addition, a plan that satisfies the ADP safe harbor requirements of § 1.401(k)-3 for a plan year using qualified matching contributions but does not satisfy the ACP safe harbor requirements of section 401(m)(11) or 401(m)(12) for such plan year is permitted to apply this section by excluding matching contributions with respect to all eligible employees that do not exceed 4 percent (3½ percent in the case of a plan that satisfies the ADP safe harbor under section 401(k)(13)) of each employee's compensation. If a plan disregards matching contributions pursuant to this paragraph (a)(5)(iv), the disregard must apply with respect to all eligible employees.

(v) *Treatment of forfeited matching contributions.*—A matching contribution that is forfeited because the contribution to which it relates is treated as an excess contribution, excess deferral, excess aggregate contribution, or default elective contribution that is distributed under section 414(w), is not taken into account for purposes of this section.

(vi) *Additional employee contributions or matching contributions pursuant to section 414(u).*—Additional employee contributions and matching contributions made by reason of an eligible employee's qualified military service under section 414(u) are not taken into account under paragraph (a)(4) of this section for the plan year for which the contributions are made, or for any other plan year.

(6) *Qualified nonelective contributions and elective contributions that may be taken into account under the ACP test.*—Qualified nonelective contributions and elective contributions may be taken into account in determining the ACR for an eligible employee for a plan year or applicable year, but only to the extent the contributions satisfy the following requirements—

(i) *Timing of allocation.*—The qualified nonelective contribution is allocated to the employee's account as of a date within that year (within the meaning of §1.401(k)-2(a)(4)(i)(A)) and the elective contribution satisfies §1.401(k)-2(a)(4)(i). Consequently, under the prior year testing method, in order to be taken into account in calculating the ACP for the group of eligible NHCEs for the applicable year, a qualified nonelective contribution must be contributed no later than the end of the 12-month period following the applicable year even though the applicable year is different than the plan year being tested.

(ii) *Elective contributions taken into account under the ACP test.*—Elective contributions may be taken into account for the ACP test only if the cash or deferred arrangement under which the elective contributions are made is required to satisfy the ADP test in §1.401(k)-2(a)(1) and, then only to the extent that the cash or deferred arrangement would satisfy that test, including such elective contributions in the ADP for the plan year or applicable year. Thus, for example, elective deferrals made pursuant to a salary reduction agreement under an annuity described in section 403(b) are not permitted to be taken into account in an ACP test. Similarly, elective contributions under a cash or deferred arrangement that is using the section 401(k) safe harbor described in §1.401(k)-3 cannot be taken into account in an ACP test. In addition, for plan years ending on or after November 8, 2007, elective contributions which are not permitted to be taken into account for the ADP test for the plan year under §1.401(k)-2(a)(5)(ii), (iii), (v), or (vi) are not permitted to be taken into account for the ACP test.

(iii) *Requirement that amount satisfy section 401(a)(4).*—The amount of nonelective contributions, including those qualified nonelective contributions taken into account under this paragraph (a)(6) and those qualified nonelective contributions taken into account for the ADP test under paragraph §1.401(k)-2(a)(6), and the amount of nonelective contributions, excluding those qualified nonelective contributions taken into account under this paragraph (a)(6) for the ACP test and those qualified nonelective contributions taken into account for the ADP test under paragraph §1.401(k)-2(a)(6), satisfies the requirements of section 401(a)(4). See §1.401(a)(4)-1(b)(2). In the case of an employer that is applying the special rule for employer-wide plans in §1.414(r)-1(c)(2)(ii) with respect to the plan, the determination of whether the qualified nonelective contributions satisfy the requirements of this paragraph (a)(6)(iii) must be made on an employer-wide basis regardless of whether the plans to which the qualified nonelective contributions are made are satisfying the requirements of section 410(b) on an employer-wide basis. Conversely, in the case of an employer that is treated as operating qualified separate lines of business, and does not apply the special rule for employer-wide plans in §1.414(r)-1(c)(2)(ii) with respect to the plan, then the determination of whether the qualified nonelective contributions satisfy the requirements of this paragraph (a)(6)(iii) is not permitted to be made on an employer-wide basis regardless of whether the plans to which the qualified nonelective contributions are made are satisfying the requirements of section 410(b) on that basis.

(iv) *Aggregation must be permitted.*—The plan that provides for employee or matching contributions and the plan or plans to which the qualified nonelective contributions or elective contributions are made are plans that would be permitted to be aggregated under §1.401(m)-1(b)(4). If the plan year of the plan that provides for employee or matching contributions is changed to satisfy the requirement under §1.410(b)-7(d)(5) that aggregated plans have the same plan year, qualified nonelective contributions and elective contributions may be taken into account in the resulting short plan year only if such qualified nonelective and elective contributions could have been taken into account under an ADP test for a plan with that same short plan year.

(v) *Disproportionate contributions not taken into account.*—(A) *General rule.*—Qualified nonelective contributions cannot be taken into account for an applicable year for an NHCE to the extent such contributions exceed the product of that NHCE's compensation and the greater of 5% and 2 times the plan's representative contribution rate. Any qualified nonelective contribution taken into account in an ADP test under §1.401(k)-2(a)(6) (including the determination of the representative contribution rate for purposes of §1.401(k)-2(a)(6)(iv)(B)) is not permitted to be taken into account for purposes of this paragraph (a)(6) (including the determination of the representative contribution rate for purposes of paragraph (a)(6)(v)(B) of this section).

(B) *Definition of representative contribution rate.*—For purposes of this paragraph (a)(6)(v), the plan's representative contribution rate is the lowest applicable contribution rate of any eligible NHCE among a group of eligible NHCEs that consists of half of all eligible NHCEs for the plan year (or, if greater, the lowest applicable contribution rate of any eligible NHCE in the group of all eligible NHCEs for the applicable year and who is employed by the employer on the last day of the applicable year).

(C) *Definition of applicable contribution rate.*—For purposes of this paragraph (a)(6)(v), the applicable contribution rate for an eligible NHCE is the sum of the matching contributions taken into account under this section for the employee for the plan year and the qualified nonelective contributions made for that employee for the plan year, divided by that employee's compensation for the same period.

(D) *Special rule for prevailing wage contributions.*—Notwithstanding paragraph (a)(6)(v)(A) of this section, qualified nonelective contributions that are made in connection with an employer's obligation to pay prevailing wages under the Davis-Bacon Act (46 Stat. 1494), Public Law 71-798, Service Contract Act of 1965 (79 Stat. 1965), Public Law 89-286, or similar legislation can be taken into account for a plan year for an NHCE to the extent such contributions do not exceed 10 percent of that NHCE's compensation

(vi) *Contribution only used once.*—Qualified nonelective contributions cannot be taken into account under this paragraph (a)(6) to the extent such contributions are taken into account for purposes of satisfying any other ACP test, any ADP test, or the requirements of §1.401(k)-3, 1.401(m)-3 or 1.401(k)-4. Thus, for example, qualified nonelective contributions that are made pursuant to §1.401(k)-3(b) cannot be taken into account under the ACP test. Similarly, if a plan switches from the current year testing method to the prior year testing method pursuant to §1.401(m)-2(c)(1), qualified nonelective contributions that are taken into account under the current year testing method for a plan year may not be taken into account under the prior year testing method for the next plan year.

(7) *Examples.*—The following examples illustrate the application of this paragraph (a). See §1.401(k)-2(a)(6) for additional examples of the parallel rules under section 401(k)(3)(A). The examples are as follows:

Example 1. (i) Employer L maintains Plan U, a profit-sharing plan under which $.50 matching contributions are made for each dollar of employee contributions. Plan U uses the current year testing method. The chart below shows the average employee contributions (as a percentage of compensation) and matching contributions (as a percentage of compensation) for Plan U's HCEs and NHCEs for the 2006 plan year:

	Employee Contributions	Matching Contributions	Actual Contribution Percentage
Highly compensated employees	4%	2%	6%
Nonhighly compensated employees	3%	1.5%	4.5%

(ii) The matching rate for all NHCEs is 50% and thus the matching contributions are not disproportionate under paragraph (a)(5)(ii) of this section. Accordingly, they are taken into account in determining the ACR of eligible employees.

(iii) Because the ACP for the HCEs (6.0%) exceeds 5.63% (4.5% × 1.25), Plan U does not satisfy the ACP test under paragraph (a)(1)(i)(A) of this section. However, because the ACP for the HCEs does not exceed the ACP for the NHCEs by more than 2 percentage points and the ACP for the HCEs does not exceed the ACP for the

NHCEs multiplied by 2 (4.5% × 2 = 9%), the plan satisfies the ACP test under paragraph (a)(1)(i)(B) of this section.

Example 2. (i) Employees A through F are eligible employees in Plan V, a profitsharing plan of Employer M that includes a cash or deferred arrangement and permits employee contributions. Under Plan V, a $.50 matching contribution is made for each dollar of elective contributions and employee contributions. Plan V uses the current year testing method and does not provide for elective contributions to be taken into account in determining an eligible employee's ACR. For the 2006 plan year, Employees A and B are HCEs and the remaining employees are NHCEs. The compensation, elective contributions, employee contributions, and matching contributions for the 2006 plan year are shown in the following table:

Employee	Compensation	Elective Contributions	Employee Contributions	Matching Contributions
A	$190,000	$15,000	$ 3,500	$ 9,250
B	100,000	$ 5,000	$10,000	$ 7,500
C	85,000	$12,000	$ 0	$ 6,000
D	70,000	$ 9,500	$ 0	$ 4,750
E	40,000	$10,000	$ 0	$ 5,000
F	10,000	$ 0	$ 0	$ 0

(ii) The matching rate for all NHCEs is 50% and thus the matching contributions are not disproportionate under paragraph (a)(5)(ii) of this section. Accordingly, they are taken into account in determining the ACR of eligible employees, as shown in the following table:

Employee	Compensation	Employee Contributions	Matching Contributions	ACR %
A	$190,000	$ 3,500	$ 9,250	6.71
B	100,000	$10,000	$ 7,500	17.50
C	85,000	$ 0	$ 6,000	7.06
D	70,000	$ 0	$ 4,750	6.79
E	40,000	$ 0	$ 5,000	12.50
F	10,000	$ 0	$ 0	0

(iii) The ACP for the HCEs is 12.11% ((6.71% + 17.50%)/2). The ACP for the NHCEs is 6.59% ((7.06% + 6.79% + 12.50% + 0.%)/4). Plan V fails to satisfy the ACP test under paragraph (a)(1)(i)(A) of this section because the ACP of HCEs is more than 125% of the ACP of the NHCEs (6.59% × 1.25 = 8.24%). In addition, Plan V fails to satisfy the ACP test under paragraph (a)(1)(i)(B) of this section because the ACP for the HCEs exceeds the ACP of the other employees by more than 2 percentage points (6.59% + 2% = 8.59%). Therefore, the plan fails to satisfy the requirements of section 401(m)(2) and paragraph (a)(1) of this section unless the ACP failure is corrected under paragraph (b) of this section.

Example 3. (i) The facts are the same as *Example 2*, except that the plan provides that the NHCEs' elective contributions may be used to meet the requirements of section 401(m) to the extent needed under that section.

(ii) Pursuant to paragraph (a)(6)(ii) of this section, the $10,000 of elective contributions for Employee E may be taken into account in determining the ACP rather than the ADP to the extent that the plan satisfies the requirements of §1.401(k)-2(a)(1) excluding from the ADP this $10,000. In this case, if the $10,000 were excluded from the ADP for the NHCEs, the ADP for the HCEs is 6.45% (7.89% + 5.00%) /2 and the ADP for the NHCEs would be 6.92% (14.12% + 13.57% + 0% +0%)/4) and the plan would satisfy the requirements of §1.401(k)-2(a)(1) excluding from the ADP the elective contributions for NHCEs that are taken into account under section 401(m).

(iii) After taking into account the $10,000 of elective contributions for Employee E in the ACP test, the ACP for the NHCEs is 12.84% (7.06% + 6.79% + 37.50 % + 0%) /4. Therefore the plan satisfies the ACP test because the ACP for the HCEs (12.11%) is less than 1.25 times the ACP for the NHCEs.

Example 4. (i) The facts are the same as *Example 2*, except that Plan V provides for a higher than 50% match rate on the elective contributions and employee contributions for all NHCEs. The match rate is defined as the rate, rounded up to the next whole percent, necessary to allow the plan to satisfy the ACP test, but not in excess of 100%. In this case, an increase in the match rate from 50% to 74% will be sufficient to allow the plan to satisfy the ACP test. Thus, for the 2006 plan year, the compensation, elective contributions, employee contributions, matching contributions at a 74% match rate of the eligible NHCEs (employees C through F) are shown in the following table:

Employee	Compensation	Elective Contributions	Employee Contributions	Matching Contributions
C	$85,000	$12,000	$ 0	$ 8,880
D	70,000	$ 9,500	$ 0	$ 7,030
E	40,000	$10,000	$ 0	$ 7,400
F	10,000	$ 0	$ 0	$ 0

(ii) The matching rate for all NHCEs is 74% and thus the matching contributions are not disproportionate under paragraph (a)(5)(ii) of this section. Therefore, the matching contributions may be taken into account in determining the ACP for the NHCEs.

(iii) The ACP for the NHCEs is 9.75% (10.45% + 10.04% + 18.50% + 0%)/4. Because the ACP for the HCEs (12.11%) is less than 1.25 times the ACP for the NHCEs, the plan satisfies the requirements of section 401(m).

Example 5. (i) The facts are the same as *Example 4*, except that: Employee E's elective contributions are $2,000 (rather than $10,000) and pursuant to paragraph (a)(6)(ii) of this section, the $2,000 of elective contributions for Employee E are taken into account in determining the ACP rather than the ADP. In addition, Plan V provides that the higher match rate is not limited to 100% and applies only for a specified group of NHCEs. The only member of that group is Employee E. Under the plan provision, the higher match rate is a 400% match. Thus, for the 2006 plan year, the compensation, elective contributions, employee contributions, matching contributions of the eligible NHCEs (employees C through F) are shown in the following table

Employee	Compensation	Elective Contributions	Employee Contributions	Matching Contributions
C	$ 85,000	$12,000	$ 0	$ 6,000
D	70,000	$ 9,500	$ 0	$ 4,750
E	40,000	$ 2,000	$ 0	$ 8,000
F	10,000	$ 0	$ 0	$ 0

(ii) If the entire matching contribution made on behalf of Employee E were taken into account under the ACP test, Plan V would satisfy the test, because the ACP for the NHCEs would be 9.71% (7.06% + 6.79% + 25.00% + 0%)/4. Because the ACP for the HCEs (12.11%) is less than 1.25 times what the ACP for the NHCEs would be, the plan would satisfy the requirements of section 401(m).

(iii) Pursuant to paragraph (a)(5)(ii) of this section, however, matching contributions for an eligible NHCE that exceed the greatest of 5% of compensation, the employee's elective deferrals and 2 times the product of the plan's representative matching rate and the employee's elective deferrals cannot be taken into account in applying the ACP test. The plan's representative matching rate is the lowest matching rate for any eligible employee in a group of NHCEs that is at least half of all eligible employees who are NHCEs in the plan for the plan year who make elective contributions for the plan year. For Plan V, the group of NHCEs who make such contributions consists of Employees C, D and E. The matching rates for these three employees are 50%, 50% and 400% respectively. The lowest matching rate for a group of NHCEs that is at least half of all the NHCEs who make elective contributions (or 2 NHCEs) is 50%. Because 400% is more than twice the plan's representative matching rate and the matching contributions exceed 5% of compensation, the full amount of matching contributions is not taken into account. Only $2,000 of the matching contributions made on behalf of Employee E (matching contributions that do not exceed the greatest of 5% of compensation, the employee's elective deferrals, or the product of 100% (2 times the representative matching rate) and the employee's elective deferrals) satisfy the requirements of paragraph (a)(5)(ii) of this section and may be taken into account under the ACP test. Accordingly, the ACP for the NHCEs is 5.96% (7.06% + 6.79% + 10% + 0%)/4 and the plan fails to satisfy the requirements of section 401(m)(2) and paragraph (a)(1) of this section unless the ACP failure is corrected under paragraph (b) of this section.

Example 6. (i) The facts are the same as *Example 2*, except that Plan V provides a QNEC equal to 13% of pay for Employee F that will be taken into account under the ACP test to the extent the contributions satisfy the requirements of paragraph (a)(6) of this section.

(ii) Pursuant to paragraph (a)(6)(v) of this section, a QNEC cannot be taken into account in determining an NHCE's ACR to the extent it exceeds the greater of 5% and the product of the employee's compensation and the plan's representative contribution rate. The plan's representative contribution rate is two times the lowest applicable contribution rate for any eligible employee in a group of NHCEs that is at least half of all eligible employees who are NHCEs in the plan for the plan year. For Plan V, the applicable contribution rates for Employees C, D, E and F are 7.06%, 6.79%, 12.5% and 13% respectively. The lowest applicable contribution rate for a group of NHCEs that is at least half of all the NHCEs is 12.50% (the lowest applicable contribution rate for the group of NHCEs that consists of Employees E and F).

(iii) Under paragraph (a)(6)(v)(B) of this section, the plan's representative contribution rate is 2 times 12.50% or 25.00%. Accordingly, the QNECs for Employee F can be taken into account under the ACP test only to the extent they do not exceed 25.00% of compensation. In this case, all of the QNECs for Employee F may be taken into account under the ACP test.

(iv) After taking into account the QNECs for Employee F, the ACP for the NHCEs is 9.84% (7.06% + 6.79% + 12.50% + 13%)/4. Because the ACP for the HCEs (12.11%) is less than 1.25 times the ACP for the NHCEs, the plan satisfies the requirements of section 401(m)(2) and paragraph (a)(1) of this section.

(b) *Correction of excess aggregate contributions.*—(1) *Permissible correction methods.*—(i) *In general.*—A plan that provides for employee contributions or matching contributions does not fail to satisfy the requirements of section 401(m)(2) and paragraph (a)(1) of this section if the employer, in accordance with the terms of the plan, uses either of the following correction methods—

(A) *Additional contributions.*—The employer makes additional contributions that are taken into account for the ACP test under this section that, in combination with the other contributions taken into account under this section, allow the plan to satisfy the requirements of paragraph (a)(1) of this section.

(B) *Excess aggregate contributions distributed or forfeited.*—Excess aggregate contributions are distributed or forfeited in accordance with paragraph (b)(2) of this section.

(ii) *Combination of correction methods.*—A plan may provide for the use of either of the correction methods described in paragraph (b)(1)(i) of this section, may limit employee contributions or matching contributions in a manner that prevents excess aggregate contributions from being made, or may use a combination of these methods, to avoid or correct excess aggregate contributions. If a plan uses a combination of correction methods, any contributions made

under paragraph (b)(1)(i)(A) of this section must be taken into account before application of the correction method in paragraph (b)(1)(i)(B) of this section.

(iii) *Exclusive means of correction.*—A failure to satisfy the requirements of paragraph (a)(1) of this section may not be corrected using any method other than one described in paragraph (b)(1)(i) or (ii) of this section. Thus, excess aggregate contributions for a plan year may not be corrected by forfeiting vested matching contributions, distributing nonvested matching contributions, recharacterizing matching contributions, or not making matching contributions required under the terms of the plan. Similarly, excess aggregate contributions for a plan year may not remain unallocated or be allocated to a suspense account for allocation to one or more employees in any future year. In addition, excess aggregate contributions may not be corrected using the retroactive correction rules of § 1.401(a)(4)-11(g). See § 1.401(a)(4)-11(g)(3)(vii) and (5).

(2) *Correction through distribution.*—(i) *General rule.*—This paragraph (b)(2) contains the rules for correction of excess aggregate contributions through a distribution from the plan. Correction through a distribution generally involves a 4-step process. First, the plan must determine, in accordance with paragraph (b)(2)(ii) of this section, the total amount of excess aggregate contributions that must be distributed under the plan. Second, the plan must apportion the total amount of excess aggregate contributions among the HCEs in accordance with paragraph (b)(2)(iii) of this section. Third, the plan must determine the income allocable to excess aggregate contributions in accordance with paragraph (b)(2)(iv) of this section. Finally, the plan must distribute the apportioned contributions, together with allocable income (or forfeit the apportioned matching contributions, if forfeitable) in accordance with paragraph (b)(2)(v) of this section. Paragraph (b)(2)(vi) of this section provides rules relating to the tax treatment of these distributions.

(ii) *Calculation of total amount to be distributed.*—The following procedures must be used to determine the total amount of the excess aggregate contributions to be distributed—

(A) *Calculate the dollar amount of excess aggregate contributions for each HCE.*—The amount of excess aggregate contributions attributable to an HCE for a plan year is the amount (if any) by which the HCE's contributions taken into account under this section must be reduced for the HCE's ACR to equal the highest permitted ACR under the plan. To calculate the highest permitted ACR under a plan, the ACR of the HCE with the highest ACR is reduced by the amount required to cause that HCE's ACR to equal the ACR of the HCE with the next highest ACR. If a lesser reduction would enable the plan to satisfy the requirements of paragraph (b)(2)(ii)(C) of this section, only this lesser reduction applies.

(B) *Determination of the total amount of excess aggregate contributions.*—The process described in paragraph (b)(2)(ii)(A) of this section must be repeated until the plan would satisfy the requirements of paragraph (b)(2)(ii)(C) of this section. The sum of all reductions for all HCEs determined under paragraph (b)(2)(ii)(A) of this section is the total amount of excess aggregate contributions for the plan year.

(C) *Satisfaction of ACP.*—A plan satisfies this paragraph (b)(2)(ii)(C) if the plan would satisfy the requirements of paragraph (a)(1)(i) of this section if the ACR for each HCE were determined after the reductions described in paragraph (b)(2)(ii)(A) of this section.

(iii) *Apportionment of total amount of excess aggregate contributions among the HCEs.*—The following procedures must be used in apportioning the total amount of excess aggregate contributions determined under paragraph (b)(2)(ii) of this section among the HCEs—

(A) *Calculate the dollar amount of excess aggregate contributions for each HCE.*—The contributions with respect to the HCE with the highest dollar amount of contributions taken into account under this section are reduced by the amount required to cause that HCE's contributions to equal the dollar amount of contributions taken into account under this section for the HCE with the next highest dollar amount of such contributions. If a lesser apportionment to the HCE would enable the plan to apportion the total amount of excess aggregate contributions, only the lesser apportionment would apply.

(B) *Limit on amount apportioned to any HCE.*—For purposes of this paragraph (b)(2)(iii), the contributions for an HCE who is an eligible employee in more than one plan of an employer to which matching contributions and employee contributions are made is determined by adding together all contributions otherwise taken into account in determining the ACR of the HCE under the rules of paragraph (a)(3)(ii) of this section. However, the amount of contributions apportioned with respect to an HCE must not exceed the amount of contributions taken into account under this section that were actually made on behalf of the HCE to the plan for the plan year. Thus, in the case of an HCE who is an eligible employee in more than one plan of the same employer to which employee contributions or matching contributions are made and whose ACR is calculated in accordance with paragraph (a)(3)(ii) of this section, the amount distributed under this paragraph (b)(2)(iii) will not exceed such contributions actually contributed to the plan for the plan year that are taken into account under this section for the plan year.

(C) *Apportionment to additional HCEs.*—The procedure in paragraph (b)(2)(iii)(A) of this section must be repeated until the total amount of excess aggregate contributions have been apportioned.

(iv) *Income allocable to excess aggregate contributions.*—(A) *General rule.*—For plan years beginning on or after January 1, 2008, the income allocable to excess aggregate contributions is equal to the allocable gain or loss through the end of the plan year. See paragraph (b)(2)(iv)(D) of this section for rules that apply to plan years beginning before January 1, 2008.

(B) *Method of allocating income.*—A plan may use any reasonable method for computing the income allocable to excess aggregate contributions, provided that the method does not violate section 401(a)(4), is used consistently for all participants and for all corrective distributions under the plan for the plan year, and is used by the plan for allocating income to participants' accounts. See §1.401(a)(4)-1(c)(8). A plan will not fail to use a reasonable method for computing the income allocable to excess contributions merely because the income allocable to excess aggregate contributions is determined on a date that is no more than 7 days before the distribution.

(C) *Alternative method of allocating income for the plan year.*—A plan may allocate income to excess aggregate contributions for the plan year by multiplying the income for the plan year allocable to employee contributions, matching contributions and other amounts taken into account under this section (including the contributions for the year), by a fraction, the numerator of which is the excess aggregate contributions for the employee for the plan year, and the denominator of which is the sum of the—

(1) Account balance attributable to employee contributions and matching contributions and other amounts taken into account under this section as of the beginning of the plan year; and

(2) Any additional such contributions for the plan year.

(D) *Plan years before 2008.*—For plan years beginning before January 1, 2008, the income allocable to excess aggregate contributions is determined under §1.401(m)-2(b)(2)(iv) (as it appeared in the April 1, 2007, edition of 26 CFR part 1).

(E) *Allocable income for recharacterized elective contributions.*—If recharacterized elective contributions are distributed as excess aggregate contributions, the income allocable to the excess aggregate contributions is determined as if recharacterized elective contributions had been distributed as excess contributions. Thus, income must be allocated to the recharacterized amounts distributed using the methods in §1.401(k)-2(b)(2)(iv).

(v) *Distribution and forfeiture.*—Within 12 months after the close of the plan year in which the excess aggregate contribution arose, the plan must distribute to each HCE the contributions apportioned to such HCE under paragraph (b)(2)(iii) of this section (and the allocable income) to the extent they are vested or forfeit such amounts, if forfeitable. Except as otherwise provided in this paragraph (b)(2)(v), a distribution of excess aggregate contributions must be in addition to any other distributions made during the year and must be designated as a corrective distribution by the employer. In the event of a complete termination of the plan during the plan year in which an excess aggregate contribution arose, the corrective distribution must be made as soon as administratively feasible after the date of termination of the plan, but in no event later than 12 months after the date of termination. If the entire account balance of an HCE is distributed prior to when the plan makes a distribution of excess aggregate contributions in accordance with this paragraph (b)(2), the distribution is deemed to have been a corrective distribution of excess aggregate contributions (and income) to the extent that a corrective distribution would otherwise have been required.

(vi) *Tax treatment of corrective distributions.*—(A) *Corrective distributions for plan years beginning on or after January 1, 2008.*—Except as otherwise provided in this paragraph (b)(2)(vi), for plan years beginning on or after January 1, 2008, a corrective distribution of excess aggregate contributions (and allocable income) is includible in the employee's gross income in the taxable year of the employee in which distributed. The portion of the distribution that is treated as an investment in the contract and is therefore not subject to tax under section 72 is determined without regard to any plan contributions other than those distributed as excess aggregate contributions. Regardless of when the corrective distribution is made, it is not subject to the early distribution tax of section 72(t). See paragraph (b)(4) of this section for additional rules relating to the employer excise tax on amounts distributed more than $2^{1}/_{2}$ months (6 months in the case of certain plans that include an eligible automatic contribution arrangement within the meaning of section 414(w)) after the end of the plan year. See also §1.402(c)-2, A-4, prohibiting rollover of distributions that are excess aggregate contributions.

(B) *Corrective distributions for plan years beginning before January 1, 2008.*—The tax treatment of corrective distributions for plan years beginning before January 1, 2008, is determined under §1.401(m)-2(b)(2)(vi) (as it appeared in the April 1, 2007, edition of 26 CFR Part 1). If the total amount of excess aggregate contributions determined under this paragraph (b)(2), and excess contributions determined under §1.401(k)-2(b)(2) distributed to a recipient under a plan for any plan year is less than $100 (excluding income), a corrective distribution of excess aggregate contributions (and income) is includible in gross income in the recipient's taxable year in which the corrective distribution is made, except to the extent the corrective distribution is a return of employee contributions, or as provided in paragraph (b)(2)(vi)(C) of this section.

(C) *Corrective distributions attributable to designated Roth contributions.*—Notwithstanding paragraphs (b)(2)(vi)(A) and (B) of this section, a distribution of excess aggregate contributions is not includible in gross income to the extent it represents a distribution of designated Roth contributions. However, the income allocable to a corrective distribution of excess aggregate contributions that are designated Roth contributions is taxed in accordance with paragraph (b)(2)(vi)(A) or (B) of this section (i.e., in the same manner as income allocable to a corrective distribution of excess aggregate contributions that are not designated Roth contributions).

(3) *Other rules.*—(i) *No employee or spousal consent required.*—A distribution of excess aggregate contributions (and income) may be made under the terms of the plan without regard to any notice or consent otherwise required under sections 411(a)(11) and 417.

(ii) *Treatment of corrective distributions and forfeited contributions as employer contributions.*—Excess aggregate contributions (other than amounts attributable to employee contributions), including forfeited matching contributions, are treated as employer contributions for purposes of sections 404 and 415 even if distributed from the plan. Forfeited matching contributions that are reallocated to the accounts of other participants for the plan year in which the forfeiture occurs are treated under section 415 as annual additions for the participants to whose accounts they are reallocated and for the participants from whose accounts they are forfeited.

(iii) *No reduction of required minimum distribution.*—A distribution of excess aggregate contributions (and income) is not treated as a distribution for purposes of determining whether the plan satisfies the minimum distribution requirements of section 401(a)(9). See §1.401(a)(9)-5, A-9(b).

(iv) *Partial correction.*—Any distribution of less than the entire amount of excess aggregate contributions (and allocable income) is treated as a pro rata distribution of excess aggregate contributions and allocable income.

(v) *Matching contributions on excess contributions, excess deferrals and excess aggregate contributions.*—(A) *Corrective distributions not permitted.*—A matching contribution may not be distributed merely because the contribution to which it relates is treated as an excess contribution, excess deferral, or excess aggregate contribution.

(B) *Coordination with section 401(a)(4).*—A matching contribution is taken into account under section 401(a)(4) even if the match is distributed, unless the distributed contribution is an excess aggregate contribution. This requires that, after correction of excess aggregate contributions, each level of matching contributions be currently and effectively available to a group of employees that satisfies section 410(b). See § 1.401(a)(4)-4(e)(3)(iii)(G). Thus, a plan that provides the same rate of matching contributions to all employees will not meet the requirements of section 401(a)(4) if employee contributions are distributed under this paragraph (b) to HCEs to the extent needed to meet the requirements of section 401(m)(2), while matching contributions attributable to employee contributions remain allocated to the HCEs' accounts. This is because the level of matching contributions will be higher for a group of employees that consists entirely of HCEs. Under section 411(a)(3)(G) and § 1.411(a)-4(b)(7), a plan may forfeit matching contributions attributable to excess contributions, excess aggregate contributions and excess deferrals to avoid a violation of section 401(a)(4). See also § 1.401(a)(4)-11(g)(3)(vii)(B) regarding the use of additional allocations to the accounts of NHCEs for the purpose of correcting a discriminatory rate of matching contributions. A plan is permitted to provide for which contributions are to be distributed to satisfy the ACP test so as to avoid discriminatory matching rates that would otherwise violate section 401(a)(4). For example, the plan may provide that unmatched employee contributions will be distributed before matched employee contributions.

(vi) *No requirement for recalculation.*—If the distributions and forfeitures described in paragraph (b)(2) of this section are made, the employee contributions and matching contributions are treated as meeting the nondiscrimination test of section 401(m)(2) regardless of whether the ACP for the HCEs, if recalculated after the distributions and forfeitures, would satisfy section 401(m)(2).

(4) *Failure to timely correct.*—(i) *Failure to correct within 2½ months after end of plan year.*—If a plan does not correct excess aggregate contributions within 2½ months after the close of the plan year for which the excess aggregate contributions are made, the employer will be liable for a 10% excise tax on the amount of the excess aggregate contributions. See section 4979 and § 54.4979-1 of this chapter. Qualified nonelective contributions properly taken into account under paragraph (a)(6) of this section for a plan year may

enable a plan to avoid having excess aggregate contributions, even if the contributions are made after the close of the 2½ month period.

(ii) *Failure to correct within 12 months after end of plan year.*—If excess aggregate contributions are not corrected within 12 months after the close of the plan year for which they were made, the plan will fail to meet the requirements of section 401(a)(4) for the plan year for which the excess aggregate contributions were made and all subsequent plan years in which the excess aggregate contributions remain in the trust.

(iii) *Special rule for eligible automatic contribution arrangements.*—In the case of excess aggregate contributions under a plan that includes an eligible automatic contribution arrangement (within the meaning of section 414(w)), 6 months is substituted for 2½ months in paragraph (b)(4)(i) of this section. The additional time described in this paragraph (b)(4)(iii) applies to a distribution of excess aggregate contributions for a plan year beginning on or after January 1, 2010 only where all the eligible NHCEs and eligible HCEs are covered employees under the eligible automatic contribution arrangement (within the meaning of § 1.414(w)-1(e)(3)) for the entire plan year (or for the portion of the plan year that the eligible NHCEs and eligible HCEs are eligible employees).

(5) *Examples.*—The following examples illustrate the application of this paragraph. See also § 1.401(k)-2(b) for additional examples of the parallel correction rules applicable to cash or deferred arrangements. For purposes of these examples, none of the plans provide for catch-up contributions under section 414(v). The examples are as follows:

Example 1. (i) Employer L maintains a plan that provides for employee contributions and fully vested matching contributions. The plan provides that failures of the ACP test are corrected by distribution. In 2006, the ACP for the eligible NHCEs is 6%. Thus, the ACP for the eligible HCEs may not exceed 8%. The three HCEs who participate have the following compensation, contributions, and ACRs:

Employee	Compensation	Employee contributions and matching contributions	Actual Contribution Ratio
A	200,000	14,000	7%
B	150,000	13,500	9
C	100,000	12,000	12
			Average 9.33%

(ii) The total amount of excess aggregate contributions for the HCEs is determined under paragraph (b)(2)(ii) of this section as follows: the matching and employee contributions of Employee C (the HCE with the highest ACR) is reduced by 3% of compensation (or $3,000) in order to reduce the ACR of that HCE to 9%, which is the ACR of Employee B.

(iii) Because the ACP of the HCEs determined after the $3,000 reduction still exceeds 8%, further reductions in matching contributions and employee contributions are necessary in order to reduce the ACP of the HCEs to 8%. The employee contributions and matching contributions for Employees B and C are reduced by an additional .5% of compensation or $1,250 ($750 and $500 respectively). Because the ACP of the HCEs determined after the reductions now equals 8%, the plan would satisfy the requirements of (a)(1)(ii) of this section.

(iv) The total amount of excess aggregate contributions ($4,250) is apportioned among the HCEs under paragraph (b)(2)(iii) of this section first to the HCE with the highest amount of matching contributions and employee contributions. Therefore, Employee A is apportioned $500 (the amount required to cause A's matching contributions and employee contributions to equal the next highest dollar amount of matching contributions and employee contributions).

(v) Because the total amount of excess aggregate contributions has not been apportioned, further apportionment is necessary. The balance ($3,750) of the total amount of excess aggregate contributions is apportioned equally among Employees A and B ($1,500 to each, the amount required to cause their contributions to equal the next

highest dollar amount of matching contributions and employee contributions).

(vi) Because the total amount of excess aggregate contributions has not been apportioned, further apportionment is necessary. The balance ($750) of the total amount of excess aggregate contributions is apportioned equally among Employees A, B and C ($250 to each, the amount required to allocate the total amount of excess aggregate contributions for the plan).

(vii) Therefore, the plan will satisfy the requirements of paragraph (a)(1) of this section if, by the end of the 12 month period following the end of the 2006 plan year, Employee A receives a corrective distribution of excess aggregate contributions equal to $2,250 ($500 + $1,500 + $250) and allocable income, Employee B receives a corrective distribution of $250 and allocable income and Employee C receives a corrective distribution of $1,750 ($1,500 + $250) and allocable income.

Example 2. (i) Employee D is the sole HCE who is eligible to participate in a cash or deferred arrangement maintained by Employer M. The plan that includes the arrangement, Plan X, permits employee contributions and provides a fully vested matching contribution equal to 50% of elective contributions. Plan X is a calendar year plan. Plan X corrects excess contributions by recharacterization and provides that failures of the ACP test are corrected by distribution. For the 2006 plan year, D's compensation is $200,000, and D's elective contributions are $15,000. The actual deferral percentages and actual contribution percentages for Employee D and the other eligible employees under Plan X are shown in the following table:

	Actual Deferral Percentage		Actual Contribution Percentage
Employee D	7.5%		3.75%
NHCEs	4%		2%

(ii) In February 2007, Employer M determines that D's actual deferral ratio must be reduced to 6%, or $12,000, which requires a recharacterization of $3,000 as an employee contribution. This increases D's actual contribution ratio to 5.25% ($7,500 in matching contributions plus $3,000 recharacterized as employee contributions,

divided by $200,000 in compensation). Since D's actual contribution ratio must be limited to 4% for Plan X to satisfy the actual contribution percentage test, Plan X must distribute 1.25% or $2,500 of D's employee contributions and matching contributions together with allocable income. If $2,500 in matching contributions and allocable income is distributed, this will correct the excess aggregate contributions and will not result in a discriminatory rate of matching contributions. See *Example 8*.

Example 3. (i) The facts are the same as in *Example 2*, except that Employee D also had elective contributions under Plan Y, maintained by an employer unrelated to M. In January 2007, D requests and receives a distribution of $1,200 in excess deferrals from Plan X. Pursuant to the terms of Plan X, D forfeits the $600 match on the excess deferrals to correct a discriminatory rate of match.

(ii) The $3,000 that would otherwise have been recharacterized for Plan X to satisfy the actual deferral percentage test is reduced by the $1,200 already distributed as an excess deferral, leaving $1,800 to be recharacterized. See §1.401(k)-2(b)(4)(i)(A). D's actual contribution ratio is now 4.35% ($7,500 in matching contributions plus $1,800 in recharacterized contributions less $600 forfeited matching contributions attributable to the excess deferrals, divided by $200,000 in compensation).

(iii) The matching and employee contributions for Employee D must be reduced by .35% of compensation in order to reduce the ACP of the HCEs to 4%. The plan must provide for forfeiture of additional matching contributions to prevent a discriminatory rate of matching contributions. See *Example 8*.

Example 4. (i) The facts are the same as in *Example 3*, except that D does not request a distribution of excess deferrals until March 2007. Employer X has already recharacterized $3,000 as employee contributions.

(ii) Under §1.402(g)-1(e)(6), the amount of excess deferrals is reduced by the amount of excess contributions that are recharacterized. Because the amount recharacterized is greater than the excess deferrals, Plan X is neither required nor permitted to make a distribution of excess deferrals, and the recharacterization has corrected the excess deferrals.

Example 5. (i) For the 2006 plan year, Employee F defers $10,000 under Plan M and $6,000 under Plan N. Plans M and N, which have calendar plan years are maintained by unrelated employers. Plan M provides a fully vested, 100% matching contribution, does not take elective contributions into account under section 401(m) or take matching contributions into account under section 401(k) and provides that excess contributions and excess aggregate contributions are corrected by distribution. Under Plan M, Employee F is allocated excess contributions of $600 and excess aggregate contributions of $1,600. Employee F timely requests and receives a distribution of the $1,000 excess deferral from Plan M and, pursuant to the terms of Plan M, forfeits the corresponding $1,000 matching contribution.

(ii) No distribution is required or permitted to correct the excess contributions because $1,000 has been distributed by Plan M as excess deferrals. The distribution required to correct the excess aggregate contributions (after forfeiting the matching contribution) is $600 ($1,600 in excess aggregate contributions minus $1,000 in forfeited matching contributions). If Employee F had corrected the excess deferrals of $1,000 by withdrawing $1,000 from Plan N, Plan M would have had to correct the $600 excess contributions in Plan M by distributing $600. Since Employee F then would have forfeited $600 (instead of $1,000) in matching contributions, Employee F would have had $1,000 ($1,600 in excess aggregate contributions minus $600 in forfeited matching contributions) remaining of excess aggregate contributions in Plan M. These would have been corrected by distributing an additional $1,000 from Plan M.

Example 6. (i) Employee G is the sole HCE in a profit sharing plan under which the employer matches 100% of employee contributions up to 2% of compensation, and 50% of employee contributions up to the next 4% of compensation. For the 2008 plan year, Employee G has compensation of $100,000 and makes a 7% employee contribution of $7,000. Employee G receives a 4% matching contribution or $4,000. Thus, Employee G's actual contribution ratio (ACR) is 11%. The actual contribution percentage for the NHCEs is 5%, and the employer determines that Employee G's ACR must be reduced to 7% to comply with the rules of section 401(m).

(ii) In this case, the plan satisfies the requirements of section if it distributes the unmatched employee contributions of $1,000, and $2,000 of matched employee contributions with their related matches of $1,000. This would leave Employee G with 4% employee contributions, and 3% matching contributions, for an ACR of 7%. Alternatively, the plan could distribute all matching contributions and satisfy this section. However, the plan could not distribute $4,000 of Employee G's employee contributions without forfeiting the related matching contributions because this would result in a discriminatory rate of matching contributions. See also *Example 7*.

Example 7. (i) Employee H is an HCE in Employer X's profit sharing plan, which matches 100% of employee contributions up to 5% of compensation. The matching contribution is vested at the rate of 20% per year. In 2006, Employee H makes $5,000 in employee contributions and receives $5,000 of matching contributions. Employee H is 60% vested in the matching contributions at the end of

the 2006 plan year. In February 2007, Employer X determines that Employee H has excess aggregate contributions of $1,000. The plan provides that only matching contributions will be distributed as excess aggregate contributions.

(ii) Employer X has two options available in distributing Employee H's excess aggregate contributions. The first option is to distribute $600 of vested matching contributions and forfeit $400 of nonvested matching contributions. These amounts are in proportion to Employee H's vested and nonvested interests in all matching contributions. The second option is to distribute $1,000 of vested matching contributions, leaving the nonvested matching contributions in the plan.

(iii) If the second option is chosen, the plan must also provide a separate vesting schedule for vesting these nonvested matching contributions. This is necessary because the nonvested matching contributions must vest as rapidly as they would have had no distribution been made. Thus, 50% must vest in each of the next 2 years.

(iv) The plan will not satisfy the nondiscriminatory availability requirement of section 401(a)(4) if only nonvested matching contributions are forfeited because the effect is that matching contributions for HCEs vest more rapidly than those for NHCEs. See §1.401(m)-2(b)(3)(v)(B).

Example 8. (i) Employer Y maintains a calendar year profit sharing plan that includes a cash or deferred arrangement. Elective contributions are matched at the rate of 100%. After-tax employee contributions are permitted under the plan only for NHCEs and are matched at the same rate. No employees make excess deferrals. Employee J, an HCE, makes an $8,000 elective contribution and receives an $8,000 matching contribution.

(ii) Employer Y performs the actual deferral percentage (ADP) and the actual contribution percentage (ACP). To correct failures of the ADP and ACP tests, the plan distributes to A $1,000 of excess contributions and $500 of excess aggregate contributions. After the distributions, Employee J's contributions for the year are $7,000 of elective contributions and $7,500 of matching contributions. As a result, Employee J has received a higher effective rate of matching contributions than NHCEs ($7,000 of elective contributions matched by $7,500 is an effective matching rate of 107 percent). If this amount remains in Employee J's account without correction, it will cause the plan to fail to satisfy section 401(a)(4), because only an HCE receives the higher matching contribution rate. The remaining $500 matching contribution may be forfeited (but not distributed) under section 411(a)(3)(G), if the plan so provides. The plan could instead correct the discriminatory rate of matching contributions by making additional allocations to the accounts of NHCEs. See §1.401(a)(4)-11(g)(3)(vii)(B) and (6), *Example 7*.—

(c) *Additional rules for prior year testing method.*—(1) *Rules for change in testing method.*—A plan is permitted to change from the prior year testing method to the current year testing method for any plan year. A plan is permitted to change from the current year testing method to the prior year testing method only in situations described in §1.401(k)-2(c)(1)(ii). For purposes of this paragraph (c)(1), a plan that uses the safe harbor method described in §1.401(m)-3 or a SIMPLE 401(k) plan is treated as using the current year testing method for that plan year

(2) *Calculation of ACP under the prior year testing method for the first plan year.*—(i) *Plans that are not successor plans.*—If, for the first plan year of any plan (other than a successor plan), a plan uses the prior year testing method, the plan is permitted to use either that first plan year as the applicable year for determining the ACP for the eligible NHCEs, or 3% as the ACP for eligible NHCEs, for applying the ACP test for that first plan year. A plan (other than a successor plan) that uses the prior year testing method but has elected for its first plan year to use that year as the applicable year for determining the ACP for the eligible NHCEs is not treated as changing its testing method in the second plan year and is not subject to the limitations on double counting under paragraph (a)(6)(vi) of this section for the second plan year.

(ii) *First plan year defined.*—For purposes of this paragraph (c)(2), the first plan year of any plan is the first year in which the plan provides for employee contributions or matching contributions. Thus, the rules of this paragraph (c)(2) do not apply to a plan (within the meaning of §1.410(b)-7) for a plan year for such plan year the plan is aggregated under §1.401(m)-1(b)(4) with any other plan that provides for employee or matching contributions in the prior year.

(iii) *Plans that are successor plans.*—A plan is a successor plan if 50% or more of the eligible employees for the first plan year were eligible employees under another plan maintained by the employer in the prior year that provides for employee contributions or matching contributions. If a plan that is a successor plan uses the prior year testing method for its first plan year, the ACP for the group of

NHCEs for the applicable year must be determined under paragraph (c)(4) of this section.

(3) *Plans using different testing methods for the ACP and ADP test.*—Except as otherwise provided in this paragraph (c)(3), a plan may use the current year testing method or prior year testing method for the ACP test for a plan year without regard to whether the current year testing method or prior year testing method is used for the ADP test for that year. For example, a plan may use the prior year testing method for the ACP test and the current year testing method for its ADP test for the plan year. However, plans that use different testing methods under this paragraph (c)(3) cannot use —

(i) The recharacterization method of §1.401(k)-2(b)(3) to correct excess contributions for a plan year;

(ii) The rules of paragraph (a)(6)(ii) of this section to take elective contributions into account under the ACP test (rather than the ADP test); or

(iii) The rules of paragraph §1.401(k)-2(a)(6) to take qualified matching contributions into account under the ADP test (rather than the ACP test).

(4) *Rules for plan coverage change.*—(i) *In general.*—A plan that uses the prior year testing method that experiences a plan coverage change during a plan year satisfies the requirements of this section for that year only if the plan provides that the ACP for the NHCEs for the plan year is the weighted average of the ACPs for the prior year subgroups.

(ii) *Optional rule for minor plan coverage changes.*—If a plan coverage change occurs and 90% or more of the total number of the NHCEs from all prior year subgroups are from a single prior year subgroup, then, in lieu of using the weighted averages described in paragraph (c)(4)(i) of this section, the plan may provide that the ACP for the group of eligible NHCEs for the prior year under the plan is the ACP of the NHCEs for the prior year of the plan under which that single prior year subgroup was eligible.

(iii) *Definitions.*—The following definitions apply for purposes of this paragraph (c)(4)—

(A) *Plan coverage change.*—The term *plan coverage change* means a change in the group or groups of eligible employees under a plan on account of—

(1) The establishment or amendment of a plan;

(2) A plan merger or spinoff under section 414(l);

(3) A change in the way plans (within the meaning of §1.410(b)-7) are combined or separated for purposes of §1.401(m)-1(b)(4) (e.g., permissively aggregating plans not previously aggregated under §1.410(b)-7(d), or ceasing to permissively aggregate plans under §1.410(b)-7(d));

(4) A reclassification of a substantial group of employees that has the same effect as amending the plan (e.g., a transfer of a substantial group of employees from one division to another division); or

(5) A combination of any of paragraphs (c)(4)(iii)(A)(1) through (4) of this section.

(B) *Prior year subgroup.*—The term *prior year subgroup* means all NHCEs for the prior plan year who, in the prior year, were eligible employees under a specific plan that provides for employee contributions or matching contributions maintained by the employer and who would have been eligible employees in the prior year under the plan being tested if the plan coverage change had first been effective as of the first day of the prior plan year instead of first being effective during the plan year. The determination of whether an NHCE is a member of a prior year subgroup is made without regard to whether the NHCE terminated employment during the prior year.

(C) *Weighted average of the ACPs for the prior year subgroups.*—The term *weighted average of the ACPs for the prior year subgroups* means the sum, for all prior year subgroups, of the adjusted ACPs for the plan year. The term *adjusted ACP with respect to a prior year subgroup* means the ACP for the prior plan year of the specific plan under which the members of the prior year subgroup were eligible employees on the first day of the prior plan year, multiplied by a fraction, the numerator of which is the number of NHCEs in the prior year subgroup and denominator of which is the total number of NHCEs in all prior year subgroups.

(iv) *Example.*—The following example illustrate the application of this paragraph (c)(4). See also §1.401(k)-2(c)(4) for examples of the parallel rules applicable to the ADP test. The example is as follows:

Example. (i) Employer B maintains two plans, Plan N and Plan P, each of which provides for employee contributions or matching contributions. The plans were not permissively aggregated under

§1.410(b)-7(d) for the 2005 testing year. Both plans use the prior year testing method. Plan N had 300 eligible employees who were NHCEs for 2005, and their ACP for that year was 6%. Plan P had 100 eligible employees who were NHCEs for 2005, and the ACP for those NHCEs for that plan was 4%. Plan N and Plan P are permissively aggregated under §1.410(b)-7(d) for the 2006 plan year.

(ii) The permissive aggregation of Plan N and Plan P for the 2006 testing year under §1.410(b)-7(d) is a plan coverage change that results in treating the plans as one plan (Plan NP). Therefore, the prior year ACP for the NHCEs under Plan NP for the 2006 testing year is the weighted average of the ACPs for the prior year subgroups.

(iii) The first step in determining the weighted average of the ACPs for the prior year subgroups is to identify the prior year subgroups. With respect to the 2006 testing year, an employee is a member of a prior year subgroup if the employee was an NHCE of Employer B for the 2005 plan year, was an eligible employee for the 2005 plan year under any section 401(k) plan maintained by Employer B, and would have been an eligible employee in the 2005 plan year under Plan N and Plan P if Plan N and Plan P had been permissively aggregated under §1.410(b)-7(d) for that plan year. The NHCEs who were eligible employees under separate plans for the 2005 plan year comprise separate prior year subgroups. Thus, there are two prior year subgroups under Plan NP for the 2006 testing year: the 300 NHCEs who were eligible employees under Plan N for the 2005 plan year and the 100 NHCEs who were eligible employees under Plan P for the 2005 plan year.

(iv) The weighted average of the ACPs for the prior year subgroups is the sum of the adjusted ACP with respect to the prior year subgroup that consists of the NHCEs who were eligible employees under Plan N, and the adjusted ACP with respect to the prior year subgroup that consists of the NHCEs who were eligible employees under Plan P. The adjusted ACP for the prior year subgroup that consists of the NHCEs who were eligible employees under Plan N is 4.5%, calculated as follows: 6% (the ACP for the NHCEs under Plan N for the prior year) × 300/400 (the number of NHCEs in that prior year subgroup divided by the total number of NHCEs in all prior year subgroups), which equals 4.5%. The adjusted ACP for the prior year subgroup that consists of the NHCEs who were eligible employees under Plan P is 1%, calculated as follows: 4% (the ACP for the NHCEs under Plan P for the prior year) × 100/400 (the number of NHCEs in that prior year subgroup divided by the total number of NHCEs in all prior year subgroups), which equals 1%. Thus, the prior year ACP for NHCEs under Plan NP for the 2006 testing year is 5.5% (the sum of adjusted ACPs for the prior year subgroups, 4.5% plus 1%).

[Reg. §1.401(m)-2.]

☐ [*T.D.* 8357, 8-8-91. *Amended by T.D.* 8581, 12-22-94; *T.D.* 9169, 12-28-2004; *T.D.* 9237, 12-30-2005 and *T.D.* 9447, 2-23-2009.]

[Reg. §1.401(m)-3]

§1.401(m)-3. Safe harbor requirements.—(a) *ACP test safe harbor.*—(1) *Section 401(m)(11) safe harbor.*—Matching contributions under a plan satisfy the ACP safe harbor provisions of section 401(m)(11) for a plan year if the plan satisfies the safe harbor contribution requirement of paragraph (b) or (c) of this section for the plan year, the limitations on matching contributions of paragraph (d) of this section, the notice requirement of paragraph (e) of this section, the plan year requirements of paragraph (f) of this section, and the additional rules of paragraphs (g), (h) and (j) of this section, as applicable.

(2) *Section 401(m)(12) safe harbor.*—For a plan year beginning on or after January 1, 2008, matching contributions under a plan satisfy the ACP safe harbor provisions of section 401(m)(12) for a plan year if the matching contributions are made with respect to an automatic contribution arrangement described in paragraph §1.401(k)-3(j) that satisfies the safe harbor requirements of §1.401(k)-3, the limitations on matching contributions of paragraph (d) of this section, the notice requirement of paragraph (e) of this section, the plan year requirements of paragraph (f) of this section, and the additional rules of paragraphs (g), (h) and (j) of this section, as applicable.

(3) *Requirements applicable to safe harbor contributions.*—Pursuant to sections 401(k)(12)(E)(ii) and 401(k)(13)(D)(iv), the safe harbor contribution requirement of paragraph (b) or (c) of this section and §1.401(k)-3(k) must be satisfied without regard to section 401(l). The contributions made under paragraphs (b) and (c) of this section and §1.401(k)-3(k) are referred to as safe harbor nonelective contributions and safe harbor matching contributions.

(b) *Safe harbor nonelective contribution requirement.*—A plan satisfies the safe harbor nonelective contribution requirement of this paragraph (b) if it satisfies the safe harbor nonelective contribution requirement of §1.401(k)-3(b).

(c) *Safe harbor matching contribution requirement.*—A plan satisfies the safe harbor matching contribution requirement of this paragraph (c) if it satisfies the safe harbor matching contribution requirement of §1.401(k)-3(c).

(d) *Limitation on contributions.*—(1) *General rule.*—A plan that provides for matching contributions meets the requirements of this section only if it satisfies the limitations on contributions set forth in this paragraph (d).

(2) *Matching rate must not increase.*—A plan that provides for matching contributions meets the requirements of this paragraph (d) only if the ratio of matching contributions on behalf of an employee under the plan for a plan year to the employee's elective deferrals and employee contributions, does not increase as the amount of an employee's elective deferrals and employee contributions increases.

(3) *Limit on matching contributions.*—A plan that provides for matching contributions satisfies the requirements of this section only if—

(i) Matching contributions are not made with respect to elective deferrals or employee contributions that exceed 6% of the employee's safe harbor compensation (within the meaning of §1.401(k)-3(b)(2)); and

(ii) Matching contributions that are discretionary do not exceed 4% of the employee's safe harbor compensation.

(4) *Limitation on rate of match.*—A plan meets the requirements of this section only if the ratio of matching contributions on behalf of an HCE to that HCE's elective deferrals or employee contributions (or the sum of elective deferrals and employee contributions) for that plan year is no greater than the ratio of matching contributions to elective deferrals or employee contributions (or the sum of elective deferrals and employee contributions) that would apply with respect to any NHCE for whom the elective deferrals or employee contributions (or the sum of elective deferrals and employee contributions) are the same percentage of safe harbor compensation. An employee is taken into account for purposes of this paragraph (d)(4) if the employee is an eligible employee under the cash or deferred arrangement with respect to which the contributions required by paragraph (b) or (c) of this section are being made for a plan year. A plan will not fail to satisfy this paragraph (d)(4) merely because the plan provides that matching contributions will be made separately with respect to each payroll period (or with respect to all payroll periods ending with or within each month or quarter of a plan year) taken into account under the plan for the plan year, provided that matching contributions with respect to any elective deferrals or employee contributions made during a plan year quarter are contributed to the plan by the last day of the immediately following plan year quarter.

(5) *HCEs participating in multiple plans.*—The rules of section 401(m)(2)(B) and §1.401(m)-2(a)(3)(ii) apply for purposes of determining the rate of matching contributions under paragraph (d)(4) of this section. However, a plan will not fail to satisfy the safe harbor matching contribution requirements of this section merely because an HCE participates during the plan year in more than one plan that provides for matching contributions, provided that —

(i) The HCE is not simultaneously an eligible employee under two plans that provide for matching contributions maintained by an employer for a plan year; and

(ii) The period used to determine compensation for purposes of determining matching contributions under each such plan is limited to periods when the HCE participated in the plan.

(6) *Permissible restrictions on elective deferrals by NHCEs.*—(i) *General rule.*—A plan does not satisfy the safe harbor requirements of this section, if elective deferrals or employee contributions by NHCEs are restricted, unless the restrictions are permitted by this paragraph (d)(6).

(ii) *Restrictions on election periods.*—A plan may limit the frequency and duration of periods in which eligible employees may make or change contribution elections under a plan. However, an employee must have a reasonable opportunity (including a reasonable period after receipt of the notice described in paragraph (e) of this section) to make or change a contribution election for the plan year. For purposes of this section, a 30-day period is deemed to be a reasonable period to make or change a contribution election.

(iii) *Restrictions on amount of contributions.*—A plan is permitted to limit the amount of contributions that may be made by an eligible employee under a plan, provided that each NHCE who is an eligible employee is permitted (unless the employee is restricted under paragraph (d)(6)(v) of this section) to make contributions in an amount that is at least sufficient to receive the maximum amount of matching contributions available under the plan for the plan year, and the employee is permitted to elect any lesser amount of contribu-

tions. However, a plan may require eligible employees to make contribution elections in whole percentages of compensation or whole dollar amounts.

(iv) *Restrictions on types of compensation that may be deferred.*—A plan may limit the types of compensation that may be deferred or contributed by an eligible employee under a plan, provided that each eligible NHCE is permitted to make contributions under a definition of compensation that would be a reasonable definition of compensation within the meaning of §1.414(s)-1(d)(2). Thus, the definition of compensation from which contributions may be made is not required to satisfy the nondiscrimination requirement of §1.414(s)-1(d)(3).

(v) *Restrictions due to limitations under the Internal Revenue Code.*—A plan may limit the amount of contributions made by an eligible employee under a plan—

(A) Because of the limitations of section 402(g) or section 415;

(B) Due to a suspension under section 414(u)(12)(B)(ii); or

(C) Because, on account of a hardship distribution made before January 1, 2020, an employee's ability to make contributions has been suspended for 6 months.

(e) *Notice requirement.*—A plan satisfies the notice requirement of this paragraph (e) if it satisfies the notice requirement of §1.401(k)-3(d).

(f) *Plan year requirement.*—(1) *General rule.*—Except as provided in this paragraph (f) or in paragraph (g) of this section, a plan will fail to satisfy the requirements of section 401(m)(11), section 401(m)(12), and this section unless plan provisions that satisfy the rules of this section are adopted before the first day of that plan year and remain in effect for an entire 12-month plan year. In addition, except as provided in paragraph (h) of this section or in guidance of general applicability published in the Internal Revenue Bulletin (see §601.601(d)(2)(ii)(b) of this chapter), a plan which includes provisions that satisfy the rules of this section will not satisfy the requirements of §1.401(m)-1(b) if it is amended to change such provisions for that plan year. Moreover, if, as described in paragraph (j)(4) of this section, safe harbor matching or nonelective contributions will be made to another plan for a plan year, provisions under that other plan specifying that the safe harbor contributions will be made and providing that the contributions will be QNECs or QMACs must also be adopted before the first day of that plan year.

(2) *Initial plan year.*—A newly established plan (other than a successor plan within the meaning of §1.401(m)-2(c)(2)(iii)) will not be treated as violating the requirements of this paragraph (f) merely because the plan year is less than 12 months, provided that the plan year is at least 3 months long (or, in the case of a newly established employer that establishes the plan as soon as administratively feasible after the employer comes into existence, a shorter period). Similarly, a plan will not fail to satisfy the requirements of this paragraph (f) for the first plan year in which matching contributions are provided under the plan provided that—

(i) The plan is not a successor plan; and

(ii) The amendment providing for matching contributions is made effective at the same time as the adoption of a cash or deferred arrangement that satisfies the requirements of §1.401(k)-3, taking into account the rules of §1.401(k)-3(e)(2).

(3) *Change of plan year.*—A plan that has a short plan year as a result of changing its plan year will not fail to satisfy the requirements of paragraph (f)(1) of this section merely because the plan year has less than 12 months, provided that—

(i) The plan satisfied the requirements of this section for the immediately preceding plan year; and

(ii) The plan satisfies the requirements of this section (determined without regard to paragraph (h) of this section) for the immediately following plan year or for the immediately following 12 months if the immediately following plan year is less than 12 months.

(4) *Final plan year.*—A plan that terminates during a plan year will not fail to satisfy the requirements of paragraph (f)(1) of this section merely because the final plan year is less than 12 months, provided that the plan satisfies the requirement of this section through the date of termination and either—

(i) The plan would satisfy the requirements of paragraph (h) of this section, treating the termination of the plan as a reduction or suspension of safe harbor contributions, other than the requirements of paragraph (h)(1)(i)(A) or (h)(1)(ii)(A) of this section (relating to the employer's financial condition and information included in the initial notice for the plan year) and paragraph (h)(1)(i)(D) or (h)(1)(ii)(D) of this section (requiring that employees have a reasonable opportunity to change their cash or deferred elections and, if applicable, employee contribution elections); or

Reg. §1.401(m)-3(f)(4)(i)

(ii) The plan termination is in connection with a transaction described in section 410(b)(6)(C) or the employer incurs a substantial business hardship, comparable to a substantial business hardship described in section 412(c).

(g) *Plan amendments adopting nonelective safe harbor contributions.*— Notwithstanding paragraph (f)(1) of this section, a plan that provides for the use of the current year testing method may be amended after the first day of the plan year and no later than 30 days before the last day of the plan year to adopt the safe harbor method of this section, effective as of the first day of the plan year, using nonelective contributions under paragraph (b) of this section if the plan satisfies the requirements of § 1.401(k)-3(f).

(h) *Permissible reduction or suspension of safe harbor contributions.*— (1) *General rule.*—(i) *Matching contributions.*—A plan that provides for safe harbor matching contributions intended to satisfy the requirements of paragraph (c) of this section for a plan year will not fail to satisfy the requirements of section 401(m)(2) merely because the plan is amended during the plan year to reduce or suspend safe harbor matching contributions on future elective deferrals (and, if applicable, employee contributions) provided that—

(A) In the case of plan years beginning on or after January 1, 2015, the employer either—

(1) Is operating at an economic loss as described in section 412(c)(2)(A) for the plan year; or

(2) Includes in the notice described in paragraph (e) of this section, a statement that the plan may be amended during the plan year to reduce or suspend safe harbor matching contributions and that the reduction or suspension will not apply until at least 30 days after all eligible employees are provided notice of the reduction or suspension;

(B) All eligible employees are provided a supplemental notice that satisfies the requirements of paragraph (h)(2) of this section;

(C) The reduction or suspension of safe harbor matching contributions is effective no earlier than the later of the date the amendment is adopted or 30 days after eligible employees are provided the supplemental notice described in paragraph (h)(2) of this section;

(D) Eligible employees are given a reasonable opportunity (including a reasonable period after receipt of the supplemental notice) prior to the reduction or suspension of safe harbor matching contributions to change their cash or deferred elections and, if applicable, their employee contribution elections;

(E) The plan is amended to provide that the ACP test will be satisfied for the entire plan year in which the reduction or suspension occurs using the current year testing method described in § 1.401(m)-2(a)(2)(ii); and

(F) The plan satisfies the requirements of this section (other than this paragraph (h)) with respect to amounts deferred through the effective date of the amendment.

(ii) *Nonelective contributions.*—For plan amendments adopted after May 18, 2009, a plan that provides for safe harbor nonelective contributions intended to satisfy the requirements of paragraph (b) of this section will not fail to satisfy the requirements of section 401(m)(2) for the plan year merely because the plan is amended during the plan year to reduce or suspend safe harbor nonelective contributions provided that—

(A) The employer either—

(1) Is operating at an economic loss as described in section 412(c)(2)(A) for the plan year; or

(2) Includes in the notice described in paragraph (e) of this section a statement that the plan may be amended during the plan year to reduce or suspend safe harbor nonelective contributions and that the reduction or suspension will not apply until at least 30 days after all eligible employees are provided notice of the reduction or suspension;

(B) All eligible employees are provided a supplemental notice that satisfies the requirements of paragraph (h)(2) of this section;

(C) The reduction or suspension of safe harbor nonelective contributions is effective no earlier than the later of the date the amendment is adopted or 30 days after eligible employees are provided the supplemental notice described in paragraph (h)(2) of this section;

(D) Eligible employees are given a reasonable opportunity (including a reasonable period after receipt of the supplemental notice) prior to the reduction or suspension of nonelective contributions to change their cash or deferred elections and, if applicable, their employee contribution elections;

(E) The plan is amended to provide that the ACP test will be satisfied for the entire plan year in which the reduction or suspension occurs using the current year testing method described in § 1.401(m)-2(a)(2)(ii); and

(F) The plan satisfies the requirements of this section (other than this paragraph (h)) with respect to safe harbor compensation paid through the effective date of the amendment.

(2) *Supplemental notice.*—The supplemental notice requirement of this paragraph (h)(2) is satisfied if each eligible employee is given a notice that satisfies the requirements of § 1.401(k)-3(g)(2).

(i) [Reserved].

(j) *Other rules.*—(1) *Contributions taken into account.*—A contribution is taken into account for purposes of this section for a plan year under the same rules as § 1.401(k)-3(h)(1).

(2) *Use of safe harbor nonelective contributions to satisfy other non-discrimination tests.*—A safe harbor nonelective contribution used to satisfy the nonelective contribution requirement under paragraph (b) of this section may also be taken into account for purposes of determining whether a plan satisfies section 401(a)(4) under the same rules as § 1.401(k)-3(h)(2).

(3) *Early participation rules.*—Section 401(m)(5)(C) and § 1.401(m)-2(a)(1)(iii)(A), which provide an alternative nondiscrimination rule for certain plans that provide for early participation, do not apply for purposes of section 401(m)(11), section 401(m)(12), and this section. Thus, a plan is not treated as satisfying this section with respect to the eligible employees who have not completed the minimum age and service requirements of section 410(a)(1)(A) unless the plan satisfies the requirements of this section with respect to such eligible employees.

(4) *Satisfying safe harbor contribution requirement under another defined contribution plan.*—Safe harbor matching or nonelective contributions may be made to another defined contribution plan under the same rules as § 1.401(k)-3(h)(4). Consequently, each NHCE under the plan providing for matching contributions must be eligible under the same conditions under the other defined contribution plan and the plan to which the contributions are made must have the same plan year as the plan providing for matching contributions.

(5) *Contributions used only once.*—Safe harbor matching or nonelective contributions cannot be used to satisfy the requirements of this section with respect to more than one plan.

(6) *Plan must satisfy ACP with respect to employee contributions.*—If the plan provides for employee contributions, in addition to satisfying the requirements of this section, it must also satisfy the ACP test of § 1.401(m)-2. See § 1.401(m)-2(a)(5)(iv) for special rules under which the ACP test is permitted to be performed disregarding some or all matching when this section is satisfied with respect to the matching contributions. [Reg. § 1.401(m)-3.]

☐ [*T.D.* 9169, 12-28-2004. *Amended by T.D.* 9447, 2-23-2009, *T.D.* 9641, 11-14-2013 *and T.D.* 9875, 9-19-2019.]

[Reg. § 1.401(m)-4]

§ 1.401(m)-4. Special rules for mergers, acquisitions and similar events.—*[Reserved]*.

☐ [*T.D.* 9169, 12-28-2004.]

[Reg. § 1.401(m)-5]

§ 1.401(m)-5. Definitions.—Unless otherwise provided, the definitions of this section govern for purposes of section 401(m) and the regulations thereunder.

Actual contribution percentage (ACP). Actual contribution percentage or *ACP* means the ACP of the group of eligible employees as defined in § 1.401(m)-2(a)(2)(i).

Actual contribution percentage (ACP) test. Actual contribution percentage test or *ACP test* means the test described in § 1.401(m)-2(a)(1).

Actual contribution ratio (ACR). Actual contribution ratio or *ACR* means the ACR of an eligible employee as defined in § 1.401(m)-2(a)(3).

Actual deferral percentage (ADP) test. Actual deferral percentage test or *ADP test* means the test described in § 1.401(k)-2(a)(1).

Compensation. Compensation means compensation as defined in section 414(s) and § 1.414(s)-1. The period used to determine an employee's compensation for a plan year must be either the plan year or the calendar year ending within the plan year. Whichever period is selected must be applied uniformly to determine the compensation of every eligible employee under the plan for that plan year. A plan may, however, limit the period taken into account under either method to that portion of the plan year or calendar year in which the employee was an eligible employee, provided that this limit is applied uniformly to all eligible employees under the plan for the plan year. See also section 401(a)(17) and § 1.401(a)(17)-1(c)(1). For this purpose, in case of an HCE whose ACR is determined under § 1.401(m)-2(a)(3)(ii), period of participation includes periods under another plan for which matching contributions or employee contributions are aggregated under § 1.401(m)-2(a)(3)(ii).

Current year testing method. Current year testing method means the testing method under which the applicable year is the current plan year, as described in § 1.401(k)-2(a)(2)(ii) or 1.401(m)-2(a)(2)(ii).

Designated Roth contributions. Designated Roth contributions means designated Roth contributions as defined in § 1.401(k)-1(f)(1).

Elective contributions. Elective contributions means elective contributions as defined in § 1.401(k)-6.

Elective deferrals. Elective deferrals means elective deferrals described in section 402(g)(3).

Eligible employee—(1) *General rule. Eligible employee* means an employee who is directly or indirectly eligible to make an employee contribution or to receive an allocation of matching contributions (including matching contributions derived from forfeitures) under the plan for all or a portion of the plan year. For example, if an employee must perform purely ministerial or mechanical acts (e.g., formal application for participation or consent to payroll withholding) in order to be eligible to make an employee contribution for a plan year, the employee is an eligible employee for the plan year without regard to whether the employee performs these acts.

(2) *Conditions on eligibility.* An employee who is unable to make employee contributions or to receive an allocation of matching contributions because the employee has not contributed to another plan is also an eligible employee. By contrast, if an employee must perform additional service (e.g., satisfy a minimum period of service requirement) in order to be eligible to make an employee contribution or to receive an allocation of matching contributions for a plan year, the employee is not an eligible employee for the plan year unless the service is actually performed. An employee who would be eligible to make employee contributions but for a suspension due to a distribution, a loan, or an election not to participate in the plan, is treated as an eligible employee for purposes of section 401(m) for a plan year even though the employee may not make employee contributions or receive an allocation of matching contributions by reason of the suspension. Finally, an employee does not fail to be treated as an eligible employee merely because the employee may receive no additional annual additions because of section 415(c)(1).

(3) *Certain one-time elections.* An employee is not an eligible employee merely because the employee, no later than the employee's first becoming eligible under any plan or arrangement described in section 219(g)(5)(A) and providing for employee or matching contributions, is given a one-time opportunity to elect, and the employee in fact does elect, not to be eligible to make employee contributions or to receive allocations of matching contributions under the plan or any other plan or arrangement maintained by the employer (including plans not yet established) for the duration of the employee's employment with the employer. In no event is an election made after December 23, 1994, treated as a one-time irrevocable election under this paragraph if the election is made by an employee who previously became eligible under another plan or arrangement (whether or not terminated) of the employer.

Eligible HCE. Eligible HCE means an eligible employee who is an HCE.

Eligible NHCE. Eligible NHCE means an eligible employee who is not an HCE.

Employee. Employee means an employee within the meaning of § 1.410(b)-9.

Employee contributions. Employee contributions means employee contributions as defined in § 1.401(m)-1(a)(3).

Employee stock ownership plan (ESOP). Employee stock ownership plan or *ESOP* means the portion of a plan that is an ESOP within the meaning of § 1.410(b)-7(c)(2).

Employer. Employer means an employer within the meaning of § 1.410(b)-9.

Excess aggregate contributions. Excess aggregate contributions means, with respect to a plan year, the amount of excess aggregate contributions apportioned to an HCE under § 1.401(m)-2(b)(2)(iii).

Excess contributions. Excess contributions means with respect to a plan year, the amount of excess contributions apportioned to an HCE under § 1.401(k)-2(b)(2)(iii).

Excess deferrals. Excess deferrals means excess deferrals as defined in § 1.402(g)-1(e)(3).

Highly compensated employee (HCE). Highly compensated employee or *HCE* has the meaning provided in section 414(q).

Matching contributions. Matching contribution is defined in § 1.401(m)-1(a)(2).

Nonelective contributions. Nonelective contributions means employer contributions (other than matching contributions) with respect to which the employee may not elect to have the contributions paid to the employee in cash or other benefits instead of being contributed to the plan.

Non-employee stock ownership plan (non-ESOP). Non-employee stock ownership plan or *non-ESOP* means the portion of a plan that is not an ESOP within the meaning of § 1.410(b)-7(c)(2).

Non-highly compensated employee (NHCE). Non-highly compensated employee or *NHCE* means an employee who is not an HCE.

Plan. Plan means plan as defined in § 1.401(m)-1(b)(4).

Prior year testing method. Prior year testing method means the testing method under which the applicable year is the prior plan year, as described in § 1.401(k)-2(a)(2)(ii) or 1.401(m)-2(a)(2)(ii).

Qualified matching contributions (QMACs). Qualified matching contributions or *QMACs* means qualified matching contributions or QMACs as defined in § 1.401(k)-6.

Qualified nonelective contributions (QNECs). Qualified nonelective contributions or *QNECs* means qualified nonelective contributions or QNECs as defined in § 1.401(k)-6.

[Reg. § 1.401(m)-5.]

☐ [T.D. 9169, 12-28-2004. Amended by T.D. 9237, 12-30-2005 and T.D. 9835, 7-19-2018.]

[Reg. § 1.402(a)-1]

§ 1.402(a)-1. Taxability of beneficiary under a trust which meets the requirements of section 401(a).—(a) *In general.*

(1)(i) Section 402 relates to the taxation of the beneficiary of an employees' trust. If an employer makes a contribution for the benefit of an employee to a trust described in section 401(a) for the taxable year of the employer which ends within or with a taxable year of the trust for which the trust is exempt under section 501(a), the employee is not required to include such contribution in his income except for the year or years in which such contribution is distributed or made available to him. It is immaterial in the case of contributions to an exempt trust whether the employee's rights in the contributions to the trust are forfeitable or nonforfeitable either at the time the contribution is made to the trust or thereafter.

(ii) The provisions of section 402(a) relate only to a distribution by a trust described in section 401(a) which is exempt under section 501(a) for the taxable year of the trust in which the distribution is made. With two exceptions, the distribution from such an exempt trust when received or made available is taxable to the distributee to the extent provided in section 72 (relating to annuities). First, for taxable years beginning before January 1, 1964, section 72(e)(3) (relating to the treatment of certain lump sums), as in effect before such date, shall not apply to such distributions. For taxable years beginning after December 31, 1963, such distributions may be taken into account in computations under sections 1301 through 1305 (relating to income averaging). Secondly, certain total distributions described in section 402(a)(2) are taxable as long-term capital gains. For the treatment of such total distributions, see subparagraph (6) of this paragraph. Under certain circumstances, an amount representing the unrealized appreciation in the value of the securities of the employer is excludable from gross income for the year of distribution. For the rules relating to such exclusion, see paragraph (b) of this section. Paragraph (e) of this section provides rules relating to use of a qualified pension, annuity, profit-sharing, or stock bonus plan to provide accident or health benefits or coverage otherwise described in sections 104, 105, or 106.

(iii) Except as provided in paragraph (b) of this section, a distribution of property by a trust described in section 401(a) and exempt under section 501(a) shall be taken into account by the distributee at its fair market value. In the case of a distribution of a life insurance contract, retirement income contract, endowment contract, or other contract providing life insurance protection, or any interest therein, the policy cash value and all other rights under such contract (including any supplemental agreements thereto and whether or not guaranteed) are included in determining the fair market value of the contract. In addition, in the case of a transfer of property that occurs on or after August 29, 2005, where a trust described in section 401(a) and exempt under section 501(a) transfers property to a plan participant or beneficiary in exchange for consideration and where the fair market value of the property transferred exceeds the value of the consideration, then the excess of the fair market value of the property transferred by the trust over the value of the consideration received by the trust is treated as a distribution to the distributee under the plan for all purposes under the Internal Revenue Code. Where such a transfer occurs before that date, the excess of the fair market value of the property transferred by the trust over the value of the consideration received by the trust is includible in the gross income of the participant or beneficiary under section 61. However, such a transfer of a life insurance contract, retirement income contract, endowment contract, or other contract providing life insurance protection occurring before that date is not treated as a distribution for purposes of applying the requirements of subchapter D of chapter 1 of subtitle A of the Internal Revenue Code.

(iv) If a trust is exempt for the taxable year in which the distribution occurs, but was not so exempt for one or more prior taxable years under section 501(a) (or under section 165(a) of the Internal Revenue Code of 1939 for years to which such section was applicable), the contributions of the employer which were includible in the gross income of the employee for the taxable year when made shall, in accordance with section 72(f), also be treated as part of the consideration paid by the employee.

(v) If the trust is not exempt at the time the distribution is received by or made available to the employee, see section 402(b) and paragraph (b) of §1.402(b)-1.

(vi) For the treatment of amounts paid to provide medical benefits described in section 401(h) as defined in paragraph (a) of §1.401-14, see paragraph (h) of §1.72-15.

(2) If a trust described in section 401(a) and exempt under section 501(a) purchases an annuity contract for an employee and distributes it to the employee in a year in which the trust is exempt, and the contract contains a cash surrender value which may be available to an employee by surrendering the contract, such cash surrender value will not be considered income to the employee unless and until the contract is surrendered. For the rule as to nontransferability of annuity contracts issued after 1962, see §1.401-9(b)(1). For additional requirements regarding distributions of annuity contracts, see, e.g., §§1.401(a)-20, Q&A-2, 1.401(a)(31)-1, Q&A-17, and 1.401(a)(9)-6, Q&A-4. However, the distribution of an annuity contract must be treated as a lump sum distribution for purposes of determining the amount of tax under the 10-year averaging rule of section 402(e) (as in effect prior to amendment by the Tax Reform Act of 1986, Public Law 99-514, 100 Stat. 2085). If, however, the contract distributed by such exempt trust is a life insurance contract, retirement income contract, endowment contract, or other contract providing life insurance protection, the fair market value of the contract at the time of distribution must be included in the distributee's income in accordance with the provisions of section 402(a), except to the extent that, within 60 days after the distribution of the contract, all or any portion of such value is irrevocably converted into a contract under which no part of any proceeds payable on death at any time would be excludable under section 101(a) (relating to life insurance proceeds), or the contract is treated as a rollover contribution under section 402(c). If the contract distributed by such trust is a transferable annuity contract, or a retirement income, endowment, or other life insurance contract and such contract is not treated as a rollover contribution under section 402(c), then, notwithstanding the preceding sentence, the fair market value of the contract is includible in the distributee's gross income unless, within such 60 days, such contract is made nontransferable.

(3) For the rules applicable to premiums paid by a trust described in section 401(a) and exempt under section 501(a) for the purchase of retirement income, endowment, or other contracts providing life insurance protection payable upon the death of the employee-participant, see paragraph (b) of §1.72-16.

(4) For the rules applicable to the amounts payable by reason of the death of an employee under a contract providing life insurance protection, or an annuity contract, purchased by a trust described in section 401(a) and exempt under section 501(a), see paragraph (c) of §1.72-16.

(5) If pension or annuity payments or other benefits are paid or made available to the beneficiary of a deceased employee or a deceased retired employee by a trust described in section 401(a) which is exempt under section 501(a), such amounts are taxable in accordance with the rules of section 402(a) and this section. In case such amounts are taxable under section 72, the "investment in the contract" shall be determined by reference to the amount contributed by the employee and by applying the applicable rules of sections 72 and 101(b)(2)(D). In case the amounts paid to, or includible in the gross income of, the beneficiaries of the deceased employee or deceased retired employee constitute a distribution to which subparagraph (6) of this paragraph is applicable, the extent to which the distribution is taxable is determined by reference to the contributions of the employee, by reference to any prior distributions which were excludable from gross income as a return of employee contributions, and by applying the applicable rules of sections 72 and 101(b).

(6)(i) If the total distributions payable with respect to any employee under a trust described in section 401(a) which in the year of distribution is exempt under section 501(a) are paid to, or includible in the gross income of, the distributee within one taxable year of the distributee on account of the employee's death or other separation from the service, or death after such separation from service, the amount of such distribution, to the extent it exceeds the net amount contributed by the employee, shall be considered a gain from the sale or exchange of a capital asset held for more than six months. The total distributions payable are includible in the gross income of the distributee within one taxable year if they are made available to such distributee and the distributee fails to make a timely election under section 72(h) to receive an annuity in lieu of such total distributions. The "net amount contributed by the employee" is the amount actu-

ally contributed by the employee plus any amounts considered to be contributed by the employee under the rules of sections 72(f), 101(b), and subparagraph (3) of this paragraph, reduced by any amounts theretofore distributed to him which were excludable from gross income as a return of employee contributions. See, however, paragraph (b) of this section for rules relating to the exclusion of amounts representing net unrealized appreciation in the value of securities of the employer corporation. In addition, all or part of the amount otherwise includible in gross income under this paragraph by a nonresident alien individual in respect of a distribution by the United States under a qualified pension plan may be excludable from gross income under section 402(a)(4). For rules relating to such exclusion, see paragraph (c) of this section. For additional rules relating to the treatment of total distributions described in this subdivision in the case of a nonresident alien individual, see sections 871 and 1441 and the regulations thereunder.

(ii) The term "total distributions payable" means the balance to the credit of an employee which becomes payable to a distributee on account of the employee's death or other separation from the service or on account of his death after separation from the service. Thus, distributions made before a total distribution (for example, annuity payments received by the employee after retirement), will not defeat application of the capital gains treatment with respect to the total distributions received by a beneficiary upon the death of the employee after retirement. However, a distribution on separation from service will not receive capital gains treatment unless it constitutes the total amount in the employee's account at the time of his separation from service. If the total amount in the employee's account at the time of his death or other separation from the service or death after separation from the service is paid or includible in the gross income of the distributee within one taxable year of the distributee, such amount is entitled to the capital gains treatment notwithstanding that in a later taxable year an additional amount, attributable to the last year of service, is credited to the account of the employee and distributed.

(iii) If an employee retires and commences to receive an annuity but subsequently, in some succeeding taxable year, is paid a lump sum in settlement of all future annuity payments, the capital gains treatment does not apply to such lump sum settlement paid during the lifetime of the employee since it is not a payment on account of separation from the service, or death after separation, but is on account of the settlement of future annuity payments.

(iv) If the "total distributions payable" are paid or includible in the gross income of several distributees within one taxable year on account of the employee's death or other separation from the service or on account of his death after separation from the service, the capital gains treatment is applicable. The total distributions payable are paid within one taxable year of the distributees when, for example, a portion of such total is distributed in cash to one distributee and the balance is used to purchase an annuity contract which is distributed to the other distributee. However, if the share of any distributee is not paid or includible in his gross income within the same taxable year in which the shares of the other distributees are paid or includible in their gross income, none of the distributees is entitled to the capital gains treatment, since the total distributions payable are not paid or includible in the distributees' gross income within one taxable year. For example, if the total distributions payable are made available to each of two distributees and one elects to receive his share in cash while the other makes a timely election under section 72(h) to receive his share in installment payments from the trust, the capital gains treatment does not apply to either distributee.

(v) [Reserved].

(vi) The term "total distributions payable" does not include United States Retirement Plan Bonds held by a trust to the credit of an employee. Thus, a distribution by a qualified trust may constitute a total distributions payable with respect to an employee even though the trust retains retirement plan bonds registered in the name of such employee. Similarly, the proceeds of a retirement plan bond received as a part of the total amount to the credit of an employee will not be entitled to capital gains treatment.

(vii) For purposes of determining whether the total distributions payable to an employee have been distributed within one taxable year, the term "total distributions payable" includes amounts held by a trust to the credit of an employee which are attributable to contributions on behalf of the employee while he was a self-employed individual in the business with respect to which the plan was established. Thus, a distribution by a qualified trust is not a total distributions payable with respect to an employee if the trust retains amounts which are so attributable.

(viii) The term "total distributions payable" does not include any amount which has been placed in a separate account for the funding of medical benefits described in section 401(h) as defined in paragraph (a) of §1.401-14. Thus, a distribution by a qualified trust may constitute a total distribution payable with respect to an employee even though the trust retains amounts attributable to the funding of medical benefits described in section 401(h).

(7) The capital gains treatment provided by section 402(a)(2) and subparagraph (6) of this paragraph is not applicable to distributions paid to a distributee to the extent such distributions are attributable to contributions made on behalf of an employee while he was a self-employed individual in the business with respect to which the plan was established. For the taxation of such amounts, see §1.72-18. For the rules for determining the amount attributable to contributions on behalf of an employee while he was self-employed, see paragraphs (b)(4) and (c)(2) of such section.

(8) For purposes of this section, the term "employee" includes a self-employed individual who is treated as an employee under section 401(c)(1), and paragraph (b) of §1.401-10, and the term "employer" means the person treated as the employer of such individual under section 401(c)(4).

(b) *Distributions including securities of the employer corporation.*— (1) *In general.*—(i) If a trust described in section 401(a) which is exempt under section 501(a) makes a distribution to a distributee, and such distribution includes securities of the employer corporation, the amount of any net unrealized appreciation in such securities shall be excluded from the distributee's income in the year of such distribution to the following extent:

(a) If the distribution constitutes a total distribution to which the rules of paragraph (a)(6) of this section are applicable, the amount to be excluded is the entire net unrealized appreciation attributable to that part of the total distribution which consists of securities of the employer corporation; and

(b) If the distribution is other than a total distribution to which paragraph (a)(6) of this section is applicable, the amount to be excluded is that portion of the net unrealized appreciation in the securities of the employer corporation which is attributable to the amount considered to be contributed by the employee to the purchase of such securities.

The amount of net unrealized appreciation which is excludable under the regulations of (a) and (b) of this subdivision shall not be included in the basis of the securities in the hands of the distributee at the time of distribution for purposes of determining gain or loss on their subsequent disposition. In the case of a total distribution the amount of net unrealized appreciation which is not included in the basis of the securities in the hands of the distributee at the time of distribution shall be considered as a gain from the sale or exchange of a capital asset held for more than six months to the extent that such appreciation is realized in a subsequent taxable transaction. However, if the net gain realized by the distributee in a subsequent taxable transaction exceeds the amount of the net unrealized appreciation at the time of distribution, such excess shall constitute a long-term or short-term capital gain depending upon the holding period of the securities in the hands of the distributee.

(ii) For purposes of section 402(a) and of this section, the term "securities" means only shares of stock and bonds or debentures issued by a corporation with interest coupons or in registered form, and the term "securities of the employer corporation" includes securities of a parent or subsidiary corporation (as defined in subsections (e) and (f) of section 425) of the employer corporation.

(2) *Determination of net unrealized appreciation.*—(i) The amount of net unrealized appreciation in securities of the employer corporation which are distributed by the trust is the excess of the market value of such securities at the time of distribution over the cost or other basis of such securities to the trust. Thus, if a distribution consists in part of securities which have appreciated in value and in part of securities which have depreciated in value, the net unrealized appreciation shall be considered to consist of the net increase in value of all of the securities included in the distribution. For this purpose, two or more distributions made by a trust to a distributee in a single taxable year of the distributee shall be treated as a single distribution.

(ii) For the purpose of determining the net unrealized appreciation on a distributed security of the employer corporation, the cost or other basis of such security to the trust shall be computed in accordance with whichever of the following rules is applicable:

(a) If a security was earmarked for the account of a particular employee at the time it was purchased by or contributed to the trust so that the cost or other basis of such security to the trust is reflected in the account of such employee, such cost or other basis shall be used.

(b) If as of the close of each taxable year of the trust (or other specified period of time not in excess of 12 consecutive calendar months) the trust allocates among the accounts of participating employees all securities acquired by the trust during the period (exclusive of securities unallocated under a plan providing for allocation in whole shares only), the cost or other basis to the trust of any securities allocated as of the close of a particular allocation period

shall be the average cost or other basis to the trust of all securities of the same type which were purchased or otherwise acquired by the trust during such allocation period. For purposes of determining the average cost to the trust of securities included in a subsequent allocation, the actual cost to the trust of the securities unallocated as of the close of a prior allocation period shall be deemed to be the average cost or other basis to the trust of securities of the same type allocated as of the close of such prior allocation period.

(c) In a case where neither (a) nor (b) of this subdivision is applicable, if the trust fund, or a specified portion thereof, is invested exclusively in one particular type of security of the employer corporation, and if during the period the distributee participated in the plan none of such securities has been sold except for the purpose of paying benefits under the trust or for the purpose of enabling the trustee to obtain funds with which to exercise rights which have accrued to the trust, the cost or other basis to the trust of all securities distributed to such distributee shall be the total amount credited to the account of such distributee (or such portion thereof as was available for investment in such securities) reduced by the amount available for investment but uninvested on the date of distribution. If at the time of distribution to a particular distributee a portion of the amount credited to his account is forfeited, appropriate adjustment shall be made with respect thereto in determining the cost or other basis to the trust of the securities distributed.

(d)(1) In all other cases, there shall be used the average cost (or other basis) to the trust of all securities of the employer corporation of the type distributed to the distributee which the trust has on hand at the time of the distribution, or which the trust had on hand on a specified inventory date which date does not precede the date of distribution by more than twelve calendar months. If a distribution includes securities of the employer corporation of more than one type, the average cost (or other basis) to the trust of each type of security distributed shall be determined. The average cost to the trust of securities of the employer corporation on hand on a specified inventory date (or on hand at the time of distribution) shall be computed on the basis of their actual cost, considering the securities most recently purchased to be those on hand, or by means of a moving average calculated by subtracting from the total cost of securities on hand immediately preceding a particular sale or distribution an amount computed by multiplying the number of securities sold or distributed by the average cost of all securities on hand preceding such sale or distribution.

(2) These methods of computing average cost may be illustrated by the following examples:

Example (1). A, a distributee who makes his income tax returns on the basis of a calendar year, receives on August 1, 1954, in a total distribution, to which paragraph (a)(6) of this section is applicable, ten shares of class D stock of the employer corporation. On July 1, 1954 (the specified inventory date of the trust), the trust had on hand 80 shares of class D stock. The average cost of the 10 shares distributed, on the basis of the actual cost method, is $100 computed as follows:

Shares	Purchase date	Cost per share	Total cost
20	June 24, 1954	$101	$2,020
40	Jan. 10, 1953	102	4,080
20	Oct. 20, 1952	95	1,900
80			$8,000

Example (2). B, a distributee who makes his income tax returns on the basis of a calendar year, receives on October 31, 1954, in a total distribution, to which paragraph (a)(6) of this section is applicable, 20 shares of class E stock of the employer corporation. The specified inventory date of the trust is the last day of each calendar year. The trust had on hand on December 31, 1952, 1,000 shares of class E stock of the employer corporation. During the calendar year 1953 the trust distributed to four distributees a total of 100 shares of such stock and acquired, through a number of purchases, a total of 120 shares. The average cost of the 20 shares distributed to B, on the basis of the moving average method, is $52 computed as follows:

	Shares	Total cost	Average cost
On hand Dec. 31, 1952	1,000	$50,000	$50
Distributed during 1953 at average cost of $50	100	5,000	. . .
	900	45,000	. . .
Purchased during 1953 . . .	120	8,040	. . .
On hand Dec. 31, 1953	1,020	53,040	52

(3) *Unrealized appreciation attributable to employee contributions.*— In any case in which it is necessary to determine the amount of net

unrealized appreciation in securities of the employer corporation which is attributable to contributions made by an employee:

(i) The cost or other basis of the securities to the trust and the amount of net unrealized appreciation shall first be determined in accordance with the regulations in subparagraph (2) of this paragraph (b);

(ii) The amount contributed by the employee to the purchase of the securities shall be solely the portion of his actual contributions to the trust properly allocable to such securities, and shall not include any part of the increment in the trust fund expended in the purchase of the securities;

(iii) The amount of net unrealized appreciation in the securities distributed which is attributable to the contributions of the employee shall be that proportion of the net unrealized appreciation determined under the regulations of subparagraph (2) of this paragraph which the contributions of the employee properly allocable to such securities bear to the cost or other basis to the trust of the securities;

(iv) If a distribution consists solely of securities of the employer corporation, the contributions of the employee expended in the purchase of such securities shall be allocated to the securities

distributed in a manner consistent with the principles set forth in subparagraph (2) (ii) (*a*), (*b*), (*c*), or (*d*) of this paragraph, whichever is applicable. Thus, the amount of the employee's contribution which can be identified as having been expended in the purchase of a particular security shall be allocated to such security, and the amount of such contribution which cannot be so identified shall be allocated ratably among the securities distributed. If a distribution consists in part of securities of the employer corporation and in part of cash or other property, appropriate allocation of a portion of the employee's contribution to such cash or other property shall be made unless such allocation is inconsistent with the terms of the plan or trust.

(v) The application of this subparagraph may be illustrated by the following example:

Example. A trust distributes ten shares of stock issued by the employer corporation each of which has an average cost to the trust of $100, consisting of employee contributions in the amount of $60 and employer contributions in the amount of $40, and on the date of distribution has a fair market value of $180. The portion of the net unrealized appreciation attributable to the contributions of the employee with respect to each of the shares of stock is $48 computed as follows:

(1)	Value of one share of stock on distribution date	$180
(2)	Employee contributions	60
(3)	Employer contributions	40
(4)	Total contributions	100
(5)	Net unrealized appreciation	80
(6)	Portion of net unrealized appreciation attributable to employee contributions, 60/100 (amount of employee contributions (item 2) over total contributions (item 4) of $80 (item 5))	48

(vi) For the purpose of determining gain or loss to the distributee in the year or years in which any share of stock referred to in the example in subdivision (v) of this subparagraph is sold or otherwise

disposed of in a taxable transaction, the basis of each such share in the hands of the distributee at the time of the distribution by the trust will be $132 computed as follows:

(*a*)	Employee contributions	$60
(*b*)	Employer contributions (taxable as ordinary income in the year the securities were distributed)	40
(*c*)	Portion of net unrealized appreciation attributable to employer contributions (item (5) minus item (6)) (taxable as ordinary income in the year the securities were distributed)	32
(*d*)	Basis of stock	132

(4) *Change in exempt status of trust.*—For principles applicable in making appropriate adjustments if the trust was not exempt for one or more years before the year of distribution, see paragraph (a) of this section.

(c) *Certain distributions by United States to nonresident alien individuals.*—(1) This paragraph applies to a distribution—

(i) Which is made by the United States under a pension plan described in section 401(a);

(ii) Which is made in respect of services performed by an employee of the United States; and

(iii) Which is received by, or made available to, a nonresident alien individual (including a nonresident alien individual who is a beneficiary of a deceased employee) during a taxable year beginning after December 31, 1959. The amount of such a distribution that is includible in the gross income of the nonresident alien individual under section 402(a)(1) or (2) shall not exceed an amount which bears the same ratio to the amount which would be includible in gross income if it were not for this paragraph, as—

(*a*) The aggregate basic salary paid by the United States to the employee for his services in respect of which the distribution is being made, reduced by the amount of such basic salary which was not includible in the employee's gross income by reason of being from sources without the United States, bears to

(*b*) The aggregate basic salary paid by the United States to the employee for his services in respect of which the distribution is being made.

See section 402(a)(4). See, also, paragraph (a) of this section for rules relating to the amount that is includible in gross income under

section 402(a)(1) or (2) in the case of a distribution under a pension plan described in section 401(a).

(2) For purposes of applying section 402(a)(4) and this paragraph to distributions under the Civil Service Retirement Act (5 U.S.C. 2251), the term "basic salary" shall have the meaning provided in section 1(d) of such Act. In applying section 402(a)(4) and this paragraph to distributions under any other qualified pension plan of the United States, such term shall have a similar meaning. Thus, for example, "basic salary" does not, in any case, include bonuses, allowances, or overtime pay.

(3) The rules in this paragraph may be illustrated by the following examples:

Example (1). A, a retired employee of the United States who performed all of his services for the United States in a foreign country, receives, in respect of such services, a monthly pension of $200 under the Civil Service Retirement Act (a pension plan described in section 401(a)). A received an aggregate basic salary for his services for the United States of $100,000. A was a nonresident alien individual during the whole of his employment with the United States and, therefore, his basic salary from the United States was not includible in his gross income by reason of being from sources without the United States. A would be required, under section 72 but without regard to section 402(a)(4) and this paragraph, to include $60 of each monthly pension payment in his gross income. The amount that is includible in A's gross income under section 402(a)(1) with respect to the monthly payments received during taxable years beginning after December 31, 1959, and while A is a nonresident alien individual, is computed as follows:

(i)	Amount of distribution includible in gross income under section 72 without regard to section 402(a)(4)	$60
(ii)	Aggregate basic salary for services for United States	100,000
(iii)	Aggregate basic salary for services for United States reduced by amount of such salary not includible in A's gross income by reason of being from sources without the United States	0
(iv)	Amount includible in A's gross income under section 402(a)(1) ((iii) ÷ (ii) × (i), or $0/$100,000 × $60)	0

Example (2). B, a retired employee of the United States who performed services for the United States both in a foreign country and in the United States, receives, in respect of such services, a monthly pension of $240 under the Civil Service Retirement Act. B received an aggregate basic salary for his services for the United

States of $120,000; $80,000 of which was for his services performed in the United States, and $40,000 of which was for his services performed in the foreign country. B was a nonresident alien individual during the whole of his employment with the United States and, consequently, the $40,000 basic salary for his services performed in the foreign country was not includible in his gross income by reason of being from sources without the United States. B would be required, under section 72 but without regard to section 402(a)(4) and this paragraph, to include $165 of each monthly pension in his gross

(i)	Amount of distribution includible in gross income under section 72 without regard to section 402(a)(4)	$165
(ii)	Aggregate basic salary for services for United States	120,000
(iii)	Aggregate basic salary for services for United States reduced by amount of such salary not includible in B's gross income by reason of being from sources without the United States ($120,000 – $40,000)	80,000
(iv)	Amount includible in B's gross income under section 402(a)(1) ((iii) ÷ (ii) × (i), or $80,000/$120,000 × $165)	$110

income. The amount that is includible in B's gross income under section 402(a)(1) with respect to the monthly payments received during taxable years beginning after December 31, 1959, and while B is a nonresident alien individual, is computed as follows:

(d) *Salary reduction, cash or deferred arrangements.*—(1) *Inclusion in income.*—Whether a contribution to an exempt trust or plan described in section 401(a) or 403(a) is made by the employer or the employee is determined on the basis of the particular facts and circumstances of each case. Nevertheless, an amount contributed to a plan or trust will, except as otherwise provided under paragraph (d)(2) of this section, be treated as contributed by the employee if it was contributed at the employee's election, even though the election was made before the year in which the amount was earned by the employee or before the year in which the amount became currently available to the employee. Any amount treated as contributed by the employee is includible in the gross income of the employee for the year in which the amount would have been received by the employee but for the election. Thus, for example, amounts contributed to an exempt trust or plan by reason of a salary reduction agreement under a cash or deferred arrangement are treated as received by the employee when they would have been received by the employee but for the election to defer. Accordingly, they are includible in the gross income of the employee for that year (except as provided under paragraph (d)(2) of this section). See § 1.401(k)-1(a)(3)(iv) and (2)(iv) for the meaning of currently available and cash or deferred arrangement, respectively.

(2) *Amounts not included in income.*—(i) *Qualified cash or deferred arrangement.*—Elective contributions as defined in § 1.401(k)-6 for a plan year made by an employer on behalf of an employee pursuant to a cash or deferred election under a qualified cash or deferred arrangement, as defined in § 1.401(k)-1(a)(4)(i), are not treated as received by or distributed to the employee or as employee contributions. For plan years beginning after December 31, 1992, whether a cash or deferred election is made under a qualified cash or deferred arrangement is determined without regard to the special rules for certain collectively bargained plans contained in § 1.401(k)-1(a)(5)(iv)(B). As a result, elective contributions under these plans are treated as employee contributions for purposes of this section if the cash or deferred arrangement does not satisfy the actual deferral percentage test of section 401(k)(3) or otherwise fails to be a qualified cash or deferred arrangement.

(ii) *Matching contributions.*—Matching contributions described in § 1.401(m)-1(a)(2) and section 401(m)(4) are not treated as contributed by an employee merely because they are made by the employer as a result of an employee's election.

(iii) *Effect of certain one-time elections.*—Amounts contributed to an exempt plan or trust described in section 401(a) or 403(a) pursuant to the one-time irrevocable employee election to participate in a plan described in § 1.401(k)-1(a)(3)(v) are not treated as contributed by an employee. Similarly, amounts contributed to an exempt plan or trust described in section 401(a) or 403(a) in which self-employed individuals may participate pursuant to the one-time irrevocable election described in § 1.401(k)-1(a)(3)(v)(B) are not treated as contributed by an employee.

(3) *Effective date and transition rules.*—(i) *Effective date.*—In the case of a plan or trust that does not include a salary reduction or cash or deferred arrangement in existence on June 27, 1974, this paragraph applies to taxable years ending after that date.

(ii) *Transition rule for cash or deferred arrangements in existence on June 27, 1974.*—(A) *General rule.*—In the case of a plan or trust that includes a salary reduction or a cash or deferred arrangement in existence on June 27, 1974, this paragraph applies to plan years beginning after December 31, 1979 (or, in the case of a pre-ERISA money purchase plan, as defined in § 1.401(k)-6, plan years beginning after July 18, 1984). For plan years beginning prior to January 1, 1980 (or, in the case of a pre-ERISA money purchase plan, plan years beginning before July 19, 1984), the taxable year of inclusion in gross income of the employee of any amount so contributed by the employer to the trust is determined in a manner consistent with Rev. Rul. 56-497, 1956-2 CB 284, Rev. Rul. 63-180, 1963-2 CB 189, and Rev. Rul. 68-89, 1968-1 CB 402.

(B) *Meaning of cash or deferred arrangement in existence on June 27, 1974.*—A cash or deferred arrangement is considered as in existence on June 27, 1974, if, on or before that date, it was reduced to writing and adopted by the employer (including, in the case of a corporate employer, formal approval by the employer's board of directors and, if required, shareholders), even though no amounts had been contributed pursuant to the terms of the arrangement as of that date.

(iii) *Reasonable interpretation for plan years beginning after 1979 and before 1992.*—For plan years beginning after December 31, 1979 (or in the case of a pre-ERISA money purchase plan, plan years beginning after July 18, 1984) and before January 1, 1992, a reasonable interpretation of the rules set forth in section 401(k) (as in effect during those years) may be relied upon to determine whether contributions were made under a qualified cash or deferred arrangement.

(iv) *Special rule for collectively bargained plans.*—For plan years beginning before January 1, 1993, a nonqualified cash or deferred arrangement will be treated as satisfying section 401(k)(3) solely for purposes of paragraph (d)(2)(i) of this section if it is part of a plan (or portion of a plan) that automatically satisfies section 401(a)(4) under § 1.401(k)-1(a)(5)(iv)(B), relating to certain collectively bargained plans.

(v) *Special rule for governmental plans.*—For plan years beginning before the later of January 1, 1996, or 90 days after the opening of the first legislative session beginning on or after January 1, 1996, of the governing body with authority to amend the plan, if that body does not meet continuously, in the case of governmental plans described in section 414(d), a nonqualified cash or deferred arrangement will be treated as satisfying section 401(k)(3) solely for purposes of paragraph (d)(2)(i) of this section if it is part of a plan adopted by a state or local government before May 6, 1986. For purposes of this paragraph (d)(3)(v), the term *governing body with authority to amend the plan* means the legislature, board, commission, council, or other governing body with authority to amend the plan.

(e) *Medical, accident, etc. benefits paid from a qualified pension, annuity, profitsharing, or stock bonus plan.*—(1) *Payment of premiums.*—(i) *General rule.*—Except as provided in paragraph (e)(1)(iii) of this section, a payment made from a qualified trust that is a premium for accident or health insurance (including a qualified long-term care insurance contract under section 7702B) constitutes a distribution under section 402(a) to the participant for whose benefit the premium is charged. The amount of the distribution equals the amount of the premium charged against the participant's benefits under the plan. If a defined contribution plan pays these premiums from a current year contribution or forfeiture that has not been allocated to a participant's account, then the amount of the premium for each participant is treated as first being allocated to the participant and then charged against the participant's benefits under the plan, so that the amount of the distribution is treated in the same manner as determined under the preceding sentence. Except as provided in paragraphs (e)(2) and (e)(3) of this section, a distribution described in this paragraph (e)(1) is not excludable from gross income.

(ii) *Treatment of amounts received through accident or health insurance.*—To the extent that the payment of a premium for accident or health insurance constitutes a distribution under this paragraph (e)(1), amounts received through accident or health insurance are neither paid by the employer nor attributable to contributions by the employer that are excludable from the gross income of the employee. Accordingly, to the extent the premium for accident or health insurance constitutes a distribution under this paragraph (e)(1), amounts received through the accident or health insurance for personal injuries or sickness are excludable from gross income under section 104(a)(3) and are not treated as distributions from the plan. If those amounts are paid to the plan instead of to the employee, those amounts are treated as having been paid to the employee and then contributed by the employee to the plan (and must satisfy the qualification requirements applicable to employee contributions).

(iii) *Exception for disability insurance that replaces retirement contributions.*—The rules of paragraph (e)(1)(i) of this section do not apply to the payment made from a qualified trust that is a premium paid to an insurance company for a contract providing for payment of benefits to be made to the trust in the event of an employee's inability to continue employment with the employer due to disability, provided that the payment of benefits with respect to the employee's account for each year does not exceed the reasonable expectation of the annual contributions that would have been made to the plan on the employee's behalf for the period of disability within that year, reduced by any other contributions made on the employee's behalf for the period of disability within that year. The payment of premiums described in the preceding sentence is not treated as a distribution under section 402(a), but instead constitutes incidental accident or health insurance as provided in § 1.401-1(b)(1)(ii). The Commissioner may issue rules of general applicability in revenue rulings, notices, or other guidance published in the Internal Revenue Bulletin further describing the tax treatment of disability coverage described in this paragraph (e)(1)(iii).

(2) *Medical benefits for retired employees provided under an account described in section 401(h).*—The payment of medical benefits under a pension or annuity plan from an account described in section 401(h) is treated in the same manner as a payment of accident or health benefits attributable to employer contributions, or employer-provided coverage under an accident or health plan. See § 1.401-14(a) for the definition of medical benefits described in section 401(h). Accordingly, amounts applied for the payment of accident or health benefits, or for the payment of accident or health coverage, from a section 401(h) account are not includible in the gross income of the participant on whose behalf such contributions are made to the extent they are excludible from gross income under section 104, 105, or 106.

(3) *Distributions to eligible retired public safety officers.*—See section 402(l) (and any guidance issued under section 402(l)) for a limited exclusion from gross income for distributions used to pay for certain accident or health premiums (including premiums for qualified long-term care insurance contracts). This limited exclusion applies to eligible retired public safety officers, as defined in section 402(l)(4)(B).

(4) *Effect of distribution of insurance premiums on plan qualification.*—See § 1.401-1(b)(1) for rules concerning the types and amount of medical coverage and benefits that are permitted to be provided under a plan that is part of a trust described in section 401(a). For example, § 1.401-1(b)(1)(ii) provides that a profit-sharing plan is primarily a plan of deferred compensation, but the amounts allocated to the account of a participant may be used to provide incidental accident or health insurance for the participant and the participant's family. See also section 401(k)(2)(B) for certain restrictions on the distribution of elective contributions.

(5) *Applicability to beneficiaries and alternate payees.*—This paragraph (e) applies to the payment of premiums charged against the benefits of a beneficiary or an alternate payee in the same manner as the payment of premiums charged against the account of a participant.

(6) *Examples.*—The provisions of this paragraph (e) are illustrated by the following examples:

Example 1. (i) *Facts.* Employer A sponsors a profit-sharing plan qualified under section 401(a). The plan provides solely for non-elective employer profit-sharing contributions. The plan's trustee enters into a contract with a third-party insurance carrier to provide health insurance for certain plan participants. The insurance contract provides for the payment of medical expenses incurred by those participants. The plan limits the amounts used to provide medical benefits to comply with the incidental benefit rules. The trustee makes monthly payments of $1,000 to pay the premiums due for Participant P's health insurance and Participant P's account balance is reduced by $1,000 at the time of each premium payment. In June 2015, Participant P is admitted to the hospital for covered medical care, and in July 2015, the health insurer pays the hospital $5,000 for the medical care provided to Participant P in June.

(ii) *Conclusion.* Under paragraph (e)(1) of this section, each of the trustee's payments of $1,000 constitutes a taxable distribution under section 402(a) to Participant P on the date of each payment. The amount of these distributions may constitute payments for medical care under section 213. The $5,000 payment to the hospital is excludable from Participant P's gross income under section 104(a)(3) and is not treated as a distribution from the plan.

Example 2. (i) *Facts.* Employer B sponsors a profit-sharing plan qualified under section 401(a). The plan provides for elective contributions described in section 401(k) and matching contributions as well as non-elective employer profit-sharing contributions. The plan does not provide that a disabled participant's compensation for purposes of determining plan contributions includes amounts that the participant would have received in the absence of the disability, and accordingly Employer B does not make any contributions to the plan for the benefit of a disabled employee for the period of disabil-

ity. The plan's trustee enters into a contract with a third-party insurance carrier to provide disability insurance for plan participants who elect to be covered under the insurance contract. The insurance contract provides for the payment of an amount to the trustee on a participant's behalf during the period of the participant's disability. Amounts to be paid to the trustee from the insurance contract with respect to a participant are equal to the sum of the elective, matching, and non-elective employer profit-sharing contributions that would have been made on the participant's behalf during the participant's disability (based on the participant's rate of compensation before becoming disabled) with the payments to continue for the duration of the disability until age 65 (or 5 years after the participant became disabled, if later). Participant Q elects to be covered under the insurance contract, and the trustee makes the periodic premium payments out of the account balance of Participant Q. In June 2015, Participant Q becomes disabled. During the period Participant Q is absent from employment due to disability, the insurer pays the trust the amount of the elective, matching, and non-elective employer profit-sharing contributions that would have been made to the trust with respect to Participant Q had Participant Q not been disabled. The amount of the premiums for the insurance contract satisfies the limitations on incidental benefits under § 1.401-1(b)(1)(ii).

(ii) *Conclusion.* The payment of premiums from the trust is described in paragraph (e)(1)(iii) of this section. Accordingly, none of the premium payments under the contract constitute a distribution under section 402(a) to Participant Q. Further, amounts paid from the insurance contract to the trust also do not constitute a distribution to Participant Q. However, when Participant Q's account balance is distributed from the trust, the distribution will be subject to taxation in the year of distribution in accordance with the rules in section 402.

(7) *Effective/applicability date.*—This paragraph (e) applies for taxable years beginning on or after January 1, 2015. [Reg. § 1.402(a)-1.]

☐ [*T.D. 6203*, 9-24-56. *Amended by T.D. 6485*, 7-29-60; *T.D. 6497*, 10-19-60; *T.D. 6676*, 9-16-63; *T.D. 6717*, 3-27-64; *T.D. 6722*, 4-13-64; *T.D. 6823*, 5-5-65; *T.D. 6885*, 6-1-66; *T.D. 6887*, 6-23-66; *T.D. 8217*, 8-5-88; *T.D. 8357*, 8-8-91; *T.D. 8581*, 12-22-94; *T.D. 9169*, 12-28-2004; *T.D. 9223*, 8-26-2005; *T.D. 9665*, 5-9-2014 (corrected 7-3-2014) and T.D. 9849*, 3-11-2019.]

[Reg. § 1.402(a)(5)-1T]

§ 1.402(a)(5)-1T. Rollovers of partial distributions from qualified trusts and annuities (Temporary).—

Q-1: Can an employee or the surviving spouse of a deceased employee roll over to an individual retirement account or annuity, described in section 408(a) or (b), the taxable portion of a partial distribution from a qualified trust described in section 401(a), a qualified plan described in section 403(a), or a tax-sheltered annuity contract under section 403(b)?

A-1: Yes. For distributions made after July 18, 1984, the taxable portion of a partial distribution may be rolled over within 60 days of the distribution to an individual retirement account or annuity.

Q-2: Are there special requirements applicable to rollovers of partial distributions?

A-2: Yes. Section 402(a)(5)(D)(i) specifies that no part of a partial distribution may be rolled over unless the distribution is equal to at least 50 percent of the balance to the credit of the employee in the contract or plan immediately before the distribution, and the distribution is not one of a series of periodic payments. For purposes of this section, the balance to the credit of an employee does not include any accumulated deductible employee contributions (within the meaning of section 72(o)). In addition, in calculating the balance to the credit for purposes of the 50 percent test, qualified plans are not to be aggregated with other qualified plans and tax-sheltered annuity contracts are not to be aggregated with other tax-sheltered annuity contracts. Also, in applying the 50 percent test to a surviving spouse, the balance to the credit is the maximum amount the spouse is entitled to receive under the plan or contract, rather than the total balance to the credit of the employee. The rollover of a partial distribution may result in adverse tax consequences; see section 402(a)(5)(D)(iii) and (iv).

Q-3: Are there any other requirements applicable to rollovers of partial distribution?

A-3: Yes. Section 402(a)(5)(D)(i)(III) requires the employee to elect, in conformance with Treasury regulations, to treat a contribution of a partial distribution to an IRA as a rollover contribution. An election is made by designating, in writing, to the trustee or issuer of the IRA at the time of the contribution that the contribution is to be treated as a rollover contribution. This requirement of a written designation to the trustee or issuer of the IRA is effective for contributions paid to the trustee or issuer of the IRA after March 20, 1986. For contributions paid to the trustee or issuer before March 21, 1986, an election is made by computing the individual's income tax liability on the income tax return for the taxable year in which the distribution occurs in a manner consistent with not including the distribution (or portion thereof) in gross income. Both such elections are irrevocable, except that an election made on an income tax return filed before March 21, 1986, is revocable.

Q-4: Does the election requirement apply to rollovers of qualified total distributions or rollover contributions described in section 402(a)(5) or (7), 403(a)(4), 403(b)(8), 405(d)(3), or 408(d)(3) to individual retirement accounts and annuities (IRAs)?

A-4: Yes. No amounts may be treated as a rollover contribution to an IRA under section 402(a)(5), 402(a)(7), 403(a)(4), 403(b)(8), 405(d)(3) (as amended by section 491(c) of the TRA of 1984), or 408(d)(3) unless the requirements described in Q&A 3 of this section are satisfied. Thus, once any portion of a total distribution is irrevocably designated as a rollover contribution, such distribution is not taxable under section 402 or 403 and, therefore, is not eligible for the special capital gains and separate tax treatment under section 402(a) and (e). Election requirements for rollover contributions to IRAs described in this Q&A 4 are subject to the same effective date rules set forth in Q&A 3. [Temporary Reg. § 1.402(a)(5)-1T.]

☐ [T.D. 8073, 1-29-86.]

[Reg. § 1.402(b)-1]

§ 1.402(b)-1. Treatment of beneficiary of trust not exempt under section 501 (a).—(a) *Taxation by reason of employer contributions made after August 1, 1969.*—(1) *Taxation of contributions.*—Section 402 (b) provides rules for taxing an employee on contributions made on his behalf by an employer to an employees' trust that is not exempt under section 501(a). In general, any such contributions made after August 1, 1969, during a taxable year of the employer which ends within or with a taxable year of the trust for which it is not so exempt shall be included as compensation in the gross income of the employee for his taxable year during which the contribution is made, but only to the extent that the employee's interest in such contribution is substantially vested at the time the contribution is made. The preceding sentence does not apply to contracts referred to in the transitional rule of paragraph (d)(1)(ii) or (iii) of this section. For the definition of the terms "substantially vested" and "substantially nonvested" see § 1.83-3(b).

(2) *Determination of amount of employer contributions.*—If, for an employee, the actual amount of employer contributions referred to in paragraph (a)(1) of this section for any taxable year of the employee is not determinable or for any other reason is not known, then, except as set forth in rules prescribed by the Commissioner in revenue rulings, notices, or other guidance published in the Internal Revenue Bulletin (see § 601.601(d)(2)(ii)(b) of this chapter), such amount shall be either—

(i) The excess of—

(A) The amount determined as of the end of such taxable year in accordance with the formula described in § 1.403(b)-1(d)(4), as it appeared in the April 1, 2006, edition of 26 CFR Part 1; over

(B) The amount determined as of the end of the prior taxable year in accordance with the formula described in paragraph (a)(2)(i)(A) of this section; or

(ii) The amount determined under any other method utilizing recognized actuarial principles that are consistent with the provisions of the plan under which such contributions are made and the method adopted by the employer for funding the benefits under the plan.

(b) *Taxability of employee when rights under nonexempt trust change from nonvested to vested.*—(1) *In general.*—If rights of an employee under a trust become substantially vested during a taxable year of the employee (ending after August 1, 1969), and a taxable year of the trust for which it is not exempt under section 501(a) ends with or within such year, the value of the employee's interest in the trust on the date of such change shall be included in his gross income for such taxable year, to the extent provided in paragraph (b) (3) of this section. When an employees' trust that was exempt under section 501 (a) ceases to be so exempt, an employee shall include in his gross income only amounts contributed to the trust during a taxable year of the employer that ends within or with a taxable year of the trust in which it is not so exempt (to the same extent as if the trust had not been so exempt in all prior taxable years).

(2) *Value of an employee's interest in a trust.*—(i) For purposes of this section, the term "the value of an employee's interest in a trust" means the amount of the employee's beneficial interest in the net fair market value of all the assets in the trust as of any date on which some or all of the employee's interest in the trust becomes substantially vested. The net fair market value of all the assets in the trust is the total amount of the fair market values (determined without regard to any lapse restriction, as defined in § 1.83-3(h)) of all the assets in the trust, less the amount of all the liabilities (including taxes) to which such assets are subject or which the trust has as-

sumed (other than the rights of any employee in such assets), as of the date on which some or all of the employee's interest in the trust becomes substantially vested.

(ii) If a separate account in a trust for the benefit of two or more employees is not maintained for each employee, the value of the employee's interest in such trust is determined in accordance with rules prescribed by the Commissioner under the authority in paragraph (a)(2) of this section.

(iii) If there is no valuation of a nonexempt trust's assets on the date of the change referred to in paragraph (b)(1) of this section, the value of an employee's interest in such trust is determined by taking the weighted average of the values on the nearest valuation dates occurring before and after the date of such change. The average is to be determined in the manner described in § 20.2031-2(b)(1).

(3) *Extent to which value of an employee's interest is includible in gross income.*—For purposes of paragraph (b)(1) of this section, there shall be included in the gross income of the employee for his taxable year in which his rights under the trust become substantially vested only that portion of the value of his interest in the trust that is attributable to contributions made by the employer after August 1, 1969. However, the preceding sentence shall not apply—

(i) To the extent such value is attributable to a contribution made on the date of such change, and

(ii) To the extent such value is attributable to contributions described in paragraph (d)(1)(ii) or iii) of this section (relating to contributions made pursuant to a binding contract entered into before April 22, 1969).

For purposes of this paragraph (3), if the value of an employee's interest in a trust which is attributable to contributions made by the employer after August 1, 1969, is not known, it shall be deemed to be an amount which bears the same ratio to the value of the employee's interest as the contributions made by the employer after such date bear to the total contributions made by the employer.

(4) *Partial vesting.*—For purposes of paragraph (b)(1) of this section, if only part of an employee's interest in the trust becomes substantially vested during any taxable year, then only the corresponding part of the value of the employee's interest in such trust is includible in his gross income for such year. In such a case, it is first necessary to compute, under the rules in paragraphs (b)(1) and (2) of this section, the amount that would be includible if his entire interest had changed to a substantially vested interest during such year. The amount that is includible under this paragraph (4) is the amount determined under the preceding sentence multiplied by the percent of the employee's interest which became substantially vested during the taxable year.

(5) *Basis.*—The basis of any employee's interest in a trust to which this section applies shall be increased by the amount included in his gross income under this section.

(6) *Treatment as owner of trust.*—In general, a beneficiary of a trust to which this section applies may not be considered to be the owner under subpart E, part I, subchapter J, chapter I of the Code of any portion of such trust which is attributable to contributions to such trust made by the employer after August 1, 1969, or to incidental contributions made by the employee after such date. However, where contributions made by the employee are not incidental when compared to contributions made by the employer, such beneficiary shall be considered to be the owner of the portion of the trust attributable to contributions made by the employee, if the applicable requirements of such subpart E are satisfied. For purposes of this paragraph (6), contributions made by an employee are not incidental when compared to contributions made by the employer if the employee's total contributions as of any date exceed the employer's total contributions on behalf of the employee as of such date.

(7) *Example.*—The provisions in this paragraph may be illustrated by the following example:

Example. On January 1, 1968 M corporation establishes an employees' trust, which is not exempt under section 501(a), for some of its employees, including A, reserving the right to discontinue contributions at any time. M corporation contributes $5,000 on A's behalf to the trust on February 1, 1968. At the time of contribution 50 percent of A's interest was substantially vested. On January 1, 1971, and January 1, 1974, M corporation makes additional $5,000 contributions to the trust on A's behalf. A's interest in the trust changed from a 50 percent substantially vested interest to a 100 percent substantially vested interest in the trust on December 31, 1974. Assume that the value of A's interest in the trust on December 31, 1974, which is attributable to employer contributions made after August 1, 1969, is calculated to be $11,000 under paragraph (b)(3) of this section. The amount includible in A's gross income for 1971 and 1974 is computed as follows:

—1971—

(i) Amount of M corporation's contribution made on January 1, 1971, to the trust which is includible in A's gross income under paragraph (b)(1) of this section (50% substantially vested interest in the trust times $5,000 contributions) $2,500

—1974—

(i) Amount of M corporation's contribution made on January 1, 1974, to the trust which is includible in A's gross income under paragraph (b)(1) of this section (50% substantially vested interest in the trust times $5,000 contribution) $2,500

(ii) Amount which would have been includible if A's entire interest had changed to a substantially vested interest (value of employee's interest in the trust attributable to employer contributions made after August 1, 1969) $11,000

(iii) Percent of A's interest that became substantially vested on December 31, 1974 . . . .   50%

(iv) Amount includible in A's gross income for 1974 in respect of his percentage change from a substantially nonvested to a substantially vested interest in the trust (50% of $11,000) $5,500

(v) Total amount includible in A's gross income for 1974 ((i) plus (iv)) $8,000

(c) *Taxation of distributions from trust not exempt under section 501(a).*—(1) *In general.*—Any amount actually distributed or made available to any distributee by an employees' trust in a taxable year in which it is not exempt under section 501(a) shall be taxable under section 72 (relating to annuities) to the distributee in the taxable year in which it is so distributed or made available. For taxable years beginning after December 31, 1963, such amounts may be taken into account in computations under sections 1301 through 1305 (relating to income averaging). If, for example, the distribution from such a trust consists of an annuity contract, the amount of the distribution shall be considered to be the entire value of the contract at the time of distribution. Such value is includible in the gross income of the distributee to the extent that such value exceeds the investment in the contract, determined by applying sections 72 and 101(b). The distributions by such a trust shall be taxed as provided in section 72 whether or not the employee's rights to the contributions become substantially vested beforehand. For rules relating to the treatment of employer contributions to a nonexempt trust as part of the consideration paid by the employee, see section 72(f). For rules relating to the treatment of the limited exclusion allowable under section 101(b)(2)(D) as additional consideration paid by the employee, see the regulations under that section.

(2) *Distributions before annuity starting date.*—Any amount distributed or made available to any distributee before the annuity starting date (as defined in section 72(c)(4)) by an employees' trust in a taxable year in which it is not exempt under section 501(a) shall be treated as distributed in the following order—

(i) First, from that portion of the employee's interest in the trust attributable to contributions made by the employer after August 1, 1969 (other than those referred to in paragraph (d)(1)(ii) or (iii) of this section) that has not been previously includible in the employee's gross income, to the extent that such a distribution is permitted under the trust (or the plan of which the trust is a part);

(ii) Second, from that portion of the employee's interest in the trust attributable to contributions made by the employer on or before August 1, 1969 (or contributions referred to in paragraph (d)(1)(ii) or (iii) of this section);

(iii) Third, from the remaining portion of the employee's interest in the trust attributable to contributions made by the employer.

If the employee has made contributions to the trust, amounts attributable thereto shall be treated as distributed prior to any amounts attributable to the employer's contributions, to the extent provided by the trust (or the plan of which the trust is a part). However, the portion of such amounts attributable to income earned on the employee's contributions made after August 1, 1969, shall be treated as distributed prior to any return of such contributions.

(d) *Taxation by reason of employer contributions made on or before August 1, 1969.*—(1) Except as provided in section 402(d) (relating to taxable years beginning before January 1, 1977), any contribution to a trust made by an employer on behalf of an employee—

(i) On or before August 1, 1969, or

(ii) After such date, pursuant to a binding contract (as defined in § 1.83-3(b)(2)) entered into before April 22, 1969, or

(iii) After August 1, 1969, pursuant to a written plan in which the employee participated on April 22, 1969, and under which the obligation of the employer on such date was essentially the same as under a binding written contract,

during a taxable year of the employer which ends within or with a taxable year of the trust for which the trust is not exempt under section 501(a) shall be included in income of the employee for his taxable year during which the contribution is made. If the employee's *beneficial interest* in the contribution is forfeitable at the time the contribution is made, even though his interest becomes nonforfeitable later the amount of such contribution is not required to be included in the income of the employee at the time his interest becomes nonforfeitable.

(2)(i) An employee's beneficial interest in the contribution is nonforfeitable, within the meaning of sections 402(b), 403(c), and 404(a)(5) prior to the amendments made thereto by the Tax Reform Act of 1969 and section 403(b), at the time the contribution is made if there is no contingency under the plan that may cause the employee to lose his rights in the contribution. Similarly, an employee's rights under an annuity contract purchased for him by his employer change from forfeitable to nonforfeitable rights within the meaning of section 403(d) prior to the repeal thereof by the Tax Reform Act of 1969 at that time when, for the first time, there is no contingency which may cause the employee to lose his rights under the contract. For example, if under the terms of a pension plan, an employee upon termination of his services before the retirement date, whether voluntarily or involuntarily, is entitled to a deferred annuity contract to be purchased with the employer's contributions made on his behalf, or is entitled to annuity payments which the trustee is obligated to make under the terms of the trust instrument based on the contributions made by the employer on his behalf, the employee's beneficial interest in such contributions is nonforfeitable.

(ii) On the other hand, if, under the terms of a pension plan, an employee will lose the right to any annuity purchased from, or to be provided by, contributions made by the employer if his services should be terminated before retirement, his beneficial interest in such contributions is forfeitable.

(iii) The mere fact that an employee may not live to the retirement date, or may live only a short period after the retirement date, and may not be able to enjoy the receipt of annuity or pension payments, does not make his beneficial interest in the contributions made by the employer on his behalf forfeitable. If the employer's contributions have been irrevocably applied to purchase an annuity contract for the employee, or if the trustee is obligated to use the employer's contributions to provide an annuity for the employee provided only that the employee is alive on the dates the annuity payments are due, the employee's rights in the employer's contributions are nonforfeitable. [Reg. § 1.402(b)-1.]

☐ [*T.D. 6203, 9-24-56. Amended by T.D. 6783, 12-23-64; T.D. 6885, 6-1-66; T.D. 7554, 7-21-78 and T.D. 9340, 7-23-2007.*]

[Reg. § 1.402(c)-1]

§ 1.402(c)-1. Taxability of beneficiary of certain foreign situs trusts.—Section 402(c) has the effect of treating for purposes of section 402, the distributions from a trust which at the time of the distribution is located outside the United States in the same manner as distributions from a trust which is located in the United States. If the trust would qualify for exemption from tax under section 501(a) except for the fact that it fails to comply with the provisions of paragraph (a)(3)(i) of § 1.401-1, which restricts qualification to trusts created or organized in the United States and maintained here, section 402(a) and § 1.402(a)-1 are applicable to the distributions from such a trust. Thus, for example, a total distribution from such a trust is entitled to the long-term capital gains treatment of section 402(a)(2), except in the case of a nonresident alien individual (see sections 871 and 1441 and the regulations thereunder). However, if the plan fails to meet any requirement of section 401 and the regulations thereunder in addition to paragraph (a)(3)(i) of § 1.401-1, section 402(b) and § 1.402(b)-1 are applicable to the distributions from such a trust. [Reg. § 1.402(c)-1.]

☐ [*T.D. 6203, 9-24-86.*]

[Reg. § 1.402(c)-2]

§ 1.402(c)-2. Eligible rollover distributions; questions and answers.—The following questions and answers relate to the rollover rules under section 402(c) of the Internal Revenue Code of 1986, as added by sections 521 and 522 of the Unemployment Compensation Amendments of 1992, Public Law 102-318, 106 Stat. 290 (UCA). For additional UCA guidance under sections 401(a)(31), 402(f), 403(b)(8) and (10), and 3405(c), see §§ 1.401(a)(31)-1, 1.402(f)-1, and 1.403(b)-7(b), and § 31.3405(c)-1 of this chapter, respectively.

LIST OF QUESTIONS

Q-1: What is the rule regarding distributions that may be rolled over to an eligible retirement plan?

Q-2: What is an *eligible retirement plan* and a *qualified plan*?

Q-3: What is an *eligible rollover distribution*?

Q-4: Are there other amounts that are not eligible rollover distributions?

Q-5: For purposes of determining whether a distribution is an eligible rollover distribution, how is it determined whether a series of payments is a series of substantially equal periodic payments over a period specified in section 402(c)(4)(A)?

Q-6: What types of variations in the amount of a payment cause the payment to be independent of a series of substantially equal periodic payments and thus not part of the series?

Q-7: When is a distribution from a plan a required minimum distribution under section 401(a)(9)?

Q-8: How are amounts that are not includible in gross income allocated for purposes of determining the required minimum distribution?

Q-9: What is a distribution of a plan loan offset amount and is it an eligible rollover distribution?

Q-10: What is a qualified plan distributed annuity contract, and is an amount paid under such a contract a distribution of the balance to the credit of the employee in a qualified plan for purposes of section 402(c)?

Q-11: If an eligible rollover distribution is paid to an employee, and the employee contributes all or part of the eligible rollover distribution to an eligible retirement plan within 60 days, is the amount contributed not currently includible in gross income?

Q-12: How does section 402(c) apply to a distributee who is not the employee?

Q-13: Must an employee's (or spousal distributee's) election to treat a contribution of an eligible rollover distribution to an individual retirement plan as a rollover contribution be irrevocable?

Q-14: How is the $5,000 death benefit exclusion under section 101(b) treated for purposes of determining the amount that is an eligible rollover distribution?

Q-15: May an employee (or spousal distributee) roll over more than the plan administrator determines to be an eligible rollover distribution using an assumption described in § 1.401(a)(31)-1, Q&A-18?

Q-16: Is a rollover from a qualified plan to an individual retirement account or individual retirement annuity treated as a rollover contribution for purposes of the one-year look-back rollover limitation of section 408(d)(3)(B)?

QUESTIONS AND ANSWERS

Q-1: What is the rule regarding distributions that may be rolled over to an eligible retirement plan?

A-1: (a) *General rule.* Under section 402(c), as added by UCA, any portion of a distribution from a qualified plan that is an eligible rollover distribution described in section 402(c)(4) may be rolled over to an eligible retirement plan described in section 402(c)(8)(B). For purposes of section 402(c) and this section, a rollover is either a direct rollover as described in § 1.401(a)(31)-1, Q&A-3 or a contribution of an eligible rollover distribution to an eligible retirement plan that satisfies the time period requirement in section 402(c)(3) and Q&A-11 of this section and the designation requirement described in Q&A-13 of this section. See Q&A-2 of this section for the definition of an eligible retirement plan and a qualified plan.

(b) *Related Internal Revenue Code provisions*—(1) *Direct rollover option.* Section 401(a)(31), added by UCA, requires qualified plans to provide a distributee of an eligible rollover distribution the option to elect to have the distribution paid directly to an eligible retirement plan in a direct rollover. See § 1.401(a)(31)-1 for further guidance concerning this direct rollover option.

(2) *Notice requirement.* Section 402(f) requires the plan administrator of a qualified plan to provide, within a reasonable time before making an eligible rollover distribution, a written explanation to the distributee of the distributee's right to elect a direct rollover and the withholding consequences of not making that election. The explanation also is required to provide certain other relevant information relating to the taxation of distributions. See § 1.402(f)-1 for guidance concerning the written explanation required under section 402(f).

(3) *Mandatory income tax withholding.* If a distributee of an eligible rollover distribution does not elect to have the eligible rollover distribution paid directly from the plan to an eligible retirement plan in a direct rollover under section 401(a)(31), the eligible rollover distribution is subject to 20-percent income tax withholding under section 3405(c). See § 31.3405(c)-1 of this chapter for provisions relating to the withholding requirements applicable to eligible rollover distributions.

(4) *Section 403(b) annuities.* See § 1.403(b)-7(b) for guidance concerning the direct rollover requirements for distributions from annuities described in section 403(b).

(c) *Effective date*—(1) *Statutory effective date.* Section 402(c), added by UCA, applies to eligible rollover distributions made on or after January 1, 1993, even if the event giving rise to the distribution occurred on or before January 1, 1993 (e.g. termination of the employee's employment with the employer maintaining the plan before January 1, 1993), and even if the eligible rollover distribution is part of a series of payments that began before January 1, 1993.

(2) *Regulatory effective date.* This section applies to any distribution made on or after October 19, 1995. For eligible rollover distributions made on or after January 1, 1993 and before October 19, 1995, § 1.402(c)-2T (as it appeared in the April 1, 1995 edition of 26 CFR part 1), applies. However, for any distribution made on or after January 1, 1993 but before October 19, 1995, any or all of the provisions of this section may be substituted for the corresponding provisions of § 1.402(c)-2T, if any.

Q-2: What is an *eligible retirement plan* and a *qualified plan*?

A-2: An eligible retirement plan, under section 402(c)(8)(B), means a qualified plan or an individual retirement plan. For purposes of section 402(c) and this section, a qualified plan is an employees' trust described in section 401(a) which is exempt from tax under section 501(a) or an annuity plan described in section 403(a). An individual retirement plan is an individual retirement account described in section 408(a) or an individual retirement annuity (other than an endowment contract) described in section 408(b).

Q-3: What is an *eligible rollover distribution*?

A-3: (a) *General rule.* Unless specifically excluded, an eligible rollover distribution means any distribution to an employee (or to a spousal distributee described in Q&A-12(a) of this section) of all or any portion of the balance to the credit of the employee in a qualified plan. Thus, except as specifically provided in Q&A-4(b) of this section, any amount distributed to an employee (or such a spousal distributee) from a qualified plan is an eligible rollover distribution, regardless of whether it is a distribution of a benefit that is protected under section 411(d)(6).

(b) *Exceptions.* An eligible rollover distribution does not include the following:

(1) Any distribution that is one of a series of substantially equal periodic payments made (not less frequently than annually) over any one of the following periods—

(i) The life of the employee (or the joint lives of the employee and the employee's designated beneficiary);

(ii) The life expectancy of the employee (or the joint life and last survivor expectancy of the employee and the employee's designated beneficiary); or

(iii) A specified period of ten years or more;

(2) Any distribution to the extent the distribution is a required minimum distribution under section 401(a)(9); or

(3) The portion of any distribution that is not includible in gross income (determined without regard to the exclusion for net unrealized appreciation described in section 402(e)(4)). Thus, for example, an eligible rollover distribution does not include the portion of any distribution that is excludible from gross income under section 72 as a return of the employee's investment in the contract (e.g., a return of the employee's after-tax contributions), but does include net unrealized appreciation.

Q-4: Are there other amounts that are not eligible rollover distributions?

A-4: Yes. The following amounts are not eligible rollover distributions:

(a) Elective deferrals (as defined in section 402(g)(3)) and employee contributions that, pursuant to rules prescribed by the Commissioner in revenue rulings, notices, or other guidance published in the Internal Revenue Bulletin (see § 601.601(d)(2) of this chapter), are returned to the employee (together with the income allocable thereto) in order to comply with the section 415 limitations.

(b) Corrective distributions of excess deferrals as described in § 1.402(g)-1(e)(3), together with the income allocable to these corrective distributions.

(c) Corrective distributions of excess contributions under a qualified cash or deferred arrangement described in § 1.401(k)-2(b)(2) and excess aggregate contributions described in § 1.401(m)-2(b)(2), together with the income allocable to these distributions.

(d) Loans that are treated as deemed distributions pursuant to section 72(p).

(e) Dividends paid on employer securities as described in section 404(k).

(f) The costs of life insurance coverage (P.S. 58 costs).

(g) Prohibited allocations that are treated as deemed distributions pursuant to section 409(p).

Reg. § 1.402(c)-2

(h) A distribution that is a permissible withdrawal from an eligible automatic contribution arrangement within the meaning of section 414(w).

(i) [Reserved]

(j) Distributions of premiums for accident or health insurance under §1.402(a)-1(e)(1)(i). This paragraph A-4(j) applies for taxable years beginning on or after January 1, 2015.

(k) Similar items designated by the Commissioner in revenue rulings, notices, and other guidance published in the Internal Revenue Bulletin. See §601.601(d)(2)(ii)(b) of this chapter.

Q-5: For purposes of determining whether a distribution is an eligible rollover distribution, how is it determined whether a series of payments is a series of substantially equal periodic payments over a period specified in section 402(c)(4)(A)?

A-5: (a) *General rule.* Generally, whether a series of payments is a series of substantially equal periodic payments over a specified period is determined at the time payments begin, and by following the principles of section 72(t)(2)(A)(iv), without regard to contingencies or modifications that have not yet occurred. Thus, for example, a joint and 50-percent survivor annuity will be treated as a series of substantially equal payments at the time payments commence, as will a joint and survivor annuity that provides for increased payments to the employee if the employee's beneficiary dies before the employee. Similarly, for purposes of determining if a disability benefit payment is part of a series of substantially equal payments for a period described in section 402(c)(4)(A), any contingency under which payments cease upon recovery from the disability may be disregarded.

(b) *Certain supplements disregarded.* For purposes of determining whether a distribution is one of a series of payments that are substantially equal, social security supplements described in section 411(a)(9) are disregarded. For example, if a distributee receives a life annuity of $500 per month, plus a social security supplement consisting of payments of $200 per month until the distributee reaches the age at which social security benefits of not less than $200 a month begin, the $200 supplemental payments are disregarded and, therefore, each monthly payment of $700 made before the social security age and each monthly payment of $500 made after the social security age is treated as one of a series of substantially equal periodic payments for life. A series of payments that are not substantially equal solely because the amount of each payment is reduced upon attainment of social security retirement age (or, alternatively, upon commencement of social security early retirement, survivor, or disability benefits) will also be treated as substantially equal as long as the reduction in the actual payments is level and does not exceed the applicable social security benefit.

(c) *Changes in the amount of payments or the distributee.* If the amount (or, if applicable, the method of calculating the amount) of the payments changes so that subsequent payments are not substantially equal to prior payments, a new determination must be made as to whether the remaining payments are a series of substantially equal periodic payments over a period specified in Q&A-3(b)(1) of this section. This determination is made without taking into account payments made or the years of payment that elapsed prior to the change. However, a new determination is not made merely because, upon the death of the employee, the spouse or former spouse of the employee becomes the distributee. Thus, once distributions commence over a period that is at least as long as either the first annuitant's life or 10 years (e.g., as provided by a life annuity with a five-year or ten-year-certain guarantee), then substantially equal payments to the survivor are not eligible rollover distributions even though the payment period remaining after the death of the employee is or may be less than the period described in section 402(c)(4)(A). For example, substantially equal periodic payments made under a life annuity with a five-year term certain would not be an eligible rollover distribution even when paid after the death of the employee with three years remaining under the term certain.

(d) *Defined contribution plans.* The following rules apply in determining whether a series of payments from a defined contribution plan constitute substantially equal periodic payments for a period described in section 402(c)(4)(A):

(1) *Declining balance of years.* A series of payments from an account balance under a defined contribution plan will be considered substantially equal payments over a period if, for each year, the amount of the distribution is calculated by dividing the account balance by the number of years remaining in the period. For example, a series of payments will be considered substantially equal payments over 10 years if the series is determined as follows. In year 1, the annual payment is the account balance divided by 10; in year 2, the annual payment is the remaining account balance divided by 9; and so on until year 10 when the entire remaining balance is distributed.

(2) *Reasonable actuarial assumptions.* If an employee's account balance under a defined contribution plan is to be distributed in annual installments of a specified amount until the account balance is ex-

hausted, then, for purposes of determining if the period of distribution is a period described in section 402(c)(4)(A), the period of years over which the installments will be distributed must be determined using reasonable actuarial assumptions. For example, if an employee has an account balance of $100,000, elects distributions of $12,000 per year until the account balance is exhausted, and the future rate of return is assumed to be 8% per year, the account balance will be exhausted in approximately 14 years. Similarly, if the same employee elects a fixed annual distribution amount and the fixed annual amount is less than or equal to $10,000, it is reasonable to assume that a future rate of return would be greater than 0% and, thus, the account will not be exhausted in less than 10 years.

(e) *Series of payments beginning before January 1, 1993.* Except as provided in paragraph (c) of this Q&A, if a series of periodic payments began before January 1, 1993, the determination of whether the post-December 31, 1992 payments are a series of substantially equal periodic payments over a specified period is made by taking into account all payments made, including payments made before January 1, 1993. For example, if a series of substantially equal periodic payments beginning on January 1, 1983, is scheduled to be paid over a period of 15 years, payments in the series that are made after December 31, 1992, will not be eligible rollover distributions even though they will continue for only five years after December 31, 1992, because the pre-January 1, 1993 payments are taken into account in determining the specified period.

Q-6: What types of variations in the amount of a payment cause the payment to be independent of a series of substantially equal periodic payments and thus not part of the series?

A-6: (a) *Independent payments.* Except as provided in paragraph (b) of this Q&A, a payment is treated as independent of the payments in a series of substantially equal payments, and thus not part of the series, if the payment is substantially larger or smaller than the other payments in the series. An independent payment is an eligible rollover distribution if it is not otherwise excepted from the definition of eligible rollover distribution. This is the case regardless of whether the payment is made before, with, or after payments in the series. For example, if an employee elects a single payment of half of the account balance with the remainder of the account balance paid over the life expectancy of the distributee, the single payment is treated as independent of the payments in the series and is an eligible rollover distribution unless otherwise excepted. Similarly, if an employee's surviving spouse receives a survivor life annuity of $1,000 per month plus a single payment on account of death of $7,500, the single payment is treated as independent of the payments in the annuity and is an eligible rollover distribution unless otherwise excepted (e.g., $5,000 of the $7,500 might qualify to be excluded from gross income as a death benefit under section 101(b)).

(b) *Special rules*—(1) *Administrative error or delay.* If, due solely to reasonable administrative error or delay in payment, there is an adjustment after the annuity starting date to the amount of any payment in a series of payments that otherwise would constitute a series of substantially equal payments described in section 402(c)(4)(A) and this section, the adjusted payment or payments will be treated as part of the series of substantially equal periodic payments and will not be treated as independent of the payments in the series. For example, if, due solely to reasonable administrative delay, the first payment of a life annuity is delayed by two months and reflects an additional two months worth of benefits, that payment will be treated as a substantially equal payment in the series rather than as an independent payment. The result will not change merely because the amount of the adjustment is paid in a separate supplemental payment.

(2) *Supplemental payments for annuitants.* A supplemental payment from a defined benefit plan to annuitants (e.g., retirees or beneficiaries) will be treated as part of a series of substantially equal payments, rather than as an independent payment, provided that the following conditions are met—

(i) The supplement is a benefit increase for annuitants;

(ii) The amount of the supplement is determined in a consistent manner for all similarly situated annuitants;

(iii) The supplement is paid to annuitants who are otherwise receiving payments that would constitute substantially equal periodic payments; and

(iv) The aggregate supplement is less than or equal to the greater of 10% of the annual rate of payment for the annuity, or $750 or any higher amount prescribed by the Commissioner in revenue rulings, notices, and other guidance published in the Federal Register. See §601.601(d)(2)(ii)(b) of this chapter.

(3) *Final payment in a series.* If a payment in a series of payments from an account balance under a defined contribution plan represents the remaining balance to the credit and is substantially less than the other payments in the series, the final payment must nevertheless be treated as a payment in the series of substantially equal payments and may not be treated as an independent payment if the other

payments in the series are substantially equal and the payments are for a period described in section 402(c)(4)(A) based on the rules provided in paragraph (d)(2) of Q&A-5 of this section. Thus, such final payment will not be an eligible rollover distribution.

Q-7: When is a distribution from a plan a required minimum distribution under section 401(a)(9)?

A-7: (a) *General rule.* Except as provided in paragraphs (b) and (c) of this Q&A, if a minimum distribution is required for a calendar year, the amounts distributed during that calendar year are treated as required minimum distributions under section 401(a)(9), to the extent that the total required minimum distribution under section 401(a)(9) for the calendar year has not been satisfied. Accordingly, these amounts are not eligible rollover distributions. For example, if an employee is required under section 401(a)(9) to receive a required minimum distribution for a calendar year of $5,000 and the employee receives a total of $7,200 in that year, the first $5,000 distributed will be treated as the required minimum distribution and will not be an eligible rollover distribution and the remaining $2,200 will be an eligible rollover distribution if it otherwise qualifies. If the total section 401(a)(9) required minimum distribution for a calendar year is not distributed in that calendar year (e.g., when the distribution for the calendar year in which the employee reaches age 70 1/2 is made on the following April 1), the amount that was required but not distributed is added to the amount required to be distributed for the next calendar year in determining the portion of any distribution in the next calendar year that is a required minimum distribution.

(b) *Distribution before age 70 1/2.* Any amount that is paid before January 1 of the year in which the employee attains (or would have attained) age 70 1/2 will not be treated as required under section 401(a)(9) and, thus, is an eligible rollover distribution if it otherwise qualifies.

(c) *Special rule for annuities.* In the case of annuity payments from a defined benefit plan, or under an annuity contract purchased from an insurance company (including a qualified plan distributed annuity contract (as defined in Q&A-10 of this section)), the entire amount of any such annuity payment made on or after January 1 of the year in which an employee attains (or would have attained) age 70 1/2 will be treated as an amount required under section 401(a)(9) and, thus, will not be an eligible rollover distribution.

Q-8: How are amounts that are not includible in gross income allocated for purposes of determining the required minimum distribution?

A-8: If section 401(a)(9) has not yet been satisfied by the plan for the year with respect to an employee, a distribution is made to the employee that exceeds the amount required to satisfy section 401(a)(9) for the year for the employee, and a portion of that distribution is excludible from gross income, the following rule applies for purposes of determining the amount of the distribution that is an eligible rollover distribution. The portion of the distribution that is excludible from gross income is first allocated toward satisfaction of section 401(a)(9) and then the remaining portion of the required minimum distribution, if any, is satisfied from the portion of the distribution that is includible in gross income. For example, assume an employee is required under section 401(a)(9) to receive a minimum distribution for a calendar year of $4,000 and the employee receives a $4,800 distribution, of which $1,000 is excludible from income as a return of basis. First, the $1,000 return of basis is allocated toward satisfying the required minimum distribution. Then, the remaining $3,000 of the required minimum distribution is satisfied from the $3,800 of the distribution that is includible in gross income, so that the remaining balance of the distribution, $800, is an eligible rollover distribution if it otherwise qualifies.

Q-9: What is a distribution of a plan loan offset amount, and is it an eligible rollover distribution?

A-9: (a) *General rule.* A distribution of a plan loan offset amount, as defined in paragraph (b) of this Q&A, is an eligible rollover distribution if it satisfies Q&A-3 of this section. Thus, an amount equal to the plan loan offset amount can be rolled over by the employee (or spousal distributee) to an eligible retirement plan within the 60-day period under section 402(c)(3), unless the plan loan offset amount fails to be an eligible rollover distribution for another reason. See §1.401(a)(31)-1, Q&A-16 for guidance concerning the offering of a direct rollover of a plan loan offset amount. See §31.3405(c)-1, Q&A-11 of this chapter for guidance concerning special withholding rules with respect to plan loan offset amounts.

(b) *Definition of plan loan offset amount.* For purposes of section 402(c), a distribution of a plan loan offset amount is a distribution that occurs when, under the plan terms governing a plan loan, the participant's accrued benefit is reduced (offset) in order to repay the loan (including the enforcement of the plan's security interest in a participant's accrued benefit). A distribution of a plan loan offset amount can occur in a variety of circumstances, e.g., where the terms governing a plan loan require that, in the event of the employee's termination of employment or request for a distribution, the loan be

repaid immediately or treated as in default. A distribution of a plan loan offset amount also occurs when, under the terms governing the plan loan, the loan is cancelled, accelerated, or treated as if it were in default (e.g., where the plan treats a loan as in default upon an employee's termination of employment or within a specified period thereafter). A distribution of a plan loan offset amount is an actual distribution, not a deemed distribution under section 72(p).

(c) *Examples.* The rules with respect to a plan loan offset amount in this Q&A-9, §1.401(a)(31)-1, Q&A-16 and §31.3405(c)-1, Q&A-11 of this chapter are illustrated by the following examples:

Example 1. (a) In 1996, Employee A has an account balance of $10,000 in Plan Y, of which $3,000 is invested in a plan loan to Employee A that is secured by Employee A's account balance in Plan Y. Employee A has made no after-tax employee contributions to Plan Y. Plan Y does not provide any direct rollover option with respect to plan loans. Upon termination of employment in 1996, Employee A, who is under age 70 1/2, elects a distribution of Employee A's entire account balance in Plan Y, and Employee A's outstanding loan is offset against the account balance on distribution. Employee A elects a direct rollover of the distribution.

(b) In order to satisfy section 401(a)(31), Plan Y must pay $7,000 directly to the eligible retirement plan chosen by Employee A in a direct rollover. When Employee A's account balance was offset by the amount of the $3,000 unpaid loan balance, Employee A received a plan loan offset amount (equivalent to $3,000) that is an eligible rollover distribution. However, under §1.401(a)(31)-1, Q&A-16 Plan Y satisfies section 401(a)(31), even though a direct rollover option was not provided with respect to the $3,000 plan loan offset amount.

(c) No withholding is required under section 3405(c) on account of the distribution of the $3,000 plan loan offset amount because no cash or other property (other than the plan loan offset amount) is received by Employee A from which to satisfy the withholding. Employee A may roll over $3,000 to an eligible retirement plan within the 60 day period provided in section 402(c)(3).

Example 2. (a) The facts are the same as in *Example 1,* except that the terms governing the plan loan to Employee A provide that, upon termination of employment, Employee A's account balance is automatically offset by the amount of any unpaid loan balance to repay the loan. Employee A terminates employment but does not request a distribution from Plan Y. Nevertheless, pursuant to the terms governing the plan loan, Employee A's account balance is automatically offset by the amount of the $3,000 unpaid loan balance.

(b) The $3,000 plan loan offset amount attributable to the plan loan in this example is treated in the same manner as the $3,000 plan loan offset amount in *Example 1.*

Example 3. (a) The facts are the same as in *Example 2,* except that, instead of providing for an automatic offset upon termination of employment to repay the plan loan, the terms governing the plan loan require full repayment of the loan by Employee A within 30 days of termination of employment. Employee A terminates employment, does not elect a distribution from Plan Y, and also fails to repay the plan loan within 30 days. The plan administrator of Plan Y declares the plan loan to Employee A in default and executes on the loan by offsetting Employee A's account balance by the amount of the $3,000 unpaid loan balance.

(b) The $3,000 plan loan offset amount attributable to the plan loan in this example is treated in the same manner as the $3,000 plan loan offset amount in *Example 1* and in *Example 2.* The result in this *Example 3* is the same even though the plan administrator treats the loan as in default before offsetting Employee A's accrued benefit by the amount of the unpaid loan.

Example 4. (a) The facts are the same as in *Example 1,* except that Employee A elects to receive the distribution of the account balance that remains after the $3,000 offset to repay the plan loan, instead of electing a direct rollover of the remaining account balance.

(b) In this case, the amount of the distribution received by Employee A is $10,000, not $3,000. Because the amount of the $3,000 offset attributable to the loan is included in determining the amount that equals 20 percent of the eligible rollover distribution received by Employee A, withholding in the amount of $2,000 (20 percent of $10,000) is required under section 3405(c). The $2,000 is required to be withheld from the $7,000 to be distributed to Employee A in cash, so that Employee A actually receives a check for $5,000.

Example 5. The facts are the same as in *Example 4,* except that the $7,000 distribution to Employee A after the offset to repay the loan consists solely of employer securities within the meaning of section 402(e)(4)(E). In this case, no withholding is required under section 3405(c) because the distribution consists solely of the $3,000 plan loan offset amount and the $7,000 distribution of employer securities. This is the result because the total amount required to be withheld does not exceed the sum of the cash and the fair market value of other property distributed, excluding plan loan offset amounts and employer securities. Employee A may roll over the employer securities and $3,000 to an eligible retirement plan within the 60-day period provided in section 402(c)(3).

Example 6. Employee B, who is age 40, has an account balance in Plan Z, a profit sharing plan qualified under section 401(a) that includes a qualified cash or deferred arrangement described in section 401(k). Plan Z provides for no after-tax employee contributions. In 1990, Employee B receives a loan from Plan Z, the terms of which satisfy section 72(p)(2), and which is secured by elective contributions subject to the distribution restrictions in section 401(k)(2)(B). In 1996, the loan fails to satisfy section 72(p)(2) because Employee B stops repayment. In that year, pursuant to section 72(p), Employee B is taxed on a deemed distribution equal to the amount of the unpaid loan balance. Under Q&A-4 of this section, the deemed distribution is not an eligible rollover distribution. Because Employee B has not separated from service or experienced any other event that permits the distribution under section 401(k)(2)(B) of the elective contributions that secure the loan, Plan Z is prohibited from executing on the loan. Accordingly, Employee B's account balance is not offset by the amount of the unpaid loan balance at the time Employee B stops repayment on the loan. Thus, there is no distribution of an offset amount that is an eligible rollover distribution in 1996.

Q-10: What is a qualified plan distributed annuity contract, and is an amount paid under such a contract a distribution of the balance to the credit of the employee in a qualified plan for purposes of section 402(c)?

A-10: (a) *Definition of a qualified plan distributed annuity contract.* A qualified plan distributed annuity contract is an annuity contract purchased for a participant, and distributed to the participant, by a qualified plan.

(b) *Treatment of amounts paid as eligible rollover distributions.* Amounts paid under a qualified plan distributed annuity contract are payments of the balance to the credit of the employee for purposes of section 402(c) and are eligible rollover distributions, if they otherwise qualify. Thus, for example, if the employee surrenders the contract for a single sum payment of its cash surrender value, the payment would be an eligible rollover distribution to the extent it is includible in gross income and not a required minimum distribution under section 401(a)(9). This rule applies even if the annuity contract is distributed in connection with a plan termination. See § 1.401(a)(31)-1, Q&A-17 and § 31.3405(c)-1, Q&A-13 of this chapter concerning the direct rollover requirements and 20-percent withholding requirements, respectively, that apply to eligible rollover distributions from such an annuity contract.

Q-11: If an eligible rollover distribution is paid to an employee, and the employee contributes all or part of the eligible rollover distribution to an eligible retirement plan within 60 days, is the amount contributed not currently includible in gross income?

A-11: Yes, the amount contributed is not currently includible in gross income, provided that it is contributed to the eligible retirement plan no later than the 60th day following the day on which the employee received the distribution. If more than one distribution is received by an employee from a qualified plan during a taxable year, the 60-day rule applies separately to each distribution. Because the amount withheld as income tax under section 3405(c) is considered an amount distributed under section 402(c), an amount equal to all or any portion of the amount withheld can be contributed as a rollover to an eligible retirement plan within the 60-day period, in addition to the net amount of the eligible rollover distribution actually received by the employee. However, if all or any portion of an amount equal to the amount withheld is not contributed as a rollover, it is included in the employee's gross income to the extent required under section 402(a), and also may be subject to the 10-percent additional income tax under section 72(t). See § 1.401(a)(31)-1, Q&A-14, for guidance concerning the qualification of a plan that accepts a rollover contribution.

Q-12: How does section 402(c) apply to a distributee who is not the employee?

A-12: (a) *Spousal distributee.* If any distribution attributable to an employee is paid to the employee's surviving spouse, section 402(c) applies to the distribution in the same manner as if the spouse were the employee. The same rule applies if any distribution attributable to an employee is paid in accordance with a qualified domestic relations order (as defined in section 414(p)) to the employee's spouse or former spouse who is an alternate payee. Therefore, a distribution to the surviving spouse of an employee (or to a spouse or former spouse who is an alternate payee under a qualified domestic relations order), including a distribution of ancillary death benefits *attributable to the employee, is an eligible rollover* distribution if it meets the requirements of section 402(c)(2) and (4) and Q&A-3 through Q&A-10 and Q&A-14 of this section. However, a qualified plan (as defined in Q&A-2 of this section) is not treated as an eligible retirement plan with respect to a surviving spouse. Only an individual retirement plan is treated as an eligible retirement plan with respect to an eligible rollover distribution to a surviving spouse.

(b) *Non-spousal distributee.* A distributee other than the employee or the employee's surviving spouse (or a spouse or former spouse who is an alternate payee under a qualified domestic relations order) is not permitted to roll over distributions from a qualified plan. Therefore, those distributions do not constitute eligible rollover distributions under section 402(c)(4) and are not subject to the 20-percent income tax withholding under section 3405(c).

Q-13: Must an employee's (or spousal distributee's) election to treat a contribution of an eligible rollover distribution to an individual retirement plan as a rollover contribution be irrevocable?

A-13: (a) *In general.* Yes. In order for a contribution of an eligible rollover distribution to an individual retirement plan to constitute a rollover and, thus, to qualify for current exclusion from gross income, a distributee must elect, at the time the contribution is made, to treat the contribution as a rollover contribution. An election is made by designating to the trustee, issuer, or custodian of the eligible retirement plan that the contribution is a rollover contribution. This election is irrevocable. Once any portion of an eligible rollover distribution has been contributed to an individual retirement plan and designated as a rollover distribution, taxation of the withdrawal of the contribution from the individual retirement plan is determined under section 408(d) rather than under section 402 or 403. Therefore, the eligible rollover distribution is not eligible for capital gains treatment, five-year or ten-year averaging, or the exclusion from gross income for net unrealized appreciation on employer stock.

(b) *Direct rollover.* If an eligible rollover distribution is paid to an individual retirement plan in a direct rollover at the election of the distributee, the distributee is deemed to have irrevocably designated that the direct rollover is a rollover contribution.

Q-14: How is the $5,000 death benefit exclusion under section 101(b) treated for purposes of determining the amount that is an eligible rollover distribution?

A-14: To the extent that a death benefit is a distribution from a qualified plan, the portion of the distribution that is excluded from gross income under section 101(b) is not an eligible rollover distribution. See § 1.401(a)(31)-1, Q&A-18 for guidance concerning assumptions that a plan administrator may make with respect to whether and to what extent a distribution of a survivor benefit is excludible from gross income under section 101(b).

Q-15: May an employee (or spousal distributee) roll over more than the plan administrator determines to be an eligible rollover distribution using an assumption described in § 1.401(a)(31)-1, Q&A-18?

A-15: Yes. The portion of any distribution that an employee (or spousal distributee) may roll over as an eligible rollover distribution under section 402(c) is determined based on the actual application of section 402 and other relevant provisions of the Internal Revenue Code. The actual application of these provisions may produce different results than any assumption described in § 1.401(a)(31)-1, Q&A-18 that is used by the plan administrator. Thus, for example, even though the plan administrator calculates the portion of a distribution that is a required minimum distribution (and thus is not made eligible for direct rollover under section 401(a)(31)), by assuming that there is no designated beneficiary, the portion of the distribution that is actually a required minimum distribution and thus not an eligible rollover distribution is determined by taking into account the designated beneficiary, if any. If, by taking into account the designated beneficiary, a greater portion of the distribution is an eligible rollover distribution, the distributee may rollover the additional amount. Similarly, even though a plan administrator assumes that a distribution from a qualified plan is the only death benefit with respect to an employee that qualifies for the $5,000 death benefit exclusion under section 101(b), to the extent that the death benefit exclusion is allocated to a different death benefit, a greater portion of the distribution may actually be includible in gross income and, thus, be an eligible rollover distribution, and the surviving spouse may roll over the additional amount if it otherwise qualifies.

Q-16: Is a rollover from a qualified plan to an individual retirement account or individual retirement annuity treated as a rollover contribution for purposes of the one-year look-back rollover limitation of section 408(d)(3)(B)?

A-16: No. A distribution from a qualified plan that is rolled over to an individual retirement account or individual retirement annuity is not treated for purposes of section 408(d)(3)(B) as an amount received by an individual from an individual retirement account or individual retirement annuity which is not includible in gross income because of the application of section 408(d)(3).

[Reg. § 1.402(c)-2.]

☐ [T.D. 8619, 9-15-95. *Amended by T.D. 8880, 4-20-2000 T.D. 9169, 12-28-2004; T.D. 9302, 12-19-2006; T.D. 9319, 4-4-2007; T.D. 9340, 7-23-2007; T.D. 9447, 2-23-2009 and T.D. 9665, 5-9-2014.*]

[Reg. §1.402(c)-3]

§1.402(c)-3. Eligible rollover distributions; Qualified plan loan offsets.—(a)(1) *Q-1.*—What special rollover rules apply to a plan loan offset amount (including a qualified plan loan offset amount)?

(2) *A-1.*—(i) *In general.*—(A) *Eligible rollover distribution.*—A distribution of a plan loan offset amount, as defined in paragraph (a)(2)(iii)(A) of this section (including a qualified plan loan offset amount, a type of plan loan offset amount defined in paragraph (a)(2)(iii)(B) of this section), is an eligible rollover distribution if it satisfies § 1.402(c)-2, Q&A-3 and 4.

(B) *Other rules relating to plan loan offset amounts.*—See § 1.401(a)(31)-1, Q&A-16, for guidance concerning the offering of a direct rollover of a plan loan offset amount. See also § 31.3405(c)-1, Q&A-11, of this chapter for guidance concerning special withholding rules with respect to plan loan offset amounts.

(ii) *Rollover period for a plan loan offset amount.*—(A) *Plan loan offset amount that is not a qualified plan loan offset amount.*—A distribution of a plan loan offset amount that is an eligible rollover distribution and not a qualified plan loan offset amount may be rolled over by the employee (or spousal distributee) to an eligible retirement plan (as defined in § 1.402(c)-2, Q&A-2) within the 60-day period set forth in section 402(c)(3)(A).

(B) *Plan loan offset amount that is a qualified plan loan offset amount.*—A distribution of a plan loan offset amount that is an eligible rollover distribution and that is a qualified plan loan offset amount may be rolled over by the employee (or spousal distributee) to an eligible retirement plan within the period set forth in section 402(c)(3)(C), which is the individual's tax filing due date (including extensions) for the taxable year in which the offset is treated as distributed from a qualified employer plan.

(iii) *Definitions.*—(A) *Plan loan offset amount.*—For purposes of section 402(c), a plan loan offset amount is the amount by which, under the plan terms governing a plan loan, an employee's accrued benefit is reduced (offset) in order to repay the loan (including the enforcement of the plan's security interest in an employee's accrued benefit). A distribution of a plan loan offset amount can occur in a variety of circumstances, for example, when the terms governing a plan loan require that, in the event of the employee's termination of employment or request for a distribution, the loan be repaid immediately or treated as in default. A distribution of a plan loan offset amount also occurs when, under the terms governing the plan loan, the loan is cancelled, accelerated, or treated as if it were in default (for example, when the plan treats a loan as in default upon an employee's termination of employment or within a specified period thereafter). A distribution of a plan loan offset amount is an actual distribution, not a deemed distribution under section 72(p).

(B) *Qualified plan loan offset amount.*—For purposes of section 402(c), a qualified plan loan offset amount is a plan loan offset amount that satisfies the following requirements:

(1) The plan loan offset amount is treated as distributed from a qualified employer plan to an employee or beneficiary solely by reason of the termination of the qualified employer plan, or the failure to meet the repayment terms of the loan because of the severance from employment of the employee; and

(2) The plan loan offset amount relates to a plan loan that met the requirements of section 72(p)(2) immediately prior to the termination of the qualified employer plan or the severance from employment of the employee, as applicable.

(C) *Qualified employer plan.*—For purposes of section 402(c) and this section, a qualified employer plan is a qualified employer plan as defined in section 72(p)(4).

(iv) *Special rules for qualified plan loan offset amounts.*—(A) *Definition of severance from employment.*—For purposes of paragraph (a)(2)(iii)(B)(1) of this section, whether an employee has a severance from employment with the employer that maintains the qualified employer plan is determined in the same manner as under § 1.401(k)-1(d)(2). Thus, an employee has a severance from employment when the employee ceases to be an employee of the employer maintaining the plan.

(B) *Offset because of severance from employment.*—A plan loan offset amount is treated as distributed from a qualified employer plan to an employee or beneficiary solely by reason of the failure to meet the repayment terms of a plan loan because of severance from employment of the employee if the plan loan offset:

(1) Relates to a failure to meet the repayment terms of the plan loan, and

(2) Occurs within the period beginning on the date of the employee's severance from employment and ending on the first anniversary of that date.

(v) *Examples.*—The following examples illustrate the rules with respect to plan loan offset amounts, including qualified plan loan offset amounts, in this paragraph (a) and in §§ 1.401(a)(31)-1, Q&A-16, and 31.3405(c)-1, Q&A-11, of this chapter. For purposes of the examples in this paragraph (a)(2)(v), each reference to a plan refers to a qualified employer plan as described in section 72(p)(4).

(A) *Example 1.*—(1) In 2020, Employee A has an account balance of $10,000 in Plan Y, of which $3,000 is invested in a plan loan to Employee A that is secured by Employee A's account balance in Plan Y. Employee A has made no after-tax employee contributions to Plan Y. The plan loan meets the requirements of section 72(p)(2). Plan Y does not provide any direct rollover option with respect to plan loans. Employee A severs from employment on June 15, 2020. After severance from employment, Plan Y accelerates the plan loan and provides Employee A 90 days to repay the remaining balance of the plan loan. Employee A, who is under the age set forth in section 401(a)(9)(C)(i)(II), does not repay the loan within the 90 days and instead elects a direct rollover of Employee A's entire account balance in Plan Y. On September 18, 2020 (within the 12-month period beginning on the date that Employee A severed from employment), Employee A's outstanding loan is offset against the account balance.

(2) In order to satisfy section 401(a)(31), Plan Y must make a direct rollover by paying $7,000 directly to the eligible retirement plan chosen by Employee A. When Employee A's account balance was offset by the amount of the $3,000 unpaid loan balance, Employee A received a plan loan offset amount (equivalent to $3,000) that is an eligible rollover distribution. However, under § 1.401(a)(31)-1, Q&A-16, Plan Y satisfies section 401(a)(31), even though a direct rollover option was not provided with respect to the $3,000 plan loan offset amount.

(3) No withholding is required under section 3405(c) on account of the distribution of the $3,000 plan loan offset amount because no cash or other property (other than the plan loan offset amount) is received by Employee A from which to satisfy the withholding.

(4) The $3,000 plan loan offset amount is a qualified plan loan offset amount within the meaning of paragraph (a)(2)(iii)(B) of this section. Accordingly, Employee A may roll over up to the $3,000 qualified plan loan offset amount to an eligible retirement plan within the period that ends on the employee's tax filing due date (including extensions) for the taxable year in which the offset occurs.

(B) *Example 2.*—(1) The facts are the same as in paragraph (a)(2)(v)(A) of this section (*Example 1*), except that, rather than accelerating the plan loan, Plan Y permits Employee A to continue making loan installment payments after severance from employment. Employee A continues making loan installment payments until January 1, 2021, at which time Employee A does not make the loan installment payment due on January 1, 2021. In accordance with § 1.72(p)-1, Q&A-10, Plan Y allows a cure period that continues until the last day of the calendar quarter following the quarter in which the required installment payment was due. Employee A does not make a plan loan installment payment during the cure period. Plan Y offsets the unpaid $3,000 loan balance against Employee A's account balance on July 1, 2021 (which is after the 12-month period beginning on the date that Employee A severed from employment).

(2) The conclusion is the same as in paragraph (a)(2)(v)(A) of this section (*Example 1*), except that the $3,000 plan loan offset amount is not a qualified plan loan offset amount (because the offset did not occur within the 12-month period beginning on the date that Employee A severed from employment). Accordingly, Employee A may roll over up to the $3,000 plan loan offset amount to an eligible retirement plan within the 60-day period provided in section 402(c)(3)(A) (rather than within the period that ends on Employee A's tax filing due date (including extensions) for the taxable year in which the offset occurs).

(C) *Example 3.*—(1) The facts are the same as in paragraph (a)(2)(v)(A) of this section (*Example 1*), except that the terms governing the plan loan to Employee A provide that, upon severance from employment, Employee A's account balance is automatically offset by the amount of any unpaid loan balance to repay the loan. Employee A severs from employment but does not request a distribution from Plan Y. Nevertheless, pursuant to the terms governing the plan loan, Employee A's account balance is automatically offset on June 15, 2020, by the amount of the $3,000 unpaid loan balance.

(2) The $3,000 plan loan offset amount is a qualified plan loan offset amount within the meaning of paragraph (a)(2)(iii)(B) of this section. Accordingly, Employee A may roll over up to the $3,000 qualified plan loan offset amount to an eligible retirement plan

within the period that ends on Employee A's tax filing due date (including extensions) for the taxable year in which the offset occurs.

(D) *Example 4.*—(1) The facts are the same as in paragraph (a)(2)(v)(A) of this section (*Example 1*), except that Employee A elects to receive a cash distribution of the account balance that remains after the $3,000 plan loan offset amount, instead of electing a direct rollover of the remaining account balance.

(2) The amount of the distribution received by Employee A is $10,000 ($3,000 relating to the plan loan offset and $7,000 relating to the cash distribution). Because the amount of the $3,000 plan loan offset amount attributable to the loan is included in determining the amount of the eligible rollover distribution to which withholding applies, withholding in the amount of $2,000 (20 percent of $10,000) is required under section 3405(c). The $2,000 is required to be withheld from the $7,000 to be distributed to Employee A in cash, so that Employee A actually receives a cash amount of $5,000.

(3) The $3,000 plan loan offset amount is a qualified plan loan offset amount within the meaning of paragraph (a)(2)(iii)(B) of this section. Accordingly, Employee A may roll over up to the $3,000 qualified plan loan offset to an eligible retirement plan within the period that ends on the Employee A's tax filing due date (including extensions) for the taxable year in which the offset occurs. In addition, Employee A may roll over up to $7,000 (the portion of the distribution that is not related to the offset) within the 60-day period provided in section 402(c)(3).

(E) *Example 5.*—(1) The facts are the same as in paragraph (a)(2)(v)(D) of this section (*Example 4*), except that the $7,000 distribution to Employee A after the offset consists solely of employer securities within the meaning of section 402(e)(4)(E).

(2) No withholding is required under section 3405(c) because the distribution consists solely of the $3,000 plan loan offset amount and the $7,000 distribution of employer securities. This is the result because the total amount required to be withheld does not exceed the sum of the cash and the fair market value of other property distributed, excluding plan loan offset amounts and employer securities.

(3) Employee A may roll over up to the $7,000 of employer securities to an eligible retirement plan within the 60-day period provided in section 402(c)(3). The $3,000 plan loan offset amount is a qualified plan loan offset amount within the meaning of paragraph (a)(2)(iii)(B) of this section. Accordingly, Employee A may roll over up to the $3,000 qualified plan loan offset amount to an eligible retirement plan within the period that ends on Employee A's tax filing due date (including extensions) for the taxable year in which the offset occurs.

(F) *Example 6.*—(1) Employee B, who is age 40, has an account balance in Plan Z. Plan Z provides for no after-tax employee contributions. In 2022, Employee B receives a loan from Plan Z, the terms of which satisfy section 72(p)(2), and which is secured by elective contributions subject to the distribution restrictions in section 401(k)(2)(B).

(2) Employee B fails to make an installment payment due on April 1, 2023, or any other monthly payments thereafter. In accordance with §1.72(p)-1, Q&A-10, Plan Z allows a cure period that continues until the last day of the calendar quarter following the quarter in which the required installment payment was due (September 30, 2023). Employee B does not make a plan loan installment payment during the cure period. On September 30, 2023, pursuant to section 72(p)(1), Employee B is taxed on a deemed distribution equal to the amount of the unpaid loan balance. Pursuant to §1.402(c)-2, Q&A-4(d), the deemed distribution is not an eligible rollover distribution.

(3) Because Employee B has not severed from employment or experienced any other event that permits the distribution under section 401(k)(2)(B) of the elective contributions that secure the loan, Plan Z is prohibited from executing on the loan. Accordingly, Employee B's account balance is not offset by the amount of the unpaid loan balance at the time of the deemed distribution. Thus, there is no distribution of an offset amount that is an eligible rollover distribution on September 30, 2023.

(G) *Example 7.*—(1) The facts are the same as in paragraph (a)(2)(v)(F) of this section (*Example 6*), except that Employee B has a severance from employment on November 1, 2023. On that date, Employee B's unpaid loan balance is offset against the account balance on distribution.

(2) The plan loan offset amount is not a qualified plan loan offset amount. Although the offset occurred within 12 months after Employee B severed from employment, the plan loan does not meet the requirement in paragraph (a)(2)(iii)(B) of this section (that the plan loan meet the requirements of section 72(p)(2) immediately prior to Employee B's severance from employment). Instead, the loan

was taxable on September 30, 2023 (prior to Employee B's severance from employment on November 1, 2023), because of the failure to meet the level amortization requirement in section 72(p)(2)(C). Accordingly, Employee B may roll over the plan loan offset amount to an eligible retirement plan within the 60-day period provided in section 402(c)(3)(A) (rather than within the period that ends on Employee B's tax filing due date (including extensions) for the taxable year in which the offset occurs).

(b)(1) *Q-2.*—When are the rules in this section applicable to plan loan offset amounts, including qualified plan loan offset amounts?

(2) *A-2.*—The rules provided in paragraph (a) of this section are applicable to plan loan offset amounts, including qualified plan loan offset amounts, treated as distributed on or after January 1, 2021. However, taxpayers (including a filer of a Form 1099-R) may choose to apply the regulations in this section with respect to plan loan offset amounts, including qualified plan loan offset amounts, treated as distributed on or after August 20, 2020. [Reg. §1.402(c)-3.]

☐ [T.D. 9937, 1-5-2021.]

[Reg. §1.402(f)-1]

§1.402(f)-1. Required explanation of eligible rollover distributions; questions and answers.—The following questions and answers concern the written explanation requirement imposed by section 402(f) of the Internal Revenue Code of 1986 relating to distributions eligible for rollover treatment. Section 402(f) was amended by section 521(a) of the Unemployment Compensation Amendments of 1992, Public Law 102-318, 106 Stat. 290 (UCA). For additional UCA guidance under sections 401(a)(31), 402(c), 403(b)(8) and (10), and 3405(c), see §§1.401(a)(31)-1, 1.402(c)-2, 1.403(b)-7(b), and 31.3405(c)-1 of this chapter.

LIST OF QUESTIONS

Q-1: What are the requirements for a written explanation under section 402(f)?

Q-2: When must the plan administrator provide the section 402(f) notice to a distributee?

Q-3: Must the plan administrator provide a separate section 402(f) notice for each distribution in a series of periodic payments that are eligible rollover distributions?

Q-4: May a plan administrator post the section 402(f) notice as a means of providing it to distributees?

QUESTIONS AND ANSWERS

Q-1: What are the requirements for a written explanation under section 402(f)?

A-1: (a) *General rule.* Under section 402(f), as amended by UCA, the plan administrator of a qualified plan is required, within a reasonable period of time before making an eligible rollover distribution, to provide the distributee with the written explanation described in section 402(f) (section 402(f) notice). The section 402(f) notice must be designed to be easily understood and must explain the following: the rules under which the distributee may elect that the distribution be paid in the form of a direct rollover to an eligible retirement plan; the rules that require the withholding of tax on the distribution if it is not paid in a direct rollover; the rules under which the distributee may defer tax on the distribution if it is contributed in a rollover to an eligible retirement plan within 60 days of the distribution; and if applicable, certain special rules regarding the taxation of the distribution as described in section 402(d) (averaging with respect to lump sum distributions) and (e) (other rules including treatment of net unrealized appreciation). See §1.401(a)(31)-1, Q&A-7 for additional information that must be provided if a plan provides a default procedure regarding the election of a direct rollover.

(b) *Model section 402(f) notice.* The plan administrator will be deemed to have complied with the requirements of paragraph (a) of this Q&A-1 relating to the contents of the section 402(f) notice if the plan administrator provides the applicable model section 402(f) notice published by the Internal Revenue Service for this purpose in a revenue ruling, notice, or other guidance published in the Internal Revenue Bulletin. See §601.601(d)(2)(ii)(b) of this chapter.

(c) *Delegation to Commissioner.* The Commissioner, in revenue rulings, notices, and other guidance, published in the Internal Revenue Bulletin, may modify, or provide any additional guidance with respect to, the notice requirement of this section. See §601.601(d)(2)(ii)(b) of this chapter.

(d) *Effective date*—(1) *Statutory effective date.* Section 402(f) applies to eligible rollover distributions made after December 31, 1992.

(2) *Regulatory effective date.* This section applies to eligible rollover distributions made on or after October 19, 1995. For eligible rollover distributions made on or after January 1, 1993 and before October 19, 1995, §1.402(c)-2T, Q&A-11 through 15 (as it appeared in the April 1, 1995 edition of 26 CFR part 1), apply. However, for any distribution made on or after January 1, 1993 but before October 19, 1995, a plan administrator or payor may satisfy the requirements of section 402(f)

by substituting any or all provisions of this section for the corresponding provisions of §1.402(c)-1T, Q&A-11 through 15, if any.

Q-2: When must the plan administrator provide the section 402(f) notice to a distributee?

A-2: The plan administrator must provide the section 402(f) notice to a distributee at a time that satisfies either paragraph (a) or (b) of this Q & A-2.

(a) This paragraph (a) is satisfied if the plan administrator provides a distributee with the section 402(f) notice no less than 30 days and no more than 90 days before the date of a distribution. However, if the distributee, after having received the section 402(f) notice, affirmatively elects a distribution, a plan will not fail to satisfy section 402(f) merely because the distribution is made less than 30 days after the section 402(f) notice was provided to the distributee, provided the plan administrator clearly indicates to the distributee that the distributee has a right to consider the decision of whether or not to elect a direct rollover for at least 30 days after the notice is provided. The plan administrator may use any method to inform the distributee of the relevant time period, provided that the method is reasonably designed to attract the attention of the distributee. For example, this information could be either provided in the section 402(f) notice or stated in a separate document (e.g., attached to the election form) that is provided at the same time as the notice. For purposes of satisfying the requirement in the first sentence of paragraph (a) of this Q & A-2, the plan administrator may substitute the annuity starting date, within the meaning of §1.401(a)-20, Q & A-10, for the date of the distribution.

(b) This paragraph (b) is satisfied if the plan administrator—

(1) Provides a distributee with the section 402(f) notice;

(2) Provides the distributee with a summary of the section 402(f) notice within the time period described in paragraph (a) of this Q & A-2; and

(3) If the distributee so requests after receiving the summary described in paragraph (b)(2) of this Q & A-2, provides the section 402(f) notice to the distributee without charge and no less than 30 days before the date of a distribution (or the annuity starting date), subject to the rules for the distributee's waiver of that 30-day period. The summary described in paragraph (b)(2) of this Q & A-2 must set forth a summary of the principal provisions of the section 402(f) notice, must refer the distributee to the most recent version of the section 402(f) notice (and, in the case of a notice provided in any document containing information in addition to the notice, must identify that document and must provide a reasonable indication of where the notice may be found in that document, such as by index reference or by section heading), and must advise the distributee that, upon request, a copy of the section 402(f) notice will be provided without charge.

Q-3: Must the plan administrator provide a separate section 402(f) notice for each distribution in a series of periodic payments that are eligible rollover distributions?

A-3: No. In the case of a series of periodic payments that are eligible rollover distributions, the plan administrator is permitted to satisfy section 402(f) with respect to each payment in the series by providing the section 402(f) notice prior to the first payment in the series, in accordance with the rules in Q&A-1 and Q&A-2 of this section, and providing the notice at least once annually for as long as the payments continue. However, see §1.401(a)(31)-1, Q&A-12 for additional guidance if the plan administrator intends to treat a distributee's election to make or not make a direct rollover with respect to one payment in a series of periodic payments as applicable to all subsequent payments in the series (absent a subsequent change of election).

Q-4: May a plan administrator post the section 402(f) notice as a means of providing it to distributees?

A-4: No. The posting of the section 402(f) notice will not be considered provision of the notice. The written notice must be provided individually to any distributee of an eligible rollover distribution within the time period described in Q&A-2 and Q&A-3 of this section.

Q-5: Will the requirements of section 402(f) be satisfied if a plan administrator provides a distributee with the section 402(f) notice or the summary of the notice described in paragraph (b)(2) of Q & A-2 of this section other than through a written paper document?

A-5. Yes. See §1.401(a)-21 of this chapter for rules permitting the use of electronic media to provide applicable notices to recipients with respect to retirement plans.

[Reg. §1.402(f)-1.]

☐ [T.D. 8219, 8-19-88. *Amended by* T.D. 8619, 9-15-95; T.D. 8873, 2-7-2000; T.D. 9294, 10-19-2006 *and* T.D. 9340, 7-23-2007.]

[Reg. §1.402(g)-0]

§1.402(g)-0. Limitation on exclusion for elective deferrals, table of contents.—This section contains the captions that appear in §1.402(g)-1.

§1.402(g)-1. Limitation on exclusion for elective deferrals.
(a) In general.
(b) Elective deferrals.
(c) Certain one-time irrevocable elections.
(d) Applicable limit.
　(1) In general.
　(2) Special adjustment for elective deferrals with respect to a section 403(b) annuity contract.
　(3) Special adjustment for elective deferrals with respect to a section 403(b) annuity contract for certain long-term employees.
　(4) Example.
(e) Treatment of excess deferrals.
　(1) Plan qualification.
　　(i) Effect of excess deferrals.
　　(ii) Treatment of excess deferrals as employer contributions.
　　(iii) Definition of excess deferrals.
　(2) Correction of excess deferrals after the taxable year.
　(3) Correction of excess deferrals during taxable year.
　(4) Plan provisions.
　(5) Income allocable to excess deferrals.
　　(i) General rule.
　　(ii) Method of allocating income.
　　(iii) Alternative method of allocating income.
　　(iv) Safe harbor method of allocating gap period income.
　(6) Coordination with distribution or recharacterization of excess contributions.
　(7) No employee or spousal consent required.
　(8) Tax treatment.
　　(i) Corrective distributions on or before April 15 after close of taxable year.
　　(ii) Special rule for 1987 and 1988 excess deferrals.
　　(iii) Distributions of excess deferrals after correction period.
　(9) No reduction of required minimum distribution.
　(10) Partial correction.
　(11) Examples.
(f) Community property laws.
(g) Effective date.
　(1) In general.
　(2) Deferrals under collective bargaining agreements.
　(3) Transition rule.
　(4) Partnership cash or deferred arrangements.
[Reg. §1.402(g)-0.]

☐ [T.D. 8357, 8-8-91.]

[Reg. §1.402(g)-1]

§1.402(g)-1. Limitation on exclusion for elective deferrals.—
(a) *In general.*—The excess of an individual's elective deferrals for any taxable year over the applicable limit for the year may not be excluded from gross income under sections 402(a)(8), 402(h)(1)(B), 403(b), 408(k)(6), or 501(c)(18). Thus, an individual's elective deferrals in excess of the applicable limit for a taxable year (that is, the individual's excess deferrals for the year) must be included in gross income for the year, except to the extent the excess deferrals are comprised of designated Roth contributions, and thus, are already includible in gross income. A designated Roth contribution is treated as an excess deferral only to the extent that the total amount of designated Roth contributions for an individual exceeds the applicable limit for the taxable year or the designated Roth contributions are identified as excess deferrals and the individual receives a distribution of the excess deferrals and allocable income under paragraph (e)(2) or (e)(3) of this section.

(b) *Elective deferrals.*—An individual's elective deferrals for a taxable year are the sum of the following:

(1) Any elective contribution under a qualified cash or deferred arrangement (as defined in section 401(k)) to the extent not includible in the individual's gross income for the taxable year on account of section 402(a)(8) (before applying the limits of section 402(g) or this section).

(2) Any employer contribution to a simplified employee pension (as defined in section 408(k)) to the extent not includible in the individual's gross income for the taxable year on account of section 402(h)(1)(B) (before applying the limits of section 402(g) or this section).

(3) Any employer contribution to an annuity contract under section 403(b) under a salary reduction agreement (within the mean-

ing of section 3121(a)(5)(D)) to the extent not includible in the individual's gross income for the taxable year on account of section 403(b) (before applying the limits of section 402(g) or this section).

(4) Any employee contribution designated as deductible under a trust described in section 501(c)(18) to the extent deductible from the individual's income for the taxable year on account of section 501(c)(18) (before applying the limits of section 402(g) or this section). For purposes of this section, the employee contribution is treated as though it were excluded from the individual's gross income.

(5) Any designated Roth contributions described in section 402A (before applying the limits of section 402(g) or this section).

(6) Any elective employer contributions to a SIMPLE retirement account, on behalf of an employee pursuant to a qualified salary reduction arrangement as described in section 408(p)(2) (before applying the limits of section 402(g) or this section).

(c) *Certain one-time irrevocable elections.*—An employer contribution is not treated as an elective deferral under paragraph (b) of this section if the contribution is made pursuant to a one-time irrevocable election made by the employee:

(1) In the case of an annuity contract under section 403(b), at the time of initial eligibility to participate in the salary reduction agreement;

(2) In the case of a qualified cash or deferred arrangement, at a time when, under § 1.401(k)-1(a)(3)(v), the election is not treated as a cash or deferred election;

(3) In the case of a trust described in section 501(c)(18), at the time of initial eligibility to have the employer contribute on the employee's behalf to the trust.

(d) *Applicable limit.*—(1) *In general.*—Except as provided under paragraph (d)(2) of this section, the applicable limit for an individual's taxable year is the applicable dollar amount set forth in section 402(g)(1)(B). This applicable dollar amount is increased for the taxable year beginning in 2007 and later years in the same manner as the dollar amount under section 415(b)(1)(A) is adjusted pursuant to section 415(d). See § 1.402(g)-2 for the treatment of catch-up contributions described in section 414(v).

(2) *Special adjustment for elective deferrals with respect to section 403(b) annuity contracts for certain long-term employees.*—The applicable limit for an individual who is a qualified employee (as defined in section 402(g)(7)(C)) and has elective deferrals described in paragraph (b)(3) or (5) of this section for a taxable year is adjusted by increasing the applicable limit otherwise determined under paragraph (d)(1) of this section in accordance with section 402(g)(7).

(e) *Treatment of excess deferrals.*—(1) *Plan qualification.*—(i) *Effect of excess deferrals.*—For plan years beginning before January 1, 1988, a plan, annuity contract, simplified employee pension, or trust does not fail to meet the requirements of section 401(a), section 403(b), section 408(k), or section 501(c)(18), respectively, merely because excess deferrals are made with respect to the plan, contract, pension, or trust. For plan years beginning after December 31, 1987, see section 401(a)(30) and § 1.401(a)-30 for the effect of excess deferrals on the qualification of a plan or trust under section 401(a). For purposes of determining whether a plan or trust complies in operation with section 401(a)(30), excess deferrals that are distributed under paragraph (e)(2) or (3) of this section are disregarded. Similar rules apply to annuity contracts under section 403(b), simplified employee pensions under section 408(k), and plans or trusts under section 501(c)(18).

(ii) *Treatment of excess deferrals as employer contributions.*—For other purposes of the Code, including sections 401(a)(4), 401(k)(3), 404, 409, 411, 412, and 416, excess deferrals must be treated as employer contributions even if they are distributed in accordance with paragraph (e)(2) or (3) of this section. However, excess deferrals of a nonhighly compensated employee are not taken into account under section 401(k)(3) (the actual deferral percentage test) to the extent the excess deferrals are prohibited under section 401(a)(30). Excess deferrals are also treated as employer contributions for purposes of section 415 unless distributed under paragraph (e)(2) or (3) of this section.

(iii) *Definition of excess deferrals.*—The term "excess deferrals" means the excess of an individual's elective deferrals for any taxable year, as defined in § 1.402(g)-1(b), over the applicable limit under section 402(g)(1) for the taxable year.

(2) *Correction of excess deferrals after the taxable year.*—A plan may provide that if any amount is an excess deferral under paragraph (a) of this section:

(i) Not later than the first April 15 (or such earlier date specified in the plan) following the close of the individual's taxable year, the individual may notify each plan under which elective deferrals

were made of the amount of the excess deferrals received by the plan. If any designated Roth contributions were made to a plan, the notification must also identify the extent, if any, to which the excess deferrals are comprised of designated Roth contributions. A plan may provide that an individual is deemed to have notified the plan of excess deferrals (including the portion of excess deferrals that are comprised of designated Roth contributions) to the extent the individual has excess deferrals for the taxable year calculated by taking into account only elective deferrals under the plan and other plans of the same employer and the plan may provide the extent to which such excess deferrals are comprised of designated Roth contributions. A plan may instead provide that the employer may notify the plan on behalf of the individual under these circumstances.

(ii) Not later than the first April 15 following the close of the taxable year, the plan may distribute to the individual the amount designated under paragraph (e)(2)(i) of this section (and any income allocable to that amount).

(3) *Correction of excess deferrals during taxable year.*—(i) A plan may provide that an individual who has excess deferrals for a taxable year may receive a corrective distribution of excess deferrals during the same year. This corrective distribution may be made only if all of the following conditions are satisfied:

(A) The individual designates the distribution as an excess deferral. If any designated Roth contributions were made to a plan, the notification must identify the extent to which, if any, the excess deferrals are comprised of designated Roth contributions. A plan may provide that an individual is deemed to have notified the plan of excess deferrals (including the portion of excess deferrals that are comprised of designated Roth contributions) for the taxable year calculated by taking into account only elective deferrals under the plan and other plans of the same employer and the plan may provide the extent to which such excess deferrals are comprised of designated Roth contributions. A plan may instead provide that the employer may make the designation on behalf of the individual under these circumstances.

(B) The correcting distribution is made after the date on which the plan received the excess deferral.

(C) The plan designates the distribution as a distribution of excess deferrals.

(ii) The provisions of this paragraph (e)(3) are illustrated by the following example:

Example. S is a 62 year old individual who participates in Employer Y's qualified cash or deferred arrangement. In January 1991, S withdraws $5,000 from Y's cash or deferred arrangement. From February through September, S defers $900 per month. On October 1, S leaves Employer Y and becomes employed by Employer Z (unrelated to Y). During the remainder of 1991, S defers $1,800 under Z's qualified cash or deferred arrangement. In January 1992, S realizes that S has deferred a total of $9,000 in 1991, and therefore has a $525 excess deferral ($9,000 minus $8,475, the applicable limit for 1991). An additional $525 must be distributed to S before April 15, 1992, to correct the excess deferral. The $5,000 withdrawal did not correct the excess deferral because it occurred before the excess deferral was made.

(4) *Plan provisions.*—In order to distribute excess deferrals pursuant to paragraphs (e)(2) or (e)(3) of this section, a plan must contain language permitting distribution of excess deferrals. A plan may require the notification in paragraphs (e)(2) and (e)(3) of this section to be in writing and may require that the employee certify or otherwise establish that the designated amount is an excess deferral. A plan need not permit distribution of excess deferrals.

(5) *Income allocable to excess deferrals.*—(i) *General rule.*—The income allocable to excess deferrals for a taxable year that begins on or after January 1, 2007 is equal to the sum of the allocable gain or loss for the taxable year of the individual and ,to the extent the excess deferrals are or will be credited with gain or loss for the period after the close of the taxable year and prior to the distribution (the gap period) if the total account were to be distributed, the allocable gain or loss during that period. The income allocable to excess deferrals for a taxable year that begins before 2007 is determined using the 1.402(g)-1(e)(5) (as it appeared in the April 1, 2006 edition of 26 CFR Part 1).

(ii) *Method of allocating income.*—A plan may use any reasonable method for computing the income allocable to excess deferrals, provided that the method does not violate section 401(a)(4), is used consistently for all participants and for all corrective distributions under a plan for the plan year, and is used by the plan for allocating income to participants' accounts. See § 1.401(a)(4)-1(c)(8). A plan will not fail to use a reasonable method for computing the income allocable to excess deferrals merely because the income allocable to excess deferrals is determined on a date that is no more than 7 days before the distribution.

(iii) *Alternative method of allocating taxable year income.*—A plan may determine the income allocable to excess deferrals for the taxable year by multiplying the income for the taxable year allocable to elective deferrals by a fraction. The numerator of the fraction is the excess deferrals by the employee for the taxable year. The denominator of the fraction is equal to the sum of:

(A) The total account balance of the employee attributable to elective deferrals as of the beginning of the taxable year, plus

(B) The employee's elective deferrals for the taxable year.

(iv) *Safe harbor method of allocating gap period income.*—Under the safe harbor method, income on excess deferrals for the gap period is equal to 10 percent of the income allocable to excess deferrals for the taxable year (calculated under the method described in paragraph (e)(5)(iii) of this section), multiplied by the number of calendar months that have elapsed since the end of the taxable year. For purposes of calculating the number of calendar months that have elapsed under the safe harbor method, a corrective distribution that is made on or before the fifteenth day of the month is treated as made on the last day of the preceding month. A distribution made after the fifteenth day of the month is treated as made on the first day of the next month.

(v) *Alternative method for allocating taxable year and gap period income.*—A plan may determine the allocable gain or loss for the aggregate of the taxable year and the gap period by applying the alternative method provided by paragraph (e)(5)(iii) of this section to this aggregate period. This is accomplished by substituting the income for the taxable year and the gap period for the income for the taxable year and by substituting the elective deferrals for the taxable year and the gap period for the elective deferrals for the taxable year in determining the fraction that is multiplied by that income.

(6) *Coordination with distribution or recharacterization of excess contributions.*—The amount of excess deferrals that may be distributed under this paragraph (e) with respect to an employee for a taxable year is reduced by any excess contributions previously distributed or recharacterized with respect to the employee for the plan year beginning with or within the taxable year. In the event of a reduction under this paragraph (e)(6), the amount of excess contributions includible in the gross income of the employee and reported by the employer as a distribution of excess contributions is reduced by the amount of the reduction under this paragraph (e)(6). See § 1.401(k)-2(b)(4)(i). In no case may an individual receive from a plan as a corrective distribution for a taxable year under paragraph (e)(2) or (e)(3) of this section an amount in excess of the individual's total elective deferrals under the plan for the taxable year.

(7) *No employee or spousal consent required.*—A corrective distribution of excess deferrals (and income) may be made under the terms of the plan without regard to any notice or consent otherwise required under sections 411(a)(11) or 417.

(8) *Tax treatment.*—(i) *Corrective distributions on or before April 15 after close of taxable year.*—A corrective distribution of excess deferrals within the period described in paragraph (e)(2) or (e)(3) of this section is excludable from the employee's gross income. However, the income allocable to excess deferrals is includible in the employee's gross income for the taxable year in which the allocable income is distributed. The corrective distribution of excess deferrals (and income) is not subject to the early distribution tax of section 72(t) and is not treated as a distribution for purposes of applying the excise tax under section 4980A.

(ii) *Special rule for 1987 and 1988 excess deferrals.*—Income on excess deferrals for 1987 or 1988 that were timely distributed on or before April 17, 1989, may be reported by the recipient either in the year described in paragraph (e)(8)(i) of this section, or in the year in which the employee would have received the elective deferrals had the employee originally elected to receive the amounts in cash.

Employee	Compensation
A	$140,000
B	70,000
C	70,000
D	45,000
E	40,000
F	35,000
G	35,000
H	30,000
I	17,500
J	17,500

(ii) Employees A, B, and C are highly compensated employees within the meaning of section 414(q). Employees D, E, F, G, H, I, and J are nonhighly compensated employees. The actual deferral percentages for the highly compensated employees and nonhighly compensated employees are 8.33 percent and 4.43 percent, respectively. These percentages do not satisfy the requirements of section

(iii) *Distributions of excess deferrals after correction period.*—If excess deferrals (and income) for a taxable year are not distributed within the period described in paragraphs (e)(2) and (e)(3) of this section, they may only be distributed when permitted under section 401(k)(2)(B). These amounts are includible in gross income when distributed, and are treated for purposes of the distribution rules otherwise applicable to the plan as elective deferrals (and income) that were excludable from the individual's gross income under section 402(g). Thus, any amount includible in gross income for any taxable year under this section that is not distributed by April 15 of the following taxable year is not treated as an investment in the contract for purposes of section 72 and is includible in the employee's gross income when distributed from the plan. Excess deferrals that are distributed under this paragraph (e)(8)(iii) are treated as employer contributions for purposes of section 415 when they are contributed to the plan.

(iv) *Distributions of excess deferrals from a designated Roth account.*—The rules of paragraph (e)(8)(iii) of this section generally apply to distributions of excess deferrals that are designated Roth contributions and the attributable income. Thus, if a designated Roth account described in section 402A includes any excess deferrals, any distribution of amounts attributable to those excess deferrals are includible in gross income (without adjustment for any return of investment in the contract under section 72(e)(8)). In addition, such distributions cannot be qualified distributions described in section 402A(d)(2) and are not eligible rollover distributions within the meaning of section 402(c)(4). For this purpose, if a designated Roth account includes any excess deferrals, any distributions from the account are treated as attributable to those excess deferrals until the total amount distributed from the designated Roth account equals the total of such deferrals and attributable income.

(9) *No reduction of required minimum distribution.*—A distribution of excess deferrals (and income) under paragraphs (e)(2) and (e)(3) of this section is not treated as a distribution for purposes of determining whether the plan meets the minimum distribution requirements of section 401(a)(9).

(10) *Partial correction.*—Any distribution under paragraphs (e)(2) or (e)(3) of this section of less than the entire amount of excess deferrals (and income) is treated as a pro rata distribution of excess deferrals and income.

(11) *Examples.*—The provisions of this paragraph are illustrated by the following examples. Assume in *Examples 1* and *2* that there is no income or loss allocable to the elective deferrals.

Example 1. Employee A is a 60-year-old highly compensated employee who participates in Employer M's cash or deferred arrangement. During the period of January through September of 1988, A contributed $7,000 to the arrangement in elective deferrals. During the same period A also contributed $813 in elective deferrals under a plan of an unrelated employer. In December of 1988, A made a withdrawal of $1,000 from Employer M's plan but did not designate this as a withdrawal of an excess deferral. In January of 1989, A notifies Employer M of an excess deferral, specifying a distribution of $500 for 1988. To correct the excess deferrals, A must receive this additional $500 even though A has already withdrawn $1,000 for 1988. A may exclude from income in 1988 only $7,313. However, if the $500 is distributed by April 15, 1989, the distribution is excludable from A's gross income in 1989. Even if A withdraws the $500, M must take into account the entire $7,000 in computing A's actual deferral percentage for 1988.

Example 2. (i) Corporation X maintains a cash or deferred arrangement. The plan year is the calendar year. For plan year 1989, all 10 of X's employees are eligible to participate in the plan. The employees' compensation, contributions, and actual deferral ratios are shown in the following table:

Contribution	Actual Deferral Ratio
$7,000	5.0 %
7,000	10.0
7,000	10.0
2,250	5.0
4,000	10.0
1,750	5.0
350	1.0
3,000	10.0
0	0.0
0	0.0

401(k)(3)(A)(ii). The actual deferral percentage for the highly compensated employees may not exceed 6.43 percent.

(iii) The plan reduces the actual deferral ratios of B and C to 7.14 percent by distributing $2,002 ($7,000 − .0714 × $70,000) to each in January 1990. Section 401(k)(3)(A)(ii) is therefore satisfied.

(iv) In February 1990, B notifies X that B made elective deferrals of $2,000 under a qualified cash or deferred arrangement maintained by an unrelated employer in 1989, and requests distribution of $2,000 from X's plan. However, since B has already received a distribution of $2,002 to meet the ADP test, no additional amounts are required or are permitted to be distributed as excess deferrals by this plan, and the prior distribution of excess contributions has corrected the excess deferrals. But X must report $2,000 as a distribution of an excess deferral and $2 as a distribution of an excess contribution.

Example 3. Employee T has excess deferrals of $1,000. The income attributable to excess deferrals is $100. T properly notifies the employer, and requests a distribution of the excess deferral (and income) on February 1. The plan distributes $1,000 to T by April 15. Because the plan did not distribute any additional amount as income, $909 is treated as a distribution of excess deferrals, and $91 is treated as a distribution of earnings. With respect to amounts remaining in the account, $91 is treated as an elective deferral and is not included in T's investment in the contract. Because it was not distributed by the required date, the $91 is includible in gross income upon distribution as well as in the year of deferral.

(f) *Community property laws.*—This section is applied without regard to community property laws.

(g) *Effective date.*—(1) *In general.*—Except as otherwise provided, the provisions of this section are effective for taxable years beginning after December 31, 1986.

(2) *Deferrals under collective bargaining agreements.*—In the case of a plan maintained pursuant to one or more collective bargaining agreements between employee representatives and one or more employers ratified before March 1, 1986, the provisions of this section do not apply to contributions made pursuant to the collective bargaining agreement for taxable years beginning before the earlier of January 1, 1989, or the date on which the agreement terminates (determined without regard to any extension thereof after February 28, 1986). These contributions under a collective bargaining agreement are taken into account for purposes of applying this section to elective deferrals under plans not described in this paragraph (g)(2).

(3) *Transition rule.*—For taxable years beginning before January 1, 1992, a plan or an individual may rely on a reasonable interpretation of the rules set forth in section 402(g), as in effect during those years.

(4) *Partnership cash or deferred arrangements.*—For purposes of section 402(g), employer contributions for any plan year beginning after December 31, 1986, and before January 1, 1989, under an arrangement that directly or indirectly permits individual partners to vary the amount of contributions made on their behalf will be treated as elective contributions only if the arrangement was intended to satisfy and did satisfy the nondiscrimination test of section 401(k)(3) and §1.401(k)-1(b) for the plan year. [Reg. §1.402(g)-1.]

☐ [*T.D. 8357, 8-8-91. Amended by T.D. 8581, 12-22-94; T.D. 9169, 12-28-2004 and T.D. 9324, 4-27-2007.*]

[Reg. §1.402(g)-2]

§1.402(g)-2. Increased limit for catch-up contributions.—(a) *General rule.*—Under section 402(g)(1)(C), in determining the amount of elective deferrals that are includible in gross income under section 402(g) for a catch-up eligible participant (within the meaning of §1.414(v)-1(g)), the otherwise applicable dollar limit under section 402(g)(1)(B) (as increased under section 402(g)(7), to the extent applicable) shall be further increased by the applicable dollar catch-up limit as set forth under §1.414(v)-1(c)(2).

(b) *Participants in multiple plans.*—Paragraph (a) of this section applies without regard to whether the applicable employer plans (within the meaning of section 414(v)(6)) treat the elective deferrals as catch-up contributions. Thus, a catch-up eligible participant who makes elective deferrals under applicable employer plans of two or more employers that in total exceed the applicable dollar amount under section 402(g)(1) by an amount that does not exceed the applicable dollar catch-up limit under either plan may exclude the elective deferrals from gross income, even if neither applicable employer plan treats those elective deferrals as catch-up contributions.

(c) *Effective date.*—(1) *Statutory effective date.*—Section 402(g)(1)(C) applies to contributions in taxable years beginning on or after January 1, 2002.

(2) *Regulatory effective date.*—Paragraphs (a) and (b) of this section apply to contributions in taxable years beginning on or after January 1, 2004. [Reg. §1.402(g)-2.]

☐ [*T.D. 9072, 7-7-2003.*]

[Reg. §1.402(g)(3)-1]

§1.402(g)(3)-1. Employer contributions to purchase a section 403(b) contract under a salary reduction agreement.—(a) *General rule.*—With respect to an annuity contract under section 403(b), except as provided in paragraph (b) of this section, an elective deferral means an employer contribution to purchase an annuity contract under section 403(b) under a salary reduction agreement within the meaning of section 3121(a)(5)(D).

(b) *Special rule.*—Notwithstanding paragraph (a) of this section, for purposes of section 403(b), an elective deferral only includes a contribution that is made pursuant to a cash or deferred election (as defined at §1.401(k)-1(a)(3)). Thus, for purposes of section 402(g)(3)(C), an elective deferral does not include a contribution that is made pursuant to an employee's one-time irrevocable election made on or before the employee's first becoming eligible to participate under the employer's plans or a contribution made as a condition of employment that reduces the employee's compensation.

(c) *Applicable date.*—This section is applicable for taxable years beginning after December 31, 2008. [Reg. §1.402(g)(3)-1.]

☐ [*T.D. 9340, 7-23-2007.*]

[Reg. §1.402A-1]

§1.402A-1. Designated Roth Accounts.
Q-1. What is a designated Roth account?
A-1. A designated Roth account is a separate account under a qualified cash or deferred arrangement under a section 401(a) plan, or under a section 403(b) plan, to which designated Roth contributions are permitted to be made in lieu of elective contributions and that satisfies the requirements of §1.401(k)-1(f) (in the case of a section 401(a) plan) or §1.403(b)-3(c) (in the case of a section 403(b) plan).
Q-2. How is a distribution from a designated Roth account taxed?
A-2. (a) The taxation of a distribution from a designated Roth account depends on whether or not the distribution is a qualified distribution. A qualified distribution from a designated Roth account is not includible in the distributee's gross income.
(b) Except as otherwise provided in paragraph (c) of this A-2, a qualified distribution is a distribution that is both—
(1) Made after the 5-taxable-year period of participation defined in A-4 of this section has been completed; and
(2) Made on or after the date the employee attains age 591/2, made to a beneficiary or the estate of the employee on or after the employee's death, or attributable to the employee's being disabled within the meaning of section 72(m)(7).
(c) A distribution from a designated Roth account is not a qualified distribution to the extent it consists of a distribution of excess deferrals and attributable income described in §1.402(g)-1(e). See A-11 of this section for other amounts that are not treated as qualified distributions, including excess contributions described in section 401(k)(8), and excess aggregate contributions described in section 401(m)(8), and income, on any of these excess amounts.
Q-3. How is a distribution from a designated Roth account taxed if it is not a qualified distribution?
A-3. Except as provided in A-11 of this section, a distribution from a designated Roth account that is not a qualified distribution is taxable to the distributee under section 402 in the case of a plan qualified under section 401(a) and under section 403(b)(1) in the case of a section 403(b) plan. For this purpose, a designated Roth account is treated as a separate contract under section 72. Thus, except as otherwise provided in A-5 of this section for a rollover, if a distribution is before the annuity starting date, the portion of any distribution that is includible in gross income as an amount allocable to income on the contract and the portion not includible in gross income as an amount allocable to investment in the contract is determined under section 72(e)(8), treating the designated Roth account as a separate contract. Similarly, in the case of any amount received as an annuity, if a distribution is on or after the annuity starting date, the portion of any annuity payment that is includible in gross income as an amount allocable to income on the contract and the portion not includible in gross income as an amount allocable to investment in the contract is determined under section 72(b) or (d), as applicable, treating the designated Roth account as a separate contract. For purposes of section 72, designated Roth contributions are described in section 72(f)(1) or 72(f)(2), to the extent applicable.
Q-4. What is the 5-taxable-year period of participation described in A-2 of this section?
A-4. (a) The 5-taxable-year period of participation described in A-2 of this section for a plan is the period of 5 consecutive taxable years that begins with the first day of the first taxable year in which the employee makes a designated Roth contribution to any designated Roth account established for the employee under the same plan and ends when 5 consecutive taxable years have been completed. For this purpose, the first taxable year in which an employee makes a desig-

nated Roth contribution is the year in which the amount is includible in the employee's gross income. Notwithstanding the preceding, however, a contribution that is returned as an excess deferral or excess contribution does not begin the 5 taxable-year period of participation. Similarly, a contribution returned as a permissible withdrawal under section 414(w) does not begin the 5 taxable-year period of participation.

(b) Generally, an employee's 5-taxable-year period of participation is determined separately for each plan (within the meaning of section 414(l)) in which the employee participates. Thus, if an employee has elective deferrals made to designated Roth accounts under two or more plans, the employee may have two or more different 5-taxable-year periods of participation, depending on when the employee first had contributions made to a designated Roth account under each plan. However, if a direct rollover contribution of a distribution from a designated Roth account under another plan is made by the employee to the plan, the 5-taxable-year period of participation begins on the first day of the employee's taxable year in which the employee first had designated Roth contributions made to such other designated Roth account, if earlier than the first taxable year in which a designated Roth contribution is made to the plan. See A-5(c) of this section for additional rules on determining the start of the 5-taxable-year of participation in the case of an indirect rollover.

(c) The beginning of the 5-taxable-year period of participation is not redetermined for any portion of an employee's designated Roth account. This is true even if the entire designated Roth account is distributed during the 5-taxable-year period of participation and the employee subsequently makes additional designated Roth contributions under the plan.

(d) The rule in paragraph (c) of this section applies if the employee dies or the account is divided pursuant to a qualified domestic relations order (QDRO), and thus, a portion of the account is not payable to the employee and is payable to the employee's beneficiary or an alternate payee. In the case of distribution to an alternate payee or beneficiary, generally, the age, death, or disability of the employee is used to determine whether the distribution to an alternate payee or beneficiary is qualified. However, if an alternate payee or a spousal beneficiary rolls the distribution into a designated Roth account in a plan maintained by his or her own employer, such individual's age, disability, or death is used to determine whether a distribution from the recipient plan is qualified. In addition, if the rollover is a direct rollover contribution to the alternate payee's or spousal beneficiary's own designated Roth account, the 5-taxable-year period of participation under the recipient plan begins on the earlier of the date the employee's 5-taxable-year period of participation began under the distributing plan or the date the 5-taxable-year period of participation applicable to the alternate payee's or spousal beneficiary's designated Roth account began under the recipient plan.

(e) If a designated Roth contribution is made by a reemployed veteran for a year of qualified military service pursuant to section 414(u) that is before the year in which the contribution is actually made, the contribution is treated as having been made in the year of qualified military service to which the contribution relates, as designated by the reemployed veteran. Reemployed veterans may identify the year of qualified military service for which a contribution is made for other purposes, such as for entitlement to a match, and the treatment for the 5-taxable-year period of participation rule follows that identification. In the absence of such designation, for purposes of determining the first year of the five years of participation under section 402A(d)(2)(B), the contribution is treated as relating to the first year of qualified military service for which the reemployed veteran could have made designated Roth contributions under the plan, or if later the first taxable year in which designated Roth contributions could be made under the plan.

Q-5. How do the taxation rules apply to a distribution from a designated Roth account that is rolled over?

A-5. (a) An eligible rollover distribution from a designated Roth account is permitted to be rolled over into another designated Roth account or a Roth IRA, and the amount rolled over is not currently includable in gross income. In accordance with section 402(c)(2), to the extent that a portion of a distribution from a designated Roth account is not includible in income (determined without regard to the rollover), if that portion of the distribution is to be rolled over into a designated Roth account, the rollover must be accomplished through a direct rollover (i.e., a 60 day rollover to another designated Roth account is not available for this portion of the distribution). If a distribution from a designated Roth account is instead made to the employee, the employee would still be able to roll over the entire amount (or any portion thereof) into a Roth IRA within the 60-day period described in section 402(c)(3). For distributions made prior to January 1, 2016, any amount paid in a direct rollover is treated as a separate distribution from any amount paid directly to the employee, except that taxpayers may choose not to apply this sentence to distributions made on or after September 18, 2014, and before January 1, 2016.

(b) In the case of an eligible rollover distribution from a designated Roth account that is not a qualified distribution and not paid as a direct rollover contribution, if less than the entire amount of the distribution is rolled over, the part that is rolled over is deemed to consist first of the portion of the distribution that is attributable to income under section 72(e)(8).

(c) If an employee receives a distribution from a designated Roth account, the portion of the distribution that would be includible in gross income is permitted to be rolled over into a designated Roth account under another plan. In such a case, §1.402A-2, A-3, provides for additional reporting by the recipient plan. In addition, the employee's period of participation under the distributing plan is not carried over to the recipient plan for purposes of satisfying the 5-taxable-year period of participation requirement under the recipient plan. Generally, the taxable year in which the recipient plan accepts such rollover contribution is the taxable year that begins the participant's new 5-taxable-year period of participation. However, if the participant is rolling over to a plan in which the participant already has a pre-existing designated Roth account with a longer period of participation, the starting date of the recipient account is used to measure the participant's 5-taxable-year period of participation.

(d) The following example illustrates the application of this A-5:

Example. Employee B receives a $14,000 eligible rollover distribution that is not a qualified distribution from B's designated Roth account, consisting of $11,000 of investment in the contract and $3,000 of income. Within 60 days of receipt, Employee B rolls over $7,000 of the distribution into a Roth IRA. The $7,000 is deemed to consist of $3,000 of income and $4,000 of investment in the contract. Because the only portion of the distribution that could be includible in gross income (the income) is rolled over, none of the distribution is includible in Employee B's gross income.

(e) This A-5 applies for taxable years beginning on or after January 1, 2006.

Q-6. In the case of a rollover contribution to a designated Roth account, how is the amount that is treated as investment in the contract under section 72 determined?

A-6. (a) If a distribution from a designated Roth account is rolled over to another designated Roth account in a direct rollover, the amount of the rollover contribution allocated to investment in the contract in the recipient designated Roth account is the amount that would not have been includible in gross income (determined without regard to section 402(e)(4)) if the distribution had not been rolled over. Thus, if an amount that is a qualified distribution is rolled over, the entire amount of the rollover contribution is allocated to investment in the contract.

(b) If the entire account balance of a designated Roth account is rolled over to another designated Roth account in a direct rollover, and, at the time of the distribution, the investment in the contract exceeds the balance in the designated Roth account, the investment in the contract in the distributing plan is included in the investment in the contract of the recipient plan.

Q-7. After a qualified distribution from a designated Roth account has been made, how is the remaining investment in the contract of the designated Roth account determined under section 72?

A-7. (a) The portion of any qualified distribution that is treated as a recovery of investment in the contract is determined in the same manner as if the distribution were not a qualified distribution. (See A-3 of this section) Thus, the remaining investment in the contract in a designated Roth account after a qualified distribution is determined in the same manner after a qualified distribution as it would be determined if the distribution were not a qualified distribution.

(b) The following example illustrates the application of this A-7:

Example. Employee C receives a $12,000 distribution, which is a qualified distribution that is attributable to the employee being disabled within the meaning of section 72(m)(7), from C's designated Roth account. Immediately prior to the distribution, the account consisted of $21,850 of investment in the contract (i.e., designated Roth contributions) and $1,150 of income. For purposes of determining recovery of investment in the contract under section 72, the distribution is deemed to consist of $11,400 of investment in the contract [$12,000 × 21,850/(1,150 − 21,850)], and $600 of income [$12,000 × 1,150/(1,150 + 21,850)]. Immediately after the distribution, C's designated Roth account consists of $10,450 of investment in the contract and $550 of income. This determination of the remaining investment in the contract will be needed if C subsequently is no longer disabled and takes a nonqualified distribution from the designated Roth account.

Q-8. What is the relationship between the accounting for designated Roth contributions as investment in the contract for purposes of section 72 and their treatment as elective deferrals available for a hardship distribution under section 401(k)(2)(B)?

A-8. (a) There is no relationship between the accounting for designated Roth contributions as investment in the contract for purposes of section 72 and their treatment as elective deferrals available for a hardship distribution under section 401(k)(2)(B). A plan that makes a hardship distribution under section 401(k)(2)(B) from elective deferrals that includes designated Roth contributions must separately determine the amount of elective deferrals available for hardship and the amount of investment in the contract attributable to designated Roth contributions for purposes of section 72. Thus, the entire amount of a hardship distribution is treated as reducing the otherwise maximum distributable amount for purposes of applying the rule in section 401(k)(2)(B) and § 1.401(k)-1(d)(3)(ii) that generally limits hardship distributions to the principal amount of elective deferrals made less the amount of elective deferrals previously distributed from the plan, even if a portion of the distribution is treated as income under section 72(e)(8).

(b) The following example illustrates the application of this A-8:

Example. The facts are the same as in the Example in A-7 of this section, except that instead of being disabled, Employee C is receiving a hardship distribution. In addition, Employee C has made elective deferrals that are not designated Roth contributions totaling $20,000 and has received no previous distributions of elective deferrals from the plan. The adjustment to the investment in the contract is the same as in A-7 of this section, but for purposes of determining the amount of elective deferrals available for future hardship distribution, the entire amount of the distribution is subtracted from the maximum distributable amount. Thus, Employee C has only $29,850 ($41,850 – $12,000) available for hardship distribution from C's designated Roth account.

Q-9. Can an employee have more than one separate contract for designated Roth contributions under a plan qualified under section 401(a) or a section 403(b) plan?

A-9. (a) Except as otherwise provided in paragraph (b) of this A-9, for purposes of section 72, there is only one separate contract for an employee with respect to the designated Roth contributions under a plan. Thus, if a plan maintains one separate account for designated Roth contributions made under the plan and another separate account for rollover contributions received from a designated Roth account under another plan (so that the rollover account is not required to be subject to the distribution restrictions otherwise applicable to the account consisting of designated Roth contributions made under the plan), both separate accounts are considered to be one contract for purposes of applying section 72 to the distributions from either account.

(b) If a separate account with respect to an employee's accrued benefit consisting of designated Roth contributions is established and maintained for an alternate payee pursuant to a qualified domestic relations order and another designated Roth account is maintained for the employee, each account is treated as a separate contract for purposes of section 72. The alternate payee's designated Roth account is also a separate contract for purposes of section 72 with respect to any other account maintained for that alternate payee. Similarly, if separate accounts are established and maintained for different beneficiaries after the death of an employee, the separate account for each beneficiary is treated as a separate contract under section 72 and is also a separate contract with respect to any other account maintained for that beneficiary under the plan that is not a designated Roth account. When the separate account is established for an alternate payee or for a beneficiary (after an employee's death), each separate account must receive a proportionate amount attributable to investment in the contract.

Q-10. What is the tax treatment of employer securities distributed from a designated Roth account?

A-10. (a) If a distribution of employer securities from a designated Roth account is not a qualified distribution, section 402(e)(4)(B) applies. Thus, in the case of a lump-sum distribution that includes employer securities, unless the taxpayer elects otherwise, net unrealized appreciation attributable to the employer securities is not includible in gross income; and such net unrealized appreciation is not included in the basis of the distributed securities and is capital gain to the extent such appreciation is realized in a subsequent taxable transaction.

(b) In the case of a qualified distribution of employer securities from a designated Roth account, the distributee's basis in the distributed securities for purposes of subsequent disposition is their fair market value at the time of distribution.

Q-11. Can an amount described in A-4 of § 1.402(c)-2 with respect to a designated Roth account be a qualified distribution?

A-11. No. An amount described in A-4 of § 1.402(c)-2 with respect to a designated Roth account cannot be a qualified distribution. Such an amount is taxable under the rules of §§ 1.72-16(b), 1.72(p)-1, A-11 through A-13, 1.402(g)-1(e)(8), 1.401(k)-2(b)(2)(vi), 1.401(m)-2(b)(2)(vi), or 1.404(k)-1T. Thus, for example, loans that are treated as deemed distributions pursuant to section 72(p), or divi-

dends paid on employer securities as described in section 404(k) are not qualified distributions even if the deemed distributions occur or the dividends are paid after the employee attains age 59 1/2 and the 5-taxable-year period of participation defined in A-4 of this section has been satisfied. However, if a dividend is reinvested in accordance with section 404(k)(2)(A)(iii)(II), the amount of such a dividend is not precluded from being a qualified distribution if later distributed. Further, an amount is not precluded from being a qualified distribution merely because it is described in section 402(c)(4) as an amount not eligible for rollover. Thus, a hardship distribution is not precluded from being a qualified distribution.

Q-12. If any amount from a designated Roth account is included in a loan to an employee, do the plan aggregation rules of section 72(p)(2)(D) apply for purposes of determining the total amount an employee is permitted to borrow from the plan, even though the designated Roth account generally is treated as a separate contract under section 72?

A-12. Yes. If any amount from a designated Roth account is included in a loan to an employee, notwithstanding the general rule that the designated Roth account is treated as a separate contract under section 72, the plan aggregation rules of section 72(p)(2)(D) apply for purposes of determining the maximum amount the employee is permitted to borrow from the plan and such amount is based on the total of the designated Roth contribution amounts and the other amounts under the plan. To the extent a loan is from a designated Roth account, the repayment requirement of section 72(p)(2)(C) must be satisfied separately with respect to that portion of the loan and with respect to the portion of the loan from other accounts under the plan.

Q-13. Does a transaction or accounting methodology involving an employee's designated Roth account and any other accounts under the plan or plans of an employer that has the effect of transferring value from the other accounts into the designated Roth account violate the separate accounting requirement of section 402A?

A-13. (a) Yes. Any transaction or accounting methodology involving an employee's designated Roth account and any other accounts under the plan or plans of an employer that has the effect of directly or indirectly transferring value from another account into the designated Roth account violates the separate accounting requirement under section 402A. However, any transaction that merely exchanges investments between accounts at fair market value will not violate the separate accounting requirement.

(b) In the case of an annuity contract which contains both a designated Roth account and any other accounts, the Commissioner may prescribe additional guidance of general applicability, published in the Internal Revenue Bulletin (see 601.601(d)(2) of this chapter), to provide additional rules for allocation of income, expenses, gains and losses among the accounts under the contract.

(c) This A-13 applies to designated Roth accounts for taxable years beginning on or after January 1, 2006.

Q-14. How is an annuity contract that is distributed from a designated Roth account treated for purposes of section 402A?

A-14. A qualified plan distributed annuity contract within the meaning of § 1.402(c)-2, A-10(a) that is distributed from a designated Roth account is not treated as a distribution for purposes of section 402 or 402A. Instead, the amounts paid under the annuity contract are treated as distributions for purposes of sections 402 and 402A. Thus, the period after the annuity contract is distributed and before a payment from the annuity contract is made is included in determining whether the five-year period of participation is satisfied. Further, for purposes of determining if a distribution is a qualified distribution, the determination of whether a distribution is made on or after the date the employee attains age 59^{1}/2, made to a beneficiary or the estate of the employee on or after the employee's death, or attributable to the employee's being disabled within the meaning of section 72(m)(7) is made based on the facts at the time the distribution is made from the annuity contract. Thus for example, if an employee first makes a designated Roth contribution to a designated Roth account in 2006 at age 56, receives a distributed annuity contract within the meaning of § 1.402(c)-2, A-10(a) in 2007 purchased only with assets from the designated Roth account, and then receives a distribution from the contract in 2011 at age 60, the distribution is a qualified distribution.

Q-15. When are section 402A and this § 1.402A-1 applicable?

A-15. Section 402A is applicable for taxable years beginning on or after January 1, 2006. Except as otherwise provided in A-5 and A-13 of this section, the rules of this § 1.402A-1 apply for taxable years beginning on or after January 1, 2007. [Reg. § 1.402A-1.]

☐ [T.D. 9324, 4-27-2007 (*corrected* 6-4-2007). *Amended by* T.D. 9340, 7-23-2007 *and* T.D. 9769, 5-17-2016.]

[Reg. §1.402A-2]

§1.402A-2. Reporting and recordkeeping requirements with respect to designated Roth accounts.

Q-1. Who is responsible for keeping track of the 5-taxable-year period of participation and the investment in the contract, i.e., the amount of unrecovered designated Roth contributions for the employee?

A-1. The plan administrator or other responsible party with respect to a plan with a designated Roth account is responsible for keeping track of the 5-taxable-year period of participation for each employee and the amount of investment in the contract (unrecovered designated Roth contributions) on behalf of such employee. For purposes of the preceding sentence, in the absence of actual knowledge to the contrary, the plan administrator or other responsible party is permitted to assume that an employee's taxable year is the calendar year. In the case of a direct rollover from another designated Roth account, the plan administrator or other responsible party of the recipient plan can rely on reasonable representations made by the plan administrator or responsible party with respect to the plan with the other designated Roth account. See A-2 of this section for statements required in the case of rollovers.

Q-2. In the case of an eligible rollover distribution from a designated Roth account, what additional information must be provided with respect to such distribution?

A-2. (a) Pursuant to section 6047(f), if an amount is distributed from a designated Roth account, the plan administrator or other responsible party with respect to the plan must provide a statement as described below in the following situations—

(1) In the case of a direct rollover of a distribution from a designated Roth account under a plan to a designated Roth account under another plan, the plan administrator or other responsible party must provide to the plan administrator or responsible party of the recipient plan either a statement indicating the first year of the 5-taxable-year period described in A-1 of this section and the portion of the distribution that is attributable to investment in the contract under section 72, or a statement that the distribution is a qualified distribution.

(2) If the distribution is not a direct rollover to a designated Roth account under another plan, the plan administrator or responsible party must provide to the employee, upon request, the same information described in paragraph (a)(1) of this A-2, except the statement need not indicate the first year of the 5-taxable-year period described in A-1 of this section.

(b) The statement described in paragraph (a) of this A-2 must be provided within a reasonable period following the direct rollover or distributee request but in no event later than 30 days following the direct rollover or distributee request.

Q-3. If a plan qualified under section 401(a) or a section 403(b) plan accepts a 60-day rollover of earnings from a designated Roth account, what report to the IRS must be provided with respect to such rollover contribution?

A-3. To the extent required in Forms and Instructions, if a plan qualified under section 401(a), or a section 403(b) plan, accepts a rollover contribution (other than a direct rollover contribution) under section 402(c)(2), or section 403(b)(8)(B), of the portion of a distribution from a designated Roth account that would have been includable in gross income, the plan administrator or other responsible party for the recipient plan must notify the Commissioner of its acceptance of the rollover contribution no later than the due date for filing Form 1099-R, "Distributions From Pensions, Annuities, Retirement or Profit-Sharing Plans, IRAs, Insurance Contracts, etc.," The Forms and Instructions will specify the address to which the notification is required to be sent and will require inclusion of the employee's name and social security number, the amount rolled over, the year in which the rollover contribution was made, and such other information as the Commissioner may prescribe in order to determine that the amount rolled over is a valid rollover contribution.

Q-4. When is this §1.402A-2 applicable?

A-4. The rules of this §1.402A-2 are applicable for taxable years beginning on or after January 1, 2007. [Reg. §1.402A-2.]

□ [*T.D.* 9324, 4-27-2007 (*corrected* 6-4-2007).]

[Reg. §1.403(a)-1]

§1.403(a)-1. Taxability of beneficiary under a qualified annuity plan.—(a) An employee or retired or former employee for whom an annuity contract is purchased by his employer is not required to include in his gross income the amount paid for the contract at the time such amount is paid, whether or not his rights to the contract are forfeitable, if the annuity contract is purchased under a plan which meets the requirements of section 404(a)(2). For purposes of the preceding sentence, it is immaterial whether the employer deducts the amounts paid for the contract under such section 404(a)(2). See §§1.403(b)-1 through 1.403(b)-10 for rules relating to annuity

contracts which are not purchased under qualified plans but which are purchased by organizations described in section 501(c)(3) and exempt under section 501(a) or which are purchased for employees who perform services for certain public schools.

(b) The amounts received by or made available to any employee referred to in paragraph (a) of this section under such annuity contract shall be included in gross income of the employee for the taxable year in which received or made available, as provided in section 72 (relating to annuities), except that certain total distributions described in section 403(a)(2) are taxable as long-term capital gains. For the treatment of such total distributions, see §1.403(a)-2. However, for taxable years beginning before January 1, 1964, section 72(e)(3) (relating to the treatment of certain lump sums), as in effect before such date, shall not apply to such amounts. For taxable years beginning after December 31, 1963, such amounts may be taken into account in computations under sections 1301 through 1305 (relating to income averaging).

(c) If upon the death of an employee or of a retired employee, the widow or other beneficiary of such employee is paid, in accordance with the terms of the annuity contract relating to the deceased employee, an annuity or other death benefit, the extent to which the amounts received by or made available to the beneficiary must be included in the beneficiary's income under section 403(a) shall be determined in accordance with the rules presented in paragraph (a)(5) of §1.402(a)-1.

(d) An individual contract issued after December 31, 1962, or a group contract, which provides incidental life insurance protection may be purchased under a qualified annuity plan. For the rules as to nontransferability of such contracts issued after December 31, 1962, see §1.401-9. For the rules relating to the taxation of the cost of the life insurance protection and the proceeds thereunder, see §1.72-16. Section 403(a) is not applicable to premiums paid after October 26, 1956, for individual contracts which were issued prior to January 1, 1963, and which provide life insurance protection.

(e) As to inclusion of full-time life insurance salesmen within the class of persons considered to be employees, see section 7701(a)(20).

(f) For purposes of this section and §1.403(a)-2, the term "employee" includes a self-employed individual who is treated as an employee under section 401(c)(1) and paragraph (b) of §1.401-10, and the term "employer" means the person treated as the employer of such individual under section 401(c)(4). For the rules relating to annuity plans covering self-employed individuals, see section 404(a)(2) and §§1.404(a)-8 and 1.401-10.

(g) The rules of §1.402(a)-1(e) apply for purposes of determining the treatment of amounts paid to provide accident and health insurance benefits. [Reg. §1.403(a)-1.]

□ [*T.D.* 6203, 9-24-56. *Amended by* T.D. 6676, 9-16-63, *by* T.D. 6722, 4-13-64, *by* T.D. 6783, 12-23-64, T.D. 6885, 6-1-66, T.D. 9340, 7-23-2007, T.D. 9665, 5-9-2014 *and T.D.* 9849, 3-11-2019.]

[Reg. §1.403(a)-2]

§1.403(a)-2. Capital gains treatment for certain distributions.— (a) If the total amounts payable with respect to any employee for whom an annuity contract has been purchased by an employer under a plan which—

(1) Is a plan described in section 403(a)(1) and §1.403(a)-1, and

(2) Requires that refunds of contributions with respect to annuity contracts purchased under such plan be used to reduce subsequent premiums on the contracts under the plan,

are paid to, or includible in gross income of, the payee within one taxable year of the payee by reason of the employee's death or other separation from the service, or death after such separation from the service, such total payments, to the extent they exceed the net amount contributed by the employee, shall be considered a gain from the sale or exchange of a capital asset held for more than six months. The "net amount contributed by the employee" is the amount actually contributed by the employee plus any amounts considered to be contributed by the employee under the rules of sections 72(f), 101(b), and paragraph (d) of §1.403(a)-1, reduced by any amounts theretofore distributed to him which were excludable from his gross income as a return of employee contributions. For example, if under an annuity contract purchased under a plan described in this section, the total distributions payable to the employee's widow are paid to her in the year in which the employee dies, in the amount of $8,000, and if $5,000 thereof is excludable under section 101(b), and if the employee made contributions of $600 and had received no payments, the remaining amount of $2,400 will be considered a gain from the sale or exchange of a capital asset held for more than six months.

(b)(1) The term "total amounts" means the balance to the credit of an employee with respect to all annuities under the annuity plan which becomes payable to the payee by reason of the employee's death or other separation from the service, or by reason of his death after separation from the service. If an employee commences to receive annuity payments on retirement and then a lump sum payment is made to his widow upon his death, the capital gains treatment applies to the lump sum payment, but it does not apply to amounts received before the time the "total amounts" become payable. However, if the total amount to the credit of the employee at the time of his death or other separation from the service or death after separation from the service is paid or includible in the gross income of the payee within one taxable year of the payee, such amount is entitled to the capital gains treatment notwithstanding that in a later taxable year an additional amount is credited to the employee and paid to the payee.

(2) If more than one annuity contract is received under the plan, the capital gains treatment does not apply to any amount received on the surrender thereof unless all contracts under the plan with respect to a particular employee are surrendered either at the time of the employee's death or other separation from the service or death after separation from the service. Thus, if an employee receives two contracts on separation from the service and surrenders one of them in the year of separation and receives payments under the other until his death, the capital gains treatment is applicable to the balance paid to his beneficiary on his death if paid within one taxable year of the beneficiary. The amount received by the employee on surrender of the contract in the year of his separation from the service, however, would not receive capital gains treatment since the balance to the credit of the employee with respect to all amounts under the plan did not become payable at that time.

(3) If an employee retires and commences to receive an annuity but subsequently in some succeeding taxable year, he is paid a lump sum in settlement of all future annuity payments, the capital gains treatment does not apply to such lump sum settlement paid during the lifetime of the employee since it is not a payment on account of separation from the service, or death after separation, but is on account of the settlement of future annuity payments.

(4) If the "total amounts" payable under all annuity contracts under the plan with respect to a particular employee are paid or includible in the gross income of several payees within one taxable year on account of the employee's death or other separation from the service or on account of his death after separation from the service, the capital gains treatment is applicable. Thus, if the balance to the credit of a deceased employee under all annuity contracts provided under an annuity plan becomes payable to two payees, the capital gains treatment is applicable provided the "total amounts" payable are received by or includible in the gross income of both payees within the same taxable year. However, if the "total amounts" payable are made available to each payee and one elects to receive his share in cash while the other makes a timely election under section 72(h) to receive his share as an annuity, the capital gains treatment does not apply to either payee.

(5) For purposes of determining whether the total amounts payable to an employee have been paid within one taxable year, the term "total amounts" includes amounts under a plan which are attributable to contributions on behalf of an individual while he was self-employed in the business with respect to which the plan was established. Thus, the "total amounts" payable are not paid within one taxable year if amounts remain payable which are so attributable.

(6) The term "total amounts" does not include any amount which has been placed in a separate account for the funding of benefits described in section 401(h). Thus, a distribution under a qualified annuity plan may constitute a distribution of the total amounts payable with respect to an employee even though amounts attributable to the funding of section 401(h) medical benefits as defined in paragraph (a) of §1.401-14 are not so distributed.

(c) The provisions of this section are not applicable to any amounts paid to a payee to the extent such amounts are attributable to contributions made on behalf of an employee while he was a self-employed individual in the business with respect to which the plan was established. For the taxation of such amounts, see §1.72-18. For the rules for determining the amount attributable to contributions on behalf of an employee while he was self-employed, see paragraphs (b)(4) and (c)(2) of such section. [Reg. §1.403(a)-2.]

☐ [T.D. 6302, 9-24-56. *Amended by T.D. 6676, 9-16-63, by T.D. 6722,* 4-13-64.]

[Reg. §1.403(b)-0]

§1.403(b)-0. Taxability under an annuity purchased by a section 501(c)(3) organization or a public school.—This section lists the headings that appear in §§1.403(b)-1 through 1.403(b)-11.

§1.403(b)-1 General overview of taxability under an annuity contract purchased by a section 501(c)(3) organization or a public school.

§1.403(b)-2 Definitions.
   (a) Application of definitions.
   (b) Definitions.

§1.403(b)-3 Exclusion for contributions to purchase section 403(b) contracts.
   (a) Exclusion for section 403(b) contracts.
   (b) Application of requirements.
   (c) Special rules for designated Roth section 403(b) contributions.
   (d) Effect of failure.

§1.403(b)-4 Contribution limitations.
   (a) Treatment of contributions in excess of limitations.
   (b) Maximum annual contribution.
   (c) Section 403(b) elective deferrals.
   (d) Employer contributions for former employees.
   (e) Special rules for determining years of service.
   (f) Excess contributions of deferrals.

§1.403(b)-5 Nondiscrimination rules.
   (a) Nondiscrimination rules for contributions other than section 403(b) elective deferrals.
   (b) Universal availability required for section 403(b) elective deferrals.
   (c) Plan required.
   (d) Church plans exception.
   (e) Other rules.

§1.403(b)-6 Timing of distributions and benefits.
   (a) Distributions generally.
   (b) Distributions from contracts other than custodial accounts or amounts attributable to section 403(b) elective deferrals.
   (c) Distributions from custodial accounts that are not attributable to section 403(b) elective deferrals.
   (d) Distribution of section 403(b) elective deferrals.
   (e) Minimum required distributions for eligible plans.
   (f) Loans.
   (g) Death benefits and other incidental benefits.
   (h) Special rule regarding severance from employment.

§1.403(b)-7 Taxation of distributions and benefits.
   (a) General rules for when amounts are included in gross income.
   (b) Rollovers to individual retirement arrangements and other eligible retirement plans.
   (c) Special rules for certain corrective distributions.
   (d) Amounts taxable under section 72(p)(1).
   (e) Special rules relating to distributions from a designated Roth account.
   (f) Certain rules relating to employment taxes.

§1.403(b)-8 Funding.
   (a) Investments.
   (b) Contributions to the plan.
   (c) Annuity contracts.
   (d) Custodial accounts.
   (e) Retirement income accounts.
   (f) Combining assets.

§1.403(b)-9 Special rules for church plans.
   (a) Retirement income accounts.
   (b) Retirement income account defined.
   (c) Special deduction rule for self-employed ministers.

§1.403(b)-10 Miscellaneous provisions.
   (a) Plan terminations and frozen plans.
   (b) Contract exchanges and plan-to-plan transfers.
   (c) Qualified domestic relations orders.
   (d) Rollovers to a section 403(b) contract.
   (e) Deemed IRAs.
   (f) Defined benefit plans.
   (g) Other rules relating to section 501(c)(3) organizations.

§1.403(b)-11 Applicable date.
   (a) General rule.
   (b) Collective bargaining agreements.
   (c) Church conventions.
   (d) Special rules for plans that exclude certain types of employees from elective deferrals.
   (e) Special rules for plans that permit in-service distributions.
   (f) Special rule for life insurance contracts.
   (g) Special rule for contracts received in an exchange.
[Reg. §1.403(b)-0.]
   ☐ [T.D. 9340, 7-23-2007.]

[Reg. § 1.403(b)-1]

§ 1.403(b)-1. General overview of taxability under an annuity contract purchased by a section 501(c)(3) organization or a public school.—Section 403(b) and § § 1.403(b)-2 through 1.403(b)-10 provide rules for the Federal income tax treatment of an annuity purchased for an employee by an employer that is either a tax-exempt entity under section 501(c)(3) (relating to certain religious, charitable, scientific, or other types of organizations) or a public school, or for a minister described in section 414(e)(5)(A). See section 403(a) (relating to qualified annuities) for rules regarding the taxation of an annuity purchased under a qualified annuity plan that meets the requirements of section 404(a)(2), and see section 403(c) (relating to nonqualified annuities) for rules regarding the taxation of other types of annuities. [Reg. § 1.403(b)-1.]

☐ [*T.D. 6203, 9-24-56. Amended by T.D. 6783, 12-23-64; T.D. 6885, 6-1-66; T.D. 7748, 12-30-80; T.D. 7836, 9-23-82; T.D. 8115, 12-16-86 and T.D. 9340, 7-23-3007.*]

[Reg. § 1.403(b)-2]

§ 1.403(b)-2. Definitions.—(a) **Application of definitions.**—The definitions set forth in this section are applicable for purposes of § 1.403(b)-1, this section and § § 1.403(b)-3 through 1.403(b)-11.

(b) *Definitions.*—(1) *Accumulated benefit* means the total benefit to which a participant or beneficiary is entitled under a section 403(b) contract, including all contributions made to the contract and all earnings thereon.

(2) *Annuity contract* means a contract that is issued by an insurance company qualified to issue annuities in a State and that includes payment in the form of an annuity. See § 1.401(f)-1(d)(2) and (e) for the definition of an annuity, and see § 1.403(b)-8(c)(3) for a special rule for certain State plans. See also § § 1.403(b)-8(d) and 1.403(b)-9(a) for additional rules regarding the treatment of custodial accounts and retirement income accounts as annuity contracts.

(3) *Beneficiary* means a person who is entitled to benefits in respect of a participant following the participant's death or an alternate payee pursuant to a qualified domestic relations order, as described in § 1.403(b)-10(c).

(4) *Catch-up* amount or *catch-up* limitation for a participant for a taxable year means a section 403(b) elective deferral permitted under section 414(v) (as described in § 1.403(b)-4(c)(2)) or section 402(g)(7) (as described in § 1.403(b)-4(c)(3)).

(5) *Church* means a church as defined in section 3121(w)(3)(A) and a qualified church-controlled organization as defined in section 3121(w)(3)(B).

(6) *Church-related organization* means a church or a convention or association of churches, including an organization described in section 414(e)(3)(A).

(7) *Elective deferral* means an elective deferral under § 1.402(g)-1 (with respect to an employer contribution to a section 403(b) contract) and any other amount that constitutes an elective deferral under section 402(g)(3).

(8)(i) *Eligible employer* means—

(A) A State, but only with respect to an employee of the State performing services for a public school;

(B) A section 501(c)(3) organization with respect to any employee of the section 501(c)(3) organization;

(C) Any employer of a minister described in section 414(e)(5)(A), but only with respect to the minister; or

(D) A minister described in section 414(e)(5)(A), but only with respect to a retirement income account established for the minister.

(ii) An entity is not an eligible employer under paragraph (a)(8)(i)(A) of this section if it treats itself as not being a State for any other purpose of the Internal Revenue Code, and a subsidiary or other affiliate of an eligible employer is not an eligible employer under paragraph (a)(8)(i) of this section if the subsidiary or other affiliate is not an entity described in paragraph (a)(8)(i) of this section.

(9) *Employee* means a common-law employee performing services for the employer, and does not include a former employee or an independent contractor. Subject to any rules in § 1.403(b)-1, this section, and § § 1.403(b)-3 through 1.403(b)-11 that are specifically applicable to ministers, an employee also includes a minister described in section 414(e)(5)(A) when performing services in the exercise of his or her ministry.

(10) *Employee performing services for a public school* means an employee performing services as an employee for a public school of a State. This definition is not applicable unless the employee's compensation for performing services for a public school is paid by the State. Further, a person occupying an elective or appointive public office is not an employee performing services for a public school unless such office is one to which an individual is elected or appointed only if the individual has received training, or is experienced, in the field of education. The term *public office* includes any elective or appointive office of a State.

(11) *Includible compensation* means the employee's compensation received from an eligible employer that is includible in the participant's gross income for Federal income tax purposes (computed without regard to section 911) for the most recent period that is a year of service. Includible compensation for a minister who is self-employed means the minister's earned income as defined in section 401(c)(2) (computed without regard to section 911) for the most recent period that is a year of service. Includible compensation does not include any compensation received during a period when the employer is not an eligible employer. Includible compensation also includes any elective deferral or other amount contributed or deferred by the eligible employer at the election of the employee that would be includible in the gross income of the employee but for the rules of sections 125, 132(f)(4), 402(e)(2), 402(h)(1)(B), 402(k), or 457(b). The amount of includible compensation is determined without regard to any community property laws. See section 415(c)(3)(A) through (D) for additional rules, and see § 1.403(b)-4(d) for a special rule regarding former employees.

(12) *Participant* means an employee for whom a section 403(b) contract is currently being purchased, or an employee or former employee for whom a section 403(b) contract has previously been purchased and who has not received a distribution of his or her entire accumulated benefit under the contract.

(13) *Plan* means a plan as described in § 1.403(b)-3(b)(3).

(14) *Public school* means a State-sponsored educational organization described in section 170(b)(1)(A)(ii) (relating to educational organizations that normally maintain a regular faculty and curriculum and normally have a regularly enrolled body of pupils or students in attendance at the place where educational activities are regularly carried on).

(15) *Retirement income account* means a defined contribution program established or maintained by a church-related organization to provide benefits under section 403(b) for its employees or their beneficiaries as described in § 1.403(b)-9.

(16) *Section 403(b) contract; section 403(b) plan.*—(i) *Section 403(b) contract* means a contract that satisfies the requirements of § 1.403(b)-3. If for any taxable year an employer contributes to more than one section 403(b) contract for a participant or beneficiary, then, under section 403(b)(5), all such contracts are treated as one contract for purposes of section 403(b) and § 1.403(b)-1, this section, and § § 1.403(b)-3 through 1.403(b)-11. See also § 1.403(b)-3(b)(1).

(ii) *Section 403(b) plan* means the plan of the employer under which the section 403(b) contracts for its employees are maintained.

(17) *Section 403(b) elective deferral; designated Roth contribution.*—(i) *Section 403(b) elective deferral* means an elective deferral that is an employer contribution to a section 403(b) plan for an employee. See § 1.403(b)-5(b) for additional rules with respect to a section 403(b) elective deferral.

(ii) *Designated Roth contribution* under a section 403(b) plan means a section 403(b) elective deferral that satisfies § 1.403(b)-3(c).

(18) *Section 501(c)(3) organization* means an organization that is described in section 501(c)(3) (relating to certain religious, charitable, scientific, or other types of organizations) and exempt from tax under section 501(a).

(19) *Severance from employment* means that the employee ceases to be employed by the employer maintaining the plan. See § 1.401(k)-1(d) for additional guidance concerning severance from employment. See also § 1.403(b)-6(h) for a special rule under which severance from employment is determined by reference to employment with the eligible employer.

(20) *State* means a State, a political subdivision of a State, or any agency or instrumentality of a State. For this purpose, the District of Columbia is treated as a State. In addition, for purposes of determining whether an individual is an employee performing services for a public school, an Indian tribal government is treated as a State, as provided under section 7871(a)(6)(B). See also section 1450(b) of the Small Business Job Protection Act of 1996 (110 Stat. 1755, 1814) for special rules treating certain contracts purchased in a plan year beginning before January 1, 1995, that include contributions by an Indian tribal government as section 403(b) contracts, whether or not those contributions are for employees performing services for a public school.

(21) *Year of service* means each full year during which an individual is a full-time employee of an eligible employer, plus fractional credit for each part of a year during which the individual is either a full-time employee of an eligible employer for a part of the year or a part-time employee of an eligible employer. See § 1.403(b)-4(e) for rules for determining years of service. [Reg. § 1.403(b)-2.]

☐ [*T.D. 8619, 9-15-95. Amended by T.D. 8880, 4-20-2000 and T.D. 9340, 7-23-2007 (corrected 9-24-2007).*]

[Reg. §1.403(b)-3]

§1.403(b)-3. Exclusion for contributions to purchase section 403(b) contracts.—(a) *Exclusion for section 403(b) contracts.*—Amounts contributed by an eligible employer for the purchase of an annuity contract for an employee are excluded from the gross income of the employee under section 403(b) only if each of the requirements in paragraphs (a)(1) through (9) of this section is satisfied. In addition, amounts contributed by an eligible employer for the purchase of an annuity contract for an employee pursuant to a cash or deferred election (as defined at §1.401(k)-1(a)(3)) are not includible in an employee's gross income at the time the cash would have been includible in the employee's gross income (but for the cash or deferred election) if each of the requirements in paragraphs (a)(1) through (9) of this section is satisfied. However, the preceding two sentences generally do not apply to designated Roth contributions; see paragraph (c) of this section and §1.403(b)-7(e) for special taxation rules that apply with respect to designated Roth contributions under a section 403(b) plan.

(1) *Not a contract issued under qualified plan or eligible governmental plan.*—The annuity contract is not purchased under a qualified plan (under section 401(a) or 403(a)) or an eligible governmental plan under section 457(b).

(2) *Nonforfeitability.*—The rights of the employee under the annuity contract (disregarding rights to future premiums) are nonforfeitable. An employee's rights under a contract fail to be nonforfeitable unless the employee for whom the contract is purchased has at all times a fully vested and nonforfeitable right (as defined in regulations under section 411) to all benefits provided under the contract. See paragraph (d)(2) of this section for additional rules regarding the nonforfeitability requirement of this paragraph (a)(2).

(3) *Nondiscrimination.*—In the case of an annuity contract purchased by an eligible employer other than a church, the contract is purchased under a plan that satisfies section 403(b)(12) (relating to nondiscrimination requirements, including universal availability). See §1.403(b)-5.

(4) *Limitations on elective deferrals.*—In the case of an elective deferral, the contract satisfies section 401(a)(30) (relating to limitations on elective deferrals). A contract does not satisfy section 401(a)(30) as required under this paragraph (a)(4) unless the contract requires that all elective deferrals for an employee not exceed the limits of section 402(g)(1), including elective deferrals for the employee under the contract and any other elective deferrals under the plan under which the contract is purchased and under all other plans, contracts, or arrangements of the employer. See §1.401(a)-30.

(5) *Nontransferability.*—The contract is not transferable. This paragraph (a)(5) does not apply to a contract issued before January 1, 1963. See section 401(g).

(6) *Minimum required distributions.*—The contract satisfies the requirements of section 401(a)(9) (relating to minimum required distributions). See §1.403(b)-6(e).

(7) *Rollover distributions.*—The contract provides that, if the distributee of an eligible rollover distribution elects to have the distribution paid directly to an eligible retirement plan, as defined in section 402(c)(8)(B), and specifies the eligible retirement plan to which the distribution is to be paid, then the distribution will be paid to that eligible retirement plan in a direct rollover. See §1.403(b)-7(b)(2).

(8) *Limitation on incidental benefits.*—The contract satisfies the incidental benefit requirements of section 401(a). See §1.403(b)-6(g).

(9) *Maximum annual additions.*—The annual additions to the contract do not exceed the applicable limitations of section 415(c) (treating contributions and other additions as annual additions). See paragraph (b) of this section and §1.403(b)-4(b) and (f).

(b) *Application of requirements.*—(1) *Aggregation of contracts.*—In accordance with section 403(b)(5), for purposes of determining whether this section is satisfied, all section 403(b) contracts purchased for an individual by an employer are treated as purchased under a single contract. Additional aggregation rules apply under section 402(g) for purposes of satisfying paragraph (a)(4) of this section and under section 415 for purposes of satisfying paragraph (a)(9) of this section.

(2) *Disaggregation for excess annual additions.*—In accordance with the last sentence of section 415(a)(2), if an excess annual addition is made to a contract that otherwise satisfies the requirements of this section, then the portion of the contract that includes such excess annual addition fails to be a section 403(b) contract (as further described in paragraph (d)(1) of this section) and the remaining portion of the contract is a section 403(b) contract. This paragraph (b)(2) is not satisfied unless, for the year of the excess and each year thereafter, the issuer of the contract maintains separate accounts for each such portion. Thus, the entire contract fails to be a section 403(b) contract if an excess annual addition is made and a separate account is not maintained with respect to the excess.

(3) *Plan in form and operation.*—(i) A contract does not satisfy paragraph (a) of this section unless it is maintained pursuant to a plan. For this purpose, a plan is a written defined contribution plan, which, in both form and operation, satisfies the requirements of §1.403(b)-1, §1.403(b)-2, this section, and §§1.403(b)-4 through 1.403(b)-11. For purposes of §1.403(b)-1, §1.403(b)-2, this section, and §§1.403(b)-4 through 1.403(b)-11, the plan must contain all the material terms and conditions for eligibility, benefits, applicable limitations, the contracts available under the plan, and the time and form under which benefit distributions would be made. For purposes of §1.403(b)-1, §1.403(b)-2, this section, and §§1.403(b)-4 through 1.403(b)-11, a plan may contain certain optional features that are consistent with but not required under section 403(b), such as hardship withdrawal distributions, loans, plan-to-plan or annuity contract-to-annuity contract transfers, and acceptance of rollovers to the plan. However, if a plan contains any optional provisions, the optional provisions must meet, in both form and operation, the relevant requirements under section 403(b), this section, and §§1.403(b)-4 through 1.403(b)-11.

(ii) The plan may allocate responsibility for performing administrative functions, including functions to comply with the requirements of section 403(b) and other tax requirements. Any such allocation must identify responsibility for compliance with the requirements of the Internal Revenue Code that apply on the basis of the aggregated contracts issued to a participant under a plan, including loans under section 72(p) and the conditions for obtaining a hardship withdrawal under §1.403(b)-6. A plan is permitted to assign such responsibilities to parties other than the eligible employer, but not to participants (other than employees of the employer a substantial portion of whose duties are administration of the plan), and may incorporate by reference other documents, including the insurance policy or custodial account, which thereupon become part of the plan.

(iii) This paragraph (b)(3) applies to contributions to an annuity contract by a church only if the annuity is part of a retirement income account, as defined in §1.403(b)-9.

(4) *Exclusion limited for former employees.*—(i) *General rule.*—Except as provided in paragraph (b)(4)(ii) of this section and in §1.403(b)-4(d), the exclusion from gross income provided by section 403(b) does not apply to contributions made for former employees. For this purpose, a contribution is not made for a former employee if the contribution is with respect to compensation that would otherwise be paid for a payroll period that begins before severance from employment.

(ii) *Exceptions.*—The exclusion from gross income provided by section 403(b) applies to contributions made for former employees with respect to compensation described in §1.415(c)-2(e)(3)(i) (relating to certain compensation paid by the later of 2 1/2 months after severance from employment or the end of the limitation year that includes the date of severance from employment), and compensation described in §1.415(c)-2(e)(4), §1.415(c)-2(g)(4), or §1.415(c)-2(g)(7) (relating to compensation paid to participants who are permanently and totally disabled or relating to qualified military service under section 414(u)).

(c) *Special rules for designated Roth section 403(b) contributions.*—(1) The rules of §1.401(k)-1(f)(1) and (2) for designated Roth contributions under a qualified cash or deferred arrangement apply to designated Roth contributions under a section 403(b) plan. Thus, a designated Roth contribution under a section 403(b) plan is a section 403(b) elective deferral that is designated irrevocably by the employee at the time of the cash or deferred election as a designated Roth contribution that is being made in lieu of all or a portion of the section 403(b) elective deferrals the employee is otherwise eligible to make under the plan; that is treated by the employer as includible in the employee's gross income at the time the employee would have received the amount in cash if the employee had not made the cash or deferred election (such as by treating the contributions as wages subject to applicable withholding requirements); and that is maintained in a separate account (within the meaning of §1.401(k)-1(f)(2)).

(2) A designated Roth contribution under a section 403(b) plan must satisfy the requirements applicable to section 403(b) elective deferrals. Thus, for example, designated Roth contributions under a section 403(b) plan must satisfy the requirements of §1.403(b)-6(d). Similarly, a designated Roth account under a section 403(b) plan is subject to the rules of sections 401(a)(9)(A) and (B) and §1.403(b)-6(e).

(d) Effect of failure.—(1) *General rules.*—(i) If a contract includes any amount that fails to satisfy the requirements of section 403(b), §1.403(b)-1, §1.403(b)-2, this section, or §§1.403(b)-4 through 1.403(b)-11, then, except as otherwise provided in paragraph (d)(2) of this section (relating to failure to satisfy nonforfeitability requirements) or §1.403(b)-4(f) (relating to excess contributions under section 415 and excess deferrals under section 402(g)), the contract is not a section 403(b) contract. In addition, section 403(b)(5) and paragraph (b)(1) of this section provide that, for purposes of determining whether a contract satisfies section 403(b), all section 403(b) contracts purchased for an individual by an employer are treated as purchased under a single contract. Thus, except as provided in paragraph (b)(2) of this section or as otherwise provided in this paragraph (d), a failure to satisfy section 403(b) with respect to any contract issued to an individual by an employer adversely affects all contracts issued to that individual by that employer.

(ii) In accordance with paragraph (b)(3) of this section, a failure to operate in accordance with the terms of a plan adversely affects all of the contracts issued by the employer to the employee or employees with respect to whom the operational failure occurred. Such a failure does not adversely affect any other contract if the failure is neither a failure to satisfy the nondiscrimination requirements of §1.403(b)-5 (a nondiscrimination failure) nor a failure of the employer to be an eligible employer as defined in §1.403(b)-2 (an employer eligibility failure). However, any failure that is not a operational failure adversely affects all contracts issued under the plan, including: a failure to have contracts issued pursuant to a written defined contribution plan which, in form, satisfies the requirements of §1.403(b)-1, §1.403(b)-2, this section, and §§1.403(b)-4 through 1.403(b)-11 (a written plan failure); a nondiscrimination failure; or an employer eligibility failure.

(iii) See other applicable Internal Revenue Code provisions for the treatment of a contract that is not a section 403(b) contract, such as sections 61, 83, 402(b), and 403(c). Thus, for example, section 403(c) (relating to nonqualified annuities) applies if any annuity contract issued by an insurance company fails to satisfy section 403(b), based on the value of the contract at the time of the failure. However, see paragraph (d)(2) of this section for special rules with respect to the nonforfeitability requirement of paragraph (a)(2) of this section.

(2) Failure to satisfy nonforfeitability requirement.—(i) *Treatment before contract becomes nonforfeitable.*—If an annuity contract issued by an insurance company would qualify as a section 403(b) contract but for the failure to satisfy the nonforfeitability requirement of paragraph (a)(2) of this section, then the contract is treated as a contract to which section 403(c) applies. See §1.403(b)-8(d)(4) for a rule under which a custodial account that fails to satisfy the nonforfeitability requirement of paragraph (a)(2) of this section is treated as a section 401(a) qualified plan for certain purposes.

(ii) *Treatment when contract becomes nonforfeitable.*—(A) *In general.*—Notwithstanding paragraph (d)(2)(i) of this section, on or after the date on which the participant's interest in a contract described in paragraph (d)(2)(i) of this section becomes nonforfeitable, the contract may be treated as a section 403(b) contract if no election has been made under section 83(b) with respect to the contract, the participant's interest in the contract has been subject to a substantial risk of forfeiture (as defined in section 83) before becoming nonforfeitable, each contribution under the contract that is subject to a different vesting schedule is maintained in a separate account, and the contract has at all times satisfied the requirements of paragraph (a) of this section other than the nonforfeitability requirement of paragraph (a)(2) of this section. Thus, for example, for the current year and each prior year, no contribution can have been made to the contract that would cause the contract to fail to be a section 403(b) contract as a result of contributions exceeding the limitations of section 415 (except to the extent permitted under paragraph (b)(2) of this section) or to fail to satisfy the nondiscrimination rules described in §1.403(b)-5. See also §1.403(b)-10(a)(1) for a special rule in connection with termination of a section 403(b) plan.

(B) *Partial vesting.*—For purposes of applying this paragraph (d), if only a portion of a participant's interest in a contract becomes nonforfeitable in a year, then the portion that is nonforfeitable and the portion that fails to be nonforfeitable are each treated as separate contracts. In addition, for purposes of applying this paragraph (d), if a contribution is made to an annuity contract in excess of the limitations of section 415(c) and the excess is maintained in a separate account, then the portion of the contract that includes the excess contributions account and the remainder are each treated as separate contracts. Thus, if an annuity contract that includes an excess contributions account changes from forfeitable to nonforfeitable during a year, then the portion that is not attributable to the excess contributions account constitutes a section 403(b) contract

(assuming it otherwise satisfies the requirements to be a section 403(b) contract) and is not included in gross income, and the portion that is attributable to the excess contributions account is included in gross income in accordance with section 403(c). See §1.403(b)-4(f) for additional rules. [Reg. §1.403(b)-3.]

☐ [*T.D. 8987, 4-16-2002. Amended by T.D. 9130, 6-14-2004 and T.D. 9340, 7-23-2007 (corrected 9-24-2007).*]

[Reg. §1.403(b)-4]

§1.403(b)-4. Contribution limitations.—(a) *Treatment of contributions in excess of limitations.*—The exclusion provided under §1.403(b)-3(a) applies to a participant only if the amounts contributed by the employer for the purchase of an annuity contract for the participant do not exceed the applicable limit under sections 415 and 402(g), as described in this section. Under §1.403(b)-3(a)(4), a section 403(b) contract is required to include the limits on elective deferrals imposed by section 402(g), as described in paragraph (c) of this section. See paragraph (f) of this section for special rules concerning excess contributions and deferrals. Rollover contributions made to a section 403(b) contract, as described in §1.403(b)-10(d), are not taken into account for purposes of the limits imposed by section 415, §1.403(b)-3(a)(9), section 402(g), §1.403(b)-3(a)(4), and this section, but after-tax employee contributions are taken into account under section 415, §1.403(b)-3(a)(9), and paragraph (b) of this section.

(b) *Maximum annual contribution.*—(1) *General rule.*—In accordance with section 415(a)(2) and §1.403(b)-3(a)(9), the contributions for any participant under a section 403(b) contract (namely, employer nonelective contributions (including matching contributions), section 403(b) elective deferrals, and after-tax employee contributions) are not permitted to exceed the limitations imposed by section 415. Under section 415(c), contributions are permitted to be made for participants in a defined contribution plan, subject to the limitations set forth therein (which are generally the lesser of a dollar limit for a year or the participant's compensation for the year). For purposes of section 415, contributions made for a participant are aggregated to the extent applicable under sections 414(b), (c), (m), (n), and (o). For purposes of section 415(a)(2), §§1.403(b)-1 through 1.403(b)-3, this section, and §§1.403(b)-5 through 1.403(b)-11, a contribution means any annual addition, as defined in section 415(c).

(2) *Special rules.*—See section 415(k)(4) for a special rule under which contributions to section 403(b) contracts are generally aggregated with contributions under other arrangements in applying section 415. For purposes of applying section 415(c)(1)(B) (relating to compensation) with respect to a section 403(b) contract, except as provided in section 415(c)(3)(C), a participant's includible compensation (as defined in §1.403(b)-2) is substituted for the participant's compensation, as described in section 415(c)(3)(E). Any age 50 catch-up contributions under paragraph (c)(2) of this section are disregarded in applying section 415.

(c) *Section 403(b) elective deferrals.*—(1) *Basic limit under section 402(g)(1).*—In accordance with section 402(g)(1)(A), the section 403(b) elective deferrals for any individual are included in the individual's gross income to the extent the amount of such deferrals, plus all other elective deferrals for the individual, for the taxable year exceeds the applicable dollar amount under section 402(g)(1)(B). The applicable annual dollar amount under section 402(g)(1)(B) is $15,000, adjusted for cost-of-living after 2006 in the manner described in section 402(g)(4). See §1.403(b)-5(b) for a universal availability rule that applies if any employee is permitted to have any section 403(b) elective deferrals made on his or her behalf.

(2) *Age 50 catch-up.*—(i) *In general.*—In accordance with section 414(v) and the regulations thereunder, a section 403(b) contract may provide for catch-up contributions for a participant who is age 50 by the end of the year, provided that such age 50 catch-up contributions do not exceed the catch-up limit under section 414(v)(2) for the taxable year. The maximum amount of additional age 50 catch-up contributions for a taxable year under section 414(v) is $5,000, adjusted for cost-of-living after 2006 in the manner described in section 414(v)(2)(C). For additional requirements, see regulations under section 414(v).

(ii) *Coordination with special section 403(b) catch-up.*—In accordance with sections 414(v)(6)(A)(ii) and 402(g)(7)(A), the age 50 catch-up described in this paragraph (c)(2) may apply for any taxable year in which a participant also qualifies for the special section 403(b) catch-up under paragraph (c)(3) of this section.

(3) *Special section 403(b) catch-up for certain organizations.*—(i) *Amount of the special section 403(b) catch-up.*—In the case of a qualified employee of a qualified organization for whom the basic section 403(b) elective deferrals for any year are not less than the applicable dollar amount under section 402(g)(1)(B), the section

403(b) elective deferral limitation of section 402(g)(1) for the taxable year of the qualified employee is increased by the least of—

(A) $3,000;

(B) The excess of—

(1) $15,000, over

(2) The total elective deferrals described in section 402(g)(7)(A)(ii) made for the qualified employee by the qualified organization for prior years; or

(C) The excess of—

(1) $5,000 multiplied by the number of years of service of the employee with the qualified organization, over

(2) The total elective deferrals (as defined at §1.403(b)-2) made for the employee by the qualified organization for prior years.

(ii) *Qualified organization.*—(A) For purposes of this paragraph (c)(3), *qualified organization* means an eligible employer that is—

(1) An educational organization described in section 170(b)(1)(A)(ii);

(2) A hospital;

(3) A health and welfare service agency (including a home health service agency);

(4) A church-related organization; or

(5) Any organization described in section 414(e)(3)(B)(ii).

(B) All entities that are in a church-related organization or an organization controlled by a church-related organization under section 414(e)(3)(B)(ii) are treated as a single qualified organization (so that years of service and any special section 403(b) catch-up elective deferrals previously made for a qualified employee for a church or other entity within a church-related organization or an organization controlled by the church-related organization are taken into account for purposes of applying this paragraph (c)(3) to the employee with respect to any other entity within the same church-related organization or organization controlled by a church-related organization).

(C) For purposes of this paragraph (c)(3)(ii), a *health and welfare service agency* means—

(1) An organization whose primary activity is to provide services that constitute medical care as defined in section 213(d)(1) (such as a hospice);

(2) A section 501(c)(3) organization whose primary activity is the prevention of cruelty to individuals or animals;

(3) An adoption agency; or

(4) An agency that provides substantial personal services to the needy as part of its primary activity (such as a section 501(c)(3) organization that either provides meals to needy individuals, is a home health service agency, provides services to help individuals who have substance abuse, or provides help to the disabled).

(iii) *Qualified employee.*—For purposes of this paragraph (c)(3), *qualified employee* means an employee who has completed at least 15 years of service (as defined under paragraph (e) of this section) taking into account only employment with the qualified organization. Thus, an employee who has not completed at least 15 years of service (as defined under paragraph (e) of this section) taking into account only employment with the qualified organization is not a qualified employee.

(iv) *Coordination with age 50 catch-up.*—In accordance with sections 402(g)(1)(C) and 402(g)(7), any catch-up amount contributed by an employee who is eligible for both an age 50 catch-up and a special section 403(b) catch-up is treated first as an amount contributed as a special section 403(b) catch-up to the extent a special section 403(b) catch-up is permitted, and then as an amount contributed as an age 50 catch-up (to the extent the catch-up amount exceeds the maximum special section 403(b) catch-up after taking into account sections 402(g) and 415(c), this paragraph (c)(3), and any limitations on the special section 403(b) catch-up that are imposed by the terms of the plan).

(4) *Coordination with designated Roth contributions.*—See regulations under section 402A for rules for determining whether an elective deferral is a pre-tax elective deferral or a designated Roth contribution.

(5) *Examples.*—The provisions of this paragraph (c) are illustrated by the following examples:

Example 1. (i) *Facts illustrating application of the basic dollar limit.* Participant B, who is 45, is eligible to participate in a State university section 403(b) plan in 2006. B is not a qualified employee, as defined in paragraph (c)(3)(iii) of this section. The plan permits section 403(b) elective deferrals, but no other employer contributions are made under the plan. The plan provides limitations on section 403(b) elective deferrals up to the maximum permitted under paragraphs (c)(1) and (3) of this section and the additional age 50 catch-up amount described in paragraph (c)(2) of this section. For 2006, B will receive includible compensation of $42,000 from the eligible employer. B desires to elect to have the maximum section 403(b) elective deferral possible contributed in 2006. For 2006, the basic dollar limit for section 403(b) elective deferrals under paragraph (c)(1) of this section is $15,000 and the additional dollar amount permitted under the age 50 catch-up is $5,000.

(ii) *Conclusion.* B is not eligible for the age 50 catch-up in 2006 because B is 45 in 2006. B is also not eligible for the special section 403(b) catch-up under paragraph (c)(3) of this section because B is not a qualified employee. Accordingly, the maximum section 403(b) elective deferral that B may elect for 2006 is $15,000.

Example 2. (i) *Facts illustrating application of the includible compensation limitation.* The facts are the same as in *Example 1*, except B's includible compensation is $14,000.

(ii) *Conclusion.* Under section 415(c), contributions may not exceed 100 percent of includible compensation. Accordingly, the maximum section 403(b) elective deferral that B may elect for 2006 is $14,000.

Example 3. (i) *Facts illustrating application of the age 50 catch-up.* Participant C, who is 55, is eligible to participate in a State university section 403(b) plan in 2006. The plan permits section 403(b) elective deferrals, but no other employer contributions are made under the plan. The plan provides limitations on section 403(b) elective deferrals up to the maximum permitted under paragraphs (c)(1) and (c)(3) of this section and the additional age 50 catch-up amount described in paragraph (c)(2) of this section. For 2006, C will receive includible compensation of $48,000 from the eligible employer. C desires to elect to have the maximum section 403(b) elective deferral possible contributed in 2006. For 2006, the basic dollar limit for section 403(b) elective deferrals under paragraph (c)(1) of this section is $15,000 and the additional dollar amount permitted under the age 50 catch-up is $5,000. C does not have 15 years of service and thus is not a qualified employee, as defined in paragraph (c)(3)(iii) of this section.

(ii) *Conclusion.* C is eligible for the age 50 catch-up in 2006 because C is 55 in 2006. C is not eligible for the special section 403(b) catch-up under paragraph (c)(3) of this section because C is not a qualified employee (as defined in paragraph (c)(3)(iii) of this section). Accordingly, the maximum section 403(b) elective deferral that C may elect for 2006 is $20,000 ($15,000 plus $5,000).

Example 4. (i) *Facts illustrating application of both the age 50 and the special section 403(b) catch-up.* The facts are the same as in *Example 3*, except that C is a qualified employee for purposes of the special section 403(b) catch-up provisions in paragraph (c)(3) of this section. For 2006, the maximum additional section 403(b) elective deferral for which C qualifies under the special section 403(b) catch-up under paragraph (c)(3) of this section is $3,000.

(ii) *Conclusion.* The maximum section 403(b) elective deferrals that C may elect for 2006 is $23,000. This is the sum of the basic limit on section 403(b) elective deferrals under paragraph (c)(1) of this section equal to $15,000, plus the $3,000 additional special section 403(b) catch-up amount for which C qualifies under paragraph (c)(3) of this section, plus the additional age 50 catch-up amount of $5,000.

Example 5. (i) *Facts illustrating calculation of years of service with a predecessor organization for purposes of the special section 403(b) catch-up.* Participant A is an employee of hospital H and is eligible to participate in a section 403(b) plan of H in 2006. A does not have 15 years of service with H, but A has previously made special section 403(b) catch-up deferrals to a section 403(b) plan maintained by hospital P which has since been acquired by H.

(ii) *Conclusion.* The special section 403(b) catch-up amount for which A qualifies under paragraph (c)(3) of this section must be calculated taking into account A's prior years of service and section 403(b) elective deferrals with the predecessor hospital if and only if A did not have any severance from service in connection with the acquisition.

Example 6. (i) *Facts illustrating application of the age 50 catch-up and the section 415(c) dollar limitation.* The facts are the same as in *Example 4*, except that the employer makes a nonelective contribution for each employee equal to 20 percent of C's compensation (which is $48,000). Thus, the employer makes a nonelective contribution for C for 2006 equal to $9,600. The plan provides that a participant is not permitted to make section 403(b) elective deferrals to the extent the section 403(b) elective deferrals would result in contributions in excess of the maximum permitted under section 415 and provides that contributions are reduced in the following order: the special section 403(b) catch-up elective deferrals under paragraph (c)(3) of this section are reduced first; the age 50 catch-up elective deferrals under paragraph (c)(2) of this section are reduced second; and then the basic section 403(b) elective deferrals under paragraph (c)(1) of this section are reduced. For 2006, the applicable dollar limit under section 415(c)(1)(A) is $44,000.

(ii) *Conclusion.* The maximum section 403(b) elective deferral that C may elect for 2006 is $23,000. This is the sum of the basic limit on section 403(b) elective deferrals under paragraph (c)(1) of this section equal to $15,000, plus the $3,000 additional special section 403(b) catch-up amount for which C qualifies under paragraph (c)(3) of this section, plus the additional age 50 catch-up amount of $5,000. The limit in paragraph (b) of this section would not be exceeded because the sum of the $9,600 nonelective contribution and the $23,000 section 403(b) elective deferrals does not exceed the lesser of $49,000 (which is the sum of $44,000 plus the $5,000 additional age 50 catch-up amount) or $53,000 (which is the sum of C's includible compensation for 2006 ($48,000) plus the $5,000 additional age 50 catch-up amount).

Example 7. (i) *Facts further illustrating application of the age 50 catch-up and the section 415(c) dollar limitation.* The facts are the same as in *Example 6,* except that C's includible compensation for 2006 is $58,000 and the plan provides for a nonelective contribution equal to 50 percent of includible compensation, so that the employer nonelective contribution for C for 2006 is $29,000 (50 percent of $58,000).

(ii) *Conclusion.* The maximum section 403(b) elective deferral that C may elect for 2006 is $20,000. A section 403(b) elective deferral in excess of this amount would exceed the sum of the limit in section 415(c)(1)(A) plus the additional age 50 catch-up amount, because the sum of the employer's nonelective contribution of $29,000 plus a section 403(b) elective deferral in excess of $20,000 would exceed $49,000 (the sum of the $44,000 limit in section 415(c)(1)(A) plus the $5,000 additional age 50 catch-up amount). (Note that a section 403(b) elective deferral in excess of $20,000 would also exceed the limitations of section 402(g) unless a special section 403(b) catch-up were permitted.)

Example 8. (i) *Facts further illustrating application of the age 50 catch-up and the section 415(c) dollar limitation.* The facts are the same as in *Example 7,* except that the plan provides for a nonelective contribution for C equal to $44,000 (which is the limit in section 415(c)(1)(A)).

(ii) *Conclusion.* The maximum section 403(b) elective deferral that C may elect for 2006 is $5,000. A section 403(b) elective deferral in excess of this amount would exceed the sum of the limit in section 415(c)(1)(A) plus the additional age 50 catch-up amount ($5,000), because the sum of the employer's nonelective contribution of $44,000 plus a section 403(b) elective deferral in excess of $5,000 would exceed $49,000 (the sum of the $44,000 limit in section 415(c)(1)(A) plus the $5,000 additional age 50 catch-up amount).

Example 9. (i) *Facts illustrating application of the age 50 catch-up and the section 415(c) includible compensation limitation.* The facts are the same as in *Example 7,* except that C's includible compensation for 2006 is $28,000, so that the employer nonelective contribution for C for 2006 is $14,000 (50 percent of $28,000).

(ii) *Conclusion.* The maximum section 403(b) elective deferral that C may elect for 2006 is $19,000. A section 403(b) elective deferral in excess of this amount would exceed the sum of the limit in section 415(c)(1)(B) plus the additional age 50 catch-up amount, because C's includible compensation is $28,000 and the sum of the employer's nonelective contribution of $14,000 plus a section 403(b) elective deferral in excess of $19,000 would exceed $33,000 (which is the sum of 100 percent of C's includible compensation plus the $5,000 additional age 50 catch-up amount).

Example 10. (i) *Facts illustrating that section 403(b) elective deferrals cannot exceed compensation otherwise payable.* Employee D is age 60, has includible compensation of $14,000, and wishes to contribute section 403(b) elective deferrals of $20,000 for the year. No nonelective contributions are made for Employee D.

(ii) *Conclusion.* Because a contribution is a section 403(b) elective deferral only if it relates to an amount that would otherwise be included in the participant's compensation, the effective limitation on section 403(b) elective deferrals for a participant whose compensation is less than the basic dollar limit for section 403(b) elective deferrals is the participant's compensation. Thus, D cannot make section 403(b) elective deferrals in excess of D's actual compensation, which is $14,000, even though the basic dollar limit exceeds that amount.

Example 11. (i) *Facts illustrating calculation of the special section 403(b) catch-up.* For 2006, employee E, who is age 53, is eligible to participate in a section 403(b) plan of hospital H, which is a section 501(c)(3) organization. H's plan permits section 403(b) elective deferrals and provides for an employer contribution of 10 percent of a participant's compensation. The plan provides limitations on section 403(b) elective deferrals up to the maximum permitted under paragraphs (c)(1), (2), and (3) of this section. For 2006, E's includible compensation is $50,000. E wishes to elect to have the maximum section 403(b) elective deferral possible contributed in 2006. E has previously made $62,000 of section 403(b) elective deferrals under the plan, but has never made an election for a special section 403(b) catch-up elective deferral. For 2006, the basic dollar limit for section 403(b) elective deferrals under paragraph (c)(1) of this section is $15,000, the additional dollar amount permitted under the age 50 catch-up is $5,000, E's employer will make a nonelective contribution

of $5,000 (10% of $50,000 compensation), and E is a qualified employee of a qualified employer as defined in paragraph (c)(3) of this section.

(ii) *Conclusion.* The maximum section 403(b) elective deferrals that E may elect under H's section 403(b) plan for 2006 is $23,000. This is the sum of the basic limit on section 403(b) elective deferrals for 2006 under paragraph (c)(1) of this section equal to $15,000, plus the $3,000 maximum additional special section 403(b) catch-up amount for which D qualifies in 2006 under paragraph (c)(3) of this section, plus the additional age 50 catch-up amount of $5,000. The limitation on the additional special section 403(b) catch-up amount is not less than $3,000 because the limitation at paragraph (c)(3)(i)(B) of this section is $15,000 ($15,000 minus zero) and the limitation at paragraph (c)(3)(i)(C) of this section is $13,000 ($5,000 times 15, minus $62,000 of total deferrals in prior years). These conclusions would be unaffected if H were an eligible governmental employer under section 457(b) that has a section 457(b) eligible governmental plan and E were in the past to have made annual deferrals to that plan, because contributions to a section 457(b) eligible governmental plan do not constitute elective deferrals; and these conclusions would also be the same if H had a section 401(k) plan and E were in the past to have made elective deferrals to that plan, assuming that those elective deferrals did not exceed $10,000 ($5,000 times 15, minus the sum of $62,000 plus $10,000, equals $3,000), so as to result in the limitation at paragraph (c)(3)(i)(C) of this section being less than $3,000.

Example 12. (i) *Facts illustrating calculation of the special section 403(b) catch-up in the next calendar year.* The facts are the same as in *Example 11,* except that, for 2007, E has includible compensation of $60,000. For 2007, E now has previously made $85,000 of section 403(b) elective deferrals ($62,000 deferred before 2006, plus the $15,000 in basic section 403(b) elective deferrals in 2006, the $3,000 maximum additional special section 403(b) catch-up amount in 2006, plus the $5,000 age 50 catch-up amount in 2006). However, the $5,000 age 50 catch-up amount deferred in 2006 is disregarded for purposes of applying the limitation at paragraph (c)(3)(i)(C) of this section to determine the special section 403(b) catch-up amount. Thus, for 2007, only $80,000 of section 403(b) elective deferrals are taken into account in applying the limitation at paragraph (c)(3)(i)(C) of this section. For 2007, the basic dollar limit for section 403(b) elective deferrals under paragraph (c)(1) of this section is assumed to be $16,000, the additional dollar amount permitted under the age 50 catch-up is assumed to be $5,000, and E's employer contributes $6,000 (10% of $60,000) as a non-elective contribution.

(ii) *Conclusion.* The maximum section 403(b) elective deferral that D may elect under H's section 403(b) plan for 2007 is $21,000. This is the sum of the basic limit on section 403(b) elective deferrals under paragraph (c)(1) of this section equal to $16,000, plus the additional age 50 catch-up amount of $5,000. E is not entitled to any additional special section 403(b) catch-up amount for 2007 under paragraph (c)(3) of this section due to the limitation at paragraph (c)(3)(i)(C) of this section (16 times $5,000 equals $80,000, minus D's total prior section 403(b) elective deferrals of $80,000 equals zero).

(d) *Employer contributions for former employees.*—(1) *Includible compensation deemed to continue for nonelective contributions.*—For purposes of applying paragraph (b) of this section, a former employee is deemed to have monthly includible compensation for the period through the end of the taxable year of the employee in which he or she ceases to be an employee and through the end of each of the next five taxable years. The amount of the monthly includible compensation is equal to one twelfth of the former employee's includible compensation during the former employee's most recent year of service. Accordingly, nonelective employer contributions for a former employee must not exceed the limitation of section 415(c)(1) up to the lesser of the dollar amount in section 415(c)(1)(A) or the former employee's annual includible compensation based on the former employee's average monthly compensation during his or her most recent year of service.

(2) *Examples.*—The provisions of paragraph (d)(1) of this section are illustrated by the following examples:

Example 1. (i) *Facts.* Private college M is a section 501(c)(3) organization operated on the basis of a June 30 fiscal year that maintains a section 403(b) plan for its employees. In 2004, M amends the plan to provide for a temporary early retirement incentive under which the college will make a nonelective contribution for any participant who satisfies certain minimum age and service conditions and who retires before June 30, 2006. The contribution will equal 110 percent of the participant's rate of pay for one year and will be payable over a period ending no later than the end of the fifth fiscal year that begins after retirement. It is assumed for purposes of this *Example 1* that, in accordance with § 1.401(a)(4)-10(b) and under the facts and circumstances, the post-retirement contributions made for participants who satisfy the minimum age and service conditions and retire before June 30, 2006, do not discriminate in favor of former employees who are highly compensated employees. Employee A retires under the early retirement incentive on March 12, 2006, and A's annual includible compensation for the period from March 1, 2005, through February 28, 2006 (which is A's most recent one year of service) is $30,000. The applicable dollar limit under section 415(c)(1)(A) is assumed to be $44,000 for 2006 and $45,000 for 2007. The college contributes $30,000 for A for 2006 and $3,000 for A for 2007 (totaling $33,000 or 110 percent of $30,000). No other contributions are made to a section 403(b) contract for A for those years.

(ii) *Conclusion.* The contributions made for A do not exceed A's includible compensation for 2006 or 2007.

Example 2. (i) *Facts.* Private college N is a section 501(c)(3) organization that maintains a section 403(b) plan for its employees. The plan provides for N to make monthly nonelective contributions equal to 20 percent of the monthly includible compensation for each eligible employee. In addition, the plan provides for contributions to continue for 5 years following the retirement of any employee after age 64 and completion of at least 20 years of service (based on the employee's average annual rate of base salary in the preceding 3 calendar years ended before the date of retirement). It is assumed for purposes of this *Example 2* that, in accordance with § 1.401(a)(4)-10(b) and under the facts and circumstances, the post-retirement contributions made for participants who satisfy the minimum age and service conditions do not discriminate in favor of former employees who are highly compensated employees. Employee B retires on July 1, 2006, at age 64 after completion of 20 or more years of service. At that date, B's annual includible compensation for the most recently ended fiscal year of N is $72,000 and B's average monthly rate of base salary for 2003 through 2005 is $5,000. N contributes $1,200 per month (20 percent of 1/12th of $72,000) from January of 2006 through June of 2006 and contributes $1,000 (20 percent of $5,000) per month for B from July of 2006 through June of 2011. The applicable dollar limit under section 415(c)(1)(A) is $44,000 for 2006 and 2011. No other contributions are made to a section 403(b) contract for B for those years.

(ii) *Conclusion.* The contributions made for B do not exceed B's includible compensation for any of the years from 2006 through 2010.

Example 3. (i) *Facts.* A public university maintains a section 403(b) under which it contributes annually 10% of compensation for participants, including for the first 5 calendar years following the date on which the participant ceases to be an employee. The plan provides that if a participant who is a former employee dies during the first 5 calendar years following the date on which the participant ceases to be an employee, a contribution is made that is equal to the lesser of—

(A) The excess of the individual's includible compensation for that year over the contributions previously made for the individual for that year; or

(B) The total contributions that would have been made on the individual's behalf thereafter if he or she had survived to the end of the 5-year period.

(ii) Individual C's annual includible compensation is $72,000 (so that C's monthly includible compensation is $6,000). A $600 contribution is made for C for January of the first taxable year following retirement (10% of individual C's monthly includible compensation of $6,000). Individual C dies during February of that year. The university makes a contribution for individual C for February equal to $11,400 (C's monthly includible compensation for January and February, reduced by $600).

(iii) *Conclusion.* The contribution does not exceed the amount of individual C's includible compensation for the taxable year for purposes of section 415(c), but any additional contributions would exceed C's includible compensation for purposes of section 415(c).

(3) *Disabled employees.*—See also section 415(c)(3)(C) which sets forth a special rule under which compensation may be treated as continuing for purposes of section 415 for certain former employees who are disabled.

(e) *Special rules for determining years of service.*—(1) *In general.*—For purposes of determining a participant's includible compensation under paragraph (b)(2) of this section and a participant's years of service under paragraphs (c)(3) (special section 403(b) catch-up for qualified employees of certain organizations) and (d) (employer contributions for former employees) of this section, an employee must be credited with a full year of service for each year during which the individual is a full-time employee of the eligible employer for the *entire* work period, and a fraction of a year for each part of a work period during which the individual is a full-time or part-time employee of the eligible employer. An individual's number of years of service equals the aggregate of the annual work periods during which the individual is employed by the eligible employer.

(2) *Work period.*—A year of service is based on the employer's annual work period, not the employee's taxable year. For example, in determining whether a university professor is employed full time, the annual work period is the school's academic year. However, in no case may an employee accumulate more than one year of service in a twelve-month period.

(3) *Service with more than one eligible employer.*—(i) *General rule.*—With respect to any section 403(b) contract of an eligible employer, except as provided in paragraph (e)(3)(ii) of this section, any period during which an individual is not an employee of that eligible employer is disregarded for purposes of this paragraph (e).

(ii) *Special rule for church employees.*—With respect to any section 403(b) contract of an eligible employer that is a church-related organization, any period during which an individual is an employee of that eligible employer and any other eligible employer that is a church-related organization that has an association (as defined in section 414(e)(3)(D)) with that eligible employer is taken into account on an aggregated basis, but any period during which an individual is not an employee of a church-related organization or is an employee of a church-related organization that does not have an association with that eligible employer is disregarded for purposes of this paragraph (e).

(4) *Full-time employee for full year.*—Each annual work period during which an individual is employed full time by the eligible employer constitutes one year of service. In determining whether an individual is employed full-time, the amount of work which he or she actually performs is compared with the amount of work that is normally required of individuals performing similar services from which substantially all of their annual compensation is derived.

(5) *Other employees.*—(i) An individual is treated as performing a fraction of a year of service for each annual work period during which he or she is a full-time employee for part of the annual work period and for each annual work period during which he or she is a part-time employee either for the entire annual work period or for a part of the annual work period.

(ii) In determining the fraction that represents the fractional year of service for an individual employed full time for part of an annual work period, the numerator is the period of time (such as weeks or months) during which the individual is a full-time employee during that annual work period, and the denominator is the period of time that is the annual work period.

(iii) In determining the fraction that represents the fractional year of service of an individual who is employed part time for the entire annual work period, the numerator is the amount of work performed by the individual, and the denominator is the amount of work normally required of individuals who perform similar services and who are employed full time for the entire annual work period.

(iv) In determining the fraction representing the fractional year of service of an individual who is employed part time for part of an annual work period, the fractional year of service that would apply if the individual were a part-time employee for a full annual work period is multiplied by the fractional year of service that would apply if the individual were a full-time employee for the part of an annual work period.

(6) *Work performed.*—For purposes of this paragraph (e), in measuring the amount of work of an individual performing particular services, the work performed is determined based on the individual's hours of service (as defined under section 410(a)(3)(C)), except that a plan may use a different measure of work if appropriate under the facts and circumstances. For example, a plan may provide for a university professor's work to be measured by the number of courses taught during an annual work period in any case in which that individual's work assignment is generally based on a specified number of courses to be taught.

(7) *Most recent one-year period of service.*—For purposes of paragraph (d) of this section, in the case of a part-time employee or a full-time employee who is employed for only part of the year determined on the basis of the employer's annual work period, the employee's most recent periods of service are aggregated to determine his or her most recent one-year period of service. In such a case, there is first taken into account his or her service during the annual work period for which the last year of service's includible compensation is being determined; then there is taken into account his or her service during his or her next preceding annual work period based on whole months; and so forth until the employee's service equals, in the aggregate, one year of service.

(8) *Less than one year of service considered as one year.*—If, at the close of a taxable year, an employee has, after application of all of the other rules in this paragraph (e), some portion of one year of service (but has accumulated less than one year of service), the employee is

deemed to have one year of service. Except as provided in the previous sentence, fractional years of service are not rounded up.

(9) *Examples.*—The provisions of this paragraph (e) are illustrated by the following examples:

Example 1. (i) *Facts.* Individual G is employed half-time in 2004 and 2005 as a clerk by H, a hospital which is a section 501(c)(3) organization. G earns $20,000 from H in each of those years, and retires on December 31, 2005.

(ii) *Conclusion.* For purposes of determining G's includible compensation during G's last year of service under paragraph (d) of this section, G's most recent periods of service are aggregated to determine G's most recent one-year period of service. In this case, since D worked half-time in 2004 and 2005, the compensation D earned in those two years are aggregated to produce D's includible compensation for D's last full year in service. Thus, in this case, the $20,000 that D earned in 2004 and 2005 for D's half-time work are aggregated, so that D has $40,000 of includible compensation for D's most recent one-year of service for purposes of applying paragraphs (b)(2), (c)(3), and (d) of this section.

Example 2. (i) *Facts.* Individual H is employed as a part-time professor by public University U during the first semester of its two-semester 2004- 2005 academic year. While H teaches one course generally for 3 hours a week during the first semester of the academic year, U's full-time faculty members generally teach for 9 hours a week during the full academic year.

(ii) *Conclusion.* For purposes of calculating how much of a year of service H performs in the 2004-2005 academic year (before application of the special rules of paragraphs (e)(7) and (8) of this section concerning less than one year of service), paragraph (e)(5)(iv) of this section is applied as follows: since H teaches one course at U for 3 hours per week for 1 semester and other faculty members at U teach 9 hours per week for 2 semesters, H is considered to have completed 3/18 or 1/6 of a year of service during the 2004-2005 academic year, determined as follows:

(A) The fractional year of service if H were a part-time employee for a full year is 3/9 (number of hours employed divided by the usual number of hours of work required for that position).

(B) The fractional year of service if H were a full-time employee for half of a year is ¹/₂ (one semester, divided by the usual 2-semester annual work period).

(C) These fractions are multiplied to obtain the fractional year of service: 3/9 times ¹/₂, or 3/18, equals 1/6 of a year of service.

(f) *Excess contributions or deferrals.*—(1) *Inclusion in gross income.*—Any contribution made for a participant to a section 403(b) contract for the taxable year that exceeds either the maximum annual contribution limit set forth in paragraph (b) of this section or the maximum annual section 403(b) elective deferral limit set forth in paragraph (c) of this section constitutes an excess contribution that is included in gross income for that taxable year. See §1.403(b)-3(d)(1)(iii) and (2)(i) for additional rules, including special rules relating to contracts that fail to be nonforfeitable. See also section 4973 for an excise tax applicable with respect to excess contributions to a custodial account and section 4979(f)(2)(B) for a special rule applicable if excess matching contributions, excess after-tax employee contributions, and excess section 403(b) elective deferrals do not exceed $100.

(2) *Separate account required for certain excess contributions; distribution of excess elective deferrals.*—A contract to which a contribution is made that exceeds the maximum annual contribution limit set forth in paragraph (b) of this section is not a section 403(b) contract unless the excess contribution is held in a separate account which constitutes a separate account for purposes of section 72. See also §1.403(b)-3(a)(4) and paragraph (f)(4) of this section for additional rules with respect to the requirements of section 401(a)(30) and any excess deferral.

(3) *Ability to distribute excess contributions.*—A contract does not fail to satisfy the requirements of §1.403(b)-3, the distribution rules of §1.403(b)-6 or 1.403(b)-9, or the funding rules of §1.403(b)-8 solely by reason of a distribution made from a separate account under paragraph (f)(2) of this section or made under paragraph (f)(4) of this section.

(4) *Excess section 403(b) elective deferrals.*—A section 403(b) contract may provide that any excess deferral as a result of a failure to comply with the limitation under paragraph (c) of this section for a taxable year with respect to any section 403(b) elective deferral made for a participant by the employer will be distributed to the participant, with allocable net income, no later than April 15 of the following taxable year or otherwise in accordance with section 402(g). See section 402(g)(2)(A) for rules permitting the participant to allocate excess deferrals among the plans in which the participant has made elective deferrals, and see section 402(g)(2)(C) for special rules to determine the tax treatment of such a distribution.

(5) *Examples.*—The provisions of this paragraph (f) are illustrated by the following examples:

Example 1. (i) *Facts.* Individual D's employer makes a $46,000 contribution for 2006 to an individual annuity insurance policy for Individual D that would otherwise be a section 403(b) contract. The contribution does not include any elective deferrals and the applicable limit under section 415(c) is $44,000 for 2006. The $2,000 section 415(c) excess is put into a separate account under the policy. Employer includes $2,000 in D's gross income as wages for 2006 and, to the extent of the amount held in the separate account for the section 415(c) excess contribution, does not treat the account as a contract to which section 403(b) applies.

(ii) *Conclusion.* The separate account for the section 415(c) excess contribution is a contract to which section 403(c) applies, but the excess contribution does not cause the rest of the contract to fail section 403(b).

Example 2. (i) *Facts.* Same facts as *Example 1*, except that the contribution is made to purchase mutual funds that are held in a custodial account, instead of an individual annuity insurance policy.

(ii) *Conclusion.* The conclusion is the same as in *Example 1*, except that the purchase constitutes a transfer described in section 83.

Example 3. (i) *Facts.* Same facts as *Example 1*, except that the amount held in the separate account for the section 415(c) excess contribution is subsequently distributed to D.

(ii) *Conclusion.* The distribution is included in gross income to the extent provided under section 72 relating to distributions from a section 403(c) contract.

Example 4. (i) *Facts.* Individual E makes section 403(b) elective deferrals totaling $15,500 for 2006, when E is age 45 and the applicable limit on section 403(b) elective deferrals is $15,000. On April 14, 2007, the plan refunds the $500 excess along with applicable earnings of $65.

(ii) *Conclusion.* The $565 payment constitutes a distribution of an excess deferral under paragraph (f)(4) of this section. Under section 402(g), the $500 excess deferral is included in E's gross income for 2006. The additional $65 is included in E's gross income for 2007 and, because the distribution is made by April 15, 2007 (as provided in section 402(g)(2)), the $65 is not subject to the additional 10 percent income tax on early distributions under section 72(t). [Reg. §1.403(b)-4.]

□ [T.D. 9340, 7-23-2007 (*corrected* 9-24-2007 *and* 10-25-2010).]

[Reg. §1.403(b)-5]

§1.403(b)-5. Nondiscrimination rules.—(a) *Nondiscrimination rules for contributions other than section 403(b) elective deferrals.*—(1) *General rule.*—Under section 403(b)(12)(A)(i), employer contributions and after-tax employee contributions to a section 403(b) plan must satisfy all of the following requirements (the nondiscrimination requirements) in the same manner as a qualified plan under section 401(a):

(i) Section 401(a)(4) (relating to nondiscrimination in contributions and benefits), taking section 401(a)(5) into account.

(ii) Section 401(a)(17) (limiting the amount of compensation that can be taken into account).

(iii) Section 401(m) (relating to matching and after-tax employee contributions).

(iv) Section 410(b) (relating to minimum coverage).

(2) *Nonapplication to section 403(b) elective deferrals.*—The requirements of this paragraph (a) do not apply to section 403(b) elective deferrals.

(3) *Compensation for testing.*—Except as may otherwise be specifically permitted under the provisions referenced in paragraph (a)(1) of this section, compliance with those provisions is tested using compensation as defined in section 414(s) (and without regard to section 415(c)(3)(E)). In addition, for purposes of paragraph (a)(1) of this section, there may be excluded employees who are permitted to be excluded under paragraph (b)(4)(ii)(D) and (E) of this section. However, as provided in paragraph (b)(4)(i) of this section, the exclusion of any employee listed in paragraph (b)(4)(ii)(D) or (E) of this section is subject to the conditions applicable under section 410(b)(4).

(4) *Employer aggregation rules.*—See regulations under section 414(b), (c), (m), and (o) for rules treating entities as a single employer for purposes of the nondiscrimination requirements.

(5) *Special rules for governmental plans.*—Paragraphs (a)(1)(i), (iii), and (iv) of this section do not apply to a governmental plan as defined in section 414(d) (but contributions to a governmental plan must comply with paragraphs (a)(1)(i) and (b) of this section).

(b) *Universal availability required for section 403(b) elective deferrals.*—(1) *General rule.*—Under section 403(b)(12)(A)(ii), all employees of the eligible employer must be permitted to have section 403(b) elective deferrals contributed on their behalf if any employee of the eligible employer may elect to have the organization make section 403(b) elective deferrals. Further, the employee's right to make elective deferrals also includes the right to designate section 403(b) elective deferrals as designated Roth contributions.

(2) *Effective opportunity required.*—For purposes of paragraph (b)(1) of this section, an employee is not treated as being permitted to have section 403(b) elective deferrals contributed on the employee's behalf unless the employee is provided an effective opportunity that satisfies the requirements of this paragraph (b)(2). Whether an employee has an effective opportunity is determined based on all the relevant facts and circumstances, including notice of the availability of the election, the period of time during which an election may be made, and any other conditions on elections. A section 403(b) plan satisfies the effective opportunity requirement of this paragraph (b)(2) only if, at least once during each plan year, the plan provides an employee with an effective opportunity to make (or change) a cash or deferred election (as defined at § 1.401(k)-1(a)(3)) between cash or a contribution to the plan. Further, an effective opportunity includes the right to have section 403(b) elective deferrals made on his or her behalf up to the lesser of the applicable limits in § 1.403(b)-4(c) (including any permissible catch-up elective deferrals under § 1.403(b)-4(c)(2) and (3)) or the applicable limits under the contract with the largest limitation, and applies to part-time employees as well as full-time employees. An effective opportunity is not considered to exist if there are any other rights or benefits (other than rights or benefits listed in § 1.401(k)-1(e)(6)(i)(A), (B), or (D)) that are conditioned (directly or indirectly) upon a participant making or failing to make a cash or deferred election with respect to a contribution to a section 403(b) contract.

(3) *Special rules.*—(i) In the case of a section 403(b) plan that covers the employees of more than one section 501(c)(3) organization, the universal availability requirement of this paragraph (b) applies separately to each common law entity (that is, applies separately to each section 501(c)(3) organization). In the case of a section 403(b) plan that covers the employees of more than one State entity, this requirement applies separately to each entity that is not part of a common payroll. An eligible employer may condition the employee's right to have section 403(b) elective deferrals made on his or her behalf on the employee electing a section 403(b) elective deferral of more than $200 for a year.

(ii) For purposes of this paragraph (b)(3), an employer that historically has treated one or more of its various geographically distinct units as separate for employee benefit purposes may treat each unit as a separate organization if the unit is operated independently on a day-to-day basis. Units are not geographically distinct if such units are located within the same Standard Metropolitan Statistical Area (SMSA).

(4) *Exclusions.*—(i) *Exclusions for special types of employees.*—A plan does not fail to satisfy the universal availability requirement of this paragraph (b) merely because it excludes one or more of the types of employees listed in paragraph (b)(4)(ii) of this section. However, the exclusion of any employee listed in paragraph (b)(4)(ii)(D) or (E) of this section is subject to the conditions applicable under section 410(b)(4). Thus, if any employee listed in paragraph (b)(4)(ii)(D) of this section has the right to have section 403(b) elective deferrals made on his or her behalf, then no employee listed in that paragraph (b)(4)(ii)(D) of this section may be excluded under this paragraph (b)(4) and, if any employee listed in paragraph (b)(4)(ii)(E) of this section has the right to have section 403(b) elective deferrals made on his or her behalf, then no employee listed in that paragraph (b)(4)(ii)(E) of this section may be excluded under this paragraph (b)(4).

(ii) *List of special types of excludible employees.*—The following types of employees are listed in this paragraph (b)(4)(ii):

(A) Employees who are eligible under another section 403(b) plan, or a section 457(b) eligible governmental plan, of the employer which permits an amount to be contributed or deferred at the election of the employee.

(B) Employees who are eligible to make a cash or deferred election (as defined at § 1.401(k)-1(a)(3)) under a section 401(k) plan of the employer.

(C) Employees who are non-resident aliens described in section 410(b)(3)(C).

(D) Subject to the conditions applicable under section 410(b)(4) (including section 410(b)(4)(B) permitting separate testing for employees not meeting minimum age and service requirements), employees who are students performing services described in section 3121(b)(10).

(E) Subject to the conditions applicable under section 410(b)(4), employees who normally work fewer than 20 hours per

week (or such lower number of hours per week as may be set forth in the plan).

(iii) *Special rules.*—(A) A section 403(b) plan is permitted to take into account coverage under another plan, as permitted in paragraphs (b)(4)(ii)(A) and (B) of this section, only if the rights to make elective deferrals with respect to that coverage would satisfy paragraphs (b)(2) and (4)(i) of this section if that coverage were provided under the section 403(b) plan.

(B) For purposes of paragraph (b)(4)(ii)(E) of this section, an employee normally works fewer than 20 hours per week if and only if—

(1) For the 12-month period beginning on the date the employee's employment commenced, the employer reasonably expects the employee to work fewer than 1,000 hours of service (as defined in section 410(a)(3)(C)) in such period; and

(2) For each plan year ending after the close of the 12-month period beginning on the date the employee's employment commenced (or, if the plan so provides, each subsequent 12-month period), the employee worked fewer than 1,000 hours of service in the preceding 12-month period. (See, however, section 202(a)(1) of the Employee Retirement Income Security Act of 1974 (ERISA) (88 Stat. 829) Public Law 93-406, and regulations under section 410(a) of the Internal Revenue Code applicable with respect to plans that are subject to Title I of ERISA.)

(c) *Plan required.*—Contributions to an annuity contract do not satisfy the requirements of this section unless the contributions are made pursuant to a plan, as defined in § 1.403(b)-3(b)(3), and the terms of the plan satisfy this section.

(d) *Church plans exception.*—This section does not apply to a section 403(b) contract purchased by a church (as defined in § 1.403(b)-2).

(e) *Other rules.*—This section only reflects requirements of the Internal Revenue Code applicable for purposes of section 403(b) and does not include other requirements. Specifically, this section does not reflect the requirements of ERISA that may apply with respect to section 403(b) arrangements, such as the vesting requirements at 29 U.S.C. 1053. [Reg. § 1.403(b)-5.]

☐ [T.D. 9340, 7-23-2007.]

[Reg. § 1.403(b)-6]

§ 1.403(b)-6. Timing of distributions and benefits.— (a) *Distributions generally.*—This section provides special rules regarding the timing of distributions from, and the benefits that may be provided under, a section 403(b) contract, including limitations on when early distributions can be made (in paragraphs (b) through (d) of this section), required minimum distributions (in paragraph (e) of this section), and special rules relating to loans (in paragraph (f) of this section) and incidental benefits (in paragraph (g) of this section).

(b) *Distributions from contracts other than custodial accounts or amounts attributable to section 403(b) elective deferrals.*—Except as provided in paragraph (c) of this section relating to distributions from custodial accounts, paragraph (d) of this section relating to distributions attributable to section 403(b) elective deferrals, § 1.403(b)-4(f) (relating to correction of excess deferrals), or § 1.403(b)-10(a) (relating to plan termination), a section 403(b) contract is permitted to distribute retirement benefits to the participant no earlier than upon the earlier of the participant's severance from employment or upon the prior occurrence of some event, such as after a fixed number of years, the attainment of a stated age, or disability. See § 1.401-1(b)(1)(ii) for additional guidance. This paragraph (b) does not apply to after-tax employee contributions or earnings thereon.

(c) *Distributions from custodial accounts that are not attributable to section 403(b) elective deferrals.*—Except as provided in § 1.403(b)-4(f) (relating to correction of excess deferrals) or § 1.403(b)-10(a) (relating to plan termination), distributions from a custodial account, as defined in § 1.403(b)-8(d)(2), may not be paid to a participant before the participant has a severance from employment, dies, becomes disabled (within the meaning of section 72(m)(7)), or attains age 59 1/2. Any amounts transferred out of a custodial account to an annuity contract or retirement income account, including earnings thereon, continue to be subject to this paragraph (c). This paragraph (c) does not apply to distributions that are attributable to section 403(b) elective deferrals.

(d) *Distribution of section 403(b) elective deferrals.*—(1) *Limitation on distributions.*—(i) *General rule.*—Except as provided in § 1.403(b)-4(f) (relating to correction of excess deferrals) or § 1.403(b)-10(a) (relating to plan termination), distributions of amounts attributable to section 403(b) elective deferrals may not be paid to a participant earlier than the earliest of the date on which the participant has a severance from employment, dies, has a hardship, becomes disabled (within the meaning of section 72(m)(7)), or attains age 591/2.

(ii) *Special rule for pre-1989 section 403(b) elective deferrals.*—For special rules relating to amounts held as of the close of the taxable year beginning before January 1, 1989 (which does not apply to earnings thereon), see section 1123(e)(3) of the Tax Reform Act of 1986 (100 Stat. 2085, 2475) Public Law 99-514, and section 1011A(c)(11) of the Technical and Miscellaneous Revenue Act of 1988 (102 Stat. 3342, 3476) Public Law 100-647.

(2) *Hardship rules.*—A hardship distribution under this paragraph (d) has the same meaning as a distribution on account of hardship under §1.401(k)-1(d)(3) and is subject to the rules and restrictions set forth in §1.401(k)-1(d)(3) (including limiting the amount of a distribution in the case of hardship to the amount necessary to satisfy the hardship). In addition, a hardship distribution is limited to the aggregate dollar amount of the participant's section 403(b) elective deferrals under the contract (and may not include any income thereon), reduced by the aggregate dollar amount of the distributions previously made to the participant from the contract.

(3) *Failure to keep separate accounts.*—If a section 403(b) contract includes both section 403(b) elective deferrals and other contributions and the section 403(b) elective deferrals are not maintained in a separate account, then distributions may not be made earlier than the later of—

(i) Any date permitted under paragraph (d)(1) of this section; and

(ii) Any date permitted under paragraph (b) or (c) of this section with respect to contributions that are not section 403(b) elective deferrals (whichever applies to the contributions that are not section 403(b) elective deferrals).

(e) *Minimum required distributions for eligible plans.*—(1) *In general.*—Under section 403(b)(10), a section 403(b) contract must meet the minimum distribution requirements of section 401(a)(9) (in both form and operation). See section 401(a)(9) for these requirements.

(2) *Treatment as IRAs.*—For purposes of applying the distribution rules of section 401(a)(9) to section 403(b) contracts, the minimum distribution rules applicable to individual retirement annuities described in section 408(b) and individual retirement accounts described in section 408(a) apply to section 403(b) contracts. Consequently, except as otherwise provided in this paragraph (e), the distribution rules in section 401(a)(9) are applied to section 403(b) contracts in accordance with the provisions in §1.408-8 for purposes of determining required minimum distributions.

(3) *Required beginning date.*—The required beginning date for purposes of section 403(b)(10) is April 1 of the calendar year following the later of the calendar year in which the employee attains age 70¹/₂ or the calendar year in which the employee retires from employment with the employer maintaining the plan. However, for any section 403(b) contract that is not part of a governmental plan or church plan, the required beginning date for a 5-percent owner is April 1 of the calendar year following the calendar year in which the employee attains age 70¹/₂.

(4) *Surviving spouse rule does not apply.*—The special rule in §1.408-8, A-5 (relating to spousal beneficiaries), does not apply to a section 403(b) contract. Thus, the surviving spouse of a participant is not permitted to treat a section 403(b) contract as the spouse's own section 403(b) contract, even if the spouse is the sole beneficiary.

(5) *Retirement income accounts.*—For purposes of §1.401(a)(9)-6, A-4 (relating to annuity contracts), annuity payments provided with respect to retirement income accounts do not fail to satisfy the requirements of section 401(a)(9) merely because the payments are not made under an annuity contract purchased from an insurance company, provided that the relationship between the annuity payments and the retirement income accounts is not inconsistent with any rules prescribed by the Commissioner in revenue rulings, notices, or other guidance published in the Internal Revenue Bulletin (see §601.601(d)(2)(ii)(b) of this chapter). See also §1.403(b)-9(a)(5) for additional rules relating to annuities payable from a retirement income account.

(6) *Special rules for benefits accruing before December 31, 1986.*—(i) The distribution rules provided in section 401(a)(9) do not apply to the undistributed portion of the account balance under the section 403(b) contract valued as of December 31, 1986, exclusive of subsequent earnings (pre-'87 account balance). The distribution rules provided in section 401(a)(9) apply to all benefits under section 403(b) contracts accruing after December 31, 1986 (post-'86 account balance), including earnings after December 31, 1986. Consequently, the post-'86 account balance includes earnings after December 31, 1986, on contributions made before January 1, 1987, in addition to the contributions made after December 31, 1986, and earnings thereon.

(ii) The issuer or custodian of the section 403(b) contract must keep records that enable it to identify the pre-'87 account balance and subsequent changes as set forth in paragraph (d)(6)(iii) of this section and provide such information upon request to the relevant employee or beneficiaries with respect to the contract. If the issuer or custodian does not keep such records, the entire account balance is treated as subject to section 401(a)(9).

(iii) In applying the distribution rules in section 401(a)(9), only the post-'86 account balance is used to calculate the required minimum distribution for a calendar year. The amount of any distribution from a contract is treated as being paid from the post-'86 account balance to the extent the distribution is required to satisfy the minimum distribution requirement with respect to that contract for a calendar year. Any amount distributed in a calendar year from a contract in excess of the required minimum distribution for a calendar year with respect to that contract is treated as paid from the pre-'87 account balance, if any, of that contract.

(iv) If an amount is distributed from the pre-'87 account balance and rolled over to another section 403(b) contract, the amount is treated as part of the post-'86 account balance in that second contract. However, if the pre-'87 account balance under a section 403(b) contract is directly transferred to another section 403(b) contract (as permitted under §1.403(b)-10(b)), the amount transferred retains its character as a pre-'87 account balance, provided the issuer of the transferee contract satisfies the recordkeeping requirements of paragraph (e)(6)(ii) of this section.

(v) The distinction between the pre-'87 account balance and the post-'86 account balance provided for under this paragraph (e)(6) of this section has no relevance for purposes of determining the portion of a distribution that is includible in income under section 72.

(vi) The pre-'87 account balance must be distributed in accordance with the incidental benefit requirement of §1.401-1(b)(1)(i). Distributions attributable to the pre-'87 account balance are treated as satisfying this requirement if all distributions from the section 403(b) contract (including distributions attributable to the post-'86 account balance) satisfy the requirements of §1.401-1(b)(1)(i) without regard to this section, and distributions attributable to the post-'86 account balance satisfy the rules of this paragraph (e) (without regard to this paragraph (e)(6)). Distributions attributable to the pre-'87 account balance are treated as satisfying the incidental benefit requirement if all distributions from the section 403(b) contract (including distributions attributable to both the pre-'87 account balance and the post-'86 account balance) satisfy the rules of this paragraph (e) (without regard to this paragraph (e)(6)).

(7) *Application to multiple contracts for an employee.*—The required minimum distribution must be separately determined for each section 403(b) contract of an employee. However, because, as provided in paragraph (e)(2) of this section, the distribution rules in section 401(a)(9) apply to section 403(b) contracts in accordance with the provisions in §1.408-8, the required minimum distribution from one section 403(b) contract of an employee is permitted to be distributed from another section 403(b) contract in order to satisfy section 401(a)(9). Thus, as provided in §1.408-8, A-9, with respect to IRAs, the required minimum distribution amount from each contract is then totaled and the total minimum distribution taken from any one or more of the individual section 403(b) contracts. However, consistent with the rules in §1.408-8, A-9, only amounts in section 403(b) contracts that an individual holds as an employee may be aggregated. Amounts in section 403(b) contracts that an individual holds as a beneficiary of the same decedent may be aggregated, but such amounts may not be aggregated with amounts held in section 403(b) contracts that the individual holds as the employee or as the beneficiary of another decedent. Distributions from section 403(b) contracts do not satisfy the minimum distribution requirements for IRAs, nor do distributions from IRAs satisfy the minimum distribution requirements for section 403(b) contracts.

(8) *Special rule for governmental plans.*—A section 403(b) contract that is part of a governmental plan (within the meaning of section 414(d)) is treated as having complied with section 401(a)(9) for all years to which section 401(a)(9) applies to the contract, if the contract complies with a reasonable and good faith interpretation of section 401(a)(9).

(9) *Special rule for qualifying longevity annuity contracts.*—The rules in A-17(b) of §1.401(a)(9)-6 (relating to limitations on premiums for a qualifying longevity annuity contract (QLAC), defined in A-17 of §1.401(a)(9)-6) and A-17(d)(1) of §1.401(a)(9)-6 (relating to reliance on representations with respect to a QLAC) apply to the purchase of a QLAC under a section 403(b) plan (rather than the rules in A-12(b) and (c) of §1.408-8).

(f) *Loans.*—The determination of whether the availability of a loan, the making of a loan, or a failure to repay a loan made from an issuer of a section 403(b) contract to a participant or beneficiary is treated as a distribution (directly or indirectly) for purposes of this section, and the determination of whether the availability of the loan, the making of the loan, or a failure to repay the loan is in any other respect a violation of the requirements of section 403(b) and §§1.403(b)-1 through 1.403(b)-5, this section, and §§1.403(b)-7 through 1.403(b)-11. depends on the facts and circumstances. Among the facts and circumstances are whether the loan has a fixed repayment schedule and bears a reasonable rate of interest, and whether there are repayment safeguards to which a prudent lender would adhere. Thus, for example, a loan must bear a reasonable rate of interest in order to be treated as not being a distribution. However, a plan loan offset is a distribution for purposes of this section. See §1.72(p)-1, Q&A-13. See also §1.403(b)-7(d) relating to the application of section 72(p) with respect to the taxation of a loan made under a section 403(b) contract. (Further, see section 408(b)(1) of Title I of ERISA and 29 CFR 2550.408b-1 of the Department of Labor regulations concerning additional requirements applicable with respect to plans that are subject to Title I of ERISA.)

(g) *Death benefits and other incidental benefits.*—An annuity is not a section 403(b) contract if it fails to satisfy the incidental benefit requirement of §1.401-1(b)(1)(ii) (in form or in operation). For purposes of this paragraph (g), to the extent the incidental benefit requirement of §1.401-1(b)(1)(ii) requires a distribution of the participant's or beneficiary's accumulated benefit, that requirement is deemed to be satisfied if distributions satisfy the minimum distribution requirements of section 401(a)(9). In addition, if a contract issued by an insurance company qualified to issue annuities in a State includes provisions under which, in the event a participant becomes disabled, benefits will be provided by the insurance carrier as if employer contributions were continued until benefit distribution commences, then that benefit is treated as an incidental benefit (as insurance for a deferred annuity benefit in the event of disability) that must satisfy the incidental benefit requirement of §1.401-1(b)(1)(ii) (taking into account any other incidental benefits provided under the plan). The rules of §1.402(a)-1(e) apply for purposes of determining when certain incidental benefits are treated as distributed and included in gross income. See §§1.72-15 and 1.72-16.

(h) *Special rule regarding severance from employment.*—For purposes of this section, severance from employment occurs on any date on which an employee ceases to be an employee of an eligible employer, even though the employee may continue to be employed either by another entity that is treated as the same employer where either that other entity is not an entity that can be an eligible employer (such as transferring from a section 501(c)(3) organization to a for-profit subsidiary of the section 501(c)(3) organization) or in a capacity that is not employment with an eligible employer (for example, ceasing to be an employee performing services for a public school but continuing to work for the same State employer). Thus, this paragraph (h) does not apply if an employee transfers from one section 501(c)(3) organization to another section 501(c)(3) organization that is treated as the same employer or if an employee transfers from one public school to another public school of the same State employer.

(i) *Certain limitations do not apply to rollover contributions.*—The limitations on distributions in paragraphs (b) through (d) of this section do not apply to amounts held in a separate account for eligible rollover distributions as described in §1.403(b)-10(d). [Reg. §1.403(b)-6.]

☐ [T.D. 9340, 7-23-2007 (*corrected* 9-24-2007 and 10-25-2010). *Amended by* T.D. 9459, 9-4-2009; T.D. 9665, 5-9-2014 *and* T.D. 9673, 7-1-2014.]

[Reg. §1.403(b)-7]

§1.403(b)-7. Taxation of distributions and benefits.—(a) *General rules for when amounts are included in gross income.*—Except as provided in this section (or in §1.403(b)-10(c) relating to payments pursuant to a qualified domestic relations order), amounts actually distributed from a section 403(b) contract are includible in the gross income of the recipient participant or beneficiary (in the year in which so distributed) under section 72 (relating to annuities). For an additional income tax that may apply to certain early distributions that are includible in gross income, see section 72(t).

(b) *Rollovers to individual retirement arrangements and other eligible retirement plans.*—(1) *Timing of taxation of rollovers.*—In accordance with sections 402(c), 403(b)(8), and 403(b)(10), a direct rollover in accordance with section 401(a)(31) is not includible in the gross income of a participant or beneficiary in the year rolled over. In addition, any payment made in the form of an eligible rollover distribution (as defined in section 402(c)(4)) is not includible in gross income in the year paid to the extent the payment is contributed to

an eligible retirement plan (as defined in section 402(c)(8)(B)) within 60 days, including the contribution to the eligible retirement plan of any property distributed. For this purpose, the rules of section 402(c)(2) through (7) and (c)(9) apply. Thus, to the extent that a portion of a distribution (including a distribution from a designated Roth account) would be excluded from gross income if it were not rolled over, if that portion of the distribution is to be rolled over into an eligible retirement plan that is not an IRA, the rollover must be accomplished through a direct rollover of the entire distribution to a plan qualified under section 401(a) or a section 403(b) plan and that plan must agree to separately account for the amount not includible in income (so that a 60-day rollover to a plan qualified under section 401(a) or another section 403(b) plan is not available for this portion of the distribution). Any direct rollover under this paragraph (b)(1) is a distribution that is subject to the distribution requirements of §1.403(b)-6.

(2) *Requirement that contract provide rollover options for eligible rollover distributions.*—As required in §1.403(b)-3(a)(7), an annuity contract is not a section 403(b) contract unless the contract provides that if the distributee of an eligible rollover distribution elects to have the distribution paid directly to an eligible retirement plan (as defined in section 402(c)(8)(B)) and specifies the eligible retirement plan to which the distribution is to be paid, then the distribution will be paid to that eligible retirement plan in a direct rollover. For purposes of determining whether a contract satisfies this requirement, the provisions of section 401(a)(31) apply to the annuity as though it were a plan qualified under section 401(a) unless otherwise provided in section 401(a)(31). Thus, the special rule in §1.401(k)-1(f)(3)(ii) with respect to distributions from a designated Roth account that are expected to total less than $200 during a year applies to designated Roth accounts under a section 403(b) plan. In applying the provisions of this paragraph (b)(2), the payor of the eligible rollover distribution from the contract is treated as the plan administrator.

(3) *Requirement that contract payor provide notice of rollover option to distributees.*—To ensure that the distributee of an eligible rollover distribution from a section 403(b) contract has a meaningful right to elect a direct rollover, section 402(f) requires that the distributee be informed of the option. Thus, within a reasonable time period before making the initial eligible rollover distribution, the payor must provide an explanation to the distributee of his or her right to elect a direct rollover and the income tax withholding consequences of not electing a direct rollover. For purposes of satisfying the reasonable time period requirement, the plan timing rule provided in section 402(f)(1) and §1.402(f)-1 applies to section 403(b) contracts.

(4) *Mandatory withholding upon certain eligible rollover distributions from contracts.*—If a distributee of an eligible rollover distribution from a section 403(b) contract does not elect to have the eligible rollover distribution paid directly to an eligible retirement plan in a direct rollover, the eligible rollover distribution is subject to 20-percent income tax withholding imposed under section 3405(c). See section 3405(c) and §31.3405(c)-1 of this chapter for provisions regarding the withholding requirements relating to eligible rollover distributions.

(5) *Automatic rollover for certain mandatory distributions under section 401(a)(31).*—In accordance with section 403(b)(10), a section 403(b) plan is required to comply with section 401(a)(31) (including automatic rollover for certain mandatory distributions) in the same manner as a qualified plan.

(c) *Special rules.*—See section 402(g)(2)(C) for special rules to determine the tax treatment of a distribution of excess deferrals, and see §1.401(m)-1(e)(3)(v) for the tax treatment of corrective distributions of after-tax employee contributions and matching contributions to comply with section 401(m). See sections 402(l) and 403(b)(2) for a special rule regarding distributions for certain retired public safety officers made from a governmental plan for the direct payment of certain premiums.

(d) *Amounts taxable under section 72(p)(1).*—In accordance with section 72(p), the amount of any loan from a section 403(b) contract to a participant or beneficiary (including any pledge or assignment treated as a loan under section 72(p)(1)(B)) is treated as having been received as a distribution from the contract under section 72(p)(1), except to the extent set forth in section 72(p)(2) (relating to loans that do not exceed a maximum amount and that are repayable in accordance with certain terms) and §1.72(p)-1. See generally §1.72(p)-1. Thus, except to the extent a loan satisfies section 72(p)(2), any amount loaned from a section 403(b) contract to a participant or beneficiary (including any pledge or assignment treated as a loan under section 72(p)(1)(B)) is includible in the gross income of the participant or beneficiary for the taxable year in which the loan is made. A deemed distribution is not an actual distribution for purposes of §1.403(b)-6, as provided at §1.72(p)-1, Q&A-12 and Q&A-13.

(Further, see section 408(b)(1) of Title I of ERISA concerning the effect of noncompliance with Title I loan requirements for plans that are subject to Title I of ERISA.)

(e) *Special rules relating to distributions from a designated Roth account.*—If an amount is distributed from a designated Roth account under a section 403(b) plan, the amount, if any, that is includible in gross income and the amount, if any, that may be rolled over to another section 403(b) plan is determined under §1.402A-1. Thus, the designated Roth account is treated as a separate contract for purposes of section 72. For example, the rules of section 72(b) must be applied separately to annuity payments with respect to a designated Roth account under a section 403(b) plan and separately to annuity payments with respect to amounts attributable to any other contributions to the section 403(b) plan.

(f) *Aggregation of contracts.*—In accordance with section 403(b)(5), the rules of this section are applied as if all annuity contracts for the employee by the employer are treated as a single contract.

(g) *Certain rules relating to employment taxes.*—With respect to contributions under the Federal Insurance Contributions Act (FICA) under Chapter 21, see section 3121(a)(5)(D) for a special rule relating to section 403(b) contracts. With respect to income tax withholding on distributions from section 403(b) contracts, see section 3405 generally. However, see section 3401 for income tax withholding applicable to annuity contracts or custodial accounts that are not section 403(b) contracts or for cases in which an annuity contract or custodial account ceases to be a section 403(b) contract. See also §1.72(p)-1, Q&A-15, and §35.3405(c)-1, Q&A-11 of this chapter, for special rules relating to income tax withholding for loans made from certain employer plans, including section 403(b) contracts. [Reg. §1.403(b)-7.]

☐ [*T.D. 9340, 7-23-2007 (corrected 10-25-2010).*]

[Reg. §1.403(b)-8]

§1.403(b)-8. Funding.—(a) *Investments.*—Section 403(b) and §1.403(b)-3(a) only apply to amounts held in an annuity contract (as defined in §1.403(b)-2), including a custodial account that is treated as an annuity contract under paragraph (d) of this section, or a retirement income account that is treated as an annuity contract under §1.403(b)-9.

(b) *Contributions to the plan.*—Contributions to a section 403(b) plan must be transferred to the insurance company issuing the annuity contract (or the entity holding assets of any custodial or retirement income account that is treated as an annuity contract) within a period that is not longer than is reasonable for the proper administration of the plan. For purposes of this requirement, the plan may provide for section 403(b) elective deferrals for a participant under the plan to be transferred to the annuity contract within a specified period after the date the amounts would otherwise have been paid to the participant. For example, the plan could provide for section 403(b) elective deferrals under the plan to be contributed within 15 business days following the month in which these amounts would otherwise have been paid to the participant.

(c) *Annuity contracts.*—(1) *Generally.*—As defined in §1.403(b)-2, and except as otherwise permitted under this section, an annuity contract means a contract that is issued by an insurance company qualified to issue annuities in a State and that includes payment in the form of an annuity. This paragraph (c) sets forth additional rules regarding annuity contracts.

(2) *Certain insurance contracts.*—Neither a life insurance contract, as defined in section 7702, an endowment contract, a health or accident insurance contract, nor a property, casualty, or liability insurance contract meets the definition of an annuity contract. See §1.401(f)-4(e). If a contract issued by an insurance company qualified to issue annuities in a State provides death benefits as part of the contract, then that coverage is permitted, assuming that those death benefits do not cause the contract to fail to satisfy any requirement applicable to section 403(b) contracts, for example, assuming that those benefits satisfy the incidental benefit requirement of §1.401-1(b)(1)(i), as required by §1.403(b)-6(g).

(3) *Special rule for certain contracts.*—This paragraph (c)(3) applies in the case of a contract issued under a State section 403(b) plan established on or before May 17, 1982, or for an employee who becomes covered for the first time under the plan after May 17, 1982, unless the Commissioner had before that date issued any written communication (either to the employer or financial institution) to the effect that the arrangement under which the contract was issued did not meet the requirements of section 403(b). The requirement that the contract be issued by an insurance company qualified to issue annuities in a State does not apply to a contract described in the preceding

sentence if one of the following two conditions is satisfied and that condition has been satisfied continuously since May 17, 1982—

(i) Benefits under the contract are provided from a separately funded retirement reserve that is subject to supervision of the State insurance department; or

(ii) Benefits under the contract are provided from a fund that is separate from the fund used to provide statutory benefits payable under a state retirement system and that is part of a State teachers retirement system (including a state university retirement system) to purchase benefits that are unrelated to the basic benefits provided under the retirement system, and the death benefit provided under the contract does not at any time exceed the larger of the reserve or the contribution made for the employee.

(d) *Custodial accounts.*—(1) *Treatment as a section 403(b) contract.*—Under section 403(b)(7), a custodial account is treated as an annuity contract for purposes of §§1.403(b)-1 through 1.403(b)-7, this section and §§1.403(b)-9 through 1.403(b)-11. See section 403(b)(7)(B) for special rules regarding the tax treatment of custodial accounts and section 4973(c) for an excise tax that applies to excess contributions to a custodial account.

(2) *Custodial account defined.*—A custodial account means a plan, or a separate account under a plan, in which an amount attributable to section 403(b) contributions (or amounts rolled over to a section 403(b) contract, as described in §1.403(b)-10(d)) is held by a bank or a person who satisfies the conditions in section 401(f)(2), if—

(i) All of the amounts held in the account are invested in stock of a regulated investment company (as defined in section 851(a) relating to mutual funds);

(ii) The requirements of §1.403(b)-6(c) (imposing restrictions on distributions with respect to a custodial account) are satisfied with respect to the amounts held in the account;

(iii) The assets held in the account cannot be used for, or diverted to, purposes other than for the exclusive benefit of plan participants or their beneficiaries (for which purpose, assets are treated as diverted to the employer if the employer borrows assets from the account); and

(iv) The account is not part of a retirement income account.

(3) *Effect of definition.*—The requirement in paragraph (d)(2)(i) of this section is not satisfied if the account includes any assets other than stock of a regulated investment company.

(4) *Treatment of custodial account.*—A custodial account is treated as a section 401 qualified plan solely for purposes of subchapter F of subtitle A and subtitle F of the Internal Revenue Code with respect to amounts received by it (and income from investment thereof). This treatment only applies to a custodial account that constitutes a section 403(b) contract under §§1.403(b)-1 through 1.403(b)-7, this section and §§1.403(b)-9 through 1.403(b)-11 or that would constitute a section 403(b) contract under §§1.403(b)-1 through 1.403(b)-7, this section and §§1.403(b)-9 through 1.403(b)-11 if the amounts held in the account were to satisfy the nonforfeitability requirement of §1.403(b)-3(a)(2).

(e) *Retirement income accounts.*—See §1.403(b)-9 for special rules under which a retirement income account for employees of a church-related organization is treated as a section 403(b) contract for purposes of §§1.403(b)-1 through 1.403(b)-7, this section and §§1.403(b)-9 through 1.403(b)-11.

(f) *Combining assets.*—To the extent permitted by the Commissioner in revenue rulings, notices, or other guidance published in the Internal Revenue Bulletin (see §601.601(d)(2)(ii)(b) of this chapter), trust assets held under a custodial account and trust assets held under a retirement income account, as described in §1.403(b)-9(a)(6), may be invested in a group trust with trust assets held under a qualified plan or individual retirement plan. For this purpose, a trust includes a custodial account that is treated as a trust under section 401(f). [Reg. §1.403(b)-8.]

☐ [*T.D. 9340, 7-23-2007.*]

[Reg. §1.403(b)-9]

§1.403(b)-9. Special rules for church plans.—(a) *Retirement income accounts.*—(1) *Treatment as a section 403(b) contract.*—Under section 403(b)(9), a retirement income account for employees of a church-related organization (as defined in §1.403(b)-2) is treated as an annuity contract for purposes of §§1.403(b)-1 through 1.403(b)-8, this section, §1.403(b)-10 and §1.403(b)-11.

(2) *Retirement income account defined.*—(i) *In general.*—A retirement income account means a defined contribution program established or maintained by a church-related organization under which—

(A) There is separate accounting for the retirement income account's interest in the underlying assets (namely, there must be sufficient separate accounting in order for it to be possible at all times to determine the retirement income account's interest in the underlying assets and to distinguish that interest from any interest that is not part of the retirement income account);

(B) Investment performance is based on gains and losses on those assets; and

(C) The assets held in the account cannot be used for, or diverted to, purposes other than for the exclusive benefit of plan participants or their beneficiaries (and for this purpose, assets are treated as diverted to the employer if there is a loan or other extension of credit from assets in the account to the employer).

(ii) *Plan required.*—A retirement income account must be maintained pursuant to a program which is a plan (as defined in §1.403(b)-3(b)(3)) and the plan document must state (or otherwise evidence in a similarly clear manner) the intent to constitute a retirement income account.

(3) *Ownership or use constitutes distribution.*—Any asset of a retirement income account that is owned or used by a participant or beneficiary is treated as having been distributed to that participant or beneficiary. See §§1.403(b)-6 and 1.403(b)-7 for rules relating to distributions.

(4) *Coordination of retirement income account with custodial account rules.*—A retirement income account that is treated as an annuity contract is not a custodial account (as defined in §1.403(b)-8(d)(2)), even if it is invested solely in stock of a regulated investment company.

(5) *Life annuities.*—A retirement income account may distribute benefits in a form that includes a life annuity only if—

(i) The amount of the distribution form has an actuarial present value, at the annuity starting date, equal to the participant's or beneficiary's accumulated benefit, based on reasonable actuarial assumptions, including regarding interest and mortality; and

(ii) The plan sponsor guarantees benefits in the event that a payment is due that exceeds the participant's or beneficiary's accumulated benefit.

(6) *Combining retirement income account assets with other assets.*—For purposes of §1.403(b)-8(f) relating to combining assets, retirement income account assets held in trust (including a custodial account that is treated as a trust under section 401(f)) are subject to the same rules regarding combining of assets as custodial account assets. In addition, retirement income account assets are permitted to be commingled in a common fund with amounts devoted exclusively to church purposes (such as a fund from which unfunded pension payments are made to former employees of the church). However, unless otherwise permitted by the Commissioner, no assets of the plan sponsor, other than retirement income account assets, may be combined with custodial account assets or any other assets permitted to be combined under §1.403(b)-8(f). This paragraph (a)(6) is subject to any additional rules issued by the Commissioner in revenue rulings, notices, or other guidance published in the Internal Revenue Bulletin (see §601.601(d)(2)(ii)(b) of this chapter).

(7) *Trust treated as tax exempt.*—A trust (including a custodial account that is treated as a trust under section 401(f)) that includes no assets other than assets of a retirement income account is treated as an organization that is exempt from taxation under section 501(a).

(b) *No compensation limitation up to $10,000.*—See section 415(c)(7) for special rules regarding certain annual additions not exceeding $10,000.

(c) *Special deduction rule for self-employed ministers.*—See section 404(a)(10) for a special rule regarding the deductibility of a contribution made by a self-employed minister. [Reg. §1.403(b)-9.]

☐ [*T.D. 9340, 7-23-2007.*]

[Reg. §1.403(b)-10]

§1.403(b)-10. Miscellaneous provisions.—(a) *Plan terminations and frozen plans.*—(1) *In general.*—An employer is permitted to amend its section 403(b) plan to eliminate future contributions for existing participants or to limit participation to existing participants and employees (to the extent consistent with §1.403(b)-5). A section 403(b) plan is permitted to contain provisions that provide for plan termination and that allow accumulated benefits to be distributed on termination. However, in the case of a section 403(b) contract that is subject to the distribution restrictions in §1.403(b)-6(c) or (d) (relating to custodial accounts and section 403(b) elective deferrals), termination of the plan and the distribution of accumulated benefits is permitted only if the employer (taking into account all entities that are treated as the same employer under section 414(b), (c), (m), or (o) on the date of the termination) does not make contributions to any section 403(b) contract that is not part of the plan during the period

beginning on the date of plan termination and ending 12 months after distribution of all assets from the terminated plan. However, if at all times during the period beginning 12 months before the termination and ending 12 months after distribution of all assets from the terminated plan, fewer than 2 percent of the employees who were eligible under the section 403(b) plan as of the date of plan termination are eligible under the alternative section 403(b) contract, the alternative section 403(b) contract is disregarded. To the extent a contract fails to satisfy the nonforfeitability requirement of §1.403(b)-3(a)(2) at the date of plan termination, the contact is not, and cannot later become, a section 403(b) contract. In order for a section 403(b) plan to be considered terminated, all accumulated benefits under the plan must be distributed to all participants and beneficiaries as soon as administratively practicable after termination of the plan. For this purpose, delivery of a fully paid individual insurance annuity contract is treated as a distribution. The mere provision for, and making of, distributions to participants or beneficiaries upon plan termination does not cause a contract to cease to be a section 403(b) contract. See §1.403(b)-7 for rules regarding the tax treatment of distributions, including §1.403(b)-7(b)(1) under which an eligible rollover distribution is not included in gross income if paid in a direct rollover to an eligible retirement plan or if transferred to an eligible retirement plan within 60 days.

(2) *Employers that cease to be eligible employers.*—An employer that ceases to be an eligible employer may no longer contribute to a section 403(b) contract for any subsequent period, and the contract will fail to satisfy §1.403(b)-3(a) if any further contributions are made with respect to a period after the employer ceases to be an eligible employer.

(b) *Contract exchanges and plan-to-plan transfers.*—(1) *Contract exchanges and transfers.*—(i) *General rule.*—If the conditions in paragraph (b)(2) of this section are met, a section 403(b) contract held under a section 403(b) plan is permitted to be exchanged for another section 403(b) contract held under that section 403(b) plan. Further, if the conditions in paragraph (b)(3) of this section are met, a section 403(b) plan is permitted to provide for the transfer of its assets (including any assets held in a custodial account or retirement income account that are treated as section 403(b) contracts) to another section 403(b) plan. In addition, if the conditions in paragraph (b)(4) of this section (relating to permissive service credit and repayments under section 415) are met, a section 403(b) plan is permitted to provide for the transfer of its assets to a qualified plan under section 401(a). However, neither a qualified plan nor an eligible governmental plan under section 457(b) may transfer assets to a section 403(b) plan, and a section 403(b) plan may not accept such a transfer. In addition, a section 403(b) contract may not be exchanged for an annuity contract that is not a section 403(b) contract. Neither a plan-to-plan transfer nor a contract exchange permitted under this paragraph (b) is treated as a distribution for purposes of the distribution restrictions at §1.403(b)-6. Therefore, such a transfer or exchange may be made before severance from employment or another distribution event. Further, no amount is includible in gross income by reason of such a transfer or exchange.

(ii) *ERISA rules.*—See §1.414(l)-1 for other rules that are applicable to section 403(b) plans that are subject to section 208 of the Employee Retirement Income Security Act of 1974 (88 Stat. 829, 865).

(2) *Requirements for contract exchange within the same plan.*—(i) *General rule.*—A section 403(b) contract of a participant or beneficiary may be exchanged under paragraph (b)(1) of this section for another section 403(b) contract of that participant or beneficiary under the same section 403(b) plan if each of the following conditions are met:

(A) The plan under which the contract is issued provides for the exchange.

(B) The participant or beneficiary has an accumulated benefit immediately after the exchange that is at least equal to the accumulated benefit of that participant or beneficiary immediately before the exchange (taking into account the accumulated benefit of that participant or beneficiary under both section 403(b) contracts immediately before the exchange).

(C) The other contract is subject to distribution restrictions with respect to the participant that are not less stringent than those imposed on the contract being exchanged, and the employer enters into an agreement with the issuer of the other contract under which the employer and the issuer will from time to time in the future provide each other with the following information:

(1) Information necessary for the resulting contract, or any other contract to which contributions have been made by the employer, to satisfy section 403(b), including information concerning the participant's employment and information that takes into account other section 403(b) contracts or qualified employer plans (such as whether a severance from employment has occurred for purposes of

the distribution restrictions in §1.403(b)-6 and whether the hardship withdrawal rules of §1.403(b)-6(d)(2) are satisfied).

(2) Information necessary for the resulting contract, or any other contract to which contributions have been made by the employer, to satisfy other tax requirements (such as whether a plan loan satisfies the conditions in section 72(p)(2) so that the loan is not a deemed distribution under section 72(p)(1)).

(ii) *Accumulated benefit.*—The condition in paragraph (b)(2)(i)(B) of this section is satisfied if the exchange would satisfy section 414(l)(1) if the exchange were a transfer of assets.

(iii) *Authority for future guidance.*—Subject to such conditions as the Commissioner determines to be appropriate, the Commissioner may issue rules of general applicability, in revenue rulings, notices, or other guidance published in the Internal Revenue Bulletin (see §601.601(d)(2)(ii)(*b*) of this chapter), permitting an exchange of one section 403(b) contract for another section 403(b) contract for an exchange that does not satisfy paragraph (b)(2)(i)(C) of this section. Any such rules must require the resulting contract to set forth procedures that the Commissioner determines are reasonably designed to ensure compliance with those requirements of section 403(b) or other tax provisions that depend on either information concerning the participant's employment or information that takes into account other section 403(b) contracts or other employer plans (such as whether a severance from employment has occurred for purposes of the distribution restrictions in §1.403(b)-6, whether the hardship withdrawal rules of §1.403(b)-6(d)(2) are satisfied, and whether a plan loan constitutes a deemed distribution under section 72(p)).

(3) *Requirements for plan-to-plan transfers.*—(i) *In general.*—A plan-to-plan transfer under paragraph (b)(1) of this section from a section 403(b) plan to another section 403(b) plan is permitted if each of the following conditions are met—

(A) In the case of a transfer for a participant, the participant is an employee or former employee of the employer (or the business of the employer) for the receiving plan.

(B) In the case of a transfer for a beneficiary of a deceased participant, the participant was an employee or former employee of the employer (or business of the employer) for the receiving plan.

(C) The transferor plan provides for transfers.

(D) The receiving plan provides for the receipt of transfers.

(E) The participant or beneficiary whose assets are being transferred has an accumulated benefit immediately after the transfer that is at least equal to the accumulated benefit of that participant or beneficiary immediately before the transfer.

(F) The receiving plan provides that, to the extent any amount transferred is subject to any distribution restrictions under §1.403(b)-6, the receiving plan imposes restrictions on distributions to the participant or beneficiary whose assets are being transferred that are not less stringent than those imposed on the transferor plan.

(G) If a plan-to-plan transfer does not constitute a complete transfer of the participant's or beneficiary's interest in the section 403(b) plan, the transferee plan treats the amount transferred as a continuation of a pro rata portion of the participant's or beneficiary's interest in the section 403(b) plan (for example, a pro rata portion of the participant's or beneficiary's interest in any after-tax employee contributions).

(ii) *Accumulated benefit.*—The condition in paragraph (b)(3)(i)(D) of this section is satisfied if the transfer would satisfy section 414(l)(1).

(4) *Purchases of permissive service credit by contract-to-plan transfers from a section 403(b) contract to a qualified plan.*—(i) *General rule.*—If the conditions in paragraph (b)(4)(ii) of this section are met, a section 403(b) plan may provide for the transfer of assets held in the plan to a qualified defined benefit plan that is a governmental plan (as defined in section 414(d)).

(ii) *Conditions for plan-to-plan transfers.*—A transfer may be made under this paragraph (b)(4) only if the transfer is either—

(A) For the purchase of permissive service credit (as defined in section 415(n)(3)(A)) under the receiving defined benefit plan; or

(B) A repayment to which section 415 does not apply by reason of section 415(k)(3).

(c) *Qualified domestic relations orders.*—In accordance with the second sentence of section 414(p)(9), any distribution from an annuity contract under section 403(b) (including a distribution from a custodial account or retirement income account that is treated as a section 403(b) contract) pursuant to a qualified domestic relations order is treated in the same manner as a distribution from a plan to which section 401(a)(13) applies. Thus, for example, a section 403(b) plan does not fail to satisfy the distribution restrictions set forth in

§1.403(b)-6(b), (c), or (d) merely as a result of distribution made pursuant to a qualified domestic relations order under section 414(p), so that such a distribution is permitted without regard to whether the employee from whose contract the distribution is made has had a severance from employment or another event permitting a distribution to be made under section 403(b). In the case of a plan that is subject to Title I of ERISA, see also section 206(d)(3) of ERISA under which the prohibition against assignment or alienation of plan benefits under section 206(d)(1) of ERISA does not apply to an order that is determined to be a qualified domestic relations order.

(d) *Rollovers to a section 403(b) contract.*—(1) *General rule.*—A section 403(b) contract may accept a contribution that is an eligible rollover distribution (as defined in section 402(c)(4)) made from another eligible retirement plan (as defined in section 402(c)(8)(B)). Any amount contributed to a section 403(b) contract as an eligible rollover distribution is not taken into account for purposes of the limits in §1.403(b)-4, but, except as otherwise specifically provided (for example, at §1.403(b)-6(i)), is otherwise treated in the same manner as an amount held under a section 403(b) contract for purposes of §§1.403(b)-3 through 1.403(b)-9 and this section.

(2) *Special rules relating to after-tax employee contributions and designated Roth contributions.*—A section 403(b) plan that receives an eligible rollover distribution that includes after-tax employee contributions or designated Roth contributions is required to obtain information regarding the employee's section 72 basis in the amount rolled over. A section 403(b) plan is permitted to receive an eligible rollover distribution that includes designated Roth contributions only if the plan permits employees to make elective deferrals that are designated Roth contributions.

(e) *Deemed IRAs.*—See regulations under section §408(q) for special rules relating to deemed IRAs.

(f) *Defined benefit plans.*—(1) *Defined benefit plans generally.*—Except for a TEFRA church defined benefit plan as defined in paragraph (f)(2) of this section, section 403(b) does not apply to any contributions or accrual under a defined benefit plan.

(2) *TEFRA church defined benefit plans.*—See section 251(e)(5) of the Tax Equity and Fiscal Responsibility Act of 1982, Public Law 97-248, for a provision permitting certain arrangements established by a church-related organization and in effect on September 3, 1982 (a TEFRA church defined benefit plan) to be treated as section 403(b) contract even though it is a defined benefit arrangement. In accordance with section 403(b)(1), for purposes of applying section 415 to a TEFRA church defined benefit plan, the accruals under the plan are limited to the maximum amount permitted under section 415(c) when expressed as an annual addition, and, for this purpose, the rules at §1.402(b)-1(a)(2) for determining the present value of an accrual under a nonqualified defined benefit plan also apply for purposes of converting the accrual under a TEFRA church defined benefit plan to an annual addition. See section 415(b) for additional limits applicable to TEFRA church defined benefit plans.

(g) *Other rules relating to section 501(c)(3) organizations.*—See section 501(c)(3) and regulations thereunder for the substantive standards for tax-exemption under that section, including the requirement that no part of the organization's net earnings inure to the benefit of any private shareholder or individual. See also sections 4941 (self dealing), 4945 (taxable expenditures), and 4958 (excess benefit transactions), and the regulations thereunder, for rules relating to excise taxes imposed on certain transactions involving organizations described in section 501(c)(3). [Reg. §1.403(b)-10.]

☐ [T.D. 9340, 7-23-2007 (corrected 10-25-2010).]

[Reg. §1.403(b)-11]

§1.403(b)-11. **Applicable dates.**—(a) *General rule.*—Except as otherwise provided in this section, §§1.403(b)-1 through 1.403(b)-10 apply for taxable years beginning after December 31, 2008.

(b) *Collective bargaining agreements.*—In the case of a section 403(b) plan maintained pursuant to one or more collective bargaining agreements that have been ratified and in effect on July 26, 2007, §§1.403(b)-1 through 1.403(b)-10 do not apply before the earlier of—

(1) The date on which the last of the collective bargaining agreements terminates (determined without regard to any extension thereof after July 26, 2007); or

(2) July 26, 2010.

(c) *Church conventions; retirement income account.*—(1) In the case of a section 403(b) plan maintained by a church-related organization for which the authority to amend the plan is held by a church convention (within the meaning of section 414(e)), §§1.403(b)-1 through 1.403(b)-10 do not apply before the first day of the first plan year that begins after December 31, 2009.

(2) In the case of a loan or other extension of credit to the employer that was entered into under a retirement income account before July 26, 2007, the plan does not fail to satisfy §1.403(b)-9(a)(2)(i)(C) on account of the loan or other extension of credit if the plan takes reasonable steps to eliminate the loan or other extension of credit to the employer before the applicable date for §1.403(b)-9(a)(2) or as promptly as practical thereafter (including taking steps after July 26, 2007 and before the applicable date).

(d) *Special rules for plans that exclude certain types of employees from elective deferrals.*—(1) If, on July 26, 2007, a plan excludes any of the following categories of employees, then the plan does not fail to satisfy §1.403(b)-5(b) as a result of that exclusion before the first day of the first taxable year that begins after December 31, 2009:

(i) Employees who make a one-time election to participate in a governmental plan described in section 414(d) that is not a section 403(b) plan.

(ii) Professors who are providing services on a temporary basis to another educational organization (as defined under section 170(b)(1)(A)(ii)) for up to one year and for whom section 403(b) contributions are being made at a rate no greater than the rate each such professor would receive under the section 403(b) plan of the original educational organization.

(iii) Employees who are affiliated with a religious order and who have taken a vow of poverty where the religious order provides for the support of such employees in their retirement from eligibility to make elective deferrals.

(2) If, on July 26, 2007, a plan excludes employees who are covered by a collective bargaining agreement from eligibility to make elective deferrals, the plan does not fail to satisfy §1.403(b)-5(b) (relating to universal availability) as a result of that exclusion before the later of—

(i) The first day of the first taxable year that begins after December 31, 2008; or

(ii) The earlier of—

(A) The date on which the related collective bargaining agreement terminates (determined without regard to any extension thereof after July 26, 2007); or

(B) July 26, 2010.

(3) In the case of a governmental plan (as defined in section 414(d)) for which the authority to amend the plan is held by a legislative body that meets in legislative session, the plan does not fail to satisfy §1.403(b)-5(b) as a result of any exclusion in paragraph (d)(1)(i), (d)(1)(ii), (d)(1)(iii), or (d)(2) of this section before the earlier of —

(i) The close of the first regular legislative session of the legislative body with the authority to amend the plan that begins on or after January 1, 2009; or

(ii) January 1, 2011.

(e) *Special rules for plans that permit in-service distributions.*—(1) Section 1.403(b)-6(b) does not apply to a contract issued by an insurance company before January 1, 2009.

(2) Any amendment to comply with the requirements of §1.403(b)-6 (disregarding paragraph (e)(1) of this section) that is adopted before January 1, 2009, or such later date as may be permitted under guidance issued by the Commissioner in revenue rulings, notices, or other guidance published in the Internal Revenue Bulletin (see §601.601(d)(2)(ii)(*b*) of this chapter), does not violate section 204(g) of the Employee Retirement Income Security Act of 1974 to the extent the amendment eliminates or reduces a right to receive benefit distributions during employment.

(f) *Special rule for life insurance contracts.*—Section 1.403(b)-8(c)(2) does not apply to a contract issued before September 24, 2007.

(g) *Special rule for contracts received in an exchange.*—Section 1.403(b)-10(b)(2) does not apply to a contract received in an exchange that occurred on or before September 24, 2007 if the exchange (including the contract received in the exchange) satisfies such rules as the Commissioner has prescribed in guidance of general applicability at the time of the exchange.

(h) *Special rule for coordination with regulations under section 415.*—Section 1.403(b)-3(b)(4)(ii) is applicable for taxable years beginning on or after July 1, 2007.

(i) *Special rule for coordination with regulations under section 402A.*—Sections 1.403(b)-3(c), 1.403(b)-7(e), and 1.403(b)-10(d)(2) are applicable with respect to taxable years beginning on or after January 1, 2007. [Reg. §1.403(b)-11.]

☐ [*T.D. 9340, 7-23-2007 (corrected 9-24-2007).*]

[Reg. §1.403(c)-1]

§1.403(c)-1. Taxability of beneficiary under a nonqualified annuity.—(a) *Taxability of vested interest in premiums.*—If after August 1,

1969, an employer (whether or not exempt under section 501(a) or 521(a)) pays premiums for an annuity contract for the benefit of an employee, the amount of such premiums shall be included as compensation in the gross income of the employee for the taxable year during which such premiums are paid, but only to the extent that the employee's rights in such premiums are substantially vested (as defined in §1.83-3(b)) at the time such premiums are paid. The preceding sentence shall not apply to contracts referred to in the transitional rule of paragraph (d)(1)(ii) or (iii) of this section, or to premiums subject to §1.403(a)-1(a) or excludible under §1.403(b)-3. If an employer has purchased annuity contracts and transferred them to a trust (other than one described in section 401(a)) that is to provide annuity contracts or benefits for his employees, the amounts so paid shall be treated as contributions to a trust described in section 402(b). For the rules relating to the taxation of the cost of life insurance protection when rights in a life insurance contract are substantially nonvested, see §1.83-1(a)(2).

(b) *Taxability of employee when rights under annuity contract change from nonvested to vested.*—(1) *In general.*—If, during a taxable year of an employee ending after August 1, 1969, the rights of such employee under an annuity contract purchased for him by an employer (whether or not exempt under section 501(a) or 521(a)) become substantially vested, the value of the annuity contract on the date of such change shall be included in the employee's gross income for such year, to the extent provided in paragraph (b)(2) of this section. The preceding sentence shall not apply, however, to an annuity contract purchased and held as part of a plan which met at the time of such purchase, and continues to meet, the requirements of section 404(a)(2) or an annuity contract referred to in paragraph (d)(1)(ii) or (iii) of this section. For purposes of this section, the value of an annuity contract on the date the employee's rights become substantially vested means the cash surrender value of such contract on such date.

(2) *Extent to which value of annuity contract is includible in employee's gross income.*—For purposes of paragraph (b)(1) of this section, the only amount includible in the gross income of the employee is that portion of the value of the contract on the date of the change that is attributable to premiums which were paid by the employer after August 1, 1969, and which were not excludible from the employee's gross income under §1.403(b)-3. However, the includible portion does not include—

(i) The value attributable to a premium paid on the date of such change, and

(ii) The value attributable to premiums described in the transitional rule of paragraph (d)(1)(ii) or (iii) of this section.

See §1.403(b)-3(c) for the treatment of an amount otherwise includible in gross income under section 403(c) as an employer contribution for purposes of the exclusion under section 403(b).

(3) *Partial vesting.*—If, during any taxable year of an employee, only part of his beneficial interest in an annuity contract becomes substantially vested, then only the corresponding part of the value of the annuity contract on the date of such change is includible in the employee's gross income for such taxable year. In such a case, it is first necessary to compute, under the rules in paragraphs (b)(1) and (2) of this section but without regard to any exclusion allowable under §1.403(b)-3, the amount which would be includible in the employee's gross income for the taxable year if his entire beneficial interest in the annuity contract had changed to a substantially vested interest during such year. The amount that is includible under this (3) (without regard to the section 403(b) exclusion) is equal to the amount determined under the preceding sentence multiplied by the percent of the employee's beneficial interest which became substantially vested during the taxable year.

(c) *Amounts paid or made available under an annuity contract.*—The amounts paid or made available to the employee under an annuity contract subject to this section shall be included in the gross income of the employee for the taxable year in which paid or made available, as provided in section 72 (relating to annuities). Such amounts may be taken into account in computations under sections 1301 through 1305 (relating to income averaging). For rules relating to the treatment of employer contributions as part of the consideration paid by the employee, see section 72(f). See also section 101(b)(2)(D) for rules relating to the treatment of the limited exclusion provided thereunder as part of the consideration paid by the employee.

(d) *Taxability of beneficiary under a nonqualified annuity on or before August 1, 1969.*—(1) Except as provided in section 402(d) (relating to taxable years beginning before January 1, 1977), if an employer purchases an annuity contract and if the amounts paid for the contract—

(i) On or before August 1, 1969, or

(ii) After such date, if pursuant to a binding written contract (as defined in §1.83-8(b)(2)) entered into before April 22, 1969, or

(iii) After August 1, 1969, pursuant to a written plan in which the employee participated on April 22, 1969 and under which the obligation of the employer is essentially the same as under a binding written contract, are not subject to paragraph (a) of §1.403(a)-1 or paragraph (a) of §1.403(b)-1, the amount of such contribution shall, to the extent it is not excludible under paragraph (b) of §1.403(b)-1, be included in the income of the employee for the taxable year during which such contribution is made if, at the time the contribution is made, the employee's rights under the annuity contract are nonforfeitable, except for failure to pay future premiums. If the annuity contract was purchased by an employer which is not exempt from tax under section 501(a) or section 521(a), and if the employee's rights under the annuity contract in such a case where forfeitable at the time the employer's contribution was made for the annuity contract, even though they become nonforfeitable later the amount of such contribution is not required to be included in the income of the employee at the time his rights under the contract become nonforfeitable. On the other hand, if the annuity contract is purchased by an employer which is exempt from tax under section 501(a) or section 521(a), all or part of the value of the contract may be includible in the employee's gross income at the time his rights under the contract become nonforfeitable (see section 403(d) prior to the repeal thereof by the Tax Reform Act of 1969 and the regulations thereunder). As to what constitutes nonforfeitable rights of an employee, see §1.402(b)-1(d)(2). The amounts received by or made available to the employee under the annuity contract shall be included in the gross income of the employee for the taxable year in which received or made available, as provided in section 72 (relating to annuities). For taxable years beginning before January 1, 1964, section 72(e)(3) (relating to the treatment of certain lump sums), as in effect before such date, shall not apply to such amounts. For taxable years beginning after December 31, 1963, such amounts may be taken into account in computations under sections 1301 through 1305 (relating to income averaging). For rules relating to the treatment of employer contributions as part of the consideration paid by the employee, see section 72(f). See also section 101(b)(2)(D) for rules relating to the treatment of the limited exclusion provided thereunder as part of the consideration paid by the employee.

(2) If an employer has purchased annuity contracts and transferred them to a trust, or if an employer has made contributions to a trust for the purpose of providing annuity contracts for his employees as provided in section 402(d) (see paragraph (a) of §1.402(d)-1), the amount so paid or contributed is not required to be included in the income of the employee, but any amount received by or made available to the employee under the annuity contract shall be includible in the gross income of the employee for the taxable year in which received or made available, as provided in section 72 (relating to annuities). For taxable years beginning before January 1, 1964, section 72(e)(3) (relating to the treatment of certain lump sums), as in effect before such date, shall not apply to any amount received by or made available to the employee under the annuity contract. For taxable years beginning after December 31, 1963, amounts received by or made available to the employee under the annuity contract may be taken into account in computations under sections 1301 through 1305 (relating to income averaging). In such case the amount paid or contributed by the employer shall not constitute consideration paid by the employee for such annuity contract in determining the amount of annuity payments required to be included in his gross income under section 72 unless the employee has paid income tax for any taxable year beginning before January 1, 1949, with respect to such payment or contribution by the employer for such year and such tax is not credited or refunded to the employee. In the event such tax has been paid and not credited or refunded the amount paid or contributed by the employer for such year shall constitute consideration paid by the employee for the annuity contract in determining the amount of the annuity required to be included in the income of the employee under section 72.

(3) For taxable years beginning before January 1, 1958, the provisions contained in section 403(c) prior to the amendment made thereto by the Tax Reform Act of 1969 were included in section 403(b) of the Internal Revenue Code of 1954. Therefore, the regulations contained in this paragraph shall, for such taxable years, be considered as the regulations under section 403(b) as in effect for such taxable years. For the rules with respect to contributions paid after August 1, 1969, see paragraph (a), (b), and (c) of this section. [Reg. §1.403(c)-1.]

☐ [*T.D. 6783*, 12-23-64. *Amended by T.D. 6885*, 6-1-66; *T.D. 7554*, 7-21-78 *and T.D. 9340*, 7-23-2007.]

[Reg. §1.404(a)-1]

§1.404(a)-1. Contributions of an employer to an employees' trust or annuity plan and compensation under a deferred payment plan;

general rule.—(a)(1) Section 404(a) prescribes limitations upon deductions for amounts contributed by an employer under a pension, annuity, stock bonus, or profit-sharing plan, or under any plan of deferred compensation. It is immaterial whether the plan covers present employees only, or present and former employees, or only former employees. Section 404(a) also governs the deductibility of unfunded pensions and death benefits paid directly to former employees or their beneficiaries (see §1.404(a)-12). For taxable years beginning after 1962, certain self-employed individuals may be covered by pension, annuity, or profit-sharing plans. For the rules relating to the deduction of contributions on behalf of such individuals, see paragraph (a)(2) of §1.404(a)-8.

(2) Section 404(a) does not apply to a plan which does not defer the receipt of compensation. Furthermore, section 404(a) does not apply to deductions for contributions under a plan which is solely a dismissal wage or unemployment benefit plan, or a sickness, accident, hospitalization, medical expense, recreation, welfare, or similar benefit plan, or a combination thereof. For example, if under a plan an employer contributes 5 percent of each employee's compensation per month to a fund out of which employees who are laid off will be paid benefits for temporary periods, but employees who are not laid off have no rights to the funds, such a plan is an unemployment benefit plan, and the deductibility of the contributions to it is determined under section 162. As to the deductibility of such contributions, see §1.162-9.

(3) If, however, the contributions to a pension, profit-sharing, stock bonus, or other plan of deferred compensation can be used to provide any of the benefits referred to in subparagraph (2) of this paragraph, then, except as provided in section 404(c), section 404(a) applies to the entire contribution to the plan. Thus, if in the example described in subparagraph (2) of this paragraph, the employer's contribution on behalf of each employee is set up as a separate account, and if any amount which remains in an employee's account at the time of retirement is paid to him at such time, the deductibility of the contributions to the plan is determined under section 404(a). For the regulations for determining whether the benefits referred to in subparagraph (2) of this paragraph can be included in a qualified pension or profit-sharing plan, see §1.401-1(b).

(4) As to inclusion of full-time life insurance salesmen within the class of persons considered to be employees, see section 7701(a)(20).

(b) In order to be deductible under section 404(a), contributions must be expenses which would be deductible under section 162 (relating to trade or business expenses) or 212 (relating to expenses for production of income) if it were not for the provision in section 404(a) that they are deductible, if at all, only under section 404(a). Contributions may therefore be deducted under section 404(a) only to the extent that they are ordinary and necessary expenses during the taxable year in carrying on the trade or business or for the production of income and are compensation for personal services actually rendered. In no case is a deduction allowable under section 404(a) for the amount of any contribution for the benefit of an employee in excess of the amount which, together with other deductions allowed for compensation for such employee's services, constitutes a reasonable allowance for compensation for the services actually rendered. What constitutes a reasonable allowance depends upon the facts in the particular case. Among the elements to be considered in determining this are the personal services actually rendered in prior years as well as the current year and all compensation and contributions paid to or for such employee in prior years as well as in the current year. Thus, a contribution which is in the nature of additional compensation for services performed in prior years may be deductible, even if the total of such contributions and other compensation for the current year would be in excess of reasonable compensation for services performed in the current year, provided that such total plus all compensation and contributions paid to or for such employee in prior years represents a reasonable allowance for all services rendered by the employee by the end of the current year. A contribution under a plan which is primarily for the benefit of shareholders of the employer is not deductible. Such a contribution may constitute a dividend within the meaning of section 316. See also §§1.162-6 and 1.162-8. In addition to the limitations referred to above, deductions under section 404(a) are also subject to further conditions and limitations particularly provided therein.

(c) Deductions under section 404(a) are generally allowable only for the year in which the contribution or compensation is paid, regardless of the fact that the taxpayer may make his returns on the accrual method of accounting. Exceptions are made in the case of overpayments as provided in paragraphs (1), (3), and (7) of section 404(a), and, as provided by section 404(a)(6), in the case of payments made by a taxpayer on the accrual method of accounting not later than the time prescribed by law for filing the return for the taxable year of accrual (including extensions thereof). This latter provision is intended to permit a taxpayer on the accrual method to deduct such accrued contribution or compensation in the year of accrual, provided payment is actually made not later than the time prescribed by law for filing the return for the taxable year of accrual (including extensions thereof), but this provision is not applicable unless, during the taxable year on account of which the contribution is made, the taxpayer incurs a liability to make the contribution, the amount of which is accruable under section 461 for such taxable year. See section 461 and the regulations thereunder. There is another exception in the case of certain taxpayers who are required to make additional contributions as a result of the Act of June 15, 1955 (Public Law 74, 84th Cong., 69 Stat. 134), and the regulations thereunder. [Reg. § 1.404(a)-1.]

☐ [*T.D.* 6203, 9-24-56. *Amended by T.D.* 6676, 9-16-63 *and T.D.* 9849, 3-11-2019.]

[Reg. § 1.404(a)-1T]

§ 1.404(a)-1T. Questions and answers relating to deductibility of deferred compensation and deferred benefits for employees (Temporary).

Q-1: How does the amendment of section 404(b) by the Tax Reform Act of 1984 affect the deduction of contributions or compensation under section 404(a)?

A-1: As amended by the Tax Reform Act of 1984, section 404(b) clarifies that section 404(a) shall govern the deduction of contributions paid and compensation paid or incurred by the employer under a plan, or method or arrangement, deferring the receipt of compensation or providing for deferred benefits to employees, their spouses, or their dependents. See section 404(b) and § 1.404(b)-1T. Section 404(a) and (d) requires that such a contribution or compensation be paid or incurred for purposes of section 162 or 212 and satisfy the requirements for deductibility under either of those sections. However, notwithstanding the above, section 404 does not apply to contributions paid or accrued with respect to a "welfare benefit fund" (as defined in section 419(e)) after July 18, 1984, in taxable years of employers (and payors) ending after that date. Also, section 463 shall govern the deduction of vacation pay by a taxpayer that has elected the application of such section. For rules relating to the deduction of contributions paid or accrued with respect to a welfare benefit fund, see section 419, § 1.419-1T and § 1.419A-2T. For rules relating to the deduction of vacation pay for which an election is made under section 463, see § 301.9100-16T of this chapter and § 1.463-1T. [Temporary Reg. § 1.404(a)-1T.]

☐ [*T.D.* 8073, 1-29-86. *Amended by T.D.* 8435, 9-18-92.]

[Reg. § 1.404(a)-3]

§ 1.404(a)-3. Contributions of an employer to or under an employees' pension trust or annuity plan that meets the requirements of section 401(a); application of section 404(a)(1).—(a) If contributions are paid by an employer to or under a pension trust or annuity plan for employees and the general conditions and limitations applicable to deductions for such contributions are satisfied (see § 1.404(a)-1), the contributions are deductible under section 404(a)(1) or (2) if the further conditions provided therein are also satisfied. As used in this section, a "pension trust" means a trust forming part of a pension plan and an "annuity plan" means a pension plan under which retirement benefits are provided under annuity or insurance contracts without a trust. This section is also applicable to contributions to a foreign situs pension trust which could qualify for exemption under section 501(a) except that it is not created or organized and maintained in the United States. For the meaning of "pension plan" as used in this section, see paragraph (b)(1)(i) of § 1.401-1. Where disability pensions, insurance, or survivorship benefits incidental and directly related to the retirement benefits under a pension or annuity plan are provided for the employees or their beneficiaries by contributions under the plan, deductions on account of such incidental benefits are also covered under section 404(a)(1) or (2). See paragraph (b)(2) of § 1.72-16 as to taxability to employees of cost of incidental life insurance protection. Similarly, where medical benefits described in section 401(h) as defined in paragraph (a) of § 1.401-14 are provided for retired employees, their spouses, or their dependents under the plan, deductions on account of such subordinate benefits are also covered under section 404(a)(1) or (2). In order to be deductible under section 404(a)(1), contributions to a pension trust must be paid in a taxable year of the employer which ends with or within a year of the trust for which it is exempt under section 501(a). Contributions paid in such a taxable year of the employer may be carried over and deducted in a succeeding taxable year of the employer in accordance with section 404(a)(1)(D), whether or not such succeeding taxable year ends with or within a taxable year of the *trust for which it is exempt under section 501(a).* See § 1.404(a)-8 as to conditions for deductions under section 404(a)(2) in the case of an annuity plan. In either case, the deductions are also subject to further limitations provided in section 404(a)(1). The limitations provided in section 404(a)(1) are, with an exception provided for certain years

under subparagraph (A) thereof, based on the actuarial costs of the plan.

(b) In determining costs for the purpose of limitations under section 404(a)(1), the effects of expected mortality and interest must be discounted and the effects of expected withdrawals, changes in compensation, retirements at various ages, and other pertinent factors may be discounted or otherwise reasonably recognized. A properly weighted retirement age based on adequate analyses of representative experience may be used as an assumed retirement age. Different basic assumptions or rates may be used for different classes of risks or different groups where justified by conditions or required by contract. In no event shall costs for the purpose of section 404(a)(1) exceed costs based on assumptions and methods which are reasonable in view of the provisions and coverage of the plan, the funding medium, reasonable expectations as to the effects of mortality and interest, reasonable and adequate regard for other factors such as withdrawal and deferred retirement (whether or not discounted) which can be expected to reduce costs materially, reasonable expenses of operation, and all other relevant conditions and circumstances. In any case, in determining the costs and limitations, an adjustment shall be made on account of any experience more favorable than that assumed in the basis of limitations for prior years. Unless such adjustments are consistently made every year by reducing the limitations otherwise determined by any decrease in liability or cost arising from experience in the next preceding taxable year which was more favorable than the assumptions on which the costs and limitations were based, the adjustment shall be made by some other method approved by the Commissioner.

(c) The amount of a contribution to a pension or annuity plan that is deductible under section 404(a)(1) or (2) depends upon the methods, factors, and assumptions which are used to compute the costs of the plan and the limitation of section 404(a)(1) which is applied. Since the amount that is deductible for one taxable year may affect the amount that is deductible for other taxable years, the methods, factors, and assumptions used in determining costs and the method of determining the limitation which have been used for determining the deduction for a taxable year for which the return has been filed shall not be changed for such taxable year, except when the Commissioner determines that the methods, factors, assumptions, or limitations were not proper, or except when a change is necessitated by reason of the use of different methods, factors, assumptions, or limitations for another taxable year. However, different methods, factors, and assumptions, or a different method of determining the limitation, if they are proper, may be used in determining the deduction for a subsequent taxable year.

(d) Any expenses incurred by the employer in connection with the plan, such as trustee's and actuary's fees, which are not provided for by contributions under the plan are deductible by the employer under section 162 (relating to trade or business expenses), or 212 (relating to expenses for production of income) to the extent that they are ordinary and necessary.

(e) In case deductions are allowable under section 404(a)(3) as well as under section 404(a)(1) or (2), the limitations under section 404(a)(1) and (3) are determined and applied without giving effect to the provisions of section 404(a)(7) but the amounts allowable as deductions are subject to the further limitations provided in section 404(a)(7). See § 1.404(a)-13.

(f)(1) Amounts contributed by an employer under the plan for the funding of medical benefits described in section 401(h) as defined in paragraph (a) of § 1.401-14 must satisfy the general requirements which are applicable to deductions allowable under section 404 and which are set forth in § 1.404(a)-1 including, for example, the requirements described in paragraph (b) of such section. Accordingly, such amounts must constitute an ordinary and necessary expense relating to either the trade or business or the production of income and must not, when added to all other compensation paid by the employer to the employee on whose behalf such a contribution is made, constitute more than reasonable compensation. However, in determining the amount which is deductible with respect to contributions to provide retirement benefits under the plan, amounts contributed for the funding of medical benefits described in section 401(h) shall not be taken into consideration.

(2) The amounts deductible with respect to employer contributions to fund medical benefits described in section 401(h) shall not exceed the total cost of providing such benefits. The total cost of providing such benefits shall be determined in accordance with any generally accepted actuarial method which is reasonable in view of the provisions and coverage of the plan, the funding medium, and other applicable considerations. The amount deductible for any taxable year with respect to such cost shall not exceed the greater of—

(i) An amount determined by distributing the remaining unfunded costs of past and current service credits as a level amount, or as a level percentage of compensation, over the remaining future service of each employee, or

(ii) 10 percent of the cost which would be required to completely fund or purchase such medical benefits.

In determining the amount deductible, an employer must apply either subdivision (i) of this subparagraph for all employees or subdivision (ii) of this subparagraph for all employees. If contributions paid by an employer in a taxable year to fund such medical benefits under a pension or annuity plan exceed the limitations of this subparagraph but otherwise satisfy the conditions for deduction under section 404, then the excess contributions are carried over and are deductible in succeeding taxable years of the employer which end with or within taxable years of the trust for which it is exempt under section 501(a) in order of time to the extent of the difference between the amount paid and deductible in each succeeding year and the limitation applicable to such year under this subparagraph. For purposes of subdivision (i) of this subparagraph, if the remaining future service of an employee is one year or less, it shall be treated as one year. [Reg. §1.404(a)-3.]

☐ [*T.D. 6203, 9-24-56. Amended by T.D. 6534, 1-19-61, by T.D. 6722, 4-13-64, T.D. 7168, 3-8-72 and T.D. 9849, 3-11-2019.*]

[Reg. §1.404(a)-4]

§1.404(a)-4. [Reserved].

☐ [*T.D. 6203, 9-24-56. Amended by T.D. 6534, 1-19-61. Removed and reserved by T.D. 9849, 3-11-2019.*]

[Reg. §1.404(a)-5]

§1.404(a)-5. [Reserved].

☐ [*T.D. 6203, 9-24-56. Amended by T.D. 6534, 1-19-61. Removed and reserved by T.D. 9849, 3-11-2019.*]

[Reg. §1.404(a)-6]

§1.404(a)-6. [Reserved].

☐ [*T.D. 6203, 9-24-56. Amended by T.D. 6534, 1-19-61. Removed and reserved by T.D. 9849, 3-11-2019.*]

[Reg. §1.404(a)-7]

§1.404(a)-7. [Reserved].

☐ [*T.D. 6203, 9-24-56. Amended by T.D. 6534, 1-19-61. Removed and reserved by T.D. 9849, 3-11-2019.*]

[Reg. §1.404(a)-8]

§1.404(a)-8. Contributions of employer under an employees' annuity plan which meets the requirements of section 401(a); application of section 404(a)(2).—(a) If contributions are paid by an employer under an annuity plan for employees and the general conditions and limitations applicable to deductions for such contributions are satisfied (see §1.404(a)-1), the contributions are deductible under section 404(a)(2) if the further conditions provided therein are satisfied. For the meaning of "annuity plan" as used here, see §1.404(a)-3. In order that contributions by the employer may be deducted under section 404(a)(2), all of the following conditions must be satisfied:

(1) The contributions must be paid toward the purchase of retirement annuities (or for disability, severance, insurance, survivorship benefits incidental and directly related to such annuities, or medical benefits described in section 401(h) as defined in paragraph (a) of §1.401(h)-1) under an annuity plan for the exclusive benefit of the employer's employees or their beneficiaries.

(2) The contributions must be paid in a taxable year of the employer which ends with or within a year of the plan for which it meets the applicable requirements set forth in section 401(a)(3), (4), (5), (6), (7), (8), (11), (12), (13), (14), (15), (16), and (19). In the case of a plan which covers a self-employed individual, the contributions must be paid in a taxable year of the employer which ends with or within a year of the plan for which it also meets the requirements of section 401(a)(9), (10), (17), and (18) and of section 401(d) (other than paragraph (1)). In the case of a plan which covers a shareholder-employee within the meaning of section 1379(d), the contributions must be paid in a taxable year of the employer which ends with or within a year of the plan for which it also meets the requirements of section 401(a)(17) and (18). See section 401(a) and the regulations thereunder for the requirements and the applicable effective dates of the respective paragraphs set forth in section 401(a). Any contributions of an employer which are paid in a taxable year of the employer ending with or within a year of the plan for which it meets the applicable requirements of section 401 may be carried over and deducted in a succeeding taxable year of the employer in accordance with section 404(a)(1)(D), whether or not such succeeding taxable year ends with or within a taxable year of the plan for which it meets the requirements set out in section 401(a) and (d). See section 401(b) and the regulations thereunder for special rules allowing certain plan amendments to be given retroactive effect. See section 404(a)(6) for a

special rule for determining the time when a contribution is deemed to have been made.

(3) There must be a definite written arrangement between the employer and the insurer that refunds of premiums, if any, shall be applied within the taxable year of the employer in which received or within the next succeeding taxable year toward the purchase of retirement annuities (or for disability, severance, insurance, survivorship benefits incidental and directly related to such annuities, or medical benefits described in section 401(h) as defined in paragraph (a) of §1.401(h)-1) under the plan. For the purpose of this condition, "refunds of premiums" means payments by the insurer on account of credits such as dividends, experience rating credits, or surrender or cancellation credits. The arrangement may be in the form of contract provisions or written directions of the employer or partly in one form and partly in another. This condition will be considered satisfied where—

(i) All credits are applied regularly, as they are determined, toward the premiums next due under the contracts before any further employer contributions are so applied, and

(ii) Under the arrangement,

(A) No refund of premiums may be made during continuance of the plan unless applied as aforesaid, and

(B) If refunds of premiums may be made after discontinuance or termination, whichever is applicable, of the plan on account of surrenders or cancellations before all retirement annuities provided under the plan with respect to service before its discontinuance or termination have been purchased, such refunds will be applied in the taxable year of the employer in which received, or in the next succeeding taxable year, to purchase retirement annuities for employees by a procedure which does not contravene the conditions of section 401(a)(4).

If the plan also includes medical benefits described in section 401(h) as defined in paragraph (a) of §1.401(h)-1, any refund of premiums attributable to such benefits must, in accordance with these rules, be applied toward the purchase of medical benefits described in section 401(h).

(4) Any amounts described in subparagraph (3) of this paragraph which are attributable to contributions on behalf of a self-employed individual must be applied toward the purchase of retirement benefits. Amounts which are so applied are not contributions and thus are not taken into consideration in determining—

(i) The amount deductible with respect to contributions on his behalf, nor

(ii) In the case of an owner-employee, the maximum amount of contributions that may be made on his behalf.

(b) Where the above conditions are satisfied, the amounts deductible under section 404(a)(2) are governed by the limitations provided in section 404(a)(1). [Reg. §1.404(a)-8.]

☐ [*T.D. 6203, 9-24-56. Amended by T.D. 6534, 1-19-61, T.D. 6676, 9-16-63, T.D. 6722, 4-13-64, T.D. 7501, 8-22-77 and T.D. 9849, 3-11-2019..*]

[Reg. §1.404(a)-9]

§1.404(a)-9. [Reserved].

☐ [*T.D. 6203, 9-24-56. Amended by T.D. 6534, 1-19-61. Removed and reserved by T.D. 9849, 3-11-2019.*]

[Reg. §1.404(a)-10]

§1.404(a)-10. Profit-sharing plan of an affiliated group; application of section 404(a)(3)(B).—(a) Section 404(a)(3)(B) allows a corporation a deduction to the extent provided in paragraphs (b) and (c) of this section for a contribution which it makes for another corporation to a profit-sharing plan or a stock bonus plan under which contributions are determined by reference to profits, provided the following tests are met:

(1) The corporation for which the contribution is made and the contributing corporation are members of an affiliated group of corporations as defined in section 1504, relating to the filing of consolidated returns, and both such corporations participate in the plan. However, it is immaterial whether all the members of such group participate in the plan.

(2) The corporation for which the contribution is made is required under the plan to make the contribution, but such corporation is prevented from making such contribution because it has neither current nor accumulated earnings or profits, or because its current and accumulated earnings or profits are insufficient to make the required contribution. To the extent that such a corporation has any current or accumulated earnings or profits, it is not considered to be prevented from making its required contribution to the plan.

(3) The contribution is made out of the current or accumulated earnings or profits of the contributing corporation.

(b) The amount that is deductible under section 404(a)(3)(B) is determined by applying the rules of section 404(a)(3)(A) as if the contribution were made by the corporation for which it is made. The contributing corporation may deduct the amount so determined subject to the limitations contained in paragraph (c) of this section. The contributing corporation shall not treat such amount as a contribution made by it in applying the rules of section 404(a)(3)(A) either for the taxable year for which the contribution is made or for succeeding taxable years. The corporation for which the contribution is made shall treat the contributions as having been made by it in applying the rules of section 404(a)(3)(A) for succeeding taxable years.

(c) The allowance of the deduction under section 404(a)(3)(B) does not depend upon whether the affiliated group does or does not file a consolidated return. If a consolidated return is filed, it is immaterial which of the participating corporations makes the contribution and takes the deduction or how the contribution or the deduction is allocated among them. However, if a consolidated return is not filed, the contribution which is deductible under section 404(a)(3)(B) by each contributing corporation shall be limited to that portion of its total current and accumulated earnings or profits (adjusted for its contribution deductible without regard to section 404(a)(3)(B)) which the prevented contribution bears to the total current and accumulated earnings or profits of all the participating members of the group having such earnings or profits (adjusted for all contributions deductible without regard to section 404(a)(3)(B)). For the purpose of this section, current earnings or profits shall be computed as of the close of the taxable year without diminution by reasons of any dividends during the taxable year, and accumulated earnings or profits shall be computed as of the beginning of the taxable year.

(d) The application of section 404(a)(3)(B) may be illustrated by the following example in which the affiliated group does not file a consolidated return:

(1)	(2)	(3)	(4)	(5)	(6)
A.	($10,000)	($140,000)	($150,000)	$ 200,000	1/5
B.	(5,000)	105,000	100,000	300,000	3/10
C.	75,000	175,000	250,000	500,000	1/2
Total	$60,000	$140,000	$200,000	$1,000,000	

(1)	(7)	(8)	(9)	(10)	(11)
A.	$ 6,000	....			
B.	9,000	$ 9,000	$ 91,000	$\left[\begin{array}{c} 6/326 \\ \times \\ 91,000 \end{array}\right]$	$1,674.85
C.	15,000	15,000	235,000	$\left[\begin{array}{c} 6/326 \\ \times \\ 235,000 \end{array}\right]$	4,325.15
Total	$30,000	$ 24,000	$326,000		$6,000.00

Column		
	(1)	Member.
	(2)	Earnings and profits of the taxable year.
	(3)	Accumulated earnings and profits at beginning of taxable year.
	(4)	Total current and accumulated earnings and profits (column 2 plus column 3).
	(5)	Compensation of participating employees.
	(6)	Contribution formula: 50% of consolidated earnings and profits, allocated among participating members in proportion of covered payroll of each to covered payroll of consolidated group.
	(7)	Individual contribution had it not been prevented.
	(8)	Individual contribution made by each employer for its own employees.
	(9)	Balance of accumulated earnings and profits (column 4 minus column 8).
	(10)	Proportion of make-up contribution.
	(11)	Make-up contribution.

[Reg. §1.404(a)-10.]

☐ [T.D. 6203, 9-24-56. Amended by T.D. 9849, 3-11-2019.]

[Reg. §1.404(a)-11]

§1.404(a)-11. Trusts created or organized outside the United States; application of section 404(a)(4).—In order that a trust may constitute a qualified trust under section 401(a) and be exempt under section 501(a), it must be created or organized in the United States and maintained at all times as a domestic trust. See paragraph (a) of §1.401-1. Paragraph (4) of section 404(a) provides, however, that an employer which is a resident, a corporation, or other entity of the United States, making contributions to a foreign stock bonus, pension, or profit-sharing trust, shall be allowed deductions for such contributions, under the applicable conditions and within the prescribed limits of section 404(a), if such foreign trust would qualify for exemption under section 501(a) except for the fact that it is a trust created, organized, or maintained outside the United States. Moreover, if a nonresident alien individual, foreign corporation, or other entity is engaged in trade or business within the United States and makes contributions to a foreign stock bonus, pension, or profit-sharing trust, which would qualify under section 401(a) and be exempt under section 501(a) except that it is created, organized, or maintained outside the United States, such contributions are deductible subject to the conditions and limitations of section 404(a) and to the extent allowed by section 873 or 882(c). [Reg. §1.404(a)-11.]

☐ [T.D. 6203, 9-24-56.]

[Reg. §1.404(a)-12]

§1.404(a)-12. Contributions of an employer under a plan that does not meet the requirements of section 401(a); application of section 404(a)(5).—(a) *In general.*—Section 404(a)(5) covers all cases for which deductions are allowable under section 404(a) (for contributions paid by an employer under a stock bonus, pension, profit-sharing, or annuity plan or for any compensation paid on account of any employee under a plan deferring the receipt of such compensation) but not allowable under paragraph (1), (2), (3), (4), or (7) of such section. For the rules with respect to the taxability of an employee when rights under a nonexempt trust become substantially vested, see section 402(b) and the regulations thereunder.

(b) *Contributions made after August 1, 1969.*—(1) *In general.*—A deduction is allowable for a contribution paid after August 1, 1969, under section 404(a)(5) only in the taxable year of the employer in which or with which ends the taxable year of an employee in which an amount attributable to such contribution is includible in his gross income as compensation, and then only to the extent allowable under section 404(a). See §1.404(a)-1. For example, if an employer A contributes $1,000 to the account of its employee E for its taxable (calendar) year 1977, but the amount in the account attributable to that contribution is not includible in E's gross income until his taxable (calendar) year 1980 (at which time the includible amount is $1,150), A's deduction for that contribution is $1,000 in 1980 (if allowable under section 404(a)). For purposes of this (1), a contribution is considered to be so includible where the employee or his beneficiary excludes it from his gross income under section 101(b) or subchapter N. To the extent that property of the employer is transferred in connection with such a contribution, such transfer will constitute a disposition of such property by the employer upon which gain or loss is recognized, except as provided in section 1032 and the regulations thereunder. The amount of gain or loss recognized from such disposition shall be the difference between the value of such property used to measure the deduction allowable under this section and the employer's adjusted basis in such property.

(2) *Special rule for unfunded pensions and certain death benefits.*—If unfunded pensions are paid directly to former employees, such payments are includible in their gross income when paid, and accordingly, such amounts are deductible under section 404(a)(5) when paid. Similarly, if amounts are paid as a death benefit to the beneficiaries of an employee (for example, by continuing his salary for a reasonable period), and if such amounts meet the requirements of section 162 or 212, such amounts are deductible under section 404(a)(5) in any case when they are not includible under the other paragraphs of section 404(a).

(3) *Separate accounts for funded plans with more than one employee.*—In the case of a funded plan under which more than one

employee participates, no deduction is allowable under section 404(a)(5) for any contribution unless separate accounts are maintained for each employee. The requirement of separate accounts does not require that a separate trust be maintained for each employee. However, a separate account must be maintained for each employee to which employer contributions under the plan are allocated, along with any income earned thereon. In addition, such accounts must be sufficiently separate and independent to qualify as separate shares under section 663(c). Nothing shall preclude a trust which loses its exemption under section 501(a) from setting up such accounts and meeting the separate account requirement of section 404(a)(5) with respect to the taxable years in which such accounts are set up and maintained.

(c) *Contributions paid on or before August 1, 1969.*—No deduction is allowable under section 404(a)(5) for any contribution paid on or before August 1, 1969, by an employer under a stock bonus, pension, profit-sharing, or annuity plan, or for any compensation paid on account of any employee under a plan deferring the receipt of such compensation, except in the year when paid, and then only to the extent allowable under section 404(a). See §1.404(a)-1. If payments are made under such a plan and the amounts are not deductible under the other paragraphs of section 404(a), they are deductible under section 404(a)(5) to the extent that the rights of individual employees to, or derived from, such employer's contribution or such compensation are nonforfeitable at the time the contribution or compensation is paid. If unfunded pensions are paid to former employees, their rights to such payments are nonforfeitable, and accordingly, such amounts are deductible under section 404(a)(5) when paid. Similarly, if amounts are paid as a death benefit to the beneficiaries of an employee (for example, by continuing his salary for a reasonable period), and if such amounts meet the requirements of section 162 or 212, such amounts are deductible under section 404(a)(5) in any case where they are not deductible under the other paragraphs of section 404(a). As to what constitutes nonforfeitable rights of an employee in other cases, see §1.402(b)-1(d)(2). If an amount is accrued but not paid during the taxable year, no deduction is allowable for such amount for such year. If an amount is paid during the taxable year to a trust or under a plan and the employee's rights to such amount are forfeitable at the time the amount is paid, no deduction is allowable for such amount for any taxable year. [Reg. §1.404(a)-12.]

□ [*T.D. 6203, 9-24-56. Amended by T.D. 7554, 7-21-78.*]

[Reg. §1.404(a)-13]

§1.404(a)-13. **Contributions of an employer where deductions are allowable under section 404(a)(1) or (2) and also under section 404(a)(3); application of section 404(a)(7).**—(a) Where deductions are allowable under section 404(a)(1) or (2) on account of contributions under a pension or annuity plan and deductions are also allowable under section 404(a)(3) for the same taxable year on account of contributions to a profit-sharing or stock bonus trust, the total deductions under these sections are subject to the provisions of section 404(a)(7) unless no employee who is a beneficiary under the trusts or plans for which deductions are allowable under section 404(a)(1) or (2) is also a beneficiary under the trusts for which deductions are allowable under section 404(a)(3). The provisions of section 404(a)(7) apply only to deductions for overlapping trusts or plans, *i.e.*, for all trusts or plans for which deductions are allowable under section 404(a)(1), (2), or (3) except (1) any trust or plan for which deductions are allowable under section 404(a)(1) or (2) and which does not cover any employee who is also covered under a trust for which deductions are allowable under section 404(a)(3), and (2) any trust for which deductions are allowable under section

404(a)(3) and which does not cover any employee who is also covered under a trust or plan for which deductions are allowable under section 404(a)(1) or (2). The limitations under section 404(a)(7) for any taxable year of the employer are based on the compensation otherwise paid or accrued during the year by the employer to all employees who, in such year, are beneficiaries of the funds accumulated under one or more of the overlapping trusts or plans. For purposes of the preceding sentence, if the taxable year of the employer with respect to which the limitation is being computed ends with or within a taxable year of any of the overlapping trusts or plans during which any such trust is not exempt under section 501(a) or, in the case of a plan, during which it does not meet the requirements of section 404(a)(2), or if such taxable year of the employer ends after any such trust or plan has terminated, then, with respect to such trust or plan, those employees, and only those employees, who, at any time during the one-year period ending on the last day of the last calendar month during which the trust was exempt under section 501(a), or the plan met the requirements of section 404(a)(2), were beneficiaries of the funds accumulated under such trust or plan shall be considered the beneficiaries of such trust or plan in the taxable year of the employer with respect to which the limitation is being computed. For purposes of this paragraph, "compensation otherwise paid or accrued" means all of the compensation paid or accrued except that for which a deduction is allowable under a plan that qualifies under section 401(a), including a plan that qualifies under section 404(a)(2).

(b) Under section 404(a)(7), any excess of the total amount otherwise deductible for the taxable year under section 404(a)(1), (2), or (3) as contributions to overlapping trusts or plans over 25 percent of the compensation otherwise paid or accrued during the year to all the employees who are beneficiaries under such trusts or plans, is not deductible for such year but is deductible for succeeding taxable year, in order of time, so that the total deduction for contributions to such trusts or plans for a succeeding taxable year is equal to the lesser of—

(1) 30 percent of the compensation otherwise paid or accrued during the taxable year to all the employees who are beneficiaries under such trusts or plans in the year, or

(2) The sum of (i) the smaller of (a) 25 percent of the compensation otherwise paid or accrued during the taxable year to all the employees who are beneficiaries under such trusts or plans in the year, or (b) the total of the amounts otherwise deductible under section 404(a)(1), (2), or (3) for the year for such trusts or plans and (ii) any carryover to the year from prior years under section 404(a)(7), i.e., any excess otherwise deductible under section 404(a)(1), (2), or (3), but not deducted for a prior taxable year because of the limitations under section 404(a)(7).

(c) The limitations under section 404(a)(7) are determined and applied after all the limitations, deductions otherwise allowable, and carryovers under section 404(a)(1), (2), and (3) have been determined and applied, and, in particular, after effect has been given to the carryover provision in section 404(a)(1)(D) and in the second and third sentences of section 404(a)(3)(A) Where the limitations under section 404(a)(7) reduce the total amount deductible, the excess deductible in succeeding years is treated as a carryover which is distinct from, and additional to, any excess contributions carried over and deductible in succeeding years under the provisions in section 404(a)(1)(D) or in the third sentence of section 404(a)(3)(A). The application of the provisions of section 404(a)(7) and the treatment of carryovers for a case where the taxable years are calendar years and the overlapping trusts or plans consist of a pension trust and a profit-sharing trust put into effect in 1954 and covering the same employees may be illustrated as follows:

Illustration of application of provisions of section 404(a)(7) and of treatment of carryovers for overlapping pension and profit-sharing trusts put into effect in 1954 and covering the same employees (all figures represent thousands of dollars and all taxable (calendar) years of the employer are years which end with or within a taxable year of the trust for which it is exempt under section 501(a))

		Taxable (calendar) years			
		1954	1955	1956	1957
BEFORE GIVING EFFECT TO SECTION 404(a)(7)					
Pension trust contributions and limitations, deductions, and carryovers under section 404(a)(1):					
1.	Contributions paid in year	$215	$85	$140	$60
2.	Contributions carried over from prior years	0	5	0	20
3.	Total deductible for years subject to limitation	215	90	140	80
4.	Limitation applicable to year	210	175	120	85
5.	Amount deductible for year	210	90	120	80
6.	Contributions carried over to succeeding years	5	0	20	0
Profit-sharing trust contributions and limitations, deductions, and carryovers under section 404(a)(3):					
7.	Contributions paid in year	$200	$125	$105	$65
8.	Contributions carried over from prior years	0	35	10	0

		Taxable (calendar) years			
		1954	1955	1956	1957
9.	Total deductible for years subject to limitation	200	160	115	65
10.	Limitation applicable to year	165	150	135	110[1]
11.	Amount deductible for year	165	150	115	65
12.	Contributions carried over to succeeding years	35	10	0	0

APPLICATION OF SECTION 404(a)(7)

Totals for pension and profit-sharing trust:

13.	Amount deductible for year under section 404(a)(7):					
	(1) 30 percent of compensation covered in year[2]	3	$300	$270	$180
	(2)(i)(a) 25 percent of compensation covered in year[2]	$275	250	225	150
	(b) Total amount otherwise deductible for year: item 5 plus item 11	375	240	235	145
	(c) Smaller of (a) or (b)	275	240	225	145
	(ii) Carryover from prior years under section 404(a)(7)	0	100	40	10
	(iii) Sum of (i)(c) and (ii)	275	340	265	155
	(3) Amount deductible: Lesser of (1) or (2)(iii)	275	300	265	155
14.	Carryover to succeeding years under section 404(a)(7): item 13(2)(ii) plus item 13(2)(i)(b) minus item 13(3)	100	40	10	0

[1] Includes carryover of 20 from 1956.

[2] Compensation otherwise paid or accrued during the year to the employees who are beneficiaries under the trusts in the year.

[3] 30 percent limitation not applicable to first year of plan.

[Reg. § 1.404(a)-13.]

☐ [T.D. 6203, 9-24-56. *Amended by T.D. 6534, 1-19-61.*]

[Reg. § 1.404(a)-14]

§ 1.404(a)-14. Special rules in connection with the Employee Retirement Income Security Act of 1974.—(a) *Purpose of this section.*—This section provides rules for determining the deductible limit under section 404(a)(1)(A) of the Internal Revenue Code of 1954 for defined benefit plans.

(b) *Definitions.*—For purposes of this section—

(1) *Section 404(a).*—The term "old section 404(a)" means section 404(a) as in effect on September 1, 1974. Any reference to section 404 without the designation "old" is a reference to section 404 as amended by the Employee Retirement Income Security Act of 1974.

(2) *Ten-year amortization base.*—The term "10-year amortization base" means either the past service and other supplementary pension and annuity credits described in section 404(a)(1)(A)(iii) or any base established in accordance with paragraph (g) of this section. A plan may have several 10-year amortization bases to reflect different plan amendments, changes in actuarial assumptions, changes in funding method, and experience gains and losses of previous years.

(3) *Limit adjustment.*—The term "limit adjustment" with respect to any 10-year amortization base is the lesser of—

(i) The level annual amount necessary to amortize the base over 10 years using the valuation rate, or

(ii) The unamortized balance of the base,

in each case using absolute values (solely for the purpose of determining which is the lesser). To compute the level amortization amount, the base may be divided by the present value of an annuity of one dollar, obtained from standard annuity tables on the basis of a given interest rate (the valuation rate) and a known period (the amortization period).

(4) *Absolute value.*—The term "absolute value" for any number is the value of that number, treating negative numbers as if they were positive numbers. For example, the absolute value of 5 is 5 and absolute value of minus 3 is 3. On the other hand, the true value of minus 3 is minus 3. This term is relevant to the computation of the limit adjustment described in paragraph (b)(3) and the remaining amortization period of combined bases described in paragraph (i)(3) of this section.

(5) *Valuation rate.*—The term "valuation rate" means the assumed interest rate used to value plan liabilities.

(c) *Use of plan in determining deductible limit for employer's taxable year.*—Although the deductible limit applies for an employer's taxable year, the deductible limit is determined on the basis of a plan year. If the employer's taxable year coincides with the plan year, the deductible limit for the taxable year is the deductible limit for the plan year that coincides with that year. If the employer's taxable year *does not coincide with the plan year,* the deductible limit under section 404(a)(1)(A)(i), (ii), or (iii) for a given taxable year of the employer is one of the following alternatives:

(1) The deductible limit determined for the plan year commencing within the taxable year.

(2) The deductible limit determined for the plan year ending within the taxable year, or

(3) A weighted average of alternatives (1) and (2). Such an average may be based, for example, upon the number of months of each plan year falling within the taxable year.

The employer must use the same alternative for each taxable year unless consent to change is obtained from the Commissioner under section 446(e).

(d) *Computation of deductible limit for a plan year.*—(1) *General rules.*—The computation of the deductible limit for a plan year is based on the funding methods, actuarial assumptions, and benefit structure used for purposes of section 412, determined without regard to section 412(g) (relating to the alternative minimum funding standard), for the plan year. The method of valuing assets for purposes of section 404 must be the same method of valuing assets used for purposes of section 412.

(2) *Special adjustments of computations under section 412.*—To apply the rules of this section (*i.e.*, rules regarding the computation of normal cost with aggregate type funding methods, unfunded liabilities, and the full funding limitation described in paragraph (k) of the section, where applicable) with respect to a given plan year in computing deductible limits under section 404(a)(1)(A), the following adjustments must be made:

(i) There must be excluded from the total assets of the plan the amount of any plan contribution for a plan year for which the plan was qualified under section 401(a), 403(a) or 405(a) that has not been previously deducted, even though that amount may have been credited to the funding standard account under section 412(b)(3). In the case of a plan using a spread gain funding method which maintains an unfunded liability (*e.g.*, the frozen initial liability method, but not the aggregate method), the amount described in the preceding sentence must be included in the unfunded liability of the plan.

(ii) There must be included in the total assets of the plan for a plan year the amount of any plan contribution that has been deducted with respect to a prior plan year, even though that amount is considered under section 412 to be contributed in a plan year subsequent to that prior plan year. In the case of a plan using a spread gain funding method which maintains an unfunded liability, the amount described in the preceding sentence must be excluded from the unfunded liability of the plan.

The special adjustments described in paragraph (d)(2)(i) and (ii) of this section apply on a year-by-year basis for purposes of section 404(a)(1)(A) only. Thus, the adjustments have no effect on the computation of the minimum funding requirement under section 412.

(e) *Special computation rules under section 404(a)(1)(A)(i).*—(1) *In general.*—For purposes of determining the deductible limit under section 404(a)(1)(A)(i), the deductible limit with respect to a plan year is the sum of—

(i) The amount required to satisfy the minimum funding standard of section 412(a) (determined without regard to section 412(g)) for the plan year and

(ii) An amount equal to the includible employer contributions.

The term "includible employer contributions" means employer contributions which were required by section 412 for the plan year immediately preceding such plan year, and which were not deductible under section 404(a) for the prior taxable year of the employer solely because they were not contributed during the prior taxable year (determined with regard to section 404(a)(6)).

(2) *Rule for an employer using alternative minimum funding standard account and computing its deduction under section 404(a)(1)(A)(i).*—This paragraph (e)(2) applies if the minimum funding requirements for the plan are determined under the alternative minimum funding standard described in section 412(g) for both the current plan year and the immediately preceding plan year. In that case, the deductible limit under section 404(a)(1)(A)(i) (regarding the minimum funding requirement of section 412) for the current year is the sum of the amount determined under the rules of paragraph (e)(1) of this section.

(i) Plus the charge under section 412(b)(2)(D), and

(ii) Less the credit under section 412(b)(3)(D),

that would be required if in the current plan year the use of the alternative method were discontinued.

(f) *Special computation rules under section 404(a)(1)(A)(ii) and (iii).*— (1) *In general.*—Subject to the full funding limitation described in paragraph (k) of this section, the deductible limit under section 404(a)(1)(A)(ii) and (iii) is the normal cost of the plan (determined in accordance with paragraph (d) of this section).

(2) *Adjustments in calculating limit under section 404(a)(1)(A)(iii).*— In calculating the deductible limit under section 404(a)(1)(A)(iii), the normal cost of the plan is—

(i) Decreased by the limit adjustments to any unamortized bases required by paragraph (g) of this section, for example, bases that are due to a net experience gain, a change in actuarial assumptions, a change in funding method, or a plan provision or amendment which decreases the accrued liability of the plan, and

(ii) Increased by the limit adjustments of any unamortized 10-year amortization bases required by paragraph (g) or (j) of this section, for example, bases that are due to a net experience loss, a change in actuarial assumptions, a change in funding method, or a plan provision or amendment which increases the accrued liability.

(3) *Timing for computations and interest adjustments under section 404(a)(1)(A)(ii) and (iii).*—Regardless of the actual time when contributions are made to a plan, in computing the deductible limit under section 404(a)(1)(A)(ii) and (iii) the normal cost and limit adjustments shall be computed as of the date when contributions are assumed to be made ("the computation date") and adjusted for interest at the valuation rate from the computation date to the earlier of—

(i) The last day of the plan year used to compute the deductible limit for the taxable year, or

(ii) The last day of that taxable year.

For additional provisions relating to the timing of computations and interest adjustments, see paragraph (h)(6) of this section (relating to the timing of computations and interest adjustments in the maintenance of 10-year amortization bases) For taxable years beginning before April 22, 1981, computations under the preceding sentence may, as an alternative, be based on prior published positions of the Internal Revenue Service under section 404(a).

(4) *Special limit under section 404(a)(1)(A)(ii).*—If the deduction for the plan year is determined solely on the basis of section 404(a)(1)(A)(ii) (that is, without regard to clauses (i) or (iii)), the special limitation contained in section 404(a)(1)(A)(ii), regarding the unfunded cost with respect to any three individuals, applies, notwithstanding the rules contained in paragraphs (d)(2) and (f)(1) of this section.

(g) *Establishment of a 10-year amortization base.*—(1) *Experience gains and losses.*—In the case of a plan valued by the use of a funding method which is an immediate gain type of funding method (and therefore separately amortizes rather than includes experience gains and losses as a part of the normal cost of the plan), a 10-year amortization base must be established in any plan year equal to the net experience gain or loss required under section 412 to be determined with respect to that plan year. The base is to be maintained in accordance with paragraph (h) of this section. Such a base must not be established if the deductible limit is determined by use of a funding method which is a spread gain type of funding method (under which experience gains and losses are spread over future periods as a part of the plan's normal cost). Examples of the immediate gain type of funding method are the unit credit method, entry age normal cost method, and the individual level premium cost method. Examples of the spread gain type of funding method are the aggregate cost method, frozen initial liability cost method, and the attained age normal cost method.

(2) *Change in actuarial assumptions.*—(i) If the creation of an amortization base is required under the rules of section 412(b)(2)(B)(v) or (3)(B)(iii) (as applied to the funding method used by the plan), a 10-year amortization base must be established at the time of a change in actuarial assumptions used to value plan liabilities. The amount of the base is the difference between the accrued liability calculated on the basis of the new assumptions and the accrued liability calculated on the basis of the old assumptions. Both computations of accrued liability are made as of the date of the change in assumptions.

(ii) A plan using a funding method of the spread gain type does not directly determine an accrued liability. If a plan using such a method is required under section 412(b)(2)(B)(v) or (3)(B)(iii) to create an amortization base, it must establish a base as described in paragraph (g)(2)(i) of this section for a change in actuarial assumptions by determining an accrued liability on the basis of another funding method (of the immediate gain type) that does determine an accrued liability. (The aggregate method is an example of a funding method that is not required under section 412(b)(2)(B)(v) or (3)(B)(iii) to create an amortization base.) The funding method chosen to determine the accrued liability of the plan in these cases must be the same method used to establish all other 10-year amortization bases maintained by the plan, if any. These bases must be maintained in accordance with paragraph (h) of this section.

(3) *Past service or supplemental credits.*—A 10-year base must be established when a plan is established or amended, if the creation of an amortizable base is required under the rules of section 412(b)(2)(B)(ii) or (iii), or (b)(3)(B)(i) (as applied to the funding method used by the plan). The amount of the base is the accrued liability arising from, or the decrease in accrued liability resulting from, the establishment or amendment of the plan. The base must be maintained in accordance with paragraph (h) of this section.

(4) *Change in funding method.*—If a change in funding method results in an increase or decrease in an unfunded liability required to be amortized under section 412, a 10-year base must be established equal to the increase or decrease in unfunded liability resulting from the change in funding method. The base must be maintained in accordance with paragraph (h) of this section.

(h) *Maintenance of 10-year amortization base.*—(1) *In general.*—Each time a 10-year amortization base is established, whether by a change in funding method, by plan amendment, by change in actuarial assumptions, or by experience gains and losses, the base must, except as provided in paragraph (i) of this section, be separately maintained in order to determine when the unamortized amount of the base is zero. The sum of the unamortized balances of all of the 10-year bases must equal the plan's unfunded liability with the adjustments described in paragraph (d) of this section, if applicable. When the unamortized amount of a base is zero, the deductible limit is no longer adjusted to reflect the amortization of the base.

(2) *First year's base.*—See either paragraph (g) or paragraph (i) of this section for rules applicable with respect to the first year of a base.

(3) *Succeeding year's base.*—For any plan year after the first year of a base, the unamortized amount of the base is equal to—

(i) The unamortized amount of the base as of the valuation date in the prior plan year, plus

(ii) Interest at the valuation rate from the valuation date in the prior plan year to the valuation date in the current plan year on the amount described in subdivision (i), minus

(iii) The contribution described in paragraph (h)(4) of this section with respect to the base for the prior plan year.

The valuation date is the date as of which plan liabilities are valued under section 412(c)(9). If such a valuation is performed less often than annually for purposes of section 412, bases must be adjusted for purposes of section 404 each year as of the date on which a section 412 valuation would be performed were it required on an annual basis. See paragraph (b)(3) of this section for the definition of valuation rate.

(4) *Contribution allocation with respect to each base.*—A portion of the total contribution for the prior plan year is allocated to each base. Generally, this portion equals the product of—

(i) The total contribution described in paragraph (h)(6) of this section with respect to all bases, and

(ii) The ratio of the amount described in paragraph (b)(3)(i) of this section with respect to the base to the sum (using true rather than absolute values) of such amounts with respect to all remaining bases.

However, if the result of this computation with respect to a particular base exceeds the amount necessary to amortize such base fully, the smaller amount shall be deemed the contribution made with respect to such base. The unallocated excess with respect to a now fully amortized base shall be allocated among the other bases as indicated above.

(5) *Other allocation methods.*—The Commissioner may authorize the use of methods other than the method described in paragraph (h)(4) of this section for allocating contributions to bases.

(6) *Total contribution for all bases.*—The contribution with respect to all bases for the prior plan year (see paragraph (h)(3)(iii) of this section) is the difference between—

(i) The sum of (A) the total deduction (including a carryover deduction) for the prior year, (B) interest on the actual contributions for the prior year (whether or not deductible) at the valuation rate for the period between the dates as of which the contributions are credited under section 412 and the valuation date in the current plan year, and (C) interest on the carryover described in section 404(a)(1)(D) that is available at the beginning of the prior taxable year at the valuation rate for the period between the current and prior valuation dates, and

(ii) The normal cost for the prior plan year and interest on it at the valuation rate from the date as of which the normal cost is calculated to the current valuation date.

(7) *Effect of failure to contribute normal cost plus interest on unamortized amounts.*—The failure to make a contribution at least equal to the sum of the normal cost plus interest on the unamortized amounts has the following effects under the preceding rules of this section—

(i) It does not create a new base.

(ii) It results in an increase in the unamortized amount of each base and consequently extends the time before the base is fully amortized.

(iii) The limit adjustment for any base is not increased (in absolute terms) even if the unamortized amount computed under paragraph (h) of this section exceeds the initial 10-year amortization base. Thus, if the total unamortized amount of the plan's bases at the beginning of the plan year is $100,000 (which is also the unfunded liability of the plan), and a required $50,000 normal cost contribution is not made for the plan year, the following effects occur. The total unamortized balance of the plan's bases increases by the $50,000 normal cost for the year (adjusted for interest), plus interest on the $100,000 balance of the bases; and, because of that increase, it will take a longer period to amortize the remaining balance of the bases. (The annual amortization amount does not change.)

(8) *Required adjustment to a 10-year base limit adjustment if valuation rate changed.*—If there is a change in the valuation rate, the limit adjustment for all unamortized 10-year amortization bases must be changed, in addition to establishing a new base as provided in paragraph (g)(2) of this section. The new limit adjustment for any base is the level amount necessary to amortize the unamortized amount of the base over the remaining amortization period using the new valuation rate. The remaining amortization period of the base is the number of years at the end of which the unamortized amount of the base would be zero if the contribution made with respect to that base equaled the limit adjustment each year. This calculation of the remaining period is made on the basis of the valuation rate used before the change. Both the remaining amortization period and the revised limit adjustment may be determined through the use of standard annuity tables. The remaining period may be computed in terms of fractional years, or it may be rounded off to a full year. The unamortized amount of the base as of the valuation date and the remaining amortization period of that base shall not be changed by any change in the valuation rate.

(i) *Combining bases.*—(1) *General method.*—For purposes of section 404 only, and not for purposes of section 412, different 10-year amortization bases may be combined into a single 10-year amortization base if such single base satisfies all of the requirements of paragraph (i)(2), (3), and (4) of this section at the time of the combining of the different bases.

(2) *Unamortized amount.*—The unamortized amount of the single base equals the sum, as of the date the combination is made, of the unamortized amount of the bases being combined (treating negative bases as having negative unamortized amounts).

(3) *Remaining amortization period.*—The remaining amortization period of the single base is equal to (i) the sum of the separate products of (A) the unamortized amount of each of these bases (using absolute values) and (B) its remaining amortization period, divided by (ii) the sum of the unamortized amounts of each of the bases (using absolute values). For purposes of this paragraph (i)(3), the remaining amortization period of each base being combined is that number of years at the end of which the unamortized amount of the base would be zero if the contribution made with respect to that base equaled the limit adjustment of that base in each year. This number may be determined through the use of standard annuity tables. The remaining amortization period described in this paragraph may be computed in terms of fractional years, or it may be rounded off to a whole year.

(4) *Limit adjustment.*—The limit adjustment for the single base is the level amount necessary to amortize the unamortized amount of the combined base over the remaining amortization period described in paragraph (i)(3) of this section, using the valuation rate. This amount may be determined through the use of standard annuity tables.

(5) *Fresh start alternative.*—In lieu of combining different 10-year amortization bases, a plan may replace all existing bases with one new 10-year amortization base equal to the unfunded liability of the plan as of the time the new base is being established. This unfunded liability must be determined in accordance with the general rules of paragraphs (d) and (f) of this section. The unamortized amount of the base and the limit adjustment for the base will be determined as though the base were newly established.

(j) *Initial 10-year amortization base for existing plan.*—(1) *In general.*—In the case of a plan in existence before the effective date of section 404(a), the 10-year amortization base on the effective date of section 404(a) is the sum of all 10 percent bases existing immediately before section 404(a) became effective for the plan, determined under the rules of old section 404(a).

(2) *Limit adjustment.*—The limit adjustment for the initial base is the lesser of the unamortized amount of such base or the sum of the amounts determined under paragraph (b)(3) of this section using original balances of the remaining bases (under old section 404(a) rules) as the amount to be amortized.

(3) *Unamortized amount.*—The employer may choose either to establish a single initial base reflecting both all prior 10-percent bases and the experience gain or loss for the immediately preceding actuarial period, or to establish a separate base for the prior 10-percent bases and another for the experience gain or loss for the immediately preceding period. If the initial 10-year amortization base reflects the net experience gain or loss from the immediately preceding actuarial period, the unamortized amount of the initial base shall equal the total unfunded liability on the effective date of section 404(a) determined in accordance with the general rules of paragraphs (d) and (f) of this section. If, however, a separate base will be used to reflect that gain or loss, the unamortized amount of the initial base shall equal such unfunded liability on the effective date of section 404(a), reduced by the net experience loss or increased by the net experience gain for the immediately preceding actuarial period. In this case, a separate 10-year amortization base must be established on the effective date equal to the net experience gain or loss. Thus, if the effective date unfunded liability is $100,000 and an experience loss of $15,000 is recognized on that date, and if the loss is to be treated as a separate base, the unamortized balances of the two bases would be $85,000 and $15,000. If the unfunded liability were the same $100,000, but a gain of $15,000 instead of a loss were recognized on that date, the unamortized balances of the two bases would be $115,000 and a credit base of $15,000. In both cases, if only one 10-year base is to be established on the effective date, its unamortized balance would be $100,000 (the unfunded liability of the plan). See paragraphs (d) and (f) for rules for determining the unfunded liability of the plan.

(k) *Effect of full funding limit on 10-year-amortization bases.*—The amount deductible under section 404(a)(1)(A)(i), (ii), or (iii) for a plan year may not exceed the full funding limitation for that year. See section 412 and paragraphs (d), (e), and (f) of this section for rules to be used in the computation of the full funding limitation. If the total deductible contribution (including carryover) for a plan year equals or exceeds the full funding limitation for the year, all 10-year amortization bases maintained by the plan will be considered fully amortized, and the deductible limit for subsequent plan years will not be adjusted to reflect the amortization of these bases.

(l) *Transitional rules.*—(1) *Plan years beginning before April 22, 1981.*—In determining the deductible limit for plan years beginning before April 22, 1981, a contribution will be deductible under section 404(a)(1)(A) if the computation of the deductible limit is based on an interpretation of section 404(a)(1)(A) that is reasonable when considered with prior published positions of the Internal Revenue Service. A computation of the deductible limit may satisfy the preceding sentence even if it does not satisfy the rules contained in paragraphs (c) through (i) of this section.

(2) *Transitional approaches.*—The deductible limit determined for the first plan year with respect to which a plan applies the rules contained in paragraphs (c) through (i) of this section must be computed using one of the following approaches—

(i) The plan (whether or not in existence before the effective date of section 404(a)) may apply the rules of paragraph (j) for establishing the initial base for an existing plan, treating 10-year bases (if any) as 10 percent bases in adding bases.

(ii) The plan may apply the fresh start alternative for combining bases under paragraph (i)(5).

(iii) The plan may retroactively establish 10-year amortization bases for years with respect to which section 404(a)(1)(A) and the rules of this section would have applied but for the transition rule contained in paragraph (l)(1) of this section. Contributions actually deducted are used in retroactively establishing and maintaining these bases under paragraph (h). However, a deduction already taken shall not be recomputed because of the retroactive establishment of a base.

(m) *Effective date of section 404(a).*—In the case of a plan which was in existence on January 1, 1974, section 404(a) generally applies for contributions on account of taxable years of an employer ending with or within plan years beginning after December 31, 1974. In the case of a plan not in existence on January 1, 1974, section 404(a) generally applies for contributions on account of taxable years of an employer ending with or within plan years beginning after September 4, 1974. See § 1.410(a)-2(c) for rules concerning the time of plan existence. See also § 1.410(a)-2(d), which provides that a plan in existence on January 1, 1974, may elect to have certain provisions, including the amendments to section 404(a) contained in section 1013 of the Employee Retirement Income Security Act of 1974, apply to a plan year beginning after September 2, 1974, and before the otherwise applicable effective date contained in that section. [Reg § 1.404(a)-14.]

☐ [*T.D. 7760,* 1-16-81.]

[Reg. § 1.404(b)-1]

§ 1.404(b)-1. Method of contribution, etc., having the effect of a plan; effect of section 404(b).—Section 404(a) is not confined to formal stock bonus, pension, profit-sharing, and annuity plans, or deferred compensation plans, but it includes any method of contributions or compensation having the effect of a stock bonus, pension, profit-sharing, or annuity plan, or similar plan deferring the receipt of compensation. Thus, where a corporation pays pensions to a retired employee or employees or to their beneficiaries in such amounts as may be determined from time to time by the board of directors or responsible officers of the company, or where a corporation is under an obligation, whether funded or unfunded, to pay a pension or other deferred compensation to an employee or his beneficiaries, there is a method having the effect of a plan deferring the receipt of compensation for which deductions are governed by section 404(a). If an employer on the accrual basis defers paying any compensation to an employee until a later year or years under an arrangement having the effect of a stock bonus, pension, profit-sharing, or annuity plan, or similar plan deferring the receipt of compensation, he shall not be allowed a deduction until the year in which the compensation is paid. This provision is not intended to cover the case where an employer on the accrual basis defers payment of compensation after the year of accrual merely because of inability to pay such compensation in the year of accrual, as, for example, where the funds of the company are not sufficient to enable payment of the compensation without jeopardizing the solvency of the company, or where the liability accrues in the earlier year, but the amount payable cannot be exactly determined until the later year. [Reg. § 1.404(b)-1.]

☐ [*T.D. 6203,* 9-24-56.]

[Reg. § 1.404(b)-1T]

§ 1.404(b)-1T. Method or arrangement of contributions, etc., deferring the receipt of compensation or providing for deferred benefits (Temporary).

Q-1: As amended by the Tax Reform Act of 1984, what does section 404(b) of the Internal Revenue Code provide?

A-1: As amended, section 404(b) clarifies that any plan, or method or arrangement, deferring the receipt of compensation or providing for deferred benefits (other than compensation) is to be treated as a plan deferring the receipt of compensation for purposes of section 404(a) and (d). Accordingly, section 404(a) and (d) (in the case of employees and nonemployees, respectively) shall govern the deduction of contributions paid or compensation paid or incurred with respect to such a plan, or method or arrangement. Section 404(a) and (d) requires that such a contribution or compensation be paid or incurred for purposes of section 162 or 212 and satisfy the requirements for deductibility under either of those sections. Thus, for example, under section 404(a)(5) and (b), if otherwise deductible under section 162 or 212, a contribution paid or incurred with respect to a nonqualified plan, or method or arrangement, providing for deferred benefits is deductible in the taxable year of the employer in which or with which ends the taxable year of the employee in which the amount attributable to the contribution is includible in the gross income of the employee (without regard to any applicable exclusion under Chapter 1, Subtitle A, of the Internal Revenue Code). Section 404(a) and (d) applies to all compensation and benefit plans, or methods or arrangements, however denominated, which defer the receipt of any amount of compensation or benefit, including fees or other payments. Thus, a limited partnership (using the accrual method of accounting) may not accrue deductions for a fee owed to an unrelated person (using the cash method of accounting) who performs services for the partnership until the partnership taxable year in which or with which ends the taxable year of the service provider in which the fee is included in income. However, notwithstanding the above, section 404 does not apply to contributions paid or accrued with respect to a "welfare benefit fund" (as defined in section 419(e)) after July 18, 1984, in taxable years of employers (and payors) ending after that date. Also, section 463 shall govern the deduction of vacation pay by a taxpayer that has elected the application of such section. For rules relating to the deduction of contributions paid or accrued with respect to a welfare benefit fund, see section 419, § 1.419-1T and § 1.419A-2T. For rules relating to the deduction of vacation pay for which an election is made under section 463, see § 301.9100-16T of this chapter and § 1.463-1T.

Q-2: When does a plan, or method or arrangement, defer the receipt of compensation or benefits for purposes of section 404(a), (b), and (d)?

A-2: (a) For purposes of section 404(a), (b), and (d), a plan, or method or arrangement, defers the receipt of compensation or benefits to the extent it is one under which an employee receives compensation or benefits more than a brief period of time after the end of the employer's taxable year in which the services creating the right to such compensation or benefits are performed. The determination of whether a plan, or method or arrangement, defers the receipts of compensation or benefits is made separately with respect to each employee and each amount of compensation or benefit. Compensation or benefits received by an employee's spouse or dependent or any other person, but taxable to the employee, are treated as received by the employee for purposes of section 404. An employee is determined to receive compensation or benefits within or beyond a brief period of time after the end of the employer's taxable year under the rules provided in this Q&A. For the treatment of expenses with respect to transactions between related taxpayers, see section 267.

(b)(1) A plan, or method or arrangement, shall be presumed to be one deferring the receipt of compensation for more than a brief period of time after the end of an employer's taxable year to the extent that compensation is received after the 15th day of the 3rd calendar month after the end of the employer's taxable year in which the related services are rendered ("the 2½ month period"). Thus, for example, salary under an employment contract or a bonus under a year-end bonus declaration is presumed to be paid under a plan, or method or arrangement, deferring the receipt of compensation, to the extent that the salary or bonus is received beyond the applicable 2½ month period. Further, salary or a year-end bonus received beyond the applicable 2½ month period by one employee shall be presumed to constitute payment under a plan, or method or arrangement, deferring the receipt of compensation for such employee even though salary or bonus payments to all other employees are not similarly treated because they are received within the 2½ month period. Benefits are "deferred benefits" if, assuming the benefits were cash compensation, such benefits would be considered deferred compensation. Thus, a plan, or method or arrangement, shall be presumed to be one providing for deferred benefits to the extent benefits for services are received by an employee after the 2½ month period following the end of the employer's taxable year in which the related services are rendered.

(2) The taxpayer may rebut the presumption established under the previous subparagraph with respect to an amount of compensation or benefits only by setting forth facts and circumstances the preponderance of which demonstrates that it was impracticable, either administratively or economically, to avoid the deferral of the receipt by an employee of the amount of compensation or benefits beyond the applicable 2½ month period and that, as of the end of the employer's taxable year such impracticability was unforeseeable. For example, the presumption may be rebutted with respect to an amount of compensation to the extent that receipt of such amount is deferred beyond the applicable 2½ month period (i) either because the funds of the employer were not sufficient to make the payment within the 2½ month period without jeopardizing the solvency of the employer or because it was not reasonably possible to determine within the 2½ month period whether payment of such amount was to be made, and (ii) the circumstance causing the deferral described in (i) was unforeseeable as of the close of the employer's taxable year. Thus, the presumption with respect to the receipt of an amount of compensation or benefit is not rebutted to the extent it was foreseeable, as of the end of the employer's taxable year, that the amount would be received after the applicable 2½ month period. For example, if, as of the end of the employer's taxable year, it is foreseeable that calculation of a year-end bonus to be paid to an employee under a given formula will not be completed and thus the bonus will not be received (and is in fact not received) by the end of the applicable 2½

month period, the presumption that the bonus is deferred compensation is not rebutted.

(c) A plan, or method or arrangement, shall not be considered as deferring the receipt of compensation or benefits for more than a brief period of time after the end of the employer's taxable year to the extent that compensation or benefits are received by the employee on or before the end of the applicable $2^1/_2$ month period. Thus, for example, salary under an employment contract or a bonus under a year-end bonus declaration is not considered paid under a plan, or method or arrangement, deferring the receipt of compensation to the extent that such salary or bonus is received by the employee on or before the end of the applicable $2^1/_2$ month period.

(d) Solely for purposes of applying the rules of paragraphs (b) and (c) of this Q&A, in the case of an employer's taxable year ending on or after July 18, 1984, and on or before March 21, 1986, compensation or benefits that relate to services rendered in such taxable year shall be deemed to have been received within the applicable $2^1/_2$ month period if such receipt actually occurs after such $2^1/_2$ month period but on or before March 21, 1986.

Q-3: When does section 404(b), as amended by the Tax Reform Act of 1984, become effective?

A-3: With the exceptions discussed below, section 404(b), as amended, and the rules under Q&A-2 are effective with respect to amounts paid or incurred after July 18, 1984, in taxable years of employers (and payors) ending after that date. In the case of an extended vacation pay plan maintained pursuant to a collective bargaining agreement (i) between employee representatives and one or more employers, and (ii) in effect on June 22, 1984, section 404(b) is not effective before the date on which such collective bargaining agreement terminates (determined without regard to any extension thereof agreed to after June 22, 1984). For purposes of the preceding sentence, any plan amendment made pursuant to a collective bargaining agreement relating to the plan which amends the plan solely to conform to any requirement added under section 512 of the Tax Reform Act of 1984 shall not be treated as a termination of such collective bargaining agreement. For purposes of this section, an "extended vacation pay plan" is one under which covered employees gradually over a specified period of years earn the right to additional vacation benefits, no part of which, under the terms of the plan, can be taken until the end of the specified period. [Temporary Reg. § 1.404(b)-1T.]

☐ [*T.D. 8073, 1-29-86. Amended by T.D. 8435, 9-18-92.*]

[Reg. § 1.404(c)-1]

§ 1.404(c)-1. Certain negotiated plans; effect of section 404(c).—(a) Section 404(a) does not apply to deductions for contributions paid by an employer under a negotiated plan which meets the following conditions:

(1) The contributions under the plan are held in trust for the purpose of paying, either from principal or income or both, for the benefit of employees and their families, at least medical or hospital care, and pensions on retirement or death of employees; and

(2) Such plan was established before January 1, 1954, as a result of an agreement between employee representatives and the Government of the United States during a period of Government operation,

under seizure powers, of a major part of the productive facilities of the industry in which such employer is engaged.

If these conditions are met, such contributions shall be deductible under section 162, to the extent that they constitute ordinary and necessary business expenses.

(b) The term "as a result of an agreement" is intended primarily to cover a trust established under the terms of an agreement referred to in paragraph (a)(2) of this section. It will also include a trust established under a plan of an employer, or group of employers, who are in competition with the employers whose facilities were seized by reason of producing the same commodity, and who would therefore be expected to establish such a trust as a reasonable measure to maintain a sound position in the labor market producing the commodity. Thus, for example, if a trust was established under such an agreement in the bituminous coal industry, a similar trust established about the same time in the anthracite coal industry would be covered by this provision.

(c) If any such trust becomes qualified for exemption under section 501(a), the deductibility of contributions by an employer to such trust on or after the date of such qualification would no longer be governed by section 404(c), even though the trust may later lose its exemption under section 501(a). [Reg. § 1.404(c)-1.]

☐ [*T.D. 6203, 9-24-56.*]

[Reg. § 1.404(d)-1T]

§ 1.404(d)-1T. Questions and answers relating to deductibility of deferred compensation and deferred benefits for independent contractors (Temporary).

Q-1: How does the amendment of section 404(b) by the Tax Reform Act of 1984 affect the deduction of contributions or compensation under section 404(d)?

A-1: As amended by the Tax Reform Act of 1984, section 404(b) clarifies that section 404(d) shall govern the deduction of contributions paid and compensation paid or incurred by a payor under a plan, or method or arrangement, deferring the receipt of compensation or providing for deferred benefits for service providers with respect to which there is no employer-employee relationship. In such a case, section 404(a) and (b) and the regulations thereunder apply as if the person providing the services were the employee and the person to whom the services are provided were the employer. Section 404(a) requires that such a contribution or compensation be paid or incurred for purposes of section 162 or 212 and satisfy the requirements for deductibility under either of those sections. However, notwithstanding the above, section 404 does not apply to contributions paid or accrued with respect to a "welfare benefit fund" (as defined in section 419(e)) after June 18, 1984, in taxable years of employers (and payors) ending after that date. Also, section 463 shall govern the deduction of vacation pay by a taxpayer that has elected under such section. For rules relating to the deduction of contributions paid or accrued with respect to a welfare benefit fund, see section 419, § 1.419-1T and § 1.419A-2T. For rules relating to the deduction of vacation pay for which an election is made under section 463, see § 301.9100-16T of this chapter and § 1.463-1T. [Temporary Reg. § 1.404(d)-1T.]

☐ [*T.D. 8073, 1-29-86. Amended by T.D. 8435, 9-18-92.*]

⟫→ *Caution: Obsolete provisions of Reg. § 1.404(e)-1A, below, are no longer reproduced.*

[Reg. § 1.404(e)-1A]

§ 1.404(e)-1A. Contributions on behalf of a self-employed individual to or under a qualified pension, annuity, or profit-sharing plan.—

* * *

(f) *Partner's distributive share of contributions and deductions.*—(1) For purposes of sections 702(a)(8) and 704 in the case of a defined contribution plan, a partner's distributive share of contributions on behalf of self-employed individuals under such a plan is the contribution made on his behalf, and his distributive share of deductions allowed the partnership under section 404 for contributions on behalf of a self-employed individual is that portion of the deduction which is attributable to contributions made on his behalf under the plan. The contribution on behalf of a partner and the deduction with respect thereto must be accounted for separately by such partner, for his taxable year with or within which the partnership's taxable year ends, as an item described in section 702(a)(8).

(2) In the case of a defined benefit plan, a partner's distributive share of contributions on behalf of self-employed individuals and his distributive share of deductions allowed the partnership under section 404 for such contributions is determined in the same manner as his distributive share of partnership taxable income. See section 704, relating to the determination of the distributive share and the regulations thereunder.

* * *

(g) *Contributions allocable to insurance protection.*—Under section 404(e)(3), for purposes of determining the amount deductible with respect to contributions on behalf of a self-employed individual, amounts allocable to the purchase of life, accident, health, or other insurance protection shall not be taken into account. Such amounts are neither deductible nor considered as contributions for purposes of determining the maximum amount of contributions that may be made on behalf of an owner-employee. The amount of a contribution allocable to insurance shall be an amount equal to a reasonable net premium cost, as determined by the Commissioner, for such amount of insurance for the appropriate period. See paragraph (b)(5) of § 1.72-16.

* * *

(i) *Definitions.*—Under section 404(a)(8), for purposes of section 404 and the regulations thereunder—

(1) The term "employee" includes an employee as defined in section 401(c)(1) and the term "employer" means the person treated as the employer of such individual under section 401(c)(4);

(2) The term "owner-employee" means an owner-employee as defined in section 401(c)(3);

(3) The term "earned income" means earned income as defined in section 401(c)(2); and

(4) The term "compensation" when used with respect to an individual who is an employee described in subparagraph (1) of this paragraph shall be considered to be a reference to the earned income

>>>→ *Caution: Obsolete provisions of Reg. §1.404(e)-1A, below, are no longer reproduced.*

of such individual derived from the trade or business with respect to which the plan is established. [Reg. § 1.404(e)-1A.]

☐ [*T.D. 7636, 8-9-79. Amended by T.D. 9849, 3-11-2019.*]

[Reg. §1.404(g)-1]

§1.404(g)-1. Deduction of employer liability payments.— (a) *General rule.*—Employer liability payments shall be treated as contributions to a stock bonus, pension, profit-sharing, or annuity plan to which section 404 applies. Such payments that satisfy the limitations of this section shall be deductible under section 404 when paid without regard to any other limitations in section 404.

(b) *Employer liability payments.*—For purposes of this section, employer liability payments mean:

(1) Any payment to the Pension Benefit Guaranty Corporation (PBGC) for termination or withdrawal liability imposed under section 4062 (without regard to section 4062(b)(2)), 4063, or 4064 of the Employee Retirement Insurance Security Act of 1974 (ERISA). Any bond or escrow payment furnished under section 4063 of ERISA shall not be considered as a payment of liability until applied against the liability of the employer.

(2) Any payment to a non-multiemployer plan pursuant to a commitment to the PBGC made in accordance with PBGC Determination of Plan Sufficiency and Termination of Sufficient Plans. See PBGC regulations, 29 C.F.R. § 2617.13(b) for rules concerning these commitments. Such payment shall not exceed an amount necessary to provide for, and used to fund, the benefits guaranteed under section 4022 of ERISA.

(3) Any payment to a multiemployer plan for withdrawal liability imposed under part 1 of subtitle E of title IV of ERISA. Any bond or escrow payment furnished under such part shall not be considered as a payment of liability until applied against the liability of the employer.

(c) *Limitations, etc.*—(1) *Permissible expenses.*—A payment shall be deductible under section 404(g) and this section only if the payment satisfies the conditions of section 162 or section 212. Payments made by an entity which is liable for such payments because it is a member of a commonly controlled group of corporations, or trades or businesses, within the meaning of section 414(b) or (c), shall not fail to satisfy such conditions merely because the entity did not directly employ participants in the plan with respect to which the liability payments were made.

(2) *Qualified plan.*—A payment shall be deductible under section 404(g) and this section only if the payment is made in a taxable year of the employer ending within or with a taxable year of the trust for which the trust is exempt under section 501(a). For purposes of this paragraph, the payment timing rules of section 404(a)(6) shall apply.

(3) *Full funding limitation.*—(i) If the employer liability payment is to a plan, the total amount deductible for such payment and for other plan contributions may not exceed an amount equal to the full funding limitation as defined in section 412(c)(7) for the taxable year with respect to which the contributions are deemed made under section 404.

(ii) If the total contributions to the plan for the taxable year including the employer liability payment exceed the amount equal to this full funding limitation, the employer liability payment shall be deductible first.

(iii) Any amount paid in a taxable year in excess of the amount deductible in such year under the full funding limitation shall be treated as a liability payment and be deductible in the succeeding taxable years in order of time to the extent of the difference between the employer liability payments made in each succeeding year and the maximum amount deductible for such year under the full funding limitation.

(4) *Maximum deduction allowable under section 404.*—The amount deductible under section 404 is limited to the higher of the maximum amount deductible by that employer under section 404(a) or the amount otherwise deductible under section 404(g). If the contributions are to a plan to which more than one employer contributes, this limit shall apply to each employer separately rather than all employers in the aggregate. Thus, each employer may deduct the greater of its allocable share of the deduction determined under sections 404(a) and 413(b)(7) or 413(c)(6) or its allocable share of the amount deductible under section 404(g). However, pursuant to the rule in subdivision (ii) of subparagraph (3), in determining each employer's allocable share under section 404(a), the total amount deductible under section 404(a) by all employers shall not exceed the difference between the full funding limitation and the total amount deductible by all employers under section 404(g).

(5) *Example.*—The provisions of this paragraph may be illustrated by the following example:

Example. In the 1983 taxable year, Employer A makes a withdrawal liability payment of $700,000 to multiemployer Plan X to which Employer A and Employer B are required to contribute. Employer A's allocable share of the deduction allowable under sections 404(a) and 413(b)(7) in the 1983 taxable year is $600,000. Employer B's allocable share of the deduction allowable under section 404(a) and 413(b)(7) in the 1983 taxable year is $400,000. The full funding limitation for the 1983 taxable year is $1,000,000. Based on paragraph (c)(4) of this section, Employer A may deduct $700,000, the amount of the withdrawal liability payment. However, the deduction of Employer B is limited to $300,000, the difference between the full funding limitation and the amount deductible under section 404(g).

(d) *Effective date, etc.*—(1) *General rule.*—This section is effective for employer payments made after September 25, 1980.

(2) *Transitional rule.*—For employer payments made before September 26, 1980, for purposes of section 404, any amount paid by an employer under section 4062, 4063, or 4064 of the Employee Retirement Income Security Act of 1974 shall be treated as a contribution to which section 404 applies by such employer to or under a stock bonus, pension, profit-sharing, or annuity plan. [Reg. § 1.404(g)-1.]

☐ [*T.D. 8085, 5-1-86.*]

[Reg. §1.404(k)-1T]

§1.404(k)-1T. Questions and answers relating to the deductibility of certain dividend distributions (Temporary).

Q-1: What does section 404(k) provide?

A-1: Section 404(k) allows a corporation a deduction for dividends actually paid in accordance with section 404(k)(2) with respect to stock of such corporation held by an employee stock ownership plan (as defined in section 4975(e)(7)) maintained by the corporation (or by any other corporation that is a member of a "controlled group of corporations" within the meaning of section 409(l)(4) that includes the corporation), but only if such dividends may be immediately distributed under the terms of the plan and all of the applicable qualification and distribution rules. The deduction is allowed under section 404(k) for the taxable year of the corporation during which the dividends are received by the participants.

Q-2: Is the deductibility of dividends paid to plan participants under section 404(k) affected by a plan provision which permits participants to elect to receive or not receive payment of dividends?

A-2: No. Dividends actually paid in cash to plan participants in accordance with section 404(k) are deductible under section 404(k) despite such an election provision.

Q-3: Are dividends paid in cash directly to plan participants by the corporation and dividends paid to the plan and then distributed in cash to plan participants under section 404(k) treated as distributions under the plan holding stock to which the dividends relate for purposes of sections 72, 401 and 402?

A-3: Generally, yes. However, a deductible dividend under section 404(k) is treated for purposes of section 72 as paid under a contract separate from any other contract that is part of the plan. Thus, a deductible dividend is treated as a plan distribution and as paid under a separate contract providing only for payment of deductible dividends. Therefore, a deductible dividend under section 404(k) is a taxable plan distribution even though an employee has unrecovered employee contributions or basis in the plan. [Temporary Reg. §1.404(k)-1T.]

☐ [*T.D. 8073, 1-29-86.*]

[Reg. §1.404(k)-3]

§1.404(k)-3. Disallowance of deduction for reacquisition payments.

Q-1: Are payments to reacquire stock held by an ESOP applicable dividends that are deductible under section 404(k)(1)?

A-1: (a) Payments to reacquire stock held by an ESOP, including reacquisition payments that are used to make benefit distributions to participants or beneficiaries, are not deductible under section 404(k) because—

(1) Those payments do not constitute applicable dividends under section 404(k)(2); and

(2) The treatment of those payments as applicable dividends would constitute, in substance, an avoidance or evasion of taxation within the meaning of section 404(k)(5).

(b) See also § 1.162(k)-1 concerning the disallowance of deductions for amounts paid or incurred by a corporation in connection with the reacquisition of its stock from an ESOP.

Q-2: What is the effective date of this section?

A-2: This section applies with respect to payments to reacquire stock that are made on or after August 30, 2006.

[Reg. § 1.404(k)-3.]

☐ [T.D. 9282, 8-29-2006.]

[Reg. § 1.406-1]

§ 1.406-1. Treatment of certain employees of foreign subsidiaries as employees of the domestic corporation.—(a) *Scope.*—(1) *General rule.*—For purposes of applying the rules in part 1 of subchapter D of chapter 1 of subtitle A of the Code and the regulations thereunder with respect to a pension, profit-sharing, or stock bonus plan described in section 401(a), an annuity plan described in section 403(a), or a bond purchase plan described in section 405(a), of a domestic corporation, an individual who is a citizen of the United States and who is an employee of a foreign subsidiary (as defined in section 3121(l)(8) and the regulations thereunder) of such domestic corporation shall be treated as an employee of such domestic corporation if the requirements of paragraph (b) of this section are satisfied.

(2) *Cross references.*—For rules relating to nondiscrimination requirements and the determination of compensation, see paragraph (c) of this section. For rules under which termination of the status of an individual as an employee of the domestic corporation in certain instances will not be considered as separation from service for certain purposes, see paragraph (d) of this section. For rules regarding deductibility of contributions, see paragraph (e) of this section. For rules regarding treatment of such individual as an employee of the domestic corporation under related provisions, see paragraph (f) of this section.

(b) *Application of this section.*—(1) *Requirements.*—This section shall apply and the employee of the foreign subsidiary shall be treated as an employee of domestic corporation for the purposes set forth in paragraph (a)(1) of this section only if each of the following requirements is satisfied:

(i) The domestic corporation must have entered into an agreement under section 3121(l) to provide social security coverage which applies to the foreign subsidiary of which such individual is an employee and which has not been terminated under section 3121(l)(3) or (4).

(ii) The plan, referred to in paragraph (a)(1) of this section, must expressly provide for contributions or benefits for individuals who are citizens of the United States and who are employees of one or more of its foreign subsidiaries to which an agreement entered into by such domestic corporation under section 3121(l) applies. The plan must apply to all of the foreign subsidiaries to which such agreement applies.

(iii) Contributions under a funded plan of deferred compensation (whether or not a plan described in section 401(a), 403(a), or 405(a)) must not be provided by any other person with respect to the remuneration paid to such individual by the foreign subsidiary.

(2) *Supplementary rules.*—Subparagraph (1)(ii) of this paragraph does not modify the requirements for qualification of a plan described in section 401(a), 403(a), or 405(a) and the regulations thereunder. It is not necessary that the plan provide benefits or contributions for all United States citizens who are employees of such foreign subsidiaries. If the plan is amended to cover individuals who are employees by reason of paragraph (a)(1) of this section, the plan will not qualify unless it meets the coverage requirements of section 410(b)(1) (section 401(a)(3), as in effect on September 1, 1974, for plan years to which section 410 does not apply; see § 1.410(a)-2 for the effective dates of section 410) and the nondiscrimination requirements of section 401(a)(4). In addition, the administrative rules contained in § 1.401(a)-3(e) (relating to the determination of the contributions or benefits provided by the employer under the Social Security Act) will also apply for purposes of determining whether the plan meets the requirements of section 401. For purposes of subparagraph (1)(iii) of this paragraph, contributions will not be considered as provided under a funded plan merely because the foreign subsidiary is required under the laws of the foreign jurisdiction to pay social insurance taxes or to make similar payments with respect to the wages paid to the employee.

(c) *Special rules.*—(1) *Nondiscrimination requirements.*—For purposes of applying sections 401(a)(4) and 410(b)(1)(B) (section 401(a)(3)(B), as in effect on September 1, 1974, for plan years to which section 410 does not apply) and the regulations thereunder (relating to nondiscrimination concerning benefits and contributions and coverage of employees) with respect to an employee of the foreign subsidiary who is treated as an employee of the domestic corporation under paragraph (a)(1) of this section—

(i) If the employee is an officer, shareholder, or (with respect to plan years to which section 410 does not apply) a person whose principal duties consist in supervising the work of other employees of the foreign subsidiary of the domestic corporation, he shall be treated as having such capacity with respect to the domestic corporation; and

(ii) The determination as to whether the employee is a highly compensated employee shall be made by comparing his total compensation (determined under subparagraph (2) of this paragraph) with the compensation of all the employees of the domestic corporation (including individuals treated as employees of the domestic corporation pursuant to section 406 and this section).

(2) *Determination of compensation.*—For purposes of applying section 401(a)(5) and the regulations thereunder, relating to classifications that will not be considered discriminatory, with respect to an employee of the foreign subsidiary who is treated as an employee of the domestic corporation under paragraph (a)(1) of this section—

(i) The total compensation of the employee shall be the remuneration of the employee from the foreign subsidiary (including any allowances that are paid to the employee because of his employment in a foreign country) which would constitute his total compensation if his services had been performed for the domestic corporation;

(ii) The basic or regular rate of compensation of the employee shall be determined for the employee in the same manner as it is determined under section 401 for other employees of the domestic corporation; and

(iii) The amount paid by the domestic corporation which is equivalent to the tax imposed with respect to the employee by section 3101 (relating to the tax on employees under the Federal Insurance Contributions Act) shall be treated as having been paid by the employee and shall be included in his compensation.

(d) *Termination of status as deemed employee not to be treated as separation from service for purposes of capital gain provisions and limitation on tax.*—For purposes of applying the rules, relating to the treatment of certain distributions which are made after an employee's separation from service, set forth in section 72(n) as in effect on September 1, 1974 (with respect to taxable years ending after December 31, 1969, and to which section 402(e) does not apply), and in sections 402(a)(2) and (e) and 403(a)(2) (with respect to distributions or payments made after December 31, 1973, and in taxable years beginning after December 31, 1973) with respect to an employee of a foreign subsidiary who is treated as an employee of a domestic corporation under paragraph (a)(1) of this section, the employee shall not be considered as separated from the service of the domestic corporation solely by reason of the occurrence of any one or more of the following events:

(1) The termination, under the provisions of section 3121(l), of the agreement entered into by the domestic corporation under that section which covers the employment of the employee;

(2) The employee's becoming an employee of another foreign subsidiary of the domestic corporation with respect to which such agreement does not apply;

(3) The employee's ceasing to be an employee of the foreign subsidiary by reason of which employment he was treated as an employee of such domestic corporation, if he becomes an employee of another corporation controlled by such domestic corporation; or

(4) The termination of the provision of the plan described in paragraph (b)(1)(ii) of this section, for coverage of United States citizens who are employees of foreign subsidiaries covered by an agreement under section 3121(l).

For purposes of subparagraph (3) of this paragraph, a corporation is considered to be controlled by a domestic corporation if such domestic corporation owns directly or indirectly more than 50 percent of the voting stock of the corporation.

(e) *Deductibility of contributions.*—(1) *In general.*—For purposes of applying sections 404 and 405(c) with respect to the deduction for contributions made to or under a pension, profit-sharing, or stock bonus plan described in section 401(a), an annuity plan described in section 403(a), or a bond purchase plan described in section 405(a), by a domestic corporation, or by another corporation which is entitled to deduct its contributions under section 404(a)(3)(B), on behalf of an employee of a foreign subsidiary treated as an employee of the domestic corporation under paragraph (a)(1) of this section—

(i) Except as provided in subdivision (ii) of this subparagraph, no deduction shall be allowed to such domestic corporation or to any other corporation which would otherwise be entitled to deduct its contributions on behalf of such employee under one of such sections;

(ii) There shall be allowed as a deduction from the gross income of the foreign subsidiary which is effectively connected with the conduct of a trade or business within the United States (within the meaning of section 882 and the regulations thereunder) an amount which is allocable and apportionable to such gross income under the rules of § 1.861-8 and which in no event may exceed the amount which (but for subdivision (i) of this subparagraph) would be deductible under section 404 of section 405(c) by the domestic corporation if the individual were an employee of the domestic corporation and if his compensation were paid by the domestic corporation; and

(iii) Any reference to compensation shall be considered to be a reference to the total compensation of such individual (determined by applying paragraph (c)(2) of this section).

(2) *Year of deduction.*—Any amount deductible by the foreign subsidiary under section 406(d) and this paragraph shall be deductible for its taxable year with or within which ends the taxable year of the domestic corporation for which the contribution is made.

(3) *Special rules.*—Whether contributions to a plan on behalf of an employee of the foreign subsidiary who is treated as an employee of the domestic corporation under paragraph (a)(1) of this section, or whether forfeitures with regard to such employee, will require an inclusion in the income of the domestic corporation or an adjustment in the basis of its stock in the foreign subsidiary, shall be determined in accordance with the rules of general application of subtitle A of chapter 1 of the Code (relating to income taxes). For example, an unreimbursed contribution by the domestic corporation to a plan which meets the requirements of section 401(a) will be treated, to the extent each employee's rights to the contribution are nonforfeitable, as a contribution of capital to the foreign subsidiary to the extent that such contributions are made on behalf of the employees of such subsidiary.

(f) *Treatment as an employee of the domestic corporation under related provisions.*—An individual who is treated as an employee of a domestic corporation under paragraph (a)(1) of this section shall also be treated as an employee of such domestic corporation, with respect to the plan having the provision described in paragraph (b)(1)(ii) of this section, for purposes of applying section 72(d) (relating to employees' annuities), section 72(f) (relating to special rules for computing employees' contributions), section 101(b) (relating to employees' death benefits), section 2039 (relating to annuities), and section 2517 (relating to certain annuities under qualified plans) and the regulations thereunder.

(g) *Nonexempt trust.*—If the plan of the domestic corporation is a qualified plan described under section 401(a), the fact that a trust which forms a part of such plan is not exempt from tax under section 510(a) shall not affect the treatment of an employee of a foreign subsidiary as an employee of a domestic corporation under section 406(a) and paragraph (a)(1) of this section. [Reg. §1.406-1.]

☐ [T.D. 7501, 8-22-77.]

[Reg. §1.407-1]

§1.407-1. Treatment of certain employees of domestic subsidiaries engaged in business outside the United States as employees of the domestic parent corporation.—(a) *Scope.*—(1) *General rule.*—For purposes of applying the rules in part 1 of the subchapter D of chapter 1 of subtitle A of the Code and the regulations thereunder with respect to a pension, profit-sharing, or stock bonus plan described in section 401(a), an annuity plan described in section 403(a), or a bond purchase plan described in section 405(a), of a domestic parent corporation (as defined in paragraph (b)(3)(ii) of this section), an individual who is a citizen of the United States and who is an employee of a domestic subsidiary (as defined in paragraph (b)(3)(i) of this section) of such domestic parent corporation shall be treated as an employee of such domestic parent corporation if the requirements of paragraph (b) of this section are satisfied.

(2) *Cross-references.*—For rules relating to nondiscrimination requirements and the determination of compensation, see paragraph (c) of this section. For rules under which termination of the status of an individual as an employee of the domestic parent corporation in certain instances will not be considered as separation from service for certain purposes, see paragraph (d) of this section. For rules regarding deductibility of contributions, see paragraph (e) of this section. For rules regarding treatment of such individual as an employee of the domestic parent corporation under related provisions, see paragraph (f) of this section.

(b) *Application of this section.*—(1) *Requirements.*—This section shall apply and the employee of the domestic subsidiary shall be treated as an employee of the domestic parent corporation for the purposes set forth in paragraph (a)(1) of this section only if each of the following requirements is satisfied:

(i) The plan, referred to in paragraph (a)(1) of this section, must expressly provide for contributions or benefits for individuals who are citizens of the United States and who are employees of one or more of the domestic subsidiaries of the domestic parent corporation. The plan must apply to every domestic subsidiary.

(ii) Contributions under a funded plan of deferred compensation (whether or not a plan described in section 401(a), 403(a), or 405(a)) must not be provided by any other person with respect to the remuneration paid to such individual by the domestic subsidiary.

(2) *Supplementary rules.*—Subparagraph (1)(i) of this paragraph does not modify the requirements for qualification of a plan described in section 401(a), 403(a), or 405(a) and the regulations thereunder. It is not necessary that the plan provide benefits or contributions for all United States citizens who are employees of such domestic subsidiaries. If the plan is amended to cover individuals who are employees by reason of paragraph (a)(1) of this section, the plan will not qualify unless it meets the coverage requirements of section 410(b)(1) (section 401(a)(3), as in effect on September 1, 1974, for plan years to which section 410 does not apply; see §1.410(a)-2 for the effective dates of section 410) and the nondiscrimination requirements of section 401(a)(4). The administrative rules contained in §1.401(a)-3(e) (relating to the determination of the contributions or benefits provided by the employer under the Social Security Act) will also apply for purposes of determining whether the plan meets the requirements of section 401. For purposes of subparagraph (1)(ii) of this paragraph, contributions will not be considered as provided under a funded plan merely because the domestic subsidiary employer pays the tax imposed by section 3111 (relating to tax on employers under the Federal Insurance Contributions Act) with respect to such employee or is required under the laws of a foreign jurisdiction to pay social insurance taxes or to make similar payments with respect to the wages paid to the employee.

(3) *Definitions.*—(i) *Domestic subsidiary.*—For purposes of this section, a corporation shall be treated as a domestic subsidiary for any taxable year only if each of the following requirements is satisfied:

(A) It is a domestic corporation 80 percent or more of the outstanding voting stock of which is owned by another domestic corporation;

(B) 95 percent of more of its gross income for the three-year period immediately preceding the close of its taxable year which ends on or before the close of the taxable year of such other domestic corporation (or for such part of such period during which it was in existence) was derived from sources without the United States, determined pursuant to sections 861 through 864 and the regulations thereunder; and

(C) 90 percent or more of its gross income for such period (or such part) was derived from the active conduct of a trade or business.

If for the period (or part thereof) referred to in (B) and (C) of this subdivision such corporation has no gross income, the provisions of (B) and (C) shall be treated as satisfied if it is reasonable to anticipate that, with respect to the first taxable year thereafter for which such corporation has gross income, such provisions will be satisfied.

(ii) *Domestic parent corporation.*—The domestic parent corporation of any domestic subsidiary is the domestic corporation which owns 80 percent or more of the outstanding voting stock of such domestic subsidiary.

(c) *Special rules.*—(1) *Nondiscrimination requirements.*—For purposes of applying sections 401(a)(4) and 410(b)(1)(B) (section 401(a)(3)(B), as in effect on September 1, 1974, for plan years to which section 410 does not apply) and the regulations thereunder (relating to nondiscrimination concerning benefits and contributions and coverage of employees) with respect to an employee of the domestic subsidiary who is treated as an employee of the domestic parent corporation under paragraph (a)(1) of this section—

(i) If the employee is an officer, shareholder, or (with respect to plan years to which section 410 does not apply) a person whose principal duties consist in supervising the work of other employees of the domestic subsidiary of the domestic parent corporation, he shall be treated as having such capacity with respect to the domestic parent corporation; and

(ii) The determination as to whether the employee is a highly compensated employee shall be made by comparing his total compensation (determined under subparagraph (2) of this paragraph) with the compensation of all the employees of the domestic parent corporation (including individuals treated as employees of the domestic parent corporation pursuant to section 407 and this section).

(2) *Determination of compensation.*—For purposes of applying section 401(a)(5) and the regulations thereunder, relating to classifications that will not be considered discriminatory, with respect to an employee of the domestic subsidiary who is treated as an employee of the domestic parent corporation under paragraph (a)(1) of this section—

(i) The total compensation of the employee shall be the remuneration of the employee from the domestic subsidiary (including any allowances that are paid to the employee because of his employment in a foreign country) which would constitute his total compensation if his services had been performed for such domestic parent corporation; and

(ii) The basic or regular rate of compensation of the employee shall be determined for the employee in the same manner as it is determined under section 401 for other employees of the domestic parent corporation.

(d) *Termination of status as deemed employee not to be treated as separation from service for purposes of capital gain provisions and limitation of tax.*—For purposes of applying the rules, relating to treatment of certain distributions which are made after an employee's separation from service, set forth in section 72(n) as in effect on September 1, 1974 (with respect to taxable years ending after December 31, 1969, and to which section 402(e) does not apply), and in sections 402(a)(2) and (e) and 403(a)(2) (with respect to distributions or payments made after December 31, 1973, and in taxable years beginning after December 31, 1973) with respect to an employee of a domestic subsidiary who is treated as an employee of a domestic parent corporation under paragraph (a)(1) of this section, the employee shall not be considered as separated from the service of the domestic parent corporation solely by reason of the occurrence of any one or more of the following events:

(1) The fact that the corporation of which such individual is an employee ceases, for any taxable year, to be a domestic subsidiary within the meaning of paragraph (b)(3)(i) of this section;

(2) The employee's ceasing to be an employee of the domestic subsidiary of such domestic parent corporation, if he becomes an employee of another corporation controlled by such domestic parent corporation; or

(3) The termination of the provision of the plan described in paragraph (b)(1)(i) of this section, requiring coverage of United States citizens who are employees of domestic subsidiaries of the domestic parent corporation. For purposes of subparagraph (2) of this paragraph, a corporation is considered to be controlled by a domestic parent corporation if the domestic parent corporation owns directly or indirectly more than 50 percent of the voting stock of the corporation.

(e) *Deductibility of contributions.*—(1) *In general.*—For purposes of applying sections 404 and 405(c) with respect to the deduction for contributions made to or under a pension, profit-sharing, or stock bonus plan described in section 401(a), an annuity plan described in section 403(a), or a bond purchase plan described in section 405(a), by a domestic parent corporation, or by another corporation which is entitled to deduct its contributions under section 404(a)(3)(B), on behalf of an employee of a domestic subsidiary treated as an employee of the domestic parent corporation under paragraph (a)(1) of this section—

(i) Except as provided in subdivision (ii) of this subparagraph, no deduction shall be allowed to the domestic parent corporation which would otherwise be entitled to deduct its contributions on behalf of such employee under one of such sections;

(ii) There shall be allowed as a deduction to the domestic subsidiary of which such individual is an employee an amount equal to the amount which (but for subdivision (i) of this subparagraph) would be deductible under section 404 or section 405(c) by the domestic parent corporation if the individual were an employee of the domestic parent corporation and if his compensation were paid by the domestic corporation; and

(iii) Any reference to compensation shall be considered to be a reference to the total compensation of such individual (determined by applying paragraph (c)(2) of this section).

(2) *Year of deduction.*—Any amount deductible by the domestic subsidiary under section 407(d) and this paragraph shall be deductible for its taxable year with or within which ends the taxable year of the domestic parent corporation for which the contribution is made.

(3) *Special rules.*—Whether contributions to a plan on behalf of an employee of the domestic subsidiary who is treated as an employee of the domestic parent corporation under paragraph (a)(1) of this section, or whether forfeitures with regard to such employee, will require an inclusion in the income of the domestic parent corporation or an adjustment in the basis of its stock in the domestic subsidiary, shall be determined in accordance with the rules of general application of subtitle A of chapter 1 of the Code (relating to income taxes). For an example, an unreimbursed contribution by the domestic parent corporation to a plan which meets the requirements of section 401(a) will be treated, to the extent each employee's rights to the contribution are nonforfeitable, as a contribution of capital to the domestic subsidiary to the extent that such contributions are made on behalf of the employees of such subsidiary.

(f) *Treatment as an employee of the domestic parent corporation under related provisions.*—An individual who is treated as an employee of a domestic parent corporation under paragraph (a)(1) of this section shall also be treated as an employee of such domestic corporation, with respect to the plan having the provision described in paragraph (b)(1)(i) of this section, for purposes of applying section 72(d) (relating to special rules for computing employees' contributions), section 72(f) (relating to special rules for computing employees' contributions), section 101(b) (relating to employees' death benefits), section 2039 (relating to annuities), and section 2517 (relating to certain annuities under qualified plans) and the regulations thereunder.

(g) *Nonexempt trust.*—If the plan of the domestic parent corporation is a qualified plan described under section 401(a), the fact that a trust which forms a part of such plan is not exempt from tax under section 501(a) shall not affect the treatment of an employee of a domestic subsidiary as an employee of a domestic parent corporation under section 407(a) and paragraph (a)(1) of this section. [Reg. §1.407-1.]

☐ [T.D. 7501, 8-22-77.]

[Reg. §1.408-1]

§1.408-1. General rules.—(a) *In general.*—Section 408 prescribes rules relating to individual retirement accounts and individual retirement annuities. In addition to the rules set forth in §§1.408-2 and 1.408-3, relating respectively to individual retirement accounts and individual retirement annuities, the rules set forth in this section shall also apply.

(b) *Exemption from tax.*—The individual retirement account or individual retirement annuity is exempt from all taxes under subtitle A of the Code other than the taxes imposed under section 511, relating to tax on unrelated business income of charitable, etc., organizations.

(c) *Sanctions.*—(1) *Excess contributions.*—If an individual retirement account or individual retirement annuity accepts and retains excess contributions, the individual on whose behalf the account is established or who is the owner of the annuity will be subject to the excise tax imposed by section 4973.

(2) *Prohibited transactions by owner or beneficiary of individual retirement account.*—(i) Under section 408(e)(2), if, during any taxable year of the individual for whose benefit any individual retirement account is established, that individual or the individual's beneficiary engages in any transaction prohibited by section 4975 with respect to such account, such account ceases to be an individual retirement account as of the first day of such taxable year. In any case in which any individual retirement account ceases to be an individual retirement account by reason of the preceding sentence as of the first day of any taxable year, section 408(d)(1) applies as if there were a distribution on such first day in an amount equal to the fair market value (on such first day) of all assets in the account (on such first day). The preceding sentence applies even though part of the fair market value of the individual retirement account as of the first day of the taxable year is attributable to excess contributions which may be returned tax-free under section 408(d)(4) or 408(d)(5).

(ii) If the trust with which the individual engages in any transaction described in subdivision (i) of this subparagraph is established by an employer or employee association under section 408(c), only the employee who engages in the prohibited transaction is subject to disqualification of his separate account.

(3) *Prohibited transaction by person other than owner or beneficiary of account.*—If any person other than the individual on whose behalf an individual retirement account is established or the individual's beneficiary engages in any transaction prohibited by section 4975 with respect to such account, such person shall be subject to the taxes imposed by section 4975.

(4) *Pledging account as security.*—Under section 408(e)(4), if, during any taxable year of the individual for whose benefit an individual retirement account is established, that individual uses the account or any portion thereof as security for a loan, the portion so used is treated as distributed to that individual.

(5) *Borrowing on annuity contract.*—Under section 408(e)(3), if during any taxable year the owner of an individual retirement annuity borrows any money under or by use of such contract, the contract ceases to be an individual retirement annuity as of the first day of such taxable year. See §1.408-3(c).

(6) *Premature distributions.*—If a distribution (whether a deemed distribution or an actual distribution) is made from an individual retirement account, or individual retirement annuity, to the individual for whose benefit the account was established, or who is the owner of the annuity, before the individual attains age 59½ (unless the individual has become disabled within the meaning of section

72(m)(7)), the tax under Chapter 1 of the Code for the taxable year in which such distribution is received is increased under section 408(f)(1) or (f)(2). The increase equals 10 percent of the amount of the distribution which is includible in gross income for the taxable year. Except in the case of the credits allowable under section 31, 39, or 42, no credit can be used to offset the increased tax described in this subparagraph. See, however, § 1.408-4(c)(3).

(d) *Limitation on contributions and benefits.*—An individual retirement account or individual retirement annuity is subject to the limitation on contributions and benefits imposed by section 415 for years beginning after December 31, 1975.

(e) *Community property laws.*—Section 408 shall be applied without regard to any community property laws. [Reg. § 1.408-1.]

☐ [T.D. 7714, 8-7-80.]

[Reg. § 1.408-2]

§ 1.408-2. Individual retirement accounts.—(a) *In general.*—An individual retirement account must be a trust or a custodial account (see paragraph (d) of this section). It must satisfy the requirements of paragraph (b) of this section in order to qualify as an individual retirement account. It may be established and maintained by an individual, by an employer for the benefit of his employees (see paragraph (c) of this section), or by an employee association for the benefit of its members (see paragraph (c) of this section).

(b) *Requirements.*—An individual retirement account must be a trust created or organized in the United States (as defined in section 7701(a)(9)) for the exclusive benefit of an individual or his beneficiaries. Such trust must be maintained at all times as a domestic trust in the United States. The instrument creating the trust must be in writing and the following requirements must be satisfied.

(1) *Amount of acceptable contributions.*—Except in the case of a contribution to a simplified employee pension described in section 408(k) and a rollover contribution described in section 408(d)(3), 402(a)(5), 402(a)(7), 403(a)(4), 403(b)(8) or 409(b)(3)(C), the trust instrument must provide that contributions may not be accepted by the trustee for the taxable year in excess of $1,500 on behalf of any individual for whom the trust is maintained. An individual retirement account maintained as a simplified employee pension may provide for the receipt of up to $7,500 for a calendar year.

(2) *Trustee.*—(i) The trustee must be a bank (as defined in section 408(n) and the regulations thereunder) or another person who demonstrates, in the manner described in paragraph (e) of this section, to the satisfaction of the Commissioner, that the manner in which the trust will be administered will be consistent with the requirements of section 408 and this section.

(ii) Section 11.408(a)(2)-1 of the Temporary Income Tax Regulations under the Employee Retirement Income Security Act of 1974 is superseded by this subparagraph (2).

(3) *Life insurance contracts.*—No part of the trust funds may be invested in life insurance contracts. An individual retirement account may invest in annuity contracts which provide, in the case of death prior to the time distributions commence, for a payment equal to the sum of the premiums paid or, if greater, the cash value of the contract.

(4) *Nonforfeitability.*—The interest of any individual on whose behalf the trust is maintained in the balance of his account must be nonforfeitable.

(5) *Prohibition against commingling.*—(i) The assets of the trust must not be commingled with other property except in a common trust fund or common investment fund.

(ii) For purposes of this subparagraph, the term "common investment fund" means a group trust created for the purpose of providing a satisfactory diversification of investments or a reduction of administrative expenses for the individual participating trust, and which group trust satisfies the requirements of section 408(c) (except that it need not be established by an employer or an association of employees) and the requirements of section 401(a) in the case of a group trust in which one of the individual participating trusts is an employees' trust described in section 401(a) which is exempt from tax under section 501(a).

(iii) For purposes of this subparagraph, the term "individual participating trust" means an employees' trust described in section 401(a) which is exempt from tax under section 501(a) or a trust which satisfies the requirements of section 408(a) provided that in the case of such an employees' trust, such trust would be permitted to participate in such a group trust if all of the other individual participating trusts were employees' trusts described in section 401(a) which are exempt from tax under section 501(a).

(6) *Distribution of interest.*—(i) The trust instrument must provide that the entire interest of the individual for whose benefit the trust is maintained must be distributed to him in accordance with paragraph (b)(6)(ii) or (iii) of this section.

(ii) Unless the provisions of paragraph (b)(6)(iii) of this section apply, the entire interest of the individual must be actually distributed to him not later than the close of his taxable year in which he attains age 70½.

(iii) In lieu of distributing the individual's entire interest as provided in paragraph (b)(6)(ii) of this section, the interest may be distributed commencing not later than the taxable year described in such paragraph (b)(6)(ii). In such case, the trust must expressly provide that the entire interest of the individual will be distributed to the individual and the individual's beneficiaries, in a manner which satisfies the requirements of paragraph (b)(6)(v) of this section, over any of the following periods (or any combination thereof)—

(A) The life of the individual,

(B) The lives of the individual and spouse,

(C) A period certain not extending beyond the life expectancy of the individual, or

(D) A period certain not extending beyond the joint life and last survivor expectancy of the individual and spouse.

(iv) The life expectancy of the individual or the joint life and last survivor expectancy of the individual and spouse cannot exceed the period computed by use of the expected return multiples in § 1.72-9, or, in the case of payments under a contract issued by an insurance company, the period computed by use of the mortality tables of such company.

(v) If an individual's entire interest is to be distributed over a period described in paragraph (b)(6)(iii) of this section, beginning in the year the individual attains 70½ the amount to be distributed each year must be not less than the lesser of the balance of the individual's entire interest or an amount equal to the quotient obtained by dividing the entire interest of the individual in the trust at the beginning of such year (including amounts not in the individual retirement account at the beginning of the year because they have been withdrawn for the purpose of making a rollover contribution to another individual retirement plan) by the life expectancy of the individual (or the joint life and last survivor expectancy of the individual and spouse (whichever is applicable)), determined in either case as of the date the individual attains age 70 in accordance with paragraph (b)(6)(iv) of this section, reduced by one for each taxable year commencing after the individual's attainment of age 70½. An annuity or endowment contract issued by an insurance company which provides for non-increasing payments over one of the periods described in paragraph (b)(6)(iii) of this section beginning not later than the close of the taxable year in which the individual attains age 70½ satisfies this provision. However, no distribution need be made in any year, or a lesser amount may be distributed, if beginning with the year the individual attains age 70½ the aggregate amounts distributed by the end of any year are at least equal to the aggregate of the minimum amounts required by this subdivision to have been distributed by the end of such year.

(vi) If an individual's entire interest is distributed in the form of an annuity contract, then the requirements of section 408(a)(6) are satisfied if the distribution of such contract takes place before the close of the taxable year described in subdivision (ii) of this subparagraph, and if the individual's interest will be paid over a period described in subdivision (iii) of this subparagraph and at a rate which satisfies the requirements of subdivision (v) of this subparagraph.

(vii) In determining whether paragraph (b)(6)(v) of this section is satisfied, all individual retirement plans maintained for an individual's benefit (except those under which he is a beneficiary described in section 408(a)(7)) at the close of the taxable year in which he reaches age 70½ must be aggregated. Thus, the total payments which such individual receives in any taxable year must be at least equal to the amount he would have been required to receive had all the plans been one plan at the close of the taxable year in which he attained age 70½.

(7) *Distribution upon death.*—(i) The trust instrument must provide that if the individual for whose benefit the trust is maintained dies before the entire interest in the trust has been distributed to him, or if distribution has been commenced as provided in paragraph (b)(6) of this section to the surviving spouse and such spouse dies before the entire interest has been distributed to such spouse, the entire interest (or the remaining part of such interest if distribution thereof has commenced) must, within 5 years after the individual's death (or the death of the surviving spouse) be distributed or applied to the purchase of an immediate annuity for this beneficiary or beneficiaries (or the beneficiary or beneficiaries of the surviving spouse) which will be payable for the life of such beneficiary or beneficiaries (or for a term certain not extending beyond the life expectancy of such beneficiary or beneficiaries) and which annuity

contract will be immediately distributed to such beneficiary or beneficiaries. A contract described in the preceding sentence is not includible in gross income upon distribution. Section 1.408-4(e) provides rules applicable to the taxation of such contracts. The first sentence of this paragraph (b)(7) shall have no application if distributions over a term certain commenced before the death of the individual for whose benefit the trust was maintained and the term certain is for a period permitted under paragraph (b)(6)(iii)(C) or (D) of this section.

(ii) Each such beneficiary (or beneficiary of a surviving spouse) may elect to treat the entire interest in the trust (or the remaining part of such interest if distribution thereof has commenced) as an account subject to the distribution requirements of section 408(a)(6) and paragraph (b)(6) of this section instead of those of section 408(a)(7) and paragraph (b)(7) of this section. Such an election will be deemed to have been made if such beneficiary treats the account in accordance with the requirements of section 408(a)(6) and paragraph (b)(6) of this section. An election will be considered to have been made by such beneficiary if either of the following occurs: (A) any amounts in the account (including any amounts that have been rolled over, in accordance with the requirements of section 408(d)(3)(A)(i), into an individual retirement account, individual retirement annuity, or retirement bond for the benefit of such individual) have not been distributed within the appropriate time period required by section 408(a)(7) and paragraph (b)(7) of this section; or (B) any additional amounts are contributed to the account (or to the account, annuity, or bond to which the beneficiary has rolled such amounts over, as described in (1) above) which are subject, or deemed to be subject, to the distribution requirements of section 408(a)(6) and paragraph (b)(6) of this section.

(8) *Definition of beneficiaries.*—The term "beneficiaries" on whose behalf an individual retirement account is established includes (except where the context indicates otherwise) the estate of the individual, dependents of the individual, and any person designated by the individual to share in the benefits of the account after the death of the individual.

(c) *Accounts established by employers and certain association of employees.*—(1) *In general.*—A trust created or organized in the United States (as defined in section 7701(a)(9)) by an employer for the exclusive benefit of his employees or their beneficiaries, or by an association of employees for the exclusive benefit of its members or their beneficiaries, is treated as an individual retirement account if the requirements of paragraphs (c)(2) and (c)(3) of this section are satisfied under the written governing instrument creating the trust. A trust described in the preceding sentence is for the exclusive benefit of employees or members even though it may maintain an account for former employees or members and employees who are temporarily on leave.

(2) *General requirements.*—The trust must satisfy the requirements of paragraphs (b)(1) through (7) of this section.

(3) *Special requirement.*—There must be a separate accounting for the interest of each employee or member.

(4) *Definitions.*—(i) *Separate accounting.*—For purposes of paragraph (c)(3) of this section, the term "separate accounting" means that separate records must be maintained with respect to the interest of each individual for whose benefit the trust is maintained. The assets of the trust may be held in a common trust fund, common investment fund, or common fund for the account of all individuals who have an interest in the trust.

(ii) *Employee association.*—For purposes of this paragraph and section 408(c), the term "employee association" means any organization composed of two or more employees, including, but not limited to, an employee association described in section 501(c)(4). Such association may include employees within the meaning of section 401(c)(1). There must be, however, some nexus between the employees (*e.g.,* employees of same employer, employees in the same industry, etc.) in order to qualify as an employee association described in this subdivision (ii).

(d) *Custodial accounts.*—For purposes of this section and section 408(a), a custodial account is treated as a trust described in section 408(a) if such account satisfies the requirements of section 408(a) except that it is not a trust and if the assets of such account are held by a bank (as defined in section 401(d)(1) and the regulations thereunder) or such other person who satisfies the requirements of paragraph (b)(2)(ii) of this section. For purposes of this chapter, in the case of a custodial account treated as a trust by reason of the preceding sentence, the custodian of such account will be treated as the trustee thereof.

(e) *Nonbank trustee.*—(1) *In general.*—The trustee of a trust described in paragraph (b) of this section may be a person other than a

bank if the person demonstrates to the satisfaction of the Commissioner that the manner in which the person will administer trusts will be consistent with the requirements of section 408. The person must demonstrate by written application that the requirements of paragraph (e)(2) to (e)(6) of this section will be met. The written application must be sent to the address prescribed by the Commissioner in revenue rulings, notices, and other guidance published in the Internal Revenue Bulletin (see §601.601(d)(2)(ii)(*b*) of this chapter). For procedural and administrative rules, see paragraph (e)(7) of this section.

(2) *Fiduciary ability.*—The applicant must demonstrate in detail its ability to act within the accepted rules of fiduciary conduct. Such demonstration must include the following elements of proof:

(i) *Continuity.*—(A) The applicant must assure the uninterrupted performance of its fiduciary duties notwithstanding the death or change of its owners. Thus, for example, there must be sufficient diversity in the ownership of the applicant to ensure that the death or change of its owners will not interrupt the conduct of its business. Therefore, the applicant cannot be an individual.

(B) Sufficient diversity in the ownership of an incorporated applicant is demonstrated in the following circumstances:

(1) Individuals each of whom owns more than 20 percent of the voting stock in the applicant own, in the aggregate, no more than 50 percent of such stock;

(2) The applicant has issued securities registered under section 12(b) of the Securities Exchange Act of 1934 (15 U.S.C. 781(b)) or required to be registered under section 12(g)(1) of that Act (15 U.S.C. 781(g)(1)); or

(3) The applicant has a parent corporation within the meaning of section 1563(a)(1) that has issued securities registered under section 12(b) of the Securities Exchange Act of 1934 (15 U.S.C. 781(b)) or required to be registered under Section 12(g)(1) of that Act (15 U.S.C. 781(g)(1)).

(C) Sufficient diversity in the ownership of an applicant that is a partnership means that—

(1) Individuals each of whom owns more than 20 percent of the profits interest in the partnership own, in the aggregate, no more than 50 percent of such profits interest, and

(2) Individuals each of whom owns more than 20 percent of the capital interest in the partnership own, in the aggregate, no more than 50 percent of such capital interest.

(D) For purposes of this subdivision, the ownership of stock and of capital and profits interests shall be determined in accordance with the rules for constructive ownership of stock provided in section 1563(e) and (f)(2). For this purpose, the rules for constructive ownership of stock provided in section 1563(e) and (f)(2) shall apply to a capital or profits interest in a partnership as if it were a stock interest.

(ii) *Established location.*—The applicant must have an established place of business in the United States where it is accessible during every business day.

(iii) *Fiduciary experience.*—The applicant must have fiduciary experience or expertise sufficient to ensure that it will be able to perform its fiduciary duties. Evidence of fiduciary experience must include proof that a significant part of the business of the applicant consists of exercising fiduciary powers similar to those it will exercise if its application is approved. Evidence of fiduciary expertise must include proof that the applicant employs personnel experienced in the administration of fiduciary powers similar to those the applicant will exercise if its application is approved.

(iv) *Fiduciary responsibility.*—The applicant must assure compliance with the rules of fiduciary conduct set out in paragraph (e)(5) of this section.

(v) *Financial responsibility.*—The applicant must exhibit a high degree of solvency commensurate with the obligations imposed by this paragraph. Among the factors to be taken into account are the applicant's net worth, its liquidity, and its ability to pay its debts as they come due.

(3) *Capacity to account.*—The applicant must demonstrate in detail its experience and competence with respect to accounting for the interests of a large number of individuals (including calculating and allocating income earned and paying out distributions to payees). Examples of accounting for the interests of a large number of individuals include accounting for the interests of a large number of shareholders in a regulated investment company and accounting for the interests of a large number of variable annuity contract holders.

(4) *Fitness to handle funds.*—(i) *In general.*—The applicant must demonstrate in detail its experience and competence with respect to other activities normally associated with the handling of retirement funds.

(ii) *Examples.*—Examples of activities normally associated with the handling of retirement funds include:

(A) To receive, issue receipts for, and safely keep securities;

(B) To collect income;

(C) To execute such ownership certificates, to keep such records, make such returns, and render such statements as are required for Federal tax purposes:

(D) To give proper notification regarding all collections;

(E) To collect matured or called principal and properly report all such collections;

(F) To exchange temporary for definitive securities;

(G) To give proper notification of calls, subscription rights, defaults in principal or interest, and the formation of protective committees;

(H) To buy, sell, receive, or deliver securities on specific directions.

(5) *Rules of fiduciary conduct.*—The applicant must demonstrate that under applicable regulatory requirements, corporate or other governing instruments, or its established operating procedures:

(i) *Administration of fiduciary powers.*—(A)(1) The owners or directors of the applicant will be responsible for the proper exercise of fiduciary powers by the applicant. Thus, all matters pertinent thereto, including the determination of policies, the investment and disposition of property held in a fiduciary capacity, and the direction and review of the actions of all employees utilized by the applicant in the exercise of its fiduciary powers, will be the responsibility of the owners or directors. In discharging this responsibility, the owners or directors may assign to designated employees, by action duly recorded, the administration of such of the applicant's fiduciary powers as may be proper to assign.

(2) A written record will be made of the acceptance and of the relinquishment or closing out of all fiduciary accounts, and of the assets held for each account.

(3) If the applicant has the authority or the responsibility to render any investment advice with regard to the assets held in or for each fiduciary account, the advisability of retaining or disposing of the assets will be determined at least once during each period of 12 months.

(B) All employees taking part in the performance of the applicant's fiduciary duties will be adequately bonded. Nothing in this subdivision (i)(B) shall require any person to be bonded in contravention of section 412(d) of the Employee Retirement Income Security Act of 1974 (29 U.S.C. 1112(d)).

(C) The applicant will employ or retain legal counsel who will be readily available to pass upon fiduciary matters and to advise the applicant.

(D) In order to segregate the performance of its fiduciary duties from other business activities, the applicant will maintain a separate trust division under the immediate supervision of an individual designated for that purpose. The trust division may utilize the personnel and facilities of other divisions of the applicant, and other divisions of the applicant may utilize the personnel and facilities of the trust division, as long as the separate identity of the trust division is preserved.

(ii) *Adequacy of net worth.*—(A) *Initial net worth requirement.*—In the case of applications received after January 5, 1995, no initial application will be accepted by the Commissioner unless the applicant has a net worth of not less than $250,000 (determined as of the end of the most recent taxable year). Thereafter, the applicant must satisfy the adequacy of net worth requirements of paragraph (e)(5)(ii)(B) and (C) of this section.

(B) No fiduciary account will be accepted by the applicant unless the applicant's net worth (determined as of the end of the most recent taxable year) exceeds the greater of—

(1) $100,000, or

(2) Four percent (or, in the case of a passive trustee described in paragraph (e)(6)(i)(A) of this section, two percent) of the value of all of the assets held by the applicant in fiduciary accounts (determined as of the most recent valuation date).

(C) The applicant will take whatever lawful steps are necessary (including the relinquishment of fiduciary accounts) to ensure that its net worth (determined as of the close of each taxable year) exceeds the greater of—

(1) $50,000, or

(2) Two percent (or, in the case of a passive trustee described in paragraph (e)(6)(i)(A) of this section, one percent) of the value of all of the assets held by the applicant in fiduciary accounts (determined as of the most recent valuation date).

(D) *Assets held by members of SIPC.*—(1) For purposes of satisfying the adequacy-of-net worth requirement of this paragraph, a special rule is provided for nonbank trustees that are members of the Securities Investor Protection Corporation (SIPC) created under the Securities Investor Protection Act of 1970 (SIPA)(15 U.S.C. §78aaa et seq, as amended). The amount that the net worth of a nonbank trustee that is a member of SIPC must exceed is reduced by two percent for purposes of paragraph (e)(5)(ii)(B)(2), and one percent for purposes of paragraph (e)(5)(ii)(C)(2), of the value of assets (determined on an account-by-account basis) held for the benefit of customers (as defined in 15 U.S.C. §78fff-2(e)(4)) in fiduciary accounts by the nonbank trustee to the extent of the portion of each account that does not exceed the dollar limit on advances described in 15 U.S.C. §78fff-3(a), as amended, that would apply to the assets in that account in the event of a liquidation proceeding under the SIPA.

(2) The provisions of this special rule for assets held in fiduciary accounts by members of SIPC are illustrated in the following example.

Example—(a) Trustee X is a broker-dealer and is a member of the Securities Investment Protection Corporation. Trustee X also has been approved as a nonbank trustee for individual retirement accounts (IRAs) by the Commissioner but not as a passive nonbank trustee. Trustee X is the trustee for four IRAs. The total assets of each IRA (for which Trustee X is the trustee) as of the most recent valuation date before the last day of Trustee X's taxable year ending in 1995 are as follows: the total assets for IRA-1 is $3,000,000 (all of which is invested in securities); the value of the total assets for IRA-2 is $500,000 ($200,000 of which is cash and $300,000 of which is invested in securities), the value of the total assets for IRA-3 is $400,000 (all of which is invested in securities); and the value of the total assets of IRA-4 is $200,000 (all of which is cash). The value of all assets held in fiduciary accounts, as defined in §1.408-2(e)(6)(viii)(A), is $4,100,000.

(b) The dollar limit on advances described in 15 U.S.C. §78fff-3(a) that would apply to the assets in each account in the event of a liquidation proceeding under the Securities Investor Protection Act of 1970 in effect as of the last day of Trustee X's taxable year ending in 1995 is $500,000 per account (no more that $100,000 of which is permitted to be cash). Thus, the dollar limit that would apply to IRA-1 is $500,000; the dollar limit for IRA-2 is $400,000 ($100,000 of the cash and the $300,000 of the value of the securities); the dollar limit for IRA-3 is $400,000 (the full value of the account because the value of the account is less than $500,000 and no portion of the account is cash); and the dollar limit for IRA-4 is $100,000 (the entire account is cash and the dollar limit per account for cash is $100,000). The aggregate dollar limits of the four IRAs is $1,400,000.

(c) For 1996, the amount determined under §1.408-2(e)(5)(ii)(B) is determined as follows for Trustee X: (1) four percent of $4,100,000 equals $164,000; (2) two percent of $1,400,000 equals $28,000; and (3) $164,000 minus $28,000 equals $136,000. Thus, because $136,000 exceeds $100,000, the minimum net worth necessary for Trustee X to accept new accounts for 1996 is $136,000.

(d) For 1996, the amount determined under §1.408-2(e)(5)(ii)(C) for Trustee X is determined as follows: (1) two percent of $4,100,000 equals $82,000; (2) one percent of $1,400,000 equals $14,000; and (3) $82,000 minus $14,000 equals $68,000. Thus, because $68,000 exceeds $50,000, the minimum net worth necessary for Trustee X to avoid a mandatory relinquishment of accounts for 1996 is $68,000.

(E) The applicant will determine the value of the assets held by it in trust at least once in each calendar year and no more than 18 months after the preceding valuation. The assets will be valued at their fair market value, except that the assets of an employee pension benefit plan to which section 103(b)(3)(A) of the Employee Retirement Income Security Act of 1974 (29 U.S.C. 1023(b)(3)(A)) applies will be considered to have the value stated in the most recent annual report of the plan.

(iii) *Audits.*—(A) At least once during each period of 12 months, the applicant will cause detailed audits of the fiduciary books and records to be made by a qualified public accountant. At that time, the applicant will ascertain whether the fiduciary accounts have been administered in accordance with law, this paragraph, and sound fiduciary principles. The audits shall be conducted in accordance with generally accepted auditing standards, and shall involve whatever tests of the fiduciary books and records of the applicant are considered necessary by the qualified public accountant.

(B) In the case of an applicant which is regulated, supervised, and subject to periodic examination by a State or Federal agency, such applicant may adopt an adequate continuous audit system in lieu of the periodic audits required by paragraph (e)(5)(iii)(A) of this section.

(C) A report of the audits and examinations required under this subdivision, together with the action taken thereon, will be noted in the fiduciary records of the applicant.

(iv) *Funds awaiting investment or distribution.*—Funds held in a fiduciary capacity by the applicant awaiting investment or distribution will not be held uninvested or undistributed any longer than is reasonable for the proper management of the account.

(v) *Custody of investments.*—(A) Except for investments pooled in a common investment fund in accordance with the provisions of paragraph (e)(5)(vi) of this section and for investments of accounts established under section 408(q) on or after August 1, 2003, the investments of each account will not be commingled with any other property.

(B) Assets of accounts requiring safekeeping will be deposited in an adequate vault. A permanent record will be kept of assets deposited in or withdrawn from the vault.

(vi) *Common investment funds.*—The assets of an account may be pooled in a common investment fund (as defined in paragraph (e)(5)(viii)(C) of this section) if the applicant is authorized under applicable law to administer a common investment fund and if pooling the assets in a common investment fund is not in contravention of the plan documents or applicable law. The common investment fund must be administered as follows:

(A) Each common investment fund must be established and maintained in accordance with a written agreement, containing appropriate provisions as to the manner in which the fund is to be operated, including provisions relating to the investment powers and a general statement of the investment policy of the applicant with respect to the fund; the allocation of income, profits and losses; the terms and conditions governing the admission or withdrawal of participations in the fund; the auditing of accounts of the applicant with respect to the fund; the basis and method of valuing assets held by the fund, setting forth specific criteria for each type of asset; the minimum frequency for valuation of assets of the fund; the period following each such valuation date during which the valuation may be made (which period in usual circumstances may not exceed 10 business days); the basis upon which the fund may be terminated; and such other matters as may be necessary to define clearly the rights of participants in the fund. A copy of the agreement must be available at the principal office of the applicant for inspection during all business hours, and upon request a copy of the agreement must be furnished to the employer, the plan administrator, any participant or beneficiary of an account, or the individual for whose benefit the account is established or that individual's beneficiary.

(B) All participations in the common investment fund must be on the basis of a proportionate interest in all of the investments.

(C) Not less frequently than once during each period of 3 months the applicant must determine the value of the assets in the fund as of the date set for the valuation of assets. No participation may be admitted to or withdrawn from the fund except (1) on the basis of such valuation and (2) as of such valuation date. No participation may be admitted to or withdrawn from the fund unless a written request for or notice of intention of taking such action has been entered on or before the valuation date in the fiduciary records of the applicant. No request or notice may be canceled or countermanded after the valuation date.

(D)(1) The applicant must at least once during each period of 12 months cause an adequate audit to be made of the common investment fund by a qualified public accountant.

(2) The applicant must at least once during each period of 12 months prepare a financial report of the fund which, based upon the above audit, must contain a list of investments in the fund showing the cost and current value of each investment; a statement for the period since the previous report showing purchases, with cost; sales, with profit or loss; any other investment changes; income and disbursements; and an appropriate notation as to any investments in default.

(3) The applicant must transmit and certify the accuracy of the financial report to the administrator of each plan participating in the common investment fund within 120 days after the end of the plan year.

(E) When participations are withdrawn from a common investment fund, distributions may be made in cash or ratably in kind, or partly in cash and partly in kind: *Provided,* That all distributions as of any one valuation date must be made on the same basis.

(F) If for any reason an investment is withdrawn in kind from a common investment fund for the benefit of all participants in the fund at the time of such withdrawal and such investment is not distributed ratably in kind, it must be segregated and administered or realized upon for the benefit ratably of all participants in the common investment fund at the time of withdrawal.

(vii) *Books and records.*—(A) The applicant must keep its fiduciary records separate and distinct from other records. All fiduciary records must be so kept and retained for as long as the contents thereof may become material in the administration of any internal revenue law. The fiduciary records must contain full information relative to each account.

(B) The applicant must keep an adequate record of all pending litigation to which it is a party in connection with the exercise of fiduciary powers.

(viii) *Definitions.*—For purposes of this paragraph (e)(5), and paragraph (e)(2)(v), and paragraph (e)(7) of this section—

(A) The term "account" or "fiduciary account" means a trust described in section 401(a) (including a custodial account described in section 401(f)), a custodial account described in section 403(b)(7), or an individual retirement account described in section 408(a) (including a custodial account described in section 408(h)).

(B) The term "plan administrator" means an administrator as defined in § 1.414(g)-1.

(C) The term "common investment fund" means a trust that satisfies the following requirements:

(1) The trust consists of all or part of the assets of several accounts that have been established with the applicant, and

(2) The trust is described in section 401(a) and is exempt from tax under section 501(a), or is a trust that is created for the purpose of providing a satisfactory diversification of investments or a reduction of administrative expenses for the participating accounts and that satisfies the requirements of section 408(c).

(D) The term "fiduciary records" means all matters which are written, transcribed, recorded, received or otherwise come into the possession of the applicant and are necessary to preserve information concerning the acts and events relevant to the fiduciary activities of the applicant.

(E) The term "qualified public accountant" means a qualified public accountant, as defined in section 103(a)(3)(D) of the Employee Retirement Income Security Act of 1974, 29 U.S.C. 1023(a)(3)(D), who is independent of the applicant.

(F) The term "net worth" means the amount of the applicant's assets less the amount of its liabilities, as determined in accordance with generally accepted accounting principles.

(6) *Special rules.*—(i) *Passive trustee.*—(A) An applicant that undertakes to act only as a passive trustee may be relieved of one or more of the requirements of this paragraph upon clear and convincing proof that such requirements are not germane, under all the facts and circumstances, to the manner in which the applicant will administer any trust. A trustee is a passive trustee only if under the written trust instrument the trustee has no discretion to direct the investment of the trust funds or any other aspect of the business administration of the trust, but is merely authorized to acquire and hold particular investments specified by the trust instrument. Thus, for example, in the case of an applicant that undertakes merely to acquire and hold the stock of regulated investment companies, the requirements of paragraph (e)(5)(i)(A)(3), (i)(D), and (vi) of this section shall not apply and no negative inference shall be drawn from the applicant's failure to demonstrate its experience or competence with respect to the activities described in paragraph (e)(4)(ii)(E) to (H) of this section.

(B) The notice of approval issued to an applicant that is approved by reason of this subdivision shall state that the applicant is authorized to act only as a passive trustee.

(ii) *Federal or State regulation.*—Evidence that an applicant is subject to Federal or State regulation with respect to one or more relevant factors shall be given weight in proportion to the extent that such regulatory standards are consonant with the requirements of section 401. Such evidence may be submitted in addition to, or in lieu of, the specific proofs required by this paragraph.

(iii) *Savings account.*—(A) An applicant will be approved to act as trustee under this subdivision if the following requirements are satisfied:

(1) The applicant is a credit union, industrial loan company, or other financial institution designated by the Commissioner;

(2) The investment of the trust assets will be solely in deposits in the applicant;

(3) Deposits in the applicant are insured (up to the dollar limit prescribed by applicable law) by an agency or instrumentality of the United States, or by an organization established under a special statute the business of which is limited to insuring deposits in financial institutions and providing related services.

(B) Any applicant that satisfies the requirements of this subdivision is hereby approved, and (notwithstanding subparagraph (2) of this paragraph) is not required to submit a written application. This approval takes effect on the first day after December 22, 1976, on which the applicant satisfies the requirements of this subdivision, and continues in effect for so long as the applicant continues to satisfy those requirements.

(C) If deposits are insured, but not in the manner provided in paragraph (e)(6)(iii)(A)(3) of this section, the applicant must submit an application. The application, notwithstanding subparagraph (2) of this paragraph, will be limited to a complete description of the insurance of applicant's deposits. The applicant will be approved if the Commissioner approves of the applicant's insurance.

(iv) *Notification of Commissioner.*—The applicant must notify the Commissioner in writing of any change that affects the continuing accuracy of any representation made in the application required by this paragraph, whether the change occurs before or after the applicant receives a notice of approval. The notification must be addressed to the address prescribed by the Commissioner in revenue rulings, notices, and other guidance published in the Internal Revenue Bulletin (see § 601.601(d)(2)(ii)(b) of this chapter).

(v) *Substitution of trustee.*—No applicant will be approved unless the applicant undertakes to act as trustee only under trust instruments which contain a provision to the effect that the grantor is to substitute another trustee upon notification by the Commissioner that such substitution is required because the applicant has failed to comply with the requirements of this paragraph or is not keeping such records, or making such returns, or rendering such statements as are required by forms or regulations.

(7) *Procedure and administration.*—(i) *Notice of approval.*—If the applicant is approved, a written notice of approval will be issued to the applicant. The notice of approval will state the day on which it becomes effective, and (except as otherwise provided therein) will remain effective until revoked. This paragraph does not authorize the applicant to accept any fiduciary account before such notice of approval becomes effective.

(ii) *Notice of disapproval.*—If the applicant is not approved, a written notice will be furnished to the applicant containing a statement of the reasons why the applicant has not been approved.

(iii) *Copy to be furnished.*—The applicant must not accept a fiduciary account until after the plan administrator or the person for whose benefit the account is to be established is furnished with a copy of the written notice of approval issued to the applicant. This provision is effective six months after April 20, 1979 for new accounts accepted thereafter. For accounts accepted before that date, the administrator must be notified before the later of the effective date of this provision or six months after acceptance of the account.

(iv) *Grounds for revocation.*—The notice of approval issued to an applicant will be revoked if the Commissioner determines that the applicant is unwilling or unable to administer fiduciary accounts in a manner consistent with the requirements of this paragraph. Generally, the notice will not be revoked unless the Commissioner determines that the applicant has knowingly, willfully, or repeatedly failed to administer fiduciary accounts in a manner consistent with the requirements of this paragraph, or has administered a fiduciary account in a grossly negligent manner.

(v) *Procedures for revocation.*—The notice of approval issued to an applicant may be revoked in accordance with the following procedures:

(A) If the Commissioner proposes to revoke the notice of approval issued to an applicant, the Commissioner will advise the applicant in writing of the proposed revocation and of the reasons therefor.

(B) Within 60 days after the receipt of such written advice, the applicant may protest the proposed revocation by submitting a written statement of facts, law, and arguments opposing such revocation to the address prescribed by the Commissioner in revenue rulings, notices, and other guidance published in the Internal Revenue Bulletin (see § 601.601(d)(2)(ii)(b) of this chapter). In addition, the applicant may request a conference in the National Office.

(C) If the applicant consents to the proposed revocation, either before or after a National Office conference, or if the applicant fails to file a timely protest, the Commissioner will revoke the notice of approval that was issued to the applicant.

(D) If, after considering the applicant's protest and any information developed in conference, the Commissioner determines that the applicant is unwilling or unable to administer fiduciary accounts in a manner consistent with the requirements of this paragraph, the Commissioner will revoke the notice of approval that was issued to the applicant and will furnish the applicant with a written statement of findings on which the revocation is based.

(E) If at any time the Commissioner determines that immediate action is necessary to protect the interest of the Internal Revenue Service or of any fiduciary account, the notice of approval issued to the applicant will be suspended at once, pending a final decision to be based on the applicant's protest and any information developed in conference.

(8) *Special rules for governmental units.*—(i) *In general.*—A governmental unit that seeks to qualify as a nonbank trustee of a deemed IRA that is part of its qualified employer plan must demonstrate to the satisfaction of the Commissioner that it is able to administer the trust in a manner that is consistent with the requirements of section 408. The demonstration must be made by written application to the Commissioner. Notwithstanding the requirement of paragraph (e)(1) of this section that a person must demonstrate by written application that the requirements of paragraphs (e)(2) through (e)(6) of this section will be met in order to qualify as a nonbank trustee, a governmental unit that maintains a plan qualified under section 401(a), 403(a), 403(b) or 457 need not demonstrate that all of these requirements will be met with respect to any individual retirement accounts maintained by that governmental unit pursuant to section 408(q). For example, a governmental unit need not demonstrate that it satisfies the net worth requirements of paragraph (e)(3)(ii) of this section if it demonstrates instead that it possesses taxing authority under applicable law. The Commissioner, in his discretion, may exempt a governmental unit from certain other requirements upon a showing that the governmental unit is able to administer the deemed IRAs in the best interest of the participants. Moreover, in determining whether a governmental unit satisfies the other requirements of paragraphs (e)(2) through (e)(6) of this section, the Commissioner may apply the requirements in a manner that is consistent with the applicant's status as a governmental unit.

(ii) *Governmental unit.*—For purposes of this special rule, the term governmental unit means a state, political subdivision of a state, and any agency or instrumentality of a state or political subdivision of a state.

(iii) *Additional rules.*—The Commissioner may in revenue rulings, notices, or other guidance of general applicability provide additional rules for governmental units seeking approval as nonbank trustees.

(iv) *Effective/applicability date.*—This section is applicable for written applications made on or after June 18, 2007. The rules in this section also may be relied on for applications submitted on or after August 1, 2003 (or such earlier application as the Commissioner deems appropriate) and before June 18, 2007. [Reg. § 1.408-2.]

☐ [T.D. 7714, 8-7-80. *Amended by* T.D. 8635, 12-19-95; T.D. 9142, 7-21-2004 *and* T.D. 9331, 6-15-2007.]

[Reg. § 1.408-3]

§ 1.408-3. Individual retirement annuities.—(a) *In general.*—An individual retirement annuity is an annuity contract or endowment contract (described in paragraph (e)(1) of this section) issued by an insurance company which is qualified to do business under the law of the jurisdiction in which the contract is sold and which satisfies the requirements of paragraph (b) of this section. A participation certificate in a group contract issued by an insurance company described in this paragraph will be treated as an individual retirement annuity if the contract satisfies the requirements of paragraph (b) of this section; the certificate of participation sets forth the requirements of paragraph (1) through (5) of section 408(b); the contract provides for a separate accounting of the benefit allocable to each participant-owner; and the group contract is for the exclusive benefit of the participant-owners and their beneficiaries. For purposes of this title, a participant-owner of a group contract described in this paragraph shall be treated as the owner of an individual retirement annuity. A contract will not be treated as other than an individual retirement annuity merely because it provides for waiver of premium on disability. An individual retirement annuity contract which satisfies the requirements of section 408(b) need not be purchased under a trust if the requirements of paragraph (b) of this section are satisfied. An individual retirement endowment contract may not be held under a trust which satisfies the requirements of section 408(a). Distribution of the contract is not a taxable event. Distributions under the contract are includible in gross income in accordance with the provisions of § 1.408-4(e).

(b) *Requirements.*—(1) *Transferability.*—The annuity or the endowment contract must not be transferable by the owner. An annuity or endowment contract is transferable if the owner can transfer any portion of his interest in the contract to any person other than the issuer thereof. Accordingly, such a contract is transferable if the owner can sell, assign, discount, or pledge as collateral for a loan or as security for the performance of an obligation or for any other purpose his interest in the contract to any person other than the issuer thereof. On the other hand, a contract is not to be considered transferable merely because the contract contains a provision permitting the individual to designate a beneficiary to receive the proceeds in the event of his death, a provision permitting the individual to elect a joint and survivor annuity, or other similar provisions.

(2) *Annual premium.*—Except in the case of a contribution to a simplified employee pension described in section 408(k), the annual premium on behalf of any individual for the annuity or the endow-

ment contract cannot exceed $1,500. Any refund of premiums must be applied before the close of the calendar year following the year of the refund toward the payment of future premiums or the purchase of additional benefits.

(3) *Distribution.*—The entire interest of the owner must be distributed to him in the same manner and over the same period as described in § 1.408-2(b)(6).

(4) *Distribution upon death.*—If the owner dies before the entire interest has been distributed to him, or if distribution has commenced to the surviving spouse, the remaining interest must be distributed in the same manner, over the same period, and to the same beneficiaries as described in § 1.408-2(b)(7).

(5) *Nonforfeitability.*—The entire interest of the owner in the annuity or endowment contract must be nonforfeitable.

(6) *Flexible premium.*—(Reserved)

(c) *Disqualification.*—If during any taxable year the owner of an annuity borrows any money under the annuity or endowment contract or by use of such contract (including, but not limited to, pledging the contract as security for any loan), such contract will cease to be an individual retirement annuity as of the first day of such taxable year, and will not be an individual retirement annuity at any time thereafter. If an annuity or endowment contract which constitutes an individual retirement annuity is disqualified as a result of the preceding sentence, an amount equal to the fair market value of the contract as of the first day of the taxable year of the owner in which such contract is disqualified is deemed to be distributed to the owner. Such owner shall include in gross income for such year an amount equal to the fair market value of such contract as of such first day. The preceding sentence applies even though part of the fair market value of the individual retirement annuity as of the first day of the taxable year is attributable to excess contributions which may be returned tax-free under section 408(d)(4) or 408(d)(5).

(d) *Premature distribution tax on deemed distribution.*—If the individual has not attained age 59½ before the beginning of the year in which the disqualification described in paragraph (c) of this section occurs, see section 408(f)(2) for additional tax on premature distributions.

(e) *Endowment contracts.*—(1) *Additional requirements for endowment contracts.*—No contract providing life insurance protection issued by a company described in paragraph (a) of this section shall be treated as an endowment contract for purposes of this section if—

(i) Such contract matures later than the taxable year in which the individual in whose name the contract is purchased attains the age of 70½;

(ii) Such contract is not for the exclusive benefit of such individual or his beneficiaries;

(iii) Premiums under the contract may increase over the term of the contract;

(iv) When all premiums are paid when due, the cash value of such contract at maturity is less than the death benefit payable under the contract at any time before maturity;

(v) The death benefit does not, at some time before maturity, exceed the greater of the cash value or the sum of premiums paid under the contract;

(vi) Such contract does not provide for a cash value;

(vii) Such contract provides that the life insurance element of such contract may increase over the term of such contract, unless such increase is merely because such contract provides for the purchase of additional benefits;

(viii) Such contract provides insurance other than life insurance and waiver of premiums upon disability; or

(ix) Such contract is issued after November 6, 1978.

(2) *Treatment of proceeds under endowment contract upon death of individual.*—In the case of the payment of a death benefit under an endowment contract upon the death of the individual in whose name the contract is purchased, the portion of such payment which is equal to the cash value immediately before the death of such individual is not excludable from gross income under section 101(a) and is treated as a distribution from an individual retirement annuity. The remaining portion, if any, of such payment constitutes current life insurance protection and is excludable under section 101(a). If a death benefit is paid under an endowment contract at a date or dates later than the death of the individual, section 101(d) is applicable only to the portion of the benefit which is attributable to the amount excludable under section 101(a). [Reg. § 1.408-3.]

☐ [*T.D. 7714, 8-7-80.*]

§ 1.408-4. Treatment of distributions from individual retirement arrangements.—(a) *General rule.*—(1) *Inclusion in income.*—Except as otherwise provided in this section, any amount actually paid or distributed or deemed paid or distributed from an individual retirement account or individual retirement annuity shall be included in the gross income of the payee or distributee for the taxable year in which the payment or distribution is received.

(2) *Zero basis.*—Notwithstanding section 1015(d) or any other provision of the Code, the basis (or investment in the contract) of any person in such an account or annuity is zero. For purposes of this section, an assignment of an individual's rights under an individual retirement account or an individual retirement annuity shall, except as provided in § 1.408-4(g) (relating to transfer incident to divorce), be deemed a distribution to such individual from such account or annuity of the amount assigned.

(b) *Rollover contribution.*—(1) *To individual retirement arrangement.*—Paragraph (a)(1) of this section shall not apply to any amount paid or distributed from an individual retirement account or individual retirement annuity to the individual for whose benefit the account was established or who is the owner of the annuity if the entire amount received (including the same amount of money and any other property) is paid into an individual retirement account, annuity (other than an endowment contract), or bond created for the benefit of such individual not later than the 60th day after the day on which he receives the payment or distribution.

(2) *To qualified plan.*—Paragraph (a)(1) of this section does not apply to any amount paid or distributed from an individual retirement account or individual retirement annuity to the individual for whose benefit the account was established or who is the owner of the annuity if—

(i) No amount in the account or no part of the value of the annuity is attributable to any source other than a rollover contribution from an employees' trust described in section 401(a) which is exempt from tax under section 501(a) or a rollover contribution from an annuity plan described in section 403(a) and the earnings on such sums, and

(ii) The entire amount received (including the same amount of money and any other property) represents the entire amount in the account and is paid into another such trust or plan (for the benefit of such individual) not later than the 60th day after the day on which the payment or distribution is received.

This subparagraph does not apply if any portion of the rollover contribution described in paragraph (b)(2)(i) of this section is attributable to an employees' trust forming part of a plan or an annuity under which the individual was an employee within the meaning of section 401(c)(1) at the time contributions were made on his behalf under the plan.

(3) *To section 403(b) contract.*—[Reserved]

(4) *Frequency limitation.*—(i) For taxable years beginning on or before December 31, 1977, paragraph (b)(1) of this section does not apply to any amount received by an individual from an individual retirement account, annuity or bond if at any time during the 3-year period ending on the day of receipt, the individual received any other amount from an individual retirement account, annuity or bond which was not includible in his gross income because of the application of paragraph (b)(1) of this section.

(ii) [Reserved]

(c) *Excess contributions returned before due date of return.*—(1) *Excess contribution.*—The rules in this paragraph (c) apply for purposes of determining net income attributable to IRA contributions made before January 1, 2004, and returned pursuant to section 408(d)(4). The rules in § 1.408-11 apply for purposes of determining net income attributable to IRA contributions made on or after January 1, 2004, and returned pursuant to section 408(d)(4). For purposes of this paragraph, excess contributions are the excess of the amounts contributed to an individual retirement account or paid for an individual retirement annuity during the taxable year over the amount allowable as a deduction under section 219 or 220 for the taxable year.

(2) *General rule.*—(i) Paragraph (a)(1) of this section does not apply to the distribution of any excess contribution paid during a taxable year to an account or annuity if: the distribution is received on or before the date prescribed by law (including extensions) for filing the individual's return for such taxable year; no deduction is allowed under section 219 or section 220 with respect to the excess contribution; and the distribution is accompanied by the amount of net income attributable to the excess contribution as of the date of the distribution as determined under subdivision (ii).

(ii) The amount of net income attributable to the excess contributions is an amount which bears the same ratio to the net income earned by the account during the computation period as the excess contribution bears to the sum of the balance of the account as of the first day of the taxable year in which the excess contribution is made and the total contribution made for such taxable year. For purposes of this paragraph, the term "computation period" means the period beginning on the first day of the taxable year in which the excess contribution is made and ending on the date of the distribution from the account.

(iii) For purposes of paragraph (c)(2)(ii), the net income earned by the account during the computation period is the fair market value of the balance of the account immediately after the distribution increased by the amount of distributions from the account during the computation period, and reduced (but not below zero) by the sum of: (A) the fair market value of the balance of the account as of the first day of the taxable year in which the excess contribution is made and (B) the contributions to the account made during the computation period.

(3) *Time of inclusion.*—(i) For taxable years beginning before January 1, 1977, the amount of net income determined under subparagraph (2) is includible in the gross income of the individual for the taxable year in which it is received. The amount of net income thus distributed is subject to the tax imposed by section 408(f)(1) for the year includible in gross income.

(ii) [Reserved]

(4) *Example.*—The provisions of this paragraph may be illustrated by the following example:

Example. On January 1, 1975, A, age 55, who is a calendar-year taxpayer, contributes $1,500 to an individual retirement account established for his benefit. For 1975, A is entitled to a deduction of $1,400 under section 219. For 1975, A does not claim as deductions any other items listed in section 62. A's gross income for 1975 is $9,334. On April 1, 1976, $107 is distributed to A from his individual retirement account. As of such date, the balance of the account is $1,498 [$1,605 − $107]. There were no other distributions from the account as of such date. The net amount of income earned by the account is $105 [$1,498 + $107 − (0 + $1,500)]. The net income attributable to the excess contribution is $7. [$105 × ($100/$1,500)]. A's adjusted gross income for 1975 is his gross income for 1975 ($9,334) reduced by the amount allowable to A as a deduction under section 219 ($1,400), or $7,934. A will include the $7 of the $107 distributed on April 1, 1976, in his gross income for 1976. Further, A will pay an additional income tax of $.70 for 1976 under section 408(f)(1).

(d) *Deemed distribution.*—(1) *General rule.*—In any case in which an individual retirement account ceases to be an individual retirement account by reason of the application of section 408(e)(2), paragraph (a)(1) of this section shall apply as if there were a distribution on the first day of the taxable year in which such account ceases to be an individual retirement account of an amount equal to the fair market value on such day of all the assets in the account on such day. In the case of a deemed distribution from an individual retirement annuity, see § 1.408-3(d).

(2) *Using account as security.*—In any case in which an individual for whose benefit an individual retirement account is established uses, directly or indirectly, all or any portion of the account as security for a loan, paragraph (a)(1) of this section shall apply as if there were distributed on the first day of the taxable year in which the loan was made an amount equal to that portion of the account used as security for such loan.

(e) *Distribution of annuity contracts.*—Paragraph (a)(1) of this section does not apply to any annuity contract which is distributed from an individual retirement account and which satisfies the requirements of paragraphs (b)(1), (3), (4) and (5) of section 408. Amounts distributed under such contracts will be taxable to the distributee under section 72. For purposes of applying section 72 to a distribution from such a contract, the investment in such contract is zero.

(f) *Treatment of assets distributed from an individual retirement account for the purchase of an endowment contract.*—Under section 408(e)(5), if all, or any portion, of the assets of an individual retirement account are used to purchase an endowment contract described in § 1.408-3(e) for the benefit of the individual for whose benefit the account is established—

(1) The excess, if any, of the total amount of assets used to purchase such contract over the portion of the assets attributable to life insurance protection shall be treated as a rollover contribution described in section 408(d)(3), and

(2) The portion of the assets attributable to life insurance protection shall be treated as a distribution described in paragraph (a)(1) of

this section, except that the provisions of section 408(f) shall not apply to such amount.

(g) *Transfer incident to divorce.*—(1) *General rule.*—The transfer of an individual's interest, in whole or in part, in an individual retirement account, individual retirement annuity, or a retirement bond, to his former spouse under a valid divorce decree or a written instrument incident to such divorce shall not be considered to be a distribution from such an account or annuity to such individual or his former spouse; nor shall it be considered a taxable transfer by such individual to his former spouse notwithstanding any other provision of Subtitle A of the Code.

(2) *Spousal account.*—The interest described in this paragraph (g) which is transferred to the former spouse shall be treated as an individual retirement account of such spouse if the interest is an individual retirement account; an individual retirement annuity of such spouse if such interest is an individual retirement annuity; and a retirement bond of such spouse if such interest is a retirement bond. [Reg. § 1.408-4.]

☐ [T.D. 7714, 8-7-80. *Amended by T.D 9056, 5-2-2003.*]

[Reg. § 1.403-5]

§ 1.408-5. Annual reports by trustees or issuers.—(a) *In general.*—The trustee of an individual retirement account or the issuer of an individual retirement annuity shall make annual calendar year reports concerning the status of the account or annuity. The report shall contain the information required in paragraph (b) and be furnished or filed in the manner and time specified in paragraph (c).

(b) *Information required to be included in the annual reports.*—The annual calendar year report shall contain the following information for transactions occurring during the calendar year—

(1) The amount of contributions;

(2) The amount of distributions;

(3) In the case of an endowment contract, the amount of the premium paid allocable to the cost of life insurance;

(4) The name and address of the trustee or issuer; and

(5) Such other information as the Commissioner may require.

(c) *Manner and time for filing.*—(1) The annual report shall be furnished to the individual on whose behalf the account is established or in whose name the annuity is purchased (or the beneficiary of the individual or owner). The report shall be furnished on or before the 30th day of June following the calendar year for which the report is required.

(2) The Commissioner may require the annual report to be filed with the Service at the time the Commissioner specifies.

(d) *Penalties.*—Section 6693 prescribes penalties for failure to file the annual report.

(e) *Effective date.*—This section shall apply to reports for calendar years after 1978.

(f) *Reports for years prior to 1979.*—For years prior to 1979, a trustee or issuer shall make reports in the time and manner as the Commissioner requires. [Reg. § 1.408-5.]

☐ [T.D. 7714, 8-7-80.]

[Reg. § 1.408-6]

§ 1.408-6. Disclosure statements for individual retirement arrangements.—(a) *In general.*—(1) *General rule.*—Trustees and issuers of individual retirement accounts and annuities are, under the authority of section 408(i), required to provide disclosure statements. This section sets forth these requirements.

(2) [Reserved]

(b) [Reserved]

(c) [Reserved]

(d) *Requirements.*—(1) [Reserved]

(2) [Reserved]

(3) [Reserved]

(4) *Disclosure statements.*—(i) Under the authority contained in section 408(i), a disclosure statement shall be furnished in accordance with the provisions of this subparagraph by the trustee of an individual retirement account described in section 408(a) or the issuer of an individual retirement annuity described in section 408(b) or of an endowment contract described in section 408(b) to the individual (hereinafter referred to as the "benefited individual") for whom such an account, annuity, or contract is, or is to be, established.

(ii)(A)*(1)* The trustee or issuer shall furnish, or cause to be furnished, to the benefited individual, a disclosure statement satisfying the requirements of subdivisions (iii) through (viii) of this subparagraph, as applicable, and a copy of the governing instrument to be used in establishing the account, annuity, or endowment contract. The copy of such governing instrument need not be filled in with financial and other data pertaining to the benefited individual; however, such copy must be complete in all other respects. The disclosure statement and copy of the governing instrument must be received by the benefited individual at least seven days preceding the earlier of the date of establishment or purchase of the account, annuity, or endowment contract. A disclosure statement or copy of the governing instrument required by this subparagraph may be received by the benefited individual less than seven days preceding, but no later than, the earlier of the date of establishment or purchase, if the benefited individual is permitted to revoke the account, annuity, or endowment contract pursuant to a procedure which satisfies the requirements of subdivision (ii)(A)(2) of this subparagraph.

(2) A procedure for revocation satisfies the requirements of this subdivision (ii)(A)(2) of this subparagraph if the benefited individual is permitted to revoke the account, or endowment contract by mailing or delivering, at his option, a notice of revocation on or before a day not less than seven days after the earlier of the date of establishment or purchase and, upon revocation, is entitled to a return of the entire amount of the consideration paid by him for the account, annuity, or endowment contract without adjustment for such items as sales commissions, administrative expenses or fluctuation in market value. The procedure may require that the notice be in writing or that it be oral, or it may require both a written and an oral notice. If an oral notice is required or permitted, the procedure must permit it to be delivered by telephone call during normal business hours. If a written notice is required or permitted, the procedure must provide that, if mailed, it shall be deemed mailed on the date of the postmark (or if sent by certified or registered mail, the date of certification or registration) if it is deposited in the mail in the United States in an envelope, or other appropriate wrapper, first class postage prepaid, properly addressed.

(B) If after a disclosure statement has been furnished, or caused to be furnished, to the benefited individual pursuant to paragraph (d)(4)(ii)(A) of this section and—

(1) On or before the earlier of the date of establishment or purchase, or

(2) On or before the last day on which the benefited individual is permitted to revoke the account, annuity, or endowment contract (if the benefited individual has a right to revoke the account, annuity, or endowment contract pursuant to the rules of subdivision (ii)(A) of this subparagraph),

there becomes effective a material adverse change in the information set forth in such disclosure statement or a material change in the governing instrument to be used in establishing the account, annuity, or contract, the trustee or issuer shall furnish, or cause to be furnished, to the benefited individual such amendments to any previously furnished disclosure statement or governing instrument as may be necessary to adequately inform the benefited individual of such change. The trustee or issuer shall be treated as satisfying this subdivision (ii)(B) of this subparagraph only if material required to be furnished by this subdivision is received by the benefited individual at least seven days preceding the earlier of the date of establishment or purchase of the account, annuity, or endowment contract or if the benefited individual is permitted to revoke the account, annuity, or endowment contract on or before a date not less than seven days after the date on which such material is received, pursuant to a procedure for revocation otherwise satisfying the provision of subdivision (ii)(A)(2) of this subparagraph.

(C) If the governing instrument is amended after the account, annuity, or endowment contract is no longer subject to revocation pursuant to subdivision (ii)(A) or (B) of this subparagraph, the trustee or issuer shall not later than the 30th day after the later of the date on which the amendment is adopted or becomes effective, deliver or mail to the last known address of the benefited individual a copy of such amendment and, if such amendment affects a matter described in subdivisions (iii) through (viii) of this subparagraph, a disclosure statement with respect to such matter meeting the requirements of subdivision (iv) of this subparagraph.

(D) For purposes of subdivision (ii)(A) and (B) of this subparagraph, if a disclosure statement, governing instrument, or an amendment to either, is mailed to the benefited individual, it shall be deemed (in the absence of evidence to the contrary) to be received by the benefited individual seven days after the date of mailing.

(E) In the case of a trust described in section 408(c) (relating to certain retirement savings arrangements for employees or members of associations of employees), the following special rule shall be applied:

(1) For purposes of this subparagraph, references to the benefited individual's account, annuity, or endowment contract shall refer to the benefited individual's interest in such trust, and

(2) The provisions of subdivision (ii) of this subparagraph shall be applied by substituting "the date on which the benefited individual's interest in such trust commences" for "the earlier of the date of establishment or purchase" wherever it appears therein.

Thus, for example, if an employer establishes a trust described in section 408(c) for the benefit of employees, and the trustee furnishes an employee with a disclosure statement and a copy of the governing instrument (as required by this subparagraph) on the date such employee's interest in the trust commences, such employee must be given a right to revoke such interest within a period of at least seven days. If any contribution has been made within such period (whether by the employee or by the employer), the full amount of such contribution must be paid to such employee pursuant to subdivision (ii)(A)(2) of this subparagraph.

(iii) The disclosure statement required by this subparagraph shall set forth in nontechnical language the following matters as such matters relate to the account, annuity, or endowment contract (as the case may be);

(A) Concise explanations of—

(1) The statutory requirements prescribed in section 408(a) (relating to an individual retirement account) or section 408(b) (relating to an individual retirement annuity and an endowment contract), and any additional requirements (whether or not required by law) that pertain to the particular retirement savings arrangement.

(2) The income tax consequences of establishing an account, annuity, or endowment contract (as the case may be) which meets the requirements of section 408(a) (relating to an individual retirement account) or section 408(b) (relating to an individual retirement annuity and an endowment contract), including the deductibility of contributions to, the tax treatment of distributions (other than premature distributions) from, the availability of income tax free rollovers to and from, and the tax status of such account, annuity, or endowment contract.

(3) The limitations and restrictions on the deduction for retirement savings under section 219, including the ineligibility of certain individuals who are active participants in a plan described in section 219(b)(2)(A) or for whom amounts are contributed under a contract described in section 219(b)(2)(B) to make deductible contributions to an account or for an annuity or endowment contract.

(4) The circumstances under which the benefited individual may revoke the account, annuity, or endowment contract, and the procedure therefor (including the name, address, and telephone number of the person designated to receive notice of such revocation). Such explanations shall be prominently displayed at the beginning of the disclosure statement.

(B) Statements to the effect that—

(1) If the benefited individual or his beneficiary engages in a prohibited transaction, described in section 4975(c) with respect to an individual retirement account, the account will lose its exemption from tax by reason of section 408(e)(2)(A), and the benefited individual must include in gross income, for the taxable year during which the benefited individual or his beneficiary engages in the prohibited transaction the fair market value of the account.

(2) If the owner of an individual retirement annuity or endowment contract described in section 408(b) borrows any money under, or by use of, such annuity or endowment contract, then, under section 408(e)(3), such annuity or endowment contract loses its section 408(b) classification, and the owner must include in gross income, for the taxable year during which the owner borrows any money under, or by use of, such annuity or endowment contract, the fair market value of the annuity or endowment contract.

(3) If a benefited individual uses all or any portion of an individual retirement account as security for a loan, then, under section 408(e)(4), the portion so used is treated as distributed to such individual and the benefited individual must include such distribution in gross income for the taxable year during which he so uses such account.

(4) An additional tax of 10 percent is imposed by section 408(f) on distributions (including amounts deemed distributed as the result of a prohibited loan or use as security for a loan) made before the benefited individual has attained age 59 1/2 unless such distribution is made on account of death or disability, or unless a rollover contribution is made with such distribution.

(5) Sections 2039(e) (relating to exemption from estate tax of annuities under certain trusts and plans) and 2517 (relating to exemption from gift tax of specified transfers of certain annuities under qualified plans) apply (including the manner in which such sections apply) to the account, annuity, or endowment contract.

(6) Section 402(a)(2) and (e) (relating to tax on lump sum distributions) is not applicable to distributions from an account, annuity, or endowment contract.

(7) A minimum distribution is required under section 408(a)(6) or (7) and 408(b)(3) or (4) (including a brief explanation of the amount of minimum distribution) and that if the amount distributed from an account, annuity, or endowment contract during the taxable year of the payee is less than the minimum required during

such year, an excise tax, which shall be paid by the payee, is imposed under section 4974, in an amount equal to 50 percent of the excess of the minimum required to be distributed over the amount actually distributed during the year.

(8) An excise tax is imposed under section 4973 on excess contributions (including a brief explanation of an excess contribution).

(9) The benefited individual must file Form 5329 (Return for Individual Retirement Savings Arrangement) with the Internal Revenue for each taxable year during which the account, annuity, or endowment contract is maintained.

(10) The account or contract has or has not (as the case may be) been approved as to form for use as an account, annuity, or endowment contract by the Internal Revenue Service. For purposes of this subdivision, if a favorable opinion or determination letter with respect to the form of a prototype trust, custodial account, annuity, or endowment contract has been issued by the Internal Revenue Service, or the instrument which establishes an individual retirement trust account or an individual retirement custodial account utilizes the precise language of a form currently provided by the Internal Revenue Service (including any additional language permitted by such form), such account or contract may be treated as approved as to form.

(11) The Internal Revenue Service approval is a determination only as to the form of the account, annuity, or endowment contract, and does not represent a determination of the merits of such account, annuity, or endowment contract.

(12) The proceeds from the account, annuity or endowment contract may be used by the benefited individual as a rollover contribution to another account or annuity or retirement bond in accordance with the provisions of section 408(d)(3).

(13) In the case of an endowment contract described in section 408(b), no deduction is allowed under section 219 for that portion of the amounts paid under the contract for the taxable year properly allocable to the cost of life insurance.

(14) If applicable, in the event that the benefited individual revokes the account, annuity, or endowment contract, pursuant to the procedure described in the disclosure statement (see subdivision (A)(4) of this subdivision (iii)), the benefited individual is entitled to a return of the entire amount of the consideration paid by him for the account, annuity or endowment contract without adjustment for such items as sales commissions, administrative expenses or fluctuation in market value.

(15) Further information can be obtained from any district office of the Internal Revenue Service.

To the extent that information on the matters described in subdivisions (iii)(A) and (B) of this subparagraph is provided in a publication of the Internal Revenue Service relating to individual retirement savings arrangements, such publication may be furnished by the trustee or issuer in lieu of providing information relating to such matters in a disclosure statement.

(C) The financial disclosure required by paragraph (d)(4)(v), (vi), and (vii) of this section.

(iv) In the case of an amendment to the terms of an account, annuity, or endowment contract described in paragraph (d)(4)(i) of this section, the disclosure statement required by this subparagraph need not repeat material contained in the statement furnished pursuant to paragraph (d)(4)(iii) of this section, but it must set forth in nontechnical language those matters described in paragraph (d)(4)(iii) of this section which are affected by such amendment.

(v) With respect to an account, annuity, or endowment contract described in paragraph (d)(4)(i) of this section (other than an account or annuity which is to receive only a rollover contribution described in paragraph (d)(4)(vi) of this section and to which no deductible contributions will be made), the disclosure statement must set forth in cases where either an amount is guaranteed over period of time (such as in the case of a nonparticipating endowment or annuity contract), or a projection of growth of the value of the account, annuity, or endowment contract can reasonably be made (such as in the case of a participating endowment or annuity contract (other than a variable annuity) or passbook savings account), the following:

(A) To the extent that an amount is guaranteed,

(1) The amount, determined without regard to any portion of a contribution which is not deductible, that would be guaranteed to be available to the benefited individual if (i) level annual contributions in the amount of $1,000 were to be made on the first day of each year, and (ii) the benefited individual were to withdraw in a single sum the entire amount of such account, annuity, or endowment contract at the end of each of the first five years during which contributions are to be made, at the end of the year in which the benefited individual attains the ages of 60, 65, and 70, and at the end of any other year during which the increase of the guaranteed available amount is less than the increase of the guaranteed available

amount during any preceding year for any reason other than decrease or cessation of contributions, and

(2) A statement that the amount described in subdivision (v)(A)(1) of this subparagraph is guaranteed, and the period for which guaranteed;

(B) To the extent a projection of growth of the value of the account, annuity, or endowment contract can reasonably be made but the amounts are not guaranteed.

(1) The amount, determined without regard to any portion of a contribution which is not deductible, and upon the basis of an earnings rate no greater than, and terms no different from, those currently in effect, that would be available to the benefited individual if (i) level annual contributions in the amount of $1,000 were to be made on the first day of each year, and (ii) the benefited individual were to withdraw in a single sum the entire amount of such account, annuity, or endowment contract at the end of each of the first five years during which contributions are to be made, at the end of each of the years in which the benefited individual attains the ages of 60, 65, and 70, and at the end of any other year during which the increase of the available amount is less than the increase of the available amount during any preceding year for any reason other than decrease or cessation of contributions, and

(2) A statement that the amount described in paragraph (d)(4)(v)(B)(1) of this section is a projection and is not guaranteed and a statement of the earnings rate and terms on the basis of which the projection is made;

(C) The portion of each $1,000 contribution attributable to the cost of life insurance, which would not be deductible, for each year during which contributions are to be made; and

(D) The sales commission (including any commission attributable to the sale of life insurance), if any, to be charged in each year, expressed as a percentage of gross annual contributions (including any portion attributable to the cost of life insurance) to be made for each year.

(vi) With respect to an account or annuity described in paragraph (d)(4)(i) of this section to which a rollover contribution described in section 402(a)(5)(A), 403(a)(4)(A), 408(d)(3)(A) or 409(b)(3)(C) will be made, the disclosure statement must set forth, in cases where an amount is guaranteed over a period of time (such as in the case of a nonparticipating annuity contract, or a projection of growth of the value of the account or annuity can reasonably be made (such as in the case of a participating annuity contract (other than a variable annuity) or passbook savings account), the following:

(A) To the extent guaranteed,

(1) The amount that would be guaranteed to be available to the benefited individual if (i) Such a rollover contribution in the amount of $1,000 were to be made on the first day of the year, (ii) No other contribution were to be made, and (iii) The benefited individual were to withdraw in a single sum the entire amount of such account or annuity at the end of each of the first five years after the contribution is made, at the end of the year in which the benefited individual attains the ages of 60, 65, and 70, and at the end of any other year during which the increase of the guaranteed available amount is less than the increase of the guaranteed available amount during any preceding year, and

(2) A statement that the amount described in paragraph (d)(4)(vi)(A)(1) of this section is guaranteed;

(B) To the extent that a projection of growth of the value of the account or annuity can reasonably be made but the amounts are not guaranteed.

(1) The amount, determined upon the basis of an earnings rate no greater than, and terms no different from, those currently in effect, that would be available to the benefited individual if (i) such a rollover contribution in the amount of $1,000 were to be made on the first day of the year, (ii) no other contribution were to be made, and (iii) the benefited individual were to withdraw in a single sum the entire amount of such account or annuity at the end of each of the first five years after the contribution is made, at the end of each of the years in which the benefited individual attains the ages 60, 65, 70, and at the end of any other year during which the increase of the available amount is less than the increase of the available amount during any preceding year, and

(2) A statement that the amount described in paragraph (d)(4)(vi)(B)(1) of this section is a projection and is not guaranteed and a statement of the earnings rate and terms on the basis of which the projection is made; and

(C) The sales commission, if any, to be charged in each year, expressed as a percentage of the assumed $1,000 contribution.

(vii) With respect to an account, annuity, or endowment contract described in paragraph (d)(4)(i) of this section, in all cases not subject to paragraph (d)(4)(v) or (vi) of this section (such as in the case of a mutual fund or variable annuity), the disclosure statement must set forth information described in subdivision (A) through (C) of this subdivision (vii) based (as applicable with respect to the type or types of contributions to be received by the account, annuity, or endowment contract) upon the assumption of (1) level annual contributions of $1,000 on the first day of each year, (2) a rollover contribution of $1,000 on the first day of the year and no other contributions, or (3) a rollover contribution of $1,000 on the first day of the year plus level annual contributions of $1,000 on the first day of each year.

(A) A description (in nontechnical language) with respect to the benefited individual's interest in the account, annuity, or endowment contract, of:

(1) Each type of charge, and the amount thereof, which may be made against a contribution.

(2) The method for computing and allocating annual earnings, and

(3) Each charge (other than those described in complying with paragraph (d)(4)(vii)(A)(1) of this section) which may be applied to such interest in determining the net amount of money available to the benefited individual and the method of computing each such charge;

(B) A statement that growth in value of the account, annuity, or endowment contract is neither guaranteed nor projected; and

(C) The portion of each $1,000 contribution attributable to the cost of life insurance, which would not be deductible, for every year during which contributions are to be made.

(viii) A disclosure statement, or an amendment thereto, furnished pursuant to the provisions of this subparagraph may contain information in addition to that required by paragraph (d)(4)(iii) through (vii) of this section. However, such disclosure statement will not be considered to comply with the provisions of this subparagraph if the substance of such additional material or the form in which it is presented causes such disclosure statement to be false or misleading with respect to the information required to be disclosed by this paragraph.

(ix) The provisions of section 6693, relating to failure to provide reports on individual retirement accounts or annuities, shall apply to any trustee or issuer who fails to furnish, or cause to be furnished, a disclosure statement, a copy of the governing instrument, or an amendment to either, as required by this paragraph.

(x) This section shall be effective for disclosure statements and copies of governing instruments mailed, or delivered without mailing, after February 14, 1977.

(xi) This section does not reflect the amendments made by section 1501 of the Tax Reform Act of 1976 (90 Stat. 1734) relating to retirement savings for certain married individuals. [Reg. § 1.408-6.]

☐ [T.D. 7714, 8-7-80.]

[Reg. § 1.408-7]

§ 1.408-7. Reports on distributions from individual retirement plans.—(a) *Requirement of report.*—The trustee of an individual retirement account or the issuer of an individual retirement annuity who makes a distribution during any calendar year to an individual from such account or under such annuity shall make a report on Form W-2P (in the case of distributions that are not total distributions) or Form 1099R (in the case of total distributions), and their related transmittal forms, for such year. The return must show the name and address of the person to whom the distribution was made, the aggregate amount of such distribution, and such other information as is required by the forms.

(b) *Amount subject to this section.*—The amounts subject to reporting under paragraph (a) include all amounts distributed or made available to which section 408(d) applies.

(c) *Time and place for filing.*—The report required under this section for any calendar year shall be filed after the close of that year and on or before February 28 of the following year with the appropriate Internal Revenue Service Center.

(d) *Statement to recipients.*—(1) Each trustee or issuer required to file Form 1099R or Form W-2P under this section shall furnish to the person whose identifying number is (or should be) shown on the forms a copy of the form.

(2) Each statement required by this paragraph to be furnished to recipients shall be furnished to such person after November 30 of the year of the distribution and on or before January 31 of the following year. However, for a distribution after December 31, 2008, the February 15 due date under section 6045 applies to the statement if the statement is furnished in a consolidated reporting statement under section 6045. *See* §§ 1.6045-1(k)(3), 1.6045-2(d)(2), 1.6045-3(e)(2), 1.6045-4(m)(3), and 1.6045-5(a)(3)(ii).

(e) *Effective date.*—This section is effective for calendar years beginning after December 31, 1977. [Reg. § 1.408-7.]

☐ [T.D. 7714, 8-7-80. Amended by T.D. 9504, 10-12-2010.]

[Reg. § 1.408-8]

§ 1.408-8. Distribution requirements for individual retirement plans.—The following questions and answers relate to the distribution rules for IRAs provided in section 408(a)(6) and 408(b)(3).

Q-1. Is an IRA subject to the distribution rules provided in section 401(a)(9) for qualified plans?

A-1. (a) Yes, an IRA is subject to the required minimum distribution rules provided in section 401(a)(9). In order to satisfy section 401(a)(9) for purposes of determining required minimum distributions for calendar years beginning on or after January 1, 2003, the rules of §§ 1.401(a)(9)-1 through 1.401(a)(9)-9 and 1.401(a)(9)-6 for defined contribution plans must be applied, except as otherwise provided in this section. For example, whether the 5-year rule or the life expectancy rule applies to distributions after death occurring before the IRA owner's required beginning date is determined in accordance with § 1.401(a)(9)-3 and the rules of § 1.401(a)(9)-4 apply for purposes of determining an IRA owner's designated beneficiary. Similarly, the amount of the minimum distribution required for each calendar year from an individual account is determined in accordance with § 1.401(a)(9)-5. For purposes of this section, the term *IRA* means an individual retirement account or annuity described in section 408(a) or (b). The IRA owner is the individual for whom an IRA is originally established by contributions for the benefit of that individual and that individual's beneficiaries.

(b) For purposes of applying the required minimum distribution rules in §§ 1.401(a)(9)-1 through 1.401(a)(9)-9 and 1.401(a)(9)-6 for qualified plans, the IRA trustee, custodian, or issuer is treated as the plan administrator, and the IRA owner is substituted for the employee.

(c) See A-14 and A-15 of § 1.408A-6 for rules under section 401(a)(9) that apply to a Roth IRA.

Q-2. Are IRAs that receive employer contributions under a simplified employee pension (defined in section 408(k)) or a SIMPLE IRA (defined in section 408(p)) treated as IRAs for purposes of section 401(a)(9)?

A-2. Yes, IRAs that receive employer contributions under a simplified employee pension (defined in section 408(k)) or a SIMPLE plan (defined in section 408(p)) are treated as IRAs, rather than employer plans, for purposes of section 401(a)(9) and are, therefore, subject to the distribution rules in this section.

Q-3. In the case of distributions from an IRA, what does the term *required beginning date* mean?

A-3. In the case of distributions from an IRA, the term *required beginning date* means April 1 of the calendar year following the calendar year in which the individual attains age 70^1/$_2$.

Q-4. What portion of a distribution from an IRA is not eligible for rollover because the amount is a required minimum distribution?

A-4. The portion of a distribution that is a required minimum distribution from an IRA and thus not eligible for rollover is determined in the same manner as provided in A-7 of § 1.402(c)-2 for distributions from qualified plans. For example, if a minimum distribution is required under section 401(a)(9) for a calendar year, an amount distributed during a calendar year from an IRA is treated as a required minimum distribution under section 401(a)(9) to the extent that the total required minimum distribution for the year under section 401(a)(9) for that IRA has not been satisfied. This requirement may be satisfied by a distribution from the IRA or, as permitted under A-9 of this section, from another IRA.

Q-5. May an individual's surviving spouse elect to treat such spouse's entire interest as a beneficiary in an individual's IRA upon the death of the individual (or the remaining part of such interest if distribution to the spouse has commenced) as the spouse's own account?

A-5. (a) The surviving spouse of an individual may elect, in the manner described in paragraph (b) of this A-5, to treat the spouse's entire interest as a beneficiary in an individual's IRA (or the remaining part of such interest if distribution thereof has commenced to the spouse) as the spouse's own IRA. This election is permitted to be made at any time after the individual's date of death. In order to make this election, the spouse must be the sole beneficiary of the IRA and have an unlimited right to withdraw amounts from the IRA. If a trust is named as beneficiary of the IRA, this requirement is not satisfied even if the spouse is the sole beneficiary of the trust. If the surviving spouse makes the election, the required minimum distribution for the calendar year of the election and each subsequent calendar year is determined under section 401(a)(9)(A) with the spouse as IRA owner and not section 401(a)(9)(B) with the surviving spouse as the deceased IRA owner's beneficiary. However, if the election is made in the calendar year containing the IRA owner's death, the spouse is not required to take a required minimum distribution as the IRA owner for that calendar year. Instead, the spouse is required to take a required minimum distribution for that year, determined with respect to the deceased IRA owner under the rules of A-4(a) of

§ 1.401(a)(9)-5, to the extent such a distribution was not made to the IRA owner before death.

(b) The election described in paragraph (a) of this A-5 is made by the surviving spouse redesignating the account as an account in the name of the surviving spouse as IRA owner rather than as beneficiary. Alternatively, a surviving spouse eligible to make the election is deemed to have made the election if, at any time, either of the following occurs—

(1) Any amount in the IRA that would be required to be distributed to the surviving spouse as beneficiary under section 401(a)(9)(B) is not distributed within the time period required under section 401(a)(9)(B); or

(2) Any additional amount is contributed to the IRA which is subject, or deemed to be subject, to the lifetime distribution requirements of section 401(a)(9)(A).

(c) The result of an election described in paragraph (b) of this A-5 is that the surviving spouse shall then be considered the IRA owner for whose benefit the trust is maintained for all purposes under the Internal Revenue Code (e.g., section 72(t)).

Q-6. How is the benefit determined for purposes of calculating the required minimum distribution from an IRA?

A-6. For purposes of determining the minimum distribution required to be made from an IRA in any calendar year, the account balance of the IRA as of December 31 of the calendar year immediately preceding the calendar year for which distributions are required to be made is substituted in A-3 of § 1.401(a)(9)-5 for the account balance of the employee. Except as provided in A-7 and A-8 of this section, no adjustments are made for contributions or distributions after that date.

Q-7. What rules apply in the case of a rollover to an IRA of an amount distributed by a qualified plan or another IRA?

A-7. If the surviving spouse of an employee rolls over a distribution from a qualified plan, such surviving spouse may elect to treat the IRA as the spouse's own IRA in accordance with the provisions in A-5 of this section. In the event of any other rollover to an IRA of an amount distributed by a qualified plan or another IRA, the rules in § 1.401(a)(9)-7 will apply for purposes of determining the account balance for the receiving IRA and the required minimum distribution from the receiving IRA. However, because the value of the account balance is determined as of December 31 of the year preceding the year for which the required minimum distribution is being determined and not as of a valuation date in the preceding year, the account balance of the receiving IRA is only adjusted if the amount is not received in the calendar year in which the amount rolled over is distributed. In that case, for purposes of determining the required minimum distribution for the calendar year in which such amount is actually received, the account balance of the receiving IRA as of December 31 of the preceding year must be adjusted by the amount received in accordance with A-2 of § 1.401(a)(9)-7.

Q-8. What rules apply in the case of a transfer (including a recharacterization) from one IRA to another?

A-8. (a) *General rule.* In the case of a trustee-to-trustee transfer from one IRA to another IRA that is not a distribution and rollover, the transfer is not treated as a distribution by the transferor IRA for purposes of section 401(a)(9). Accordingly, the minimum distribution requirement with respect to the transferor IRA must still be satisfied. Except as provided in paragraph (b) of this A-8 for recharacterizations, after the transfer the employee's account balance and the required minimum distribution under the transferee IRA are determined in the same manner as an account balance and required minimum distribution are determined under an IRA receiving a rollover contribution under A-7 of this section.

(b) *Recharacterizations.* If an amount is contributed to a Roth IRA that is a conversion contribution or failed conversion contribution and that amount (plus net income allocable to that amount) is transferred to another IRA (transferee IRA) in a subsequent year as a recharacterized contribution, the recharacterized contribution (plus allocable net income) must be added to the December 31 account balance of the transferee IRA for the year in which the conversion or failed conversion occurred.

Q-9. Is the required minimum distribution from one IRA of an owner permitted to be distributed from another IRA in order to satisfy section 401(a)(9)?

A-9. Yes, the required minimum distribution must be calculated separately for each IRA. The separately calculated amounts may then be totaled and the total distribution taken from any one or more of the individual's IRAs under the rules set forth in this A-9. Generally, only amounts in IRAs that an individual holds as the IRA owner may be aggregated. However, amounts in IRAs that an individual holds as a beneficiary of the same decedent and which are being distributed under the life expectancy rule in section 401(a)(9)(B)(iii) or (iv) may be aggregated, but such amounts may not be aggregated with amounts held in IRAs that the individual holds as the IRA owner or

as the beneficiary of another decedent. Distributions from section 403(b) contracts or accounts will not satisfy the distribution requirements from IRAs, nor will distributions from IRAs satisfy the distribution requirements from section 403(b) contracts or accounts. Distributions from Roth IRAs (defined in section 408A) will not satisfy the distributions requirements applicable to IRAs or section 403(b) accounts or contracts and distributions from IRAs or section 403(b) contracts or accounts will not satisfy the distribution requirements from Roth IRAs.

Q-10. Is any reporting required by the trustee, custodian, or issuer of an IRA with respect to the minimum amount that is required to be distributed from that IRA?

A-10. Yes, the trustee, custodian, or issuer of an IRA is required to report information with respect to the minimum amount required to be distributed from the IRA for each calendar year to individuals or entities, at the time, and in the manner, prescribed by the Commissioner in revenue rulings, notices, and other guidance published in the Internal Revenue Bulletin (see § 601.601(d)(2)(ii)(b) of this chapter) as well as the applicable Federal tax forms and accompanying instructions.

Q-11. Which amounts distributed from an IRA are taken into account in determining whether section 401(a)(9) is satisfied?

A-11. (a) *General rule.* Except as provided in paragraph (b) of this A-11, all amounts distributed from an IRA are taken into account in determining whether section 401(a)(9) is satisfied, regardless of whether the amount is includible in income.

(b) *Amounts not taken into account.* The following amounts are not taken into account in determining whether the required minimum amount with respect to an IRA for a calendar year has been distributed—

(1) Contributions returned pursuant to section 408(d)(4), together with the income allocable to these contributions;

(2) Contributions returned pursuant to section 408(d)(5);

(3) Corrective distributions of excess simplified employee pension contributions under section 408(k)(6)(C), together with the income allocable to these distributions; and

(4) Similar items designated by the Commissioner in revenue rulings, notices, and other guidance published in the Internal Revenue Bulletin. See § 601.601(d)(2)(ii)(b) of this chapter.

Q-12. How does the special rule in A-3(d) of § 1.401(a)(9)-5 for a qualifying longevity annuity contract (QLAC) apply to an IRA?

A-12. (a) *General rule.* The special rule in A-3(d) of § 1.401(a)(9)-5 for a QLAC, defined in A-17 of § 1.401(a)(9)-6, applies to an IRA, subject to the exceptions set forth in this A-12. See A-14(d) of § 1.408A-6 for special rules relating to Roth IRAs.

(b) *Limitations on premiums*—(1) *In general.* In lieu of the limitations described in A-17(b) of § 1.401(a)(9)-6, the premiums paid with respect to the contract on a date are not permitted to exceed the lesser of the dollar limitation in paragraph (b)(2) of this A-12 or the percentage limitation in paragraph (b)(3) of this A-12.

(2) *Dollar limitation.* The dollar limitation is an amount equal to the excess of—

(i) $125,000 (as adjusted under A-17(d)(2) of § 1.401(a)(9)-6), over

(ii) The sum of—

(A) The premiums paid before that date with respect to the contract, and

(B) The premiums paid on or before that date with respect to any other contract that is intended to be a QLAC and that is purchased for the IRA owner under the IRA, or any other plan, annuity, or account described in section 401(a), 403(a), 403(b), or 408 or eligible governmental plan under section 457(b).

(3) *Percentage limitation.* The percentage limitation is an amount equal to the excess of—

(i) 25 percent of the total account balances of the IRAs (other than Roth IRAs) that an individual holds as the IRA owner (including the value of any QLAC held under those IRAs) as of December 31 of the calendar year immediately preceding the calendar year in which a premium is paid, over

(ii) The sum of—

(A) The premiums paid before that date with respect to the contract, and

(B) The premiums paid on or before that date with respect to any other contract that is intended to be a QLAC and that is held or was purchased for the individual under those IRAs.

(c) *Reliance on representations.* For purposes of the limitations described in paragraphs (b)(2) and (3) of this A-12, unless the trustee, custodian, or issuer of an IRA has actual knowledge to the contrary, the trustee, custodian, or issuer may rely on the IRA owner's representation (made in writing or such other form as may be prescribed by the Commissioner) of—

(1) The amount of the premiums described in paragraphs (b)(2)(ii)(B) and (b)(3)(ii)(B) of this A-12 that are not paid under the IRA, and

(2) The amount of the account balances described in paragraph (b)(3)(i) of this A-12 (other than the account balance under the IRA).

(d) *Permitted delay in setting beneficiary designation.* In case of a contract that is rolled over from a plan to an IRA before the required beginning date under the plan, the contract will not violate the rule in A-17(c)(2)(v) of § 1.401(a)(9)-6 that a non-spouse beneficiary must be irrevocably selected on or before the later of the date of purchase or the required beginning date under the IRA, provided that the contract requires a beneficiary to be irrevocably selected by the end of the year following the year of the rollover.

(e) *Roth IRAs.* A contract that is purchased under a Roth IRA is not treated as a contract that is intended to be a QLAC for purposes of applying the dollar and percentage limitation rules in paragraphs (b)(2)(ii)(B) and (b)(3)(ii)(B) of this A-12. See A-14(d) of § 1.408A-6. If a QLAC is purchased or held under a plan, annuity, account, or traditional IRA, and that contract is later rolled over or converted to a Roth IRA, the contract is not treated as a contract that is intended to be a QLAC after the date of the rollover or conversion. Thus, premi-

ums paid with respect to the contract will not be taken into account under paragraph (b)(2)(ii)(B) or paragraph (b)(3)(ii)(B) of this A-12 after the date of the rollover or conversion.

(f) *Effective/applicability date.* This A-12 applies to contracts purchased on or after July 2, 2014. [Reg. § 1.408-8.]

☐ [*T.D. 8987, 4-16-2002. Amended by T.D. 9130, 6-14-2004 and T.D. 9673, 7-1-2014.*]

[Reg. § 1.408-11]

§ 1.408-11. Net income calculation for returned or recharacterized IRA contributions.—(a) *Net income calculation for returned IRA contributions.*—(1) *General rule.*—For purposes of returned contributions under section 408(d)(4), the net income attributable to a contribution made to an IRA is determined by allocating to the contribution a pro-rata portion of the earnings on the assets in the IRA during the period the IRA held the contribution. This attributable net income is calculated by using the following formula:

$$\text{Net Income} = \text{Contribution} \times \frac{(\text{Adjusted Closing Balance} - \text{Adjusted Opening Balance})}{\text{Adjusted Opening Balance}}.$$

(2) *Special rule.*—If an IRA is established with a contribution and no other contributions, distributions or transfers are made to or from that IRA, then the subsequent distribution of the entire account balance of the IRA pursuant to section 408(d)(4) will satisfy the requirement of that Internal Revenue Code section that the return of a contribution be accompanied by the amount of net income attributable to the contribution.

(b) *Definitions.*—For purposes of this section the following definitions apply:

(1) *Adjusted opening balance.*—The term *adjusted opening balance* means the fair market value of the IRA at the beginning of the computation period plus the amount of any contributions or transfers (including the contribution that is distributed as a returned contribution pursuant to section 408(d)(4) and recharacterizations of contributions pursuant to section 408A(d)(6)) made to the IRA during the computation period.

(2) *Adjusted closing balance.*—The term *adjusted closing balance* means the fair market value of the IRA at the end of the computation period plus the amount of any distributions or transfers (including recharacterizations of contributions pursuant to section 408A(d)(6)) made from the IRA during the computation period.

(3) *Computation period.*—The term *computation period* means the period beginning immediately prior to the time that the contribution being returned was made to the IRA and ending immediately prior to the removal of the contribution. If more than one contribution was made as a regular contribution and is being returned from the IRA, the computation period begins immediately prior to the time the first contribution being returned was contributed.

(4) *Regular contribution.*—The term *regular contribution* means an IRA contribution made by the IRA owner that is neither a trustee-to-trustee transfer from another IRA nor a rollover from another IRA or retirement plan.

(c) *Additional rules.*—(1) When an IRA asset is not normally valued on a daily basis, the fair market value of the asset at the beginning of the computation period is deemed to be the most recent, regularly determined, fair market value of the asset, determined as of a date that coincides with or precedes the first day of the computation period. In addition, solely for purposes of this section, notwithstanding A-3 of § 1.408A-5, recharacterized contributions are taken into account for the period they are actually held in a particular IRA.

(2) In the case of an IRA that has received more than one regular contribution for a particular taxable year, the last regular contribution made to the IRA for the year is deemed to be the contribution that is distributed as a returned contribution under section 408(d)(4), up to the amount of the contribution identified by the IRA owner as the amount distributed as a returned contribution.

(3) In the case of an individual who owns multiple IRAs, the net income calculation is performed only on the IRA containing the contribution being returned, and that IRA is the IRA that must distribute the contribution.

(d) *Examples.*—The following examples illustrate the net income calculation under section 408(d)(4) and this section:

Example 1. (i) On May 1, 2004, when her IRA is worth $4,800, Taxpayer A makes a $1,600 regular contribution to her IRA. Taxpayer A requests that $400 of the May 1, 2004, contribution be returned to her pursuant to section 408(d)(4). Pursuant to this request, on February 1, 2005, when the IRA is worth $7,600, the IRA trustee distributes

to Taxpayer A the $400 plus attributable net income. During this time, no other contributions have been made to the IRA and no distributions have been made.

(ii) The adjusted opening balance is $6,400 [$4,800 + $1,600]and the adjusted closing balance is $7,600. Thus, the net income attributable to the $400 May 1, 2004, contribution is $75 [$400 × ($7,600 – $6,400)/$6,400]. Therefore, the total to be distributed on February 1, 2005, pursuant to § 408(d)(4) is $475.

Example 2. (i) Beginning in January 2004, Taxpayer B contributes $300 on the 15th of each month to an IRA for 2004, resulting in an excess regular contribution of $600 for that year. Taxpayer B requests that the $600 excess regular contribution be returned to her pursuant to section 408(d)(4). Pursuant to this request, on March 1, 2005, when the IRA is worth $16,000, the IRA trustee distributes to Taxpayer B the $600 plus attributable net income. The excess regular contributions to be returned are deemed to be the last two made in 2004: the $300 December 15 contribution and the $300 November 15 contribution. On November 15 the IRA was worth $11,000 immediately prior to the contribution. No distributions or transfers have been made from the IRA and no contributions or transfers, other than the monthly contributions (including $300 in January and February 2005), have been made.

(ii) As of the beginning of the computation period (November 15), the adjusted opening balance is $12,200 [$11,000 + $300 + $300 + $300 + $300] and the adjusted closing balance is $16,000. Thus, the net income attributable to the excess regular contributions is $187 [$600 × ($16,000 – $12,200)/$12,200]. Therefore, the total to be distributed as returned contributions on March 1, 2005, to correct the excess regular contribution is $787 [$600 + $187].

[Reg. § 1.408-11.]

☐ [*T.D. 9056, 5-2-2003.*]

[Reg. § 1.408(q)-1]

§ 1.408(q)-1. Deemed IRAs in qualified employer plans.—(a) *In general.*—Under section 408(q), a qualified employer plan may permit employees to make voluntary employee contributions to a separate account or annuity established under the plan. If the requirements of section 408(q) and this section are met, such account or annuity is treated in the same manner as an individual retirement plan under section 408 or 408A (and contributions to such an account or annuity are treated as contributions to an individual retirement plan and not to the qualified employer plan). The account or annuity is referred to as a deemed IRA.

(b) *Types of IRAs.*—If the account or annuity meets the requirements applicable to traditional IRAs under section 408, the account or annuity is deemed to be a traditional IRA, and if the account or annuity meets the requirements applicable to Roth IRAs under section 408A, the account or annuity is deemed to be a Roth IRA. Simplified employee pensions (SEPs) under section 408(k) and SIMPLE IRAs under section 408(p) may not be used as deemed IRAs.

(c) *Separate entities.*—Except as provided in paragraphs (d) and (g) of this section, the qualified employer plan and the deemed IRA are treated as separate entities under the Internal Revenue Code and are subject to the separate rules applicable to qualified employer plans and IRAs, respectively. Issues regarding eligibility, participation, disclosure, nondiscrimination, contributions, distributions, investments, a nd plan administration are generally to be resolved under the separate rules (if any) applicable to each entity under the Internal Revenue Code.

(d) *Exceptions.*—The following exceptions to treatment of a deemed IRA and the qualified employer plan as separate entities apply:

(1) The plan document of the qualified employer plan must contain the deemed IRA provisions and a deemed IRA must be in effect at the time the deemed IRA contributions are accepted. Notwithstanding the preceding sentence, employers that provided deemed IRAs for plan years beginning before January 1, 2004, (but after December 31, 2002) are not required to have such provisions in their plan documents before the end of such plan years.

(2) The requirements of section 408(a)(5) regarding commingling of assets do not apply to deemed IRAs. Accordingly, the assets of a deemed IRA may be commingled for investment purposes with those of the qualified employer plan. However, the restrictions on the commingling of plan and IRA assets with other assets apply to the assets of the qualified employer plan and the deemed IRA.

(e) *Application of distribution rules.*—(1) Rules applicable to distributions from qualified employer plans under the Internal Revenue Code and regulations do not apply to distributions from deemed IRAs. Instead, the rules applicable to distributions from IRAs apply to distributions from deemed IRAs. Also, any restrictions that a trustee, custodian, or insurance company is permitted to impose on distributions from traditional and Roth IRAs may be imposed on distributions from deemed IRAs (for example, early withdrawal penalties on annuities).

(2) The required minimum distribution rules of section 401(a)(9) must be met separately with respect to the qualified employer plan and the deemed IRA. The determination of whether a qualified employer plan satisfies the required minimum distribution rules of section 401(a)(9) is made without regard to whether a participant satisfies the required minimum distribution requirements with respect to the deemed IRA that is established under such plan.

(f) *Additional rules.*—(1) *Trustee.*—The trustee or custodian of an individual retirement account must be a bank, as required by section 408(a)(2), or, if the trustee is not a bank, as defined in section 408(n), the trustee must have received approval from the Commissioner to serve as a nonbank trustee or nonbank custodian pursuant to § 1.408-2(e). For further guidance regarding governmental units serving as nonbank trustees of deemed IRAs established under section 408(q), see § 1.408-2T(e)(8).

(2) *Trusts.*—(i) *General rule.*—Deemed IRAs that are individual retirement accounts may be held in separate individual trusts, a single trust separate from a trust maintained by the qualified employer plan, or in a single trust that includes the qualified employer plan. A deemed IRA trust must be created or organized in the United States for the exclusive benefit of the participants. If deemed IRAs are held in a single trust that includes the qualified employer plan, the trustee must maintain a separate account for each deemed IRA. In addition, the written governing instrument creating the trust must satisfy the requirements of section 408(a) (1), (2), (3), (4), and (6).

(ii) *Application of section 408(a)(3).*—If deemed IRAs are held in a single trust that includes the qualified employer plan, section 408(a)(3) is treated as satisfied if no part of the separate accounts of any of the deemed IRAs is invested in life insurance contracts, regardless of whether the separate account for the qualified employer plan invests in life insurance contracts.

(iii) *Separate accounts for traditional and Roth deemed IRAs.*—The rules of section 408A(b) and the regulations thereunder, requiring each Roth IRA to be clearly designated as a Roth IRA, will not fail to be satisfied solely because Roth deemed IRAs and traditional deemed IRAs are held in a single trust, provided that the trustee maintains separate accounts for the Roth deemed IRAs and traditional deemed IRAs of each participant, and each of those accounts is clearly designated as such.

(3) *Annuity contracts.*—Deemed IRAs that are individual retirement annuities may be held under a single annuity contract or under separate annuity contracts. However, the contract must be separate from any annuity contract or annuity contracts of the qualified employer plan. In addition, the contract must satisfy the requirements of section 408(b) and there must be separate accounting for the interest of each participant in those cases where the individual retirement annuities are held under a single annuity contract.

(4) *Deductibility.*—The deductibility of voluntary employee contributions to a traditional deemed IRA is determined in the same manner as if they were made to any other traditional IRA. Thus, for example, taxpayers with compensation that exceeds the limits imposed by section 219(g) may not be able to make contributions to deemed IRAs, or the deductibility of such contributions may be limited in accordance with sections 408 and 219(g). However, section 219(f)(5), regarding the taxable year in which amounts paid by an employer to an individual retirement plan are includible in the employee's income, is not applicable to deemed IRAs.

(5) *Rollovers and transfers.*—The same rules apply to rollovers and transfers to and from deemed IRAs as apply to rollovers and transfers to and from other IRAs. Thus, for example, the plan may provide that an employee may request and receive a distribution of his or her deemed IRA account balance and may roll it over to an eligible retirement plan in accordance with section 408(d)(3), regardless of whether that employee may receive a distribution of any other plan benefits.

(6) *Nondiscrimination.*—The availability of a deemed IRA is not a benefit, right or feature of the qualified employer plan under § 1.401(a)(4)-4.

(7) *IRA assets and benefits not taken into account in determining benefits under or funding of qualified employer plan.*—Neither the assets held in the deemed IRA portion of the qualified employer plan, nor any benefits attributable thereto, shall be taken into account for purposes of:

(i) determining the benefits of employees and their beneficiaries under the plan (within the meaning of section 401(a)(2)); or

(ii) determining the plan's assets or liabilities for purposes of section 404 or 412.

(g) *Disqualifying defects.*—(1) *Single trust.*—If the qualified employer plan fails to satisfy the qualification requirements applicable to it, either in form or operation, any deemed IRA that is an individual retirement account and that is included as part of the trust of that qualified employer plan does not satisfy section 408(q). Accordingly, any account maintained under such a plan as a deemed IRA ceases to be a deemed IRA at the time of the disqualifying event. In addition, the deemed IRA also ceases to satisfy the requirements of sections 408(a) and 408A. Also, if any one of the deemed IRAs fails to satisfy the applicable requirements of sections 408 or 408A, and the assets of that deemed IRA are included as part of the trust of the qualified employer plan, section 408(q) does not apply and the plan will fail to satisfy the plan's qualification requirements.

(2) *Separate trusts and annuities.*—If the qualified employer plan fails to satisfy its qualification requirements, either in form or operation, but the assets of a deemed IRA are held in a separate trust (or where a deemed IRA is an individual retirement annuity), then the deemed IRA does not automatically fail to satisfy the applicable requirements of section 408 or 408A. Instead, its status as an IRA will be determined by considering whether the account or the annuity satisfies the applicable requirements of sections 408 and 408A (including, in the case of individual retirement accounts, the prohibition against the commingling of assets under section 408(a)(5)). Also, if a deemed IRA fails to satisfy the requirements of a qualified IRA and the assets of the deemed IRA are held in a separate trust (or where the deemed IRA is an individual retirement annuity), the qualified employer plan will not fail the qualification requirements applicable to it under the Code solely because of the failure of the deemed IRA.

(h) *Definitions.*—The following definitions apply for purposes of this section:

(1) *Qualified employer plan.*—A *qualified employer plan* is a plan described in section 401(a), an annuity plan described in section 403(a), a section 403(b) plan, or a governmental plan under section 457(b).

(2) *Voluntary employee contribution.*—A *voluntary employee contribution* is any contribution (other than a mandatory contribution within the meaning of section 411(c)(2)(C)) which is made by an individual as an employee under a qualified employer plan that allows employees to elect to make contributions to deemed IRAs and with respect to which the individual has designated the contribution as a contribution to which section 408(q) applies.

(3) *Employee.*—An *employee* includes any individual who is an employee under the rules applicable to the qualified employer plan under which the deemed IRA is established.

(i) *Effective date.*—This section applies to accounts or annuities established under section 408(q) on or after August 1, 2003. [Reg. § 1.408(q)-1.]

☐ [T.D. 9142, 7-21-2004.]

[Reg. § 1.408A-0]

§ 1.408A-0. Roth IRAs; Table of contents.—This table of contents lists the regulations relating to Roth IRAs under section 408A of the Internal Revenue Code as follows:

§ 1.408A-1 Roth IRAs in general.

§ 1.408A-2 Establishing Roth IRAs.

§ 1.408A-3 Contributions to Roth IRAs.

§ 1.408A-4 Converting amounts to Roth IRAs.

§ 1.408A-5 Recharacterized contributions.

§ 1.408A-6 Distributions.

§ 1.408A-7 Reporting.

§ 1.408A-8 Definitions.

§ 1.408A-9 Effective date.
[Reg. § 1.408A-0.]
☐ [T.D. 8816, 2-3-99.]

[Reg. § 1.408A-1]

§ 1.408A-1. Roth IRAs in general.—This section sets forth the following questions and answers that discuss the background and general features of Roth IRAs:

Q-1 What is a Roth IRA?

A-1. (a) A Roth IRA is a new type of individual retirement plan that individuals can use, beginning in 1998. Roth IRAs are described in section 408A, which was added by the Taxpayer Relief Act of 1997 (TRA 97), Public Law 105-34 (111 Stat. 788).

(b) Roth IRAs are treated like traditional IRAs except where the Internal Revenue Code specifies different treatment. For example, aggregate contributions (other than by a conversion or other rollover) to all an individual's Roth IRAs are not permitted to exceed $2,000 for a taxable year. Further, income earned on funds held in a Roth IRA is generally not taxable. Similarly, the rules of section 408(e), such as the loss of exemption of the account where the owner engages in a prohibited transaction, apply to Roth IRAs in the same manner as to traditional IRAs.

Q-2. What are the significant differences between traditional IRAs and Roth IRAs?

A-2. There are several significant differences between traditional IRAs and Roth IRAs under the Internal Revenue Code. For example, eligibility to contribute to a Roth IRA is subject to special modified AGI (adjusted gross income) limits; contributions to a Roth IRA are never deductible; qualified distributions from a Roth IRA are not includible in gross income; the required minimum distribution rules under section 408(a)(6) and (b)(3) (which generally incorporate the provisions of section 401(a)(9)) do not apply to a Roth IRA during the lifetime of the owner; and contributions to a Roth IRA can be made after the owner has attained age 70 1/2.
[Reg. § 1.408A-1.]
☐ [T.D. 8816, 2-3-99.]

[Reg. § 1.408A-2]

§ 1.408A-2. Establishing Roth IRAs.—This section sets forth the following questions and answers that provide rules applicable to establishing Roth IRAs:

Q-1. Who can establish a Roth IRA?

A-1. Except as provided in A-3 of this section, only an individual can establish a Roth IRA. In addition, in order to be eligible to contribute to a Roth IRA for a particular year, an individual must satisfy certain compensation requirements and adjusted gross income limits (see § 1.408A-3 A-3).

Q-2. How is a Roth IRA established?

A-2. A Roth IRA can be established with any bank, insurance company, or other person authorized in accordance with § 1.408-2(e) to serve as a trustee with respect to IRAs. The document establishing the Roth IRA must clearly designate the IRA as a Roth IRA, and this designation cannot be changed at a later date. Thus, an IRA that is designated as a Roth IRA cannot later be treated as a traditional IRA. However, see § 1.408A-4 A-1(b)(3) for certain rules for converting a traditional IRA to a Roth IRA with the same trustee by redesignating the traditional IRA as a Roth IRA, and see § 1.408A-5 for rules for recharacterizing certain IRA contributions.

Q-3. Can an employer or an association of employees establish a Roth IRA to hold contributions of employees or members?

A-3. Yes. Pursuant to section 408(c), an employer or an association of employees can establish a trust to hold contributions of employees or members made under a Roth IRA. Each employee's or member's account in the trust is treated as a separate Roth IRA that is subject to the generally applicable Roth IRA rules. The employer or association of employees may do certain acts otherwise required by an individual, for example, establishing and designating a trust as a Roth IRA.

Q-4. What is the effect of a surviving spouse of a Roth IRA owner treating an IRA as his or her own?

A-4. If the surviving spouse of a Roth IRA owner treats a Roth IRA as his or her own as of a date, the Roth IRA is treated from that date forward as though it were established for the benefit of the surviving spouse and not the original Roth IRA owner. Thus, for example, the surviving spouse is treated as the Roth IRA owner for purposes of applying the minimum distribution requirements under section 408(a)(6) and (b)(3). Similarly, the surviving spouse is treated as the Roth IRA owner rather than a beneficiary for purposes of determining the amount of any distribution from the Roth IRA that is includible in gross income and whether the distribution is subject to the 10-percent additional tax under section 72(t).
[Reg. § 1.408A-2.]
☐ [T.D. 8816, 2-3-99.]

[Reg. § 1.408A-3]

§ 1.408A-3. Contributions to Roth IRAs.—This section sets forth the following questions and answers that provide rules regarding contributions to Roth IRAs:

Q-1. What types of contributions are permitted to be made to a Roth IRA?

A-1. There are two types of contributions that are permitted to be made to a Roth IRA: regular contributions and qualified rollover contributions (including conversion contributions). The term regular contributions means contributions other than qualified rollover contributions.

Q-2. When are contributions permitted to be made to a Roth IRA?

A-2. (a) The provisions of section 408A are effective for taxable years beginning on or after January 1, 1998. Thus, the first taxable year for which contributions are permitted to be made to a Roth IRA by an individual is the individual's taxable year beginning in 1998.

(b) Regular contributions for a particular taxable year must generally be contributed by the due date (not including extensions) for filing a Federal income tax return for that taxable year. (See § 1.408A-5 regarding recharacterization of certain contributions.)

Q-3. What is the maximum aggregate amount of regular contributions an individual is eligible to contribute to a Roth IRA for a taxable year?

A-3. (a) The maximum aggregate amount that an individual is eligible to contribute to all his or her Roth IRAs as a regular contribution for a taxable year is the same as the maximum for traditional IRAs: $2,000 or, if less, that individual's compensation for the year.

(b) For Roth IRAs, the maximum amount described in paragraph (a) of this A-3 is phased out between certain levels of modified AGI. For an individual who is not married, the dollar amount is phased out ratably between modified AGI of $95,000 and $110,000; for a married individual filing a joint return, between modified AGI of $150,000 and $160,000; and for a married individual filing separately, between modified AGI of $0 and $10,000. For this purpose, a married individual who has lived apart from his or her spouse for the entire taxable year and who files separately is treated as not married. Under section 408A(c)(3)(A), in applying the phase-out, the maximum amount is rounded up to the next higher multiple of $10 and is not reduced below $200 until completely phased out.

(c) If an individual makes regular contributions to both traditional IRAs and Roth IRAs for a taxable year, the maximum limit for the Roth IRA is the lesser of—

(1) The amount described in paragraph (a) of this A-3 reduced by the amount contributed to traditional IRAs for the taxable year; and

(2) The amount described in paragraph (b) of this A-3. Employer contributions, including elective deferrals, made under a SEP or SIMPLE IRA Plan on behalf of an individual (including a self-employed individual) do not reduce the amount of the individual's maximum regular contribution.

(d) The rules in this A-3 are illustrated by the following examples:

Example 1. In 1998, unmarried, calendar-year taxpayer B, age 60, has modified AGI of $40,000 and compensation of $5,000. For 1998, B can contribute a maximum of $2,000 to a traditional IRA, a Roth IRA or a combination of traditional and Roth IRAs.

Example 2. The facts are the same as in *Example 1.* However, assume that B violates the maximum regular contribution limit by contributing $2,000 to a traditional IRA and $2,000 to a Roth IRA for 1998. The $2,000 to B's Roth IRA would be an excess contribution to B's Roth IRA for 1998 because an individual's contributions are applied first to a traditional IRA, then to a Roth IRA.

Example 3. The facts are the same as in *Example 1,* except that B's compensation is $900. The maximum amount B can contribute to either a traditional IRA or a Roth (or a combination of the two) for 1998 is $900.

Example 4. In 1998, unmarried, calendar-year taxpayer C, age 60, has modified AGI of $100,000 and compensation of $5,000. For 1998, C contributes $800 to a traditional IRA and $1,200 to a Roth IRA.

Because C's $1,200 Roth IRA contribution does not exceed the phased-out maximum Roth IRA contribution of $1,340 and because C's total IRA contributions do not exceed $2,000, C's Roth IRA contribution does not exceed the maximum permissible contribution.

Q-4. How is compensation defined for purposes of the Roth IRA contribution limit?

A-4. For purposes of the contribution limit described in A-3 of this section, an individual's compensation is the same as that used to determine the maximum contribution an individual can make to a traditional IRA. This amount is defined in section 219(f)(1) to include wages, commissions, professional fees, tips, and other amounts received for personal services, as well as taxable alimony and separate maintenance payments received under a decree of divorce or separate maintenance. Compensation also includes earned income as defined in section 401(c)(2), but does not include any amount received as a pension or annuity or as deferred compensation. In addition, under section 219(c), a married individual filing a joint return is permitted to make an IRA contribution by treating his or her spouse's higher compensation as his or her own, but only to the extent that the spouse's compensation is not being used for purposes of the spouse making a contribution to a Roth IRA or a deductible contribution to a traditional IRA.

Q-5. What is the significance of modified AGI and how is it determined?

A-5. Modified AGI is used for purposes of the phase-out rules described in A-3 of this section and for purposes of the $100,000 modified AGI limitation described in §1.408A-4 A-2(a) (relating to eligibility for conversion). As defined in section 408A(c)(3)(C)(i), modified AGI is the same as adjusted gross income under section 219(g)(3)(A) (used to determine the amount of deductible contributions that can be made to a traditional IRA by an individual who is an active participant in an employer-sponsored retirement plan), except that any conversion is disregarded in determining modified AGI. For example, the deduction for contributions to an IRA is not taken into account for purposes of determining adjusted gross income under section 219 and thus does not apply in determining modified AGI for Roth IRA purposes.

Q-6. Is a required minimum distribution from an IRA for a year included in income for purposes of determining modified AGI?

A-6. (a) Yes. For taxable years beginning before January 1, 2005, any required minimum distribution from an IRA under section 408(a)(6) and (b)(3) (which generally incorporate the provisions of section 401(a)(9)) is included in income for purposes of determining modified AGI.

(b) For taxable years beginning after December 31, 2004, and solely for purposes of the $100,000 limitation applicable to conversions, modified AGI does not include any required minimum distributions from an IRA under section 408(a)(6) and (b)(3).

Q-7. Does an excise tax apply if an individual exceeds the aggregate regular contribution limits for Roth IRAs?

A-7. Yes. Section 4973 imposes an annual 6-percent excise tax on aggregate amounts contributed to Roth IRAs that exceed the maximum contribution limits described in A-3 of this section. Any contribution that is distributed, together with net income, from a Roth IRA on or before the tax return due date (plus extensions) for the taxable year of the contribution is treated as not contributed. Net income described in the previous sentence is includible in gross income for the taxable year in which the contribution is made. Aggregate excess contributions that are not distributed from a Roth IRA on or before the tax return due date (with extensions) for the taxable year of the contributions are reduced as a deemed Roth IRA contribution for each subsequent taxable year to the extent that the Roth IRA owner does not actually make regular IRA contributions for such years. Section 4973 applies separately to an individual's Roth IRAs and other types of IRAs.

[Reg. §1.408A-3.]

☐ [T.D. 8816, 2-3-99.]

[Reg. §1.408A-4]

§1.408A-4. Converting amounts to Roth IRAs.—This section sets forth the following questions and answers that provide rules applicable to Roth IRA conversions:

Q-1. Can an individual convert an amount in his or her traditional IRA to a Roth IRA?

A-1. (a) Yes. An amount in a traditional IRA may be converted to an amount in a Roth IRA if two requirements are satisfied. First, the IRA owner must satisfy the modified AGI limitation described in A-2(a) of this section and, if married, the joint filing requirement described in A-2(b) of this section. Second, the amount contributed to the Roth IRA must satisfy the definition of a qualified rollover contribution in section 408A(e) (i.e., it must satisfy the requirements for a rollover contribution as defined in section 408(d)(3), except that the one-rollover-per-year limitation in section 408(d)(3)(B) does not apply).

(b) An amount can be converted by any of three methods—

(1) An amount distributed from a traditional IRA is contributed (rolled over) to a Roth IRA within the 60-day period described in section 408(d)(3)(A)(i);

(2) An amount in a traditional IRA is transferred in a trustee-to-trustee transfer from the trustee of the traditional IRA to the trustee of the Roth IRA; or

(3) An amount in a traditional IRA is transferred to a Roth IRA maintained by the same trustee. For purposes of sections 408 and 408A, redesignating a traditional IRA as a Roth IRA is treated as a transfer of the entire account balance from a traditional IRA to a Roth IRA.

(c) Any converted amount is treated as a distribution from the traditional IRA and a qualified rollover contribution to the Roth IRA for purposes of section 408 and section 408A, even if the conversion is accomplished by means of a trustee-to-trustee transfer or a transfer between IRAs of the same trustee.

(d) A transaction that is treated as a failed conversion under §1.408A-5 A-9(a)(1) is not a conversion.

Q-2. What are the modified AGI limitation and joint filing requirements for conversions?

A-2. (a) An individual with modified AGI in excess of $100,000 for a taxable year is not permitted to convert an amount to a Roth IRA during that taxable year. This $100,000 limitation applies to the taxable year that the funds are paid from the traditional IRA, rather than the year they are contributed to the Roth IRA.

(b) If the individual is married, he or she is permitted to convert an amount to a Roth IRA during a taxable year only if the individual and the individual's spouse file a joint return for the taxable year that the funds are paid from the traditional IRA. In this case, the modified AGI subject to the $100,000 limit is the modified AGI derived from the joint return using the couple's combined income. The only exception to this joint filing requirement is for an individual who has lived apart from his or her spouse for the entire taxable year. If the married individual has lived apart from his or her spouse for the entire taxable year, then such individual can treat himself or herself as not married for purposes of this paragraph, file a separate return and be subject to the $100,000 limit on his or her separate modified AGI. In all other cases, a married individual filing a separate return is not permitted to convert an amount to a Roth IRA, regardless of the individual's modified AGI.

Q-3. Is a remedy available to an individual who makes a failed conversion?

A-3. (a) Yes. See §1.408A-5 for rules permitting a failed conversion amount to be recharacterized as a contribution to a traditional IRA. If the requirements in §1.408A-5 are satisfied, the failed conversion amount will be treated as having been contributed to the traditional IRA and not to the Roth IRA.

(b) If the contribution is not recharacterized in accordance with §1.408A-5, the contribution will be treated as a regular contribution to the Roth IRA and, thus, an excess contribution subject to the excise tax under section 4973 to the extent that it exceeds the individual's regular contribution limit. This is the result regardless of which of the three methods described in A-1(b) of this section applies to this transaction. Additionally, the distribution from the traditional IRA will not be eligible for the 4-year spread and will be subject to the additional tax under section 72(t) (unless an exception under that section applies).

Q-4. Do any special rules apply to a conversion of an amount in an individual's SEP IRA or SIMPLE IRA to a Roth IRA?

A-4. (a) An amount in an individual's SEP IRA can be converted to a Roth IRA on the same terms as an amount in any other traditional IRA.

(b) An amount in an individual's SIMPLE IRA can be converted to a Roth IRA on the same terms as a conversion from a traditional IRA, except that an amount distributed from a SIMPLE IRA during the 2-year period described in section 72(t)(6), which begins on the date that the individual first participated in any SIMPLE IRA Plan maintained by the individual's employer, cannot be converted to a Roth IRA. Pursuant to section 408(d)(3)(G), a distribution of an amount from an individual's SIMPLE IRA during this 2-year period is not eligible to be rolled over into an IRA that is not a SIMPLE IRA and thus cannot be a qualified rollover contribution. This 2-year period of section 408(d)(3)(G) applies separately to the contributions of each of an individual's employers maintaining a SIMPLE IRA Plan.

(c) Once an amount in a SEP IRA or SIMPLE IRA has been converted to a Roth IRA, it is treated as a contribution to a Roth IRA for all purposes. Future contributions under the SEP or under the SIMPLE IRA Plan may not be made to the Roth IRA.

Q-5. Can amounts in other kinds of retirement plans be converted to a Roth IRA?

A-5. No. Only amounts in another IRA can be converted to a Roth IRA. For example, amounts in a qualified plan or annuity plan described in section 401(a) or 403(a) cannot be converted directly to a

Roth IRA. Also, amounts held in an annuity contract or account described in section 403(b) cannot be converted directly to a Roth IRA.

Q-6. Can an individual who has attained at least age 70 1/2 by the end of a calendar year convert an amount distributed from a traditional IRA during that year to a Roth IRA before receiving his or her required minimum distribution with respect to the traditional IRA for the year of the conversion?

A-6. (a) No. In order to be eligible for a conversion, an amount first must be eligible to be rolled over. Section 408(d)(3) prohibits the rollover of a required minimum distribution. If a minimum distribution is required for a year with respect to an IRA, the first dollars distributed during that year are treated as consisting of the required minimum distribution until an amount equal to the required minimum distribution for that year has been distributed.

(b) As provided in A-1(c) of this section, any amount converted is treated as a distribution from a traditional IRA and a rollover contribution to a Roth IRA and not as a trustee-to-trustee transfer for purposes of section 408 and section 408A. Thus, in a year for which a minimum distribution is required (including the calendar year in which the individual attains age 70 1/2), an individual may not convert the assets of an IRA (or any portion of those assets) to a Roth IRA to the extent that the required minimum distribution for the traditional IRA for the year has not been distributed.

(c) If a required minimum distribution is contributed to a Roth IRA, it is treated as having been distributed, subject to the normal rules under section 408(d)(1) and (2), and then contributed as a regular contribution to a Roth IRA. The amount of the required minimum distribution is not a conversion contribution.

Q-7. What are the tax consequences when an amount is converted to a Roth IRA?

A-7. (a) Any amount that is converted to a Roth IRA is includible in gross income as a distribution according to the rules of section 408(d)(1) and (2) for the taxable year in which the amount is distributed or transferred from the traditional IRA. Thus, any portion of the distribution or transfer that is treated as a return of basis under section 408(d)(1) and (2) is not includible in gross income as a result of the conversion.

(b) The 10-percent additional tax under section 72(t) generally does not apply to the taxable conversion amount. But see § 1.408A-6 A-5 for circumstances under which the taxable conversion amount would be subject to the additional tax under section 72(t).

(c) Pursuant to section 408A(e), a conversion is not treated as a rollover for purposes of the one-rollover-per-year rule of section 408(d)(3)(B).

Q-8. Is there an exception to the income-inclusion rule described in A-7 of this section for 1998 conversions?

A-8. Yes. In the case of a distribution (including a trustee-to-trustee transfer) from a traditional IRA on or before December 31, 1998, that is converted to a Roth IRA, instead of having the entire taxable conversion amount includible in income in 1998, an individual includes in gross income for 1998 only one quarter of that amount and one quarter of that amount for each of the next 3 years. This 4-year spread also applies if the conversion amount was distributed in 1998 and contributed to the Roth IRA within the 60-day period described in section 408(d)(3)(A)(i), but after December 31, 1998. However, see § 1.408A-6 A-6 for special rules requiring acceleration of inclusion if an amount subject to the 4-year spread is distributed from the Roth IRA before 2001.

Q-9. Is the taxable conversion amount included in income for all purposes?

A-9. Except as provided below, any taxable conversion amount includible in gross income for a year as a result of the conversion (regardless of whether the individual is using a 4-year spread) is included in income for all purposes. Thus, for example, it is counted for purposes of determining the taxable portion of social security payments under section 86 and for purposes of determining the phase-out of the $25,000 exemption under section 469(i) relating to the disallowance of passive activity losses from rental real estate activities. However, as provided in § 1.408A-3 A-5, the taxable conversion amount (and any resulting change in other elements of adjusted gross income) is disregarded for purposes of determining modified AGI for section 408A.

Q-10. Can an individual who makes a 1998 conversion elect not to have the 4-year spread apply and instead have the full taxable conversion amount includible in gross income for 1998?

A-10. Yes. Instead of having the taxable conversion amount for a 1998 conversion included over 4 years as provided under A-8 of this section, an individual can elect to include the full taxable conversion amount in income for 1998. The election is made on Form 8606 and cannot be made or changed after the due date (including extensions) for filing the 1998 Federal income tax return.

Q-11. What happens when an individual who is using the 4-year spread dies, files separately, or divorces before the full taxable conversion amount has been included in gross income?

A-11. (a) If an individual who is using the 4-year spread described in A-8 of this section dies before the full taxable conversion amount has been included in gross income, then the remainder must be included in the individual's gross income for the taxable year that includes the date of death.

(b) However, if the sole beneficiary of all the decedent's Roth IRAs is the decedent's spouse, then the spouse can elect to continue the 4-year spread. Thus, the spouse can elect to include in gross income the same amount that the decedent would have included in each of the remaining years of the 4-year period. Where the spouse makes such an election, the amount includible under the 4-year spread for the taxable year that includes the date of the decedent's death remains includible in the decedent's gross income and is reported on the decedent's final Federal income tax return. The election is made on either Form 8606 or Form 1040, in accordance with the instructions to the applicable form, for the taxable year that includes the decedent's date of death and cannot be changed after the due date (including extensions) for filing the Federal income tax return for the spouse's taxable year that includes the decedent's date of death.

(c) If a Roth IRA owner who is using the 4-year spread and who was married in 1998 subsequently files separately or divorces before the full taxable conversion amount has been included in gross income, the remainder of the taxable conversion amount must be included in the Roth IRA owner's gross income over the remaining years in the 4-year period (unless accelerated because of distribution or death).

Q-12. Can an individual convert a traditional IRA to a Roth IRA if he or she is receiving substantially equal periodic payments within the meaning of section 72(t)(2)(A)(iv) from that traditional IRA?

A-12. Yes. Not only is the conversion amount itself not subject to the early distribution tax under section 72(t), but the conversion amount is also not treated as a distribution for purposes of determining whether a modification within the meaning of section 72(t)(4)(A) has occurred. Distributions from the Roth IRA that are part of the original series of substantially equal periodic payments will be nonqualified distributions from the Roth IRA until they meet the requirements for being a qualified distribution, described in § 1.408A-6 A-1(b). The additional 10-percent tax under section 72(t) will not apply to the extent that these nonqualified distributions are part of a series of substantially equal periodic payments. Nevertheless, to the extent that such distributions are allocable to a 1998 conversion contribution with respect to which the 4-year spread for the resultant income inclusion applies (see A-8 of this section) and are received during 1998, 1999, or 2000, the special acceleration rules of § 1.408A-6 A-6 apply. However, if the original series of substantially equal periodic payments does not continue to be distributed in substantially equal periodic payments from the Roth IRA after the conversion, the series of payments will have been modified and, if this modification occurs within 5 years of the first payment or prior to the individual becoming disabled or attaining age 59 1/2, the taxpayer will be subject to the recapture tax of section 72(t)(4)(A).

Q-13. Can a 1997 distribution from a traditional IRA be converted to a Roth IRA in 1998?

A-13. No. An amount distributed from a traditional IRA in 1997 that is contributed to a Roth IRA in 1998 would not be a conversion contribution. See A-3 of this section regarding the remedy for a failed conversion.

Q-14. What is the amount that is treated as a distribution, for purposes of determining income inclusion, when a conversion involves an annuity contract?

A-14. (a) *In general*—(1) *Distribution of Fair Market Value Upon Conversion.* Notwithstanding § 1.408-4(e), when part or all of a traditional IRA that is an individual retirement annuity described in section 408(b) is converted to a Roth IRA, for purposes of determining the amount includible in gross income as a distribution under § 1.408A-4, A-7, the amount that is treated as distributed is the fair market value of the annuity contract on the date the annuity contract is converted. Similarly, when a traditional IRA that is an individual retirement account described in section 408(a) holds an annuity contract as an account asset and the traditional IRA is converted to a Roth IRA, for purposes of determining the amount includible in gross income as a distribution under § 1.408A-4, A-7, the amount that is treated as distributed with respect to the annuity contract is the fair market value of the annuity contract on the date that the annuity contract is distributed or treated as distributed from the traditional IRA. The rules in this A-14 also apply to conversions from SIMPLE IRAs.

(2) *Annuity contract surrendered.* Paragraph (a)(1) of this paragraph A-14 does not apply to a conversion of a traditional IRA to the extent the conversion is accomplished by the complete surrender of an annuity contract for its cash value and the reinvestment of the cash

proceeds in a Roth IRA, but only if the surrender extinguishes all benefits and other characteristics of the contract. In such a case, the cash from the surrendered contract is the amount reinvested in the Roth IRA.

(3) *Definitions.* The definitions set forth in §1.408A-8 apply for purposes of this paragraph A-14.

(b) *Determination of fair market value*—(1) *Overview*—(i) *Use of alternative methods.* This paragraph (b) sets forth methods which may be used to determine the fair market value of an individual retirement annuity for purposes of paragraph (a)(1) of this paragraph A-14. However, if, because of the unusual nature of the contract, the value determined under one of these methods does not reflect the full value of the contract, that method may not be used.

(ii) *Additional guidance.* Additional guidance regarding the fair market value of an individual retirement annuity, including formulas to be used for determining fair market value, may be issued by the Commissioner in revenue rulings, notices, or other guidance published in the Internal Revenue Bulletin (see §601.601(d)(2)(ii)(b)).

(2) *Gift tax method*—(i) *Cost of contract or comparable contract.* If with respect to an annuity, there is a comparable contract issued by the company which sold the annuity, the fair market value of the annuity may be established by the price of the comparable contract. If the conversion occurs soon after the annuity was sold, the comparable contract may be the annuity itself, and thus, the fair market value of the annuity may be established through the sale of the particular contract by the company (that is, the actual premiums paid for such contract).

(ii) *Use of reserves where no comparable contract available.* If with respect to an annuity, there is no comparable contract available in order to make the comparison described in paragraph (b)(2)(i) of this paragraph A-14, the fair market value may be established through an approximation that is based on the interpolated terminal reserve at the date of the conversion, plus the proportionate part of the gross premium last paid before the date of the conversion which covers the period extending beyond that date.

(3) *Accumulation method.* As an alternative to the gift tax method described in paragraph (b)(2) of this paragraph A-14, this paragraph (b)(3) provides a method that may be used for an annuity contract which has not been annuitized. The fair market value of such an annuity contract is permitted to be determined using the methodology provided in §1.401(a)(9)-6, A-12, with the following modifications:

(i) All front-end loads and other non-recurring charges assessed in the twelve months immediately preceding the conversion must be added to the account value.

(ii) Future distributions are not to be assumed in the determination of the actuarial present value of additional benefits.

(iii) The exclusions provided under §1.401(a)(9)-6, A-12(c)(1) and (c)(2), are not to be taken into account.

(c) *Effective/applicability date.* The provisions of this paragraph A-14 are applicable to any conversion in which an annuity contract is distributed or treated as distributed from a traditional IRA on or after August 19, 2005. However, for annuity contracts distributed or treated as distributed from a traditional IRA on or before December 31, 2008, taxpayers may instead apply the valuation methods in §1.408A-4T (as it appeared in the April 1, 2008, edition of 26 CFR

part 1) and Revenue Procedure 2006-13 (2006-1 CB 315) (See §601.601(d)(2)(ii)(b)).
[Reg. §1.408A-4.]

☐ [T.D. 8816, 2-3-99. *Amended by T.D. 9220, 8-19-2005 and T.D. 9418, 7-28-2008.*]

[Reg. §1.408A-5]

§1.408A-5. Recharacterized contributions.—This section sets forth the following questions and answers that provide rules regarding recharacterizing IRA contributions:

Q-1. Can an IRA owner recharacterize certain contributions (i.e., treat a contribution made to one type of IRA as made to a different type of IRA) for a taxable year?

A-1. (a) Yes. In accordance with section 408A(d)(6), except as otherwise provided in this section, if an individual makes a contribution to an IRA (the FIRST IRA) for a taxable year and then transfers the contribution (or a portion of the contribution) in a trustee-to-trustee transfer from the trustee of the FIRST IRA to the trustee of another IRA (the SECOND IRA), the individual can elect to treat the contribution as having been made to the SECOND IRA, instead of to the FIRST IRA, for Federal tax purposes. A transfer between the FIRST IRA and the SECOND IRA will not fail to be a trustee-to-trustee transfer merely because both IRAs are maintained by the same trustee. For purposes of section 408A(d)(6), redesignating the FIRST IRA as the SECOND IRA will be treated as a transfer of the entire account balance from the FIRST IRA to the SECOND IRA.

(b) This recharacterization election can be made only if the trustee-to-trustee transfer from the FIRST IRA to the SECOND IRA is made on or before the due date (including extensions) for filing the individual's Federal income tax return for the taxable year for which the contribution was made to the FIRST IRA. For purposes of this section, a conversion that is accomplished through a rollover of a distribution from a traditional IRA in a taxable year that, 60 days after the distribution (as described in section 408(d)(3)(A)(i)), is contributed to a Roth IRA in the next taxable year is treated as a contribution for the earlier taxable year.

Q-2. What is the proper treatment of the net income attributable to the amount of a contribution that is being recharacterized?

A-2. (a) The net income attributable to the amount of a contribution that is being recharacterized must be transferred to the SECOND IRA along with the contribution.

(b) If the amount of the contribution being recharacterized was contributed to a separate IRA and no distributions or additional contributions have been made from or to that IRA at any time, then the contribution is recharacterized by the trustee of the FIRST IRA transferring the entire account balance of the FIRST IRA to the trustee of the SECOND IRA. In this case, the net income (or loss) attributable to the contribution being recharacterized is the difference between the amount of the original contribution and the amount transferred.

(c)(1) If paragraph (b) of this A-2 does not apply, then, for purposes of determining net income attributable to IRA contributions, the net income attributable to the amount of a contribution is determined by allocating to the contribution a pro-rata portion of the earnings on the assets in the IRA during the period the IRA held the contribution. This attributable net income is calculated by using the following formula:

$$\text{Net Income} = \text{Contribution} \times \frac{(\text{Adjusted Closing Balance} - \text{Adjusted Opening Balance})}{\text{Adjusted Opening Balance}}.$$

(2) For purposes of this paragraph (c), the following definitions apply:

(i) The term *adjusted opening balance* means the fair market value of the IRA at the beginning of the computation period plus the amount of any contributions or transfers (including the contribution that is being recharacterized pursuant to section 408A(d)(6) and any other recharacterizations) made to the IRA during the computation period.

(ii) The term *adjusted closing balance* means the fair market value of the IRA at the end of the computation period plus the amount of any distributions or transfers (including contributions returned pursuant to section 408(d)(4) and recharacterizations of contributions pursuant to section 408A(d)(6)) made from the IRA during the computation period.

(iii) The term *computation period* means the period beginning immediately prior to the time the particular contribution being recharacterized is made to the IRA and ending immediately prior to the recharacterizing transfer of the contribution. If a series of regular contributions was made to the IRA, and consecutive contributions in that series are being recharacterized, the computation period begins immediately prior to the time the first of the regular contributions being recharacterized was made.

(3) When an IRA asset is not normally valued on a daily basis, the fair market value of the asset at the beginning of the computation period is deemed to be the most recent, regularly determined, fair

market value of the asset, determined as of a date that coincides with or precedes the first day of the computation period. In addition, solely for purposes of this paragraph (c), notwithstanding A-3 of this section, recharacterized contributions are taken into account for the period they are actually held in a particular IRA.

(4) In the case of an individual with multiple IRAs, the net income calculation is performed only on the IRA containing the particular contribution to be recharacterized and that IRA is the IRA from which the recharacterizing transfer must be made.

(5) In the case of multiple contributions made to an IRA for a particular year that are eligible for recharacterization, the IRA owner can choose (by date and by dollar amount, not by specific assets acquired with those dollars) which contribution, or portion thereof, is to be recharacterized.

(6) The following examples illustrate the net income calculation under section 408A(d)(6) and this paragraph:

Example 1. (i) On March 1, 2004, when her Roth IRA is worth $80,000, Taxpayer A makes a $160,000 conversion contribution to the Roth IRA. Subsequently, Taxpayer A discovers that she was ineligible to make a Roth conversion contribution in 2004 and so she requests that the $160,000 be recharacterized to a traditional IRA pursuant to section 408A(d)(6). Pursuant to this request, on March 1, 2005, when the IRA is worth $225,000, the Roth IRA trustee transfers to a traditional IRA the $160,000 plus allocable net income. No other contributions have been made to the Roth IRA and no distributions have been made.

(ii) The adjusted opening balance is $240,000 [$80,000 + $160,000]and the adjusted closing balance is $225,000. Thus the net income allocable to the $160,000 is –$10,000 [$160,000 × ($225,000 – $240,000)/$240,000]. Therefore, in order to recharacterize the March 1, 2004, $160,000 conversion contribution on March 1, 2005, the Roth IRA trustee must transfer from Taxpayer A's Roth IRA to her traditional IRA $150,000 [$160,000 – $10,000].

Example 2. (i) On April 1, 2004, when her traditional IRA is worth $100,000, Taxpayer B converts the entire amount, consisting of 100 shares of stock in ABC Corp. and 100 shares of stock in XYZ Corp., by transferring the shares to a Roth IRA. At the time of the conversion, the 100 shares of stock in ABC Corp. are worth $50,000 and the 100 shares of stock in XYZ Corp. are also worth $50,000. Taxpayer B decides that she would like to recharacterize the ABC Corp. shares back to a traditional IRA. However, B may choose only by dollar amount the contribution or portion thereof that is to be recharacterized. On the date of transfer, November 1, 2004, the 100 shares of stock in ABC Corp. are worth $40,000 and the 100 shares of stock in XYZ Corp. are worth $70,000. No other contributions have been made to the Roth IRA and no distributions have been made.

(ii) If B requests that $50,000 (which was the value of the ABC Corp. shares at the time of conversion) be recharacterized, the net income allocable to the $50,000 is $5,000 [$50,000 × ($110,000 – $100,000)/$100,000]. Therefore, in order to recharacterize $50,000 of the April 1, 2004, conversion contribution on November 1, 2004, the Roth IRA trustee must transfer from Taxpayer B's Roth IRA to a traditional IRA assets with a value of $55,000 [$50,000 + $5,000].

(iii) If, on the other hand, B requests that $40,000 (which was the value of the ABC Corp. shares on November 1) be recharacterized, the net income allocable to the $40,000 is $4,000 [$40,000 × ($110,000 – $100,000)/$100,000]. Therefore, in order to recharacterize $40,000 of the April 1, 2004, conversion contribution on November 1, 2004, the Roth IRA trustee must transfer from Taxpayer B's Roth IRA to a traditional IRA assets with a value of $44,000 [$40,000 + $4,000].

(iv) Regardless of the amount of the contribution recharacterized, the determination of that amount (or of the net income allocable thereto) is not affected by whether the recharacterization is accomplished by the transfer of shares of ABC Corp. or of shares of XYZ Corp.

(7) This paragraph (c) applies for purposes of determining net income attributable to IRA contributions, made on or after January 1, 2004. For purposes of determining net income attributable to IRA contributions made before January 1, 2004, see paragraph (c) of this A-2 of § 1.408A-5 (as it appeared in the April 1, 2003, edition of 26 CFR part 1).

Q-3. What is the effect of recharacterizing a contribution made to the FIRST IRA as a contribution made to the SECOND IRA?

A-3. The contribution that is being recharacterized as a contribution to the SECOND IRA is treated as having been originally contributed to the SECOND IRA on the same date and (in the case of a regular contribution) for the same taxable year that the contribution was made to the FIRST IRA. Thus, for example, no deduction would be allowed for a contribution to the FIRST IRA, and any net income transferred with the recharacterized contribution is treated as earned in the SECOND IRA, and not the FIRST IRA.

Q-4. Can an amount contributed to an IRA in a tax-free transfer be recharacterized under A-1 of this section?

A-4. No. If an amount is contributed to the FIRST IRA in a tax-free transfer, the amount cannot be recharacterized as a contribution to the SECOND IRA under A-1 of this section. However, if an amount is erroneously rolled over or transferred from a traditional IRA to a SIMPLE IRA, the contribution can subsequently be recharacterized as a contribution to another traditional IRA.

Q-5. Can an amount contributed by an employer under a SIMPLE IRA Plan or a SEP be recharacterized under A-1 of this section?

A-5. No. Employer contributions (including elective deferrals) under a SIMPLE IRA Plan or a SEP cannot be recharacterized as contributions to another IRA under A-1 of this section. However, an amount converted from a SEP IRA or SIMPLE IRA to a Roth IRA may be recharacterized under A-1 of this section as a contribution to a SEP IRA or SIMPLE IRA, including the original SEP IRA or SIMPLE IRA.

Q-6. How does a taxpayer make the election to recharacterize a contribution to an IRA for a taxable year?

A-6. (a) An individual makes the election described in this section by notifying, on or before the date of the transfer, both the trustee of the FIRST IRA and the trustee of the SECOND IRA, that the individual has elected to treat the contribution as having been made to the SECOND IRA, instead of the FIRST IRA, for Federal tax purposes. The notification of the election must include the following information: the type and amount of the contribution to the FIRST IRA that is to be recharacterized; the date on which the contribution was made

to the FIRST IRA and the year for which it was made; a direction to the trustee of the FIRST IRA to transfer, in a trustee-to-trustee transfer, the amount of the contribution and net income allocable to the contribution to the trustee of the SECOND IRA; and the name of the trustee of the FIRST IRA and the trustee of the SECOND IRA and any additional information needed to make the transfer.

(b) The election and the trustee-to-trustee transfer must occur on or before the due date (including extensions) for filing the individual's Federal income tax return for the taxable year for which the recharacterized contribution was made to the FIRST IRA, and the election cannot be revoked after the transfer. An individual who makes this election must report the recharacterization, and must treat the contribution as having been made to the SECOND IRA, instead of the FIRST IRA, on the individual's Federal income tax return for the taxable year described in the preceding sentence in accordance with the applicable Federal tax forms and instructions.

(c) The election to recharacterize a contribution described in this A-6 may be made on behalf of a deceased IRA owner by his or her executor, administrator, or other person responsible for filing the final Federal income tax return of the decedent under section 6012(b)(1).

Q-7. If an amount is initially contributed to an IRA for a taxable year, then is moved (with net income attributable to the contribution) in a tax-free transfer to another IRA (the FIRST IRA for purposes of A-1 of this section), can the tax-free transfer be disregarded, so that the initial contribution that is transferred from the FIRST IRA to the SECOND IRA is treated as a recharacterization of that initial contribution?

A-7. Yes. In applying section 408A(d)(6), tax-free transfers between IRAs are disregarded. Thus, if a contribution to an IRA for a year is followed by one or more tax-free transfers between IRAs prior to the recharacterization, then for purposes of section 408A(d)(6), the contribution is treated as if it remained in the initial IRA. Consequently, an individual may elect to recharacterize an initial contribution made to the initial IRA that was involved in a series of tax-free transfers by making a trustee-to-trustee transfer from the last IRA in the series to the SECOND IRA. In this case the contribution to the SECOND IRA is treated as made on the same date (and for the same taxable year) as the date the contribution being recharacterized was made to the initial IRA.

Q-8. If a contribution is recharacterized, is the recharacterization treated as a rollover for purposes of the one-rollover-per-year limitation of section 408(d)(3)(B)?

A-8. No, recharacterizing a contribution under A-1 of this section is never treated as a rollover for purposes of the one-rollover-per-year limitation of section 408(d)(3)(B), even if the contribution would have been treated as a rollover contribution by the SECOND IRA if it had been made directly to the SECOND IRA, rather than as a result of a recharacterization of a contribution to the FIRST IRA.

Q-9. If an IRA owner converts an amount from a traditional IRA to a Roth IRA and then transfers that amount back to a traditional IRA in a recharacterization, may the IRA owner subsequently reconvert that amount from the traditional IRA to a Roth IRA?

A-9. (a)(1) Except as otherwise provided in paragraph (b) of this A-9, an IRA owner who converts an amount from a traditional IRA to a Roth IRA during any taxable year and then transfers that amount back to a traditional IRA by means of a recharacterization may not reconvert that amount from the traditional IRA to a Roth IRA before the beginning of the taxable year following the taxable year in which the amount was converted to a Roth IRA or, if later, the end of the 30-day period beginning on the day on which the IRA owner transfers the amount from the Roth IRA back to a traditional IRA by means of a recharacterization (regardless of whether the recharacterization occurs during the taxable year in which the amount was converted to a Roth IRA or the following taxable year). Thus, any attempted reconversion of an amount prior to the time permitted under this paragraph (a)(1) is a failed conversion of that amount. However, see § 1.408A-4 A-3 for a remedy available to an individual who makes a failed conversion.

(2) For purposes of paragraph (a)(1) of this A-9, a failed conversion of an amount resulting from a failure to satisfy the requirements of § 1.408A-4 A-1(a) is treated as a conversion in determining whether an IRA owner has previously converted that amount.

(b)(1) An IRA owner who converts an amount from a traditional IRA to a Roth IRA during taxable year 1998 and then transfers that amount back to a traditional IRA by means of a recharacterization may reconvert that amount once (but no more than once) on or after November 1, 1998 and on or before December 31, 1998; the IRA owner may also reconvert that amount once (but no more than once) during 1999. The rule set forth in the preceding sentence applies without regard to whether the IRA owner's initial conversion or recharacterization of the amount occurred before, on, or after November 1, 1998. An IRA owner who converts an amount from a traditional IRA to a Roth IRA during taxable year 1999 that has not been converted previously and then transfers that amount back to a traditional IRA by means of a recharacterization may reconvert that amount once (but no more than once) on or before December 31, 1999. For purposes of this paragraph (b)(1), a failed conversion of an amount resulting from a failure to satisfy the requirements of §1.408A-4 A-1(a) is not treated as a conversion in determining whether an IRA owner has previously converted that amount.

(2) A reconversion by an IRA owner during 1998 or 1999 for which the IRA owner is not eligible under paragraph (b)(1) of this A-9 will be deemed an excess reconversion (rather than a failed conversion) and will not change the IRA owner's taxable conversion amount. Instead, the excess reconversion and the last preceding recharacterization will not be taken into account for purposes of determining the IRA owner's taxable conversion amount, and the IRA owner's taxable conversion amount will be based on the last reconversion that was not an excess reconversion (unless, after the excess reconversion, the amount is transferred back to a traditional IRA by means of a recharacterization). An excess reconversion will otherwise be treated as a valid reconversion.

(3) For purposes of this paragraph (b), any reconversion that an IRA owner made before November 1, 1998 will not be treated as an excess reconversion and will not be taken into account in determining whether any later reconversion is an excess reconversion.

(c) In determining the portion of any amount held in a Roth IRA or a traditional IRA that an IRA owner may not reconvert under this A-9, any amount previously converted (or reconverted) is adjusted for subsequent net income thereon.

Q-10. Are there examples to illustrate the rules in this section?

A-10. The rules in this section are illustrated by the following examples:

Example 1. In 1998, Individual C converts the entire amount in his traditional IRA to a Roth IRA. Individual C thereafter determines that his modified AGI for 1998 exceeded $100,000 so that he was ineligible to have made a conversion in that year. Accordingly, prior to the due date (plus extensions) for filing the individual's Federal income tax return for 1998, he decides to recharacterize the conversion contribution. He instructs the trustee of the Roth IRA (FIRST IRA) to transfer in a trustee-to-trustee transfer the amount of the contribution, plus net income, to the trustee of a new traditional IRA (SECOND IRA). The individual notifies the trustee of the FIRST IRA and the trustee of the SECOND IRA that he is recharacterizing his IRA contribution (and provides the other information described in A-6 of this section). On the individual's Federal income tax return for 1998, he treats the original amount of the conversion as having been contributed to the SECOND IRA and not the Roth IRA. As a result, for Federal tax purposes, the contribution is treated as having been made to the SECOND IRA and not to the Roth IRA. The result would be the same if the conversion amount had been transferred in a tax-free transfer to another Roth IRA prior to the recharacterization.

Example 2. In 1998, an individual makes a $2,000 regular contribution for 1998 to his traditional IRA (FIRST IRA). Prior to the due date (plus extensions) for filing the individual's Federal income tax return for 1998, he decides that he would prefer to contribute to a Roth IRA instead. The individual instructs the trustee of the FIRST IRA to transfer in a trustee-to-trustee transfer the amount of the contribution, plus attributable net income, to the trustee of a Roth IRA (SECOND IRA). The individual notifies the trustee of the FIRST IRA and the trustee of the SECOND IRA that he is recharacterizing his $2,000 contribution for 1998 (and provides the other information described in A-6 of this section). On the individual's Federal income tax return for 1998, he treats the $2,000 as having been contributed to the Roth IRA for 1998 and not to the traditional IRA. As a result, for Federal tax purposes, the contribution is treated as having been made to the Roth IRA for 1998 and not to the traditional IRA. The result would be the same if the conversion amount had been transferred in a tax-free transfer to another traditional IRA prior to the recharacterization.

Example 3. The facts are the same as in *Example 2*, except that the $2,000 regular contribution is initially made to a Roth IRA and the recharacterizing transfer is made to a traditional IRA. On the individual's Federal income tax return for 1998, he treats the $2,000 as having been contributed to the traditional IRA for 1998 and not the Roth IRA. As a result, for Federal tax purposes, the contribution is treated as having been made to the traditional IRA for 1998 and not the Roth IRA. The result would be the same if the contribution had been transferred in a tax-free transfer to another Roth IRA prior to the recharacterization, except that the only Roth IRA trustee the individual must notify is the one actually making the recharacterization transfer.

Example 4. In 1998, an individual receives a distribution from traditional IRA 1 and contributes the entire amount to traditional IRA 2 in a rollover contribution described in section 408(d)(3). In this case, the individual cannot elect to recharacterize the contribution by transferring the contribution amount, plus net income, to a Roth IRA,

because an amount contributed to an IRA in a tax-free transfer cannot be recharacterized. However, the individual may convert (other than by recharacterization) the amount in traditional IRA 2 to a Roth IRA at any time, provided the requirements of §1.408A-4 A-1 are satisfied.

[Reg. §1.408A-5.]

☐ [*T.D.* 8816, 2-3-99. *Amended by T.D.* 9056, 5-2-2003.]

[Reg. §1.408A-6]

§1.408A-6. Distributions.—This section sets forth the following questions and answers that provide rules regarding distributions from Roth IRAs:

Q-1. How are distributions from Roth IRAs taxed?

A-1. (a) The taxability of a distribution from a Roth IRA generally depends on whether or not the distribution is a qualified distribution. This A-1 provides rules for qualified distributions and certain other nontaxable distributions. A-4 of this section provides rules for the taxability of distributions that are not qualified distributions.

(b) A distribution from a Roth IRA is not includible in the owner's gross income if it is a qualified distribution or to the extent that it is a return of the owner's contributions to the Roth IRA (determined in accordance with A-8 of this section). A qualified distribution is one that is both—

(1) Made after a 5-taxable-year period (defined in A-2 of this section); and

(2) Made on or after the date on which the owner attains age 59 1/2, made to a beneficiary or the estate of the owner on or after the date of the owner's death, attributable to the owner's being disabled within the meaning of section 72(m)(7), or to which section 72(t)(2)(F) applies (exception for first-time home purchase).

(c) An amount distributed from a Roth IRA will not be included in gross income to the extent it is rolled over to another Roth IRA on a tax-free basis under the rules of sections 408(d)(3) and 408A(e).

(d) Contributions that are returned to the Roth IRA owner in accordance with section 408(d)(4) (corrective distributions) are not includible in gross income, but any net income required to be distributed under section 408(d)(4) together with the contributions is includible in gross income for the taxable year in which the contributions were made.

Q-2. When does the 5-taxable-year period described in A-1 of this section (relating to qualified distributions) begin and end?

A-2. The 5-taxable-year period described in A-1 of this section begins on the first day of the individual's taxable year for which the first regular contribution is made to any Roth IRA of the individual or, if earlier, the first day of the individual's taxable year in which the first conversion contribution is made to any Roth IRA of the individual. The 5-taxable-year period ends on the last day of the individual's fifth consecutive taxable year beginning with the taxable year described in the preceding sentence. For example, if an individual whose taxable year is the calendar year makes a first-time regular Roth IRA contribution any time between January 1, 1998, and April 15, 1999, for 1998, the 5-taxable-year period begins on January 1, 1998. Thus, each Roth IRA owner has only one 5-taxable-year period described in A-1 of this section for all the Roth IRAs of which he or she is the owner. Further, because of the requirement of the 5-taxable-year period, no qualified distributions can occur before taxable years beginning in 2003. For purposes of this A-2, the amount of any contribution distributed as a corrective distribution under A-1(d) of this section is treated as if it was never contributed.

Q-3. If a distribution is made to an individual who is the sole beneficiary of his or her deceased spouse's Roth IRA and the individual is treating the Roth IRA as his or her own, can the distribution be a qualified distribution based on being made to a beneficiary on or after the owner's death?

A-3. No. If a distribution is made to an individual who is the sole beneficiary of his or her deceased spouse's Roth IRA and the individual is treating the Roth IRA as his or her own, then, in accordance with §1.408A-2 A-4, the distribution is treated as coming from the individual's own Roth IRA and not the deceased spouse's Roth IRA. Therefore, for purposes of determining whether the distribution is a qualified distribution, it is not treated as made to a beneficiary on or after the owner's death.

Q-4. How is a distribution from a Roth IRA taxed if it is not a qualified distribution?

A-4. A distribution that is not a qualified distribution, and is neither contributed to another Roth IRA in a qualified rollover contribution nor constitutes a corrective distribution, is includible in the owner's gross income to the extent that the amount of the distribution, when added to the amount of all prior distributions from the owner's Roth IRAs (whether or not they were qualified distributions) and reduced by the amount of those prior distributions previously includible in gross income, exceeds the owner's contributions to all his or her Roth IRAs. For purposes of this A-4, any amount distributed as a corrective distribution is treated as if it was never contributed.

Q-5. Will the additional tax under 72(t) apply to the amount of a distribution that is not a qualified distribution?

A-5. (a) The 10-percent additional tax under section 72(t) will apply (unless the distribution is excepted under section 72(t)) to any distribution from a Roth IRA includible in gross income.

(b) The 10-percent additional tax under section 72(t) also applies to a nonqualified distribution, even if it is not then includible in gross income, to the extent it is allocable to a conversion contribution, if the distribution is made within the 5-taxable-year period beginning with the first day of the individual's taxable year in which the conversion contribution was made. The 5-taxable-year period ends on the last day of the individual's fifth consecutive taxable year beginning with the taxable year described in the preceding sentence. For purposes of applying the tax, only the amount of the conversion contribution includible in gross income as a result of the conversion is taken into account. The exceptions under section 72(t) also apply to such a distribution.

(c) The 5-taxable-year period described in this A-5 for purposes of determining whether section 72(t) applies to a distribution allocable to a conversion contribution is separately determined for each conversion contribution, and need not be the same as the 5-taxable-year period used for purposes of determining whether a distribution is a qualified distribution under A-1(b) of this section. For example, if a calendar-year taxpayer who received a distribution from a traditional IRA on December 31, 1998, makes a conversion contribution by contributing the distributed amount to a Roth IRA on February 25, 1999 in a qualifying rollover contribution and makes a regular contribution for 1998 on the same date, the 5-taxable-year period for purposes of this A-5 begins on January 1, 1999, while the 5-taxable-year period for purposes of A-1(b) of this section begins on January 1, 1998.

Q-6. Is there a special rule for taxing distributions allocable to a 1998 conversion?

A-6. Yes. In the case of a distribution from a Roth IRA in 1998, 1999 or 2000 of amounts allocable to a 1998 conversion with respect to which the 4-year spread for the resultant income inclusion applies (see §1.408A-4 A-8), any income deferred as a result of the election to years after the year of the distribution is accelerated so that it is includible in gross income in the year of the distribution up to the amount of the distribution allocable to the 1998 conversion (determined under A-8 of this section). This amount is in addition to the amount otherwise includible in the owner's gross income for that taxable year as a result of the conversion. However, this rule will not require the inclusion of any amount to the extent it exceeds the total amount of income required to be included over the 4-year period. The acceleration of income inclusion described in this A-6 applies in the case of a surviving spouse who elects to continue the 4-year spread in accordance with §1.408A-4 A-11(b).

Q-7. Is the 5-taxable-year period described in A-1 of this section redetermined when a Roth IRA owner dies?

A-7. (a) No. The beginning of the 5-taxable-year period described in A-1 of this section is not redetermined when the Roth IRA owner dies. Thus, in determining the 5-taxable-year period, the period the Roth IRA is held in the name of a beneficiary, or in the name of a surviving spouse who treats the decedent's Roth IRA as his or her own, includes the period it was held by the decedent.

(b) The 5-taxable-year period for a Roth IRA held by an individual as a beneficiary of a deceased Roth IRA owner is determined independently of the 5-taxable-year period for the beneficiary's own Roth IRA. However, if a surviving spouse treats the Roth IRA as his or her own, the 5-taxable-year period with respect to any of the surviving spouse's Roth IRAs (including the one that the surviving spouse treats as his or her own) ends at the earlier of the end of either the 5-taxable-year period for the decedent or the 5-taxable-year period applicable to the spouse's own Roth IRAs.

Q-8. How is it determined whether an amount distributed from a Roth IRA is allocated to regular contributions, conversion contributions, or earnings?

A-8. (a) Any amount distributed from an individual's Roth IRA is treated as made in the following order (determined as of the end of a taxable year and exhausting each category before moving to the following category)—

(1) From regular contributions;
(2) From conversion contributions, on a first-in-first-out basis; and
(3) From earnings.

(b) To the extent a distribution is treated as made from a particular conversion contribution, it is treated as made first from the portion, if any, that was includible in gross income as a result of the conversion.

Q-9. Are there special rules for determining the source of distributions under A-8 of this section?

A-9. Yes. For purposes of determining the source of distributions, the following rules apply:

(a) All distributions from all an individual's Roth IRAs made during a taxable year are aggregated.

(b) All regular contributions made for the same taxable year to all the individual's Roth IRAs are aggregated and added to the undistributed total regular contributions for prior taxable years. Regular contributions for a taxable year include contributions made in the following taxable year that are identified as made for the taxable year in accordance with §1.408A-3 A-2. For example, a regular contribution made in 1999 for 1998 is aggregated with the contributions made in 1998 for 1998.

(c) All conversion contributions received during the same taxable year by all the individual's Roth IRAs are aggregated. Notwithstanding the preceding sentence, all conversion contributions made by an individual during 1999 that were distributed from a traditional IRA in 1998 and with respect to which the 4-year spread applies are treated for purposes of A-8(b) of this section as contributed to the individual's Roth IRAs prior to any other conversion contributions made by the individual during 1999.

(d) A distribution from an individual's Roth IRA that is rolled over to another Roth IRA of the individual in accordance with section 408A(e) is disregarded for purposes of determining the amount of both contributions and distributions.

(e) Any amount distributed as a corrective distribution (including net income), as described in A-1(d) of this section, is disregarded in determining the amount of contributions, earnings, and distributions.

(f) If an individual recharacterizes a contribution made to a traditional IRA (FIRST IRA) by transferring the contribution to a Roth IRA (SECOND IRA) in accordance with §1.408A-5, then, pursuant to §1.408A-5 A-3, the contribution to the Roth IRA is taken into account for the same taxable year for which it would have been taken into account if the contribution had originally been made to the Roth IRA and had never been contributed to the traditional IRA. Thus, the contribution to the Roth IRA is treated as contributed to the Roth IRA on the same date and for the same taxable year that the contribution was made to the traditional IRA.

(g) If an individual recharacterizes a regular or conversion contribution made to a Roth IRA (FIRST IRA) by transferring the contribution to a traditional IRA (SECOND IRA) in accordance with §1.408A-5, then, pursuant to §1.408A-5 A-3, the contribution to the Roth IRA and the recharacterizing transfer are disregarded in determining the amount of both contributions and distributions for the taxable year with respect to which the original contribution was made to the Roth IRA.

(h) Pursuant to §1.408A-5 A-3, the effect of income or loss (determined in accordance with §1.408A-5 A-2) occuring after the contribution to the FIRST IRA is disregarded in determining the amounts described in paragraphs (f) and (g) of this A-9. Thus, for purposes of paragraphs (f) and (g), the amount of the contribution is determined based on the original contribution.

Q-10. Are there examples to illustrate the ordering rules described in A-8 and A-9 of this section?

A-10. Yes. The following examples illustrate these ordering rules:

Example 1. In 1998, individual B converts $80,000 in his traditional IRA to a Roth IRA. B has a basis of $20,000 in the conversion amount and so must include the remaining $60,000 in gross income. He decides to spread the $60,000 income by including $15,000 in each of the 4 years 1998-2001, under the rules of §1.408A-4 A-8. B also makes a regular contribution of $2,000 in 1998. If a distribution of $2,000 is made to B anytime in 1998, it will be treated as made entirely from the regular contributions, so there will be no Federal income tax consequences as a result of the distribution.

Example 2. The facts are the same as in *Example 1*, except that the distribution made in 1998 is $5,000. The distribution is treated as made from $2,000 of regular contributions and $3,000 of conversion contributions that were includible in gross income. As a result, B must include $18,000 in gross income for 1998: $3,000 as a result of the acceleration of amounts that otherwise would have been included in later years under the 4-year-spread rule and $15,000 includible under the regular 4-year-spread rule. In addition, because the $3,000 is allocable to a conversion made within the previous 5 taxable years, the 10-percent additional tax under section 72(t) would apply to this $3,000 distribution for 1998, unless an exception applies. Under the 4-year-spread rule, B would now include in gross income $15,000 for 1999 and 2000, but only $12,000 for 2001, because of the accelerated inclusion of the $3,000 distribution.

Example 3. The facts are the same as in *Example 1*, except that B makes an additional $2,000 regular contribution in 1999 and he does not take a distribution in 1998. In 1999, the entire balance in the account, $90,000 ($84,000 of contributions and $6,000 of earnings), is distributed to B. The distribution is treated as made from $4,000 of regular contributions, $60,000 of conversion contributions that were includible in gross income, $20,000 of conversion contributions that were not includible in gross income, and $6,000 of earnings. Because a distribution has been made within the 4-year-spread period, B must accelerate the income inclusion under the 4-year-spread rule and must include in gross income the $45,000 remaining under the 4-year-spread rule in addition to the $6,000 of earnings. Because $60,000 of the distribution is allocable to a conversion made within the previous 5 taxable years, it is subject to the 10-percent additional tax under section 72(t) as if it were includible in gross income for 1999, unless an exception applies. The $6,000 allocable to earnings would be subject to the tax under section 72(t), unless an exception applies. Under the 4-year-spread rule, no amount would be includible in gross income for 2000 or 2001 because the entire amount of the conversion that was includible in gross income has already been included.

Example 4. The facts are the same as in *Example 1,* except that B also makes a $2,000 regular contribution in each year 1999 through 2002 and he does not take a distribution in 1998. A distribution of $85,000 is made to B in 2002. The distribution is treated as made from the $10,000 of regular contributions (the total regular contributions made in the years 1998-2002), $60,000 of conversion contributions that were includible in gross income, and $15,000 of conversion contributions that were not includible in gross income. As a result, no amount of the distribution is includible in gross income; however, because the distribution is allocable to a conversion made within the previous 5 years, the $60,000 is subject to the 10-percent additional tax under section 72(t) as if it were includible in gross income for 2002, unless an exception applies.

Example 5. The facts are the same as in *Example 4,* except no distribution occurs in 2002. In 2003, the entire balance in the account, $170,000 ($90,000 of contributions and $80,000 of earnings), is distributed to B. The distribution is treated as made from $10,000 of regular contributions, $60,000 of conversion contributions that were includible in gross income, $20,000 of conversion contributions that were not includible in gross income, and $80,000 of earnings. As a result, for 2003, B must include in gross income the $80,000 allocable to earnings, unless the distribution is a qualified distribution; and if it is not a qualified distribution, the $80,000 would be subject to the 10-percent additional tax under section 72(t), unless an exception applies.

Example 6. Individual C converts $20,000 to a Roth IRA in 1998 and $15,000 (in which amount C had a basis of $2,000) to another Roth IRA in 1999. No other contributions are made. In 2003, a $30,000 distribution, that is not a qualified distribution, is made to C. The distribution is treated as made from $20,000 of the 1998 conversion contribution and $10,000 of the 1999 conversion contribution that was includible in gross income. As a result, for 2003, no amount is includible in gross income; however, because $10,000 is allocable to a conversion contribution made within the previous 5 taxable years, that amount is subject to the 10-percent additional tax under section 72(t) as if the amount were includible in gross income for 2003, unless an exception applies. The result would be the same whichever of C's Roth IRAs made the distribution.

Example 7. The facts are the same as in *Example 6,* except that the distribution is a qualified distribution. The result is the same as in Example 6, except that no amount would be subject to the 10-percent additional tax under section 72(t), because, to be a qualified distribution, the distribution must be made on or after the date on which the owner attains age 59 1/2, made to a beneficiary or the estate of the owner on or after the date of the owner's death, attributable to the owner's being disabled within the meaning of section 72(m)(7), or to which section 72(t)(2)(F) applies (exception for a first-time home purchase). Under section 72(t)(2), each of these conditions is also an exception to the tax under section 72(t).

Example 8. Individual D makes a $2,000 regular contribution to a traditional IRA on January 1, 1999, for 1998. On April 15, 1999, when the $2,000 has increased to $2,500, D recharacterizes the contribution by transferring the $2,500 to a Roth IRA (pursuant to § 1.408A-5 A-1). In this case, D's regular contribution to the Roth IRA for 1998 is $2,000. The $500 of earnings is not treated as a contribution to the Roth IRA. The results would be the same if the $2,000 had decreased to $1,500 prior to the recharacterization.

Example 9. In December 1998, individual E receives a distribution from his traditional IRA of $300,000 and in January 1999 he contributes the $300,000 to a Roth IRA as a conversion contribution. In April 1999, when the $300,000 has increased to $350,000, E recharacterizes the conversion contribution by transferring the $350,000 to a traditional IRA. In this case, E's conversion contribution for 1998 is $0, because the $300,000 conversion contribution and the earnings of $50,000 are disregarded. The results would be the same if the $300,000 had decreased to $250,000 prior to the recharacterization. Further, since the conversion is disregarded, the $300,000 is not includible in gross income in 1998.

Q-11. If the owner of a Roth IRA dies prior to the end of the 5-taxable-year period described in A-1 of this section (relating to qualified distributions) or prior to the end of the 5-taxable-year period described in A-5 of this section (relating to conversions), how

are different types of contributions in the Roth IRA allocated to multiple beneficiaries?

A-11. Each type of contribution is allocated to each beneficiary on a pro-rata basis. Thus, for example, if a Roth IRA owner dies in 1999, when the Roth IRA contains a regular contribution of $2,000, a conversion contribution of $6,000 and earnings of $1,000, and the owner leaves his Roth IRA equally to four children, each child will receive one quarter of each type of contribution. Pursuant to the ordering rules in A-8 of this section, an immediate distribution of $2,000 to one of the children will be deemed to consist of $500 of regular contributions and $1,500 of conversion contributions. A beneficiary's inherited Roth IRA may not be aggregated with any other Roth IRA maintained by such beneficiary (except for other Roth IRAs the beneficiary inherited from the same decedent), unless the beneficiary, as the spouse of the decedent and sole beneficiary of the Roth IRA, elects to treat the Roth IRA as his or her own (see A-7 and A-14 of this section).

Q-12. How do the withholding rules under section 3405 apply to Roth IRAs?

A-12. Distributions from a Roth IRA are distributions from an individual retirement plan for purposes of section 3405 and thus are designated distributions unless one of the exceptions in section 3405(e)(1) applies. Pursuant to section 3405(a) and (b), nonperiodic distributions from a Roth IRA are subject to 10-percent withholding by the payor and periodic payments are subject to withholding as if the payments were wages. However, an individual can elect to have no amount withheld in accordance with section 3405(a)(2) and (b)(2).

Q-13. Do the withholding rules under section 3405 apply to conversions?

A-13. Yes. A conversion by any method described in § 1.408A-4 A-1 is considered a designated distribution subject to section 3405. However, a conversion occurring in 1998 by means of a trustee-to-trustee transfer of an amount from a traditional IRA to a Roth IRA established with the same or a different trustee is not required to be treated as a designated distribution for purposes of section 3405. Consequently, no withholding is required with respect to such a conversion (without regard to whether or not the individual elected to have no withholding).

Q-14. What minimum distribution rules apply to a Roth IRA?

A-14. (a) No minimum distributions are required to be made from a Roth IRA under section 408(a)(6) and (b)(3) (which generally incorporate the provisions of section 401(a)(9)) while the owner is alive. The post-death minimum distribution rules under section 401(a)(9)(B) that apply to traditional IRAs, with the exception of the at-least-as-rapidly rule described in section 401(a)(9)(B)(i), also apply to Roth IRAs.

(b) The minimum distribution rules apply to the Roth IRA as though the Roth IRA owner died before his or her required beginning date. Thus, generally, the entire interest in the Roth IRA must be distributed by the end of the fifth calendar year after the year of the owner's death unless the interest is payable to a designated beneficiary over a period not greater than that beneficiary's life expectancy and distribution commences before the end of the calendar year following the year of death. If the sole beneficiary is the decedent's spouse, such spouse may delay distributions until the decedent would have attained age 70 1/2 or may treat the Roth IRA as his or her own.

(c) Distributions to a beneficiary that are not qualified distributions will be includible in the beneficiary's gross income according to the rules in A-4 of this section.

(d) The special rules in A-3 of § 1.401(a)(9)-5 and A-12 of § 1.408-8 for a qualifying longevity annuity contract (QLAC), defined in A-17 of § 1.401(a)(9)-6, do not apply to a Roth IRA.

Q-15. Does section 401(a)(9) apply separately to Roth IRAs and individual retirement plans that are not Roth IRAs?

A-15. Yes. An individual required to receive minimum distributions from his or her own traditional or SIMPLE IRA cannot choose to take the amount of the minimum distributions from any Roth IRA. Similarly, an individual required to receive minimum distributions from a Roth IRA cannot choose to take the amount of the minimum distributions from a traditional or SIMPLE IRA. In addition, an individual required to receive minimum distributions as a beneficiary under a Roth IRA can only satisfy the minimum distributions for one Roth IRA by distributing from another Roth IRA if the Roth IRAs were inherited from the same decedent.

Q-16. How is the basis of property distributed from a Roth IRA determined for purposes of a subsequent disposition?

A-16. The basis of property distributed from a Roth IRA is its fair market value (FMV) on the date of distribution, whether or not the distribution is a qualified distribution. Thus, for example, if a distribution consists of a share of stock in XYZ Corp. with an FMV of $40.00 on the date of distribution, for purposes of determining gain or loss on the subsequent sale of the share of XYZ Corp. stock, it has a basis of $40.00.

Q-17. What is the effect of distributing an amount from a Roth IRA and contributing it to another type of retirement plan other than a Roth IRA?

A-17. Any amount distributed from a Roth IRA and contributed to another type of retirement plan (other than a Roth IRA) is treated as a distribution from the Roth IRA that is neither a rollover contribution for purposes of section 408(d)(3) nor a qualified rollover contribution within the meaning of section 408A(e) to the other type of retirement plan. This treatment also applies to any amount transferred from a Roth IRA to any other type of retirement plan unless the transfer is a recharacterization described in § 1.408A-5.

Q-18. Can an amount be transferred directly from an education IRA to a Roth IRA (or distributed from an education IRA and rolled over to a Roth IRA)?

A-18. No amount may be transferred directly from an education IRA to a Roth IRA. A transfer of funds (or distribution and rollover) from an education IRA to a Roth IRA constitutes a distribution from the education IRA and a regular contribution to the Roth IRA (rather than a qualified rollover contribution to the Roth IRA).

Q-19. What are the Federal income tax consequences of a Roth IRA owner transferring his or her Roth IRA to another individual by gift?

A-19. A Roth IRA owner's transfer of his or her Roth IRA to another individual by gift constitutes an assignment of the owner's rights under the Roth IRA. At the time of the gift, the assets of the Roth IRA are deemed to be distributed to the owner and, accordingly, are treated as no longer held in a Roth IRA. In the case of any such gift of a Roth IRA made prior to October 1, 1998, if the entire interest in the Roth IRA is reconveyed to the Roth IRA owner prior to January 1, 1999, the Internal Revenue Service will treat the gift and reconveyance as never having occurred for estate tax, gift tax, and generation-skipping tax purposes and for purposes of this A-19.
[Reg. § 1.408A-6.]

☐ [*T.D.* 8816, 2-3-99. *Amended by T.D. 9673, 7-1-2014.*]

[Reg. § 1.408A-7]

§ 1.408A-7. Reporting.—This section sets forth the following questions and answers that relate to the reporting requirements applicable to Roth IRAs:

Q-1. What reporting requirements apply to Roth IRAs?

A-1. Generally, the reporting requirements applicable to IRAs other than Roth IRAs also apply to Roth IRAs, except that, pursuant to section 408A(d)(3)(D), the trustee of a Roth IRA must include on Forms 1099-R and 5498 additional information as described in the instructions thereto. Any conversion of amounts from an IRA other than a Roth IRA to a Roth IRA is treated as a distribution for which a Form 1099-R must be filed by the trustee maintaining the non-Roth IRA. In addition, the owner of such IRAs must report the conversion by completing Form 8606. In the case of a recharacterization described in § 1.408A-5 A-1, IRA owners must report such transactions in the manner prescribed in the instructions to the applicable Federal tax forms.

Q-2. Can a trustee rely on reasonable representations of a Roth IRA contributor or distributee for purposes of fulfilling reporting obligations?

A-2. A trustee maintaining a Roth IRA is permitted to rely on reasonable representations of a Roth IRA contributor or distributee for purposes of fulfilling reporting obligations.
[Reg. § 1.408A-7.]

☐ [*T.D.* 8816, 2-3-99.]

[Reg. § 1.408A-8]

§ 1.408A-8. Definitions.—This section sets forth the following question and answer that provides definitions of terms used in the provisions of § § 1.408A-1 through 1.408A-7 and this section:

Q-1. Are there any special definitions that govern in applying the provisions of § § 1.408A-1 through 1.408A-7 and this section?

A-1. Yes, the following definitions govern in applying the provisions of § § 1.408A-1 through 1.408A-7 and this section. Unless the context indicates otherwise, the use of a particular term excludes the use of the other terms.

(a) *Different types of IRAs*—(1) *IRA*. Sections 408(a) and (b), respectively, describe an individual retirement account and an individual retirement annuity. The term IRA means an IRA described in either section 408(a) or (b), including each IRA described in paragraphs (a)(2) through (5) of this A-1. However, the term IRA does not include an education IRA described in section 530.

(2) *Traditional IRA*. The term traditional IRA means an individual retirement account or individual retirement annuity described in section 408(a) or (b), respectively. This term includes a SEP IRA but does not include a SIMPLE IRA or a Roth IRA.

(3) *SEP IRA*. Section 408(k) describes a simplified employee pension (SEP) as an employer-sponsored plan under which an employer

can make contributions to IRAs established for its employees. The term SEP IRA means an IRA that receives contributions made under a SEP. The term SEP includes a salary reduction SEP (SARSEP) described in section 408(k)(6).

(4) *SIMPLE IRA*. Section 408(p) describes a SIMPLE IRA Plan as an employer-sponsored plan under which an employer can make contributions to SIMPLE IRAs established for its employees. The term SIMPLE IRA means an IRA to which the only contributions that can be made are contributions under a SIMPLE IRA Plan or rollovers or transfers from another SIMPLE IRA.

(5) *Roth IRA*. The term Roth IRA means an IRA that meets the requirements of section 408A.

(b) *Other defined terms or phrases*—(1) *4-year spread*. The term 4-year spread is described in § 1.408A-4 A-8.

(2) *Conversion*. The term conversion means a transaction satisfying the requirements of § 1.408A-4 A-1.

(3) *Conversion amount or conversion contribution*. The term conversion amount or conversion contribution is the amount of a distribution and contribution with respect to which a conversion described in § 1.408A-4 A-1 is made.

(4) *Failed conversion*. The term failed conversion means a transaction in which an individual contributes to a Roth IRA an amount transferred or distributed from a traditional IRA or SIMPLE IRA (including a transfer by redesignation) in a transaction that does not constitute a conversion under § 1.408A-4 A-1.

(5) *Modified AGI*. The term modified AGI is defined in § 1.408A-3 A-5.

(6) *Recharacterization*. The term recharacterization means a transaction described in § 1.408A-5 A-1.

(7) *Recharacterized amount or recharacterized contribution*. The term recharacterized amount or recharacterized contribution means an amount or contribution treated as contributed to an IRA other than the one to which it was originally contributed pursuant to a recharacterization described in § 1.408A-5 A-1.

(8) *Taxable conversion amount*. The term taxable conversion amount means the portion of a conversion amount includible in income on account of a conversion, determined under the rules of section 408(d)(1) and (2).

(9) *Tax-free transfer*. The term tax-free transfer means a tax-free rollover described in section 402(c), 402(e)(6), 403(a)(4), 403(a)(5), 403(b)(8), 403(b)(10) or 408(d)(3), or a tax-free trustee-to-trustee transfer.

(10) *Treat an IRA as his or her own*. The phrase treat an IRA as his or her own means to treat an IRA for which a surviving spouse is the sole beneficiary as his or her own IRA after the death of the IRA owner in accordance with the terms of the IRA instrument or in the manner provided in the regulations under section 408(a)(6) or (b)(3).

(11) *Trustee*. The term trustee includes a custodian or issuer (in the case of an annuity) of an IRA (except where the context clearly indicates otherwise).
[Reg. § 1.408A-8.]

☐ [*T.D.* 8816, 2-3-99.]

[Reg. § 1.408A-9]

§ 1.408A-9. Effective date.—This section contains the following question and answer providing the effective date of § § 1.408A-1 through 1.408A-8:

Q-1. To what taxable years do § § 1.408A-1 through 1.408A-8 apply?

A-1 Sections 1.408A-1 through 1.408A-8 apply to taxable years beginning on or after January 1, 1998.
[Reg. § 1.408A-9.]

☐ [*T.D.* 8816, 2-3-99.]

[Reg. § 1.408A-10]

§ 1.408A-10. Coordination between designated Roth accounts and Roth IRAs.

Q-1. Can an eligible rollover distribution, within the meaning of section 402(c)(4), from a designated Roth account, as defined in A-1 of § 1.402A-1, be rolled over to a Roth IRA?

A-1. Yes. An eligible rollover distribution, within the meaning of section 402(c)(4), from a designated Roth account may be rolled over to a Roth IRA. For purposes of this section, a designated Roth account means a designated Roth account as defined in A-1 of § 1.402A-1.

Q-2. Can an eligible rollover distribution from a designated Roth account be rolled over to a Roth IRA even if the distributee is not otherwise eligible to make regular or conversion contributions to a Roth IRA?

A-2. Yes. An individual may establish a Roth IRA and roll over an eligible rollover distribution from a designated Roth account to that Roth IRA even if such individual is not eligible to make regular contributions or conversion contributions (as described in section

408A(c)(2) and (d)(3), respectively) because of the modified adjusted gross income limits in section 408A(b)(3).

Q-3. For purposes of the ordering rules on distributions from Roth IRAs, what portion of a distribution from a rollover contribution from a designated Roth account is treated as contributions?

A-3. (a) Under section 408A(d)(4), distributions from Roth IRAs are deemed to consist first of regular contributions, then of conversion contributions, and finally, of earnings. For purposes of section 408A(d)(4), the amount of a rollover contribution that is treated as a regular contribution is the portion of the distribution that is treated as investment in the contract under A-6 of §1.402A-1, and the remainder of the rollover contribution is treated as earnings. Thus, the entire amount of any qualified distribution from a designated Roth account that is rolled over into a Roth IRA is treated as a regular contribution to the Roth IRA. Accordingly, a subsequent distribution from the Roth IRA in the amount of that rollover contribution is not includible in gross income under the rules of A-8 of §1.408A-6.

(b) If the entire account balance of a designated Roth account is distributed to an employee and only a portion of the distribution is rolled over to a Roth IRA within the 60-day period described in section 402(c)(3), and at the time of the distribution, the investment in the contract exceeds the balance in the designated Roth account, the portion of investment in the contract that exceeds the amount used to determine the taxable amount of the distribution is treated as a regular contribution for purposes of section 408A(d)(4).

Q-4. In the case of a rollover from a designated Roth account to a Roth IRA, when does the 5-taxable-year period (described in section 408A(d)(2)(B) and A-1 of §1.408A-6) for determining qualified distributions from a Roth IRA begin?

A-4. (a) The 5-taxable-year period for determining a qualified distribution from a Roth IRA (described in section 408A(d)(2)(B) and A-1 of §1.408A-6) begins with the earlier of the taxable year described in A-2 of §1.408A-6 or the taxable year in which a rollover contribution from a designated Roth account is made to a Roth IRA. The 5-taxable-year period described in this A-4 and the 5-taxable-year period of participation described in A-4 of §1.402A-1 are determined independently.

(b) The following examples illustrate the application of this A-4:

Example 1. Employee D began making designated Roth contributions under his employer's 401(k) plan in 2006. Employee D, who is over age 59¹/₂, takes a distribution from D's designated Roth account in 2008, prior to the end of the 5-taxable-year period of participation used to determine qualified distributions from a designated Roth account. The distribution is an eligible rollover distribution and D rolls it over in accordance with sections 402(c) and 402A(c)(3) to D's Roth IRA, which was established in 2003. Any subsequent distribution from the Roth IRA of the amount rolled in, plus earnings thereon, would not be includible in gross income (because it would be a qualified distribution within the meaning of section 408A(d)(2)).

Example 2. The facts are the same as in *Example 1*, except that the Roth IRA is D's first Roth IRA and is established with the rollover in 2008, which is the only contribution made to the Roth IRA. If a distribution is made from the Roth IRA prior to the end of the 5-taxable-year period used to determine qualified distributions from a Roth IRA (which begins in 2008, the year of the rollover which established the Roth IRA) the distribution would not be a qualified distribution within the meaning of section 408A(d)(2), and any amount of the distribution that exceeded the portion of the rollover contribution that consisted of investment in the contract is includible in D's gross income.

Example 3. The facts are the same as in *Example 2*, except that the distribution from the designated Roth account and the rollover to the Roth IRA occurin 2011 (after the end of the 5-taxable-year period of participation used to determine qualified distributions from a designated Roth account). If a distribution is made from the Roth IRA prior to the expiration of the 5-taxable-year period used to determine qualified distributions from a Roth IRA, the distribution would not be a qualified distribution within the meaning of section 408A(d)(2), and any amount of the distribution that exceeded the amount rolled in is includible in D's gross income.

Q-5. Can amounts distributed from a Roth IRA be rolled over to a designated Roth account as defined in A-1 of §1.402A-1?

A-5. No. Amounts distributed from a Roth IRA may be rolled over or transferred only to another Roth IRA and are not permitted to be rolled over to a designated Roth account under a section 401(a) or section 403(b) plan. The same rule applies even if all the amounts in the Roth IRA are attributable to a rollover distribution from a designated Roth account in a plan.

Q-6. When is this §1.408A-10 applicable?

A-6. The rules of this §1.408A-10 apply for taxable years beginning on or after January 1, 2006. [Reg. §1.408A-10.]

☐ [*T.D. 9324, 4-27-2007.*]

§1.409(p)-1. Prohibited allocation of securities in an S corporation.—(a) *Organization of this section and definition.*—(1) *Organization of this section.*—Section 409(p) applies if a nonallocation year occurs in an ESOP that holds shares of stock of an S corporation that are employer securities. Paragraph (b) of this section sets forth the general rule under section 409(p)(1) and (2) prohibiting any accrual or allocation to a disqualified person in a nonallocation year. Paragraph (c) of this section sets forth rules under section 409(p)(3), (5), and (7) for determining whether a year is a nonallocation year, generally based on whether disqualified persons own at least 50 percent of the shares of the S corporation, either taking into account only the outstanding shares of the S corporation (including shares held by the ESOP) or taking into account both the outstanding shares and synthetic equity of the S corporation. Paragraphs (d), (e), and (f) of this section contain definitions of disqualified person under section 409(p)(4) and (5), deemed-owned ESOP shares under section 409(p)(4)(C), and synthetic equity under section 409(p)(6)(C). Paragraph (g) of this section contains a standard for determining when the principal purpose of the ownership structure of an S corporation constitutes an avoidance or evasion of section 409(p).

(2) *Definitions.*—The following definitions apply for purposes of section 409(p) and this section, as well as for purposes of section 4979A, which imposes an excise tax on certain events.

(i) *Deemed-owned ESOP shares* has the meaning set forth in paragraph (e) of this section.

(ii) *Disqualified person* has the meaning set forth in paragraph (d) of this section.

(iii) *Employer* has the meaning set forth in §1.410(b)-9.

(iv) *Employer securities* means employer securities within the meaning of section 409(l).

(v) *ESOP* means an employee stock ownership plan within the meaning of section 4975(e)(7).

(vi) *Prohibited allocation* has the meaning set forth in paragraph (b)(2) of this section.

(vii) *S corporation* means S corporation within the meaning of section 1361.

(viii) *Synthetic equity* has the meaning set forth in paragraph (f) of this section.

(b) *Prohibited allocation in a nonallocation year.*—(1) *General rule.*—Section 409(p)(1) provides that an ESOP holding employer securities consisting of stock in an S corporation must provide that no portion of the assets of the plan attributable to (or allocable in lieu of) such employer securities may, during a nonallocation year, accrue under the ESOP, or be allocated directly or indirectly under any plan of the employer (including the ESOP) meeting the requirements of section 401(a), for the benefit of any disqualified person.

(2) *Additional rules.*—(i) *Prohibited allocation definition.*—For purposes of section 409(p) and this section, a prohibited allocation means an impermissible accrual or an impermissible allocation. Whether there is impermissible accrual is determined under paragraph (b)(2)(ii) of this section and whether there is an impermissible allocation is determined under paragraph (b)(2)(iii) of this section. The amount of the prohibited allocation is equal to the sum of the amount of the impermissible accrual plus the amount of the impermissible allocation.

(ii) *Impermissible accrual.*—There is an impermissible accrual to the extent that employer securities consisting of stock in an S corporation owned by the ESOP and any assets attributable thereto are held under the ESOP for the benefit of a disqualified person during a nonallocation year. For this purpose, assets attributable to stock in an S corporation owned by an ESOP include any distributions, within the meaning of section 1368, made on S corporation stock held in a disqualified person's account in the ESOP (including earnings thereon), plus any proceeds from the sale of S corporation securities held for a disqualified person's account in the ESOP (including any earnings thereon). Thus, in the event of a nonallocation year, all S corporation shares and all other ESOP assets attributable to S corporation stock, including distributions, sales proceeds, and earnings on either distributions or proceeds, held for the account of such disqualified person in the ESOP during that year are an impermissible accrual for the benefit of that person, whether attributable to contributions in the current year or in prior years.

(iii) *Impermissible allocation.*—An impermissible allocation occurs during a nonallocation year to the extent that a contribution or other annual addition (within the meaning of section 415(c)(2)) is made with respect to the account of a disqualified person, or the disqualified person otherwise accrues additional benefits, directly or indirectly under the ESOP or any other plan of the employer qualified under section 401(a) (including a release and allocation of assets from a suspense account, as described at §54.4975-11(c) and (d) of this chapter) that, for the nonallocation year, would have been added to the account of the disqualified person under the ESOP and invested in employer securities consisting of stock in an S corporation owned by the ESOP but for a provision in the ESOP that precludes such addition to the account of the disqualified person, and investment in employer securities during a nonallocation year.

(iv) *Effects of prohibited allocation.*—(A) *Deemed distribution.*—If a plan year is a nonallocation year, the amount of any prohibited allocation in the account of a disqualified person as of the first day of the plan year, as determined under this paragraph (b)(2), is treated as distributed from the ESOP (or other plan of the employer) to the disqualified person on the first day of the plan year. In the case of an impermissible accrual or impermissible allocation that is not in the account of the disqualified person as of the first day of the plan year, the amount of the prohibited allocation, as determined under this paragraph (b)(2), is treated as distributed on the date of the prohibited allocation. Thus, the fair market value of assets in the disqualified person's account that constitutes an impermissible accrual or allocation is included in gross income (to the extent in excess of any investment in the contract allocable to such amount) and is subject to any additional income tax that applies under section 72(t). A deemed distribution under this paragraph (b)(2)(iv)(A) is not an actual distribution from the ESOP. Thus, the amount of the prohibited allocation is not an eligible rollover distribution under section 402(c). However, for purposes of applying sections 72 and 402 with respect to any subsequent distribution from the ESOP, the amount that the disqualified person previously took into account as income as a result of the deemed distribution is treated as investment in the contract.

(B) *Other effects.*—If there is a prohibited allocation, then the plan fails to satisfy the requirements of section 4975(e)(7) and ceases to be an ESOP. In such a case, the exemption from the excise tax on prohibited transactions for loans to leveraged ESOPs contained in section 4975(d)(3) would cease to apply to any loan (with the result that the employer would owe an excise tax with respect to the previously exempt loan). As a result of these failures, the plan would lose the prohibited transaction exemption for loans to an ESOP under section 4975(d)(3) of the Code and section 408(b)(3) of Title I of the Employee Retirement Income Security Act of 1974, as amended (ERISA). Finally, a plan that does not operate in accordance with its terms to reflect section 409(p) fails to satisfy the qualification requirements of section 401(a), which would cause the corporation's S election to terminate under section 1362. See also section 4979A(a) which imposes an excise tax in certain events, including a prohibited allocation under section 409(p).

(C) *Example.*—The rules of this paragraph (b)(2)(iv) are illustrated by the following example:

Example. (i) *Facts.* Corporation M, an S corporation under section 1361, establishes Plan P as an ESOP in 2006, with a calendar plan year. Plan P is a qualified plan that includes terms providing that a prohibited allocation will not occur during a nonallocation year in accordance with section 409(p). On December 31, 2006, all of the 1,000 outstanding shares of stock of Corporation M, with a fair market value of $30 per share, are contributed to Plan P and allocated among accounts established within Plan P for the benefit of Corporation M's three employees, individuals A, B, and C, based on their compensation for 2006. As a result, on December 31, 2006, participant A's account includes 800 of the shares ($24,000); participant B's account includes 140 of the shares ($4,200); and participant C's account includes the remaining 60 shares ($1,800). The plan year 2006 is a nonallocation year, participants A and B are disqualified persons on December 31, 2006, and a prohibited allocation occurs for A and B on December 31, 2006.

(ii) *Conclusion.* On December 31, 2006, participants A and B each have a deemed distribution as a result of the prohibited allocation, resulting in income of $24,000 for participant A and $4,200 for participant B. Corporation M owes an excise tax under section 4979A, based on an amount involved of $28,200. Plan P ceases to be an ESOP on the date of the prohibited allocation (December 31, 2006) and also fails to satisfy the qualification requirements of section 401(a) on that date due to the failure to comply with the provisions requiring compliance with section 409(p). As a result of having an ineligible shareholder under section 1361(b)(1)(B), Corporation M ceases to be an S corporation under section 1361 on December 31, 2006.

(v) *Prevention of prohibited allocation.*—(A) *Transfer of account to non-ESOP.*—An ESOP may prevent a nonallocation year or a prohibited allocation during a nonallocation year by providing for assets (including S corporation securities) allocated to the account of a disqualified person (or a person reasonably expected to become a disqualified person absent a transfer described in this paragraph (b)(2)(v)(A)) to be transferred into a separate portion of the plan that is not an ESOP, as described in §54.4975-11(a)(5) of this chapter, or to

another plan of the employer that satisfies the requirements of section 401(a) and that is not an ESOP. Any such transfer must be effectuated by an affirmative action taken no later than the date of the transfer, and all subsequent actions (including benefit statements) generally must be consistent with the transfer having occurred on that date. In the event of such a transfer involving S corporation securities, the recipient plan is subject to tax on unrelated business taxable income under section 512.

(B) *Relief from nondiscrimination requirement.*—Pursuant to this paragraph (b)(2)(v)(B), if a transfer described in paragraph (b)(2)(v)(A) of this section is made from an ESOP to a separate portion of the plan or to another qualified plan of the employer that is not an ESOP, then both the ESOP and the plan or portion of a plan that is not an ESOP do not fail to satisfy the requirements of §1.401(a)(4)-4 merely because of the transfer. Further, subsequent to the transfer, that plan will not fail to satisfy the requirements of §1.401(a)(4)-4 merely because of the benefits, rights, and features with respect to the transferred benefits if those benefits, rights, and features would satisfy the requirements of §1.401(a)(4)-4 if the mandatory disaggregation rule for ESOPs at §1.410(b)-7(c)(2) did not apply.

(c) *Nonallocation year.*—A year is a nonallocation year if it is described in the general definition in paragraph (c)(1) of this section or if the special rule of paragraph (c)(3) of this section applies.

(1) *General definition.*—For purposes of section 409(p) and this section, a nonallocation year means a plan year of an ESOP during which, at any time, the ESOP holds any employer securities that are shares of an S corporation and either—

(i) Disqualified persons own at least 50 percent of the number of outstanding shares of stock in the S corporation (including deemed-owned ESOP shares); or

(ii) Disqualified persons own at least 50 percent of the sum of:

(A) The outstanding shares of stock in the S corporation (including deemed-owned ESOP shares); and

(B) The shares of synthetic equity in the S corporation owned by disqualified persons.

(2) *Attribution rules.*—For purposes of this paragraph (c), the rules of section 318(a) apply to determine ownership of shares in the S corporation (including deemed-owned ESOP shares) and synthetic equity. However, for this purpose, section 318(a)(4) (relating to options to acquire stock) is disregarded and, in applying section 318(a)(1), the members of an individual's family include members of the individual's family under paragraph (d)(2) of this section. In addition, an individual is treated as owning deemed-owned ESOP shares of that individual notwithstanding the employee trust exception in section 318(a)(2)(B)(i). If the attribution rules in paragraph (f)(1) of this section apply, then the rules of paragraph (f)(1) of this section are applied before (and in addition to) the rules of this paragraph (c)(2).

(3) *Special rule for avoidance or evasion.*—(i) Any ownership structure described in paragraph (g)(3) of this section results in a nonallocation year. In addition, each individual referred to in paragraph (g)(3) of this section is treated as a disqualified person and the individual's interest in the separate entity described in paragraph (g)(3) of this section is treated as synthetic equity.

(ii) Pursuant to section 409(p)(7)(B), the Commissioner, in revenue rulings, notices, and other guidance published in the Internal Revenue Bulletin (see §601.601(d)(2)(ii)(b) of this chapter), may provide that a nonallocation year occurs in any case in which the principal purpose of the ownership structure of an S corporation constitutes an avoidance or evasion of section 409(p). For any year that is a nonallocation year under this paragraph (c)(3), the Commissioner may treat any person as a disqualified person. See paragraph (g) of this section for guidance regarding when the principal purpose of an ownership structure of an S corporation involving synthetic equity constitutes an avoidance or evasion of section 409(p).

(4) *Special rule for certain stock rights.*—(i) For purposes of paragraph (c)(1) of this section, a person is treated as owning stock if the person has an exercisable right to acquire the stock, the stock is both issued and outstanding, and the stock is held by persons other than the ESOP, the S corporation, or a related entity (as defined in paragraph (f)(3) of this section).

(ii) This paragraph (c)(4) applies only if treating persons as owning the shares described in paragraph (c)(4)(i) of this section results in a nonallocation year. This paragraph (c)(4) does not apply to a right to acquire stock of an S corporation held by a shareholder that is subject to Federal income tax that, under §1.1361-1(l)(2)(iii)(A) or (l)(4)(iii)(C), would not be taken into account in determining if an S corporation has a second class of stock, provided that a principal purpose of the right is not the avoidance or evasion of section 409(p). Under the last sentence of paragraph (f)(2)(i) of this section, this paragraph (c)(4)(ii) does not apply for purposes of determining ownership of deemed-owned ESOP shares or whether an interest constitutes synthetic equity.

(5) *Application with respect to shares treated as owned by more than one person.*—For purposes of applying paragraph (c)(1) of this section, if, by application of the rules of paragraph (c)(2), (c)(4), or (f)(1) of this section, any share is treated as owned by more than one person, then that share is counted as a single share and that share is treated as owned by disqualified persons if any of the owners is a disqualified person.

(6) *Effect of nonallocation year.*—See paragraph (b) of this section for a prohibition applicable during a nonallocation year. See also section 4979A for an excise tax applicable in certain cases, including section 4979A(a)(3) and (4) which applies during a nonallocation year (whether or not there is a prohibited allocation during the year).

(d) *Disqualified persons.*—A person is a disqualified person if the person is described in paragraph (d)(1), (d)(2), or (d)(3) of this section.

(1) *General definition.*—For purposes of section 409(p) and this section, a disqualified person means any person for whom—

(i) The number of such person's deemed-owned ESOP shares of the S corporation is at least 10 percent of the number of the deemed-owned ESOP shares of the S corporation;

(ii) The aggregate number of such person's deemed-owned ESOP shares and synthetic equity shares of the S corporation is at least 10 percent of the sum of—

(A) The total number of deemed-owned ESOP shares of the S corporation; and

(B) The person's synthetic equity shares of the S corporation;

(iii) The aggregate number of the S corporation's deemed-owned ESOP shares of such person and of the members of such person's family is at least 20 percent of the number of deemed-owned ESOP shares of the S corporation; or

(iv) The aggregate number of the S corporation's deemed-owned ESOP shares and synthetic equity shares of such person and of the members of such person's family is at least 20 percent of the sum of—

(A) The total number of deemed-owned ESOP shares of the S corporation; and

(B) The synthetic equity shares of the S corporation owned by such person and the members of such person's family.

(2) *Treatment of family members; definition.*—(i) *Rule.*—Each member of the family of any person who is a disqualified person under paragraph (d)(1)(iii) or (iv) of this section and who owns any deemed-owned ESOP shares or synthetic equity shares is a disqualified person.

(ii) *General definition.*—For purposes of section 409(p) and this section, member of the family means, with respect to an individual—

(A) The spouse of the individual;

(B) An ancestor or lineal descendant of the individual or the individual's spouse;

(C) A brother or sister of the individual or of the individual's spouse and any lineal descendant of the brother or sister; and

(D) The spouse of any individual described in paragraph (d)(2)(ii)(B) or (C) of this section.

(iii) *Spouse.*—A spouse of an individual who is legally separated from such individual under a decree of divorce or separate maintenance is not treated as such individual's spouse under paragraph (d)(2)(ii) of this section.

(3) *Special rule for certain nonallocation years.*—See paragraph (c)(3) of this section (relating to avoidance or evasion of section 409(p)) for special rules under which certain persons are treated as disqualified persons.

(4) *Example.*—The rules of this paragraph (d) are illustrated by the following examples:

Example 1. (i) *Facts.* An S corporation has 800 outstanding shares, of which 100 are owned by individual O and 700 are held in an employee stock ownership plan (ESOP) during 2006, including 200 shares held in the ESOP account of 0, 65 shares held in the ESOP account of participant P, 65 shares held in the ESOP account of participant Q who is P's spouse, and 14 shares held in the ESOP account of R, who is the daughter of P and Q. There are no unallocated suspense account shares in the ESOP. The S corporation has no synthetic equity.

(ii) *Conclusion.* Under paragraph (d)(1)(i) of this section, O is a disqualified person during 2006 because O's account in the ESOP holds at least 10% of the shares owned by the ESOP (200 is 28.6% of

700). During 2006, neither P, Q, nor R is a disqualified person under paragraph (d)(1)(i) of this section, because each of their accounts holds less than 10% of the shares owned by the ESOP. However, each of P, Q, and R is a disqualified person under paragraph (d)(1)(iii) of this section because P and members of P's family own at least 20% of the deemed-owned ESOP shares (144 (the sum of 65, 65 and 14) is 20.6% of 700). As a result, disqualified persons own at least 50% of the outstanding shares of the S corporation during 2006 (O's 100 directly owned shares, O's 200 deemed-owned shares, P's 65 deemed-owned shares, Q's 65 deemed-owned shares, and R's 14 deemed-owned shares are 55.5% of 800).

Example 2. (i) *Facts.* An S corporation has shares that are owned by an ESOP and various individuals. Individuals S and T are married and have a son, U. Individuals V and W are married and have a daughter, X. Individuals U and X are married. Individual V has a brother Y. Their percentages of the deemed-owned ESOP shares of the S corporation are as follows: T has 6%; U has 7%; and V has 8%. Neither S, W, X, nor Y has any deemed-owned ESOP shares and the S corporation has no synthetic equity. However, individual S and individual Y each own directly a number of shares of the outstanding shares of the S corporation.

(ii) *Conclusion.* In this example, individual U is a disqualified person under paragraph (d)(1) of this section (because U's family consists of S, T, U, V, W, and X, and, in the aggregate, those persons own more than 20% of the deemed-owned ESOP shares) and individual X is also a disqualified person under paragraph (d)(1) of this section (because T's family consists of S, T, U, V, W, and X, and, in the aggregate, those persons own more than 20% of the deemed-owned ESOP shares). Further, individuals T and V are each a disqualified person under paragraph (d)(2) of this section because each is a member of a family that includes one or more disqualified persons and each has deemed-owned ESOP shares. However, individuals S, W, and Y are not disqualified persons under this paragraph (d). For example, S does not own more than 10% of the deemed-owned ESOP shares, and S's family, which consists of S, T, U, and X, owns, in the aggregate, only 13% of the deemed-owned ESOP shares (X's parents are not members of S's family because the family members of a person do not include the parents-in-law of the person's descendants). Further, note that, for purposes of determining whether the ESOP has a nonallocation year under paragraph (c) of this section, the shares directly owned by S and Y would be taken into account as shares owned by disqualified persons under the attribution rules in paragraph (c)(2) of this section.

(e) *Deemed-owned ESOP shares.*—For purposes of section 409(p) and this section, a person is treated as owning his or her deemed-owned ESOP shares. Deemed-owned ESOP shares owned by a person mean, with respect to any person—

(1) Any shares of stock in the S corporation constituting employer securities that are allocated to such person's account under the ESOP; and

(2) Such person's share of the stock in the S corporation that is held by the ESOP but is not allocated to the account of any participant or beneficiary (with such person's share to be determined in the same proportion as the shares released and allocated from a suspense account, as described at §54.4975-11(c) and (d) of the Excise Tax Regulations, under the ESOP for the most recently ended plan year for which there were shares released and allocated from a suspense account, or if there has been no such prior release and allocation from a suspense account, then determined in proportion to a reasonable estimate of the shares that would be released and allocated in the first year of a loan repayment).

(f) *Synthetic equity and rights to acquire stock of the S corporation.*—
(1) *Ownership of synthetic equity.*—For purposes of section 409(p) and this section, synthetic equity means the rights described in paragraph (f)(2) of this section. Synthetic equity is treated as owned by the person that has any of the rights specified in paragraph (f)(2) of the section. In addition, the attribution rules as set forth in paragraph (c)(2) of this section apply for purposes of attributing ownership of synthetic equity.

(2) *Synthetic equity.*—(i) *Rights to acquire stock of the S corporation.*—(A) *General rule.*—Synthetic equity includes any stock option, warrant, restricted stock, deferred issuance stock right, stock appreciation right payable in stock, or similar interest or right that gives the holder the right to acquire or receive stock of the S corporation in the future. Rights to acquire stock in an S corporation with respect to stock that is, at all times during the period when such rights are effective, both issued and outstanding, and held by a person other than the ESOP, the S corporation, or a related entity are not synthetic equity but only if that person is subject to federal income taxes. (See also paragraph (c)(4) of this section.)

(B) *Exception for certain rights of first refusal.*—A right of first refusal to acquire stock held by an ESOP is not treated as a right to acquire stock of an S corporation under this paragraph if the right to acquire stock would not be taken into account under §1.1361-1(1)(2)(iii)(A) in determining if an S corporation has a second class of stock and the price at which the stock is acquired under the right of first refusal is not less than the price determined under section 409(h). See §54.4975-11(d)(5) of the Excise Tax Regulations. The right of first refusal must also comply with the requirements of §54.4975-7(b)(9) of the Excise Tax Regulations. This paragraph (f)(2)(i)(B) does not apply if, based on the facts and circumstances, the Commissioner finds that the right to acquire stock held by the ESOP constitutes an avoidance or an evasion of section 409(p). See also section 408(d) of ERISA, under which the exemption provided by section 408(e) of ERISA (and the related exemption at section 4975(d)(13) of the Code) does not apply to an owner-employee, including an employee or officer of an S corporation who is a 5 percent owner.

(ii) *Special rule for certain stock rights.*—Synthetic equity also includes a right to a future payment (payable in cash or any other form other than stock of the S corporation) from an S corporation that is based on the value of the stock of the S corporation, such as appreciation in such value. Thus, for example, synthetic equity includes a stock appreciation right with respect to stock of an S corporation that is payable in cash or a phantom stock unit with respect to stock of an S corporation that is payable in cash.

(iii) *Rights to acquire interests in or assets of an S corporation or a related entity.*—Synthetic equity includes a right to acquire stock or other similar interests in a related entity to the extent of the S corporation's ownership. Synthetic equity also includes a right to acquire assets of an S corporation or a related entity other than either rights to acquire goods, services, or property at fair market value in the ordinary course of business or fringe benefits excluded from gross income under section 132.

(iv) *Special rule for nonqualified deferred compensation.*—(A) Synthetic equity also includes any of the following with respect to an S corporation or a related entity: any remuneration to which section 404(a)(5) applies; remuneration for which a deduction would be permitted under section 404(a)(5) if separate accounts were maintained; any right to receive property, as defined in §1.83-3(e) of the Income Tax Regulations (including a payment to a trust described in section 402(b) or to an annuity described in section 403(c)) in a future year for the performance of services; any transfer of property in connection with the performance of services to which section 83 applies to the extent that the property is not substantially vested within the meaning of §1.83-3(i) by the end of the plan year in which transferred; and a split-dollar life insurance arrangement under §1.61-22(b) entered into in connection with the performance of services (other than one under which, at all times, the only economic benefit that will be provided under the arrangement is current life insurance protection as described in §1.61-22(d)(3)). Synthetic equity also includes any other remuneration for services under a plan, method, or arrangement deferring the receipt of compensation to a date that is after the 15th day of the 3rd calendar month after the end of the entity's taxable year in which the related services are rendered. However, synthetic equity does not include benefits under a plan that is an eligible retirement plan within the meaning of section 402(c)(8)(B).

(B) For purposes of applying paragraph (f)(2)(iv)(A) of this section with respect to an ESOP, synthetic equity does not include any interest described in such paragraph (f)(2)(iv)(A) of this section to the extent that—

(1) The interest is nonqualified deferred compensation (within the meaning of section 3121(v)(2)) that was outstanding on December 17, 2004;

(2) The interest is an amount that was taken into account (within the meaning of §31.3121(v)(2)-1(d) of this chapter) prior to January 1, 2005, for purposes of taxation under chapter 21 of the Internal Revenue Code (or income attributable thereto); and

(3) The interest was held before the first date on which the ESOP acquires any employer securities.

(v) *No overlap among shares of deemed-owned ESOP shares or synthetic equity.*—Synthetic equity under this paragraph (f)(2) does not include shares that are deemed-owned ESOP shares (or any rights with respect to deemed-owned ESOP shares to the extent such rights are specifically provided under section 409(h)). In addition, synthetic equity under a specific subparagraph of this paragraph (f)(2) does not include anything that is synthetic equity under a preceding provision of paragraph (f)(2)(i), (ii), (iii), or (iv) of this section.

(3) *Related entity.*—For purposes of this paragraph (f), related entity means any entity in which the S corporation holds an interest and which is a partnership, a trust, an eligible entity that is disregarded as an entity that is separate from its owner under §301.7701-3 of this chapter, or a qualified subchapter S subsidiary under section 1361(b)(3).

(4) *Number of synthetic shares.*—(i) *Synthetic equity determined by reference to S corporation shares.*—In the case of synthetic equity that is determined by reference to shares of stock of the S corporation, the person who is entitled to the synthetic equity is treated as owning the number of shares of stock deliverable pursuant to such synthetic equity. In the case of synthetic equity that is determined by reference to shares of stock of the S corporation, but for which payment is made in cash or other property (besides stock of the S corporation), the number of shares of synthetic equity treated as owned is equal to the number of shares of stock having a fair market value equal to the cash or other property (disregarding lapse restrictions as described in §1.83-3(i)). Where such synthetic equity is a right to purchase or receive S corporation shares, the corresponding number of shares of synthetic equity is determined without regard to lapse restrictions as described in §1.83-3(i) or to any amount required to be paid in exchange for the shares. Thus, for example, if a corporation grants an employee of an S corporation an option to purchase 100 shares of the corporation's stock, exercisable in the future only after the satisfaction of certain performance conditions, the employee is the deemed owner of 100 synthetic equity shares of the corporation as of the date the option is granted. If the same employee were granted 100 shares of restricted S corporation stock (or restricted stock units), subject to forfeiture until the satisfaction of performance or service conditions, the employee would likewise be the deemed owner of 100 synthetic equity shares from the grant date. However, if the same employee were granted a stock appreciation right with regard to 100 shares of S corporation stock (whether payable in stock or in cash), the number of synthetic equity shares the employee is deemed to own equals the number of shares having a value equal to the appreciation at the time of measurement (determined without regard to lapse restrictions).

(ii) *Synthetic equity determined by reference to shares in a related entity.*—In the case of synthetic equity that is determined by reference to shares of stock (or similar interests) in a related entity, the person who is entitled to the synthetic equity is treated as owning shares of stock of the S corporation with the same aggregate value as the number of shares of stock (or similar interests) of the related entity (with such value determined without regard to any lapse restriction as defined at §1.83-3(i)).

(iii) *Other synthetic equity.*—(A) *General rule.*—In the case of any synthetic equity to which neither paragraph (f)(4)(i) of this section nor paragraph (f)(4)(ii) of this section apply, the person who is entitled to the synthetic equity is treated as owning on any date a number of shares of stock in the S corporation equal to the present value (on that date) of the synthetic equity (with such value determined without regard to any lapse restriction as defined at §1.83-3(i)) divided by the fair market value of a share of the S corporation's stock as of that date.

(B) *Use of annual or more frequent determination dates.*—A year is a nonallocation year if the thresholds in paragraph (c) of this section are met at any time during that year. However, for purposes of this paragraph (f)(4)(iii), an ESOP may provide that the number of shares of S corporation stock treated as owned by a person who is entitled to synthetic equity to which this paragraph (f)(4)(iii) applies is determined annually (or more frequently), as of the first day of the ESOP's plan year or as of any other reasonable determination date or dates during a plan year. If the ESOP so provides, the number of shares of synthetic equity to which this paragraph (f)(4)(iii) applies that are treated as owned by that person for any period from a given determination date through the date immediately preceding the next following determination date is the number of shares treated as owned on the given determination date.

(C) *Use of triennial recalculations.*—(1) Although an ESOP must have a determination date that is no less frequent than annually, if the terms of the ESOP so provide, then the number of shares of synthetic equity with respect to grants of synthetic equity to which this paragraph (f)(4)(iii) applies may be fixed for a specified period from a determination date identified under the ESOP through the day before a determination date that is not later than the third anniversary of the identified determination date. Thus, the ESOP must provide for the number of shares of synthetic equity to which this paragraph (f)(4)(iii) applies to be re-determined not less frequently than every three years, based on the S corporation share value on a determination date that is not later than the third anniversary of the identified determination date and the aggregate present value of the synthetic equity to which this paragraph (f)(4)(iii) applies (including all grants made during the three-year period) on that determination date.

(2) However, additional accruals, allocations, or grants (to which this paragraph (f)(4)(iii) applies) that are made during such

three-year period are taken into account on each determination date during that period, based on the number of synthetic equity shares resulting from the additional accrual, allocation, or grant (determined as of the determination date on or next following the date of the accrual, allocation, or grant). See *Example 3* of paragraph (h) of this section for an example illustrating this paragraph (f)(4)(iii)(C).

(3) If, as permitted under this paragraph (f)(4)(iii)(C), an ESOP provides for the number of shares of synthetic equity to be fixed for a specified period from a determination date to a subsequent determination date, then that subsequent determination date can be changed to a new determination date, subject to the following conditions:

(i) The change in the subsequent determination date must be effectuated through a plan amendment adopted before the new determination date;

(ii) The new determination date must be earlier than the prior determination date (that is, the new determination date must be earlier than the determination date applicable in the absence of the plan amendment);

(iii) The conditions in paragraph (f)(4)(iii)(C)(2) of this section must be satisfied measured from the new determination date; and

(iv) Except to the extent permitted by the Commissioner in revenue rulings, notices, or other guidance published in the Internal Revenue Bulletin (see § 601.601(d)(2)(ii)(b) of this chapter), the change must be adopted in connection with either a change in the plan year of the ESOP or a merger, consolidation, or transfer of plan assets of the ESOP under section 414(1) (and the new determination date must consistent with that plan year change or section 414(1) event).

(4) *Conditions for application of rules.*—This paragraph (f)(4)(iii)(C) only applies with respect to grants of synthetic equity to which this paragraph (f)(4)(iii) applies. In addition, paragraph (f)(4)(iii)(C) of this section applies only if the fair market value of a share of the S corporation securities on any determination date is not unrepresentative of the value of the S corporation securities throughout the rest of the plan year and only if the terms of the ESOP include provisions conforming to paragraph (f) (4) (iii) (C) (1) of this section which are consistently used by the ESOP for all persons. In addition, paragraph (f)(4)(iii)(C)(1) of this section applies only if the terms of the ESOP include provisions conforming to paragraphs (f) (4) (iii) (C) (1) of this section which are consistently used by the ESOP for all persons.

(iv) *Adjustment of number of synthetic equity shares where ESOP owns less than 100 Percent of S corporation.*— The number of synthetic shares otherwise determined under this paragraph (f)(4) is decreased ratably to the extent that shares of the S corporation are owned by a person who is not an ESOP and who is subject to Federal income taxes. For example, if an S corporation has 200 outstanding shares, of which individual A owns 50 shares and the ESOP owns the other 150 shares, and individual B would be treated under this paragraph (f)(4) as owning 100 synthetic equity shares of the S corporation but for this paragraph (f)(4)(iv), then, under the rule of this paragraph (f)(4)(iv), the number of synthetic shares treated as owned by B under this paragraph (f)(4) is decreased from 100 to 75 (because the ESOP only owns 75 percent of the outstanding stock of the S corporation, rather than 100 percent).

(v) *Special rule for shares with greater voting power than ESOP shares.*—Notwithstanding any other provision of this paragraph (f)(4), if a synthetic equity right includes (directly or indirectly) a right to purchase or receive shares of S corporation stock that have per-share voting rights greater than the per-share voting rights of one or more shares of S corporation stock held by the ESOP, then the number of shares of deemed owned synthetic equity attributable to such right is not less than the number of shares that would have the same voting rights if the shares had the same per-share voting rights as shares held by the ESOP with the least voting rights. For example, if shares of S corporation stock held by the ESOP have one voting right per share, then an individual who holds an option to purchase one share with 100 voting rights is treated as owning 100 shares of synthetic equity.

(g) *Avoidance or evasion of section 409 (p) involving synthetic equity.*— (1) *General rule.*—Paragraph (g)(2) of this section sets forth a stan-

dard for determining whether the principal purpose of the ownership structure of an S corporation involving synthetic equity constitutes an avoidance or evasion of section 409(p). Paragraph (g)(3) of this section identifies certain specific ownership structures that constitute an avoidance or evasion of section 409(p). See also paragraph (c)(3) of this section for a rule under which the ownership structures in paragraph (g)(3) of this section result in a nonallocation year for purposes of section 409(p).

(2) *Standard for determining when there is an avoidance or evasion of section 409(p) involving synthetic equity.*—For purposes of section 409(p) and this section, whether the principal purpose of the ownership structure of an S corporation involving synthetic equity constitutes an avoidance or evasion of section 409(p) is determined by taking into account all the surrounding facts and circumstances, including all features of the ownership of the S corporation's outstanding stock and related obligations (including synthetic equity), any shareholders who are taxable entities, and the cash distributions made to shareholders, to determine whether, to the extent of the ESOP's stock ownership, the ESOP receives the economic benefits of ownership in the S corporation that occur during the period that stock of the S corporation is owned by the ESOP. Among the factors indicating that the ESOP receives those economic benefits include shareholder voting rights, the right to receive distributions made to shareholders, and the right to benefit from the profits earned by the S corporation, including the extent to which actual distributions of profits are made from the S corporation to the ESOP and the extent to which the ESOP's ownership interest in undistributed profits and future profits is subject to dilution as a result of synthetic equity. For example, the ESOP's ownership interest is not subject to dilution if the total amount of synthetic equity is a relatively small portion of the total number of shares and deemed-owned shares of the S corporation.

(3) *Specific transactions that constitute an avoidance or evasion of section 409(p) involving segregated profits.*—Taking into account the standard in paragraph (g)(2) of this section, the principal purpose of the ownership structure of an S corporation constitutes an avoidance or evasion of section 409(p) in any case in which—

(i) The profits of the S corporation generated by the business activities of a specific individual or individuals are not provided to the ESOP, but are instead substantially accumulated and held for the benefit of the individual or individuals on a tax-deferred basis within an entity related to the S corporation, such as a partnership, trust, or corporation (such as in a subsidiary that is a disregarded entity), or any other method that has the same effect of segregating profits for the benefit of such individual or individuals (such as nonqualified deferred compensation described in paragraph (f)(2)(iv) of this section);

(ii) The individual or individuals for whom profits are segregated have rights to acquire 50 percent or more of those profits directly or indirectly (for example, by purchase of the subsidiary); and

(iii) A nonallocation year would occur if this section were separately applied with respect to either the separate entity or whatever method has the effect of segregating profits of the individual or individuals, treating such entity as a separate S corporation owned by an ESOP (or in the case of any other method of segregation of profits by treating those profits as the only assets of a separate S corporation owned by an ESOP).

(h) *Examples.*—The rules of this section are illustrated by the following examples:

Example 1. Relating to determination of disqualified persons and nonallocation year if there is no synthetic equity. (i) *Facts.* Corporation X is a calendar year S corporation that maintains an ESOP. X has a single class of common stock, of which there are a total of 1,200 shares outstanding. X has no synthetic equity. In 2006, individual A, who is not an employee of X (and is not related to any employee of X), owns 100 shares directly, B, who is an employee of X, owns 100 shares directly, and the remaining 1,000 shares are owned by an ESOP maintained by X for its employees. The ESOP's 1,000 shares are allocated to the accounts of individuals who are employees of X (none of whom are related), as set forth in columns 1 and 2 in the following table:

1 Shareholders	2 Deemed-Owned ESOP Shares (total of 1,000)	3 Percentage Deemed-Owned ESOP Shares	4 Disqualified Person
B	330	33%	Yes
C	145	14.5%	Yes

1 Shareholders	2 Deemed-Owned ESOP Shares (total of 1,000)	3 Percentage Deemed-Owned ESOP Shares	4 Disqualified Person
D	75	7.5%	No
E	30	3%	No
F	20	2%	No
Other participants	400 (none exceed 10 shares)	1% or less	No

(ii) *Conclusion with respect to disqualified persons.* As shown in column 4 in the table contained in paragraph (i) of *Example 1*, individuals B and C are disqualified persons for 2006 under paragraph (d)(1) of this section because each owns at least 10% of X's deemed-owned ESOP shares. However, the synthetic equity shares owned by any person do not affect the calculation for any other person's ownership of shares.

(iii) *Conclusion with respect to nonallocation year.* 2006 is not a nonallocation year under section 409(p) because disqualified persons do not own at least 50% of X's outstanding shares (the 100 shares owned directly by B, B's 330 deemed-owned ESOP shares, plus C's 145 deemed-owned ESOP shares equal only 47.9% of the 1,200 outstanding shares of X).

Example 2. Relating to determination of disqualified persons and nonallocation year if there is synthetic equity. (i) *Facts.* The facts are the same as in *Example 1*, except that, as shown in column 4 of the table in this *Example 2*, individuals E and F have options to acquire 110 and 130 shares, respectively, of the common stock of X from X:

1 Shareholders	2 Deemed-Owned ESOP Shares (total of 1,000)	3 Percentage Deemed-Owned ESOP Shares	4 Options (240)	5 Shareholder Percentage of Deemed-Owned ESOP plus Synthetic Equity Shares	6 Disqualified Person
B	330	33%			Yes (col. 3)
C	145	14.5%			Yes (col.3)
D	75	7.5%			No
E	30	3%	110	11.1% ([30+ 91.7] divided by 1,091.7)	Yes (col. 5)
F	20	2%	130	11.6% ([20 +108.3] divided by 1,108.3)	Yes (col. 5)
Other participants	400 (none exceeds 10 shares)	1% or less			No

(ii) *Conclusion with respect to disqualified persons.* Individual E's synthetic equity shares are counted in determining whether E is a disqualified person for 2006, and individual F's synthetic equity shares are counted in determining whether F is a disqualified person for 2006. Applying the rule of paragraph (f)(4)(iv) of this section, E's option to acquire 110 shares of the S corporation converts under paragraph (f)(4)(iv) of this section, into 91.7 shares of synthetic equity (110 times the ratio of the 1,000 deemed-owned ESOP shares to the sum of the 1,000 deemed-owned ESOP shares plus the 200 shares held outside the ESOP by A and B). Similarly, F's option to acquire 130 shares of the S corporation converts into 108.3 shares of synthetic equity (130 times the ratio of the 1,000 deemed-owned ESOP shares to the sum of the 1,000 deemed-owned ESOP shares plus the 200 shares held outside the ESOP by A and B). However, the synthetic equity shares owned by any person do not affect the calculation for any other person's ownership of shares. Accordingly, as shown in column 6 in the table contained in paragraph (i) of *Example 2*, individuals B, C, E, and F are disqualified persons for 2006.

(iii) *Conclusion with respect to nonallocation year.* The 100 shares owned directly by B, B's 330 deemed-owned ESOP shares, C's 145 deemed-owned ESOP shares, E's 30 deemed-owned ESOP shares, E's 91.7 synthetic equity shares, F's 20 deemed-owned ESOP shares, plus F's 108.3 synthetic equity shares total 825, which equals 58.9% of 1,400, which is the sum of the 1,200 outstanding shares of X and the 200 shares of synthetic equity shares of X held by disqualified persons. Thus, 2006 is a nonallocation year for X's ESOP under section 409(p) because disqualified persons own at least 50% of the total shares of outstanding stock of X and the total synthetic equity shares of X held by disqualified persons. In addition, independent of the preceding conclusion, 2006 would be a nonallocation year because disqualified persons own at least 50% of X's outstanding shares because the 100 shares owned directly by B, B's 330 deemed-owned ESOP shares, C's 145 deemed-owned ESOP shares, E's 30 deemed-owned ESOP shares, plus F's 20 deemed-owned ESOP shares equal 52.1% of the 1,200 outstanding shares of X.

Example 3. Relating to determination of number of shares of synthetic equity. (i) *Facts.* Corporation Y is a calendar year S corporation that maintains an ESOP. Y has a single class of common stock, of which there are a total of 1,000 shares outstanding, all of which are owned by the ESOP. Y has no synthetic equity, except for four grants of nonqualified deferred compensation that are made to an individual during the period from 2005 through 2011, as set forth in column 2 in the following table. The ESOP provides for the special rules in paragraph (f)(4)(iii) of this section to determine the number of shares of synthetic equity owned by that individual with a determination date of January 1 and the triennial rule redetermining value, as shown in columns 4 and 5:

1 Determination Date	2 Present Value of Nonqualified Deferred Compensation on Determination Date	3 Share Value on Determination Date	4 New Shares of Synthetic Equity on Determination Date	5 Aggregate Number of Synthetic Equity Shares on Determination Date
January 1, 2005	A grant is made on January 1, 2005, with a present value of $1,000. An additional grant of nonqualified deferred compensation with a present value of $775 is made on March 1, 2005.	$10 per share	100	100

1 Determination Date	2 Present Value of Nonqualified Deferred Compensation on Determination Date	3 Share Value on Determination Date	4 New Shares of Synthetic Equity on Determination Date	5 Aggregate Number of Synthetic Equity Shares on Determination Date
January 1, 2006	An additional grant is made on December 31, 2005, which has a present value of $800 on January 1, 2006. The March 1, 2005, grant has a present value on January 1, 2006, of $800.	$8 per share	200	300
January 1, 2007	No new grants made.	$12 per share		300
January 1, 2008	An additional grant is made on December 31, 2007, which has a present value of $3,000 on January 1, 2008. The grants made during 2005 through 2007 have an aggregate present value on January 1, 2008, of $3,750.	$15 per share	200	450
January 1, 2009	No new grants are made.	$11 per share		450
January 1, 2010	No new grants are made.	$22 per share		450
January 1, 2011	No new grants are made. The grants made during 2005 through 2008 have an aggregate present value on January 1, 2011, of $7,600.	$20 per share		380

(ii) *Conclusion.* The grant made on January 1, 2005, is treated as 100 shares until the determination date in 2008. The grant made on March 1, 2005, is not taken into account until the 2006 determination date and its present value on that date, along with the then present value of the grant made on December 31, 2005, is treated as a number of shares that are based on the $8 per share value on the 2006 determination date, with the resulting number of shares continuing to apply until the determination date in 2008. On the January 1, 2008, determination date, the grant made on the preceding day is taken into account at its present value of $3,000 on January 1, 2008 and the $15 per share value on that date with the resulting number of shares (200) continuing to apply until the next determination date. In addition, on the January 1, 2008, determination date, the number of shares determined under other grants made between January 1, 2005 and December 31, 2007, must be revalued. Accordingly, the aggregate value of all nonqualified deferred compensation granted during that period is determined to be $3750 on January 1, 2008, and the corresponding number of shares of synthetic equity based on the $15 per share value is determined to be 250 shares on the 2008 determination date, with the resulting aggregate number of shares (450) continuing to apply until the determination date in 2011. On the January 1, 2011,

determination date, the aggregate value of all nonqualified deferred compensation is determined to be $7,600 and the corresponding number of shares of synthetic equity based on the $20 per share value on the 2011 determination date is determined to be 380 shares (with the resulting number of shares continuing to apply until the day before the determination date in 2014, assuming no further grants are made).

(i) *Effective dates.*—(1) *Statutory effective date.*—(i) Except as otherwise provided in paragraph (i)(1)(ii) of this section, section 409(p) applies for plan years ending after March 14, 2001.

(ii) If an ESOP holding stock in an S corporation was established on or before March 14, 2001, and the election under section 1362(a) with respect to that S corporation was in effect on March 14, 2001, section 409(p) applies for plan years beginning on or after January 1, 2005.

(2) *Regulatory effective date.*—This section applies for plan years beginning on or after January 1, 2006. For plan years beginning before January 1, 2006, §1.409(p)-1 (as it appeared in the April 1, 2005, edition of 26 CFR part 1) applies. [Reg. §1.409(p)-1.]

☐ [T.D. 9302, 12-19-2006.]

⋙→ *Caution: Temporary Reg. §1.409(p)-1T, below, applies for plan years beginning before January 1, 2006 (see Reg. §1.409(p)-1(i)(2)).*

[Reg. §1.409(p)-1T]

§1.409(p)-1T. Prohibited allocation of securities in an S corporation (temporary).—(a) *Organization of this section.*—Section 409(p) applies if a nonallocation year occurs in an employee stock ownership plan (ESOP), as defined in section 4975(e)(7), that holds shares of stock of an S corporation, as defined in section 1361, that are employer securities as defined in section 409(1). Paragraph (b) of this section sets forth the general rule under section 409(p)(1) and (2) prohibiting any accrual or allocation to a disqualified person in a nonallocation year. Paragraph (c) of this section sets forth rules under section 409(p)(3), (5), and (7) for determining whether a year is a nonallocation year, generally based on whether disqualified persons own at least 50 percent of the shares of the S corporation, either taking into account only the outstanding shares of the S corporation (including shares held by the ESOP) or taking into account both the outstanding shares and synthetic equity of the S corporation. Paragraphs (d), (e), and (f) of this section contain definitions of disqualified person under section 409(p)(4) and (5), deemed-owned ESOP shares under section 409(p)(4)(C), and synthetic equity under section 409(p)(6)(C). Paragraph (g) of this section contains a standard for determining when the principal purpose of the ownership structure of an S corporation constitutes an avoidance or evasion of section 409(p). The definitions used in section 409(p) and this section are also applicable for purposes of section 4979A, which imposes an excise tax on certain events, including a nonallocation year under section 409(p).

(b) *Prohibited allocation in a nonallocation year.*—(1) *General rule.*—An ESOP holding employer securities consisting of stock in an S corporation must provide that no portion of the assets of the plan attributable to (or allocable in lieu of) such employer securities may, during a nonallocation year, accrue under the ESOP, or be allocated directly or indirectly under any plan of the employer (including the ESOP) meeting the requirements of section 401(a), for the benefit of any disqualified person (a prohibited allocation).

(2) *Additional rules.*—(i) *Prohibited allocation definition.*—For purposes of section 409(p)(2)(A) and paragraph (b)(1) of this section, there is a prohibited allocation (i.e. assets accrue or are allocated as prohibited under paragraph (b)(1) of this section) if there is either an impermissible accrual as defined in paragraph (b)(2)(ii) of this section or an impermissible allocation as defined in paragraph (b)(2)(iii) of this section. The amount of the prohibited allocation is equal to the sum of the impermissible accrual plus the amount of the impermissible allocation (if any).

(ii) *Impermissible accrual.*—There is an impermissible accrual to the extent (and only to the extent) that employer securities consisting of stock in an S corporation owned by the ESOP and any assets attributable thereto are held under the ESOP for the benefit of a disqualified person during a nonallocation year. For this purpose, assets attributable to S corporation securities include any distributions, within the meaning of section 1368, made on S corporation stock held in a disqualified person's account in the ESOP (including earnings thereon), plus any proceeds from the sale of S corporation

>>>→ *Caution: Temporary Reg. §1.409(p)-1T, below, applies for plan years beginning before January 1, 2006 (see Reg. §1.409(p)-1(i)(2)).*

securities held for a disqualified person's account in the ESOP (including any earnings thereon). Thus, for example, in the event of a nonallocation year, all S corporation shares and all other ESOP assets attributable to S corporation stock, including distributions, sales proceeds, and earnings on either the distribution or proceeds, held for the account of such disqualified person in the ESOP during that year are an impermissible accrual for the benefit of that person, whether attributable to contributions in the current year or in prior years.

(iii) *Impermissible allocation.*—An impermissible allocation means any allocation for a disqualified person directly or indirectly under any plan of the employer qualified under section 401(a) that occurs during a nonallocation year to the extent that a contribution or other annual addition is made, or the disqualified person otherwise accrues additional benefits, under the ESOP or any other plan of the employer qualified under section 401(a) (including a release and allocation of assets from a suspense account, as described at §54.4975-11(c) and (d) of their chapter) that, for the nonallocation year, would otherwise have been added to the account of the disqualified person under the ESOP and invested in employer securities consisting of stock in an S corporation owned by the ESOP but for a provision in the ESOP to comply with section 409(p).

(iv) *Effects of prohibited allocation.*—(A) *Deemed distribution.*—If there is a prohibited allocation, the amount of the prohibited allocation, as determined under this paragraph (b)(2), is treated as distributed from the ESOP (or other plan of the employer) to the disqualified person on the first day of the plan year on which there is an impermissible accrual or on the date of the allocation in the case of an additional impermissible accrual or impermissible allocation during the plan year but after the first day of the plan year. Thus, the fair market value of assets in the disqualified person's account that constitutes an impermissible accrual or allocation is included in gross income (to the extent in excess of any investment in the contract allocable to such amount) and is subject to any additional income tax that applies under section 72(t). A deemed distribution under this paragraph (b)(2)(iv)(A) is not an actual distribution from the ESOP. Thus, the amount of the prohibited allocation is not an eligible rollover distribution under section 402(c). However, for purposes of applying sections 72 and 402 with respect to any subsequent distribution from the ESOP, the amount that the disqualified person previously took into account as income as a result of the deemed distribution is treated as an investment in the contract.

(B) *Other effects.*—If there is a prohibited allocation, then the plan fails to satisfy the requirements of section 4975(e)(7) and ceases to be an ESOP. In such a case, the exemption from the excise tax on prohibited transactions for loans to leveraged ESOPs contained in section 4975(d)(3) would cease to apply to any loan (with the result that the employer would owe an excise tax with respect to the previously exempt loan) and, further, the exception in section 512(e)(3) would not apply to the plan (with the result that the plan may owe income tax as a result of unrelated business taxable income under section 512 with respect to S corporation stock held by the plan). See also section 4979A(a) which imposes an excise tax in certain events, including a prohibited allocation under section 409(p).

(v) *Prevention of prohibited allocation.*—(A) *Transfer of account to non-ESOP.*—An ESOP may prevent a nonallocation year or a prohibited allocation during a nonallocation year by permitting assets (including S corporation securities) allocated to the account of a disqualified person (or a person reasonably expected to become a disqualified person absent a transfer described in this paragraph (b)(2)(v)(A)) to be transferred into a separate portion of the plan that is not an ESOP, as described in §54.4975-11 (a)(5) of this chapter, or to another plan of the employer that satisfies the requirements of section 401(a) (and that is not an ESOP). In the event of such a transfer involving S corporation securities, the recipient plan is subject to tax on unrelated business taxable income under section 512.

(B) *Relief from nondiscrimination requirement.*—Pursuant to this paragraph (b)(2)(v)(B), if a transfer described in paragraph (b)(2)(v)(A) of this section is made from an ESOP to a separate portion of the plan or to another qualified plan of the employer that is not an ESOP, then both the ESOP and the plan or portion of a plan that is not an ESOP will not fail to satisfy the requirements of §1.401(a)(4)-4 merely because of the transfer. Further, subsequent to the transfer, that plan will not fail to satisfy the requirements of §1.401(a)(4)-4 merely because of the benefits, rights, or features with respect to the transferred benefits if those benefits, rights, or features would satisfy the requirements of §1.401(a)(4)-4 if the mandatory disaggregation rule for ESOPs at §1.410(b)-7(c)(2) did not apply.

(c) *Nonallocation year.*—(1) *Definition generally.*—For purposes of section 409(p) and this section, a *nonallocation year* means a plan year

of an ESOP during which, at any time, the ESOP holds any employer securities that are shares of an S corporation and either —

(i) Disqualified persons own at least 50 percent of the number of outstanding shares of stock in the S corporation (including deemed-owned ESOP shares); or

(ii) Disqualified persons own at least 50 percent of the sum of:

(A) The outstanding shares of stock in the S corporation (including deemed-owned ESOP shares), plus

(B) The shares of synthetic equity in the S corporation owned by disqualified persons.

(2) *Attribution rules.*—For purposes of this paragraph (c), the rules of section 318(a) apply to determine ownership of shares in the S corporation (including deemedowned ESOP shares) and synthetic equity. However, for this purpose, section 318(a)(4) (relating to options to acquire stock) is disregarded and, in applying section 318(a)(1), the members of an individual's family include members of the individual's family under paragraph (d)(2) of this section. In addition, an individual is treated as owning deemed-owned ESOP shares of that individual notwithstanding the employee trust exception in section 318(a)(2)(B)(i). If the attribution rules in paragraph (f)(1) of this section apply, then the rules of paragraph (f)(1) of this section are applied before the rules of this paragraph (c)(2).

(3) *Special rule for avoidance or evasion.*—(i) The ownership structures described in paragraph (g)(3) of this section result in a nonallocation year. In addition, under the ownership structures described in paragraph (g)(3) of this section, the individual referred to in paragraph (g)(3) of this section is treated as a disqualified person and that person's interest in the separate entity is treated as synthetic equity.

(ii) Under section 409(p)(7)(B), the Commissioner, in revenue rulings, notices, and other guidance published in the Internal Revenue Bulletin (see §601.601(d)(2)(ii)(b) of this chapter), may provide that a nonallocation year occurs in any case in which the principal purpose of the ownership structure of an S corporation constitutes an avoidance or evasion of section 409(p). For any year that is a nonallocation year under this paragraph (c)(3), the Commissioner may treat any person as a disqualified person. See paragraph (g) of this section for guidance regarding when the principal purpose of an ownership structure of an S corporation involving synthetic equity constitutes an avoidance or evasion of section 409(p).

(4) *Special rule for certain stock rights.*—(i) For purposes of paragraph (c)(1) of this section, a person is treated as owning stock that the person has a right to acquire if, at all times during the period when such right is effective, the stock that the person has the right to acquire is both issued and outstanding and is held by persons other than the ESOP, the S corporation, or a related entity (as defined in paragraph (f)(3) of this section).

(ii) This paragraph (c)(4) applies only if treating persons as owning the shares described in paragraph (c)(4)(i) of this section results in a nonallocation year. This paragraph (c)(4) does not apply to a right to acquire stock of an S corporation held by a shareholder subject to Federal income tax that, under §1.1361-1(1)(2)(iii) or (1)(4)(iii)(C), would not be taken into account in determining if an S corporation has a second class of stock provided that a principal purpose of the right is not the avoidance or evasion of section 409(p). Under the last sentence of paragraph (f)(2)(i) of this section, this paragraph (c)(4)(ii) does not apply for purposes of determining ownership of deemed-owned ESOP shares or whether an interest constitutes synthetic equity.

(5) *Application with respect to shares treated as owned by more than one person.*—For purposes of applying paragraph (c)(1) of this section, if, by application of the rules of paragraph (c)(2), (c)(4), or (f)(1) of this section, any share is treated as owned by more than one person, then that share is counted as a single share and that share is treated as owned by disqualified persons if any of the owners is a disqualified person.

(6) *Effect of nonallocation year.*—See paragraph (b) of this section for a prohibition applicable during a nonallocation year. See also section 4979A for an excise tax applicable in certain cases, including section 4979A(a)(3) and (4) which applies during a nonallocation year (whether or not there is a prohibited allocation during the year).

(d) *Disqualified persons.*—(1) *General definition.*—For purposes of section 409(p) and this section, a *disqualified person* means any person for whom —

(i) The number of such person's deemed-owned ESOP shares of the S corporation is at least 10 percent of the number of the deemed-owned ESOP shares of the S corporation;

(ii) The aggregate number of such person's deemed-owned ESOP shares and synthetic equity shares of the S corporation is at least 10 percent of the sum of:

»»→ *Caution: Temporary Reg. §1.409(p)-1T, below, applies for plan years beginning before January 1, 2006 (see Reg. §1.409(p)-1(i)(2)).*

(A) The total number of deemed-owned ESOP shares, and

(B) The person's synthetic equity shares of the S corporation;

(iii) The aggregate number of the S corporation's deemed-owned ESOP shares of such person and of the members of such person's family is at least 20 percent of the number of deemed-owned ESOP shares of the S corporation; or

(iv) The aggregate number of the S corporation's deemed-owned ESOP shares and synthetic equity shares of such person and of the members of such person's family is at least 20 percent of the sum of:

(A) The total number of deemed-owned ESOP shares, and

(B) The synthetic equity shares of the S corporation owned by such person and the members of such person's family.

(2) *Treatment of family members; definition.*—(i) *Rule.*—Each member of the family of any person who is a disqualified person under paragraph (d)(1)(iii) or (iv) of this section is a disqualified person.

(ii) *General definition.*—For purposes of section 409(p) and this section, *member of the family* means, with respect to an individual —

(A) The spouse of the individual;

(B) An ancestor or lineal descendant of the individual or the individual's spouse;

(C) A brother or sister of the individual or of the individual's spouse and any lineal descendant of the brother or sister; and

(D) The spouse of any individual described in paragraph (d)(2)(ii)(B) or (C) of this section.

(iii) *Spouse.*—A spouse of an individual who is legally separated from such individual under a decree of divorce or separate maintenance is not treated as such individual's spouse under paragraph (d)(2)(ii)(A) of this section.

(3) *Special rule for certain nonallocation years.*—See paragraph (c)(3) of this section (relating to avoidance or evasion of section 409(p)) for special rules permitting certain persons to be treated as disqualified persons in certain nonallocation years.

(4) *Example.*—The rules of this paragraph (d) are illustrated by the following example:

Example. (i) *Facts.* An S corporation has 800 outstanding shares of which 100 are owned by individual O and 700 are held in an employee stock ownership plan (ESOP) during 2005, including 200 shares held in the ESOP account of O, 65 shares held in the ESOP account of participant P, and 40 shares held in the ESOP account of participant Q who is P's spouse. The S corporation has no synthetic equity.

(ii) *Conclusion.* O is a disqualified person during 2005 because O's account in the ESOP holds at least 10 percent of the shares owned by the ESOP (200 is 28.6 percent of 700). In addition, P is a disqualified person during 2005 because, under paragraph (d)(2) of this section, P is treated as owning the shares held by Q and P's total deemed-owned shares are thus at least 10 percent of the shares owned by the plan (65 plus 40 is more than 10 percent of 700). In addition, Q is a disqualified person as a result of the rules in paragraph (d)(2) of this section. As a result, disqualified persons own at least 50 percent of the outstanding shares of the S corporation during 2005 (O's 100 directly owned shares, O's 200 deemed-owned shares, P's 65 deemed-owned shares, plus Q's 40 deemed owned shares are 50.6 percent of 800).

(e) *Deemed-owned ESOP shares.*—For purposes of section 409(p) and this section, a person is treated as owning his or her deemed-owned ESOP shares. *Deemed-owned ESOP shares* mean, with respect to any person —

(1) Any shares of stock in the S corporation constituting employer securities that are allocated to such person's account under the ESOP; and

(2) Such person's share of the stock in the S corporation that is held by the ESOP but is not allocated to the account of any participant or beneficiary (with such person's share to be determined in the same proportion as the shares released and allocated from a suspense account, as described at §54.4975-11(c) and (d) of this chapter, under the ESOP for the most recently ended plan year for which there were shares released and allocated from a suspense account, or if there has been no such prior release and allocation from a suspense account, then determined in proportion to a reasonable estimate of the shares that would be released and allocated in the first year of loan repayment).

(f) *Synthetic equity.*—(1) *Ownership of synthetic equity.*—For purposes of section 409(p) and this section, synthetic equity is treated as owned by a person in the same manner as stock is treated as owned by a person, directly or under the rules of section 318(a)(2) and (3).

Synthetic equity means the rights described in paragraph (f)(2) of this section.

(2) *Synthetic equity.*—(i) *Rights to acquire stock of the S corporation.*—Synthetic equity includes any stock option, warrant, restricted stock, deferred issuance stock right, stock appreciation right payable in stock, or similar interest or right that gives the holder the right to acquire or receive stock of the S corporation in the future. Rights to acquire stock in an S corporation with respect to stock that is, at all times during the period when such rights are effective, both issued and outstanding and held by persons (who are subject to federal income taxes) other than the ESOP, the S corporation, or a related entity are not synthetic equity (but see paragraph (c)(4) of this section).

(ii) *Special rule for certain stock rights.*—Synthetic equity also includes a right to a future payment (payable in cash or any other form other than stock of the S corporation) from an S corporation that is based on the value of the stock of the S corporation, such as appreciation in such value. Thus, synthetic equity includes a stock appreciation right with respect to stock of an S corporation that is payable in cash or a phantom stock unit with respect to stock of an S corporation that is payable in cash.

(iii) *Rights to acquire interests in or assets of an S corporation or a related entity.*—Synthetic equity includes a right to acquire stock or other similar interests in a related entity to the extent of the S corporation's ownership. Synthetic equity also includes a right to acquire assets of an S corporation or a related entity other than either rights to acquire goods, services, or property at fair market value in the ordinary course of business or fringe benefits excluded from gross income under section 132.

(iv) *Special rule for nonqualified deferred compensation.*—(A) Synthetic equity also includes any of the following with respect to an S corporation or a related entity: any remuneration to which section 404(a)(5) applies; remuneration for which a deduction would be permitted under section 404(a)(5) if separate accounts were maintained; any right to receive property to which section 83 applies (including a payment to a trust described in section 402(b) or to an annuity described in section 403(c)) in a future year for the performance of services; any transfer of property (to which section 83 applies) in connection with the performance of services to the extent that the property is not substantially vested within the meaning of §1.83-3(i) by the end of the plan year in which transferred; and a split-dollar life insurance arrangement under §1.61-22(b) entered into in connection with the performance of services (other than one under which, at all times, the only economic benefit that will be provided under the arrangement is current life insurance protection as described in §1.61-22(d)(3)). Synthetic equity also includes any other remuneration for services under a plan, or method or arrangement, deferring the receipt of compensation to a date that is after the 15th day of the 3rd calendar month after the end of the entity's taxable year in which the related services are rendered. However, synthetic equity does not include benefits under a plan that is an eligible retirement plan within the meaning of section 402(c)(8)(B).

(B) For purposes of applying paragraph (f)(2)(iv)(A) of this section with respect to an ESOP, synthetic equity does not include any interest described in such paragraph (f)(2)(iv)(A) of this section to the extent that—

(1) The interest is nonqualified deferred compensation (within the meaning of section 3121(v)(2)) that was outstanding on December 17, 2004;

(2) The interest is an amount that was taken into account (within the meaning of §31.3121(v)(2)-1(d) of this chapter) prior to January 1, 2005, for purposes of taxation under chapter 21 of the Internal Revenue Code (or income attributable thereto); and

(3) The interest was held before the first date on which the ESOP acquires any employer securities.

(v) *No overlap among shares of deemed-owned ESOP shares or synthetic equity.*—Synthetic equity under this paragraph (f)(2) does not include shares that are deemed-owned ESOP shares (or any rights with respect to deemed-owned ESOP shares to the extent such rights are specifically permitted under section 409(h)). In addition, synthetic equity under a specific subparagraph of this paragraph (f)(2) does not include anything that is synthetic equity under paragraph (b)(2)(i), (ii), (iii) or (iv) of this section.

(3) *Related entity.*—For purposes of this paragraph (f), *related entity* means any entity in which the S corporation holds an interest and which is a partnership, a trust, an eligible entity that is disregarded as an entity that is separate from its owner under §301.7701-3 of this chapter, or a Qualified Subchapter S Subsidiary under section 1361(b)(3).

>>→ *Caution: Temporary Reg. §1.409(p)-1T, below, applies for plan years beginning before January 1, 2006 (see Reg. §1.409(p)-1(i)(2)).*

(4) *Number of synthetic shares.*—(i) *Synthetic equity determined by reference to S corporation shares.*—In the case of synthetic equity that is determined by reference to shares of stock of the S corporation, the person who is entitled to the synthetic equity is treated as owning the number of shares of stock deliverable pursuant to such synthetic equity. In the case of synthetic equity that is determined by reference to shares of stock of the S corporation, but for which payment is made in cash or other property (besides stock of the S corporation), the number of shares of synthetic equity treated as owned is equal to the number of shares of stock having a fair market value equal to the cash or other property (disregarding lapse restrictions as described in §1.83-3(i)). Where such synthetic equity is a right to purchase or receive S corporation shares, the corresponding number of shares of synthetic equity is determined without regard to lapse restrictions as described in §1.83-3(i) or to any amount required to be paid in exchange for the shares. Thus, for example, if a corporation grants an employee of an S corporation an option to purchase 100 shares of the corporation's stock, exercisable in the future only after the satisfaction of certain performance conditions, the employee is the deemed owner of 100 synthetic equity shares of the corporation as of the date the option is granted. If the same employee were granted 100 shares of restricted S corporation stock (or restricted stock units), subject to forfeiture until the satisfaction of performance or service conditions, the employee would likewise be the deemed owner of 100 synthetic equity shares from the grant date. However, if the same employee were granted a stock appreciation right with regard to 100 shares of S corporation stock (whether payable in stock or in cash), the number of synthetic equity shares the employee is deemed to own equals the number of shares having a value equal to the appreciation at the time of measurement (determined without regard to lapse restrictions).

(ii) *Synthetic equity determined by reference to shares in a related entity.*—In the case of synthetic equity that is determined by reference to shares of stock (or similar interests) in a related entity, the person who is entitled to the synthetic equity is treated as owning shares of stock of the S corporation with the same aggregate value as the number of shares of stock (or similar interests) of the related entity (with such value determined without regard to any lapse restriction as defined at §1.83-3(i)).

(iii) *Other synthetic equity.*—(A) *General rule.*—In the case of any synthetic equity to which neither paragraph (f)(4)(i) nor paragraph (f)(4)(ii) of this section apply, the person who is entitled to the synthetic equity is treated as owning on any date a number of shares of stock in the S corporation equal to the present value (on that date) of the synthetic equity (with such value determined without regard to any lapse restriction as defined at §1.83-3(i)) divided by the fair market value of a share of the S corporation's stock as of that date.

(B) *Special rules.*—(1) *Use of annual or more frequent determination dates.*—For purposes of this paragraph (b)(4)(iii), while the determination of whether there is a nonallocation year depends on day-by-day determinations under paragraph (c) of this section, the number of shares of S corporation stock treated as owned by a person who is entitled to synthetic equity to which this paragraph (b)(4)(iii) applies is permitted to be determined only annually (or more frequently), as of the first day of the ESOP's plan year or as of any other reasonable determination date or dates during a plan year. If the ESOP so provides, the number of shares of synthetic equity to which this paragraph (f)(4)(iii) applies that are treated as owned by that person for any period from a given determination date through the date immediately preceding the next following determination date is the number of shares treated as owned on the given determination date.

(2) *Use of triannual recalculations.*—In addition, if the terms of the ESOP so provide, then the number of shares of synthetic equity with respect to grants of synthetic equity to which this paragraph (f)(4)(iii) applies may be fixed for a specified period from a determination date identified under the ESOP through a date that is not later than the day before the determination date that is on or immediately preceding the third anniversary of the identified determination date. Additional accruals, allocations, or grants (to which this paragraph (f)(4)(iii) applies) that are made during such three-year period are taken into account on each determination date during that period, based on the number of synthetic equity shares resulting from the additional accrual, allocation, or grant (determined as of the determination date on or next following the date of the accrual, allocation, or grant). However, the ESOP must provide for the number of shares of synthetic equity to which this paragraph (f)(4)(iii) applies to be re-determined not less frequently than every three years, based on the S corporation share value on a determination date that is not later than the third anniversary of the identified determination date and the aggregate present value of the synthetic equity to which this paragraph (f)(4)(iii) applies (including all grants

made during the three-year period) on that determination date. See *Example 3* of paragraph (h) of this section for an example illustrating this paragraph (f)(4)(iii)(B)(2).

(3) *Conditions for application of rules.*—Paragraph (f)(4)(iii)(B) of this section only applies with respect to grants of synthetic equity to which this paragraph (f)(4)(iii) applies. In addition, paragraph (f)(4)(iii)(B)(1) of this section applies only if the fair market value of a share of the S corporation securities on any determination date is not unrepresentative of the value of the S corporation securities throughout the rest of the plan year and only if the terms of the ESOP include provisions conforming to paragraph (f)(4)(iii)(B)(1) of this section which are consistently used by the ESOP for all persons. In addition, paragraph (f)(4)(iii)(B)(2) of this section applies only if the terms of the ESOP include provisions conforming to paragraphs (f)(4)(iii)(B)(1) and (2) of this section which are consistently used by the ESOP for all persons.

(iv) *Adjustment of number of synthetic equity shares where ESOP owns less than 100% of S corporation.*—Under this paragraph (f)(4)(iv), the number of synthetic shares otherwise determined under this paragraph (f)(4) is decreased ratably to the extent that shares of the S corporation are owned by a person who is not an ESOP (and who is subject to federal income taxes). For example, if an S corporation has 200 outstanding shares, of which individual A owns 50 shares and the ESOP owns the other 150 shares, and individual B would be treated under this paragraph (f)(4) as owning 200 synthetic equity shares of the S corporation but for this paragraph (f)(4)(iv), then, under the rule of this paragraph (f)(4)(iv), the number of synthetic shares treated as owned by B under this paragraph (f)(4) is decreased from 200 to 150 (because the ESOP only owns 75% of the outstanding stock of the S corporation, rather than 100%).

(v) *Special rule for shares with greater voting power than ESOP shares.*—Notwithstanding any other provision of this paragraph (f)(4), if a synthetic equity right includes (directly or indirectly) a right to purchase or receive shares of S corporation stock that have per-share voting rights greater than the per-share voting rights of one or more shares of S corporation stock held by the ESOP, then the number of shares of deemed owned synthetic equity attributable to such right is not less than the number of shares that would have the same voting rights if the shares had the same per-share voting rights as shares held by the ESOP with the least voting rights. For example, if shares of S corporation stock held by the ESOP have one voting right per share, then an individual who holds an option to purchase one share with 100 voting rights is treated as owning 100 shares of synthetic equity.

(g) *Avoidance or evasion of section 409(p) involving synthetic equity.*—(1) *General rule.*—Paragraph (g)(2) of this section sets forth a standard for determining whether the principal purpose of the ownership structure of an S corporation involving synthetic equity constitutes an avoidance or evasion of section 409(p). Paragraph (g)(3) of this section identifies certain specific ownership structures that constitute an avoidance or evasion of section 409(p). See also paragraph (c)(3) of this section for a rule under which the ownership structures in paragraph (g)(3) result in a nonallocation year for purposes of section 409(p).

(2) *Standard for determining when there is an avoidance or evasion of section 409(p) involving synthetic equity.*—For purposes of section 409(p) and this section, whether the principal purpose of the ownership structure of an S corporation involving synthetic equity constitutes an avoidance or evasion of section 409(p) is determined by taking into account all the surrounding facts and circumstances, including all features of the ownership of the S corporation's outstanding stock and related obligations (including synthetic equity), any shareholders who are taxable entities, and the cash distributions made to shareholders, to determine whether, to the extent of the ESOP's stock ownership, the ESOP receives the economic benefits of ownership in the S corporation that occur during the period that stock of the S corporation is owned by the ESOP. Among the factors indicating that the ESOP receives these economic benefits include shareholder voting rights, the right to receive distributions made to shareholders, and the right to benefit from the profits earned by the S corporation, including the extent to which actual distributions of profits are made from the S corporation to the ESOP and the extent to which the ESOP's ownership interest in undistributed profits and future profits is subject to dilution as a result of synthetic equity, for example, the ESOP's ownership interest is not subject to dilution if the total amount of synthetic equity is a relatively small portion of the total number of shares and deemed-owned shares of the S corporation.

(3) *Specific transactions that constitute an avoidance or evasion of section 409(p) involving segregated profits.*—Taking into account the

>>>→ *Caution: Temporary Reg. §1.409(p)-1T, below, applies for plan years beginning before January 1, 2006 (see Reg. §1.409(p)-1(i)(2)).*

standard in paragraph (g)(2) of this section, the principal purpose of the ownership structure of an S corporation constitutes an avoidance or evasion of section 409(p) in any case in which—

(i) The profits of the S corporation generated by the business activities of a specific individual or individuals are not provided to the ESOP, but are instead substantially accumulated and held for the benefit of that individual or individuals on a tax-deferred basis within an entity related to the S corporation, such as a partnership, trust, or corporation (such as in a subsidiary that is a disregarded entity), or any other method that has the same effect of segregating profits for the benefit of such individual or individuals (such as nonqualified deferred compensation described in paragraph (f)(2)(iv) of this section);

(ii) The individual or individuals for whom profits are segregated have rights to acquire 50 percent or more of those profits directly or indirectly (for example, by purchase of the subsidiary); and

(iii) A nonallocation year would occur if this section were separately applied with respect to either the separate entity or whatever method has the effect of segregating profits of the individual or individuals, treating such entity as a separate S corporation owned by an ESOP (or in the case of any other method of segregation of profits by treating those profits as the only assets of a separate S corporation owned by an ESOP).

(h) *Examples.*—The rules of this section are illustrated by the following examples:

Example 1. Relating to determination of disqualified persons and nonallocation year if there is no synthetic equity. (i) *Facts.* Corporation X is a calendar year S corporation that maintains an ESOP. X has a single class of common stock, of which there are a total of 1,200 shares outstanding. X has no synthetic equity. In 2006, individual A, who is not an employee of X (and is not related to any employee of X), owns 100 shares directly, individual B owns 100 shares directly, and the remaining 1,000 shares are owned by an ESOP maintained by X for its employees. The ESOP's 1,000 shares are allocated to the accounts of individuals who are employees of X (none of whom are related), as set forth in columns 1 and 2 in the following table:

1 Shareholders	2 Deemed-Owned ESOP Shares (total of 1,000)	3 Percentage Deemed-Owned ESOP Shares	4 Disqualified Person
B	330	33%	Yes
C	145	14.5%	Yes
D	75	7.5%	No
E	30	3%	No
F	20	2%	No
Other participants	400 (none exceed 10 shares)	1% or less	No

(ii) *Conclusion with respect to disqualified persons.* As shown in column 4 in the table above, individuals B and C are disqualified persons for 2006 under paragraph (d)(1) of this section because each owns at least 10% of X's deemed-owned ESOP shares.

(iii) *Conclusion with respect to nonallocation year.* However, 2006 is not a nonallocation year under section 409(p) because disqualified persons do not own at least 50% of X's outstanding shares (the 100 shares owned directly by B, B's 330 deemed-owned ESOP shares, plus C's 145 deemed-owned ESOP shares equal only 47.9% of the 1,200 outstanding shares of X).

Example 2. Relating to determination of disqualified persons and nonallocation year if there is synthetic equity. (i) *Facts.* The facts are the same as in *Example 1*, except that, as shown in column 4 of the table in this *example 2*, individuals E and F have options to acquire 110 and 130 shares, respectively, of the common stock of X from X:

1 Shareholders	2 Deemed-Owned ESOP Shares (total of 1,000)	3 Percentage Deemed-Owned ESOP Shares	4 Options (240)	5 Shareholder Percentage of Deemed-Owned ESOP plus Synthetic Equity Shares	6 Disqualified Person
B	330	33%			Yes (col. 3)
C	145	14.5%			Yes (col.3)
D	75	7.5%			No
E	30	3%	110	11.1% ([30+ 91.7] divided by 1,091.7)	Yes (col. 5)
F	20	2%	130	11.6% ([20 +108.3] divided by 1,108.3)	Yes (col. 5)
Other participants	400 (none exceeds 10 shares)	1% or less			No

(ii) *Conclusion with respect to disqualified persons.* Applying the rule of paragraph (f)(4)(iv) of this section, E's option to acquire 110 shares of the S corporation converts into 91.7 shares of synthetic equity (110 times the ratio of the 1,000 deemed-owned ESOP shares to the sum of the 1,000 deemed-owned ESOP shares plus the 200 shares held outside the ESOP by A and B). Similarly, F's option to acquire 130 shares of the S corporation converts into 108.3 shares of synthetic equity (130 times the ratio of the 1,000 deemed-owned ESOP shares to the sum of the 1,000 deemed-owned ESOP shares plus the 200 shares held outside the ESOP by A and B). Accordingly, as shown in column 6 in the table above, individual E's synthetic equity shares are counted in determining whether E is a disqualified person for 2006, and individual F's synthetic equity shares are counted in determining whether F is a disqualified person for 2006, but the synthetic equity shares owned by any person do not affect the calculation for any other person's ownership of shares. Accordingly, individuals B, C, E, and F are disqualified persons for 2006.

(iii) *Conclusion with respect to nonallocation year.* The 100 shares owned directly by B, B's 330 deemed-owned ESOP shares, C's 145 deemed-owned ESOP shares, E's 30 deemed-owned ESOP shares, E's 91.7 synthetic equity shares, F's 20 deemed-owned ESOP shares, plus F's 108.3 synthetic equity shares total 825, which equals 58.9% of 1,400, which is the sum of the 1,200 outstanding shares of X and the 200 shares of synthetic equity shares of X held by disqualified persons. Thus, 2006 is a nonallocation year for X's ESOP under section 409(p) because disqualified persons own at least 50% of the total shares of outstanding stock of X and the total synthetic equity shares of X held by disqualified persons. In addition, independent of the preceding conclusion, 2006 would be a nonallocation year because disqualified persons own at least 50% of X's outstanding shares because the 100 shares owned directly by B, B's 330 deemed-owned ESOP shares, C's 145 deemed-owned ESOP shares, E's 30 deemed-owned ESOP shares, plus F's 20 deemed-owned ESOP shares equal 52.1% of the 1,200 outstanding shares of X.

Example 3. Relating to determination of number of shares of synthetic equity. (i) *Facts.* Corporation Y is a calendar year S corporation that maintains an ESOP. Y has a single class of common stock, of which there are a total of 1,000 shares outstanding, all of which are owned by the ESOP. Y has no synthetic equity, except for four grants of nonqualified deferred compensation that are made to an individual

>>>→ *Caution: Temporary Reg. §1.409(p)-1T, below, applies for plan years beginning before January 1, 2006 (see Reg. §1.409(p)-1(i)(2)).*

during the period from 2005 through 2011, as set forth in column 2 in the following table, and the ESOP uses the special rules in paragraph (f)(4)(iii) of this section to determine the number of shares of synthetic equity owned by that individual, as shown in columns 4 and 5:

1 Determination Date	2 Present Value of Nonqualified Deferred Compensation on Determination Date	3 Share Value on Determination Date	4 New Shares of Synthetic Equity on Determination Date	5 Aggregate Number of Synthetic Equity Shares on Determination Date
January 1, 2005	A grant is made on January 1, 2005 with a present value of $1,000. An additional grant of nonqualified deferred compensation with a present value of $775 is made on March 1, 2005.	$10 per share	100	100
January 1, 2006	An additional grant is made on December 31, 2005 which has a present value of $800 on January 1, 2006. The March 1, 2005 grant has a present value on January 1, 2006 of $800.	$8 per share	200	300
January 1, 2007	No new grants made.	$12 per share		300
January 1, 2008	An additional grant is made on December 31, 2007 which has a present value of $3,000 on January 1, 2008. The grants made during 2005 through 2007 have an aggregate present value on January 1, 2008 of $3,750.	$15 per share	200	450
January 1, 2009	No new grants are made.	$11 per share		450
January 1, 2010	No new grants are made.	$22 per share		450
January 1, 2011	No new grants are made. The grants made during 2005 through 2008 have an aggregate present value on January 1, 2011 of $7,600.	$20 per share		380

(ii) *Conclusion.* The grant made on January 1, 2005, is treated as 100 shares until the determination date in 2008. The grant made on March 1, 2005, is not taken into account until the 2006 determination date and its present value on that date, along with the then present value of the grant made on the preceding day, is treated as a number of shares that are based on the $8 per share value on the 2006 determination date, with the resulting number of shares continuing to apply until the determination date in 2008. On the January 1, 2008, determination date, the grant made on the preceding day is taken into account at its present value of $3,000 on January 1, 2008 and the $15 per share value on that date with the resulting number of shares (200) continuing to apply until the next determination date. In addition, on the January 1, 2008, determination date, the number of shares determined under other grants made between January 1, 2005 and December 31, 2007, must be revalued. Accordingly, the aggregate value of all nonqualified deferred compensation granted during that period is determined to be $3750 on January 1, 2008, and the corresponding number of shares of synthetic equity based on the $15 per share value is determined to be 250 shares on the 2008 determination date, with the resulting aggregate number of shares (450) continuing to apply until the determination date in 2011. On the January 1, 2011, determination date, the aggregate value of all nonqualified deferred compensation is determined to be $7,600 and the corresponding number of shares of synthetic equity based on the $20 per share value on the 2011 determination date is determined to be 380 shares (with the resulting number of shares continuing to apply until the determination date in 2014, assuming no further grants are made).

(i) *Effective dates.*—(1) *Statutory effective date.*—(i) Except as otherwise provided in paragraph (i)(1)(ii) of this section, section 409(p) applies for plan years ending after March 14, 2001.

(ii) If an *ESOP holding stock in an S corporation was established on or before March 14, 2001, and the election under section 1362(a) with respect to that S corporation was in effect on March 14, 2001,* section 409(p) applies for plan years beginning on or after January 1, 2005.

(2) *Regulation effective date.*—(i) *General effective date.*—Except as otherwise provided in paragraph (i)(2)(ii) of this section, this section applies for plan years beginning on or after January 1, 2005.

(ii) *Rules for plan years beginning before January 1, 2005.*—(A) Except as provided in this paragraph (i)(2)(ii), §1.409(p)-1T as in effect prior to December 17, 2004 (see §1.409(p)-1T in 26 CFR Part 1 revised as of April 1, 2004) applies for plan years ending after October 20, 2003, and beginning before January 1, 2005.

(B) Paragraphs (c)(3) and (g) of this section apply for plan years ending on or after December 31, 2004, but do not apply with respect to an interest held in a qualified subchapter S subsidiary (QSUB) of an S corporation or another entity to which paragraph (g)(3) of this section applies before March 15, 2004 if:

(1) All interests in the entity held by individuals who would be disqualified persons under paragraph (g)(3) of this section or under guidance issued by the Commissioner before March 15, 2004 are distributed to those individuals as compensation on or before March 15, 2004 and

(2) No such individual has been a participant in the ESOP of the S corporation at any time after October 20, 2003 and before March 15, 2004.

(C) Paragraph (f)(2)(iv)(B) of this section (providing that synthetic equity does not include certain preexisting nonqualified deferred compensation) applies for plan years ending before January 1, 2005.

(D) Paragraph (f)(4)(iv) of this section (permitting an adjustment of the number of synthetic equity shares where an ESOP owns less than 100% of an S corporation) applies for plan years ending before January 1, 2005.

(E) In no event does this paragraph (i)(2)(ii) apply for any plan year ending before January 1, 2005, for an ESOP holding stock in an S corporation that was established on or before March 14, 2001, if the election under section 1362(a) with respect to that S Corporation was in effect on March 14, 2001.

(iii) *Transition rules.*—(A) Assets held in the account of a disqualified person as of the last day of the first plan year beginning before January 1, 2005, will not be treated as an impermissible accrual

>>>→ *Caution: Temporary Reg. §1.409(p)-1T, below, applies for plan years beginning before January 1, 2006 (see Reg. §1.409(p)-1(i)(2)).*

with respect to that disqualified person under paragraph (b)(2)((ii) of this section for the first plan year beginning on or after January 1, 2005, to the extent those assets are not held in that person's account on or after July 1, 2005. Thus, for example, to the extent the assets allocated to the account of a disqualified person as of the last day of the first plan year beginning before January 1, 2005, are transferred to a non-ESOP portion of the plan as described in paragraph (b)(2)(v)(A) of this section before July 1, 2005, those assets will not be treated as an impermissible accrual under paragraph (b)(2)((ii) of this section for the period from the first day of the first plan year beginning on or after January 1, 2005 through June 30, 2005. However, see section 4979A(a)(3), (a)(4), and (e)(2)(C) for excise tax provisions that apply to all deemed-owned shares during the first nonallocation year for the ESOP.

(B) An individual is not treated as a disqualified person during the period from the first day of the first plan year beginning on or after January 1, 2005 through June 30, 2005 if that person would not be a disqualified person during that period under the modified rules of this paragraph (i)(2)(iii)(B) as of any date during that same period. Further, solely for the purpose of determining whether the first plan year beginning on or after January 1, 2005 is a nonallocation year under section 409(p) and this section, if that plan year would not have been a nonallocation year under the modified rules of this paragraph (i)(2)(iii)(B), then synthetic equity that is not owned by a person on July 1, 2005 is disregarded during the period from the first day of the first plan year beginning on or after January 1, 2005 through June 30, 2005. For purposes of this paragraph (i)(2)(iii)(B), the *modified rules of this paragraph (i)(2)(iii)(B)* are the rules in §1.409(p)-1T as in effect prior to December 17, 2004 (see §1.409(p)-1T in 26 CFR Part 1 revised as of April 1, 2004), modified to exclude from the definition of synthetic equity any stock option, stock appreciation right (payable in cash or stock), or similar rights with respect to shares of the S corporation or a related entity where the facts and circumstances indicate that there is no reasonable likelihood that the holder of the right will receive the shares (or equivalent value). For this purpose, there is no reasonable likelihood that the holder of the right will receive the shares (or equivalent value) in any case in which the option is based on an exercise price that is more than 200% of the fair market value of the shares on the date of grant or the right (in the case of a stock appreciation right or similar right to acquire shares of the S corporation or a related entity) is payable only if the appreciation exceeds 100% of the fair market value of the shares on the date of grant.

(C) For the period from the first day of the first plan year beginning on or after January 1, 2005 through June 30, 2005, there is no nonallocation year under this section if there would be no nonallocation year under this section during that period if this section were applied without regard to paragraph (f)(4)(v) of this section (relating to voting rights).

(D) This paragraph (iii) does not apply to an ESOP for which the first plan year beginning on or after January 1, 2005 begins after June 30, 2005. [Temporary Reg. §1.409(p)-1T.]

☐ [T.D. 9081, 7-18-2003. *Amended by* T.D. 9164, 12-16-2004 (*corrected* 3-7-2005).]

[Reg. §1.409A-0]

§1.409A-0. Table of contents.—This section lists captions contained in §§1.409A-1, 1.409A-2, 1.409A-3, 1.409A-4, 1.409A-5 and 1.409A-6.

(iii) Separation pay due to involuntary separation from service or participation in a window program.

(iv) Foreign separation pay plans.

(v) Reimbursements and certain other separation payments.

(A) In general.

(B) Medical benefits.

(C) In-kind benefits and direct service recipient payments.

(D) Limited payments.

(E) Limited period of time.

(vi) Window programs — definition.

(10) Certain indemnification and liability insurance plans.

(11) Legal settlements.

(12) Certain educational benefits.

(c) Plan.

(1) In general.

(2) Plan aggregation rules.

(i) In general.

(ii) Dual status.

(3) Establishment of plan.

(i) In general.

(ii) Initial deferral election provisions.

(iii) Subsequent deferral election provisions.

(iv) Payment accelerations.

(v) Six-month delay for specified employees.

(vi) Plan amendments.

(vii) Transition rule for written plan requirement.

(viii) Plan aggregation rules.

(d) Substantial risk of forfeiture

(1) In general.

(2) Stock rights.

(3) Enforcement of forfeiture condition.

(i) In general.

(ii) Examples.

(e) Performance-based compensation.

(1) In general.

(2) Payments based upon subjective performance criteria.

(3) Equity-based compensation.

(f) Service provider.

(1) In general.

(2) Independent contractors.

(i) In general.

(ii) Related person.

(iii) Significant services.

(iv) Management services.

(v) Services provided to related persons.

(g) Service recipient.

(h) Separation from service.

(1) Employees.

(i) In general.

(ii) Termination of employment.

(2) Independent contractors.

(i) In general.

(ii) Special rule.

(3) Definition of service recipient and employer.

(4) Asset purchase transactions.

(5) Dual status.

(6) Collectively bargained plans covering multiple employers.

(i) Specified employee.

(1) In general.

(2) Definition of compensation.

(3) Specified employee identification date.

(4) Specified employee effective date.

(5) Alternative methods of satisfying the six-month delay rule.

(6) Corporate transactions.

(i) Mergers and acquisitions of public service recipients.

(ii) Mergers and acquisitions of nonpublic service recipients.

(iii) Spinoffs.

(iv) Public offerings and other corporate transactions.

(v) Alternative methods of compliance.

(7) Nonresident alien employees.

(8) Elections affecting the identification of specified employees.

(j) Nonresident alien.

(k) Established securities market.

(l) Stock right.

(m) Separation pay plan.

(n) Involuntary separation from service.

(1) In general.

(2) Separations from service for good reason.

(i) In general.

(ii) Safe harbor.

(3) Special rule for certain collectively bargained plans.

(o) Earnings.

(p) In-kind benefits.

(q) Application of definitions and rules.

§1.409A-2. *Deferral elections.*

(a) Initial elections as to the time and form of payment.

(1) In general.

(2) Service recipient elections.

(3) General rule.

(4) Initial deferral election with respect to short-term deferrals.

(5) Initial deferral election with respect to certain forfeitable rights.

(6) Initial deferral election with respect to fiscal year compensation.

(7) First year of eligibility.

(i) In general.

(ii) Eligibility to participate.

(iii) Application to excess benefit plans.

(8) Initial deferral election with respect to performance-based compensation.

(9) Nonqualified deferred compensation plans linked to qualified employer plans or certain other arrangements.

(10) Changes in elections under a cafeteria plan.

(11) Initial deferral election with respect to certain separation pay.

(12) Initial deferral election with respect to certain commissions.

(i) Sales commission compensation.

(ii) Investment commission compensation.

(iii) Commission compensation and related persons.

(13) Initial deferral election with respect to compensation paid for final payroll period.

(i) In general.

(ii) Transition rule.

(14) Elections to annualize recurring part-year compensation.

(15) USERRA rights.

(b) Subsequent changes in time and form of payment.

(1) In general.

(2) Definition of payments for purposes of subsequent changes in the time and form of payment.

(i) In general.

(ii) Life annuities.

(A) In general.

(B) Certain features disregarded.

(C) Subsidized joint and survivor annuities.

(D) Actuarial assumptions and methods.

(iii) Installment payments.

(iv) Transition rule.

(3) Beneficiaries.

(4) Domestic relations orders.

(5) Coordination with prohibition against acceleration of payments.

(6) Application to multiple payment events.

(7) Delay of payments under certain circumstances.

(i) Payments subject to section 162(m).

(ii) Payments that would violate Federal securities laws or other applicable law.

(iii) Other events and conditions.

(8) USERRA rights.

(9) Examples.

(c) Special rules for certain resident aliens.

§1.409A-3. *Permissible payments.*

(a) In general.

(b) Designation of payment upon a permissible payment event.

(c) Designation of alternative specified dates or payment schedules based upon date of permissible event.

(d) When a payment is treated as made upon the designated payment date.

(e) Designation of time and form of payment with respect to earnings.

(f) Substitutions.

(g) Disputed payments and refusals to pay.

(h) Special rule for certain resident aliens.

Reg. §1.409A-0

(i) Definitions and special rules.
(1) Specified time or fixed schedule.
(i) In general.
(ii) Payment schedules with formula and fixed limitations.
(A) Individual limitations.
(B) Limitations on aggregate payments to all participants in substantially identical plans.
(iii) Payment schedules determined by timing of payments received by the service recipient.
(iv) Reimbursement or in-kind benefit plans.
(A) General rule.
(B) Medical reimbursement arrangements.
(v) Tax gross-up payments.
(vi) Examples.
(2) Separation from service—required delay in payment to a specified employee pursuant to a separation from service.
(i) In general.
(ii) Application of payment rules to delayed payments.
(3) Unforeseeable emergency.
(i) Definition.
(ii) Amount of payment permitted upon an unforeseeable emergency.
(iii) Payments due to an unforeseeable emergency.
(4) Disability.
(i) In general.
(ii) Limited plan definition of disability.
(iii) Determination of disability.
(5) Change in the ownership or effective control of a corporation, or a change in the ownership of a substantial portion of the assets of a corporation.
(i) In general.
(ii) Identification of relevant corporation.
(A) In general.
(B) Majority shareholder.
(C) Example.
(iii) Attribution of stock ownership.
(iv) Special rules for certain delayed payments pursuant to a change in control event.
(A) Certain transaction-based compensation
(B) Certain nonvested compensation
(v) Change in the ownership of a corporation.
(A) In general.
(B) Persons acting as a group.
(vi) Change in the effective control of a corporation.
(A) In general.
(B) Multiple change in control events.
(C) Acquisition of additional control.
(D) Persons acting as a group.
(vii) Change in the ownership of a substantial portion of a corporation's assets.
(A) In general.
(B) Transfers to a related person.
(C) Persons acting as a group.
(6) Certain back-to-back arrangements.
(i) In general.
(ii) Example.
(j) Prohibition on acceleration of payments.
(1) In general.
(2) Application to multiple payment events.
(3) Beneficiaries.
(4) Exceptions.
(i) In general.
(ii) Domestic relations order.
(iii) Conflicts of interest.
(A) Compliance with ethics agreements with the Federal government.
(B) Compliance with ethics laws or conflicts of interest laws.
(iv) Section 457 plans.
(v) Limited cashouts.
(vi) Payment of employment taxes.
(vii) Payment upon income inclusion under section 409A.
(viii) Cancellation of deferrals following an unforeseeable emergency or hardship distribution.
(ix) Plan terminations and liquidations.
(x) Certain distributions to avoid a nonallocation year under section 409(p).
(xi) Payment of state, local, or foreign taxes.
(xii) Cancellation of deferral elections due to disability.
(xiii) Certain offsets.

(xiv) Bona fide disputes as to a right to a payment.
(5) Nonqualified deferred compensation plans linked to qualified employer plans or certain other arrangements.
(6) Changes in elections under a cafeteria plan.

§1.409A-4. *Calculation of income inclusion.* [Reserved]

§1.409A-5. *Funding.* [Reserved]

§1.409A-6. *Application of section 409A and effective dates.*
(a) Statutory application and effective dates
(1) Application to amounts deferred.
(i) In general.
(ii) Collectively bargained plans.
(2) Identification of date of deferral for statutory effective date purposes.
(3) Calculation of amount of compensation deferred for statutory effective date purposes.
(i) Nonaccount balance plans.
(ii) Account balance plans.
(iii) Equity-based compensation plans.
(iv) Earnings.
(v) Definition of plan.
(4) Material modifications.
(i) In general.
(ii) Adoptions of new plans.
(iii) Suspension or termination of a plan.
(iv) Changes to investment measures - account balance plans.
(v) Stock rights.
(vi) Rescission of modifications.
(vii) Definition of plan.
(b) Regulatory applicability date.
[Reg. §1.409A-0.]
☐ [*T.D. 9321,* 4-10-2007.]

[Reg. §1.409A-1]

§1.409A-1. Definitions and covered plans.—(a) *Nonqualified deferred compensation plan.*—(1) *In general.*—Except as otherwise provided in this paragraph (a), the term *nonqualified deferred compensation plan* means any plan (within the meaning of paragraph (c) of this section) that provides for the deferral of compensation (within the meaning of paragraph (b) of this section). Whether a plan provides for the deferral of compensation generally is determined at the time the service provider obtains a legally binding right to the compensation under the plan, and is not affected by any retroactive change to the plan to characterize the right as one that does not provide for the deferral of compensation. For example, amounts deferred under a nonqualified deferred compensation plan do not become an excluded death benefit if the plan is amended so that the amounts are payable only upon the death of the service provider. If a principal purpose of a plan is to achieve a result with respect to a deferral of compensation that is inconsistent with the purposes of section 409A, the Commissioner may treat the plan as a nonqualified deferred compensation plan for purposes of section 409A and the regulations thereunder.

(2) *Qualified employer plans.*—The term *nonqualified deferred compensation plan* does not include a qualified employer plan. The term *qualified employer plan* means any of the following plans:
(i) Any plan described in section 401(a) and a trust exempt from tax under section 501(a) or that is described in section 402(d).
(ii) Any annuity plan described in section 403(a).
(iii) Any annuity contract described in section 403(b).
(iv) Any simplified employee pension (within the meaning of section 408(k)).
(v) Any simple retirement account (within the meaning of section 408(p)).
(vi) Any plan under which an active participant makes deductible contributions to a trust described in section 501(c)(18).
(vii) Any eligible deferred compensation plan (within the meaning of section 457(b)).
(viii) Any plan described in section 415(m).
(ix) Any plan described in §1022(i)(2) of the Employee Retirement Income Security Act of 1974, Public Law 93-406 (88 Stat. 829, 942) (Sept. 2, 1974) (ERISA).

(3) *Certain foreign plans.*—(i) *Participation addressed by treaty.*—With respect to an individual for a taxable year, the term *nonqualified deferred compensation plan* does not include any scheme, trust, arrangement, or plan maintained with respect to such individual, to the extent contributions made by or on behalf of such individual to such scheme, trust, arrangement, or plan, or credited allocations, accrued benefits, earnings, or other amounts constituting income, of such individual under such scheme, trust, arrangement, or plan, are ex-

cludable by such individual for Federal income tax purposes pursuant to any bilateral income tax convention, or other bilateral or multilateral agreement, to which the United States is a party.

(ii) *Participation by nonresident aliens, certain resident aliens, and bona fide residents of possessions.*—With respect to an alien individual for a taxable year during which such individual is a nonresident alien, a resident alien classified as a resident alien solely under section 7701(b)(1)(A)(ii) (and not section 7701(b)(1)(A)(i)), or a bona fide resident of a possession (within the meaning of section 937(a)), the term *nonqualified deferred compensation plan* does not include any broad-based foreign retirement plan (within the meaning of paragraph (a)(3)(v) of this section).

(iii) *Participation by U.S. citizens and lawful permanent residents.*—With respect to an individual for a given taxable year during which such individual is a U.S. citizen or a resident alien classified as a resident alien under section 7701(b)(1)(A)(i), other than an individual who is also a bona fide resident of a possession (within the meaning of section 937(a)), the term *nonqualified deferred compensation plan* does not include a broad-based foreign retirement plan (within the meaning of paragraph (a)(3)(v) of this section), but only with respect to a plan, or a portion of a plan where such portion may be distinguished, providing for nonelective deferrals of modified foreign earned income, and earnings with respect to such nonelective deferrals, and only to the extent that the amounts deferred under all such plans of the service recipient, or all portions of such plans, in which the service provider participates in such taxable year, do not exceed the applicable limits under section 415(b) (applied to nonaccount balance plans as defined in paragraph (c)(2)(i)(C) of this section) and section 415(c) (applied to account balance plans as defined in paragraph (c)(2)(i)(A) of this section) that would be applicable if such plans were plans subject to section 415 and the modified foreign earned income of such individual were treated as compensation for purposes of applying section 415(b) and (c). For purposes of this paragraph (a)(3)(iii), the term *modified foreign earned income* means foreign earned income as defined in section 911(b)(1) without regard to section 911(b)(1)(B)(iv) and without regard to the requirement that the income be attributable to services performed during the period described in section 911(d)(1)(A) or (B). The provisions of this paragraph (a)(3)(iii) do not apply to any individual with respect to any taxable year in which the individual is simultaneously eligible to participate in a broad-based foreign retirement plan and a qualified employer plan described in paragraph (a)(2) of this section. For purposes of this paragraph (a)(3)(iii), an individual is eligible to participate in a qualified employer plan if under the terms of the plan and without further amendment or action by the plan sponsor, the individual is eligible to make or receive contributions or accrue benefits under the plan (regardless of whether the individual has elected to participate in the plan).

(iv) *Plans subject to a totalization agreement and similar plans.*—The term *nonqualified deferred compensation plan* does not include any social security system of a jurisdiction to the extent that benefits provided under or contributions made to the system are subject to an agreement entered into pursuant to section 233 of the Social Security Act (42 U.S.C. 433) with any foreign jurisdiction. In addition, the term *nonqualified deferred compensation plan* does not include a social security system of a foreign jurisdiction to the extent that benefits are provided under or contributions are made to a government-mandated plan as part of that foreign jurisdiction's social security system.

(v) *Broad-based foreign retirement plan.*—The term *broad-based foreign retirement plan* means a scheme, trust, arrangement, or plan (regardless of whether sponsored by a U.S. person) that is written and that, in the case of an employer-maintained plan, satisfies the following conditions:

(A) The plan is nondiscriminatory insofar as the employees who, under the terms of the plan (alone or in combination with other comparable plans) and without further amendment or action by the employer, are eligible to make or receive contributions or accrue benefits under the plan other than earnings (regardless of whether the employee has elected to participate in the plan), are a wide range of employees, substantially all of whom are nonresident aliens, resident aliens classified as resident aliens solely under section 7701(b)(1)(A)(ii) (and not section 7701(b)(1)(A)(i)), or bona fide residents of a possession (within the meaning of section 937(a)), including rank and file employees.

(B) The plan (alone or in combination with other comparable plans) actually provides significant benefits for a substantial majority of such covered employees.

(C) The benefits actually provided under the plan to such covered employees are nondiscriminatory.

(D) The plan contains provisions or is the subject of tax law provisions or other legal restrictions that generally discourage employees from using plan benefits for purposes other than retirement

or restrict access to plan benefits before separation from service, including (but not limited to), restricting in-service distributions except in events similar to an unforeseeable emergency (as defined in § 1.409A-3(i)(3)(i)) or hardship (as defined for purposes of section 401(k)(2)(B)(i)(IV)), or for educational purposes or the purchase of a primary residence.

(4) *Section 457 plans.*—A nonqualified deferred compensation plan under section 457(f) may constitute a nonqualified deferred compensation plan for purposes of this paragraph (a). The rules of section 409A apply to nonqualified deferred compensation plans separately and in addition to any requirements applicable to such plans under section 457(f). In addition, nonelective deferred compensation of non-employees described in section 457(e)(12) and a grandfathered plan or arrangement described in § 1.457-2(k)(4) may constitute a nonqualified deferred compensation plan for purposes of this paragraph (a). The term *nonqualified deferred compensation plan* does not include a length of service award to a bona fide volunteer under section 457(e)(11)(A)(ii). For purposes of the application of section 409A to a plan to which section 457 applies, a payment under the plan generally means the provision of cash or property to the service provider, provided that for purposes of the application of the short-term deferral rule set forth in paragraph (b)(4) of this section, the inclusion in income of an amount under section 457(f) is treated as a payment of the amount.

(5) *Certain welfare benefits.*—The term *nonqualified deferred compensation plan* does not include a plan, or a portion of a plan, to the extent that the plan provides bona fide vacation leave, sick leave, compensatory time, disability pay, or death benefits. For these purposes, the terms "disability pay" and "death benefits" have the same meanings as provided in § 31.3121(v)(2)-1(b)(4)(iv)(C) of this chapter, provided that for purposes of this paragraph, such disability pay and death benefits may be provided through insurance and the lifetime benefits payable under the plan are not treated as including the value of any taxable term life insurance coverage or taxable disability insurance coverage provided under the plan. The term *nonqualified deferred compensation plan* also does not include any Archer Medical Savings Account as described in section 220, any Health Savings Account as described in section 223, or any other medical reimbursement arrangement, including a health reimbursement arrangement, that satisfies the requirements of section 105 and section 106 such that the benefits or reimbursements provided under such arrangement are not includible in income.

(b) *Deferral of compensation.*—(1) *In general.*—Except as otherwise provided in paragraphs (b)(3) through (b)(12) of this section, a plan provides for the deferral of compensation if, under the terms of the plan and the relevant facts and circumstances, the service provider has a legally binding right during a taxable year to compensation that, pursuant to the terms of the plan, is or may be payable to (or on behalf of) the service provider in a later taxable year. Such compensation is deferred compensation for purposes of section 409A, this section and §§ 1.409A-2 through 1.409A-6. A legally binding right to an amount that will be excluded from income when and if received does not constitute a deferral of compensation, unless the service provider has received the right in exchange for, or has the right to exchange the right for, an amount that will be includible in income (other than due to participation in a cafeteria plan described in section 125). A service provider does not have a legally binding right to compensation to the extent that compensation may be reduced unilaterally or eliminated by the service recipient or other person after the services creating the right to the compensation have been performed. However, if the facts and circumstances indicate that the discretion to reduce or eliminate the compensation is available or exercisable only upon a condition, or the discretion to reduce or eliminate the compensation lacks substantive significance, a service provider will be considered to have a legally binding right to the compensation. Whether the discretion to reduce or eliminate the compensation lacks substantive significance depends on all the relevant facts and circumstances. However, where the service provider to whom the compensation may be paid has effective control of the person retaining the discretion to reduce or eliminate the compensation, or has effective control over any portion of the compensation of the person retaining the discretion to reduce or eliminate the compensation, or is a member of the family (as defined in section 267(c)(4) applied as if the family of an individual includes the spouse of any member of the family) of the person retaining the discretion to reduce or eliminate the compensation, the discretion to reduce or eliminate the compensation will not be treated as having substantive significance. For this purpose, compensation is not considered subject to unilateral reduction or elimination merely because it may be reduced or eliminated by operation of the objective terms of the plan, such as the application of a nondiscretionary, objective provision creating a substantial risk of forfeiture. Similarly, a service provider does not fail to have a legally binding right to compensation merely because the amount of compensation is determined under a formula that provides for benefits to be offset by benefits provided under another plan (including a plan that is qualified under section 401(a)), or because benefits are reduced due to actual or notional investment losses, or, in a final average pay plan, subsequent decreases in compensation.

(2) *Earnings.*—References to the deferral of compensation or deferred compensation include references to earnings. When the right to earnings is specified under the terms of the plan, the legally binding right to earnings arises at the time of the deferral of the compensation to which the earnings relate. A plan may provide that the time and form of payment of earnings is treated separately from the time and form of payment of the underlying compensation, so that, provided that the rules of section 409A are otherwise met, a plan may provide that earnings will be paid at a separate time or in a separate form from the payment of the underlying compensation. For the application of the deferral election rules to current payments of earnings and dividend equivalents, see § 1.409A-3(e).

(3) *Compensation payable pursuant to the service recipient's customary payment timing arrangement.*—A deferral of compensation does not occur solely because compensation is paid after the last day of the service provider's taxable year pursuant to the timing arrangement under which the service recipient normally compensates service providers for services performed during a payroll period described in section 3401(b), or with respect to a non-employee service provider, a period not longer than the payroll period described in section 3401(b) or if no such payroll period exists, a period not longer than the earlier of the normal timing arrangement under which the service provider normally compensates non-employee service providers or 30 days after the end of the service provider's taxable year.

(4) *Short-term deferrals.*—(i) *In general.*—A deferral of compensation does not occur under a plan with respect to any payment (as defined in § 1.409A-2(b)(2)) that is not a deferred payment, provided that the service provider actually or constructively receives such payment on or before the last day of the applicable 2 ¹/₂ month period. The following rules apply for purposes of this paragraph (b)(4)(i):

(A) The applicable 2 ¹/₂ month period is the period ending on the later of the 15th day of the third month following the end of the service provider's first taxable year in which the right to the payment is no longer subject to a substantial risk of forfeiture or the 15th day of the third month following the end of the service recipient's first taxable year in which the right to the payment is no longer subject to a substantial risk of forfeiture.

(B) A payment is treated as actually or constructively received if the payment is includible in income, including if the payment is includible in income under section 83, the economic benefit doctrine, section 402(b), or section 457(f).

(C) A right to a payment that is never subject to a substantial risk of forfeiture is considered to be no longer subject to a substantial risk of forfeiture on the first date the service provider has a legally binding right to the payment.

(D) A payment is a deferred payment if it is made pursuant to a provision of a plan that provides for the payment to be made or completed on or after any date, or upon or after the occurrence of any event, that will or may occur later than the end of the applicable 2 ¹/₂ month period, such as a separation from service, death, disability, change in control event, specified time or schedule of payment, or unforeseeable emergency, regardless of whether an amount is actually paid as a result of the occurrence of such a payment date or event during the applicable 2 ¹/₂ month period. If a plan provides that the service provider or service recipient may make an election under the plan (including an election under § 1.409A-2(a)(4)) of a different payment date, schedule, or event, such right is disregarded for this purpose. In such cases, whether a plan provides for a deferred payment is determined based on the payment date, schedule, or event that would apply if no such election were made, except that if the plan would not provide for a deferred payment absent such an election, and the service provider or service recipient makes such an election, whether the plan provides for a deferred payment is determined based upon the payment date, schedule, or event that the service provider or service recipient in fact elected.

(E) A stock right provides for a deferred payment if such right includes any provision pursuant to which the holder of the stock right will or may have the right to exercise the stock right after the applicable 2 ¹/₂ month period.

(F) This paragraph (b)(4)(i) is applied separately to each payment (as defined in § 1.409A-2(b)(2)) required to be made under a plan.

(G) If a plan provides for a deferred payment with respect to part of a payment (for example a life annuity or a series of installment amounts treated as a single payment), the plan provides for a deferred payment with respect to the entire payment.

(ii) *Certain delayed payments.*—A payment that otherwise qualifies as a short-term deferral under paragraph (b)(4)(i) of this section but is made after the applicable 2 ¹/₂ month period may continue to qualify as a short-term deferral if the taxpayer establishes that it was administratively impracticable to make the payment by the end of the applicable 2 ¹/₂ month period and, as of the date upon which the legally binding right to the compensation arose, such impracticability was unforeseeable, or the taxpayer establishes that making the payment by the end of the applicable 2 ¹/₂ month period would have jeopardized the ability of the service recipient to continue as a going concern, and provided further that the payment is made as soon as administratively practicable or as soon as the payment would no longer have such effect. For purposes of this paragraph (b)(4)(ii), an action or failure to act of the service provider or a person under the service provider's control, such as a failure to provide necessary information or documentation, is not an unforeseeable event. In addition, a payment that otherwise qualifies as a short-term deferral under paragraph (b)(4)(i) of this section but is made after the applicable 2 ¹/₂ month period may continue to qualify as a short-term deferral if the taxpayer establishes that the service recipient reasonably anticipated that the service recipient's deduction with respect to such payment otherwise would not be permitted by application of section 162(m), and, as of the date the legally binding right to the payment arose, a reasonable person would not have anticipated the application of section 162(m) at the time of the payment, and provided further that the payment is made as soon as reasonably practicable following the first date on which the service recipient anticipates or reasonably should anticipate that, if the payment were made on such date, the service recipient's deduction with respect to such payment would no longer be restricted due to the application of section 162(m). For additional rules applicable to certain transaction-based compensation, see § 1.409A-3(i)(5)(iv)(A).

(iii) *Examples.*—The following examples illustrate the provisions of this paragraph (b)(4). In these examples, except as otherwise noted, each employee and each employer has a calendar year taxable year and each employee is an individual who is employed by the specified employer.

Example 1. On November 1, 2008, Employer Z awards a bonus to Employee A such that Employee A has a legally binding right to the payment as of November 1, 2008, that is not subject to a substantial risk of forfeiture. The bonus plan does not provide for a payment date or a deferred payment. The bonus plan will not be considered to have provided for a deferral of compensation if the bonus is paid or made available to Employee A on or before March 15, 2009.

Example 2. Employer Y has a taxable year ending August 31. On November 1, 2008, Employer Y awards a bonus to Employee B so that Employee B has a legally binding right to the payment as of November 1, 2008, that is not subject to a substantial risk of forfeiture. The bonus plan does not provide for a payment date or a deferred payment. The bonus plan will not be considered to have provided for a deferral of compensation if the bonus is paid or made available to Employee B on or before November 15, 2009.

Example 3. On November 1, 2008, Employer X awards a bonus to Employee C such that Employee C has a legally binding right to the payment as of November 1, 2008. Under the bonus plan, Employee C will forfeit the bonus unless Employee C continues performing services through December 31, 2010. The right to the payment is subject to a substantial risk of forfeiture through December 31, 2010. Employee C has the right to make a written election not later than December 31, 2009, to receive the bonus on or after December 31, 2015, but Employee C does not make such election. The bonus plan does not provide for a default payment date or a deferred payment in the absence of an election by Employee C. The bonus plan will not be considered to have provided for a deferral of compensation if the bonus is paid or made available to Employee C on or before March 15, 2011.

Example 4. On November 1, 2008, Employer W awards a bonus to Employee D such that Employee D has a legally binding right to the payment as of November 1, 2008. Under the bonus plan, the bonus will be determined based on services performed during the period from January 1, 2009 through December 31, 2010. The bonus is scheduled to be paid as a lump sum payment on February 15, 2011. Under the bonus plan, Employee D will forfeit the bonus unless Employee D continues performing services through the scheduled payment date (February 15, 2011). Provided that at all times before the scheduled payment date Employee D is required to continue to perform services to retain the right to the bonus, and the bonus is paid on or before March 15, 2012, the bonus plan will not be considered to have provided for a deferral of compensation.

Example 5. On November 1, 2008, Employer V awards a bonus to Employee E such that Employee E has a legally binding right to the payment as of November 1, 2008. Under the bonus plan, Employee E will forfeit the bonus unless Employee E continues performing services through December 31, 2010. Under the bonus plan, the bonus is scheduled to be paid as a lump sum payment on July 1, 2011. By specifying a payment date after the applicable 2 1/2 month period, the bonus plan provides for a deferred payment. The bonus plan provides for a deferral of compensation, and will not qualify as a short-term deferral regardless of whether the bonus is paid or made available on or before March 15, 2011 (and generally any payment before June 1, 2011 would constitute an impermissible acceleration of a payment).

Example 6. On November 1, 2008, Employer U awards a bonus to Employee F such that Employee F has a legally binding right to the payment as of November 1, 2008, that is not subject to a substantial risk of forfeiture. The bonus plan provides for a lump sum payment upon Employee F's separation from service. Because the separation from service is an event that may occur after the applicable 2 1/2 month period, the bonus plan provides for a deferred payment and therefore provides for a deferral of compensation. Accordingly, the bonus plan will not qualify as a short-term deferral regardless of whether Employee F separates from service and the bonus is paid or made available on or before March 15, 2009.

Example 7. On November 1, 2008, Employer T grants Employee G a legally binding right to the payment of a life annuity with the first annuity payment on November 1, 2013, provided that Employee G continues performing services for Employer T continuously through November 1, 2013. Because the life annuity is treated as a single payment, and because all payments of the life annuity may not occur during the applicable 2 1/2 month period, the plan provides for a deferred payment and none of the amounts payable under the annuity will qualify as a short-term deferral, so that section 409A applies to all amounts that are payable under the plan.

Example 8. On November 1, 2008, Employer S grants Employee H a stock right providing for an exercise price less than the fair market value of the underlying stock on November 1, 2008. The stock right is subject to a substantial risk of forfeiture requiring services through November 1, 2010. The stock right becomes exercisable when the substantial risk of forfeiture lapses and expires on November 1, 2013. Employee H continues providing services through November 1, 2010, at which time the substantial risk of forfeiture lapses. The stock right provides for a deferred payment and will not qualify as a short-term deferral regardless of whether Employee H exercises the stock right on or before March 15, 2011.

(5) *Stock options, stock appreciation rights, and other equity-based compensation.*—(i) *Stock rights.*—(A) *Nonstatutory stock options not providing for the deferral of compensation.*—An option to purchase service recipient stock does not provide for a deferral of compensation if—

(1) The exercise price may never be less than the fair market value of the underlying stock (disregarding lapse restrictions as defined in § 1.83-3(i)) on the date the option is granted and the number of shares subject to the option is fixed on the original date of grant of the option;

(2) The transfer or exercise of the option is subject to taxation under section 83 and § 1.83-7; and

(3) The option does not include any feature for the deferral of compensation other than the deferral of recognition of income until the later of the following:

(i) The exercise or disposition of the option under § 1.83-7.

(ii) The time the stock acquired pursuant to the exercise of the option first becomes substantially vested (as defined in § 1.83-3(b)).

(B) *Stock appreciation rights not providing for the deferral of compensation.*—A right to compensation based on the appreciation in value of a specified number of shares of service recipient stock occurring between the date of grant and the date of exercise of such right (a stock appreciation right) does not provide for a deferral of compensation if—

(1) Compensation payable under the stock appreciation right cannot be greater than the excess of the fair market value of the stock (disregarding lapse restrictions as defined in § 1.83-3(i)) on the date the stock appreciation right is exercised over an amount specified on the date of grant of the stock appreciation right (the stock appreciation right exercise price), with respect to a number of shares fixed on or before the date of grant of the right;

(2) The stock appreciation right exercise price may never be less than the fair market value of the underlying stock (disregarding lapse restrictions as defined in § 1.83-3(i)) on the date the right is granted; and

(3) The stock appreciation right does not include any feature for the deferral of compensation other than the deferral of recognition of income until the exercise of the stock appreciation right.

(C) *Stock rights that may provide for the deferral of compensation.*—An option to purchase stock other than service recipient stock, or a stock appreciation right with respect to stock other than service recipient stock, generally will provide for the deferral of compensation within the meaning of this paragraph (b). If under the terms of an option to purchase service recipient stock (other than an incentive stock option described in section 422 or a stock option granted under an employee stock purchase plan described in section 423), the exercise price is or could become less than the fair market value of the stock (disregarding lapse restrictions as defined in § 1.83-3(i)) on the date of grant, the grant of the option generally will provide for the deferral of compensation within the meaning of this paragraph (b). If under the terms of a stock appreciation right with respect to service recipient stock, the compensation payable under the stock appreciation right is or could be any amount greater than, with respect to a predetermined number of shares, the excess of the fair market value of the stock (disregarding lapse restrictions as defined in § 1.83-3(i)) on the date the stock appreciation right is exercised over the fair market value of the stock (disregarding lapse restrictions as defined in § 1.83-3(i)) on the date of grant of the stock appreciation right, the grant of the stock appreciation right generally will provide for a deferral of compensation within the meaning of this paragraph (b).

(D) *Feature for the deferral of compensation.*—To the extent a stock right provides a right other than the right to receive cash or stock on the date of exercise and such additional right would otherwise allow compensation to be deferred beyond the date of exercise, the entire arrangement (including the underlying stock right) provides for the deferral of compensation. For purposes of this paragraph (b)(5)(i), neither the right to receive substantially nonvested stock (as defined in § 1.83-3(b)) upon the exercise of a stock right, nor the right to pay the exercise price with previously acquired shares, constitutes a feature for the deferral of compensation.

(E) *Rights to dividends.*—For purposes of this paragraph (b)(5)(i), the right, directly or indirectly contingent upon the exercise of a stock right, to receive an amount equal to all or part of the dividends or other distributions (other than stock dividends described in paragraph (b)(5)(v)(H) of this section) declared and paid on the number of shares underlying the stock right between the date of grant and the date of exercise of the stock right constitutes an offset to the exercise price of the stock option or an increase in the amount payable under the stock appreciation right (generally causing such stock right to be subject to section 409A). A plan providing a right to dividends or other distributions declared and paid on the number of shares underlying a stock right, the payment of which is not contingent upon, or otherwise payable on, the exercise of the stock right, may provide for a deferral of compensation, but the existence of the right to receive such an amount will not be treated as a reduction to the exercise price of (or an increase to the compensation payable under) the stock right. Thus, a right to such dividends or distributions that is not contingent, directly or indirectly, upon the exercise of a stock right will not cause the related stock right to fail to satisfy the requirements of the exclusion from the definition of a deferral of compensation provided in paragraphs (b)(5)(i)(A) and (B) of this section.

(ii) *Statutory stock options.*—The grant of an incentive stock option as described in section 422, or the grant of an option under an employee stock purchase plan described in section 423 (including the grant of an option with an exercise price discounted in accordance with section 423(b)(6) and the accompanying regulations), does not constitute a deferral of compensation. However, the exclusion for statutory stock options under this paragraph (b)(5)(ii) does not apply to a modification, extension, or renewal of a statutory option that is treated as the grant of a new option that is not a statutory option. See § 1.424-1(e). In such event, the option is treated for purposes of this paragraph (b) as if it had been a nonstatutory stock option from the date of the original grant. Accordingly, if such modification, extension, or renewal of the stock option would have been treated as the grant of a new option or as causing the option to have had a deferral feature from the date of grant under paragraph (b)(5)(v) of this section, the modification, extension, or renewal of the stock option is treated as the grant of a new option or as causing the option to have had a deferral feature from the date of grant for purposes of this paragraph (b)(5).

(iii) *Service recipient stock.*—(A) *In general.*—Except as otherwise provided in paragraphs (b)(5)(iii)(B), (C), and (D) of this section, the term *service recipient stock* means a class of stock that, as of the date of grant, is common stock for purposes of section 305 and the regulations thereunder of a corporation that is an eligible issuer of service recipient stock (as defined in paragraph (b)(5)(iii)(E) of this section). Notwithstanding the foregoing, the term *service recipient stock* does not include a class of stock that has any preference as to distributions other than distributions of service recipient stock and distributions in liquidation of the issuer. The term *service recipient stock* also does not include any stock that is subject to a mandatory repurchase obligation (other than a right of first refusal), or a put or call right that is not a lapse restriction as defined in § 1.83-3(i), if the stock price under such right or obligation is based on a measure other than the fair market value (disregarding lapse restrictions as defined in § 1.83-3(i)) of the equity interest in the corporation represented by the stock.

(B) *American depositary receipts.*—An American depositary receipt or American depositary share may constitute service recipient stock, to the extent that the stock traded on a foreign securities market to which the American depositary receipt or American depositary share relates qualifies as service recipient stock.

(C) *Mutual company units.*—Mutual company units may constitute service recipient stock. For this purpose, the term *mutual company unit* means a fixed percentage of the overall value of a non-stock mutual company or association. For purposes of determining the value of the mutual company unit, the unit may be valued in accordance with the rules set forth in paragraph (b)(5)(iv)(B) of this section governing valuation of service recipient stock the shares of which are not traded on an established securities market, applied as if the mutual company were a stock corporation with one class of common stock and the number of shares of such stock determined according to such fixed percentage. For example, an appreciation right based on the appreciation of 10 mutual company units, where each unit is defined as one percent of the overall value of the mutual company, would be valued as if the appreciation right were based upon 10 shares of a corporation, with 100 shares of common stock (and no other class of stock), the shares of which are not readily tradable on an established securities market.

(D) *Other entities.*—An interest in an entity other than a corporation or non-stock mutual company or association may constitute service recipient stock to the extent designated by the Commissioner in revenue procedures, notices, or other guidance published in the Internal Revenue Bulletin (see § 601.601(d)(2) of this chapter).

(E) *Eligible issuer of service recipient stock.*—(1) *In general.*— The term *eligible issuer of service recipient stock* means only the corporation for which the service provider provides direct services on the date of grant of the stock right (if the entity receiving such services is a corporation), and any corporation in a chain of corporations or other entities in which each corporation or other entity has a controlling interest in another corporation or other entity in the chain, ending with the corporation or other entity that has a controlling interest in the corporation or other entity for which the service provider provides direct services on the date of grant of the stock right. For this purpose, the term *controlling interest* has the same meaning as provided in § 1.414(c)-2(b)(2)(i), provided that the language "at least 50 percent" is used instead of "at least 80 percent" each place it appears in § 1.414(c)-2(b)(2)(i). In addition, where the use of such stock with respect to the grant of a stock right to such service provider is based upon legitimate business criteria, the term *controlling interest* has the same meaning as provided in § 1.414(c)-2(b)(2)(i), provided that the language "at least 20 percent" is used instead of "at least 80 percent" each place it appears in § 1.414(c)-2(b)(2)(i). For purposes of determining ownership of an interest in an organization, the rules of §§ 1.414(c)-3 and 1.414(c)-4 apply. The determination of whether a grant is based on legitimate business criteria is based on the facts and circumstances, focusing primarily on whether there is a sufficient nexus between the service provider and the issuer of the stock right so that the grant serves a legitimate non-tax business purpose other than simply providing compensation to the service provider that is excluded from the requirements of section 409A. For example, stock of a corporation that owns an interest in a joint venture involving an operating business, used with respect to stock rights granted to service providers of the joint venture who are former service providers of such corporation, generally will constitute use of service recipient stock based upon legitimate business criteria, and therefore could constitute service recipient stock with respect to such service providers if the corporation owns at least 20 percent of the joint venture and the other requirements of this paragraph (b)(5)(iii) are met. Similarly, the legitimate business criteria requirement generally would be met if the corporate venturer issued such a right to an employee of the joint venture who it reasonably expected would in the future become an employee of the corporate venturer. However, where a service provider has no real nexus with a corporate venturer, such as generally happens when the corporate venturer is a passive investor in the service recipient joint venture, a stock right issued to that employee on the investor corporation's stock generally would not be based upon legitimate business criteria. Similarly, where a corporation holds only a minority interest in an entity that in turn holds a minority interest in the entity for which the service provider performs services, such that the corporation holds only an insubstantial indirect interest in the entity receiving the services, legitimate business criteria generally would not exist for issuing a stock right on the corporation's stock to the service provider.

(2) *Investment vehicles.*—Notwithstanding the provisions of paragraph (b)(5)(iii)(E)(1) of this section, except as to a service provider providing services directly to such corporation, for purposes of this paragraph (b)(5), an eligible issuer of service recipient stock does not include any corporation whose primary purpose is to serve as an investment vehicle with respect to the corporation's minority ownership interests in entities other than the service recipient.

(3) *Corporate structures established or transactions undertaken for purposes of avoiding coverage under section 409A.*—Notwithstanding the provisions of paragraph (b)(5)(iii)(E)(1) of this section, an eligible issuer of service recipient stock does not include any corporation within a group of entities treated as a single service recipient if a purpose of the establishment of the structure of the ownership, or a purpose of a significant transaction between or among two or more entities comprising a single service recipient, is to provide deferred compensation not subject to the application of section 409A. If an entity becomes a member of a group of corporations or other entities treated as a single service recipient, and the primary source of income or value of such entity arises from the provision of management services to other members of the service recipient group, it is presumed that such structure was established for purposes of avoiding the application of section 409A if any stock rights are issued with respect to such entity.

(4) *Substitutions and assumptions by reason of a corporate transaction.*—If the requirements of paragraph (b)(5)(v)(D) of this section are met such that the substitution of a new stock right pursuant to a corporate transaction for an outstanding stock right, or the assumption of an outstanding stock right pursuant to a corporate transaction, would not be treated as the grant of a new stock right or a change in the form of payment for purposes of this section and §§ 1.409A-2 through 1.409A-6, the stock underlying the stock right that replaced the stock right that is substituted or assumed will be treated as service recipient stock for purposes of applying this paragraph (b)(5) to the replacement stock rights if such underlying stock otherwise satisfies the requirements of paragraph (b)(5)(iii)(A) of this section. For example, if by reason of a spinoff transaction (under which the stock of a subsidiary corporation is distributed to the stockholders of a distributing corporation), a stock option to purchase distributing corporation stock is replaced with a stock option to purchase distributing corporation stock and a stock option to purchase the spun off subsidiary corporation's stock (each otherwise satisfying the requirements of paragraph (b)(5)(iii)(A) of this section), and where such substitution is not treated as a modification of the original stock option pursuant to paragraph (b)(5)(v)(D) of this section, both the distributing corporation stock and the subsidiary corporation stock are treated as service recipient stock for purposes of applying this paragraph (b)(5) to the replacement stock options.

(iv) *Determination of the fair market value of service recipient stock.*—(A) *Stock readily tradable on an established securities market.*— For purposes of paragraph (b)(5)(i) of this section, in the case of service recipient stock that is readily tradable on an established securities market, the fair market value of the stock may be determined based upon the last sale before or the first sale after the grant, the closing price on the trading day before or the trading day of the grant, the arithmetic mean of the high and low prices on the trading day before or the trading day of the grant, or any other reasonable method using actual transactions in such stock as reported by such market. The determination of fair market value also may be determined using an average selling price during a specified period that is within 30 days before or 30 days after the applicable valuation date, provided that the program under which the stock right is granted, including a program with a single participant, must irrevocably specify the commitment to grant the stock right with an exercise price set using such an average selling price before the beginning of the specified period. For this purpose, the term *average selling price* refers to the arithmetic mean of such selling prices on all trading days during the specified period, or the average of such prices over the specified period weighted based on the volume of trading such stock on each trading day during such specified period. To satisfy this requirement, the service recipient must designate the recipient of the stock right, the number and class of shares of stock that are subject to the stock right, and the method for determining the exercise price including the period over which the averaging will occur, before the beginning of the specified averaging period. Notwithstanding the forgoing provisions of this paragraph (b)(5)(iv)(A), where applicable foreign law requires that a compensatory stock right be priced based upon a specific price averaging method and period, a stock right granted in accordance with such applicable foreign law will be treated as meeting the requirements of this paragraph (b)(5)(iv)(A), provided that the averaging period does not exceed 30 days.

(B) *Stock not readily tradable on an established securities market.—(1) In general.*—For purposes of paragraph (b)(5)(i) of this section, in the case of service recipient stock that is not readily tradable on an established securities market, the fair market value of the stock as of a valuation date means a value determined by the reasonable application of a reasonable valuation method. The determination whether a valuation method is reasonable, or whether an application of a valuation method is reasonable, is made based on the facts and circumstances as of the valuation date. Factors to be considered under a reasonable valuation method include, as applicable, the value of tangible and intangible assets of the corporation, the present value of anticipated future cash-flows of the corporation, the market value of stock or equity interests in similar corporations and other entities engaged in trades or businesses substantially similar to those engaged in by the corporation the stock of which is to be valued, the value of which can be readily determined through nondiscretionary, objective means (such as through trading prices on an established securities market or an amount paid in an arm's length private transaction), recent arm's length transactions involving the sale or transfer of such stock or equity interests, and other relevant factors such as control premiums or discounts for lack of marketability and whether the valuation method is used for other purposes that have a material economic effect on the service recipient, its stockholders, or its creditors. The use of a valuation method is not reasonable if such valuation method does not take into consideration in applying its methodology all available information material to the value of the corporation. Similarly, the use of a value previously calculated under a valuation method is not reasonable as of a later date if such calculation fails to reflect information available after the date of the calculation that may materially affect the value of the corporation (for example, the resolution of material litigation or the issuance of a patent) or the value was calculated with respect to a date that is more than 12 months earlier than the date for which the valuation is being used. The service recipient's consistent use of a valuation method to determine the value of its stock or assets for other purposes, including for purposes unrelated to compensation of service providers, is also a factor supporting the reasonableness of such valuation method.

(2) *Presumption of reasonableness.*—For purposes of this paragraph (b)(5)(iv)(B), the use of any of the following methods of valuation is presumed to result in a reasonable valuation, provided that the Commissioner may rebut such a presumption upon a showing that either the valuation method or the application of such method was grossly unreasonable:

(i) A valuation of a class of stock determined by an independent appraisal that meets the requirements of section 401(a)(28)(C) and the regulations as of a date that is no more than 12 months before the relevant transaction to which the valuation is applied (for example, the date of grant of a stock option).

(ii) A valuation based upon a formula that, if used as part of a nonlapse restriction (as defined in §1.83-3(h)) with respect to the stock, would be considered to be the fair market value of the stock pursuant to §1.83-5, provided that such stock is valued in the same manner for purposes of any transfer of any shares of such class of stock (or any substantially similar class of stock) to the issuer or any person that owns stock possessing more than 10 percent of the total combined voting power of all classes of stock of the issuer (applying the stock attribution rules of §1.424-1(d)), other than an arm's length transaction involving the sale of all or substantially all of the outstanding stock of the issuer, and such valuation method is used consistently for all such purposes, and provided further that this paragraph (b)(5)(iv)(B)(2)(ii) does not apply with respect to stock subject to a stock right payable in stock, where the stock acquired pursuant to the exercise of the stock right is transferable other than through the operation of a nonlapse restriction.

(iii) A valuation, made reasonably and in good faith and evidenced by a written report that takes into account the relevant factors described in paragraph (b)(5)(iv)(B)(1) of this section, of illiquid stock of a start-up corporation. For this purpose, illiquid stock of a start-up corporation means service recipient stock of a corporation that has no material trade or business that it or any predecessor to it has conducted for a period of 10 years or more and has no class of equity securities that are traded on an established securities market (as defined in paragraph (k) of this section), where such stock is not subject to any put, call, or other right or obligation of the service recipient or other person to purchase such stock (other than a right of first refusal upon an offer to purchase by a third party that is unrelated to the service recipient or service provider and other than a

right or obligation that constitutes a lapse restriction as defined in §1.83-3(i)), and provided that this paragraph (b)(5)(iv)(B)(2)(iii) does not apply to the valuation of any stock if the service recipient or service provider may reasonably anticipate, as of the time the valuation is applied, that the service recipient will undergo a change in control event as described in §1.409A-3(i)(5)(v) or §1.409A-3(i)(5)(vii) within the 90 days following the action to which the valuation is applied, or make a public offering of securities within the 180 days following the action to which the valuation is applied. For purposes of this paragraph (b)(5)(iv)(B)(2)(iii), a valuation will not be treated as made reasonably and in good faith unless the valuation is performed by a person or persons that the corporation reasonably determines is qualified to perform such a valuation based on the person's or persons' significant knowledge, experience, education, or training. Generally, a person will be qualified to perform such a valuation if a reasonable individual, upon being apprised of such knowledge, experience, education, and training, would reasonably rely on the advice of such person with respect to valuation in deciding whether to accept an offer to purchase or sell the stock being valued. For this purpose, significant experience generally means at least five years of relevant experience in business valuation or appraisal, financial accounting, investment banking, private equity, secured lending, or other comparable experience in the line of business or industry in which the service recipient operates.

(3) *Use of alternative methods.*—For purposes of this paragraph (b)(5), a different valuation method may be used for each separate action for which a valuation is relevant, provided that a single valuation method is used for each separate action and, once used, may not retroactively be altered. For example, one valuation method may be used to establish the exercise price of a stock option, and a different valuation method may be used to determine the value at the date of the repurchase of stock pursuant to a put or call right. However, once an exercise price or amount to be paid has been established, the exercise price or amount to be paid may not be changed through the retroactive use of another valuation method. In addition, notwithstanding the foregoing, where after the date of grant, but before the date of exercise or transfer, of the stock right, the service recipient stock to which the stock right relates becomes readily tradable on an established securities market, the service recipient must use the valuation method set forth in paragraph (b)(5)(iv)(A) of this section for purposes of determining the payment at the date of exercise or the purchase of the stock, as applicable.

(v) *Modifications, extensions, substitutions, and assumptions of stock rights.—(A) Treatment of modified and extended stock rights.*—A modification of the terms of a stock right within the meaning of paragraph (b)(5)(v)(B) of this section is considered to be the grant of a new stock right. The new stock right may or may not constitute a deferral of compensation under paragraph (b)(5)(i) of this section, determined at the date of grant of the new stock right. If there is an extension of a stock right (within the meaning of paragraph (b)(5)(v)(C) of this section), the stock right is treated as having had an additional deferral feature from the original date of grant of the stock right, and therefore will be treated as a plan providing for the deferral of compensation from the original grant date for purposes of this paragraph (b).

(B) *Modification in general.*—Except as otherwise provided in paragraph (b)(5)(v) of this section, the term *modification* means any change in the terms of the stock right (or change in the terms of the plan pursuant to which the stock right was granted or in the terms of any other agreement governing the stock right) that may provide the holder of the stock right with a direct or indirect reduction in the exercise price of the stock right regardless of whether the holder in fact benefits from the change in terms. A change in the terms of the stock right shortening the period during which the stock right is exercisable is not a modification. It is not a modification to add a feature providing the ability to tender previously acquired stock for the stock purchasable under the stock right, or to withhold or have withheld shares of stock to facilitate the payment of the exercise price or the employment taxes or required withholding taxes resulting from the exercise of the stock right. In addition, it is not a modification for the grantor to exercise discretion specifically reserved under a stock right with respect to the transferability of the stock right.

(C) *Extensions.—(1) In general.*—An extension of a stock right refers to the provision to the holder of an additional period of time within which to exercise the stock right beyond the time originally prescribed under the terms of the stock right, the conversion or exchange of a stock right for a legally binding right to compensation in a future taxable year, or the addition of any feature for the deferral of compensation not permitted in paragraph (b)(5)(i)(A)(3) of this section (in the case of a stock option) or not permitted in paragraph (b)(5)(i)(B)(3) of this section (in the case of a stock appreciation right) to the terms of the stock right, other than at a time when the exercise price of the stock right equals or exceeds the fair market value of the service recipient stock that could be purchased (in the case of an option) or the fair market value of the service recipient stock used to determine the payment to the service provider (in the case of a stock appreciation right), and includes a renewal of such right that has such effect. It is not an extension if the exercise period of a stock right is extended to a date no later than the earlier of the latest date upon which the stock right could have expired by its original terms under any circumstances or the 10th anniversary of the original date of grant of the stock right. If the exercise period of a stock right is extended at a time when the exercise price of the stock right equals or exceeds the fair market value of the service recipient stock that could be purchased (in the case of an option) or the fair market value of the service recipient stock used to determine the payment to the service provider (in the case of a stock appreciation right), it is not an extension of the original stock right. Instead, in such a case, the original stock right is treated as modified rather than extended and a new stock right is treated as having been granted for purposes of this section. In addition, it is not an extension of a stock right if the expiration of the stock right is tolled while the holder cannot exercise the stock right because such an exercise would violate an applicable Federal, state, local, or foreign law, or would jeopardize the ability of the service recipient to continue as a going concern, provided that the period during which the stock right may be exercised is not extended more than 30 days after the exercise of the stock right first would no longer violate an applicable Federal, state, local, and foreign laws or would first no longer jeopardize the ability of the service recipient to continue as a going concern. For this purpose, a provision of foreign law shall be considered applicable only to foreign earned income (as defined under section 911(b)(1) without regard to section 911(b)(1)(B)(iv) and without regard to the requirement that the income be attributable to services performed during the period described in section 911(d)(1)(A) or (B)) from sources within the foreign country that promulgated such law.

(2) Certain extensions before April 10, 2007. An extension of a stock right before April 10, 2007 solely in order to provide the holder of such stock right an additional period of time beyond the time originally prescribed under the terms of such stock right within which to exercise the stock right is disregarded for purposes of applying the rules contained in paragraph (b)(5)(v)(C)(*1*) of this section. For purposes of applying the rules contained in paragraph (b)(5)(v)(C)(*1*) of this section on and after April 10, 2007, such a stock right is treated as having specified at the date of grant the time within which to exercise such stock right that was prescribed under the terms of such stock right in effect on April 9, 2007. Nothing in this paragraph (b)(5)(v)(C)(2) affects any other action treated as the extension of a stock right, including the addition of a deferral feature.

(3) Examples.—The following examples illustrate the provisions of this paragraph (b)(5)(v)(C). In the examples, each employee is an individual employed by the specified employer, and each employee and each employer has a calendar year taxable year.

Example 1. On July 1, 2009, Employer Z grants Employee A a nonstatutory stock option that does not provide for the deferral of compensation in accordance with paragraph (b)(5)(i)(A) of this section. The terms of the nonstatutory stock option provide that the exercise period of the stock option expires on the earlier of July 1, 2019, or 3 months after Employee A's separation from service. On July 1, 2011, Employee A separates from service. On the same day, Employee A and Employer Z change the exercise period of the option so that it expires on July 1, 2013. Because the exercise period of the stock right is not extended beyond July 1, 2019, the change is not an extension for purposes of this paragraph (b)(5)(v)(C).

Example 2. The facts are the same as in *Example 1* except that Employee A separates from service on July 1, 2018, and on the same day, Employee A and Employer Z change the exercise period of the option so that it expires on July 1, 2020. As of July 1, 2018, the fair market value of the underlying stock exceeds the exercise price. Because the exercise period of the stock right is extended beyond July 1, 2019, the change is an extension for purposes of this paragraph (b)(5)(v)(C).

Example 3. The facts are the same as in *Example 2* except that as of July 1, 2018, the fair market value of the underlying stock is less than the exercise price of the option. Because the exercise period of the stock right is extended at a time when the fair market value of the underlying stock is less than the exercise price, the change is not an extension for purposes of this paragraph (b)(5)(v)(C) and the change is treated as a modification of the option, resulting in the extension of the exercise period being treated as the grant of a new option on July 1, 2018.

Example 4. On July 1, 2009, Employer Y grants to Employee B a stock appreciation right with respect to 200 shares of Employer Y common stock that does not provide for the deferral of compensation in accordance with paragraph (b)(5)(i)(B) of this section. Upon exercise of the stock appreciation right, Employee B is entitled to receive the excess of the fair market value of a share of Employer Y common stock on the date of exercise over $100 (the fair market value of a share of Employer Y common stock on July 1, 2009), multiplied by the number of shares with respect to which Employee B is exercising the right. The exercise period of the right expires on the earlier of July 1, 2019, or 3 months after Employee B separates from service. Employee B cannot exercise the stock appreciation right with respect to more than 100 shares unless Employee B continues to be employed by Employer Y through June 30, 2014. On July 1, 2011, when the fair market value of a share of Employer Y common stock is $200, Employee B and Employer Y amend the stock appreciation right to provide that the right will be exercisable only during calendar year 2018, except that before January 1, 2017, Employee B may elect to designate calendar year 2023 or any subsequent calendar year before 2033 as the year in which the right will be exercisable. The amendment constitutes an extension of the stock appreciation right under paragraph (b)(5)(v)(C)(*1*) of this section. Under paragraph (b)(5)(v)(A) of this section, the stock appreciation right is treated as having had an additional deferral feature from the original date of grant (July 1, 2009) of the right, and therefore is treated as a plan providing for the deferral of compensation from that date. During the period from July 1, 2009, through June 30, 2011, the provisions of the stock appreciation right relating to the time and form of payment did not satisfy the requirements of §1.409A-3(a). Therefore, the stock appreciation right provides for a deferral of compensation that does not comply with section 409A.

(D) *Substitutions and assumptions of stock rights by reason of a corporate transaction.*—If the requirements of §1.424-1 (without regard to the requirement described in §1.424-1(a)(2) that an eligible corporation be the employer of the optionee) would be met if the stock right were a statutory option, the substitution of a new stock right pursuant to a corporate transaction (as defined in §1.424-1(a)(3)) for an outstanding stock right or the assumption of an outstanding stock right pursuant to a corporate transaction will not be treated as the grant of a new stock right or a change in the form of payment for purposes of this section and §§1.409A-2 through 1.409A-6. For purposes of the preceding sentence, the requirement of §1.424-1(a)(5)(iii) will be deemed to be satisfied if the ratio of the exercise price to the fair market value of the shares subject to the stock right immediately after the substitution or assumption is not greater than the ratio of the exercise price to the fair market value of the shares subject to the stock right immediately before the substitution or assumption. In the case of a transaction described in section 355 in which the stock of the distributing corporation and the stock distributed in the transaction are both readily tradable on an established securities market immediately after the transaction, for purposes of this paragraph (b)(5)(v), the requirements of §1.424-1(a)(5) related to the fair market value of the stock may be satisfied by—

(*1*) Using the last sale before or the first sale after the specified date as of which such valuation is being made, the closing price on the last trading day before or the trading day of a specified date, the arithmetic mean of the high and low prices on the last trading day before or the trading day of such specified date, or any other reasonable method using actual transactions in such stock as reported by such market on a specified date, for the stock of the distributing corporation and the stock distributed in the transaction, provided the specified date is designated before such specified date, and such specified date is not more than 60 days after the transaction;

(*2*) Using the arithmetic mean of such market prices on trading days during a specified period designated before the beginning of such specified period, where such specified period is not longer than 30 days and ends no later than 60 days after the transaction; or

(*3*) Using an average of such prices during such prespecified period weighted based on the volume of trading of such stock on each trading day during such prespecified period.

(E) *Acceleration of date when exercisable.*—Although with respect to a stock right not immediately exercisable in full, a change in the terms of the right solely to accelerate or delay, within the original term of the stock right, the time at which the stock right (or any portion of such stock right) may be exercised is not a modification for purposes of this section, with respect to a stock right subject to section 409A, such an acceleration may constitute an impermissible acceleration of a payment date under §1.409A-3(j) or a subsequent deferral under §1.409A-2(b).

(F) *Discretionary added benefits.*—If a change to a stock right provides, either by its terms or in substance, that the holder may receive an additional benefit under the stock right at the future discretion of the grantor, and the addition of such benefit would constitute a modification or extension, then the addition of such discretion is a modification or extension at the time that the stock right is changed to provide such discretion.

Reg. §1.409A-1(b)(5)(v)(F)

(G) Change in underlying stock increasing value.—A change in the terms of the stock subject to a stock right that increases the value of the stock is a modification of such stock right, except to the extent that a new stock right is substituted for such stock right by reason of the change in the terms of the stock in accordance with paragraph (b)(5)(v)(D) of this section.

(H) Change in the number of shares purchasable.—If a stock right is amended solely to increase the number of shares subject to the stock right, the increase is not considered a modification of the stock right but is treated as the grant of a new additional stock right to which the additional shares are subject. Notwithstanding the previous sentence, if the exercise price and number of shares subject to a stock right are proportionally adjusted to reflect a stock split (including a reverse stock split) or stock dividend, and the only effect of the stock split or stock dividend is to increase (or decrease) on a pro rata basis the number of shares owned by each shareholder of the class of stock subject to the stock right, then there is no modification of the stock right if it is proportionally adjusted to reflect the stock split or stock dividend and the aggregate exercise price of the stock right is not less than the aggregate exercise price before the stock split or stock dividend.

(I) Rescission of changes.—A change to the terms of a stock right (or change in the terms of the plan pursuant to which the stock right was granted or in the terms of any other agreement governing the right) is not considered a modification or extension of the stock right to the extent the change in the terms of the stock right is rescinded by the earlier of the date the stock right is exercised or the last day of the service provider's taxable year during which such change occurred. Thus, for example, if the terms of a stock right granted to an individual employee with a calendar year taxable year are changed on March 1 in a manner that would result in an extension of the stock right, and the change is rescinded on November 1 of the same year, and the stock right is not exercised before the change is rescinded, the stock right is not considered extended under this paragraph (b)(5)(v).

(J) Successive modifications and extensions.—The rules of this paragraph (b)(5)(v) apply as well to successive modifications and extensions.

(K) Modifications and extensions in effect on October 23, 2004.—For purposes of the application of section 409A and these regulations to a stock right, if a legally binding right to a modification or extension of such stock right existed on October 23, 2004, such modification or extension is disregarded, and the stock right is treated as if granted with the terms and conditions in effect on October 23, 2004.

(vi) Meaning and use of certain terms.—(A) *Option.*—The term *option* means the right or privilege of an individual to purchase stock from a corporation by virtue of an offer of the corporation continuing for a stated period of time, whether or not irrevocable, to sell such stock at a price determined under paragraph (b)(5)(vi)(D) of this section, such individual being under no obligation to purchase. While no particular form of words is necessary, the option must express an offer to sell at the option price, the maximum number of shares purchasable under the option, and the period of time during which the offer remains open. The term *option* includes a warrant that meets the requirements of this paragraph (b)(5)(vi)(A). An option may be granted as part of or in conjunction with an employee stock purchase plan or subscription contract. An option must be in writing (in paper or electronic form) provided that such writing is adequate to establish an option right or privilege that is enforceable under applicable law.

(B) Date of grant of option.—(1) The language the *date of grant of the option*, and similar phrases, refer to the date when the granting corporation completes the corporate action necessary to create the legally binding right constituting the option. A corporate action creating the legally binding right constituting the option is not considered complete until the date on which the maximum number of shares that can be purchased under the option and the minimum exercise price are fixed or determinable, and the class of underlying stock and the identity of the service provider is designated. Ordinarily, if the corporate action provides for an immediate offer of stock for sale to a service provider, or provides for a particular date on which such offer is to be made, the date of the granting of the option is the date of such corporate action if the offer is to be made immediately, or the date provided as the date of the offer, as the case may be. However, an unreasonable delay in the giving of notice of such offer to the service provider will be taken into account as indicating that the corporation provided that the offer was to be made at the subsequent date on which such notice is given.

(2) If the corporation imposes a condition on the granting of an option (as distinguished from a condition governing the exercise of the option), such condition generally will be given effect in accordance with the intent of the corporation. However, if the grant of an option is subject to approval by stockholders, the date of grant of the option will be determined as if the option had not been subject to such approval. A condition that does not require corporate action, such as the approval of, or registration with, some regulatory or government agency, for example, a stock exchange or the Securities and Exchange Commission, is ordinarily considered a condition upon the exercise of the option unless the corporate action clearly indicates that the option is not to be granted until such condition has been satisfied.

(3) In general, a condition imposed upon the exercise of an option will not operate to make ineffective the granting of the option. For example, on June 1, 2008, Corporation A grants to X, an employee, an option to purchase 5,000 shares of the corporation's common stock, exercisable by X on or after June 1, 2009, provided X is employed by the corporation on June 1, 2009, and provided that A's profits during the fiscal year preceding the year of exercise exceed $200,000. Such an option is granted to X on June 1, 2008, and will be treated as outstanding as of such date.

(C) Stock.—The term *stock* means capital stock of any class, including voting or nonvoting common or preferred stock. Except as otherwise provided, the term stock includes both treasury stock and stock of original issue. Special classes of stock authorized to be issued to and held by employees are within the scope of the term stock for this purpose, provided such stock otherwise possesses the rights and characteristics of capital stock.

(D) Exercise price.—The term *exercise price* means the consideration in cash or property that, pursuant to the terms of the option, is the price at which the stock subject to the option is purchased. The term *exercise price* does not include any amounts paid as interest under a deferred payment plan or treated as interest.

(E) Exercise.—The term *exercise*, when used in reference to an option, means the act of acceptance by the holder of the option of the offer to sell contained in the option. In general, the time of exercise is the time when there is a sale or a contract to sell between the corporation and the individual. A promise to pay the exercise price does not constitute an exercise of the option unless the holder of the option is subject to personal liability on such promise. An agreement or undertaking by the service provider to make payments under a stock purchase plan does not constitute the exercise of an option to the extent the payments made remain subject to withdrawal by or refund to the service provider.

(F) Transfer.—The term *transfer*, when used in reference to the transfer to an individual of a share of stock pursuant to the exercise of an option, means the transfer of ownership of such share, or the transfer of substantially all the rights of ownership. Such transfer must, within a reasonable time, be evidenced on the books of the corporation. A transfer may occur even if a share of stock is subject to a substantial risk of forfeiture or is not otherwise transferable immediately after the date of exercise. A transfer does not fail to occur merely because, under the terms of the arrangement, the individual may not dispose of the share for a specified period of time, or the share is subject to a right of first refusal or a right to acquire the share at the share's fair market value at the time of the sale.

(G) Readily tradable.—For purposes of this section and §§1.409A-2 through 1.409A-6, stock is treated as readily tradable if it is regularly quoted by brokers or dealers making a market in such stock.

(H) Application to stock appreciation rights.—For purposes of this section and §§1.409A-2 through 1.409A-6, the definitions provided in paragraphs (b)(5)(vi)(A) through (G) of this section may be applied by analogy to the issuance of, exercise of, or payment upon the exercise of, a stock appreciation right.

(6) Restricted property, section 402(b) trusts, and section 403(c) annuities.—(i) *In general.*—If a service provider receives property from, or pursuant to, a plan maintained by a service recipient, there is no deferral of compensation merely because the value of the property is not includible in income by reason of the property being substantially nonvested (as defined in §1.83-3(b)), or is includible in income solely due to a valid election under section 83(b). For purposes of this paragraph (b)(6)(i), a transfer of property includes the transfer of a beneficial interest in a trust or annuity plan, or a transfer to or from a trust or under an annuity plan, to the extent such a transfer is subject to section 83, section 402(b) or section 403(c). In addition, for purposes of this paragraph (b), a right to compensation income that will be required to be included in income under section 402(b)(4)(A) is not a deferral of compensation.

(ii) *Promises to transfer property.*—A plan under which a service provider obtains a legally binding right to receive property in a future taxable year where the property will be substantially vested (as defined in § 1.83-3(b)) at the time of transfer of the property may provide for the deferral of compensation and, accordingly, may constitute a nonqualified deferred compensation plan. A legally binding right to receive property in a future taxable year where the property will be substantially nonvested (as defined in § 1.83-3(b)) at the time of transfer of the property will not provide for the deferral of compensation and, accordingly, will not constitute a nonqualified deferred compensation plan unless offered in conjunction with another legally binding right that constitutes a deferral of compensation.

(7) *Arrangements between partnerships and partners.*—[Reserved.]

(8) *Certain foreign plans.*—(i) *Plans with respect to compensation covered by treaty or other international agreement.*—A plan in which a service provider participates does not provide for a deferral of compensation for purposes of this paragraph (b) to the extent that the compensation under the plan would have been excluded from gross income for Federal income tax purposes under the provisions of any bilateral income tax convention or other bilateral or multilateral agreement to which the United States is a party if the compensation had been paid to the service provider at the time that the legally binding right to the compensation first arose or, if later, the time that the legally binding right was no longer subject to a substantial risk of forfeiture.

(ii) *Plans with respect to certain other compensation.*—A plan in which a service provider participates does not provide for a deferral of compensation for purposes of this paragraph (b) to the extent that compensation under the plan would not have been includible in gross income for Federal tax purposes if it had been paid to the service provider at the time that the legally binding right to the compensation first arose or, if later, the time that the legally binding right was no longer subject to a substantial risk of forfeiture, due to one of the following:

(A) The service provider was a nonresident alien at such time and the compensation would not have been includible in gross income under section 872.

(B) The service provider was a qualified individual (as defined in section 911(d)(1)) at such time, the compensation would have been foreign earned income within the meaning of section 911(b)(1) (without regard to section 911(b)(1)(B)(iv)) if paid at such time, and the amount of such compensation was equal to or less than the excess (if any) of the maximum exclusion amount under section 911(b)(2)(D) for such taxable year over the amount of foreign earned income actually excluded from gross income by such qualified individual for such taxable year under section 911(a)(1).

(C) The compensation would have been excludible from gross income under section 893.

(D) The compensation would have been excludible from gross income under section 931 or section 933.

(iii) *Tax equalization agreements.*—A tax equalization agreement does not provide for a deferral of compensation if payments made under such tax equalization agreement are made no later than the end of the second taxable year of the service provider beginning after the taxable year of the service provider in which the service provider's U.S. Federal income tax return is required to be filed (including any extensions) for the year to which the compensation subject to the tax equalization payment relates, or, if later, the second taxable year of the service provider beginning after the latest such taxable year in which the service provider's foreign tax return or payment is required to be filed or made for the year to which the compensation subject to the tax equalization payment relates. Where such payments arise due to an audit, litigation or similar proceeding, the right to the payments will not be treated as resulting in a deferral of compensation if the payments are scheduled and made in accordance with the provisions of § 1.409A-3(i)(1)(v) (timing of tax gross-up payments). For purposes of this paragraph (b)(8)(iii), the term *tax equalization agreement* refers to an agreement, method, program, or other arrangement that provides payments intended to compensate the service provider for some or all of the excess of the taxes actually imposed by a foreign jurisdiction on the compensation paid by the service recipient to the service provider over the taxes that would be imposed if the compensation were subject solely to United States Federal, state, and local income tax, or some or all of the excess of the United States Federal, state, and local income tax actually imposed on the compensation paid by the service to the service provider over the taxes that would be imposed if the compensation were subject solely to taxes in the foreign jurisdiction, provided that the payment made under such agreement, method, program, or other arrangement may not exceed such excess and the amount necessary to compensate for the additional taxes on the amount paid under the agreement, method, program, or other arrangement.

(iv) *Certain limited deferrals of a nonresident alien.*—With respect to a nonresident alien, a foreign plan does not provide for a deferral of compensation if the amounts deferred under the foreign plan based upon services performed by the nonresident alien in the United States (including amounts deferred based upon service credits or compensation received due to services performed in the United States) do not exceed the applicable dollar amount under section 402(g)(1)(B) for the taxable year. If the amounts deferred under the foreign plan based upon the services performed by the nonresident alien in the United States exceed the applicable dollar amount, an amount of such deferrals equal to such amount is treated as not deferred under a nonqualified deferred compensation plan. For purposes of this paragraph (b)(8)(iv), the term *foreign plan* means a plan that, together with all substantially similar plans, is maintained by a service recipient for a substantial number of participants, substantially all of whom are nonresident aliens or resident aliens classified as resident aliens solely under section 7701(b)(1)(A)(ii) (and not section 7701(b)(1)(A)(i)).

(v) *Additional foreign plans.*—A plan in which a service provider participates does not provide for a deferral of compensation for purposes of this paragraph (b) to the extent designated by the Commissioner in revenue procedures, notices, or other guidance published in the Internal Revenue Bulletin (see § 601.601(d)(2) of this chapter).

(vi) *Earnings.*—Earnings on compensation excluded from the definition of deferral of compensation pursuant to this paragraph (b)(8) are also not treated as a deferral of compensation.

(9) *Separation pay plans.*—(i) *In general.*—A plan that otherwise provides for a deferral of compensation under this paragraph (b) does not fail to provide a deferral of compensation merely because the right to payment of the compensation is conditioned upon a separation from service. However, paragraphs (b)(9)(ii), (iii), (iv), and (v) of this section provide rules concerning the extent to which certain separation pay plans do not provide for the deferral of compensation. The exceptions contained in paragraphs (b)(9)(ii), (iii), (iv), and (v) of this section may be used in combination, such that compensation under a plan that would be excepted under one of those paragraphs may be treated as excepted under another of those paragraphs, so that other compensation under a plan may be treated as excepted under the first of such paragraphs. Notwithstanding any other provision of this paragraph (b)(9), any payment or benefit, or entitlement to a payment or benefit, that acts as a substitute for, or replacement of, amounts deferred by the service recipient under a separate nonqualified deferred compensation plan constitutes a payment or a deferral of compensation under the separate nonqualified deferred compensation plan, and does not constitute a payment or deferral of compensation under a separation pay plan. If a service provider receives a payment at separation from service and also has a legally binding right to an amount of deferred compensation that would be forfeited upon the separation from service, whether the payment acts as an acceleration of vesting and substitute payment for the amount of deferred compensation forfeited, or whether the deferred compensation is treated as forfeited and the amount paid is treated as a separate payment of current compensation, is determined based on the facts and circumstances, provided that, where the separation from service is voluntary, it is presumed that the payment results from an acceleration of vesting followed by a payment of the deferred compensation that is subject to section 409A. Accordingly, any change in the payment schedule to accelerate or defer the payments would be subject to the rules of section 409A. The presumption that a right to a payment is not a new right, but is instead a right substituted for a pre-existing forfeited right, may be rebutted by demonstrating that the service provider would have obtained the right to the payment regardless of the forfeiture of the nonvested right. A factor indicating that the service provider would have obtained a right to a payment regardless of the forfeiture of the nonvested right is that the amount to which the service provider obtains a right is materially less than an amount equal to the present value of the forfeited amount multiplied by a fraction, the numerator of which is the period of service the service provider actually completed, and the denominator of which is the full period of service the service provider would have been required to complete to receive the full amount of the payment. For example, where a service provider is entitled to a future payment only if the service provider completes three years of service and at the time of termination the service provider has completed one year of service, the presumption could be rebutted if the payment to the service provider is materially less than the present value of one-third of the nonvested amount. Another such factor is that the payment to the service provider is of a type customarily made to service providers who separate from ser-

vice with the service recipient and do not forfeit nonvested rights to deferred compensation (for example, a payment of accrued but unused leave or a payment for a release of actual or potential claims).

(ii) *Collectively bargained separation pay plans.*—A separation pay plan does not provide for a deferral of compensation to the extent the plan is a collectively bargained separation pay plan that provides for separation pay only upon an involuntary separation from service or pursuant to a window program. Only the portion of the separation pay plan attributable to employees covered by a bona fide collective bargaining agreement is considered to be provided under a collectively bargained separation pay plan. A collectively bargained separation pay plan is a separation pay plan that meets the following conditions:

(A) The separation pay plan is contained within an agreement that the Secretary of Labor determines to be a collective bargaining agreement.

(B) The separation pay provided by the collective bargaining agreement was the subject of arm's length negotiations between employee representatives and one or more employers, and the agreement between employee representatives and one or more employers satisfies section 7701(a)(46).

(C) The circumstances surrounding the agreement evidence good faith bargaining between adverse parties over the separation pay to be provided under the agreement.

(iii) *Separation pay due to involuntary separation from service or participation in a window program.*—A separation pay plan that is not described in paragraph (b)(9)(ii) of this section and that provides for separation pay only upon an involuntary separation from service (as defined in paragraph (n) of this section) or pursuant to a window program does not provide for a deferral of compensation to the extent that the separation pay, or portion of the separation pay, provided under the plan meets the following requirements:

(A) The separation pay (other than amounts described in paragraphs (b)(9)(iv) and (v) of this section) does not exceed two times the lesser of—

(1) The sum of the service provider's annualized compensation based upon the annual rate of pay for services provided to the service recipient for the taxable year of the service provider preceding the taxable year of the service provider in which the service provider has a separation from service with such service recipient (adjusted for any increase during that year that was expected to continue indefinitely if the service provider had not separated from service); or

(2) The maximum amount that may be taken into account under a qualified plan pursuant to section 401(a)(17) for the year in which the service provider has a separation from service.

(B) The plan provides that the separation pay described in paragraph (b)(9)(iii)(A) of this section must be paid no later than the last day of the second taxable year of the service provider following the taxable year of the service provider in which occurs the separation from service.

(iv) *Foreign separation pay plans.*—A separation pay plan (including a plan providing payments upon a voluntary separation from service) does not provide for deferred compensation to the extent the plan provides for amounts of separation pay required to be provided under the applicable law of a foreign jurisdiction. For this purpose, a provision of foreign law shall be considered applicable only to foreign earned income (as defined under section 911(b)(1) without regard to section 911(b)(1)(B)(iv) and without regard to the requirement that the income be attributable to services performed during the period described in section 911(d)(1)(A) or (B)) from sources within the foreign country that promulgated such law.

(v) *Reimbursements and certain other separation payments.*—(A) *In general.*—To the extent a separation pay plan (including a plan providing payments upon a voluntary separation from service) entitles a service provider to payment by the service recipient of reimbursements that are not otherwise excludible from gross income for expenses that the service provider could otherwise deduct under section 162 or section 167 as business expenses incurred in connection with the performance of services (ignoring any applicable limitation based on adjusted gross income), or of reasonable outplacement expenses and reasonable moving expenses actually incurred by the service provider and directly related to the termination of services for the service recipient, such plan does not provide for a deferral of compensation to the extent such rights apply during a limited period of time (regardless of whether such rights extend beyond the limited period of time). For purposes of this paragraph (b)(9)(v)(A), the reimbursement of reasonable moving expenses includes the reimbursement of all or part of any loss the service provider actually incurs due to the sale of a primary residence in connection with a separation from service.

(B) *Medical benefits.*—To the extent a separation pay plan (including a plan providing payments due to a voluntary separation from service) entitles a service provider to reimbursement by the service recipient of payments of medical expenses incurred and paid by the service provider but not reimbursed by a person other than the service recipient and allowable as a deduction under section 213 (disregarding the requirement of section 213(a) that the deduction is available only to the extent that such expenses exceed 7.5 percent of adjusted gross income), such plan does not provide for a deferral of compensation to the extent such rights apply during the period of time during which the service provider would be entitled (or would, but for such plan, be entitled) to continuation coverage under a group health plan of the service recipient under section 4980B (COBRA) if the service provider elected such coverage and paid the applicable premiums.

(C) *In-kind benefits and direct service recipient payments.*—A service provider's entitlement to in-kind benefits from the service recipient, or a payment by the service recipient directly to the person providing the goods or services to the service provider, is treated as not providing for a deferral of compensation for purposes of this paragraph (b), if a right to reimbursement by the service recipient for a payment for such benefits, goods, or services by the service provider would not be treated as providing for a deferral of compensation under this paragraph (b)(9)(v).

(D) *Limited payments.*—If not otherwise excluded, a taxpayer may treat a right or rights under a separation pay plan to a payment or payments as not providing for a deferral of compensation to the extent such payments in the aggregate do not exceed the applicable dollar amount under section 402(g)(1)(B) for the year of the separation from service.

(E) *Limited period of time.*—For purposes of paragraphs (b)(9)(v)(A) and (C) of this section, a limited period of time in which expenses may be incurred, or in-which in-kind benefits may be provided by the service recipient or a third party that the service recipient will pay, does not include periods beyond the last day of the second taxable year of the service provider following the taxable year of the service provider in which the separation from service occurred, provided that the period during which the reimbursements for such expenses must be paid may not extend beyond the third taxable year of the service provider following the taxable year of the service provider in which the separation from service occurred.

(vi) *Window programs — definition.*—The term *window program* refers to a program established by a service recipient in connection with an impending separation from service to provide separation pay, where such program is made available by the service recipient for a limited period of time (no longer than 12 months) to service providers who separate from service during that period or to service providers who separate from service during that period under specified circumstances. A program will not be considered a window program if a service recipient establishes a pattern of repeatedly providing for similar separation pay in similar situations for substantially consecutive, limited periods of time. Whether the recurrence of these programs constitutes a pattern is determined based on the facts and circumstances. Although no one factor is determinative, relevant factors include whether the benefits are on account of a specific business event or condition, the degree to which the separation pay relates to the event or condition, and whether the event or condition is temporary or discrete or is a permanent aspect of the employer's business.

(10) *Certain indemnification and liability insurance plans.*—A plan in which a service provider participates does not provide for a deferral of compensation for purposes of this paragraph (b) to the extent that the plan provides (to the extent permissible under applicable law), for the indemnification of, or the purchase of an insurance policy providing for payments of, all or part of the expenses incurred or damages paid or payable by a service provider with respect to a bona fide claim against the service provider or service recipient, including amounts paid or payable by the service provider upon the settlement of a bona fide claim against the service provider or service recipient, where such claim is based on actions or failures to act by the service provider in his or her capacity as a service provider of the service recipient.

(11) *Legal settlements.*—An agreement to which a service provider is a party does not provide for a deferral of compensation for purposes of this paragraph (b) to the extent that the agreement provides for amounts paid as settlements or awards resolving bona fide legal claims based on wrongful termination, employment discrimination, the Fair Labor Standards Act, or worker's compensation statutes, including claims under applicable Federal, state, local, or foreign laws, or for reimbursements or payments of reasonable attorneys fees or other reasonable expenses incurred by the service pro-

vider related to such bona fide legal claims, regardless of whether such settlements, awards, or reimbursement or payment of expenses pursuant to such claims are treated as compensation or wages for Federal tax purposes. Whether the execution of a waiver of any or all of such types of claims indicates that the amounts are paid as an award or settlement of an actual bona fide claim for damages under applicable law is determined based on the facts and circumstances. This paragraph (b)(11) does not apply to any deferred amounts that did not arise as a result of an actual bona fide claim for damages under applicable law, such as amounts that would have been deferred or paid regardless of the existence of such claim, even if such amounts are paid or modified as part of a settlement or award resolving an actual bona fide claim. For this purpose, a provision of foreign law shall be considered applicable only to foreign earned income (as defined under section 911(b)(1) without regard to section 911(b)(1)(B)(iv) and without regard to the requirement that the income be attributable to services performed during the period described in section 911(d)(1)(A) or (B)) from sources within the foreign country that promulgated such law.

(12) *Certain educational benefits.*—A plan in which a service provider participates does not provide for a deferral of compensation to the extent the plan provides for taxable educational benefits. For purposes of this paragraph (b)(12), the term *educational benefits* refers solely to benefits provided to a service provider, consisting solely of educational assistance for the education of the service provider, as defined in section 127(c) and the accompanying regulations, and does not refer to any benefits provided for the education of any other person, including any spouse, child, or other family member of the service provider.

(c) *Plan.*—(1) *In general.*—The term *plan* includes any agreement, method, program, or other arrangement, including an agreement, method, program, or other arrangement that applies to one person or individual. A plan may be adopted unilaterally by the service recipient or may be negotiated or agreed to by the service recipient and one or more service providers or service provider representatives. An agreement, method, program, or other arrangement may constitute a plan regardless of whether it is an employee benefit plan under section 3(3) of ERISA, as amended (29 U.S.C. 1002(3)). The requirements of section 409A are applied as if a separate plan or plans is maintained for each service provider. For purposes of determining the terms of a plan, general provisions of the plan that purport to nullify noncompliant plan terms, or to supply any specific plan terms required by this section, § 1.409A-2 or § 1.409A-3, are disregarded.

(2) *Plan aggregation rules.*—(i) *In general.*—Except as otherwise provided, the following rules apply with respect to the application of this section and §§ 1.409A-2 through 1.409A-6 to deferrals of compensation with respect to a service provider:

(A) All deferrals of compensation at the election of that service provider under all plans of the service recipient that are account balance plans, except to the extent that the plan is described in paragraph (c)(2)(i)(D), (E), (F), (G), or (H) of this section, are treated as deferred under a single plan. For purposes of this paragraph, the term *account balance plan* means—

(1) An agreement, method, program, or other arrangement that is an account balance plan as defined in § 31.3121(v)(2)-1(c)(1)(ii)(A) of this chapter, including mandatorily bifurcating the agreement, method, program, or other arrangement in accordance with the rules provided in § 31.3121(v)-1(c)(1)(iii)(B) of this chapter; or

(2) An agreement, method, program, or other arrangement that would be described in paragraph (c)(2)(i)(A)(1) of this section if the service provider were an employee.

(B) All deferrals of compensation other than at the election of that service provider, including deferrals reflecting matching by the service recipient with respect to amounts a service provider elects to defer, under all plans of the service recipient that are account balance plans, except to the extent the plan is described in paragraph (c)(2)(i)(D), (E), (F), (G), or (H) of this section, are treated as deferred under a single plan. For purposes of this paragraph (c)(2)(i)(B), the term "account balance plan" has the same meaning as provided in paragraph (c)(2)(i)(A) of this section.

(C) All deferrals of compensation with respect to that service provider under all plans of the service recipient that are nonaccount balance plans, except to the extent such plan is described in paragraph (c)(2)(i)(D), (E), (F), (G), or (H) of this section, are treated as deferred under a single plan. For purposes of this paragraph (c)(2)(i)(C), the term *nonaccount balance plan* means—

(1) An agreement, method, program, or other arrangement that is a nonaccount balance plan as defined in § 31.3121(v)(2)-1(c)(2)(i) of this chapter, including mandatorily bifurcating the agreement, method, program, or other arrangement in accordance with the rules provided in § 31.3121(v)-1(c)(1)(iii)(B) of this chapter; or

(2) An agreement, method, program, or other arrangement that would be described in paragraph (c)(2)(i)(C)(1) of this section if the service provider were an employee.

(D) All deferrals of compensation with respect to that service provider under all separation pay plans (as defined in paragraph (m) of this section) of the service recipient to the extent an amount deferred under the plans is not described in paragraph (c)(2)(i)(E) of this section and is payable solely upon an involuntary separation from service within the meaning of paragraph (n) of this section or as a result of participation in a window program, are treated as deferred under a single plan.

(E) All deferrals of compensation with respect to that service provider under all plans of the service recipient to the extent such amounts deferred consist of rights to in-kind benefits or reimbursements of expenses, such as membership fees, or expenses related to aircraft or vehicle usage, to the extent that the right to the in-kind benefit or reimbursement, separately or in the aggregate, does not constitute a substantial portion of either the overall compensation earned by the service provider for performing services for the service recipient or the overall compensation received due to a separation from service, are treated as deferred under a single plan.

(F) All deferrals of compensation with respect to that service provider under all plans of the service recipient to the extent that the taxation of such compensation is governed by § 1.61-22 or § 1.7872-15 (split-dollar life insurance arrangements), or the taxation of such compensation would be governed by § 1.61-22 or § 1.7872-15 but for the operation of § 1.61-22(j) (effective date provisions), are treated as deferred under a single plan.

(G) All deferrals of compensation with respect to that service provider under all agreements, methods, programs, or other arrangements of the service recipient to the extent the deferrals under the agreements, methods, programs, or other arrangements are deferrals of amounts that would be treated as modified foreign earned income (meaning foreign earned income as defined under section 911(b)(1) without regard to section 911(b)(1)(B)(iv) and without regard to the requirement that the income be attributable to services performed during the period described in section 911(d)(1)(A) or (B)) if paid to the service provider at the time the amount is first deferred, and provided further that substantially all the participants in such agreements, methods, programs, or other arrangements and any substantially similar agreements, methods, programs, or other arrangements are nonresident aliens and that the service provider does not participate in a substantially identical agreement, method, program, or other arrangement that does not meet the requirements of this paragraph (c)(2)(i)(G) (a domestic arrangement), are treated as deferred under a single plan.

(H) All deferrals of compensation with respect to that service provider under all plans of the service recipient to the extent such plans are stock rights (as defined in paragraph (1) of this section) subject to section 409A, are treated as deferred under a single plan.

(I) All deferrals of compensation with respect to that service provider under all plans of the service recipient to the extent such plans are not described in paragraph (c)(2)(i)(A), (B), (C), (D), (E), (F), (G), or (H) of this section are treated as deferred under a single plan.

(ii) *Dual status.*—Agreements, methods, programs, and other arrangements in which a service provider participates are not aggregated with other agreements, methods, programs, and other arrangements to the extent the service provider participates in one set of agreements, methods, programs, and other arrangements due to status as an employee of the service recipient (employee arrangements) and another set of agreements, methods, programs, and other arrangements due to status as an independent contractor of the service recipient (independent contractor arrangements). For example, where a service provider deferred amounts under an independent contractor arrangement while providing services as an independent contractor, and then becomes eligible for and defers amounts under a separate employee arrangement after being hired as an employee, the two arrangements will not be aggregated for purposes of this paragraph (c)(2). Where an employee also is a member of the board of directors of the service recipient (or a similar position with respect to a non-corporate service recipient), the arrangements under which the employee participates as a director (director arrangements) are not aggregated with employee arrangements, provided that the director arrangements are substantially similar to arrangements provided to service providers providing services only as directors (or similar positions with respect to non-corporate service recipients). For example, an employee director who participates in an employee arrangement and a director arrangement generally may treat the two arrangements as separate plans, provided that the director arrangement is substantially similar to arrangements providing benefits to non-employee directors. To the extent a plan in which an employee director participates is not substantially similar to arrangements in which non-employee directors participate, such plan is treated as an employee plan for purposes of this paragraph (c)(2). Director plans and independent contractor plans are aggregated for purposes of this paragraph (c)(2).

(3) *Establishment of plan.*—(i) *In general.*—A plan does not satisfy the requirements of section 409A and this section and §§ 1.409A-2 through 1.409A-3 and §§ 1.409A-5 through 1.409A-6, unless the plan is established and maintained by a service recipient in accordance with the requirements of this section, §§ 1.409A-2 through 1.409A-3 and §§ 1.409A-5 through 1.409A-6. For purposes of this paragraph (c)(3), a plan is established on the latest of the date on which it is adopted, the date on which it is effective, and the date on which the material terms of the plan are set forth in writing. The material terms of the plan may be set forth in writing in one or more documents. For purposes of this paragraph (c)(3)(i), a plan will be deemed to be set forth in writing if it is set forth in any other form that is approved by the Commissioner. The material terms of the plan include the amount (or the method or formula for determining the amount) of deferred compensation to be provided under the plan and the time and form of payment. Notwithstanding the foregoing, a plan will be deemed to be established as of the date the participant obtains a legally binding right to a deferral of compensation, provided that the plan is otherwise established under the rules of this paragraph (c)(3)(i) by the end of the taxable year of the service provider in which the legally binding right arises, or with respect to an amount not payable in the year immediately following the taxable year of the service provider in which the legally binding right arises (the subsequent year), the 15th day of the third month of the subsequent year.

(ii) *Initial deferral election provisions.*—If a plan provides a service provider or a service recipient with an initial deferral election, the plan satisfies the requirements of this paragraph (c)(3) if the plan sets forth in writing, on or before the date the applicable election is required to be irrevocable to satisfy the requirements of § 1.409A-2(a), the conditions under which such election may be made.

(iii) *Subsequent deferral election provisions.*—If a plan permits a subsequent deferral election described in § 1.409A-2(b), the plan satisfies the requirements of this paragraph (c)(3) if the plan sets forth in writing, on or before the date the election is required to be irrevocable to meet the requirements of § 1.409A-2(b), the conditions under which such election may be made.

(iv) *Payment accelerations.*—Except as explicitly provided in § 1.409A-3, a plan is not required to set forth in writing the conditions under which a payment may be accelerated if such acceleration is permitted under § 1.409A-3(j)(4).

(v) *Six-month delay for specified employees.*—A plan must provide that distributions to a specified employee may not be made before the date that is six months after the date of separation from service or, if earlier, the date of death (the six-month delay rule). The six-month delay rule, required for payments due to the separation from service of a specified employee, must be written in the plan. A plan does not fail to be established and maintained merely because it does not contain the six-month delay rule when the service provider who has a right to compensation deferred under such plan is not a specified employee. However, such provision must be set forth in writing on or before the date such service provider first becomes a specified employee. In general, this means the provision must be set forth in writing on or before the specified employee effective date (as defined in paragraph (i)(3) of this section) for the first list of specified employees that includes such service provider.

(vi) *Plan amendments.*—In the case of an amendment that increases the amount deferred under a nonqualified deferred compensation plan, the plan is not considered established with respect to the additional amount deferred until the plan, as amended, is established in accordance with paragraph (c)(3)(i) of this section.

(vii) *Transition rule for written plan requirement.*—For purposes of this paragraph (c)(3), a legally enforceable unwritten plan that was adopted and effective before December 31, 2007, is treated as established under this section as of the later of the date on which it was adopted or became effective, provided that the material terms of the plan are set forth in writing on or before December 31, 2007.

(viii) *Plan aggregation rules.*—The plan aggregation rules of paragraph (c)(2)(i) of this section do not apply to the written plan requirements of this paragraph (c)(3). Accordingly, deferrals of compensation under an agreement, method, program, or other arrangement that fails to meet the requirements of section 409A solely due to a failure to meet the written plan requirements of this paragraph (c)(3) are not aggregated with deferrals of compensation under other agreements, methods, programs, or other arrangements that meet such requirements.

(d) *Substantial risk of forfeiture.*—(1) *In general.*—Compensation is subject to a substantial risk of forfeiture if entitlement to the amount is conditioned on the performance of substantial future services by any person or the occurrence of a condition related to a purpose of the compensation, and the possibility of forfeiture is substantial. For purposes of this paragraph (d), a condition related to a purpose of the compensation must relate to the service provider's performance for the service recipient or the service recipient's business activities or organizational goals (for example, the attainment of a prescribed level of earnings or equity value or completion of an initial public offering). For purposes of this paragraph (d), if a service provider's entitlement to the amount is conditioned on the occurrence of the service provider's involuntary separation from service without cause, the right is subject to a substantial risk of forfeiture if the possibility of forfeiture is substantial. An amount is not subject to a substantial risk of forfeiture merely because the right to the amount is conditioned, directly or indirectly, upon the refraining from the performance of services. Except as provided with respect to certain transaction-based compensation under § 1.409A-3(i)(5)(iv), the addition of any risk of forfeiture after the legally binding right to the compensation arises, or any extension of a period during which compensation is subject to a risk of forfeiture, is disregarded for purposes of determining whether such compensation is subject to a substantial risk of forfeiture. An amount will not be considered subject to a substantial risk of forfeiture beyond the date or time at which the recipient otherwise could have elected to receive the amount of compensation, unless the present value of the amount subject to a substantial risk of forfeiture (disregarding, in determining the present value, the risk of forfeiture) is materially greater than the present value of the amount the recipient otherwise could have elected to receive absent such risk of forfeiture. For this purpose, compensation that the service provider would receive for continuing to perform services regardless of whether the service provider elected to receive the amount that is subject to a substantial risk of forfeiture is not taken into account in determining whether the present value of the right to the amount subject to a substantial risk of forfeiture is materially greater than the amount the recipient otherwise could have elected to receive absent such risk of forfeiture. For example, a salary deferral generally may not be made subject to a substantial risk of forfeiture. But, for example, where a bonus plan provides an election between a cash payment or restricted stock units with a present value that is materially greater (disregarding the risk of forfeiture) than the present value of such cash payment and that will be forfeited absent continued services for a period of years, the right to the restricted stock units generally will be treated as subject to a substantial risk of forfeiture.

(2) *Stock rights.*—A stock right is not subject to a substantial risk of forfeiture at the earlier of the first date the holder may exercise the stock right and receive cash or property that is substantially vested (as defined in § 1.83-3(b)) or the first date that the stock right is not subject to a forfeiture condition that would constitute a substantial risk of forfeiture. Accordingly, a stock option that the service provider may exercise immediately and receive substantially vested stock is not subject to a substantial risk of forfeiture, even if the stock option automatically terminates upon the service provider's separation from service.

(3) *Enforcement of forfeiture condition.*—(i) *In general.*—In determining whether the possibility of forfeiture is substantial in the case of rights to compensation granted by a service recipient to a service provider that owns a significant amount of the total combined voting power or value of all classes of equity of the service recipient (where the service provider's ownership is determined with application of the attribution rules under section 318 if the service recipient is a corporation, or if the service recipient is an entity that is not a corporation, with application by analogy of the attribution rules under section 318), all relevant facts and circumstances will be taken into account in determining whether the probability of the service recipient enforcing such condition is substantial, including—

(A) The service provider's relationship to other equity holders and the extent of their control, potential control and possible loss of control of the service recipient;

(B) The position of the service provider in the service recipient and the extent to which the service provider is subordinate to other service providers;

(C) The service provider's relationship to the officers and directors of the service recipient (or similar positions with respect to a noncorporate service recipient);

(D) The person or persons who must approve the service provider's discharge; and

(E) Past actions of the service recipient in enforcing the restrictions.

(ii) *Examples.*—The following examples illustrate the rules of paragraph (d)(3)(i) of this section:

Example 1. A service provider would be considered as having deferred compensation subject to a substantial risk of forfeiture, but for the fact that the service provider owns 20 percent of the single class of stock in the transferor corporation. If the remaining 80 percent of the class of stock is owned by an unrelated individual (or members of such an individual's family) so that the possibility of the corporation enforcing a restriction on such rights is substantial, then such rights are subject to a substantial risk of forfeiture.

Example 2. A service provider would be considered as having deferred compensation subject to a substantial risk of forfeiture, but for the fact that the service provider, who is president of the corporation, also owns 4 percent of the voting power of all the stock of a corporation. If the remaining stock is so diversely held by the public that the president, in effect, controls the corporation, then the possibility of the corporation enforcing a restriction on the right to deferred compensation of the president is not substantial, and such rights are not subject to a substantial risk of forfeiture.

(e) *Performance-based compensation.*—(1) *In general.*—The term *performance-based compensation* means compensation the amount of which, or the entitlement to which, is contingent on the satisfaction of preestablished organizational or individual performance criteria relating to a performance period of at least 12 consecutive months. Organizational or individual performance criteria are considered preestablished if established in writing by not later than 90 days after the commencement of the period of service to which the criteria relates, provided that the outcome is substantially uncertain at the time the criteria are established. Performance-based compensation may include payments based on performance criteria that are not approved by a compensation committee of the board of directors (or similar entity in the case of a non-corporate service recipient) or by the stockholders or members of the service recipient. Performance-based compensation does not include any amount or portion of any amount that will be paid either regardless of performance, or based upon a level of performance that is substantially certain to be met at the time the criteria is established. In addition, except as provided in paragraph (e)(3) of this section, compensation is not performance-based compensation merely because the amount of such compensation is determined by reference to the value of the service recipient or the stock of the service recipient. Where a portion of an amount of compensation would qualify as performance-based compensation if the portion were the sole amount available under the plan, that portion of the award will not fail to qualify as performance-based compensation if that portion is designated separately or otherwise separately identifiable under the terms of the plan, and the amount of each portion is determined independently of the other. Compensation may be performance-based compensation where the amount will be paid regardless of satisfaction of the performance criteria due to the service provider's death, disability, or a change in control event (as defined in § 1.409A-3(i)(5)(i)), provided that a payment made under such circumstances without regard to the satisfaction of the performance criteria will not constitute performance-based compensation. For purposes of this paragraph (e)(1), a disability refers to any medically determinable physical or mental impairment resulting in the service provider's inability to perform the duties of his or her position or any substantially similar position, where such impairment can be expected to result in death or can be expected to last for a continuous period of not less than six months.

(2) *Payments based upon subjective performance criteria.*—The term *performance-based compensation* includes payments based upon subjective performance criteria, provided that—

(i) The subjective performance criteria are bona fide and relate to the performance of the participant service provider, a group of service providers that includes the participant service provider, or a business unit for which the participant service provider provides services (which may include the entire organization); and

(ii) The determination that any subjective performance criteria have been met is not made by the participant service provider or a family member of the participant service provider (as defined in section 267(c)(4) applied as if the family of an individual includes the spouse of any member of the family), or a person under the effective control of the participant service provider or such a family member, and no amount of the compensation of the person making such determination is effectively controlled in whole or in part by the service provider or such a family member.

(3) *Equity-based compensation.*—Compensation is performance-based compensation if it is based solely on an increase in the value of the service recipient, or a share of stock in the service recipient, after the date of a grant or award. However, compensation payable for a service period that is equal to the value of a predetermined number of shares of stock, and is variable only to the extent that the value of such shares appreciates or depreciates, generally will not be performance-based compensation. Notwithstanding the foregoing, the attainment of a prescribed value for the service recipient (or a portion

thereof), or a share of stock in the service recipient, may be used as a preestablished organizational criterion for purposes of providing performance-based compensation, provided that the other requirements of paragraph (e)(1) of this section are satisfied. In addition, an award of equity-based compensation may constitute performance-based compensation if entitlement to the compensation is subject to a condition that would cause the award to otherwise qualify as performance-based compensation, such as a performance-based vesting condition. A provision that allows a service provider to defer compensation that would be realized upon the exercise of a stock right generally constitutes an additional deferral feature for purposes of the definition of a deferral of compensation under paragraph (b)(5) of this section.

(f) *Service provider.*—(1) *In general.*—The term *service provider* includes an individual, corporation, subchapter S corporation, partnership, personal service corporation (as defined in section 269A(b)(1)), noncorporate entity that would be a personal service corporation if it were a corporation, qualified personal service corporation (as defined in section 448(d)(2)), and noncorporate entity that would be a qualified personal service corporation if it were a corporation, for any taxable year in which such individual, corporation, subchapter S corporation, partnership, or other entity accounts for gross income from the performance of services under the cash receipts and disbursements method of accounting. The term *service provider* generally includes a person who has separated from service (a former service provider).

(2) *Independent contractors.*—(i) *In general.*—Except as otherwise provided in paragraph (f)(2)(iv) of this section, section 409A does not apply to an amount deferred under a plan between a service provider and service recipient with respect to a particular trade or business in which the service provider participates, including earnings credited to such deferred amount, if during the service provider's taxable year in which the service provider obtains a legally binding right to the payment of the amount deferred each of the following applies:

(A) The service provider is actively engaged in the trade or business of providing services, other than as an employee or as a member of the board of directors of a corporation (or similar position with respect to an entity that is not a corporation).

(B) The service provider provides significant services to two or more service recipients to which the service provider is not related and that are not related to one another (as defined in paragraph (f)(2)(ii) of this section).

(C) The service provider is not related to the service recipient, applying the definition of related person contained in paragraph (f)(2)(ii) of this section subject to the modification that the language "20 percent" is not used instead of "50 percent" each place "50 percent" appears in sections 267(b) and 707(b)(1).

(ii) *Related person.*—For purposes of this paragraph (f)(2), a person is related to another person if the persons bear a relationship to each other that is specified in section 267(b) or 707(b)(1), subject to the modifications that the language "20 percent" is used instead of "50 percent" each place it appears in sections 267(b) and 707(b)(1), and section 267(c)(4) is applied as if the family of an individual includes the spouse of any member of the family; or the persons are engaged in trades or businesses under common control (within the meaning of section 52(a) and (b)). In addition, an individual is related to an entity if the individual is an officer of an entity that is a corporation, or holds a position substantially similar to an officer of a corporation with an entity that is not a corporation.

(iii) *Significant services.*—Whether a service provider is providing significant services depends on the facts and circumstances of each case. However, for purposes of paragraph (f)(2)(i) of this section, a service provider who provides services to two or more service recipients to which the service provider is not related and that are not related to one another is deemed to be providing significant services to two or more of such service recipients for a given taxable year, if the revenues generated from the services provided to any service recipient or group of related service recipients during such taxable year do not exceed 70 percent of the total revenue generated by the service provider from the trade or business of providing such services. In addition, in the case of a service provider who has been providing services in a trade or business for a period of not less than three consecutive years, for purposes of paragraph (f)(2)(i) of this section, a service provider who provides services to two or more service recipients to which the service provider is not related and that are not related to one another is deemed to be providing significant services to two or more of such service recipients for a given taxable year if in each of the prior three taxable years the revenues generated from the services provided to any service recipient or group of related service recipients during such prior taxable years did not exceed 70 percent of the total revenue generated by the service provider from the trade or business of providing such services and, at the time an amount is deferred, the service provider does not know or have reason to anticipate that the revenues generated from the services provided to any service recipient or group of related service recipients during the current year will exceed 70 percent of the total revenue generated by the service provider from the trade or business of providing such services.

(iv) *Management services.*—This paragraph (f)(2) does not apply to a service provider to the extent the service provider provides management services to a service recipient. For purposes of this paragraph (f)(2)(iv), the term *management services* means services that involve the actual or de facto direction or control of the financial or operational aspects of a trade or business of the service recipient, or investment management or advisory services provided to a service recipient whose primary trade or business includes the investment of financial assets (including investments in real estate), such as a hedge fund or a real estate investment trust.

(v) *Services provided to related persons.*—Section 409A does not apply to an amount deferred under a plan that is a bona fide agreement, method, program, or other arrangement between a service provider and a related service recipient arising in the ordinary course of a particular trade or business in which the service provider is engaged to the extent that—

(A) The service provider provides services to the service recipient as an independent contractor;

(B) During the service provider's taxable year in which the amount is deferred, the service provider qualifies for the safe harbor provided in paragraph (f)(2)(iii) of this section with respect to such trade or business; and

(C) Such agreement, method, program, or other arrangement and the practices thereunder (including billing and collection practices), are substantially similar to the agreements, methods, programs, or other arrangements and practices applicable to one or more unrelated service recipients to whom the service provider provides substantial services and that produce a majority of the total revenue that the service provider earns from the trade or business of providing such services during the taxable year.

(g) *Service recipient.*—Except as otherwise specifically provided in these regulations, the term *service recipient* means the person for whom the services are performed and with respect to whom the legally binding right to compensation arises, and all persons with whom such person would be considered a single employer under section 414(b) (employees of controlled group of corporations), and all persons with whom such person would be considered a single employer under section 414(c) (employees of partnerships, proprietorships, etc., under common control). For example, if the service provider is an employee, the service recipient generally is the employer (including all persons treated as a single employer under section 414(b) or (c)). Notwithstanding the foregoing, section 409A applies to a plan that provides for the deferral of compensation, even if the payment of the compensation is not made by the person for whom services are performed.

(h) *Separation from service.*—(1) *Employees.*—(i) *In general.*—An employee separates from service with the employer if the employee dies, retires, or otherwise has a termination of employment with the employer. However, for purposes of this paragraph (h)(1), the employment relationship is treated as continuing intact while the individual is on military leave, sick leave, or other bona fide leave of absence if the period of such leave does not exceed six months, or if longer, so long as the individual retains a right to reemployment with the service recipient under an applicable statute or by contract. For purposes of this paragraph (h)(1), a leave of absence constitutes a bona fide leave of absence only if there is a reasonable expectation that the employee will return to perform services for the employer. If the period of leave exceeds six months and the individual does not retain a right to reemployment under an applicable statute or by contract, the employment relationship is deemed to terminate on the first date immediately following such six-month period. Notwithstanding the foregoing, where a leave of absence is due to any medically determinable physical or mental impairment that can be expected to result in death or can be expected to last for a continuous period of not less than six months, where such impairment causes the employee to be unable to perform the duties of his or her position of employment or any substantially similar position of employment, a 29-month period of absence may be substituted for such six-month period.

(ii) *Termination of employment.*—Whether a termination of employment has occurred is determined based on whether the facts and circumstances indicate that the employer and employee reasonably anticipated that no further services would be performed after a certain date or that the level of bona fide services the employee

would perform after such date (whether as an employee or as an independent contractor) would permanently decrease to no more than 20 percent of the average level of bona fide services performed (whether as an employee or an independent contractor) over the immediately preceding 36-month period (or the full period of services to the employer if the employee has been providing services to the employer less than 36 months). Facts and circumstances to be considered in making this determination include, but are not limited to, whether the employee continues to be treated as an employee for other purposes (such as continuation of salary and participation in employee benefit programs), whether similarly situated service providers have been treated consistently, and whether the employee is permitted, and realistically available, to perform services for other service recipients in the same line of business. An employee is presumed to have separated from service where the level of bona fide services performed decreases to a level equal to 20 percent or less of the average level of services performed by the employee during the immediately preceding 36-month period. An employee will be presumed not to have separated from service where the level of bona fide services performed continues at a level that is 50 percent or more of the average level of service performed by the employee during the immediately preceding 36-month period. No presumption applies to a decrease in the level of bona fide services performed to a level that is more than 20 percent and less than 50 percent of the average level of bona fide services performed during the immediately preceding 36-month period. The presumption is rebuttable by demonstrating that the employer and the employee reasonably anticipated that as of a certain date the level of bona fide services would be reduced permanently to a level less than or equal to 20 percent of the average level of bona fide services provided during the immediately preceding 36-month period or full period of services provided to the employer if the employee has been providing services to the service recipient for a period of less than 36 months (or that the level of bona fide services would not be so reduced). For example, an employee may demonstrate that the employer and employee reasonably anticipated that the employee would cease providing services, but that, after the original cessation of services, business circumstances such as termination of the employee's replacement caused the employee to return to employment. Although the employee's return to employment may cause the employee to be presumed to have continued in employment because the employee is providing services at a rate equal to the rate at which the employee was providing services before the termination of employment, the facts and circumstances in this case would demonstrate that at the time the employee originally ceased to provide services, the employee and the service recipient reasonably anticipated that the employee would not provide services in the future. Notwithstanding the foregoing provisions of this paragraph (h)(1)(ii), a plan may treat another level of reasonably anticipated permanent reduction in the level of bona fide services as a separation from service, provided that the level of reduction required must be designated in writing as a specific percentage, and the reasonably anticipated reduced level of bona fide services must be greater than 20 percent but less that 50 percent of the average level of bona fide services provided in the immediately preceding 36 months. The plan must specify the definition of separation from service on or before the date on which a separation from service is designated as a time of payment of the applicable amount deferred, and once designated, any change to the definition of separation from service with respect to such amount deferred will be subject to the rules regarding subsequent deferrals and the acceleration of payments. For purposes of this paragraph (h)(1)(ii), for periods during which an employee is on a paid bona fide leave of absence (as defined in paragraph (h)(1)(i) of this section) and has not otherwise terminated employment pursuant to paragraph (h)(1)(i) of this section, the employee is treated as providing bona fide services at a level equal to the level of services that the employee would have been required to perform to receive the compensation paid with respect to such leave of absence. Periods during which an employee is on an unpaid bona fide leave of absence (as defined in paragraph (h)(1)(i) of this section) and has not otherwise terminated employment pursuant to paragraph (h)(1)(i) of this section, are disregarded for purposes of this paragraph (h)(1)(ii) (including for purposes of determining the applicable 36-month (or shorter) period).

(2) *Independent contractors.*—(i) *In general.*—An independent contractor is considered to have a separation from service with the service recipient upon the expiration of the contract (or in the case of more than one contract, all contracts) under which services are performed for the service recipient if the expiration constitutes a good-faith and complete termination of the contractual relationship. An expiration does not constitute a good faith and complete termination of the contractual relationship if the service recipient anticipates a renewal of a contractual relationship or the independent contractor becoming an employee. For this purpose, a service recipient is considered to anticipate the renewal of the contractual relationship with

an independent contractor if it intends to contract again for the services provided under the expired contract, and neither the service recipient nor the independent contractor has eliminated the independent contractor as a possible provider of services under any such new contract. Further, a service recipient is considered to intend to contract again for the services provided under an expired contract if the service recipient's doing so is conditioned only upon incurring a need for the services, the availability of funds, or both.

(ii) *Special rule.*—Notwithstanding paragraph (h)(2)(i) of this section, a plan is considered to satisfy the requirement described in §1.409A-3(a)(1) with respect to an amount payable upon a separation from service if, with respect to amounts payable to a service provider who is an independent contractor, the plan provides that—

(A) No amount will be paid to the service provider before a date at least 12 months after the day on which the contract expires under which the service provider performs services for the service recipient (or, in the case of more than one contract, all such contracts expire); and

(B) No amount payable to the service provider on that date will be paid to the service provider if, after the expiration of the contract (or contracts) and before that date, the service provider performs services for the service recipient as an independent contractor or an employee.

(3) *Definition of service recipient and employer.*—For purposes of this paragraph (h), the term *service recipient* or *employer* means the service recipient as defined in paragraph (g) of this section, provided that in applying section 1563(a)(1), (2), and (3) for purposes of determining a controlled group of corporations under section 414(b), the language "at least 50 percent" is used instead of "at least 80 percent" each place it appears in section 1563(a)(1), (2), and (3), and in applying §1.414(c)-2 for purposes of determining trades or businesses (whether or not incorporated) that are under common control for purposes of section 414(c), "at least 50 percent" is used instead of "at least 80 percent" each place it appears in §1.414(c)-2. A plan may provide with respect to a deferral of compensation under the plan that in applying sections 1563(a)(1), (2), and (3) for purposes of determining a controlled group of corporations under section 414(b), another defined percentage greater than 50 percent, but not greater than 80 percent, is used instead of "at least 80 percent" at each place it appears in sections 1563(a)(1), (2), and (3), and in applying §1.414(c)-2 for purposes of determining trades or businesses (whether or not incorporated) that are under common control for purposes of section 414(c), another defined percentage greater than 50 percent, but not greater than 80 percent, is used instead of "at least 80 percent" at each place it appears in §1.414(c)-2. In addition, where the use of such definition of service recipient for purposes of determining a separation from service is based upon legitimate business criteria, the plan may provide that for purposes of a deferral of compensation under the plan that in applying sections 1563(a)(1), (2), and (3) for purposes of determining a controlled group of corporations under section 414(b), the language "at least 20 percent" or another defined percentage not less than 20 percent but not greater than 50 percent is used instead of "at least 80 percent" at each place it appears in sections 1563(a)(1), (2), and (3), and in applying §1.414(c)-2 for purposes of determining trades or businesses (whether or not incorporated) that are under common control for purposes of section 414(c), the language "at least 20 percent" or another defined percentage not less than 20 percent but not greater than 50 percent is used instead of "at least 80 percent" at each place it appears in §1.414(c)-2. Where a definition of service recipient or employer other than the definition provided in the first sentence of this paragraph (h)(3) (the 50 percent standard) is used, the plan must designate in writing the alternate definition no later than the last date at which the time and form of payment of the applicable amount deferred must be elected in accordance with §1.409A-2(a), and any change in the definition for such amounts deferred will constitute a change in the time and form of payment subject to the rules governing subsequent deferral elections under §1.409A-2(b) and the acceleration of payments under §1.409A-3(j).

(4) *Asset purchase transactions.*—Where as part of a sale or other disposition of assets by one service recipient (seller) to an unrelated service recipient (buyer), a service provider of the seller would otherwise experience a separation from service with the seller, the seller and the buyer may retain the discretion to specify, and may specify, whether a service provider providing services to the seller immediately before the asset purchase transaction and providing services to the buyer after and in connection with the asset purchase transaction has experienced a separation from service for purposes of this paragraph (h), provided that the asset purchase transaction results from bona fide, arm's length negotiations, all service providers providing services to the seller immediately before the asset purchase transaction and providing services to the buyer after and in connection with the asset purchase transaction are treated consist-

ently (regardless of position at the seller) for purposes of applying the provisions of any nonqualified deferred compensation plan, and such treatment is specified in writing no later than the closing date of the asset purchase transaction. For purposes of this paragraph (h)(4), references to a sale or other disposition of assets, or an asset purchase transaction, refer only to a transfer of substantial assets, such as a plant or division or substantially all the assets of a trade or business. For purposes of this paragraph (h)(4), whether a service recipient is related to another service recipient is determined under the rules provided in paragraph (f)(2)(ii) of this section.

(5) *Dual status.*—If a service provider provides services both as an employee of a service recipient and as an independent contractor of a service recipient, the service provider must separate from service both as an employee and as an independent contractor to be treated as having separated from service. If a service provider ceases providing services as an independent contractor and begins providing services as an employee, or ceases providing services as an employee and begins providing services as an independent contractor, the service provider will not be considered to have a separation from service until the service provider has ceased providing services in both capacities. Notwithstanding the foregoing, if a service provider provides services both as an employee of a service recipient and a member of the board of directors of a corporate service recipient (or an analogous position with respect to a non-corporate service recipient), the services provided as a director are not taken into account in determining whether the service provider has a separation from service as an employee for purposes of a nonqualified deferred compensation plan in which the service provider participates as an employee that is not aggregated with any plan in which the service provider participates as a director under paragraph (c)(2)(ii) of this section. In addition, if a service provider provides services both as an employee of a service recipient and a member of the board of directors of a corporate service recipient (or an analogous position with respect to a non-corporate service recipient), the services provided as an employee are not taken into account in determining whether the service provider has a separation from service as a director for purposes of a nonqualified deferred compensation plan in which the service provider participates as a director that is not aggregated with any plan in which the service provider participates as an employee under paragraph (c)(2)(ii) of this section.

(6) *Collectively bargained plans covering multiple employers.*—Notwithstanding the foregoing provisions of this paragraph (h), to the extent a plan is established pursuant to a bona fide collective bargaining agreement covering services performed by employees for multiple employers, such plan may define a separation from service in a reasonable manner that treats the employee as not having separated from service during periods in which the employee is not providing services but is available to perform services covered by the collective bargaining agreement for one or more employers, provided that the definition also provides that the employee must be deemed to have separated from service at a specified date not later than the end of any period of at least 12 consecutive months during which the employee has not provided any services covered by the collective bargaining agreement to any participating employer. This paragraph (h)(6) applies only if the definition of separation from service provided by the collective bargaining agreement was the subject of arm's length negotiations between employee representatives and two or more employers, the agreement between employee representatives and such employers satisfies section 7701(a)(46), and the circumstances surrounding the agreement evidence good faith bargaining between adverse parties over such definition.

(i) *Specified employee.*—(1) *In general.*—The term *specified employee* means a service provider who, as of the date of the service provider's separation from service, is a key employee of a service recipient any stock of which is publicly traded on an established securities market or otherwise. For purposes of this paragraph (i)(1), a service provider is a key employee if the service provider meets the requirements of section 416(i)(1)(A)(i), (ii), or (iii) (applied in accordance with the regulations thereunder and disregarding section 416(i)(5)) at any time during the 12-month period ending on a specified employee identification date. If a service provider is a key employee as of a specified employee identification date, the service provider is treated as a key employee for purposes of this paragraph (i) for the entire 12-month period beginning on the specified employee effective date.

(2) *Definition of compensation.*—For purposes of identifying a specified employee by applying the requirements of section 416(i)(1)(A)(i), (ii), and (iii), the definition of compensation under §1.415(c)-2(a) is used, applied as if the service recipient were not using any safe harbor provided in §1.415(c)-2(d), were not using any of the elective special timing rules provided in §1.415(c)-2(e), and were not using any of the elective special rules provided in §1.415(c)-2(g). Notwithstanding the foregoing, a service recipient

may elect to use any available definition of compensation under section 415 and the regulations thereunder in accordance with the election requirements set forth in paragraph (i)(8) of this section, including any available safe harbor and any available election under the timing rules or special rules, provided that the definition is applied consistently to all employees of the service recipient for purposes of identifying specified employees. A service recipient may elect to use such an alternative definition regardless of whether another definition of compensation is being used for purposes of a qualified plan sponsored by the service recipient. However, once a list of specified employees has become effective, the service recipient cannot change the definition of compensation for purposes of identifying specified employees for the period with respect to which such list is effective.

(3) *Specified employee identification date.*—Unless another date is designated in accordance with the requirements of this paragraph (i)(3) and paragraph (i)(8) of this section, the specified employee identification date is December 31. A service recipient may designate in accordance with the requirements of paragraph (i)(8) of this section any other date as the specified employee identification date, provided that a service recipient must use the same specified employee identification date with respect to all nonqualified deferred compensation plans, and any change to the specified employee identification date may not be effective for a period of at least 12 months. The service recipient may designate a specified employee identification date in each plan or in a separate document applicable to all plans, provided that the service recipient will not be treated as having designated a specified employee identification date before the designation is legally binding on the service recipient and all affected service providers. Any designation of a specified employee identification date made on or before December 31, 2007, may be applied to any separation from service occurring on or after January 1, 2005, unless and until subsequently changed pursuant to this paragraph (i)(3).

(4) *Specified employee effective date.*—Unless another date is designated in accordance with the requirements of this paragraph (i)(4) and paragraph (i)(8) of this section, the specified employee effective date is the first day of the fourth month following the specified employee identification date. A service recipient may designate in accordance with the requirements of paragraph (i)(8) of this section any date following the specified employee identification date as the specified employee effective date, provided that such date may not be later than the first day of the fourth month following the specified employee identification date, and provided further that a service recipient must use the same specified employee effective date with respect to all nonqualified deferred compensation plans, and any change to the specified employee effective date may not be effective for a period of at least 12 months. The service recipient may designate a specified employee effective date through inclusion in each plan document or through a separate document applicable to all plans, provided that the service recipient will not be treated as having designated a specified employee effective date on any date before the designation is legally binding on the service recipient and all affected service providers. Any designation of a specified employee effective date made on or before December 31, 2007, may be applied to any separation from service occurring on or after January 1, 2005, unless and until subsequently changed pursuant to this paragraph (i)(4).

(5) *Alternative methods of satisfying the six-month delay rule.*—A plan may provide, in accordance with the requirements of paragraph (i)(8) of this section, for an alternative method to identify service providers who will be subject to the six-month delay rule provided in section 409A(a)(2)(B)(i), provided that the alternative method is reasonably designed to include all specified employees (determined without respect to any available service recipient elections), the alternative method is an objectively determinable standard providing no direct or indirect election to any service provider regarding its application, and the alternative method results in either all service providers or no more than 200 service providers being identified in the class as of any date. Use of such an alternative method will not be treated as a change in the time and form of payment for purposes of §1.409A-2(b) (the subsequent deferral rules), even if the service provider is not a specified employee when the payment is delayed.

(6) *Corporate transactions.*—(i) *Mergers and acquisitions of public service recipients.*—If as a result of a corporate transaction, two or more separate service recipients, more than one of which has stock outstanding that is publicly traded on an established securities market or otherwise immediately before the transaction, become one service recipient, any stock of which is publicly traded on an established securities market or otherwise immediately after the transaction (resulting public service recipient), the resulting public service recipient's next specified employee identification date and specified

employee effective date following the corporate transaction are the specified employee identification date and specified employee effective date that the acquiring service recipient would have been required to use absent such transaction. For this purpose, in the case of a corporate merger, the acquiring service recipient is the service recipient that included the surviving corporation in such merger, in the case of an acquisition by a corporation of the stock of another corporation, the acquiring service recipient is the service recipient that included the corporation that acquired such stock, and in all other cases, the surviving service recipient is determined on the basis of all of the facts and circumstances. For the period between the transaction and the next specified employee effective date, the list of specified employees of the resulting public service recipient is determined by combining the lists of specified employees of all service recipients participating in the transaction that were in effect at the date of the corporate transaction, ranking such specified employees in order of the amount of compensation used to determine each specified employee's status as a specified employee, and treating the top 50 of such specified employees, plus any employees described in section 416(i)(1)(ii) or section 416(i)(1)(iii) and the regulations thereunder (relating to 1-percent and 5-percent owners) who are not included in such top 50 specified employees, as specified employees for the period between the corporate transaction and the next specified employee effective date. Alternatively, the resulting service recipient may elect in accordance with the requirements of paragraph (i)(8) of this section to use any reasonable method to determine the specified employees of the resulting service recipient, including the use of an alternative method of compliance described in paragraph (i)(5) of this section, provided that such method is adopted no later than 90 days after the corporate transaction and applied prospectively from the date the method is adopted.

(ii) *Mergers and acquisitions of nonpublic service recipients.*—If as part of a corporate transaction a service recipient that does not have outstanding stock that is publicly traded on an established securities market or otherwise immediately before the transaction (initial private service recipient), and a service recipient with stock outstanding that is publicly traded on an established securities market or otherwise immediately before the transaction (initial public service recipient), become a single service recipient having stock that is publicly traded on an established securities market or otherwise immediately after the transaction (resulting public service recipient), the resulting public service recipient's next specified employee identification date and specified employee effective date following the corporate transaction are the specified employee identification date and specified employee effective date that the initial public service recipient would have been required to use absent such transaction. For the period after the date of the corporate transaction and before the next specified employee effective date, the specified employees of the initial public service recipient immediately before the transaction continue to be the specified employees of the resulting public service recipient, and no service providers of the initial private service recipient are required to be treated as specified employees.

(iii) *Spinoffs.*—If as part of a corporate transaction, a service recipient with stock outstanding that is publicly traded on an established securities market or otherwise immediately before the transaction (initial public service recipient), becomes two or more separate service recipients, each with stock outstanding that is publicly traded on an established securities market or otherwise immediately after the transaction (post-transaction public service recipients), the next specified employee identification date of each of the post-transaction public service recipients is the specified employee identification date that the initial public service recipient would have been required to use absent such transaction. For the period after the date of the corporate transaction and before the next specified employee effective date, the specified employees of the initial public service recipient immediately before the transaction continue to be the specified employees of the post-transaction public service recipients.

(iv) *Public offerings and other corporate transactions.*—If as part of an initial public offering or corporate transaction not described in paragraph (i)(6)(ii) or (iii) of this section, a service recipient with no outstanding stock that is publicly traded on an established securities market or otherwise immediately before such offering or other transaction (initial private service recipient), becomes one or more service recipients with stock outstanding that is publicly traded on an established securities market or otherwise immediately after such offering or other transaction (post-transaction public service recipient), each post-transaction public service recipient has a specified employee identification date of December 31 and a specified employee effective date of April 1, effective retroactively to the December 31 and April 1 next preceding the offering or other transaction for purposes of identifying the specified employees between the corporation transaction and the next December 31. Alternatively, a post-transaction public service recipient may elect in accordance with the requirements of paragraph (i)(8) of this section, a specified employee identification date and specified employee effective date on or before the date of the offering or other transaction. If a public service recipient makes such an election, for the period after the offering or other transaction and before the next specified employee effective date, the specified employees of the post-transaction public service recipient consist of the service providers that at the time of the offering or other transaction would have been classified as specified employees of the initial private service recipient, had the initial private service recipient elected the same specified employee identification date and specified employee effective date as selected by the post-transaction public service recipient, and had such initial private service recipient had stock publicly traded on an established securities market or otherwise as of the specified employee identification date preceding the transaction.

(v) *Alternative methods of compliance.*—For purposes of this paragraph (i)(6), references to specified employees as of a corporate transaction or offering include any specified employees identified through the use of an alternative method described in paragraph (i)(5) of this section, where the use of such alternative method was established and effective at the time of the corporate transaction or offering.

(7) *Nonresident alien employees.*—For purposes of determining whether an employee meets the requirements of section 416(i)(1)(A)(i), (ii), or (iii) (applied in accordance with the regulations thereunder and disregarding section 416(i)(5)), and therefore is a key employee, the incorporation of the rules of § 1.415(c)-2(g)(5) regarding the definition of compensation applies. Accordingly, the rule of § 1.415(c)-2(g)(5)(i), generally requiring the treatment as compensation of certain compensation excludible from an employee's gross income due to the location of the services or the identity of the employer, applies. In addition, a service recipient may elect in accordance with paragraph (i)(8) of this section to apply the rule of § 1.415(c)-2(g)(5)(ii) to not treat as compensation certain compensation excludible from an employee's gross income on account of the location of the services or the identity of the employer that is not effectively connected with the conduct of a trade or business within the United States. A service recipient may elect to apply the rule of § 1.415-2(g)(5)(ii) regardless of whether the service recipient has elected to apply the rule to a qualified plan sponsored by the service recipient; however, once a list of specified employees has become effective, any election of the rule for that period may not be changed. Notwithstanding the foregoing, any election of the rule made before January 1, 2008, may be effective with respect to any specified employee identification date on or before December 31, 2007.

(8) *Elections affecting the identification of specified employees.*—The elections described in paragraphs (i)(2) through (7) of this section are effective only as of the date that all necessary corporate action has been taken to make such elections binding for purposes of all affected nonqualified deferred compensation plans in which the service providers of the service recipient that would become a specified employee due to the application of such election participate. Where a taxpayer attempts to make an election under paragraph (i)(2), (3), (4), (5), (6), or (7) of this section but such election is not binding on all the affected nonqualified deferred compensation plans and applied consistently to all such service providers, the election is not effective and the rule under paragraph (i)(2), (3), (4), (5), (6), or (7) of this section, as applicable, that would apply absent an election is applicable for identifying specified employees.

(j) *Nonresident alien.*—(1) Except as provided in paragraph (j)(2) of this section, the term *nonresident alien* means an individual who is—

(i) A nonresident alien within the meaning of section 7701(b)(1)(B); or

(ii) A dual resident taxpayer within the meaning of § 301.7701(b)-7(a)(1) of this chapter with respect to any taxable year in which such individual is treated as a nonresident alien for purposes of computing the individual's U.S. income tax liability.

(2) *The term nonresident alien does not include.*—(i) A nonresident alien with respect to whom an election is in effect for the taxable year under section 6013(g) to be treated as a resident of the United States;

(ii) A former citizen or long-term resident (within the meaning of section 877(e)(2)) who expatriated after June 3, 2004, and has not complied with the requirements of section 7701(n); or

(iii) An individual who is treated as a citizen or resident of the United States for the taxable year under section 877(g).

(k) *Established securities market.*—The term *established securities market* means an established securities market within the meaning of § 1.897-1(m).

(l) *Stock right.*—The term *stock right* means a stock option (other than an incentive stock option described in section 422 or an option

granted pursuant to an employee stock purchase plan described in section 423) or a stock appreciation right.

(m) *Separation pay plan.*—The term *separation pay plan* means any plan that provides separation pay or, where a plan provides both amounts that are separation pay and that are not separation pay, that portion of the plan that provides separation pay. The term *separation pay* means any deferral of compensation (before the application of the exclusions from the definition of a deferral of compensation set forth in paragraph (b)(9) of this section) that will not be paid under any circumstances unless the service provider has had a separation from service, whether voluntary or involuntary, including payments in the form of reimbursements of expenses incurred, and the provision of in-kind benefits. A deferral of compensation that the service provider may receive without a separation from service does not become separation pay merely because the service provider elects to receive or receives the payment after or upon a separation from service. A deferral of compensation does not fail to be separation pay merely because the payment is conditioned upon the execution of a release of claims, noncompetition or nondisclosure provisions, or other similar requirements. Notwithstanding the foregoing, any amount, or entitlement to any amount, that acts as a substitute for, or replacement of, amounts deferred by the service recipient under a nonqualified deferred compensation plan constitutes a payment of compensation or deferral of compensation under such nonqualified deferred compensation plan.

(n) *Involuntary separation from service.*—(1) *In general.*—An involuntary separation from service means a separation from service due to the independent exercise of the unilateral authority of the service recipient to terminate the service provider's services, other than due to the service provider's implicit or explicit request, where the service provider was willing and able to continue performing services. An involuntary separation from service may include the service recipient's failure to renew a contract at the time such contract expires, provided that the service provider was willing and able to execute a new contract providing terms and conditions substantially similar to those in the expiring contract and to continue providing such services. The determination of whether a separation from service is involuntary is based on all the facts and circumstances. Any characterization of the separation from service as voluntary or involuntary by the service provider and the service recipient in the documentation of the separation from service is presumed to properly characterize the nature of the separation from service. However, the presumption may be rebutted where the facts and circumstances indicate otherwise. For example, if a separation from service is designated as a voluntary separation from service or resignation, but the facts and circumstances indicate that absent such voluntary separation from service the service recipient would have terminated the service provider's services, and that the service provider had knowledge that the service provider would be so terminated, the separation from service is involuntary.

(2) *Separations from service for good reason.*—(i) *In general.*—Notwithstanding paragraph (n)(1) of this section, a service provider's voluntary separation from service will be treated for purposes of this section and § § 1.409A-2 through 1.409A-6 as an involuntary separation from service if the separation from service occurs under certain limited bona fide conditions, where the avoidance of the requirements of section 409A is not a purpose of the inclusion of these conditions in the plan or of the actions by the service recipient in connection with the satisfaction of these conditions, and a voluntary separation from service under such conditions effectively constitutes an involuntary separation from service. Generally such conditions will be prespecified under an agreement to provide compensation upon a separation from service for good reason. Such a good reason (or a similar condition) must be defined to require actions taken by the service recipient resulting in a material negative change to the service provider in the service relationship, such as the duties to be performed, the conditions under which such duties are to be performed, or the compensation to be received for performing such services. Other factors taken into account in determining whether a separation from service for good reason effectively constitutes an involuntary separation from service include the extent to which the payments upon a separation from service for good reason are in the same amount and are to be made at the same time and in the same form as payments available upon an actual involuntary separation from service, and whether the service provider is required to give the service recipient notice of the existence of the condition that would result in treatment as a separation from service for good reason and a reasonable opportunity to remedy the condition.

(ii) *Safe harbor.*—For purposes of this section and § § 1.409A-2 through 1.409A-6, if a plan provides that a voluntary separation from service will be treated as an involuntary separation from service if the separation from service occurs under certain express conditions, a separation from service satisfying the conditions set forth in the plan will be treated as an involuntary separation from the service if the necessary conditions (or set of conditions) require the following:

(A) The separation from service must occur during a pre-determined limited period of time not to exceed two years following the initial existence of one or more of the following conditions arising without the consent of the service provider:

(1) A material diminution in the service provider's base compensation.

(2) A material diminution in the service provider's authority, duties, or responsibilities.

(3) A material diminution in the authority, duties, or responsibilities of the supervisor to whom the service provider is required to report, including a requirement that a service provider report to a corporate officer or employee instead of reporting directly to the board of directors of a corporation (or similar governing body with respect to an entity other than a corporation).

(4) A material diminution in the budget over which the service provider retains authority.

(5) A material change in the geographic location at which the service provider must perform the services.

(6) Any other action or inaction that constitutes a material breach by the service recipient of the agreement under which the service provider provides services.

(B) The amount, time, and form of payment upon the separation from service must be substantially identical to the amount, time and form of payment payable due to an actual involuntary separation from service, to the extent such a right exists.

(C) The service provider must be required to provide notice to the service recipient of the existence of the condition described in paragraph (n)(2)(ii)(A) of this section within a period not to exceed 90 days of the initial existence of the condition, upon the notice of which the service recipient must be provided a period of at least 30 days during which it may remedy the condition and not be required to pay the amount.

(3) *Special rule for certain collectively bargained plans.*—Notwithstanding the foregoing, for purposes of this paragraph (n), to the extent a plan is subject to a bona fide collective bargaining agreement covering services performed for multiple employers under which an employee must separate from service with all such employers in order to receive a payment, such plan may use any reasonable definition of involuntary separation from service, provided that such definition is consistent with any definition of a separation from service adopted under paragraph (h)(6) of this section, and provided further that the definition of an involuntary separation from service provided by the collective bargaining agreement was the subject of arm's length negotiations between employee representatives and two or more employers, the agreement between employee representatives and such employers satisfies section 7701(a)(46), and the circumstances surrounding the agreement evidence good faith bargaining between adverse parties over such definition.

(o) *Earnings.*—Whether a deferred amount constitutes earnings on an amount deferred, or actual or notional income attributable to an amount deferred, is determined under the principles defining income attributable to the amount taken into account under §31.3121(v)(2)-1(d)(2) of this chapter. Accordingly, with respect to an account balance plan, earnings on an amount deferred generally include an amount credited on behalf of a service provider under the terms of the plan that reflects a rate of return that does not exceed either the rate of return on a predetermined actual investment or, if the income does not reflect the rate of return on a predetermined actual investment, a reasonable rate of interest. With respect to nonaccount balance plans, earnings on an amount deferred generally include an increase, due solely to the passage of time, in the present value of the future payments to which the service provider has obtained a legally binding right, the present value of which constituted the amount deferred (determined as of the date such amount was deferred), but only if the amount deferred was determined using reasonable actuarial assumptions and methods. A right to earnings on an amount deferred generally is treated as a right to a deferral of compensation for purposes of this section and §§1.409A-2 through 1.409A-6. However, for purposes of any provision of this section and §§1.409A-2 through 1.409A-6 referring to earnings on deferred compensation (or similar terms), the use of an unreasonable rate of return, or unreasonable actuarial assumptions and methods, generally will result in the treatment of some or all of such a right to *deferred compensation as a right only to deferred compensation*, and not a right to earnings on deferred compensation, so that the provision will not be applicable. With respect to plans that are neither account balance plans nor nonaccount balance plans, these rules apply by analogy.

(p) *In-kind benefits.*—The term *in-kind benefits* refers to services provided to or on behalf of a service provider, such as financial planning services, or tangible personal or real property made available for use by or on behalf of the service provider, such as the use of an aircraft or vehicle, and does not refer to a transfer of property within the meaning of section 83 and the regulations thereunder, or a promise to transfer, or an option to purchase or receive, property in the future.

(q) *Application of definitions and rules.*—The definitions and rules set forth in paragraphs (a) through (p) of this section apply for purposes of section 409A, this section, and §§1.409A-2 through 1.409A-6. [Reg. §1.409A-1.]

☐ [T.D. 9321, 4-10-2007 (corrected 7-30-2007).]

[Reg. §1.409A-2]

§1.409A-2. Deferral elections.—(a) *Initial elections as to the time and form of payment.*—(1) *In general.*—A plan that is, or constitutes part of, a nonqualified deferred compensation plan meets the requirements of section 409A(a)(4)(B) only if under the terms of the plan, compensation for services performed during a service provider's taxable year (the service year) may be deferred at the service provider's election only if the election to defer such compensation is made and becomes irrevocable not later than the latest date permitted in this paragraph (a). An election will not be considered to be revocable merely because the service provider or service recipient may make an election to change the time and form of payment pursuant to paragraph (b) of this section, or the service recipient may accelerate the time of payment pursuant to §1.409A-3(j)(4) (exceptions to prohibition on accelerated payments). Whether a plan provides a service provider an opportunity to elect the time or form of payment of compensation is determined based upon all the facts and circumstances surrounding the determination of the time and form of payment of the compensation. For purposes of this section, an election to defer includes an election as to the time of the payment, an election as to the form of the payment or an election as to both the time and the form of the payment, but does not include an election as to the medium of payment (for example, an election between a payment of cash or a payment of property). Except as otherwise expressly provided in this section, an election will not be considered made until such election becomes irrevocable under the terms of the applicable plan. Accordingly, a plan may provide that an election to defer may be changed at any time before the last permissible date for making such an election. Where a plan provides the service provider a right to make an initial deferral election, and further provides that the election remains in effect until terminated or modified by the service provider, the election will be treated as made as of the date such election becomes irrevocable as to compensation for services performed during the relevant service year. For example, where a plan provides that a service provider's election to defer a set percentage will remain in effect until changed or revoked, but that as of each December 31 the election becomes irrevocable with respect to salary payable in connection with services performed in the immediately following year, the initial deferral election with respect to salary payable with respect to services performed in the immediately following year will be deemed to have been made as of the December 31 upon which the election became irrevocable. For purposes of this paragraph (a), the reference to a service period or a performance period refers to the period of service for which the right to the compensation arises, and may include periods before the grant of a legally binding right to the compensation. For example, where a service recipient grants a bonus based upon services performed in the calendar year 2010, but retains the discretion to rescind the bonus until 2011 such that the promise of the bonus is not a legally binding right, the period of service or performance period to which the compensation relates is the calendar year 2010.

(2) *Service recipient elections.*—A plan that provides for a deferral of compensation for services performed during a service provider's taxable year that does not provide the service provider with an opportunity to elect the time or form of payment of such compensation must designate the time and form of payment by no later than the later of the time the service provider first has a legally binding right to the compensation or, if later, the time the service provider would be required under this section to make such an election if the service provider were provided such an election. Such designation is treated as an initial deferral election for purposes of this section. Where a plan permits a service recipient to exercise discretion to disregard a service provider election as to the time or form of a payment, any service provider election that is subject to such discretion will be treated as revocable so long as such discretion may be exercised.

(3) *General rule.*—A plan that is, or constitutes part of, a nonqualified deferred compensation plan meets the requirements of

section 409A(a)(4)(B) if under the terms of the plan, compensation for services performed during a service provider's taxable year (the service year) may be deferred at the service provider's election only if the election to defer such compensation is made not later than the close of the service provider's taxable year next preceding the service year.

(4) *Initial deferral election with respect to short-term deferrals.*—If a service provider has a legally binding right to a payment of compensation in a subsequent taxable year that, absent a deferral election, would be treated as a short-term deferral within the meaning of §1.409A-1(b)(4), an election to defer such compensation may be made in accordance with the requirements of paragraph (b) of this section, applied as if the amount were a deferral of compensation and the scheduled payment date for the amount were the date the substantial risk of forfeiture lapses. Notwithstanding the requirements of paragraph (b) of this section, such a deferral election may provide that the deferred amounts will be payable upon a change in control event (as defined in §1.409A-3(i)(5)) without regard to the five-year additional deferral requirement in paragraph (b) of this section.

(5) *Initial deferral election with respect to certain forfeitable rights.*—If a service provider has a legally binding right to a payment in a subsequent year that is subject to a condition requiring the service provider to continue to provide services for a period of at least 12 months from the date the service provider obtains the legally binding right to avoid forfeiture of the payment, an election to defer such compensation may be made on or before the 30th day after the service provider obtains the legally binding right to the compensation, provided that the election is made at least 12 months in advance of the earliest date at which the forfeiture condition could lapse. For purposes of this paragraph (a)(5), a condition will not be treated as failing to require the service provider to continue to provide services for a period of at least 12 months from the date the service provider obtains the legally binding right merely because the condition immediately lapses upon the death or disability (as defined in §1.409A-1(i)(4)) of the service provider, or upon a change in control event (as defined in §1.409A-3(i)(5)), provided that if death, disability, or a change in control event occurs and the condition lapses before the end of such 12-month period, a deferral election may be given effect only if the deferral election is permitted under this section without regard to this paragraph (a)(5).

(6) *Initial deferral election with respect to fiscal year compensation.*— In the case of a service recipient with a taxable year that is not the same as the taxable year of the service provider, a plan may provide that fiscal year compensation may be deferred at the service provider's election if the election to defer such compensation is made not later than the close of the service recipient's taxable year immediately preceding the first taxable year of the service recipient in which any services are performed for which such compensation is payable. For purposes of this paragraph (a)(6), the term *fiscal year compensation* means compensation relating to a period of service coextensive with one or more consecutive taxable years of the service recipient, of which no amount is paid or payable during the service recipient's taxable year or years constituting the period of service. For example, fiscal year compensation generally would include a bonus to an individual employee with a calendar year taxable year that is based on a service period consisting of the service recipient's two consecutive taxable years ending September 30, 2011, where the amount will be paid after the end of the second of such taxable years, but would not include either a bonus based on a service period consisting of one or more calendar years or salary that would otherwise be paid during such taxable years of the service recipient.

(7) *First year of eligibility.*—(i) *In general.*—In the case of the first year in which a service provider becomes eligible to participate in a plan, the service provider may make an initial deferral election within 30 days after the date the service provider becomes eligible to participate in such plan, with respect to compensation paid for services to be performed after the election. In the case of a plan that does not provide for service provider elections with respect to the time or form of a payment, the time and form of the payment must be specified on or before the date that is 30 days after the date the service provider first becomes eligible to participate in such plan. For compensation that is earned based upon a specified performance period (for example, an annual bonus), where a deferral election is made in the first year of eligibility but after the beginning of the performance period, the election must apply only to the compensation paid for services performed after the election. For this purpose, an election will be deemed to apply to compensation paid for services performed after the election if the election applies to no more than an amount equal to the total amount of the compensation for the performance period multiplied by the ratio of the number of days

remaining in the performance period after the election over the total number of days in the performance period.

(ii) *Eligibility to participate.*—For purposes of this paragraph (a)(7), a service provider is eligible to participate in a plan at any time during which, under the plan's terms and without further amendment or action by the service recipient, the service provider is eligible to accrue an amount of deferred compensation under the plan other than earnings on amounts previously deferred, even if the service provider has elected not to accrue (or has not elected to accrue) an amount of deferred compensation. Where a service provider has been paid all amounts deferred under a plan, and on and before the date of the last payment was not eligible to continue (or to elect to continue) to participate in the plan for periods after the last payment (other than through an election of a different time and form of payment with respect to the amounts paid), the service provider may be treated as initially eligible to participate in a plan as of the first date following such payment that the service provider becomes eligible to accrue an additional amount of deferred compensation. Where a service provider has ceased being eligible to participate in a plan (other than the accrual of earnings), regardless of whether all amounts deferred under the plan have been paid, and subsequently becomes eligible to participate in the plan again, the service provider may be treated as being initially eligible to participate in the plan if the service provider had not been eligible to participate in the plan (other than the accrual of earnings) at any time during the 24-month period ending on the date the service provider again becomes eligible to participate in the plan.

(iii) *Application to excess benefit plans.*—For purposes of this paragraph (a)(7), a service provider is treated as initially eligible to participate in an excess benefit plan as of the first day of the service provider's taxable year immediately following the first year the service provider accrues a benefit under the excess benefit plan; and any election made within 30 days following such date is treated as applying to benefits accrued under such plan for services performed before the election. For purposes of this paragraph (a)(7), the term *excess benefit plan* means all nonqualified deferred compensation plans in which a service provider participates, to the extent such plans do not provide for an election between current compensation (including a short-term deferral) and deferred compensation and solely provide deferred compensation equal to the excess of the benefits the service provider would have accrued under a qualified employer plan (as defined in §1.409A-1(a)(2)) in which the service provider also participates, in the absence of one or more of the limits incorporated into the plan to reflect one or more of the limits on contributions or benefits applicable to the qualified employer plan under the Internal Revenue Code, over the benefits the service provider actually accrues under the qualified employer plan. For purposes of this paragraph (a)(7), once a service provider has accrued a benefit or deferred compensation under a plan in any year, the service provider will not become eligible for an initial deferral election based upon an accrual or deferral under an excess benefit plan in a subsequent year, even if the benefit or deferred compensation accrued in a previous year is forfeited or eliminated.

(8) *Initial deferral election with respect to performance-based compensation.*—In the case of any performance-based compensation (as defined in §1.409A-1(e)), an initial deferral election may be made with respect to such performance-based compensation on or before the date that is six months before the end of the performance period, provided that the service provider performs services continuously from the later of the beginning of the performance period or the date the performance criteria are established through the date an election is made under this paragraph (a)(8), and provided further that in no event may an election to defer performance-based compensation be made after such compensation has become readily ascertainable. For purposes of this paragraph (a)(8), if the performance-based compensation is a specified or calculable amount, the compensation is readily ascertainable if and when the amount is first substantially certain to be paid. If the performance-based compensation is not a specified or calculable amount because, for example, the amount may vary based upon the level of performance, the compensation, or any portion of the compensation, is readily ascertainable when the amount is first both calculable and substantially certain to be paid. For this purpose, the performance-based compensation is bifurcated between the portion that is readily ascertainable and the amount that is not readily ascertainable. Accordingly, in general any minimum amount that is both calculable and substantially certain to be paid will be treated as readily ascertainable.

(9) *Nonqualified deferred compensation plans linked to qualified employer plans or certain other arrangements.*—If a nonqualified deferred compensation plan provides that the amount deferred under the plan is determined under the formula for determining benefits under a qualified employer plan (as defined in §1.409A-1(a)(2)) or a broad-

based foreign retirement plan (as defined in § 1.409A-1(a)(3)(v)) maintained by the service recipient but applied without regard to one or more limitations applicable to the qualified employer plan under the Internal Revenue Code or to the broad-based foreign retirement plan under other applicable law, or that the amount deferred under the nonqualified deferred compensation plan is determined as an amount offset by some or all of the benefits provided under the qualified employer plan or the broad-based foreign retirement plan, an increase in amounts deferred under the nonqualified deferred compensation plan that results directly from the operation of the qualified employer plan or broad-based foreign retirement plan (other than service provider actions described in paragraphs (a)(9)(iii) and (iv) of this section) including changes in benefit limitations applicable to the qualified employer plan or the broad-based foreign retirement plan under the Internal Revenue Code or other applicable law does not constitute a deferral election under the nonqualified deferred compensation plan, provided that such operation does not otherwise result in a change in the time or form of a payment under the nonqualified deferred compensation plan, and provided further that such change in the amounts deferred under the nonqualified deferred compensation plan does not exceed that change in the amounts deferred under the qualified employer plan or the broad-based foreign retirement plan, as applicable. In addition, with respect to such a nonqualified deferred compensation plan, the following actions or failures to act will not constitute a deferral election under the nonqualified deferred compensation plan even if in accordance with the terms of the nonqualified deferred compensation plan, the actions or inactions result in an increase in the amounts deferred under the plan, provided that such actions or inactions do not otherwise affect the time or form of payment under the nonqualified deferred compensation plan and provided further that with respect to actions or inactions described in paragraphs (a)(9)(i) or (ii), the change in the amount deferred under the nonqualified deferred compensation plan does not exceed the change in the amounts deferred under the qualified employer plan or the broad-based foreign retirement plan, as applicable:

(i) A service provider's action or inaction under the qualified employer plan or broad-based foreign retirement plan with respect to whether to elect to receive a subsidized benefit or an ancillary benefit under the qualified employer plan or broad-based foreign retirement plan.

(ii) The amendment of a qualified employer plan or broad-based foreign retirement plan to add or remove a subsidized benefit or an ancillary benefit, or to freeze or limit future accruals of benefits under the qualified plan or freeze or limit future accruals of benefits or reduce existing benefits under the broad-based foreign retirement plan.

(iii) A service provider's action or inaction under a qualified employer plan with respect to elective deferrals and other employee pre-tax contributions subject to the contribution restrictions under section 401(a)(30) or section 402(g), including an adjustment to a deferral election under such qualified employer plan, provided that for any given taxable year, the service provider's action or inaction does not result in an increase in the amounts deferred under all nonqualified deferred compensation plans in which the service provider participates (other than amounts described in paragraph (a)(9)(iv) of this section) in excess of the limit with respect to elective deferrals under section 402(g)(1)(A), (B), and (C) in effect for the taxable year in which such action or inaction occurs.

(iv) A service provider's action or inaction under a qualified employer plan with respect to elective deferrals and other employee pre-tax contributions subject to the contribution restrictions under section 401(a)(30) or section 402(g), and after-tax contributions by the service provider to a qualified employer plan that provides for such contributions, that affects the amounts that are credited under one or more nonqualified deferred compensation plans as matching amounts or other similar amounts contingent on such elective deferrals, employee pre-tax contributions, or after-tax contributions, provided that the total of such matching or contingent amounts, as applicable, never exceeds 100 percent of the matching or contingent amounts that would be provided under the qualified employer plan absent any plan-based restrictions that reflect limits on qualified plan contributions under the Internal Revenue Code.

(10) *Changes in elections under a cafeteria plan.*—A change in an election under a cafeteria plan does not constitute a deferral election with respect to an amount deferred under a nonqualified deferred compensation plan to the extent that the change in the amount deferred under the nonqualified deferred compensation plan results solely from the application of the change in amount eligible to be treated as compensation under the terms of the nonqualified deferred compensation plan resulting from the election change under the cafeteria plan, to a benefit formula under the nonqualified deferred compensation plan based upon the service provider's eligible compensation, and only to the extent that such change applies in the

same manner as any other increase or decrease in compensation would apply to such benefit formula.

(11) *Initial deferral election with respect to certain separation pay.*—In the case of separation pay (as defined in § 1.409A-1(m)), where such separation pay is the subject of bona fide, arm's length negotiations at the time of the separation from service, an initial deferral election may be made at any time up to the time the service provider obtains a legally binding right to the payment. This paragraph (a)(11) does not apply to any separation pay to which the service provider obtained a legally binding right before the negotiations at the time of the separation from service, including a right to a payment subject to a condition such as that the service provider separate from service other than for cause. In the case of separation pay due to participation in a window program (as defined in § 1.409A-1(b)(9)(vi)), an initial deferral election may be made at any time before the time the election to participate in the window program becomes irrevocable.

(12) *Initial deferral election with respect to certain commissions.*—(i) *Sales commission compensation.*—For purposes of this paragraph (a), a service provider earning sales commission compensation is treated as providing the services to which such compensation relates only in the service provider's taxable year in which the customer remits payment to the service recipient or, if applied consistently to all similarly situated service providers, the service provider's taxable year in which the sale occurs. For purposes of this paragraph (a)(12), the term *sales commission compensation* means compensation or portions of compensation earned by a service provider if a substantial portion of the services provided by such service provider to a service recipient consist of the direct sale of a product or service to an unrelated customer, the compensation paid by the service recipient to the service provider consists of either a portion of the purchase price for the product or service or an amount substantially all of which is calculated by reference to the volume of sales, and payment of the compensation is either contingent upon the service recipient receiving payment from an unrelated customer for the product or services or, if applied consistently to all similarly situated service providers, is contingent upon the closing of the sales transaction and such other requirements as may be specified by the service recipient before the closing of the sales transaction. For this purpose, a customer is treated as an unrelated customer only if the customer is not related to either the service provider or the service recipient. A person is treated as related to another person if the person would be treated as related to the other person under § 1.409A-1(f)(2)(ii) or the person would be treated as providing management services to the other person under § 1.409A-1(f)(2)(iv).

(ii) *Investment commission compensation.*—For purposes of this paragraph (a), a service provider earning investment commission compensation is treated as providing the services to which such compensation relates over the 12 months preceding the date as of which the overall value of the assets or asset accounts is determined for purposes of the calculation of the investment commission compensation. For purposes of this paragraph (a)(12), the term *investment commission compensation* means the compensation or the portion of compensation earned by a service provider if a substantial portion of the services provided by such service provider to a service recipient to which such compensation relates consists of sales of financial products or other direct customer services to an unrelated customer with respect to customer assets or customer asset accounts, the customer retains the right to terminate the customer relationship and may move or liquidate the assets or asset accounts without undue delay (which may be subject to a reasonable notice period), such compensation consists of a portion of the value of the overall assets or asset account balance, an amount substantially all of which is calculated by reference to the increase in the value of the overall assets or account balance during a specified period, or both, and the value of the overall assets or account balance and investment commission compensation is determined at least annually. For this purpose, a customer is treated as an unrelated customer only if the customer is not related to either the service provider or the service recipient. A person is treated as related to another person if the person would be treated as related to the other person under § 1.409A-1(f)(2)(ii) or the person would be treated as providing management services to the other person under § 1.409A-1(f)(2)(iv).

(iii) *Commission compensation and related persons.*—The rules of paragraphs (a)(12)(i) and (ii) of this section apply to sales commission compensation and investment commission compensation involving a related customer, provided that substantial sales from which commission compensation arises are made, or substantial services from which commission compensation arises are provided, to unrelated customers by the service recipient, the sales and service arrangement and the commission arrangement with respect to the related customer are bona fide, arise from the service recipient's ordinary course of business, and are substantially the same, both in terms and in practice, as the terms and practices applicable to unrelated customers (as defined in such paragraphs) to which individually or in the aggregate substantial sales are made or substantial services provided by the service recipient.

(13) *Initial deferral election with respect to compensation paid for final payroll period.*—(i) *In general.*—Unless a plan provides otherwise, compensation payable after the last day of the service provider's taxable year solely for services performed during the final payroll period described in section 3401(b) containing the last day of the service provider's taxable year or, with respect to a non-employee service provider, a period not longer than the payroll period described in section 3401(b), where such amount is payable pursuant to the timing arrangement under which the service recipient normally compensates service providers for services performed during a payroll period described in section 3401(b), or with respect to a non-employee service provider, a period not longer than the payroll period described in section 3401(b), is treated as compensation for services performed in the subsequent taxable year in which the payment is made. The preceding sentence does not apply to any compensation paid during such period for services performed during any period other than such final payroll period, such as a payment of an annual bonus. Any amendment of a plan after December 31, 2007, to add a provision providing for a differing treatment of such compensation may not be effective for 12 months from the date the amendment is executed and enacted.

(ii) *Transition rule.*—For purposes of this paragraph (a)(13), a plan that was adopted and effective before December 31, 2007, whether written or unwritten, will be treated as designating such compensation for services performed in the taxable year in which the payroll period ends, unless otherwise set forth in writing before December 31, 2007.

(14) *Elections to annualize recurring part-year compensation.*—In the case of a service provider receiving recurring part-year compensation, an election to defer all or a portion of the recurring part-year compensation to be earned during a particular service period is considered to meet the requirements of this paragraph (a) if the election is made before the services for which the recurring part-year compensation is paid begin, and the election does not defer payment of any of the recurring part-year compensation to a date beyond the last day of the 13th month following the first date of the service period. For purposes of this paragraph (a)(14), the term *recurring part-year compensation* means compensation paid for services rendered in a position that the service recipient and service provider reasonably anticipate will continue on similar terms and conditions in subsequent years, and will require services to be provided during successive service periods each of which comprises less than 12 months (for example, a teacher providing services during a school year comprised of 10 consecutive months), and each of which periods begins in one taxable year of the service provider and ends in the next such taxable year. The rules of this paragraph (a)(14) apply to a particular amount of compensation only once, so that an amount deferred under this rule may not again be treated as recurring part-year compensation for purposes of this paragraph and subject to a second deferral election under this paragraph (a)(14).

(15) *USERRA rights.*—The requirements of this paragraph (a) are deemed satisfied to the extent an initial deferral election is provided to satisfy the requirements of the Uniformed Service Employment and Reemployment Rights Act of 1994, as amended, 38 U.S.C. 4301-4334.

(b) *Subsequent changes in time and form of payment.*—(1) *In general.*—A plan that permits under a subsequent election a delay in a payment or a change in the form of payment (a subsequent deferral election), including a subsequent deferral election made by a service provider or a service recipient, satisfies the requirements of section 409A(a)(4)(C) only if the conditions of this paragraph (b) are met. For purposes of this paragraph (b), except as otherwise expressly provided in this section, a subsequent deferral election is not considered made until such election becomes irrevocable under the terms of the plan. Accordingly, a plan may provide that a subsequent deferral election may be changed at any time before the last permissible date for making such a subsequent deferral election. Where a plan permits a subsequent deferral election, the requirements of this paragraph are satisfied only if the following conditions are met:

(i) The plan requires that such election not take effect until at least 12 months after the date on which the election is made.

(ii) In the case of an election related to a payment not described in § 1.409A-3(a)(2) (payment on account of disability), § 1.409A-3(a)(3) (payment on account of death), or § 1.409A-3(a)(6) (payment on account of the occurrence of an unforeseeable emergency), the plan requires that the payment with respect to which such election is made be deferred for a period of not less than five

years from the date such payment would otherwise have been paid (or in the case of a life annuity or installment payments treated as a single payment, five years from the date the first amount was scheduled to be paid).

(iii) The plan requires that any election related to a payment described in § 1.409A-3(a)(4) (payment at a specified time or pursuant to a fixed schedule) be made not less than 12 months before the date the payment is scheduled to be paid (or in the case of a life annuity or installment payments treated as a single payment, 12 months before the date the first amount was scheduled to be paid).

(2) *Definition of payments for purposes of subsequent changes in the time or form of payment.*—(i) *In general.*—Except as provided in paragraphs (b)(2)(ii) and (iii) of this section, the term *payment* refers to each separately identified amount to which a service provider is entitled to payment under a plan on a determinable date, and includes amounts applied for the benefit of the service provider. An amount is separately identified only if the amount may be objectively determined under a nondiscretionary formula. For example, an amount identified as 10 percent of the account balance as of a specified payment date would be a separately identified amount. A payment includes the provision of any taxable benefit, including payment in cash or in kind. In addition, a payment includes, but is not limited to, the transfer, cancellation, or reduction of an amount of deferred compensation in exchange for benefits under a welfare benefit plan, a fringe benefit excludible under section 119 or section 132, or any other benefit that is excludible from gross income. For additional rules relating to the application of this paragraph (b) to amounts payable at a fixed time or pursuant to a fixed schedule, see § 1.409A-3(i)(1).

(ii) *Life annuities.*—(A) *In general.*—The entitlement to a life annuity is treated as the entitlement to a single payment. Accordingly, an election to delay payment of a life annuity, or to change the form of payment of a life annuity, must be made at least 12 months before the scheduled commencement of the life annuity, and must defer the payment for a period of not less than five years from the originally scheduled commencement of the life annuity. For purposes of § 1.409A-1, this section, and §§ 1.409A-3 through 1.409A-6, the term *life annuity* means a series of substantially equal periodic payments, payable not less frequently than annually, for the life (or life expectancy) of the service provider, or a series of substantially equal periodic payments, payable not less frequently than annually, for the life (or life expectancy) of the service provider, followed upon the death or end of the life expectancy of the service provider by a series of substantially equal periodic payments, payable not less frequently than annually, for the life (or life expectancy) of the service provider's designated beneficiary (if any). Notwithstanding the foregoing, a schedule of payments does not fail to be an annuity solely because such plan provides for an immediate payment of the actuarial present value of all remaining annuity payments if the actuarial present value of the remaining annuity payments falls below a predetermined amount, and the immediate payment of such amount does not constitute an accelerated payment for purposes of § 1.409A-3(j), provided that such feature, including the predetermined amount, is established by no later than the time and form of payment is otherwise required to be established, and provided further that any change in such feature, including the predetermined amount, is a change in the time and form of payment. A change in designated beneficiary before any annuity payment has been made under the plan is not a change in the time or form of payment. A change in the form of a payment before any annuity payment has been made under the plan, from one type of life annuity to another type of life annuity with the same scheduled date for the first annuity payment, is not considered a change in the time and form of a payment, provided that the annuities are actuarially equivalent applying reasonable actuarial methods and assumptions. For purposes of this paragraph (b)(2)(ii), a requirement that a service provider obtain the consent of a spouse or other potential recipient of a survivor annuity to change a beneficiary or form of payment is disregarded, so that any annuity form that the service recipient could elect to receive with such consent is considered currently available.

(B) *Certain features disregarded.*—Notwithstanding the foregoing provisions of this paragraph (b)(2)(ii), the following features are disregarded for purposes of determining whether a payment form is a life annuity within the meaning of this paragraph (b)(2)(ii), but are not disregarded for purposes of determining whether a life annuity is the actuarial equivalent of another life annuity except as otherwise provided in this paragraph (b)(2)(ii):

(1) Term certain features under which annuity payments continue for the longer of the life of the annuitant or a fixed period of time.

(2) Pop-up features under which payments increase upon the death of the beneficiary or another event that eliminates the right to a survivor annuity.

(3) Cash refund features under which payment is provided upon the death of the last annuitant in an amount that is not greater than the excess of the present value of the annuity at the annuity starting date over the total of payments before the death of the last annuitant.

(4) Features under which an annuity form of payment provides higher periodic payments before the expected commencement of benefits under the Social Security Act (42 U.S.C. ch. 7) or the Railroad Retirement Act (45 U.S.C. 231 et. seq.) and lower periodic payments after such expected commencement date, so that the combined periodic payments under the arrangement and the Social Security Act or the Railroad Retirement Act, as applicable, are approximately level before and after such expected commencement date (Social Security or Railroad Retirement leveling features).

(5) Features providing for an increase in the annuity payment in a manner described in §1.401(a)(9)-6, Q&A-14(a)(1) or (2) (eligible cost-of-living adjustments).

(C) *Subsidized joint and survivor annuities.*—For purposes of this paragraph (b)(2)(ii), a joint and survivor annuity will not fail to be treated as actuarially equivalent to a single life annuity due solely to the value of a subsidized survivor annuity benefit, provided that the annual lifetime annuity benefit available to the service provider under the joint and survivor annuity is not greater than the annual lifetime annuity benefit available to the service provider under the single life annuity alternative, and provided that the annual survivor annuity benefit is not greater than the annual lifetime annuity benefit available to the service provider under the joint and survivor annuity.

(D) *Actuarial assumptions and methods.*—For purposes of this paragraph (b)(2)(ii), at any given time the same actuarial assumptions and methods must be used in valuing each annuity payment option, in determining whether the payments are actuarially equivalent and such assumptions must be reasonable. This requirement applies over the entire term of the service provider's participation in the plan, such that the annuity payment must be actuarially equivalent at all times for the annuity payment options to be treated as one time and form of payment. There is no requirement that the same actuarial methods and assumptions be used over the term of a service provider's participation in a plan. Accordingly, a plan may change the actuarial assumptions and methods used to determine the life annuity payments provided that all of the actuarial assumptions and methods are reasonable.

(iii) *Installment payments.*—The entitlement to a series of installment payments that is not a life annuity is treated as the entitlement to a single payment, unless the plan provides at all times with respect to the amount deferred that the right to the series of installment payments is to be treated as a right to a series of separate payments. For purposes of §1.409A-1, this section, and §§1.409A-3 through 1.409A-6, a series of installment payments refers to an entitlement to the payment of a series of substantially equal periodic amounts to be paid over a predetermined period of years, except to the extent any increase (or decrease) in the amount reflects reasonable earnings (or losses) through the date the amount is paid. For this purpose, a series of installment payments over a predetermined period and a series of installment payments over a shorter or longer period, or a series of installment payments over the same predetermined period but with a different commencement date, are different times and forms of payment. Accordingly, a change in the predetermined period or the commencement date is a change in the time and form of payment. Notwithstanding the foregoing, a schedule of payments does not fail to be an installment payment solely because such plan provides for an immediate payment of all remaining installments if the present value of the deferred amount to be paid in the remaining installment payments falls below a predetermined amount, and the immediate payment of such amount does not constitute an accelerated payment for purposes of §1.409A-3(j), provided that such feature including the predetermined amount is established by no later than the time and form of payment is otherwise required to be established, and provided further that any change in such feature including the predetermined amount is a change in the time and form of payment.

(iv) *Transition rule.*—For purposes of this section, a plan that was adopted and effective before December 31, 2007, whether written or unwritten, that fails to make a designation as to whether the entitlement to a series of payments is to be treated as an entitlement to a series of separate payments under paragraph (b)(2)(iii) of this section, may make such designation on or before December 31, 2007, *provided such designation is set forth in writing on or before December 31, 2007.*

(3) *Beneficiaries.*—The rules of this paragraph (b) governing changes in the time and form of payment apply to elections by

beneficiaries with respect to the time and form of payment, as well as elections by service providers or service recipients with respect to the time and form of payment to beneficiaries. An election to change the identity of a beneficiary does not constitute a change in the time and form of payment merely because the election changes the identity of the recipient of the payment, if the time and form of the payment is not otherwise changed. In addition, an election to change the identity of a beneficiary before the initial payment of a life annuity does not constitute a change in the time and form of payment if the change in the time of payments stems solely from the different life expectancy of the new beneficiary, such as in the case of a joint and survivor annuity.

(4) *Domestic relations orders.*—The rules of this paragraph (b) governing changes in the time and form of payment do not apply to elections by individuals other than a service provider, with respect to payments to a person other than the service provider, to the extent such elections are reflected in, or made in accordance with, the terms of a domestic relations order (as defined in section 414(p)(1)(B)).

(5) *Coordination with prohibition against acceleration of payments.*—For purposes of applying the prohibition against the acceleration of payments in §1.409A-3(j), the definition of payment is the same as the definition in paragraph (b)(2) of this section. Accordingly, a change in the form of a payment that results in a more rapid schedule for payments generally will not constitute an acceleration of a payment, if the change in the form of payment is made in compliance with the subsequent deferral rules. For example, a change in form from a 10-year installment payment treated as a single payment to a lump-sum payment would not constitute an acceleration if the change in the form of the payment is made in compliance with the requirements of paragraph (b)(1) of this section, generally meaning that the election to change to a lump-sum payment must be made at least 12 months before the installment payments were scheduled to commence and the lump-sum payment could not be made until at least five years after the date the installment payments were scheduled to commence. See §1.409A-3(j)(4)(i) with respect to situations in which the failure to accelerate a payment or the modification of a plan term relating to certain accelerated payments will not be subject to the rules of this paragraph (b).

(6) *Application to multiple payment events.*—In the case of a plan that permits a payment upon each of a number of potential permissible payment events, such as the earlier of a fixed date or separation from service, the requirements of paragraph (b)(1) of this section are applied separately to each payment (as defined in paragraph (b)(2) of this section) due upon each payment event. Notwithstanding the foregoing, the addition or deletion of a permissible payment event to a plan under which amounts were previously deferred is subject to the rules of this paragraph (b) where the addition or deletion of the permissible payment event may result in a change in the time or form of payment of the amount deferred. For application of the rules governing accelerations of payments to the addition of a permissible payment event to amounts deferred, see §1.409A-3(j).

(7) *Delay of payments under certain circumstances.*—A payment may be delayed to a date after the designated payment date under any of the circumstances described in this paragraph (b)(7), and the provision will not fail to meet the requirements of establishing a permissible payment event and the delay in the payment will not constitute a subsequent deferral election, so long as the service recipient treats all payments to similarly situated service providers on a reasonably consistent basis.

(i) *Payments subject to section 162(m).*—A payment may be delayed to the extent that the service recipient reasonably anticipates that if the payment were made as scheduled, the service recipient's deduction with respect to such payment would not be permitted due to the application of section 162(m), provided that the payment is made either during the service provider's first taxable year in which the service recipient reasonably anticipates, or should reasonably anticipate, that if the payment is made during such year, the deduction of such payment will not be barred by application of section 162(m) or during the period beginning with the date of the service provider's separation from service and ending on the later of the last day of the taxable year of the service recipient in which the service provider separates from service or the 15th day of the third month following the service provider's separation from service, and provided further that where any scheduled payment to a specific service provider in a service recipient's taxable year is delayed in accordance with this paragraph, the delay in payment will be treated as a subsequent deferral election unless all scheduled payments to that service provider that could be delayed in accordance with this paragraph are also delayed. Where the payment is delayed to a date on or after the service provider's separation from service, the payment will be considered a payment upon a separation from service for purposes of the rules under §1.409A-3(i)(2) (payments to specified employees upon a separation from service) and, in the case of a specified employee, the date that is six months after a service provider's separation from service is substituted for any reference to a service provider's separation from service in the first sentence of this paragraph. No election may be provided to the service provider with respect to the timing of the payment under this paragraph (b)(7)(i).

(ii) *Payments that would violate Federal securities laws or other applicable law.*—A payment may be delayed where the service recipient reasonably anticipates that the making of the payment will violate Federal securities laws or other applicable law; provided that the payment is made at the earliest date at which the service recipient reasonably anticipates that the making of the payment will not cause such violation. The making of a payment that would cause inclusion in gross income or the application of any penalty provision or other provision of the Internal Revenue Code is not treated as a violation of applicable law.

(iii) *Other events and conditions.*—A service recipient may delay a payment upon such other events and conditions as the Commissioner may prescribe in generally applicable guidance published in the Internal Revenue Bulletin (see § 601.601(d)(2) of this chapter). For additional rules applicable to certain delayed payments pursuant to a change in control event, see § 1.409A-3(i)(5)(iv). For additional rules applicable to amounts payable because of an unforeseeable emergency, see § 1.409A-3(i)(3).

(8) *USERRA rights.*—The requirements of this paragraph (b) are deemed met to the extent an election to change the time or form of a payment of deferred compensation is provided to satisfy the requirements of the Uniformed Services Employment and Reemployment Rights Act of 1994, as amended, 38 U.S.C. 4301-4344.

(9) *Examples.*—The following examples illustrate the application of the provisions of this section. For purposes of these examples, each employee is an individual with a calendar year taxable year, and is employed by the specified employer:

Example 1. Initial election to defer salary. Employer ZZ sponsors a plan under which Employee A may elect to defer a percentage of Employee A's salary. Employee A has participated in the plan in prior years. To satisfy the requirements of this section with respect to salary earned in calendar year 2008, if Employee A elects to defer any amount of such salary, the deferral election (including an election as to the time and form of payment) must be made no later than December 31, 2007.

Example 2. Designation of time and form of payment where an initial deferral election is not provided. Employer YY has a taxable year ending September 30. On July 1, 2008, Employer YY enters into a legally binding obligation to pay Employee B a $10,000 bonus. The amount is not subject to a substantial risk of forfeiture and does not qualify as performance-based compensation as described in § 1.409A-1(e). Employer YY does not provide Employee B an election as to the time and form of payment. Unless the amount is to be paid in accordance with the short-term deferral rule of § 1.409A-1(b)(4), Employer YY must specify the time and form of payment on or before July 1, 2008, to satisfy the requirements of this section.

Example 3. Initial election to defer bonus payable based on services during calendar year. Employer XX has a taxable year ending September 30. Employee C participates in a bonus plan under which Employee C is entitled to a bonus for services performed during the calendar year that, absent an election by Employee C, will be paid on March 15 of the following year. The amount is not subject to a substantial risk of forfeiture and does not qualify as performance-based compensation as described in § 1.409A-1(e). If Employee C elects to defer the payment of the bonus with respect to services rendered during calendar year 2008, Employee C must elect the time and form of payment not later than December 31, 2007, to satisfy the requirements of this section.

Example 4. Initial election to defer bonus payable based on services during fiscal year other than calendar year. Employer WW has a taxable year ending September 30. Employee D participates in a bonus plan under which Employee D is entitled to a bonus for services performed during Employer WW's fiscal year that, absent an election by Employee D, will be paid on December 15 of the calendar year in which the fiscal year ends. The amount is not subject to a substantial risk of forfeiture and does not qualify as performance-based compensation as described in § 1.409A-1(e). The amount qualifies as fiscal year compensation. If Employee D elects to defer the payment of the amount related to the fiscal year ending September 30, 2009, to satisfy the requirements of this section Employee D must elect the time and form of payment not later than September 30, 2008.

Example 5. Initial election to defer bonus payable only if service provider completes at least 12 months of services after the election. Employer VV has a calendar year taxable year. On March 1, 2008, Employer VV grants Employee E a $10,000 bonus, payable on March 1, 2010 (with reasonable interest), provided that Employee E contin-

ues performing services as an employee of Employer VV through March 1, 2010. The amount does not qualify as performance-based compensation as described in § 1.409A-1(e), and Employee E already participates in another account balance nonqualified deferred compensation plan. Employee E may make an initial deferral election on or before March 31, 2008 (within 30 days after obtaining a legally binding right), because at least 12 months of additional services are required after the date of election for the risk of forfeiture to lapse.

Example 6. Initial election to defer bonus that would otherwise constitute a short-term deferral. The same facts as *Example 5*, except that Employee E does not make an initial deferral election on or before March 31, 2008. Because the right to the compensation would not be treated as a deferral of compensation pursuant to § 1.409A-1(b)(4) absent a deferral election (because the arrangement would be treated as a short-term deferral), Employee E may make an initial deferral election provided that the election may not become effective for 12 months and must defer the payment at least 5 years from March 1, 2010 (the first date the payment could become substantially vested). Accordingly, Employee E may make an election before March 1, 2009, provided that the election defers the payment to a date on or after March 1, 2015 (other than a payment due to death, disability, unforeseeable emergency, or a change in control event).

Example 7. Initial election to defer sales commissions. Employer UU has a calendar year taxable year. As part of Employee F's services for Employer UU, Employee F sells refrigerators to customers unrelated to Employee F or Employer UU. Under the employment arrangement, Employee F is entitled to 10% of the sales price of any refrigerator Employee F sells, payable only upon the receipt of payment from the customer who purchased the refrigerator. For purposes of the initial deferral rule, Employee F is treated as performing the services related to each refrigerator sale in the calendar year in which each customer pays for the refrigerator.

Example 8. Initial election to defer renewal sales commissions. The same facts as *Example 7*, except that Employee F also sells warranties related to the refrigerators sold. Under the warranty arrangement, refrigerator warranty customers are entitled in a future year to extend the warranty for an additional cost to be paid at the time of the extension. Under Employee F's arrangement with Employer UU, Employee F is entitled to 10% of the amount paid for an extension of any warranty, payable upon the receipt of payment from the customer extending the warranty. For purposes of the initial deferral election rule, Employee F is treated as performing the services related to the amount paid for the extension of the warranty in the taxable year in which the customer pays for the warranty extension.

Example 9. Initial election to defer investment commissions. Employer TT is in the trade or business of managing financial assets for customer accounts. Customers who deposit funds in an account with Employer TT are entitled to remove the account balance of such account upon 60 days notice to Employer TT. Employee G sells financial products and provides continuing customer service to certain unrelated customers involving the deposit and maintenance of funds in customer accounts managed by Employer TT. Under the employment arrangement, Employee G is entitled to a set percentage of the aggregate value of the assets held in the accounts of customers to whom Employee G sold financial products and provides customer service. Under the arrangement, the aggregate value of the assets held in the accounts is determined as of June 30 of each year, and unless Employee G elects to defer the payment, the amount is payable to Employee G in a lump sum on December 31 of the year in which the valuation is made. Employee G has no control over the valuation of the assets held in the accounts, or the calculation of the amount due Employee G. For purposes of the initial deferral rule, Employee G is treated as providing the services to which a payment relates during the July 1 through June 30 period ending on the June 30 date as of which the assets held in the account are valued.

Example 10. Initial election to defer part-year compensation. Employee H provides services as a teacher to Employer SS, a school system. The period of services routinely begins on the second Monday of August of one year and ends on the first Friday of June of the subsequent year. Employer SS provides an election to Employee H to receive the compensation for the period of services ratably over the period beginning on the second Monday of August of one year and ending on the last day of August of the subsequent year. Because the compensation constitutes recurring part-year compensation, as defined in paragraph (a)(14) of this section, and because the schedule will provide that all of the recurring part-year compensation is paid no later than September 30 of the subsequent year, Employee H will be deemed to have made a timely deferral election with respect to such recurring part-year compensation if Employee H elects before the first day of the service period to have the recurring part-year compensation paid under such schedule.

Example 11. Initial election to defer negotiated separation pay. Employer RR decides to terminate Employee J's employment involuntarily. As part of the process of terminating Employee J, Employer RR enters into bona fide, arm's length negotiations with respect to the terms of Employee J's termination of employment. As part of the process, Employer RR offers Employee J an amount that is in addition to any amounts to which Employee J is otherwise entitled, payable either as a lump sum payment at the end of 3 years or in 3 annual payments starting at the date of termination of employment. The election of the time and form of payment by Employee J may be made at any time before Employee J accepts the offer and obtains a legally binding right to the additional amount. The election may not apply to any amount to which Employee J already had a legally binding right.

Example 12. Election of time and form of payments under a window program. Employer QQ establishes a window program, as defined in §1.409A-1(b)(9)(vi). Individuals who elect to terminate employment under the window program are entitled to receive an amount equal to 2 weeks pay multiplied by every year of service with Employer QQ. The individuals participating in the window program may elect to receive the payment as either a lump sum payment payable on the first day of the month after making the election to participate in the window program, or as a payment of 3 equal annual installments on each January 1 of the first 3 years following the election to participate in the window program. Employee K is eligible to participate in the window program. Employee K will be treated as making a timely deferral election if the election as to the time and form of payment is made on or before the date Employee K's election to participate in the window program becomes irrevocable.

Example 13. Initial election to defer salary earned during final payroll period beginning in one calendar year and ending in the subsequent calendar year. Employer PP pays the salary of its employees, including Employee L, on a bi-weekly basis. One bi-weekly payroll period runs from December 24, 2008, through January 6, 2009, with a scheduled payment date of January 13, 2009. Employer PP sponsors, and Employee L participates in, a nonqualified deferred compensation plan under which Employee L may defer a specified percentage of his annual salary. The plan does not specify that any salary compensation paid for the payroll period in which falls January 1 is to be treated as compensation for services performed during the year preceding the year in which falls January 1. For purposes of applying the initial deferral election rules, Employee L is deemed to have performed the services for the payroll period December 24, 2008, through January 6, 2009, during the calendar year 2009.

Example 14. Application of deferral election rules and anti-acceleration rules to a nonqualified deferred compensation plan linked to a qualified plan. Employee M participates in a qualified retirement plan that is a defined benefit plan that offers a subsidized early retirement benefit to employees who have attained age 55 and completed 30 years of service. Employee M, who has attained age 55 and completed 30 years of service, also participates in a nonqualified deferred compensation plan, under which the benefit payable is calculated under a formula, with that benefit then reduced by any benefit that Employee M has accrued under the qualified retirement plan. In 2008, Employee M fails to elect the subsidized early retirement benefit under the qualified retirement plan, with the effect that the amounts payable under the nonqualified deferred compensation plan are increased by an amount equal to the reduction in the benefit payable under the qualified plan. In 2009, Employer NN amends the qualified retirement plan to increase benefits under the plan, resulting in a decrease in the amounts payable under the nonqualified deferred compensation plan equal to the increase in the benefit payable under the qualified plan. Neither of these actions constitutes a deferral election or an acceleration of a payment under the nonqualified deferred compensation plan.

Example 15. Subsequent deferral election. Employee N participates in a nonqualified deferred compensation plan. Employee N elects to be paid in a lump sum payment at the earlier of age 65 or separation from service. Employee N anticipates that he will work after age 65, and wishes to defer payment to a later date. Provided that Employee N continues in employment and makes the election by his 64th birthday, Employee N may elect to receive a lump sum payment at the earlier of age 70 or separation from service.

Example 16. Subsequent deferral election rule — change in form of payment from lump sum payment to life annuity. Employee P participates in a nonqualified deferred compensation plan. Employee P elects to be paid in a lump sum payment at age 65. Employee P wishes to change the payment form to a life annuity. Provided that Employee P makes the election on or before his 64th birthday, Employee P may elect to receive a life annuity commencing at age 70.

Example 17. Subsequent deferral election rule — change in form of payment from life annuity to lump sum payment. Employee Q participates in a nonqualified deferred compensation plan. Employee Q elects to be paid in a life annuity at age 65. Employee Q wishes to change the payment form to a lump sum payment. Provided that Employee Q makes the election on or before his 64th birthday, Employee Q may elect to receive a lump sum payment at age 70.

Example 18. Subsequent deferral election rule — installment payments designated as separate payments. Employee R, whose taxable year is the calendar year, participates in a nonqualified deferred compensation plan that provides for payment in a series of 5 equal annual amounts, each designated as a separate payment. The first payment is scheduled to be made on January 1, 2010. Provided that Employee R makes the election on or before January 1, 2009, Employee R may elect for the first payment scheduled to be made on January 1, 2010, to be made on January 1, 2015. If Employee R makes that election, but does not elect to defer the remaining payments, the remaining payments continue to be due upon January 1 of the 4 consecutive calendar years commencing on January 1, 2011.

Example 19. Subsequent deferral election rule — change in form of payment from installment payments not designated as separate payments to lump sum payment. Employee S participates in a nonqualified deferred compensation plan that provides for payment in a series of 5 equal annual amounts that are not designated as a series of 5 separate payments. The first amount is scheduled to be paid on January 1, 2010. Employee S wishes to receive the entire amount equal to the sum of all 5 of the amounts to be paid as a lump sum payment. Provided that Employee S makes the election on or before January 1, 2009, Employee S may elect to receive a lump sum payment on or after January 1, 2015.

Example 20. Subsequent deferral election rule — change in form of payment from installment payments designated as separate payments to lump sum payment. Employee T participates in a nonqualified deferred compensation plan that provides for payment in a series of 5 equal annual amounts each of which is designated as a separate payment. The first amount is scheduled to be paid on January 1, 2010. Employee T wishes to receive the entire amount equal to the sum of all 5 of the amounts in a single lump sum payment. Provided that Employee T makes the election on or before January 1, 2009, Employee T may elect to receive a lump sum payment on or after January 1, 2019.

Example 21. Subsequent deferral election rule — change in form of payment from one life annuity form to another life annuity form. Employee U participates in a nonqualified deferred compensation plan that permits Employee U to elect before Employee U's separation from service whether to be paid in the form of a single life annuity beginning on the first day of the month following Employee U's separation from service, or an annuity beginning on the first day of the month following Employee U's separation from service under which annuity payments continue for Employee U's lifetime but not less than 10 years. The two types of annuities are actuarially equivalent at all times applying reasonable actuarial methods and assumptions. For purposes of this section, the two types of annuities are treated as a single form of payment. Accordingly, the election provided under the plan is not treated as providing a subsequent deferral election or accelerated payment, and an election by Employee U under the plan between the two annuity options made before the first scheduled payment date for an annuity payment is not treated as a subsequent deferral election or an acceleration of a payment.

Example 22. Subsequent deferral election rule — change in time of payment from payment at specified age to payment at later of specified age or separation from service. Employee V participates in a nonqualified deferred compensation plan that provides for a lump sum payment at age 65. Employee V wishes to modify the plan so that the deferred amount will be payable upon the later of Employee V's attainment of a specified age or separation from service. Provided that Employee V makes such election on or before his 64th birthday, Employee V may modify the plan so Employee V will receive a lump sum payment upon the later of age 70 or separation from service.

Example 23. Subsequent deferral election rule — change in time of payment from payment at separation from service to payment at later of separation from service or specified age. Employee W participates in a nonqualified deferred compensation plan that provides for a lump sum payment at separation from service. Employee W wishes to make the payment payable upon the later of separation from service or a predetermined age. Provided that Employee W makes such election on or before the date 1 year before a separation from service, Employee W may elect to receive a lump sum payment upon the later of the date 5 years following a separation from service or at a specified age.

Example 24. Subsequent deferral election rule — change in time of payment from payment at separation from service to payment at a change in control event. Employee X participates in a nonqualified deferred compensation plan that provides for a lump sum payment at separation from service. Employee X wishes to change the payment provision such that the payment is payable upon a change in control event. A change in the distribution provision to provide for a payment only upon a change in control event will violate the rules governing payment provisions, because the change could result in an acceleration if the change in control event occurs before Employee X separates from service, or a subsequent deferral if the change in control does not occur until after Employee X separates from service. However, provided that Employee X makes such election on or before the date 1 year before a separation from service, Employee X may elect to receive a payment upon the later of a change in control event or 5 years following a separation from service.

(c) *Special rules for certain resident aliens.*—For the first taxable year of an individual in which such individual is a resident alien, a nonqualified deferred compensation plan is deemed to meet the requirements of paragraph (a) of this section if, with respect to compensation payable for services performed during that first taxable year or with respect to compensation the right to which is subject to a substantial risk of forfeiture as of the first day of that first taxable year, an initial deferral election is made by the end of such first taxable year, provided that the initial deferral election may not apply to amounts that have already been paid or made available to the service provider before the election is made. For any year after the first taxable year in which an individual is classified as a resident alien, this paragraph (c) does not apply, provided that a taxable year may again be treated as the first taxable year in which an individual is classified as a resident alien if such individual is classified as a resident alien in that taxable year and has not been classified as a resident alien for the three consecutive taxable years immediately preceding that taxable year. [Reg. §1.409A-2.]

☐ [T.D. 9321, 4-10-2007 (corrected 7-30-2007).]

§1.409A-3. Permissible payments.—(a) *In general.*—The requirements of section 409A(a)(2)(A) are met only if the plan provides that an amount of deferred compensation under the plan may be paid only upon an event or at a time set forth in this paragraph (a):

(1) The service provider's separation from service (as defined in §1.409A-1(h) and in accordance with paragraph (i)(2) of this section).

(2) The service provider becoming disabled (in accordance with paragraph (i)(4) of this section).

(3) The service provider's death.

(4) A time or a fixed schedule specified under the plan (in accordance with paragraph (i)(1) of this section).

(5) A change in the ownership or effective control of the corporation, or in the ownership of a substantial portion of the assets of the corporation (in accordance with paragraph (i)(5) of this section).

(6) The occurrence of an unforeseeable emergency (in accordance with paragraph (i)(3) of this section).

(b) *Designation of payment upon a permissible payment event.*—Except as otherwise specified in this section, a plan provides for the payment upon an event described in paragraph (a)(1), (2), (3), (5), or (6) of this section if the plan provides the date of the event is the payment date, or specifies another payment date that is objectively determinable and nondiscretionary at the time the event occurs. A plan may also provide that a payment upon an event described in paragraph (a)(1), (2), (3), (5), or (6) of this section is to be made in accordance with a schedule that is objectively determinable and nondiscretionary based on the date the event occurs and that would qualify as a fixed schedule under paragraph (i)(1) of this section if the payment event were instead a fixed date, provided that the schedule must be fixed at the time the permissible payment event is designated. In addition, a plan may provide that a payment, including a payment that is part of a schedule, is to be made during a designated taxable year of the service provider that is objectively determinable and nondiscretionary at the time the payment event occurs such as, for example, a schedule of three substantially equal payments payable during the first three taxable years following the taxable year in which a separation from service occurs. A plan may also provide that a payment, including a payment that is part of a schedule, is to be made during a designated period objectively determinable and nondiscretionary at the time the payment event occurs, but only if the designated period both begins and ends within one taxable year of the service provider or the designated period is not more than 90 days and the service provider does not have a right to designate the taxable year of the payment (other than an election that complies with the subsequent deferral election rules of §1.409A-2(b)). Where a plan provides for a period of more than one day following a payment event during which a payment may be made, such as within 90 days following the date of the event, the payment date for purposes of the subsequent deferral rules under §1.409A-2(b) is treated as the first possible date upon which a payment could be made under the terms of the plan. A plan may provide for payment upon the earliest or latest of more than one event or time, provided that each event or time is described in paragraphs (a)(1) through (6) of this section. For examples illustrating the provisions of this paragraph, see paragraph (i)(1)(vi) of this section.

(c) *Designation of alternative specified dates or payment schedules based upon date of permissible event.*—Except as otherwise provided in this paragraph (c), for an amount of deferred compensation under a plan, the plan may designate only one time and form of payment upon the

occurrence of each event described in paragraph (a)(1), (2), (3), (5), or (6) of this section. For example, a plan does not satisfy the requirements of this paragraph (c) if it provides for one payment date or schedule of payments if a specified event occurs on a Monday, but another payment date or schedule of payments if the event occurs on any other day of the week. However, a plan that provides for a payment upon an event described in paragraph (a)(2), (3), (5), or (6) of this section may allow for an alternative payment schedule if the event occurs on or before one (but not more than one) specified date, provided that the addition or deletion of such a different time and form of payment applicable to an existing deferral is subject to §1.409A-2(b) (subsequent deferral elections) and paragraph (j) of this section (accelerated payments). For example, a plan may provide that a service provider will receive a lump sum payment of the service provider's entire benefit under the plan on the first day of the month following a change in control event that occurs before the service provider attains age 55, but will receive 5 substantially equal annual payments commencing on the first day of the month following a change in control event that occurs on or after the service provider attains age 55. In the case of a plan that provides that a payment upon an event described in paragraph (a)(1) of this section (a payment upon a separation from service), a different time and form of payment may be designated with respect to a separation from service under each of the following conditions, provided that the addition or deletion of such a different time and form of payment applicable to an existing deferral is subject to §1.409A-2(b) and paragraph (j) of this section:

(1) A separation from service during a limited period of time not to exceed two years following a change in control event (as defined in paragraph (i)(5) of this section).

(2) A separation from service before or after a specified date (for example, the attainment of a specified age), or a separation from service before or after a combination of a specified date, such as attaining a specified age, and a specified period of service determined under a predetermined, nondiscretionary, objective formula or pursuant to the method for crediting service under a qualified plan sponsored by the service recipient.

(3) A separation from service not described in paragraphs (c)(1) or (c)(2) of this section.

(d) *When a payment is treated as made upon the designated payment date.*—Except as otherwise specified in this section, a payment is treated as made upon the date specified under the plan (including a date specified under paragraph (a)(4) of this section) if the payment is made at such date or a later date within the same taxable year of the service provider or, if later, by the 15th day of the third calendar month following the date specified under the plan and the service provider is not permitted, directly or indirectly, to designate the taxable year of the payment. In addition, a payment is treated as made upon the date specified under the plan (including a date specified under paragraph (a)(4) of this section) and is not treated as an accelerated payment if the payment is made no earlier than 30 days before the designated payment date and the service provider is not permitted, directly or indirectly to designate the taxable year of the payment. For purposes of this paragraph, if the date specified is only a designated taxable year of the service provider, or a period of time during such a taxable year, the date specified under the plan is treated as the first day of such taxable year or the first day of the period of time during such taxable year, as applicable. The payment with respect to a stock right generally occurs upon the exercise of the stock right, so that where a stock right designates a fixed exercise date, the stock right will be deemed to have been paid at such date if the exercise and payment occur on such date or a later date within the same taxable year of the service provider or, if later, by the 15th day of the third calendar month following the exercise date specified under the plan. If calculation of the amount of the payment is not administratively practicable due to events beyond the control of the service provider (or service provider's beneficiary), the payment will be treated as made upon the date specified under the plan if the payment is made during the first taxable year of the service provider in which the calculation of the amount of the payment is administratively practicable. For purposes of this paragraph, the inability of a service recipient to calculate the amount or timing of a payment due to a failure of a service provider (or service provider's beneficiary) to provide reasonably available information necessary to make such calculation does not constitute an event beyond the control of the service provider. Similarly, if the making of the payment at the date specified under the plan would jeopardize the ability of the service recipient to continue as a going concern, the payment will be treated as made upon the date specified under the plan if the payment is made during the first taxable year of the service provider in which the making of the payment would not have such effect.

(e) *Designation of time and form of payment with respect to earnings.*—A nonqualified deferred compensation plan that provides for actual or notional earnings to be credited on amounts of deferred compensation may specify, in accordance with the requirements of §1.409A-2(a) (initial deferral elections), that such earnings are treated separately from the right to the other amounts deferred under the plan for purposes of designating the time and form of payments under such plan, provided that to satisfy the requirements of this paragraph (e), actual or notional earnings must be credited at least annually. For these purposes, a right to dividend equivalents may be treated analogously to a right to actual or notional earnings on an amount of deferred compensation. For purposes of this paragraph (e), the term *dividend equivalents* means the right to an amount equal to all or a specified portion of dividends declared and paid, if any, on a specified number of shares of stock.

(f) *Substitutions.*—Except as otherwise provided under these regulations, the payment of an amount as a substitute for a payment of deferred compensation will be treated as a payment of the deferred compensation. A forfeiture or voluntary relinquishment of an amount of deferred compensation will not be treated as a payment of the compensation, but there is no forfeiture or voluntary relinquishment for this purpose if an amount is paid, or a legally binding right to a payment is created, that acts as a substitute for the forfeited or voluntarily relinquished amount. Whether a payment or a right to a payment acts as a substitute for a payment of deferred compensation is determined based on all the facts and circumstances. However, where the payment of an amount results in an actual or potential reduction of, or current or future offset to, an amount of deferred compensation, or if the service provider receives a loan the repayment of which is secured by or may be accomplished through an offset of or a reduction in an amount deferred under a nonqualified deferred compensation plan, the payment or loan is a substitute for the deferred compensation. In addition, where a service provider's right to deferred compensation is made subject to anticipation, alienation, sale, transfer, assignment, pledge, encumbrance, attachment, or garnishment by creditors of the service provider or the service provider's beneficiary, the deferred compensation is treated as having been paid. For the treatment of certain offsets, see paragraph (j)(4)(xiii) of this section. Even where there is no explicit reduction or offset, the payment of an amount or creation of a new right to a payment proximate to the purported forfeiture or voluntary relinquishment of a right to deferred compensation is presumed to be a substitute for the deferred compensation. The presumption is rebuttable by a showing that the compensation paid would have been received regardless of the forfeiture or voluntary relinquishment of the right to deferred compensation. Factors indicating that a payment would have been received regardless of such forfeiture or voluntarily relinquishment include that the amount paid is materially less than the forfeited or relinquished amount, or consists of a type of payment customarily made in the ordinary course of business of the service recipient to service providers who do not forfeit or relinquish deferred compensation (for example, a payment of accrued but unused leave or a payment for a release of actual or potential claims). See §1.409A-1(b)(9)(i) with respect to certain separation pay plans.

(g) *Disputed payments and refusals to pay.*—If a service recipient fails to make a payment in whole or in part as of the date specified under a plan, either intentionally or unintentionally, other than with the express or implied consent of the service provider, the payment will be treated as made upon the date specified under the plan if the service provider accepts the portion (if any) of the payment that the service recipient is willing to make (unless such acceptance will result in a relinquishment of the claim to all or part of the remaining amount), makes prompt and reasonable, good faith efforts to collect the remaining portion of the payment, and any further payment (including payment of a lesser amount that satisfies the obligation to make the payment) is made no later than the end of the first taxable year of the service provider in which the service recipient and the service provider enter into a legally binding settlement of such dispute, the service recipient concedes that the amount is payable, or the service recipient is required to make such payment pursuant to a final and nonappealable judgment or other binding decision. For purposes of this paragraph (g), efforts to collect the payment will be presumed not to be prompt, reasonable, good faith efforts, unless the service provider provides notice to the service recipient within 90 days of the latest date upon which the payment could have been timely made in accordance with the terms of the plan and these regulations, and unless, if not paid, the service provider takes further enforcement measures within 180 days after such latest date. For purposes of this paragraph (g), a service recipient is not treated as having failed to make a payment where pursuant to the terms of the plan the service provider is required to request payment, or otherwise provide information or take any other action, and the service provider has failed to take such action. In addition, for purposes of this paragraph (g), the service provider is deemed to have requested that a payment not be made, rather than the service recipient having failed to make such payment, where the service recipient's decision

to refuse to make the payment is made by the service provider or a member of the service provider's family (as defined in section 267(c)(4) applied as if the family of an individual includes the spouse of any member of the family), or any person or group of persons over whom the service provider or service provider's family member has effective control, or any person any portion of whose compensation is controlled the service provider or service provider's family member.

(h) *Special rule for certain resident aliens.*—An agreement, method, program, or other arrangement that is, or constitutes part of, a nonqualified deferred compensation plan is deemed to meet the requirements of this section with respect to any amount payable in the first taxable year of the service provider in which a service provider is a resident alien, and with respect to any amount payable in a subsequent taxable year if no later than the last day of the first taxable year of the service provider in which the service provider is a resident alien, the plan is amended as necessary so that the times and forms of payment of amounts payable in a subsequent year comply with the provisions of this section. For any year after the first taxable year of an individual in which the individual is a resident alien, this paragraph (h) does not apply, provided that a taxable year may again be treated as the first taxable year in which an individual is a resident alien if such individual has not been a resident alien for at least three consecutive taxable years immediately preceding the taxable year in which the service provider is again a resident alien.

(i) *Definitions and special rules.*—(1) *Specified time or fixed schedule.*—(i) *In general.*—Amounts are payable at a specified time or pursuant to a fixed schedule if objectively determinable amounts are payable at a date or dates that are nondiscretionary and objectively determinable at the time the amount is deferred. An amount is objectively determinable for this purpose if the amount is specifically identified or if the amount may be determined at the time payment is due pursuant to an objective, nondiscretionary formula specified at the time the amount is deferred (for example, 50 percent of a specified account balance). Except as otherwise provided in paragraph (i)(1) of this section, an amount is not objectively determinable if the amount of the payment is based all or in part upon the occurrence of an event, including the consummation of a transaction by, or a payment of an amount to, a service recipient. If an amount is payable in a service provider's taxable year (or pursuant to a fixed schedule of taxable years of the service provider) that is designated at the time the amount is deferred and that is objectively determinable, the amount is treated as payable at a specified time (or pursuant to a fixed schedule), provided that for purposes of the application of the subsequent deferral rules contained in §1.409A-2(b), the specified time or fixed schedule of payments is deemed to refer to the first day of the relevant taxable year or years. A specified time or fixed schedule also includes the designation at the time the amount is deferred of a defined period or periods within the service provider's taxable year or taxable years that are objectively determinable, provided that no such defined period may begin within one taxable year and end within another taxable year, and provided further that for purposes of the application of the subsequent deferral rules contained in §1.409A-2(b), the specified time or fixed schedule of payments is deemed to refer to the first day of the relevant period in which the payment will be made. A plan may provide that a payment upon the lapse of a substantial risk of forfeiture is to be made in accordance with a fixed schedule that is objectively determinable based on the date the substantial risk of forfeiture lapses (disregarding any discretionary acceleration of the lapse of the substantial risk of forfeiture), provided that the schedule must be fixed on the date the time and form of payment are designated, and any change in the fixed schedule will constitute a change in the time and form of payment. For example, a plan that provides for a bonus payment subject to the condition that the service provider complete three years of service, and subject to the further condition that such requirement of continued services will lapse upon the occurrence of an initial public offering, which condition if applied alone would constitute a substantial risk of forfeiture, may provide that a service provider is entitled to substantially equal payments on each of the first three anniversaries of the date the substantial risk of forfeiture lapses (the earlier of three years of service or the date of an initial public offering).

(ii) *Payment schedules with formula and fixed limitations.*—(A) *Individual limitations.*—A schedule of payments does not fail to be a fixed schedule of payments where the amount of a payment or payments that may be paid at a specified time or during a specified period is limited by an objective nondiscretionary formula or a specified amount that is not under the effective control of the service provider and is not subject to the exercise of discretion by the service recipient, where such limitation is established on or before the date the time and form of payment is otherwise required to be set under these regulations, and the plan specifies the time and form of any payment that will be made or completed after its original payment date due to the application of the limitation. A change in the limitation or a change in the time and form of any payment that exceeds the limitation is subject to the requirements of §1.409A-2(b) (subsequent deferral elections) and paragraph (j) of this section (accelerated payments). For purposes of this paragraph, a plan provision that reduces a schedule of periodic payments on a dollar-for-dollar basis by the amount of Social Security payments received or receivable may be treated as a nondiscretionary, objective formula limitation, if such reduction does not otherwise affect the time of payment of the deferred compensation (other than a forfeiture due to the reduction), including changes based on the service provider's eligibility or elections related to Social Security benefits. Similarly, a plan provision that reduces a schedule of periodic payments on a dollar-for-dollar basis by the amount of bona fide disability pay (within the meaning of §1.409A-1(a)(5)) received or receivable may be treated as a nondiscretionary, objective formula limitation, if the disability payments are made pursuant to a plan sponsored by the service recipient that covers a substantial number of service providers and was established before the service provider became disabled, and if such reduction does not otherwise affect the time of payment of the deferred compensation (other than a forfeiture due to the reduction). Whether an amendment to, or other change in the benefit payable under, such bona fide disability plan results in an acceleration of a payment for purposes of paragraph (j) of this section or a subsequent election to delay the time or change the form of payment for purposes of §1.409A-2(b) is determined based on all of the relevant facts and circumstances.

(B) *Limitations on aggregate payments to all participants in substantially identical plans.*—A schedule of payments does not fail to be a fixed schedule of payments where the amount of the aggregate payments that will be made during a specified period of time to all participants in substantially identical plans is limited by an objective nondiscretionary formula or specified amount that is not under the effective control of the service provider and is not subject to the exercise of discretion by the service recipient, where the limit is established on or before the date the time and form of payment of the amount deferred is otherwise required to be set under these regulations, the method of allocating payments among the participants where there is an overall limitation on the aggregate amount that may be paid to a group of service providers during a specified period is an objective nondiscretionary allocation method that is not under the effective control of the service provider and is not subject to the exercise of discretion by the service recipient, the method is established on or before the date the time and form of payment of the amount deferred is otherwise required to be set, and the plan specifies the time and form of any payment of any amount that will be paid after its original payment date due to the application of the limitation. A change in the limitation or a change in the time and form of payment of any payment that is not otherwise made at the scheduled payment date due to application of the formula limitation is subject to the requirements of §1.409A-2(b) (subsequent deferral elections) and paragraph (j) of this section (accelerated payments).

(iii) *Payment schedules determined by timing of payments received by the service recipient.*—A payment schedule determined by reference to the timing of payments received by the service recipient (not including payments from one entity to another entity where both entities are treated as part of a single service recipient), meets the requirements of a specified date or fixed schedule of payments if the following conditions are met:

(A) The payments due to the service recipient arise from bona fide and routine transactions in the ordinary course of business of the service recipient.

(B) The service provider does not have effective control of the service recipient, the person from whom such amounts are due, or the collection of any of the amounts due to the service recipient.

(C) The payment schedule provides an objective, nondiscretionary method of identification of the payments to the service recipient from which the amount of the payment from the service recipient to the service provider is determined.

(D) The payment schedule provides an objective, nondiscretionary schedule under which the payments will be made to the service provider.

(E) The payments to the service recipient from which the amount of the payments from service recipient to the service provider are determined result from sales of a type that the service recipient is in the trade or business of making and makes frequently, and either all such sales by the service recipient are taken into account for purposes of determining the payment to the service provider, or there is a legitimate, non-tax business reason for identifying the specific sales taken into account.

(iv) *Reimbursement or in-kind benefit plans.*—(A) *General rule.*—A plan that provides for reimbursements of expenses incurred by a service provider, or in-kind benefits, meets the requirements of a specified date or fixed schedule of payments with respect to such reimbursements or benefits if the following conditions are met:

(1) The plan provides an objectively determinable nondiscretionary definition of the expenses eligible for reimbursement or of the in-kind benefits to be provided.

(2) The plan provides for the reimbursement of expenses incurred or for the provision of the in-kind benefits during an objectively and specifically prescribed period (including the lifetime of the service provider).

(3) The plan provides that the amount of expenses eligible for reimbursement, or in-kind benefits provided, during a service provider's taxable year may not affect the expenses eligible for reimbursement, or in-kind benefits to be provided, in any other taxable year.

(4) The reimbursement of an eligible expense is made on or before the last day of the service provider's taxable year following the taxable year in which the expense was incurred.

(5) The right to reimbursement or in-kind benefits is not subject to liquidation or exchange for another benefit.

(B) *Medical reimbursement arrangements.*—Notwithstanding the foregoing, an arrangement providing for the reimbursement of expenses referred to in section 105(b) will not be deemed to fail to meet the requirements of paragraph (i)(1)(iv)(A)(3) of this section solely because the arrangement provides for a limit on the amount of expenses that may be reimbursed under such arrangement over some or all of the period in which the reimbursement arrangement remains in effect.

(v) *Tax gross-up payments.*—A plan providing a right to a tax gross-up payment will be treated as providing for payment at a specified time or on a fixed schedule of payments if the plan provides that payment will be made, and the payment is made, by the end of the service provider's taxable year next following the service provider's taxable year in which the service provider remits the related taxes. For purposes of this paragraph (i)(1)(v), the term *tax gross-up payment* refers to a payment to reimburse the service provider in an amount equal to all or a designated portion of the Federal, state, local, or foreign taxes imposed upon the service provider as a result of compensation paid or made available to the service provider by the service recipient, including the amount of additional taxes imposed upon the service provider due to the service recipient's payment of the initial taxes on such compensation. In addition, a right to the reimbursement of expenses incurred due to a tax audit or litigation addressing the existence or amount of a tax liability, whether Federal, state, local, or foreign, satisfies the requirement of a fixed time and form of payment if the right to the reimbursement provides that payment will be made, and the payment is made, by the end of the service provider's taxable year following the service provider's taxable year in which the taxes that are the subject of the audit or litigation are remitted to the taxing authority, or where as a result of such audit or litigation no taxes are remitted, the end of the service provider's taxable year following the service provider's taxable year in which the audit is completed or there is a final and nonappealable settlement or other resolution of the litigation. Nothing in this paragraph (i)(1)(v) otherwise alters the application of section 409A to the underlying compensation arrangement or other arrangement that results in the taxes subject to the right to the tax gross-up payment.

(vi) *Examples.*—The following examples (in which each employee is an individual whose taxable year is the calendar year) illustrate the principles of paragraphs (a), (b), (c), (d), and (i)(1) of this section:

Example 1. Employee A provides services as an employee of Employer Z, but is not a specified employee. Employee A participates in a nonqualified deferred compensation plan providing for a lump sum payment payable on or before December 31 of the calendar year in which Employee A separates from service. The plan provides for a payment upon a separation from service in compliance with this section.

Example 2. Employee B provides services as an employee of Employer Y, but is not a specified employee. Employee B participates in a nonqualified deferred compensation plan providing for a lump sum payment payable on or before the 90th day immediately following the date upon which Employee B separates from service. Employer Y retains the sole discretion to determine when during the 90-day period the payment will be made. Although the plan does not specify a period during one calendar year in which the payment will be made, the plan provides for a payment upon a separation from service in compliance with this section because the period over which the payment may be made is not longer than 90 days.

Example 3. Employee C provides services as an employee of Employer X, but is not a specified employee. Employee C participates in a nonqualified deferred compensation plan providing for a lump sum payment payable on or before the 180th day following the date upon which Employee C separates from service. Employer X retains the sole discretion to determine when during the 180-day period the payment will be made. Because the plan does not specify a period during one calendar year in which the payment will be made, and because the period over which the payment may be made is longer than 90 days, the plan does not provide for a payment upon a separation from service that complies with this section.

Example 4. Employee D provides services as an employee of Employer W, but is not a specified employee. Employee D participates in a nonqualified deferred compensation plan providing for 10 installment payments payable on the first 10 anniversaries of the date Employee D separates from service, provided that no installment payment in any year may be more than 1% of Employer W's net income for the previous calendar year, and provided further that the excess over such limit that would otherwise be payable but is not paid due to application of the limit will become payable as of the first installment payment date at which time such amount, in combination with any installment payment otherwise due Employee D, does not exceed 1% of Employer W's net income for the previous calendar year. Provided that Employee D does not retain effective control of the calculation of Employer W's net income or the amount that Employee D will not be paid due to application of the limit, the plan provides for a schedule of payments upon a separation from service that complies with this section.

Example 5. Employee E and Employee F provide services as employees of Employer V, but neither is a specified employee. Employee E and Employee F both participate in substantially identical nonqualified deferred compensation plans providing for 10 installment payment payable on the first 10 anniversaries of the date the respective employee separates from service, provided that the total amount of installment payments in any year may not be more than 1% of Employer V's net income for the previous year, that where any payments are not made due to application of the limit the determination of the amount not paid to a particular employee will be made by applying the overall limit proportionately based upon the installment payment due the employee that year, and that the excess over such limit that would otherwise be payable but is not paid due to application of the limit will become payable as of the first installment payment date at which time such amount, in combination with any installment payments otherwise due the participants, does not exceed 1% of Employer V's net income for the previous calendar year. Provided that neither Employee E nor Employee F retains effective control of the calculation of Employer V's net income or the amount that the respective employee will not be paid due to application of the limit, the plan provides for a schedule of payments upon a separation from service that complies with this section.

Example 6. Employee G provides services as an employee of Employer U, but is not a specified employee. As a bona fide part of this employment relationship, Employee G provides professional services to clients of Employer U as part of the bona fide, ordinary course of Employer U's trade or business. Under an arrangement between Employee G and Employer U, Employer U agrees to pay Employee G upon Employee G's separation from service an amount equal to 5% of any amount collected from Company T, a client of Employer U for which Employee G performed services during his employment with Employer U, during the 36 months following Employee G's separation from service. Under the arrangement, the amounts due to Employee G based upon payments received by Employer U during any calendar year are payable to Employee G on April 1 of the subsequent calendar year. Provided that Employee G does not have effective control of Employer U, Company T, or the collection of any amounts due Employer Y from Company T, the arrangement provides for a schedule of payments upon a separation from service that complies with this section.

Example 7. Employee H provides services as an employee of Employer S, but is not a specified employee. Under a plan sponsored by Employer S, Employee H has a legally binding right upon a separation from service to the reimbursement of country club dues paid in the calendar year of the separation from service and each of the next 3 calendar years following the separation from service in an amount not to exceed $30,000 in any calendar year, provided that the amount of dues paid in any calendar year that are eligible for reimbursement equals only the amount actually expended during such calendar year, and the maximum amount available for reimbursement in any calendar year will not be increased or decreased to reflect the amount expended or reimbursed in a prior or subsequent calendar year. The plan further provides that any reimbursement must be paid to Employee H by December 31 of the calendar year following the year in which Employee H pays the country club dues. The reimbursement plan provides for a schedule of payments upon a separation from service that complies with this section.

Example 8. Employee J provides services as an employee of Employer Q, but is not a specified employee. Under a plan sponsored by Employer Q, Employee J has a legally binding right upon a separation from service to the reimbursement of country club dues paid during the calendar year in which the separation from service occurs and the next 3 calendar years in a total amount not to exceed $90,000. The plan further provides that any reimbursement must be paid to Employee J by December 31 of the calendar year following the year in which Employee J pays the country club dues. Because the reimbursement of a payment of country club dues in one calendar year may affect the amount of country club dues available for reimbursement in another calendar year, the plan does not provide for a schedule of payments upon a separation from service that complies with this section.

(2) *Separation from service—required delay in payment to a specified employee pursuant to a separation from service.—(i) In general.—*In the case of any service provider who is a specified employee (as defined in §1.409A-1(i)) as of the date of a separation from service, the requirements of paragraph (a)(1) of this section permitting a payment upon a separation from service are satisfied only if payments may not be made before the date that is six months after the date of separation from service (or, if earlier than the end of the six-month period, the date of death of the specified employee). For this purpose, a service provider who is not a specified employee as of the date of a separation from service will not be treated as subject to this requirement even if the service provider would have become a specified employee if the service provider had continued to provide services through the next specified employee effective date. Similarly, a service provider who is treated as a specified employee as of the date of a separation from service will be subject to this requirement even if the service provider would not have been treated as a specified employee after the next specified employee effective date had the specified employee continued providing services through the next specified employee effective date. Notwithstanding the foregoing, this paragraph (i)(2)(i) does not apply to a payment made under the circumstances described in paragraph (j)(4)(ii) (domestic relations order), (j)(4)(iii) (conflicts of interest), or (j)(4)(vi) (payment of employment taxes) of this section.

(ii) *Application of payment rules to delayed payments.—*The required delay in payment is met if payments to which a specified employee would otherwise be entitled during the first six months following the date of separation from service are accumulated and paid on the first day of the seventh month following the date of separation from service, or if each payment to which a specified employee is otherwise entitled upon a separation from service is delayed by six months. A service recipient may retain discretion to choose which method will be implemented, provided that no direct or indirect election as to the method may be provided to the service provider. For an affected specified employee, a date upon which the plan or the service recipient designates that the payment will be made after the six-month delay is treated as a fixed payment date for purposes of paragraph (d) of this section once the separation from service has occurred.

(3) *Unforeseeable emergency.—(i) Definition.—*For purposes of §§1.409A-1 and 1.409A-2, this section, and §§1.409A-4 through 1.409A-6, an *unforeseeable emergency* is a severe financial hardship to the service provider resulting from an illness or accident of the service provider, the service provider's spouse, the service provider's beneficiary, or the service provider's dependent (as defined in section 152, without regard to section 152(b)(1), (b)(2), and (d)(1)(B)); loss of the service provider's property due to casualty (including the need to rebuild a home following damage to a home not otherwise covered by insurance, for example, not as a result of a natural disaster); or other similar extraordinary and unforeseeable circumstances arising as a result of events beyond the control of the service provider. For example, the imminent foreclosure of or eviction from the service provider's primary residence may constitute an unforeseeable emergency. In addition, the need to pay for medical expenses, including non-refundable deductibles, as well as for the costs of prescription drug medication, may constitute an unforeseeable emergency. Finally, the need to pay for the funeral expenses of a spouse, a beneficiary, or a dependent (as defined in section 152, without regard to section 152(b)(1), (b)(2), and (d)(1)(B)) may also constitute an unforeseeable emergency. Except as otherwise provided in this paragraph (i)(3)(i), the purchase of a home and the payment of college tuition are not unforeseeable emergencies. Whether a service provider is faced with an unforeseeable emergency permitting a distribution under this paragraph (i)(3)(i) is to be determined based on the relevant facts and circumstances of each case, but, in any case, a distribution on account of unforeseeable emergency may not be made to the extent that such emergency is or may be relieved through reimbursement or compensation from insurance or otherwise, by liquidation of the service provider's assets, to the extent the liquidation of such assets would not cause severe financial hardship, or by cessation of deferrals under the plan. A plan may provide for a payment upon a specific type or types of unforeseeable emergency,

without providing for payment upon all unforeseeable emergencies, provided that any event upon which a payment may be made qualifies as an unforeseeable emergency.

(ii) *Amount of payment permitted upon an unforeseeable emergency.*—Distributions because of an unforeseeable emergency must be limited to the amount reasonably necessary to satisfy the emergency need (which may include amounts necessary to pay any Federal, state, local, or foreign income taxes or penalties reasonably anticipated to result from the distribution). Determinations of amounts reasonably necessary to satisfy the emergency need must take into account any additional compensation that is available if the plan provides for cancellation of a deferral election upon a payment due to an unforeseeable emergency. See paragraph (j)(4)(viii) of this section. However, the determination of amounts reasonably necessary to satisfy the emergency need is not required to take into account any additional compensation that is available from a qualified employer plan as defined in § 1.409A-1(a)(2) (including any amount available by obtaining a loan under the plan), or that due to the unforeseeable emergency is available under another nonqualified deferred compensation plan (including a plan that would provide for deferred compensation except due to the application of the effective date provisions under § 1.409A-6). The payment may be made from any plan in which the service provider participates that provides for payment upon an unforeseeable emergency, provided that the plan under which the payment was made must be designated at the time of payment.

(iii) *Payments due to an unforeseeable emergency.*—A service provider may retain discretion with respect to whether to apply for a payment upon an unforeseeable emergency, and a service recipient may retain discretion with respect to whether to make a payment available under the plan due to an unforeseeable emergency. A service provider who has experienced an unforeseeable emergency will not be treated as making a subsequent deferral election under § 1.409A-2(b) (subsequent deferral election rules) if the service provider does not apply for or elect to receive a payment available under the plan. A service recipient will not be treated as making a subsequent deferral election under § 1.409A-2(b) (subsequent deferral election rules) if the service recipient exercises its discretion not to make a payment otherwise available due to an unforeseeable emergency.

(4) *Disability.*—(i) *In general.*—For purposes of §§ 1.409A-1 and 1.409A-2, this section, and §§ 1.409A-4 through 1.409A-6, except as otherwise specifically provided, a service provider is considered disabled if the service provider meets one of the following requirements:

(A) The service provider is unable to engage in any substantial gainful activity by reason of any medically determinable physical or mental impairment that can be expected to result in death or can be expected to last for a continuous period of not less than 12 months.

(B) The service provider is, by reason of any medically determinable physical or mental impairment that can be expected to result in death or can be expected to last for a continuous period of not less than 12 months, receiving income replacement benefits for a period of not less than three months under an accident and health plan covering employees of the service provider's employer.

(ii) *Limited plan definition of disability.*—A plan may provide for a payment upon any disability, and need not provide for a payment upon all disabilities, provided that any disability upon which a payment may be made under the plan complies with the provisions of this paragraph (i)(4).

(iii) *Determination of disability.*—A plan may provide that a service provider will be deemed disabled if determined to be totally disabled by the Social Security Administration or Railroad Retirement Board. A plan may also provide that a service provider will be deemed disabled if determined to be disabled in accordance with a disability insurance program, provided that the definition of disability applied under such disability insurance program complies with the requirements of this paragraph (i)(4).

(5) *Change in the ownership or effective control of a corporation, or a change in the ownership of a substantial portion of the assets of a corporation.*—(i) *In general.*—Pursuant to section 409A(a)(2)(A)(v), a plan may permit a payment upon the occurrence of a change in the ownership of the corporation (as defined in paragraph (i)(5)(v) of this section), a change in effective control of the corporation (as defined in paragraph (i)(5)(vi) of this section), or a change in the ownership of a substantial portion of the assets of the corporation (as defined in paragraph (i)(5)(vii) of this section) (collectively referred to as a change in control event). To qualify as a change in control event, the occurrence of the event must be objectively determinable and any requirement that any other person or group, such as a plan administrator or compensation committee, certify the occurrence of a change

in control event must be strictly ministerial and not involve any discretionary authority. The plan may provide for a payment on a particular type or types of change in control events, and need not provide for a payment on all such events, provided that each event upon which a payment is provided qualifies as a change in control event. For rules regarding the ability of the service recipient to terminate the plan and pay amounts of deferred compensation upon a change in control event, see paragraph (j)(4)(ix)(B) of this section.

(ii) *Identification of relevant corporation.*—(A) *In general.*—To constitute a change in control event with respect to the service provider, the change in control event must relate to—

(1) The corporation for whom the service provider is performing services at the time of the change in control event;

(2) The corporation that is liable for the payment of the deferred compensation (or all corporations liable for the payment if more than one corporation is liable) but only if either the deferred compensation is attributable to the performance of service by the service provider for such corporation (or corporations) or there is a bona fide business purpose for such corporation or corporations to be liable for such payment and, in either case, no significant purpose of making such corporation or corporations liable for such payment is the avoidance of Federal income tax; or

(3) A corporation that is a majority shareholder of a corporation identified in paragraph (i)(5)(ii)(A)(1) or (2) of this section, or any corporation in a chain of corporations in which each corporation is a majority shareholder of another corporation in the chain, ending in a corporation identified in paragraph (i)(5)(ii)(A)(1) or (2) of this section.

(B) *Majority shareholder.*—For purposes of this paragraph (i)(5)(ii), a majority shareholder is a shareholder owning more than 50 percent of the total fair market value and total voting power of such corporation.

(C) *Example.*—The following example illustrates the rules of this paragraph (i)(5)(ii):

Example. Corporation A is a majority shareholder of Corporation B, which is a majority shareholder of Corporation C. A change in ownership of Corporation B constitutes a change in control event to service providers performing services for Corporation B or Corporation C, and to service providers for which Corporation B or Corporation C is solely liable for payments under the plan (for example, former employees), but is not a change in control event as to Corporation A or any other corporation of which Corporation A is a majority shareholder unless the sale constitutes a change in the ownership of a substantial portion of Corporation A's assets (see paragraph (i)(5)(vii) of this section).

(iii) *Attribution of stock ownership.*—For purposes of paragraph (i)(5) of this section, section 318(a) applies to determine stock ownership. Stock underlying a vested option is considered owned by the individual who holds the vested option (and the stock underlying an unvested option is not considered owned by the individual who holds the unvested option). For purposes of the preceding sentence, however, if a vested option is exercisable for stock that is not substantially vested (as defined by § 1.83-3(b) and (j)), the stock underlying the option is not treated as owned by the individual who holds the option.

(iv) *Special rules for certain delayed payments pursuant to a change in control event.*—(A) *Certain transaction-based compensation.*—Payments of compensation related to a change in control event described in paragraph (i)(5)(v) of this section (change in the ownership of a corporation) or paragraph (i)(5)(vii) of this section (change in the ownership of a substantial portion of a corporation's assets), that occur because a service recipient purchases its stock held by the service provider or because the service recipient or a third party purchases a stock right held by a service provider, or that are calculated by reference to the value of stock of the service recipient (collectively, transaction-based compensation), may be treated as paid at a designated date or pursuant to a payment schedule that complies with the requirements of section 409A if the transaction-based compensation is paid on the same schedule and under the same terms and conditions as apply to payments to shareholders generally with respect to stock of the service recipient pursuant to a change in control event described in paragraph (i)(5)(v) of this section (change in the ownership of a corporation) or as apply to payments to the service recipient pursuant to a change in control event described in paragraph (i)(5)(vii) of this section (change in the ownership of a substantial portion of a corporation's assets), and to the extent that the transaction-based compensation is paid not later than five years after the change in control event, the payment of such compensation will not violate the initial or subsequent deferral election rules set out in § 1.409A-2(a) and (b) solely as a result of such transaction-based compensation being paid pursuant to such schedule and terms and conditions. If before and in connection with a change in control event described in paragraph (i)(5)(v) or (i)(5)(vii) of this section, transaction-based compensation that would otherwise be payable as a result of such event is made subject to a condition on payment that constitutes a substantial risk of forfeiture (as defined in § 1.409A-1(d), without regard to the provisions of that section under which additions or extensions of forfeiture conditions are disregarded) and the transaction-based compensation is payable under the same terms and conditions as apply to payments made to shareholders generally with respect to stock of the service recipient pursuant to a change in control event described in paragraph (i)(5)(v) of this section or to payments to the service recipient pursuant to a change in control event described in paragraph (i)(5)(vii) of this section, for purposes of determining whether such transaction-based compensation is a short-term deferral the requirements of § 1.409A-1(b)(4) are applied as if the legally binding right to such transaction-based compensation arose on the date that it became subject to such substantial risk of forfeiture.

(B) *Certain nonvested compensation.*—Notwithstanding the provisions of § 1.409A-1(d) (definition of a substantial risk of forfeiture) that disregard the extension or modification of a condition for purposes of determining whether a condition on payment constitutes a substantial risk of forfeiture, a condition that is a substantial risk of forfeiture that otherwise would lapse as a result of a change in control event described in paragraph (i)(5)(v) or (i)(5)(vii) of this section may be extended or modified before and in connection with such event to provide for a condition on payment that will not lapse as a result of such change in control event, and such extended or modified condition will be treated as continuing to subject the amount to a substantial risk of forfeiture, provided that the transaction constituting the change in control event is a bona fide arm's length transaction between the service recipient or its shareholders and one or more parties who are unrelated to the service recipient and service provider (applying the rules of § 1.409A-1(f)(2)(ii)) and the modified or extended condition to which the payment is subject would otherwise be treated as a substantial risk of forfeiture under § 1.409A-1(d) (without regard to the provisions disregarding additions or extensions of forfeiture conditions). In such a case, the continued application of a fixed schedule of payments based upon the lapse of the substantial risk of forfeiture, so that payments commence upon the lapse of the modified or extended condition on payment, will not be treated as a change in the fixed schedule of payments for purposes of § 1.409A-2(b) (subsequent deferral elections) or paragraph (j) of this section (prohibition on the acceleration of payments).

(v) *Change in the ownership of a corporation.*—(A) *In general.*—Except as provided in paragraph (i)(5)(vi)(C) of this section, a change in the ownership of a corporation occurs on the date that any one person, or more than one person acting as a group (as defined in paragraph (i)(5)(v)(B) of this section), acquires ownership of stock of the corporation that, together with stock held by such person or group, constitutes more than 50 percent of the total fair market value or total voting power of the stock of such corporation. A nonqualified deferred compensation plan may provide that amounts payable upon a change in the ownership of a corporation will be paid only if the conditions in the preceding sentence are satisfied but substituting a percentage specified in the plan that is higher than 50 percent for the words "50 percent" in the preceding sentence, but only if the provision is set forth in the plan no later than the date by which the time and form of payment must be established under § 1.409A-2. However, if any one person, or more than one person acting as a group, is considered to own more than 50 percent of the total fair market value or total voting power of the stock of a corporation (or such higher percentage specified in accordance with the preceding sentence), the acquisition of additional stock by the same person or persons is not considered to cause a change in the ownership of the corporation (or to cause a change in the effective control of the corporation (within the meaning of paragraph (i)(5)(vi) of this section)). An increase in the percentage of stock owned by any one person, or persons acting as a group, as a result of a transaction in which the corporation acquires its stock in exchange for property will be treated as an acquisition of stock for purposes of this section. This section applies only when there is a transfer of stock of a corporation (or issuance of stock of a corporation) and stock in such corporation remains outstanding after the transaction (see paragraph (i)(5)(vii) of this section for rules regarding the transfer of assets of a corporation). See § 1.280G-1, Q&A-27(d), *Example 1*, *Example 2*, *Example 5*, and *Example 6*.

(B) *Persons acting as a group.*—For purposes of paragraph (i)(5)(v)(A) of this section, persons will not be considered to be acting as a group solely because they purchase or own stock of the same corporation at the same time, or as a result of the same public

offering. However, persons will be considered to be acting as a group if they are owners of a corporation that enters into a merger, consolidation, purchase or acquisition of stock, or similar business transaction with the corporation. If a person, including an entity, owns stock in both corporations that enter into a merger, consolidation, purchase or acquisition of stock, or similar transaction, such shareholder is considered to be acting as a group with other shareholders only with respect to the ownership in that corporation before the transaction giving rise to the change and not with respect to the ownership interest in the other corporation. See § 1.280G-1, Q&A-27(d), *Example 3* and *Example 4*.

(vi) *Change in the effective control of a corporation.*—(A) *In general.*—Notwithstanding that a corporation has not undergone a change in ownership under paragraph (i)(5)(v) of this section, a change in the effective control of the corporation occurs only on either of the following dates:

(1) The date any one person, or more than one person acting as a group (as determined under paragraph (i)(5)(v)(B) of this section), acquires (or has acquired during the 12-month period ending on the date of the most recent acquisition by such person or persons) ownership of stock of the corporation possessing 30 percent or more of the total voting power of the stock of such corporation. A nonqualified deferred compensation plan may provide that amounts payable upon an effective change in control of a corporation will be paid only if the conditions in the preceding sentence are satisfied but substituting a percentage specified in the plan that is higher than 30 percent for the word "30 percent" in the preceding sentence, but only if the percentage is set forth in the plan no later than the date by which the time and form of payment must be established under § 1.409A-2).

(2) The date a majority of members of the corporation's board of directors is replaced during any 12-month period by directors whose appointment or election is not endorsed by a majority of the members of the corporation's board of directors before the date of the appointment or election, provided that for purposes of this paragraph (i)(5)(vi)(A) the term *corporation* refers solely to the relevant corporation identified in paragraph (i)(5)(ii) of this section for which no other corporation is a majority shareholder for purposes of that paragraph. For example, if Corporation A is a publicly held corporation with no majority shareholder, and Corporation A is the majority shareholder of Corporation B, which is the majority shareholder of Corporation C, the term *corporation* for purposes of this paragraph (i)(5)(vi)(A)(2) would refer solely to Corporation A. A nonqualified deferred compensation plan may provide that amounts payable upon a change in the effective control of a corporation will be paid only if the conditions in the first sentence of this paragraph are satisfied substituting a portion of the members of the corporation's board of directors that is higher than the words "a majority of the members of the corporation's board of directors" in the first sentence of this paragraph, but only if the higher portion is set forth in the plan no later than the date by which the time and form of payment must be established under § 1.409A-2(a)).

(B) *Multiple change in control events.*—A change in effective control may occur in a transaction in which one of the two corporations involved in the transaction has a change in control event under paragraph (i)(5)(v) or (i)(5)(vii) of this section. Thus, for example, assume Corporation P transfers more than 40 percent of the total gross fair market value of its assets to Corporation O in exchange for 35 percent of O's stock. P has undergone a change in ownership of a substantial portion of its assets under paragraph (i)(5)(vii) of this section and O has a change in effective control under this paragraph (i)(5)(vi).

(C) *Acquisition of additional control.*—If any one person, or more than one person acting as a group, is considered to effectively control a corporation (within the meaning of this paragraph (i)(5)(vi)), the acquisition of additional control of the corporation by the same person or persons is not considered to cause a change in the effective control of the corporation (or to cause a change in the ownership of the corporation within the meaning of paragraph (i)(5)(v) of this section).

(D) *Persons acting as a group.*—Persons will not be considered to be acting as a group solely because they purchase or own stock of the same corporation at the same time, or as a result of the same public offering. However, persons will be considered to be acting as a group if they are owners of a corporation that enters into a merger, consolidation, purchase or acquisition of stock, or similar business transaction with the corporation. If a person, including an entity, owns stock in both corporations that enter into a merger, consolidation, purchase or acquisition of stock, or similar transaction, such shareholder is considered to be acting as a group with other shareholders in a corporation only with respect to the ownership in that corporation before the transaction giving rise to the change and not with respect to the ownership interest in the other corporation. See § 1.280G-1, Q&A-27(d), *Example 4*.

(vii) *Change in the ownership of a substantial portion of a corporation's assets.*—(A) *In general.*—A change in the ownership of a substantial portion of a corporation's assets occurs on the date that any one person, or more than one person acting as a group (as determined in paragraph (i)(5)(v)(B) of this section), acquires (or has acquired during the 12-month period ending on the date of the most recent acquisition by such person or persons) assets from the corporation that have a total gross fair market value equal to or more than 40 percent of the total gross fair market value of all of the assets of the corporation immediately before such acquisition or acquisitions (or such higher amount specified by the plan no later than the date by which the time and form of payment must be established under § 1.409A-2). For this purpose, gross fair market value means the value of the assets of the corporation, or the value of the assets being disposed of, determined without regard to any liabilities associated with such assets.

(B) *Transfers to a related person.*—(1) There is no change in control event under this paragraph (i)(5)(vii) when there is a transfer to an entity that is controlled by the shareholders of the transferring corporation immediately after the transfer, as provided in this paragraph (i)(5)(vii)(B). A transfer of assets by a corporation is not treated as a change in the ownership of such assets if the assets are transferred to—

(i) A shareholder of the corporation (immediately before the asset transfer) in exchange for or with respect to its stock;

(ii) An entity, 50 percent or more of the total value or voting power of which is owned, directly or indirectly, by the corporation;

(iii) A person, or more than one person acting as a group, that owns, directly or indirectly, 50 percent or more of the total value or voting power of all the outstanding stock of the corporation; or

(iv) An entity, at least 50 percent of the total value or voting power of which is owned, directly or indirectly, by a person described in paragraph (i)(5)(vii)(B)(1)(iii) of this section.

(2) For purposes of this paragraph (i)(5)(vii)(B) and except as otherwise provided in this paragraph (i), a person's status is determined immediately after the transfer of the assets. For example, a transfer to a corporation in which the transferor corporation has no ownership interest before the transaction, but that is a majority-owned subsidiary of the transferor corporation after the transaction is not treated as a change in the ownership of the assets of the transferor corporation.

(C) *Persons acting as a group.*—Persons will not be considered to be acting as a group solely because they purchase assets of the same corporation at the same time. However, persons will be considered to be acting as a group if they are owners of a corporation that enters into a merger, consolidation, purchase or acquisition of assets, or similar business transaction with the corporation. If a person, including an entity shareholder, owns stock in both corporations that enter into a merger, consolidation, purchase or acquisition of assets, or similar transaction, such shareholder is considered to be acting as a group with other shareholders in a corporation only to the extent of the ownership in that corporation before the transaction giving rise to the change and not with respect to the ownership interest in the other corporation. See § 1.280G-1, Q&A-27(d), *Example 4*.

(6) *Certain back-to-back arrangements.*—(i) *In general.*—This paragraph (i)(6) applies where a service provider is providing services to a service recipient (the intermediate service recipient), who in turn is providing services to another service recipient (the ultimate service recipient), the services provided by the service provider to the intermediate service recipient are closely related to the services provided by the intermediate service recipient to the ultimate service recipient, there is a nonqualified deferred compensation plan providing for payments by the ultimate service recipient to the intermediate service recipient (the ultimate service recipient plan), there is a nonqualified deferred compensation plan or other agreement, method, program, or other arrangement providing for payments of compensation by the intermediate service recipient to the service provider (the intermediate service recipient plan), and the intermediate service recipient plan provides for a payment upon the occurrence of an event described in paragraph (a)(1), (2), (3), (5), or (6) of this section. In such a case, notwithstanding the generally applicable limits on payments in paragraph (a) of this section, the ultimate service recipient plan may provide for a payment to the intermediate service recipient upon the occurrence of a payment event under the intermediate service recipient plan described in paragraph (a)(1), (2), (3), (5), or (6) of this section if the time and form of payment is defined as the same time and form of payment provided under the intermediate service recipi-

ent plan, the amount of the payment under the ultimate service recipient plan does not exceed the amount of the payment under the intermediate service recipient plan, and the ultimate service recipient plan and the intermediate service recipient plan otherwise satisfy the requirements of section 409A (regardless of whether such plan is subject to section 409A).

(ii) *Example.*—The provisions of paragraph (i)(6)(i) of this section are illustrated by the following example:

Example. Company B (intermediate service recipient) provides services to Company C (ultimate service recipient). Employee A (service provider) provides services to Company B that are closely related to the services Company B provides to Company C. Pursuant to a nonqualified deferred compensation plan meeting the requirements of section 409A, Employee A is entitled to a payment of deferred compensation upon a separation from service with Company B (the intermediate service recipient plan). Under an arrangement between Company B and Company C (the ultimate service recipient plan), Company C agrees to pay an amount of deferred compensation to Company B upon Employee A's separation from service with Company B, in accordance with the time, form and amount of payment provided in the intermediate service recipient plan. Provided that the intermediate service recipient plan and the ultimate service recipient plan otherwise comply with the requirements of section 409A (regardless of whether such arrangements are subject to section 409A), Company C's payment to Company B of the amount due under the ultimate service recipient plan upon the separation from service of Employee A from Company B may constitute a permissible payment event for purposes of paragraph (a) of this section.

(j) *Prohibition on acceleration of payments.*—(1) *In general.*—Except as provided in paragraph (j)(4) of this section, a nonqualified deferred compensation plan may not permit the acceleration of the time or schedule of any payment or amount scheduled to be paid pursuant to the terms of the plan, and no such accelerated payment may be made whether or not provided for under the terms of such plan. For purposes of determining whether a payment of deferred compensation has been made, the rules of paragraph (f) of this section (substituted payments) apply. For purposes of this paragraph (j), an impermissible acceleration does not occur if payment is made in accordance with plan provisions or an election as to the time and form of payment in effect at the time of initial deferral (or added in accordance with the rules applicable to subsequent deferral elections under § 1.409A-2(b)) pursuant to which payment is required to be made on an accelerated schedule as a result of an intervening event that is an event described in paragraph (a)(1), (2), (3), (5), or (6) of this section. For example, a plan may provide that a participant will receive six installment payments commencing at separation from service, and also provide that if the participant dies after such payments commence but before all payments have been made, all remaining amounts will be paid in a lump sum payment. Additionally, it is not an acceleration of the time or schedule of payment of a deferral of compensation if a service recipient waives or accelerates the satisfaction of a condition constituting a substantial risk of forfeiture applicable to such deferral of compensation, provided that the requirements of section 409A (including the requirement that the payment be made upon a permissible payment event) are otherwise satisfied with respect to such deferral of compensation. For example, if a nonqualified deferred compensation plan provides for a lump sum payment of the vested benefit upon separation from service, and the benefit vests under the plan only after 10 years of service, it is not a violation of the requirements of section 409A if the service recipient reduces the vesting requirement to five years of service, even if a service provider becomes vested as a result and receives a payment in connection with a separation from service before the service provider would have completed 10 years of service. However, if the plan in this example had provided for a payment at a fixed date, rather than at separation from service, the date of payment could not be accelerated due to the accelerated vesting. For the definition of a payment for purposes of this paragraph (j), see § 1.409A-2(b)(5) (coordination of the subsequent deferral election rules with the prohibition on acceleration of payments). For other permissible payments, see § 1.409A-2(b)(2)(iii) (certain immediate payments of remaining installments) and paragraph (d) of this section (certain payments made no more than 30 days before the designated payment date).

(2) *Application to multiple payment events.*—Generally, the addition of a permissible payment event, the deletion of a permissible payment event, or the substitution of one permissible payment event for another permissible payment event, results in an acceleration of a payment if the addition, deletion, or substitution could result in the payment being made at an earlier date than such payment would have been made absent such addition, deletion, or substitution. Notwithstanding the previous sentence, the addition of death, disability (as defined in paragraph (i)(4) of this section), or an unforesee-

able emergency (as defined in paragraph (i)(3) of this section), as a potentially earlier alternative payment event to an amount previously deferred will not be treated as resulting in an acceleration of a payment, even if such addition results in the payment being paid at an earlier time than such payment would have been made absent the addition of the payment event. However, the addition of such a payment event as a potentially later alternative payment event generally is subject to the rules governing changes in the time and form of payment (see § 1.409A-2(b)).

(3) *Beneficiaries.*—The rules of this paragraph (j) apply to elections by beneficiaries with respect to the time and form of payment, as well as elections by service providers or service recipients with respect to the time and form of payment to beneficiaries. An election to change the identity of a beneficiary does not constitute an acceleration of a payment merely because the election changes the identity of the recipient of the payment, if the time and form of the payment is not otherwise changed. In addition, an election before the commencement of a life annuity to change the identity of a beneficiary does not constitute an acceleration of a payment if the change in the time of payments stems solely from the different life expectancy of the new beneficiary, such as in the case of a joint and survivor annuity, and does not change the commencement date of the life annuity.

(4) *Exceptions.*—(i) *In general.*—Except as otherwise expressly provided, a plan may provide for the acceleration of a payment in accordance with paragraphs (j)(4)(ii) through (xiv) of this section, or may provide a service recipient discretion to accelerate payments in accordance with the provisions of paragraphs (j)(4)(ii) through (xiv) of this section. A plan may not provide a service provider discretion with respect to whether a payment will be accelerated, and a service recipient may not provide a service provider a direct or indirect election as to whether the service recipient's discretion to accelerate a payment will be exercised, even if such acceleration would be permitted under paragraphs (j)(4)(ii) through (xiv) of this section. Whether a service recipient has provided a service provider an election as to whether the service recipient's discretion to accelerate a payment will be exercised is determined based on all the facts and circumstances, including whether similarly situated service providers have been treated differently. Except as otherwise provided in paragraphs (j)(4)(ii) through (xiv) of this section, the plan need not set forth the exception in writing, and provided all other requirements of this section are met, the making of such a payment or the addition of a plan term permitting the making of such a payment will not constitute the acceleration of a payment, and the failure to make such a payment or the deletion or modification of a plan term permitting the making of such a payment will not be subject to the rules regarding a change in the time and form of payment under § 1.409A-2(b).

(ii) *Domestic relations order.*—A plan may provide for acceleration of the time or schedule of a payment under the plan to an individual other than the service provider, or a payment under such plan may be made to an individual other than the service provider, to the extent necessary to fulfill a domestic relations order (as defined in section 414(p)(1)(B)).

(iii) *Conflicts of interest.*—(A) *Compliance with ethics agreements with the Federal government.*—A plan may provide for acceleration of the time or schedule of a payment under the plan, or a payment may be made under a plan, to the extent necessary for any Federal officer or employee in the executive branch to comply with an ethics agreement with the Federal government.

(B) *Compliance with ethics laws or conflicts of interest laws.*—A plan may provide for acceleration of the time or schedule of a payment under the plan, or a payment may be made under a plan, to the extent reasonably necessary to avoid the violation of an applicable Federal, state, local, or foreign ethics law or conflicts of interest law (including where such payment is reasonably necessary to permit the service provider to participate in activities in the normal course of his or her position in which the service provider would otherwise not be able to participate under an applicable rule). A payment is reasonably necessary to avoid the violation of a Federal, state, local, or foreign ethics law or conflicts of interest law if the payment is a necessary part of a course of action that results in compliance with a Federal, state, local, or foreign ethics law or conflicts of interest law that would be violated absent such course of action, regardless of whether other actions would also result in compliance with the Federal, state, local, or foreign ethics law or conflicts of interest law. For this purpose, a provision of foreign law is considered applicable only to foreign earned income (as defined under section 911(b)(1) without regard to section 911(b)(1)(B)(iv) and without regard to the requirement that the income be attributable to services performed during the period described in section 911(d)(1)(A) or (B)) from sources within the foreign country that promulgated such law.

(iv) *Section 457 plans.*—A plan subject to section 457(f) may provide for an acceleration of the time or schedule of a payment to a service provider, or a payment may be made under such a plan, to pay Federal, state, local, and foreign income taxes due upon a vesting event, provided that the amount of such payment is not more than an amount equal to the Federal, state, local, and foreign income tax withholding that would have been remitted by the employer if there had been a payment of wages equal to the income includible by the service provider under section 457(f) at the time of the vesting.

(v) *Limited cashouts.*—A plan may require or provide a service recipient discretion to require (or be amended to require or to provide a service recipient discretion to require), a mandatory lump sum payment of amounts deferred under the plan that do not exceed a specified amount, provided that such plan term or amendment is executed and effective, and any required exercise of service recipient discretion is evidenced in writing, no later than the date of such payment, and provided that—

(A) The payment results in the termination and liquidation of the entirety of the service provider's interest under the plan, including all agreements, methods, programs, or other arrangements with respect to which deferrals of compensation are treated as having been deferred under a single nonqualified deferred compensation plan under § 1.409A-1(c)(2); and

(B) The payment is not greater than the applicable dollar amount under section 402(g)(1)(B).

(vi) *Payment of employment taxes.*—A plan may provide for the acceleration of the time or schedule of a payment, or a payment may be made under the plan, to pay the Federal Insurance Contributions Act (FICA) tax imposed under section 3101, section 3121(a), and section 3121(v)(2), or the Railroad Retirement Act tax imposed under section 3201, section 3211, section 3231(e)(1), and section 3231(e)(8), where applicable, on compensation deferred under the plan (the FICA or RRTA amount). Additionally, a plan may provide for the acceleration of the time or schedule of a payment, or a payment may be made under the plan, to pay the income tax at source on wages imposed under section 3401 or the corresponding withholding provisions of applicable state, local, or foreign tax laws as a result of the payment of the FICA or RRTA amount, and to pay the additional income tax at source on wages attributable to the pyramiding section 3401 wages and taxes. However, the total payment under this acceleration provision must not exceed the aggregate of the FICA or RRTA amount, and the income tax withholding related to such FICA or RRTA amount.

(vii) *Payment upon income inclusion under section 409A.*—A plan may provide for the acceleration of the time or schedule of a payment, or a payment under such plan may be made, at any time the plan fails to meet the requirements of section 409A and these regulations. Such payment may not exceed the amount required to be included in income as a result of the failure to comply with the requirements of section 409A and these regulations.

(viii) *Cancellation of deferrals following an unforeseeable emergency or hardship distribution.*—A plan may provide for a cancellation of a service provider's deferral election, or such a cancellation may be made, due to an unforeseeable emergency or a hardship distribution pursuant to § 1.401(k)-1(d)(3). The deferral election must be cancelled, not merely postponed or otherwise delayed. Accordingly, any later deferral election will be subject to the provisions governing initial deferral elections. See § 1.409A-2(a).

(ix) *Plan terminations and liquidations.*—A plan may provide for the acceleration of the time and form of a payment, or a payment under such plan may be made, where the acceleration of the payment is made pursuant to a termination and liquidation of the plan in accordance with one of the following:

(A) The service recipient's termination and liquidation of the plan within 12 months of a corporate dissolution taxed under section 331, or with the approval of a bankruptcy court pursuant to 11 U.S.C. § 503(b)(1)(A), provided that the amounts deferred under the plan are included in the participants' gross incomes in the latest of the following years (or, if earlier, the taxable year in which the amount is actually or constructively received):

(1) The calendar year in which the plan termination and liquidation occurs.

(2) The first calendar year in which the amount is no longer subject to a substantial risk of forfeiture.

(3) The first calendar year in which the payment is administratively practicable.

(B) The service recipient's termination and liquidation of the plan pursuant to irrevocable action taken by the service recipient within the 30 days preceding or the 12 months following a change in control event (as defined in paragraph (i)(5) of this section), provided that this paragraph will only apply to a payment under a plan if all agreements, methods, programs, and other arrangements sponsored by the service recipient immediately after the time of the change in control event with respect to which deferrals of compensation are treated as having been deferred under a single plan under §1.409A-1(c)(2) are terminated and liquidated with respect to each participant that experienced the change in control event, so that under the terms of the termination and liquidation all such participants are required to receive all amounts of compensation deferred under the terminated agreements, methods, programs, and other arrangements within 12 months of the date the service recipient irrevocably takes all necessary action to terminate and liquidate the agreements, methods, programs, and other arrangements. Solely for purposes of this paragraph (j)(4)(ix)(B), the applicable service recipient with the discretion to liquidate and terminate the agreements, methods, programs, and other arrangements is the service recipient that is primarily liable immediately after the transaction for the payment of the deferred compensation.

(C) The service recipient's termination and liquidation of the plan, provided that—

(1) The termination and liquidation does not occur proximate to a downturn in the financial health of the service recipient;

(2) The service recipient terminates and liquidates all agreements, methods, programs, and other arrangements sponsored by the service recipient that would be aggregated with any terminated and liquidated agreements, methods, programs, and other arrangements under §1.409A-1(c) if the same service provider had deferrals of compensation under all of the agreements, methods, programs, and other arrangements that are terminated and liquidated;

(3) No payments in liquidation of the plan are made within 12 months of the date the service recipient takes all necessary action to irrevocably terminate and liquidate the plan other than payments that would be payable under the terms of the plan if the action to terminate and liquidate the plan had not occurred;

(4) All payments are made within 24 months of the date the service recipient takes all necessary action to irrevocably terminate and liquidate the plan; and

(5) The service recipient does not adopt a new plan that would be aggregated with any terminated and liquidated plan under §1.409A-1(c) if the same service provider participated in both plans, at any time within three years following the date the service recipient takes all necessary action to irrevocably terminate and liquidate the plan.

(D) Such other events and conditions as the Commissioner may prescribe in generally applicable guidance published in the Internal Revenue Bulletin (see §601.601(d)(2) of this chapter).

(x) *Certain distributions to avoid a nonallocation year under section 409(p).*—A plan may provide for an acceleration of the time and form of a payment, or a payment may be made under such plan, to prevent the occurrence of a nonallocation year (within the meaning of section 409(p)(3)) in the plan year of an employee stock ownership plan next following the plan year in which such payment is made, provided that the amount distributed may not exceed 125 percent of the minimum amount of distribution necessary to avoid the occurrence of a nonallocation year. Solely for purposes of determining permissible distributions under this paragraph (j)(4)(x), synthetic equity (within the meaning of section 409(p)(6)(C) and §1.409(p)-1(f)) granted during the plan year of the employee stock ownership plan in which such payment is made is disregarded for purposes of determining whether the subsequent plan year would result in a nonallocation year.

(xi) *Payment of state, local, or foreign taxes.*—A plan may provide for an acceleration of the time and form of a payment, or a payment may be made under such plan, to reflect payment of state, local, or foreign tax obligations arising from participation in the plan that apply to an amount deferred under the plan before the amount is paid or made available to the participant (the state, local, or foreign tax amount). Such payment may not exceed the amount of such taxes due as a result of participation in the plan. Such payment may be made by distributions to the participant in the form of withholding pursuant to provisions of applicable state, local, or foreign law or by distribution directly to the participant. Additionally, an arrangement may provide for the acceleration of the time or schedule of payment, or a payment may be made under such arrangement, to pay the income tax at source on wages imposed under section 3401 as a result of such payment and to pay the additional income tax at source on wages imposed under section 3401 attributable to such additional section 3401 wages and taxes. However, the total payment under this acceleration provision must not exceed the aggregate of the state, local, and foreign tax amount, and the income tax withholding related to such state, local, and foreign tax amount.

(xii) *Cancellation of deferral elections due to disability.*—A plan may provide for a cancellation of a service provider's deferral election, or a cancellation of such election may be made, where such cancellation occurs by the later of the end of the taxable year of the service provider or the 15th day of the third month following the date the service provider incurs a disability. For purposes of this paragraph, a disability refers to any medically determinable physical or mental impairment resulting in the service provider's inability to perform the duties of his or her position or any substantially similar position, where such impairment can be expected to result in death or can be expected to last for a continuous period of not less than six months.

(xiii) *Certain offsets.*—A plan may provide for the acceleration of the time or schedule of a payment, or a payment may be made under such plan, as satisfaction of a debt of the service provider to the service recipient, where such debt is incurred in the ordinary course of the service relationship between the service recipient and the service provider, the entire amount of reduction in any of the service recipient's taxable years does not exceed $5,000, and the reduction is made at the same time and in the same amount as the debt otherwise would have been due and collected from the service provider.

(xiv) *Bona fide disputes as to a right to a payment.*—A plan may provide for the acceleration of the time or schedule of one or more payments, or a payment may be made under such plan, where such payments occur as part of a settlement between the service provider and the service recipient of an arm's length, bona fide dispute as to the service provider's right to the deferred amount. Discretion to accelerate payments, other than due to an arm's length settlement of a bona fide dispute as to the service provider's right to the deferred amount, is not permitted under this paragraph (j)(4)(xiv). Whether a payment qualifies for the exception under this paragraph is based on all relevant facts and circumstances. A payment will be presumed not to meet this exception unless the payment is subject to a substantial reduction in the value of the payment made in relation to the amount that would have been payable had there been no dispute as to the service provider's right to the payment. For this purpose, a reduction that is less than 25 percent of the present value of the deferred amount in dispute generally is not a substantial reduction. In addition, a payment will be presumed not to meet this exception if the payment is made proximate to a downturn in the financial health of the service recipient.

(5) *Nonqualified deferred compensation plans linked to qualified employer plans or certain other arrangements.*—If a nonqualified deferred compensation plan provides that the amount deferred under the plan is the amount determined under the formula determining benefits under a qualified employer plan (as defined in §1.409A-1(a)(2)), or a broad-based foreign retirement plan (as defined in §1.409A-1(a)(3)(v)) maintained by the service recipient but applied without regard to one or more limitations applicable to the qualified employer plan under the Internal Revenue Code or to the broad-based foreign retirement plan under other applicable law, or that the amount deferred under the nonqualified deferred compensation plan is determined as an amount offset by some or all of the benefits provided under the qualified employer plan or broad-based foreign retirement plan, a decrease in amounts deferred under the nonqualified deferred compensation plan that results directly from the operation of the qualified employer plan or broad-based foreign retirement plan (other than service provider actions described in paragraphs (j)(5)(iii) and (iv) of this section) including changes in benefit limitations applicable to the qualified employer plan or the broad-based foreign retirement plan under the Internal Revenue Code or other applicable law does not constitute an acceleration of a payment under the nonqualified deferred compensation plan, provided that such operation does not otherwise result in a change in the time or form of a payment under the nonqualified deferred compensation plan, and provided further that the change in the amounts deferred under the nonqualified deferred compensation plan does not exceed such change in the amounts deferred under the qualified employer plan or the broad-based foreign retirement plan, as applicable. In addition, with respect to such a nonqualified deferred compensation plan, the following actions or failures to act will not constitute an acceleration of a payment under the nonqualified deferred compensation plan even if in accordance with the terms of the nonqualified deferred compensation plan, the actions or inactions result in a decrease in the amounts deferred under the plan, provided that such actions or inactions do not otherwise affect the time or form of payment under the nonqualified deferred compensation plan, and provided further that with respect to actions or inactions described in paragraphs (j)(5)(i) and (ii) of this section, the change in the amount deferred under the nonqualified deferred compensation plan does not exceed the change in the amounts deferred under the qualified

employer plan or the broad-based foreign retirement plan, as applicable:

(i) A service provider's action or inaction under the qualified employer plan or broad-based foreign retirement plan with respect to whether to elect to receive a subsidized benefit or an ancillary benefit under the qualified employer plan or broad-based foreign retirement plan.

(ii) The amendment of a qualified employer plan or broad-based foreign retirement plan to increase benefits provided under such plan, or to add or remove a subsidized benefit or an ancillary benefit.

(iii) A service provider's action or inaction under a qualified employer plan with respect to elective deferrals and other employee pre-tax contributions subject to the contribution restrictions under section 401(a)(30) or section 402(g), including an adjustment to a deferral election under such qualified employer plan, provided that for any given taxable year, the service provider's action or inaction does not result in a decrease in the amounts deferred under all nonqualified deferred compensation plans in which the service provider participates (other than amounts described in paragraph (j)(5)(iv) of this section) in excess of the limit with respect to elective deferrals under section 402(g)(1)(A), (B), and (C) in effect for the taxable year in which such action or inaction occurs.

(iv) A service provider's action or inaction under a qualified employer plan with respect to elective deferrals and other employee pre-tax contributions subject to the contributions restrictions under section 401(a)(30) or section 402(g), and after-tax contributions by the service provider to a qualified employer plan that provides for such contributions, that affects the amounts that are credited under one or more nonqualified deferred compensation plans as matching amounts or other similar amounts contingent on such elective deferrals, pre-tax contributions, or after-tax contributions, provided that the total of such matching or contingent amounts, as applicable, never exceeds 100 percent of the matching or contingent amounts that would be provided under the qualified employer plan absent any plan-based restrictions that reflect limits on qualified plan contributions under the Internal Revenue Code.

(6) *Changes in elections under a cafeteria plan.*—A change in an election under a cafeteria plan (as defined in section 125(d)) does not result in an accelerated payment of an amount deferred under a nonqualified deferred compensation plan to the extent that the change in the amount deferred under the nonqualified deferred compensation plan results solely from the application of the change in amount eligible to be treated as compensation under the terms of the nonqualified deferred compensation plan resulting from the election change under the cafeteria plan, to a benefit formula under the nonqualified deferred compensation plan based upon the service provider's eligible compensation, and only to the extent that such change applies in the same manner as any other increase or decrease in compensation would apply to such benefit formula. [Reg. §1.409A-3.]

☐ [*T.D.* 9321, 4-10-2007 (corrected 7-30-2007).]

[Reg. §1.409A-4]

§1.409A-4. Calculation of income inclusion.—[Reserved].

☐ [*T.D.* 9321, 4-10-2007.]

[Reg. §1.409A-5]

§1.409A-5. Funding.—[Reserved].

☐ [*T.D.* 9321, 4-10-2007.]

[Reg. §1.409A-6]

§1.409A-6. Application of section 409A and effective dates.— (a) *Statutory application and effective dates.*—(1) *Application to amounts deferred.*—(i) *In general.*—Except as otherwise provided in this section, section 409A applies with respect to amounts deferred in taxable years beginning after December 31, 2004, and with respect to amounts deferred in taxable years beginning before January 1, 2005, if the plan under which the deferral is made is materially modified after October 3, 2004. For amounts deferred in taxable years beginning before January 1, 2005, under a plan that is materially modified after October 3, 2004, whether the plan complies with the requirements of section 409A and these regulations is determined by reference to the terms of the plan in effect as of, and any actions taken under the plan on or after, the date of the material modification. Section 409A is applicable with respect to earnings on amounts deferred only to the extent that section 409A is applicable with respect to the amounts deferred. Accordingly, section 409A does not apply with respect to earnings on amounts deferred before January 1, 2005, unless section 409A applies with respect to the amounts deferred. For this purpose, a right to earnings that is subject to a substantial risk of forfeiture (as defined in §1.83-3(c)) or a require-

ment to perform further services, on an amount deferred that is not subject to a substantial risk of forfeiture (as defined in §1.83-3(c)) or a requirement to perform further services, is not treated as earnings on the amount deferred, but a separate right to compensation. Except as otherwise provided in applicable guidance (see §601.601(d)(2) of this chapter), the provisions of §§1.409A-1 through 1.409A-5 and this section provide the exclusive means of identifying agreements, methods, programs, or other arrangements subject to section 409A, and the exclusive means of satisfying the requirements of section 409A with respect to such agreements, methods, programs, or other arrangements.

(ii) *Collectively bargained plans.*—Section 409A does not apply with respect to amounts deferred under a plan maintained pursuant to one or more bona fide collective bargaining agreements in effect on October 3, 2004, for the period ending on the earlier of the date on which the last of such collective bargaining agreements terminates (determined without regard to any extension thereof after October 3, 2004) or December 31, 2009.

(2) *Identification of date of deferral for statutory effective date purposes.*—For purposes of determining whether section 409A is applicable with respect to an amount, the amount is considered deferred before January 1, 2005, if before January 1, 2005, the service provider had a legally binding right to be paid the amount, and the right to the amount was earned and vested. For purposes of this paragraph (a)(2), a right to an amount was earned and vested only if the amount was not subject to a substantial risk of forfeiture (as defined in §1.83-3(c)) or a requirement to perform further services. Amounts to which the service provider did not have a legally binding right before January 1, 2005 (for example because the service recipient retained discretion to reduce the amount), will not be considered deferred before January 1, 2005. In addition, amounts to which the service provider had a legally binding right before January 1, 2005, but the right to which was subject to a substantial risk of forfeiture or a requirement to perform further services after December 31, 2004, are not considered deferred before January 1, 2005, for purposes of the effective date. Notwithstanding the foregoing, an amount to which the service provider had a legally binding right before January 1, 2005, but for which the service provider was required to continue performing services to retain the right only through the completion of the payroll period (as defined in §1.409A-1(b)(3)) that includes December 31, 2004, is not treated as subject to a requirement to perform further services (or a substantial risk of forfeiture) for purposes of the effective date. For purposes of this paragraph (a)(2), a stock option, stock appreciation right, or similar compensation that on or before December 31, 2004, was immediately exercisable for cash or substantially vested property (as defined in §1.83-3(b)) is treated as earned and vested, regardless of whether the right would terminate if the service provider ceased providing services for the service recipient.

(3) *Calculation of amount of compensation deferred for statutory effective date purposes.*—(i) *Nonaccount balance plans.*—The amount of compensation deferred before January 1, 2005, under a nonqualified deferred compensation plan that is a nonaccount balance plan (as defined in §1.409A-1(c)(2)(i)(C)), equals the present value of the amount to which the service provider would have been entitled under the plan if the service provider voluntarily terminated services without cause on December 31, 2004, and received a payment of the benefits available from the plan on the earliest possible date allowed under the plan to receive a payment of benefits following the termination of services, and received the benefits in the form with the maximum value. Notwithstanding the foregoing, for any subsequent taxable year of the service provider, the grandfathered amount may increase to equal the present value of the benefit the service provider actually becomes entitled to, in the form and at the time actually paid, determined under the terms of the plan (including applicable limits under the Internal Revenue Code), as in effect on October 3, 2004, without regard to any further services rendered by the service provider after December 31, 2004, or any other events affecting the amount of or the entitlement to benefits (other than a participant election with respect to the time or form of an available benefit). For purposes of calculating the present value of a benefit under this paragraph (a)(3)(i), reasonable actuarial assumptions and methods must be used. Whether assumptions and methods are reasonable for this purpose is determined as of each date the benefit is valued for purposes of determining the grandfathered benefit, provided that any reasonable actuarial assumptions and methods that were used by the service recipient with respect to such benefit as of December 31, 2004, will continue to be treated as reasonable assumptions and methods for purposes of calculating the grandfathered benefit. Actuarial assumptions and methods will be presumed reasonable if they are the same as those used to value benefits under a qualified plan sponsored by the service recipient the benefits under which are part of the benefit formula under, or otherwise impact the amount of

benefits under, the nonaccount balance nonqualified deferred compensation plan.

(ii) *Account balance plans.*—The amount of compensation deferred before January 1, 2005, under a nonqualified deferred compensation plan that is an account balance plan (as defined in §1.409A-1(c)(2)(i)(A)), equals the portion of the service provider's account balance as of December 31, 2004, the right to which was earned and vested (as defined in paragraph (a)(2) of this section) as of December 31, 2004, plus any future contributions to the account, the right to which was earned and vested (as defined in paragraph (a)(2) of this section) as of December 31, 2004, to the extent such contributions are actually made.

(iii) *Equity-based compensation plans.*—For purposes of determining the amounts deferred before January 1, 2005, under an equity-based compensation plan, the rules of paragraph (a)(3)(ii) of this section governing account balance plans are applied except that the account balance is deemed to be the amount of the payment available to the service provider on December 31, 2004 (or that would be available to the service provider if the right were immediately exercisable) the right to which is earned and vested (as defined in paragraph (a)(2) of this section) as of December 31, 2004. For this purpose, the payment available to the service provider excludes any exercise price or other amount that must be paid by the service provider.

(iv) *Earnings.*—Earnings on amounts deferred under a plan before January 1, 2005, include only income (whether actual or notional) attributable to the amounts deferred under a plan as of December 31, 2004, or to such income. For example, notional interest earned under the plan on amounts deferred in an account balance plan as of December 31, 2004, generally will be treated as earnings on amounts deferred under the plan before January 1, 2005. Similarly, an increase in the amount of payment available pursuant to a stock option, stock appreciation right, or other equity-based compensation above the amount of payment available as of December 31, 2004, due to appreciation in the underlying stock after December 31, 2004, or accrual of other earnings such as dividends, is treated as earnings on the amount deferred. In the case of a nonaccount balance plan, earnings include the increase, due solely to the passage of time, in the present value of the future payments to which the service provider has obtained a legally binding right, the present value of which constituted the amounts deferred under the plan before January 1, 2005. Thus, for each year, there will be an increase (determined using the same interest rate used to determine the amounts deferred under the plan before January 1, 2005) resulting from the shortening of the discount period before the future payments are made, plus, if applicable, an increase in the present value resulting from the service provider's survivorship during the year. However, an increase in the potential benefits under a nonaccount balance plan due to, for example, an application of an increase in compensation after December 31, 2004, to a final average pay plan or subsequent eligibility for an early retirement subsidy, does not constitute earnings on the amounts deferred under the plan before January 1, 2005.

(v) *Definition of plan.*—For purposes of paragraphs (a)(1), (2), and (3) of this section, the term "plan" has the meaning provided in §1.409A-1(c), except that the plan aggregation rules do not apply for purposes of the actuarial assumptions and methods used in paragraph (a)(3)(i) of this section. Accordingly, different reasonable actuarial assumptions and methods may be used to calculate the amounts deferred by a service provider in two different agreements, methods, programs, or other arrangements each of which constitutes a nonaccount balance plan.

(4) *Material modifications.*—(i) *In general.*—Except as otherwise provided, a modification of a plan is a material modification if a benefit or right existing as of October 3, 2004, is materially enhanced or a new material benefit or right is added, and such material enhancement or addition affects amounts earned and vested before January 1, 2005. Such material benefit enhancement or addition is a material modification whether it occurs pursuant to an amendment or to the service recipient's exercise of discretion under the terms of the plan. For example, an amendment to a plan to add a provision that payments of deferred amounts earned and vested before January 1, 2005, may be allowed upon request if service providers are required to forfeit 20 percent of the amount of the payment (a haircut) would be a material modification to the plan. Similarly, a material modification would occur if a service recipient exercised discretion to accelerate vesting of a benefit under the plan to a date on or before December 31, 2004. However, it is not a material modification for a service recipient to exercise discretion over the time and manner of payment of a benefit to the extent such discretion is provided under the terms of the plan as of October 3, 2004. It is not a material modification for a service provider to exercise a right permitted under the plan as in effect on October 3, 2004. The amendment of a

plan to bring the plan into compliance with the provisions of section 409A will not be treated as a material modification. However, a plan amendment or the exercise of discretion under the terms of the plan that materially enhances an existing benefit or right or adds a new material benefit or right will be considered a material modification even if the enhanced or added benefit would be permitted under section 409A. For example, the addition of a right to a payment upon an unforeseeable emergency of an amount earned and vested before January 1, 2005, would be considered a material modification. The reduction of an existing benefit is not a material modification. For example, the removal of a haircut provision generally would not constitute a material modification. The following modifications also are not material modifications for purposes of this paragraph (a)(4)(i):

(A) The establishment of or contributions to a trust or other arrangement from which benefits under the plan are to be paid is not a material modification of the plan, provided that the contribution to the trust or other arrangement would not otherwise cause an amount to be includible in the service provider's gross income.

(B) The modification of a provision requiring the immediate cancellation of a current deferral election, to require the cancellation of deferrals for the same length of time beginning with the first date at which the application of such cancellation would not violate section 409A (for example, the first date of the service provider's first taxable year following the cancellation).

(C) Compliance with a domestic relations order (as defined in §1.409A-3(j)(4)(ii)) with respect to payments to an individual other than the service provider, or an amendment to a plan to require compliance with a domestic relations order with respect to payments to an individual other than the service provider.

(D) The modification of a plan providing a life annuity form of payment to permit an election between the existing life annuity form of payment and other forms of annuity payments that would be treated as a single form of payment with the existing life annuity form of payment under §1.409A-2(b)(2)(ii).

(E) The modification of a grandfathered plan to add a limited cashout feature consistent with §1.409A-3(j)(4)(v) (exception to prohibition on accelerated payments).

(ii) *Adoptions of new plans.*—It is presumed that the adoption of a new plan or the grant of an additional benefit under an existing plan after October 3, 2004, and before January 1, 2005, constitutes a material modification of a plan. However, the presumption may be rebutted by demonstrating that the adoption of the plan or grant of the additional benefit was consistent with the service recipient's historical compensation practices. For example, the presumption that the grant of a discounted stock option on November 1, 2004, is a material modification of a plan may be rebutted by demonstrating that the grant was consistent with the historic practice of granting substantially similar discounted stock options (both as to terms and amounts) each November for a significant number of years. Notwithstanding paragraph (a)(4)(i) of this section and this paragraph (a)(4)(ii), the grant of an additional benefit under an existing plan that consists of a deferral of additional compensation not otherwise provided under the plan as of October 3, 2004, will be treated as a material modification of the plan only as to the additional deferral of compensation, if the plan explicitly identifies the additional deferral of compensation and provides that the additional deferral of compensation is subject to section 409A. Accordingly, amendments to conform a plan to the requirements of section 409A with respect to deferrals under a plan occurring after December 31, 2004, will not constitute a material modification of the plan with respect to amounts deferred that are earned and vested on or before December 31, 2004, provided that there is no concurrent material modification with respect to the amount of, or rights to, amounts deferred that were earned and vested on or before December 31, 2004. Similarly, a grant of an additional benefit under a new plan adopted after October 3, 2004, and before January 1, 2005, will not be treated as a material modification of an existing plan to the extent that the new plan explicitly identifies additional deferrals of compensation and provides that the additional deferrals of compensation are subject to section 409A.

(iii) *Suspension or termination of a plan.*—A cessation of deferrals under, or termination of, a plan, pursuant to the provisions of such plan, is not a material modification. Amending a plan to provide participants an election whether to terminate participation in a plan generally constitutes a material modification of the plan.

(iv) *Changes to investment measures—account balance plans.*—With respect to an account balance plan (as defined in §1.409A-1(c)(2)(i)(A)), it is not a material modification to change a notional investment measure to, or to add to an existing investment measure, an investment measure that qualifies as a predetermined actual investment within the meaning of §31.3121(v)(2)-1(d)(2) of this chapter or, for any given taxable year, reflects a reasonable rate of interest (determined in accordance with § 31.3121(v)(2)-1(d)(2)(i)(C) of this chapter).

(v) *Stock rights.*—The modification, extension, or renewal of a stock right will not constitute a material modification of the stock right, if the modification, extension, or renewal would not be treated as the grant of a new stock right under § 1.409A-1(b)(5)(v)(A), and would not result in the stock right being treated as having had a deferral feature from the date of grant pursuant to § 1.409A-1(b)(5)(v)(C).

(vi) *Rescission of modifications.*—Any modification to the terms of a plan that would inadvertently result in treatment as a material modification under this section is not considered a material modification of the plan to the extent the modification in the terms of the plan is rescinded by the earlier of a date before the right is exercised (if the change grants a discretionary right) or the last day of the taxable year of the service provider during which such change occurred. Thus, for example, if a service recipient modifies the terms of a plan on March 1 to allow an individual employee to elect a new change in the time or form of payment without realizing that such a change constituted a material modification that would subject the plan to the requirements of section 409A, and the modification is rescinded on November 1, then if no change in the time or form of payment has been made pursuant to the modification before November 1, the plan is not considered materially modified under this section.

(vii) *Definition of plan.*—For purposes of this paragraph (a)(4), the term "plan" has the same meaning provided in § 1.409A-1(c), except that the plan aggregation rules of § 1.409A-1(c)(2) do not apply.

(b) *Regulatory applicability date.*—§ 1.409A-1, § 1.409A-2, § 1.409A-3 and this section are applicable for taxable years beginning on or after January 1, 2008. [Reg. § 1.409A-6.]

☐ [*T.D. 9321, 4-10-2007 (corrected 7-30-2007, 9-23-2008 and 10-6-2008).*]

[Reg. § 1.410(a)-1]

§ 1.410(a)-1. Minimum participation standards; general rules.—(a) *In general.*—A plan is not a qualified plan (and a trust forming a part of such plan is not a qualified trust) unless the plan satisfies—

(1) The minimum age and service requirements of section 410(a)(1) and § 1.410(a)-3,

(2) The maximum age requirements of section 410(a)(2) and § 1.410(a)-4, and

(3) The minimum coverage requirements of section 410(b)(1) and §§ 1.410(b)-2 through 1.410(b)-10.

(b) *Organization of regulations relating to minimum participation standards.*—(1) *General rules.*—This section prescribes general rules relating to the minimum participation standards provided by section 410.

(2) *Effective dates.*—Section 1.410(a)-2 provides rules under section 1017 of the Employee Retirement Income Security Act of 1974 relating to effective dates under section 410.

(3) *Age and service conditions.*—Section 1.410(a)-3 provides rules under Section 410(a)(1) relating to minimum age and service conditions.

(4) *Maximum age and time of participation.*—Section 1.410(a)-4 provides rules under section 410(a)(2) and (4) relating to maximum age and time of participation.

(5) *Year of service; breaks in service.*—For rules relating to years of service and breaks in service, see 29 CFR Part 2530 (Department of Labor regulations relating to minimum standards for employee pension benefit plans). See § 1.410(a)-5 for rules under section 410(a)(3)(B) relating to seasonal industries and for certain rules under section 410(a)(5) relating to breaks in service.

(6) *Breaks in service.*—Section 1.410(a)-6 provides special rules under section 1017(f) of the Employee Retirement Income Security Act of 1974 relating to amendment of break in service rules.

(7) *Elapsed time.*—Section 1.410(a)-7 provides rules under sections 410 and 411 relating to the elapsed time method of crediting years of service.

(8) *Coverage.*—Sections 1.410(b)-2 through 1.410(b)-10 provides rules relating to the minimum coverage requirements provided by section 410(b)(1).

(9) *Church election.*—Section 1.410(d)-1 provides rules relating to the election by a church to have participation, vesting, funding, etc., provisions apply.

(c) *Application of participation standards to certain plans.*—(1) *General rule.*—Except as provided in subparagraph (2) of this paragraph, section 410 does not apply to—

(i) A governmental plan (within the meaning of section 414(d) and the regulations thereunder),

(ii) A church plan (within the meaning of section 414(e) and the regulations thereunder) which has not made the elections provided by section 410(d) and the regulations thereunder,

(iii) A plan which has not provided for employer contributions at any time after September 2, 1974, and

(iv) A plan established and maintained by a society, order, or association described in section 501(c)(8) or (9), if no part of the contributions to or under such plan are made by employers of participants in such plan.

(2) *Participation requirements.*—A plan described in subparagraph (1) of this paragraph shall, for purposes of section 401(a), be treated as meeting the requirements of section 410 if such plan meets the coverage requirements resulting from the application of section 401(a)(3) as in effect on September 1, 1974. In applying the rules of that paragraph (d) to plans described in this paragraph (c), employees whose principal duties consist in supervising the work of other employees shall be treated as officers, shareholders, and highly compensated employees.

(d) *Supersession.*—Section 11.410(a)-1 through 11.410(d)-1 (other than § 11.410(b)-1(d)(2)), inclusive, of the Temporary Income Tax Regulations under the Employee Retirement Income Security Act of 1974 are superseded by this section and §§ 1.410(a)-2 through 1.410(d)-1. [Reg. § 1.410(a)-1.]

☐ [*T.D. 7508, 9-14-77. Amended by T.D. 7703, 6-16-80, T.D. 7735, 11-10-80 and T.D. 9849, 3-11-2019.*]

[Reg. § 1.410(a)-2]

§ 1.410(a)-2. Effective dates.—(a) *Plans not in existence on January 1, 1974.*—Under section 1017(a) of the Employee Retirement Income Security Act of 1974, in the case of a plan which was not in existence on January 1, 1974, section 410 and the regulations thereunder apply for plan years beginning after September 2, 1974. See paragraph (c) of this section for time plan is considered in existence.

(b) *Plans in existence on January 1, 1974.*—Under section 1017(b) of the Employee Retirement Income Security Act of 1974, in the case of a plan which was in existence on January 1, 1974, section 410 and the regulations thereunder apply for plan years beginning after December 31, 1975. See paragraph (c) of this section for time plan is considered to be in existence.

(c) *Time of plan existence.*—(1) *General rule.*—For purposes of this section, a plan is considered to be in existence on a particular day if—

(i) The plan on or before that day was reduced to writing and adopted by the employer (including, in the case of a corporate employer, formal approval by the employer's board of directors and, if required, shareholders), even though no amounts had been contributed under the plan as of such day, and

(ii) The plan was not terminated on or before that day.

(2) *Collectively bargained plan.*—Notwithstanding subparagraph (1) of this paragraph, a plan described in section 413(a), relating to a plan maintained pursuant to a collective bargaining agreement, is considered to be in existence on a particular day if—

(i) On or before that day there is a legally enforceable agreement to establish such a plan signed by the employer, and

(ii) The employer contributions to be made to the plan are set forth in the agreement.

(3) *Special rule.*—If a plan is considered to be in existence on January 1, 1974, under subparagraph (1) of this paragraph, any other plan with which such existing plan is merged or consolidated shall also be considered to be in existence on such date.

(d) *Certain existing plans may elect new provisions.*—(1) *In general.*—The plan administrator (as defined in section 414(g)) of a plan that was in existence on January 1, 1974, may elect to have the provisions of the Code relating to participation, vesting, funding, and form of benefit (as in effect from time to time) apply to a plan year selected by the plan administrator which begins after September 2, 1974, but before the otherwise applicable effective dates determined under section 1017(b) or (c), 1021, or 1024 of the Employee Retirement Income Security Act of 1974, and to all subsequent plan years. The provisions referred to are the amendments to the Code made by sections 1011, 1012, 1013, 1015, 1016(a)(1) through (11) and (13) through (27), 1021, and 1022(b) of the Employee Retirement Income Security Act of 1974.

(2) *Election is irrevocable.*—Any election made under this paragraph, once made, shall be irrevocable.

(3) *Procedure and time for making election.*—An election under this paragraph shall be made by attaching a statement to either the annual return required under section 6058(a) (or an amended return) with respect to the plan which is filed for the first plan year for which the election is effective or to a written request for a determination letter relating to the qualification of the plan under section 401(a), 403(a), or 405(a) of the Code and, if trusteed, the exempt status under section 501(a) of the Code of a trust constituting a part of the plan. If the election is made with a written request for a determination letter, the election may be conditioned upon issuance of a favorable determination letter and will become irrevocable upon issuance of such letter. The statement shall indicate that the election is made under section 1017(d) of the Employee Retirement Income Security Act of 1974 and the first plan year for which the election is effective.

(e) *Examples.*—The rules of this section are illustrated by the following examples:

Example (1). A plan is adopted on January 2, 1974, effective as of January 1, 1974. The plan is not considered to have been in existence on January 1, 1974.

Example (2). A plan was in existence on January 1, 1974, and was amended on November 1, 1974, to increase benefits. The fact that the plan was amended is not relevant and the amended plan is considered to be in existence on January 1, 1974.

Example (3). (i) A subsidiary business corporation is a member of a controlled group of corporations within the meaning of IRC section 1563(a). On November 1, 1974, the plan of the parent corporation is amended to provide coverage for employees of the subsidiary corporation. This amendment of the parent corporation's plan does not affect the effective date of section 410 with respect to the parent corporation's plan. No distinction is made for this purpose between employees of the parent corporation and employees of the subsidiary corporation.

(ii) If the subsidiary adopted a separate plan on November 1, 1974, under paragraph (a) of this section, section 410 would apply to that plan for its first plan year beginning after September 2, 1974. However, the adoption of a different plan by the subsidiary would not affect the time section 410 applies to the plan of the parent corporation. If, instead of adopting its own separate plan, the subsidiary merely executed an adoption agreement under the terms of the parent plan providing that a subsidiary, upon the execution of an adoption agreement, will become part of the parent plan, the effective date of section 410 with respect to such plan will not be affected by the adoption of the plan by the subsidiary. [Reg. § 1.410(a)-2.]

☐ [T.D. 7508, 9-14-77.]

[Reg. § 1.410(a)-3]

§ 1.410(a)-3. **Minimum age and service conditions.**—(a) *General rule.*—Except as provided by paragraph (b) or (c) of this section, a plan is not a qualified plan (and a trust forming a part of such plan is not a qualified trust) if the plan requires, as a condition of participation in the plan, that an employee complete a period of service with the employer or employers maintaining the plan extending beyond the later of—

(1) *Age 25.*—The date on which the employee attains the age of 25; or

(2) *One year of service.*—The date on which the employee completes 1 year of service.

(b) *Special rule for plan with 3 year-100 percent vesting.*—A plan which provides that after not more than 3 years of service each participant's right to his accrued benefit under the plan is completely nonforfeitable (within the meaning of section 411 and the regulations thereunder) at the time such benefit accrues satisfies the requirements of paragraph (a) of this section if the period of service required by the plan as a condition of participation does not extend beyond the later of—

(1) *Age 25.*—The date on which the employee attains the age of 25; or

(2) *Three years of service.*—The date on which the employee completes 3 years of service.

(c) *Special rule for employees of certain educational institutions.*—A plan maintained exclusively for employees of an educational institution (as defined in section 170(b)(1)(A)(ii)) by an employer exempt from tax under section 501(a) which provides that after 1 year of service each participant's right to his accrued benefit under the plan is completely nonforfeitable (within the meaning of section 411 and the regulations thereunder) at the time such benefit accrues satisfies the requirements of paragraph (a) of this section if the period of

service required by the plan as a condition of participation does not extend beyond the later of—

(1) *Age 30.*—The date on which the employee attains the age of 30; or

(2) *One year of service.*—The date on which the employee completes 1 year of service.

(d) *Other conditions.*—Section 410(a), § 1.410(a)-4, and this section relate solely to age and service conditions and do not preclude a plan from establishing conditions, other than conditions relating to age or service, which must be satisfied by plan participants. For example, such provisions would not preclude a qualified plan from requiring, as a condition of participation, that an employee be employed within a specified job classification. See section 410(b) and the regulations thereunder for rules with respect to coverage of employees under qualified plans.

(e) *Age and service requirements.*—(1) *General rule.*—For purposes of applying the rules of this section, plan provisions may be treated as imposing age or service requirements even though the provisions do not specifically refer to age or service. Plan provisions which have the effect of requiring an age or service requirement with the employer or employers maintaining the plan will be treated as if they imposed an age or service requirement. In general, a plan under which an employee cannot participate unless he retires will impose an age and service requirement. However, a plan may provide benefits which supplement benefits provided for employees covered under a pension plan, as defined in section 3(2) of the Employee Retirement Income Security Act of 1974, satisfying the requirements of section 410(a)(1) without violating the age and service rules.

(2) *Examples.*—The rules of this paragraph are illustrated by the following examples:

Example (1). Corporation A is divided into two divisions. In order to work in division 2 an employee must first have been employed in division 1 for 5 years. A plan provision which required division 2 employment for participation will be treated as a service requirement because such a provision has the effect of requiring 5 years of service.

Example (2). Plan B requires as a condition of participation that each employee have had a driver's license for 15 years or more. This provision will be treated as an age requirement because such a provision has the effect of requiring an employee to attain a specified age.

Example (3). A plan which requires 1 year of service as a condition of participation also excludes a part-time or seasonal employee if his customary employment is for not more than 20 hours per week or 5 months in any plan year. The plan does not qualify because the provision could result in the exclusion by reason of a minimum service requirement of an employee who has completed a year of service. The plan would not qualify even though after excluding all such employees, the plan satisfied the coverage requirements of section 410(b).

Example (4). Employer A establishes a plan which covers employees after they retire and does not cover current employees unless they retire. Any employee who works past age 60 is treated as retired. The plan fails to satisfy the requirements of section 410(a) because the plan imposes a minimum age and service requirement in excess of that allowed by this section.

Example (5). Employer B establishes plan X, which provides that employees covered by qualified plan Y will receive benefits supplementing their benefits under plan Y to take into account cost of living increases after retirement. Plan X is not treated as imposing an age or service requirement.

Example (6). Employer C establishes a qualified plan satisfying the minimum age and service requirements. At a later time, entry into the plan is frozen so that employees not covered at that time cannot participate in the plan. The limitation on new participants is not treated as imposing a minimum age and service requirement. [Reg. § 1.410(a)-3.]

☐ [T.D. 7508, 9-14-77.]

[Reg. § 1.410(a)-3T]

§ 1.410(a)-3T. **Minimum age and service conditions (Temporary).**—(a) [Reserved.]

(b) *Special rule for plan with 2-year 100 percent vesting.*—A plan which provides that after not more than 2 years of service each participant's right to his or her accrued benefit under the plan is completely nonforfeitable (within the meaning of section 411 and the regulations thereunder) at the time such benefit accrues satisfies the requirements of paragraph (a) of this section if the period of service required by the plan as a condition of participation does not extend beyond the later of—

(1) [Reserved.]

(2) *Two years of service.*—The date on which the employee completes 2 years of service. For employees not described in §1.411(a)-3T(e)(1), which describes employees with one hour of service in any plan year beginning after December 31, 1988, or later in the case of certain collectively bargained plans, the preceding sentence shall be applied by substituting "3 years of service" for "2 years of service". [Temporary Reg. §1.410(a)-3T.]

□ [*T.D.* 8170, 1-5-88.]

[Reg. §1.410(a)-4]

§1.410(a)-4. Maximum age conditions and time of participation.—(a) *Maximum age conditions.*—(1) *General rule.*—A plan is not a qualified plan (and a trust forming a part of such plan is not a qualified trust) if the plan excludes from participation (on the basis of age) an employee who has attained an age specified by the plan unless—

(i) The plan is a defined benefit plan or a target benefit plan, and

(ii) The employee begins employment with the employer after the employee has attained an age specified by the plan, which age is not more than 5 years before normal retirement age (within the meaning of section 411(a)(8) and §1.411(a)-7). For purposes of this paragraph, a target benefit plan is a defined contribution plan under which the amount of employer contributions allocated to each participant is determined under a plan formula which does not allow employer discretion and on the basis of the amount necessary to provide a target benefit specified by the plan for such participant. Such target benefit must be the type of benefit which is provided by a defined benefit plan and the targeted benefit must not discriminate in favor of employees who are officers, shareholders, or highly compensated. For purposes of this paragraph, in the determination of the time an employee begins employment, any such time which is included in a period of service which may be disregarded under the break in service rules need not be taken into account.

(2) *Examples.*—The rules provided by this paragraph are illustrated by the following examples:

Example (1). A defined benefit plan provides that an employee will become a participant upon completion of 3 years of service if at such time the employee is less than age 60. The normal retirement age under the plan is age 65. The plan also provides full and immediate vesting for each of the plan's participants. Under the plan, an employee hired at age 58 would be denied participation on account of service for the first 3 years and on account of maximum age for the remaining years even though the employee was hired more than 5 years prior to the normal retirement date. The plan therefore does not satisfy section 410(a)(2).

Example (2). A defined benefit plan provides a normal retirement age of the later of age 65 or completion of 10 years of service. Because no employee could ever be hired within 5 years of his normal retirement age, the plan could not exclude employees for being over a specified age.

Example (3). Prior to the effective date of section 410, a defined benefit plan with a normal retirement age of 65 contained a maximum age 55 requirement for participation. Because of the maximum age requirement, an employee hired at age 58 was excluded from the plan. This employee is age 61 at the time that section 410 first applies to the plan. The employee cannot be excluded from participation because of age. The exclusion under section 410(a)(2) is not applicable in this instance because the employee's age at the time of hire, 58, was not within 5 years of the normal retirement age specified in the plan.

Example (4). Employee A was hired at age 50 and participated in a defined benefit plan until separating from service at age 55 with 5 years of service and with no vested benefit. At age 61, employee A was rehired within 5 years of the normal retirement age of 65 after he incurred 6 consecutive breaks in service. Because A's consecutive number of 1-year breaks (6) exceeds his year of service prior to such breaks (5), his service before the breaks may be disregarded. Consequently, A's initial employment date falling within such period may be disregarded and the plan could exclude A on account of his age because his employment commenced within 5 years of normal retirement age.

(b) *Time of participation.*—(1) *General rule.*—A plan is not a qualified plan (and a trust forming a part of such plan is not a qualified trust) unless under the plan any employee who has satisfied the applicable minimum age and service requirements specified in §1.410(a)-3, and who is otherwise entitled to participate in the plan, commences participation in the plan no later than the earlier of—

(i) The first day of the first plan year beginning after the date on which such employee first satisfied such requirements, or

(ii) The date 6 months after the date on which he first satisfied such requirements,

unless such employee was separated from service and has not returned before the date referred to in subdivision (i) or (ii), whichever is applicable. If such separated employee returns to service after either of such dates without incurring a 1-year break in service, the employee must commence participation immediately upon his return. In the case of a plan using the elapsed time method described in §1.410(a)-7, such an employee who has a period of absence commencing before the date referred to in subdivision (i) or (ii) (whichever is applicable) must commence participation as of such applicable date no later than the date such absence ended. However, if an employee's prior service is disregarded on account of the plant's break-in-service rules, then, for purposes of this subparagraph, such service is also disregarded for purposes of determining the date on which such employee first satisfied the minimum age and service requirements.

(2) *Examples.*—The rules provided by this paragraph are illustrated by the following examples:

Example (1). A calendar year plan provides that an employee may enter the plan only on the first semi-annual entry date, January 1 or July 1, after he has satisfied the applicable minimum age and service requirements specified in section 410(a)(1). The plan satisfies the requirements of this paragraph because an employee is eligible to participate no later than the earlier of (1) the first day of the first plan year beginning after he satisfied the applicable minimum age and service requirements, or (2) the date 6 months after he satisfied such requirements.

Example (2). A plan provides that an employee is not eligible to participate until the first day of the first plan year beginning after he has satisfied the minimum age and service requirements of section 410(a)(1). In this case, an employee who satisfies the "6 month" rule described in subparagraph (1) of this paragraph will not be eligible to participate in the plan. Therefore, the plan does not satisfy the requirements of this paragraph.

Example (3). A calendar year plan provides that an employee may enter the plan only on the first semi-annual entry date, January 1 or July 1, after he has satisfied the applicable minimum age and service requirements specified in section 410(a)(1). Employee A after 10 years of service separated from service in 1976 with a vested benefit. On February 1, 1990, A returns to employment covered by the plan. Assuming A completes a year of service after his return, A must participate immediately on his return, February 1. A's prior service cannot be disregarded, because he had a vested benefit when he separated from service. Therefore, the plan may not postpone his participation until July 1.

Example (4). Assume the same facts as in example (3). The plan has the break-in-service rule described in section 410(a)(5)(D) and §1.410(a)-5(c)(4). Employee B, after he had 5 years of service but no vested benefit incurs 5 consecutive 1-year breaks. Because B's prior service can be disregarded, the plan may postpone B's participation in the plan under the rule described in section 410(a)(4) and this paragraph. [Reg. §1.410(a)-4.]

□ [*T.D.* 7508, 9-14-77. *Amended by T.D.* 7703, 6-16-80.]

[Reg. §1.410(a)-5]

§1.410(a)-5. Year of service; break in service.—(a) *Year of service.*—For the rules relating to years of service under subparagraphs (A), (C), and (D) of section 410(a)(3), see regulations prescribed by the Secretary of Labor under 29 CFR Part 2530, relating to minimum standards for employee pension benefit plans. Rules relating to a general rule for a year of service, hours of service, and maritime industries apply for purposes of section 410(a) and the regulations thereunder.

(b) *Seasonal industries.*—For rules which relate to seasonal industries under section 410(a)(3)(B), see regulations prescribed by the Secretary of Labor under 29 CFR Part 2530, relating to minimum standards for employee pension benefit plans.

(c) *Breaks in service.*—(1) *General rule.*—This paragraph provides rules with respect to breaks in service under section 410(a)(5). Except as provided in subparagraphs (2), (3), (4), and (5) of this paragraph, all of an employee's years of service with the employer or employers maintaining a plan are taken into account in computing his period of service under the plan for purposes of section 410(a)(1) and §1.410(a)-3.

(2) *Employees under 3-year 100 percent vesting schedule.*—(i) *General rule.*—In the case of an employee who incurs a 1-year break in service under a plan which provides that after not more than 3 years of service, each participant's right to his accrued benefit under the plan is completely nonforfeitable (within the meaning of section 411 and the regulations thereunder) at the time such benefit

accrues, the employee's service before the break in service is not required to be taken into account after the break in service in determining the employee's years of service under section 410(a)(1) and §1.410(a)-3 if such employee has not satisfied such service requirement.

(ii) *Example.*—The rules of this subparagraph are illustrated by the following example:

Example. A qualified plan computing service by the actual counting of hours provides full and immediate vesting. The plan cannot require as a condition of participation that an employee complete 3 consecutive years of service with the employer because the requirement as to consecutive years is not permitted under section 410(a)(5). However, such a plan can require 3 years without a break in service, i.e., 3 years with no intervening years in which the employee fails to complete more than 500 hours of service. Under a plan containing such a participation requirement, the following example illustrates when employees would become eligible to participate.

| Year | Hours of service completed | | |
	Employee A	Employee B	Employee C
1	1,000	1,000	1,000
2	1,000	1,000	500
3	1,000	700	1,000
4	1,000	1,000	700
5	1,000	1,000	1,000
6	1,000	1,000	1,000

NOTE.—Employee A will have satisfied the plan's service requirement at the end of year 3, Employee B at the end of year 4, and Employee C at the end of year 6.

(3) *One-year break in service.*—(i) *In general.*—In computing the period of service of an employee who has incurred a 1-year break in service, for purposes of section 410(a)(1) and §1.410(a)-3, a plan may disregard the employee's service before the break until the employee completes a year of service after such break in service.

(ii) *Examples.*—The rules provided by this subparagraph are illustrated by the following examples:

Example (1). Employee A completes a year of service under a plan computing service by the actual counting of hours for the 12-month period ending December 31, 1980, and incurs a 1-year break in service for the 12-month period ending December 31, 1981. The plan does not contain the provisions permitted by section 410(a)(5)(B) (relating to 3-year 100 percent vesting) and section 410(a)(5)(D) (relating to nonvested participants). Thereafter, he does not complete a year of service. As of January 1, 1982, in computing his period of service under the plan his service prior to December 31, 1981, is not required to be taken into account for purposes of section 410(a)(1) and §1.410(a)-3.

Example (2). The employee in example (1) completes a year of service for the 12-month period ending December 31, 1982. Prior to December 31, 1982, in computing the employee's period of service as of any date occurring in 1982, the employee's service before December 31, 1981, is not required to be taken into account for purposes of section 410(a)(1) and §1.410(a)-3. Because the employee completed a year of service for the 12-month period ending December 31, 1982, however, his period of service is redetermined as of January 1, 1982. Upon completion of a year of service for 1982, the employee's period of service, determined as of any date occurring in 1982, includes service prior to December 31, 1981.

(4) *Nonvested participants.*—(i) *General rule.*—In the case of a participant in a plan who does not have any nonforfeitable right under the plan to his employer-derived accrued benefit and who incurs a 1-year break in service, for purposes of section 410(a)(1) and §1.410(a)-3 the plan may disregard his years of service prior to such break if the number of his consecutive 1-year breaks in service equals or exceeds his aggregate number of years of service prior to such break. In the case of a plan using the elapsed time method described in Department of Labor regulations, the plan may disregard such years of service prior to such break if the period of severance is at least one year and the period of severance equals or exceeds the prior period of service, whether or not consecutive, completed before such period of severance. The plan may in computing such aggregate number of years of service prior to such break disregard any years of service which could have been disregarded under this subparagraph by reason of any prior break in service.

(ii) *Examples.*—The rules of this subparagraph are illustrated by the following example:

Example. In 1980, A, who was hired at age 35, separates from the service of X Corporation after completing 4 years of service. At this time A had no vested benefits. In 1985, after incurring 5 consecutive one-year breaks in service, A was reemployed. Under section 410(a)(5)(D), A's 4 years of service may be disregarded because they

are exceeded by the number of years of consecutive one-year breaks (5) after such service.

(d) *Special continuity rule for certain plans.*—For special rules for computing years of service in the case of certain plans maintained by more than one employer, see regulations prescribed by the Secretary of Labor under 29 CFR Part 2530, relating to minimum standards for employee pension plans. [Reg. §1.410(a)-5.]

☐ [*T.D. 7508, 9-14-77. Amended by T.D. 7703, 6-16-80.*]

[Reg. §1.410(a)-6]

§1.410(a)-6. Amendment of break in service rules; Transitional period.—(a) *In general.*—Under section 1017(f)(1) of the Employee Retirement Income Security Act of 1974, a plan is not a qualified plan (and a trust forming a part of such plan is not a qualified trust) if the rules of the plan relating to breaks in service are amended, and—

(1) Such amendment is effective after January 1, 1974, and before the date on which section 410 becomes applicable to the plan, and

(2) Under such amendment, any employee's participation in the plan commences at any date later than the later of—

(i) The date on which his participation would commence under the break in service rules of section 410(a)(5), or

(ii) The earliest date on which his participation would commence under the plan as in effect on or after January 1, 1974.

(b) *Break in service rules.*—For purposes of paragraph (a), the term "break in service rules" means the rules provided by a plan relating to circumstances under which a period of an employee's service or plan participation is disregarded for purposes of determining his rights to participate in the plan, if under such rules such service is disregarded by reason of the employee's failure to complete a required period of service within a specified period of time. [Reg. §1.410(a)-6.]

☐ [*T.D. 7508, 9-14-77.*]

[Reg. §1.410(a)-7]

§1.410(a)-7. Elapsed time.—(a) *In general.*—(1) *Introduction to elapsed time method of crediting service.*—(i) 29 CFR §2530.200b-2 sets forth the general method of crediting service for an employee. The general method is based upon the actual counting of hours of service during the applicable 12-consecutive-month computation period. The equivalencies set forth in 29 CFR §2530.200b-3 are also methods for crediting hours of service during computation periods. Under the general method and the equivalencies, an employee receives a year's credit (in units of years of service or years of participation) for a computation period during which the employee is credited with a specified number of hours of service. In general, an employee's statutory entitlement with respect to eligibility to participate, vesting and benefit accrual is determined by totalling the number of years' credit to which an employee is entitled.

(ii) Under the alternative method set forth in this section, by contrast, an employee's statutory entitlement with respect to eligibility to participate, vesting and benefit accrual is not based upon the actual completion of a specified number of hours of service during a 12-consecutive-month period. Instead, such entitlement is determined generally with reference to the total period of time which elapses while the employee is employed (*i.e.*, while the employment relationship exists) with the employer or employers maintaining the plan. The alternative method set forth in this section is designed to enable a plan to lessen the administrative burdens associated with the maintenance of records of an employee's hours of service by permitting each employee to be credited with his or her total period of service with the employer or employers maintaining the plan, irrespective of the actual hours of service completed in any 12-consecutive-month period.

(2) *Overview of the operation of the elapsed time method.*—(i) Under the elapsed time method of crediting service, a plan is generally required to take into account the period of time which elapses while the employee is employed (*i.e.*, while the employment relationship exists) with the employer or employers maintaining the plan, regardless of the actual number of hours he or she completes during such period. Under this alternative method of crediting service, an employee's service is required to be taken into account for purposes of eligibility to participate and vesting as of the date he or she first performs an hour of service within the meaning of 29 CFR §2530.200b-2(a)(1) for the employer or employers maintaining the plan. Service is required to be taken into account for the period of time from the date the employee first performs such an hour of service until the date he or she severs from service with the employer or employers maintaining the plan.

(ii) The date the employee severs from service is the earlier of the date the employee quits, is discharged, retires or dies, or the first anniversary of the date the employee is absent from service for any other reason (*e.g.*, disability, vacation, leave of absence, layoff, etc.). Thus, for example, if an employee quits, the severance from service date is the date the employee quits. On the other hand, if an employee is granted a leave of absence (and if no intervening event occurs), the severance from service date will occur one year after the date the employee was first absent on leave, and this one year of absence is required to be taken into account as service for the employer or employers maintaining the plan. Because the severance from service date occurs on the earlier of two possible dates (*i.e.*, quit, discharge, retirement or death *or* the first anniversary of an absence from service for any other reason), a quit, discharge, retirement or death within the year after the beginning of an absence for any other reason results in an immediate severance from service. Thus, for example, if an employee dies at the end of a four-week absence resulting from illness, the severance from service date is the date of death, rather than the first anniversary date of the first day of absence for illness.

(iii) In addition, for purposes of eligibility to participate and vesting under the elapsed time method of crediting service, an employee who has severed from service by reason of a quit, discharge or retirement may be entitled to have a period of time of 12 months or less taken into account by the employer or employers maintaining the plan if the employee returns to service within a certain period of time and performs an hour of service within the meaning of 29 CFR § 2530.200b-2(a)(1). In general, the period of time during which the employee must return to service begins on the date the employee severs from service as a result of a quit, discharge or retirement and ends on the first anniversary of such date. However, if the employee is absent for any other reason (*e.g.*, layoff) and then quits, is discharged or retires, the period of time during which the employee may return and receive credit begins on the severance from service date and ends one year after the first day of absence (*e.g.*, first day of layoff). As a result of the operation of these rules, a severance from service (*e.g.*, a quit), or an absence (*e.g.*, layoff) followed by a severance from service, never results in a period of time of more than one year being required to be taken into account after an employee severs from service or is absent from service.

(iv) For purposes of benefit accrual under the elapsed time method of crediting service, an employee is entitled to have his or her service taken into account from the date he or she begins to participate in the plan until the severance from service date. Periods of severance under any circumstances are not required to be taken into account. For example, a participant who is discharged on December 14, 1980 and rehired on October 14, 1981 is not required to be credited with the 10 month period of severance for benefit accrual purposes.

(3) *Overview of certain concepts relating to the elapsed time method.*—(i) *In general.*—The rules with respect to the elapsed time method of crediting service are based on certain concepts which are defined in paragraph (b) of this section. These concepts are applied in the substantive rules contained in paragraphs (c), (d), (e), (f) and (g) of this section. The purpose of this subparagraph is to summarize these concepts.

(ii) *Employment commencement date.*—(A) A concept which is necessary in order to credit service accurately under any service crediting method is the establishment of a starting point for crediting service. The employment commencement date, which is the date on which an employee first performs an hour of service within the meaning of 29 CFR § 2530.200b-2(a)(1) for the employer or employers maintaining the plan, is used to establish the date upon which an employee must begin to receive credit for certain purposes (*e.g.*, eligibility to participate and vesting).

(B) In order to credit accurately an employee's total service with an employer or employers maintaining the plan, a plan also may provide for an "adjusted" employment commencement date (*i.e.*, a recalculation of the employment commencement date to reflect noncreditable periods of severance) or a reemployment commencement date as defined in paragraph (b)(3) of this section. Fundamentally, all three concepts rely upon the performance of an hour of service to provide a starting point for crediting service. One purpose of these three concepts is to enable plans to satisfy the requirements of this section in a variety of ways.

(C) The fundamental rule with respect to these concepts is that any plan provision is permissible so long as it satisfies the minimum standards. Thus, for example, although the rules of this section provide that credit must begin on the employment commencement date, *a plan is permitted to "adjust"* the employment commencement date to reflect periods of time for which service is not required to be credited. Similarly, a plan may wish to credit service under the elapsed time method as discrete periods of service and provide for a reemployment commencement date. Certain plans may

wish to provide for both concepts, although it is not a requirement of this section that plans so provide.

(iii) *Severance from service date.*—Another fundamental concept of the elapsed time method of crediting service is the severance from service date, which is defined as the earlier of the date on which an employee quits, retires, is discharged or dies, or the first anniversary of the first date of absence for any other reason. One purpose of the severance from service date is to provide the endpoint for crediting service under the elapsed time method. As a general proposition, service is credited from the employment commencement date (*i.e.*, the starting point) until the severance from service date (*i.e.*, the endpoint). A complementary purpose of the severance from service date is to establish the starting point for measuring a period of severance from service in order to determine a "break in service" (see paragraph (a)(3)(v) of this section). A third purpose of such date is to establish the starting point for measuring the period of time which may be required to be taken into account under the service spanning rules (see paragraph (a)(3)(vi) of this section).

(iv) *Period of service.*—A third elapsed time concept is the use of the "period of service" rather than the "year of service" in determining service to be taken into account for purposes of eligibility to participate, vesting and benefit accrual. For purposes of eligibility to participate and vesting, the period of service runs from the employment commencement date or reemployment commencement date until the severance from service date. For purposes of benefit accrual, a period of service runs from the date that a participant commences participation under the plan until the severance from service date. Because the endpoint of the period of service is marked by the severance from service date, an employee is credited with the period of time which runs during any absence from service (other than for reason of a quit, retirement, discharge or death) which is 12 months or less. Thus, for example, a three week absence for vacation is taken into account as part of a period of service and does not trigger a severance from service date.

(v) *Period of severance.*—A period of severance begins on the severance from service date and ends when an employee returns to service with the employer or employers maintaining the plan. The purpose of the period of severance is to apply the statutory "break in service" rules to an elapsed time method of crediting service.

(vi) *Service spanning.*—Under the elapsed time method of crediting service, a plan is required to credit periods of service and, under the service spanning rules, certain periods of severance of 12 months or less for purposes of eligibility to participate and vesting. Under the first service spanning rule, if an employee severs from service as a result of quit, discharge or retirement and then returns to service within 12 months, the period of severance is required to be taken into account. Also, a situation may arise in which an employee is absent from service for any reason other than quit, discharge, retirement or death and during the absence a quit, discharge or retirement occurs. The second service spanning rule provides in that set of circumstances that a plan is required to take into account the period of time between the severance from service date (*i.e.*, the date of quit, discharge or retirement) and the first anniversary of the date on which the employee was first absent, if the employee returns to service on or before such first anniversary date.

(4) *Organization and applicability.*—(i) The substantive rules for crediting service under the elapsed time method with respect to eligibility to participate are contained in paragraph (c), the rules with respect to vesting are contained in subparagraph (d), and the rules with respect to benefit accrual are contained in paragraph (e). The format of the rules is designed to enable a plan to use the elapsed time method of crediting service either for all purposes or for any one or combination of purposes under sections 410 and 411. Thus, for example, a plan may credit service for eligibility to participate purposes by the use of the general method of crediting service set forth in 29 CFR § 2530.200b-2 or by the use of any of the equivalencies set forth in 29 CFR § 2530.200b-3, while the plan may credit service for vesting and benefit accrual purposes by the use of the elapsed time method of crediting service.

(ii) A plan using the elapsed time method of crediting service for one or more classifications of employees covered under the plan may use the general method of crediting service set forth in 29 CFR § 2530.200b-2 or any of the equivalencies set forth in 29 CFR § 2530.200b-3 for other classifications of employees, provided that such classifications are reasonable and are consistently applied. Thus, for example, a plan may provide that part-time employees are credited under the general method of crediting service set forth in 29 CFR § 2530.200b-2 and full-time employees are credited under the elapsed time method. A classification, however, will not be deemed to be reasonable or consistently applied if such classification is designed with an intent to preclude an employee or employees from attaining his or her statutory entitlement with respect to eligibility to participate, vesting or benefit accrual. For example, a classification applied so that any full-time employee credited with less than 1,000 hours of service during a given 12-consecutive-month period would be considered part-time and subject to the general method of crediting service rather than the elapsed time method would not be reasonable.

(iii) Notwithstanding paragraph (a)(4)(i) and (ii) of this section, the use of the elapsed time method for some purposes or the use of the elapsed time method for some employees may, under certain circumstances, result in discrimination prohibited under section 401(a)(4), even though the use of the elapsed time method for such purposes, and for such employees, is permitted under this section.

(5) *More than one employer plans.*—For special rules for computing years of service in the case of a plan maintained by more than one employer, see 29 CFR Part 2530 (Department of Labor regulations relating to minimum standards for employee pension benefit plans).

(b) *Definitions.*—(1) *Employment commencement date.*—For purposes of this section, the term "employment commencement date" shall mean the date on which the employee first performs an hour of service within the meaning of 29 CFR § 2530.200b-2(a)(1) for the employer or employers maintaining the plan.

(2) *Severance from service date.*—For purposes of this section, a "severance from service" shall occur on the earlier of—

(i) The date on which an employee quits, retires, is discharged or dies; or

(ii) The first anniversary of the first date of a period in which an employee remains absent from service (with or without pay) with the employer or employers maintaining the plan for any reason other than quit, retirement, discharge or death, such as vacation, holiday, sickness, disability, leave of absence or layoff.

(3) *Reemployment commencement date.*—For purposes of this section, the term "reemployment commencement date" shall mean the first date, following a period of severance from service which is not required to be taken into account under the service spanning rules in paragraphs (c)(2)(iii) and (d)(1)(iii) of this section, on which the employee performs an hour of service within the meaning of 29 CFR § 2530.200b-2(a)(1) for the employer or employers maintaining the plan.

(4) *Participation commencement date.*—For purposes of this section, the term "participation commencement date" shall mean the date a participant first commences participation under the plan.

(5) *Period of severance.*—For purposes of this section, the term "period of severance" shall mean the period of time commencing on the severance from service date and ending on the date on which the employee again performs an hour of service within the meaning of 29 CFR § 2530.200b-2(a)(1) for an employer or employers maintaining the plan.

(6) *Period of service.*—(i) *General rule.*—For purposes of this section, the term "period of service" shall mean a period of service commencing on the employee's employment commencement date or reemployment commencement date, whichever is applicable, and ending on the severance from service date.

(ii) *Aggregation rule.*—Unless a plan provides in some manner for an "adjusted" employment commencement date or similar method of consolidating periods of service, periods of service shall be aggregated unless such periods may be disregarded under section 410(a)(5) or 411(a)(4).

(iii) *Other federal law.*—Nothing in this section shall be construed to alter, amend, modify, invalidate, impair or supersede any law of the United States or any rule or regulation issued under such law. Thus, for example, nothing in this section shall be construed as denying an employee credit for a "period of service" if credit is required by a separate federal law. Furthermore, the nature and extent of such credit shall be determined under such law.

(c) *Eligibility to participate.*—(1) *General rule.*—For purposes of section 410(a)(1)(A), a plan generally may not require as a condition of participation in the plan that an employee complete a period of service with the employer or employers maintaining the plan extending beyond the later of—

(i) The date on which the employee attains the age of 25; or

(ii) The date on which the employee completes a one-year period of service.
See the regulations under section 410(a) (relating to eligibility to participate).

(2) *Determination of one-year period of service.*—(i) For purposes of determining the date on which an employee satisfies the service requirement for initial eligibility to participate under the plan, a plan

using the elapsed time method of crediting service shall provide that an employee who completes the 1-year period of service requirement on the first anniversary of his employment commencement date satisfies the minimum service requirement as of such date. In the case of an employee who fails to complete a one-year period of service on the first anniversary of his employment commencement date, a plan which does not contain a provision permitted by section 410(a)(5)(D) (rule of parity) shall provide for the aggregation of periods of service so that a one-year period of service shall be completed as of the date the employee completes 12 months of service (30 days are deemed to be a month in the case of the aggregation of fractional months) or 365 days of service.

(ii) For purposes of section 410(a)(1)(B)(i), a "3-year period of service" shall be deemed to be "3 years of service".

(iii) *Service spanning rules.*—In determining a 1-year period of service for purposes of initial eligibility to participate and a period of service for purposes of retention of eligibility to participate, in addition to taking into account an employee's period of service, a plan shall take into account the following periods of severance—

(A) If an employee severs from service by reason of a quit, discharge or retirement and the employee then performs an hour of service within the meaning of 29 CFR § 2530.200b-2(a)(1) within 12 months of the severance from service date, the plan is required to take into account the period of severance; and

(B) Notwithstanding paragraph (c)(2)(iii)(A) of this section, if an employee severs from service by reason of a quit, discharge or retirement during an absence from service of 12 months or less for any reason other than a quit, discharge, retirement or death, and then performs an hour of service within the meaning of 29 CFR § 2530.200b-2(a)(1) within 12 months of the date on which the employee was first absent from service, the plan is required to take into account the period of severance.

(iv) For purposes of determining an employee's retention of eligibility to participate in the plan, a plan shall take into account an employee's entire period of service unless certain periods of service may be disregarded under section 410(a)(5) of the Code.

(v) *Example.*—Employee W, age 31, completed 6 months of service and was laid off. After 2 months of layoff, W quit. Five months later, W returned to service. For purposes of eligibility to participate, W was required to be credited with 13 months of service (8 months of service and 5 months of severance). If, on the other hand, W had not returned to service within the first 10 months of severance (*i.e.,* within 12 months after the first day of layoff), W would be required to be credited with only 8 months of service.

(3) *Entry date requirements.*—(i) *General rule.*—For purposes of section 410(a)(4), it is necessary for a plan to provide that any employee who has satisfied the minimum age and service requirements, and who is otherwise entitled to participate in the plan, commences participation in the plan no later than the earlier of—

(A) The first day of the first plan year beginning after the date on which such employee satisfied such requirements, or

(B) The date six months after the date on which he satisfied such requirements,
unless such employee was separated from service before the date referred to in subdivision (i)(A) or (B), whichever is applicable. See the regulations under section 410(a) (relating to eligibility to participate).

(ii) *Separation from service.*—(A) *Definition.*—For purposes of this section, the term "separated from service" includes a severance from service or an absence from service for any reason other than a quit, discharge, retirement or death, regardless of the duration of such absence. Accordingly, if an employee is laid off for a period of six weeks, the employee shall be deemed to be "separated from service" during such period for purposes of the entry date requirements.

(B) *Application.*—A period of severance which is taken into account under the service spanning rules in paragraph (c)(2)(iii) of this section or an absence of 12 months or less may result in an employee satisfying the plan's minimum service requirement during such period of time. In addition, once an employee satisfies the plan's minimum service requirement, either before or during such period of time, such period of time may contain an entry date applicable to such employee. In the case of an employee whose period of severance is taken into account and such period contains an entry date applicable to the employee, he or she shall be made a participant in the plan (if otherwise eligible) no later than the date on which he or she ended the period of severance. In the case of an employee whose period of absence contains an entry date applicable to such employee, he or she, no later than the date such absence ended, shall be made a participant in the plan (if otherwise eligible) as of the first applicable entry date which occurred during such absence from service.

(iii) *Examples.*—For purposes of the following examples, assume that the plan provides for a minimum age requirement of 25 and a minimum service requirement of one year, and provides for semi-annual entry dates.

(A) Employee A, age 35, worked for 10 months in a job classification covered under the plan, became disabled for nine consecutive months and then returned to service. During the period of absence, A completed a 1-year period of service and passed a semi-annual entry date after satisfying the minimum service requirement. Accordingly, the plan is required to make A a participant no later than his return to service effective as of the applicable entry date.

(B) Employee B, after satisfying the minimum age and service requirements, quit work before the next semi-annual entry date, and then returned to service before incurring a 1-year period of severance, but after such semi-annual entry date. Employee B is entitled to become a participant immediately upon his return to service effective as of the date of his return.

(4) *Break in service.*—For purposes of applying the break in service rules under section 410(a)(5)(B) and (C), the term "1-year period of severance" shall be substituted for the term "1-year break in service". A 1-year period of severance shall be determined on the basis of a 12-consecutive-month period beginning on the severance from service date and ending on the first anniversary of such date, provided that the employee during such 12-consecutive-month period does not perform an hour of service within the meaning of 29 CFR § 2530.200b-2(a)(1) for the employer or employers maintaining the plan.

(5) *One-year hold-out.*—(i) *General rule.*—(A) For purposes of section 410(a)(5)(C), in determining the period of service of an employee who has incurred a 1-year period of severance, a plan may disregard the employee's period of service before such period of severance until the employee completes a 1-year period of service after such period of severance.

(B) *Example.*—Assume that a plan provides for a minimum service requirement of 1 year and provides for semi-annual entry dates, but does not contain the provisions permitted by section 410(a)(5)(D) (relating to the rule of parity). Employee G, age 40, completed a seven-month period of service, quit and then returned to service 15 months later, thereby incurring a 1-year period of severance. After working four months, G was laid off for nine months and then returned to work again. Although the plan may hold employee G out from participation in the plan until the completion of a 1-year period of service after the 1-year (or greater) period of severance, once the 1-year hold-out is completed, the plan is required to provide the employee with such statutory entitlement as arose during the 1-year hold-out. Accordingly, employee G satisfied the 1-year hold-out requirement as of the eighth month of layoff, and G is entitled to become a participant in the plan immediately upon his return to service after the nine-month layoff effective as of the first applicable entry date occurring after the date on which he satisfied the 1-year of service requirement (*i.e.*, the first applicable entry date after the first month of layoff). See the regulations under section 410(a) (relating to eligibility to participate).

(6) *Rule of parity.*—(i) *General rule.*—For purposes of section 410(a)(5)(D), in the case of a participant who does not have any nonforfeitable right under the plan to his accrued benefit derived from employer contributions and who incurs a 1-year period of severance, a plan, in determining an employee's period of service for purposes of section 410(a)(1), may disregard his period of service if his latest period of severance equals or exceeds his prior periods of service, whether or not consecutive, completed before such period of severance. See the regulations under section 410(a) (relating to eligibility to participate).

(ii) In determining whether a completely nonvested employee's service may be disregarded under the rule of parity, a plan is not permitted to apply the rule until the employee incurs a 1-year period of severance. Accordingly, a plan may not disregard a period of service of less than one year until an employee has incurred a period of severance of at least one year.

(iii) *Example.*—Assume that a plan provides for a minimum service requirement of one year and provides for the rule of parity. An employee works for three months, quits and then is rehired 10 months later. Such employee is entitled to receive 13 months of credit for purposes of eligibility to participate and vesting (see the service spanning rules). Although the period of severance exceeded the period of service, the three months of service may not be disregarded because no 1-year period of severance occurred.

(d) *Vesting.*—(1) *General rule.*—(i) For purposes of section 411(a)(2), relating to vesting in accrued benefits derived from employer contributions, a plan which determines service to be taken into account on the basis of elapsed time shall provide that an employee is credited with a number of years of service equal to at least the number of whole years of the employee's period of service, whether or not such periods of service were completed consecutively.

(ii) In order to determine the number of whole years of an employee's period of service, a plan shall provide that nonsuccessive periods of service must be aggregated and that less than whole year periods of service (whether or not consecutive) must be aggregated on the basis that 12 months of service (30 days are deemed to be a month in the case of the aggregation of fractional months) or 365 days of service equal a whole year of service.

(iii) *Service spanning rules.*—In determining a participant's period of service for vesting purposes, a plan shall take into account the following periods of severance—

(A) If an employee severs from service by reason of a quit, discharge or retirement and the employee then performs an hour of service within the meaning of 29 CFR § 2530.200b-2(a)(1) within 12 months of the severance from service date, the plan is required to take into account the period of severance; and

(B) Notwithstanding paragraph (d)(1)(iii)(A) of this section, if an employee severs from service by reason of a quit, discharge or retirement during an absence from service of 12 months or less for any reason other than a quit, discharge, retirement or death, and then performs an hour of service within the meaning of 29 CFR § 2530.200b-2(a)(1) within 12 months of the date on which the employee was first absent from service, the plan is required to take into account the period of severance.

(iv) For purposes of determining an employee's nonforfeitable percentage of accrued benefits derived from employer contributions, a plan, after calculating an employee's period of service in the manner prescribed in this paragraph, may disregard any remaining less than whole year, 12-month or 365-day period of service. Thus, for example, if a plan provides for the statutory five to fifteen year graded vesting, an employee with a period (or periods) of service which yield 5 whole year periods of service and an additional 321-day period of service is twenty-five percent vested in his or her employer-derived accrued benefits (based solely on the 5 whole year periods of service).

(2) *Service which may be disregarded.*—(i) for purposes of section 411(a)(4), in determining the nonforfeitable percentage of an employee's right to his or her accrued benefits derived from employer contributions, all of an employee's period or periods of service with an employer or employers maintaining the plan shall be taken into account unless such service may be disregarded under paragraph (d)(2)(ii) of this section.

(ii) For purposes of paragraph (d)(2)(i) of this section, the following periods of service may be disregarded—

(A) The period of service completed by an employee before the date on which he attains age 22;

(B) In the case of a plan which requires mandatory employee contributions, the period of service which falls within the period of time to which a particular employee contribution relates, if the employee had the opportunity to make a contribution for such period of time and failed to do so;

(C) The period of service during any period for which the employer did not maintain the plan or a predecessor plan;

(D) The period of service which is not required to be taken into account by reason of a period of severance which constitutes a break in service within the meaning of paragraph (d)(4) of this section;

(E) The period of service completed by an employee prior to January 1, 1971, unless the employee completes a period of service of at least 3 years at any time after December 31, 1970; and

(F) The period of service completed before the first plan year for which this section applies to the plan, if such service would have been disregarded under the plan rules relating to breaks in service in effect at that time.

See the regulations under section 411(a) (relating to vesting).

(3) *Seasonal industry.*—[Reserved.]

(4) *Break in service.*—For purposes of applying the break in service rules, the term "1-year period of severance" shall be substituted for the term "1-year break in service". A 1-year period of severance shall be a 12-consecutive-month period beginning on the severance from service date and ending on the first anniversary of such date, provided that the employee during such 12-consecutive-month periods fails to perform an hour of service within the meaning of 29 CFR § 2530.200b-2(a)(1) for an employer or employers maintaining the plan.

(5) *One-year hold-out.*—For purposes of section 411(a)(6)(B), in determining the nonforfeitable percentage of the right to accrued benefits derived from employer contributions of an employee who has incurred a 1-year period of severance, the period of service completed before such period of severance is not required to be taken into account until the employee has completed a 1-year period of service after his return to service. See the regulations under section 411(a) (relating to vesting).

(6) *Vesting in pre-break accruals.*—For purposes of section 411(a)(6)(C), a "1-year period of severance" shall be deemed to constitute a "1-year break in service." See the regulations under section 411(a) (relating to vesting).

(7) *Rule of parity.*—(i) *General rule.*—For purposes of section 411(a)(6)(D), in the case of an employee who is a nonvested participant in employer-derived benefits at the time he incurs a 1-year period of severance, the period of service completed by such participant before such period of severance is not required to be taken into account for purposes of determining the vested percentage of his or her right to employer-derived benefits if at such time the consecutive period of severance equals or exceeds his prior periods of service, whether or not consecutive, completed before such period of severance. See the regulations under section 411(a) (relating to vesting).

(e) *Benefit accrual.*—(1) For purposes of section 411(b), a plan may provide that a participant's service with an employer or employers maintaining the plan shall be determined on the basis of the participant's total period of service beginning on the participation commencement date and ending on the severance from service date.

(2) Under section 411(b)(3)(A), a defined benefit pension plan may determine an employee's service for purposes of benefit accrual on any basis which is reasonable and consistent and which takes into account all service during the employee's participation in the plan which is included in a period of service required to be taken into account under section 410(a)(5) (relating to service which must be taken into account for purposes of determining an employee's eligibility to participate). A plan which provides for the determination of an employee's service with an employer or employers maintaining the plan on the basis permitted under paragraph (e)(1) of this section will be deemed to meet the requirements of section 411(b)(3)(A), provided that the plan meets the requirements of 29 CFR § 2530.204-3, relating to plans which determine an employee's service for purposes of benefit accrual on a basis other than computation periods. Specifically, under 29 CFR § 2530.204-3, it must be possible to prove that, despite the fact that benefit accrual under such a plan is not based on computation periods, the plan's provisions meet at least one of the three benefit accrual rules of section 411(b)(1) under all circumstances. Further, 29 CFR § 2530.204-3 prohibits such a plan from disregarding service under section 411(b)(3)(C) (which would otherwise permit a plan to disregard service performed by an employee during a computation period in which the employee is credited with less than 1,000 hours). See the regulations under section 411(b) (relating to benefit accrual).

(f) *Transfers between methods of crediting service.*—(1) *Single plan.*—A plan may provide that an employee's service for purposes of eligibility to participate, vesting or benefit accrual shall be determined on the basis of computation periods under the general method set forth in 29 CFR § 2530.200b-2 for certain classes of employees but under the alternative method permitted under this section for other classes of employees if the plan provides as follows:

(i) In the case of an employee who transfers from a class of employees whose service is determined on the basis of computation periods to a class of employees whose service is determined on the alternative basis permitted under this section, the employee shall receive credit for a period of service consisting of—

(A) A number of years equal to the number of years of service credited to the employee before the computation period during which the transfer occurs; and

(B) The greater of *(1)* the period of service that would be credited to the employee under the elapsed time method for his service during the entire computation period in which the transfer occurs or *(2)* the service taken into account under the computation periods method as of the date of the transfer.
In addition, the employee shall receive credit for service subsequent to the transfer commencing on the day after the last day of the computation period in which the transfer occurs.

(ii) In the case of an employee who transfers from a class of employees whose service is determined on the alternative basis permitted under this section to a class of employees whose service is determined on the basis of computation periods—

(A) The employee shall receive credit, as of the date of the transfer, for a number of years of service equal to the number of 1-year periods of service credited to the employee as of the date of the transfer, and

(B) The employee shall receive credit, in the computation period which includes the date of the transfer, for a number of hours of service determined by applying one of the equivalencies set forth in 29 CFR § 2530.200b-3(e)(1) to any fractional part of a year credited to the employee under this section as of the date of the transfer. Such equivalency shall be set forth in the plan and shall apply to all similarly situated employees.

(2) *More than one plan.*—In the case of an employee who transfers from a plan using either the general method of determining service on the basis of computation periods set forth in 29 CFR § 2530.200b-2 or the method of determining service permitted under this section to a plan using the other method of determining service, all service required to be credited under the plan to which the employee transfers shall be determined by applying the rules of paragraph (f)(1) of this section.

(g) *Amendments to change method of crediting service.*—A plan may be amended to change the method of crediting service for any purpose or for any class of employees between the general method set forth in 29 CFR § 2530.200b-2 and the method permitted under this section, if such amendment contains provisions under which each employee with respect to whom the method of crediting service is changed is treated in the same manner as an employee who transfers from one class of employees to another under paragraph (f)(1) of this section.

(h) *Transitional rule.*—For plans in existence on [insert the date of the publication of this document], the provisions of paragraph (f) of this section are effective for plan years beginning after December 31, 1983. [Reg. § 1.410(a)-7.]

☐ [*T.D.* 7703, 6-16-80.]

[Reg. § 1.410(a)-8]

§ 1.410(a)-8. Five consecutive 1-year breaks in service, transitional rules under the Retirement Equity Act of 1984.—Sections 410(a)(5)(D) and 411(a)(6)(D), as amended by the Retirement Equity Act of 1984 (REA 1984), permit a plan to disregard years of service that were disregarded under the plan provisions satisfying those sections (as in effect on August 22, 1984) as of the day before the REA amendments apply to the plan. Under section 302(a) of REA 1984, the new break-in-service rules generally apply to plan years beginning after December 31, 1984. Thus, for example, assume a plan has a calendar plan year and disregarded years of service as permitted by sections 410(a)(5)(D) and 411(a)(6)(D) as in effect on August 22, 1984. An employee completed two years of service in 1981 and 1982, and then incurred two consecutive 1-year breaks in service in 1983 and 1984. The plans may disregard the prior years of service even though the employee did not incur five consecutive 1-year breaks in service. On the other hand, assume the employee completed three consecutive years of service beginning in 1980, and incurred two 1-year breaks in service in 1983 and 1984. Because, as of December 31, 1984, the years of service credited before 1983 could not be disregarded, whether the plan may subsequently disregard those years of service would be governed by the rules enacted by REA 1984. [Reg. § 1.410(a)-8.]

☐ [*T.D.* 8219, 8-19-88.]

[Reg. § 1.410(a)-8T]

§ 1.410(a)-8T. Year of service; break in service (Temporary).—
(a) [Reserved.]
(b) [Reserved.]

(c) *Breaks in service*—
(1) [Reserved.]

(2) *Employees under 2-year 100 percent vesting schedule.*—(i) *General rule.*—In the case of an employee who incurs a 1-year break in service under a plan which provides that after not more than 2 years of service each participant's right to his accrued benefit under the plan is completely nonforfeitable (within the meaning of section 411 and the regulations thereunder) at the time such benefit accrues, the employee's service before the break in service is not required to be taken into account after the break in service in determining the employee's years of service under section 410(a)(1) and § 1.410(a)-3 if such employee has not satisfied such service requirement.

(ii) *Example.*—The rules of this subparagraph are illustrated by the following example:

Example. A qualified plan computing service by the actual counting of hours provides full and immediate vesting. The plan can not require as a condition of participation that an employee complete 2 consecutive years of service with the employer because the requirement as to consecutive years is not permitted under section 410(a)(5). However, such a plan can require 2 years without a break in service, i.e., 2 years with no intervening years in which the employee fails to complete more than 500 hours of service. Under a plan containing such a participation requirement, the following example illustrates when employees would become eligible to participate.

Year	Hours of service completed Employee A	Employee B	Employee C
1	1,000	1,000	1,000
2	1,000	700	500
3	1,000	1,000	1,000
4	1,000	1,000	700
5	1,000	1,000	1,000

Note.—Employee A will have satisfied the plan's service requirement at the end of year 2, Employee B at the end of year 3, and Employee C at the end of year 5.

(3) *One-year break in service*—

(i) [Reserved.]

(ii) *Examples.*—The rules provided by this subparagraph are illustrated by the following examples:

Example (1). Employee A completes a year of service under a plan computing service by the actual counting of hours for the 12-month period ending December 31, 1989, and incurs a 1-year break in service for the 12-month period ending December 31, 1990. The plan does not contain the provisions permitted by section 410(a)(5)(B) (relating to 2-year 100 percent vesting) and section 410(a)(5)(D) (relating to nonvested participants). Thereafter, he does not complete a year of service. As of January 1, 1991, in computing his period of service under the plan his service prior to December 31, 1990, is not required to be taken into account for purposes of section 410(a)(1) and §1.410(a)-3.

Example (2). [Reserved.]

[Temporary Reg. §1.410(a)-8T.]

☐ [T.D. 8170, 1-5-88.]

[Reg. §1.410(a)-9]

§1.410(a)-9. Maternity and paternity absence.—(a) *Elapsed Time.*—(1) *Rule.*—For purposes of applying the rules of §1.410(a)-7 (relating to the elapsed time method of crediting service) to absences described in sections 410(a)(5)(E) and 411(a)(6)(E) (relating to maternity or paternity absence), the severance from service date of an employee who is absent from service beyond the first anniversary of the first day of absence by reason of a maternity or paternity absence described in section 410(a)(5)(i)(E) or 411(a)(6)(E)(i) is the second anniversary of the first day of such absence. The period between the first and second anniversaries of the first day of absence from work is neither a period of service nor a period of severance. This rule applies to maternity and paternity absences beginning on or after the first day of the first plan year in which the plan is required to credit service under sections 410(a)(5)(E) and 411(a)(6)(E).

(2) *Example.*—The rules of this section are illustrated by the following example:

Assume an individual works until June 30, 1986; is first absent from employment on July 1, 1986, on account of maternity or paternity absence; and on July 1, 1989, performs an hour of service. The period of service must include the period from employment commencement date until June 30, 1987 (one year after the date of separation for any reason other than a quit, discharge, retirement, or death). The period from July 1, 1987, to June 30, 1988, is neither a period of service nor a period of severance. The period of severance would be from July 1, 1988 to June 30, 1989.

(b) *Other methods.*—This paragraph provides a safe harbor for plans that compute years of service under the hours of service methods or permitted equivalencies. Such a plan will be treated as satisfying the requirements of sections 410(a)(5)(E) and 411(a)(6)(E) if the plan increases the minimum period of consecutive 1-year breaks required to disregard any service (or deprive any employee of any right) by one. Thus, a plan will satisfy sections 410(a)(5)(E) and 411(a)(6)(E) without having to compute service for maternity or paternity and sections 410(a)(5)(D) and 411(a)(4)(D) and (a)(6)(C), by increasing the period of consecutive breaks in service from 5 to 6. [Reg. §1.410(a)-9.]

☐ [T.D. 8219, 8-19-88.]

[Reg. §1.410(a)-9T]

§1.410(a)-9T. Elapsed time (Temporary).—(a) [Reserved.]

(b) [Reserved.]

(c) *Eligibility to participate*—

(1) [Reserved.]

(2) *Determination of one-year period of service.*

(i) [Reserved.]

(ii) For purposes of section 410(a)(1)(B)(i), a "2-year period of service" shall be deemed to be "2 years of service."

(d) *Vesting.*—(1) *General rule.*

(i) [Reserved.]

(ii) [Reserved.]

(iii) [Reserved.]

(iv) For purposes of determining an employee's nonforfeitable percentage of accrued benefits derived from employer contributions, a plan, after calculating an employee's period of service in the manner prescribed in this paragraph, may disregard any remaining less than whole year, 12-month or 365-day period of service. Thus, for example, if a plan provides for the statutory three to seven year graded vesting, an employee with a period (or periods) of service which yields 3 whole year periods of service and an additional 321-day period of service is twenty percent vested in his or her employer-derived accrued benefits (based solely on the 3 whole year periods of service).

(2) [Reserved.]

[Temporary Reg. §1.410(a)-9T.]

☐ [T.D. 8170, 1-5-88.]

[Reg. §1.410(b)-0]

§1.410(b)-0. Table of contents.—This section contains a listing of the headings of §§1.410(b)-2 through 1.410(b)-10.

☐ [*T.D.* 8363, 9-12-91. *Amended by T.D.* 8487, 8-31-93, *T.D.* 8548, 6-23-94, *T.D.* 9275, 7-20-2006 *and T.D.* 9849, 3-11-2019.]

Reg. § 1.410(b)-0

[Reg. §1.410(b)-1]

§1.410(b)-1. [Reserved].

☐ [*T.D. 7508, 9-14-77. Amended by T.D. 7735, 11-10-80; T.D. 8363, 9-12-91 and T.D. 8487, 8-31-93. Removed and reserved by T.D. 9849, 3-11-2019.*]

[Reg. §1.410(b)-2]

§1.410(b)-2. Minimum coverage requirements (after 1993).—

(a) *In general.*—A plan is a qualified plan for a plan year only if the plan satisfies section 410(b) for the plan year. A plan satisfies section 410(b) for a plan year if and only if it satisfies paragraph (b) of this section with respect to employees for the plan year and paragraph (c) of this section with respect to former employees for the plan year. The rules in paragraphs (a), (b), and (c) of this section apply to all plans as a condition of qualification, including plans under which no employee is able to accrue any additional benefits (for example, frozen plans). Paragraphs (d), (e), and (f) of this section provide special rules for nonelective section 403(b) plans subject to section 403(b)(12)(A)(i), for governmental and church plans subject to section 410(c), and for certain acquisitions or dispositions, respectively. See §1.410(b)-7 for rules for determining the "plan" subject to section 410(b).

(b) *Requirements with respect to employees.*—(1) *In general.*—A plan satisfies this paragraph (b) for a plan year if and only if it satisfies at least one of the tests in paragraphs (b)(2) through (b)(7) of this section for the plan year.

(2) *Ratio percentage test.*—(i) *In general.*—A plan satisfies this paragraph (b)(2) for a plan year if and only if the plan's ratio percentage for the plan year is at least 70 percent. This test incorporates both the percentage test of section 410(b)(1)(A) and the ratio test of section 410(b)(1)(B). See §1.410(b)-9 for the definition of ratio percentage.

(ii) *Examples.*—The following examples illustrate the ratio percentage test of this paragraph (b)(2).

Example 1. For a plan year, Plan A benefits 70 percent of an employer's nonhighly compensated employees and 100 percent of an employer's highly compensated employees. The plan's ratio percentage for the year is 70 percent (70 percent/100 percent), and thus the plan satisfies the ratio percentage test.

Example 2. For a plan year, Plan B benefits 40 percent of the employer's nonhighly compensated employees and 60 percent of the employer's highly compensated employees. Plan B fails to satisfy the ratio percentage test because the plan's ratio percentage is only 66.67 percent (40 percent/60 percent).

(3) *Average benefit test.*—A plan satisfies this paragraph (b)(3) for a plan year if and only if the plan satisfies both the nondiscriminatory classification test of §1.410(b)-4 and the average benefit percentage test of §1.410(b)-5 for the plan year.

(4) *Certain tax credit employee stock ownership plans.*—A plan satisfies this paragraph (b)(4) for a plan year if and only if the plan—

(i) Is a tax credit employee stock ownership plan (as defined in section 409(a)),

(ii) Is the only plan of the employer that is intended to qualify under section 401(a), and

(iii) Is a plan that satisfies the rule set forth in section 410(b)(6)(D).

This paragraph (b)(4) is available only for plan years for which the tax credit employee stock ownership plan receives contributions for which the employer is allowed a tax credit under section 41 (as in effect prior to its repeal by the Tax Reform Act of 1986) or section 48(n) (as in effect prior to its amendment by the Tax Reform Act of 1984). The requirement of this paragraph (b)(4) that the plan be the only plan of the employer that is intended to qualify under section 401(a) is not satisfied if the employer has only one plan, but that plan is treated as two or more separate plans under the mandatory disaggregation rules of §1.410(b)-7(c).

(5) *Employers with no nonhighly compensated employees.*—A plan satisfies this paragraph (b)(5) for a plan year if and only if the plan is maintained by an employer that has no nonhighly compensated employees at any time during the plan year.

(6) *Plans benefiting no highly compensated employees.*—A plan satisfies this paragraph (b)(6) for a plan year if and only if the plan benefits no highly compensated employees for the plan year.

(7) *Plans benefiting collectively bargained employees.*—A plan that benefits solely collectively bargained employees for a plan year satisfies this paragraph (b)(7) for the plan year. If a plan (within the meaning of §1.410(b)-7(b)) benefits both collectively bargained employees and noncollectively bargained employees for a plan year,

§1.410(b)-7(c)(4) provides that the portion of the plan that benefits collectively bargained employees is treated as a separate plan from the portion of the plan that benefits noncollectively bargained employees. Thus, the mandatorily disaggregated portion of the plan that benefits the collectively bargained employees automatically satisfies this paragraph (b)(7) for the plan year and hence section 410(b). See §1.410(b)-9 for the definitions of collectively bargained employee and noncollectively bargained employee.

(c) *Requirements with respect to former employees.*—(1) *Former employees tested separately.*—Former employees are tested separately from employees for purposes of section 410(b). Thus, former employees are disregarded in applying the ratio percentage test, the nondiscriminatory classification test, and the average benefit percentage test with respect to the coverage of employees under a plan, and employees are disregarded in applying this section with respect to the coverage of former employees under a plan.

(2) *Testing former employees.*—A plan satisfies section 410(b) with respect to former employees if and only if, under all of the relevant facts and circumstances (including the group of nonexcludable former employees not benefiting under the plan), the group of former employees benefiting under the plan does not discriminate significantly in favor of highly compensated former employees.

(d) *Nonelective contributions under section 403(b) plans.*—For plan years beginning on or after January 1, 1989, a plan subject to section 403(b)(12)(A)(i) with respect to nonelective contributions (i.e., contributions not made pursuant to a salary reduction agreement) is treated as a plan subject to the requirements of this section. For this purpose, a plan described in the preceding sentence must satisfy the requirements of this section without regard to section 410(c) and paragraph (e) of this section. For plan years beginning before the effective date set forth in §1.410(b)-10(d), any plan described in section 410(c)(1)(A) (regarding governmental plans) satisfies the requirements of this section.

(e) *Certain governmental and church plans.*—The requirements of section 410(b) do not apply to a plan described in section 410(c)(1) (other than a plan subject to section 403(b)(12)(A)(i) or a plan with respect to which an election has been made under section 410(d)). Such a plan must satisfy section 401(a)(3) as in effect on September 1, 1974. For this purpose, a plan that satisfies section 410(b) (without regard to this paragraph (e)) is treated as satisfying section 401(a)(3) as in effect on September 1, 1974. For plan years beginning before the effective date set forth in §1.410(b)-10(d), any plan described in section 410(c)(1)(A) (regarding governmental plans) satisfies the requirements of this section and is thus treated as satisfying the requirements of section 401(a)(3) as in effect on September 1, 1974. See §1.410(b)-10(b)(2) for a special rule for plans of tax-exempt organizations.

(f) *Certain acquisitions or dispositions.*—Section 410(b)(6)(C) (relating to certain acquisitions or dispositions) provides a special rule whereby a plan may be treated as satisfying section 410(b) for a limited period of time after an acquisition or disposition if it satisfies section 410(b) (without regard to the special rule) immediately before the acquisition or disposition and there is no significant change in the plan or in the coverage of the plan other than the acquisition or disposition. For purposes of section 410(b)(6)(C) and this paragraph (f), the terms "acquisition" and "disposition" refer to an asset or stock acquisition, merger, or other similar transaction involving a change in employer of the employees of a trade or business.

(g) *Additional rules.*—The Commissioner may, in revenue rulings, notices, and other guidance of general applicability, provide any additional rules that may be necessary or appropriate in applying the minimum coverage requirements of section 410(b), including (without limitation) additional rules limiting or expanding the methods in §1.410(b)-5(d) and (e) for determining employee benefit percentages. [Reg. §1.410(b)-2.]

☐ [*T.D. 8363, 9-12-91. Amended by T.D. 8487, 8-31-93 and T.D. 8548, 6-23-94.*]

[Reg. §1.410(b)-3]

§1.410(b)-3. Employees and former employees who benefit under a plan.—

(a) *Employees benefiting under a plan.*—(1) *In general.*—Except as provided in paragraph (a)(2) of this section, an employee is treated as benefiting under a plan for a plan year if and only if for that plan year, in the case of a defined contribution plan, the employee receives an allocation taken into account under §1.401(a)(4)-2(c)(2)(ii), or in the case of a defined benefit plan, the employee has an increase in a benefit accrued or treated as an accrued benefit under section 411(d)(6).

(2) *Exceptions to allocation or accrual requirement.*—(i) *Section 401(k) and 401(m) plans.*—Notwithstanding paragraph (a)(1) of this

section, an employee is treated as benefiting under a section 401(k) plan for a plan year if and only if the employee is an eligible employee as defined in §1.401(k)-6 under the plan. Similarly, an employee is treated as benefiting under a section 401(m) plan for a plan year if and only if the employee is an eligible employee as defined in §1.401(m)-5 under the plan for the plan year.

(ii) *Section 415 limits.*—(A) *General rule for defined benefit plans.*—In determining whether an employee is treated as benefiting under a defined benefit plan for a plan year, plan provisions that implement the limits of section 415 are disregarded. Any plan provision that provides for increases in an employee's accrued benefit under the plan due solely to adjustments under section 415(d)(1), additional years of participation or service under section 415(b)(5), or changes in the defined contribution fraction under section 415(e) is also disregarded, but only if such provision applies uniformly to all employees in the plan.

(B) *Defined benefit plans taking section 415 limits into account under section 401(a)(4) testing.*—Paragraph (a)(2)(ii)(A) of this section does not apply in the case of a defined benefit plan that uses the option in §1.401(a)(4)-3(d)(2)(ii)(B) to take into account plan provisions implementing the provisions of section 415 in determining accrual rates under the section 401(a)(4) general test.

(C) *Defined contribution plans.*—A defined contribution plan is permitted to apply the rule in the first sentence of paragraph (a)(2)(ii)(A) of this section in determining whether an employee is treated as benefiting under the plan, provided it applies the rule on a consistent basis for all employees in the plan.

(iii) *Certain employees treated as benefiting.*—(A) *In general.*—An employee is treated as benefiting under a plan for a plan year if the employee satisfies all of the applicable conditions for accruing a benefit or receiving an allocation for the plan year but fails to have an increase in accrued benefit or to receive an allocation solely because of one or more of the conditions set forth in paragraphs (a)(2)(iii)(B) through (F) of this section.

(B) *Certain plan limits.*—The employee's benefit would otherwise exceed a limit that is applicable on a uniform basis to all employees in the plan. Thus, for example, if the formula under a defined benefit plan takes into account only the first 30 years of service for accrual purposes, an employee who has completed more than 30 years of service is still treated as benefiting under the plan.

(C) *Benefits previously accrued.*—The benefit previously accrued by the employee is greater than the benefit that would be determined under the plan if the benefit previously accrued were disregarded. This could happen, for example, when the plan is applying the wear-away formula of §1.401(a)(4)-13(c)(4)(ii) and the employee's frozen accrued benefit exceeds the benefit determined under the current formula.

(D) *Benefit offset arrangements.*—The plan offsets the employee's current benefit accrual under an offset arrangement described in §1.401(a)(4)-3(f)(9) (without regard to whether the offset is attributable to pre-participation service or past service).

(E) *Target benefit plans.*—In the case of a target benefit plan that satisfies the nondiscriminatory amount requirement of §1.401(a)(4)-8(b)(3) by satisfying the safe harbor in §1.401(a)(4)-1(b)(2), the employee's theoretical reserve is greater than or equal to the actuarial present value of the fractional rule benefit.

(F) *Post-normal retirement age adjustments.*—The employee has attained normal retirement age under a defined benefit plan and fails to accrue a benefit because of the provisions of section 411(b)(1)(H)(iii) regarding adjustments for delayed retirement.

(iv) *Section 412(i) plans.*—(A) *General rule.*—Notwithstanding paragraph (a)(1) of this section, an employee is treated as benefiting under an insurance contract plan within the meaning of section 412(i) for a plan year if and only if a premium is paid on behalf of the employee for the plan year.

(B) *Exceptions.*—Notwithstanding paragraph (a)(2)(iv)(A) of this section, an employee is treated as benefiting under an insurance contract plan within the meaning of section 412(i) for a plan year if the sole reason that a premium is not paid on behalf of the employee is one of the reasons described in paragraph (a)(2)(iii) of this section. In addition, an employee is treated as benefiting under an insurance contract plan, within the meaning of section 412(i), that is a defined benefit plan if a premium is not paid on behalf of the employee solely because the insurance contracts that have previously been purchased on behalf of the employee guarantee to provide for the employee's projected normal retirement benefit without regard to future premium payments.

(3) *Examples.*—The following examples illustrate the determination of whether an employee is benefiting under a plan for purposes of section 410(b).

Example 1. An employer has 35 employees who are eligible under a defined benefit plan. The plan requires 1,000 hours of service to accrue a benefit. Only 30 employees satisfy the 1,000-hour requirement and accrue a benefit. The five employees who do not satisfy the 1,000-hour requirement during the plan year are taken into account in testing the plan under section 410(b) but are treated as not benefiting under the plan.

Example 2. An employer maintains a section 401(k) plan. Only employees who are at least age 21 and who complete one year of service are eligible employees under the plan within the meaning of §1.401(k)-6. Under the rule of paragraph (a)(2)(i) of this section, only employees who have satisfied these age and service conditions are treated as benefiting under the plan.

Example 3. The facts are the same as in *Example 2*, except that the employer also maintains a section 401(m) plan that provides matching contributions contingent on elective contributions under the section 401(k) plan. The matching contributions are contingent on employment on the last day of the plan year. Under §1.401(m)-5, because matching contributions are contingent on employment on the last day of the plan year, not all employees who are eligible employees under the section 401(k) plan are eligible employees under the section 401(m) plan. Thus, employees who have satisfied the age and service conditions but who do not receive a matching contribution because they are not employed on the last day of the plan year are treated as not benefiting under the section 401(m) portion of the plan.

(b) *Former employees benefiting under a plan.*—(1) *In general.*—A former employee is treated as benefiting for a plan year if and only if the plan provides an allocation or benefit increase described in paragraph (a)(1) of this section to the former employee for the plan year. Thus, for example, a former employee benefits under a defined benefit plan for a plan year if the plan is amended to provide an ad hoc cost-of-living adjustment in the former employee's benefits. In contrast, because an increase in benefits payable under a plan pursuant to an automatic cost-of-living provision adopted and effective before the beginning of the plan year is previously accrued, a former employee is not treated as benefiting in a subsequent plan year merely because the former employee receives an increase pursuant to such an automatic cost-of-living provision. Any accrual or allocation for an individual during the plan year that arises from the individual's status as an employee is treated as an accrual or allocation of an employee. Similarly, any accrual or allocation for an individual during the plan year that arises from the individual's status as a former employee is treated as an accrual or allocation of a former employee. It is possible for an individual to accrue a benefit both as an employee and as a former employee in a given plan year. During the plan year in which an individual ceases performing services for the employer, the individual is treated as an employee in applying section 410(b) with respect to employees and is treated as a former employee in applying section 410(b) with respect to former employees.

(2) *Examples.*—The following examples illustrate the determination of whether a former employee benefits under a plan for purposes of section 410(b).

Example 1. Employer A amends its defined benefit plan in the 1995 plan year to provide an ad hoc cost-of-living increase of 5 percent for all retirees. Former employees who receive this increase are treated as benefiting under the plan for the 1995 plan year.

Example 2. Employer B maintains a defined benefit plan with a calendar plan year. In the 1995 plan year, Employer B amends the plan to provide that an employee who has reached early retirement age under the plan and who retires before July 31 of the 1995 plan year will receive an unreduced benefit, even though the employee has not yet reached normal retirement age. This early retirement window benefit is provided to employees based on their status as employees. Thus, although individuals who take advantage of the benefit become former employees, the window benefit is treated as provided to employees and is not treated as a benefit for former employees.

Example 3. The facts are the same as *Example 2*, except that on September 1, 1995, Employer B also amends the defined benefit plan to provide an ad hoc cost-of-living increase effective for all former employees. An individual who ceases performing services for the employer before July 31, 1995, under the early retirement window, and then receives the ad hoc cost-of-living increase, is treated as benefiting for the 1995 plan year both as an employee with respect to the early retirement window, and as a former employee with respect to the ad hoc COLA. [Reg. §1.410(b)-3.]

□ [*T.D.* 8363, 9-12-91. *Amended by T.D.* 8487, 8-31-93 *and T.D.* 9169, 12-28-2004.]

[Reg. § 1.410(b)-4]

§ 1.410(b)-4. Nondiscriminatory classification test.—(a) *In general.*—A plan satisfies the nondiscriminatory classification test of this section for a plan year if and only if, for the plan year, the plan benefits the employees who qualify under a classification established by the employer in accordance with paragraph (b) of this section, and the classification of employees is nondiscriminatory under paragraph (c) of this section.

(b) *Reasonable classification established by the employer.*—A classification is established by the employer in accordance with this paragraph (b) if and only if, based on all the facts and circumstances, the classification is reasonable and is established under objective business criteria that identify the category of employees who benefit under the plan. Reasonable classifications generally include specified job categories, nature of compensation (i.e., salaried or hourly), geographic location, and similar bona fide business criteria. An enumeration of employees by name or other specific criteria having substantially the same effect as an enumeration by name is not considered a reasonable classification.

(c) *Nondiscriminatory classification.*—(1) *General rule.*—A classification is nondiscriminatory under this paragraph (c) for a plan year if and only if the group of employees included in the classification benefiting under the plan satisfies the requirements of either paragraph (c)(2) or (c)(3) of this section for the plan year.

(2) *Safe harbor.*—A plan satisfies the requirement of this paragraph (c)(2) for a plan year if and only if the plan's ratio percentage is greater than or equal to the employer's safe harbor percentage, as defined in paragraph (c)(4)(i) of this section. See § 1.410(b)-9 for the definition of a plan's ratio percentage.

(3) *Facts and circumstances.*—(i) *General rule.*—A plan satisfies the requirements of this paragraph (c)(3) if and only if—

(A) The plan's ratio percentage is greater than or equal to the unsafe harbor percentage, as defined in paragraph (c)(4)(ii) of this section, and

(B) The classification satisfies the factual determination of paragraph (c)(3)(ii) of this section.

(ii) *Factual determination.*—A classification satisfies this paragraph (c)(3)(ii) if and only if, based on all the relevant facts and circumstances, the Commissioner finds that the classification is nondiscriminatory. No one particular fact is determinative. Included among the facts and circumstances relevant in determining whether a classification is nondiscriminatory are the following—

(A) The underlying business reason for the classification. The greater the business reason for the classification, the more likely the classification is to be nondiscriminatory. Reducing the employer's cost of providing retirement benefits is not a relevant business reason.

(B) The percentage of the employer's employees benefiting under the plan. The higher the percentage, the more likely the classification is to be nondiscriminatory.

(C) Whether the number of employees benefiting under the plan in each salary range is representative of the number of employees in each salary range of the employer's workforce. In general, the more representative the percentages of employees benefiting under the plan in each salary range, the more likely the classification is to be nondiscriminatory.

(D) The difference between the plan's ratio percentage and the employer's safe harbor percentage. The smaller the difference, the more likely the classification is to be nondiscriminatory.

(E) The extent to which the plan's average benefit percentage (determined under § 1.410(b)-5) exceeds 70 percent.

(4) *Definitions.*—(i) *Safe harbor percentage.*—The safe harbor percentage of an employer is 50 percent, reduced by $3/4$ of a percentage point for each whole percentage point by which the nonhighly compensated employee concentration percentage exceeds 60 percent. See paragraph (c)(4)(iv) for a table that illustrates the safe harbor percentage and unsafe harbor percentage.

(ii) *Unsafe harbor percentage.*—The unsafe harbor percentage of an employer is 40 percent, reduced by $3/4$ of a percentage point for each whole percentage point by which the nonhighly compensated employee concentration percentage exceeds 60 percent. However, in no case is the unsafe harbor percentage less than 20 percent.

(iii) *Nonhighly compensated employee concentration percentage.*—The nonhighly compensated employee concentration percentage of an employer is the percentage of all the employees of the employer who are nonhighly compensated employees. Employees who are excludable employees for purposes of the average benefit test are not taken into account.

(iv) *Table.*—The following table sets forth the safe harbor and unsafe harbor percentages at each nonhighly compensated employee concentration percentage:

Nonhighly compensated employee concentration percentage	Safe harbor percentage	Unsafe harbor percentage
0-60	50.00	40.00
61	49.25	39.25
62	48.50	38.50
63	47.75	37.75
64	47.00	37.00
65	46.25	36.25
66	45.50	35.50
67	44.75	34.75
68	44.00	34.00
69	43.25	33.25
70	42.50	32.50
71	41.75	31.75
72	41.00	31.00
73	40.25	30.25
74	39.50	29.50
75	38.75	28.75
76	38.00	28.00
77	37.25	27.25
78	36.50	26.50
79	35.75	25.75
80	35.00	25.00
81	34.25	24.25
82	33.50	23.50
83	32.75	22.75
84	32.00	22.00
85	31.25	21.25
86	30.50	20.50
87	29.75	20.00
88	29.00	20.00
89	28.25	20.00
90	27.50	20.00
91	26.75	20.00
92	26.00	20.00
93	25.25	20.00
94	24.50	20.00
95	23.75	20.00
96	23.00	20.00
97	22.25	20.00
98	21.50	20.00
99	20.75	20.00

(5) *Examples.*—The following examples illustrate the rules in this paragraph (c).

Example 1. Employer A has 200 nonexcludable employees, of whom 120 are nonhighly compensated employees and 80 are highly compensated employees. Employer A maintains a plan that benefits 60 nonhighly compensated employees and 72 highly compensated employees. Thus, the plan's ratio percentage is 55.56 percent ([60/120]/ [72/80]= 50%/90% = 0.5556), which is below the percentage necessary to satisfy the ratio percentage test of §1.410(b)-2(b)(2). The employer's nonhighly compensated employee concentration percentage is 60 percent (120/200); thus, Employer A's safe harbor percentage is 50 percent and its unsafe harbor percentage is 40 percent. Because the plan's ratio percentage is greater than the safe harbor percentage, the plan's classification satisfies the safe harbor of paragraph (c)(2) of this section.

Example 2. The facts are the same as in *Example 1*, except that the plan benefits only 40 nonhighly compensated employees. The plan's ratio percentage is thus 37.03 percent ([40/120]/ [72/80] = 33.33%/90% = 0.3703). Under these facts, the plan's classification is below the unsafe harbor percentage and is thus considered discriminatory.

Example 3. The facts are the same as in *Example 1*, except that the plan benefits 45 nonhighly compensated employees. The plan's ratio percentage is thus 41.67 percent ([45/120]/ [72/80] = 37.50%/90% = 0.4167), above the unsafe harbor percentage (40 percent) and below the safe harbor percentage (50 percent). The Commissioner may determine that the classification is nondiscriminatory after considering all the relevant facts and circumstances.

Example 4. Employer B has 10,000 nonexcludable employees, of whom 9,600 are nonhighly compensated employees and 400 are highly compensated employees. Employer B maintains a plan that benefits 600 nonhighly compensated employees and 100 highly compensated employees. Thus, the plan's ratio percentage is 25.00 percent ([600/9,600] / [100/400] = 6.25%/25% = 0.2500), which is below the percentage necessary to satisfy the ratio percentage test of §1.410(b)-2(b)(2). Employer B's nonhighly compensated employee concentration percentage is 96 percent (9,600/10,000); thus, Employer B's safe harbor percentage is 23 percent, and its unsafe harbor percentage is 20 percent. Because the plan's ratio percentage (25.00 percent) is greater than the safe harbor percentage (23.00 percent), the plan's classification satisfies the safe harbor of paragraph (c)(2) of this section.

Example 5. The facts are the same as in *Example 4*, except that the plan benefits only 400 nonhighly compensated employees. The plan's ratio percentage is thus 16.67 percent ([400/9,600] / [100/400]= 4.17%/25% = 0.1667). The plan's ratio percentage is below the unsafe harbor percentage and thus the classification is considered discriminatory.

Example 6. The facts are the same as in *Example 4*, except that the plan benefits 500 nonhighly compensated employees. The plan's ratio percentage is thus 20.83 percent ([500/9,600] / [100/400] = 5.21%/25% = 0.2083), above the unsafe harbor percentage (20 percent) and below the safe harbor percentage (23 percent). The Commissioner may determine that the classification is nondiscriminatory after considering all the facts and circumstances. [Reg. §1.410(b)-4.]

□ [T.D. 8363, 9-12-91.]

[Reg. §1.410(b)-5]

§1.410(b)-5. Average benefit percentage test.—(a) *General rule.*—A plan satisfies the average benefit percentage test of this section for a plan year if and only if the average benefit percentage of the plan for the plan year is at least 70 percent. A plan is deemed to satisfy this requirement if it satisfies paragraph (f) of this section for the plan year.

(b) *Determination of average benefit percentage.*—The average benefit percentage of a plan for a plan year is the percentage determined by dividing the actual benefit percentage of the nonhighly compensated employees in plans in the testing group for the testing period that includes the plan year by the actual benefit percentage of the highly compensated employees in plans in the testing group for that testing period. See paragraph (d)(3)(ii) of this section for the definition of testing period.

(c) *Determination of actual benefit percentage.*—The actual benefit percentage of a group of employees for a testing period is the average of the employee benefit percentages, calculated separately with respect to each of the employees in the group for the testing period. All nonexcludable employees of the employer are taken into account for this purpose, even if they are not benefiting under any plan that is taken into account.

(d) *Determination of employee benefit percentages.*—(1) *Overview.*—This paragraph (d) provides rules for determining employee benefit percentages. See paragraph (e) of this section for alternative methods for determining employee benefit percentages.

(2) *Employee contributions and employee-provided benefits disregarded.*—Only employer-provided contributions and benefits are taken into account in determining employee benefit percentages. Therefore, employee contributions (including both employee contributions allocated to separate accounts and employee contributions not allocated to separate accounts), and benefits derived from such contributions, are not taken into account in determining employee benefit percentages.

(3) *Plans and plan years taken into account.*—(i) *Testing group.*—All plans included in the testing group under §1.410(b)-7(e)(1), and only those plans, are taken into account in determining an employee's employee benefit percentage.

(ii) *Testing period.*—An employee's employee benefit percentage is determined on the basis of plan years ending with or within the same calendar year. These plan years are referred to in this section as the relevant plan years or, in the aggregate, as the testing period.

(4) *Contributions or benefits basis.*—Employee benefit percentages may be determined on either a contributions or a benefits basis. Employee benefit percentages for any testing period must be determined on the same basis (contributions or benefits) for all plans in the testing group.

(5) *Determination of employee benefit percentage.*—(i) *General rule.*—The employee benefit percentage for an employee for a testing period is the rate that would be determined for that employee for purposes of applying the general test for nondiscrimination in §§1.401(a)(4)-2, 1.401(a)(4)-3, 1.401(a)(4)-8 or 1.401(a)(4)-9, if all the plans in the testing group were aggregated for purposes of section 410(b). Thus, if employee benefit percentages are determined on a contributions basis, each employee's employee benefit percentage is the aggregate normal allocation rate that would be determined for the employee under §1.401(a)(4)-9(b)(2)(ii)(A) (if the plans in the testing group include both defined benefit and defined contribution plans), the allocation rate that would be determined for the employee under §1.401(a)(4)-2(c)(2) (if the plans in the testing group include only defined contribution plans), or the equivalent normal allocation rate that would be determined for the employee under §1.401(a)(4)-8(c)(2) (if the plans in the testing group include only defined benefit plans). Similarly, if employee benefit percentages are determined on a benefits basis, each employee's employee benefit percentage is the aggregate normal accrual rate that would be determined for the employee under §1.401(a)(4)-9(b)(2)(ii)(B), the normal accrual rate that would be determined for the employee under §1.401(a)(4)-3(d), or the equivalent accrual rate that would be determined for the employee under §1.401(a)(4)-8(b)(2), depending on whether the plans in the testing group include both defined benefit and defined contribution plans, only defined benefit plans, or only defined contribution plans.

(ii) *Plans with differing plan years.*—If not all the plans in the testing group share the same plan year, §1.410(b)-7(d)(5) would ordinarily prohibit them from being aggregated for purposes of section 410(b). In such a case, employee benefit percentages are determined by applying the rules of paragraph (d)(5)(i) of this section separately to each subset of plans in the testing group that share the same plan year (or the same accrual computation period) and aggregating the results for all plans in the testing group. Thus, an employee's employee benefit percentage is determined as the sum of these separate employee benefit percentages that are determined consistently for all the plans in the testing group (except for differences attributable solely to the differences in plan years).

(iii) *Options and consistency requirements.*—In determining employee benefit percentages under this paragraph (d)(5), any optional or alternative methods or rules available for determining rates in §§1.401(a)(4)-2, 1.401(a)(4)-3, 1.401(a)(4)-8, or 1.401(a)(4)-9, whichever is applicable, may be applied. Thus, for example, employee benefit percentages may generally be calculated using any of the alternative methods of determining average annual compensation or plan year compensation under §1.401(a)(4)-12, and using any underlying definition of compensation that satisfies section 414(s). Except as otherwise specifically permitted, the determination of employee benefit percentages must be made on a consistent basis for all employees and for all plans in the testing group as required by

§§ 1.401(a)(4)-2(c)(2)(vi), 1.401(a)(4)-3(d)(2)(i), 1.401(a)(4)-8(b)(2)(iv), 1.401(a)(4)-8(c)(2)(iv) or 1.401(a)(4)-9(b)(2)(iv).

(6) *Permitted disparity.*—(i) *In general.*—Permitted disparity may be imputed in determining employee benefit percentages as provided in §§ 1.401(a)(4)-2, 1.401(a)(4)-3, 1.401(a)(4)-8, or 1.401(a)(4)-9, whichever is applicable. When separate employee benefit percentages are determined for individual plans under paragraph (e)(2) of this section (or for subsets of plans that have the same plan year as described in paragraph (d)(5)(ii) of this section), permitted disparity may be imputed for an employee only in one individual plan (or subset of plans) and may not be imputed for the same employee in another individual plan (or subset of plans). However, if the same average annual compensation or plan year compensation is used to determine employee benefit percentages in more than one plan, the employee's employee benefit percentages for those plans may be summed prior to imputing permitted disparity.

(ii) *Plans which may not use permitted disparity.*—Permitted disparity may be reflected in the determination of rates only to the extent that the plans for which rates are being determined are plans for which the permitted disparity of section 401(l) is available. Thus, for example, if a section 401(k) plan is included in the testing group and permitted disparity is imputed under § 1.401(a)(4)-2(c)(iv), then employee benefit percentages are determined by first calculating an adjusted allocation rate (within the meaning of § 1.401(a)(4)-7(b)(1)) without regard to the amount of allocations under the section 401(k) plan and adding to it the allocation rate for the section 401(k) plan. See § 1.401(l)-1(a)(4) for a list of types of plans for which permitted disparity is not available.

(7) *Requirements for certain plans providing early retirement benefits.*—(i) *General rule.*—If any defined benefit plan in the testing group provides for early retirement benefits in addition to normal retirement benefits to any highly compensated employee, and the average actuarial reduction for any one of these benefits commencing in the five years prior to the plan's normal retirement age is less than four percent per year, then the aggregate most valuable allocation rate, equivalent most valuable allocation rate, aggregate most valuable accrual rate, or most valuable accrual rate must be substituted for the related normal rates in paragraph (d)(5) of this section.

(ii) *Exception.*—Paragraph (d)(7)(i) of this section does not apply if early retirement benefits with average actuarial reductions described in that paragraph are currently available, within the meaning of § 1.401(a)(4)-4(b), under plans in the testing group to a percentage of nonhighly compensated employees that is at least 70 percent of the highly compensated employees to whom these benefits are currently available.

(e) *Additional optional rules.*—(1) *Overview.*—This paragraph (e) contains various alternative methods for determining employee benefit percentages for a testing period.

(2) *Determination of employee benefit percentages as the sum of separately determined rates.*—(i) *In general.*—Employee benefit percentages may be determined as the sum of separately determined employee benefit percentages for each of the plans in the testing group that are aggregated under paragraphs (d)(5)(i) or (ii) of this section, provided that these employee benefit percentages are determined on a consistent basis for all of these plans pursuant to paragraph (d)(5)(iii) of this section.

(ii) *Exception from consistency requirement.*—The consistency requirement of paragraph (e)(2)(i) of this section is not violated merely because employee benefit percentages are not determined in a consistent manner for all of the plans in the testing group and the inconsistencies in determination of rates among plans are described in paragraph (e)(2)(iii) of this section. The exception in this paragraph (e)(2)(ii) applies only if it is reasonable to believe that the inconsistencies do not result in an average benefit percentage that is significantly higher than the average benefit percentage that would be determined had employee benefit percentages been determined on a consistent basis pursuant to paragraph (d)(5)(iii) of this section.

(iii) *Permitted inconsistencies.*—The following inconsistencies between plans are permitted under this paragraph (e)(2)—

(A) Use of different underlying definitions of section 414(s) compensation in the determination of rates;

(B) Use of different definitions of average annual compensation;

(C) Use of different testing ages;

(D) Use of different fresh-start dates;

(E) Use of different actuarial assumptions for normalization; or

(F) Disregard of actuarial increases after normal retirement age and QPSA charges without regard to any requirement for uniformity in the actuarial increases or QPSA charges.

(3) *Determination of employee benefit percentages without regard to plans of another type.*—(i) *General rule.*—Employee benefit percentages may be determined under plans of one type (i.e., defined benefit plans or defined contribution plans) by treating all plans of the other type (i.e., defined contribution plans or defined benefit plans, respectively) as if they were not part of the testing group, using the method provided in this paragraph (e)(3). If this method is used to determine whether a defined contribution plan satisfies the average benefit percentage test, employee benefit percentages under all defined contribution plans in the testing group must be determined on a contributions basis, and benefits under any defined benefit plan may not be included in the employee benefit percentage. Similarly, if this method is used to determine whether a defined benefit plan satisfies the average benefit percentage test, employee benefit percentages under all defined benefit plans in the testing group must be determined on a benefits basis, and allocations under any defined contribution plan may not be included in the employee benefit percentage.

(ii) *Restriction on use of separate testing group determination method.*—A plan does not satisfy the average benefit percentage test using the method provided in this paragraph (e)(3) unless each of the plans in the testing group of the other type (i.e., defined benefit plan or defined contribution plan) than the plan being tested satisfies the average benefit test of § 1.410(b)-2(b)(3) using the method in this paragraph (e)(3) or satisfies the ratio percentage test of § 1.410(b)-2(b)(2).

(iii) *Treatment of permitted disparity.*—Although under the general rule of this paragraph (e)(3) plans of another type are disregarded in determining employee benefit percentages, the permitted disparity used by those plans (including any permitted disparity that is used by those plans to satisfy § 1.401(a)(4)-1(b)(2)) is nonetheless taken into account in determining the extent to which permitted disparity may be used in determining employee benefit percentages.

(iv) *Example.*—The following example illustrates the rules of this paragraph (e)(3):

Example. Employer A maintains two defined benefit plans, neither of which covers a group of employees that satisfies the ratio percentage test of § 1.410(b)-2(b)(2), and a profit-sharing plan and a section 401(k) plan, each of which benefits a group of employees that satisfies the ratio percentage test of § 1.410(b)-2(b)(2). The defined benefit plans will satisfy the average benefit percentage test if the actual benefit percentage of all nonexcludable nonhighly compensated employees, computed on a benefits basis without regard to contributions under the profit-sharing plan or the section 401(k) plan, is at least 70 percent of the actual benefit percentage of all nonexcludable highly compensated employees, computed on a benefits basis without regard to contributions under the profit-sharing plan or the section 401(k) plan.

(4) *Simplified method for determining employee benefit percentages for certain defined benefit plans.*—(i) *In general.*—An employee's employee benefit percentage with respect to a plan may be determined under the simplified method of paragraph (e)(4)(ii) of this section, provided the following conditions are satisfied:

(A) The only plans included in the testing group are defined benefit plans, and employee benefit percentages under these plans are determined on a benefits basis.

(B) Employee benefit percentages under the plans in the testing group are not required to be determined by taking into account early retirement benefits under paragraph (d)(7) of this section.

(C) The plan is a safe harbor defined benefit plan described in § 1.401(a)(4)-3(b).

(ii) *Simplified method.*—(A) *Section 401(l) plans.*—Under the simplified method of this paragraph (e)(4)(ii), an employee's employee benefit percentage with respect to a section 401(l) plan described in § 1.401(a)(4)-3(b)(3) (i.e., a unit credit plan) may be deemed equal to the employee's excess benefit percentage or gross benefit percentage (as defined in § 1.401(l)-1(c)(14) or (18), respectively), whichever is applicable under the plan's benefit formula in the plan year. In the case of a section 401(l) plan described in § 1.401(a)(4)-3(b)(4) (i.e., a fractional accrual plan), an employee's employee benefit percentage with respect to that plan may be deemed equal to the rate at which the excess or gross benefit, whichever is applicable, accrues for the employee in the plan year, taking into account the plan's benefit formula and the employee's projected service at normal retirement age. The use of this simplified method will be treated as an imputation of permitted disparity. See paragraph (d)(6) of this section for a restriction on multiple use of permitted disparity.

(B) *Other plans.*—Under the simplified method of this paragraph (e)(4)(ii), an employee's employee benefit percentage with respect to a plan described in §1.401(a)(4)-3(b)(3) that is not a section 401(*l*) plan and that is not imputing permitted disparity may be deemed equal to the employee's benefit rate in the plan year under the plan's benefit formula. In the case of a plan described in §1.401(a)(4)-3(b)(4) that is not a section 401(*l*) plan and that is not imputing permitted disparity, an employee's employee benefit percentage with respect to that plan may be deemed equal to the rate at which the benefit accrues for the employee in the plan year, taking into account the plan's benefit formula and an employee's projected service at normal retirement age.

(5) *Three-year averaging period.*—An employee's employee benefit percentage may be determined for a testing period as the average of the employee's employee benefit percentages determined separately for the testing period and for the immediately preceding one or two testing periods (referred to in this section as an averaging period). Employee benefit percentages of a particular employee that are averaged together within an averaging period must be determined on a consistent basis for all testing periods within the averaging period.

(6) *Alternative methods of determining compensation.*—Employee benefit percentages may be determined on the basis of any definition of compensation that satisfies §1.414(s)-1(d) (without regard to whether the definition satisfies §1.414(s)-1(d)(3)), provided that the same definition is used for all employees and it is reasonable to believe that the definition does not result in an average benefit percentage that is significantly higher than the average benefit percentage that would be determined had employee benefit percentages been determined using a definition of compensation that also satisfies §1.414(s)-1(d)(3).

(f) *Special rule for certain collectively bargained plans.*—A plan (as determined without regard to the mandatory disaggregation rule of §1.410(b)-7(c)(5)) that benefits both collectively bargained employees and noncollectively bargained employees is deemed to satisfy the average benefit percentage test of this section if—

(1) The provisions of the plan applicable to each employee in the plan are identical to the provisions of the plan applicable to every other employee in the plan, including the plan benefit or allocation formula, any optional forms of benefit, any ancillary benefit, and any other right or feature under the plan, and

(2) The plan would satisfy the ratio percentage test of §1.410(b)-2(b)(2), if §§1.410(b)-6(d) and 1.410(b)-7(c)(5) (the excludable employee and mandatory disaggregation rules for collectively bargained and noncollectively bargained employees) did not apply. [Reg. §1.410(b)-5.]

☐ [*T.D. 8363, 9-12-91. Amended by T.D. 8487, 8-31-93.*]

[Reg. §1.410(b)-6]

§1.410(b)-6. Excludable employees.—(a) *Employees.*—(1) *In general.*—For purposes of applying section 410(b) with respect to employees, all employees of the employer, other than the excludable employees described in paragraphs (b) through (i) of this section, are taken into account. Excludable employees are not taken into account with respect to a plan even if they are benefiting under the plan, except as otherwise provided in paragraph (b) of this section.

(2) *Rules of application.*—Except as specifically provided otherwise, excludable employees are determined separately with respect to each plan for purposes of testing that plan under section 410(b). Thus, in determining whether a particular plan satisfies the ratio percentage test of §1.410(b)-2(b)(2), paragraphs (b) through (i) of this section are applied solely with reference to that plan. Similarly, in determining whether two or more plans that are permissively aggregated and treated as a single plan under §1.410(b)-7(d) satisfy the ratio percentage test of §1.410(b)-2(b)(2), paragraphs (b) through (i) of this section are applied solely with reference to the deemed single plan. In determining whether a plan satisfies the average benefit percentage test of §1.410(b)-5, the rules of this section are applied by treating all plans in the testing group as a single plan.

(b) *Minimum age and service exclusions.*—(1) *In general.*—If a plan applies minimum age and service eligibility conditions permissible under section 410(a)(1) and excludes all employees who do not meet those conditions from benefiting under the plan, then all employees who fail to satisfy those conditions are excludable employees with respect to that plan. An employee is treated as meeting the age and service requirements on the date that any employee with the same age and service (including service permitted to be taken into account for purposes of nondiscrimination testing under

§1.401(a)(4)-11(d)(3)) would be eligible to commence participation in the plan, as provided in section 410(b)(4)(C).

(2) *Multiple age and service conditions.*—If a plan, including a plan for which an employer chooses the treatment under paragraph (b)(3) of this section, has two or more different sets of minimum age and service eligibility conditions, those employees who fail to satisfy all of the different sets of age and service conditions are excludable employees with respect to the plan. Except as provided in paragraph (b)(3) of this section, an employee who satisfies any one of the different sets of conditions is not an excludable employee with respect to the plan. Differences in the manner in which service is credited (e.g., hours of service calculated in accordance with 29 CFR 2530.200b-2 for hourly employees and elapsed time calculated in accordance with §1.410(a)-7 for salaried employees) for purposes of applying a service condition are not taken into account in determining whether multiple age and service eligibility conditions exist.

(3) *Plans benefiting certain otherwise excludable employees.*—(i) *In general.*—An employer may treat a plan benefiting otherwise excludable employees as two separate plans, one for the otherwise excludable employees and one for the other employees benefiting under the plan. See §1.410(b)-7(c)(3) regarding permissive disaggregation of plans benefiting otherwise excludable employees. The effect of this rule is that employees who would be excludable under paragraph (b)(1) of this section (applied without regard to section 410(a)(1)(B)) but for the fact that the plan does not apply the greatest permissible minimum age and service conditions may be treated as excludable employees with respect to the plan. This treatment is available only if the plan satisfies section 410(b) and §1.410(b)-2 with respect to these otherwise excludable employees in the manner described in paragraph (b)(3)(ii) of this section.

(ii) *Testing portion of plan benefiting otherwise excludable employees.*—In determining whether the plan that benefits employees who would otherwise be excludable under paragraph (b)(1) of this section (applied without regard to section 410(a)(1)(B)) satisfies section 410(b) and §1.410(b)-2, employees who have satisfied the greatest permissible minimum age and service conditions with respect to the plan are excludable employees. In addition, if the plan being tested applies minimum age and service conditions and those conditions are less than the maximum permissible minimum age and service conditions, employees who have not satisfied the lower minimum age and service conditions actually provided for in the plan are excludable employees. Thus, for example, if the plan requires attainment of age 18 and 3 months of service, employees who have not attained age 18 or 3 months of service with the employer are excludable employees.

(4) *Examples.*—The following examples illustrate the minimum age and service condition rules of this paragraph (b). In each example, the employer is not treated as operating qualified separate lines of business under section 414(r).

Example 1. An employer maintains Plan A for hourly employees and Plan B for salaried employees. Plan A has no minimum age or service condition. Plan B has no minimum age condition and requires 1 year of service. The employer treats Plans A and B as a single plan for purposes of section 410(b). Because Plan A imposes no minimum age or service condition, all employees of the employer automatically satisfy the minimum age and service conditions of Plan A. Therefore, no employees are excludable under this paragraph (b) in testing Plans A and B for purposes of section 410(b).

Example 2. An employer maintains three plans. Plan C benefits employees in Division C who satisfy the plan's minimum age and service condition of age 21 and 1 year of service. Plan D benefits employees in Division D who satisfy the plan's minimum age and service condition of age 18 and 1 year of service. Plan E benefits employees in Division E who satisfy the plan's minimum age and service condition of age 21 and 6 months of service. The employer treats Plans D and E as a single plan for purposes of section 410(b). In testing Plan C under the ratio percentage test or the nondiscriminatory classification test of section 410(b), employees who are not at least age 21 or who do not have at least 1 year of service are excludable employees under paragraph (b)(1) of this section. In testing Plans D and E, employees who do not satisfy the age and service requirements of either of the two plans are excludable employees under paragraph (b)(2) of this section. Thus, an employee is excludable with respect to Plans D and E only if the employee is not at least age 18 with at least 1 year of service or is not at least age 21 with at least 6 months of service. Thus, an employee who is 19 years old and has 11 months of service is excludable. Similarly, an employee who is 17 years old and has performed 2 years of service is also excludable.

Example 3. An employer maintains three plans. Plan F benefits all employees in Division F (the plan does not apply any minimum age or service condition). Plan G benefits employees in Division G who satisfy the plan's minimum age and service condition of age 18 and 1 year of service. Plan H benefits employees in Division H who satisfy the plan's minimum age and service condition of age 21 and 6 months of service. In testing the employer's plans under the average benefit percentage test provided in § 1.410(b)-5, Plans F, G, and H are treated as a single plan and, as such, use the lowest minimum age and service condition under the rule of paragraph (b)(2) of this section. Therefore, because Plan F does not apply any minimum age or service condition, no employee is excludable under this paragraph (b).

Example 4. An employer maintains Plan J, which does not apply any minimum age or service conditions. Plan J benefits all employees in Division 1 but does not benefit employees in Division 2. Although Plan J has no minimum age or service condition, the employer wants to exclude employees whose age and service is below the permissible minimums provided in section 410(b)(1)(A). The employer has 110 employees who either do not have 1 year of service or are not at least age 21. Of these 110 employees, 10 are highly compensated employees and 100 are nonhighly compensated employees. Five of these highly compensated employees, or 50 percent, work in Division 1 and thus benefit under Plan J. Thirty-five of these nonhighly compensated employees, or 35 percent, work in Division 1 and thus benefit under Plan J. Plan J satisfies the ratio percentage test of section 410(b) with respect to employees who do not satisfy the greatest permissible minimum age and service requirement because the ratio percentage of that group of employees is 70 percent. Thus, in determining whether or not Plan J satisfies section 410(b), the 110 employees may be treated as excludable employees in accordance with paragraph (b)(3)(i) of this section.

(c) *Certain nonresident aliens.*—(1) *General rule.*—An employee who is a nonresident alien (within the meaning of section 7701(b)(1)(B)) and who receives no earned income (within the meaning of section 911(d)(2)) from the employer that constitutes income from sources within the United States (within the meaning of section 861(a)(3)) is treated as an excludable employee.

(2) *Special treaty rule.*—In addition, an employee who is a non-resident alien (within the meaning of section 7701(b)(1)(B)) and who does receive earned income (within the meaning of section 911(d)(2)) from the employer that constitutes income from sources within the United States (within the meaning of section 861(a)(3)) is permitted to be excluded, if all of the employee's earned income from the employer from sources within the United States is exempt from United States income tax under an applicable income tax convention. This paragraph (c)(2) applies only if all employees described in the preceding sentence are so excluded.

(d) *Collectively bargained employees.*—(1) *General rule.*—A collectively bargained employee is an excludable employee with respect to a plan that benefits solely noncollectively bargained employees. If a plan (within the meaning of § 1.410(b)-7(b)) benefits both collectively bargained employees and noncollectively bargained employees for a plan year, § 1.410(b)-7(c)(4) provides that the portion of the plan that benefits the collectively bargained employees is treated as a separate plan from the portion of the plan that benefits the noncollectively bargained employees. Thus, a collectively bargained employee is always an excludable employee with respect to the mandatorily disaggregated portion of any plan that benefits noncollectively bargained employees.

(2) *Definition of collectively bargained employee.*—(i) *In general.*—A collectively bargained employee is an employee who is included in a unit of employees covered by an agreement that the Secretary of Labor finds to be a collective bargaining agreement between employee representatives and one or more employers, provided that there is evidence that retirement benefits were the subject of good faith bargaining between employee representatives and the employer or employers. An employee is a collectively bargained employee regardless of whether the employee benefits under any plan of the employer. See section 7701(a)(46) and § 301.7701-17T of this Chapter for additional requirements applicable to the collective bargaining agreement. An employee who performs hours of service during the plan year as both a collectively bargained employee and a noncollectively bargained employee is treated as a collectively bargained employee with respect to the hours of service performed as a collectively bargained employee and a noncollectively bargained employee with respect to the hours of service performed as a noncollectively bargained employee. See § 1.410(b)-7(c) for disaggregation rules for plans benefiting collectively bargained and noncollectively bargained employees.

(ii) *Special rules for certain employees in multiemployer plans.*—(A) *In general.*—For purposes of this paragraph (d), in testing the disaggregated portion of a multiemployer plan benefiting noncollectively bargained employees, a noncollectively bargained employee

who benefits under the plan may be treated as a collectively bargained employee with respect to all of the employee's hours of service under the rules of paragraphs (d)(2)(ii)(B) through (E) of this section, if the employee is or was a member of a unit of employees covered by a collective bargaining agreement and that agreement or a successor agreement provides for the employee to benefit under the plan in the current plan year. For this purpose, provisions of a participation agreement or similar document are taken into account in determining whether a collective bargaining agreement provides for an employee to benefit under a multiemployer plan.

(B) *Employees who were collectively bargained employees during a portion of the current plan year.*—An employee described in paragraph (d)(2)(ii)(A) of this section who performs services for one or more employers that are parties to the collective bargaining agreement, for the plan, or for the employee representative both as a collectively bargained employee and as a noncollectively bargained employee during a plan year may be treated as a collectively bargained employee for the plan year, provided that at least half of the employee's hours of service during the plan year are performed as a collectively bargained employee.

(C) *Employees who were collectively bargained employees during the collective bargaining agreement.*—An employee described in paragraph (d)(2)(ii)(A) of this section who was a collectively bargained employee with respect to all of the employee's hours of service during a plan year (including employees who are treated as collectively bargained employees with respect to all of their hours of service during a plan year under paragraph (d)(2)(ii)(B) or (E) of this section) may be treated as a collectively bargained employee with respect to all of the employee's hours of service for the duration of the collective bargaining agreement applicable for such plan year or, if later, until the end of the following plan year. For this purpose, a collective bargaining agreement is applicable for a plan year if it provided for the employee to benefit in the plan and was effective for any portion of that plan year. This paragraph (d)(2)(ii)(C) does not apply unless the terms of the plan providing for benefit accruals treat the employee in a manner that is generally no more favorable than similarly-situated employees who are collectively bargained employees.

(D) *Employees who previously were collectively bargained employees.*—An employee who was treated as a collectively bargained employee pursuant to paragraph (d)(2)(ii)(C) of this section may be treated as a collectively bargained employee with respect to all of the employee's hours of service after the end of the period described in paragraph (d)(2)(ii)(C) of this section, provided that the employee is performing services for one or more employers that are parties to the collective bargaining agreement, for the plan, or for the employee representative. This paragraph (d)(2)(ii)(D) does not apply unless the terms of the plan providing for benefit accruals treat the employee in a manner that is generally no more favorable than similarly-situated employees who are collectively bargained employees, and no more than five percent of the employees covered under the multiemployer plan are noncollectively bargained employees (determined without regard to this paragraph (d)(2)(ii)(D)). In determining whether more than five percent of the employees covered under the multiemployer plan are noncollectively bargained employees, those employees who are described in paragraphs (d)(2)(ii)(B) and (C) of this section are treated as collectively bargained employees.

(E) *Transition rule.*—For a plan year beginning before the applicable effective date of these regulations as set forth in § 1.410(b)-10(b) or (d), any employee described in paragraph (d)(2)(ii)(A) of this section may be treated as a collectively bargained employee with respect [to]all of the employee's hours of service for that plan year.

(F) *Consistency requirement.*—The rules in paragraphs (d)(2)(i) and (ii) of this section must be applied to all employees on a reasonable and consistent basis for the plan year.

(iii) *Covered by a collective bargaining agreement.*—(A) *General rule.*—For purposes of paragraph (d)(2)(i) of this section, an employee is included in a unit of employees covered by a collective bargaining agreement if and only if the employee is represented by a bona fide employee representative that is a party to the collective bargaining agreement under which the plan is maintained. Thus, for example, an employee of either a plan or the employee representative that is a party to the collective bargaining agreement under which the plan is maintained is not included in a unit of employees covered by the collective bargaining agreement under which the plan is maintained merely because the employee is covered under the plan pursuant to an agreement entered into by the plan or employee representative on behalf of the employee (other than in the capacity of an employee representative with respect to the employee). This is the case even if all of such employees benefiting under the plan constitute only a de minimis percentage of the total employees benefiting under the plan.

(B) *Plans covering professional employees.*—(1) *In general.*—An employee is not considered included in a unit of employees covered by a collective bargaining agreement for a plan year for purposes of paragraph (d)(2)(iii)(A) of this section if, for the plan year, more than 2 percent of the employees who are covered pursuant to the agreement are professionals. This rule applies to all employees under the agreement, nonprofessionals as well as professionals. Thus, no employees covered by such an agreement are excludable employees with respect to employees who are not covered by a collective bargaining agreement.

(2) *Multiple collective bargaining agreements.*—This paragraph (d)(2)(iii)(B) is applied separately with respect to each collective bargaining agreement. Thus, for example, if a plan benefits two groups of employees, one included in a unit of employees covered by collective bargaining agreement X, more than 2 percent of whom are professionals, and another included in a unit of employees covered by collective bargaining agreement Y, none of whom are professionals, the group covered by collective bargaining agreement X is not considered covered by a collective bargaining agreement and the group covered by agreement Y is considered covered by a collective bargaining agreement.

(3) *Application of minimum coverage tests.*—If a plan covers more than 2 percent professional employees, no employees in the plan are treated as covered by a collective bargaining agreement. A plan that covers more than 2 percent professional employees must satisfy section 410(b) without regard to section 413(b) and the special rule in § 1.410(b)-2(b)(7) of this section (regarding collectively bargained plans). In such cases, all nonexcludable employees must be taken into account. For this purpose, employees included in other collective bargaining units are excludable employees. However, the employees who are not covered by a collective bargaining agreement and the employees who are covered by an agreement that has more than 2 percent professionals are not excludable employees.

(iv) *Examples.*—The following examples illustrate the collective bargaining unit rules of this section.

Example 1. An employer has 700 collectively bargained employees (none of whom is a professional employee) and 300 noncollectively bargained employees (200 of whom are highly compensated employees). For purposes of applying the ratio percentage test of § 1.410(b)-2(b)(2) to Plan X, which benefits only the 300 noncollectively bargained employees, the 700 collectively bargained employees are treated as excludable employees pursuant to paragraph (d) of this section.

Example 2. (i) An employer has 1,500 employees in the following categories:

	Noncollectively Bargained Employees	Collectively Bargained Employees	Total
Highly Compensated Employees	100	100	200
Nonhighly Compensated Employees	900	400	1,300
Total	1,000	500	1,500

The employer maintains Plan Y, which benefits 1,100 employees, including all of the noncollectively bargained employees (except for 100 nonhighly compensated employees who are noncollectively bargained employees), and 200 of the collectively bargained employees (including the 100 highly compensated employees who are collectively bargained employees). There are no professional employees covered by the collective bargaining agreement. In accordance with § 1.410(b)-7(c)(4), the employer must apply the ratio percentage test of § 1.410(b)-2(b)(2) to Plan Y as if the plan were two separate plans, one benefiting the noncollectively bargained employees and the other benefiting the collectively bargained employees.

(ii) In testing the portion of Plan Y that benefits the noncollectively bargained employees, the collectively bargained employees are excludable employees. That portion's ratio percentage is 88.89 percent ([800/900]/[100/100]= 88.89%/100% = 0.8889), and thus it satisfies the ratio percentage test. The portion of Plan Y that benefits collectively bargained employees automatically satisfies section 410(b) under the special rule in § 1.410(b)-2(b)(7).

(e) *Employees of qualified separate lines of business.*—If an employer is treated as operating qualified separate lines of business for purposes of section 410(b) in accordance with § 1.414(r)-1(b), in testing a plan that benefits employees of one qualified separate line of business, the employees of the other qualified separate lines of business of the employer are treated as excludable employees. The rule in this paragraph (e) does not apply for purposes of satisfying the nondiscriminatory classification requirement of section 410(b)(5)(B). See §§ 1.414(r)-1(c)(2) and 1.414(r)-8 (separate application of section 410(b) to the employees of a qualified separate line of business). In addition, the rule in this paragraph (e) does not apply to a plan that is tested under the special rule for employer-wide plans in § 1.414(r)-1(c)(2)(ii) for a plan year.

(f) *Certain terminating employees.*—(1) *In general.*—An employee may be treated as an excludable employee for a plan year with respect to a particular plan if—

(i) The employee does not benefit under the plan for the plan year,

(ii) The employee is eligible to participate in the plan,

(iii) The plan has a minimum period of service requirement or a requirement that an employee be employed on the last day of the plan year (last-day requirement) in order for an employee to accrue a benefit or receive an allocation for the plan year,

(iv) The employee fails to accrue a benefit or receive an allocation under the plan solely because of the failure to satisfy the minimum period of service or last-day requirement,

(v) The employee terminates employment during the plan year with no more than 500 hours of service, and the employee is not an employee as of the last day of the plan year (for purposes of this

paragraph (f)(1)(v), a plan that uses the elapsed time method of determining years of service may use either 91 consecutive calendar days or 3 consecutive calendar months instead of 500 hours of service, provided it uses the same convention for all employees during a plan year), and

(vi) If this paragraph (f) is applied with respect to any employee with respect to a plan for a plan year, it is applied with respect to all employees with respect to the plan for the plan year.

(2) *Hours of service.*—For purposes of this paragraph (f), the term "hours of service" has the same meaning as provided for such term by 29 CFR 2530.200b-2 under the general method of crediting service for the employee. If one of the equivalencies set forth in 29 CFR 2530.200b-3 is used for crediting service under the plan, the 500-hour requirement must be adjusted accordingly.

(3) *Examples.*—The following examples illustrate the provision of this paragraph (f).

Example 1. An employer has 35 employees who are eligible to participate under a defined contribution plan. The plan provides that an employee will not receive an allocation of contributions for a plan year unless the employee is employed by the employer on the last day of the plan year. Only 30 employees are employed by the employer on the last day of the plan year. Two of the five employees who terminated employment before the last day of the plan year had 500 or fewer hours of service during the plan year, and the remaining three had more than 500 hours of service during the year. Of the five employees who were no longer employed on the last day of the plan year, the two with 500 hours of service or less during the plan year are treated as excludable employees for purposes of section 410(b), and the remaining three who had over 500 hours of service during the plan year are taken into account in testing the plan under section 410(b) but are treated as not benefiting under the plan.

Example 2. An employer has 30 employees who are eligible to participate under a defined contribution plan. The plan requires 1,000 hours of service to receive an allocation of contributions or forfeitures. Ten employees do not receive an allocation because of their failure to complete 1,000 hours of service. Three of the 10 employees who failed to satisfy the minimum service requirement completed 500 or fewer hours of service and terminated their employment. Two of the employees completed more than 500, but fewer than 1,000 hours of service and terminated their employment. The remaining five employees did not terminate employment. Under the rule in paragraph (f) of this section, the three terminated employees who completed 500 or fewer hours of service are treated as excludable employees for the portion of the plan year they are employed. The other seven employees who do not receive an allocation are taken into account in testing the plan under section 410(b) but are treated as not benefiting under the plan.

Reg. § 1.410(b)-6(f)(3)

Example 3. An employer maintains two plans, Plan A for salaried employees and Plan B for hourly employees. Of the 100 salaried employees, two do not receive an allocation under Plan A for the plan year because they terminate employment before completing 500 hours of service. Of the 300 hourly employees, 50 do not receive an allocation under Plan B for the plan year because they terminate employment before completing 500 hours. In applying section 410(b) to Plan A, the two employees who did not receive an allocation under Plan A are excludable employees, but the 50 who did not receive an allocation under Plan B are not excludable employees, because they were not eligible to participate under Plan A.

(g) *Employees of certain governmental or tax-exempt entities.*— (1) *Plans covered.*—For purposes of testing either a section 401(k) plan, or a section 401(m) plan that is provided under the same general arrangement as a section 401(k) plan, an employer may treat as excludable those employees described in paragraphs (g)(2) and (3) of this section.

(2) *Employees of governmental entities.*—Employees of governmental entities who are precluded from being eligible employees under a section 401(k) plan by reason of section 401(k)(4)(B)(ii) may be treated as excludable employees if more than 95 percent of the employees of the employer who are not precluded from being eligible employees by reason of section 401(k)(4)(B)(ii) benefit under the plan for the year.

(3) *Employees of tax-exempt entities.*—Employees of an organization described in section 403(b)(1)(A)(i) who are eligible to make salary reduction contributions under section 403(b) may be treated as excludable with respect to a section 401(k) plan, or a section 401(m) plan that is provided under the same general arrangement as a section 401(k) plan, if—

(i) No employee of an organization described in section 403(b)(1)(A)(i) is eligible to participate in such section 401(k) plan or section 401(m) plan; and

(ii) At least 95 percent of the employees who are neither employees of an organization described in section 403(b)(1)(A)(i) nor employees of a governmental entity who are precluded from being eligible employees under a section 401(k) plan by reason of section 401(k)(4)(B)(ii) are eligible to participate in such section 401(k) plan or section 401(m) plan.

(h) *Former employees.*—(1) *In general.*—For purposes of applying section 410(b) with respect to former employees, all former employees of the employer are taken into account, except that the employer may treat a former employee described in paragraph (h)(2) or (h)(3) of this section as an excludable former employee. If either or both of the former employee exclusion rules under paragraphs (h)(2) and (h)(3) of this section is applied, it must be applied to all former employees for the plan year on a consistent basis.

(2) *Employees terminated before a specified date.*—The employer may treat a former employee as excludable if—

(i) The former employee became a former employee either prior to January 1, 1984, or prior to the tenth calendar year preceding the calendar year in which the current plan year begins, and

(ii) The former employee became a former employee in a calendar year that precedes the earliest calendar year in which any former employee who benefits under the plan in the current plan year became a former employee.

(3) *Previously excludable employees.*—The employer may treat a former employee as excludable if the former employee was an excludable employee (or would have been an excludable employee if these regulations had been in effect) under the rules of paragraphs (b) through (g) of this section during the plan year in which the former employee became a former employee. If the employer treats a former employee as excludable pursuant to this paragraph (h)(3), the former employee is not taken into account with respect to a plan even if the former employee is benefiting under the plan.

(i) *Former employees treated as employees.*—An employer may treat as excludable employees all formerly nonhighly compensated employees who are treated as employees of the employer under § 1.410(b)-9 solely because they have increases in accrued benefits under a defined benefit plan that are based on ongoing service or compensation credits (including imputed service or compensation) after they cease to perform services for the employer. [Reg. § 1.410(b)-6.]

☐ [*T.D. 8363, 9-12-91. Amended by T.D. 8376, 12-2-91; T.D. 8487, 8-31-93; T.D. 8548, 6-23-94 and T.D. 9275, 7-20-2006.*]

[Reg. § 1.410(b)-7]

§ 1.410(b)-7. Definition of plan and rules governing plan disaggregation and aggregation.—(a) *In general.*—This section provides a

definition of "plan." First, this section sets forth a definition of plan within the meaning of section 401(a) or 403(a). Then certain mandatory disaggregation and permissive aggregation rules are applied. The result is the definition of plan that applies for purposes of sections 410(b) and 401(a)(4). Thus, in general, the term "plan" as used in this section initially refers to a plan described in section 414(*l*) and to an annuity plan described in section 403(a), and the term "plan" as used in other sections under these regulations means the plan determined after application of this section. Paragraph (b) of this section provides that each single plan under section 414(*l*) is treated as a single plan for purposes of section 410(b). Paragraph (c) of this section describes the rules for certain plans that must be treated as comprising two or more separate plans, each of which is a single plan subject to section 410(b). Paragraph (d) of this section provides a rule permitting an employer to aggregate certain separate plans to form a single plan for purposes of section 410(b). Paragraph (e) of this section provides rules for determining the testing group of plans taken into account in determining whether a plan satisfies the average benefit percentage test of § 1.410(b)-5.

(b) *Separate asset pools are separate plans.*—Each single plan within the meaning of section 414(*l*) is a separate plan for purposes of section 410(b). See § 1.414(*l*)-1(b). For example, if only a portion of the assets under a defined benefit plan is available, on an ongoing basis, to provide the benefits of certain employees, and the remaining assets are available only in certain limited cases to provide such benefits (but are available in all cases for the benefit of other employees), there are two separate plans. Similarly, the defined contribution portion of a plan described in section 414(k) is a separate plan from the defined benefit portion of that same plan. A single plan under section 414(*l*) is a single plan for purposes of section 410(b), even though the plan comprises separate written documents and separate trusts, each of which receives a separate determination letter from the Internal Revenue Service. A defined contribution plan does not comprise separate plans merely because it includes more than one trust, or merely because it provides for separate accounts and permits employees to direct the investment of the amounts allocated to their accounts. Further, a plan does not comprise separate plans merely because assets are separately invested in individual insurance or annuity contracts for employees.

(c) *Mandatory disaggregation of certain plans.*—(1) *Section 401(k) and 401(m) plans.*—The portion of a plan that is a section 401(k) plan and the portion that is not a section 401(k) plan are treated as separate plans for purposes of section 410(b). Similarly, the portion of a plan that is a section 401(m) plan and the portion that is not a section 401(m) plan are treated as separate plans for purposes of section 410(b). Thus, a plan that consists of elective contributions under a section 401(k) plan, employee and matching contributions under a section 401(m) plan, and contributions other than elective, employee, or matching contributions is treated as three separate plans for purposes of section 410(b). In addition, the portion of a plan that consists of contributions described in § 1.401(k)-2(a)(5) (i.e., contributions that fail to satisfy the allocation or compensation requirements applicable to elective contributions and are therefore required to be tested separately) and the portion of the plan that does not consist of such contributions are treated as separate plans for purposes of section 410(b). Similarly, the portion of a plan that consists of contributions described in § 1.410(m)-1(b)(4)(ii) (i.e., matching contributions that fail to satisfy the allocation and other requirements applicable to matching contributions and are therefore required to be tested separately) and the portion of the plan that does not consist of such contributions are treated as separate plans for purposes of section 410(b).

(2) *ESOPs and non-ESOPs.*—The portion of a plan that is an ESOP and the portion of the plan that is not an ESOP are treated as separate plans for purposes of section 410(b), except as otherwise permitted under § 54.4975-11(e) of this Chapter.

(3) *Plans benefiting otherwise excludable employees.*—If an employer applies section 410(b) separately to the portion of a plan that benefits only employees who satisfy age and service conditions under the plan that are lower than the greatest minimum age and service conditions permissible under section 410(a), the plan is treated as comprising separate plans, one benefiting the employees who have satisfied the lower minimum age and service conditions but not the greatest minimum age and service conditions permitted under section 410(a) and one benefiting employees who have satisfied the greatest minimum age and service conditions permitted under section 410(a). See § 1.410(b)-6(b)(3)(ii) for rules about testing otherwise excludable employees.

(4) *Plans benefiting certain disaggregation populations of employees.*—(i) *In general.*—(A) *Single plan must be treated as separate plans.*—If a plan (i.e., a single plan within the meaning of section 414(l)) benefits employees of more than one disaggregation population, the

plan must be disaggregated and treated as separate plans, each separate plan consisting of the portion of the plan benefiting the employees of each disaggregation population. See paragraph (c)(4)(ii) of this section for the definition of disaggregation population.

(B) *Benefit accruals or allocations attributable to current status.*—Except as otherwise provided in paragraph (c)(4)(i)(C) of this section, in applying the rule of paragraph (c)(4)(i)(A) of this section, the portion of the plan benefiting employees of a disaggregation population consists of all benefits accrued by, or all allocations made to, employees while they were members of the disaggregation population.

(C) *Exceptions for certain benefit accruals.*—(1) *Attribution of benefits to first disaggregation population.*—If employees benefiting under a plan change from one disaggregation population to a second disaggregation population, benefits that accrue while members of the second disaggregation population that are attributable to years of service previously credited while the employees were members of the first disaggregation population may be treated as provided to them in their status as members of the first disaggregation population and thus included in the portion of the plan benefiting employees of the first disaggregation population. This special treatment is available only if it is applied on a consistent basis, if it does not result in significant discrimination in favor of highly compensated employees, and if the plan provision providing the additional benefits applies on the same terms to all similarly-situated employees. For example, if all formerly collectively bargained employees accrue additional benefits under a plan after becoming noncollectively bargained employees, then those benefit increases may be treated as included in the portion of the plan benefiting collectively bargained employees if they are attributable to years of service credited while the employees were collectively bargained (e.g., where the additional benefits result from compensation increases that occur while the employees are noncollectively bargained or from plan amendments affecting benefits earned while collectively bargained that are adopted while the employees are noncollectively bargained) and if such treatment does not result in significant discrimination in favor of highly compensated employees.

(2) *Attribution of benefits to current disaggregation population.*—If employees benefiting under a plan change from one disaggregation population to another disaggregation population, benefits they accrue while members of the first disaggregation population may be treated as provided to them in their current status and thus included in the portion of the plan benefiting employees of the disaggregation population of which they are currently members. This special treatment is available only if it is applied on a consistent basis and if it does not result in significant discrimination in favor of highly compensated employees.

(D) *Change in disaggregation populations.*—(1) *Reasonable treatment.*—If, in previous years, the configuration of a plan's disaggregation populations differed from their configuration for the current year, for purposes of the benefits accrued by, or allocations made to, an employee for those years, the employee's status as a member of a current disaggregation population for those years must be determined on a reasonable basis. A different configuration occurs, for example, if disaggregation populations exist for the first time, such as when an employer is first treated as operating qualified separate lines of business, or if the existing disaggregation populations change, such as when an employer redesignates its qualified separate lines of business.

(2) *Example.*—The following example illustrates the application of this paragraph (c)(4)(i)(D).

Example. (a) Employer X operates Divisions M and N, which are treated as qualified separate lines of business for the first time in 1998. Thus, the disaggregation populations of employees of Division M and employees of Division N exist for the first time. Since 1981 Employer X has maintained a defined benefit plan, Plan P, for employees of Division M. Plan P provides a normal retirement benefit of one percent of average annual compensation for each year of service up to 25. Employee A has worked for Division M since 1981 and has never worked for Division N. Employee B has worked for Division N since 1989 and worked for Division M from 1981 to 1988. Employee C has worked in the headquarters of Employer X since 1981. For the period 1981 to 1988 Employee C was credited with years of service under Plan P.

(b) For purposes of the benefits accrued by Employee A under Plan P during years 1981 through 1997, Employee A is reasonably treated as having been a member of the Division M disaggregation population for those years. For purposes of the benefits accrued by Employee B under Plan P during years 1981 through 1988, Employee B is reasonably treated as having been a member of the Division M disaggregation population for 1981 through 1988 and as

having changed to the Division N disaggregation population for 1989 through 1997. For purposes of the benefits accrued by Employee C under Plan P during years 1981 through 1988, Employee C is reasonably treated as having been a member of the Division M disaggregation population for those years. Moreover, any benefit accruals for Employee B and Employee C in years after 1988, that result from increases in average annual compensation after 1988 and that are attributable to years of service credited for 1981 through 1988, may be treated as provided to Employee B and Employee C in their status as members of the Division M disaggregation population if the requirements of paragraph (c)(4)(i)(C)(_) of this section are otherwise met.

(ii) *Definition of disaggregation population.*—(A) *Plan benefiting employees of qualified separate lines of business.*—If an employer is treated as operating qualified separate lines of business for purposes of section 410(b) in accordance with §1.414(r)-1(b), and a plan benefits employees of more than one qualified separate line of business, the employees of each qualified separate line of business are separate disaggregation populations. In this case, the portion of the plan benefiting the employees of each qualified separate line of business is treated as a separate plan maintained by that qualified separate line of business. However, employees of different qualified separate lines of business who are benefiting under a plan that is tested under the special rule for employer-wide plans in §1.414(r)-1(c)(2)(ii) for a plan year are not separate disaggregation populations merely because they are employees of different qualified separate lines of business.

(B) *Plan benefiting collectively bargained employees.*—If a plan benefits both collectively bargained employees and noncollectively bargained employees, the collectively bargained employees are one disaggregation population and the noncollectively bargained employees are another disaggregation population. If the population of collectively bargained employees includes employees covered under different collective bargaining agreements, the population of employees covered under each collective bargaining agreement is also a separate disaggregation population.

(C) *Plan maintained by more than one employer.*—If a plan benefits employees of more than one employer, the employees of each employer are separate disaggregation populations. In this case, the portion of the plan benefiting the employees of each employer is treated as a separate plan maintained by that employer, which must satisfy section 410(b) by reference only to that employer's employees. However, for purposes of this paragraph (c)(4)(ii)(C), if the plan of one employer (or, in the case of a plan maintained by more than one employer, the plan provisions applicable to the employees of one employer) treats compensation or service with another employer as compensation or service with the first employer, then the current accruals attributable to that compensation or service are treated as provided to an employee of the first employer under the plan of the first employer (or the portion of a plan maintained by more than one employer benefiting employees of the first employer), and the provisions of paragraph (c)(4)(i)(C) of this section do not apply to those accruals. Thus, for example, if Plan A maintained by Employer X imputes service or compensation for an employee of Employer Y, then Plan A is not treated as benefiting the employees of more than one employer merely because of this imputation.

(5) *Additional rule for plans benefiting employees of more than one qualified separate line of business.*—If a plan benefiting employees of more than one qualified separate line of business satisfies the reasonable classification requirement of §1.410(b)-4(b) before the application of paragraph (c)(4) of this section, then any portion of the plan that is treated as a separate plan as a result of the application of paragraphs (c)(4)(i)(A) and (ii)(A) of this section is deemed to satisfy that requirement.

(d) *Permissive aggregation for ratio percentage and nondiscriminatory classification tests.*—(1) *In general.*—Except as provided in paragraphs (d)(2) and (d)(3) of this section, for purposes of applying the ratio percentage test of §1.410(b)-2(b)(2) or the nondiscriminatory classification test of §1.401(b)-4, an employer may designate two or more separate plans (determined after application of paragraph (b) of this section) as a single plan. If an employer treats two or more separate plans as a single plan under this paragraph, the plans must be treated as a single plan for all purposes under sections 401(a)(4) and 410(b).

(2) *Rules of disaggregation.*—An employer may not aggregate portions of a plan that are disaggregated under the rules of paragraph (c) of this section. Similarly, an employer may not aggregate two or more separate plans that would be disaggregated under the rules of paragraph (c) of this section if they were portions of the same plan. In addition, an employer may not aggregate an ESOP with another ESOP, except as permitted under §54.4975-11(e) of this Chapter.

(3) *Duplicative aggregation.*—A plan may not be combined with two or more plans to form more than one single plan. Thus, for example, an employer that maintains plans A, B, and C may not aggregate plans A and B and plans A and C to form two single plans. However, the employer may apply the permissive aggregation rules of this paragraph (d) to form any one (and only one) of the following combinations: plan ABC, plans AB and C, plans AC and B, or plans A and BC.

(4) *Special rule for plans benefiting employees of a qualified separate line of business.*—For purposes of paragraph (d)(1) of this section, an employer that is treated as operating qualified separate lines of business for purposes of section 410(b) in accordance with §1.414(r)-1(b) is permitted to aggregate the portions of two or more plans that benefit employees of the same qualified separate line of business (regardless of whether the employer elects to aggregate the portions of the same plans that benefit employees of the other qualified separate lines of business of the employer), provided that none of the plans is tested under the special rule for employer-wide plans in §1.414(r)-1(c)(2)(ii). Thus, the employer is permitted to apply paragraph (d)(1) of this section with respect to two or more separate plans determined after the application of paragraphs (b) and (c)(4) of this section, but may not aggregate a plan that is tested under the special rule for employer-wide plans in §1.414(r)-1(c)(2)(ii) for a plan year with any portion of a plan that does not rely on that special rule for the plan year. In all other respects, the provisions of this paragraph (d) regarding permissive aggregation apply, including (but not limited to) the disaggregation rules under paragraph (d)(2) of this section (including the mandatory disaggregation rule of paragraph (c)(4) of this section), and the prohibition on duplicative aggregation under paragraph (d)(3) of this section. This paragraph (d)(4) applies only in the case of an employer that is treated as operating qualified separate lines of business for purposes of section 410(b) in accordance with §1.414(r)-1(b). See §§1.414(r)-1(c)(2) and 1.414(r)-8 (separate application of section 410(b) to the employees of a qualified separate line of business).

(5) *Same plan year requirement.*—Two or more plans may not be aggregated and treated as a single plan under this paragraph (d) unless they have the same plan year.

(e) *Determination of plans in testing group for average benefit percentage test.*—(1) *In general.*—For purposes of applying the average benefit percentage test of §1.410(b)-5 with respect to a plan, all plans in the testing group must be taken into account. For this purpose, the plans in the testing group are the plan being tested and all other plans of the employer that could be permissively aggregated with that plan under paragraph (d) of this section. Whether two or more plans could be permissively aggregated under paragraph (d) of this section is determined (i) without regard to the rule in paragraph (d)(4) of this section that portions of two or more plans benefiting employees of the same line of business may not be aggregated if any of the plans is tested under the special rule for employer-wide plans in §1.414(r)-1(c)(2)(ii), (ii) without regard to paragraph (d)(5) of this section, and (iii) by applying paragraph (d)(2) of this section without regard to paragraphs (c)(1) and (c)(2) of this section.

(2) *Examples.*—The following example illustrates the rules of this paragraph (e).

Example 1. Employer X is treated as operating two qualified separate lines of business for purposes of section 410(b) in accordance with section 414(r), QSLOB1 and QSLOB2. Employer X must apply the rules in §1.414(r)-8 to determine whether its plans satisfy section 410(b) on a qualified-separate-line-of-business basis. Employer X maintains the following plans:

(a) Plan A, the portion of Employer X's employer-wide section 401(k) plan that benefits all noncollectively bargained employees of QSLOB1,

(b) Plan B, the portion of Employer X's employer-wide section 401(k) plan that benefits all noncollectively bargained employees of QSLOB2,

(c) Plan C, a defined benefit plan that benefits all hourly noncollectively bargained employees of QSLOB1,

(d) Plan D, a defined benefit plan that benefits all collectively bargained employees of QSLOB1,

(e) Plan E, an ESOP that benefits all noncollectively bargained employees of QSLOB1,

(f) Plan F, a profit-sharing plan that benefits all salaried noncollectively bargained employees of QSLOB1.

Assume that Plan F does not satisfy the ratio percentage test of §1.410(b)-2(b)(2) on a qualified-separate-line-of-business basis, but does satisfy the nondiscriminatory classification test of §1.410(b)-4 on both an employer-wide and a qualified-separate-line-of-business basis. Therefore, to satisfy section 410(b), Plan F must satisfy the average benefit percentage test of §1.410(b)-5 on a qualified-separate-line-of-business basis. The plans in the testing group used to deter-

mine whether Plan F satisfies the average benefit percentage test of §1.410(b)-5 are Plans A, C, E, and F.

Example 2. The facts are the same as in *Example 1*, except that Employer X applies the special rule for employer-wide plans in §1.414(r)-1(c)(2)(ii) to its employer-wide section 401(k) plan. To satisfy section 410(b), Plan F must satisfy the average benefit percentage test of §1.410(b)-5. Since paragraph (c)(4) of this section no longer applies to Plans A and B, they are treated as a single plan (Plan AB). The plans in the testing group used to determine whether Plan F satisfies the average benefit percentage test of §1.410(b)-5 are therefore Plans AB, C, E, and F. However, the employees of QSLOB 2 continue to be excludable employees for purposes of determining whether Plan F satisfies the average benefit percentage test. See §1.410(b)-6(e).

(f) *Section 403(b) plans.*—In determining whether a plan satisfies section 410(b), a plan subject to section 403(b)(12)(A)(i) is disregarded. However, in determining whether a plan subject to section 403(b)(12)(A)(i) satisfies section 410(b), plans that are not subject to section 403(b)(12)(A)(i) may be taken into account. [Reg. §1.410(b)-7.]

☐ [*T.D. 8363, 9-12-91. Amended by T.D. 8376, 12-2-91; T.D. 8487, 8-31-93; T.D. 8548, 6-23-94 and T.D. 9169, 12-28-2004.*]

[Reg. §1.410(b)-8]

§1.410(b)-8. Additional rules.—(a) *Testing methods.*—(1) *In general.*—A plan must satisfy section 410(b) for a plan year using one of the testing options in paragraphs (a)(2) through (a)(4) of this section. Whichever testing option is used for the plan year must also be used for purposes of applying section 401(a)(4) to the plan for the plan year. The annual testing option in paragraph (a)(4) of this section must be used in applying section 410(b) to a section 401(k) plan or a section 401(m) plan, and in applying the average benefit percentage test of §1.410(b)-5. For purposes of this paragraph (a), the plan provisions and other relevant facts as of the last day of the plan year regarding which employees benefit under the plan for the plan year are applied to the employees taken into account under the testing option used for the plan year. For this purpose, amendments retroactively correcting a plan in accordance with §1.401(a)(4)-11(g) are taken into account as plan provisions in effect as of the last day of the plan year.

(2) *Daily testing option.*—A plan satisfies section 410(b) for a plan year if it satisfies §1.410(b)-2 on each day of the plan year, taking into account only those employees (or former employees) who are employees (or former employees) on that day.

(3) *Quarterly testing option.*—A plan is deemed to satisfy section 410(b) for a plan year if the plan satisfies §1.410(b)-2 on at least one day in each quarter of the plan year, taking into account for each of those days only those employees (or former employees) who are employees (or former employees) on that day. The preceding sentence does not apply if the plan's eligibility rules or benefit formula operate to cause the four quarterly testing days selected by the employer not to be reasonably representative of the coverage of the plan over the entire plan year.

(4) *Annual testing option.*—A plan satisfies section 410(b) for a plan year if it satisfies §1.410(b)-2 as of the last day of the plan year, taking into account all employees (or former employees) who were employees (or former employees) on any day during the plan year.

(5) *Example.*—The following example illustrates this paragraph (a).

Example. Plan A is a defined contribution plan that is not a section 401(k) plan or a section 401(m) plan, and that conditions allocations on an employee's employment on the last day of the plan year. Plan A is being tested for the 1995 calendar plan year using the daily testing option in paragraph (a)(2) of this section. In testing the plan for compliance with section 410(b) on March 11, 1995, Employee X is taken into account because he was an employee on that day and was not an excludable employee with respect to Plan A on that day. Employee X was a participant in Plan A on March 11, 1995, was employed on December 31, 1995, and received an allocation under Plan A for the 1995 plan year. Under these facts, Employee X is treated as benefiting under Plan A on March 11, 1995, even though Employee X had not satisfied all of the conditions for receiving an allocation on that day, because Employee X satisfied all of those conditions as of the last day of the plan year.

(b) *Family member aggregation rule.*—For purposes of section 410(b), and in accordance with section 414(q)(6), a highly compensated employee who is a 5-percent owner or one of the ten most highly compensated employees and any family member (or members) of such a highly compensated employee who is also an employee of the employer are to be treated as a single highly compensated employee. If any member of that group is benefiting under a plan, the deemed single employee is treated as benefiting under the plan. If no member of that group is benefiting under a plan, the deemed single employee is treated as not benefiting under the plan. [Reg. § 1.410(b)-8.]

☐ [T.D. 8363, 9-12-91.]

[Reg. § 1.410(b)-9]

§ 1.410(b)-9. Definitions.—In applying this section and §§ 1.410(b)-2 through 1.410(b)-10, the definitions in this section govern unless otherwise provided.

Collectively bargained employee. "Collectively bargained employee" means a collectively bargained employee within the meaning of § 1.410(b)-6(d)(2).

Defined benefit plan. "Defined benefit plan" means a defined benefit plan within the meaning of section 414(j). The portion of a plan described in section 414(k) that does not consist of separate accounts is treated as a defined benefit plan.

Defined contribution plan. "Defined contribution plan" means a defined contribution plan within the meaning of section 414(i). The portion of a plan described in section 414(k) that consists of separate accounts is treated as a defined contribution plan.

Employee. Employee means an individual who performs services for the employer who is either a common law employee of the employer, a self-employed individual who is treated as an employee pursuant to section 401(c)(1), or a leased employee (not excluded under section 414(n)(5)) who is treated as an employee of the employer-recipient under section 414(n)(2) or 414(o)(2). Individuals that an employer treats as employees under section 414(n) pursuant to the requirements of section 414(o) are considered to be leased employees for purposes of this rule. In addition, an individual must be treated as an employee with respect to allocations under a defined contribution plan taken into account under § 1.401(a)(4)-2(c)(ii) and with respect to increases in accrued benefits (within the meaning of [section]411(a)(7)) under a defined benefit plan that are based on ongoing service or compensation (including imputed service or compensation) credits.

Employer. "Employer" means the employer maintaining the plan and those employers required to be aggregated with the employer under sections 414(b), (c), (m), or (o). An individual who owns the entire interest of an unincorporated trade or business is treated as an employer. Also, a partnership is treated as the employer of each partner and each employee of the partnership.

ESOP. "ESOP" or "employee stock ownership plan" means an employee stock ownership plan within the meaning of section 4975(e)(7) or a tax credit employee stock ownership plan within the meaning of section 409(a).

Former employee. Former employee means an individual who was, but has ceased to be, an employee of the employer (i.e., the individual has ceased performing services as an employee for the employer). An individual is treated as a former employee beginning on the day after the day on which the individual ceases performing services as an employee for the employer. Thus, an individual who ceases performing services as an employee for an employer during a plan year is both an employee and a former employee for the plan year. Notwithstanding the foregoing, an individual is an employee (and not a former employee) to the extent that the individual is treated as an employee with respect to the plan for the plan year under the definition of employee in this section.

Highly compensated employee. Highly compensated employee means an employee who is a highly compensated employee within the meaning of section 414(q) or a former employee treated as an employee under the definition of employee in this section who is a highly compensated former employee within the meaning of section 414(q).

Highly compensated former employee. Highly compensated former employee means a former employee who is a highly compensated former employee within the meaning of section 414(q).

Multiemployer plan. "Multiemployer plan" means a multiemployer plan within the meaning of section 414(f).

Noncollectively bargained employee. "Noncollectively bargained employee" means an employee who is not a collectively bargained employee.

Nonhighly compensated employee. "Nonhighly compensated employee" means an employee who is not a highly compensated employee.

Nonhighly compensated former employee. "Nonhighly compensated former employee" means a former employee who is not a highly compensated former employee.

Plan year. "Plan year" means the plan year of the plan as defined in the written plan document. In the absence of a specifically designated plan year, the plan year is deemed to be the calendar year.

Plan year compensation. "Plan year compensation" means plan year compensation within the meaning of § 1.401(a)(4)-12.

Professional employee. "Professional employee" means any highly compensated employee who, on any day of the plan year, performs professional services for the employer as an actuary, architect, attor-

ney, chiropodist, chiropractor, dentist, executive, investment banker, medical doctor, optometrist, osteopath, podiatrist, psychologist, certified or other public accountant, stockbroker, or veterinarian, or in any other professional capacity determined by the Commissioner in a notice or other document of general applicability to constitute the performance of services as a professional.

Ratio percentage. With respect to a plan for a plan year, a plan's "ratio percentage" means the percentage (rounded to the nearest hundredth of a percentage point) determined by dividing the percentage of the nonhighly compensated employees who benefit under the plan by the percentage of the highly compensated employees who benefit under the plan. The percentage of the nonhighly compensated employees who benefit under the plan is determined by dividing the number of nonhighly compensated employees benefiting under the plan by the total number of nonhighly compensated employees of the employer. The percentage of the highly compensated employees who benefit under the plan is determined by dividing the number of highly compensated employees benefiting under the plan by the total number of highly compensated employees of the employer.

Section 401(k) plan. "Section 401(k) plan" means a plan consisting of elective contributions described in § 1.401(k)-6 under a qualified cash or deferred arrangement described in § 1.401(k)-1(a)(4)(i). Thus, a section 401(k) plan does not include a plan (or portion of a plan) that consists of contributions under a nonqualified cash or deferred arrangement, or qualified nonelective or qualified matching contributions treated as elective contributions under § 1.401(k)-1(a)(6).

Section 401(l) plan. "Section 401 (l) plan" means a plan that—

(1) Provides for a disparity in employer-provided benefits or contributions that satisfies section 401(l) in form, and

(2) Relies on one of the safe harbors of § 1.401(a)(4)-2(b)(2), 1.401(a)(4)-3(b), 1.401(a)(4)-8(b)(3), or 1.401(a)(4)-8(c)(3)(iii)(B) to satisfy section 401(a)(4).

Section 401(m) plan. "Section 401(m) plan" means a plan consisting of employee contributions described in § 1.401(m)-1(f)(6) or matching contributions described in § 1.401(m)-1(a)(2), or both. Thus, a section 401(m) plan does not include a plan (or portion of a plan) that consists of elective contributions or qualified nonelective contributions treated as matching contributions under § 1.401(m)-1(b)(5). [Reg. § 1.410(b)-9.]

☐ [T.D. 8363, 9-12-91. *Amended by T.D. 8487, 8-31-93 and T.D. 9169*, 12-28-2004.]

[Reg. § 1.410(b)-10]

§ 1.410(b)-10. Effective dates and transition rules.—(a) *Statutory effective dates.*—(1) *In general.*—Except as set forth in paragraph (a)(2) of this section, the minimum coverage rules of section 410(b) as amended by section 1112 of the Tax Reform Act of 1986 apply to plan years beginning on or after January 1, 1989.

(2) *Special statutory effective date for collective bargaining agreements.*—(i) *In general.*—As provided for by section 1112(e)(2) of the Tax Reform Act of 1986, in the case of a plan maintained pursuant to one or more collective bargaining agreements between employee representatives and one or more employers ratified before March 1, 1986, the minimum coverage rules of section 410(b) as amended by section 1112 of the Tax Reform Act of 1986 do not apply to employees covered by any such agreement in plan years beginning before the earlier of—

(A) January 1, 1991; or

(B) The later of January 1, 1989, or the date on which the last of such collective bargaining agreements terminates (determined without regard to any extension thereof after February 28, 1986). For purposes of this paragraph (a)(2), any extension or renegotiation of a collective bargaining agreement, which extension or renegotiation is ratified after February 28, 1986, is to be disregarded in determining the date on which the agreement terminates.

(ii) *Example.*—The following example illustrates this paragraph (a)(2).

Example. Employer A maintains Plan 1 pursuant to a collective bargaining agreement. Plan 1 covers 100 of Employer A's noncollectively bargained employees and 900 of Employer A's collectively bargained employees. Employer A also maintains Plan 2, which covers Employer A's other 400 noncollectively bargained employees. The collective bargaining agreement under which Plan 1 is maintained was entered into on January 1, 1986, and expires December 31, 1992. Because Plan 1 is a plan maintained pursuant to a collective bargaining agreement, section 410(b) applies to the first plan year beginning on or after January 1, 1991. In applying section 410(b) to Plan 2, the 100 noncollectively bargained employees in Plan 1 must be taken into account. The deferred effective date for plans maintained pursuant to a collective bargaining agreement is not applicable in determining how section 410(b) is applied to a plan that is not maintained pursuant to a collective bargaining agreement.

(iii) *Plan maintained pursuant to a collective bargaining agreement.*—For purposes of this paragraph (a)(2), a plan is maintained pursuant to one or more collective bargaining agreements between employee representatives and one or more employers, if one or more of the agreements were ratified before March 1, 1986. Only plans maintained pursuant to agreements that the Secretary of Labor finds to be collective bargaining agreements and that satisfy section 7701(a)(46) are eligible for the deferred effective date under this paragraph (a)(2). A plan will not be treated as a plan maintained pursuant to one or more collective bargaining agreements eligible for the deferred effective date under this paragraph (a)(2) unless the plan would be a plan maintained pursuant to one or more collective bargaining agreements under the principles applied under section 1017(c) of the Employee Retirement Income Security Act of 1974. See H.R. Rep. No. 1280, 93rd Cong. 2d Sess. 266 (1974).

(b) *Regulatory effective dates.*—(1) *In general.*—Except as otherwise provided in this section, § § 1.410(b)-2 through 1.410(b)-9 apply to plan years beginning on or after January 1, 1994.

(2) *Plans of tax-exempt organizations.*—In the case of plans maintained by organizations exempt from income taxation under section 501(a), including plans subject to section 403(b)(12)(A)(i) (nonelective plans), § § 1.410(b)-2 through 1.410(b)-9 apply to plan years beginning on or after January 1, 1996, to the extent such plans are subject to section 410(b).

(c) *Compliance during transition period.*—For plan years beginning before the effective date of these regulations, as set forth in paragraph (b) of this section, and on or after the statutory effective date as set forth in paragraph (a) of this section, a plan must be operated in accordance with a reasonable, good faith interpretation of section 410(b). Whether a plan is operated in accordance with a reasonable, good faith interpretation of section 410(b) will generally be determined based on all of the relevant facts and circumstances, including the extent to which an employer has resolved unclear issues in its favor. If a plan's classification has been determined by the Commissioner to be nondiscriminatory and there have been no significant changes in or omissions of a material fact, the classification will be treated as nondiscriminatory for the relevant plan year. A plan will be deemed to be operated in accordance with a reasonable, good faith interpretation of section 410(b) if it is operated in accordance with the terms of § § 1.410(b)-2 through 1.410(b)-9.

(d) *Effective date for governmental plans.*—In the case of governmental plans described in section 414(d), including plans subject to section 403(b)(12)(A)(i) (nonelective plans) § 1.410(b)-2 through § 1.410(b)-10 apply to plan years beginning on or after January 1, 1996, or 90 days after the opening of the first legislative session beginning on or after January 1, 1996, of the governing body with authority to amend the plan, if that body does not meet continuously. Such plans are deemed to satisfy section 410(b) (and in the case of such plans that are not subject to section 403(b)(12)(A)(i), section 401(a)(3) as in effect on September 1, 1974) for plan years before that effective date. For purposes of this section, the governing body with authority to amend the plan is the legislature, board, commission, council, or other governing body with authority to amend the plan. See § 1.410(b)-2(d) and (e).

(e) *Effective date for provisions relating to exclusion of employees of certain tax-exempt entities.*—The provisions in § 1.410(b)-6(g) apply to plan years beginning after December 31, 1996. For plan years to which § 1.410(b)-6 applies that begin before January 1, 1997, § 1.410(b)-6(g) (as it appeared in the April 1, 2005 edition of 26 CFR part 1) applies. [Reg. § 1.410(b)-10.]

☐ [*T.D. 8363, 9-12-91. Amended by T.D. 8487, 8-31-93 and T.D. 9275, 7-20-2006.*]

[Reg. § 1.410(d)-1]

§ 1.410(d)-1. Election by church to have participation, vesting, funding, etc. provisions apply.—(a) *In general.*—If a church or convention or association of churches which maintains any church plan, as defined in section 414(e), makes an election under this section, certain provisions of the Code and Title I of the Employee Retirement Income Security Act of 1974 (the "Act") shall apply to such church plan as if such plan were not a church plan. The provisions of the Code referred to are section 410 (relating to minimum participation standards), section 411 (relating to minimum vesting standards), section 412 (relating to minimum funding standards), section 4975 (relating to prohibited transactions), and paragraphs (11), (12), (13), (14), (15), and (19) of section 401(a) (relating to joint and survivor annuities, mergers and consolidations, assignment or alienation of benefits, time of benefit commencement, certain social security increases, and withdrawals of employee contributions, respectively).

(b) *Election is irrevocable.*—An election under this section with respect to any church plan shall be binding with respect to such plan and, once made, shall be irrevocable.

(c) *Procedure for making election.*—(1) *Time of election.*—An election under this section may be made for plan years for which the provisions of section 410(d) of the Code apply to the church plan. By reason of section 1017(b) of the Act section 410(d) does not apply to a plan in existence on January 1, 1974, for plan years beginning before January 1, 1976. Section 1017(d) of the Act permits a plan administrator to elect to have certain provisions of the Code (including section 410(d)) apply to a plan before the otherwise applicable effective dates of such provisions. See § 1.410(a)-2(d). Therefore, for a plan in existence on January 1, 1974, an election under section 410(d) of the Code may be made for a plan year beginning before January 1, 1976, only if an election has been made under section 1017(d) of the Act with respect to that plan year.

(2) *By whom election is to be made.*—The election provided by this section may be made only by the plan administrator of the church plan.

(3) *Manner of making election.*—The plan administrator may elect to have the provisions of the Code described in paragraph (a) of this section apply to the church plan as if it were not a church plan by attaching the statement described in subparagraph (5) of this paragraph to either (i) the annual return required under section 6058(a) (or an amended return) with respect to the plan which is filed for the first plan year for which the election is effective or (ii) a written request for a determination letter relating to the qualification of the plan under section 401(a), 403(a), or 405(a) of the Code and, if trusteed, the exempt status under section 501(a) of the Code of a trust constituting a part of the plan.

(4) *Conditional election.*—If an election is made with a written request for a determination letter, the election may be conditioned upon issuance of a favorable determination letter and will become irrevocable upon issuance of such letter.

(5) *Statement.*—The statement described in subparagraph (3) of this paragraph shall indicate (i) that the election is made under section 410(d) of the Code and (ii) the first plan year for which it is effective. [Reg. § 1.410(d)-1.]

☐ [*T.D. 7508, 9-14-77.*]

[Reg. § 1.411(a)-1]

§ 1.411(a)-1. Minimum vesting standards; general rules.—(a) *In general.*—A plan is not a qualified plan (and a trust forming a part of such plan is not a qualified trust) unless—

(1) The plan provides that an employee's right to his normal retirement benefit (see § 1.411(a)-7(c)) is nonforfeitable (see § 1.411(a)-4) upon and after the attainment of normal retirement age (see § 1.411(a)-7(b)),

(2) The plan provides that an employee's rights in his accrued benefit derived from his own contributions (see § 1.411(c)-1) are nonforfeitable at all times, and

(3) The plan satisfies the requirements of—

(A) Section 411(a)(2) and § 1.411(a)-3 (relating to vesting in accrued benefit derived from employer contributions), and

(B) In the case of a defined benefit plan, section 411(b)(1) and § 1.411(b)-1 (relating to accrued benefit).

(b) *Organization of regulations relating to minimum vesting standards.*—(1) *General rules.*—This section prescribes general rules relating to the minimum vesting standards provided by section 411.

(2) *Effective dates.*—Section 1.411(a)-2 provides rules under section 1017 of the Employee Retirement Income Security Act of 1974 relating to effective dates under section 411.

(3) *Employer contributions.*—Section 1.411(a)-3 provides rules under section 411(a)(2) relating to vesting in employer-derived accrued benefits.

(4) *Certain forfeitures.*—Section 1.411(a)-4 provides rules under section 411(a)(3) relating to certain permitted forfeitures, suspensions, etc. under qualified plans.

(5) *Nonforfeitable percentage.*—Section 1.411(a)-5 provides rules under section 411(a)(4) relating to service included in the determination of an employee's nonforfeitable percentage under section 411(a)(2) and § 1.411(a)-3.

(6) *Years of service; break in service.*—Section 1.411(a)-6 provides rules under section 411(a)(5) and (6) of the Internal Revenue Code of 1954 relating to years of service and breaks in service. Rules prescribed by the Secretary of Labor, relating to years of service and breaks in service under part 2 of subtitle B of title 1 of the Employee Retirement Income Security Act of 1974 are provided under 29 CFR Part 2530 (Department of Labor regulations relating to minimum standards for employee pension benefit plans).

(7) *Definitions and special rules.*—Section 1.411(a)-7 provides definitions and special rules under section 411(a)(7), (8), and (9), for purposes of section 411 and the regulations thereunder.

(8) *Changes in vesting schedule.*—Section 1.411(a)-8 provides rules under section 411(a)(10) relating to changes in the vesting schedule of a plan.

(9) [Reserved].

(10) *Accrued benefits.*—See 1.411(b)-1 for rules under section 411(b) relating to accrued benefit requirements under defined benefit plans.

(11) *Allocation of accrued benefits.*—See § 1.411(c)-1 for rules under section 411(c) relating to allocation of accrued benefits between employer and employee contributions.

(12) *Discrimination, etc.*—See § 1.411(d)-1 for rules relating to the coordination of section 411 with section 401(a)(4) (relating to discrimination) and other rules under section 411(d).

(c) *Application of standards to certain plans.*—(1) *General rule.*—Except as provided in subparagraph (2) of this paragraph, section 411 does not apply to—

(i) A governmental plan (within the meaning of section 414(d) and the regulations thereunder),

(ii) A church plan (within the meaning of section 414(c) and the regulations thereunder) which has not made the election provided by section 410(d) and the regulations thereunder,

(iii) A plan which has not provided for employer contributions at any time after September 2, 1974, and

(iv) A plan established and maintained by a society, order, or association described in section 501(c)(8) or (9), if no part of the contributions to or under such plan are made by employers of participants in such plan.

(2) *Vesting requirements.*—A plan described in subparagraph (1) of this paragraph shall, for purposes of section 401(a), be treated as meeting the requirements of section 411 if such plan meets the vesting requirements resulting from the application of section 401(a)(4) and section 401(a)(7) as in effect on September 1, 1974.

(d) *Supersession.*—Sections 11.411(a)-1 through 11.411(d)-3, inclusive, of the Temporary Income Tax Regulations under the Employee Retirement Income Security Act of 1974 are superseded by this section and §§ 1.411(a)-2 through 1.411(d)-3. [Reg. § 1.411(a)-1.]

☐ [*T.D. 7501, 8-22-77. Amended by T.D. 9849, 3-11-2019.*]

[Reg. § 1.411(a)-2]

§1.411(a)-2. Effective dates.—(a) *Plan not in existence on January 1, 1974.*—Under section 1017(a) of the Employee Retirement Income Security Act of 1974, in the case of a plan which was not in existence on January 1, 1974, section 411 and the regulations thereunder apply for plan years beginning after September 2, 1974. See paragraph (c) of this section for time plan is considered in existence.

(b) *Plans in existence on January 1, 1974.*—Under section 1017(b) of the Employee Retirement Income Security Act of 1974, in the case of a plan which was in existence on January 1, 1974, section 411 and the regulations thereunder apply for plan years beginning after December 31, 1975. See paragraph (c) of this section for time plan is considered to be in existence.

(c) *Time of plan existence.*—(1) *General rule.*—For purposes of this section, a plan is considered to be in existence on a particular day if—

(i) The plan on or before that day was reduced to writing and adopted by the employer (including, in the case of a corporate employer, formal approval by the employer's board of directors and, if required, shareholders), even though no amounts had been contributed under the plan as of such day, and

(ii) The plan was not terminated on or before that day.
For example, if a plan was adopted on January 2, 1974, effective as of January 1, 1974, the plan is not considered to have been in existence on January 1, 1974, because it was not both adopted and in writing on January 1, 1974.

(2) *Collectively-bargained plan.*—Notwithstanding subparagraph (1) of this paragraph, a plan described in section 413(a), relating to a plan maintained pursuant to a collective bargaining agreement, is considered to be in existence on a particular day if—

(i) On or before that day there is a legally enforceable agreement to establish such a plan signed by the employer, and

(ii) The employer contributions to be made to the plan are set forth in the agreement.

(3) *Special rule.*—If a plan is considered to be in existence under subparagraph (1) of this paragraph, any other plan with which such existing plan is merged or consolidated shall also be considered to be in existence on such date.

(d) *Existing plans under collective bargaining agreements.*—For a special effective date rule for certain plans maintained pursuant to a collective bargaining agreement, see section 1017(c)(1) of the Employee Retirement Income Security Act of 1974 (88 Stat. 932).

(e) *Certain existing plans may elect new provisions.*—The plan administrator may elect to have the provisions of the Code relating to participation, vesting, funding, and form of benefit apply to a selected plan year. See § 1.410(a)-2(d) for rules relating to such an election.

(f) *Application of rules.*—The requirements of section 411 do not apply to employees who separate from service with the employer prior to the first plan year which such requirements apply and who never return to service with the employer in a plan year to which section 411 applies. [Reg. § 1.411(a)-2.]

☐ [*T.D. 7501, 8-22-77.*]

[Reg. § 1.411(a)-3]

§1.411(a)-3. Vesting in employer-derived benefits.—(a) *In general.*—(1) *Alternative requirements.*—A plan is not a qualified plan (and a trust forming a part of such plan is not qualified trust) unless the plan satisfies the requirements of section 411(a)(2) and this section. A plan satisfies the requirements of this section if it satisfies the requirements of paragraph (b), (c), or (d) of this section.

(2) *Composite arrangements.*—A plan will not be considered to satisfy the requirements of paragraph (b), (c), or (d) of this section unless it satisfies all requirements of a particular one of such paragraphs with respect to all of an employee's years of service. A plan which, for example, satisfies the requirements of paragraph (b) (but not (c) or (d)) for an employee's first 9 years of service and satisfies the requirements of paragraph (c) (but not (b)) for all of his remaining years of service, does not satisfy the requirements of this section. A plan is not precluded from satisfying the requirement of one such paragraph with respect to one group of employees and another such paragraph with respect to another group provided that the groups are not so structured as to evade the requirements of this paragraph. For example, if plan A provides that employees who commence participation before age 30 are subject to the "rule of 45" vesting schedule and employees who commence participation after age 30 are subject to the full vesting after 10 years schedule, plan A would be so structured as to evade the requirements of this paragraph.

(3) *Plan amendments.*—A plan which satisfies the requirements of a particular one of such paragraphs for each of an employee's years of service and which is amended so that, as amended, it satisfies the requirements of another such paragraph for all such years of service, satisfies the requirements of this section even though, as amended, it does not satisfy the requirements of the paragraph which were satisfied prior to the amendment. See § 1.411(a)-8 for rules relating to employee election where the vesting schedule is amended.

(b) *10-year vesting.*—A plan satisfies the requirements of section 411(a)(2)(A) and this paragraph if an employee who has completed 10 years of service has a nonforfeitable right to 100 percent of his accrued benefit derived from employer contributions.

(c) *5- to 15-year vesting.*—A plan satisfies the requirements of section 411(a)(2)(B) and this paragraph if an employee who has completed at least 5 years of service has a nonforfeitable right to a percentage of his accrued benefit derived from employer contributions, which percentage is not less than the nonforfeitable percentage determined under the following table:

Completed years of service	Nonforfeitable percentage
5	25
6	30
7	35
8	40
9	45
10	50
11	60
12	70
13	80
14	90
15 or more	100

(d) *Rule of 45.*—A plan satisfies the requirements of section 411(a)(2)(C) and this paragraph if an employee is entitled to the greater of the two percentages determined under subparagraph (1) or (2) of this paragraph.

(1) *Age and service test.*—An employee who is not separated from the service, who has completed at least 5 years of service, and with respect to whom the sum of his age and years of service equals or

exceeds 45, has a nonforfeitable right to a percentage of his accrued benefit derived from employer contributions which is not less than the nonforfeitable percentage corresponding to his number of completed years of service or to the sum of his age and completed years of service (whichever percentage is the lesser) determined under the following table:

Completed years of service	Sum of age and service	Nonforfeitable percentage
5	45 or 46	50
6	47 or 48	60
7	49 or 50	70
8	51 or 52	80
9	53 or 54	90
10 or more	55 or more	100

(2) *Service test.*—An employee who has completed at least 10 years of service has a nonforfeitable right to a percentage of his accrued benefit derived from employer contributions determined under the following table:

Completed years of service	Nonforfeitable percentage
10	50
11	60
12	70
13	80
14	90
15	100

(3) *Computation of age.*—For purposes of subparagraph (1) of this paragraph, the age of an employee is his age on his last birthday.

(e) *Examples.*—The rules provided by this section are illustrated by the following examples:

Example (1). Plan B provides that each employee's rights to his employer-derived accrued benefit are nonforfeitable as follows:

Completed years of service	Nonforfeitable percentage
2 or less	0
3	30
4	35
5	40
6	45
7	50
8	55
9	60
10	65
11	70
12	75
13	80
14	85
15	100

Plan B does not satisfy the requirements of paragraph (c) of this section (relating to 5-15-year vesting) because the nonforfeitable percentage provided by the plan after completion of 14 years of service (85%) is less than the percentage required by paragraph (c) of this section at that time (90%). The fact that the nonforfeitable percentage provided by the plan for years prior to the 13th year of service is greater than the percentage required under paragraph (c) of this section is immaterial. The plan fails to satisfy the requirements of paragraph (c) of this section even if it is demonstrated that the value of the vesting provided by the plan to the employee is at least equal to the value of the vesting rate required by that paragraph.

Example (2). Plan C provides for plan participation after the completion of 1 year of service. The plan provides that each employee's rights to his employer-derived accrued benefit are 100% nonforfeitable after 10 years of plan participation rather than service. The plan does not satisfy the requirements of paragraph (b) of this section because, under the plan, an employee obtains a 100% nonforfeitable right to his employer-derived accrued benefit only after completion of more than 10 years of service.

Example (3). Plan D provides that each employee's rights to his employer-derived accrued benefit are nonforfeitable in accordance with the following schedule:

Completed years of service	Nonforfeitable percentage
0-9	0
10	50
11	60
12	70
13	80
14	90
15	100

The plan does not satisfy the requirements of paragraph (b) of this section after the 9th year of service. It does not satisfy the requirements of paragraph (c) of this section for years prior to the 10th year of service. It does not satisfy the requirements of paragraph (d)(1) of this section for any year of service prior to the 10th year. The plan does not satisfy the requirements of this section because it does not satisfy the requirements of a particular one of the three paragraphs for each of an employee's years of service.

Example (4). Plan G provides that each employee's rights to his employer-derived accrued benefit are 100% nonforfeitable upon completion of 5 years of service. The plan satisfies the requirements of paragraphs (b), (c), and (d) of this section and, because it satisfies the requirements of at least one of such paragraphs for all of an employee's years of service, it satisfies the requirements of this section. [Reg. § 1.411(a)-3.]

☐ [T.D. 7501, 8-22-77.]

[Reg. § 1.411(a)-3T]

§ 1.411(a)-3T. Vesting in employer-derived benefits (Temporary).—(a) *In general.*
(1) [Reserved.]

(2) *Composite arrangements.*—A plan will not be considered to satisfy the requirements of paragraph (b), (c), or (d) of this section unless it satisfies all requirements of a particular one of such paragraphs with respect to all of an employee's years of service. A plan which, for example, satisfies the requirements of paragraph (b) (but not (c) or (d)) for an employee's first 4 years of service and satisfies the requirements of paragraph (c) (but not (b)) for all of his remaining years of service does not satisfy the requirements of this section. A plan is not precluded from satisfying the requirements of one such paragraph with respect to one group of employees and another such paragraph with respect to another group provided that the groups are not so structured as to evade the requirements of this paragraph.

(3) [Reserved.]

(b) *5-year vesting.*—A plan satisfies the requirements of section 411(a)(2)(A) and this paragraph if an employee who has completed 5 years of service has a nonforfeitable right to 100 percent of his or her accrued benefits derived from employer contributions.

(c) *3-to 7-year vesting.*—A plan satisfies the requirements of section 411(a)(2)(B) and this paragraph if an employee who has completed at least 3 years of service has a nonforfeitable right to a percentage of his accrued benefit derived from employer contributions, which percentage is not less than the nonforfeitable percentage determined under the following table:

Completed years of service	Nonforfeitable percentage
3	20
4	40
5	60
6	80
7 or more	100

(d) *Multiemployer plans.*—A plan satisfies the requirements of section 411 (a)(2)(C) and this paragraph if—

(1) The plan is a multiemployer plan (within the meaning of section 414(f)), and

(2) Under the plan—

(i) An employee who is covered pursuant to a collective bargaining agreement described in section 414(f)(1)(B) has a nonforfeitable right to 100 percent of the employee's accrued benefit derived from employer contributions not later than upon completion of 10 years of service, and

(ii) The requirements of paragraph (b) or (c) of this section are met with respect to employees who are not covered pursuant to a collective bargaining agreement described in section 414(f)(1)(B).

(iii) For purposes of this provision, an employee is not covered pursuant to a collective bargaining agreement unless the employee is represented by a bona fide employee representative that is a party to the collective bargaining agreement pursuant to which the multiemployer plan is maintained. Thus, for example, an employee of either the multiemployer plan or the employee representative is not covered pursuant to the collective bargaining agreement under which the plan is maintained even if the employee is covered pursuant to an agreement entered into by the multiemployer plan or employee representative on behalf of the employee and even if all such employees covered under the plan constitute only a de minimis percentage of the total employees covered under the plan.

(e) *Effective date.*—(1) The provisions of this section apply to all employees who have one hour of service in any plan year beginning after—

(i) December 31, 1988, or

(ii) In the case of a plan maintained pursuant to one or more collective bargaining agreements between employee representatives and one or more employers ratified before March 1, 1986, for employees covered by any such agreement, the earlier of—

(A) the later of—

(1) January 1, 1989, or

(2) The date on which the last of such collective bargaining agreements terminates (determined without regard to any extension thereof after February 28, 1986), or

(B) January 1, 1991.

(2) For employees not described in paragraph (e)(1), above, the regulations in effect prior to January 1, 1989, shall be applied to determine the requirements of this section.

(f) *Examples.*—The rules provided by this section are illustrated by the following examples:

Example (1). Plan B provides that each employee's rights to his employer-derived accrued benefit are nonforfeitable as follows:

Completed years of service	Nonforfeitable percentage
1	0
2	10
3	25
4	45
5	65
6	75
7	100

Plan B does not satisfy the requirements of paragraph (c) of this section (relating to 3-to 7-year vesting) because the nonforfeitable percentage provided by the plan after completion of 6 years of service (75 percent) is less than the percentage required by paragraph (c) of this section at that time (80 percent). The fact that the nonforfeitable percentage provided by the plan for years prior to the 6th year of service is greater than the percentage required under paragraph (c) of this section is immaterial. The plan fails to satisfy the requirements of paragraph (c) of this section even if it is demonstrated that the value of the vesting provided by the plan to the employees is at least equal to the value of the vesting rate required by this paragraph.

Example (2). Plan C provides for plan participation after the completion of 1 year of service. The plan provides that each employee's rights to his employer-derived accrued benefits are 100 percent nonforfeitable after 5 years of plan participation rather than service. The plan does not satisfy the requirements of paragraph (b) of this section because, under the plan, an employee obtains a 100 percent nonforfeitable right to his or her employer-derived accrued benefit only after completion of more than 5 years of service.

Example (3). Plan D provides that each employee's rights to his employer-derived accrued benefits are nonforfeitable in accordance with the following schedule:

Completed years of service	Nonforfeitable percentage
0-4	0
5	60
6	80
7	100

The plan does not satisfy the requirements of paragraph (b) of this section after the 4th year of service. It does not satisfy the requirements of paragraph (c) of this section for years prior to the 5th year of service. The plan does not satisfy the requirements of this section because it does not satisfy the requirements of a particular one of the two paragraphs for each of an employee's years of service.

Example (4). Plan G provides that each employee's rights to his employer-derived accrued benefit are 100 percent nonforfeitable upon completion of 3 years of service. The plan satisfies the requirements of paragraphs (b) and (c) of this section and, because it satisfies the requirements of at least one of such paragraphs for all of an employee's years of service, it satisfies the requirements of this section. [Temporary Reg. §1.411(a)-3T.]

☐ [*T.D.* 8170, 1-5-88.]

§1.411(a)-4. Forfeitures, suspensions, etc.—(a) *Nonforfeitability.*—Certain rights in an accrued benefit must be nonforfeitable to satisfy the requirements of section 411(a). This section defines the term "nonforfeitable" for purposes of these requirements. For purposes of section 411 and the regulations thereunder, a right to an accrued benefit is considered to be nonforfeitable at a particular time if, at that time and thereafter, it is an unconditional right. Except as provided by paragraph (b) of this section, a right which, at a particular time, is conditioned under the plan upon a subsequent event, subsequent performance, or subsequent forbearance which will cause the loss of such right, is a forfeitable right at that time. Certain adjustments to plan benefits, such as adjustments in excess of reasonable actuarial reductions, can result in rights being forfeitable. Rights which are conditioned upon a sufficiency of plan assets in the event of a termination or partial termination are considered to be forfeitable because of such condition. However, a plan does not violate the nonforfeitability requirements merely because in the event of a termination an employee does not have any recourse towards satisfaction of his nonforfeitable benefits from other than the plan assets or the Pension Benefit Guaranty Corporation. Furthermore, nonforfeitable rights are not considered to be forfeitable by reason of the fact that they may be reduced to take into account benefits which are provided under the Social Security Act or under any other Federal or State law and which are taken into account in determining plan benefits. To the extent that rights are not required to be nonforfeitable to satisfy the minimum vesting standards, or the nondiscrimination requirements of section 401(a)(4), they may be forfeited without regard to the limitations on forfeitability required by this section. The right of an employee to repurchase his accrued benefit, for example under section 411(a)(3)(D), is an example of a right which is required to satisfy such standards. Accordingly, such a right is subject to the limitations on forfeitability. Rights which are required to be prospectively nonforfeitable under the vesting standards are nonforfeitable and may not be forfeited until it is determined that such rights are, in fact, in excess of the vesting standards. Thus, employees have a right to vest in the accrued benefits if they continue in employment of employers maintaining the plan unless a forfeitable event recognized by section 411 occurs. For example, if a plan covered employees in Division A of Corporation X under a plan utilizing a 10-year-100 percent vesting schedule, the plan could not forfeit employees' rights on account of their moving to service in Division B of Corporation X prior to completion of 10 years of service even though employees are not vested at that time.

(b) *Special rules.*—For purposes of paragraph (a) of this section, a right is not treated as forfeitable—

(1) *Death.*—(i) *General rule.*—In the case of a participant's right to his employer-derived accrued benefit, merely because such accrued benefit is forfeitable by the participant to the extent that it has not been paid or distributed to him prior to his death. This subparagraph shall not apply to a benefit which must be paid to a survivor in order to satisfy the requirements of section 401(a)(11).

(ii) *Employee contributions.*—A participant's right in his accrued benefit derived from his own contributions must be nonforfeitable at all times. Such a right is not treated as forfeitable merely because, after commencement of annuity or pension payments in a benefit form provided under the plan, the participant dies without receiving payments equal in amount to his nonforfeitable accrued benefit derived from his contributions determined at the time of commencement.

(2) *Suspension of benefits upon reemployment of retiree.*—In the case of certain suspensions of benefits under section 411(a)(3)(B), see regulations prescribed by the Secretary of Labor under 29 CFR Part 2530 (Department of Labor regulations relating to minimum standards for employee pension benefit plans).

(3) *Retroactive plan amendment.*—In the case of a participant's right to his employer-derived accrued benefit, merely because such benefit is subject to reduction to the extent provided by a plan amendment described in section 412(c)(8) and the regulations thereunder, which amendment is given retroactive effect in accordance with such section.

(4) *Other forfeiture rules.*—(i) *Withdrawal of mandatory contributions.*—For rules allowing forfeitures on account of the withdrawal of mandatory contributions, see §1.411(a)-7(d)(2) and (3).

(ii) *Additional requirements.*—For additional requirements relating to nonforfeitability of benefits in the event of a withdrawal by the employee, see section 401(a)(19) and §1.401(a)-19.

(5) *Multiemployer plan.*—In the case of a multiemployer plan described in section 414(f), merely because an employee's accrued benefit which results from service with an employer before such employer was required to contribute to the plan is forfeitable on account of the cessation of contributions by the employer of the employee. This subparagraph shall not apply to an employee's accrued benefit with respect to an employer which accrued under a plan maintained by that employer prior to the adoption by that employer of the multiemployer plan.

(6) *Lost beneficiary; escheat.*—In the case of a benefit which is payable, merely because the benefit is forfeitable on account of the inability to find the participant or beneficiary to whom payment is due, provided that the plan provides for reinstatement of the benefit if a claim is made by the participant or beneficiary for the forfeited benefit. In addition, a benefit which is lost by reason of escheat under applicable state law is not treated as a forfeiture.

(7) *Certain matching contributions.*—A matching contribution (within the meaning of section 401(m)(4)(A) and §1.401(m)-1(a)(2)) is not treated as forfeitable even if under the plan it may be forfeited under §1.401(m)-2(b)(1) because the contribution to which it relates is treated as an excess contribution (within the meaning of §§1.401(k)-2(b)(2)(ii) and 1.401(k)-6), excess deferral (within the meaning of §1.402(g)-1(e)(1)(iii)), excess aggregate contribution (within the meaning of §1.401(m)-5), or a default elective contribution (within the meaning of §1.414(w)-1(e)) that is withdrawn in accordance with the requirements of §1.414(w)-1(c).

(c) *Examples.*—The rules of this section are illustrated by the following examples:

Example (1). Corporation A's plan provides that an employee is fully vested in his employer-derived accrued benefit [plan] after completion of 5 years of service. The plan also provides that, if an employee works for a competitor he forfeits his rights in the plan. Such provision could result in the forfeiture of an employee's rights which are required to be nonforfeitable under section 411 and therefore the plan would not satisfy the requirements of section 411. If the plan limited the forfeiture to employees who completed less than 10 years of service, the plan would not fail to satisfy the requirements of section 411 because the forfeitures under this provision are limited to rights which are in excess of the minimum required to be nonforfeitable under section 411(a)(2)(A).

Example (2). Plan B provides that if an employee does not apply for benefits within 5 years after the attainment of normal retirement age, the employee loses his plan benefits. Such a plan provision could result in forfeiture of an employee's rights which are required to be nonforfeitable under section 411 and, therefore, the plan would not satisfy the requirements of section 411. [Reg. §1.411(a)-4.]

☐ [*T.D. 7501, 8-22-77. Amended by T.D. 8357, 8-8-91; T.D. 9169, 12-28-2004; T.D. 9219, 8-11-2005 and T.D 9447, 2-23-2009.*]

[Reg. §1.411(a)-4T]

§1.411(a)-4T. Forfeitures, suspensions, etc. (temporary).—(a) *Nonforfeitability.*—Certain rights in an accrued benefit must be nonforfeitable to satisfy the requirements of section 411(a). This section defines the term "nonforfeitable" for purposes of these requirements. For purposes of section 411 and the regulations thereunder, a right to an accrued benefit is considered to be nonforfeitable at a particular time if, at that time and thereafter, it is an unconditional right. Except as provided by paragraph (b) of this section, a right which, at a particular time, is conditioned under the plan upon a subsequent event, subsequent performance, or subsequent forbearance which will cause the loss of such right is a forfeitable right at that time. Certain adjustments to plan benefits, such as adjustments in excess of reasonable actuarial reductions, can result in rights being forfeitable. Rights which are conditioned upon a sufficiency of plan assets in the event of a termination or partial termination are considered to be forfeitable because of such condition. However, a plan does not violate the nonforfeitability requirements merely because in the event of a termination an employee does not have any recourse toward satisfaction of his nonforfeitable benefits from other than the plan assets, the Pension Benefit Guaranty Corporation, or a trust *established and maintained pursuant to sections 4041(c)(3)(B)(ii) or* (iii) and section 4049 of ERISA with respect to the plan. Furthermore, nonforfeitable rights are not considered to be forfeitable by reason of the fact that they may be reduced as allowed under sections 401(a)(5) and 401(l). To the extent that rights are not required to be nonforfeit-

able to satisfy the minimum vesting standards, or the nondiscrimination requirements of section 401(a)(4), they may be forfeited without regard to the limitations on forfeitability required by this section. The right of an employee to repurchase his accrued benefit, for example under section 411(a)(3)(D), is an example of a right which is required to satisfy such standards. Accordingly, such a right is subject to the limitations on forfeitability. Rights which are required to be prospectively nonforfeitable under the vesting standards are nonforfeitable and may not be forfeited until it is determined that such rights are, in fact, in excess of the vesting standards. Thus, employees have a right to vest in the accrued benefits if they continue in employment of employers maintaining the plan unless a forfeitable event recognized by section 411 occurs. For example, if a plan covered employees in Division A of Corporation X under a plan utilizing a 5-year 100 percent vesting schedule, the plan could not forfeit employees' rights on account of their moving to service in Division B of Corporation X prior to completion of 5 years of service even though employees are not vested at that time.

(b) [Reserved.]

(c) *Examples.*—The rules of this section are illustrated by the following examples:

Example (1). Corporation A's plan provides that an employee is fully vested in his employer-derived accrued benefit after completion of 3 years of service. The plan also provides that if the employee works for a competitor he forfeits his rights in the plan. Such provision could result in the forfeiture of an employee's rights which are required to be nonforfeitable under section 411 and therefore the plan would not satisfy the requirements of section 411. If the plan limited the forfeiture to employees who completed less than 5 years of service, the plan would not fail to satisfy the requirements of section 411 because the forfeitures under this provision are limited to rights which are in excess of the minimum required to be nonforfeitable under section 411(a)(2)(A).

Example (2). [Reserved.] [Temporary Reg. §1.411(a)-4T.]

☐ [*T.D. 8170, 1-5-88.*]

[Reg. §1.411(a)-5]

§1.411(a)-5. Service included in determination of nonforfeitable percentage.—(a) *In general.*—Under section 411(a)(4), for purposes of determining the nonforfeitable percentage of an employee's right to his employer-derived accrued benefit under section 411(a)(2) and §1.411(a)-3, all of an employee's years of service with an employer or employers maintaining the plan shall be taken into account except that years of service described in paragraph (b) of this section may be disregarded.

(b) *Certain service.*—For purposes of paragraph (a) of this section, the following years of service may be disregarded:

(1) *Service before age 22.*—(i) In the case of a plan which satisfies the requirements of section 411(a)(2)(A) or (B) (relating to 10-year vesting and 5-15-year vesting, respectively), a year of service completed by an employee before he attains age 22.

(ii) In the case of a plan which does not satisfy the requirements of section 411(a)(2)(A) or (B), a year of service completed by an employee before he attains age 22 if the employee is not a participant (for purposes of section 410) in the plan at any time during such year.

(iii) For purposes of this subparagraph in the case of a plan utilizing computation periods, service during a computation period described in section 411(a)(5)(A) within which the employee attains age 22 may not be disregarded. In the case of a plan utilizing the elapsed time method described in §1.410(a)-7, service on or after the date on which the employee attains age 22 may not be disregarded.

(2) *Contributory plans.*—In the case of a plan utilizing computation periods, a year of service completed by an employee under a plan which requires mandatory contributions (within the meaning of section 411(c)(2)(C) and §1.411(c)-1(c)(4)) to be made by the employee for such year, if the employee does not participate for such year solely because of his failure to make all mandatory contributions to the plan for such year. If the employee contributes any part of the mandatory contributions for the year, such year may not be excluded by reason of this subparagraph. In the case of a plan utilizing the elapsed time method described in §1.410(a)-7, the service which may be disregarded is the period with respect to which the mandatory contribution is not made.

(3) *Plan not maintained.*—(i) *In general.*—An employee's years of service with an employer during any period for which the employer did not maintain the plan or a predecessor plan may be disregarded for purposes of section 411(a)(2). Paragraph (b)(3)(ii) of this section provides rules regarding the period prior to the adoption of a plan. Paragraph (b)(3)(iii) of this section provides rules regarding the period after the termination of a plan. Paragraph (b)(3)(iv) of this

section provides rules regarding employers who have certain relationships with other employers maintaining the plan.

    (ii) *Period prior to adoption.*—The period for which a plan is not maintained by an employer includes the period before the plan was established. For purposes of this subdivision, a plan is established on the first day of the plan year in which the plan is adopted even though the plan is adopted after such first day. Except as provided in paragraph (b)(3)(iv) of this section, if an employer adopts a plan which has previously been established by another employer or group of employers, the plan is not maintained by the adopting employer prior to the first day of the plan year in which the plan is adopted by the adopting employer. In the case of a transfer of assets or liabilities (including a merger or consolidation) involving two plans maintained by a single employer, the successor (or transferee) plan is treated as if it was established at the same time as the date of the establishment of the earliest component plan. In the case of a plan merger, consolidation, or transfer of plan assets or liabilities involving plans of two or more employers, the successor plan is treated as if it were established on each of the separate dates on which such component plan was established for the employee of each employer. Thus, for example, if employer A establishes a plan January 1, 1970, and employer B establishes a plan January 1, 1980, and the plans were subsequently merged, then the merged plan would be treated as if it were in existence on January 1, 1970, with respect to A's employees and as if it were in existence on January 1, 1980, with respect to B's employees.

    (iii) *Period after termination or withdrawal.*—The period for which a plan is not maintained by an employer includes the period after the plan is terminated. For purposes of this section, a plan is terminated at the date there is a termination of the plan within the meaning of section 411(d)(3)(A) and the regulations thereunder. Notwithstanding the preceding sentence, if contributions to or under a plan are made after termination, the plan is treated as being maintained until such contributions cease, whether or not accruals are made after such termination. If, after termination of a plan in circumstances under which the employer may be liable to the Pension Benefit Guaranty Corporation under section 4062 of the Act, employer contributions are made to or under the plan to fund benefits accrued at the time of termination, such contributions shall, for purposes of this paragraph, be deemed to be payments in satisfaction of employer liability to such Corporation rather than contributions to or under the plan. In the case of a plan maintained by more than one employer, the period for which the plan is not maintained by the withdrawing employer includes the period after the withdrawal from the plan.

    (iv) *Certain employers.*—For purposes of this subparagraph—

    (A) *Predecessor employers.*—Service with a predecessor employer who maintained the plan of the current employer is treated as service with such current employer (see section 414(a)(1) and the regulations thereunder), and certain service with a predecessor employer who did not maintain the plan of the current employer is treated as service with the current employer (see section 414(a)(2) and the regulations thereunder).

    (B) *Related employers.*—Service with an employer is treated as service for certain related employers for the period during which the employers are related. These related employers include members of a controlled group of corporations (within the meaning of section 1563(a), determined without regard to subsections (a)(4) and (e)(3)(C) thereof) and trades or businesses (whether or not incorporated) which are under common control (see section 414(b) and (c) and 29 CFR Part 2530, Department of Labor regulations relating to minimum standards for employee pension benefit plans).

    (C) *Plan maintained by more than one employer.*—Service with an employer who maintains a plan is treated as service for each other employer who maintains that plan for the period during which the employers are maintaining the plan (see section 413(b)(4) and (c)(3) and 29 CFR Part 2530, Department of Labor regulations relating to minimum standards for employee pension benefit plans).

    (v) *Predecessor plan.*—(A) *General rule.*—In the case of an employee who was covered by a predecessor plan, the time the successor of such plan is maintained for such employee includes the time the predecessor plan was maintained if, as of the later of the time the predecessor plan is terminated or the successor plan is established, the employee's years of service under the predecessor plan are not equalled or exceeded by the aggregate number of consecutive 1-year breaks in service occurring after such years of service. Years of service and breaks in service, without regard to whether the employee has nonforfeitable rights under the predecessor plan, are determined under section 411(a)(5) and (6) except that years between

the termination date of the predecessor plan and the date of establishment of the successor plan do not count as years of service.

    (B) *Definition of predecessor plan.*—For purposes of this section, if—

    (1) An employer establishes a retirement plan (within the meaning of section 7476(d)) qualified under subchapter D of chapter 1 of the Code within the 5-year period immediately preceding or following the date another such plan terminates, and

    (2) The other plan is terminated during a plan year to which this section applies, the terminated plan is a predecessor plan with respect to such other plan.

    (C) *Example.*—The rules provided by this subparagraph are illustrated by the following example:
    Example. (1) Employer X's qualified plan A terminated on January 1, 1977. Employer X established qualified plan B on January 1, 1981. Under paragraph (b)(3)(v)(B) of this section, plan A is a predecessor plan with respect to plan B because plan B is established within the 5-year period immediately following the date plan A terminated.
    (2) Employee C was not covered by the A plan. Under the general rule in subdivision (v)(A) of this subparagraph, plan B is not maintained until January 1, 1981, with respect to Employee C.
    (3) Employee D was covered by the A plan. On December 31, 1976, D had 4 years of service. D had 4 consecutive 1-year breaks in service because, during the years between the termination of plan A and the establishment of plan B, he did not have more than 500 hours of service in any applicable computation period. Because D's consecutive 1-year breaks (4) equal his years of service prior to his breaks (4), plan B is not maintained until January 1, 1981, with respect to Employee D.
    (4) Employee E was covered by the A plan. On December 31, 1975, E had 6 years of service. E had a 1-year break in service in 1976. E also had 4 consecutive 1-year breaks in service for the period between plan A's termination and plan B's establishment. Because E's years of service (6) are not less than his consecutive 1-year breaks (5), plan B is maintained for E as of the establishment date of plan A.

    (4) *Break in service.*—A year of service which is not required to be taken into account by reason of a break in service (within the meaning of section 411(a)(6) and § 1.411(a)(6)).

    (5) *Service before January 1, 1971.*—A year of service completed by an employee prior to January 1, 1971, unless the employee completes at least 3 years of service at any time after December 31, 1970. For purposes of determining if an employee completes 3 years of service, whether or not consecutive, the exceptions of section 411(a)(4) are not applicable. For the meaning of the term "year of service", see regulations prescribed by the Secretary of Labor under 29 CFR Part 2530, relating to minimum standards for employee pension benefit plans.

    (6) *Service before effective date.*—(i) *General rule.*—A year of service completed before the first plan year for which this section applies to the plan, if such service would have been disregarded under the plan rules relating to breaks in service (whether or not such rules are so designated in the plan) as such rules were in effect from time to time under the plan. For this purpose, plan rules which result in the loss of prior vesting or benefit accruals of an employee, or which deny an employee eligibility to participate, by reason of separation or failure to complete a required period of service within a specified period of time (*e.g.*, 300 hours in one year) will be considered break in service rules.

    (ii) *Examples.*—The rules of this subparagraph are illustrated by the following examples:
    Example 1. The A plan in 1971 provides for immediate participation and vesting at normal retirement age. Employees accrue a unit benefit based on their compensation in each year. The plan provides that if an employee is not employed on the last day of the calendar year, he loses all accrued benefits. The requirement of employment on the last day of the year is a break in service rule because employees can lose benefits by reason of their separation. Accordingly, in the case of employees who separate and do not return by the close of the year, service which is completed prior to separation may be disregarded.
    Example 2. The B plan in 1971 excludes from plan participation employees who work less than 1,200 hours per year. Because years of less than 1,200 hours are not taken into account under the B plan for eligibility to participate, such years are excluded under rules relating to breaks in service. Therefore, the years can be disregarded under this subparagraph.
    Example 3. The C plan in 1971 provides for immediate participation and provides accruals and vesting credit for 1,200 hours or more in a given year. The plan provides that if a participant works

less than 300 hours in a given year, he loses all prior vesting and benefit credits. The 300 hour rule is a break in service rule because the failure to complete 300 hours results in the loss of vesting and prior service credit. The 1,200 hour requirement is not a break in service rule because even though employees do not increase vesting or accrue benefits for service between 300 and 1,200 hours, they can not lose prior vesting or benefits for such service. Accordingly, the C plan can disregard completed years only on account of less than 300 hours of service by an employee.

(c) *Special continuity rule for certain plans.*—For special rules for computing years of service in the case of a plan maintained by more than one employer, see 29 CFR Part 2530 (Department of Labor regulations relating to minimum standards for employee pension benefit plans). [Reg. § 1.411(a)-5.]

[T.D. 7501, 8-22-77. *Amended by T.D. 7703, 6-16-80 and T.D. 9849,* 3-11-2019.]

[Reg. § 1.411(a)-6]

§ 1.411(a)-6. Year of service; hour of service; breaks in service.—(a) *Year of service.*—Under section 411(a)(5)(A), for purposes of the regulations thereunder, the term "year of service" is defined in regulations prescribed by the Secretary of Labor under section 203(b)(2)(A) of the Employee Retirement Income Security Act of 1974. For special rules applicable to seasonal industries and maritime industries, see regulations prescribed by the Secretary of Labor under subparagraphs (C) and (D) of section 203(b)(2) of the Employee Retirement Income Security Act of 1974.

(b) *Hours of service.*—Under section 411(a)(5)(B), for purposes of the regulations thereunder, the term "hours of service" has the meaning provided by section 410(a)(3)(C). See regulations prescribed by the Secretary of Labor under 29 CFR Part 2530, relating to minimum standards for employee pension benefit plans.

(c) *Breaks in service.*—Under section 411(a)(6), for purposes of § 1.411(a)-5(b)(4) and of this paragraph—

(1) *In general.*—(i) *Year of service after 1-year break in service.*—In the case of any employee who has incurred a 1-year break in service, years of service completed before such break are not required to be taken into account until the employee has completed one year of service after his return to service.

(ii) *Defined contribution plan.*—In the case of a participant in a defined contribution plan or in an insured defined benefit plan (which plan satisfies the requirements of section 411(b)(1)(F) and § 1.411(b)-1) who has incurred a 1-year break in service, years of service completed after such break are not required to be taken into account for purposes of determining the nonforfeitable percentage of the participant's right to employer-derived benefits which accrued before such break. This subdivision does not permit any years of service completed before a 1-year break in service to be disregarded in determining the nonforfeitable percentage of a participant's right to employer-derived benefits which accrue after such break.

(iii) *Nonvested participants.*—In the case of an employee who is a nonvested participant in employer-derived benefits at the time he incurs a 1-year break in service, years of service completed by such participant before such break are not required to be taken into account for purposes of determining the nonforfeitable percentage of his right to employer-derived benefits if at such time the number of consecutive 1-year breaks in service included in his most recent break in service equals or exceeds the aggregate number of his years of service, whether or not consecutive, completed before such break. In the case of a plan utilizing the elapsed time method described in § 1.410(a)-7, the condition in the preceding sentence shall be satisfied if the period of severance is at least one year and the consecutive period of severance equals or exceeds his prior period of service, whether or not consecutive, completed before such period of severance. In computing the aggregate number of years of service prior to such break, years of service which could have been disregarded under this subdivision by reason of any prior break in service may be disregarded.

(2) *One-year break in service defined.*—The term "1-year break in service" means a calendar year, plan year, or other 12-consecutive month period designated by a plan (and not prohibited under regulations prescribed by the Secretary of Labor) during which the participant has not completed more than 500 hours of service. In the case of a plan utilizing the elapsed time method, the term "1-year break in service" means a 12-consecutive month period beginning on the severance from service date or any anniversary thereof and ending on the next succeeding anniversary of such date; provided, however, that the employee during such 12-consecutive-month period does not complete any hours of service within the meaning of 29 CFR Part

2530.200b-2(a) for the employer or employers maintaining the plan. See regulations prescribed by the Secretary of Labor under 29 CFR Part 2530, relating to minimum standards for employee pension benefit plans.

(d) *Examples.*—The rules provided by this section are illustrated by the following examples:

Example (1). (i) X Corporation maintains a defined contribution plan to which section 411 applies. The plan uses the calendar year as the vesting computation period. In 1980, Employee A, who was hired at age 35, separates from the service of X Corporation after completing 4 years of service. At the time of his separation, Employee A had a nonforfeitable right to 25% of his employer-derived accrued benefit which was not distributed. In 1985, after incurring 5 consecutive one-year breaks in service, Employee A is re-employed by X Corporation and becomes an active participant in the plan. The plan provides that, for 1985 and all subsequent years, Employee A's previous years of service will not be taken into account for purposes of computing the nonforfeitable percentage of his employer-derived accrued benefit, solely because of his break in service.

(ii) The plan fails to satisfy section 411. Section 411(a)(6)(B) would permit the plan to disregard Employee A's prior service for purposes of computing his nonforfeitable percentage in 1985 only, but such service must be taken into account in subsequent years unless there is another break in service. Under section 411(a)(6)(C), the plan is not required to take Employee A's post-break service into account for purposes of computing his nonforfeitable right to his pre-break employer-derived accrued benefits. This provision, however, would not permit the plan to disregard pre-break service in determining his nonforfeitable right to his benefit accrued after the break. The exception provided by section 411(a)(6)(D) does not apply in the case of a participant who has any nonforfeitable right to his accrued benefit derived from employer contributions.

Example (2). (i) X Corporation maintains a qualified plan to which sections 410 and 411 (relating to minimum participation standards and minimum vesting standards, respectively) apply. The plan permits participation upon completion of a year of service and provides that 100% of an employee's employer-derived accrued benefit vests after 10 years of service. The plan uses the calendar year as the vesting computation period. The plan provides that an employee who completes at least 1,000 hours of service in a 12-month period is credited with a year of service for participation and vesting purposes. The plan also provides that an employee who does not complete more than 500 hours of service in that 12-month period incurs a one-year break in service. The plan includes the rule described in section 411(a)(6)(D) for participation and vesting purposes. Under this rule, an employee's years of service prior to a break in service may be disregarded under certain circumstances if he has no vested right to any employer-derived benefit under the plan. The plan does not contain the rule described in section 411(a)(6)(B) (relating to the requirement of one year of service after a one-year break in service).

(ii) Employee A commences employment with the X Corporation on January 1, 1977. Employee A's employment history for 1977 through 1989 is as follows:

Year Ending 12/31	Hours of Service Completed
1977	1,000
1978	800
1979	1,000
1980	400
1981	1,000
1982	0
1983	400
1984	1,000
1985	0
1986	0
1987	500
1988	200
1989	1,000

Employee A's status as a participant during this period is determined as follows:

1978: Employee A was a plan participant on January 1, 1978 because he completed a year of service (1,000 hours) in 1977. He did not complete a year of service in 1978 because he completed fewer than 1,000 hours in that year. Because he completed more than 500 hours of service in 1978, however, Employee A did not incur a one-year break in service that year.

1979: Employee A completes a year of service in 1979. Because he did not incur a one-year break in service in 1978, the plan may not disregard his 1977 service for purposes of determining his years of service as of January 1, 1979.

1980: Employee A incurs a one-year break in service in 1980.

1981: Because Employee A had completed 2 years of service prior to 1981 and had incurred one 1-year break in service prior to 1981, under section 411(a)(6)(D), the plan may not disregard his pre-1980 service in 1981. Employee A completes a year of service in 1981.

1982: Employee A incurs a one-year break in service in 1982.

1983: Employee A incurs a one-year break in service in 1983. As of the end of 1983, he has completed 3 years of service and has incurred 2 consecutive one-year breaks in service.

1984: Employee A completes a year of service in 1984. Under section 411(a)(6)(D), his pre-1982 service may not be disregarded in 1984 because, as of the beginning of 1984, his pre-1984 years of service (3) exceed his consecutive one-year breaks in service (2).

1985—1988: Employee A incurs 4 consecutive one-year breaks in service during the years 1985 through 1988.

1989: Employee A's pre-1989 service is disregarded in 1989 and all subsequent plan years because his years of service as of January 1, 1989, equal the number of consecutive one-year breaks he has incurred as of that date. Therefore, as of the beginning of 1989, Employee A is not a plan participant. Employee A completes a year of service in 1989. (Although section 411(a)(6)(D) does not prohibit the plan provision under which Employee A's pre-1989 service is disregarded, that section does not require such a provision in a qualified plan.) [Reg. § 1.411(a)-6.]

☐ [T.D. 7501, 8-22-77. Amended by T.D. 7703, 6-16-80.]

[Reg. § 1.411(a)-7]

§1.411(a)-7. Definitions and special rules.—(a) *Accrued benefit.*—For purposes of section 411 and the regulations thereunder, the term "accrued benefit" means—

(1) *Defined benefit plan.*—In the case of a defined benefit plan—

(i) If the plan provides an accrued benefit in the form of an annual benefit commencing at normal retirement age, such accrued benefit, or

(ii) If the plan does not provide an accrued benefit in the form described in subdivision (i) of this subparagraph, an annual benefit commencing at normal retirement age which is the actuarial equivalent (determined under section 411(c)(3) and §1.411(c)-5) of the accrued benefit determined under the plan.

In general, the term "accrued benefit" refers only to pension or retirement benefits. Consequently, accrued benefits do not include ancillary benefits not directly related to retirement benefits such as payment of medical expenses (or insurance premiums for such expenses), disability benefits not in excess of the qualified disability benefit (see section 411(a)(9) and paragraph (c)(3) of this section), life insurance benefits payable as a lump sum, incidental death benefits, current life insurance protection, or medical benefits described in section 401(h). For purposes of this subparagraph a subsidized early retirement benefit which is provided by a plan is not taken into account, except to the extent of determining the normal retirement benefit under the plan (see section 411(a)(9) and paragraph (c) of this section). The accrued benefit includes any optional settlement at normal retirement age under actuarial assumptions no less favorable than those which would be applied if the employee were terminating his employment at normal retirement age. The accrued benefit does not include any subsidized value in a joint and survivor annuity to the extent that the annual benefit of the joint and survivor annuity does not exceed the annual benefit of a single life annuity.

(2) *Defined contribution plan.*—In the case of a defined contribution plan, the balance of the employee's account held under the plan.

(b) *Normal retirement age.*—(1) *General rule.*—For purposes of section 411 and the regulations thereunder, the term "normal retirement age" means the earlier of—

(i) The time specified by a plan at which a plan participant attains normal retirement age, or

(ii) The later of—

(A) The time the plan participant attains age 65, or

(B) The 10th anniversary of the date the plan participant commences participation in the plan.

If a plan, or the employer sponsoring the plan, imposes a requirement that an employee retire upon reaching a certain age, the normal retirement age may not exceed that mandatory retirement age. The preceding sentence will apply if the employer consistently enforces a mandatory retirement age rule, whether or not set forth in the plan or any related document. For purposes of subdivision (i) of this subparagraph, if an age is not specified by a plan as the normal retirement age, then the normal retirement age under the plan is the earliest age beyond which the participant's benefits under the plan are not greater solely on account of his age or service. For purposes of subdivision (ii)(B) of this subparagraph, participation commences on the first day of the first year in which the participant commenced his participation in the plan, except that years which may be disregarded under section 410(a)(5)(D) may be disregarded in determining when participation commenced.

(2) *Examples.*—The provisions of this paragraph are illustrated by the following examples:

Example (1). Plan A defines normal retirement age as age 65. Under the plan, benefits payable to participants who retire at or after age 60 are not reduced on account of early retirement. For purposes of section 411 and the vesting regulations, normal retirement age under Plan A is age 65 (determined under subparagraph (1)(i) of this paragraph). This is true even if in operation all participants retire at age 60.

Example (2). Plan B does not specify any age as the normal retirement age. Under the plan, participants who have attained age 55 are entitled to benefits commencing upon retirement but the benefits of participants who retire before attaining age 70 are subject to reduction on account of early retirement. For purposes of section 411 and the vesting regulations the normal retirement age under plan B is the later of (i) age 65, or (ii) the 10th anniversary of the date a plan participant commences participation in the plan (assuming such date is prior to age 70).

Example (3). The facts are the same as in example (2). Employee X first became a participant in Plan B on January 1, 1980 at age 53. His participation continued until December 31, 1980, when he separated from the service with no vested benefits. After incurring 5 consecutive 1-year breaks in service, Employee X again becomes an employee and a plan participant on January 1, 1986, at age 59. For purposes of section 411, Employee X's normal retirement age under Plan B is age 69, the 10th anniversary of the date on which his year of plan participation commenced. His participation in 1980 may be disregarded under the last sentence of subparagraph (1) of this paragraph.

(c) *Normal retirement benefit.*—(1) *In general.*—For purposes of section 411 and the regulations thereunder, the term "normal retirement benefit" means the periodic benefit under the plan commencing upon early retirement (if any) or at normal retirement age, whichever benefit is greater.

(2) *Periodic benefit.*—For purposes of subparagraph (1) of this paragraph—

(i) In the case of a plan under which a benefit is payable as an annuity in the same form upon early retirement and at normal retirement age, the greater benefit is determined by comparing the amount of such annuity payments.

(ii) In the case of a plan under which an annuity benefit payable upon early retirement is not in the same form as an annuity benefit payable at normal retirement age, the greater benefit is determined by converting the annuity benefit payable upon early retirement age into the same form of annuity benefit as is payable at normal retirement age and by comparing the amount of the converted early retirement benefit payment with the amount of the normal retirement benefit payment.

(iii) In the case of a plan which is integrated with the Social Security Act or any other Federal or State law, the periodic benefit payable upon and after early retirement age is adjusted for any increases in such benefits occurring on or after early retirement age which are taken into account under the plan. See however, section 401(a)(15) and the regulations thereunder.

(3) *Benefits included.*—For purposes of this paragraph, the normal retirement benefit under a plan shall be determined without regard to ancillary benefits not directly related to retirement benefits such as medical benefits or disability benefits not in excess of the qualified disability benefit; see section 411(a)(7) and paragraph (a)(1) of this section. For this purpose, a qualified disability benefit is a disability benefit which is not in excess of the amount of the benefit which would be payable to the participant if he separated from service at normal retirement age.

(4) *Early retirement benefit; social security supplement.*—(i) For purposes of this paragraph, the early retirement benefit under a plan shall be determined without regard to any social security supplement.

(ii) For purposes of this subparagraph, a social security supplement is a benefit for plan participants which—

(A) Commences before the age and terminates before the age when participants are entitled to old-age insurance benefits, unreduced on account of age, under title II of the Social Security Act, as amended (see section 202(a) and (g) of such Act), and

(B) Does not exceed such old-age insurance benefit.

(5) *Special limitation.*—If a defined benefit plan bases its normal retirement benefits on employee compensation, the compensation must reflect the compensation which would have been paid for a full year of participation within the meaning of section 411(b)(3). If an employee works less than a full year of participation, the compensation used to determine benefits under the plan for such year of participation must be multiplied by the ratio of the number of hours

for a complete year of participation to the number of hours worked in such year. A plan whose benefit formula is computed on a computation base which cannot decrease is not required to adjust employee compensation in the manner described in the previous sentence. Thus, for example, if a plan provided a benefit based on an employee's compensation for his highest five consecutive years or a separate benefit for each year of participation based on the employee's compensation for such year, the plan would not have to so adjust compensation. However, if a plan provided a benefit based on an employee's compensation for the employee's last five years or the five highest consecutive years out of the last 10 years, the compensation would have to be so adjusted. For special rules for applying the limitations on proration of a year of participation for benefit accrual, see regulations prescribed by the Secretary of Labor under 29 CFR Part 2530, relating to minimum standards for employee pension benefit plans.

(6) *Examples.*—The provisions of this paragraph are illustrated by the following examples:

Example (1). Plan A provides for a benefit equal to 1% of high 5 years compensation for each year of service and a normal retirement age of 65. The plan also provides for a full unreduced accrued benefit without any actuarial reduction for any employee at age 55 with 30 years of service. Even though the actuarial value of the early retirement benefit could exceed the value of the benefit at the normal retirement age, the normal retirement benefit would not include the greater value of the early retirement benefit because actuarial subsidies are ignored.

Example (2). Plan B provides the following benefits: (1) at normal retirement age 65, $300/mo. for life and (2) at early retirement age 60, $400/mo. for life. The normal retirement benefit is $400/mo., the greater of the benefit payable at normal retirement age ($300) or early retirement ($400).

Example (3). Assume the same facts as example (2) except that the early retirement benefit of $400 is reduced to $300 upon attainment of age 65. If each employee's social security benefit at age 65 is not less than $100, the $100 would be considered to be a social security supplement and would therefore be ignored. Consequently, the normal retirement benefit would be $300.

Example (4). Plan C provides a benefit at normal retirement age equal to 1% per year of service, multiplied by the participant's compensation averaged over the 5 years immediately prior to retirement. An early retirement benefit is provided upon attainment of age 60 equal to the benefit accrued to date of early retirement reduced by 4 percent for each year by which the early retirement date precedes the normal retirement age of 65. Employee A was hired at age 30, participated immediately, and retired at age 65. Employee A's annual compensation was $50,000 between ages 55-60 and was reduced to $33,000 after age 60. The following table indicates the amount of annual benefit that would have been provided by the plan formula if the employee retired at or after age 60:

Age	Final average computed (1)—	Percent accrued benefit (2)—	Reduction (3)—	Annual benefit (4)—
60 ..	$50,000	30	0.80	$12,000
61 ..	46,600	31	.84	12,135
62 ..	43,200	32	.88	12,165
63 ..	39,800	33	.92	12,083
64 ..	36,400	34	.96	11,881
65 ..	33,000	35	1.00	11,550

NOTE.—Col. (1) times col. (2) times col. (3) equals col. (4).
The normal retirement benefit is the greater of the benefit payable at normal retirement age or the early retirement benefit. Employee A's normal retirement benefit is $12,165, the greatest annual benefit Employee A would be entitled to.

(d) *Rules relating to certain distributions and cash-outs of accrued benefits.*—(1) *In general.*—This paragraph sets forth vesting rules applicable to certain distributions from qualified plans and their related trusts (other than class year plans). Subparagraphs (2) and (3) set forth the exceptions to nonforfeitability on account of withdrawal of mandatory contributions provided by section 411(a)(3)(D). When a plan utilizes these exceptions with respect to a given participant's accrued benefit, such accrued benefit is not subject to the cash-out rules or vesting rules of subparagraphs (4) or (5), respectively. Section 411 prescribes certain requirements with respect to accrued benefits under a qualified plan. These requirements would generally not be satisfied if the plan disregarded service in computing accrued benefits even though amounts were distributed on account of such service. Subparagraph (4) of this paragraph sets forth rules under section 411(a)(7)(B) which allow a plan to make distributions and compute accrued benefits without regard to the accrued benefit

attributable to the distribution. When a defined contribution plan utilizes this exception with respect to an accrued benefit, the plan is not required to satisfy the rules of subparagraph (5) of this paragraph. Subparagraph (5) of this paragraph sets forth a vesting requirement applicable to certain distributions from defined contribution plans. Subparagraph (6) sets forth other rules which pertain to the distribution rules of this paragraph.

(2) *Withdrawal of mandatory contribution.*—(i) *General rule.*—In the case of a participant's right to his employer-derived accrued benefit, a right is not treated as forfeitable merely because all or a portion of such benefit may be forfeited on account of the withdrawal by the participant of any amount attributable to his accrued benefit derived from his mandatory contributions (within the meaning of section 411(c)(2)(C) and §1.411(c)-1 before he has become a 50 percent vested participant (within the meaning of §1.401(a)-19(b)(2)). For purposes of determining the vested percentage, the plan may disregard service after the withdrawal. For example, assume that a plan utilizes 1000 hours for computing years of service and that for the computation period employee A had 1000 hours of service. If A was 40 percent vested at the beginning of the period but only had 800 hours at the time of the withdrawal, the plan could treat A as only 40 percent vested because service after the withdrawal can be disregarded. On the other hand, if A had 1000 hours at the time of the withdrawal, he must receive a year of service for the computation period, even though service is not taken into account until the end of such period.

(ii) *Plan repayment provision.*—(A) Subdivision (i) of this subparagraph shall not apply unless, at the time the amount described in such subdivision is withdrawn by the participant, the plan provides the employee with a right to restoration of his employer-derived accrued benefit to the extent forfeited in accordance with such subdivision upon repayment to the plan of the full amount of the withdrawal.

(B) In the case of a defined benefit plan (as defined in section 414(j)) the restoration of the employee's employer-derived accrued benefit may be conditioned upon repayment of interest on the full amount of the distribution. Such interest shall be computed on the amount of the distribution from the date of such distribution to the date of repayment, compounded annually from the date of distribution, at the rate determined under section 411(c)(2)(C) in effect on the date of repayment. A plan may provide for repayment of interest which is less than the amount determined under the preceding sentence.

(C) In the case of both defined benefit plans and defined contribution plans, the plan repayment provision described in this subparagraph may provide that the employee must repay the full amount of the distribution in order to have the forfeited benefit restored. The plan provision may not require that such repayment be made sooner than the time described in paragraph (d)(2)(ii)(D) of this section.

(D)(1) If a distribution is on account of separation from service, the time for repayment may not end before the earlier of—

(i) 5 years after the first day the employee is subsequently employed or

(ii) The close of the first period of consecutive 1-year breaks in service commencing after the distribution.
If the distribution occurs for any other reason, the time for repayment may not end earlier than 5 years after the date of distribution. Nevertheless, a plan provision may provide for a longer period in which the employee may repay. For example, a plan could allow repayments to be made at any time before normal retirement age.

(2) In the case of a plan utilizing the elapsed time method, described in §1.410(a)-7, the minimum time for repayment shall be determined as in paragraph (d)(2)(ii)(D)(1) above except as provided in this subdivision. The 5 consecutive 1-year break periods shall be determined by substituting the term "1-year period of severance" for the term "1-year break in service". Also, the repayment period both commences and closes in a manner determined by the Commissioner that is consistent with the rules in §1.410(a)-7 and the substitution in section 411(a)(6)(C) and (D) of a 5-year break in service rule for the former 1-year break in service rule.

(E) A defined benefit plan using the break in service rule described in section 410(a)(5)(D) or a defined contribution plan using the break in service rule described in section 411(a)(6)(C) for determining employees' accrued benefits is not required to provide for repayment by an employee whose accrued benefit is disregarded by reason of a plan provision using these rules.

(iii) *Computation of benefit.*—In the case of a defined contribution plan, the employer-derived accrued benefit required to be restored by this subparagraph shall not be less than the amount in the account balance of the employee which was forfeited, unadjusted by any subsequent gains or losses.

(iv) *Delayed forfeiture.*—A defined contribution plan may, in lieu of the forfeiture and restoration described in this subparagraph, provide that the forfeiture does not occur until the expiration of the time for repayment described in subdivision (ii) of this subparagraph provided that the conditions of this subparagraph are satisfied.

(3) *Withdrawal of mandatory contributions; accruals before September 2, 1974.*—(i) *General rule.*—In the case of a participant's right to the portion of the employer-derived benefit which accrued prior to September 2, 1974, a right is not treated as forfeitable merely because all or part of such portion may be forfeited on account of the withdrawal by the participant of an amount attributable to his benefit derived from mandatory contributions (within the meaning of section 411(c)(2)(C) and §1.411(c)-1(c)(4)) made by the participant before September 2, 1974, if the amount so subject to forfeiture is no more than proportional to such amounts withdrawn. This subparagraph shall not apply to any plan to which any mandatory contribution (within the meaning of section 411(c)(2)(C) and §1.411(c)-1(c)(4)) is made after September 2, 1974.

(ii) *Defined contribution plan.*—In the case of a defined contribution plan, the portion of a participant's employer-derived benefit which accrued prior to September 2, 1974, shall be determined on the basis of a separate accounting between benefits accruing before and after such date. Gains, losses, withdrawals, forfeitures, and other credits or charges must be separately allocated to such benefits. Any allocation made on a reasonable and consistent basis prior to September 1, 1977, shall satisfy the requirements of this subdivision.

(iii) *Defined benefit plan.*—In the case of a defined benefit plan, the portion of a participant's employer-derived benefit which accrued prior to September 2, 1974, shall be determined in a manner consistent with the determination of an accrued benefit under section 411(b)(1)(D) (see §1.411(b)-1(c)). Any method of determining such accrued benefit which the Commissioner finds to be reasonable shall satisfy the requirements of this subdivision.

(4) *Certain cash-outs of accrued benefits.*—(i) *Involuntary cash-outs.*—For purposes of determining an employee's right to an accrued benefit derived from employer contributions under a plan, the plan may disregard service performed by the employee with respect to which—

(A) The employee receives a distribution of the present value of his entire nonforfeitable benefit at the time of the distribution;

(B) The requirements of section 411(a)(11) are satisfied at the time of the distribution;

(C) The distribution is made due to the termination of the employee's participation in the plan; and

(D) The plan has a repayment provision which satisfies the requirements of paragraph (d)(4)(iv) of this section in effect at the time of the distribution.

(ii) *Voluntary cash-outs.*—For purposes of determining an employee's accrued benefit derived from employer contributions under a plan, the plan may disregard service performed by the employee with respect to which—

(A) The employee receives a distribution of the present value of his nonforfeitable benefit attributable to such service at the time of such distribution,

(B) The employee voluntarily elects to receive such distribution,

(C) The distribution is made on termination of the employee's participation in the plan, and

(D) The plan has a repayment provision in effect at the time of the distribution which satisfies the requirements of subdivision (iv) of this subparagraph.

A distribution shall be deemed to be made on termination of participation in the plan if it is made not later than the close of the second plan year following the plan year in which such termination occurs. For purposes of determining the nonforfeitable benefit, the plan may disregard service after the distribution as illustrated in subparagraph (2)(i) of this subparagraph.

(iii) *Disregard of service.*—Service of an employee permitted to be disregarded under subdivision (i) or (ii) of this subparagraph is not required to be taken into account in computing the employee's accrued benefit under the plan. In the case of a voluntary distribution described in subdivision (ii) of this subparagraph which is less than the present value of the employee's total nonforfeitable benefit immediately prior to the distribution, the accrued benefit not required to be taken into account is such total accrued benefit multiplied by a fraction, the numerator of which is the amount of the distribution and the denominator of which is the present value of his total nonforfeitable benefit immediately prior to such distribution. For example, A who is 50 percent vested in an account balance of $1,000

receives a voluntary distribution of $250. The accrued benefit which can be disregarded equals $1,000 times $250/$500, or $500. However, such service may not by reason of this paragraph be disregarded for purposes of determining an employee's years of service under sections 410(a)(3) and 411(a)(4).

(iv) *Plan repayment provision.*—(A) A plan repayment provision satisfies the requirements of this subdivision if, under the provision, the accrued benefit of an employee that is disregarded by a plan under this subparagraph is restored upon repayment to the plan by the employee of the full amount of the distribution. An accrued benefit is not restored unless all of the optional forms of benefit and subsidies relating to such benefit are also restored. A plan is not required to provide for repayment of an accrued benefit unless the employee—

(1) Received a distribution that is in a plan year to which section 411 applies (see §1.411(a)-2), which distribution is less than the amount of his accrued benefit determined under the same optional form of benefit as the distribution was made, and

(2) Resumes employment covered under the plan.

(B) *Example.*—Plan A provides a single sum distribution equal to the present value of the normal form of the accrued benefit payable at normal retirement age which is a single life annuity. Plan A also provides a subsidized joint and survivor annuity and a subsidized early retirement annuity benefit. A participant who is fully vested and receives a single sum distribution equal to the present value of the single life annuity normal retirement benefit is not required to be provided the right under the plan to repay the distribution upon subsequent reemployment even though the participant received a distribution that did not reflect the value of the subsidy in the joint and survivor annuity or the value of the early retirement annuity subsidy. This is true whether or not the participant had satisfied at the time of the distribution all of the conditions necessary to receive the subsidies. However, if a participant does not receive his total accrued benefit in the optional form of benefit under which his benefit was distributed, the plan must provide for repayment. If the employee repays the distribution in accordance with section 411(a)(7), the plan must restore the employee's accrued benefit which would include the right to receive the subsidized joint and survivor annuity and the subsidized early retirement annuity benefit.

(C) A plan may impose the same conditions on repayments for the restoration of employer-derived accrued benefits that are allowed as conditions for restoration of employer-derived accrued benefits upon repayment of mandatory contributions under paragraph (d)(2)(ii)(B), (C), (D) and (E) of this section.

(v) In the case of a defined contribution plan, the employer-derived accrued benefit required to be restored by this subparagraph shall not be less than the amount in the account balance of the employee, both the amount distributed and the amount forfeited, unadjusted by any subsequent gains or losses. Thus, for example, if an employee received a distribution of $250 when he was 25 percent vested in an account balance of $1,000, upon repayment of $250 the account balance may not be less than $1,000 even if, because of plan losses, the account balance, if not distributed, would have been reduced to $500.

(vi) For purposes of paragraph (d)(4)(i) of this section, a distribution shall be deemed to be made due to the termination of an employee's participation in the plan if it is made no later than the close of the second plan year following the plan year in which such termination occurs, or if such distribution would have been made under the plan by the close of such second plan year but for the fact that the present value of the nonforfeitable accrued benefit then exceeded the cash-out limit in effect under §1.411(a)-11(c)(3)(ii). For purposes of determining the entire nonforfeitable benefit, the plan may disregard service after the distribution, as illustrated in paragraph (d)(2)(i) of this section.

(vii) *Effective date.*—Paragraphs (d)(4)(i) and (vi) of this section apply to distributions made on or after March 22, 1999. However, an employer is permitted to apply paragraphs (d)(4)(i) and (vi) of this section to plan years beginning on or after August 6, 1997. Otherwise, for distributions prior to March 22, 1999, §§1.411(a)-7 and 1.411(a)-7T, in effect prior to October 17, 2000 (as contained in 26 CFR part 1, revised as of April 1, 2000) apply.

(5) *Vesting requirement for defined contribution plans.*—(i) *Application.*—The requirements of this subparagraph apply to a defined contribution plan which makes distributions to employees from their accounts attributable to employer contributions at a time when—

(A) Employees are less than 100 percent vested in such accounts, and

(B) Under the plan, employees can increase their percentage of vesting in such accounts after the distributions.

Reg. §1.411(a)-7(d)(5)(i)(B)

(ii) *Requirements.*—In order for a plan, to which this subparagraph applies, to satisfy the vesting requirements of section 411, account balances under the plan (with respect to which percentage vesting can increase) must be computed in a manner which satisfies either subdivision (iii)(A) or (B) of this subparagraph.

(iii) *Permissible methods.*—A plan may provide for either of the following methods, but not both, for computing account balances with respect to which percentage vesting can increase and from which distributions are made:

(A)(1) A separate account is established for the employee's interest in the plan as of the time of the distribution, and

(2) At any relevant time the employee's vested portion of the separate account is not less than an amount ("X") determined by the formula: $X = P (AB + (R \times D)) - (R \times D)$. For purposes of applying the formula: P is the vested percentage at the relevant time; AB is the account balance at the relevant time; D is the amount of the distribution; R is the ratio of the account balance at the relevant time to the account balance after distribution; and the relevant time is the time at which, under the plan, the vested percentage in the account can not increase.

$$\frac{\$1,500}{\$750}\ \text{or 2.}$$

A's separate account must equal 60 percent ($\$1,500 + (2 \times \$250)) - (2 \times \$250)$ or 60 percent ($\$1,500 + \$500) - \$500$, or $\$1,200 - \$500$ equals \$700.

Example (2). The Y defined contribution plan uses the method described in subdivision (iii)(B) of this subparagraph for computing account balances and the break in service rule described in section 411(a)(6)(C). The plan distributes $250 to B when B's account balance prior to the distribution equals $1,000 and he is 25 percent vested. At the time of the distribution, B has not incurred a 1-year break so that his vesting percentage can increase. Six years later, when A is 60 percent vested, he incurs a 1-year break so that his vesting percentage cannot increase. At this time his account balance equals $1,500. B's separate account must equal 60 percent ($1,500 + $250) – $250, 60% of $1,750 – $250 equals $800.

(6) *Other rules.*—(i) *Distributions on separation or other event.*—None of the rules of this paragraph preclude distributions to employees upon separation from service of any other event recognized by the plan for commencing distributions. Such a distribution must, of course, satisfy the applicable qualification requirements pertaining to such distributions. For example, a profit-sharing plan could pay the vested portion of an account balance to an employee when he separated from service, but in order to satisfy section 411 the plan might not be able to forfeit the nonvested account balance until the employee has a 1-year break in service. Similarly, the fact that a plan can not disregard an accrued benefit attributable to service for which an employee has received a distribution because the plan does not satisfy the cash-out requirements of subparagraph (4) does not mean that the employee's accrued benefit (computed by taking into account such service) cannot be offset by the accrued benefit attributable to the distribution.

(ii) *Joint and survivor requirements.*—See § 1.401(a)-11(a)(2) (relating to joint and survivor annuities) for special rules applicable to certain distributions described in this paragraph.

(iii) *Plan repayments.*—(A) Under subparagraphs (2) and (4) of this paragraph, a plan may be required to restore accrued benefits in the event of repayment by an employee.

(B) For purposes of applying the limitations of section 415 (c) and (e), in the case of a defined contribution plan, the repayment by the employee and the restoration by the employer shall not be treated as annual additions.

(C) In the case of a defined contribution plan, the permissible sources for restoration of the accrued benefit are: income or gain to the plan, forfeitures, or employer contributions. Notwithstanding the provisions of § 1.401-1(b)(1)(ii), contributions may be made for such an accrued benefit by a profit-sharing plan even though there are no profits. In order for such a plan to be qualified, account balances (accrued benefits) generally must correspond to assets in the plan. Accordingly, there can not be an unfunded account balance. However, an account balance will not be deemed to be unfunded in the case of a restoration if assets for the restored benefit are provided by the end of the plan year following the plan year in which the repayment occurs. [Reg. § 1.411(a)-7.]

☐ [T.D. 7501, 8-22-77. Amended by T.D. 8038, 7-18-85; T.D. 8218, 8-19-88; T.D. 8794, 12-18-98 and T.D. 8891, 7-18-2000.]

Reg. § 1.411(a)-7(d)(5)(ii)

A plan is not required to provide for separate accounts provided that account balances are maintained under a method that has the same effect as under this subdivision.

(B) At any relevant time the employee's vested portion is not less than an amount ("X") determined by the formula: $X = P (AB + D) - D$. For purposes of applying the formula, the terms have the same meaning as under subdivision (iii)(A)(2) of this subparagraph.

(C) An application of the methods described in subdivisions (iii)(A) and (B) of this subparagraph is illustrated by the following examples:

Example (1). The X defined contribution plan uses the method described in subdivision (iii)(A) of this subparagraph for computing account balances and the break in service rule described in section 411(a)(6)(C) (service after a 1-year break does not increase the vesting percentage in account balances accrued prior to the break). The plan distributes $250 to A when A's account balance prior to the distribution equals $1,000 and he is 25 percent vested. At the time of the distribution, A has not incurred a 1-year break so that his vesting percentage can increase. Six years later, when A is 60 percent vested, he incurs a 1-year break so that his vesting percentage cannot increase. At this time his separate account balance equals $1,500. R equals

[Reg. § 1.411(a)-8]

§ 1.411(a)-8. Changes in vesting schedule.—(a) *Requirement of prior schedule.*—Under section 411(a)(10)(A), for plan years for which section 411 applies, a plan will be treated as not meeting the minimum vesting standards of section 411(a)(2) if the plan does not satisfy the requirements of this paragraph. If the vesting schedule of a plan is amended, then as of the date such amendment is adopted, the plan satisfies the requirements of this paragraph if, under the plan as amended, in the case of an employee who is a participant on—

(1) The date the amendment is adopted, or

(2) The date the amendment is effective, if later,

the nonforfeitable percentage (determined as of such date) of such employee's right to his employer-derived accrued benefit is not less than his percentage computed under the plan without regard to such amendment.

(b) *Election of former schedule.*—(1) *In general.*—Under section 411(a)(10)(B), for plan years for which section 411 applies, if the vesting schedule of a plan is amended, the plan will not be treated as meeting the minimum vesting standards of section 411(a)(2) unless the plan, as amended, provides that each participant whose nonforfeitable percentage of his accrued benefit derived from employer contributions is determined under such schedule, and who has completed at least 5 years of service with the employer, may elect, during the election period, to have the nonforfeitable percentage of his accrued benefit derived from employer contributions determined without regard to such amendment. Notwithstanding the preceding sentence, no election need be provided for any participant whose nonforfeitable percentage under the plan, as amended, at any time cannot be less than such percentage determined without regard to such amendment.

(2) *Election period.*—For purposes of subparagraph (1) of this paragraph, the election period under the plan must begin no later than the date the plan amendment is adopted and end no earlier than the latest of the following dates:

(i) The date which is 60 days after the day the plan amendment is adopted,

(ii) The date which is 60 days after the day the plan amendment becomes effective, or

(iii) The date which is 60 days after the day the participant is issued written notice of the plan amendment by the employer or plan administration.

(3) *Service requirement.*—For purposes of subparagraph (1) of this paragraph, a participant shall be considered to have completed 5 years of service if such participant has completed 5 years of service, whether or not consecutive, without regard to the exceptions of section 411(a)(4) prior to the expiration of the election period described in subparagraph (2) of this paragraph. For the meaning of the term "year of service," see regulations prescribed by the Secretary of Labor under 29 CFR Part 2530, relating to minimum standards for employee pension benefit plans.

(4) *Election only by participant.*—The election described in subparagraph (1) of this paragraph is available only to an individual who is a participant in the plan at the time such election is made.

(5) *Election may be irrevocable.*—A plan, as amended, shall not fail to meet the minimum vesting standards of section 411(a)(2) by reason of section 411(a)(10)(B) merely because such plan provides that the election described in subparagraph (1) of this paragraph is irrevocable.

(6) *Relationship with section 411(a)(2).*—The election described in subparagraph (1) of this paragraph is available for a vesting schedule which does not satisfy the requirements of section 411(a)(2) only if under such schedule all participants have a 50 percent nonforfeitable right after 10 years of service, and a 100 percent nonforfeitable right after 15 years of service, in their employer-derived accrued benefit. If the vesting schedule provides less vesting than the percentages required by the preceding sentence, the plan can be amended to provide for such vesting.

(c) *Special rules.*—(1) *Amendment of vesting schedule.*—For purposes of this section, an amendment of a vesting schedule is each plan amendment which directly or indirectly affects the computation of the nonforfeitable percentage of employees' rights to employer-derived accrued benefits. Consequently, such an amendment, for example, includes each change in the plan which affects either the plan's computation of years of service or of vesting percentages for years of service.

(2) *Aggregation of amendments.*—All plan amendments which are: (i) amendments of a vesting schedule within the meaning of subparagraph (1) of this paragraph and (ii) adopted and effective at the same time, shall be deemed to be a single amendment for purposes of applying the rules in paragraphs (a) and (b) of this section.

(3) *Relationship with section 411(d)(6).*—For additional requirements relating to section 411(d)(6), see § 1.411(d)-3(a)(3). [Reg. § 1.411(a)-8.]

☐ [*T.D. 7501, 8-22-77. Amended by T.D. 9280, 8-8-2006.*]

[Reg. § 1.411(a)-8T]

§ 1.411(a)-8T. Changes in vesting schedule (Temporary).—
(a) [Reserved.]

(b) *Election of former schedule.*—(1) *In general.*—Under section 411(a)(10)(B), for plan years for which section 411 applies, if the vesting schedule of a plan is amended, the plan will not be treated as meeting the minimum vesting standards of section 411(a)(2) unless the plan as amended provides that each participant whose nonforfeitable percentage of his accrued benefit derived from employer contributions is determined under such schedule, and who has completed at least 3 years of service with the employer, may elect, during the election period, to have the nonforfeitable percentage of his accrued benefit derived from employer contributions determined without regard to such amendment. Notwithstanding the preceding sentence, no election need be provided for any participant whose nonforfeitable percentage under the plan, as amended, at any time cannot be less than such percentage determined without regard to such amendment. For employees not described in § 1.411(a)-3T(e)(1), this section shall be applied by substituting "5 years of service" for "3 years of service" where such language appears.

(2) *Election period.*—For purposes of subparagraph (1) of this paragraph, the election period under the plan must begin no later than the date the plan amendment is adopted and end no earlier than the latest of the following dates:

(i) The date which is 60 days after the day the plan amendment is adopted,

(ii) The date which is 60 days after the day the plan amendment becomes effective, or

(iii) The date which is 60 days after the day the participant is issued written notice of the plan amendment by the employer or plan administrator.

(3) *Service requirement.*—For purposes of subparagraph (1) of this paragraph, a participant shall be considered to have completed 3 years of service if such participant has completed 3 years of service, whether or not consecutive, without regard to the exceptions of section 411(a)(4) prior to the expiration of the election period described in subparagraph (2) of this paragraph. For the meaning of the term "year of service", see regulations prescribed by the Secretary of Labor under 29 CFR Part 2530, relating to minimum standards for employee pension benefit plans. [Temporary Reg. § 1.411(a)-8T.]

☐ [*T.D. 8170, 1-5-88.*]

[Reg. § 1.411(a)-9]

§ 1.411(a)-9. [Reserved].
☐ [*T.D. 7501, 8-22-77. Removed and reserved by T.D. 9849, 3-11-2019.*]

[Reg. § 1.411(a)-11]

§ 1.411(a)-11. Restriction and valuation of distributions.—
(a) *Scope.*—(1) *In general.*—Section 411(a)(11) restricts the ability of a plan to distribute any portion of a participant's accrued benefit without the participant's consent. Section 411(a)(11) also restricts the ability of defined benefit plans to distribute any portion of a participant's accrued benefit in optional forms of benefit without complying with specified valuation rules for determining the amount of the distribution. If the consent requirements or the valuation rules of this section are not satisfied, the plan fails to satisfy the requirements of section 411(a).

(2) *Accrued benefit.*—For purposes of this section, an accrued benefit is valued taking into consideration the particular optional form in which the benefit is to be distributed. The value of an accrued benefit is the present value of the benefit in the distribution form determined under the plan. For example, a plan that provides a subsidized early retirement annuity benefit may specify that the optional single sum distribution form of benefit available at early retirement age is the present value of the subsidized early retirement annuity benefit. In this case, the subsidized early retirement annuity benefit must be used to apply the valuation requirements of this section and the resulting amount of the single sum distribution. However, if a plan that provides a subsidized early retirement annuity benefit specifies that the single sum distribution benefit available at early retirement age is the present value of the normal retirement annuity benefit, then the normal retirement annuity benefit is used to apply the valuation requirements of this section and the resulting amount of the single sum distribution available at early retirement age.

(b) *General consent rules.*—A plan must satisfy the participant consent requirement with respect to the distribution of a participant's nonforfeitable accrued benefit with a present value in excess of the cash-out limit in effect under paragraph (c)(3)(ii) of this section. See paragraph (c)(3) and (4) for situations where no consent is required.

(c) *Consent, etc. requirements.*—(1) *General rule.*—If an accrued benefit is immediately distributable, section 411(a)(11) permits plans to provide for the distribution of any portion of a participant's nonforfeitable accrued benefits only if the applicable consent requirements are satisfied.

(2) *Consent.*—(i) No consent is valid unless the participant has received a general description of the material features of the optional forms of benefit available under the plan. In addition, so long as a benefit is immediately distributable, a participant must be informed of the right, if any, to defer receipt of the distribution. Furthermore, consent is not valid if a significant detriment is imposed under the plan on any participant who does not consent to a distribution. Whether or not a significant detriment is imposed shall be determined by the Commissioner by examining the particular facts and circumstances.

(ii) Consent of the participant to the distribution must not be made before the participant receives the notice of his or her rights specified in this paragraph (c)(2) and must not be made more than 90 days before the date the distribution commences.

(iii) A plan must provide a participant with notice of the rights specified in this paragraph (c)(2) at a time that satisfies either paragraph (c)(2)(iii)(A) or (B) of this section:

(A) This paragraph (c)(2)(iii)(A) is satisfied if the plan provides a participant with notice of the rights specified in this paragraph (c)(2) no less than 30 days and no more than 90 days before the date the distribution commences. However, if the participant, after having received this notice, affirmatively elects a distribution, a plan will not fail to satisfy the consent requirement of section 411(a)(11) merely because the distribution commences less than 30 days after the notice was provided to the participant, provided the plan administrator clearly indicates to the participant that the participant has a right to at least 30 days to consider whether to consent to the distribution.

(B) This paragraph (c)(2)(iii)(B) is satisfied if the plan—

(1) Provides the participant with notice of the rights specified in this paragraph (c)(2);

(2) Provides the participant with a summary of the notice within the time period described in paragraph (c)(2)(iii)(A) of this section; and

(3) If the participant so requests after receiving the summary described in paragraph (c)(2)(iii)(B)(2) of this section, provides the notice to the participant without charge and no less than 30 days before the date the distribution commences, subject to the rules for

the participant's waiver of that 30-day period. The summary described in paragraph (c)(2)(iii)(B)(2) of this section must advise the participant of the right, if any, to defer receipt of the distribution, must set forth a summary of the distribution options under the plan, must refer the participant to the most recent version of the notice (and, in the case of a notice provided in any document containing information in addition to the notice, must identify that document and must provide a reasonable indication of where the notice may be found in that document, such as by index reference or by section heading), and must advise the participant that, upon request, a copy of the notice will be provided without charge.

(iv) For purposes of satisfying the requirements of this paragraph (c)(2), the plan administrator may substitute the annuity starting date, within the meaning of §1.401(a)-20, Q&A-10, for the date the distribution commences.

(v) See §1.401(a)-20, Q&A-24 for a special rule applicable to consents to plan loans.

(3) *Cash-out limit.*—(i) Consent of the participant is required before the commencement of the distribution of any portion of an accrued benefit if the present value of the nonforfeitable total accrued benefit is greater than the cash-out limit in effect under paragraph (c)(3)(ii) of this section on the date the distribution commences. The consent requirements are deemed satisfied if such value does not exceed the cash-out limit, and the plan may distribute such portion to the participant as a single sum. Present value for this purpose must be determined in the same manner as under section 417(e); see §1.417(e)-1(d).

(ii) The cash-out limit in effect for a date is the amount described in section 411(a)(11)(A) for the plan year that includes that date. The cash-out limit in effect for dates in plan years beginning on or after August 6, 1997, is $5,000. The cash-out limit in effect for dates in plan years beginning before August 6, 1997, is $3,500.

(iii) *Effective date.*—Paragraphs (c)(3)(i) and (ii) of this section apply to distributions made on or after October 17, 2000. However, an employer is permitted to apply the $5,000 cash-out limit described in paragraph (c)(3)(ii) of this section to plan years beginning on or after August 6, 1997. Otherwise, for distributions prior to October 17, 2000, §§1.411(a)-11 and 1.411(a)-11T in effect prior to October 17, 2000 (as contained in 26 CFR Part 1 revised as of April 1, 2000) apply.

(4) *Immediately distributable.*—Participant consent is required for any distribution while it is immediately distributable, *i.e.*, prior to the later of the time a participant has attained normal retirement age (as defined in section 411(a)(8)) or age 62. Once a distribution is no longer immediately distributable, a plan may distribute the benefit in the form of a QJSA in the case of a benefit subject to section 417 or in the normal form in other cases without consent.

(5) *Death of participant.*—The consent requirements of section 411(a)(11) do not apply after the death of the participant.

(6) *QDROs.*—The consent requirements of section 411(a)(11) do not apply to payments to an alternate payee, defined in section 414(p)(8), except as provided in a qualified domestic relations order pursuant to section 414(p).

(7) *Section 401(a)(9), etc.*—The consent requirements of section 411(a)(11) do not apply to the extent that a distribution is required to satisfy the requirements of section 401(a)(9) or 415. See section 401(a)(9) and the regulations thereunder and §1.401(a)-20 Q&A 23 for guidance on these requirements. Notwithstanding any provision to the contrary in section 401(a)(14) or §1.401(a)-14, a plan may not distribute a participant's nonforfeitable accrued benefit with a present value in excess of the cash-out limit in effect under paragraph (c)(3)(ii) of this section while the benefit is immediately distributable unless the participant consents to such distribution. The failure of a participant to consent is deemed to be an election to defer commencement of payment of the benefit for purposes of section 401(a)(14) and §1.401(a)-14.

(8) *Delegation to Commissioner.*—The Commissioner, in revenue rulings, notices, and other guidance published in the Internal Revenue Bulletin, may modify, or provide additional guidance with respect to, the notice and consent requirements of this section. See §601.601(d)(2)(ii)(b) of this chapter.

»»→ *Caution: Reg. §1.411(a)(13)-1(b)(2) generally applies to plan years that begin on or after January 1, 2017.*

(2) *General rules with respect to current account balance or current value.*—(i) *Benefit after normal retirement age.*—The relief of section 411(a)(13) does not override the requirement for a plan that, with respect to a participant with an annuity starting date after normal retirement age, the plan either provide an actuarial increase after normal retirement age or satisfy the requirements for suspension of benefits under section 411(a)(3)(B). Accordingly, with respect to such a participant, a plan with a lump sum based benefit formula violates

(d) *Distribution valuation requirements.*—In determining the present value of any distribution of any accrued benefit from a defined benefit plan, the plan must take into account specified valuation rules. For this purpose, the valuation rules are the same valuation rules for valuing distributions as set forth in section 417(e); see §1.417(e)-1(d). This paragraph (d) applies both before and after the participant's death regardless of whether the accrued benefit is immediately distributable. This paragraph also applies whether or not the participant's consent is required under paragraphs (b) and (c) of this section.

(e) *Special rules.*—(1) *Plan termination.*—The requirements of this section apply before, on and after a plan termination. If a defined contribution plan terminates and the plan does not offer an annuity option (purchased from a commercial provider), then the plan may distribute a participant's accrued benefit without the participant's consent. The preceding sentence does not apply if the employer or any entity within the same controlled group as the employer maintains another defined contribution plan, other than an employee stock ownership plan (as defined in section 4975(e)(7)). In such a case, the participant's accrued benefit may be transferred without the participant's consent to the other plan if the participant does not consent to an immediate distribution from the terminating plan. See section 411(d)(6) and the regulations thereunder for other rules applicable to transferee plans and plan terminations.

(2) *ESOP dividends.*—The requirements of this section do not apply to any distribution of dividends to which section 404(k) applies.

(3) *Other rules.*—See §1.401(a)-20 Q&As 14, 17 and 24 for other rules that apply to the section 411(a)(11) requirements.

(f) *Medium for notice and consent.*—(1) *Notice.*—The notice of a participant's rights described in paragraph (c)(2) of this section or the summary of that notice described in paragraph (c)(2)(iii)(B)(2) of this section must be provided on a written paper document. However, see §1.401(a)-21 of this chapter for rules permitting the use of electronic media to provide applicable notices to recipients with respect to retirement plans.

(2) *Consent.*—The consent described in paragraphs (c)(2) and (3) of this section must be given on a written paper document. However, see §1.401(a)-21 of this chapter for rules permitting the use of electronic media to make participant elections with respect to retirement plans.
[Reg. §1.411(a)-11.]

☐ [*T.D.* 8219, 8-19-88. *Amended by T.D.* 8620, 9-15-95; *T.D.* 8794, 12-18-98; *T.D.* 8796, 12-17-98; *T.D.* 8873, 2-7-2000; *T.D.* 8891, 7-18-2000 *and T.D.* 9294, 10-19-2006.]

[Reg. §1.411(a)(13)-1]

§1.411(a)(13)-1. **Statutory hybrid plans.**—(a) *In general.*—This section sets forth certain rules that apply to statutory hybrid plans under section 411(a)(13). Paragraph (b) of this section describes special rules for certain statutory hybrid plans that determine benefits under a lump sum-based benefit formula. Paragraph (c) of this section describes the vesting requirement for statutory hybrid plans. Paragraphs (d) and (e) of this section contain definitions and effective/applicability dates, respectively.

(b) *Calculation of benefit by reference to hypothetical account balance or accumulated percentage.*—(1) *Payment of a current balance or current value under a lump sum-based benefit formula.*—Pursuant to section 411(a)(13)(A), a statutory hybrid plan that determines any portion of a participant's benefits under a lump sum-based benefit formula is not treated as failing to meet the following requirements solely because, with respect to benefits determined under that formula, the present value of those benefits is, under the terms of the plan, equal to the then-current balance of the hypothetical account maintained for the participant or to the then-current value of the accumulated percentage of the participant's final average compensation under that formula—

(i) Section 411(a)(2); or

(ii) With respect to the participant's accrued benefit derived from employer contributions, section 411(a)(11), 411(c), or 417(e).

the requirements of section 411(a) if the balance of the hypothetical account or the value of the accumulated percentage of the participant's final average compensation is not increased sufficiently to satisfy the requirements of section 411(a)(2) for distributions commencing after normal retirement age, unless the plan suspends benefits in accordance with section 411(a)(3)(B).

(ii) *Reductions limited.*—The relief of section 411(a)(13) does not permit the accumulated benefit under a lump sum-based benefit

»»→ *Caution: Reg. §1.411(a)(13)-1(b)(2) generally applies to plan years that begin on or after January 1, 2017.*

formula to be reduced in a manner that would be prohibited if that reduction were applied to the accrued benefit. Accordingly, the only reductions that can apply to the balance of the hypothetical account or accumulated percentage of the participant's final average compensation are reductions as a result of—

(A) Benefit payments;

(B) Qualified domestic relations orders under section 414(p);

(C) Forfeitures that are permitted under section 411(a) (such as charges for providing a qualified preretirement survivor annuity);

(D) Amendments that would reduce the accrued benefit but that are permitted under section 411(d)(6);

(E) Adjustments resulting in a decrease in the balance of the hypothetical account due to the application of interest credits (as defined in § 1.411(b)(5)-1(d)(1)(ii)(A)) that are negative for an interest crediting period;

(F) In the case of a formula that expresses the accumulated benefit as an accumulated percentage of the participant's final average compensation, adjustments resulting in a decrease in the dollar amount of the accumulated percentage of the participant's final average compensation—

(1) Due to a decrease in the dollar amount of the participant's final average compensation; or

(2) Due to an increase in the integration level, under a formula that is integrated with Social Security (for example, as a result of an increase in the Social Security taxable wage base or in Social Security covered compensation); or

(G) Other reductions to the extent provided by the Commissioner in revenue rulings, notices, or other guidance published in the Internal Revenue Bulletin (see § 601.601(d)(2)(ii)(b)).

»»→ *Caution: Reg. §1.411(a)(13)-1(b)(3) generally applies to plan years that begin on or after January 1, 2017.*

(3) *Payment of benefits based on current account balance or current value.*—(i) *Optional forms that are actuarially equivalent.*—With respect to the benefits under a lump sum-based benefit formula, the relief of paragraph (b)(1) of this section applies to an optional form of benefit that is determined as of the annuity starting date as the actuarial equivalent, using reasonable actuarial assumptions, of the then-current balance of a hypothetical account maintained for the participant or the then-current value of an accumulated percentage of the participant's final average compensation.

(ii) *Optional forms that are subsidized.*—With respect to the benefits under a lump sum-based benefit formula, if an optional form of benefit is payable in an amount that is greater than the actuarial equivalent, determined using reasonable actuarial assumptions, of the then-current balance of a hypothetical account maintained for the participant or the then-current value of an accumulated percentage of the participant's final average compensation, then the plan satisfies the requirements of sections 411(a)(2), 411(a)(11), 411(c) and 417(e) with respect to the amount of that optional form of benefit. However, see § 1.411(b)(5)-1(b)(1)(iii) for rules relating to early retirement subsidies.

(iii) *Optional forms that are less valuable.*—Except as otherwise provided in paragraph (b)(4)(i) of this section, if an optional form of benefit is not at least the actuarial equivalent, using reasonable actuarial assumptions, of the then-current balance of a hypothetical account maintained for the participant or the then-current value of an accumulated percentage of the participant's final average compensation, then the relief under section 411(a)(13) (permitting a plan to treat the account balance or accumulated percentage as the actuarial equivalent of the portion of the accrued benefit determined under the lump sum-based benefit formula) does not apply in determining whether the optional form of benefit is the actuarial equivalent of the portion of the accrued benefit determined under the lump sum-based benefit formula. As a result, payment of that optional form of benefit must satisfy the rules applicable to payment of the accrued benefit generally under a defined benefit plan (without regard to the special rules of section 411(a)(13)(A) and paragraph (b)(1) of this section), including the requirements of section 411(a)(2) and, for optional forms subject to the minimum present value requirements of section 417(e)(3), those minimum present value requirements.

»»→ *Caution: Reg. §1.411(a)(13)-1(b)(4) generally applies to plan years that begin on or after January 1, 2017.*

(4) *Rules of application.*—(i) *Relief applies on proportionate basis with respect to payment of only a portion of the benefit under a lump sum-based benefit formula.*—The relief of paragraph (b)(1) of this section applies on a proportionate basis to a payment of a portion of the benefit under a lump sum-based benefit formula, such as a payment of a specified dollar amount or percentage of the then-current balance of a hypothetical account maintained for the participant or then-current value of an accumulated percentage of the participant's final average compensation. Thus, for example, if a plan that expresses the participant's entire accumulated benefit as the balance of a hypothetical account distributes 40 percent of the participant's then-current hypothetical account balance in a single payment, the plan is treated as satisfying the requirements of section 411(a) and the minimum present value rules of section 417(e) with respect to 40 percent of the participant's then-current accrued benefit.

(ii) *Relief applies only to portion of benefit determined under lump sum-based benefit formula.*—The relief of paragraph (b)(1) of this section generally applies only to the portion of the participant's benefit that is determined under a lump sum-based benefit formula and generally does not apply to any portion of the participant's benefit that is determined under a formula that is not a lump sum-based benefit formula. The following rules apply for purposes of satisfying section 417(e):

(A) *"Greater-of" formulas.*—If the participant's accrued benefit equals the greater of the accrued benefit under a lump sum-based benefit formula and the accrued benefit under another formula that is not a lump-sum based benefit formula, a single-sum payment of the participant's entire benefit must be no less than the greater of the then-current accumulated benefit under the lump sum-based benefit formula and the present value, determined in accordance with section 417(e), of the benefit under the other formula. For example, assume that the accrued benefit under a plan is determined as the greater of the accrued benefit attributable to the balance of a hypothetical account and the accrued benefit equal to a pro rata portion of a normal retirement benefit determined by projecting the hypothetical account balance (including future principal and interest credits) to normal retirement age. In such a case, a single-sum payment of the participant's entire benefit must be no less than the greater of the then-current balance of the hypothetical account and the present value, determined in accordance with section 417(e), of the pro rata benefit determined by projecting the hypothetical account balance to normal retirement age.

(B) *"Sum-of" formulas.*—If the participant's accrued benefit equals the sum of the accrued benefit under a lump sum-based benefit formula and the accrued benefit under another formula that is not a lump-sum based benefit formula, a single-sum payment of the participant's entire benefit must be no less than the sum of the then-current accumulated benefit under the lump sum-based benefit formula and the present value, determined in accordance with section 417(e), of the benefit under the other formula. For example, assume that the accrued benefit under a plan is determined as the sum of the accrued benefit attributable to the balance of a hypothetical account and the accrued benefit equal to the excess of the benefit under another formula over the benefit under the hypothetical account formula. In such a case, a single-sum payment of the participant's entire benefit must be no less than the sum of the then-current balance of the hypothetical account and the present value, determined in accordance with section 417(e), of the excess of the benefit under the other formula over the benefit under the hypothetical account formula.

(C) *"Lesser-of" formulas.*—If the participant's accrued benefit equals the lesser of the accrued benefit under a lump sum-based benefit formula and the accrued benefit under another formula that is not a lump-sum based benefit formula, a single-sum payment of the participant's entire benefit must be no less than the lesser of the then-current accumulated benefit under the lump sum-based benefit formula and the present value, determined in accordance with section 417(e), of the benefit under the other formula. For example, assume that the accrued benefit under a plan is determined as the accrued benefit attributable to the balance of a hypothetical account, but no greater than an accrued benefit payable at normal retirement age in the form of a straight life annuity of $100,000 per year. In such a case, a single-sum payment of the participant's entire benefit must be no less than the lesser of the then-current balance of the hypothetical account and the present value, determined in accordance with section 417(e), of a benefit payable at normal retirement age in the form of a straight life annuity of $100,000 per year. If the formula that is not a lump sum-based benefit formula is the maximum annual benefit described in section 415(b), then the single-sum payment of the participant's entire benefit must not exceed the then-current accumulated benefit under the lump sum-based benefit formula.

(c) *Three-year vesting requirement.*—(1) *In general.*—Pursuant to section 411(a)(13)(B), if any portion of the participant's accrued benefit under a defined benefit plan is determined under a statutory hybrid benefit formula, the plan is treated as failing to satisfy the requirements of section 411(a)(2) unless the plan provides that the participant has a nonforfeitable right to 100 percent of the participant's accrued benefit if the participant has three or more years of service. Thus, this 3-year vesting requirement applies with respect to the entire accrued benefit of a participant under a defined benefit plan even if only a portion of the participant's accrued benefit under the plan is determined under a statutory hybrid benefit formula. Similarly, if the participant's accrued benefit under a defined benefit plan is, under the plan's terms, the larger of two (or more) benefit amounts, where each amount is determined under a different benefit formula (including a benefit determined pursuant to an offset among formulas within the plan or a benefit determined as the greater of a protected benefit under section 411(d)(6) and another benefit amount) and at least one of those formulas is a statutory hybrid benefit formula, the participant's entire accrued benefit under the defined benefit plan is subject to the 3-year vesting rule of section 411(a)(13)(B) and this paragraph (c). The rule described in the preceding sentence applies even if the larger benefit is ultimately the benefit determined under a formula that is not a statutory hybrid benefit formula.

(2) *Examples.*—The provisions of this paragraph (c) are illustrated by the following examples:

Example 1. Employer M sponsors Plan X, a defined benefit plan under which each participant's accrued benefit is equal to the sum of the benefit provided under two benefit formulas. The first benefit formula is a statutory hybrid benefit formula, and the second formula is not. Because a portion of each participant's accrued benefit provided under Plan X is determined under a statutory hybrid benefit formula, the 3-year vesting requirement described in paragraph (c)(1) of this section applies to each participant's entire accrued benefit provided under Plan X.

Example 2. The facts are the same as in *Example 1*, except that the benefit formulas described in *Example 1* only apply to participants for service performed in Division A of Employer M and a different benefit formula applies to participants for service performed in Division B of Employer M. Pursuant to the terms of Plan X, the accrued benefit of a participant attributable to service performed in Division B is based on a benefit formula that is not a statutory hybrid benefit formula. Therefore, the 3-year vesting requirement described in paragraph (c)(1) of this section does not apply to a participant with an accrued benefit under Plan X if the participant's benefit is solely attributable to service performed in Division B.

Example 3. Employer N sponsors defined benefit Plan Y, an independent plan that provides benefits based solely on a lump sum-based benefit formula, and defined benefit Plan Z, which provides benefits based on a formula which is not a statutory hybrid benefit formula, but which is a floor plan that provides for the benefits payable to a participant under Plan Z to be reduced by the amount of the vested accrued benefit payable under Plan Y. The formula under Plan Y is a statutory hybrid benefit formula. Accordingly, Plan Y is subject to the 3-year vesting requirement described in paragraph (c)(1) of this section. The formula provided under Plan Z, even taking into account the offset for vested accrued benefits under Plan Y, is not a statutory hybrid benefit formula. Therefore, Plan Z is not subject to the 3-year vesting requirement in paragraph (c)(1) of this section.

(d) *Definitions.*—(1) *In general.*—The definitions in this paragraph (d) apply for purposes of this section.

(2) *Accumulated benefit.*—A participant's accumulated benefit at any date means the participant's benefit, as expressed under the terms of the plan, accrued to that date. For this purpose, if a participant's benefit is expressed under the terms of the plan as the current balance of a hypothetical account or the current value of an accumulated percentage of the participant's final average compensation, the participant's accumulated benefit is expressed in that manner regardless of how the plan defines the participant's accrued benefit. Thus, for example, the accumulated benefit of a participant may be expressed under the terms of the plan as either the current balance of a hypothetical account or the current value of an accumulated percentage of the participant's final average compensation, even if the plan defines the participant's accrued benefit as an annuity beginning at normal retirement age that is actuarially equivalent to that balance or value.

(3) *Lump sum-based benefit formula.*—(i) *In general.*—A lump sum-based benefit formula means a benefit formula used to determine all or any part of a participant's accumulated benefit under a defined benefit plan under which the accumulated benefit provided under the formula is expressed as the current balance of a hypothetical account maintained for the participant or as the current value of an accumulated percentage of the participant's final average compensation. A benefit formula is expressed as the current balance of a

hypothetical account maintained for the participant if it is expressed as a current single-sum dollar amount equal to that balance. A benefit formula is expressed as the current value of an accumulated percentage of the participant's final average compensation if it is expressed as a current single-sum dollar amount equal to a percentage of the participant's final average compensation or, for plan years described in paragraph (e)(2)(ii)(A) or (e)(2)(ii)(B) of this section, as applicable (or any earlier date as elected by the taxpayer), a percentage of the participant's highest average compensation (regardless of whether the plan applies a limitation on the past period for which compensation is taken into account in determining highest average compensation). Whether a benefit formula is a lump sum-based benefit formula is determined based on how the accumulated benefit of a participant is expressed under the terms of the plan, and does not depend on whether the plan provides an optional form of benefit in the form of a single-sum payment. However, for plan years described in paragraph (e)(2)(ii)(A) or (e)(2)(ii)(B) of this section (as applicable), a benefit formula does not constitute a lump sum-based benefit formula unless a distribution of the benefits under that formula in the form of a single-sum payment equals the accumulated benefit under that formula (except to the extent the single-sum payment is greater to satisfy the requirements of section 411(d)(6)). In addition, for plan years described in paragraph (e)(2)(ii)(A) or (e)(2)(ii)(B) of this section (as applicable), a benefit formula does not constitute a lump sum-based benefit formula unless the portion of the participant's accrued benefit that is determined under that formula and the then-current balance of the hypothetical account or the then-current value of the accumulated percentage of the participant's final average compensation are actuarially equivalent (determined using reasonable actuarial assumptions) either—

(A) Upon attainment of normal retirement age; or

(B) At the annuity starting date for a distribution with respect to that portion.

(ii) *Exception for employee contributions.*—For purposes of the definition of a lump sum-based benefit formula in paragraph (d)(3)(i) of this section, the benefit properly attributable to after-tax employee contributions, rollover contributions from eligible retirement plans under section 402(c)(8), and other similar employee contributions (such as repayments of distributions pursuant to section 411(a)(7)(C) and employee contributions that are pickup contributions pursuant to section 414(h)(2)) is disregarded. However, a benefit is not properly attributable to contributions described in this paragraph (d)(3)(ii) if the contributions are credited with interest at a rate that exceeds a reasonable rate of interest or if the conversion factors used to calculate such benefit are not actuarially reasonable. See section 411(c) for an example of a calculation of a benefit that is properly attributable to employee contributions.

(4) *Statutory hybrid benefit formula.*—(i) *In general.*—A statutory hybrid benefit formula means a benefit formula that is either a lump sum-based benefit formula or a formula that is not a lump sum-based benefit formula but that has an effect similar to a lump sum-based benefit formula.

(ii) *Effect similar to a lump sum-based benefit formula.*—(A) *In general.*—Except as provided in paragraphs (d)(4)(ii)(B) through (E) of this section, a benefit formula under a defined benefit plan that is not a lump sum-based benefit formula has an effect similar to a lump sum-based benefit formula if the formula provides that a participant's accumulated benefit is expressed as a benefit that includes the right to adjustments (including a formula that provides for indexed benefits under §1.411(b)(5)-1(b)(2)) for a future period and the total dollar amount of those adjustments is reasonably expected to be smaller for the participant than for any similarly situated, younger individual (within the meaning of §1.411(b)(5)-1(b)(5)) who is or could be a participant in the plan. For this purpose, the right to adjustments for a future period means, for plan years described in paragraph (e)(2)(ii)(A) or (e)(2)(ii)(B) of this section (as applicable), the right to any changes in the dollar amount of benefits over time, regardless of whether those adjustments are denominated as interest credits. A benefit formula that does not include adjustments for any future period is treated as a formula with an effect similar to a lump sum-based benefit formula if the formula would be described in this paragraph (d)(4)(ii)(A) except for the fact that the adjustments are provided pursuant to a pattern of repeated plan amendments. See §1.411(d)-4, A-1(c)(1).

(B) *Exception for post-retirement benefit adjustments.*—Post-annuity starting date adjustments in the amount payable to a participant (such as cost-of-living increases) are disregarded in determining whether a benefit formula under a defined benefit plan has an effect similar to a lump sum-based benefit formula.

(C) *Exception for certain variable annuity benefit formulas.*—If a variable annuity benefit formula adjusts benefits by reference to the difference between a rate of return on plan assets (or specified market indices) and a specified assumed interest rate of 5 percent or higher, then the variable annuity benefit formula is not treated as being reasonably expected to provide a smaller total dollar amount of future adjustments for the participant than for any similarly situated, younger individual who is or could be a participant in the plan, and thus such a variable annuity benefit formula does not have an effect similar to a lump sum-based benefit formula. For plan years described in paragraph (e)(2)(ii)(A) or (e)(2)(ii)(B) of this section (as applicable) (or any earlier date as elected by the taxpayer), the rate of return on plan assets (or specified market index) by reference to which the benefit formula adjusts must be a rate of return described in § 1.411(b)(5)-1(d)(5) (which includes, in the case of a benefit formula determined with reference to an annuity contract for an employee issued by an insurance company licensed under the laws of a State, the rate of return on the market index specified under that contract).

(D) *Exception for employee contributions.*—Benefits that are disregarded under paragraph (d)(3)(ii) of this section (benefits properly attributable to certain employee contributions) are also disregarded for purposes of determining whether a benefit formula has an effect similar to a lump sum-based benefit formula.

(E) *Exception for certain actuarial reductions for early commencement under traditional formula.*—A defined benefit formula is not treated as having an effect similar to a lump sum-based benefit formula with respect to a participant merely because the formula provides for a reduction in the benefit payable at early retirement due to early commencement (with the result that the benefit payable at normal retirement age is greater than the benefit payable at early retirement), provided that the benefit payable at normal retirement age to the participant cannot be less than the benefit payable at normal retirement age to any similarly situated, younger individual who is or could be a participant in the plan. Thus, for example, a plan that provides a benefit equal to 1 percent of final average pay per year of service, payable as a life annuity at normal retirement age, is not treated as having an effect similar to a lump sum-based benefit formula by reason of an actuarial reduction in the benefit payable under the plan for early commencement.

(5) *Statutory hybrid plan.*—A statutory hybrid plan means a defined benefit plan that contains a statutory hybrid benefit formula.

(6) *Variable annuity benefit formula.*—A variable annuity benefit formula means any benefit formula under a defined benefit plan which provides that the amount payable is periodically adjusted by reference to the difference between a rate of return and a specified assumed interest rate.

(e) *Effective/applicability date.*—(1) *Statutory effective/applicability date.*—(i) *In general.*—Except as provided in paragraphs (e)(1)(ii) and (e)(1)(iii) of this section, section 411(a)(13) applies for periods beginning on or after June 29, 2005.

(ii) *Calculation of benefits.*—Section 411(a)(13)(A) applies to distributions made after August 17, 2006.

(iii) *Vesting.*—(A) *Plans in existence on June 29, 2005.*—(1) *General rule.*—In the case of a plan that is in existence on June 29, 2005 (regardless of whether the plan is a statutory hybrid plan on that date), section 411(a)(13)(B) applies to plan years that begin on or after January 1, 2008.

(2) *Exception for plan sponsor election.*—See § 1.411(b)(5)-1(f)(1)(iii)(A)(2) for a special election for early application of section 411(a)(13)(B).

(B) *Plans not in existence on June 29, 2005.*—In the case of a plan not in existence on June 29, 2005, section 411(a)(13)(B) applies to plan years that end on or after June 29, 2005.

(C) *Collectively bargained plans.*—Notwithstanding paragraphs (e)(1)(iii)(A) and (B) of this section, in the case of a collectively bargained plan maintained pursuant to one or more collective bargaining agreements between employee representatives and one or more employers ratified on or before August 17, 2006, the requirements of section 411(a)(13)(B) do not apply to plan years that begin before the earlier of—

(1) The later of—

(i) The date on which the last of those collective bargaining agreements terminates (determined without regard to any extension thereof on or after August 17, 2006); or

(ii) January 1, 2008; or

(2) January 1, 2010.

(D) *Treatment of plans with both collectively bargained and non-collectively bargained employees.*—In the case of a plan with respect to which a collective bargaining agreement applies to some, but not all, of the plan participants, the plan is considered a collectively bargained plan for purposes of paragraph (e)(1)(iii)(C) of this section if it is considered a collectively bargained plan under the rules of § 1.436-1(a)(5)(ii)(B).

(E) *Hour of service required.*—Section 411(a)(13)(B) does not apply to a participant who does not have an hour of service after section 411(a)(13)(B) would otherwise apply to the participant under the rules of paragraph (e)(1)(iii)(A), (B), or (C) of this section.

(2) *Effective/applicability date of regulations.*—(i) *In general.*—Except as provided in paragraph (e)(2)(ii) of this section, this section applies to plan years that begin on or after January 1, 2011. For the periods after the statutory effective date set forth in paragraph (e)(1) of this section and before the regulatory effective date set forth in the preceding sentence, the relief of section 411(a)(13)(A) applies and the 3-year vesting requirement of section 411(a)(13)(B) must be satisfied. During these periods, a plan is permitted to rely on the provisions of this section for purposes of applying the relief of section 411(a)(13)(A) and satisfying the requirements of section 411(a)(13)(B).

(ii) *Special effective date.*—(A) *In general.*—Except as otherwise provided in this paragraph (e)(2)(ii), paragraphs (b)(2), (3), and (4) of this section apply to plan years that begin on or after January 1, 2017.

(B) *Collectively bargained plans.*—In the case of a plan maintained pursuant to one or more collective bargaining agreements between employee representatives and one or more employers ratified on or before November 13, 2015, that constitutes a collectively bargained plan under the rules of § 1.436-1(a)(5)(ii)(B), paragraphs (b)(2), (3), and (4) of this section apply to plan years that begin on or after the later of—

(1) January 1, 2017; and

(2) The earlier of—

(i) January 1, 2019; and

(ii) The date on which the last of those collective bargaining agreements terminates (determined without regard to any extension thereof on or after November 13, 2015).

(iii) *Hour of service required.*—A benefit formula is not treated as having an effect similar to a lump sum-based benefit formula under paragraph (d)(4)(ii) of this section with respect to a participant who does not have an hour of service after the regulatory effective date set forth in paragraph (e)(2)(i) of this section. [Reg. § 1.411(a)(13)-1.]

☐ [T.D. 9505, 10-18-2010. Amended by T.D. 9693, 9-18-2014 and T.D. 9743, 11-13-2015.]

[Reg. §1.411(b)-1]

§1.411(b)-1. Accrued benefit requirements.—(a) *Accrued benefit requirements.*—(1) *In general.*—Under section 411(b), for plan years beginning after the applicable effective date of section 411, rules are provided for the determination of the accrued benefit to which a participant is entitled under a plan. Under a defined contribution plan, a participant's accrued benefit is the balance to the credit of the participant's account. Under a defined benefit plan, a participant's accrued benefit is his accrued benefit determined under the plan. A defined benefit plan is not a qualified plan unless the method provided by the plan for determining accrued benefits satisfies at least one of the alternative methods (described in paragraph (b) of this section) for determining accrued benefits with respect to all active participants under the plan. A defined benefit plan may provide that accrued benefits for participants are determined under more than one plan formula. In such a case, the accrued benefits under all such formulas must be aggregated in order to determine whether or not the accrued benefits under the plan for participants satisfy one of the alternative methods. A plan may satisfy different methods with respect to different classifications of employees, or separately satisfy one method with respect to the accrued benefits for each such classification, provided that such classifications are not so structured as to evade the accrued benefit requirements of section 411(b) and this section. (For example, if a plan provides that employees who commence participation at or before age 40 accrue benefits in a manner which satisfies the 133¹/₃ percent method of determining accrued benefits and employees who commence participation after age 40 accrue benefits in a manner which satisfies the 3 percent method of determining accrued benefits, the plan would be so structured as to evade the requirements of section 411(b).) A defined benefit plan does not satisfy the requirements of section 411(b) and this section merely because the accrued benefit is defined as the "accrued liability" or the "reserve under the plan". Special rules are provided for the first two years of service by a participant, certain insured defined benefit plans, and certain reductions in accrued benefits due to increasing age or service. In addition, a special rule is provided with respect to accruals for service before the effective date of section 411.

(2) *Cross references—*

(i) *3 percent method.*—For rules relating to the 3 percent method of determining accrued benefits, see paragraph (b)(1) of this section.

(ii) *133⅓ percent method.*—For rules relating to the 133⅓ percent method of determining accrued benefits, see paragraph (b)(2) of this section.

(iii) *Fractional method.*—For rules relating to the fractional method of determining accrued benefits, see paragraph (b)(3) of this section.

(iv) *Accruals before effective date.*—For rules relating to accruals for service before the effective date of section 411, see paragraph (c) of this section.

(v) *First 2 years of service.*—For special rules relating to determination of accrued benefit for first 2 continuous years of service, see paragraph (d)(1) of this section.

(vi) *Certain insured plans.*—For special rules relating to determination of accrued benefit under a defined benefit plan funded exclusively by insurance contracts, see paragraph (d)(2) of this section.

(vii) *Accruals decreased by increasing age or service.*—For special rules relating to prohibition of decrease in accrued benefit on account of increasing age or service, see paragraph (d)(3) of this section.

(viii) *Separate accounting.*—For rules relating to requirements for separate accounting, see paragraph (e) of this section.

(ix) *Year of participation.*—For definition of "year of participation", see paragraph (f) of this section.

(b) *Defined benefit plans.*—A defined benefit plan satisfies the requirements of section 411(b)(1) and this paragraph for a plan year to which section 411 and this section apply if it satisfies the requirements of subparagraph (1), (2), or (3) of this paragraph for such year.

(1) *3 percent method.*—(i) *General rule.*—A defined benefit plan satisfies the requirements of this paragraph for a plan year if, as of the close of the plan year, the accrued benefit to which each participant is entitled, computed as if the participant separated from the service as of the close of such plan year, is not less than 3 percent of the 3 percent method benefit, multiplied by the number of years (not in excess of 33⅓) of his participation in the plan including years after his normal retirement age. For purposes of this subparagraph, the "3 percent method benefit" is the normal retirement benefit to which the participant would be entitled if he commenced participation at the earliest possible entry age for any individual who is or could be a participant under the plan and served continuously until the earlier of age 65 or the normal retirement age under the plan.

(ii) *Special rules.*—(A) *Compensation.*—In the case of a plan providing a retirement benefit based upon compensation during any period, the normal retirement benefit to which a participant would be entitled is determined as if he continued to earn annually the average rate of compensation which he earned during consecutive years of service, not in excess of 10, for which his compensation was the highest. For purposes of this subdivision (A), the number of consecutive years of service used in computing average compensation shall be the number of years of service specified under the plan (not in excess of 10) for computing normal retirement benefits.

(B) *Social security, etc.*—For purposes of this subparagraph, for any plan year, social security benefits and all relevant factors used to compute benefits, *e.g.,* consumer price index, are treated as remaining constant as of the beginning of the current plan year for all subsequent plan years.

(C) *Computation in certain cases.*—In the case of any plan to which the provisions of section 411(b)(1)(D) and paragraph (c) of this section are applicable, for any plan year the accrued benefit of any participant shall not be less than the accrued benefit otherwise determined under this subparagraph, reduced by the excess of the accrued benefit determined under this subparagraph as of the first day of the first plan year to which section 411 applies over the accrued benefit determined under section 411(b)(1)(D) and paragraph (c) of this section and increased by the amount determined under paragraph (c)(2)(v) of this section.

(iii) *Examples.*—The application of this subparagraph is illustrated by the following examples.

Example (1). The M Corporation's defined benefit plan provides an annual retirement benefit commencing at age 65 of $4 per month for each year of participation. As a condition of participation, the plan requires that an employee have attained age 25. The normal

retirement age specified under the plan is age 65. The plan provides for no limit on the number of years of credited service. A, age 40, is a participant in the M Corporation's plan. A has completed 12 years of participation in the plan of the M Corporation as of the close of the plan year. Under subdivision (i) of this subparagraph, the normal retirement benefit commencing at age 65 to which a participant would be entitled if he commenced participation at the earliest possible entry age (25) under the plan and served continuously until normal retirement age (65) is an annual benefit of $1,920 [40 × (12 × $4)]. Under subdivision (i) of this subparagraph, the plan does not satisfy the requirements of this subparagraph unless A has accrued an annual benefit of at least $691 [0.03 × ($1,920 × 12)] as of the close of the plan year. Under the M Corporation plan, A is entitled to an accrued benefit of $576 [(12 × 12) × $4] as of the close of the plan year. Thus, with respect to A, the accrued benefit provided under the M Corporation plan does not satisfy the requirements of this subparagraph.

Example (2). Assume the same facts as in example (1) except that the M Corporation's plan provides that only the first 30 years of participation are taken into account. Under subdivision (i) of this subparagraph, the normal retirement benefit commencing at age 65 to which a participant would be entitled if he commenced participation at the earliest possible entry age under the plan (25) and served continuously until normal retirement age (65) is an annual benefit of $1,440 [30 × $48]. Under subdivision (i) of this subparagraph, the plan does not satisfy the requirements of this subparagraph unless A has accrued an annual benefit of at least $518 [0.03 × ($1,440 × 12)] as of the close of the plan year. Under the M Corporation plan, A is entitled to an accrued benefit of $576 [12 × $48]. Thus, with respect to A, the accrued benefit provided under the M Corporation plan satisfies the requirements of this subparagraph.

Example (3). The N Corporation's defined benefit plan provides an annual retirement benefit commencing at age 65 of 50 percent of average compensation for the highest 3 consecutive years of compensation for an employee with 25 years of participation. A participant who separates from service before age 65 is entitled to 2 percent of average compensation for the highest 3 consecutive years of compensation for each year of participation not in excess of 25. The plan has no minimum age or service requirement for participation. The normal retirement age specified under the plan is age 65. On December 31, 1990, B, age 40, is a participant in the N Corporation's plan. B began employment with the N Corporation and became a participant in the N Corporation's plan on January 1, 1980. Under this subparagraph, the normal retirement benefit to which a participant would be entitled if he commenced participation at the earliest possible entry age (0) under the plan and served continuously until normal retirement age (65) is 50 percent of average compensation for the highest 3 consecutive years of compensation per year commencing at age 65. Under this subparagraph, B must have accrued an annual benefit of at least 16.5 percent of his highest 3 consecutive years of compensation per year commencing at age 65 [0.03 × 50 percent of average compensation for the highest 3 consecutive years of compensation × 11] as of the close of the plan year. Under the N Corporation plan, B has accrued an annual benefit of 22 percent of average compensation for his highest 3 consecutive years of compensation per year commencing at age 65. Thus, with respect to B, the accrued benefit under the N Corporation plan satisfies the requirements of this subparagraph.

Example (4). The P Corporation's defined benefit plan provides an annual retirement benefit commencing at age 65 of 50 percent of average compensation for the 3 consecutive years of compensation from the P corporation next preceding normal retirement age. The plan has no minimum age or service requirement for participation. The normal retirement age under the plan is age 65. On December 31, 1990, C, age 55, separates from service with the P Corporation. C began employment with the P Corporation and became a participant in the P Corporation's plan on January 1, 1980. As of December 31, 1990, C's average compensation for the 3 consecutive years preceding his separation from service is $15,000. Under this subparagraph, the normal retirement benefit to which a participant would be entitled if he commenced participation at the earliest possible entry age (0) under the plan and served continuously until normal retirement age (65) is an annual benefit of 50 percent of average compensation for the 3 consecutive years of compensation from the P Corporation next preceding normal retirement age commencing at age 65. C must have accrued an annual benefit of at least $2,475 commencing at age 65 [0.03 × (0.50 × $15,000) × 11] as of his separation from the service with the P Corporation in order for the P Corporation's plan to satisfy the requirements of this subparagraph with respect to C.

Example (5). On December 31, 1985, the R Corporation's defined benefit plan provided an annual retirement benefit commencing at age 65 of $100 for each year of participation not to exceed 30. As a condition of participation, the plan requires that an employee have attained age 25. The normal retirement age specified under the plan is age 65. The appropriate computation period is the calendar year. On January 1, 1986, the plan is amended to provide an annual retirement benefit commencing at age 65 of $200 for each year of participation (before and after the amendment), not to exceed 30. B, age 40, is a participant in the R Corporation's plan. B has completed 15 years of participation in the plan of the R Corporation as of December 31, 1990. Under subdivision (i) of this subparagraph, the normal retirement benefit commencing at age 65 to which a participant would be entitled if he commenced participation at the earliest possible entry age (25) under the plan and served continuously until normal retirement age (65) is an annual benefit of $6,000 [30 × $200]. Under subdivision (i) of this subparagraph, the plan does not satisfy the requirements of this subparagraph unless B has accrued an annual benefit of at least $2,700 [0.03 × $6,000 × 15] as of December 31, 1990. Under the R Corporation plan, B is entitled to an accrued benefit of $3,000 [$200 × 15] as of December 31, 1990. Thus, with respect to B, the accrued benefit provided under the R Corporation plan satisfies the requirements of this subparagraph.

Example (6). On December 31, 1995, the J Corporation's defined benefit plan provided an annual retirement benefit commencing at age 65 of $4,800 after 30 years of participation. The normal retirement age specified under the plan is age 65. The appropriate computation period is the calendar year. On January 1, 1996, the plan is amended to provide an annual retirement benefit commencing at age 65 of $6,000. A, age 40, is a participant in the J Corporation's plan since its adoption on January 1, 1986. Under subdivision (i) of this subparagraph, on December 31, 1995, the normal retirement benefit commencing at age 65 to which a participant would be entitled if he commenced participation at the earliest possible entry age (0) under the plan and served continuously until normal retirement age (65) is an annual benefit of $4,800. Under subdivision (i) of this subparagraph, on January 1, 1996, the normal retirement benefit commencing at age 65 to which a participant would be entitled if he commenced participation at the earliest possible entry age (0) under the plan and served continuously until normal retirement age (65) is an annual benefit of $6,000. Under subdivision (i) of this subparagraph, the plan does not satisfy the requirements of this subparagraph unless A has an accrued benefit on December 31, 1995 of at least $1,440 [$4,800 × 0.03 × 10] and an accrued benefit on January 1, 1996 of at least $2,000 [$6,000 × 0.03 × 10].

Example (7). The X Company's defined benefit plan provides an annual retirement benefit commencing at age 65 of $4 per month for each year of participation (not to exceed 30). As a condition of participation, the plan requires that an employee have attained age 25. The normal retirement age specified under the plan is age 65. D, age 68, is a participant in the X Company's plan. D has completed 20 years of participation in the X Company plan as of the close of the plan year. Under subdivision (i) of this subparagraph, the normal retirement benefit commencing at age 65 to which a participant would be entitled if he commenced participation at the earliest possible entry age (25) under the plan and served continuously until normal retirement age (65) is an annual benefit, commencing at age 65, of $1,440 [30 × $48]. Under subdivision (i) of this subparagraph, the plan does not satisfy the requirements of this subparagraph unless D has accrued an annual benefit, commencing at age 65, of $864 [0.03 × $1,440 × 20] as of the close of the plan year. Under the X Company plan, D has accrued an annual benefit, commencing at age 65, of $960 [20 × $48]. Thus, with respect to D the accrued benefit provided under the X Company plan satisfies the requirements of this subparagraph.

Example (8). Assume the same facts as in example (7) except that for purposes of determining accrued benefits under the plan the X Company's plan disregards all years of participation after normal retirement age. Under subdivision (i) of this subparagraph, the normal retirement benefit commencing at age 65 to which a participant would be entitled if he commenced participation at the earliest possible entry age (25) under the plan and served continuously until normal retirement age (65) is an annual benefit of $1,440 [30 × $48]. Under subdivision (i) of this subparagraph, the plan does not satisfy the requirements of this subparagraph unless D has accrued an annual benefit, commencing at age 65, of $864 [0.03 × $1,440 × 20] as of the close of the plan year. Under the X Company's plan, D has accrued an annual benefit commencing at age 65, of $816 [17 × $48]. Thus, with respect to D, the accrued benefit provided under the X *Company plan does not satisfy the requirements of this* subparagraph.

(2) *133¹/₃ percent rule.*—(i) *General rule.*—A defined benefit plan satisfies the requirements of this subparagraph for a particular plan year if—

(A) Under the plan the accrued benefit payable at the normal retirement age (determined under the plan) is equal to the normal retirement benefit (determined under the plan), and

(B) The annual rate at which any individual who is or could be a participant can accrue the retirement benefits payable at normal retirement age under the plan for any later plan year cannot be more than 133¹/₃ percent of the annual rate at which he can accrue benefits for any plan year beginning on or after such particular plan year and before such later plan year.

(ii) *Special rules.*—For purposes of this subparagraph—

(A) *Plan amendments.*—Any amendment to the plan which is in effect for the current plan year shall be treated as if it were in effect for all other plan years.

(B) *Change in accrual rate.*—Any change in an accrual rate which change does not apply to any individual who is or could be a participant in the plan year is disregarded. Thus, for example, if for its plan year beginning January 1, 1980, a defined benefit plan provides an accrued benefit in plan year 1980 of 2 percent of a participant's average compensation for his highest 3 years of compensation for each year of service and provides that in plan year 1981 the accrued benefit will be 3 percent of such average compensation, the plan will not be treated as failing to satisfy the requirements of this subparagraph for plan year 1980 because in plan year 1980 the change in the accrual rate does not apply to any individual who is or could be a participant in plan year 1980. However, if, for example, a defined benefit plan provided for an accrued benefit of 1 percent of a participant's average compensation for his highest 3 years of compensation for each of the first 10 years of service and 1.5 percent of such average compensation for each year of service thereafter, the plan will be treated as failing to satisfy the requirements of this subparagraph for the plan year even though no participant is actually accruing at the 1.5 percent rate because an individual who could be a participant and who had over 10 years of service would accrue at the 1.5 percent rate, which rate exceeds 133¹/₃ percent of the 1 percent rate.

(C) *Early retirement benefits.*—The fact that certain benefits under the plan may be payable to certain participants before normal retirement age is disregarded. Thus, the requirements of subdivision (i) of this subparagraph must be satisfied without regard to any benefit payable prior to the normal retirement benefit (such as an early retirement benefit which is not the normal retirement benefit (see § 1.411(a)-7(c))).

(D) *Social security, etc.*—For purposes of this subparagraph, for any plan year, social security benefits and all relevant factors used to compute benefits, *e.g.,* consumer price index, are treated as remaining constant as of the beginning of the current plan year for all subsequent plan years.

(E) *Postponed retirement.*—A plan shall not be treated as failing to satisfy the requirements of this subparagraph for a plan year merely because no benefits under the plan accrue to a participant who continues service with the employer after such participant has attained normal retirement age.

(F) *Computation of benefit.*—A plan shall not satisfy the requirements of this subparagraph if the case for the computation of retirement benefits changes solely by reason of an increase in the number of years of participation. Thus, for example, a plan will not satisfy the requirements of this subparagraph if it provides a benefit, commencing at normal retirement age, of the sum of (*1*) 1 percent of average compensation for a participant's first 3 years of participation multiplied by his first 10 years of participation (or, if less than 10 his total years of participation) and (*2*) 1 percent of average compensation for a participant's 3 highest years of participation multiplied by each year of participation subsequent to the 10th year.

(G) *Variable interest crediting rate under a statutory hybrid benefit formula.*—For plan years that begin on or after January 1, 2012 (or an earlier date as elected by the taxpayer), a plan that determines any portion of the participant's accrued benefit pursuant to a statutory hybrid benefit formula (as defined in § 1.411(a)(13)-1(d)(4)) that utilizes an interest crediting rate described in § 1.411(b)(5)-1(d) that is a variable rate that was less than zero for the prior plan year is not treated as failing to satisfy the requirements of paragraph (b)(2) of this section for the current plan year merely because the plan assumes for purposes of paragraph (b)(2) of this section that the variable rate is zero for the current plan year and all future plan years.

(H) *Special rule for multiple formulas.*—[Reserved]

(iii) *Examples.*—The application of this subparagraph is illustrated by the following examples:

Example (1). On January 1, 1980, the R Corporation's defined benefit plan provides for an annual benefit (commencing at age 65) of a percentage of a participant's average compensation for the period of 5 consecutive years of participation for which his compensation is the highest. The percentage is 2 percent for each of the first 20 years of participation and 1 percent per year thereafter. The appropriate computation period is the calendar year. The R Corporation's plan satisfies the requirements of this subparagraph because the $133\frac{1}{3}$ percent rule does not restrict subsequent accrual rate decreases.

Example (2). On January 1, 1980, the J Corporation's defined benefit plan provides for an annual benefit (commencing at age 65) of a percentage of a participant's average compensation for the period of his final 5 consecutive years of participation. The percentage is 1 percent for each of the first 5 years of participation; $1\frac{1}{3}$ percent for each of the next 5 years of participation; and $1\text{-}7/9$ percent for each year thereafter. The appropriate computation period is the calendar year. Even though no single accrual rate under the J Corporation's plan exceeds $133\frac{1}{3}$ percent of the immediately preceding accrual rate, the J Corporation's plan does not satisfy the requirements of this subparagraph because the rate of accrual for all years of participation in excess of 10 ($1\text{-}7/9$ percent) exceeds $133\frac{1}{3}$ percent of the rate of accrual for any of the first 5 years of participation (1 percent).

Example (3). On January 1, 1980, the C Corporation's defined benefit plan provides for an annual benefit (commencing at age 65) of a percentage of a participant's average compensation for the period of 3 consecutive years of participation for which his compensation is the highest. The percentage is 2 percent for each of the first 5 years of participation; 1 percent for each of the next 5 years of participation; and $1\frac{1}{2}$ percent for each year thereafter. The appropriate computation period is the calendar year. Even though the average rate of accrual under the C Corporation's plan is not less rapidly than ratably, the C Corporation's plan does not satisfy the requirements of this subparagraph because the rate of accrual for all years of participation in excess of 10 ($1\frac{1}{2}$ percent) for any employee who is actually accruing benefits or who could accrue benefits exceeds $133\frac{1}{3}$ percent of the rate of accrual for the sixth through tenth years of participation, respectively (1 percent).

(3) *Fractional rule.*—(i) *In general.*—A defined benefit plan satisfies the requirements of this paragraph if the accrued benefit to which any participant is entitled is not less than the fractional rule benefit multiplied by a fraction (not exceeding 1)—

(A) The numerator of which is his total number of years of participation in the plan, and

(B) The denominator of which is the total number of years he would have participated in the plan if he separated from the service at the normal retirement age under the plan.

(ii) *Special rules.*—For purposes of this subparagraph—

(A) *Fractional rule benefit.*—The "fractional rule benefit" is the annual benefit commencing at the normal retirement age under the plan to which a participant would be entitled if he continued to earn annually until such normal retirement age the same rate of compensation upon which his normal retirement benefit would be computed. Such rate of compensation shall be computed on the basis of compensation taken into account under the plan (but taking into account average compensation for no more than the 10 years of service immediately preceding the determination). For purposes of this subdivision (A), the normal retirement benefit shall be determined as if the participant had attained normal retirement age on the date any such determination is made.

(B) *Social security, etc.*—For purposes of this subparagraph, for any plan year, social security benefits and all relevant factors used to compute benefits, *e.g.*, consumer price index, are treated as remaining constant as of the beginning of the current plan year for all subsequent plan years.

(C) *Postponed retirement.*—A plan shall not be treated as failing to satisfy the requirements of this subparagraph merely because no benefits under the plan accrue to a participant who continues service with the employer after such participant has attained normal retirement age under the plan.

(D) *Computation in certain cases.*—In the case of any plan to which the provisions of section 411(b)(1)(D) and paragraph (c) of this section are applicable, for any plan year the accrued benefit of any participant shall not be less than the accrued benefit otherwise determined under this subparagraph, reduced by the excess of the accrued benefit determined under this subparagraph as of the first day of the first plan year to which section 411 applies over the accrued benefit determined under section 411(b)(1)(D) and paragraph (c) of this section and increased by the amount determined under paragraph (c)(2)(v) of this section.

(iii) *Examples.*—The application of this subparagraph is illustrated by the following examples:

Example (1). The R Corporation's defined benefit plan provides an annual retirement benefit commencing at age 65 of 30 percent of a participant's average compensation for his highest 3 consecutive years of participation. If a participant separates from service prior to normal retirement age, the R Corporation's plan provides a benefit

equal to an amount which bears the same ratio to 30 percent of such average compensation as the participant's actual number of years of participation in the plan bears to the number of years the participant would have participated in the plan had he separated from service at age 65. The plan further provides that normal retirement age is age 65. A, age 55, is a participant in the R Corporation's plan for the current year, and A has 15 years of participation in the R Corporation's plan. As of the current year, A's average compensation for his highest 3 years of compensation is $20,000. The R Corporation's plan satisfies the requirements of this subparagraph because if A separates from the service in the current year he will be entitled to an annual benefit of $3,600 commencing at age 65 [$(0.3 \times \$20,000) \times 15/25$].

Example (2). The J Corporation's defined benefit plan provides a normal retirement benefit of 1 percent per year of a participant's average compensation from the employer. In the case of a participant who separates from service prior to normal retirement age (65), the plan provides that the annual benefit is an amount which is equal to 1 percent of such compensation multiplied by the number of years of plan participation actually completed by the participant. The plan year of the J Corporation's plan is the calendar year. B, age 55, is a participant in the J Corporation's plan for the current year. B became a participant in the J Corporation's plan on January 1, 1980. As of December 31, 1990, B's compensation history is as follows:

Year	Compensation
1980	$17,000
1981	18,000
1982	20,000
1983	20,000
1984	21,000
1985	22,000
1986	23,000
1987	25,000
1988	26,000
1989	29,000
1990	32,000

If B separates from service on December 31, 1990, he would [be] entitled to an annual benefit of $2,530 commencing at age 65. Because the J Corporation's plan does not limit the number of years of compensation to be taken into account in determining the normal retirement benefit, B's rate of compensation for purposes of determining his normal retirement benefit is $23,600 [$18,000 + $20,000 + $20,000 + $21,000 + $22,000 + $23,000 + $25,000 + $26,000 + $29,000 + $32,000] ÷ 10. Under this subparagraph, B's accrued benefit under the J Corporation's plan as of December 31, 1990 must be not less than $2,561 per year commencing at age 65 [$0.01 \times$ ($17,000 + $18,000 + $20,000 + $20,000 + $21,000 + $22,000 + $23,000 + $25,000 + $26,000 + $29,000 + $32,000 + ($23,600 × 10)) × 11/21]. Thus, the J Corporation's plan would not satisfy the requirements of this subparagraph.

(c) *Accruals for service before effective date.*—(1) *General rule.*—For a plan year to which section 411 applies, a defined benefit plan does not satisfy the requirements of section 411(b)(1) and this section unless, under the plan, the accrued benefit of each participant for plan years beginning before section 411 applies is not less than the greater of—

(i) Such participant's accrued benefit (as of the day before section 411 applies) determined under the plan as in effect from time to time prior to September 2, 1974 (without regard to any amendment adopted after such date), or

(ii) One-half of the accrued benefit that would be determined with respect to the participant as of the day before section 411 applies if the participant's accrued benefit were computed for such prior plan years under a method which satisfies the requirements of section 411(b)(1)(A), (B), or (C) and paragraph (b)(1), (2), or (3) of this section. See 29 CFR Part 2530, Department of Labor regulations relating to minimum standards for employee pension benefit plans, for time participation deemed to begin.

(2) *Special rules.*—(i) A plan shall not be deemed to fail to satisfy the requirements of section 411(b) and this section merely because the method for computing the accrued benefit of a participant for years of participation prior to the first plan year for which section 411 is effective with respect to the plan is not the same method for computing the accrued benefit of a participant for years of participation subsequent to such plan year.

(ii) For purposes of subparagraph (1)(ii) of this paragraph, section 411(b)(1)(A) and paragraph (b)(1) of this section shall be applied as if the participant separated from service with the employer on the day before the first day of the first plan year to which section 411 applies.

(iii) For purposes of subparagraph (1)(ii) this paragraph, section 411(b)(1)(B) and paragraph (b)(2) of this section shall be applied in the following manner:

(A) Except as provided in (B) of this subdivision, section 411(b)(1)(B) and paragraph (b)(2) of this section shall be applied as if the participant separated from service with the employer on the day before the first day of the first plan year to which section 411 applies.

(B) In the case that the plan does not satisfy the requirements of section 411(b)(1)(B) and paragraph (b)(2) of this section at any time prior to the day specified in (A) of this subdivision, the plan shall be deemed revised to the extent necessary to satisfy the requirements of section 411(b)(1)(B) and paragraph (b)(2) of this section for all plan years beginning before the applicable effective date of section 411 and this section. For purposes of the preceding sentence, a plan shall not be deemed revised to the extent necessary to satisfy the requirements of section 411(b)(1)(B) and paragraph (b)(2) of this section for a plan year if the benefit a participant would receive if he were employed until normal retirement age is reduced by such revision or if the revised rate of accrual with respect to such accrued benefit does not otherwise satisfy the requirements of section 411(b)(1)(B) and paragraph (b)(2) of this section.

(iv) For purposes of subparagraph (1)(ii) of this paragraph, section 411(b)(1)(C) and paragraph (b)(3) of this section shall be applied as if the participant separated from service on the day before the first day of the first plan year to which section 411 applies.

(v) The excess of the accrued benefit payable at normal retirement age of any participant determined under section 411(b)(1)(A), (B), or (C) (without regard to section 411(b)(1)(D)), and paragraph (b)(1), (2), or (3) of this section (without regard to this paragraph) as of the day before the first day of the first plan year to which section 411 and this section applies over the accrued benefit determined under subparagraph (1) of this paragraph shall be accrued in accordance with the provisions of the plan as in effect after the applicable effective date of section 411, as if the plan had been initially adopted on such effective date.

(d) *Special rules.*—(1) *First 2 years of service.*—Notwithstanding subparagraphs (1), (2), and (3) of paragraph (b) of this section, under section 411(b)(1)(E) and this subparagraph, a plan shall not be treated as failing to satisfy the requirements of paragraph (b) of this section solely because the accrual of benefits under the plan does not become effective until the employee has completed 2 continuous years of service. For purposes of this subparagraph, continuous years of service are years of service (within the meaning of section 410(a)(3)(A)) which are not separated by a break in service (within the meaning of section 410(a)(5)). For years of service beginning after such 2 years of service, the accrued benefit of an employee shall not be less than that to which the employee would be entitled if section 411(b)(1)(E) and this subparagraph did not apply. Thus, for example, a plan which otherwise satisfies the requirements of paragraph (b)(2) of this section provides for a rate of accrual of 1 percent of average compensation for the highest 3 years of compensation beginning with the third year of service of a participant shall not be treated as satisfying paragraph (b)(2) of this section because as of the time the employee completes 3 continuous years of service there is no accrual during the first 2 years of service. In addition, a plan which otherwise satisfies the requirements of paragraph (b)(1) of this section and which requires that an employee must attain age 25 and complete 1 year of service prior to becoming a participant will not satisfy the requirements of paragraph (b)(1) of this section if an employee who completes 2 years of service prior to attaining age 25 does not begin accruals immediately upon commencement of participation in the plan. For rules relating to years of service, see 29 CFR Part 2530, Department of Labor regulations relating to minimum standards for employee pension benefit plans.

(2) *Certain insured defined benefit plans.*—Notwithstanding paragraphs (b)(1), (2), and (3) of this section, a defined benefit plan satisfies the requirements of paragraph (b) of this section if such plan is funded exclusively by the purchase of contracts from a life insurance company and such contracts satisfy the requirements of sections 412(i)(2) and (3) and the regulations thereunder. The preceding sentence is applicable only if an employee's accrued benefit as of any applicable date is not less than the cash surrender value such employee's insurance contracts would have on such applicable date if the requirements of section 412(i)(4), (5), and (6) and the regulations thereunder were satisfied.

(3) *Accrued benefit may not decrease on account of increasing age or service.*—Notwithstanding paragraphs (b)(1), (2), and (3) of this section and subparagraphs (1) and (2) of this paragraph, a defined benefit plan shall be treated as not satisfying the requirements of paragraph (b) and this paragraph of this section if the participant's accrued benefit is reduced on account of any increase in his age or years of service. The preceding sentence shall not apply to social security supplements described in §1.411(a)-7(c)(4).

(e) *Separate accounting.*—A plan satisfies the requirements of this paragraph if the requirements of subparagraph (1) or (2) of this paragraph are met.

(1) *Defined benefit plan.*—In the case of a defined benefit plan, the requirements of this paragraph are satisfied if the plan requires separate accounting for the portion of each employee's accrued benefit derived from any voluntary employee contributions permitted under the plan. For purposes of this subparagraph the term "voluntary employee contributions" means all employee contributions which are not mandatory contributions within the meaning of section 411(c)(2)(C) and the regulations thereunder. See §1.411(c)-1(b)(1) for rules requiring the determination of such an accrued benefit by the use of a separate account.

(2) *Defined contribution plan.*—In the case of a defined contribution plan, the requirements of this paragraph are not satisfied unless the plan requires separate accounting for each employee's accrued benefit. If a plan utilizes the break in service rule of section 411(a)(6)(C), an employee could have different percentages of vesting between pre-break and post-break accrued benefits. In such a case, the requirements of this paragraph are not satisfied unless the plan computes accrued benefits in a manner which takes into account different percentages. A plan which provides separate accounts for pre-break and post-break accrued benefits will be deemed to compute benefits in a reasonable manner.

(f) *Year of participation.*—(1) *In general.*—This paragraph is inapplicable to a defined contribution plan. For purposes of determining an employee's accrued benefit, a "year of participation" is a period of service determined under regulations prescribed by the Secretary of Labor in 29 CFR Part 2530, relating to minimum standards for employee pension benefit plans.

(2) *Additional rule relating to year of participation.*—A trust shall not constitute a qualified trust if the plan of which such trust is a part provides for the crediting of a year of participation, or part thereof, and such credit results in the discrimination prohibited by section 401(a)(4).

(g) *Additional illustrations.*—The application of this section may be illustrated by the following example:

Example. (i) The S Corporation established a defined benefit plan on January 1, 1980. The plan provides a minimum age for participation of age 25. The normal retirement age under the plan is age 65. The appropriate computation periods are the calendar year. The plan provides an annual benefit, commencing at age 65, equal to $96 per year of service for the first 25 years of service, and $48 per year of service for each additional year of service.

(ii) The plan of the S Corporation does not satisfy the requirements of section 411(b)(1)(A) and paragraph (b)(1) of this section because the accrued benefit under the plan at some point will be less than the accrued benefit required under section 411(b)(1)(A) and paragraph (b)(1) of this section (i.e., 3 percent × normal retirement benefit × years of participation).

(iii) The plan of the S Corporation does satisfy the requirements of Section 411(b)(1)(B) and paragraph (b)(2) of this section because the rate of benefit accrual is equal in each of the first 25 years of service and the rate decreases thereafter.

(iv) The plan of the S Corporation does satisfy the requirements of section 411(b)(1)(C) and paragraph (b)(3) of this section because the accrued benefit under the plan will equal or exceed the normal retirement benefit multiplied by the fraction described in paragraph (b)(3)(i) of this section. [Reg. §1.411(b)-1.]

☐ [*T.D. 7501, 8-22-77. Amended by T.D. 9693, 9-18-2014.*]

[Reg. §1.411(b)(5)-1]

§1.411(b)(5)-1. Reduction in rate of benefit accrual under a defined benefit plan.—(a) *In general.*—(1) *Organization of regulation.*—This section sets forth certain rules for determining whether a reduction occurs in the rate of benefit accrual under a defined benefit plan because of the attainment of any age for purposes of section 411(b)(1)(H)(i). Paragraph (b) of this section describes safe harbors for certain plan designs (including statutory hybrid plans) that are deemed to satisfy the age discrimination rules under section 411(b)(1)(H). Paragraph (c) of this section describes rules relating to statutory hybrid plan conversion amendments. Paragraph (d) of this section describes rules restricting interest credits (or equivalent amounts) under a statutory hybrid plan to a market rate of return. Paragraph (e) of this section contains additional rules related to market rates of return. Paragraph (f) of this section contains effective/applicability dates.

(2) *Definitions.*—The definitions of accumulated benefit, lump sum-based benefit formula, statutory hybrid benefit formula, statu-

tory hybrid plan, and variable annuity benefit formula in § 1.411(a)(13)-1(d) apply for purposes of this section.

(b) *Safe harbors for certain plan designs.*—(1) *Accumulated benefit testing.*—(i) *In general.*—Pursuant to section 411(b)(5)(A), and subject to paragraph (b)(1)(ii) of this section, a plan is not treated as failing to meet the requirements of section 411(b)(1)(H)(i) with respect to an individual who is or could be a participant if, as of any date, the accumulated benefit of the individual would not be less than the accumulated benefit of any similarly situated, younger individual who is or could be a participant. Thus, this test involves a comparison of the accumulated benefit of an individual who is or could be a participant in the plan with the accumulated benefit of each similarly situated, younger individual who is or could be a participant in the plan. See paragraph (b)(5) of this section for rules regarding whether a younger individual who is or could be a participant is similarly situated to a participant. The comparison described in this paragraph (b)(1)(i) is based on any of one the following benefit measures, each of which is referred to as a *safe-harbor formula measure*:

(A) The annuity payable at normal retirement age (or current age, if later) if the accumulated benefit of the participant under the terms of the plan is an annuity payable at normal retirement age (or current age, if later).

(B) The current balance of a hypothetical account maintained for the participant if the accumulated benefit of the participant is the current balance of a hypothetical account.

(C) The current value of an accumulated percentage of the participant's final average compensation if the accumulated benefit of the participant is the current value of an accumulated percentage of the participant's final average compensation.

(ii) *Benefit formulas for comparison.*—(A) *In general.*—Except as provided in paragraphs (b)(1)(ii)(B), (C), (D) and (E) of this section, the safe harbor provided by section 411(b)(5)(A) and paragraph (b)(1)(i) of this section is available only with respect to a participant if the participant's accumulated benefit under the plan is expressed in terms of only one safe-harbor formula measure and no similarly situated, younger individual who is or could be a participant has an accumulated benefit that is expressed in terms of any measure other than that same safe-harbor formula measure. Thus, for example, if a plan provides that the accumulated benefit of participants who are age 55 or older is expressed under the terms of the plan as a life annuity payable at normal retirement age (or current age if later) as described in paragraph (b)(1)(i)(A) of this section and the plan provides that the accumulated benefit of participants who are younger than age 55 is expressed as the current balance of a hypothetical account as described in paragraph (b)(1)(i)(B) of this section, then the safe harbor described in section 411(b)(5)(A) and paragraph (b)(1)(i) of this section does not apply to individuals who are or could be participants and who are age 55 or older.

(B) *Sum-of benefit formulas.*—If a plan provides that a participant's accumulated benefit is expressed as the sum of benefits determined in terms of two or more benefit formulas, each of which is expressed in terms of a different safe-harbor formula measure, then the plan is deemed to satisfy paragraph (b)(1)(i) of this section with respect to the participant, provided that the plan satisfies the comparison described in paragraph (b)(1)(i) of this section separately for benefits determined in terms of each safe-harbor formula measure and no accumulated benefit of a similarly situated, younger individual who is or could be a participant is expressed other than as—

(1) The sum of benefits under two or more benefit formulas, each of which is expressed in terms of one of those same safe-harbor formula measures as is used for the participant's "sum-of" benefit;

(2) The greater of benefits under two or more benefit formulas, each of which is expressed in terms of any one of those same safe-harbor formula measures;

(3) The choice of benefits under two or more benefit formulas, each of which is expressed in terms of any one of those same safe-harbor formula measures;

(4) A benefit that is determined in terms of only one of those same safe-harbor formula measures; or

(5) The lesser of benefits under two or more benefit formulas, at least one of which is expressed in terms of one of those same safe-harbor formula measures.

(C) *Greater-of benefit formulas.*—If a plan provides that a participant's accumulated benefit is expressed as the greater of benefits under two or more benefit formulas, each of which is determined in terms of a different safe-harbor formula measure, then the plan is deemed to satisfy paragraph (b)(1)(i) of this section with respect to the participant, provided that the plan satisfies the comparison described in paragraph (b)(1)(i) of this section separately for benefits determined in terms of each safe-harbor formula measure and no

accumulated benefit of a similarly situated, younger individual who is or could be a participant is expressed other than as—

(1) The greater of benefits determined under two or more benefit formulas, each of which is expressed in terms of one of those same safe-harbor formula measures as is used for the participant's "greater-of" benefit;

(2) The choice of benefits determined under two or more benefit formulas, each of which is expressed in terms of one of those same safe-harbor formula measures;

(3) A benefit that is determined in terms of only one of those same safe-harbor formula measures; or

(4) The lesser of benefits under two or more benefit formulas, at least one of which is expressed in terms of one of those same safe-harbor formula measures.

(D) *Choice-of benefit formulas.*—If a plan provides that a participant's accumulated benefit is determined pursuant to a choice by the participant between benefits determined in terms of two or more different safe-harbor formula measures, then the plan is deemed to satisfy paragraph (b)(1)(i) of this section with respect to the participant, provided that the plan satisfies the comparison described in paragraph (b)(1)(i) of this section separately for benefits determined in terms of each safe-harbor formula measure and no accumulated benefit of a similarly situated, younger individual who is or could be a participant is expressed other than as—

(1) The choice of benefits determined under two or more benefit formulas, each of which is expressed in terms of one of those same safe-harbor formula measures as is used for the participant's "choice-of" benefit;

(2) A benefit that is determined in terms of only one of those same safe-harbor formula measures; or

(3) The lesser of benefits under two or more benefit formulas, at least one of which is expressed in terms of one of those same safe-harbor formula measures.

(E) *Lesser-of benefit formulas.*—If a plan provides that a participant's accumulated benefit is expressed as a single safe-harbor formula measure and no accumulated benefit of a similarly situated, younger individual who is or could be a participant is expressed other than as a benefit that is determined under the same safe-harbor formula measure or as the lesser of benefits under two or more benefit formulas, at least one of which is expressed in terms of the same safe-harbor formula measure, then the plan is deemed to satisfy paragraph (b)(1)(i) of this section with respect to the participant only if the plan satisfies the comparison described in paragraph (b)(1)(i) of this section for benefits determined in terms of the same safe-harbor formula measure. Similarly, if a plan provides that a participant's accumulated benefit is expressed as the lesser of benefits under two or more benefit formulas, each of which is determined in terms of a different safe-harbor formula measure, then the plan is deemed to satisfy paragraph (b)(1)(i) of this section with respect to the participant only if the plan satisfies the comparison described in paragraph (b)(1)(i) of this section separately for benefits determined in terms of each safe-harbor formula measure and no accumulated benefit of a similarly situated, younger individual who is or could be a participant is expressed other than as the lesser of benefits under two or more benefit formulas, expressed in terms of all of those same safe-harbor formula measures (and any other additional formula measures).

(F) *Limitations on plan formulas that provide for hypothetical accounts or accumulated percentages of final average compensation.*—For plan years described in paragraph (f)(2)(i)(B)(1) or (f)(2)(i)(B)(3) of this section (as applicable), a benefit measure is a safe harbor formula measure described in paragraph (b)(1)(i)(B) or (C) of this section only if the formula under which the balance of a hypothetical account or the accumulated percentage of final average compensation is determined is a lump-sum based benefit formula.

(iii) *Disregard of certain subsidized benefits.*—For purposes of paragraph (b)(1)(i) of this section, any subsidized portion of an early retirement benefit that is included in a participant's accumulated benefit is disregarded. For this purpose, an early retirement benefit includes a subsidized portion only if it provides a higher actuarial present value on account of commencement before normal retirement age. However, for plan years described in paragraph (f)(2)(i)(B)(1) or (f)(2)(i)(B)(3) of this section (as applicable), if the annual benefit payable before normal retirement age is greater for a participant than the annual benefit under the corresponding form of benefit for any similarly situated, older individual who is or could be a participant and who is currently at or before normal retirement age, then that excess is not part of the subsidized portion of an early retirement benefit and, accordingly, is not disregarded under this paragraph (b)(1)(iii). For purposes of determining whether the annual benefit payable before normal retirement age is greater for a participant than the annual benefit under the corresponding form of benefit for any

Pension, Profit-Sharing, Stock Bonus Plans, Etc.
See p. 20,601 for regulations not amended to reflect law changes

33,669

similarly situated, older individual who is or could be a participant, social security leveling options and social security supplements are disregarded. In addition, a plan is not treated as providing a greater annual benefit to a participant than to a similarly situated, older individual who is or could be a participant merely because the reduction (based on actuarial equivalence, using reasonable actuarial assumptions) in the amount of an annuity to reflect a survivor benefit is smaller for the participant than for a similarly situated, older individual who is or could be a participant.

(iv) *Examples.*—The provisions of this paragraph (b)(1) are illustrated by the following examples:

Example 1. (i) *Facts relating to formulas described in paragraph (b)(1)(i)(A) of this section.* Employer X maintains a defined benefit plan that provides a straight life annuity payable commencing at normal retirement age (which is age 65) equal to 1 percent of the participant's highest 3 consecutive years' compensation times years of service and provides for suspension of benefits as permitted under section 411(a)(3)(B). In the case of a participant whose service continues after normal retirement age, the amount payable is the greater of (i) the benefit payable at normal retirement age, and for each year thereafter, actuarially increased to account for delayed commencement and (ii) the retirement benefit determined under the formula at the date the employee's service ceases (calculated by including years of service and increases in compensation after normal retirement age).

(ii) *Conclusion.* Under these facts, the plan formula is a formula described in paragraph (b)(1)(i)(A) of this section. The formula is not a statutory hybrid benefit formula merely because the plan formula includes a benefit that is based on the participant's benefit at normal retirement age (and each year thereafter) that is actuarially increased for commencement after attainment of normal retirement age. In addition, the plan formula would satisfy the comparison under paragraph (b)(1)(i) of this section for each individual who is or could be a participant because, as of any date (including any date after normal retirement age), the accumulated benefit of the individual would not be less than the accumulated benefit of any similarly situated, younger individual who is or could be a participant.

Example 2. (i) *Facts relating to formulas described in paragraph (b)(1)(i)(B) of this section.* Employer Y maintains a defined benefit plan that expresses each participant's accumulated benefit as the balance of a hypothetical account. Under the formula, the hypothetical account balance of each participant is credited monthly with interest at a specified rate and the hypothetical account balance of each employee who is a participant is also credited with a pay credit under the plan equal to 7 percent of the participant's compensation for the month.

(ii) *Conclusion.* The plan formula is a lump sum-based benefit formula described in paragraph (b)(1)(i)(B) of this section and the formula would satisfy the comparison under paragraph (b)(1)(i) of this section for each individual who is or could be a participant because, as of any date, the hypothetical account balance of the individual would not be less than the hypothetical account balance of any similarly situated, younger individual who is or could be a participant.

Example 3. (i) *Facts where plan suspends interest credits after normal retirement age.* The facts are the same as in *Example 2* except that the plan provides for suspension of benefits as permitted under section 411(a)(3)(B). Pursuant to the plan's suspension of benefits provision, the plan provides for interest credits to cease during service after normal retirement age or for the amount of the interest credits during this service to be reduced to reflect principal credits credited.

(ii) *Conclusion.* The plan does not satisfy the safe harbor in paragraph (b)(1)(i) of this section. Applying the rule of paragraph (b)(1)(i) of this section, the plan formula would fail to satisfy the safe harbor comparison under paragraph (b)(1)(i) of this section with respect to an individual whose benefits have been suspended because, as of any date after attainment of normal retirement age, the hypothetical account balance of this individual would be less than the hypothetical account balance of one or more similarly situated individuals who have not attained normal retirement age.

Example 4. (i) *Facts providing greater-of benefits as described in paragraph (b)(1)(ii)(C) of this section.* Employer Z sponsors a defined benefit plan that provides an accumulated benefit expressed as a straight life annuity commencing at the plan's normal retirement age (age 65), based on a percentage of average annual compensation times the participant's years of service. On November 2, 2011, the plan is amended effective as of January 1, 2012, to provide participants who have attained age 55 by January 1, 2012, with a benefit that is the greater of the benefit under the average annual compensation formula and a benefit that is based on the balance of a hypothetical account, which provides for annual pay credits of a specified percentage of the participant's compensation and annual interest credits based on the third segment rate.

(ii) *Conclusion where plan provides greater-of benefits to older participants.* The plan satisfies the safe harbor of paragraph (b)(1)(i) of this section with respect to all individuals who are or could be participants. Pursuant to the rules of paragraph (b)(1)(ii)(C) of this section, the plan satisfies the safe harbor with respect to individuals who have attained age 55 by January 1, 2012, because (A) with respect to the benefit described in paragraph (b)(1)(i)(A) of this section (the benefit based on average annual compensation, disregarding the benefit based on the balance of a hypothetical account), the accumulated benefit for any individual who is or could be a participant and who is at least age 55 on January 1, 2012, would in no event be less than the accumulated benefit for a similarly situated, younger individual who is or could be a participant and who has not yet attained age 55 by January 1, 2012, (B) with respect to the benefit described in paragraph (b)(1)(i)(B) of this section (the benefit based on the balance of a hypothetical account, disregarding the benefit based on average annual compensation), the accumulated benefit for any individual who is or could be a participant and who is at least age 55 on January 1, 2012, would in no event be less than the accumulated benefit for a similarly situated, younger individual who is or could be a participant and who has not yet attained age 55 by January 1, 2012, and (C) the benefit of any individual who is or could be a participant who has not yet attained age 55 by January 1, 2012, is only expressed as an annuity payable at normal retirement age as described in paragraph (b)(1)(i)(A) of this section, and this safe-harbor formula measure applies also to participants who have attained age 55 by January 1, 2012. Furthermore, the plan satisfies the safe harbor with respect to individuals who have not yet attained age 55 by January 1, 2012, because the benefit of these individuals satisfies the general rule of paragraph (b)(1)(ii)(A) of this section.

(iii) *Conclusion where plan provides greater-of benefits only to younger participants.* If, instead of the facts in paragraph (i) of this *Example 4,* the plan had been amended to provide only participants who have not yet attained age 55 by January 1, 2012, with a benefit that is the greater of the benefit under the average annual compensation formula and a benefit that is based on the balance of a hypothetical account, then the safe harbor would not be satisfied with respect to individuals who have attained age 55 by January 1, 2012. Under paragraph (b)(1)(ii)(A) of this section, except as provided in paragraphs (b)(1)(ii)(B), (C), and (D) of this section, the safe harbor of paragraph (b)(1)(i) of this section is available only with respect to individuals over age 55, whose benefit is expressed in terms of only one safe-harbor formula measure, if no similarly situated, younger individual has an accumulated benefit that is expressed in terms of any measure other than that same safe-harbor formula measure. This is not the case under these facts. The greater-of rule of paragraph (b)(1)(ii)(C) of this section would not apply to individuals who have attained age 55 because the accumulated benefits of these individuals is not equal to the greater of benefits under two or more benefit formulas.

Example 5. (i) *Facts where plan provides choice-of benefits to older participants.* The facts are the same as in paragraph (i) of *Example 4,* except that for service after December 31, 2011, the amendment permits participants who have attained age 55 by January 1, 2012, to choose between benefits under the average annual compensation benefit formula or benefits under the hypothetical account balance formula (but, if a participant chooses the hypothetical account balance formula, his or her benefit under the plan is in no event to be less than the benefit determined under the average annual compensation benefit formula for service before January 1, 2012), while other participants receive benefits solely under the hypothetical account balance formula (but individuals who are participants on December 31, 2011, are in no event to receive less than the benefit determined under the average annual compensation benefit formula for service before January 1, 2012).

(ii) *Conclusion where plan provides choice to older participants.* The plan satisfies the safe harbor with respect to all individuals who are or could be participants. Pursuant to the rule of paragraph (b)(1)(ii)(D) of this section, the plan satisfies the safe harbor of paragraph (b)(1)(i) of this section with respect to individuals who have attained age 55 by January 1, 2012, and, pursuant to the rule of paragraph (b)(1)(ii)(A), the plan satisfies the safe harbor with respect to individuals who have not yet attained 55 by January 1, 2012.

(iii) *Conclusion where plan provides choice-of benefits to older workers and greater-of benefits to younger participants.* If, in addition to the facts in paragraph (i) of this *Example 5,* the plan were also to provide participants who had not yet attained age 55 by January 1, 2012, the greater of the benefits under the average annual compensation benefit formula or the benefits under the hypothetical account balance formula, then pursuant to the rules of paragraph (b)(1)(ii)(A) and (D) of this section, the safe harbor would not be satisfied with respect to participants who have attained age 55 by January 1, 2012.

(2) *Indexed benefits.*—(i) *In general.*—Except as provided in paragraph (b)(2)(iii) of this section, pursuant to section 411(b)(5)(E) and

this paragraph (b)(2)(i), a defined benefit plan is not treated as failing to meet the requirements of section 411(b)(1)(H) with respect to a participant solely because a benefit formula (other than a lump sum-based benefit formula) under the plan provides for the periodic adjustment of the participant's accrued benefit under the plan by means of the application of a recognized index or methodology. An indexing rate that does not exceed a market rate of return, as defined in paragraph (d) of this section, is deemed to be a recognized index or methodology for purposes of the preceding sentence. In addition, for plan years described in paragraph (f)(2)(i)(B)(*1*) or (f)(2)(i)(B)(*3*) of this section, as applicable (or an earlier date as elected by the taxpayer), any subsidized portion of any early retirement benefit under such a plan that meets the requirements of paragraph (b)(1)(iii) is disregarded in determining whether the plan meets the requirements of section 411(b)(1)(H). However, such a plan must satisfy the qualification requirements otherwise applicable to statutory hybrid plans, including the requirements of § 1.411(a)(13)-1(c) (relating to minimum vesting standards) and paragraph (c) of this section (relating to plan conversion amendments) if the plan has an effect similar to a lump sum-based benefit formula, pursuant to the rules of § 1.411(a)(13)-1(d)(4)(ii).

(ii) *Similarly situated participant test.*—Paragraph (b)(2)(i) of this section does not apply unless the aggregate adjustments made to a participant's accrued benefit under the plan (determined as a percentage of the unadjusted accrued benefit) in a period would not be less than the aggregate adjustments for any similarly situated, younger participant. This test requires a comparison, for each period, of the aggregate adjustments for each individual who is or could be a participant in the plan for the period with the aggregate adjustments of each other similarly situated, younger individual who is or could be a participant in the plan for that period. See paragraph (b)(5) of this section for rules regarding whether each younger individual who is or could be a participant is similarly situated to a participant.

(iii) *Protection against loss.*—(A) *In general.*—Paragraph (b)(2)(i) of this section does not apply unless the plan satisfies section 411(b)(5)(E)(ii) and paragraph (d)(2) of this section (relating to preservation of capital).

(B) *Exception for variable annuity benefit formulas.*—The requirement to satisfy section 411(b)(5)(B)(i)(II), as set forth in paragraph (d)(2) of this section, as well as section 411(b)(5)(E)(ii), as set forth in this paragraph (b)(2)(iii), does not apply in the case of a benefit provided under a variable annuity benefit formula as defined in § 1.411(a)(13)-1(d)(6).

(3) *Certain offsets permitted.*—A plan is not treated as failing to meet the requirements of section 411(b)(1)(H) solely because the plan provides offsets against benefits under the plan to the extent the offsets are allowable in applying the requirements of section 401(a) and the applicable requirements of the Employee Retirement Income Security Act of 1974, Public Law 93-406 (88 Stat. 829 (1974)), and the Age Discrimination in Employment Act of 1967, Public Law 90-202 (81 Stat. 602 (1967)).

(4) *Permitted disparities in plan contributions or benefits.*—A plan is not treated as failing to meet the requirements of section 411(b)(1)(H) solely because the plan provides a disparity in contributions or benefits with respect to which the requirements of section 401(l) are met.

(5) *Definition of similarly situated.*—For purposes of paragraphs (b)(1) and (b)(2) of this section, an individual is similarly situated to another individual if the individual is identical to that other individual in every respect that is relevant in determining a participant's benefit under the plan (including period of service, compensation, position, date of hire, work history, and any other respect) except for age. In determining whether an individual is similarly situated to another individual, any characteristic that is relevant for determining benefits under the plan and that is based directly or indirectly on age is disregarded. For example, if a particular benefit formula applies to a participant on account of the participant's age, an individual to whom the benefit formula does not apply and who is identical to the participant in all other respects is similarly situated to the participant. By contrast, an individual is not similarly situated to a participant if a different benefit formula applies to the individual and the application of the different formula is not based directly or indirectly on age.

(c) *Special rules for plan conversion amendments.*—(1) *In general.*—Pursuant to section 411(b)(5)(B)(ii), (iii), and (iv), if there is a conversion amendment within the meaning of paragraph (c)(4) of this section with respect to a defined benefit plan, then the plan is treated as failing to meet the requirements of section 411(b)(1)(H) unless the plan, after the amendment, satisfies the requirements of paragraph (c)(2) of this section.

(2) *Separate calculation of post-conversion benefit.*—(i) *In general.*—A statutory hybrid plan satisfies the requirements of this paragraph (c)(2) if the plan provides that, in the case of an individual who was a participant in the plan immediately before the date of adoption of the conversion amendment, the participant's benefit at any subsequent annuity starting date is not less than the sum of—

(A) The participant's section 411(d)(6) protected benefit (as defined in § 1.411(d)-3(g)(14)) with respect to service before the effective date of the conversion amendment, determined under the terms of the plan as in effect immediately before the effective date of the conversion amendment; and

(B) The participant's section 411(d)(6) protected benefit with respect to service on and after the effective date of the conversion amendment, determined under the terms of the plan as in effect after the effective date of the conversion amendment.

(ii) *Rules of application.*—For purposes of this paragraph (c)(2), except as provided in paragraph (c)(3) of this section, the benefits under paragraphs (c)(2)(i)(A) and (c)(2)(i)(B) of this section must each be determined in the same manner as if they were provided under separate plans that are independent of each other (for example, without any benefit offsets), and, except to the extent permitted under § 1.411(d)-3 or § 1.411(d)-4 (or other applicable law), each optional form of payment provided under the terms of the plan with respect to a participant's section 411(d)(6) protected benefit as in effect before the conversion amendment must be available thereafter to the extent of the plan's benefits for service prior to the effective date of the conversion amendment.

(3) *Establishment of opening hypothetical account balance or opening accumulated percentage.*—(i) *In general.*—Provided that the requirements of paragraph (c)(3)(ii) of this section are satisfied, a statutory hybrid plan under which an opening hypothetical account balance or opening accumulated percentage of the participant's final average compensation is established as of the effective date of the conversion amendment does not fail to satisfy the requirements of paragraph (c)(2) of this section merely because benefits attributable to that opening hypothetical account balance or opening accumulated percentage (that is, benefits that are not described in paragraph (c)(2)(i)(B) of this section) are substituted for benefits described in paragraph (c)(2)(i)(A) of this section.

(ii) *Comparison of benefits at annuity starting date.*—(A) *Testing requirement.*—The requirements of this paragraph (c)(3)(ii) are satisfied with respect to an optional form of benefit payable at an annuity starting date only if the plan provides that the amount of the benefit payable in that optional form under the lump sum-based benefit formula that is attributable to the opening hypothetical account balance or opening accumulated percentage as described in paragraph (c)(3)(i) of this section is not less than the benefit under the comparable optional form of benefit under paragraph (c)(2)(i)(A) of this section. To satisfy this requirement, if the benefit under the optional form attributable to the opening hypothetical account balance or opening accumulated percentage is less than the benefit under the comparable optional form of benefit described in paragraph (c)(2)(i)(A) of this section, then the benefit attributable to the opening hypothetical account balance or opening accumulated percentage must be increased to the extent necessary to provide the minimum benefit described in this paragraph (c)(3)(ii). Thus, if a plan is using the option under this paragraph (c)(3)(ii) to satisfy paragraph (c)(2) of this section with respect to a participant, the participant must receive a benefit equal to not less than the sum of—

(*1*) The benefit described in paragraph (c)(2)(i)(B) of this section; and

(*2*) The greater of—

(*i*) The benefit attributable to the opening hypothetical account balance or attributable to the opening accumulated percentage of the participant's final average compensation as described in this paragraph (c)(3)(ii); or

(*ii*) The benefit described in paragraph (c)(2)(i)(A) of this section.

(B) *Comparable optional form of benefit.*—If there was an optional form of benefit within the same generalized optional form of benefit (within the meaning of § 1.411(d)-3(g)(8)) that would have been available to the participant at that annuity starting date under the terms of the plan as in effect immediately before the effective date of the conversion amendment, then that optional form of benefit is the comparable optional form of benefit.

(C) *Special rule for new post-conversion optional forms of benefit.*—If an optional form of benefit is available on the annuity starting date with respect to the benefit attributable to the opening hypothetical account balance or opening accumulated percentage, but no optional form within the same generalized optional form of benefit (within the meaning of § 1.411(d)-3(g)(8)) was available at that annuity starting date under the terms of the plan as in effect immediately prior to the effective date of the conversion amendment, then, for purposes of this paragraph (c)(3)(ii), the plan is treated as if such an optional form of benefit were available immediately prior to the effective date of the conversion amendment for purposes of this paragraph (c)(3)(ii). Thus, for example, if a single-sum optional form of payment is not available under the plan terms applicable to the accrued benefit described in paragraph (c)(2)(i)(A) of this section, but a single-sum optional form of payment is available with respect to the benefit attributable to the opening hypothetical account balance or opening accumulated percentage as of the annuity starting date, then, for purposes of this paragraph (c)(3)(ii), the plan is treated as if a single sum (which satisfies the requirements of section 417(e)(3)) were available under the terms of the plan as in effect immediately prior to the effective date of the conversion amendment.

(4) *Conversion amendment.*—(i) *In general.*—An amendment is a conversion amendment that is subject to the requirements of this paragraph (c) with respect to a participant if—

(A) The amendment reduces or eliminates the benefits that, but for the amendment, the participant would have accrued after the effective date of the amendment under a benefit formula that is not a statutory hybrid benefit formula (and under which the participant was accruing benefits prior to the amendment); and

(B) After the effective date of the amendment, all or a portion of the participant's benefit accruals under the plan are determined under a statutory hybrid benefit formula.

(ii) *Rules of application.*—(A) *In general.*—Paragraphs (c)(4)(iii), (iv), and (v) of this section describe special rules that treat certain arrangements as conversion amendments. The rules described in those paragraphs apply both separately and in combination. Thus, for example, in an acquisition described in § 1.410(b)-2(f), if the buyer adopts an amendment under which a participant's benefits under the seller's plan that is not a statutory hybrid plan are coordinated with a separate plan of the buyer that is a statutory hybrid plan, such as through an offset of the participant's benefit under the buyer's plan by the participant's benefit under the seller's plan, the seller and buyer are treated as a single employer under paragraph (c)(4)(iv) of this section and they are treated as having adopted a conversion amendment under paragraph (c)(4)(iii) of this section. However, pursuant to paragraph (c)(4)(iii) of this section, if there is no coordination between the two plans, there is no conversion amendment.

(B) *Covered amendments.*—Only amendments that eliminate or reduce accrued benefits described in section 411(a)(7), or a retirement-type subsidy described in section 411(d)(6)(B)(i), that would otherwise accrue as a result of future service are treated as amendments described in paragraph (c)(4)(i)(A) of this section.

(C) *Operation of plan terms treated as covered amendment.*—If, under the terms of a plan, a change in the conditions of a participant's employment results in a reduction of the participant's benefits that would have accrued in the future under a benefit formula that is not a statutory hybrid benefit formula, the plan is treated for purposes of this paragraph (c)(4) as if such plan terms constitute an amendment that reduces the participant's benefits that would have accrued after the effective date of the change under a benefit formula that is not a statutory hybrid benefit formula. Thus, for example, if a participant transfers from an operating division that is covered by a non-statutory hybrid benefit formula to an operating division that is covered by a statutory hybrid benefit formula, there has been a conversion amendment and the effective date of the conversion amendment is the date of the transfer. For purposes of applying the effective date rule of paragraph (f)(1)(ii) of this section, the date that the relevant plan terms were adopted is treated as the adoption date of the amendment.

(iii) *Multiple plans.*—An employer is treated as having adopted a conversion amendment if the employer adopts an amendment under which a participant's benefits under a plan that is not a statutory hybrid plan are coordinated with a separate plan that is a statutory hybrid plan, such as through a reduction (offset) of the benefit under the plan that is not a statutory hybrid plan.

(iv) *Multiple employers.*—If the employer of an employee changes as a result of a transaction described in § 1.410(b)-2(f), then the two employers are treated as a single employer for purposes of this paragraph (c)(4).

(v) *Multiple amendments.*—(A) *In general.*—(1) *General rule.*—For purposes of this paragraph (c)(4), a conversion amendment includes multiple amendments that result in a conversion amendment even if the amendments are not conversion amendments individually. For example, an employer is treated as having adopted a conversion amendment if the employer first adopts an amendment described in paragraph (c)(4)(i)(A) of this section and, at a later date,

adopts an amendment that adds a benefit under a statutory hybrid benefit formula as described in paragraph (c)(4)(i)(B) of this section, if they are consolidated under paragraph (c)(4)(v)(A)(2) of this section.

(2) *Delay between plan amendments.*—In determining whether a conversion amendment has been adopted, an amendment to provide a benefit under a statutory hybrid benefit formula is consolidated with a prior amendment to reduce non-statutory hybrid benefit formula benefits if the amendment providing benefits under a statutory hybrid benefit formula is adopted within three years after adoption of the amendment reducing non-statutory hybrid benefit formula benefits. Thus, the later adoption of the statutory hybrid benefit formula will cause the earlier amendment to be treated as part of a conversion amendment. In the case of an amendment to provide a benefit under a statutory hybrid benefit formula that is adopted more than three years after adoption of an amendment to reduce benefits under a non-statutory hybrid benefit formula, there is a presumption that the amendments are not consolidated unless the facts and circumstances indicate that adoption of the amendment to provide a benefit under a statutory hybrid benefit formula was intended at the time of reduction in the nonstatutory hybrid benefit formula.

(B) *Multiple conversion amendments.*—If an employer adopts multiple amendments reducing benefits described in paragraph (c)(4)(i)(A) of this section, each amendment is treated as a separate conversion amendment, provided that paragraph (c)(4)(i)(B) of this section is applicable at the time of the amendment (taking into account the rules of this paragraph (c)(4)).

(vi) *Effective date of a conversion amendment.*—The effective date of a conversion amendment is, with respect to a participant, the date as of which the reduction of the participant's benefits described in paragraph (c)(4)(i)(A) of this section occurs. In accordance with section 411(d)(6), the date of a reduction of those benefits cannot be earlier than the date of adoption of the conversion amendment.

(5) *Examples.*—The following examples illustrate the application of this paragraph (c):

Example 1. (i) *Facts where plan does not establish opening hypothetical account balance for participants and participant elects life annuity at normal retirement age.* Employer N sponsors Plan E, a defined benefit plan that provides an accumulated benefit, payable as a straight life annuity commencing at age 65 (which is Plan E's normal retirement age), based on a percentage of highest average compensation times the participant's years of service. Plan E permits any participant who has had a severance from employment to elect payment in the following optional forms of benefit (with spousal consent if applicable), with any payment not made in a straight life annuity converted to an equivalent form based on reasonable actuarial assumptions: a straight life annuity; and a 50 percent, 75 percent, or 100 percent joint and survivor annuity. The payment of benefits may commence at any time after attainment of age 55, with an actuarial reduction if the commencement is before normal retirement age. In addition, the plan offers a single-sum payment after attainment of age 55 equal to the present value of the normal retirement benefit using the applicable interest rate and mortality table under section 417(e)(3) in effect under the terms of the plan on the annuity starting date.

(ii) *Facts relating to the conversion amendment.* On January 1, 2012, Plan E is amended to eliminate future accruals under the highest average compensation benefit formula and to base future benefit accruals under a hypothetical account balance formula. For service on or after January 1, 2012, each participant's hypothetical account balance is credited monthly with a pay credit equal to a specified percentage of the participant's compensation during the month and also with interest based on the third segment rate described in section 430(h)(2)(C)(iii). With respect to benefits under the hypothetical account balance attributable to service on and after January 1, 2012, a participant is permitted to elect (with spousal consent if applicable) payment in the same generalized optional forms of benefit (even though different actuarial factors apply) as under the terms of the plan in effect before January 1, 2012, and also as a single-sum distribution. The plan provides for the benefit attributable to service before January 1, 2012, to be determined under the terms of the plan as in effect immediately before the effective date of the amendment, and the benefit attributable to service on and after January 1, 2012, to be determined separately, under the terms of the plan as in effect after the effective date of the amendment, with neither benefit offsetting the other in any manner. Thus, each participant's benefit is equal to the sum of the benefit attributable to service before January 1, 2012 (to be determined under the terms of the plan as in effect immediately before the effective date of the amendment), plus the benefit attributable to the participant's hypothetical account balance.

(iii) *Facts relating to an affected participant.* Participant A is age 62 on January 1, 2012. On December 31, 2011, A's benefit for years of service before January 1, 2012, payable as a straight life annuity commencing at A's normal retirement age (age 65), which is January 1, 2015, is $1,000 per month. On January 1, 2015, when Participant A has a severance from employment, the then-current hypothetical account balance, with pay credits and interest from January 1, 2012, to January 1, 2015, is $11,000. Using the conversion factors applicable under the plan on January 1, 2015, that balance is equivalent to a straight life annuity of $100 per month commencing on January 1, 2015. This benefit is in addition to the benefit attributable to service before January 1, 2012. Participant A elects (with spousal consent) a straight life annuity of $1,100 per month commencing January 1, 2015.

(iv) *Conclusion.* Participant A's benefit satisfies the requirements of paragraph (c) of this section because Participant A's benefit is not less than the sum of Participant A's section 411(d)(6) protected benefit (as defined in § 1.411(d)-3(g)(14)) with respect to service before the effective date of the conversion amendment, determined under the terms of the plan as in effect immediately before the effective date of the amendment, and Participant A's section 411(d)(6) protected benefit with respect to service on and after the effective date of conversion amendment, determined under the terms of the plan as in effect after the effective date of the amendment.

Example 2. (i) *Facts involving plan's establishment of opening hypothetical account balance and payment of pre-conversion accumulated benefit in life annuity at normal retirement age.* Except as indicated in this *Example 2,* the facts are the same as the facts under paragraph (i) of *Example 1.*

(ii) *Facts relating to the conversion amendment.* On January 1, 2012, Plan E is amended to eliminate future accruals under the highest average compensation benefit formula and to provide future benefit accruals under a hypothetical account balance formula. An opening hypothetical account balance is established for each participant, and, under the plan's terms, that balance is equal to the present value of the participant's accumulated benefit on December 31, 2011 (payable as a straight life annuity at normal retirement age or immediately, if later), using the applicable interest rate and applicable mortality table under section 417(e)(3) on January 1, 2012. Under Plan E, the account based on this opening hypothetical account balance is maintained as a separate account from the account for accruals on or after January 1, 2012. The hypothetical account balance maintained for each participant for accruals on or after January 1, 2012, is credited monthly with a pay credit equal to a specified percentage of the participant's compensation during the month. A participant's hypothetical account balance (including both of the separate accounts) is credited monthly with interest based on the third segment rate described in section 430(h)(2)(C)(iii).

(iii) *Facts relating to optional forms of benefit.* Following severance from employment and attainment of age 55, a participant is permitted to elect (with spousal consent if applicable) payment in the same generalized optional forms of benefit as under the plan in effect prior to January 1, 2012, with the amount payable calculated based on the hypothetical account balance on the annuity starting date and the applicable interest rate and applicable mortality table on the annuity starting date. The single-sum distribution is equal to the hypothetical account balance.

(iv) *Facts relating to conversion protection.* The plan provides that, as of a participant's annuity starting date, the plan will determine whether the benefit attributable to the opening hypothetical account balance payable in the particular optional form of benefit selected is equal to or greater than the benefit accrued under the plan through the date of conversion and payable in the same generalized optional form of benefit with the same annuity starting date. If the benefit attributable to the opening hypothetical account balance is equal to or greater than the pre-conversion benefit, the plan provides that such benefit is paid in lieu of the pre-conversion benefit, together with the benefit attributable to post-conversion pay-based principal credits. If the benefit attributable to the opening hypothetical account balance is less than the pre-conversion benefit, the plan provides that such benefit is increased sufficiently to provide the pre-conversion benefit, together with the benefit attributable to post-conversion pay-based principal credits.

(v) *Facts relating to an affected participant.* On January 1, 2012, the opening hypothetical account balance established for Participant A is $80,000, which is the present value of Participant A's straight life annuity of $1,000 per month commencing at January 1, 2015, using the applicable interest rate and applicable mortality table under section 417(e)(3) in effect on January 1, 2012. On January 1, 2012, the applicable interest rate for Participant A is equivalent to a level rate of 5.5 percent. Thereafter, Participant A's hypothetical account balance for subsequent accruals is credited monthly with a pay credit equal to a specified percentage of the participant's compensation during the month. In addition, Participant A's hypothetical account balance (including both of the separate accounts) is credited monthly with interest based on the third segment rate described in section 430(h)(2)(C)(iii).

(vi) *Facts relating to calculation of the participant's benefit.* Participant A has a severance from employment on January 1, 2015 at age 65, and elects (with spousal consent) a straight life annuity commencing January 1, 2015. On January 1, 2015, the opening hypothetical account balance, with interest credits from January 1, 2012, to January 1, 2015, has become $95,000, which, using the conversion factors under the plan on January 1, 2015, is equivalent to a straight life annuity of $1,005 per month commencing on January 1, 2015 (which is greater than the $1,000 a month payable at age 65 under the terms of the plan in effect before January 1, 2012). This benefit is in addition to the benefit determined using the hypothetical account balance for service after January 1, 2012.

(vii) *Conclusion.* The benefit satisfies the requirements of paragraph (c)(3)(ii)(A) of this section with respect to Participant A because A's benefit is not less than the sum of (A) the greater of Participant A's benefits attributable to the opening hypothetical account balance and A's section 411(d)(6) protected benefit (as defined in § 1.411(d)-3(g)(14)) with respect to service before the effective date of the conversion amendment, determined under the terms of the plan as in effect immediately before the effective date of the amendment, and (B) Participant A's section 411(d)(6) protected benefit with respect to service on and after the effective date of the conversion amendment, determined under the terms of the plan as in effect after the effective date of the amendment.

Example 3. (i) *Facts involving a subsequent decrease in interest rates.* The facts are the same as in *Example 2,* except that, because of a decrease in bond rates after January 1, 2012, and before January 1, 2015, the rate of interest credited in that period averages less than 5.5 percent, and, on January 1, 2015, the effective applicable interest rate under section 417(e)(3) under the plan's terms is 4.7 percent. As a result, Participant A's opening hypothetical account balance plus attributable interest credits has increased to only $87,000 on January 1, 2015, and, using the conversion factors under the plan on January 1, 2015, is equivalent to a straight life annuity commencing on January 1, 2015, of $775 per month. Under the terms of Plan E, the benefit attributable to A's opening hypothetical account balance is increased so that A's straight life annuity commencing on January 1, 2015, is $1,000 per month. This benefit is in addition to the benefit attributable to the hypothetical account balance for service after January 1, 2012.

(ii) *Conclusion.* The benefit satisfies the requirements of paragraph (c)(3)(ii)(A) of this section with respect to Participant A because A's benefit is not less than the sum of—

(A) The greater of A's benefits attributable to the opening hypothetical account balance and A's section 411(d)(6) protected benefit (as defined in § 1.411(d)-3(g)(14)) with respect to service before the effective date of the conversion amendment, determined under the terms of the plan as in effect immediately before the effective date of the amendment; and

(B) A's section 411(d)(6) protected benefit with respect to service on and after the effective date of the conversion amendment, determined under the terms of the plan as in effect after the effective date of the amendment.

Example 4. (i) *Facts involving payment of a subsidized early retirement benefit.* The facts are the same as in *Example 2,* except that under the terms of Plan E on December 31, 2011, a participant who retires before age 65 and after age 55 with 30 years of service has only a 3 percent per year actuarial reduction. Participant A has a severance from employment on January 1, 2013, when A is age 63 and has 30 years of service. On January 1, 2013, A's opening hypothetical account balance, with interest from January 1, 2012, to January 1, 2013, has become $86,000, which, using the conversion factors under the plan (as amended) on January 1, 2013, is equivalent to a straight life annuity commencing on January 1, 2013, of $850 per month.

(ii) *Facts relating to calculation of the participant's benefit.* Under the terms of Plan E on December 31, 2011, Participant A is entitled to a straight life annuity commencing on January 1, 2013, equal to at least $940 per month ($1,000 reduced by 3 percent for each of the 2 years that A's benefits commence before normal retirement age). Under the terms of Plan E, the benefit attributable to A's opening account balance is increased so that A is entitled to a straight life annuity of $940 per month commencing on January 1, 2015. This benefit is in addition to the benefit determined using the hypothetical account balance for service after January 1, 2012.

(iii) *Conclusion.* The benefit satisfies the requirements of paragraph (c)(3)(ii)(A) of this section with respect to Participant A because A's benefit is not less than the sum of—

(A) The greater of Participant A's benefits attributable to the opening hypothetical account balance (increased by attributable interest credits) and A's section 411(d)(6) protected benefit (as defined in § 1.411(d)-3(g)(14)) with respect to service before the effective date of the conversion amendment, determined under the terms of the plan as in effect immediately before the effective date of the amendment; and

(B) Participant A's section 411(d)(6) protected benefit with respect to service on and after the effective date of the conversion amendment, determined under the terms of the plan as in effect after the effective date of the amendment.

Example 5. (i) *Facts involving addition of a single-sum payment option.* The facts are the same as in *Example 2*, except that, before January 1, 2012, Plan E did not offer payment in a single-sum distribution for amounts in excess of $5,000. Plan E, as amended on January 1, 2012, offers payment in any of the available annuity distribution forms commencing at any time following severance from employment as were provided under Plan E before January 1, 2012. In addition, Plan E, as amended on January 1, 2012, offers payment in the form of a single sum attributable to service before January 1, 2012, which is the greater of the opening hypothetical account balance (increased by attributable interest credits) or a single-sum distribution of the straight life annuity payable at age 65 using the same actuarial factors as are used for mandatory cashouts for amounts equal to $5,000 or less under the terms of the plan on December 31, 2011. Participant B is age 40 on January 1, 2012, and B's opening hypothetical account balance (increased by attributable interest credits) is $33,000 (which is the present value, using the conversion factors under the plan (as amended) on January 1, 2012, of Participant B's straight life annuity of $1,000 per month commencing at January 1, 2037, which is when B will be age 65). Participant B has a severance from employment on January 1, 2015, and elects (with spousal consent) an immediate single-sum distribution. Participant B's opening hypothetical account balance (increased by attributable interest) on January 1, 2015, is $45,000. The present value, on January 1, 2015, of Participant B's benefit of $1,000 per month, commencing immediately using the actuarial factors for mandatory cashouts under the terms of the plan on December 31, 2011, would result in a single-sum payment of $44,750. Participant B is paid a single-sum distribution equal to the sum of $45,000 plus an amount equal to B's January 1, 2015, hypothetical account balance for benefit accruals for service after January 1, 2012.

(ii) *Conclusion.* Because, under Plan E, Participant B is entitled to the sum of—

(A) The greater of the $45,000 opening hypothetical account balance (increased by attributable interest credits) and $44,750 (present value of the benefit with respect to service prior to January 1, 2012, using the actuarial factors for mandatory cashout distributions under the terms of the plan on December 31, 2011); and

(B) An amount equal to B's hypothetical account balance for benefit accruals for service after January 1, 2012, the benefit satisfies the requirements of paragraph (c)(3)(ii)(A) of this section with respect to Participant B. If Participant B's hypothetical account balance under Plan E was instead less than $44,750 on January 1, 2015, Participant B would be entitled to a single-sum payment equal to the sum of $44,750 and an amount equal to B's hypothetical account balance for benefit accruals for service after January 1, 2012.

Example 6. (i) *Facts involving addition of new annuity optional form of benefit.* The facts are the same as in *Example 2*, except that, after December 31, 2011, and before January 1, 2015, Plan E is amended to offer payment in a 5-, 10-, or 15-year term certain and life annuity, using the same actuarial assumptions that apply for other optional forms of distribution. When Participant A has a severance from employment on January 1, 2015, A elects (with spousal consent) a 5-year term certain and life annuity commencing immediately equal to $935 per month. Application of the same actuarial assumptions to Participant A's benefit of $1,000 per month (under Plan E as in effect on December 31, 2011), commencing immediately on January 1, 2015, would result in a 5-year term certain and life annuity commencing immediately equal to $955 per month. Under the terms of Plan E, the benefit attributable to A's opening account balance is increased so that, using the conversion factors under the plan (as amended) on January 1, 2015, A's opening hypothetical account balance (increased by attributable interest credits) produces a 5-year term certain and life annuity commencing immediately equal to $955 per month commencing on January 1, 2015. This benefit is in addition to the benefit determined using the January 1, 2015, hypothetical account balance for service after January 1, 2012.

(ii) *Conclusion.* This benefit satisfies the requirements of paragraph (c)(3)(ii)(A) of this section with respect to Participant A.

Example 7. (i) *Facts involving addition of distribution option before age 55.* The facts are the same as in *Example 5*, except that Participant B (age 43) elects (with spousal consent) a straight life annuity commencing immediately on January 1, 2015. Under Plan E, the straight life annuity attributable to Participant B's opening hypothetical account balance at age 43 is $221 per month. Application of the same actuarial assumptions to Participant B's benefit of $1,000 per month commencing at age 65 (under Plan E as in effect on December 31, 2011) would result in a straight life annuity commencing immediately on January 1, 2015, equal to $219 per month.

(ii) *Conclusion.* Because, under its terms, Plan E provides that Participant B is entitled to an amount not less than the present value (using the same actuarial assumptions as apply on January 1, 2015, in converting the $45,000 hypothetical account balance attributable to the opening hypothetical account balance to the $221 straight life annuity) of Participant B's straight life annuity of $1,000 per month commencing at age 65, and the $221 straight life annuity is in addition to the benefit accruals for service after January 1, 2012, payment of the $221 monthly annuity would satisfy the requirements of paragraph (c)(3)(ii)(A) of this section with respect to Participant B.

Example 8. (i) *Facts involving establishment of opening hypothetical account balance.* A defined benefit plan provides an accrued benefit expressed as a straight life annuity commencing at the plan's normal retirement age (age 65), based on a percentage of average annual compensation multiplied by the participant's years of service. On January 1, 2009, a conversion amendment is adopted that converts the plan to a statutory hybrid plan. Participant A, age 55, had an accrued benefit under the pre-conversion formula of $1,500 per month payable at normal retirement age. In conjunction with this conversion, the plan provides each participant with an opening hypothetical account balance equal to the present value, determined in accordance with section 417(e)(3) of the participant's pre-conversion benefit. Participant A's opening hypothetical account balance was calculated as $121,146. The opening account balance (along with any subsequent amounts credited to the hypothetical account) is credited annually with interest credits at the rate of 5.0 percent up to the annuity starting date of each participant.

(ii) *Facts relating to changes between establishment of opening hypothetical account balance and age 65.* Upon attainment of age 65, Participant A elects to receive Participant A's entire benefit under the plan as a single sum distribution. At the annuity starting date, Participant A's hypothetical account balance attributable to Participant A's opening account balance has increased to $197,334. However, under the terms of the plan and in accordance with section 417(e)(3), the present value at the annuity starting date of Participant A's pre-conversion benefit of $1,500 per month is $221,383.

(iii) *Conclusion.* Pursuant to paragraph (c)(3)(ii)(A) of this section, Participant A must receive the benefit attributable to post-conversion service, plus the greater of the benefit attributable to the opening hypothetical account balance and the pre-conversion benefit (with the determination as to which is greater made at the annuity starting date). Accordingly the single-sum distribution must equal the benefit attributable to post-conversion service plus $221,383.

(d) *Market rate of return.*—(1) *In general.*—(i) *Basic test.*—Subject to the rules of paragraph (e) of this section, a statutory hybrid plan satisfies the requirements of section 411(b)(1)(H) and this paragraph (d) only if, for any plan year, the interest crediting rate with respect to benefits determined under a statutory hybrid benefit formula is not greater than a market rate of return.

(ii) *Definitions relating to market rate of return.*—(A) *Interest credit.*—Subject to other rules in this paragraph (d), an interest credit for purposes of this paragraph (d) and section 411(b)(5)(B) means the following adjustments to a participant's accumulated benefit under a statutory hybrid benefit formula, to the extent not conditioned on current service and not made on account of imputed service (as defined in § 1.401(a)(4)-11(d)(3)(ii)(B))—

(1) Any increase or decrease for a period, under the terms of the plan at the beginning of the period, that is calculated by applying a rate of interest or rate of return (including a rate of increase or decrease under an index) to the participant's accumulated benefit (or a portion thereof) as of the beginning of the period; and

(2) Any other increase for a period, under the terms of the plan at the beginning of the period.

(B) *Treatment of plan amendments.*—An increase to a participant's accumulated benefit is not treated as an interest credit to the extent the increase is made as a result of a plan amendment providing for a one-time adjustment to the participant's accumulated benefit. However, a pattern of repeated plan amendments each of which provides for a one-time adjustment to a participant's accumulated benefit will cause such adjustments to be treated as provided on a permanent basis under the terms of the plan. See § 1.411(d)-4, A-1(c)(1).

(C) *Interest crediting rate.*—Except as otherwise provided in this paragraph (d), the interest crediting rate, or effective rate of return, for a period with respect to a participant equals the total amount of interest credits for the period divided by the participant's accumulated benefit at the beginning of the period.

(D) *Principal credit.*—For purposes of this paragraph (d), a principal credit means any increase to a participant's accumulated benefit under a statutory hybrid benefit formula that is not an interest credit. Thus, for example, a principal credit includes an increase to a participant's accumulated benefit to the extent the increase is conditioned on current service or made on account of imputed service. As a result, a principal credit includes an increase to the value of an accumulated percentage of the participant's final average compensation. For indexed benefits described in paragraph (b)(2) of this section, a principal credit includes an increase to the participant's accrued benefit other than an increase provided by indexing. In addition, pursuant to the rule in paragraph (d)(1)(ii)(B)

of this section, a principal credit generally includes an increase to a participant's accumulated benefit to the extent the increase is made as a result of a plan amendment providing for a one-time adjustment to the participant's accumulated benefit. As a result, a principal credit includes an opening hypothetical account balance or opening accumulated percentage of the participant's final average compensation, as described in paragraph (c)(3) of this section.

>>>→ *Caution: Reg. §1.411(b)(5)-1(d)(1)(iii) generally applies to plan years that begin on or after January 1, 2017 (or an earlier date as elected by the taxpayer).*

(iii) *Market rate of return for single rates.*—Except as otherwise provided in this paragraph (d)(1), an interest crediting rate is not in excess of a market rate of return only if the plan terms provide that the interest credit for each plan year is determined using one of the following specified interest crediting rates:

(A) The interest rate on long-term investment grade corporate bonds (as described in paragraph (d)(3) of this section).

(B) An interest rate that, under paragraph (d)(4) of this section, is deemed to be not in excess of the interest rate described in paragraph (d)(3) of this section.

(C) A rate of return that, under paragraph (d)(5) of this section, is not in excess of a market rate of return.

(iv) *Timing and other rules related to interest crediting rate.*—(A) *In general.*—A plan that provides interest credits must specify how the plan determines interest credits and must specify how and when interest credits are credited. The plan must specify the method for determining interest credits in accordance with the requirements of paragraph (d)(1)(iv)(B) of this section, the frequency of interest crediting in accordance with the requirements of paragraph (d)(1)(iv)(C) of this section, and the treatment of interest credits on distributed amounts, as well as other debits and credits during the period, in accordance with the rules of paragraph (d)(1)(iv)(D) of this section. In addition, a plan is permitted to round the calculated interest rate or rate of return in accordance with paragraph (d)(1)(iv)(E) of this section. See paragraph (e) of this section for additional rules that apply to changes in the interest crediting rate.

(B) *Methods to determine interest credits.*—A plan that is using any specified interest crediting rate can determine interest credits for each current interest crediting period based on the effective periodic interest crediting rate that applies over the period. Alternatively, a plan that is using one of the interest crediting rates described in paragraph (d)(3) or (d)(4) of this section can determine interest credits for a stability period based on the interest crediting rate for a specified lookback month with respect to that stability period. For purposes of the preceding sentence, the stability period and lookback

month must satisfy the rules for selecting the stability period and lookback month under §1.417(e)-1(d)(4), although the interest crediting rate can be any one of the rates in paragraph (d)(3) or (d)(4) of this section and the stability period and lookback month need not be the same as those used under the plan for purposes of section 417(e)(3).

(C) *Frequency of interest crediting.*—Interest credits under a plan must be provided on an annual or more frequent periodic basis and interest credits for each interest crediting period must be credited as of the end of the period. If a plan provides for the crediting of interest more frequently than annually (for example, daily, monthly or quarterly) based on one of the annual interest rates described in paragraph (d)(3) or (d)(4) of this section, then the plan generally provides an above market rate of return unless each periodic interest credit is determined using an interest crediting rate that is no greater than a pro rata portion of the applicable annual interest crediting rate. However, a plan that credits interest daily based on one of the annual interest rates described in paragraph (d)(3) or (d)(4) of this section is not treated as providing an above market rate of return merely because the plan determines each daily interest credit using a daily interest crediting rate that is 1/360 of the applicable annual interest crediting rate. In addition, interest credits determined, under the terms of a plan, based on one of the annual interest rates described in paragraph (d)(3) or (d)(4) of this section are not treated as creating an effective rate of return that is in excess of a market rate of return merely because an otherwise permissible interest crediting rate for a plan year is compounded more frequently than annually. Thus, for example, if a plan's terms provide for interest to be credited monthly and for the interest crediting rate to be equal to the interest rate on long-term investment grade corporate bonds (as described in paragraph (d)(3) of this section) and the applicable annual rate on these bonds for the plan year is 6 percent, then the accumulated benefit at the beginning of each month could be increased as a result of interest credits by as much as 0.5 percent per month during the plan year without resulting in an interest crediting rate that is in excess of a market rate of return.

>>>→ *Caution: Reg. §1.411(b)(5)-1(d)(1)(iv)(D) generally applies to plan years that begin on or after January 1, 2017 (or an earlier date as elected by the taxpayer).*

(D) *Debits and credits during the interest crediting period.*—A plan is not treated as failing to meet the requirements of this paragraph (d) merely because the plan does not provide for interest credits on amounts distributed prior to the end of the interest crediting period. Furthermore, a plan is not treated as failing to meet the requirements of this paragraph (d) merely because the plan calculates increases or decreases to the participant's accumulated benefit by applying a rate of interest or rate of return (including a rate of increase or decrease under an index) to the participant's adjusted accumulated benefit (or portion thereof) for the period. For this purpose, the participant's adjusted accumulated benefit equals the participant's accumulated benefit as of the beginning of the period, adjusted for debits and credits (other than interest credits) made to

the accumulated benefit prior to the end of the interest crediting period, with appropriate weighting for those debits and credits based on their timing within the period. For plans that calculate increases or decreases to the participant's accumulated benefit by applying a rate of interest or rate of return to the participant's adjusted accumulated benefit (or portion thereof) for the period, interest credits include these increases and decreases, to the extent provided under the terms of the plan at the beginning of the period and to the extent not conditioned on current service and not made on account of imputed service (as defined in §1.401(a)(4)-11(d)(3)(ii)(B)), and the interest crediting rate with respect to a participant equals the total amount of interest credits for the period divided by the participant's adjusted accumulated benefit for the period.

>>>→ *Caution: Reg. §1.411(b)(5)-1(d)(1)(iv)(E) generally applies to plan years that begin on or after January 1, 2017 (or an earlier date as elected by the taxpayer).*

(E) *Rounding of interest crediting rate.*—A plan is not treated as failing to meet the requirements of this paragraph (d) merely because the plan determines interest credits for an interest crediting period by rounding the calculated interest rate or rate of return in accordance with this paragraph (d)(1)(iv)(E). An annual rate may be rounded to the nearest multiple of 25 basis points (or a smaller rounding interval). If a plan provides for the crediting of interest more frequently than annually, then the rounding interval must not exceed a pro-rata portion of 25 basis points. Notwithstanding the preceding sentence, a plan is permitted to round to the nearest basis point regardless of the length of the interest crediting period.

(v) *Lesser rates.*—An interest crediting rate is not in excess of a market rate of return if the rate can never be in excess of a particular rate that is described in paragraph (d)(1)(iii) of this section. Thus, for example, an interest crediting rate that always equals the rate described in paragraph (d)(3) of this section minus 200 basis points is not in excess of a market rate of return because it can never be in excess of the rate described in paragraph (d)(3) of this section. Similarly, an interest crediting rate that always equals the lesser of the yield on 30-year Treasury Constant Maturities and a fixed 7 percent interest rate is not in excess of a market rate of return because it can never be in excess of the yield on 30-year Treasury Constant Maturities.

>>>→ *Caution: Reg. §1.411(b)(5)-1(d)(1)(vi) generally applies to plan years that begin on or after January 1, 2017 (or an earlier date as elected by the taxpayer).*

(vi) *Greater-of rates.*—If a statutory hybrid plan determines an interest credit by applying the greater of 2 or more different rates to the accumulated benefit, the effective interest crediting rate is not in

excess of a market rate of return only if each of the different rates would separately satisfy the requirements of this paragraph (d) and the requirements of paragraph (d)(6) of this section are also satisfied.

(vii) *Blended rates.*—A statutory hybrid plan does not provide an effective interest crediting rate that is in excess of a market rate of return merely because the plan determines an interest credit by applying different rates to different predetermined portions of the accumulated benefit, provided each rate would separately satisfy the requirements of this paragraph (d) if the rate applied to the entire accumulated benefit.

(viii) *Increases to existing rates and addition of other rates.*—(A) *Increases to existing rates.*—The Commissioner may, in guidance published in the Internal Revenue Bulletin, see §601.601(d)(2)(ii)(*b*) of this chapter, increase an interest crediting rate set forth in this paragraph (d), so that the increased rate is treated as satisfying the requirement that the rate not exceed a market rate of return for purposes of this paragraph (d) and section 411(b)(5)(B). For this purpose, these increases can include increases to the maximum permitted margin that can be added to one or more of the safe harbor rates set forth in paragraph (d)(4) of this section, increases to the maximum permitted fixed rate set forth in paragraph (d)(4)(v) of this section, or increases to a maximum permitted annual floor set forth in paragraph (d)(6) of this section.

(B) *Additional rates.*—The Commissioner may, in guidance published in the Internal Revenue Bulletin, see §601.601(d)(2)(ii)(*b*) of this chapter, provide for additional interest crediting rates that

satisfy the requirement that they not exceed a market rate of return for purposes of this paragraph (d) and section 411(b)(5)(B) (including providing for additional combinations of rates, such as annual minimums in conjunction with rates that are based on rates described in paragraph (d)(5) of this section but that are reduced in order to ensure that the effective rate of return does not exceed a market rate of return).

(2) *Preservation of capital requirement.*—(i) *General rule.*—A statutory hybrid plan satisfies the requirements of section 411(b)(1)(H) only if the plan provides that the participant's benefit under the statutory hybrid benefit formula determined as of the participant's annuity starting date is no less than the benefit determined as if the accumulated benefit were equal to the sum of all principal credits (as described in paragraph (d)(1)(ii)(D) of this section) credited under the plan to the participant as of that date (including principal credits that were credited before the applicable statutory effective date of paragraph (f)(1) of this section). This paragraph (d)(2) applies only as of an annuity starting date, within the meaning of §1.401(a)-20, A-10(b), with respect to which a distribution of the participant's entire vested benefit under the plan's statutory hybrid benefit formula as of that date commences. For a participant who has more than one annuity starting date, paragraph (d)(2)(ii) of this section provides rules to account for prior annuity starting dates when applying this paragraph (d)(2)(i).

»»→ Caution: Reg. §1.411(b)(5)-1(d)(2)(ii) generally applies to plan years that begin on or after January 1, 2017 (or an earlier date as elected by the taxpayer).

(ii) *Application to multiple annuity starting dates.*—(A) *In general.*—If the comparison under paragraph (d)(2)(ii)(B) of this section results in the sum of all principal credits credited to the participant (as of the current annuity starting date) exceeding the sum of the amounts described in paragraphs (d)(2)(ii)(B)(*1*) through (d)(2)(ii)(B)(3) of this section, then the participant's benefit to be distributed at the current annuity starting date must be no less than would be provided if that excess were included in the current accumulated benefit.

(B) *Comparison to reflect prior distributions.*—For a participant who has more than one annuity starting date, the sum of all principal credits credited to the participant under the plan, as of the current annuity starting date, is compared to the sum of—

(*1*) The remaining balance of the participant's accumulated benefit as of the current annuity starting date;

(*2*) The amount of the reduction to the participant's accumulated benefit under the statutory hybrid benefit formula that is attributable to any prior distribution of the participant's benefit under that formula; and

(*3*) Any amount that was treated as included in the accumulated benefit under the rules of this paragraph (d)(2) as of any prior annuity starting date.

(C) *Special rule for participants with 5 or more breaks in service.*—A plan is permitted to provide that, in the case of a participant who receives a distribution of the entire vested benefit under the plan and thereafter completes 5 consecutive 1-year breaks in service, as defined in section 411(a)(6)(A), the rules of this paragraph (d)(2) are applied without regard to the prior period of service. Thus, in the case of such a participant, the plan is permitted to provide that the

rules of this paragraph (d)(2) are applied disregarding the principal credits and distributions that occurred before the breaks in service.

(iii) *Exception for variable annuity benefit formulas.*—See paragraph (b)(2)(iii)(B) of this section for an exception to this paragraph (d)(2).

(3) *Long-term investment grade corporate bonds.*—For purposes of this paragraph (d), the rate of interest on long-term investment grade corporate bonds means the third segment rate described in section 417(e)(3)(D) or 430(h)(2)(C)(iii) (determined with or without regard to section 430(h)(2)(C)(iv) and with or without regard to the transition rules of section 417(e)(3)(D)(ii) or 430(h)(2)(G)). However, for plan years beginning prior to January 1, 2008, the rate of interest on long-term investment grade corporate bonds means the rate described in section 412(b)(5)(B)(ii)(II) prior to amendment by the Pension Protection Act of 2006, Public Law 109-280 (120 Stat. 780 (2006)) (PPA '06).

(4) *Safe harbor rates of interest.*—(i) *In general.*—This paragraph (d)(4) identifies interest rates that are deemed to be not in excess of the interest rate described in paragraph (d)(3) of this section. The Commissioner may, in guidance of general applicability, specify additional interest crediting rates that are deemed to be not in excess of the rate described in paragraph (d)(3) of this section. See §601.601(d)(2)(ii)(*b*).

(ii) *Rates based on government bonds with margins.*—An interest crediting rate is deemed to be not in excess of the interest rate described in paragraph (d)(3) of this section if the rate is equal to the sum of any of the following rates of interest for bonds and the associated margin for that interest rate:

Interest Rate Bond Index	Associated Margin
The discount rate on 3-month Treasury Bills	175 basis points
The discount rate on 12-month or shorter Treasury Bills	150 basis points
The yield on 1-year Treasury Constant Maturities	100 basis points
The yield on 3-year or shorter Treasury Constant Maturities	50 basis points
The yield on 7-year or shorter Treasury Constant Maturities	25 basis points
The yield on 30-year or shorter Treasury Constant Maturities	0 basis points

(iii) *Eligible cost-of-living indices.*—An interest crediting rate is deemed to be not in excess of the interest rate described in paragraph (d)(3) of this section if the rate is adjusted no less frequently than annually and is equal to the rate of increase with respect to an eligible cost-of-living index described in §1.401(a)(9)-6, A-14(b), except that, for purposes of this paragraph (d)(4)(iii), the eligible cost-of-living index described in §1.401(a)(9)-6, A-14(b)(2) is increased by 300 basis points.

(iv) *Short and mid-term investment grade corporate bonds.*—An interest crediting rate equal to the first segment rate is deemed to be

not in excess of the interest rate described in paragraph (d)(3) of this section. Similarly, an interest crediting rate equal to the second segment rate is deemed to be not in excess of the interest rate described in paragraph (d)(3) of this section. For this purpose, the first and second segment rates mean the first and second segment rates described in section 417(e)(3)(D) or 430(h)(2)(C), determined with or without regard to section 430(h)(2)(C)(iv) and with or without regard to the transition rules of section 417(e)(3)(D)(ii) or 430(h)(2)(G).

»»→ Caution: Reg. §1.411(b)(5)-1(d)(4)(v) generally applies to plan years that begin on or after January 1, 2017 (or an earlier date as elected by the taxpayer).

(v) *Fixed rate of interest.*—An annual interest crediting rate equal to a fixed 6 percent is deemed to be not in excess of the interest rate described in paragraph (d)(3) of this section.

(5) *Other rates of return.*—(i) *General rule.*—This paragraph (d)(5) sets forth additional methods for determining an interest crediting rate that is not in excess of a market rate of return.

(ii) *Actual rate of return on plan assets.*—(A) *In general.*—An interest crediting rate equal to the actual rate of return on the aggregate assets of the plan, including both positive returns and negative returns, is not in excess of a market rate of return if the plan's assets are diversified so as to minimize the volatility of returns. This requirement that plan assets be diversified so as to minimize the volatility of returns does not require greater diversification than is required under section 404(a)(1)(C) of Title I of the Employee Retirement Income Security Act of 1974, Public Law 93-406 (88 Stat. 829 (1974)), as amended (ERISA), with respect to defined benefit pension plans.

>>>→ *Caution: Reg. §1.411(b)(5)-1(d)(5)(ii)(B) generally applies to plan years that begin on or after January 1, 2017 (or an earlier date as elected by the taxpayer).*

(B) *Subset of plan assets.*—An interest crediting rate equal to the actual rate of return on the assets within a specified subset of plan assets, including both positive and negative returns, is not in excess of a market rate of return if—

(1) The subset of plan assets is diversified so as to minimize the volatility of returns, within the meaning of paragraph (d)(5)(ii)(A) of this section (thus, this requirement is satisfied if the subset of plan assets is diversified such that it would meet the requirements of paragraph (d)(5)(ii)(A) of this section if the subset were aggregate plan assets);

(2) The aggregate fair market value of qualifying employer securities and qualifying employer real property (within the meaning of section 407 of ERISA) held in the subset of plan assets does not exceed 10 percent of the fair market value of the aggregate assets in the subset; and

(3) The fair market value of the assets within the subset of plan assets approximates the liabilities for benefits that are adjusted by reference to the rate of return on the assets within the subset, determined using reasonable actuarial assumptions.

(C) *Examples.*—The following examples illustrate the application of paragraph (d)(5)(ii)(B) of this section:

Example 1. (i) *Facts.* (a) Employer A sponsors a defined benefit plan under which benefit accruals are determined under a formula that is not a statutory hybrid benefit formula. Effective January 1, 2015, the plan is amended to cease future benefit accruals under the existing formula and to provide future benefit accruals under a statutory hybrid benefit formula that uses hypothetical accounts. For service on or after January 1, 2015, the terms of the plan provide that each participant's hypothetical account balance is credited monthly with a pay credit equal to a specified percentage of the participant's compensation during the month. The plan also provides that hypothetical account balance is increased or decreased by an interest credit, which is calculated as the product of the account balance at the beginning of the period and the net rate of return on the assets within a specified subset of plan assets during that period. Under the terms of the plan, the net rate of return is equal to the actual rate of return adjusted to reflect a reduction for specified plan expenses. The plan does not provide for interest credits on amounts that are distributed prior to the end of an interest crediting period.

(b) As of the effective date of the amendment, there are no assets in the specified subset of plan assets. Under the terms of the plan, an amount is added to the specified subset at the time each subsequent contribution for any plan year starting on or after the effective date of the amendment is made to the plan. The amount added (the formula contribution) is the amount deemed necessary to fund benefit accruals under the statutory hybrid benefit formula. Investment of the specified subset is diversified so as to minimize the volatility of returns, within the meaning of paragraph (d)(5)(ii)(A) of this section, and no qualifying employer securities or qualifying employer real property (within the meaning of section 407 of ERISA) are held in the subset. Benefits accrued under the statutory hybrid benefit formula are paid from the specified subset. However, if assets of the specified subset are insufficient to pay benefits accrued under the statutory hybrid benefit formula, the plan provides that assets of the residual legacy subset of plan assets (from which benefits accrued before January 1, 2015 are paid) are available to pay those benefits in accordance with the requirement that all assets of the plan be available to pay all plan benefits. Except as described in this paragraph, no other amounts are added to or subtracted from the specified subset of plan assets.

(c) The formula contribution for each plan year that is added to the specified subset of plan assets is an amount equal to the sum of the target normal cost of the statutory hybrid benefit formula for the plan year plus an additional amount intended to reflect gains or losses. This additional amount is equal to the annual amount necessary to amortize the difference between the funding target attributable to the statutory hybrid benefit formula portion of the plan for the plan year over the value of plan assets included in the specified subset of plan assets for the plan year in level annual installments over a 7-year period. For this purpose, target normal cost and funding target are determined under the rules of §1.430(d)-1 as if the statutory hybrid benefit formula portion of the plan were the entire plan and without regard to special rules that are applicable to a plan in at-risk status, even if the plan is in at-risk status for a plan year. If the formula contribution for a plan year exceeds the amount of the actual contribution to the plan for a year (such as could be the case if all or a portion of the contribution is offset by all or a portion of the plan's prefunding balance), then an amount equal to the excess of the formula contribution over the actual contribution is transferred from the residual legacy subset of plan assets to the specified subset of plan assets on the plan's due date for the minimum required contribution for the year.

(ii) *Conclusion.* The specified subset is diversified so as to minimize the volatility of returns (within the meaning of paragraph (d)(5)(ii)(A) of this section). The aggregate fair market value of qualifying employer securities and qualifying employer real property (within the meaning of section 407 of ERISA) held in the specified subset do not exceed 10 percent of the fair market value of the aggregate assets in the subset. The fair market value of the assets within the specified subset of plan assets approximates the liabilities for benefits that are adjusted by reference to the rate of return on the assets within the subset, determined using reasonable actuarial assumptions, within the meaning of paragraph (d)(5)(ii)(B)(3) of this section. Therefore, the interest crediting rate under the statutory hybrid benefit formula portion of Employer A's defined benefit plan is not in excess of a market rate of return.

Example 2. (i) *Facts.* (a) Pursuant to a collective bargaining agreement, Employer X, Employer Y and Employer Z maintain and contribute to a multiemployer plan (as defined in section 414(f)) that is established as of January 1, 2015 under which benefit accruals are determined under a variable annuity benefit formula. The plan provides that, on an annual basis, the benefit of each participant who has not yet retired is adjusted by reference to the difference between the actual return on the assets within a specified subset of plan assets and 4 percent. A participant's benefits are fixed at retirement and thereafter are not adjusted.

(b) As of the effective date of the plan, there are no assets in the specified subset. Under the terms of the plan, any amount contributed to the plan by a contributing employer is added to the specified subset at the time of the contribution. Investment of the specified subset is diversified so as to minimize the volatility of returns, within the meaning of paragraph (d)(5)(ii)(A) of this section, and no qualifying employer securities or qualifying employer real property (within the meaning of section 407 of ERISA) are held in the subset. The plan provides that, at the time of a participant's retirement, an amount equal to the present value of the liability for benefits payable to that participant is transferred to a separate subset of plan assets (the retiree pool). The retiree pool is invested in high-quality bonds in an attempt to achieve cash-flow matching of the retiree liabilities. Benefits are paid from the retiree pool. However, if assets of the retiree pool are insufficient to pay benefits, the plan provides that assets of the specified subset are available to pay benefits in accordance with the requirement that all assets of the plan be available to pay all plan benefits. Except as described in this paragraph, no other amounts are added to or subtracted from the specified subset of plan assets.

(ii) *Conclusion.* The specified subset is diversified so as to minimize the volatility of returns (within the meaning of paragraph (d)(5)(ii)(A) of this section). The aggregate fair market value of qualifying employer securities and qualifying employer real property (within the meaning of section 407 of ERISA) held in the specified subset do not exceed 10 percent of the fair market value of the aggregate assets in the subset. The fair market value of the assets within the specified subset of plan assets approximates the liabilities for benefits that are adjusted by reference to the rate of return on the assets within the subset, determined using reasonable actuarial assumptions, within the meaning of paragraph (d)(5)(ii)(B)(3) of this section. Therefore, the methodology used to adjust participant benefits under the plan's variable annuity benefit formula, which is a statutory hybrid benefit formula under §1.411(a)(13)-1(d)(4), is not in excess of a market rate of return.

(iii) *Annuity contract rates.*—The rate of return on the annuity contract for the employee issued by an insurance company licensed under the laws of a State is not in excess of a market rate of return. However, this paragraph (d)(5)(iii) does not apply if the Commissioner determines that the annuity contract has been structured to provide an interest crediting rate that is in excess of a market rate of return.

»»→ *Caution: Reg. §1.411(b)(5)-1(d)(5)(iv) generally applies to plan years that begin on or after January 1, 2017 (or an earlier date as elected by the taxpayer).*

(iv) *Rate of return on certain RICs.*—An interest crediting rate is not in excess of a market rate of return if it is equal to the rate of return on a regulated investment company (RIC), as defined in section 851, that is reasonably expected to be not significantly more volatile than the broad United States equities market or a similarly broad international equities market. For example, a RIC that has most of its assets invested in securities of issuers (including other RICs) concentrated in an industry sector or a country other than the United States generally would not meet this requirement. Likewise a RIC that uses leverage, or that has significant investment in derivative financial products, for the purpose of achieving returns that amplify the returns of an unleveraged investment, generally would not meet this requirement. Thus, a RIC that has most of its investments concentrated in the semiconductor industry or that uses leverage in order to provide a rate of return that is twice the rate of return on the Standard & Poor's 500 index (S&P 500) would not meet this requirement. On the other hand, a RIC with investments that track the rate of return on the S&P 500, a broad-based "small-cap" index (such as the Russell 2000 index), or a broad-based international equities index would meet this requirement.

»»→ *Caution: Reg. §1.411(b)(5)-1(d)(6) generally applies to plan years that begin on or after January 1, 2017 (or an earlier date as elected by the taxpayer).*

(6) *Combinations of rates of return.*—(i) *In general.*—A plan that determines interest credits based, in whole or in part, on the greater of two or more different interest crediting rates provides an effective interest crediting rate in excess of a market rate of return unless the combination of rates is described in paragraph (d)(6)(ii), (d)(6)(iii), (e)(3)(iii), or (e)(4) of this section. However, a plan is not treated as providing the greater of two or more interest crediting rates merely because the plan satisfies the requirements of paragraph (d)(2) of this section. In addition, a plan is not treated as providing the greater of two or more interest crediting rates merely because a rate of return described in paragraph (d)(5)(iii) of this section is itself based on the greater of two or more rates.

(ii) *Annual or more frequent floor.*—(A) *Application to segment rates.*—An interest crediting rate under a plan does not fail to be described in paragraph (d)(3) or (d)(4)(iv) of this section for an interest crediting period merely because the plan provides that the interest crediting rate for that interest crediting period equals the greater of—

(1) An interest crediting rate described in paragraph (d)(3) or (d)(4)(iv) of this section; and

(2) An annual interest rate of 4 percent or less (or a pro rata portion of an annual interest rate of 4 percent or less for plans that provide interest credits more frequently than annually).

(B) *Application to other bond-based rates.*—An interest crediting rate under a plan does not fail to be described in paragraph (d)(4) of this section for an interest crediting period merely because the plan provides that the interest crediting rate for that interest crediting period equals the greater of—

(1) An interest crediting rate described in paragraph (d)(4)(ii) or (d)(4)(iii) of this section; and

(2) An annual interest rate of 5 percent or less (or a pro rata portion of an annual interest rate of 5 percent or less for plans that provide interest credits more frequently than annually).

(iii) *Cumulative floor applied to investment-based or bond-based rates.*—(A) *In general.*—A plan that determines interest credits under a statutory hybrid benefit formula using a particular interest crediting rate described in paragraph (d)(3), (d)(4), or (d)(5) of this section (or an interest crediting rate that can never be in excess of a particular interest crediting rate described in paragraph (d)(3), (d)(4) or (d)(5) of this section) does not provide an effective interest crediting rate in excess of a market rate of return merely because the plan provides that the participant's benefit under the statutory hybrid benefit formula determined as of the participant's annuity starting date is equal to the benefit determined as if the accumulated benefit were equal to the greater of—

(1) The accumulated benefit determined using the interest crediting rate; and

(2) The accumulated benefit determined as if the plan had used a fixed annual interest crediting rate equal to 3 percent (or a lower rate) for all principal credits that are credited under the plan to the participant during the guarantee period (minimum guarantee amount).

(B) *Guarantee period defined.*—The guarantee period is the prospective period that begins on the date the cumulative floor described in this paragraph (d)(6)(iii) begins to apply to the participant's benefit and that ends on the date on which that cumulative floor ceases to apply to the participant's benefit.

(C) *Application to multiple annuity starting dates.*—The determination under this paragraph (d)(6)(iii) is made only as of an annuity starting date, within the meaning of §1.401(a)-20, A-10(b), with respect to which a distribution of the participant's entire vested benefit under the plan's statutory hybrid benefit formula as of that date commences. For a participant who has more than one annuity starting date, paragraph (d)(6)(iii)(D) of this section provides rules to account for prior annuity starting dates when applying paragraph (d)(6)(iii)(A) of this section. If the comparison under paragraph (d)(6)(iii)(D) of this section results in the minimum guarantee amount exceeding the sum of the amounts described in paragraphs (d)(6)(iii)(D)(1) through (d)(6)(iii)(D)(3) of this section, then the participant's benefit to be distributed at the current annuity starting date must be no less than would be provided if that excess were included in the current accumulated benefit.

(D) *Comparison to reflect prior distributions.*—For a participant who has more than one annuity starting date, the minimum guarantee amount (described in paragraph (d)(6)(iii)(A)(2) of this section), as of the current annuity starting date, is compared to the sum of—

(1) The remaining balance of the participant's accumulated benefit, as of the current annuity starting date, to which a minimum guaranteed rate described in paragraph (d)(6)(iii)(A)(2) of this section applies;

(2) The amount of the reduction to the participant's accumulated benefit under the statutory hybrid benefit formula that is attributable to any prior distribution of the participant's benefit under that formula and to which a minimum guaranteed rate described in paragraph (d)(6)(iii)(A)(2) of this section applied, together with interest at that minimum guaranteed rate annually from the prior annuity starting date to the current annuity starting date; and

(3) Any amount that was treated as included in the accumulated benefit under the rules of this paragraph (d)(6)(iii) as of any prior annuity starting date, together with interest annually at the minimum guaranteed rate that applied to the prior distribution from the prior annuity starting date to the current annuity starting date.

(E) *Application to portion of participant's benefit.*—A cumulative floor described in this paragraph (d)(6)(iii) may be applied to a portion of a participant's benefit, provided the requirements of this paragraph (d)(6)(iii) are satisfied with respect to that portion of the benefit. If a cumulative floor described in this paragraph (d)(6)(iii) applies to a portion of a participant's benefit, only the principal credits that are attributable to that portion of the participant's benefit are taken into account in determining the amount of the guarantee described in paragraph (d)(6)(iii)(A)(2) of this section.

(e) *Other rules regarding market rates of return.*—(1) *In general.*—This paragraph (e) sets forth additional rules regarding the application of the market rate of return requirement with respect to benefits determined under a statutory hybrid benefit formula.

»»→ *Caution: Reg. §1.411(b)(5)-1(e)(2) generally applies to plan years that begin on or after January 1, 2017 (or an earlier date as elected by the taxpayer).*

(2) *Plan termination.*—(i) *In general.*—This paragraph (e)(2) provides special rules that apply for purposes of determining certain plan factors under a statutory hybrid benefit formula after the plan termination date of a statutory hybrid plan. The terms of a statutory hybrid plan must reflect the requirements of this paragraph (e)(2). Paragraph (e)(2)(ii) of this section sets forth rules relating to the interest crediting rate for interest crediting periods that end after the plan termination date. Paragraph (e)(2)(iii) of this section sets forth rules for converting a participant's accumulated benefit to an annuity after the plan termination date. Paragraph (e)(2)(iv) of this section sets forth rules of application. Paragraph (e)(2)(v) of this section contains examples. The Commissioner may, in revenue rulings, notices, or other guidance published in the Internal Revenue Bulletin, provide for additional rules that apply for purposes of this paragraph (e)(2) and the plan termination provisions of section 411(b)(5)(B)(vi). See §601.601(d)(2)(ii)(b) of this chapter. See also regulations of the Pension Benefit Guaranty Corporation for additional rules that apply when a pension plan subject to Title IV of ERISA is terminated.

»»→ *Caution: Reg. §1.411(b)(5)-1(e)(2) generally applies to plan years that begin on or after January 1, 2017 (or an earlier date as elected by the taxpayer).*

(ii) *Interest crediting rates used to determine accumulated benefits.*—(A) *General rule.*—The interest crediting rate used under the plan to determine a participant's accumulated benefit for interest crediting periods that end after the plan termination date must be equal to the average of the interest rates used under the plan during the 5-year period ending on the plan termination date. Except as otherwise provided in this paragraph (e)(2)(ii), the actual annual interest rate (taking into account minimums, maximums, and other adjustments) used to determine interest credits under the plan for each of the interest crediting periods is used for purposes of determining the average of the interest rates.

(B) *Special rule for variable interest crediting rates that are other rates of return.*—(1) *Application to interest crediting periods.*—This paragraph (e)(2)(ii)(B) applies for an interest crediting period if the interest crediting rate that was used for that interest crediting period was a rate of return described in paragraph (d)(5) of this section. This paragraph (e)(2)(ii)(B) also applies for an interest crediting period that begins before the first plan year described in paragraph (f)(2)(i)(B)(1) or (f)(2)(i)(B)(3) of this section (as applicable), if the interest crediting rate that was used for that interest crediting period had the potential to be negative. For this purpose, a rate is not treated as having the potential to be negative if it is a rate described in paragraph (d)(3) or (d)(4) of this section or is any other rate that is based solely on current bond yields.

(2) *Use of substitution rate.*—For any interest crediting period to which this paragraph (e)(2)(ii)(B) applies, for purposes of determining the average of the interest rates under this paragraph (e)(2)(ii), the interest rate used under the plan for the interest crediting period is deemed to be equal to the substitution rate (as described in paragraph (e)(2)(ii)(C) of this section) for the period.

(C) *Definition of substitution rate.*—The substitution rate for any interest crediting period equals the second segment rate under section 430(h)(2)(C)(ii) (determined without regard to section 430(h)(2)(C)(iv)) for the last calendar month ending before the beginning of the interest crediting period, as adjusted to account for any minimums or maximums that applied in the period (other than cumulative floors under paragraph (d)(6)(iii) of this section), but without regard to other reductions that applied in the period. Thus, for example, if the actual interest crediting rate in an interest crediting period is equal to the rate of return on plan assets, but not greater than 5 percent, then the substitution rate for that interest crediting period is equal to the lesser of the applicable second segment rate for the period and 5 percent. However, if the actual interest crediting rate for an interest crediting period is equal to the rate of return on plan assets minus 200 basis points, then the substitution rate for that interest crediting period is equal to the applicable second segment rate for the period.

(D) *Cumulative floors.*—Cumulative floors under paragraph (d)(6)(iii) of this section that applied during the 5-year period ending on the plan termination date are not taken into account for purposes of determining the average of the interest rates under this paragraph (e)(2)(ii). However, the rules of paragraph (d)(6)(iii) of this section continue to apply to determine benefits as of annuity starting dates on or after the plan termination date. Thus, if, as of an annuity starting date on or after the plan termination date, the benefit provided by applying an applicable cumulative minimum rate under paragraph (d)(6)(iii)(A)(2) of this section exceeds the benefit determined by applying interest credits to the participant's accumulated benefit (with interest credits for interest crediting periods that end after the plan termination date determined under this paragraph (e)(2)), then that cumulative minimum rate is used to determine benefits as of that annuity starting date.

(iii) *Annuity conversion rates and factors.*—(A) *Conversion factors where a separate mortality table was used prior to plan termination.*—(1) *Use of a separate mortality table.*—This paragraph (e)(2)(iii)(A) applies for purposes of converting a participant's accumulated benefit to an annuity after the plan termination date if, for the entire 5-year period ending on the plan termination date, the plan provides for a mortality table in conjunction with an interest rate to be used to convert a participant's accumulated benefit (or a portion thereof) to an annuity. If this paragraph (e)(2)(iii)(A) applies, then the plan is treated as meeting the requirements of section 411(b)(5)(B)(i) and paragraph (d)(1) of this section only if, for purposes of converting a participant's accumulated benefit (or portion thereof) to an annuity for annuity starting dates after the plan termination date, the mortality table used is the table described in paragraph (e)(2)(iii)(A)(2) of this section and the interest rate is the rate described in paragraph (e)(2)(iii)(A)(3) of this section.

(2) *Specific mortality table.*—The mortality table used is the mortality table specified under the plan for purposes of converting a participant's accumulated benefit to an annuity as of the termination date. This mortality table is used regardless of whether it was used during the entire 5-year period ending on the plan termination date. For purposes of applying this paragraph (e)(2)(iii)(A)(2), if the mortality table specified in the plan, as of the plan termination date, is a mortality table that is updated to reflect expected improvements in mortality experience (such as occurs with the applicable mortality table under section 417(e)(3)), then the table used for an annuity starting date after the plan termination date takes into account updates through the annuity starting date.

(3) *Specific interest rate.*—The interest rate used is the interest rate specified under the plan for purposes of converting a participant's accumulated benefit to an annuity for annuity starting dates after the plan termination date. However, if the interest rate used under the plan for purposes of converting a participant's accumulated benefit to an annuity has not been the same fixed rate during the 5-year period ending on the plan termination date, then the interest rate used for purposes of converting a participant's accumulated benefit to an annuity for annuity starting dates after the plan termination date is the average interest rate that applied for this purpose during the 5-year period ending on the plan termination date.

(B) *Tabular factors.*—If, as of the plan termination date, a tabular annuity conversion factor (i.e., a single conversion factor that combines the effect of interest and mortality) is used to convert a participant's accumulated benefit (or a portion thereof) to an annuity and that same fixed tabular annuity conversion factor has been used during the entire 5-year period ending on the plan termination date, then the plan satisfies the requirements of this paragraph (e)(2)(iii) only if that same tabular annuity conversion factor continues to apply after the plan termination date. However, if the tabular annuity conversion factor used to convert a participant's accumulated benefit (or a portion thereof) to an annuity is not described in the preceding sentence (including any case in which the tabular annuity conversion factor was a fixed conversion factor that changed during the 5-year period ending on the plan termination date), then the plan satisfies the requirements of this paragraph (e)(2)(iii) only if the tabular annuity conversion factor used to convert a participant's accumulated benefit (or a portion thereof) to an annuity for annuity starting dates after the plan termination date is equal to the average of the tabular annuity conversion factors used under the plan for that purpose during the 5-year period ending on the plan termination date.

(C) *Factor applicable where a separate mortality table was not used for entire 5-year period prior to plan termination.*—If paragraph (e)(2)(iii)(A) of this section does not apply (including any case in which a separate mortality table was used in conjunction with a separate interest rate to convert a participant's accumulated benefit (or a portion thereof) to an annuity for only a portion of the 5-year period ending on the plan termination date), then the plan is treated as having used a tabular annuity conversion factor to convert a participant's accumulated benefit (or a portion thereof) to an annuity for the entire 5-year period ending on the plan termination date. As a result, the rules of paragraph (e)(2)(iii)(B) of this section apply to determine the annuity conversion factor used for purposes of converting a participant's accumulated benefit (or portion thereof) to an annuity for annuity starting dates after the plan termination date. For this purpose, if a separate mortality table and separate interest rate applied for a portion of the 5-year period, that mortality table and interest rate are used to calculate an annuity conversion factor and that factor is treated as having been the tabular annuity conversion factor that applied for that portion of the 5-year period for purposes of this paragraph (e)(2)(iii).

(D) *Separate application with respect to optional forms.*—This paragraph (e)(2)(iii) applies separately with respect to each optional form of benefit on the date of plan termination. For this purpose, the term optional form of benefit has the meaning given that term in §1.411(d)-3(g)(6)(ii), except that a change in the annuity conversion factor used to determine a particular benefit is disregarded in determining whether different optional forms exist. Thus, for example, if, for the entire 5-year period ending on the plan termination date, the plan provides for a mortality table in conjunction with an interest rate to be used to determine annuities other than qualified joint and survivor annuities, but for specified tabular factors to apply to determine annuities that are qualified joint and survivor annuities, then paragraph (e)(2)(iii)(A) of this section applies for purposes of annuities other than qualified joint and survivor annuities and paragraph (e)(2)(iii)(B) of this section applies for purposes of annuities that are

»»→ Caution: Reg. §1.411(b)(5)-1(e)(2) generally applies to plan years that begin on or after January 1, 2017 (or an earlier date as elected by the taxpayer).

qualified joint and survivor annuities. In addition, if the annuity conversion factor used to determine a particular qualified joint and survivor annuity has changed in the 5-year period ending on the plan termination date, the different factors are averaged for purposes of determining the annuity conversion factor that applies after plan termination for that particular qualified joint and survivor annuity.

(iv) *Rules of application.*—(A) *Average of interest rates for crediting interest.*—(1) *In general.*—For purposes of determining the average of the interest rates under paragraph (e)(2)(ii) of this section, an interest crediting period is taken into account if the interest crediting date for the interest crediting period is within the 5-year period ending on the plan termination date. The average of the interest rates is determined as the arithmetic average of the annual interest rates used for those interest crediting periods. If the interest crediting periods taken into account are not all the same length, then each rate is weighted to reflect the length of the interest crediting period in which it applied. If the plan provides for the crediting of interest more frequently than annually, then interest credits after the plan termination date must be prorated in accordance with the rules of paragraph (d)(1)(iv)(C) of this section.

(2) *Section 411(d)(6) protected accumulated benefit.*—In general, the interest rate that was used for each interest crediting period is the ongoing interest crediting rate that was specified under the plan for that period, without regard to any interest rate that was used prior to an amendment changing the interest crediting rate with respect to a section 411(d)(6) protected benefit. However, if, as of the end of the last interest crediting period that ends on or before the plan termination date, the participant's accumulated benefit is based on a section 411(d)(6) protected benefit that results from a prior amendment to change the rate of interest crediting applicable under the plan, then the pre-amendment interest rate is treated as having been used for each interest crediting period after the date of the interest crediting rate change (so that the amendment is disregarded).

(B) *Average annuity conversion rates and factors.*—(1) *In general.*—For purposes of determining average annuity conversion interest rates and average tabular annuity conversion factors under paragraph (e)(2)(iii) of this section, an interest rate or tabular annuity conversion factor is taken into account if the rate or conversion factor applied under the terms of the plan to convert a participant's accumulated benefit (or a portion thereof) to a benefit payable in the form of an annuity during the 5-year period ending on the plan termination date. The average is determined as the arithmetic average of the interest rates or tabular factors used during that period. If the periods in which the rates or factors that are averaged are not all the same length, then each rate or factor is weighted to reflect the length of the period in which it applied.

(2) *Section 411(d)(6) protected annuity conversion factors.*—In general, the annuity conversion interest rate or tabular annuity conversion factor that was used for each period is the ongoing interest rate or tabular factor that was specified under the plan for that period, without regard to any rate or factor that was used under the plan prior to an amendment changing the rate or factor with respect to a section 411(d)(6) protected benefit. However, if, as of the plan termination date, the participant's annuity benefit for an annuity commencing at that date would be based on a section 411(d)(6) protected benefit that results from a prior amendment to change the rate or factor under the plan, then the pre-amendment rate or factor is treated as having been used after the date of the amendment (so that the amendment is disregarded).

(C) *Blended rates.*—If, as of the plan termination date, the plan determines interest credits by applying different rates to two or more different predetermined portions of the accumulated benefit, then the interest crediting rate that applies after the plan termination date is determined separately with respect to each portion under the rules of paragraph (e)(2)(ii) of this section.

(D) *Participants with less than 5 years of interest credits upon plan termination.*—If the plan provided for interest credits for any interest crediting period in which, pursuant to the terms of the plan, an individual was not eligible to receive interest credits (including because the individual was not a participant or beneficiary in the relevant interest crediting period), then, for purposes of determining the individual's average interest crediting rate under paragraph (e)(2)(ii) of this section, the individual is treated as though the individual received interest credits in that period using the interest crediting rate that applied in that period under the terms of the plan to a similarly situated participant or beneficiary who was eligible to receive interest credits.

(E) *Plan termination date.*—(1) *Plans subject to Title IV of ERISA.*—In the case of a plan that is subject to Title IV of ERISA, the plan termination date for purposes of this paragraph (e)(2) means the plan's termination date established under section 4048(a) of ERISA.

(2) *Other plans.*—In the case of a plan that is not subject to Title IV of ERISA, the plan termination date for purposes of this paragraph (e)(2) means the plan's termination date established by the plan administrator, provided that the plan termination date may be no earlier than the date on which the actions necessary to effect the plan termination - other than the distribution of plan benefits - are taken. However, a plan is not treated as terminated on the plan's termination date if the assets are not distributed as soon as administratively feasible after that date. See Rev. Rul. 89-87 (1989-2 CB 2), (see §601.601(d)(2)(ii)(*b*) of this chapter).

(v) *Examples.*—The following examples illustrate the rules of this paragraph (e)(2). In each case, it is assumed that the plan is terminated in a standard termination.

Example 1. (i) *Facts.* (A) Plan A is a defined benefit plan with a calendar plan year that expresses each participant's accumulated benefit in the form of a hypothetical account balance to which principal credits are made at the end of each calendar quarter and to which interest is credited at the end of each calendar quarter based on the balance at the beginning of the quarter. Interest credits under Plan A are based on a rate of interest fixed at the beginning of each plan year equal to the third segment rate for the preceding December, except that the plan used the rate of interest on 30-year Treasury bonds (instead of the third segment rate) for plan years before 2013. The plan is terminated on March 3, 2017.

(B) The third segment rate credited under Plan A from January 1, 2013, through December 31, 2016, is assumed to be: 6 percent annually for each of the four quarters in 2016; 6.5 percent annually for each of the four quarters in 2015; 6 percent annually for each of the four quarters in 2014; and 5.5 percent annually for each of the four quarters in 2013. The rate of interest on 30-year Treasury bonds credited under Plan A for each of the four quarters in 2012 is assumed to be 4.4 percent annually.

(ii) *Conclusion.* Pursuant to paragraph (e)(2)(ii) of this section, the interest crediting rate used to determine accrued benefits under the plan on and after the date of plan termination is an annual rate of 5.68 percent (which is the arithmetic average of 6 percent, 6.5 percent, 6 percent, 5.5 percent, and 4.4 percent). In accordance with the rules of paragraph (d)(1)(iv)(C) of this section, the quarterly interest crediting rate after the plan termination date is 1.42 percent (5.68 divided by 4).

Example 2. (i) *Facts.* The facts are the same as *Example 1.* Participant S, who terminated employment before January 1, 2017, has a hypothetical account balance of $100,000 when the plan is terminated on March 3, 2017. Participant S commences distribution in the form of a straight life annuity commencing on January 1, 2020. For the entire 5-year period ending on the plan termination date, the plan has provided that the applicable section 417(e) rates for the preceding August are applied on the annuity starting date in order to convert the hypothetical account balance to an annuity. Based on the 5-year averages of the first segment rates, the second segment rates, and the third segment rates as of the plan termination date, and the applicable mortality table for the year 2020, the resulting conversion rate at the January 1, 2020 annuity starting date is 166.67 for a monthly straight life annuity payable to a participant whose age is the age of Participant S on January 1, 2020.

(ii) *Conclusion.* In accordance with the conclusion in *Example 1,* the interest crediting rate after the plan termination date is 1.42 percent for each of the 12 quarterly interest crediting dates in the period from March 3, 2017, through December 31, 2019, so that Participant S's account balance is $118,436 on December 31, 2019. As a result, using the annuity conversion rate of 166.67, the amount payable to Participant S commencing on January 1, 2020 is $711 per month.

Example 3. (i) *Facts.* The facts are the same as *Example 1.* In addition, Participant T commenced participation in Plan A on April 17, 2014.

(ii) *Conclusion.* In accordance with the conclusion in *Example 1* and the rule of paragraph (e)(2)(iv)(D) of this section, the quarterly interest crediting rate used to determine Participant T's accrued benefits under Plan A on and after the date of plan termination is 1.42 percent, which is the same rate that applies to all participants and beneficiaries in Plan A after the termination date (and that would have applied to Participant T if Participant T had participated in the plan during the 5-year period preceding the date of plan termination).

Example 4. (i) *Facts.* (A) Plan B is a defined benefit plan with a calendar plan year that expresses each participant's accumulated

⟫⟫→ *Caution: Reg. §1.411(b)(5)-1(e)(2) generally applies to plan years that begin on or after January 1, 2017 (or an earlier date as elected by the taxpayer).*

benefit in the form of a hypothetical account balance to which principal credits are made at the end of each calendar year and to which interest is credited at the end of each calendar year based on the balance at the end of the preceding year. The plan is terminated on January 27, 2018.

(B) The plan's interest crediting rate for each calendar year during the entire 5-year period ending on the plan termination date is equal to (A) 50 percent of the greater of the rate of interest on 3-month Treasury Bills for the preceding December and an annual rate of 4 percent, plus (B) 50 percent of the rate of return on plan assets. The rate of interest on 3-month Treasury Bills credited under Plan B is assumed to be: 3.4 percent for 2017; 4 percent for 2016; 4.5 percent for 2015; 3.5 percent for 2014; and 4.2 percent for 2013. Each of these rates applied under Plan B for purposes of determining the interest credits described in clause (A) of this paragraph (i), except that the 4 percent minimum rate applied for 2017 and 2014. The second segment rate is assumed to be: 6 percent for December 2016; 6 percent for December 2015; 6.5 percent for December 2014; 6 percent for December 2013; and 5.5 percent for December 2012.

(ii) *Conclusion.* Pursuant to paragraph (e)(2)(ii) of this section, the interest crediting rate used to determine accrued benefits under the plan on and after the date of plan termination is 5.07 percent. This number is equal to the sum of 50 percent of 4.14 percent (which is the sum of 4 percent, 4 percent, 4.5 percent, 4 percent, and 4.2 percent, divided by 5), and 50 percent of 6 percent (which is the average second segment rate applicable for the 5 interest crediting periods ending within the 5-year period, as applied pursuant to the substitution rule described in paragraphs (e)(2)(ii)(B) and (C) of this section).

Example 5. (i) *Facts.* The facts are the same as in *Example 4*, except that the plan had credited interest before January 1, 2016, using the rate of return on a specified RIC and had been amended effective January 1, 2016, to base interest credits for all plan years after 2015 on the interest rate formula described in paragraph (i) of *Example 4*. In order to comply with section 411(d)(6), the plan provides that, for each participant or beneficiary who was a participant on December 31, 2015, benefits at any date are based on either the ongoing hypothetical account balance on that date (which is based on the December 31, 2015 balance, with interest credited thereafter at the rate described in the first sentence of paragraph (i) of *Example 4* and taking principal credits after 2015 into account) or a special hypothetical account balance (the pre-2016 balance) on that date, whichever balance is greater. For each participant, the pre-2016 balance is a hypothetical account balance equal to the participant's December 31, 2015 balance, with interest credited thereafter at the RIC rate of return, but with no principal credits after 2015. There are 10 participants for whom the pre-2016 balance exceeds the ongoing hypothetical account balance at the end of 2017 (which is the end of the last interest crediting period that ends on or before the January 27, 2018, plan termination date).

(ii) *Conclusion.* Because Plan B credited interest prior to 2016 using the rate of return on a RIC (a rate described in paragraph (d)(5) of this section), for purposes of determining the average interest crediting rate upon plan termination, the interest crediting rate used to determine accrued benefits under Plan B for all participants during those periods (for the calendar years 2013, 2014, and 2015) is equal to the second segment rate for December of the calendar year preceding each interest crediting period. In addition, because the pre-2016 balances exceeded the ongoing hypothetical account balance for 10 participants in the last interest crediting period prior to plan termination, for purposes of determining the average interest crediting rate upon plan termination, the interest crediting rate used to determine accrued benefits under Plan B for 2016 and 2017 for those participants is equal to the second segment rate for December 2015 and December 2016, respectively. For all other participants, for purposes of determining the average interest crediting rate upon plan termination, the interest crediting rate used to determine accrued benefits under Plan B for 2016 and 2017 is based on the ongoing interest crediting rate (as described in *Example 4*).

(3) *Rules relating to section 411(d)(6).*—(i) *General rule.*—The right to future interest credits determined in the manner specified under the plan and not conditioned on future service is a factor that is used to determine the participant's accrued benefit, for purposes of section 411(d)(6). Thus, to the extent that benefits have accrued under the terms of a statutory hybrid plan that entitle the participant to future interest credits, an amendment to the plan to change the interest crediting rate must satisfy section 411(d)(6) if the revised rate under any circumstances could result in interest credits that are smaller as of any date after the applicable amendment date (within the meaning of §1.411(d)-3(g)(4)) than the interest credits that would be provided without regard to the amendment. For additional rules, see §1.411(d)-3(b). Paragraphs (e)(3)(ii) through (e)(3)(vi) of this section set forth special rules that apply regarding the interaction of section 411(d)(6) and changes to a plan's interest crediting rate. The Commissioner may, in guidance of general applicability, prescribe additional rules regarding the interaction of section 411(d)(6) and section 411(b)(5), including changes to a plan's interest crediting rate. See §601.601(d)(2)(ii)(*b*).

(ii) *Adoption of long-term investment grade corporate bond rate.*— For purposes of applying section 411(d)(6) and this paragraph (e) to an amendment to change to the interest crediting rate described in paragraph (d)(3) of this section, a plan is not treated as providing interest credits that are smaller as of any date after the applicable amendment date than the interest credits that would be provided using an interest crediting rate described in paragraph (d)(4) of this section merely because the plan credits interest after the applicable amendment date using the interest crediting rate described in paragraph (d)(3) of this section, provided—

(A) The amendment only applies to interest credits to be credited after the effective date of the amendment;

(B) The effective date of the amendment is at least 30 days after adoption of the amendment;

(C) On the effective date of the amendment, the new interest crediting rate is not lower than the interest crediting rate that would have applied in the absence of the amendment; and

(D) For plan years described in paragraph (f)(2)(i)(B)(*1*) or (f)(2)(i)(B)(3) of this section (as applicable), if prior to the amendment the plan used a fixed annual floor in connection with a rate described in paragraph (d)(4)(ii), (iii) or (iv) of this section (as permitted under paragraph (d)(6)(ii) of this section), the floor is retained after the amendment to the maximum extent permissible under paragraph (d)(6)(ii)(A) of this section.

⟫⟫→ *Caution: Reg. §1.411(b)(5)-1(e)(3)(iii) generally applies to plan years that begin on or after January 1, 2017 (or an earlier date as elected by the taxpayer).*

(iii) *Coordination of section 411(d)(6) and market rate of return limitation.*—(A) *In general.*—An amendment to a statutory hybrid plan that preserves a section 411(d)(6) protected benefit is subject to the rules under paragraph (d) of this section relating to market rate of return. However, in the case of an amendment to change a plan's interest crediting rate for periods after the applicable amendment date from one interest crediting rate (the old rate) that satisfies the requirements of paragraph (d) of this section to another interest crediting rate (the new rate) that satisfies the requirements of paragraph (d) of this section, the plan's effective interest crediting rate is not in excess of a market rate of return for purposes of paragraph (d) of this section merely because the plan provides for the benefit of any participant who is benefiting under the plan (within the meaning of §1.410(b)-3(a)) on the applicable amendment date to never be less than what it would be if the old rate had continued but without taking into account any principal credits (as defined in paragraph (d)(1)(ii)(D) of this section) after the applicable amendment date.

(B) *Multiple amendments.*—A pattern of repeated plan amendments each of which provides for a prospective change in the plan's interest crediting rate with respect to the benefit as of the applicable amendment date will be treated as resulting in the ongoing plan terms providing for an effective interest crediting rate that is in excess of a market rate of return. See §1.411(d)-4, A-1(c)(1).

⟫⟫→ *Caution: Reg. §1.411(b)(5)-1(e)(3)(iv) generally applies to plan years that begin on or after January 1, 2017 (or an earlier date as elected by the taxpayer).*

(iv) *Change in lookback month or stability period used to determine interest credits.*—(A) *Section 411(d)(6) anti-cutback relief.*—With respect to a plan using an interest crediting rate described in paragraph (d)(3) or (d)(4) of this section, notwithstanding the general rule of paragraph (e)(3)(i) of this section, if a plan amendment changes the lookback month or stability period used to determine interest credits, the amendment is not treated as reducing accrued benefits in violation of section 411(d)(6) merely on account of this change if the conditions of this paragraph (e)(3)(iv)(A) are satisfied. If the plan amendment is effective on or after the adoption date, any interest credits credited for the one-year period commencing on the date the amendment is effective must be determined using the lookback month and stability period provided under the plan before the amendment or the lookback month and stability period after the amendment, whichever results in the larger interest credits. If the plan amendment is adopted retroactively (that is, the amendment is

⋙→ *Caution: Reg. §1.411(b)(5)-1(e)(3)(iv) generally applies to plan years that begin on or after January 1, 2017 (or an earlier date as elected by the taxpayer).*

effective prior to the adoption date), the plan must use the lookback month and stability period resulting in the larger interest credits for the period beginning with the effective date and ending one year after the adoption date.

(B) *Section 411(b)(5)(B)(i)(I) market rate of return relief.*—The plan's effective interest crediting rate is not in excess of a market rate of return for purposes of paragraph (d) of this section merely because

⋙→ *Caution: Reg. §1.411(b)(5)-1(e)(3)(v) generally applies to plan years that begin on or after January 1, 2017 (or an earlier date as elected by the taxpayer).*

(v) *RIC ceasing to exist.*—This paragraph (e)(3)(v) applies in the case of a statutory hybrid plan that credits interest using an interest crediting rate equal to the rate of return on a RIC (pursuant to paragraph (d)(5)(iv) of this section) that ceases to exist, whether as a result of a name change, liquidation, or otherwise. In such a case, the plan is not treated as violating section 411(d)(6) provided that the rate of return on the successor RIC is substituted for the rate of return on the RIC that no longer exists, for purposes of crediting interest for periods after the date the RIC ceased to exist. In the case of a name change or merger of RICs, the successor RIC means the RIC that results from the name change or merger involving the RIC that no longer exists. In all other cases, the successor RIC is a RIC selected by the plan sponsor that has reasonably similar characteristics, including characteristics related to risk and rate of return, as the RIC that no longer exists.

(vi) *Transitional amendments needed to satisfy the market rate of return rules.*—(A) *In general.*—Notwithstanding the requirements of section 411(d)(6), if the requirements set forth in this paragraph (e)(3)(vi) are satisfied, a plan may be amended to change its interest crediting rate with respect to benefits that have already accrued in order to comply with the requirements of section 411(b)(5)(B)(i) and paragraph (d) of this section. A plan amendment is eligible for the treatment provided under this paragraph (e)(3)(vi)(A) to the extent that the amendment modifies an interest crediting rate that does not satisfy the requirements of section 411(b)(5)(B)(i) and paragraph (d) of this section in the manner specified in paragraph (e)(3)(vi)(C) of this section.

(B) *Rules of application.*—(1) *Multiple noncompliant features.*—If a plan's interest crediting rate has more than one noncompliant feature as described in paragraph (e)(3)(vi)(C) of this section, then each noncompliant feature must be addressed separately in the manner specified in paragraph (e)(3)(vi)(C) of this section.

(2) *Definition of investment-based rate.*—The application of the rules of paragraph (e)(3)(vi)(C) of this section to an interest crediting rate depends on whether the interest crediting rate is an investment-based rate. For purposes of this paragraph (e)(3)(vi), an investment-based rate is a rate based on either a rate of return provided by actual investments (taking into account the return attributable to any change in the value of the underlying investments) or a rate of return for an index that measures the change in the value of investments. A rate is an investment-based rate even if it is based only in part on a rate described in the preceding sentence.

(3) *Timing rules for permitted amendments.*—The rules under this paragraph (e)(3)(vi) apply only to a plan amendment that is adopted prior to and effective no later than the first day of the first plan year described in paragraph (f)(2)(i)(B)(1) or (f)(2)(i)(B)(3) of this section, as applicable. In addition, the rules under this paragraph (e)(3)(vi) apply to a plan amendment only with respect to interest credits that are credited for interest crediting periods that begin on or after the applicable amendment date (within the meaning of §1.411(d)-3(g)(4)).

(4) *Amendments that provide for greater interest crediting rates.*—If a plan is amended in accordance with paragraphs (e)(3)(vi)(C)(1) through (10) of this section to switch from a noncompliant rate to a compliant rate and is subsequently amended to switch to a second compliant rate that can never be less than the first compliant rate, then the second amendment does not violate section 411(d)(6). If, instead, the plan is amended to switch from the noncompliant rate to the second compliant rate in a single amendment, that amendment also does not violate section 411(d)(6). For example, if it is permitted under paragraph (e)(3)(vi)(C) of this section to first amend the plan to credit interest using the lesser of the current rate and a rate described in paragraph (d)(3) of this section, it is then permissible to amend the plan to credit interest using that rate described in paragraph (d)(3) of this section. In such a case, it is also permissible to amend the plan to switch from the current rate to a rate described in paragraph (d)(3) of this section in a single amendment.

a plan amendment complies with the requirements of paragraph (e)(3)(iv)(A) of this section. However, a pattern of repeated plan amendments each of which provides for a change in the lookback month or stability period used to determine interest credits will be treated as resulting in the ongoing plan terms providing for an effective interest crediting rate that is in excess of a market rate of return. See §1.411(d)-4, A-1(c)(1).

(5) *Cumulative floors, including floors resulting from a prior change in rates with section 411(d)(6) protection.*—This paragraph (e)(3)(vi)(B)(5) applies to a plan that takes into account a minimum rate of return that applies less frequently than annually. This paragraph (e)(3)(vi)(B)(5) also applies to a plan that determines the participant's benefit as of the annuity starting date as the benefit provided by the greatest of two or more account balances (for example, in order to comply with section 411(d)(6) in connection with a prior amendment to change the plan's interest crediting rate). In either case, this paragraph (e)(3)(vi)(3)(5) applies with respect to a participant only if the requirements of paragraph (d)(6) of this section are not satisfied with respect to that participant. If this paragraph (e)(3)(vi)(B)(5) applies with respect to a participant, the plan must be amended to provide that the benefit for the participant is based solely on the benefit (and the associated interest crediting rate with respect to that benefit) that is greatest for that participant as of the applicable amendment date for the amendment made pursuant to this paragraph (e)(3)(vi). In addition, the plan must be further amended pursuant to the other rules in this paragraph (e)(3)(vi) if the remaining interest crediting rate does not satisfy the requirements of paragraph (d) of this section.

(6) *Plans that permit participant direction of interest crediting rates.*—This paragraph (e)(3)(vi)(B)(6) applies in the case in which a plan permits a participant to choose an interest crediting rate from among a menu of hypothetical investment options and at least one of those hypothetical investment options provides for an interest crediting rate that is not permitted under paragraph (d) of this section (so that the plan fails to satisfy the requirements of paragraph (d) of this section). In such a case, the rules of this paragraph (e)(3)(vi) may be applied separately to correct each impermissible investment option. Alternatively, with respect to such a plan that permitted a participant to choose an interest crediting rate from among a menu of hypothetical investment options on September 18, 2014, pursuant to plan provisions that were adopted on or before September 18, 2014, the entire menu of investment options may be treated as an impermissible investment-based rate for which there is no permitted investment-based rate with similar risk and return characteristics (so that the rule of paragraph (e)(3)(vi)(C)(7) of this section does not apply). As a result, plans described in the preceding sentence may be amended to eliminate a participant's ability to choose an interest crediting rate from among a menu of hypothetical investment options in accordance with paragraph (e)(3)(vi)(C)(9) of this section.

(C) *Noncompliant feature and amendment to bring plan into compliance.*—(1) *Timing or other rules related to determining interest credits not satisfied.*—If a plan has an underlying interest rate that generally satisfies the rules of paragraph (d) of this section but that does not satisfy the rules relating to how interest credits are determined and credited as set forth in paragraph (d)(1)(iv) of this section, then the plan must be amended either—

(i) To correct the aspect of the plan's interest crediting rate that fails to comply with the rules of paragraph (d)(1)(iv) of this section with respect to its underlying interest crediting rate; or

(ii) If the plan's interest crediting rate is a variable rate that is not an investment-based rate of return, to provide that the plan's interest crediting rate is the lesser of that variable rate and a rate described in paragraph (d)(3) of this section that satisfies the rules of paragraph (d)(1)(iv) of this section.

(2) *Fixed rate in excess of 6 percent.*—If a plan's interest crediting rate is a fixed rate in excess of the rate described in paragraph (d)(4)(v) of this section, then the plan must be amended to reduce the interest crediting rate to an annual interest crediting rate of 6 percent.

(3) *Bond-based rate with margin exceeding maximum permitted margin.*—If a plan's interest crediting rate is a noncompliant rate that consists of an underlying rate described in paragraph (d)(3) or (d)(4) of this section except that the plan applies a margin that exceeds the maximum permitted margin under paragraph (d)(3) or (d)(4) of this section to the underlying rate, then the plan must be amended either—

(*i*) To reduce the margin to the maximum permitted margin for the underlying rate used by the plan; or

(*ii*) To provide that the plan's interest crediting rate is the lesser of the plan's noncompliant rate and a rate described in paragraph (d)(3) of this section (together with any fixed minimum rate that was part of the noncompliant rate, reduced to the extent necessary to comply with paragraph (d)(6)(ii) of this section).

(*4*) *Bond-based rate with fixed minimum rate applied on an annual or more frequent basis in excess of the highest permitted fixed minimum rate.*—If a plan's interest crediting rate is a composite rate that consists of a variable rate described in paragraph (d)(3) or (d)(4) of this section in combination with a fixed minimum rate in excess of the highest permitted fixed minimum rate under paragraph (d)(6)(ii)(A)(2) or (B)(2) of this section (as applicable), then the plan must be amended in one of the following manners:

(*i*) To reduce the fixed minimum rate to the highest permitted fixed minimum rate that may be used in combination with the plan's variable rate;

(*ii*) To credit interest using an annual interest crediting rate of 6 percent; or

(*iii*) To provide that the plan's interest crediting rate is the lesser of the plan's noncompliant composite rate and a rate described in paragraph (d)(3) of this section (together with a fixed minimum rate of 4 percent).

(*5*) *Greatest of two or more variable bond-based rates.*—If a plan's interest crediting rate is a composite rate that is the greatest of two or more variable rates described in paragraph (d)(3) or (d)(4) of this section, then the plan must be amended to provide for an interest crediting rate that is the lesser of the composite rate and a rate described in paragraph (d)(3) of this section.

(*6*) *Other impermissible bond-based rates.*—If, after application of the rules of paragraphs (e)(3)(vi)(C)(*1*) through (*5*) of this section, a plan's interest crediting rate is a variable rate that is not an investment-based rate of return and is not described in paragraph (d)(3) or (d)(4) of this section, then the plan must be amended either—

(*i*) To provide for an interest crediting rate based on a variable rate described in paragraph (d)(3) or (d)(4) of this section that has similar duration and quality characteristics as the plan's variable rate, if such a rate can be selected; or

(*ii*) To provide for an interest crediting rate that is the lesser of the plan's variable rate and a rate described in paragraph (d)(3) of this section.

(*7*) *Impermissible investment-based rate that can be replaced with a permissible rate that has similar risk and return characteristics.*—If a plan's interest crediting rate is an investment-based rate of return that is not described in paragraph (d)(5) of this section and a permitted investment-based rate described in paragraph (d)(5)(ii)(A), (d)(5)(ii)(B), or (d)(5)(iv) of this section that has similar risk and return characteristics as the plan's impermissible investment-based rate can be selected, then the plan must be amended to provide for an interest crediting rate based on such a permitted investment-based rate.

(*8*) *Investment-based rate with an annual or more frequent minimum rate that is either a fixed rate or a non-investment based variable rate.*—If a plan's interest crediting rate is an investment-based rate of return that would be described in paragraph (d)(5) of this section except that the plan uses an annual or more frequent minimum rate that is either a fixed rate or a non-investment based variable rate in conjunction with the investment-based rate, then the plan must be amended either—

(*i*) To credit interest using that investment-based rate of return described in paragraph (d)(5) of this section without the minimum rate and eliminating any reduction (or other adjustment) to the investment-based rate; or

(*ii*) To provide that the plan's interest crediting rate is a rate described in paragraph (d)(3) of this section (together with any fixed minimum rate, reduced to the extent necessary to comply with paragraph (d)(6)(ii) of this section).

(*9*) *Other impermissible investment-based rates.*—If, after application of the rules of paragraphs (e)(3)(vi)(C)(*1*), (*7*), and (*8*) of this section, a plan's interest crediting rate is an investment-based rate that is not described in paragraph (d)(5) of this section, then the plan must be amended either—

(*i*) To provide for an interest crediting rate that is an investment-based rate that is described in paragraph (d)(5) of this section and that is otherwise similar to the plan's impermissible investment-based rate but without the risk and return characteristics of the impermissible investment-based rate that caused it to be impermissible (generally requiring the use of a rate that is less

volatile than the plan's impermissible investment-based rate but is otherwise similar to that rate); or

(*ii*) To provide that the plan's interest crediting rate is a rate described in paragraph (d)(3) of this section with a fixed minimum rate of 4 percent.

(D) *Examples.*—The following examples illustrate the application of the rules of this paragraph (e)(3)(vi). Each plan has a plan year that is the calendar year, and all amendments are adopted on October 1, 2016, and become effective for interest crediting periods beginning on or after January 1, 2017. Except as otherwise provided, the interest crediting rate under the plan satisfies the timing and other rules related to crediting interest under paragraph (d)(1)(iv) of this section.

Example 1. (i) *Facts.* A plan determines interest credits for a plan year using the average yield on 30-year Treasury Constant Maturities for the last week of the preceding plan year (which is an impermissible lookback period for this purpose pursuant to paragraph (d)(1)(iv)(B) of this section because it is not a month).

(ii) *Conclusion.* Pursuant to paragraph (e)(3)(vi)(C)(*1*) of this section, the plan must be amended in one of two manners. It may be amended to determine interest credits for a plan year using the average yield on 30-year Treasury Constant Maturities for a lookback month that complies with the requirements of paragraph (d)(1)(iv)(B) of this section. Alternatively, the plan may be amended to cap the existing rate so that it cannot exceed a third segment rate described in paragraph (d)(3) of this section for a period that complies with the requirements of paragraph (d)(1)(iv)(B) of this section.

Example 2. (i) *Facts.* A plan determines interest credits for a plan year using the average yield on 30-year Treasury Constant Maturities for the last week of the preceding plan year, plus 50 basis points.

(ii) *Conclusion.* Pursuant to paragraph (e)(3)(vi)(B)(*1*) of this section, the plan must be amended to correct both the impermissible lookback period and the excess margin. Accordingly, pursuant to paragraph (e)(3)(vi)(C)(*1*) and (*3*) of this section, the plan may be amended to determine interest credits for a plan year using the average yield on 30-year Treasury Constant Maturities (with no margin) for a period that complies with the requirements of paragraph (d)(1)(iv)(B) of this section. Alternatively, the plan may be amended to cap the existing rate so that it cannot exceed a third segment rate described in paragraph (d)(3) of this section for a period that complies with the requirements of paragraph (d)(1)(iv)(B) of this section.

Example 3. (i) *Facts.* A plan credits interest for a plan year using the rate of return on plan assets for the preceding plan year.

(ii) *Conclusion.* Pursuant to paragraph (e)(3)(vi)(C)(*1*) of this section, the plan must be amended to determine interest credits for each plan year using the rate of return on plan assets for that plan year.

Example 4. (i) *Facts.* A plan credits interest using the average yield on 30-year Treasury Constant Maturities for December of the preceding plan year with a minimum rate of 5.5 percent per year.

(ii) *Conclusion.* Pursuant to paragraph (e)(3)(vi)(C)(*4*) of this section, the plan must be amended to change the plan's interest crediting rate. The new interest crediting rate under the plan may be the average yield on 30-year Treasury Constant Maturities for December of the preceding plan year with a minimum rate of 5 percent per year. Alternatively, the new interest crediting rate under the plan may be an annual interest crediting rate of 6 percent. As another alternative, the existing noncompliant composite rate may be capped so that it cannot exceed a third segment rate described in paragraph (d)(3) of this section, with a minimum rate of 4 percent as a floor on the entire resulting rate.

Example 5. (i) *Facts.* A plan credits interest using the greater of the unadjusted yield on 30-year Treasury Constant Maturities and the yield on 1-year Treasury Constant Maturities plus 100 basis points.

(ii) *Conclusion.* Pursuant to paragraph (e)(3)(vi)(C)(*5*) of this section, the plan must be amended to cap the existing composite "greater-of" rate so that the composite rate cannot exceed a third segment rate described in paragraph (d)(3) of this section.

Example 6. (i) *Facts.* A plan credits interest using a broad-based index that measures the yield to maturity on a group of intermediate-term investment grade corporate bonds.

(ii) *Conclusion.* Pursuant to paragraph (e)(3)(vi)(C)(*6*) of this section, the plan must be amended in one of two manners. The plan may be amended to credit interest using a second segment rate described in paragraph (d)(4)(iv) of this section. Alternatively, the plan may be amended to cap the existing rate so that it cannot exceed a third segment rate described in paragraph (d)(3) of this section.

Example 7. (i) *Facts.* A plan credits interest using the rate of return for a broad-based index that measures the yield to maturity on a group of short-term non-investment grade corporate bonds.

(ii) *Conclusion.* Pursuant to paragraph (e)(3)(vi)(C)(*6*)(*ii*) of this section, the plan must be amended to cap the existing rate so that it cannot exceed a third segment rate described in paragraph (d)(3) of this section.

Example 8. (i) *Facts.* A plan credits interest using the rate of return for the S&P 500 index. To bring the plan into compliance with the market rate of return rules, the plan sponsor amends the plan to credit interest based on the rate of return on a RIC that is designed to track the rate of return on the S&P 500 index.

(ii) *Conclusion.* The amendment satisfies the rule of paragraph (e)(3)(vi)(C)(7) of this section.

Example 9. (i) *Facts.* A plan credits interest based on the rate of return on a collective trust that holds a portfolio of equity investments, which provides a rate of return that is reasonably expected to be not significantly more volatile than the broad U.S. equities market or a similarly broad international equities market. To bring the plan into compliance with the market rate of return rules, the plan sponsor amends the plan to credit interest based on the actual rate of return on the assets within a specified subset of the plan's assets that is invested in the collective trust and that satisfies the requirements of paragraph (d)(5)(ii)(B) of this section.

(ii) *Conclusion.* The amendment satisfies the rule of paragraph (e)(3)(vi)(C)(7) of this section.

Example 10. (i) *Facts.* A plan credits interest for a plan year using the rate of return on a RIC that has most of its investments concentrated in the semiconductor industry.

(ii) *Conclusion.* Pursuant to paragraph (e)(3)(vi)(C)(*9*) of this section, the plan must be amended in one of two manners. The plan may be amended to provide for an interest crediting rate that is an investment-based rate that is described in paragraph (d)(5) of this section and that is similar to the plan's impermissible investment-based rate except to the extent that the risk and return characteristics of the impermissible investment-based rate caused it to be impermissible. Thus, the plan may be amended to provide for an interest crediting rate based on the rate of return on a RIC that is invested in a broader sector of the market than the semiconductor industry (such as the overall technology sector of the market), provided that the sector in which the RIC is invested is broad enough that the volatility requirements of paragraph (d)(5)(iv) of this section are satisfied. Alternatively, the plan may be amended to provide that the plan's interest crediting rate is a third segment rate described in paragraph (d)(3) of this section with a fixed minimum rate of 4 percent.

Example 11. (i) *Facts.* A plan was amended in 2014 to change its interest crediting rate for all interest crediting periods after the applicable amendment date of the amendment. The amendment changed the rate from the yield on 30-year Treasury Constant Maturi-

ties to the rate of return on aggregate plan assets under paragraph (d)(5)(ii)(A) of this section. The amendment also provided for section 411(d)(6) protection with respect to the account balance as of the applicable amendment date (by providing that the account balance after the applicable amendment date will never be smaller than the account balance as of the applicable amendment date credited with interest using the yield on 30-year Treasury Constant Maturities).

(ii) *Conclusions.* (A) *Participants benefiting under the plan.* With respect to those participants who were benefiting under the plan as of the applicable amendment date of the amendment described in paragraph (i) of this *Example 11,* the requirements of paragraph (e)(3)(iii) of this section (which provides a special market rate of return rule to permit certain changes in rates for participants benefiting under the plan) are satisfied. Accordingly, no amendment is required under this paragraph (e)(3)(vi) with respect to those participants.

(B) *Participants not benefiting under the plan.* With respect to those participants who were not benefiting under the plan as of the applicable amendment date of the amendment described in paragraph (i) of this *Example 11,* the requirements of paragraph (e)(3)(iii) of this section are not satisfied and, accordingly, the "greater-of" rate resulting from the section 411(d)(6) protection does not satisfy the requirements of paragraph (d)(6) of this section. As a result, pursuant to paragraph (e)(3)(vi)(B)(5) of this section, it must be determined on a participant-by-participant basis which account balance provides the benefit that is greater as of the applicable amendment date for the amendment made pursuant to this paragraph (e)(3)(iv) (the transitional amendment). If, as of the applicable amendment date for the transitional amendment, the account balance credited with interest after the change in rates using the yield on 30-year Treasury Constant Maturities is greater, then the plan must be amended to provide that the participant's benefit is based solely on that account balance credited with interest using the yield on 30-year Treasury Constant Maturities. On the other hand, if, as of the applicable amendment date for the transitional amendment, the account balance using the rate of return on aggregate plan assets is greater, then the plan must be amended to provide that the participant's benefit is based solely on that account balance credited with interest at the rate of return on aggregate plan assets.

(vii) *Plan termination amendments.*—A plan amendment with an applicable amendment date on or before the first day of the first plan year described in paragraph (f)(2)(i)(B)(*1*) or (3) of this section (as applicable) is not treated as reducing accrued benefits in violation of section 411(d)(6) merely because the amendment changes the rules that apply upon plan termination in order to satisfy the requirements of paragraph (e)(2) of this section.

»»→ Caution: *Reg. §1.411(b)(5)-1(e)(4) generally applies to plan years that begin on or after January 1, 2017 (or an earlier date as elected by the taxpayer).*

(4) *Actuarial increases after normal retirement age.*—A statutory hybrid plan is not treated as providing an effective interest crediting rate that is in excess of a market rate of return for purposes of paragraph (d) of this section merely because the plan provides that the participant's benefit, as of each annuity starting date after normal retirement age, is equal to the greater of—

(i) The benefit based on the accumulated benefit determined using an interest crediting rate that is not in excess of a market rate of return under paragraph (d) of this section; and

(ii) The benefit that satisfies the requirements of section 411(a)(2).

(5) *Plans that permit participant direction of interest crediting rates.*—[Reserved]

(f) *Effective/applicability date.*—(1) *Statutory effective/applicability dates.*—(i) *In general.*—Except as provided in paragraph (f)(1)(iii) of this section, section 411(b)(5) applies for periods beginning on or after June 29, 2005.

(ii) *Conversion amendments.*—The requirements of section 411(b)(5)(B)(ii), 411(b)(5)(B)(iii), and 411(b)(5)(B)(iv) apply to a conversion amendment (as defined in paragraph (c)(4) of this section) that both is adopted on or after June 29, 2005, and takes effect on or after June 29, 2005.

(iii) *Market rate of return.*—(A) *Plans in existence on June 29, 2005.*—(*1*) *In general.*—In the case of a plan that was in existence on June 29, 2005 (regardless of whether the plan was a statutory hybrid plan on that date), section 411(b)(5)(B)(i) applies to plan years that begin on or after January 1, 2008.

(*2*) *Exception for plan sponsor election.*—Notwithstanding paragraph (f)(1)(iii)(A)(*1*) of this section, a plan sponsor of a plan that was in existence on June 29, 2005 (regardless of whether the plan was a statutory hybrid plan on that date) may elect to have the requirements of section 411(a)(13)(B) and section 411(b)(5)(B)(i) apply for

any period on or after June 29, 2005, and before the first plan year beginning after December 31, 2007. In accordance with section 1107 of the PPA '06, an employer is permitted to adopt an amendment to make this election as late as the last day of the first plan year that begins on or after January 1, 2009 (January 1, 2011, in the case of a governmental plan as defined in section 414(d)) if the plan operates in accordance with the election.

(B) *Plans not in existence on June 29, 2005.*—In the case of a plan not in existence on June 29, 2005, section 411(b)(5)(B)(i) applies to the plan on and after the later of June 29, 2005, and the date the plan becomes a statutory hybrid plan.

(iv) *Collectively bargained plans.*—(A) *In general.*—Notwithstanding paragraph (f)(1)(iii) of this section, in the case of a collectively bargained plan maintained pursuant to one or more collective bargaining agreements between employee representatives and one or more employers ratified on or before August 17, 2006, the requirements of section 411(b)(5)(B)(i) do not apply to plan years that begin before the earlier of—

(*1*) The later of—

(*i*) The date on which the last of those collective bargaining agreements terminates (determined without regard to any extension thereof on or after August 17, 2006); or

(*ii*) January 1, 2008; or

(*2*) January 1, 2010.

(B) *Treatment of plans with both collectively bargained and non-collectively bargained employees.*—In the case of a plan with respect to which a collective bargaining agreement applies to some, but not all, of the plan participants, the plan is considered a collectively bargained plan for purposes of this paragraph (f)(1)(iv) if it is considered a collectively bargained plan under the rules of §1.436-1(a)(5)(ii)(B).

(2) *Effective/applicability date of regulations.*—(i) *In general.*—(A) *General effective date.*—Except as provided in paragraph

Reg. §1.411(b)(5)-1(f)(2)(i)(A)

(f)(2)(i)(B) of this section, this section applies to plan years that begin on or after January 1, 2011.

(B) *Special effective date.*—*(1) In general.*—Except as otherwise provided in this paragraph (f)(2)(i)(B), paragraphs (d)(1)(iii), (d)(1)(iv)(D) and (E), (d)(1)(vi), (d)(2)(ii) and (v), (d)(5)(ii)(B), (d)(5)(iv), (d)(6), (e)(2), (e)(3)(iii), (iv) and (v), and (e)(4) of this section apply to plan years that begin on or after January 1, 2017 (or an earlier date as elected by the taxpayer).

(2) *Transitional amendments.*—Paragraphs (e)(3)(vi) and (vii) of this section apply to plan amendments made on or after September 18, 2014 (or an earlier date as elected by the taxpayer).

(3) *Collectively bargained plans.*—In the case of a plan maintained pursuant to one or more collective bargaining agreements between employee representatives and one or more employers ratified on or before November 13, 2015, that constitutes a collectively bargained plan under the rules of §1.436-1(a)(5)(ii)(B), the paragraphs referenced in paragraph (f)(2)(i)(B)(1) of this section apply to plan years that begin on or after the later of—

(i) January 1, 2017; and

(ii) The earlier of January 1, 2019; and the date on which the last of those collective bargaining agreements terminates (determined without regard to any extension thereof on or after November 13, 2015).

(ii) *Conversion amendments.*—With respect to a conversion amendment (within the meaning of paragraph (c)(4) of this section), where the effective date of the conversion amendment (as defined in paragraph (c)(4)(vi) of this section) is on or after the statutory effective date set forth in paragraph (f)(1)(ii) of this section, the requirements of paragraph (c)(2) of this section apply only to a participant who has an hour of service on or after the regulatory effective date set forth in paragraph (f)(2)(i) of this section.

(iii) *Reliance before regulatory effective date.*—For the periods after the statutory effective date set forth in paragraph (f)(1) of this section and before the regulatory effective date set forth in paragraph (f)(2)(i) of this section, the safe harbor and other relief of section 411(b)(5) apply and the market rate of return and other requirements of section 411(b)(5) must be satisfied. During these periods, a plan is permitted to rely on the provisions of this section for purposes of applying the relief and satisfying the requirements of section 411(b)(5). [Reg. §1.411(b)(5)-1.]

☐ [*T.D.* 9505, 10-18-2010 *(corrected* 12-27-2010). *Amended by T.D.* 9693, 9-18-2014 *and T.D.* 9743, 11-13-2015.]

[Reg. §1.411(c)-1]

§1.411(c)-1. Allocation of accrued benefits between employer and employee contributions.—(a) *Accrued benefit derived from employer contributions.*—For purposes of section 411 and the regulations thereunder, under section 411(c)(1), an employee's accrued benefit derived from employer contributions under a plan as of any applicable date is the excess, if any, of—

(1) The total accrued benefit under the plan provided for the employee as of such date, over

(2) The accrued benefit provided for the employee, derived from contributions made by the employee under the plan as of such date.

For computation of accrued benefit derived from employee contributions to a defined contribution plan or from voluntary employee contributions to a defined benefit plan, see paragraph (b) of this section. For computation of accrued benefit derived from mandatory employee contributions to a defined benefit plan, see paragraph (c) of this section.

(b) *Accrued benefit derived from employee contribution to defined contribution plan, etc.*—For purposes of section 411 and the regulations thereunder, under section 411(c)(2)(A) the accrued benefit derived from employee contributions to a refund contribution plan is determined under subparagraph (1) or (2) of this paragraph, whichever applies. Under section 411(d)(5), the accrued benefit derived from voluntary employee contributions to a defined benefit plan is determined under subparagraph (1) of this paragraph.

(1) *Separate accounts maintained.*—If a separate account is maintained with respect to an employee's contributions and all income, expenses, gains, and losses attributable thereto, the accrued benefit determined under this subparagraph as of any applicable date is the balance of such account as of such date.

(2) *Separate accounts not maintained.*—If a separate account is not maintained with respect to an employee's contributions and the income, expenses, gains, and losses attributable thereto, the accrued benefit determined under this subparagraph is the employee's total accrued benefit determined under the plan multiplied by a fraction—

(i) The numerator of which is the total amount of the employee's contributions under the plan less withdrawals, and

(ii) The denominator of which is the sum of (A) the amount described in subdivision (i) of this subparagraph, and (B) the total contributions made under the plan by the employer on behalf of the employee less withdrawals.

For purposes of this subparagraph, contributions include all amounts which are contributed to the plan even if such amounts are used to provide ancillary benefits, such as incidental life insurance, health insurance, or death benefits, and withdrawals include only amounts distributed to the employee and do not reflect the cost of any death benefits under the plan.

(c) *Accrued benefit derived from mandatory employee contributions to a defined benefit plan.*—(1) *General rule.*—In the case of a defined benefit plan (as defined in section 414(j)) the accrued benefit derived from contributions made by an employee under the plan as of any applicable date is an annual benefit, in the form of a single life annuity (without ancillary benefits) commencing at normal retirement age, equal to the amount of the employee's accumulated contributions (determined under subparagraph (3) of this paragraph) multiplied by the appropriate conversion factor (determined under subparagraph (2) of this paragraph). Paragraph (e) of this section provides rules for actuarial adjustments where the benefit is to be determined in a form other than the form described in this subparagraph.

(2) *Appropriate conversion factor.*—For purposes of this paragraph, the term "appropriate conversion factor" means the factor necessary to convert an amount equal to the accumulated contributions to a single life annuity (without ancillary benefits) commencing at normal retirement age and shall be 10 percent for a normal retirement age of 65 years. For other normal retirement ages the appropriate conversion factor shall be the factor as determined by the Commissioner.

(3) *Accumulated contributions.*—For purposes of section 411(c) and this section, the term "accumulated contributions" means the total of—

(i) All mandatory contributions made by the employee (determined under subparagraph (4) of this paragraph),

(ii) Interest (if any) on such contributions, computed at the rate provided by the plan to the end of the last plan year to which section 411(a)(2) does not apply (by reason of the applicable effective date), and

(iii) Interest on the sum of the amounts determined under subdivisions (i) and (ii) of this subparagraph compounded annually at the rate of 5 percent per annum from the beginning of the first plan year to which section 411(a)(2) applies (by reason of the applicable effective date) to the date on which the employee would attain normal retirement age.

For example, if under section 1017 of the Employee Retirement Income Security Act of 1974, section 411(a)(2) of the Code applies for plan years beginning after December 31, 1975, and for plan years beginning before 1975, the plan provided for 3 percent interest on employee contributions, an employee's accumulated contributions would be computed by crediting interest at the rate provided by the plan (3 percent) for plan years beginning before 1976 and by crediting interest at the rate of 5 percent (or another rate prescribed under section 411(c)(2)(D)) thereafter. Section 1017 of the Employee Retirement Income Security Act of 1974 and §1.411(a)-2 provide the effective dates for the application of section 411(a)(2).

(4) *Mandatory contributions.*—For purposes of section 411(c) and this section the term "mandatory contributions" means amounts contributed to the plan by the employee which are required as a condition of his employment, as a condition of his participation in the plan, or as a condition of obtaining benefits (or additional benefits) under the plan attributable to employer contributions. For example, if the benefit derived from employer contributions depends upon a specified level of employee contributions, employee contributions up to that level would be treated as mandatory contributions. Mandatory contributions, otherwise satisfying the requirements of this subparagraph, include amounts contributed to the plan which are used to provide ancillary benefits such as incidental life insurance, health insurance, or death benefits.

(d) *Limitation on accrued benefit.*—The accrued benefit derived from mandatory employee contributions under a defined benefit plan (determined under paragraph (c) of this section) shall not exceed the greater of—

(1) The accrued benefit of the employee under the plan, or

(2) The accrued benefit derived from employee contributions determined without regard to any interest under section 411(c)(2)(C)(ii) and (iii) and under subdivisions (ii) and (iii) of paragraph (c)(3) of this section.

(e) *Actuarial adjustments for defined benefit plans.*—(1) *Accrued benefit.*—In the case of a defined benefit plan (as defined in section 414(j)) if an employee's accrued benefit is to be determined as an amount other than an annual benefit commencing at normal retirement age, such benefit (determined under section 411(c)(1) and paragraph (a) of this section) shall be the actuarial equivalent of such benefit, as determined by the Commissioner.

(2) *Accrued benefit derived from mandatory employee contributions.*—In the case of a defined benefit plan (as defined in section 414(j)) if the accrued benefit derived from mandatory contributions made by an employee is to be determined with respect to a benefit other than an annual benefit in the form of a single life annuity (without ancillary benefits) commencing at normal retirement age, such benefit shall be the actuarial equivalent of such benefit (determined under section 411(c)(2)(B) and paragraph (c) of this section), as determined by the Commissioner.

(f) *Suspension of benefits, etc.*—(1) *Suspensions.*—No adjustment to an accrued benefit is required on account of any suspension of benefits if such suspension is permitted under section 203(a)(3)(B) of the Employee Retirement Income Security Act of 1974 (88 Stat. 855) (Code Section 411(a)(3)(B)).

(2) *Employment after retirement.*—No actuarial adjustment to an accrued benefit is required on account of employment after normal retirement age. For example, if a plan with a normal retirement age of 65 provides a benefit of $400 a month payable at age 65, the same $400 benefit (with no upward adjustment) could be paid to an employee who retires at age 68. [Reg. § 1.411(c)-1.]

☐ [T.D. 7501, 8-22-77.]

[Reg. § 1.411(d)-2]

§ 1.411(d)-2. Termination or partial termination; discontinuance of contributions.—(a) *General rule.*—(1) *Required nonforfeitability.*—A plan is not a qualified plan (and a trust forming a part of such plan is not a qualified trust) unless the plan provides that—

(i) Upon the termination or partial termination of the plan, or

(ii) In addition, in the case of a plan to which section 412 (relating to minimum funding standards) does not apply, upon the complete discontinuance of contributions under the plan,

the rights of each affected employee to benefits accrued to the date of such termination or partial termination (or, in the case of a plan to which section 412 does not apply, discontinuance), to the extent funded, or the rights of each employee to the amounts credited to his account at such time, are nonforfeitable (within the meaning of § 1.411(a)-4).

(2) *Required allocation.*—(i) A plan is not a qualified plan (and a trust forming a part of such plan is not a qualified trust) unless the plan provides for the allocation of any previously unallocated funds to the employees covered by the plan upon the termination or partial termination of the plan (or, in the case of a plan to which section 412 does not apply, upon the complete discontinuance of contributions under the plan). Such provision may be incorporated in the plan at its inception or by an amendment made prior to the termination or partial termination of the plan or the discontinuance of contributions thereunder. In the case of a defined contribution plan under which unallocated forfeitures are held in a suspense account in order to satisfy the requirements of section 415, this subdivision shall not require such plan to provide for allocations from the suspense account to the extent that such allocations would result in annual additions to participants' accounts in excess of amounts permitted under section 415 for the year for which such allocations would be made.

(ii) Any provision for the allocation of unallocated funds which is found by the Secretary of Labor or the Pension Benefit Guaranty Corporation (whichever is appropriate) to satisfy the requirements of section 4044 or section 403(d)(1) of the Employee Retirement Income Security Act of 1974 is acceptable if it specifies the method to be used and does not conflict with the provisions of section 401(a)(4) of the Internal Revenue Code of 1954 and the regulations thereunder. Any allocation of funds required by paragraph (1), (2), (3), or (4)(A) of section 4044 (a) of such Act shall be deemed not to result in discrimination prohibited by section 401(a)(4) of the Code (see, however, paragraph (e) of this section). Notwithstanding the preceding sentence, in the case of a plan which establishes subclasses or categories pursuant to section 4044(b)(6) of such Act, the allocation of funds by the use of such subclasses or categories shall not be deemed not to result in discrimination prohibited by the Code. The allocation of unallocated funds may be in cash or in the form of other benefits provided under the plan. However, the allocation of the funds contributed by the employer among the employees need not necessarily benefit all the employees covered by the plan.

(iii) Subdivisions (i) and (ii) of this subparagraph do not require the allocation of amounts to the account of any employee if such amounts are not required to be used to satisfy the liabilities with respect to employees and their beneficiaries under the plan (see section 401(a)(2)).

(b) *Partial termination.*—(1) *General rule.*—Whether or not a partial termination of a qualified plan occurs (and the time of such event) shall be determined by the Commissioner with regard to all the facts and circumstances in a particular case. Such facts and circumstances include: the exclusion, by reason of a plan amendment or severance by the employer, of a group of employees who have previously been covered by the plan; and plan amendments which adversely affect the rights of employees to vest in benefits under the plan.

(2) *Special rule.*—If a defined benefit plan ceases or decreases future benefit accruals under the plan, a partial termination shall be deemed to occur if, as a result of such cessation or decrease, a potential reversion to the employer, or employers, maintaining the plan (determined as of the date such cessation or decrease is adopted) is created or increased. If no such reversion is created or increased, a partial termination shall be deemed not to occur by reason of such cessation or decrease. However, the Commissioner may determine that a partial termination of such a plan occurs pursuant to subparagraph (1) of this paragraph for reasons other than such cessation or decrease.

(3) *Effect of partial termination.*—If a termination of a qualified plan occurs, the provisions of section 411(d)(3) apply only to the part of the plan that is terminated.

(c) *Termination.*—(1) *Application.*—This paragraph applies to a plan other than a plan described in section 411(e)(1) (relating to governmental, certain church plans, etc.).

(2) *Plans subject to termination insurance.*—For purposes of this section, a plan to which title IV of the Employee Retirement Income Security Act of 1974 applies is considered terminated on a particular date if, as of that date—

(i) The plan is voluntarily terminated by the plan administrator under section 4041 of the Employee Retirement Income Security Act of 1974, or

(ii) The Pension Benefit Guaranty Corporation terminates the plan under section 4042 of the Employee Retirement Income Security Act of 1974.

For purposes of this subparagraph, the particular date of termination shall be the date of termination determined under section 4048 of such Act.

(3) *Other plans.*—In the case of a plan not described in subparagraph (2) of this paragraph, a plan is considered terminated on a particular date if, as of that date, the plan is voluntarily terminated by the employer, or employers, maintaining the plan.

(d) *Complete discontinuance.*—(1) *General rule.*—For purposes of this section, a complete discontinuance of contributions under the plan is contrasted with a suspension of contributions under the plan which is merely a temporary cessation of contributions by the employer. A complete discontinuance of contributions may occur although some amounts are contributed by the employer under the plan if such amounts are not substantial enough to reflect the intent on the part of the employer to continue to maintain the plan. The determination of whether a complete discontinuance of contributions under the plan has occurred will be made with regard to all the facts and circumstances in the particular case, and without regard to the amount of any contributions made under the plan by employees. Among the factors to be considered in determining whether a suspension constitutes a discontinuance are:

(i) Whether the employer may merely be calling an actual discontinuance of contributions a suspension of such contributions in order to avoid the requirement of full vesting as in the case of a discontinuance, or for any other reason;

(ii) Whether contributions are recurring and substantial; and

(iii) Whether there is any reasonable probability that the lack of contributions will continue indefinitely.

(2) *Time of discontinuance.*—In any case in which a suspension of a profit-sharing plan maintained by a single employer is considered a discontinuance, the discontinuance becomes effective not later than the last day of the taxable year of the employer following the last taxable year of such employer for which a substantial contribution was made under the profit-sharing plan. In the case of a profit-sharing plan maintained by more than one employer, the discontinuance becomes effective not later than the last day of the plan year following the plan year within which any employer made a substantial contribution under the plan.

(e) *Contributions or benefits which remain forfeitable.*—Under section 411(d)(2) and (3), section 411(a) and this section do not apply to plan benefits which may not be provided for designated employees in the event of early termination of the plan under provisions of the plan adopted pursuant to regulations prescribed by the Secretary or his delegate to preclude the discrimination prohibited by section 401(a)(4). Accordingly, in such a case, plan benefits may be required to be reallocated without regard to this section. [Reg. § 1.411(d)-2.]

☐ [*T.D. 7501, 8-22-77. Amended by T.D. 9849, 3-11-2019.*]

[Reg. § 1.411(d)-3]

§ 1.411(d)-3. Section 411(d)(6) protected benefits.—(a) *Protection of accrued benefits.*—(1) *General rule.*—Under section 411(d)(6)(A), a plan is not a qualified plan (and a trust forming a part of such plan is not a qualified trust) if a plan amendment decreases the accrued benefit of any plan participant, except as provided in section 412(d)(2) (section 412(c)(8) for plan years beginning before January 1, 2008), section 4281 of the Employee Retirement Income Security Act of 1974 as amended (ERISA), or other applicable law (see, for example, sections 418D and 418E of the Internal Revenue Code, and section 1107 of the Pension Protection Act of 2006, Public Law 109-280 (120 Stat. 780, 1063)). For purposes of this section, a plan amendment includes any changes to the terms of a plan, including changes resulting from a merger, consolidation, or transfer (as defined in section 414(l)) or a plan termination. The protection of section 411(d)(6) applies to a participant's entire accrued benefit under the plan as of the applicable amendment date, without regard to whether the entire accrued benefit was accrued before a participant's severance from employment or whether any portion was the result of an increase in the accrued benefit of the participant pursuant to a plan amendment adopted after the participant's severance from employment.

(2) *Plan provisions taken into account.*—(i) *Direct or indirect reduction in accrued benefit.*—For purposes of determining whether a participant's accrued benefit is decreased, all of the amendments to the provisions of a plan affecting, directly or indirectly, the computation of accrued benefits are taken into account. Plan provisions indirectly affecting the computation of accrued benefits include, for example, provisions relating to years of service and compensation.

(ii) *Amendments effective with the same applicable amendment date.*—In determining whether a reduction in a participant's accrued benefit has occurred, all plan amendments with the same applicable amendment date are treated as one amendment. Thus, if two amendments have the same applicable amendment date and one amendment, standing alone, increases participants' accrued benefits and the other amendment, standing alone, decreases participants' accrued benefits, the amendments are treated as one amendment and will only violate section 411(d)(6) if, for any participant, the net effect is to decrease participants' accrued benefit as of that applicable amendment date.

(iii) *Multiple amendments.*—(A) *General rule.*—A plan amendment violates the requirements of section 411(d)(6) if it is one of a series of plan amendments that, when taken together, have the effect of reducing or eliminating a section 411(d)(6) protected benefit in a manner that would be prohibited by section 411(d)(6) if accomplished through a single amendment.

(B) *Determination of the time period for combining plan amendments.*—For purposes of applying the rule in paragraph (a)(2)(iii)(A) of this section, generally only plan amendments adopted within a 3-year period are taken into account.

(3) *Application of section 411(a) nonforfeitability provisions with respect to section 411(d)(6) protected benefits.*—(i) *In general.*—The rules of this paragraph (a) apply to a plan amendment that decreases a participant's accrued benefits, or otherwise places greater restrictions or conditions on a participant's rights to section 411(d)(6) protected benefits, even if the amendment merely adds a restriction or condition that is permitted under the vesting rules in section 411(a)(3) through (11). However, such an amendment does not violate section 411(d)(6) to the extent it applies with respect to benefits that accrue after the applicable amendment date. See section 411(a)(10) and § 1.411(a) - 8 for additional rules relating to changes in a plan's vesting schedule.

(ii) *Exception for changes in a plan's vesting computation period.*—Notwithstanding paragraph (a)(3)(i) of this section, a plan amendment that satisfies the applicable requirements under 29 CFR 2530.203-2(c) (rules relating to vesting computation periods) does not fail to satisfy the requirements of section 411(d)(6) merely because the plan amendment changes the plan's vesting computation period.

(4) *Examples.*—The following examples illustrate the application of this paragraph (a):

Example 1. (i) *Facts.* Plan A provides an annual benefit of 2% of career average pay times years of service commencing at normal retirement age (age 65). Plan A is amended on November 1, 2006, effective as of January 1, 2007, to provide for an annual benefit of 1.3% of final pay times years of service, with final pay computed as the average of a participant's highest 3 consecutive years of compensation. As of January 1, 2007, Participant M has 16 years of service, M's career average pay is $37,500, and the average of M's highest 3 consecutive years of compensation is $67,308. Thus, Participant M's accrued benefit as of the applicable amendment date is increased from $12,000 per year at normal retirement age (2% times $37,500 times 16 years of service) to $14,000 per year at normal retirement age (1.3% times $67,308 times 16 years of service). As of January 1, 2007, Participant N has 6 years of service, N's career average pay is $50,000, and the average of N's highest 3 consecutive years of compensation is $51,282. Participant N's accrued benefit as of the applicable amendment date is decreased from $6,000 per year at normal retirement age (2% times $50,000 times 6 years of service) to $4,000 per year at normal retirement age (1.3% times $51,282 times 6 years of service).

(ii) *Conclusion.* While the plan amendment increases the accrued benefit of Participant M, the plan amendment fails to satisfy the requirements of section 411(d)(6)(A) because the amendment decreases the accrued benefit of Participant N below the level of the accrued benefit of Participant N immediately before the applicable amendment date.

Example 2. (i) *Facts.* The facts are the same as *Example 1*, except that Plan A includes a provision under which Participant N's accrued benefit cannot be less than what it was immediately before the applicable amendment date (so that Participant N's accrued benefit could not be less than $6,000 per year at normal retirement age).

(ii) *Conclusion.* The amendment does not violate the requirements of section 411(d)(6)(A) with respect to Participant M (whose accrued benefit has been increased) or with respect to Participant N (although Participant N would not accrue any benefits until the point in time at which the new formula amount would exceed the amount payable under the minimum provision, approximately 3 years after the amendment becomes effective).

Example 3. (i) *Facts.* Employer N maintains Plan C, a qualified defined benefit plan under which an employee becomes a participant upon completion of 1 year of service and is vested in 100% of the employer-derived accrued benefit upon completion of 5 years of service. Plan C provides that a former employee's years of service prior to a break in service will be reinstated upon completion of 1 year of service after being rehired. Plan C has participants who have fewer than 5 years of service and who are accordingly 0% vested in their employer-derived accrued benefits. On December 31, 2007, effective January 1, 2008, Plan C is amended, in accordance with section 411(a)(6)(D), to provide that any nonvested participant who has at least 5 consecutive 1-year breaks in service and whose number of consecutive 1-year breaks in service exceeds his or her number of years of service before the breaks will have his or her pre-break service disregarded in determining vesting under the plan.

(ii) *Conclusion.* Under paragraph (a)(3) of this section, the plan amendment does not satisfy the requirements of this paragraph (a), and thus violates section 411(d)(6), because the amendment places greater restrictions or conditions on the rights to section 411(d)(6) protected benefits, as of January 1, 2008, for participants who have fewer than 5 years of service, by restricting the ability of those participants to receive further vesting protections on benefits accrued as of that date.

Example 4. (i) *Facts.* (A) Employer O sponsors Plan D, a qualified profit sharing plan under which each employee has a nonforfeitable right to a percentage of his or her employer-derived accrued benefit based on the following table:

Completed years of service	Nonforfeitable percentage
Fewer than 3	0%
3	20%
4	40%
5	60%
6	80%
7	100%

(B) In January 2006, Employer O acquires Company X, which maintains Plan E, a qualified profit sharing plan under which each employee who has completed 5 years of service has a nonforfeitable right to 100% of the employer-derived accrued benefit. In 2007, Plan E is merged into Plan D. On the effective date for the merger, Plan D is amended to provide that the vesting schedule for participants of Plan E is the 7-year graded vesting schedule of Plan D. In accordance with section 411(a)(10)(A), the plan amendment provides that any participant of Plan E who had completed 5 years of service prior to the amendment is fully vested. In addition, as required under section

411(a)(10)(B), the amendment provides that any participant in Plan E who has at least 3 years of service prior to the amendment is permitted to make an irrevocable election to have the vesting of his or her nonforfeitable right to the employer-derived accrued benefit determined under either the 5-year cliff vesting schedule or the 7-year graded vesting schedule. Participant G, who has an account balance of $10,000 on the applicable amendment date, is a participant in Plan E with 2 years of service as of the applicable amendment date. As of the date of the merger, Participant G's nonforfeitable right to G's employer-derived accrued benefit is 0% under both the 7-year graded vesting schedule of Plan D and the 5-year cliff vesting schedule of Plan E.

(ii) *Conclusion.* Under paragraph (a)(3) of this section, the plan amendment does not satisfy the requirements of this paragraph (a) and violates section 411(d)(6), because the amendment places greater restrictions or conditions on the rights to section 411(d)(6) protected benefits with respect to G and any participant who has fewer than 5 years of service and who elected (or was made subject to) the new vesting schedule. A method of avoiding a section 411(d)(6) violation with respect to account balances attributable to benefits accrued as of the applicable amendment date and earnings thereon would be for Plan D to provide for the vested percentage of G and each other participant in Plan E to be no less than the greater of the vesting percentages under the two vesting schedules (for example, for G and each other participant in Plan E to be 20% vested upon completion of 3 years of service, 40% vested upon completion of 4 years of service, and fully vested upon completion of 5 years of service) for those account balances and earnings.

(b) *Protection of section 411(d)(6)(B) protected benefits.*—(1) *General rule.*—(i) *Prohibition against plan amendments eliminating or reducing section 411(d)(6)(B) protected benefits.*—Except as provided in this section, a plan is treated as decreasing an accrued benefit if it is amended to eliminate or reduce a section 411(d)(6)(B) protected benefit as defined in paragraph (g)(15) of this section. This paragraph (b)(1) applies to participants who satisfy (either before or after the plan amendment) the preamendment conditions for a section 411(d)(6)(B) protected benefit.

(ii) *Contingent benefits.*—The rules of paragraph (b)(1)(i) of this section apply to participants who satisfy (either before or after the plan amendment) the preamendment conditions for the section 411(d)(6)(B) protected benefit even if the condition on which the eligibility for the section 411(d)(6)(B) protected benefit depends is an unpredictable contingent event (e.g., a plant shutdown).

(iii) *Application of general rules in paragraph (a) of this section to section 411(d)(6)(B) protected benefits.*—For purposes of determining whether a participant's section 411(d)(6)(B) protected benefit is eliminated or reduced, the rules of paragraph (a) of this section apply to section 411(d)(6)(B) protected benefits in the same manner as they apply to accrued benefits described in section 411(d)(6)(A). As an example of the application of paragraph (a)(2)(ii) of this section to section 411(d)(6)(B) protected benefits, if there are two amendments with the same applicable amendment date and one amendment increases accrued benefits and the other amendment decreases the early retirement factors that are used to determine the early retirement annuity, the amendments are treated as one amendment and only violate section 411(d)(6) if, after the two amendments, the net dollar amount of any early retirement annuity with respect to the accrued benefit of any participant as of the applicable amendment date is lower than it would have been without the two amendments. As an example of the application of paragraph (a)(2)(iii) of this section to section 411(d)(6)(B) protected benefits, a series of amendments made within a 3-year period that, when taken together, have the effect of reducing or eliminating early retirement benefits or retirement-type subsidies in a manner that adversely affects the rights of any participant in a more than de minimis manner violates section 411(d)(6)(B) even if each amendment would be permissible pursuant to paragraphs (c), (d), or (f) of this section.

(2) *Permissible elimination of section 411(d)(6)(B) protected benefits.*—(i) *In general.*—A plan is permitted to be amended to eliminate a section 411(d)(6)(B) protected benefit if the elimination is in accordance with this section or §1.411(d)-4.

(ii) *Increases in payment amounts do not eliminate an optional form of benefit.*—An amendment is not treated as eliminating an optional form of benefit or eliminating or reducing an early retirement benefit or retirement-type subsidy under the plan, if, effective after the plan amendment, there is another optional form of benefit available to the participant under the plan that is of inherently equal or greater value (within the meaning of §1.401(a)(4)-4(d)(4)(i)(A)). Thus, for example, a change in the method of calculating a joint and survivor annuity from using a 90% adjustment factor on account of the survivorship payment at particular ages for a participant and a spouse to using a 91% adjustment factor at the same ages is not treated as an elimina-

tion of an optional form of benefit. Similarly, a plan that offers a subsidized qualified joint and survivor annuity option for married participants under which the amount payable during the participant's lifetime is not less than the amount payable under the plan's straight life annuity is permitted to be amended to eliminate the straight life annuity option for married participants.

(3) *Permissible elimination of benefits that are not section 411(d)(6) protected benefits.*—(i) *In general.*—Section 411(d)(6) does not provide protection for benefits that are ancillary benefits, other rights and features, or any other benefits that are not described in section 411(d)(6). See §1.411(d)-4, Q&A-1(d). However, a plan may not be amended to recharacterize a retirement-type benefit as an ancillary benefit. Thus, for example, a plan amendment to recharacterize any portion of an early retirement subsidy as a social security supplement that is an ancillary benefit violates section 411(d)(6).

(ii) *No protection for future benefit accruals.*—Section 411(d)(6) only protects benefits that accrue before the applicable amendment date. Thus, a plan is permitted to be amended to eliminate or reduce an early retirement benefit, a retirement-type subsidy, or an optional form of benefit with respect to benefits that accrue after the applicable amendment date without violating section 411(d)(6). However, section 4980F(e) of the Internal Revenue Code and section 204(h) of ERISA require notice of an amendment to an applicable pension plan that either provides for a significant reduction in the rate of future benefit accrual or that eliminates or significantly reduces an early retirement benefit or a retirement-type subsidy. See §54.4980F-1 of this chapter generally, and see §54.4980F-1, Q&A-7(b) and Q&A-8(c) of this chapter, with respect to the circumstances under which such notice is required for a reduction in an early retirement benefit or retirement-type subsidy.

(4) *Examples.*—The following examples illustrate the application of this paragraph (b):

Example 1. (i) *Facts involving amendments to an early retirement subsidy.* Plan A provides an annual benefit of 2% of career average pay times years of service commencing at normal retirement age (age 65). Plan A is amended on November 1, 2006, effective as of January 1, 2007, to provide for an annual benefit of 1.3% of final pay times years of service, with final pay computed as the average of a participant's highest 3 consecutive years of compensation. Participant M is age 50, M has 16 years of service, M's career average pay is $37,500, and the average of M's highest 3 consecutive years of compensation is $67,308. Thus, M's accrued benefit as of the effective date of the amendment is increased from $12,000 per year at normal retirement age (2% times $37,500 times 16 years of service) to $14,000 per year at normal retirement age (1.3% times $67,308 times 16 years of service). (These facts are similar to the facts in *Example 1* in paragraph (a)(4) of this section.) Before the amendment, Plan A permitted a former employee to commence distribution of benefits as early as age 55 and, for a participant with at least 15 years of service, actuarially reduced the amount payable in the form of a straight life annuity commencing before normal retirement age by 3% per year from age 60 to age 65 and by 7% per year from age 55 through age 59. Thus, before the amendment, the amount of M's early retirement benefit that would be payable for commencement at age 55 was $6,000 per year ($12,000 per year minus 3% for 5 years and minus 7% for 5 more years). The amendment also alters the actuarial reduction factor so that, for a participant with at least 15 years of service, the amount payable in a straight life annuity commencing before normal retirement age is reduced by 6% per year. As a result, the amount of M's early retirement benefit at age 55 becomes $5,600 per year after the amendment ($14,000 minus 6% for 10 years).

(ii) *Conclusion.* The straight life annuity payable under Plan A at age 55 is an optional form of benefit that includes an early retirement subsidy. The plan amendment fails to satisfy the requirements of section 411(d)(6)(B) because the amendment decreases the optional form of benefit payable to Participant M below the level that Participant M was entitled to receive immediately before the effective date of the amendment. If instead Plan A had included a provision under which M's straight life annuity payable at any age could be not be less than what it was immediately before the amendment (so that M's straight life annuity payable at age 55 could not be less than $6,000 per year), then the amendment would not fail to satisfy the requirements of section 411(d)(6)(B) with respect to M's straight life annuity payable at age 55 (although the straight life annuity payable to M at age 55 would not increase until the point in time at which the new formula amount with the new actuarial reduction factors exceeds the amount payable under the minimum provision, approximately 14 months after the amendment becomes effective).

Example 2. (i) *Facts involving plant shutdown benefits.* Plan B permits participants who have a severance from employment before normal retirement age (age 65) to commence distributions at any time after age 55 with the amount payable to be actuarially reduced using reasonable actuarial assumptions regarding interest and mortality specified in the plan, but provides that the annual reduction for any participant who has at least 20 years of service and who has a severance from employment after age 55 is only 3% per year (which is a smaller reduction than would apply under reasonable actuarial reductions). Plan B also provides two plant shutdown benefits to participants who have a severance of employment as a result of a plant shutdown. First, the favorable 3% per year actuarial reduction applies for commencement of benefits after age 55 and before age 65 for any participant who has at least 10 years of service and who has a severance from employment as a result of a plant shutdown. Second, all participants who have at least 20 years of service and who have a severance from employment after age 55 (and before normal retirement age at age 65) as a result of a plant shutdown will receive supplemental payments. Under the supplemental payments, an additional amount equal to the participant's estimated old-age insurance benefit under the Social Security Act is payable until age 65. The supplemental payments are not a QSUPP, as defined in §1.401(a)(4)-12, because the plan's terms do not state that the supplement is treated as an early retirement benefit that is protected under section 411(d)(6).

(ii) *Conclusion with respect to plant shutdown benefits.* The benefits payable with the 3% annual reduction are retirement-type benefits. The excess of the actuarial present value of the early retirement benefit using the 3% annual reduction over the actuarial present value of the normal retirement benefit is a retirement-type subsidy and the right to receive payments of the benefit at age 55 is an early retirement benefit. These conclusions apply not only with respect to the rights that apply to participants who have at least 20 years of service, but also to participants with at least 10 years of service who have a severance from employment as a result of a plant shutdown. Thus, the right to receive benefits based on a 3% annual reduction for participants with at least 10 years of service at the time of a plant shutdown is an early retirement benefit that provides a retirement-type subsidy and is a section 411(d)(6)(B) protected benefit (even though no plant shutdown has occurred). Therefore, a plan amendment cannot eliminate this benefit with respect to benefits accrued before the applicable amendment date, even before the occurrence of the plant shutdown. Because the plan provides that the supplemental payments cannot exceed the OASDI benefit under the Social Security Act, the supplemental payments constitute a social security supplement (but not a QSUPP as defined in §1.401(a)(4)-12), which is an ancillary benefit that is not a section 411(d)(6)(B) protected benefit and accordingly is not taken into account in determining whether a prohibited reduction has occurred.

Example 3. (i) *Facts.* Plan C, a multiemployer defined benefit plan in which participation is limited to electricians in the construction industry, provides that a participant may elect to commence distributions only if the participant is not currently employed by a participating employer and provides that, if the participant has a specified number of years of service and attains a specified age, the distribution is without any actuarial reduction for commencement before normal retirement age. Since the plan's inception, Plan C has provided for suspension of pension benefits during periods of disqualifying employment (ERISA section 203(a)(3)(B) service). Before 2007, the plan defined disqualifying employment to include any job as an electrician in the particular industry and geographic location to which Plan C applies. This definition of disqualifying employment did not cover a job as an electrician supervisor. In 2005, Participant E, having rendered the specified number of years of service and attained the specified age to retire with a fully subsidized early retirement benefit, retires from E's job as an electrician with Employer Y and starts a position with Employer Z as an electrician supervisor. Employer Z is not a participating employer in Plan C but is an employer in the same industry and geographic location as Employer Y. When E left service with Employer Y, E's position as an electrician supervisor was not disqualifying employment for purposes of Plan C's suspension of pension benefit provision, and E elected to commence benefit payments in 2005. In 2006, effective January 1, 2007, Plan C is amended to expand the definition of disqualifying employment to include any job (including supervisory positions) as an electrician in the same industry and geographic location to which Plan C applies. The plan's definition of disqualifying employment satisfies the requirements of section 411(a)(3)(B). On January 1, 2007, E's pension benefits are suspended because of E's disqualifying employment as an electrician supervisor.

(ii) *Conclusion.* Under paragraphs (a)(3) and (b)(1) of this section, the 2007 plan amendment violates section 411(d)(6), because the amendment places greater restrictions or conditions on a participant's rights to section 411(d)(6) protected benefits to the extent it applies with respect to benefits that accrued before January 1, 2007. The result would be the same even if the amendment did not apply to former employees and instead applied only to participants who were actively employed at the time of the applicable amendment.

(c) *Permissible elimination of optional forms of benefit that are redundant.*—(1) *General rule.*—Except as otherwise provided in paragraph (c)(5) of this section, a plan is permitted to be amended to eliminate an optional form of benefit for a participant with respect to benefits accrued before the applicable amendment date if—

(i) The optional form of benefit is redundant with respect to a retained optional form of benefit, within the meaning of paragraph (c)(2) of this section;

(ii) The plan amendment is not applicable with respect to an optional form of benefit with an annuity commencement date that is earlier than the number of days in the maximum QJSA explanation period (as defined in paragraph (g)(9) of this section) after the date the amendment is adopted; and

(iii) The requirements of paragraph (e) of this section are satisfied in any case in which either:

(A) The retained optional form of benefit for the participant does not commence on the same annuity commencement date as the optional form of benefit that is being eliminated, or

(B) As of the date the amendment is adopted, the actuarial present value of the retained optional form of benefit for the participant is less than the actuarial present value of the optional form of benefit that is being eliminated.

(2) *Similar types of optional forms of benefit are redundant.*—(i) *General rule.*—An optional form of benefit is redundant with respect to a retained optional form of benefit if, after the amendment becomes applicable—

(A) There is a retained optional form of benefit available to the participant that is in the same family of optional forms of benefit, within the meaning of paragraphs (c)(3) and (4) of this section, as the optional form of benefit being eliminated; and

(B) The participant's rights with respect to the retained optional form of benefit are not subject to materially greater restrictions (such as conditions relating to eligibility, restrictions on a participant's ability to designate the person who is entitled to benefits following the participant's death, or restrictions on a participant's right to receive an in-kind distribution) than applied to the optional form of benefit being eliminated.

(ii) *Special rule for core options.*—An optional form of benefit that is a core option as defined in paragraph (g)(5) of this section may not be eliminated as a redundant benefit under the rules of this paragraph (c) unless the retained optional form of benefit and the eliminated core option are identical except for differences described in paragraph (c)(3)(ii) of this section. Thus, for example, a particular 10-year term certain and life annuity may not be eliminated by plan amendment unless the retained optional form of benefit is another 10-year term certain and life annuity.

(3) *Family of optional forms of benefit.*—(i) *In general.*—Paragraph (c)(4) of this section describes certain families of optional forms of benefits. Not every optional form of benefit that is offered under a plan necessarily fits within a family of optional forms of benefit as described in paragraph (c)(4) of this section. Each optional form of benefit that is not included in any particular family of optional forms of benefit listed in paragraph (c)(4) of this section is in a separate family of optional forms of benefit with other optional forms of benefit that would be identical to that optional form of benefit but for differences that are disregarded under paragraph (c)(3)(ii) of this section.

(ii) *Certain differences among optional forms of benefit.*—(A) *Differences in actuarial factors and annuity starting dates.*—The determination of whether two optional forms of benefit are within a family of optional forms of benefit is made without regard to actuarial factors or annuity starting dates. Thus, any optional forms of benefit that are part of the same generalized optional form (within the meaning of paragraph (g)(8) of this section) are in the same family of optional forms of benefit. For example, if a plan has a single-sum distribution option for some participants that is calculated using a 5% interest rate and a specific mortality table (but no less than the minimum present value as determined under section 417(e)) and another single-sum distribution option for other participants that is calculated using the applicable interest rate as defined in section 417(e)(3)(A)(ii)(II) and the applicable mortality table as defined in section 417(e)(3)(A)(ii)(I), both single-sum distribution options are part of the same generalized optional form and thus in the same family of optional forms of benefit under the rules of paragraph (c)(3)(i) of this section. However, differences in actuarial factors and annuity starting dates are taken into account for purposes of the requirements in paragraph (e)(3) of this section.

(B) *Differences in pop-up provisions and cash refund features for joint and contingent options.*—The determination of whether two optional forms of benefit are within a family of optional forms of benefit relating to joint and contingent families (as described in paragraph (c)(4)(i) and (ii) of this section) is made without regard to the following features—

 (1) Pop-up provisions (under which payments increase upon the death of the beneficiary or another event that causes the beneficiary not to be entitled to a survivor annuity);

 (2) Cash refund features (under which payment is provided upon the death of the last annuitant in an amount that is not greater than the excess of the present value of the annuity at the annuity starting date over the total of payments before the death of the last annuitant); or

 (3) Term-certain provisions for optional forms of benefit within a joint and contingent family.

 (C) *Differences in social security leveling features, refund of employee contributions features, and retroactive annuity starting date features.*—The determination of whether two optional forms of benefit are within a family of optional forms of benefit is made without regard to social security leveling features, refund of employee contributions features, or retroactive annuity starting date features. But see paragraph (c)(5) of this section for special rules relating to social security leveling, refund of employee contributions, and retroactive annuity starting date features in optional forms of benefit.

 (4) *List of families.*—The following are families of optional forms of benefit for purposes of this paragraph (c):

 (i) *Joint and contingent options with continuation percentages of 50% to 100%.*—An optional form of benefit is within the 50% or more joint and contingent family if it provides a life annuity to the participant and a survivor annuity to an individual that is at least 50% and no more than 100% of the annuity payable during the joint lives of the participant and the participant's survivor.

 (ii) *Joint and contingent options with continuation percentages less than 50%.*—An optional form of benefit is within the less than 50% joint and contingent family if it provides a life annuity to the participant and a survivor annuity to an individual that is less than 50% of the annuity payable during the joint lives of the participant and the participant's survivor.

 (iii) *Term certain and life annuity options with a term of 10 years or less.*—An optional form of benefit is within the 10 years or less term certain and life family if it is a life annuity with a guarantee that payments will continue to the participant's beneficiary for the remainder of a fixed period that is 10 years or less if the participant dies before the end of the fixed period.

 (iv) *Term certain and life annuity options with a term longer than 10 years.*—An optional form of benefit is within the longer than 10 years term certain and life family if it is a life annuity with a guarantee that payments will continue to the participant's beneficiary for the remainder of a fixed period that is in excess of 10 years if the participant dies before the end of the fixed period.

 (v) *Level installment payment options over a period of 10 years or less.*—An optional form of benefit is within the 10 years or less installment family if it provides for substantially level payments to the participant for a fixed period of at least two years and not in excess of 10 years with a guarantee that payments will continue to the participant's beneficiary for the remainder of the fixed period if the participant dies before the end of the fixed period.

 (vi) *Level installment payment options over a period of more than 10 years.*—An optional form of benefit is within the more than 10 years installment family if it provides for substantially level payments to the participant for a fixed period that is in excess of 10 years with a guarantee that payments will continue to the participant's beneficiary for the remainder of the fixed period if the participant dies before the end of the fixed period.

 (5) *Special rules for certain features included in optional forms of benefit.*—For purposes of applying this paragraph (c), to the extent an optional form of benefit that is being eliminated includes either a social security leveling feature or a refund of employee contributions feature, the retained optional form of benefit must also include that feature, and, to the extent that the optional form of benefit that is being eliminated does not include a social security leveling feature or a refund of employee contributions feature, the retained optional form of benefit must not include that feature. For purposes of applying this paragraph (c), to the extent an optional form of benefit that is being eliminated does not include a retroactive annuity starting date feature, the retained optional form of benefit must not include the feature.

 (6) *Separate application of redundancy rules for bifurcated benefits.*—If a plan permits the participant to make different distribution elections with respect to two or more separate portions of the participant's benefit, the rules of this paragraph (c) are permitted to be

applied separately to each such portion of the participant's benefit as if that portion were the participant's entire benefit. Thus, for example, if one set of distribution elections applies to a portion of the participant's accrued benefit and another set of distribution elections applies to the other portion of the participant's accrued benefit, then with respect to one portion of the participant's benefit, the determination of whether any optional form of benefit is within a family of optional forms of benefit is permitted to be made disregarding elections that apply to the other portion of the participant's benefit. Similarly, if a participant can elect to receive any portion of the accrued benefit in a single sum and the remainder pursuant to a set of distribution elections, the rules of this paragraph (c) are permitted to be applied separately to the set of distribution elections that apply to the portion of the participant's accrued benefit that is not payable in a single sum (for example, for the portion of a participant's benefit that is not paid in a single sum, the determination of whether any optional form of benefit is within a family of optional forms of benefit is permitted to be made disregarding the fact that the other portion of the participant's benefit is paid in a single sum).

 (d) *Permissible elimination of noncore optional forms of benefit where core options are offered.*—(1) *General rule.*—Except as otherwise provided in paragraph (d)(2) of this section, a plan is permitted to be amended to eliminate an optional form of benefit for a participant with respect to benefits accrued before the applicable amendment date if—

 (i) After the amendment becomes applicable, each of the core options described in paragraph (g)(5) of this section is available to the participant with respect to benefits accrued before and after the amendment;

 (ii) The plan amendment is not applicable with respect to an optional form of benefit with an annuity commencement date that is earlier than 4 years after the date the amendment is adopted; and

 (iii) The requirements of paragraph (e) of this section are satisfied in any case in which either:

 (A) One or more of the core options are not available commencing on the same annuity commencement date as the optional form of benefit that is being eliminated, or

 (B) As of the date the amendment is adopted, the actuarial present value of the benefit payable under any core option with the same annuity commencement date is less than the actuarial present value of benefits payable under the optional form of benefit that is being eliminated.

 (2) *Special rules.*—(i) *Treatment of certain features included in optional forms of benefit.*—For purposes of applying this paragraph (d), to the extent an optional form of benefit that is being eliminated includes either a social security leveling feature or a refund of employee contributions feature, at least one of the core options must also be available with that feature, and, to the extent that the optional form of benefit that is being eliminated does not include a social security leveling feature or a refund of employee contributions feature, each of the core options must be available without that feature. For purposes of applying this paragraph (d), to the extent an optional form of benefit that is being eliminated does not include a retroactive annuity starting date feature, each of the core options must be available without that feature.

 (ii) *Eliminating the most valuable option for a participant with a short life expectancy.*—For purposes of applying this paragraph (d), if the most valuable option for a participant with a short life expectancy (as defined in paragraph (g)(5)(iii) of this section) is eliminated, then, after the plan amendment, an optional form of benefit that is identical, except for differences described in paragraph (c)(3)(ii) of this section, must be available to the participant. However, such a plan amendment cannot eliminate a refund of employee contributions feature from the most valuable option for a participant with a short life expectancy.

 (iii) *Single-sum distributions.*—A plan amendment is not treated as satisfying this paragraph (d) if it eliminates an optional form of benefit that includes a single-sum distribution that applies with respect to at least 25% of the participant's accrued benefit as of the date the optional form of benefit is eliminated. But see § 1.411(d)-4, Q&A-2(b)(2)(v), relating to involuntary single-sum distributions for benefits with a present value not in excess of the maximum dollar amount in section 411(a)(11).

 (iv) *Application of multiple amendment rule to core option rule.*—Notwithstanding paragraph (a)(2)(iii)(B) of this section, if a plan is amended to eliminate an optional form of benefit using the core options rule in this paragraph (d), then the employer must wait 3 years after the first annuity commencement date for which the optional form of benefit is no longer available before making any changes to the core options offered under the plan (other than a change that is not treated as an elimination under paragraph (b)(2)(ii) of this section). Thus, for example, if a plan amendment eliminates an optional form of benefit for a participant using the core options rule under this paragraph (d), with an adoption date of January 1, 2006 and an effective date of January 1, 2010, the plan would not be permitted to be amended to make changes to the core options offered under the plan (and the core options would continue to apply with respect to the participant's accrued benefit) until January 1, 2013.

(v) *Special rule for joint and contingent annuity core option.*—If a plan offers joint and contingent annuities under which a participant is entitled to a life annuity with a survivor annuity for the individual designated by the participant (including a non-spousal contingent annuitant) with continuation percentage options of both 50% and 100% (after adjustments permitted under paragraph (g)(5)(ii) of this section to comply with applicable law), the plan is permitted to treat both of these options as core options for purposes of this paragraph (d), in lieu of a 75% joint and contingent annuity. Thus, such a plan is permitted to use the rules of this paragraph (d) if the plan satisfies all of the requirements of this paragraph (d) (taking into account the modification rule in paragraph (g)(5)(ii) of this section) other than the requirement of offering a 75% joint and contingent annuity as described in paragraph (g)(5)(i)(B) of this section.

(e) *Permissible plan amendments under paragraphs (c) and (d) eliminating or reducing section 411(d)(6)(B) protected benefits that are burdensome and of de minimis value.*—(1) *In general.*—A plan amendment that, pursuant to paragraph (c)(1)(iii) or (d)(1)(iii) of this section, is required to satisfy this paragraph (e) satisfies this paragraph (e) if—

(i) The amendment eliminates section 411(d)(6)(B) protected benefits that create significant burdens or complexities for the plan and its participants as described in paragraph (e)(2) of this section; and

(ii) The amendment does not adversely affect the rights of any participant in a more than de minimis manner as described in paragraph (e)(3) of this section.

(2) *Plan amendments eliminating section 411(d)(6)(B) protected benefits that create significant burdens and complexities.*—(i) *Facts and circumstances analysis.*—(A) *In general.*—The determination of whether a plan amendment eliminates section 411(d)(6)(B) protected benefits that create significant burdens or complexities for the plan and its participants is based on facts and circumstances.

(B) *Early retirement benefits.*—In the case of an amendment that eliminates an early retirement benefit, relevant factors include whether the annuity starting dates under the plan considered in the aggregate are burdensome or complex (e.g., the number of categories of early retirement benefits, whether the terms and conditions applicable to the plan's early retirement benefits are difficult to summarize in a manner that is concise and readily understandable to the average plan participant, and whether those different early retirement benefits were added to the plan as a result of a plan merger, transfer, or consolidation), and whether the effect of the plan amendment is to reduce the number of categories of early retirement benefits.

(C) *Retirement-type subsidies and actuarial factors.*—In the case of a plan amendment eliminating a retirement-type subsidy or changing the actuarial factors used to determine optional forms of benefit, relevant factors include whether the actuarial factors used for determining optional forms of benefit available under the plan considered in the aggregate are burdensome or complex (e.g., the number of different retirement-type subsidies and other actuarial factors available under the plan, whether the terms and conditions applicable to the plan's retirement-type subsidies are difficult to summarize in a manner that is concise and readily understandable to the average plan participant, whether the plan is eliminating one or more generalized optional forms, whether the plan is replacing a complex optional form of benefit that contains a retirement-type subsidy with a simpler form, and whether the different retirement-type subsidies and other actuarial factors were added to the plan as a result of a plan merger, transfer, or consolidation), and whether the effect of the plan amendment is to reduce the number of categories of retirement-type subsidies or other actuarial factors.

(D) *Example.*—The following example illustrates the application of this paragraph (e)(2)(i):

Example. (i) *Facts.* Plan A is a defined benefit plan under which employees may select a distribution in the form of a straight life annuity, a straight life annuity with cost-of-living increases, a 50% qualified joint and survivor annuity with a pop-up provision, or a 10-year term certain and life annuity. On January 15, 2007, Plan A is amended, effective June 1, 2007, to eliminate the 50% qualified joint and survivor annuity with a pop-up provision as described in paragraph (c)(3)(ii)(B)(*1*) of this section and replace it with a 50% qualified joint and survivor annuity without the pop-up provision (and using the same actuarial factor).

(ii) *Conclusion.* Plan A satisfies the requirements of paragraph (e)(2)(i)(B) of this section because, based on the relevant facts and circumstances (e.g., the amendment replaces a complex optional form of benefit with a simpler form), the amendment eliminates section 411(d)(6)(B) protected benefits that create significant burdens and complexities. Accordingly, the plan amendment is permitted to eliminate the pop-up provision, provided that the plan amendment satisfies all the other applicable requirements in paragraph (c) or (d) of this section. For example, the plan amendment must not eliminate the most valuable option for a participant with a short life expectancy (as defined in paragraph (g)(5)(iii) of this section) and the plan amendment must not adversely affect the rights of any participant in a more than de minimis manner, taking into account the actuarial factors for the joint and survivor annuity with the pop-up provision and the joint and survivor annuity without the pop-up provision, as described in paragraph (e)(3) of this section.

(ii) *Presumptions for certain amendments.*—(A) *Presumption for amendments eliminating certain annuity starting dates.*—If the annuity starting dates under the plan considered in the aggregate are burdensome or complex, then elimination of any one of the annuity starting dates is presumed to eliminate section 411(d)(6)(B) protected benefits that create significant burdens or complexities for the plan and its participants. However, if the effect of a plan amendment with respect to a set of optional forms of benefit is merely to substitute one set of annuity starting dates for another set of annuity starting dates, without any reduction in the number of different annuity starting dates, then the plan amendment does not satisfy the requirements of this paragraph (e)(2).

(B) *Presumption for amendments changing certain actuarial factors.*—If the actuarial factors used for determining benefit distributions available under a generalized optional form considered in the aggregate are burdensome or complex, then replacing some of the actuarial factors for the generalized optional form is presumed to eliminate section 411(d)(6)(B) protected benefits that create significant burdens or complexities for the plan and its participants. However, if the effect is merely to substitute one set of actuarial factors for another set of actuarial factors, without any reduction in the number of different actuarial factors or the complexity of those factors, then the plan amendment does not satisfy the requirements of this paragraph (e)(2) unless the change of actuarial factors is merely to replace one or more of the plan's actuarial factors for determining optional forms of benefit with new actuarial factors that are more accurate (e.g., reflecting more recent mortality experience or more recent market rates of interest).

(iii) *Restrictions against creating burdens or complexities.*—See paragraphs (a)(2)(iii) and (b)(1)(iii) of this section for general rules applicable to multiple amendments. In accordance with these rules, a plan amendment does not eliminate a section 411(d)(6)(B) protected benefit that creates burdens and complexities for a plan and its participants if, less than 3 years earlier, a plan was previously amended to add another retirement-type subsidy in order to facilitate the elimination of the original retirement-type subsidy, even if the elimination of the other subsidy would not adversely affect the rights of any plan participant in a more than de minimis manner as provided in paragraph (e)(3) of this section.

(3) *Elimination of early retirement benefits or retirement-type subsidies that are de minimis.*—(i) *Rules for retained optional forms of benefit under paragraph (c) of this section.*—For purposes of paragraph (c) of this section, the elimination of an optional form of benefit does not adversely affect the rights of any participant in a more than de minimis manner if—

(A) The retained optional form of benefit described in paragraph (c) of this section has substantially the same annuity commencement date as the optional form of benefit that is being eliminated, as described in paragraph (e)(4) of this section; and

(B) Either the actuarial present value of the benefit payable in the optional form of benefit that is being eliminated does not exceed the actuarial present value of the benefit payable in the retained optional form of benefit by more than a de minimis amount, as described in paragraph (e)(5) of this section, or the amendment satisfies the requirements of paragraph (e)(6) of this section relating to a delayed effective date.

(ii) *Rules for core options under paragraph (d) of this section.*—For purposes of paragraph (d) of this section, the elimination of an optional form of benefit does not adversely affect the rights of any participant in a more than de minimis manner if, with respect to each of the core options—

(A) The core option is available after the amendment with substantially the same annuity commencement date as the optional form of benefit that is being eliminated, as described in paragraph (e)(4) of this section; and

(B) Either the actuarial present value of the benefit payable in the optional form of benefit that is being eliminated does not exceed the actuarial present value of the benefit payable under the core option by more than a de minimis amount, as described in paragraph (e)(5) of this section, or the amendment satisfies the requirements of paragraph (e)(6) of this section.

(4) *Definition of substantially the same annuity starting dates.*—For purposes of applying paragraphs (e)(3)(i)(A) and (ii)(A) of this section, annuity starting dates are considered substantially the same if they are within 6 months of each other.

(5) *Definition of de minimis difference in actuarial present value.*—For purposes of applying paragraph (e)(3)(i)(B) and (ii)(B) of this section, a difference in actuarial present value between the optional form of benefit being eliminated and the retained optional form of benefit or core option is not more than a de minimis amount if, as of the date the amendment is adopted, the difference between the actuarial present value of the eliminated optional form of benefit and the actuarial present value of the retained optional form of benefit or core option is not more than the greater of—

(i) 2% of the present value of the retirement-type subsidy (if any) under the eliminated optional form of benefit prior to the amendment; or

(ii) 1% of the greater of the participant's compensation (as defined in section 415(c)(3)) for the prior plan year or the participant's average compensation for his or her high 3 years (within the meaning of section 415(b)(1)(B) and (b)(3)).

(6) *Delayed effective date.*—(i) *General rule.*—For purposes of applying paragraph (e)(3)(i)(B) and (ii)(B) of this section, an amendment that eliminates an optional form of benefit satisfies the requirements of this paragraph (e)(6) if the elimination of the optional form of benefit is not applicable to any annuity commencement date before the end of the expected transition period for that optional form of benefit.

(ii) *Determination of expected transition period.*—(A) *General rule.*—The expected transition period for a plan amendment eliminating an optional form of benefit is the period that begins when the amendment is adopted and ends when it is reasonable to expect, with respect to a section 411(d)(6)(B) protected benefit (i.e., not taking into account benefits that accrue in the future), that the form being eliminated would be subsumed by another optional form of benefit after taking into account expected future benefit accruals.

(B) *Determination of expected transition period using conservative actuarial assumptions.*—The expected transition period for a plan amendment eliminating an optional form of benefit must be determined in accordance with actuarial assumptions that are reasonable at the time of the amendment and that are conservative (i.e., reasonable actuarial assumptions that are likely to result in the longest period of time until the eliminated optional form of benefit would be subsumed). For this purpose, actuarial assumptions are not treated as conservative unless they include assumptions that a participant's compensation will not increase and that future benefit accruals will not exceed accruals in recent periods.

(C) *Effect of subsequent amendments reducing future benefit accruals on the expected transition period.*—If, during the expected transition period for a plan amendment eliminating an optional form of benefit, the plan is subsequently amended to reduce the rate of future benefit accrual (or otherwise to lengthen the expected transition period), thus that subsequent plan amendment must provide that the elimination of the optional form of benefit is void or must provide for the effective date for elimination of the optional form of benefit to be further extended to a new expected transition period that satisfies this paragraph (e)(6) taking into account the subsequent amendment.

(iii) *Applicability of the delayed effective date rule limited to employees who continue to accrue benefits through the end of expected transition period.*—An amendment eliminating an optional form of benefit under this paragraph (e)(6) must be limited to participants who continue to accrue benefits under the plan through the end of the expected transition period. Thus, for example, the plan amendment may not apply to any participant who has a severance from employment during the expected transition period.

(iv) *Special rule for section 204(h) notice.*—See § 54.4980F-1(b), Q&A-8(c) of this chapter for a special rule relating to this paragraph (e)(6).

(f) *Utilization test.*—(1) *General rule.*—A plan is permitted to be amended to eliminate all of the optional forms of benefit that comprise a generalized optional form (as defined in paragraph (g)(8) of this section) for a participant with respect to benefits accrued before the applicable amendment date if—

(i) None of the optional forms of benefit being eliminated is a core option, within the meaning of paragraph (g)(5) of this section;

(ii) The plan amendment is not applicable with respect to an optional form of benefit with an annuity commencement date that is earlier than the number of days in the maximum Qualified Joint and Survivor Annuity explanation period (as defined in paragraph (g)(9) of this section) after the date the amendment is adopted;

(iii) During the look-back period—

(A) The generalized optional form has been available to at least the applicable number of participants who are taken into account under paragraph (f)(3) and (4) of this section; and

(B) No participant has elected any optional form of benefit that is part of the generalized optional form with an annuity commencement date that is within the look-back period.

(2) *Look-back period.*—(i) *In general.*—For purposes of this paragraph (f), the look-back period is the period that includes—

(A) The portion of the plan year in which such plan amendment is adopted that precedes the date of adoption (the pre-adoption period); and

(B) The 2 plan years immediately preceding the pre-adoption period.

(ii) *Special look-back period rules.*—(A) *12-month plan year.*—In the look-back period, at least 1 of the plan years must be a 12-month plan year.

(B) *Permitted 3-month exclusion in the pre-adoption period.*—A plan is permitted to exclude from the look-back period the calendar month in which the amendment is adopted and the preceding 1 or 2 calendar months to the extent those preceding months are contained within the pre-adoption period.

(C) *Permission to extend the look-back period.*—In order to have a look-back period that satisfies the minimum applicable number of participants requirement in paragraph (f)(1)(iii)(A) of this section, the look-back period described in paragraph (f)(2)(i)(B) of this section is permitted to be expanded, so as to include the 3, 4, or 5 plan years immediately preceding the plan year in which the amendment is adopted. Thus, in determining the look-back period, a plan is permitted to substitute the 3, 4, or 5 plan years immediately preceding the pre-adoption period for the 2 plan years described in paragraph (f)(2)(i)(B) of this section. However, if a plan does not satisfy the minimum applicable number of participants requirement of paragraph (f)(1)(iii)(A) of this section using the pre-adoption period and the immediately preceding 5 plan years, the plan is not permitted to be amended in accordance with the utilization test in this paragraph (f).

(3) *Participants taken into account.*—A participant is taken into account for purposes of this paragraph (f) only if the participant was eligible to elect to commence payment of an optional form of benefit that is part of the generalized optional form being eliminated with an annuity commencement date that is within the look-back period. However, a participant is not taken into account if the participant—

(i) Did not elect any optional form of benefit with an annuity commencement date that was within the look-back period;

(ii) Elected an optional form of benefit that included a single-sum distribution that applied with respect to at least 25% of the participant's accrued benefit;

(iii) Elected an optional form of benefit that was only available during a limited period of time and that contained a retirement-type subsidy where the subsidy that is part of the generalized optional form being eliminated was not extended to any optional form of benefit with the same annuity commencement date; or

(iv) Elected an optional form of benefit with an annuity commencement date that was more than 10 years before normal retirement age.

(4) *Determining the applicable number of participants.*—For purposes of applying the rules in this paragraph (f), the applicable number of participants is 50 participants. However, notwithstanding paragraph (f)(3)(ii) of this section, a plan is permitted to take into account any participant who elected an optional form of benefit that included a single-sum distribution that applied with respect to at least 25% of the participant's accrued benefit, but only if the applicable number of participants is increased to 1,000 participants.

(5) *Default elections.*—For purposes of this paragraph (f), an election includes the payment of an optional form of benefit that applies in the absence of an affirmative election.

(g) *Definitions and use of terms.*—The definitions in this paragraph (g) apply for purposes of this section.

(1) *Actuarial present value.*—The term *actuarial present value* means actuarial present value (within the meaning of § 1.401(a)(4)-12) determined using reasonable actuarial assumptions.

(2) *Ancillary benefit.*—The term *ancillary benefit* means—
(i) A social security supplement under a defined benefit plan (other than a QSUPP as defined in § 1.401(a)(4)-12);

(ii) A benefit payable under a defined benefit plan in the event of disability (to the extent that the benefit exceeds the benefit otherwise payable), but only if the total benefit payable in the event of disability does not exceed the maximum qualified disability benefit, as defined in section 411(a)(9);

(iii) A life insurance benefit;

(iv) A medical benefit described in section 401(h);

(v) A death benefit under a defined benefit plan other than a death benefit which is a part of an optional form of benefit; or

(vi) A plant shutdown benefit or other similar benefit in a defined benefit plan that does not continue past retirement age and does not affect the payment of the accrued benefit, but only to the extent that such plant shutdown benefit, or other similar benefit (if any), is permitted in a qualified pension plan (see § 1.401-1(b)(1)(i)).

(3) *Annuity commencement date.*—The term *annuity commencement date* generally means the annuity starting date, except that, in the case of a retroactive annuity starting date under section 417(a)(7), *annuity commencement date* means the date of the first payment of benefits pursuant to a participant election of a retroactive annuity starting date, as defined in § 1.417(e)-1(b)(3)(iv).

(4) *Applicable amendment date.*—The term *applicable amendment date*, with respect to a plan amendment, means the later of the effective date of the amendment or the date the amendment is adopted.

(5) *Core options.*—(i) *General rule.*—With respect to a plan, the term *core options* means—

(A) A straight life annuity generalized optional form under which the participant is entitled to a level life annuity with no benefit payable after the participant's death;

(B) A 75% joint and contingent annuity generalized optional form under which the participant is entitled to a life annuity with a survivor annuity for any individual designated by the participant (including a non-spousal contingent annuitant) that is 75% of the amount payable during the participant's life (but see paragraph (d)(2)(v) of this section for a special rule relating to the joint and contingent annuity core option);

(C) A 10-year term certain and life annuity generalized optional form under which the participant is entitled to a life annuity with a guarantee that payments will continue to any person designated by the participant for the remainder of a fixed period of 10 years if the participant dies before the end of the 10-year period; and

(D) The most valuable option for a participant with a short life expectancy (as defined in paragraph (g)(5)(iii) of this section).

(ii) *Modification of core options to satisfy other requirements.*—An annuity does not fail to be a core option (e.g., a joint and contingent annuity described in paragraph (g)(5)(i)(B) of this section or a 10-year term certain and life annuity described in paragraph (g)(5)(i)(C) of this section) as a result of differences to comply with applicable law, such as limitations on death benefits to comply with the incidental benefit requirement of (1.401-1(b)(1)(i) or on account of the spousal consent rules of section 417.

(iii) *Most valuable option for a participant with a short life expectancy.*—(A) *General definition.*—Except as provided in paragraph (g)(5)(iii)(B) of this section, *most valuable option for a participant with a short life expectancy* means, for an annuity starting date, the optional form of benefit that is reasonably expected to result in payments that have the largest actuarial present value in the case of a participant who dies shortly after the annuity starting date, taking into account both payments due to the participant prior to the participant's death and any payments due after the participant's death. For this purpose, a plan is permitted to assume that the spouse of the participant is the same age as the participant. In addition, a plan is permitted to assume that the optional form of benefit that is the most valuable option for a participant with a short life expectancy when the participant is age 701/2 also is the most valuable option for a participant with a short life expectancy at all older ages, and that the most valuable option for a participant with a short life expectancy at age 55 is the most valuable option for a participant with a short life expectancy at all younger ages.

(B) *Safe harbor hierarchy.*—(1) A plan is permitted to treat a single-sum distribution option with an actuarial present value that is not less than the actuarial present value of any optional form of benefit eliminated by the plan amendment as the most valuable option for a participant with a short life expectancy for all of a participant's annuity starting dates if such single-sum distribution option is available at all such dates, without regard to whether the option was available before the plan amendment.

(2) If the plan before the amendment does not offer a single-sum distribution option as described in paragraph (g)(5)(iii)(B)(1) of this section, a plan is permitted to treat a joint and contingent annuity with a continuation percentage that is at least 75% and that is at least as great as the highest continuation percent-

age available before the amendment as the most valuable option for a participant with a short life expectancy for all of a participant's annuity starting dates if such joint and contingent annuity is available at all such dates, without regard to whether the option was available before the plan amendment.

(3) If the plan before the amendment offers neither a single-sum distribution option as described in paragraph (g)(5)(iii)(B)(1) of this section nor a joint and contingent annuity with a continuation percentage as described in paragraph (g)(5)(iii)(B)(2) of this section, a plan is permitted to treat a term certain and life annuity with a term certain period no less than 15 years as the most valuable option for a participant with a short life expectancy for each annuity starting date if such 15-year term certain and life annuity is available at all annuity starting dates, without regard to whether the option was available before the plan amendment.

(6) *Definitions of types of section 411(d)(6)(B) protected benefits.*—(i) *Early retirement benefit.*—The term *early retirement benefit* means the right, under the terms of a plan, to commence distribution of a retirement-type benefit at a particular date after severance from employment with the employer and before normal retirement age. Different early retirement benefits result from differences in terms relating to timing.

(ii) *Optional form of benefit.*—(A) *In general.*—The term *optional form of benefit* means a distribution alternative (including the normal form of benefit) that is available under the plan with respect to an accrued benefit or a distribution alternative with respect to a retirement-type benefit. Different optional forms of benefit exist if a distribution alternative is not payable on substantially the same terms as another distribution alternative. The relevant terms include all terms affecting the value of the optional form, such as the method of benefit calculation and the actuarial factors or assumptions used to determine the amount distributed. Thus, for example, different optional forms of benefit may result from differences in terms relating to the payment schedule, timing, commencement, medium of distribution (e.g., in cash or in kind), election rights, differences in eligibility requirements, or the portion of the benefit to which the distribution alternative applies. Likewise, differences in the normal retirement ages of employees or in the form in which the accrued benefit of employees is payable at normal retirement age under a plan are taken into account in determining whether a distribution alternative constitutes one or more optional forms of benefit.

(B) *Death benefits.*—If a death benefit is payable after the annuity starting date for a specific optional form of benefit and the same death benefit would not be provided if another optional form of benefit were elected by a participant, then that death benefit is part of the specific optional form of benefit and is thus protected under section 411(d)(6). A death benefit is not treated as part of a specific optional form of benefit merely because the same benefit is not provided to a participant who has received his or her entire accrued benefit prior to death. For example, a $5,000 death benefit that is payable to all participants except any participant who has received his or her accrued benefit in a single-sum distribution is not part of a specific optional form of benefit.

(iii) *Retirement-type benefit.*—The term *retirement-type benefit* means—

(A) The payment of a distribution alternative with respect to an accrued benefit; or

(B) The payment of any other benefit under a defined benefit plan (including a QSUPP as defined in § 1.401(a)(4)-12) that is permitted to be in a qualified pension plan, continues after retirement, and is not an ancillary benefit.

(iv) *Retirement-type subsidy.*—The term *retirement-type subsidy* means the excess, if any, of the actuarial present value of a retirement-type benefit over the actuarial present value of the accrued benefit commencing at normal retirement age or at actual commencement date, if later, with both such actuarial present values determined as of the date the retirement-type benefit commences. Examples of retirement-type subsidies include a subsidized early retirement benefit and a subsidized qualified joint and survivor annuity.

(v) *Subsidized early retirement benefit or early retirement subsidy.*—The terms *subsidized early retirement benefit* or *early retirement subsidy* mean the right, under the terms of a plan, to commence distribution of a retirement-type benefit at a particular date after severance from employment with the employer and before normal retirement age where the actuarial present value of the optional forms of benefit available to the participant under the plan at that annuity starting date exceeds the actuarial present value of the accrued benefit commencing at normal retirement age (with such actuarial present values determined as of the annuity starting date). Thus, an early retirement subsidy is an early retirement benefit that provides a retirement-type subsidy.

(7) *Eliminate; elimination; reduce; reduction.*—The terms *eliminate* or *elimination* when used in connection with a section 411(d)(6)(B) protected benefit mean to eliminate or the elimination of an optional form of benefit or an early retirement benefit and to reduce or a reduction in a retirement-type subsidy. The terms *reduce* or *reduction* when used in connection with a retirement-type subsidy mean to reduce or a reduction in the amount of the subsidy. For purposes of this section, an *elimination* includes a *reduction* and a *reduction* includes an *elimination.*

(8) *Generalized optional form.*—The term *generalized optional form* means a group of optional forms of benefit that are identical except for differences due to the actuarial factors that are used to determine the amount of the distributions under those optional forms of benefit and the annuity starting dates.

(9) *Maximum QJSA explanation period.*—The term *maximum QJSA explanation period* means the maximum number of days before an annuity starting date for a qualified joint and survivor annuity for which a written explanation relating to the qualified joint and survivor annuity would satisfy the timing requirements of section 417(a)(3) and §1.417(e)-1(b)(3)(ii).

(10) *Other right and feature.*—The term *other right or feature* has the meaning set forth at §1.401(a)(4)-4(e)(3)(ii).

(11) *Refund of employee contributions feature.*—The term *refund of employee contributions feature* means a feature with respect to an optional form of benefit that provides for employee contributions and interest thereon to be paid in a single sum at the annuity starting date with the remainder to be paid in another form beginning on that date.

(12) *Retirement; retirement age.*—For purposes of this section, the date of *retirement* means the annuity starting date. Thus, *retirement age* means a participant's age at the annuity starting date.

(13) *Retroactive annuity starting date feature.*—The term *retroactive annuity starting date* feature means a feature with respect to an optional form of benefit under which the annuity starting date for the distribution occurs on or before the date the written explanation required by section 417(a)(3) is provided to the participant.

(14) *Section 411(d)(6) protected benefit.*—The term *section 411(d)(6) protected benefit* means the accrued benefit of a participant as of the applicable amendment date described in section 411(d)(6)(A) and any section 411(d)(6)(B) protected benefit.

(15) *Section 411(d)(6)(B) protected benefit.*—The term *section 411(d)(6)(B) protected benefit* means the portion of an early retirement benefit, a retirement-type subsidy, or an optional form of benefit attributable to benefits accrued before the applicable amendment date.

(16) *Social security leveling feature.*—The term *social security leveling feature* means a feature with respect to an optional form of benefit commencing prior to a participant's expected commencement of social security benefits that provides for a temporary period of higher payments which is designed to result in an approximately level amount of income when the participant's estimated old age benefits from Social Security are taken into account.

(h) *Examples.*—The following examples illustrate the application of paragraphs (c) through (g) of this section:

Example 1. (i) *Facts involving elimination of optional forms of benefit as redundant.* Plan C is a defined benefit plan under which employees may elect to commence distributions at any time after the later of termination of employment or attainment of age 55. At each potential annuity commencement date, Plan C permits employees to select, with spousal consent where required, a straight life annuity or any of a number of actuarially equivalent alternative forms of payment, including a straight life annuity with cost-of-living increases and a joint and contingent annuity with the participant having the right to select any beneficiary and any continuation percentage from 1% to 100%, subject to modification to the extent necessary to satisfy the requirements of the incidental benefit requirement of (1.401-1(b)(1)(i). The amount of any alternative payment is determined as the actuarial equivalent of the straight life annuity payable at the same age using reasonable actuarial assumptions. On June 2, 2006, Plan C is amended to delete all continuation percentages for joint and contingent options other than 25%, 50%, 75%, or 100%, effective with respect to annuity commencement dates that are on or after January 1, 2007.

(ii) *Conclusion*—(A) *Categorization of family members under the redundancy rule.* The optional forms of benefit described in paragraph (i) of this *Example 1* are members of 4 families: a straight life annuity; a straight life annuity with cost-of-living increases; joint and contingent options with continuation percentages of less than 50%; and joint and contingent options with continuation percentages of 50% or

more. The amendment does not affect either of the first two families, but affects the two families relating to joint and contingent options.

(B) *Conclusion for elimination of optional forms of benefit as redundant.* The amendment satisfies the requirements of paragraph (c) of this section. First, the eliminated optional forms of benefit are redundant with respect to the retained optional forms of benefit because each eliminated joint and contingent annuity option with a continuation percentage of less than 50% is redundant with respect to the 25% continuation option and each eliminated joint and contingent annuity option with a continuation percentage of 50% or higher is redundant with respect to any one of the retained 50%, 75%, or 100% continuation options. In addition, to the extent the optional form of benefit that is being eliminated does not include a social security leveling feature, return of employee contribution feature, or retroactive annuity starting date feature, the retained optional form of benefit does not include that feature. Second, the amendment is not effective with respect to annuity commencement dates before September 1, 2006, as required under paragraph (c)(1)(ii) of this section. Third, the plan amendment does not eliminate any available core option, including the most valuable option for a participant with a short life expectancy, treating a joint and contingent annuity with a 100% continuation percentage as this optional form of benefit pursuant to paragraph (g)(5)(iii)(B)(2) of this section. Finally, the amendment need not satisfy the requirements of paragraph (e) of this section because the retained optional forms of benefit are available on the same annuity commencement dates and have the same actuarial present value as the optional forms of benefit that are being eliminated.

Example 2. (i) *Facts involving elimination of optional forms of benefit as redundant if additional restrictions are imposed.* The facts are the same as *Example 1,* except that the plan amendment also restricts the class of beneficiaries that may be elected under the 4 retained joint and contingent annuities to the employee's spouse.

(ii) *Conclusion.* The amendment fails to satisfy the requirements of paragraph (c)(2)(i)(B) of this section because the retained joint and contingent annuities have materially greater restrictions on the beneficiary designation than did the eliminated joint and contingent annuities. Thus, the joint and contingent annuities being eliminated are not redundant with respect to the retained joint and contingent annuities. In addition, the amendment fails to satisfy the requirements of the core option rules in paragraph (d) of this section because the amendment fails to be limited to annuity commencement dates that are at least 4 years after the date the amendment is adopted, the amendment fails to include the core option in paragraph (g)(5)(i)(B) of this section because the participant does not have the right to designate any beneficiary, and the amendment fails to include the core option described in paragraph (g)(5)(i)(C) of this section because the plan does not provide a 10-year term certain and life annuity.

Example 3. (i) *Facts involving elimination of a social security leveling feature and a period certain annuity as redundant.* Plan D is a defined benefit plan under which participants may elect to commence distributions in the following actuarially equivalent forms, with spousal consent if applicable: a straight life annuity; a 50%, 75%, or 100% joint and contingent annuity; a 5-year, 10-year, or a 15-year term certain and life annuity; and an installment refund annuity (i.e., an optional form of benefit that provides a period certain, the duration of which is based on the participant's age), with the participant having the right to select any beneficiary. In addition, each annuity offered under the plan, if payable to a participant who is less than age 65, is available both with and without a social security leveling feature. The social security leveling feature provides for an assumed commencement of social security benefits at any age selected by the participant between age 62 and 65. Plan D is amended on June 2, 2006, effective as of January 1, 2007, to eliminate the installment refund form of benefit and to restrict the social security leveling feature to an assumed social security commencement age of 65.

(ii) *Conclusion.* The amendment satisfies the requirements of paragraph (c) of this section. First, the installment refund annuity option is redundant with respect to the 15-year certain and life annuity (except for advanced ages where, because of shorter life expectancies, the installment refund annuity option is redundant with respect to the 5-year certain and life annuity and also redundant with respect to the 10-year certain and life annuity). Second, with respect to restricting the social security leveling feature to an assumed social security commencement age of 65, under paragraph (c)(3)(ii)(C) of this section, straight life annuities with social security leveling features that have different social security commencement ages are treated as members of the same family as straight life annuities without social security leveling features. To the extent an optional form of benefit that is being eliminated includes a social security leveling feature, the retained optional form of benefit must also include that feature, but it is permitted to have a different assumed age for commencement of social security benefits. Third, to the extent that the optional form of benefit that is being eliminated does not include a social security leveling feature, a return of employee contribution feature, or retroactive annuity starting date feature, the retained optional form of benefit must not include that feature. Fourth, the plan amendment does not eliminate any available core option, including the most valuable option for a participant with a short life expectancy, treating a joint and contingent annuity with a 100% continuation percentage as this optional form of benefit pursuant to paragraph (g)(5)(iii)(B)(2) of this section. Fifth, the amendment is not effective with respect to annuity commencement dates before September 1, 2006, as required under paragraph (c)(1)(ii) of this section. The amendment need not satisfy the requirements of paragraph (e) of this section because the retained optional forms of benefit are available on the same annuity commencement dates and have the same actuarial present value as the optional forms of benefit that are being eliminated.

Example 4. (i) *Facts involving elimination of noncore options.* Employer N sponsors Plan E, a defined benefit plan that permits every participant to elect payment in the following actuarially equivalent optional forms of benefit (Plan E's uniformly available options), with spousal consent if applicable: a straight life annuity; a 50%, 75%, or 100% joint and contingent annuity with no restrictions on designation of beneficiaries; and a 5-, 10-, or 15-year term certain and life annuity. In addition, each can be elected in conjunction with a social security leveling feature, with the participant permitted to select a social security commencement age from age 62 to age 67. None of Plan E's uniformly available options include a single-sum distribution. The plan has been in existence for over 30 years, during which time Employer N has acquired a large number of other businesses, including merging over 20 defined benefit plans of acquired entities into Plan E. Many of the merged plans offered optional forms of benefit that were not among Plan E's uniformly available options, including some plans funded through insurance products, often offering all of the insurance annuities that the insurance carrier offers, and with some of the merged plans offering single-sum distributions. In particular, under the XYZ acquisition that occurred in 1990, the XYZ acquired plan offered a single-sum distribution option that was frozen at the time of the acquisition. On April 1, 2006, each single-sum distribution option applies to less than 25% of the XYZ participants' accrued benefits. Employer N has generally, but not uniformly, followed the practice of limiting the optional forms of benefit for an acquired unit to an employee's service before the date of the merger, and has uniformly followed this practice with respect to each of the early retirement subsidies in the acquired unit's plan. As a result, as of April 1, 2007, Plan E includes a large number of generalized optional forms which are not members of families of optional forms of benefit identified in paragraph (c)(4) of this section, but there are no participants who are entitled to any early retirement subsidies because any subsidies have been subsumed by the actuarially reduced accrued benefit. Plan E is amended in April of 2007 to eliminate all of the optional forms of benefit that Plan E offers other than Plan E's uniformly available options, except that the amendment does not eliminate any single-sum distribution option except with respect to XYZ participants and permits any commencement date that was permitted under Plan E before the amendment. Plan E also eliminates the single-sum distribution option for XYZ participants. Further, each of Plan E's uniformly available options has an actuarial present value that is not less than the actuarial present value of any optional form of benefit offered before the amendment. The amendment is effective with respect to annuity commencement dates that are on or after May 1, 2011.

(ii) *Conclusion.* The amendment satisfies the requirements of paragraph (d) of this section. First, Plan E, as amended, does not eliminate any single-sum distribution option as provided in paragraph (d)(2)(iii) of this section except for single-sum distribution options that apply to less than 25% of a plan participant's accrued benefit as of the date the option is eliminated (May 1, 2011). Second, Plan E, as amended, includes each of the core options as defined in paragraph

(g)(5) of this section, including offering the most valuable option for a participant with a short life expectancy (treating the 100% joint and contingent annuity as this benefit, under paragraph (g)(5)(iii)(B)(2) of this section). The 100% joint and contingent annuity option (and not the grandfathered single-sum distribution option) is the most valuable option for a participant with a short life expectancy because the grandfathered single-sum distribution option is not available with respect to a participant's entire accrued benefit. In addition, as required under paragraph (d)(2) of this section, to the extent an optional form of benefit that is being eliminated includes either a social security leveling feature or a refund of employee contributions feature, at least one of the core options is available with that feature and, to the extent that the optional form of benefit that is being eliminated does not include a social security leveling feature or a refund of employee contributions feature, each of the core options is available without that feature. Third, the amendment is not effective with respect to annuity commencement dates that are less than 4 years after the date the amendment is adopted. Finally, the amendment need not satisfy the requirements of paragraph (e) of this section because the retained optional forms of benefit are available on the same annuity commencement date and have the same actuarial present value as the optional forms of benefit that are being eliminated. The conclusion that the amendment satisfies the requirements of paragraph (d) of this section assumes that no amendments are made to change the core options before May 1, 2014.

Example 5. (i) *Facts involving reductions in actuarial present value.* (A) Plan F is a defined benefit plan providing an accrued benefit of 1% of the average of a participant's highest 3 consecutive years' pay times years of service, payable as a straight life annuity beginning at the normal retirement age at age 65. Plan F permits employees to elect to commence actuarially reduced distributions at any time after the later of termination of employment or attainment of age 55. At each potential annuity commencement date, Plan F permits employees to select, with spousal consent, either a straight life annuity, a joint and contingent annuity with the participant having the right to select any beneficiary and a continuation percentage of 50%, 66 2/3%, 75%, or 100%, or a 10-year certain and life annuity with the participant having the right to select any beneficiary, subject to modification to the extent necessary to satisfy the requirements of the incidental benefit requirement of § 1.401-1(b)(1)(i). The amount of any joint and contingent annuity and the 10-year certain and life annuity is determined as the actuarial equivalent of the straight life annuity payable at the same age using reasonable actuarial assumptions. The plan covers employees at 4 divisions, one of which, Division X, was acquired on January 1, 1999. The plan provides for distributions before normal retirement age to be actuarially reduced, but, if a participant retires after attainment of age 55 and completion of 10 years of service, the applicable early retirement reduction factor is 3% per year for the years between age 65 and 62 and 6% per year for the ages from 62 to 55 for all employees at any division, except for employees who were in Division X on January 1, 1999, for whom the early retirement reduction factor for retirement after age 55 and 10 years of service is 5% for each year before age 65. On June 2, 2006, effective January 1, 2007, Plan F is amended to change the early retirement reduction factors for all employees of Division X to be the same as for other employees, effective with respect to annuity commencement dates that are on or after January 1, 2008, but only with respect to participants who are employees on or after January 1, 2008 and only if Plan F continues accruals at the current rate through January 1, 2008 (or the effective date of the change in reduction factors is delayed to reflect the change in the accrual rate). For purposes of this *Example 5*, it is assumed that an actuarially equivalent early retirement factor would have a reduction shown in column 4 of the following table, which compares the reduction factors for Division X before and after the amendment:

1	2	3	4	5
Age	Old Division X Factor (as a %)	New Factor (as a %)	Actuarially Equivalent Factor (as a %)	Column 3 minus Column 2
65	NA	NA	NA	NA
64	95	97	91.1	+2
63	90	94	83.2	+4
62	85	91	76.1	+5
61	80	85	69.8	+5
60	75	79	64.1	+4
59	70	73	59.0	+3
58	65	67	54.3	+2
57	60	61	50.1	+1
56	55	55	46.3	0
55	50	49	42.8	−1

Reg. § 1.411(d)-3(h)

(B) On January 1, 2007, the employee with the largest number of years of service is Employee E, who is age 54 and has 20 years of service. For 2006, Employee E's compensation is $80,000 and E's highest 3 consecutive years of pay on January 1, 2007 is $75,000. Employee E's accrued benefit as of the January 1, 2007 effective date of the amendment is a life annuity of $15,000 per year at normal retirement age (1% times $75,000 times 20 years of service) and E's early retirement benefit commencing at age 55 has a present value of $91,397 as of January 1, 2007. It is assumed for purposes of this example that the longest expected transition period for any active employee does not exceed 5 months (20 years and 5 months, times 1% times 49% exceeds 20 years times 1% times 50%). Finally, it is assumed for purposes of this example that the amendment reduces optional forms of benefit which are burdensome or complex.

(ii) *Conclusion concerning application of section 411(d)(6)(B).* The amendment reducing the early retirement factors has the effect of eliminating the existing optional forms of benefit (where the amount of the benefit is based on preamendment early retirement factors in any case where the new factors result in a smaller amount payable) and adding new optional forms of benefit (where the amount of benefit is based on the different early retirement factors). Accordingly, the elimination must satisfy the requirements of paragraph (c) or (d) of this section if the amount payable at any date is less than would have been payable under the plan before the amendment.

(iii) *Conclusion concerning application of redundancy rules.* The amendment satisfies the requirements of paragraph (c)(1)(i) and (ii) of this section (see paragraphs (iv) through (vi) of this *Example 5* below for the requirements of paragraph (c)(1)(iii) of this section). First, with respect to each eliminated optional form of benefit (i.e., with respect to each optional form of benefit with the Old Division X Factor), after the amendment there is a retained optional form of benefit that is in the same family of optional forms of benefit (i.e., the optional form of benefit with the New Factor). Second, the amendment is not effective with respect to annuity commencement dates that are less than the time period required under paragraph (c)(1)(ii) of this section. Third, to the extent that the plan amendment eliminates the most valuable option for a participant with a short life expectancy, the retained optional form of benefit is identical except for differences in actuarial factors.

(iv) *Conclusion concerning application of the requirements under paragraph (e) of this section.* The plan amendment must satisfy the requirements of paragraph (e) of this section because, as of the December 2, 2006 adoption date, the actuarial present value of the early retirement subsidy is less than the actuarial present value of the early retirement subsidy being eliminated. The plan amendment satisfies the requirements under paragraph (e)(1)(i) and (2) of this section because the amendment eliminates optional forms of benefit that create significant burdens or complexities for the plan and its participants. See below for the de minimis requirement under paragraph (e)(1)(ii) and (3) of this section.

(v) *Conclusion concerning application of de minimis rules under paragraph (e)(5) of this section.* In order to satisfy the requirements under paragraph (e)(1)(ii) and (3) of this section, the amendment must satisfy the requirements of either paragraph (e)(5) or paragraph (e)(6) of this section. The amendment does not satisfy the requirements of paragraph (e)(5) of this section because the reduction in the actuarial present value is more than a de minimis amount under paragraph (e)(5) of this section. For example, for Employee E, the amount of the joint and contingent annuity payable at age 55 is reduced from $7,500 (50% of $15,000) to $7,350 (49% of $15,000) and the reduction in present value as a result of the amendment is $1,828 ($91,397 – $89,569). In this case, the retirement-type subsidy at age 55 is the excess of the present value of the 50% early retirement benefit over the present value of the deferred payment of the accrued benefit, or $13,921 ($97,269 – $83,348) and the present value at age 54 of the retirement-type subsidy is $13,081. The reduction in present value is more than the greater of 2% of the present value of the retirement-type subsidy and 1% of E's compensation because the reduction in present value exceeds $800 (the greater of $262, which is 2% of the present value of the retirement-type subsidy for the benefit being eliminated, and $800, which is 1% of E's compensation of $80,000).

(vi) *Conclusion involving application of de minimis rules under paragraph (e)(6) of this section relating to expected transition period.* The amendment satisfies the requirements of paragraph (e)(6) of this section and, thus, satisfies the requirements of paragraph (c) of this section, including the requirement in paragraph (c)(1)(iii) of this section that paragraph (e) of this section be satisfied. First, as assumed under the facts above, the amendment reduces optional forms of benefit that are burdensome or complex. Second, the plan amendment is not effective for annuity commencement dates before January 1, 2008, and that date is not earlier than the longest expected transition period for any participant in Plan F on the date of the amendment. Third, the amendment does not apply to any participant who has a severance from employment during the transition period. If,

however, a later plan amendment reduces accruals under Plan F, the initial plan amendment will no longer satisfy the requirements of paragraph (e)(6) of this section (and must be voided) unless, as part of the later amendment, the expected transition period is extended to reflect the reduction in accruals under Plan F.

Example 6. (i) *Facts involving elimination of noncore options using utilization test*—(A) *In general.* Plan G is a calendar year defined benefit plan under which participants may elect to commence distributions after termination of employment in the following actuarially equivalent forms, with spousal consent, if applicable: a straight life annuity; a 50%, 75%, or 100% joint and contingent annuity; or a 5-year, 10-year, or a 15-year term certain and life annuity. A participant is permitted to elect a single-sum distribution if the present value of the participant's nonforfeitable accrued benefit is not greater than $5,000. The annuities offered under the plan are generally available both with and without a social security leveling feature. The social security leveling feature provides for an assumed commencement of social security benefits at any age selected by the participant between the ages of 62 and 67. Under Plan G, the normal retirement age is defined as age 65.

(B) *Utilization test.* In 2007, the plan sponsor of Plan G, after reviewing participants' benefit elections, determines that, during the period from January 1, 2005, through June 30, 2007, no participant has elected a 5-year term certain and life annuity with a social security leveling option. During that period, Plan G has made the 5-year term certain and life annuity with a social security leveling option available to 142 participants who were at least age 55 and who elected optional forms of benefit with an annuity commencement dates during that period. In addition, during that period, 20 of the 142 participants elected a single-sum distribution and there was no retirement-type subsidy available for a limited period of time. Plan G, in accordance with paragraph (f)(1) of this section, is amended on September 15, 2007, effective as of January 1, 2008, to eliminate all 5-year term certain and life annuities with a social security leveling option for all annuity commencement dates on or after January 1, 2008.

(ii) *Conclusion.* The amendment satisfies the requirements of paragraph (f) of this section. First, the 5-year term certain and life annuity with a social security leveling option is not a core option as defined in paragraph (g)(5) of this section. Second, the plan amendment is not applicable with respect to an optional form of benefit with an annuity commencement date that is earlier than the number of days in the maximum QJSA explanation period after the date the amendment is adopted. Third, the 5-year term certain and life annuity with a social security leveling option has been available to at least 50 participants who are taken into account for purposes of paragraph (f) of this section during the look-back period. Fourth, during the look-back period, no participant elected any optional form that is part of the generalized optional form being eliminated (for example, the 5-year term and life annuity with a social security leveling option).

(i) [Reserved].

(j) *Effective dates.*—(1) *General effective date.*—Except as otherwise provided in this paragraph (j), the rules of this section apply to amendments adopted on or after August 12, 2005.

(2) *Effective date for rules relating to contingent event benefits.*—Paragraph (b)(1)(ii) of this section applies to amendments adopted after December 31, 2005.

(3) *Effective dates for rules relating to section 411 (a) nonforfeitability provisions.*—(i) *Application of suspension of benefit rules to section 411 (d) (6) protected benefits.*—With respect to a plan amendment that places greater restrictions or conditions on a participant's rights to section 411 (d) (6) protected benefits by adding or modifying a plan provision relating to suspension of benefit payments during a period of employment or reemployment, the rules provided in paragraph (a) (3) of this section apply to periods beginning on or after June 7, 2004.

(ii) *Application of section 411(a) nonforfeitability provisions to section 411 (d) (6) protected benefits.*—With respect to a plan amendment that places greater restrictions or conditions on a participant's rights to section 411 (d) (6) protected benefits other than a plan amendment described in paragraph (j)(3)(i) of this section, the rules provided in paragraph (a) (3) of this section apply to plan amendments adopted after August 9, 2006.

(4) *Effective date for change to redundancy rule regarding bifurcation of benefits.*—The rules provided in paragraph (c)(6) of this section are applicable for amendments adopted after August 9, 2006.

(5) *Effective date for rules relating to utilization test.*—The rules provided in paragraph (f) of this section are applicable for amendments adopted after December 31, 2006. [Reg. § 1.411(d)-3.]

☐ [T.D. 7501, 8-22-77. Amended by T.D. 8038, 7-18-85; T.D. 8219, 8-19-88; T.D. 9219, 8-11-2005; T.D. 9280, 8-8-2006 (corrected 9-20-2006) and T.D. 9472, 11-23-2009.]

[Reg. §1.411(d)-4]

§1.411(d)-4. Section 411(d)(6) protected benefits.

Q-1: What are "section 411(d)(6) protected benefits"?

A-1: (a) *In general.* The term "section 411(d)(6) protected benefit" includes any benefit that is described in one or more of the following categories—

(1) Benefits described in section 411(d)(6)(A),

(2) Early retirement benefits (as defined in §1.411(d)-3(g)(6)(i)) and retirement-type subsidies (as defined in §1.411(d)-3(g)(6)(iv)), and

(3) Optional forms of benefit described in section 411(d)(6)(B)(ii).

Such benefits, to the extent they have accrued, are subject to the protection of section 411(d)(6) and, where applicable, the definitely determinable requirement of section 401(a) (including section 401(a)(25)) and cannot, therefore, be reduced, eliminated or made subject to employer discretion except to the extent permitted by regulations.

(b) *Optional forms of benefit*—(1) *In general.* The term *optional form of benefit* has the same meaning as in §1.411(d)-3(g)(6)(ii). Under this definition, different optional forms of benefit exist if a distribution alternative is not payable on substantially the same terms as another distribution alternative. Thus, for example, different optional forms of benefit may result from differences in terms relating to the payment schedule, timing, commencement, medium of distribution (e.g., in cash or in kind), election rights, differences in eligibility requirements, or the portion of the benefit to which the distribution alternative applies.

(2) *Examples.* The following examples illustrate the meaning of the term "optional form of benefit." Other issues, such as the requirement that the optional forms satisfy section 401(a)(4), are not addressed in these examples and no inferences are intended with respect to such requirements. Assume that the distribution forms, including those not described in these examples, provided under the plan in each of the following examples are identical in all respects not described.

Example 1. A plan permits each participant to receive his benefit under the plan as a single sum distribution; a level monthly distribution schedule over 15 years; a single life annuity; a joint and 50 percent survivor annuity; a joint and 75 percent survivor annuity; a joint and 50 percent survivor annuity with a benefit increase for the participant if the beneficiary dies before a specified date; and joint and 50 percent survivor annuity with a 10 year certain feature. Each of these benefit distribution options is an optional form of benefit (without regard to whether the values of these options are actuarially equivalent).

Example 2. A plan permits each participant who is employed by division A to receive his benefit in a single sum distribution payable upon termination from employment and each participant who is employed by division B in a single sum distribution payable upon termination from employment on or after the attainment of age 50. This plan provides two single sum optional forms of benefit.

Example 3. A plan permits each participant to receive his benefit in a single life annuity that commences in the month after the participant's termination from employment or in a single life annuity that commences upon the completion of five consecutive one year breaks in service. These are two optional forms of benefit.

Example 4. A profit-sharing plan permits each participant who is employed by division A to receive an in-service distribution upon the satisfaction of objective criteria set forth in the plan designed to determine whether the participant has a heavy and immediate financial need, and each participant who is employed by division B to receive an in-service distribution upon the satisfaction of objective criteria set forth in the plan designed to determine whether the participant has a heavy and immediate financial need attributable to extraordinary medical expenses. These in-service distribution options are two optional forms of benefit.

Example 5. A profit-sharing plan permits each participant who is employed by division A to receive an in-service distribution up to $5,000 and each participant who is employed by division B to receive an in-service distribution of up to his total benefit. These in-service distribution options differ as to the portion of the accrued benefit that may be distributed in a particular form and are, therefore, two optional forms of benefit.

Example 6. A profit-sharing plan provides for a single sum distribution on termination of employment. The plan is amended in 1991 to eliminate the single sum optional form of benefit with respect to benefits accrued after the date of amendment. This single sum optional form of benefit continues to be a single optional form of benefit although, over time, the percentage of various employees' accrued benefits that are potentially payable under this single sum may vary because the form is only available with respect to benefits accrued up to and including the date of the amendment.

Example 7. A profit-sharing plan permits each participant to receive a single sum distribution of his benefit in cash or in the form of a specified class of employer stock. This plan provides two single sum distribution optional forms of benefit.

Example 8. A stock bonus plan permits each participant to receive a single sum distribution of his benefit in cash or in the form of the property in which such participant's benefit was invested prior to the distribution. This plan's single sum distribution option provides two optional forms of benefit.

Example 9. A defined benefit plan provides for an early retirement benefit payable upon termination of employment after attainment of age 55 and either after ten years of service or, if earlier, upon plan termination to employees of Division A and provides for an identical early retirement benefit payable on the same terms with the exception of payment on plan termination to employees of Division B. The plan provides for two optional forms of benefit.

Example 10. A profit-sharing plan provides for loans secured by an employee's account balance. In the event of default on such a loan, there is an execution on such account balances. Such execution is a distribution of the employee's accrued benefits under the plan. A distribution of an accrued benefit contingent on default under a plan loan secured by such accrued benefits is an optional form of benefit under the plan.

(c) *Plan terms*—(1) *General rule.* Generally, benefits described in section 411(d)(6)(A), early retirement benefits, retirement-type subsidies, and optional forms of benefit are section 411(d)(6) protected benefits only if they are provided under the terms of a plan. However, if an employer establishes a pattern of repeated plan amendments providing for similar benefits in similar situations for substantially consecutive, limited periods of time, such benefits will be treated as provided under the terms of the plan, without regard to the limited periods of time, to the extent necessary to carry out the purposes of section 411(d)(6) and, where applicable, the definitely determinable requirement of section 401(a), including section 401(a)(25). A pattern of repeated plan amendments providing that a particular optional form of benefit is available to certain named employees for a limited period of time is within the scope of this rule and may result in such optional form of benefit being treated as provided under the terms of the plan to all employees covered under the plan without regard to the limited period of time and the limited group of named employees.

(2) *Effective date.* The provisions of paragraph (c)(1) of this Q&A-1 are effective as of July 11, 1988. Thus, patterns of repeated plan amendments adopted and effective before July 11, 1988, will be disregarded in determining whether such amendments have created an ongoing optional form of benefit under the plan.

(d) *Benefits that are not section 411(d)(6) protected benefits.* The following benefits are examples of items that are not section 411(d)(6) protected benefits: (1) ancillary life insurance protection; (2) accident or health insurance benefits; (3) social security supplements described in section 411(a)(9), except qualified social security supplements as defined in §1.401(a)(4)-12; (4) the availability of loans (other than the distribution of an employee's accrued benefit upon default under a loan); (5) the right to make after-tax employee contributions or elective deferrals described in section 402(g)(3); (6) the right to direct investments; (7) the right to a particular form of investment (e.g., investment in employer stock or securities or investment in certain types of securities, commercial paper, or other investment media); (8) the allocation dates for contributions, forfeitures, and earnings, the time for making contributions (but not the conditions for receiving an allocation of contributions or forfeitures for a plan year after such conditions have been satisfied), and the valuation dates for account balances; (9) administrative procedures for distributing benefits, such as provisions relating to the particular dates on which notices are given and by which elections must be made; and (10) rights that derive from administrative and operational provisions, such as mechanical procedures for allocating investment experience among accounts in defined contribution plans.

Q-2: To what extent may section 411(d)(6) protected benefits under a plan be reduced or eliminated?

A-2: (a) *Reduction or elimination of section 411(d)(6) protected benefits*—(1) *In general.* A plan is not permitted to be amended to eliminate or reduce a section 411(d)(6) protected benefit that has already accrued, except as provided in §1.411(d)-3 or this section. This is generally the case even if such elimination or reduction is contingent upon the employee's consent. However, a plan may be amended to eliminate or reduce section 411(d)(6) protected benefits with respect to benefits not yet accrued as of the later of the amendment's adoption date or effective date without violating section 411(d)(6).

(2) *Selection of optional forms of benefit*—(i) *General rule.* A plan may treat a participant as receiving his entire nonforfeitable accrued benefit under the plan if the participant receives his benefit in an optional

form of benefit in an amount determined under the plan that is at least the actuarial equivalent of the employee's nonforfeitable accrued benefit payable at normal retirement age under the plan. This is true even though the participant could have elected to receive an optional form of benefit with a greater actuarial value than the value of the optional form received, such as an optional form including retirement-type subsidies, and without regard to whether such other, more valuable optional form could have commenced immediately or could have become available only upon the employee's future satisfaction of specified eligibility conditions.

(ii) *Election of an optional form.* Except as provided in paragraph (a)(2)(iii) of this Q&A-2, a plan does not violate section 411(d)(6) merely because an employee's election to receive a portion of his nonforfeitable accrued benefit in one optional form of benefit precludes the employee from receiving that portion of his benefit in another optional form of benefit. Such employee retains all 411(d)(6) protected rights with respect to the entire portion of such employee's nonforfeitable accrued benefit for which no distribution election was made. For purposes of this rule, an elective transfer of an otherwise distributable benefit is treated as the selection of an optional form of benefit. See Q&A-3 of this section.

(iii) *Buy-back rule.* Notwithstanding paragraph (a)(2)(ii) of this Q&A-2, an employee who received a distribution of his nonforfeitable benefit from a plan that is required to provide a repayment opportunity to such employee if he returns to service within the applicable period pursuant to the requirements of section 411(a)(7) and who, upon subsequent reemployment, repays the full amount of such distribution in accordance with section 411(a)(7)(C) must be reinstated in the full array of section 411(d)(6) protected benefits that existed with respect to such benefit prior to distribution.

(iv) *Examples.* The rules in this paragraph (a)(2) can be illustrated by the following examples:

Example 1. Defined benefit plan X provides, among its optional forms of benefit, for a subsidized early retirement benefit payable in the form of an annuity and available to employees who terminate from employment on or after their 55th birthdays. In addition plan X provides for a single sum distribution available on termination from employment or termination of the plan. The single sum distribution is determined on the basis of the present value of the accrued normal retirement benefit and does not take the early retirement subsidy into account. Plan X is terminated December 31, 1991. Employees U, age 47, V, age 55, and W, age 47, all continue in the service of the employer. Employees X, age 47, Y, age 55 and Z, age 47, terminate from employment with the employer during 1991. Employees U and V elect to take the single sum optional form of distribution at the time of plan termination. Employees X and Y elect to take the single sum distribution on termination from employment with the employer. The elimination of the subsidized early retirement benefit with respect to employees U, V, X and Y does not result in a violation of section 411(d)(6). This is the result even though employees U and X had not yet satisfied the conditions for the subsidized early retirement benefit. Because employees W and Z have not selected an optional form of benefit, they continue to have a 411(d)(6) protected right to the full array of section 411(d)(6) protected benefits provided under the plan, including the single sum distribution form and the subsidized early retirement benefit.

Example 2. A partially vested employee receives a single sum distribution of the present value of his entire nonforfeitable benefit on account of separation from service under a defined benefit plan providing for a repayment provision. Upon reemployment with the employer such employee makes repayment in the required amount in accordance with section 411(a)(7). Such employee may, upon subsequent termination of employment, elect to take such repaid benefits in any optional form provided under the plan as of the time of the employee's initial separation from service. If the plan was amended prior to such repayment, to eliminate the single sum optional form of benefit with respect to benefits accrued after the date of the amendment, such participant has a 411(d)(6) protected right to take distribution of the repaid benefit in the form of a single sum distribution.

(3) *Certain transactions*—(i) *Plan mergers and benefit transfers.* The prohibition against the reduction or elimination of section 411(d)(6) protected benefits already accrued applies to plan mergers, spinoffs, transfers, and transactions amending or having the effect of amending a plan or plans to transfer plan benefits. Thus, for example, if Plan A, a profit-sharing plan that provides for distribution of plan benefits in annual installments over ten or twenty years, is merged with Plan B, a profit-sharing plan that provides for distribution of plan benefits in annual installments over life expectancy at time of retirement, the merged plan must retain the ten or twenty year installment option for participants with respect to benefits already accrued under Plan A as of the merger and the installments over life expectancy for participants with benefits already accrued under Plan B. Similarly, for example, if an employee's benefit under a defined contribution plan is transferred to another defined contribution plan (whether or not of the same employer), the optional forms of benefit available with respect to the employee's benefit accrued under the transferor plan may not be eliminated or reduced except as otherwise permitted under this regulation. See Q&A-3 of this section with respect to the transfer of benefits between and among defined benefit and defined contribution plans.

(ii) *Annuity contracts*—(A) *General rule.* The right of a participant to receive a benefit in the form of cash payments from the plan and the right of a participant to receive that benefit in the form of the distribution of an annuity contract that provides for cash payments that are identical in all respects to the cash payments from the plan except with respect to the source of the payments are not separate optional forms of benefit. Therefore, for example, if a plan includes an optional form of benefit under which benefits are distributed in the medium of an annuity contract that provides for cash payments, that optional form of benefit may be modified by a plan amendment that substitutes cash payments from the plan for the annuity contract, where those cash payments from the plan are identical to the cash payments payable from the annuity contract in all respects except with respect to the source of the payments. The protection provided by section 411(d)(6) may not be avoided by the use of annuity contracts. Thus, section 411(d)(6) protected benefits already accrued may not be eliminated or reduced merely because a plan uses annuity contracts to provide such benefits, without regard to whether the plan, a participant, or a beneficiary of a participant holds the contract or whether such annuity contracts are purchased as a result of the termination of the plan. However, to the extent that an annuity contract constitutes payment of benefits in a particular optional form elected by the participant, the plan does not violate section 411(d)(6) merely because it provides that other optional forms are no longer available with respect to such participant. See paragraph (a)(2) of this Q&A-2.

(B) *Examples.* The provisions of this paragraph (a)(3)(ii) can be illustrated by the following examples:

Example 1. A profit-sharing plan that is being terminated satisfies section 411(d)(6) only if the plan makes available to participants annuity contracts that provide for all section 411(d)(6) protected benefits under the plan that may not otherwise be reduced or eliminated pursuant to this Q&A-2. Thus, if such a plan provided for a single sum distribution upon attainment of early retirement age, and a provision for payment in the form of 10 equal annual installments, the plan would satisfy section 411(d)(6) only if the participants had the opportunity to elect to have their benefits provided under an annuity contract that provided for the same single sum distribution upon the attainment of the participant's early retirement age and the same 10 year installment optional form of benefit.

Example 2. A defined benefit plan permits each participant who separates from service on or after age 62 to receive a qualified joint and survivor annuity or a single life annuity commencing 45 days after termination from employment. For a participant who separates from service before age 62, payments under these optional forms of benefit commence 45 days after the participant's 62nd birthday. Under the plan, a participant is to elect among these optional forms of benefit during the 90-day period preceding the annuity starting date. However, during such period, a participant may defer both benefit commencement and the election of a particular benefit form to any later date, subject to section 401(a)(9). In January 1990, the employer decides to terminate the plan as of July 1, 1990. The plan will fail to satisfy section 411(d)(6) unless the optional forms of benefit provided under the plan are preserved under the annuity contract purchased on plan termination. Thus, such annuity contract must provide a participant the same optional benefit commencement rights that the plan provided. In addition, such contract must provide the same election rights with respect to such benefit options. This is the case even if, for example, in conjunction with the termination, the employer amended the plan to permit participants to elect a qualified joint and survivor annuity, single life annuity, or single sum distribution commencing on July 1, 1990.

(4) *Benefits payable to a spouse or beneficiary.* Section 411(d)(6) protected benefits may not be eliminated merely because they are payable with respect to a spouse or other beneficiary.

(b) *Section 411(d)(6) protected benefits that may be eliminated or reduced only as permitted by the Commissioner*—(1) *In general.* The Commissioner may, consistent with the provisions of this section, provide for the elimination or reduction of section 411(d)(6) protected benefits that have already accrued only to the extent that such elimination or reduction does not result in the loss to plan participants of either a valuable right or an employer-subsidized optional form of benefit where a similar optional form of benefit with a comparable subsidy is not provided or to the extent such elimination or reduction is necessary to permit compliance with other requirements of section 401(a) (e.g., sections 401(a)(4), 401(a)(9) and 415). The Commissioner may exercise this authority only through the publication of revenue rulings, notices, and other documents of general applicability.

(2) *Section 411(d)(6) protected benefits that may be eliminated or reduced.* The elimination or reduction of certain section 411(d)(6) protected benefits that have already accrued in the following situations does not violate section 411(d)(6). The rules with respect to permissible eliminations and reductions provided in this paragraph (b)(2) generally are effective January 30, 1986; however, the rules of paragraphs (b)(2)(iii)(A) and (B) and (b)(2)(viii) of this Q&A-2 are effective for plan amendments that are adopted and effective on or after September 6, 2000. These exceptions create no inference with respect to whether any other applicable requirements are satisfied (for example, requirements imposed by section 401(a)(9) and section 401(a)(14)).

(i) *Change in statutory requirement.* A plan may be amended to eliminate or reduce a section 411(d)(6) protected benefit if the following three requirements are met: the amendment constitutes timely compliance with a change in law affecting plan qualification; there is an exercise of section 7805(b) relief by the Commissioner; and the elimination or reduction is made only to the extent necessary to enable the plan to continue to satisfy the requirements for qualified plans. In general, the elimination or reduction of a section 411(d)(6) protected benefit will not be treated as necessary if it is possible through other modifications to the plan (e.g., by expanding the availability of an optional form of benefit to additional employees) to satisfy the applicable qualification requirement.

(ii) *Joint and survivor annuity.* A plan that provides a range of three or more actuarially equivalent joint and survivor annuity options may be amended to eliminate any of such options, other than the options with the largest and smallest optional survivor payment percentages, even if the effect of such amendment is to change which of the options is the qualified joint and survivor annuity under section 417. Thus, for example, if a money purchase pension plan provides three joint and survivor annuity options with survivor payments of 50%, 75% and 100%, respectively, that are uniform with respect to age and are actuarially equivalent, then the employer may eliminate the option with the 75% survivor payment, even if this option had been the qualified joint and survivor annuity under the plan.

(iii) *In-kind distributions*—(A) *In-kind distributions payable under defined contribution plans in the form of marketable securities other than employer securities.* If a defined contribution plan includes an optional form of benefit under which benefits are distributed in the form of marketable securities, other than securities of the employer, that optional form of benefit may be modified by a plan amendment that substitutes cash for the marketable securities as the medium of distribution. For purposes of this paragraph (b)(2)(iii)(A) and paragraph (b)(2)(iii)(B) of this Q&A-2, the term *marketable securities* means marketable securities as defined in section 731(c)(2), and the term *securities of the employer* means securities of the employer as defined in section 402(e)(4)(E)(ii).

(B) *Amendments to defined contribution plans to specify medium of distribution.* If a defined contribution plan includes an optional form of benefit under which benefits are distributable to a participant in a medium other than cash, the plan may be amended to limit the types of property in which distributions may be made to the participant to the types of property specified in the amendment. For this purpose, the types of property specified in the amendment must include all types of property (other than marketable securities that are not securities of the employer) that are allocated to the participant's account on the effective date of the amendment and in which the participant would be able to receive a distribution immediately before the effective date of the amendment if a distributable event occurred. In addition, a plan amendment may provide that the participant's right to receive a distribution in the form of specified types of property is limited to the property allocated to the participant's account at the time of distribution that consists of property of those specified types.

(C) *In-kind distributions after plan termination.* If a plan includes an optional form of benefit under which benefits are distributed in specified property, that optional form of benefit may be modified for distributions after plan termination by substituting cash for the specified property as the medium of distribution to the extent that, on plan termination, an employee has the opportunity to receive the optional form of benefit in the form of the specified property. This exception is not available, however, if the employer that maintains the terminating plan also maintains another plan that provides an optional form of benefit under which benefits are distributed in the specified property.

(D) *Examples.* The following examples illustrate the application of this paragraph (b)(2)(iii):

Example 1. (i) An employer maintains a profit-sharing plan under which participants may direct the investment of their accounts. One investment option available to participants is a fund invested in common stock of the employer. The plan provides that the participant has the right to a distribution in the form of cash upon termination of employment. In addition, the plan provides that, to the extent a participant's account is invested in the employer stock fund, the participant may receive an in-kind distribution of employer stock upon termination of employment. On October 18, 2000, the plan is amended, effective on January 1, 2001, to remove the fund invested in employer common stock as an investment option under the plan and to provide for the stock held in the fund to be sold. The amendment permits participants to elect how the sale proceeds are to be reallocated among the remaining investment options, and provides for amounts not so reallocated as of January 1, 2001, to be allocated to a specified investment option.

(ii) The plan does not fail to satisfy section 411(d)(6) solely on account of the plan amendment relating to the elimination of the employer stock investment option, which is not a section 411(d)(6) protected benefit. See paragraph (d)(7) of Q&A-1 of this section. Moreover, because the plan did not provide for distributions of employer securities except to the extent participants' accounts were invested in the employer stock fund, the plan is not required operationally to offer distributions of employer securities following the amendment. In addition, the plan would not fail to satisfy section 411(d)(6) on account of a further plan amendment, effective after the plan has ceased to provide for an employer stock fund investment option (and participants' accounts have ceased to be invested in employer securities), to eliminate the right to a distribution in the form of employer stock. See paragraph (b)(2)(iii)(B) of this Q&A-2.

Example 2. (i) An employer maintains a profit-sharing plan under which a participant, upon termination of employment, may elect to receive benefits in a single-sum distribution either in cash or in kind. The plan's investments are limited to a fund invested in employer stock, a fund invested in XYZ mutual funds (which are marketable securities), and a fund invested in shares of PQR limited partnership (which are not marketable securities).

(ii) The following alternative plan amendments would not cause the plan to fail to satisfy section 411(d)(6):

(A) A plan amendment that limits non-cash distributions to a participant on termination of employment to a distribution of employer stock and shares of PQR limited partnership. See paragraph (b)(2)(iii)(A) of this Q&A-2.

(B) A plan amendment that limits non-cash distributions to a participant on termination of employment to a distribution of employer stock and shares of PQR limited partnership, and that also provides that only participants with employer stock allocated to their accounts as of the effective date of the amendment have the right to distributions in the form of employer stock, and that only participants with shares of PQR limited partnership allocated to their accounts as of the effective date of the amendment have the right to distributions in the form of shares of PQR limited partnership. To comply with the plan amendment, the plan administrator retains a list of participants with employer stock allocated to their accounts as of the effective date of the amendment, and a list of participants with shares of PQR limited partnership allocated to their accounts as of the effective date of the amendment. See paragraphs (b)(2)(iii)(A) and (B) of this Q&A-2.

(C) A plan amendment that limits non-cash distributions to a participant on termination of employment to a distribution of employer stock and shares of PQR limited partnership to the extent that those assets are allocated to the participant's account at the time of the distribution. See paragraphs (b)(2)(iii)(A) and (B) of this Q&A-2.

(D) A plan amendment that limits non-cash distributions to a participant on termination of employment to a distribution of employer stock and shares of PQR limited partnership, and that provides that only participants with employer stock allocated to their accounts as of the effective date of the amendment have the right to distributions in the form of employer stock, and that only participants with shares of PQR limited partnership allocated to their accounts as of the effective date of the amendment have the right to distributions in the form of shares of PQR limited partnership, and that further provides that the distribution of that stock or those shares is available only to the extent that those assets are allocated to those participants' accounts at the time of the distribution. To comply with the plan amendment, the plan administrator retains a list of participants with employer stock allocated to their accounts as of the effective date of the amendment, and a list of participants with shares of PQR limited partnership allocated to their accounts as of the effective date of the amendment. See paragraphs (b)(2)(iii)(A) and (B) of this Q&A-2.

Example 3. (i) An employer maintains a stock bonus plan under which a participant, upon termination of employment, may elect to receive benefits in a single-sum distribution in employer stock. This is the only plan maintained by the employer under which distributions in employer stock are available. The employer decides to terminate the stock bonus plan.

(ii) If the plan makes available a single-sum distribution in employer stock on plan termination, the plan will not fail to satisfy section 411(d)(6) solely because the optional form of benefit providing a single-sum distribution in employer stock on termination of employment is modified to provide that such distribution is available only in cash. See paragraph (b)(2)(iii)(C) of this Q&A-2.

(iv) *Coordination with diversification requirement.* A tax credit employee stock ownership plan (as defined in section 409(a)) or an employee stock ownership plan (as defined in section 4975(e)(7)) may be amended to provide that a distribution is not available in employer securities to the extent that an employee elects to diversify benefits pursuant to section 401(a)(28).

(v) *Involuntary distributions.* A plan may be amended to provide for the involuntary distribution of an employee's benefit to the extent such involuntary distribution is permitted under sections 411(a)(11) and 417(e). Thus, for example, an involuntary distribution provision may be amended to require that an employee who terminates from employment with the employer receive a single sum distribution in the event that the present value of the employee's benefit is not more than $3,500, by substituting the cash-out limit in effect under §1.411(a)-11(c)(3)(ii) for $3,500, without violating section 411(d)(6). In addition, for example, the employer may amend the plan to reduce the involuntary distribution threshold from the cash-out limit in effect under §1.411(a)-11(c)(3)(ii) to any lower amount and to eliminate the involuntary single sum option for employees with benefits between the cash-out limit in effect under §1.411(a)-11(c)(3)(ii) and such lower amount without violating section 411(d)(6). This rule does not permit a plan provision permitting employer discretion with respect to optional forms of benefit for employees the present value of whose benefit is less than the cash-out limit in effect under §1.411(a)-11(c)(3)(ii).

(vi) *Distribution exception for certain profit-sharing plans—(A) In general.* If a defined contribution plan that is not subject to section 412 and does not provide for an annuity option is terminated, the plan may be amended to provide for the distribution of a participant's accrued benefit upon termination in a single sum optional form without the participant's consent. The preceding sentence does not apply if the employer maintains any other defined contribution plan (other than an employee stock ownership plan as defined in section 4975(e)(7)).

(B) *Examples.* The provisions of this paragraph (b)(2)(vi) can be illustrated by the following examples:

Example 1. Employer X maintains a defined contribution plan that is not subject to section 412. The plan provides for distribution in the form of equal installments over five years or equal installments over twenty years. X maintains no other defined contribution plans. X terminates its defined contribution plan after amending the plan to provide for the distribution of all participants' accrued benefits in the form of single sum distributions, without obtaining participant consent. Pursuant to the rule in this paragraph (b)(2)(vi), this amendment does not violate the requirements of section 411(d)(6).

Example 2. Corporations X and Y are members of controlled group employer XY. Both X and Y maintain defined contribution plans. X's plan, which is not subject to section 412, covers only employees working for X. Y's plan, which is subject to section 412, covers only employees working for Y. X terminates its defined contribution plan. Because employer XY maintains another defined contribution plan, plan X may not provide for the distribution of participants' accrued benefits upon termination without a participants' consent.

(vii) *Distribution of benefits on default of loans.* Notwithstanding that the distribution of benefits arising from an execution on an account balance used to secure a loan on which there has been a default is an optional form of benefit, a plan may be amended to eliminate or change a provision for loans, even if such loans would be secured by an employee's account balance.

(viii) *Provisions for transfer of benefits between and among defined contribution plans and defined benefit plans.* A plan may be amended to eliminate provisions permitting the transfer of benefits between and among defined contribution plans and defined benefit plans.

(ix) *De minimis change in the timing of an optional form of benefit.* A plan may be amended to modify an optional form of benefit by changing the timing of the availability of such optional form if, after the change, the optional form is available at a time that is within two months of the time such optional form was available before the amendment. To the extent the optional form of benefit is available prior to termination of employment, six months may be substituted

for two months in the prior sentence. Thus, for example, a plan that makes in-service distributions available to employees once every month may be amended to make such in-service distributions available only once every six months. This exception to section 411(d)(6) relates only to the timing of the availability of the optional form of benefit. Other aspects of an optional form of benefit may not be modified and the value of such optional form may not be reduced merely because of an amendment permitted by this exception.

(x) *Amendment of hardship distribution standards.* A qualified cash or deferred arrangement that permits hardship distributions under §1.401(k)-1(d)(3) may be amended to specify or modify nondiscriminatory and objective standards for determining the existence of an immediate and heavy financial need, the amount necessary to meet the need, or other conditions relating to eligibility to receive a hardship distribution. For example, a plan will not be treated as violating section 411(d)(6) merely because it is amended to specify or modify the resources an employee must exhaust to qualify for a hardship distribution or to require employees to provide additional statements or representations to establish the existence of a hardship. A qualified cash or deferred arrangement may also be amended to eliminate hardship distributions. The provisions of this paragraph also apply to profit-sharing or stock bonus plans that permit hardship distributions, whether or not the hardship distributions are limited to those described in §1.401(k)-1(d)(3).

(xi) *Section 415 benefit limitations.* Accrued benefits under a plan as of the first day of the first limitation year beginning after December 31, 1986, that exceed the benefit limitations under section 415(b) or (e), effective on the first day of the plan's first limitation year beginning after December 31, 1986, because of a change in the terms and conditions of the plan made after May 5, 1986, or the establishment of a plan after that date, may be reduced to the level permitted under section 415(b) or (e).

(xii) *Prohibited payment option under single-employer defined benefit plan of plan sponsor in bankruptcy.* A single-employer plan that is covered under section 4021 of the Employee Retirement Income Security Act of 1974, Public Law 93-406 (88 Stat. 829 (1974)), as amended (ERISA), may be amended, effective for a plan amendment that is both adopted and effective after November 8, 2012, to eliminate an optional form of benefit that includes a prohibited payment described in section 436(d)(5), provided that the following conditions are satisfied on the applicable amendment date (as defined in §1.411(d)-3(g)(4)):

(A) The enrolled actuary of the plan has certified that the plan's adjusted funding target attainment percentage (as defined in section 436(j)(2)) for the plan year that contains the applicable amendment date is less than 100 percent.

(B) The plan is not permitted to pay any prohibited payment, due to application of the requirements of section 436(d)(2) of the Internal Revenue Code and section 206(g)(3)(B) of ERISA, because the plan sponsor is a debtor in a bankruptcy case (that is, a case under title 11, United States Code, or under similar Federal or State law).

(C) The court overseeing the bankruptcy case has issued an order, after notice to the affected parties (as defined in section 4001(a)(21) of ERISA) and a hearing, within the meaning of 11 U.S.C. 102(1), finding that the adoption of the amendment eliminating that optional form of benefit is necessary to avoid a distress termination of the plan pursuant to section 4041(c) of ERISA or an involuntary termination of the plan pursuant to section 4042 of ERISA before the plan sponsor emerges from bankruptcy (or before the bankruptcy case is otherwise completed).

(D) The Pension Benefit Guaranty Corporation has issued a determination that—

(*1*) The adoption of the amendment eliminating that optional form of benefit is necessary to avoid a distress or involuntary termination of the plan before the plan sponsor emerges from bankruptcy (or before the bankruptcy case is otherwise completed); and

(*2*) The plan is not sufficient for guaranteed benefits within the meaning of section 4041(d)(2) of ERISA.

(c) *Multiple amendments*—(1) *General rule.* A plan amendment violates the requirements of section 411(d)(6) if it is one of a series of plan amendments that, when taken together, have the effect of reducing or eliminating a section 411(d)(6) protected benefit in a manner that would be prohibited by section 411(d)(6) if accomplished through a single amendment.

(2) *Determination of time period for combining plan amendments.* For purposes of paragraph (c)(1) of this Q&A-2, generally only plan amendments adopted within a 3-year period are taken into account. But see Q&A-1(c)(1) of this section for rules relating to repeated plan amendments.

(d) *ESOP and stock bonus plan exception*—(1) *In general.* Subject to the limitations in paragraph (d)(2) of this Q&A-2, a tax credit employee stock ownership plan (as defined in section 409(a)) or an employee stock ownership plan (as defined in section 4975(e)(7)) will not be treated as violating the requirements of section 411(d)(6) merely because of any of the circumstances described in paragraphs (d)(1)(i) through (d)(1)(iv) of this Q&A-2. In addition, a stock bonus plan that is not an employee stock ownership plan will not be treated as violating the requirements of section 411(d)(6) merely because of any of the circumstances described in paragraphs (d)(1)(ii) and (d)(1)(iv) of this Q&A-2.

(i) *Single sum or installment optional forms of benefit.* The employer eliminates, or retains the discretion to eliminate, with respect to all participants, a single sum optional form or installment optional form with respect to benefits that are subject to section 409(h)(1)(B), provided such elimination or retention of discretion is consistent with the distribution and payment requirements otherwise applicable to such plans (e.g., those required by section 409).

(ii) *Employer becomes substantially employee-owned or is an S corporation.* The employer eliminates, or retains the discretion to eliminate, with respect to all participants, optional forms of benefit by substituting cash distributions for distributions in the form of employer stock with respect to benefits subject to section 409(h) in the circumstances described in paragraph (d)(1)(ii)(A) or (B) of this Q&A-2, but only if the employer otherwise meets the requirements of section 409(h)(2)—

(A) The employer becomes substantially employee-owned; or

(B) For taxable years of the employer beginning after December 31, 1997, the employer is an S corporation as defined in section 1361.

(iii) *Employer securities become readily tradable.* The employer eliminates, or retains the discretion to eliminate, with respect to all participants, in cases in which the employer securities become readily tradable, optional forms of benefit by substituting distributions in the form of employer securities for distributions in cash with respect to benefits that are subject to section 409(h).

(iv) *Employer securities cease to be readily tradable or certain sales.* The employer eliminates, or retains the discretion to eliminate, with respect to all participants, optional forms of benefit by substituting cash distributions for distributions in the form of employer stock with respect to benefits that are subject to section 409(h) in the following circumstances:

(A) The employer stock ceases to be readily tradable;

(B) The employer stock continues to be readily tradable but there is a sale of substantially all of the stock of the employer or a sale of substantially all of the assets of a trade or business of the employer and, in either situation, the purchasing employer continues to maintain the plan.

In the situation described in paragraph (d)(1)(iv)(B) of this Q&A-2, the employer may also substitute distributions in the purchasing employer's stock for distributions in the form of employer stock of the predecessor employer.

(2) *Limitations on ESOP and stock bonus plan exceptions—*(i) *Nondiscrimination requirement.* Plan amendments and the retention and exercise of discretion permitted under the exceptions in paragraph (d)(1) must meet the nondiscrimination requirements of section 401(a)(4).

(ii) *ESOP investment requirement.* Except as provided in paragraph (d)(2)(iii) of this Q & A-2, benefits provided by employee stock ownership plans will not be eligible for the exceptions in paragraph (d)(1) of this Q & A-2 unless the benefits have been held in a tax credit employee stock ownership plan (as defined in section 409(a)) or an employee stock ownership plan (as defined in section 4975(e)(7)) subject to section 409(h) for the five-year period prior to the exercise of employer discretion or any amendment affecting such benefits and permitted under paragraph (d)(1) of this Q & A-2. For purposes of the preceding sentence, if benefits held under an employee stock ownership plan are transferred to a plan that is an employee stock ownership plan at the time of transfer, then the consecutive periods under the transferor and transferee employee stock ownership plans may be aggregated for purposes of meeting the five-year requirement. If the benefits are held in an employee stock ownership plan throughout the entire period of their existence, and such total period of existence is less than five years, then such lesser period may be substituted for the five year requirement.

(3) *Effective date.* The provisions of this paragraph (d) are effective beginning with the first day of the first plan year commencing on or after January 1, 1989. Prior to this effective date the reduction or elimination of a section 411(d)(6) protected benefit by a tax credit employee stock ownership plan (as defined in section 409(a)) or an employee stock ownership plan (as defined in section 4975(e)(7)) will not be treated as violating the requirements of section 411(d)(6) if such reduction or elimination reflects a reasonable interpretation of the statutory language of section 411(d)(6)(C).

(4) *Additional exceptions and requirements.* The Commissioner may, in revenue rulings, notices or other documents of general applicability, prescribe such additional rules and exceptions, consistent with the purposes of this section, as may be necessary or appropriate.

(e) *Permitted plan amendments affecting alternative forms of payment under defined contribution plans—*(1) *General rule.* A defined contribution plan does not violate the requirements of section 411(d)(6) merely because the plan is amended to eliminate or restrict the ability

of a participant to receive payment of accrued benefits under a particular optional form of benefit for distributions with annuity starting dates after the date the amendment is adopted if, after the plan amendment is effective with respect to the participant, the alternative forms of payment available to the participant include payment in a single-sum distribution form that is otherwise identical to the optional form of benefit that is being eliminated or restricted.

(2) *Otherwise identical single-sum distribution.* For purposes of this paragraph (e), a single-sum distribution form is otherwise identical to an optional form of benefit that is eliminated or restricted pursuant to paragraph (e)(1) of this Q&A-2 only if the single-sum distribution form is identical in all respects to the eliminated or restricted optional form of benefit (or would be identical except that it provides greater rights to the participant) except with respect to the timing of payments after commencement. For example, a single-sum distribution form is not otherwise identical to a specified installment form of benefit if the single-sum distribution form is not available for distribution on the date on which the installment form would have been available for commencement, is not available in the same medium of distribution as the installment form, or imposes any condition of eligibility that did not apply to the installment form. However, an otherwise identical distribution form need not retain rights or features of the optional form of benefit that is eliminated or restricted to the extent that those rights or features would not be protected from elimination or restriction under section 411(d)(6) or this section.

(3) *Example.* The following example illustrates the application of this paragraph (e):

Example. (i) P is a participant in Plan M, a qualified profit-sharing plan with a calendar plan year that is invested in mutual funds. The distribution forms available to P under Plan M include a distribution of P's vested account balance under Plan M in the form of distribution of various annuity contract forms (including a single life annuity and a joint and survivor annuity). The annuity payments under the annuity contract forms begin as of the first day of the month following P's severance from employment (or as of the first day of any subsequent month, subject to the requirements of section 401(a)(9)). P has not previously elected payment of benefits in the form of a life annuity, and Plan M is not a direct or indirect transferee of any plan that is a defined benefit plan or a defined contribution plan that is subject to section 412. Distributions on the death of a participant are made in accordance with plan provisions that comply with section 401(a)(11)(B)(iii)(l). On September 2, 2005, Plan M is amended so that, effective for payments that begin on or after November 1, 2005, P is no longer entitled to any distribution in the form of the distribution of an annuity contract. However, after the amendment is effective, P is entitled to receive a single-sum cash distribution of P's vested account balance under Plan M payable as of the first day of the month following P's severance from employment (or as of the first day of any subsequent month, subject to the requirements of section 401(a)(9)).

(ii) Plan M does not violate the requirements of section 411(d)(6) (or section 401(a)(11)) merely because, as of November 1, 2005, the plan amendment has eliminated P's option to receive a distribution in any of the various annuity contract forms previously available.

(4) *Effective date.* This paragraph (e) is applicable on January 25, 2005.

Q-3: Does the transfer of benefits between and among defined benefit plans and defined contribution plans (or similar transactions) violate the requirements of section 411(d)(6)?

A-3: (a) *Transfers and similar transactions—*(1) *General rule.* Section 411(d)(6) protected benefits may not be eliminated by reason of transfer or any transaction amending or having the effect of amending a plan or plans to transfer benefits. Thus, for example, except as otherwise provided in this section, an employer who maintains a money purchase pension plan that provides for a single sum optional form of benefit may not establish another plan that does not provide for this optional form of benefit and transfer participants' account balances to such new plan.

(2) *Defined benefit feature and separate account feature.* The defined benefit feature of an employee's benefit under a defined benefit plan and the separate account feature of an employee's benefit under a defined contribution plan are section 411(d)(6) protected benefits. Thus, for example, the elimination of the defined benefit feature of an employee's benefit under a defined benefit plan, through transfer of benefits from a defined benefit plan to a defined contribution plan or plans, will violate section 411(d)(6).

(3) *Waiver prohibition.* In general, except as provided in paragraph (b) of this Q&A-3, a participant may not elect to waive section 411(d)(6) protected benefits. Thus, for example, the elimination of the defined benefit feature of a participant's benefit under a defined benefit plan by reason of a transfer of such benefits to a defined contribution plan pursuant to a participant election, at a time when the benefit is not distributable to the participant, violates section 411(d)(6).

Reg. §1.411(d)-4

(4) Direct rollovers. A direct rollover described in Q&A-3 of §1.401(a)(31)-1 that is paid to a qualified plan is not a transfer of assets and liabilities that must satisfy the requirements of section 414(l), and is not a transfer of benefits for purposes of applying the requirements under section 411(d)(6) and paragraph (a)(1) of this Q&A-3. Therefore, for example, if such a direct rollover is made to another qualified plan, the receiving plan is not required to provide, with respect to amounts paid to it in a direct rollover, the same optional forms of benefit that were provided under the plan that made the direct rollover. See §1.401(a)(31)-1, Q&A-14.

(b) Elective transfers of benefits between defined contribution plans—(1) *General rule.* A transfer of a participant's entire benefit between qualified defined contribution plans (other than any direct rollover described in Q&A-3 of §1.401(a)(31)-1) that results in the elimination or reduction of section 411(d)(6) protected benefits does not violate section 411(d)(6) if the following requirements are met—

(i) *Voluntary election.* The plan from which the benefits are transferred must provide that the transfer is conditioned upon a voluntary, fully-informed election by the participant to transfer the participant's entire benefit to the other qualified defined contribution plan. As an alternative to the transfer, the participant must be offered the opportunity to retain the participant's section 411(d)(6) protected benefits under the plan (or, if the plan is terminating, to receive any optional form of benefit for which the participant is eligible under the plan as required by section 411(d)(6)).

(ii) *Types of plans to which transfers may be made.* To the extent the benefits are transferred from a money purchase pension plan, the transferee plan must be a money purchase pension plan. To the extent the benefits being transferred are part of a qualified cash or deferred arrangement under section 401(k), the benefits must be transferred to a qualified cash or deferred arrangement under section 401(k). To the extent the benefits being transferred are part of an employee stock ownership plan as defined in section 4975(e)(7), the benefits must be transferred to another employee stock ownership plan. Benefits transferred from a profit-sharing plan other than from a qualified cash or deferred arrangement, or from a stock bonus plan other than an employee stock ownership plan, may be transferred to any type of defined contribution plan.

(iii) *Circumstances under which transfers may be made.* The transfer must be made either in connection with an asset or stock acquisition, merger, or other similar transaction involving a change in employer of the employees of a trade or business (i.e., an acquisition or disposition within the meaning of §1.410(b)-2(f)) or in connection with the participant's change in employment status to an employment status with respect to which the participant is not entitled to additional allocations under the transferor plan.

(2) *Applicable qualification requirements.* A transfer described in this paragraph (b) is a transfer of assets or liabilities within the meaning of section 414(l)(1) and, thus, must satisfy the requirements of section 414(l). In addition, this paragraph (b) only provides relief under section 411(d)(6); a transfer described in this paragraph must satisfy all other applicable qualification requirements. Thus, for example, if the survivor annuity requirements of sections 401(a)(11) and 417 apply to the plan from which the benefits are transferred, as described in this paragraph (b), but do not otherwise apply to the receiving plan, the requirements of sections 401(a)(11) and 417 must be met with respect to the transferred benefits under the receiving plan. In addition, the vesting provisions under the receiving plan must satisfy the requirements of section 411(a)(10) with respect to the amounts transferred.

(3) *Status of elective transfer as other right or feature.* A right to a transfer of benefits from a plan pursuant to the elective transfer rules of this paragraph (b) is an other right or feature within the meaning of §1.401(a)(4)-4(e)(3), the availability of which is subject to the nondiscrimination requirements of section 401(a)(4) and §1.401(a)(4)-4. However, for purposes of applying the rules of §1.401(a)(4)-4, the following conditions are to be disregarded in determining the employees to whom the other right or feature is available—

(i) A condition restricting the availability of the transfer to benefits of participants who are transferred to a different employer in connection with a specified asset or stock disposition, merger, or other similar transaction involving a change in employer of the employees of a trade or business (i.e., a disposition within the meaning of §1.410(b)-2(f)), or in connection with any such disposition, merger, or other similar transaction.

(ii) A condition restricting the availability of the transfer to benefits of participants who have a change in employment status to an employment status with respect to which the participant is not entitled to additional allocations under the transferor plan.

(c) Elective transfers of certain distributable benefits between qualified plans—(1) *In general.* A transfer of a participant's benefits between qualified plans that results in the elimination or reduction of section 411(d)(6) protected benefits does not violate section 411(d)(6) if—

(i) The transfer occurs at a time at which the participant's benefits are distributable (within the meaning of paragraph (c)(3) of this Q&A-3);

(ii) For a transfer that occurs on or after January 1, 2002, the transfer occurs at a time at which the participant is not eligible to receive an immediate distribution of the participant's entire nonforfeitable accrued benefit in a singlesum distribution that would consist entirely of an eligible rollover distribution within the meaning of section 401(a)(31)(C);

(iii) The voluntary election requirements of paragraph (b)(1)(i) of this Q&A-3 are met;

(iv) The participant is fully vested in the transferred benefit in the transferee plan;

(v) In the case of a transfer from a defined contribution plan to a defined benefit plan, the defined benefit plan provides a minimum benefit, for each participant whose benefits are transferred, equal to the benefit, expressed as an annuity payable at normal retirement age, that is derived solely on the basis of the amount transferred with respect to such participant; and

(vi) The amount of the benefit transferred, together with the amount of any contemporaneous section 401(a)(31) direct rollover to the transferee plan, equals the entire nonforfeitable accrued benefit under the transferor plan of the participant whose benefit is being transferred, calculated to be at least the greater of the single-sum distribution provided for under the plan for which the participant is eligible (if any) or the present value of the participant's accrued benefit payable at normal retirement age (calculated by using interest and mortality assumptions that satisfy the requirements of section 417(e) and subject to the limitations imposed by section 415).

(2) *Treatment of transfer*—(i) *In general.* A transfer of benefits pursuant to this paragraph (c) generally is treated as a distribution for purposes of section 401(a). For example, the transfer is subject to the cash-out rules of section 411(a)(7), the early termination requirements of section 411(d)(2), and the survivor annuity requirements of sections 401(a)(11) and 417. A transfer pursuant to the elective transfer rules of this paragraph (c) is not treated as a distribution for purposes of the minimum distribution requirements of section 401(a)(9).

(ii) *Status of elective transfer as optional form of benefit.* A right to a transfer of benefits from a plan pursuant to the elective transfer rules of this paragraph (c) is an optional form of benefit under section 411(d)(6), the availability of which is subject to the nondiscrimination requirements of section 401(a)(4) and §1.401(a)(4)-4.

(3) *Distributable benefits.* For purposes of paragraph (c)(1)(i) of this Q&A-3, a participant's benefits are distributable on a particular date if, on that date, the participant is eligible, under the terms of the plan from which the benefits are transferred, to receive an immediate distribution of these benefits (e.g., in the form of an immediately commencing annuity) from that plan under provisions of the plan not inconsistent with section 401(a).

(d) Effective date. This Q&A-3 is applicable for transfers made on or after September 6, 2000.

Q-4: May a plan provide that the employer may, through the exercise of discretion, deny a participant a section 411(d)(6) protected benefit for which the participant is otherwise eligible?

A-4: (a) *In general.* Except as provided in paragraph (d) of Q&A-2 of this section with respect to certain employee stock ownership plans, a plan that permits the employer, either directly or indirectly, through the exercise of discretion, to deny a participant a section 411(d)(6) protected benefit provided under the plan for which the participant is otherwise eligible (but for the employer's exercise of discretion) violates the requirements of section 411(d)(6). A plan provision that makes a section 411(d)(6) protected benefit available only to those employees as the employer may designate is within the scope of this prohibition. Thus, for example, a plan provision under which only employees who are designated by the employer are eligible to receive a subsidized early retirement benefit constitutes an impermissible provision under section 411(d)(6). In addition, a pension plan that permits employer discretion to deny the availability of a section 411(d)(6) protected benefit violates the definitely determinable requirement of section 401(a), including section 401(a)(25). See §1.401-1(b)(1)(i). This is the result even if the plan specifically limits the employer's discretion to choosing among section 411(d)(6) protected benefits, including optional forms of benefit, that are actuarially equivalent. In addition, the provisions of sections 411(a)(11) and 417(e) that allow a plan to make involuntary distributions of certain amounts are not excepted from this limitation on employer discretion. Thus, for example, a plan may not permit employer discretion with respect to whether benefits will be distributed involuntarily in the event that the present value of the employee's benefit is not more than the cash-out limit in effect under §1.411(a)-11(c)(3)(ii) within the meaning of sections 411(a)(11) and 417(e). (An exception is provided for such provisions with respect to the nondiscrimination requirements of section 401(a)(4). See §1.401(a)(4)-4(b)(2)(ii)(C).)

(b) *Exception for administrative discretion.* A plan may permit limited discretion with respect to the ministerial or mechanical administration of the plan, including the application of objective plan criteria specifically set forth in the plan. Such plan provisions do not violate the requirements of section 411(d)(6) or the definitely determinable requirement of section 401(a), including section 401(a)(25). For example, these requirements are not violated by the following provisions that permit limited administrative discretion: (1) commencement of benefit payments as soon as administratively feasible after a stated date or event; (2) employer authority to determine whether objective criteria specified in the plan (e.g., objective criteria designed to identify those employees with a heavy and immediate financial need or objective criteria designed to determine whether an employee has a permanent and total disability) have been satisfied; and (3) employer authority to determine, pursuant to specific guidelines set forth in the plan, whether the participant or spouse is dead or cannot be located.

Q-5: When will the exercise of discretion by some person or persons, other than the employer, be treated as employer discretion?

A-5: For purposes of applying the rules of this section and §1.401(a)-4, the term "employer" includes plan administrator, fiduciary, trustee, actuary, independent third party, and other persons. Thus, if a plan permits any person, other than the participant (and other than the participant's spouse), the discretion to deny or limit the availability of a section 411(d)(6) protected benefit for which the employee is otherwise eligible under the plan (but for the exercise of such discretion), such plan violates the requirements of sections 401(a), including section 411(d)(6) and, where applicable, the definitely determinable requirement of section 401(a), including section 401(a)(25).

Q-6: May a plan condition the availability of a section 411(d)(6) protected benefit on the satisfaction of objective conditions that are specifically set forth in the plan?

A-6: (a) *Certain objective conditions permissible*—(1) *In general.* The availability of a section 411(d)(6) protected benefit may be limited to employees who satisfy certain objective conditions provided the conditions are ascertainable, clearly set forth in the plan and not subject to the employer's discretion except to the extent reasonably necessary to determine whether the objective conditions have been met. Also, the availability of the section 411(d)(6) protected benefit must meet the nondiscrimination requirements of section 401(a)(4). See §1.401(a)-4.

(2) *Examples of permissible conditions.* The following examples illustrate permissible objective conditions: a plan may deny a single sum distribution form to employees for whom life insurance is not available at standard rates as defined under the terms of the plan at the time the single sum distribution would otherwise be payable; a plan may provide that a single sum distribution is available only if the employee is in extreme financial need as defined under the terms of the plan at the time the single sum distribution would otherwise be payable; a plan may condition the availability of a single sum distribution on the execution of a covenant not to compete, provided that objective conditions with respect to the terms of such covenant and the employees and circumstances requiring execution of such covenant are set forth in the plan.

(b) *Conditions based on factors within employer's discretion generally impermissible.* A plan may not limit the availability of section 411(d)(6) protected benefits permitted under the plan on objective conditions that are within the employer's discretion. For example, the availability of section 411(d)(6) protected benefits in a plan may not be conditioned on a determination with respect to the level of the plan's funded status, because the amount of plan funding is within the employer's discretion. However, for example, although conditions based on the plan's funded status are impermissible, a plan may limit the availability of a section 411(d)(6) protected benefit (e.g., a single sum distribution) in an objective manner, such as the following: (1) single sum distributions of $25,000 and less are available without limit; and (2) single sum distributions in excess of $25,000 are available for a year only to the extent that the total amount of such single sum distributions for the year is not greater than $5,000,000; and (3) an objective and nondiscriminatory method for determining which particular single sum distributions will not be available during a year in order for the $5,000,000 limit to be satisfied is set forth in the plan.

Q-7: May a plan be amended to add employer discretion or conditions restricting the availability of a section 411(d)(6) protected benefit?

A-7: No. The addition of employer discretion or objective conditions with respect to a section 411(d)(6) protected benefit that has already accrued violates section 411(d)(6). Also, the addition of conditions (whether or not objective) or any change to existing conditions with respect to section 411(d)(6) protected benefits that results in any further restriction violates section 411(d)(6). However, the addition of objective conditions to a section 411(d)(6) protected benefit may be made with respect to benefits accrued after the later of the adoption or effective date of the amendment. In addition, objective conditions may be imposed on section 411(d)(6) protected benefits accrued as of the date of an amendment where permitted under the transitional rules of §1.401(a)-4 Q&A-5 and Q&A-8 of this section. Finally, objective conditions may be imposed on section 411(d)(6) protected benefits to the extent permitted by the permissible benefit cutback provisions of Q&A-2 of this section.

Q-8: If a plan contains an impermissible employer discretion provision with respect to a section 411(d)(6) protected benefit, what acceptable alternatives exist for amending the plan without violating the requirements of section 411(d)(6)?

A-8: (a) *In general.* The following rules apply for purposes of making necessary amendments to existing plans (as defined in Q&A-9 of this section) that contain discretion provisions with respect to the availability of section 411(d)(6) protected benefits that violate the requirements of section 401(a), including sections 401(a)(25) and 411(d)(6), and this section. These transitional rules are provided under the authority of section 411(d)(6) and section 7805(b).

(b) *Transitional alternatives.* If the availability of an optional form of benefit, early or late retirement benefit, or retirement-type subsidy under an existing plan is conditioned on the exercise of employer discretion, the plan must be amended either to eliminate the optional form of benefit, early or late retirement benefit, or retirement-type subsidy to make such benefit available to all participants without limitation, or to apply objective and nondiscriminatory conditions to the availability of the optional form of benefit, early or late retirement benefit, or retirement-type subsidy. See paragraph (d) of this Q&A-8 for rules limiting the period during which section 411(d)(6) protected benefits may be eliminated or reduced under this paragraph.

(c) *Compliance and amendment date provisions*—(1) *Operational compliance requirement.* On or before the applicable effective date for the plan (as determined under Q&A-9 of this section), the plan sponsor must select one of the alternatives permitted under paragraph (b) of this Q&A-8 with respect to each affected section 411(d)(6) protected benefit and the plan must be operated in accordance with this selection. This is an operational requirement and does not require a plan amendment prior to the period set forth in paragraph (c)(2) of this Q&A-8. There are no special reporting requirements under the Code or this section with respect to this selection.

(2) *Deferred amendment date.* If paragraph (c)(1) of this Q&A-8 is satisfied, a plan amendment conforming the plan to the particular alternative selected under paragraph (b) of this Q&A-8 must be adopted within the time period permitted for amending plans in order to meet the requirements of section 410(b) as amended by TRA `86. The plan amendment to conform the plan to these regulations may be made at an earlier date. Such conforming amendment must be consistent with the sponsor's selection as reflected by plan practice during the period from the effective date to the date the amendment is adopted. Thus, for example, if an existing calendar year noncollectively bargained defined benefit plan has a single sum distribution option that is subject to employer discretion as of August 1, 1986, and such employer makes one or more single sum distributions available on or after January 1, 1989 and before the effective date by which plan amendment is required pursuant to this section, then such employer may not adopt a plan amendment eliminating the single sum distribution, but rather must adopt an amendment eliminating the discretion provision. Any objective conditions that are adopted as part of such amendment must not be inconsistent with the plan practice for the applicable period prior to the amendment. A conforming amendment under this paragraph (c)(2) must be made with respect to each section 411(d)(6) protected benefit for which such amendment is required and must be retroactive to the applicable effective date.

(d) *Limitation on transitional alternatives.* The transitional alternatives permitting the elimination or reduction of section 411(d)(6) protected benefits are only permissible until the applicable effective date for the plan (see Q&A-9 of this section). After the applicable effective date, any amendment (other than one permitted under paragraph (c)(2) of this Q&A-8) that eliminates or reduces a section 411(d)(6) protected benefit or imposes new objective conditions on the availability of such benefit will fail to qualify for the exception to section 411(d)(6) provided in this Q&A-8. This is the case without regard to whether the section 411(d)(6) protected benefit is subject to employer discretion.

Q-9: What are the applicable effective date rules for purposes of this section?

A-9: (a) *General effective date.* Except as otherwise provided in this section, the provisions of this section are effective January 30, 1986.

(b) *New plans*—(1) *In general.* Unless otherwise provided in paragraph (b)(2) of this Q&A-9, plans that are either adopted or made effective on or after August 1, 1986, are "new plans". With respect to such new plans, this section is effective August 1, 1986. This effective date is applicable to such plans whether or not they are collectively bargained.

(2) *Exception with respect to certain new plans.* Plans that are new plans as defined in paragraph (b)(1) of this Q&A-9, under which the availability of a section 411(d)(6) protected benefit is subject to employer discretion, and that receive a favorable determination letter that covered such plan provisions with respect to an application submitted prior to July 11, 1988, will be treated as existing plans with respect to such section 411(d)(6) protected benefit for purposes of the transitional rules of this section. Thus, such plans are eligible for the compliance and amendment alternatives set forth in the transitional rule in Q&A-8 of this section.

(c) *Existing plans*—(1) *In general.* Plans, including plans that are adoptions of master or prototype plans, that are both adopted and in effect prior to August 1, 1986, are "existing plans" for purposes of this section. In addition, a plan that is established after July 31, 1986, but before January 1, 1989, as an initial adoption of a master or prototype plan for which a favorable opinion letter was issued by the Service after July 18, 1985, and before January 1, 1989, will be deemed to be an existing plan for purposes of this section. See sections 4.01 and 4.02 of Rev. Proc. 84-23, 1984-1 C.B. 457, 459, for the definitions of master and prototype plans. However, if such plan ceases to be covered under an opinion letter of the type described above, as a result of amendment of the plan or adoption of a new plan, prior to the first day of the first plan year beginning on or after January 1, 1989, then the effective date for such plan will be determined as though the plan were a new plan initially adopted as of the date of such amendment or adoption of a new plan. Finally, new plans described in paragraph (b)(2) of this Q&A-9 are treated as existing plans with respect to certain section 411(d)(6) protected benefits. Subject to the limitations in paragraph (c) of this Q&A-9, the effective dates set forth in paragraphs (c)(2), (c)(3), and (c)(4) of this Q&A-9 apply to these existing plans for purposes of this section.

(2) *Existing noncollectively bargained plans.* With respect to existing plans other than collectively bargained plans this section is effective for the first day of the first plan year commencing on or after January 1, 1989.

(3) *Existing collectively bargained plans.* With respect to existing collectively bargained plans this section is effective for the later of the first day of the first plan year commencing on or after January 1, 1989, or the first day of the first plan year that the requirements of section 410(b) as amended by TRA '86 apply to such plan.

(4) *Existing master and prototype plans.* With respect to existing plans that are adoptions of master or prototype plans the effective date will be the first day of the first plan year commencing on or after January 1, 1989.

(d) *Delayed effective date not applicable to new alternatives or conditions*—(1) *In general.* The delayed effective dates in paragraphs (c)(2) and (c)(3) of this Q&A-9 for existing plans are only applicable with respect to a section 411(d)(6) protected benefit if both the section 411(d)(6) protected benefit and the condition providing employer discretion as to the availability of such benefit are both adopted and in effect prior to August 1, 1986. If the preceding sentence is not satisfied with respect to a particular section 411(d)(6) protected benefit, this section is effective with respect to such section 411(d)(6) protected benefit as if the plan were a new plan.

(2) *Addition of discretion on or after January 30, 1986.* The delayed effective dates in paragraphs (c)(2) and (c)(3) of this Q&A-9 are not available with respect to any section 411(d)(6) protected benefit if the section 411(d)(6) protected benefit was provided for in the plan prior to January 30, 1986, and the availability of such benefit was made subject to the exercise of employer discretion on or after January 30, 1986. If the conditions set forth in this paragraph are not satisfied with respect to a particular section 411(d)(6) protected benefit, this section is effective with respect to such section 411(d)(6) protected benefit as if the plan were a new plan. A limited exception is provided with respect to existing plans that provided a particular section 411(d)(6) protected benefit prior to January 30, 1986, and then amended the plan after January 30, 1986, and before August 1, 1986, to add a provision for employer discretion with respect to the availability of such benefit. Such plans are required to have been amended retroactively by December 31, 1987, to remove such provision for employer discretion, and, if the benefit made subject to such discretion was subsequently eliminated, the plan is required to have been further amended, by the same date, to retroactively reinstate the benefit.

(3) *Exception for certain amendments covered by a favorable determination letter.* If an amendment adding a section 411(d)(6) protected benefit subject to employer discretion was adopted or made effective after August 1, 1986, and the plan receives a favorable determination letter covering such provision with respect to an application for such letter made prior to July 11, 1988, then the effective date for purposes of amending such provision under the transitional rules is the appli-

cable effective date determined under the rules with respect to existing plans.

(e) *Transitional rule effective date.* The transitional rule provided in Q&A-8 of this section is effective January 30, 1986.

Q-10. If a plan provides for an age 70¹/₂ distribution option that commences prior to retirement from employment with the employer maintaining the plan, to what extent may the plan be amended to eliminate this distribution option?

A-10. (a) *In general.* The right to commence benefit distributions in a particular form and at a particular time prior to retirement from employment with the employer maintaining the plan is a separate optional form of benefit within the meaning of section 411(d)(6)(B) and Q&A-1 of this section, even if the plan provision creating this right was included in the plan solely to comply with section 401(a)(9), as in effect for years before January 1, 1997. Therefore, except as otherwise provided in paragraph (b) of this Q&A-10 or any other Q&A in this section, a plan amendment violates section 411(d)(6) if it eliminates an age 70¹/₂ distribution option (within the meaning of paragraph (c) of this Q&A-10) to the extent that it applies to benefits accrued as of the later of the adoption date or effective date of the amendment.

(b) *Permitted elimination of age 70¹/₂ distribution option.* An amendment of a plan will not violate the requirements of section 411(d)(6) merely because the amendment eliminates an age 70¹/₂ distribution option to the extent that the option provides for distribution to an employee prior to retirement from employment with the employer maintaining the plan, provided that—

(1) The amendment eliminating this optional form of benefit applies only to benefits with respect to employees who attain age 70¹/₂ in or after a calendar year, specified in the amendment, that begins after the later of—

(i) December 31, 1998; or

(ii) The adoption date of the amendment;

(2) The plan does not, except to the extent required by section 401(a)(9), preclude an employee who retires after the calendar year in which the employee attains age 70¹/₂ from receiving benefits in any of the same optional forms of benefit (except for the difference in the timing of the commencement of payments) that would have been available had the employee retired in the calendar year in which the employee attained age 70¹/₂; and

(3) The amendment is adopted no later than—

(i) The last day of the remedial amendment period that applies to the plan for changes under the Small Business Job Protection Act of 1996 (110 Stat. 1755); or

(ii) Solely in the case of a plan maintained pursuant to one or more collective bargaining agreements between employee representatives and one or more employers ratified before September 3, 1998, the last day of the twelfth month beginning after the date on which the last of such collective bargaining agreements terminates (determined without regard to any extension thereof on or after September 3, 1998), if later than the date described in paragraph (b)(3)(i) of this Q&A-10. For purposes of this paragraph (b)(3)(ii), the rules of § 1.410(b)-10(a)(2) apply for purposes of determining whether a plan is maintained pursuant to one or more collective bargaining agreements, except that September 3, 1998, is substituted for March 1, 1986, as the date before which the collective bargaining agreements must be ratified.

(c) *Age 70¹/₂ distribution option.* For purposes of this Q&A-10, an age 70¹/₂ distribution option is an optional form of benefit under which benefits payable in a particular distribution form (including any modifications that may be elected after benefit commencement) commence at a time during the period that begins on or after January 1 of the calendar year in which an employee attains age 70¹/₂ and ends April 1 of the immediately following calendar year.

(d) *Examples.* The provisions of this Q&A-10 are illustrated by the following examples:

Example 1. Plan A, a defined benefit plan, provides each participant with a qualified joint and survivor annuity (QJSA) that is available at any time after the later of age 65 or retirement. However, in accordance with section 401(a)(9) as in effect prior to January 1, 1997, Plan A provides that if an employee does not retire by the end of the calendar year in which the employee attains age 70¹/₂, then the QJSA commences on the following April 1. On October 1, 1998, Plan A is amended to provide that, for an employee who is not a 5-percent owner and who attains age 70¹/₂ after 1998, benefits may not commence before the employee retires but must commence no later than the April 1 following the later of the calendar year in which the employee retires or the calendar year in which the employee attains age 70¹/₂. This amendment satisfies this Q&A-10 and does not violate section 411(d)(6).

Example 2. Plan B, a money purchase pension plan, provides each participant with a choice of a QJSA or a single sum distribution commencing at any time after the later of age 65 or retirement. In addition, in accordance with section 401(a)(9) as in effect prior to

January 1, 1997, Plan B provides that benefits will commence in the form of a QJSA on April 1 following the calendar year in which the employee attains age 70½, except that, with spousal consent, a participant may elect to receive annual installment payments equal to the minimum amount necessary to satisfy section 401(a)(9) (calculated in accordance with a method specified in the plan) until retirement, at which time a participant may choose between a QJSA and a single sum distribution (with spousal consent). On June 30, 1998, Plan B is amended to provide that, for an employee who is not a 5-percent owner and who attains age 70½ after 1998, benefits may not commence prior to retirement but benefits must commence no later than April 1 after the later of the calendar year in which the employee retires or the calendar year in which the employee attains age 70½. The amendment further provides that the option described above to receive annual installment payments prior to retirement will not be available under the plan to an employee who is not a 5-percent owner and who attains age 70½ after 1998. This amendment satisfies this Q&A-10 and does not violate section 411(d)(6).

Example 3. Plan C, a profit-sharing plan, contains two distribution provisions. Under the first provision, in any year after an employee attains age 59 1/2, the employee may elect a distribution of any specified amount not exceeding the balance of the employee's account. In addition, the plan provides a section 401(a)(9) override provision under which, if, during any year following the year that the employee attains age 70½, the employee does not elect an amount at least equal to the minimum amount necessary to satisfy section 401(a)(9) (calculated in accordance with a method specified in the plan), Plan C will distribute the difference by December 31 of that year (or for the year the employee attains age 70½, by April 1 of the following year). On December 31, 1996, Plan C is amended to provide that, for an employee other than an employee who is a 5-percent owner in the year the employee attains age 70½, in applying the section 401(a)(9) override provision, the later of the year of retirement or year of attainment of age 70½, is substituted for the year of attainment of age 70½. After the amendment, Plan C still permits each employee to elect to receive the same amount as was available before the amendment. Because this amendment does not eliminate an optional form of benefit, the amendment does not violate section 411(d)(6). Accordingly, the amendment is not required to satisfy the conditions of paragraph (b) of this Q&A-10.

(e) *Effective date.* This Q&A-10 applies to amendments adopted and effective after June 5, 1998.

Q-11: To what extent may a plan amendment that is made pursuant to the Taxpayer Relief Act of 1997 (TRA '97) (Public Law 105-34, 111 Stat. 788), reduce or eliminate section 411(d)(6) protected benefits?

A-11: A plan amendment does not violate the requirements of section 411(d)(6) merely because the plan amendment reduces or eliminates section 411(d)(6) protected benefits as of the effective date of the plan amendment, provided that—

(a) The plan amendment is made pursuant to an amendment made by title XV, or subtitle H of title X, of TRA '97; and

(b) The plan amendment is adopted no later than the last day of any remedial amendment period that applies to the plan pursuant to §§ 1.401(b)-1 and 1.401(b)-1T for changes under TRA '97.

Q-12. Is there a transition period during which a plan is permitted to eliminate a right to in-service distributions in connection with an amendment to ensure that the plan's normal retirement age satisfies the requirements of § 1.401(a)-1(b)(2)?

A-12. (a) *In general.* A plan amendment that changes the normal retirement age under the plan to a later normal retirement age pursuant to § 1.401(a)-1(b)(2) does not violate section 411(d)(6) merely because it eliminates a right to an in-service distribution prior to the amended normal retirement age. However, this paragraph does not provide relief from any other applicable requirements; for example, this relief does not permit the amendment to violate section 411(a)(9) (requiring that the normal retirement benefit not be less than the greater of any early retirement benefit payable under the plan or the benefit under the plan commencing at normal retirement age), section 411(a)(10) (if the amendment changes the plan's vesting rules), section 411(d)(6) (other than elimination of the right to an in-service distribution prior to the amended normal retirement age), or section 4980F (relating to an amendment that reduces the rate of future benefit accrual). This paragraph only applies to a plan amendment that is adopted after May 22, 2007 and on or before the last day of the applicable remedial amendment period under § 1.401(b)-1 with respect to the requirements of § 1.401(a)-1(b)(2) and (3).

(b) *Example.* The following example illustrates the application of this section:

(i) *Facts.* (A) Plan A is a defined benefit plan intended to be qualified under section 401(a). Plan A is maintained by a calendar year taxpayer and has a normal retirement age that is age 45. For employees who cease employment before normal retirement age with a vested benefit, Plan A permits benefits to commence at any

date after the attainment of normal retirement age through attainment of age 70 1/2 and provides for benefits to be actuarially increased to the extent they commence after normal retirement age. For employees who continue employment after attainment of normal retirement age, Plan A provides for benefits to continue to accrue and permits benefits to commence at any time, with an actuarial increase in benefits to apply to the extent benefits do not commence after normal retirement age. Age 45 is an age that is earlier than the earliest age that is reasonably representative of the typical retirement age for the industry in which the covered workforce is employed.

(B) On February 18, 2008, Plan A is amended, effective May 21, 2007, to change its normal retirement age to the later of age 65 or the fifth anniversary of participation in the plan. The amendment provides full vesting for any participating employee who is employed on May 21, 2007, and who terminates employment on or after attaining age 45. The amendment provides employees who cease employment before the revised normal retirement age and who are entitled to a vested benefit with the right to be able to commence benefits at any date from age 45 to age 70 1/2. The plan amendment also revises the plan's benefit accrual formula so that the benefit for prior service (payable commencing at the revised normal retirement age or any other age after age 45) is not less than would have applied under the plan's formula before the amendment (also payable commencing at the corresponding dates), based on the benefit accrued on May 21, 2007, and provides for service thereafter to have the same rate of future benefit accrual. Thus, for any participant employed on May 21, 2007, with respect to benefits accrued for service after May 21, 2007, the amount payable under the plan (as amended) at any benefit commencement date after age 45 is the same amount that would have been payable at that benefit commencement date under the plan prior to amendment. The plan amendment also eliminates the right to an in-service distribution between age 45 and the revised normal retirement age. Plan A has been operated since May 22, , in conformity with the amendment adopted on February 18, 2008.

(ii) *Conclusion.* The plan amendment does not violate section 411(d)(6). Although the amendment eliminates the right to commence benefits in-service between age 45 and the revised normal retirement age, the amendment is made before the last day of the remedial amendment period applicable to the plan under § 1.401(b)-1 with respect to the requirements of § 1.401(a)-1(b)(2) and (3), and therefore the amendment is permitted under paragraph (a) of this A-12. Further, the amendment does not result in a reduction in any benefit for service after May 22, 2007.

Thus, the amendment does not result in a reduction in any benefit for future service, and advance notice of a significant reduction in the rate of future benefit accrual is not required under section 4980F. [Reg. § 1.411(d)-4.]

☐ [*T.D.* 8212, 7-8-88. *Amended by T.D.* 8357, 8-8-91; *T.D.* 8360, 9-12-91; *T.D.* 8485, 8-30-93; *T.D.* 8581, 12-22-94; *T.D.* 8769, 6-4-98; *T.D.* 8781, 9-3-98; *T.D.* 8794, 12-18-98; *T.D.* 8806, 1-7-99 (*corrected 7-19-99*); *T.D.* 8891, 7-18-2000; *T.D.* 8900, 8-31-2000; *T.D.* 9169, 12-28-2004; *T.D.* 9176, 1-24-2005 (*corrected 3-7-2005*); *T.D.* 9219, 8-11-2005; *T.D.* 9325, 5-21-2007 *and T.D.* 9601, 11-7-2012.]

[Reg. § 1.411(d)-5]

§ 1.411(d)-5. [Reserved].

☐ [*T.D.* 8219, 8-19-88. *Removed and reserved by T.D.* 9849, 3-11-2019.]

[Reg. § 1.412(b)-2]

§ 1.412(b)-2. Amortization of experience gains in connection with certain group deferred annuity contracts.—(a) *Experience gain treatment.*—Dividends, rate credits, and credits for forfeitures arising in a plan described in paragraph (b) of this section are experience gains described in section 412(b)(3)(B)(ii) (relating to the amortization of experience gains).

(b) *Plan.*—A plan is described in this paragraph (b) if—

(1) The plan is funded solely through a group deferred annuity contract,

(2) The annual single premium required under the contract for the purchase of the benefits accruing during the plan year is treated as the normal cost of the plan for that year, and

(3) The amount necessary to pay in equal annual installments, over the appropriate amortization period, an amount equal to the single premium necessary to provide all past service benefits not initially funded, together with interest thereon, is treated as the annual amortization amount determined under section 412(b)(2)(B)(i), (ii) or (iii).

(c) *Effective date.*—This section applies for the first plan year to which section 412 applies that begins after May 22, 1981. [Reg. § 1.412(b)-2.]

☐ [*T.D.* 7764, 1-19-81.]

[Reg. §11.412(c)-7]

§11.412(c)-7. **Election to treat certain retroactive plan amendments as made on the first day of the plan year (Temporary).**— (a) *General rule.*—Under section 412(c)(8), a plan administrator may elect to have any amendment which is adopted after the close of the plan year to which it applies deemed to have been made on the first day of such plan year if the amendment—

(1) Is adopted no later than 2 and one-half months after the close of such plan year (or, in the case of a multi-employer plan, no later than 2 years after the close of such plan year),

(2) Does not reduce the accrued benefit of any participant determined as of the beginning of such plan year, and

(3) Does not reduce the accrued benefit of any participant determined as of the time of adoption of the amendment, or, if it does so reduce such accrued benefit, it is shown that the plan administrator filed a notice with the Secretary of Labor notifying him of the amendment, and—

(i) The Secretary of Labor approved the amendment, or

(ii) The Secretary of Labor failed to disapprove the amendment within 90 days after the date on which the notice was filed.

(b) *Time and manner of making election.*—(1) The election under section 412(c)(8) shall be made by the plan administrator by a statement of election described in subparagraph (3) of this paragraph, attached to the annual return relating to minimum funding standards required to be filed under section 6058 with respect to the plan year to which the election relates.

(2) In the event that an amendment to which paragraph (a) of this section applies is adopted after the filing of the annual return required under section 6058, the plan administrator may make the election under section 412(c)(8) by attaching a statement of election, described in subparagraph (3) of this paragraph, to a copy of such annual return, and filing such copy no later than the time allowed for the filing of such returns under section 6058. (In the case of multiemployer plans, such copy may be filed within a 24 month period beginning with the date prescribed for the filing of such returns.)

(3) The statement of election filed by or on behalf of the plan administrator shall—

(i) State the date of the close of the first plan year to which the amendment applies and the date on which the amendment was adopted;

(ii) Contain a statement that the amendment does not reduce the accrued benefit of any participant determined as of the beginning of the plan year preceding the plan year in which the amendment is adopted; and

(iii) Contain either—

(A) A statement that the amendment does not reduce the accrued benefit of any participant determined as of the time of adoption of such amendment, or

(B) A copy of the notice filed with the Secretary of Labor under section 412(c)(8) and a statement that either the Secretary of Labor has approved the amendment or he has failed to act within 90 days after notification of the amendment. [Temporary Reg. §11.412(c)-7.]

☐ [*T.D. 7338, 12-26-74.*]

[Reg. §11.412(c)-11]

§11.412(c)-11. **Election with respect to bonds (Temporary).**— (a) *In general.*—Section 412(c)(2)(B) provides that, at the election of the administrator of a plan which includes a trust qualified under section 401(a) or of a plan which satisfies the requirements of section 403(a) or section 405(a), the value of a bond or other evidence of indebtedness which is held by the plan and which is not in default as to principal or interest may be determined on an amortized basis running from initial cost at purchase to the amount payable at maturity (or, in the case of a bond which is callable prior to maturity, the earliest call date). So long as this election is in effect, the value of any such evidence of indebtedness shall, for purposes of section 412, be determined on such an amortized basis rather than on a method taking into account fair market value as described in section 412(c)(2)(A).

(b) *Manner of making election.*—The election to value evidences of indebtedness in accordance with paragraph (a) of this section shall be made by a statement to that effect attached to and filed as a part of the annual return of the plan required under section 6058 of the Code.

(c) *Effect of election.*—The election provided by section 412(c)(2)(B), once made, will affect the valuation of all evidences of indebtedness, not in default as to principal or interest, which are held by the plan for the plan year for which the election is made and any evidences of indebtedness which are subsequently acquired by the plan. The value of any evidence of indebtedness which is in default as of the

valuation date for the plan year must be determined on the basis of any reasonable actuarial method of valuation which takes into account fair market value in accordance with section 412(c)(2)(A) and must continue to be so valued until the indebtedness is no longer in default.

(d) *Consent to revoke required.*—(1) *In general.*—An election made in accordance with paragraph (a) of this section may be revoked only if consent to revoke the election is obtained from the Secretary or his delegate.

(2) *Manner of obtaining permission for revocation.*—[Reserved.] [Temporary Reg. §11.412(c)-11.]

☐ [*T.D. 7335, 12-19-74.*]

[Reg. §11.412(c)-12]

§11.412(c)-12. **Extension of time to make contributions to satisfy requirements of section 412 (Temporary).**—(a) *In general.*—Section 412(c)(10) of the Internal Revenue Code of 1954 provides that for purposes of section 412 a contribution for a plan year made after the end of such plan year but not later than two and one-half months after the last day of such plan year shall be deemed to have been made on such last day. Section 412(c)(10) further provides that the two and one-half month period may be extended for not more than six months under regulations.

(b) *Six month extension of two and one-half month period.*—(1) For purposes of section 412 a contribution for a plan year to which section 412 applies that is made not more than eight and one-half months after the end of such plan year shall be deemed to have been made on the last day of such year.

(2) The rules of this section relating to the time a contribution to a plan is deemed made for purposes of the minimum funding standard under section 412 are independent from the rules contained in section 404(a)(6) relating to the time a contribution to a plan is deemed made for purposes of claiming a deduction for such contribution under section 404. [Temporary Reg. §11.412(c)-12.]

☐ [*T.D. 7439, 10-21-76.*]

[Reg. §1.412(c)(1)-1]

§1.412(c)(1)-1. **Determinations to be made under funding method—Terms defined.**—(a) *Actuarial cost method and funding method.*—Section 3(31) of the Employee Retirement Income Security Act of 1974 ("ERISA") provides certain acceptable (and unacceptable) actuarial cost methods which may (or may not) be used by employee plans. The term "funding method" when used in section 412 has the same meaning as the term "actuarial cost method" in section 3(31) of ERISA. For shortfall method for certain collectively bargained plans, see §1.412(c)(1)-2; for principles applicable to funding methods in general, see regulations under section 412(c)(3).

(b) *Computations included in funding method.*—The funding method of a plan includes not only the overall funding method used by the plan but also each specific method of computation used in applying the overall method. However, the choice of which actuarial assumptions are appropriate to the overall method or to the specific method of computation is not a part of the funding method. For example, the decision to use or not to use a mortality factor in the funding method of a plan is not a part of such funding method. Similarly, the specific mortality rate determined to be applicable to a particular plan year is not part of the funding method. See section 412(c)(5) for the requirement of approval to change the funding method used by a plan. [Reg. §1.412(c)(1)-1.]

☐ [*T.D. 7733, 11-13-80.*]

[Reg. §1.412(c)(1)-2]

§1.412(c)(1)-2. **Shortfall method.**—(a) *In general.*—(1) *Shortfall method.*—The shortfall method is a funding method that adapts a plan's underlying funding method for purposes of section 412. As such, the use of the shortfall method is subject to section 412(c)(3). A plan described in paragraph (a)(2) of this section may elect to determine the charges to the funding standard account required by section 412(b) under the shortfall method. These charges are computed on the basis of an estimated number of units of service or production (for which a certain amount per unit is to be charged). The difference between the net amount charged under this method and the net amount that otherwise would have been charged under section 412 for the same period is a shortfall loss (gain) and is to be amortized over certain subsequent plan years.

(2) *Eligibility for use of shortfall.*—No plan may use the shortfall method unless—

(i) The plan is a collectively bargained plan described in section 413(a), and

(ii) Contributions to the plan are made at a rate specified under the terms of a legally binding agreement applicable to the plan.

For purposes of this section, a plan maintained by a labor organization which is exempt from tax under section 501(c)(5) is treated as a collectively bargained plan and the governing rules of the organization (such as its constitution, bylaws, or other document that can be altered only through action of a convention of the organization) are treated as a collectively bargained agreement.

(b) *Computation and effect of net shortfall charge.*—(1) *In general.*—The "net shortfall charge" to the funding standard account under the shortfall method is the product of (i) the estimated unit charge described in paragraph (c) of this section that applies for a particular plan year, multiplied by (ii) the actual number of base units (for example, units of service or production) which occurred during that plan year. When the shortfall method is used, the net shortfall charge is a substitute for the specific charges and credits to the funding standard account described in section 412(b)(2) and (3)(B).

(2) *Example.*—Paragraph (b)(1) of this section may be illustrated by the following example:

Example. A pension plan uses the calendar year as the plan year and the shortfall method. Its estimated unit charge applicable to 1980 is 80 cents per hour of covered employment. During 1980, there were 125,000 hours of covered employment. The net shortfall charge for the plan year is $100,000 (*i.e.*, 125,000 × $.80), regardless of the amount which would be charged and credited to the funding standard account under section 412(b)(2) and (3)(B) had the shortfall method not applied. The funding standard account for 1980 will be separately credited for the amount considered contributed for the plan year under section 412(b)(3)(A). The other items which may be credited, if applicable, are a waived funding deficiency and the alternative minimum funding standard credit adjustment under section 412(b)(3)(C) and (D) because these items are not credits under section 412(b)(3)(B).

(3) *Plans with more than one contract, contribution rate, employer, or benefit level.*—(i) *General rule.*—A single plan with more than one contract, contribution rate, employer, or benefit level may compute a separate net shortfall charge for each contract, contribution rate, each employer, or each benefit level. The sum of these charges is the plan's total net shortfall charge. Under §1.412(c)(1)-1(b), the use of separate computations would be a specific method of computation used in applying the overall funding method. See also paragraph (f)(5) of this section.

(ii) *Single valuation.*—Only one actuarial valuation shall be made for the single plan on each actuarial valuation date.

(iii) *Reasonableness test.*—The specific method of computation of the net shortfall charge must be reasonable, determined in the light of the facts and circumstances.

(c) *Estimated unit charge.*—The estimated unit charge is the annual computation charge described in paragraph (d) of this section divided by the estimated base units of service or production described in paragraph (e) of this section.

(d) *Annual computation charge.*—The annual computation charge for a plan year is the sum of the following amounts:

(1) The net charges and credits which, but for using the shortfall method, would be made under section 412(b)(2) and (b)(3)(B).

(2) The amount described in paragraph (g)(3) of this section, if applicable, for amortization of shortfall gain or loss.

(e) *Estimated base units.*—(1) *In general.*—The estimated base units are the expected units of service or production for a plan year (hours, days, tons, dollars of compensation, etc.), determined as of the base unit estimation date for that plan year under paragraph (f) of this section. This estimate must be based on the past experience of the plan and the reasonable expectations of the plan for the plan year. The specific type of unit used must be described in the statement of funding method for the plan year. (See paragraph (i)(3) of this section for reporting requirements.)

(2) *Reasonable expectations.*—The reasonableness of expectations used under paragraph (e)(1) of this section is determined under the facts and circumstances of the plan for each plan year as of the relevant base unit estimation date. Expectations will be considered unreasonable if, for example, they do not reflect a consistent and substantial decline or growth in actual base units that has occurred over the course of recent years and that is likely to continue beyond the base unit estimation date. This determination of reasonableness is independent of determinations made under section 412(c)(3) of the reasonableness of actuarial assumptions.

(f) *Base unit estimation date.*—(1) *In general.*—The base unit estimation date for the current plan year is determined under this paragraph (f). This date shall be an actuarial valuation date no earlier than the last actuarial valuation date occurring at least one year before the earliest date any current collectively bargained agreement in existence during the plan year came into effect.

(2) *Four-month rule.*—For purposes of this paragraph (f), a current collectively bargained agreement is one in effect during at least four months of the current plan year.

(3) *Effective date of agreement.*—For purposes of this paragraph (f), a collectively bargained agreement shall be deemed to have come into effect on the effective date of the agreement containing the currently effective provision for contributions to the plan or the benefits provided under the plan.

(4) *Long-term contract rule.*—The effective date of a collectively bargained agreement shall be deemed not to occur prior to the first day of the third plan year preceding the current year.

(5) *Special rule for plans computing separate net shortfall charge.*—A plan that computes a separate net shortfall charge for each contract, contribution rate, employer, or benefit level under paragraph (b)(3) of this section shall determine the base unit estimation date for each separate charge without regard to any collectively bargained agreement that does not relate to that contract, contribution rate, employer, or benefit level. If a collective bargaining agreement requiring contributions by a certain employer, or prescribing a certain benefit level, is in effect on December 31, 1980, the preceding sentence shall not apply to the computation of a separate net shortfall charge for that employer or benefit level until the earlier of—

(i) The first plan year beginning after the date on which expires the collective bargaining agreement requiring contributions by that employer (or the last collective bargaining agreement relating to that benefit level), or

(ii) The first plan year beginning after December 31, 1983.

(6) *Example.*—The rules contained in paragraph (f) of this section are illustrated by the following table. In the table, "V" signifies actuarial valuation date (January 1 in each case shown); "B" signifies beginning of a contract; and "E" signifies end of a contract. The table shows the resulting earliest base unit estimation date with respect to the following assumed items:

COMPUTATION OF BASE UNIT ESTIMATION DATE

Example	Plan year (calendar year basis)								
	1976	1977	1978	1979	1980	1981	1982	1983	1984
Plan A [2]	V			V			V		
Contract A	......	......	E/B	......	E/B	......	......	......	E/B
Base unit estimation date [1]	1976	1976	1976	1979	1979	1979	1982	1982	1982
Plan B—C [3]	V			V			V		
Contract B	B*	......	......	E/B	......	......	E/B*	......	E
Contract C	E/B	......	......	E/B	......	......	E/B	......	......
Base unit estimation date [1]	1976	1976	1976	1976	1976	1976	1976	1979	1979
Plan D—E [3]	V	V	V	V	V	V	V	V	V
Contract D	......	......	......	E/B*	......	......	......	E/B	......
Contract E	......	......	......	E/B*	......	......	......	......	E/B
Base unit estimation date [1]	1976	1976	1976	1978	1978	1978	1978	1979	1982

[1] The base unit estimation date may be on or any time after the actuarial valuation date in the year indicated on this line.
[2] Plan A is maintained by only one employer.
[3] Plans B-C and D-E are maintained by more than one employer.
* Denotes that a prior contract ends and a new contract begins prior to the fifth month of a plan year.

(g) *Amortization of shortfall gain or loss.*—(1) *Definition.*—The shortfall gain for a plan is the excess for the plan year of—

(i) The net shortfall charge computed under paragraph (b) of this section over

(ii) The annual computation charge described in paragraph (d) of this section.

The shortfall loss for a plan is the excess for the plan year of the annual computation charge over the net shortfall charge.

(2) *Shortfall amortization period.*—(i) *First year.*—The plan year in which the amortization of a shortfall gain or loss must begin is the earlier of two years: the fifth plan year following the plan year in which the shortfall gain or loss arose, or the first plan year beginning after the latest scheduled expiration date of a collectively bargained agreement in effect with respect to the plan during the plan year in which the shortfall gain or loss arose. For purposes of this subparagraph, a contract expiring on the last day of a plan year shall be deemed to be renewed on such last day for the same period of years as the contract that succeeds the expiring contract.

(ii) *Last year.*—The plan year in which the amortization of a shortfall gain or loss must end is the 15th plan year following the plan year in which the shortfall gain or loss arose. For a multiemployer plan described in section 414(f), the amortization must end with the 20th plan year instead of the 15th.

(3) *Annual amortization amount.*—The shortfall gain or loss must be amortized in equal annual installments. The total amount to be amortized must be adjusted for interest at the rate used for determining the plan's normal cost.

(4) *Shortfall gain or loss under spread gain type of funding method.*—(i) *In general.*—A spread gain type of funding method spreads experience gains and losses over future periods as part of a plan's normal cost. (Examples of spread gain types of funding methods are the aggregate cost method, the frozen initial liability method, and the attained age normal method.) However, a shortfall gain or loss is not an experience gain or loss. Therefore, a plan using a spread gain type of funding method together with the shortfall method must amortize shortfall gains and losses and otherwise meet the requirements of paragraph (g) of this section.

(ii) *Asset adjustment for aggregate method.*—A plan using the shortfall method with the aggregate cost method of funding must adjust its plan assets for a shortfall gain or loss in calculating normal cost. The unamortized portion of any shortfall gain is subtracted from plan assets. The unamortized portion of any shortfall loss is added to plan assets.

(5) *Reconciliation of shortfall gain or loss with funding standard account.*—At the beginning of each plan year, the actual unfunded liability under the method used by the plan must equal the outstanding balance of all amortization bases, including bases for shortfall gains and losses, less the credit balance under the funding standard account at the end of the prior year.

(6) *Examples.*—This paragraph is illustrated by the following examples:

Example (1). A multiemployer plan described in section 414(f) is maintained with the calendar year as the plan year and uses the shortfall method. The plan uses the frozen initial liability funding method. A five percent interest assumption is used by the plan, with payments computed as of the first day of each plan year for all items. The expiration dates of contracts in effect during plan years 1976, 1977, and 1978 are such that the amortization of gains or losses for each year must begin in the fifth following plan year. The assumed plan costs and estimated base units for selected years, and the computations under this section which follow from such assumptions, are shown in the following table. In the table, "*" denotes an assumed item. The remaining figures have been calculated on the basis of these assumptions.

(a) *Computation of net shortfall charge and shortfall gain or loss.*

Plan year	1976	1977	1978
1. Normal Cost*	$100,000	$100,000	$100,000
2. Amortization of unfunded liability*	50,000	50,000	50,000
3. Total annual computation charges	$150,000	$150,000	$150,000
4. Estimated base units*	100,000	100,000	100,000
5. Estimated unit charge (line 3 ÷ line 4)	$1.50	$1.50	$1.50
6. Actual units during year*	80,000	90,000	110,000
7. Net shortfall charge for year (line 5 × line 6)	$120,000	$135,000	$165,000
8. Shortfall (gain) or loss (line 3 – line 7)	$30,000	$15,000	($15,000)

(b) *Annual amortization amount*

9. Year of shortfall gain or loss	1976	1977	1978
10. First year of amortization	1981	1982	1983
11. Last year of amortization	1996	1997	1998
12. (Gain) or loss adjusted for interest to year amortization begins (1-1-76 to 1-1-81, etc.)	$38,288	$19,144	($19,144)
13. Annual amortization (16 years)	$3,364	$1,682	($1,682)

(c) *Computation of net shortfall charges for selected years (including shortfall amortization).*

Plan year	1981	1982	1983
14. Normal cost*	$120,000	$125,000	$130,000
15. Amortization of unfunded liability*	50,000	50,000	50,000
16. Shortfall amortization (see line 13) from			
1976	3,364	3,364	3,364
1977	. . .	1,682	1,682
1978	. . .	. . .	(1,682)
17. Total annual computation charges	$173,364	$180,046	$183,364
18. Estimated base units*	$110,000	$110,000	$110,000
19. Estimated unit charge (line 17 ÷ line 18)	$1.576	$1.637	$1.667
20. Actual units during year*	105,000	110,000	105,000
21. Net shortfall charge for year (line 19 × line 20)	$165,480	$180,070	$175,035
22. Shortfall (gain) loss (line 17 – line 21)	$7,884	$(24)	$8,329

The amounts in line 22 will be amortized beginning 1986, 1987, and 1988, respectively. The $24 gain in 1982 results from rounding the estimated unit charge.

Example (2). Assume the facts in Example (1). Also assume that the plan uses the frozen initial liability funding method, that the unfunded liability as of January 1, 1976 (corresponding to a 40-year charge of $50,000 due at the beginning of the year) is $900,850, and that actual contributions at the rate of $1.75 per unit are paid at mid-year in 1976.

(a) *Computation of the unfunded liability as of December 31, 1976.*

1.	Unfunded liability as of 1/1/76 .	$900,850
2.	Normal cost (that used in the calculation of the total annual computation charges)	100,000
3.	Interest at 5% due on items 1 and 2	50,043
4.	Contribution with interest: $1.75 × 80,000 × 1.025 (actual contribution rate times actual base units times interest adjustment from mid-year)	143,500
5.	Unfunded liability as of 12/31/76: item 1 + item 2 + item 3 – item 4 .	907,393

(b) *Computation of the outstanding balance of the bases as of December 31, 1976.*

1.	Original base: ($900,850 – $50,000) × 1.05	$893,393
2.	Shortfall loss $30,000 × 1.05	31,500
3.	Total	924,893

(c) *Computation of the credit balance as of December 31, 1976.*

1.	Net shortfall charge (§ 1.412(c)(1)-2(b)) adjusted for interest: $120,000 × 1.05	$126,000
2.	Actual contributions with interest	143,500
3.	Credit balance as of 12/31/76: item 2 – item 1	17,500

(d) *Reconciliation of computations.* As of January 1, 1977, the unfunded liability ($907,393) equals the outstanding balance of the bases minus the credit balance ($924,893 – $17,500 = $907,393).

(h) *Amortization of experience gain or loss.*—(1) *General rule.*—In the case of a plan using an immediate gain type of funding method, an experience gain or loss shall be amortized pursuant to section 412(b)(2)(B)(iv) or (b)(3)(B)(ii). (Examples of the immediate gain type of funding method are the unit credit method, the entry age normal cost method, and the individual level premium cost method.) For purposes of this section, a shortfall gain or loss is not an experience gain or loss. The amount of the experience gain or loss must be adjusted for interest at the rate used for determining the plan's normal cost.

(2) *Experience amortization period under shortfall method.*—(i) *First year.*—The plan year in which the amortization of an experience gain or loss must begin in the case of a plan using the shortfall method is the earlier of two years: the fifth plan year following the plan year in which the experience gain or loss arose, or the first plan year beginning after the latest scheduled expiration date of a contract in effect during the plan year in which the experience gain or loss arose. For purposes of this subparagraph a contract expiring on the last day of the plan year shall be deemed to be renewed on such last day for the same period of years as the contract that succeeds the expiring contract.

(ii) *Last year.*—The plan year in which the amortization of an experience gain or loss must end in the case of a plan using the shortfall method is the 15th plan year following the plan year in which the experience gain or loss arose. For a multi-employer plan

described in section 414(f), the amortization must end with the 20th plan year instead of the 15th.

(3) *Use of annual computation charge in determining experience gain or loss.*—In the case of a plan using an immediate gain type of funding method, an experience gain or loss is the difference between the expected unfunded liability and the actual unfunded liability under the plan. The expected unfunded liability as of the end of a plan year equals the actual unfunded liability as of the beginning of the year plus normal cost, minus contributions, all adjusted for interest. If the plan adopts the shortfall method, the expected unfunded liability is computed by using the normal cost applicable for the plan year in determining the annual computation charge under paragraph (d) of this section. The same normal cost is used in computing the unfunded liability under the frozen initial liability funding method.

(4) *Example.*—This paragraph is illustrated by the following example:

Example. Assume the facts as in Example (2) from paragraph (g)(6) of this section, except that the entry age normal funding method is used. Also assume that as of December 31, 1976, the actual unfunded liability is $900,000.

(a) *Computation of expected unfunded liability.*

1.	Actual unfunded liability as of 1-1-76 . .	$900,850
2.	Normal cost portion of annual computation charge as of 1-1-76	100,000
3.	Interest at 5% due on items 1 and 2 . . .	50,043
4.	Contribution received with interest: $1.75 × 80,000 × 1.025 (actual contribution rate times actual base units times interest adjustment at mid-year)	143,500
5.	Expected unfunded liability as of 12-31-76 (item 1 + item 2 + item 3 – item 4)	907,393

(b) *Computation of gain or loss.*

1.	Expected unfunded liability as of 12-31-76	$907,393
2.	Actual unfunded liability as of 12-31-76	900,000
3.	Gain (or loss) (item 1 — item 2) .	7,393

(i) *Election procedure.*—(1) *In general.*—To elect the shortfall method, a collectively bargained plan must attach a statement to the annual report required under section 6058(a) for the first plan year to which it is applied. The statement shall state that the shortfall method is adopted, beginning with the plan year covered by such report. Advance approval from the Internal Revenue Service is not required if the shortfall method is first adopted on or before the later of—

(i) The first plan year to which section 412 applies or

(ii) The last plan year commencing before December 31, 1981. However, approval must be received pursuant to section 412(c)(5) prior to the adoption of the shortfall method at a later time, or the discontinuance of such method, once adopted.

(2) *Use of specific computation method.*—A specific method of computation under the shortfall method is described in paragraph (b)(3) of this section, regarding the treatment of more than one contract, employer, or benefit level under the plan. This specific method may be adopted with respect to any plan year to which the shortfall method applies. Approval from the Commissioner must be received under section 412(c)(5) prior to the adoption of this specific computation method for a plan year subsequent to the first plan year to which the shortfall method applies, or prior to the discontinuance of a specific computation method, once adopted.

(3) *Reporting requirements.*—Each annual report required by section 6058(a) and periodic report of the actuary required by section 6059 must include all additional information relevant to the use of the shortfall method as may be required by the applicable forms and the instructions for such forms.

(j) *Transitional rule.*—In lieu of paragraphs (g)(2) and (h)(2) of this section relating to the amortization period for shortfall and experience gains and losses, for gains and losses arising in plan years beginning before January 1, 1981, a plan may rely on the prior published position of the Internal Revenue Service with respect to the amortization period for shortfall and experience gains and losses.

(k) *Supersession.*—This section and § 1.412(c)(1)-1 supersede §§ 11.412(c)(1)-1 and (c)(1)-2 of the Temporary Income Tax Regulations Under the Employee Retirement Income Security Act of 1974. [Reg. § 1.412(c)(1)-2.]

☐ [*T.D. 7733, 11-13-80.*]

[Reg. § 1.412(c)(1)-3]

§ 1.412(c)(1)-3. Applying the minimum funding requirements to restored plans.—(a) *In general.*—(1) *Restoration method.*—The restoration method is a funding method that adapts the underlying funding method of section 412 in the case of certain plans that are or have been terminated and are later restored by the Pension Benefit Guaranty Corporation (PBGC). The normal operation of the funding standard account, and all other provisions of section 412 and the regulations thereunder, are unchanged except as provided in this § 1.412(c)(1)-3. Under the restoration method, the PBGC shall determine a restoration payment schedule, extending over no more than 30 years, that replaces all charges and credits to the funding standard account attributable to pre-restoration amortization bases. The restoration payment schedule is determined on the basis of an actuarial valuation of the accrued liability of the plan on the initial post-restoration valuation date less the actuarial value of the plan assets on that date. The initial post-restoration valuation date is the date of the valuation that falls in the first plan year beginning on or after the date of the restoration order.

(2) *Applicability of restoration method.*—A plan must use the restoration method if, and only if—

(i) The plan is being or has been terminated pursuant to section 4041(c) or section 4042 of the Employee Retirement Income Security Act of 1974 (ERISA); and

(ii) The plan has been restored by the PBGC pursuant to its authority under section 4047 of ERISA.

(b) *Computation and effect of the initial restoration amortization base.*—(1) *In general.*—The initial restoration amortization base is determined under the underlying funding method used by the plan. When the plan uses a spread gain funding method that does not maintain an unfunded liability, the plan must change either to an immediate gain method that directly calculates an accrued liability or to a spread gain method that maintains an unfunded liability. A plan may adopt any cost method that satisfies this requirement and that is acceptable under section 412 and the regulations thereunder, provided that the plan administrator follows the procedures established by the Commissioner for changes in funding methods. The initial restoration amortization base is determined using the valuation for the plan year in which the initial post-restoration valuation date falls. The initial restoration amortization base equals the accrued liability with respect to plan benefit liabilities returned by the PBGC less the value of the plan assets returned by the PBGC. The initial restoration amortization base replaces all prior amortization bases including those under section 412(b)(2)(B), (C), and (D) and under section 412(b)(3)(B). Any base resulting from a change in funding method, including a change required under this paragraph, is treated as a prior amortization base within the meaning of this paragraph (b). Any accumulated funding deficiency or credit balance in the funding standard account is set equal to zero when the initial restoration amortization base is established.

(2) *Example.*—The following example illustrates the provisions of this paragraph (b):

Example. A pension plan uses the calendar year as its plan year, makes its annual periodic valuation as of January 1, and uses the unit credit actuarial cost method for funding purposes. The plan is in the process of being terminated. By order of the PBGC the plan is restored as of July 1, 1991. The initial post-restoration valuation date is January 1, 1992, and a restoration payment schedule order is issued on October 31, 1992. If, as of January 1, 1992, the accrued liability of the plan is $1,000,000 and the value of the plan assets is $200,000, the initial restoration amortization base is $800,000.

(c) *Establishment of a restoration payment schedule.*—(1) *Certification requirement.*—When the PBGC establishes a restoration payment schedule, the Executive Director of the PBGC must certify to the PBGC's Board of Directors, and to the Internal Revenue Service, that the PBGC has reviewed the funding of the plan, the financial condition of the plan sponsor and its controlled group members, the payments required under the restoration payment schedule (taking into account the availability of deferrals authorized under paragraph (c)(4) of this section), and any other factor that the PBGC deems relevant, and, based on that review, determines that it is in the best interests of participants and beneficiaries of the plan and the pension insurance program that the restored plan not be reterminated.

(2) *Requirements for restoration payment schedule.*—(i) *Amortization of base over period of no more than 30 years.*—The restoration payment schedule must be prescribed in an order requiring the employer to make stated contributions to the plan sufficient to amortize the initial restoration amortization base over a period extending not more than 30 years after the initial post-restoration valuation date (the restoration payment period). Payments included in the restoration payment schedule order are charged to the funding standard account of the plan at the end of each plan year in accordance with paragraph (d) of this section. The restoration payment schedule must provide for total charges that are sufficient to amortize the entire amount of the initial restoration amortization base by the end of the restoration payment period. The scheduled charges need not be in level amounts, but the present value of the prescribed charges on the initial post-restoration valuation date, computed with interest at the valuation rate, must equal the initial restoration amortization base.

(ii) *Minimum annual charge.*—The restoration payment schedule must prescribe annual charges that are sufficient to prevent the outstanding balance of the initial restoration amortization base from exceeding whichever of the following amounts is applicable—

(A) During the first 10 plan years on the restoration payment schedule, the amount of the initial restoration amortization base on the date the base was established; or

(B) During plan years 11 through 20 on the restoration payment schedule, the maximum permitted outstanding balance of the initial restoration amortization base at the end of the tenth plan year, as calculated under paragraph (c)(2)(iii) of this section; or

(C) During plan years 21 through the end of the restoration payment schedule, the maximum permitted outstanding balance of the initial restoration amortization base at the end of the twentieth plan year, as calculated under paragraph (c)(2)(iii) of this section.

(iii) *Interim amortization requirements.*—The restoration payment schedule must provide for sufficient periodic charges so that the outstanding balance of the initial restoration amortization base at the end of the tenth plan year and at the end of the twentieth plan year of the restoration payment period will not be larger than the outstanding balance that would have remained at the end of the tenth plan year and at the end of the twentieth plan year, respectively, if the initial restoration amortization base had been amortized in level annual amounts over the restoration payment period at the valuation rate.

(3) *Amendments to the restoration payment schedule.*—The order establishing the restoration payment schedule may be amended by the PBGC from time to time with respect to any remaining payments, provided that no amendment may extend the restoration payment period beyond 30 years from the initial post-restoration valuation date, and provided further that the restoration payment schedule, as amended, satisfies the requirements of paragraph (c)(2) of this section.

(4) *Deferral of minimum scheduled annual payment amounts.*—(i) *Authority to grant deferral.*—Not later than $2\frac{1}{2}$ months following the end of the plan year, the PBGC may grant a deferral of the charges required in the restoration payment schedule for that plan year if the requirements in paragraph (c)(4)(ii) of this section are satisfied. The PBGC may require the plan sponsor and its controlled group members to provide security to the plan as a condition to granting a deferral.

(ii) *Determination of business hardship.*—Before granting a deferral under this paragraph (c)(4), the PBGC must make a determination that the granting of the deferral is in the best interests of plan participants and the plan termination insurance system, and that the plan sponsor and its controlled group members are unable to make the scheduled restoration payments without experiencing temporary substantial business hardship. In making these determinations, the factors the PBGC shall consider, include, but are not limited to, the following—

(A) Whether the plan sponsor and its controlled group members are operating at an economic loss;

(B) Whether there is substantial unemployment or underemployment in the trades or businesses of the plan sponsor and its controlled group members;

(C) Whether the sales and profits of the industry or industries are depressed or declining; and

(D) Whether it is reasonable to expect that the plan termination insurance system will suffer a greater loss if the plan is terminated than if it is continued as a restored plan.

(iii) *Amount of deferral.*—The amount of the deferral for any particular plan year may not exceed the lesser of the amount that would have been required to be contributed under the restoration payment schedule for that year or interest at the valuation rate on the outstanding balance of the initial restoration amortization base for that year. An amortization payment for a deferral granted for a prior plan year may not be deferred. No deferral may extend the overall restoration payment period beyond 30 years.

(iv) *Modification of payment schedule.*—The restoration payment schedule must be adjusted to reflect any deferral granted for a plan year in the manner prescribed in this paragraph (c). The charge otherwise specified in the schedule is reduced by the amount of any deferral. The charges under the restoration payment schedule for the subsequent plan years are increased by the amounts in paragraph (c)(4)(v) of this section.

(v) *Amortization of deferred amount.*—The amount of any deferral granted by the PBGC for any plan year must be amortized in level amounts over five years or such shorter period as may be prescribed by the PBGC, at the valuation rate, beginning with the plan year following the year of the deferral.

(vi) *Number of deferrals permitted.*—The PBGC may not grant more than five deferrals of the minimum scheduled payments as required by this section during the restoration payment period and no more than three of these deferrals may be granted during the first ten years of that period.

(vii) *Deferrals override minimum annual charges and interim amortization requirements.*—In determining the minimum annual charge under paragraph (c)(2)(ii) of this section and in applying the interim amortization requirements of paragraph (c)(2)(iii) of this section, the unamortized balances of any deferrals granted by the PBGC under this paragraph shall be added to the outstanding balance of the initial restoration amortization base otherwise allowable.

(d) *Charging the scheduled restoration payments to the funding standard account.*—In addition to any other charges and credits prescribed in the normal operation of the funding standard account under section 412, the amount of each payment specified in the restoration payment schedule shall be charged against the funding standard account of the plan for the plan year to which that payment is attributed in the restoration payment schedule. To the extent that the restoration payment schedule provides for payments before the end of the plan year, the annual charge to the funding standard account attributable to the restoration payment schedule is equal to the sum of the periodic payments for the plan year accumulated with interest at the valuation rate to the last day of the plan year.

(e) *Changes in actuarial assumptions or methods.*—The plan administrator must notify the PBGC of any changes in the actuarial assumptions or methods used by the plan. Upon notification of any such change, the PBGC may make any changes to the restoration payment schedule that it deems appropriate.

(f) *Change to restoration method.*—A plan that has been restored must use the restoration method until the initial restoration amortization base has been fully amortized. The use of this method does not require prior approval from the Commissioner. A plan using the restoration method must compute the charges to the funding standard account to amortize the initial restoration amortization base in accordance with the order of the PBGC and in accordance with this section.

(g) *Deficit reduction contribution.*—(1) *Calculation of deficit reduction contribution.*—For any plan using the restoration method, the deficit reduction contribution under section 412(l)(2) is equal to the sum of—

(i) The unfunded section 412(l) restoration liability amount; plus

(ii) The unfunded new liability amount.

(2) *Unfunded section 412(l) restoration liability amount.*—The unfunded section 412(l) restoration liability amount is the amount necessary to amortize fully the unfunded section 412(l) restoration liability in installments, as prescribed by the PBGC, over not more than 30 years. The annual amount need not be level, but at all times

the present value of the future amortization charges prescribed under the restoration payment schedule, at the current liability interest rate, must equal the outstanding balance of the unfunded section 412(l) restoration liability and the schedule must provide that at the end of no more than 30 years the entire amount of the unfunded section 412(l) restoration liability base will have been fully amortized. The schedule prescribed for amortization of the unfunded section 412(l) restoration liability must comply with the requirements imposed in paragraph (c) of this section on the restoration payment schedule, except as provided in paragraph (g)(7) of this section and except that the maximum permitted outstanding balance of the unfunded section 412(l) restoration liability at the end of the tenth plan year must not be greater than the outstanding balance of the section 412(l) restoration liability that would have remained at the end of the tenth plan year if the unfunded section 412(l) restoration liability had been amortized in level amounts over the restoration payment period at the actual current liability interest rate for each year, increased by the current liability interest rate differential as defined under paragraph (g)(7) of this section. The unfunded section 412(l) restoration liability amount for the tenth plan year otherwise prescribed under the restoration payment schedule is increased by any outstanding current liability interest rate differential. By issuing an appropriate order, the PBGC may permit the outstanding current liability interest rate differential to be amortized over the tenth through the fourteenth plan years. If the PBGC permits the amortization of the outstanding current liability interest rate differential, then the unfunded section 412(l) restoration liability amount for each year to which an amortization payment is attributed under the order shall be increased by such payment. The outstanding balance otherwise required by paragraph (g)(2) of this section is increased by the outstanding balance, if any, of the base resulting from the amortization of the current liability interest rate differential. The PBGC may amend the amortization schedule for the unfunded section 412(l) restoration liability subject to the limits on amendments to the amortization schedule prescribed for the initial restoration amortization base.

(3) *Establishment of unfunded section 412(l) restoration liability.*—In the plan year in which the initial post-restoration valuation date falls, the unfunded section 412(l) restoration liability is equal to the unfunded current liability of the plan.

(4) *Unfunded new liability amount.*—In the case of a plan using the restoration method, the unfunded new liability amount is the applicable percentage, as defined in section 412(l)(4)(C), of the unfunded new liability determined under paragraph (g)(5) of this section.

(5) *Unfunded new liability.*—The unfunded new liability of a plan using the restoration method is the excess, if any, of the unfunded current liability of the plan, within the meaning of section 412(l)(8)(A) for the plan year (determined without taking into account any unpredictable contingent event benefits, even if the event has occurred) over the outstanding balance of the unfunded section 412(l) restoration liability determined under paragraph (g)(3) of this section.

(6) *Offset of amortization charges.*—The amounts charged to the funding standard account pursuant to the restoration payment schedule in order to amortize the initial restoration base, as described in paragraph (d) of this section, must be offset against the deficit reduction contribution in paragraph (g)(1) of this section along with any other applicable amounts provided in section 412(l)(1)(A)(ii).

(7) *Interest rate differential.*—During the first 10 plan years after the initial post-restoration valuation date, the restoration payment schedule must prescribe an unfunded section 412(l) restoration liability amount for each plan year that is sufficient to prevent the outstanding balance of the unfunded section 412(l) restoration liability from exceeding the initial amount of the unfunded section 412(l) restoration liability increased by the current liability interest rate differential. The current liability interest rate differential at any point during the first ten years of the restoration payment period is the excess, if any, of the outstanding balance of the unfunded section 412(l) restoration liability determined using the actual current liability interest rate for each year, taking into account the charges described in paragraph (d) of this section, over the outstanding balance of the unfunded section 412(l) restoration liability determined using the lowest, for each year, of the initial current liability interest rate, the current liability interest rate for the computation year, and the valuation interest rate, taking into account the charges described in paragraph (d) of this section.

(h) *Election of the alternative minimum funding standard.*—A plan using the restoration method may not elect the alternative minimum funding standard under section 412(g).

(i) *Funding review by the PBGC.*—The PBGC must review the funding of any plan using the restoration method at least once in each plan year. As a result of a funding review, the PBGC may amend the restoration payment schedule as provided in paragraph (c)(3) of this section. As part of the funding review, the Executive Director of the PBGC must certify to the PBGC's Board of Directors, and to the Internal Revenue Service, that the PBGC has reviewed the funding of the plan, the financial condition of the plan sponsor and its controlled group members, the payments required under the restoration payment schedule (taking into account the availability of deferrals authorized under paragraph (c)(4) of this section), and any other factor that the PBGC deems relevant, and, based on that review, determines that it is in the best interests of participants and beneficiaries of the plan and the pension insurance program that the restored plan not be reterminated. [Reg. §1.412(c)(1)-3.]

☐ *[T.D. 8494, 10-21-93.]*

[Reg. §1.412(c)(2)-1]

§1.412(c)(2)-1. Valuation of plan assets; reasonable actuarial valuation methods.—(a) *Introduction.*—(1) *In general.*—This section prescribes rules for valuing plan assets under an actuarial valuation method which satisfies the requirements of section 412(c)(2)(A). An actuarial valuation method is a funding method within the meaning of section 412(c)(3) and the regulations thereunder. Therefore, certain changes affecting the actuarial valuation method are identified in this section as changes in a plan's funding method.

(2) *Exception for certain bonds, etc.*—The rules of this section do not apply to bonds or other evidences of indebtedness for which the election described in section 412(c)(2)(B) has been made, nor are such assets counted in applying paragraphs (b) or (c) of this section. Also, an election under section 412(c)(2)(B) is not a change in funding method within the meaning of section 412(c)(5).

(3) *Money purchase pension plan.*—A money purchase pension plan must value assets for the purpose of satisfying the requirements of section 412(c)(2)(A) solely on the basis of their fair market value (under paragraph (c) of this section).

(4) *Defined benefit plans.*—(i) To satisfy the requirements of section 412(c)(2)(A), an actuarial method of valuing assets of a defined benefit plan must meet the requirements of paragraph (b) of this section.

(ii) In general, the purpose of paragraph (b) of this section is to permit use of reasonable actuarial valuation methods designed to mitigate short-run changes in the fair market value of plan assets. The funding of plan benefits and the charges and credits to the funding standard account required by section 412 are generally based upon the assumption that the defined benefit plan will be continued by the employer. Thus, short-run changes in the value of plan assets presumably will offset one another in the long term. Accordingly, in the determination of the amount required to be contributed under section 412 it is generally not necessary to recognize fully each change in fair market value of the assets in the period in which it occurs.

(iii) The asset valuation rules contained in paragraph (b) produce a "smoothing" effect. Thus, investment performance, including appreciation or depreciation in the market value of the assets occurring in each plan year, may be recognized gradually over several plan years. This "smoothing" is in addition to the "smoothing" effect which results, for example, from amortizing experience losses and gains over 15 to 20 years under section 412(b)(2)(B)(iv) and (3)(B)(ii).

(b) *Asset valuation method requirements.*—(1) *Consistent basis.*—(i) The actuarial asset valuation method must be applied on a consistent basis. Any change in meeting the requirements of this paragraph (b) is a change in funding method subject to section 412(c)(5).

(ii) A method may satisfy the consistency requirement even though computations are based only on the period elapsed since the adoption of the method or on asset values occurring during that period.

(2) *Statement of plan's method.*—The method of determining the actuarial value (but not fair market value) of the assets must be specified in the plan's actuarial report (required under section 6059). The method must be described in sufficient detail so that another actuary employing the method described would arrive at a reasonably similar result. Whether a deviation from the stated actuarial valuation method is a change in funding method is to be determined in accordance with section 412(c)(5) and the regulations thereunder. A deviation to include a type of asset not previously held by the plan would not be a change in funding method.

(3) *Consistent valuation dates.*—The same day or days (such as the first or the last day of a plan year) must be used for all purposes to value the plan's assets for each plan year, or portion of plan year, for which a valuation is made. For purposes of this section, each such day is a valuation date. A change in the day or days used is a change in funding method.

(4) *Reflect fair market value.*—The valuation method must take into account fair market value by making use of the—

(i) Fair market value (determined under paragraph (c) of this section), or

(ii) Average value (determined under paragraph (b)(7) of this section)

of the plan's assets as of the applicable asset valuation date. This is done either directly in the computation of their actuarial value or indirectly in the computation of upper or lower limits placed on that value.

(5) *Results above and below fair market or average value.*—A method will not satisfy the requirements of this paragraph (b) if it is designed to produce a result which will be consistently above or below the values described in paragraph (b)(4)(i) and (ii). However, a method designed to produce a result which consistently falls between fair market value and average value will satisfy this requirement. See Example (5) in paragraph (b)(9) of this section for an illustration of a method described in the preceding sentence.

(6) *Corridor limits.*—(i) Regardless of how the method reflects fair market value under paragraph (b)(4), the method must result in an actuarial value of the plan's assets which is not less than a minimum amount and not more than a maximum amount. The minimum amount is the lesser of 80 percent of the current fair market value of plan assets as of the applicable asset valuation date or 85 percent of the average value (as described in subparagraph (7)) of plan assets as of that date. The maximum amount is the greater of 120 percent of the current fair market value of plan assets as of the applicable asset valuation date or 115 percent of the average value of plan assets as of that date.

(ii) Under a plan's method, a preliminary computation of the expected actuarial value may fall outside the prescribed corridor. A method meets the requirements of paragraph (b)(6)(i) of this section in such a case only by adjusting the expected actuarial value to the nearest corridor limit applicable under the method. A plan may use an actuarial valuation method with a narrower corridor than the general corridor required under paragraph (b)(6)(i). The adjustment to the nearest corridor limit of such a method for purposes of this subdivision (ii) would be determined by the narrower corridor stated in the description of the plan's method.

(7) *Average value.*—The average value of plan assets is computed by—

(i) Determining the fair market value of plan assets at least annually,

(ii) Adding the current fair market value of the assets (as of the applicable valuation date) and their adjusted values (as described in paragraph (b)(8) of this section) for a stated period not to exceed the five most recent plan years (including the current year), and

(iii) Dividing this sum by the number of values (including the current fair market value) considered in computing the sum described in subdivision (ii).

(8) *Adjusted value.*—(i) The adjusted value of plan assets for a prior valuation date is their fair market value on that date with certain positive and negative adjustments. These adjustments reflect changes that occur between the prior asset valuation date and the current valuation date. However, no adjustment is made for increases or decreases in the total value of plan assets that result from the purchase, sale, or exchange of plan assets or from the receipt of payment on a debt obligation held by the plan.

(ii) In determining the adjusted value of plan assets for a prior valuation date, there is added to the fair market value of the plan assets on that date the sum of all additions to the plan assets since that date, excluding appreciation in the fair market value of the assets. The additions would include, for example, any contribution to the plan; any interest or dividend paid to the plan; and any asset not taken into account in a prior valuation of assets, but taken into account for the current year, in computing the fair market value of plan assets under paragraph (c) of this section.

(iii) In determining the adjusted value of plan assets for a prior valuation date, there is subtracted from the fair market value of the plan assets on that date the sum of all reductions in plan assets since that date, excluding depreciation in the fair market value of the assets. The reductions would include, for example, any benefit paid from plan assets; any expense paid from plan assets; and any asset taken into account in a prior valuation of assets but not taken into account for the current year, in computing the fair market value of plan assets under paragraph (c) of this section.

(9) *Examples.*—This paragraph (b) may be illustrated by the following examples. In each example, assume that the pension plan uses a consistent actuarial method of valuing its assets within the meaning of paragraph (b)(1), (2), and (3) of this section.

Example (1). Plan A considers the value of its assets to be initial cost, increased by an assumed rate of growth of X percent annually. Under the circumstances, the X-percent factor used by the plan is a reasonable assumption. Thus, this method is not designed to produce results consistently above or below fair market value as prohibited by paragraph (b)(5) of this section. Also, the method requires that the actuarial value be adjusted as required to fall within the corridor under paragraph (b)(6) and (7) of this section. Therefore, the method reflects fair market value as required by paragraph (b)(4) of this section.

Example (2). Plan B computes the actuarial value of its assets as follows: It determines the fair market value of the plan assets. Then the fair market value is adjusted to the extent necessary to make the actuarial value fall within a "5 percent" corridor. This corridor is plus or minus 5 percent of the following amount: the fair market value of the assets at the beginning of the valuation period plus an assumed annual growth of 4 percent with adjustments for contributions and benefit payments during the period. This method reflects fair market value in a manner prescribed by paragraph (b)(4) of this section. If the 4 percent factor used by the plan is a reasonable assumption, this method is not designed to produce results consistently above or below fair market value, and thus it satisfies paragraph (b)(5). However, this method is unacceptable because in some instances it may result in an actuarial value outside the corridor described in paragraph (b)(6) of this section. This method would be permitted if a second corridor were imposed which would adjust the value of the total plan assets to the corridor limits as required by paragraph (b)(6).

Example (3). Plan C values its assets by multiplying their fair market value by an index number. The use of the index results in the hypothetical average value that plan assets present on the valuation date would have had if they had been held during the current and four preceding years, and had appreciated or depreciated at the actual yield rates including appreciation and depreciation experienced by the plan during that period. However, the method requires an adjustment to the extent necessary to bring the resulting actuarial value of the assets inside the corridor described in the statement of the plan's actuarial valuation method. In this case, the stated corridor is 90 to 110 percent of fair market value, a corridor narrower than that described in paragraph (b)(7) of this section. This method is permitted.

Example (4). Plan D values its assets by multiplying their fair market value by 95 percent. Although the method reflects fair market value and the results of this method will always be within the required corridor, it is not acceptable because it will consistently result in a value less than fair market value.

Example (5). Plan E values its assets by using a five-year average method with appropriate adjustments for the period. Under the particular method used by Plan E, assets are not valued below 80 percent of fair market value or above 100 percent of fair market value. If the average produces a value that exceeds 100 percent of fair market value, the excess between 100 and 120 percent is recorded in a "value reserve account." In years after one in which the average exceeds 100 percent of fair market value, amounts are subtracted from this account and added, to the extent necessary, to raise the value produced by the average for that year to 100 percent of fair market value. This method is permitted because it reflects fair market value under paragraph (b)(4) of this section by appropriately computing an average value, it satisfies paragraph (b)(5) by producing a result that falls consistently between fair market value and average value, and it properly reflects the corridor described in paragraph (b)(7).

Example (6). All assets of Plan F are invested in a trust fund and the plan year is the calendar year. The actuarial value is determined by averaging fair market value over 4 years. An actuarial valuation is performed as of December 31, 1988.

(i) The average value as of December 31, 1988, is computed as follows:

	1986		1987		1988	
Fair market value:						
Jan. 1		$150,000		$196,500		$238,000
Contributions	$65,000		$62,000		$66,000	
Benefit payments	(22,000)		(24,000)		(25,000)	
Expenses	(6,500)		(7,000)		(7,500)	
Interest and dividends	8,000	44,500	7,500	38,500	7,000	40,500
Net realized gains (losses)		(2,000)		6,000		(8,000)
Balancing item*		4,000		(3,000)		(42,500)
Fair market value:						
Dec. 31		$196,500		$238,000		$228,000

* This equals the increase (decrease) in unrealized appreciation.

Adjusted values:	1985	1986	1987	1988
Fair market value:				
December 31	$150,000	$196,500	$238,000	$228,000
Net adjustments:				
1988	40,500	40,500	40,500	...
1987	38,500	38,500	...	...
1986	44,500	...	...	...
	$273,500	$275,500	$278,500	$228,000

$$\text{Average value: 1988} = \frac{\$273,500 + \$275,500 + \$278,500 + \$228,000}{4} = \$263,875$$

(ii) Plan F properly determines an average value under paragraph (b)(7) of this section for use as an actuarial value. Therefore, the valuation method meets the requirements of this section.

Example (7). Plan G computes the actuarial value of the plan assets as follows: The current fair market value of the plan assets is averaged with the most recent prior adjusted actuarial value. This average value is adjusted up or down toward the current fair market value by 20 percent of the difference between it and the current fair market value of the assets. This value is further adjusted to the extent necessary to fall within the corridor described in the statement of the plan's actuarial valuation method. The lower end of the corridor is the lesser of 80 percent of the fair market value of the plan assets or 85 percent of the average value of the plan assets. The higher end of the corridor is the greater of 120 percent of the fair market value of plan assets or 115 percent of the average value of plan assets. Average value for purposes of the corridor is determined under paragraph (b)(7) of this section. Assuming the numerical data of Example (6), the application of the corridor is as follows. The actuarial asset value as of December 31, 1988, must not be less than $182,400 (80 percent of current fair market value, $228,000) nor greater than $303,456 (115 percent of average value, $263,875). This method is permitted because it reflects fair market value in a manner permitted by paragraph (b)(4) of this section, it produces an actuarial value which is neither consistently above nor consistently below fair market or average value to satisfy paragraph (b)(5), and it is appropriately limited by the corridor described in paragraph (b)(6).

(c) *Fair market value of assets.*—(1) *General rules.*—Except as otherwise provided in this paragraph (c), the fair market value of a plan's assets for purposes of this section is the price at which the property would change hands between a willing buyer and a willing seller, neither being under any compulsion to buy nor sell and both having reasonable knowledge of relevant facts.

(2) [Reserved]

(d) *Methods for taking into account the fair market value of certain agreements.*—[Reserved]

(e) *Effective date and transition rules.*—(1) *Effective date.*—This section applies to plan years to which section 412, or section 302 of the Employee Retirement Income Security Act of 1974, applies.

(2) *Special rule for certain plan years.*—For plan years beginning prior to November 12, 1980, the amounts required to be determined under section 412 may be computed on the basis of any reasonable actuarial method of asset valuation which takes into account the fair

market value of the plan's assets, even if the method does not meet all of the requirements of paragraphs (a) through (c) of this section.

(3) *Plan years beginning on or after November 12, 1980.*— Paragraphs (a) through (c) of this section apply beginning with the first valuation of plan assets made for a plan year to which section 412 applies that begins on or after [the publication date of this section]. The statement of the plan's actuarial asset valuation method required by paragraph (b)(2) of this section must be included with the plan's actuarial report for that year, in addition to any subsequent reports.

(4) *Effect of change of asset valuation method.*—A plan which is required to change its asset valuation method to comply with paragraphs (a) through (c) of this section must make the change no later than the time when the plan is first required to comply with this section under paragraph (e)(3). A method of adjustment must be used to take account of any difference in the actuarial value of the plan's assets based on the old and new valuation methods. The plan may use either—

(i) A method of adjustment described in paragraph (e)(5) or (e)(6) of this section without prior approval by the Commissioner, or

(ii) Any other method of adjustment if the Commissioner gives prior approval under section 412(c)(5).

(5) *Retroactive recomputation method.*—(i) Under this method of adjustment, the plan recomputes the balance of the funding standard account as of the beginning of the first plan year for which it uses its new asset valuation method to comply with paragraphs (a) through (c) of this section. This new balance is recomputed by retroactively applying the plan's new method as of the first day of the first plan year to which section 412 applies.

(ii) Beginning with the first plan year for which it uses its new method, the plan computes the normal cost and amortization charges and credits to the funding standard account based on the retroactive application of its new method as of the first day of the first plan year to which section 412 applies.

(iii) If the recomputed aggregate charges exceed the recomputed aggregate credits to the funding standard account as of the end of the first plan year for which the plan uses its new method, an additional contribution to the plan may be necessary to avoid an accumulated funding deficiency in that year. The use of the retroactive recomputation method may also result in an accumulated funding deficiency for years prior to that first year. In such cases, the rules of section 412(c)(10), relating to the time when certain contributions are deemed to have been made, apply.

(6) *Prospective gain or loss adjustment method.*—(i) Under this method of adjustment the plan values its assets under its new method no later than the valuation date for the first plan year beginning after November 12, 1980.

(ii) Regardless of the type of funding method used by a plan, the difference in the value of the assets under the old and the new asset valuation methods may be treated as arising from an experience loss or gain; or alternatively it may be treated as arising from a change in actuarial assumptions.

(iii) The treatment of this difference as an experience gain or loss or as a change in actuarial assumptions must be consistent with the treatment of such gains, losses, or changes under the funding method used by the plan. Thus, if a plan uses a spread gain type funding method other than the aggregate cost method, the difference in the value of assets under the old and the new asset valuation methods may be either amortized or spread over future periods as a part of normal cost. Examples of this type of funding method are the frozen initial liability cost method and the attained age normal cost method. With an aggregate method, the difference in the value of assets under the old and the new asset valuation methods must be spread over future periods as a part of normal cost. [Reg. §1.412(c)(2)-1.]

☐ [T.D. 7734, 11-11-80.]

[Reg. §1.412(c)(3)-1]

§1.412(c)(3)-1. Reasonable funding methods.—(a) *Introduction.*— (1) *In general.*—This section prescribes rules for determining whether or not, in the case of an ongoing plan, a funding method is reasonable for purposes of section 412(c)(3). A method is unreasonable only if it is found to be inconsistent with a rule prescribed in this section. The term "reasonable funding method" under this section has the same meaning as the term "acceptable actuarial cost method" under section 3(31) of the Employee Retirement Income Security Act of 1974 (ERISA).

(2) *Computations included in method.*—See §1.412(c)(1)-1(b) for a discussion of matters that are, and are not, included in the funding method of a plan.

(3) *Plans using shortfall.*—The shortfall method is a method of determining charges to the funding standard account by adapting the underlying funding method of certain collectively bargained plans in the manner described in §1.412(c)(1)-2. As such, the shortfall method is a funding method. The underlying method of a plan that uses the shortfall method must be a reasonable funding method under this section. The rules contained in this section, relating to cost under a reasonable funding method, apply in the shortfall method to the annual computation charge under §1.412(c)(1)-2(d).

(4) *Scope of funding method.*—Except for the shortfall method, a reasonable funding method is applied to the computation of—

(i) The normal cost of a plan for a plan year; and, if applicable,

(ii) The bases established under section 412(b)(2)(B), (C), and (D), and (3)(B) ("amortizable bases").

(b) *General rules for reasonable funding methods.*—(1) *Basic funding formula.*—At any time, except as provided by the Commissioner, the present value of future benefits under a reasonable funding method must equal the sum of the following amounts:

(i) The present value of normal costs (taking into account future mandatory employee contributions, within the meaning of section 411(c)(2)(C), in the case of a contributory plan) over the future working lifetime of participants;

(ii) The sum of the unamortized portions of amoritzable bases, if any, treating credit bases under section 412(b)(3)(B) as negative numbers; and

(iii) The plan assets, decreased by a credit balance (and increased by a debit balance) in the funding standard account under section 412(b).

(2) *Normal cost.*—Normal cost under a reasonable funding method must be expressed as—

(i) A level dollar amount, or a level percentage of pay, that is computed from year to year on either an individual basis or an aggregate basis; or

(ii) An amount equal to the present value of benefits accruing under the method for a particular plan year.

(3) *Application to shortfall.*—Paragraph (b)(2) will not fail to be satisfied merely because an amount described in (i) or (ii) is expressed as permitted under the shortfall method.

(c) *Additional requirements.*—(1) *Inclusion of all liabilities.*—Under a reasonable funding method, all liabilities of the plan for benefits, whether vested or not, must be taken into account.

(2) *Production of experience gains and losses.*—If each actuarial assumption is exactly realized under a reasonable funding method, no experience gains or losses are produced.

(3) *Plan population.*—(i) *In general*—Under a reasonable funding method, the plan population must include three classes of individuals: participants currently employed in the service of the employer; former participants who either terminated service with the employer, or retired, under the plan; and all other individuals currently entitled to benefits under the plan. See §1.412(c)(3)-1(d)(2) for rules concerning anticipated future participants.

(ii) *Limited exclusion for certain recent participants.*—Under a reasonable funding method, certain individuals may be excluded from the first class of individuals described in paragraph (c)(3)(i) of this section unless otherwise provided by the Commissioner. The excludable individuals are participants who would be excluded from participation by the minimum age or service requirement of section 410 but who, under the terms of the plan, participate immediately upon entering the service of the employer.

(iii) *Special exclusion for "rule of parity" cases.*—Under a reasonable funding method, certain individuals may be excluded from the second class of individuals described in paragraph (c)(3)(i) of this section. The excludable individuals are those former participants who have terminated service with the employer without vested benefits and whose service might be taken into account in future years because the "rule of parity" of section 411(a)(6)(D) does not permit that service to be disregarded. However, if the plan's experience as to separated employees' returning to service has been such that the exclusion described in this subparagraph would be unreasonable, the exclusion would no longer apply.

(4) *Use of salary scale.*—(i) *General acceptability.*—The use of a salary scale assumption is not inappropriate merely because of the funding method with which it is used. Therefore, in determining whether actuarial assumptions are reasonable, a salary scale will not be considered to be prohibited merely because a particular funding method is being used.

(ii) *Protection to appropriate salary.*—Under a reasonable funding method, salary scales reflected in projected benefits must be the expected salary on which benefits would be based under the plan at the age when the receipt of benefits is expected to begin.

(5) *Treatment of allocable items.*—Under a reasonable funding method that allocates assets to individual participants to determine costs, the allocation of assets among participants must be reasonable. An initial allocation of assets among participants will be considered reasonable only if it is in proportion to related liabilities. However, the Commissioner may determine, based on the facts and circumstances, that it is unreasonable to continue to allocate assets on this basis beyond the initial year. Under a reasonable funding method that allocates liabilities among different elements of past and future service, the allocation of liabilities must be reasonable.

(d) *Prohibited considerations under a reasonable funding method.*—(1) *Anticipated benefit changes.*—(i) *In general.*—Except as otherwise provided by the Commissioner, a reasonable funding method does not anticipate changes in plan benefits that become effective, whether or not retroactively, in a later plan year or that become effective after the first day of, but during, a current plan year.

(ii) *Exception for collectively bargained plans.*—A collectively bargained plan described in section 413(a) may on a consistent basis anticipate benefit increases scheduled to take effect during the term of the collective-bargaining agreement applicable to the plan. A plan's treatment of benefit increases scheduled in a collective bargaining agreement is part of its funding method. Accordingly, a change in a plan's treatment of such benefit increases (for example, ignoring anticipated increases after taking them into account) is a change of funding method.

(2) *Anticipated future participants.*—A reasonable funding method must not anticipate the affiliation with the plan of future participants not employed in the service of the employer on the plan valuation date. However, a reasonable funding method may anticipate the affiliation with the plan of current employees who have not satisfied the participation requirements of the plan.

(e) *Special rules for certain funding methods.*—(1) *Applicability of special rules.*—Paragraph (e) of this section applies to a funding method that determines normal cost under paragraph (b)(2)(ii) of this section.

(2) *Use of salary scale.*—For rules relating to use of a salary scale assumption, see paragraph (c)(4) of this section.

(3) *Allocation of liabilities.*—In determining a plan's normal cost and accrued liability for a particular plan year, the projected benefits of the plan must be allocated between past years and future years. Except in the case of a career average pay plan, this allocation must be in proportion to the applicable rates of benefit accrual under the plan. Thus, the allocation to past years is effected by multiplying the projected benefit by a fraction. The numerator of the fraction is the participant's credited years of service. The denominator is the participant's total credited years of service at the anticipated benefit commencement date. Adjustments are made to account for changes in the rate of benefit accrual. An allocation based on compensation is not permitted. In the case of a career average pay plan, an allocation between past and future service benefits must be reasonable.

(f) *Treatment of ancillary benefit costs.*—(1) *General rule.*—Under a reasonable funding method, except as otherwise provided by this paragraph (f), ancillary benefit costs must be computed by using the same method used to compute retirement benefit costs under a plan.

(2) *Ancillary benefit defined.*—For purposes of this paragraph an ancillary benefit is a benefit that is paid as a result of a specified event which—

(i) Occurs not later than a participant's separation from service, and

(ii) Was detrimental to the participant's health.

Thus, for example, benefits payable if a participant dies or becomes disabled prior to separation from service are ancillary benefits because the events giving rise to the benefits are detrimental to the participant's health. However, an early retirement benefit, a social security supplement (as defined in § 1.411(a)-7(c)(4)(ii)), and the vesting of plan benefits (even if more rapid than is required by section 411) are not ancillary benefits because those benefits do not result from an event which is detrimental to the participant's health.

(3) *Exception for certain insurance contracts.*—Under a reasonable funding method, regardless of the method used to compute retirement benefit costs, the cost of an ancillary benefit may equal the premium paid for that benefit under an insurance contract if—

(i) The ancillary benefit is provided under the contract, and

(ii) The benefit is guaranteed under the contract.

(4) *Exception for 1-year term funding and other approved methods.*—[Reserved]

(5) *Section 401(h) benefits.*—Section 412 does not apply to benefits that are described in section 401(h) and for which a separate account is maintained.

(g) *Examples.*—The principles of this section are illustrated by the following examples:

Example (1). Assume that a plan, using funding method A, is in its first year. No contributions have been made to the plan, other than a nominal contribution to establish a corpus for the plan's trust. There is no past service liability, and the normal cost is a constant percentage of an annually determined amount. The constant percentage is 99 percent, and the annually determined amount is the excess of the present value of future benefits over plan assets. The present value of future benefits is $10,000. Under paragraph (b)(1) of this section, the present value of future benefits must equal the present value of future normal costs plus plan assets. (No amortizable bases exist, nor are there credit or debit balances.) Under method A, the present value of future normal costs would equal the sum of a series of annually decreasing amounts. Because of the constant percentage factor, the present value of future normal costs over the years can never equal $10,000, the present value of future benefits. In effect, then, assets under method A can never equal the present value of future benefits if all assumptions are exactly realized. Therefore, method A is not a reasonable funding method.

Example (2). Assume that a plan, using funding method B, determines normal cost by computing the present value of benefits expected to be accrued under the plan by the end of 10 years after the valuation date and adding to this the present value of benefits expected to be paid within these 10 years. Plan assets are subtracted from the sum of the two present value amounts. The difference then is divided by the present value of salaries projected over the 10 years. Under paragraph (c)(1) of this section, all liabilities of a plan must be taken into account. Because method B takes into account only benefits paid or accrued by the end of 10 years, it is not a reasonable funding method.

Example (3). Assume that a plan, using funding method C, determines normal cost as a constant percentage of compensation. (This percentage is determined as follows: The excess of projected benefits over accrued benefits is computed. Then the present value of this excess is divided by the present value of future salaries.) However, the accrued liability is computed each year as the present value of accrued benefits. (This computation does not reflect normal cost as a constant percentage of compensation. Thus, normal cost under the plan does not link accrued liabilities under the plan for consecutive years as would be the case, for example, under a unit credit cost method.) In determining gains and losses, method C compares the actual unfunded liability (the accrued liability less assets) with the expected unfunded liability (the sum of the actual unfunded liability in the previous year and the normal cost for the previous year less the contribution made for the previous year, all adjusted for interest). Under paragraph (c)(2) of this section, if actuarial assumptions are exactly realized, experience gains and losses must not be produced. Under method C, the use of a constant percentage in computing normal cost (and the expected unfunded liability) coupled with the manner of computing the accrued liability (and the actual unfunded liability) generally produces gains in the earlier years and losses in the later years if each actuarial assumption is exactly realized. Therefore, method C is not a reasonable funding method.

Example (4). Assume that a plan, using funding method D, bases benefits on final average pay. Under method D, the past service liability on any date equals the present value of the accrued benefit on that date based on compensation as of that date. The normal cost for any year equals the present value of a certain amount. That amount is the excess of the projected accrued benefit as of the end of the year over the actual accrued benefit at the beginning of the year. Accrued benefits, projected as of the end of a year, reflect a 1-year salary projection. Under paragraph (c)(4) of this section, salary scales reflected in projected benefits must project salaries to the salary on which benefits would be based under the plan at the age when the receipt of benefits under the plan is expected to begin. Because the plan is not a career average pay plan and compensation is projected only 1 year, method D is not a reasonable funding method. (Under paragraph (c)(4) of this section, the use of a salary scale assumption could be required with a unit credit method if, without the use of a salary scale, assumptions in the aggregate are unreasonable.)

Example (5). Assume that a plan using method E, a unit credit funding method, calculates a participant's accrued benefit according to the following formula: 2 percent of final salary for the first 10 years of service and 1 percent of final salary for the years of service in excess of 10. Under the plan, no employee may be credited with more than 25 years of service. The actuarial assumptions for the valuation include a salary scale of 5 percent per year. For a participant at age 40 with 15 years of service, a current salary of $20,000 and a normal retirement age of 65, the accrued liability for the retirement benefit is

$$\$20,000 \times 3.3864 \times 35\% \times \underline{\hspace{8cm}}$$

(3.3864 is 1.05 raised to the 25th power; the 25th power reflects the difference between normal retirement age and attained age (65–40).) Salary under this method is projected to the age when the receipt of benefits is expected to begin. Therefore, method E meets the requirement of paragraph (c)(4) of this section. Also, the allocation of benefits under method E between past and future years of service meets the requirements of paragraph (e)(3) of this section.

Example (6). Assume that a plan that has two participants and that previously used the unit credit cost method wishes to change the funding method at the beginning of the plan year to funding method F, a modification of the aggregate cost method. The modification involves determining normal cost for each of the two participants under the plan. Therefore, it requires an allocation of assets to each participant for valuation purposes. The actuary proposes to allocate the assets on hand at the beginning of the plan year of the change in funding method in proportion to the accrued liabilities calculated under the unit credit cost method. The relevant results of the calculations are shown below:

Accrued Liabilities	Employees		
(unit credit method)	M	N	Totals
$ Amount	15,670	906	16,576
% of Total	94.53	5.47	100.00
Assets			
$ Amount	7,835	453	8,288
% of Total	94.53	5.47	100.00

The proposed allocation in proportion to the accrued liabilities under the unit credit cost method satisfies the requirements of paragraph (c)(5) of this section at the beginning of the first plan year for which the new method is used.

Example (7). The facts are the same as in Example (6). However, the actuary proposes to allocate all the assets to employee M, the older employee. Method F, under these facts, is not an acceptable funding method because the allocation is not in proportion of related liabilities as required under paragraph (c)(5) of this section. [Reg. §1.412(c)(3)-1.]

☐ [*T.D. 7746, 12-29-80.*]

[Reg. §1.412(c)(3)-2]

§1.412(c)(3)-2. Effective dates and transitional rules relating to reasonable funding methods.—(a) *Introduction.*—This section prescribes effective dates for rules relating to reasonable funding methods, under section 412(c)(3) and §1.412(c)(3)-1. Also, this section sets forth rules concerning adjustments to a plan's funding standard account that are necessitated by a change in funding method, and a provision setting forth procedural requirements for use of an optional phase-in of required changes.

(b) *Effective date.*—(1) *General rule.*—Except as otherwise provided by subparagraph (2) of this paragraph, §1.412(c)(3)-1 applies to any valuation of a plan's liabilities (within the meaning of section 412(c)(9)) as of a date after April 30, 1981.

(2) *Exception.*—If a collective bargaining agreement which determines contributions to a plan is in effect on April 30, 1981, then §1.412(c)(3)-1 applies to any valuation of that plan's liabilities as of a date after the earlier of the date on which the last such collective bargaining agreement expires or April 30, 1981.

(3) *Transitional rule.*—The reasonableness of a funding method used in making a valuation of a plan's liability as of a date before the effective date determined under subparagraph (1) or (2) of this paragraph is determined on the basis of such published guidance as was available on the date as of which the valuation was made.

(c) *Change of funding method without approval.*—(1) *In general.*—A plan that is required to change its funding method to comply with §1.412(c)(3)-1 is not required to submit the change of funding method for approval as otherwise required by section 412(c)(5). However, this change must be described on Form 5500, Schedule B for the plan year with respect to which the change is first effective.

(2) *Amortization base.*—An amortization base must be established in the plan year of the change in method equal to the change in the unfunded liability due to the change (where both unfunded liabilities are based on the same actuarial assumptions). Such a base must be amortized over 30 years in determining the charges or

the present value of an annuity of $16,932 per year, commencing at age 65. The $16,932 is calculated as follows:

$$\frac{(10 \times 2) + (5 \times 1)}{(10 \times 2) - (15 \times 1) + (15 \times 0)}.$$

credits to the funding standard account, unless the Commissioner upon application permits amortization over a shorter period.

(d) *Phase-in of additional funding required by new method.*—(1) *In general.*—A plan that is required to change its funding method to comply with §1.412(c)(3)-1 may elect to charge and credit the funding standard account as provided in this paragraph. An election under this paragraph shall be irrevocable.

(2) *Credit in year of change.*—In the plan year of the change in method the funding standard account may be credited with an amount not in excess of 0.8 multiplied by the excess (if any) of—

(i) The normal cost under the new method plus the amortization charge (or minus the amortization credit) computed as described in §1.412(c)(3)-2(c)(2), over

(ii) The normal cost under the prior method, for the plan year of the change in method.

(3) *Credits in the next three years.*—In the three years following the year of the change the funding standard account may be credited with an amount not in excess of 0.6, 0.4, and 0.2 respectively in the first, second, and third years, multiplied by either of the following amounts, computed as of the last day of the year of credit—

(i) The excess described in §1.412(c)(3)-2(d)(2) multiplied by a fraction (not greater than 1), the numerator of which is the number of participants in the year of the credit and the denominator of which is the number of participants in the year of the change, or, at the option of the plan,

(ii) The excess (if any) in the year of credit of—

(A) The net charge to the funding standard account based on the new method, over

(B) The net charge to the funding standing account based on the prior method.

(4) *Computational rules.*—For purposes of the calculation described in §1.412(c)(3)-2(d)(3)(ii), the net charge is the excess of charges under section 412(b)(2)(A) and (B) over the credits under section 412(b)(3)(B) (including the charge or credit described in §1.412(c)(3)-2(c)) which would be required using the actuarial assumptions and plan benefit structure in effect on the last day of the plan year of change.

(5) *Fifteen-year amortization of credits.*—The funding standard account shall be charged with 15-year amortization of each credit described in §1.412(c)(3)-2(d)(2) and (3) beginning in the year following each such credit.

(6) *Manner of election.*—An election under this paragraph shall be made by the claiming of the credits described in §1.412(c)(3)-2(d)(2) and (3) on Schedule B to Form 5500 and by filing such other information as may be required by the Commissioner.

(e) *Effect on shortfall method.*—The charges and credits described in this section apply in the shortfall method to the annual computation charge described in §1.412(c)(1)-2(d). The amounts described in §1.412(c)(3)-2(d) shall be determined before the application of the shortfall method. [Reg. §1.412(c)(3)-2.]

☐ [*T.D. 7746, 12-29-80.*]

[Reg. §1.412(i)-1]

§1.412(i)-1. Certain insurance contract plans.—(a) *In general.*—Under section 412(h)(2) of the Internal Revenue Code of 1954, as added by section 1013(a) of the Employee Retirement Income Security Act of 1974 (88 Stat. 914) (hereinafter referred to as "the Act"), an insurance contract plan described in section 412(i) for a plan year is not subject to the minimum funding requirements of section 412 for that plan year. Consequently, if an individual or group insurance contract plan satisfies all of the requirements of paragraph (b)(2) or (c)(2) of this section, whichever are applicable for the plan year, the plan is not subject to the requirements of section 412 for that plan year. The effective date for section 412 of the Code is determined under section 1017 of the Act. In general, in the case of a plan which was not in existence on January 1, 1974, this section applies for plan years beginning after September 2, 1974, and in the case of a plan in existence on January 1, 1974, to plan years beginning after December 31, 1975.

(b) *Individual insurance contract plans.*—(1) An individual insurance contract plan is described in section 412(i) during a plan year if the plan satisfies the requirements of paragraph (b)(2) of this section for the plan year.

(2) The requirements of this paragraph are:

(i) The plan must be funded exclusively by the purchase from an insurance company or companies (licensed under the law of a State or the District of Columbia to do business with the plan) of individual annuity or individual insurance contracts, or a combination thereof. The purchase may be made either directly by the employer or through the use of a custodial account or trust. A plan shall not be considered to be funded otherwise than exclusively by the purchase of individual annuity or individual insurance contracts merely because the employer makes a payment necessary to comply with the provisions of section 411(c)(2) (relating to accrued benefit from employee contributions).

(ii) The individual annuity or individual insurance contracts issued under the plan must provide for level annual, or more frequent, premium payments to be paid under the plan for the period commencing with the date each individual participating in the plan became a participant and ending not later than the normal retirement age for that individual or, if earlier, the date the individual ceases his participation in the plan. Premium payments may be considered to be level even though items such as experience gains and dividends are applied against premiums. In the case of an increase in benefits, the contracts must provide for level annual payments with respect to such increase to be paid for the period commencing at the time the increase becomes effective. If payment commences on the first payment date under the contract occurring after the date an individual becomes a participant or after the effective date of an increase in benefits, the requirements of this subdivision will be satisfied even though payment does not commence on the date on which the individual's participation commenced or on the effective date of the benefit increase, whichever is applicable. If an individual accrues benefits after his normal retirement age, the requirements of this subdivision are satisfied if payment is made at the time such benefits accrue. If the provisions required by this subdivision are set forth in a separate agreement with the issuer of the individual contracts, they need not be included in the individual contracts.

(iii) The benefits provided by the plan for each individual participant must be equal to the benefits provided under his individual contracts at his normal retirement age under the plan provisions.

(iv) The benefits provided by the plan for each individual participant must be guaranteed by the life insurance company, described in paragraph (b)(2)(i) of this section, issuing the individual contracts to the extent premiums have been paid.

(v) Except as provided in the following sentence, all premiums payable for the plan year, and for all prior plan years, under the insurance or annuity contracts must have been paid before lapse. If the lapse has occurred during the plan year, the requirements of this subdivision will be considered to have been met if reinstatement of the insurance policy, under which the individual insurance contracts are issued, occurs during the year of the lapse and before distribution is made or benefits commence to any participant whose benefits are reduced because of the lapse.

(vi) No rights under the individual contracts may have been subject to a security interest at any time during the plan year. This subdivision shall not apply to contracts which have been distributed to participants if the security interest is created after the date of distribution.

(vii) No policy loans, including loans to individual participants, on any of the individual contracts may be outstanding at any time during the plan year. This subdivision shall not apply to contracts which have been distributed to participants if the loan is made after the date of distribution. An application of funds by the issuer to pay premiums due under the contracts shall be deemed not to be a policy loan if the amount of the funds so applied, and interest thereon, is repaid during the plan year in which the funds are applied and before distribution is made or benefits commence to any participant whose benefits are reduced because of such application.

(c) *Group insurance contract plans.*—(1) A group insurance contract plan is described in section 412(i) during a plan year if the plan satisfies the requirements of subparagraph (2) for the plan year.

(2) The requirements of this subparagraph are:

(i) The plan must be funded exclusively by the purchase from an insurance company or companies, described in paragraph (b)(2)(i) of this section, of group annuity or group insurance contracts, or a combination thereof. The purchase may be made either directly by the employer or through the use of a custodial account or trust. A plan shall not be considered to be funded otherwise than exclusively by the purchase of group annuity or group insurance contracts merely because the employer makes a payment necessary to comply with the provisions of section 411(c)(2) (relating to accrued benefit derived from employee contributions).

(ii) In the case of a plan funded by a group insurance contract or a group annuity contract the requirements of paragraph (b)(2)(ii) of this section must be satisfied by the group contract issued under

the plan. Thus, for example, each individual participant's benefits under the group contract must be provided for by level annual, or more frequent, payments equivalent to the payments required to satisfy such paragraph. The requirements of this subdivision will not be satisfied if benefits for any individual are not provided for by level payments made on his behalf under the group contract.

(iii) The group annuity or group insurance contract must satisfy the requirements of clauses (iii), (iv), (v), (vi), and (vii) of paragraph (b)(2). Thus, for example, each participant's benefits provided by the plan must be equal to his benefits provided under the group contract at his normal retirement age.

(iv)(A) If the plan is funded by a group annuity contract, the value of the benefits guaranteed by the insurance company issuing the contract under the plan with respect to each participant under the contract must not be less than the value of such benefits which the cash surrender value would provide for that participant under any individual annuity contract plan satisfying the requirements of paragraph (b) and approved for sale in the State where the principal office of the plan is located.

(B) If the plan is funded by a group insurance contract, the value of the benefits guaranteed by the insurance company issuing the contract under the plan with respect to each participant under the contract must not be less than the value of such benefits which the cash surrender value would provide for that participant under any individual insurance contract plan satisfying the requirements of paragraph (b) and approved for sale in the State where the principal office of the plan is located.

(v) Under the group annuity or group insurance contract, premiums or other consideration received by the insurance company (and, if a custodial account or trust is used, the custodian or trustee thereof) must be allocated to purchase individual benefits for participants under the plan. A plan which maintains unallocated funds in an auxiliary trust fund or which provides that an insurance company will maintain unallocated funds in a separate account, such as a group deposit administration contract, does not satisfy the requirements of this subdivision.

(d) *Combination of plans.*—A plan which is funded by a combination of individual contracts and a group contract shall be treated as a plan described in section 412(i) for the plan year if the combination, in the aggregate, satisfies the requirements of this section for the plan year. [Reg. § 1.412(i)-1.]

☐ [T.D. 7706, 7-14-80.]

[Reg. § 1.413-1]

§ 1.413-1. Special rules for collectively bargained plans.— (a) *Application of section 413(b) to certain collectively bargained plans.*— (1) *In general.*—Section 413(b) sets forth special rules applicable to certain pension, profit-sharing, and stock bonus plans (and each trust which is a part of such a plan), hereinafter referred to as "section 413(b) plans", described in paragraph (a)(2) of this section. Notwithstanding any other provision of the Code, a section 413(b) plan is subject to the special rules of section 413(b)(1) through (8) and paragraphs (b) through (i) of this section.

(2) *Requirements.*—Section 413(b) applies to a plan (and each trust which is a part of such plan) if the plan is a single plan which is maintained pursuant to one or more agreements which the Secretary of Labor finds to be a collective bargaining agreement between employee representatives and one or more employers. A plan which provides benefits for employees of more than one employer is considered a single plan subject to the requirements of section 413(b) and this section if the plan is considered a single plan for purposes of applying section 414(l) (see § 1.414(l)-1(b)(1)). For purposes of determining whether one or more plans (or agreements) are a single plan, under sections 413(a) and 414(l) it is irrelevant that there are in form two or more separate plans (or agreements). For example, a single plan will be considered to exist where agreements are entered into separately by a national labor organization (or one or more local units of such organization), on one hand, and individual employers, on the other hand, if the plan is considered a single plan for purposes of applying section 414(l).

(3) *Additional rules and effective dates.*—(i) If a plan is a section 413(b) plan at a relevant time, the rules of section 413(b) and this section apply, and the rules of section 413(c) and § 1.413-2 do not apply to the plan.

(ii) The qualification of a section 413(b) plan, at any relevant time, under section 401(a), 403(a), or 405(a), as modified by sections 413(b) and this section, is determined with respect to all employers maintaining the plan. Consequently, the failure by one employer maintaining the plan (or by the plan itself) to satisfy an applicable qualification requirement will result in the disqualification of the plan for all employers maintaining the plan.

(iii) Except as otherwise provided, section 413(a) and (b) and this section apply to a plan for plan years beginning after December 31, 1953.

(b) *Participation.*—Section 410 and the regulations thereunder shall be applied as if all employees of each of the employers who are parties to the collective-bargaining agreement and all such employees who are subject to the same benefit computation formula under the plan were employed by a single employer.

(c) *Discrimination, etc.*—(1) *General rule.*—Section 401(a)(4) (relating to prohibited discrimination) and section 411(d)(3) (relating to vesting required on termination, partial termination, or discontinuance of contributions) shall be applied as if all the participants in the plan, who are subject to the same benefit computation formula and who are employed by employers who are parties to the collective bargaining agreement, are employed by a single employer.

(2) *Application of discrimination rules.*—Under section 401(a)(4) and the regulations thereunder a plan is not qualified unless the contributions or benefits provided under the plan do not discriminate in favor of officers, shareholders or highly compensated employees (hereinafter referred to collectively as "the prohibited group"). The presence or absence of such discrimination under a plan to which this section applies at any time shall not be determined on an employer-by-employer basis, but rather by testing separately each group of employees who are subject to the same benefit computation formula to determine if there is discrimination within such group. Consequently, discrimination in contributions or benefits among two or more different groups or among employees in different groups covered by the plan may be present without causing the plan to be disqualified. However, the presence of prohibited discrimination within one such group will result in the disqualification of the plan for all groups. Section 401(a)(4) and the regulations thereunder provide rules relating to the determination of which employees are members of the prohibited group and to the determination of discrimination in contributions or benefits which are applicable to a plan to which this section applies. The determination of whether or not an individual employee is a highly compensated employee shall be based on the relationship of the compensation of the employee to the compensation of all the other employees of all employers who are maintaining the plan and have employees covered under the same

	Employer X
Local union 1	20
Local union 2	30

Under the rules of subparagraph (2) of this paragraph, the determination of whether contributions or benefits provided under the plan discriminate in favor of the prohibited group is made by applying the rules of section 401(a)(4) separately to participants who are members of local union 1 and local union 2. Thus, plan A will satisfy the qualification requirements of section 401(a)(4) if, within local union 1 and local union 2, respectively, plan benefits do not discriminate in favor of participants who are prohibited group employees within local union 1 and local union 2. Under the rules of subparagraph (2) of this paragraph, the determination under section 401(a)(4) of whether or not any individual employee, included within the 300 participants in plan A, is a highly compensated employee is based on the relationship of the compensation of such individual employee to the compensation of all the employees of Employers X, Y, and Z, whether or not such employees are participants in plan A. Thus, if there are 20 participants who are prohibited group employees within the 100 participants of local union 1, discrimination is determined by comparing the benefits of the 20 prohibited group participants to the benefits of the other 80 participants within local union 1. The same comparison would have to be made for the local union 2 participants between the prohibited group participants and the other participants in local union 2. Discrimination in benefits, if any, between the participants in local union 1 and local union 2, or among the employees of X, Y, or Z, would not affect the qualification of plan A under section 401(a)(4).

Example (2). Assume the same facts as in example (1). Employer X withdraws from the plan. Under subparagraph (3) of this paragraph, whether or not as a result of the withdrawal there is a partial termination under section 411(d)(3) is to be determined by applying the requirements of such section separately to the local union 1 and local union 2 participants. See §1.411 (d)-2 for the requirements relating to partial terminations. The application of such requirements raises the following possibilities with respect to the plan: (1) A partial termination as to local union 1, (2) a partial termination as to local union 2, (3) a partial termination as to both local unions 1 and 2, or (4) no partial termination for either local union.

Example (3). Assume the same facts as in example (1). Plan A is amended to cease future benefit accruals under the plan for local union 1 participants. Under subparagraph (3) of the paragraph, whether or not as a result of the cessation there is a partial termina-

benefit computation formula, whether or not such other employees are covered by the plan or are covered under the same benefit computation formula, rather than to the compensation of all the other employees of the employer of such individual employee.

(3) *Application of termination, etc. rules.*—Section 411(d)(3) and the regulations thereunder (relating to vesting required in the case of a termination, partial termination, or complete discontinuance of contributions) apply to a plan subject to the provisions of this section. The requirements of section 411(d)(3) shall be applied as if all participants in the plan who are subject to the same benefit computation formula and who are employed by employers who are parties to the collective bargaining agreement are employed by a single employer. The determination of whether or not there is a termination, partial termination, or complete discontinuance of contributions shall be made separately for each such group of participants who are treated as employed by a single employer. Consequently, if there are two or more groups of participants, a termination, partial termination, or complete discontinuance can take place under a plan with respect to one group of participants but not with respect to another such group of participants or for the entire plan. See §1.411(d)-2 for rules prescribed under section 411(d)(3).

(4) *Effective dates and transitional rules.*—(i) Section 413(b)(2) and this paragraph apply to a plan for plan years beginning after December 31, 1953.

(ii) In applying the rules of this paragraph to a plan for plan years to which section 411 does not apply, section 401(a)(7) (as in effect on September 1, 1974) shall be substituted for section 411(d)(3). See §1.401-6 for rules prescribed under section 401(a)(7) as in effect on September 1, 1974. See §1.411(a)-2 for the effective dates of section 411.

(5) *Examples.*—The provisions of this paragraph are illustrated by the following examples:

Example (1). Plan A is a defined benefit plan subject to the provisions of this section and covers two groups of participants, local unions 1 and 2. Each local union has negotiated its own bargaining agreement with employers X, Y, and Z to provide its own benefit computation formula. The following table indicates the composition of the plan A participants:

Employer Y	Employer Z	Total
10	70	100
70	100	200

tion under section 411(d)(3) is to be determined by applying the requirements of such section separately to the local union 1 and local union 2 participants.

Example (4). Plan A is a defined benefit plan that provides for two normal retirement benefits, X and 2X. A participant receives benefit X if the collective bargaining agreement covering his employment provides for a contribution rate, M. If such agreement provides for a contribution rate of N, the participant receives benefit 2X. Benefit X and benefit 2X constitute separate benefit computation formulas.

Example (5). Plan B is a defined benefit plan that provides for a normal retirement benefit, X. Benefit X is provided for all plan participants even though there are two collective bargaining agreements providing for different contribution rates, M and N. Plan B has a single benefit computation formula, even though there are two contribution rates.

(d) *Exclusive benefit.*—Under section 401(a), a plan is not qualified unless the plan is for the exclusive benefit of the employees (and their beneficiaries) of the employer establishing and maintaining the plan. Other qualification requirements under section 401(a) require the application of the exclusive benefit rule (for example, section 401(a)(2), which precludes diversion of plan assets). For purposes of applying the requirements of section 401(a) in determining whether a plan subject to this section is, with respect to each employer establishing and maintaining the plan, for the exclusive benefit of its employees (and their beneficiaries), all of the employees participating in the plan shall be treated as employees of each such employer. Thus, for example, contributions by employer A to a plan subject to this section could be allocated to employees of other employers maintaining the plan without violating the requirements of section 401(a)(2), because all the employees participating in the plan are deemed to be employees of A.

(e) *Vesting.*—Section 411 (other than section 411(d)(3) relating to termination or partial termination; discontinuance of contributions) and the regulations thereunder shall be applied as if all employers who have been parties to the collective-bargaining agreement constituted a single employer. The application of any rules with respect to breaks in service under section 411 shall be made under regulations prescribed by the Secretary of Labor. Thus, for example, all the hours which an employee worked for each employer in a collectively-bargained plan would be aggregated in computing the employee's hours of service under the plan. See also 29 CFR Part 2530 (Department of Labor regulations relating to minimum standards for employee pension benefit plans).

(f) through (h) [Reserved].

(i) *Employees of labor unions.*—(1) *General rule.*—For purposes of section 413(b) and this section, employees of employee representatives shall be treated as employees of an employer establishing and maintaining a plan to which section 413(b) and this section apply if, with respect to the employees of such representatives, the plan satisfies the nondiscrimination requirements of section 401(a)(4) (determined without regard to section 413(b)(2)) and the minimum participation and coverage requirements of section 410 (determined without regard to section 413(b)(1)). For purposes of the preceding sentence, the plan and any affiliated employee health or welfare plan shall be deemed to be an employee representative. If employees of employee representatives, the plan, or an affiliated employee health or welfare plan are covered by the plan and are not treated as employees of an employer establishing and maintaining the plan under the provisions of this paragraph, the plan fails to satisfy the qualification requirements of section 401(a). In addition, in order for such a plan to be qualified, the plan must satisfy the requirements of section 413(b)(1) and (2), relating to participation and discrimination, respectively; see paragraphs (b) and (c) of this section. For purposes of this paragraph, an affiliated health or welfare plan is a health or welfare plan that is maintained under the same collective bargaining agreement or agreements, and that covers the same membership.

(2) *Effective dates and transitional rules.*—(i) Section 413(b)(8) and this paragraph apply to a plan for plan years beginning after December 31, 1953.

(ii) In applying the rules of this paragraph to a plan for plan years to which section 410 does not apply, section 401(a)(3) (as in effect on September 1, 1974) shall be substituted for section 410. See § 1.401-3 for rules prescribed under section 401(a)(3) as in effect on September 1, 1974. See § 1.410(a)-2 for the effective dates of section 410.

(3) *Examples.*—The provisions of this paragraph are illustrated by the following examples:

Example (1). Plan A is a defined benefit plan, maintained pursuant to a collective bargaining agreement between employers, X, Y, and Z and labor union, L, which covers members of L employed by X, Y, and Z. In 1978, plan A is amended to cover, under the same benefit formula, all five employees of L who have satisfied the minimum age and service requirements of the plans (age 25 and 1 year of service). Assume that plan A is subject to section 413(b) and satisfies the requirements of section 413(b)(1) and (2). Assume further that with respect to employees of L, plan A (i) satisfies the nondiscrimination requirements of section 401(a)(4), (ii) meets the minimum participation requirements of section 410(a), and (iii) meets the minimum coverage requirements of section 410(b)(1)(A). Under the rules of subparagraph (1) of this paragraph, because such requirements are all satisfied, the employees of L are treated as employees of an employer establishing and maintaining plan A.

Example (2). Assume the same facts as example (1), except that plan A is amended to cover only one of the five employees of L, none of whom is covered by any other plan. Assume further that, under plan A, L does not satisfy the minimum percentage coverage requirement of section 410(b)(1)(A) with respect to employees of L. Assume further that the compensation of the one L employee who is covered by the plan is such that he is highly compensated relative to the four employees of L not covered by the plan. Consequently, L does not satisfy the minimum coverage requirements of section 410(b)(1)(B), with respect to employees of L. Under the rules of subparagraph (1) of this paragraph, the employees of L cannot be treated as employees of an employer establishing and maintaining the A plan because such coverage requirements are not satisfied by L. Consequently, the A plan fails to satisfy the qualification requirements of section 401(a). [Reg. § 1.413-1.]

☐ [*T.D. 7501, 8-22-77. Amended by T.D. 7508, 9-14-77 and by T.D. 7654, 8-8-79.*]

[Reg. § 1.413-2]

§ 1.413-2. Special rules for plans maintained by more than one employer.—(a) *Application of section 413(c).*—(1) *In general.*—Section 413(c) describes certain plans (and each trust which is a part of any such plan) hereinafter referred to as "section 413(c) plans." A plan (and each trust which is a part of such plan) is deemed to be a section 413(c) plan if it is described in subparagraph (2) of this paragraph. Notwithstanding any other provision of the code (not specifically in conflict with the special rules hereinafter mentioned), a section 413(c)

plan is subject to the special rules of section 413(c)(1) through (6) and paragraphs (b) through (g) of this section.

(2) *Section 413(c) plan.*—A plan (and each trust which is a part of such plan) is a section 413(c) plan if—

(i) The plan is a single plan, within the meaning of section 413(a) and § 1.413-1(a)(2), and

(ii) The plan is maintained by more than one employer.

For purposes of subdivision (ii) of this subparagraph, the number of employers maintaining the plan is determined by treating any employers described in section 414(b) (relating to a controlled group of corporations) or any employers described in section 414(c) (relating to trades or businesses under common control), whichever is applicable, as if such employers are a single employer. See § 1.411(a)-5(b)(3) for rules relating to the time when an employer maintains a plan. A master or prototype plan is not a section 413(c) plan unless such a plan is described in this subparagraph. Similarly, the mere fact that a plan, or plans, utilizes a common trust fund or otherwise pools plan assets for investment purposes does not, by itself, result in a particular plan being treated as a section 413(c) plan.

(3) *Additional rules.*—(i) If a plan is a collectively bargained plan described in § 1.413-1(a), the rules of section 413(c) and this section do not apply, and the rules of section 413(b) and § 1.413-1 do apply to the plan.

(ii) The special rules of section 413(b)(1) and § 1.413-1(b) relating to the application of section 410, other than the rules of section 410(a), do not apply to a section 413(c) plan. Thus, for example, the minimum coverage requirements of section 410(b) are generally applied to a section 413(c) plan on an employer-by-employer basis, taking into account the generally applicable rules such as section 401(a)(5) and section 414(b) and (c).

(iii) The special rules of section 413(b)(2) and § 1.413-1(c) (relating to (A) section 401(a)(4) and prohibited discrimination, and (B) 411(d)(3) and vesting required on termination, partial termination, or discontinuance of contributions) do not apply to a section 413(c) plan. Thus, for example, the determination of whether or not there is a termination, within the meaning of section 411(d)(3), of a section 413(c) plan is made solely by reference to the rules of sections 411(d)(3) and 413(c)(3).

(iv) The qualification of a section 413(c) plan, at any relevant time, under section 401(a), 403(a) or 405(a), as modified by section 413(c) and this section, is determined with respect to all employers maintaining the section 413(c) plan. Consequently, the failure by one employer maintaining the plan (or by the plan itself) to satisfy an applicable qualification requirement will result in the disqualification of the section 413(c) plan for all employers maintaining the plan.

(4) *Effective dates.*—Except as otherwise provided, section 413(c) and this section apply to a plan for plan years beginning after December 31, 1953.

(b) *Participation.*—Section 410(a) and the regulations thereunder shall be applied as if all employees of each of the employers who maintain the plan were employed by a single employer.

(c) *Exclusive benefit.*—In the case of a plan subject to this section, the exclusive benefit requirements of section 401(a) shall be applied to the plan in the same manner as under section 413(b)(3) and § 1.413-1(d).

(d) *Vesting.*—Section 411 and the regulations thereunder shall be applied as if all employers who maintain the plan constituted a single employer. The application of any rules with respect to breaks in service under section 411 shall be made under regulations prescribed by the Secretary of Labor. Thus, for example, all the hours which an employee worked for each employer maintaining the plan would be aggregated in computing the employee's hours of service under the plan. See also 29 CFR Part 2530 (Department of Labor regulations relating to minimum standards for employee pension benefit plans). [Reg. § 1.413-2.]

☐ [*T.D. 7501, 8-22-77. Amended by T.D. 7508, 9-14-77 and by T.D. 7654, 11-8-79.*]

[Reg. § 1.414(b)-1]

§ 1.414(b)-1. Controlled group of corporations.—(a) *Definition of controlled group of corporations.*—For purposes of this section, the term "controlled group of corporations" has the same meaning as is assigned to the term in section 1563(a) and the regulations thereunder, except that (1) the term "controlled group of corporations" shall not include an "insurance group" described in section 1563(a)(4), and (2) section 1563(e)(3)(C) (relating to stock owned by certain employees' trusts) shall not apply. For purposes of this section, the term "members of a controlled group" means two or more corporations connected through stock ownership described in section 1563(a)(1), (2), or (3), whether or not such corporations are "component members of a controlled group" within the meaning of section 1563(b). Two or more corporations are members of a controlled group at any time such corporations meet the requirements of section 1563(a) (as modified by this paragraph). For purposes of this section, if a corporation is a member of more than one controlled group of corporations, such corporation shall be treated as a member of each controlled group.

(b) *Single plan adopted by two or more members.*—If two or more members of a controlled group of corporations adopt a single plan for a plan year, then the minimum funding standard provided in section 412, the tax imposed by section 4971, and the applicable limitations provided by section 404(a) shall be determined as if such members were a single employer. In such a case, the amount of such items and the allocable portion attributable to each member shall be determined in the manner provided in regulations under sections 412, 4971, and 404(a).

(c) *Cross reference.*—For rules relating to the application of sections 401, 408(k) 410, 411, 415, and 416 with respect to two or more trades or businesses which are under common control, see section 414(c) and the regulations thereunder. [Reg. § 1.414(b)-1.]

□ [T.D. 8179, 3-1-88.]

[Reg. § 1.414(c)-1]

§ 1.414(c)-1. Commonly controlled trades or businesses.—For purposes of applying the provisions of sections 401 (relating to qualified pension, profit-sharing, and stock bonus plans), 408(k) (relating to simplified employee pensions), 410 (relating to minimum participation standards), 411 (relating to minimum vesting standards), 415 (relating to limitations on benefits and contributions under qualified plans), and 416 (relating to top-heavy plans), all employees of two or more trades or businesses under common control within the meaning of § 1.414(c)-2 for any period shall be treated as employed by a single employer. See sections 401, 408(k), 410, 411, 415, and 416 and the regulations thereunder for rules relating to employees of trades or businesses which are under common control. See § 1.414(c)-5 for effective date. [Reg. § 1.414(c)-1.]

□ [T.D. 8179, 3-1-88.]

[Reg. § 1.414(c)-2]

§ 1.414(c)-2. Two or more trades or businesses under common control.—(a) *In general.*—For purposes of this section, the term "two or more trades or businesses under common control" means any group of trades or businesses which is either a "parent-subsidiary group of trades or businesses under common control" as defined in paragraph (b) of this section, a "brother-sister group of trades or businesses under common control" as defined in paragraph (c) of this section, or a "combined group of trades or businesses under common control" as defined in paragraph (d) of this section. For purposes of this section and §§ 1.414(c)-3 and 1.414(c)-4, the term "organization" means a sole proprietorship, a partnership (as defined in section 7701(a)(2)), a trust, an estate, or a corporation.

(b) *Parent-subsidiary group of trades or businesses under common control.*—(1) *In general.*—The term "parent-subsidiary group of trades or businesses under common control" means one or more chains of organizations conducting trades or businesses connected through ownership of a controlling interest with a common parent organization if—

(i) A controlling interest in each of the organizations, except the common parent organization, is owned (directly and with the application of § 1.414(c)-4(b)(1), relating to options) by one or more of the other organizations; and

(ii) The common parent organization owns (directly and with the application of § 1.414(c)-4(b)(1), relating to options) a controlling interest in at least one of the other organizations, excluding, in computing such controlling interest, any direct ownership interest by such other organizations.

(2) *Controlling interest defined.*—(i) *Controlling interest.*—For purposes of paragraphs (b) and (c) of this section, the phrase "controlling interest" means:

(A) In the case of an organization which is a corporation, ownership of stock possessing at least 80 percent of total combined voting power of all classes of stock entitled to vote of such corporation or at least 80 percent of the total value of shares of all classes of stock of such corporation;

(B) In the case of an organization which is a trust or estate, ownership of an actuarial interest of at least 80 percent of such trust or estate;

(C) In the case of an organization which is a partnership, ownership of at least 80 percent of the profits interest or capital interest of such partnership; and

(D) In the case of an organization which is a sole proprietorship, ownership of such sole proprietorship.

(ii) *Actuarial interest.*—For purposes of this section, the actuarial interest of each beneficiary of trust or estate shall be determined by assuming the maximum exercise of discretion by the fiduciary in favor of such beneficiary. The factors and methods prescribed in § 20.2031-7 or, for certain prior periods, § 20.2031-7A (Estate Tax Regulations) for use in ascertaining the value of an interest in property for estate tax purposes shall be used for purposes of this subdivision in determining a beneficiary's actuarial interest.

(c) *Brother-sister group of trades or businesses under common control.*—(1) *In general.*—The term "brother-sister group of trades or businesses under common control" means two or more organizations conducting trades or businesses if (i) the same five or fewer persons who are individuals, estates, or trusts own (directly and with the application of § 1.414(c)-4) a controlling interest in each organization, and (ii) taking into account the ownership of each such person only to the extent such ownership is identical with respect to each such organization, such persons are in effective control of each organization. The five or fewer persons whose ownership is considered for purposes of the controlling interest requirement for each organization must be the same persons whose ownership is considered for purposes of the effective control requirement.

(2) *Effective control defined.*—For purposes of this paragraph, persons are in "effective control" of an organization if—

(i) In the case of an organization which is a corporation, such persons own stock possessing more than 50 percent of the total combined voting power of all classes of stock entitled to vote or more than 50 percent of the total value of shares of all classes of stock of such corporation;

(ii) In the case of an organization which is a trust or estate, such persons own an aggregate actuarial interest of more than 50 percent of such trust or estate;

(iii) In the case of an organization which is a partnership, such persons own an aggregate of more than 50 percent of the profits interest or capital interest of such partnership; and

(iv) In the case of an organization which is a sole proprietorship, one of such persons owns such sole proprietorship.

(d) *Combined group of trades or businesses under common control.*—The term "combined group of trades or businesses under common control" means any group of three or more organizations, if (1) each such organization is a member of either a parent-subsidiary group of trades or businesses under common control or a brother-sister group of trades or businesses under common control, and (2) at least one such organization is the common parent organization of a parent-subsidiary group of trades or businesses under common control and is also a member of a brother-sister group of trades or businesses under common control.

(e) *Examples.*—The definitions of parent-subsidiary group of trades or businesses under common control, brother-sister group of trades or businesses under common control, and combined group of trades or businesses under common control may be illustrated by the following examples.

Example (1). (a) The ABC partnership owns stock possessing 80 percent of the total combined voting power of all classes of stock entitled to voting of S corporation. ABC partnership is the common parent of a parent-subsidiary group of trades or businesses under common control consisting of the ABC partnership and S Corporation.

(b) Assume the same facts as in (a) and assume further that S owns 80 percent of the profits interest in the DEF Partnership. The ABC Partnership is the common parent of a parent-subsidiary group of trades or businesses under common control consisting of the ABC Partnership, S Corporation, and the DEF Partnership. The result would be the same if the ABC Partnership, rather than S, owned 80 percent of the profits interest in the DEF Partnership.

Example (2). L Corporation owns 80 percent of the only class of stock of T Corporation, and T, in turn, owns 40 percent of the capital interest in the GHI Partnership. L also owns 80 percent of the only class of stock of N Corporation and N, in turn, owns 40 percent of the capital interest in the GHI Partnership. L is the common parent of a parent-subsidiary group of trades or businesses under common control consisting of L Corporation, T Corporation, N Corporation, and the GHI Partnership.

Example (3). ABC Partnership owns 75 percent of the only class of stock of X and Y Corporations; X owns all the remaining stock of Y, and Y owns all the remaining stock of X. Since interorganization ownership is excluded (that is, treated as not outstanding) for purposes of determining whether ABC owns a controlling interest of at least one of the other organizations, ABC is treated as the owner of stock possessing 100 percent of the voting power and value of all classes of stock of X and Y for purposes of paragraph (b)(1)(ii) of this section. Therefore, ABC is the common parent of a parent-subsidiary group of trades or businesses under common control consisting of the ABC Partnership, X Corporation, and Y Corporation.

Example (4). Unrelated individuals A, B, C, D, E, and F own an interest in sole proprietorship A, a capital interest in the GHI Partnership, and stock of corporations M, W, X, Y, and Z (each of which has only one class of stock outstanding) in the following proportions:

ORGANIZATIONS

Individuals	A	GHI	M	W	X	Y	Z
A	100 %	50 %	100 %	60 %	40 %	20 %	60 %
B	—	40 %	—	15 %	40 %	50 %	30 %
C	—	—	—	—	10 %	10 %	10 %
D	—	—	—	25 %	—	20 %	—
E	—	10 %	—	—	10 %	—	—
	100 %	100 %	100 %	100 %	100 %	100 %	100 %

Under these facts the following four brother-sister groups of trades or businesses under common control exist: GHI, X and Z; X, Y and Z; W and Y; A and M. In the case of GHI, X, and Z, for example, A and B together have effective control of each organization because their combined identical ownership of GHI, X and Z is greater than 50%. (A's identical ownership of GHI, X and Z is 40% because A owns at least a 40% interest in each organization. B's identical ownership of GHI, X and Z is 30% because B owns at least a 30% interest in each organization.) A and B (the persons whose ownership is considered for purposes of the effective control requirement) together own a controlling interest in each organization because they own at least 80% of the capital interest of partnership GHI and at least 80% of the total combined voting power of corporations X and Z. Therefore, GHI, X and Z comprise a brother-sister group of trades or businesses under common control. Y is not a member of this group because neither the effective control requirement nor the 80% controlling interest requirement are met. (The effective control requirement is not met because A's and B's combined identical ownership in GHI, X, Y and Z (20% for A and 30% for B) does not exceed 50%. The 80% controlling interest test is not met because A and B together only own 70% of the total combined voting power of the stock of Y.) A and M are not members of this group because B owns no interest in either organization and A's ownership of GHI, X and Z, considered alone, is less than 80%.

Example (5). The outstanding stock of corporations U and V, which have only one class of stock outstanding, is owned by the following unrelated individuals:

CORPORATIONS

Individuals	U	V
	(percent)	(percent)
A	12	12
B	12	12
C	12	12
D	12	12
E	13	13
F	13	13
G	13	13
H	13	13
	100	100

Any group of five of the shareholders will own more than 50 percent of the stock in each corporation, in identical holdings. However, U and V are not members of a brother-sister group of trades or businesses under common control because at least 80 percent of the stock of each corporation is not owned by the same five or fewer persons.

Example (6). A, an individual, owns a controlling interest in ABC Partnership and DEF Partnership. ABC, in turn, owns a controlling interest in X Corporation. Since ABC, DEF, and X are each members of either a parent-subsidiary group or a brother-sister group of trades or businesses under common control, and ABC is the common parent of a parent-subsidiary group of trades or businesses under common control consisting of ABC and X, and also a member of a brother-sister group of trades or businesses under common control consisting of ABC and DEF, ABC Partnership, DEF Partnership, and X Corporation are members of the same combined group of trades or businesses under common control. [Reg. §1.414(c)-2.]

☐[T.D. 8179, 3-1-88. *Amended by T.D. 8540, 6-9-94.*]

[Reg. §1.414(c)-3]

§1.414(c)-3. Exclusion of certain interests or stock in determining control.—(a) *In general.*—For purposes of §1.414(c)-2(b)(2)(i) and (c)(2), the term "interest" and the term "stock" do not include an interest which is treated as not outstanding under paragraph (b) of this section in the case of a parent-subsidiary group of trades or businesses under common control or under paragraph (c) of this section in the case of a brother-sister group of trades or businesses under common control. In addition, the term "stock" does not include treasury stock or nonvoting stock which is limited and pre-

ferred as to dividends. For definitions of certain terms used in this section, see paragraph (d) of this section.

(b) *Parent-subsidiary group of trades or businesses under common control.*—(1) *In general.*—If an organization (hereinafter in this section referred to as "parent organization") owns (within the meaning of paragraph (b)(2) of this section)—

(i) In the case of a corporation, 50 percent or more of the total combined voting power of all classes of stock entitled to vote or 50 percent or more of the total value of shares of all classes of stock of such corporation.

(ii) In the case of a trust or an estate, an actuarial interest (within the meaning of §1.414(c)-2(b)(2)(ii)) of 50 percent or more of such trust or estate, and

(iii) In the case of a partnership, 50 percent or more of the profits or capital interest of such partnership, then for purposes of determining whether the parent organization or such other organization (hereinafter in this section referred to as "subsidiary organization") is a member of a parent-subsidiary group of trades or businesses under common control, an interest in such subsidiary organization excluded under paragraph (b)(3), (4), (5), or (6) of this section shall be treated as not outstanding.

(2) *Ownership.*—For purposes of paragraph (b)(1) of this section, a parent organization shall be considered to own an interest in or stock of another organization which it owns directly or indirectly with the application of paragraph (b)(1) of §1.414(c)-4 and—

(i) In the case of a parent organization which is a partnership, a trust, or an estate, with the application of paragraphs (b)(2), (3), and (4) of §1.414(c)-4, and

(ii) In the case of a parent organization which is a corporation, with the application of paragraph (b)(4) of §1.414(c)-4.

(3) *Plan of deferred compensation.*—An interest which is an interest in or stock of the subsidiary organization held by a trust which is part of a plan of deferred compensation (within the meaning of section 406(a)(3) and the regulations thereunder) for the benefit of the employees of the parent organization or the subsidiary organization shall be excluded.

(4) *Principal owners, officers, etc.*—An interest which is an interest in or stock of the subsidiary organization owned (directly and with the application of §1.414(c)-4) by an individual who is a principal owner, officer, partner, or fiduciary of the parent organization shall be excluded.

(5) *Employees.*—An interest which is an interest in or stock of the subsidiary organization owned (directly and with the application of §1.414(c)-4) by an employee of the subsidiary organization shall be excluded if such interest or such stock is subject to conditions which substantially restrict or limit the employee's right (or if the employee constructively owns such interest or such stock, the direct or record owner's right) to dispose of such interest or such stock and which run in favor of the parent or subsidiary organization.

(6) *Controlled exempt organization.*—An interest which is an interest in or stock of the subsidiary organization shall be excluded if owned (directly and with the application of §1.414(c)-4) by an organization (other than the parent organization):

(i) To which section 501 (relating to certain educational and charitable organizations which are exempt from tax) applies, and

(ii) Which is controlled directly or indirectly (within the meaning of paragraph (d)(7) of this section) by the parent organization or subsidiary organization, by an individual, estate, or trust that is a principal owner of the parent organization, by an officer, partner, or fiduciary of the parent organization, or by any combination thereof.

(c) *Brother-sister group of trades or businesses under common control.*—(1) *In general.*—If five or fewer persons (hereinafter in this section referred to as "common owners") who are individuals, estates, or trusts own (directly and with the application of §1.414(c)-4)—

(i) In the case of a corporation, 50 percent or more of the total combined voting power of all classes of stock entitled to vote or 50 percent or more of the total value of shares of all classes of stock of such corporation.

(ii) In the case of a trust or an estate, an actuarial interest (within the meaning of §1.414(c)-2(b)(2)(ii)) of 50 percent or more of such trust or estate, and

(iii) In the case of a partnership, 50 percent or more of the profits or capital interest of such partnership, then for purposes of determining whether such organization is a member of a brother-sister group of trades or businesses under common control, an interest in such organization excluded under paragraph (c)(2), (3), or (4) of this section shall be treated as not outstanding.

(2) *Exempt employees' trust.*—An interest which is an interest in or stock of such organization held by an employees' trust described in section 401(a) which is exempt from tax under section 501(a) shall be excluded if such trust is for the benefit of the employees of such organization.

(3) *Employees.*—An interest which is an interest in or stock of such organization owned (directly and with the application of §1.414(c)-4) by an employee of such organization shall be excluded if such interest or stock is subject to conditions which run in favor of a common owner of such organization or in favor of such organization and which substantially restrict or limit the employee's right (or if the employee constructively owns such interest or stock, the direct or record owner's right) to dispose of such interest or stock.

(4) *Controlled exempt organization.*—An interest which is an interest in or stock of such organization shall be excluded if owned (directly and with the application of §1.414(c)-4) by an organization:

(i) To which section 501(c)(3) (relating to certain educational and charitable organizations which are exempt from tax) applies, and

(ii) Which is controlled directly or indirectly (within the meaning of paragraph (d)(7) of this section) by such organization, by an individual, estate, or trust that is a principal owner of such organization, by an officer, partner, or fiduciary of such organization, or by any combination thereof.

(d) *Definitions.*—(1) *Employee.*—For purposes of this section, the term "employee" has the same meaning such term is given in section 3306(i) of the Code (relating to definitions for purposes of the Federal Unemployment Tax Act).

(2) *Principal owner.*—For purposes of this section, the term "principal owner" means a person who owns (directly and with the application of §1.414(c)-4)—

(i) In the case of a corporation, 5 percent or more of the total combined voting power of all classes of stock entitled to vote in such corporation or 5 percent or more of the total value of shares of all classes of stock of such corporation;

(ii) In the case of a trust or estate, an actuarial interest of 5 percent or more of such trust or estate; or

(iii) In the case of a partnership, 5 percent or more of the profits or capital interest of such partnership.

(3) *Officer.*—For purposes of this section, the term "officer" includes the president, vice-presidents, general manager, treasurer, secretary, and comptroller of a corporation, and any other person who performs duties corresponding to those normally performed by persons occupying such positions.

(4) *Partner.*—For purposes of this section, the term "partner" means any person defined in section 7701(a)(2) (relating to definitions of partner).

(5) *Fiduciary.*—For purposes of this section and §1.414(c)-4, the term "fiduciary" has the same meaning as such term is given in section 7701(a)(6) and the regulations thereunder.

(6) *Substantial conditions.*—(i) *In general.*—For purposes of this section, an interest in or stock of an organization is subject to conditions which substantially restrict or limit the right to dispose of such interest or stock and which run in favor of another person if the condition extends directly or indirectly to such person preferential rights with respect to the acquisition of the direct owner's (or the record owner's) interest or stock. For a condition to be in favor of another person it is not necessary that such person be extended a discriminatory concession with respect to price. A right of first refusal with respect to an interest or stock in favor of another person is a condition which substantially restricts or limits the direct or record owner's right of disposition which runs in favor of such person. Further, any legally enforceable condition which prohibits the direct or record owner from disposing of his or her interest or stock without the consent of another person will be considered to be a substantial limitation running in favor of such person.

(ii) *Special rule.*—For purposes of paragraph (c)(3) of this section only, if a condition which restricts or limits an employee's right (or direct or record owner's right) to dispose of his or her interest or stock also applies to the interest or stock in such organization held by a common owner pursuant to a bonafide reciprocal purchase arrangement, such condition shall not be treated as a substantial limitation or restriction. An example of a reciprocal purchase arrangement is an agreement whereby a common owner and the employee are given a right of first refusal with respect to stock of the employer corporation owned by the other party. If, however, the agreement also provides that the common owner has the right to purchase the stock of the employer corporation owned by the employee in the event the corporation should discharge the employee for reasonable cause, the purchase arrangement would not be reciprocal within the meaning of this subdivision.

(7) *Control.*—For purposes of paragraphs (b)(6) and (c)(4) of this section, the term "control" means control in fact. The determination of whether there exists control in fact will depend upon all of the facts and circumstances of each case, without regard to whether such control is legally enforceable and irrespective of the method by which such control is exercised or exercisable.

(e) *Examples.*—The provisions of this section may be illustrated by the following examples:

Example (1). ABC Partnership owns 70 percent of the capital interest and of the profits interest in the DEF Partnership. The remaining capital interest and profits interest in DEF is owned as follows: 4 percent by A (a general partner in ABC), and 26 percent by D (a limited partner in ABC). ABC satisfies the 50-percent capital interest or profits interest ownership requirement of paragraph (b)(1)(iii) of this section with respect to DEF. Since A and D are partners in ABC, under paragraph (b)(4) of this section the capital and profits interests in DEF owned by A and D are treated as not outstanding for purposes of determining whether ABC and DEF are members of a parent-subsidiary group of trades or businesses under common control under §1.414(c)-2(b). Thus, ABC is considered to own 100 percent (70 ÷ 70) of the capital interest and profits interest in DEF. Accordingly, ABC and DEF are members of a parent-subsidiary group of trades or businesses under common control.

Example (2). Assume the same facts as in example (1) and assume further that A owns 15 shares of the 100 shares of the only class of stock of S Corporation and DEF Partnership owns 75 shares of such stock. ABC satisfies the 50 percent stock requirement of paragraph (b)(1)(i) of this section with respect to S since ABC is considered as owning 52.5 percent (70 percent × 75 percent) of the S stock with the application of §1.414(c)-4(b)(2). Since A is a partner of ABC, the S stock owned by A is treated as not outstanding for purposes of determining whether S is a member of a parent-subsidiary group of trades or businesses under common control. Thus, DEF Partnership is considered to own stock possessing 88.2 percent (75 ÷ 85) of the voting power and value of the S stock. Accordingly, ABC Partnership, DEF Partnership, and S Corporation are members of a parent-subsidiary group of trades or businesses under common control.

Example (3). ABC Partnership owns 60 percent of the only class of stock of Corporation Y. D, the president of Y, owns the remaining 40 percent of the stock of Y. D has agreed that if she offers her stock in Y for sale she will first offer the stock to ABC at a price equal to the fair market value of the stock on the first date the stock is offered for sale. Since D is an employee of Y within the meaning of section 3306(i) of the Code and her stock in Y is subject to a condition which substantially restricts or limits her right to dispose of such stock and runs in favor of ABC Partnership, under paragraph (b)(5) of this section such stock is treated as not outstanding for purposes of determining whether ABC and Y are members of a parent-subsidiary group of trades or businesses under common control. Thus, ABC Partnership is considered to own stock possessing 100 percent of the voting power and value of the stock of Y. Accordingly, ABC Partnership and Y Corporation are members of a parent-subsidiary group of trades or businesses under common control. The result would be the same if D's husband, instead of D, owned directly the 40 percent stock interest in Y and such stock was subject to a right of first refusal running in favor of ABC Partnership.

(f) *Exception.*—(1) *In general.*—If an interest in an organization (including stock of a corporation) is owned by a person directly or with the application of the rules of paragraph (b) of §1.414(c)-4 and such ownership results in the membership of that organization in a group of two or more trades or businesses under common control for any period, then the interest will not be treated as an excluded interest under paragraph (b) or (c) of this section if the result of applying such provisions is that the organization is not a member of a group of two or more trades or businesses under common control for the period.

(2) *Example.*—The provisions of this paragraph may be illustrated by the following example:

Example. Corporation P owns directly 50 of the 100 shares of the only class of stock of corporation S. A, an officer of P, owns directly 30 shares of S stock which P has an option to acquire. If, under paragraph (b)(4) of this section, the 30 shares owned directly by A are treated as not outstanding, P would be treated as owning stock possessing only 71 percent (50/70) of the total voting power and value of S stock, and S should not be a member of a parent-subsidiary group of trades or businesses under common control. However, because the 30 shares owned by A that P has an option to purchase are considered as owned by P under paragraph (b)(2) of this section, and that ownership plus P's direct ownership of 50 shares result in S's membership in a parent-subsidiary group of trades or businesses under common control for 1985, the provisions of this paragraph apply. Therefore, A's stock is not treated as an excluded interest and S is a member of a parent-subsidiary group consisting of P and S. [Reg. § 1.414(c)-3.]

☐ [*T.D.* 8179, 3-1-88.]

[Reg. § 1.414(c)-4]

§1.414(c)-4. Rules for determining ownership.—(a) *In general.*— In determining the ownership of an interest in an organization for purposes of §1.414(c)-2 and §1.414(c)-3, the constructive ownership rules of paragraph (b) of this section shall apply, subject to the operating rules contained in paragraph (c). For purposes of this section the term "interest" means: in the case of a corporation, stock; in the case of a trust or estate, an actuarial interest; in the case of a partnership, an interest in the profits or capital; and in the case of a sole proprietorship, the proprietorship.

(b) *Constructive ownership.*—(1) *Options.*—If a person has an option to acquire any outstanding interest in an organization, such interest shall be considered as owned by such person. For this purpose, an option to acquire an option, and each one of a series of such options shall be considered as an option to acquire such interest.

(2) *Attribution from partnerships.*—(i) *General.*—An interest owned, directly or indirectly, by or for a partnership shall be considered as owned by any partner having an interest of 5 percent or more in either the profits or capital of the partnership in proportion to such partner's interest in the profits or capital, whichever such proportion is greater.

(ii) *Example.*—The provisions of paragraph (b)(2)(i) of this section may be illustrated by the following example:

Example. A, B, and C, unrelated individuals, are partners in the ABC Partnership. The partners' interest in the capital and profits of ABC are as follows:

(In percent)

Partner	Capital	Profits
A	36	25
B	60	71
C	4	4

The ABC Partnership owns the entire outstanding stock (100 shares) of X Corporation. Under paragraph (b)(2)(i) of this section, A is considered to own the stock of X owned by the partnership in proportion to his interest in capital (36 percent) or profits (25 percent), whichever such proportion is greater. Therefore, A is considered to own 36 shares of X stock. Since B has a greater interest in the profits of the partnership than in the capital, B is considered to own X stock in proportion to his interest in such profits. Therefore, B is considered to own 71 shares of X stock. Since C does not have an interest of 5 percent or more in either the capital or profits of ABC, he is not considered to own any shares of X stock.

(3) *Attribution from estates and trusts.*—(i) *In general.*—An interest in an organization (hereinafter called an "organization interest") owned, directly or indirectly, by or for an estate or trust shall be considered as owned by any beneficiary of such estate or trust who has an actuarial interest of 5 percent or more in such organization interest, to the extent of such actuarial interest. For purposes of this subparagraph, the actuarial interest of each beneficiary shall be determined by assuming the maximum exercise of discretion by the fiduciary in favor of such beneficiary and the maximum use of the organization interest to satisfy the beneficiary's rights. A beneficiary of an estate or trust who cannot under any circumstances receive any part of an organization interest held by the estate or trust, including the proceeds from the disposition thereof, or the income therefrom, does not have an actuarial interest in such organization interest. Thus, where stock owned by a decedent's estate has been specifically bequeathed to certain beneficiaries and the remainder of the estate has been specifically bequeathed to other beneficiaries, the stock is attributable only to the beneficiaries to whom it is specifically bequeathed. Similarly a remainderman of a trust who cannot under any

circumstances receive any interest in the stock of a corporation which is a part of the corpus of the trust (including any accumulated income therefrom or the proceeds from a disposition thereof) does not have an actuarial interest in such stock. However, an income beneficiary of a trust does have an actuarial interest in stock if he has any right to the income from such stock even though under the terms of the trust instrument such stock can never be distributed to him. The factors and methods prescribed in § 20.2031-7 or, for certain prior periods, § 20.2031-7A (Estate Tax Regulations) for use in ascertaining the value of an interest in property for estate tax purposes shall be used for purposes of this subdivision in determining a beneficiary's actuarial interest in an organization interest owned directly or indirectly by or for an estate or trust.

(ii) *Special rules for estates.*—(A) For purposes of this paragraph (b)(3) with respect to an estate, property of a decedent shall be considered as owned by his or her estate if such property is subject to administration by the executor or administrator for the purposes of paying claims against the estate and expenses of administration notwithstanding that, under local law, legal title to such property vests in the decedent's heirs, legatees or devisees immediately upon death.

(B) For purposes of this paragraph (b)(3) with respect to an estate, the term "beneficiary" includes any person entitled to receive property of a decedent pursuant to a will or pursuant to laws of descent and distribution.

(C) For purposes of this paragraph (b)(3) with respect to an estate, a person shall no longer be considered a beneficiary of an estate when all the property to which he or she is entitled has been received by him or her, when he or she no longer has a claim against the estate arising out of having been a beneficiary, and when there is only a remote possibility that it will be necessary for the estate to seek the return of property from him or her or to seek payment from him or her by contribution or otherwise to satisfy claims against the estate or expenses of administration.

(iii) *Grantor trusts, etc.*—An interest owned, directly or indirectly, by or for any portion of a trust of which a person is considered the owner under subpart E, part I, subchapter J of the Code (relating to grantors and others treated as substantial owners) is considered as owned by such person.

(4) *Attribution from corporations.*—(i) *General.*—An interest owned, directly or indirectly, by or for a corporation shall be considered as owned by any person who owns (directly and, in the case of a parent-subsidiary group of trades or businesses under common control, with the application of paragraph (b)(1) of this section, or in the case of a brother-sister group of trades or business under common control, with the application of this section), 5 percent or more in value of the stock in that proportion which the value of the stock which such person so owns bears to the total value of all the stock in such corporation.

(ii) *Example.*—The provisions of paragraph (b)(4)(i) of this section may be illustrated by the following example:

Example. B, an individual, owns 60 of the 100 shares of the only class of outstanding stock of corporation P. C, an individual, owns 4 shares of the P stock, and corporation X owns 36 shares of the P stock. Corporation P owns, directly and indirectly, 50 shares of the stock of corporation S. Under this subparagraph, B is considered to own 30 shares of the S stock (60/100 × 50), and X is considered to own 18 shares of S stock (36/100 × 50). Since C does not own 5 percent or more in the value of P stock, he is not considered as owning any of the S stock owned by P. If in this example, C's wife had owned directly 1 share of the P stock, C and his wife would each be considered as owning 5 shares of the P stock, and therefore C and his wife would be considered as owning 2.5 shares of the S stock (5/100 × 50).

(5) *Spouse.*—(i) *General rule.*—Except as provided in paragraph (b)(5)(ii) of this section, an individual shall be considered to own an interest owned, directly or indirectly, by or for his or her spouse, other than a spouse who is legally separated from the individual under a decree of divorce, whether interlocutory or final, or a decree of separate maintenance.

(ii) *Exception.*—An individual shall not be considered to own an interest in an organization owned, directly or indirectly, by or for his or her spouse on any day of a taxable year of such organization, provided that each of the following conditions are satisfied with respect to such taxable year:

(A) Such individual does not, at any time during such taxable year, own directly any interest in such organization;

(B) Such individual is not a member of the board of directors, a fiduciary, or an employee of such organization and does not participate in the management of such organization at any time during such taxable year;

(C) Not more than 50 percent of such organization's gross income for such taxable year was derived from royalties, rents, dividends, interest, and annuities; and

(D) Such interest in such organization is not, at any time during such taxable year, subject to conditions which substantially restrict or limit the spouse's right to dispose of such interest and which run in favor of the individual or the individual's children who have not attained the age of 21 years. The principles of § 1.414(c)-3(d)(6)(i) shall apply in determining whether a condition is a condition described in the preceding sentence.

(iii) *Definitions.*—For purposes of paragraph (b)(5)(ii)(C) of this section, the gross income of an organization shall be determined under section 61 and the regulations thereunder. The terms "interest", "royalties", "rents", "dividends", and "annuities" shall have the same meaning such terms are given for purposes of section 1244(c) and § 1.1244(c)-1(e)(1).

(6) *Children, grandchildren, parents, and grandparents.*—(i) *Children and parents.*—An individual shall be considered to own an interest owned, directly or indirectly, by or for the individual's children who have not attained the age of 21 years, and if the individual has not attained the age of 21 years, an interest owned, directly or indirectly, by or for the individual's parents.

(ii) *Children, grandchildren, parents, and grandparents.*—If an individual is in effective control (within the meaning of § 1.414(c)-2(c)(2)), directly and with the application of the rules of this paragraph without regard to this subdivision, of an organization, then such individual shall be considered to own an interest in such organization owned, directly or indirectly, by or for the individual's parents, grandparents, grandchildren, and children who have attained the age of 21 years.

(iii) *Adopted children.*—For purposes of this section, a legally adopted child of an individual shall be treated as a child of such individual.

(iv) *Example.*—The provisions of this subparagraph (6) may be illustrated by the following example:

Example—(A) *Facts.* Individual F owns directly 40 percent of the profits interest of the DEF Partnership. His son, M, 20 years of age, owns directly 30 percent of the profits interest of DEF, and his son, A, 30 years of age, owns directly 20 percent of the profits interest of DEF. The 10 percent remaining of the profits interest and 100 percent of the capital interest of DEF is owned by an unrelated person.

(B) *F's ownership.* F owns 40 percent of the profits interest in DEF directly and is considered to own the 30 percent profits interest owned directly by M. Since, for purposes of the effective control test contained in paragraph (b)(6)(ii) of this section, F is treated as owning 70 percent of the profits interest of DEF, F is also considered as owning the 20 percent profits interest of DEF owned by his adult son, A. Accordingly, F is considered as owning a total of 90 percent of the profits interest in DEF.

(C) *M's ownership.* Minor son, M, owns 30 percent of the profits interest in DEF directly, and is considered to own the 40 percent profits interest owned directly by his father, F. However, M is not considered to own the 20 percent profits interest of DEF owned directly by his brother, A, and constructively by F, because an interest constructively owned by F by reason of family attribution is not considered as owned by him for purposes of making another member of his family the constructive owner of such interest. (See paragraph (c)(2) of this section.) Accordingly, M is considered as owning a total of 70 percent of the profits interest of the DEF Partnership.

(D) *A's ownership.* Adult son, A, owns 20 percent of the profits interest in DEF directly. Since, for purposes of determining whether A effectively controls DEF under paragraph (b)(6)(ii) of this section, A is treated as owning only the percentage of profits interest he owns directly, he does not satisfy the condition precedent for the attribution of the DEF profits interest from his father. Accordingly, A is considered as owning only the 20 percent profits interest in DEF which he owns directly.

(c) *Operating rules.*—(1) *In general.*—Except as provided in paragraph (c)(2) of this section, an interest constructively owned by a person by reason of the application of paragraph (b)(1), (2), (3), (4), (5), or (6) of this section shall, for the purposes of applying such paragraph, be treated as actually owned by such person.

(2) *Members of family.*—An interest constructively owned by an individual by reason of the application of paragraph (b)(5) or (6) of this section shall not be treated as owned by such individual for purposes of again applying such subparagraphs in order to make another the constructive owner of such interest.

(3) *Precedence of option attribution.*—For purposes of this section, if an interest may be considered as owned under paragraph (b)(1) of this section (relating to option attribution) and under any other subparagraph of paragraph (b) of this section, such interest shall be considered as owned by such person under paragraph (b)(1) of this section.

(4) *Examples.*—The provisions of this paragraph may be illustrated by the following examples:

Example (1). A, 30 years of age, has a 90 percent interest in the capital and profits of DEF Partnership. DEF owns all the outstanding stock of corporation X and X owns 60 shares of the 100 outstanding shares of corporation Y. Under paragraph (c)(1) of this section, the 60 shares of Y constructively owned by DEF by reason of paragraph (b)(4) of this section are treated as actually owned by DEF for purposes of applying paragraph (b)(2) of this section. Therefore, A is considered as owning 54 shares of the Y stock (90 percent of 60 shares).

Example (2). Assume the same facts as in example (1). Assume further that B, who is 20 years of age and the brother of A, directly owns 40 shares of Y stock. Although the stock of Y owned by B is considered as owned by C (the father of A and B) under paragraph (b)(6)(i) of this section, under paragraph (c)(2) of this section such stock may not be treated as owned by C for purposes of applying paragraph (b)(6)(ii) of this section in order to make A the constructive owner of such stock.

Example (3). Assume the same facts as in example (2), and further assume that C has an option to acquire the 40 shares of Y stock owned by his son, B. The rule contained in paragraph (c)(2) of this section does not prevent the reattribution of such 40 shares to A because, under paragraph (c)(3) of this section, C is considered as owning the 40 shares by reason of option attribution and not by reason of family attribution. Therefore, since A is in effective control of Y under paragraph (b)(6)(ii) of this section, the 40 shares of Y stock constructively owned by C are reattributed to A. A is considered as owning a total of 94 shares of Y stock. [Reg. § 1.414(c)-4.]

☐ [*T.D. 8179, 3-1-88. Amended by T.D. 8540, 6-9-94.*]

[Reg. § 1.414(c)-5]

§ 1.414(c)-5. Certain tax-exempt organizations.—(a) *Application.*—This section applies to an organization that is exempt from tax under section 501(a). The rules of this section only apply for purposes of determining when entities are treated as the same employer for purposes of section 414(b), (c), (m), and (o) (including the sections referred to in section 414(b), (c), (m), (o), and (t)), and are in addition to the rules otherwise applicable under section 414(b), (c), (m), and (o) for determining when entities are treated as the same employer. Except to the extent set forth in paragraphs (d), (e), and (f) of this section, this section does not apply to any church, as defined in section 3121(w)(3)(A), or any qualified church-controlled organization, as defined in section 3121(w)(3)(B).

(b) *General rule.*—In the case of an organization that is exempt from tax under section 501(a) (an exempt organization) whose employees participate in a plan, the employer with respect to that plan includes the exempt organization whose employees participate in the plan and any other organization that is under common control with that exempt organization. For this purpose, common control exists between an exempt organization and another organization if at least 80 percent of the directors or trustees of one organization are either representatives of, or directly or indirectly controlled by, the other organization. A trustee or director is treated as a representative of another exempt organization if he or she also is a trustee, director, agent, or employee of the other exempt organization. A trustee or director is controlled by another organization if the other organization has the general power to remove such trustee or director and designate a new trustee or director. Whether a person has the power to remove or designate a trustee or director is based on facts and circumstances. To illustrate the rules of this paragraph (b), if exempt organization A has the power to appoint at least 80 percent of the trustees of exempt organization B (which is the owner of the outstanding shares of corporation C, which is not an exempt organization) and to control at least 80 percent of the directors of exempt organization D, then, under this paragraph (b) and § 1.414(b)-1, entities A, B, C, and D are treated as the same employer with respect to any plan maintained by A, B, C, or D for purposes of the sections referenced in section 414(b), (c), (m), (o), and (t).

(c) *Permissive aggregation with entities having a common exempt purpose.*—(1) *General rule.*—For purposes of this section, exempt organizations that maintain a plan to which section 414(c) applies that covers one or more employees from each organization may treat themselves as under common control for purposes of section 414(c) (and, thus, as a single employer for all purposes for which section 414(c) applies) if each of the organizations regularly coordinates their day-to-day exempt activities. For example, an entity that provides a type of emergency relief within one geographic region and another exempt organization that provides that type of emergency relief within another geographic region may treat themselves as under common control if they have a single plan covering employees of both entities and regularly coordinate their day-to-day exempt activities. Similarly, a hospital that is an exempt organization and another exempt organization with which it coordinates the delivery of medical services or medical research may treat themselves as under common control if there is a single plan covering employees of the hospital and employees of the other exempt organization and the coordination is a regular part of their day-to-day exempt activities.

(2) *Authority to permit aggregation.*—(i) For determining when entities are treated as the same employer under section 414(b), (c), (m), and (o), the Commissioner may issue rules of general applicability, in revenue rulings, notices, or other guidance published in the Internal Revenue Bulletin (see §601.601(d)(2)(ii)(*b*) of this chapter), permitting other types of combinations of entities that include exempt organizations to elect to be treated as under common control for one or more specified purposes if—

(A) There are substantial business reasons for maintaining each entity in a separate trust, corporation, or other form; and

(B) Such treatment would be consistent with the anti-abuse standards in paragraph (f) of this section.

(ii) For example, this authority might be exercised in any situation in which the organizations are so integrated in their operations as to effectively constitute a single coordinated employer for purposes of section 414(b), (c), (m), and (o), including common employee benefit plans.

(d) *Permissive disaggregation between qualified church controlled organizations and other entities.*—In the case of a church plan (as defined in section 414(e)) to which contributions are made by more than one common law entity, any employer may apply paragraphs (b) and (c) of this section to those entities that are not a church (as defined in section 403(b)(12)(B) and §1.403(b)-2) separately from those entities that are churches. For example, in the case of a group of entities consisting of a church (as defined in section 3121(w)(3)(A)), a secondary school (that is treated as a church under §1.403(b)-2), and several nursing homes each of which receives more than 25 percent of its support from fees paid by residents (so that none of them is a qualified church-controlled organization under §1.403(b)-2 and section 3121(w)(3)(B)), the nursing homes may treat themselves as being under common control with each other, but not as being under common control with the church and the school, even though the nursing homes would be under common control with the school and the church under paragraph (b) of this section.

(e) *Application to certain church entities under section 3121(w)(3).*—[Reserved].

(f) *Anti-abuse rule.*—In any case in which the Commissioner determines that the structure of one or more exempt organizations (which may include an exempt organization and an entity that is not exempt from income tax) or the positions taken by those organizations has the effect of avoiding or evading any requirements imposed under section 401(a), 403(b), or 457(b), or any applicable section (as defined in section 414(t)), or any other provision for which section 414(c) applies, the Commissioner may treat an entity as under common control with the exempt organization.

(g) *Examples.*—The provisions of this section are illustrated by the following examples:

Example 1. (i) *Facts.* Organization A is a tax-exempt organization under section 501(c)(3) which owns 80% or more of the total value of all classes of stock of corporation B, which is a for profit organization.

(ii) *Conclusion.* Under paragraph (a) of this section, this section does not alter the rules of section 414(b) and (c), so that organization A and corporation B are under common control under §1.414(c)-2(b).

Example 2. (i) *Facts.* Organization M is a hospital which is a tax-exempt organization under section 501(c)(3) and organization N is a medical clinic which is also a tax-exempt organization under section 501(c)(3). N is located in a city and M is located in a nearby suburb. There is a history of regular coordination of day-to-day activities between M and N, including periodic transfers of staff, coordination of staff training, common sources of income, and coordination of budget and operational goals. A single section 403(b) plan covers professional and staff employees of both the hospital and the medical clinic. While a number of members of the board of directors of M are also on the board of directors of N, there is less than 80% overlap in board membership. Both organizations have approximately the same percentage of employees who are highly compensated and have appropriate business reasons for being maintained in separate entities.

(ii) *Conclusion.* M and N are not under common control under this section, but, under paragraph (c) of this section, may chose to treat themselves as under common control, assuming both of them act in a manner that is consistent with that choice for purposes of §1.403(b)-5(a), sections 401(a), 403(b), and 457(b), and any other applicable section (as defined in section 414(t)), or any other provision for which section 414(c) applies.

Example 3. (i) *Facts.* Organizations O and P are each tax-exempt organizations under section 501(c)(3). Each organization maintains a qualified plan for it employees, but one of the plans would not satisfy section 410(b) (or section 401(a)(4)) if the organizations were under common control. The two organizations are closely related and, while the organizations have several trustees in common, the common trustees constitute fewer than 80 percent of the trustees of either organization. Organization O has the power to remove any of the trustees of P and to select the slate of replacement nominees.

(ii) *Conclusion.* Under these facts, pursuant to paragraphs (b) and (f) of this section, the Commissioner treats the entities as under common control.

(h) *Applicable date.*—This section applies for plan years beginning after December 31, 2008. [Reg. §1.414(c)-5.]

☐ [*T.D. 9340, 7-23-2007 (corrected 9-24-2007).*]

[Reg. §1.414(c)-6]

§1.414(c)-6. **Effective date.**—(a) *General rule.*—Except as provided in paragraph (b), (c), (e), or (f) of this section, the provisions of §1.414(b)-1 and §§1.414(c)-1 through 1.414(c)-4 shall apply for plan years beginning after September 2, 1974.

(b) *Existing plans.*—In the case of a plan in existence on January 1, 1974, unless paragraph (c) of this section applies, the provisions of §1.414(b)-1 and §§1.414(c)-1 through 1.414(c)-4 shall apply for plan years beginning after December 31, 1975. For definition of the term "existing plan", see §1.410(a)-2(c).

(c) *Existing plans electing new provisions.*—In the case of a plan in existence on January 1, 1974, for which the plan administrator makes an election under §1.410(a)-2(d), the provisions of §1.414(b)-1 and §§1.414(c)-1 through 1.414(c)-4 shall apply to the plan years elected under §1.410(a)-2(d).

(d) *Application.*—For purposes of the Employee Retirement Income Security Act of 1974, the provisions of §1.414(b)-1 and §§1.414(c)-1 through 1.414(c)-4 do not apply for any period of time before the plan years described in paragraph (a), (b), or (c) of this section, whichever is applicable.

(e) *Special rule.*—Notwithstanding paragraph (a), (b), or (c) of this section, §1.414(c)-3(f) is effective April 1, 1988.

(f) *Transitional rule.*—(1) *In general.*—The amendments made by T.D. 8179 apply to the plan years or period described in paragraphs (a), (b), or (c) of this section, whichever is applicable.

(2) *Exception.*—In the case of a plan year or period beginning before March 2, 1988, if an organization—

(i) Is a member of a brother-sister group of trades or businesses under common control under §11.414(c)-2(c), as in effect before removal by T.D. 8179 ("old group"), for such plan year or period, and

(ii) Is not such a member for such plan year or period because of the amendments made by such Treasury decision,

such member (whether or not a corporation) nevertheless will be treated as a member of such old group for purposes of section 414(c) for that plan year or period to the extent provided in §1.1563-1(d)(2). Also, such member will be treated as a member of an old group for all purposes of the Code for such plan year or period if all the organizations (whether or not corporations) that are members of the old group meet all the requirements of §1.1563-1(d)(3) with respect to such plan year or period. [Reg. §1.414(c)-6.]

☐ [*T.D. 8179, 3-1-88. Redesignated by T.D. 9340, 7-23-2007.*]

[Reg. §1.414(e)-1]

§1.414(e)-1. **Definition of church plan.**—(a) *General rule.*—For the purposes of part I of subchapter D of chapter 1 of the Code and the regulations thereunder, the term "church plan" means a plan established and at all times maintained for its employees by a church or by a convention or association of churches (hereinafter included within the term "church") which is exempt from tax under section 501(a), provided that such plan meets the requirements of paragraphs (b) and (if applicable) (c) of this section. If at any time during its existence a plan is not a church plan because of a failure to meet the requirements set forth in this section, it cannot thereafter become a church plan.

(b) *Unrelated businesses.*—(1) *In general.*—A plan is not a church plan unless it is established and maintained primarily for the benefit of employees (or their beneficiaries) who are not employed in connection with one or more unrelated trades or businesses (within the meaning of section 513).

(2) *Establishment or maintenance of a plan primarily for persons not employed in connection with one or more unrelated trades or businesses.*—(i)(A) A plan, other than a plan in existence on September 2, 1974, is established primarily for the benefit of employees (or their beneficiaries) who are not employed in connection with one or more unrelated trades or businesses if on the date the plan is established the number of employees employed in connection with the unrelated trades or businesses eligible to participate in the plan is less than 50 percent of the total number of employees of the church eligible to participate in the plan.

(B) A plan in existence on September 2, 1974, is to be considered established as a plan primarily for the benefit of employees (or their beneficiaries) who are not employed in connection with one or more unrelated trades or businesses if it meets the requirements of both paragraphs (b)(2)(ii)(A) and (B) (if applicable) in either of its first 2 plan years ending after September 2, 1974.

(ii) For plan years ending after September 2, 1974, a plan will be considered maintained primarily for the benefit of employees of a church who are not employed in connection with one or more unrelated trades or businesses if in 4 out of 5 of its most recently completed plan years—

(A) Less than 50 percent of the persons participating in the plan (at any time during the plan year) consist of, and in the same year

(B) Less than 50 percent of the total compensation paid by the employer during the plan year (if benefits or contributions are a function of compensation) to employees participating in the plan is paid to,

employees employed in connection with an unrelated trade or business. The determination that the plan is not a church plan will apply to the second year (within a 5 year period) for which the plan fails to meet paragraph (b)(2)(ii)(A) or (B) (if applicable) and to all plan years thereafter unless, taking into consideration all of the facts and circumstances as described in paragraph (b)(2)(iii) of this section, the plan is still considered to be a church plan. A plan that has not completed 5 plan years ending after September 2, 1974, shall be considered maintained primarily for the benefit of employees not employed in connection with an unrelated trade or business unless it fails to meet paragraphs (b)(2)(ii)(A) and (B) in at least 2 such plan years.

(iii) Even though a plan does not meet the provisions of paragraph (b)(2)(ii) of this section, it nonetheless will be considered maintained primarily for the benefit of employees who are not employed in connection with one or more unrelated trades or businesses if the church maintaining the plan can demonstrate that based on all of the facts and circumstances such is the case. Among the facts and circumstances to be considered in evaluating each case are:

(A) The margin by which the plan fails to meet the provisions of paragraph (b)(2)(ii) of this section, and

(B) Whether the failure to meet such provisions was due to a reasonable mistake as to what constituted an unrelated trade or business or whether a particular person or group of persons were employed in connection with one or more unrelated trades or businesses.

(iv) For purposes of this section, an employee will be considered eligible to participate in a plan if such employee is a participant in the plan or could be a participant in the plan upon making mandatory employee contributions to the plan.

(3) *Employment in connection with one or more unrelated trades or businesses.*—An employee is employed in connection with one or more unrelated trades or businesses of a church if a majority of such employee's duties and responsibilities in the employ of the church are directly or indirectly related to the carrying on of such trades or businesses. Although an employee's duties and responsibilities may be insignificant with respect to any one unrelated trade or business, such employee will nonetheless be considered as employed in connection with one or more unrelated trades or businesses if such employee's duties and responsibilities with respect to all of the unrelated trades or businesses of the church represent a majority of the total of such person's duties and responsibilities in the employ of the church.

(c) *Plans of two or more employers.*—The term "church plan" does not include a plan which, during the plan year, is maintained by two or more employers unless—

(1) Each of the employers is a church that is exempt from tax under section 501(a), and

(2) With respect to the employees of each employer, the plan meets the provisions of paragraph (b)(2)(ii) of this section or would be determined to be a church plan based on all the facts and circumstances described in paragraph (b)(2)(iii) of this section.

Thus, if with respect to a single employer the plan fails to meet any provision of this paragraph, the entire plan ceases to be a church plan unless that employer ceases maintaining the plan for all plan years beginning after the plan year in which it receives a final notification from the Internal Revenue Service that it does not meet the provisions of this paragraph. If the employer does cease maintaining the plan in accordance with this paragraph, the fact that the employer formerly did maintain the plan will not prevent the plan from being a church plan for prior years.

(d) *Special rule.*—(1) Notwithstanding paragraph (c)(1) of this section, a plan maintained by a church and one or more agencies of such church for the employees of such church and of such agency or agencies, that is in existence on January 1, 1974, shall be treated as a church plan for plan years ending after September 2, 1974, and beginning before January 1, 1983, provided that the plan is described in paragraph (c) of this section without regard to paragraph (c)(1) of this section, and the plan is not maintained by an agency which did not maintain the plan on January 1, 1974.

(2) For the purposes of section 414(e) and this section, an agency of a church means an organization which is exempt from tax under section 501 and which is either controlled by, or associated with, a church. For example, an organization, a majority of whose officers or directors are appointed by a church's governing board or by officials of a church, is controlled by a church within the meaning of this paragraph. An organization is associated with a church if it shares common religious bonds and convictions with that church.

(e) *Religious orders and religious organizations.*—For the purpose of this section the term "church" includes a religious order or a religious organization if such order or organization (1) is an integral part of a church, and (2) is engaged in carrying out the functions of a church, whether as a civil law corporation or otherwise.

(f) *Separately incorporated fiduciaries.*—A plan which otherwise meets the provisions of this section shall not lose its status as a church plan because of the fact that it is administered by a separately incorporated fiduciary such as a pension board or a bank.

(g) *Cross reference.*—(1) For rules relating to treatment of church plans, see section 410(d), 411(e), 412(h), 4975(g) and the regulations thereunder.

(2) For rules relating to church plan elections, see section 410(d) and the regulations thereunder. [Reg. §1.414(e)-1.]

☐ [T.D. 7688, 3-28-80.]

[Reg. §1.414(f)-1]

§1.414(f)-1. Definition of multiemployer plan.—(a) *General rule.*—For purposes of part I of subchapter D of chapter 1 of the Code and the regulations thereunder, a plan is a multiemployer plan for a plan year if all of the following requirements are satisfied:

(1) *Number of contributing employers.*—More than one employer is required by the plan instrument or other agreement to contribute (or to have contributions made on its behalf) to the plan for the plan year.

(2) *Collective bargaining agreement.*—The plan is maintained for the plan year pursuant to one or more collective bargaining agreements between employee representatives and more than one employer.

(3) *Amount of contributions.*—Except as provided by paragraph (c) of this section (relating to the special rule for contributions exceeding 50 percent), the amount of contributions made under the plan for the plan year by or on behalf of each employer is less than 50 percent of the total amount of contributions made under the plan for such plan year by or on behalf of all employers.

(4) *Benefits.*—The plan provides that the amount of benefits payable with respect to each employee participating in the plan is determined without regard to whether or not his employer continues as a member of the plan. If benefits accrued as a result of the participant's service with his employer during a period before such employer was a member of the plan, this requirement does not apply to the amount of those benefits, except that this requirement does apply to the amount of those benefits (i) which are accrued benefits derived from employee contributions, or (ii) which are accrued under a plan maintained by an employer prior to the time such employer became a member of the plan to which the requirements of this paragraph (a) are applied.

(5) *Other requirements.*—The plan satisfies such other requirements as the Secretary of Labor by regulations prescribes under the authority of section 414(f)(1)(E) of the Code and section 3(37) of the Employee Retirement Income Security Act of 1974 (Public Law 93-406, 88 Stat. 839). See 29 CFR 2510.3-37.

(b) *Special rules.*—(1) *Amount of contributions.*—For purposes of paragraphs (a)(3) and (c) of this section, the amount of contributions made under the plan for the plan year by or on behalf of each employer shall be the sum of such contributions made on or before the last day of the plan year. For purposes of determining whether contributions are made on or before the last day of the plan year, the rule of section 412(c)(10) and the regulations thereunder (relating to the treatment of certain contributions made after the last day of the plan year as made on such last day) shall apply.

(2) *Benefits.*—(i) For purposes of paragraph (a)(4) of this section, certain benefit amounts are treated as accrued as a result of the participant's service with an employer during a period before such employer was a member of the plan. The amount of such a benefit so treated is the difference (if any) between two calculated amounts. The first calculated amount is the participant's total accrued benefit calculated under the plan as of the date the employer ceased to be a member of the plan. The second calculated amount is the participant's accrued benefit calculated without regard to his service with such employer during the period before such employer was a member of the plan. However, under a special limitation, this difference may not exceed the benefit a participant accrued from service before

Years	Monthly Accrued Benefit Retained	
Before January 1, 1976		
January 1, 1976-		
December 31, 1979	$4 × 4 years =	$16
January 1, 1980-		
December 31, 1990	$12 × 11 years =	$132
Total		$148

The XYZ Plan does not satisfy the requirements of paragraphs (a)(4) and (b)(2)(i) of this section because no benefit can be forfeited with respect to service after W began participating in the plan. Thus, the maximum accrued benefit that may be forfeited is $180 per month (the accrued benefit with respect to A's service prior to January 1, 1976). Therefore, in order for the plan to meet the requirements of paragraphs (a)(4) and (b)(2)(i) of this section, the plan must provide for A's accrued benefit after W ceased to be a member of the plan to be at least $180 per month ($360 per month total accrued benefit less $180 per month benefit accrued for service prior to W's membership in the plan).

(iii) For purposes of paragraphs (a)(4) and (b)(2) of this section, if an employer for a period employs two or more individuals who, solely by reason of their employment, are participants in the plan and who do not belong to the same collective bargaining unit, the dates on which the employer became and ceased to be a member of the plan shall be determined separately on a class basis for individuals who belong to separate collective bargaining units, as separate classes, and for individuals who do not belong to a collective bargaining unit, as a further single separate class. Thus, such dates shall be determined with respect to individuals as a class who belong to the same collective bargaining unit (or who do not belong to a collective bargaining unit) without consideration of the employment by the employer of, or the participation in the plan by, other individuals (who do not belong to such collective bargaining unit and who may belong to another collective bargaining unit) or whether the employer is a member of the plan with respect to such other individuals. In no event, however, may service not attributable to service with a particular collective bargaining unit be disregarded under paragraphs (a)(4) and (b)(2) of this section merely because the employer ceases to maintain the plan with respect to such unit. Thus, for example, paragraphs (a)(4) and (b)(2) of this section do not permit the disregard of a period of service of an individual belonging to a collective bargaining unit prior to the time the employer became a member of the plan with respect to such unit to the extent that, during such period of service, the individual belonged to another collective bargaining unit with respect to which the employer was a member of the plan.

(3) *Controlled groups.*—For purposes of section 414(f) and this section, all corporations which are members of a controlled group of corporations (within the meaning of section 1563(a) and the regulations thereunder, but determined without regard to section 1563(e)(3)(C) *and the regulations thereunder*) are deemed to be one employer.

(c) *Contributions exceeding 50 percent.*—If a plan was a multiemployer plan as defined in this section for any plan year (including plan years ending prior to September 3, 1974), "75 percent" shall be

his employer became a member of the plan. For purposes of this limitation, this benefit is the benefit accrued as of the date the employer ceases to be a member of the plan. An employer shall be deemed to be a member of the plan in a plan year if the employer is required by the plan instrument or other agreement to contribute (or to have contributions made on its behalf) to the plan for such plan year or if an employee of the employer accrues a benefit, on account of service with the employer during such plan year, under the plan for that plan year.

(ii) The provisions of paragraphs (a)(4) and (b)(2)(i) of this section are illustrated by the following example:

Example. On January 1, 1976, Employer W became a member of the noncontributory XYZ pension plan which uses the calendar year as the plan year. W did not maintain any plan prior to that date. The plan provided for benefits of $4 per month per year of service (including service with W before January 1, 1976). On January 1, 1980, following adoption of a new collective bargaining agreement, the benefits were increased to $12 per month per year of service for all years of service (including service with W before January 1, 1976). On January 1, 1991, W ceased to be a member of the plan.

A, an employee of W, had 15 years of service before January 1, 1976, 4 years of service between January 1, 1976, and December 31, 1979, and 11 years of service between January 1, 1980, and December 31, 1990. On December 31, 1990, A's accrued benefit was $360 per month ($12 per month × 30). On January 1, 1991 the portion of A's accrued benefit retained and the portion forfeited under the terms of the XYZ Pension Plan were determined as follows:

	Monthly Accrued Benefit Forfeited	
	$12 × 15 years =	$180
	$8 × 4 years =	$32
		$212

substituted for "50 percent" in applying paragraph (a)(3) of this section for subsequent plan years until the first plan year following a plan year in which the amount contributed by or on behalf of one employer is 75 percent or more of the total amount of contributions made under the plan for that plan year by or on behalf of all of the employers making contributions. In such case "75 percent" shall not again be substituted for "50 percent" until the plan has met the requirements of paragraph (a) of this section (determined without regard to this paragraph) for one plan year.

(d) *Examples.*—The application of this section is illustrated by the following examples. For purposes of these examples, assume that the plan meets the requirements of paragraphs (a)(1), (2), (4), and (5) of this section for each plan year.

Example (1). On January 1, 1979, U, V, and W, three employers none of which is a member of a controlled group of corporations with any of the other two employers, establish a plan with a plan year corresponding to the calendar year. U, V, and W each contribute less than one-half of the total contributions made under the plan for each of the years 1970, 1971, and 1972. For the years 1973, 1974, and 1975, U contributes 70 percent and V and W each contribute 15 percent of the total contributions made under the plan for each year. The plan is a multiemployer plan under section 414(f) and this section for 1975 because no employer has contributed 75 percent or more of the total amount contributed for each of the plan years subsequent to 1972.

Example (2). (i) *First plan year.* On January 1, 1975, X, Y, and Z, three employers none of which is a member of a controlled group of corporations with any of the other two employers, establish a plan with a plan year corresponding to the calendar year. X, Y, and Z each contribute less than one-half of the total contributions made under the plan for 1975. The plan is a multiemployer plan for 1975 because it meets the 50 percent contribution requirement of paragraph (a)(3) of this section.

(ii) *Second plan year.* For the second plan year, 1976, X contributes 70 percent and Y and Z each contribute 15 percent of the total contributions made under the plan. The plan is a multiemployer plan for 1976 because it was a multiemployer plan for the preceding plan year and satisfies the 75 percent contribution requirement of paragraph (c) of this section.

(iii) *Third plan year.* For the third plan year, 1977, X contributes 80 percent and Y and Z each contribute 10 percent of the total contributions made under the plan. The plan is not a multiemployer plan for 1977 because it fails to satisfy the 75 percent contribution requirement of paragraph (c) of this section.

(iv) *Fourth plan year.* For the fourth plan year, 1978, Y contributes 60 percent and X and Z each contribute 20 percent of the total contributions made under the plan. The 75 percent contribution requirement of paragraph (c) of this section does not apply. The plan is not a multiemployer plan for 1978 because it fails to satisfy the 50 percent contribution requirement of paragraph (a)(3) of this section.

(v) *Fifth plan year.* For the fifth plan year, 1979, X, Y, and Z each contribute less than one-half of the total contributions made under the plan. The 75 percent contribution requirement of paragraph (c) of this section does not apply. The plan is a multiemployer plan for 1979 because it again meets the 50 percent contribution requirement of paragraph (a)(3) of this section.

(vi) *Sixth plan year.* For the sixth plan year, 1980, the plan will continue to be a multiemployer plan, provided that no employer contributes 75 percent or more of the total amount of contributions made under the plan for the plan year.

(e) *Retention of records.*—(1) For plan years ending prior to September 3, 1974, a plan may be required to furnish proof that it met the requirements of section 414(f) and this section for each plan year ending prior to that date to the extent necessary to show the applicability of the 75 percent test provided in paragraph (c) of this section.

(2) For plan years ending after September 2, 1974, a plan may be required to furnish proof that it met the requirements of section 414(f) and this section for 6 immediately preceding plan years. [Reg. §1.414(f)-1.]

☐ [T.D. 7552, 7-11-78.]

[Reg. §1.414(g)-1]

§1.414(g)-1. **Definition of plan administrator.**—(a) *In general.*—For purposes of part I of subchapter D of chapter 1 of the Code and the regulations thereunder, if the instrument under which the plan is operated for a plan year specifically designates a person or a group of persons as plan administrator, the person or group of persons collectively is the plan administrator for the plan year. The instrument may specifically designate a plan administrator—

(1) By name,

(2) By reference to the person or group of persons holding a named position or positions,

(3) By reference to a procedure established under the terms of the instrument pursuant to which a plan administrator is designated, or

(4) By reference to the person or group of persons charged with specific responsibilities of plan administrator.

Consistent with the provisions of section 405(c)(1) of the Employee Retirement Income Security Act of 1974 (29 U.S. 1105(c)(1)), a plan may provide for the allocation of specific responsibilities of plan administrator among named persons and for named persons to designate others to carry out such responsibilities. A person or group of persons may be designated as plan administrator in accordance with the rules of this paragraph even though the person or group of persons does not carry the specific title "plan administrator." In the absence of a person or group of persons designated as the plan administrator (individually, collectively, or by designation of different specific administrative responsibilities), the plan administrator for the plan year is the person or group of persons specified in paragraph (b) of this section.

(b) *Plan administrator not specifically designated.*—If no person or group of persons is specifically designated as the plan administrator for a plan year by the instrument under which the plan is operated, the plan administrator for such year is the person or group of persons determined under the following rules:

(1) *Single employer.*—In the case of a plan maintained by a single employer, the employer is the plan administrator. If the employer is a corporation, the corporation is the plan administrator. However, the corporation's board of directors may authorize a person or group of persons to fulfill responsibilities of the corporation as plan administrator. In the absence of such authorization, any corporate officer authorized under law, corporate by-laws, or resolution of the board of directors to act on behalf of the corporation with respect to contracts of a value equivalent to the fair market value of the assets of the plan shall be presumed to have authority to fulfill responsibilities of the corporation as plan administrator. For purposes of this paragraph (b)(1), "employer" means the "employer" as defined in section 3(5) of the Employee Retirement Income Security Act of 1974 (29 U.S.C. 1003(5)).

(2) *Employee organization.*—In the case of a plan maintained by an employee organization, the employee organization is the plan administrator.

(3) *Group representing the parties.*—In the case of a plan maintained by two or more employers, or jointly by one or more employers and one or more employee organizations, the association, committee, joint board of trustees, or other similar group of representatives of the parties who maintain the plan, as the case may be, is the plan administrator. For purposes of this subparagraph (3), a plan

shall be considered maintained by two or more employers or jointly by one or more employers and one or more employee organizations only if none of the parties has the express power, under the terms of the instrument under which the plan is operated, to terminate the plan unilaterally.

(4) *Person in control of assets.*—In any case where a plan administrator may not be determined by application of paragraphs (a) and (b)(1), (2) and (3) of this section, the plan administrator is the person or persons actually responsible, whether or not under the terms of the plan, for the control, disposition, or management of the cash or property received by or contributed to the plan, irrespective of whether such control, disposition, or management is exercised directly by such person or persons or indirectly through an agent or trustee designated by such person or persons. [Reg. §1.414(g)-1.]

☐ [T.D. 7618, 5-8-79.]

[Reg. §1.414(l)-1]

§1.414(l)-1. **Mergers and consolidations of plans or transfers of plan assets.**—(a) *In general.*—(1) *Scope of the regulations.*—Sections 401(a)(12) and 414(l) apply only to plans to which section 411 applies without regard to section 411(e)(2). Thus, for example, these sections do not apply to a governmental plan within the meaning of section 414(d); a church plan, within the meaning of section 414(e), for which there has not been made the election under section 410(d) to have the participation, vesting, funding, etc. requirements apply; or a plan which at no time after September 2, 1974, provided for employer contributions.

(2) *General rule.*—Under section 414(l),

(i) A trust which forms a part of a plan will not constitute a qualified trust under section 401, and

(ii) A plan will not be treated as being qualified under section 403(a) and 405(a),

unless, in the case of a merger or consolidation (as defined in paragraph (b)(2) of this section), or a transfer of assets or liabilities (as defined in paragraph (b)(3) of this section), the following condition is satisfied. This condition requires that each participant receive benefits on a termination basis (as defined in paragraph (b)(5) of this section) from the plan immediately after the merger, consolidation or transfer which are equal to or greater than the benefits the participant would receive on a termination basis immediately before the merger, consolidation, or transfer.

(b) *Definitions.*—For purposes of this section:

(1) *Single plan.*—A plan is a "single plan" if and only if, on an ongoing basis, all of the plan assets are available to pay benefits to employees who are covered by the plan and their beneficiaries. For purposes of the preceding sentence, all the assets of a plan will not fail to be available to provide all the benefits of a plan merely because the plan is funded in part or in whole with allocated insurance instruments. A plan will not fail to be a single plan merely because of the following:

(i) The plan has several distinct benefit structures which apply either to the same or different participants,

(ii) The plan has several plan documents,

(iii) Several employers, whether or not affiliated, contribute to the plan,

(iv) The assets of the plan are invested in several trusts or annuity contracts, or

(v) Separate accounting is maintained for purposes of cost allocation but not for purposes of providing benefits under the plan. However, more than one plan will exist if a portion of the plan assets is not available to pay some of the benefits. This will be so even if each plan has the same benefit structure or plan document, or if all or part of the assets are invested in one trust with separate accounting with respect to each plan.

(2) *Merger or consolidation.*—The terms "merger" or "consolidation" means the combining of two or more plans into a single plan. A merger or consolidation will not occur merely because one or more corporations undergo a reorganization (whether or not taxable). Furthermore, a merger or consolidation will not occur if two plans are not combined into a single plan, such as by using one trust which limits the availability of assets of one plan to provide benefits to participants and beneficiaries of only that plan.

(3) *Transfer of assets or liabilities.*—A "transfer of assets or liabilities" occurs when there is a diminution of assets or liabilities with respect to one plan and the acquisition of these assets or the assumption of these liabilities by another plan. For example, the shifting of assets or liabilities pursuant to a reciprocity agreement between two plans in which one plan assumes liabilities of another plan is a transfer of assets or liabilities. However, the shifting of assets between several funding media used for a single plan (such as between

trusts, between annuity contracts, or between trusts and annuity contracts) is not a transfer of assets or liabilities.

(4) *Spinoff.*—The term "spinoff" means the splitting of a single plan into two or more plans.

(5) *Benefits on a termination basis.*—(i) The term "benefits on a termination basis" means the benefits that would be provided exclusively by the plan assets pursuant to section 4044 of the Employee Retirement Income Security Act of 1974 ("ERISA") and the regulations thereunder if the plan terminated. Thus, the term does not include benefits that are guaranteed by the Pension Benefit Guaranty Corporation, but not provided by the plan assets.

(ii) For purposes of determining the benefits on a termination basis, the allocation of assets to various priority categories under section 4044 of ERISA must be made on the basis of reasonable actuarial assumptions. The assumptions used by the Pension Benefit Guaranty Corporation as of the date of the merger or spinoff are deemed reasonable for this purpose.

(iii) If a change in the benefit structure of a plan in conjunction with a merger, consolidation, or transfer of assets or liabilities alters the benefits on a termination basis, the change should be designated, at the time the merger, consolidation, or transfer occurs, to be effective either immediately before or immediately after that occurrence. In the event that no designation is made, the change in the benefit structure will be deemed to occur immediately after the merger, consolidation, or transfer of assets or liabilities.

(6) *Lower funded plan.*—(i) The term "lower funded plan" generally means the plan which, immediately prior to the merger, would have its assets exhausted in a higher priority category than the other plan.

(ii) Where two plans, immediately prior to the merger, would have their assets exhausted in the same priority category of section 4044 of ERISA in the event of termination, the lower funded plan is the one in which the assets would satisfy a lesser proportion of the liability allocated to that priority category.

(7) *Priority category.*—The term "priority category" means the category of benefits described in each paragraph of section 4044(a) of ERISA. References to higher or highest priority categories refer to those priority categories which receive the first allocation of assets, i.e., the lowest paragraph numbers in section 4044(a).

(8) *Separate accounting of assets.*—The term "separate accounting of assets" means the maintenance of an asset account with respect to a given group of participants which is:

(i) Credited with contributions made to the plan on behalf of the participants and with its allocable share of investment income, if any, and

(ii) Charged with benefits paid to the participants, and with its allocable share of investment losses or expenses.

(9) *Present value of accrued benefit.*—For purposes of this section, the present value of an accrued benefit must be determined on the basis of reasonable actuarial assumptions. For this purpose, the assumptions used by the Pension Benefit Guaranty Corporation as of the date of the merger or spinoff are deemed reasonable.

(10) *Valuation of plan assets.*—In determining the value of a plan's assets, the standards set forth in regulations prescribed by the Pension Benefit Guaranty Corporation (29 CFR Part 2611) shall be applied.

(11) *Date of merger or spinoff.*—The actual date of a merger or spinoff shall be determined on the basis of the facts and circumstances of the particular situation. For purposes of this determination, the following factors, none of which is necessarily controlling, are relevant:

(i) The date on which the affected employees stop accruing benefits under one plan and begin coverage and benefit accruals under another plan.

(ii) The date as of which the amount of assets to be eventually transferred is calculated.

(iii) If the merger or spinoff agreement provides that interest is to accrue from a certain date to the date of actual transfer, the date from which such interest will accrue.

(c) *Application of section 414(l).*—(1) *Two or more plans.*—(i) Section 414(l) does not apply unless more than a single plan is involved. It also does not apply unless at least a single plan assumes liabilities from another plan or obtains assets from another plan (as in a merger or spinoff). For purposes of section 414(l), a transfer of assets or liabilities will not be deemed to occur merely because a defined contribution plan is amended to become a defined benefit plan. This rule will apply even if, under the facts and circumstances of a particular case, a termination of the defined contribution plan will be

considered to have occurred for purposes of other provisions of the Code.

(ii) The requirements of this subparagraph may be illustrated as follows:

Example. After acquiring Corporation B, Corporation A amends Corporation B's defined benefit plan (Plan B) to provide the same benefits as Corporation A's defined benefit plan (Plan A). The assets of Plan B are transferred to the trust containing the assets of Plan A in such a manner that the assets of each plan: (1) are separately accounted for, and (2) are not available to pay benefits of the other plan. Because of condition (2) there are still two plans and, therefore, a merger did not occur. As a result, section 414(l) does not apply. If at some later date Corporation A were to sell Corporation B and transfer the assets of Plan B that were separately accounted for to another trust or to an annuity contract solely for the purpose of providing Plan B's benefits, this transfer would also not involve section 414(l). This is so because Plan B was a separate plan before the entire transaction and because no plan assumed liabilities or obtained assets from another plan. If, on the other hand, Corporation A merged Plan A and Plan B at the time of the acquisition of Corporation B by deleting condition (2) above, then section 414(l) would apply both to the merger of Plan A and Plan B and to the spinoff of Plan B from the merged plan. The spinoff would have to satisfy the requirements of paragraph (n) of this section, even if the assets attributable to Plan A and Plan B were separately accounted for in order to allocate funding costs.

(2) *Multiemployer plans.*—Except to the extent provided by regulations of the Pension Benefit Guaranty Corporation, section 414(l) does not apply to any transaction to the extent that participants either before or after that transaction are covered under a multiemployer plan within the meaning of section 414(f). Until these regulations are issued, section 414(l) does not apply to any of the following situations:

(i) A multiemployer plan is split into two or more plans, one or more of which are not multiemployer plans, or

(ii) A single employer plan is merged into a multiemployer plan. Therefore, if some (but not all) of the participants in a single employer plan become participants in a multiemployer plan under an agreement in which the multiemployer plan assumes all the liabilities of the single employer plan with respect to these participants and in which some or all of the assets of the single employer plan are transferred to the multiemployer plan, section 414(l) applies, but only with respect to the participants in the single employer plan who did not transfer to the multiemployer plan.

(d) *Merger of defined contribution plans.*—In the case of a merger of two or more defined contribution plans, the requirements of section 414(l) will be satisfied if all of the following conditions are met:

(1) The sum of the account balances in each plan equals the fair market value (determined as of the date of the merger) of the entire plan assets.

(2) The assets of each plan are combined to form the assets of the plan as merged.

(3) Immediately after the merger, each participant in the plan as merged has an account balance equal to the sum of the account balances the participant had in the plans immediately prior to merger.

(e) *Merger of defined benefit plans.*—(1) *General rule.*—Section 414(l) compares the benefits on a termination basis before and after the merger. If the sum of the assets of all plans is not less than the sum of the present values of the accrued benefit (whether or not vested) of all plans, the requirements of section 414(l) will be satisfied merely by combining the assets and preserving each participant's accrued benefits. This is so because all the accrued benefits of the plan as merged are provided on a termination basis by the plan as merged. However, if the sum of the assets of all plans is less than the sum of the present values of the accrued benefits (whether or not vested) in all plans, the accrued benefits in the plan as merged are not provided on a termination basis.

(2) *Special schedule of benefits.*—Generally, for some participants, the benefits provided on a termination basis for the plan as merged would be different from the benefits provided on a termination basis in the plans prior to merger if the assets were merely combined and if each participant retained his accrued benefit. Some participants would, therefore, receive greater benefits on a termination basis as a result of the merger and some other participants would receive smaller benefits. Accordingly, the requirements of section 414(l) would not be satisfied unless the distribution on termination were modified in some manner to prevent any participant from receiving smaller benefits on a termination basis as a result of the merger. This is accomplished through modifying the application of section 4044 of ERISA by inserting a special schedule of benefits.

(f) *Operational rules for the special schedule.*—The application of section 4044 of ERISA as modified by the schedule of benefits is accomplished by the following steps:

(1) Section 4044 is applied in the plan as merged through the priority categories fully satisfied by the assets of the lower funded plan immediately prior to the merger.

(2) The assets in the plan as merged are then allocated to the next priority category as a percentage of the value of the benefits that would otherwise be allocated to that priority category. That percentage is the ratio of (i) the assets allocated to the first priority category not fully satisfied by the lower funded plan immediately prior to the merger to (ii) the assets that would have been allocated had that priority category been fully satisfied.

(3) A schedule of benefits is formed listing participants and scheduled accrued benefits. The scheduled accrued benefit is the excess of the benefits provided on a termination basis with respect to any participant from the plans immediately prior to the merger, over the benefits provided on a termination basis in subparagraphs (1) and (2) of this paragraph immediately after the merger. After allocating the assets in accordance with subparagraph (2) of this paragraph, the assets are allocated to the schedule of benefits as follows:

(i) First the assets are allocated to the scheduled benefits to the extent that the participant would have benefits provided in subparagraph (4) of this paragraph if there were no scheduled benefits.

(ii) Then the assets are allocated to the scheduled benefits to the extent that the participant would have benefits provided pursuant to subparagraph (5) of this paragraph if there were no scheduled benefits.

These assets should be allocated first to those scheduled benefits that are in the highest priority category under section 4044.

(4) The assets are then allocated to those benefits in the priority category described in subparagraph (2) of this paragraph with respect to which assets were not allocated. This allocation is made to the extent that these benefits are not associated with benefits in the schedule.

(5) Finally, the assets are allocated in accordance with section 4044 with respect to priority categories lower than the priority category described in subparagraph (4) of this paragraph. This allocation is made to the extent that these benefits are not associated with benefits in the schedule.

(g) *Successive mergers.*—(1) *In general.*—In the case of a current merger of a defined benefit plan with another defined benefit plan which as a result of a previous merger has a special schedule, the rules of paragraphs (e) and (f) of this section apply as if the schedule were considered a category described in section 4044 of ERISA. Thus, a second schedule may be formed as a result of the current merger. The second schedule will be inserted in the priority category of section 4044 described in paragraph (f)(2) of this section as of the date of the current merger. This priority category may be higher, lower, or within the schedule of benefits existing on account of a previous merger. If this priority schedule is inserted within a schedule of benefits, a new single schedule of benefits replacing the old schedule of benefits would in effect be created.

(2) *Allocation of assets.*—Assets in the new schedule of benefits are allocated as follows:

(i) First to the benefits remaining in the old schedule to the extent that there are assets immediately prior to the second merger to satisfy the original benefits,

(ii) Then to the benefits provided on a termination basis from the plans immediately prior to the second merger to the extent that they are not provided before the schedule after the second merger or in subdivision (i) of this subparagraph,

(iii) Then to benefits remaining in the original schedule not included in subdivision (i) of this subparagraph.

(h) *De minimis rule for merger of defined benefit plan.*—(1) *In general.*—In the case of a merger of a defined benefit plan ("smaller plan") whose liabilities (*i.e.,* the present value of accrued benefits, whether or not vested) are less than 3 percent of the assets of another defined benefit plan ("larger plan") as of at least one day in the larger

plan's plan year in which the merger of the two plans occurs, section 414(l) will be deemed satisfied if the following condition is met. The condition requires that a special schedule of benefits (consisting of all the benefits that would be provided by the smaller plan on a termination basis just prior to the merger) be payable in a priority category higher than the highest priority category in section 4044 of ERISA. Assets will be allocated to that schedule in accordance with the allocation of assets to scheduled benefits in paragraph (f)(3) of this section.

(2) *Application to a series of mergers.*—In the case of a series of such mergers in a given plan year of the larger plan, the rule described in subparagraph (1) of this paragraph will apply only if the sum of the liabilities (whether or not vested) assumed by the larger plan are less than 3 percent of the assets of the larger plan as of at least one day in the plan year of the larger plan in which the mergers occurred.

(3) *Application to a merger occurring over more than one plan year.*—In the case of a merger of a smaller plan or a portion thereof with a larger plan designed to occur in steps over more than one plan year of the larger plan, the entire transaction will be deemed to occur in the plan year of the larger plan which contains the first of these steps.

(4) *Liabilities of the smaller plan.*—For purposes of subparagraphs (2) and (3) of this paragraph, mergers satisfying paragraphs (e), (f) or (g) of this section will be ignored in determining the sum of the liabilities assumed by the larger plan.

(i) *Data maintenance.*—(1) *Alternative to the special schedule.*—In the case of a merger which would require the creation of a special schedule in order to satisfy section 414(l), the schedule need not be created at the time of the merger if data sufficient to create the schedule is maintained. The schedule would only have to be created in the event of a subsequent plan termination or a subsequent spinoff. In that case the schedule must be determined as of the date of the merger.

(2) *Required data.*—The data that must be maintained depends on the plan, and care should be taken to ensure that all necessary data is maintained. Furthermore, in order to take advantage of the data maintenance alternative provided in this paragraph, an enrolled actuary must certify to the plan administrator that each element of data necessary to determine the schedule as of the date of the merger is maintained. This certification must be based either upon the enrolled actuary's independent examination of the data, or upon his reliance, which under the circumstances of the particular situation must be reasonable, upon a written statement of the plan administrator concerning what data is actually being maintained.

(j) *Five year rule.*—(1) *Limitation on the required use of the special schedule.*—A plan will not fail to satisfy the requirements of section 414(l) merely because the effects of the special schedule created pursuant to paragraph (e)(2) or (h) of this section are ignored 5 years after the date of a merger. Furthermore, the data maintained pursuant to paragraph (i) of this section need not be maintained for more than 5 years after the merger, if the plan does not have a spinoff or a termination within 5 years.

(2) *Illustration.*—If Plans A and B merge to form Plan AB and if Plan AB merges with Plan C 3 years later to form Plan ABC and if Plan ABC terminates 4 years later, the data relating to the merger of Plans A and B need not be maintained for more than 5 years after the merger of Plans A and B. In addition. after 5 years have elapsed after the merger of Plans A and B, the effect of any special schedule created by the merger of Plans A and B on the schedule created by the merger of Plans AB and C may be ignored in determining the later schedule.

(k) *Examples.*—The provisions of paragraphs (e) through (j) of this section may be illustrated by the following examples:

Example (1). Plan A, whose assets are $220,000, is to be merged with Plan B, whose assets are $200,000. Plan A has three employees. Plan B has two employees. If Plans A and B were to terminate just prior to the merger, the benefits provided on a termination basis would be as follows:

Plan A

Priority category of sec. 4044 of ERISA	(1) Annual accrued benefits			(2) Present value of accrued benefits			(3) Fair market value of assets allocated to priority category			(4) Benefits on a termination basis		
	EE_1	EE_2	EE_3	EE_1	EE_2	EE_3	EE_1	EE_2	EE_3	EE_1	EE_2	EE_3
3	$10,000	$4,000	$4,000	$120,000	$44,000	$40,000	$10,000	$4,000		$10,000	$4,000	
4	2,000	3,000	1,000	24,000	33,000	10,000	2,000	1,315	2 $1,753	2,000	1,315	2 $1,753
5												
6												
Total							$12,000	$5,315	$1,753	$12,000	$5,315	$1,753

Plan B

	(1)			(2)			(3)			(4)		
	EE_4	EE_5		EE_4	EE_5		EE_4	EE_5		EE_4	EE_5	
3	$15,000	$5,000		$195,000	$50,000		$15,000	5,000		$15,000	3 $500	
4		8,000			80,000		$195,000					
5												
Total							$200,000			$15,000	$500	

Assets available for priority category 5

Total present value of accrued benefits in category 5

i.e. Accrued benefit ×

1 $3,000 × $32,000 / $73,000 = $32,000

2 $4,000 × $73,000 / $5,000 = $5,000

3 $5,000 × $73,000 / $5,000 = $50,000

Because Plan B's assets are exhausted in a higher priority category than Plan A's assets, Plan B is the lower funded plan. A schedule will, therefore, be inserted in Priority Category 4 of the plan as merged after providing 10% of the benefits provided in category 4,

i.e., the ratio of $5,000 assets in Plan B allocated to category 4 to the $50,000 liability in category 4. The schedule would be constructed as follows:

	(1) Benefits on a termination basis before merger	(2) Benefits provided from priority categories higher than category 4	(3) 10 percent of benefits provided in priority category 4	(4) Benefits provided before schedule (2) + (3)	(5) Schedule of benefits (1) – (4)
EE:					
1	$12,000	$10,000	$200	$10,200	$1,800
2	5,315	—	400	400	4,915
3	1,753	—	—	—	1,753
4	15,000	15,000	—	15,000	—
5	500	—	500	500	—

Example (2). The facts are the same as in Example (1). The plan, however, terminates one year later. Furthermore, no employee has accrued additional benefits during the year except that the $2,000

benefit of EE1 that was originally in category 4 is now in category 3. The assets would be allocated to the priority categories to the extent that there are assets to cover the following benefits.

Priority termination category	EE$_1$	EE$_2$	EE$_3$	EE$_4$	EE$_5$
3	$12,000	—	—	$15,000	—
10% of 4	—	$400	—	—	$500
Schedule of benefits included in balance of category 4	—	3,600	—	—	—
Schedule of benefits included in category 5	—	1,315	$1,753	—	—
Schedule of benefits included in category 6	—	—	—	—	—
Balance of category 4 not included in schedule	—	—	—	—	4,500
Balance of category 5 not included in schedule	—	1,685	2,247	—	8,000
Balance of category 6 not included in schedule	—	—	1,000	—	—

(l) *Merger of defined benefit and defined contribution plan.*—In the case of a merger of a defined benefit plan with a defined contribution plan, one of the plans before the merger should be converted into the other type of plan (i.e., the defined benefit converted into a defined contribution or the defined contribution converted into a defined benefit) and either paragraph (d) or paragraphs (e) through (j) of this section, whichever is appropriate, should be applied.

(m) *Spinoff of a defined contribution plan.*—In the case of a spinoff of a defined contribution plan, the requirements of section 414(l) will be satisfied if after the spinoff—

(1) The sum of the account balances for each of the participants in the resulting plans equals the account balance of the participant in the plan before the spinoff, and

(2) The assets in each of the plans immediately after the spinoff equals the sum of the account balances for all participants in that plan.

(n) *Spinoff of a defined benefit plan.*—(1) *General rule.*—In the case of a spinoff of a defined benefit plan, the requirements of section 414(l) will be satisfied if—

(i) All of the accrued benefits of each participant are allocated to only one of the spun off plans, and

(ii) The value of the assets allocated to each of the spunoff plans is not less than the sum of the present value of the benefits on a termination basis in the plan before the spinoff for all participants in that spunoff plan.

(2) *De minimis rule.*—In the case of a spinoff, the requirements of section 414(l) will be deemed to be satisfied if the value of the assets spun off—

(i) Equals the present value of the accrued benefits spun off (whether or not vested), and

(ii) In conjunction with other assets spun off during the plan year in which the spinoff occurs in accordance with this subparagraph, is less than 3 percent of the assets as of at least one day in that year.

Spinoffs occurring in previous or subsequent plan years are ignored if they are not part of a single spinoff designed to occur in steps over more than one plan year.

(3) *Special temporary rule.*—In the case of a defined benefit plan maintained for different groups of employees, which is a single plan (as defined in paragraph (b)(1) of this section) and under which there has been separate accounting of assets for each group, a spinoff of the plan on or before July 1, 1978, into a separate plan for each group will be deemed to satisfy section 414(l) if—

(i) All the liabilities with respect to each group of employees are allocated to a separate plan for the group of employees, and

(ii) The assets that are separately accounted for with respect to each group of employees are allocated to the separate plan for that group of employees.

For purposes of this subparagraph, a separate accounting of assets will not be considered to have occurred to the extent that the assets allocated to each single plan are determined by an historical re-creation of benefits, contributions, investment gains, etc.

(o) *Transfers of assets or liabilities.*—Any transfer of assets or liabilities will for purposes of section 414(l) be considered as a combination of separate mergers and spinoffs using the rules of paragraphs (d), (e) through (j), (l), (m), or (n) of this section, whichever is appropriate. Thus, for example, if in accordance with the transfer of one or more employees, a block of assets and liabilities are transferred from Plan A to Plan B, each of which is a defined benefit plan, the transaction will be considered as a spinoff from Plan A and a merger of one of the spinoff plans with Plan B. The spinoff and merger described in the previous sentence would be subject to the requirements of paragraphs (n) and (e) through (j) of this section, respectively.

(p) *Effective date.*—The provisions of this section apply to mergers, consolidations and transfers of assets or liabilities which occur after September 2, 1974. [Reg. §1.414(l)-1.]

□ [T.D. 7638, 8-16-79.]

[Reg. §1.414(q)-1]

§1.414(q)-1. Highly compensated employee.—Q&A-1 through Q&A-8: [Reserved] See §1.414(q)-1T, Q&A-1 through Q&A-8 for further guidance.

Q-9: How is the top-paid group determined?

A-9: (a) [Reserved] See §1.414(q)-1T, Q&A-9(a) for further guidance.

(b) *Number of employees in the top-paid group*—(1) *Exclusions.* The number of employees who are in the top-paid group for a year is equal to 20 percent of the total number of active employees of the employer for such year. However, solely for purposes of determining the total number of active employees in the top-paid group for a year, the employees described in §1.414(q)-1T, A-9(b)(1)(i), (ii) and (iii)(B) are disregarded. Paragraph (g) of this A-9 provides rules for determining those employees who are excluded for purposes of applying section 414(r)(2)(A), relating to the 50-employee requirement applicable to a qualified separate line of business.

(i) through (iii) [Reserved] See §1.414(q)-1T, Q&A-9(b)(1)(i) through (iii) for further guidance.

(2) *Alternative exclusion provisions*—(i) and (ii) [Reserved] See §1.414(q)-1T, Q&A-9(b)(2)(i) and (ii) for further guidance.

(iii) *Method of election.* The elections in this paragraph (b)(2) must be provided for in all plans of the employer and must be uniform and consistent with respect to all situations in which the section 414(q) definition is applicable to the employer. Thus, with respect to all plan years beginning in the same calendar year, the employer must apply the test uniformly for purposes of determining its top-paid group with respect to all its qualified plans and employee benefit plans. If either election is changed during the determination year, no recalculation of the look-back year based on the new election is required, provided the change in election does not result in discrimination in operation.

(c) through (f) [Reserved] See § 1.414(q)-1T, Q&A-9(c) through (f) for further guidance.

(g) *Excluded employees under section 414(r)(2)(A)*—(1) *In general.* This paragraph (g) provides the rules for determining which employees are excluded employees for purposes of applying section 414(r)(2)(A), relating to the 50-employee requirement applicable to a qualified separate line of business.

(2) *Excluded employees*—(i) *Age and service exclusion.* All employees are excluded who are described in § 1.414(q)-1T, A-9(b)(1)(i) (relating to exclusions based on age or service). For this purpose, the rules in § 1.414(q)-1T, A-9(e) and (f) (relating respectively to the 17 1/2-hour rule and the 6-month rule) apply. However, the election in § 1.414(q)-1T, A-9(b)(2)(i) (permitting the employer to elect reduced minimum age or service requirements) does not apply.

(ii) *Nonresident alien exclusion.* All employees are excluded who are described in § 1.414(q)-1T, A-9(b)(1)(ii) (relating to the exclusion of nonresident aliens with no U.S.-source income from the employer).

(iii) *Inclusion of employees covered under a collective bargaining agreement.* All employees are included who are described in § 1.414(q)-1T, A-9(b)(1)(iii)(A) (relating to employees covered under a collective bargaining agreement) and who are not otherwise described in paragraph (g)(2)(i) or (ii) of this A-9. For this purpose, the exclusion in § 1.414(q)-1T, A-9(b)(1)(iii)(B) and the related election in § 1.414(q)-1T, A-9(b)(2)(ii) do not apply.

(3) *Applicable period.* The determination of which employees are excluded employees is made on the basis of the testing year specified in the regulations under section 414(r) and not on the basis of the determination year or the look-back year under section 414(q).

(h) *Effective date.* The provisions of this A-9 apply to plan years and testing years beginning on or after January 1, 1994.

Q&A-10 through Q&A-15: [Reserved] See § 1.414(q)-1T, Q&A-10 through Q&A-15 for further guidance. [Reg. § 1.414(q)-1.]

☐ [*T.D. 8548, 6-23-94.*]

[Reg. § 1.414(q)-1T]

§ 1.414(q)-1T. Highly compensated employee (Temporary).—The following questions and answers relate to the definition of "highly compensated employee" provided in section 414(q). The definitions and rules provided in these questions and answers are provided solely for purposes of determining the group of highly compensated employees.

Table of contents.

Q-1: To what employee benefit plans and statutory provisions is the definition of highly compensated employee contained in section 414(q) applicable?

A-1: (a) *In general.* This definition is applicable to statutory provisions that incorporate the definition by reference.

(b) *Qualified retirement plans*—(1) *In general.* Generally, this definition is incorporated in many of the nondiscrimination requirements applicable to pension, profit-sharing, and stock bonus plans qualified under section 401(a). *See, e.g.,* the nondiscrimination provisions of sections 401(a)(4) and (5), 401(k)(3), 401(l), 401(m), 406(b), 407(b), 408(k), 410(b) and 411(d)(1). The definition is also incorporated by certain other provisions with respect to such plans, including the aggregation rules of section 414(m) and section 4975 (tax on prohibited transactions).

(2) *Not applicable where not incorporated by reference.* This definition is not applicable to qualified plan provisions that do not incorporate it. *See, e.g.,* section 415 (limitations on contributions and benefits), with the exception of section 415(c)(3)(C) and 415(c)(6) (special rules for permanent and total disability and employee stock ownership plans respectively).

(c) *Other employee benefit plans or arrangements.* This definition is incorporated by various sections relating to employee benefit provisions. *See, e.g.,* section 89 (certain other employee benefit plans), section 106 (accident and health plans), 117(d) (qualified tuition reduction), section 125 (cafeteria plans), section 129 (dependent care assistance programs), section 132 (certain fringe benefits), section 274 (certain entertainment, etc. expenses), section 423(b) (employee stock purchase plan provisions), section 501(c)(17) and (18) (certain exempt trusts providing benefits to employees), and section 505 (certain exempt organizations or trusts providing benefits to individuals). See the respective sections for the applicable effective dates.

(d) *ERISA.* This definition is not determinative with respect to any provisions of Title I of the Employee Retirement Income Security Act of 1974 (ERISA), unless it is explicitly incorporated by reference (e.g., section 408(b)(1)(B)).

Q-2: Who is a highly compensated employee?

A-2: The group of employees (including former employees) who are highly compensated employees consists of both highly compensated active employees (see A-3 of this § 1.414(q)-1T) and highly compensated former employees (see A-4 of this § 1.414(q)-1T). In many circumstances, highly compensated active employees and highly compensated former employees are considered separately in applying the provisions for which the definition of highly compensated employees in section 414(q) is applicable. Specific rules with respect to the treatment of highly compensated active employees and highly compensated former employees will be provided in the regulations with respect to the sections to which the definition of highly compensated employees is applicable.

Q-3: Who is a highly compensated active employee?

A-3: (a) *General rule.* For purposes of the year for which the determination is being made (the determination year), a highly compensated active employee is any employee who, with respect to the employer, performs services during the determination year and is described in any one or more of the following groups applicable with respect to the look-back year calculation and/or determination year calculation for such determination year. See A-14 for rules relating to the periods for which the look-back year calculation and determination year calculation are to be made.

(1) *Look-back year calculation.*

(i) *5-percent owner.* The employee is a 5-percent owner at any time during the look-back year (i.e., generally, the 12-month period immediately preceding the determination year; see A-14. (See A-8 of this § 1.414(q)-1T.)

(ii) *Compensation above $75,000.* The employee receives compensation in excess of $75,000 during the look-back year.

(iii) *Compensation above $50,000 and top-paid group.* The employee receives compensation in excess of $50,000 during the look-back year and is a member of the top-paid group for the look-back year. (See A-9 of this § 1.414(q)-1T.)

(iv) *Officer.* The employee is an "includible officer" during the look-back year. (See A-10 of this § 1.414(q)-1T.)

(2) *Determination year calculation.*

(i) *5-percent owner.* The employee is a 5-percent owner at any time during the determination year. (See A-8 of this § 1.414(q)-1T.)

(ii) *Top-100 employees.* The employee is both (A) described in paragraph (a)(1)(i), (ii) and/or (iv) of this A-3, when such paragraphs are modified to substitute the determination year for the look-back year, and (B) one of the 100 employees who receive the most compensation from the employer during the determination year.

(b) *Rounding and tie-breaking rules.* In making the look-back year and determination year calculations for a determination year, it may be necessary for an employer to adopt a rule for rounding calculations (e.g., in determining the number of employees in the top-paid group). In addition, it may be necessary to adopt a rule breaking ties among two or more employees (e.g., in identifying those particular employees who are in the top-paid group or who are among the 100 most highly compensated employees). In such cases, the employer may adopt any rounding or tie-breaking rules it desires, so long as such rules are reasonable, nondiscriminatory, and uniformly and consistently applied.

(c) *Adjustments to dollar thresholds*—(1) *Indexing of dollar thresholds.* The dollar amounts in paragraph (a)(1)(i) and (ii) of this A-3 are indexed at the same time and in the same manner as the section 415(b)(1)(A) dollar limitation for defined benefit plans.

(2) *Applicable dollar threshold.* The applicable dollar amount for a particular determination year or look-back year is the dollar amount for the calendar year in which such determination year or look-back year begins. Thus, the dollar amount for purposes of determining the highly compensated active employees for a particular look-back year is based on the calendar year in which such look-back year begins, not the calendar year in which such look-back year ends or in which the determination year with respect to such look-back year begins.

(d) *Employees described in more than one group.* An individual who is a highly compensated active employee for a determination year, by reason of being described in one group in paragraph (a) of this A-3, under either the look-back year calculation or the determination year calculation, is not disregarded in determining whether another indi-

vidual is a highly compensated active employee by reason of being described in another group under paragraph (a). For example, an individual who is a highly compensated active employee for a determination year, by reason of being a 5-percent owner during such year, who receives compensation in excess of $50,000 during both the look-back year and the determination year, is taken into account in determining the group of employees who are highly compensated active employees for such determination year by reason of receiving more than $50,000, and being in the top-paid group under either or both the look-back year calculation or determination year calculation for such determination year.

(e) *Examples.* The following examples, in which the determination year and look-back year are the calendar year, are illustrative of the rules in paragraph (a) of this A-3. For purposes of these examples, the threshold dollar amounts in paragraph (a)(1)(ii) and (iii) of this A-3 are not increased pursuant to paragraph (c) of this A-3.

Example (1). Employee A, who is not at any time a 5-percent owner, an officer, or a member of the top-100 within the meaning of paragraph (a)(1)(i), or (iv), or (a)(2)(i) or (ii), but who was a member of the top-paid group for each year, is included in or excluded from the highly compensated groups as specified below for the following years:

Year	Compensation	Status	Comments
1986	$45,000	N/A	Although prior to 414(q) effective date, 1986 constitutes the look-back year for purposes of determining the highly compensated group for the 1987 determination year.
1987	$80,000	Excl.	Excluded because A was not an employee described in paragraph (a)(1)(ii) or (iii) of this A-3 for the look-back year (1986).
1988	$80,000	Incl.	Included because A was an employee described in paragraph (a)(1)(ii) or (iii) of this A-3 for the look-back year (1987).
1989	$45,000	Incl.	Included because A was an employee described in paragraph (a)(1)(ii) or (iii) of this A-3 for the look-back year (1988).
1990	$45,000	Excl.	Excluded because A was not an employee described in paragraph (a)(1)(ii) or (iii) of this A-3 for the look-back year (1989).

Example (2). Assuming the same facts as those given in *Example (1)*, except that A is a member of the top-100 employees within the meaning of paragraph (a)(2)(ii) of this A-3 for the 1987 year and 1990 year, the results are as follows:

Year	Compensation	Status	Comments
1986	$45,000	N/A	Although prior to 414(q) effective date, 1986 constitutes the look-back year for purposes of determining the highly compensated group for the 1987 determination year.
1987	$80,000	Incl.	Included because A was an employee described in paragraph (a)(1)(ii) or (iii) of this A-3 for the determination year (1987) and was described in paragraph (a)(2)(ii) of this A-3 in that year.
1988	$80,000	Incl.	Included because A was an employee described in paragraph (a)(1)(ii) or (iii) of this A-3 for the look-back year (1987).
1989	$45,000	Incl.	Included because A was an employee described in paragraph (a)(1)(ii) or (iii) of this A-3 for the look-back year (1988).
1990	$45,000	Excl.	Excluded even though in top-100 employees during 1990 determination year because A was not an employee described in paragraph (a)(1)(ii) or (iii) of this A-3 for the look-back year (1989) or for the determination year (1990).

Q-4: Who is a highly compensated former employee?

A-4: (a) *General rule.* Except to the extent provided in paragraph (d) of this A-4, a highly compensated former employee for a determination year is any former employee who, with respect to the employer, had a separation year (as defined in A-5 of this §1.414(q)-1T) prior to the determination year and was a highly compensated active employee as defined in A-3 of this §1.414(q)-1T for either such employee's separation year or any determination year ending on or after the employee's 55th birthday. Thus, for example, an employee who is a highly compensated active employee for such employee's separation year, by reason of receiving over $75,000 during the look-back year, is a highly compensated former employee for determination years after such employee's separation year.

(b) *Special rule for employees who perform no services for the employer in the determination year.* For purposes of this rule, employees who perform no services for an employer during a determination year are treated as former employees. Thus, for example, an employee who performed no services for the employer during a determination year, by reason of a leave of absence during such year, is treated as a former employee for such year.

(c) *Dollar amounts for pre-1987 determination years.* For determination years beginning before January 1, 1987, the dollar amounts in paragraph (a)(1)(B) and (C) of A-2 of this §1.414(q)-1T are $75,000 and $50,000 respectively.

(d) *Special rule for employees who separated from service before January 1, 1987*—(1) *Election of special rule.* Employers may elect to apply paragraph (d)(2) of this A-4 in lieu of paragraph (a) of this A-4 in determining whether former employees who separated from service prior to January 1, 1987, are highly compensated former employees. If this election is made with respect to any qualified plan, it must be provided for in the plan. If the employer makes this election with respect to any employee benefit plan, such election must be used uniformly for all purposes for which the section 414(q) definition is

applicable. The election, once made, cannot be changed without the consent of the Commissioner.

(2) *Special definition of highly compensated former employee.* A highly compensated former employee includes any former employee who separated from service with the employer prior to January 1, 1987, and was described in any one or more of the following groups during either the employee's separation year (or the year preceding such separation year) or any year ending on or after such individual's 55th birthday (or the last year ending before such employee's 55th birthday):

(i) *5-percent owner.* The employee was a 5-percent owner of the employer at any time during the year.

(ii) *Compensation amount.* The employee received compensation in excess of $50,000 during the year.

The determinations provided for in this paragraph (b)(2) may be made on the basis of the calendar year, the plan year, or any other twelve month period selected by the employer and applied on a reasonable and consistent basis.

(e) *Rules with respect to former employees*—(1) *In general.* For specific provisions with respect to the treatment of former employees and of highly compensated former employees, refer to the rules with respect to which the section 414(q) definition of highly compensated employee is applicable.

(2) *Former employees excluded in determining top-paid group, top-100 employees and includible officers.* Former employees are not included in the top-paid group, the group of the top-100 employees, or the group of includible officers for purposes of applying section 414(q) to active employees. In addition, former employees are not counted as employees for purposes of determining the number of employees in the top-paid group.

Q-5: What is a separation year for purposes of section 414(q)?

A-5: (a) *Separation year*—(1) *In general.* The separation year generally is the determination year during which the employee separates from service with the employer. For purposes of this rule, an employee who performs no services for the employer during a determination year will be treated as having separated from service with the employer in the year in which such employee last performed services for the employer. Thus, for example, an employee who performs no services for the employer by reason of being on a leave of absence throughout the determination year is considered to have separated from service with the employer in the year in which such employee last performed services prior to beginning the leave of absence.

(2) *Deemed separation.* An employee who performs services for the employer during a determination year may be deemed to have separated from service with the employer during such year pursuant to the rules in paragraph (a)(3) of this A-5. Such deemed separation year is relevant for purposes of determining whether such employee is a highly compensated former employee after such employee actually separates from service, not for purposes of identifying such employee as either an active or former employee. Because employees to whom the provisions of paragraph (a)(2) of this A-5 apply are still performing services for the employer during the determination year, they are treated as active employees. Thus, for example, an employee who has a deemed separation year in 1989, a year during which he was a highly compensated employee, who continues to work for the employer until he retires from employment in 1995, is an active employee of the employer until 1995 and is either highly compensated or not highly compensated for any determination year during such period based on the rules with respect to highly compensated active employees. For determination years after the year of such employee's retirement, such employee is a highly compensated former employee because such employee was a highly compensated active employee for the deemed separation year.

(3) *Deemed separation year.* An employee will be deemed to have a separation year if, in a determination year prior to attainment of age 55, the employee receives compensation in an amount less than 50% of the employee's average annual compensation for the three consecutive calendar years preceding such determination year during which the employee received the greatest amount of compensation from the employer (or the total period of the employee's service with the employer, if less).

(4) *Leave of absence.* The deemed separation rules contained in paragraph (a)(2) and (3) of this A-5 apply without regard to whether the reduction in compensation occurs on account of a leave of absence.

(b) *Deemed resumption of employment.* An employee who is treated as having a deemed separation year by reason of the provisions of paragraph (a) of this A-5 will not be treated as a highly compensated former employee (by reason of such deemed separation year) after such employee actually separates from service with the employer if, after such deemed separation year, and before the year of actual separation, such employee's services for and compensation from the employer for a determination year increase significantly so that such employee is treated as having a deemed resumption of employment. The determination of whether an employee who has incurred a deemed separation year has an increase in services and compensation sufficient to result in a deemed resumption of employment will be made on the basis of all the surrounding facts and circumstances pertaining to each individual case. At a minimum, there must be an increase in compensation from the employer to the extent that such compensation would not result in a deemed separation year under the tests in paragraph (a)(2) of this A-5 using the same three-year period taken into account in such paragraph.

(c) *Examples.* Paragraphs (a) and (b) of this A-5 are illustrated by the following examples based on calendar years. For purposes of these examples the threshold dollar amounts in A-5(a) of this §1.414(q)-1T have not been increased pursuant to A-5(b) of this §1.414(q)-1T.

Example (1). Assume that in 1990 A is a highly compensated employee of X by reason of having earned more than $75,000 during the 1989 look-back year. In 1987, 1988 and 1989, A's years of greatest compensation received from X, A received $76,000, $80,000 and $79,000 respectively. In February of 1990, A received $30,000 in compensation. Because A's compensation during the 1990 determination year is less than 50% of A's average annual compensation from X during A's high three prior determination years, A is deemed to have a separation year during the 1990 determination year pursuant to the provisions of paragraph (a) of this A-5. Since A is a highly compensated employee for X in 1990, A's deemed separation year, A will be treated as a highly compensated former employee after A actually separates from service with the employer unless A experiences a deemed resumption of employment within the meaning of paragraph (b) of this A-5.

Example (2). Assume that in 1990 A is a highly compensated employee by reason of having been an officer (with annual compensation in excess of the section 415(c)(1)(A) dollar limitation) during the 1989 look-back year. A's compensation from X during 1990 is

$37,000. A's average compensation from X for the three-year period ending with or within January, 1990, was $60,000. A's compensation during the 1990 determination year is not less than 50% of the compensation earned during the test period. Therefore, A is not deemed to have a separation year under paragraph (a)(2)(i) of this A-5.

Example (3). Assume that in 1990 C is 35 and a highly compensated employee of Z for the reasons given in *Example (1)* with the same compensation set forth in that example. During 1990, C leaves C's 40 hour a week position as director of the actuarial division of Z and starts working as an actuary for the same division, producing actuarial reports approximately 15 to 20 hours a week, approximately half of these hours at home. C contemplates returning to full-time employment with Z when C's child enters school. During the 1990 determination year, C's compensation is less than 50% of C's compensation during her high three preceding determination years. Therefore, C has a deemed separation year during the 1990 determination year. In 1991 C commences working 32 hours a week for X at X's place of business and receives compensation in an amount equal to 80 percent of her average annual compensation during her high three prior determination years. The C's increased compensation, considered in conjunction with the reasons for the reduction in service, the nature and extent of the services performed before and after the reduction in services, and the lack of proximity of C's age to age 55 at the time of the reduction are sufficient to establish that C has a deemed resumption of employment within the meaning of paragraph (b) of this A-5. Therefore, when C separates from service with the employer, C will not be treated as a highly compensated former employee by reason of C's deemed separation year in 1990.

Q-6: Who is the employer?

A-6: (a) *Aggregation of certain entities.* The employer is the entity employing the employees and includes all other entities aggregated with such employing entity under the aggregation requirements of section 414(b), (c), (m) and (o). Thus, the following entities must be taken into account as a single employer for purposes of determining the employees who are "highly compensated employees" within the meaning of section 414(q):

(1) All corporations that are members of a controlled group of corporations (as defined in section 414(b)) that includes the employing entity.

(2) All trades or businesses (whether or not incorporated) that are under common control (as defined in section 414(c)) which group includes the employing entity.

(3) All organizations (whether or not incorporated) that are members of an affiliated service group (as defined in section 414(m)) that includes the employing entity.

(4) Any other entities required to be aggregated with the employing entity pursuant to section 414(o) and the regulations thereunder.

(b) *Priority of aggregation provisions.* The aggregation requirements of paragraph (a) of this A-6 and of A-7(b) of this section with respect to leased employees are applied before the application of any of the other provisions of section 414(q) and this section.

(c) *Line of business rules.* The section 414(r) rules with respect to separate lines of business are not applicable in determining the group of highly compensated employees.

Q-7: Who is an employee for purposes of section 414(q)?

A-7: (a) *General rule.* Except as provided in paragraph (b) of this A-7, the term "employee" for purposes of section 414(q) refers to individuals who perform services for the employer and are either common-law employees of the employer or self-employed individuals who are treated as employees pursuant to section 401(c)(1). This rule with respect to the inclusion of certain self-employed individuals in the group of highly compensated employees is applicable whether or not such individuals are eligible to participate in the plan or benefit arrangement being tested.

(b) *Leased employees*—(1) *In general.* The term "employee" includes a leased employee who is treated as an employee of the recipient pursuant to the provisions of section 414(n)(2) or 414(o)(2). Employees that an employer treats as leased employees under section 414(n), pursuant to the requirements of section 414(o), are considered to be leased employees for purposes of this rule.

(2) *Safe-harbor exception.* For purposes of qualified retirement plans, if an employee who would be a leased employee within the meaning of section 414(n)(2) is covered in a safe-harbor plan described in section 414(n)(5) (a qualified money purchase pension plan maintained by the leasing organization), and not otherwise covered under a qualified retirement plan of the employer, then such employee is excluded from the term "employee" unless the employer elects to include such employee pursuant to the provisions of subparagraph (4) of this paragraph (b).

(3) *Other employee benefit plans.* The exception in paragraph (b)(2) of this A-7 is not applicable to the determination of the highly compensated employee group for purposes of the sections enumerated in section 414(n)(3)(C). Thus, for example, a leased employee covered

by a safe-harbor plan is considered to be an employee in applying the nondiscrimination provisions of section 89 to statutory benefit plans. Consequently, an employer with leased employees covered in a safe-harbor plan may have 2 groups of highly compensated employees, one with respect to its retirement plans and another with respect to its statutory benefit plans.

(4) *Election with respect to leased employee exclusion.* An employer may elect to include the employees excepted under the provisions of paragraph (b)(2) of this A-7 in determining the highly compensated group with respect to an employer's retirement plans. Thus, for example, by electing to forego the exception in paragraph (b)(2) of this A-7, an employer may achieve more uniform highly compensated employee groups for purposes of its retirement plans and welfare benefit plans. The election to include such employees must be made on a reasonable and consistent basis and must be provided for in the plan.

Q-8: Who is a 5-percent owner of the employer?

A-8: An employee is a 5-percent owner of the employer for a particular year if, at any time during such year, such employee is a 5-percent owner as defined in section 416(i)(B)(i) and §1.416-1 A T-17&18. Thus, if the employer is a corporation, a 5-percent owner is any employee who owns (or is considered as owning within the meaning of section 318) more than 5 percent of the value of the outstanding stock of the corporation or stock possessing more than 5 percent of the total combined voting power of all stock of the corporation. If the employer is not a corporation, a 5-percent owner is any employee who owns more than 5 percent of the capital or profits interest in the employer. The rules of subsections (b), (c), and (m) of section 414 do not apply for purposes of determining who is a 5-percent owner. Thus, for example, an individual who is a 5-percent owner of a subsidiary corporation that is part of a controlled group of corporations within the meaning of section 414(b) is treated as a 5-percent owner for purposes of these rules.

Q-9: How is the "top-paid group" determined?

A-9: (a) *General rule.* An employee is in the top-paid group of employees for a particular year if such employee is in the group consisting of the top 20 percent of the employer's employees when ranked on the basis of compensation received from the employer during such year. The identification of the particular employees who are in the top-paid group for a year involves a two-step procedure:

(1) The determination of the number of employees that corresponds to 20 percent of the employer's employees, and

(2) The identification of the particular employees who are among the number of employees who receive the most compensation during this year.

Employees who perform no services for the employer during a year are not included in making either of these determinations for such year.

(b) *Number of employees in the top-paid group*—(1) *Exclusions.* [Reserved] See §1.414(q)-1, Q&A-9(b)(1) for further information.

(i) *Age and service exclusion.* The following employees are excluded on the basis of age or service absent an election by the employer pursuant to the rules in paragraph (b)(2) of this A-9:

(A) Employees who have not completed 6 months of service by the end of such year. For purposes of this subdivision (A), an employee's service in the immediately preceding year is added to service in the current year in determining whether the exclusion is applicable with respect to a particular employee in the current year. For example, given a plan with a calendar determination year, if employee A commences work August 1, 1989, and terminates employment May 31, 1990, A may be excluded under this paragraph (b)(1)(i)(A) in 1989 because A completed only 5 months of service by December 31, 1989. However, A cannot be excluded pursuant to this rule in 1990 because A has completed 10 months of service, for purposes of this rule, by the end of 1990.

(B) Employees who normally work less than $17^1/_2$ hours per week as defined in paragraph (d) of this A-9 for such year.

(C) Employees who normally work during less than 6 months during any year as defined in paragraph (e) of this A-9 for such year.

(D) Employees who have not had their 21st birthdays by the end of such year.

(ii) *Nonresident alien exclusion.* Employees who are nonresident aliens and who receive no earned income (within the meaning of section 911(d)(2)) from the employer that constitutes income from sources within the United States (within the meaning of section 861(a)(3)) are excluded.

(iii) *Collective bargaining exclusion*—(A) *In general.* Except as provided in subdivision (B) of this paragraph (b)(1)(iii), employees who are included in a unit of employees covered by an agreement that the Secretary of Labor finds to be a collective bargaining agreement between employee representatives and the employer, which agreement satisfies section 7701(a)(46) and §301.7701-17T (Temporary), are included in determining the number of employees in the top-paid group.

(B) *Percentage exclusion provision.* If 90 percent or more of the employees of the employer are covered under collective bargaining agreements that the Secretary of Labor finds to be collective bargaining agreements between employee representatives and the employer, which agreements satisfy section 7701(a)(46) and §301.7701-17T (Temporary), and the plan being tested covers only employees who are not covered under such agreements, then the employees who are covered under such collective bargaining agreements are not counted in determining the number of noncollective bargaining employees who will be included in the top-paid group for purposes of testing such plan. In addition, such employees are not included in the top-paid group for such purposes. Thus, if the conditions of this paragraph (b)(1)(iii)(B) are satisfied, a separate calculation is required to determine the number and identity of noncollective bargaining employees who will be highly compensated employees by reason of receiving over $50,000 and being in the top-paid group of employees for purposes of testing those plans that cover only noncollective bargaining employees.

(2) *Alternative exclusion provisions*—(i) *Age and service exclusion election.* An employer may elect, on a consistent and uniform basis, to modify the permissible exclusions set forth in paragraph (b)(1)(i)(A), (B), (C), and (D) of this A-9 by substituting any shorter period of service or lower age than that specified in such paragraph. These exclusions may be modified to substitute a zero service or age requirement.

(ii) *Election not to apply percentage exclusion provision.* An employer may elect not to exclude employees under the rules in paragraph (b)(1)(iii)(B) of this A-9.

(iii) *Method of election.* [Reserved] See §1.414(q)-1, Q&A-9(b)(2)(iii) for further information.

(c) *Identification of top-paid group members.* With the exception of the paragraph (b)(1)(iii) of this A-9 exclusion for certain employees covered by collective bargaining agreements, the exclusions in paragraph (b)(1) of this A-9 are not applicable for purposes of identifying the particular employees in the top-paid group. Thus, for example, even if an employee who normally works for less than $17^1/_2$ hours is excluded in determining the number of employees in the top-paid group, such employee may be a member of the top-paid group. Similarly, if during a determination year, employee A receives over $75,000 and is one of the top-100 employees ranked by compensation, then employee A is a highly compensated active employee for such determination year. This is true even though employee A has worked less than six months and thus may be excluded in determining the number of persons in the top-paid group for the determination year.

(d) *Example.* Paragraphs (b) and (c) of this A-9 are illustrated by the following example:

Example. Employer X has 200 active employees during the 1989 determination year, 100 of whom normally work less than $17^1/_2$ hours per week during such year and 80 of whom normally work less than 15 hours per week during such year. X elects to exclude all employees who normally work less than 15 hours per week in determining the number of employees in the top-paid group. Thus, X excludes 80 employees in determining the number of employees in the top-paid group. X's top-paid group for the 1989 determination year consists of 20% of 120 or 24 employees. All 200 of X's employees must then be ranked in order by compensation received during the year, and the 24 employees X paid the greatest amount of compensation during the year are top-paid employees with respect to X for the 1989 determination year.

(e) *$17^1/_2$ hour rule*—(1) *In general.* The determination of whether an employee normally works less than $17^1/_2$ hours per week is made independently for each year based on the rules in paragraph (e)(2) and (3) of this A-9. In making this determination, weeks during which the employee did not work for the employer are not considered. Thus, for example, if an employee normally works twenty hours a week for twenty-five weeks during the fall and winter school quarters, 10 hours a week for the 12 week spring quarter, and does not work for the employer during the three-month summer quarter, such employee is treated as normally working more than $17^1/_2$ hours per week under the rule of this paragraph (e).

(2) *Deemed above $17^1/_2$.* An employee who works $17^1/_2$ hours a week or more, for more than fifty percent of the total weeks worked by such employee during the year, is deemed to normally work more than $17^1/_2$ hours a week for purposes of this rule.

(3) *Deemed below $17^1/_2$.* An employee who works less than $17^1/_2$ hours a week for fifty percent or more of the total weeks worked by such employee during the year is deemed to normally work less than $17^1/_2$ hours a week for purposes of this rule.

(4) *Application.* The determination provided for in paragraph (e)(1), (2), and (3) of this A-9 may be made separately with respect to each employee, or on the basis of groups of employees who fall within particular job categories as established by the employer on a reasonable basis. For example, under the rule of this paragraph (e)(4) an

employer may exclude all office cleaning personnel if, for the year in question, the employees performing this function normally work less than $17^1/_2$ hours a week. This is true even though one or more employees within this group normally work in excess of $17^1/_2$ hours. The election to make this determination on the basis of individuals or groups is operational and does not require a plan provision.

(5) *Application based on groups.* (i) Groups of employees who perform the same job are not required to be considered as one category for purposes of the rule in paragraph (e)(4) of this A-9. Thus, for example, an employer supermarket may determine its highly compensated employees by excluding part-time grocery checkers if such personnel normally work less than $17^1/_2$ hours a week while continuing to include full-time personnel performing this function. In general, 80 percent of the positions within a particular job category must be filled by employees who normally work less than $17^1/_2$ hours a week before any employees may be excluded under this rule on the basis of their membership in that job category.

(ii) Alternatively, an employer may exclude employees who are members of a particular job category if the median number of hours of service credited to employees in that category during a determination or look-back year is 500 or less.

(f) *6-month rule*—(1) *In general.* The determination of whether employees normally work during not more than 6 months in any year is made on the basis of the facts and circumstances of the particular employer as evidenced by the employer's customary experience in the years preceding the determination year. An employee who works on one day during a month is deemed to have worked during that month.

(2) *Application of prior year experience.* In making the determination under this paragraph (f), the experience for years immediately preceding the determination year will generally be weighed more heavily than that of earlier years. However, this emphasis on more recent years is not appropriate if the data for a particular year reflects unusual circumstances. For example, if fishermen working for employer X worked 9 months in 1987 and 1988, 8 months in 1989, and then, because of abnormal ice conditions, worked only 5 months in 1990, such fishermen could not be excluded under this rule in 1990. Furthermore, the data with respect to 1990 would not be weighed more heavily in making a determination with respect to subsequent years.

(3) *Individual or group basis.* This determination may be made separately with respect to each employee or on the basis of groups of employees who fall within particular job categories in the manner set forth in paragraph (e)(4) of this A-8.

Q-10: For purposes of determining the group of highly compensated employees, which employees are officers and which officers must be included in the highly compensated group?

A-10: (a) *In general.* Subject to the limitations set forth in paragraph (b) of this A-10 and the top-100 employee rule set forth in A-2, an employee is an includible officer for purposes of this section and is a member of the group of highly compensated employees if such employee is an officer of the employer (within the meaning of section 416(i) and §1.416-1 A-T 13 & A-T 15) at any time during the determination year or look-back year and receives compensation during such year that is greater than 150 percent of the dollar limitation in effect under section 415(c)(1)(A) for the calendar year in which the determination or look-back year begins. In addition, an officer who does not meet the 415(c)(1)(A) dollar limitation requirement may be an includible officer based on the minimum inclusion rules set forth in paragraph (c) of this A-10.

(b) *Maximum limitation*—(1) *In general.* No more than 50 employees (or, if lesser, the greater of 3 employees or 10 percent of the employees without regard to any exclusions) shall be treated as officers for purposes of this provision in determining the group of highly compensated employees for any determination year or look-back year.

(2) *Total number of employees.* The total number of employees for purposes of the limitation in this paragraph (b) is the number of employees the employer has during the particular determination year or look-back year. For purposes of this A-10, employees include only those individuals who perform services for the employer during the determination or look-back year. The exclusions applicable for purposes of determining the number of employees in the top-paid group are not applicable for purposes of the limitations in this paragraph (b).

(3) *Inclusion ranking.* If the number of the employer's officers who satisfy paragraph (a) of this A-10 during either the determination year or the look-back year exceeds the limitation under this paragraph (b), then the officers who will be considered as includible officers for purposes of this rule are those who receive the greatest compensation from the employer during such determination or look-back year. The definition of compensation in A-13 is to be used for this purpose.

(c) *Minimum inclusion rule.* This paragraph (c) is applicable when no officer of the employer satisfies the compensation requirements of

paragraph (a) of this A-10 during either a determination year or look-back year. In such case, the highest paid officer of the employer for such year is treated as a highly compensated employee by reason of being an officer, without regard to the amount of compensation paid to such officer in relation to the section 415(c)(1)(A) dollar amount for the year. This is true whether or not such employee is also a highly compensated employee on any other basis. Thus, for example, if no officer of employer X meets the compensation requirements of paragraph (a) of this A-10 during the 1989 look-back year, and employee A is both the highest paid officer during such year and a 5-percent owner, employee A is treated as an includible officer satisfying the minimum inclusion rules of this paragraph.

(d) *Separate application.* The maximum and minimum officer inclusion rules of paragraphs (b) and (c) of this A-10 apply separately with respect to the determination year calculation and the look-back year calculation. Thus, for example, if no officer of employer X receives compensation above the threshold amount in paragraph (a) of this A-10 during either the determination year or look-back year, application of the minimum inclusion rule would result in the officer of employer X who received the greatest compensation during the look-back year being treated as a highly compensated employee and, in addition, the officer of employer X who receives the most compensation during the determination year would be included in the highly compensated group if such officer is also in the top-100 employees of employer X for such year. Thus, two officers may be treated as highly compensated active employees for a determination year by reason of the provisions of the minimum inclusion rule.

Q-11: To what extent must family members who are employed by the same employer be aggregated for purposes of section 414(q)?

A-11: (a) *Family aggregation*—(1) *In general.* Aggregation is required with respect to an employee who is, during a particular determination year or look-back year, a family member (as defined in A-12) of either (i) a 5-percent owner who is an active or former employee or (ii) a highly compensated employee who is one of the ten most highly compensated employees ranked on the basis of compensation paid by the employer during such year.

(2) *Aggregation of contributions or benefits.* As prescribed in regulations under the provisions to which section 414(q) is applicable, a family member and a 5-percent owner or top-10 highly compensated employee aggregated under this rule are generally treated as a single employee receiving an amount of compensation and a plan contribution or benefit that is based on the compensation, contributions, and benefits of such family member and 5-percent owner or top-10 highly compensated employee.

(b) *Exclusion status irrelevant.* Family members are subject to this aggregation rule whether or not they fall within the categories of employees that may be excluded for purposes of determining the number of employees in the top-paid group and whether or not they are highly compensated employees when considered separately.

(c) *Order of determination*—(1) *Determination of highly compensated employees.* The determination of which employees are highly compensated employees and which highly compensated employees are among the ten most highly compensated employees in making the look-back year calculation or the determination year calculation for a determination year will be made prior to the application of the rules in paragraph (a) of this A-11.

(2) *Determination of top-paid group and top-100 employees.* The determination of the number and identity of employees in the top-paid group under the look-back year calculation or the determination year calculation for a determination year and the identity of individuals in the top-100 employees under the determination year calculation for a determination year is made prior to application of the rules in paragraph (a) of this A-11.

(d) *Determination period.* The rules under paragraph (a) of this A-11 apply separately to the determination year and the look-back year. Thus, assuming there are no 5-percent owners, if employees A, B, C, D, E, F, G, H, I and J are the top 10 highly compensated employees in the 1988 look-back year, and employees F, G, H, I, J, K, L, M, N and O are the top 10 highly compensated employees in the 1989 determination year, then family aggregation would be required with respect to all fifteen of such employees (i.e. employees A, B, C, D, E, F, G, H, I, J, K, L, M, N, and O).

Q-12: Which individuals are family members for purposes of the aggregation rules in section 414(a)(6)(A) and A-11?

A-12: (a) *Definition of family member.* Individuals who are family members for purposes of these provisions include, with respect to any employee or former employee, such employee's or former employee's spouse and lineal ascendants or descendants and the spouses of such lineal ascendants and descendants. In determining whether an individual is a family member with respect to an employee or former employee, legal adoptions shall be taken into account.

(b) *Test period.* If an individual is a family member with respect to an employee or former employee on any day during the year, such individual is treated as a family member for the entire year. Thus, for example, if an individual is a family member with respect to an employee on the first day of a year, such individual continues to be a family member with respect to such employee throughout the year even though their relationship changes as a result of death or divorce.

Q-13: How is "compensation" determined for purposes of determining the group of "highly compensated employees."

A-13: (a) *In general.* For purposes of section 414(q), the term "compensation" means compensation within the meaning of section 415(c)(3) without regard to sections 125, 402(a)(8), and 402(h)(1)(B) and, in the case of employer contributions made pursuant to a salary reduction agreement, without regard to section 403(b). Thus, compensation includes elective or salary reduction contributions to a cafeteria plan, cash or deferred arrangement or tax-sheltered annuity.

(b) *Determination period.* For purposes of determining the group of highly compensated employees, compensation must be calculated on the basis of the applicable period for the determination year and look-back year respectively.

(c) *Compensation taken into account.* Only compensation received by an employee during the determination year or during the look-back year is considered in determining whether such employee is a highly compensated active employee under either the look-back year calculation or determination year calculation for such determination year. Thus, compensation is not annualized for purposes of determining an employee's compensation in the determination year or the look-back year in applying the rules of paragraph (a) of this A-13.

Q-14: What periods must be used for determining who is a highly compensated employee for a determination year?

A-14: (a) *Determination year and look-back year*—(1) *In general.* For purposes of determining the group of highly compensated employees for a determination year, the determination year calculation is made on the basis of the applicable year of the plan or other entity for which a determination is being made and the look-back year calculation is made on the basis of the twelve month period immediately preceding such year. Thus, in testing plans X and Y of an employer, if plan X has a calendar year plan year and plan Y has a July 1 to June 30 plan year, the determination year calculation and look-back year calculation for plan X must be made on the basis of the calendar year. Similarly, the determination year calculation and look-back year calculation for plan Y must be made on the basis of the July 1 to June 30 year.

(2) *Applicable year.* For purposes of this A-14, the applicable year is the plan year of the qualified plan or other employee benefit arrangement to which the definition of highly compensated employees is applicable as defined in the written plan document or otherwise identified in regulations pursuant to sections to which the definition of highly compensated employees is applicable. To the extent that the definition of highly compensated employees is applicable to entities or other arrangements that do not have an otherwise identified plan year, then either the calendar year or the employer's fiscal year may be treated as the plan year.

(3) *Look-back year.* The look-back year is never less than a twelve month period.

(b) *Calendar year calculation election*—(1) *In general.* An employer may elect to make the look-back year calculation for a determination year on the basis of the calendar year ending with or within the applicable determination year (or, in the case of a determination year that is shorter than twelve months, the calendar year ending with or within the twelve-month period ending with the end of the applicable determination year). In such case, the employer must make the determination year calculation for the determination year on the basis of the period (if any) by which the applicable determination year extends beyond such calendar year (i.e., the lag period). If the applicable year for which the determination is being made is the calendar year, the employer still may elect to make the calendar year calculation election under this A-14(b). In such case, the look-back year calculation is made on the basis of the calendar year determination year and, because there is no lag period, a separate determination year calculation under A-3(a)(2) of this §1.414(q)-1 is not required.

(2) *Lag period calculation.* In making the determination year calculation under A-3(a)(2) of this §1.414(q)-1 on the basis of the lag period, the dollar amounts applicable under A-3(a)(1)(B) and (C) of this §1.414(q)-1 are to be adjusted by multiplying such dollar amounts by a fraction, the numerator of which is the number of calendar months that are included in the lag period and the denominator of which is twelve.

(3) *Determination of active employees.* An employee will be considered an active employee for purposes of a determination year for which the calendar year calculation election is in effect so long as such employee performs services for the employer during the appli-

cable year for which the determination is being made. This is the case even if such employee does not perform services for the employer during the lag-period for such determination year.

(4) *Election requirement.* If the employer elects to make the calendar year calculation election with respect to one plan, entity, or arrangement, such election must apply with respect to all plans, entities, and arrangements of the employer. In addition, such election must be provided for in the plan.

(c) *Change in applicable years.* Where there is a change in the applicable year for which a determination is being made with respect to a plan entity, or other arrangement that is not subject to the calendar year calculation election, the look-back year calculation for the short applicable year is to be made on the basis of the twelve month period preceding the short applicable year (i.e., generally, the old applicable year) and the determination year calculation for the short applicable year is to be made on the basis of the short applicable year. In addition, the dollar amounts under A-3(a)(1)(B) and (C) are to be adjusted for such determination year calculation as if the short applicable year were a lag period under paragraph (b)(2) of this A-14.

(d) *Example.* The following examples illustrate the rules of this A-14:

Example 1.

Employer X has a single plan (Plan A) with an April 1 to March 31 plan year. Employer X makes no election to use the calendar year for the determination period. Therefore, in determining the group of highly compensated employees for the April 1, 1989 to March 31, 1990 plan year, the determination year is the plan year ending March 31, 1990 and the look-back year is the plan year ending March 31, 1989.

Example 2.

Assume the same facts given above. With respect to the plan year beginning in 1990, employer X elects to use the calendar year for the determination period. Therefore, in determining the group of highly compensated employees for the April 1, 1990 to March 31, 1991 plan year, the lag-period determination year is the period from January 1, 1991, through March 31, 1991, and the applicable look-back year is the 1990 calendar year.

Example 3.

Employer Y has a single plan (Plan B) with a calendar plan year. With respect to the plan year beginning in 1990, employer Y elects to make the look-back year calculation for the 1990 determination year on the basis of the calendar year ending with or within the 1990 determination year. Because employer Y's determination year is the 1990 calendar year there is no lag period and employer Y determines the group of highly compensated employees for purposes of the 1990 calendar plan year on the basis of such plan year alone.

Q-15: Is there any transition rule in determining the group of highly compensated employees for 1987 and 1988?

A-15: (a) *In general.* Solely for purposes of section 401(k)(3) and (m)(2) and solely for twelve-month plan years beginning in 1987 and 1988, an eligible employer may elect to define the group of highly compensated employees as the group consisting of 5-percent owners of the employer at any time during the plan year and employees who receive compensation in excess of $50,000 during the plan year. This rule would apply in lieu of the look-back year calculation and determination year calculation otherwise applicable under A-3(a) of this §1.414(q)-1. In addition, an eligible employer may elect to make the determinations permitted under this transition rule on the basis of the calendar year ending in the plan year and the period by which such plan year extends beyond such calendar year, in accordance with the rules of A-14(b), in lieu of making the determinations under this transition rule on the basis of the plan year for which the determinations are being made.

(b) *Eligible employers.* An employer is an eligible employer under this A-15 if such employer satisfies both of the following requirements:

(1) The employer does not maintain any top-heavy plan within the meaning of section 416 at any time during 1987 and 1988; and

(2) Under each plan of the employer to which section 401(k)(3) or 401(m)(2) is applicable, the group of eligible employees that comprises the highest 25% of eligible employees ranked on the basis of compensation includes at least one employee whose compensation is $50,000 or below. This requirement must be met separately with respect to each such plan of the employer.

(c) *Uniformity requirement.* An eligible employer may not make the election under paragraph (a) of this A-15 unless the election applies to all of the plans maintained by the employer to which section 401(k)(3) or 401(m)(2) applies.

(d) *Election requirements.* This election is operational and does not require a plan provision. [Temporary Reg. §1.414(q)-1T.]

☐ [*T.D.* 8173, 2-18-88. *Amended by T.D.* 8334, 1-31-91 *and T.D.* 8548, 6-23-94.]

(ii) Requirement

(4) Employees taken into account

(5) Example

(g) Safe harbor for separate lines of business that provide minimum or maximum benefits

(1) In general

(2) Minimum benefit required

(i) Applicability

(ii) Requirement

(iii) Defined benefit minimum

(A) In general

(B) Normal form and equivalent benefits

(C) Compensation definition

(D) Average compensation requirement

(E) Special rules

(iv) Defined contribution minimum

(A) In general

(B) Modified allocation definition for averaging

(3) Maximum benefit permitted

(i) Applicability

(ii) Requirement

(iii) Defined benefit maximum

(A) In general

(B) Determination of defined benefit maximum

(C) Adjustment for different compensation definitions

(D) Adjustment for certain subsidies

(iv) Defined contribution maximum

(4) Duplication of benefits or contributions

(i) Plans of the same type

(ii) Plans of different types

(iii) Special rule for floor-offset arrangements

(5) Certain contingency provisions ignored

(6) Employees taken into account

§ 1.414(r)-6. Qualified separate line of business—administrative scrutiny requirement—individual determinations.

(a) In general

(b) Authority to establish procedures.

§ 1.414(r)-7. Determination of the employees of an employer's qualified separate lines of business.

(a) Introduction

(1) In general

(2) Purposes for which this section applies

(b) Assignment procedure

(1) In general

(2) Assignment for the first testing day

(3) Assignment of new employees for subsequent testing days

(4) Special rule for employers using annual option under section 410(b)

(c) Assignment and allocation of residual shared employees

(1) In general

(2) Dominant line of business method of allocation

(i) In general

(ii) Dominant line of business

(iii) Employee assignment percentage

(A) *Determination of percentage*

(B) Employees taken into account

(iv) Option to apply reduced percentage

(v) Examples

(3) Pro-rata method of allocation

(i) In general

(ii) Allocation procedure

(iii) Examples

(4) HCE percentage ratio method of allocation

(i) In general

(ii) Highly compensated employee percentage assignment ratio

(iii) Allocation procedure

(5) Small group method

(i) In general

(ii) Size of group

(iii) Composition of qualified separate line of business

(iv) Reasonable allocation

§ 1.414(r)-8. Separate application of section 410(b).

(a) General rule

(b) Rules of separate application

(1) In general

(2) Satisfaction of section 410(b)(5)(B) on an employer-wide basis

(i) General rule

(ii) Application of facts and circumstances requirements under nondiscriminatory classification test

(iii) Modification of unsafe harbor percentage for plans satisfying ratio percentage test at 90 percent level

(A) General Rule

(B) Facts and circumstances alternative

(3) Satisfaction of section 410(b) on a qualified-separate-line-of-business basis

(4) Examples

(c) Coordination of section 401(a)(4) with section 410(b)

(1) General rule

(2) Examples

(d) Supplementary rules

(1) In general

(2) Definition of plan

(3) Employees of a qualified separate line of business

(4) Consequences of failure

§ 1.414(r)-9. Separate application of section 401(a)(26).

(a) General rule

(b) Requirements applicable to a plan

(c) Supplementary rules

(1) In general

(2) Definition of plan

(3) Employees of a qualified separate line of business

(4) Consequences of failure

§ 1.414(r)-10. Separate application of section 129(d)(8).—[Reserved]

§ 1.414(r)-11. Definitions and special rules.

(a) In general

(b) Definitions

(1) In general

(2) Substantial-service employee

(3) Top-paid employee

(4) Residual shared employee

(5) Testing year

(6) Testing day

(7) First testing day

(8) Section 401(a)(26) testing day

(c) Averaging rules

(1) In general

(2) Specified provisions

(3) Averaging of large fluctuations not permitted

(4) Consistency requirements

(c) *Flowchart.*—The following is a flowchart showing how the major provisions of §§ 1.414(r)-1 through 1.414(r)-6 are applied. [Reg. § 1.414(r)-0.]

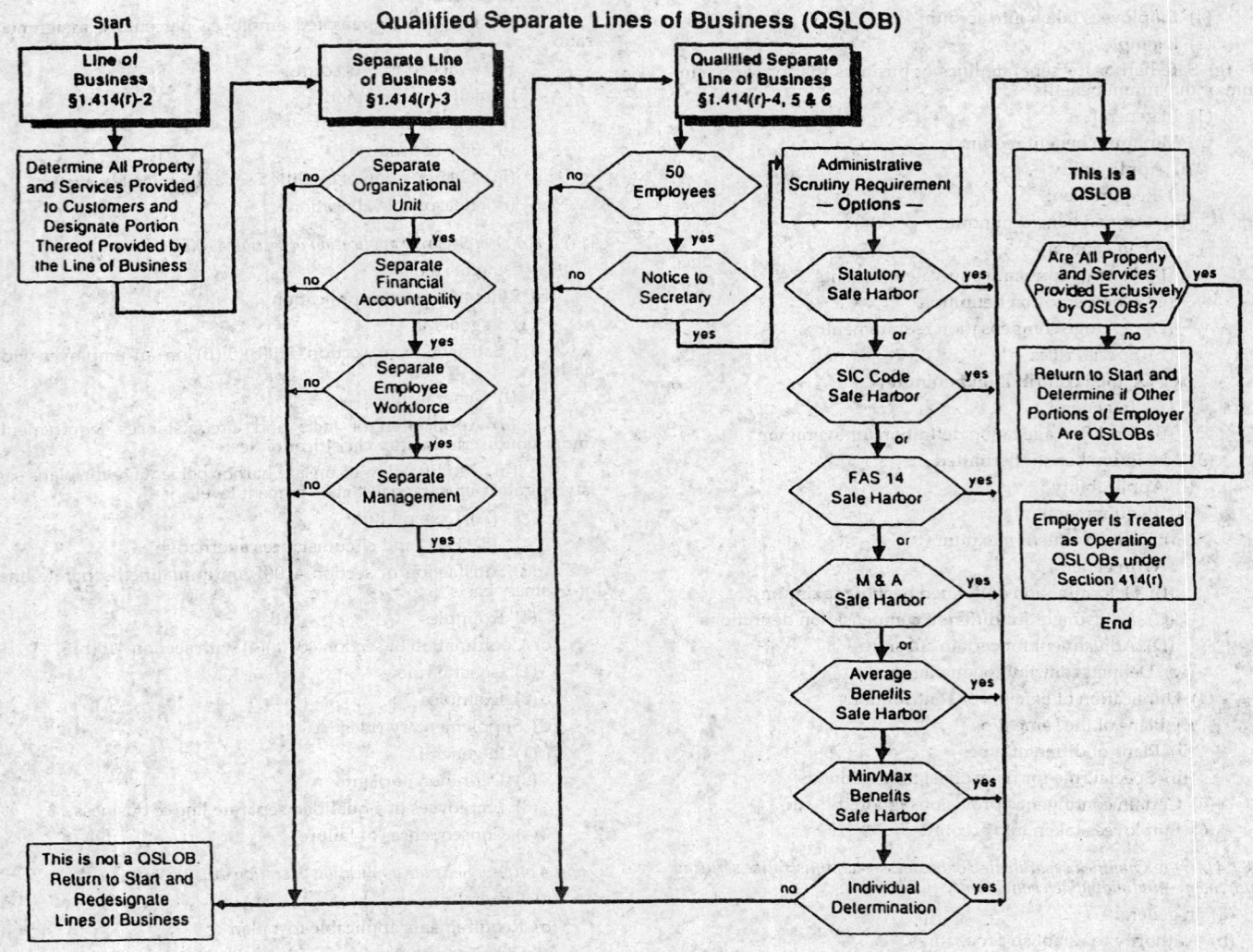

Qualified Separate Lines of Business (QSLOB)

☐ [*T.D. 8376, 12-2-91. Amended by T.D. 8548, 6-23-94.*]

[Reg. §1.414(r)-1]

§1.414(r)-1. Requirements applicable to qualified separate lines of business.—(a) *In general.*—Section 414(r) prescribes the conditions under which an employer is treated as operating qualified separate lines of business. If an employer is treated as operating qualified separate lines of business under section 414(r), certain requirements under the Code may be applied separately with respect to the employees of each qualified separate line of business. These requirements are limited to the minimum coverage requirements of section 410(b) (including the nondiscrimination requirements of section 401(a)(4)), the minimum participation requirements of section 401(a)(26), and the 55-percent average benefits test of section 129(d)(8). This section provides the exclusive rules for determining whether an employer is treated as operating qualified separate lines of business under section 414(r), as well as rules for applying the requirements of sections 410(b), 401(a)(26), and 129(d)(8) separately with respect to the employees of a qualified separate line of business.

(b) *Conditions under which an employer is treated as operating qualified separate lines of business.*—(1) *In general.*—An employer is treated as operating qualified separate lines of business under section 414(r) only if all property and services provided by the employer to its customers are provided exclusively by qualified separate lines of business. Thus, once an employer has determined its qualified separate lines of business under paragraph (b)(2) of this section, no portion of the employer may remain that is not included in a qualified separate line of business. In addition, once the employer has determined the employees of its qualified separate lines of business under paragraph (b)(3) of this section, every employee must be treated as an employee of a qualified separate line of business, and no employee may be treated as an employee of more than one qualified separate line of business.

(2) *Qualified separate line of business.*—(i) *In general.*—A qualified separate line of business is a portion of the employer that is a line of business within the meaning of paragraph (b)(2)(ii) of this section, that is also a separate line of business within the meaning of paragraph (b)(2)(iii) of this section, and, finally, that satisfies the requirements of section 414(r)(2) in accordance with paragraph (b)(2)(iv) of this section.

(ii) *Line of business.*—A line of business is a portion of an employer that is identified by the property or services it provides to customers of the employer. For this purpose, the employer is permitted to determine the lines of business it operates by designating the property and services that each of its lines of business provides to customers of the employer. Rules for determining an employer's lines of business are provided in §1.414(r)-2.

(iii) *Separate line of business.*—A separate line of business is a line of business that is organized and operated separately from the remainder of the employer. The determination of whether a line of business is organized and operated separately from the remainder of the employer is made on the basis of objective criteria. These criteria generally require that the line of business be organized into one or more separate organizational units (e.g., corporations, partnerships, or divisions), that the line of business constitute one or more distinct profit centers within the employer, and that no more than a moderate overlap exist between the employee workforce and management employed by the line of business and those employed by the remainder of the employer. Rules for determining whether a line of business is organized and operated separately from the remainder of the employer and thus constitutes a separate line of business are provided in §1.414(r)-3. These rules include an optional rule for vertically integrated lines of business.

(iv) *Qualified separate line of business.*—(A) *In general.*—A qualified separate line of business must satisfy the three statutory requirements in section 414(r)(2). A separate line of business that satisfies these three statutory requirements in accordance with paragraphs (b)(2)(iv)(B) through (b)(2)(iv)(D) of this section constitutes a qualified separate line of business.

(B) *Fifty-employee requirement.*—Under section 414(r)(2)(A), a separate line of business must have at least 50 employees. Rules for determining whether this requirement is satisfied are provided in §1.414(r)-4(b).

(C) *Notice requirement.*—Under section 414(r)(2)(B), the employer must notify the Secretary that it treats itself as operating qualified separate lines of business under section 414(r) for purposes of applying the requirements of section 410(b), 401(a)(26), or 129(d)(8) separately with respect to the employees of the separate line of business. Rules and procedures for complying with this requirement are provided in §1.414(r)-4(c).

(D) *Requirement of administrative scrutiny.*—Under section 414(r)(2)(C), a separate line of business must pass administrative scrutiny. A separate line of business may satisfy this requirement in one of two ways. First, a separate line of business that satisfies any of the safe harbors in §1.414(r)-5 satisfies the requirement of administrative scrutiny. These safe harbors implement the statutory safe harbor of section 414(r)(3) as well as the guidelines prescribed under section 414(r)(2)(C). Second, a separate line of business that does not satisfy any of the safe harbors in §1.414(r)-5 nonetheless satisfies the requirement of administrative scrutiny if the employer requests and receives an individual determination from the Commissioner that the separate line of business satisfies the requirement of administrative scrutiny. Rules and procedures applicable to requesting and receiving an individual determination are provided in §1.414(r)-6. A separate line of business is permitted to satisfy the requirement of administrative scrutiny in any manner permitted under this paragraph (b)(2)(iv)(D), regardless of how any other separate line of business of the employer satisfies the requirement.

(3) *Determining the employees of a qualified separate line of business.*—In order to apply certain provisions under these regulations, it is necessary to determine the employees of a qualified separate line of business. For these purposes, the employees of a qualified separate line of business consist of all employees who are substantial-service employees with respect to the qualified separate line of business, and all other employees who are assigned to the qualified separate line of business. Rules for making these determinations are provided in §1.414(r)-7. These rules apply solely for the purposes specified in these regulations (see §1.414(r)-7(a)(2) for a comprehensive listing of these purposes). These rules do not apply for any other purpose (e.g., the determination under §1.414(r)-3 of whether a line of business is organized and operated separately from the remainder of the employer).

(c) *Separate application of certain Code requirements to employees of a qualified separate line of business.*—(1) *In general.*—If an employer is treated as operating qualified separate lines of business under section 414(r) in accordance with paragraph (b) of this section, the requirements of sections 410(b), 401(a)(26), and 129(d)(8) may be applied separately with respect to the employees of each qualified separate line of business. Paragraphs (c)(2) through (c)(4) of this section provide for the separate application of these requirements. In general, the requirements of a Code section are applied separately with respect to the employees of a qualified separate line of business by treating those employees as if they were the only employees of the employer. Paragraph (c)(5) of this section prescribes the limited conditions under which other Code requirements may be applied separately with respect to the employees of a qualified separate line of business.

(2) *Separate application of section 410(b).*—(i) *General rule.*—Except as provided in paragraph (c)(2)(ii) of this section, an employer is permitted to apply the requirements of section 410(b) separately with respect to the employees of each qualified separate line of business operated by the employer only if the employer does so with respect to all its plans, all its employees, and all its qualified separate lines of business. For this purpose, the requirements of section 410(b) encompass the requirements of section 401(a)(4) (including, but not limited to, the permitted disparity rules of section 401(l), the actual deferral percentage test of section 401(k)(3) and the actual contribution percentage test of section 401(m)(2)). Rules for applying section 410(b) separately with respect to the employees of a qualified separate line of business are provided in §1.414(r)-8. An employer may apply the

rules of section 414(r) for purposes of section 410(b) even if it does not apply the rules of section 414(r) for purposes of section 401(a)(26).

(ii) *Special rule for employer-wide plans.*—Notwithstanding paragraph (c)(2)(i) of this section, an employer that is treated as operating qualified separate lines of business for purposes of section 410(b) in accordance with paragraph (b) of this section may apply the requirements of section 410(b) on an employer-wide rather than a qualified-separate-line-of-business basis with respect to any plan (within the meaning of §1.414(r)-8(d)(2), but without regard to the mandatory disaggregation rule of §1.410(b)-7(c)(4) for portions of a plan that benefit employees of different qualified separate lines of business) that benefits a group of employees that satisfies the percentage test of section 410(b)(1)(A) (i.e., benefits at least 70 percent of the employer's nonexcludable nonhighly compensated employees). If section 401(a)(4) requires that a group of employees under the plan described in the preceding sentence satisfy section 410(b) for purposes of satisfying section 401(a)(4), the percentage test of section 410(b)(1)(A) must be satisfied by each such group of employees. See §1.414(r)-8(c). The rules of this paragraph (c)(2)(ii) are illustrated by the following example.

Example. Employer A maintains a single profit-sharing plan, Plan W, and three pension plans, Plans X, Y and Z, each benefiting employees of a different one of Employer A's three qualified separate lines of business. Contributions to the profit-sharing plan are made pursuant to a cash or deferred arrangement in which all employees of Employer A are eligible to participate. Assume that, as a result, Plan W satisfies the requirements to be tested under this paragraph (c)(2)(ii). None of the pension plans benefits more than 70 percent of the nonexcludable nonhighly compensated employees of Employer A. Employer A is treated as operating qualified separate lines of business for purposes of applying section 410(b) to its qualified plans. The requirements of sections 410(b) and 401(a)(4) must therefore be applied to Plans X, Y and Z separately with respect to the employees of each of the three qualified separate line of business operated by Employer A. Since Plan W benefits at least 70 percent of the nonexcludable nonhighly compensated employees of Employer A, however, the requirements of sections 410(b) and 401(a)(4)(including section 401(k)) may be applied to Plan W on an employer-wide basis.

(3) *Separate application of section 401(a)(26).*—(i) *General rule.*—Except as provided in paragraph (c)(3)(ii) of this section, an employer is permitted to apply the requirements of section 401(a)(26) separately with respect to the employees of each qualified separate line of business operated by the employer only if the employer does so with respect to all its plans, all its employees, and all its qualified separate lines of business. Rules for applying the requirements of section 401(a)(26) separately with respect to the employees of a qualified separate line of business are provided in §1.414(r)-9. An employer may apply the rules of section 414(r) for purposes of section 401(a)(26) even if it does not apply the rules of section 414(r) for purposes of section 410(b).

(ii) *Special rule for employer-wide plans.*—Notwithstanding the first sentence of paragraph (c)(3)(i) of this section, an employer that is treated as operating qualified separate lines of business in accordance with paragraph (b) of this section for purposes of both sections 410(b) and 401(a)(26) may apply the requirements of section 401(a)(26) on an employer-wide rather than a qualified-separate-line-of-business basis with respect to any plan (within the meaning of §1.414(r)-9(c)(2), but without regard to the mandatory disaggregation rule of §1.401(a)(26)-2(d)(1)(iv) for portions of a plan that benefit employees of different qualified separate lines of business), but only if the special rule for employer-wide plans in paragraph (c)(2)(ii) of this section is applied to the same plan for the same plan year.

(4) *Separate application of section 129(d)(8).*—[Reserved]

(5) *Separate application of other Code requirements.*—Under no circumstance may the requirements of any section of the Code (other than a section described in paragraphs (c)(2) through (c)(4) of this section) be applied separately with respect to the employees of a qualified separate line of business unless the section specifically cross-references, or is specifically cross-referenced by, section 414(r). The Code sections whose requirements may not be applied separately with respect to the employees of a qualified separate line of business include, but are not limited to, sections 79(d)(3), 105(h), 117(d)(3), 120(c)(2), 125(g)(3), 127(b)(2), 129(d)(3), 132, 195, 401(a)(3) (as in effect on September 1, 1974), 414(q)(4), 501(c)(17)(A)(ii), 501(c)(17)(B)(iii), 501(c)(18)(B), and 505(b)(1)(A).

(d) *Application of requirements.*—(1) *In general.*—The requirements of paragraphs (b) and (c) of this section must be applied in accordance with the rules in this paragraph (d).

(2) *Interpretation.*—The provisions of this section and of §§1.414(r)-2 through 1.414(r)-11 are to be interpreted in a reasonable manner consistent with the purpose of section 414(r) to recognize an employer's operation of qualified separate lines of business for bona fide business reasons and not for reasons of evading the requirements of any section of the Code, including sections 410(b), 401(a)(26), and 129(d)(8). See section 414(r)(1) and (r)(7). Thus, for example, an employer is not permitted to apply these regulations in a manner that may literally comply with the other provisions of this section and of §§1.414(r)-2 through 1.414(r)-11, but that does not reflect the employer's operation of qualified separate lines of business for bona fide business reasons.

(3) *Separate operating units.*—No additional requirements beyond those provided in these regulations apply to a separate operating unit. Thus, a separate operating unit that satisfies the requirements of paragraph (b)(2) of this section is deemed to satisfy the geographic separation requirement of section 414(r)(7) and accordingly is treated as a qualified separate line of business for all purposes under this section, including the separate application of section 401(a)(26).

(4) *Certain mergers and acquisitions.*—A portion of an employer that is acquired in a transaction described in section 410(b)(6)(C) and §1.410(b)-2(f) (i.e., an asset or stock acquisition, merger, or other similar transaction involving a change in the employer of the employees of a trade or business) is deemed to satisfy the requirements to be a qualified separate line of business, other than the 50-employee requirement and the notice requirement of paragraphs (b)(2)(iv)(B) and (b)(2)(iv)(C) of this section, respectively. In addition, the acquired employees are not taken into account, and the property and services provided by the acquired portion to customers of the employer are disregarded, for purposes of determining whether the employer's remaining lines of business satisfy the requirements of §§1.414(r)-3 through 1.414(r)-6. The rules in this paragraph (d)(4) apply only for those testing years with first testing days that fall within the transition period described in section 410(b)(6)(C). For this purpose, the transition period described in section 410(b)(6)(C) lasts only for so long as the conditions in that section are satisfied. For the definition of "first testing day," see §1.414(r)-11(b)(7). See §1.414(r)-5(d)(4), *Example 1,* for an example of the application of the rule in this paragraph (d)(4). See also §1.414(r)-5(d) for an administrative scrutiny safe harbor applicable to certain separate lines of business acquired in a transaction described in this section.

(5) *Governmental and tax-exempt employers.*—(i) *General rule.*—Except as provided in paragraph (d)(5)(ii) of this section, the rules of this section are applicable in determining whether section 401(a)(26) is satisfied by a plan maintained by an employer that is exempt from tax under Subtitle A of the Internal Revenue Code (including a governmental plan within the meaning of section 414(d)). Similarly, except as provided in paragraph (d)(5)(ii) of this section, the rules of this section are applicable in determining whether section 410(b) is satisfied by a plan that is subject to section 410(b)(including by virtue of §1.410(b)-2(e)) and is maintained by an employer that is exempt from tax under Subtitle A of the Internal Revenue Code (including a governmental plan within the meaning of section 414(d)).

(ii) *Additional rules.*—[Reserved]

(6) *Testing year basis of application.*—(i) *Section 414(r).*—Whether an employer is treated as operating qualified separate lines of business under section 414(r) in accordance with paragraph (b) of this section is determined on a year-by-year basis with respect to the testing year. It is therefore possible for an employer to satisfy paragraph (b) of this section for one testing year and to fail to satisfy it for another testing year. It is also possible for an employer to satisfy paragraph (b) of this section for two testing years but to have designated its lines of business differently in each of those two testing years. In determining whether an employer satisfies paragraph (b) of this section for a testing year, the requirements of that paragraph are applied solely with respect to the testing year. Thus, all property and services provided by the employer to its customers during the testing year must be provided exclusively by portions of the employer that for the testing year constitute qualified separate lines of business. Furthermore, each employee of the employer must respectively be treated as an employee of one and only one of those qualified separate lines of business for all purposes with respect to the testing year.

(ii) *Sections 410(b), 401(a)(26), and 129(d)(8).*—For purposes of paragraph (c) of this section, relating to the separate application of sections 410(b), 401(a)(26), and 129(d)(8) to the employees of a qualified separate line of business, the determination whether an employer operates qualified separate lines of business in accordance with paragraph (b) of this section for a testing year generally applies for all plan years beginning in the testing year. Rules for the separate

application of sections 410(b), 401(a)(26), and 129(d)(8) are respectively provided in §§1.414(r)-8, 1.414(r)-9, and 1.414(r)-10.

(7) *Averaging rules.*—The employer is permitted to apply certain provisions of these regulations on the basis of a consecutive-year average (not to exceed five consecutive years) under the averaging rules of §1.414(r)-11(c).

(8) *Definitions.*—In applying the provisions of this section and of §§1.414(r)-2 through 1.414(r)-11, the definitions in §§1.414(r)-11(b) and 1.410(b)-9 govern, unless otherwise provided.

(9) *Effective date.*—(i) *General rule.*—The provisions of this section and of §§1.414(r)-2 through 1.414(r)-11 apply to plan years and testing years beginning on or after January 1, 1994 (on January 1, 1996, in the case of plans maintained by organizations exempt from income taxation under section 501(a), including plans subject to section 403(b)(12)(A)(i) (nonelective plans)).

(ii) *Reasonable compliance.*—(A) *In general.*—With respect to plan years beginning before the date on which the Commissioner begins issuing determinations under section 414(r)(2)(C), and on or after the first day of the first plan year to which section 414(r) applies under section 1112(a) of the Tax Reform Act of 1986, an employer is treated as operating qualified separate lines of business if the employer reasonably determines that it meets the requirements of section 414(r)(other than the requirement of administrative scrutiny under section 414(r)(2)(C)).

(B) *Determination of reasonable compliance.*—Whether an employer reasonably determines that it meets the requirements of section 414(r) generally will be determined on the basis of all relevant facts and circumstances, including the extent to which the employer has resolved unclear issues in its favor. For the period described in paragraph (d)(9)(ii)(A) of this section, the Internal Revenue Service will consider the employer's compliance with the terms of these final regulations (other than the requirement of administrative scrutiny under paragraph (b)(2)(iv)(D) of this section) to constitute a reasonable determination that the employer meets the requirements of section 414(r)(other than the requirement of administrative scrutiny under section 414(r)(2)(C)).

(C) *Effect on other plans.*—If an employer sponsors a plan that has a plan year beginning within the period described in paragraph (d)(9)(ii)(A) of this section, the employer's reasonable determination of its qualified separate lines of business for the testing year in which that plan year begins, and the allocation of employees to those qualified separate lines of business, must also be used for purposes of applying §1.414(r)-8 and §1.414(r)-9 for plan years that begin in that testing year but after the end of the period described in paragraph (d)(9)(ii)(A) of this section.

(e) *Additional rules.*—The Commissioner may, in revenue rulings, notices, and other guidance of general applicability, provide any additional rules that may be necessary or appropriate in applying the qualified separate line of business requirements of section 414(r). These additional rules may include, for example, new safe harbors in §1.414(r)-5. [Reg. §1.414(r)-1.]

☐ [*T.D. 8376, 12-2-91. Amended by T.D. 8548, 6-23-94.*]

[Reg. §1.414(r)-2]

§1.414(r)-2. Line of business.—(a) *General rule.*—A line of business is a portion of an employer that is identified by the property or services it provides to customers of the employer. For this purpose, an employer is permitted to determine its lines of business by designating the property or services that each of its lines of business provides to customers of the employer. Paragraph (b) of this section explains how an employer determines its lines of business for a testing year. Paragraph (c) of this section provides examples illustrating the application of this section.

(b) *Employer determination of its lines of business.*—(1) *In general.*—An employer determines its lines of business for a testing year first by identifying all the property and services it provides to its customers during the testing year, and then by designating which portion of the property and services is provided by each of its lines of business.

(2) *Property and services provided to customers.*—(i) *In general.*—Property, whether real or personal, tangible or intangible, is provided by an employer to a customer if the employer provides the property to or on behalf of the customer for consideration. Similarly, services are provided by an employer to a customer if the employer renders the services to or on behalf of the customer for consideration. An individual item of property or service is taken into account under this paragraph (b)(2) only if the employer provides the item to a person other than the employer in the ordinary course of a trade or business conducted by the employer and the person to whom the

employer provides the item is acting in the capacity of a customer of the employer. A type of tangible property is deemed to be provided to customers of the employer for purposes of this section if, with respect to a business that produces or manufactures that type of tangible property, the employer satisfies the special rule in §1.414(r)-3(d)(2)(iii)(B) for vertically integrated businesses.

(ii) *Timing of provision of property or services.*—Generally an employer determines its lines of business on the basis of the property and services it provides to its customers for consideration during the testing year. However, it is not necessary both that property or services actually be provided, and that consideration for the property or services actually be paid, during the current testing year. For an employer to be considered to provide property or services to customers for consideration during a testing year under this paragraph (b)(2), it is sufficient that the property or services actually be provided to customers during the testing year, the consideration actually be paid during the testing year, or the employer actually incur significant costs during the testing year associated with the provision of the property or services to a specified customer or specified customers.

(3) *Employer designation.*—(i) *In general.*—Once the employer has identified all the property and services it provides to its customers during the testing year under paragraph (b)(2) of this section, the employer determines its lines of business for the testing year by designating which portion of those property and services is provided by each of its lines of business. For this purpose, the employer must apportion all the property and services identified under paragraph (b)(2) of this section among its lines of business. An employer generally is not required to designate its lines of business for the testing year in the same manner as it designates its lines of business for any other testing year.

(ii) *Ability to combine unrelated types of property or services in a single line of business.*—For purposes of this paragraph (b)(3), there is no requirement that a line of business provide only one type of property or service, or only related types of property or services. Nor is there any requirement that a line of business provide solely property or solely services. Thus, the employer is permitted to combine in a single line of business dissimilar types of property or services that are otherwise unrelated to one another.

(iii) *Ability to separate related types of property or services into two or more lines of business.*—For purposes of this paragraph (b)(3), there is no requirement that all property or services of related types or the same type be provided by a single line of business. Thus, the employer is permitted to designate two or more lines of business that provide related types of property or services, or the same type of property or service. An employer might designate two or more lines of business that provide property or services of related types or the same type, for example, where the lines of business manufacture, prepare, or provide the property or services in different geographic areas (e.g., in different regions of the country or the world), or at different levels in the chain of commercial distribution (e.g., wholesale versus retail), or in different types of transactions (e.g., sale versus lease), or for different types of customers (e.g., governmental versus private), or subject to different legal constraints (e.g., regulated versus unregulated), or if the lines of business have developed differently (e.g., one line of business was acquired while another line of business developed internally). Notwithstanding the foregoing, an employer is not permitted to designate two or more lines of business that provide property or services of related types or the same type, if the employer's designation is unreasonable. An employer's designation would be unreasonable, for example, if the designation separated two types of property or services in different lines of business, but the employer did not provide those types of property or services separately from one another to its customers. Similarly, an employer's designation would be unreasonable if it separated two types of property or services in different lines of business, but the provision of one type of property or service was merely ancillary or incidental to, or regularly associated with, the provision of the other type of property or service. See generally §1.414(r)-1(d)(2) (requiring an employer's operation of qualified separate lines of business to be for bona fide business reasons).

(iv) *Affiliated service groups.*—An employer is not permitted to designate its lines of business in a manner that results in separating employees of an affiliated service group (within the meaning of section 414(m)) from other employees of the employer. See section 414(r)(8).

(c) *Examples.*—(1) *In general.*—Paragraphs (c)(2) and (c)(3) of this section provide examples that illustrate the application of this section.

(2) *Examples illustrating employer designation.*—The following examples illustrate the application of paragraph (b)(3) of this section relating to an employer's designation of the property or services provided to customers by each of its lines of business.

Example 1. Employer A is a domestic conglomerate engaged in the manufacture and sale of consumer food and beverage products and the provision of data processing services to private industry. Employer A provides no other property or services to its customers. Pursuant to paragraph (b)(3) of this section, Employer A apportions all the property and services it provides to its customers among three lines of business, one providing all its consumer food products, a second providing all its consumer beverage products, and a third providing all its data processing services. Employer A has three lines of business for purposes of this section.

Example 2. The facts are the same as in *Example 1*, except that Employer A determines that neither the consumer food products line of business nor the consumer beverage products line of business would satisfy the separateness criteria of §1.414(r)-3 for recognition as a separate line of business. Accordingly, pursuant to paragraph (b)(3) of this section, Employer A apportions all the property and services it provides to its customers between only two lines of business, one providing all its consumer food and beverage products, and a second providing all its data processing services. Employer A has two lines of business for purposes of this section.

Example 3. The facts are the same as in *Example 2*, except that Employer A also owns and operates a regional commuter airline, a professional basketball team, a pharmaceutical manufacturer, and a leather tanning company. Pursuant to paragraph (b)(3) of this section, Employer A apportions all the property and services it provides to its customers among three lines of business, one providing all its consumer food and beverage products, a second providing all its data processing services, and a third providing all the other property and services provided to customers through Employer A's regional commuter airline, professional basketball team, pharmaceutical manufacturer, and leather tanning company. Even though the third line of business includes dissimilar types of property and services that are otherwise unrelated to one another, paragraph (b)(3)(ii) of this section permits Employer A to combine these property and services in a single line of business. Employer A has three lines of business for purposes of this section.

Example 4. The facts are the same as in *Example 2*, except that Employer A has recently acquired Corporation L, whose only product is a well-known brand of gourmet ice cream. Although Employer A manufactures and sells other ice cream products, it does not manufacture or market the newly acquired brand of gourmet ice cream except through Corporation L. Pursuant to paragraph (b)(3) of this section, Employer A apportions all the property and services it provides to its customers among three lines of business, one providing only the newly acquired brand of gourmet ice cream, a second providing all its other consumer food and beverage products (including the other ice cream products manufactured and sold by Employer A), and a third providing all its data processing services. Even though the gourmet ice cream line of business provides the same type of property as the consumer food and beverage line of business (i.e., ice cream), paragraph (b)(3)(iii) of this section permits Employer A to separate its ice cream products between two different lines of business. Employer A has three lines of business for purposes of this section.

Example 5. The facts are the same as in *Example 2*, except that Employer A operates the data processing services portion of its business in two separate subsidiaries, one serving customers in the eastern half of the United States and the other serving customers in the western half of the United States. Pursuant to paragraph (b)(3) of this section, Employer A apportions all the property and services it provides to its customers among three lines of business, one providing all its consumer food and beverage products, a second providing data processing services to customers in the eastern half of the United States, and a third providing data processing services to customers in the western half of the United States. Even though the second and third lines of business provide the same type of service (i.e., data processing services), paragraph (b)(3)(iii) of this section permits Employer A to separate its data processing services into two lines of business. Employer A has three lines of business for purposes of this section.

Example 6. Employer B is a diversified engineering firm offering civil, chemical, and aeronautical engineering services to government and private industry. Employer B provides no other property or services to its customers. Employer B operates the aeronautical engineering services portion of its business as two separate divisions, one serving federal government customers and the other serving customers in private industry. Pursuant to paragraph (b)(3) of this section, Employer B apportions all the property and services it provides to its customers among four lines of business, one providing all its civil engineering services, a second providing all its chemical engineering services, a third providing aeronautical engineering services to federal government customers, and a fourth providing aeronautical engineering services to customers in private industry. Even though the third and fourth lines of business include the same type of service (i.e., aeronautical engineering services), paragraph (b)(3)(iii) of this section permits Employer B to separate its aeronautical engineering services into two lines of business. Employer B has four lines of business for purposes of this section.

Example 7. Among its other business activities, Employer C manufactures industrial diesel generators. At no additional cost to its buyers, Employer C warrants the proper functioning of its diesel generators for a one-year period following sale. Pursuant to its warranty, Employer C provides labor and parts to repair or replace any components that malfunction within the one-year warranty period. Because Employer C does not provide the industrial diesel generators, on the one hand, and the warranty repair services and replacement parts, on the other hand, separately from one another to its customers, under paragraph (b)(3)(iii) of this section it would be unreasonable for Employer C to separate these property and services in different lines of business.

Example 8. Among its other business activities, Employer D leases office photocopying equipment. Employer D also provides photo-copying supplies and repair services to its lessees for a separate charge. Employer D generally does not provide such supplies and repair services to persons other than its lessees. Lessees of Employer D's equipment are permitted to use photo-copying supplies and repair services from suppliers other than Employer D. Because the provision of the photo-copying supplies and repair services are merely ancillary or incidental to the provision of the leased photo-copiers, under paragraph (b)(3)(iii) of this section it would be unreasonable for Employer D to separate these property and services in different lines of business.

Example 9. Employer E operates a medical clinic. The employees of the clinic include physicians, nurses, and laboratory technicians, all of whom participate in providing medical and related services to patients of the clinic. Under paragraph (b)(3)(iii) of this section, it would be unreasonable for Employer E to separate the services of the physicians, nurses, and laboratory technicians in different lines of business.

Example 10. Employer F is a law firm. The employees of the firm include lawyers, paralegals, and secretaries, all of whom participate in rendering legal and related services to clients of the firm. Under paragraph (b)(3)(iii) of this section, it would be unreasonable for Employer F to separate the services of the lawyers, paralegals, and secretaries in different lines of business.

Example 11. Employer G is a management consulting firm. The employees of the firm include management consultants, secretaries, and other support staff personnel, all of whom participate in rendering management consulting and related services to clients of the firm. Under paragraph (b)(3)(iii) of this section, it would be unreasonable for Employer G to separate the services of the management consultants, secretaries, and other support staff personnel in different lines of business.

(3) *Examples illustrating property and services provided to customers.*—The following examples illustrate the application of paragraph (b)(2) of this section relating to property and services provided to customers of the employer.

Example 1. Employer H operates several dairy farms and dairy product processing plants. The dairy farms provide part of their output of milk and milk by-products to Employer H's dairy product processing plants and also sell part to retail distributors unrelated to Employer H. The dairy farms' provision of milk and milk by-products to Employer H's dairy product processing plants does not constitute the provision of property or services to customers of Employer H because the milk and milk by-products are not provided to a person other than employer H. However, the dairy farms' provision of milk and milk by-products to independent retail distributors does constitute the provision of property or services to customers of Employer H under paragraph (b)(2) of this section.

Example 2. The facts are the same as in *Example 1*, except that the dairy farms provide their entire output of milk and milk by-products to Employer H's dairy product processing plants. The dairy farms' provision of milk and milk by-products to the dairy product processing plants generally does not constitute the provision of property or services to customers of Employer H because the milk and milk by-products are not provided to a person other than Employer H. However, paragraph (b)(2)(i) of this section provides a special rule for vertically integrated businesses that satisfy §1.414(r)-3(d)(2)(iii)(B). If §1.414(r)-3(d)(2)(iii)(B) is satisfied, then, under the special rule of paragraph (b)(2)(i) of this section, the milk and milk by-products are deemed to be provided to customers of *Employer H.*

Example 3. Among its other business activities, Employer J manufactures automobiles. Employer J operates a cafeteria at one of its automobile manufacturing facilities. The cafeteria is intended primarily for use by employees of Employer J, but non-employees are not prohibited from using the cafeteria. The cafeteria charges the same prices to employees and non-employees. Under paragraph (b)(2) of this section, the provision of cafeteria services to employees of Employer J does not constitute the provision of property or services to customers of Employer J, because the cafeteria services are provided to the employees in their capacity as employees of Employer J and not as customers of Employer J.

Example 4. Employer K sells books and periodicals to members of the public and provides telecommunications services to private industry. Employer K periodically acquires and disposes of businesses in both asset and stock transactions. In addition, for its own investment purposes, Employer K acquires and disposes of corporate and other securities. Under paragraph (b)(2) of this section, the sale by Employer K of businesses and investment securities does not constitute the provision of property or services to customers of Employer K, because the sales are not made in the ordinary course of a trade or business conducted by Employer K. However, the sale of published materials and the provision of telecommunications services to persons unrelated to Employer K does constitute the provision of property or services to customers of Employer K.

Example 5. Employer L is active in the financial services industry. Subsidiary 1 of Employer L is a brokerage firm that is regulated as a broker-dealer under applicable federal and state law. In its capacity as a dealer, Subsidiary 1 holds in its own inventory securities of unrelated corporations and regularly sells these securities to unrelated persons. Under paragraph (b)(2) of this section, the sale by Subsidiary 1 of the securities to unrelated persons constitutes the provision of property or services to customers of Employer L, because the sales are made in the ordinary course of Subsidiary 1's trade or business as a broker-dealer.

Example 6. The facts are the same as in *Example 5.* Subsidiary 2 of Employer L is an insurance company that is regulated under applicable state insurance laws. In managing its investments, Subsidiary 2 regularly makes use of the brokerage services of Subsidiary 1 (which Subsidiary 1 regularly provides to unrelated persons as well). Under paragraph (b)(2) of this section, Subsidiary 1's provision of brokerage services to Subsidiary 2 does not constitute the provision of property or services to customers of Employer L, because the brokerage services are not provided to a person other than Employer L. However, Subsidiary 1's provision of brokerage services to unrelated persons does constitute the provision of property or services to customers of Employer L.

Example 7. Employer M is a shipbuilder. In a testing year, Employer M enters into a contract with a customer to construct a new cargo ship for delivery two years later. Employer M incurs significant costs designing and planning for the production of the new ship during the testing year, but receives no payments from the customer during that year. Under paragraph (b)(2) of this section, Employer M is treated as providing the cargo ship to the customer during the testing year.

Example 8. The facts are the same as in *Example 7*, except that, pursuant to a request from the customer, Employer M also incurred significant costs developing a prototype and submitting a bid on the new cargo ship in the prior testing year, and that these costs were not reimbursed by the customer. Under paragraph (b)(2) of this section, Employer M is also treated as providing the cargo ship to the customer in the prior testing year. [Reg. §1.414(r)-2.]

☐ [*T.D. 8376, 12-2-91. Amended by T.D. 8548, 6-23-94.*]

[Reg. §1.414(r)-3]

§1.414(r)-3. Separate line of business.—(a) *General rule.*—A separate line of business is a line of business (as determined under §1.414(r)-2) that is organized and operated separately from the remainder of the employer. Paragraph (b) of this section sets forth the rules for determining whether a line of business is organized and operated separately from the remainder of the employer. Paragraph (c) of this section provides certain supplementary rules necessary to apply the requirements of paragraph (b) of this section, as well as examples illustrating the application of those requirements. Paragraph (d) of this section provides an optional rule for lines of business that are vertically integrated.

(b) *Separate organization and operation.*—(1) *In general.*—A line of business is organized and operated separately from the remainder of the employer for a testing year only if it satisfies all the requirements of paragraphs (b)(2) through (b)(5) of this section for the testing year.

(2) *Separate organizational unit.*—The line of business must be formally organized as a separate organizational unit or group of separate organizational units within the employer. For this purpose, an organizational unit is a corporation, partnership, division, or other unit having a similar degree of organizational formality. This requirement must be satisfied on every day of the testing year.

(3) *Separate financial accountability.*—The line of business must be a separate profit center or group of separate profit centers within the employer. This requirement must be satisfied on every day of the testing year. In addition, the employer must maintain books and records that provide separate revenue and expense information that is used for internal planning and control with respect to each profit center comprising the line of business.

(4) *Separate employee workforce.*—The line of business must have its own separate employee workforce. A line of business has its own separate workforce only if at least 90 percent of the employees who provide services to the line of business, and who are not substantial-service employees with respect to any other line of business, are substantial-service employees with respect to the line of business. See paragraph (c)(2) of this section to determine how the percentage in the preceding sentence is calculated for the testing year.

(5) *Separate management.*—The line of business must have its own separate management. A line of business has its own separate management only if at least 80 percent of the employees who are top-paid employees with respect to the line of business are substantial-service employees with respect to the line of business. See paragraph (c)(3) of this section to determine how the percentage in the preceding sentence is calculated for the testing year.

(c) *Supplementary rules.*—(1) *In general.*—This paragraph (c) provides certain supplementary rules necessary to apply the requirements of paragraph (b) of this section, as well as examples illustrating the application of those requirements.

(2) *Determination of separate employee workforce.*—The percentage in paragraph (b)(4) of this section is the fraction (expressed as a percentage)—

(i) The numerator of which is the number of substantial-service employees with respect to the line of business within the meaning of §1.414(r)-11(b)(2); and

(ii) The denominator of which is the total number of employees who provide services to the line of business within the meaning of paragraph (c)(5) of this section and who are not substantial-service employees with respect to any other line of business.

(3) *Determination of separate management.*—The percentage in paragraph (b)(5) of this section is the fraction (expressed as a percentage)—

(i) The numerator of which is the number of employees who are both top-paid employees and substantial-service employees with respect to the line of business within the meaning of §1.414(r)-11(b)(3) and (2), respectively; and

(ii) The denominator of which is the total number of top-paid employees with respect to the line of business within the meaning of §1.414(r)-11(b)(3).

(4) *Employees taken into account.*—For purposes of applying this paragraph (c), only employees who are employees on the first testing day are taken into account. For this purpose, there are no excludable employees except nonresident aliens described in section 410(b)(3)(C). Consequently, all other employees who are employees on the first testing day are taken into account, including collectively bargained employees. For the definition of first testing day, see §1.414(r)-11(b)(7).

(5) *Services taken into account.*—(i) *Provision of services to a line of business.*—An employee provides services to a line of business if more than a negligible portion of the employee's services contributes to providing the property or services provided by the line of business to customers of the employer. All of the services of each employee who provides services to the employer contribute, whether directly or indirectly, to the provision of property or services to customers of the employer, and therefore each employee who provides services to the employer must be treated as providing more than a negligible portion of the employee's services to one or more lines of business operated by the employer.

(ii) *Period for which services are provided.*—Only services performed by an employee during the testing year that contribute to providing the property or services provided by a line of business to customers are taken into account. An employee's services during the testing year are considered to contribute to providing the property or services provided by a line of business to customers of the employer if—

(A) The employee's services during the testing year contribute to providing such property or services to customers of the employer during the testing year; or

(B) It is reasonably anticipated that the employee's services during the testing year will contribute to providing such property and services to customers of the employer after the close of the testing year.

(iii) *Optional rule for employees who change status.*—(A) *In general.*—Solely for purposes of the separateness rules of this section and the assignment rules of §1.414(r)-7, if an employee changes status as described in paragraph (c)(5)(iii)(B) of this section, an employer may, for up to three consecutive testing years after the base year (within the meaning of paragraph (c)(5)(iii)(B)(*1*) or (*2*) of this section), treat the employee as providing the same level of service to its lines of business as the employee provided in the base year.

(B) *Change in employee's status.*—An employee changes status as described in this paragraph (c)(5)(iii)(B) if—

(*1*) For a testing year (the base year), the employee was a substantial-service employee with respect to a qualified separate line of business of the employer (prior line of business) and, for the immediately succeeding testing year, the employee is not a substantial-service employee with respect to that prior line of business; or

(*2*) For a testing year (the base year), the employee was a residual shared employee and, for the immediately succeeding testing year, the employee is a substantial-service employee with respect to a qualified separate line of business.

(6) *Examples of the separate employee workforce requirement.*—The following examples illustrate the application of the separate employee workforce requirement in paragraph (b)(4) of this section and the supplementary rules of this paragraph (c). Unless otherwise specified, it is assumed that the employees and their services described in these examples are taken into account under paragraphs (c)(4) and (5) of this section for the testing year and that the employer does not use the option under §1.414(r)-11(b)(2) to treat employees who provide less than 75 percent of their services to a line of business as substantial-service employees with respect to the line of business.

Example 1. Employer A operates three lines of business as determined under §1.414(r)-2. One of Employer A's lines of business manufactures and sells tires and other automotive products. Employee M is a tire press operator in Employer A's tire factory. Employee N is the manager of the tire factory. Under these facts, the services of Employees M and N contribute to providing tires to customers of Employer A. Both employees therefore provide services to Employer A's tire and automotive products line of business within the meaning of paragraph (c)(5) of this section.

Example 2. The facts are the same as in *Example 1.* In addition, none of the services of Employees M and N that contribute to providing property or services to customers contribute to providing any property or service other than tires to customers of Employer A. Under these facts, Employees M and N provide at least 75 percent of their respective services to Employer A's tire and automotive products line of business. Therefore Employees M and N are substantial-service employees with respect to Employer A's tire and automotive products line of business within the meaning of §1.414(r)-11(b)(2), and do not provide any services within the meaning of paragraph (c)(5) of this section to any of Employer A's other lines of business. Moreover, because Employees M and N provide at least 75 percent of their services to Employer A's tire and automotive products line of business and are substantial-service employees with respect to that line, they are disregarded in applying paragraph (b)(4) of this section to any other line of business, even if they provide services to the other line.

Example 3. The facts are the same as in *Example 2.* Employer A's second line of business manufactures and sells construction machinery, and Employer A's third line of business manufactures and sells agricultural equipment. As part of these lines of business, Employer A operates a construction machinery factory and an agricultural equipment factory on the same site as the tire factory described in *Example 2.* Employer A's facilities at the site include a health clinic and a fitness center that serve the employees of the construction machinery factory, the agricultural equipment factory, and the tire factory. Employee O is a nurse in the health clinic, and Employee P is a fitness instructor in the fitness center. Both employees therefore provide services within the meaning of paragraph (c)(5) of this section to Employer A's tire and automotive products line of business, construction machinery line of business, and agricultural equipment line of business. In addition, under these facts, Employer A determines that approximately 33 percent of the services of Employees O and P are provided to each of Employer A's three lines of business. As a result, neither Employee O or P provide at least 75 percent of their respective services to any of Employer A's lines of business. Therefore, Employees O and P are not substantial-service employees with respect to any of Employer A's three lines of business within the meaning of §1.414(r)-11(b)(2).

Example 4. The facts are the same as in *Example 3.* Employee Q is the president and chief executive officer of Employer A and is responsible for reviewing the performance of all Employer A's lines of business. Under these facts, the services of Employee Q contributes to providing property and services to customers of each of Employer A's three lines of business. Employee Q therefore provides services to each of these three lines of business. Employer A determines that Employee Q provides the following percentages of his services to Employer A's three lines of business: tire and automotive products—40 percent; construction machinery—40 percent, and agricultural equipment—20 percent. Employee Q does not provide at least 75 percent of his services to any of Employer A's lines of business. Therefore, Employee Q is not a substantial-service employee with respect to any of Employer A's three lines of business within the meaning of § 1.414(r)-11(b)(2).

Example 5. The facts are the same as in *Example 4,* except that Employer A also owns 75 percent of Corporation X. Corporation X is not treated as part of Employer A within the meaning of § 1.410(b)-9. Employee R is an accountant in the accounting department of Employer A. Employee R devotes all of his time to maintaining the accounting book and records of the tire and automotive products line of business of Employer A and the accounting books and records of Corporation X. Employer A determines that Employee R provides 40 percent of his services directly to the tire and automotive products line of business. Employer A also determines that Employee R provides the following percentages of the remainder of Employee R's services (i.e., his provision of services of maintaining the accounting books and records of Corporation X) indirectly to Employer A's three lines of business by virtue of the services he provides to Corporation X: tire and automotive products—25 percent; construction machinery—20 percent, and agricultural equipment—15 percent. Therefore, Employee R provides 65 percent of his services to the tire and automotive products line of business of Employer A (i.e., 40 percent directly and 25 percent indirectly). Under the definition of substantial-service employee in § 1.414(r)-11(b)(2), Employer A may treat Employee R as a substantial-service employee with respect to the tire and automotive products line of business because Employee R provides at least 50 percent of his services to that line. In that case, Employee R would be disregarded in applying paragraph (b)(4) of this section to the construction machinery and agricultural equipment lines of business.

Example 6. The facts are the same as in *Example 5.* Employee S is a lawyer in the legal department located at the headquarters who devotes all her time to product liability suits filed against the construction machinery line of business. Under these facts, the services of Employee S contribute to providing property and services to customers of Employer A in the construction machinery line of business, and therefore Employee S provides services to that line of business. Because Employee S's services do not contribute to providing property or services in any other of Employer A's lines of business within the meaning of paragraph (c)(5) of this section, Employee S provides more than 75 percent of her services to the construction machinery line of business and therefore is a substantial-service employee with respect to Employer A's construction machinery line of business within the meaning of § 1.414(r)-11(b)(2).

Example 7. The facts are the same as in *Example 6.* Employer A also maintains a separate facility that houses a centralized procurement, marketing, and billing operation for all of its lines of business. None of the procurement, marketing, or billing employees specializes in any particular line of business. Under these facts, the services of the procurement, marketing, and billing employees contribute to providing property and services to customers of Employer A in each of Employer A's three lines of business. Employer A determines that each of the procurement, marketing, and billing employees provides approximately an equal proportion of their services to each of Employer A's three lines of business. These employees therefore provide services to all of Employer A's lines of business within the meaning of paragraph (c)(5) of this section. However, none of them provides at least 75 percent of his services to any line of business. Therefore, these employees are not substantial-service employees with respect to any of Employer A's three lines of business within the meaning of § 1.414(r)-11(b)(2).

Example 8. The facts are the same as in *Example 7.* Employee T works for the construction machinery line of business. During the testing year, he is temporarily detailed to the agricultural equipment line of business. His temporary detail lasts for one week, after which he returns to his regular duties with the construction machinery line of business. Under these facts, Employee T does not provide more than a negligible portion of his services during the testing year to the agricultural equipment line of business. Accordingly, Employee T does not provide services to the agricultural equipment line of business within the meaning of paragraph (c)(5) of this section. In addition, because Employee T provides at least 75 percent of his services to the construction machinery line of business, Employee T is a substantial-service employee with respect to Employer A's agricultural equipment line of business within the meaning of § 1.414(r)-11(b)(2).

Example 9. The facts are the same as in *Example 8,* except that, during the testing year but before the first testing day, Employee T retires from employment with Employer A. Under paragraph (c)(5)(ii) of this section, Employee T is not taken into account in

determining whether Employer A's construction machinery line of business has its own separate employee workforce within the meaning of paragraph (b)(4) of this section.

Example 10. Employer B is a multinational controlled group of corporations that engages in the exploration, production, refining, and marketing of petrochemical products. Employer B operates two lines of business as determined under § 1.414(r)-2. The first line of business (the "exploration, production, and refining line of business") provides lubricating oil, gasoline, and other petrochemical products to wholesale customers of Employer B as well as to the second line of business. The wholesale customers of Employer B include independent jobbers, independent franchisees that operate retail filling stations under Employer B's trademark and tradename, as well as chemical and plastics manufacturers. The second line of business (the "retail marketing line of business") provides lubricating oil and gasoline products to retail customers of Employer B through filling stations owned and operated by Employer B. Employee U is an attendant at a filling station owned and operated by Employer B. Employee U performs no other services for Employer B. Under these facts, Employee U provides at least 75 percent of his services to Employer B's retail marketing line of business and therefore is a substantial-service employee with respect to that line of business within the meaning of § 1.414(r)-11(b)(2), and does not provide any services within the meaning of paragraph (c)(5) of this section to any of Employer B's other lines of business.

Example 11. The facts are the same as in *Example 10.* Employer B operates a refinery that produces lubricating oil, gasoline, and other petrochemical products. Employee V is an operating engineer at the refinery who is involved at a stage in the refining process before lubricating oil and gasoline products have been separated from other types of petrochemical products. Employee V performs no other services for Employer B. Under these facts, Employee V's services contribute to providing property and services to customers of Employer B in both the exploration, production, and refining line of business and the retail marketing line of business. Employee V therefore provides services to both lines of business within the meaning of paragraph (c)(5) of this section. See paragraph (d) of this section, however, for an optional rule for vertically integrated lines of business.

Example 12. The facts are the same as in *Example 11.* Employee W is a petroleum engineer who conducts geological studies of potential future drilling sites. Although Employee W's services during the testing year will not contribute to providing lubricating oil, gasoline, and other petrochemical products to customers of Employer B during the testing year, it is reasonably anticipated (in accordance with paragraph (c)(5)(ii)(B) of this section) that her services during the testing year will contribute to providing such products to customers of Employer B after the close of the testing year. Under these facts, Employee W provides her services to both of Employer B's lines of business within the meaning of paragraph (c)(5) of this section.

(7) *Examples of the separate management requirement.*—The following examples illustrate the application of the separate management requirement in paragraph (b)(5) of this section and the supplementary rules of this paragraph (c). Unless otherwise specified, it is assumed that employees who provide services to a line of business are not substantial-service employees with respect to any other line of business and that, in determining the top-paid employees with respect to a line of business, the employer is using the option under § 1.414(r)-11(b)(3) to disregard all employees who provide less than 25 percent of their services to that line of business.

Example 1. (a) Employer C operates three lines of business as determined under § 1.414(r)-2. One of its lines of business is the operation of a chain of athletic equipment and apparel stores. Of Employer C's total workforce, 12,000 employees provide more than a negligible amount of the services they provide to Employer C to the athletic equipment and apparel stores line of business, within the meaning of paragraph (c)(5) of this section. Of the 1,200 employees who constitute the top ten percent by compensation of those 12,000 employees, 930 are substantial-service employees with respect to that line of business. Because 930 is 77.5 percent of 1,200, less than 80 percent of the top-paid employees with respect to the line of business are substantial-service employees with respect to that line of business. Therefore, Employer C's athletic equipment and apparel stores line of business does not have its own separate management under paragraph (b)(5) of this section.

(b) Assume that, in determining the top-paid employees with respect to the athletic equipment and apparel stores line of business, Employer C chooses to disregard all employees who provide less than 25 percent of their services to the line of business as permitted under the definition in § 1.414(r)-11(b)(3). Of the 12,000 employees who provide more than a negligible amount of their services to the athletic equipment and apparel stores line of business, 10,000 provide at least 25 percent of their services to that line. Of the 1,000 employees who constitute the top ten percent by compensation of those

10,000 employees, 930 are substantial-service employees with respect to the athletic equipment and apparel stores line of business. Because 930 is 93 percent of 1,000, at least 80 percent of the top-paid employees with respect to the line of business are substantial-service employees with respect to that line of business. Therefore, Employer C's athletic equipment and apparel stores line of business has its own separate management and satisfies the requirement of paragraph (b)(5) of this section.

Example 2. The facts are the same as in *Example 1.* Employee X is a vice president of the accounting department located at the headquarters, who devotes all of his time supervising the staff of Employer C's accounting department. Employer C determines that 10 percent of Employee X's services contribute to providing property and services to customers of Employer C's athletic equipment and apparel stores line of business and 45 percent of Employee X's services contribute to providing property and services to customers to each of Employer C's other two lines of business. Because Employee X does not provide at least 25 percent of his services to Employer C's athletic equipment and apparel stores line of business, Employee X is not one of the 10,000 employees described in *Example 1* and therefore cannot be a top paid employee within the meaning of § 1.414(r)-11(b)(3) with respect to the athletic equipment and apparel stores line of business. Therefore, Employee X is not taken into account in determining whether the athletic equipment and apparel stores line of business satisfies the separate management requirement of paragraph (b)(5) of this section.

Example 3. The facts are the same as in *Example 2* except that Employee X provides 60 percent of his services to Employer C's second line of business, an athletic equipment factory, and 30 percent of his service to Employer C's third line of business, a fast-food chain. Because Employer X provides at least 50 percent of his services to the athletic equipment factory line of business, Employer C chooses to treat him as a substantial-service employee with respect to that line of business, as permitted under § 1.414(r)-11(b)(2). Thus, Employee X is taken into account as a substantial-service employee with respect to the athletic equipment factory line of business and is disregarded in applying the separate workforce and separate management requirements under paragraphs (b)(4) and (5) to the fast-food chain line of business.

Example 4. Employer D operates four lines of business as determined under § 1.414(r)-2. One of its lines of business is a machine tool shop. Sixty of Employer D's employees provide at least 25 percent of their services to the machine tool shop line of business. Of the six employees who constitute the top 10 percent by compensation of those 60 employees, four are substantial-service employees with respect to the line of business. Because four is 67 percent of six, 80 percent of the top-paid employees with respect to the machine tool shop line of business are not substantial-service employees with respect to that line of business. Therefore the machine tool shop line of business does not satisfy the separate management requirement of paragraph (b)(5) of this section.

Example 5. The facts are the same as in *Example 4,* except that, in addition, another of Employer D's lines of business is an automotive repair shop, and 80 of Employer D's employees provide at least 25 percent of their services to that line of business. Employer D combines the machine shop line of business with the automotive repair shop line of business and treats them as a single line of business. As a result, Employer D has three lines of business as determined under § 1.414(r)-2. Assume that 150 of employer D's employees provide more than 25 percent of their services to the machine tool shop/automotive repair shop line of business within the meaning of paragraph (c)(5) of this section. Of the 15 employees who constitute the top 10 percent by compensation of these 150 employees, 12 are substantial-service employees with respect to that line of business. Because 12 is 80 percent of 15, at least 80 percent of the top-paid employees with respect to the machine tool shop/automotive repair shop line of business are substantial-service employees with respect to that line of business. Therefore, the machine tool shop/automotive repair shop line of business satisfies the separate management requirement of paragraph (b)(5) of this section.

(d) *Optional rule for vertically integrated lines of business.*—(1) *In general.*—If two lines of business satisfy the requirements of this paragraph (d) with respect to a type of property or service for a testing year, the employer is permitted to apply the optional rule in this paragraph (d) for the testing year.

(2) *Requirements.*—Two lines of business satisfy the requirements of this paragraph (d) with respect to a type of property or service only if—

(i) One of the lines of business (the upstream line of business) provides a type of property or service to the other line of business (the downstream line of business);

(ii) The downstream line of business either—

(A) Uses, consumes, or substantially modifies the property or service in the course of itself providing property or services to customers of the employer; or

(B) Provides the same property or service to customers of the employer at a different level in the chain of commercial distribution from the upstream line of business (e.g., retail versus wholesale); and

(iii) The upstream line of business either—

(A) Provides the same type of property or service to customers of the employer, and at least 25 percent of the total number of units of the same type of property or service provided by the upstream line of business to all persons (including customers of the employer, the downstream line of business, and all other lines of business of the employer) are provided to customers of the employer by the upstream line of business, when measured on a uniform basis; or

(B) Provides to the downstream line of business property consisting primarily of a type of tangible property (i.e., goods, not services) that it produces or manufactures, and some entities outside the employer's controlled group that are engaged in a similar business as the upstream line of business provide the same type of tangible property to unrelated customers (i.e., customers outside those entities' respective controlled groups).

(3) *Optional rule.*—(i) *Treatment of employees.*—For purposes of determining the lines of business to which an employee provides services under paragraph (c)(5) of this section, an employee is not treated as providing services to the downstream line of business if—

(A) The employee is considered to provide services to the downstream line of business under paragraph (c)(5) of this section (applied without regard to the optional rule in this paragraph (d)); and

(B) The employee is so considered solely because the employee's services contribute to providing the property or service from the upstream line of business to the downstream line of business.

(ii) *Purposes for which optional rule applies.*—If an employer applies the optional rule in this paragraph (d), the treatment specified in paragraphs (d)(3)(i)(A) and (B) of this section applies for all the following purposes and only for the following purposes—

(A) The separate employee workforce and separate management requirements of paragraphs (b)(4) and (b)(5) of this section;

(B) The 50-employee requirement of § 1.414(r)-4(b); and

(C) The determination of the employees of a qualified separate line of business under § 1.414(r)-7.

(4) *Examples.*—The following examples illustrate the application of the optional rule in this paragraph (d).

Example 1. Employer E operates two lines of business as determined under § 1.414(r)-2, one engaged in upholstery textile manufacturing and the other in furniture manufacturing. During the testing year, the upholstery textile line of business provides its entire output of upholstery textiles to the furniture line of business. The furniture line of business uses the upholstery textiles in the manufacture of upholstered furniture for sale to customers of Employer E. The furniture line of business thus substantially modifies the upholstery textiles provided to it by the upholstery textile line of business in providing upholstered furniture products to customers of Employer E. In addition, although the upholstery textile line of business does not provide upholstery textiles to customers of Employer E, some entities engaged in upholstery textile manufacturing provide upholstery textiles to customers outside their controlled groups. Under these facts, Employer E's two lines of business satisfy the requirements of this paragraph (d) with respect to upholstery textiles for the testing year.

Example 2. Employer B is a multinational controlled group of corporations that engages in the exploration, production, refining, and marketing of petrochemical products. See *Example 10* under paragraph (c)(7) of this section. Employer B operates two lines of business as determined under § 1.414(r)-2. The first line of business ("the exploration, production, and refining line of business") provides lubricating oil, gasoline, and other petrochemical products to wholesale customers of Employer B as well as the second line of business. The wholesale customers of Employer B include independent jobbers, independent franchisees that operate retail filling stations under Employer B's trademark and tradename, as well as chemical and plastics manufacturers. The second line of business (the "retail marketing line of business") provides lubricating oil and gasoline products to retail customers of Employer B through filling stations owned and operated by Employer B. During the testing year, the exploration, production, and refining line of business provides 25,000 gallons of lubricating oil, 100,000 gallons of unleaded and 150,000 gallons of leaded gasoline to the retail marketing line of business, and 75,000 gallons of lubricating oil, 500,000 gallons of unleaded gasoline and 15,000 gallons of leaded gasoline to wholesale customers of Employer B. Thus, the exploration, production, and refining line of business provides 75 percent of its output of lubricating oil during the testing year to wholesale customers of Employer B. In addition, because unleaded and leaded gasoline is the same type of property (i.e., gasoline), the exploration, production, and refining line of business provides 67 percent of its output of gasoline products during the testing year to wholesale customers of Employer B. Furthermore, the retail line of business provides lubricating oil and gasoline products to customers of Employer B at different levels in the chain of commercial distribution than the exploration, production, and refining line of business. Under these facts, Employer B's two lines of business satisfy the requirements of this paragraph (d) with respect to both lubricating oil and gasoline products for the testing year.

Example 3. The facts are the same as in *Example 2.* Employer B operates a refinery that produces lubricating oil, gasoline, and other petrochemical products. Employee V is an operating engineer at the refinery who is involved at a stage in the refining process before lubricating oil and gasoline products have been separated from other types of petrochemical products. Employee V performs no other services for Employer B. Absent application of the optional rule in this paragraph (d), Employee V would be considered to provide services to both of Employer B's lines of business. See *Example 11* under paragraph (c)(7) of this section. However, because Employee V's services to the retail marketing line of business contribute solely to providing lubricating oil and gasoline products from the exploration, production, and refining line of business to the retail marketing line of business, under the optional rule in paragraph (d)(3)(i) of this section Employee V is not treated as providing services to the retail marketing line of business.

Example 4. The facts are the same as in *Example 3.* Employee W is a petroleum engineer who conducts geological studies of potential future drilling sites. Employee W performs no other services for Employer B. Absent application of the optional rule in this paragraph (d), Employee W would be considered to provide services to both of Employer B's lines of business. See *Example 12* under paragraph (c)(7) of this section. However, because Employee W's services to the retail marketing line of business contribute solely to providing lubricating oil and gasoline products from the exploration, production, and refining line of business to the retail marketing line of business, under the optional rule in paragraph (d)(3)(i) of this section Employee W is not treated as providing services to the retail marketing line of business.

Example 5. The facts are the same as in *Example 4.* Employee Y is a vice president in Employer B's home office. As part of his senior management responsibilities, Employee Y helps to set the rate of production at Employer B's refineries in the United States and also helps to set the price charged at the pump at the retail filling stations owned and operated by Employer B in this country. Absent application of the optional rule in this paragraph (d), Employee X would be considered to provide services to both of Employer B's lines of business within the meaning of paragraph (c)(5) of this section for purposes of satisfying the separate workforce requirement of paragraph (b)(4) of this section. Because Employee X helps to set the price charged at the pump by Employer B's retail marketing line of business, Employee X's services to the retail marketing line of business are not limited to contributing solely to providing lubricating oil and gasoline products from the exploration, production, and refining line of business to the retail marketing line of business, as required under paragraph (d)(3)(i)(B) of this section. Accordingly, even though Employer B's two lines of business satisfy the requirements of this paragraph (d) with respect to both lubricating oil and gasoline products for the testing year, and even though Employer B applies the optional rule in this paragraph (d), Employee X is still considered to provide services to both of Employer B's lines of business. [Reg. §1.414(r)-3.]

☐ [*T.D. 8376, 12-2-91. Amended by T.D. 8548, 6-23-94.*]

[Reg. §1.414(r)-4]

§1.414(r)-4. Qualified separate line of business—fifty employee and notice requirement.—(a) *In general.*—This section sets forth the rules for determining whether a separate line of business (as determined under §1.414(r)-3) satisfies the 50-employee and notice requirements of §1.414(r)-1(b)(2)(iv)(B) and (C), respectively.

(b) *Fifty-employee requirement.*—A separate line of business satisfies the 50-employee requirement of §1.414(r)-1(b)(2)(iv)(B) for a testing year only if on each day of the testing year there are at least 50 employees who provide services to the separate line of business for the testing year and do not provide services to any other separate line of business of the employer for the testing year within the meaning of §1.414(r)-3(c)(5). For this purpose, all employees of the employer are taken into account (including collectively bargained employees), except employees described in §1.414(q)-1, Q&A-9(g)(i.e., the same employees, subject to certain modifications,

who are excluded in determining the number of employees in the top-paid group under section 414(q)(4)).

(c) *Notice requirement.*—(1) *General rule.*—A separate line of business satisfies the notice requirement of §1.414(r)-1(b)(2)(iv)(C) for a testing year only if the employer notifies the Secretary that it treats itself as operating qualified separate lines of business for the testing year in accordance with §1.414(r)-1(b). The employer's notice for the testing year must specify each of the qualified separate lines of business operated by the employer and the section or sections of the Code to be applied on a qualified-separate-line-of-business basis. See §1.414(r)-1(c). The employer's notice must take the form, must be filed at the time and the place, and must contain any additional information prescribed by the Commissioner in revenue procedures, notices, or other guidance of general applicability. No other notice, whether actual or constructive, satisfies the requirement of this paragraph (c).

(2) *Effect of notice.*—Once an employer has provided the notice prescribed in this paragraph (c) for a testing year, and the time for filing the notice for the testing year has expired without its being modified, withdrawn, or revoked, the employer is deemed to have irrevocably elected to apply the requirements of the section or sections of the Code specified in the notice separately with respect to the employees of each qualified separate line of business specified in the notice for all plan years that begin in the testing year. The Commissioner may, in revenue procedures, notices, or other guidance of general applicability, provide for exceptions to the rule in this paragraph (c)(2) as well as for the effect that will be given to the employer's notice for purposes of any future testing year. [Reg. §1.414(r)-4.]

☐ [*T.D. 8376, 12-2-91. Amended by T.D. 8548, 6-23-94.*]

[Reg. §1.414(r)-5]

§1.414(r)-5. Qualified separate line of business—administrative scrutiny requirement— safe harbors.—(a) *In general.*—A separate line of business (as determined under §1.414(r)-3) satisfies the administrative scrutiny requirement of §1.414(r)-1(b)(2)(iv)(D) for a testing year if the separate line of business satisfies any of the safe harbors in paragraphs (b) through (g) of this section for the testing year. The safe harbor in paragraph (b) of this section implements the statutory safe harbor of section 414(r)(3). The safe harbors in paragraphs (c) through (g) of this section constitute the guidelines provided for under section 414(r)(2)(C). A separate line of business that does not satisfy any of the safe harbors in this section nonetheless satisfies the requirement of administrative scrutiny if the employer requests and receives an individual determination from the Commissioner under §1.414(r)-6 that the separate line of business satisfies the requirement of administrative scrutiny.

(b) *Statutory safe harbor.*—(1) *General rule.*—A separate line of business satisfies the safe harbor in this paragraph (b) for the testing year only if the highly compensated employee percentage ratio of the separate line of business is—

(i) At least 50 percent; and
(ii) No more than 200 percent.

(2) *Highly compensated employee percentage ratio.*—For purposes of this paragraph (b), the highly compensated employee percentage ratio of a separate line of business is the fraction (expressed as a percentage), the numerator of which is the percentage of the employees of the separate line of business who are highly compensated employees, and the denominator of which is the percentage of all employees of the employer who are highly compensated employees.

(3) *Employees taken into account.*—For purposes of this paragraph (b), the employees taken into account are the same employees who are taken into account for purposes of applying section 410(b) with respect to the first testing day. For this purpose, employees described in section 410(b)(3) and (b)(4) are excluded. However, section 410(b)(4) is applied with reference to the lowest minimum age requirement applicable under any plan of the employer, and with reference to the lowest service requirement applicable under any plan of the employer, as if all the plans were a single plan under §1.410(b)-6(b)(2). The employees of the separate line of business are determined by applying §1.414(r)-7 to the employees taken into account under this paragraph (b)(3). An employee is treated as a highly compensated employee for purposes of this paragraph (b) if the employee is treated as a highly compensated employee for purposes of applying section 410(b) with respect to the first testing day. For the definition of "first testing day," see §1.414(r)-11(b)(7).

(4) *Ten-percent exception.*—A separate line of business is deemed to satisfy paragraph (b)(1)(i) of this section for the testing year if at least 10 percent of all highly compensated employees of the employer provide services to the separate line of business during the testing

year and do not provide services to any other separate line of business of the employer during the testing year within the meaning of § 1.414(r)-3(c)(5).

(5) *Determination based on preceding testing year.*—A separate line of business that satisfied this safe harbor for the immediately preceding testing year (without taking into account the special rule in this paragraph (b)(5)) is deemed to satisfy the safe harbor for the current testing year. The preceding sentence applies to a separate line of business only if the employer designated the same line of business in the immediately preceding testing year as in the current testing year and either—

(i) The highly compensated employee percentage ratio of the separate line of business for the current testing year does not deviate by more than 10 percent (not 10 percentage points) from the highly compensated employee percentage ratio of the separate line of business for the immediately preceding testing year; or

	Employer-Wide	Railroad	Insurance Company	Newspaper
Number of Employees	400	100	150	150
Number of HCEs	100	20	50	30
Number of Non-HCEs	300	80	100	120
HCE Percentage	25% (100/400)	20% (20/100)	33% (50/150)	20% (30/150)
HCE Percentage Ratio	N/A	80% (20%/25%)	133% (33%/25%)	80% (20%/25%)

(ii) Because the highly compensated employee percentage ratio of each separate line of business is at least 50 percent and no more than 200 percent, each of Employer A's separate lines of business satisfies the requirements of the safe harbor in this paragraph (b).

Example 2. (i) Employer B operates three separate lines of business as determined under § 1.414(r)-3, that respectively consist of a

(ii) No more than five percent of the employees of the separate line of business for the current testing year were employees of a different separate line of business for the immediately preceding testing year, and no more than five percent of the employees of the separate line of business for the immediately preceding testing year are employees of a different separate line of business for the current testing year.

(6) *Examples.*—The following examples illustrate the application of the safe harbor in this paragraph (b).

Example 1. (i) Employer A operates three separate lines of business as determined under § 1.414(r)-3, that respectively consist of a railroad, an insurance company, and a newspaper. Employer A employs a total of 400 employees, 100 of whom are highly compensated employees. Thus, the percentage of all employees of Employer A who are highly compensated employees is 25 percent. After applying § 1.414(r)-7, the distribution of highly and nonhighly compensated employees among Employer A's separate lines of business is as follows:

dairy products manufacturer, a candy manufacturer, and a chain of housewares stores. Employer B employs a total of 1,000 employees, 100 of whom are highly compensated employees. Thus, the percentage of all employees of Employer B who are highly compensated employees is 10 percent. After applying § 1.414(r)-7, the distribution of highly and nonhighly compensated employees among Employer B's separate lines of business is as follows:

	Employer-Wide	Dairy Products	Candy	Housewares Stores
Number of Employees	1,000	200	500	300
Number of HCEs	100	5	50	45
Number of Non-HCEs	900	195	450	255
HCE Percentage	10% (100/1,000)	2.5% (5/200)	10% (50/500)	15% (45/300)
HCE Percentage Ratio	N/A	25% (2.5%/10%)	100% (10%/10%)	150% (15%/10%)

(ii) Because the highly compensated employee percentage ratio for the dairy products line of business is less than 50 percent, it does not satisfy the requirements of the statutory safe harbor in this paragraph (b). However, because Employer B's other two separate lines of business (candy manufacturing and housewares stores) each has a highly compensated employee percentage ratio that is no less than 50 percent and no greater than 200 percent, they each satisfy the statutory safe harbor in this paragraph (b).

Example 3. (i) The facts are the same as in *Example 2*, except that Employer B operates only two separate lines of business as determined under § 1.414(r)-3, one consisting of the dairy products manufacturer and the candy manufacturer, and the other consisting of the chain of housewares stores. After applying § 1.414(r)-7, the distribution of highly and nonhighly compensated employees among Employer B's separate lines of business is as follows:

	Employer-Wide	Candy/Dairy Products	Housewares Stores
Number of Employees	1,000	700	300
Number of HCEs	100	55	45
Number of Non-HCEs	900	645	255
HCE Percentage	10% (100/1,000)	7.9% (55/700)	15% (45/300)
HCE Percentage Ratio	N/A	79% (7.9%/10%)	150% (15%/10%)

(ii) Because the highly compensated employee percentage ratio for both of Employer B's separate lines of business is at least 50 percent and no more than 200 percent, they each satisfy the requirements of the statutory safe harbor in this paragraph (b).

(c) *Safe harbor for separate lines of business in different industries.*—(1) *In general.*—A separate line of business satisfies the safe harbor in this paragraph (c) for the testing year if it is in a different industry or industries from every other separate line of business of the employer. For this purpose, a separate line of business is in a different industry or industries from every other separate line of business of the employer only if—

(i) The property or services provided to customers of the employer by the separate line of business (as designated by the employer for the testing year under § 1.414(r)-2) fall exclusively within one or more industry categories established by the Commissioner for purposes of this paragraph (c); and

(ii) None of the property or services provided to customers of the employer by any of the employer's other separate lines of business (as designated by the employer for the testing year under § 1.414(r)-2) falls within the same industry category or categories.

(2) *Optional rule for foreign operations.*—For purposes of satisfying this paragraph (c), an employer is permitted to disregard any property or services provided to customers of the employer during the

testing year by a foreign corporation or foreign partnership (as defined in section 7701(a)(5)), to the extent that income from the provision of the property or services is not effectively connected with the conduct of the trade or business within the United States within the meaning of section 864(c). Thus, for example, an employer is permitted to take into account only property and services provided to customers of the employer by its domestic subsidiaries and property and services provided by its foreign subsidiaries that generate income effectively connected with the conduct of a trade or business within the United States in determining whether the property or services provided to customers of the employer by a separate line of business fall exclusively within one or more industry categories and also whether the property or services provided by any other separate line of business fall within the same industry category or categories.

(3) *Establishment of industry categories.*—The Commissioner shall, by revenue procedure or other guidance of general applicability, establish industry categories for purposes of this paragraph (c).

(4) *Examples.*—The following examples illustrate the application of the safe harbor in this paragraph (c). For purposes of these examples, it is assumed that, pursuant to paragraph (c)(3) of this section, the Commissioner has established the following industry categories (among others): transportation equipment and services; banking, insurance, and finance; machinery and electronics; and entertainment, sports, and hotels.

Example 1. Among its other business activities, Employer C operates a commercial airline that constitutes a separate line of business under §1.414(r)-3. In addition, no other separate line of business of Employer C provides to customers of Employer C any property or services in the transportation equipment and services industry category. Under these facts, the separate line of business described in this example satisfies the safe harbor in this paragraph (c).

Example 2. The facts are the same as in *Example 1*, except that Employer C also operates a trucking company that constitutes another separate line of business of Employer C under §1.414(r)-3. Because the commercial airline and the trucking company both provide to customers of Employer C services in the transportation equipment and services industry category, neither separate line of business satisfies the safe harbor in this paragraph (c).

Example 3. Among its other business activities, Employer D operates a commercial bank and a luxury hotel that together constitute a single separate line of business under §1.414(r)-3. No other separate line of business of Employer D provides to customers of Employer D property or services in either the banking, insurance, or financial industry category, or the entertainment, sports, or hotel industry category. Under these facts, the separate line of business described in this example satisfies the safe harbor in this paragraph (c).

Example 4. The facts are the same as in *Example 3*, except that Employer D also manufactures computers in the United States and abroad. Employer D apportions its computer operations by designating these operations between two separate lines of business, one consisting of its domestic operations located in the United States and the second consisting of its foreign operations by a foreign subsidiary. Because both lines of business provide property and services in the machinery and electronics industry category to customers of Employer D , neither separate line of business would satisfy the safe harbor in this paragraph (c). However, pursuant to the optional rule in paragraph (c)(2) of this section, Employer D disregards the property and services provided by its foreign computer subsidiary. As a result, no other separate line of business of Employer D provides to customers of Employer D any property or services in the machinery and electronics industry category. Under these facts, Employer D's domestic computer operations separate line of business satisfies the safe harbor in this paragraph (c).

(d) *Safe harbor for separate lines of business that are acquired through certain mergers and acquisitions.*—(1) *General rule.*—A portion of the employer that is acquired through a transaction described in section 410(b)(6)(C) and §1.410(b)-2(f) (i.e., an asset or stock acquisition, merger, or other similar transaction involving a change in the employer of the employees of a trade or business) (the "acquired line of business") satisfies the safe harbor in this paragraph (d) for each testing year in the transition period provided in paragraph (d)(3) of this section if each of the following requirements is satisfied—

(i) For each testing year within the transition period the employer designates the acquired line of business as a line of business within the meaning of §1.414(r)-2;

(ii) On the first testing day in each testing year in the transition period:

(A) The acquired line business constitutes a separate line of business within the meaning of §1.414(r)-3 (taking into account §1.414(r)-1(d)(4));

(B) No more than 10 percent of the employees who are substantial-service employees with respect to the acquired line of business were substantial-service employees with respect to a different separate line of business for the immediately preceding testing year; and

(C) No more than 10 percent of the employees who were substantial-service employees with respect to the acquired line of business for the immediately preceding testing year are substantial-service employees with respect to a different separate line of business in the respective testing year.

(iii) If the transaction described in paragraph (d)(1) of this section occurs after the first testing day in a testing year, the determinations required by paragraphs (d)(1)(ii)(B) and (C) of this section with respect to that testing year are made as of the date of the transaction.

(2) *Employees taken into account.*—For purposes of this paragraph (d), the employees taken into account are the same employees who are taken into account for purposes of applying section 410(b) with respect to the first testing day. For this purpose, employees described in section 410(b)(3) and (b)(4) are excluded. However, section 410(b)(4) is applied with reference to the lowest minimum age requirement, and with reference to the lowest service requirement applicable under any plan of the employer that benefits employees of the separate line of business, as if all the plans were a single plan under §1.410(b)-6(b)(2). The employees of the separate line of business are determined by applying §1.414(r)-7 to the employees taken into account under this paragraph (d)(2).

(3) *Transition period.*—The transition period for purposes of this safe harbor is the period that begins with the first testing year beginning after the date that the transaction described in paragraph (d)(1) of this section occurs. The employer is permitted, but not required, to extend the transition period to include one, two, or three of the testing years immediately succeeding that first testing year.

(4) *Examples.*—The following examples illustrate the application of the safe harbor in this paragraph (d).

Example 1. Employer E is treated as operating three qualified separate lines of business pursuant to §1.414(r)-1(b). In 1996, Employer E acquires a company that employs 4,000 employees who manufacture and sell pharmaceutical supplies, and designates that portion as a line of business under §1.414(r)-2. Under §1.414(r)-1(d)(4), the pharmaceutical supplies line of business is deemed to satisfy the requirements to be a qualified separate line of business (other than the 50-employee and notice requirements) for testing year 1996. In addition, the determination of whether Employer E's remaining three lines of business constitute qualified separate lines of business for testing year 1996 is made without taking into account the acquired employees and by disregarding the property and services provided to customers of Employer E by the pharmaceutical supplies line of business.

Example 2. The facts are the same as in *Example 1* except that, by the first testing day in 1997 (Transition Year 1), there are 300 additional substantial-service employees with respect to the pharmaceutical supplies line of business, increasing the total number to 4,300. Of those 300 employees, 250 were substantial-service employees with respect to a different separate line of business for testing year 1996 and 50 are new hires. Assume that, on the first testing day in Transition Year 1, the pharmaceutical supplies line of business satisfies the requirements of §1.414(r)-3 (taking into account §1.414(r)-1(d)(4)) and therefore constitutes a separate line of business. Because 250 is 6 percent of 4,300, no more than ten percent of the employees who are substantial-service employees with respect to the pharmaceutical supplies line of business were substantial-service employees with respect to a different separate line of business for the immediately preceding testing year. The 50 newly hired employees are disregarded in making this determination. Under these facts, the pharmaceutical supplies separate line of business satisfies the safe harbor in this paragraph (d) for Transition Year 1.

Example 3. The facts are the same as in *Example 2*, except that, before the first day of the next testing year ("Transition Year 2"), Employer E permanently transfers 200 of the 4,300 employees who were substantial-service employees with respect to the pharmaceutical line of business on the first testing day in Transition Year 1 to a different line of business and does not hire any additional employees for the pharmaceutical supplies line of business. Therefore, by the first testing day in Transition Year 2, the number of employees who are substantial-service employees with respect to the pharmaceutical line of business of Employer E has decreased from 4,300 to 4,100. Assume that, on that first testing day in Transition Year 2, the pharmaceutical supplies line of business constitutes a separate line of business within the meaning of §1.414(r)-3. Because 200 is approximately 5 percent of 4,300, no more than 10 percent of the employees who were substantial-service employees of the pharmaceutical line of business for Transition Year 1 are not substantial-service employees of the pharmaceutical line of business in Transition Year 2. Under these facts, the pharmaceutical supplies separate line of business continues to satisfy the safe harbor in this paragraph (d) for Transition Year 2.

(e) *Safe harbor for separate lines of business reported as industry segments.*—(1) *In general.*—A separate line of business satisfies the safe harbor in this paragraph (e) for the testing year if, for the employer's fiscal year ending latest in the testing year, the separate line of business is reported as one or more industry segments on its annual report required to be filed in conformity with either—

    (i) Form 10-K, Annual Report Pursuant to Section 13 or 15(d) of the Securities Exchange Act of 1934 ("Form 10-K"); or

    (ii) Form 20-F, Annual Report Pursuant to Section 13(a) or 15(d) of the Securities Exchange Act of 1934 with Item 18 financials ("Form 20-F"),

and the employer timely files either the Form 10-K or Form 20-F with the Securities and Exchange Commission ("SEC").

(2) *Reported as an industry segment in conformity with Form 10-K or Form 20-F.*—For purposes of this paragraph (e), a separate line of business is reported as one or more industry segments in conformity with either Form 10-K or Form 20-F only if—

    (i) The separate line of business consists of one or more industry segments within the meaning of paragraphs 10(a), 11(b), and 12 through 14 of the Statement of Financial Accounting Standards No. 14, Financial Reporting for Segments of a Business Enterprise ("FAS 14"); and

    (ii) The property or services provided to customers of the employer by the separate line of business (as designated by the employer for the testing year under § 1.414(r)-2) is identical to the property or services provided to customers of the employer by the industry segment or segments (as determined under paragraphs 10(a), 11(b), and 12 through 14 of FAS 14).

(3) *Timely filing of Form 10-K or Form 20-F.*—For purposes of this paragraph (e), a Form 10-K or Form 20-F is timely filed with the SEC if it is filed within the required period as provided under 17 C.F.R. § 240.12b-25(b)(2)(ii). Therefore, the required period for timely filing of the Form 10-K is the 90-day period after the end of the fiscal year covered by the annual report (including the 15-day extension), and the required period for timely filing of the Form 20-F is the six month period after the end of the fiscal year covered by the annual report (including the 15-day extension).

(4) *Examples.*—The following examples illustrate the application of the safe harbor in this paragraph (e).

Example 1. Among its other business activities, Employer F operates a bearing manufacturing firm that constitutes a separate line of business under § 1.414(r)-3. Employer F is required to file an annual Form 10-K with the SEC. On its timely filed Form 10-K, Employer F reports its bearing manufacturing operations as an industry segment in accordance of FAS 14 (as determined under paragraphs 10(a), 11(b), and 12 through 14 of FAS 14). The group of bearing products provided by the separate line of business (as designated by Employer F under § 1.414(r)-2) is identical to the group of bearing products provided by the industry segment (as determined under paragraphs 10(a), 11(b), and 12 through 14 of FAS 14). Under these facts, the separate line of business described in this example satisfies the safe harbor in this paragraph (e).

Example 2. The facts are the same as in *Example 1*, except that Employer F has apportioned its bearing manufacturing operations between two separate lines of business as determined under § 1.414(r)-3, one engaged in the manufacture of bearings for use in the automotive industry, and a second engaged in the manufacture of bearings for use in the aerospace industry. Because neither separate line of business provides a group of property or services to customers of Employer F that is identical to the group of bearing products provided by the industry segment reported on Employer F's annual Form 10-K, neither separate line of business described in this example satisfies the safe harbor in this paragraph (e).

(f) *Safe harbor for separate lines of business that provide the same average benefits as other separate lines of business.*—(1) *General rule.*—A separate line of business satisfies the safe harbor in this paragraph (f) for the testing year only if the level of benefits provided to employees of the separate line of business satisfies paragraph (f)(2) or (f)(3) of this section, whichever is applicable.

(2) *Separate lines of business with a disproportionate number of nonhighly compensated employees.*—(i) *Applicability of safe harbor.*—This paragraph (f)(2) applies to a separate line of business that for the testing year has a highly compensated employee percentage ratio of less than 50 percent (as determined under paragraph (b)(2) of this section).

    (ii) *Requirement.*—A separate line of business satisfies this paragraph (f)(2) only if the actual benefit percentage of the group of nonhighly compensated employees of the separate line of business for the testing period that ends with or within the testing year is at least as great as the actual benefit percentage of the group of all other nonhighly compensated employees of the employer for the same testing period. See § 1.410(b)-5(c) and (d)(3)(ii) for the definitions of actual benefit percentage and testing period, respectively. In determining actual benefit percentages for purposes of this paragraph (f)(2)(ii), the special rule in § 1.410(b)-5(e)(3) (permitting an employer to determine employee benefit percentages separately for defined contribution and defined benefit plans) may not be used.

(3) *Separate lines of business with a disproportionate number of highly compensated employees.*—(i) *Applicability of safe harbor.*—This paragraph (f)(3) applies to a separate line of business that for the testing year has a highly compensated employee percentage ratio of more than 200 percent (as determined under paragraph (b)(2) of this section).

    (ii) *Requirement.*—A separate line of business satisfies this paragraph (f)(3) only if the actual benefit percentage of the group of highly compensated employees of the separate line of business for the testing period that ends with or within the testing year is no greater than the actual benefit percentage of the group of all other highly compensated employees of the employer for the same testing period. See § 1.410(b)-5(c) and (d)(3)(ii) for the definitions of actual benefit percentage and testing period, respectively. In determining actual benefit percentages for purposes of this paragraph (f)(3)(ii), the special rule in § 1.410(b)-5(e)(3) (permitting an employer to determine employee benefit percentages separately for defined contribution and defined benefit plans) may not be used.

(4) *Employees taken into account.*—An employee of a separate line of business (as determined under § 1.414(r)-7) is taken into account for a testing period for purposes of this paragraph (f) only if the employee is an employee of the separate line of business on the first testing day, and would not be an excludable employee for purposes of applying the average benefit percentage test of § 1.410(b)-5 to a plan for a plan year included in that testing period. In determining whether an employee is an excludable employee for purposes of the average benefit percentage test, the employer is assumed not to be operating qualified separate lines of business under § 1.414(r)-1(b). An employee is treated as a highly compensated employee for purposes of this paragraph (f) if the employee is treated as a highly compensated employee for purposes of applying section 410(b) on the first testing day. See § 1.414(r)-11(b)(7) for the definition of "first testing day".

(5) *Example.*—The rules of this paragraph (f) are illustrated by the following example.

Example. (i) Employer G is treated as operating two separate lines of business, Line 1 and Line 2, in accordance with § 1.414(r)-1(b). Employer G maintains three qualified plans. Plan A is a calendar-year profit-sharing plan that benefits all employees of Employer G. Plan B is a defined benefit plan with a plan year ending March 31 that benefits all employees of Line 1. Plan C is a defined benefit plan with a plan year ending November 30 that benefits all employees of Line 2.

    (ii) In 1995, Line 1 has a highly compensated employee percentage ratio of 25 percent. Employer G's first testing day is March 31. After applying the rules of § 1.414(r)-7, the nonhighly compensated employees of Line 1 and Line 2 on March 31, 1995, are N1-N80 and N81-N100, respectively. N1 is an excludable employee under § 1.410(b)-6 for purposes of the average benefit percentage test during the testing period that includes the plan years of Plans A, B, and C that end in 1995 (the "1995 testing period"), and would therefore not be taken into account in determining whether any of those plans satisfied the average benefit percentage test of § 1.410(b)-5 for plan years included in that testing period, because N1 does not satisfy the minimum age and service conditions under any plan of the employer. All other employees of Line 1 and Line 2 on March 31, 1995, are nonexcludable employees for purposes of the average benefit percentage test during the 1995 testing period.

    (iii) In order for Line 1 to satisfy the requirements of this paragraph (f) for 1995, the actual benefit percentage of N2-N80 for the 1995 testing period under Plans A, B and C must be at least as great as the actual benefit percentage of N81-N100 for the same testing period under the same plans. N1 is not taken into account because N1 is an excludable employee for purposes of the average benefit percentage test for the 1995 testing period. Any other employees who were taken into account for purposes of the average benefit percentage test for the 1995 testing period are excluded because they are not employees of Line 1 or Line 2 on March 31, 1995.

(g) *Safe harbor for separate lines of business that provide minimum or maximum benefits.*—(1) *In general.*—A separate line of business satisfies the safe harbor in this paragraph (g) for the testing year only if the level of benefits provided to employees of the separate line of business satisfies paragraph (g)(2) or (g)(3) of this section, whichever is applicable. For this purpose, the level of benefits is determined with respect to all qualified plans of the employer that benefit employees of the separate line of business for plan years that begin in the testing year.

(2) *Minimum benefit required.*—(i) *Applicability.*—This paragraph (g)(2) applies to a separate line of business that for the testing year has a highly compensated employee percentage ratio of less than 50 percent (as determined under paragraph (b)(2) of this section).

(ii) *Requirement.*—A separate line of business satisfies this paragraph (g)(2) only if one of the following requirements is satisfied—

(A) At least 80 percent of all nonhighly compensated employees of the separate line of business either accrue a benefit for the plan year that equals or exceeds the defined benefit minimum in paragraph (g)(2)(iii) of this section, receive an allocation for the plan year that equals or exceeds the defined contribution minimum in paragraph (g)(2)(iv) of this section, or accrue a benefit and receive an allocation that together equal or exceed the combined plan minimum in paragraph (g)(4) of this section. The defined benefit minimum must be provided in a defined benefit plan, and the defined contribution minimum must be provided in a defined contribution plan.

(B) The separate line of business would satisfy the requirements of paragraph (g)(2)(ii)(A) of this section if the 80 percent threshold were reduced to 60 percent, and the average of the accrual rates or allocation rates of all nonhighly compensated employees in the separate line of business equals or exceeds the minimum amount described for each individual employee in paragraph (g)(2)(ii)(A) of this section.

(iii) *Defined benefit minimum.*—(A) *In general.*—The defined benefit minimum for a plan year is the employer-derived accrual that would result in a normal accrual rate for the plan year equal to 0.75 percent of compensation. For purposes of this paragraph (g)(2)(iii), the normal accrual rate is the percentage (not less than 0) determined by subtracting the employee's normalized accrued benefit as of the end of the prior plan year (expressed as a percentage of average annual compensation as of the end of the prior plan year) from the employee's normalized accrued benefit as of the end of the plan year (expressed as a percentage of average annual compensation as of the end of the plan year).

(B) *Normal form and equivalent benefits.*—The benefit that is tested for purposes of this paragraph (g)(2)(iii) is the accrued retirement benefit commencing at normal retirement age. If the normal form of benefit for a plan being tested is other than a straight life annuity beginning at a normal retirement age of 65, the benefit must be normalized (within the meaning of §1.401(a)(4)-12) to a straight life annuity commencing at age 65. No adjustment is permitted for early retirement benefits or for any ancillary benefit, including disability benefits.

(C) *Compensation definition.*—The underlying definition of compensation used for purposes of determining accrual rates under this paragraph (g)(2)(iii) must be a definition of compensation that automatically satisfies section 414(s) without a test for nondiscrimination (see §1.414(s)-1(c)).

(D) *Average compensation requirement.*—For purposes of determining accrual rates, compensation must be average annual compensation within the meaning of §1.401(a)(4)-3(e)(2) determined using a five-year averaging period. The compensation history to be taken into account are all years beginning with the first year in which the employee benefits under the plan, and ending with the last plan year in which the employee participates in the plan. However, a plan may disregard in a reasonable and consistent manner: years before the effective date of these regulations as set forth in §1.414(r)-1(d)(9)(i), years more than 10 years preceding the current plan year, and years for which the employer does not use this paragraph (g)(2) to satisfy this safe harbor with respect to the separate line of business. If a plan provides a defined benefit minimum that uses three consecutive years (in lieu of five) for calculating average annual compensation, the 0.75 percent annual accrual rate in paragraph (g)(2)(iii)(A) of this section is multiplied by 93.3 percent, resulting in a normal accrual rate equal to 0.70 percent. If a plan *provides a defined benefit minimum that uses more than five consecutive years for calculating average annual compensation or the plan is an accumulation plan as defined in §1.401(a)(4)-12, the 0.75 percent annual accrual rate in paragraph (g)(2)(iii)(A) of this section is multiplied by 133.3 percent, resulting in a normal accrual rate equal to 1.0 percent.*

(E) *Special rules.*—The special rules of §1.401(a)(4)-3(f) apply for purposes of determining whether a benefit accrual satisfies the minimum benefit requirement. For example, benefits may be determined on other than a plan year basis as permitted by §1.401(a)(4)-3(f)(6). A plan described in section 412(i) may be used to provide the defined benefit minimum described in this paragraph (g)(2). In such case, the rules in §1.416-1, M-17, apply to such a plan. For purposes of this paragraph (g)(2)(iii) an employee is treated as accruing a benefit equal to the minimum benefit in paragraph (g)(2)(iii)(A) of this section if the reason that the employee does not accrue such a benefit is either—

(1) The application of a plan provision that applies uniformly to all employees in the plan and limits the service used for purposes of benefit accrual to a specified maximum no less than 25 years, or

(2) The employee has attained normal retirement age and fails to accrue a benefit solely because of the provisions of section 411(b)(1)(H)(iii) regarding adjustments for delayed retirement.

(iv) *Defined contribution minimum.*—(A) *In general.*—The defined contribution minimum for a plan year is an allocation that results in an allocation rate for the plan year (within the meaning of §1.401(a)(4)-2(c)) equal to three percent of an employee's plan year compensation. Plan year compensation must be based on a definition of compensation that automatically satisfies section 414(s) without a test for nondiscrimination (see §1.414(s)-1(c)). For this purpose, allocations that are taken into account do not include matching contributions described in §1.401(m)-1(a)(2), elective contributions described in §1.401(k)-6, any adjustment in allocation rates permitted under section 401(*l*) or imputed disparity under §1.401(a)(4)-7.

(B) *Modified allocation definition for averaging.*—For purposes of determining whether the average allocation rates for all nonhighly compensated employees of the separate line of business satisfy the minimum benefit requirement in paragraph (g)(2)(ii)(B) of this section, matching contributions described in §1.401(m)-1(a)(2) are treated as employer allocations.

(3) *Maximum benefit permitted.*—(i) *Applicability.*—This paragraph (g)(3) applies to a separate line of business that for the testing year has a highly compensated employee percentage ratio that exceeds 200 percent (as determined under paragraph (b)(2) of this section).

(ii) *Requirement.*—A separate line of business satisfies this paragraph (g)(3) only if one of the following requirements is satisfied—

(A) No highly compensated employee of the separate line of business accrues a benefit for the plan year that results in an accrual rate that exceeds the defined benefit maximum in paragraph (g)(3)(iii) of this section, receives an allocation that exceeds the defined contribution maximum in paragraph (g)(3)(iv) of this section, or accrues a benefit and receives an allocation that together exceed the combined plan maximum in paragraph (g)(4) of this section. All benefits provided by qualified defined benefit plans are subject to the defined benefit maximum, and all benefits provided by qualified defined contribution plans are subject to the defined contribution maximum.

(B) The average of the accrual rates or allocation rates of all highly compensated employees of the separate line of business is no more than 80 percent of the maximum amount described for any individual employee in paragraph (g)(3)(ii)(A) of this section.

(iii) *Defined benefit maximum.*—(A) *In general.*—The defined benefit maximum is the employer-derived accrued benefit that would result from calculating a normal accrual rate equal to 2.5 percent of compensation.

(B) *Determination of defined benefit maximum.*—The accrual rate used for the defined benefit maximum is determined in the same manner as the normal accrual rate used for the defined benefit minimum is determined under paragraph (g)(2)(iii) of this section, except as provided below. Thus, a defined benefit plan may provide, in addition to the defined benefit maximum, any benefit the value of which is not taken into account under paragraph (g)(2)(iii) of this section. For example, a plan may provide qualified disability benefits described in section 411(a)(9) or ancillary benefits described in §1.401(a)(4)-4(e)(2).

(C) *Adjustment for different compensation definitions.*—If a plan subject to the defined benefit maximum determines accrual rates by using three consecutive years (in lieu of five) for purposes of determining average annual compensation, the 2.5 percent annual accrual rate in paragraph (g)(3)(iii)(B) of this section is multiplied by 93.3 percent, resulting in a maximum accrual rate equal to 2.33 percent. Compensation may be less inclusive than the compensation described in paragraph (g)(2)(iii)(C) of this section. However, no adjustment is made to the maximum normal accrual rate because of the use of a definition of compensation that is less inclusive than the compensation described in paragraph (g)(2)(iii)(C) of this section. In addition, no adjustment is made to the maximum normal accrual rate because the plan uses more than five consecutive years for calculating average annual compensation or the plan is an accumulation plan as defined in § 1.401(a)(4)-12.

(D) *Adjustment for certain subsidies.*—If the plan provides subsidized optional forms of benefit, the accrual rate for purposes of this paragraph (g)(3) must be determined by taking those subsidies into account. An optional form of benefit is considered subsidized if the normalized optional form of benefit is larger than the normalized normal retirement benefit under the plan. In the case of a plan with subsidized optional forms, the determination of accrual rate for the plan year under paragraph (g)(2)(iii)(A) of this section is the percentage (not less than 0) determined by subtracting the largest of the sums of the employee's normalized QJSAs and QSUPPs determined for each age under § 1.401(a)(4)-3(d)(1)(ii) as of the end of the prior plan year (expressed as a percentage of average annual compensation as of the end of the prior plan year) from the largest of the sums of the employee's normalized QJSAs and QSUPPs determined for each age under § 1.401(a)(4)-3(d)(1)(ii) as of the end of the plan year (expressed as a percentage of average annual compensation as of the end of the plan year).

(iv) *Defined contribution maximum.*—The defined contribution maximum is an allocation that results in an allocation rate for the plan year (within the meaning of § 1.401(a)(4)-2(c)) equal to 10 percent of an employee's plan year compensation. Compensation may be less inclusive than the compensation described in paragraph (g)(2)(iv)(A) of this section. However, no adjustment is made to the defined contribution maximum because of the use of a definition of compensation that is less inclusive than the compensation described in paragraph (g)(2)(iv)(A) of this section. For this purpose, allocations that are taken into account do not include elective contributions described in § 1.401(k)-6, any adjustment in allocation rates permitted under section 401(*l*) or imputed disparity under § 1.401(a)(4)-7 but do include employer matching contributions under § 1.401(m)-1(f)(12).

(4) *Duplication of benefits or contributions.*—(i) *Plans of the same type.*—In the case of an employee who benefits under more than one defined benefit plan, the defined benefit minimum required or the defined benefit maximum permitted under this paragraph (g) is determined by reference to the employee's aggregate employer-provided benefit under all qualified defined benefit plans of the employer. In the case of an employee who benefits under more than one defined contribution plan, the defined contribution minimum required or the defined contribution maximum permitted under this paragraph (g) is determined by reference to the employee's aggregate employer-provided allocations under all qualified defined contribution plans of the employer.

(ii) *Plans of different types.*—In the case of an employee who benefits under both a defined benefit plan and a defined contribution plan, a percentage of the minimum benefit required or the maximum benefit permitted under this paragraph (g) may be provided in each type of plan as long as the combined percentage equals at least 100 percent in the case of the minimum benefit required and does not exceed 100 percent in the case of the maximum benefit permitted. Thus, for example, if a highly compensated employee benefits under both types of plans and accrues an aggregate adjusted normal accrual rate equal to 1.25 percent of average annual compensation under all defined benefit plans of the employer (i.e., 50 percent of the defined benefit maximum described in paragraph (g)(3)(iii) of this section), in order to comply with the maximum benefit safe harbor, the employee may not receive an aggregate allocation under all defined contribution plans of the employer in excess of five percent of plan year compensation (i.e., 50 percent of the defined contribution maximum described in paragraph (g)(3)(iv) of this section).

(iii) *Special rule for floor-offset arrangements.*—In the case of a floor-offset arrangement (as described in § 1.401(a)(4)-8(d)), the minimum or maximum benefit rules are applied to each plan as if the other plan did not exist. Thus, the defined benefit plan must provide at least 100 percent of the defined benefit minimum (or no more than 100 percent of the defined benefit maximum) based on the gross benefit prior to offset, and the defined contribution plan must provide at least 100 percent of the defined contribution minimum (or no more than 100 percent of the defined contribution maximum).

(5) *Certain contingency provisions ignored.*—For purposes of this paragraph (g), an employee's accrual or allocation rate is determined without regard to any minimum benefit or any maximum benefit limitation that is applicable to the employee only if the separate line of business fails otherwise to satisfy the requirement of administrative scrutiny.

(6) *Employees taken into account.*—For purposes of this paragraph (g), an employee is taken into account if the employee is taken into account for purposes of applying section 410(b) with respect to any testing day for the testing year. For this purpose, employees described in section 410(b)(3) and (b)(4) are excluded. However, section 410(b)(4) is applied with reference to the lowest minimum age requirement applicable, and with reference to the lowest service requirement applicable under any plan of the employer that benefits employees of the separate line of business, as if all the plans were a single plan under § 1.410(b)-6(b)(2). For purposes of the minimum benefit requirement of paragraph (g)(2) of this section, section 410(b)(4) may be applied with reference to the lowest minimum age requirement, and with reference to the lowest minimum service requirement, applicable under any plan of the employer that benefits highly compensated employees of the separate line of business, as if all the plans were a single plan under § 1.410(b)-6(b)(2), or, if no plan of the employer benefits highly compensated employees of the separate line of business, with reference to the greatest age and service requirements permitted under section 410(a)(1)(A). The employees of the separate line of business are determined by applying § 1.414(r)-7 to the employees taken into account under this paragraph (g)(6). An employee is treated as a highly compensated employee for purposes of this paragraph (g) if the employee is treated as a highly compensated employee for purposes of applying section 410(b) on any testing day for the testing year. For the definition of "testing day," see § 1.414(r)-11(b)(6). [Reg. § 1.414(r)-5.]

☐ [T.D. 8376, 12-2-91. *Amended by T.D. 8548, 6-23-94 and T.D. 9169, 12-28-2004.*]

[Reg. § 1.414(r)-6]

§ 1.414(r)-6. Qualified separate line of business—administrative scrutiny requirement— individual determinations.—(a) *In general.*—A separate line of business (as determined under § 1.414(r)-3) that does not satisfy any of the safe harbors in § 1.414(r)-5 for a testing year nonetheless satisfies the administrative scrutiny requirement of § 1.414(r)-1(b)(2)(iv)(D) if the employer requests and receives from the Commissioner an individual determination under this section that the separate line of business satisfies the requirement of administrative scrutiny for the testing year. This section implements the individual determinations provided for under section 414(r)(2)(C). The Commissioner shall issue such an individual determination only when it is consistent with the purpose of section 414(r), taking into account the nondiscrimination requirements of sections 401(a)(4) and 410(b). Paragraph (b) of this section authorizes the Commissioner to establish procedures for requesting and granting individual determinations.

(b) *Authority to establish procedures.*—The Commissioner may, in revenue rulings and procedures, notices, and other guidance, published in the Internal Revenue Bulletin (see § 601.601(d)(2)(ii)(*b*) of this chapter), provide any additional guidance that may be necessary or appropriate for requesting and granting individual determinations under this section. For example, such guidance may specify the circumstances in which an employer may request an individual determination and factors to be taken into account in deciding whether to grant a favorable individual determination. In addition, such guidance may describe situations that automatically fail the administrative scrutiny requirement. [Reg. § 1.414(r)-6.]

☐ [T.D. 8376, 12-2-91. *Amended by T.D. 8548, 6-23-94.*]

[Reg. § 1.414(r)-7]

§ 1.414(r)-7. Determination of the employees of an employer's qualified separate lines of business —(a) *Introduction.*—(1) *In general.*—This section provides the rules for determining the employees of each qualified separate line of business operated by an employer. Paragraph (a)(2) of this section lists the specific provisions of the regulations for which these rules apply. Paragraph (b) of this section provides the procedure for assigning the employees of the employer among the qualified separate lines of business of the employer and for determining the day or days on which such assignments must be made. Under this procedure, each employee (i.e., a substantial-service employee or a residual shared employee as defined in § 1.414(r)-11(b)(2) and (4)) is assigned to a single qualified separate line of business in a consistent manner for all purposes listed in paragraph (a)(2) of this section with respect to the testing year and plan years beginning within the testing year. Paragraph (c) of this section provides methods for allocating residual shared employees among qualified separate lines of business.

(2) *Purposes for which this section applies.*—This section applies solely for purposes of determining whether—

(i) A separate line of business satisfies the statutory safe harbor of § 1.414(r)-5(b) for a testing year (see § 1.414(r)-5(b)(3) for the employees taken into account for this purpose);

(ii) A separate line of business satisfies the merger and acquisition safe harbor of §1.414(r)-5(d) for a testing year (see §1.414(r)-5(d)(2) for the employees taken into account for this purpose);

(iii) A separate line of business satisfies the average benefits safe harbor of §1.414(r)-5(f) for a testing year (see §1.414(r)-5(f)(4) for the employees taken into account for this purpose);

(iv) A separate line of business satisfies the minimum or maximum benefits safe harbor of §1.414(r)-5(g) for a testing year (see §1.414(r)-5(g)(6) for the employees taken into account for this purpose);

(v) A plan of the employer satisfies sections 410(b) and 401(a)(4) for a plan year (see §1.414(r)-8(d)(3) for the employees taken into account for this purpose); or

(vi) A plan of the employer satisfies section 401(a)(26) for a plan year (see §1.414(r)-9(c)(3) for the employees taken into account for this purpose).

(b) *Assignment procedure.*—(1) *In general.*—To apply the provisions listed in paragraph (a)(2) of this section with respect to a testing year or plan year, as the case may be, each of the employees taken into account under that provision must be assigned to a qualified separate line of business of the employer on one or more testing days (or section 401(a)(26) testing days) during the year. The first day for which this assignment procedure is required for a testing year is the first testing day. See §1.414(r)-11(b)(6), (7) and (8) (definitions of "testing day", "first testing day" and "section 401(a)(26) testing day"). Section 1.414(r)-8 may require that the assignment procedure be repeated for testing days that fall after the first testing day (including testing days that fall after the close of the testing year in a plan year that begins in the testing year). Accordingly, new employees may be taken into account for the first time on these later testing days who were not taken into account on the first testing day. Section 1.414(r)-9 may have the same effect with respect to section 401(a)(26) testing days that fall after the first testing day.

(2) *Assignment for the first testing day.*—The employees taken into account under a provision described in paragraph (a)(2) of this section with respect to the first testing day for a testing year are assigned among the employer's qualified separate lines of business by applying the following procedure to each of those employees—

(i) An employee who is a substantial-service employee with respect to a qualified separate line of business within the meaning of §1.414(r)-11(b)(2) must be assigned to that qualified separate line of business;

(ii) An employee who is a residual shared employee within the meaning of §1.414(r)-11(b)(4) must be assigned to a qualified separate line of business under paragraph (c) of this section.

Each employee assigned to a qualified separate line of business under paragraph (b)(2)(i) of this section or this paragraph (b)(2)(ii) remains assigned to the same qualified separate line of business for all purposes with respect to the testing year listed in paragraph (a)(2) of this section and for all plan years beginning in that testing year. Once an employee is assigned to a qualified separate line of business with respect to a particular testing day or section 401(a)(26) testing day, that employee remains assigned to that qualified separate line of business after the employee terminates employment. However, after the employee terminates employment, that employee will in most cases not be taken into account with respect to a subsequent testing day or section 401(a)(26) testing day for purposes of applying one or more of the provisions in paragraph (a)(2) of this section.

(3) *Assignment of new employees for subsequent testing days.*—After the first testing day for the testing year, the employees taken into account under a provision described in paragraph (a)(2) of this section with respect to a subsequent testing day (or a section 401(a)(26) testing day) for the testing year may include one or more employees who previously have not been assigned to a qualified separate line of business for any purpose listed in paragraph (a)(2) of this section with respect to the testing year. An employee may not previously have been assigned to a qualified separate line of business for any purpose with respect to the testing year if, for example, the employee has just been hired or has just become a nonexcludable employee. Previously unassigned employees are assigned among the employer's qualified separate lines of business by applying the procedure in paragraph (b)(2) of this section to those employees. In determining whether an employee who is not employed by the employer during the testing year is a substantial-service or a residual shared employee with respect to a qualified separate line of business, §1.414(r)-3(c)(5) is applied with reference to services performed by the employee during a period in the immediately succeeding testing year that are reasonably representative of the employee's services for the employer.

(4) *Special rule for employers using annual option under section 410(b).*—Notwithstanding the fact that paragraphs (b)(1) through (b)(3) of this section generally only require employees to be assigned on testing days beginning with the first testing day, if a plan is tested under section 410(b) using the annual option of §1.410(b)-8(a)(4) (including for purposes of the average benefit percentage test), employees must be assigned on every day of the plan year of that plan for purposes of this paragraph (b). Thus, all employees who provide services at any time during the plan year of a plan that is tested using the annual option of §1.410(b)-8(a)(4) must be assigned to a line of business even if they terminate employment before the first testing day within the meaning of §1.414(r)-11(b)(7) of the testing year in which the plan year begins.

(c) *Assignment and allocation of residual shared employees.*—(1) *In general.*—All residual shared employees must be allocated among an employer's qualified separate lines of business under one of the allocation methods provided in paragraphs (c)(2) through (5) of this section. An employer is permitted to select which method of allocation to apply for the testing year to residual shared employees. However, the same allocation method must be used for all of the employer's residual shared employees and for all purposes listed in paragraph (a)(2) of this section with respect to the testing year.

(2) *Dominant line of business method of allocation.*—(i) *In general.*—Under the method of allocation in this paragraph (c)(2), all residual shared employees are allocated to the employer's dominant line of business. This method does not apply unless the employer has a dominant line of business within the meaning of paragraph (c)(2)(ii) or (c)(2)(iv) of this section. If an employer has more than one dominant line of business under this paragraph (c), the employer must select which qualified separate lines of business is its dominant line of business.

(ii) *Dominant line of business.*—An employer's dominant line of business is that qualified separate line of business that has an employee assignment percentage of at least 50 percent.

(iii) *Employee assignment percentage.*—(A) *Determination of percentage.*—The employee assignment percentage of a qualified separate line of business is the fraction (expressed as a percentage)—

(1) The numerator of which is the number of substantial-service employees with respect to the qualified separate line of business who are assigned to that line of business under paragraph (b) of this section; and

(2) The denominator of which is the total number of substantial-service employees who are assigned to all qualified separate lines of business of the employer under paragraph (b) of this section.

(B) *Employees taken into account.*—The employee assignment percentage is calculated solely with respect to employees who are taken into account for purposes of satisfying section 410(b) with respect to the first testing day. Therefore, this percentage is calculated only once for all purposes with respect to a testing year. The employees described in section 410(b)(3) and (4) are excluded. However, section 410(b)(4) is applied with reference to the lowest minimum age requirement applicable under any plan of the employer, and with reference to the lowest service requirement applicable under any plan of the employer, as if all the plans were a single plan under §1.410(b)-6(b)(2).

(iv) *Option to apply reduced percentage.*—An employer is permitted to determine whether it has a dominant line of business by substituting 25 percent for 50 percent in paragraph (c)(2)(ii) of this section. This option is available for a testing year only if the qualified separate line of business satisfies one of the following requirements:

(A) The qualified separate line of business accounts for at least 60 percent of the employer's gross revenues for the employer's latest fiscal year ending in the testing year.

(B) The employee assignment percentage of the qualified separate line of business would be at least 60 percent if collectively bargained employees were taken into account.

(C) Each qualified separate line of business of the employer satisfies the statutory safe harbor of §1.414(r)-5(b), the average benefits safe harbor of §1.414(r)-5(f), or the minimum or maximum benefits safe harbor of §1.414(r)-5(g). Whether a qualified separate line of business satisfies one of these safe harbors is determined after the application of this section, including the assignment of all residual shared employees under this paragraph (c)(2).

(D) The employee assignment percentage of the qualified separate line of business is at least twice the employee assignment percentages of each of the employer's other qualified separate lines of business.

(v) *Examples.*—The following examples illustrate the application of the method of allocation in this paragraph (c)(2).

Example 1. (i) Employer A operates four qualified separate lines of business as determined under §1.414(r)-1(b) for the testing year, consisting of a software developer, a health food products supplier, a real estate developer, and a ski equipment manufacturer. In applying this section for the first testing day with respect to the testing year, Employer A determines that it has a total of 21,000

employees, of whom 10,000 are substantial-service employees not excludable under section 410(b)(3) or (b)(4). Pursuant to paragraph (b) of this section, these 10,000 employees are assigned among Employer A's qualified separate lines of business as follows:

	Software Developer	Health Food	Real Estate	Ski Equipment
Substantial-Service Employees	2,500	1,000	2,500	4,000
Percentage Assigned to QSLOB	25 %	10 %	25 %	40 %

(ii) Under these facts, Employer A is not permitted to apply the method of allocation in paragraph (c)(3)(ii) of this section, because none of its qualified separate lines of business satisfies the 50 percent requirement in paragraph (c)(2)(ii) of this section.

Example 2. The facts are the same as in *Example 1*, except that, after allocating all residual shared employees to the ski equipment line of business, the software, ski equipment and health food supplier lines of business each would satisfy the statutory safe harbor of §1.414(r)-5(b), and that the real estate development line of business would satisfy the minimum or maximum benefits safe harbor of §1.414(r)-5(g). Under these facts, Employer A is permitted to apply the method of allocation in this paragraph (c)(2) to allocate all its residual shared employees to the ski equipment line of business, because the employee assignment percentage of the ski equipment

line of business exceeds 25 percent and each qualified separate line of business satisfies either the statutory safe harbor of §1.414(r)-5(b) or the minimum or maximum benefits safe harbor of §1.414(r)-5(g).

Example 3. (i) The facts are the same as in *Example 1*, except that, Employer A chooses not to satisfy the minimum or maximum benefits safe harbor of §1.414(r)-5(g). Instead, Employer A combines the real estate developer and ski equipment manufacturer into a single line of business. As a result, Employer A has three qualified separate lines of business as determined under §1.414(r)-1(b). Assume that no residual shared employee becomes a substantial-service employee as a result of the new combination. Employer A's substantial-service employees are assigned among Employer A's qualified separate lines of business as follows:

	Software Developer	Health Food	Real Estate/ Ski Equipment
Substantial-Service Employees	2,500	1,000	6,500
Percentage Assigned to QSLOB	25 %	10 %	65 %

(ii) Under these facts, Employer A is permitted to apply the method of allocation in this paragraph (c)(2) to allocate all its residual shared employees to the combined real estate development and ski equipment manufacturing line of business, because more than 50 percent of Employer A's substantial-service employees that are taken into account for the first testing day are assigned to that qualified separate line of business.

Example 4. (i) The facts are the same as in *Example 1*, except that, of the remaining 11,000 employees of Employer A, 10,000 employees are substantial-service employees who are collectively bargained employees. Pursuant to paragraph (b) of this section, the 10,000 substantial-service employees and the 10,000 substantial-service employees who are collectively bargained employees are assigned among Employer A's qualified separate lines of business as follows:

	Software Developer	Health Food	Real Estate	Ski Equipment
Substantial-Service Employees	2,500	1,000	2,500	4,000
Percentage of total substantial-service employees asssigned to QSLOB	25 %	10 %	25 %	40 %
Substantial-Service Employees (including collectively bargained employees)	2,500	1,000	2,500	14,000
Percentage of total employees (including collectively bargained employees) assigned to QSLOB	12.5 %	5 %	12.5 %	70 %

(ii) Thus, the ski equipment line of business satisfies the 25-percent threshold in paragraph (c)(2)(iv) of this section. In addition, the ski equipment's percentage of substantial-service employees is at least 60 percent when taking into account substantial-service employees who are collectively bargained employees and therefore satisfies the requirement under paragraph (c)(2)(iv)(B) of this section. Under these facts, Employer A is permitted to apply the method of allocation in this paragraph (c)(2) to allocate all its residual shared employees to the ski equipment line of business.

(3) *Pro-rata method of allocation.*—(i) *In general.*—Under the method of allocation in this paragraph (c)(3), all residual shared employees are allocated among an employer's qualified separate lines of business in proportion to the employee assignment percentage of each qualified separate line of business, as determined under paragraph (c)(2)(iii) of this section.

(ii) *Allocation procedure.*—The procedure for allocating residual shared employees under the method in this paragraph (c)(3) is as follows—

(A) The number of highly compensated residual shared employees who are allocated to each qualified separate line of business is equal to the product determined by multiplying the total number of highly compensated residual shared employees of the employer by the employee assignment percentage determined with respect to the qualified separate line of business under paragraph (c)(3)(i) of this section;

(B) The number of nonhighly compensated residual shared employees who are allocated to each qualified separate line of business is equal to the product determined by multiplying the total number of nonhighly compensated residual shared employees of the employer by the employee assignment percentage determined with respect to the qualified separate line of business under paragraph (c)(3)(i) of this section;

(C) For purposes of this procedure, the employer is permitted to determine which highly compensated residual shared employees and which nonhighly compensated residual shared employees are allocated to each qualified separate line of business, provided that the required number of highly and nonhighly compensated residual shared employees are allocated to each qualified separate line of business.

(iii) *Examples.*—The following example illustrates the application of the method of allocation in this paragraph (c)(3).

Example 1. The facts are the same as in *Example 1* under paragraph (c)(2)(v) of this section except that there are no additional residual shared employees after the first testing day. Of Employer A's 1,000 residual shared employees, 800 are highly compensated employees and 200 are nonhighly compensated employees. Employer A applies the pro-rata method of allocation in this paragraph (c)(3). Under these facts, the 1,000 residual shared employees are allocated among Employer A's qualified separate lines of business as follows:

	Software Developer	Health Food	Real Estate	Ski Equipment
Substantial-Service Employees	2,500	1,000	2,500	4,000
Percentage Assigned to QSLOB ("employee assignment percentage")	25%	10%	25%	40%
Residual Shared HCEs Allocated to QSLOB	200 (25% × 800)	80 (10% × 800)	200 (25% × 800)	320 (40% × 800)
Residual Shared NHCEs Allocated to QSLOB	50 (25% × 200)	20 (10% × 200)	50 (25% × 200)	80 (40% × 200)

(4) *HCE percentage ratio method of allocation.*—(i) *In general.*—Under the method of allocation in this paragraph (c)(4), all residual shared employees are allocated among an employer's qualified separate lines of business according to the highly compensated employee percentage assignment ratio of each qualified separate line of business.

(ii) *Highly compensated employee percentage assignment ratio.*—For purposes of this paragraph (c)(4), the highly compensated employee percentage assignment ratio of a qualified separate line of business is the fraction (expressed as a percentage)—

(A) The numerator of which is the percentage of all employees who have previously been assigned to the qualified separate line of business under this section with respect to the testing year who are highly compensated employees; and

(B) The denominator of which is the percentage of all employees who have previously been assigned to any qualified separate line of business under this section with respect to the testing year who are highly compensated employees.

Thus, the highly compensated employee percentage assignment ratio of each of the employer's qualified separate lines of business is recalculated each time a residual shared employee is allocated to a qualified separate line of business under this paragraph (c)(4).

(iii) *Allocation procedure.*—The procedure for allocating all residual shared employees under the method in this paragraph (c)(4) is as follows—

(A) If there are any qualified separate lines of business with a highly compensated employee percentage assignment ratio of less than 50 percent (as determined immediately before the employee is allocated to a qualified separate line of business), the highly compensated residual shared employee must be allocated to one of these qualified separate lines of business;

(B) If there are any qualified separate lines of business with a highly compensated employee percentage assignment ratio greater than 200 percent (as determined immediately before the employee is allocated to a qualified separate line of business), the nonhighly compensated residual shared employee must be allocated to one of these qualified separate lines of business;

(C) If there are no qualified separate lines of business with a highly compensated employee percentage assignment ratio less than 50 percent, a highly compensated residual shared employee may be allocated to any qualified separate line of business with a highly compensated employee percentage assignment ratio of no more than 200 percent, provided that the employee's allocation to the qualified separate line of business does not cause its highly compensated employee percentage assignment ratio to exceed 200 percent (as determined immediately after the employee is allocated to the qualified separate line of business);

(D) If there are no qualified separate lines of business with a highly compensated employee percentage assignment ratio greater than 200 percent, a nonhighly compensated residual shared employee may be allocated to any qualified separate line of business with a highly compensated employee percentage assignment ratio of no less than 50 percent, provided that the employee's allocation to the qualified separate line of business does not cause its highly compensated employee percentage assignment ratio to fall below 50 percent (as determined immediately after the employee is allocated to the qualified separate line of business);

(E) For purposes of this procedure, the employer is permitted to determine which highly compensated residual shared employees and which nonhighly compensated residual shared employees are allocated to each qualified separate line of business, provided that the requirements of this paragraph (c)(4)(iii) are satisfied.

(5) *Small group method.*—(i) *In general.*—Under the method of allocation provided for in this paragraph (c)(5), each residual shared employee is allocated to a qualified separate line of business chosen by the employer. This method does not apply unless all of the requirements of paragraphs (c)(5)(ii), (iii), and (iv) of this section are satisfied.

(ii) *Size of group.*—The total number of the employer's residual shared employees allocated under this paragraph (c) must not exceed three percent of all of the employer's employees. For this purpose, the employer's employees include only those employees taken into account under paragraph (c)(2)(iii)(B) of this section.

(iii) *Composition of qualified separate line of business.*—The qualified separate line of business to which the residual shared employee is allocated must have an employee assignment percentage under paragraph (c)(2)(iii) of this section of at least ten percent. In addition, the qualified separate line of business to which the residual shared employee is allocated must satisfy the statutory safe harbor under § 1.414(r)-5(b) after the employee is so allocated.

(iv) *Reasonable allocation.*—The allocation of residual shared employees under the small group method provided for in this paragraph (c)(5) must be reasonable. Reasonable allocations generally include allocations that are based on the level of services that the residual shared employees provide to the employer's qualified separate lines of business, the similar treatment of similarly-situated residual shared employees, and other bona fide business criteria; in contrast, an allocation that is designed to maximize benefits for select employees is not considered a reasonable allocation. For example, allocation of all residual shared employees who work in the same department, or at the same location, to the same qualified separate line of business would be an indication of reasonableness. However, allocation of a group of similarly-situated residual shared employees to a qualified separate line of business for which they provide minimal services might not be considered reasonable. In addition, the allocation of the professional employees of a department to one qualified separate line of business and the allocation of the support staff of the same department to a different qualified separate line of business would not be reasonable. [Reg. § 1.414(r)-7.]

☐ [*T.D. 8376, 12-2-91. Amended by T.D. 8548, 6-23-94.*]

[Reg. § 1.414(r)-8]

§ 1.414(r)-8. Separate application of section 410(b).—(a) *General rule.*—If an employer is treated as operating qualified separate lines of business for purposes of section 410(b) in accordance with § 1.414(r)-1(b) for a testing year, the requirements of section 410(b) must be applied in accordance with this section separately with respect to the employees of each qualified separate line of business for purposes of testing all plans of the employer for plan years that begin in the testing year (other than a plan tested under the special rule for employer-wide plans in § 1.414(r)-1(c)(2)(ii) for such a plan year). Conversely, if an employer is not treated as operating qualified separate lines of business for purposes of section 410(b) in accordance with § 1.414(r)-1(b) for a testing year, the requirements of section 410(b) must be applied on an employer-wide basis for purposes of testing all plans of the employer for plan years that begin in the testing year. See § 1.414(r)-1(c)(2) and (d)(6). Paragraph (b) of this section explains how the requirements of section 410(b) are applied separately with respect to the employees of a qualified separate line of business for purposes of testing a plan. Paragraph (c) of this section explains the coordination between sections 410(b) and 401(a)(4). Paragraph (d) of this section provides certain supplementary rules necessary for the application of this section.

(b) *Rules of separate application.*—(1) *In general.*—If the requirements of section 410(b) are applied separately with respect to the employees of each qualified separate line of business operated by the employer for a testing year, a plan (other than a plan that is tested under the special rule for employer-wide plans in § 1.414(r)-1(c)(2)(ii) for a plan year) satisfies the requirements of section 410(b) only if—

(i) The plan satisfies section 410(b)(5)(B) on an employer-wide basis; and

(ii) The plan satisfies section 410(b) on a qualified-separate-line-of-business basis.

(2) *Satisfaction of section 410(b)(5)(B) on an employer-wide basis.*—(i) *General rule.*—Section 410(b)(5)(B) provides that a plan is not permitted to be tested separately with respect to the employees of a qualified separate line of business unless the plan benefits a classification of employees found by the Secretary to be nondiscriminatory. A plan satisfies this requirement only if the plan satisfies either the ratio percentage test of § 1.410(b)-2(b)(2) or the nondiscriminatory classification test of § 1.410(b)-4 (without regard to the average benefit percentage test of § 1.410(b)-5), taking into account the other applicable provisions of §§ 1.410(b)-2 through 1.410(b)-10. For this purpose, the nonexcludable employees of the employer taken into account in testing the plan under section 410(b) are determined under § 1.410(b)-6, without regard to the exclusion in § 1.410(b)-6(e) for employees of other qualified separate lines of business of the employer. Thus, in testing a plan separately with respect to the employees of one qualified separate line of business under this paragraph (b)(2), the otherwise nonexcludable employees of the employer's other qualified separate lines of business are not treated as excludable employees. However, under the definition of "plan" in paragraph (d)(2) of this section, these employees are not treated as benefiting under the plan for purposes of applying this paragraph (b)(2).

(ii) *Application of facts and circumstances requirements under nondiscriminatory classification test.*—The fact that an employer has satisfied the qualified-separate-line-of-business requirements in §§ 1.414(r)-1 through 1.414(r)-7 is taken into account in determining whether a classification of employees benefiting under a plan that falls between the safe and unsafe harbors satisfies § 1.410(b)-4(c)(3) (facts and circumstances requirements). Except in unusual circumstances, this fact will be determinative.

(iii) *Modification of unsafe harbor percentage for plans satisfying ratio percentage test at 90 percent level.*—(A) *General rule.*—If a plan benefits a group of employees for a plan year that would satisfy the ratio percentage test of § 1.410(b)-2(b)(2) on a qualified-separate-line-of-business basis under paragraph (b)(3) of this section if the percentage in § 1.410(b)-2(b)(2) were increased to 90 percent, the unsafe harbor percentage in § 1.410(b)-4(c)(4)(ii) for the plan is reduced by five percentage points (not five percent) for the plan year and is applied without regard to the requirement that the unsafe harbor percentage not be less than 20 percent. Thus, if the requirements of this paragraph (b)(2)(iii)(A) are satisfied, the unsafe harbor percentage in § 1.410(b)-4(c)(4)(ii) is treated as 35 percent, reduced by 3/4 of a percentage point for each whole percentage point by which the nonhighly compensated employee concentration percentage exceeds 60 percent.

(B) *Facts and circumstances alternative.*—If a plan satisfies the requirements of paragraph (b)(2)(iii)(A) of this section, but has a ratio percentage on an employer-wide basis that falls below the unsafe harbor percentage determined under paragraph (b)(2)(iii)(A) of this section, the plan nonetheless is deemed to satisfy section 410(b)(5)(B) on an employer-wide basis if the Commissioner determines that, on the basis of all of the relevant facts and circumstances, the plan benefits such employees as qualify under a classification of employees that does not discriminate in favor of highly compensated employees.

(3) *Satisfaction of section 410(b) on a qualified-separate-line-of-business basis.*—A plan satisfies section 410(b) on a qualified-separate-line-of-business basis only if the plan satisfies either the ratio percentage test of § 1.410(b)-2(b)(2) or the average benefit test of § 1.410(b)-2(b)(3) (including the nondiscriminatory classification test of § 1.410(b)-4 and the average benefit percentage test of § 1.410(b)-5), taking into account the other applicable provisions of §§ 1.410(b)-2 through 1.410(b)-10. For this purpose, the nonexcludable employees of the employer taken into account in testing the plan under section 410(b) are determined under § 1.410(b)-6, taking into account the exclusion in § 1.410(b)-6(e) for employees of other qualified separate lines of business of the employer. Thus, in testing a plan separately

with respect to the employees of one qualified separate line of business under this paragraph (b)(3), all employees of the employer's other qualified separate lines of business are treated as excludable employees.

(4) *Examples.*—The following examples illustrate the application of this paragraph (b).

Example 1. (i) Employer A is treated as operating qualified separate lines of business for purposes of section 410(b) in accordance with § 1.414(r)-1(b) for the 1994 testing year with respect to all of its plans. Employer A operates two qualified separate lines of business as determined under § 1.414(r)-1(b)(2), Line 1 and Line 2. Employer A maintains only two plans, Plan X which benefits solely employees of Line 1, and Plan Y which benefits solely employees of Line 2. In testing Plan X under section 410(b) with respect to the first testing day for the plan year of Plan X beginning in the 1994 testing year, it is determined that Employer A has 2,100 nonexcludable employees, of whom 100 are highly compensated employees and 2,000 are nonhighly compensated employees. After applying § 1.414(r)-7 to these employees, 50 of the highly compensated employees and 100 of the nonhighly compensated employees are treated as employees of Line 2, and the remaining 50 highly compensated employees and the remaining 1,900 nonhighly compensated employees are treated as employees of Line 1.

(ii) All of the highly compensated employees and 1,300 of the nonhighly compensated employees who are treated as employees of Line 1 benefit under Plan X. Thus, on an employer-wide basis, Plan X benefits 50 percent of all Employer A's highly compensated employees (50 out of 100) and 65 percent of all Employer A's nonhighly compensated employees (1,300 out of 2,000). Plan X consequently has a ratio percentage determined on an employer-wide basis of 130 percent (65% ÷ 50%), see § 1.410(b)-9, and could satisfy section 410(b) under the ratio percentage test of § 1.410(b)-2(b)(2) if that section were applied on an employer-wide basis without regard to the provisions of this paragraph (b). Under paragraph (a) of this section, however, the requirements of section 410(b) must be applied separately with respect to the employees of each qualified separate line of business operated by Employer A for all plans of Employer A for plan years that begin in the 1994 testing year. This rule does not apply to plans tested under the special rule for employer-wide plans in § 1.414(r)-1(c)(2)(ii). Plan X benefits only 65 percent of the nonhighly compensated employees of Employer A, however, and therefore cannot satisfy the 70 percent requirement necessary to be tested under that rule. As a result, for the plan year of Plan X beginning in the 1994 testing year, Plan X is not permitted to satisfy section 410(b) on an employer-wide basis and, instead, is only permitted to satisfy section 410(b) separately with respect to the employees of each qualified separate line of business operated by Employer A, in accordance with paragraphs (b)(2) and (b)(3) of this section.

Example 2. The facts are the same as in *Example 1.* All of the 50 highly compensated employees treated as employees of Line 2 benefit under Plan Y, and 80 of the 100 nonhighly compensated employees treated as employees of Line 2 benefit under Plan Y. Thus, Plan Y benefits 50 percent of all Employer A's highly compensated employees (50 out of 100) and only 4 percent of all Employer A's nonhighly compensated employees (80 out of 2,000). Thus, while Plan Y has a ratio percentage of 80 percent (80% ÷ 100%) on a qualified-separate-line-of-business basis, it has a ratio percentage of only 8 percent (4% ÷ 50%) on an employer-wide basis. See § 1.410(b)-9. Under § 1.410(b)-4(c)(4)(iii), the nonhighly compensated employee concentration percentage is 2,000/2,100 or 95 percent. Because 8 percent is less than 20 percent (the unsafe harbor percentage applicable to Employer A under § 1.410(b)-4(c)(4)(ii)), Plan Y does not satisfy the nondiscriminatory classification test of § 1.410(b)-4 on an employer-wide basis. Nor does Plan Y satisfy the ratio percentage test of § 1.410(b)-2(b)(2) on an employer-wide basis, since 8 percent is less than 70 percent. Under these facts, Plan Y does not satisfy section 410(b)(5)(B) on an employer-wide basis in accordance with paragraph (b)(2) of this section for the plan year of Plan Y beginning in the 1994 testing year, and therefore fails to satisfy section 410(b) for that year. This is true even though Plan Y satisfies section 410(b) on a qualified-separate-line-of-business basis in accordance with paragraph (b)(3) of this section.

Example 3. The facts are the same as in *Example 2*, except that all of the employees treated as employees of Line 2 benefit under Plan Y. Thus, Plan Y benefits 50 percent of all of Employer A's highly compensated employees (50 out of 100) and 5 percent of all of Employer A's nonhighly compensated employees (100 out of 2,000). Plan Y therefore has a ratio percentage of 100 percent (100% ÷ 100%) on a qualified-separate-line-of-business basis and a ratio percentage of 10 percent (5% ÷ 50%) on an employer-wide basis. Because Plan Y has a ratio percentage of at least 90 percent on a qualified-separate-line-of-business basis, a reduced unsafe harbor percentage applies to Plan Y under paragraph (b)(2)(iii)(A) of this section. The reduced unsafe harbor percentage applicable to Plan Y is 8.75 percent because

Employer A's nonhighly compensated employee concentration percentage is 95 percent. Plan Y's employer-wide ratio percentage of 10 percent therefore exceeds the unsafe harbor percentage. Plan Y thus satisfies section 410(b)(5)(B) on an employer-wide basis in accordance with paragraph (b)(2) of this section for the plan year of Plan Y beginning in the 1994 testing year. Plan Y also satisfies section 410(b) on a qualified-separate-line-of-business basis in accordance with paragraph (b)(3) of this section.

Example 4. The facts are the same as in *Example 3*, except that Employer A's total nonexcludable nonhighly compensated employees are 2,500 (rather than 2,000), of whom 100 are treated as employees of Line 2 and of whom 90 benefit under Plan Y. Plan Y has a ratio percentage of 90 percent (90% ÷ 100%) on a qualified-separate-line-of-business basis, and Employer A's nonhighly compensated employee concentration percentage is 2,500/2,600 or 96 percent. Thus, the reduced unsafe harbor percentage applicable to Plan Y under paragraph (b)(2)(iii)(A) of this section is 8 percent. Plan Y benefits 50 percent of all of Employer A's highly compensated employees (50 out of 100) and 3.6 percent of all of Employer A's nonhighly compensated employees (90 out of 2,500). Plan Y therefore has a ratio percentage of only 7.2 percent (3.6% ÷ 50%) on an employer-wide basis, which falls below the reduced unsafe harbor percentage of 8 percent. Nonetheless, under paragraph (b)(2)(iii)(B) of this section, Plan Y will be deemed to satisfy section 410(b)(5)(B) on an employer-wide basis if the Commissioner determines that, on the basis of all of the relevant facts and circumstances, the plan benefits such employees as qualify under a classification of employees that does not discriminate in favor of highly compensated employees.

Example 5. (i) The facts are the same as in *Example 1*, except that Plan X benefits only 950 of the employees of Line 1. Assume Plan X satisfies the reasonable classification requirement of §1.410(b)-4(b) on an employer-wide basis. Plan X benefits 50 percent of all Employer A's highly compensated employees (50 out of 100) and 47.5 percent of all Employer A's nonhighly compensated employees (950 out of 2,000). Plan X consequently has a ratio percentage determined on an employer-wide basis of 95 percent (47.5% ÷ 50%), see §1.410(b)-9, and thus satisfies section 410(b)(5)(B) on an employer-wide basis.

(ii) Plan X has a ratio percentage determined on a qualified-separate-line-of-business basis of 50 percent (50% ÷ 100%). Because 50 percent is less than 70 percent, Plan X must satisfy the nondiscriminatory classification test of §1.410(b)-4 and the average benefit percentage test of §1.410(b)-5 on a qualified-separate-line-of-business basis in order to satisfy the other requirements of section 410(b). Plan X satisfies the nondiscriminatory classification requirement of §1.410(b)-4(c) on a qualified-separate-line-of-business because its ratio percentage determined on a qualified-separate-line-of-business basis is more than 22.25 percent, the safe harbor percentage applicable to Line 1 under §1.410(b)-4(c)(4)(i). Because Plan X satisfies the reasonable classification requirement of §1.410(b)-4(b) on an employer-wide basis, it is also deemed to satisfy this requirement on a qualified-separate-line-of-business basis. See §1.410(b)-7(c)(5). In determining whether Plan X satisfies the average benefit percentage test of §1.410(b)-5, only Plan X and only employees of Line 1 are taken into account. See §§1.410(b)-6(e) and 1.410(b)-7(e).

Example 6. The facts are the same as in *Example 2*, except that, prior to the 1994 testing year, Employer A merges Plan X and Plan Y so that they form a single plan within the meaning of section 414(*l*). Under the definition of "plan" in paragraph (d)(2) of this section, however, the portion of the newly merged plan that benefits employees of Line 2 (former Plan Y) is still treated as a separate plan from the portion of the newly merged plan that benefits employees of Line 1 (former Plan X). The portion of the newly merged plan that benefits employees of Line 2 (former Plan Y) fails to satisfy section 410(b) for the reasons stated in Example 2. Under these facts, because the portion of the newly merged plan that benefits employees of Line 2 fails to satisfy section 410(b), the entire newly merged plan fails to satisfy section 410(b) for the plan year of the newly merged plan that begins in the 1994 testing year. See paragraph (d)(5) of this section.

(c) *Coordination of section 401(a)(4) with section 410(b).*—(1) *General rule.*—For purposes of these regulations, the requirements of section 410(b) encompass the requirements of section 401(a)(4) (including, but not limited to, the permitted disparity rules of section 401(*l*), the actual deferral percentage test of section 401(k)(3), and the actual contribution percentage test of section 401(m)(2)). Therefore, if the requirements of section 410(b) are applied separately with respect to the employees of each qualified separate line of business of an employer for purposes of testing one or more plans of the employer for plan years that begin in a testing year, the requirements of section *401(a)(4)* must also be applied separately with respect to the employees of the same qualified separate lines of business for purposes of testing the same plans for the same plan years. Furthermore, if section 401(a)(4) requires that a group of employees under the plan satisfy section 410(b) for purposes of satisfying section 401(a)(4),

section 410(b) must be applied for this purpose in the same manner provided in paragraph (b) of this section. See, for example, §§1.401(a)(4)-2(c)(1) and 1.401(a)(4)-3(c)(1) (requiring each rate group of employees under a plan to satisfy section 410(b)), §1.401(a)(4)-4(b) (requiring the group of employees to whom each benefit, right, or feature is currently available under a plan to satisfy section 410(b)), and §1.401(a)(4)-9(c)(1) (requiring the group of employees included in each component plan into which a plan is restructured to satisfy section 410(b)). Thus, the group of employees must satisfy section 410(b)(5)(B) on an employer-wide basis in accordance with paragraph (b)(2) of this section and also must satisfy section 410(b) on a qualified-separate-line-of-business basis in accordance with paragraph (b)(3) of this section, in both cases as if the group of employees were the only employees benefiting under the plan.

(2) *Examples.*—The following examples illustrate the application of the rule in this paragraph (c).

Example 1. Employer B is treated as operating qualified separate lines of business for purposes of section 410(b) in accordance with §1.414(r)-1(b) for the 1993 testing year. Employer B operates two qualified separate lines of business as determined under §1.414(r)-1(b)(2), Line 1 and Line 2. Employer B maintains Plan Z, which benefits employees in both Line 1 and Line 2. Under the definition of "plan" in paragraph (d)(2) of this section, the portion of Plan Z that benefits employees of Line 1 is treated as a separate plan from the portion of Plan Z that benefits employees of Line 2. Under this paragraph (c), this result applies for purposes of both section 410(b) and section 401(a)(4).

Example 2. The facts are the same as in *Example 1*, except that Plan Z benefits solely employees of Line 1. In testing Plan Z under section 401(a)(4) for the plan year of Plan Z beginning in the 1993 testing year, Employer B restructures Plan Z into several component plans (within the meaning of §1.401(a)(4)-9(c)). Under §1.401(a)(4)-9(c)(1), each of these component plans is required to satisfy section 410(b). This paragraph (c) requires that each of the component plans be tested separately with respect to the employees of each qualified separate line of business operated by Employer B. This testing must be done in accordance with paragraph (b) of this section. Consequently, each component plan must satisfy section 410(b)(5)(B) on an employer-wide basis in accordance with paragraph (b)(2) of this section and must also satisfy section 410(b) on a qualified-separate-line-of-business basis in accordance with paragraph (b)(3) of this section.

Example 3. The facts are the same as in *Example 1*, except that Plan Z is a profit-sharing plan, and contributions to Plan Z are made pursuant to cash or deferred arrangement in which all employees of Employer B are eligible to participate. Assume that, as a result, Plan Z satisfies the requirements to be tested under the special rule for employer-wide plans in §1.414(r)-1(c)(2)(ii). Under these facts, the requirements of sections 410(b), 401(a)(4) and 401(k), including the actual deferral percentage test of section 401(k)(3) and §1.401(k)-1(b), would generally be required to be applied separately to the portions of Plan Z that benefit the employees of Line 1 and Line 2, respectively. However, if Plan Z is tested under the special rule in §1.414(r)-1(c)(2)(ii), these requirements must be applied on an employer-wide basis.

(d) *Supplementary rules.*—(1) *In general.*—This paragraph (d) provides certain supplementary rules necessary for the application of this section.

(2) *Definition of plan.*—For purposes of this section, the term "plan" means a plan within the meaning of §1.410(b)-7(a) and (b), after application of the mandatory disaggregation rules of §1.410(b)-7(c) (including the mandatory disaggregation rule for portions of a plan that benefit employees of different qualified separate lines of business) and the permissive aggregation rules of §1.410(b)-7(d). Thus, for purposes of this section, the portion of a plan that benefits employees of one qualified separate line of business is treated as a separate plan from the other portions of the same plan that benefit employees of other qualified separate lines of business of the employer, unless the plan is tested under the special rule for employer-wide plans in §1.414(r)-1(c)(2)(ii) for the plan year.

(3) *Employees of a qualified separate line of business.*—For purposes of applying paragraph (b) of this section with respect to a testing day, the employees of each qualified separate line of business of the employer are determined by applying §1.414(r)-7 to the employees of the employer otherwise taken into account under section 410(b) for the testing day. For purposes of applying paragraph (c) of this section with respect to a testing day, the employees of each qualified separate line of business of the employer are determined by applying §1.414(r)-7 to the employees of the employer otherwise taken into account under section 401(a)(4) for the testing day. For the definition of "testing day," see §1.414(r)-11(b)(6).

(4) *Consequences of failure.*—If a plan fails to satisfy either paragraph (b)(2), (b)(3), or (c)(1) of this section, the plan (and any plan of which it constitutes a portion) fails to satisfy section 401(a). However, this failure alone does not cause the employer to fail to be treated as operating qualified separate lines of business in accordance with §1.414(r)-1(b), unless the employer is relying on benefits provided under the plan to satisfy the minimum benefit portion of the safe harbor in §1.414(r)-5(g)(2) with respect to at least one of its qualified separate lines of business. [Reg. §1.414(r)-8.]

☐ [*T.D. 8376, 12-2-91. Amended by T.D. 8548, 6-23-94 and T.D. 9849, 3-11-2019.*]

[Reg. §1.414(r)-9]

§1.414(r)-9. Separate application of section 401(a)(26).—(a) *General rule.*—If an employer is treated as operating qualified separate lines of business for purposes of section 401(a)(26) in accordance with §1.414(r)-1(b) for a testing year, the requirements of section 401(a)(26) must be applied separately with respect to the employees of each qualified separate line of business for purposes of testing all plans of the employer for plan years that begin in the testing year (other than a plan tested under the special rule for employer-wide plans in §1.414(r)-1(c)(3)(ii) for such a plan year). Conversely, if an employer is not treated as operating qualified separate lines of business for purposes of section 401(a)(26) in accordance with §1.414(r)-1(b) for a testing year, the requirements of section 401(a)(26) must be applied on an employer-wide basis for purposes of testing all plans of the employer for plan years that begin in the testing year. See §1.414(r)-1(c)(3) and (d)(6). Paragraph (b) of this section explains how the requirements of section 401(a)(26) are applied separately with respect to the employees of a qualified separate line of business for purposes of testing a plan. Paragraph (c) of this section provides certain supplementary rules necessary for the application of this section.

(b) *Requirements applicable to a plan.*—If the requirements of section 401(a)(26) are applied separately with respect to the employees of a qualified separate line of business for a testing year, a plan (other than a plan that is tested under the special rule for employer-wide plans in §1.414(r)-1(c)(3)(ii) for a plan year) satisfies section 401(a)(26) only if it satisfies the requirements of §§1.401(a)(26)-1 through 1.401(a)(26)-9 on a qualified-separate-line-of-business basis. For this purpose, the nonexcludable employees of the employer taken into account in testing the plan under section 401(a)(26) are determined under §1.401(a)(26)-6(b), taking into account the exclusion in §1.401(a)(26)-6(b)(8) for employees of other qualified separate lines of business of the employer. Thus, in testing a plan separately with respect to the employees of one qualified separate line of business under this paragraph (b), all employees of the employer's other qualified separate lines of business are treated as excludable employees.

(c) *Supplementary rules.*—(1) *In general.*—This paragraph (c) provides certain supplementary rules necessary for the application of this section.

(2) *Definition of plan.*—For purposes of this section, the term "plan" means a plan within the meaning of §1.401(a)(26)-2(c) and (d), including the mandatory disaggregation rule of §1.401(a)(26)-2(d)(6) for portions of a plan that benefit employees of different qualified separate lines of business. Thus, for purposes of this section, the portion of a plan that benefits employees of one qualified separate line of business is treated as a separate plan from the other portions of the same plan that benefit employees of other qualified separate lines of business of the employer, unless the plan is tested under the special rule for employer-wide plans in §1.414(r)-1(c)(3)(ii) for the plan year.

(3) *Employees of a qualified separate line of business.*—For purposes of applying paragraph (b)(2) of this section with respect to a section 401(a)(26) testing day, the employees of each qualified separate line of business of the employer are determined by applying §1.414(r)-7 to the employees of the employer otherwise taken into account under section 401(a)(26) for the section 401(a)(26) testing day. For the definition of "section 401(a)(26) testing day," see §1.414(r)-11(b)(8).

(4) *Consequences of failure.*—If a plan fails to satisfy paragraph (b)(2) of this section, the plan (and any plan of which it constitutes a portion) fails to satisfy section 401(a). However, this failure alone would not cause the employer to fail to be treated as operating qualified separate lines of business in accordance with §1.414(r)-1(b), unless the employer is relying on benefits provided under the plan to satisfy the minimum benefit portion of the safe harbor in §1.414(r)-5(g)(2) with respect to at least one of its qualified separate lines of business. [Reg. §1.414(r)-9.]

☐ [*T.D. 8376, 12-2-91.*]

[Reg. §1.414(r)-10]

§1.414(r)-10. Separate application of section 129(d)(8).—[Reserved]

☐ [*T.D. 8376, 12-2-91.*]

[Reg. §1.414(r)-11]

§1.414(r)-11. Definitions and special rules.—(a) *In general.*—This section contains certain definitions and special rules applicable under these regulations. Paragraph (b) of this section provides certain definitions that apply for purposes of these regulations. Paragraph (c) of this section provides averaging rules under which certain provisions of these regulations may be applied on the basis of a two-year or a three-year average.

(b) *Definitions.*—(1) *In general.*—In applying the provisions of this section and of §§1.414(r)-1 through 1.414(r)-10, unless otherwise provided, the definitions in this paragraph (b) govern in addition to the definitions in §1.410(b)-9.

(2) *Substantial-service employee.*—An employee is a substantial-service employee with respect to a line of business for a testing year if at least 75 percent of the employee's services are provided to that line of business for that testing year within the meaning of §1.414(r)-3(c)(5). In addition, if an employee provides at least 50% and less than 75% of the employee's services to a line of business for the testing year within the meaning of §1.414(r)-3(c)(5), the employer may treat that employee as a substantial service employee with respect to that line of business provided the employee is so treated for all purposes of these regulations. The employer may choose such treatment separately with respect to each employee.

(3) *Top-paid employee.*—Generally, an employee is a top-paid employee with respect to a line of business for a testing year if the employee is among the top 10 percent by compensation of those employees who provide services to that line of business for that testing year within the meaning of §1.414(r)-3(c)(5) and who are not substantial-service employees within the meaning of paragraph (b)(2) of this section with respect to any other line of business. In addition, in determining the group of top-paid employees, the employer may choose to disregard all employees who provide less than 25 percent of their services to the line of business. For purposes of this paragraph (b)(3), an employee's compensation is the compensation used to determine the employee's status as a highly or nonhighly compensated employee under section 414(q) for purposes of applying section 410(b) with respect to the first testing day. For this purpose, only compensation received during the determination year (within the meaning of §1.414(q)-1T, Q&A-13) is taken into account. See §1.414(r)-3(c)(7) for examples of the determination of top-paid employee.

(4) *Residual shared employee.*—An employee is a residual shared employee for a testing year if the employee is not a substantial-service employee with respect to any line of business for the testing year.

(5) *Testing year.*—The term "testing year" means the calendar year.

(6) *Testing day.*—The term "testing day" means any day on which §1.410(b)-8(a)(1) requires any plan (within the meaning of §1.414(r)-8(d)(2)) of the employer actually to satisfy section 410(b) with respect to a plan year that begins in the testing year. Thus, if a plan is required to satisfy section 410(b) on one day within each quarter of the plan year under the quarterly testing option of §1.410(b)-8(a)(3), each of those four days is a testing day. Similarly, if a plan is required to satisfy section 410(b) on every day of the plan year under the daily testing option of §1.410(b)-8(a)(2), every day of the plan year is a testing day.

(7) *First testing day.*—The term "first testing day" means the testing day that occurs earliest in time of all the testing days under all plans of the employer with respect to the testing year. If a plan is tested under the annual testing option of §1.410(b)-8(a)(4) (other than for purposes of the average benefit percentage test of §1.410(b)-5) for a plan year that begins in a testing year, then, solely for purposes of determining the first testing day in a testing year, the employer may treat any day in the plan year as a testing day, provided that the coverage of each plan of the employer on the day selected is reasonably representative of the coverage of the plan over the entire plan year. The first testing day with respect to a testing year must fall within that testing year.

(8) *Section 401(a)(26) testing day.*—The term "section 401(a)(26) testing day" means any day on which §1.401(a)(26)-7(a) or (b) requires any plan of the employer actually to satisfy section 401(a)(26) with respect to a plan year that begins in the testing year. In no event

may a section 401(a)(26) testing day with respect to a testing year fall before the first testing day for that testing year. For purposes of this paragraph (b)(8), the term "plan" has the same meaning as in §1.414(r)-9(c)(2).

(c) *Averaging rules.*—(1) *In general.*—The provisions specified in this paragraph (c) are permitted to be applied based on the average of the percentages for the current testing year and the consecutive testing years (not to exceed four consecutive testing years) immediately preceding the current testing year.

(2) *Specified provisions.*—The provisions specified in this paragraph (c) are—

(i) The 90-percent separate employee workforce requirement of §1.414(r)-3(b)(4);

(ii) The 80-percent separate management requirement of §1.414(r)-3(b)(5);

(iii) The 25-percent provision-to-customers requirement of §1.414(r)-3(d)(2)(iii);

(iv) The minimum and maximum highly compensated employee percentage ratios under the statutory safe harbor of §1.414(r)-5(b)(1)(i) and (ii) (50 percent and 200 percent, respectively), but not the 10-percent exception in §1.414(r)-5(b)(4);

(v) The employee assignment percentage applied for purposes of the dominant line of business method of allocating residual shared employees under §1.414(r)-7(c)(2) and the pro-rata method for allocating residual shared employees under §1.414(r)-7(c)(3).

(3) *Averaging of large fluctuations not permitted.*—A provision is not permitted to be applied based on an average determined under this paragraph (c) if the percentage for any testing year taken into account in calculating the average falls below a minimum percentage, or exceeds a maximum percentage, by more than 10 percent (not 10 percentage points) of the respective minimum or maximum percentage. Thus, for example, the statutory safe harbor of §1.414(r)-5(b) is not permitted to be applied based on an average determined under this paragraph (c) if the percentage for any testing year taken into account in calculating the average falls below 45 percent (which is 10 percent below the 50-percent minimum) or exceeds 220 percent (which is 10 percent above the 200-percent maximum).

(4) *Consistency requirements.*—A provision is permitted to be applied on an averaging basis under this paragraph (c) regardless of how any other provision is applied, except in the case of the separate employee workforce and separate management requirements of §1.414(r)-3(b)(4) and (5), which each must be applied on the same basis as the other. A provision is also permitted to be applied on an averaging basis under this paragraph (c) for a testing year, regardless of how the provision is applied for any other testing year. However, once a provision is applied on an averaging basis under this paragraph (c) for a testing year, it must be applied on the same basis to all the employer's lines of business to which the provision is applied for the testing year. The percentage for a preceding testing year may be taken into account under this paragraph (c) only if—

(i) The employer calculates the percentage for the preceding testing year in the same manner as the employer calculates the percentage for the current testing year;

(ii) The employer is treated as operating qualified separate lines of business in accordance with §1.414(r)-1(b) for the preceding testing year; and

(iii) The employer designated the same lines of business in the preceding testing year as in the current testing year. [Reg. §1.414(r)-11.]

☐ [T.D. 8376, 12-2-91. *Amended by* T.D. 8548, 6-23-94.]

[Reg. §1.414(s)-1]

§1.414(s)-1. Definition of compensation.—(a) *Introduction.*—(1) *In general.*—Section 414(s) and this section provide rules for defining compensation for purposes of applying any provision that specifically refers to section 414(s) or this section. For example, section 414(s) is referred to in many of the nondiscrimination provisions applicable to pension, profit-sharing, and stock bonus plans qualified under section 401(a). In accordance with section 414(s)(1), this section defines compensation as compensation within the meaning of section 415(c)(3). It also implements the election provided in section 414(s)(2) to treat certain deferrals as compensation and exercises the authority granted to the Secretary in section 414(s)(3) to prescribe alternative nondiscriminatory definitions of compensation.

(2) *Limitations on scope of section 414(s).*—Section 414(s) and this section do not apply unless a provision specifically refers to section 414(s) or this section. For example, even though a definition of compensation permitted under section 414(s) must be used in determining whether the contributions or benefits under a pension, profit-sharing, or stock bonus plan satisfy a certain applicable provision

(such as section 401(a)(4)), except as otherwise specified, the plan is not required to use a definition of compensation that satisfies section 414(s) in calculating the amount of contributions or benefits actually provided under the plan.

(3) *Overview.*—Paragraph (b) of this section provides rules of general application that govern a definition of compensation that satisfies section 414(s). Paragraph (c) of this section contains specific definitions of compensation that satisfy section 414(s) without satisfying any additional nondiscrimination requirement under section 414(s). Paragraph (d) of this section provides rules permitting the use of alternative definitions of compensation that satisfy section 414(s) as long as the nondiscrimination requirement and other requirements described in paragraph (d) of this section are satisfied. Paragraphs (e) and (f) of this section provide special rules permitting the use of rate of compensation, or prior-employer compensation or imputed compensation, rather than actual compensation, under a definition of compensation that satisfies section 414(s). Paragraph (g) of this section provides other special rules, including a special rule for determining the compensation of a self-employed individual under an alternative definition of compensation. Paragraph (h) of this section provides definitions for certain terms used in this section.

(b) *Rules of general application.*—(1) *Use of a definition.*—Any definition of compensation that satisfies section 414(s) may be used when a provision explicitly refers to section 414(s) unless the reference or this section specifically indicates otherwise.

(2) *Consistency rule.*—(i) *General rule.*—A definition of compensation selected by an employer for use in satisfying an applicable provision must be used consistently to define the compensation of all employees taken into account in satisfying the requirements of the applicable provision for the determination period. For example, although any definition of compensation that satisfies section 414(s) may be used for section 401(a)(4) purposes, the same definition of compensation generally must be used consistently to define the compensation of all employees taken into account in determining whether a plan satisfies section 401(a)(4). Furthermore, a different definition of compensation that satisfies section 414(s) is permitted to be used to determine whether another plan maintained by the same employer separately satisfies the requirements of section 401(a)(4). Although a definition of compensation must be used consistently, an employer may change its definition of compensation for a subsequent determination period with respect to the applicable provision. Rules provided under any applicable provision may modify the consistency requirements of this paragraph (b)(2).

(ii) *Scope of consistency rule.*—Compensation will not fail to be defined consistently for a group of employees merely because some employees do not receive one or more of the types of compensation included in the definition. For example, a definition of compensation that includes salary, regular or scheduled pay, overtime, and specified types of bonuses will not fail to define compensation consistently merely because only salaried employees receive salary and these specified types of bonuses and only hourly employees receive regular or scheduled pay and overtime.

(3) *Self-employed individuals.*—Notwithstanding paragraph (b)(1) of this section, self-employed individuals' compensation can only be determined under paragraph (c)(2) of this section (with or without the modification permitted by paragraph (c)(4) of this section or a modification permitted by paragraph (c)(5) of this secion) or by using an equivalent alternative compensation amount determined in accordance with paragraph (g)(1) of this section. These limitations on self-employed individuals do not affect their common-law employees. Thus, the compensation of common-law employees of a partnership or sole proprietorship may be defined using an alternative definition, provided the definition otherwise satisfies paragraph (c)(3), (d), (e), or (f) of this section. If an alternative definition of compensation under paragraph (c)(3), (d), (e), or (f) of this section is used for other employees to satisfy an applicable provision, the consistency requirement is only met if paragraph (g) of this section is used for the self-employed individuals.

(c) *Specific definitions of compensation that satisfy section 414(s).*—(1) *General rules.*—The definitions of compensation provided in paragraphs (c)(2) and (c)(3) of this section satisfy section 414(s) and need not satisfy any additional requirements under section 414(s). Paragraph (c)(2) of this section describes definitions of compensation within the meaning of section 415(c)(3). Paragraph (c)(3) of this section provides a safe harbor alternative definition that excludes certain additional items of compensation. Paragraph (c)(4) of this section permits any definition provided in paragraph (c)(2) or (c)(3) of this section to include certain types of elective contributions and deferred compensation. Paragraph (c)(5) of this section permits certain modifications to a definition otherwise provided under this paragraph (c).

(2) *Compensation within the meaning of section 415(c)(3).*—A definition of compensation that includes all compensation within the meaning of section 415(c)(3) and excludes all other compensation satisfies section 414(s). Sections 1.415(c)-2(b) and (c) provide rules for determining items of compensation included in and excluded from compensation within the meaning of section 415(c)(3). In addition, section 414(s) is satisfied by the safe harbor definitions provided in § 1.415(c)-2(d)(2), (d)(3) and (d)(4) and any additional definitions of compensation prescribed by the Commissioner under the authority provided in § 1.415(c)-2(d)(1) that are treated as satisfying section 415(c)(3).

(3) *Safe harbor alternative definition.*—Under the safe harbor alternative definition in this paragraph (c)(3), compensation is compensation as defined in paragraph (c)(2) of this section, reduced by all of the following items (even if includible in gross income): reimbursements or other expense allowances, fringe benefits (cash and non-cash), moving expenses, deferred compensation, and welfare benefits.

(4) *Inclusion of certain deferrals in compensation.*—Any definition of compensation provided in paragraph (c)(2) or (c)(3) of this section satisfies section 414(s) even though it is modified to include all of the following types of elective contributions and all of the following types of deferred compensation—

(i) Elective contributions that are made by the employer on behalf of its employees that are not includible in gross income under section 125, section 402(e)(3), section 402(h), and section 403(b);

(ii) Compensation deferred under an eligible deferred compensation plan within the meaning of section 457(b) (deferred compensation plans of state and local governments and tax-exempt organizations); and

(iii) Employee contributions (under governmental plans) described in section 414(h)(2) that are picked up by the employing unit and thus are treated as employer contributions.

(5) *Exclusions applicable solely to highly compensated employees.*—Any definition of compensation that satisfies paragraph (c)(2) or (c)(3) of this section, with or without the modification permitted by paragraph (c)(4) of this section, may be modified to exclude any portion of the compensation of some or all of the employer's highly compensated employees (including, for example, any one or more of the types of elective contributions or deferred compensation described in paragraph (c)(4) of this section). This paragraph (c)(5) only permits modifications that apply to the compensation of highly compensated employees. See paragraph (d) of this section for requirements with respect to any modifications in defining the compensation of nonhighly compensated employees.

(d) *Alternative definitions of compensation that satisfy section 414(s).*— (1) *General rule.*—In addition to the definitions provided in paragraph (c) of this section, any definition of compensation satisfies section 414(s) with respect to employees (other than self-employed individuals treated as employees under section 401(c)(1)) if the definition of compensation does not by design favor highly compensated employees, is reasonable within the meaning of paragraph (d)(2) of this section, and satisfies the nondiscrimination requirement in paragraph (d)(3) of this section.

(2) *Reasonable definition of compensation.*—(i) *General rule.*—An alternative definition of compensation under this paragraph (d) is reasonable under section 414(s) if it is a definition of compensation provided in paragraph (c) of this section, modified to exclude all or any portion of one or more of the types of compensation described in paragraph (d)(2)(ii) of this section. See paragraph (e) of this section, however, for special rules that permit definitions of compensation based on employees' rates of compensation and paragraph (f) of this section for special rules that permit definitions of compensation that include prior-employer compensation or imputed compensation.

(ii) *Items that may be excluded.*—A reasonable definition of compensation is permitted to exclude, on a consistent basis, all or any portion of irregular or additional compensation, including (but not limited to) one or more of the following: any type of additional compensation for employees working outside their regularly scheduled tour of duty (such as overtime pay, premiums for shift differential, and call-in premiums), bonuses, or any one or more of the types of compensation excluded under the safe harbor alternative definition in paragraph (c)(3) of this section. Whether a type of compensation is irregular or additional is determined based on all the relevant facts and circumstances. A reasonable definition is also permitted to include, on a consistent basis, all or any portion of the types of elective contributions or deferred compensation described in paragraph (c)(4) of this section and, thus, need not include all those types of elective contributions or deferred compensation as otherwise required under paragraph (c)(4) of this section.

(iii) *Limits on the amount excluded from compensation.*—A definition of compensation is not reasonable if it provides that each employee's compensation is a specified portion of the employee's compensation measured for the otherwise applicable determination period under another definition. For example, a definition of compensation that specifically limits each employee's compensation for a determination period to 95 percent of the employee's compensation using a definition provided in paragraph (c) of this section is not reasonable. Similarly, a definition of compensation that limits each employee's compensation used to satisfy an applicable provision with a 12-month determination period to compensation under a definition provided in paragraph (c) of this section for one month is not a reasonable definition of compensation. However, a definition of compensation is not unreasonable merely because it excludes all compensation in excess of a specified dollar amount.

(3) *Nondiscrimination requirement.*—(i) *In general.*—An alternative definition of compensation under this paragraph (d) is nondiscriminatory under section 414(s) for a determination period if the average percentage of total compensation included under the alternative definition of compensation for an employer's highly compensated employees as a group for the determination period does not exceed by more than a de minimis amount the average percentage of total compensation included under the alternative definition for the employer's nonhighly compensated employees as a group.

(ii) *Total compensation.*—(A) *General rule.*—For purposes of this paragraph (d)(3), total compensation must be determined using a definition of compensation provided in paragraph (c)(2) of this section, either with or without the modification permitted by paragraph (c)(4) of this section. Thus, total compensation does not include prior-employer compensation or imputed compensation described in paragraph (f)(1) of this section (including imputed compensation for a period during which an employee performs services for another employer). Total compensation taken into account for each employee (including, if added, the elective contributions and deferred compensation described in paragraph (c)(4) of this section) may not exceed the annual compensation limit of section 401(a)(17).

(B) *Alternative definitions with exclusions applicable solely to highly compensated employees.*—If an alternative definition of compensation contains a provision that excludes amounts from compensation and, as described in paragraph (c)(5) of this section, the provision only applies in defining the compensation of some highly compensated employees, then, for purposes of this paragraph (d)(3), the total compensation of any highly compensated employee subject to the provision must be reduced by any amount excluded from the employee's compensation as a result of the provision. However, if the provision applies consistently in defining the compensation of all highly compensated employees, this adjustment to total compensation is not required.

(iii) *Employees taken into account.*—(A) *General rule.*—In applying the requirement of this paragraph (d)(3), the employees taken into account are the same employees taken into account in satisfying the requirements of the applicable provision for the determination period. For example, in determining whether a plan satisfies section 401(a)(4), an alternative definition must satisfy this paragraph (d)(3) taking into account all employees who benefit under the plan for the plan year (within the meaning of § 1.410(b)-3(a)). If an employer is using the same alternative definition of compensation to determine whether more than one separate plan satisfies section 401(a)(4), the employer is permitted to take into account all the employees who benefit under all of those plans for the plan year in determining whether the alternative definition of compensation being used satisfies this paragraph (d)(3).

(B) *Exclusion of self-employed individuals.*—In applying the requirement of this paragraph (d)(3), self-employed individuals are disregarded.

(C) *Certain employees disregarded.*—If an employee's total compensation for the determination period, determined under paragraph (d)(3)(ii) and (d)(3)(vi)(B) of this section, is zero, the employee is disregarded in determining whether the nondiscrimination requirement of paragraph (d)(3) of this section is satisfied for that determination period. For example, an employee who does not receive any actual compensation during a determination period because the employee is on unpaid leave of absence for the entire period, but who is credited with imputed compensation described in paragraph (f)(1) of this section, is disregarded in determining whether the nondiscrimination requirement of this paragraph (d)(3) is satisfied for that determination period.

(iv) *Calculation of average percentages.*—(A) *General rule.*—To determine the average percentages described in paragraph (d)(3)(i) of this section, an individual compensation percentage must be calculated for each employee in a group, and then the average of the separately calculated compensation percentages for each employee in the group must be determined. The individual compensation percentage for an employee is calculated by dividing the amount of the employee's compensation that is included under the alternative definition by the amount of the employee's total compensation.

(B) *Other reasonable methods.*—Notwithstanding paragraph (d)(3)(iv)(A) of this section, any other reasonable method is permitted to be used to determine the average percentages described in paragraph (d)(3)(i) of this section for either or both of the groups (i.e., highly compensated employees and nonhighly compensated employees), provided that the method cannot reasonably be expected to create a significant variance from the average percentage for that group determined using the individual-percentage method provided in paragraph (d)(3)(iv)(A) of this section. The same method is not required to be used for calculating the two average percentages. For example, to determine the average percentage for nonhighly compensated employees as a group, an employer may calculate an aggregate compensation percentage by dividing the aggregate amount of compensation of nonhighly compensated employees that is included under the alternative definition by the aggregate amount of total compensation of nonhighly compensated employees, provided the resulting percentage is not reasonably expected to vary significantly from the average percentage produced using the individual-percentage method provided in paragraph (d)(3)(iv)(A) of this section because of the extra weight given employees with higher compensation.

(v) *Facts and circumstances determination.*—The determination of whether the average percentage of total compensation included for the employer's highly compensated employees as a group for a determination period exceeds by more than a de minimis amount the average percentage of total compensation included for the employer's nonhighly compensated employees as a group is based on all the relevant facts and circumstances. The differences between the percentages for prior determination periods may be considered in determining whether the amount of the difference between the percentages is more than de minimis. In addition, an isolated instance of a more than de minimis difference between the compensation percentages that is due to an extraordinary unforeseeable event (such as overtime payments to employees of a public utility due to a major hurricane) will be disregarded if the amount of the difference in prior determination periods was de minimis.

(vi) *Special rules for definitions of compensation based on rate of compensation or that include prior-employer or imputed compensation.*—(A) *Special rule for determining compensation included under an alternative definition.*—If an alternative definition uses rate of compensation or includes prior-employer compensation or imputed compensation, the amount of each employee's compensation for a determination period that is treated as included under the alternative definition for purposes of determining the average percentages for the nondiscrimination requirement (i.e., the amount used in the numerator) must not be more than 100 percent of the employee's total compensation for that period, determined under paragraph (d)(3)(ii) and (d)(3)(vi)(B) of this section. This limit on the amount of compensation treated as included under the alternative definition applies even if the amount of compensation actually credited to the employee for the determination period under the definition and, thus, used as compensation within the meaning of section 414(s), exceeds the employee's total compensation for the period.

(B) *Special rule for determining total compensation.*—If an alternative definition uses rate of compensation or includes prior-employer compensation or imputed compensation, each employee's total compensation for purposes of determining the average percentages for the nondiscrimination requirement (i.e., the amount used in the denominator) must include all the types of elective contributions and deferred compensation described in paragraph (c)(4) of this section.

(e) *Rate of compensation.*—(1) *General rule.*—A definition of compensation satisfies section 414(s) as a reasonable definition of compensation even though it defines the amount of each employee's basic or regular compensation using the employee's basic or regular rate of compensation rather than using the employee's actual basic or regular compensation from the employer if the definition satisfies the requirements specified in paragraph (e)(3) of this section and otherwise satisfies the requirements of paragraph (d) of this section, including the nondiscrimination test in paragraph (d)(3) of this section. For this purpose, the employee's rate of compensation must be determined using an hourly pay scale, weekly salary, or similar unit of basic or regular compensation applicable to the employee. A definition will not fail to satisfy the requirements of this paragraph (e) merely because it defines compensation as including each employee's basic or regular compensation, the amount of which is

determined using each employee's basic or regular rate of compensation, plus actual amounts of irregular or additional compensation, such as overtime or bonuses. In addition, a definition of compensation will not fail to satisfy section 414(s) merely because it defines compensation for each employee as the greater of the employee's actual compensation, the amount of which is determined using a definition that would otherwise satisfy paragraph (c) or (d)(2) of this section, or the employee's basic or regular compensation, the amount of which is determined using the employee's basic or regular rate of compensation.

(2) *Not applicable to certain contributions.*—This paragraph (e) does not apply to a definition of compensation used in determining whether elective deferrals (as defined in section 402(g)(3)), matching contributions (as defined in section 401(m)(4)), or employee contributions subject to section 401(m) satisfy any applicable provision. Thus, for example, a definition of compensation that defines compensation based on each employee's basic or regular rate of compensation may not be used to measure compensation for purposes of determining if a qualified cash or deferred arrangement satisfies the actual deferral percentage test in section 401(k)(3).

(3) *Requirements for definitions of compensation based on rate of compensation.*—(i) *Benefit determination.*—The definition of compensation must actually be used to calculate the benefits, contributions, or other amounts, that are subject to the applicable provision. For example, a definition of compensation that defines compensation based on each employee's basic or regular rate of compensation may not be used to determine whether a plan satisfies section 401(a)(4) unless the benefits, contributions, or other amounts for each employee in the plan are determined using that definition of compensation.

(ii) *Period for determining compensation.*—The amount of each employee's basic or regular compensation for the determination period must be determined using the employee's basic or regular rate of compensation as of a designated date in the determination period. For example, if the determination period is a calendar year, this requirement would be satisfied if the amount of each employee's basic or regular compensation for the calendar year is determined using the employee's basic or regular rate of compensation as of January 1 of the calendar year. Alternatively, the amount of each employee's basic or regular compensation for a determination period can be the sum of the amounts separately determined for shorter specified periods (e.g., weeks or months) within the determination period provided the amount of each employee's basic or regular compensation for each specified period is determined using the employee's basic or regular rate of compensation as of a designated date within the specified period.

(iii) *Dates for determining rate of compensation.*—One or more dates may be used to determine employees' rates of compensation for a determination period or specified period provided that, if the same date is not used for all employees, the dates selected are designed to determine the rates of compensation for that period on a consistent basis for all employees taken into account for the determination period. For example, if annual compensation increases are provided to different groups of employees on different dates during the year, it would be consistent to choose a different date for each group in order to include the annual increase in the employees' rates of compensation for the determination period. In addition, the date or dates selected, by themselves, must not cause the portion of total compensation included to vary significantly among employees.

(iv) *Periods without compensation or with reduced compensation.*—An employee's compensation may generally only be determined using the employee's rate of compensation for employment periods during which the employer actually compensates the employee. However, if an employee terminates employment or otherwise stops performing services (such as for a leave of absence, lay off or similar event) either without compensation or with reduced compensation during a determination period, the employer may continue to credit the employee with compensation based on the employee's rate of compensation for a period of up to 31 days after the event, but not beyond the end of the determination period. Paragraph (f) of this section contains special rules for crediting imputed compensation for periods extending beyond 31 days during which an employee is not compensated or an employee's compensation is reduced. See also the definition of *Section 414(s) compensation* in § 1.401(a)(4)-12 that, for purposes of satisfying section 401(a)(4), permits adjustments to compensation to reflect the equivalent of full-time compensation to the extent necessary to satisfy the requirements of 29 CFR 2530.204-2(d) (regarding double proration of service and compensation).

(f) *Prior-employer compensation and imputed compensation.*—(1) *General rule.*—Solely for purposes of determining whether a defined benefit plan, as defined in § 1.410(b)-9, satisfies section 401(a)(4) or

410(b), an alternative definition that includes prior-employer compensation or imputed compensation satisfies section 414(s) as a reasonable alternative definition if the definition satisfies the requirements specified in paragraphs (f)(2) and (3) of this section. For this purpose, prior-employer compensation is compensation from an employer other than the employer (determined at the time that the compensation is paid) maintaining the plan that is credited for periods prior to the employee's employment with the employer maintaining the plan and during which the employee performed services for the other employer. For this purpose, imputed compensation is compensation credited for periods after an employee has commenced or recommenced participation in a plan while the employee is not compensated by the employer maintaining the plan or is compensated at a reduced rate by that employer because the employee is not performing services as an employee for the employer (including a period in which the employee performs services for another employer, e.g., a joint venture) or because the employee has a reduced work schedule.

(2) *Requirements for definitions of compensation crediting prior-employer compensation or imputed compensation.*—(i) *General requirement.*—The definition must otherwise be described in paragraph (c) of this section or must otherwise satisfy the requirements of paragraph (d) or (e) of this section for alternative definitions of compensation, including the nondiscrimination requirement in paragraph (d)(3) of this section.

(ii) *Benefit determination.*—A definition of compensation that credits prior-employer compensation or imputed compensation must actually be used to calculate the benefits under the plan. For example, the definition may not be used to determine whether a defined benefit plan satisfies section 401(a)(4) unless the benefits for each employee in the plan are determined using that definition of compensation.

(iii) *Provision applied to all similarly-situated employees.*—A provision in a plan's definition of compensation crediting prior-employer compensation or imputed compensation must apply on the same terms to all similarly-situated employees in the plan. The criteria for determining whether employees are similarly situated for this purpose are the same as the criteria for determining whether a plan provision crediting pre-participation or imputed service satisfies the requirements of §1.401(a)(4)-11(d)(3)(iii)(A).

(iv) *Legitimate business purpose.*—There must be a legitimate business purpose, based on all of the relevant facts and circumstances, for crediting prior-employer compensation or imputed compensation to an employee for the period being credited. The standard for determining whether crediting prior-employer compensation or imputed compensation satisfies this requirement is the same as the standard for determining whether crediting pre-participation or imputed service under a plan satisfies the requirements of §1.401(a)(4)-11(d)(3)(iii)(B) and whether crediting imputed service satisfies the additional requirements of §1.401(a)(4)-11(d)(3)(iv)(A). However, if the legitimate business reason for crediting imputed compensation relates to the services the employee is performing for another employer and the reason satisfies the standard in §1.401(a)(4)-11(d)(3)(iii)(B), the additional requirements of §1.401(a)(4)-11(d)(3)(iv)(A) are deemed to be satisfied. For example, if an employee becomes employed by another employer as a result of a merger, acquisition or similar transaction with the other employer and imputed compensation is credited to the employee while the employee is performing services for the other employer, the crediting of imputed compensation to the employee satisfies the standard in §1.401(a)(4)-11(d)(3)(iii)(B). Thus, under that example, crediting the imputed compensation to the employee is deemed to satisfy the additional requirements of §1.401(a)(4)-11(d)(3)(iv)(A), even if the employee is not performing those services under an arrangement that provides an ongoing business benefit to the employer maintaining the plan.

(v) *No significant discrimination.*—Based on all of the relevant facts and circumstances, crediting prior-employer compensation or imputed compensation must not by design or in operation discriminate significantly in favor of highly compensated employees. The standard for determining whether crediting prior-employer compensation or imputed compensation satisfies this requirement is the same as the standard for determining whether crediting pre-participation or imputed service satisfies the requirement in §1.401(a)(4)-11(d)(3)(iii)(C) and whether crediting imputed service satisfies the additional requirement of §1.401(a)(4)-11(d)(3)(iv)(B).

(3) *Reasonable method.*—(i) *General rule.*—Any reasonable method may be used to determine the amount of prior-employer compensation or imputed compensation provided that the requirements of paragraph (f)(3)(ii) or (iii) of this section are satisfied, whichever is applicable.

(ii) *Requirements for prior-employer compensation.*—Prior-employer compensation credited to an employee for a period that an employee is performing services for another employer must be compensation for the employee from the other employer (or be based on the employee's basic or regular rate of compensation from the other employer) for that period. In addition, prior employer compensation credited to an employee must not exceed the amount of compensation from the other employer that would have been included under the definition of compensation in effect for that period for compensation from the employer maintaining the plan. Reasonable assumptions may be made in determining the amount of compensation received from another employer for a period that would have been included under the definition of compensation in effect for that period for compensation from the employer maintaining the plan.

(iii) *Requirements for imputed compensation.*—(A) *General rule.*—The amount of imputed compensation credited to an employee during any period, when combined with the amount of any actual compensation being included, must not exceed an amount that, based on all of the relevant facts and circumstances, is reasonably representative of the amount of compensation that the employee would have received and that would have been included under the definition of compensation in effect for the period if the employee had continued to perform services for the employer during that period at the same level as the employee was performing before the employee stopped performing services or changed to a reduced work schedule. The relevant facts and circumstances include the compensation that the employee was receiving immediately before the employee stopped performing services or changed to a reduced work schedule, and, if applicable, the rate of compensation in effect while the employee is not performing services or has a reduced work schedule that is applicable to the employee's specific job grade immediately before the change occurred.

(B) *Imputed compensation from another employer.*—Imputed compensation credited for a period that an employee is performing services for another employer is deemed to satisfy paragraph (f)(3)(iii)(A) of this section if the amount of compensation credited satisfies the requirements of paragraph (f)(3)(ii) of this section for prior-employer compensation. Thus, for example, the amount of imputed compensation credited to an employee for a period that the employee is performing services for another employer is deemed to satisfy paragraph (f)(3)(iii)(A) of this section if the amount credited is compensation for the employee from the other employer (or is based on the employee's basic or regular rate of compensation from the other employer) for that period, and the amount credited does not exceed the compensation from the other employer that would be included for the employee under the definition of compensation in effect for that period for compensation from the employer maintaining the plan.

(4) *Special nondiscrimination rule for safe harbor definitions.*—If a definition of compensation crediting prior-employer or imputed compensation is otherwise described in paragraph (c) of this section, and the prior-employer compensation or imputed compensation credited satisfies the requirements of paragraphs (f)(1), (2), and (3) of this section, then the definition is deemed to satisfy paragraph (d) of this section (i.e., it is deemed to be nondiscriminatory).

(g) *Special rules.*—(1) *Self-employed individuals.*—(i) *General rule.*—If an alternative definition of compensation under paragraph (c)(3), (d), (e), or (f) of this section is used to satisfy an applicable provision, an equivalent alternative compensation amount must be determined for any self-employed individual who is in the group of employees for whom paragraph (b) of this section requires a single definition of compensation to be used. This equivalent alternative compensation amount is determined by multiplying the self-employed individual's total earned income (as defined in section 401(c)(2)) for the determination period by the percentage of total compensation (as defined in paragraph (d)(3)(ii) of this section) included under the alternative definition for the employer's nonhighly compensated common-law employees as a group (determined in a manner consistent with the rules in paragraph (d)(3)(iii) of this section and, if applicable, paragraph (d)(3)(vi) of this section). Thus, for purposes of this determination, highly compensated common-law employees must be disregarded. This equivalent alternative compensation amount will be treated as the self-employed individual's compensation under the alternative definition of compensation for the determination period.

(ii) *Inclusion of elective contributions.*—If the alternative definition of compensation includes any types of elective contributions described in paragraph (c)(4) of this section, the self-employed individual's earned income for this determination must be increased by the amount of elective contributions made by the employer on behalf of the self-employed individual, and the definition of total compensation for this determination must include all the types of elective contributions described in paragraph (c)(4) of this section made by the employer on behalf of common-law employees (other than highly compensated employees).

(iii) *Reductions in equivalent alternative compensation amount applicable only to highly compensated employees.*—An alternative definition of compensation may provide that compensation under the alternative definition for some or all self-employed individuals who are highly compensated employees is a specified portion of, rather than equal to, the equivalent compensation amount determined under paragraph (g)(1)(i).

(2) *Leased employees.*—[Reserved]

(h) *Definitions.*—The following definitions apply for purposes of this section:

(1) *Applicable provision.*—Applicable provision means a provision that specifically refers to section 414(s) or this section.

(2) *Determination period.*—Determination period means a period during which the amount of compensation is measured for use in determining whether the requirements of an applicable provision are satisfied. If no period is provided under the applicable provision for measuring compensation, the determination period is the period for which the applicable provision must be satisfied. The applicable provision may provide additional rules concerning the determination period to be used for satisfying the nondiscrimination requirement in paragraph (d) of this section.

(3) *Employee.*—Employee means employee within the meaning of § 1.410(b)-9.

(4) *Highly compensated employee.*—Highly compensated employee means highly compensated employee within the meaning of § 1.410(b)-9.

(5) *Nonhighly compensated employee.*—Nonhighly compensated employee means nonhighly compensated employee within the meaning of § 1.410(b)-9.

(6) *Self-employed individual.*—Self-employed individual means self-employed individual within the meaning of section 401(c)(1).

(i) *Additional rules.*—The Commissioner may in revenue rulings, notices, and other guidance of general applicability provide additional rules for defining compensation within the meaning of section 414(s), including additional definitions of compensation that satisfy section 414(s).

(j) *Effective date and transition rules.*—(1) *Statutory effective date.*—Section 414(s) applies to years beginning on or after January 1, 1987.

(2) *Regulatory effective date.*—(i) *In general.*—Except as otherwise provided in paragraph (j)(2)(ii) of this section, § 1.414(s)-1(a) through (i) apply to years beginning on or after January 1, 1994.

(ii) *Plans of tax-exempt organizations.*—In the case of a plan maintained by an organization that is exempt from income taxation pursuant to section 501(a), including plans subject to section 403(b)(12)(A)(i) (nonelective plans), § 1.414(s)-1(a) through (i) apply to plan years beginning on or after January 1, 1996.

(3) *Compliance during transition period.*—For plan years beginning before the effective date of these regulations, as set forth in paragraph (j)(2) of this section, and on or after the statutory effective date as set forth in paragraph (j)(1) of this section, a plan must be operated in accordance with a reasonable, good faith interpretation of section 414(s). Whether a plan is operated in accordance with a reasonable, good faith interpretation of section 414(s) will generally be determined based on all relevant facts and circumstances, including the extent to which an employer has resolved unclear issues in its favor. A plan will be deemed to be operated in accordance with a reasonable, good faith interpretation of section 414(s)(1) and (2) if it is operated in accordance with the terms of § 1.414(s)-1(a) through (i). For years beginning on or after the statutory effective date and before the effective date of these regulations, a definition of compensation is also deemed to satisfy section 414(s) as an alternative method of determining compensation under section 414(s)(3) if the definition satisfies the requirements of § 1.414(s)-1(a) through (i) or if the definition satisfies the prior regulation provisions of § 1.414(s)-1T. (See § 1.414(s)-1T as contained in the CFR edition revised as of April 1, 1991.) In addition, for those transition years, a definition of compensation is deemed to satisfy section 414(s) as an alternative method of determining compensation under section 414(s)(3) if, based on all the relevant facts and circumstances in effect for the year, use of the definition does not cause discrimination in favor of highly compensated employees. [Reg. § 1.414(s)-1.]

☐ [*T.D. 8361, 9-12-91. Amended by T.D. 8488, 9-1-93 and T.D. 9319, 4-4-2007.*]

[Reg. § 1.414(v)-1]

§ 1.414(v)-1. Catch-up contributions.—(a) *Catch-up contributions.*—(1) *General rule.*—An applicable employer plan shall not be treated as failing to meet any requirement of the Internal Revenue Code solely because the plan permits a catch-up eligible participant to make catch-up contributions in accordance with section 414(v) and this section. With respect to an applicable employer plan, catch-up contributions are elective deferrals made by a catch-up eligible participant that exceed any of the applicable limits set forth in paragraph (b) of this section and that are treated under the applicable employer plan as catch-up contributions, but only to the extent they do not exceed the catch-up contribution limit described in paragraph (c) of this section (determined in accordance with the special rules for employers that maintain multiple applicable employer plans in paragraph (f) of this section, if applicable). To the extent provided under paragraph (d) of this section, catch-up contributions are disregarded for purposes of various statutory limits. In addition, unless otherwise provided in paragraph (e) of this section, all catch-up eligible participants of the employer must be provided the opportunity to make catch-up contributions in order for an applicable employer plan to comply with the universal availability requirement of section 414(v)(4). The definitions in paragraph (g) of this section apply for purposes of this section and § 1.402(g)-2.

(2) *Treatment as elective deferrals.*—Except as specifically provided in this section, elective deferrals treated as catch-up contributions remain subject to statutory and regulatory rules otherwise applicable to elective deferrals. For example, catch-up contributions under an applicable employer plan that is a section 401(k) plan are subject to the distribution and vesting restrictions of section 401(k)(2)(B) and (C). In addition, the plan is permitted to provide a single election for catch-up eligible participants, with the determination of whether elective deferrals are catch-up contributions being made under the terms of the plan.

(3) *Coordination with section 457(b)(3).*—In the case of an applicable employer plan that is a section 457 eligible governmental plan, the catch-up contributions permitted under this section shall not apply to a catch-up eligible participant for any taxable year for which a higher limitation applies to such participant under section 457(b)(3). For additional guidance, see regulations under section 457.

(b) *Elective deferrals that exceed an applicable limit.*—(1) *Applicable limits.*—An applicable limit for purposes of determining catch-up contributions for a catch-up eligible participant is any of the following:

(i) *Statutory limit.*—A statutory limit is a limit on elective deferrals or annual additions permitted to be made (without regard to section 414(v) and this section) with respect to an employee for a year provided in section 401(a)(30), 402(h), 403(b), 408, 415(c), or 457(b)(2) (without regard to section 457(b)(3)), as applicable.

(ii) *Employer-provided limit.*—An employer-provided limit is any limit on the elective deferrals an employee is permitted to make (without regard to section 414(v) and this section) that is contained in the terms of the plan, but which is not required under the Internal Revenue Code. Thus, for example, if, in accordance with the terms of the plan, highly compensated employees are limited to a deferral percentage of 10% of compensation, this limit is an employer-provided limit that is an applicable limit with respect to the highly compensated employees.

(iii) *Actual deferral percentage (ADP) limit.*—In the case of a section 401(k) plan that would fail the ADP test of section 401(k)(3) if it did not correct under section 401(k)(8), the ADP limit is the highest amount of elective deferrals that can be retained in the plan by any highly compensated employee under the rules of section 401(k)(8)(C) (without regard to paragraph (d)(2)(iii) of this section). In the case of a simplified employee pension (SEP) with a salary reduction arrangement (within the meaning of section 408(k)(6)) that would fail the requirements of section 408(k)(6)(A)(iii) if it did not correct in accordance with section 408(k)(6)(C), the ADP limit is the highest amount of elective deferrals that can be made by any highly compensated employee under the rules of section 408(k)(6) (without regard to paragraph (d)(2)(iii) of this section).

(2) *Contributions in excess of applicable limit.*—(i) *Plan year limits.*—(A) *General rule.*—Except as provided in paragraph (b)(2)(ii) of this section, the amount of elective deferrals in excess of an applicable limit is determined as of the end of the plan year by comparing the total elective deferrals for the plan year with the applicable limit for the plan year. In addition, except as provided in paragraph (b)(2)(i)(B) of this section, in the case of a plan that provides for separate employer-provided limits on elective deferrals for separate portions of plan compensation within the plan year, the applicable limit for the plan year is the sum of the dollar amounts of the limits

for the separate portions. For example, if a plan sets a deferral percentage limit for each payroll period, the applicable limit for the plan year is the sum of the dollar amounts of the limits for the payroll periods.

(B) *Alternative method for determining employer-provided limit.*—(1) *General rule.*—If the plan limits elective deferrals for separate portions of the plan year, then, solely for purposes of determining the amount that is in excess of an employer-provided limit, the plan is permitted to provide that the applicable limit for the plan year is the product of the employee's plan year compensation and the time-weighted average of the deferral percentage limits, rather than determining the employer-provided limit as the sum of the limits for the separate portions of the year. Thus, for example, if, in accordance with the terms of the plan, highly compensated employees are limited to 8% of compensation during the first half of the plan year and 10% of compensation for the second half of the plan year, the plan is permitted to provide that the applicable limit for a highly compensated employee is 9% of the employee's plan year compensation.

(2) *Alternative definition of compensation permitted.*—A plan using the alternative method in this paragraph (b)(2)(i)(B) is permitted to provide that the applicable limit for the plan year is determined as the product of the catch-up eligible participant's compensation used for purposes of the ADP test and the time-weighted average of the deferral percentage limits. The alternative calculation in this paragraph (b)(2)(i)(B)(2) is available regardless of whether the deferral percentage limits change during the plan year.

(ii) *Other year limit.*—In the case of an applicable limit that is applied on the basis of a year other than the plan year (e.g., the calendar-year limit on elective deferrals under section 401(a)(30)), the determination of whether elective deferrals are in excess of the applicable limit is made on the basis of such other year.

(c) *Catch-up contribution limit.*—(1) *General rule.*—Elective deferrals with respect to a catch-up eligible participant in excess of an applicable limit under paragraph (b) of this section are treated as catch-up contributions under this section as of a date within a taxable year only to the extent that such elective deferrals do not exceed the catch-up contribution limit described in paragraphs (c)(1) and (2) of this section, reduced by elective deferrals previously treated as catch-up contributions for the taxable year, determined in accordance with paragraph (c)(3) of this section. The catch-up contribution limit for a taxable year is generally the applicable dollar catch-up limit for such taxable year, as set forth in paragraph (c)(2) of this section. However, an elective deferral is not treated as a catch-up contribution to the extent that the elective deferral, when added to all other elective deferrals for the taxable year under any applicable employer plan of the employer, exceeds the participant's compensation (determined in accordance with section 415(c)(3)) for the taxable year. See also paragraph (f) of this section for special rules for employees who participate in more than one applicable employer plan maintained by the employer.

(2) *Applicable dollar catch-up limit.*—(i) *In general.*—The applicable dollar catch-up limit for an applicable employer plan, other than a plan described in section 401(k)(11) or 408(p), is determined under the following table:

For Taxable Years Beginning in	Applicable Dollar Catch-up Limit
2002	$1,000
2003	$2,000
2004	$3,000
2005	$4,000
2006	$5,000

(ii) *SIMPLE plans.*—The applicable dollar catch-up limit for a SIMPLE 401(k) plan described in section 401(k)(11) or a SIMPLE IRA plan as described in section 408(p) is determined under the following table:

For Taxable Years Beginning in	Applicable Dollar Catch-up Limit
2002	$500
2003	$1,000
2004	$1,500
2005	$2,000
2006	$2,500

(iii) *Cost of living adjustments.*—For taxable years beginning after 2006, the applicable dollar catch-up limit is the applicable dollar

catch-up limit for 2006 described in paragraph (c)(2)(i) or (ii) of this section increased at the same time and in the same manner as adjustments under section 415(d), except that the base period shall be the calendar quarter beginning July 1, 2005, and any increase that is not a multiple of $500 shall be rounded to the next lower multiple of $500.

(3) *Timing rules.*—For purposes of determining the maximum amount of permitted catch-up contributions for a catch-up eligible participant, the determination of whether an elective deferral is a catch-up contribution is made as of the last day of the plan year (or in the case of section 415, as of the last day of the limitation year), except that, with respect to elective deferrals in excess of an applicable limit that is tested on the basis of the taxable year or calendar year (e.g., the section 401(a)(30) limit on elective deferrals), the determination of whether such elective deferrals are treated as catch-up contributions is made at the time they are deferred.

(d) *Treatment of catch-up contributions.*—(1) *Contributions not taken into account for certain limits.*—Catch-up contributions are not taken into account in applying the limits of section 401(a)(30), 402(h), 403(b), 408, 415(c), or 457(b)(2) (determined without regard to section 457(b)(3)) to other contributions or benefits under an applicable employer plan or any other plan of the employer.

(2) *Contributions not taken into account in application of ADP test.*—(i) *Calculation of ADR.*—Elective deferrals that are treated as catch-up contributions pursuant to paragraph (c) of this section with respect to a section 401(k) plan because they exceed a statutory or employer-provided limit described in paragraph (b)(1)(i) or (ii) of this section, respectively, are subtracted from the catch-up eligible participant's elective deferrals for the plan year for purposes of determining the actual deferral ratio (ADR) (as defined in regulations under section 401(k)) of a catch-up eligible participant. Similarly, elective deferrals that are treated as catch-up contributions pursuant to paragraph (c) of this section with respect to a SEP because they exceed a statutory or employer-provided limit described in paragraph (b)(1)(i) or (ii) of this section, respectively, are subtracted from the catch-up eligible participant's elective deferrals for the plan year for purposes of determining the deferral percentage under section 408(k)(6)(D) of a catch-up eligible participant.

(ii) *Adjustment of elective deferrals for correction purposes.*—For purposes of the correction of excess contributions in accordance with section 401(k)(8)(C), elective deferrals under the plan treated as catch-up contributions for the plan year and not taken into account in the ADP test under paragraph (d)(2)(i) of this section are subtracted from the catch-up eligible participant's elective deferrals under the plan for the plan year.

(iii) *Excess contributions treated as catch-up contributions.*—A section 401(k) plan that satisfies the ADP test of section 401(k)(3) through correction under section 401(k)(8) must retain any elective deferrals that are treated as catch-up contributions pursuant to paragraph (c) of this section because they exceed the ADP limit in paragraph (b)(1)(iii) of this section. In addition, a section 401(k) plan is not treated as failing to satisfy section 401(k)(8) merely because elective deferrals described in the preceding sentence are not distributed or recharacterized as employee contributions. Similarly, a SEP is not treated as failing to satisfy section 408(k)(6)(A)(iii) merely because catch-up contributions are not treated as excess contributions with respect to a catch-up eligible participant under the rules of section 408(k)(6)(C). Notwithstanding the fact that elective deferrals described in this paragraph (d)(2)(iii) are not distributed, such elective deferrals are still considered to be excess contributions under section 401(k)(8), and accordingly, matching contributions with respect to such elective deferrals are permitted to be forfeited under the rules of section 411(a)(3)(G).

(3) *Contributions not taken into account for other nondiscrimination purposes.*—(i) *Application for top-heavy.*—Catch-up contributions with respect to the current plan year are not taken into account for purposes of section 416. However, catch-up contributions for prior years are taken into account for purposes of section 416. Thus, catch-up contributions for prior years are included in the account balances that are used in determining whether the plan is top-heavy under section 416(g).

(ii) *Application for section 410(b).*—Catch-up contributions with respect to the current plan year are not taken into account for purposes of section 410(b). Thus, catch-up contributions are not taken into account in determining the average benefit percentage under §1.410(b)-5 for the year if benefit percentages are determined based on current year contributions. However, catch-up contributions for prior years are taken into account for purposes of section 410(b). Thus, catch-up contributions for prior years would be included in the account balances that are used in determining the average benefit percentage if allocations for prior years are taken into account.

(4) *Availability of catch-up contributions.*—An applicable employer plan does not violate § 1.401(a)(4)-4 merely because the group of employees for whom catch-up contributions are currently available (i.e., the catch-up eligible participants) is not a group of employees that would satisfy section 410(b) (without regard to § 1.410(b)-5). In addition, a catch-up eligible participant is not treated as having a right to a different rate of allocation of matching contributions merely because an otherwise nondiscriminatory schedule of matching rates is applied to elective deferrals that include catch-up contributions. The rules in this paragraph (d)(4) also apply for purposes of satisfying the requirements of section 403(b)(12).

(e) *Universal availability requirement.*—(1) *General rule.*—(i) *Effective opportunity.*—An applicable employer plan that offers catch-up contributions and that is otherwise subject to section 401(a)(4) (including a plan that is subject to section 401(a)(4) pursuant to section 403(b)(12)) will not satisfy the requirements of section 401(a)(4) unless all catch-up eligible participants who participate under any applicable employer plan maintained by the employer are provided with an effective opportunity to make the same dollar amount of catch-up contributions. A plan fails to provide an effective opportunity to make catch-up contributions if it has an applicable limit (e.g., an employer-provided limit) that applies to a catch-up eligible participant and does not permit the participant to make elective deferrals in excess of that limit. An applicable employer plan does not fail to satisfy the universal availability requirement of this paragraph (e) solely because an employer-provided limit does not apply to all employees or different limits apply to different groups of employees under paragraph (b)(2)(i) of this section. However, a plan may not provide lower employer-provided limits for catch-up eligible participants.

(ii) *Certain practices permitted.*—(A) *Proration of limit.*—A applicable employer plan does not fail to satisfy the universal availability requirement of this paragraph (e) merely because the plan allows participants to defer an amount equal to a specified percentage of compensation for each payroll period and for each payroll period permits each catch-up eligible participant to defer a pro-rata share of the applicable dollar catch-up limit in addition to that amount.

(B) *Cash availability.*—An applicable employer plan does not fail to satisfy the universal availability requirement of this paragraph (e) merely because it restricts the elective deferrals of any employee (including a catch-up eligible participant) to amounts available after other withholding from the employee's pay (e.g., after deduction of all applicable income and employment taxes). For this purpose, an employer limit of 75% of compensation or higher will be treated as limiting employees to amounts available after other withholdings.

(2) *Certain employees disregarded.*—An applicable employer plan does not fail to satisfy the universal availability requirement of this paragraph (e) merely because employees described in section 410(b)(3) (e.g., collectively bargained employees) are not provided the opportunity to make catch-up contributions.

(3) *Exception for certain plans.*—An applicable employer plan does not fail to satisfy the universal availability requirement of this paragraph (e) merely because another applicable employer plan that is a section 457 eligible governmental plan does not provide for catch-up contributions to the extent set forth in section 414(v)(6)(C) and paragraph (a)(3) of this section.

(4) *Exception for section 410(b)(6)(C)(ii) period.*—If an applicable employer plan satisfies the universal availability requirement of this paragraph (e) before an acquisition or disposition described in § 1.410(b)-2(f) and would fail to satisfy the universal availability requirement of this paragraph (e) merely because of such event, then the applicable employer plan shall continue to be treated as satisfying this paragraph (e) through the end of the period determined under section 410(b)(6)(C)(ii).

(f) *Special rules for an employer that sponsors multiple plans.*—(1) *General rule.*—For purposes of paragraph (c) of this section, all applicable employer plans, other than section 457 eligible governmental plans, maintained by the same employer are treated as one plan and all section 457 eligible governmental plans maintained by the same employer are treated as one plan. Thus, the total amount of catch-up contributions under all applicable employer plans of an employer (other than section 457 eligible governmental plans) is limited to the applicable dollar catch-up limit for the taxable year, and the total amount of catch-up contributions for all section 457 eligible governmental plans of an employer is limited to the applicable dollar catch-up limit for the taxable year.

(2) *Coordination of employer-provided limits.*—An applicable employer plan is permitted to allow a catch-up eligible participant to defer amounts in excess of an employer-provided limit under that plan without regard to whether elective deferrals made by the participant have been treated as catch-up contributions for the taxable year under another applicable employer plan aggregated with such plan under this paragraph (f). However, to the extent elective deferrals under another plan maintained by the employer have already been treated as catch-up contributions during the taxable year, the elective deferrals under the plan may be treated as catch-up contributions only up to the amount remaining under the catch-up limit for the year. Any other elective deferrals that exceed the employer-provided limit may not be treated as catch-up contributions and must satisfy the otherwise applicable nondiscrimination rules. For example, the right to make contributions in excess of the employer-provided limit is an other right or feature which must satisfy § 1.401(a)(4)-4 to the extent that the contributions are not catch-up contributions. Also, contributions in excess of the employer provided limit are taken into account under the ADP test to the extent they are not catch-up contributions.

(3) *Allocation rules.*—If a catch-up eligible participant makes additional elective deferrals in excess of an applicable limit under paragraph (b)(1) of this section under more than one applicable employer plan that is aggregated under the rules of this paragraph (f), the applicable employer plan under which elective deferrals in excess of an applicable limit are treated as catch-up contributions is permitted to be determined in any manner that is not inconsistent with the manner in which such amounts were actually deferred under the plan.

(g) *Definitions.*—(1) *Applicable employer plan.*—The term applicable employer plan means a section 401(k) plan, a SIMPLE IRA plan as defined in section 408(p), a simplified employee pension plan as defined in section 408(k) (SEP), a plan or contract that satisfies the requirements of section 403(b), or a section 457 eligible governmental plan.

(2) *Elective deferral.*—The term elective deferral means an elective deferral within the meaning of section 402(g)(3) or any contribution to a section 457 eligible governmental plan.

(3) *Catch-up eligible participant.*—An employee is a catch-up eligible participant for a taxable year if—

(i) The employee is eligible to make elective deferrals under an applicable employer plan (without regard to section 414(v) or this section); and

(ii) The employee's 50th or higher birthday would occur before the end of the employee's taxable year.

(4) *Other definitions.*—(i) The terms employer, employee, section 401(k) plan, and highly compensated employee have the meanings provided in § 1.410(b)-9.

(ii) The term section 457 eligible governmental plan means an eligible deferred compensation plan described in section 457(b) that is established and maintained by an eligible employer described in section 457(e)(1)(A).

(h) *Examples.*—The following examples illustrate the application of this section. For purposes of these examples, the limit under section 401(a)(30) is $15,000 and the applicable dollar catch-up limit is $5,000 and, except as specifically provided, the plan year is the calendar year. In addition, it is assumed that the participant's elective deferrals under all plans of the employer do not exceed the participant's section 415(c)(3) compensation, that the taxable year of the participant is the calendar year and that any correction pursuant to section 401(k)(8) is made through distribution of excess contributions. The examples are as follows:

Example 1. (i) Participant A is eligible to make elective deferrals under a section 401(k) plan, Plan P. Plan P does not limit elective deferrals except as necessary to comply with sections 401(a)(30) and 415. In 2006, Participant A is 55 years old. Plan P also provides that a catch-up eligible participant is permitted to defer amounts in excess of the section 401(a)(30) limit up to the applicable dollar catch-up limit for the year. Participant A defers $18,000 during 2006.

(ii) Participant A's elective deferrals in excess of the section 401(a)(30) limit ($3,000) do not exceed the applicable dollar catch-up limit for 2006 ($5,000). Under paragraph (a)(1) of this section, the $3,000 is a catch-up contribution and, pursuant to paragraph (d)(2)(i) of this section, it is not taken into account in determining Participant A's ADR for purposes of section 401(k)(3).

Example 2. (i) Participants B and C, who are highly compensated employees each earning $120,000, are eligible to make elective deferrals under a section 401(k) plan, Plan Q. Plan Q limits elective deferrals as necessary to comply with section 401(a)(30) and 415, and also provides that no highly compensated employee may make an elective deferral at a rate that exceeds 10% of compensation. However, Plan Q also provides that a catch-up eligible participant is permitted to defer amounts in excess of 10% during the plan year up to the applicable dollar catch-up limit for the year. In 2006, Participants B and C are both 55 years old and, pursuant to the catch-up provision in Plan Q, both elect to defer 10% of compensation plus a pro-rata portion of the $5,000 applicable dollar catch-up limit for 2006. Participant B continues this election in effect for the entire year, for a total elective contribution for the year of $17,000. However, in July 2006, after deferring $8,500, Participant C discontinues making elective deferrals.

(ii) Once Participant B's elective deferrals for the year exceed the section 401(a)(30) limit ($15,000), subsequent elective deferrals are treated as catch-up contributions as they are deferred, provided that such elective deferrals do not exceed the catch-up contribution limit for the taxable year. Since the $2,000 in elective deferrals made after Participant B reaches the section 402(g) limit for the calendar year does not exceed the applicable dollar catch-up limit for 2006, the entire $2,000 is treated as a catch-up contribution.

(iii) As of the last day of the plan year, Participant B has exceeded the employer-provided limit of 10% (10% of $120,000 or $12,000 for Participant B) by an additional $3,000. Since the additional $3,000 in elective deferrals does not exceed the $5,000 applicable dollar catch-up limit for 2006, reduced by the $2,000 in elective deferrals previously treated as catch-up contributions, the entire $3,000 of elective deferrals is treated as a catch-up contribution.

(iv) In determining Participant B's ADR, the $5,000 of catch-up contributions are subtracted from Participant B's elective deferrals for the plan year under paragraph (d)(2)(i) of this section. Accordingly, Participant B's ADR is 10% ($12,000/$120,000). In addition, for purposes of applying the rules of section 401(k)(8), Participant B is treated as having elective deferrals of $12,000.

(v) Participant C's elective deferrals for the year do not exceed an applicable limit for the plan year. Accordingly, Participant C's $8,500 of elective deferrals must be taken into account in determining Participant C's ADR for purposes of section 401(k)(3).

Example 3. (i) The facts are the same as in *Example 2*, except that Plan Q is amended to change the maximum permitted deferral percentage for highly compensated employees to 7%, effective for deferrals after April 1, 2006. Participant B, who has earned $40,000 in the first 3 months of the year and has been deferring at a rate of 10% of compensation plus a pro-rata portion of the $5,000 applicable dollar catch-up limit for 2006). During those 9 months, Participant B earns $80,000. Thus, Participant B's total elective deferrals for the year are $14,600 ($4,000 for the first 3 months of the year plus $5,600 for the last 9 months of the year plus an additional $5,000 throughout the year).

(ii) The employer-provided limit for Participant B for the plan year is $9,600 ($4,000 for the first 3 months of the year, plus $5,600 for the last 9 months of the year). Accordingly, Participant B's elective deferrals for the year that are in excess of the employer-provided limit are $5,000 (the excess of $14,600 over $9,600), which does not exceed the applicable dollar catch-up limit of $5,000.

(iii) Alternatively, Plan Q may provide that the employer-provided limit is determined as the time-weighted average of the different deferral percentage limits over the course of the year. In this case, the time-weighted average limit is 7.75% for all participants, and the applicable limit for Participant B is 7.75% of $120,000, or $9,300. Accordingly, Participant B's elective deferrals for the year that are in excess of the employer-provided limit are $5,300 (the excess of $14,600 over $9,300). Since the amount of Participant B's elective deferrals in excess of the employer-provided limit ($5,300) exceeds the applicable dollar catch-up limit for the taxable year, only $5,000 of Participant B's elective deferrals may be treated as catch-up contributions. In determining Participant B's actual deferral ratio, the $5,000 of catch-up contributions are subtracted from Participant B's elective deferrals for the plan year under paragraph (d)(2)(i) of this section. Accordingly, Participant B's actual deferral ratio is 8% ($9,600/$120,000). In addition, for purposes of applying the rules of section 401(k)(8), Participant B is treated as having elective deferrals of $9,600.

Example 4. (i) The facts are the same as in *Example 1*. In addition to Participant A, Participant D is a highly compensated employee who is eligible to make elective deferrals under Plan P. During 2006, Participant D, who is 60 years old, elects to defer $14,000.

(ii) The ADP test is run for Plan P (after excluding the $3,000 in catch-up contributions from Participant A's elective deferrals), but Plan P needs to take corrective action in order to pass the ADP test. After applying the rules of section 401(k)(8)(C) to allocate the total excess contributions determined under section 401(k)(8)(B), the maximum deferrals which may be retained by any highly compensated employee in Plan P is $12,500.

(iii) Pursuant to paragraph (b)(1)(iii) of this section, the ADP limit under Plan P of $12,500 is an applicable limit. Accordingly, $1,500 of Participant D's elective deferrals exceed the applicable limit. Similarly, $2,500 of Participant A's elective deferrals (other than the $3,000 of elective deferrals treated as catch-up contributions because they exceed the section 401(a)(30) limit) exceed the applicable limit.

(iv) The $1,500 of Participant D's elective deferrals that exceed the applicable limit are less than the applicable dollar catch-up limit and are treated as catch-up contributions. Pursuant to paragraph (d)(2)(iii) of this section, Plan P must retain Participant D's $1,500 in elective deferrals and Plan P is not treated as failing to satisfy section 401(k)(8) merely because the elective deferrals are not distributed to Participant D.

(v) The $2,500 of Participant A's elective deferrals that exceed the applicable limit are greater than the portion of the applicable dollar catch-up limit ($2,000) that remains after treating the $3,000 of elective deferrals in excess of the section 401(a)(30) limit as catch-up contributions. Accordingly, $2,000 of Participant A's elective deferrals are treated as catch-up contributions. Pursuant to paragraph (d)(2)(iii) of this section, Plan P must retain Participant A's $2,000 in elective deferrals and Plan P is not treated as failing to satisfy section 401(k)(8) merely because the elective deferrals are not distributed to Participant A. However, $500 of Participant A's elective deferrals can not be treated as catch-up contributions and must be distributed to Participant A in order to satisfy section 401(k)(8).

Example 5. (i) Participant E is a highly compensated employee who is a catch-up eligible participant under a section 401(k) plan, Plan R, with a plan year ending October 31, 2006. Plan R does not limit elective deferrals except as necessary to comply with section 401(a)(30) and section 415. Plan R permits all catch-up eligible participants to defer an additional amount equal to the applicable dollar catch-up limit for the year ($5,000) in excess of the section 401(a)(30) limit. Participant E did not exceed the section 401(a)(30) limit in 2005 and did not exceed the ADP limit for the plan year ending October 31, 2005. Participant E made $3,200 of deferrals in the period November 1, 2005 through December 31, 2005 and an additional $16,000 of deferrals in the first 10 months of 2006, for a total of $19,200 in elective deferrals for the plan year.

(ii) Once Participant E(s elective deferrals for the calendar year 2006 exceed $15,000, subsequent elective deferrals are treated as catch-up contributions at the time they are deferred, provided that such elective deferrals do not exceed the applicable dollar catch-up limit for the taxable year. Since the $1,000 in elective deferrals made after Participant E reaches the section 402(g) limit for the calendar year does not exceed the applicable dollar catch-up limit for 2006, the entire $1,000 is a catch-up contribution. Pursuant to paragraph (d)(2)(i) of this section, $1,000 is subtracted from Participant E(s $19,200 in elective deferrals for the plan year ending October 31, 2006 in determining Participant E's ADR for that plan year.

(iii) The ADP test is run for Plan R (after excluding the $1,000 in elective deferrals in excess of the section 401(a)(30) limit), but Plan R needs to take corrective action in order to pass the ADP test. After applying the rules of section 401(k)(8)(C) to allocate the total excess contributions determined under section 401(k)(8)(C), the maximum deferrals that may be retained by any highly compensated employee under Plan R for the plan year ending October 31, 2006 (the ADP limit) is $14,800.

(iv) Under paragraph (d)(2)(ii) of this section, elective deferrals that exceed the section 401(a)(30) limit under Plan R are also subtracted from Participant E's elective deferrals under Plan R for purposes of applying the rules of section 401(k)(8). Accordingly, for purposes of correcting the failed ADP test, Participant E is treated as having contributed $18,200 of elective deferrals in Plan R. The amount of elective deferrals that would have to be distributed to Participant E in order to satisfy section 401(k)(8)(C) is $3,400 ($18,200 minus $14,800), which is less than the excess of the applicable dollar catch-up limit ($5,000) over the elective deferrals previously treated as catch-up contributions under Plan R for the taxable year ($1,000). Under paragraph (d)(2)(iii) of this section, Plan R must retain Participant E(s $3,400 in elective deferrals and is not treated as failing to satisfy section 401(k)(8) merely because the elective deferrals are not distributed to Participant E.

(v) Even though Participant E's elective deferrals for the calendar year 2006 have exceeded the section 401(a)(30) limit, Participant E can continue to make elective deferrals during the last 2 months of the calendar year, since Participant E's catch-up contributions for the taxable year are not taken into account in applying the section 401(a)(30) limit for 2006. Thus, Participant E can make an additional contribution of $3,400 ($15,000 minus ($16,000 minus $4,400)) without exceeding the section 401(a)(30) for the calendar year and without regard to any additional catch-up contributions. In addition, Participant E may make additional catch-up contributions of $600 (the $5,000 applicable dollar catch-up limit for 2006, reduced by the $4,400 ($1,000 plus $3,400) of elective deferrals previously treated as catch-up contributions during the taxable year). The $600 of catch-up contributions will not be taken into account in the ADP test for the plan year ending October 31, 2007.

Example 6. (i) The facts are the same as in *Example 5*, except that Participant E exceeded the section 401(a)(30) limit for 2005 by $1,300 prior to October 31, 2005, and made $600 of elective deferrals in the period November 1, 2005, through December 31, 2005 (which were catch-up contributions for 2005). Thus, Participant E made $16,600 of elective deferrals for the plan year ending October 31, 2006.

(ii) Once Participant E's elective deferrals for the calendar year 2006 exceed $15,000, subsequent elective deferrals are treated as catch-up contributions as they are deferred, provided that such elective deferrals do not exceed the applicable dollar catch-up limit for the taxable year. Since the $1,000 in elective deferrals made after Participant E reaches the section 402(g) limit for calendar year 2006 does not exceed the applicable dollar catch-up limit for 2006, the entire $1,000 is a catch-up contribution. Pursuant to paragraph (d)(2)(i) of this section, $1,000 is subtracted from Participant E(s elective deferrals in determining Participant E's ADR for the plan year ending October 31, 2006. In addition, the $600 of catchup contributions from the period November 1, 2005 to December 31, 2005 are subtracted from Participant E's elective deferrals in determining Participant E's ADR. Thus, the total elective deferrals taken into account in determining Participant E(s ADR for the plan year ending October 31, 2006, is $15,000 ($16,600 in elective deferrals for the current plan year, less $1,600 in catch-up contributions).

(iii) The ADP test is run for Plan R (after excluding the $1,600 in elective deferrals in excess of the section 401(a)(30) limit), but Plan R needs to take corrective action in order to pass the ADP test. After applying the rules of section 401(k)(8)(C) to allocate the total excess contributions determined under section 401(k)(8)(C), the maximum deferrals that may be retained by any highly compensated employee under Plan R (the ADP limit) is $14,800.

(iv) Under paragraph (d)(2)(ii) of this section, elective deferrals that exceed the section 401(a)(30) limit under Plan R are also subtracted from Participant E's elective deferrals under Plan R for purposes of applying the rules of section 401(k)(8). Accordingly, for purposes of correcting the failed ADP test, Participant E is treated as having contributed $15,000 of elective deferrals in Plan R. The amount of elective deferrals that would have to be distributed to Participant E in order to satisfy section 401(k)(8)(C) is $200 ($15,000 minus $14,800), which is less than the excess of the applicable dollar catch-up limit ($5,000) over the elective deferrals previously treated as catch-up contributions under Plan R for the taxable year ($1,000). Under paragraph (d)(2)(iii) of this section, Plan R must retain Participant E(s $200 in elective deferrals and is not treated as failing to satisfy section 401(k)(8) merely because the elective deferrals are not distributed to Participant E.

(v) Even though Participant E's elective deferrals for calendar year 2006 have exceeded the section 401(a)(30) limit, Participant E can continue to make elective deferrals during the last 2 months of the calendar year, since Participant E's catch-up contributions for the taxable year are not taken into account in applying the section 401(a)(30) limit for 2006. Thus Participant E can make an additional contribution of $200 ($15,000 minus ($16,000 minus $1,200)) without exceeding the section 401(a)(30) for the calendar year and without regard to any additional catch-up contributions. In addition, Participant E may make additional catch-up contributions of $3,800 (the $5,000 applicable dollar catch-up limit for 2006, reduced by the $1,200 ($1,000 plus $200) of elective deferrals previously treated as catch-up contributions during the taxable year). The $3,800 of catch-up contributions will not be taken into account in the ADP test for the plan year ending October 31, 2007.

Example 7. (i) Participant F, who is 58 years old, is a highly compensated employee who earns $100,000 per year. Participant F participates in a section 401(k) plan, Plan S, for the first 6 months of the year and then transfers to another section 401(k) plan, Plan T, sponsored by the same employer, for the second 6 months of the year. Plan S limits highly compensated employees' elective deferrals to 6% of compensation for the period of participation, but permits catch-up eligible participants to defer amounts in excess of 6% during the plan year, up to the applicable dollar catch-up limit for the year. Plan T limits highly compensated employees' elective deferrals to 8% of compensation for the period of participation, but permits catch-up eligible participants to defer amounts in excess of 8% during the plan year, up to the applicable dollar catch-up limit for the year. Participant F earned $50,000 in the first 6 months of the year and deferred $6,000 under Plan S. Participant F also deferred $6,500 under Plan T.

(ii) As of the last day of the plan year, Participant F has $3,000 in elective deferrals under Plan S that exceed the employer-provided limit of $3,000. Under Plan T, Participant F has $2,500 in elective deferrals that exceed the employer-provided limit of $4,000. The total amount of elective deferrals in excess of employer-provided limits, $5,500, exceeds the applicable dollar catch-up limit by $500. Accordingly, $500 of the elective deferrals in excess of the employer-provided limits are not catch-up contributions and are treated as regular elective deferrals (and are taken into account in the ADP test). The

determination of which elective deferrals in excess of an applicable limit are treated as catch-up contributions is permitted to be made in any manner that is not inconsistent with the manner in which such amounts were actually deferred under Plan S and Plan T.

Example 8. (i) Employer X sponsors Plan P, which provides for matching contributions equal to 50% of elective deferrals that do not exceed 10% of compensation. Elective deferrals for highly compensated employees are limited, on a payroll-by-payroll basis, to 10% of compensation. Employer X pays employees on a monthly basis. Plan P also provides that elective contributions are limited in accordance with section 401(a)(30) and other applicable statutory limits. Plan P also provides for catch-up contributions. Under Plan P, for purposes of calculating the amount to be treated as catch-up contributions (and to be excluded from the ADP test), amounts in excess of the 10% limit for highly compensated employees are determined at the end of the plan year based on compensation used for purposes of ADP testing (testing compensation), a definition of compensation that is different from the definition used under the plan for purposes of calculating elective deferrals and matching contributions during the plan year (deferral compensation).

(ii) Participant A, a highly compensated employee, is a catch-up eligible participant under Plan P with deferral compensation of $10,000 per monthly payroll period. Participant A defers 10% per payroll period for the first 10 months of the year, and is allocated a matching contribution each payroll period of $500. In addition, Participant A defers an additional $4,000 during the first 10 months of the year. Participant A then reduces deferrals during the last 2 months of the year to 5% of compensation. Participant A is allocated a matching contribution of $250 for each of the last 2 months of the plan year. For the plan year, Participant A has $15,000 in elective deferrals and $5,500 in matching contributions.

(iii) A's testing compensation is $118,000. At the end of the plan year, based on 10% of testing compensation, or $11,800, Plan P determines that A has $3,200 in deferrals that exceed the 10% employer provided limit. Plan P excludes $3,200 from ADP testing and calculates A's ADR as $11,800 divided by $118,000, or 10%. Although A has not been allocated a matching contribution equal to 50% of $11,800, because Plan P provides that matching contributions are calculated based on elective deferrals during a payroll period as a percentage of deferral compensation, Plan P is not required to allocate an additional $400 of matching contributions to A.

(i) *Effective date.*—(1) *Statutory effective date.*—Section 414(v) applies to contributions in taxable years beginning on or after January 1, 2002.

(2) *Regulatory effective date.*—Paragraphs (a) through (h) of this section apply to contributions in taxable years beginning on or after January 1, 2004. [Reg. § 1.414(v)-1.]

☐ [T.D. 9072, 7-7-2003.]

[Reg. § 1.414(w)-1]

§ 1.414(w)-1. Permissible withdrawals from eligible automatic contribution arrangements.—(a) *Overview.*—Section 414(w) provides rules under which certain employees are permitted to elect to make a withdrawal of default elective contributions from an eligible automatic contribution arrangement. This section sets forth the rules applicable to permissible withdrawals from an eligible automatic contribution arrangement within the meaning of section 414(w). Paragraph (b) of this section defines an eligible automatic contribution arrangement. Paragraph (c) of this section describes a permissible withdrawal and addresses which employees are eligible to elect a withdrawal, the timing of the withdrawal election, and the amount of the withdrawal. Paragraph (d) of this section describes the tax and other consequences of the withdrawal. Paragraph (e) of this section includes the definitions applicable to this section.

(b) *Eligible automatic contribution arrangement.*—(1) *In general.*—An eligible automatic contribution arrangement is an automatic contribution arrangement under an applicable employer plan that is intended to be an eligible automatic contribution arrangement for the plan year and that satisfies the uniformity requirement under paragraph (b)(2) of this section, and the notice requirement under paragraph (b)(3) of this section. An eligible automatic contribution arrangement need not cover all employees who are eligible to elect to have contributions made on their behalf under the applicable employer plan.

(2) *Uniformity requirement.*—(i) *In general.*—An eligible automatic contribution arrangement must provide that the default elective contribution is a uniform percentage of compensation.

(ii) *Exception to uniform percentage requirement.*—An arrangement does not violate the uniformity requirement of paragraph (b)(2)(i) of this section merely because the percentage varies in a manner that is permitted under § 1.401(k)-3(j)(2)(iii), except that the rule of §1.401(k)-3(j)(2)(iii)(B) is applied without regard to whether the arrangement is intended to be a qualified automatic contribution arrangement.

(iii) *Rules of application.*—For purposes of this paragraph (b)(2), all automatic contribution arrangements that are intended to be eligible automatic contribution arrangements within a plan (or within the disaggregated plan under §1.410(b)-7, in the case of a plan subject to section 410(b)) are aggregated. Thus, for example, if a single plan within the meaning of section 414(l) covering employees in two separate divisions has two different automatic contribution arrangements that are intended to be eligible automatic contributions arrangements, the two automatic contribution arrangements can constitute eligible automatic contribution arrangements only if the default elective contributions under the arrangements are the same percentage of compensation. However, if the different automatic contribution arrangements cover employees in portions of the plan that are mandatorily disaggregated under the rules of section 410(b), then there is no requirement to aggregate those automatic contribution arrangements under the uniformity requirements of this paragraph (b)(2).

(3) *Notice requirement.*—(i) *General rule.*—The notice requirement of this paragraph (b)(3) is satisfied for a plan year if each covered employee is given notice of the employee's rights and obligations under the arrangement. The notice must be sufficiently accurate and comprehensive to apprise the employee of such rights and obligations, and be written in a manner calculated to be understood by the average employee to whom the arrangement applies. The notice must be in writing; however, see §1.401(a)-21 for rules permitting the use of electronic media to provide applicable notices.

(ii) *Content requirement.*—The notice must include the provisions found in §1.401(k)-3(d)(2)(ii) to the extent those provisions apply to the arrangement. A notice is not considered sufficiently accurate and comprehensive unless the notice accurately describes—

(A) The level of the default elective contributions which will be made on the employee's behalf if the employee does not make an affirmative election;

(B) The employee's rights to elect not to have default elective contributions made to the plan on his or her behalf or to have a different percentage of compensation or different amount of contribution made to the plan on his or her behalf;

(C) How contributions made under the arrangement will be invested in the absence of any investment election by the employee; and

(D) The employee's rights to make a permissible withdrawal, if applicable, and the procedures to elect such a withdrawal.

(iii) *Timing.*—(A) *General rule.*—The timing requirement of this paragraph (b)(3)(iii) is satisfied if the notice is provided within a reasonable period before the beginning of each plan year or, in the plan year the employee is first eligible to make a cash or deferred election (or first becomes covered under the automatic contribution arrangement as a result of a change in employment status), within a reasonable period before the employee becomes a covered employee. In addition, a notice satisfies the timing requirements of paragraph (b)(3) of this section only if it is provided sufficiently early so that the employee has a reasonable period of time after receipt of the notice in order to make the election described under paragraph (e)(2)(i) or (e)(2)(ii) of this section.

(B) *Deemed satisfaction of timing requirement.*—The timing requirement of this paragraph (b)(3)(iii) is satisfied if at least 30 days (and no more than 90 days) before the beginning of each plan year, the notice is given to each employee covered under the automatic contribution arrangement for the plan year. In the case of an employee who does not receive the notice within the period described in the previous sentence because the employee becomes eligible to make a cash or deferred election (or becomes covered under the automatic contribution arrangement as a result of a change in employment status) after the 90th day before the beginning of the plan year, the timing requirement is deemed to be satisfied if the notice is provided no more than 90 days before the employee becomes eligible to make a cash or deferred election (or becomes covered under the automatic contribution arrangement as a result of a change in employment status), and no later than the date that affords the employee a reasonable period of time after receipt of the notice to make the election described under paragraph (e)(2)(i) or (e)(2)(ii) of this section. If it is not practicable for the notice to be provided on or before the date specified in the plan that an employee becomes eligible to make a cash or deferred election, the notice will nonetheless be treated as provided timely if it is provided as soon as practicable after that date and the employee is permitted to elect to defer from all types of compensation that may be deferred under the plan earned beginning on that date.

(c) *Permissible withdrawal.*—(1) *In general.*—If the plan so provides, any employee who has default elective contributions made under the eligible automatic contribution arrangement may elect to make a withdrawal of such contributions (and earnings attributable thereto) in accordance with the requirements of this paragraph (c). An applicable employer plan that includes an eligible automatic contribution arrangement will not fail to satisfy the prohibition on in-service withdrawals under section 401(k)(2)(3), 403(b)(7), 403(b)(11), or 457(d)(1) merely because it permits withdrawals that satisfy the timing requirement of paragraph (c)(2) of this section and the amount requirement of paragraph (c)(3) of this section.

(2) *Timing.*—(i) *Last date to make election.*—A covered employee's election to withdraw default elective contributions must be made no later than 90 days after the date of the first default elective contribution under the eligible automatic contribution arrangement and must be effective no later than the date set forth in paragraph (c)(2)(iii) of this section. A plan is permitted to set an earlier deadline for making this election, but if a plan provides that a covered employee may withdraw default elective contributions, then the election period for the covered employee must be at least 30 days.

(ii) *Determination of date of first default elective contribution.*—For purposes of this paragraph (c)(2), the date of the first default elective contribution is the date that the compensation that is subject to the cash or deferred election would otherwise have been included in gross income.

(iii) *Latest effective date of the election.*—The effective date of an election described in this paragraph (c)(2) cannot be after the earlier of—

(A) The pay date for the second payroll period that begins after the date the election is made; and

(B) The first pay date that occurs at least 30 days after the election is made.

(iv) *Special rules.*—(A) *Treatment of periods without default elective contributions.*—For purposes of determining the date of the first default elective contribution under the eligible automatic contribution arrangement, a plan is permitted to treat an employee who for an entire plan year did not have default elective contributions made under the eligible automatic contribution arrangement as if the employee had not had such contributions for any prior plan year as well.

(B) *Treatment relating to aggregation of arrangements.*—The determination of whether an election is made no later than 90 days after the date of the first default elective contribution under the eligible automatic contribution arrangement must take into account any other eligible automatic contribution arrangement that is required to be aggregated with the eligible automatic contribution arrangement under the rules of paragraph (b)(2)(iii) of this section.

(3) *Amount and timing of distributions.*—(i) *In general.*—A distribution satisfies the requirement of this paragraph (c)(3) if the distribution is equal to the amount of default elective contributions made under the eligible automatic contribution arrangement through the effective date of the election described in paragraph (c)(2) of this section (adjusted for allocable gains and losses to the date of distribution). If default elective contributions are separately accounted for in the participant's account, the amount of the distribution will be the total amount in that account. However, if default elective contributions are not separately accounted for under the plan, the amount of the allocable gains and losses will be determined under rules similar to those provided under §1.401(k)-2(b)(2)(iv) for the distribution of excess contributions.

(ii) *Fees.*—The distribution amount as determined under this paragraph (c)(3) may be reduced by any generally applicable fees. However, the plan may not charge a higher fee for a distribution under section 414(w) than would apply to any other distributions of cash.

(iii) *Date of distribution.*—The distribution must be made in accordance with the plan's ordinary timing procedures for processing distributions and making distributions.

(d) *Consequences of the withdrawal.*—(1) *Income tax consequences.*—(i) *Year of inclusion.*—The amount of the withdrawal is includible in the eligible employee's gross income for the taxable year in which the distribution is made. However, any portion of the distribution consisting of designated Roth contributions is not included in an employee's gross income a second time. The portion of the withdrawal that is treated as an investment in the contract is determined without regard to any plan contributions other than those distributed as a withdrawal of default elective contributions.

(ii) *No additional tax on early distributions from qualified retirement plans.*—The withdrawal is not subject to the additional tax under section 72(t).

(iii) *Reporting.*—The amount of the withdrawal is reported on Form 1099-R, "Distributions From Pensions, Annuities, Retirement or Profit-Sharing Plans, IRAs, Insurance Contracts, etc.," as described in the applicable instructions.

(iv) *Disregarded for purposes of section 402(g).*—The amount of the withdrawal is not taken into account in determining the limitation on elective deferrals under section 402(g).

(2) *Forfeiture of matching contributions.*—In the case of any withdrawal made under paragraph (c) of this section, employer matching contributions with respect to the amount withdrawn that have been allocated to the participant's account (adjusted for allocable gains and losses) must be forfeited. A plan is permitted to provide that employer matching contributions will not be made with respect to any withdrawal made under paragraph (c) of this section if the withdrawal has been made prior to the date as of which the match would otherwise be allocated.

(3) *Consent rules.*—A withdrawal made under paragraph (c) of this section may be made without regard to any notice or consent otherwise required under section 401(a)(11) or 417.

(e) *Definitions.*—Unless indicated otherwise, the following definitions apply for purposes of section 414(w) and this section.

(1) *Applicable employer plan.*—An applicable employer plan means a plan that—

(i) Is qualified under section 401(a);

(ii) Satisfies the requirements of section 403(b);

(iii) Is a section 457(b) eligible governmental plan described in §1.457-2(f);

(iv) Is a simplified employee pension the terms of which provide for a salary reduction arrangement described in section 408(k)(6); or

(v) Is a SIMPLE described in section 408(p).

(2) *Automatic contribution arrangement.*—An automatic contribution arrangement means an arrangement that provides for a cash or deferred election and which specifies that, in the absence of a covered employee's affirmative election, a default election applies under which the employee is treated as having elected to have default elective contributions made on his or her behalf under the plan. The default election begins to apply with respect to an eligible employee no earlier than a reasonable period of time after receipt of the notice describing the automatic contribution arrangement. This default election ceases to apply with respect to an eligible employee for periods of time with respect to which the employee has an affirmative election that is currently in effect to—

(i) Not have any default elective contributions made on his or her behalf; or

(ii) Have contributions made in a different amount or percentage of compensation.

(3) *Covered employee.*—Covered employee means an employee who is covered under the automatic contribution arrangement, determined under the terms of the plan. A plan must provide whether an employee who makes an affirmative election remains a covered employee. If a plan provides that an employee who makes an affirmative election described in paragraph (e)(2)(i) or (e)(2)(ii) of this section remains a covered employee, then the employee must continue to receive the notice described in paragraph (b)(3) of this section and the plan may be eligible for the excise tax relief with respect to excess amounts distributed within 6 months after the end of the plan year under section 4979(f)(1). Such an employee will also have the default election reapply if the plan provides that the employee's prior affirmative election no longer remains in effect and the employee does not make a new affirmative election.

(4) *Default elective contributions.*—Default elective contributions means the contributions that are made at a specified level or amount under an automatic contribution arrangement in the absence of a covered employee's affirmative election that are—

(i) Contributions described in section 402(g)(3); or

(ii) Contributions made to an eligible governmental plan within the meaning of §1.457-2(f) that would be elective contributions if they were made under a qualified plan.

(f) *Effective/applicability date.*—(1) *Statutory effective date.*—Section 414(w) applies to plan years beginning on or after January 1, 2008.

(2) *Regulatory effective date.*—This section applies to plan years beginning on or after January 1, 2010. For plan years that begin in 2008, a plan must operate in accordance with a good faith interpretation of section 414(w). For this purpose, a plan that operates in accordance with this section will be treated as operating in accordance with a good faith interpretation of section 414(w). [Reg. §1.414(w)-1.]

☐ [*T.D. 9447, 2-23-2009.*]

[Reg. §1.415(a)-1]

§1.415(a)-1. General rules with respect to limitations on benefits and contributions under qualified plans.—(a) *Trusts.*—Under sections 415 and 401(a)(16), a trust that forms part of a pension, profit-sharing, or stock bonus plan will not be qualified under section 401(a) if any of the following conditions exists:

(1) In the case of a defined benefit plan, the annual benefit with respect to any participant for any limitation year exceeds the limitations of section 415(b) and §1.415(b)-1.

(2) In the case of a defined contribution plan, the annual additions credited with respect to any participant for any limitation year exceed the limitations of section 415(c) and §1.415(c)-1.

(3) The trust has been disqualified under section 415(g) and §1.415(g)-1 for any year.

(b) *Certain annuities and accounts.*—(1) *In general.*—Under section 415, an employee annuity plan described in section 403(a), an annuity contract described in section 403(b), or a simplified employee pension described in section 408(k) will not be considered to be described in the otherwise applicable section if any of the following conditions exists:

(i) The annual benefit under a defined benefit plan with respect to any participant for any limitation year exceeds the limitations of section 415(b) and §1.415(b)-1.

(ii) The contributions and other additions credited under a defined contribution plan with respect to any participant for any limitation year exceed the limitations of section 415(c) and §1.415(c)-1.

(iii) The employee annuity plan, annuity contract, or simplified employee pension has been disqualified under section 415(g) and §1.415(g)-1 for any year.

(2) *Special rule for section 403(b) annuity contracts.*—If the contributions and other additions under an annuity contract that otherwise satisfies the requirements of section 403(b) exceed the limitations of section 415(c) and §1.415(c)-1 with respect to any participant for any limitation year (regardless of whether the annuity contract is a defined contribution plan or a defined benefit plan), then the portion of the contract that includes such excess annual addition fails to be a section 403(b) annuity contract, and the remaining portion of the contract is a section 403(b) annuity contract. However, the status of the remaining portion of the contract as a section 403(b) annuity contract is not retained unless, for the year of the excess and each year thereafter, the issuer of the contract maintains separate accounts for each such portion. In addition, if the benefit under an annuity contract that is a defined benefit plan and that otherwise satisfies the requirements of section 403(b) exceeds the limitations of section 415(b) and §1.415(b)-1 with respect to any participant for any limitation year, then the contract fails to be a section 403(b) annuity contract.

(3) *Section 403(b) annuity contract.*—For purposes of section 415 and regulations promulgated under section 415, the term *section 403(b) annuity contract* includes arrangements that are treated as annuity contracts for purposes of section 403(b). Thus, such term includes custodial accounts described in section 403(b)(7) and retirement income accounts described in section 403(b)(9).

(c) *Regulations.*—(1) *In general.*—This section provides general rules regarding the application of section 415. For further rules regarding the application of section 415, see—

(i) Section 1.415(b)-1 (for general rules regarding the limits applicable to defined benefit plans);

(ii) Section 1.415(b)-2 (for special rules for defined benefit plans where a participant has multiple annuity starting dates);

(iii) Section 1.415(c)-1 (for general rules regarding the limits applicable to defined contribution plans);

(iv) Section 1.415(c)-2 (for rules regarding the definition of compensation for purposes of section 415);

(v) Section 1.415(d)-1 (for rules regarding cost-of-living adjustments to the various limits of section 415);

(vi) Section 1.415(f)-1 (for rules for aggregating plans for purposes of section 415);

(vii) Section 1.415(g)-1 (for rules regarding disqualification of plans that fail to satisfy the requirements of section 415); and

(viii) Section 1.415(j)-1 (for rules regarding limitation years).

(2) *Cross references to special rules for section 403(b) annuity contracts.*—For special rules relating to section 403(b) annuity contracts, see—

(i) Section 1.415(c)-2(g)(1) and (3) (relating to the definition of compensation for section 403(b) annuity contracts);

(ii) Section 1.415(f)-1(f) (relating to rules for section 403(b) annuity contracts for purposes of aggregating plans);

(iii) Section 1.415(g)-1(b)(1)(iv)(C) (regarding disqualification of a section 403(b) annuity contract aggregated with a qualified defined contribution plan if the aggregated plans exceed the limitations of section 415(c));

(iv) Section 1.415(g)-1(c) (relating to the plan year for section 403(b) annuity contracts); and

(v) Section 1.415(j)-1(e) (relating to the limitation year for section 403(b) annuity contracts).

(3) *Cross references to special rules for governmental plans.*—For special rules relating to governmental plans, see—

(i) Paragraph (f)(4) of this section (regarding permissive service credits);

(ii) Paragraph (g)(2) of this section (providing a delayed effective date for governmental plans);

(iii) Section 1.415(b)-1(a)(6)(i) (providing an exception from the compensation-based limit of section 415(b)(1)(B) for governmental plans);

(iv) Section 1.415(b)-1(a)(7)(ii) (regarding a special limitation for certain governmental plans making an election during 1990);

(v) Section 1.415(b)-1(b)(4) (regarding qualified governmental excess benefit arrangements);

(vi) Section 1.415(b)-1(d)(3) and (4) (regarding age adjustments to the dollar limit of section 415(b)(1)(A) for employees of police and fire departments and members of the Armed Forces of the United States, and for survivor and disability benefits);

(vii) Section 1.415(b)-1(g)(3) (regarding adjustments to applicable limitations for years of participation, and adjustments to applicable limitations for years of service for survivor and disability benefits under governmental plans);

(viii) Section 1.415(c)-1(b)(2)(ii) and (3)(iii) (regarding amounts not treated as annual additions under governmental plans); and

(ix) Section 1.415(c)-2(e)(5) (providing an alternative rule for inclusion of compensation after a severance from employment for governmental plans).

(4) *Cross references to special rules for multiemployer plans.*—For special rules relating to multiemployer plans as defined in section 414(f), see—

(i) Paragraph (e) of this section (regarding benefits or contributions taken into account where a plan is maintained by more than one employer);

(ii) Paragraph (f)(5)(ii) of this section (providing a special definition of severance from employment for multiemployer plans);

(iii) Section 1.415(b)-1(a)(6)(ii) (providing an exception from the compensation-based limit for multiemployer plans);

(iv) Section 1.415(b)-1(f)(3) (regarding the application of the minimum $10,000 limitation on benefits in the case of a multiemployer plan);

(v) Section 1.415(f)-1(g) (providing special rules for aggregating multiemployer plans with other plans); and

(vi) Section 1.415(g)-1(b)(3)(ii) (regarding plan disqualification rules where a multiemployer plan is aggregated with a plan that is not a multiemployer plan and the aggregated plans exceed the limitations of section 415).

(5) *Cross references to special rules for plans that are not subject to the requirements of section 411.*—For special rules relating to plans that are not subject to the requirements of section 411, see—

(i) Paragraph (d)(1) of this section and §1.415(b)-1(a)(7)(iii) (providing that the rule limiting accruals to the section 415(b) limits does not apply to plans that are not subject to the requirements of section 411); and

(ii) Section 1.415(b)-1(b)(2)(iii) (providing rules for applying the section 411(c) factors in determining the annual benefit attributable to employee contributions for plans that are not subject to the requirements of section 411).

(6) *Cross references to special rules for plans maintained by churches.*—For special rules relating to plans maintained by churches as defined in section 3121(w)(3)(A), see §§1.415(b)-1(a)(6)(iv) and 1.415(b)-1(a)(7)(iv) (providing an exception from the compensation-based limit for participants who have never been a highly compensated employee of the church).

(d) *Plan provisions.*—(1) *In general.*—Although no specific plan provision is required under section 415 in order for a plan to establish or maintain its qualification, the plan provisions must preclude the possibility that any distribution under a defined benefit plan or annual addition under a defined contribution plan will exceed the limitations of section 415. In addition, a defined benefit plan that is subject to the requirements of section 411 must preclude the possibility that any accrual under the plan will exceed the limitations of section 415. A defined benefit plan may include provisions that automatically freeze or reduce the rate of benefit accrual (or limit the benefit payable in the case of a plan that is not subject to the requirements of section 411), and a defined contribution plan may include provisions that automatically limit the annual addition to a level necessary to prevent the limitations of section 415 from being exceeded with respect to any participant. For rules relating to this type of plan provision and the definitely determinable benefit requirement for pension plans, see §1.401(a)-1(b)(1)(iii). Because §1.401(a)-1(b)(1)(iii) requires that the operation of such a provision preclude discretion by the employer, if two defined benefit plans that are aggregated under the rules of section 415(f) would otherwise provide for aggregate benefits that might exceed the limits of section 415(b), the plan provisions must specify (without involving employer discretion) how benefits will be limited to prevent a violation of section 415(b).

(2) *Special rule for profit-sharing and stock bonus plans.*—A provision of a profit-sharing or stock bonus plan that automatically freezes or reduces the amount of annual additions to ensure that the limitations of section 415 will not be exceeded must comply with the requirement set forth in §1.401-1(b)(1)(ii) or (iii) (as applicable) that such plans provide a definite predetermined formula for allocating the contributions made to the plan among the participants. If the operation of a provision that automatically freezes or reduces the amount of annual additions to ensure that the limitations of section 415 are not exceeded does not involve discretionary action on the part of the employer, the definite predetermined allocation formula requirement is not violated by the provision. If the operation of such a provision involves discretionary action on the part of the employer, the definite predetermined allocation formula requirement is violated. For example, if two profit-sharing plans of one employer otherwise provide for aggregate contributions which may exceed the limits of section 415(c), the plan provisions must specify (without involving employer discretion) under which plan contributions and allocations will be reduced to prevent an excess annual addition and how the reduction will occur.

(3) *Incorporation by reference.*—(i) *In general.*—A plan is permitted to incorporate by reference the limitations of section 415, and will not fail to meet the definitely determinable benefit requirement or the definite predetermined allocation formula requirement, whichever applies to the plan, merely because it incorporates the limits of section 415 by reference.

(ii) *Section 415 can be applied in more than one manner, but a statutory or regulatory default rule exists.*—Where a provision of section 415 is permitted to be applied in more than one manner but is to be applied in a specified manner in the absence of contrary plan provisions (in other words, a default rule exists), if a plan incorporates the limitations of section 415 by reference with respect to that provision of section 415 and does not specifically vary from the default rule, then the default rule applies. With respect to a provision of section 415 for which a default rule exists, if the limitations of section 415 are to be applied in a manner other than using the default rule, the plan must specify the manner in which the limitation is to be applied in addition to generally incorporating the limitations of section 415 by reference. For example, if a plan generally incorporates the limitations of section 415 by reference and does not restrict the accrued benefits to which the amendments to section 415(b)(2)(E) made by the Uruguay Round Agreements Act of 1994, Public Law 103-465 (108 Stat. 4809) (GATT), apply (as permitted by Q&A-12 of Rev. Rul. 98-1 (1998-1 CB 249) (see §601.601(d)(2) of this chapter), which reflects the amendments to section 767 of GATT made by section 1449 of the Small Business Job Protection Act of 1996, Public Law 104-188 (110 Stat. 1755)), then the amendments to section 415(b)(2)(E) made by GATT apply to all benefits under the plan.

(iii) *Section 415 can be applied in more than one manner with no statutory or regulatory default.*—If a limitation of section 415 may be applied in more than one manner, and if there is no governing principle pursuant to which that limitation is applied in the absence of contrary plan provisions, then the plan must specify the manner in which the limitation is to be applied in addition to generally incorporating the limitations of section 415 by reference. For example, if an employer maintains two profit-sharing plans, and if any participant participates in more than one such plan, then both plans must specify (in a consistent manner) under which of the employer's two profit-sharing plans annual additions must be reduced if aggregate annual additions would otherwise exceed the limitations of section 415(c).

(iv) *Former requirements.*—A plan is not permitted to incorporate by reference formerly applicable requirements of section 415 that are no longer in force (such as the limits of former section 415(e)).

(v) *Cost-of-living adjustments.*—(A) *In general.*—A plan is permitted to incorporate by reference the annual adjustments to the limitations of section 415 that are made pursuant to section 415(d). See § 1.415(d)-1 for additional rules relating to cost-of-living adjustments under section 415(d).

(B) *Cost-of-living adjustments not included in accrued benefit until effective.*—Notwithstanding that a plan incorporates the increases to the applicable limits under section 415(d) by reference, the accrued benefit of a participant for purposes of section 411 and any amount payable to a participant for purposes of § 1.415(b)-1(a)(1) are not permitted to reflect increases pursuant to the annual increase under section 415(d) of the dollar limitation described in section 415(b)(1)(A) or the compensation limit described in section 415(b)(1)(B) for any period before the annual increase becomes effective. See § 1.415(d)-1(a)(3) for rules relating to when the annual adjustments to the dollar and compensation limitations are effective. A plan amendment does not violate the requirements of section 411(d)(6) merely because it eliminates the incorporation by reference of the increases under section 415(d) with respect to increases that have not yet occurred.

(C) *Application of increase in defined benefit dollar limit to participants who have incurred a severance from employment or commenced receiving benefits.*—If a plan incorporates by reference the annual adjustments to the limitations of section 415 pursuant to this paragraph (d)(3)(v), the plan will be treated as applying the section 415(d) cost-of-living adjustments to the maximum extent permitted under the safe harbor described in § 1.415(d)-1(a)(5), except to the extent provided in this paragraph (d)(3)(v)(C). Thus, such a plan is not subject to the requirements of § 1.415(b)-1(b)(1)(iii) (providing special rules for determining the annual benefit of an employee in the case of multiple annuity starting dates) with respect to benefit increases that result solely from an increase in the section 415(b) limits pursuant to section 415(d). If a plan incorporates by reference the annual adjustments to the limitations of section 415 pursuant to this paragraph (d)(3)(v), the annual increase under section 415(d) of the dollar limitation described in section 415(b)(1)(A) does not apply with respect to a participant if the increase is effective after the participant's severance from employment with the employer maintaining the plan (or, if earlier, after the annuity starting date in the case of a participant who has commenced receiving benefits), unless the plan specifies that this annual increase applies. Similarly, if a plan incorporates by reference the annual adjustments to the limitations of section 415 pursuant to this paragraph (d)(3)(v), the annual increase under section 415(d) of the compensation-based limitation described in section 415(b)(1)(B) does not apply with respect to a participant for increases that are effective after the participant's severance from employment with the employer maintaining the plan (or, if earlier, after the annuity starting date in the case of a participant who has commenced receiving benefits), unless the plan specifies that this annual increase applies.

(D) *Treatment of cost-of-living adjustments for funding and deduction purposes.*—In general, the annual increase under section 415(d) of the dollar limitation described in section 415(b)(1)(A) and the compensation limitation described in section 415(b)(1)(B) is treated as a plan amendment, regardless of whether the plan reflects the increase automatically through operation of plan provisions in accordance with this paragraph (d)(3)(v) or the plan is amended to reflect the increase (pursuant to § 1.415(d)-1(a)(5)). However, where a plan reflects the annual increase under section 415(d) of the dollar limitation described in section 415(b)(1)(A) or the compensation limitation described in section 415(b)(1)(B) automatically through operation of plan provisions pursuant to this paragraph (d)(3)(v), the funding method for the plan is permitted to provide for this annual increase to be treated as an experience loss for purposes of applying sections 404, 412, and 431.

(e) *Rules for plans maintained by more than one employer.*—Except as provided in § 1.415(f)-1(g)(2)(i) (regarding aggregation of multiemployer plans with plans other than multiemployer plans), for purposes of applying the limitations of section 415 with respect to a participant in a plan maintained by more than one employer, benefits and contributions attributable to such participant from all of the employers maintaining the plan must be taken into account. Furthermore, in applying the limitations of section 415 with respect to a participant in such a plan, the total compensation received by the participant from all of the employers maintaining the plan is taken into account under the plan, unless the plan specifies otherwise.

(f) *Special rules.*—(1) *Affiliated employers.*—Pursuant to section 414(b) and § 1.414(b)-1, all employees of all corporations that are

members of a controlled group of corporations (within the meaning of section 1563(a), as modified by section 1563(f)(5), and determined without regard to section 1563(a)(4) and (e)(3)(C)) are treated as employed by a single employer for purposes of section 415. Similarly, pursuant to section 414(c) and regulations promulgated under section 414(c), all employees of trades or businesses that are under common control are treated as employed by a single employer. Thus, any defined benefit plan or defined contribution plan maintained by any member of a controlled group of corporations (within the meaning of section 414(b)) or by any trade or business (whether or not incorporated) that is part of a group of trades or businesses that are under common control (within the meaning of section 414(c)) is deemed maintained by all such members or such trades or businesses. Pursuant to section 415(h), for purposes of section 415, sections 414(b) and 414(c) are applied by using the phrase "more than 50 percent" instead of the phrase "at least 80 percent" each place the latter phrase appears in section 1563(a)(1) and in the regulations under section 414(c) (except for purposes of determining whether two or more organizations are a brother-sister group of trades or businesses under common control under the rules in § 1.414(c)-2(c)).

(2) *Affiliated service groups.*—Any defined benefit plan or defined contribution plan maintained by any member of an affiliated service group (within the meaning of section 414(m)) is deemed maintained by all members of that affiliated service group.

(3) *Leased employees.*—(i) *In general.*—Pursuant to section 414(n), except as provided in paragraph (f)(3)(ii) of this section, with respect to any person (referred to as the recipient) for whom a leased employee (within the meaning of section 414(n)(2)) performs services, the leased employee is treated as an employee of the recipient, but contributions or benefits provided by the leasing organization that are attributable to services performed for the recipient are treated as provided under a plan maintained by the recipient.

(ii) *Exception for leased employees covered by safe harbor plans.*—Pursuant to section 414(n)(5), the rule of paragraph (f)(3)(i) of this section does not apply to a leased employee with respect to services performed for a recipient if—

(A) The leased employee is covered by a plan that is maintained by the leasing organization and that meets the requirements of section 414(n)(5)(B); and

(B) Leased employees (determined without regard to this paragraph (f)(3)(ii)) do not constitute more than 20 percent of the recipient's nonhighly compensated workforce.

(4) *Permissive service credit under governmental plans.*—See section 415(n) for rules regarding the application of the limitations of sections 415(b) and (c) where a participant makes contributions (including a transfer described in section 403(b)(13) or section 457(e)(17)) to a defined benefit governmental plan to purchase permissive service credit under the plan.

(5) *Definition of severance from employment.*—(i) *General rule.*—For purposes of this section and §§ 1.415(b)-1, 1.415(b)-2, 1.415(c)-1, 1.415(c)-2, 1.415(d)-1, 1.415(f)-1, 1.415(g)-1, and 1.415(j)-1, whether an employee has a severance from employment with the employer that maintains a plan is determined in the same manner as under § 1.401(k)-1(d)(2) except that, for purposes of determining the employer of an employee, the modifications provided under section 415(h) (described in paragraph (f)(1) of this section) to the employer aggregation rules apply. Thus, an employee has a severance from employment when the employee ceases to be an employee of the employer maintaining the plan, and an employee does not have a severance from employment if, in connection with a change of employment, the employee's new employer maintains such plan with respect to the employee. The determination of whether an employee ceases to be an employee of the employer maintaining the plan is based on all of the relevant facts and circumstances.

(ii) *Multiemployer plans.*—A participant in a multiemployer plan (within the meaning of section 414(f)) is not treated as having incurred a severance from employment with the employer maintaining the multiemployer plan for purposes of this section and §§ 1.415(b)-1, 1.415(b)-2, 1.415(c)-1, 1.415(c)-2, 1.415(d)-1, 1.415(f)-1, 1.415(g)-1, and 1.415(j)-1 if the participant continues to be an employee of another employer maintaining the multiemployer plan.

(6) *Qualified domestic relations orders.*—A benefit provided to an alternate payee (as defined in section 414(p)(8)) of a participant pursuant to a qualified domestic relations order (as defined in section 414(p)(1)(A)) is treated as if it were provided to the participant for purposes of applying the limitations of section 415. See § 1.401(a)-13(g)(4)(iv).

(7) *Effect on other requirements.*—Except as provided in § 1.417(e)-1(d)(1), the application of section 415 does not relieve a

plan from the obligation to satisfy other applicable qualification requirements. Accordingly, the terms of the plan must provide for the plan to satisfy section 415 as well as all other applicable requirements. For example, if a defined benefit plan has a normal retirement age of 62, and if a participant's benefit remains unchanged between the ages of 62 and 65 because of the application of the section 415(b)(1)(A) dollar limit, the plan satisfies the requirements of section 411 only if the plan either commences distribution of the participant's benefit at normal retirement age (without regard to severance from employment) or provides for a suspension of benefits at normal retirement age that satisfies the requirements of section 411(a)(3)(B) and 29 CFR 2530.203-3. Similarly, if the increase to a participant's benefit under a defined benefit plan in a year after the participant has attained normal retirement age is less than the actuarial increase to the participant's previously accrued benefit because of the application of the section 415(b)(1)(B) compensation limitation (which is not adjusted for commencement after age 65), the plan satisfies the requirements of section 411 only if the plan either commences distribution of the participant's benefit at normal retirement age (without regard to severance from employment) or provides for a suspension of benefits at normal retirement age that satisfies the requirements of section 411(a)(3)(B) and 29 CFR 2530.203-3.

(g) *Effective date.*—(1) *General rule.*—Except as otherwise provided, this section and §§1.415(b)-1, 1.415(c)-1, 1.415(c)-2, 1.415(d)-1, 1.415(f)-1, 1.415(g)-1, and 1.415(j)-1 apply to limitation years beginning on or after July 1, 2007.

(2) *Governmental plans.*—In the case of a governmental plan as defined in section 414(d), this section and §§1.415(b)-1, 1.415(c)-1, 1.415(c)-2, 1.415(d)-1, 1.415(f)-1, 1.415(g)-1, and 1.415(j)-1 apply to limitation years that begin more than 90 days after the close of the first regular legislative session of the legislative body with authority to amend the plan that begins on or after July 1, 2007. A governmental plan is permitted to apply the provisions of this section and §§1.415(b)-1, 1.415(c)-1, 1.415(c)-2, 1.415(d)-1, 1.415(f)-1, 1.415(g)-1, and 1.415(j)-1 to limitation years beginning on or after July 1, 2007, provided the plan applies all the applicable provisions of this section and §§1.415(b)-1, 1.415(c)-1, 1.415(c)-2, 1.415(d)-1, 1.415(f)-1, 1.415(g)-1, and 1.415(j)-1 for such limitation years.

(3) *Option to apply regulations earlier.*—A plan may apply the rules in §1.415(c)-2(e) regarding post-severance compensation payments for limitation years prior to the effective date described in paragraphs (g)(1) and (2) of this section. This early application affects the rules relating to the definition of compensation in §1.401(k)-1(e)(8) and §1.457-4(d).

(4) *Grandfather rule for preexisting benefits.*—A defined benefit plan is considered to satisfy the limitations of section 415(b) for a participant with respect to benefits accrued or payable under the plan as of the end of the limitation year that is immediately prior to the effective date of final regulations under this section and §§1.415(b)-1, 1.415(c)-1, 1.415(c)-2, 1.415(d)-1, 1.415(f)-1, 1.415(g)-1, and 1.415(j)-1 (as provided under paragraph (g)(1) or (2) of this section) pursuant to plan provisions (including plan provisions relating to the plan's limitation year) that were both adopted and in effect before April 5,2007, but only if such plan provisions meet the applicable requirements of statutory provisions, regulations, and other published guidance relating to section 415 in effect immediately before the effective date of final regulations under this section and §§1.415(b)-1, 1.415(c)-1, 1.415(c)-2, 1.415(d)-1, 1.415(f)-1, 1.415(g)-1, and 1.415(j)-1 (as provided under paragraph (g)(1) or (2) of this section). Plan provisions will not be treated as failing to satisfy these requirements merely because the plan has not been amended to reflect changes to section 415(b) made by the Pension Funding Equity Act of 2004, Public Law 108-218 (118 Stat. 596), and the Pension Protection Act of 2006, Public Law 109-280 (120 Stat. 780). In addition, plan provisions will not be treated as failing to satisfy these requirements merely because the plan's definition of compensation for a limitation year that is used for purposes of applying the limitations of section 415(b)(1)(B) reflects compensation for a plan year that is in excess of the limitation under section 401(a)(17) that applies to that plan year. If benefits under a plan are accrued after the applicable effective date under paragraph (g)(1) or (2) of this section, then the sum of the benefits grandfathered under the first sentence of this paragraph (g)(4) and benefits accrued after the applicable effective date must satisfy the requirements of section 415, taking into account the requirements of this section and §§1.415(b)-1, 1.415(c)-1, 1.415(c)-2, 1.415(d)-1, 1.415(f)-1, 1.415(g)-1, and 1.415(j)-1. [Reg. §1.415(a)-1.]

☐ [*T.D. 9319, 4–4–2007.*]

[Reg. §1.415(b)-1]

§1.415(b)-1. Limitations for defined benefit plans.—(a) *General rules.*—(1) *Maximum limitations.*—Except as otherwise provided

under this section, a defined benefit plan fails to satisfy the requirements of section 415(a) for a limitation year if, during the limitation year, either the annual benefit (as defined in paragraph (b)(1)(i) of this section) accrued by a participant (whether or not the benefit is vested) or the annual benefit payable to a participant at any time under the plan exceeds the lesser of—

(i) $160,000 (as adjusted pursuant to section 415(d), §1.415(d)-1(a), and this section); or

(ii) 100 percent of the participant's average compensation for the period of the participant's high-3 years of service (as adjusted pursuant to section 415(d), §1.415(d)-1(a), and this section).

(2) *Defined benefit plan.*—For purposes of section 415 and regulations promulgated under section 415, a defined benefit plan is any plan, contract, or account to which section 415 applies pursuant to §1.415(a)-1(a) or (b) (or any portion thereof) that is not a defined contribution plan within the meaning of §1.415(c)-1(a)(2). In addition, a section 403(b) annuity contract that is not described in section 414(i) is treated as a defined benefit plan for purposes of section 415 and regulations promulgated under section 415.

(3) *Plan provisions.*—As required in §1.415(a)-1(d)(1), in order to satisfy the limitations on benefits under this section, the plan provisions (including the provisions of any annuity) must preclude the possibility that any annual benefit exceeding these limitations will be accrued (except as provided in paragraph (a)(7)(iii) of this section), distributed, or otherwise payable in any optional form of benefit (including the normal form of benefit) at any time (from the plan, from an annuity contract that will make distributions to the participant on behalf of the plan, or from an annuity contract that has been distributed under the plan). Thus, for example, a plan that is subject to the requirements of section 411 will fail to satisfy the limitations of this section if the plan does not contain terms that preclude the possibility that any annual benefit exceeding these limitations will be accrued or payable in any optional form of benefit (including the normal form of benefit) at any time, even though no participant has actually accrued a benefit in excess of these limitations.

(4) *Adjustments to dollar limitation for commencement before age 62 or after age 65.*—The age-adjusted section 415(b)(1)(A) dollar limit computed pursuant to paragraph (d) or (e) of this section is used in place of the dollar limitation described in section 415(b)(1)(A) and paragraph (a)(1)(i) of this section in the case of a benefit with an annuity starting date that occurs before the participant attains age 62 or after the participant attains age 65.

(5) *Average compensation for period of high-3 years of service.*—(i) *In general.*—Except as otherwise provided in this paragraph (a)(5), for purposes of applying the limitation on benefits described in this section, the period of a participant's high-3 years of service is the period of 3 consecutive calendar years taking into account the rule in paragraph (a)(5)(iii) of this section) during which the employee had the greatest aggregate compensation (as defined in §1.415(c)-2) from the employer, and the average compensation for the period of a participant's high-3 years of service is determined by dividing the aggregate compensation for this period by 3. For purposes of this paragraph (a)(5), in determining a participant's high-3 years of service, the plan may use any 12-month period to determine a year of service instead of the calendar year, provided that it is uniformly and consistently applied in a manner that is specified under the terms of the plan. As provided under §1.415(c)-2(f), because a plan is not permitted to base benefits on compensation in excess of the limitation under section 401(a)(17), a plan's definition of compensation for a year that is used for purposes of applying the limitations of section 415 is not permitted to reflect compensation for a year that is in excess of the limitation under section 401(a)(17) that applies to that year. See §§1.401(a)(17)-1(a)(3)(i) and 1.401(a)(17)-1(b)(3)(ii) for rules regarding the effective date of increases in the section 401(a)(17) compensation limitation for a plan year and for a 12-month period other than the plan year.

(ii) *Short periods of service.*—For a participant who is employed with an employer for less than 3 consecutive years, the period of the participant's high-3 years of service is the actual number of consecutive years of service (including fractions of years, but not less than one year). In such a case, the limitation of section 415(b)(1)(B) of 100 percent of the participant's average compensation for the period of the participant's high-3 years of service is computed by dividing the participant's compensation during the participant's longest consecutive period of service by the number of years in that period (including fractions of years, but not less than one year). The rule in paragraph (a)(5)(iii) of this section is used for purposes of determining a participant's consecutive years of service.

(iii) *Break in service.*—In the case of a participant who has had a severance from employment with an employer that maintains the plan and who is subsequently rehired by the employer, the period of the participant's high-3 years of service is calculated by excluding all years for which the participant performs no services for and receives no compensation from the employer maintaining the plan (referred to as the break period), and by treating the year of service immediately prior to and the year of service immediately after the break period as if such years of service were consecutive. See § 1.415(d)-1(a)(2)(iii) for a special rule for determining a rehired participant's section 415(b)(1)(B) compensation limit in the case of a plan that adjusts the compensation limit for limitation years after the limitation year in which the participant incurs a severance from employment.

(iv) *Examples.*—For purposes of these examples, except as otherwise stated, the plan year and the limitation year are the calendar year, and the plan uses the calendar year for purposes of determining the period of high-3 years of service. In addition, except as otherwise stated, it is assumed that the plan's normal retirement age is 65, and all participants discussed in these examples have at least ten years of service with the employer and at least ten years of participation in the plan at issue. It is also assumed that none of the plans in the examples are governmental plans. The following examples illustrate the rules of this paragraph (a)(5):

Example 1. (i) *Facts.* Plan A, which was established on January 1, 2008, covers Participant M, who was hired on January 1, 1990. Participant M's compensation (as defined in § 1.415(c)-2) from the employer maintaining the plan is $140,000 each year for 1990 through 1992, is $120,000 each year for 1993 through 2007, and is $165,000 for 2008 and 2009. Assume that for Plan A's 2008 and 2009 limitation years, the section 415(b)(1)(A) age-adjusted dollar limit for M is $185,000 and $190,000, respectively, prior to the reduction of the age-adjusted dollar limit pursuant to paragraph (g)(1) of this section (which requires a reduction in the dollar limit if a participant has less than 10 years of participation in the plan).

(ii) *Conclusion.* As of the end of the 2008 limitation year, the period of M's high-3 consecutive years of service runs from January 1, 1990, through December 31, 1992, and M's average compensation for this period is $140,000. Thus, the limitation under section 415(b)(1)(B) for the 2008 limitation year is $140,000. As of the end of the 2009 limitation year, the period of M's high-3 consecutive years of service runs from January 1, 2007, through December 31, 2009, and M's average compensation for this period is $150,000. Thus, the limitation under section 415(b)(1)(B) for the 2009 limitation year is $150,000.

Example 2. (i) *Facts.* Participant N is a participant in Plan B. N's compensation for 2008, 2009, and 2010 is $300,000 for each year. N's average compensation for the period of N's high-3 years of service (determined before the application of section 401(a)(17)) is $300,000, based on N's compensation for 2008, 2009, and 2010. For all years before 2008, Participant N's compensation was less than the then-applicable section 401(a)(17) limit. On January 1, 2011, N commences receiving benefits from Plan B at the age of 75, 10 years after attaining N's normal retirement age under Plan B, when the age-adjusted section 415(b)(1)(A) dollar limit for benefits commencing at that age is $293,453.

(ii) *Conclusion.* Pursuant to § 1.415(c)-2(f) and section 401(a)(17), Plan B is not permitted to provide for a definition of compensation that includes compensation for a year that is in excess of the limitation under section 401(a)(17) that applies to that year. Accordingly, the limitation under section 415(b)(1)(B) based on N's average compensation for the period of N's high three years of service must not reflect compensation for a year that is in excess of the limitation under section 401(a)(17) that applies to that year. Thus, if the limitation under section 401(a)(17) for years beginning in 2008, 2009, and 2010 is $230,000, $235,000, and $240,000, respectively, then the limitation under section 415(b)(1)(B) based on N's average compensation for the period of N's high three years of service is $235,000.

Example 3. (i) *Facts.* The facts are the same as in *Example 2*, except that N commences receiving benefits from Plan B on January 1, 2008, at the age of 75, 10 years after attaining N's normal retirement age under Plan B. In addition, N's period of high three years of service is from January 1, 2003, through December 31, 2005, and N's average compensation for this period is $300,000. The section 401(a)(17) limits for 2003, 2004 and 2005 are $200,000, $205,000, and $210,000, respectively. As of December 31, 2007, pursuant to plan provisions adopted and in effect on January 1, 2007, N's accrued benefit under Plan B, payable in the form of a straight life annuity, actuarially adjusted to reflect commencement 10 years after normal retirement age, is $300,000. Plan B has not been amended during 2007, and that as of December 31, 2007, Plan B satisfied all of the requirements of section 415(b) with respect to N's accrued benefit, pursuant to statutory provisions, regulations, and other published guidance in effect immediately before the limitation year beginning on January 1, 2008.

(ii) *Conclusion.* Under § 1.415(a)-1(g)(4), Plan B is considered to satisfy the section 415(b)(1)(B) compensation limit with respect to N's benefit payable at age 75 of $300,000 (which N accrued prior to January 1, 2008), for limitation years beginning after December 31, 2007. This is because § 1.415(a)-1(g)(4) provides that plan provisions will not be treated as failing to satisfy the requirements of section 415(b)(1)(B) merely because the plan's definition of compensation that is used for purposes of applying the limitations of section 415(b)(1)(B) reflects compensation in excess of the section 401(a)(17) limitation for limitation years beginning before January 1, 2008. N, however, cannot accrue any additional benefits under Plan B for limitation years beginning after December 31, 2007, until N's section 415(b)(1)(B) compensation limit, as limited by § 1.415(c)-2(f) and section 401(a)(17), increases above $300,000.

Example 4. (i) *Facts.* Participant O participates in Plan C, maintained by Employer X. Plan C does not adjust a participant's section 415(b)(1)(B) compensation limit for limitation years after the limitation year in which the participant incurs a severance from employment. Prior to separating from employment with X in 2010, O's average compensation for O's period of high-3 years of service is $50,000, based on O's compensation for 2007, 2008, and 2009, which was $50,000 for each year. O's compensation for 2010 was $45,000. O's compensation is $0 for 2011. In 2012, O is rehired by X and resumes participation in Plan C. O's compensation in 2012 is $45,000, and is $70,000 in 2013.

(ii) *Conclusion.* As of the end of the 2013 limitation year, O's average compensation for O's period of high-3 years of service is $53,333, based on O's compensation in 2010, 2012, and 2013. See paragraph (a)(5)(iii) of this section.

Example 5. (i) *Facts.* The facts are the same as in *Example 4*, except that, in accordance with § 1.415(a)-1(d)(3)(v), Plan C incorporates by reference section 415(d) adjustments to a participant's section 415(b)(1)(B) compensation limit for limitation years after the limitation year in which the participant incurs a severance from employment. Assume that the annual adjustment factor described in § 1.415(d)-1(a)(2)(ii) for 2011 through 2013 is 1.03 for each year. Thus, disregarding O's rehire by X, O's average compensation for O's period of high-3 years of service for the 2013 limitation year is equal to $54,636 ($50,000 * 1.03 * 1.03 * 1.03).

(ii) *Conclusion.* Under § 1.415(d)-1(a)(2)(iii), O's average compensation for O's period of high-3 years of service for the 2013 limitation year is $54,636.

(6) *Exceptions from compensation limit.*—The limit under paragraph (a)(1)(ii) of this section (100 percent of the participant's average compensation for the participant's high-3 years of service) does not apply to—

(i) A governmental plan (as defined in section 414(d));

(ii) A multiemployer plan (as defined in section 414(f));

(iii) A collectively bargained plan that is described in section 415(b)(7); or

(iv) A participant in a plan maintained by an organization described in section 3121(w)(3)(A) who has never been a highly compensated employee (within the meaning of section 414(q)) of the organization.

(7) *Special rules.*—(i) *Total benefits not in excess of $10,000.*—See section 415(b)(4) and paragraph (f) of this section for an exception from the limits of section 415(b)(1) and paragraph (a)(1) of this section with respect to retirement benefits that do not exceed $10,000 for the limitation year.

(ii) *Governmental plans electing during 1990.*—For a special limitation applicable to certain governmental plans electing the application of this rule during the first plan year beginning after December 31, 1989, see section 415(b)(10).

(iii) *Defined benefit plans not subject to the requirements of section 411.*—In the case of a defined benefit plan that is not subject to the requirements of section 411, the limitations described in this paragraph (a) are not required to be applied to the annual benefit accrued by a participant before the benefit is payable. However, such a defined benefit plan is subject to the limitations described in this paragraph (a) with respect to the annual benefit payable to a participant at any time under the plan.

(iv) *Application of compensation limitation exception to a church employee who becomes a highly compensated employee.*—(A) *In general.*—If a participant who was described in paragraph (a)(6)(iv) of this section for a prior limitation year later becomes a highly compensated employee (within the meaning of section 414(q)) of the organization that maintains the defined benefit plan, the plan is not treated as failing to satisfy the compensation-based limitation described in paragraph (a)(1)(ii) of this section with respect to the participant if the requirements of paragraph (a)(7)(iv)(B) of this section are satisfied with respect to the participant.

(B) *Limitation on accruals.*—The requirements of this paragraph (a)(7)(iv)(B) are satisfied with respect to a participant if no plan amendments increasing the participant's benefits are adopted during the limitation year in which the participant first becomes a highly compensated employee (within the meaning of section 414(q)) of the organization that maintains the plan, and there is no increase in the participant's accrued benefit derived from employer contributions (including increases as a result of increased compensation or service) in subsequent limitation years.

(b) *Annual benefit.*—(1) *In general.*—(i) *Definition of annual benefit.*—(A) *Straight life annuities.*—For purposes of this section and § 1.415(b)-2, the term *annual benefit* means a benefit that is payable in the form of a straight life annuity. A *straight life annuity* means an annuity payable in equal installments for the life of the participant that terminates upon the participant's death. Examples of benefits that are not in the form of a straight life annuity include an annuity with a post-retirement death benefit and an annuity providing a guaranteed number of payments. If a benefit is payable in the form of a straight life annuity, no adjustment is made to the benefit to account for differences in the timing of payments during a year (for example, no adjustment is made on account of the annuity being payable in annual or monthly installments).

(B) *Other benefit forms.*—With respect to a benefit payable in a form other than a straight life annuity, the annual benefit is determined as the straight life annuity payable on the first day of each month that is actuarially equivalent to the benefit payable in such other form, determined under the rules of paragraph (c) of this section.

(ii) *Rules for determination of annual benefit.*—The annual benefit does not include the annual benefit attributable to either employee contributions or rollover contributions (as described in sections 401(a)(31), 402(c)(1), 403(a)(4), 403(b)(8), 408(d)(3), and 457(e)(16)), determined pursuant to the rules of paragraph (b)(2) of this section. The treatment of transferred benefits is determined under the rules of paragraph (b)(3) of this section. Paragraph (b)(4) of this section discusses the treatment of qualified governmental excess benefit arrangements.

(iii) *Determination of annual benefit in the case of multiple annuity starting dates.*—(A) *General rule.*—If a participant has or will have distributions commencing at more than one annuity starting date, then the limitations of section 415 must be satisfied as of each of the annuity starting dates, taking into account the benefits that have been or will be provided at all of the annuity starting dates. This will happen, for example, where benefit distributions to a participant have previously commenced under a plan that is aggregated for purposes of section 415 with a plan under which the participant receives current accruals. In determining the annual benefit for such a participant as of a particular annuity starting date, the plan must actuarially adjust the past and future distributions with respect to the benefits that commenced at the other annuity starting dates. For limitation years to which § 1.415(b)-2 applies, these adjustments must be made using the rules of § 1.415(b)-2. For purposes of this paragraph (b)(1)(iii) and § 1.415(b)-2, the determination of whether a new annuity starting date has occurred is made without regard to the rule of § 1.401(a)-20, Q&A-10(d) (under which the commencement of certain distributions may not give rise to a new annuity starting date).

(B) *Scope of multiple annuity starting date rules.*—The rules provided in this paragraph (b)(1)(iii) and § 1.415(b)-2 apply for purposes of determining the annual benefit of a participant where a new distribution election is effective during the current limitation year with respect to a distribution that previously commenced. The rules of this paragraph (b)(1)(iii) and § 1.415(b)-2 also apply for determining the annual benefit of a participant for purposes of applying the limitations of section 415(b) and this section where benefit payments are increased as a result of plan terms or a plan amendment applying a cost-of-living adjustment or similar benefit increase, unless the increase is described in paragraph (b)(1)(iii)(C) of this section.

(C) *Safe harbors for certain benefit increases.*—An increase to benefit payments as a result of plan terms or a plan amendment applying a cost-of-living adjustment or similar benefit increase is described in this paragraph (b)(1)(iii)(C) if the increase—

(1) Has previously been accounted for as part of the annual benefit under the rules of paragraph (c) of this section;

(2) Is not required to be accounted for as part of the annual benefit, pursuant to the exception for certain automatic benefit increase features under paragraph (c)(5) of this section;

(3) Is pursuant to a plan provision that automatically incorporates section 415(d) cost-of-living adjustments under § 1.415(a)-1(d)(3)(v); or

(4) Complies with one of the safe harbors described in § 1.415(d)-1(a)(5) or (6) (providing safe harbors for annual and other periodic adjustments to distributions).

(2) *Determination of annual benefit attributable to employee contributions and rollover contributions.*—(i) *In general.*—If employee contributions (other than contributions described in paragraph (b)(2)(ii) of this section) or rollover contributions are made to the plan, the annual benefit attributable to these contributions is determined as provided in this paragraph (b)(2).

(ii) *Certain employee contributions disregarded.*—For purposes of this paragraph (b)(2), the following are not treated as employee contributions:

(A) Contributions that are picked up by a governmental employer as provided under section 414(h)(2).

(B) Repayment of any loan made to a participant from the plan.

(C) Repayment of a previously distributed amount as described in section 411(a)(7)(B) in accordance with section 411(a)(7)(C).

(D) Repayment of a withdrawal of employee contributions as provided under section 411(a)(3)(D).

(E) Repayments that would have been described in paragraph (b)(2)(ii)(C) or (b)(2)(ii)(D) of this section except that the plan does not restrict the timing of repayments to the maximum extent permitted by section 411(a).

(iii) *Annual benefit attributable to mandatory employee contributions.*—In the case of mandatory employee contributions as defined in section 411(c)(2)(C) and § 1.411(c)-1(c)(4) (or contributions that would be mandatory employee contributions if section 411 applied to the plan), the annual benefit attributable to those contributions is determined by applying the factors applicable to mandatory employee contributions as described in section 411(c)(2)(B) and (C) and regulations promulgated under section 411 to those contributions to determine the amount of a straight life annuity commencing at the annuity starting date, regardless of whether the requirements of sections 411 and 417 apply to that plan. For purposes of applying such factors to a plan that is not subject to the requirements of section 411, the applicable effective date of section 411(a)(2) (which is used under § 1.411(c)-1(c)(3) to determine the beginning date from which statutorily specified interest must be credited to mandatory employee contributions) must be determined as if section 411 applied to the plan, and in determining the annual benefit that is actuarially equivalent to these accumulated contributions, the plan must determine the interest rate that would have been required under section 417(e)(3) as if section 417 applied to the plan. See § 1.415(c)-1(a)(2)(ii)(B) and (b)(3) for rules regarding treatment of mandatory employee contributions to a defined benefit plan as annual additions under a defined contribution plan.

(iv) *Voluntary employee contributions.*—If voluntary employee contributions are made to the plan, the portion of the plan to which voluntary employee contributions are made is treated as a defined contribution plan pursuant to section 414(k) and, accordingly, is a defined contribution plan pursuant to § 1.415(c)-1(a)(2)(i). Accordingly, the portion of a plan to which voluntary employee contributions are made is not a defined benefit plan within the meaning of paragraph (a)(2) of this section and is not taken into account in determining the annual benefit under the portion of the plan that is a defined benefit plan.

(v) *Annual benefit attributable to rollover contributions.*—The annual benefit attributable to rollover contributions from an eligible retirement plan, as defined in section 402(c)(8)(B) (for example, a contribution received pursuant to a direct rollover under section 401(a)(31)(A)), is determined in the same manner as the annual benefit attributable to mandatory employee contributions if the plan provides for a benefit derived from the rollover contribution (other than a benefit derived from a separate account to be maintained with respect to the rollover contribution and actual earnings and losses thereon). Thus, in the case of rollover contributions from a defined contribution plan to a defined benefit plan to provide an annuity distribution, the annual benefit attributable to those rollover contributions for purposes of section 415(b) is determined by applying the rules of section 411(c) as described in paragraph (b)(2)(iii) of this section, regardless of the assumptions used to compute the annuity distribution under the plan and regardless of whether the plan is subject to the requirements of sections 411 and 417. Accordingly, in such a case, if the plan uses more favorable factors than those specified in section 411(c) to determine the amount of annuity payments arising from rollover contributions, the annual benefit under the plan would reflect the excess of those annuity payments over the amounts that would be payable using the factors specified in section 411(c). See § 1.415(c)-1(b)(3)(i) for rules excluding rollover contributions maintained in a separate account that is treated as a defined contribution plan pursuant to section 414(k) from annual additions to a defined contribution plan.

(3) *Treatment of transferred benefits.*—(i) *In general.*—(A) *Treatment of transferor plan if transferred benefits are aggregated with transferor plan.*—Except as provided in paragraph (b)(3)(ii) of this section, when there has been a transfer of benefits from one defined benefit plan to another plan, to the extent the benefits transferred to the transferee plan are otherwise required to be taken into account pursuant to section 415(f) and § 1.415(f)-1 in determining whether the transferor plan satisfies the limitations of section 415(b) for a limitation year, the transferred benefits are not treated as being provided under the transferor plan. This will occur, for example, if the employer sponsoring the transferor plan and the employer sponsoring the transferee plan are in the same controlled group within the meaning of section 414(b).

(B) *Treatment of transferor plan if transferred benefits are not aggregated with transferor plan.*—Except as provided in paragraph (b)(3)(ii) of this section, when there has been a transfer of benefits from one defined benefit plan to another plan, to the extent the benefits transferred to the transferee plan are not otherwise required to be taken into account pursuant to section 415(f) and § 1.415(f)-1 in determining whether the transferor plan satisfies the limitations of section 415(b) for a limitation year, the transferred benefits are treated by the transferor plan as if such benefits were provided under annuities purchased to provide benefits under a plan that must be aggregated with the transferor plan and that terminated immediately prior to the transfer with sufficient assets to pay all benefit liabilities under the plan, in accordance with the rules of paragraph (b)(5)(i) of this section. This will occur, for example, in the case of a transfer of benefits between defined benefit plans maintained by employers that are not required to be aggregated under sections 414(b) and (c) (as modified by section 415(h)) or sections 414(m).

(C) *Treatment of transferee plan.*—Except as provided in paragraph (b)(3)(ii) of this section, where there has been a transfer of benefits from one defined benefit plan to another defined benefit plan, the transferee plan must take into account the transferred benefits in determining whether it satisfies the limitations of section 415(b).

(ii) *Elective transfer of distributable benefit.*—Where, as described in § 1.411(d)-4, Q&A-3(c) (permitting certain elective transfers of distributable benefits), a distributable benefit is transferred to a defined benefit plan from either a defined contribution plan or a defined benefit plan, the amount transferred is treated as a benefit paid from the transferor plan, and the annual benefit provided by the transferee defined benefit plan does not include the annual benefit attributable to the amount transferred (determined as if the transferred amount were a rollover contribution subject to the rules of paragraph (b)(2)(v) of this section). The rule in the preceding sentence applies regardless of whether the requirements of section 411 apply to the plan and, in the case of a transfer from a defined contribution plan that is not subject to the requirements of section 411 (such as a governmental plan) to a defined benefit plan, the rule applies even if the participant's benefits are not distributable from the defined contribution plan at the time of the transfer.

(4) *Treatment of qualified governmental excess benefit arrangements.*—Pursuant to section 415(m), in determining whether a governmental plan (as defined in section 414(d)) meets the requirements of this section, the annual benefit does not include benefits provided under a qualified governmental excess benefit arrangement, as defined in section 415(m)(3). Thus, the limitation of section 415(b) does not apply to benefits to the extent the benefits are provided under a qualified governmental excess benefit arrangement.

(5) *Treatment of benefits provided under a terminated plan.*—(i) *Terminated plan with sufficient assets.*—If a defined benefit plan is terminated with sufficient assets for the payment of the benefit liabilities of all plan participants and a participant in the plan has not yet commenced benefits under the plan, for purposes of satisfying section 415(b) with respect to the participant, all other defined benefit plans maintained by the employer that maintained the terminated plan are required to take into account the benefits provided pursuant to the annuities purchased to provide benefits under the terminated plan at each possible annuity starting date. In such a case, see paragraph (b)(1)(iii) of this section for rules regarding the determination of a participant's annual benefit if the participant commences receiving benefits under the terminated plan.

(ii) *Terminated plan with insufficient assets.*—If a defined benefit plan is terminated and there are not sufficient assets for the payment of the benefit liabilities of all plan participants, for purposes of satisfying section 415(b) with respect to a participant, all other defined benefit plans maintained by the employer that maintained the

terminated plan are required to take into account the benefits that are actually provided to the participant under the terminated plan. For example, in the case of a plan that is subject to Title IV of the Employee Retirement Income Security Act of 1974 (88 Stat. 829), Public Law 93-406 (ERISA), and that terminates with insufficient assets for the payment of the benefit liabilities of all plan participants, all other defined benefit plans maintained by the employer that maintained the terminating plan must take into account benefits that are paid by the Pension Benefit Guaranty Corporation. In such a case, see paragraph (b)(1)(iii) of this section for rules regarding the determination of a participant's annual benefit if the participant commences receiving benefits under the terminated plan.

(iii) *Other guidance.*—The Commissioner may provide guidance regarding the rules applicable to terminated plans (and plans that are deemed to have been terminated pursuant to paragraph (b)(3)(i)(B) of this section) in revenue rulings, notices, and other guidance published in the Internal Revenue Bulletin. See § 601.601(d) of this chapter.

(c) *Adjustment to form of benefit for forms other than a straight life annuity.*—(1) *In general.*—This paragraph (c) provides rules for adjusting a form of benefit other than a straight life annuity to an actuarially equivalent straight life annuity beginning at the same time for purposes of determining the annual benefit described in paragraph (b) of this section. Paragraph (c)(2) of this section describes how to adjust a benefit paid in a form to which section 417(e)(3) does not apply. Paragraph (c)(3) of this section describes how to adjust a benefit paid in a form to which section 417(e)(3) applies. Paragraph (c)(4) of this section describes benefit forms for which no adjustment is required. Paragraph (c)(5) of this section provides an exception from the requirements of this paragraph (c) with respect to certain automatic benefit increase features. Paragraph (c)(6) of this section sets forth examples illustrating the application of this paragraph (c). The Commissioner may, in revenue rulings, notices, or other guidance published in the Internal Revenue Bulletin set forth simplified methods for adjusting a form of benefit other than a straight life annuity to an actuarially equivalent straight life annuity beginning at the same time for purposes of determining the annual benefit described in paragraph (b) of this section. See § 601.601(d)(2) of this chapter.

(2) *Benefits paid in a form to which section 417(e)(3) does not apply.*—For a benefit paid in a form to which section 417(e)(3) does not apply, the actuarially equivalent straight life annuity benefit is the greater of—

(i) The annual amount of the straight life annuity (if any) payable to the participant under the plan commencing at the same annuity starting date as the form of benefit payable to the participant; or

(ii) The annual amount of the straight life annuity commencing at the same annuity starting date that has the same actuarial present value as the form of benefit payable to the participant, computed using a 5 percent interest assumption and the applicable mortality table described in § 1.417(e)-1(d)(2) for that annuity starting date.

(3) *Benefits paid in a form to which section 417(e)(3) applies.*—(i) *In general.*—Except as otherwise provided in this paragraph (c)(3), for a benefit paid in a form to which section 417(e)(3) applies, the actuarially equivalent straight life annuity benefit is the greatest of:

(A) The annual amount of the straight life annuity commencing at the annuity starting date that has the same actuarial present value as the particular form of benefit payable, computed using the interest rate and mortality table, or tabular factor, specified in the plan for actuarial equivalence;

(B) The annual amount of the straight life annuity commencing at the annuity starting date that has the same actuarial present value as the particular form of benefit payable, computed using a 5.5 percent interest assumption and the applicable mortality table for the distribution under § 1.417(e)-1(d)(2); or

(C) The annual amount of the straight life annuity commencing at the annuity starting date that has the same actuarial present value as the particular form of benefit payable (computed using the applicable interest rate for the distribution under § 1.417(e)-1(d)(3) and the applicable mortality table for the distribution under § 1.417(e)-1(d)(2)), divided by 1.05.

(ii) *Special rule for distributions in plan years beginning in 2004 and 2005.*—For a distribution to which section 417(e)(3) applies and which has an annuity starting date occurring in plan years beginning in 2004 or 2005, except as provided in section 101(d)(3) of the Pension Funding Equity Act of 2004, Public Law 108-218 (118 Stat. 596), the actuarially equivalent straight life annuity benefit is the greater of—

(A) The annual amount of the straight life annuity commencing at the annuity starting date that has the same actuarial present value as the particular form of benefit payable, computed using the interest rate and mortality table, or tabular factor, specified in the plan for actuarial equivalence; or

(B) The annual amount of the straight life annuity commencing at the annuity starting date that has the same actuarial present value as the particular form of benefit payable, computed using a 5.5 percent interest assumption and the applicable mortality table for the distribution under § 1.417(e)-1(d)(2).

(4) *Certain benefit forms for which no adjustment is required.*—(i) *In general.*—For purposes of the adjustments described in this paragraph (c), the following benefits are not taken into account:

(A) Survivor benefits payable to a surviving spouse under a qualified joint and survivor annuity (as defined in section 417(b)) to the extent that such benefits would not be payable if the participant's benefit were not paid in the form of a qualified joint and survivor annuity.

(B) Ancillary benefits that are not directly related to retirement benefits, such as preretirement disability benefits not in excess of the qualified disability benefit, preretirement incidental death benefits (including a qualified preretirement survivor annuity), and post-retirement medical benefits.

(ii) *Rules of application.*—(A) *Social security supplements.*—Although a social security supplement described in section 411(a)(9) and § 1.411(a)-7(c)(4) may be an ancillary benefit, it is included in determining the annual benefit because it is payable upon retirement and therefore is directly related to retirement income benefits.

(B) *Qualified joint and survivor annuities combined with other distributions.*—If benefits are paid partly in the form of a qualified joint and survivor annuity (QJSA) and partly in some other form (such as a single-sum distribution), the rule of paragraph (c)(4)(i)(A) of this section (under which survivor benefits are not included in determining the annual benefit) applies to the survivor annuity payments under the portion of the benefit that is paid in the form of a QJSA.

(5) *Exception for certain automatic benefit increase features.*—(i) *General rule.*—Notwithstanding paragraph (b)(1)(i)(B) of this section, no adjustment is required to a benefit that is paid in a form that is not a straight life annuity to take into account the inclusion in that form of an automatic benefit increase feature, as described in paragraph (c)(5)(ii) of this section, if:

(A) The benefit is paid in a form to which section 417(e)(3) does not apply.

(B) The plan satisfies the requirements of paragraph (c)(5)(iii) of this section.

(ii) *Definition of automatic benefit increase feature.*—An automatic benefit increase feature is included in a form of benefit if that form provides for automatic, periodic increases to the benefits paid in that form, such as a form of benefit that automatically increases the benefit paid under that form annually according to a specified percentage or objective index, or a form of benefit that automatically increases the benefit paid in that form to share favorable investment returns on plan assets.

(iii) *Requirements.*—A plan satisfies the requirements of this paragraph (c)(5)(iii) with respect to a form of benefit that includes an automatic benefit increase feature if the form of benefit without regard to the automatic benefit increase feature satisfies the requirements of section 415(b) and this section, and the plan provides that in no event will the amount payable to the participant under the form of benefit in any limitation year be greater than the section 415(b) limit applicable at the annuity starting date (which is the lesser of the age-adjusted section 415(b)(1)(A) dollar limit described in paragraph (a)(1)(i) of this section or the section 415(b)(1)(B) compensation limit described in paragraph (a)(1)(ii) of this section, as increased in subsequent years pursuant to section 415(d) and § 1.415(d)-1. If the form of benefit without regard to the automatic benefit increase feature is not a straight life annuity, then the preceding sentence is applied by reducing the section 415(b) limit applicable at the annuity starting date to an actuarially equivalent amount (determined using the assumptions specified in paragraph (c)(2)(ii) of this section) that takes into account the death benefits under the form of benefit (other than the survivor portion of a QJSA).

(6) *Examples.*—The following examples illustrate the provisions of this paragraph (c). For purposes of these examples, except as otherwise stated, actuarial equivalence under the plan is determined using a 5 percent interest assumption and the mortality table that applies under section 417(e)(3) as of January 1, 2003. It is assumed for purposes of these examples that the interest rate that applies under section 417(e)(3) and § 1.417(e)-1(d)(3) for relevant time periods is 5.25 percent and that the mortality table that applies under section 417(e)(3) and § 1.417(e)-1(d)(2) for relevant time periods is the mortal-

ity table that applies under section 417(e)(3) as of January 1, 2003. In addition, it is assumed that all participants discussed in these examples have at least ten years of service with the employer and at least ten years of participation in the plan at issue, all payments other than a payment of a single sum are made monthly, on the first day of each calendar month, and each plan's normal retirement age is 65. The examples are as follows:

Example 1. (i) *Facts.* Plan A provides a single-sum distribution determined as the actuarial present value of the straight life annuity payable at the actual retirement date. Plan A provides that a participant's single sum is determined as the greater of the present value determined using the otherwise applicable actuarial assumptions of the plan and the present value determined using the applicable interest rate and the applicable mortality table for the distribution under section 417(e)(3). In accordance with § 1.417(e)-1(d)(1), Plan A also provides that the single sum is not less than the actuarial present value of the accrued benefit payable at normal retirement age, determined using the applicable interest rate and the applicable mortality table under section 417(e)(3) and § 1.417(e)-1(d). Participant M retires at age 65 with a benefit under the plan formula (and before the application of section 415) of $152,619 and elects to receive a distribution in the form of a single sum. Under the plan and before the application of section 415, the amount of the single sum is $1,800,002 (which is based on the 5 percent interest rate and applicable mortality table as of January 1, 2003, since that present value is greater than the present value that would have been determined using the applicable interest rate (5.25 percent) and the applicable mortality table (the January 1, 2003, table) for the distribution under section 417(e)(3)).

(ii) *Conclusion.* For purposes of this section, the annual benefit is the greatest of the annual amount of the actuarially equivalent straight life annuity commencing at the same age (determined using the plan's actuarial factors), the annual amount of the actuarially equivalent straight life annuity commencing at the same age (determined using a 5.5 percent interest assumption and the applicable mortality table for the distribution under § 1.417(e)-1(d)(2)), and the annual amount of the actuarially equivalent straight life annuity commencing at the same age (determined using the applicable interest rate and applicable mortality table for the distribution under §§ 1.417(e)-1(d)(2) and (d)(3)) divided by 1.05. Based on the factors used in the plan to determine the actuarially equivalent lump sum (in this case, an interest rate of 5 percent and the applicable mortality table as of January 1, 2003), $1,800,002 payable as a single sum is actuarially equivalent to an immediate straight life annuity at age 65 of $152,619. A single sum payment of $1,800,002 is actuarially equivalent to an immediate straight life annuity at age 65 of $159,105, using a 5.5 percent interest assumption and the applicable mortality table under § 1.417(e)-1(d)(2). Based on the applicable interest rate and the applicable mortality table for the distribution under §§ 1.417(e)-1(d)(2) and (d)(3), $1,800,002 payable as a single sum is actuarially equivalent to an immediate straight life annuity at age 65 of $155,853. $148,432 is the result when this annual amount is divided by 1.05. With respect to the single-sum distribution, M's annual benefit for purposes of section 415(b) is equal to the greatest of the three resulting amounts ($152,619, $159,105, and $148,432), or $159,105.

Example 2. (i) *Facts.* The facts are the same as in *Example 1*, except that Participant M elects to receive his benefit in the form of a 10-year certain and life annuity. Applying the plan's actuarial equivalence factors, the benefit payable in this form is $146,100.

(ii) *Conclusion.* Since the form of benefit elected by M is a form of benefit to which section 417(e)(3) does not apply, the annual benefit for purposes of this section is the greater of the annual amount of the plan's straight life annuity commencing at the same age or the annual amount of the actuarially equivalent straight life annuity commencing at the same age, determined using a 5 percent interest rate and the applicable mortality table described in § 1.417(e)-1(d)(2) for that annuity starting date. In this case, the straight life annuity payable under the plan commencing at the same age is $152,619. Because the plan's factors for actuarial equivalence in this case are the same standardized actuarial factors required to be applied to determine the actuarially equivalent straight life annuity, the actuarially equivalent straight life annuity using the required standardized factors is also $152,619. With respect to the 10-year certain and life annuity distribution, M's annual benefit is equal to the greater of the two resulting amounts ($152,619 and $152,619), or $152,619.

Example 3. (i) *Facts.* The facts are the same as in *Example 1*. Participant M retires at age 62 with a benefit under the plan (before the application of section 415) of $100,000 (after application of the plan's early retirement factors) and a Social Security supplement of $10,000 per year payable until age 65. N chooses to receive the accrued benefit in the form of a straight life annuity. The Plan has no provisions under which the actuarial value of the Social Security supplement can be paid as a level annuity for life.

(ii) *Conclusion.* Because the form of benefit elected by M is a form of benefit to which section 417(e)(3) does not apply and because the plan does not provide for a straight life annuity beginning at age 62, the annual benefit for purposes of this section is the annual amount of the straight life annuity commencing at age 62 that is actuarially equivalent to the distribution stream of $110,000 for three years and $100,000 thereafter, where actuarial equivalence is determined using a 5 percent interest rate and the applicable mortality table described in § 1.417(e)-1(d)(2) for the annuity starting date. In this case, the actuarially equivalent straight life annuity is $102,180. Accordingly, with respect to this distribution stream, N's annual benefit is equal to $102,180. The results are the same without regard to whether the Social Security supplement is a QSUPP (as defined in § 1.401(a)(4)-12).

Example 4. (i) *Facts.* Plan B is a defined benefit plan that provides a benefit equal to 100 percent of a participant's average compensation for the period of the participant's high-3 years of service, payable as a straight life annuity. For a married participant who does not elect another form of benefit, the benefit is payable in the form of a joint and 100 percent survivor annuity benefit that is a QJSA within the meaning of section 417 and that is reduced from the straight life annuity. For purposes of determining the amount of this QJSA, the plan provides that the reduction is only half of the reduction that would normally apply under the actuarial assumptions specified in the plan for determining actuarial equivalence of optional forms. The plan also provides that a married participant can elect to receive the plan benefits as a straight life annuity, or in the form of a single sum distribution that is the actuarial equivalent of the joint and 100 percent survivor annuity determined using the applicable interest rate and the applicable mortality table under section 417(e)(3) and § 1.417(e)-1(d). Participant O elects, with spousal consent, a single-sum distribution.

(ii) *Conclusion.* The special rule that disregards the value of the survivor portion of a QJSA set forth in paragraph (c)(4)(i) of this section only applies to a benefit that is payable in the form of a qualified joint and survivor annuity. Any other form of benefit must be adjusted to a straight life annuity in accordance with paragraph (c)(1) of this section. Accordingly, because the benefit payable under the plan in the form of a single-sum distribution is actuarially equivalent to a straight life annuity that is greater than 100 percent of a participant's average compensation for the period of the participant's high-3 years of service, the limitation of section 415(b)(1)(B) has been exceeded.

Example 5. (i) *Facts.* Plan C is a defined benefit plan that provides an option to receive the benefit in the form of a joint and 100 percent survivor annuity with a 10-year certain feature, where the survivor beneficiary is the participant's spouse.

(ii) *Conclusion.* Since this form of benefit is not subject to section 417(e)(3), for a participant at age 65, the annual benefit with respect to the joint and 100 percent survivor annuity with a 10-year certain feature is determined for purposes of this section as the greater of the annual amount of the straight life annuity payable to the participant under the plan at age 65 (if any), or the annual amount of the straight life annuity commencing at age 65 that has the same actuarial present value as the joint and 100 percent survivor annuity with a 10-year certain feature (but excluding the survivor annuity payments pursuant to paragraph (c)(4)(i)(A) of this section), computing using a 5 percent interest assumption and the applicable mortality table described in § 1.417(e)-1(d)(2) for the annuity starting date. This latter amount is equal to the product of the annual payments under this optional form of benefit and the factor that provides for actuarial equivalence between a straight life annuity and a 10-year certain and life annuity (with no annuity for the survivor) computed using a 5 percent interest rate and the applicable mortality table described in § 1.417(e)-1(d)(2) for the annuity starting date.

Example 6. (i) *Facts.* Plan E provides a benefit at age 65 of a straight life annuity equal to the lesser of 90 percent of the participant's average compensation for the period of the participant's high-3 years of service and $148,500. Upon retirement at age 65, the optional forms of benefit available to a participant include payment of a QJSA with annual payments equal to 50 percent of the annual payments under the straight life annuity, along with a single-sum distribution that is actuarially equivalent (determined as the greater of the single sum calculated using a 5 percent interest assumption and the section 417(e)(3)(A)(ii)(I) mortality table in effect on January 1, 2003, and the single sum calculated using the section 417(e)(3)(A)(ii)(II) applicable interest rate and the section 417(e)(3)(A)(ii)(I) applicable mortality table for the distribution) to 50 percent of the annual payments under the straight life annuity. Participant Q retires at age 65. Q's average compensation for the period of Q's high-3 years of service is $100,000. Q elects to receive a distribution in the optional form of benefit described above, under which the annual payments under the QJSA are $45,000 and the single-sum distribution is equal to $530,734. Q's spouse is 3 years younger than Q.

(ii) *Determination of annual benefit.* Q's annual benefit under Plan E for purposes of section 415(b) is determined as the sum of the annual benefit attributable to the QJSA portion of the distribution and the annual benefit attributable to the single-sum portion of the distribution.

(iii) *Annual benefit attributable to QJSA portion.* Because survivor benefits are not taken into account in determining the annual benefit attributable to the QJSA portion of the distribution, the annual benefit attributable to the QJSA portion of the distribution is determined as if that distribution were a straight life annuity of $45,000 per year commencing at age 65. Thus, no form adjustment is needed to determine the annual benefit attributable to the QJSA portion of the distribution, and the annual benefit attributable to the QJSA portion of the benefit is $45,000.

(iv) *Annual benefit attributable to single sum portion.* The annual benefit attributable to the single sum portion of the distribution is determined as the greatest of the annual amount of the actuarially equivalent straight life annuity commencing at the same age (determined using the plan's actuarial factors), the annual amount of the actuarially equivalent straight life annuity commencing at the same age (determined using a 5.5 percent interest assumption and the applicable mortality table under § 1.417(e)-1(d)(2) for the distribution), and the annual amount of the actuarially equivalent straight life annuity commencing at the same age (determined using the applicable interest rate and applicable mortality table under section 417(e)(3) and § § 1.417(e)-1(d)(2) and (d)(3) for the distribution) divided by 1.05. With respect to the single-sum distribution, the annual amount of the actuarially equivalent straight life annuity commencing at the same age determined using the plan's actuarial factors is equal to $45,000. The annual amount of the actuarially equivalent straight life annuity commencing at the same age determined using a 5.5 percent interest assumption and the applicable mortality table under § 1.417(e)-1(d)(2) for the distribution is $46,912. The actuarially equivalent straight life annuity commencing at the same age determined using the applicable interest rate and applicable mortality table under section 417(e)(3) and § § 1.417(e)-1(d)(2) and (d)(3) for the distribution is equal to $45,954. This amount divided by 1.05 is equal to $43,766. Thus, the annual benefit attributable to the single sum portion of the benefit is $46,912.

(v) *Conclusion.* Q's annual benefit under the optional form of benefit for purposes of section 415(b) is equal to the sum of the annual benefit attributable to the QJSA portion of the distribution and the annual benefit attributable to the single sum portion of the distribution, or $91,912. Because Q's average compensation for the period of Q's high-3 years of service is $100,000, the distribution satisfies the compensation limit of section 415(b)(1)(B).

Example 7. (i) *Facts.* Plan D is a defined benefit plan with a normal retirement age of 65. The normal retirement benefit under Plan D (and the only life annuity available under Plan D) is a life annuity with a fixed increase of 2 percent per year. The increase applies to the benefit provided in the prior year and is thus compounded. The plan provides that the benefit is limited to the lesser of 84 percent of the participant's average compensation for the period of the participant's high-3 years of service or 84 percent of the age-adjusted section 415(b)(1)(A) dollar limit (which is assumed to be $180,000 at age 65). Plan D does not incorporate the section 415(d) cost-of-living adjustments to the section 415(b) limits for limitation years following the limitation year in which a participant incurs a severance from employment. Participant P's retires at age 65, at which time P's average compensation for the period of P's high-3 years of service is $165,000. Under Plan D, P commences receiving benefits in the form of a life annuity of $138,600 with a fixed increase of 2 percent per year.

(ii) *Conclusion.* Because Plan D does not provide for a straight life annuity and the form of benefit is not subject to section 417(e)(3), P's annual benefit for purposes of section 415(b) is the annual amount of the straight life annuity, commencing at age 65, that is actuarially equivalent to the distribution stream of $138,600 with a fixed increase of 2 percent per year, where actuarial equivalence is determined using a 5 percent interest rate and the applicable mortality table for the distribution under section 417(e)(3) and § 1.417(e)-1(d)(2). In order to satisfy the requirements of section 415 and this section, this annual benefit must not exceed 100 percent of the average compensation for the period of the participant's high-3 years of service, or $165,000. Using a 5 percent interest rate and the section 417(e)(3) applicable mortality table for the distribution, the actuarially equivalent straight life annuity is $165,453, which exceeds $165,000. Accordingly, the plan fails to satisfy the compensation-based limitation of section 415(b)(1)(B).

Example 8. (i) *Facts.* The facts are the same as in *Example 7*, except that Plan D incorporates by reference the section 415(d) cost-of-living adjustments to the section 415(b) limits as described in § 1.415(a)-1(d)(3)(v) and Plan D provides that the benefit is limited to the applicable section 415(b) limit. Under Plan D, P commences receiving benefits at age 65 in the form of a life annuity of $138,221 with a fixed increase of 2 percent per year.

(ii) *Conclusion.* Because Plan D does not provide for a straight life annuity and the form of benefit is not subject to section 417(e)(3), P's annual benefit for purposes of section 415(b) is the annual amount of the straight life annuity, commencing at age 65, that is actuarially equivalent to the distribution stream of $138,221 with a fixed increase of 2 percent per year, where actuarial equivalence is determined using a 5 percent interest rate and the applicable mortality table for P's annuity starting date under section 417(e)(3) and § 1.417(e)-1(d)(2). In order to satisfy the requirements of section 415(b) and this section, this annual benefit must not exceed 100 percent of P's average compensation for the period of P's high-3 years of service, or $165,000. Using a 5 percent interest rate and the section 417(e)(3) applicable mortality table for the distribution, the actuarially equivalent straight life annuity is $165,000, which does not exceed $165,000. Accordingly, the plan satisfies the compensation-based limitation of section 415(b)(1)(B).

(iii) *Section 415(d) adjustments.* In addition to the fixed 2 percent per year automatic increase, P's benefit will be increased in limitation years following the limitation year in which P retires in accordance with the plan provisions that incorporate by reference the section 415(d) cost-of-living adjustments to the section 415(b) limits (or, if Plan D did not incorporate by reference the section 415(d) adjustments, P's benefit may be increased pursuant to plan amendments that comply with the safe harbors provided in § 1.415(d)-1(a)(5) or (6)), and such increases will not cause P's benefit to violate the requirements of section 415(b). For example, if in a later limitation year the applicable section 415(b) limit is increased by 3 percent pursuant to section 415(d) and § 1.415(d)-1, P's benefit payable under Plan D will be increased by both the fixed automatic 2 percent per year increase and by the 3 percent section 415(d) cost-of-living adjustment. The effect of the combined increases may result in P's benefits for a year exceeding the then applicable dollar limit under section 415(b), but the plan will not violate section 415(b).

Example 9. (i) *Facts.* The facts are the same as in *Example 7*, except that the plan provides that benefits are limited to the lesser of 100 percent of the participant's average compensation for the period of the participant's high-3 years of service or 100 percent of the age-adjusted section 415(b)(1)(A) dollar limit. Assume that P retires at age 65 with a benefit in the form of a life annuity of $165,000 per year with a fixed increase of 2 percent per year. Additionally, assume that Plan D incorporates by reference the section 415(d) cost-of-living adjustments to the section 415(b) limits as described in § 1.415(a)-1(d)(3)(v) and the plan provides pursuant to paragraph (c)(5) of this section that in no event will a benefit payable from the plan, as increased by the fixed increase of 2 percent per year, be greater than the section 415(b) limit applicable as of the annuity starting date for the benefit (increased pursuant to the rules of section 415(d) and § 1.415(d)-1).

(ii) *Conclusion.* The benefit payable to P at age 65 is not required to be adjusted to take into account the fixed increase of 2 percent per year. This is because the benefit payable to P satisfies the requirements of section 415(b) without regard to the fixed increase of 2 percent per year, and pursuant to paragraph (c)(5) of this section, the plan provides that the benefit payable to P, as increased by the fixed increase of 2 percent per year, will never be greater than the section 415(b) limit applicable as of P's annuity starting date (increased in subsequent limitation years pursuant to the rules of section 415(d) and § 1.415(d)-1).

(iii) *Section 415(d) adjustments.* In addition to the fixed 2 percent per year automatic increase, P's benefit will be increased in limitation years following the limitation year in which P retires in accordance with the plan provisions that incorporate by reference the section 415(d) cost-of-living adjustments to the section 415(b) limits (or, if Plan D did not incorporate by reference the section 415(d) adjustments, P's benefit may be increased pursuant to plan amendments that comply with the safe harbors provided in § 1.415(d)-1(a)(5) or (6)), and such increases will not cause P's benefit to violate the requirements of section 415(b). However, pursuant to paragraph (c)(5)(iii) of this section, P's benefit during any limitation year, as increased by the 2 percent per year automatic increase feature and any plan provisions that incorporate by reference the section 415(d) cost-of-living adjustments or any plan amendments that increase P's benefits, cannot exceed the then applicable section 415(b) limit (as increased pursuant to section 415(d) and § 1.415(d)-1).

Example 10. (i) *Facts.* Employer T maintains a defined benefit plan. Under the terms of the plan, all benefits in pay status (other than single sum payments) are adjusted upwards or downwards annually depending on an annual comparison of actual return on plan assets and an assumed interest rate of 4 percent. Thus, the plan does not offer a straight life annuity form of benefit, and the plan must determine for purposes of applying the section 415(b) limits the actuarially equivalent straight life annuity for benefits provided under the plan.

(ii) *Conclusion.* Benefits under the plan are paid in a form to which section 417(e)(3) does not apply. In determining the actuarially equivalent straight life annuity of benefits that are subject to the annual investment performance adjustment, the plan must assume a 5 percent return on plan assets. See paragraph (c)(2) of this section. Therefore, in determining the actuarially equivalent straight life annuity, the plan must assume that the form of benefit payable under the plan will be an annuity that increases annually by a factor equal to 1.05 divided by 1.04. This increasing annuity is then converted to an actuarially equivalent straight life annuity under paragraph (c)(2) of this section using a 5 percent interest rate and the applicable mortality table described in § 1.417(e)-1(d)(2) for the relevant annuity starting date.

Example 11. (i) *Facts.* R is a participant in a defined benefit plan maintained by R's employer. Under the terms of the plan, R must make contributions to the plan in a stated amount to accrue benefits derived from employer contributions.

(ii) *Conclusion.* R's contributions are mandatory employee contributions within the meaning of section 411(c)(2)(C) and, thus, the annual benefit attributable to these contributions is not taken into account for purposes of testing the annual benefit derived from employer contributions against the applicable limitation on benefits. However, these contributions are treated as contributions to a defined contribution plan maintained by R's employer for purposes of section 415(c). See § 1.415(c)-1(a)(2)(ii)(B). Accordingly, with respect to the current limitation year, the limitation on benefits (as described in paragraph (a)(1) of this section) is applicable to the annual benefit attributable to employer contributions to the defined benefit plan, and the limitation on contributions and other additions (as described in § 1.415(c)-1) is applicable to the portion of the plan treated as a defined contribution plan, which consists of R's mandatory contributions. These same limitations would also apply if, instead of providing for mandatory employee contributions, the plan permitted voluntary employee contributions, because the portion of the plan attributable to voluntary employee contributions and earnings thereon is treated as a defined contribution plan maintained by the employer pursuant to section 414(k), and thus is not subject to the limitations of section 415(b).

Example 12. (i) *Facts.* V is a participant in a defined benefit plan maintained by V's employer. Under the terms of the plan, V must make contributions to the plan in a stated amount to accrue benefits derived from employer contributions. V's contributions are mandatory employee contributions within the meaning of section 411(c)(2)(C). Thus, the annual benefit attributable to these contributions is not taken into account for purposes of testing the annual benefit derived from employer contributions against the applicable limitation on benefits. V terminates employment and receives a distribution from the plan that includes V's mandatory employee contributions. Subsequently, V resumes employment with the employer maintaining the plan. V recommences participation in the plan and repays the prior distribution from the plan (including the portion of the distribution that included V's prior mandatory employee contributions to the plan) with reasonable interest.

(ii) *Conclusion.* In determining V's annual benefit under the plan for purposes of applying the limitations of section 415(b), no portion of V's repayment of the prior distribution is treated as employee contributions. See paragraphs (b)(2)(ii)(C), (D) and (E) of this section. However, V's annual benefit under the plan is determined by excluding the portion of the annual benefit attributable to V's employee contributions to the plan made both prior to the first distribution and during V's subsequent recommencement of plan participation.

(d) *Adjustment to section 415(b)(1)(A) dollar limit for commencement before age 62.*—(1) *General rule.*—(i) *Calculation using statutory factors.*—For a distribution with an annuity starting date that occurs before the participant attains the age of 62, the age-adjusted section 415(b)(1)(A) dollar limit generally is determined as the actuarial equivalent of the annual amount of a straight life annuity commencing at the annuity starting date that has the same actuarial present value as a deferred straight life annuity commencing at age 62, where annual payments under the straight life annuity commencing at age 62 are equal to the dollar limitation of section 415(b)(1)(A) (as adjusted pursuant to section 415(d) and § 1.415(d)-1 for the limitation year), and where the actuarially equivalent straight life annuity is computed using a 5 percent interest rate and the applicable mortality table under § 1.417(e)-1(d)(2) that is effective for that annuity starting date (and expressing the participant's age based on completed calendar months as of the annuity starting date). However, if the plan has an immediately commencing straight life annuity payable both at age 62 and the age of benefit commencement, then the age-adjusted section 415(b)(1)(A) dollar limit is equal to the lesser of—

(A) The limit as otherwise determined under this paragraph (d)(1)(i); and

(B) The amount determined under paragraph (d)(1)(ii) of this section.

(ii) *Calculation using plan factors.*—The amount determined under this paragraph (d)(1)(ii) is equal to the section 415(b)(1)(A) dollar limit (as adjusted pursuant to section 415(d) and §1.415(d)-1 for the limitation year) multiplied by the ratio of the annual amount of the immediately commencing straight life annuity under the plan to the annual amount of the straight life annuity under the plan commencing at age 62, with both annual amounts determined without applying the rules of section 415.

(2) *Mortality adjustments.*—(i) *In general.*—For purposes of determining the actuarially equivalent amount described in paragraph (d)(1)(i) of this section, to the extent that a forfeiture does not occur upon the participant's death before the annuity starting date, no adjustment is made to reflect the probability of the participant's death between the annuity starting date and the participant's attainment of age 62, unless the plan provides for such an adjustment. To the extent that a forfeiture occurs upon the participant's death before the annuity starting date, an adjustment must be made to reflect the probability of the participant's death between the annuity starting date and the participant's attainment of age 62.

(ii) *No forfeiture deemed to occur where qualified preretirement survivor annuity payable.*—For purposes of paragraphs (d)(2)(i) and (e)(2)(i) of this section, a plan is permitted to treat no forfeiture as occurring upon a participant's death if the plan does not charge participants for providing a qualified preretirement survivor annuity (QPSA) (as defined in section 417(c)) on the participant's death, but only if the plan applies this treatment both for adjustments before age 62 and adjustments after age 65. Thus, in such a case, the plan is permitted to provide that, in computing the adjusted dollar limitation under section 415(b)(1)(A), no adjustment is made to reflect the probability of a participant's death after the annuity starting date and before age 62 or after age 65 and before the annuity starting date.

(3) *Exception for certain participants of certain governmental plans.*—Pursuant to section 415(b)(2)(G) and (H), no age adjustment is made to the dollar limit for commencement before age 62 for any qualified participant. For this purpose, a qualified participant is a participant in a defined benefit plan that is maintained by a state, Indian tribal government (as defined in section 7701(a)(40)), or any political subdivision of a state or Indian tribal government with respect to whom the service taken into account in determining the amount of the benefit under the defined benefit plan includes at least 15 years of service of the participant—

(i) As a full-time employee of any police department or fire department that is organized and operated by the state, Indian tribal government, or political subdivision maintaining such defined benefit plan to provide police protection, firefighting services, or emergency medical services for any area within the jurisdiction of such state, Indian tribal government, or political subdivision; or

(ii) As a member of the Armed Forces of the United States.

(4) *Exception for survivor and disability benefits under governmental plans.*—Pursuant to section 415(b)(2)(I), no age adjustment is made to the dollar limit for commencement before age 62 for a distribution from a governmental plan (as defined in section 414(d)) on account of the participant's becoming disabled by reason of personal injuries or sickness, or as a result of the death of the participant.

(5) *Special rule for commercial airline pilots.*—Pursuant to section 415(b)(9), no age adjustment is made to the dollar limit for early commencement on or after age 60 for a participant if—

(i) The participant is a commercial airline pilot;

(ii) The participant separates from service upon or after attaining age 60; and

(iii) As of the time of the participant's retirement, regulations prescribed by the Federal Aviation Administration require an individual to separate from service as a commercial airline pilot after attaining any age occurring on or after age 60 and before age 62.

(6) *No decrease in age-adjusted section 415(b)(1)(A) dollar limit on account of age or service.*—Notwithstanding any other provision of this paragraph (d), the age-adjusted section 415(b)(1)(A) dollar limit applicable to a participant does not decrease on account of an increase in age or the performance of additional service.

(7) *Examples.*—The following examples illustrate the application of this paragraph (d). For purposes of these examples, it is assumed that the dollar limitation under section 415(b)(1)(A) for all relevant years is $180,000, that the normal form of benefit under the plan is a straight life annuity payable beginning at age 65, and that all payments other than a payment of a single sum are made monthly, on the first day of each calendar month. The examples are as follows:

Example 1. (i) Plan A provides that early retirement benefits are determined by reducing the accrued benefit by 4 percent for each year that the early retirement age is less than age 65. Participant M retires at age 60 with exactly 30 years of service with a benefit (prior

to the application of section 415) in the form of a straight life annuity of $100,000 payable at age 65, and is permitted to elect to commence benefits at any time between M's retirement and M's attainment of age 65. For example, M can elect to commence benefits at age 60 in the amount of $80,000, can wait until age 62 and commence benefits in the amount of $88,000, or can wait until age 65 and commence benefits in the amount of $100,000. Plan A provides a QPSA to all married participants without charge. Plan A provides (consistent with paragraph (d)(2)(ii) of this section) that, for purposes of adjusting the dollar limitation under section 415(b)(1)(A) for commencement before age 62 or after age 65, no forfeiture is treated as occurring upon a participant's death before retirement and, therefore, in computing the adjusted dollar limitation under section 415(b)(1)(A), no adjustment is made to reflect the probability of a participant's death after the annuity starting date and before age 62 or after age 65 and before the annuity starting date.

(ii) The age-adjusted section 415(b)(1)(A) dollar limit that applies for commencement of M's benefit at age 60 is the lesser of the section 415(b)(1)(A) dollar limit multiplied by the ratio of the annuity payable at age 60 to the annuity payable at age 62, or the straight life annuity payable at age 60 that is actuarially equivalent, using 5 percent interest and the applicable mortality table effective for that annuity starting date under section 417(e)(3)(A)(ii)(I) and §1.417(e)-1(d)(2), to the deferred annuity payable at age 62 of $180,000 per year. In this case, the age-adjusted section 415(b)(1)(A) dollar limit at age 60 is $156,229 (the lesser of $163,636 ($180,000* $80,000/$88,000) and $156,229 (the straight life annuity at age 60 that is actuarially equivalent to a deferred annuity of $180,000 commencing at age 62, determined using 5 percent interest and the applicable mortality table, without a mortality decrement for the period between 60 and 62)).

Example 2. (i) The facts are the same as in *Example 1*, except that participant M elects to retire at age 60, 6 months, and 21 days.

(ii) Under paragraph (d)(1)(i) of this section, M is treated as age 60 and 6 months (or, age 60.5). Absent the rule provided in paragraph (d)(6) of this section, the age-adjusted section 415(b)(1)(A) dollar limit that applies for commencement of M's benefit at age 60.5 is the lesser of the section 415(b)(1)(A) dollar limit multiplied by the ratio of the annuity payable at age 60.5 to the annuity payable at age 62, or the straight life annuity payable at age 60.5 that is actuarially equivalent, using 5 percent interest and the applicable mortality table for that annuity starting date under section 417(e)(3)(A)(ii)(I) and §1.417(e)-1(d)(2), to the deferred annuity payable at age 62 of $180,000 per year. The age-adjusted section 415(b)(1)(A) dollar limit at age 60.5 is $161,769 (the lesser of $167,727 ($180,000* $82,000/$88,000) and $161,769 (the straight life annuity at age 60.5 that is actuarially equivalent to a deferred annuity of $180,000 commencing at age 62, determined using 5 percent interest and the applicable mortality table, without a mortality decrement for the period between 60.5 and 62).

Example 3. (i) The facts are the same as in *Example 1*, except the plan provides that, if a participant has 30 or more years of service, no reduction applies for benefits commencing at age 62 and later.

(ii) Absent the rule provided in paragraph (d)(6) of this section, the age-adjusted section 415(b)(1)(A) dollar limit that applies for commencement of M's benefit at age 60 is the lesser of the section 415(b)(1)(A) dollar limit multiplied by the ratio of the annuity payable at age 60 to the annuity payable at age 62, or the straight life annuity payable at age 60 that is actuarially equivalent, using 5 percent interest and the applicable mortality table for that annuity starting date under section 417(e)(3)(A)(ii)(I) and §1.417(e)-1(d)(2), to the deferred annuity payable at age 62 of $180,000 per year. In this case, because M has 30 years of service and would be eligible for the unreduced early retirement benefit at age 62, the age-adjusted section 415(b)(1)(A) dollar limit at age 60 would be $144,000 (the lesser of $144,000 ($180,000* $80,000/$100,000) and $156,229 (the straight life annuity at age 60 that is actuarially equivalent to a deferred annuity of $180,000 commencing at age 62, determined using 5 percent interest and the applicable mortality table, without a mortality decrement for the period between 60 and 62).

(iii) However, at age 59 11/12 with 29 11/12 years of service, the age-adjusted section 415(b)(1)(A) dollar limit for M is $155,311 (the lesser of $162,955 ($180,000* $79,667/$88,000) and $155,311 (the straight life annuity at age 59 11/12 that is actuarially equivalent to a deferred annuity of $180,000 commencing at age 62, determined using 5 percent interest and the applicable mortality table, without a mortality decrement for the period between 59 and 62). Thus, after applying the rule provided in paragraph (d)(6) of this section, the age-adjusted section 415(b)(1)(A) dollar limit that applies for commencement of M's benefit at age 60 is $155,311.

Example 4. (i) The facts are the same as in *Example 1*, except that the plan provides that, if a participant has 30 or more years of service, then no reduction is made in early retirement benefits if the early retirement age is at least age 62 and, in the case of an early retirement age before age 62, the early retirement benefit is determined by reducing the accrued benefit by 4 percent for each year that the early retirement age is less than age 62.

(ii) The age-adjusted section 415(b)(1)(A) dollar limit that applies for commencement of M's benefit at age 60 is the lesser of the section 415(b)(1)(A) dollar limit multiplied by the ratio of the annuity payable at age 60 to the annuity payable at age 62, or the straight life annuity payable at age 60 that is actuarially equivalent, using 5 percent interest and the applicable mortality table for that annuity starting date under section 417(e)(3)(A)(ii)(I) and § 1.417(e)-1(d)(2), to the deferred annuity payable at age 62 of $180,000 per year. In this case, because M has 30 years of service and would be eligible for the unreduced early retirement benefit at age 62, the age-adjusted section 415(b)(1)(A) dollar limit at age 60 is $156,229 (the lesser of $165,600 ($180,000* $92,000/$100,000) and $156,229 (the straight life annuity at age 60 that is actuarially equivalent to a deferred annuity of $180,000 commencing at age 62, determined using 5 percent interest and the applicable mortality table, without a mortality decrement for the period between 60 and 62).

Example 5. (i) The facts are the same as in *Example 1*, except that Participant M chooses to receive benefits in the form of a 10-year certain and life annuity under which payments are 97 percent of the periodic payments that would be made under the immediately commencing straight life annuity. Annual payments to M are 97 percent of $80,000, or $77,600. Additionally, M's average compensation for the period of M's high-3 years of service is $120,000. As in *Example 1*, the age-adjusted section 415(b)(1)(A) dollar limit at age 60 is $156,229.

(ii) In the case of a form of benefit to which section 417(e)(3) does not apply, the annual benefit for purposes of this section is the greater of the annual amount of the plan's straight life annuity commencing at the same age or the annual amount of the actuarially equivalent straight life annuity commencing at the same age, determined using a 5 percent interest rate and the applicable mortality table for that annuity starting date under section 417(e)(3)(A)(ii)(I) and § 1.417(e)-1(d)(2). In this case, the straight life annuity payable under the plan commencing at the same age is $80,000. The annual amount of the straight life annuity that is actuarially equivalent to the $77,600 benefit payable as a 10-year certain and life annuity is determined by applying the required standardized factors (a 5 percent interest assumption and the applicable mortality under section 417(e)(3)(A)(ii)(I) and § 1.417(e)-1(d)(2), and is $79,416. With respect to the 10-year certain and life annuity commencing at age 62, M's annual benefit is equal to the greater of the two resulting amounts ($80,000 and $79,416), or $80,000. Because M's annual benefit is less than the age-adjusted section 415(b)(1)(A) dollar limit and is less than the section 415(b)(1)(B) compensation limit, M's benefit satisfies section 415.

Example 6. (i) Participant O is a full-time civilian employee of the Harbor Police Division of the State of X Port Authority. The Harbor Police Division provides police protection services. O performs clerical services for the Harbor Police Division. O is a participant in the defined benefit plan that is maintained by the State of X with respect to whom the years of service taken into account in determining the amount of the benefit under the plan includes 10 years of service working for the Harbor Police Division and 5 years of service as a member of the Armed Forces of the United States.

(ii) For a distribution with an annuity starting date that occurs before O attains the age of 62, there is no age adjustment to the section 415(b)(1)(A) dollar limit.

Example 7. (i) Participant R is a full-time employee of the Emergency Medical Service Department of County Y (which is not a part of a police or fire department) who performs services as a driver of an ambulance. R is a participant in the defined benefit plan that is maintained by County Y with respect to whom the years of service taken into account in determining the amount of the benefit under the plan includes 15 years of service working for County Y. R does not have service credit for time in the Armed Forces of the United States.

(ii) The age adjustments to the limitations of section 415(b)(1)(A) pursuant to section 415(b)(2)(C) and (D) will apply if R commences receiving a distribution at an age to which either of those adjustments applies.

(e) *Adjustment to section 415(b)(1)(A) dollar limit for commencement after age 65.*—(1) *General rule.*—(i) *Calculation using statutory factors.*—For a distribution with an annuity starting date that occurs after the participant attains the age of 65, the age-adjusted section 415(b)(1)(A) dollar limit generally is determined as the actuarial equivalent of the annual amount of a straight life annuity commencing at the annuity starting date that has the same actuarial present value as a straight life annuity commencing at age 65, where annual payments under the straight life annuity commencing at age 65 are equal to the dollar limitation of section 415(b)(1)(A) (as adjusted pursuant to section

415(d) and § 1.415(d)-1 for the limitation year), and where the actuarially equivalent straight life annuity is computed using a 5 percent interest rate and the applicable mortality table under § 1.417(e)-1(d)(2) that is effective for that annuity starting date (and expressing the participant's age based on completed calendar months as of the annuity starting date). However, if the plan has an immediately commencing straight life annuity payable as of the annuity starting date and an immediately commencing straight life annuity payable at age 65, then the age-adjusted section 415(b)(1)(A) dollar limit is equal to the lesser of—

(A) The limit as otherwise determined under this paragraph (e)(1)(i); and

(B) The amount determined under paragraph (e)(1)(ii) of this section.

(ii) *Calculation using plan factors.*—The amount determined under this paragraph (e)(1)(ii) is equal to the section 415(b)(1)(A) dollar limit (as adjusted pursuant to section 415(d) and § 1.415(d)-1 for the limitation year) multiplied by the adjustment ratio described in paragraph (e)(2)(i) of this section.

(2) *Adjustment ratio.*—(i) *General rule.*—For purposes of applying the rule of paragraph (e)(1)(ii) of this section, the adjustment ratio is equal to the ratio of the annual amount of the adjusted immediately commencing straight life annuity under the plan described in paragraph (e)(2)(ii) of this section to the adjusted age 65 straight life annuity described in paragraph (e)(2)(iii) of this section.

(ii) *Adjusted immediately commencing straight life annuity.*—The adjusted immediately commencing straight life annuity that is used for purposes of paragraph (e)(2)(i) of this section is the annual amount of the immediately commencing straight life annuity payable to the participant, computed disregarding the participant's accruals after age 65 but including actuarial adjustments even if those actuarial adjustments are applied to offset accruals. For this purpose, the annual amount of the immediately commencing straight life annuity is determined without applying the rules of section 415.

(iii) *Adjusted age 65 straight life annuity.*—The adjusted age 65 straight life annuity that is used for purposes of paragraph (e)(2)(i) of this section is the annual amount of the straight life annuity that would be payable under the plan to a hypothetical participant who is 65 years old and has the same accrued benefit (with no actuarial increases for commencement after age 65) as the participant receiving the distribution (determined disregarding the participant's accruals after age 65 and without applying the rules of section 415).

(3) *Mortality adjustments.*—(i) *In general.*—For purposes of determining the actuarially equivalent amount described in paragraph (e)(1)(i) of this section, to the extent that a forfeiture does not occur upon the participant's death before the annuity starting date, no adjustment is made to reflect the probability of the participant's death between the participant's attainment of age 65 and the annuity starting date. To the extent that a forfeiture occurs upon the participant's death before the annuity starting date, an adjustment must be made to reflect the probability of the participant's death between the participant's attainment of age 65 and the annuity starting date.

(ii) *No forfeiture deemed to occur where QPSA payable.*—See paragraph (d)(2)(ii) of this section for a rule deeming no forfeiture to occur if the plan does not charge participants for providing a QPSA on the participant's death.

(4) *Examples.*—The following examples illustrate the application of this paragraph (e):

Example 1. (i) Plan A provides that monthly benefits payable upon commencement after normal retirement age (which is age 65) are increased by 0.5 percent for each month of delay in commencement after attainment of normal retirement age. Plan A provides a QPSA to all married participants without charge. Plan A provides (consistent with paragraph (d)(2)(ii) of this section) that, for purposes of adjusting the dollar limitation under section 415(b)(1)(A) for commencement before age 62 or after age 65, no adjustment is made to reflect the probability of a participant's death between the annuity starting date and the participant's attainment of age 62 or between the age of 65 and the annuity starting date. The normal form of benefit under Plan A is a straight life annuity commencing at age 65. Plan A does not provide additional benefit accruals once a participant is credited with 30 years of service. Participant M was credited with 30 years of service under Plan A when M attained age 65. M retires at age 70 on January 1, 2008, with a benefit (prior to the application of section 415) that is payable monthly in the form of a straight life annuity of $195,000, which reflects the actuarial increase of 30 percent applied to the accrued benefit of $150,000. It is assumed that all payments under Plan A, other than a payment of a single sum, are made monthly, on the first day of each calendar month. It is also assumed that the dollar limit in 2008 is $185,000.

(ii) The age-adjusted section 415(b)(1)(A) dollar limit at age 70 is the lesser of the section 415(b)(1)(A) dollar limit multiplied by the ratio of the adjusted immediately commencing straight life annuity payable at age 70 (computed disregarding the rules of section 415 and accruals after age 65, but including actuarial adjustments) to the adjusted age 65 straight life annuity (computed disregarding the rules of section 415 and any accruals after age 65), or the straight life annuity payable at age 70 that is actuarially equivalent, using 5 percent interest and the applicable mortality table for that annuity starting date under section 417(e)(3)(A)(ii)(I) and § 1.417(e)-1(d)(2), to the straight life annuity payable at age 65, where annual payments under the straight life annuity payable at age 65 are equal to the dollar limitation of section 415(b)(1)(A). In this case, the age-adjusted section 415(b)(1)(A) dollar limit at age 70 is $240,500 (the lesser of $240,500 ($185,000* $195,000/$150,000) and $271,444 (the straight life annuity at age 70 that is actuarially equivalent to an annuity of $185,000 commencing at age 65, determined using 5 percent interest and the applicable mortality table, without a mortality decrement for the period between 65 and 70)).

Example 2. (i) The facts are the same as in *Example 1*, except that Plan A does not limit benefit accruals to 30 years of credited service, and thus M accrues benefits between ages 65 and 70.

(ii) Since M's accruals after attaining age 65 are disregarded for purposes of determining the age-adjusted section 415(b)(1)(A) dollar limit applicable to M at age 70, the result is the same as in *Example 1*.

Example 3. (i) The facts are the same as in *Example 1*, except that Plan A does not limit benefit accruals to 30 years of credited service. However, benefit accruals after an employee has reached normal retirement age (age 65), are offset by the actuarial increase that the plan provides for commencement of benefits after normal retirement age.

(ii) The result is the same as in *Example 1*, even if the actuarial increases for post-age 65 benefit commencement provided under Plan A do or do not fully offset M's benefit accruals after attaining age 65. This is because benefit accruals after age 65 are disregarded for purposes of determining the age-adjusted section 415(b)(1)(A) dollar limit applicable to M after age 65.

(f) *Total annual payments not in excess of $10,000.*—(1) *In general.*— Pursuant to section 415(b)(4), the annual benefit (without regard to the age at which benefits commence) payable with respect to a participant under any defined benefit plan is not considered to exceed the limitations on benefits described in section 415(b)(1) and in paragraph (a)(1) of this section if—

(i) The benefits (other than benefits not taken into account in the computation of the annual benefit under the rules of paragraph (b) or (c) of this section) payable with respect to the participant under the plan and all other defined benefit plans of the employer do not in the aggregate exceed $10,000 (as adjusted under paragraph (g) of this section) for the limitation year, or for any prior limitation year; and

(ii) The employer (or a predecessor employer) has not at any time maintained a defined contribution plan in which the participant participated.

(2) *Computation of benefits for purposes of applying the $10,000 amount.*—For purposes of paragraph (f)(1)(i) of this section, the benefits payable with respect to the participant under a plan for a limitation year reflect all amounts payable under the plan for the limitation year (other than benefits not taken into account in the computation of the annual benefit under the rules of paragraph (b) or (c) of this section), and are not adjusted for form of benefit or commencement date.

(3) *Special rule with respect to participants in multiemployer plans.*— The special $10,000 exception set forth in paragraph (f)(1) of this section applies to a participant in a multiemployer plan described in section 414(f) without regard to whether that participant ever participated in one or more other plans maintained by an employer who also maintains the multiemployer plan, provided that none of such other plans were maintained as a result of collective bargaining involving the same employee representative as the multiemployer plan.

(4) *Special rule with respect to employee contributions.*—Notwithstanding §§ 1.415(c)-1(a)(2)(ii)(B) and 1.415(c)-1(b)(3), mandatory employee contributions under a defined benefit plan described in paragraph (b)(2)(iii) of this section are not considered a separate defined contribution plan maintained by the employer for purposes of paragraph (f)(1)(ii) of this section. Thus, the special dollar limitation provided for in this paragraph (f) applies to a contributory *defined benefit plan. Similarly, for* purposes of this paragraph (f), an individual medical account under section 401(h) or an account for postretirement medical benefits established pursuant to section 419A(d)(1) is not considered a separate defined contribution plan maintained by the employer.

(5) *Examples.*—The application of this paragraph (f) may be illustrated by the following examples. For purposes of these examples, it is assumed that each participant has 10 years of participation in the plan and service with the employer. The examples are as follows:

Example 1. (i) B is a participant in a defined benefit plan maintained by X Corporation, which provides for a benefit payable in the form of a straight life annuity beginning at age 65. B's average compensation for the period of B's high-3 years of service is $6,000. The plan does not provide for mandatory employee contributions, and at no time has B been a participant in a defined contribution plan maintained by X. With respect to the current limitation year, B's benefit under the plan (before the application of section 415) is $9,500.

(ii) Because annual payments under B's benefit do not exceed $10,000, and because B has at no time participated in a defined contribution plan maintained by X, the benefits payable under the plan are not considered to exceed the limitation on benefits otherwise applicable to B ($6,000).

(iii) This result would remain the same even if, under the terms of the plan, B's benefit of $9,500 were payable at age 60, or if the plan provided for mandatory employee contributions.

Example 2. (i) The facts are the same as in *Example 1*, except that the plan provides for a benefit payable in the form of a life annuity with a 10-year certain feature with annual payments of $9,500. Assume that, after the adjustment described in paragraph (c) of this section, B's actuarially equivalent straight life annuity (which is the annual benefit used for demonstrating compliance with section 415) for the current limitation year is $10,400.

(ii) For purposes of applying the special rule provided in this paragraph for total benefits not in excess of $10,000, there is no adjustment required if the retirement benefit payable under the plan is not in the form of a straight life annuity. Therefore, because B's retirement benefit does not exceed $10,000, B may receive the full $9,500 benefit without the otherwise applicable benefit limitations of this section being exceeded.

Example 3. (i) The facts are the same as in *Example 1*, except that the plan provides for a benefit payable in the form of a single sum and the amount of the single sum that is the actuarial equivalent of the straight life annuity payable to B ($9,500 annually), determined in accordance with the rules of section 417(e)(3) and § 1.417(e)-1(d), is $95,000.

(ii) Because the amount payable to B for the limitation year would exceed $10,000, the rule of this paragraph (f) does not provide an exception from the generally applicable limits of section 415(b)(1) for the single-sum distribution. Thus, the otherwise applicable limits apply to the single-sum distribution, and a single-sum distribution of $95,000 would not satisfy the requirements of section 415(b). Limiting the single-sum distribution to $60,000 (the present value of the annuity that complies with the compensation-based limitation of section 415(b)(1)(B)) in order to satisfy section 415 would be an impermissible forfeiture under the requirements of section 411(a). Accordingly, the plan should not provide for a single-sum distribution in these circumstances.

(g) *Special rule for participation or service of less than 10 years.*— (1) *Proration of dollar limit based on years of participation.*—(i) *In general.*—Pursuant to section 415(b)(5)(A), where a participant has less than 10 years of participation in the plan, the dollar limit described in paragraph (a)(1)(i) of this section (as adjusted pursuant to section 415(d), § 1.415(d)-1, and paragraphs (d) and (e) of this section) is reduced by multiplying the otherwise applicable limitation by a fraction—

(A) The numerator of which is the number of years of participation in the plan (or 1, if greater); and

(B) The denominator of which is 10.

(ii) *Years of participation.*—The following rules apply for purposes of determining a participant's years of participation for purposes of this paragraph (g)(1)—

(A) A participant is credited with a year of participation (computed to fractional parts of a year) for each accrual computation period for which the participant is credited with at least the number of hours of service (or period of service if the elapsed time method is used for benefit accrual purposes) required under the terms of the plan in order to accrue a benefit for the accrual computation period, and the participant is included as a plan participant under the eligibility provisions of the plan for at least one day of the accrual computation period. If these two conditions are met, the portion of a year of participation credited to the participant is equal to the amount of benefit accrual service credited to the participant for such accrual computation period. For example, if under the terms of a plan, a participant receives 1/10 of a year of benefit accrual service for an accrual computation period for each 200 hours of service, and the participant is credited with 1,000 hours of service for the period, the participant is credited with 1/2 a year of participation for purposes of section 415(b)(5)(A) and this paragraph (g)(1).

(B) A participant who is permanently and totally disabled within the meaning of section 415(c)(3)(C)(i) for an accrual computation period is credited with a year of participation with respect to that period for purposes of section 415(b)(5)(A) and this paragraph (g)(1).

(C) For a participant to receive a year of participation (or part thereof) for an accrual computation period for purposes of section 415(b)(5)(A) and this paragraph (g)(1), the plan must be established no later than the last day of such accrual computation period.

(D) No more than one year of participation may be credited for any 12-month period for purposes of section 415(b)(5)(A) and this paragraph (g)(1).

(2) *Proration of compensation limit and special rule for total annual payments less than $10,000 based on years of service.*—(i) *In general.*—Pursuant to section 415(b)(5)(B), where a participant has less than 10 years of service with the employer, the compensation limit described in paragraph (a)(1)(ii) of this section and the $10,000 amount under the special rule for small annual payments under paragraph (f) of this section are reduced by multiplying the otherwise applicable limitation by a fraction—

(A) The numerator of which is the number of years of service with the employer (or 1, if greater); and

(B) The denominator of which is 10.

(ii) *Years of service.*—(A) *In general.*—For purposes of applying this paragraph (g)(2), years of service must be determined on a reasonable and consistent basis. A plan is considered to be determining years of service on a reasonable and consistent basis for this purpose if, subject to the limits of paragraph (g)(2)(ii)(B) of this section, a participant is credited with a year of service (computed to fractional parts of a year) for each accrual computation period for which the participant is credited with at least the number of hours of service (or period of service if the elapsed time method is used for benefit accrual purposes) required under the terms of the plan in order to accrue a benefit for the accrual computation period.

(B) *Rules of application.*—No more than one year of service may be credited for any 12-month period for purposes of section 415(b)(5)(B). In addition, only the participant's service with the employer or a predecessor employer (as defined in §1.415-1(c)) may be taken into account in determining the participant's years of service for this purpose. Thus, if an employer does not maintain a former employer's plan, a participant's service with the former employer may be taken into account in determining the participant's years of service for purposes of this paragraph (g)(2) only if the former employer is a predecessor employer with respect to the employer pursuant to §1.415(f)-1(c)(2) (which defines predecessor employer to include, under certain circumstances, a former entity that antedates the employer).

(C) *Period of disability.*—Notwithstanding the rules of paragraph (g)(2)(ii)(B) of this section, a plan is permitted to provide that a participant who is permanently and totally disabled within the meaning of section 415(c)(3)(C)(i) for an accrual computation period is credited with service with respect to that period for purposes of section 415(b)(5)(B).

(3) *Exception for survivor and disability benefits under governmental plans.*—The requirements of this paragraph (g) (regarding participation or service of less than 10 years) do not apply to a distribution from a governmental plan (as defined in section 414(d)) on account of the participant's becoming disabled by reason of personal injuries or sickness, or as a result of the death of the participant.

(4) *Examples.*—The provisions of this paragraph (g) may be illustrated by the following examples:

Example 1. (i) C begins employment with Employer A on January 1, 2005, at the age of 58. Employer A maintains only a noncontributory defined benefit plan which provides for a straight life annuity beginning at age 65 and uses the calendar year for the limitation and plan year. Employer A has never maintained a *defined contribution* plan. C becomes a participant in Employer A's plan on January 1, 2006, and works through December 31, 2011, when C is age 65. C begins to receive benefits under the plan in 2012. C's average compensation for the period of C's high-3 years of service is $40,000. Furthermore, under the terms of Employer A's plan, for purposes of computing C's nonforfeitable percentage in C's accrued benefit derived from employer contributions, C has only 7 years of service with Employer A (2005-2011).

(ii) Because C has only 7 years of service with Employer A at the time he begins to receive benefits under the plan, the maximum permissible annual benefit payable with respect to C is $28,000 ($40,000 multiplied by 7/10).

Example 2. (i) The facts are the same as in *Example 1*, except that C's average compensation for the period of his high-3 years of service is $8,000.

(ii) Because C has only 7 years of service with Employer A at the time he begins to receive benefits, the maximum benefit payable with respect to C would be reduced to $5,600 ($8,000 multiplied by 7/10). However, the special rule for total benefits not in excess of $10,000, provided in paragraph (f) of this section, is applicable in this case. Accordingly, C may receive an annual benefit of $7,000 ($10,000 multiplied by 7/10) without the benefit limitations of this section being exceeded.

Example 3. (i) Employer B maintains a defined benefit plan. Benefits under the plan are computed based on months of service rather than on years of service. Accordingly, for purposes of applying the reduction based on years of service less than 10 to the limitations under section 415(b), the plan provides that the otherwise applicable limitation is multiplied by a fraction, the numerator of which is the number of completed months of service with the employer (but not less than 12 months), and the denominator of which is 120. The plan further provides that months of service are computed in the same manner for this purpose as for purposes of computing plan benefits.

(ii) The manner in which the plan applies the reduction based on years of service less than 10 to the limitations under section 415(b) is consistent with the requirements of this paragraph (g).

Example 4. (i) G begins employment with Employer D on January 1, 2003, at the age of 58. Employer D maintains a noncontributory defined benefit plan which provides for a straight life annuity beginning at age 65 and uses the calendar year for the limitation and plan year. G becomes a participant in Employer D's plan on January 1, 2004, and works through December 31, 2009, when G is age 65. G performs sufficient service to be credited with a year of service under the plan for each year during 2003 through 2009 (although G is not credited with a year of service for 2003 because G is not yet a plan participant). G begins to receive benefits under the plan during 2010. The plan's accrual computation period is the plan year. The plan provides that, for purposes of applying the rules of section 415(b)(5)(B), a participant is credited with a year of service (computed to fractional parts of a year) for each plan year for which the participant is credited with sufficient service to accrue a benefit for the plan year. G's average compensation for the period of G's high-3 years of service is $200,000. It is assumed for purposes of this example that the dollar limitation of section 415(b)(1)(A) for limitation years ending in 2010 is $195,000.

(ii) G has 7 years of service and 5 years of participation in the plan at the time G begins to receive benefits under the plan. Accordingly, the limitation under section 415(b)(1)(B) based on G's average compensation for the period of G's high-3 years of service that applies pursuant to the adjustment required under section 415(b)(5)(B) is $140,000 ($200,000 multiplied by 7/10), and the dollar limitation under section 415(b)(1)(A) that applies to G pursuant to the adjustment required under section 415(b)(5)(A) is $117,000 ($195,000 multiplied by 6/10).

(h) *Retirement Protection Act of 1994 transition rules.*—For special rules affecting the actuarial adjustment for form of benefit under paragraph (c) of this section and the adjustment to the dollar limit for early or late commencement under paragraphs (d) and (e) of this section for certain plans adopted and in effect before December 8, 1994, see section 767(d)(3)(A) of the Uruguay Round Agreements Act of 1994, Public Law 103-465 (108 Stat. 4809) as amended by section 1449(a) of the Small Business Job Protection Act of 1996, Public Law 104-188 (110 Stat. 1755). The Commissioner may provide guidance regarding these special rules in revenue rulings, notices, and other guidance published in the Internal Revenue Bulletin. See §601.601(d) of this chapter. [Reg. §1.415(b)-1.]

☐ [T.D. 9319, 4-4-200 (*corrected* 5-22-2007).]

[Reg. §1.415(b)-2]

§1.415(b)-2. Multiple annuity starting dates .—[Reserved].

☐ [T.D. 9319, 4-4-2007.]

[Reg. §1.415(c)-1]

§1.415(c)-1. Limitations for defined contribution plans.—(a) *General rules.*—(1) *Maximum limitations.*—Under section 415(c) and this section, to satisfy the provisions of section 415(a) for any limitation year, except as provided by paragraph (a)(3) of this section, the annual additions (as defined in paragraph (b) of this section) credited to the account of a participant in a defined contribution plan for the limitation year must not exceed the lesser of—

(i) $40,000 (adjusted pursuant to section 415(d) and §1.415(d)-1(b)); or

(ii) 100 percent of the participant's compensation (as defined in § 1.415(c)-2) for the limitation year.

(2) *Defined contribution plan.*—(i) *Definition.*—For purposes of section 415 and regulations promulgated under section 415, the term *defined contribution plan* means a defined contribution plan within the meaning of section 414(i) (including the portion of a plan treated as a defined contribution plan under the rules of section 414(k)) that is—

(A) A plan described in section 401(a) which includes a trust which is exempt from tax under section 501(a);

(B) An annuity plan described in section 403(a); or

(C) A simplified employee pension described in section 408(k).

(ii) *Additional plans treated as defined contribution plans.*—(A) *In general.*—Contributions to the types of arrangements described in paragraphs (a)(2)(ii)(B) through (D) of this section are treated as contributions to defined contribution plans for purposes of section 415 and regulations promulgated under section 415.

(B) *Employee contributions to a defined benefit plan.*—Mandatory employee contributions (as defined in section 411(c)(2)(C) and § 1.411(c)-1(c)(4), regardless of whether the plan is subject to the requirements of section 411) to a defined benefit plan are treated as contributions to a defined contribution plan. For this purpose, contributions that are picked up by the employer as described in section 414(h)(2) are not considered employee contributions.

(C) *Individual medical benefit accounts under section 401(h).*—Pursuant to section 415(l)(1), contributions allocated to any individual medical benefit account which is part of a pension or annuity plan established pursuant to section 401(h) are treated as contributions to a defined contribution plan.

(D) *Post-retirement medical accounts for key employees.*—Pursuant to section 419A(d)(2), amounts attributable to medical benefits allocated to an account established for a key employee (any employee who, at any time during the plan year or any preceding plan year, is or was a key employee as defined in section 416(i)) pursuant to section 419A(d)(1) are treated as contributions to a defined contribution plan.

(iii) *Section 403(b) annuity contracts.*—Annual additions under an annuity contract described in section 403(b) are treated as annual additions under a defined contribution plan for purposes of this section.

(3) *Alternative contribution limitations.*—(i) *Church plans.*—For alternative contribution limitations relating to church plans, see paragraph (d) of this section.

(ii) *Special rules for medical benefits.*—For additional rules relating to certain medical benefits, see paragraph (e) of this section.

(iii) *Employee stock ownership plans.*—For additional rules relating to employee stock ownership plans, see paragraph (f) of this section.

(b) *Annual additions.*—(1) *In general.*—(i) *General definition.*—The term *annual addition* means, for purposes of this section, the sum, credited to a participant's account for any limitation year, of—

(A) Employer contributions;

(B) Employee contributions; and

(C) Forfeitures.

(ii) *Certain excess amounts treated as annual additions.*—Contributions do not fail to be annual additions merely because they are excess contributions (as described in section 401(k)(8)(B)) or excess aggregate contributions (as described in section 401(m)(6)(B)), or merely because excess contributions or excess aggregate contributions are corrected through distribution.

(iii) *Direct transfers.*—The direct transfer of a benefit or employee contributions from a qualified plan to a defined contribution plan does not give rise to an annual addition.

(iv) *Reinvested employee stock ownership plan dividends.*—The reinvestment of dividends on employer securities under an employee stock ownership plan pursuant to section 404(k)(2)(A)(iii)(II) does not give rise to an annual addition.

(2) *Employer contributions.*—(i) *Amounts treated as an annual addition.*—For purposes of paragraph (b)(1)(i)(A) of this section, the term *annual addition* includes employer contributions credited to the participant's account for the limitation year and other allocations described in paragraph (b)(4) of this section that are made during the limitation year. See paragraph (b)(6) of this section for timing rules applicable to annual additions with respect to employer contributions.

(ii) *Amounts not treated as annual additions.*—(A) *Certain restorations of accrued benefits.*—The restoration of an employee's accrued benefit by the employer in accordance with section 411(a)(3)(D) or section 411(a)(7)(C) or resulting from the repayment of cashouts (as described in section 415(k)(3)) under a governmental plan (as defined in section 414(d)) is not considered an annual addition for the limitation year in which the restoration occurs. This treatment of a restoration of an employee's accrued benefit as not giving rise to an annual addition applies regardless of whether the plan restricts the timing of repayments to the maximum extent allowed by section 411(a).

(B) *Catch-up contributions.*—A catch-up contribution made in accordance with section 414(v) and § 1.414(v)-1 does not give rise to an annual addition.

(C) *Restorative payments.*—A restorative payment that is allocated to a participant's account does not give rise to an annual addition for any limitation year. For this purpose, restorative payments are payments made to restore losses to a plan resulting from actions by a fiduciary for which there is reasonable risk of liability for breach of a fiduciary duty under Title I of the Employee Retirement Income Security Act of 1974 (88 Stat. 829), Public Law 93-406 (ERISA) or under other applicable federal or state law, where plan participants who are similarly situated are treated similarly with respect to the payments. Generally, payments to a defined contribution plan are restorative payments only if the payments are made in order to restore some or all of the plan's losses due to an action (or a failure to act) that creates a reasonable risk of liability for such a breach of fiduciary duty (other than a breach of fiduciary duty arising from failure to remit contributions to the plan). This includes payments to a plan made pursuant to a Department of Labor order, the Department of Labor's Voluntary Fiduciary Correction Program, or a court-approved settlement, to restore losses to a qualified defined contribution plan on account of the breach of fiduciary duty (other than a breach of fiduciary duty arising from failure to remit contributions to the plan). Payments made to a plan to make up for losses due merely to market fluctuations and other payments that are not made on account of a reasonable risk of liability for breach of a fiduciary duty under Title I of ERISA are not restorative payments and generally constitute contributions that give rise to annual additions under paragraph (b)(4) of this section.

(D) *Excess deferrals.*—Excess deferrals that are distributed in accordance with § 1.402(g)-1(e)(2) or (3) do not give rise to annual additions.

(3) *Employee contributions.*—For purposes of paragraph (b)(1)(i)(B) of this section, the term *annual addition* includes mandatory employee contributions (as defined in section 411(c)(2)(C) and regulations promulgated under section 411) as well as voluntary employee contributions. The term *annual addition* does not include—

(i) Rollover contributions (as described in sections 401(a)(31), 402(c)(1), 403(a)(4), 403(b)(8), 408(d)(3), and 457(e)(16));

(ii) Repayments of loans made to a participant from the plan;

(iii) Repayments of amounts described in section 411(a)(7)(B) (in accordance with section 411(a)(7)(C)) and section 411(a)(3)(D) or repayment of contributions to a governmental plan (as defined in section 414(d)) as described in section 415(k)(3);

(iv) Repayments that would have been described in paragraph (b)(3)(iii) of this section except that the plan does not restrict the timing of repayments to the maximum extent permitted by section 411(a); or

(v) Employee contributions to a qualified cost of living arrangement within the meaning of section 415(k)(2)(B).

(4) *Transactions with plan.*—The Commissioner may in an appropriate case, considering all of the facts and circumstances, treat transactions between the plan and the employer, transactions between the plan and the employee, or certain allocations to participants' accounts as giving rise to annual additions. Further, where an employee or employer transfers assets to a plan in exchange for consideration that is less than the fair market value of the assets transferred to the plan, there is an annual addition in the amount of the difference between the value of the assets transferred and the consideration. A transaction described in this paragraph (b)(4) may constitute a prohibited transaction with the meaning of section 4975(c)(1).

(5) *Contributions other than cash.*—For purposes of this paragraph (b), a contribution by the employer or employee of property rather than cash is considered to be a contribution in an amount equal to the fair market value of the property on the date the contribution is made. For this purpose, the fair market value is the price at which the property would change hands between a willing buyer and a willing seller, neither being under any compulsion to buy or to sell and both having reasonable knowledge of relevant facts. In addition, a contri-

bution described in this paragraph (b)(5) may constitute a prohibited transaction within the meaning of section 4975(c)(1).

(6) *Timing rules.*—(i) *In general.*—(A) *Date of allocation.*—For purposes of this paragraph (b), an annual addition is credited to the account of a participant for a particular limitation year if it is allocated to the participant's account under the terms of the plan as of any date within that limitation year. Similarly, an annual addition that is made pursuant to a corrective amendment that complies with the requirements of §1.401(a)(4)-11(g) is credited to the account of a participant for a particular limitation year if it is allocated to the participant's account under the terms of the corrective amendment as of any date within that limitation year. However, if the allocation of an annual addition is dependent upon the satisfaction of a condition (such as continued employment or the occurrence of an event) that has not been satisfied by the date as of which the annual addition is allocated under the terms of the plan, then the annual addition is considered allocated for purposes of this paragraph (b) as of the date the condition is satisfied.

(B) *Date of employer contributions.*—For purposes of this paragraph (b), employer contributions are not treated as credited to a participant's account for a particular limitation year unless the contributions are actually made to the plan no later than 30 days after the end of the period described in section 404(a)(6) applicable to the taxable year with or within which the particular limitation year ends. If, however, contributions are made by an employer exempt from Federal income tax (including a governmental employer), the contributions must be made to the plan no later than the 15th day of the tenth calendar month following the end of the calendar year or fiscal year (as applicable, depending on the basis on which the employer keeps its books) with or within which the particular limitation year ends. If contributions are made to a plan after the end of the period during which contributions can be made and treated as credited to a participant's account for a particular limitation year, allocations attributable to those contributions are treated as credited to the participant's account for the limitation year during which those contributions are made.

(C) *Date of employee contributions.*—For purposes of this paragraph (b), employee contributions, whether voluntary or mandatory, are not treated as credited to a participant's account for a particular limitation year unless the contributions are actually made to the plan no later than 30 days after the close of that limitation year.

(D) *Date for forfeitures.*—A forfeiture is treated as an annual addition for the limitation year that contains the date as of which it is allocated to a participant's account as a forfeiture.

(E) *Treatment of elective contributions as plan assets.*—The extent to which elective contributions constitute plan assets for purposes of the prohibited transaction provisions of section 4975 and Title I of ERISA, is determined in accordance with regulations and rulings issued by the Department of Labor. See 29 CFR 2510.3-102.

(ii) *Special timing rules.*—(A) *Corrective contributions.*—For purposes of this section, if, in a particular limitation year, an employer allocates an amount to a participant's account because of an erroneous forfeiture in a prior limitation year, or because of an erroneous failure to allocate amounts in a prior limitation year, the corrective allocation will not be considered an annual addition with respect to the participant for that particular limitation year, but will be considered an annual addition for the prior limitation year to which it relates. An example of a situation in which an employer contribution might occur under the circumstances described in the preceding sentence is a retroactive crediting of service for an employee under 29 CFR 2530.200b-2(a)(3) in accordance with an award of back pay. For purposes of this paragraph (b)(6)(ii), if the amount so contributed in the particular limitation year takes into account actual investment gains attributable to the period subsequent to the year to which the contribution relates, the portion of the total contribution that consists of such gains is not considered as an annual addition for any limitation year.

(B) *Contributions for accumulated funding deficiencies and previously waived contributions.*—(1) *Accumulated funding deficiency.*—In the case of a defined contribution plan to which the rules of section 412 apply, a contribution made to reduce an accumulated funding deficiency will be treated as if it were timely made for purposes of determining the limitation year in which the annual additions arising from the contribution are made, but only if the contribution is allocated to those participants who would have received an annual addition if the contribution had been timely made.

(2) *Previously waived contributions.*—In the case of a defined contribution plan to which the rules of section 412 apply and for which there has been a waiver of the minimum funding standard in a prior limitation year in accordance with section 412(d), that portion of an employer contribution in a subsequent limitation year which, if not for the waiver, would have otherwise been required in the prior limitation year under section 412(a) will be treated as if it were timely made (without regard to the funding waiver) for purposes of determining the limitation year in which the annual additions arising from the contribution are made, but only if the contribution is allocated to those participants who would have received an annual addition if the contribution had been timely made (without regard to the funding waiver).

(3) *Interest.*—For purposes of determining the amount of the annual addition under paragraphs (b)(6)(ii)(B)(1) and (2) of this section, a reasonable amount of interest paid by the employer is disregarded. However, any interest paid by the employer that is in excess of a reasonable amount, as determined by the Commissioner, is taken into account as an annual addition for the limitation year during which the contribution is made.

(C) *Simplified employee pensions.*—For purposes of this paragraph (b), amounts contributed to a simplified employee pension described in section 408(k) are treated as allocated to the individual's account as of the last day of the limitation year ending with or within the taxable year for which the contribution is made.

(D) *Treatment of certain contributions made pursuant to veterans' reemployment rights.*—If, in a particular limitation year, an employer contributes an amount to an employee's account with respect to a prior limitation year and such contribution is required by reason of such employee's rights under chapter 43 of title 38, United States Code, resulting from qualified military service, as specified in section 414(u)(1), then such contribution is not considered an annual addition with respect to the employee for that particular limitation year in which the contribution is made, but, in accordance with section 414(u)(1)(B), is considered an annual addition for the limitation year to which the contribution relates.

(c) *Examples.*—The following examples illustrate the rules of paragraphs (a) and (b) of this section:

Example 1. (i) P is a participant in a qualified profit-sharing plan maintained by his employer, ABC Corporation. The limitation year for the plan is the calendar year. P's compensation (as defined in §1.415(c)-2) for the current limitation year is $30,000.

(ii) Because the compensation limitation described in section 415(c)(1)(B) applicable to P for the current limitation year is lower than the dollar limitation described in section 415(c)(1)(A), the maximum annual addition which can be allocated to P's account for the current limitation year is $30,000 (100 percent of $30,000).

Example 2. (i) The facts are the same as in *Example 1*, except that P's compensation for the current limitation year is $140,000.

(ii) The maximum amount of annual additions that may be allocated to P's account in the current limitation year is the lesser of $140,000 (100 percent of P's compensation) or the dollar limitation of section 415(c)(1)(A) as in effect as of January 1 of the calendar year in which the current limitation year ends. If, for example, the dollar limitation of section 415(c)(1)(A) in effect as of January 1 of the calendar year in which the current limitation year ends is $45,000, then the maximum annual addition that can be allocated to P's account for the current limitation year is $45,000.

Example 3. (i) Employer N maintains a qualified profit-sharing plan that uses the calendar year as its plan year and its limitation year. N's taxable year is a fiscal year beginning June 1 and ending May 31. Under the terms of the profit-sharing plan maintained by N, employer contributions are made to the plan two months after the close of N's taxable year and are allocated as of the last day of the plan year ending within the taxable year (and are not dependent on the satisfaction of a condition). Thus, employer contributions for the 2008 calendar year limitation year are made on July 31, 2009 (the date that is two months after the close of N's taxable year ending May 31, 2009) and are allocated as of December 31, 2008.

(ii) Because the employer contributions are actually made to the plan no later than 30 days after the end of the period described in section 404(a)(6) with respect to N's taxable year ending May 31, 2009, the contributions will be considered annual additions for the 2008 calendar year limitation year.

Example 4. (i) The facts are the same as in *Example 3*, except that the plan year for the profit-sharing plan maintained by N is the 12-month period beginning on February 1 and ending on January 31. The limitation year continues to be the calendar year. Under the terms of the plan, an employer contribution which is made to the plan on July 31, 2009, is allocated to participants' accounts as of January 31, 2009.

(ii) Because the last day of the plan year is in the 2009 calendar year limitation year, and because, under the terms of the plan, employer contributions are allocated to participants' accounts as of the last day of the plan year, the contributions are considered annual additions for the 2009 calendar year limitation year.

Example 5. (i) XYZ Corporation maintains a profit-sharing plan to which a participant may make voluntary employee contributions for any year not to exceed 10 percent of the participant's compensation for the year. The plan permits a participant to make retroactive make-up contributions for any year for which the participant contributed less than 10 percent of compensation. XYZ uses the calendar year as the plan year and the limitation year. Under the terms of the plan, voluntary employee contributions are credited to a participant's account for a particular limitation year if such contributions are allocated to the participant's account as of any date within that limitation year. Participant A's compensation is as follows—

Limitation year	Compensation
2008	$30,000
2009	$32,000
2010	$34,000
2011	$36,000

(ii) Participant A makes no voluntary employee contributions during limitation years 2008, 2009, and 2010. On October 1, 2011, participant A makes a voluntary employee contribution of $13,200 (10 percent of A's aggregate compensation for limitation years 2008, 2009, 2010, and 2011 of $132,000). Under the terms of the plan, $3,000 of this 2011 contribution is allocated to A's account as of limitation year 2008; $3,200 is allocated to A's account of limitation year 2009; $3,400 is allocated to A's account as of limitation year 2010, and $3,600 is allocated to A's account as of limitation year 2011.

(iii) Under the rule set forth in paragraph (b)(6)(i)(C) of this section, employee contributions will not be considered credited to a participant's account for a particular limitation year for section 415 purposes unless the contributions are actually made to the plan no later than 30 days after the close of that limitation year. Thus, A's voluntary employee contribution of $13,200 made on October 1, 2011, would be considered as credited to A's account only for the 2011 calendar year limitation year, notwithstanding the plan provisions.

(d) *Special rules relating to church plans.*—(1) *Alternative contribution limitation.*—(i) *In general.*—Pursuant to section 415(c)(7)(A), notwithstanding the general rule of paragraph (a)(1) of this section, additions for a section 403(b) annuity contract for a year with respect to a participant who is an employee of a church or a convention or association of churches, including an organization described in section 414(e)(3)(B)(ii), when expressed as an annual addition to such participant's account, are treated as not exceeding the limitation of paragraph (a)(1) of this section if such annual additions for the year are not in excess of $10,000.

(ii) *$40,000 aggregate limitation.*—With respect to any participant, the total amount of annual additions that are in excess of the limitation of paragraph (a)(1) of this section but, pursuant to the rule of paragraph (d)(1)(i) of this section, are treated as not exceeding that limitation (taking into account the rule of paragraph (d)(3) of this section) cannot exceed $40,000. Thus, the aggregate of annual additions for all limitation years that would exceed the limitation of this section but for this paragraph (d)(1) is limited to $40,000.

(2) *Years of service taken into account for duly ordained, commissioned, or licensed ministers or lay employees.*—For purposes of this paragraph (d)—

(i) All years of service by an individual as an employee of a church, or a convention or association of churches, including an organization described in section 414(e)(3)(B)(ii), are considered as years of service for one employer; and

(ii) All amounts contributed for annuity contracts by each such church (or convention or association of churches) during such years for the employee are considered to have been contributed by one employer.

(3) *Foreign missionaries.*—Pursuant to section 415(c)(7)(C), in the case of any individual described in paragraph (d)(1) of this section performing any services for the church outside the United States during the limitation year, additions for an annuity contract under section 403(b) for any year are not treated as exceeding the limitation of paragraph (a)(1) of this section if such annual additions for the year do not exceed $3,000. The preceding sentence shall not apply with respect to any taxable year to any individual whose adjusted gross income for such taxable year (determined separately and without regard to community property law) exceeds $17,000.

(4) *Church, convention or association of churches.*—For purposes of this paragraph (d), the terms "church" and "convention or association of churches" have the same meaning as when used in section 414(e).

(5) *Examples.*—The following examples illustrate the rules of this paragraph (d):

Example 1. (i) E is an employee of ABC Church earning $7,000 during each calendar year. E participates in a section 403(b) annuity contract maintained by ABC Church beginning in the year 2008. E's taxable year is the calendar year, and the limitation year for the plan coincides with the calendar year. ABC Church contributes $10,000 to be allocated to E's account under the plan for the year 2008.

(ii) Under paragraph (d)(1) of this section, this allocation is treated as not violating the limits established in paragraph (a)(1) of this section because it does not exceed $10,000. Moreover, since an annual addition of $10,000 would otherwise exceed the limitation of paragraph (a)(1) of this section by $3,000, $3,000 is counted toward the aggregate limitation specified in paragraph (d)(1)(ii) of this section for year 2008. Accordingly, ABC Church may make such allocations for 13 years (for example, for years 2008 through 2020) without exceeding the aggregate limitation of $40,000 specified in paragraph (d) of this section. For the fourteenth year, ABC Church could allocate only $8,000 to E's account (the sum of the $7,000 limitation computed under paragraph (a)(1)(ii) of this section and the remaining $1,000 of the $40,000 aggregate limitation under paragraph (d)(1)(ii) of this section on annual additions in excess of the limits under paragraph (a)(1) of this section).

Example 2. (i) F is an employee of XYZ Church and F's taxable year is the calendar year. F earns $2,000 during each calendar year for services he provides to XYZ Church, all of which are performed outside the United States during each calendar year. F participates in a section 403(b) annuity contract maintained by ABC Church beginning in the year 2008. The limitation year for the plan coincides with the calendar year. ABC Church contributes $10,000 to be allocated to F's account under the plan for the year 2008. F's adjusted gross income for each taxable year (determined separately and without regard to community property law) does not exceed $17,000.

(ii) Under paragraph (d)(1) of this section, this allocation is treated as not violating the limits established in paragraph (a)(1) of this section because it does not exceed $10,000. Moreover, since an annual addition of $10,000 would otherwise exceed the limitation of paragraph (a)(1) of this section by $7,000 (the excess of $10,000 over the greater of the $2,000 compensation limitation under section 415(c)(1)(B) or the $3,000 section 415(c)(7)(C) amount), XYZ Church may make such allocations for 5 years (for example, for years 2008 through 2012) without exceeding the aggregate limitation of $40,000 specified in paragraph (d) of this section. In year 2013, XYZ church may contribute $8,000 to be allocated to F's account under the plan (the sum of the $3,000 limitation computed under paragraph (d)(3) of this section and the remaining $5,000 of the $40,000 aggregate limitation under paragraph (d)(1)(ii) of this section on annual additions in excess of the limits under paragraph (a)(1) of this section). For years after 2013, pursuant to paragraph (d)(3) of this section, XYZ Church could allocate $3,000 per year to F's account.

(e) *Special rules for medical benefits.*—The limit under paragraph (a)(1)(ii) of this section (100 percent of the participant's compensation for the limitation year) does not apply to—

(1) An individual medical benefit account (as defined in section 415(l)); or

(2) A post-retirement medical benefits account for a key employee (as defined in section 419A(d)(1)).

(f) *Special rules for employee stock ownership plans.*—(1) *In general.*—Special rules apply to employee stock ownership plans, as provided in paragraphs (f)(2) through (f)(4) of this section.

(2) *Determination of annual additions for leveraged employee stock ownership plans.*—(i) *In general.*—Except as provided in this paragraph (f) of this section, in the case of an employee stock ownership plan to which an exempt loan as described in § 54.4975-7(b) of this chapter has been made, the amount of employer contributions that is considered an annual addition for the limitation year is calculated with respect to employer contributions of both principal and interest used to repay that exempt loan for the limitation year.

(ii) *Employer stock that has decreased in value.*—A plan may provide that, in lieu of computing annual additions in accordance with paragraph (f)(2)(i) of this section, annual additions with respect to a loan repayment described in paragraph (f)(2)(i) of this section are determined as the fair market value of shares released from the suspense account on account of the repayment and allocated to participants for the limitation year if that amount is less than the amount determined in accordance with paragraph (f)(2)(i) of this section.

(3) *Exclusions from annual additions for certain employee stock ownership plans that allocate to a broad range of participants.*—(i) *General rule.*—Pursuant to section 415(c)(6), in the case of an employee stock ownership plan (as described in section 4975(e)(7)) that meets the requirements of paragraph (f)(3)(ii) of this section for a limitation year, the limitations imposed by this section do not apply to—

(A) Forfeitures of employer securities (within the meaning of section 409(l)) under such an employee stock ownership plan if such securities were acquired with the proceeds of a loan (as described in section 404(a)(9)(A)); or

(B) Employer contributions to such an employee stock ownership plan which are deductible under section 404(a)(9)(B) and charged against the participant's account.

(ii) *Employee stock ownership plans to which the special exclusion applies.*—An employee stock ownership plan meets the requirements of this paragraph (f)(3)(ii) for a limitation year if no more than one-third of the employer contributions for the limitation year that are deductible under section 404(a)(9) are allocated to highly compensated employees (within the meaning of section 414(q)).

(4) *Gratuitous transfers under section 664(g)(1).*—The amount of any qualified gratuitous transfer (as defined in section 664(g)(1)) allocated to a participant for any limitation year is not taken into account in determining whether any other annual addition exceeds the limitations imposed by this section, but only if the amount of the qualified gratuitous transfer does not exceed the limitations imposed by section 415. [Reg. § 1.415(c)-1.]

☐ [T.D. 9319, 4–4–2007.]

[Reg. § 1.415(c)-2]

§ 1.415(c)-2. Compensation.—(a) *General definition.*—Except as otherwise provided in this section, compensation from the employer within the meaning of section 415(c)(3), which is used for purposes of section 415 and regulations promulgated under section 415, means all items of remuneration described in paragraph (b) of this section, but excludes the items of remuneration described in paragraph (c) of this section. Paragraph (d) of this section provides safe harbor definitions of compensation that are permitted to be provided in a plan in lieu of the generally applicable definition of compensation. Paragraph (e) of this section provides timing rules relating to compensation. Paragraph (f) of this section provides rules regarding the application of the rules of section 401(a)(17) to the definition of compensation for purposes of section 415. Paragraph (g) of this section provides special rules relating to the determination of compensation, including rules for determining compensation for a section 403(b) annuity contract, rules for determining the compensation of employees of controlled groups or affiliated service groups, rules for disabled employees, rules relating to foreign compensation, rules regarding deemed section 125 compensation, rules for employees in qualified military service, and rules relating to back pay.

(b) *Items includible as compensation.*—For purposes of applying the limitations of section 415, except as otherwise provided in this section, the term *compensation* means remuneration for services of the following types—

(1) The employee's wages, salaries, fees for professional services, and other amounts received (without regard to whether or not an amount is paid in cash) for personal services actually rendered in the course of employment with the employer maintaining the plan, to the extent that the amounts are includible in gross income (or to the extent amounts would have been received and includible in gross income but for an election under section 125(a), 132(f)(4), 402(e)(3), 402(h)(1)(B), 402(k), or 457(b)). These amounts include, but are not limited to, commissions paid to salespersons, compensation for services on the basis of a percentage of profits, commissions on insurance premiums, tips, bonuses, fringe benefits, and reimbursements or other expense allowances under a nonaccountable plan as described in § 1.62-2(c).

(2) In the case of an employee who is an employee within the meaning of section 401(c)(1) and regulations promulgated under section 401(c)(1), the employee's earned income (as described in section 401(c)(2) and regulations promulgated under section 401(c)(2)), plus amounts deferred at the election of the employee that would be includible in gross income but for the rules of section 402(e)(3), 402(h)(1)(B), 402(k), or 457(b).

(3) Amounts described in section 104(a)(3), 105(a), or 105(h), but only to the extent that these amounts are includible in the gross income of the employee.

(4) Amounts paid or reimbursed by the employer for moving expenses incurred by an employee, but only to the extent that at the time of the payment it is reasonable to believe that these amounts are not deductible by the employee under section 217.

(5) The value of a nonstatutory option (which is an option other than a statutory option as defined in § 1.421-1(b)) granted to an employee by the employer, but only to the extent that the value of the option is includible in the gross income of the employee for the taxable year in which granted.

(6) The amount includible in the gross income of an employee upon making the election described in section 83(b).

(7) Amounts that are includible in the gross income of an employee under the rules of section 409A or section 457(f)(1)(A) or because the amounts are constructively received by the employee.

(c) *Items not includible as compensation.*—The term *compensation* does not include—

(1) Contributions (other than elective contributions described in section 402(e)(3), section 408(k)(6), section 408(p)(2)(A)(i), or section 457(b)) made by the employer to a plan of deferred compensation (including a simplified employee pension described in section 408(k) or a simple retirement account described in section 408(p), and whether or not qualified) to the extent that the contributions are not includible in the gross income of the employee for the taxable year in which contributed. In addition, any distributions from a plan of deferred compensation (whether or not qualified) are not considered as compensation for section 415 purposes, regardless of whether such amounts are includible in the gross income of the employee when distributed. However, if the plan so provides, any amounts received by an employee pursuant to a nonqualified unfunded deferred compensation plan are permitted to be considered as compensation for section 415 purposes in the year the amounts are actually received, but only to the extent such amounts are includible in the employee's gross income.

(2) Amounts realized from the exercise of a nonstatutory option (which is an option other than a statutory option as defined in § 1.421-1(b)), or when restricted stock or other property held by an employee either becomes freely transferable or is no longer subject to a substantial risk of forfeiture (see section 83 and regulations promulgated under section 83).

(3) Amounts realized from the sale, exchange, or other disposition of stock acquired under a statutory stock option (as defined in § 1.421-1(b)).

(4) Other amounts that receive special tax benefits, such as premiums for group-term life insurance (but only to the extent that the premiums are not includible in the gross income of the employee and are not salary reduction amounts that are described in section 125).

(5) Other items of remuneration that are similar to any of the items listed in paragraphs (c)(1) through (c)(4) of this section.

(d) *Safe harbor rules with respect to plan's definition of compensation.*—(1) *In general.*—Paragraphs (d)(2) through (4) of this section contain safe harbor definitions of compensation that are automatically considered to satisfy section 415(c)(3) if specified in the plan. The Commissioner may, in revenue rulings, notices, and other guidance of general applicability published in the Internal Revenue Bulletin (see § 601.601(d)(2) of this chapter), provide additional definitions of compensation that are treated as satisfying section 415(c)(3).

(2) *Simplified compensation.*—The safe harbor definition of compensation under this paragraph (d)(2) includes only those items specified in paragraph (b)(1) or (2) of this section and excludes all those items listed in paragraph (c) of this section.

(3) *Section 3401(a) wages.*—The safe harbor definition of compensation under this paragraph (d)(3) includes wages within the meaning of section 3401(a) (for purposes of income tax withholding at the source), plus amounts that would be included in wages but for an election under section 125(a), 132(f)(4), 402(e)(3), 402(h)(1)(B), 402(k), or 457(b). However, any rules that limit the remuneration included in wages based on the nature or location of the employment or the services performed (such as the exception for agricultural labor in section 3401(a)(2)) are disregarded for this purpose.

(4) *Information required to be reported under sections 6041, 6051 and 6052.*—The safe harbor definition of compensation under this paragraph (d)(4) includes amounts that are compensation under the safe harbor definition of paragraph (d)(3) of this section, plus all other payments of compensation to an employee by his employer (in the course of the employer's trade or business) for which the employer is required to furnish the employee a written statement under sections 6041(d), 6051(a)(3), and 6052. See §§ 1.6041-1(a), 1.6041-2(a)(1), 1.6052-1, and 1.6052-2, and also see § 31.6051-1(a)(1)(i)(C) of this chapter. This safe harbor definition of compensation may be modified to exclude amounts paid or reimbursed by the employer for moving expenses incurred by an employee, but only to the extent that, at the time of the payment, it is reasonable to believe that these amounts are deductible by the employee under section 217.

(e) *Timing rules.*—(1) *In general.*—(i) *Payment during the limitation year.*—Except as otherwise provided in this paragraph (e), in order to be taken into account for a limitation year, compensation within the meaning of section 415(c)(3) must be actually paid or made available to an employee (or, if earlier, includible in the gross income of the employee) within the limitation year. For this purpose, compensation is treated as paid on a date if it is actually paid on that date or it would have been paid on that date but for an election under section 125, 132(f)(4), 401(k), 403(b), 408(k), 408(p)(2)(A)(i), or 457(b).

(ii) *Payment prior to severance from employment.*—Except as otherwise provided in this paragraph (e), in order to be taken into account for a limitation year, compensation within the meaning of section 415(c)(3) must be paid or treated as paid to the employee (in accordance with the rules of paragraph (e)(1)(i) of this section) prior to the employee's severance from employment with the employer maintaining the plan See §1.415(a)-1(f)(5) for the definition of severance from employment.

(2) *Certain minor timing differences.*—Notwithstanding the provisions of paragraph (e)(1)(i) of this section, a plan may provide that compensation for a limitation year includes amounts earned during that limitation year but not paid during that limitation year solely because of the timing of pay periods and pay dates if—

(i) These amounts are paid during the first few weeks of the next limitation year;

(ii) The amounts are included on a uniform and consistent basis with respect to all similarly situated employees; and

(iii) No compensation is included in more than one limitation year.

(3) *Compensation paid after severance from employment.*—(i) *In general.*—Any compensation described in paragraph (e)(3)(ii) of this section does not fail to be compensation (within the meaning of section 415(c)(3)) pursuant to the rule of paragraph (e)(1)(ii) of this section merely because it is paid after the employee's severance from employment with the employer maintaining the plan, provided the compensation is paid by the later of 2 1/2 months after severance from employment with the employer maintaining the plan or the end of the limitation year that includes the date of severance from employment with the employer maintaining the plan. In addition, the plan may provide that amounts described in paragraph (e)(3)(iii) of this section are included in compensation (within the meaning of section 415(c)(3)) if—

(A) Those amounts are paid by the later of 2 1/2 months after severance from employment with the employer maintaining the plan or the end of the limitation year that includes the date of severance from employment with the employer maintaining the plan; and

(B) Those amounts would have been included in the definition of compensation if they were paid prior to the employee's severance from employment with the employer maintaining the plan.

(ii) *Regular pay after severance from employment.*—An amount is described in this paragraph (e)(3)(ii) if—

(A) The payment is regular compensation for services during the employee's regular working hours, or compensation for services outside the employee's regular working hours (such as overtime or shift differential), commissions, bonuses, or other similar payments; and

(B) The payment would have been paid to the employee prior to a severance from employment if the employee had continued in employment with the employer.

(iii) *Leave cashouts and deferred compensation.*—An amount is described in this paragraph (e)(3)(iii) if the amount is either—

(A) Payment for unused accrued bona fide sick, vacation, or other leave, but only if the employee would have been able to use the leave if employment had continued; or

(B) Received by an employee pursuant to a nonqualified unfunded deferred compensation plan, but only if the payment would have been paid to the employee at the same time if the employee had continued in employment with the employer and only to the extent that the payment is includible in the employee's gross income.

(iv) *Other post-severance payments.*—Any payment that is not described in paragraph (e)(3)(ii) or (iii) of this section is not considered compensation under paragraph (e)(3)(i) of this section if paid after severance from employment with the employer maintaining the plan, even if it is paid within the time period described in paragraph (e)(3)(i) of this section. Thus, compensation does not include severance pay, or parachute payments within the meaning of section 280G(b)(2), if they are paid after severance from employment with the employer maintaining the plan, and does not include post-severance payments under a nonqualified unfunded deferred compensation plan unless the payments would have been paid at that time without regard to the severance from employment.

(4) *Salary continuation payments for military service and disabled participants.*—The rule of paragraph (e)(1)(ii) of this section does not apply to payments to an individual who does not currently perform services for the employer by reason of qualified military service (as

that term is used in section 414(u)(1)) to the extent those payments do not exceed the amounts the individual would have received if the individual had continued to perform services for the employer rather than entering qualified military service, but only if the plan so provides. In addition, the rule of paragraph (e)(1)(ii) of this section does not apply to compensation paid to a participant who is permanently and totally disabled (as defined in section 22(e)(3)) if the conditions set forth in paragraph (g)(4)(ii)(A) of this section are satisfied (applied by substituting a continuation of compensation for the continuation of contributions), but only if the plan so provides.

(5) *Special rule for governmental plans.*—For purposes of applying the rules of paragraph (e)(3) of this section, a governmental plan (as defined in section 414(d)) may provide for the substitution of the calendar year in which the severance from employment with the employer maintaining the plan occurs for the limitation year in which the severance from employment with the employer maintaining the plan occurs.

(6) *Examples.*—The provisions of this paragraph (e) are illustrated by the following examples:

Example 1. (i) *Facts.* Participant A was a common law employee of Employer X, performing services as a script writer for Employer X from January 1, 2005 to December 31, 2005. Pursuant to a collective bargaining agreement, Employer X, Employer Y and Employer Z maintain and contribute to Plan T, a multiemployer plan (as defined in section 414(f)) in which Participant A participates. Under the collective bargaining agreement, Participant A is entitled to residual payments whenever television shows that Participant A wrote are reused commercially (These residual payments constitute compensation described in paragraph (b) of this section and do not constitute compensation described in paragraph (c) of this section.). In the year 2008, Participant A receives residual payments from Employer X for television programs using the scripts that Participant A wrote in the year 2005 that were rebroadcast in the year 2008. In the years 2006, 2007, and 2008, Participant A was a common law employee of Employer Y, and did not perform any services for Employer X.

(ii) *Conclusion.* The residual payments received from Employer X by Participant A in the year 2008 are compensation for purposes of section 415(c)(3). The payments are not treated as made after severance from employment because Plan T is a multiemployer plan (as defined in section 414(f)) and Participant A continues to be employed by an employer maintaining Plan T.

Example 2. (i) *Facts.* The facts are the same as in *Example 1,* except that Participant A: ceased employment with Employer Y in the year 2006; subsequently moved away from the area in which A formerly worked; performs no services as an employee for any employer; and commenced receiving distributions under Plan T in March, 2006.

(ii) *Conclusion.* Based on the facts and circumstances, A has ceased employment with any employer maintaining Plan T. Pursuant to paragraph (e)(1)(ii) of this section, compensation must be paid prior to an employee's severance from employment with the employer maintaining the plan. Accordingly, the residual payments received by Participant A in the year 2008 are not compensation for purposes of section 415(c)(3).

(f) *Interaction with section 401(a)(17).*—Because a plan may not base allocations (in the case of a defined contribution plan) or benefits (in the case of a defined benefit plan) on compensation in excess of the limitation under section 401(a)(17), a plan's definition of compensation for a year that is used for purposes of applying the limitations of section 415 is not permitted to reflect compensation for a year that is in excess of the limitation under section 401(a)(17) that applies to that year. See §§1.401(a)(17)-1(a)(3)(i) and 1.401(a)(17)-1(b)(3)(ii) for rules regarding the effective date of increases in the section 401(a)(17) compensation limitation for a plan year and for a 12-month period other than the plan year.

(g) *Special rules.*—(1) *Compensation for section 403(b) annuity contract.*—In the case of an annuity contract described in section 403(b), the term *participant's compensation* means the participant's includible compensation determined under section 403(b)(3). Accordingly, the rules for determining a participant's compensation pursuant to section 415(c)(3) (other than section 415(c)(3)(E)) and this section do not apply to a section 403(b) annuity contract.

(2) *Employees of controlled groups of corporations, etc.*—In the case of an employee of two or more corporations which are members of a controlled group of corporations (as defined in section 414(b) as modified by section 415(h)), the term *compensation* for such employee includes compensation from all employers that are members of the group, regardless of whether the employee's particular employer has a qualified plan. This special rule is also applicable to an employee of two or more trades or businesses (whether or not incorporated) that are under common control (as defined in section 414(c) as modified by section 415(h)), to an employee of two or more members of an

affiliated service group as defined in section 414(m), and to an employee of two or more members of any group of employers who must be aggregated and treated as one employer pursuant to section 414(o).

(3) *Aggregation of section 403(b) annuity with qualified plan of controlled employer.*—If a section 403(b) annuity contract is aggregated with a qualified plan of a controlled employer in accordance with §1.415(f)-1(f)(2), then, in applying the limitations of section 415(c) in connection with the aggregation of the section 403(b) annuity with a qualified plan, the total compensation from both employers is permitted to be taken into account.

(4) *Permanent and total disability of defined contribution plan participant.*—(i) *In general.*—Pursuant to section 415(c)(3)(C), if the conditions set forth in paragraph (g)(4)(ii) of this section are satisfied, then, in the case of a participant in any defined contribution plan who is permanently and totally disabled (as defined in section 22(e)(3)), the *participant's compensation* means the compensation the participant would have received for the year if the participant was paid at the rate of compensation paid immediately before becoming permanently and totally disabled, if such compensation is greater than the participant's compensation determined without regard to this paragraph (g)(4).

(ii) *Conditions for deemed disability compensation.*—The rule of paragraph (g)(4)(i) of this section applies only if the following conditions are satisfied—

(A) Either the participant is not a highly compensated employee (as defined in section 414(q)) immediately before becoming disabled, or the plan provides for the continuation of contributions on behalf of all participants who are permanently and totally disabled for a fixed or determinable period;

(B) The plan provides that the rule of this paragraph (g)(4) (treating certain amounts as compensation for a disabled participant) applies with respect to the participant; and

(C) Contributions made with respect to amounts treated as compensation under this paragraph (g)(4) are nonforfeitable when made.

(5) *Foreign compensation, etc.*—(i) *In general.*—Amounts paid to an individual as compensation for services do not fail to be treated as compensation under paragraphs (b)(1) and (2) of this section (and are not excluded from the definition of compensation pursuant to paragraph (c)(4) of this section) merely because those amounts are not includible in the individual's gross income on account of the location of the services. Similarly, compensation for services do not fail to be treated as compensation under paragraphs (b)(1) and (2) of this section (and are not excluded from the definition of compensation pursuant to paragraph (c)(4) of this section) merely because those amounts are paid by an employer with respect to which all compensation paid to the participant by such employer is excluded from gross income. Thus, for example, the determination of whether an amount is treated as compensation under paragraph (b)(1) or (2) of this section is made without regard to the exclusions from gross income under sections 872, 893, 894, 911, 931, and 933.

(ii) *Exclusion of non-participant compensation by the plan.*—With respect to a nonresident alien who is not a participant in a plan, the plan may provide that the compensation described in paragraph (g)(5)(i) of this section is not treated as compensation for purposes of paragraphs (b)(1) and (b)(2) of this section to the extent the compensation is excludable from gross income and is not effectively connected with the conduct of a trade or business within the United States, but only if the plan applies this rule uniformly to all such employees. For purposes of this paragraph (g)(5)(ii), nonresident alien has the same meaning as in section 7701(b)(1)(B).

(6) *Deemed section 125 compensation.*—(i) *General rule.*—A plan is permitted to provide that deemed section 125 compensation (as defined in paragraph (g)(6)(ii) of this section) is compensation within the meaning of section 415(c)(3), but only if the plan applies this rule uniformly to all employees with respect to whom amounts subject to section 125 are included in compensation.

(ii) *Definition of deemed section 125 compensation.*—Deemed section 125 compensation is an amount that is excludable from the income of the participant under section 106 that is not available to the participant in cash in lieu of group health coverage under a section 125 arrangement solely because that participant is not able to certify that the participant has other health coverage. Under this definition, amounts are deemed section 125 compensation only if the employer does not otherwise request or collect information regarding the participant's other health coverage as part of the enrollment process for the health plan.

(7) *Employees in qualified military service.*—See section 414(u)(7) for special rules regarding compensation of employees who are in qualified military service within the meaning of section 414(u)(5).

(8) *Back pay.*—Payments awarded by an administrative agency or court or pursuant to a bona fide agreement by an employer to compensate an employee for lost wages are compensation within the meaning of section 415(c)(3) for the limitation year to which the back pay relates, but only to the extent such payments represent wages and compensation that would otherwise be included in compensation under this section. [Reg. §1.415(c)-2.]

☐ [*T.D.* 9319, 4–4–2007.]

[Reg. §1.415(d)-1]

§1.415(d)-1. Cost-of-living adjustments.—(a) *Defined benefit plans.*—(1) *Dollar limitation.*—(i) *Determination of adjusted limit.*—Under section 415(d)(1)(A), the dollar limitation described in section 415(b)(1)(A) applicable to defined benefit plans is adjusted annually to take into account increases in the cost of living. The adjustment of the dollar limitation is made by multiplying the adjustment factor for the year, as described in paragraph (a)(1)(ii)(A) of this section, by $160,000, and rounding the result in accordance with paragraph (a)(1)(iii) of this section. The adjusted dollar limitation is prescribed by the Commissioner and published in the Internal Revenue Bulletin. See §601.601(d)(2) of this chapter.

(ii) *Determination of adjustment factor.*—(A) *Adjustment factor.*—The adjustment factor for a calendar year is equal to a fraction, the numerator of which is the value of the applicable index for the calendar quarter ending September 30 of the preceding calendar year, and the denominator of which is the value of such index for the base period. The applicable index is determined consistent with the procedures used to adjust benefit amounts under section 215(i)(2)(A) of the Social Security Act, Public Law 92-336 (86 Stat. 406), as amended. If, however, the value of that fraction is less than one for a calendar year, then the adjustment factor for the calendar year is equal to one.

(B) *Base period.*—For the purpose of adjusting the dollar limitation pursuant to paragraph (a)(1)(ii)(A) of this section, the base period is the calendar quarter beginning July 1, 2001.

(iii) *Rounding.*—Any increase in the $160,000 amount specified in section 415(b)(1)(A) which is not a multiple of $5,000 is rounded to the next lowest multiple of $5,000.

(2) *Average compensation for high-3 years of service limitation.*—(i) *Determination of adjusted limit.*—Under section 415(d)(1)(B), with regard to participants who have had a severance from employment with the employer maintaining the plan, the compensation limitation described in section 415(b)(1)(B) is permitted to be adjusted annually to take into account increases in the cost of living. For any limitation year beginning after the severance occurs, the adjustment of the compensation limitation is made by multiplying the annual adjustment factor (as defined in paragraph (a)(2)(ii) of this section) by the compensation limitation applicable to the participant in the prior limitation year. The annual adjustment factor is prescribed by the Commissioner and published in the Internal Revenue Bulletin. See §601.601(d)(2) of this chapter.

(ii) *Annual adjustment factor.*—The annual adjustment factor for a calendar year is equal to a fraction, the numerator of which is the value of the applicable index for the calendar quarter ending September 30 of the preceding calendar year, and the denominator of which is the value of such index for the calendar quarter ending September 30 of the calendar year prior to that preceding calendar year. The applicable index is determined consistent with the procedures used to adjust benefit amounts under section 215(i)(2)(A) of the Social Security Act. If the value of the fraction described in the first sentence of this paragraph (a)(2)(ii) is less than one for a calendar year, then the adjustment factor for the calendar year is equal to one. In such a case, the annual adjustment factor for future calendar years will be determined in accordance with revenue rulings, notices, or other published guidance prescribed by the Commissioner and published in the Internal Revenue Bulletin. See §601.601(d)(2) of this chapter.

(iii) *Special rule for rehired employees.*—If, after having a severance from employment with the employer maintaining the plan, an employee is rehired by the employer maintaining the plan, the employee's compensation limit under section 415(b)(1)(B) is the greater of—

(A) 100 percent of the participant's average compensation for the period of the participant's high-3 years of service, as determined prior to the employee's severance from employment with the employer maintaining the plan, as adjusted pursuant to paragraph (a)(2)(i) of this section (if the plan so provides); or

(B) 100 percent of the participant's average compensation for the period of the participant's high-3 years of service, with the period of the participant's high-3 years of service determined pursuant to § 1.415(b)-1(a)(5)(iii).

(3) *Effective date of adjustment.*—The adjusted dollar limitation applicable to defined benefit plans and the adjusted compensation limit applicable to a participant are effective as of January 1 of each calendar year and apply with respect to limitation years ending with or within that calendar year. However, benefit payments (and, in the case of plans that are subject to the requirements of section 411, accrued benefits for a limitation year) cannot exceed the currently applicable dollar limitation or compensation limitation (as in effect before the January 1 adjustment) prior to January 1. Thus, where there is an increase in the limitation under section 415(b)(1), any increase in a participant's benefits associated with the limitation increase is permitted to occur as of a date no earlier than January 1 of the calendar year for which the increase in the limitation is effective, and can only be applied for payments due on or after January 1 of such calendar year. For example, assume that a participant in a defined benefit plan is currently receiving a benefit in the form of a straight life annuity, payable monthly, in an amount equal to the section 415(b)(1)(A) dollar limit, and the defined benefit plan has a limitation year that runs from July 1 to June 30. If the plan is amended to reflect the section 415(d) increase to the section 415(b)(1)(A) dollar limit that is effective as of January 1, 2009, the associated increase in the participant's monthly benefit payments is only effective for payments due on or after January 1, 2009, and the participant's benefit cannot be increased to reflect the section 415(d) increase that is effective January 1, 2009, with respect to any monthly payment due prior to January 1, 2009.

(4) *Application of adjusted figure.*—(i) *In general.*—If the dollar limitation of section 415(b)(1)(A) or the compensation limitation of section 415(b)(1)(B) is adjusted pursuant to section 415(d) for a limitation year, the adjustment is applied as provided in this paragraph (a)(4).

(ii) *Application of adjusted limitations to benefits that have not commenced.*—An adjustment to the dollar limitation of section 415(b)(1)(A) is permitted to be applied to a participant who has not commenced benefits before the date on which the adjustment is effective. Annual adjustments to the compensation limit of section 415(b)(1)(B) as described in paragraph (a)(2) of this section are permitted to be made for all limitation years that begin after the participant's severance from employment, and apply to distributions that commence after the effective dates of such adjustments. However, no adjustment to the compensation limit of section 415(b)(1)(B) is made for any limitation year that begins on or before the date of the participant's severance from employment with the employer maintaining the plan.

(iii) *Application of adjusted dollar limitation to remaining payments under benefits that have commenced.*—With respect to a distribution of accrued benefits that commenced before the date on which an adjustment to the section 415(b)(1)(A) dollar limitation is effective, a plan is permitted to apply the adjusted limitations to that distribution, but only to the extent that benefits have not been paid. Thus, for example, a plan cannot provide that the adjusted dollar limitation applies to a participant who has previously received the entire plan benefit in a single-sum distribution. However, a plan can provide for an increase in benefits to a participant who accrues additional benefits under the plan that could have been accrued without regard to the adjustment of the dollar limitation (including benefits that accrue as a result of a plan amendment) on or after the effective date of the adjusted limitation.

(iv) *Manner of adjustment for benefits that have commenced.*—If a plan is amended to increase benefits payable under the plan in accordance with paragraphs (a)(5) or (a)(6) of this section (or the plan is treated as applying paragraph (a)(5) of this section because the plan incorporates the section 415(d) cost-of-living adjustments automatically by reference pursuant to § 1.415(a)-1(d)(3)(v)), or if benefits payable under the plan are increased pursuant to a form of benefit that is described in § 1.415(b)-1(c)(5), then the distribution as increased will be treated as continuing to satisfy the requirements of section 415(b). If benefits payable under a plan are increased in a manner other than as described in the preceding sentence, the plan must satisfy the requirements of § 1.415(b)-1(b)(1)(iii), treating the commencement of the additional benefit as the commencement of a new distribution that gives rise to a new annuity starting date.

(5) *Safe harbor for annual adjustments to distributions.*—An amendment to a plan to incorporate adjustments to the section 415(b) limits that increases a distribution that has previously commenced is described in this paragraph (a)(5) if—

(i) The employee has received one or more distributions that satisfy the requirements of section 415(b) before the date the adjustment to the applicable limits is effective (as determined under paragraph (a)(3) of this section);

(ii) The increased distribution is solely as a result of the amendment of the plan to reflect the adjustment to the applicable limits pursuant to section 415(d); and

(iii) The amounts payable to the employee on and after the effective date of the adjustment (as determined under paragraph (a)(3) of this section) are not greater than the amounts that would otherwise be payable without regard to the adjustment, multiplied by a fraction determined for the limitation year, the numerator of which is the limitation under section 415(b) (which is the lesser of the applicable dollar limitation under section 415(b)(1)(A), as adjusted for age at commencement, and the applicable compensation-based limitation under section 415(b)(1)(B)) in effect with respect to the distribution taking into account the section 415(d) adjustment, and the denominator of which is the limitation under section 415(b) in effect for the distribution immediately before the adjustment.

(6) *Safe harbor for periodic adjustments to distributions.*—(i) *General rule.*—An amendment to a plan that increases a distribution that has previously commenced is made using the safe harbor methodology of this paragraph (a)(6) if—

(A) The employee has received one or more distributions that satisfy the requirements of section 415(b) before the date on which the increase is effective; and

(B) The amounts payable to the employee on and after the effective date of the increase are not greater than the amounts that would otherwise be payable without regard to the increase, multiplied by the cumulative adjustment fraction.

(ii) *Cumulative adjustment fraction.*—The cumulative adjustment fraction for purposes of this paragraph (a)(6) is equal to the product of all of the fractions described in paragraph (a)(5)(iii) of this section that would have applied after benefits commence if the plan had been amended each year to incorporate the section 415(d) adjustments to the applicable section 415(b) limits and had otherwise satisfied the safe harbor methodology described in paragraph (a)(5) of this section. For purposes of the preceding sentence, if for the limitation year for which the increase to the section 415(b)(1)(A) dollar limitation pursuant to section 611(a)(1)(A) of the Economic Growth and Tax Relief Reconciliation Act of 2001 (115 Stat. 38), Public Law 107-16 (EGTRRA), is first effective (generally, the first limitation year beginning after December 31, 2001), the section 415(b)(1)(A) dollar limit applicable to a participant is less than the section 415(b)(1)(B) compensation limit for the participant, then the fraction described in paragraph (a)(5)(iii) of this section for that limitation year is 1.0.

(7) *Examples.*—The following examples illustrate the application of this paragraph (a):

Example 1. (i) X is a participant in a qualified defined benefit plan maintained by X's employer. The plan has a calendar year limitation year. Under the terms of the plan, X is entitled to a benefit consisting of a straight life annuity equal to 100 percent of X's average compensation for the period of X's high-3 years of service. X's average compensation for the period of X's high-3 years of service is $50,000. X incurs a severance from employment with the employer maintaining the plan on October 3, 2007, at age 65 with a nonforfeitable right to the accrued benefit after more than 10 years of participation in the plan. X begins to receive annual benefit payments (payable monthly) of $50,000, commencing on November 1, 2007. The dollar limitation for the 2007 limitation year (as adjusted pursuant to section 415(d)) is $180,000. Assume that the dollar limitation for the 2008 limitation year (as adjusted pursuant to section 415(d)) is $185,000 and the annual adjustment factor for adjusting the compensation limitation of section 415(b)(1)(B) for the 2008 limitation year is 1.0334. Effective January 1, 2008, the plan is amended to incorporate these adjustments to the dollar and compensation limitations, and accordingly, X's annual benefit payment is increased, effective for payments due on or after January 1, 2008. Prior to the plan amendment incorporating the application of the adjusted dollar and compensation limitations, X has received one or more distributions that satisfy the requirements of section 415(b). In addition, the adjustment to X's annual benefit payments is solely on account of the plan amendment incorporating the adjusted limitations.

(ii) For the limitation year beginning January 1, 2008, the dollar limit applicable to X under section 415(b)(1)(A) is $185,000, and the compensation limit applicable to X under section 415(b)(1)(B) is $51,670 ($50,000 multiplied by the annual adjustment factor of 1.0334). Accordingly, the adjustment to X's benefit satisfies the safe harbor for cost-of-living adjustments under paragraph (a)(5) of this section if, after the adjustment, X's benefit payable in the 2008 limitation year is no greater than $50,000 multiplied by $51,670 (X's section 415(b) limitation for 2008)/$50,000 (X's section 415(b) limitation for 2007).

Example 2. (i) The facts are the same as in *Example 1*, except that X's average compensation for the period of X's high-3 consecutive years of service is $200,000. Consequently, X's annual benefit payments commencing on November 1, 2007, are limited to $180,000.

(ii) For the limitation year beginning January 1, 2008, the dollar limit applicable to X under section 415(b)(1)(A) is $185,000, and the compensation limit applicable to X under section 415(b)(1)(B) is $206,680 ($200,000 multiplied by the annual adjustment factor of 1.0334). Accordingly, the adjustment to X's benefit satisfies the safe harbor for cost-of-living adjustments under paragraph (a)(5) of this section if, after the adjustment, X's benefit payable in 2008 is no greater than $180,000 multiplied by $185,000 (X's section 415(b) limitation for 2008)/$180,000 (X's section 415(b) limitation for 2007).

Example 3. (i) X is a participant in Plan T, a qualified defined benefit plan maintained by X's employer. In the year 2008, X receives a single-sum distribution of X's entire accrued benefit under the plan. At the time that X receives the single-sum distribution, X's accrued benefit under Plan T is limited by the section 415(b)(1)(A) age-adjusted dollar limit. X accrues no further benefits under Plan T after X receives the single-sum distribution. In the 2009 limitation year, pursuant to section 415(d) and §1.415(d)-1, the section 415(b)(1)(A) dollar limit is increased.

(ii) In the 2009 limitation year, Plan T may not provide additional benefits to X on account of the increase in the section 415(b)(1)(A) dollar limit pursuant to section 415(d) and §1.415(d)-1.

Example 4. (i) X is a participant in Plan T, a qualified defined benefit plan maintained by X's employer, Employer S. Plan T has a calendar limitation year. In 2008, X incurs a severance from employment with Employer S and X commences receiving distributions from Plan T in the form of a single life annuity in an annual amount of $30,000. At the time that X commences receiving distributions from Plan T, X's accrued benefit under Plan T is limited by the section 415(b)(1)(B) compensation limit. In 2009, the annual adjustment factor described in paragraph (a)(2) of this section (which is the factor for adjusting the compensation limit described in section 415(b)(1)(B)) is 1.03. Employer S amends Plan T, effective as of January 1, 2009, to increase the annual benefit of all participants who, prior to January 1, 2009, incurred a severance from employment with Employer S and who have commenced receiving benefits from Plan T by a factor of 1.015. Assume that for limitation years prior to 2009, X's distributions from Plan T satisfy the requirements of section 415(b).

(ii) The increase in X's annual benefit pursuant to the amendment effective January 1, 2009, is within the safe harbor described in paragraph (a)(6) of this section. This is because the amount payable to X under Plan T for the 2009 limitation year and limitation years thereafter (as increased by the amendment effective January 1, 2009) is not greater than the product of the amount payable to X under Plan T for such limitation years (as determined without regard to the amendment increasing X's benefit effective January 1, 2009) and the cumulative adjustment fraction (which, in X's case, is 1.03). Thus, X's annual benefit, as increased by the amendment, is not determined pursuant to the rules of §1.415(b)-1(b)(1)(iii).

Example 5. (i) Participant P participated in Plan A, maintained by Employer M, for more than 10 years. Plan A uses a calendar year limitation year and Plan A automatically adjusts a participant's section 415(b)(1)(B) compensation limit for limitation years after the limitation year in which the participant incurs a severance from employment as described in §1.415(a)-1(d)(3)(v). Prior to separating from employment with M in 2010, P's average compensation for P's period of high-3 years while a participant in Plan A is $50,000, based on P's compensation for 2007, 2008, and 2009, which was $50,000 for each year. P's compensation for year 2010 was $45,000. In year 2012, P is rehired by M and resumes participation in Plan A. P's compensation in year 2012 is $45,000, and is $70,000 in year 2013. Assume that the annual adjustment factor described in §1.415(d)-1(a)(2)(ii) for the limitation years 2011 through 2013 is 1.03 for each year. Thus, disregarding P's rehire by M, P's average compensation for P's period of high-3 years while a participant in Plan A for the 2013 limitation year *would be equal to* $54,636 (or 1.03 * 1.03 * 1.03 * $50,000). See §1.415(b)-1(a)(5)(iii).

(ii) Under §1.415(d)-1(a)(2)(iii), P's average compensation for P's period of high-3 years while a participant in Plan A for the 2013 limitation year is $54,636.

(b) *Defined contribution plans.*—(1) *In general.*—Under section 415(d)(1)(C), the dollar limitation described in section 415(c)(1)(A) is adjusted annually to take into account increases in the cost of living. The adjusted dollar limitation is prescribed by the Commissioner and published in the Internal Revenue Bulletin. See §601.601(d)(2) of this chapter.

(2) *Determination of adjusted limit.*—(i) *Base period.*—The base period taken into account for purposes of adjusting the dollar limitation pursuant to paragraph (b)(2)(ii) of this section is the calendar quarter beginning July 1, 2001.

(ii) *Method of adjustment.*—(A) *In general.*—The dollar limitation is adjusted with respect to a calendar year based on the increase in the applicable index for the calendar quarter ending September 30 of the preceding calendar year over such index for the base period. Adjustment procedures similar to the procedures used to adjust benefit amounts under section 215(i)(2)(A) of the Social Security Act will be used.

(B) *Rounding.*—Any increase in the $40,000 amount specified in section 415(c)(1)(A) which is not a multiple of $1,000 shall be rounded to the next lowest multiple of $1,000.

(iii) *Effective date of adjustment.*—The adjusted dollar limitation applicable to defined contribution plans is effective as of January 1 of each calendar year and applies with respect to limitation years ending with or within that calendar year. Annual additions for a limitation year cannot exceed the currently applicable dollar limitation (as in effect before the January 1 adjustment) prior to January 1. However, after a January 1 adjustment is made, annual additions for the entire limitation year are permitted to reflect the dollar limitation as adjusted on January 1.

(c) *Application of rounding rules to other cost-of-living adjustments.*—Pursuant to section 415(d)(4)(A), the $5,000 rounding methodology of paragraph (a)(1)(iii) of this section is used for purposes of any provision of chapter 1 of subtitle A of the Internal Revenue Code that provides for adjustments in accordance with section 415(d), except to the extent provided by that provision. Thus, the $5,000 rounding methodology of paragraph (a)(1)(iii) of this section is used for purposes of—

(1) Determining the level of compensation specified in section 414(q)(1)(B) that is used to determine whether an employee is a highly compensated employee;

(2) Calculating the amounts used pursuant to section 409(o)(1)(C) to determine the maximum period over which distributions from an employee stock ownership plan may be made without participant consent; and

(3) Determining the levels of compensation specified in §1.61-21(f)(5)(i) and (iii) used in determining whether an employee is a control employee of a nongovernmental employer for purposes of the commuting valuation rule of §1.61-21(f).

(d) *Implementation of cost-of-living adjustments.*—A plan is permitted to be amended to reflect any of the adjustments described in this section at any time after those limitations become applicable. Alternatively, a plan is permitted to incorporate by reference any of the adjustments described in this section in accordance with the rules of §1.415(a)-1(d)(3)(v). Because the accrued benefit of a participant can reflect increases in the applicable limitations only after those increases become effective, a pattern of repeated plan amendments increasing annual benefits to reflect the increases in the section 415(b) limitations pursuant to section 415(d) does not result in any protection under section 411(d)(6) for future increases to reflect increases in the section 415(b) limitations pursuant to §1.411(d)-4, Q&A-1(c)(1). Thus, a plan does not violate the requirements of section 411(d)(6) merely because the plan has been amended annually for a number of years to increase annual benefits to reflect the increases in the section 415(b) limitations pursuant to section 415(d) and subsequently is not amended to reflect later increases in the section 415(b) limitations. [Reg. §1.415(d)-1.]

☐ [*T.D.* 9319, 4-4-2007 (*corrected* 5-22-2007).]

[Reg. §1.415(f)-1]

§1.415(f)-1. Aggregating plans.—(a) *In general.*—Except as provided in paragraph (g) of this section (regarding multiemployer plans), and taking into account the rules of paragraph (b)(2) (regarding the break-up of affiliated employers and affiliated service groups), paragraph (c) (regarding predecessor employers), and paragraph (d)(1) (regarding nonduplication rules) of this section, section 415(f) and this section require that for purposes of applying the limitations of sections 415(b) and (c) applicable to a participant for a particular limitation year—

(1) All defined benefit plans (without regard to whether a plan has been terminated) ever maintained by the employer (or a predecessor employer within the meaning of paragraphs (c)(1) and (c)(2) of this section) under which the participant has accrued a benefit are treated as one defined benefit plan;

(2) All defined contribution plans (without regard to whether a plan has been terminated) ever maintained by the employer (or a predecessor employer within the meaning of paragraphs (c)(1) and

(c)(2) of this section) under which the participant receives annual additions are treated as one defined contribution plan; and

(3) All section 403(b) annuity contracts purchased by an employer (including plans purchased through salary reduction contributions) for the participant are treated as one section 403(b) annuity contract.

(b) *Affiliated employers, affiliated service groups, and leased employees.*—(1) *General rule.*—See § 1.415(a)-1(f)(1) and (2) for rules regarding aggregation of employers in the case of affiliated employers and affiliated service groups. See § 1.415(a)-1(f)(3) for rules regarding the treatment of leased employees.

(2) *Special rule in the case of the break-up of an affiliated employer or an affiliated service group.*—(i) *In general.*—A formerly affiliated plan of an employer is taken into account for purposes of applying paragraph (a) of this section to the employer, but the formerly affiliated plan is treated as if it had terminated immediately prior to the cessation of affiliation with sufficient assets to pay benefit liabilities under the plan, and had purchased annuities to provide plan benefits. See § 1.415(b)-1(b)(5)(i) for rules determining annual benefits under a terminated defined benefit plan under which annuities are purchased to provide plan benefits.

(ii) *Definitions.*—For purposes of this paragraph (b)(2), a *formerly affiliated plan of an employer* is a plan that, immediately prior to the cessation of affiliation, was actually maintained by one or more of the entities that constitute the employer (as determined under the employer affiliation rules described in § 1.415(a)-1(f)(1) and (2)), and immediately after the cessation of affiliation, is not actually maintained by any of the entities that constitute the employer (as determined under the employer affiliation rules described in § 1.415(a)-1(f)(1) and (2)). For purposes of this paragraph (b)(2), a *cessation of affiliation* means the event that causes an entity to no longer be aggregated with one or more other entities as a single employer under the employer affiliation rules described in § 1.415(a)-1(f)(1) and (2) (such as the sale of a subsidiary outside a controlled group), or that causes a plan to not actually be maintained by any of the entities that constitute the employer under the employer affiliation rules of § 1.415(a)-1(f)(1) and (2) (such as a transfer of plan sponsorship outside of a controlled group).

(c) *Predecessor employer.*—(1) *Where plan is maintained by successor.*—For purposes of section 415 and regulations promulgated under section 415, a former employer is a predecessor employer with respect to a participant in a plan maintained by an employer if the employer maintains a plan under which the participant had accrued a benefit while performing services for the former employer (for example, the employer assumed sponsorship of the former employer's plan, or the employer's plan received a transfer of benefits from the former employer's plan), but only if that benefit is provided under the plan maintained by the employer. In such a case, in applying the limitations of section 415 to a participant in a plan maintained by the employer, paragraph (a) of this section requires the plan to take into account benefits provided to the participant under plans that are maintained by the predecessor employer and that are not maintained by the employer. For this purpose, the formerly affiliated plan rules in paragraph (b)(2) of this section apply as if the employer and predecessor employer constituted a single employer under the rules described in § 1.415(a)-1(f)(1) and (2) immediately prior to the cessation of affiliation (and as if they constituted two, unrelated employers under the rules described in § 1.415(a)-1(f)(1) and (2) immediately after the cessation of affiliation) and cessation of affiliation was the event that gives rise to the predecessor employer relationship, such as a transfer of benefits or plan sponsorship.

(2) *Where plan is not maintained by successor.*—With respect to an employer of a participant, a former entity that antedates the employer is a predecessor employer with respect to the participant if, under the facts and circumstances, the employer constitutes a continuation of all or a portion of the trade or business of the former entity. This will occur, for example, where formation of the employer constitutes a mere formal or technical change in the employment relationship and continuity otherwise exists in the substance and administration of the business operations of the former entity and the employer.

(d) *Special rules.*—(1) *Nonduplication.*—In applying the limitations of section 415 to a plan maintained by an employer, if the plan is aggregated with another plan pursuant to the aggregation rules of paragraph (a) of this section, a participant's benefits are not counted more than once in determining the participant's aggregate annual benefit or annual additions. For example, if a defined benefit plan is treated as if it terminated immediately prior to a cessation of affiliation under paragraph (b)(2) of this section, the plans maintained by the employer (as determined after the cessation of affiliation) that

actually maintains the plan do not double count the annual benefit provided under the plan by aggregating under paragraph (a) of this section both the participant's annual benefit provided under the plan and the participant's annual benefit under the plan as a formerly affiliated plan (which is a plan that the employers formerly affiliated with the employer must take into account as a terminated plan under the rules of paragraph (b)(2) of this section). Instead, the plans maintained by the employer include the annual benefit provided to the participant under the actual plan that the employer maintains. Similarly, if a defined benefit plan maintained by an employer (the transferee plan) receives a transfer of benefits from a defined benefit plan maintained by a predecessor employer (the transferor plan) and the transfer is described in § 1.415(b)-1(b)(3)(i)(B) (which requires the transferred benefits to be treated by the transferor plan as if the benefits were provided under a plan that must be aggregated with the transferor plan that terminated immediately prior to the transfer), the transferee plan does not double count the transferred benefits under paragraph (a) of this section by taking into account both the actual benefit provided under the transferee plan and the benefit provided under the deemed terminated plan that the predecessor employer is treated as maintaining (and that otherwise would have to be taken into account by the transferee plan under the predecessor employer aggregation rules of paragraph (a) of this section). Instead, the transferee plan takes into account the transferred benefits that are actually provided under the transferee plan (see § 1.415(b)-1(b)(3)(i)(C)) and, pursuant to paragraph (c)(1) of this section, any nontransferred benefits provided under plans maintained by the predecessor employer with respect to a participant whose benefits have been transferred to the transferee plan.

(2) *Determination of years of participation for multiple plans.*—If two or more defined benefit plans are aggregated under section 415(f) and this section for a particular limitation year, in applying the reduction for participation of less than ten years (as described in section 415(b)(5)(A)) to the dollar limitation under section 415(b)(1)(A), time periods that are counted as years of participation under any of the plans are counted in computing the limitation of the aggregated plans under this section.

(3) *Determination of years of service for multiple plans.*—If two or more defined benefit plans are aggregated under section 415(f) and this section for a particular limitation year, in applying the reduction for service of less than ten years (as described in section 415(b)(5)(B)) to the compensation limitation under section 415(b)(1)(B), time periods that are counted as years of service under any of the plans are counted in computing the limitation of the aggregated plans under this section.

(e) *Previously unaggregated plans.*—(1) *In general.*—This paragraph (e) provides rules for those situations in which two or more existing plans, which previously were not required to be aggregated pursuant to section 415(f) and this section, are aggregated during a particular limitation year and, as a result, the limitations of section 415(b) or (c) are exceeded for that limitation year. Paragraph (e)(2) of this section provides rules for defined contribution plans that are first required to be aggregated pursuant to section 415(f) and this section in a plan year. Paragraph (e)(3) of this section provides rules for defined benefit plans that are first required to be aggregated pursuant to section 415(f) and this section, and for defined benefit plans under which a participant's benefit is frozen following aggregation.

(2) *Defined contribution plans.*—Two or more defined contribution plans that are not required to be aggregated pursuant to section 415(f) and this section as of the first day of a limitation year do not fail to satisfy the requirements of section 415 with respect to a participant for the limitation year merely because they are aggregated later in that limitation year, provided that no annual additions are credited to the participant's account after the date on which the plans are required to be aggregated.

(3) *Defined benefit plans.*—(i) *First year of aggregation.*—Two or more defined benefit plans that are not required to be aggregated pursuant to section 415(f) and this section as of the first day of a limitation year do not fail to satisfy the requirements of section 415 for the limitation year merely because they are aggregated later in that limitation year, provided that no plan amendments increasing benefits with respect to the participant under either plan are made after the occurrence of the event causing the plan to be aggregated.

(ii) *All years of aggregation in which accrued benefits are frozen.*—Two or more defined benefit plans that are required to be aggregated pursuant to section 415(f) and this section during a limitation year subsequent to the limitation year during which the plans were first aggregated do not fail to satisfy the requirements of section 415 with respect to a participant for the limitation year merely because they are aggregated if there have been no increases in the participant's accrued benefit derived from employer contributions (including increases as a result of increased compensation or service) under any of the plans within the period during which the plans have been aggregated.

(f) *Section 403(b) annuity contracts.*—(1) *In general.*—In the case of a section 403(b) annuity contract, except as provided in paragraph (f)(2) of this section, the participant on whose behalf the annuity contract is purchased is considered for purposes of section 415 to have exclusive control of the annuity contract. Accordingly, except as provided in paragraph (f)(2) of this section, the participant, and not the participant's employer who purchased the section 403(b) annuity contract, is deemed to maintain the annuity contract, and such a section 403(b) annuity contract is not aggregated with a qualified plan that is maintained by the participant's employer.

(2) *Special rules under which the employer is deemed to maintain the annuity contract.*—(i) *In general.*—Where a participant on whose behalf a section 403(b) annuity contract is purchased is in control of any employer for a limitation year as defined in paragraph (f)(2)(ii) of this section (regardless of whether the employer controlled by the participant is the employer maintaining the section 403(b) annuity contract), the annuity contract for the benefit of the participant is treated as a defined contribution plan maintained by both the controlled employer and the participant for that limitation year. Accordingly, where a participant on whose behalf a section 403(b) annuity contract is purchased is in control of any employer for a limitation year, the section 403(b) annuity contract is aggregated with all other defined contribution plans maintained by that employer. In addition, in such a case, the section 403(b) annuity contract is aggregated with all other defined contribution plans maintained by the employee or any other employer that is controlled by the employee. Thus, for example, if a doctor is employed by a non-profit hospital to which section 501(c)(3) applies and which provides him with a section 403(b) annuity contract, and the doctor also maintains a private practice as a shareholder owning more than 50 percent of a professional corporation, then any qualified defined contribution plan of the professional corporation must be aggregated with the section 403(b) annuity contract for purposes of applying the limitations of section 415(c) and § 1.415(c)-1. For purposes of this paragraph (f)(2), it is immaterial whether the section 403(b) annuity contract is purchased as a result of a salary reduction agreement between the employer and the participant.

(ii) *Determination of when a participant is in control of an employer.*—For purposes of paragraph (f)(2)(i) of this section, a participant is in control of an employer for a limitation year if, pursuant to § 1.415(a)-1(f)(1) and (2), a plan maintained by that employer would have to be aggregated with a plan maintained by an employer that is 100 percent owned by the participant. Thus, for example, if a participant owns 60 percent of the common stock of a corporation, the participant is considered to be in control of that employer for purposes of applying paragraph (f)(2)(i) of this section.

(3) *Aggregation of section 403(b) annuity with qualified plan of controlled employer.*—If a section 403(b) annuity contract is aggregated with a qualified plan of a controlled employer in accordance with paragraph (f)(2) of this section, the plans must satisfy the limitations of section 415(c) both separately and on an aggregate basis. In applying separately the limitations of section 415 to the qualified plan and to the section 403(b) annuity contract, compensation from the controlled employer may not be aggregated with compensation from the employer purchasing the section 403(b) annuity contract (that is, without regard to § 1.415(c)-2(g)(3)).

(g) *Multiemployer plans.*—(1) *Multiemployer plan aggregated with another multiemployer plan.*—Pursuant to section 415(f)(3)(B), multiemployer plans, as defined in section 414(f), are not aggregated with other multiemployer plans for purposes of applying the limits of section 415.

(2) *Multiemployer plan aggregated with other plan.*—(i) *Aggregation only for benefits provided by the employer.*—Notwithstanding the rule of § 1.415(a)-1(e), a multiemployer plan, as defined in section 414(f), is permitted to provide that only the benefits under that multiemployer plan that are provided by an employer are aggregated with benefits under plans maintained by that employer that are not multiemployer plans. If the multiemployer plan so provides, then, where an employer maintains both a plan which is not a multiemployer plan and a multiemployer plan, only the benefits under the multiemployer plan that are provided by the employer are aggregated with benefits under the employer's plans other than multiemployer plans (in lieu of including benefits provided by all employers under the multiemployer plan pursuant to the generally applicable rule of § 1.415(a)-1(e)).

(ii) *Exception from aggregation for purposes of applying section 415(b)(1)(B) compensation limit.*—Pursuant to section 415(f)(3)(A), a multiemployer plan, as defined in section 414(f), is not aggregated with any other plan that is not a multiemployer plan for purposes of applying the compensation limit of section 415(b)(1)(B) and § 1.415(b)-1(a)(1)(ii).

(h) *Special rules for aggregating certain plans, etc.*—If a plan, annuity contract or arrangement is subject to a special limitation in addition to, or instead of, the regular limitations described in section 415(b) or (c), and is aggregated under this section with a plan which is subject only to the regular section 415(b) or (c) limitations, the following rules apply:

(1) Each plan, annuity contract or arrangement which is subject to a special limitation must meet its own applicable limitation and each plan subject to the regular limitations of section 415 must meet its applicable limitation.

(2) The limitation for the aggregated plans is the larger of the applicable limitations for the separate plans.

(i) [Reserved.]

(j) *Examples.*—The following examples illustrate the rules of this section. Except to the extent otherwise stated in an example, each entity is not and has never been affiliated with another entity under the employer affiliation rules of § 1.415(a)-1(f)(1) and (2), each entity has never maintained a qualified plan (other than the plans specifically mentioned in the example), and the limitation year for each qualified plan is the calendar year.

Example 1. (i) *Facts.* M was formerly an employee of ABC Corporation and is currently an employee of XYZ Corporation. ABC maintains a qualified defined benefit plan (Plan ABC) and a qualified defined contribution plan in which M participates and XYZ maintains a qualified defined benefit plan (Plan XYZ) and a qualified defined contribution plan in which M participates. ABC Corporation owns 60 percent of XYZ Corporation.

(ii) *Treatment as a single employer.* ABC Corporation and XYZ Corporation are members of a controlled group of corporations within the meaning of section 414(b) as modified by section 415(h). Because ABC Corporation and XYZ Corporation are members of a controlled group of corporations within the meaning of section 414(b) as modified by section 415(h), M is treated as being employed by a single employer under § 1.415(a)-1(f)(1).

(iii) *Plan aggregation.* Under paragraph (a)(1) of this section, the sum of M's annual benefit under Plan ABC and M's annual benefit under Plan XYZ is not permitted to exceed the limitations of section 415(b) and § 1.415(b)-1; and, under paragraph (a)(2) of this section, the sum of the annual additions to M's account under the defined contribution plans maintained by ABC and XYZ may not exceed the limitations of section 415(c) and § 1.415(c)-1. For purposes of determining the limitations of section 415(b) and § 1.415(b)-1 for the aggregated plans, a year of service for either employer is considered as a year of service for purposes of § 1.415(b)-1(g)(2) (phase-in rules for the compensation limit) and a year of participation under either plan is considered as a year of participation for purposes of § 1.415(b)-1(g)(1) (phase-in rules for the dollar limit).

Example 2. (i) *Facts.* The facts are the same as in *Example 1*, except that ABC Corporation and XYZ Corporation do not maintain defined contribution plans. In addition, Participant O was formerly an employee of ABC Corporation and is currently an employee of XYZ Corporation. Participant O has an accrued benefit under the ABC Plan, but Participant O has no accrued benefit under the XYZ Plan. Effective January 1, 2010, ABC Corporation sells all of its shares of stock of XYZ Corporation to an unaffiliated entity, LMN Corporation (the 2010 stock sale). After the 2010 stock sale, XYZ Corporation continues to maintain Plan XYZ. LMN Corporation maintains a qualified defined benefit plan (Plan LMN). After the 2010 stock sale, M begins to accrue benefits under Plan LMN, but O does not participate in Plan LMN.

(ii) *Affiliated employer status of the corporations.* Immediately after the 2010 stock sale, ABC Corporation and XYZ Corporation are no longer members of a controlled group of corporations under section 414(b) (as modified by section 414(h)) and accordingly are no longer treated as a single employer under the employer affiliation rules of § 1.415(a)-1(f)(1). Immediately after the 2010 stock sale, LMN Corporation and XYZ Corporation are members of a controlled group of corporations under section 414(b) (as modified by section 414(h)) and accordingly are treated as a single employer under the employer affiliation rules of § 1.415(a)-1(f)(1).

(iii) *Treatment of plans maintained by ABC Corporation after the 2010 stock sale.* Under § 1.415(a)-1(f)(1), any plan maintained by any member of a controlled group of corporations is deemed maintained by all members of the controlled group, and paragraph (a)(1) of this section requires that, for purposes of applying the limitations of section 415(b), all defined benefit plans ever maintained by an employer (as determined under the affiliation rules of § 1.415(a)-1(f)(1) and (2)) are treated as one defined benefit plan. Therefore, defined benefit plans maintained by ABC Corporation must take into account the annual benefit of a participant provided under Plan XYZ in applying the limitations of section 415(b) to the participant because Plan XYZ is a plan that had once been maintained by ABC Corporation. However, beginning with the 2010 limitation year, the aggregation of the annual benefit accrued by a participant under Plan XYZ for purposes of testing defined benefit plans maintained by ABC Corporation is limited to the annual benefit accrued by the participant under Plan XYZ immediately prior to the 2010 stock sale. This is because paragraph (b)(2)(i) of this section provides that a formerly affiliated plan of an employer is treated as if it had terminated immediately prior to the cessation of affiliation with sufficient assets to pay benefit liabilities under the plan, and had purchased annuities to provide plan benefits. The 2010 stock sale is a cessation of affiliation under paragraph (b)(2)(ii) of this section because this event caused XYZ Corporation to no longer be affiliated with ABC Corporation under the employer affiliation rules of §1.415(a)-1(f)(1) and (2). Immediately after the 2010 stock sale, Plan XYZ is a formerly affiliated plan with respect to ABC Corporation under paragraph (b)(2)(ii) of this section because immediately prior to the cessation of affiliation, Plan XYZ was actually maintained by XYZ Corporation (which together with ABC Corporation constituted a single employer under the employer affiliation rules of §1.415(a)-1(f)(1) and (2)), and immediately after the cessation of affiliation, Plan XYZ is not actually maintained by ABC Corporation or any other entity affiliated with it.

(iv) *Application of rules to Participants M and O with respect to plans maintained by ABC Corporation after the 2010 stock sale.* In applying the limitations of section 415(b) to Participant M for the 2010 limitation year and later limitation years, Plan ABC must take into account the annual benefit provided under Plan ABC to Participant M and the annual benefit provided under Plan XYZ to Participant M, but treating Plan XYZ as if it had terminated immediately prior to the 2010 stock sale with sufficient assets to pay benefit liabilities under the plan, and had purchased annuities to provide plan benefits. The aggregation of Plan XYZ with Plan ABC is irrelevant for purposes of Participant O because Participant O does not have any accrued benefit under Plan XYZ (as determined prior to the 2010 stock sale).

(v) *Treatment of plans maintained by LMN Corporation and XYZ Corporation after the 2010 stock sale.* Under §1.415(a)-1(f)(1) and paragraph (a)(1) of this section, when applying the limitations of section 415(b) to a participant under Plans LMN and XYZ for the 2010 limitation year and later years, the annual benefit provided to the participant under Plans LMN, XYZ and ABC must be aggregated. Benefits under Plan ABC must be included in this aggregation because XYZ Corporation is deemed to have once maintained Plan ABC pursuant to §1.415(a)-1(f)(1), and since LMN Corporation and XYZ Corporation constitute a single employer under §1.415(a)-1(f)(1), paragraph (a)(1) of this section requires the aggregation of all defined benefit plans ever maintained by LMN Corporation and XYZ Corporation. However, in performing this aggregation, a participant's annual benefit under Plan ABC is limited to the annual benefit accrued by the participant immediately prior to the 2010 stock sale. This is because, pursuant to paragraph (b)(2)(i) of this section, Plan ABC is a formerly affiliated plan of LMN Corporation and XYZ Corporation.

(vi) *Application of rules to Participants M and O with respect to plans maintained by LMN Corporation and XYZ Corporation after the 2010 stock sale.* In applying the limitation of section 415(b) to Participant M for the 2010 limitation year and later limitation years, Plan LMN and Plan XYZ must take into account the annual benefit provided under Plans LMN and XYZ to Participant M and the annual benefit provided under Plan ABC to Participant M as if Plan ABC had terminated immediately prior to the 2010 stock sale with sufficient assets to pay benefit liabilities under the plan, and had purchased annuities to provide plan benefits. Participant O does not have an accrued benefit under Plan LMN or Plan XYZ, so the aggregation of Plan ABC with Plans LMN and XYZ is currently irrelevant with respect to Participant O. However, if Participant O were to ever participate in Plans LMN or XYZ after the 2010 stock sale, Participant O's annual benefit under Plan ABC (determined as if Plan ABC terminated immediately prior to the 2010 stock sale) would have to be aggregated with any annual benefit that Participant O accrues under Plan LMN or Plan XYZ.

(vii) *Application of nonduplication rule.* In applying paragraph (a)(1) of this section to plans maintained by ABC Corporation after 2010 stock sale, plans maintained by ABC Corporation do not take into account the deemed termination of Plan ABC since ABC Corporation maintains Plan ABC after the cessation of affiliation. Similarly, in applying paragraph (a)(1) of this section to plans maintained by LMN Corporation and XYZ Corporation after the 2010 stock sale, plans maintained by LMN Corporation and XYZ Corporation do not take into account the deemed termination of Plan XYZ since XYZ Corporation maintains Plan XYZ after the cessation of affiliation. See paragraph (d)(1) of this section.

Example 3. (i) *Facts.* The facts are the same as in *Example 2*, except that on January 1, 2009, Plan ABC transfers Participant M's benefit to Plan XYZ.

(ii) *Treatment of plans maintained by ABC Corporation.* Pursuant to §1.415(b)-1(b)(3)(i)(A), M's benefit that is transferred from Plan ABC to Plan XYZ is not treated as being provided under Plan ABC for the limitation year in which the transfer occurs (2009). This is because M's transferred benefit is otherwise required to be taken into account by Plan ABC for the 2009 limitation year since Plan XYZ must be aggregated with Plan ABC pursuant to paragraph (a)(1) of this section. This result does not change for the 2010 limitation year and later limitation years, where pursuant to paragraph (b)(2)(i) of this section, Plan XYZ becomes a formerly affiliated plan with respect to ABC Corporation due to the 2010 stock sale. Under paragraph (b)(2)(i) of this section, Plan XYZ (the formerly affiliated plan) is treated from the perspective of plans maintained by ABC Corporation (Plan ABC) as if Plan XYZ terminated immediately prior to the 2010 stock sale with sufficient assets to pay benefit liabilities under the plan, and had purchased annuities to provide plan benefits. However, the pre-2010 stock sale benefits of Plan XYZ include the January 1, 2009, transfer of Participant M's benefit. Thus, in the 2010 limitation year, M's transferred benefit is still otherwise required to be taken into account by Plan ABC on account of the aggregation of Plan XYZ with Plan ABC pursuant to paragraph (a)(1) of this section, and therefore the transferred benefit is not treated as being provided by Plan ABC.

(iii) *Treatment of plans maintained by LMN Corporation and XYZ Corporation.* Pursuant to §1.415(b)-1(b)(3)(i)(C), Participant M's benefit that is transferred to Plan XYZ from Plan ABC must be treated as provided under Plan XYZ for purposes of applying the limitations of section 415 to Plan XYZ with respect to Participant M for the limitation year in which the transfer occurs and later years. This result does not change on account of the 2010 stock sale. When applying the limitation of section 415 to Plans LMN and XYZ for the 2010 limitation year and later years, Plans LMN and XYZ must aggregate the annual benefit provided to a participant under each plan along with the participant's benefit under Plan ABC pursuant to §1.415(a)-1(f)(1) and paragraph (a)(1) of this section. However, under paragraph (b)(2)(i) of this section, for the 2010 limitation year and later years, this aggregation of M's Plan ABC benefit only includes the annual benefit attributable to a participant's accrued benefit under Plan ABC immediately prior to the 2010 stock sale, which (due to the 2009 transfer) is zero.

Example 4. (i) *Facts.* The facts are the same as in *Example 2*, except that on January 1, 2011, Plan ABC transfers Participant M's benefit to Plan XYZ.

(ii) *Treatment of plans maintained by ABC Corporation for the 2011 limitation year and later years.* Pursuant to §1.415(b)-1(b)(3)(i)(B), M's benefit that is transferred from Plan ABC to Plan XYZ during the 2011 limitation year is treated by Plan ABC for the 2011 limitation year and later years as if the transferred benefit were provided under a plan that must be aggregated with Plan ABC that terminated immediately prior to the transfer with sufficient assets to pay benefit liabilities under the plan, and had purchased annuities to provide plan benefits. This is because M's transferred benefit is not otherwise required to be taken into account by Plan ABC for the 2011 limitation year and later years pursuant to paragraphs (a)(1) and (b)(2)(i) of this section. While Plan ABC must take into account Participant M's annual benefit under Plan XYZ under paragraph (a)(1) of this section, Participant M's annual benefit for this purpose is limited under paragraph (b)(2)(i) of this section to M's accrued benefit under Plan XYZ immediately prior to the 2010 stock sale, and Participant M's pre-2010 stock sale accrued benefit under Plan XYZ excludes the 2011 transfer.

(iii) *Treatment of plans maintained by LMN Corporation and XYZ Corporation for the 2011 limitation year and later years.* Pursuant to §1.415(b)-1(b)(3)(i)(C), Participant M's benefit that is transferred to Plan XYZ from Plan ABC must be treated as provided under Plan XYZ for purposes of applying the limitations of section 415 to Plan XYZ with respect to Participant M for the limitation year in which the transfer occurs and later years. In applying the limitations of section 415(b) to Plans LMN and XYZ with respect to Participant M for the 2010 limitation year and later years, the annual benefit of Participant M under Plans ABC, LMN, and XYZ must be aggregated pursuant to §1.415(a)-1(f)(1) and paragraph (a)(1) of this section, but for this purpose, Participant M's benefit under Plan ABC is treated as if it were provided under a plan that terminated immediately prior to the cessation of affiliation of ABC Corporation and XYZ Corporation with sufficient assets to pay benefit liabilities under the plan, and had purchased an annuity to provide Participant M's benefits. (See paragraph (b)(2)(i) of this section and *Example 2*.) In applying the limitations of section 415(b) to Plans LMN and XYZ with respect to Participant M for the 2011 limitation year and later years, the annual benefit of Participant M under Plans ABC, LMN, and XYZ still must be aggregated pursuant to §1.415(a)-1(f)(1) and paragraph (a)(1) of this section. However, beginning with the 2011 limitation year, ABC Corporation is a predecessor employer with respect to LMN Corporation and XYZ Corporation with respect to Participant M on account of the transfer of benefits from Plan ABC to Plan XYZ, pursuant to paragraph (c)(1) of this section. Therefore, Plans LMN and XYZ must take into account benefits that Participant M accrued under Plan ABC after the January 1, 2010, cessation of affiliation of ABC Corporation and XYZ Corporation that were not transferred to Plan XYZ on January 1, 2011, pursuant to paragraphs (c)(1) and (d)(1) of this section. Since all of Participant M's benefit in Plan ABC is transferred to Plan XYZ on January 1, 2011, Participant M's annual benefit from Plan ABC for purposes of aggregating Plan ABC with Plans LMN and XYZ is zero.

Example 5. (i) *Facts.* The facts are the same as in *Example 2,* except that instead of the 2010 stock sale, XYZ Corporation sells some of its operating assets to LMN Corporation (and, under the facts and circumstances, the sale does not result in XYZ Corporation constituting a predecessor employer of LMN Corporation under the rules of paragraph (c)(2) of this section), and in connection with the asset sale, LMN Corporation assumes sponsorship of Plan XYZ in place of XYZ Corporation, effective January 1, 2010.

(ii) *Treatment of plans maintained by ABC Corporation and XYZ Corporation.* Pursuant to paragraph (a)(1) of this section, all defined benefit plans ever maintained by ABC Corporation and XYZ Corporation must be aggregated as a single defined benefit plan for purposes of applying the limitations of section 415(b). However, for purposes of determining the annual benefit under Plan XYZ for the 2010 limitation year and later years, the aggregation of a participant's benefit under Plan XYZ is limited to the participant's annual benefit accrued immediately prior to the January 1, 2010, transfer of sponsorship of Plan XYZ. This is because paragraph (b)(2)(i) of this section provides that a formerly affiliated plan of an employer is treated as if it were a plan that terminated immediately prior to the cessation of affiliation with sufficient assets to pay benefit liabilities under the plan, and had purchased annuities to provide plan benefits. The January 1, 2010, transfer of sponsorship of Plan XYZ is a cessation of affiliation under paragraph (b)(2)(ii) of this section because this event causes Plan XYZ to no longer actually be maintained by either ABC Corporation or XYZ Corporation. Effective immediately after the January 1, 2010, transfer of sponsorship, Plan XYZ is a formerly affiliated plan with respect to ABC Corporation and XYZ Corporation under paragraph (b)(2)(ii) of this section because immediately prior to the cessation of affiliation, Plan XYZ was actually maintained by XYZ Corporation, and immediately after the cessation of affiliation, Plan XYZ is not actually maintained by either XYZ Corporation or ABC Corporation. Therefore, in applying the limitation of section 415(b) to Participant M for the 2010 limitation year and later limitation years, Plan ABC must take into account the annual benefit provided under Plan ABC to Participant M and the annual benefit provided under Plan XYZ to Participant M as if Plan XYZ had terminated immediately prior to the 2010 stock sale with sufficient assets to pay benefit liabilities under the plan, and had purchased annuities to provide plan benefits. The aggregation of Plan XYZ with Plan ABC is irrelevant for purposes of Participant O because Participant O does not have any accrued benefit under Plan XYZ (as determined prior to the 2010 transfer of sponsorship).

(iii) *Treatment of plans maintained by LMN Corporation.* Under paragraph (a)(1) of this section, all defined benefit plans ever maintained by LMN Corporation or a predecessor employer must be aggregated as a single plan for purposes of applying the limitations of section 415(b). ABC Corporation and XYZ Corporation constitute a predecessor employer pursuant to paragraph (c)(1) of this section with respect to the participants who participate in Plan XYZ on the date of the transfer of sponsorship of Plan XYZ (the transferred participants) from XYZ Corporation to LMN Corporation, such as Participant M. This is because, effective with the January 1, 2010, transfer of sponsorship, LMN Corporation maintains a plan (Plan XYZ) under which the participants accrued a benefit while performing services for XYZ Corporation (which is in turn affiliated with ABC Corporation under §1.415(a)-1(f)(1)) and such benefits are provided under a plan maintained by LMN Corporation. Therefore, for the 2010 limitation year and later years, the annual benefit under Plan ABC of the transferred participants (such as Participant M) must be aggregated with the annual benefit provided to such participants under Plans XYZ and LMN for purposes of determining whether Plan LMN or Plan XYZ satisfies the limitations of section 415(b). However, the aggregation of the transferred participants' Plan ABC annual benefits is limited to the annual benefit accrued under Plan ABC immediately prior to January 1, 2010, transfer of sponsorship. This is because, pursuant to paragraph (c)(1) of this section, Plan ABC is treated from the perspective of plans maintained by LMN Corporation as if Plan ABC had terminated immediately prior to the transfer of sponsorship of Plan ABC to LMN Corporation with sufficient assets to pay benefit liabilities under the plan, and had purchased annuities to provide plan

benefits. ABC Corporation and XYZ Corporation do not constitute a predecessor employer with respect to Participant O. Thus, if Participant O is a participant in Plan LMN or becomes a participant in Plan XYZ after the 2010 transfer of sponsorship, neither plan aggregates Participant O's Plan ABC benefits for purposes of satisfying section 415(b). In applying paragraph (a)(1) of this section to a participant, plans maintained by LMN Corporation do not double count the participant's annual benefit. See paragraph (d)(1) of this section. Thus, such plans do not aggregate the annual benefit provided under Plan XYZ with the annual benefit from the deemed termination of Plan XYZ that LMN Corporation's predecessor employer (which is ABC and XYZ Corporations) must take into account in applying paragraph (a)(1) of this section, and instead consider the annual benefit actually provided under Plan XYZ.

Example 6. (i) *Facts.* N is employed by a hospital which purchases an annuity contract described in section 403(b) on N's behalf for the current limitation year. N is in control of the hospital within the meaning of section 414(b) or (c), as modified by section 415(h). The hospital also maintains a qualified defined contribution plan during the current limitation year in which N participates.

(ii) *Conclusion.* Under section 415(k)(4), the hospital, as well as N, is considered to maintain the annuity contract. Accordingly, for N the sum of the annual additions under the qualified defined contribution plan and the annuity contract must satisfy the limitations of section 415(c) and §1.415(c)-1.

Example 7. (i) *Facts.* The facts are the same as in *Example 6,* except that instead of being in control of the hospital, N is the 100 percent owner of a professional corporation P, which maintains a qualified defined contribution plan in which N participates.

(ii) *Conclusion.* Under section 415(k)(4), the professional corporation, as well as N, is considered to maintain the annuity contract. Accordingly, the sum of the annual additions under the qualified defined contribution plan maintained by professional corporation P and the annuity contract must satisfy the limitations of section 415(c) and §1.415(c)-1. See §1.415(g)-1(b)(3)(iv)(C)(2) for an example of the treatment of a contribution to a section 403(b) annuity contract that exceeds the limits of section 415(c) by reason of the aggregation required by this section.

Example 8. (i) *Facts.* J is an employee of two corporations, N and M, each of which has employed J for more than 10 years. N and M are not required to be aggregated pursuant to section 415(f) and this section. Each corporation has a qualified defined benefit plan in which J has participated for more than 10 years. Each plan provides a benefit which is equal to 75 percent of a participant's average compensation for the period of the participant's high-3 years of service and is payable in the form of a straight life annuity beginning at age 65. J's average compensation for the period of his high-3 years of service from each corporation is $160,000. In July 2008, N Corporation becomes a wholly owned subsidiary of M Corporation.

(ii) *Plan aggregation analysis.* As a result of the acquisition of N Corporation by M Corporation, J is treated as being employed by a single employer under section 414(b). Therefore, because section 415(f)(1)(A) requires that all defined benefit plans of an employer be treated as one defined benefit plan, the two plans must be aggregated for purposes of applying the limitations of section 415. However, under paragraph (e)(3)(i) of this section, since the plans were not aggregated as of the first day of the 2008 limitation year (January 1, 2008), they will not be considered aggregated until the limitation year beginning January 1, 2009, provided that no plan amendment increasing benefits with respect to participant J is made after the acquisition of N by M.

(iii) *Application to Participant J.* J has a total benefit under the two plans of $240,000, which, as a result of the plan aggregation, is in excess of the section 415(b) limit. However, under paragraph (e)(3)(ii) of this section, the limitations of section 415(b) and §1.415(b)-1 applicable to J may be exceeded in this situation without plan disqualification so long as J's accrued benefit derived from employer contributions is not increased (that is, J's accrued benefit does not increase on account of increased compensation, service, participation, or other accruals) during the period within which the limitations are being exceeded.

Example 9. (i) *Facts.* A, age 30, owns all of the stock of X Corporation and also owns 10 percent of the stock of Z Corporation. F, A's father, directly owns 75 percent of the stock of Z Corporation. Both corporations have qualified defined contribution plans in which A participates. A's compensation (within the meaning of §1.415(c)-2) for 2008 is $20,000 from Z Corporation and $150,000 from X Corporation. During the period January 1, 2008 through June 30, 2008, annual additions of $20,000 are credited to A's account under the plan of Z Corporation, while annual additions of $40,000 are credited to A's account under the plan of X Corporation. In both instances, the amount of annual additions represent the maximum allowable under section 415(c) and §1.415(c)-1. On July 15, 2008, F dies, and A inherits all of F's stock in Z in 2008.

(ii) *Conclusion.* As of July 15, 2008, A is considered to be in control of X and Z Corporations, and the two plans must be aggregated for purposes of applying the limitations of section 415. However, even though A's total annual additions for 2008 are $60,000, the limitations of section 415(c) and §1.415(c)-1 are not violated for 2008, provided no annual additions are credited to A's accounts after July 15, 2008 (the date that A is first in control of Z) for the remainder of the 2008 limitation year.

Example 10. (i) *Facts.* P is a key employee of employer XYZ who participates in a qualified defined contribution plan (Plan X). P is also provided post-retirement medical benefits, and XYZ has taken into account a reserve for those benefits under section 419A(c)(2). In the 2008 limitation year, P's compensation is $30,000 and P's annual additions under Plan X are $5,000. Pursuant to section 419A(d), a separate account is maintained for P, and that account is credited with an allocation of $32,000 for the 2008 limitation year. It is assumed that the section 415(c)(1)(A) dollar limit for 2008 is $46,000.

(ii) *Separate testing analysis.* Under paragraph (h)(1) of this section, Plan X and the individual medical account must separately satisfy the requirements of section 415(c), taking into account any special limit applicable to that arrangement. In this case, the contributions to Plan X separately satisfy the limitations of section 415(c). While the individual medical account is treated as a defined contribution plan subject to the rules of section 415(c), it is not subject to the 100 percent of compensation limit of section 415(c)(1)(B), so the contributions to that account satisfy the limitations of section 415(c).

(iii) *Aggregation analysis.* The sum of the annual additions under Plan X and the amounts contributed to the separate account on P's behalf must satisfy the requirements of section 415(c). Under paragraph (h)(2) of this section, the limit applicable to the aggregated plan is equal to the greater of the limits applicable to the separate plans. In this case, the limit applicable to the medical account is $46,000 (which is greater than the limit of $30,000 applicable to the qualified plan), so the limit that applies to the aggregated plan is $46,000, and the aggregated plan satisfies the requirements of section 415. [Reg. §1.415(f)-1.]

☐ [T.D. 9319, 4–4–2007 (*corrected* 5-22-2007).]

[Reg. §1.415(g)-1]

§1.415(g)-1. Disqualification of plans and trusts.— (a) *Disqualification of plans.*—(1) *In general.*—Under section 415(g) and this section, with respect to a particular limitation year, a plan (and the trust forming part of the plan) is disqualified in accordance with the rules provided in paragraph (b) of this section, if the conditions described in paragraph (a)(2) or (a)(3) of this section apply. For purposes of this paragraph (a), the determination of whether a plan or a group of aggregated plans exceeds the limitations imposed by section 415 for a particular limitation year is, except as otherwise provided, made by taking into account the aggregation of plan rules provided in section 415(f) and §1.414(f)-1.

(2) *Defined contribution plans.*—A plan is disqualified in accordance with the rules provided in paragraph (b) of this section if annual additions (as defined in §1.415(c)-1(b)) with respect to the account of any participant in a defined contribution plan maintained by the employer exceed the limitations of section 415(c) and §1.415(c)-1.

(3) *Defined benefit plans.*—A plan is disqualified in accordance with the rules provided in paragraph (b) of this section if the annual benefit (as defined in §1.415(b)-1(b)(1)) of a participant in a defined benefit plan maintained by the employer exceeds the limitations of section 415(b) and §1.415(b)-1.

(b) *Rules for disqualification of plans and trusts.*—(1) *In general.*—If any plan (including a trust which forms part of such plan) is disqualified for a particular limitation year under the rules set forth in this paragraph (b), then the disqualification is effective as of the first day of the first plan year containing any portion of the particular limitation year.

(2) *Single plan.*—In the case of a single qualified defined benefit plan (determined without regard to section 415(f) and §1.415(f)-1) maintained by the employer that provides an annual benefit (as defined in §1.415(b)-1(b)(1)) in excess of the limitations of section 415(b) and §1.415(b)-1 for any particular limitation year, such plan is disqualified in that limitation year. Similarly, if the employer only maintains a single defined contribution plan (determined without regard to section 415(f) and §1.415(f)-1) under which annual additions (as defined in §1.415(c)-1(b)) allocated to the account of any participant exceed the limitations of section 415(c) and §1.415(c)-1 for *any particular limitation year, such plan is also disqualified in that* limitation year.

(3) *Multiple plans.*—(i) *In general.*—If the limitations of section 415(b) and §1.415(b)-1, or section 415(c) and §1.415(c)-1, are ex-

ceeded for a particular limitation year with respect to any participant solely because of the application of the aggregation rules of section 415(f)(1) and §1.415(f)-1 (taking into account the rules of §1.415(a)-1(f)), then one or more of the plans is disqualified in accordance with the ordering rules set forth in paragraph (b)(3)(ii) of this section, applied in accordance with the rules of application set forth in paragraph (b)(3)(iii) of this section, subject to the special rules set forth in paragraph (b)(3)(iv) of this section, until, without regard to annual benefits or annual additions under the disqualified plan or plans, the remaining plans satisfy the applicable limitations of section 415.

(ii) *Ordering rules.*—(A) *Disqualification of ongoing plans other than multiemployer plans.*—If there are two or more plans that have not been terminated at any time including the last day of the particular limitation year, and if one or more of those plans is a multiemployer plan described in section 414(f), then one or more of the plans (as needed to satisfy the limitations of section 415) that has not been terminated and is not a multiemployer plan is disqualified in that limitation year. For purposes of the preceding sentence, the determination of whether a plan is a multiemployer plan described in section 414(f) is made as of the last day of the particular limitation year.

(B) *Disqualification of ongoing multiemployer plans.*—If, after the application of paragraph (b)(3)(ii)(A) of this section, there are two or more plans and one or more of the plans has been terminated at any time including the last day of the particular limitation year, then one or more of the plans (as needed to satisfy the applicable limitations of section 415) that has not been so terminated (regardless of whether the plan is a multiemployer plan described in section 414(f)) is disqualified in that limitation year.

(iii) *Rules of application.*—(A) *Employer elects which plan is disqualified.*—If there are two or more plans of an employer within a group of plans one or more of which is to be disqualified pursuant to paragraph (b)(3)(ii)(A) or (B) of this section, then the employer may elect, in a manner determined by the Commissioner, which plan or plans are disqualified. If those two or more plans are involved because of the application of §1.415(a)-1(f), the employers involved may elect, in a manner determined by the Commissioner, which plan or plans are disqualified. However, the election described in the preceding sentence is not effective unless made by all of those employers.

(B) *Commissioner determines which plan is disqualified.*—If the election described in paragraph (b)(3)(iii)(A) of this section is not made with respect to the two plans described in paragraph (b)(3)(iii)(A) of this section, then the Commissioner, taking into account all of the facts and circumstances, has the discretion to determine the plan that is disqualified in the particular limitation year. In making this determination, some of the factors that will be taken into account include, but are not limited to, the number of participants in each plan, the amount of benefits provided on an overall basis by each plan, and the extent to which benefits are distributed or retained in each plan.

(iv) *Special rules.*—(A) *Simplified employee pensions.*—If there are two or more plans one or more of which is to be disqualified pursuant to paragraph (b)(3)(ii)(A) or (B) of this section, and if one of the plans is a simplified employee pension (as defined in section 408(k)), then the simplified employee pension is not disqualified until all of the other plans have been disqualified. However, if one of the plans has been terminated, then the simplified employee pension is disqualified before the terminated plan. For purposes of this paragraph (b)(3)(iv)(A), the disqualification of a simplified employee pension means that the simplified employee pension is no longer described under section 408(k).

(B) *Aggregating medical accounts with defined contribution plans.*—In the event that aggregating a medical account described in §1.415(c)-1(a)(2)(ii)(C) or (D) and a defined contribution plan other than such a medical account causes the limitations of section 415(c) and §1.415(c)-1 applicable to a participant to be exceeded for a particular limitation year, the defined contribution plan other than the medical account is disqualified for the limitation year.

(C) *Aggregating section 403(b) annuity contract and qualified defined contribution plan.*—(1) *In general.*—In the event that aggregating a section 403(b) annuity contract and a qualified defined contribution plan under the provisions of section 415(f)(1)(B) causes the limitations of section 415(c) and §1.415(c)-1 applicable to a participant under the aggregated defined contribution plans to be exceeded for a particular limitation year, the excess of the contributions to the annuity contract plus the annual additions to the qualified plan over such limitations is attributed to the annuity contract and therefore includable in the gross income of the participant for the taxable year with or within which that limitation year ends. See §1.415(a)-1(b)(2) for rules regarding the treatment of a contribution to a section 403(b) annuity contract that exceeds the limitations of section 415.

(2) *Example.*—The following example illustrates the application of this paragraph (b)(3)(iv)(C). It is assumed for purposes of this example that the dollar limitation under section 415(c)(1)(A) that applies for all relevant limitation years is $45,000. The example is as follows:

Example. (i) N is employed by a hospital which purchases an annuity contract described in section 403(b) on N's behalf for the current limitation year. N is also the 100 percent owner of a professional corporation P that maintains a qualified defined contribution plan during the current limitation year in which N participates. (The facts of this example are the same as in §1.415(f)-1(j) *Example 7.*) N's compensation (within the meaning of §1.415(c)-2) from the hospital for the current limitation year is $150,000. For the current limitation year, the hospital contributes $30,000 for the section 403(b) annuity contract on N's behalf, which is within the limitations applicable to N under the annuity contract (specifically, the limit under the annuity contract is $45,000)). Professional corporation P also contributes $20,000 to the qualified defined contribution plan on N's behalf for the current limitation year (which represents the only annual additions allocated to N's account under the plan for such year), which is within the $45,000 limitation of section 415(c)(1) applicable to N under the plan.

(ii) Under section 415(k)(4), the professional corporation, as well as N, is considered to maintain the annuity contract. Accordingly, the sum of the annual additions under the qualified defined contribution plan maintained by professional corporation P and the annuity contract must satisfy the limitations of section 415(c) and §1.415(c)-1.

(iii) Because the total aggregate contributions ($50,000) exceed the section 415(c) limitation applicable to N ($45,000), $5,000 of the $30,000 contributed to the section 403(b) annuity contract is considered an excess contribution and therefore currently includable in N's gross income. The contract continues to be a section 403(b) annuity contract only if, for the current limitation year and all years thereafter, the issuer of the contract maintains separate accounts for each portion attributable to such excess contributions. See §§1.415(a)-1(b)(2).

(c) *Plan year for certain annuity contracts and individual retirement plans.*—For purposes of this section, unless the plan under which the annuity contract or individual retirement plan is provided specifies that a different twelve-month period is considered to be the plan year—

(1) An annuity contract described in section 403(b) is considered to have a plan year coinciding with the taxable year of the individual on whose behalf the contract has been purchased; and

(2) A simplified employee pension described in section 408(k) is considered to have a plan year coinciding with the year under the plan that is used pursuant to section 408(k)(7)(C). [Reg. §1.415(g)-1.]

□ [*T.D. 9319, 4-4-2007.*]

[Reg. §1.415(j)-1]

§1.415(j)-1. Limitation year.—(a) *In general.*—Unless the terms of a plan provide otherwise, the limitation year, with respect to any qualified plan maintained by the employer, is the calendar year.

(b) *Alternative limitation year election.*—The terms of a plan may provide for the use of any other consecutive twelve month period as the limitation year. This includes a fiscal year with an annual period varying from 52 to 53 weeks, so long as the fiscal year satisfies the requirements of section 441(f). A plan may only provide for one limitation year regardless of the number or identity of the employers maintaining the plan.

(c) *Multiple limitation years.*—(1) *In general.*—Where an employer maintains more than one qualified plan, those plans may provide for different limitation years. The rule described in this paragraph (c) also applies to a controlled group of employers (within the meaning of section 414(b) or (c), as modified by section 415(h)). If the plans of an employer (or a controlled group of employers whose plans are aggregated) have different limitation years, section 415 is applied in accordance with the rule of paragraphs (c)(2) and (3) of this section.

(2) *Testing rule for defined contribution plans.*—If a participant is credited with annual additions in only one defined contribution plan, in determining whether the requirements of section 415(c) are satisfied, only the limitation year applicable to that plan is considered. However, if a participant is credited with annual additions in more than one defined contribution plan, each such plan satisfies the requirements of section 415(c) only if the limitations of section 415(c) are satisfied with respect to amounts that are annual additions for the limitation year with respect to the participant under the plan, plus amounts credited to the participant's account under all other plans

required to be aggregated with the plan pursuant to section 415(f) and §1.415(f)-1 that would have been considered annual additions for the limitation year under the plan if they had been credited under the plan rather than an aggregated plan.

(3) *Testing rule for defined benefit plans.*—If a participant has participated in only one defined benefit plan, in determining whether the requirements of section 415(b) are satisfied, only the limitation year applicable to that plan is considered. However, if a participant has participated in more than one defined benefit plan, a plan satisfies the requirements of section 415(b) only if the annual benefit under all plans required to be aggregated pursuant to section 415(f) and §1.415(f)-1 for the limitation year of that plan with respect to the participant satisfy the applicable limitations of section 415(b). Thus, for example, the dollar limitation of section 415(b)(1)(A) applicable to the limitation year for each plan must be applied to annual benefits under all aggregated plans to determine whether the plan satisfies the requirements of section 415(b).

(d) *Change of limitation year.*—(1) *In general.*—Once established, the limitation year may be changed only by amending the plan. Any change in the limitation year must be a change to a 12-month period commencing with any day within the current limitation year. For purposes of this section, the limitations of section 415 are to be applied in the normal manner to the new limitation year.

(2) *Application to short limitation period.*—Where there is a change of limitation year, the limitations of section 415 are to be separately applied to a limitation period which begins with the first day of the current limitation year and which ends on the day before the first day of the first limitation year for which the change is effective. In the case of a defined contribution plan, the dollar limitation with respect to this limitation period is determined by multiplying the applicable dollar limitation for the calendar year in which the limitation period ends by a fraction, the numerator of which is the number of months (including any fractional parts of a month) in the limitation period, and the denominator of which is 12. In the case of a defined benefit plan, no adjustment is made to the section 415(b) limitations to reflect a short limitation period.

(3) *Deemed change of limitation year.*—If a defined contribution plan is terminated effective as of a date other than the last day of the plan's limitation year, the plan is treated for purposes of this section as if the plan was amended to change its limitation year. Thus, the rules of this paragraph (d) apply to the terminating plan's final limitation year.

(e) *Limitation year for individuals on whose behalf section 403(b) annuity contracts have been purchased.*—The limitation year of an individual on whose behalf a section 403(b) annuity contract has been purchased by an employer is determined in the following manner.

(1) If the individual is not in control of any employer (within the meaning of §1.415(f)-1(f)(2)(ii)), the limitation year is the calendar year. However, the individual may elect to change the limitation year to another twelve-month period. To do this, the individual must attach a statement to his or her income tax return filed for the taxable year in which the change is made. Any change in the limitation year must comply with the rules set forth in paragraph (d) of this section.

(2) If the individual is in control of an employer (within the meaning of §1.415(f)-1(f)(2)(ii)), the limitation year is the limitation year of that employer.

(f) *Limitation year for individuals on whose behalf individual retirement plans are maintained.*—The limitation year of an individual on whose behalf an individual retirement plan (within the meaning of section 7701(a)(37)) is maintained is determined in the manner described in paragraph (e) of this section.

(g) *Examples.*—The following examples illustrate the application of this section:

Example 1. (i) Participant M is employed by both Employer A and Employer B, each of which maintains a qualified defined contribution plan. M participates in both of these plans. The limitation year for Employer A's plan is January 1 through December 31, and the limitation year for Employer B's plan is April 1 through March 31. Employer A and Employer B are both corporations, and Corporation X owns 100 percent of the stock of Employer A and Employer B.

(ii) The two plans in which M participates are required under section 415(f) to be aggregated for purposes of applying the limitations of section 415(c) to annual additions made with respect to M. Thus, for example, for the limitation year of Employer A's plan that begins January 1, 2008, annual additions with respect to M that are subject to the limitations of section 415(c) include both amounts that are annual additions with respect to M under Employer A's plan for the period beginning January 1, 2008, and ending December 31, 2008, and amounts contributed to Employer B's plan with respect to M that would have been considered annual additions for the period beginning January 1, 2008, and ending December 31, 2008, under Employer A's plan if those amounts had instead been contributed to Employer A's plan.

Example 2. In 2008, an employer with a qualified defined contribution plan using the calendar year as the limitation year elects to change the limitation year to a period beginning July 1 and ending June 30. Because of this change, the plan must satisfy the limitations of section 415(c) for the limitation period beginning January 1, 2008, and ending June 30, 2008. In applying the limitations of section 415(c) to this limitation period, the amount of compensation taken into account may only include compensation for this period. Furthermore, the dollar limitation for this period is the otherwise applicable dollar limitation for calendar year 2008, multiplied by 6/12. [Reg. §1.415(j)-1.]

☐ [T.D. 9319, 4-4-2007.]

[Reg. §1.416-1]

§1.416-1. Questions and answers on top-heavy plans.—The following questions and answers relate to special rules for top-heavy plans under section 416 of the Internal Revenue Code of 1954, as added by section 240 of the Tax Equity and Fiscal Responsibility Act of 1982 (Pub. L. 97-248) (TEFRA), and amended by sections 524 and 713(f) of the Tax Reform Act of 1984 (Pub. L. 98-369):

TABLE OF CONTENTS
G—General Provisions
T—Top-Heaviness Determinations
V—Vesting Rules for Top-Heavy Plans
M—Minimum Benefits Under Top-Heavy Plans

G. General Provisions

G-1 Q. What retirement plans are subject to the top-heavy rules added to the Code by the Tax Equity and Fiscal Responsibility Act and amended by the Tax Reform Act of 1984?

A. All stock bonus, pension, or profit-sharing plans intended to qualify under section 401(a), annuity contracts described in section 403(a), and simplified employee pensions described in section 408(k) are subject to the new top-heavy rules added to the Code by the Tax Equity and Fiscal Responsibility Act and amended by the Tax Reform Act ("TRA") of 1984.

G-2 Q. Is a multiple employer plan subject to the top-heavy requirements of section 416?

A. A multiple employer plan is subject to the requirements of section 416, but only with respect to each individual employer. Thus, if twelve employers contribute to a multiple employer plan and the accrued benefits for the key employees of one employer exceed 60 percent of the accrued benefits of all employees for such employer, the plan is top-heavy with respect to that employer. A failure by the multiple employer plan to satisfy section 416 with respect to the employees of such employer means that all employers are maintaining a plan that is not a qualified plan.

G-3 Q. As of what date must plan amendments to comply with top-heavy rules be effective?

A. Amendments required to comply with the top-heavy rules must be effective as of the first day of the first plan year which begins after 1983. See §1.401(b)-1 for the date by which such amendments must be adopted.

T. Top-Heaviness Determinations

T-1 Q. What factors must be considered in determining whether a plan is top-heavy?

A. (a) In order to determine whether a plan is top-heavy for a plan year, it is necessary to determine which employers will be treated as a single employer for purposes of section 416; what the determination date is for the plan year; which employees are or formerly were key employees; which former employees have not performed any service for the employer maintaining the plan at any time during the five-year period ending on the determination date; which plans of such employers are required or permitted to be aggregated to determine top-heavy status; and the present value of the accrued benefits (including distributions made during the plan year containing the determination date and the four preceding plan years) of key employees, former key employees, and non-key employees.

(b) All employers that are aggregated under section 414(b), (c), and (m) must be taken into account as a single employer for the plan year in question, and those employees in all plans maintained by the employers that are aggregated must be categorized as key employees, as former key employees, or as non-key employees. See Question and Answer T-12 for the determination of which employees are or were key employees. All plans maintained by the employers in which a key employee participates, and certain other plans, must then be aggregated (the required aggregation group). See Question and Answer T-6 for rules concerning required aggregation. Other plans may in some cases be aggregated with the required aggregation group. See Question and Answer T-7 for rules concerning such permissive aggregation.

(c) Once aggregated, all plans that are required to be aggregated will either be top-heavy or not top-heavy, depending upon whether the aggregation group is top-heavy. A plan or aggregation group will be considered top-heavy if the sum of the present value of the accrued benefits for key employees is more than 60 percent of the sum of the present value of accrued benefits of all employees.

(d) Except as otherwise stated, for purposes of section 416(g), an employee is an individual currently or formerly employed by an employer. Former key employees are non-key employees and are excluded entirely from the calculation to determine top-heaviness. In all cases, the present value of accrued benefits includes distributions made during the plan year containing the determination date and the preceding four plan years. See Questions and Answers T-24 and T-25 for rules concerning the account balances and present value of accrued benefits. For plan years beginning after December 31, 1984, the accrued benefit of an employee who has not performed any service for the employer maintaining the plan at any time during the five-year period ending on the determination date is excluded from the calculation to determine top-heaviness. However, if an employee performs no services for five years and then performs services, such employee's total accrued benefit is included in the calculation for top-heaviness.

T-2 Q. To what extent are multiemployer plans and multiple employer plans to which an employer makes contributions on behalf of its employees treated as plans of that employer for top-heavy purposes?

A. Multiemployer plans described in section 414(f) and multiple employer plans described in section 413(c) to which an employer makes contributions on behalf of its employees are treated as plans of that employer to the extent that benefits under the plan are provided to employees of the employer because of service with that employer.

T-3 Q. Must a collectively-bargained plan be aggregated with other plans of the employer to determine whether some or all of the employer's plans are top-heavy?

A. A collectively-bargained plan that includes a key employee of an employer must be included in the required aggregation group for that employer. See Question and Answer T-6 for rules concerning required aggregation. A collectively-bargained plan that does not include a key employee may be included in a permissive aggregation group. See Question and Answer T-7 for rules concerning permissive aggregation. However, the special rules in section 416(b), (c), or (d) applicable to top-heavy plans do not apply with respect to any employee included in a unit of employees covered by an agreement which the Secretary of Labor finds to be a collective-bargaining agreement between employee representatives and one or more employers if there is evidence that retirement benefits were the subject of good faith bargaining between such employee representatives and such employer or employers. In determining whether there is a collective-bargaining agreement between employee representatives and one or more employers, the additional condition of section 7701(a)(46) must be satisfied after March 31, 1984.

T-4 Q. How is a terminated plan treated for purposes of the top-heavy rules?

A. A terminated plan is treated like any other plan for purposes of the top-heavy rules. For purposes of section 416, a terminated plan is one that has been formerly terminated, has ceased crediting service for benefit accruals and vesting, and has been or is distributing all plan assets to participants or their beneficiaries as soon as administratively feasible. Such a plan must be aggregated with other plans of the employer if it was maintained within the last five years ending on the determination date for the plan year in question and would, but for the fact that it terminated, be part of a required aggregation group for such plan year. Distributions which have taken place within the five years ending on the determination date must be accounted for in accordance with section 416(g)(3). No additional vesting, benefit accruals or contributions must be provided for participants in a terminated plan.

T-5 Q. How are frozen plans treated for purposes of the top-heavy rules?

A. For purposes of section 416, a frozen plan is one in which benefit accruals have ceased but all assets have not been distributed to participants or their beneficiaries. Such plans are treated, for purposes of the top-heavy rules, as any non-frozen plan. That is, such plans must provide minimum contributions or benefit accruals, limit the amount of compensation which can be taken into account in providing benefits, and provide top-heavy vesting. A frozen defined contribution plan may not be required to provide additional contributions because of the rule in section 416(c)(2)(B).

T-6 Q. What is a required aggregate group?

A. For purposes of determining whether the plans of an employer are top-heavy for a particular plan year, the required aggregation group includes each plan of the employer in which a key employee participates in the plan year containing the determination date, or any of the four preceding plan years. In addition, each other plan of the employer which, during this period, enables any plan in which a key employee participates to meet the requirements of section 401(a)(4) or 410 is part of the required aggregation group. This concept may be illustrated by the following examples:

Example (1). An employer maintains two plans. Key employees participate in one plan, but not in the other. If the plan containing key employees independently satisfies the coverage and nondiscrimination rules of sections 410 and 401(a)(4), it may be tested independently to determine whether it is top-heavy. Also, the plan not covering key employees would not be part of a required aggregation group and would not need to be tested to determine whether it is top-heavy. However, if the plan containing key employees satisfies the coverage requirements of section 410(b) or the nondiscrimination requirements of section 401(a)(4) only when it is considered together with the other plan in accordance with §1.410(b)-7(d), the plan not covering key employees would be part of the required aggregation group.

Example (2). A sole proprietor terminated a Keogh plan in 1981. In 1982, the sole proprietor incorporated and established a corporate plan with a calendar-year plan year. For purposes of determining whether the corporate plan is top-heavy for its 1984 plan year, the terminated Keogh plan and the corporate plan would be part of a required aggregation group. The sole proprietor and the corporation would be treated as a single employer under section 414(c). Under Question and Answer T-4, the terminated plan would be aggregated with the corporate plan because it was maintained within the five-year period ending on the determination date for the 1984 plan year and because, but for the fact that it terminated, it would be aggregated with the corporate plan because it covered a key employee.

T-7 Q. What is a permissive aggregation group?

A. A permissive aggregation group consists of plans of the employer that are required to be aggregated, plus one or more plans of the employer that are not part of a required aggregation group but that satisfy the requirements of sections 401(a)(4) and 410 when considered together with the required aggregation group. This concept may be illustrated by the following examples:

Example (1). (a) An employer maintains two plans:

1. Plan A covers key employees and independently satisfies the requirements of section 410 and 401(a)(4).

2. Plan B covers no key employees. It also independently satisfies the requirements of section 410 and 401(a)(4).

(b) As indicated in Question and Answer T-6, Plan B is not required to be aggregated with Plan A. Further, if Plan B provided contributions or benefits that were not at least comparable to the contributions or benefits provided under Plan A, then Plan B could not be permissively aggregated with Plan A because the contributions and benefits would discriminate if the two plans were considered as a unit. However, if the benefits or contributions under Plan B were comparable to those under Plan A, the two plans would be permitted to be aggregated to determine whether or not the group consisting of both plans is top-heavy. If Plan A and B are permitted to be aggregated, and if the permissive aggregation group is not top-heavy, then neither Plan A nor B would be considered top-heavy.

Example (2). (a) Employer W maintains two plans.

1. Plan C covers salaried employees and independently satisfies the requirements of sections 410 and 401(a)(4).

2. Plan D covers employees who are included in a unit of employees covered by an agreement which the Secretary of Labor has found to be a collective-bargaining agreement between employee representatives and the employer and retirement benefits were bargained for between employee representatives and the employer.

(b) The fact that Plan D is a collectively-bargained plan does not necessarily mean that it may be permissively aggregated with Plan C. In order to be permissively aggregated with Plan C, Plan D must provide contributions or benefits with respect to service with Employer W that are at least comparable to the contributions or benefits provided under Plan C.

T-8 Q. May an employer permissively aggregate multiemployer plans, multiple employer plans and simplified employee pension plans to which the employer contributes with a plan covering key employees or a required aggregated group?

A. Yes. Multiemployer plans, multiple employer plans and simplified employee pensions to which an employer makes contributions may be permissively aggregated with a plan covering key employees or with a required aggregation group if the contributions or benefits provided under the multiemployer plan, multiple employer plan or simplified employee pension by the employer are comparable to the contributions or benefits provided under the plan covering key employees or the plans in the required aggregation group. In making this determination, only the employer's contribution to the simplified employee pension may be used.

T-9 Q. What plans will be treated as top-heavy if they are part of a required aggregation group that is top-heavy?

A. In the case of plans that are required to be aggregated, each plan in the required aggregation group will be top-heavy if the group is top-heavy. No plan in the required aggregation group will be top-heavy if the group is not top-heavy.

T-10 Q. If a required aggregation group is top-heavy, and one plan of the group satisfies the requirements of sections 416(b), (c), and (d), may other plans in the group include provisions which do not satisfy sections 416(b), (c) and (d)?

A. No. Each plan in a required aggregation group is top-heavy if the group is top-heavy. Thus, each plan must contain provisions satisfying the requirements of sections 416(b) and (d). If all the plans are defined contribution plans, only one plan need satisfy the requirements of section 416(c)(2) with respect to any non-key employee who participates in more than one of the plans. If all the plans are defined benefit plans, only one plan need satisfy the requirements of section 416(c)(1) with respect to any non-key employee who participates in more than one of the plans. However, in the case of non-key employees who do not participate in more than one plan, each plan must separately provide the application minimum contribution or benefit with respect to each such employee. See Question and Answer M-12 in the case of employees who are covered under both a defined benefit and a defined contribution plan.

T-11 Q. What plans will be treated as top-heavy if a permissive aggregation group is top-heavy?

A. If a permissive aggregation group is top-heavy, only those plans that are part of the required aggregation group will be subject to the requirements of section 416(b), (c) and (d). Plans that are not part of the required aggregation group will not be subject to these requirements. Thus, if an employer wishes to demonstrate that the plans maintained by the employer are not top-heavy, the employer need consider only the required aggregation group. If, after considering the required aggregation group, it is determined that the plans are not top-heavy, the requirements of section 416(b), (c) and (d) will not apply to any of the plans. If, on the other hand, the plans required to be aggregated are top-heavy, the employer may wish to determine whether there are any plans that may be permissively aggregated to demonstrate that the plans are not top-heavy. Assuming that there are plans that are eligible for permissive aggregation, the employer may take these plans into consideration. If, after taking such plans into consideration, the net result is that the entire group is not top-heavy, the top-heavy requirements do not apply to any plan in the group.

T-12 Q. For purposes of determining whether a plan is top-heavy for a plan year, who is a key employee?

A. Under section 416(i)(1), a key employee is any employee (including any deceased employee) who at any time during the plan year containing the determination date for the plan year in question or the four preceding plan years (including plan years before 1984) is:

1. An officer of the employer having annual compensation from the employer for a plan year greater than 150 percent of the dollar limitation in effect under section 415(c)(1)(A) for the calendar year in which such plan year ends (see Questions and Answers T-13, T-14, and T-15),

2. One of the ten employees having annual compensation from the employer for a plan year greater than the dollar limitation in effect under section 415(c)(1)(A) for the calendar year in which such plan year ends and owning (or considered as owning within the meaning of section 318) both more than a $1/2$ percent interest and the largest interests in the employer (see Question and Answer T-19),

3. A 5-percent owner of the employer, or

4. A 1-percent owner of the employer having annual compensation from the employer for a plan year more than $150,000 (see Questions and Answers T-16 and T-21).

An individual may be considered a key employee in a plan year for more than one reason. For example, an individual may be both an officer and one of the ten largest owners. However, in testing whether a plan or group is top-heavy, an individual's accrued benefit is counted only once. The terms key employee, former key employee, and non-key employee include the beneficiaries of such individuals. This Question and Answer is illustrated by the following examples:

Example (1). An employer maintains a calendar-year plan. An individual who was an employee of the employer and a 5-percent owner of the employer in 1986 was neither an employee nor an owner in 1987 or thereafter. Even though the individual is no longer an employee or owner of the employer, the individual would be treated as a key employee for purposes of determining whether the plan is top-heavy for each plan year through the 1991 plan year. However, for purposes of determining whether the plan is top-heavy for the 1992 plan year and for subsequent plan years, the individual would be treated as a former key employee.

Example (2). The facts are the same as in example (1), except that the individual died in early 1987 and his total benefit under the plan was distributed to his beneficiary in 1987. Such distribution would be treated as the accrued benefit of the individual for each year through the 1991 plan year. However, such individual would be treated as a former key employee for purposes of determining whether the plan is top-heavy for the 1992 plan year and for subsequent plan years. The conclusions are not affected by whether the beneficiary of the individual is a non-key employee or a key employee of the employer.

T-13 Q. For purposes of defining a key employee, who is an officer?

A. Whether an individual is an officer shall be determined upon the basis of all the facts, including, for example, the source of his authority, the term for which elected or appointed, and the nature and extent of his duties. Generally, the term officer means an administrative executive who is in regular and continued service. The term officer implies continuity of service and excludes those employed for a special and single transaction. An employee who merely has the title of an officer but not the authority of an officer is not considered an officer for purposes of the key employee test. Similarly, an employee who does not have the title of an officer but has the authority of an officer is an officer for purposes of the key employee test. In the case of one or more employers treated as a single employer under sections 414(b), (c), or (m), whether or not an individual is an officer shall be determined based upon his responsibilities with respect to the employer or employers for which he is directly employed, and not with respect to the controlled group of corporations, employers under common control or affiliated service group.

A partner of a partnership will not be treated as an officer for purposes of the key employee test merely because he owns a capital or profits interest in the partnership, exercises his voting rights as a partner, and may, for limited purposes, be authorized and does in fact act as an agent of the partnership.

T-14 Q. For purposes of determining whether a plan is top-heavy for a plan year, how many officers must be taken into account?

A. There is no minimum number of officers that must be taken into account. Only individuals who are in fact officers within the meaning of Question and Answer T-13 must be considered. For example, a corporation with only one officer and two employees would have only one officer for purposes of section 416(i)(1)(A)(i). After aggregating all employees (including leased employees within the meaning of section 414(n)) of employers required to be aggregated under section 414(b), (c) or (m), there is a maximum limit to the number of officers that are to be taken into account as officers for the entire group of employers that are so aggregated. The number of employees an employer (including all employers required to be aggregated under section 414(b), (c), or (m)) has for the plan year containing the determination date is the greatest number of employees it had during that plan year or any of the four preceding plan years. For purposes of this Question and Answer, employees include only those individuals who perform services for the employer during a plan year. If the number of employees (including part-time employees) of all the employers aggregated under section 414(b), (c) or (m) is less than 30 employees, no more than three individuals shall be treated as key employees for the plan year containing the determination date by reason of being officers. If the number of employees of all organizations aggregated under section 414(b), (c) or (m) is greater than 30 but less than 500, no more than 10% of the number of employees will be treated as key employees by reason of being officers. (If 10% of the number of employees is not an integer, the maximum number of individuals to be treated as key employees by reason of being officers shall be increased to the next integer.) If the number of employees of employers aggregated under section 414(b), (c) and (m) exceeds 500, no more than 50 employees are to be considered as key employees by reason of being officers. This limited number of officers is comprised of the individual officers, selected from the group of all individuals who were officers in the plan year containing the determination date or any one of the four preceding plan years, who had annual plan year compensation (in the other year) in excess of 150 percent of the dollar limitation in effect under section 415(c)(1)(A) for the calendar year in which the plan year ends and who had the largest annual plan-year compensation in that five-year period. (The definition of compensation contained in Question and Answer T-21 is to be used for this purpose.) In determining the officers of an employer, an employee who is an officer shall be counted as an officer for key employee purposes without regard to whether the employee is a key employee for any other reason. However, in testing whether the plan(s) is top-heavy, an individual's present value of accrued benefits is counted only once.

Example. A company is testing to see if its plan is top-heavy for the 1985 plan year. In each year from 1980 through 1984 it has more than 500 employees. Assume that (1) because of rapid turnover among officers, the individuals who are officers each year are different from the individuals who are officers in any preceding year, and (2) the annual plan year compensation of each officer exceeds 150 percent of the dollar limitation in effect under section 415(c)(1)(A) for the calen-

dar year in which the plan year ends. Under the limitations, only a total of 50 individuals would be considered to be key employees by virtue of being officers in testing for top-heaviness for the 1985 plan year. Further, the 50 individuals considered as key employees under this test would be determined by selecting the 50 out of 250 individuals (50 different officers each year) who had the highest annual plan-year compensation during the 1980-1984 period (while officers).

T-15 Q. For purposes of section 416, do organizations other than corporations have officers?

A. Yes. For purposes of the top-heavy rules, sole proprietorships, partnerships, associations, trusts, and labor organizations may have officers. This rule is effective for purposes of determining whether a plan is top-heavy for plan years which begin after February 28, 1985.

T-16 Q. Who is a 1-percent owner of the employer?

A. (a) If the employer is a corporation, a 1-percent owner is any employee who owns (or is considered as owning within the meaning of section 318) more than 1 percent of the value of the outstanding stock of the corporation or stock possessing more than 1 percent of the total combined voting power of all stock of the corporation. If the employer is not a corporation, a 1-percent owner is any employee who owns more than 1-percent of the capital or profits interest in the employer. The rules of subsections (b), (c), and (m) of section 414 do not apply for purposes of determining who is a 1-percent owner.

(b) For purposes of determining who is a 1-percent owner, 5-percent owner, or top-ten owner, value means fair market value taking into account all facts and circumstances.

T-17 Q. Who is a 5-percent owner of the employer?

A. If the employer is a corporation, a 5-percent owner is any employee who owns (or is considered as owning within the meaning of section 318) more than 5 percent of the value of the outstanding stock of the corporation or stock possessing more than 5 percent of the total combined voting power of all stock of the corporation. If the employer is not a corporation, a 5-percent owner is any employee who owns more than 5 percent of the capital or profits interest in the employer. The rules of subsections (b), (c), and (m) of section 414 do not apply for purposes of determining who is a 5-percent owner.

T-18 Q. How do the rules of section 318 apply for purposes of determining ownership in an entity other than a corporation?

A. For purposes of determining ownership in an entity other than a corporation, the rules of section 318 apply in a manner similar to the way in which they apply for purposes of determining ownership in a corporation. For non-corporate interests, capital or profits interest must be substituted for stock.

T-19 Q. Which employees will be considered one of the top ten owners?

A. (a) For purposes of determining whether a plan is top-heavy for a plan year, the top ten owners are the ten employees who (1) own (or are considered as owning within the meaning of section 318) during the plan year containing the determination date or any of the four preceding plan years both more than a $1/2$ percent ownership interest in value and the largest percentage ownership interests in value of any of the employers required to be aggregated under section 414(b), (c), or (m), and (2) have during the plan year of ownershp annual plan year compensation from the employer more than the limitation in effect under section 415(c)(1)(A) for the calendar year in which such plan year ends. The five years for which the test is made will be referred to as the "testing period." An employee whose annual plan year compensation exceeds the section 415(c)(1)(A) limit in effect for the calendar year in which a plan year in the testing period ends who has an ownership interest greater than $1/2$ percent in that plan year is considered to be one of the top ten owners unless at least ten other employees own a greater interest in the employer during any year of the testing period and have annual plan year compensation during such plan year of ownership greater than the section 415(c)(1)(A) limit in effect for the calendar year in which such plan year ends. Ownership each plan year is determined on the basis of percentage of ownership interest in total ownership value and not dollar amounts. Thus, an employee whose stock interest is valued at 15 percent of the total stock value of a corporation in year one that was worth $15,000 is ranked higher than an employee whose stock interest is valued at 5 percent of the total stock value of the same corporation in year three which is now worth $50,000.

(b) If an employee's ownership interest changes during a plan year, his ownership interest for the year is the largest interest owned at any time during the year. If two employees have the same ownership interest in the employer during the testing period, the employee having the largest annual compensation from the employer for the plan year during any part of which that ownership interest existed shall be treated as having a larger interest. Thus, if 25 employees each own four percent in value of the employer during the testing period, the 10 employees with the largest single plan year compensation during this period will be considered the top ten owners. For purposes of this Question and Answer, compensation has the meaning set forth in Question and Answer T-21. This Question and Answer is illustrated by the following examples:

Example 1. Corporation K maintains a calendar year defined contribution plan. On January 1, 1986, Corporation K has five owners who owned the following value percentages of K stock: A = 50%, B = 20%, C = 15%, D = 10% and E = 5%. On June 30, 1987, the five owners of Corporation K sold all of their shares of stock. The new owners and their respective ownership percentages were: F = 40%, G = 30%, H = 10%, I = 10%, and J = 10%. Assume that, for 1986, A, B, C, D, and E had annual compensation from Corporation K greater than the section 415(c)(1)(A) limit and that, for 1987, F, G, H, I, and J also had compensation from Corporation K greater than the section 415(c)(1)(A) limit. For purposes of determining whether the plan is top-heavy for the 1991 plan year, the top ten owners will include A, B, C, D, E, F, G, H, I and J because no 10 individuals during the testing period, 1986-1990, had a greater ownership interest than these individuals.

Example 2. Assume the same facts in *Example 1*, except that on June 1, 1988, F, G, H, I and J sold their interests to new owners, K, L, M, N, and O. K, L, M, N and O owned, respectively, 30%, 30%, 30%, 5% and 5% of the value of the shares of X. Assume also that for 1988 K, L, M, N, and O earned more than the section 415(c)(1)(A) limitation. For purposes of determining whether the plan is top-heavy for the 1991 plan year, the top ten owners will include: A, B, F, K, G, L, M, and C because these eight individuals owned the highest value percentages of the Corporation K stock. Since D, H, I, and J owned equal 10% interests in value, the two employees of this group who had the largest annual plan year compensation during the plan years of their ownership will be the last 2 top ten owners.

T-20 Q. For purposes of determining whether an employee is a key employee under section 416(i)(1)(A), what aggregation rules apply?

A. In the case of ownership percentages, each employer that would otherwise be aggregated under section 414(b), (c) and (m) is treated as a separate employer. (See section 416(i)(1)(C).) However, for purposes of determining whether an individual has compensation of $150,000, or whether an individual is a key employee by reason of being an officer or a top ten owner, compensation from each entity required to be aggregated under sections 414(b), (c) and (m) is taken into account. These rules may be illustrated by the following example:

Example. An individual owns two percent of the value of a professional corporation, which in turn owns a 1/10th of 1 percent interest in a partnership. The entities must be aggregated in accordance with section 414(m). The individual performs services for the professional corporation and for the partnership. The individual receives compensation of $125,000 from the professional corporation and $26,000 from the partnership. The individual is considered to be a key employee with respect to the employer that comprises both the professional corporation and the partnership because he has a two percent interest in the professional corporation and because his combined compensation from both the professional corporation and the partnership is more than $150,000.

T-21 Q. For purposes of testing whether an individual has compensation of more than $150,000, what definition of compensation must be used?

A. The definition of compensation to be used is the definition in §1.415(c)-2, however, compensation must be determined for a plan year, not a limitation year. Alternatively, compensation that would be stated on an employee's Form W-2, "Wage and Tax Statement," for the calendar year that ends with or within the plan year may be used, although amounts that would have been stated on the employee's Form W-2 but for an election under section 125, 132(f)(4), 401(k), 403(b), 408(k), 408(p)(2)(A)(i), or 457(b) must be included. A plan must use the same definition of compensation for all top-heavy plan purposes for which the definition in this Q and A must be used.

T-22 Q. In the case of an employer who maintains a single plan, when must the determination whether the plan is top-heavy be made?

A. Whether a plan is top-heavy for a particular plan year is determined as of the determination date for such plan year. The determination date with respect to a plan year is defined in section 416(g)(4)(C) as (1) the last day of the preceding plan year, or (2) in the case of the first plan year, the last day of such plan year. Distributions made and the present value of accrued benefits are generally determined as of the determination date. (See Questions and Answers T-24 and T-25 for more specific rules.)

T-23 Q. In the case of an aggregation group, when must the determination whether the group is top-heavy be made?

A. When two or more plans constitute an aggregation group in accordance with section 416(g)(2), the following procedures are used to determine whether the plans are top-heavy for a particular plan year. First, the present value of the accrued benefits (including distributions for key employees and all employees) is determined separately for each plan as of each plan's determination date. The plans are then aggregated by adding together the results for each plan as of the determination dates for such plans that fall within the same calendar year. The combined results will indicate whether or not the plans so aggregated are top-heavy. These rules may be illustrated by the following example:

Example. An employer maintains Plan A and Plan B, each containing a key employee. Plan A's plan year commences July 1 and ends June 30. Plan B's plan year is the calendar year. For Plan A's plan year commencing July 1, 1984, the determination date is June 30, 1984. For Plan B's plan year in 1985 the determination date is December 31, 1984. These plans are required to be aggregated. For each of these plans as of their respective determination dates, the present value of the accrued benefits for key employees and all employees are separately determined. The two determination dates, June 30, 1984, and December 31, 1984, fall within the same calendar year. Accordingly, the present values of accrued benefits as of each of these determination dates are combined for purposes of determining whether the group is top-heavy. If, after combining the two present values, the total results show that the group is top-heavy, Plan A will be top-heavy for the plan year commencing July 1, 1984, and Plan B will be top-heavy for the 1985 calendar year.

T-24 Q. How is the present value of an accrued benefit determined in a defined contribution plan?

A. The present value of accrued benefits as of the determination date for any individual is the sum of (a) the account balance as of the most recent valuation date occurring within a 12-month period ending on the determination date, and (b) an adjustment for contributions due as of the determination date. In the case of a plan not subject to the minimum funding requirements of section 412, the adjustment in (b) is generally the amount of any contributions actually made after the valuation date but on or before the determination date. However, in the first plan year of the plan, the adjustment in (b) should also reflect the amount of any contributions made after the determination date that are allocated as of a date in that first plan year. In the case of a plan that is subject to the minimum funding requirements, the account balance in (a) should include contributions that would be allocated as of a date not later than the determination date, even though those amounts are not yet required to be contributed. Thus, the account balance will include contributions waived in prior years as reflected in the adjusted account balance and contributions not paid that resulted in a funding deficiency. The adjusted account balance is described in Rev. Rul. 78-223, 1978-1 C.B. 125. Also, the adjustment in (b) should reflect the amount of any contribution actually made (or due to be made) after the valuation date but before the expiration of the extended payment period in section 412(c)(10).

T-25 Q. How is the present value of an accrued benefit determined in a defined benefit plan?

A. The present value of an accrued benefit as of a determination date must be determined as of the most recent valuation date which is within a 12-month period ending on the determination date. In the first plan year of a plan, the accrued benefit for a current employee must be determined either (i) as if the individual terminated service as of the determination date or (ii) as if the individual terminated service as of the valuation date, but taking into account the estimated accrued benefit as of the determination date. For the second plan year of a plan, the accrued benefit taken into account for a current participant must not be less than the accrued benefit taken into account for the first plan year unless the difference is attributable to using an estimate of the accrued benefit as of the determination date for the first plan year and using the actual accrued benefit as of the determination date for the second plan year. For any other plan year, the accrued benefit for a current employee must be determined as if the individual terminated service as of such valuation date. For this purpose, the valuation date must be the same valuation date for computing plan costs for minimum funding, regardless of whether a valuation is performed that year.

T-26 Q. What actuarial assumptions are used for determining the present value of accrued benefits for defined benefit plans?

A. (a) There are no specific prescribed actuarial assumptions that must be used for determining the present value of accrued benefits. The assumptions used must be reasonable and need not relate to the actual plan and investment experience. The assumptions need not be the same as those used for minimum funding purposes or for purposes of determining the actuarial equivalence of optional benefits under the plan. The accrued benefit for each current employee is computed as if the employee voluntarily terminated service as of the valuation date. The present value must be computed using an interest and a post-retirement mortality assumption. Pre-retirement mortality and future increases in cost of living (but not in the maximum dollar amount permitted by section 415) may also be assumed. However, assumptions as to future withdrawals or future salary increases may not be used. In the case of a plan providing a qualified joint and survivor annuity within the meaning of section 401(a)(11) as a normal form of benefit, for purposes of determining the present value of the accrued benefit, the spouse of the participant may be assumed to be the same age as the participant.

(b) Except in the case where the plan provides for a nonproportional subsidy, the present value should reflect a benefit payable commencing at normal retirement age (or attained age, if later). Thus, benefits not relating to retirement benefits, such as pre-retirement death and disability benefits and post-retirement medical benefits, must not be taken into account. Further, subsidized early retirement benefits and subsidized benefit options must not be taken into account unless they are nonproportional subsidies. See Question and Answer T-27.

(c) Where the plan provides for a nonproportional subsidy, the benefit should be assumed to commence at the age at which the benefit is most valuable. In the case of two or more defined benefit plans which are being tested for determining whether an aggregation group is top-heavy, the actuarial assumptions used for all plans within the group must be the same. Any assumptions which reflect a reasonable mortality experience and an interest rate not less than five percent or greater than six percent will be considered as reasonable. Plans, however, are not required to use an interest rate in this range.

T-27 Q. In determining the present value of accrued benefits in a defined benefit plan, what standards are applied toward determining whether a subsidy is nonproportional?

A. A subsidy is nonproportional unless the subsidy applies to a group of employees that would independently satisfy the requirements of section 410(b). If two or more plans are considered as a unit for comparability purposes under § 1.410(b)-1(d)(3), subsidies may be necessary in both plans or else the subsidy may be nonproportional. Thus, for example, in the case of a plan which provides an early retirement benefit after age 55 and 20 years of service equal to the normal retirement benefit without actuarial reduction and if the employees who may conceivably reach age 55 with 20 years of service would, as a group, satisfy the requirements of section 410(b), that subsidy is proportional. However, in contrast, consider a plan that provides an early retirement benefit that is the actuarial equivalent of the normal retirement benefit. In determining the early retirement benefit, the plan imposes the section 415 limits only on the early retirement benefit (not on the normal retirement benefit before applying the early retirement reduction factors). In such a plan, a participant with a normal retirement benefit (before limitation by section 415) in excess of the section 415 limits will receive a subsidized early retirement benefit, whereas a participant with a lower normal retirement benefit will not. Thus, such a benefit would be a nonproportional subsidy if the group of individuals who are limited by the limitations under section 415 do not, by themselves, constitute a cross section of employees that could satisfy section 410(b).

T-28 Q. For purposes of determining the present value of accrued benefits in either a defined benefit or defined contribution plan, are the accrued benefits attributable to employee contributions considered to be part of the accrued benefits?

A. The accrued benefits attributable to employee contributions are considered to be part of the accrued benefits without regard to whether such contributions are mandatory or voluntary. However, the amounts attributable to deductible employee contributions (as defined in section 72(o)(5)(A)) are not considered to be part of the accrued benefits.

T-29 Q. How are plans described in section 401(k) treated for purposes of the top-heavy rules?

A. No special top-heavy rules are provided for plans described in section 401(k), except a transitional rule. For plan years beginning after December 31, 1984, amounts which an employee elects to defer are treated as employer contributions for purposes of determining minimum required contributions under section 416(c)(2). However, for plan years beginning prior to January 1, 1985, amounts which an employee elects to have contributed to a plan described in section 401(k) are not treated as employer contributions for these purposes. A plan described in section 401(k) which is top-heavy must provide minimum contributions by the employer and limit the amount of compensation which can be taken into account in providing benefits under the plan.

T-30 Q. What distributions are added to the present value of accrued benefits in determining whether a plan is top-heavy for a particular plan year?

A. Under section 416(g)(3)(A), distributions made within the plan year that includes the determination date and within the four preceding plan years are added to the present value of accrued benefits of key employees and non-key employees in testing for top-heaviness. However, in the case of distributions made after the valuation date and prior to the determination date, such distributions are not included as distributions in section 416(g)(3)(A) to the extent that such distributions are included in the present value of the accrued benefits as of the valuation date. In the case of the distribution of an annuity

contract, the amount of such distribution is deemed to be the current actuarial value of the contract, determined on the date of the distribution. Certain distributions that are rolled over by the employee are not included as distributions. See Question and Answer T-32. A distribution will not fail to be considered in determining the present value of accrued benefits merely because it was made before the effective date of section 416. For purposes of this question and answer, distributions mean all distributions made by a plan, including all distributions of employee contributions made during and before the plan year.

T-31 Q. Are benefits paid on account of death treated as distributions for purposes of section 416(g)(3)?

A. Benefits paid on account of death are treated as distributions for purposes of section 416(g)(3) to the extent such benefits do not exceed the present value of accrued benefits existing immediately prior to death; benefits paid on account of death are not treated as distributions for purposes of section 416(g)(3) to the extent such benefits exceed the present value of accrued benefits existing immediately prior to death. The distribution from a defined contribution plan (including the cash value of life insurance policies) of a participant's account balance on account of death will be treated as a distribution for purposes of section 416(g)(3).

T-32 Q. How are rollovers and plan-to-plan transfers treated in testing whether a plan is top-heavy?

A. The rules for handling rollovers and transfers depend upon whether they are unrelated (both initiated by the employee and made from a plan maintained by one employer to a plan maintained by another employer) or related (a rollover or transfer either not initiated by the employee or made to a plan maintained by the same employer). Generally, a rollover or transfer made incident to a merger or consolidation of two or more plans or the division of a single plan into two or more plans will not be treated as being initiated by the employee. The fact that the employer initiated the distribution does not mean that the rollover was not initiated by the employee. For purposes of determining whether two employers are to be treated as the same employer, all employers aggregated under section 414(b), (c) or (m) are treated as the same employer. In the case of unrelated rollovers and transfers, (1) the plan making the distribution or transfer is to count the distribution as a distribution under section 416(g)(3), and (2) the plan accepting the rollover or transfer is not to consider the rollover or transfer as part of the accrued benefit if such rollover or transfer was accepted after December 31, 1983, but is to consider it as part of the accrued benefit if such rollover or transfer was accepted prior to January 1, 1984. In the case of related rollovers and transfers, the plan making the distribution or transfer is not to count the distribution or transfer under section 416(g)(3) and the plan accepting the rollover or transfer counts the rollover or transfer in the present value of the accrued benefits. Rules for related rollovers and transfers do not depend on whether the rollover or transfer was accepted prior to January 1, 1984.

T-33 Q. How are the aggregate defined benefit and defined contribution limits under section 415(e) affected by the top-heavy rules?

A. Section 416(h) modifies the aggregate limits in section 415(e) for super top-heavy plans and for top-heavy plans that are not super top-heavy but do not provide for an additional minimum contribution or benefit. A plan is a super top-heavy plan if the present value of accrued benefits for key employees exceeds 90% of the present value of the accrued benefits for all employees. In the case of a top-heavy aggregation group, the test is applied to all plans in the group as a whole. These present values are computed using the same rules as are used for determining whether the plan is top-heavy. In the case of a super top-heavy plan, in computing the denominators of the defined benefit and defined contribution fractions under section 415(e), a factor of 1.0 is used instead of 1.25 for all employees. In the case of a top-heavy plan that is not super top-heavy, the same rule applies unless each non-key employer who is entitled to a minimum contribution or benefit receives an additional minimum contribution or benefit. In the case of a defined benefit plan, the additional minimum benefit is one percentage point (up to a maximum of ten percentage points) for each year of service described in Question and Answer M-2 of the participant's average compensation for the years described in Question and Answer M-2. In the case of a defined contribution plan, the additional minimum contribution is one percent of the participant's compensation. If a plan does not provide the applicable additional one percent minimum or if a plan is super top-heavy, the factor of 1.25 may be used for an individual only if there are both no further accruals for that individual under any defined benefit plan and no further annual additions for that individual under any defined contribution plan until the combined fraction satisfies the rules of section 415(e) using the 1.0 factor for that individual. The rules contained in this Question and Answer apply for each limitation year that contains any portion of a plan year for which the plan is top-heavy. This Question and Answer may be illustrated by the following example:

Example. A Corporation maintains a profit-sharing plan and a defined benefit plan, and these plans constitute a required aggregation group. Both plans use the calendar year for the plan year and the limitation year under section 415. The plans were determined to be top-heavy for plan year 1986. The plans use the 1.25 factor under section 415(e), and non-key employees covered by both the profit-sharing and the defined benefit plan accrue, under the defined benefit plan, 3% of compensation for each year of service (up to a maximum of 30%). The plans become super top-heavy for the 1990 plan year. In order to satisfy section 415, no further accruals and no further annual additions may take place for any employee covered by both plans until the combined defined benefit-defined contribution fraction for such employee is less than 1.0, using the 1.0 factor in place of 1.25.

T-34. Q. May plans be permissively aggregated to avoid being super top-heavy?

A. Yes, plans may be permissively aggregated to avoid being super top-heavy.

T-35. Q. What provisions must be contained in a plan to comply with the top-heavy requirements?

A. Section 401(a)(10)(B) provides that a plan will qualify only if it contains provisions which will take effect if the plan becomes top-heavy and which meet the requirements of section 416. See Questions and Answers T-39 and T-40 for rules on what provisions must be included. Under section 401(a)(10(B)(ii), regulations may waive this requirement for some plans. See Question and Answer T-38 for a description of plans that need not include such provisions.

T-36 Q. For an employer who has no employee who has participated or is eligible to participate in both a defined benefit and defined contribution plan (or a simplified employee pension, "SEP") of that employer, what provisions must be in the plan(s) to comply with the top-heavy requirements?

A. (a) If the defined benefit plan has no participants who are or could be participants in a defined contribution plan of the employer (or vice versa), the defined benefit plan (or defined contribution plan) need not include provisions describing the defined benefit or defined contribution fractions for purposes of section 415 and, thus, the plan need not contain provisions to determine whether the plan is super top-heavy or to change any plan provisions if the plan becomes super top-heavy. Furthermore, if the plan contains a single benefit structure that satisfies the requirements of section 416(b), (c), and (d) for each plan year without regard to whether the plan is top-heavy for such year, the plan need not include separate provisions to determine whether the plan is top-heavy or that apply if the plan is top-heavy. If the plan's single benefit structure does not assure that section 416(b), (c), and (d) will be satisfied in all cases, then the plan must include three types of provisions.

(b) First, the plan must contain provisions describing how to determine whether the plan is top-heavy. These provisions must include (1) the criteria for determining which employees are key employees (or non-key employees), (2) in the case of a defined benefit plan, the actuarial assumptions and benefits considered to determine the present value of accrued benefits, (3) a description of how the top-heavy ratio is computed, (4) a description of what plans (or types of plans) will be aggregated in testing whether the plan is top-heavy, and (5) a definition of the determination date and the valuation date applicable to the determination date. These determinations must be based on standards that are uniformly and consistently applied and that satisfy the rules set forth in section 416 and these Questions and Answers. The provisions in (1) and (3) above may be incorporated in the plan by reference to the applicable sections of the Internal Revenue Code without adversely affecting the qualification of the plan. However, the plan must state the definition of compensation for purposes of determining who is a key employee.

(c) Second, the plan must specifically contain the following provisions that will become effective if the plan becomes top-heavy: vesting that satisfies the minimum vesting requirements of section 416(b), benefits that will not be less than the minimum benefits set forth in section 416(c), and the compensation limitation described in section 416(d). The compensation limitation described in section 416(d) may be incorporated by reference. If a plan always meets the requirements of *either* section 416(b), (c) or (d), the plan need not include additional provisions to meet any such requirements.

(d) Third, the plan must include provisions insuring that any change in the plan's benefit structure (including vesting schedules) resulting from a change in the plan's top-heavy status will not violate section 411(a)(10). Thus, if a plan ceases being top-heavy, certain restrictions apply with respect to the change in the applicable vesting schedule.

T-37 Q. For an employer who maintains or has maintained both a defined benefit and a defined contribution plan (or a simplified employee pension, "SEP") and some participants do or could partici-

pate in both types of plan, what provisions must be in the plans to comply with the top-heavy requirements?

A. If an employer maintains (or has maintained) both a defined benefit plan and a defined contribution plan (or SEP), and the plans have or could have participants who participate in both types of plans, then the plans must contain more provisions than those described in Question and Answer T-36. First, the plans may exclude rules to determine whether the plan is top- heavy (or to apply when the plan is top-heavy) only if both plans contain a single benefit structure that satisfies sections 416(b), (c), and (d) without regard to whether the plans are top-heavy. Second, unless the plans always satisfy the requirements of section 415(e) using the 1.0 factor in the defined benefit and defined contribution fractions as described in section 416(h)(1), the plans must include provisions similar to those in Question and Answer T-36 (for top-heavy) to determine whether the plan is super top-heavy and to satisfy section 416(h) if it is.

T-38 Q. Are any plans exempted from including top-heavy provisions?

A. Section 401(a)(10)(B) exempts governmental plans (as defined in section 414(d)) from the top-heavy requirements and provides that regulations may exempt certain plans from including the top-heavy provisions. A plan need not include any top-heavy provisions if the plan: (1) is not top-heavy, and (2) covers only employees who are included in a unit of employees covered by a collective-bargaining agreement (if retirement benefits were the subject of good faith bargaining) or employees of employee representatives. The requirement set forth in section 7701(a)(46) must be met before an agreement will be considered a collective-bargaining agreement after March 31, 1984.

T-39 Q. Must ratios be computed each year to determine whether a plan is top-heavy?

A. No. In order to administer the plan, the plan administrator must know whether the plan is top-heavy. However, precise top-heavy ratios need not be computed every year. If, on examination, the Internal Revenue Service requests a demonstration as to whether the plan is top-heavy (or super top-heavy; see Question and Answer T-33) the employer must demonstrate to the Service's satisfaction that the plan is not operating in violation of section 401(a)(10)(B). For purposes of any demonstration, the employer may use computations that are not precisely in accordance with this section but which mathematically prove that the plan is not top-heavy. For example, if the employer determined the present value of accrued benefits for key employees in a simplified manner which overstated that value, determined the present value for non-key employees in a simplified manner which understated that value, and the ratio of the key employee present value divided by the sum of the present values was less than 60 percent, the plan would not be considered top-heavy. This would be a sufficient demonstration because the simplified fraction could be shown to be greater than the exact fraction and, thus, the exact fraction must also be less than 60 percent.

Several methods that may be used to simplify the determinations are indicated below.

(1) If the top-heavy ratio, computed considering all the key employees and only some of the non-key employees, is less than 60 percent, then it is not necessary to accumulate employee data on the remaining non-key employees. Inclusion of additional non-key employees would only further decrease the ratio.

(2) If the number of key employees is known but the identity of the key employees is not known (i.e. if the only key employees are officers and the limit on officers is applicable), the numerator may be determined by using a hypothetical "worst case" basis. Thus, in the case of a defined benefit plan, if the numerator of the top-heavy ratio were determined assuming each key employee's present value of accrued benefits were equal to the maximum section 415 benefits at the age that would maximize such present value, that assumption would only overstate the present value of accrued benefits for key employees. Thus, if that ratio is less than 60 percent, the plan is not top-heavy and accurate data on the key employees need not be collected.

(3) If the employer has available present value of accrued benefit computations for key and non-key employees in a defined benefit plan, and these values differ from those that would be produced under Question and Answer T-25 only by inclusion of a withdrawal assumption, the present value for the key employees (but not the non-key employees) may be adjusted to a "worst case" value by dividing by the lowest possible probability of not withdrawing from plan participation before normal retirement age. If the top-heavy ratio based on this inflated key employee value is less than 60 percent, the present value need not be recomputed without the withdrawal assumption. The methods set forth in this answer may also be used to determine whether a plan is super top-heavy by inserting "90%" for "60%" in the appropriate places.

T-40 Q. Will a plan fail to qualify if it provides that the $200,000 maximum amount of annual compensation taken into account under section 416(d) for any plan year that the plan is top-heavy may be automatically increased in accordance with regulations under section 416?

A. No.

T-41 Q. If a plan provides benefits based on compensation in excess of $200,000 and the plan becomes top-heavy, must any accrued benefits attributable to this excess compensation be eliminated?

A. No. For any year that a plan is top-heavy, section 416(d) provides that compensation in excess of $200,000 must not be taken into account. However, a top-heavy plan may continue to provide for any benefits attributable to compensation in excess of $200,000 to the extent such benefits were accrued before the plan was top-heavy. Furthermore, section 411(d)(6) will be violated if any individual's pre-top-heavy benefit is reduced by either (1) a plan amendment adding the $200,000 restriction, or (2) an automatic change in the plan benefit structure imposing the $200,000 restriction due to the plan's becoming top-heavy.

T-42 Q. Under a top-heavy defined benefit plan, are the requirements of section 416(d) satisfied if the annual compensation of an employee taken into account to determine plan benefits is limited to the amount currently described in section 416(d) for years during which the plan is top-heavy but higher compensation is taken into account for years before the plan became top-heavy?

A. No. For the top-heavy plan to meet the requirements of section 416(d), compensation for all years, including years before the plan became top-heavy, that is taken into account to determine plan benefits must not exceed the amount currently described in section 416(d). However, if the accrued benefit as of the end of the last plan year before the plan became top-heavy (ignoring any plan amendments after that date) is greater than the accrued benefit determined by limiting compensation in accordance with section 416(d), that higher accrued benefit as of the end of the last plan year before the plan became top-heavy must not be reduced. Providing such higher accrued benefit will not cause the plan to violate section 416(d).

T-43 Q. What happens to an individual who has ceased employment before a plan becomes top-heavy?

A. If an individual has ceased employment before a plan becomes top-heavy, such individual would not be required to receive any additional benefit accruals, contributions, or vesting, unless the individual returned to employment with the employer. See Questions and Answers V-3, M-4, and M-10. In addition, if the individual is receiving benefits based on annual compensation greater than $200,000, such benefits cannot be decreased.

V. Vesting Rules for Top-heavy Plans

V-1 Q. What vesting must be provided under a top-heavy plan?

A. Under section 416(b), the accrued benefits attributable to employer contributions must be nonforfeitable in accordance with one of two statutory standards. Either such accrued benefits must be nonforfeitable after 3 years of service or the nonforfeitable portion of accrued benefits must be at least 20 percent after 2 years of service, 40 percent after 3 years of service, 60 percent after 4 years of service, 80 percent after 5 years of service, and 100 percent after 6 years of service. The accrued benefits attributable to employer contributions has the same meaning as under section 411(c) of the Code. As under section 411(a), the accrued benefits attributable to employee contributions must be nonforfeitable at all times.

V-2 Q. What service must be counted in determining vesting requirements?

A. All service required to be counted under section 411(a) must be counted for these purposes. All service permitted to be disregarded under section 411(a)(4) may similarly be disregarded under the schedules of section 416(b).

V-3 Q. What benefits must be subject to the minimum vesting schedule of section 416(b)?

A. All accrued benefits within the meaning of section 411(a)(7) must be subject to the minimum vesting schedule. These accrued benefits include benefits accrued before the effective date of section 416 and benefits accrued before a plan becomes top-heavy. However, when a plan becomes top-heavy, the accrued benefits of any employee who does not have an hour of service after the plan becomes top-heavy are not required to be subject to the minimum vesting schedule. Accrued benefits which have been forfeited before a plan becomes top-heavy need not vest when a plan becomes top-heavy.

V-4 Q. May a top heavy plan provide a minimum eligibility requirement of the later of age 21 or the completion of 3 years of service and provide that all benefits are nonforfeitable when accrued?

A. Yes. For plan years which begin after December 31, 1984, a top-heavy plan may provide a minimum eligibility requirement of the later of age 21, or the completion of 3 years of service, and provide that all benefits are nonforfeitable when accrued. For plan years which begin before January 1, 1985, "25" may be substituted for "21" in the preceding sentence.

V-5 Q. What does nonforfeitable mean?

A. In general, nonforfeitable has the same meaning as in section 411(a). However, the minimum benefits required under section 416 (to the extent required to be nonforfeitable under section 416(b)) may not be forfeited under section 411(a)(3)(B) or (D). Thus, if benefits are suspended (ceased) during a period of reemployment, the benefit payable upon the subsequent resumption of payments must be actuarially increased to reflect the nonpayment of benefits during such period of re-employment.

V-6 Q. Will a class-year plan automatically satisfy the minimum vesting requirements in section 416(b) if it provides that contributions with respect to any plan year become nonforfeitable no later than the end of the third plan year following the plan year for which the contribution was made?

A. No. Although this vesting schedule is similar to the 3-year minimum vesting schedule permitted by section 416(b)(1)(A), it does not satisfy that minimum. The 3-year vesting schedule in section 416(b)(1)(A) requires that, after completion of 3 years of service, the entire accrued benefit of a participant be nonforfeitable. Under the class-year vesting schedule described above, a portion of a participant's accrued benefit (that portion attributable to contributions for the prior 3 years) is forfeitable regardless of the participant's years of service.

V-7 Q. When a top-heavy plan ceases to be top-heavy, may the vesting schedule be altered to a vesting schedule permitted without regard to section 416?

A. When a top-heavy plan ceases to be top-heavy, the vesting schedule may be changed to one that would otherwise be permitted. However, in changing the vesting schedule, the rules described in section 411(a)(10) apply. Thus, the nonforfeitable percentage of the accrued benefit before the plan ceased to be top-heavy must not be reduced; also, any employee with five or more years of service must be given the option of remaining under the prior (i.e., top-heavy) vesting schedule.

M. Minimum Benefits under Top-Heavy Plans

M-1 Q. Which employees must receive minimum contributions or benefits in a plan?

A. Generally, every non-key employee who is a participant in a top-heavy plan must receive minimum contributions or benefits under such plan. However, see Questions and Answers M-4 and M-10 for certain exceptions. Different minimums apply for defined benefit and defined contribution plans.

M-2 Q. What is the defined benefit minimum?

A. (a) The defined benefit minimum requires that the accrued benefit at any point in time must equal at least the product of (i) an employee's average annual compensation for the period of consecutive years (not exceeding five) when the employee had the highest aggregate compensation from the employer and (ii) the lesser of 2% per year of service with the employer or 20%.

(b) For purposes of the defined benefit minimum, years of service with the employer are generally determined under the rules of section 411(a)(4), (5) and (6). However, a plan may disregard any year of service if the plan was not top-heavy for any plan year ending during such year of service, or if the year of service was completed in a plan year beginning before January 1, 1984.

(c) In determining the average annual compensation for a period of consecutive years during which the employee had the largest aggregate compensation, years for which the employee did not earn a year of service under the rules of section 411(a)(4), (5), and (6) are to be disregarded. Thus, if an employee has received compensation from the employer during years one, two, and three, and for each of these years the employee earned a year of service, then the employee's average annual compensation is determined by dividing the employee's aggregate compensation for these three years by three. If the employee fails to earn a year of service in the next year, but does earn a year of service in the fifth year, the employee's average annual compensation is calculated by dividing the employee's aggregate compensation for years one, two, three, and five by four. The compensation required to be taken into account is the compensation described in Question and Answer T-21. In addition, compensation received for years ending in plan years beginning before January 1, 1984 and compensation received for years beginning after the close of the last plan year in which the plan is top-heavy may be disregarded.

(d) The defined benefit minimum is expressed as a life annuity (with no ancillary benefits) commencing at normal retirement age. Thus, if post-retirement death benefits are also provided, the 2% minimum annuity benefit may be adjusted. (See Question and Answer M-3.) The 2% minimum annuity benefit may not be adjusted due to the provision of pre-retirement ancillary benefits. Normal retirement age has the same meaning as under section 411(a)(8).

(e) Any accruals of employer-derived benefits, whether or not attributable to years for which the plan is top-heavy, may be used to satisfy the defined benefit minimums. Thus, if a non-key employee had already accrued a benefit of 20 percent of final average pay at the time the plan became top-heavy, no additional minimum accruals are required (although the accrued benefit would increase as final average pay increased). Accrued benefits attributable to employee contributions must be ignored. Accrued benefits attributable to employer and employee contributions have the same meaning as under section 411(c).

M-3 Q. What defined benefit minimum must be received if an employee receives a benefit in a form other than a single life annuity or a benefit other than at normal retirement age?

A. If the form of benefit is other than a single life annuity, the employee must receive an amount that is the actuarial equivalent of the minimum single life annuity benefit. If the benefit commences at a date other than at normal retirement age, the employee must receive at least an amount that is the actuarial equivalent of the minimum single life annuity benefit commencing at normal retirement age. Thus, the employee may receive a lower benefit if the benefit commences before the normal retirement age and the employee must receive a higher benefit if the benefit commences after the normal retirement age. No specific actuarial assumptions are mandated providing different actuarial equivalents. However, the assumptions must be reasonable.

M-4 Q. Which employees must accrue a minimum benefit in a top-heavy defined benefit plan?

A. Each non-key employee who is a participant in a top-heavy defined benefit plan and who has at least one thousand hours of service (or equivalent service as determined under Department of Labor regulations, 29 CFR 2530.200b-3) for an accrual computation period must accrue a minimum benefit in a top-heavy defined benefit plan for that accrual computation period. If the accrual computation period does not coincide with the plan year, a minimum benefit must be provided, if required, for both accrual periods within the top-heavy plan year. For a top-heavy plan that does not base accruals on accrual computation periods, minimum benefits must be credited for all periods of service required to be credited for benefit accrual. (See § 1.410(a)-7). A non-key employee may not fail to accrue a minimum benefit merely because the employee was not employed on a specified date. Similarly, a non-key employee may not fail to accrue a minimum benefit because either (1) an employee is excluded from participation (or accrues no benefit) merely because the employee's compensation is less than a stated amount, or (2) the employee is excluded from participation (or accrues no benefit) merely because of a failure to make mandatory employee contributions.

M-5 Q. Would the defined benefit minimum be satisfied if the plan provides a normal retirement benefit equal to the greater of the plan's projected formula or the projected minimum benefit and if benefits accrue in accordance with the fractional rule described in section 411(b)(1)(C)?

A. No. The fact that this fractional rule would not satisfy the defined benefit minimum may be illustrated by the following example. Consider a non-key employee, age 25, entering a top-heavy plan in which the projected minimum for the employee is greater than the projected benefit under the normal formula. Under the fractional rule, the employee's accrued benefit ten years later at age 35 would be 5% (20% × (10/40)). Under section 416, the employee's minimum accrued benefit after ten years of service must be at least 20%. Thus, because the 5% benefit is less than the 20% benefit required under section 416, such benefit would not satisfy the required minimum.

M-6 Q. What benefit must an employer provide in a top-heavy defined benefit employee pay-all plan?

A. The defined benefit minimum in an employee pay-all top-heavy plan is the same as that for a plan which has employer contributions. That is, the employer must provide the benefits specified in Question and Answer M-2.

M-7 Q. What is the defined contribution minimum?

A. The sum of the contributions and forfeitures allocated to the account of any non-key employee who is a participant in a top-heavy defined contribution plan must equal at least 3% of such employee's compensation (see Question and Answer T-21 for the definition of compensation) for that plan year or for the calendar year ending within the plan year. However, a lower minimum is permissible where the largest contribution made or required to be made for key employees is less than 3%. The preceding sentence does not apply to any plan required to be included in an aggregation group if such plan enables a defined benefit plan required to be included in such group to meet the requirements of section 401(a)(4) or 410. The contribution made or required to be made on behalf of any key employee is equal to the ratio of the sum of the contributions made or required to be made and forfeitures allocated for such key employee divided by the compensation (nor in excess of $200,000) for such key employee. Thus, the defined contribution minimum that must be provided for any non-key employee for a top-heavy plan year is the largest percentage of compensation (not in excess of $200,000) provided on behalf of any key employee for that plan year

(if the largest percentage of compensation provided on behalf of any key employee for that plan year is less than 3%).

M-8 Q. If an employer maintains two top-heavy defined contribution plans, must both plans provide the defined contribution minimum for each non-key employee who is a participant in both plans?

A. No. If one of the plans provides the defined contribution minimum for each non-key employee who participates in both plans, the other plan need not provide an additional contribution for such employees. However, the other plan must provide the vesting required by section 416(b) and must limit compensation (based on all compensation from all aggregated employers) in providing benefits as required by section 416(d).

M-9 Q. In the case of the waiver of minimum funding standards of section 412(d), how does section 416 treat the defined contribution minimum?

A. For purposes of determining the contribution that is required to be made on behalf of a key employee, a waiver of the minimum funding requirements is disregarded. Thus, if a defined contribution plan receives a waiver of the minimum funding requirement, and if the minimum contribution required under the plan without regard to the waiver exceeds 3%, the exception described in Question and Answer M-7 does not apply even though no key employee receives a contribution in excess of 3% and even though the amount required to be contributed on behalf of the key employee has been waived. Also, a waiver of the minimum funding requirements will not alter the requirements of section 416. Thus, in the case of a top-heavy defined contribution plan in which the non-key employee must receive an allocation, a waiver of the minimum funding requirements may eliminate a funding violation and such waiver will preclude a violation under section 416 even though the required contribution is not made. However, the adjusted account balance (as described in Rev. Rul. 78-223, 1978-1 C.B. 125) of the non-key employees must reflect the required minimum contribution even though such contribution was not made.

M-10 Q. Which employees must receive the defined contribution minimum?

A. Those non-key employees who are participants in a top-heavy defined contribution plan who have not separated from service by the end of the plan year must receive the defined contribution minimum. Non-key employees who have become participants but who subsequently fail to complete 1,000 hours of service (or the equivalent) for an accrual computation period must receive the defined contribution minimum. A non-key employee may not fail to receive a defined contribution minimum because either (1) the employee is excluded from participation (or accrues no benefit) merely because the employee's compensation is less than a stated amount, or (2) the employee is excluded from participation (or accrues no benefit) merely because of a failure to make mandatory employee contributions or, in the case of a cash or deferred arrangement, elective contributions.

M-11 Q. May either the defined benefit minimum or the defined contribution minimum be integrated with social security?

A. No.

M-12 Q. What minimum contribution or benefit must be received by a non-key employee who participates in a top-heavy plan?

A. In the case of an employer maintaining only one plan, if such plan is a defined benefit plan, each non-key employee covered by that plan must receive the defined benefit minimum. If such plan is a defined contribution plan (including a target benefit plan), each non-key employee covered by the plan must receive the defined contribution minimum. In the case of an employer who maintains more than one plan, employees covered under only the defined benefit plan must receive the defined benefit minimum. Employees covered under only the defined contribution plan must receive the defined contribution minimum. In the case of employees covered under both defined benefit and defined contribution plans, the rules are more complicated. Section 416(f) precludes, in the case of employees covered under both defined benefit and defined contribution plans, either required duplication or inappropriate omission. Therefore, such employees need not receive both the defined benefit and the defined contribution minimums. There are four safe harbor rules a plan may use in determining which minimum must be provided to a non-key employee who is covered by both defined benefit and defined contribution plans. Since the defined benefit minimums are generally more valuable, if each employee covered under both a top-heavy defined benefit plan and a top-heavy defined contribution plan receives the defined benefit minimum, the defined benefit and defined contribution minimums will be satisfied. Another approach that may be used is a floor offset approach (see Rev. Rul. 76-259, 1976-2 C.B. 111) under which the defined benefit minimum is provided in the defined benefit plan and is offset by the benefits provided under the defined contribution plan. Another approach that may be used in the case of employees covered under both defined benefit and defined contribution plans is to prove, using a comparability analysis (see Rev. Rul. 81-202, 1981-2 C.B. 93) that the plans are providing benefits at least equal to the defined benefit minimum. Finally, in order to preclude the cost of providing the defined benefit minimum alone, the complexity of a floor offset plan and the annual fluctuation of a comparability analysis, a safe haven minimum defined contribution is being provided. If the contributions and forfeitures under the defined contribution plan equal 5% of compensation for each plan year the plan is top-heavy, such minimum will be presumed to satisfy the section 416 minimums.

M-13 Q. An employer maintains a defined benefit plan and a profit-sharing plan. Both plans are top-heavy and are members of a required aggregation group. In order to meet the minimum contribution/minimum benefit requirements, the employer decides to contribute 5% of compensation to the profit-sharing plan. What happens if for a particular plan year there are no profits out of which to make contributions to the profit-sharing plan?

A. In this particular situation, in order to satisfy the requirements of section 416(c), the employer must provide the defined contribution minimum, 5% of compensation. This rule is an exception to the general rule that an employer cannot make a contribution to a profit-sharing plan if there are no profits. Alternatively, the employer may provide the defined benefit minimum for this year.

M-14 Q. What minimum contribution or benefit must be received by a non-key employee when he is covered under both a defined benefit plan and defined contribution plan (both of which are top-heavy) of an employer and the employer desires to use a factor of 1.25 in computing the denominators of the defined benefit and defined contribution fractions under section 415(e)?

A. In this particular situation, the employer may use one of the four rules set forth in Question and Answer M-12, subject to the following modifications. The defined benefit minimum must be increased by one percentage point (up to a maximum of ten percentage points) for each year of service described in Question and Answer M-2 of the participant's average compensation for the years described in Question and Answer M-2. The defined contribution minimum is increased to $7^1/_2$ percent of compensation. If the floor offset or comparability analysis approach is used, the defined benefit minimum must be increased by one percentage point (up to a maximum of ten percentage points) for each year of service described in Question and Answer M-2 of the participant's average compensation for the years described in Question and Answer M-2.

M-15 Q. May an employer use a different method each year to meet the requirements of Question and Answer M-12 or Question and Answer M-14 without amending the plans each year?

A. No. An employer must set forth in the plan document the method he will use to meet the requirements of Question and Answer M-12 or M-14, as the case may be. If an employer desires to change the method, the plan document must be amended.

M-16 Q. Will target benefit plans be treated as defined benefit or defined contribution plans for purposes of the top-heavy rules?

A. Target benefit plans will be treated as defined contribution plans for purposes of the top-heavy rules.

M-17 Q. Can a plan described in section 412(i) (funded exclusively by level premium insurance contracts) also satisfy the minimum benefit requirements of section 416?

A. The accrued benefits provided for a non-key employee under most level premium insurance contracts might not provide a benefit satisfying the defined benefit minimum because of the lower cash values in early years under most level premium insurance contracts, and because such contracts normally provide for level premiums until normal retirement age. However, a plan will not be considered to violate the requirements of section 412(i) merely because it funds certain benefits through either an auxiliary fund or deferred annuity contracts, if the following conditions are met:

(1) The targeted benefit at normal retirement age under the level premium insurance contract is determined, taking into account the defined benefit minimum that would be required assuming the current top-heavy (or non top-heavy) status of the plan continues until normal retirement age; and

(2) The benefits provided by the auxiliary fund or deferred annuity contracts do not exceed the excess of the defined benefit minimum benefits over the benefits provided by the level premium insurance contract.

If the above conditions are satisfied, then the plan is still exempt from the minimum funding requirements under section 412 and may still utilize the special accrued benefit rule in section 411(b)(1)(F) subject to the following modifications: Although the portion of the plan funded by the level premium annuity contract is exempt from the minimum funding requirements, the portion funded by an auxiliary fund is subject to those requirements. (Thus, a funding standard account must be maintained and a Schedule B must be filed with the annual report). The accrued benefit for any participant may be determined using the rule in section 411(b)(1)(F) but must not be less than the defined benefit minimum.

M-18 Q. May qualified nonelective contributions described in section 401(m)(4)(C) be treated as employer contributions for purposes of the minimum contribution or benefit requirement of section 416?

A. Yes. This is the case even if the qualified nonelective contributions are taken into account under the actual deferral percentage test of § 1.401(k)-1(b)(2) or under the actual contribution percentage test of § 1.401(m)-1(b).

M-19 Q. May matching contributions described in section 401(m)(4)(A) be treated as employer contributions for purposes of the minimum contribution or benefit requirement of section 416?

A. Matching contributions allocated to key employees are treated as employer contributions for purposes of determining the minimum contribution or benefit under section 416. However, if a plan uses contributions allocated to employees other than key employees on the basis of employee contributions or elective contributions to satisfy the minimum contribution requirement, these contributions are not treated as matching contributions for purposes of applying the requirements of sections 401(k) and 401(m) for plan years beginning after December 31, 1988. Thus these contributions must meet the nondiscrimination requirements of section 401(a)(4) without regard to section 401(m). See § 1.401(m)-1(f)(12) (iii).

M-20 Q. May elective contributions be treated as employer contributions for purposes of satisfying the minimum contribution or benefit requirement of section 416(c)(2)?

A. Elective contributions on behalf of key employees are taken into account in determining the minimum required contribution under section 416(c)(2). However, elective contributions on behalf of employees other than key employees may not be treated as employer contributions for purposes of the minimum contribution or benefit requirement of section 416. See section 401(k)(4)(C) and the regulations thereunder. This Question and Answer is effective for plan years beginning after December 31, 1988. [Reg. § 1.416-1.]

☐ [*T.D. 7997*, 12-28-84. *Amended by T.D. 8357*, 8-8-91, *T.D. 9319*, 4-4-2007 *and T.D. 9849*, 3-11-2019.]

[Reg. § 1.417(a)(3)-1]

§ 1.417(a)(3)-1. Required explanation of qualified joint and survivor annuity and qualified preretirement survivor annuity.—
(a) *Written explanation requirement.*—(1) *General rule.*—A plan meets the survivor annuity requirements of section 401(a)(11) only if the plan meets the requirements of section 417(a)(3) and this section regarding the written explanation required to be provided a participant with respect to a QJSA or a QPSA. A written explanation required to be provided to a participant with respect to either a QJSA or a QPSA under section 417(a)(3) and this section is referred to in this section as a section 417(a)(3) explanation. See § 1.401(a)-20, Q&A-37, for exceptions to the written explanation requirement in the case of a fully subsidized QPSA or QJSA, and § 1.401(a)-20, Q&A-38, for the definition of a fully subsidized QPSA or QJSA.

(2) *Time for providing section 417(a)(3) explanation.*—(i) *QJSA explanation.*—See § 1.417(e)-1(b)(3)(ii) for rules governing the timing of the QJSA explanation.

(ii) *QPSA explanation.*—See § 1.401(a)-20, Q&A-35, for rules governing the timing of the QPSA explanation.

(3) *Required method for providing section 417(a)(3) explanation.*—A section 417(a)(3) explanation must be a written explanation. First class mail to the last known address of the participant is an acceptable delivery method for a section 417(a)(3) explanation. Likewise, hand delivery is acceptable. However, the posting of the explanation is not considered provision of the section 417(a)(3) explanation. But see § 1.401(a)-21 of this chapter for rules permitting the use of electronic media to provide applicable notices to recipients with respect to retirement plans.

(4) *Understandability.*—A section 417(a)(3) explanation must be written in a manner calculated to be understood by the average participant.

(b) *Required content of section 417(a)(3) explanation.*—(1) *Content of QPSA explanation.*—The QPSA explanation must contain a general description of the QPSA, the circumstances under which it will be paid if elected, the availability of the election of the QPSA, and, except as provided in paragraph (d)(3) of this section, a description of the financial effect of the election of the QPSA on the participant's benefits (i.e., an estimate of the reduction to the participant's estimated normal retirement benefit that would result from an election of the QPSA).

(2) *Content of QJSA explanation.*—The QJSA explanation must satisfy either paragraph (c) or paragraph (d) of this section. Under paragraph (c) of this section, the QJSA explanation must contain certain specific information relating to the benefits available under the plan to the particular participant. Alternatively, under paragraph

(d) of this section, the QJSA explanation can contain generally applicable information in lieu of specific participant information, provided that the participant has the right to request additional information regarding the participant's benefits under the plan.

(c) *Participant-specific information required to be provided.*—(1) *In general.*—A QJSA explanation satisfies this paragraph (c) if it provides the following information with respect to each of the optional forms of benefit presently available to the participant (i.e., optional forms of benefit for which the QJSA explanation applies that have an annuity starting date after the providing of the QJSA explanation and optional forms of benefit with retroactive annuity starting dates that are available with payments commencing at that same time)—

(i) A description of the optional form of benefit;

(ii) A description of the eligibility conditions for the optional form of benefit;

(iii) A description of the financial effect of electing the optional form of benefit (i.e., the amounts and timing of payments to the participant under the form of benefit during the participant's lifetime, and the amounts and timing of payments after the death of the participant);

(iv) In the case of a defined benefit plan, a description of the relative value of the optional form of benefit compared to the value of the QJSA, in the manner described in paragraph (c)(2) of this section; and

(v) A description of any other material features of the optional form of benefit.

(2) *Requirement for numerical comparison of relative values.*—(i) *In general.*—The description of the relative value of an optional form of benefit compared to the value of the QJSA under paragraph (c)(1)(iv) of this section must be expressed to the participant in a manner that provides a meaningful comparison of the relative economic values of the two forms of benefit without the participant having to make calculations using interest or mortality assumptions. Thus, in performing the calculations necessary to make this comparison, the benefits under one or both optional forms of benefit must be converted, taking into account the time value of money and life expectancies, so that the values of both optional forms of benefit are expressed in the same form. For example, such a comparison may be expressed to the participant using any of the following techniques—

(A) Expressing the actuarial present value of the optional form of benefit as a percentage or factor of the actuarial present value of the QJSA;

(B) Stating the amount of the annuity that is the actuarial equivalent of the optional form of benefit and that is payable at the same time and under the same conditions as the QJSA; or

(C) Stating the actuarial present value of both the optional form of benefit and the QJSA.

(ii) *Use of one form for both married and unmarried individuals.*—(A) *In general.*—Under the rules of this paragraph (c)(2)(ii), in lieu of providing different QJSA explanations for married and unmarried individuals, the plan may provide a QJSA explanation to an individual that does not vary based on the participant's marital status. Except as specifically provided in this section, any reference in this section to comparing the relative value of an optional form of benefit to the value of the QJSA may be satisfied using the substitution permitted under paragraph (c)(2)(ii)(B) or (C) of this section.

(B) *Substitution of single life annuity for married individual.*—For a married participant, in lieu of comparing the value of each optional form of benefit presently available to the participant to the value of the QJSA, the plan can compare the value of each optional form of benefit (including the QJSA) to the value of a QJSA for an unmarried participant (i.e., a single life annuity), but only if that same single life annuity is available to that married participant.

(C) *Substitution of joint and survivor annuity for unmarried individual.*—For an unmarried participant, in lieu of comparing the value of each optional form of benefit presently available to the participant to the value of the QJSA for that individual (which is a single life annuity), the plan can compare the value of each optional form of benefit (including the single life annuity) to the value of the joint and survivor annuity that is the QJSA for a married participant, but only if that same joint and survivor annuity is available to that unmarried participant.

(iii) *Simplified presentations permitted.*—(A) *Grouping of certain optional forms.*—Two or more optional forms of benefit that have approximately the same value may be grouped for purposes of a required numerical comparison described in this paragraph (c)(2). For this purpose, two or more optional forms of benefit have approximately the same value if none of those optional forms of benefit vary in relative value in comparison to the value of the QJSA by more than 5 percentage points when the relative value comparison is made by

expressing the actuarial present value of each of those optional forms of benefit as a percentage of the actuarial present value of the QJSA. For such a group of optional forms of benefit, the requirement relating to disclosing the relative value of each optional form of benefit compared to the value of the QJSA can be satisfied by disclosing the relative value of any one of the optional forms in the group compared to the value of the QJSA, and disclosing that the other optional forms of benefit in the group are of approximately the same value. If a single-sum distribution is included in such a group of optional forms of benefit, the single-sum distribution must be the distribution form that is used for purposes of this comparison.

(B) *Representative relative value for grouped optional forms.*—If, in accordance with paragraph (c)(2)(iii)(A) of this section, two or more optional forms of benefits are grouped, the relative values for all of the optional forms of benefit in the group can be stated using a representative relative value as the approximate relative value for the entire group. For this purpose, a representative relative value is any relative value that is not less than the relative value of the member of the group of optional forms of benefit with the lowest relative value and is not greater than the relative value of the member of that group with the highest relative value when measured on a consistent basis. For example, if three grouped optional forms have relative values of 87.5%, 89%, and 91% of the value of the QJSA, all three optional forms can be treated as having a relative value of approximately 90% of the value of the QJSA. As required under paragraph (c)(2)(iii)(A) of this section, if a single-sum distribution is included in the group of optional forms of benefit, the 90% relative factor of the value of the QJSA must be disclosed as the approximate relative value of the single sum, and the other forms can be described as having the same approximate value as the single sum.

(C) *Special rule for optional forms of benefit that are close in value to the QJSA.*—The relative value of all optional forms of benefit that have an actuarial present value that is at least 95% of the actuarial present value of the QJSA and no greater than 105% of the actuarial present value of the QJSA is permitted to be described by stating that those optional forms of benefit are approximately equal in value to the QJSA, or that all of those forms of benefit and the QJSA are approximately equal in value.

(iv) *Actuarial assumptions used to determine relative values.*—For the purpose of providing a numerical comparison of the value of an optional form of benefit to the value of the immediately commencing QJSA under this paragraph (c)(2), the following rules apply—

(A) If an optional form of benefit is subject to the requirements of section 417(e)(3) and §1.417(e)-1(d), any comparison of the value of the optional form of benefit to the value of the QJSA must be made using the applicable mortality table and the applicable interest rate as defined in §1.417(e)-1(d)(2) and (3) (or, at the option of the plan, another reasonable interest rate and reasonable mortality table used under the plan to calculate the amount payable under the optional form of benefit); and

(B) All other optional forms of benefit payable to the participant must be compared with the QJSA using a single set of interest and mortality assumptions that are reasonable and that are applied uniformly with respect to all such optional forms payable to the participant (regardless of whether those assumptions are actually used under the plan for purposes of determining benefit payments). For this purpose, the reasonableness of interest and mortality assumptions is determined without regard to the circumstances of the individual participant. In addition, the applicable mortality table and the applicable interest rate as defined in §1.417(e)-1(d)(2) and (3) are considered reasonable actuarial assumptions for this purpose and thus are permitted (but not required) to be used.

(v) *Required disclosure of assumptions.*—(A) *Explanation of concept of relative value.*—The notice must provide an explanation of the concept of relative value, communicating that the relative value comparison is intended to allow the participant to compare the total value of distributions paid in different forms, that the relative value comparison is made by converting the value of the optional forms of benefit presently available to a common form (such as the QJSA or a single-sum distribution), and that this conversion uses interest and life expectancy assumptions. The explanation of relative value must include a general statement that all comparisons provided are based on average life expectancies, and that the relative value of payments ultimately made under an annuity optional form of benefit will depend on actual longevity.

(B) *Disclosure of assumptions.*—A required numerical comparison of the value of the optional form of benefit to the value of the QJSA under this paragraph (c)(2) is required to include a disclosure of the interest rate that is used to develop the comparison. If all optional forms of benefit are permitted to be grouped under paragraph (c)(2)(iii)(A) of this section, then the requirement of this paragraph (c)(2)(v)(B) does not apply for any optional form of benefit not subject to the requirements of section 417(e)(3) and § 1.417(e)-1(d)(3).

(C) *Offer to provide actuarial assumptions.*—If the plan does not disclose the actuarial assumptions used to calculate the numerical comparison required under paragraph (c)(2) of this section, then, the notice must be accompanied by a statement that includes an offer to provide, upon the participant's request, the actuarial assumptions used to calculate the relative value of optional forms of benefit under the plan.

(3) *Permitted estimates of financial effect and relative value.*—(i) *General rule.*—For purposes of providing a description of the financial effect of the distribution forms available to a participant as required under paragraph (c)(1)(iii) of this section, and for purposes of providing a description of the relative value of an optional form of benefit compared to the value of the QJSA for a participant as required under paragraph (c)(1)(iv) of this section, the plan is permitted to provide reasonable estimates (e.g., estimates based on data as of an earlier date than the annuity starting date, a reasonable assumption for the age of the participant's spouse, or, in the case of a defined contribution plan, reasonable estimates of amounts that would be payable under a purchased annuity contract), including reasonable estimates of the applicable interest rate under section 417(e)(3).

(ii) *Right to more precise calculation.*—If a QJSA notice uses a reasonable estimate under paragraph (c)(3)(i) of this section, the QJSA explanation must identify the estimate and explain that the plan will, upon the request of the participant, provide a more precise calculation and the plan must provide the participant with a more precise calculation if so requested. Thus, for example, if a plan provides an estimate of the amount of the QJSA that is based on a reasonable assumption concerning the age of the participant's spouse, the participant can request a calculation that takes into account the actual age of the spouse, as provided by the participant.

(iii) *Revision of prior information.*—If a more precise calculation described in paragraph (c)(3)(ii) of this section materially changes the relative value of an optional form compared to the value of the QJSA, the revised relative value of that optional form must be disclosed, regardless of whether the financial effect of selecting the optional form is affected by the more precise calculation. For example, if a participant provides a plan with the age of the participant's spouse and that information materially changes the relative value of an optional form of benefit (such as a single sum) compared to the value of the QJSA, then the revised relative value of the optional form of benefit and the value of the QJSA must be disclosed, regardless of whether the amount of the payment under that optional form of benefit is affected by the more precise calculation.

(4) *Special rules for disclosure of financial effect for defined contribution plans.*—For a written explanation provided by a defined contribution plan, a description of financial effect required by paragraph (c)(1)(iii) of this section with respect to an annuity form of benefit must include a statement that the annuity will be provided by purchasing an annuity contract from an insurance company with the participant's account balance under the plan. If the description of the financial effect of the optional form of benefit is provided using estimates rather than by assuring that an insurer is able to provide the amount disclosed to the participant, the written explanation must also disclose this fact.

(5) *Simplified presentations of financial effect and relative value to enhance clarity for participants.*—(i) *In general.*—This paragraph (c)(5) permits certain simplified presentations of financial effect and relative value of optional forms of benefit to permit more useful presentations of information to be provided to participants in certain cases in which a plan offers a range of optional forms of benefit. Paragraph (c)(5)(ii) of this section permits simplified presentations of financial effect and relative value for a plan that offers a significant number of substantially similar optional forms of benefit. Paragraph (c)(5)(iii) of this section permits simplified presentations of financial effect and relative value for a plan that permits the participant to make separate benefit elections with respect to parts of a benefit.

(ii) *Disclosure for plans offering a significant number of substantially similar optional forms of benefit.*—(A) *In general.*—If a plan offers a significant number of substantially similar optional forms of benefit within the meaning of paragraph (c)(5)(ii)(B) of this section and disclosing the financial effect and relative value of each such optional form of benefit would provide a level of detail that could be over-*whelming rather than helpful to participants,* then the financial effect and relative value of those optional forms of benefit can be disclosed by disclosing the relative value and financial effect of a representative range of examples of those optional forms of benefit as described in paragraph (c)(5)(ii)(C) of this section if the requirements of paragraph

(c)(5)(ii)(D) of this section (relating to additional information available upon request) are satisfied.

(B) *Substantially similar optional forms of benefit.*—For purposes of this paragraph (c)(5)(ii), optional forms of benefit are substantially similar if those optional forms of benefit are identical except for a particular feature or features (with associated adjustment factors) and the feature or features vary linearly. For example, if a plan offers joint and survivor annuity options with survivor payments available in every whole number percentage between 50% and 100%, those joint and survivor annuity options are substantially similar optional forms of benefit. Similarly, if a participant is entitled under the plan to receive a particular form of benefit with an annuity starting date that is the first day of any month beginning three years before commencement of a distribution and ending on the date of commencement of the distribution, those forms of benefit are substantially similar optional forms of benefit.

(C) *Representative range of examples.*—A range of examples with respect to substantially similar optional forms of benefit as permitted under this paragraph (c)(5) is representative only if it includes examples illustrating the financial effect and relative value of the optional forms of benefit that reflect each varying feature at both extremes of its linear range, plus at least one example illustrating the financial effect and relative value of the optional forms of benefit that reflects each varying feature at an intermediate point. However, if one intermediate example is insufficient to illustrate the pattern of variation in relative value with respect to a varying feature, examples sufficient to illustrate such pattern must be provided. Thus, for example, if a plan offers joint and survivor annuity options with survivor payments available in every whole number percentage between 50% and 100%, and if all such optional forms of benefit would be permitted to be disclosed as approximately equal in value as described in paragraph (c)(5)(ii)(B) of this section, the plan could satisfy the requirement to disclose the financial effect and relative value of a representative range of examples of those optional forms of benefit by disclosing the financial effect and relative value with respect to the joint and 50% survivor annuity, the joint and 75% survivor annuity, and the joint and 100% survivor annuity.

(D) *Requirement to provide information with respect to other optional forms of benefit upon request.*—If a QJSA explanation discloses the financial effect and relative value of substantially similar optional forms of benefit by disclosing the financial effect and relative value of a representative range of examples in accordance with this paragraph (c)(5)(ii), the QJSA explanation must explain that the plan will, upon the request of the participant, disclose the financial effect and relative value of any particular optional form of benefit from among the substantially similar optional forms of benefit and the plan must provide the participant with the financial effect and relative value of any such optional form of benefit if the participant so requests.

(iii) *Separate presentations permitted for elections that apply to parts of a benefit.*—If the plan permits the participant to make separate benefit elections with respect to two or more portions of the participant's benefit, the description of the financial effect and relative values of optional forms of benefit can be made separately for each such portion of the benefit, rather than for each optional form of benefit (i.e., each combination of possible elections).

(d) *Substitution of generally applicable information for participant information in the section 417(a)(3) explanation.*—(1) *Forms of benefit available.*—In lieu of providing the information required under paragraphs (c)(1)(i) through (v) of this section for each optional form of benefit presently available to the participant as described in paragraph (c) of this section, the QJSA explanation may contain the information required under paragraphs (c)(1)(i) through (v) of this section for the QJSA and each other optional form of benefit generally available under the plan, along with a reference to where a participant may readily obtain the information required under paragraphs (c)(1)(i) through (v) of this section for any other optional form of benefit that are presently available to the participant.

(2) *Financial effect and comparison of relative values.*—(i) *General rule.*—In lieu of providing a statement of the financial effect of electing an optional form of benefit as required under paragraph (c)(1)(iii) of this section, or a comparison of relative values as required under paragraph (c)(1)(iv) of this section, based on the actual age and benefit of the participant, the QJSA explanation is permitted to include a chart (or other comparable device) showing the financial effect and relative value of optional forms of benefit in a series of examples specifying the amount of the optional form of benefit payable to a hypothetical participant at a representative range of ages and the comparison of relative values at those same representative ages. Each example in this chart must show the financial effect of electing the optional form of benefit pursuant to the rules of paragraph (c)(1)(iii) of this section, and a comparison of the relative value

of the optional form of benefit to the value of the QJSA pursuant to the rules of paragraph (c)(2) of this section, using reasonable assumptions for the age of the hypothetical participant's spouse and any other variables that affect the financial effect, or relative value, of the optional form of benefit. The requirement to show the financial effect of electing an optional form can be satisfied through the use of other methods (e.g., expressing the amount of the optional form as a percentage or a factor of the amount payable under the normal form of benefit), provided that the method provides sufficient information so that a participant can determine the amount of benefits payable in the optional form. The chart (or other comparable device) must be accompanied by the disclosures described in paragraph (c)(2)(v) of this section explaining the concept of relative value and disclosing certain interest assumptions. In addition, the chart (or other comparable device) must be accompanied by a general statement describing the effect of significant variations between the assumed ages or other variables on the financial effect of electing the optional form of benefit and the comparison of the relative value of the optional form of benefit to the value of the QJSA.

(ii) *Actual benefit must be disclosed.*—The generalized notice described in this paragraph (d)(2) will satisfy the requirements of paragraph (b)(2) of this section only if the notice includes either the amount payable to the participant under the normal form of benefit or the amount payable to the participant under the normal form of benefit adjusted for immediate commencement. For this purpose, the normal form of benefit is the form under which payments due to the participant under the plan are expressed under the plan, prior to adjustments for form of benefit. For example, assuming that a plan's benefit accrual formula is expressed as a straight life annuity, the generalized notice must provide the amount of either the straight life annuity commencing at normal retirement age or the straight life annuity commencing immediately. Reasonable estimates of the type described in paragraph (c)(3)(i) of this section may be used to determine the amount payable to the participant under the normal form of benefit for purposes of this paragraph (d)(2)(ii) if the requirements of paragraphs (c)(3)(ii) and (iii) of this section are satisfied with respect to those estimates.

(iii) *Ability to request additional information.*—The generalized notice described in this paragraph (d)(2) must be accompanied by a statement that includes an offer to provide, upon the participant's request, a statement of financial effect and a comparison of relative values that is specific to the participant for any presently available optional form of benefit, and a description of how a participant may obtain this additional information.

(3) *Financial effect of QPSA election.*—In lieu of providing a specific description of the financial effect of the QPSA election, the QPSA explanation may provide a general description of the financial effect of the election. Thus, for example, the description can be in the form of a chart showing the reduction to a hypothetical participant's normal retirement benefit at a representative range of participant ages as a result of the QPSA election (using a reasonable assumption for the age of the hypothetical participant's spouse relative to the age of the hypothetical participant). In addition, this chart must be accompanied by a statement that includes an offer to provide, upon the participant's request, an estimate of the reduction to the participant's estimated normal retirement benefit, and a description of how a participant may obtain this additional information.

(4) *Additional information required to be furnished at the participant's request.*—The generalized notice described in paragraph (d)(2) of this section must be accompanied by a statement that includes an offer to provide, upon the participant's request, information described in this paragraph (d)(4)(i) and (ii), and a description of how a participant may obtain this additional information.

(i) *Explanation of QJSA.*—If, as permitted under paragraphs (d)(1) and (2) of this section, the content of a QJSA explanation does not include all the items described in paragraph (c) of this section, then, upon a participant's request for any of the information required under paragraphs (c)(1)(i) through (v) of this section for one or more presently available optional forms (including a request for all optional forms presently available to the participant), the plan must furnish the information required under paragraphs (c)(1)(i) through (v) of this section with respect to those optional forms. Thus, with respect to those optional forms of benefit, the participant must receive a QJSA explanation specific to the participant that is based on the participant's actual age and benefit. In addition, the plan must comply with paragraph (c)(3)(iii) of this section. Further, if as permitted under paragraph (c)(2)(v)(B) of this section, the plan does not disclose the actuarial assumptions used to calculate the numerical comparison required under paragraph (c)(2) of this section, then, upon request, the plan must provide the actuarial assumptions used to calculate the relative value of optional forms of benefit under the plan.

(ii) *Explanation of QPSA.*—If, as permitted under paragraph (d)(3) of this section, the content of a QPSA explanation does not include all the items described in paragraph (b)(1) of this section, then, upon a participant's request, the plan must furnish an estimate of the reduction to the participant's estimated normal retirement benefit that would result from a QPSA election.

(5) *Use of participant-specific information in generalized notice.*—A QJSA explanation does not fail to satisfy the requirements of this paragraph (d) merely because it contains an item of participant-specific information in place of the corresponding generally applicable information.

(e) *Examples.*—The following examples illustrate the application of this section. Solely for purposes of these examples, the applicable interest rate that applies to any distribution that is subject to the rules of section 417(e)(3) is assumed to be $5\frac{1}{2}\%$, and the applicable mortality table under section 417(e)(3) and §1.417(e)-1(d)(2) is assumed to be the table that applies as of January 1, 2003. In addition, solely for purposes of these examples, assume that a plan which determines actuarial equivalence using 6% interest and the applicable mortality table under section 417(e)(3) and §1.417(e)-1(d)(2) that applies as of January 1, 1995, is using reasonable actuarial assumptions. The examples are as follows:

Example 1. (i) Participant M participates in Plan A, a qualified defined benefit plan. Under Plan A, the QJSA is a joint and 100% survivor annuity, which is actuarially equivalent to the single life annuity determined using 6% interest and the section 417(e)(3) applicable mortality table that applies as of January 1, 1995. On October 1, 2004, M will terminate employment at age 55. When M terminates employment, M will be eligible to elect an unreduced early retirement benefit, payable as either a single life annuity or the QJSA. M will also be eligible to elect a single-sum distribution equal to the actuarial present value of the single life annuity payable at normal retirement age (age 65), determined using the applicable mortality table and the applicable interest rate under section 417(e)(3).

(ii) Consistent with paragraph (c) of this section, Participant M is provided with a QJSA explanation that describes the single life annuity, the QJSA, and single-sum distribution options under the plan, and any eligibility conditions associated with these options. Participant M is married when the explanation is provided. The explanation indicates that, if Participant M commenced benefits at age 55 and had a spouse age 55, the monthly benefit under an immediately commencing single life annuity is $3,000, the monthly benefit under the QJSA is estimated to be 89.96% of the monthly benefit under the immediately commencing single life annuity or $2,699, and the single sum is estimated to be 74.7645 times the monthly benefit under the immediately commencing single life annuity or $224,293.

(iii) The QJSA explanation indicates that the single life annuity and the QJSA are of approximately the same value, but that the single-sum option is equivalent in value to a monthly benefit under the QJSA of $1,215. (This amount is 45% of the value of the QJSA at age 55 ($1,215 divided by 89.96% of $3,000 equals 45%).) The explanation states that the relative value comparison converts the value of the single life annuity and the single-sum options to the value of each if paid in the form of the QJSA and that this conversion uses interest and life expectancy assumptions. The explanation specifies that the calculations relating to the single-sum distribution were prepared using 5.5% interest and average life expectancy, that the other calculations were prepared using a 6% interest rate and that the relative value of actual annuity payments for an individual can vary depending on how long the individual and spouse live. The explanation notes that the calculation of the QJSA assumed that the spouse was age 55, that the amount of the QJSA will depend on the actual age of the spouse (for example, annuity payments will be significantly lower if the spouse is significantly younger than the participant), and that the amount of the single-sum payment will depend on the interest rates that apply when the participant actually takes a distribution. The explanation also includes an offer to provide a more precise calculation to the participant taking into account the spouse's actual age.

(iv) In accordance with paragraph (c)(3)(ii) of this section, Participant M requests a more precise calculation of the financial effect of choosing a QJSA taking into account that Participant M's spouse is 50 years of age. Using the actual age of Participant M's spouse, Plan A determines that the monthly payments under the QJSA are 87.62% of the monthly payments under the single life annuity, or $2,628.60 per month, and provides this information to M. Plan A is not required to provide an updated calculation of the relative value of the single sum because the value of single sum continues to be 45% of the value of the QJSA.

Example 2. (i) The facts are the same as in *Example 1*, except that the comparison of the relative values of optional forms of benefit to the value of the QJSA is not expressed as a percentage of the actuarial present value of the QJSA, but instead is expressed by disclosing the actuarial present values of the optional forms and the QJSA. In addition, the Plan uses the applicable interest rate and the applicable mortality table under section 417(e)(3) for all comparison purposes.

(ii) Accordingly, the QJSA explanation indicates that the QJSA has an actuarial present value of $498,089, while the single-sum payment has an actuarial present value of $224,293 (i.e. the amount of the single sum is $224,293) and that the single life annuity is approximately equal in value to the QJSA. The explanation states that the relative value comparison converts the value of single life annuity and the QJSA into an amount payable in the form of the single-sum option (even though a single-sum distribution in that amount is not available under the plan) and that this conversion uses interest and life expectancy assumptions. The explanation specifies that the calculations were prepared using 5.5% interest and average life expectancy, and that the relative value of actual annuity payments for an individual can vary depending on how long the individual and spouse live. The explanation notes that the calculation of the QJSA assumed that the spouse was age 55, that the amount of the QJSA will depend on the actual age of the spouse (for example, annuity payments will be significantly lower if the spouse is significantly younger than the participant), and that the amount of the single-sum payment will depend on the interest rates that apply when the participant actually takes a distribution. The explanation also includes an offer to provide a more precise calculation to the participant taking into account the spouse's actual age.

Example 3. (i) The facts are the same as in *Example 1*, except that, in lieu of providing information specific to Participant M in the QJSA notice as set forth in paragraph (c) of this section, Plan A satisfies the QJSA explanation requirement in accordance with paragraph (d)(2) of this section by providing M with a statement that M's monthly benefit under an immediately commencing single life annuity (which is the normal form of benefit under Plan A, adjusted for immediate commencement) is $3,000, along with the following chart. The chart shows the financial effect of electing each optional form of benefit for a hypothetical participant with a $1,000 benefit and a spouse who is the same age as the participant. Instead of showing the relative value of these optional forms of benefit compared to the value of the QJSA, the chart shows the relative value of these optional forms of benefit compared to the value of the single life annuity. Separate charts are provided for ages 55, 60, and 65 as follows:

Age 55 Commencement

Optional Form	Amount of distribution per $1,000 of immediate single life annuity	Relative Value
Life Annuity	$1,000 per month	n/a
QJSA (Joint and 100% survivor annuity)	$900 per month ($900 per month for survivor annuity)	approximately the same value as the Life Annuity
Lump sum	$ 74,764	approximately 45% of the value of the Life Annuity

Age 60 Commencement

Optional Form	Amount of distribution per $1,000 of immediate single life annuity	Relative Value
Life annuity	$1,000 per month	n/a
QJSA (Joint and 100% survivor annuity)	$878 per month ($878 per month for survivor annuity)	approximately the same value as the Life Annuity
Lump sum	$99,792	approximately 66% of the value of the Life Annuity

Age 65 Commencement

Optional Form	Amount of distribution per $1,000 of immediate single life annuity	Relative Value
Life Annuity	$1,000 per month	n/a
QJSA (Joint and 100% survivor annuity)	$852 per month ($852 per month for survivor annuity)	approximately the same value as the Life Annuity
Lump sum	$135,759	approximately the same value as the Life Annuity

(ii) In accordance with paragraph (d)(4)(i) of this section, when Participant M requests specific information regarding the amounts payable under the QJSA, the joint and 100% survivor annuity, and the single-sum distribution and provides the age of M's spouse, Plan A determines that M's QJSA is $2,628.60 per month and the single-sum distribution is $224,293. The actuarial present value of the QJSA (determined using the 5.5% interest and the section 417(e)(3) applicable mortality table) is $498,896 and the actuarial present value of the single life annuity is $497,876. Accordingly, the specific information discloses that the single-sum distribution has a value that is 45% of the value of the single life annuity available to M on October 1, 2004. In accordance with paragraph (c)(2)(iii)(C) of this section, the QJSA notice provides that the QJSA is of approximately the same value as the single life annuity.

Example 4. (i) The facts are the same as in *Example 1*, except that under Plan A, the single-sum distribution is determined as the actuarial present value of the immediately commencing single life annuity. In addition, Plan A provides a joint and 75% survivor annuity that is reduced from the single life annuity and that is the QJSA under Plan A. For purposes of determining the amount of the QJSA, if the participant is married the reduction is only half of the reduction that would normally apply under the actuarial assumptions specified in Plan A for determining actuarial equivalence of optional forms.

(ii) In lieu of providing information specific to Participant M in the QJSA notice as set forth in paragraph (c) of this section, Plan A satisfies the QJSA explanation requirement in accordance with paragraph (d)(2) of this section by providing M with a statement that M's monthly benefit under an immediately commencing single life annuity (which is the normal form of benefit under Plan A, adjusted for immediate commencement) is $3,000, along with the following chart showing the financial effect and the relative value of the optional forms of benefit compared to the QJSA for a hypothetical participant with a $1,000 benefit and a spouse who is three years younger than the participant. For each optional form generally available under the plan, the chart shows the financial effect and the relative value, using the grouping rules of paragraph (c)(2)(iii) of this section. Separate charts are provided for ages 55, 60, and 65, as follows:

Age 55 Commencement

Optional Form	Amount of distribution per $1,000 of immediate single life annuity	Relative Value
Life Annuity	$1,000 per month	approximately the same value as the QJSA
QJSA (joint and 75% survivor annuity for a participant who is married)	$956 per month ($717 per month for survivor annuity)	n/a
Joint and 100% survivor annuity	$886 per month ($886 per month for survivor annuity)	approximately the same value as the QJSA
Lump sum	$165,959	approximately the same value as the QJSA

Age 60 Commencement

Optional Form	Amount of distribution per $1,000 of immediate single life annuity	Relative Value
Life annuity	$1,000 per month	approximately 94% of the value of the QJSA
QJSA (joint and 75% survivor annuity for a participant who is married)	$945 per month ($709 per month for survivor annuity)	n/a
Joint and 100% survivor annuity	$859 per month ($859 per month for survivor annuity)	approximately 94% of the value of the QJSA
Lump sum	$151,691	approximately the same value as the QJSA
Age 65 Commencement		
Optional Form	Amount of distribution per $1,000 of immediate single life annuity	Relative Value
Life Annuity	$1,000 per month	approximately 93% of the value of the QJSA
QJSA (joint and 75% survivor annuity for a participant who is married)	$932 per month ($699 per month for survivor annuity)	n/a
Joint and 100% survivor annuity	$828 per month ($828 per month for survivor annuity)	approximately 93% of the value of the QJSA
Lump sum	$135,759	approximately 93% of the value of the QJSA

(iii) The chart disclosing the financial effect and relative value of the optional forms specifies that the calculations were prepared assuming that the spouse is three years younger than the participant, that the calculations relating to the single-sum distribution were prepared using 5.5% interest and average life expectancy, that the other calculations were prepared using a 6% interest rate, and that the relative value of actual payments for an individual can vary depending on how long the individual and spouse live. The explanation states that the relative value comparison converts the single life annuity, the joint and 100% survivor annuity, and the single-sum options to value of each if paid in the form of the QJSA and that this conversion uses interest and life expectancy assumptions. The explanation notes that the calculation of the QJSA depends on the actual age of the spouse (for example, annuity payments will be significantly lower if the spouse is significantly younger than the participant), and that the amount of the single-sum payment will depend on the interest rates that apply when the participant actually takes a distribution. The explanation also includes an offer to provide a calculation specific to the participant upon request, and an offer to provide mortality tables used in preparing calculations upon request.

(iv) In accordance with paragraph (d)(4)(i) of this section, Participant M requests specific information regarding the amounts payable under the QJSA, the joint and 100% survivor annuity, and the single sum.

(v) Based on the information about the age of Participant M's spouse, Plan A determines that M's QJSA is $2,856.30 per month, the joint and 100% survivor annuity is $2,628.60 per month, and the single sum is $497,876. The actuarial present value of the QJSA (determined using the 5.5% interest and the section 417(e)(3) applicable mortality table, the actuarial assumptions required under section 417) is $525,091. Accordingly, the value of the single-sum distribution available to M on October 1, 2004, is 94.8% of the actuarial present value of the QJSA. In addition, the actuarial present value of the life annuity and the 100% joint and survivor annuity are 95.0% of the actuarial present value of the QJSA.

(vi) Plan A provides M with a QJSA explanation that incorporates these more precise calculations of the financial effect and relative value of the optional forms for which M requested information.

(f) *Effective date.*—(1) *General effective date for QJSA explanations.*—(i) *In general.*—Except as otherwise provided in this paragraph (f), this section applies to a QJSA explanation with respect to any distribution with an annuity starting date that is on or after February 1, 2006.

(ii) *Reasonable, good faith transition rule.*—Except with respect to any portion of a QJSA explanation that is subject to the earlier effective date rule of paragraph (f)(2) of this section, a reasonable, good faith effort to comply with these regulations will be deemed to satisfy the requirements of these regulations for QJSA explanations provided before January 1, 2007, with respect to distributions with annuity starting dates that are on or after February 1, 2006. For this purpose, a reasonable, good faith effort to comply with these regulations includes substantial compliance with § 1.417(a)(3)-1 as it appeared in 26 CFR Part 1 revised April 1, 2004.

(2) *Special effective date for certain QJSA explanations.*—(i) *Application to QJSA explanations with respect to certain optional forms that are less valuable than the QJSA.*—This section also applies to a QJSA explanation with respect to any distribution with an annuity starting date that is on or after October 1, 2004, and before February 1, 2006, if the actuarial present value of any optional form of benefit that is subject to the requirements of section 417(e)(3) is less than the actuarial present value (as determined under § 1.417(e)-1(d)) of the

QJSA. For purposes of this paragraph (f)(2)(i), the actuarial present value of an optional form is treated as not less than the actuarial present value of the QJSA if—

(A) Using the applicable interest rate and applicable mortality table under § 1.417(e)-1(d)(2) and (3), the actuarial present value of that optional form is not less than the actuarial present value of the QJSA for an unmarried participant; and

(B) Using reasonable actuarial assumptions, the actuarial present value of the QJSA for an unmarried participant is not less than the actuarial present value of the QJSA for a married participant.

(ii) *Requirement to disclose differences in value for certain optional forms.*—A QJSA explanation with respect to any distribution with an annuity starting date that is on or after October 1, 2004, and before February 1, 2006, is only required to be provided under this section with respect to—

(A) An optional form of benefit that is subject to the requirements of section 417(e)(3) and that has an actuarial present value that is less than the actuarial present value of the QJSA (as described in paragraph (f)(2)(i) of this section); and

(B) The QJSA (determined without application of paragraph (c)(2)(ii) of this section).

(iii) *Application to QJSA explanations with respect to optional forms that are approximately equal in value to the QJSA.*—Paragraph (c)(2)(iii)(C) of this section, relating to disclosures of optional forms of benefit that are permitted to be described as approximately equal in value to the QJSA, is not applicable to a QJSA explanation provided before January 1, 2007. However, § 1.417(a)(3)-1(c)(2)(iii)(C), as it appeared in 26 CFR part 1 revised April 1, 2004, applies to a QJSA explanation with respect to any distribution with an annuity starting date that is on or after October 1, 2004, and that is provided before January 1, 2007.

(3) *Annuity starting date.*—For purposes of paragraphs (f)(1) and (2) of this section, in the case of a retroactive annuity starting date under section 417(a)(7), as described in § 1.417(e)-1(b)(3)(vi), the date of commencement of the actual payments based on the retroactive annuity starting date is substituted for the annuity starting date.

(4) *Effective date for QPSA explanations.*—This section applies to any QPSA explanation provided on or after July 1, 2004. [Reg. § 1.417(a)(3)-1.]

☐ [*T.D. 9099, 12-16-2003. Amended by T.D. 9256, 3-23-2006 (corrected 5-5-2006) and T.D. 9294, 10-19-2006.*]

[Reg. § 1.417(e)-1]

§ 1.417(e)-1. Restrictions and valuations of distributions from plans subject to sections 401(a)(11) and 417.—(a) *Scope.*—(1) *In general.*—A plan does not satisfy the requirements of sections 401(a)(11) and 417 unless it satisfies the consent requirements, the determination of present value requirements and the other requirements set forth in this section. See section 401(a)(11) and § 1.401(a)-11A for other rules regarding the survivor annuity requirements.

(2) *Additional requirements.*—See § 1.411(a)-11 for other rules applicable to the consent requirements.

(3) *Accrued benefit.*—The definition of "accrued benefit" in § 1.411(a)-11 applies when that term is used in this section.

(b) *Consent, etc. requirements.*—(1) *General rule.*—Generally, plans may not commence the distribution of any portion of a participant's accrued benefit in any form unless the applicable consent requirements are satisfied. No consent of the participant or spouse is needed for distribution of a QJSA or QPSA after the benefit is no longer immediately distributable (after the participant attains (or would have attained if not dead) the later of normal retirement age (as defined in section 411(a)(8)) or age 62). No consent of the spouse is needed for distribution of a QJSA at any time. After the participant's death, a benefit may be paid to a nonspouse beneficiary without the beneficiary's consent. A distribution cannot be made at any time in a form other than a QJSA unless such QJSA has been waived by the participant and such waiver has been consented to by the spouse. A QJSA is an annuity that commences immediately. Thus, for example, a plan may not offer a participant separating from service at age 45 a choice only between a single sum distribution at separation of service and a joint and survivor annuity that satisfies all the requirements of a QJSA except that it commences at normal retirement age rather than immediately. To satisfy this section, the plan must also offer a QJSA (i.e., an annuity that satisfies all the requirements for a QJSA including the requirement that it commences immediately).

(2) *Consent.*—(i) Written consent of the participant and, if the participant is married at the annuity starting date and the benefit is to be paid in a form other than a QJSA, the participant's spouse (or, if either the participant or the spouse has died, the survivor) is required before the commencement of the distribution of any part of an accrued benefit if the present value of the nonforfeitable benefit is greater than the cash-out limit in effect under §1.411(a)-11(c)(3)(ii). No consent is valid unless the participant has received a general description of the material features, and an explanation of the relative values of, the optional forms of benefit available under the plan in a manner which would satisfy the notice requirements of section 417(a)(3). See §1.417(a)(3)-1. No consent is required before the annuity starting date if the present value of the nonforfeitable benefit is not more than the cash-out limit in effect under §1.411(a)-11(c)(3)(ii). After the annuity starting date, consent is required for the immediate distribution of the present value of the accrued benefit being distributed in any form, including a qualified joint and survivor annuity or a qualified preretirement survivor annuity, regardless of the amount of such present value.

(ii) In determining the present value of any nonforfeitable accrued benefit, a defined benefit plan is limited by the interest rate restriction as set forth in paragraph (d) of this section.

(iii) Paragraph (b)(2)(i) of this section applies to distributions made on or after October 17, 2000. For distributions prior to October 17, 2000, §1.417(e)-1(b)(2)(i) in effect prior to October 17, 2000 (as contained in 26 CFR part 1 revised as of April 1, 2000) applies.

(3) *Time of consent.*—(i) Written consent of the participant and the participant's spouse to the distribution must be made not more than 90 days before the annuity starting date, and, except as otherwise provided in paragraphs (b)(3)(iii) and (b)(3)(iv) of this section, no later than the annuity starting date.

(ii) A plan must provide participants with the written explanation of the QJSA required by section 417(a)(3) no less than 30 days and no more than 90 days before the annuity starting date, except as provided in paragraph (b)(3)(iv) of this section regarding retroactive annuity starting dates. However, if the participant, after having received the written explanation of the QJSA, affirmatively elects a form of distribution and the spouse consents to that form of distribution (if necessary), a plan will not fail to satisfy the requirements of section 417(a) merely because the written explanation was provided to the participant less than 30 days before the annuity starting date, provided that the following conditions are met:

(A) The plan administrator provides information to the participant clearly indicating that (in accordance with the first sentence of this paragraph (b)(3)(ii)) the participant has a right to at least 30 days to consider whether to waive the QJSA and consent to a form of distribution other than a QJSA.

(B) The participant is permitted to revoke an affirmative distribution election at least until the annuity starting date, or, if later, at any time prior to the expiration of the 7-day period that begins the day after the explanation of the QJSA is provided to the participant.

(C) The annuity starting date is after the date that the explanation of the QJSA is provided to the participant.

(D) Distribution in accordance with the affirmative election does not commence before the expiration of the 7-day period that begins the day after the explanation of the QJSA is provided to the participant.

(iii) The plan may permit the annuity starting date to be before the date that any affirmative distribution election is made by the participant (and before the date that distribution is permitted to commence under paragraph (b)(3)(ii)(D) of this section), provided that, except as otherwise provided in paragraph (b)(3)(vii) of this section regarding administrative delay, distributions commence not more than 90 days after the explanation of the QJSA is provided.

(iv) *Retroactive annuity starting dates.*—(A) Notwithstanding the requirements of paragraphs (b)(3)(i) and (ii) of this section, pursuant to section 417(a)(7), a defined benefit plan is permitted to provide benefits based on a retroactive annuity starting date if the requirements described in paragraph (b)(3)(v) of this section are satisfied. A defined benefit plan is not required to provide for retroactive annuity starting dates. If a plan does provide for a retroactive annuity starting date, it may impose conditions on the availability of a retroactive annuity starting date in addition to those imposed by paragraph (b)(3)(v) of this section, provided that imposition of those additional conditions does not violate any of the rules applicable to qualified plans. For example, a plan that includes a single sum payment as a benefit option may limit the election of a retroactive annuity starting date to those participants who do not elect the single sum payment. A defined contribution plan is not permitted to have a retroactive annuity starting date.

(B) For purposes of this section, a "retroactive annuity starting date" is an annuity starting date affirmatively elected by a participant that occurs on or before the date the written explanation required by section 417(a)(3) is provided to the participant. In order for a plan to treat a participant as having elected a retroactive annuity starting date, future periodic payments with respect to a participant who elects a retroactive annuity starting date must be the same as the future periodic payments, if any, that would have been paid with respect to the participant had payments actually commenced on the retroactive annuity starting date. The participant must receive a make-up payment to reflect any missed payment or payments for the period from the retroactive annuity starting date to the date of the actual make-up payment (with an appropriate adjustment for interest from the date the missed payment or payments would have been made to the date of the actual make-up payment). Thus, the benefit determined as of the retroactive annuity starting date must satisfy the requirements of sections 417(e)(3), if applicable, and section 415 with the applicable interest rate and applicable mortality table determined as of that date. Similarly, a participant is not permitted to elect a retroactive annuity starting date that precedes the date upon which the participant could have otherwise started receiving benefits (e.g., in the case of an ongoing plan, the earlier of the participant's termination of employment or the participant's normal retirement age) under the terms of the plan in effect as of the retroactive annuity starting date. A plan does not fail to treat a participant as having elected a retroactive annuity starting date as described in this paragraph (b)(3)(iv)(B) merely because the distributions are adjusted to the extent necessary to satisfy the requirements of paragraph (b)(3)(v)(B) and (C) of this section relating to sections 415 and 417(e)(3).

(C) If the participant's spouse as of the retroactive annuity starting date would not be the participant's spouse determined as if the date distributions commence was the participant's annuity starting date, consent of that former spouse is not needed to waive the QJSA with respect to the retroactive annuity starting date, unless otherwise provided under a qualified domestic relations order (as defined in section 414(p)).

(D) A distribution payable pursuant to a retroactive annuity starting date election is treated as excepted from the present value requirements of paragraph (d) of this section under paragraph (d)(6) of this section if the distribution form would have been described in paragraph (d)(6) of this section had the distribution actually commenced on the retroactive annuity starting date. Similarly, annuity payments that otherwise satisfy the requirements of a QJSA under section 417(b) will not fail to be treated as a QJSA for purposes of section 415(b)(2)(B) merely because a retroactive annuity starting date is elected and a make-up payment is made. Also, for purposes of section 72(t)(2)(A)(iv), a distribution that would otherwise be one of a series of substantially equal periodic payments will be treated as one of a series of substantially equal periodic payments notwithstanding the distribution of a make-up payment provided for in paragraph (b)(3)(iv)(B) of this section.

(E) The following example illustrates the application of paragraph (b)(3)(ivi)(D) of this section:

Example. Under the terms of a defined benefit plan, participant A is entitled to a QJSA with a monthly payment of $1,500 beginning as of his annuity starting date. Due to administrative error, the QJSA explanation is provided to A after the annuity starting date. After receiving the QJSA explanation A elects a retroactive annuity starting date. Pursuant to this election, A begins to receive a monthly payment of $1,500 and also receives a make-up payment of $10,000. Under these circumstances the monthly payments may be treated as a QJSA for purposes of section 415(b)(2)(B). In addition, the monthly payments of $1,500 and the make-up payment of $10,000 may be treated as part of as series of substantially equal periodic payments for purpose of section 72(t)(2)(A)(iv).

(v) *Requirements applicable to retroactive annuity starting dates.*— A distribution is permitted to have a retroactive annuity starting date with respect to a participant's benefit only if the following requirements are met:

(A) The participant's spouse (including an alternate payee who is treated as the spouse under a qualified domestic relations order (QDRO), as defined in section 414(p)), determined as if the date distributions commence were the participant's annuity starting date, consents to the distribution in a manner that would satisfy the requirements of section 417(a)(2). The spousal consent requirement of this paragraph (b)(3)(v)(A) is satisfied if such spouse consents to the distribution under paragraph (b)(2)(i) of this section. The spousal consent requirement of this paragraph (b)(3)(v)(A) does not apply if the amount of such spouses survivor annuity payments under the retroactive annuity starting date election is no less than the amount that the survivor payments to such spouse would have been under an optional form of benefit that would satisfy the requirements to be a QJSA under section 417(b) and that has an annuity starting date after the date that the explanation was provided.

(B) The distribution (including appropriate interest adjustments) provided based on the retroactive annuity starting date would satisfy the requirements of section 415 if the date the distribution commences is substituted for the annuity starting date for all purposes, including for purposes of determining the applicable interest rate and the applicable mortality table. However, in the case of a form of benefit that would have been excepted from the present value requirements of paragraph (d) of this section under paragraph (d)(6) of this section if the distribution had actually commenced on the retroactive annuity starting date, the requirement to apply section 415 as of the date distribution commences set forth in this paragraph (b)(3)(v)(B) does not apply if the date distribution commences is twelve months or less from the retroactive annuity starting date.

(C) In the case of a form of benefit that would have been subject to section 417(e)(3) and paragraph (d) of this section if distributions had commenced as of the retroactive annuity starting date, the distribution is no less than the benefit produced by applying the applicable interest rate and the applicable mortality table determined as of the date the distribution commences to the annuity form that corresponds to the annuity form that was used to determine the benefit amount as of the retroactive annuity starting date. Thus, for example, if a distribution paid pursuant to an election of a retroactive annuity starting date is a single-sum distribution that is based on the present value of the straight life annuity payable at normal retirement age, then the amount of the distribution must be no less than the present value of the annuity payable at normal retirement age, determined as of the distribution date using the applicable mortality table and applicable interest rate that apply as of the distribution date. Likewise, if a distribution paid pursuant to an election of a retroactive annuity starting date is a single-sum distribution that is based on the present value of the early retirement annuity payable as of the retroactive annuity starting date, then the amount of the distribution must be no less than the present value of the early retirement annuity payable as of the distribution date, determined as of the distribution date using the applicable mortality table and applicable interest rate that apply as of the distribution date.

(vi) *Timing of notice and consent requirements in the case of retroactive annuity starting dates.*—In the case of a retroactive annuity starting date, the date of the first actual payment of benefits based on the retroactive annuity starting date is substituted for the annuity starting date for purposes of satisfying the timing requirements for giving consent and providing an explanation of the QJSA provided in paragraphs (b)(3)(i) and (ii) of this section, except that the substitution does not apply for purposes of paragraph (b)(3)(iii) of this section. Thus, the written explanation required by section 417(a)(3)(A) must generally be provided no less than 30 days and no more than 90 days before the date of the first payment of benefits and the election to receive the distribution must be made after the written explanation is provided and on or before the date of the first payment. Similarly, the written explanation may also be provided less than 30 days prior to the first payment of benefits if the requirements of paragraph (b)(3)(ii) of this section would be satisfied if the date of the first payment is substituted for the annuity starting date.

(vii) *Administrative delay.*—A plan will not fail to satisfy the 90-day timing requirements of paragraphs (b)(3)(iii) and (vi) of this section merely because, due solely to administrative delay, a distribution commences more than 90 days after the written explanation of the QJSA is provided to the participant.

(viii) The following example illustrates the provisions of this paragraph (b)(3):

Example. Employee E, a married participant in a defined benefit plan who has terminated employment, is provided with the explanation of the QJSA on November 28. Employee E elects (with spousal consent) on December 2 to waive the QJSA and receive an immediate distribution in the form of a single life annuity. The plan may permit Employee E to receive payments with an annuity start-

ing date of December 1, provided that the first payment is made no earlier than December 6 and the participant does not revoke the election before that date. The plan can make the remaining monthly payments on the first day of each month thereafter in accordance with its regular payment schedule.

(ix) The additional rules of this paragraph (b)(3) concerning the notice and consent requirements of section 417 apply to distributions on or after September 22, 1995. For distributions before September 22, 1995, the additional rules concerning the notice and consent requirements of section 417 in § 1.417(e)-1(b)(3) in effect prior to September 22, 1995 (see § 1.417(e)-1 (b)(3) in 26 CFR Part 1 revised as of April 1, 1995) apply.

(4) *Delegation to Commissioner.*—The Commissioner, in revenue rulings, notices, and other guidance published in the Internal Revenue Bulletin, may modify, or provide additional guidance with respect to, the notice and consent requirements of this section. See § 601.601(d)(2)(ii)(*b*) of this chapter.

(c) *Permitted distributions.*—A plan may not require that a participant or surviving spouse begin to receive benefits without satisfying paragraph (b) of this section while such benefits are immediately distributable, (see paragraph (b)(1) of this section). Once benefits are no longer immediately distributable, all benefits that the plan requires to begin must be provided in the form of a QJSA and QPSA unless the applicable written explanation, election and consent requirement of section 417 are satisfied.

(d) *Present value requirement.*—(1) *General rule.*—(i) *Defined benefit plans.*—Except as provided in section 401(a)(13) and the regulations thereunder, a defined benefit plan must provide that the present value of any accrued benefit and the amount (subject to sections 411(c)(3) and 415) of any distribution, including a single sum, must not be less than the amount calculated using the applicable interest rate described in paragraph (d)(3) of this section (determined for the month described in paragraph (d)(4) of this section) and the applicable mortality table described in paragraph (d)(2) of this section. The present value of any optional form of benefit cannot be less than the present value of the normal retirement benefit determined in accordance with the preceding sentence. The same rules used for the plan under this paragraph (d) must also be used to compute the present value of the benefit for purposes of determining whether consent for a distribution is required under paragraph (b) of this section.

(ii) *Defined contribution plans.*—Because the accrued benefit under a defined contribution plan equals the account balance, a defined contribution plan is not subject to the requirements of this paragraph (d), regardless of whether the requirements of section 401(a)(11) apply to the plan.

(2) *Applicable mortality table.*—The applicable mortality table is the mortality table based on the prevailing commissioners' standard table (described in section 807(d)(5)(A)) used to determine reserves for group annuity contracts issued on the date as of which present value is being determined (without regard to any other subparagraph of section 807(d)(5)), that is prescribed by the Commissioner in revenue rulings, notices, or other guidance published in the Internal Revenue Bulletin (see § 601.601(d)(2)(ii)(*b*) of this chapter). The Commissioner may prescribe rules that apply in the case of a change to the prevailing commissioners' standard table (described in section 807(d)(5)(A)) used to determine reserves for group annuity contracts, in revenue rulings, notices, or other guidance published in the Internal Revenue Bulletin (see § 601.601(d)(2)(ii)(*b*) of this chapter).

(3) *Applicable interest rate.*—(i) *General rule.*—The applicable interest rate for a month is the annual interest rate on 30-year Treasury securities as specified by the Commissioner for that month in revenue rulings, notices or other guidance published in the Internal Revenue Bulletin (see § 601.601(d)(2)(ii)(*b*) of this chapter).

(ii) *Example.*—This example illustrates the rules of this paragraph (d)(3):

Example. Plan A is a calendar year plan. For its 1995 plan year, Plan A provides that the applicable mortality table is the table described in Rev. Rul. 95-6 (1995-1 C.B. 80), and that the applicable interest rate is the annual interest rate on 30-year Treasury securities as specified by the Commissioner for the first full calendar month preceding the calendar month that contains the annuity starting date. Participant P is age 65 in January 1995, which is the month that contains P's annuity starting date. P has an accrued benefit payable monthly of $1,000 and has elected to receive a distribution in the form of a single sum in January 1995. The annual interest rate on 30-year Treasury securities as published by the Commissioner for December 1994 is 7.87 percent. To satisfy the requirements of section 417(e)(3) and this paragraph (d), the single sum received by P may not be less than $111,351.

(4) *Time for determining interest rate.*—(i) *General rule.*—Except as provided in paragraph (d)(4)(iv) or (v) of this section, the applicable interest rate to be used for a distribution is the rate determined under paragraph (d)(3) of this section for the applicable lookback month. The applicable lookback month for a distribution is the lookback month (as described in paragraph (d)(4)(iii) of this section) for the month (or other longer stability period described in paragraph (d)(4)(ii) of this section) that contains the annuity starting date for the distribution. The time and method for determining the applicable interest rate for each participant's distribution must be determined in a consistent manner that is applied uniformly to all participants in the plan.

(ii) *Stability period.*—A plan must specify the period for which the applicable interest rate remains constant. This stability period may be one calendar month, one plan quarter, one calendar quarter, one plan year, or one calendar year.

(iii) *Lookback month.*—A plan must specify the lookback month that is used to determine the applicable interest rate. The lookback month may be the first, second, third, fourth, or fifth full calendar month preceding the first day of the stability period.

(iv) *Permitted average interest rate.*—A plan may apply the rules of paragraph (d)(4)(i) of this section by substituting a permitted average interest rate with respect to the plan's stability period for the rate determined under paragraph (d)(3) of this section for the applicable lookback month for the stability period. For this purpose, a permitted average interest rate with respect to a stability period is an interest rate that is computed by averaging the applicable interest rates determined under paragraph (d)(3) of this section for two or more consecutive months from among the first, second, third, fourth, and fifth calendar months preceding the first day of the stability period. For this paragraph (d)(4)(iv) to apply, a plan must specify the manner in which the permitted average interest rate is computed.

(v) *Additional determination dates.*—The Commissioner may prescribe, in revenue rulings, notices or other guidance published in the Internal Revenue Bulletin (see § 601.601(d)(2)(ii)(*b*)), other times that a plan may provide for determining the applicable interest rate.

(vi) *Example.*—This example illustrates the rules of this paragraph (d)(4):

Example. Employer X maintains Plan A, a calendar year plan. Employer X wishes to amend Plan A so that the applicable interest rate will remain fixed for each plan quarter, and so that the applicable interest rate for distributions made during each plan quarter can be determined approximately 80 days before the beginning of the plan quarter. To comply with the provisions of this paragraph (d)(4), Plan A is amended to provide that the applicable interest rate is the annual interest rate on 30-year Treasury securities as specified by the Commissioner for the fourth calendar month preceding the first day of the plan quarter during which the annuity starting date occurs.

(5) *Use of alternative interest rate and mortality table.*—If a plan provides for use of an interest rate or mortality table other than the applicable interest rate or the applicable mortality table, the plan must provide that a participant's benefit must be at least as great as the benefit produced by using the applicable interest rate and the applicable mortality table. For example, if a plan provides for use of an interest rate of 7% and the UP-1984 Mortality Table (see § 1.401(a)(4)-12, *Standard mortality table*) in calculating single-sum distributions, the plan must provide that any single-sum distribution is calculated as the greater of the single-sum benefit calculated using 7% and the UP-1984 Mortality Table and the single-sum benefit calculated using the applicable interest rate and the applicable mortality table.

(6) *Exceptions.*—This paragraph (d) (other than the provisions relating to section 411(d)(6) requirements in paragraph (d)(10) of this section) does not apply to the amount of a distribution paid in the form of an annual benefit that—

(i) Does not decrease during the life of the participant, or, in the case of a QPSA, the life of the participant's spouse; or

(ii) Decreases during the life of the participant merely because of—

(A) The death of the survivor annuitant (but only if the reduction is to a level not below 50% of the annual benefit payable before the death of the survivor annuitant); or

(B) The cessation or reduction of Social Security supplements or qualified disability benefits (as defined in section 411(a)(9)).

(7) *Application to portion of a participant's benefit.*—(i) *In general.*— This paragraph (d)(7) provides rules under which the requirements of this paragraph (d) apply to the distribution of only a portion of a participant's accrued benefit. Paragraph (d)(7)(ii) of this section provides rules for how a participant's accrued benefit may be bifurcated

into separate components for purposes of applying this paragraph (d). Paragraph (d)(7)(iii) of this section provides rules of application. Paragraph (d)(7)(iv) of this section provides certain limited section 411(d)(6) relief, and paragraph (d)(7)(v) of this section provides examples of the application of the rules of this paragraph (d)(7).

(ii) *Bifurcation of accrued benefit.*—(A) *Explicit plan-specified bifurcation.*—A plan is permitted to provide that the requirements of this paragraph (d) apply to a specified portion of a participant's accrued benefit as if that portion were the participant's entire accrued benefit. For example, a plan is permitted to provide that a distribution in the form of a single-sum payment described in this paragraph (d)(7)(ii)(A) is made to settle a specified percentage of the participant's accrued benefit. As another example, a plan is permitted to provide that a distribution in the form of a single-sum payment described in this paragraph (d)(7)(ii)(A) is made to settle the accrued benefit derived from contributions made by an employee. In both examples, the distribution must satisfy the requirements of this paragraph (d) with respect to the specified portion of the accrued benefit, and the remaining portion of the accrued benefit (the participant's total accrued benefit less the portion of the accrued benefit settled by the single-sum payment) can be paid in some other form of distribution that is available under the plan.

(B) *Distribution of specified amount.*—A plan that provides for a distribution of a single-sum payment that is not described in paragraph (d)(7)(ii)(A) of this section satisfies the requirements of this paragraph (d) with respect to that distribution if the portion of the participant's accrued benefit, expressed in the normal form of benefit under the plan and commencing at normal retirement age (or at the current date, if later), that is not settled by the distribution is no less than the excess of—

(1) The participant's total accrued benefit expressed in that form; over

(2) The annuity payable in that form that is actuarially equivalent to the single-sum payment, determined using the applicable interest rate and the applicable mortality table.

(iii) *Rules of operation.*—(A) *Multiple distribution options.*—If a participant selects different distribution options with respect to two separate portions of the participant's accrued benefit that were determined in accordance with paragraph (d)(7)(ii) of this section, then the two different distribution options are treated as two separate optional forms of benefit for purposes of applying the requirements of section 417(e)(3) and this paragraph (d), even if the distribution options have the same annuity starting date. Thus, if the exception from the requirements of section 417(e)(3) and this paragraph (d) that is contained in paragraph (d)(6) of this section applies to one of those optional forms of benefit, then this paragraph (d) applies only to the other optional form of benefit.

(B) *Repeated application of rule.*—If a participant's accrued benefit has been bifurcated in accordance with paragraph (d)(7)(ii) of this section, then the provisions of paragraph (d)(7)(ii) of this section may be applied again to bifurcate the remaining accrued benefit.

(C) *Requirement to use explicit plan-specified bifurcation in certain cases.*—(1) *Section 411(d)(6)-protected optional form.*—If the amount of a distribution in an optional form of benefit to which this paragraph (d) applies is determined by reference to the portion of a participant's accrued benefit as of the applicable amendment date for an amendment that eliminates that optional form of benefit (but, in accordance with section 411(d)(6), retains the optional form of benefit with respect to benefits accrued as of the applicable amendment date), then the plan must provide for explicit bifurcation of the accrued benefit as described in paragraph (d)(7)(ii)(A) of this section.

(2) *Single-sum available with respect to entire accrued benefit.*—If a plan provides that a single-sum distribution is available to settle a participant's entire accrued benefit, then, in order to also provide for a distribution in the form of a single-sum payment that settles only a portion of a participant's accrued benefit, the plan must provide for explicit bifurcation of the accrued benefit as described in paragraph (d)(7)(ii)(A) of this section.

(D) *Application of different factors to different portions of the accrued benefit.*—If a plan provides for an early retirement benefit, a retirement-type subsidy, an optional form of benefit, or an ancillary benefit, that applies only to a portion of a participant's accrued benefit, and the plan provides for a distribution that settles some, but not all, of the participant's accrued benefit, then the plan must specify which portion of the participant's total accrued benefit is settled by that distribution. For example, if a plan had one set of early retirement factors that applied to the accrued benefit as of December 31, 2005, but a different set of early retirement factors that applied to benefit accruals earned after that date, and the plan provides for a single-sum distribution that settles only a portion of a participant's accrued benefit, then the plan must specify which portion of the accrued benefit is settled by that distribution (in order to determine which early retirement factors apply to the remaining portion of the accrued benefit).

(iv) *Limited section 411(d)(6) anti-cutback relief.*—This paragraph (d)(7)(iv) applies in the case of a plan that, for plan years beginning before January 1, 2017, uses the section 417(e)(3) applicable interest rate and applicable mortality table to calculate the amount of a distribution that is made to settle a portion of the accrued benefit if, pursuant to this paragraph (d)(7), the requirements of section 417(e)(3) and this paragraph (d) need not apply to the distribution. In such a case, section 411(d)(6) is not violated merely because, in accordance with this paragraph (d)(7), the plan is amended on or before December 31, 2017, to provide that the amount of a distribution described in the preceding sentence is determined for an annuity starting date on or after the applicable amendment date (within the meaning of § 1.411(d)-3(g)(4)) using the same actuarial assumptions that apply to calculate the amount of a distribution in the same form of benefit that is made to settle the participant's entire accrued benefit.

(v) *Examples.*—The following examples illustrate the rules of this paragraph (d)(7). Unless otherwise indicated, these examples are based on the following assumptions: The taxpayers elect to apply the rules of this paragraph (d)(7) in 2016; each plan is a noncontributory defined benefit plan with a calendar-year plan year and a normal retirement age of age 65; a one-year stability period coinciding with the calendar year and a two-month lookback are used for determining the applicable interest rate; and all participant elections are made with proper spousal consent. The November 2015 segment rates are 1.76%, 4.15% and 5.13%.

Example 1. (i) Plan A offers a number of optional forms of payment, including a qualified joint and survivor annuity and a single-sum payment. The single-sum payment is equal to the present value of the participant's immediate benefit (but not less than the present value of the participant's accrued benefit payable at normal retirement age) using the applicable interest and mortality rates under section 417(e)(3). The amount of the joint and survivor annuity is determined using plan factors that are not based on the applicable interest and mortality rates under section 417(e)(3). Plan A permits a participant to elect to receive a percentage of the accrued benefit as a single sum and the remainder in any annuity form provided under the plan, with the amount of the single-sum payment determined by multiplying the amount that would be payable if the entire benefit were paid as a single sum by the percentage of the accrued benefit settled by the single-sum payment.

(ii) Participant S retires at age 62 in 2016, with an accrued benefit of $1,000 per month payable as a straight life annuity at normal retirement age. Participant S is eligible for an unreduced early retirement benefit and can therefore collect a straight life annuity benefit of $1,000 per month beginning immediately. Alternatively, Participant S can elect to receive the benefit in other forms, including a single-sum payment of $168,516 (based on the applicable interest and mortality rates under section 417(e), which are the November 2015 segment rates and the 2016 applicable mortality table), or a 100% joint and survivor annuity of $850 per month (based on the plan's actuarial equivalence factors). Participant S elects to receive 25% of the accrued benefit in the form of a single-sum payment and the remaining 75% of the accrued benefit as a 100% joint and survivor annuity.

(iii) Participant S receives a single-sum payment with respect to 25% of the accrued benefit. Accordingly, this single-sum payment is equal to 25% of the full single-sum amount, or $42,129. The remaining portion of the accrued benefit is 75% of the total accrued benefit, or $750 per month payable as a straight life annuity at normal retirement age.

(iv) To settle the remaining portion of the accrued benefit, in addition to the single-sum payment of $42,129, Participant S receives a 100% joint and survivor annuity in the amount of $637.50 per month, which is determined by applying the plan's unreduced early retirement and actuarial equivalence factors to the remaining portion of the accrued benefit of $750 per month payable as a straight life annuity at normal retirement age. The joint and survivor annuity benefit is not subject to the minimum present value requirements of section 417(e)(3) because it is treated as a separate optional form of benefit under paragraph (d)(7)(iii)(A) of this section.

Example 2. (i) Plan B is a contributory defined benefit plan that permits a participant to elect a single sum distribution equal to the participant's employee contributions, accumulated with interest, with the remainder payable as an annuity. Plan B provides that the probability of death before normal retirement age is not taken into account for purposes of determining actuarial equivalence between the single-sum payment and an annuity at normal retirement age. Based on the applicable mortality table for 2016 and the November

2015 segment rates, the deferred annuity factor at age 60 for lifetime payments commencing at age 65 (determined without taking mortality before age 65 into account) is 10.209.

(ii) Participant T retires at age 60 in 2016 with an accrued benefit of $1,500 per month payable as a straight life annuity commencing at normal retirement age. For benefits commencing at age 60, Plan B provides for an early retirement reduction factor of 75% and an actuarial equivalence factor of 98% for adjusting a straight life annuity to a 10-year certain and life annuity, neither of which is based on the applicable interest and mortality rates under section 417(e)(3). Participant T's benefit commencing at age 60 in the form of a 10-year certain and life annuity would be $1,500 × 75% × 98% = $1,102.50 per month. Participant T elects to receive a single sum payment of $32,000 equal to T's accumulated contributions with interest, and the remainder as a 10-year certain and life annuity.

(iii) The single-sum payment elected by Participant T is a distribution that is determined by reference to Participant T's contributions and interest, and not by reference to a specified portion of the participant's accrued benefit. Therefore, the single-sum payment is not described in paragraph (d)(7)(ii)(A) of this section. In order to satisfy paragraph (d)(7)(ii)(B) of this section, the portion of the participant's accrued benefit that is not settled by the single-sum payment must be no less than the excess of (A) the participant's total accrued benefit over (B) the annuity that is actuarially equivalent to the single-sum payment, (determined using the applicable interest and mortality rates under section 417(e)(3) as applicable), both expressed in the normal form of benefit commencing at normal retirement age. The amount of that actuarially equivalent annuity is determined by dividing Participant T's single-sum payment of $32,000 by the deferred annuity factor for lifetime payments commencing at age 65 under the terms of Plan B (10.209, not considering mortality for the deferral period) and dividing by 12 for an actuarially equivalent monthly benefit commencing at age 65 of $261.21. Thus, in order to satisfy paragraph (d)(7)(ii)(B) of this section, the remaining portion of T's accrued benefit must be at least $1,238.79 per month ($1,500.00 - $261.21) payable as a straight life annuity at normal retirement age.

(iv) Based on Plan B's early retirement and optional form factors applied to the remaining portion, the annuity benefit payable to Participant T in the form of a 10-year certain and life annuity beginning at age 60 cannot be less than $910.51 per month ($1,238.79 × 75% × 98%). Participant T receives this in addition to the single-sum payment of $32,000. The 10-year certain and life benefit is not subject to the minimum present value requirements of section 417(e)(3) because it is treated as a separate optional form of benefit under paragraph (d)(7)(iii)(A) of this section.

(v) If, instead, Plan B's terms had provided for a single-sum payment equal to the present value of the participant's employee-provided accrued benefit as determined under section 411(c)(3), then the plan is determining the single-sum payment as the present value of a specified portion of the accrued benefit. In such a case, the plan is using explicit bifurcation as described in paragraph (d)(7)(ii)(A) of this section and the single-sum payment would have to be set equal to the present value, determined under Plan B's terms, of T's employee-provided accrued benefit (which may or may not be equal to T's accumulated contributions and interest, depending on the plan's terms). The remaining annuity benefit payable to Participant T would have been based on an accrued benefit equal to $1,500 per month minus the amount of T's employee-provided accrued benefit.

Example 3. (i) The facts are the same as in *Example 2* of this paragraph (d)(7)(v), except that Plan B also offers a single-sum payment option with respect to a participant's entire benefit. The single-sum payment is determined as the present value of the participant's early retirement benefit (but no less than the present value of the participant's accrued benefit) using the applicable interest and mortality rates under section 417(e)(3). Based on the applicable mortality table for 2016 and the November 2015 segment rates, the immediate annuity factor for lifetime payments commencing at age 60 is 14.632. Under the terms of the plan, the early retirement benefit payable as a straight life annuity to Participant T at age 60 with respect to T's full accrued benefit is $1,125 ($1,500 × 75%), and the corresponding single-sum amount payable to T is $1,125 × 14.632 × 12 = $197,532. (Note that this amount is larger than the age-60 present value of T's accrued benefit without taking mortality before age 65 into account, $1,500 × 10.209 × 12 = $183,762.) Participant T elects to receive a partial single-sum payment of $32,000, equal to T's accumulated contributions with interest and to take the remaining accrued benefit in the form of a 10-year certain and life annuity commencing at age 60.

(ii) Because the plan also provides for a single-sum payment option with respect to a participant's entire benefit, pursuant to paragraph (d)(7)(iii)(C)(2) of this section the partial single-sum payment must be determined pursuant to the explicit bifurcation rules of paragraph (d)(7)(ii)(A) of this section.

(iii) The portion of the participant's accrued benefit that is settled by the single-sum payment of $32,000 is determined as the amount that bears the same ratio to the total accrued benefit as that single-sum payment bears to the single-sum payment with respect to the entire accrued benefit (($32,000 ÷ $197,532) × $1,500), which is $243 per month payable as a straight life annuity at normal retirement age. Thus, the remaining portion of the accrued benefit is $1,257.00 per month payable as a straight life annuity at normal retirement age.

(iv) Based on Plan B's early retirement and optional form factors applied to the remaining portion, the annuity benefit payable to Participant T in the form of a 10-year certain and life annuity beginning at age 60 is $923.90 per month ($1,257 × 75% × 98%). Participant T receives this benefit in addition to the single sum payment of $32,000. The 10-year certain and life benefit is not subject to the minimum present value requirements of section 417(e)(3) because it is treated as a separate optional form of benefit under paragraph (d)(7)(iii)(A) of this section.

Example 4. (i) Plan C was amended to freeze benefits under a traditional defined benefit formula as of December 31, 2016, and to provide benefits under a cash balance formula beginning January 1, 2017. The plan provides that participants may elect separate distribution options for the portion of the benefit accrued under the traditional formula as of December 31, 2016, and the portion of the benefit earned under the cash balance formula. Furthermore, the plan provides that a participant may elect to receive a single-sum payment only with respect to the portion of the benefit earned under the cash balance formula.

(ii) In accordance with paragraph (d)(7)(ii)(A) of this section, Plan C provides for an explicitly bifurcated accrued benefit because the portion of the accrued benefit settled by a distribution is determined separately for the portion under the traditional formula and the portion under the cash balance formula. As provided under paragraph (d)(7)(iii)(A) of this section, a single-sum payment under the cash balance formula and a distribution option under the traditional formula are treated as two separate optional forms of benefit for purposes of applying the provisions of the plan implementing the requirements of section 417(e)(3) and this paragraph (d). Therefore, whether a participant elects to receive a single-sum payment of the portion of the benefit earned under the cash balance formula does not affect whether the distribution elected with respect to the portion of the benefit earned as of December 31, 2016, is subject to the minimum present value requirements of section 417(e)(3).

Example 5. (i) The facts are the same as in *Example 4* of this paragraph (d)(7)(v), except that Plan C also permits a participant to elect, with respect to the cash balance portion of the benefit, to receive a percentage of that portion as a single sum and the remainder in any annuity form provided under the plan, with the amount of the single-sum payment determined by multiplying the amount that would be payable if the entire cash balance portion were paid as a single sum by the percentage of the cash balance portion settled by the single-sum payment. Participant W retires at age 65, with an accrued benefit under the traditional defined benefit formula (earned as of December 31, 2016) of $500 per month payable as a straight life annuity at normal retirement age and a cash balance hypothetical account balance of $45,000. Based on Plan C's actuarial equivalence factors, Participant W's accrued benefit derived from the cash balance hypothetical account is $320 per month, payable as a straight life annuity at normal retirement age. Participant W elects to receive 1/3 or $15,000 of the current hypothetical account balance in the form of a single sum and to receive the remainder of the total accrued benefit as a straight life annuity.

(ii) Under the analysis set forth in *Example 4* of this paragraph (d)(7)(v), Plan C provides for an explicitly bifurcated accrued benefit with respect to the traditional defined benefit portion and the cash balance portion because the portion of the accrued benefit settled by a distribution is determined separately for the portion under the traditional formula and the portion under the cash balance formula. As provided under paragraph (d)(7)(iii)(A) of this section, a single-sum payment under the cash balance formula and a distribution option under the traditional formula are treated as two separate optional forms of benefit for purposes of applying the provisions of the plan implementing the requirements of section 417(e)(3) and this paragraph (d). Thus, a separate distribution option may be chosen for each of these two portions, and section 417(e)(3) applies separately to each portion.

(iii) In accordance with paragraph (d)(7)(ii)(A) of this section, Plan C also provides for an explicitly bifurcated accrued benefit with respect to the cash balance benefit because the plan provides that a distribution in the form of a single-sum payment is made to settle a *specified percentage of the cash balance benefit.* As provided under paragraph (d)(7)(iii)(A) of this section, the single-sum payment and the annuity selected by Participant W with respect to the cash balance benefit are treated as two separate optional forms of benefit for purposes of applying the provisions of the plan implementing the

requirements of section 417(e)(3) and this paragraph (d). Thus, in accordance with paragraph (d)(7)(ii)(A) of this section, 1/3 of the cash balance hypothetical account is settled by the distribution paid out as a single sum (that is, $15,000 ÷ $45,000). After the single-sum payment, the remaining portion of the accrued benefit derived from the cash balance account is 2/3 of the initial accrued benefit derived from the cash balance account, or a straight life annuity at normal retirement age of $213.33 per month (2/3 × $320).

(iv) To settle the remaining portion of the entire accrued benefit (the portion of the benefit attributable to service as of December 31, 2016 plus the remaining portion of the cash balance benefit), Participant W receives a monthly life annuity of $713.33 per month payable as a straight life annuity at normal retirement age (equal to the $500 straight life annuity at normal retirement age earned as of December 31, 2016 plus the remaining benefit derived from the cash balance portion of a straight life annuity payable at normal retirement age of $213.33 per month). Participant W's election to receive a single-sum payment of part of the benefit earned under the cash balance formula does not affect whether the remainder of Participant W's distribution is subject to the minimum present value requirements of section 417(e)(3).

Example 6. (i) Plan D permits participants to elect a single-sum payment of up to $10,000 with the remaining benefit payable in the form of an annuity. Participant X retires in 2016 at age 55 with an accrued benefit of $1,000 per month payable as a straight life annuity at normal retirement age. Participant X is eligible for an unreduced early retirement benefit of $1,000 per month payable as a straight life annuity. Alternatively, based on Plan D's definition of actuarial equivalence (which is not based on the applicable interest and mortality rates under section 417(e)(3)), Participant X can receive an immediate benefit in the form of a 100% joint and survivor annuity of $800 per month. Participant X elects to receive a single-sum payment of $10,000, with the balance of the benefit payable as a 100% joint and survivor annuity beginning at age 55. Based on the applicable mortality table for 2016 and the November 2015 segment rates, the deferred annuity factor at age 55 for lifetime payments commencing at age 65 is 7.602.

(ii) Plan D provides for a single-sum distribution of a portion of the participant's accrued benefit but, because the plan initially specifies the amount of the single-sum distribution (rather than the portion of the accrued benefit that is being settled by that distribution), Plan D is described in paragraph (d)(7)(ii)(B) of this section. As provided under paragraph (d)(7)(iii)(A) of this section, the single-sum payment and the joint-and-survivor annuity selected by Participant X are treated as two separate optional forms of benefit for purposes of applying the provisions of the plan implementing the requirements of section 417(e)(3) and this paragraph (d).

(iii) A straight life annuity of $109.62 per month payable at normal retirement age is actuarially equivalent to the $10,000 single-sum payment, determined using the applicable mortality table for 2016 and the November 2015 segment rates ($10,000 ÷ 12 ÷ 7.602). Therefore, pursuant to paragraph (d)(7)(ii)(B) of this section, in order to satisfy this paragraph (d) the remaining portion of the accrued benefit after the single-sum payment of $10,000 must be no less than $890.38 per month payable as a straight life annuity at normal retirement age ($1,000.00 - $109.62).

(iv) Based on Plan D's early retirement and optional form factors, in order to satisfy this paragraph (d), the annuity benefit payable to Participant X in the form of a 100% joint-and-survivor annuity beginning at age 55 must be no less than $712.30 per month ($890.38 × .8). Participant X receives this benefit in addition to the single sum payment of $10,000. The joint and survivor annuity benefit is not subject to the minimum present value requirements of section 417(e)(3) because it is treated as a separate optional form of benefit under paragraph (d)(7)(iii)(A) of this section.

Example 7. (i) Plan E provides for an unreduced early retirement benefit for participants who have met certain age and service requirements. Prior to amendment, Plan E permitted participants to elect a single-sum payment equal to the present value of the participant's unreduced early retirement benefit, determined using the applicable interest rate and applicable mortality table under section 417(e)(3). Plan E did not permit participants to elect a single-sum payment with respect to only a portion of their benefits. Effective December 31, 2012, Plan E was amended to eliminate the single-sum payment with respect to benefits accrued after that date.

(ii) Participant Y retires on December 31, 2016, at age 60, after meeting Plan E's age and service requirements for an unreduced early retirement benefit. Participant Y's accrued benefit is $1,000 per month payable as a straight life annuity commencing at normal retirement age, of which $800 per month was accrued as of December 31, 2012. Participant Y elects to take a single-sum payment based on the benefit accrued as of December 31, 2012, with the remainder paid as a lifetime annuity commencing at age 60. Based on the applicable mortality table for 2016 and the November 2015 segment rates, the immediate annuity factor for lifetime payments commencing at age 60 is 14.632, so Y's single-sum payment is $800 × 12 × 14.632 = $140,467.20.

(iii) In accordance with paragraph (d)(7)(iii)(C)(1) of this section, Plan E provides for explicit bifurcation of the accrued benefit as described in paragraph (d)(7)(ii)(A) of this section. Therefore, Participant Y must receive an annuity of $200 earned after December 31, 2012 in addition to the single-sum payment of $140,467. Plan E is not permitted to use the approach described in paragraph (d)(7)(ii)(B) of this section to reduce or eliminate the $200 annuity earned after December 31, 2012.

(8) *Effective/applicability date.*—(i) *In general.*—Except as otherwise provided in this paragraph (d)(8), this paragraph (d) applies to distributions with annuity starting dates in plan years beginning on or after January 1, 1995.

(ii) *Optional delayed effective date of Retirement Protection Act of 1994 (RPA '94) (108 Stat. 5012) rules for plans adopted and in effect before December 8, 1994.*—For a plan adopted and in effect before December 8, 1994, the application of the rules relating to the applicable mortality table and applicable interest rate under paragraphs (d)(2) through (4) of this section is delayed to the extent provided in this paragraph (d)(8)(ii), if the plan provisions in effect on December 7, 1994, met the requirements of section 417(e)(3) and §1.417(e)-1(d) as in effect on December 7, 1994 (as contained in 26 CFR part 1 revised April 1, 1995). In the case of a distribution from such a plan with an annuity starting date that precedes the optional delayed effective date described in paragraph (d)(8)(iv) of this section, and that precedes the first day of the first plan year beginning after December 31, 1999, the rules of paragraph (d)(9) of this section (which generally apply to distributions with annuity starting dates in plan years beginning before January 1, 1995) apply in lieu of the rules of paragraphs (d)(2) through (4) of this section. The interest rate under the rules of paragraph (d)(9) of this section is determined under the provisions of the plan as in effect on December 7, 1994, reflecting the interest rate or rates published by the Pension Benefit Guaranty Corporation (PBGC) and the provisions of the plan for determining the date on which the interest rate is fixed. The above described interest rate or rates published by the PBGC are those determined by the PBGC (for the date determined under those plan provisions) pursuant to the methodology under the regulations of the PBGC for determining the present value of a lump sum distribution on plan termination under 29 CFR part 2619 that were in effect on September 1, 1993 (as contained in 29 CFR part 2619 revised July 1, 1994).

(iii) *Optional accelerated effective date of RPA '94 rules.*—This paragraph (d) is also effective for a distribution with an annuity starting date after December 7, 1994, during a plan year beginning before January 1, 1995, if the employer elects, on or before the annuity starting date, to make the rules of this paragraph (d) effective with respect to the plan as of the optional accelerated effective date described in paragraph (d)(8)(iv) of this section. An employer is treated as making this election by making the plan amendments described in paragraph (d)(8)(iv) of this section.

(iv) *Determination of delayed or accelerated effective date by plan amendment adopting RPA '94 rules.*—The optional delayed effective date of paragraph (d)(8)(ii) of this section, or the optional accelerated effective date of paragraph (d)(8)(iii) of this section, whichever is applicable, is the date plan amendments applying both the applicable mortality table of paragraph (d)(2) of this section and the applicable interest rate of paragraph (d)(3) of this section are adopted or, if later, are made effective.

(v) *Effective date for special rules applicable to the payment of a portion of a participant's benefit.*—Paragraph (d)(7) of this section applies to distributions with annuity starting dates in plan years beginning on or after January 1, 2017. However, taxpayers may elect to apply the rules of paragraph (d)(7) of this section to earlier periods.

(9) *Plan years beginning before January 1, 1995.*—(i) *Interest rate.*—(A) For distributions made in plan years beginning after December 31, 1986, and before January 1, 1995, the following interest rate described in paragraph (d)(9)(i)(A)(1) or (2) of this section, whichever applies, is substituted for the applicable interest rate for purposes of this section—

(1) The rate or rates that would be used by the PBGC for a trusteed single-employer plan to value the participant's (or beneficiary's) vested benefit (PBGC interest rate) if the present value of such benefit does not exceed $25,000; or

(2) 120 percent of the PBGC interest rate, as determined in accordance with paragraph (d)(9)(i)(A)(1) of this section, if such present value exceeds $25,000. In no event shall the present value determined by use of 120 percent of the PBGC interest rate result in a present value less than $25,000.

(B) The PBGC interest rate may be a series of interest rates for any given date. For example, the PBGC interest rate for immediate annuities for November 1994 is 6% and the PBGC interest rates for the deferral period for that month are as follows: 5.25% for the first 7 years of the deferral period, 4% for the following 8 years of the deferral period, and 4% for the remainder of the deferral period. For November 1994, 120 percent of the PEGC interest rate is 7.2% (1.2 times 6%) for an immediate annuity, 6.3% (1.2 times 5.25%) for the first 7 years of the deferral period, 4.8% (1.2 times 4%) for the following 8 years of the deferral period, and 4.8% (1.2 times 4%) for the remainder of the deferral period. The PBGC interest rates are the interest rates that would be used (as of the date of the distribution) by the PBGC for purposes of determining the present value of that benefit upon termination of an insufficient trusteed single employer plan. Except as otherwise provided by the Commissioner, the PBGC interest rates are determined by PBGC regulations. See subpart B of 29 CFR part 4044 for the applicable PBGC rates.

(ii) *Time for determining interest rate.*—(A) Except as provided in paragraph (d)(9)(ii)(B) of this section, the PBGC interest rate or rates are determined on either the annuity starting date or the first day of the plan year that contains the annuity starting date. The plan must provide which date is applicable.

(B) The plan may provide for the use of any other time for determining the PBGC interest rate or rates provided that such time is not more than 120 days before the annuity starting date if such time is determined in a consistent manner and is applied uniformly to all participants.

(C) The Commissioner may, in revenue rulings, notices or other guidance published in the Internal Revenue Bulletin (see §601.601(d)(2)(ii)(*b*)), prescribe other times for determining the PBGC interest rate or rates.

(iii) *No applicable mortality table.*—In the case of a distribution to which this paragraph (d)(9) applies, the rules of this paragraph (d) are applied without regard to the applicable mortality table described in paragraph (d)(2) of this section.

(10) *Relationship with section 411(d)(6).*—(i) *In general.*—A plan amendment that changes the interest rate, the time for determining the interest rate, or the mortality assumptions used for the purposes described in paragraph (d)(1) of this section is subject to section 411(d)(6). But see §1.411(d)-4, Q&A-2(b)(2)(v) (regarding plan amendments relating to involuntary distributions). In addition, a plan amendment that changes the interest rate or the mortality assumptions used for the purposes described in paragraph (d)(1) of this section merely to eliminate use of the interest rate described in paragraph (d)(3) or paragraph (d)(9) of this section, or the applicable mortality table, with respect to a distribution form described in paragraph (d)(6) of this section, for distributions with annuity starting dates occurring after a specified date that is after the amendment is adopted, does not violate the requirements of section 411(d)(6) if the amendment is adopted on or before the last day of the last plan year ending before January 1, 2000.

(ii) *Section 411(d)(6) relief for change in time for determining interest rate.*—Notwithstanding the general rule of paragraph (d)(10)(i) of this section, if a plan amendment changes the time for determining the applicable interest rate (including an indirect change as a result of a change in plan year), the amendment will not be treated as reducing accrued benefits in violation of section 411(d)(6) merely on account of this change if the conditions of this paragraph (d)(10)(ii) are satisfied. If the plan amendment is effective on or after the adoption date, any distribution for which the annuity starting date occurs in the one-year period commencing at the time the amendment is effective must be determined using the interest rate provided under the plan determined at either the date for determining the interest rate before the amendment or the date for determining the interest rate after the amendment, whichever results in the larger distribution. If the plan amendment is adopted retroactively (that is, the amendment is effective prior to the adoption date), the plan must use the interest rate determination date resulting in the larger distribution for the period beginning with the effective date and ending one year after the adoption date.

(iii) *Section 411(d)(6) relief for plan amendments pursuant to changes to section 417 made by RPA '94 providing for statutory interest rate determination date.*—Notwithstanding the general rule of paragraph (d)(10)(i) of this section, except as provided in paragraph (d)(10)(vi)(B) of this section, a participant's accrued benefit is not considered to be reduced in violation of section 411(d)(6) merely because of a plan amendment that changes any interest rate or mortality assumption used to calculate the present value of a participant's benefit under the plan, if the following conditions are satisfied—

(A) The amendment replaces the PBGC interest rate (or an interest rate or rates based on the PBGC interest rate) as the interest rate used under the plan in determining the present value of a participant's benefit under this paragraph (d); and

(B) After the amendment is effective, the present value of a participant's benefit under the plan cannot be less than the amount calculated using the applicable mortality table and the applicable interest rate for the first full calendar month preceding the calendar month that contains the annuity starting date.

(iv) *Section 411(d)(6) relief for plan amendments pursuant to changes to section 417 made by RPA '94 providing for prior determination date or up to two months earlier.*—Notwithstanding the general rule of paragraph (d)(10)(i) of this section, except as provided in paragraph (d)(10)(vi)(B) of this section, a participant's accrued benefit is not considered to be reduced in violation of section 411(d)(6) merely because of a plan amendment that changes any interest rate or mortality assumption used to calculate the present value of a participant's benefit under the plan, if the following conditions are satisfied—

(A) The amendment replaces the PBGC interest rate (or an interest rate or rates based on the PBGC interest rate) as the interest rate used under the plan in determining the present value of a participant's benefit under this paragraph (d); and

(B) After the amendment is effective, the present value of a participant's benefit under the plan cannot be less than the amount calculated using the applicable mortality table and the applicable interest rate, but only if the applicable interest rate is the annual interest rate on 30-year Treasury securities for the calendar month that contains the date as of which the PBGC interest rate (or an interest rate or rates based on the PBGC interest rate) was determined immediately before the amendment, or for one of the two calendar months immediately preceding such month.

(v) *Section 411(d)(6) relief for plan amendments pursuant to changes to section 417 made by RPA '94 providing for other interest rate determination date.*—Notwithstanding the general rule of paragraph (d)(10)(i) of this section, except as provided in paragraph (d)(10)(vi)(B) of this section, a participant's accrued benefit is not considered to be reduced in violation of section 411(d)(6) merely because of a plan amendment that changes any interest rate or mortality assumption used to calculate the present value of a participant's benefit under the plan, if the following conditions are satisfied—

(A) The amendment replaces the PBGC interest rate (or an interest rate or rates based on the PBGC interest rate) as the interest rate used under the plan in determining the present value of a participant's benefit under this paragraph (d);

(B) After the amendment is effective, the present value of a participant's benefit under the plan cannot be less than the amount calculated using the applicable mortality table and the applicable interest rate; and

(C) The plan amendment satisfies either the condition of paragraph (d)(10)(ii) of this section (determined using the interest rate provided under the terms of the plan after the effective date of the amendment) or the special early transition interest rate rule of paragraph (d)(10)(vi)(C) of this section.

(vi) *Special rules.*—(A) *Provision of temporary additional benefits.*—A plan amendment described in paragraph (d)(10)(iii), (iv), or (v) of this section is not considered to reduce a participant's accrued benefit in violation of section 411(d)(6) even if the plan amendment provides for temporary additional benefits to accommodate a more gradual transition from the plan's old interest rate to the new rules.

(B) *Replacement of non-PBGC interest rate.*—The section 411(d)(6) relief provided in paragraphs (d)(10)(iii) through (v) of this section does not apply to a plan amendment that replaces an interest rate other than the PBGC interest rate (or an interest rate or rates based on the PBGC interest rate) as an interest rate used under the plan in determining the present value of a participant's benefit under this paragraph (d). Thus, the accrued benefit determined using that interest rate and the associated mortality table is protected under section 411(d)(6). For purposes of this paragraph (d), an interest rate is based on the PBGC interest rate if the interest rate is defined as a specified percentage of the PBGC interest rate, the PBGC interest rate minus a specified number of basis points, or an average of such interest rates over a specified period.

(C) *Special early transition interest rate rule for paragraph (d)(10)(v).*—A plan amendment satisfies the special rule of this paragraph (d)(10)(vi)(C) if any distribution for which the annuity starting date occurs in the one-year period commencing at the time the plan amendment is effective is determined using whichever of the following two interest rates results in the larger distribution—

(1) The interest rate as provided under the terms of the plan after the effective date of the amendment, but determined at a date that is either one month or two months (as specified in the plan) before the date for determining the interest rate used under the terms of the plan before the amendment; or

(2) The interest rate as provided under the terms of the plan after the effective date of the amendment, determined at the date for determining the interest rate after the amendment.

(vii) *Examples.*—The provisions of this paragraph (d)(10) are illustrated by the following examples:

Example 1. On December 31, 1994, Plan A provided that all single-sum distributions were to be calculated using the UP-1984 Mortality Table and 100% of the PBGC interest rate for the date of distribution. On January 4, 1995, and effective on February 1, 1995, Plan A was amended to provide that all single-sum distributions are calculated using the applicable mortality table and the annual interest rate on 30-year Treasury securities for the first full calendar month preceding the calendar month that contains the annuity starting date. Pursuant to paragraph (d)(10)(iii) of this section, this amendment of Plan A is not considered to reduce the accrued benefit of any participant in violation of section 411(d)(6).

Example 2. On December 31, 1994, Plan B provided that all single-sum distributions were to be calculated using the UP-1984 Mortality Table and an interest rate equal to the lesser of 100% of the PBGC interest rate for the date of distribution, or 6%. On January 4, 1995, and effective on February 1, 1995, Plan B was amended to provide that all single-sum distributions are calculated using the applicable mortality table and the annual interest rate on 30-year Treasury securities for the second full calendar month preceding the calendar month that contains the annuity starting date. Pursuant to paragraph (d)(10)(iv) of this section, this amendment of Plan B is not considered to reduce the accrued benefit of any participant in violation of section 411(d)(6) merely because of the replacement of the PBGC interest rate. However, under paragraph (d)(10)(vi)(B) of this section, the section 411(d)(6) relief provided in paragraphs (d)(10)(iii) through (v) of this section does not apply to a plan amendment that replaces an interest rate other than the PBGC interest rate (or a rate based on the PBGC interest rate). Therefore, pursuant to paragraph (d)(10)(vi)(B) of this section, to satisfy the requirements of section 411(d)(6), the plan must provide that the single-sum distribution payable to any participant must be no less than the single-sum distribution calculated using the UP-1984 Mortality Table and an interest rate of 6%, based on the participant's benefits under the plan accrued through January 31, 1995, and based on the participant's age at the annuity starting date.

Example 3. On December 31, 1994, Plan C, a calendar year plan, provided that all single sum distributions were to be calculated using the UP-1984 Mortality Table and an interest rate equal to the PBGC interest rate for January 1 of the plan year. On March 1, 1995, and effective on July 1, 1995, Plan C was amended to provide that all single-sum distributions are calculated using the applicable mortality table and the annual interest rate on 30-year Treasury securities for August of the year before the plan year that contains the annuity starting date. The plan amendment provides that each distribution with an annuity starting date after June 30, 1995, and before July 1, 1996, is calculated using the 30-year Treasury rate for August of the year before the plan year that contains the annuity starting date, or the 30-year Treasury rate for January of the plan year that contains the annuity starting date, whichever produces the larger benefit. Pursuant to paragraph (d)(10)(v) of this section, the amendment of Plan C is not considered to have reduced the accrued benefit of any participant in violation of section 411(d)(6).

Example 4. (a) Employer X maintains Plan D, a calendar year plan. As of December 7, 1994, Plan D provided for single-sum distributions to be calculated using the PBGC interest rate as of the annuity starting date for distributions not greater than $25,000, and 120% of that interest rate (but not an interest rate producing a present value less than $25,000) for distributions over $25,000. Employer X wishes to delay the effective date of the RPA '94 rules for a year, and to provide for an extended transition from the use of the PBGC interest rate to the new applicable interest rate under section 417(e)(3). On December 1, 1995, and effective on January 1, 1996, Employer X amends Plan D to provide that single-sum distributions are determined as the sum of—

(i) The single-sum distribution calculated based on the applicable mortality table and the annual interest rate on 30-year Treasury securities for the first full calendar month preceding the calendar month that contains the annuity starting date; and

(ii) A transition amount.

(b) The amendment provides that the transition amount for distributions in the years 1996-99 is a transition percentage of the excess, if any, of the amount that the single-sum distribution would have been under the plan provisions in effect prior to this amendment over the amount of the single sum described in paragraph (a)(i) of this *Example 4*. The transition percentages are 80% for 1996, decreasing to 60% for 1997, 40% for 1998 and 20% for 1999. The amendment also provides that the transition amount is zero for plan years beginning on or after the year 2000. Pursuant to paragraphs (d)(10)(iii) and (vi)(A) of this section, the amendment of Plan D is not considered to have reduced the accrued benefit of any participant in violation of section 411(d)(6).

Example 5. On December 31, 1994, Plan E, a calendar year plan, provided that all single sum distributions were to be calculated using the UP-1984 Mortality Table and an interest rate equal to the PBGC interest rate for January 1 of the plan year. On March 1, 1995, and effective on July 1, 1995, Plan E was amended to provide that all single-sum distributions are calculated using the applicable mortality table and the annual interest rate on 30-year Treasury securities for August of the year before the plan year that contains the annuity starting date. The plan amendment provides that each distribution with an annuity starting date after June 30, 1995, and before July 1, 1996, is calculated using the 30-year Treasury rate for August of the year before the plan year that contains the annuity starting date, or the 30-year Treasury rate for November of the plan year preceding the plan year that contains the annuity starting date, whichever produces the larger benefit. Pursuant to paragraphs (d)(10)(v) and (vi)(C) of this section, the amendment of Plan E is not considered to have reduced the accrued benefit of any participant in violation of section 411(d)(6).

(e) *Special rules for annuity contracts.*—(1) *General rule.*—Any annuity contract purchased by a plan subject to section 401(a)(11) and distributed to or owned by a participant must provide that benefits under the contract are provided in accordance with the applicable consent, present value, and other requirements of sections 401(a)(11) and 417 applicable to the plan.

(f) *Effective dates.*—(1) *Annuity contracts.*—(i) Paragraph (e) of this section does not apply to contracts distributed to or owned by a participant prior to September 17, 1985, unless additional contributions are made under the plan by the employer with respect to such contracts.

(ii) In the case of a contract owned by the employer or distributed to or owned by a participant prior to the first plan year beginning after December 31, 1988, paragraph (e) of this section shall be satisfied if the annuity contracts described therein satisfy the requirements in §§ 1.401(a)-11T and 1.417(e)-1T. The preceding sentence shall not apply if additional contributions are made under the plan by the employer with respect to such contracts on or after the beginning of the first plan year beginning after December 31, 1988.

(2) *Interest rates.*—(i) A plan that uses the PBGC immediate interest rate as required by § 1.417(e)-1T(e) for distributions commencing in plan years beginning before January 1, 1987 shall be deemed to satisfy paragraph (d) of this section for such years.

(ii) For a special exception to the requirements of section 411(d)(6) for certain plan amendments that incorporate applicable interest rates, see section 1139(d)(2) of the Tax Reform Act of 1986.

(3) *Other effective dates and transitional rules.*—(i) Except as otherwise provided, a plan will be treated as satisfying sections 401(a)(11) and 417 for plan years beginning before the first plan year that the requirements of section 410(b) as amended by TRA '86 apply to such plan, if the plan satisfied the requirements in §§ 1.401(a)-11T and 1.417(e)-1T.

(ii) See § 1.401(a)-20 for other effective dates and transitional rules that apply to plans subject to sections 401(a)(11) and 417. [Reg. § 1.417(e)-1.]

☐ [T.D. 8219, 8-19-88. *Amended by T.D. 8591, 4-4-95; T.D. 8620, 9-15-95; T.D. 8768, 4-3-98; T.D. 8794, 12-18-98; T.D. 8796, 12-17-98; T.D. 8891, 7-18-2000; T.D. 9076, 7-15-2003; T.D. 9099, 12-16-2003 and T.D. 9783, 9-8-2016.]*

[Reg. § 1.417(e)-1T]

§ 1.417(e)-1T. Restrictions and valuations of distributions from plans subject to sections 401(a)(11) and 417 (Temporary).—(a) through [*sic*] (c) [Reserved].

(b) *Consent, etc. requirements.*—(1) *General rule.*—[Reserved]

(2) *Consent.*—[Reserved]

(d) For rules regarding the present value of a participant's accrued benefit and related matters, see § 1.417(e)-1(d). [Temporary Reg. § 1.417(e)-1T.]

☐ [T.D. 8591, 4-4-95, *Amended by T.D. 8620, 9-15-95; T.D. 8768, 4-3-98 and T.D. 8796, 12-17-98.]*

[Reg. § 1.419-1T]

§ 1.419-1T. Treatment of welfare benefit funds (Temporary).

Q-1: What does section 419 of the Internal Revenue Code provide?

A-1: Section 419 prescribes limitations upon deductions for contributions paid or accrued with respect to a welfare benefit fund. Under section 419(a) and (b), an employer's contributions to a welfare benefit fund are not deductible under section 162 (relating to trade or business expenses) or section 212 (relating to expenses for production of income) but, if the requirements of section 162 or 212 are otherwise met, are deductible under section 419 for the taxable year of the employer in which paid to the extent of the welfare benefit fund's qualified cost (within the meaning of section 419(c)(1)) for the taxable year of the fund that relates to such taxable year of the employer. Under section 419(g), section 419 and this section shall also apply to the deduction by a taxpayer of contributions with respect to a fund that would be a welfare benefit fund but for the fact that there is no employer-employee relationship between the person providing the services and the person for whom the services are provided. Contributions paid to a welfare benefit fund after section 419 becomes effective with respect to such contributions are deemed to relate, first, to amounts accrued and deducted (but not paid) by the employer with respect to such fund before section 419 becomes effective with respect to such contributions and thus shall not be treated as satisfying the payment requirement of section 419. See paragraph (b) of Q&A-5 for special deduction limits applicable to employer contributions to welfare benefit funds with excess reserves.

Q-2: When do the deduction rules of section 419, as enacted by the Tax Reform Act of 1984, become effective?

A-2: (a) Section 419 generally applies to contributions paid or accrued with respect to a welfare benefit fund after December 31, 1985, in taxable years of employers ending after that date. See Q&A-9 of this regulation for special rules relating to the deduction limit for the first taxable year of a fiscal year employer ending after December 31, 1985.

(b) In the case of a welfare benefit fund which is part of a plan maintained pursuant to one or more collective bargaining agreements (a) between employee representatives and one or more employers, and (b) that are in effect on July 1, 1985 (or ratified on or before such date), section 419 shall not apply to contributions paid or accrued in taxable years beginning before the termination of the last of the collective bargaining agreements pursuant to which the plan is maintained (determined without regard to any extension thereof agreed to after July 1, 1985). For purposes of the preceding sentence, any plan amendment made pursuant to a collective bargaining agreement relating to the plan which amends the plan solely to conform to any requirement added under section 511 of the Tax Reform Act of 1984 (i.e., requirements under section 419, 419A, 512(a)(3)(E), and 4976) shall not be treated as a termination of such collective bargaining agreement. See § 1.419A-2T for special rules relating to the application of section 419 to collectively bargained welfare benefit funds.

(c) Notwithstanding paragraphs (a) and (b), section 419 applies to any contribution of a facility to a welfare benefit fund (or other contribution, such as cash, which is used to acquire, construct, or improve such a facility) after June 22, 1984, unless such facility is placed in service by the fund before January 1, 1987, and either (a) is acquired or improved by the fund (or contributed to the fund) pursuant to a binding contract in effect on June 22, 1984, and at all times thereafter, or (b) the construction of which was begun by or for the welfare benefit fund before June 22, 1984. See Q&A-11 of this regulation for special rules relating to the application of section 419 to the contribution of a facility to a welfare benefit fund (and to the contribution of other amounts, such as cash, used to acquire, construct, or improve such a facility) before section 419 generally becomes effective with respect to contributions to the fund.

Q-3: What is a "welfare benefit fund" under section 419?

A-3: (a) A "welfare benefit fund" is any fund which is part of a plan, or method or arrangement, of an employer and through which the employer provides welfare benefits to employees or their beneficiaries. For purposes of this section, the term "welfare benefit" includes any benefit other than a benefit with respect to which the employer's deduction is governed by section 83(h), section 404 (determined without regard to section 404(b)(2)), section 404A, or section 463.

(b) Under section 419(e)(3)(A) and (B), the term "fund" includes any organization described in section 501(c)(7), (9), (17) or (20), and any trust, corporation, or other organization not exempt from tax imposed by chapter 1, subtitle A, of the Internal Revenue Code. Thus, a taxable trust or taxable corporation that is maintained for the purpose or providing welfare benefits to an employer's employees is a "welfare benefit fund."

(c) Section 419(e)(3)(C) also provides that the term "fund" includes, to the extent provided in regulations, any account held for an employer by any person. Pending the issuance of further guidance, only the following accounts, and arrangements that effectively constitute accounts, as described below, are "funds" within section 419(e)(3)(C). A retired lives reserve or a premium stabilization reserve maintained by an insurance company is a "fund," or part of a "fund," if it is maintained for a particular employer and the employer has the right to have any amount in the reserve applied against its future years' benefit costs or insurance premiums. Also, if an employer makes a payment to an insurance company under an "administrative services only" arrangement with respect to which the life insurance company maintains a separate account to provide benefits, then the arrangement would be considered to be a "fund." Finally, an insurance or premium arrangement between an employer and an insurance company is a "fund" if, under the arrangement, the employer has a right to a refund, credit, or additional benefits (including upon termination of the arrangement) based on the benefit or claims experience, administrative cost experience, or investment experience attributable to such employer. However, an arrangement with an insurance company is not a "fund" under the previous sentence merely because the employer's premium for a renewal year reflects the employer's own experience for an earlier year if the arrangement is both cancellable by the insurance company and cancellable by the employer as of the end of any policy year and, upon cancellation by either of the parties, neither of the parties can receive a refund or additional amounts or benefits and neither of the parties can incur a residual liability beyond the end of the policy year (other than, in the case of the insurer, to provide benefits with respect to claims incurred before cancellation). The determination whether either of the parties can receive a refund or additional amounts or benefits or can incur a residual liability upon cancellation of an arrangement will be made by examining both the contractual rights and obligations of the parties under the arrangement and the actual practice of the insurance company (and other insurance companies) with respect to other employers upon cancellation of similar arrangements. Similarly, a disability income policy does not constitute a "fund" under the preceding provisions merely because, under the policy, an employer pays an annual premium so that employees who became disabled in such year may receive benefit payments for the duration of the disability.

Q-4: For purposes of determining the section 419 limit on the employer's deduction for contributions to the fund for a taxable year of the employer, which taxable year of the welfare benefit fund is related to the taxable year of the employer?

A-4: The amount of an employer's deduction for contributions to a welfare benefit fund for a taxable year of the employer is limited to the "qualified cost" of the welfare benefit fund for the taxable year of the fund that is related to such taxable year of the employer. The taxable year of the welfare benefit fund that ends with or within the taxable year of the employer is the taxable year of the fund that is related to the taxable year of the employer. Thus, for example, if an employer has a calendar taxable year and it makes contributions to a fund having a taxable year ending June 30, the "qualified cost" of the fund for the taxable year of the fund ending on June 30, 1986, applies to limit the employer's deduction for contributions to the fund in the employer's 1986 taxable year. In the case of employer contributions paid directly to an account or arrangement with an insurance company that is treated as a welfare benefit fund for the purposes of section 419, the policy year will be treated as the taxable year of the fund. See Q&A-7 of this regulation for special section 419 rules relating to the coordination of taxable years for the taxable year of the employer in which a welfare benefit fund is established and for the next following taxable year of the employer.

Q-5: What is the "qualified cost" of a welfare benefit fund for a taxable year under section 419?

A-5: (a) Under section 419(c), the "qualified cost" of a welfare benefit fund for a taxable year of the fund is the sum of (1) the "qualified direct cost" of such fund for such taxable year of the fund, and (2) the amount that may be added to the qualified asset account for such taxable year of the fund to the extent that such addition does not result in a total amount in such account as of the end of such taxable year of the fund that exceeds the applicable account limit under section 419A(c). However, in calculating the qualified cost of a welfare benefit fund for a taxable year of the fund, this sum is reduced by the fund's "after-tax income" (as defined in section 419(c)(4)) for such taxable year of the fund. Also, the qualified cost of a welfare benefit fund is reduced further under the provisions of paragraph (b) of this Q&A.

(b)(1) Pursuant to section 419A(i), notwithstanding section 419 and §1.419-1T, contributions to a welfare benefit fund during any taxable year of the employer beginning after December 31, 1985, shall not be deductible for such taxable year to the extent that such contributions result in the total amount in the fund as of the end of the last taxable year of the fund ending with or within such taxable year of the employer exceeding the account limit applicable to such taxable year of the fund (as adjusted under section 419A(f)(7)). Solely for purposes of this subparagraph, (i) contributions paid to a welfare benefit fund during the taxable year of the employer but after the end of the

last taxable year of the fund that relates to such taxable year of the employer, and (ii) contributions accrued with respect to a welfare benefit fund during the taxable year of the employer or during any prior taxable year of the employer (but not actually paid to such fund on or before the end of a taxable year of the employer) and deducted by the employer for such or any prior taxable year of the employer, shall be treated as an amount in the fund as of the end of the last taxable year of the fund that relates to the taxable year of the employer. Contributions that are not deductible under this subparagraph are in excess of the qualified cost of the welfare benefit fund for the taxable year of the fund that relates to the taxable year of the employer and thus are treated as contributed to the fund on the first day of the employer's next taxable year.

(2) Subparagraph (1) shall not apply to contributions with respect to a collectively bargained welfare benefit fund within the meaning of §1.419A-2T. In addition, subparagraph (1) shall not apply to any taxable year of an employer beginning after the end of the earlier of the following taxable years: (i) the first taxable year of the employer beginning after December 31, 1985, for which the employer's deduction limit under section 419 (after the application of subparagraph (1)) is at least equal to the qualified direct cost of the fund for the taxable year (or years) of the fund that relates to such first taxable year of the employer, or (ii) the first taxable year of the employer beginning after December 31, 1985, with or within which ends the first taxable year of the fund with respect to which the total amount in the fund as of the end of such taxable year of the fund does not exceed the account limit for such taxable year of the fund (as adjusted under section 419A(f)(7)).

(3) For example, assume an employer with a taxable year ending June 30 and a welfare benefit fund with a taxable year ending January 31. During its taxable year ending June 30, 1987, and on or before January 31, 1987, the employer contributes $250,000 to the fund, and during the remaining portion of its taxable year ending June 30, 1987, the employer contributes $200,000. The qualified direct cost of the fund for its taxable year ending January 31, 1987, is $500,000, the account limit applicable to such taxable year (after the adjustment under section 419A(f)(7)) is $750,000, and the total amount in the fund as of January 31, 1987, is $800,000. Before the application of this paragraph, the employer may deduct the entire $450,000 contribution for its taxable year ending June 30, 1987. However, under this paragraph, the excess of (i) the sum of the total amount in the fund as of January 31, 1987 ($800,000), and employer contributions to the fund after January 31, 1987, and on or before June 30, 1987 ($200,000), over (ii) the account limit applicable to the fund for its taxable year ending January 31, 1987 ($750,000), is $250,000. Thus, under this paragraph, only $200,000 of the $450,000 contribution the employer made during its taxable year ending June 30, 1987, is deductible for such taxable year. If the excess were $450,000 or greater, no portion of the $450,000 contribution would be deductible by the employer for its taxable year ending June 30, 1987. Such nondeductible contributions are in excess of the fund's qualified cost for the taxable year related to the employer's taxable year and thus are deemed to be contributed on the first day of the employer's next taxable year.

(c) See Q&A-7 of this regulation for special rules relating to the calculation of the qualified cost of a welfare benefit fund for an Initial Fund Year and an Overlap Fund Year (as defined in Q&A-7). See Q&A-11 of this regulation for special rules relating to the application of section 419 to the contribution to a welfare benefit fund of a facility (and to the contribution of other amounts, such as cash, used to acquire, construct, or improve a facility) before section 419 generally becomes effective with respect to contributions to the fund. See §1.419A-2T for special rules relating to certain collectively bargained welfare benefit funds.

Q-6: What is the "qualified direct cost" of a welfare benefit fund under section 419(c)(3)?

A-6: (a) Under section 419(c)(3), the "qualified direct cost" of a welfare benefit fund for any taxable year of the fund is the aggregate amount which would have been allowable as a deduction to the employer for benefits provided by such fund during such year (including insurance coverage for such year) if (1) such benefits were provided directly by the employer and (2) the employer used the cash receipts and disbursements method of accounting and had the same taxable year as the fund. In this regard, a benefit is treated as provided when such benefit would be includible in the gross income of the employee if provided directly by the employer (or would be so includible but for a provision of chapter 1, subtitle A, of the Internal Revenue Code excluding it from gross income). Thus, for example, if a calendar year welfare benefit fund pays an insurance company in July 1986 the full premium for coverage of its current employees under a term health insurance policy for the twelve month period ending June 30, 1987, the insurance coverage will be treated as provided by the fund over such twelve month period. Accordingly, only the portion of the premium for coverage during 1986 will be treated as a "qualified direct cost" of the fund for 1986; the remaining portion of the premium will be treated as a "qualified direct cost" of the fund for 1987. The "qualified direct cost" for a taxable year of the fund includes the administrative expenses incurred by the welfare benefit fund in delivering the benefits for such year.

(b) If, in a taxable year of a welfare benefit fund, the fund holds an asset with a useful life extending substantially beyond the end of the taxable year (e.g., buildings, vehicles, tangible assets, and licenses) and, for such taxable year of the fund, the asset is used in the provision of welfare benefits to employees, the "qualified direct cost" of the fund for such taxable year of the fund includes the amount that would have been allowable to the employer as a deduction under the applicable Code provisions (e.g., sections 168 and 179) with respect to the portion of the asset used in the provision of welfare benefits for such year if the employer had acquired and placed in service the asset at the same time the fund received and placed in service the asset, and the employer had the same taxable year as the fund. This rule applies regardless of whether the fund received the asset through a contribution of the asset by the employer or through an acquisition or the construction by the fund of the asset. For example, assume that in 1986 a calendar year employer contributes recovery property under section 168(c) to a welfare benefit fund with a calendar taxable year to be used in the provision of welfare benefits. The employer will be treated as having sold the property in such year and thus will recognize gain to the extent that the fair market value of the property exceeds the employer's adjusted basis in the property. In this regard, see section 1239(d). Also, the employer will be treated as having made a contribution to the fund in such year equal to the fair market value of the property. Finally, the qualified direct cost of the welfare benefit fund for 1986 will include the amount that the employer could have deducted in 1986 with respect to the portion of the property used in the provision of welfare benefits if the employer had acquired the property in 1986 and had placed the property in service when the fund actually placed the property in service. Similarly, for example, assume that in 1986 a welfare benefit fund purchases and places in service a facility to be used in the provision of welfare benefits. The qualified direct cost of the fund for 1986 will include the amount that the employer could have deducted with respect to such facility if the employer had purchased and placed in service the facility at the same time that the fund purchased and placed in service the facility.

(c) The qualified direct cost of a welfare benefit fund does not include expenditures by the fund that would not have been deductible if they had been made directly by the employer. For example, a fund's purchase of land in a year for an employee recreational facility will not be treated as a qualified direct cost because, if made directly by the employer, the purchase would not have been deductible under section 263. See also sections 264 and 274.

(d) Notwithstanding the preceding paragraphs, the qualified direct cost of a welfare benefit fund with respect to that portion of a child care facility used in the provision of welfare benefits for a year will include the amount that would have been allowable to the employer as a deduction for the year under a straight-line depreciation schedule for a period of 60 months beginning with the month in which the facility is placed in service under rules similar to those provided for section 188 property under § 1.188-1(a). For purposes of this section, a "child care facility" is tangible property of a character subject to depreciation that is located in the United States and specifically used as an integral part of a "qualified child care center facility" within the meaning of § 1.188-1(d)(4).

(e) See Q&A-7 of this regulation for special section 419 rules relating to the calculation of the qualified direct cost of a welfare benefit fund for an Initial Fund Year and an Overlap Fund Year (as defined in Q&A-7). See Q&A-11 of this regulation for special rules relating to the contribution to a welfare benefit fund of a facility (and to the contribution of other amounts, such as cash, used to acquire, construct, or improve a facility) before section 419 generally becomes effective with respect to contributions to the fund.

Q-7: What special rules apply for purposes of determining the section 419 limit on the employer's deduction for contributions to a welfare benefit fund for the taxable year of the employer in which the fund is established and for the next following taxable year of the employer?

A-7: (a) If the taxable year of a welfare benefit fund is the same as the taxable year of the employer, there are no special rules that apply for purposes of determining the section 419 limit on an employer's deduction for contributions to the fund for either the taxable year of the employer in which the fund is established or the next following taxable year of the employer. However, if the taxable year of a welfare benefit fund is different from the taxable year of the employer, the general section 419 rules are modified by the special rules set forth below for purposes of determining the section 419 deduction limit for the taxable year of the employer in which a fund is established and for the next following taxable year of the employer.

(b) If a welfare benefit fund is established after December 31, 1985, during a taxable year of an employer and either (i) the first taxable year of the fund ends after the close of such taxable year of the employer, or (ii) the first taxable year of the fund is six months or less and ends before the close of such taxable year of the employer and the second taxable year of the fund begins before and ends after the close of such taxable year of the employer, the taxable year of the fund that contains the closing day of such taxable year of the employer will be treated as an "Overlap Fund Year." For purposes of determining the limit on the employer's deduction for contributions to a welfare benefit fund for the taxable year of the employer in which the fund was established, the period between the beginning of the fund's Overlap Fund Year and the end of the employer's taxable year in which the Overlap Fund Year began will be treated as a taxable year of the fund ("Initial Fund Year").

(c) The qualified cost of a welfare benefit fund for its Initial Fund Year will be equal to the qualified direct cost of the fund for such Initial Fund Year. The qualified cost of a fund for its Overlap Fund Year will be determined under the general rules of Q&A-5 of this regulation and section 419(c), with the exception that such qualified cost will be reduced by the employer contributions made during the Initial Fund Year and deductible by the employer for the taxable year of the employer in which the Overlap Fund Year of the fund begins.

(d) Assume that an employer with a calendar taxable year establishes on July 1, 1986, a welfare benefit fund with a taxable year ending on June 30. The fund's first taxable year from July 1, 1986, to June 30, 1987, is an Overlap Fund Year. The employer contributes $1,000 to the fund during its taxable year ending December 31, 1986 (i.e., during the period between July 1, 1986, and December 31, 1986, which is also the Initial Fund Year) and another $1500 to the fund during its taxable year ending December 31, 1987. Assume further that the qualified direct cost of the fund for the Initial Fund Year is $900 and that the qualified cost for the Overlap Fund Year is $2500 (prior to the reduction required by paragraph (c) of this Q&A). Under the special rules of paragraphs (b) and (c), the employer may deduct $900 for its taxable year ending on December 31, 1986, and $1600 for its taxable year ending on December 31, 1987. If the qualified direct cost of the fund for the Initial Fund Year had been $1050 and the qualified cost for the Overlap Fund Year had been $2500 (prior to the reduction required by paragraph (c) of this Q&A), the employer's deduction for its taxable year ending December 31, 1986, would have been $1000 and its deduction for its taxable year ending December 31, 1987, would have been $1500.

(e) Assume that an employer with a calendar taxable year establishes on March 1, 1986, a welfare benefit fund with a taxable year ending June 30. Thus, the fund has a short first taxable year ending June 30, 1986, an Overlap Fund Year from July 1, 1986, until June 30, 1987, and an ongoing June 30 taxable year. The employer contributes $1750 to the fund during the employer's taxable year ending December 31, 1986—$750 during the short first taxable year of the fund and $1000 during the Initial Fund Year (i.e., the period between July 1, 1986, and December 31, 1986)—and $1500 to the fund during its taxable year ending December 31, 1987. Assume that the qualified cost of the fund for the short first taxable year of the fund is $800, the qualified direct cost for the Initial Fund Year is $900, and the qualified cost for the Overlap Fund Year is $2500 (prior to the reduction required by paragraph (c) of this Q&A). Under the special rules of paragraphs (b) and (c), the employer may deduct $1700 for its taxable year ending December 31, 1986, and $1550 for its taxable year ending December 31, 1987.

Q-8: How does section 419 treat an employer's contribution with respect to a welfare benefit fund in excess of the applicable deduction limit for a taxable year of the employer?

A-8: (a) If an employer makes contributions to a welfare benefit fund in a taxable year of the employer and such contributions (when combined with prior contributions that are deemed under the rule of this Q&A and section 419(d) to have been made in such taxable year) exceed the section 419 deduction limit for such taxable year of the employer, the excess amounts are deemed to be contributed to the fund on the first day of the next taxable year of the employer. Such deemed contributions are combined with amounts actually contributed by the employer to the fund during the next taxable year and may be deductible for such year, subject to the otherwise applicable section 419 deduction limit for such year.

(b) Contributions to a welfare benefit fund on or before December 31, 1985, that were not deductible by the employer for any taxable year of the employer ending on or before December 31, 1985, or for the first taxable year of the employer ending after December 31, 1985, as pre-1986 contributions (see Q&A-9 of this regulation) are deemed to be contributed to the fund on January 1, 1986. However, see Q&A-11 of this regulation for special rules relating to the contribution to a welfare benefit fund of amounts (such as cash) used to acquire, construct, or relating to the contribution to a welfare benefit fund of a facility (and to the contribution of other amounts, such as cash, used to acquire, construct, or improve such a facility) before section 419 generally becomes effective with respect to contributions to such fund.

Q-9: How does an employer with a fiscal taxable year calculate its deduction limit for contributions with respect to a welfare benefit fund for the first taxable year of the employer ending after December 31, 1985?

A-9: (a) If the first taxable year of an employer ending after December 31, 1985 (or, if applicable under paragraph (b) of Q&A-2 of this section, the first taxable year of an employer beginning after termination of the last of the collective bargaining agreements pursuant to which the fund is maintained) is a fiscal year, the employer's deduction for such taxable year for contributions to a welfare benefit fund that is not a collectively bargained welfare benefit fund under § 1.419A-2T is limited to the greater of the following two amounts: (1) The contributions paid to the fund during such first taxable year up to the qualified cost of the welfare benefit fund for the taxable year of the fund that relates to such taxable year of the employer, and (2) the contributions paid to the fund during the 1985 portion of such first taxable year of the employer ("the pre-1986 contributions") to the extent that such pre-1986 contributions are deductible under the rules governing the deduction of such contributions before section 419 generally becomes effective (including the rules set forth in Q&A-10 of this regulation, modified for purposes of this Q&A-9 by substituting "December 31, 1986" for "December 31, 1985" in paragraph (c)). See Q&A-11 of this regulation for special rules relating to the contribution to a welfare benefit fund of a facility (and to the contribution of other amounts, such as cash, used to acquire, construct, or improve such a facility) before section 419 generally becomes effective with respect to contributions to such fund.

(b) For example, assume that an employer with a taxable year ending June 30 contributes to a welfare benefit fund with a taxable year ending January 31. This employer contributes $1000 to the fund between July 1, 1985, and December 31, 1985, and an additional $500 to the fund between January 1, 1986, and June 30, 1986. Assume further that the qualified direct cost of the fund for the taxable year of the fund ending January 31, 1986, is $500 and that the qualified cost for such taxable year is $800. Under the deduction rule set forth above, the employer's deduction for its taxable year ending June 30, 1986, is the greater of two amounts: (i) the contributions made during such full taxable year ($1500) up to the qualified cost of the fund with respect to such taxable year ($800), and (ii) the pre-1986 contributions ($1000) to the extent that such pre-1986 contributions are deductible under the pre-section 419 rules. In determining the extent to which the pre-1986 contributions are deductible under the pre-section 419 rules, the rules contained in Q&A-10 apply as though December 31, 1985, in paragraph (c) were December 31, 1986. Assuming that only $875 is deductible under the pre-section 419 rules, because $875 is greater than $800, this employer may deduct $875 for its first taxable year ending after December 31, 1985. This full $875 deduction for 1985 is deemed to consist entirely of pre-1986 contributions.

Q-10: How do the rules of sections 263, 446(b), 461(a), and 461(h) apply in determining whether contributions with respect to a welfare benefit fund are deductible for a taxable year?

A-10: (a) Both before and after the effective date of section 419 (see Q&A-2 of this regulation), an employer is allowed a deduction for a taxable year for contributions paid or accrued with respect to a "welfare benefit fund" (as defined in Q&A-3 of this regulation and section 419(e)) only to the extent that such contributions satisfy the requirements of section 162 or 212. These requirements must be satisfied after the effective date of section 419 because section 419 requires that (among other requirements) contributions to a welfare benefit fund satisfy the requirements of section 162 or 212.

(b) Except as provided in paragraphs (c) and (d), in determining the extent to which contributions paid or accrued with respect to a welfare benefit fund satisfy the requirements of section 162 or 212 for a taxable year (both before and after section 419 generally becomes effective with respect to such contributions), the rules of sections 263, 446(b), 461(a) (including the rules that relate to the creation of an asset with a useful life extending substantially beyond the close of the taxable year), and 461(h) (to the extent that such section is effective with respect to such contributions) are generally applicable.

(c) Notwithstanding paragraph (b), under the authority of section 7805(b), the rules of sections 263, 446(b), and 461(a) shall not be applied in determining the extent to which an employer's contribution with respect to a welfare benefit fund is deductible under section 162 or 212 with respect to any taxable year of the employer ending on or before Deember 31, 1985, to the extent that, for such taxable year, (1) the contribution was made pursuant to a bona fide collective bargaining agreement requiring fixed and determinable contributions to a collectively bargained welfare benefit fund (as defined in § 1.419A-2T), or (2) the contribution was not in excess of the amount deductible under the principles of Revenue Rulings 69-382, 1969-2 C.B. 28; 69-478, 1969-2 C.B. 29; and 73-599, 1973-2 C.B. 40, modified as appropriate for benefits for active employees.

(d) Notwithstanding paragraph (b), in determining the extent to which contributions paid or accrued with respect to a welfare benefit fund are deductible under section 419, the rules of sections 263, 446(b), and 461(a) will be treated as having been satisfied to the extent that such contributions satisfy the otherwise applicable rules of section 419. Thus, for example, contributions to a welfare benefit fund will not fail to be deductible under section 419 merely because they create an asset with a useful life extending substantially beyond the close of the taxable year if such contributions satisfy the otherwise applicable requirements of section 419.

(e) In determining the extent to which contributions with respect to a welfare benefit fund satisfy the requirements of section 461(h) for any taxable year for which section 461(h) is effective, pursuant to the authority under section 461(h)(2), economic performance occurs as contributions to the welfare benefit fund are made. Solely for purposes of section 461(h), in the case of an employer's taxable year ending on or after July 18, 1984, and on or before March 21, 1986, contributions made to the welfare benefit fund after the end of such taxable year and on or before March 21, 1986, shall be deemed to have been made on the last day of such taxable year.

Q-11: What special section 419 rules apply to the payment or accrual with respect to a welfare benefit fund of a facility (and the payment or accrual of other amounts, such as cash, used to acquire, construct, or improve such a facility)?

A-11: (a)(1) In the case of an employer's payment or accrual with respect to a welfare benefit fund after June 22, 1984, and on or before December 31, 1985, (or, if applicable under paragraph (b) of Q&A-2 of this regulation, before section 419 generally becomes effective with respect to contributions to such fund) of a facility, the rules of section 419, § 1.419-1T, and § 1.419A-2T generally apply to determine the extent to which such contribution is deductible by the employer for its taxable year of contribution. For this purpose, however, the facility is to be treated as the only contribution made to the fund and the qualified cost of the fund for the taxable year of the fund in which the facility was contributed is to be equal to the qualified direct cost directly attributable to the facility (as determined under Q&A-6 of this regulation). Also, for this purpose, the welfare benefit fund to which the facility was contributed may not be aggregated with any other fund. For purposes of this Q&A, "facility" means any tangible asset with a useful life extending substantially beyond the end of the taxable year (e.g., vehicles, buildings) and any intangible asset (e.g., licenses) related to a tangible asset, whether or not such asset is used in the provision of welfare benefits. See, however, paragraph (c) of Q&A-2 of this regulation for a binding contract exception.

(2) For example, assume that an employer and a welfare benefit fund each has a calendar taxable year and that, during 1985, the employer contributes to the fund $200,000 in cash and a facility with a fair market value of $100,000. Such facility is used in the provision of welfare benefits under the fund. The employer is treated as having sold the facility in such year and thus will recognize gain to the extent that the fair market value of the facility exceeds the employer's adjusted basis in the facility. In this regard, see section 1239(d). The extent to which the facility contribution is deductible by the employer for its 1985 taxable year is determined as though it were the only contribution made by the employer to the fund during such year and the qualified cost of the fund for the taxable year of the fund in which the contribution was made (i.e., the 1985 taxable year) were equal to the amount that would have been allowable to the employer as a deduction for such year under the applicable Code provisions with respect to the portion of the facility used in the provision of welfare benefits for such year if the employer had placed in service the facility at the time the fund placed in service the facility and if the employer had the same taxable year as the fund. If, under these assumptions, the employer would have been allowed a $10,000 deduction with respect to the facility for the 1985 taxable year, the fund's qualified cost for its 1985 taxable year would be only $10,000. Thus, only $10,000 of the $100,000 facility contribution would be deductible by the employer for its 1985 taxable year (i.e., the taxable year of the employer with or within which the applicable taxable year of the fund ends). However, in determining the extent to which the $200,000 in cash is deductible by the employer for its 1985 taxable year, the $100,000 facility is not to be disregarded. Thus, if under the applicable pre-section 419 rules the employer is allowed for 1985 a total deduction of only $175,000, the employer would be permitted a deduction for 1985 of $175,000 ($10,000 with respect to the facility and $165,000 of the cash contribution). The nondeductible portion of the cash contribution is to be treated as contributed to the fund on the first day of the next taxable year of the employer. If under the applicable pre-section 419 rules the employer were allowed a total deduction of $300,000 for 1985, the employer would be permitted a deduction for 1985 of only $210,000 ($10,000 with respect to the facility and the full $200,000 cash contribution).

(3) For example, assume that an employer has a June 30 taxable year and maintains a welfare benefit fund with a taxable year ending January 31. During the 1985 portion of its taxable year ending June

30, 1986, the employer contributes $50,000 in cash and a facility with a fair market value of $100,000; and during the 1986 portion of such taxable year, the employer contributes another $75,000 in cash to the fund. The facility is used in the provision of welfare benefits under the fund. Under the rules of Q&A-9 of this regulation, the employer's deduction for its June 30, 1986, taxable year is limited to the greater of the following two amounts: (i) the contributions paid to the fund during such taxable year ($225,000) up to the qualified cost of the fund for the taxable year of the fund ending January 31, 1986, and (ii) the contributions paid to the fund during the 1985 portion of the employer's taxable year ending June 30, 1986 ("the pre-1986 contributions") ($150,000) to the extent that such pre-1986 contributions are deductible under the rules governing the deduction of such contributions before section 419 is generally effective with respect to the fund. For purposes of this rule, the contribution of the facility on or before December 31, 1985, is to be treated as a pre-1986 contribution and the rules of section 419 and this Q&A are to be treated as rules governing the deduction of such contribution before section 419 generally becomes effective with respect to the fund. Thus, in determining the extent to which the facility is deductible as a pre-1986 contribution under the rules before section 419 generally becomes effective, the facility is treated as the only contribution to the welfare benefit fund and the qualified cost of such fund for the taxable year of the fund in which the facility was contributed is the amount that would have been allowable to the employer as a deduction with respect to the portion of the facility used in the provision of welfare benefits if the employer had placed in service the facility at the same time that the fund placed in service the facility and the employer's taxable year ended on January 31, 1986.

(b)(1) The preceding rules shall also apply for purposes of determining when and the extent to which an employer may deduct contributions or other items and amounts after June 22, 1984 and on or before December 31, 1985 (or, if applicable under paragraph (b) of Q&A-2 of this regulation, before section 419 generally becomes effective with respect to contributions to the fund) that are not facilities (e.g., cash contributions) to a welfare benefit fund that are used by the fund to acquire, construct, or improve a facility. The most recent non-facility contributions made to a welfare benefit fund before the facility in question is placed in service by the fund (up to the fair market value of the facility at such time) are to be treated as used by the fund for the acquisition, construction, or improvement (as the case may be) of such facility. To the extent that contributions before such a facility is placed in service are not at least equal to the value of the facility at such time, contributions after such date (up to the value of the facility at the time it is placed in service) are treated as used for acquisition, construction, or improvement of the facility. Such non-facility contributions, to the extent that they were made after June 22, 1984, and on or before December 31, 1985 (or, if applicable under paragraph (b) of Q&A-2 of this regulation, before section 419 generally becomes effective with respect to contributions to the fund), are not deductible by the employer as non-facility contributions for any year. Instead, the employer is permitted a deduction with respect to such contributions only under the rules of this Q&A as though the employer had contributed a facility to the fund at the same time that the fund placed in service the facility in question and, at such time, the facility had a fair market value equal to the total of such non-facility contributions.

(2) For example, assume that an employer and a welfare benefit fund each has a calendar taxable year and during 1985 the fund acquired and placed in service a facility with a fair market value of $100,000 to be used in the provision of welfare benefits. Further,

during July 1984 the employer contributed $150,000 in cash to the fund and, during the portion of 1985, before the facility was placed in service by the fund, the employer contributed another $75,000 in cash to the fund; during the remaining portion of 1985, the employer contributed $125,000 in cash. The facility is used in the provision of welfare benefits under the fund. Because $25,000 of the employer's 1984 contribution is treated under this rule as used for the acquisition of a facility, such $25,000 is not deductible by the employer for 1984. For purposes of determining the employer's deduction for 1985, the employer will be treated as having contributed $125,000 in cash and a facility with a fair market value of $100,000. The employer's deduction for its 1985 taxable year will be determined under the rules relating to the contribution of a facility after June 22, 1984, and on or before December 31, 1985.

(3) For example, assume that an employer and a welfare benefit fund each has a calendar taxable year and during 1986 the fund placed in service a facility with a fair market value of $100,000 to be used in the provision of welfare benefits. During 1985, the employer contributed $125,000 in cash to the fund. During the portion of 1986 before the facility was placed in service, the employer contributed $60,000 in cash, and during the remaining portion of 1986, the employer contributed another $75,000 in cash. The facility is used in the provision of welfare benefits under the fund. Because $40,000 of its 1985 cash contribution is treated under this rule as used for the acquisition of the facility, such $40,000 is not deductible by the employer for 1985. For purposes of determining the employer's deduction for 1986, the employer will be treated as though it had contributed a $40,000 facility to the fund at the time the fund placed the facility in service.

(c) For purposes of calculating the "existing excess reserve amount" under Q&A-1 of §1.419A-1T and the "existing reserves for post-retirement medical or life insurance benefits" under Q&A-4 of §1.512(a)-5T (but not the exempt function income under Q&A-3 of §1.512(a)-5T), the amount set aside as of any applicable date is to be reduced to the extent that contributions originally included in such amount are subsequently treated under this Q&A as used for the acquisition, construction, or improvement of an asset excluded from the calculation of the total amount set aside under paragraph (b) of §1.512(a)-5T (or would be so treated under this Q&A if it applied to such asset). The reduction required under this paragraph applies for purposes of calculating the "existing excess reserve amount" and the "existing reserves for post-retirement medical or life insurance benefits" for all taxable years of the welfare benefit fund. [Temporary Reg. §1.419-1T.]

☐ [*T.D.* 8073, 1-29-86.]

[Reg. §1.419A-1T]

§1.419A-1T. Qualified asset account limitation of additions to account (Temporary).

Q-1: What does the transition rule under section 419A(f)(7) provide?

A-1: Section 419A(f)(7) provides that, in the case of a welfare benefit fund that was in existence on July 18, 1984, the account limit (as determined under section 419A(c)) for each of the first four taxable years of the fund that relate to taxable years of the employer ending after December 31, 1985 (or, if applicable under paragraph (b) of Q&A-2 of §1.419-1T, taxable years of the employer beginning after the termination of the last of the collective bargaining agreements pursuant to which the plan is maintained) shall be increased by the following percentages of the "existing excess reserve amount":

First taxable year	80 percent
Second taxable year	60 percent
Third taxable year	40 percent
Fourth taxable year	20 percent .

For purposes of this section, the "existing excess reserve amount" for any taxable year of a fund is the excess of (1) the assets actually set aside for purposes described in section 419A(a) at the close of the first taxable year of the fund ending after July 18, 1984 (calculated in the manner set forth in Q&A-3 of §1.512(a)-3T, and adjusted under paragraph (c) of Q&A-11 of §1.419-1T), reduced by employer contributions to the fund before the close of such first taxable year to the extent that such contributions are not deductible for the taxable year of the employer with or within which such taxable year of the fund ends and for any prior taxable year of the employer, over (2) the account limit which would have applied to the taxable year of the fund for which the excess is being computed (without regard to this transition rule). A welfare benefit fund is treated as in existence on July 18, 1984, for purposes of this transition rule only if amounts were actually set aside in such fund on such date to provide welfare benefits enumerated under section 419A. [Temporary Reg. §1.419A-1T.]

☐ [*T.D.* 8073, 1-29-86.]

[Reg. §1.419A-2T]

§1.419A-2T. Qualified asset account limitation for collectively bargained funds (Temporary).

Q-1: What account limits apply to welfare benefit funds that are maintained pursuant to a collective bargaining agreement?

A-1: Contributions to a welfare benefit fund maintained pursuant to one or more collective bargaining agreements and the reserves of such a fund generally are subject to the rules of sections 419, 419A, and 512. However, neither contributions to nor reserves of such a collectively bargained welfare benefit fund shall be treated as exceeding the otherwise applicable limits of section 419(b), 419A(b), or 512(a)(3)(E) until the earlier of: (i) The date on which the last of the collective bargaining agreements relating to the fund in effect on, or ratified on or before, the date of issuance of final regulations concerning such limits for collectively bargained welfare benefit funds terminates (determined without regard to any extension thereof agreed to after the date of issuance of such final regulations), or (ii) the date 3 years after the issuance of such final regulations.

Q-2: What is a welfare benefit fund maintained pursuant to a collective bargaining agreement for purposes of Q&A-1?

A-2: (1) For purposes of Q&A-1, a collectively bargained welfare benefit fund is a welfare benefit fund that is maintained pursuant to an agreement which the Secretary of Labor determines to be a collective bargaining agreement and which meets the requirements of the Secretary of the Treasury as set forth in paragraph 2 below.

(2) Notwithstanding a determination by the Secretary of Labor that an agreement is a collective bargaining agreement, a welfare benefit fund is considered to be maintained pursuant to a collective bargaining agreement only if the benefits provided through the fund were the subject of arms-length negotiations between employee representatives and one or more employers, and if such agreement between employee representatives and one or more employers satisfies section 7701(a)(46) of the Code. Moreover, the circumstances surrounding a collective bargaining agreement must evidence good faith bargaining between adverse parties over the welfare benefits to be provided through the fund. Finally, a welfare benefit fund is not considered to be maintained pursuant to a collective bargaining agreement unless at least 50 percent of the employees eligible to receive benefits under the fund are covered by the collective bargaining agreement.

(3) In the case of a collectively bargained welfare benefit fund, only the portion of the fund (as determined under allocation rules to be provided by the Commissioner) attributable to employees covered by a collective bargaining agreement, and from which benefits for such employees are provided, is considered to be maintained pursuant to a collective bargaining agreement.

(4) Notwithstanding the preceding paragraphs and pending the issuance of regulations setting account limits for collectively bargained welfare benefit funds, a welfare benefit fund will not be treated as a collectively bargained welfare benefit fund for purposes of Q&A-1 if and when, after July 1, 1985, the number of employees who are not covered by a collective bargaining agreement and are eligible to receive benefits under the fund increases by reason of an amendment, merger, or other action of the employer or the fund. In addition, pending the issuance of such regulations, for purposes of applying the 50 percent test of paragraph (2) to a welfare benefit fund that is not in existence on July 1, 1985, "90 percent" shall be substituted for "50 percent". [Temporary Reg. §1.419A-2T.]

☐ [T.D. 8034, 7-1-85.]

[Reg. §1.419A(f)(6)-1]

§1.419A(f)(6)-1. Exception for 10 or more employer plan.— (a) *Requirements.*—(1) *In general.*—Sections 419 and 419A do not apply in the case of a welfare benefit fund that is part of a 10 or more employer plan described in section 419A(f)(6). A plan is a 10 or more employer plan described in section 419A(f)(6) only if it is a single plan—

(i) To which more than one employer contributes;

(ii) To which no employer normally contributes more than 10 percent of the total contributions contributed under the plan by all employers;

(iii) That does not maintain an experience-rating arrangement with respect to any individual employer; and

(iv) That satisfies the requirements of paragraph (a)(2) of this section.

(2) *Compliance information.*—A plan satisfies the requirements of this paragraph (a)(2) if the plan is maintained pursuant to a written document that requires the plan administrator to maintain records sufficient for the Commissioner or any participating employer to readily verify that the plan satisfies the requirements of section 419A(f)(6) and this section and that provides the Commissioner and each participating employer (or a person acting on the participating employer's behalf) with the right, upon written request to the plan administrator, to inspect and copy all such records. See §1.414(g)-1 for the definition of plan administrator.

(3) *Application of rules.*—(i) *In general.*—The requirements described in paragraph (a)(1) and (2) of this section must be satisfied both in form and in operation.

(ii) *Arrangement is considered in its entirety.*—The determination of whether a plan is a 10 or more employer plan described in section 419A(f)(6) is based on the totality of the arrangement and all related facts and circumstances, including any related insurance contracts. Accordingly, all agreements and understandings (including promotional materials and policy illustrations) and the terms of any insurance contract will be taken into account in determining whether the requirements are satisfied in form and in operation.

(b) *Experience-rating arrangements.*—(1) *General rule.*—A plan maintains an experience-rating arrangement with respect to an individual employer and thus does not satisfy the requirement of paragraph (a)(1)(iii) of this section if, with respect to that employer, there is any period for which the relationship of contributions under the plan to the benefits or other amounts payable under the plan (the *cost of coverage*) is or can be expected to be based, in whole or in part, on the benefits experience or overall experience (or a proxy for either type of experience) of that employer or one or more employees of that employer. For purposes of this paragraph (b)(1), an employer's contributions include all contributions made by or on behalf of the employer or the employer's employees. See paragraph (d) of this section for the definitions of *benefits experience, overall experience,* and *benefits or other amounts payable.* The rules of this paragraph (b) apply under all circumstances, including employer withdrawals and plan terminations.

(2) *Adjustment of contributions.*—An example of a plan that maintains an experience-rating arrangement with respect to an individual employer is a plan that entitles an employer to (or for which the employer can expect) a reduction in future contributions if that employer's overall experience is positive. Similarly, a plan maintains an experience-rating arrangement with respect to an individual employer where an employer can expect its future contributions to be increased if the employer's overall experience is negative. A plan also maintains an experience-rating arrangement with respect to an individual employer where an employer is entitled to receive (or can expect to receive) a rebate of all or a portion of its contributions if that employer's overall experience is positive or, conversely, where an employer is liable to make additional contributions if its overall experience is negative.

(3) *Adjustment of benefits.*—An example of a plan that maintains an experience-rating arrangement with respect to an individual employer is a plan under which benefits for an employer's employees are (or can be expected to be) increased if that employer's overall experience is positive or, conversely, under which benefits are (or can be expected to be) decreased if that employer's overall experience is negative. A plan also maintains an experience-rating arrangement with respect to an individual employer if benefits for an employer's employees are limited by reference, directly or indirectly, to the overall experience of the employer (rather than having all the plan assets available to provide the benefits).

(4) *Special rules.*—(i) *Treatment of insurance contracts.*—(A) *In general.*—For purposes of this section, insurance contracts under the arrangement will be treated as assets of the fund. Accordingly, the value of the insurance contracts (including non-guaranteed elements) is included in the value of the fund, and amounts paid between the fund and the insurance company are disregarded, except to the extent they generate gains or losses as described in paragraph (b)(4)(i)(C) of this section.

(B) *Payments to and from an insurance company.*—Payments from a participating employer or its employees to an insurance company pursuant to insurance contracts under the arrangement will be treated as contributions made to the fund, and amounts paid under the arrangement from an insurance company will be treated as payments from the fund.

(C) *Gains and losses from insurance contracts.*—As of any date, if the sum of the benefits paid by the insurer and the value of the insurance contract (including non-guaranteed elements) is greater than the cumulative premiums paid to the insurer, the excess is treated as a gain to the fund. As of any date, if the cumulative premiums paid to the insurer are greater than the sum of the benefits paid by the insurer and the value of the insurance contract (including non-guaranteed elements), the excess is treated as a loss to the fund.

(ii) *Treatment of flexible contribution arrangements.*—Solely for purposes of determining the cost of coverage under a plan, if contributions for any period can vary with respect to a benefit package, the Commissioner may treat the employer as contributing the minimum amount that would maintain the coverage for that period.

(iii) *Experience rating by group of employers or group of employees.*—A plan will not be treated as maintaining an experience-rating arrangement with respect to an individual employer merely because the cost of coverage under the plan with respect to the employer is based, in whole or in part, on the benefits experience or the overall experience (or a proxy for either type of experience) of a rating group, provided that no employer normally contributes more than 10 percent of all contributions with respect to that rating group. For this purpose, a *rating group* means a group of participating employers that includes the employer or a group of employees covered under the plan that includes one or more employees of the employer.

(iv) *Family members, etc.*—For purposes of this section, contributions with respect to an employee include contributions with respect to any other person (e.g., a family member) who may be covered by reason of the employee's coverage under the plan and amounts provided with respect to an employee include amounts provided with respect to such a person.

(v) *Leased employees.*—In the case of an employer that is the recipient of services performed by a leased employee described in section 414(n)(2) who participates in the plan, the leased employee is treated as an employee of the recipient and contributions made by the leasing organization attributable to service performed with the recipient are treated as made by the recipient.

(c) *Characteristics indicating a plan is not a 10 or more employer plan.*—(1) *In general.*—The presence of any of the characteristics described in paragraphs (c)(2) through (c)(6) of this section generally indicates that the plan is not a 10 or more employer plan described in section 419A(f)(6). Accordingly, unless established to the satisfaction of the Commissioner that the plan satisfies the requirements of section 419A(f)(6) and this section, a plan having any of the following characteristics is not a 10 or more employer plan described in section 419A(f)(6). A plan's lack of all the following characteristics does not create any inference that the plan is a 10 or more employer plan described in section 419A(f)(6).

(2) *Allocation of plan assets.*—Assets of the plan or fund are allocated to a specific employer or employers through separate accounting of contributions and expenditures for individual employers, or otherwise.

(3) *Differential pricing.*—The amount charged under the plan is not the same for all the participating employers, and those differences are not merely reflective of differences in current risk or rating factors that are commonly taken into account in manual rates used by insurers (such as current age, gender, geographic locale, number of covered dependents, and benefit terms) for the particular benefit or benefits being provided.

(4) *No fixed welfare benefit package.*—The plan does not provide for fixed welfare benefits for a fixed coverage period for a fixed cost, within the meaning of paragraph (d)(5) of this section.

(5) *Unreasonably high cost.*—The plan provides for fixed welfare benefits for a fixed coverage period for a fixed cost, but that cost is unreasonably high for the covered risk for the plan as a whole.

(6) *Nonstandard benefit triggers.*—Benefits or other amounts payable can be paid, distributed, transferred, or otherwise provided from a fund that is part of the plan by reason of any event other than the illness, personal injury, or death of an employee or family member, or the employee's involuntary separation from employment. Thus, for example, a plan exhibits this characteristic if the plan provides for the payment of benefits or the distribution of an insurance contract to an employer's employees on the occasion of the employer's withdrawal from the plan. A plan will not be treated as having the characteristic described in this paragraph merely because, upon cessation of participation in the plan, an employee is provided with the right to convert coverage under a group life insurance contract to coverage under an individual life insurance contract without demonstrating evidence of insurability, but only if there is no additional economic value associated with the conversion right.

(d) *Definitions.*—For purposes of this section:

(1) *Benefits or other amounts payable.*—The term *benefits or other amounts payable* includes all amounts that are payable or distributable (or that will be otherwise provided) directly or indirectly to employers, to employees or their beneficiaries, or to another fund as a result of a spinoff or transfer, and without regard to whether payable or distributable as welfare benefits, cash, dividends, rebates of contributions, property, promises to pay, or otherwise.

(2) *Benefits experience.*—The *benefits experience* of an employer (or of an employee or a group of employers or employees) means the benefits and other amounts incurred, paid, or distributed (or otherwise provided) directly or indirectly, including to another fund as a result of a spinoff or transfer, with respect to the employer (or employee or group of employers or employees), and without regard to whether provided as welfare benefits, cash, dividends, credits, rebates of contributions, property, promises to pay, or otherwise.

(3) *Overall experience.*—(i) *Employer's overall experience.*—The term *overall experience* means, with respect to an employer (or group of employers), the balance that would have accumulated in a welfare benefit fund if that employer (or those employers) were the only employer (or employers) providing welfare benefits under the plan. Thus, the overall experience is credited with the sum of the contributions under the plan with respect to that employer (or group of

employers), less the benefits and other amounts paid or distributed (or otherwise provided) with respect to that employer (or group of employers) or the employees of that employer (or group of employers), and adjusted for gain or loss from insurance contracts (as described in paragraph (b)(4)(i) of this section), investment return, and expenses. Overall experience as of any date may be either a positive or a negative number.

(ii) *Employee's overall experience.*—The term *overall experience* means, with respect to an employee (or group of employees, whether or not employed by the same employer), the balance that would have accumulated in a welfare benefit fund if the employee (or group of employees) were the only employee (or employees) being provided welfare benefits under the plan. Thus, the overall experience is credited with the sum of the contributions under the plan with respect to that employee (or group of employees), less the benefits and other amounts paid or distributed (or otherwise provided) with respect to that employee (or group of employees), and adjusted for gain or loss from insurance contracts (as described in paragraph (b)(4)(i) of this section), investment return, and expenses. Overall experience as of any date may be either a positive or a negative number.

(4) *Employer.*—The term *employer* means the employer whose employees are participating in the plan and those employers required to be aggregated with the employer under section 414(b), (c), or (m).

(5) *Fixed welfare benefit package.*—(i) *In general.*—A plan provides for fixed welfare benefits for a fixed coverage period for a fixed cost, if it—

(A) Defines one or more welfare benefits, each of which has a fixed amount that does not depend on the amount or type of assets held by the fund;

(B) Specifies fixed contributions to provide for those welfare benefits; and

(C) Specifies a coverage period during which the plan agrees to provide specified welfare benefits, subject to the payment of the specified contributions by the employer.

(ii) *Treatment of actuarial gains or losses.*—A plan will not be treated as failing to provide for fixed welfare benefits for a fixed coverage period for a fixed cost merely because the plan does not pay the promised benefits (or requires all participating employers to make proportionate additional contributions based on the fund's shortfall) when there are insufficient assets under the plan to pay the promised benefits. Similarly, a plan will not be treated as failing to provide for fixed welfare benefits for a fixed coverage period for a fixed cost merely because the plan provides a period of extended coverage after the end of the coverage period with respect to employees of all participating employers at no cost to the employers (or provides a proportionate refund of contributions to all participating employers) because of the plan-wide favorable actuarial experience during the coverage period.

(e) *Maintenance of records.*—The plan administrator of a plan that is intended to be a 10 or more employer plan described in section 419A(f)(6) shall maintain permanent records and other documentary evidence sufficient to substantiate that the plan satisfies the requirements of section 419A(f)(6) and this section. (See §1.414(g)-1 for the definition of plan administrator.)

(f) *Examples.*—The provisions of paragraph (c) of this section and the provisions of section 419A(f)(6) and this section relating to experience-rating arrangements may be illustrated by the following examples. Unless stated otherwise, it should be assumed that any life insurance contract described in an example is non-participating and has no value other than the value of the policy's current life insurance protection plus its cash value, and that no employer normally contributes more than 10 percent of the total contributions contributed under the plan by all employers. Paragraph (ii) of each example applies the characteristics listed in paragraph (c) of this section to the facts described in that example. Paragraphs (iii) and (iv) of each example analyze the facts described in the example to determine whether the plan maintains experience-rating arrangements with respect to individual employers. Paragraphs (iii) and (iv) of each example illustrate only the meaning of *experience-rating arrangements*. No inference should be drawn from these examples about whether these plans are otherwise described in section 419A(f)(6) or about the applicability or nonapplicability of any other Internal Revenue Code provision that may limit or deny the deduction of contributions to the arrangements. Further, no inference should be drawn from the examples concerning the tax treatment of employees as a result of the employer contributions or the provision of the benefits. The examples are as follows:

Example 1. (i) An arrangement provides welfare benefits to employees of participating employers. Each year a participating employer is required to contribute an amount equal to the claims and other expenses expected with respect to that employer for the year (based on current age, gender, geographic locale, number of participating employees, benefit terms, and other risk or rating factors commonly taken into account in manual rates used by insurers for the benefits being provided), multiplied by the ratio of actual claims with respect to that employer for the previous year over the expected claims with respect to that employer for the previous year.

(ii) This arrangement exhibits at least one of the characteristics listed in paragraph (c) of this section generally indicating that an arrangement is not a 10 or more employer plan described in section 419A(f)(6). Differential pricing exists under this arrangement because the amount charged under the plan is not the same for all the participating employers, and those differences are not merely reflective of differences in current risk or rating factors that are commonly taken into account in manual rates used by insurers for the particular benefit or benefits being provided.

(iii) This arrangement does not satisfy the requirements of section 419A(f)(6) and this section because, at a minimum, the requirement of paragraph (a)(1)(iii) of this section is not satisfied. Under the arrangement, an employer's cost of coverage for each year is based, in part, on that employer's benefits experience (i.e., the benefits and other amounts provided in the past with respect to one or more employees of that employer). Accordingly, pursuant to paragraph (b)(1) of this section, the arrangement maintains experience-rating arrangements with respect to individual employers.

Example 2. (i) The facts are the same as in *Example 1*, except that the amount charged to an employer each year is equal to claims and other expenses expected with respect to that employer for the year (determined the same as in *Example 1*), multiplied by the ratio of actual claims for the previous year (determined on a plan-wide basis) over the expected claims for the previous year (determined on a plan-wide basis).

(ii) Based on the limited facts described above, this arrangement exhibits none of the characteristics listed in paragraph (c) of this section generally indicating that an arrangement is not a 10 or more employer plan described in section 419A(f)(6). Unlike the arrangement discussed in *Example 1*, there is no differential pricing under the arrangement because the only differences in the amounts charged to the employers are solely reflective of differences in current risk or rating factors that are commonly taken into account in manual rates used by insurers for the particular benefit or benefits being provided.

(iii) Nothing in the facts described in this *Example 2* indicates that the arrangement maintains experience-rating arrangements prohibited under section 419A(f)(6) and this section. An employer's cost of coverage under the arrangement is based, in part, on the benefits experience of that employer (as well as of all the other participating employers). However, pursuant to paragraph (b)(4)(iii) of this section, the arrangement will not be treated as maintaining experience-rating arrangements with respect to the individual employers merely because the employers' cost of coverage is based on the benefits experience of a group of employees eligible under the plan, provided no employer normally contributes more than 10 percent of all contributions with respect to the rating group that includes the employees of an individual employer. Under the arrangement described in this *Example 2*, the rating group includes all the participating employers (or all of their employees), and no employer normally contributes more than 10 percent of the contributions made under the arrangement by all the employers. Accordingly, absent other facts, the arrangement will not be treated as maintaining experience-rating arrangements with respect to individual employers.

Example 3. (i) Arrangement A provides welfare benefits to employees of participating employers. Each year an employer is required to contribute an amount equal to the claims and other expenses expected with respect to that employer for the year (based on current risk or rating factors commonly taken into account in manual rates used by insurers for the benefits being provided), adjusted based on the employer's national account. An employer's notional account is determined as follows. The account is credited with the sum of the employer's contributions previously paid under the plan less the benefit claims for that employer's employees. The notional account is further increased by a fixed five percent investment return (regardless of the actual investment return earned on the funds). If an employer's notional account is positive, the employer's contributions are reduced by a specified percentage of the notional account. If an employer's notional account is negative, the employer's contributions are increased by a specified percentage of the notional account.

(ii) Arrangement A exhibits at least two of the characteristics listed in paragraph (c) of this section generally indicating that an arrangement is not a 10 or more employer plan described in section 419A(f)(6). First, assets under the plan are allocated to specific employers. Second, differential pricing exists because the amount charged under the plan is not the same for all the participating employers, and those differences are not merely reflective of differ-

ences in current risk or rating factors that are commonly taken into account in manual rates used by insurers for the particular benefit or benefits being provided.

(iii) Arrangement A does not satisfy the requirements of section 419A(f)(6) and this section because, at a minimum, the requirement of paragraph (a)(1)(iii) of this section is not satisfied. Under the arrangement, a participating employer's cost of coverage for each year is based on a proxy for that employer's overall experience. An employer's *overall experience*, as that term is defined in paragraph (d)(3) of this section, includes the balance that would have accumulated in the fund if that employer's employees were the only employees being provided benefits under the plan. Under that definition, the overall experience is credited with the sum of the contributions paid under the plan by or on behalf of that employer less the benefits or other amounts provided to with respect to that employer's employees, and adjusted for gain or loss from insurance contracts, expenses, and investment return. Under the formula used by the arrangement in this example to determine employer contributions, expenses are disregarded and a fixed investment return of five percent is used instead of actual investment return. The disregard of expenses and substitution of the fixed investment return for the actual investment return merely results in an employer's notional account that is a proxy for the overall experience of that employer. Accordingly, the arrangement maintains experience-rating arrangements with respect to individual employers.

Example 4. (i) Under Arrangement B, death benefits are provided for eligible employees of each participating employer. Individual level premium whole life insurance policies are purchased to provide the death benefits. Each policy has a face amount equal to the death benefit payable with respect to the individual employee. Each year, a participating employer is charged an amount equal to the level premiums payable with respect to the employees of that employer. One participating employer, F, has an employee, P, whose coverage under the arrangement commenced at the beginning of 2000, when P was age 50. P is covered under the arrangement for $1 million of death benefits, and a life insurance policy with a face amount of $1 million has been purchased on P's life. The level annual premium on the policy is $23,000. At the beginning of 2005, when P is age 55, the $23,000 premium amount has been paid for five years and the policy, which continues to have a face amount of $1 million, has a cash value of $92,000. Another employer, G, has an employee, R, who is also 55 years old at the beginning of 2005 and is covered under Arrangement B for $1 million, for which a level premium life insurance policy with a face amount of $1 million has been purchased. However, R did not become covered under Arrangement B until the beginning of 2005. Because R's coverage began at age 55, the level annual premium charged for the policy on R's life is $30,000, or $7,000 more than the premiums payable on the policy in effect on P's life. Employer F is charged $23,000 and employer G is charged $30,000 for the death benefit for employees P and R, respectively. Assume that employees P and R are the only covered employees of their respective employers and that they are identical with respect to current risk and rating factors that are commonly taken into account in manual rates used by insurers for death benefits.

(ii) Arrangement B exhibits at least three of the characteristics listed in paragraph (c) of this section generally indicating that an arrangement is not a 10 or more employer plan described in section 419A(f)(6). First, assets of the plan are effectively allocated to specific employers. Second, there is differential pricing under the arrangement. That is, the amount charged under the plan during the year for a specific amount of death benefit coverage is not the same for all the employers (employer F is charged $23,000 each year for $1 million of death benefit coverage while employer G is charged $30,000 each year for the same coverage), and the difference is not merely reflective of differences in current risk or rating factors that are commonly taken into account in manual rates used by insurers for the death benefit being provided. (The differences in amounts charged are attributable to differences in issue age and not to differences in current risk or rating factors, as employees P and R are the same age). Third, during the early years of the arrangement, the amounts charged are unreasonably high for the covered risk for the plan as a whole.

(iii) Arrangement B does not satisfy the requirements of section 419A(f)(6) and this section because, at a minimum, the requirement of paragraph (a)(1)(iii) of this section is not satisfied. Arrangement B maintains experience-rating arrangements with respect to individual employers because the cost of coverage for each year for any employer participating in the arrangement is based on a proxy for the overall experience of that employer. Under Arrangement B, employer F's cost of coverage for 2005 is $23,000 for $1 million of coverage. The $92,000 cash value at the beginning of 2005 in the policy insuring P's life is a proxy for employer F's overall experience. (The $92,000 is essentially the balance that would have accumulated in the fund if employer F were the only employer providing welfare benefits under Arrangement B.) Further, the $23,000 charged to F for the $1 million of coverage in 2005 is based on the $92,000 since, in the absence of the $92,000, employer F would have been charged $30,000 for P's $1 million death benefit coverage. (Note that the conclusion that the $92,000 balance is the basis for the lower premium charged to employer F is consistent with the fact that a $92,000 balance, if converted to a life annuity using the same actuarial assumptions as were used to calculate the cash value amount, would be sufficient to provide for annual annuity payments of $7,000 for the life of P—an amount equal to the $7,000 difference from the premium charged in 2005 to employer G for the $1 million of coverage on employee R's life.) Thus, F's cost of coverage for 2005 is based on a proxy for F's overall experience. Accordingly, Arrangement B maintains an experience-rating arrangement with respect to employer F.

(iv) Arrangement B also maintains an experience-rating arrangement with respect to employer G because it can be expected that each year G will be charged $30,000 for the $1 million of coverage on R's life. Each year, G's cost of coverage will reflect G's prior contributions and allocable earnings, so that G's cost of coverage will be based on a proxy for G's overall experience. Accordingly, Arrangement B maintains an experience-rating arrangement with respect to employer G. Similarly, Arrangement B maintains an experience-rating arrangement with respect to each other participating employer. Accordingly, Arrangement B maintains experience-rating arrangements with respect to individual employers. This would also be the result if Arrangement B maintained an experience-rating arrangement with respect to only one individual employer.

Example 5. (i) The facts are the same as in *Example 4* except that the death benefits are provided under 10-year level term life insurance policies. One participating employer, H, has an employee, M, whose coverage under the arrangement commenced at the beginning of 2000, when M was age 35. M is covered under the arrangement for $1 million of death benefits, and a 10-year level term life insurance policy with a face amount of $1 million has been purchased on M's life. The level annual premium on the policy for the first 10 years is $700. At the beginning of 2007, when M is age 42, the $700 premium amount has been paid for seven years. Another employer, J, has an employee, N, who is also 42 years old at the beginning of 2007 and is covered under the arrangement for $1 million, for which a 10-year level term life insurance policy with a face amount of $1 million has been purchased. However, N did not become covered under the arrangement until the beginning of 2007. Because N's coverage began at age 42, the 10-year level term premium charged for the policy on N's life is $1,100, or $400 more than the premiums then payable on the policy in effect on M's life. Neither the policy on employee M nor the policy on employee N has any cash value at any point during its term. Assume that employees M and N are the only covered employees of their respective employers and that they are identical with respect to any current risk and rating factors that are commonly taken into account in manual rates used by insurers for the death benefit being provided.

(ii) Based on the facts described in this *Example 5*, this arrangement exhibits at least two of the characteristics listed in paragraph (c) of this section generally indicating that an arrangement is not a 10 or more employer plan described in section 419A(f)(6). First, for the same reasons as described in paragraph (ii) of *Example 4*, there is differential pricing under the arrangement. Second, assets of the plan are effectively allocated to specific employers. This is the case even though the insurance policies used by employers H and J have no accessible cash value.

(iii) The facts described in this *Example 5* indicate that the arrangement does not satisfy the requirements of section 419A(f)(6) and this section because, at a minimum, the requirement of paragraph (a)(1)(iii) of this section is not satisfied. This arrangement maintains experience-rating arrangements with respect to individual employers because the cost of coverage for each year for any employer participating in the arrangement is based on a proxy for the overall experience of that employer. Under this arrangement employer H's cost of coverage in 2007 is $700 for $1 million of coverage. Although the policy insuring M's life has no cash value accessible to employer H, the accumulation of the excesses of the amounts paid by employer H on behalf of employee M over each year's underlying mortality and expense charges for providing life insurance coverage to employee M provide economic value to employer H (i.e., the ability to purchase future coverage on M's life at a premium that is less than the underlying mortality and expense charges as those underlying charges increase with M's increasing age). Thus, H's cost of coverage for 2007 is based on a proxy for H's overall experience. Accordingly, this arrangement maintains an experience-rating arrangement with respect to employer H.

(iv) This arrangement also maintains an experience-rating arrangement with respect to employer J because it can be expected that for each of the next nine years J will be charged $1,100 for the $1 million of coverage on N's life. Each year, J's cost of coverage will reflect J's prior contributions, so that J's cost of coverage will be based on a proxy for J's overall experience. Accordingly, this arrangement main-

tains an experience-rating arrangement with respect to employer J. Similarly, this arrangement maintains an experiencing-rating arrangement with respect to each other participating employer. Accordingly, this arrangement maintains experience-rating arrangements with respect to individual employers. This would also be the result if this arrangement maintained an experience-rating arrangement with respect to only one individual employer.

Example 6. (i) Under Arrangement C, death benefits are provided for eligible employees of each participating employer. Flexible premium universal life insurance policies are purchased to provide the death benefits. Each policy has a face amount equal to the death benefit payable with respect to the individual employee. Each participating employer can make any contributions to the arrangement provided that the amount paid for each employee is at least the amount needed to prevent the lapse of the policy. The amount needed to prevent the lapse of the universal life insurance policy is the excess, if any, of the mortality and expense charges for the year over the policy balance. All contributions made by an employer are paid as premiums to the universal life insurance policies purchased on the lives of the covered employees of that employer. Participating employers S and V each have a 50-year-old employee covered under Arrangement C for death benefits of $1 million, which is the face amount of the respective universal life insurance policies on the lives of the employees. In the first year of coverage employer S makes a contribution of $23,000 (the amount of a level premium) while employer V contributes only $6,000, which is the amount of the mortality and expense charges for the first year. At the beginning of year two, the balance in employer S's policy (including earnings) is $18,000, but the balance in V's policy is zero. Although S is not required to contribute anything in the second year of coverage, S contributes an additional $15,000 in the second year. Employer V contributes $7,000 in the second year.

(ii) Arrangement C exhibits at least two of the characteristics listed in paragraph (c) of this section generally indicating that an arrangement is not a 10 or more employer plan described in section 419A(f)(6). First, assets of the plan are effectively allocated to specific employers. Second, the arrangement does not provide for fixed welfare benefits for a fixed coverage period for a fixed cost.

(iii) Arrangement C does not satisfy the requirements of section 419A(f)(6) and this section because, at a minimum, the requirement of paragraph (a)(1)(iii) of this section is not satisfied. Arrangement C maintains experience-rating arrangements with respect to individual employers because the cost of coverage of an employer participating in the arrangement is based on a proxy for the overall experience of that employer. Pursuant to paragraph (b)(4)(ii) of this section (concerning treatment of flexible contribution arrangements), solely for purposes of determining an employer's cost of coverage, the Commissioner may treat an employer as contributing the minimum amount needed to maintain the coverage. Applying this treatment, H's cost of coverage for the first year of coverage under Arrangement C is $6,000 for $1 million of death benefit coverage, but for the second year it is zero for the same amount of coverage because that is the minimum amount needed to keep the insurance policy from lapsing. Employer H's overall experience at the beginning of the second year of coverage is $18,000, because that is the balance that would have accumulated in the fund if H were the only employer providing benefits under Arrangement C. (The special rule of paragraph (b)(4)(ii) of this section only applies to determine cost of coverage; it does not apply in determining overall experience.) The $18,000 balance in the policy insuring the life of employer H's employee is a proxy for H's overall experience. Employer H can choose not to make any contributions in the second year of coverage due to the $18,000 policy balance. Thus, H's cost of coverage for the second year is based on a proxy for H's overall experience. Accordingly, Arrangement C maintains an experience-rating arrangement with respect to employer H.

(iv) Arrangement C also maintains an experience-rating arrangement with respect to employer J because in each year J can contribute more than the amount needed to prevent a lapse of the policy on the life of its employee and can expect that its cost of coverage for subsequent years will reflect its prior contributions and allocable earnings. Accordingly, Arrangement C maintains an experience-rating arrangement with respect to employer J.

Example 7. (i) Arrangement D provides death benefits for eligible employees of each participating employer. Each employer can choose to provide a death benefit of either one, two, or three times the annual compensation of the covered employees. Under Arrangement D, the death benefit is payable only if the employee dies while employed by the employer. If an employee terminates employment with the employer or if the employer withdraws from the arrangement, the death benefit is no longer payable, no refund or other credit is payable to the employer or to the employees, and no policy or other property is transferrable to the employer or the employees. Furthermore, the employees are not provided with any right under Arrangement D to coverage under any other arrangement, nor with any right to purchase or to convert to an individual insurance policy, other than any conversion rights the employees may have in accordance with state law (and which provide no additional economic benefit). Arrangement D determines the amount required to be contributed by each employer for each month of coverage by aggregating the amount required to be contributed for each covered employee of the employer. The amount required to be contributed for each covered employee is determined by multiplying the amount of the death benefit coverage (in thousands) for the employee by five-year age bracket rates in a table specified by the plan, which is used uniformly for all covered employees of all participating employers. The rates in the specified table do not exceed the rates set forth in Table I of §1.79-3(d)(2), and differences in the rates in the table are merely reflective of differences in mortality risk for the various age brackets. The rates in the table are not based in whole or in part on the experience of the employers participating in Arrangement D. Arrangement D uses the amount contributed by each employer to purchase one-year term insurance coverage on the lives of the covered employees with a face amount equal to the death benefit provided by the plan. No employer is entitled to any rebates or refunds provided under the insurance contract.

(ii) Arrangement D does not exhibit any of the characteristics listed in paragraph (c) of this section generally indicating that an arrangement is not a 10 or more employer plan described in section 419A(f)(6). Under Arrangement D, assets are not allocated to a specific employer or employers. Differences in the amounts charged to the employers are solely reflective of differences in risk or rating factors that are commonly taken into account in manual rates used by insurers for the particular benefit or benefits being provided. The arrangement provides for fixed welfare benefits for a fixed coverage period for a fixed cost, within the meaning of paragraph (d)(5) of this section. The cost charged under the arrangement is not unreasonably high for the covered risk of the plan as a whole. Finally, benefits and other amounts payable can be paid, distributed, transferred, or otherwise made available only by reason of the death of the employee, so that there is no nonstandard benefit trigger under the arrangement.

(iii) Nothing in the facts of this *Example 7* indicates that Arrangement D fails to satisfy the requirements of section 419A(f)(6) or this section by reason of maintaining experience-rating arrangements with respect to individual employers. Based solely on the facts described above, Arrangement D does not maintain an experience rating-arrangement with respect to any individual employer because for each participating employer there is no period for which the employer's cost of coverage under the arrangement is based, in whole or in part, on either the benefits experience or the overall experience (or a proxy for either type of experience) of that employer or its employees.

Example 8. (i) The facts are the same as in *Example 7*, except that under the arrangement, any refund or rebate provided under that year's insurance contract is allocated among all the employers participating in the arrangement in proportion to their contributions, and is used to reduce the employers' contributions for the next year.

(ii) This arrangement exhibits at least one of the characteristics listed in paragraph (c) of this section generally indicating that an arrangement is not a 10 or more employer plan described in section 419A(f)(6). The arrangement includes nonstandard benefit triggers because amounts are made available to an employer by reason of the insurer providing a refund or rebate to the plan, an event that is other than the illness, personal injury, or death of an employee or family member, or an employee's involuntary separation from employment.

(iii) Based on the limited and specific facts described in this *Example 8*, an employer participating in this arrangement should be able to establish to the satisfaction of the Commissioner that the plan does not maintain experience-rating arrangements with respect to individual employers. A participating employer's cost of coverage is the relationship of its contributions to the death benefit coverage or other amounts payable with respect to that employer, including the employer's portion of the insurance company rebate and refund amounts. The rebate and refund amounts are allocated to an employer based on that employer's contribution for the prior year. However, even though an employer's overall experience includes its past contributions, contributions alone are not a proxy for an employer's overall experience under the particular facts described in this Example 8. As a result, a participating employer's cost of coverage under the arrangement for each year (or any other period) is not based on that employer's benefits experience or its overall experience (or a proxy for either type of experience), except as follows: If the total of the insurance company refund or rebate amounts is a proxy for the overall experience of all participating employers, a participating employer's cost of coverage will be based in part on that employer's overall experience (or a proxy therefor) by reason of that employer's overall experience being a portion of the overall experience of all participating employers. Under the special rule of paragraph (b)(2)(iii) of this section, however, that fact alone will not cause the arrangement to be treated as maintaining an experience-rating

arrangement with respect to an individual employer because no employer normally contributes more than 10 percent of the total contributions under the plan by all employers (the rating group). Accordingly, the arrangement will not be treated as maintaining experience-rating arrangements with respect to individual employers.

Example 9. (i) Arrangement E provides medical benefits for covered employees of 90 participating employers. The level of medical benefits is determined by a schedule set forth in the trust document and does not vary by employer. Other than any rights an employee may have to COBRA continuation coverage, the medical benefits cease when an employee terminates employment with the employer. If an employer withdraws from the arrangement, there is no refund of any contributions and there is no transfer of anything of value to employees of the withdrawing employer, to the withdrawing employer, or to another plan or arrangement maintained by the withdrawing employer. Arrangement E determines the amount required to be contributed by each employer for each year of coverage, and the aggregate amounts charged are not unreasonably high for the covered risk for the plan as a whole. To determine the amount to be contributed for each employer, Arrangement E classifies an employer based on the employer's location. These geographic areas are not changed once established under the arrangement. The amount charged for the coverage under the arrangement to the employers in a geographic area is determined from a rate-setting manual based on the benefit package and geographic area, and differences in the rates in the manual are merely reflective of current differences in those risk or rating factors. The rates in the rate-setting manual are not based in whole or in part on the experience of the employers participating in Arrangement E.

(ii) Arrangement E does not exhibit any of the characteristics listed in paragraph (c) of this section generally indicating that an arrangement is not a 10 or more employer plan described in section 419A(f)(6). Although the amounts charged under the arrangement to an employer in one geographic area can be expected to differ from those charged to an employer in another geographic area, the differences are merely reflective of differences in current risk or rating factors that are commonly taken into account in manual rates used by insurers for medical benefits.

(iii) Nothing in the facts of this *Example 9* indicates that Arrangement E fails to satisfy the requirements of section 419A(f)(6) or this section by reason of maintaining experience-rating arrangements with respect to individual employers. Based solely on the facts described above, Arrangement E does not maintain an experience rating-arrangement with respect to any individual employer because for each participating employer there is no period for which the employer's cost of coverage under the arrangement is based, in whole or in part, on either the benefits experience or the overall experience (or a proxy for either type of experience) of that employer or its employees.

Example 10. (i) The facts are the same as in *Example 9*, except that the amount charged for the coverage under the arrangement to the employers in a geographic area is initially determined from a rate-setting manual based on the benefit package and then adjusted to reflect the claims experience of the employers in that classification as a whole. The arrangement does not have any geographic areas classification for which one of the employers in the classification normally contributes more than 10 percent of the contributions made by all the employers in that classification.

(ii) This arrangement exhibits at least one of the characteristics listed in paragraph (c) of this section generally indicating that an arrangement is not a 10 or more employer plan described in section 419A(f)(6). There is differential pricing under the arrangement because the amounts charged to an employer in one geographic area can be expected to differ from those charged to an employer in another geographic area, and the differences are not merely reflective of current risk or rating factors that are commonly taken into account in manual rates used by insurers for medical benefits.

(iii) Based on the facts described in this *Example 10*, an employer participating in this arrangement should be able to establish to the satisfaction of the Commissioner that the plan does not maintain experience-rating arrangements with respect to individual employers even though there is differential pricing. Although an employer's cost of coverage for each year is based, in part, on its benefits experience (as well as the benefits experience of the other employers in its geographic area), that does not result in experience-rating arrangements with respect to any individual employer because the employers in each geographic area are a rating group and no employer normally contributes more than 10 percent of the contributions made by all the employers in its rating group. (See paragraph (b)(4)(iii) of this section.)

Example 11. (i) The facts of Arrangement F are the same as those described in *Example 10*, except that K, an employer in one of Arrangement F's geographic areas, normally contributes more than 10 percent of the contributions made by the employers in that geographic area.

(ii) For the same reasons as described in *Example 10*, Arrangement F results in differential pricing.

(iii) Arrangement F does not satisfy the requirements of section 419A(f)(6) and this section because, at a minimum, the requirement of paragraph (a)(1)(iii) of this section is not satisfied. An employer's cost of coverage for each year is based, in part, on its benefits experience (as well as the benefits experience of the other employers in its geographic area) and the special rule for experience-rating by a rating group does not apply to Arrangement F because employer K normally contributes more than 10 percent of the contributions made by the employers in its rating group. Accordingly, Arrangement F maintains experience-rating arrangements with respect to individual employers.

Example 12. (i) The facts of Arrangement G are the same as those described in Example 10, except for the way that the arrangement classifies the employers. Under Arrangement G, the experience of each employer for the prior year is reviewed and then the employer is assigned to one of three classifications (low cost, intermediate cost, or high cost) based on the ratio of actual claims with respect to that employer to expected claims with respect to that employer. No employer in any classification normally contributes more than 10 percent of the contributions of all employers in that classification.

(ii) For the same reasons as described in *Example 10*, Arrangement G results in differential pricing.

(iii) Arrangement G does not satisfy the requirements of section 419A(f)(6) and this section because, at a minimum, the requirement of paragraph (a)(1)(iii) of this section is not satisfied. The special rule in paragraph (b)(4)(iii) of this section for rating groups can prevent a plan from being treated as maintaining experience-rating arrangements with respect to individual employers if the mere use of a rating group is the only reason a plan would be so treated. Under Arrangement G, however, an employer's cost of coverage for each year is based on the employer's benefits experience in two ways: the employer's benefits experience is part of the benefits experience of a rating group that is otherwise permitted under the special rule of paragraph (b)(4)(iii) of this section, and the employer's benefits experience is considered annually in redetermining the rating group to which the employer is assigned. Accordingly, Arrangement G maintains experience-rating arrangements with respect to individual employers.

Example 13. (i) Arrangement H provides a death benefit equal to a multiple of one, two, or three times compensation as elected by the participating employer for all of its covered employees. Universal life insurance contracts are purchased on the lives of the covered employees. The face amount of each contract is the amount of the death benefit payable upon the death of the covered employee. Under the arrangement, each employer is charged annually an amount equal to 200 percent of the mortality and expense charges under the contracts for that year covering the lives of the covered employees of that employer. Arrangement H pays the amount charged each employer to the insurance company. Thus, the insurance company receives an amount equal to 200 percent of the mortality and expense charges under the policies. The excess amounts charged and paid to the insurance company increase the policy value of the universal life insurance contracts. When an employer ceases to participate in Arrangement H, the insurance policies are distributed to each of the covered employees of the withdrawing employer.

(ii) Arrangement H exhibits at least three of the characteristics listed in paragraph (c) of this section generally indicating that an arrangement is not a 10 or more employer plan described in section 419A(f)(6). First, assets are effectively allocated to specific employers. Second, because the amount of the withdrawal benefit (i.e., the value of the life insurance policies to be distributed) is unknown, the arrangement does not provide for fixed welfare benefits for a fixed coverage period for a fixed cost. Finally, Arrangement H includes nonstandard benefit triggers because amounts can be distributed under the arrangement for a reason other than the illness, personal injury, or death of an employee or family member, or an employee's involuntary separation from employment.

(iii) Arrangement H does not satisfy the requirements of section 419A(f)(6) and this section because, at a minimum, the requirement of paragraph (a)(1)(iii) of this section is not satisfied. Pursuant to paragraph (b)(1) of this section, the prohibition against maintaining experience-rating arrangements applies under all circumstances, including employer withdrawals. Arrangement H maintains experience-rating arrangements with respect to individual employers because the cost of coverage for a participating employer is based on a proxy for the overall experience of that employer. Under Arrangement H, the contributions of a participating employer are fixed. The benefits or other amounts payable with respect to an employer include the value of the life insurance policies that are distributable to the employees of that employer upon the withdrawal of that

employer from the plan. Thus, the cost of coverage for any period of an employer's participation in Arrangement H is the relationship between the fixed contributions for that period and the variable benefits payable under the arrangement. The value of those variable benefits depends on the value of the policies that would be distributed if the employer were to withdraw at the end of the period. (Each year the insurance policies to be distributed to the employees in the event of the employer's withdrawal will increase in value due to the premium amounts paid on the policy in excess of current mortality and expense charges.) For reasons similar to those discussed above in *Example 6*, the aggregate value of the life insurance policies on the lives of an employer's employees is a proxy for that employer's overall experience. Thus, a participating employer's cost of coverage for any period is based on a proxy for the overall experience of that employer. Accordingly, Arrangement H maintains experience-rating arrangements with respect to individual employers.

(iv) The result would be the same if, rather than distributing the policies, Arrangement H distributed cash amounts equal to the cash values of the policies. The result would also be the same if the distribution of policies or cash values is triggered by employees terminating their employment rather than by employers ceasing to participate in the arrangement.

Example 14. (i)(1) The facts of Arrangement J are the same as those described in *Example 13* for Arrangement H, except that—

(A) Arrangement J purchases a special term insurance policy on the life of each covered employee with a face amount equal to the death benefit payable upon the death of the covered employee; and

(B) there is no benefit distributable upon an employer's withdrawal.

(2) The special term policy includes a rider that extends the term protection for a period of time beyond the term provided on the policy's face. The length of the extended term is not guaranteed, but is based on the excess of premiums over mortality and expense charges during the period of original term protection, increased by any investment return credited to the policies.

(ii) Arrangement J exhibits two of the characteristics listed in paragraph (c) of this section generally indicating that an arrangement is not a 10 or more employer plan described in section 419A(f)(6). First, assets of the plan are effectively allocated to specific employers. Second, the plan does not provide for fixed welfare benefits for a fixed coverage period for a fixed cost because the coverage period is not fixed.

(iii) Arrangement J does not satisfy the requirements of section 419A(f)(6) and this section because, at a minimum, the requirement of paragraph (a)(1)(iii) of this section is not satisfied. Arrangement J maintains experience-rating arrangements with respect to individual employers because the cost of coverage for a participating employer is based on a proxy for the overall experience of that employer. Under Arrangement J, the contributions of a participating employer are fixed. The benefits or other amounts payable with respect to an employer are the one-, two-, or three-times-compensation death benefit for each employee of the employer for the current year, plus the extended term protection coverage for future years. Thus, for any period extending to or beyond the end of the original term of one or more of the policies on the lives of an employer's employees, the employer's cost of coverage is the relationship between the fixed contributions for that period and the variable benefits payable under the arrangement. The value of those variable benefits depends on the aggregate value of the policies insuring the employer's employees (i.e., the total of the premiums paid on the policies by Arrangement J to the insurance company, reduced by the mortality and expense charges that were needed to provide the original term protection, and increased by any investment return credited to the policies). The aggregate value of the policies insuring an employer's employees is, at any time, a proxy for the employer's overall experience. Thus, a participating employer's cost of coverage for any period described above is based on a proxy for the overall experience of that employer. Accordingly, Arrangement J maintains experience-rating arrangements with respect to individual employers.

Example 15. (i) Arrangement K provides a death benefit to employees of participating employers equal to a specified multiple of compensation. Under the arrangement, a flexible-premium universal life insurance policy is purchased on the life of each covered employee in the amount of that employee's death benefit. Each policy has a face amount equal to the employee's death benefit under the arrangement. Each participating employer is charged annually with the aggregate amount (if any) needed to maintain the policies covering the lives of its employees. However, each employer is permitted to make additional contributions to the arrangement and, upon doing so, the additional contributions are paid to the insurance company and allocated to one or more contracts covering the lives of the employer's employees. In the event that any policy covering the life of an employee would lapse in the absence of new contributions from that employee's employer, and if at the same time there are policies covering the lives of other employees of the employer that have cash values in excess of the amounts needed to prevent their lapse, the employer has the option of reducing its otherwise-required contribution by amounts withdrawn from those other policies.

(ii) Arrangement K exhibits at least two of the characteristics listed in paragraph (c) of this section generally indicating that an arrangement is not a 10 or more employer plan described in section 419A(f)(6). First, assets of the plan are allocated to specific employers. Second, because the plan allows an employer to choose to contribute an amount that is different than that contributed by another employer for the same benefit, the amount charged under the plan is not the same for all participating employers (and the differences in the amounts are not merely reflective of differences in current risk or rating factors that are commonly taken into account in manual rates used by insurers for the particular benefit or benefits being provided), resulting in differential pricing.

(iii) Arrangement K does not satisfy the requirements of section 419A(f)(6) and this section because, at a minimum, the requirement of paragraph (a)(1)(iii) of this section is not satisfied. Arrangement K maintains experience-rating arrangements with respect to individual employers because the cost of coverage for any employer participating in the arrangement is based on a proxy for the overall experience of that employer. Under Arrangement K the benefits with respect to an employer for any year are a fixed amount. For purposes of determining the employer's cost of coverage for that year, the Commissioner may treat the employer's contribution under the special rule of paragraph (b)(4)(ii) of this section (concerning treatment of flexible contribution arrangements) as being the minimum contribution amount needed to maintain the universal life policies with respect to that employer for the death benefit coverage for that year. Because the employer has the option to prevent the lapse of one policy by having amounts withdrawn from other policies, that minimum contribution amount will be based in part on the aggregate value of the policies on the lives of that employer's employees. That aggregate value is a proxy for the employer's overall experience. Accordingly, Arrangement K maintains experience-rating arrangements with respect to individual employers.

(g) *Effective date.*—(1) *In general.*—Except as set forth in paragraph (g)(2) of this section, this section applies to contributions paid or incurred in taxable years of an employer beginning on or after July 11, 2002.

(2) *Compliance information and recordkeeping.*—Paragraphs (a)(1)(iv), (a)(2), and (e) of this section apply for taxable years of a welfare benefit fund beginning after July 17, 2003. [Reg. §1.419A(f)(6)-1.]

☐ [*T.D.* 9079, 7-16-2003.]

[Reg. §1.420-1]

§1.420-1. Significant reduction in retiree health coverage during the cost maintenance period.—(a) *In general.*—Notwithstanding section 420(c)(3)(A), the minimum cost requirements of section 420(c)(3) are not met if the employer significantly reduces retiree health coverage during the cost maintenance period.

(b) *Significant reduction.*—(1) *In general.*—An employer significantly reduces retiree health coverage during the cost maintenance period if, for any taxable year beginning on or after January 1, 2002, that is included in the cost maintenance period, either—

(i) The employer-initiated reduction percentage for that taxable year exceeds 10 percent; or

(ii) The sum of the employer-initiated reduction percentages for that taxable year and all prior taxable years during the cost maintenance period exceeds 20 percent.

(2) *Employer-initiated reduction percentage.*—The employer-initiated reduction percentage for any taxable year is the fraction B/A, expressed as a percentage, where:

A = The total number of individuals (retired employees plus their spouses plus their dependents) receiving coverage for applicable health benefits as of the day before the first day of the taxable year.

B = The total number of individuals included in A whose coverage for applicable health benefits ended during the taxable year by reason of employer action.

(3) *Special rules for taxable years beginning before January 1, 2002.*—The following rules apply for purposes of computing the amount in paragraph (b)(1)(ii) of this section if any portion of the cost maintenance period precedes the first day of the first taxable year beginning on or after January 1, 2002—

(i) *Aggregation of taxable years.*—The portion of the cost maintenance period that precedes the first day of the first taxable year beginning on or after January 1, 2002 (the initial period) is treated as

a single taxable year and the employer-initiated reduction percentage for the initial period is computed as set forth in paragraph (b)(2) of this section, except that the words "initial period" apply instead of "taxable year."

(ii) *Loss of coverage.*—If coverage for applicable health benefits for an individual ends by reason of employer action at any time during the initial period, an employer may treat that coverage as not having ended if the employer restores coverage for applicable health benefits to that individual by the end of the initial period.

(4) *Employer action.*—(i) *General rule.*—For purposes of paragraph (b)(2) of this section, an individual's coverage for applicable health benefits ends during a taxable year by reason of employer action, if on any day within the taxable year, the individual's eligibility for applicable health benefits ends as a result of a plan amendment or any other action of the employer (e.g., the sale of all or part of the employer's business) that, in conjunction with the plan terms, has the effect of ending the individual's eligibility. An employer action is taken into account for this purpose regardless of when the employer action actually occurs (e.g., the date the plan amendment is executed), except that employer actions occurring before the later of December 18, 1999, and the date that is 5 years before the start of the cost maintenance period are disregarded.

(ii) *Special rule.*—Notwithstanding paragraph (b)(4)(i) of this section, coverage for an individual will not be treated as having ended by reason of employer action merely because such coverage ends under the terms of the plan if those terms were adopted contemporaneously with the provision under which the individual became eligible for retiree health coverage. This paragraph (b)(4)(ii) does not apply with respect to plan terms adopted contemporaneously with a plan amendment that restores coverage for applicable health benefits before the end of the initial period in accordance with paragraph (b)(3)(ii) of this section.

(iii) *Sale transactions.*—If a purchaser provides coverage for retiree health benefits to one or more individuals whose coverage ends by reason of a sale of all or part of the employer's business, the employer may treat the coverage of those individuals as not having ended by reason of employer action. In such a case, for the remainder of the year of the sale and future taxable years of the cost maintenance period—

(A) For purposes of computing the applicable employer cost under section 420(c)(3), those individuals are treated as individuals to whom coverage for applicable health benefits was provided (for as long as the purchaser provides retiree health coverage to them), and any amounts expended by the purchaser of the business to provide for health benefits for those individuals are treated as paid by the employer;

(B) For purposes of determining whether a subsequent termination of coverage is by reason of employer action under this paragraph (b)(4), the purchaser is treated as the employer. However, the special rule in paragraph (b)(4)(ii) of this section applies only to the extent that any terms of the plan maintained by the purchaser that have the effect of ending retiree health coverage for an individual are the same as terms of the plan maintained by the employer that were adopted contemporaneously with the provision under which the individual became eligible for retiree health coverage under the plan maintained by the employer.

(c) *Definitions.*—The following definitions apply for purposes of this section:

(1) *Applicable health benefits.*—Applicable health benefits means applicable health benefits as defined in section 420(e)(1)(C).

(2) *Cost maintenance period.*—Cost maintenance period means the cost maintenance period as defined in section 420(c)(3)(D).

(3) *Sale.*—A sale of all or part of an employer's business means a sale or other transfer in connection with which the employees of a trade or business of the employer become employees of another person. In the case of such a transfer, the term *purchaser* means a transferee of the trade or business.

(d) *Examples.*—The following examples illustrate the application of this section:

Example 1. (i) Employer W maintains a defined benefit pension plan that includes a 401(h) account and permits qualified transfers that satisfy section 420. The number of individuals receiving coverage for applicable health benefits as of the day before the first day of Year 1 is 100. In Year 1, Employer W makes a qualified transfer under section 420. There is no change in the number of individuals receiving health benefits during Year 1. As of the last day of Year 2, applicable health benefits are provided to 99 individuals, because 2 individuals became eligible for coverage due to retirement and 3 individuals died in Year 2. During Year 3, Employer W amends its health plan to eliminate coverage for 5 individuals, 1 new retiree becomes eligible for coverage and an additional 3 individuals are no longer covered due to their own decision to drop coverage. Thus, as of the last day of Year 3, applicable health benefits are provided to 92 individuals. During Year 4, Employer W amends its health plan to eliminate coverage under its health plan for 8 more individuals, so that as of the last day of Year 4, applicable health benefits are provided to 84 individuals. During Year 5, Employer W amends its health plan to eliminate coverage for 8 more individuals.

(ii) There is no significant reduction in retiree health coverage in either Year 1 or Year 2, because there is no reduction in health coverage as a result of employer action in those years.

(iii) There is no significant reduction in Year 3. The number of individuals whose health coverage ended during Year 3 by reason of employer action (amendment of the plan) is 5. Since the number of individuals receiving coverage for applicable health benefits as of the last day of Year 2 is 99, the employer-initiated reduction percentage for Year 3 is 5.05 percent (5/99), which is less than the 10 percent annual limit.

(iv) There is no significant reduction in Year 4. The number of individuals whose health coverage ended during Year 4 by reason of employer action is 8. Since the number of individuals receiving coverage for applicable health benefits as of the last day of Year 3 is 92, the employer-initiated reduction percentage for Year 4 is 8.70 percent (8/92), which is less than the 10 percent annual limit. The sum of the employer-initiated reduction percentages for Year 3 and Year 4 is 13.75 percent, which is less than the 20 percent cumulative limit.

(v) In Year 5, there is a significant reduction under paragraph (b)(1)(ii) of this section. The number of individuals whose health coverage ended during Year 5 by reason of employer action (amendment of the plan) is 8. Since the number of individuals receiving coverage for applicable health benefits as of the last day of Year 4 is 84, the employer-initiated reduction percentage for Year 5 is 9.52 percent (8/84), which is less than the 10 percent annual limit. However, the sum of the employer-initiated reduction percentages for Year 3, Year 4, and Year 5 is 5.05 percent + 8.70 percent + 9.52 percent = 23.27 percent, which exceeds the 20 percent cumulative limit.

Example 2. (i) Employer X, a calendar year taxpayer, maintains a defined benefit pension plan that includes a 401(h) account and permits qualified transfers that satisfy section 420. X also provides lifetime health benefits to employees who retire from Division A as a result of a plant shutdown, no health benefits to employees who retire from Division B, and lifetime health benefits to all employees who retire from Division C. In 2000, X amends its health plan to provide coverage for employees who retire from Division B as a result of a plant shutdown, but only for the 2-year period coinciding with their severance pay. Also in 2000, X amends the health plan to provide that employees who retire from Division A as a result of a plant shutdown receive health coverage only for the 2-year period coinciding with their severance pay. A plant shutdown that affects Division A and Division B employees occurs in 2000. The number of individuals receiving coverage for applicable health benefits as of the last day of 2001 is 200. In 2002, Employer X makes a qualified transfer under section 420. As of the last day of 2002, applicable health benefits are provided to 170 individuals, because the 2-year period of benefits ends for 10 employees who retired from Division A and 20 employees who retired from Division B as a result of the plant shutdown that occurred in 2000.

(ii) There is no significant reduction in retiree health coverage in 2002. Coverage for the 10 retirees from Division A who lose coverage as a result of the end of the 2-year period is treated as having ended by reason of employer action, because coverage for those Division A retirees ended by reason of a plan amendment made after December 17, 1999. However, the terms of the health plan that limit coverage for employees who retired from Division B as a result of the 2000 plant shutdown (to the 2-year period) were adopted contemporaneously with the provision under which those employees became eligible for retiree coverage under the health plan. Accordingly, under the rule provided in paragraph (b)(4)(ii) of this section, coverage for those 20 retirees from Division B is not treated as having ended by reason of employer action. Thus, the number of individuals whose health benefits ended by reason of employer action in 2002 is 10. Since the number of individuals receiving coverage for applicable health benefits as of the last day of 2001 is 200, the employer-initiated reduction percentage for 2002 is 5 percent (10/200), which is less than the 10 percent annual limit.

(e) *Regulatory effective date.*—This section is applicable to transfers of excess pension assets occurring on or after December 18, 1999. [Reg. § 1.420-1.]

☐ [*T.D.* 8948, 6-14-2001.]

Certain Stock Options

[Reg. § 1.421-1]

§ 1.421-1. Meaning and use of certain terms.—(a) *Option.*— (1) For purposes of this section and §§ 1.421-2 through 1.424-1, the term "option" means the right or privilege of an individual to purchase stock from a corporation by virtue of an offer of the corporation continuing for a stated period of time, whether or not irrevocable, to sell such stock at a price determined under paragraph (e) of this section, such individual being under no obligation to purchase. The individual who has such right or privilege is referred to as the optionee and the corporation offering to sell stock under such an arrangement is referred to as the optionor. While no particular form of words is necessary, the option must express, among other things, an offer to sell at the option price, the maximum number of shares purchasable under the option, and the period of time during which the offer remains open. The term *option* includes a warrant that meets the requirements of this paragraph (a)(1).

(2) An option may be granted as part of or in conjunction with an employee stock purchase plan or subscription contract. See section 423.

(3) An option must be in writing (in paper or electronic form), provided that such writing is adequate to establish an option right or privilege that is enforceable under applicable law.

(b) *Statutory options.*—(1) The term *statutory option,* for purposes of this section and §§ 1.421-2 through 1.424-1, means an *incentive stock option,* as defined in § 1.422-2(a), or an option granted under an *employee stock purchase plan,* as defined in § 1.423-2.

(2) An option qualifies as a statutory option only if the option is not transferable (other than by will or by the laws of descent and distribution) by the individual to whom the option was granted, and is exercisable, during the lifetime of such individual, only by such individual. See §§ 1.422-2(a)(2)(v) and 1.423-2(j). Accordingly, an option which is transferable or transferred by the individual to whom the option is granted during such individual's lifetime, or is exercisable during such individual's lifetime by another person, is not a statutory option. However, if the option or the plan under which the option was granted contains a provision permitting the individual to designate the person who may exercise the option after such individual's death, neither such provision, nor a designation pursuant to such provision, disqualifies the option as a statutory option. A pledge of the stock purchasable under an option as security for a loan that is used to pay the option price does not cause the option to violate the nontransferability requirements of this paragraph (b). Also, the transfer of an option to a trust does not disqualify the option as a statutory option if, under section 671 and applicable State law, the individual is considered the sole beneficial owner of the option while it is held in the trust. If an option is transferred incident to divorce (within the meaning of section 1041) or pursuant to a domestic relations order, the option does not qualify as a statutory option as of the day of such transfer. For the treatment of nonstatutory options, see § 1.83-7.

(3)(i) The determination of whether an option is a statutory option is made as of the date such option is granted. An option which is a statutory option when granted does not lose its character as such an option by reason of subsequent events, and an option which is not a statutory option when granted does not become such an option by reason of subsequent events. See, however, paragraph (e) of § 1.424-1, relating to modification, extension, or renewal of an option. For rules concerning options that are not statutory options, see § 1.83-7.

(ii) The application of this subparagraph may be illustrated by the following examples:

Example (1). X Corporation is a subsidiary of S Corporation which, in turn, is a subsidiary of P Corporation. On June 1, 2004, P grants to an employee of P a statutory option to purchase a share of stock of X. On January 1, 2005, S sells a portion of the X stock which it owns to an unrelated corporation and, as of that date, X ceases to be a subsidiary of S. On May 1, 2005, while still employed by P, the employee exercises his option to purchase a share of X stock. Because X was a subsidiary of P on the date of the grant of the statutory option, the option does not fail to be a statutory option even though X ceases to be a subsidiary of P.

Example (2). Assume P grants an option to an employee under the same facts as in example (1) above, except that on June 1, 2004, X is not a subsidiary of either S or P. Such option is not a statutory option on June 1, 2004. On January 1, 2005, S purchases from an unrelated corporation a sufficient number of shares of X stock to make X, as of that date, a subsidiary of S. On May 1, 2005, while still employed by P, the employee exercises his option to purchase a share of X stock. Because X was not a subsidiary of S or P on the date of the grant of the option, the option is not a statutory option even though X later becomes a subsidiary of P. See §§ 1.422-2(a)(2) and 1.423-2(b).

(c) *Time and date of granting option.*—

> »→ Caution: Reg. §1.421-1(c)(1), below, prior to amendment by T.D. 9471, is applicable to statutory options granted before January 1, 2010.

(1) For purposes of this section and §§ 1.421-2 through 1.424-1, the language "the date of the granting of the option" and "the time such option is granted," and similar phrases refer to the date or time when the granting corporation completes the corporate action constituting an offer of stock for sale to an individual under the terms and conditions of a statutory option. A corporate action constituting an offer of stock for sale is not considered complete until the date on which the maximum number of shares that can be purchased under the option and the minimum option price are fixed or determinable. Ordinarily, if the corporate action contemplates an immediate offer

of stock for sale to an individual or to a class including such individual, or contemplates a particular date on which such offer is to be made, the time or date of the granting of the option is the time or date of such corporate action if the offer is to be made immediately, or the date contemplated as the date of the offer, as the case may be. However, an unreasonable delay in the giving of notice of such offer to the individual or to the class will be taken into account as indicating that the corporation contemplated that the offer was to be made at the subsequent date on which such notice is given.

> »→ Caution: Reg. §1.421-1(c)(1), below, as amended by T.D. 9471, is applicable to statutory options granted on or after January 1, 2010.

(1) For purposes of this section and §§ 1.421-2 through 1.424-1, the language "the date of the granting of the option" and "the time such option is granted," and similar phrases refer to the date or time when the granting corporation completes the corporate action constituting an offer of stock for sale to an individual under the terms and conditions of a statutory option. Except as set forth in § 1.423-2(h)(2), a corporate action constituting an offer of stock for sale is not considered complete until the date on which the maximum number of shares that can be purchased under the option and the minimum option price are fixed or determinable.

(2) If the corporation imposes conditions on the granting of an option (as distinguished from conditions governing the exercise of the option), such conditions shall be given effect in accordance with the intent of the corporation. However, under section 424(i), if the grant of an option is subject to approval by stockholders, the date of grant of the option shall be determined as if the option had not been subject to such approval. A condition which does not require corporate action, such as the approval of, or registration with, some regulatory or governmental agency, for example, a stock exchange or the Securities and Exchange Commission, is ordinarily considered a condition upon the exercise of the option unless the corporate action clearly indicates that the option is not to be granted until such condition is satisfied. If an option is granted to an individual upon the condition that such individual will become an employee of the corporation granting the option or of a related corporation, such option is not granted prior to the date the individual becomes such an employee.

(3) In general, conditions imposed upon the exercise of an option will not operate to make ineffective the granting of the option. For example, on June 1, 2004, the A Corporation grants to X, an employee, an option to purchase 5,000 shares of the corporation's stock, exercisable by X on or after June 1, 2005, provided he is employed by the corporation on June 1, 2005, and provided that A's profits during the fiscal year preceding the year of exercise exceed $200,000. Such an option is granted to X on June 1, 2004, and will be treated as outstanding as of such date.

(d) *Stock and voting stock.*—(1) For purposes of this section and §§ 1.421-2 through 1.424-1, the term *stock* means capital stock of any class, including voting or nonvoting common or preferred stock. Except as otherwise provided, the term includes both treasury stock and stock of original issue. Special classes of stock authorized to be issued to and held by employees are within the scope of the term *stock* as used in such sections, provided such stock otherwise possesses the rights and characteristics of capital stock.

(2) For purposes of determining what constitutes voting stock in ascertaining whether a plan has been approved by stockholders under § 1.422-2(b) or 1.423-2(c) or whether the limitations pertaining to voting power contained in §§ 1.422-2(f) and 1.423-2(d) have been met, stock which does not have voting rights until the happening of an event, such as the default in the payment of dividends on preferred stock, is not voting stock until the happening of the specified event. Generally, stock which does not possess a general voting power, and may vote only on particular questions, is not voting stock. However, if such stock is entitled to vote on whether a stock option plan may be adopted, it is voting stock.

(3) In general, for purposes of this section and §§ 1.421-2 through 1.424-1, ownership interests other than capital stock are considered stock.

(e) *Option price.*—(1) For purposes of this section and §§ 1.421-2 through 1.424-1, the term *option price, price paid under the option*, or *exercise price* means the consideration in cash or property which, pursuant to the terms of the option, is the price at which the stock subject to the option is purchased. The term *option price* does not include any amounts paid as interest under a deferred payment arrangement or treated as interest.

(2) Any reasonable valuation method may be used to determine whether, at the time the option is granted, the option price satisfies the pricing requirements of sections 422(b)(4), 422(c)(5), 422(c)(7), and 423(b)(6) with respect to the stock subject to the option. Such methods include, for example, the valuation method described in § 20.2031-2 of this chapter (Estate Tax Regulations).

(f) *Exercise.*—For purposes of this section and §§ 1.421-2 through 1.424-1, the term "exercise", when used in reference to an option, means the act of acceptance by the optionee of the offer to sell contained in the option. In general, the time of exercise is the time when there is a sale or a contract to sell between the corporation and the individual. A promise to pay the option price does not constitute an exercise of the option unless the optionee is subject to personal liability on such promise. An agreement or undertaking by the employee to make payments under a stock purchase plan does not constitute the exercise of an option to the extent the payments made remain subject to withdrawal by or refund to the employee.

(g) *Transfer.*—For purposes of this section and §§ 1.421-2 through 1.424-1, the term "transfer", when used in reference to the transfer to an individual of a share of stock pursuant to his exercise of a statutory option, means the transfer of ownership of such share, or the transfer of substantially all the rights of ownership. Such transfer must, within a reasonable time, be evidenced on the books of the corporation. For purposes of section 422, a transfer may occur even if a share of stock is subject to a substantial risk of forfeiture or is not otherwise transferable immediately after the date of exercise. See § 1.422-1(b)(3) *Example 2*. A transfer does not fail to occur merely because, under the terms of the arrangement, the individual may not dispose of the share for a specified period of time, or the share is subject to a right of first refusal or a right to reacquire the share at the share's fair market value at the time of sale.

(h) *Employment relationship.*—(1) An option is a statutory option only if, at the time the option is granted, the optionee is an employee of the corporation granting the option, or a related corporation of such corporation. If the option has been assumed or a new option has been substituted in its place under § 1.424-1(a), the optionee must, at the time of such substitution or assumption, be an employee (or a former employee within the 3-month period following termination of the employment relationship) of the corporation so substituting or assuming the option, or a related corporation of such corporation. The determination of whether the optionee is an employee at the time the option is granted (or at the time of the substitution or assumption under § 1.424-1(a)) is made in accordance with section 3401(c) and the regulations thereunder. As to the granting of an option conditioned upon employment, see paragraph (c)(2) of this section. A statutory option must be granted for a reason connected with the individual's employment by the corporation or by its related corporation.

(2) In addition, § 1.421-2(a) is applicable to the transfer of a share pursuant to the exercise of the statutory option only if the optionee is, at all times during the period beginning with the date of the granting of such option and ending on the day 3 months before the date of such exercise, an employee of either the corporation granting such option, a related corporation of such corporation, or a corporation (or a related corporation of such corporation) substituting or assuming a stock option in a transaction to which § 1.424-1(a) applies. For purposes of the preceding sentence, the employment relationship is treated as continuing intact while the individual is on military leave, sick leave, or other bona fide leave of absence (such as temporary employment by the Government) if the period of such leave does not exceed 3 months, or if longer, so long as the individual's right to reemployment with the corporation granting the option (or a related corporation of such corporation) or a corporation (or a related corporation of such corporation) substituting or assuming a stock option in a transaction to which § 1.424-1(a) applies, is provided either by statute or by contract. If the period of leave exceeds 3 months and the

individual's right to reemployment is not provided either by statute or by contract, the employment relationship is deemed to terminate on the first day immediately following such three-month period. Thus, if the option is not exercised before such deemed termination of employment, §1.421-2(a) applies to the transfer of a share pursuant to an exercise of the option only if the exercise occurs within 3 months from the date the employment relationship is deemed terminated.

(3) For purposes of determining whether an individual meets the requirements of this paragraph, the term "employer corporation", as used in section 424(e) and (f), shall be read as "grantor corporation" or "corporation issuing or assuming a stock option in a transaction to which section 424(a) is applicable", as the case may be. For purposes of the employment requirement, a corporation employing an optionee is considered a related corporation if it was a parent or subsidiary of the corporation granting the option or substituting or assuming the option during the entire portion of the requisite period of employment during which it was the employer of such optionee.

(4) The application of this paragraph may be illustrated by the following examples:

Example (1). On June 1, 2004, X Corporation granted a statutory option to A, an employee of X Corporation, to purchase a share of X stock. On February 1, 2005, X sold the plant where A was employed to M Corporation, an unrelated corporation, and A was employed by M. If A exercises his statutory option on June 1, 2005, section 421 is not applicable to such exercise, because on June 1, 2005, A is not employed by the corporation which granted the option or by a related corporation of such corporation, nor was he employed by any of such corporations within 3 months before June 1, 2005.

Example (2). Assume the facts to be the same as in example (1), except that when A was employed by M Corporation, the option to purchase X stock was terminated and was replaced by an option to buy M stock in such circumstances that M Corporation is treated as a corporation substituting an option under section 424(a). If A exercises the option to purchase the share of M stock on June 1, 2005, section 421 is applicable to the transfer of the M stock because, at all times during the period beginning with the date of grant of the X option and ending with the date of exercise of the M option, A was an employee of the corporation granting the option or substituting or assuming the option under §1.424–1(a).

Example (3). E is an employee of P Corporation. On June 1, 2004, P grants E a statutory option to purchase a share of P stock. On June 1, 2005, P acquires 100 percent of the stock of S Corporation; on such date S becomes a subsidiary of P. On July 1, 2005, E ceases to be employed by P and becomes employed by S. On October 10, 2005, while still employed by S, E exercises his option to buy P stock. Since E was at all times during the requisite period of employment an employee of either P, the corporation granting the option, or S, a subsidiary of the grantor during the period in which such corporation was E's employer, section 421 is applicable to the exercise of the option.

Example (4). Assume the same facts as in example (3) except assume that at the time E became an employee of S Corporation, S assumed E's option to purchase P stock under section 424(a). Section 421 is applicable to E's exercise of his option to buy P stock.

Example (5). M Corporation grants a statutory option to E, an employee of such corporation. E is an officer in a reserve Air Force unit. E goes on military leave with his unit for three weeks. Regardless of whether E is an employee of M within the meaning of section 3401(c) and the regulations thereunder during such 3-week period, E's employment relationship with M is treated as uninterrupted during the period of E's military leave.

Example (6). Assume the same facts as in example (5) and assume further that E's active duty status is extended indefinitely, but that E has a right to reemployment with M or a related corporation on the termination of any military duty E may be required to serve. E exercises his M option while on active military duty. Irrespective of whether E is an employee of M or a related corporation within the meaning of section 3401(c) and the regulations thereunder at the time of such exercise or within 3 months before such exercise, section 421 applies to such exercise.

Example (7). X Corporation grants an incentive option to A, an employee of X Corporation, whose employment contract provides that in the event of illness, A's right to reemployment with X, or a related corporation of X, will continue for 1 year after the time A becomes unable to perform his duties for X. A falls ill for 90 days. For purposes of section 422(a)(2), A's employment relationship with X will be treated as uninterrupted during the 90-day period. If A's incapacity extends beyond 90 days, then, for purposes of section 422(a)(2), A's employment relationship with X will be treated as continuing uninterrupted until A's reemployment rights terminate. Under section 422(a)(2), A has 3 months in which to exercise an incentive option after his employment relationship with X (and related corporations) is deemed terminated.

(i) *Additional definitions.*—(1) *Corporation.*—For purposes of this section and §§1.421-2 through 1.424-1, the term *corporation* has the meaning prescribed by section 7701(a)(3) and §301.7701-2(b) of this chapter. For example, a *corporation* for purposes of the preceding sentence includes an S corporation (as defined in section 1361), a foreign corporation (as defined in section 7701(a)(5)), and a limited liability company that is treated as a corporation for all Federal tax purposes.

(2) *Parent corporation and subsidiary corporation.*—For the definition of the terms *parent corporation* (and *parent*) and *subsidiary corporation* (and *subsidiary*), for purposes of this section and §§1.421-2 through 1.424-1, see §1.424-1(f)(i) and (ii), respectively. *Related corporation* as used in this section and in §§1.421-2 through 1.424-1 means either a parent corporation or subsidiary corporation.

(j) *Effective/applicability date.*—(1) *In general.*—Except for paragraph (c)(1) of this section, the regulations under this section are effective on August 3, 2004. Paragraph (c)(1) of this section is effective on November 17, 2009. Paragraph (c)(1) of this section applies to statutory options granted on or after January 1, 2010.

(2) *Reliance and transition period.*—For statutory options granted on or before June 9, 2003, taxpayers may rely on the 1984 proposed regulations LR-279-81 (49 FR 4504), the 2003 proposed regulations REG-122917-02 (68 FR 34344), or this section until the earlier of January 1, 2006, or the first regularly scheduled stockholders meeting of the granting corporation occurring 6 months after August 3, 2004. For statutory options granted after June 9, 2003, and before the earlier of January 1, 2006, or the first regularly scheduled stockholders meeting of the granting corporation occurring at least 6 months after August 3, 2004, taxpayers may rely on either REG-122917-02 or this section. Taxpayers may not rely on LR-279-81 or REG-122917-02 after December 31, 2005. Reliance on LR-279-81, REG-122917-02, or this section must be in its entirety, and all statutory options granted during the reliance period must be treated consistently. [Reg. §1.421-1.]

☐ [*T.D. 6887, 6-23-66. Amended by T.D. 6975, 10-2-68 and T.D. 7554, 7-21-78. Redesignated and amended by T.D. 9144, 8-2-2004 (corrected 10-15-2004 and 12-6-2004) and T.D. 9471, 11-16-2009.*]

[Reg. §1.421-2]

§1.421-2. General rules.—(a) *Effect of qualifying transfer.*—(1) If a share of stock is transferred to an individual pursuant to the individual's exercise of a statutory option, and if the requirements of §1.422-1(a) (relating to incentive stock options) or §1.423-1(a) (relating to employee stock purchase plans) whichever is applicable, are met, then—

(i) No income results under section 83 at the time of the transfer of such share to the individual upon the exercise of the option with respect to such share;

(ii) No deduction under sections 83(h) or 162 or the regulations thereunder (relating to trade or business expenses) is allowable at any time with respect to the share so transferred; and

(iii) No amount other than the price paid under the option is considered as received by the employer corporation, a related corporation of such corporation, or a corporation substituting or assuming a stock option in a transaction to which §1.424-1(a) (relating to corporate reorganizations, liquidations, etc.) applies, for the share so transferred.

(2) For the purpose of this paragraph, each share of stock transferred pursuant to a statutory option is treated separately. For example, if an individual, while employed by a corporation granting him a statutory option, exercises the option with respect to part of the stock covered by the option, and if such individual exercises the balance of the option more than three months after leaving such employment, the application of section 421 to the stock obtained upon the earlier exercise of the option is not affected by the fact that the income taxes of the employer and the individual with respect to the stock obtained upon the later exercise of the option are not determined under section 421.

(b) *Effect of disqualifying disposition.*—(1)(i) The disposition (as defined in §1.424-1(c)) of a share of stock acquired by the exercise of a statutory option before the expiration of the applicable holding periods as determined under §1.422-1(a) or 1.423-1(a) is a disqualifying disposition and makes paragraph (a) of this section inapplicable to the transfer of such share. See section 83(a) to determine the amount includible on a disqualifying disposition. The income attributable to such transfer (determined without reduction for any brokerage fees or other costs paid in connection with the disposition) is treated by the individual as compensation income received in the taxable year in which such disqualifying disposition occurs. A deduction attributable to such transfer is allowable, to the extent otherwise allowable under section 162, for the taxable year in which such disqualifying disposition occurs to the employer corporation, or a related corporation of such corporation, or a corporation substituting or assuming an option in a transaction to which § 1.424-1(a) applies. Additionally, the amount allowed as a deduction must be determined as if the requirements of section 83(h) and § 1.83-6(a) apply. No amount is treated as income, and no amount is allowed as a deduction, for any taxable year other than the taxable year in which the disqualifying disposition occurs If the amount realized on the disposition exceeds (or is less than) the sum of the amount paid for the share and the amount of compensation income recognized as a result of such disposition, the extent to which the difference is treated as gain (or loss) is determined under the rules of section 302 or 1001, as applicable.

(ii) The following examples illustrate the principles of this paragraph (b):

Example 1. On June 1, 2006, X Corporation grants an incentive stock option to A, an employee of X, entitling A to purchase 100 shares of X stock at $10 per share. On August 1, 2006, A exercises the option when the fair market value of X stock is $20 per share, and 100 shares of X stock are transferred to A on that date. On December 15, 2007, A sells the stock for $20 per share. Because A disposed of the stock before June 2, 2008, A did not satisfy the holding period requirements of § 1.422-1(a). Under paragraph (b)(1)(i) of this section, A therefore made a disqualifying disposition of the stock. Thus, paragraph (a) of this section is inapplicable to the transfer of the shares, and A must include the compensation income attributable to the transfer of the shares in gross income in the year of the disqualifying disposition. The amount of compensation income A must include in income is $1,000 ($2,000, the fair market value of X stock on transfer less $1,000, the exercise price per share). If the requirements of § 83(h) and § 1.83-6(a) are satisfied and otherwise allowable under section 162, X is allowed a deduction of $1,000 for its taxable year in which the disqualifying disposition occurs.

Example 2. Y Corporation grants an incentive stock option for 100 shares of its stock to E, an employee of Y. The option has an exercise price of $10 per share. E exercises the option and is transferred the shares when the fair market value of a share of Y stbck is $30. Before the applicable holding periods are met, Y redeems the shares for $70 per share. Because the holding period requirements of § 1.422-1(a) are not met, the redemption of the shares is a disqualifying disposition of the shares. Under paragraph (b)(1)(i) of this section, A made a disqualifying disposition of the stock. Thus, paragraph (a) of this section is inapplicable to the transfer of the shares, and E must include the compensation income attributable to the transfer of the shares in gross income in the year of the disqualifying disposition. The amount of compensation income that E must include in income is $2,000 ($3,000, the fair market value of Y stock on transfer, less $1,000, the exercise price paid by E). The character of the additional gain that is includible in E's income as a result of the redemption is determined under the rules of section 302. If the requirements of § 83(h) and § 1.83-6(a) are satisfied and otherwise allowable under section 162, Y is allowed a deduction for the taxable year in which the disqualifying disposition occurs for the compensation income of $2,000. Y is not allowed a deduction for the additional gain includible in E's income as a result of the redemption.

(2) If an optionee transfers stock acquired through the optionee's exercise of a statutory option prior to the expiration of the applicable holding periods, paragraph (a) of this section continues to apply to the transfer of the stock pursuant to the exercise of the option if such transfer is not a disposition of the stock as defined in § 1.424-1(c) (for example, a transfer from a decedent to the decedent's estate or a transfer by bequest or inheritance). Similarly, a subsequent transfer by the executor, administrator, heir, or legatee is not a disqualifying disposition by the decedent. If a statutory option is exercised by the estate of the optionee or by a person who acquired the option by bequest or inheritance or by reason of the death of such optionee, see paragraph (c) of this section. If a statutory option is exercised by the individual to whom the option was granted and the individual dies before the expiration of the holding periods, see paragraph (d) of this section.

(3) For special rules relating to the disqualifying disposition of a share of stock acquired by exercise of an incentive stock option, see §§ 1.422-5(b)(2) and 1.424-1(c)(3).

(c) *Exercise by estate.*—(1) If a statutory option is exercised by the estate of the individual to whom the option was granted (or by any person who acquired such option by bequest or inheritance or by reason of the death of such individual), paragraph (a) of this section applies to the transfer of stock pursuant to such exercise in the same manner as if the option had been exercised by the deceased optionee. Consequently, neither the estate nor such person is required to include any amount in gross income as a result of a transfer of stock pursuant to the exercise of the option. Paragraph (a) of this section applies even if the executor, administrator, or such person disposes of the stock so acquired before the expiration of the applicable

holding periods as determined under § 1.422-1(a) or 1.423-1(a). This special rule does not affect the applicability of section 423(c), relating to the estate's or other qualifying person's recognition of compensation income, or section 1222, relating to what constitutes a short-term and long-term capital gain or loss. Paragraph (a) of this section also applies even if the executor, administrator, or such person does not exercise the option within three months after the death of the individual or is not employed as described in § 1.421-1(h), either when the option is exercised or at any time. However, paragraph (a) of this section does not apply to a transfer of shares pursuant to an exercise of the option by the estate or by such person unless the individual met the employment requirements described in § 1.421-1(h) either at the time of the individual's death or within three months before such time (or, if applicable, within the period described in § 1.422-1(a)(3). Additionally, paragraph (a) of this section does not apply if the option is exercised by a person other than the executor or administrator, or other than a person who acquired the option by bequest or inheritance or by reason of the death of such deceased individual. For example, if the option is sold by the estate, paragraph (a) of this section does not apply to the transfer of stock pursuant to an exercise of the option by the buyer, but if the option is distributed by the administrator to an heir as part of the estate, paragraph (a) of this section applies to the transfer of stock pursuant to an exercise of the option by such heir.

(2) Any transfer by the estate, whether a sale, a distribution of assets, or otherwise, of the stock acquired by its exercise of the option under this paragraph is a disposition of the stock for purposes of section 423(c). Therefore, if section 423(c) is applicable, the estate must include an amount as compensation in its gross income. Similarly, if section 423(c) is applicable in case of an exercise of the option under this paragraph by a person who acquired the option by bequest or inheritance or by reason of the death of the individual to whom the option was granted, there must be included in the gross income of such person an amount as compensation, either when such person disposes of the stock, or when he dies owning the stock.

(3)(i) If, under section 423(c), an amount is required to be included in the gross income of the estate or of such person, the estate or such person shall be allowed a deduction as a result of the inclusion of the value of the option in the estate of the individual to whom the option was granted. Such deduction shall be computed under section 691(c) by treating the option as an item of gross income in respect of a decedent under section 691 and by treating the amount required to be included in gross income under section 423(c), as an amount included in gross income under section 691 in respect of such item of gross income. No such deduction shall be allowable with respect to any amount other than an amount includible under section 423(c). For the rules relating to the computation of a deduction under section 691(c), see § 1.691(c)-1.

(ii) The application of subdivision (i) may be illustrated by the following example:

Example. On June 1, 2004, E was granted an option under an employee stock purchase plan to purchase for $85 one share of the stock of his employer. On such day, the fair market value of such stock was $100 per share. E died on February 1, 2006, without having exercised such option. The option was, however, exercisable by his estate, and for purposes of the estate tax was valued at $30. On March 1, 2006, the estate exercised the option, and on March 15, 2006, sold for $150 the share of stock so acquired. For its taxable year including March 15, 2006, the estate is required by sections 421(c)(1)(B) and 423(c) to include in its gross income as compensation the amount of $15. During such taxable year, no amounts of income were properly paid, credited, or distributable to the beneficiaries of the estate. However, under section 421(c)(2), the estate is entitled to a deduction determined in the following manner. E's estate includes no other items of income in respect of a decedent referred to in section 691(a), and no deductions referred to in section 691(b), so that the value for estate tax purposes of the option, $30, is also the net value of all items of income in respect of the decedent. The estate tax attributable to the inclusion of the option in the estate of E is $10. Since $15, the amount includible in gross income by reason of sections 421(c)(1)(B) and 423(c), is less than the value for estate tax purposes of the option, only 15/30 of the estate tax attributable to the inclusion of the option in the estate is deductible; that is, 15/30 of $10, or $5. No deduction under section 421(c)(2) is allowable with respect to any capital gain.

(4)(i)(a) In the case of the death of an optionee, the basis of any share of stock acquired by the exercise of an option under this paragraph (c), determined under section 1011, shall be increased by an amount equal to the portion of the basis of the option attributable to such share. For example, if a statutory option to acquire 10 shares of stock has a basis of $100, the basis of one share acquired by a partial exercise of the option, determined under section 1011, would be increased by 1/10th of $100, or $10. The option acquires a basis, determined under section 1014(a) or under section 1022, if applicable, only if the transfer of the share pursuant to the exercise of such option qualifies for the special tax treatment provided by section 421(a). To the extent the option is so exercised, in whole or in part, it will acquire a basis equal to its fair market value (or the basis as determined under section 1022, if applicable) at the date of the employee's death or, if an election is made under section 2032, its value at its applicable valuation date. In certain cases, the basis of the share is subject to the adjustments provided by paragraphs (c)(4)(i)(b) and (c) of this section, but such adjustments are only applicable in the case of an option that is subject to section 423(c).

(b) If the amount which would have been includible in gross income under section 423(c) had the employee exercised the option on the date of his death and held the share at the time of his death exceeds the amount which is includible in gross income under such section, the basis of the share, determined under (a) of this subdivision, shall be reduced by such excess. For example, if $15 would have been includible in the gross income of the employee had he exercised the option and held such share at the time of his death, and only $10 is includible under section 423(c), the basis of the share, determined under (a) of this subdivision, would be reduced by $5. For purposes of determining the amount which would have been includible in gross income under section 423(c), if the employee had exercised the option and held such share at the time of his death, the amount which would have been paid for the share shall be computed as if the option had been exercised on the date the employee died.

(c) If the amount includible in gross income under section 423(c), exceeds the portion of the basis of the option attributable to the share, the basis of the share, determined under (a) of this subdivision, shall be increased by such excess. Thus, if $15 is includible in gross income under such section, and the basis of the option with respect to the share is $10, the basis of the share, determined under (a) of this subdivision, will be increased by $5.

(ii) If a statutory option is not exercised by the estate of the individual to whom the option was granted, or by the person who acquired such option by bequest or inheritance or by reason of the death of such individual, the option shall be considered to be property that constitutes a right to receive an item of income in respect of a decedent to which the rules of sections 691 and 1014(c) (or section 1022(f), if applicable) apply.

(iii) The application of this subparagraph may be illustrated by the following examples:

Example (1). On June 1, 2005, the X Corporation granted to E, an employee, an option under its employee stock purchase plan to purchase a share of X Corporation stock for $85. The fair market value of X Corporation stock on such date was $100 per share. On June 1, 2006, E died. The fair market value of X Corporation stock on such date exceeded $100 per share and the fair market value of the option on the applicable valuation date was $35. On August 1, 2006, the estate of E exercised the option and sold the share of X Corporation stock at a time when the fair market value of the share was $120. The basis of the share is $120 (the $85 paid for the stock plus the $35 basis of the option). When the share is sold for $120, the estate is required to include $15 in its gross income as compensation. Since $15 would have been includible in E's gross income if he had exercised the option and held such share at the time of his death, paragraph (c)(4)(1)(b) of this section does not apply. Moreover, since the $15 includible in the gross income of the estate does not exceed the basis of the option ($35), paragraph (c)(4)(i)(c) of this section does not apply. Since the basis of the stock and the sale price are the same, no gain or loss is realized by the estate on the disposition of the share.

Example (2). Assume the same facts as in Example 1, except that the fair market value of the share of stock at the time of its sale was $90. The basis of the share, determined under paragraph (c)(4)(i)(a) of this section, is $120 (the $85 paid for the stock plus the $35 basis of the option). When the share is sold for $90, the estate is required to include $5 in its gross income as compensation. If the employee had exercised the option and held the share at the time of his death, $15 would have been includible in gross income as compensation for the taxable year ending with his death. Since such amount exceeds by $10 the amount which the estate is required to include in its gross income, paragraph (c)(4)(i)(b) of this section applies, and the basis of the share ($120), determined under paragraph (c)(4)(i)(a) of this section is reduced by $10. Accordingly, the basis is $110, and a capital loss of $20 is realized on the disposition of the share.

Example (3). Assume the same facts as in Example 1, except that the fair market value of the option on the applicable valuation date was $5, and that the fair market value of X Corporation stock on the date the employee died did not exceed $100. The basis of the share, determined under paragraph (c)(4)(i)(a) of this section, is $90 (the $85 paid for the stock plus the $5 basis of the option). When the share is sold for $120, the estate is required to include $15 in its gross income as compensation. Since such amount exceeds by $10 the basis of the option, paragraph (c)(4)(i)(c) of this section applies, and the

basis of the share ($90), determined under paragraph (c)(4)(i)(a) of this section, is increased by $10. Accordingly, the basis is $100 and a capital gain of $20 is realized on the disposition of the share.

Example (4). Assume the same facts as in Example 1, except that on June 1, 2006, the date the employee died, the fair market value of X Corporation stock was $98, and that on June 1, 2007, the alternate valuation date, the fair market value of the stock had declined substantially, and the fair market value of the option was $5. On August 1, 2007, the estate of E exercised the option and sold the share when its fair market value was $92. The basis of the share, determined under paragraph (c)(4)(i)(a) of this section, is $90 (the $85 paid for the stock plus the $5 basis of the option). When the share is sold for $92, the estate is required to include $7 in its gross income as compensation. Since $13 would have been includible in E's gross income if he had exercised the option and held such share at the time of his death, paragraph (c)(4)(i)(b) of this section applies, and the basis of the share ($90), determined under paragraph (c)(4)(i)(a) of this section, is reduced by $6 to $84. Furthermore, since the $7 that the estate is required to include in its gross income when the share is sold for $92 exceeds by $2 the basis of the option, paragraph (c)(4)(i)(c) of this section applies, and the basis of the share ($84), determined under paragraph (c)(4)(i)(a) of this section and paragraph (c)(4)(i)(b) of this section, is increased by $2. Accordingly, the basis is $86 and a capital gain of $6 is realized on the disposition of the share.

(d) *Option exercised by the individual to whom the option was granted if the individual dies before expiration of the applicable holding periods.*—If a statutory option is exercised by the individual to whom the option was granted and such individual dies before the expiration of the applicable holding periods as determined under §1.422-1(a) or 1.423-1(a), paragraph (a) of this section does not become inapplicable if the executor or administrator of the estate of such individual, or any person who acquired such stock by bequest or inheritance or by reason of the death of such individual, disposes of such stock before the expiration of such applicable holding periods. This rule does not affect the applicability of section 423(c), relating to the individual's recognition of compensation income, or section 1222, relating to what constitutes a short-term and long-term capital gain or loss.

(e) *Incorporation by reference.*—Any requirement that an option expressly contain or state a prescribed limitation or term will be considered met if such limitation or term is set forth in a statutory option plan and is incorporated by reference by the option. Thus, if a statutory option plan expressly provides that no option granted thereunder shall be exercisable after five years from the date of grant, and if an option granted thereunder expressly provides that the option is granted subject to the terms and limitations of such plan, the option will be regarded as being, by its terms, not exercisable after the expiration of five years from the date such option is granted.

(f) *Effective/applicability date.*—(1) *In general.*—These regulations are effective on August 3, 2004.

(2) *Reliance and transition period.*—For statutory options granted on or before June 9, 2003, taxpayers may rely on the 1984 proposed regulations LR-279-81 (49 FR 4504), the 2003 proposed regulations REG-122917-02 (68 FR 34344), or this section until the earlier of January 1, 2006, or the first regularly scheduled stockholders meeting of the granting corporation occurring 6 months after August 3, 2004. For statutory options granted after June 9, 2003, and before the earlier of January 1, 2006, or the first regularly scheduled stockholders meeting of the granting corporation occurring at least 6 months after August 3, 2004, taxpayers may rely on either REG-122917-02 or this section. Taxpayers may not rely on LR-279-81 or REG-122917-02 after December 31, 2005. Reliance on LR-279-81, REG-122917-02, or this section must be in its entirety, and all statutory options granted during the reliance period must be treated consistently.

(3) *Application of section 1022.*—The provisions of paragraph (c) of this section relating to section 1022 are effective on and after January 19, 2017. [Reg. §1.421-2.]

☐ [T.D. 6887, 6-23-66. *Redesignated and amended by T.D. 9144,* 8-2-2004 *(corrected* 10-15-2004 *and* 12-6-2004) *and T.D. 9811,* 1-18-2017.]

[Reg. §1.422-1]

§1.422-1. Incentive stock options; general rules.—(a) *Applicability of section 421(a).*—(1)(i) Section 1.421-2(a) applies to the transfer of a share of stock to an individual pursuant to the individual's exercise of an incentive stock option if the following conditions are satisfied—

(A) The individual makes no disposition of such share before the later of the expiration of the 2-year period from the date of grant of the option pursuant to which such share was transferred, or the expiration of the 1-year period from the date of transfer of such share to the individual; and

(B) At all times during the period beginning on the date of grant of the option and ending on the day 3 months before the date of exercise, the individual was an employee of either the corporation granting the option, a related corporation of such corporation, or a corporation (or a related corporation of such corporation) substituting or assuming a stock option in a transaction to which § 1.424-1(a) applies.

(ii) For rules relating to the disposition of shares of stock acquired pursuant to the exercise of a statutory option, see § 1.424-1(c). For rules relating to the requisite employment relationship, see § 1.421-1(h).

(2)(i) The holding period requirement of section 422(a)(1), described in paragraph (a)(1)(i)(A) of this section, does not apply to the transfer of shares by an insolvent individual described in this paragraph (a)(2). If an insolvent individual holds a share of stock acquired pursuant to the individual's exercise of an incentive stock option and if such share is transferred to a trustee, receiver, or other similar fiduciary in any proceeding under the Bankruptcy Act or any other similar insolvency proceeding, neither such transfer, nor any other transfer of such share for the benefit of the individual's creditors in such proceeding is a disposition of such share for purposes of this paragraph (a). For purposes of this paragraph (a)(2), an individual is insolvent only if the individual's liabilities exceed the individual's assets or the individual is unable to satisfy the individual's liabilities as they become due. See section 422(c)(3).

(ii) A transfer by the trustee or other fiduciary that is not treated as a disposition for purposes of this paragraph (a) may be a sale or exchange for purposes of recognizing capital gain or loss with respect to the share transferred. For example, if the trustee transfers the share to a creditor in an insolvency proceeding, capital gain or loss must be recognized by the insolvent individual to the extent of the difference between the amount realized from such transfer and the adjusted basis of such share.

(iii) If any transfer by the trustee or other fiduciary (other than a transfer back to the insolvent individual) is not for the exclusive benefit of the creditors in an insolvency proceeding, then whether such transfer is a disposition of the share by the individual for purposes of this paragraph (a) is determined under § 1.424-1(c). Similarly, if the trustee or other fiduciary transfers the share back to the insolvent individual, any subsequent transfer of the share by such individual which is not made in respect of the insolvency proceeding may be a disposition of the share for purposes of this paragraph (a).

(3) If the employee exercising an option ceased employment because of permanent and total disability, within the meaning of section 22(e)(3), 1 year is used instead of 3 months in the employment period requirement of paragraph (a)(1)(i)(B) of this section.

(b) *Failure to satisfy holding period requirements.*—(1) *General rule.*—For general rules concerning a disqualifying disposition of a share of stock acquired pursuant to the exercise of an incentive stock option, see § 1.421-2(b)(1).

(2)(i) *Special rule.*—If an individual makes a disqualifying disposition of a share of stock acquired by the exercise of an incentive stock option, and if such disposition is a sale or exchange with respect to which a loss (if sustained) would be recognized to the individual, then, under this paragraph (b)(2)(i), the amount includible (determined without reduction for brokerage fees or other costs paid in connection with the disposition) in the gross income of such individual, and deductible from the income of the employer corporation (or a related corporation of such corporation, or of a corporation substituting or assuming the option in a transaction to which § 1.424-1(a) applies) as compensation attributable to the exercise of such option, shall not exceed the excess (if any) of the amount realized on such sale or exchange over the adjusted basis of such share. Subject to the special rule provided by this paragraph (b)(2)(i), the amount of compensation attributable to the exercise of the option is determined under section 83(a); see § 1.421-2(b)(1)(i).

(ii) *Limitation to special rule.*—The special rule described in paragraph (b)(2)(i) of this section does not apply if the disposition is a sale or exchange with respect to which a loss (if sustained) would not be recognized by the individual. Thus, for example, if a disqualifying disposition is a sale described in section 1091 (relating to loss from wash sales of stock or securities), a gift (or any other transaction which is not at arm's length), or a sale described in section 267(a)(1) (relating to sales between related persons), the special rule described in paragraph (b)(2)(i) of this section does not apply because a loss sustained in any such transaction would not be recognized.

(3) *Examples.*—The following examples illustrate the principles of this paragraph (b):

Example 1. Disqualifying disposition of vested stock. On June 1, 2006, X Corporation grants an incentive stock option to A, an employee of X Corporation, entitling A to purchase one share of X Corporation stock. On August 1, 2006, A exercises the option, and the share of X Corporation stock is transferred to A on that date. The option price is $100 (the fair market value of a share of X Corporation stock on June

1, 2006), and the fair market value of a share of X Corporation stock on August 1, 2006 (the date of transfer) is $200. The share transferred to A is transferable and not subject to a substantial risk of forfeiture. A makes a disqualifying disposition by selling the share on June 1, 2007, for $250. The amount of compensation attributable to A's exercise is $100 (the difference between the fair market value of the share at the date of transfer, $200, and the amount paid for the share, $100). Because the amount realized ($250) is greater than the value of the share at transfer ($200), paragraph (b)(2)(i) of this section does not apply and thus does not affect the amount includible as compensation in A's gross income and deductible by X. A must include in gross income for the taxable year in which the sale occurred $100 as compensation and $50 as capital gain ($250, the amount realized from the sale, less A's basis of $200 (the $100 paid for the share plus the $100 increase in basis resulting from the inclusion of that amount in A's gross income as compensation attributable to the exercise of the option)). If the requirements of section 83(h) and § 1.83-6(a) are satisfied and the deduction is otherwise allowable under section 162, for its taxable year in which the disqualifying disposition occurs, X Corporation is allowed a deduction of $100 for compensation attributable to A's exercise of the incentive stock option.

Example 2. Disqualifying disposition of unvested stock. Assume the same facts as in *Example 1*, except that the share of X Corporation stock received by A is subject to a substantial risk of forfeiture and not transferable for a period of six months after such exercise. Assume further that the fair market value of X Corporation stock is $225 on February 1, 2007, the date on which the six-month restriction lapses. Because section 83 does not apply for ordinary income tax purposes on the date of exercise, A cannot make an effective section 83(b) election at that time (although such an election is permissible for alternative minimum tax purposes). Additionally, at the time of the disposition, section 422 and § 1.422-1(a) no longer apply, and thus, section 83(a) is used to measure the consequences of the disposition, and the holding period for capital gain purposes begins on the vesting date, six months after exercise. The amount of compensation attributable to A's exercise of the option and disqualifying disposition of the share is $125 (the difference between the fair market value of the share on the date that the restriction lapsed, $225, and the amount paid for the share, $100). Because the amount realized ($225) is greater than the value of the share at transfer ($200), paragraph (b)(2)(i) of this section does not apply and thus does not affect the amount includible as compensation in A's gross income and deductible by X. A must include $125 of compensation income and $25 of capital gain in gross income for the taxable year in which the disposition occurs ($250, the amount realized from the sale, less A's basis of $225 (the $100 paid for the share plus the $125 increase in basis resulting from the inclusion of that amount of compensation in A's gross income)). If the requirements of section 83(h) and § 1.83-6(a) are satisfied and the deduction is otherwise allowable under section 162, for its taxable year in which the disqualifying disposition occurs, X Corporation is allowed a deduction of $125 for the compensation attributable to A's exercise of the option.

Example 3. (i) *Disqualifying disposition and application of special rule.* Assume the same facts as in *Example 1*, except that A sells the share for $150 to M.

(ii) If the sale to M is a disposition that meets the requirements of paragraph (b)(2)(i) of this section, instead of $100 which otherwise would have been includible as compensation under § 1.83-7, under paragraph (b)(2)(i) of this section, A must include only $50 (the excess of the amount realized on such sale, $150, over the adjusted basis of the share, $100) in gross income as compensation attributable to the exercise of the incentive stock option. Because A's basis for the share is $150 (the $100 which A paid for the share, plus the $50 increase in basis resulting from the inclusion of that amount in A's gross income as compensation attributable to the exercise of the option), A realizes no capital gain or loss as a result of the sale. If the requirements of section 83(h) and § 1.83-6(a) are satisfied and the deduction is otherwise allowable under section 162, for its taxable year in which the disqualifying disposition occurs, X Corporation is allowed a deduction of $50 for the compensation attributable to A's exercise of the option and disqualifying disposition of the share.

(iii) Assume the same facts as in paragraph (i) of this *Example 3*, except that 10 days after the sale to M, A purchases substantially identical stock. Because under section 1091(a) a loss (if it were sustained on the sale) would not be recognized on the sale, under paragraph (b)(2)(ii) of this section, the special rule described in paragraph (b)(2)(i) of this section does not apply. A must include $100 (the difference between the fair market value of the share on the date of transfer, $200, and the amount paid for the share, $100) in gross income as compensation attributable to the exercise of the option for the taxable year in which the disqualifying disposition occurred. A recognizes no capital gain or loss on the transaction. If the requirements of section 83(h) and § 1.83-6(a) are satisfied and the deduction is otherwise allowable under section 162, for its taxable year in which the disqualifying disposition occurs X Corporation is allowed a $100 deduction for compensation attributable to A's exercise of the option and disqualifying disposition of the share.

(iv) Assume the same facts as in paragraph (ii) of this *Example 3*, except that A sells the share for $50. Under paragraph (b)(2)(i) of this section, A is not required to include any amount in gross income as compensation attributable to the exercise of the option. A is allowed a capital loss of $50 (the difference between the amount realized on the sale, $50, and the adjusted basis of the share, $100). X Corporation is not allowed any deduction attributable to A's exercise of the option and disqualifying disposition of the share.

(c) *Failure to satisfy employment requirement.*—Section 1.421-2(a) does not apply to the transfer of a share of stock pursuant to the exercise of an incentive stock option if the employment requirement, as determined under paragraph (a)(1)(i)(B) of this section, is not met at the time of the exercise of such option. Consequently, the effects of such a transfer are determined under the rules of §1.83-7. For rules relating to the employment relationship, see §1.421-1(h). [Reg. §1.422-1.]

☐ [*T.D. 9144, 8-2-2004 (corrected 10-15-2004 and 12-6-2004).*]

[Reg. §1.422-2]

§1.422-2. Incentive stock options defined.—(a) *Incentive stock option defined.*—(1) *In general.*—The term *incentive stock option* means an option that meets the requirements of paragraph (a)(2) of this section on the date of grant. An incentive stock option is also subject to the $100,000 limitation described in §1.422-4. An incentive stock option may contain a number of permissible provisions that do not affect the status of the option as an incentive stock option. See §1.422-5 for rules relating to permissible provisions of an incentive stock option.

(2) *Option requirements.*—To qualify as an incentive stock option under this section, an option must be granted to an individual in connection with the individual's employment by the corporation granting such option (or by a related corporation as defined in §1.421-1(i)(2)), and granted only for stock of any of such corporations. In addition, the option must meet all of the following requirements—

(i) It must be granted pursuant to a plan that meets the requirements described in paragraph (b) of this section;

(ii) It must be granted within 10 years from the date of the adoption of the plan or the date such plan is approved by the stockholders, whichever is earlier (see paragraph (c) of this section);

(iii) It must not be exercisable after the expiration of 10 years from the date of grant (see paragraph (d) of this section);

(iv) It must provide that the option price per share is not less than the fair market value of the share on the date of grant (see paragraph (e) of this section);

(v) By its terms, it must not be transferrable by the individual to whom the option is granted other than by will or the laws of descent and distribution, and must be exercisable, during such individual's lifetime, only by such individual (see §§1.421-1(b)(2) and 1.421-2(c); and

(vi) Except as provided in paragraph (f) of this section, it must be granted to an individual who, at the time the option is granted, does not own stock possessing more than 10 percent of the total combined voting power of all classes of stock of the corporation employing such individual or of any related corporation of such corporation.

(3) *Amendment of option terms.*—Except as otherwise provided in §1.424-1, the amendment of the terms of an incentive stock option may cause it to cease to be an option described in this section. If the terms of an option that has lost its status as an incentive stock option are subsequently changed with the intent to re-qualify the option as an incentive stock option, such change results in the grant of a new option on the date of the change. See §1.424-1(e).

(4) *Terms provide option not an incentive stock option.*—If the terms of an option, when granted, provide that it will not be treated as an incentive stock option, such option is not treated as an incentive stock option.

(b) *Option plan.*—(1) *In general.*—An incentive stock option must be granted pursuant to a plan that meets the requirements of this paragraph (b). The authority to grant other stock options or other stock-based awards pursuant to the plan, where the exercise of such other options or awards does not affect the exercise of incentive stock options granted pursuant to the plan, does not disqualify such incentive stock options. The plan must be in writing or electronic form, provided that such writing or electronic form is adequate to establish the terms of the plan. See §1.422-5 for rules relating to permissible provisions of an incentive stock option.

(2) *Stockholder approval.*—(i) The plan required by this paragraph (b) must be approved by the stockholders of the corporation

granting the incentive stock option within 12 months before or after the date such plan is adopted. Ordinarily, a plan is adopted when it is approved by the granting corporation's board of directors, and the date of the board's action is the reference point for determining whether stockholder approval occurs within the applicable 24-month period. However, if the board's action is subject to a condition (such as stockholder approval) or the happening of a particular event, the plan is adopted on the date the condition is met or the event occurs, unless the board's resolution fixes the date of approval as the date of the board's action.

(ii) For purposes of paragraph (b)(2)(i) of this section, the stockholder approval must comply with the rules described in §1.422-3.

(iii) The provisions relating to the maximum aggregate number of shares to be issued under the plan (described in paragraph (b)(3) of this section) and the employees (or class or classes of employees) eligible to receive options under the plan (described in paragraph (b)(4) of this section) are the only provisions of a stock option plan that, if changed, must be re-approved by stockholders for purposes of section 422(b)(1). Any increase in the maximum aggregate number of shares that may be issued under the plan (other than an increase merely reflecting a change in the number of outstanding shares, such as a stock dividend or stock split), or change in the designation of the employees (or class or classes of employees) eligible to receive options under the plan is considered the adoption of a new plan requiring stockholder approval within the prescribed 24-month period. In addition, a change in the granting corporation or the stock available for purchase or award under the plan is considered the adoption of a new plan requiring new stockholder approval within the prescribed 24-month period. Any other changes in the terms of an incentive stock option plan are not considered the adoption of a new plan and, thus, do not require stockholder approval.

(3) *Maximum aggregate number of shares.*—(i) The plan required by this paragraph (b) must designate the maximum aggregate number of shares that may be issued under the plan through incentive stock options. If nonstatutory options or other stock-based awards may be granted, the plan may separately designate terms for each type of option or other stock-based awards and designate the maximum number of shares that may be issued under such option or other stock-based awards. Unless otherwise specified, all terms of the plan apply to all options and other stock-based awards that may be granted under the plan.

(ii) A plan that merely provides that the number of shares that may be issued as incentive stock options under such plan may not exceed a stated percentage of the shares outstanding at the time of each offering or grant under such plan does not satisfy the requirement that the plan state the maximum aggregate number of shares that may be issued under the plan. However, the maximum aggregate number of shares that may be issued under the plan may be stated in terms of a percentage of the authorized, issued, or outstanding shares at the date of the adoption of the plan. The plan may specify that the maximum aggregate number of shares available for grants under the plan may increase annually by a specified percentage of the authorized, issued, or outstanding shares at the date of the adoption of the plan. A plan which provides that the maximum aggregate number of shares that may be issued as incentive stock options under the plan may change based on any other specified circumstances satisfies the requirements of this paragraph (b)(3) only if the stockholders approve an immediately determinable maximum aggregate number of shares that may be issued under the plan in any event.

(iii) It is permissible for the plan to provide that, shares purchasable under the plan may be supplied to the plan through acquisitions of stock on the open market; shares purchased under the plan and forfeited back to the plan; shares surrendered in payment of the exercise price of an option; shares withheld for payment of applicable employment taxes and/or withholding obligations resulting from the exercise of an option.

(iv) If there is more than one plan under which incentive stock options may be granted and stockholders of the granting corporation merely approve a maximum aggregate number of shares that are available for issuance under such plans, the stockholder approval requirements described in paragraph (b)(2) of this section are not satisfied. A separate maximum aggregate number of shares available for issuance pursuant to incentive stock options must be approved for each plan.

(4) *Designation of employees.*—The plan described in this paragraph (b), as adopted and approved, must indicate the employees (or class or classes of employees) eligible to receive the options or other stock-based awards to be granted under the plan. This requirement is satisfied by a general designation of the employees (or the class or classes of employees) eligible to receive options or other stock-based awards under the plan. Designations such as "key employees of the

grantor corporation"; "all salaried employees of the grantor corporation and its subsidiaries, including subsidiaries which become such after adoption of the plan;" or "all employees of the corporation" meet this requirement. This requirement is considered satisfied even though the board of directors, another group, or an individual is given the authority to select the particular employees who are to receive options or other stock-based awards from a described class and to determine the number of shares to be optioned or granted to each such employee. If individuals other than employees may be granted options or other stock-based awards under the plan, the plan must separately designate the employees or classes of employees eligible to receive incentive stock options.

(5) *Conflicting option terms.*—An option on stock available for purchase or grant under the plan is treated as having been granted pursuant to a plan even if the terms of the option conflict with the terms of the plan, unless such option is granted to an employee who is ineligible to receive options under the plan, options have been granted on stock in excess of the aggregate number of shares which may be issued under the plan, or the option provides otherwise.

(6) The following examples illustrate the principles of this paragraph (b):

Example 1. Stockholder approval. (i) S Corporation is a subsidiary of P Corporation, a publicly traded corporation. On January 1, 2006, S adopts a plan under which incentive stock options for S stock are granted to S employees.

(ii) To meet the requirements of paragraph (b)(2) of this section, the plan must be approved by the stockholders of S (in this case, P) within 12 months before or after January 1, 2006.

(iii) Assume the same facts as in paragraph (i) of this *Example 1,* except that the plan was adopted on January 1, 2010. Assume further that the plan was approved by the stockholders of S (in this case, P) on March 1, 2010. On January 1, 2012, S changes the plan to provide that incentive stock options for P stock will be granted to S employees under the plan. Because there is a change in the stock available for grant under the plan, the change is considered the adoption of a new plan that must be approved by the stockholder of S (in this case, P) within 12 months before or after January 1, 2012.

Example 2. Stockholder approval. (i) Assume the same facts as in paragraph (i) of *Example 1,* except that on March 15, 2007, P completely disposes of its interest in S. Thereafter, S continues to grant options for S stock to S employees under the plan.

(ii) The new S options are granted under a plan that meets the stockholder approval requirements of paragraph (b)(2) of this section without regard to whether S seeks approval of the plan from the stockholders of S after P disposes of its interest in S.

(iii) Assume the same facts as in paragraph (i) of this *Example 2,* except that under the plan as adopted on January 1, 2006, only options for P stock are granted to S employees. Assume further that after P disposes of its interest in S, S changes the plan to provide for the grant of options for S stock to S employees. Because there is a change in the stock available for purchase or grant under the plan, under paragraph (b)(2)(ii) of this section, the stockholders of S must approve the plan within 12 months before or after the change to the plan to meet the stockholder approval requirements of paragraph (b) of this section.

Example 3. Stockholder approval. (i) Corporation X maintains a plan under which incentive stock options may be granted to all eligible employees. Corporation Y does not maintain an incentive stock option plan. On May 15, 2006, Corporation X and Corporation Y consolidate under state law to form one corporation. The new corporation will be named Corporation Y. The consolidation agreement describes the Corporation X plan, including the maximum aggregate number of shares available for issuance pursuant to incentive stock options after the consolidation and the employees eligible to receive options under the plan. Additionally, the consolidation agreement states that the plan will be continued by Corporation Y after the consolidation and incentive stock options will be issued by Corporation Y. The consolidation agreement is unanimously approved by the shareholders of Corporations X and Y on May 1, 2006. Corporation Y assumes the plan formerly maintained by Corporation X and continues to grant options under the plan to all eligible employees.

(ii) Because there is a change in the granting corporation (from Corporation X to Corporation Y), under paragraph (b)(2)(iii) of this section, Corporation Y is considered to have adopted a new plan. Because the plan is fully described in the consolidation agreement, including the maximum aggregate number of shares available for issuance pursuant to incentive stock options and employees eligible to receive options under the plan, the approval of the consolidation *agreement by the shareholders constitutes* approval of the plan. Thus, the shareholder approval of the consolidation agreement satisfies the shareholder approval requirements of paragraph (b)(2) of this section, and the plan is considered to be adopted by Corporation Y and approved by its shareholders on May 1, 2006.

Example 4. Maximum aggregate number of shares. X Corporation maintains a plan under which statutory options and nonstatutory options may be granted. The plan designates the number of shares that may be used for incentive stock options. Because the maximum aggregate number of shares that will be used for incentive stock options is designated in the plan, the requirements of paragraph (b)(3) of this section are satisfied.

Example 5. Maximum aggregate number of shares. Y Corporation adopts an incentive stock option plan on November 1, 2006. On that date, there are two million outstanding shares of Y Corporation stock. The plan provides that the maximum aggregate number of shares that may be issued under the plan may not exceed 15% of the outstanding number of shares of Y Corporation on November 1, 2006. Because the maximum aggregate number of shares that may be issued under the plan is designated in the plan, the requirements of paragraph (b)(3) of this section are met.

Example 6. Maximum aggregate number of shares. (i) B Corporation adopts an incentive stock option plan on March 15, 2005. The plan provides that the maximum aggregate number of shares available for issuance under the plan is 50,000, increased on each anniversary date of the adoption of the plan by 5 percent of the then-outstanding shares.

(ii) Because the maximum aggregate number of shares is not designated under the plan, the requirements of paragraph (b)(3) of this section are not met.

(iii) Assume the same facts as in paragraph (i) of this *Example 6,* except that the plan provides that the maximum aggregate number of shares available under the plan is the lesser of (a) 50,000 shares, increased each anniversary date of the adoption of the plan by 5 percent of the then-outstanding shares, or (b) 200,000 shares. Because the maximum aggregate number of shares that may be issued under the plan is designated as the lesser of one of two numbers, one of which provides an immediately determinable maximum aggregate number of shares that may be issued under the plan in any event, the requirements of paragraph (b)(3) of this section are met.

(c) *Duration of option grants under the plan.*—An incentive stock option must be granted within 10 years from the date that the plan under which it is granted is adopted or the date such plan is approved by the stockholders, whichever is earlier. To grant incentive stock options after the expiration of the 10-year period, a new plan must be adopted and approved.

(d) *Period for exercising options.*—An incentive stock option, by its terms, must not be exercisable after the expiration of 10 years from the date such option is granted, or 5 years from the date such option is granted to an employee described in paragraph (f) of this section. An option that does not contain such a provision when granted is not an incentive stock option.

(e) *Option price.*—(1) Except as provided by paragraph (e)(2) of this section, the option price of an incentive stock option must not be less than the fair market value of the stock subject to the option at the time the option is granted. The option price may be determined in any reasonable manner, including the valuation methods permitted under § 20.2031-2 of this chapter, so long as the minimum price possible under the terms of the option is not less than the fair market value of the stock on the date of grant. For general rules relating to the option price, see § 1.421-1(e). For rules relating to the determination of when an option is granted, see § 1.421-1(c).

(2)(i) If a share of stock is transferred to an individual pursuant to the exercise of an option which fails to qualify as an incentive stock option merely because there was a failure of an attempt, made in good faith, to meet the option price requirements of paragraph (e)(1) of this section, the requirements of such paragraph are considered to have been met. Whether there was a good-faith attempt to set the option price at not less than the fair market value of the stock subject to the option at the time the option was granted depends on the relevant facts and circumstances.

(ii) For publicly held stock that is actively traded on an established market at the time the option is granted, determining the fair market value of such stock by the appropriate method described in § 20.2031-2 of this chapter establishes that a good-faith attempt to meet the option price requirements of this paragraph (e) was made.

(iii) For non-publicly traded stock, if it is demonstrated, for example, that the fair market value of the stock at the date of grant was based upon an average of the fair market values as of such date set forth in the opinions of completely independent and well-qualified experts, such a demonstration generally establishes that there was a good-faith attempt to meet the option price requirements of this paragraph (e). The optionee's status as a majority or minority stockholder may be taken into consideration.

(iv) Regardless of whether the stock offered under an option is publicly traded, a good-faith attempt to meet the option price requirements of this paragraph (e) is not demonstrated unless the fair market value of the stock on the date of grant is determined with regard to *nonlapse restrictions* (as defined in §1.83-3(h)) and without regard to *lapse restrictions* (as defined in §1.83-3(i)).

(v) Amounts treated as interest and amounts paid as interest under a deferred payment arrangement are not includible as part of the option price. See §1.421-1(e)(1). An attempt to set the option price at not less than fair market value is not regarded as made in good faith where an adjustment of the option price to reflect amounts treated as interest results in the option price being lower than the fair market value on which the option price was based.

(3) Notwithstanding that the option price requirements of paragraphs (e)(1) and (2) of this section are satisfied by an option granted to an employee whose stock ownership exceeds the limitation provided by paragraph (f) of this section, such option is not an incentive stock option when granted unless it also complies with paragraph (f) of this section. If the option, when granted, does not comply with the requirements described in paragraph (f) of this section, such option can never become an incentive stock option, even if the employee's stock ownership does not exceed the limitation of paragraph (f) of this section when such option is exercised.

(f) *Options granted to certain stockholders.*—(1) If, immediately before an option is granted, an individual owns (or is treated as owning) stock possessing more than 10 percent of the total combined voting power of all classes of stock of the corporation employing the optionee or of any related corporation of such corporation, then an option granted to such individual cannot qualify as an incentive stock option unless the option price is at least 110 percent of the stock's fair market value on the date of grant and such option by its terms is not exercisable after the expiration of 5 years from the date of grant. For purposes of determining the minimum option price for purposes of this paragraph (f), the rules described in paragraph (e)(2) of this section, relating to the good-faith determination of the option price, do not apply.

(2) For purposes of determining the stock ownership of the optionee, the stock attribution rules of §1.424-1(d) apply. Stock that the optionee may purchase under outstanding options is not treated as stock owned by the individual. The determination of the percentage of the total combined voting power of all classes of stock of the employer corporation (or of its related corporations) that is owned by the optionee is made with respect to each such corporation in the related group by comparing the voting power of the shares owned (or treated as owned) by the optionee to the aggregate voting power of all shares of each such corporation actually issued and outstanding immediately before the grant of the option to the optionee. The aggregate voting power of all shares actually issued and outstanding immediately before the grant of the option does not include the voting power of treasury shares or shares authorized for issue under outstanding options held by the individual or any other person.

(3) *Examples.*—The rules of this paragraph (f) are illustrated by the following examples:

Example 1. (i) E, an employee of M Corporation, owns 15,000 shares of M Corporation common stock, which is the only class of stock outstanding. M has 100,000 shares of its common stock outstanding. On January 1, 2005, when the fair market value of M stock is $100, E is granted an option with an option price of $100 and an exercise period of 10 years from the date of grant.

(ii) Because E owns stock possessing more than 10 percent of the total combined voting power of all classes of M Corporation stock, M cannot grant an incentive stock option to E unless the option is granted at an option price of at least 110 percent of the fair market value of the stock subject to the option and the option, by its terms, expires no later than 5 years from its date of grant. The option granted to E fails to meet the option-price and term requirements described in paragraph (f)(1) of this section and, thus, the option is not an incentive stock option.

(iii) Assume the same facts as in paragraph (i) of this *Example 1*, except that E's father and brother each owns 7,500 shares of M Corporation stock, and E owns no M stock in E's own name. Because under the attribution rules of §1.424-1(d), E is treated as owning stock held by E's parents and siblings, M cannot grant an incentive stock option to E unless the option price is at least 110 percent of the fair market value of the stock subject to the option, and the option, by its terms, expires no later than 5 years from the date of grant.

Example 2. Assume the same facts as in paragraph (i) of this *Example 1*. Assume further that M is a subsidiary of P Corporation. Regardless of whether E owns any P stock and the number of P shares outstanding, if P Corporation grants an option to E which purports to be an incentive stock option, but which fails to meet the 110-percent-option-price and 5-year-term requirements, the option is not an incentive stock option because E owns more than 10 percent of the total combined voting power of all classes of stock of a related corporation of P Corporation (i.e., M Corporation). An individual who owns (or is treated as owning) stock in excess of the ownership

specified in paragraph (f)(1) of this section, in any corporation in a group of corporations consisting of the employer corporation and its related corporations, cannot be granted an indentive stock option by any corporation in the group unless such option meets the 110-per-cent-option-price and 5-year-term requirements of paragraph (f)(1) of this section.

Example 3. (i) F is an employee of R Corporation. R has only one class of stock, of which 100,000 shares are issued and outstanding. F owns no stock in R Corporation or any related corporation of R Corporation. On January 1, 2005, R grants a 10-year incentive stock option to F to purchase 50,000 shares of R stock at $3 per share the fair market value of R stock on the date of grant of the option. On April 1, 2005, F exercises half of the January option and receives 25,000 shares of R stock that previously were not outstanding. On July 1, 2005, R grants a second 50,000 share option to F which purports to be an incentive stock option. The terms of the July option are identical to the terms of the January option, except that the option price is $3.25 per share, which is the fair market value of R stock on the date of grant of the July option.

(ii) Because F does not own more than 10% of the total combined voting power of all classes of stock of R Corporation or any related corporation on the date of the grant of the January option and the pricing requirements of paragraph (e) of this section are satisfied on the date of grant of such option, the unexercised portion of the January option remains an incentive stock option regardless of the changes in F's percentage of stock ownership in R after the date of grant. However, the July option is not an incentive stock option because, on the date that it is granted, F owns 20 percent (25,000 shares owned by F divided by 125,000 shares of R stock issued and outstanding) of the total combined voting power of all classes of R Corporation stock and, thus the pricing requirements of paragraph (f)(1) of this section are not met.

(iii) Assume the same facts as in paragraph (i) of this *Example 3* except that the partial exercise of the January incentive stock option on April 1, 2003, is for only 10,000 shares. Under these circumstances, the July option is an incentive stock option, because, on the date of grant of the July option, F does not own more than 10 percent of the total combined voting power (10,000 shares owned by F divided by 110,000 shares of R issued and outstanding) of all classes of R Corporation stock. [Reg. §1.422-2.]

☐ [*T.D.* 9144, 8-2-2004. *Amended by T.D* 9471, 11-16-2009.]

[Reg. §1.422-3]

§1.422-3. **Stockholder approval of incentive stock option plans.**—This section addresses the stockholder approval of incentive stock option plans required by section 422(b)(1) of the Internal Revenue Code. (Section 422 was added to the Code as section 422A by section 251 of the Economic Recovery Tax Act of 1981, and was redesignated as section 422 by section 11801 of the Omnibus Budget Reconciliation Act of 1990.) The approval of stockholders must comply with all applicable provisions of the corporate charter, bylaws, and applicable State law prescribing the method and degree of stockholder approval required for the issuance of corporate stock or options. If the applicable State law does not prescribe a method and degree of stockholder approval in such cases an incentive stock option plan must be approved:

(a) By a majority of the votes cast at a duly held stockholders' meeting at which a quorum representing a majority of all outstanding voting stock is, either in person or by proxy, present and voting on the plan; or

(b) By a method and in a degree that would be treated as adequate under applicable State law in the case of an action requiring stockholder approval (i.e., an action on which stockholders would be entitled to vote if the action were taken at a duly held stockholders' meeting). [Reg. §1.422-3.]

☐ [*T.D.* 8235, 12-1-88. *Redesignated and amended by T.D.* 8374, 11-29-91. *Redesignated and amended by T.D.* 9144, 8-2-2004.]

[Reg. §1.422-4]

§1.422-4. **$100,000 limitation for incentive stock options.**—(a) *$100,000 per year limitation.*—(1) *General rule.*—An option that otherwise qualifies as an incentive stock option nevertheless fails to be an incentive stock option to the extent that the $100,000 limitation described in paragraph (a)(2) of this section is exceeded.

(2) *$100,000 per year limitation.*—To the extent that the aggregate fair market value of stock with respect to which an incentive stock option (determined without regard to this section) is exercisable for the first time by any individual during any calendar year (under all plans of the employer corporation and related corporations) exceeds $100,000, such option is treated as a nonstatutory option. See §1.83-7 for rules applicable to nonstatutory options.

(b) *Application.*—To determine whether the limitation described in paragraph (a)(2) of this section has been exceeded, the following rules apply:

(1) An option that does not meet the requirements of § 1.422-2 when granted (including an option which, when granted, contains terms providing that it will not be treated as an incentive stock option) is disregarded. See § 1.422-2(a)(4).

(2) The fair market value of stock is determined as of the date of grant of the option for such stock.

(3) Except as otherwise provided in paragraph (b)(4) of this section, options are taken into account in the order in which they are granted.

(4) For purposes of this section, an option is considered to be first exercisable during a calendar year if the option will become exercisable at any time during the year assuming that any condition on the optionee's ability to exercise the option related to the performance of services is satisfied. If the optionee's ability to exercise the option in the year is subject to an acceleration provision, then the option is considered first exercisable in the calendar year in which the acceleration provision is triggered. After an acceleration provision is triggered, the options subject to such provision are then taken into account in accordance with paragraph (b)(3) of this section for purposes of applying the limitation described in paragraph (a)(2) of this section to all options first exercisable during a calendar year. However, because an acceleration provision is not taken into account prior to its triggering, an incentive stock option that becomes exercisable for the first time during a calendar year by operation of such a provision does not affect the application of the $100,000 limitation with respect to any option (or portion thereof) exercised prior to such acceleration. For purposes of this paragraph (b)(4), an acceleration provision includes, for example, a provision that accelerates the exercisability of an option on a change in ownership or control or a provision that conditions exercisability on the attainment of a performance goal. See paragraph (d), *Example 4* of this section.

(5)(i) An option (or portion thereof) is disregarded if, prior to the calendar year during which it would otherwise have become exercisable for the first time, the option (or portion thereof) is modified and thereafter ceases to be an incentive stock option described in § 1.422-2, is canceled, or is transferred in violation of § 1.421-1(b)(2).

(ii) If an option (or portion thereof) is modified, canceled, or transferred at any other time, such option (or portion thereof) is treated as outstanding according to its original terms until the end of the calendar year during which it would otherwise have become exercisable for the first time.

(6) A disqualifying disposition has no effect on the determination of whether an option exceeds the $100,000 limitation.

(c) *Bifurcation.*—(1) *Options.*—The application of the rules described in paragraph (b) of this section may result in an option being treated, in part, as an incentive stock option and, in part, as a nonstatutory option. See § 1.83-7 for the treatment of nonstatutory options.

	Date of Grant	Fair Market Value of Stock	First Exercisable
Option 1	April 1, 2004	$60,000	2004
Option 2	May 1, 2004	$50,000	2006
Option 3	June 1, 2004	$40,000	2004

(ii) In July of 2004, a change in control of X Corporation occurs, and, under the terms of its option plan, all outstanding options become immediately exercisable. Under the rules of this section, Option 1 is treated as an incentive stock option in its entirety; Option 2 exceeds the $100,000 aggregate fair market value limitation for calendar year 2004 by $10,000 (Option 1's $60,000 + Option 2's $50,000 = $110,000) and is, therefore, bifurcated into an incentive stock option for stock with a fair market value of $40,000 as of the date of grant and a nonstatutory option for stock with a fair market

	Date of Grant	Fair Market Value of Stock	First Exercisable
Option 1	April 1, 2004	$60,000	2005
Option 2	May 1, 2004	$40,000	2006
Option 3	June 1, 2004	$20,000	2005

(ii) On June 1, 2005, E exercises Option 3. At the time of exercise of Option 3, the fair market value of X stock (at the time of grant) with respect to which options held by E are first exercisable in 2005 does not exceed $100,000. On September 1, 2005, a change of control of X

(2) *Stock.*—A corporation may issue a separate certificate for incentive option stock or designate such stock as incentive stock option stock in the corporation's transfer records or plan records. In such a case, the issuance of separate certificates or designation in the corporation's transfer records or plan records is not a modification under § 1.424-1(e). In the absence of such an issuance or designation, shares are treated as first purchased under an incentive stock option to the extent of the $100,000 limitation, and the excess shares are treated as purchased under a nonstatutory option. See § 1.83-7 for the treatment of nonstatutory options.

(d) *Examples.*—The following examples illustrate the principles of this section. In each of the following examples E is an employee of X Corporation. The examples are as follows:

Example 1. General rule. Effective January 1, 2004, X Corporation adopts a plan under which incentive stock options may be granted to its employees. On January 1, 2004, and each succeeding January 1 through January 1, 2013, E is granted immediately exercisable options for X Corporation stock with a fair market value of $100,000 determined on the date of grant. The options qualify as incentive stock options (determined without regard to this section). On January 1, 2014, E exercises all of the options. Because the $100,000 limitation has not been exceeded during any calendar year, all of the options are treated as incentive stock options.

Example 2. Order of grant. X Corporation is a parent corporation of Y Corporation, which is a parent corporation of Z Corporation. Each corporation has adopted its own separate plan, under which an employee of any member of the adopted its own separate plan, under which an employee of any member of the corporate group may be granted options for stock of any member of the group. On January 1, 2004, X Corporation grants E an incentive stock option (determined without regard to this section) for stock of Y Corporation with a fair market value of $100,000 on the date of grant. On December 31, 2004, Y Corporation grants E an incentive stock option (determined without regard to this section) for stock of Z Corporation with a fair market value of $75,000 as of the date of grant. Both of the options are immediately exercisable. For purposes of this section, options are taken into account in the order in which granted using the fair market value of stock as of the date on the option is granted. During calendar year 2004, the aggregate fair market value of stock with respect to which E's options are exercisable for the first time exceeds $100,000. Therefore, the option for Y Corporation stock is treated as an incentive stock option, and the option for Z Corporation stock is treated as a nonstatutory option.

Example 3. Acceleration provision. (i) In 2004, X Corporation grants E three incentive stock options (determined without regard to this section) to acquire stock with an aggregate fair market value of $150,000 on the date of grant. The dates of grant, the fair market value of the stock (as of the applicable date of grant) with respect to which the options are exercisable, and the years in which the options are first exercisable (without regard to acceleration provisions) are as follows:

value of $10,000 as of the date of grant. Option 3 is treated as a nonstatutory option in its entirety.

Example 4. Exercise of option and acceleration provision. (i) In 2004, X Corporation grants E three incentive stock options (determined without regard to this section) to acquire stock with an aggregate fair market value of $120,000 on the date of grant. The dates of grant, the fair market value of the stock (as of the applicable date of grant) with respect to which the options are exercisable, and the years in which the options are first exercisable (without regard to acceleration provisions) are as follows:

Corporation occurs, and, under the terms of its option plan, Option 2 becomes immediately exercisable. Under the rules of this section, because E's exercise of Option 3 occurs before the change of control and the effects of an acceleration provision are not taken into account until it is triggered, Option 3 is treated as an incentive stock option in its entirety. Option 1 is treated as an incentive stock option in its entirety. Option 2 is bifurcated into an incentive stock option for stock with a fair market value of $20,000 on the date of grant and a nonstatutory option for stock with a fair market value of $20,000 on the date of grant because it exceeds the $100,000 limitation for 2003 by $20,000 (Option 1 for $60,000 + Option 3 for $20,000 + Option 2 for $40,000 = $120,000).

(iii) Assume the same facts as in paragraph (ii) of this *Example 4*, except that the change of control occurs on May 1, 2005. Because options are taken into account in the order in which they are granted, Option 1 and Option 2 are treated as incentive stock options in their

	Date of Grant
Option 1	April 1, 2004
Option 2	May 1, 2004
Option 3	June 1, 2004

(ii) On December 31, 2004, Option 2 is canceled. Because Option 2 is canceled before the calendar year during which it would have become exercisable for the first time, it is disregarded. As a result, Option 1 and Option 3 are treated as incentive stock options in their entirety.

(iii) Assume the same facts as in paragraph (ii) of this *Example 5*, except that Option 2 is canceled on January 1, 2005. Because Option 2 is not canceled prior to the calendar year during which it would have become exercisable for the first time (2005), it is treated as an outstanding option for purposes of determining whether the $100,000 limitation for 2005 has been exceeded. Because options are taken into account in the order in which granted, Option 1 is treated as an incentive stock option in its entirety. Because Option 3 exceeds the $100,000 limitation by $40,000 (Option 1 for $60,000 + Option 2 for $40,000 + Option 3 for $40,000 = $140,000), it is treated as a nonstatutory option in its entirety.

(iv) Assume the same facts as in paragraph (i) of this *Example 5*, except that on January 1, 2005, E exercises Option 2 and immediately sells the stock in a disqualifying disposition. A disqualifying disposition has no effect on the determination of whether the underlying option is considered outstanding during the calendar year during which it is first exercisable. Because options are taken into account in the order in which granted, Option 1 is treated as an incentive stock option in its entirety. Because Option 3 exceeds the $100,000 limitation by $40,000 (Option 1 for $60,000 + Option 2 for $40,000 + Option 3 for $40,000 = $140,000), it is treated as a nonstatutory option in its entirety.

Example 6. Designation of stock. On January 1, 2004, X grants E an immediately exercisable incentive stock option (determined without regard to this section) to acquire X stock with a fair market value of $150,000 on that date. Under the rules of this section, the option is bifurcated and treated as an incentive stock option for X stock with a fair market value of $100,000 and a nonstatutory option for X stock with a fair market value of $50,000. In these circumstances, X may designate the stock that is treated as stock acquired pursuant to the exercise of an incentive stock option by issuing a separate certificate (or certificates) for $100,000 of stock and identifying such certificates as Incentive Stock Option Stock in its transfer records. In the absence of such a designation (or a designation in the corporation's transfer records or the plan records) shares with a fair market value of $100,000 are deemed purchased first under an incentive stock option, and shares with a fair market value of $50,000 are deemed purchased under a nonstatutory option.

[Reg. §1.422-4.]

☐ [T.D. 9144, 8-2-2004 (*corrected* 12-6-2004).]

[Reg. §1.422-5]

§1.422-5. Permissible provisions.—(a) *General rule.*—An option that otherwise qualifies as an incentive stock option does not fail to be an incentive stock option merely because such option contains one or more of the provisions described in paragraphs (b), (c), and (d) of this section.

(b) *Cashless exercise.*—(1) An option does not fail to be an incentive stock option merely because the optionee may exercise the option with previously acquired stock of the corporation that granted the option or stock of the corporation whose stock is being offered for purchase under the option. For special rules relating to the use of statutory option stock to pay the option price of an incentive stock option, see §1.424-1(c)(3).

(2) All shares acquired through the exercise of an incentive stock option are individually subject to the holding period requirements described in §1.422-1(a) and the disqualifying disposition rules of

entirety. Because the exercise of Option 3 (on June 1, 2005) takes place after the acceleration provision is triggered, Option 3 is treated as a nonstatutory option in its entirety.

Example 5. Cancellation of option. (i) In 2004, X Corporation grants E three incentive stock options (determined without regard to this section) to acquire stock with an aggregate fair market value of $140,000 as of the date of grant. The dates of grant, the fair market value of the stock (as of the applicable date of grant) with respect to which the options are exercisable, and the years in which the options are first exercisable (without regard to acceleration provisions) are as follows:

Fair Market Value of Stock	First Exercisable
$60,000	2005
$40,000	2005
$40,000	2005

§1.422-1(b), regardless of whether the option is exercised with previously acquired stock of the corporation that granted the option or stock of the corporation whose stock is being offered for purchase under the option. If an incentive stock option is exercised with such shares, and the exercise results in the basis allocation described in paragraph (b)(3) of this section, the optionee's disqualifying disposition of any of the stock acquired through such exercise is treated as a disqualifying disposition of the shares with the lowest basis.

(3) If the exercise of an incentive stock option with previously acquired shares is comprised in part of an exchange to which section 1036 (and so much of section 1031 as relates to section 1036) applies, then:

(i) The optionee's basis in the incentive stock option shares received in the section 1036 exchange is the same as the optionee's basis in the shares surrendered in the exchange, increased, if applicable, by any amount included in gross income as compensation pursuant to sections 421 through 424 or section 83. Except for purposes of §1.422-1(a), the holding period of the shares is determined under section 1223. For purposes of §1.422-1 and sections 421(b) and 83 and the regulations thereunder, the amount paid for the shares purchased under the option is the fair market value of the shares surrendered on the date of the exchange.

(ii) The optionee's basis in the incentive stock option shares not received pursuant to the section 1036 exchange is zero. For all purposes, the holding period of such shares begins as of the date that such shares are transferred to the optionee. For purposes of §1.422-1(b) and sections 421(b) and 83 and the regulations thereunder, the amount paid for the shares is considered to be zero.

(c) *Additional compensation.*—An option does not fail to be an incentive stock option merely because the optionee has the right to receive additional compensation, in cash or property, when the option is exercised, provided such additional compensation is includible in income under section 61 or section 83. The amount of such additional compensation may be determined in any manner, including by reference to the fair market value of the stock at the time of exercise or to the option price.

(d) *Option subject to a condition.*—(1) An option does not fail to be an incentive stock option merely because the option is subject to a condition, or grants a right, that is not inconsistent with the requirements of §§1.422-2 and 1.422-4.

(2) An option that includes an alternative right is not an incentive stock option if the requirements of §1.422-2 are effectively avoided by the exercise of the alternative right. For example, an alternative right extending the option term beyond ten years, setting an option price below fair market value, or permitting transferability prevents an option from qualifying as an incentive stock option. If either of two options can be exercised, but not both, each such option is a disqualifying alternative right with respect to the other, even though one or both options would individually satisfy the requirements of §§1.422-2, 1.422-4, and this section.

(3) An alternative right to receive a taxable payment of cash and/or property in exchange for the cancellation or surrender of the option does not disqualify the option as an incentive stock option if the right is exercisable only when the then fair market value of the stock exceeds the exercise price of the option and the option is otherwise exercisable, the right is transferable only when the option is otherwise transferable, and the exercise of the right has economic and tax consequences no more favorable than the exercise of the option followed by an immediate sale of the stock. For this purpose, the exercise of the alternative right does not have the same economic and tax consequences if the payment exceeds the difference between

the then fair market value of the stock and the exercise price of the option.

(e) *Examples.*—The principles of this section are illustrated by the following examples:

Example 1. On June 1, 2004, X Corporation grants an incentive stock option to A, an employee of X Corporation, entitling A to purchase 100 shares of X Corporation common stock at $10 per share. The option provides that A may exercise the option with previously acquired shares of X Corporation common stock. X Corporation has only one class of common stock outstanding. Under the rules of section 83, the shares transferable to A through the exercise of the option are transferable and not subject to a substantial risk of forfeiture. On June 1, 2005, when the fair market value of an X Corporation share is $25, A uses 40 shares of X Corporation common stock, which A had purchased on the open market on June 1, 2002, for $5 per share, to pay the full option price. After exercising the option, A owns 100 shares of incentive stock option stock. Under section 1036 (and so much of section 1031 as relates to section 1036), 40 of the shares have a $200 aggregate carryover basis (the $5 purchase price × 40 shares) and a three-year holding period for purposes of determining capital gain, and 60 of the shares have a zero basis and a holding period beginning on June 1, 2005, for purposes of determining capital gain. All 100 shares have a holding period beginning on June 1, 2005, for purposes of determining whether the holding period requirements of §1.422-1(a) are met.

Example 2. Assume the same facts as in *Example 1.* Assume further that, on September 1, 2005, A sells 75 of the shares that A acquired through exercise of the incentive stock option for $30 per share. Because the holding period requirements were not satisfied, A made a disqualifying disposition of the 75 shares on September 1, 2005. Under the rules of paragraphs (b)(2) and (b)(3) of this section, A has sold all 60 of the non-section-1036 shares and 15 of the 40 section-1036 shares. Therefore, under paragraph (b)(3) of this section and section 83(a), the amount of compensation attributable to A's exercise of the option and subsequent disqualifying disposition of 75 shares is $1,500 (the difference between the fair market value of the stock on the date of transfer, $1,875 (75 shares at $25 per share), and the amount paid for the stock, $375 (60 shares at $0 per share plus 15 shares at $25 per share)). In addition, A must recognize a capital gain of $675, which consists of $375 ($450, the amount realized from the sale of 15 shares less A's basis of $75) plus $300 ($1,800, the amount realized from the sale of 60 shares, less A's basis of $1,500 resulting from the inclusion of that amount in income as compensation). Accordingly, A must include in gross income for the taxable year in which the sale occurs $1,500 as compensation and $675 as capital gain. For its taxable year in which the disqualifying disposition occurs, if otherwise allowable under section 162 and if the requirements of §1.83-6(a) are met, X Corporation is allowed a deduction of $1,500 for the compensation paid to A.

Example 3. Assume the same facts as in *Example 2,* except that, instead of selling the 75 shares of incentive stock option stock on September 1, 2005, A uses those shares to exercise a second incentive stock option. The second option was granted to A by X Corporation on January 1, 2005, entitling A to purchase 100 shares of X Corporation common stock at $22.50 per share. As in *Example 2,* A has made a disqualifying disposition of the 75 shares of stock pursuant to §1.424-1(c). Under paragraph (b) of this section, A has disposed of all 60 of the non-section-1036 shares and 15 of the 40 section-1036 shares. Therefore, pursuant to paragraph (b)(3) of this section and section 83(a), the amount of compensation attributable to A's exercise of the first option and subsequent disqualifying disposition of 75 shares is $1,500 (the difference between the fair market value of the stock on the date of transfer, $1,875 (75 shares at $25 per share), and the amount paid for the stock, $375 (60 shares at $0 per share plus 15 shares at $25 per share)). Unlike *Example 2,* A does not recognize any capital gain as a result of exercising the second option because, for all purposes other than the determination of whether the exercise is a disposition pursuant to section 424(c), the exercise is considered an exchange to which section 1036 applies. Accordingly, A must include in gross income for the taxable year in which the disqualifying disposition occurs $1,500 as compensation. If the requirements of §83(h) and §1.83-6(a) are satisfied and the deduction is otherwise allowable under section 162, for its taxable year in which the disqualifying disposition occurs, X Corporation is allowed a deduction of $1,500 for the compensation paid to A. After exercising the second option, A owns a total of 125 shares of incentive stock option stock. Under section 1036 (and so much of section 1031 as relates to section 1036), the 100 "new" shares of incentive stock option stock have the *following bases and holding periods:* 15 shares have a $75 carryover basis and a three-year-and-three-month holding period for purposes of determining capital gain, 60 shares have a $1,500 basis resulting from the inclusion of that amount in income as compensation and a three-month holding period for purposes of determining capital gain,

and 25 shares have a zero basis and a holding period beginning on September 1, 2005, for purposes of determining capital gain. All 100 shares have a holding period beginning on September 1, 2005, for purposes of determining whether the holding period requirements of §1.422-1(a) are met.

Example 4. Assume the same facts as in *Example 2,* except that, instead of selling the 75 shares of incentive stock option stock on September 1, 2005, A uses those shares to exercise a nonstatutory option. The nonstatutory option was granted to A by X Corporation on January 1, 2005, entitling A to purchase 100 shares of X Corporation common stock at $22.50 per share. Unlike *Example 3,* A has not made a disqualifying disposition of the 75 shares of stock. After exercising the nonstatutory option A owns a total of 100 shares of incentive stock option stock and 25 shares of nonstatutory stock option stock. Under section 1036 (and so much of section 1031 as relates to section 1036), the 75 new shares of incentive stock option stock have the same basis and holding period as the 75 old shares used to exercise the nonstatutory option The additional 25 shares of stock received upon exercise of the nonstatutory option are taxed under the rules of section 83(a). Accordingly, A must include in gross income for the taxable year in which the transfer of such shares occurs $750 (25 shares at $30 per share) as compensation. A's basis in such shares is the same as the amount included in gross income. For its taxable year in which the transfer occurs, X Corporation is allowed a deduction of $750 for the compensation paid to A to the extent the requirements of section 83(h) and §1.83-6(a) are satisfied and the deduction is otherwise allowable under section 162.

Example 5. Assume the same facts in *Example 1,* except that the shares transferred pursuant to the exercise of the incentive stock option are subject to a substantial risk of forfeiture and not transferable (substantially nonvested) for a period of six months after such transfer. Assume further that the shares that A uses to exercise the indentive stock option are similarly restricted. Such shares were transferred to A on January 1, 2005, through A's exercise of a nonstatutory stock option which was granted to A on January 1, 2004. A paid $5 per share for the stock when its fair market value was $22.50 per share. A did not file a section 83(b) election to include the $700 spread (the difference between the option price and the fair market value of the stock on date of exercise of the nonstatutory option) in gross income as compensation. After exercising the indentive stock option with the 40 substantially-nonvested shares, A owns 100 shares of substantially-nonvested incentive stock option stock. Section 1036 (and so much of section 1031 as relates to section 1036) applies to the 40 shares exchanged in exercise of the incentive stock option. However, pursuant to section 83(g), the stock received in such exchange, because it is incentive stock option stock, is not subject to restrictions and conditions substantially similar to those to which the stock given in such exchange was subject. For purposes of section 83(a) and §1.83-1(b)(1), therefore, A has disposed of the 40 shares of substantially-nonvested stock on June 1, 2005, and must include in gross income as compensation $800 (the difference between the amount realized upon such disposition, $1,000, and the amount paid for the stock, $200). Accordingly, 40 shares of the incentive stock option stock have a $1,000 basis (the $200 original basis plus the $800 included in income as compensation) and 60 shares of the incentive stock option stock have a zero basis. For its taxable year in which the disposition of the substantially-nonvested stock occurs, X Corporation is allowed a deduction of $800 for the compensation paid to A, provided the requirements of section 83(h) and §1.83-6(a) are satisfied and the deduction is otherwise allowable under section 162.

(f) *Effective/applicability date.*—(1) *In general.*—Except for §1.422-2(b)(6) *Example 1* (iii), the regulations under this section are effective on August 3, 2004. Section 1.422-2(b)(6) *Example 1* (iii) is effective on November 17, 2009. Section 1.422-2(b)(6) *Example 1* (iii) applies to statutory options granted on or after January 1, 2010.

(2) *Reliance and transition period.*—For statutory options granted on or before June 9, 2003, taxpayers may rely on the 1984 proposed regulations LR-279-81 (49 FR 4504), the 2003 proposed regulations REG-122917-02 (68 FR 34344), or this section until the earlier of January 1, 2006, or the first regularly scheduled stockholders meeting of the granting corporation occurring 6 months after August 3, 2004. For statutory options granted after June 9, 2003, and before the earlier of January 1, 2006, or the first regularly scheduled stockholders meeting of the granting corporation occurring at least 6 months after August 3, 2004, taxpayers may rely on either REG-122917-02 or this section. Taxpayers may not rely on LR-279-81 or REG-122917-02 after December 31, 2005. Reliance on LR-279-81, REG-122917-02, or this section must be in its entirety, and all statutory options granted during the reliance period must be treated consistently. [Reg. §1.422-5.]

☐ [T.D. 9144, 8-2-2004 (*corrected* 10-15-2004 *and* 12-6-2004) *Amended by* T.D. 9471, 11-16-2009.]

»»→ *Caution: Reg. §1.423-1, below, prior to amendment by T.D. 9471, is applicable to statutory options granted before January 1, 2010.*

[Reg. §1.423-1]

§1.423-1. Applicability of section 421(a).—(a) *General rule.*—Subject to the provisions of section 423(c) and §1.423-2(k), the special rules of income tax treatment provided in section 421(a) apply with respect to the transfer of a share of stock to an individual pursuant to the individual's exercise of an option granted under an employee stock purchase plan, as defined in §1.423-2, if the following conditions are satisfied—

(1) The individual makes no disposition of such share before the later of the expiration of the two-year period from the date of the grant of the option pursuant to which such share was transferred or the expiration of the one-year period from the date of transfer of such share to the individual; and

»»→ *Caution: Reg. §1.423-1, below, as amended by T.D. 9471, is applicable to statutory options granted on or after January 1, 2010.*

[Reg. §1.423-1]

§1.423-1. Applicability of section 421(a).—(a) *General rule.*—Subject to the provisions of section 423(c) and §1.423-2(k), the special rules of income tax treatment provided in section 421(a) apply with respect to the transfer of a share of stock to an individual pursuant to the individual's exercise of an option granted under an employee stock purchase plan, as defined in §1.423-2, if the following conditions are satisfied—

(1) The individual makes no disposition of such share before the later of the expiration of the two-year period from the date of the grant of the option pursuant to which such share was transferred or the expiration of the one-year period from the date of transfer of such share to the individual; and

(2) At all times during the period beginning on the date of the grant of the option and ending on the day three months before the date of exercise, the individual was an employee of the corporation

»»→ *Caution: Reg. §1.423-2, below, prior to amendment by T.D. 9471, is applicable to statutory options granted before January 1, 2010.*

[Reg. §1.423-2]

§1.423-2. Employee stock purchase plan defined.—(a) *In general.*—(1) The term "employee stock purchase plan" means a plan which meets the requirements of paragraphs (1) through (9) of section 423(b). If the terms of an option do not satisfy the requirements of paragraphs (3) through (9) of section 423(b), such requirements may be satisfied by the terms of an offering made under such plan. However, in such a case, such requirements will be treated as satisfied only with respect to options exercised under such offering.

(2) The determination of whether a particular option is an option granted under an employee stock purchase plan is made at the time such option is granted. If the terms of an option are inconsistent with the terms of the employee stock purchase plan or an offering under such a plan, the option will not be treated as granted under an employee stock purchase plan. If such an option is granted to an employee who is entitled to the grant of an option under the terms of the plan or offering, and such employee is not granted an option under such offering which qualifies as an option granted under an employee stock purchase plan, such offering will not meet the requirements of section 423(b)(4). Accordingly, none of the options granted under such offering will be eligible for the special tax treatment of section 423(b)(4). If such an option is granted to an individual who is not entitled to the grant of an option under the terms of the plan or offering, such option will not be treated as an option granted under an employee stock purchase plan, and the grant of the option will not disqualify the plan or the options granted under such plan or offering. For example, an option granted to an individual who is ineligible to receive an option under an employee stock purchase plan by reason of his ownership of 5 percent or more of the voting power or value of the stock of the grantor corporation (or a related corporation of such corporation), will not be treated as an option granted under an employee stock purchase plan, and the grant of such an option will not disqualify options granted under such plan from the special tax treatment of section 421. If all the options granted under an offering do not give the respective optionees the same rights and privileges, none of the options granted under such offering will be treated as having been granted under an employee stock purchase plan. If, *at the time an option is granted,* it qualifies as an option granted under an employee stock purchase plan, but the terms of the option are not in fact met, the option will not qualify for the special tax treatment of section 421. However, the failure of such an option to qualify for the special tax treatment of section 421, will not disqualify other options granted under the plan.

(b) *Options restricted to employees.*—An employee stock purchase plan must provide that options are to be granted only to employees of the employer corporation or of its related corporations to purchase stock in any such corporation. If such a provision is not included in the terms of the plan, the plan will not be an employee stock

(2) At all times during the period beginning on the date of the grant of the option and ending on the day three months before the date of exercise, the individual was an employee of the corporation granting the option, a related corporation, or a corporation (or a related corporation) substituting or assuming the stock option in a transaction to which section 424(a) applies.

(b) *Cross-references.*—For rules relating to the employment relationship, see paragraph (h) of §1.421-1. For rules relating to the effect of a disqualifying disposition, see section 421(b) and paragraph (b) of §1.421-2. For definition of the term "disposition", see section 424(c) and paragraph (c) of §1.424-1. [Reg. §1.423-1.]

☐ [*T.D. 6887, 6-23-66. Amended by T.D. 7728, 10-31-80 and T.D. 9144, 8-2-2004.*]

granting the option, a related corporation, or a corporation (or a related corporation) substituting or assuming the stock option in a transaction to which section 424(a) applies.

(b) *Cross-references.*—For rules relating to the requisite employment relationship, see §1.421-1(h). For rules relating to the effect of a disqualifying disposition, see section 421(b) and §1.421-2(b). For the definition of the term "disposition," see section 424(c) and §1.424-1(c). For the definition of the term "related corporation," see §1.421-1(i).

(c) *Effective/applicability date.*—The regulations under this section are effective on November 17, 2009. The regulations under this section apply to options granted under an employee stock purchase plan on or after January 1, 2010. [Reg. §1.423-1.]

☐ [*T.D. 6887, 6-23-66. Amended by T.D. 7728, 10-31-80; T.D. 9144, 8-2-2004 and T.D. 9471, 11-16-2009.*]

purchase plan and options granted under such plan will not qualify for the special tax treatment of section 421. For rules relating to the employment requirement, see paragraph (h) of §1.421-7.

(c) *Stockholder approval.*—(1) An employee stock purchase plan must be approved by the stockholders of the granting corporation within 12 months before or after the date such plan is adopted. The approval of stockholders must comply with all applicable provisions of the corporate charter, bylaws and applicable State law prescribing the method and degree of stockholder approval required for the issuance of corporate stock or options. If the applicable State law does not prescribe a method and degree of stockholder approval in such cases an employee stock purchase plan must be approved—

(i) By a majority of the votes cast at a duly held stockholders' meeting at which a quorum representing a majority of all outstanding voting stock is, either in person or by proxy, present and voting on the plan; or

(ii) By a method and in a degree that would be treated as adequate under applicable State law in the case of an action requiring stockholder approval (i.e., an action on which stockholders would be entitled to vote if the action were taken at a duly held stockholders' meeting).

(2) The plan required by section 423 must be approved within 12 months before or after the date the plan is adopted. Ordinarily, a plan is adopted when approved by the board of directors and the date of such board action will be reference point for determining whether stockholder approval comes within the 12-month period.

(3) The plan as adopted and approved must designate the aggregate number of shares which may be issued under the plan, and the corporations or class of corporations whose employees will be offered options under such plan. A plan which merely provides that the number of shares which may be issued under options shall not exceed a stated percentage of the shares outstanding at the time of each offering or grant under the plan will not satisfy the requirement that the plan state the aggregate number of shares which may be issued under the plan. However, the maximum number of shares which may be issued under the plan may be stated in terms of a percentage of either the authorized, issued or outstanding shares at the date of the adoption of the plan. The provisions relating to the aggregate number of shares to be issued under the plan and the employees (or class of employees) eligible to receive options under the plan, are the only provisions of a stock option plan which require stockholder approval for purposes of section 423(b)(1).

(4) Any increase in the aggregate number of shares which may be issued under the plan (other than an increase merely reflecting a change in capitalization such as a stock dividend or stock split-up) will be treated as the adoption of a new plan requiring approval of the stockholders within 12 months of such adoption. Similarly, a change in the designation of corporations whose employees may be

⫸→ *Caution: Reg. §1.423-2, below, prior to amendment by T.D. 9471, is applicable to statutory options granted before January 1, 2010.*

offered options under the plan will be treated as the adoption of a new plan requiring stockholder approval unless the plan provides that designations of participating corporations may be made from time to time from among a group consisting of the grantor corporation and its parent or subsidiary corporations. The group from among which such changes and designations are permitted without additional stockholder approval may include corporations having become parents or subsidiaries of the grantor after the adoption and approval of the plan. Any other changes in the terms of an employee stock purchase plan may be made without such changes being considered the adoption of a new plan.

(5) A plan which otherwise meets the requirements of section 423(b) and this section may be used as an employee stock purchase plan although the adoption and approval of such plan occurred before January 1, 1964.

(d) *Options granted to certain shareholders.*—(1) An employee stock purchase plan must by its terms provide that no employee can be granted an option if such employee, immediately after the option is granted, owns stock possessing 5 percent or more of the total combined voting power or value of all classes of stock of the employer corporation or its parent or subsidiary corporation. In determining whether the stock ownership of an employee equals or exceeds this 5 percent limit, the rules of section 424(d) (relating to attribution of stock ownership) shall apply, and stock which the employee may purchase under outstanding options (whether or not such options qualify for the special tax treatment afforded by section 421(a)) shall be treated as stock owned by the employee. An option is outstanding for purposes of section 423(b)(3) although under its terms it may be exercised only in installments or after the expiration of a fixed period of time. If an option is granted to an individual whose stock ownership (as determined under this paragraph for purposes of section 423(b)(3)) exceeds the limitation of section 423(b)(3), no portion of such option will be treated as having been granted under an employee stock purchase plan.

(2) The determination of the percentage of the total combined voting power or value of all classes of stock of his employer corporation (or a related corporation of such corporation) that is owned by the individual is made by comparing the voting power or value of the shares owned (or treated as owned) by the individual to the aggregate voting power or value of all shares actually issued and outstanding immediately after the grant of the option to such individual. The aggregate voting power or value of all shares actually issued and outstanding immediately after the grant of the option does not include the voting power or value of treasury shares or shares authorized for issue under outstanding options held by the individual or any other person.

(3) The application of this paragraph may be illustrated by the following examples:

Example (1). E, an employee of M Corporation, owns 6,000 shares of the common stock of M Corporation, the only class of M stock outstanding. M has 100,000 shares of its common stock outstanding. Since E owns 6 percent of the combined voting power or value of all classes of M Corporation stock, M cannot grant an option to E under M's employee stock purchase plan. If E's father and brother each owned 3,000 shares of M stock and E owned no M stock in his own name, the result in this case would be the same, since under section 424(d) a person is treated as owning stock held by his father and his brother. Similarly, the result would be the same if, instead of actually owning 6,000 shares, E merely held an option on 6,000 shares of M stock, irrespective of whether the transfer of stock under such option could qualify for the special tax treatment of section 421, since section 423(b)(3) provides that stock which the employee may purchase under outstanding options shall be treated as stock owned by such employee.

Example (2). Assume the same facts as in example (1) and assume further that M is a subsidiary corporation of P Corporation. Irrespective of whether E owns any P stock, E cannot receive an option from P under P's employee stock purchase plan since he owns 5 percent of the total combined voting power of all classes of stock of a subsidiary of P Corporation, *i.e.,* M Corporation. Thus, an individual who owns (or is treated as owning) stock in excess of the limitation of section 423(b)(3), in any corporation in a group of corporations, consisting of a parent and its subsidiary corporations, cannot receive an option under an employee stock purchase plan from any corporation in the group.

Example (3). F is an employee of R Corporation. R has only one class of stock, of which 100,000 shares are issued and outstanding. Assuming F owns no stock in R or in any parent or subsidiary of R for purposes of section 423(b)(3), R can grant an option to F under its employee stock purchase plan for 4,999 shares, since immediately after the grant of the option, F would not own 5 percent or more of the combined voting power or value of all classes of R stock actually

issued and outstanding at such time. The 4,999 shares which F would be treated as owning under section 423(b)(3) would not be added to the 100,000 shares actually issued and outstanding immediately after the grant for purposes of determining whether F's stock ownership exceeds the limitation of section 423(b)(3).

Example (4). Assume the same facts as in example (3) and assume further that on June 1, 1965, R grants F an option, purportedly under its employee stock purchase plan, for 5,000 shares. No portion of this option will be treated as granted under an employee stock purchase plan.

(e) *Employees covered by plan.*—(1) Subject to the limitations of section 423(b)(3), (5) and (8), an employee stock purchase plan must, by its terms, provide the options are to be granted to all employees of any corporation which grants options to any of its employees by reason of their employment by such corporation, except that one or more of the following categories of employees may be excluded from the coverage of the plan:

(i) Employees who have been employed less than 2 years;

(ii) Employees whose customary employment is 20 hours or less per week;

(iii) Employees whose customary employment is for not more than 5 months in any calendar year;

(iv) Officers;

(v) Persons whose principal duties consist of supervising the work of other employees; and

(vi) Highly compensated employees.

No option granted under a plan or offering which excludes from participation any employees, other than those who may be excluded under section 423(b)(4) and this paragraph, and those barred from participation by reason of section 423(b)(3), (5), and (8) and paragraphs (d), (f) and (i) of this section, can be regarded as having been granted under an employee stock purchase plan. If an option is not granted to any employee who is entitled to the grant of an option under the terms of the plan or offering, none of the options granted under such offering will be treated as having been granted under an employee stock purchase plan. Furthermore, no option will be considered as having been granted under an employee stock purchase plan if the option was granted in connection with an offering made after [insert date these regulations are published in final form in the Federal Register]with respect to which employees, otherwise eligible, are denied participation to any extent because of their continuing participation or eligibility for participation in a prior plan or offering (including a prior plan or offering of a related corporation). However, a plan which, by its terms, permits all eligible employees to elect to participate in an offering will not violate the requirements of this paragraph solely because eligible employees who elect not to participate in the offering are not granted options pursuant to such offering.

(2) For purposes of section 423(b)(3) the existence of the employment relationship between an individual and the corporation participating under the plan will be determined under paragraph (h) of §1.421-1 (relating to employment relationship).

(3) The application of this paragraph may be illustrated by the following examples:

Example (1). M Corporation has a stock purchase plan which meets all the requirements of section 423(b) except that by its terms, options are not required to be granted to employees whose weekly rate of pay is less than $100. As a matter of corporate practice, M grants options under its plan to all employees, irrespective of their weekly rate of pay. M's plan is not an employee stock purchase plan.

Example (2). Assume the same facts as in example (1) and assume further that the first offering under M's plan provides by its terms that options will be granted to all employees of M Corporation. With respect to options exercised under such offering the terms of such offering will be treated as part of the terms of M's plan. Accordingly, stock transferred pursuant to options exercised under such offering will be treated as stock transferred pursuant to the exercise of options granted under an employee stock purchase plan for purposes of section 421.

(f) *Equal rights and privileges.*—(1) An employee stock purchase plan must, by its terms, provide that all employees granted under such plan shall have the same rights and privileges; however, a plan will not fail to satisfy this requirement merely because the amount of stock which may be purchased by any employee under such plan is determined on the basis of a uniform relationship to the total compensation, or the basic or regular rate of compensation of employees, or because the plan provides that no employee may purchase more than a maximum amount of stock fixed under the plan. Thus, the provisions applying to one option under an offering (such as the provisions relating to the method of payment for the stock and the determination of the purchase price per share) must apply to all

➤➤➤ *Caution: Reg. §1.423-2, below, prior to amendment by T.D. 9471, is applicable to statutory options granted before January 1, 2010.*

other options under such offering in the same manner. If all the options granted under a plan or offering do not, by their terms, give the respective optionees the same rights and privileges, none of such options shall be treated as having been granted under an employee stock purchase plan for purposes of section 421.

(2) The requirements of section 423(b)(5) and this paragraph do not prevent the maximum amount of stock which an employee may purchase from being determined on the basis of a uniform relationship to the total compensation, or the basic or regular rate of compensation, of all employees. For example, if an employee stock purchase plan provides that the maximum amount of stock which each employee may purchase under the offering is one share for each $100 of annual gross pay, options granted under such offering will be treated as meeting the requirement of section 423(b)(5). However, such a provision must not exclude employees from participation under the plan or offering. For example, a plan which provides for the grant of options based on one share for each $100 of annual gross pay in excess of $10,000 will not meet the requirements of section 423(b)(5).

(3)(i) Except as provided in paragraph (f)(3)(ii) of this section, a plan permitting one or more employees to apply sums which were withheld under an earlier plan or offering towards the purchase of additional stock under the current plan or offering will be a violation of equal rights and privileges unless all employees in the current plan or offering are permitted to make payments in an amount not less than that which any employee is allowed to carry over, to be applied to the purchase of shares under the current plan or offering.

(ii) A plan will not fail to satisfy the requirements of this section merely because one or more employees are permitted to apply sums, in an amount representing a fractional share, which were withheld under an earlier plan or offering toward the purchase of additional stock under the current plan or offering.

(4)(i) Section 423(b)(5) does not prohibit the delaying of the grant of an option to any employee who is barred from being granted an option solely by reason of such employee's failing to meet a minimum service requirement until such employee meets such requirement.

(ii) The provisions of this paragraph (4) may be illustrated by the following example:

Example. N Corporation has an employee stock purchase plan which provides that options to purchase stock in an amount equal to ten percent of an employee's annual salary at a price equal to 85 percent of the fair market value at the time the option is granted will be granted to all employees other than those who have been employed less than 18 months. In addition, the plan provides that employees who have not yet met the minimum service requirements on the date the options are initially granted will be granted similar options on the date such employment has been attained. Such plan meets the requirements of section 423(b)(5).

(g) *Option price.*—(1) An employee stock purchase plan must, by its terms, provide that the option price will not be less than the lesser of—

(i) An amount equal to 85 percent of the fair market value of the stock at the time such option is granted, or

(ii) An amount which under the terms of the option may not be less than 85 percent of the fair market value of the stock at the time such option is exercised.

For definition of the term "option price", and general rules relating to such term, see paragraph (e) of §1.421-1. For rules relating to the determination of when an option is granted, see paragraph (c) of §1.421-1. Any option which does not meet the minimum pricing requirements of section 423(b)(6) and this paragraph will not be treated as granted under an employee stock purchase plan irrespective of whether the plan itself or the offering satisfies such requirements. If such an option is granted to an employee who is entitled to the grant of an option under the terms of the plan or offering, and such employee is not granted an option under such offering which qualifies as an option granted under an employee stock purchase plan, such offering will not meet the requirements of section 423(b)(4). Accordingly, none of the options granted under such offering will be eligible for the special tax treatment of section 423(b)(4).

(2) The option price may be stated either as a percentage or as a dollar amount. If the option price is stated as a dollar amount, the requirement of section 423(b)(6) and this paragraph can only be met by a plan or offering in which the price is fixed at not less than 85 percent of the fair market value of the stock at the time the option is granted. If the fixed price is less than 85 percent of the fair market value of the stock at grant, the option cannot meet the requirement of section 423(b)(6) even if a decline in the fair market value of the stock results in such fixed price being not less than 85 percent of the fair market value of the stock at the time the option is exercised, since such a result was not certain to occur under the terms of the option.

(3) The application of this paragraph may be illustrated by the following examples:

Example (1). M Corporation has an employee stock purchase plan which provides that the option price will be 85 percent of the fair market value of the stock at grant, or 85 percent of the stock at exercise, whichever amount is the lesser. Upon the exercise of an option issued under M's plan, M agrees to accept an amount which is less than the minimum amount allowable under the terms of such plan. Notwithstanding that the option was issued under an employee stock purchase plan, the transfer of stock pursuant to the exercise of such option does not satisfy the requirement of section 423(b)(6) and cannot qualify for the special tax treatment of section 421.

Example (2). Assume the same facts as in example (1) and assume further that at the time of grant, the fair market value of M Corporation stock is $100 per share and that the option price is set at 85 percent of the fair market value of M stock at exercise, but not less than $80 per share. The option satisfies the requirement of section 422(b)(6), and can qualify for the special tax treatment of section 421.

Example (3). Assume the same facts as in example (2), except assume that the option price is set at 85 percent of the fair market value of M stock at exercise, but not more than $80 per share. This option cannot satisfy the requirement of section 423(b)(6) irrespective of whether, at the time the option is exercised, 85 percent of the fair market value of M stock is $80 or less.

(h) *Option period.*—An employee stock purchase plan must, by its terms, provide that options granted under such plan cannot be exercised after the expiration of 27 months from the date of grant unless, under the terms of such plan, the option price is to be not less than 85 percent of the fair market value of the stock at the time of the exercise of the option. If the option price is to be not less than 85 percent of the fair market value of the stock at the time the option is exercised, then the option period provided under the plan must not exceed 5 years from the date of grant. If the requirement of section 423(b)(7) is not met by the terms of the plan or offering, options issued under such plan or offering will not be treated as options granted under an employee stock purchase plan irrespective of whether such options, by their terms, are exercisable beyond the period allowable under section 423(b)(7) and this paragraph. An option which provides that the option price is to be not less than 85 percent of the fair market value of the stock at exercise may have an option period of 5 years irrespective of whether the fair market value of the stock at exercise is more or less than the fair market value of such stock at grant. However, if the option provides that the option price is to be 85 percent of the fair market value of the stock at exercise, but not more than some other fixed amount, then irrespective of the price paid on exercise, the option period must not be more than 27 months.

(i) *Restriction on amount of optioned stock.*—(1) Under section 423(b)(8), an employee stock purchase plan must, by its terms, provide that no employee may be permitted to purchase stock under all the employee stock purchase plans of his employer corporation and its related corporations at a rate which exceeds $25,000 in fair market value of such stock (determined at the time the option is granted) for each calendar year in which any such option granted to such individual is outstanding at any time. In applying the limitation of section 423(b)(8)—

(i) The right to purchase stock under an option is deemed to accrue when the option (or any portion thereof) first becomes exercisable during the calendar year;

(ii) The right to purchase stock under an option accrues at the rate provided in the option, but in no case may such rate exceed $25,000 of fair market value of such stock (determined at the time such option is granted) for any one calendar year; and

(iii) A right to purchase stock which has accrued under one option granted pursuant to the plan may not be carried over to any other option. If an option is granted under an employee stock purchase plan which satisfies the requirement of section 423(b)(8), but such option gives the optionee the right to buy stock in excess of the maximum rate allowable under such section and this paragraph, no portion of such option will be treated as having been granted under an employee stock purchase plan. Furthermore, if the option was granted to an employee entitled to the grant of an option under the terms of the plan or offering, and such employee is not granted an option under such offering which qualifies as an option granted under an employee stock purchase plan, such offering will not meet the requirements of section 423(b)(4). Accordingly, none of the options granted under such offering will be eligible for the special tax treatment of section 421.

(2) The limitation of section 423(b)(8) and this paragraph applies only to options granted under employee stock purchase plans and does not limit the amount of stock which an employee may purchase under qualified stock options (as defined in section 422(b)), restricted

⋙→ *Caution: Reg. §1.423-2, below, prior to amendment by T.D. 9471, is applicable to statutory options granted before January 1, 2010.*

stock options (as defined in section 424(b)), or any other stock options (except those to which section 423 applies). Stock purchased under options to which section 423 does not apply will not limit the amount which an employee may purchase under an employee stock purchase plan, except for purposes of the 5-percent stock ownership provision of section 423(b)(3).

(3) Under the limitation of section 423(b)(8), an individual may purchase up to $25,000 of stock (based on the fair market value of such stock at the time the option was granted) in each calendar year during which an option granted to such individual under an employee stock purchase plan is outstanding. Alternatively, an individual may purchase more than $25,000 of stock (based on the fair market value of such stock at the time the option was granted) in a calendar year, so long as the total amount of stock which he purchases does not exceed $25,000 in fair market value of such stock (determined at the time the option was granted) for each calendar year in which the option was outstanding. If in any calendar year the individual holds two or more outstanding options granted under employee stock purchase plans of his employer corporation, or a related corporation of such corporation, his purchase of stock attributable to such year under all such options must not exceed $25,000 in fair market value of such stock (determined at the time such options were granted). Under an employee stock purchase plan, an individual may not purchase stock in anticipation that the option will be outstanding for some future year. Thus, the individual may purchase only the amount of stock which does not exceed the limitation of section 423(b)(8) for the year of the purchase and for preceding years during which the option was outstanding. Thus, the amount of stock which may be purchased under an option depends on the number of years in which the option is actually outstanding. The amount of stock which may be purchased under an employee stock purchase plan may not be increased by reason of the failure to grant an option in an earlier year under such plan, or by reason of the failure to exercise an earlier option. For example, if an option is granted to an individual and expires without having been exercised at all, the failure to exercise the option does not increase the amount of stock which such individual may be permitted to purchase under an option granted in a year following the year of such expiration. If an option granted under an employee stock purchase plan is outstanding in more than one calendar year, stock purchased pursuant to the exercise of such option will be applied first, to the extent allowable under section 423(b)(8) and this paragraph, against the $25,000 limitation for the earliest year in which such option was outstanding, then, against the $25,000 limitation for each succeeding year, in order. For example, if an individual purchases $60,000 in fair market value of stock (determined at the time the option was granted) by the exercise of an option granted under an employee stock purchase plan of his employer corporation, and if such option was outstanding in 3 calendar years, then $25,000 in fair market value of such stock (determined at the time the option was granted) will be attributed to the first calendar year in which such option was outstanding, another $25,000 in fair market value of such stock will be attributed to the second calendar year in which such option was outstanding, and the remaining $10,000 in fair market value of such stock will be attributed to the last calendar year in which such option was outstanding. Thus, the individual may receive a right under another option granted under such employee stock purchase plan (or under an employee stock purchase plan of a parent or subsidiary corporation of his employer corporation) entitling him to purchase another $15,000 in fair market value of such stock (determined as of the date such option is granted) for such last calendar year.

(4) The application of section 423(b)(8) and this paragraph may be illustrated by the following examples:

Example (1). Assume that P Corporation maintains an employee stock purchase plan and that E is employed by P. On June 1, 1964, P grants E an option under the plan to purchase a total of 750 shares of P stock at $85 per share. On such date, the fair market value of P stock is $100 per share. The option provides that it cannot be exercised after May 31, 1966. Under section 423(b)(8), the option must not permit E to purchase more than 250 shares of P stock during the calendar year 1964, since 250 shares are equal to $25,000 in fair market value of P stock determined at the time of grant. During the calendar year 1965, E may purchase under such option an amount of P stock equal to the difference between $50,000 in fair market value of P stock (determined at the time the option was granted) and the fair market value of P stock (determined at the time of grant of the option) purchased during 1964. During the calendar year 1966, E may purchase an amount of P stock equal to the difference between $75,000 in fair market value of such stock (determined at the time of grant of the option) and the total amount of the fair market value of such stock (determined at the time of grant of the option) purchased under such option during the calendar years 1964 and 1965. E may purchase $25,000 of stock for the year 1964 and $25,000 of stock for

the year 1966, although the option was outstanding for only a part of each of such years. However, E may not be granted another option under an employee stock purchase plan of P or a related corporation to purchase stock of any of such corporations during the calendar years 1964, 1965, and 1966, so long as the option granted June 1, 1964, is outstanding. If this option permitted E to purchase only $15,000 of P's stock for each year it is outstanding, then E could be granted another option by P, or by a related corporation, in 1964, permitting him to purchase an additional $10,000 of stock for each year it is outstanding.

Example (2). Assume the same facts as in example (1), and assume further that the option granted to E in 1964 is terminated in 1965 without any part of such option having been exercised, and that subsequent to such termination and during 1965, E is granted another option under P's employee stock purchase plan. Under such option, E may be permitted to purchase $25,000 of stock for 1965. On the other hand, if, in 1966, E exercised the option granted to him in 1964 and purchased 600 shares of P stock, 500 shares, the maximum amount of stock which could have been purchased in 1965 under the option, is treated as having been purchased for the years 1964 and 1965. Thus, only 100 shares of the stock are treated as having been purchased for 1966, and E may be permitted under the new option to purchase for 1966 stock having a fair market value of $15,000 at the time the new option is granted.

(j) *Restriction on transferability.*—An employee stock purchase plan must, by its terms, provide that options granted under such plan are not transferable by the optionee otherwise than by will or the laws of descent and distribution, and must be exercisable, during his lifetime, only by him. For general rules relating to the restriction on transferability required by section 423(b)(9), see paragraph (b)(2) of §1.421-1. For a limited exception to the requirement of section 423(b)(9), see section 424(h)(3).

(k) *Special rule where option price is between 85 percent and 100 percent of value of stock.*—(1)(i) If all the conditions necessary for the application of section 421(a) exist, section 423(c) provides additional rules which are applicable in cases where, at the time the option is granted, the option price per share is less than 100 percent (but not less than 85 percent) of the fair market value of such share. In such case, upon the disposition of such share by the individual after the expiration of the 2-year and the 1-year (6-month for taxable years beginning before 1977; 9-month for taxable years beginning in 1977) holding periods, or upon his death while owning such share (whether occurring before or after the expiration of such periods), there shall be included in the individual's gross income as compensation (and not as gain upon the sale or exchange of a capital asset) the lesser of—

    (a) The amount, if any, by which the price paid under the option was exceeded by the fair market value of the share at the time the option was granted, or

    (b) The amount, if any, by which the price paid under the option was exceeded by the fair market value of the share at the time of such disposition or death.

For purposes of applying the rules of section 423(c) and this paragraph, if the option price is not fixed or determinable at the time the option is granted, the option price will be computed as if the option had been exercised at such time. The amount of compensation resulting from the application of section 423(c) and this paragraph shall be included in the individual's gross income for the taxable year in which the disposition occurs, or for the taxable year closing with his death, whichever event results in the application of section 423(c).

    (ii) The application of the special rules provided in section 423(c) shall not affect the rules provided in section 421(a) with respect to the individual exercising the option, the employer corporation, or its parent or subsidiary corporation. Thus, notwithstanding the inclusion of an amount as compensation in the gross income of an individual, as provided in section 423(c), no income results to the individual at the time the stock is transferred to him, and no deduction under section 162 is allowable at any time to the employer corporation or its parent or subsidiary with respect to such amount.

    (iii) If, during his lifetime, the individual exercises an option granted under an employee stock purchase plan, but such individual dies before the stock is transferred to him pursuant to his exercise of the option, the transfer of such stock to the individual's executor, administrator, heir, or legatee is deemed, for the purpose of section 421 and 423, to be a transfer of the stock to the individual exercising the option and a further transfer by reason of death from such individual to his executor, administrator, heir, or legatee.

    (2) If the special rules provided in section 423(c) are applicable to the disposition of a share of stock by an individual, the basis of such share in the individual's hands at the time of such disposition, determined under section 1011, shall be increased by an amount equal to the amount includible as compensation in his gross income under section 423(c). However, the basis of a share of stock acquired

⟫⟫→ *Caution: Reg. §1.423-2, below, prior to amendment by T.D. 9471, is applicable to statutory options granted before January 1, 2010.*

after the death of an employee by the exercise of an option granted to such employee under an employee stock purchase plan shall be determined in accordance with the rules of section 421(c) and paragraph (c) of §1.421-2. If the special rules provided in section 423(c) are applicable to a share of stock upon the death of an individual, the basis of such share in the hands of the estate or the person receiving the stock by bequest or inheritance shall be determined under section 1014, and shall not be increased by reason of the inclusion upon the decedent's death of any amount in his gross income under section 423(c). See example (9) of this paragraph with respect to the determination of basis of the share in the hands of a surviving joint owner.

(3) The application of this paragraph may be illustrated by the following examples:

Example (1). On June 1, 1964, the X Corporation grants to E, an employee, an option under X's employee stock purchase plan to purchase a share of X Corporation's stock for $85. The fair market value of the X Corporation stock on such date is $100 per share. On June 1, 1965, E exercises the option and on that date the X Corporation transfers the share of stock to E. On January 1, 1967, E sells the share for $150, its fair market value on that date. E makes his income tax return on the basis of the calendar year. The income tax consequences to E and X Corporation are as follows: (i) compensation in the amount of $15 is includible in E's gross income for 1967, the year of the disposition of the share. The $15 represents the difference between the option price ($85) and the fair market value of the share on the date the option was granted ($100), since such value is less than the fair market value of the share on the date of disposition ($150). For the purpose of computing E's gain or loss on the sale of the share, E's cost basis of $85 is increased by $15, the amount includible in E's gross income as compensation. Thus, E's basis for the share is $100. Since the share was sold for $150, E realizes a gain of $50, which is treated as long-term capital gain; (ii) the X Corporation is entitled to no deduction under section 162 at any time with respect to the share transferred to E.

Example (2). Assume the same facts as in example (1), except assume that E sells the share of X Corporation stock on January 1, 1968, for $75, its fair market value on that date. Since $75 is less than the option price ($85), no amount in respect of the sale is includible as compensation in E's gross income for 1968. E's basis for determining gain or loss on the sale is $85. Since E sold the share for $75, E realized a loss of $10 on the sale, which loss is treated as a long-term capital loss.

Example (3). Assume the same facts as in example (1), except assume that the option provides that the option price shall be 90 percent of the fair market value of the stock on the day the option is exercised. On June 1, 1965, when the option is exercised, the fair market value of the stock is $120 per share so that E pays $108 for the share of stock. Compensation in the amount of $10 is includible in E's gross income for 1967, the year of the disposition of the share. This is determined in the following manner: The excess of the fair market value of the stock at the time of the disposition ($150) over the price paid for the share ($108) is $42; and the excess of the fair market value of the stock at the time the option was granted ($100) over the option price, computed as if the option had been exercised at such time ($90), is $10. Accordingly, $10, the lesser, is includible in gross income. In this situation, E's cost basis of $108 is increased by $10, the amount includible in E's gross income as compensation. Thus, E's basis for the share is $118. Since the share was sold for $150, E realizes a gain of $32, which is treated as long-term capital gain.

Example (4). Assume the same facts as in example (1), except assume that instead of selling the share on January 1, 1967, E makes a gift of the share on that day. In such case, $15 is includible as compensation in E's gross income for 1967. E's cost basis of $85 is increased by $15, the amount includible in E's gross income as compensation. Thus, E's basis for the share is $100, which becomes the donee's basis, as of the time of the gift, for determining gain or loss.

Example (5). Assume the same facts as in example (2) except assume that instead of selling the share on January 1, 1968, E makes a gift of the share on that date. Since the fair market value of the share on that day ($75) is less than the option price ($85), no amount in respect of the disposition by way of gift is includible as compensation in E's gross income for 1968. E's basis for the share is $85, which becomes the donee's basis, as of the time of the gift, for the purpose of determining gain. The donee's basis for the purpose of determining loss, determined under section 1015'a), is $75 (fair market value of the share at the date of gift).

Example (6). Assume the same facts as in example (1), except assume that after acquiring the share of stock on June 1, 1965, E dies on August 1, 1966, at which time the share has a fair market value of $150. Compensation in the amount of $15 is includible in E's gross income for the taxable year closing with his death, such $15 being the difference between the option price ($85) and the fair market value of the share when the option was granted ($100), since such value is less than the fair market value at date of death ($150). The basis of the share in the hands of E's estate is determined under section 1014 without regard to the $15 includible in the decedent's gross income.

Example (7). Assume the same facts as in example (6), except assume that E dies on August 1, 1965, at which time the share has a fair market value of $150. Although E's death occurred within six months after the transfer of the share to him, the income tax consequences are the same as in example (6).

Example (8). Assume the same facts as in example (1), except assume that the share of stock was issued in the names of E and his wife jointly with right of survivorship, and that E and his wife sold the share on June 15, 1965, for $150, its fair market value on that date. Compensation in the amount of $15 is includible in E's gross income for 1966, the year of the disposition of the share. The basis of the share in the hands of E and his wife for the purpose of determining gain or loss on the sale is $100, that is, the cost of $85 increased by the amount of $15 includible as compensation in E's gross income. The gain of $50 on the sale is treated as long-term capital gain, and is divided equally between E and his wife.

Example (9). Assume the same facts as in example (1), except assume that the share of stock was issued in the names of E and his wife jointly with right of survivorship, and that E predeceased his wife on August 1, 1966, at which time the share had a fair market value of $150. Compensation in the amount of $15 is includible in E's gross income for the taxable year closing with his death. See example (6). The basis of the share in the hands of E's wife as survivor is determined under section 1014 without regard to the $15 includible in the decedent's gross income.

Example (10). Assume the same facts as in example (9), except assume that E's wife predeceased him on July 1, 1966. Section 423(c) does not apply in respect of her death. Upon the subsequent death of E on August 1, 1966, the income tax consequences in respect of E's taxable year closing with the date of his death, and in respect of the basis of the share in the hands of his estate, are the same as in example (6). If E had sold the share on July 15, 1966 (after the death of his wife), for $150, its fair market value at that time, the income tax consequences would be the same as in example (1). [Reg. §1.423-2.]

☐ [*T.D. 6887, 6-23-66. Amended by T.D. 7645, 9-27-79; T.D. 7728, 10-31-80; T.D. 8235, 12-1-88 and T.D. 9144, 8-2-2004.*]

⟫⟫→ *Caution: Reg. §1.423-2, below, as amended by T.D. 9471, is applicable to statutory options granted on or after January 1, 2010.*

[Reg. §1.423-2]

§1.423-2. Employee stock purchase plan defined.—(a) *In general.*—(1) The term "employee stock purchase plan" means a plan that meets the requirements of paragraphs (a)(2) and (a)(3) of this section. If the terms of the plan do not satisfy the requirements of paragraph (a)(3) of this section, then such requirements may be satisfied by the terms of an offering made under the plan. However, where the requirements of paragraph (a)(3) of this section are satisfied by the terms of an offering, such requirements will be treated as satisfied only with respect to options exercised under that offering. One or more offerings may be made under an employee stock purchase plan. Offerings may be consecutive or overlapping, and the terms of each offering need not be identical provided the terms of the plan and the offering together satisfy the requirements of paragraphs (a)(2) and (a)(3) of this section. The plan and the terms of an offering must be in writing or electronic form, provided that such writing or electronic form is adequate to establish the terms of the plan or offering, as applicable.

(2) To satisfy the requirements of this paragraph (a)(2) and §1.423-1, the plan must meet both of the following requirements—

(i) The plan must provide that options can be granted only to employees of the employer corporation or of a related corporation (as defined in paragraph (i) of §1.421-1) to purchase stock in any such corporation (see paragraph (b) of this section); and

(ii) The plan must be approved by the stockholders of the granting corporation within 12 months before or after the date the plan is adopted (see paragraph (c) of this section).

(3) To satisfy the requirements of this paragraph (a)(3) and §1.423-1, the terms of the plan or offering must meet all of the following requirements—

(i) An employee cannot be granted an option if, immediately after the option is granted, the employee owns stock possessing 5 percent or more of the total combined voting power or value of all classes of stock of the employer corporation or of a related corporation (see paragraph (d) of this section);

>>→ Caution: Reg. §1.423-2, below, as amended by T.D. 9471, is applicable to statutory options granted on or after January 1, 2010.

(ii) Options must be granted to all employees of any corporation whose employees are granted any options by reason of their employment by the corporation (see paragraph (e) of this section);

(iii) All employees granted options must have the same rights and privileges (see paragraph (f) of this section);

(iv) The option price cannot be less than the lesser of—

(A) An amount equal to 85 percent of the fair market value of the stock at the time the option is granted, or

(B) An amount not less than 85 percent of the fair market value of the stock at the time the option is exercised (see paragraph (g) of this section).

(v) Options cannot be exercised after the expiration of—

(A) Five years from the date the option is granted if, under the terms of such plan, the option price cannot be less than 85 percent of the fair market value of the stock at the time the option is exercised, or

(B) Twenty-seven months from the date the option is granted, if the option price is not determined in the manner described in paragraph (a)(3)(v)(A) of this section (see paragraph (h) of this section).

(vi) No employee may be granted an option that permits the employee's rights to purchase stock under all employee stock purchase plans of the employer corporation and its related corporations to accrue at a rate that exceeds $25,000 of fair market value of the stock (determined at the time the option is granted) for each calendar year in which the option is outstanding at any time (see paragraph (i) of this section); and

(vii) Options are not transferable by the optionee other than by will or the laws of descent and distribution, and are exercisable, during the lifetime of the optionee, only by the optionee (see paragraph (j) of this section).

(4) The determination of whether a particular option is an option granted under an employee stock purchase plan is made at the time the option is granted. If the terms of an option are inconsistent with the terms of the employee stock purchase plan or the offering under the plan pursuant to which the option is granted, the option will not be treated as granted under an employee stock purchase plan. If an option with terms that are inconsistent with the terms of the plan or an offering under the plan is granted to an employee who is entitled to the grant of an option under the terms of the plan or offering, and the employee is not granted an option under the offering that qualifies as an option granted under an employee stock purchase plan, the offering will not meet the requirements of paragraph (e) of this section. Accordingly, none of the options granted under the offering will be eligible for the special tax treatment of section 421. However, if an option with terms that are inconsistent with the terms of the plan or an offering under the plan is granted to an individual who is not entitled to the grant of an option under the terms of the plan or offering, the option will not be treated as an option granted under an employee stock purchase plan but the grant of the option will not disqualify the options granted under the plan or offering. If, at the time of grant, an option qualifies as an option granted under an employee stock purchase plan, but after the time of grant one or more of the requirements of paragraph (a)(3) of this section is not satisfied with respect to the option, the option will not be treated as granted under an employee stock purchase plan but this failure to comply with the terms of the option will not disqualify the other options granted under the plan or offering.

(5) *Examples.*—The following examples illustrate the principles of paragraph (a):

Example 1. Corporation A operates an employee stock purchase plan under which options for A stock are granted to employees of A. The terms of an offering provide that the option price will be 90 percent of the fair market value of A stock on the date of exercise. A grants an option under the offering to Employee Z, an employee of A. The terms of the option provide that the option price will be 85 percent of the fair market value of A stock on the date of exercise. Because the terms of Z's option are inconsistent with the terms of the offering, the option granted to Z will not be treated as an option granted under the employee stock purchase plan. Further, unless Z is granted an option under the offering that qualifies as an option granted under the employee stock purchase plan, the offering will not meet the requirements of paragraph (e) of this section and none of the options granted under the offering will be eligible for the special tax treatment of section 421.

Example 2. Corporation B operates an employee stock purchase plan that provides that options for B stock may only be granted to *employees of B.* Under the terms of the plan, options may not be granted to consultants and other non-employees. B grants an option to Consultant Y, a consultant of B. Because Y is ineligible to receive an option under the plan because Y is not an employee, the grant of the option to Y is inconsistent with the terms of the plan and the

option granted to Y will not be treated as an option granted under the employee stock purchase plan. However, the grant of the option to Y will not disqualify the options granted under the plan or any offering because Y was not entitled to the grant of an option under the plan.

Example 3. Corporation C operates an employee stock purchase plan under which options for C stock are granted to employees of C. C grants an option pursuant to an offering under the plan to Employee X, an employee of C who is a highly compensated employee. The terms of the employee stock purchase plan exclude highly compensated employees from participation in the plan. Because X is ineligible to receive an option under the plan by reason of X's exclusion from participation in the plan, the option granted to X will not be treated as an option granted under the employee stock purchase plan. However, the grant of the option to X will not disqualify the options granted under the plan or offering because X was not entitled to the grant of an option under the plan.

Example 4. Corporation D operates an employee stock purchase plan under which options for D stock are granted to employees of D. D grants an option pursuant to an offering under the plan to Employee W, an employee of D. The terms of the option provide that the option price will be 90 percent of the fair market value of D stock on the date of exercise. On the date of exercise, W pays only 85 percent of the fair market value of D stock. Because the terms of W's option are not satisfied, the option granted to W will not be treated as an option granted under the employee stock purchase plan. However, the failure to comply with the terms of the option granted to W will not disqualify the options granted under the plan or offering.

(b) *Options restricted to employees.*—An employee stock purchase plan must provide that options can be granted only to employees of the employer corporation (or employees of its related corporations) to purchase stock in the employer corporation (or one of its related corporations). If such a provision is not included in the terms of the plan, the plan will not be an employee stock purchase plan and options granted under the plan will not qualify for the special tax treatment of section 421. For rules relating to the employment requirement, see §1.421-1(h).

(c) *Stockholder approval.*—(1) An employee stock purchase plan must be approved by the stockholders of the granting corporation within 12 months before or after the date such plan is adopted. The approval of the stockholders must comply with all applicable provisions of the corporate charter and bylaws and of applicable State law prescribing the method and degree of stockholder approval required for the issuance of corporate stock or options. If the applicable State law does not prescribe a method and degree of stockholder approval, then an employee stock purchase plan must be approved—

(i) By a majority of the votes cast at a duly held stockholder's meeting at which a quorum representing a majority of all outstanding voting stock is, either in person or by proxy, present and voting on the plan; or

(ii) By a method and in a degree that would be treated as adequate under applicable State law in the case of an action requiring stockholder approval (such as, an action on which stockholders would be entitled to vote if the action were taken at a duly held stockholders' meeting).

(2) For purposes of the stockholder approval required by this paragraph (c), ordinarily, a plan is adopted when it is approved by the granting corporation's board of directors, and the date of the board's action is the reference point for determining whether stockholder approval occurs within the applicable 24-month period. However, if the board's action is subject to a condition (such as stockholder approval) or the happening of a particular event, the plan is adopted on the date the condition is met or the event occurs, unless the board's resolution fixes the date of adoption as the date of the board's action.

(3) An employee stock purchase plan, as adopted and approved, must designate the maximum aggregate number of shares that may be issued under the plan, and the corporations or class of corporations whose employees may be offered options under the plan. A plan that merely provides that the number of shares that may be issued under the plan may not exceed a stated percentage of the shares outstanding at the time of each offering or grant under the plan does not satisfy the requirements of this paragraph (c)(3). However, the maximum aggregate number of shares that may be issued under the plan may be stated in terms of a percentage of the authorized, issued, or outstanding shares on the date of the adoption of the plan. The plan may specify that the maximum aggregate number of shares available for grants under the plan may increase annually by a specified percentage of the authorized, issued, or outstanding shares on the date of the adoption of the plan. A plan that provides that the maximum aggregate number of shares that may be issued as options under the plan may change based on any other specific circum-

>>>→ *Caution: Reg. §1.423-2, below, as amended by T.D. 9471, is applicable to statutory options granted on or after January 1, 2010.*

stances satisfies the requirements of this paragraph only if the stockholders approve an immediately determinable maximum number of shares that may be issued under the plan in any event. If there is more than one employee stock purchase plan under which options may be granted and stockholders of the granting corporation merely approve a maximum aggregate number of shares that are available for issuance under the plans, the stockholder approval requirements described in paragraph (c)(1) of this section are not satisfied. A separate maximum aggregate number of shares available for issuance pursuant to options must be specified and approved for each plan.

(4) Once an employee stock purchase plan is approved by the stockholders of the granting corporation, the plan need not be reapproved by the stockholders of the granting corporation unless the plan is amended or changed in a manner that is considered the adoption of a new plan, in which case the plan must be reapproved within the prescribed 24-month period. Any increase in the aggregate number of shares that may be issued under the plan (other than an increase merely reflecting a change in the number of outstanding shares, such as a stock dividend or stock split) will be considered the adoption of a new plan requiring stockholder approval within the prescribed 24-month period. Similarly, a change in the designation of corporations whose employees may be offered options under the plan will be considered the adoption of a new plan requiring stockholder approval within the prescribed 24-month period unless the plan provides that designations of participating corporations may be made from time to time from among a group consisting of the granting corporation and its related corporations. The group from among which such changes and designations are permitted without additional stockholder approval may include corporations having become parents or subsidiaries of the granting corporation after the adoption and approval of the plan. In addition, a change in the granting corporation or the stock available for purchase under the plan will be considered the adoption of a new plan requiring stockholder approval within the prescribed 24-month period. Any other changes in the terms of an employee stock purchase plan are not considered the adoption of a new plan and, thus, do not require stockholder approval.

(5) *Examples.*—The following examples illustrate the principles of this paragraph (c):

Example 1. (i) Corporation E is a subsidiary of Corporation F, a publicly traded corporation. On January 1, 2010, E adopts an employee stock purchase plan under which options for E stock are granted to E employees.

(ii) To meet the requirements of paragraph (c)(1) of this section, the plan must be approved by the stockholders of E (in this case, F) within 12 months before or after January 1, 2010.

(iii) Assume the same facts as in paragraph (i) of this *Example 1*, except that the plan was approved by the stockholders of E (in this case, F) on March 1, 2010. On January 1, 2012, E changes the plan to provide that options for F stock will be granted to E employees under the plan. Because there is a change in the stock available for grant under the plan, under paragraph (c)(4) of this section, the change is considered the adoption of a new plan that must be approved by the stockholders of E (in this case, F) within 12 months before or after January 1, 2012.

Example 2. (i) Assume the same facts as in paragraph (i) of *Example 1*, except that on March 15, 2011, F completely disposes of its interest in E. Thereafter, E continues to grant options for E stock to E employees under the plan.

(ii) The new E options are granted under a plan that meets the stockholder approval requirements of paragraph (c)(1) of this section without regard to whether E seeks approval of the plan from the stockholders of E after F disposes of its interest in E.

(iii) Assume the same facts as in paragraph (i) of this *Example 2*, except that under the plan as adopted on January 1, 2010, only options for F stock are granted to E employees. Assume further that, after F disposes of its interest in E, E changes the plan to provide for the grant of options for E stock to E employees. Because there is a change in the stock available for purchase or grant under the plan, under paragraph (c)(4) of this section, the stockholders of E must approve the plan within 12 months before or after the change to the plan to meet the *stockholder approval requirements of paragraph (c)* of this section.

Example 3. (i) Corporation G maintains an employee stock purchase plan providing options for G stock. Corporation H does not maintain an employee stock purchase plan. On May 15, 2010, G and H consolidate under State law to form one corporation. The new corporation is named Corporation H. The consolidation agreement describes the G plan, including the maximum aggregate number of shares available for issuance under the plan after the consolidation. Additionally, the consolidation agreement states that the plan will be continued by H after the consolidation. The consolidation agreement

is approved by the stockholders of G and H on May 1, 2010. H assumes the plan formerly maintained by G and continues to grant options under the plan to all eligible employees, but the options are for H stock.

(ii) Because there is a change in the granting corporation (from G to H) and the stock available for purchase, under paragraph (c)(4) of this section, H is considered to have adopted a new plan. Because the plan is fully described in the consolidation agreement, including the maximum aggregate number of shares available for issuance under the plan, the approval of the consolidation agreement by the stockholders constitutes approval of the plan. Thus, the stockholder approval of the consolidation agreement satisfies the stockholder approval requirements of paragraph (c)(1) of this section, and the plan is considered to be adopted by H and approved by its stockholders on May 1, 2010.

Example 4. Corporation I adopts an employee stock purchase plan on November 1, 2010. On that date, there are two million shares of I stock outstanding. The plan provides that the maximum aggregate number of shares that may be issued under the plan may not exceed 15 percent of the number of shares of I stock outstanding on November 1, 2010. Because the maximum aggregate number of shares that may be issued under the plan is designated in the plan, the requirements of paragraph (c)(3) of this section are met.

Example 5. (i) Corporation J adopts an employee stock purchase plan on March 15, 2010. The plan provides that the maximum aggregate number of shares of J stock available for issuance under the plan is 50,000, increased on each anniversary date of the adoption of the plan by 5 percent of the then outstanding shares. Because the maximum aggregate number of shares is not designated under the plan, the requirements of paragraph (c)(3) of this section are not met.

(ii) Assume the same facts as in paragraph (i) of this *Example 5*, except that the plan provides that the maximum aggregate number of shares available under the plan is the lesser of (a) 50,000 shares, increased each anniversary date of the adoption of the plan by 5 percent of the then-outstanding shares, or (b) 200,000 shares. Because the maximum aggregate number of shares that may be issued under the plan is designated as the lesser of two numbers, one of which provides an immediately determinable maximum aggregate number of shares that may be issued under the plan in any event, the requirements of paragraph (c)(3) of this section are met.

(d) *Options granted to certain shareholders.*—(1) An employee stock purchase plan or offering must, by its terms, provide that an employee cannot be granted an option if the employee, immediately after the option is granted, owns stock possessing 5 percent or more of the total combined voting power or value of all classes of stock of the employer corporation or a related corporation. In determining whether the stock ownership of an employee equals or exceeds this 5 percent limit, the rules of section 424(d) (relating to attribution of stock ownership) shall apply, and stock that the employee may purchase under outstanding options (whether or not the options qualify for the special tax treatment afforded by section 421(a)) shall be treated as stock owned by the employee. An option is outstanding for purposes of this paragraph (d) although under its terms it may be exercised only in installments or after the expiration of a fixed period of time. If an option is granted to an employee whose stock ownership (as determined under this paragraph (d)) exceeds the limitation set forth in this paragraph (d), no portion of the option will be treated as having been granted under an employee stock purchase plan.

(2) The determination of the percentage of the total combined voting power or value of all classes of stock of the employer corporation (or a related corporation) that is owned by the employee is made by comparing the voting power or value of the shares owned (or treated as owned) by the employee to the aggregate voting power or value of all shares actually issued and outstanding immediately after the grant of the option to the employee. The aggregate voting power or value of all shares actually issued and outstanding immediately after the grant of the option does not include the voting power or value of treasury shares or shares authorized for issue under outstanding options held by the employee or any other person.

(3) *Examples.*—The following examples illustrate the principles of this paragraph (d):

Example 1. Employee V, an employee of Corporation K, owns 6,000 shares of K common stock, the only class of K stock outstanding. K has 100,000 shares of its common stock outstanding. Because V owns 6 percent of the combined voting power or value of all classes of K stock, K cannot grant an option to V under K's employee stock purchase plan. If V's father and brother each owned 3,000 shares of K stock and V did not own any K stock, then the result would be the same because, under section 424(d), an individual is treated as owning stock held by the person's father and brother. Similarly, the result would be the same if, instead of actually owning 6,000 shares, V merely held an option on 6,000 shares of K stock, irrespective of

➤➤➤ *Caution: Reg. §1.423-2, below, as amended by T.D. 9471, is applicable to statutory options granted on or after January 1, 2010.*

whether the transfer of stock under the option could qualify for the special tax treatment of section 421, because this paragraph (d) provides that stock the employee may purchase under outstanding options is treated as stock owned by such employee.

Example 2. Assume the same facts as in *Example 1*, except that K is a 50 percent subsidiary corporation of Corporation L. Irrespective of whether V owns any L stock, V cannot receive an option from L under L's employee stock purchase plan because he owns 5 percent of the total combined voting power of all classes of stock of a subsidiary of L, in this example, K. An employee who owns (or is treated as owning) stock in excess of the limitation of this paragraph (d), in any corporation in a group of related corporations, consisting of a parent and its subsidiary corporations, cannot receive an option under an employee stock purchase plan from any corporation in the group.

Example 3. Employee U is an employee of Corporation M. M has only one class of stock, of which 100,000 shares are issued and outstanding. Assuming U does not own (and is not treated as owning) any stock in M or in any related corporation of M, M may grant an option to U under its employee stock purchase plan for 4,999 shares, because immediately after the grant of the option, U would not own 5 percent or more of the combined voting power or value of all classes of M stock actually issued and outstanding at such time. The 4,999 shares that U would be treated as owning under this paragraph (d) would not be added to the 100,000 shares actually issued and outstanding immediately after the grant for purposes of determining whether U's stock ownership exceeds the limitation of this paragraph (d).

Example 4. Assume the same facts as in *Example 3* but instead of an option for 4,999 shares, M grants U an option, purportedly under its employee stock purchase plan, for 5,000 shares. No portion of this option will be treated as granted under an employee stock purchase plan because U's stock ownership exceeds the limitation of this paragraph (d).

(e) *Employees covered by plan.*—(1) Subject to the provisions of this paragraph (e) and the limitations of paragraphs (d), (f) and (i) of this section, an employee stock purchase plan or offering must, by its terms, provide that options are to be granted to all employees of any corporation whose employees are granted any of such options by reason of their employment by that corporation, except that one or more of the following categories of employees may be excluded from the coverage of the plan or offering—

(i) Employees who have been employed less than two years;

(ii) Employees whose customary employment is 20 hours or less per week;

(iii) Employees whose customary employment is for not more than five months in any calendar year; and

(iv) Highly compensated employees (within the meaning of section 414(q)).

(2) A plan or offering does not fail to satisfy the coverage provision of paragraph (e)(1) of this section in the following circumstances—

(i) The plan or offering excludes employees who have completed a shorter period of service or whose customary employment is for fewer hours per week or fewer months in a calendar year than is specified in paragraphs (e)(1)(i), (ii) and (iii) of this section, provided the exclusion is applied in an identical manner to all employees of every corporation whose employees are granted options under the plan or offering.

(ii) The plan or offering excludes highly compensated employees (within the meaning of section 414(q)) with compensation above a certain level or who are officers or subject to the disclosure requirements of section 16(a) of the Securities Exchange Act of 1934, provided the exclusion is applied in an identical manner to all highly compensated employees of every corporation whose employees are granted options under the plan or offering.

(3) Notwithstanding paragraph (e)(1) of this section, employees who are citizens or residents of a foreign jurisdiction (without regard to whether they are also citizens of the United States or resident aliens (within the meaning of section 7701(b)(1)(A))) may be excluded from the coverage of an employee stock purchase plan or offering under the following circumstances—

(i) The grant of an option under the plan or offering to a citizen or resident of the foreign jurisdiction is prohibited under the laws of such jurisdiction; or

(ii) Compliance with the laws of the foreign jurisdiction would cause the plan or offering to violate the requirements of *section 423.*

(4) No option granted under a plan or offering that excludes from participation any employees, other than those who may be excluded under this paragraph (e), and those barred from participation by reason of paragraphs (d), (f) and (i) of this section, can be

regarded as having been granted under an employee stock purchase plan. If an option is not granted to any employee who is entitled to the grant of an option under the terms of the plan or offering, none of the options granted under such offering will be treated as having been granted under an employee stock purchase plan. However, a plan that, by its terms, permits all eligible employees to elect to participate in an offering will not violate the requirements of this paragraph solely because eligible employees who elect not to participate in the offering are not granted options pursuant to such offering.

(5) For purposes of this paragraph (e), the existence of the employment relationship between an individual and the corporation participating under the plan will be determined under § 1.421-1(h).

(6) *Examples.*—The following examples illustrate the principles of this paragraph (e):

Example 1. Corporation N has a stock purchase plan that meets all the requirements of paragraphs (a)(2) and (a)(3) of this section except that options are not required to be granted to employees whose weekly rate of pay is less than $1,000. As a matter of corporate practice, however, N grants options under its plan to all employees, irrespective of their weekly rate of pay. Even though N's plan is operated in compliance with the requirements of this paragraph (e), N's plan is not an employee stock purchase plan because the terms of the plan exclude a category of employees that is not permitted under this paragraph (e).

Example 2. Assume the same facts as in *Example 1*, except that the first offering under N's plan provides that options will be granted to all employees of N. The terms of the first offering will be treated as part of the terms of N's plan, but only for purposes of the first offering. Because the terms of the first offering satisfy the requirements of this paragraph (e), stock transferred pursuant to options exercised under the first offering will be treated as stock transferred pursuant to the exercise of options granted under an employee stock purchase plan for purposes of section 421.

Example 3. Corporation O has a stock purchase plan that excludes from participation all employees who have been employed less than one year. Assuming all other requirements of paragraphs (a)(2) and (a)(3) of this section are satisfied, O's plan qualifies as an employee stock purchase plan under section 423.

Example 4. Corporation P has a stock purchase plan that excludes from participation clerical employees who have been employed less than two years. However, non-clerical employees with less than two years of service are permitted to participate in the plan. P's plan is not an employee stock purchase plan because the exclusion of employees who have been employed less than two years applies only to certain employees of P and is not applied in an identical manner to all employees of P. If, instead, P's plan excludes from participation all employees (both clerical and non-clerical) who have been employed less than two years, then P's plan would qualify as an employee stock purchase plan under section 423 assuming all other requirements of paragraphs (a)(2) and (a)(3) of this section are satisfied.

Example 5. Corporation Q has a stock purchase plan that excludes from participation all officers who are highly compensated employees (within the meaning of section 414(q)). Assuming all other requirements of paragraphs (a)(2) and (a)(3) of this section are satisfied, Q's plan qualifies as an employee stock purchase plan under section 423.

Example 6. Corporation R maintains an employee stock purchase plan that excludes from participation all highly compensated employees (within the meaning of section 414(q)), except highly compensated employees who are officers of R. R's plan is not an employee stock purchase plan because the exclusion of all highly compensated employees except highly compensated employees who are officers of R is not a permissible exclusion under paragraph (e)(2)(ii) of this section.

Example 7. Corporation S is the parent corporation of Subsidiary YY and Subsidiary ZZ. S maintains an employee stock purchase plan with both YY and ZZ participating in the same offering under the plan. Under the terms of the offering under the plan, all employees of YY and ZZ are permitted to participate in the plan with the exception of ZZ's highly compensated employees with annual compensation greater than $300,000. None of the options granted under the offering will be considered granted under an employee stock purchase plan because the exclusion of highly compensated employees with annual compensation greater than $300,000 is not applied in an identical manner to all employees of YY and ZZ granted options in the same offering.

Example 8. Assume the same facts as in *Example 7*, except that Corporation S establishes separate offerings under the plan for YY and ZZ. Under the terms of the separate offering for YY, all employees of YY are permitted to participate in the plan. Under the terms of the separate offering established for ZZ, all employees of ZZ are permitted to participate in the plan with the exception of ZZ's highly

>>>→ *Caution: Reg. §1.423-2, below, as amended by T.D. 9471, is applicable to statutory options granted on or after January 1, 2010.*

compensated employees with annual compensation greater than $300,000. The options granted under the separate offering for YY will be considered granted under an employee stock purchase plan. Further, the options granted under the separate offering for ZZ will be considered granted under an employee stock purchase plan because the exclusion of highly compensated employees with annual compensation greater than $300,000 is applied in an identical manner to all employees of ZZ granted options in the same offering.

Example 9. The laws of Country A require that options granted to residents of Country A be transferable during the lifetime of the option recipient. Corporation T has a stock purchase plan that excludes residents of Country A from participation in the plan. Because compliance with the laws of Country A would cause options granted to residents of Country A to violate paragraph (j) of this section, T may exclude residents of Country A from participation in the plan. Assuming all other requirements of paragraph (a)(2) of this section are satisfied, T's plan qualifies as an employee stock purchase plan under section 423.

(f) *Equal rights and privileges.*—(1) Except as otherwise provided in paragraphs (f)(2) through (f)(6) of this section, an employee stock purchase plan or offering must, by its terms, provide that all employees granted options under the plan or offering shall have the same rights and privileges. Thus, the provisions applying to one option under an offering (such as the provisions relating to the method of payment for the stock and the determination of the purchase price per share) must apply to all other options under the offering in the same manner. If all the options granted under a plan or offering do not, by their terms, give the respective optionees the same rights and privileges, none of the options will be treated as having been granted under an employee stock purchase plan for purposes of section 421.

(2) The requirements of this paragraph (f) do not prevent the maximum amount of stock that an employee may purchase from being determined on the basis of a uniform relationship to the total compensation, or the basic or regular rate of compensation, of all employees.

(3) A plan or offering will not fail to satisfy the requirements of this paragraph (f) because the plan or offering provides that no employee may purchase more than a maximum amount of stock fixed under the plan or offering.

(4) A plan or offering will not fail to satisfy the requirements of this paragraph (f) if, in order to comply with the laws of a foreign jurisdiction, the terms of an option granted under a plan or offering to citizens or residents of such foreign jurisdiction (without regard to whether they are also citizens of the United States or resident aliens (within the meaning of section 7701(b)(1)(A))) are less favorable than the terms of options granted under the same plan or offering to employees resident in the United States.

(5)(i) Except as provided in this paragraph and paragraph (f)(5)(ii) of this section, a plan or offering permitting one or more employees to carry forward amounts that were withheld but not applied toward the purchase of stock under an earlier plan or offering and apply the amounts towards the purchase of additional stock under a subsequent plan or offering will be a violation of the equal rights and privileges under paragraph (f)(1) of this section. However, the carry forward of amounts withheld but not applied toward the purchase of stock under an earlier plan or offering will not violate the equal rights and privileges requirement of paragraph (f)(1) of this section, if all other employees participating in the current plan or offering are permitted to make direct payments toward the purchase of shares under a subsequent plan or offering in an amount equal to the excess of the greatest amount which any employee is allowed to carry forward from an earlier plan or offering over the amount, if any, the employee will carry forward from an earlier plan or offering.

(ii) A plan or offering will not fail to satisfy the requirements of this section merely because employees are permitted to carry forward amounts representing a fractional share, that were withheld but not applied toward the purchase of stock under an earlier plan or offering and apply the amounts toward the purchase of additional stock under a subsequent plan or offering.

(6) Paragraph (f) does not prohibit the delaying of the grant of an option to any employee who is barred from being granted an option solely by reason of the employee's failing to meet a minimum service requirement set forth in paragraph (e)(1) of this section until the employee meets such requirement.

(7) *Examples.*—The following examples illustrate the principles of this paragraph (f):

Example 1. Corporation U has an employee stock purchase plan that provides that the maximum amount of stock that each employee may purchase under the offering is one share for each $100 of annual gross pay. The plan meets the requirements of this paragraph (f).

Example 2. Corporation V has an employee stock purchase plan that provides that the maximum amount of stock that each employee may purchase under the offering is one share for each $100 of annual gross pay up to and including $10,000, and two shares for each $100 of annual gross pay in excess of $10,000. The plan will not meet the requirements of this paragraph (f) because the amount of stock that may be purchased under the plan is not based on a uniform relationship to the total compensation of all employees.

Example 3. Corporation W has an employee stock purchase plan that provides that options to purchase stock in an amount equal to ten percent of an employee's annual salary at a price equal to 85 percent of the fair market value on the first day of the offering will be granted to all employees other than those who have been employed less than 18 months. In addition, the plan provides that employees who have not yet met the minimum service requirements on the first day of the offering will be granted similar options on the date the 18 month service requirement has been attained. The plan meets the requirements of this paragraph (f).

Example 4. Corporation X is the parent corporation of Subsidiary AA, Subsidiary BB and Subsidiary CC. X maintains an employee stock purchase plan with AA, BB and CC participating in the same offering under the plan. Under the terms of the offering under the plan, options to purchase stock at a price equal to 90 percent of the fair market value at the time the option is exercised will be granted to all employees. Certain employees of AA are residents of Country B. The laws of Country B provide that options granted to employees who are residents of Country B must have a purchase price not less than 95 percent of the fair market value at the time the option is exercised. The plan will not fail to satisfy the requirements of this paragraph (f) merely because the residents of Country B are granted options under the plan to purchase stock at a price equal to 95 percent of the fair market value at the time the option is exercised.

Example 5. Assume the same facts as in *Example 4*, except that Corporation X establishes two separate offerings under the plan: a separate offering for the employees of AA and a separate offering for the employees of BB and CC. Under the separate offering for the employees of BB and CC, options are granted to all employees with an exercise price equal to 90 percent of the fair market value at the time the option is exercised. Under the separate offering for the employees of AA, options are granted to all employees with an exercise price equal to 95 percent of the fair market value at the time the option is exercised. The plan does not violate the equal rights and privileges requirement of this paragraph (f) merely because the exercise price of options granted under one offering is less than the exercise price of options granted under a separate offering.

Example 6. Corporation Y maintains an employee stock purchase plan. Employee T is employed by Y. T is granted an option under the current offering to purchase a maximum of 100 shares of Y stock at an option price equal to 85 percent of the fair market value of the stock at exercise. The plan permits the carry forward of withheld but unused amounts from an earlier offering. Prior to the exercise date, $2000 of T's salary has been withheld and is available to be applied toward the purchase of Y stock. On the exercise date, the fair market value of Y stock is $20 per share. T is able to purchase 100 shares of Y stock at $17 per share for an aggregate purchase price of $1700. T can carry forward $300 to the subsequent offering. Each employee in the subsequent offering other than T will be permitted to make direct payments toward the purchase of shares under the subsequent offering in a maximum amount of $300 less any amount the employee has carried forward from an earlier offering. The plan does not violate the equal rights and privileges requirement of this paragraph (f).

(g) *Option price.*—(1) An employee stock purchase plan or offering must, by its terms, provide that the option price will not be less than the lesser of—

(i) An amount equal to 85 percent of the fair market value of the stock at the time the option is granted, or

(ii) An amount that under the terms of the option may not be less than 85 percent of the fair market value of the stock at the time the option is exercised.

(2) For purposes of determining the option price, the fair market value of the stock may be determined in any reasonable manner, including the valuation methods permitted under §20.2031-2. However, the option price must meet the minimum pricing requirements of this paragraph (g). For general rules relating to the option price, see §1.421-1(e). For rules relating to the determination of when an option is granted, see §§1.421-1(c) and 1.423-2(h)(2). Any option that does not meet the minimum pricing requirements of this paragraph (g) will not be treated as an option granted under an employee stock purchase plan irrespective of whether the plan or offering satisfies those requirements. If an option that does not meet the minimum pricing requirements is granted to an employee who is entitled to the grant of an option under the terms of the plan or offering, and the employee is not granted an option under such offering that qualifies as an option granted under an employee stock purchase plan, the

>>>→ *Caution: Reg. §1.423-2, below, as amended by T.D. 9471, is applicable to statutory options granted on or after January 1, 2010.*

offering will not meet the requirements of paragraph (e) of this section. Accordingly, none of the options granted under the offering will be eligible for the special tax treatment of section 421.

(3) The option price may be stated either as a percentage or as a dollar amount. If the option price is stated as a dollar amount, then the requirement of this paragraph (g) can only be met by a plan or offering in which the price is fixed at not less than 85 percent of the fair market value of the stock at the time the option is granted. If the fixed price is less than 85 percent of the fair market value of the stock at grant, then the option cannot meet the requirement of this paragraph (g) even if a decline in the fair market value of the stock results in such fixed price being not less than 85 percent of the fair market value of the stock at the time the option is exercised, because that result was not certain to occur under the terms of the option.

(4) *Examples.*—The following examples illustrate the principles of this paragraph (g):

Example 1. Corporation Z has an employee stock purchase plan that provides that the option price will be 85 percent of the fair market value of the stock on the first day of the offering (which is the date of grant in this case), or 85 percent of the fair market value of the stock at exercise, whichever amount is the lesser. Upon the exercise of an option issued under Z's plan, Z agrees to accept an option price that is less than the minimum amount allowable under the terms of such plan. Notwithstanding that the option was issued under an employee stock purchase plan, the transfer of stock pursuant to the exercise of such option does not satisfy the requirement of this paragraph (g) and cannot qualify for the special tax treatment of section 421.

Example 2. Corporation AA has an employee stock purchase plan that provides that the option price is set at 85 percent of the fair market value of AA stock at exercise, but not less than $80 per share. On the first day of the offering (which is the date of grant in this case), the fair market value of AA stock is $100 per share. The option satisfies the requirement of this paragraph (g), and can qualify for the special tax treatment of section 421.

Example 3. Assume the same facts as in *Example 2*, except that the option price is set at 85 percent of the fair market value of AA stock at exercise, but not more than $80 per share. This option cannot satisfy the requirement of this paragraph (g) irrespective of whether, at the time the option is exercised, 85 percent of the fair market value of AA stock is $80 or less.

(h) *Option period.*—(1) An employee stock purchase plan or offering must, by its terms, provide that options granted under the plan cannot be exercised after the expiration of 27 months from the date of grant unless, under the terms of the plan or offering, the option price is not less than 85 percent of the fair market value of the stock at the time of the exercise of the option. If the option price is not less than 85 percent of the fair market value of the stock at the time the option is exercised, then the option period provided under the plan must not exceed five years from the date of grant. If the requirements of this paragraph (h) are not met by the terms of the plan or offering, then options issued under such plan or offering will not be treated as options granted under an employee stock purchase plan irrespective of whether the options, by their terms, are exercisable beyond the period allowable under this paragraph (h). An option that provides that the option price is not less than 85 percent of the fair market value of the stock at exercise may have an option period of 5 years irrespective of whether the fair market value of the stock at exercise is more or less than the fair market value of the stock at grant. However, if the option provides that the option price is 85 percent of the fair market value of the stock at exercise, but not more than some other fixed amount determined in accordance with the provisions of paragraph (g) of this section, then irrespective of the price paid on exercise, the option period must not be more than 27 months.

(2) Section 1.421-1(c) provides that, for purposes of §§1.421-1 through 1.424-1, the language "the date of the granting of the option" and the "time such option is granted," and similar phrases refer to the date or time when the granting corporation completes the corporate action constituting an offer of stock for sale to an individual under the terms and conditions of a statutory option. With respect to options granted under an employee stock purchase plan, the principles of §1.421-1(c) shall be applied without regard to the requirement that the minimum option price must be fixed or determinable in order for the corporate action constituting an offer of stock to be considered complete.

(3) The date of grant will be the first day of an offering if the terms of an employee stock purchase plan or offering designate a *maximum number of shares that may be purchased* by each employee during the offering. Similarly, the date of grant will be the first day of an offering if the terms of the plan or offering require the application of a formula to establish, on the first day of the offering, the maximum number of shares that may be purchased by each

employee during the offering. It is not required that an employee stock purchase plan or offering designate a maximum number of shares that may be purchased by each employee during the offering or incorporate a formula to establish a maximum number of shares that may be purchased by each employee during the offering. If the maximum number of shares that can be purchased under an option is not fixed or determinable until the date the option is exercised, then the date of exercise will be the date of grant of the option.

(4) *Examples.*—The following examples illustrate the principles of this paragraph (h):

Example 1. (i) Corporation BB has an employee stock purchase plan that provides that the option price will be the lesser of 85 percent of the fair market value of the stock on the first day of an offering or 85 percent of the fair market value of the stock on the last day of the offering. Options are exercised on the last day of the offering. One million shares of BB stock are reserved for issuance under the plan. The plan provides that no employee may be permitted to purchase stock under the plan at a rate that exceeds $25,000 in fair market value of the BB stock (determined on the date of grant) for each calendar year during which an option granted to the employee is outstanding. The terms of each option granted under an offering provide that a maximum of 500 shares may be purchased by the option recipient during the offering. Because the maximum number of shares that can be purchased under the option is fixed and determinable on the first day of the offering, the date of grant for the option is the first day of the offering.

(ii) Assume the same facts as in paragraph (i) of *Example 1,* except that BB's plan excludes all employees who have been employed less than 18 months. The plan provides that employees who have not yet met the minimum service requirements on the first day of an offering will be granted an option on the date the 18-month service requirement has been attained. With respect to those employees who have been employed less than 18 months on the first day of an offering, the date of grant for the option is the date the 18-month service requirement has been attained.

Example 2. Assume the same facts as in paragraph (i) of *Example 1*, except that the terms of each option granted do not provide that a maximum of 500 shares may be purchased by the option recipient during the offering. Notwithstanding the fixed number of shares reserved for issuance under the plan and the $25,000 limitation set forth in the plan, the maximum number of shares that can be purchased under the option is not fixed or determinable until the last day of the offering when the option is exercised. Therefore the date of grant for the option is the last day of the offering when the option is exercised.

Example 3. Corporation CC has an employee stock purchase plan that provides that the option price will be 85 percent of the fair market value of the stock on the last day of the offering. Options are exercised on the last day of the offering. Each offering under the plan begins on January 1 and ends on December 31 of the same calendar year. The terms of each option granted under an offering provide that the maximum number of shares that may be purchased by any employee during the offering equals $25,000 divided by the fair market value of the stock on the first day of the offering. The maximum number of shares that can be purchased under the option is fixed and determinable on the first day of the offering and therefore the date of grant for the option is the first day of the offering.

Example 4. Assume the same facts as in *Example 3* except that the terms of each option granted under an offering provide that the maximum number of shares that may be purchased by any employee during the offering equals 10 percent of the employee's annual salary (determined as of January 1 of the year in which the offering commences) divided by the fair market value of the stock on the first day of the offering. The maximum number of shares that can be purchased under the option is fixed and determinable on the first day of the offering and therefore the date of grant for the option is the first day of the offering.

(i) *Annual $25,000 limitation.*—(1) An employee stock purchase plan or offering must, by its terms, provide that no employee may be permitted to purchase stock under all the employee stock purchase plans of the employer corporation and its related corporations at a rate that exceeds $25,000 in fair market value of the stock (determined at the time the option is granted) for each calendar year in which any option granted to the employee is outstanding at any time. In applying the foregoing limitation—

(i) The right to purchase stock under an option accrues when the option (or any portion thereof) first becomes exercisable during the calendar year;

(ii) The right to purchase stock under an option accrues at the rate provided in the option, but in no case may such rate exceed $25,000 of fair market value of such stock (determined at the time such option is granted) for any one calendar year; and

>>>→ *Caution: Reg. §1.423-2, below, as amended by T.D. 9471, is applicable to statutory options granted on or after January 1, 2010.*

(iii) A right to purchase stock that has accrued under one option granted pursuant to the plan may not be carried over to any other option.

(2) If an option is granted under an employee stock purchase plan that satisfies the requirement of this paragraph (i), but the option gives the optionee the right to buy stock in excess of the maximum rate allowable under this paragraph (i), then no portion of the option will be treated as having been granted under an employee stock purchase plan. Furthermore, if the option was granted to an employee entitled to the grant of an option under the terms of the plan or offering, and the employee is not granted an option under the offering that qualifies as an option granted under an employee stock purchase plan, then the offering will not meet the requirements of paragraph (e) of this section. Accordingly, none of the options granted under the offering will be eligible for the special tax treatment of section 421.

(3) The limitation of this paragraph (i) applies only to options granted under employee stock purchase plans and does not limit the amount of stock that an employee may purchase under incentive stock options (as defined in section 422(b)) or any other stock options except those to which section 423 applies. Stock purchased under options to which section 423 does not apply will not limit the amount that an employee may purchase under an employee stock purchase plan, except for purposes of the 5-percent stock ownership provision of paragraph (d) of this section.

(4) Under the limitation of this paragraph (i), an employee may purchase up to $25,000 of stock (based on the fair market value of the stock at the time the option was granted) in each calendar year during which an option granted to the employee under an employee stock purchase plan is outstanding. Alternatively, an employee may purchase more than $25,000 of stock (based on the fair market value of such stock at the time the option was granted) in a calendar year, so long as the total amount of stock that the employee purchases does not exceed $25,000 in fair market value of the stock (determined at the time the option was granted) for each calendar year in which any option was outstanding. If, in any calendar year, the employee holds two or more outstanding options granted under employee stock purchase plans of the employer corporation, or a related corporation, then the employee's purchases of stock attributable to that year under all options granted under employee stock purchase plans must not exceed $25,000 in fair market value of the stock (determined at the time the options were granted). Under an employee stock purchase plan, an employee may not purchase stock in anticipation that the option will be outstanding in some future year. Thus, the employee may purchase only the amount of stock that does not exceed the limitation of this paragraph (i) for the year of the purchase and for preceding years during which the option was outstanding. Thus, the amount of stock that may be purchased under an option depends on the number of years in which the option is actually outstanding. The amount of stock that may be purchased under an employee stock purchase plan may not be increased by reason of the failure to grant an option in an earlier year under such plan, or by reason of the failure to exercise an earlier option. For example, if an option is granted to an individual and expires without having been exercised at all, then the failure to exercise the option does not increase the amount of stock which such individual may be permitted to purchase under an option granted in a year following the year of such expiration. If an option granted under an employee stock purchase plan is outstanding in more than one calendar year, then stock purchased pursuant to the exercise of such an option will be applied first, to the extent allowable under this paragraph (i), against the $25,000 limitation for the earliest year in which the option was outstanding, then, against the $25,000 limitation for each succeeding year, in order.

(5) *Examples.*—The following examples illustrate the principles of this paragraph (i):

Example 1. Assume that Corporation DD maintains an employee stock purchase plan and that Employee S is employed by DD. On June 1, 2010, DD grants S an option under the plan to purchase a total of 750 shares of DD stock at $85 per share. On that date, the fair market value of DD stock is $100 per share. The option provides that it may be exercised at any time but cannot be exercised after May 31, 2012. Under this paragraph (i), the option must not permit S to purchase more than 250 shares of DD stock during the calendar year 2010, because 250 shares are equal to $25,000 in fair market value of DD stock determined at the time of grant. During the calendar year 2011, S may purchase under the option an amount of DD stock equal to the difference between $50,000 in fair market value of DD stock (determined at the time the option was granted) and the fair market value of DD stock (determined at the time of grant of the option) purchased during the year 2010. During the calendar year 2012, S may purchase an amount of DD stock equal to the difference between

$75,000 in fair market value of the stock (determined at the time of grant of the option) and the total amount of the fair market value of the stock (determined at the time of grant of the option) purchased under the option during the calendar years 2010 and 2011. S may purchase $25,000 of stock for the year 2010, and $25,000 of stock for the year 2012, although the option was outstanding for only a part of each of such years. However, S may not be granted another option under an employee stock purchase plan of DD or a related corporation to purchase stock of DD or a related corporation during the calendar years 2010, 2011, and 2012, so long as the option granted June 1, 2010, is outstanding.

Example 2. Assume the same facts as in *Example 1*, except that the option granted to S in 2010 is terminated in 2011 without any part of the option having been exercised, and that subsequent to the termination and during 2011, S is granted another option under DD's employee stock purchase plan. Under that option, S may be permitted to purchase $25,000 of stock for 2011. The failure of S to exercise the option granted to S in 2010, does not increase the amount of stock that S may be permitted to purchase under the option granted to S in 2011.

Example 3. Assume the same facts as in *Example 1*, except that, on May 31, 2012, S exercised the option granted to S in 2010, and purchased 600 shares of DD stock. Five hundred shares, the maximum amount of stock that could have been purchased in 2011, under the option, are treated as having been purchased for the years 2010 and 2011. Only 100 shares of the stock are treated as having been purchased for 2012. After S's exercise of the option on May 31, 2012, S is granted another option under DD's employee stock purchase plan. S may be permitted under the new option to purchase for 2012 stock having a fair market value of no more than $15,000 at the time the new option is granted.

Example 4. Corporation EE maintains an employee stock purchase plan and Employee R is employed by EE. On August 1, 2010, EE grants R an option under the plan to purchase 150 shares of EE stock at $85 per share during each of the calendar years 2010, 2011, and 2012. On that date, the fair market value of EE stock is $100 per share. The option provides that it may be exercised at any time during years 2010, 2011, and 2012. Because this option permits R to purchase only $15,000 of EE's stock for each year the option is outstanding, R could be granted another option by EE, or by a related corporation, in year 2010, permitting R to purchase an additional $10,000 of stock during each of the calendar years 2010, 2011, and 2012.

Example 5. Corporation FF maintains an employee stock purchase plan and Employee Q is employed by FF. On September 1, 2010, FF grants Q an option under the plan that will be automatically exercised on August 31, 2011, and August 31, 2012. The terms of the option provide that no more than 150 shares may be purchased on each date that the option is automatically exercised. On August 31, 2011, Q may purchase under the option an amount of FF stock equal to $50,000 in fair market value of FF stock (determined at the time the option was granted). On August 31, 2012, Q may purchase under the option an amount of FF stock equal to the difference between $75,000 in fair market value of FF stock (determined at the time the option was granted) and the fair market value of FF stock (determined at the time of grant of the option) purchased during year 2011.

(j) *Restriction on transferability.*—An employee stock purchase plan or offering must, by its terms, provide that options granted under the plan are not transferable by the optionee other than by will or the laws of descent and distribution, and must be exercisable, during the optionee's lifetime, only by the optionee. For general rules relating to the restriction on transferability required by this paragraph (j), see § 1.421-1(b)(2). For a limited exception to the requirement of this paragraph (j), see section 424(h)(3).

(k) *Special rule where option price is between 85 percent and 100 percent of value of stock.*—(1)(i) If all the conditions necessary for the application of section 421(a) exist, this paragraph (k) provides additional rules that are applicable in cases where, at the time the option is granted, the option price per share is less than 100 percent (but not less than 85 percent) of the fair market value of the share. In that case, upon the disposition of the share by the employee after the expiration of the two-year and the one-year holding periods, or upon the employee's death while owning the share (whether occurring before or after the expiration of such periods), there shall be included in the employee's gross income as compensation (and not as gain upon the sale or exchange of a capital asset) the lesser of—

(A) The amount, if any, by which the price paid under the option was exceeded by the fair market value of the share at the time the option was granted, or

(B) The amount, if any, by which the price paid under the option was exceeded by the fair market value of the share at the time of such disposition or death.

Reg. §1.423-2(k)(1)(i)(B)

➤➤➤ Caution: Reg. §1.423-2, below, as amended by T.D. 9471, is applicable to statutory options granted on or after January 1, 2010.

(ii) For purposes of applying the rules of this paragraph (k), if the option price is not fixed or determinable at the time the option is granted, the option price will be computed as if the option had been exercised at such time. The amount of compensation resulting from the application of this paragraph (k) shall be included in the employee's gross income for the taxable year in which the disposition occurs, or for the taxable year closing with the employee's death, whichever event results in the application of this paragraph (k).

(iii) The application of the special rules provided in this paragraph (k) shall not affect the rules provided in section 421(a) with respect to the employee exercising the option, the employer corporation, or a related corporation. Thus, notwithstanding the inclusion of an amount as compensation in the gross income of an employee, as provided in this paragraph (k), no income results to the employee at the time the stock is transferred to the employee, and no deduction under section 162 is allowable at any time to the employer corporation or a related corporation with respect to such amount.

(iv) If, during the employee's lifetime, the employee exercises an option granted under an employee stock purchase plan, but the employee dies before the stock is transferred to the employee pursuant to the exercise of the option, then for the purpose of sections 421 and 423, on the employee's death, the stock is deemed to be transferred immediately to the employee, and immediately thereafter, the employee is deemed to have transferred the stock to the employee's executor, administrator, trustee, beneficiary by operation of law, heir, or legatee, as the case may be.

(2) If the special rules provided in this paragraph (k) are applicable to the disposition of a share of stock by an employee, then the basis of the share in the employee's hands at the time of the disposition, determined under section 1011, shall be increased by an amount equal to the amount includible as compensation in the employee's gross income under this paragraph (k). However, the basis of a share of stock acquired after the death of an employee by the exercise of an option granted to the employee under an employee stock purchase plan shall be determined in accordance with the rules of section 421(c) and §1.421-2(c). If the special rules provided in this paragraph (k) are applicable to a share of stock upon the death of an employee, then the basis of the share in the hands of the estate or the person receiving the stock by bequest or inheritance shall be determined under section 1014 or under section 1022, if applicable, and shall not be increased by reason of the inclusion upon the decedent's death of any amount in the decedent's gross income under this paragraph (k). See *Example (9)* of this paragraph (k) with respect to the determination of basis of the share in the hands of a surviving joint owner.

(3) *Examples.*—The following examples illustrate the principles of this paragraph (k):

Example 1. On June 1, 2010, Corporation GG grants to Employee P, an employee of GG, an option under GG's employee stock purchase plan to purchase a share of GG stock for $85. The fair market value of GG stock on such date is $100 per share. On June 1, 2011, P exercises the option and on that date GG transfers the share of stock to P. On January 1, 2013, P sells the share for $150, its fair market value on that date. P's income tax return is filed on the basis of the calendar year. The income tax consequences to P and GG are as follows—

(i) Compensation in the amount of $15 is includible in P's gross income for the year 2013, the year of the disposition of the share. The $15 represents the difference between the option price ($85) and the fair market value of the share on the date the option was granted ($100), because the value is less than the fair market value of the share on the date of disposition ($150). For the purpose of computing P's gain or loss on the sale of the share, P's cost basis of $85 is increased by $15, the amount includible in P's gross income as compensation. Thus, P's basis for the share is $100. Because the share was sold for $150, P realizes a gain of $50, which is treated as long-term capital gain; and

(ii) GG is not entitled to any deduction under section 162 at any time with respect to the share transferred to P.

Example 2. Assume the same facts as in *Example 1,* except that P sells the share of GG stock on January 1, 2014, for $75, its fair market value on that date. Because $75 is less than the option price ($85), no amount in respect of the sale is includible as compensation in P's gross income for the year 2014. P's basis for determining gain or loss on the sale is $85. Because P sold the share for $75, P realized a loss of $10 on the sale that is treated as a long-term capital loss.

Example 3. Assume the same facts as in *Example 1,* except that the option provides that the option price shall be 90 percent of the fair market value of the stock on the day the option is exercised. On June 1, 2011, when the option is exercised, the fair market value of the stock is $120 per share so that P pays $108 for the share of the stock. Compensation in the amount of $10 is includible in P's gross income for the year 2013, the year of the disposition of the share. This is

determined in the following manner: the excess of the fair market value of the stock at the time of the disposition ($150) over the price paid for the share ($108) is $42; and the excess of the fair market value of the stock at the time the option was granted ($100) over the option price, computed as if the option had been exercised at such time ($90), is $10. Accordingly, $10, the lesser, is includible in gross income. In this situation, P's cost basis of $108 is increased by $10, the amount includible in P's gross income as compensation. Thus, P's basis for the share is $118. Because the share was sold for $150, P realizes a gain of $32 that is treated as long-term capital gain.

Example 4. Assume the same facts as in *Example 1,* except that the option provides that the option price shall be the lesser of 95 percent of the fair market value of the stock on the first day of the offering period and 95 percent of the fair market value of the stock on the day the option is exercised. On June 1, 2011, when the option is exercised, the fair market value of the stock is $120 per share. P pays $95 for the share of the stock. Compensation in the amount of $5 is includible in P's gross income for the year 2013, the year of the disposition of the share. This is determined in the following manner: the excess of the fair market value of the stock at the time of the disposition ($150) over the price paid for the share ($95) is $55; and the excess of the fair market value of the stock at the time the option was granted ($100) over the option price, computed as if the option had been exercised at such time ($95), is $5. Accordingly, $5, the lesser, is includible in gross income. In this situation, P's cost basis of $95 is increased by $5, the amount includible in P's gross income as compensation. Thus, P's basis for the share is $100. Because the share was sold for $150, P realizes a gain of $50 that is treated as long-term capital gain.

Example 5. Assume the same facts as in *Example 1,* except that instead of selling the share on January 1, 2013, P makes a gift of the share on that day. In that case $15 is includible as compensation in P's gross income for 2013. P's cost basis of $85 is increased by $15, the amount includible in P's gross income as compensation. Thus, P's basis for the share is $100, which becomes the donee's basis, as of the time of the gift, for determining gain or loss.

Example 6. Assume the same facts as in *Example 2,* except that instead of selling the share on January 1, 2014, P makes a gift of a share on that date. Because the fair market value of the share on that day ($75) is less than the option price ($85), no amount in respect of the disposition by way of gift is includible as compensation in P's gross income for 2014. P's basis for the share is $85, which becomes the donee's basis, as of the time of the gift, for the purpose of determining gain. The donee's basis for the purpose of determining loss, determined under section 1015(a), is $75 (fair market value of the share at the date of gift).

Example 7. Assume the same facts as in *Example 1,* except that after acquiring the share of stock on June 1, 2011, P dies on August 1, 2012, at which time the share has a fair market value of $150. Compensation in the amount of $15 is includible in P's gross income for the taxable year closing with P's death, $15 being the difference between the option price ($85) and the fair market value of the share when the option was granted ($100), because such value is less than the fair market value at date of death ($150). The basis of the share in the hands of P's estate is determined under section 1014 without regard to the $15 includible in the decedent's gross income.

Example 8. Assume the same facts as in *Example 7,* except that P dies on August 1, 2011, at which time the share has a fair market value of $150. Although P's death occurred within one year after the transfer of the share to P, the income tax consequences are the same as in *Example 7.*

Example 9. Assume the same facts as in *Example 1,* except that the share of stock was issued in the names of P and P's spouse jointly with right of survivorship, and that P and P's spouse sold the share on June 15, 2012, for $150, its fair market value on that date. Compensation in the amount of $15 is includible in P's gross income for the year 2012, the year of the disposition of the share. The basis of the share in the hands of P and P's spouse for the purpose of determining gain or loss on the sale is $100, that is, the cost of $85 increased by the amount of $15 includible as compensation in P's gross income. The gain of $50 on the sale is treated as long-term capital gain, and is divided equally between P and P's spouse.

Example 10. Assume the same facts as in *Example 1,* except that the share of stock was issued in the names of P and P's spouse jointly with right of survivorship, and that P predeceased P's spouse on August 1, 2012, at which time the share had a fair market value of $150. Compensation in the amount of $15 is includible in P's gross income for the taxable year closing with his death. See *Example 7.* The basis of the share in the hands of P's spouse as survivor is determined under section 1014 without regard to the $15 includible in the decedent's gross income.

Example 11. Assume the same facts as in *Example 10,* except that P's spouse predeceased P on July 1, 2012. Section 423(c) does not apply in respect of the death of P's spouse. Upon the subsequent

⟫⟶ *Caution:* Reg. §1.423-2, below, as amended by T.D. 9471, is applicable to statutory options granted on or after January 1, 2010.

death of P on August 1, 2012, the income tax consequences in respect of P's taxable year closing with the date of P's death, and in respect of the basis of the share in the hands of P's estate, are the same as in *Example 7*. If P had sold the share on July 15, 2012 (after the death of P's spouse), for $150, its fair market value at that time, the income tax consequences would be the same as in *Example 1*.

(l) *Effective/applicability date.*—The regulations under this section are effective on November 17, 2009. The regulations under this section apply to options granted under an employee stock purchase plan on or after January 1, 2010. The provisions of this section relating to section 1022 are effective on and after January 19, 2017. [Reg. §1.423-2.]

☐ [*T.D.* 6887, 6-23-66. *Amended by T.D.* 7645, 9-27-79; *T.D.* 7728, 10-31-80; *T.D.* 8235, 12-1-88; *T.D.* 9144, 8-2-2004, *T.D.* 9471, 11-16-2009 (*corrected* 12-21-2009) *and T.D.* 9811, 1-18-2017.]

[Reg. §1.424-1]

§1.424-1. Definitions and special rules applicable to statutory options.—(a) *Substitutions and assumptions of options.*—(1) *In general.*—(i) This paragraph (a) provides rules under which an *eligible corporation* (as defined in paragraph (a)(2) of this section) may, by reason of a *corporate transaction* (as defined in paragraph (a)(3) of this section), substitute a new statutory option (new option) for an outstanding statutory option (old option) or assume an old option without such substitution or assumption being considered a modification of the old option. For the definition of *modification*, see paragraph (e) of this section.

(ii) For purposes of §§1.421-1 through 1.424-1, the phrase "substituting or assuming a stock option in a transaction to which section 424 applies," "substituting or assuming a stock option in a transaction to which §1.424-1a) applies," and similar phrases means a substitution of a new option for an old option or an assumption of an old option that meets the requirements of this paragraph (a). For a substitution or assumption to qualify under this paragraph (a), the substitution or assumption must meet all of the requirements described in paragraphs (a)(4) and (a)(5) of this section.

(2) *Eligible corporation.*—For purposes of this paragraph (a), the term *eligible corporation* means a corporation that is the employer of the optionee or a related corporation of such corporation. For purposes of this paragraph (a), the determination of whether a corporation is the employer of the optionee or a related corporation of such corporation is based upon all of the relevant facts and circumstances existing immediately after the corporate transaction. See §1.421-1(h) for rules concerning the employment relationship.

(3) *Corporate transaction.*—For purposes of this paragraph (a), the term *corporate transaction* includes—

(i) A corporate merger, consolidation, acquisition of property or stock, separation, reorganization, or liquidation;

(ii) A distribution (excluding an ordinary dividend or a stock split or stock dividend described in §1.424-1(e)(4)(v)) or change in the terms or number of outstanding shares of such corporation; and

(iii) Such other corporate events prescribed by the Commissioner in published guidance.

(4) *By reason of.*—(i) For a change in an option or issuance of a new option to qualify as a substitution or assumption under this paragraph (a), the change must be made by an *eligible corporation* (as defined in paragraph (a)(2) of this section) and occur by reason of a *corporate transaction* (as defined in paragraph (a)(3) of this section).

(ii) Generally, a change in an option or issuance of a new option is considered to be by reason of a corporate transaction, unless the relevant facts and circumstances demonstrate that such change or issuance is made for reasons unrelated to such corporate transaction. For example, a change in an option or issuance of a new option will be considered to be made for reasons unrelated to a corporate transaction if there is an unreasonable delay between the corporate transaction and such change in the option or issuance of a new option, or if the corporate transaction serves no substantial corporate business purpose independent of the change in options. Similarly, a change in the number or price of shares purchasable under an option merely to reflect market fluctuations in the price of the stock purchasable under an option is not by reason of a corporate transaction.

(iii) A change in an option or issuance of a new option is by reason of a distribution or change in the terms or number of the outstanding shares of a corporation (as described in paragraph (a)(3)(ii) of this section) only if the option as changed, or the new option issued, is an option on the same stock as under the old option (or if such class of stock is eliminated in the change in capital structure, on other stock of the same corporation).

(5) *Other requirements.*—For a change in an option or issuance of a new option to qualify as a substitution or assumption under this paragraph (a), all of the requirements described in this paragraph (a)(5) must be met.

(i) In the case of an issuance of a new option (or a portion thereof) in exchange for an old option (or portion thereof), the optionee's rights under the old option (or portion thereof) must be canceled, and the optionee must lose all rights under the old option (or portion thereof). There cannot be a substitution of a new option for an old option within the meaning of this paragraph (a) if the optionee may exercise both the old option and the new option. It is not necessary to have a complete substitution of a new option for the old option. However, any portion of such option which is not substituted or assumed in a transaction to which this paragraph (a) applies is an outstanding option to purchase stock or, to the extent paragraph (e) of this section applies a modified option.

(ii) The excess of the aggregate fair market value of the shares subject to the new or assumed option immediately after the change in the option or issuance of a new option over the aggregate option price of such shares must not exceed the excess of the aggregate fair market value of all shares subject to the old option (or portion thereof) immediately before the change in the option or issuance of a new option over the aggregate option price of such shares.

(iii) On a share by share comparison, the ratio of the option price to the fair market value of the shares subject to the option immediately after the change in the option or issuance of a new option must not be more favorable to the optionee than the ratio of the option price to the fair market value of the stock subject to the old option (or portion thereof) immediately before the change in the option or issuance of a new option. The number of shares subject to the new or assumed option may be adjusted to compensate for any change in the aggregate spread between the aggregate option price and the aggregate fair market value of the shares subject to the option immediately after the change in the option or issuance of the new option as compared to the aggregate spread between the option price and the aggregate fair market value of the shares subject to the option immediately before the change in the option or issuance of the new option.

(iv) The new or assumed option must contain all terms of the old option, except to the extent such terms are rendered inoperative by reason of the corporate transaction.

(v) The new option or assumed option must not give the optionee additional benefits that the optionee did not have under the old option.

(6) *Obligation to substitute or assume not necessary.*—For a change in the option or issuance of a new option to meet the requirements of this paragraph (a), it is not necessary to show that the corporation changing an option or issuing a new option is under any obligation to do so. In fact, this paragraph (a) may apply even when the option that is being replaced or assumed expressly provides that it will terminate upon the occurrence of certain corporate transactions. However, this paragraph (a) cannot be applied to revive a statutory option which, for reasons not related to the corporate transaction, expires before it can properly be replaced or assumed under this paragraph (a).

(7) *Issuance of stock without meeting the requirements of this paragraph (a).*—A change in the terms of an option resulting in a modification of such option occurs if an optionee's new employer (or a related corporation of the new employer) issues its stock (or stock of a related corporation) upon exercise of such option without satisfying all of the requirements described in paragraphs (a)(4) and (5) of this section.

(8) *Date of grant.*—For purposes of applying the rules of this paragraph (a), a substitution or assumption is considered to occur on the date that the optionee would, but for this paragraph (a), be considered to have been granted the option that the eligible corporation is substituting or assuming. A substitution or an assumption that occurs by reason of a corporate transaction may occur before or after the corporate transaction.

(9) Any reasonable methods may be used to determine the fair market value of the stock subject to the option immediately before the assumption or substitution and the fair market value of the stock subject to the option immediately after the assumption or substitution. Such methods include the valuation methods described in §20.2031-2 of this chapter (the Estate Tax Regulations). In the case of stock listed on a stock exchange, the fair market value may be based on the last sale before and the first sale after the assumption or substitution if such sales clearly reflect the fair market value of the stock, or may be based upon an average selling price during a longer period, such as the day or week before, and the day or week after, the assumption or substitution. If the stocks are not listed, or if they are

newly issued, it will be reasonable to base the determination on experience over even longer periods. In the case of a merger, consolidation, or other reorganization which is arrived at by arm's-length negotiations, the fair market value of the stock subject to the option before and after the assumption or substitution may be based upon the values assigned to the stock for purposes of the reorganization. For example, if in the case of a merger the parties treat each share of the merged company as being equal in value to a share of the surviving company, it will be reasonable to assume that the stocks are of equal value so that the substituted option may permit the employee to purchase at the same price one share of the surviving company for each share he could have purchased of the merged company.

(10) *Examples.*—The principles of this paragraph (a) are illustrated by the following examples:

Example 1. Eligible corporation. X Corporation acquires a new subsidiary, Y Corporation, and transfers some of its employees to Y. Y Corporation wishes to grant to its new employees and to the employees of X Corporation new options for Y shares in exchange for old options for X shares that were previously granted by X Corporation. Because Y Corporation is an employer with respect to its own employees and a related corporation of X Corporation, Y Corporation is an eligible corporation under paragraph (a)(2) of this section with respect to both the employees of X and Y Corporations.

Example 2. Corporate transaction. (i) On January 1, 2004, Z Corporation grants E, an employee of Z, an option to acquire 100 shares of Z common stock. At the time of grant, the fair market value of Z common stock is $200 per share. E's option price is $200 per share. On July 1, 2005, when the fair market value of Z common stock is $400, Z declares a stock dividend of preferred stock distributed on common stock that causes the fair market value of Z common stock to decrease to $200 per share. On the same day, Z grants to E a new option to acquire 200 shares of Z common stock in exchange for E's old option. The new option has an exercise price of $100 per share.

(ii) A stock dividend other than that described in §1.424-1(e)(4)(v) is a corporate transaction under paragraph (a)(3)(ii) of this section. Generally, the issuance of a new option is considered to be by reason of a corporate transaction. None of the facts in this *Example 2* indicate that the new option is not issued by reason of the stock dividend. In addition, the new option is issued on the same stock as the old option. Thus, the substitution occurs by reason of the corporate transaction. Assuming the other requirements of this section are met, the issuance of the new option is a substitution that meets the requirements of this paragraph (a) and is not a modification of the option.

(iii) Assume the same facts as in paragraph (i) of this *Example 2.* Assume further that on December 1, 2005, Z declares an ordinary cash dividend. On the same day, Z grants E a new option to acquire Z stock in substitution for E's old option. Under paragraph (a)(3)(ii) of this section, an ordinary cash dividend is not a corporate transaction. Thus, the exchange of the new option for the old option does not meet the requirements of this paragraph (a) and is a modification of the option.

Example 3. Corporate transaction. On March 15, 2004, A Corporation grants E, an employee of A, an option to acquire 100 shares of A stock at $50 per share, the fair market value of A stock on the date of grant. On May 2, 2005, A Corporation transfers several employees, including E, to B Corporation, a related corporation. B Corporation arranges to purchase some assets from A on the same day as E's transfer to B. Such purchase is without a substantial business purpose independent of making the exchange of E's old options for the new options appear to be by reason of a corporate transaction. The following day, B Corporation grants to E, one of its new employees, an option to acquire shares of B stock in exchange for the old option held by E to acquire A stock. Under paragraph (a)(3)(i) of this section, the purchase of assets is a corporate transaction. Generally, the substitution of an option is considered to occur by reason of a corporate transaction. However, in this case, the relevant facts and circumstances demonstrate that the issuance of the new option in exchange for the old option occurred by reason of the change in E's employer rather than a corporate transaction and that the sale of assets is without a substantial corporate business purpose independent of the change in the options. Thus, the exchange of the new option for the old option is not by reason of a corporate transaction that meets the requirements of this paragraph (a) and is a modification of the old option.

Example 4. Corporate transaction. (i) E, an employee of Corporation A, holds an option to acquire 100 shares of Corporation A stock. On September 1, 2006, Corporation A has one class of stock outstanding and declares a stock dividend of one share of common stock for each outstanding share of common stock. The rights associated with the common stock issued as a dividend are the same as the rights under existing shares of stock. In connection with the stock dividend, E's option is exchanged for an otion to acquire 200 shares of Corpora-

tion A stock. The per-share exercise price is equal to one half of the per-share exercise price of the original option. The stock dividend merely changes the number of shares of Corporation A outstanding and effects no other change to the stock of Corporation A. The option is proportionally adjusted and the aggregate exercise price remains the same and therefore satisfies the requirements described in §1.424-1(e)(4)(v).

(ii) The stock dividend is not a corporate transaction under paragraph (a)(3) of this section, and the declaration of the stock dividend is not a modification of the old option under paragraph (a) of this section. Pursuant to §1.424-1(e)(4)(v), the exercise price of the old option may be adjusted proportionally with the change in the number of outstanding shares of Corporation A such that the ratio of the aggregate exercise price of the option to the number of shares covered by the option is the same both before and after the stock dividend. The adjustment of E's option is not treated as a modification of the option.

Example 5. Additional benefit. On June 1, 2004, P Corporation acquires 100 percent of the shares of S Corporation and issues a new option to purchase P shares in exchange for an old option to purchase S shares that is held by E, an employee of S. On the date of the exchange, E's old option is exercisable for 3 more years, and, after the exchange, E's new option is exercisable for 5 years. Because the new option is exercisable for an additional period of time beyond the time allowed under the old option, the effect of the exchange of the new option for the old option is to give E an additional benefit that E did not enjoy under the old option. Thus, the requirements of paragraph (a)(5) of this section are not met, and this paragraph (a) does not apply to the exchange of the new option for the old option. Therefore, the exchange is a modification of the old options.

Example 6. Spread and ratio tests. E is an employee of S Corporation. E holds an old option that was granted to E by S to purchase 60 shares of S at $12 per share. On June 1, 2005, S Corporation is merged into P Corporation, and on such date P issues a new option to purchase P shares in exchange for E's old option to purchase S shares. Immediately before the exchange, the fair market value of an S share is $32; immediately after the exchange, the fair market value of a P share is $24. The new option entitles E to buy P shares at $9 per share. Because, on a share-by-share comparison, the ratio of the new option price ($9 per share) to the fair market value of a P share immediately after the exchange ($24 per share) is not more favorable to E than the ratio of the old option price ($12 per share) to the fair market value of an S share immediately before the exchange ($32 per share) (9/24 = 12/32), the requirements of paragraph (a)(5)(iii) of this section are met. The number of shares subject to E's option to purchase P stock is set at 80. Because the excess of the aggregate fair market value over the aggregate option price of the shares subject to E's new option to purchase P stock, $1,200 (80 × $24 minus 80 × $9), is not greater than the excess of the aggregate fair market value over the aggregate option price of the shares subject to E's old option to purchase S stock, $1,200 (60 × $32 minus 60 × $12), the requirements of paragraph (a)(5)(ii) of this section are met.

Example 7. Ratio test and partial substitution. Assume the same facts as in *Example 6,* except that the fair market value of an S share immediately before the exchange of the new option for the old option is $8, that the option price is $10 per share, and that the fair market value of a P share immediately after the exchange is $12. P sets the new option price at $15 per share. Because, on a share-by-share comparison, the ratio of the new option price ($15 per share) to the fair market value of a P share immediately after the exchange ($12) is not more favorable to E than the ratio of the old option price ($10 per share) to the fair market value of an S share immediately before the substitution ($8 per share) (15/12 = 10/8), the requirements of paragraph (a)(5)(iii) of this section are met. Assume further that the number of shares subject to E's P option is set at 20, as compared to 60 shares under E's old option to buy S stock. Immediately after the exchange, 2 shares of P are worth $24, which is what 3 shares of S were worth immediately before the exchange (2 × $12 = 3 × $8). Thus, to achieve a complete substitution of a new option for E's old option, E would need to receive a new option to purchase 40 shares of P (*i.e.*, 2 shares of P for each 3 shares of S that E could have purchased under the old option (2/3 = 40/60)). Because E's new option is for only 20 shares of P, P has replaced only ¹/₂ of E's old option, and the other ¹/₂ is still outstanding.

Example 8. Partial substitution. X Corporation forms a new corporation, Y Corporation, by a transfer of certain assets and, in a spin-off, distributes the shares of Y Corporation to the stockholders of X Corporation. E, an employee of X Corporation, is thereafter an employee of Y. Y wishes to substitute a new option to purchase some of its stock for E's old option to purchase 100 shares of X. E's old option to purchase shares of X, at $50 a share, was granted when the fair market value of an X share was $50, and an X share was worth $100 just before the distribution of the Y shares to X's stockholders. Immediately after the spin-off, which is also the time of the substitution, each share of X and each share of Y is worth $50. Based on these facts, a new option to purchase 200 shares of Y at an option price of $25 per share could be granted to E in complete substitution of E's old option. In the alternative, it would also be permissible in connection with the spin off, to grant E a new option to purchase 100 shares of Y, at an option price of $25 per share, and for E to retain an option to purchase 100 shares of X under the old option, with the option price adjusted to $25. However, because X is no longer a related corporation with respect to Y, E must exercise the option for 100 shares of X within three months from the date of the spin off for the option to be treated as a statutory option. See §1.421-1(h). It would also be permissible to grant E a new option to purchase 100 shares of Y, at an option price of $25 per share, in substitution for E's right to purchase 50 of the shares under the old option.

Example 9. Stockholder approval requirements. (i) X Corporation, a publicly traded corporation, adopts an incentive stock option plan that meets the requirements of §1.422-2. Under the plan, options to acquire X stock are granted to X employees. X Corporation is acquired by Y Corporation and becomes a subsidiary corporation of Y Corporation. After the acquisition, X employees remain employees of X. In connection with the acquisition, Y Corporation substitutes new options to acquire Y stock for the old options to acquire X stock previously granted to the employees of X. As a result of this substitution, on exercise of the new options, X employees receive Y Corporation stock.

(ii) Because the requirements of §1.422-2 were met on the date of grant, the substitution of the new Y options for the old X options does not require new stockholder approval. If the other requirements of paragraphs (a)(4) and (5) of this section are met, the issuance of new options for Y stock in exchange for the old options for X stock meets the requirements of this paragraph (a) and is not a modification of the old options.

(iii) Assume the same facts as in paragraphs (i) and (ii) of this *Example 9.* Assume further that as part of the acquisition, X amends its plan to allow future grants under the plan to be grants to acquire Y stock. Because the amendment of the plan to allow options on a different stock is considered the adoption of a new plan under §1.422-2(b)(2)(iii), the stockholders of X (in this case, Y) must approve the plan within 12 months before or after the date of the amendment of the plan. If the stockholders of X (in this case, Y) timely approve the plan, the future grants to acquire Y stock will be incentive stock options (assuming the other requirements of §1.422-2 have been met).

Example 10. Modification. X Corporation merges into Y Corporation. Y Corporation retains employees of X who hold old options to acquire X Corporation stock. When the former employees of X exercise the old options, Y Corporation issues Y stock to the former employees of X. Under paragraph (a)(7) of this section, because Y issues its stock on exercise of the old options for X stock, there is a change in the terms of the old options for X stock. Thus, the issuance of Y stock on exercise of the old options is a modification of the old options.

Example 11. Eligible corporation. (i) D Corporation grants an option to acquire 100 shares of D Corporation stock to E, an employee of D Corporation. S Corporation is a subsidiary of D Corporation. On March 1, 2005, D Corporation spins off S Corporation. E remains an employee of D Corporation. In connection with the spin off, D Corporation substitutes a new option to acquire D Corporation stock and a new option to acquire S Corporation stock for the old option in a manner that meets the requirements of paragraph (a) of this section.

(ii) The substitution of the new option to acquire S and D stock for the old option to acquire D stock is not a modification of the old option. However, because S is no longer a related corporation with respect to D Corporation, E must exercise the option for S stock within three months from March 1, 2005, for the option to be treated as a statutory option. See §1.421-1(h).

(iii) Assume the same facts as in paragraph (i) of this *Example 11* except that E's employment with D Corporation is terminated on February 20, 2005. The substitution of the new option to acquire S and D stock for the old option to acquire D stock is not a modification of the old option. However, because the employment relationship between E and D Corporation terminated on February 20, 2005, E must exercise the option for the D and S stock within three months from February 20, 2005, for the option to be treated as a statutory option. See §1.421-1(h).

(b) *Acquisition of new stock.*—(1) Section 424(b) provides that the rules provided by sections 421 through 424 which are applicable with respect to stock transferred to an individual upon his exercise of an option, shall likewise be applicable with respect to stock acquired by a distribution or an exchange to which sections 305, 354, 355, 356, or 1036 (or so much of section 1031 as relates to section 1036) applies. Stock so acquired shall, for purposes of sections 421 through 424, be considered as having been transferred to the individual upon his exercise of the option. A similar rule shall be applied in the case of a series of such acquisitions. With respect to such acquisitions, section 424(b) does not make inapplicable any of the provisions of section 305, 354, 355, 356, or 1036 (or so much of section 1031 as relates to section 1036).

(2) The application of this paragraph may be illustrated by the following example:

Example. If, with respect to stock transferred pursuant to the timely exercise of a statutory option, there is a distribution of new stock to which section 305(a) is applicable, and if there is a disposition of such new stock before the expiration of the applicable holding period required with respect to the stock originally acquired pursuant to the exercise of such option, such disposition makes section 421 inapplicable to the transfer of the original stock pursuant to the exercise of the option to the extent that the disposition effects a reduction of the individual's total interest in the old and new stock. However, if the new stock, as well as the old stock, is not disposed of before the expiration of the holding period required with respect to the original stock acquired pursuant to the exercise of the option, the special tax treatment provided by section 421 is applicable to both the original shares and the shares acquired by virtue of the distribution to which section 305(a) applies.

(c) *Disposition of stock.*—(1) For purposes of section 421 through 424, the term "disposition of stock" includes a sale, exchange, gift, or any transfer of legal title, but does not include—

(i) A transfer from a decedent to his estate or a transfer by bequest or inheritance; or

(ii) An exchange to which is applicable section 354, 355, 356, or 1036 (or so much of section 1031 as relates to section 1036); or

(iii) A mere pledge or hypothecation.

(iv) A transfer between spouses or incident to divorce (described in section 1041(a)). The special tax treatment of §1.421-2(a) with respect to the transferred stock applies to the transferee. However, see §1.421-1(b)(2) for the treatment of the transfer of a statutory option incident to divorce.

However, a disposition of the stock pursuant to a pledge or hypothecation is a disposition by the individual, even though the making of the pledge or hypothecation is not such a disposition.

(2) A share of stock acquired by an individual pursuant to the exercise of a statutory option is not considered disposed of by the individual if such share is taken in the name of the individual and another person jointly with right of survivorship, or is subsequently transferred into such joint ownership, or is retransferred from such joint ownership to the sole ownership of the individual. However, any termination of such joint ownership (other than a termination effected by the death of a joint owner) is a disposition of such share, except to the extent the individual reacquires ownership of the share. For example, if such individual and his joint owner transfer such share to another person, the individual has made a disposition of such share. Likewise, if a share of stock held in the joint names of such individual and another person is transferred to the name of such other person, there is a disposition of such share by the individual. If an individual exercises a statutory option and a share of stock is transferred to another or is transferred to such individual in his name as trustee for another, the individual has made a disposition of such share. However, a termination of joint ownership resulting from the death of one of the owners is not a disposition of such share. For determination of basis in the hands of the survivor where joint ownership is terminated by the death of one of the owners, see section 1014 or section 1022, if applicable.

(3) If an optionee exercises an incentive stock option with statutory option stock and the applicable holding period requirements (under §1.422-1(a) or §1.423-1(a)) with respect to such statutory option stock are not met before such transfer, then sections 354, 355, 356, or 1036 (or so much of 1031 as relates to 1036) do not apply to determine whether there is a disposition of those shares. Therefore, there is a disposition of the statutory option stock, and the special tax treatment of §1.421-2(a) does not apply to such stock.

(4) The application of this paragraph may be illustrated by the following examples:

Example (1). On June 1, 2004, the X Corporation grants to E, an employee, a statutory option to purchase 100 shares of X Corporation stock at $100 per share, the fair market value of X Corporation stock on that date. On June 1, 2005, while employed by X Corporation, E exercises the option in full and pays X Corporation $10,000, and on that day X Corporation transfers to E 100 shares of its stock having a fair market value of $12,000. Before June 1, 2006, E makes no disposition of the 100 shares so purchased. E realizes no income on June 1, 2005, with respect to the transfer to him of the 100 shares of X Corporation stock. X Corporation is not entitled to any deduction at any time with respect to its transfer to E of the stock. E's basis for such 100 shares is $10,000.

Example (2). Assume the same facts as in example (1), except assume that on August 1, 2006, three years and two months after the transfer of the shares to him, E sells the 100 shares of X Corporation stock for $13,000 which is the fair market value of the stock on that date. For the taxable year in which the sale occurs, E realizes a gain of $3,000 ($13,000 minus E's basis of $10,000), which is treated as capital gain.

Example (3). Assume the same facts as in example (2), except assume that on August 1, 2006, E makes a gift of the 100 shares of Y Corporation stock to his son. Such disposition results in no realization of gain to E either for the taxable year in which the option is exercised or the taxable year in which the gift is made. E's basis of $10,000 becomes the donee's basis for determining gain or loss.

Example (4). Assume the same facts as in example (1), except assume that on May 1, 2006, E sells the 100 shares of X Corporation stock for $13,000. The special rules of section 421(a) are not applicable to the transfer of the stock by X Corporation to E, because disposition of the stock was made by E within two years from the date the options were granted and within one year of the date that the shares were transferred to him.

Example (5). Assume the same facts as in example (1), except assume that E dies on September 1, 2005, owning the 100 shares of X Corporation stock acquired by him pursuant to his exercise on June 1, 2005, of the statutory option. On the date of death, the fair market value of the stock is $12,500. No income is realized by E by reason of the transfer of the 100 shares to his estate. If the stock is valued as of the date of E's death for estate tax purposes, the basis of the 100 shares in the hands of the executor is $12,500.

Example (6). Assume the same facts as in example (1), except assume that on June 1, 2005, when the option is exercised by E the 100 shares are transferred by X to E and his wife W, as joint owners with right of survivorship, and that E dies on July 1, 2005. Neither the transfer into joint ownership nor the termination of such joint ownership by E's death is a disposition. Because E has made no disqualifying disposition of the shares, section 421(a) is applicable and E realizes no compensation income at death with respect to the shares even though he held the stock less than 2 years after the transfer of the shares to him pursuant to his exercise of the option. See § 1.421-2(b)(2).

Example (7). On January 1, 2004, X Corporation grants to E, an employee of X Corporation, an incentive stock option to purchase 100 shares of X Corporation stock at $100 per share (the fair market value of an X Corporation share on that date). On January 1, 2005, when the fair market value of a share of X Corporation stock is $200, E exercises half of the option, pays X Corporation $5,000 in cash, and is transferred 50 shares of X Corporation stock with an aggregate fair market value of $10,000. E makes no disposition of the shares before January 2, 2006. Under § 1.421-2(a), no income is recognized by E on the transfer of shares pursuant to the exercise of the incentive stock option and X Corporation is not entitled to any deduction at any time with respect to its transfer of the shares to E. E's basis in the shares is $5,000.

Example (8). Assume the same facts as in *Example 7*, except that on December 1, 2005, one year and 11 months after the grant of the option and 11 months after the transfer of the 50 shares to E, E uses 25 of those shares, with a fair market value of $5,000, to pay for the remaining 50 shares purchasable under the option. On that day, X Corporation transfers 50 of its shares, with an aggregate fair market value of $10,000, to E. Because E disposed of the 25 shares before the expiration of the applicable holding periods, § 1.421-2(a) does not apply to the January 1, 2005, transfer of the 25 shares used by E to exercise the remainder of the option. As a result of the disqualifying disposition of the 25 shares, E recognizes compensation income under the rules of § 1.421-2(b).

Example (9). On January 1, 2005, X Corporation grants an incentive stock option to E, an employee of X Corporation. The exercise price of the option is $10 per share. On June 1, 2005, when the fair market value of an X Corporation share is $20, E exercises the option and purchases 5 shares with an aggregate fair market value of $100. On January 1, 2006, when the fair market value of an X Corporation share is $50, X Corporation is acquired by Y Corporation in a section 368(a)(1)(A) reorganization. As part of the acquisition, all X Corporation shares are converted into Y Corporation shares. After the conversion, if an optionee holds a fractional share of Y Corporation stock, Y Corporation will purchase the fractional share for cash equal to its fair market value. After applying the conversion formula to the shares held by E, E has 10 ¹/₂ Y Corporation shares. Y Corporation purchases E's one-half share for $25, the fair market value of one-half of a Y Corporation share on the conversion date. Because E sells the one-half share prior to expiration of the holding periods described in § 1.422-1(a), the sale is a disqualifying disposition of the one-half share. Thus, in 2006, E must recognize compensation income of $5 (one-half of the fair market value of an X Corporation share on the date of exercise of the option, or $10, less one-half of the exercise price per share, or $5). For purposes of computing any additional gain, E's basis in the one-half share increases to $10 (reflecting the $5

included in income as compensation). E recognizes an additional gain of $15 ($25, the fair market value of the one-half share, less $10, the basis in such share). The extent to which the additional $15 of gain is treated as a redemption of Y Corporation stock is determined under section 302.

(d) *Attribution of stock ownership.*—To determine the amount of stock owned by an individual for purposes of applying the percentage limitations relating to certain stockholders described in § § 1.422-2(f) and 1.423-2(d), shares of the employer corporation or of a related corporation that are owned (directly or indirectly) by or for the individual's brothers and sisters (whether by the whole or half blood), spouse, ancestors, and lineal descendants, are considered to be owned by the individual. Also, for such purposes, if a domestic or foreign corporation, partnership, estate, or trust owns (directly or indirectly) shares of the employer corporation or of a related corporation, the shares are considered to be owned proportionately by or for the stockholders, partners, or beneficiaries of the corporation, partnership, estate, or trust. The extent to which stock held by the optionee as a trustee of a voting trust is considered owned by the optionee is determined under all of the facts and circumstances.

(e) *Modification, extension, or renewal of option.*—(1) This paragraph (e) provides rules for determining whether a share of stock transferred to an individual upon the individual's exercise of an option after the terms of the option have been changed is transferred pursuant to the exercise of a statutory option.

(2) Any modification, extension, or renewal of the terms of an option to purchase shares is considered the granting of a new option. The new option may or may not be a statutory option. To determine the date of grant of the new option for purposes of section 422 or 423, see § 1.421-1(c).

(3) If section 423(c) applies to an option then, in case of a modification, extension, or renewal of an option, the highest of the following values shall be considered to be the fair market value of the stock at the time of the granting of such option for purposes of applying the rules of sections 423(b)(6)—

(i) The fair market value on the date of the original granting of the option,

(ii) The fair market value on the date of the making of such modification, extension, or renewal, or

(iii) The fair market value at the time of the making of any intervening modification, extension, or renewal.

(4)(i) For purposes of § § 1.421-1 through 1.424-1 the term *modification* means any change in the terms of the option (or change in the terms of the plan pursuant to which the option was granted or in the terms of any other agreement governing the arrangement) that gives the optionee additional benefits under the option regardless of whether the optionee in fact benefits from the change in terms. In contrast, for example, a change in the terms of the option shortening the period during which the option is exercisable is not a modification. However, a change providing an extension of the period during which an option may be exercised (such as after termination of employment) or a change providing an alternative to the exercise of the option (such as a stock appreciation right) is a modification regardless of whether the optionee in fact benefits from such extension or alternative right. Similarly, a change providing an additional benefit upon exercise of the option (such as the payment of a cash bonus) or a change providing more favorable terms for payment for the stock purchased under the option (such as the right to tender previously acquired stock) is a modification.

(ii) If an option is not immediately exercisable in full, a change in the terms of the option to accelerate the time at which the option (or any portion thereof) may be exercised is not a modification for purposes of this section. Additionally, no modification occurs if a provision accelerating the time when an option may first be exercised is removed prior to the year in which it would otherwise be triggered. For example, if an acceleration provision is timely removed to avoid exceeding the $100,000 limitation described in § 1.422-4, a modification of the option does not occur.

(iii) A change to an option which provides, either by its terms or in substance, that the optionee may receive an additional benefit under the option at the future discretion of the grantor, is a modification at the time that the option is changed to provide such discretion. In addition, the exercise of discretion to provide an additional benefit is a modification of the option. However, it is not a modification for the grantor to exercise discretion specifically reserved under an option with respect to the payment of a cash bonus at the time of exercise, the availability of a loan at exercise, the right to tender previously acquired stock for the stock purchasable under the option, or the payment of employment taxes and/or required withholding taxes resulting from the exercise of a statutory option. An option is not modified merely because an optionee is offered a change in the terms of an option if the change to the option is not made. An offer to change the terms of an option that remains open less than 30 days is not a modification of the option. However, if an offer to change the terms of an option remains outstanding for 30 days or more, there is a modification of the option as of the date the offer to change the option is made.

(iv) A change in the terms of the stock purchasable under the option that increases the value of the stock is a modification of such option, except to the extent that a new option is substituted for such option by reason of the change in the terms of the stock in accordance with paragraph (a) of this section.

(v) If an option is amended solely to increase the number of shares subject to the option, the increase is not considered a modification of the option but is treated as the grant of a new option for the additional shares. Notwithstanding the previous sentence, if the exercise price and number of shares subject to an option are proportionally adjusted to reflect a stock split (including a reverse stock split) or stock dividend, and the only effect of the stock split or stock dividend is to increase (or decrease) on a pro rata basis the number of shares owned by each shareholder of the class of stock subject to the option, then the option is not modified if it is proportionally adjusted to reflect the stock split or stock dividend and the aggregate exercise price of the option is not less than the aggregate exercise price before the stock split or stock dividend.

(vi) Any change in the terms of an option made in an attempt to qualify the option as a statutory option grants additional benefits to the optionee and is, therefore, a modification.

(vii) An extension of an option refers to the granting by the corporation to the optionee of an additional period of time within which to exercise the option beyond the time originally prescribed. A renewal of an option is the granting by the corporation of the same rights or privileges contained in the original option on the same terms and conditions. The rules of this paragraph apply as well to successive modifications, extensions, and renewals.

(viii) Any inadvertent change to the terms of an option (or change in the terms of the plan pursuant to which the option was granted or in the terms of any other agreement governing the arrangement) that is treated as a modification under this paragraph (e) is not considered a modification of the option to the extent the change in the terms of the option is removed by the earlier of the date the option is exercised or the last day of the calendar year during which such change occurred. Thus, for example, if the terms of an option are inadvertently changed on March 1 to extend the exercise period and the change is removed on November 1, then if the option is not exercised prior to November 1, the option is not considered modified under this paragraph (e).

(5) A statutory option may, as a result of a modification, extension, or renewal, thereafter cease to be a statutory option, or any option may, by modification, extension, or renewal, thereafter become a statutory option.

(6) [Reserved.]

(7) The application of this paragraph may be illustrated by the following examples:

Example (1). On June 1, 2004, the X Corporation grants to an employee an option under X's employee stock purchase plan to purchase 100 shares of the stock of X Corporation at $90 per share, such option to be exercised on or before June 1, 2006. At the time the option is granted, the fair market value of the X Corporation stock is $100 per share. On February 1, 2005, before the employee exercises the option, X Corporation modifies the option to provide that the price at which the employee may purchase the stock shall be $80 per share. On February 1, 2005, the fair market value of the X Corporation stock is $90 per share. Under section 424(h), the X Corporation is deemed to have granted an option to the employee on February 1, 2005. Such option shall be treated as an option to purchase at $80 per share 100 shares of stock having a fair market value of $100 per share, that is, the higher of the fair market value of the stock on June 1, 2004, or on February 1, 2005. Because the requirements of §1.424-1(e)(3) and §1.423-2(g) have not been met, the exercise of such option by the employee after February 1, 2005, is not the exercise of a statutory option.

Example (2). On June 1, 2004, the X Corporation grants to an employee an option under X's employee stock purchase plan to purchase 100 shares of X Corporation stock at $90 per share, exercisable after December 31, 2005, and on or before June 1, 2006. On June 1, 2004, the fair market value of X Corporation's stock is $100 per share. On February 1, 2005, X Corporation modifies the option to provide that the option shall be exercisable on or before September 1, 2006. On February 1, 2005, the fair market value of X Corporation stock is $110 per share. Under section 424(h), X Corporation is deemed to have granted an option to the employee on February 1, 2005, to purchase at $90 per share 100 shares of stock having a fair market value of $110 per share, that is, the higher of the fair market value of the stock on June 1, 2004, or on February 1, 2005. Because the requirements of §1.424-1(e)(3) and §1.423-2(g) have not been met, the exercise of such option by the employee is not the exercise of a statutory option.

Example (3). The facts are the same as in example (1), except that the employee exercised the option to the extent of 50 shares on January 15, 2005, before the date of the modification of the option. Any exercise of the option after February 1, 2005, the date of the modification, is not the exercise of a statutory option. See example (1) in this subparagraph. The exercise of the option on January 15, 2005, pursuant to which 50 shares were acquired, is the exercise of a statutory option.

(f) *Definitions.*—The following definitions apply for purposes of §§1.421-1 through 1.424-1:

(1) *Parent corporation.*—The term *parent corporation*, or *parent*, means any corporation (other than the employer corporation) in an unbroken chain of corporations ending with the employer corporation if, at the time of the granting of the option, each of the corporations other than the employer corporation owns stock possessing 50 percent or more of the total combined voting power of all classes of stock in one of the other corporations in such chain.

(2) *Subsidiary corporation.*—The term *subsidiary corporation*, or *subsidiary*, means any corporation (other than the employer corporation) in an unbroken chain of corporations beginning with the employer corporation if, at the time of the granting of the option, each of the corporations other than the last corporation in an unbroken chain owns stock possessing 50 percent or more of the total combined voting power of all classes of stock in one of the other corporations in such chain.

(g) *Effective/applicability date.*—(1) *In general.*—Except for §1.424-1(a)(10) *Example 9* (iii), the regulations under this section are effective on August 3, 2004. Section 1.424-1(a)(10) *Example 9* (iii) is effective on November 17, 2009. Section 1.424-1(a)(10) *Example 9* (iii) applies to statutory options granted on or after January 1, 2010.

(2) *Reliance and transition period.*—For statutory options granted on or before June 9, 2003, taxpayers may rely on the 1984 proposed regulations LR-279-81 (49 FR 4504), the 2003 proposed regulations REG-122917-02 (68 FR 34344), or this section until the earlier of January 1, 2006, or the first regularly scheduled stockholders meeting of the granting corporation occurring 6 months after August 3, 2004. For statutory options granted after June 9, 2003, and before the earlier of January 1, 2006, or the first regularly scheduled stockholders meeting of the granting corporation occurring at least 6 months after August 3, 2004, taxpayers may rely on either REG-122917-02 or this section. Taxpayers may not rely on LR-279-81 or REG-122917-02 after December 31, 2005. Reliance on LR-279-81, REG-122917-02, or this section must be in its entirety, and all statutory options granted during the reliance period must be treated consistently.

(3) *Application of section 1022.*—The provisions of paragraph (c)(2) of this section relating to section 1022 are effective on and after January 19, 2017. [Reg. §1.424-1.]

☐ [T.D. 6887, 6-23-66. *Redesignated and amended by T.D. 9144, 8-2-2004 (corrected 10-15-2004 and 12-6-2004), T.D. 9471, 11-16-2009 and T.D. 9811, 1-18-2017.]*

Minimum Funding Standards and Benefit Limitations

[Reg. §1.430(a)-1]

§1.430(a)-1. Determination of minimum required contribution.—(a) *In general.*—(1) *Overview.*—This section sets forth rules for determining a plan's minimum required contribution for a plan year under section 430(a). Section 430 and this section apply to single-employer defined benefit plans (including multiple employer plans as defined in section 413(c)) that are subject to section 412 but do not apply to multiemployer plans (as defined in section 414(f)). Paragraph (b) of this section defines a plan's minimum required contribu-

tion for a plan year. Paragraph (c) of this section provides rules for determining shortfall amortization installments. Paragraph (d) of this section provides rules for determining waiver amortization installments. Paragraph (e) of this section provides for early deemed amortization of shortfall and waiver amortization bases for fully funded plans. Paragraph (f) of this section provides definitions that apply for purposes of this section. Paragraph (g) of this section provides examples that illustrate the application of this section. Paragraph (h) of this section provides effective/applicability dates and transition rules.

(2) *Special rules for multiple employer plans.*—(i) *In general.*—In the case of a multiple employer plan to which section 413(c)(4)(A) applies, the rules of section 430 and this section are applied separately for each employer under the plan, as if each employer maintained a separate plan. Thus, the minimum required contribution is computed separately for each employer under such a multiple employer plan. In the case of a multiple employer plan to which section 413(c)(4)(A) does not apply (that is, a plan described in section 413(c)(4)(B) that has not made the election for section 413(c)(4)(A) to apply), the rules of section 430 and this section are applied as if all participants in the plan were employed by a single employer.

(ii) *CSEC plans.*—A CSEC plan (that is, a plan that fits within the definition of a CSEC plan in section 414(y) for plan years beginning on or after January 1, 2014 and for which the election under section 414(y)(3)(A) has not been made) is not subject to the rules of section 430. See section 433 for the minimum funding rules that apply to CSEC plans.

(b) *Definition of minimum required contribution.*—(1) *In general.*—In the case of a defined benefit plan that is subject to section 430, except as offset under section 430(f) and §1.430(f)-1, the minimum required contribution for a plan year is determined as the applicable amount determined under paragraph (b)(2) of this section or paragraph (b)(3) of this section, reduced by the amount of any funding waiver under section 412(c) that is granted for the plan year. See paragraph (b)(4) of this section for special rules for a plan maintained by a commercial passenger airline (or other eligible employer) for which an election under section 402 of the Pension Protection Act of 2006, Public Law 109-280 (120 Stat. 780), as amended (PPA '06), has been made, and see section 430(j) and §1.430(j)-1(b) for rules regarding the required interest adjustment for a contribution that is paid on a date other than the valuation date for the plan year. See also §1.430(j)-1(d)(3)(iv)(B) for rules regarding an increase to the minimum required contribution in certain circumstances for a plan with an unpaid liquidity amount.

(2) *Plan assets less than funding target.*—(i) *General rule.*—For any plan year in which the value of plan assets (as reduced to reflect the subtraction of certain funding balances as provided under §1.430(f)-1(c), but not below zero) is less than the funding target for the plan year, the minimum required contribution for that plan year is equal to the sum of—

(A) The target normal cost for the plan year;

(B) The total (not less than zero) of the shortfall amortization installments as described in paragraph (c) of this section determined with respect to any shortfall amortization base for the plan year and for each preceding plan year for which the shortfall amortization base has not been fully taken into account (generally, the 6 preceding plan years); and

(C) The total of the waiver amortization installments as described in paragraph (d) of this section determined with respect to any waiver amortization base for all preceding plan years for which the waiver amortization base has not been fully taken into account (generally, the 5 preceding plan years).

(ii) *Special rule for short plan years.*—(A) *Proration of amortization installments.*—In determining the minimum required contribution in the case of a plan year that is shorter than 12 months (and is not a 52-week plan year of a plan that uses a 52-53 week plan year), the shortfall amortization installments and waiver amortization installments that are taken into account under paragraphs (b)(2)(i)(B) and (C) of this section are determined by multiplying the amount of those installments that would be taken into account for a 12-month plan year by a fraction, the numerator of which is the duration of the short plan year and the denominator of which is 1 year.

(B) *Effect on subsequent years.*—In plan years after the short plan year, installments with respect to a shortfall amortization base or waiver amortization base continue to be taken into account under paragraphs (b)(2)(i)(B) and (C) of this section until the total amount of those installments, as originally determined when the base was established, has been taken into account. Thus, in the case of a plan that has a short plan year, an additional partial installment will be taken into account under paragraphs (b)(2)(i)(B) and (C) of this section for the plan year that ends after the end of the original amortization period (generally 7 years for shortfall amortization bases and 5 years for waiver amortization bases) in an amount determined so that the total of the amortization installments (including the prorated installment payable for the short plan year and the additional partial installment) is equal to the total of the amortization installments as originally determined.

(3) *Plan assets equal or exceed funding target.*—For any plan year in which the value of plan assets (as reduced to reflect the subtraction of certain funding balances as provided under §1.430(f)-1(c), but not

below zero) equals or exceeds the funding target for the plan year, the minimum required contribution for that plan year is equal to the target normal cost for the plan year reduced (but not below zero) by that excess.

(4) *Special rules for commercial passenger airlines.*—(i) *In general.*—This paragraph (b)(4) provides special rules for a plan maintained by a commercial passenger airline (or an employer whose principal business is providing catering services to a commercial passenger airline) for which an election under section 402(a)(1) of PPA '06 has been made. See paragraph (c)(4) of this section for special rules for a plan maintained by a commercial passenger airline (or an employer whose principal business is providing catering services to a commercial passenger airline) for which an election under section 402(a)(2) of PPA '06 has been made.

(ii) *Determinations during 17-year amortization period.*—If an election described in section 402(a)(1) of PPA '06 applies for the plan year with respect to an eligible plan described in section 402(c)(1) of PPA '06, then the plan's minimum required contribution for purposes of section 430 of the Internal Revenue Code (Code) for the plan year is equal to the amount necessary to amortize (at an interest rate of 8.85 percent) the unfunded liability of the plan in equal installments over the remaining amortization period. For this purpose, the unfunded liability means the excess of the accrued liability under the plan determined using the unit credit funding method and an interest rate of 8.85 percent over the value of assets (as determined under section 430(g)(3) and §1.430(g)-1(c)), and the remaining amortization period is the 17-plan-year period beginning with the first plan year for which the election was made, reduced by 1 year for each plan year after the first plan year for which the election was made. In addition, the section 430(f)(3) election to apply funding balances against the minimum required contribution does not apply to a plan to which the election described in section 402(a)(1) of PPA '06 applies for the plan year.

(iii) *Determinations following the election period.*—If an election described in section 402(a)(1) of PPA '06 applied to the plan for any preceding plan year but does not apply for the current plan year, then the plan's minimum required contribution for purposes of section 430 of the Code for the plan year is determined without regard to that election. For the first plan year for which that election no longer applies to the plan, any prefunding balance or funding standard carryover balance is reduced to zero.

(5) *Terminated plans.*—(i) *Short plan year.*—If a plan's termination date occurs during a plan year but before the last day of a plan year, then, for purposes of section 430, the plan is treated as having a short plan year that ends on the termination date.

(ii) *Valuation date.*—If a plan's termination date is before the date that would otherwise have been the valuation date for a plan year, then the valuation date for the plan year must be changed so that it falls within the short plan year pursuant to §1.430(g)-1(b)(2)(i). See §1.430(g)-1(b)(2)(iv) for a rule providing automatic approval of changes in the valuation date that are required by section 430.

(c) *Shortfall amortization installments.*—(1) *In general.*—Except as otherwise provided in paragraphs (c)(3) and (4) of this section, the shortfall amortization installments with respect to a shortfall amortization base established for a plan year are the annual amounts necessary to amortize that shortfall amortization base in level annual installments over the 7-year period beginning with that plan year. See §1.430(h)(2)-1(e) and (f) for rules regarding interest rates used for determining shortfall amortization installments and the date within each plan year on which the installments are assumed to be paid. The shortfall amortization installments are determined using the interest rates that apply for the plan year for which the shortfall amortization base is established and are not redetermined in subsequent plan years to reflect any changes in the valuation date or changes in interest rates under section 430(h)(2) for those subsequent plan years.

(2) *Shortfall amortization base.*—(i) *In general.*—Unless the value of plan assets (as reduced to reflect the subtraction of certain funding balances as provided under §1.430(f)-1(c)(2), but not below zero) is equal to or greater than the funding target for the plan year, a shortfall amortization base is established for the plan year equal to—

(A) The funding shortfall for the plan year; minus

(B) The amount attributable to future installments determined under paragraph (c)(2)(ii) of this section.

(ii) *Amount attributable to future installments.*—The amount attributable to future installments is equal to the sum of the present values (determined in accordance with §1.430(h)(2)-1(e) and (f) using the interest rates that apply for the current plan year) of—

(A) The shortfall amortization installments that have been determined for the plan year and any succeeding plan year with respect to the shortfall amortization bases for any plan year preceding the plan year; and

(B) The waiver amortization installments that have been determined for the plan year and any succeeding plan year with respect to the waiver amortization bases for any plan year preceding the plan year.

(iii) *Timing assumption for installments after change in valuation date.*—For purposes of determining the present value in paragraph (c)(2)(ii) of this section, the shortfall amortization installments and waiver amortization installments are assumed to be paid on the valuation date for the current plan year and anniversaries thereof even if the valuation date for a subsequent plan year is not the same as the valuation date for the plan year for which a shortfall amortization base or waiver amortization base was established. For example, assume that a plan has a July 1 to June 30 plan year and a valuation date that is the first day of the plan year, and that the plan year for the plan is changed to the calendar year, so that the plan has a short plan year beginning July 1, 2017 and ending December 31, 2017 and a calendar plan year thereafter. In this case—

(A) For the July 1, 2017 actuarial valuation, the shortfall amortization payments with respect to shortfall amortization bases established for all prior plan years are assumed to be paid on July 1, 2017 and anniversaries thereof; and

(B) For the January 1, 2018 actuarial valuation, the shortfall amortization payments with respect to shortfall amortization bases established for all prior plan years are assumed to be paid on January 1, 2018 and anniversaries thereof.

(iv) *Transition rule.*—See paragraph (h)(4) of this section for a transition rule under which only a portion of the funding target is taken into account in determining whether a shortfall amortization base is established under this paragraph (c)(2).

(3) *Election of funding relief for certain plans.*—(i) *Funding relief under the Preservation of Access to Care for Medicare Beneficiaries and Pension Relief Act of 2010.*—See section 430(c)(2)(D) and section 430(c)(7) for special rules that apply to determine the amount of shortfall amortization installments with respect to shortfall amortization bases established for plan years ending on or after October 10, 2009 and beginning before January 1, 2012, for which the relief under section 430(c)(2)(D) is elected.

(ii) *Funding relief related to eligible charity plans.*—See section 104(d)(3)(B) through (F) of PPA '06, which reflects amendments made by section 103(b)(2) of the Cooperative and Small Employer Charity Pension Flexibility Act of 2014, Public Law 113-97 (128 Stat. 1137), for special rules that apply to determine the amount of shortfall amortization installments with respect to plan years beginning on or after January 1, 2014, in the case of an eligible charity plan for which the relief under section 104(d)(3)(A) of PPA '06 is elected.

(iii) *Election by commercial passenger airline under section 402(a)(2) of PPA '06.*—If an election described in section 402(a)(2) of PPA '06 has been made for an eligible plan described in section 402(c)(1) of PPA '06, then the minimum required contribution for purposes of section 430 is determined under generally applicable rules, except that the shortfall amortization base for the first plan year for which section 430 applies to the plan is amortized over 10 years (rather than over 7 years as provided in paragraph (c)(1) of this section) in accordance with § 1.430(h)(2)-1(e) and (f) using the interest rates that apply for purposes of determining the target normal cost for the first plan year for which section 430 applies to the plan. In such a case, the shortfall amortization installments with respect to the shortfall amortization base for that plan year will continue to be included in determining the minimum required contribution for 10 years rather than 7 years. See also § 1.430(h)(2)-1(b)(6) for a special rule for determining the funding target in the case of a plan for which an election under section 402(a)(2) of PPA '06 has been made.

(d) *Waiver amortization installments.*—(1) *In general.*—For purposes of this section, the waiver amortization installments with respect to a waiver amortization base established for a plan year are the annual amounts necessary to amortize that waiver amortization base in level annual installments over the 5-year period beginning with the following plan year. See § 1.430(h)(2)-1(e) and (f) for rules regarding interest rates used for determining waiver amortization installments and the date within each plan year on which the installments are assumed to be paid. The waiver amortization installments established with respect to a waiver amortization base are determined using the interest rates that apply for the plan year for which the waiver is granted (even though the first installment with respect to the waiver amortization base is not due until the subsequent plan year) and are not redetermined in subsequent plan years to reflect any changes in the valuation date or changes in interest rates under section 430(h)(2) for those subsequent plan years.

(2) *Waiver amortization base.*—(i) *In general.*—For purposes of this section, a waiver amortization base is established for each plan year for which a waiver of the minimum funding standard has been granted in accordance with section 412(c). The amount of the waiver amortization base is equal to the waived funding deficiency under section 412(c)(3) for the plan year.

(ii) *Transition rule.*—See paragraph (h)(3) of this section for the treatment of funding waivers granted for plan years beginning before 2008.

(e) *Early deemed amortization upon attainment of funding target.*—In any case in which the funding shortfall for a plan year is zero, for purposes of determining the minimum required contribution for that plan year and subsequent plan years—

(1) The shortfall amortization bases for all preceding plan years (and all shortfall amortization installments determined with respect to those bases) are reduced to zero; and

(2) The waiver amortization bases for all preceding plan years (and all waiver amortization installments determined with respect to those bases) are reduced to zero.

(f) *Definitions.*—(1) *In general.*—The definitions set forth in this paragraph (f) apply for purposes of this section.

(2) *Funding shortfall.*—The term *funding shortfall* means the excess (if any) of—

(i) The funding target for a plan year; over

(ii) The value of plan assets for the plan year (as reduced to reflect the subtraction of the funding standard carryover balance and prefunding balance to the extent provided under § 1.430(f)-1(c), but not below zero).

(3) *Funding target.*—The term *funding target* means the plan's funding target for a plan year determined under § 1.430(d)-1(b)(2), § 1.430(i)-1(c), or § 1.430(i)-1(e)(1), whichever applies to the plan for the plan year.

(4) *Target normal cost.*—The term *target normal cost* means the plan's target normal cost for a plan year determined under § 1.430(d)-1(b)(1), § 1.430(i)-1(d), or § 1.430(i)-1(e)(2), whichever applies to the plan for the plan year.

(5) *Termination date.*—(i) *Plans subject to Title IV of ERISA.*—In the case of a plan subject to Title IV of the Employee Retirement Income Security Act of 1974, as amended (ERISA), the termination date means the plan's termination date established under section 4048(a) of ERISA.

(ii) *Other plans.*—(A) *In general.*—In the case of a plan not subject to Title IV of ERISA, the termination date means the plan's termination date established by the plan administrator, provided that the termination date may be no earlier than the date on which all actions necessary to effect the plan termination (other than the distribution of plan assets) are taken.

(B) *Requirement for prompt distribution.*—A plan is not treated as terminated on the applicable date described in paragraph (f)(5)(ii)(A) of this section if the assets are not distributed as soon as administratively feasible after that date. Whether distribution of plan assets is made as soon as administratively feasible is to be determined under all the relevant facts and circumstances. In general, distribution of plan assets is deemed to have been made as soon as administratively feasible to the extent that any delay in distribution was because of circumstances outside the control of the plan administrator. However, distribution of plan assets that was delayed merely for the purpose of obtaining a higher value than current market value is generally not deemed to have been made as soon as administratively feasible.

(C) *Presumption applicable to prompt distribution requirement.*—Except as provided in paragraph (f)(5)(ii)(D) of this section, distribution of plan assets which is not completed within one year following the applicable date described in paragraph (f)(5)(ii)(A) of this section is presumed not to have been made as soon as administratively feasible.

(D) *Exception to prompt distribution presumption for obtaining determination letter from Commissioner.*—A plan is not treated as failing to meet the requirement to distribute plan assets as soon as administratively feasible after the proposed termination date if the delay is attributable to the period of time necessary to obtain a determination letter from the Commissioner on the plan's qualified status upon its termination, provided that the request for a determination letter is timely and the distribution of plan assets is made as soon as administratively feasible after the letter is obtained.

(6) *Transition funding shortfall.*—(i) *In general.*—The term *transition funding shortfall* means the excess, if any, of—

(A) The applicable percentage of the funding target for a plan year; over

(B) The value of plan assets for the plan year (as reduced to reflect the subtraction of the funding standard carryover balance and

prefunding balance to the extent provided under §1.430(f)-1(c), but not below zero).

(ii) *Applicable percentage.*—For purposes of this paragraph (f)(6), the applicable percentage is determined in accordance with the following table:

Calendar year in which the plan year begins	Applicable percentage
2008	92
2009	94
2010	96

(g) *Examples.*—The following examples illustrate the rules of this section. Unless otherwise indicated, these examples are based on the following assumptions: section 430 applies to determine the minimum required contribution for plan years beginning on or after January 1, 2008; the plan year is the calendar year; the valuation date is January 1; the plan's prefunding balance and funding standard carryover balance are equal to $0; the plan sponsor did not elect any funding relief under section 430(c)(2)(D) for any plan year; and the plan has not received any funding waivers for any relevant time periods.

Example 1. (i) Plan A has a funding target of $2,500,000 and assets totaling $1,800,000 as of January 1, 2016. For purposes of this example, the segment interest rates used for the January 1, 2016 valuation are assumed to be 5.26% for the first segment interest rate and 5.82% for the second segment interest rate. No shortfall or waiver amortization bases have been established for prior plan years.

(ii) A $700,000 shortfall amortization base is established for 2016, which is equal to the $2,500,000 funding target less $1,800,000 of assets.

(iii) With respect to the new shortfall amortization base of $700,000, there is a shortfall amortization installment of $116,852 (which is the amount necessary to amortize the $700,000 shortfall amortization base over 7 years) for each year from 2016 through 2022. The amount of this shortfall amortization installment is determined by discounting the first five installments using the first segment interest rate of 5.26%, and by discounting the sixth and seventh installments using the second segment rate of 5.82%.

Example 2. (i) The facts are the same as in *Example 1*, except that the plan was granted a funding waiver for 2014, resulting in five annual waiver amortization installments of $70,000 each, beginning with the 2015 plan year.

(ii) As of January 1, 2016, the present value of the remaining waiver amortization installments is $259,702, which is determined by discounting the remaining four waiver amortization installments of $70,000 each to January 1, 2016, using the first segment rate of 5.26%. See paragraph (c)(2)(ii) of this section.

(iii) A $440,298 shortfall amortization base is established for 2016, which is equal to the $2,500,000 funding target, less $1,800,000 of assets, less $259,702 (which is the present value of the remaining four waiver amortization installments).

(iv) With respect to this shortfall amortization base of $440,298, there is a shortfall amortization installment of $73,500 (which is equal to the $440,298 shortfall amortization base amortized over 7 years) for each year from 2016 through 2022.

Example 3. (i) The facts are the same as in *Example 2*. Plan A has a $100,000 target normal cost for the 2016 plan year and was granted a funding waiver for 2016 to the largest extent permitted under section 412(c).

(ii) If the funding waiver for 2016 had not been granted, the minimum required contribution for 2016 would have been $243,500. This is equal to the $100,000 target normal cost, plus the $70,000 waiver amortization installment from the 2014 waiver, plus the $73,500 January 1, 2016 shortfall amortization installment.

(iii) In accordance with section 412(c)(1)(C), the portion of the minimum required contribution attributable to the amortization of the 2014 funding waiver cannot be waived. Therefore, the maximum amount of the January 1, 2016 minimum required contribution that can be waived is $173,500.

(iv) In accordance with paragraph (d) of this section, a waiver amortization base of $173,500 is established as of January 1, 2016 to be amortized over 5 years beginning with the 2017 plan year. Although the waiver amortization installments for the 2016 funding waiver are not included in the minimum required contribution until 2017, the amount of those installments is determined based on the interest rates used for the 2016 plan year.

(v) The waiver amortization installments with respect to the 2016 funding waiver are calculated using the first segment interest rate of 5.26% for the first four installments (calculated as of January 1, 2017 through January 1, 2020) and the second segment interest rate of 5.82% for the final installment payable as of January 1, 2021. Accord-

ingly, the waiver amortization installments with respect to the 2016 funding waiver are $40,554 each, payable beginning January 1, 2017.

Example 4. (i) The facts are the same as in *Example 3*. As of January 1, 2017, Plan A has a funding target of $2,750,000 and assets totaling $1,900,000. For purposes of this example, the first segment rate used for the 2017 valuation is assumed to be 5.50%, the second segment rate is assumed to be 6.00%, and the third segment rate is assumed to be 6.50%.

(ii) As of January 1, 2017, the present value of the remaining three waiver amortization installments with respect to the 2014 waiver is $199,242, which is determined using the first segment rate of 5.50%.

(iii) As of January 1, 2017, the present value of the remaining five waiver amortization installments with respect to the 2016 waiver is $182,701, which is determined using the first segment rate of 5.50%.

(iv) As of January 1, 2017, the present value of the remaining six shortfall amortization installments with respect to the 2016 shortfall amortization base is $386,052, which is determined using the first segment rate of 5.50% for the first five installments and the second segment rate of 6.00% for the sixth installment.

(v) A shortfall amortization base of $82,005 is established for 2017, which is equal to the $2,750,000 funding target, reduced by the sum of $1,900,000 of assets, $199,242 (the present value of the remaining waiver amortization installments with respect to the 2014 waiver), $182,701 (the present value of the remaining waiver amortization installments with respect to the 2016 waiver), and $386,052 (the present value of the remaining installments with respect to the 2016 shortfall amortization base).

(vi) With respect to this shortfall amortization base of $82,005, there is a shortfall amortization installment of $13,766 (which is the amount necessary to amortize the $82,005 shortfall amortization base over 7 years) for each year from 2017 through 2023.

Example 5. (i) As of January 1, 2016, a plan has a funding target of $2,500,000, a target normal cost of $175,000, and assets totaling $2,450,000. As of January 1, 2016, there are six remaining installments of $60,000 each with respect to the only shortfall amortization base for the plan, which was established for the 2015 plan year. Also as of January 1, 2016, there are five remaining installments of $25,000 each with respect to the only waiver amortization base for the plan, which was established for the 2015 plan year. For purposes of this example, the segment interest rates used for the January 1, 2016, valuation are assumed to be 5.26% for the first segment interest rate and 5.82% for the second segment interest rate.

(ii) A shortfall amortization base of -$379,812 is established for 2016, which is equal to the $2,500,000 funding target, reduced by the sum of $2,450,000 of assets, $316,696 (the present value of the remaining installments with respect to the 2015 shortfall amortization base) and $113,116 (the present value of the remaining installments with respect to the 2015 funding waiver).

(iii) The shortfall amortization installment for the 2016 shortfall amortization base is -$63,403, which is the amount necessary to amortize the -$379,812 shortfall amortization base over seven years. The first five shortfall amortization installments are discounted using the first segment rate of 5.26% and the sixth and seventh shortfall amortization installments are discounted using the second segment rate of 5.82%.

(iv) The sum of the shortfall amortization installments is equal to -$3,403 ($60,000 plus -$63,403). However, in accordance with paragraph (b)(2)(i)(B) of this section, for purposes of determining the minimum required contribution for a plan year, the total of the shortfall amortization installments for a plan year is limited so that it is not less than zero.

(v) The minimum required contribution as of January 1, 2016 is $200,000. This is equal to the sum of the target normal cost of $175,000, the total of the shortfall amortization installments (as limited) of $0, and the waiver amortization installment of $25,000.

(vi) The shortfall amortization bases are not set to zero as of January 1, 2016, even though the sum of the shortfall amortization installments was set to zero for the 2016 plan year. Therefore, as of January 1, 2017 (unless the plan has a funding shortfall of zero as of that date), the shortfall amortization base established as of January 1, 2015 will have five remaining installments of $60,000 each and the shortfall amortization base established as of January 1, 2016 will have six remaining installments of -$ 63,403 each. Similarly, the waiver amortization base will have four remaining installments of $25,000 each.

Example 6. (i) The facts are the same as in *Example 5*, except that Plan A has assets totaling $2,550,000 as of January 1, 2016.

(ii) Because the assets of $2,550,000 exceed the funding target of $2,500,000, no new shortfall amortization base is established under paragraph (c)(2) of this section.

(iii) Furthermore, under paragraph (e) of this section, all shortfall amortization bases and waiver amortization bases (and all shortfall amortization installments and waiver amortization installments associated with those bases) are reduced to zero as of January 1, 2016.

(iv) The minimum required contribution for the 2016 plan year is $125,000, which is equal to the $175,000 target normal cost less the excess of the assets over the funding target ($2,550,000 minus $2,550,000).

Example 7. (i) The actuarial valuation for Plan B as of January 1, 2016, based on a 12-month plan year, results in a target normal cost of $110,000 and a shortfall amortization installment for 2016 of $185,000, attributable to a shortfall amortization base established January 1, 2016. There are no other shortfall or waiver amortization bases for Plan B as of January 1, 2016. The plan year for Plan B is changed to April 1 through March 31, effective April 1, 2016, resulting in a short plan year beginning January 1, 2016 and ending March 31, 2016.

(ii) The target normal cost for the short plan year is redetermined in order to reflect the fact that there is a short plan year. An actuarial valuation shows that the target normal cost is $25,000 for the short plan year based on the accruals for that short plan year (determined in accordance with 29 CFR 2530.204-2(e)).

(iii) In accordance with paragraph (b)(2)(ii)(A) of this section, the shortfall amortization base is prorated to reflect the three months covered by the short plan year. Accordingly, the shortfall amortization installment for the short plan year is $46,250 (that is, $185,000 multiplied by 3/12).

(iv) The total minimum required contribution for the short plan year is $71,250 (that is, the sum of the target normal cost of $25,000 plus the shortfall amortization installment of $46,250).

Example 8. (i) The facts are the same as in *Example 7*. For purposes of this example, assume that the first segment rate for the plan year beginning April 1, 2016 is 5.30%, and the second segment rate is 5.80%.

(ii) The present value of the remaining shortfall amortization installments with respect to the January 1, 2016 shortfall amortization base is equal to $1,074,937. This is determined by discounting the remaining installments (6 full-year installments of $185,000 each due April 1, 2016 through April 1, 2021, and a final 9-month installment of $138,750 due April 1, 2022) using the first segment rate of 5.30% for the first five installments and the second segment rate of 5.80% for the remaining installments.

Example 9. (i) As of January 1, 2016, Plan C has a funding target of $1,100,000, a target normal cost of $20,000, and an actuarial value of assets of $1,150,000. Prior to establishing any shortfall amortization base for 2016, the total of the shortfall amortization installments for 2016 is $30,000 and the present value of the remaining shortfall amortization installments (including installments for the 2016 plan year) is $150,000. Based on the segment rates used for the 2016 plan year, the 7-year amortization factor for any shortfall amortization base established for 2016 is 5.9887. The funding standard carryover balance as of January 1, 2016 is $40,000 and the prefunding balance is $60,000. The plan sponsor intends to use both balances to offset the minimum required contribution for 2016.

(ii) In accordance with sections 430(c) and 430(f)(4)(A), the test to determine whether Plan C is exempt from establishing a new shortfall amortization base for 2016 is initially applied based on assets reduced by the prefunding balance, because the plan sponsor intends to use the prefunding balance to offset the minimum required contribution. Therefore, the actuarial value of assets used for this purpose is $1,150,000 minus $60,000, or $1,090,000. This is less than the funding target of $1,100,000, so a new shortfall amortization base is established for 2016.

(iii) The funding shortfall as of January 1, 2016 is the difference between the funding target and the actuarial value of assets, where the actuarial value of assets is reduced by both the funding standard carryover balance and the prefunding balance. Accordingly, the value of assets used for this calculation is $1,050,000 (that is, $1,150,000 - $40,000 - $60,000), and the funding shortfall is $50,000 (that is, $1,100,000 - $1,050,000).

(iv) The shortfall amortization base established as of January 1, 2016 is the difference between the funding shortfall of $50,000 and the $150,000 present value of remaining shortfall amortization installments for bases established in prior years (that is, - $100,000). The

shortfall amortization installment attributable to this base is - $100,000 ÷ 5.9887, or - $16,698.

(v) The preliminary minimum required contribution is the sum of the target normal cost, the shortfall amortization installments for bases established prior to 2016, and the shortfall amortization installment for the new base established for 2016, or $33,302 (that is, $20,000 + $30,000 - $16,698). However, this amount is less than the funding standard carryover balance. Because section 430(f)(3)(B) and §1.430(f)-1(d)(2) require that the funding standard carryover balance be used before using the prefunding balance, this means that the full minimum required contribution will be offset without using the prefunding balance. Accordingly, the plan sponsor will not be electing to use any portion of the prefunding balance to offset the minimum required contribution for 2016.

(vi) Because the plan sponsor is not using the prefunding balance to offset the minimum required contribution, the test to determine whether Plan C is exempt from establishing a new shortfall amortization base for 2016 must be applied without subtracting the prefunding balance from the actuarial value of plan assets. Because the full actuarial value of assets of $1,150,000 is higher than the funding target of $1,100,000, the plan is exempt from establishing a new shortfall amortization base for 2016. However, the actuarial value of plan assets is reduced by both balances when determining the funding shortfall, which is used to determine whether the shortfall amortization bases established prior to 2016 are reduced to zero. Because the funding shortfall is greater than zero as of January 1, 2016 (as calculated in paragraph (iii) of this *Example 9*), the shortfall amortization bases established before the 2016 plan year are retained.

(vii) The minimum required contribution for 2016 is the sum of the target normal cost and the shortfall amortization installments, or $50,000 ($20,000 + $30,000). Because this is larger than the funding standard account carryover balance of $40,000, the plan sponsor can only offset $40,000 of the minimum required contribution and must contribute $10,000 to meet the minimum funding requirements. The prefunding balance cannot be used to offset the remaining $10,000 minimum funding requirement because doing so would require recalculating the minimum required contribution as illustrated in paragraphs (ii) through (v) of this *Example 9* and the minimum required contribution would be too small to use the prefunding balance.

Example 10. (i) The facts are the same as in *Example 9*, except that, in lieu of making the cash contribution required in *Example 9*, the plan sponsor elects to reduce the funding standard carryover balance by $9,000.

(ii) Because the plan sponsor intends to use the prefunding balance to offset the minimum required contribution, the test to determine whether Plan C is exempt from establishing a shortfall amortization base for 2016 is based on the actuarial value of assets reduced by the prefunding balance. The actuarial value of assets reduced for the prefunding balance ($1,090,000) is less than the funding target ($1,100,000), so a new shortfall amortization base is established for 2016.

(iii) The remaining funding standard carryover balance is $31,000 (that is, $40,000 minus the elected reduction of $9,000). The funding shortfall as of January 1, 2016 is the difference between the funding target and the actuarial value of assets, where the actuarial value of assets is reduced by both the remaining funding standard carryover balance and the prefunding balance. Accordingly, the value of assets used for this calculation is $1,059,000 (that is, $1,150,000 - $31,000 - $60,000), and the funding shortfall is $41,000 (that is, $1,100,000 - $1,059,000).

(iv) The shortfall amortization base established as of January 1, 2016 is the difference between the funding shortfall of $41,000 and the $150,000 present value of remaining shortfall amortization installments for bases established in prior years (that is, - $109,000). The shortfall amortization installment attributable to this base is - $109,000 ÷ 5.9887, or - $18,201.

(v) The minimum required contribution is the sum of the target normal cost, the shortfall amortization installments for bases established prior to 2016, and the shortfall amortization installment for the new base established for 2016, or $31,799 (that is, $20,000 + $30,000 - $18,201). This amount is larger than the remaining funding standard carryover balance of $31,000. Therefore, the plan sponsor can offset the full minimum required contribution using the remaining $31,000 of the funding standard carryover balance and $799 of the prefunding balance. Because a portion of the prefunding balance is used to offset the minimum required contribution, the test under section 430(c)(5) is applied by subtracting the prefunding balance from the actuarial value of assets as illustrated in paragraph (ii) of this *Example 10*, and no further adjustments are required to the minimum required contribution.

Example 11. (i) An amendment to Plan D was adopted during 2015, scheduled to be effective February 1, 2016. The actuary determines that, as of January 1, 2016, the amendment would increase Plan D's funding target by $300,000, if the amendment is permitted to take effect. As of February 1, 2016, prior to taking into account the amendment, the presumed adjusted funding target attainment percentage (AFTAP) for Plan D is less than 80% but not less than 60%. Plan D's sponsor makes a section 436 contribution (under section 436(c)(2)(A)) of $300,000, adjusted for interest as required under §1.436-1(f)(2)(i)(A)(2), to allow the amendment to take effect.

(ii) Because the plan amendment was adopted prior to the valuation date for 2016 and becomes effective during the 2016 plan year, under §1.430(d)-1(d)(1)(i), the plan amendment must be taken into account in the funding target as of January 1, 2016. However, because the section 436 contribution is made for the 2016 plan year, it is not included in Plan D's actuarial value of assets as of January 1, 2016.

(iii) The funding shortfall as of January 1, 2016 is calculated as the amount of the funding target (taking into account the plan amendment) minus the actuarial value of assets, where the value of assets is reduced by any funding standard carryover balance and prefunding balance as of that date. Because the funding target takes into account the increase of $300,000 attributable to the plan amendment but the actuarial value of assets does not include the section 436 contribution, the funding shortfall is $300,000 higher than it would have been had the plan amendment not been allowed to take effect.

(iv) The funding shortfall as of January 1, 2017 will reflect both the cost of the plan amendment and the value of the section 436 contribution made during 2016. Therefore, in the absence of any other factors affecting the shortfall amortization base, it is expected that a negative shortfall amortization base will be established as of January 1, 2017 as a result of the section 436 contribution made during 2016.

Example 12. (i) Plan E has a calendar year plan year and in 2015 had 97 participants. Plan E has a valuation date of July 1. A shortfall amortization base of $300,000 was established with the July 1, 2016 valuation. The plan had no other shortfall or waiver amortization bases. For purposes of this example, assume that the first segment rate for the 2016 plan year is 5.50% and the second segment rate is 6.00%. Accordingly, the shortfall amortization installments are determined as seven annual installments of $50,358 each, payable as of each July 1 beginning July 1, 2016.

(ii) Sometime after January 1, 2016, the number of participants in Plan E increased to over 100 during 2016, and therefore the valuation date was changed to January 1 effective with the 2017 plan year. As of January 1, 2017, Plan E has a funding target of $2,000,000, plan assets of $1,600,000, and a zero funding standard carryover balance and prefunding balance. For purposes of this example, assume that as of January 1, 2017, the first segment rate is 5.75% and the second segment rate is 6.25%.

(iii) In accordance with paragraph (c)(1) of this section, the amount of the shortfall amortization installments for the base established July 1, 2016 is not adjusted for the change in valuation date. As of January 1, 2017, the outstanding balance of the shortfall amortization base established as of July 1, 2016 is $263,047, determined as the present value of the remaining shortfall amortization installments, calculated as if the shortfall amortization installments of $50,358 are payable annually on January 1 instead of July 1.

(iv) A new shortfall amortization base of $136,953 is established effective January 1, 2017 equal to the difference between the funding shortfall of $400,000 and the outstanding balance of the shortfall amortization base established as of July 1, 2016 ($263,047). The shortfall amortization installment for this base is calculated as $23,139.

(v) The total shortfall amortization installment for the 2017 plan year is $73,497, equal to the sum of the installments for the shortfall amortization base established July 1, 2016 ($50,358) and the base established January 1, 2017 ($23,139). The total amortization installment is determined as an amount payable as of January 1 regardless of the fact that the installment for the first base was initially calculated as an amount payable on July 1.

Example 13. (i) A funding waiver of $300,000 was granted for Plan F for the 2006 plan year. The valuation interest rate for the January 1, 2007 actuarial valuation is 8.50% (which exceeds 150% of the applicable federal mid-term rate). The first segment rate for the January 1, 2008 valuation of Plan F is 5.26%.

(ii) The waiver amortization charge for the plan year beginning January 1, 2007 is $70,166, which is equal to the $300,000 funding waiver base amortized over 5 years at the valuation interest rate of 8.50%.

(iii) The annual waiver amortization installment for 2008 and later years is equal to the amortization charge for the 2007 plan year, or $70,166. As of January 1, 2008, the present value of the remaining *waiver amortization installments is $260,318, which is determined by discounting* the remaining four waiver amortization installments of $70,166 to January 1, 2008, using the first segment rate of 5.26%.

Example 14. (i) As of January 1, 2008, Plan G has a funding target of $2,500,000, plan assets of $1,800,000 and a funding standard carry-

over balance of $100,000. Plan G has not received a funding waiver for any past plan year. Plan G was in existence during 2007, and in the 2007 plan year was not subject to the deficit reduction contribution in section 412(l) of the Code as it existed prior to PPA '06.

(ii) Plan G qualifies for the transition rule in section 430(c)(5) of the Code (as in effect prior to amendments made by the Tax Increase Prevention Act of 2014, Public Law 113-295, 128 Stat. 4010) and paragraph (h)(4) of this section. Because Plan G's assets are less than 92% of its funding target, a shortfall amortization base must be established as of January 1, 2008.

(iii) Under the transition rule in paragraph (h)(4) of this section, the shortfall amortization base for 2008 is determined using only 92% of Plan G's funding target, or $2,300,000. For purposes of this calculation, the value of assets is reduced by the funding standard carryover balance for a net asset figure of $1,700,000 (that is, $1,800,000 minus $100,000). Accordingly, the shortfall amortization base as of January 1, 2008 is equal to $600,000.

(h) *Effective/applicability dates and transition rules.*—(1) *Statutory effective date/applicability date.*—Section 430 generally applies to plan years beginning on or after January 1, 2008. The applicability of section 430 for purposes of determining the minimum required contribution is delayed for certain plans in accordance with sections 104 through 106 of PPA '06.

(2) *Effective date/applicability date of regulations.*—This section applies to plan years beginning on or after January 1, 2016. For plan years beginning before January 1, 2016, plans are permitted to rely on the provisions set forth in this section for purposes of satisfying the requirements of section 430(a).

(3) *Treatment of pre-PPA '06 funding waivers.*—In the case of a plan that has received a funding waiver under section 412 for a plan year for which section 430 was not yet effective with respect to the plan for purposes of determining the minimum required contribution, the waiver is treated as giving rise to a waiver amortization base and the amortization charges with respect to that funding waiver are treated as waiver amortization installments as described in paragraph (d) of this section. With respect to such a pre-existing funding waiver, the amount of the waiver amortization installment is equal to the amortization charge with respect to that waiver determined using the interest rate or rates that applied for the pre-effective plan year.

(4) *Transition rule for determining shortfall amortization base.*—(i) *In general.*—Except as provided in paragraph (h)(4)(ii) of this section, in the case of plan years beginning after December 31, 2007 and before January 1, 2011, for purposes of applying the rules of paragraph (c)(2) of this section—

(A) The applicable percentage (as described in paragraph (f)(6)(ii) of this section) of the funding target is substituted for the funding target; and

(B) The transition funding shortfall is substituted for the funding shortfall.

(ii) *Transition rule not available for new plans or deficit reduction plans.*—The transition rule of paragraph (h)(4)(i) of this section does not apply to a plan—

(A) That was not in effect for a plan year beginning in 2007; or

(B) That was subject to section 412(l) for the last plan year beginning during 2007, determined after the application of sections 412(l)(6) and (9) (regardless of whether the deficit reduction contribution for that plan year was equal to zero).

(5) *Pre-effective plan year.*—(i) *In general.*—For purposes of this section, the pre-effective plan year for a plan is the last plan year beginning before section 430 applies to the plan to determine the minimum required contribution. Thus, except for plans with a delayed effective date as described in paragraph (h)(1) of this section, the pre-effective plan year for a plan is the last plan year beginning before January 1, 2008.

(ii) *Eligible charity plans.*—An eligible charity plan (as described in section 104(d) of PPA '06, which reflects amendments made by section 202(b)(2) of PRA 2010, Public Law No.111-192, 124 Stat. 1280 (June 25, 2010)) that applies section 430 to the first plan year beginning on or after January 1, 2008 has a pre-effective plan year that is the last plan year beginning before January 1, 2008 and a second pre-effective plan year that is the last plan year that precedes the plan year for which section 430 again applies to the plan. (Section 430 does not apply to such a plan for plan years beginning on or after January 1, 2009 and before January 1, 2017, unless the plan ceases to be an eligible charity plan, or an election under section 104(d)(2) or 104(d)(4) of PPA '06 is made for the plan not to be treated as an eligible charity plan, as of an earlier date.) [Reg. §1.430(a)-1.]

☐ [*T.D.* 9732, 9-8-2015.]

[Reg. §1.430(d)-1]

§1.430(d)-1. Determination of target normal cost and funding target.—(a) *In general.*—(1) *Overview.*—This section sets forth rules for determining a plan's target normal cost and funding target under sections 430(b) and 430(d), including guidance relating to the rules regarding actuarial assumptions under sections 430(h)(1), 430(h)(4), and 430(h)(5). Section 430 and this section apply to single employer defined benefit plans (including multiple employer plans as defined in section 413(c)) that are subject to section 412, but do not apply to multiemployer plans (as defined in section 414(f)). For further guidance on actuarial assumptions, *see* §1.430(h)(2)-1 (relating to interest rates) and §§1.430(h)(3)-1 and 1.430(h)(3)-2 (relating to mortality tables). *See* also §1.430(i)-1 for the determination of the funding target and the target normal cost for a plan that is in at-risk status.

(2) *Organization of regulation.*—Paragraph (b) of this section sets forth certain definitions that apply for purposes of section 430. Paragraph (c) of this section provides rules regarding which benefits are taken into account in determining a plan's target normal cost and funding target. Paragraph (d) of this section sets forth the rules regarding the plan provisions that are taken into account in making these determinations, and paragraph (e) of this section provides rules on the plan population that is taken into account for this purpose. Paragraph (f) of this section provides rules relating to the actuarial assumptions and the plan's funding method that are used to determine present values. Paragraph (g) of this section contains effective/applicability dates and transition rules.

(3) *Special rules for multiple employer plans.*—In the case of a multiple employer plan to which section 413(c)(4)(A) applies, the rules of section 430 and this section are applied separately for each employer under the plan, as if each employer maintained a separate plan. Thus, the plan's funding target and target normal cost are computed separately for each employer under such a multiple employer plan. In the case of a multiple employer plan to which section 413(c)(4)(A) does not apply (that is, a plan described in section 413(c)(4)(B) that has not made the election for section 413(c)(4)(A) to apply), the rules of section 430 and this section are applied as if all participants in the plan were employed by a single employer.

(b) *Definitions.*—(1) *Target normal cost.*—(i) *In general.*—For a plan that is not in at-risk status under section 430(i) for a plan year, subject to the adjustments described in paragraph (b)(1)(iii) of this section, the *target normal cost* of the plan for the plan year is the present value (determined as of the valuation date) of all benefits under the plan that accrue during, are earned during, or are otherwise allocated to service for the plan year under the applicable rules of this section, including paragraph (c)(1)(ii)(B), (C), or (D) of this section. *See* §1.430(i)-1(d) and (e)(2) for the determination of the target normal cost for a plan that is in at-risk status.

(ii) *Benefits allocated to a plan year.*—The benefits that accrue, are earned, or are otherwise allocated to service for the plan year are based on the actual benefits accrued, earned, or otherwise allocated to service for the plan year through the valuation date and benefits expected to accrue, be earned, or be otherwise allocated to service for the plan year for the period from the valuation date through the end of the plan year. The benefits that are allocated to the plan year under the rules of paragraph (c) of this section include any increase in benefits during the plan year that is attributable to increases in compensation for the current plan year even if that increase in benefits is with respect to benefits attributable to service performed in a preceding plan year. In addition, the benefits that are allocated to the plan year under the rules of paragraph (c) of this section include any increase in benefits during the plan year that arises on account of mandatory employee contributions (within the meaning of §1.411(c)-1(c)(4)) that are made during the plan year.

(iii) *Special adjustments.*—(A) *In general.*—The target normal cost of the plan for the plan year (determined under paragraph (b)(1)(i) of this section) is adjusted (not below zero) by adding the amount of plan-related expenses expected to be paid from plan assets during the plan year and subtracting the amount of mandatory employee contributions (within the meaning of §1.411(c)-1(c)(4)) that are expected to be made during the plan year.

(B) *Plan-related expenses.*—[Reserved.]

(2) *Funding target.*—For a plan that is not in at-risk status under section 430(i) for a plan year, the funding target of the plan for the plan year is the present value (determined as of the valuation date) of all benefits under the plan that have been accrued, earned, or otherwise allocated to years of service prior to the first day of the plan year under the applicable rules of this section, including paragraph (c)(1)(ii)(B), (C), or (D) of this section. *See* §1.430(i)-1(c) and (e)(1) for the determination of the funding target for a plan that is in at-risk status.

(3) *Funding target attainment percentage.*—(i) *In general.*—Except as otherwise provided in this paragraph (b)(3), the funding target attainment percentage of a plan for a plan year is a fraction (expressed as a percentage)—

(A) The numerator of which is the value of plan assets for the plan year (determined under the rules of §1.430(g)-1) after subtraction of the prefunding balance and the funding standard carryover balance under section 430(f)(4)(B) and §1.430(f)-1(c); and

(B) The denominator of which is the funding target of the plan for the plan year (determined without regard to the at-risk rules of section 430(i) and §1.430(i)-1).

(ii) *Determination of funding target attainment percentage for plans with delayed effective dates.*—If section 430 does not apply for purposes of determining the plan's minimum required contribution for a plan year that begins on or after January 1, 2008 (as is the case for a plan described in section 104, 105, or 106 of the Pension Protection Act of 2006 (PPA '06), Public Law 109-280 (120 Stat. 780)), then the funding target attainment percentage is determined for that plan year in accordance with the rules of paragraph (b)(3)(i) of this section in the same manner as for a plan to which section 430 applies to determine the plan's minimum required contribution, except that the value of plan assets that forms the numerator under paragraph (b)(3)(i)(A) of this section is determined without subtraction of the funding standard carryover balance or the credit balance under the funding standard account.

(iii) *Special rule for plans with zero funding target.*—If the funding target of the plan is equal to zero for a plan year, then the funding target attainment percentage under this paragraph (b)(3) is equal to 100 percent for the plan year.

(4) *Present value.*—The present value of a benefit (including a portion of a benefit) with respect to a participant that is taken into account under the rules of paragraph (c) of this section is determined as of the valuation date by multiplying the amount of that benefit by the probability that the benefit will be paid at a future date and then discounting the resulting product using the appropriate interest rate under §1.430(h)(2)-1. The probability that the benefit will be paid with respect to the participant at such future date is determined using the actuarial assumptions that satisfy the standards of paragraph (f) of this section as to the probability of future service, advancement in age, and other events (such as death, disability, termination of employment, and selection of optional form of benefit) that affect whether the participant or beneficiary will be eligible for the benefit and whether the benefit will be paid at that future date.

(c) *Benefits taken into account.*—(1) *In general.*—(i) *Benefits earned or accrued.*—The benefits taken into account in determining the target normal cost and the funding target under paragraph (b) of this section are all benefits earned or accrued under the plan that have not yet been paid as of the valuation date, including retirement-type and ancillary benefits (within the meaning of §1.411(d)-3(g)). The benefits taken into account are based on the participant's or beneficiary's status (such as active employee, vested or partially vested terminated employee, or disabled participant) as of the valuation date, and those benefits are allocated to the funding target or the target normal cost under paragraph (c)(1)(ii) of this section.

(ii) *Allocation of benefits.*—(A) *In general.*—To the extent that the amount of a participant's benefit that is expected to be paid is a function of the accrued benefit, the allocation of the benefit for purposes of determining the funding target and the target normal cost is made using the rules of paragraph (c)(1)(ii)(B) of this section. To the extent that the amount of a participant's benefit that is expected to be paid is not a function of the accrued benefit, but is a function of the participant's years of service (or is the excess of a function of the participant's years of service over a function of the participant's accrued benefit), the allocation of the benefit for purposes of determining the funding target and the target normal cost is made using the rules of paragraph (c)(1)(ii)(C) of this section. To the extent that the amount of a participant's benefit that is expected to be paid is not allocated under the rules of paragraph (c)(1)(ii)(B) or (C) of this section, the allocation of the benefit for purposes of determining the funding target and the target normal cost is made using the rules of paragraph (c)(1)(ii)(D) of this section.

(B) *Benefits that are based on accrued benefits.*—If the allocation of the benefit for purposes of determining the funding target and the target normal cost is made under this paragraph (c)(1)(ii)(B), then the portion of a participant's benefit that is taken into account in the funding target for a plan year is determined by applying the function to the accrued benefit as of the first day of the plan year, and the portion of the benefit that is taken into account in determining the target normal cost for the plan year is determined by applying that function to the increase in the accrued benefit during the plan year. For example, a benefit that is assumed to be payable at a particular early retirement age in the amount of 90 percent of the accrued benefit is taken into account in the funding target in the amount of 90 percent of the accrued benefit as of the beginning of the plan year, and that benefit is taken into account in the target normal cost in the amount of 90 percent of the increase in the accrued benefit during the plan year.

(C) *Benefits that are based on service.*—If the allocation of the benefit for purposes of determining the funding target and the target normal cost is made under this paragraph (c)(1)(ii)(C), then the portion of a participant's benefit that is taken into account in determining the funding target for a plan year is determined by applying the function to the participant's years of service as of the first day of the plan year, and the portion of the benefit that is taken into account in determining the target normal cost for the plan year is determined by applying that function to the increase in the participant's years of service during the plan year. For example, if a plan provides a post-retirement death benefit of $500 per year of service, then the funding target is determined based on a death benefit of $500 multiplied by a participant's years of service at the beginning of the year, and if the participant earns or is expected to earn a full year of service during the plan year, the target normal cost is based on the additional $500 in death benefits attributable to that additional year of service.

(D) *Other benefits.*—If the allocation of the benefit for purposes of determining the funding target and the target normal cost is made under this paragraph (c)(1)(ii)(D), then the portion of a participant's benefit that is taken into account in determining the funding target for a plan year is equal to the total benefit multiplied by the ratio of the participant's years of service as of the first day of the plan year to the years of service the participant will have at the time of the event that causes the benefit to be payable (whether the benefit is expected to be paid at the time of that decrement or at a future time), and the portion of the benefit that is taken into account in determining the target normal cost for the plan year is the increase in the proportionate benefit attributable to the increase in the participant's years of service during the plan year. For example, if a plan provides a Social Security supplement for a participant who retires after 30 years of service that is equal to a participant's Social Security benefit, the funding target with respect to the benefit payable beginning at a particular age (which reflects the probability of retirement at that age) is determined based on the projected Social Security benefit payable at the particular age multiplied by a fraction, the numerator of which is the participant's years of service as of the first day of the plan year and the denominator of which is the participant's projected years of service at the particular age. In such a case, if the participant earns or is expected to earn a full year of service during the plan year, the target normal cost is determined based on the projected Social Security benefit payable at the particular age multiplied by a fraction, the numerator of which is one and the denominator of which is the participant's projected years of service at the particular age.

(iii) *Application of section 436 limitations to funding target and target normal cost determination.*—(A) *Effect of limitation on unpredictable contingent event benefits.*—The determination of the funding target and the target normal cost of a plan for a plan year must take into account any limitation on unpredictable contingent event benefits under section 436(b) with respect to unpredictable contingent events which occurred before the valuation date, but must not take into account anticipated funding-based limitations on unpredictable contingent event benefits under section 436(b) with respect to unpredictable contingent events which are expected to occur on or after the valuation date.

(B) *Effect of limitation on applicability of plan amendments.*—See paragraph (d) of this section for rules regarding the treatment of plan amendments that take effect during the plan year taking into account the restrictions under section 436(c).

(C) *Effect of limitation on prohibited payments.*—The determination of the funding target and the target normal cost of a plan for a plan year must take into account any limitation on prohibited payments under section 436(d) with respect to any annuity starting date that was before the valuation date, but must not take into account any limitation on prohibited payments under section 436(d) for any annuity starting date on or after the valuation date (however, the determination must take into account benefit distributions under plan provisions that allow new annuity starting dates with respect to distributions that were limited under section 436(d)).

(D) *Effect of limitation on benefit accruals.*—Except as otherwise provided in this paragraph (c)(1)(iii)(D), the determination of the funding target of a plan for a plan year must take into account any limitation on benefit accruals under section 436(e) applicable before the valuation date. However, if the plan terms provide for the automatic restoration of benefit accruals as permitted under

§ 1.436-1(a)(4)(ii)(B), and the restoration of benefits as of the valuation date will not be treated as resulting from a plan amendment under the rules of § 1.436-1(c)(3) (because the period of limitation as of the valuation date does not exceed 12 months and the adjusted funding target attainment percentage for the plan would not be less than 60 percent taking into account the restored benefit accruals), then the determination of the funding target of a plan for a plan year must not take into account the limitation on benefit accruals under section 436(e) for that period. The determination of the target normal cost of a plan for a plan year must not take into account any limitation on benefit accruals under section 436(e). Thus, if an employer wishes to take a plan freeze into account in determining the target normal cost, the plan must be specifically amended to cease accruals.

(iv) *Effect of other limitations of benefits.*—(A) *Liquidity shortfalls.*—The determination of the funding target and the target normal cost of a plan for a plan year must take into account any restrictions on payments under section 401(a)(32) on account of a liquidity shortfall (as defined in section 430(j)(4)) for periods preceding the valuation date. The determination of the funding target and the target normal cost must not take into account any restrictions on payments under section 401(a)(32) on account of a liquidity shortfall or possible liquidity shortfall for any period on or after the valuation date.

(B) *High 25 limitation.*—The determination of the funding target and the target normal cost of a plan for a plan year must take into account any restrictions on payments under § 1.401(a)(4)-5(b) to highly compensated employees to the extent that benefits were not paid or will not be paid because of a limitation that applied prior to the valuation date. If a benefit that was otherwise restricted was paid prior to the valuation date but with suitable security (such as an escrow account) provided to the plan in the event of a plan termination, the benefit is treated as distributed for purposes of section 430 and this section. Accordingly, the funding target does not include any liability for the benefit and the plan assets do not include the security. The determination of the funding target and the target normal cost of a plan for a plan year must not take into account any restrictions on payments under § 1.401(a)(4)-5(b) to highly compensated employees that are anticipated with respect to annuity starting dates on or after the valuation date on account of the funded status of the plan.

(2) *Benefits provided by insurance.*—(i) *General rule.*—A plan generally is required to reflect in the plan's funding target and target normal cost the liability for benefits that are funded through insurance contracts held by the plan, and to include the corresponding insurance contracts in plan assets. Paragraph (c)(2)(ii) of this section sets forth an alternative to this general approach. A plan's treatment of benefits funded through insurance contracts pursuant to this paragraph (c)(2) is part of the plan's funding method. Accordingly, that treatment can be changed only with the consent of the Commissioner.

(ii) *Separate funding of insured benefits.*—As an alternative to the treatment described in paragraph (c)(2)(i) of this section, in the case of benefits that are funded through insurance contracts, the liability for benefits provided under such contracts is permitted to be excluded from the plan's funding target and target normal cost, provided that the corresponding insurance contracts are excluded from plan assets. This treatment is only available with respect to insurance purchased from an insurance company licensed under the laws of a State and only to the extent that a participant's or beneficiary's right to receive those benefits is an irrevocable contractual right under the insurance contracts, based on premiums paid to the insurance company prior to the valuation date. For example, in the case of a retired participant receiving benefits from an annuity contract in pay status under which no premiums are required on or after the valuation date, the liability for benefits provided by the contract is permitted to be excluded from the plan's funding target provided that the value of the contract is also excluded from the value of plan assets. Similarly, in the case of an active or deferred vested participant whose benefits are funded by a life insurance or annuity contract under which further premiums are required on or after the valuation date, the liability for benefits, if any, that would be paid from the contract if no further premiums were to be paid (for example, if the contract were to go on reduced paid-up status) is permitted to be excluded from the plan's funding target and target normal cost, provided that the value of the contract is excluded from the value of plan assets. By contrast, if the plan trustee can surrender a contract to the insurer for its cash value, then the participant's or beneficiary's right to receive those benefits is not an irrevocable contractual right and, therefore, the liability for benefits provided under the contract must be taken into account in determining the plan's funding target and target normal cost and the contracts cannot be excluded from plan assets.

(d) *Plan provisions taken into account.*—(1) *General rule.*—(i) *Plan provisions adopted by valuation date.*—Except as otherwise provided in this paragraph (d), a plan's funding target and target normal cost for a plan year are determined based on plan provisions that are adopted no later than the valuation date for the plan year and that take effect on or before the last day of the plan year. For example, in the case of a plan amendment adopted on or before the valuation date for the plan year that has an effective date occurring in the current plan year, the plan amendment is taken into account in determining the funding target and the target normal cost for the current plan year if it is permitted to take effect under the rules of section 436(c) for the current plan year, but the amendment is not taken into account for the current plan year if it does not take effect until a future plan year.

(ii) *Plan provisions adopted after valuation date.*—If a plan administrator makes the election described in section 412(d)(2) with respect to a plan amendment, then the plan amendment is treated as having been adopted on the first day of the plan year for purposes of this paragraph (d). Section 412(d)(2) applies to any plan amendment adopted no later than 2-1/2 months after the close of the plan year, including an amendment adopted during the plan year. Thus, if an amendment is adopted after the valuation date for a plan year (and no later than 2-1/2 months after the close of the plan year), but takes effect by the last day of the plan year, the amendment is taken into account in determining the plan's funding target and target normal cost for the plan year if the plan administrator makes the election described in section 412(d)(2) with respect to such amendment.

(iii) *Determination of when an amendment takes effect.*—For purposes of this paragraph (d)(1), the determination of whether an amendment that increases benefits takes effect and when it takes effect is determined in accordance with the rules of section 436(c) and §1.436-1(c)(5). For purposes of this paragraph (d)(1), in the case of an amendment that decreases benefits, the amendment takes effect under a plan on the first date on which the benefits of any individual who is or could be a participant or beneficiary under the plan would be less than those benefits would be under the preamendment plan provisions if the individual were on that date to satisfy the applicable conditions for the benefits. In either case, the determination of when an amendment takes effect is unaffected by an election under section 412(d)(2).

(2) *Special rule for certain amendments increasing liabilities.*—In the case of a plan amendment that is not required to be taken into account under the rules of paragraph (d)(1) of this section because it is adopted after the valuation date for the plan year, the plan amendment must be taken into account in determining a plan's funding target and target normal cost for the plan year if the plan amendment—

(i) Takes effect by the last day of the plan year;

(ii) Increases the liabilities of the plan by reason of increases in benefits, establishment of new benefits, changing the rate of benefit accrual, or changing the rate at which benefits become nonforfeitable; and

(iii) Would not be permitted to take effect under the rules of section 436(c) if those rules were applied—

(A) By treating the increase in the target normal cost for the plan year attributable to the amendment (and all other amendments that must be taken into account solely because of the application of the rules in this paragraph (d)(2)) as if the increase were an increase in the funding target for the plan year; and

(B) By taking into account all unpredictable contingent event benefits permitted to be paid for unpredictable contingent events that occurred during the current plan year and all plan amendments that took effect in the current plan year (including all amendments to which this paragraph (d)(2) applies for the plan year).

(3) *Allocation of benefits attributable to plan amendments.*—If a plan amendment is taken into account for a plan year under the rules of this paragraph (d), then the allocation of benefits that is used to determine the funding target and the target normal cost for that plan year is based on the plan as amended. Thus, if an amendment that is taken into account for a plan year increases a participant's accrued benefit for service prior to the beginning of the plan year, then the present value of that increase is included in the funding target for the plan year.

(e) *Plan population taken into account.*—(1) *In general.*—In making any determination of the funding target or target normal cost under paragraph (b) of this section, the plan population is determined as of the valuation date. The plan population must include three classes of individuals—

(i) Participants currently employed in the service of the employer;

(ii) Participants who are retired under the plan or who are otherwise no longer employed in the service of the employer; and

(iii) All other individuals currently entitled to benefits under the plan.

(2) *Assumption regarding rehiring of former employees.*—(i) *Special exclusion for "rule of parity" cases.*—Certain individuals may be excluded from the class of individuals described in paragraph (e)(1)(ii) of this section. The excludable individuals are those former employees who, prior to the valuation date for the plan year, have terminated service with the employer without vested benefits and whose service might be taken into account in future years because the "rule of parity" of section 411(a)(6)(D) does not permit that service to be disregarded. However, if the plan's experience as to separated employees returning to service has been such that the exclusion described in this paragraph (e)(2) would be unreasonable, then no such exclusion is permitted.

(ii) *Application to partially vested participants.*—Whether former employees who are terminated with partially vested benefits are assumed to return to service is determined under the same rules that apply to former employees without vested benefits under paragraph (e)(2)(i) of this section.

(3) *Anticipated future participants.*—In making any determination of the funding target or target normal cost under paragraph (b) of this section, the actuarial assumptions and funding method used for the plan must not anticipate the affiliation with the plan of future participants not employed in the service of the employer on the plan's valuation date. However, any such determination may anticipate the affiliation with the plan of current employees who have not yet satisfied the participation (age and service) requirements of the plan as of the valuation date.

(f) *Actuarial assumptions and funding method used in determination of present value.*—(1) *Selection of actuarial assumptions and funding method.*—(i) *General rules.*—The determination of any present value or other computation under section 430 and this section must be made on the basis of actuarial assumptions and a funding method. Except as otherwise specifically provided (for example, in §1.430(h)(2)-1(b)(6) or section 4006(a)(3)(E)(iv) of the Employee Retirement Income Security Act of 1974, as amended (ERISA)), the same actuarial assumptions and funding method must be used for all computations under sections 430 and 436. For example, the actuarial assumptions and the funding method used in making a certification of the adjusted funding target attainment percentage for a plan year must be the same as those disclosed on the actuarial report under section 6059 (Schedule SB, "Single-Employer Defined Benefit Plan Actuarial Information" of Form 5500, "Annual Return/Report of Employee Benefit Plan").

(ii) *Changes in actuarial assumptions and funding method.*—Actuarial assumptions established for a plan year cannot subsequently be changed for that plan year unless the Commissioner determines that the assumptions that were used are unreasonable. Similarly, a funding method established for a plan year cannot subsequently be changed for that plan year unless the Commissioner determines that the use of that funding method for that plan year is impermissible.

(iii) *Procedures for establishing actuarial assumptions and funding method.*—For purposes of this paragraph (f)(1), in the case of a plan for which an actuarial report under section 6059 (Schedule SB of Form 5500) is required to be filed for a plan year, actuarial assumptions and the funding method are established by the filing of the actuarial report if it is filed no later than the due date (with extensions) for the report. In the case of a plan for which an actuarial report for a plan year is not required to be filed, actuarial assumptions and the funding method are established by the delivery of the completed report to the employer if it is delivered no later than what would be the due date (with extensions) for filing the actuarial report were such a filing required. If the actuarial report is not filed or delivered by the applicable date described in the two preceding sentences, then the same actuarial assumptions (such as the same interest rate and mortality table elections) and funding method as were used for the preceding plan year apply for all computations under sections 430 and 436 for the current plan year, unless the Commissioner permits or requires other actuarial assumptions or another funding method permitted under section 430 to be used for the current plan year.

(iv) *Scope of funding method.*—A plan's funding method includes not only the overall funding method used by the plan but also each specific method of computation used in applying the overall method. However, the choice of which actuarial assumptions are appropriate to the overall method or to the specific method of computation is not a part of the funding method. The assumed earnings rate used for purposes of determining the actuarial value of assets under section 430(g)(3)(B) is treated as an actuarial assumption, rather than as part of the funding method.

(2) *Interest and mortality rates.*—Section 430(h)(2) and §1.430(h)(2)-1 set forth the interest rates, and section 430(h)(3) and §§1.430(h)(3)-1 and 1.430(h)(3)-2 set forth the mortality tables, that must be used for purposes of determining any present value under this section. However, notwithstanding the requirement to use the mortality tables, in the case of a plan which has fewer than 100 participants and beneficiaries who are not in pay status, the actuarial assumptions may assume no pre-retirement mortality, but only if that assumption would be a reasonable assumption.

(3) *Other assumptions.*—In the case of actuarial assumptions other than those specified in sections 430(h)(2), 430(h)(3), and 430(i), each of those actuarial assumptions must be reasonable (taking into account the experience of the plan and reasonable expectations). In addition, the actuarial assumptions (other than those specified in sections 430(h)(2), 430(h)(3), and 430(i)) must, in combination, offer the plan's enrolled actuary's best estimate of anticipated experience under the plan based on information determined as of the valuation date. *See* paragraph (f)(4)(iii) of this section for special rules for determining the present value of a single-sum and similar distributions.

(4) *Probability of benefit payments in single sum or other optional forms.*—(i) *In general.*—This paragraph (f)(4) provides rules relating to the probability that benefit payments will be paid as single sums or other optional forms under a plan and the impact of that probability on the determination of the present value of those benefit payments under section 430.

(ii) *General rules of application.*—Any determination of present value or any other computation under this section must take into account—

(A) The probability that future benefit payments under the plan will be made in the form of any optional form of benefit provided under the plan (including single-sum distributions), determined on the basis of the plan's experience and other related assumptions, in accordance with paragraph (f)(3) of this section; and

(B) Any difference in the present value of future benefit payments that results from the use of actuarial assumptions in determining the amount of benefit payments in any such optional form of benefit that are different from those prescribed by section 430(h).

(iii) *Single-sum and similar distributions.*—(A) *Distributions using section 417(e) assumptions.*—In the case of a distribution that is subject to section 417(e)(3) and that is determined using the applicable interest rates and applicable mortality table under section 417(e)(3), for purposes of applying paragraph (f)(4)(ii) of this section, the computation of the present value of that distribution is treated as having taken into account any difference in present value that results from the use of actuarial assumptions that are different from those prescribed by section 430(h) (as required under paragraph (f)(4)(ii)(B) of this section) if and only if the present value of the distribution is determined in accordance with this paragraph (f)(4)(iii).

(B) *Substitution of annuity form.*—Except as otherwise provided in this paragraph (f)(4)(iii), the present value of a distribution is determined in accordance with this paragraph (f)(4)(iii) if that present value is determined as the present value, using special actuarial assumptions, of the annuity (either the deferred or immediate annuity) which is used under the plan to determine the amount of the distribution. Under these special assumptions, for the period beginning with the expected annuity starting date for the distribution, the current applicable mortality table under section 417(e)(3) that would apply to a distribution with an annuity starting date occurring on the valuation date is substituted for the mortality table under section 430(h)(3) that would otherwise be used. In addition, under these special assumptions, the valuation interest rates under section 430(h)(2) are used for purposes of discounting the projected annuity payments from their expected payment dates to the valuation date (as opposed to the interest rates under section 417(e)(3) which the plan uses to determine the amount of the benefit).

(C) *Optional application of generational mortality and phase-in of interest rates.*—In determining the present value of a distribution under this paragraph (f)(4)(iii), if a plan uses the generational mortality tables under §1.430(h)(3)-1(a)(4) or §1.430(h)(3)-2, the plan is permitted to use a 50-50 male-female blend of the annuitant mortality rates under the §1.430(h)(3)-1(a)(4) generational mortality tables in *lieu of the applicable mortality table under section 417(e)(3)* that would apply to a distribution with an annuity starting date occurring on the valuation date. Similarly, a plan is permitted to make adjustments to the interest rates in order to reflect differences between the phase-in of the section 430(h)(2) segment rates under section

430(h)(2)(G) and the adjustments to the segment rates under section 417(e)(3)(D)(iii).

(D) *Distributions subject to section 417(e)(3) using other assumptions.*—In the case of a distribution that is subject to section 417(e)(3) but that is determined on a basis other than using the applicable interest rates and the applicable mortality table under section 417(e)(3), for purposes of applying paragraph (f)(4)(ii)(B) of this section, the computation of present value must take into account the extent to which the present value of the distribution is different from the present value determined using the rules of paragraph (f)(4)(iii)(B) of this section, based on actuarial assumptions that satisfy the requirements of paragraph (f)(3) of this section. If the plan provides that the amount of the benefit is based on a comparison of the section 417(e)(3) benefit (that is, the benefit determined using the applicable interest rates and the applicable mortality table under section 417(e)(3)) with another benefit determined using some other basis, then paragraph (f)(4)(ii)(B) of this section is applied as of the valuation date by comparing the present value of the section 417(e)(3) benefit determined under the rules of paragraph (f)(4)(iii)(B) of this section with the present value of the other benefit. The rule of this paragraph (f)(4)(iii)(D) applies, for example, where a distribution that is subject to section 417(e)(3) is determined as the greater of the benefit determined using the applicable interest rates and the applicable mortality table under section 417(e)(3) and the benefit determined using some other basis, or where the amount of a distribution that is subject to section 417(e)(3) is determined using an interest rate other than the applicable interest rates as required under section 415(b)(2)(E)(ii) (see §1.417(e)-1(d)(1)).

(5) *Distributions from applicable defined benefit plans under section 411(a)(13)(C).*—(i) *In general.*—In the case of an applicable defined benefit plan described in section 411(a)(13)(C), if the amount of a future distribution is based on an interest adjustment applied to the current accumulated benefit, then the amount of that distribution is determined by projecting the future interest credits or equivalent amount under the plan's interest crediting rules using actuarial assumptions that satisfy the requirements of paragraph (f)(3) of this section. Thus, if a plan provides for a singlesum distribution equal to the balance of a participant's hypothetical account under a cash balance plan, then the amount of that future distribution is equal to the projected account balance at the expected date of payment determined using actuarial assumptions that satisfy the requirements of paragraph (f)(3) of this section.

(ii) *Annuity distributions.*—(A) *General rule.*—In the case of an applicable defined benefit plan described in section 411(a)(13)(C), if the amount of an annuity distribution is based on either the balance of a hypothetical account maintained for a participant or the accumulated percentage of a participant's final average compensation, then the amount of that annuity distribution is calculated by converting the projected account balance (or accumulated percentage of final average compensation), in accordance with paragraph (f)(5)(i) of this section, to an annuity by applying the plan's annuity conversion provisions using the rules of this paragraph (f)(5)(ii).

(B) *Use of current annuity factors.*—Except as otherwise provided in paragraph (f)(5)(ii)(C) of this section, if the plan bases the conversion of the projected account balance (or accumulated percentage of final average compensation) to an annuity using the applicable interest rates and applicable mortality table under section 417(e)(3), then the amount of the annuity distribution is determined by dividing the projected account balance (or accumulated percentage of final average compensation) by an annuity factor corresponding to the assumed form of payment using, for the period beginning with the annuity starting date, the current applicable mortality table under section 417(e)(3) that would apply to a distribution with an annuity starting date occurring on the valuation date (in lieu of the mortality table under section 430(h)(3) that would otherwise be used) and the valuation interest rates under section 430(h)(2) (as opposed to the interest rates under section 417(e)(3) which the plan uses to determine the amount of the annuity).

(C) *Optional application of generational mortality and phase-in of segment rates.*—In determining the amount of an annuity distribution under paragraph (f)(5)(ii)(B) of this section, a plan is permitted to apply the options described in paragraph (f)(4)(iii)(C) of this section.

(D) *Distributions using assumptions other than assumptions under section 417(e)(3).*—In applying this paragraph (f)(5)(ii), in the case of a plan that determines an annuity using a basis other than the applicable interest rates and applicable mortality table under section 417(e)(3), the amount of the annuity distribution must be based on actuarial assumptions that satisfy the requirements of paragraph (f)(3) of this section.

(6) *Unpredictable contingent event benefits.*—Any determination of present value or any other computation under this section must take into account, based on information as of the valuation date, the probability that future benefits (or increased benefits) will become payable under the plan due to the occurrence of an unpredictable contingent event (as described in §1.436-1(j)(9)). For this purpose, this probability with respect to an unpredictable contingent event may be assumed to be zero if there is not more than a de minimis likelihood that the unpredictable contingent event will occur.

(7) *Reasonable techniques permitted.*—(i) *Determination of benefits to be paid during the plan year.*—Any reasonable technique can be used to determine the present value of the benefits expected to be paid during a plan year, based on the interest rates and mortality assumptions applicable for the plan year. For example, the present value of a monthly retirement annuity payable at the beginning of each month can be determined—

(A) Using the standard actuarial approximation that reflects 13/24ths of the discounted expected payments for the year as of the beginning of the year and 11/24ths of the discounted expected payments for the year as of the end of the year;

(B) By assuming a uniform distribution of death during the year; or

(C) By assuming that the payment is made in the middle of the year.

(ii) *Determination of target normal cost.*—In the case of a participant for whom there is a less than 100 percent probability that the participant will terminate employment during the plan year, for purposes of determining the benefits expected to accrue, be earned, or otherwise allocated to service during the plan year which are used to determine the target normal cost, it is permissible to assume the participant will not terminate during the plan year, unless using this method of calculation would be unreasonable.

(8) *Approval of significant changes in actuarial assumptions for large plans.*—(i) *In general.*—Except as otherwise provided in paragraph (f)(8)(iii) of this section, any actuarial assumptions used to determine the funding target of a plan for a plan year during which the plan is described in paragraph (f)(8)(ii) of this section cannot be changed from the actuarial assumptions that were used for the preceding plan year without the approval of the Commissioner if the changes in assumptions result in a decrease in the plan's funding shortfall (within the meaning of section 430(c)(4)) for the current plan year (disregarding the effect on the plan's funding shortfall resulting from changes in interest and mortality assumptions under sections 430(h)(2) and (h)(3)) that either exceeds $50,000,000, or exceeds $5,000,000 and is 5 percent or more of the funding target of the plan before such change.

(ii) *Affected plans.*—A plan is described in this paragraph (f)(8)(ii) for a plan year if—

(A) The plan is a defined benefit plan (other than a multiemployer plan) to which Title IV of ERISA applies; and

(B) The aggregate unfunded vested benefits used to determine variable-rate premiums for the plan year (as determined under section 4006(a)(3)(E)(iii) of ERISA) of the plan and all other plans maintained by the contributing sponsors (as defined in section 4001(a)(13) of ERISA) and members of such sponsors' controlled groups (as defined in section 4001(a)(14) of ERISA) which are covered by Title IV of ERISA (disregarding multiemployer plans and disregarding plans with no unfunded vested benefits) exceed $50,000,000.

(iii) *Automatic approval to resume use of previously used assumptions upon exiting at-risk status during phase-in.*—A plan that is not in at-risk status for the current plan year and that was in at-risk status for the prior plan year (but not for a period of 5 or more consecutive plan years) is granted automatic approval to use the actuarial assumptions that were applied before the plan entered at-risk status and that were used in combination with the required at-risk assumptions during the period the plan was in at-risk status.

(9) *Examples.*—The following examples illustrate the rules of this section. Unless otherwise indicated, these examples are based on the following assumptions: the normal retirement age is 65, the minimum required contribution for the plan is determined under the rules of section 430 starting in 2008, the plan year is the calendar year, the valuation date is January 1, no plan-related expenses are paid or expected to be paid from plan assets, and the plan does not provide for mandatory employee contributions. The examples are as follows:

Example 1. (i) Plan P provides an accrued benefit equal to 1.0% of a participant's highest 3-year average compensation for each year of service. Plan P provides that an early retirement benefit can be received at age 60 equal to the participant's accrued benefit reduced by 0.5% per month for early commencement. On January 1, 2010,

Participant A is age 60 and has 12 years of past service. Participant A's compensation for the years 2007 through 2009 was $47,000, $50,000, and $52,000, respectively. Participant A's rate of compensation at December 31, 2009, is $54,000 and A's rate of compensation for 2010 is assumed not to increase at any point during 2010. Decrements are applied at the beginning of the plan year.

(ii) Participant A's annual accrued benefit as of January 1, 2010, is $5,960 [0.01 × 12 × ($47,000 + $50,000 + $52,000) ÷ 3]. Participant A's expected benefit accrual for 2010 is $800 [0.01 × 13 × ($50,000 + $52,000 + $54,000) ÷ 3 − $5,960], to the extent that Participant A is expected to continue in employment for the full 2010 plan year.

(iii) Because the early retirement benefit is a function of the participant's accrued benefit, the allocation of the benefit for purposes of determining the target normal cost and funding target is made under paragraph (c)(1)(ii)(B) of this section. Accordingly, for Participant A, the early retirement benefit that is taken into account with respect to the decrement at age 60 when determining the 2010 funding target is $4,172 [$5,960 accrued benefit × (1 − 0.005 × 60 months)]. The expected accrual of the early retirement benefit during 2010 that is taken into account for Participant A with respect to the decrement at age 60 when determining the 2010 target normal cost is zero, because in this example the age-60 decrement would be applied as of January 1, 2010, before Participant A would earn any additional benefits. (But see paragraph (f)(7)(ii) of this section for an alternative approach for determining the expected accrual with respect to the decrement at age 60.)

(iv) The early retirement benefit for Participant A with respect to the decrement at age 61 that is taken into account in determining the funding target for the 2010 plan year is $4,529.60 [$5,960 accrued benefit × (1 − 0.005 × 48 months)]. The portion of the early retirement benefit that is taken into account for Participant A with respect to the decrement at age 61 that is taken into account in determining the target normal cost for the 2010 plan year is $608 [$800 expected annual accrual × (1 − 0.005 × 48 months)].

Example 2. (i) The facts are the same as in *Example 1*. In addition, the plan offers a $500 temporary monthly supplement to participants who complete 15 years of service and retire from active employment after attaining age 60. The temporary supplement is payable until the participant turns age 62. In addition, the supplement is limited so that it does not exceed the participant's Social Security benefit payable at age 62. On January 1, 2010, Participant B is age 55 and has 20 years of past service, and Participant C is age 60 and has 14 years of past service. For Participants B and C, the projected Social Security benefit is greater than $500 per month.

(ii) Because the temporary supplement is not a function of the participant's accrued benefit or service, the allocation of the benefit for purposes of determining the target normal cost and funding target is made under paragraph (c)(1)(ii)(D) of this section. The portion of the annual temporary supplement for Participant B with respect to the early retirement decrement occurring at age 60 that is taken into account in determining the funding target for the 2010 plan year is $4,800 [($500 × 12 months) × 20 years of past service ÷ 25 years of service at assumed early retirement age]. The portion of the annual temporary supplement for Participant B with respect to the early retirement decrement occurring at age 61 that is taken into account in determining the funding target for the 2010 plan year is $4,615 [($500 × 12 months) × 20 years of past service ÷ 26 years of service at assumed early retirement age]. In each case, the allocable portion of the benefit is assumed to be payable until age 62 (or the participant's death, if earlier).

(iii) For Participant B, the portion of the annual temporary supplement with respect to the early retirement decrement occurring at age 60 that is taken into account in determining the target normal cost for the 2010 plan year is $240 [($500 × 12 months) × 1 year of service expected to be earned during the plan year ÷ 25 years of service at assumed early retirement age]. The portion of the annual temporary supplement with respect to the early retirement decrement occurring at age 61 that is taken into account in determining the target normal cost for the 2010 plan year is $230.77 [($500 × 12 months) × 1 year of service expected to be earned during the plan year ÷ 26 years of service at assumed early retirement age]. The present value of these amounts reflects a payment period beginning with the decrement at age 60 or 61, as applicable, until age 62 (or assumed death, if earlier).

(iv) For Participant C, the portion of the annual temporary supplement with respect to the early retirement decrement occurring at age 61 (when the participant is first eligible for the benefit) that is taken into account in determining the funding target for the 2010 plan year is $5,600 [($500 × 12 months) × 14 years of past service ÷ 15 years of service at assumed early retirement age]. The present value of this amount reflects a payment period beginning with the decrement at age 61 until age 62 (or death if earlier).

Example 3. (i) The facts are the same as in *Example 1*. The plan also provides a single-sum death benefit (in addition to the qualified preretirement spouse's benefit) equal to the greater of the participant's annual accrued benefit at the time of death, or $10,000. The benefit is limited as necessary to ensure that the plan meets the incidental death benefit requirements of section 401(a).

(ii) The determination of the portion of the death benefit that is taken into account in determining the target normal cost and funding target is made under paragraph (c)(1)(ii)(B) of this section to the extent that it is a function of the participant's accrued benefit and under paragraph (c)(1)(ii)(D) of this section to the extent that it relates to the part of the death benefit that is not a function of the participant's accrued benefit.

(iii) The portion of the single-sum death benefit corresponding to the accrued benefit, or $5,960, is taken into account when determining the 2010 funding target for Participant A.

(iv) The excess of the death benefit over Participant A's accrued benefit is $4,040 (that is, $10,000 − $5,960). Because this part of the death benefit is not a function of the participant's accrued benefit nor is it a function of service, the determination of the corresponding portion of the death benefit taken into account in determining the target normal cost and funding target for 2010 is made under paragraph (c)(1)(ii)(D) of this section. For example, for Participant A, the portion of this benefit with respect to the death decrement occurring at age 64 that is taken into account for purposes of determining the funding target for the 2010 plan year is $3,030 ($4,040 × 12 years of past service ÷ 16 years of service at assumed age of death).

(v) The total single-sum death benefit for Participant A with respect to the death decrement at age 64 that is taken into account in determining the funding target for the 2010 plan year is $8,990 ($5,960 + $3,030).

(vi) Similarly, the portion of the single-sum death benefit for Participant A that is taken into account in determining the target normal cost for the 2010 plan year is equal to the sum of the expected increase in the accrued benefit during 2010, and the expected change in the allocable portion of the excess death benefit attributable to service during 2010 as determined in accordance with paragraph (c)(1)(ii)(D) of this section. As described in *Example 1*, the expected increase in Participant A's accrued benefit during 2010 is $800, to the extent that Participant A is expected to continue in employment for the full 2010 plan year.

(vii) At the end of 2010, Participant A's accrued benefit is expected to be $6,760 ($5,960 + $800). The excess portion of the single-sum death benefit to be allocated in accordance with paragraph (c)(1)(ii)(D) of this section is $3,240 ($10,000 − $6,760), and the allocable portion of the excess benefit for Participant A as of December 31, 2010, with respect to the death decrement at age 64, is $2,632.50 ($3,240 × 13 years of service as of December 31, 2010 ÷ 16 years of service at assumed age of death). The change in the allocable portion of Participant A's excess death benefit due to an additional year of service, with respect to the death decrement at age 64, is a decrease of $397.50. Therefore, the target normal cost for the 2010 plan year attributable to Participant A, with respect to the death decrement at age 64, will reflect a single-sum death benefit of $402.50 ($800 expected increase in Participant A's accrued benefit minus a $397.50 expected decrease in the allocable portion of the death benefit in excess of the accrued benefit).

Example 4. (i) The facts are the same as in *Example 3*, except that the plan provides a single-sum death benefit equal to the greater of the present value of the qualified pre-retirement survivor annuity or 100 times the amount of the participant's monthly retirement benefit with service projected to normal retirement age. The valuation is based on the assumption that all surviving spouses choose to receive their benefit in the form of a single sum. For Participant A, the value of the qualified pre-retirement survivor annuity is less than 100 times Participant A's projected monthly retirement benefit.

(ii) The allocation of the death benefit that is a function of Participant A's accrued benefit is based on service and compensation to the first day of the plan year for purposes of determining the funding target, and the allocation of the death benefit that is a function of the increase in Participant A's accrued benefit during the plan year for purposes of determining the target normal cost is made in accordance with paragraph (c)(1)(ii)(B) of this section. As described in *Example 1*, Participant A's accrued benefit based on service and compensation as of January 1, 2010, is $5,960, or $496.67 per month. Accordingly, the portion of the single-sum death benefit corresponding to the accrued benefit, or $49,667 (100 times $496.67), is taken into account when determining the 2010 funding target for Participant A.

(iii) In addition, the funding target and the target normal cost *reflect a portion of Participant A's death benefit* in excess of the amount based on Participant A's accrued benefit. Based on Participant A's average compensation as of the first day of the plan year, Participant A's accrued benefit with service projected to normal retirement is $8,443 [.01 × 17 years of service at age 65 × ($47,000 +

$50,000 + $52,000) ÷ 3], or $703.61 per month. The corresponding death benefit is $70,361.

(iv) The excess of the death benefit over Participant A's accrued benefit as of January 1, 2010, is $20,694 (that is, $70,361 − $49,667). Because this part of the death benefit is not a function of Participant A's accrued benefit or service, the portion that is taken into account in determining the funding target is determined under paragraph (c)(1)(ii)(D) of this section. For Participant A, the portion of this benefit with respect to the death decrement occurring at age 64 that is taken into account when determining the funding target for the 2010 plan year is $15,521 ($20,694 × 12 years of past service ÷16 years of service at assumed age of death). The total single-sum death benefit for Participant A with respect to the death decrement at age 64 reflected in the funding target for the 2010 plan year is $65,188 ($49,667 + $15,521).

(v) Similarly, the portion of the single-sum death benefit for Participant A that is taken into account when determining the target normal cost for 2010 is equal to the sum of the death benefit based on the expected increase in the accrued benefit during 2010 and the expected change in the allocable portion of the excess death benefit attributable to service during 2010 as determined in accordance with paragraph (c)(1)(ii)(D) of this section.

(vi) At the end of 2010, Participant A's accrued benefit is expected to be $6,760 ($5,960 + $800), or $563.33 per month, and the associated death benefit is $56,333. The expected increase in the amount of the death benefit attributable to the increase in Participant A's accrued benefit is therefore $6,666 ($56,333 − $49,667).

(vii) Participant A's projected accrued benefit at normal retirement based on average compensation as of the end of 2010 is $8,840 [.01 × 17 years of service at age 65 × ($50,000 + $52,000 + $54,000) ÷ 3], or $736.67 per month. The corresponding death benefit is $73,667. The excess portion of the single-sum death benefit to be allocated in accordance with paragraph (c)(1)(ii)(D) of this section is $17,334 ($73,667 − $56,333), and the allocable portion of the excess benefit for Participant A as of December 31, 2010, with respect to the death decrement at age 64, is $14,084 ($17,334 × 13 years of service as of December 31, 2010 ÷ 16 years of service at assumed age of death).

(viii) The change in the allocable portion of Participant A's excess death benefit during 2010, with respect to the death decrement at age 64, is a decrease of $1,437 ($14,084 − $15,521). Therefore, the target normal cost for the 2010 plan year attributable to Participant A, with respect to the death decrement at age 64, will reflect a single-sum death benefit of $5,229 ($6,666 expected increase in Participant A's death benefit based on the expected increase in the accrued benefit, minus an expected decrease of $1,437 in the amount of the death benefit in excess of the amount attributable to the accrued benefit).

Example 5. (i) The facts are the same as in *Example 1*. In addition, the plan provides a disability benefit to participants who become disabled after completing 15 years of service. The disability benefit is payable at normal retirement age or an earlier date if elected by a participant. For purposes of calculating the disability benefit, service continues to accrue until normal retirement age (unless recovery or commencement of retirement benefits occurs earlier). Further, compensation is deemed to continue at the same rate as when the disability began.

(ii) Participant A will be eligible for the disability benefit at age 63 after completion of 15 years of service. Participant A's annual disability benefit at normal retirement age is $9,180 (that is, 1% of highest 3-year average compensation of $54,000 multiplied by 17 years of deemed service at normal retirement age).

(iii) The portion of the disability benefit based on the participant's accrued benefit as of the valuation date that is taken into account in determining the target normal cost and funding target is determined in accordance with paragraph (c)(1)(ii)(B) of this section. Accordingly, the portion of the disability benefit corresponding to Participant A's accrued benefit as of January 1, 2010, or $5,960, is taken into account when determining the 2010 funding target.

(iv) The excess of Participant A's disability benefit over the accrued benefit as of January 1, 2010, is $3,220 ($9,180 minus $5,960). Because this portion of the disability benefit is not based on Participant A's accrued benefit or service, the portion that is taken into account in determining the funding target is determined under paragraph (c)(1)(ii)(D) of this section. The portion of Participant A's excess disability benefit with respect to the disability decrement occurring at age 63 that is taken into account when determining the 2010 funding target is $2,576 [$3,220 × (12 years of past service ÷ 15 years of service at assumed date of disability)]. The total disability benefit for Participant A, with respect to the disability decrement occurring at age 63, that is taken into account in determining the funding target for the 2010 plan year is $8,536 ($5,960 + $2,576).

(v) The portion of Participant A's disability benefit with respect to the disability decrement occurring at age 64 that is taken into account when determining the 2010 funding target is $8,375 [$5,960 +

$3,220 × (12 years of past service ÷ 16 years of service at assumed date of disability)].

(vi) If in fact Participant A becomes disabled at age 63, the funding target will reflect the full disability benefit to which Participant A will be entitled at normal retirement age, based on service projected to normal retirement age (17 years) and final average compensation reflecting compensation projected to normal retirement age at the rate Participant A was earning at the time of disablement.

Example 6. (i) The facts are the same as in *Example 5*, except that the disability benefit is based on the accrued benefit calculated using service and compensation earned to the date of disability.

(ii) Because the disability benefit is a function of the participant's accrued benefit, the portion of Participant A's disability benefit that is taken into account when determining the funding target for the 2010 plan year is Participant A's annual accrued benefit as of January 1, 2010, or $5,960, as determined in *Example 1*. This amount is taken into account for both the disability decrement occurring at age 63 and the disability decrement occurring at age 64.

(iii) Similarly, the benefit accrual for Participant A with respect to the disability decrements occurring at age 63 and age 64 that is taken into account when determining the target normal cost for the 2010 plan year is equal to Participant A's expected benefit accrual for 2010 determined in *Example 1*, or $800.

Example 7. (i) Retiree D, a participant in Plan P, is a male age 72 and is receiving a $100 monthly straight life annuity. The 2009 actuarial valuation is performed using the segment rates applicable for September 2008 (determined without regard to the transition rule of section 430(h)(2)(G)), and the 2009 annuitant and nonannuitant (male and female) mortality tables (published in Notice 2008-85). See §601.601(d)(2) relating to objectives and standards for publishing regulations, revenue rulings and revenue procedures in the Internal Revenue Bulletin.

(ii) The present value of Retiree D's straight life annuity on the valuation date is $10,535.79. This is equal to the sum of: $5,029.99, which is the present value of payments expected to be made during the first 5 years, using the first segment interest rate of 5.07%; $5,322.26, which is the present value of payments expected to be made during the next 15 years, using the second segment interest rate of 6.09%; and $183.54, which is the present value of payments expected to be made after 20 years, using the third segment interest rate of 6.56%.

Example 8. (i) The facts are same as in *Example 7*. Plan P does not provide for early retirement benefits or single-sum distributions. The actuary assumes that no participants terminate employment prior to age 50 (other than by death), there is a 5% probability of withdrawal at age 50, and that those participants who withdraw receive a deferred annuity starting at age 65. Participant E is a male age 46 on January 1, 2009, and has an annual accrued benefit of $23,000 beginning at age 65.

(ii) Before taking into account the 5% probability of withdrawal, the funding target associated with Participant E's assumed age 50 withdrawal benefit in the 2009 actuarial valuation is $68,396.75. This is equal to the sum of: $6,925.29, which is the present value of payments expected to be made during the year the participant turns age 65 (the 20th year after the valuation date), using the second segment interest rate of 6.09%; and $61,471.46, which is the present value of payments expected to be made after the 20th year, using the third segment interest rate of 6.56%.

(iii) Taking the 5% probability of withdrawal into account, the funding target for the 2009 plan year associated with Participant E's assumed age 50 withdrawal benefit is $3,419.84 ($68,396.75 × 5%).

Example 9. (i) The facts are the same as in *Example 8*, except the plan offers a single-sum distribution payable at normal retirement age (age 65) determined based on the applicable interest rates and the applicable mortality table under section 417(e)(3). The actuary assumes that 70% of the participants will elect a single sum upon retirement and the remaining 30% will elect a straight life annuity.

Age	Maturity
65	19.5
66	20.5
67	21.5
68 and over	Varies
Total	

(iii) Applying the 5% probability of withdrawal, the portion of the funding target for the 2009 plan year attributable to Participant E's assumed withdrawal at age 50 is $3,369.71 ($67,394.12 × 5%).

Example 12. (i) The facts are the same as in *Example 10*, except that the plan determines the amount of the immediate single-sum distribution upon withdrawal at age 50 based on the applicable interest rates under section 417(e)(3) or an interest rate of 6.25%,

(ii) Before taking into account the 5% probability of withdrawal or the 70% probability of electing a single-sum payment, the portion of the 2009 funding target that is attributable to Participant E's assumed single-sum payment, deferred to age 65, is $70,052.30. This is calculated in the same manner as the present value of annuity payments, except that, for the period after the annuity starting date, the 2009 applicable mortality rates are substituted for the 2009 male annuitant mortality rates. This portion of the funding target for the 2009 plan year is equal to the sum of: $6,929.00, which is the present value of annuity payments expected to be made between age 65 and 66 (during the 20th year after the valuation date), using the second segment interest rate of 6.09%; and $63,123.30, which is the present value of annuity payments expected to be made after the 20th year following the valuation date, using the third segment interest rate of 6.56%. These present value amounts reflect the 2009 male nonannuitant mortality rates prior to the assumed commencement of benefits at age 65 and the 100% probability of retiring at age 65.

(iii) Taking the 5% probability of withdrawal and the 70% probability of electing a single-sum payment into account, the portion of the 2009 funding target attributable to Participant E's assumed single-sum payment based on withdrawal at age 50 is $2,451.83 ($70,052.30 × 5% × 70%). After taking into account the 5% probability of withdrawal and the 30% probability of electing a straight life annuity, the portion of the 2009 funding target that is attributable to Participant E's assumed straight life annuity (based on assumed withdrawal at age 50), deferred to age 65, is equal to 30% of the result obtained in *Example 8*.

Example 10. (i) The facts are the same as in *Example 9*, except the plan offers an immediate single sum upon withdrawal at age 50 determined based on the applicable interest rates and the applicable mortality table under section 417(e)(3). The actuary assumes that 70% of the participants will elect to receive a single-sum distribution upon withdrawal.

(ii) Before taking into account the 5% probability of withdrawal and the 70% probability of electing a single-sum payment, the portion of the funding target for the 2009 plan year that is attributable to Participant E's assumed single-sum payment based on withdrawal at age 50 is $68,908.39. This is calculated in the same manner as the present value of annuity payments, except that the 2009 applicable mortality rates are substituted for the 2009 male annuitant and nonannuitant mortality rates after the annuity starting date. This portion of the 2009 funding target is equal to the sum of $6,815.85, which is the present value of annuity payments expected to be made between age 65 and 66 (during the 20th year after the valuation date), using the second segment interest rate of 6.09%, and $62,092.54, which is the present value of annuity payments expected to be made after the 20th year following the valuation date, using the third segment interest rate of 6.56%. These present value amounts reflect the 2009 male nonannuitant mortality rates prior to the assumed single-sum distribution age of 50.

(iii) Applying the 5% probability of withdrawal at age 50 and the 70% probability of electing a single-sum payment, the portion of the funding target for the 2009 plan year that is attributable to Participant E's assumed single-sum payment (based on withdrawal at age 50) is $2,411.79 ($68,908.39 × 5% × 70%).

Example 11. (i) The facts are the same as in *Example 8*, except that the plan sponsor elects under section 430(h)(2)(D)(ii) to use the monthly corporate bond yield curve instead of segment rates. The enrolled actuary assumes payments are made monthly throughout the year and uses the interest rate from the middle of the monthly corporate bond yield curve because this mid-year yield rate most closely matches the average timing of benefits paid. In accordance with §1.430(h)(2)-1(e)(4), the applicable monthly corporate bond yield curve is the yield curve derived from December 2008 rates.

(ii) Before taking into account the 5% probability of withdrawal, the funding target associated with Participant E's assumed age 50 withdrawal benefit in the 2009 actuarial valuation is $67,394.12. This reflects the sum of each year's expected payments, discounted at the yield rates described in paragraph (i) of this *Example 11*, as shown below:

Yield rate	Present value
6.97%	$5,897.88
6.90%	5,524.69
6.84%	5,164.63
Varies	50,806.92
	$67,394.12

whichever produces the higher amount. The applicable mortality table under section 417(e)(3) is used for both calculations.

(ii) Before taking into account the 5% probability of withdrawal and the 70% probability of electing a single-sum payment, the present value of Participant E's singlesum distribution as of January 1, 2009, using an interest rate of 6.25%, based on withdrawal at age 50, is $77,391.88. This amount is determined by calculating the projected single-sum distribution at age 50 using the applicable mortality rate under section 417(e)(3) and an interest rate of 6.25%, or $94,789.10, and discounting the result to the January 1, 2009, valuation date using the first segment rate of 5.07% because the single-sum distribution is assumed to be paid 4 years after the valuation date) and the male non-annuitant mortality rates for 2009.

(iii) Before taking into account the 5% probability of withdrawal and the 70% probability of electing a single-sum payment, the present value as of January 1, 2009, of Participant E's age-50 single-sum distribution using the applicable interest rates and applicable mortality table under section 417(e)(3) is $68,908.39, as developed in *Example 10.* Corresponding to plan provisions, the present value reflected in the funding target is the larger of this amount or the present value of the amount based on a 6.25% interest rate, or $77,391.88.

(iv) Applying the 5% probability of withdrawal at age 50 and the 70% probability of electing a single-sum payment, the portion of the funding target for the 2009 plan year that is attributable to Participant E's assumed single-sum payment (based on withdrawal at age 50) is $2,708.72 ($77,391.88 × 5% × 70%).

Example 13. (i) Plan Q is a cash balance plan that permits an immediate payment of a single sum equal to the participant's hypothetical account balance upon termination of employment. Plan Q's terms provide that the hypothetical account is credited with interest at a market-related rate, based on a specified index. The January 1, 2009, actuarial valuation is performed using the 24-month average segment rates applicable for September 2008 (determined without regard to the transition rule of section 430(h)(2)(G)). Participant F is a male age 61 on January 1, 2009, and has a hypothetical account balance equal to $150,000 on that date. In the 2009 actuarial valuation, the enrolled actuary assumes that the hypothetical account balances will increase with annual interest credits of 7% until the participant commences receiving his or her benefit, corresponding to the actuary's best estimate of future interest rates credited under the terms of the plan. The actuary also assumes that all participants will retire on the first day of the plan year in which they attain age 65 (that is, no participant will terminate employment prior to age 65 other than by death), and that 100% of participants will elect a single sum upon retirement.

(ii) Participant F's hypothetical account balance projected to January 1, 2013 (the plan year in which F attains age 65) is $196,619.40 based on the assumed annual interest crediting rate of 7%. The funding target for the 2009 plan year attributable to Participant F's benefit at age 65 is $158,525.81, which is calculated by discounting the projected hypothetical account balance of $196,619.40 using the first segment rate of 5.07% and the male non-annuitant mortality rates.

Example 14. (i) The facts are the same as in *Example 13*, except that the actuary assumes that 10% of the participants will choose to collect their benefits in the form of a straight life annuity. The plan provides that the participant's account balance at retirement is converted to an annuity using the applicable interest rates and applicable mortality table under section 417(e)(3).

(ii) Participant F's hypothetical account balance projected to January 1, 2013 (the plan year in which F attains age 65) is $196,619.40, as outlined in *Example 13*. This amount is converted to an annuity payable commencing at age 65 by dividing the projected account balance by an annuity factor based on the applicable mortality table for 2009 under section 417(e)(3) (corresponding to the valuation date) and the interest rates used for the valuation. The resulting annuity factor is 10.8321, reflecting one year of interest at the first segment rate (5.07%) corresponding to the first year of the expected annuity payments (the fifth year after the valuation date), 15 years of interest at the second segment rate (6.09%) and all remaining years at the third segment rate (6.56%). The projected future annuity is therefore $196,619.40 divided by 10.8321, or $18,151.55 per year.

(iii) Before taking into account the 10% probability that the participant will elect to take the distribution in the form of a lifetime annuity, the funding target associated with the future annuity payout for Participant F is $149,120.41. This is equal to the sum of $14,242.79, which is the present value of the annuity payment expected to made during the year the participant turns age 65 (the 5th year after the valuation date), using the first segment interest rate of 5.07%; $116,321.72, which is the present value of payments expected to be made during the 6th through the 20th years following the valuation date, using the second segment interest rate of 6.09%; and $18,555.90, which is the present value of payments expected to be made after the 20th year following the valuation date, using the third segment interest rate of 6.56%.

(iv) Applying the 10% probability of electing a lifetime annuity, the portion of the 2009 funding target attributable to Participant F's assumed lifetime annuity payable at age 65 is $14,912.04. The portion of the 2009 funding target attributable to Participant F's assumed single-sum payment is 90% of the result obtained in *Example 13*.

Example 15. (i) Plan H provides a monthly benefit of $50 times service for all participants. Plan H has a funding target of $1,000,000 and an actuarial value of assets of $810,000 as of January 1, 2010. No annuity contracts have been purchased, and Plan H has no funding standard carryover balance or prefunding balance as of January 1, 2010. The enrolled actuary certifies that the January 1, 2010, AFTAP is 81%. Effective July 1, 2010, Plan H is amended on June 14, 2010, to increase the plan's monthly benefit to $55 for years of service earned on or after July 1, 2010. The present value of the increase in plan benefits during 2010 (reflecting benefit accruals attributable to the six months between July 1, 2010, and December 31, 2010) is $25,000.

(ii) The amendment increases benefits for future service only, and so the funding target is unaffected. Since section 436(c) only restricts plan amendments that increase plan liabilities, the plan amendment can take effect.

(iii) If the $25,000 present value of the increase in plan benefits during 2010 were included in Plan H's funding target of $1,000,000, the total would be $1,025,000, and the AFTAP would be 79.02% (that is, $810,000 / $1,025,000). Since this is less than 80%, the amendment would not have been permitted to take effect if the 2010 increase were included in the funding target instead of target normal cost.

(iv) Because the amendment was adopted after the January 1, 2010, valuation date, the plan sponsor would generally have the option of deciding whether to reflect this amendment in the January 1, 2010, valuation or defer recognition of the amendment to the January 1, 2011, valuation. However, under paragraph (d)(2) of this section, because the plan amendment would not have been permitted to take effect under the provisions of section 436 if the increase in the target normal cost for the plan year had been taken into account in the funding target, the actuary must take into account the amendment in the January 1, 2010, valuation for purposes of section 430. Thus, the target normal cost for the plan year includes the $25,000 that results from the plan amendment.

(g) *Effective/applicability dates and transition rules.*—(1) *Statutory effective date/applicability date.*—(i) *In general.*—Section 430 generally applies to plan years beginning on or after January 1, 2008. The applicability of section 430 for purposes of determining the minimum required contribution is delayed for certain plans in accordance with sections 104 through 106 of PPA '06.

(ii) *Applicability of special adjustments.*—The special adjustments of paragraph (b)(1)(iii) of this section (relating to adjustments to the target normal cost for plan-related expenses and mandatory employee contributions) apply to plan years beginning after December 31, 2008. In addition, a plan sponsor may elect to make the special adjustments of paragraph (b)(1)(iii) of this section for a plan year beginning in 2008. This election must take into account both adjustments described in paragraph (b)(1)(iii) of this section. This election is subject to the same rules that apply to an election to add an amount to the plan's prefunding balance pursuant to §1.430(f)-1(f), and it must be made in the same manner as the election made under §1.430(f)-1(f). Thus, the election can be made no later than the last day for making the minimum required contribution for the plan year to which the election relates.

(2) *Effective date/applicability date of regulations.*—This section applies to plan years beginning on or after January 1, 2010, regardless of whether section 430 applies to determine the minimum required contribution for the plan year. For plan years beginning before January 1, 2010, plans are permitted to rely on the provisions set forth in this section for purposes of satisfying the requirements of section 430.

(3) *Approval for changes in funding method.*—(i) *2008 plan year.*—Any changes in a plan's funding method that are made for the first plan year beginning in 2008 that are not inconsistent with the requirements of section 430 are treated as having been approved by the Commissioner and do not require the Commissioner's specific prior approval.

(ii) *Application of this section.*—(A) *First plan year for which regulations are effective.*—Except as otherwise provided in paragraph (g)(3)(ii)(B) of this section, any change in a plan's funding method for the first plan year that begins on or after January 1, 2010, is treated as having been approved by the Commissioner and does not require the Commissioner's specific prior approval.

(B) *Optional earlier application of regulations.*—For the first plan year that a plan applies all the provisions of this section, §§1.430(f)-1, 1.430(g)-1, 1.430(i)-1, and 1.436-1, any change in a plan's funding method for that plan year is treated as having been approved by the Commissioner and does not require the Commissioner's specific prior approval. For example, if the change in funding method includes a change in the valuation software, the change in the valuation software is treated as having been approved by the Commissioner and does not require the Commissioner's specific prior approval. If that plan year begins before January 1, 2010, the automatic approval for a change in funding method under paragraph (g)(3)(ii)(A) of this section does not apply to the plan.

(C) *Special rule for changes in allocation.*—Any change in a plan's funding method for a plan year earlier than the first plan year beginning on or after January 1, 2010, that is necessary to apply the rules of paragraph (c)(1)(ii) of this section is treated as having been approved by the Commissioner and does not require the Commissioner's specific prior approval.

(iii) *First plan year for which section 430 applies to determine minimum funding.*—For a plan for which the minimum required contribution is not determined under section 430 for the first plan year that begins on or after January 1, 2008, pursuant to sections 104 through 106 of PPA '06, any change in a plan's funding method for the first plan year to which section 430 applies to determine the plan's minimum required contribution is treated as having been approved by the Commissioner and does not require the Commissioner's specific prior approval.

(4) *Approval for changes in actuarial assumptions.*—The Commissioner's specific prior approval is not required with respect to any actuarial assumptions that are adopted for the first plan year for which section 430 applies to determine the minimum required contribution for the plan and that are not inconsistent with the requirements of section 430.

(5) *Transition rule for determining funding target attainment percentage for the 2007 plan year.*—(i) *In general.*—For purposes of the first plan year beginning on or after January 1, 2008, the funding target attainment percentage for the plan's prior plan year (the 2007 plan year) is determined as the fraction (expressed as a percentage), the numerator of which is the value of plan assets determined under paragraph (g)(5)(ii) of this section, and the denominator of which is the plan's current liability determined pursuant to section 412(l)(7) (as in effect prior to amendment by PPA '06) as of the valuation date for the 2007 plan year.

(ii) *Determination of value of plan assets.*—(A) *In general.*—The value of plan assets for the 2007 plan year under this paragraph (g)(5)(ii)(A) is determined as the value of plan assets as described in paragraph (g)(5)(ii)(B) of this section, reduced by the plan's funding standard account credit balance for the 2007 plan year as described in paragraph (g)(5)(iii)(A) of this section except to the extent provided in paragraph (g)(5)(iii)(B) of this section.

(B) *Value of plan assets.*—The value of plan assets for the 2007 plan year under this paragraph (g)(5)(ii)(B) is determined under section 412(c)(2) as in effect for the 2007 plan year, except that the value of plan assets prior to subtracting the plan's funding standard account credit balance described in paragraph (g)(5)(iii)(A) of this section must be adjusted so that it is neither less than 90 percent of the fair market value of plan assets nor greater than 110 percent of the fair market value of plan assets on the valuation date for that plan year. If the value of plan assets prior to adjustment under this paragraph (g)(5)(ii)(B) is less than 90 percent of the fair market value of plan assets on the valuation date, then the value of plan assets under this paragraph (g)(5)(ii)(B) is equal to 90 percent of the fair market value of plan assets. If the value of plan assets determined under this paragraph (g)(5)(ii)(B) is greater than 110 percent of the fair market value of plan assets on the valuation date, then the value of plan assets under this paragraph (g)(5)(ii)(B) is equal to 110 percent of the fair market value of plan assets.

(iii) *Subtraction of credit balance.*—(A) *In general.*—If a plan has a funding standard account credit balance as of the valuation date for the 2007 plan year, then, except as described in paragraph (g)(5)(iii)(B) of this section, that balance is subtracted from the value of plan assets described in paragraph (g)(5)(ii)(B) of this section as of that valuation date to determine the value of plan assets for the 2007 plan year. However, the value of plan assets is not reduced below zero.

(B) *Effect of funding standard carryover balance reduction for the 2008 plan year.*—Notwithstanding the rules of paragraph (g)(5)(iii)(A) of this section, for the first plan year beginning in 2008, if the employer has made an election to reduce some or all of the funding standard carryover balance as of the first day of that year in accordance with §1.430(f)-1(e), then the present value (determined as of the valuation date for the 2007 plan year using the valuation interest rate for that 2007 plan year) of the amount so reduced is not treated as part of the funding standard account credit balance when that balance is subtracted from the value of plan assets pursuant to paragraph (g)(5)(iii)(A) of this section. [Reg. §1.430(d)-1.]

☐ [*T.D. 9467*, 10-14-2009.]

[Reg. §1.430(f)-1]

§1.430(f)-1. Effect of prefunding balance and funding standard carryover balance.—(a) *In general.*—(1) *Overview.*—This section provides rules relating to the application of prefunding and funding standard carryover balances under section 430(f). Section 430 and this section apply to single employer defined benefit plans (including multiple employer plans) that are subject to section 412, but do not apply to multiemployer plans (as defined in section 414(f)). Paragraph (b) of this section sets forth rules regarding a plan's prefunding balance and a plan sponsor's election to maintain a funding standard carryover balance. Paragraph (c) of this section provides rules under which those balances must be subtracted from plan assets. Paragraph (d) of this section describes a plan sponsor's election to use those balances to offset the minimum required contribution. Paragraph (e) of this section describes a plan sponsor's election to reduce those balances (which will affect the determination of the value of plan assets for purposes of sections 430 and 436). Paragraph (f) of this section sets forth rules regarding elections under this section. Paragraph (g) of this section contains examples. Paragraph (h) of this section contains effective/applicability dates and transition rules.

(2) *Special rules for multiple employer plans.*—In the case of a multiple employer plan to which section 413(c)(4)(A) applies, the rules of this section are applied separately for each employer under the plan, as if each employer maintained a separate plan. Thus, each employer under such a multiple employer plan may have a separate funding standard carryover balance and a prefunding balance for the plan. In the case of a multiple employer plan to which section 413(c)(4)(A) does not apply (that is, a plan described in section 413(c)(4)(B) that has not made the election for section 413(c)(4)(A) to apply), the rules of this section are applied as if all participants in the plan were employed by a single employer.

(b) *Maintenance of balances.*—(1) *Prefunding balance.*—(i) *In general.*—A plan sponsor is permitted to elect to maintain a prefunding balance for a plan. A prefunding balance maintained for a plan consists of a beginning balance of zero, increased by the amount of excess contributions to the extent the employer elects to do so as described in paragraph (b)(1)(ii) of this section, and decreased to the extent provided in paragraph (b)(1)(iii) of this section. The plan sponsor's initial election to add to the prefunding balance under paragraph (b)(1)(ii) of this section constitutes an election to maintain a prefunding balance. The prefunding balance is adjusted further for investment return and interest as provided in paragraphs (b)(3) and (b)(4) of this section.

(ii) *Increases.*—(A) *In general.*—If the plan sponsor of a plan elects to add to the plan's prefunding balance, as of the first day of a plan year following the first effective plan year for the plan, the prefunding balance is increased by the amount so elected by the plan sponsor for the plan year. The amount added to the prefunding balance cannot exceed the present value of the excess contributions for the preceding plan year determined under paragraph (b)(1)(ii)(B) of this section, increased for interest in accordance with paragraph (b)(1)(iv)(A) of this section.

(B) *Present value of excess contribution.*—The present value of the excess contribution for the preceding plan year is the excess, if any, of—

(1) The present value (determined under the rules of paragraph (b)(1)(iv)(B) of this section) of the employer contributions (other than contributions to avoid or terminate benefit limitations described in §1.436-1(f)(2)) to the plan for such preceding plan year; over

(2) The minimum required contribution for such preceding plan year.

(C) *Treatment of unpaid minimum required contributions.*—For purposes of this paragraph (b)(1)(ii), a contribution made during a plan year to correct an unpaid minimum required contribution (within the meaning of section 4971(c)(4)) for a prior plan year is not treated as a contribution for the current plan year.

(iii) *Decreases.*—As of the first day of each plan year, the prefunding balance of a plan is decreased (but not below zero) by the sum of—

(A) Any amount of the prefunding balance that was used under paragraph (d) of this section to offset the minimum required contribution of the plan for the preceding plan year; and

(B) Any reduction in the prefunding balance under paragraph (e) of this section for the plan year.

(iv) *Adjustments for interest.*—(A) *Adjustment of excess contribution.*—The present value of the excess contribution for the preceding year (as determined under paragraph (b)(1)(ii)(B) of this section) is increased for interest accruing for the period between the valuation date for the preceding plan year and the first day of the current plan year. For this purpose, interest is determined by using the plan's effective interest rate under section 430(h)(2)(A) for the preceding plan year, except to the extent provided in paragraph (b)(3)(iii) of this section.

(B) *Determination of present value.*—The present value of the contributions described in paragraph (b)(1)(ii)(B)(*1*) of this section is determined as of the valuation date for the preceding plan year, using the plan's effective interest rate under section 430(h)(2)(A) for the preceding plan year.

(2) *Funding standard carryover balance.*—(i) *In general.*—A funding standard carryover balance is automatically established for a plan that had a positive balance in the funding standard account under section 412(b) (as in effect prior to amendment by the Pension Protection Act of 2006 (PPA '06), Public Law 109-280 (120 Stat. 780)) as of the end of the pre-effective plan year for the plan. The funding standard carryover balance as of the beginning of the first effective plan year for the plan is the positive balance in the funding standard account under section 412(b) (as in effect prior to amendment by PPA '06) as of the end of the pre-effective plan year for the plan. After that date, the funding standard carryover balance is decreased to the extent provided in paragraph (b)(2)(ii) of this section and adjusted further for investment return and interest as provided in paragraphs (b)(3) and (b)(4) of this section.

(ii) *Decreases.*—As of the first day of each plan year, the funding standard carryover balance of a plan is decreased (but not below zero) by the sum of—

(A) Any amount of the funding standard carryover balance that was used under paragraph (d) of this section to offset the minimum required contribution of the plan for the preceding plan year; and

(B) Any reduction in the funding standard carryover balance under paragraph (e) of this section for the plan year.

(3) *Adjustments for investment experience.*—(i) *In general.*—A plan's prefunding balance under paragraph (b)(1) of this section and a plan's funding standard carryover balance under paragraph (b)(2) of this section as of the first day of a plan year must be adjusted to reflect the actual rate of return on plan assets for the preceding plan year. For this purpose, the actual rate of return on plan assets for the preceding plan year is determined on the basis of fair market value and must take into account the amount and timing of all contributions, distributions, and other plan payments made during that period.

(ii) *Ordering rules for adjustments.*—In general, the adjustment for actual rate of return on plan assets is applied to the balance after any reduction of prefunding and funding standard carryover balances for that preceding plan year under paragraph (e) of this section and after subtracting amounts used to offset the minimum required contribution for the preceding plan year pursuant to paragraph (d) of this section. However, see paragraph (d)(1)(ii)(D) of this section for a special ordering rule when adjusting for investment experience.

(iii) *Special rule for excess contributions attributable to use of funding balances.*—Notwithstanding paragraph (b)(1)(iv)(A) of this section, to the extent that a contribution is included in the present value of excess contributions solely because the minimum required contribution has been offset under paragraph (d) of this section, the contribution is adjusted for investment experience under the rules of this paragraph (b)(3).

(4) *Valuation date other than the first day of the plan year.*—(i) *In general.*—If a plan's valuation date is not the first day of the plan year, then, solely for purposes of applying paragraphs (c), (d), and (e) of this section, the plan's prefunding and funding standard carryover balances (if any) determined under this paragraph (b) are increased from the first day of the plan year to the valuation date using the plan's effective interest rate under section 430(h)(2)(A) for the plan year.

(ii) *Special rule for adjustments for investment experience.*—In the case of a plan with a valuation date that is not the first day of the plan year, for purposes of applying the subtraction under paragraph (b)(3)(ii) of this section for amounts used to offset the minimum required contribution for the preceding plan year and the decreases under paragraphs (b)(1)(iii) and (b)(2)(ii) of this section, the amount of the prefunding balance or funding standard carryover balance that *is used to offset the minimum required contribution* under paragraph (d) of this section or reduced under paragraph (e) of this section is discounted from the valuation date to the first day of the plan year using the effective interest rate under section 430(h)(2)(A) for the plan year.

(5) *Special rule for quarterly contributions.*—For purposes of applying a prefunding balance or funding standard carryover balance to required installments described in section 430(j)(3), the respective balances are increased from the beginning of the year to the date of the election (using the plan's effective interest rate for the plan year) to determine the amount available to offset the required quarterly installment. The amounts used to offset required quarterly installments are then discounted from that date to the first day of the plan year for purposes of the subtraction under paragraph (b)(3)(ii) of this section and the decreases under paragraphs (b)(1)(iii) and (b)(2)(ii) of this section, using the effective interest rate for the plan year. However, see paragraph (d)(1)(i)(B) of this section for a special rule regarding late quarterly installments when determining the amount that is used to offset the minimum required contribution for the plan year.

(c) *Effect of balances on the value of plan assets.*—(1) *In general.*—In the case of any plan with a prefunding balance or a funding standard carryover balance, the amount of those balances is subtracted from the value of plan assets for purposes of sections 430 and 436, except as otherwise provided in paragraphs (c)(2), (c)(3), and (d)(3) of this section and § 1.436-1(j)(1)(ii)(B).

(2) *Subtraction of balances in determining new shortfall amortization base.*—(i) *Prefunding balance.*—For purposes of determining whether a plan is exempt from the requirement to establish a new shortfall amortization base under section 430(c)(5), the amount of the prefunding balance is subtracted from the value of plan assets only if an election under paragraph (d) of this section to use the prefunding balance to offset the minimum required contribution is made for the plan year.

(ii) *Funding standard carryover balance.*—For purposes of determining whether a plan is exempt from the requirement to establish a new shortfall amortization base under section 430(c)(5), the funding standard carryover balance is not subtracted from the value of plan assets regardless of whether any portion of either the funding standard carryover balance or the prefunding balance is used to offset the minimum required contribution for the plan year under paragraph (d) of this section.

(3) *Special rule for certain binding agreements with PBGC.*—If there is in effect for a plan year a binding written agreement with the Pension Benefit Guaranty Corporation (PBGC) which provides that all or a portion of the prefunding balance or funding standard carryover balance (or both balances) is not available to offset the minimum required contribution for a plan year, that specified amount is not subtracted from the value of plan assets for purposes of determining the funding shortfall under section 430(c)(4). For example, if a plan has no prefunding balance and a $20 million funding standard carryover balance, a PBGC agreement provides that $5 million of a plan's funding standard carryover balance is unavailable to offset the minimum required contribution for a plan year, and the plan's assets are $100 million, then the value of plan assets for purposes of determining the funding shortfall under section 430(c)(4) is reduced by $15 million ($20 million less $5 million) to $85 million. For purposes of this paragraph (c)(3), an agreement with the PBGC is taken into account with respect to a plan year only if the agreement was executed prior to the valuation date for the plan year.

(d) *Election to apply balances against minimum required contribution.*—(1) *In general.*—(i) *Amount of offset to minimum required contribution.*—(A) *Effect of use of balances.*—Subject to the limitations provided in this paragraph (d), in the case of any plan year with respect to which the plan sponsor elects to use all or a portion of the prefunding balance or the funding standard carryover balance to offset the minimum required contribution for the plan year, the minimum required contribution for the plan year (determined after taking into account any waiver under section 412(c)) is offset as of the valuation date for the plan year by the amount so used.

(B) *Special rule for late election with respect to quarterly contributions.*—Notwithstanding paragraph (d)(1)(i)(A) of this section, if the plan sponsor elects to use all or a portion of the prefunding balance or the funding standard carryover balance to satisfy a required installment under section 430(j)(3), the amount used to offset the minimum required contribution for the plan year is the portion of the balance so used, adjusted in accordance with the rules of paragraph (b)(5) of this section, unless the date of the election is after the due date of the required installment. If the election to use all or a portion of the prefunding balance or the funding standard carryover balance to satisfy the required installments under section 430(j)(3) is made after the due date for the required installment, then the amount used to offset the minimum required contribution for the plan year is the portion of the balance so used, discounted from the date of the election to the due date of the required installment at the effective interest rate plus 5 percentage points, and then further adjusted from the installment due date to the valuation date at the effective interest rate. For example, if a quarterly installment of $20,250 is due on April 15 for a calendar year plan with a valuation date on January 1 and an effective interest rate of 6 percent, and the installment is satisfied by an election to apply the funding standard carryover balance that is made on July 1 (2 $^{1}/_{2}$ months after the April 15 due date), then the amount used to offset the minimum required contribution under this paragraph (d)(1)(i) is $19,481 (that is, $20,250 ÷ $1.11^{(2.5/12)}$ ÷ $1.06^{(3.5/12)}$). However, the amount by which the funding standard carryover balance is reduced under paragraph (b)(2)(ii) of this section is $19,669 (that is, $20,250 ÷ $1.06^{(6/12)}$).

(ii) *Maximum amount of available balances and coordination of elections.*—(A) *General requirement to follow chronology.*—In general, the amount of prefunding and funding standard carryover balances that may be used to offset the minimum required contribution for a plan year must take into account any decrease in those balances which results from a prior election either to use the prefunding balance or funding standard carryover balance under section 430(f)(3) and this paragraph (d) or to reduce those balances under section 430(f)(5) and paragraph (e) of this section (including deemed elections under section 436(f)(3) and §1.436-1(a)(5)). For example, for a calendar plan year with a January 1 valuation date, a deemed election under section 436(f)(3) and §1.436-1(a)(5) on April 1, 2010 (the first day of the 4th month of the plan year) will reduce the available prefunding balance or funding standard carryover balance that can be used with respect to an election made after April 1, 2010.

(B) *Exception to chronological rule.*—Notwithstanding the general rule of paragraph (d)(1)(ii)(A) of this section, all elections under section 430(f)(5) and paragraph (e) of this section to reduce the prefunding balance or funding standard carryover balance for the current plan year (including deemed elections under section 436(f)(3) and §1.436-1(a)(5)) are deemed to occur on the valuation date for the plan year and before any election under section 430(f)(3) and this paragraph (d) to offset the minimum required contribution for the current plan year. Accordingly, if an election to use the prefunding balance or funding standard carryover balance to offset the minimum required contribution for the plan year (including an election to satisfy the quarterly contribution requirement) has been made prior to the election to reduce the prefunding balance or funding standard carryover balance, then the amount available for use to offset the otherwise applicable minimum required contribution for the plan year under this paragraph (d) will be retroactively reduced. However, an election to reduce a prefunding balance or funding standard carryover balance for a plan year does not affect a prior election to use a prefunding balance or funding standard carryover balance to offset a minimum required contribution for a prior plan year.

(C) *Investment experience.*—In addition to reflecting any decrease in the prefunding balance or the funding standard carryover balance which results from a prior election for the previous year either to use the prefunding balance or funding standard carryover balance under section 430(f)(3) and this paragraph (d) to offset the minimum required contribution for such prior plan year or to reduce those balances under section 430(f)(5) and paragraph (e) of this section (including deemed elections under section 436(f)(3) and §1.436-1(a)(5)), the prior plan year's prefunding and funding standard carryover balances must be adjusted under the rules of paragraph (b)(3) of this section for investment experience for that prior plan year before determining the amount of those balances available for such an election for the current plan year.

(D) *Special rule for current year elections that are made before prior year elections.*—This paragraph (d)(1)(ii)(D) sets forth a special rule that applies if, for the current plan year, a plan sponsor makes an election under this paragraph (d) or paragraph (e) of this section (including a deemed election under section 436(f)(3) and §1.436-1(a)(5)), and then subsequently makes an election under this paragraph (d) to offset the minimum required contribution for the prior plan year. This special rule applies solely for purposes of determining the amount of prefunding and funding standard carryover balances available for that subsequent election. Under this special rule, in lieu of decreasing the funding standard carryover balance or prefunding balance as of the valuation date for the current year to take into account the current year election, the funding standard carryover balance or prefunding balance as of the valuation date for the prior plan year is decreased by the amount of the prior year equivalent of the current year election. The prior year equivalent of the current year election is determined by dividing the amount of the current year election (as of the first day of the current plan year) by a number equal to 1 plus the rate of investment return for the prior plan year determined under paragraph (b)(3) of this section. If this paragraph (d)(1)(ii)(D) applies for a plan year, then the funding standard carryover balance and prefunding balance are nonetheless adjusted in accordance with the rules of paragraph (b) of this section,

after the application of the rules of this paragraph (d)(1)(ii)(D). Thus, the amount used to offset the minimum required contribution for the earlier plan year is subtracted from the prefunding balance or funding standard carryover balance as of the valuation date for that year prior to the adjustment for investment return under paragraph (b)(3) of this section for that plan year, and the amount by which the prefunding balance or funding standard carryover balance is decreased for the second year is based on the elections made for the second year.

(2) *Requirement to use funding standard carryover balance before prefunding balance.*—To the extent that a plan has a funding standard carryover balance greater than zero, no amount of the plan's prefunding balance may be used to offset the minimum required contribution. Thus, a plan's funding standard carryover balance must be exhausted before the plan's prefunding balance may be applied under paragraph (d)(1) of this section to offset the minimum required contribution.

(3) *Limitation for underfunded plans.*—(i) *In general.*—An election to use the prefunding balance or funding standard carryover balance to offset the minimum required contribution under this paragraph (d) is not available for a plan year if the plan's prior plan year funding ratio is less than 80 percent. For purposes of this paragraph (d)(3), except as otherwise provided in this paragraph (d)(3) or paragraph (h)(3) of this section, the plan's prior plan year funding ratio is the fraction (expressed as a percentage)—

(A) The numerator of which is the value of plan assets on the valuation date for the preceding plan year, reduced by the amount of any prefunding balance (but not the amount of any funding standard carryover balance); and

(B) The denominator of which is the funding target of the plan for the preceding plan year (determined without regard to the at-risk rules of section 430(i)(1)).

(ii) *Special rule for second year of a new plan with no past service.*—In the case of a new plan that was neither the result of a merger nor involved in a spinoff, if the prior plan year was the first year of the plan and the funding target for the prior plan year was zero, then the plan's prior plan year funding ratio is deemed to be 80 percent for purposes of this paragraph (d)(3).

(iii) *Special rule for plans that are the result of a merger.*— [Reserved.]

(iv) *Special rules for plans that are involved in a spinoff.*— [Reserved.]

(e) *Election to reduce balances.*—(1) *In general.*—A plan sponsor may make an election for a plan year to reduce any portion of a plan's prefunding and funding standard carryover balances under this paragraph (e). If such an election is made, the amount of those balances that must be subtracted from the value of plan assets pursuant to paragraph (c)(1) of this section will be smaller and, accordingly, the value of plan assets taken into account for purposes of sections 430 and 436 will be larger. Thus, this election to reduce a plan's prefunding and funding standard carryover balances is taken into account in the determination of the value of plan assets for the plan year and applies for all purposes under sections 430 and 436, including for purposes of determining the plan's prior plan year funding ratio under paragraph (d)(3) of this section for the following plan year. *See also* section 436(f)(3) and §1.436-1(a)(5) for a rule under which the plan sponsor is deemed to make the election described in this paragraph (e). The rules of paragraph (d)(1)(ii) of this section also apply for purposes of determining the maximum amount of prefunding balance or funding standard carryover balance that is available for an election under this paragraph (e).

(2) *Requirement to reduce funding standard carryover balance before prefunding balance.*—To the extent that a plan has a funding standard carryover balance greater than zero, no election under paragraph (e)(1) of this section is permitted to be made that reduces the plan's prefunding balance. Thus, a plan must exhaust its funding standard carryover balance before it is permitted to make an election under paragraph (e)(1) of this section with respect to its prefunding balance.

(f) *Elections.*—(1) *Method of making elections.*—(i) *In general.*—Any election under this section by the plan sponsor must be made by providing written notification of the election to the plan's enrolled actuary and the plan administrator. The written notification must set forth the relevant details of the election, including the specific dollar amount involved in the election (except as provided in this paragraph (f)(1)). Thus, except as provided in this paragraph (f)(1), a conditional or formula-based election generally does not satisfy the requirements of this paragraph (f).

(ii) *Standing elections to increase or use balances.*—A plan sponsor may provide a standing election in writing to the plan's enrolled actuary to use the funding standard carryover balance and the prefunding balance to offset the minimum required contribution for the plan year to the extent needed to avoid an unpaid minimum required contribution under section 4971(c)(4) taking into account any contributions that are or are not made. In addition, a plan sponsor may provide a standing election in writing to the plan's enrolled actuary to add the maximum amount possible each year to the prefunding balance. Any election made pursuant to a standing election under this paragraph (f)(1)(ii) is deemed to occur on the last day available to make the election for the plan year as provided under paragraph (f)(2)(i) of this section. Any standing election under this paragraph (f)(1)(ii) remains in effect for the plan with respect to the enrolled actuary named in the election, unless—

(A) The standing election is revoked under the rules of paragraph (f)(3) of this section; or

(B) The enrolled actuary who signs the actuarial report under section 6059 (Schedule SB, "Single-Employer Defined Benefit Plan Actuarial Information" of Form 5500, "Annual Return/Report of Employee Benefit Plan") for the plan for the plan year is not the enrolled actuary named in the standing election.

(iii) *Standing election to satisfy installments through use of funding balances.*—(A) *In general.*—A plan sponsor may provide a standing election in writing to the plan's enrolled actuary to use (to the extent available) the funding standard carryover balance and the prefunding balance to satisfy any otherwise unpaid portion of a required installment under section 430(j)(3). Any use pursuant to a standing election under this paragraph (f)(1)(iii) is deemed to occur on the later of the last date for making the required installment and the date the standing election is provided to the enrolled actuary.

(B) *Otherwise unpaid portion of a required installment.*—For purposes of paragraph (f)(1)(iii)(A) of this section, the otherwise unpaid portion of a required installment equals the amount necessary to satisfy the required installment rules under section 430(j) based on the installment amounts determined as if the required annual payment were the amount described in § 1.430(j)-1(c)(5)(ii)(B). Thus, the amount of the prefunding and funding standard carryover balances used under a standing election is the amount that is needed to satisfy an installment in the amount of 25 percent of the minimum required contribution for the prior plan year, plus installments in that amount with respect to all earlier required installment due dates for the plan year, taking into account prior contributions for the plan year and prior elections to use the funding standard carryover balance and prefunding balance for the plan year.

(C) *Duration of standing election.*—Generally, any standing election under this paragraph (f)(1)(iii) remains in effect for the plan with respect to the enrolled actuary named in the election, unless either of the events described in paragraph (f)(1)(ii)(A) or (B) of this section occurs with respect to the standing election. However, a plan sponsor may suspend application of a standing election for the remaining installments with respect to a plan year by providing, in writing to the plan's enrolled actuary, notice that the standing election is not to apply for the remainder of the plan year. In addition, once the current year's minimum required contribution has been determined, a plan sponsor may modify application of a standing election for the remaining installments with respect to a plan year by providing, in writing to the plan's enrolled actuary, a replacement formula election to use the funding standard carryover balance and prefunding balance (to the extent available) so that the otherwise unpaid portions of the remaining required installments satisfy the required installment rules under section 430(j), taking into account the determination of the current year's minimum required contribution pursuant to § 1.430(j)-1(c)(5)(ii)(A), prior contributions for the plan year and prior elections to use the prefunding and funding standard carryover balances.

(2) *Timing of elections.*—(i) *General rule.*—Except as otherwise provided in paragraph (f)(2)(ii) or (iii) of this section, any election under this section with respect to a plan year must be made no later than the last date for making the minimum required contribution for the plan year as described in section 430(j)(1), or such later date as prescribed in guidance published in the Internal Revenue Bulletin. For this purpose, an election to add to the prefunding balance relates to the plan year for which excess contributions were made. For example, an election to add to the prefunding balance as of the first day of the plan year that begins on January 1, 2010 (in an amount not in excess of the present value of the excess contribution as of the valuation date in 2009, adjusted for interest under the rules of paragraph (b)(1)(ii) of this section), must be made no later than September 15, 2010, *even though the election is reported on the 2010 Schedule SB of Form 5500, which is not due until 2011.* Except for the standing elections covered by paragraph (f)(1)(ii) of this section, an election under this section may not be made prior to the first day of the plan year to which the election relates.

(ii) *Special rule for standing election revoked by a change in enrolled actuary.*—If there is a change in enrolled actuary for the plan year which would result in a revocation of the standing election under the rule of paragraph (f)(1)(ii)(B) of this section, then the plan sponsor may reinstate the revoked standing election by providing a replacement to the new enrolled actuary by the due date of the Schedule SB of Form 5500.

(iii) *Election to reduce balances.*—Any election under paragraph (e) of this section to reduce the prefunding balance or funding standard carryover balance for a plan year (for example, in order to avoid or terminate a benefit restriction under section 436) must be made by the end of the plan year to which the election relates.

(iv) *Earlier elections.*—This paragraph (f)(2) sets forth the latest date that an election can be made. A plan sponsor is permitted to make an earlier election, and in certain circumstances may need to make such an election in order to timely satisfy a quarterly contribution requirement under section 430(j)(3).

(3) *Irrevocability of elections.*—(i) *In general.*—Except as otherwise provided in this paragraph (f)(3) or in guidance published in the Internal Revenue Bulletin, a plan sponsor's election under this section with respect to the plan's prefunding balance or funding standard carryover balance is irrevocable (and must be unconditional). A standing election by the plan sponsor may be revoked by providing written notification of the revocation to the plan's enrolled actuary and the plan administrator on or before the date the corresponding election is deemed to occur pursuant to paragraph (f)(1)(ii) of this section.

(ii) *Exception for certain elections.*—An election to use the prefunding balance or funding standard carryover balance to offset the minimum required contribution for a plan year (including an election to satisfy the quarterly contribution requirements for a plan year) is permitted to be revoked to the extent the amount the plan sponsor elected to use to offset the minimum contribution requirements (including an election used to satisfy the quarterly contribution requirements) exceeds the minimum required contribution for a plan year (determined without regard to the election under paragraph (d) of this section) if and only if the election is revoked by providing written notification of the revocation to the plan's enrolled actuary and the plan administrator by the deadline set forth in paragraph (f)(3)(iii) of this section. If no such revocation is made, then, under paragraph (b) of this section, the funding standard carryover balance or prefunding balance is decreased by the entire amount that the plan sponsor elected to use to offset the minimum required contribution for a plan year (including an election to satisfy the quarterly contribution requirements for a plan year).

(iii) *Deadline for revoking election.*—The deadline for revoking the election described in paragraph (f)(3)(ii) of this section is generally the end of the plan year. However, for plans with a valuation date other than the first day of the plan year, the deadline for the revocation is the deadline for contributions for the plan year as described in section 430(j)(1). In addition, for the first plan year beginning in 2008, the deadline for the revocation for all plans is deferred to the due date (including extensions) of the Schedule SB, "Single-Employer Defined Benefit Plan Actuarial Information" of Form 5500, "Annual Return/Report of Employee Benefit Plan".

(4) *Plan sponsor.*—(i) *In general.*—For purposes of the elections described in this section, except as otherwise provided in paragraph (f)(4)(ii) of this section, any reference to the plan sponsor means the employer or employers responsible for making contributions to or under the plan.

(ii) *Certain multiple employer plans.*—For purposes of the elections described in this section, in the case of plans that are multiple employer plans to which section 413(c)(4)(A) does not apply, any reference to the plan sponsor means the plan administrator within the meaning of section 414(g).

(g) *Examples.*—The following examples illustrate the rules of this section:

Example 1. (i) Plan P is a defined benefit plan with a plan year that is the calendar year and a valuation date of January 1. The funding standard carryover balance of Plan P is $25,000 and the prefunding balance is zero as of the beginning of the 2010 plan year. The sponsor of Plan P, Sponsor S, does not elect to use any portion of the balance to offset the minimum required contribution for 2010 pursuant to paragraph (d)(1) of this section, or to reduce any portion of the funding standard carryover balance prior to the determination of the value of plan assets for 2010, pursuant to paragraph (e)(1) of this section. The actual rate of return on Plan P's assets for 2010 is 2%. Plan P's effective interest rate for 2010 is 6%. The minimum required contribution for Plan P under section 430 for 2010 is $100,000, and no quarterly installments are required for Plan P for the 2010 plan year.

As of January 1, 2010, the value of plan assets is $1,100,000 and the funding target is $1,000,000. Therefore, the prior plan year funding ratio for Plan P for 2010, as determined under paragraph (d)(3) of this section, is 110%.

(ii) Sponsor S makes a contribution to Plan P of $150,000 on December 1, 2010, for the 2010 plan year and makes no other contributions for the 2010 plan year. Because this contribution was made on a date other than the valuation date for the 2010 plan year, the contribution must be adjusted to reflect interest that would otherwise have accrued between the valuation date and the date of the contribution, at the effective interest rate for the 2010 plan year. The amount of the contribution after adjustment is $142,198, determined as $150,000 discounted for 11 months of compound interest at an effective annual interest rate of 6%.

(iii) The excess of employer contributions for 2010 over the minimum required contribution for 2010, as of the valuation date, is $42,198 ($142,198 less $100,000). Accordingly, the increase in Plan P's prefunding balance as of January 1, 2011, cannot exceed $44,730 (which is the present value of the excess contribution of $42,198 adjusted for 12 months of interest at an effective interest rate of 6%).

(iv) Plan P's funding standard carryover balance as of January 1, 2011, is $25,500 (which is the funding standard carryover balance as of January 1, 2010, adjusted for investment experience during 2010 at a rate of 2%).

Example 2. (i) The facts are the same as in *Example 1*, except that the contribution of $150,000 is made on February 1, 2011, for the 2010 plan year.

(ii) The amount of the contribution after adjustment is $140,824, which is determined as $150,000 discounted for 13 months of interest at an effective interest rate of 6%. Accordingly, the increase in Plan P's prefunding balance as of January 1, 2011, cannot exceed $43,273 (which is the present value of the excess contribution of $40,824 adjusted for 12 months of interest at an effective interest rate of 6%).

(iii) Plan P's funding standard carryover balance as of January 1, 2011, is $25,500, as developed in *Example 1* of this section. If Sponsor S elects to increase the prefunding balance as of January 1, 2011, by the present value of the excess contribution adjusted for interest, or $43,273, the total of the funding standard carryover balance and prefunding balance as of January 1, 2011, is $68,773.

Example 3. (i) The facts are the same as in *Example 1*, except that Sponsor S contributes $90,539 to Plan P on February 1, 2011, for the 2010 plan year and makes no other contributions to Plan P for the 2010 plan year. In addition, on February 1, 2011, Sponsor S elects to use $15,000 of the funding standard carryover balance to offset P's minimum required contribution for 2010, pursuant to paragraph (d)(1) of this section. This is permitted because Plan P's prior-year funding ratio determined under paragraph (d)(3) of this section is 110%, and is therefore not less than 80%.

(ii) Because the contribution was made on a date other than the valuation date for the 2010 plan year, the contribution must be adjusted to reflect interest that would otherwise have accrued between the valuation date and the date of the contribution, at the effective interest rate for the 2010 plan year. The amount of the contribution after adjustment is $85,000, determined as $90,539 discounted for 13 months of compound interest at an effective interest rate of 6%. The adjusted contribution of $85,000 plus the $15,000 of the funding standard carryover balance used to offset the minimum required contribution equals the minimum required contribution for the 2010 plan year of $100,000. Therefore, no excess contributions are available to increase the prefunding balance, and the prefunding balance as of January 1, 2011, remains zero.

(iii) The funding standard carryover balance as of January 1, 2011, is adjusted for investment experience during the 2010 plan year, in accordance with paragraph (b)(3) of this section. The amount of the adjustment is $200, determined as the actual rate of return on plan assets for 2010 as applied to the 2010 funding standard carryover balance after reduction for the amount of that balance used under paragraph (d)(1) of this section (that is, $25,000 less $15,000, multiplied by the actual rate of return of 2%).

(iv) The funding standard carryover balance, as of January 1, 2011, is $10,200, determined as the 2010 funding standard carryover balance less the amount used to offset the 2010 minimum required contribution, adjusted for investment experience during the 2010 year ($25,000 less $15,000 plus $200).

Example 4. (i) The facts are the same as in *Example 3*, except that Sponsor S contributes $150,000 (instead of $90,539) to Plan P on February 1, 2011, for the 2010 plan year.

(ii) Because the contribution was made on a date other than the valuation date for the 2010 plan year, the contribution must be adjusted to reflect interest that would otherwise have accrued between the valuation date and the date of the contribution, at the effective interest rate for the 2010 plan year. The amount of the contribution after adjustment is $140,824, determined as $150,000

discounted for 13 months of interest at an effective interest rate of 6%.

(iii) Because Sponsor S elected to use $15,000 of the funding standard carryover balance to offset the minimum required contribution for 2010 of $100,000, the cash contribution requirement for 2010, adjusted with interest to January 1, 2010, is $85,000. The adjusted contribution of $140,824 exceeds this amount by $55,824. Of this amount, $15,000 exceeds the minimum required contribution only because of Sponsor S's election to use the funding standard carryover balance to offset the minimum required contribution as provided in paragraph (d)(1) of this section. The remaining $40,824 ($140,824 minus $100,000) results from cash contributions made in excess of the minimum required contribution before offset by the funding standard carryover balance.

(iv) The portion of the excess contribution resulting solely because the minimum required contribution was offset by a portion of the funding standard carryover balance is adjusted for investment experience during 2009, pursuant to paragraph (b)(3)(iii) of this section. Accordingly, this portion of the present value of the excess contribution adjusted for interest as of January 1, 2011, is $15,300 ($15,000 adjusted for investment experience during 2010 at a rate of 2%).

(v) The excess contribution resulting from cash contributions in excess of the minimum required contribution before offset by the funding standard carryover balance is adjusted for interest at the effective interest rate for 2010, pursuant to paragraph (b)(1)(iv)(A) of this section. Accordingly, this portion of the present value of the excess contribution adjusted for interest as of January 1, 2011, is $43,273 ($40,824 increased by the effective interest rate of 6%). The increase in Plan P's prefunding balance as of January 1, 2011, cannot exceed the total present value of the excess contribution adjusted for interest of $58,573 ($15,300 plus $43,273).

(vi) The funding standard carryover balance as of January 1, 2011, is $10,200, determined as the 2010 funding standard carryover balance less the $15,000 used to offset the 2010 minimum required contribution, adjusted for investment experience during the 2010 plan year as developed in *Example 3* ($25,000 less $15,000 plus $200).

(vii) Sponsor S elects to increase the prefunding balance by the maximum amount of the present value of the excess contribution adjusted for interest of $58,573, resulting in a total of the funding standard carryover balance and the prefunding balance as of January 1, 2011, of $68,773, the same amount as that developed in *Example 2*.

Example 5. (i) Plan Q is a defined benefit plan with a plan year that is the calendar year and a valuation date of July 1. The funding standard carryover balance of Plan Q is $50,000 as of January 1, 2010, the beginning of the 2010 plan year. The prefunding balance of Plan Q as of the beginning of the 2010 plan year is $0. The actual rate of return on Plan Q's assets for 2010 is 10%. Plan Q's effective interest rate for 2010 is 6.25%. The funding ratio for Plan Q for 2009 (the prior plan year funding ratio with respect to 2010, as determined under paragraph (d)(3) of this section) is 85%, which is not less than 80%. The minimum required contribution for Plan Q for 2010 is $200,000. Sponsor T makes a contribution to Plan Q of $190,000 on July 1, 2010, for the 2010 plan year, and makes no other contributions for the 2010 plan year. Sponsor T elects to use $10,000 of the funding standard carryover balance to offset Plan Q's minimum required contribution in 2010.

(ii) Pursuant to paragraph (b)(4) of this section, the funding standard carryover balance is increased to $51,539 as of July 1, 2010 (that is, an increase to reflect 6 months of interest at an effective interest rate of 6.25%) for the purpose of adjusting plan assets under paragraph (c) of this section, and for applying any election to use or reduce Plan Q's funding standard carryover balance under paragraph (d) or (e) of this section. However, Sponsor T does not elect in 2010 to reduce any portion of the funding standard carryover balance pursuant to paragraph (e) of this section. The funding standard carryover balance ($51,539) is subtracted from the value of plan assets, as of July 1, 2010, prior to the determination of the minimum funding contribution, and $51,539 is the maximum amount that may applied against the minimum required contribution.

(iii) The value of the funding standard carryover balance as of January 1, 2011, is determined by first discounting the amount used to offset the minimum required contribution for 2010 from July 1, 2010, to January 1, 2010, using the effective interest rate of 6.25%, and subtracting the discounted amount from the January 1, 2010, funding standard carryover balance. The resulting amount is adjusted for investment experience to January 1, 2011, using a rate equal to the actual rate of return on plan assets of 10% during 2010. Thus, the $10,000 used to offset Plan Q's minimum required contribution as of July 1, 2010, is discounted for 6 months of interest, at an effective interest rate of 6.25%, to obtain an amount of $9,701 as of January 1, 2010. The remaining funding standard carryover balance as of January 1, 2010, solely for purposes of determining the adjustment for investment experience during 2010, is $40,299 ($50,000 − $9,701), and the adjustment for investment experience is $4,030 ($40,299 × 10%).

The value of the funding standard carryover balance as of January 1, 2011, is $44,329 (that is, $50,000 − $9,701 + $4,030).

Example 6. (i) The facts are the same as in *Example 5*, except that Sponsor T contributes $200,000 on July 1, 2010, for the 2010 plan year.

(ii) The cash contribution required for 2010, after offsetting the minimum required contribution by $10,000 of the funding standard carryover balance in accordance with T's election, is $190,000. The difference, or $10,000, must be adjusted to January 1, 2011, to determine the maximum amount that can be added to the prefunding balance as of that date.

(iii) The excess contribution is first adjusted to January 1, 2010, by discounting for 6 months of interest using the effective interest rate for 2010 of 6.25%. This results in an excess contribution of $9,701 ($10,000 ÷ 1.0625$^{0.5}$). Because this amount is an excess contribution solely because of Sponsor T's election to offset the minimum required contribution for 2010 by a portion of the funding standard carryover balance, the amount is then adjusted for investment experience during 2010 at a rate of 10%, in accordance with paragraph (b)(3)(iii) of this section, for a present value of the excess contribution adjusted for interest of $10,671 ($9,701 × 1.10) as of January 1, 2011.

Example 7. (i) The facts are the same as in *Example 4*. Plan P's effective interest rate for 2011 is 6.5%, and the rate of return on investments during 2011 is 7%. All required quarterly installments for the 2011 plan year were made by the applicable due dates. On February 1, 2012, Sponsor S elects to use $50,000 of Plan P's prefunding and funding standard carryover balances to offset the minimum required contribution for the 2011 plan year. On April 15, 2012, Sponsor S elects to use Plan P's prefunding and funding standard carryover balances to offset the 2012 minimum required contribution by $20,000, in accordance with paragraph (d) of this section, in order to offset the required quarterly installment then due.

(ii) When adjusting Plan P's prefunding and funding standard carryover balances to reflect Sponsor S's election to use them to offset the 2011 minimum required contribution, the remaining $10,200 in the funding standard carryover balance as of January 1, 2011, must be used before any portion of the prefunding balance. The prefunding balance is reduced by the remaining $39,800 ($50,000 total election minus $10,200 from the funding standard carryover balance).

(iii) The amount available for Sponsor S's election to use Plan P's prefunding and funding standard carryover balances to offset the 2012 minimum required contribution is determined by reducing the January 1, 2011, prefunding and funding standard carryover balances to reflect the election to use the prefunding and funding standard carryover balances to offset the 2011 minimum required contribution, and by adjusting the resulting amount to January 1, 2012, using the rate of investment return for Plan P during 2011. Accordingly, the available amount in Plan P's funding standard carryover balance as of January 1, 2012, is zero. The available amount in Plan P's prefunding balance as of January 1, 2012, is $20,087 ($58,573 minus $39,800, increased by 7%). Therefore, Sponsor S has $20,087 available to offset the minimum required contribution for the 2012 plan year.

Example 8. (i) The facts are the same as in *Example 7*, except that based on the enrolled actuary's certification of the AFTAP on July 1, 2012, Sponsor S is deemed to elect to reduce the January 1, 2012, prefunding balance by $15,000 under section 436(f)(3).

(ii) In accordance with paragraph (d)(1)(ii)(B) of this section, the deemed election to reduce the prefunding balance is deemed to occur on the first day of the plan year, and before the date of any election to offset the minimum required contribution for the 2012 plan year. The deemed election does not affect Sponsor S's election to offset the 2011 minimum contribution because that election was made on February 1, 2012, before the date of the deemed election, July 1, 2012.

(iii) As shown in *Example 7*, the available prefunding balance as of January 1, 2012, after reflecting the February 1, 2012, election to offset the 2011 minimum required contribution but before reflecting the April 15, 2012, election to offset the 2012 minimum required contribution, is $20,087. Adjusting this amount to reflect the deemed election to reduce the prefunding balance by $15,000 leaves a balance of $5,087 available to offset the minimum required contribution for 2012.

(iv) The portion of the quarterly installment due April 15, 2012 that was not covered by the remaining $5,087 prefunding balance is considered unpaid retroactive to April 15, 2012.

Example 9. (i) The facts are the same as in *Example 8*, except that Sponsor S does not make the election to offset the 2011 minimum required contribution until August 1, 2012, and the deemed election as of July 1, 2012, reduces Plan P's prefunding and funding standard carryover balances as of January 1, 2012, by $68,500. Sponsor S does not elect to use Plan P's prefunding and funding standard carryover balances to offset the 2012 minimum contribution.

(ii) In accordance with paragraph (d)(1)(ii)(A) of this section, the July 1, 2012, deemed election to reduce Plan P's prefunding and funding standard carryover balances must be taken into account before determining the amount available to offset the 2011 minimum

required contribution because the election to offset the 2011 minimum required contribution was made after the date of the deemed election, July 1, 2012.

(iii) Pursuant to paragraph (d)(1)(ii)(C) of this section, the January 1, 2011, prefunding and funding standard carryover balances are adjusted to January 1, 2012, using Plan P's rate of investment return for 2011 of 7%. This results in an available funding standard carryover balance of $10,914 ($10,200 × 1.07) and an available prefunding balance of $62,673 (58,573 × 1.07) as of January 1, 2012.

(iv) Paragraph (d)(2) of this section requires that the funding standard carryover balance must be used before reducing Plan P's prefunding balance. Accordingly, the funding standard carryover balance is eliminated, and the prefunding balance is reduced by the remaining $57,586 ($68,500 − $10,914), resulting in an available prefunding balance of $5,087 ($62,673 − $57,586) as of January 1, 2012.

(v) In accordance with paragraph (d)(1)(ii)(D) of this section, the remaining balance is adjusted to January 1, 2011, to determine the amount available to offset the 2011 minimum required contribution. This adjustment is done by dividing the remaining balance by 1 plus the rate of investment return for 2011. Accordingly, the amount available to offset the 2011 minimum required contribution is $4,754 ($5,087 ÷ 1.07).

(vi) If the plan sponsor elects to use the $4,754 available balance to offset the 2011 minimum required contribution, the funding standard carryover balance as of January 1, 2012 (prior to the deemed reduction under section 436(f)(3)) is $5,827 ($10,200 less $4,754, plus $381 for investment experience at a rate of 7%). The prefunding balance as of January 1, 2012 (prior to the deemed reduction under section 436(f)(3)) is $62,673 (that is, $58,573 × 1.07). The deemed election to reduce Plan P's balance is first applied to eliminate the funding standard carryover balance, and the remaining $62,673 ($68,500 less $5,827) reduces the January 1, 2012, prefunding balance to zero.

Example 10. (i) Plan V is a defined benefit plan with a plan year that is the calendar year and a valuation date of December 31. The valuation is based on the fair market value of plan assets, which amounts to $1,000,000 as of December 31, 2010, before any adjustments. As of January 1, 2010, Plan V's funding standard carryover balance is $0 and its prefunding balance is $125,000. Plan V's effective interest rate for 2010 is 5.5%. The enrolled actuary's certification of AFTAP for 2010 on March 31, 2010, results in a deemed reduction of $15,000 in the plan's prefunding balance as of January 1, 2010. Plan V's sponsor elected to use the prefunding balance to offset any portion of the minimum required contribution for 2010 not covered by cash contributions.

(ii) In accordance with paragraph (b)(4)(i) of this section, the amount of the prefunding balance subtracted from plan assets is increased from the first day of the plan year to the valuation date using the effective interest rate of 5.5% for 2009. Accordingly, the prefunding balance used for this purpose is $116,050 [($125,000 − $15,000 deemed reduction) × 1.055].

(iii) The fair market value of plan assets used for the December 31, 2010, valuation is $883,950 ($1,000,000 − $116,050).

Example 11. (i) The facts are the same as in *Example 10*. The minimum contribution for Plan V for the 2010 plan year is $45,000; no quarterly installments are required for Plan V for 2010. Plan V's sponsor makes a contribution of $20,000 for the 2010 plan year on July 1, 2011. The actual rate of return on assets for Plan V during 2010 is 10%.

(ii) The contribution of $20,000 is discounted to December 31, 2010, using the effective interest rate of 5.5% to determine the remaining balance of the 2010 minimum required contribution. Accordingly, the contribution is adjusted to $19,472 ($20,000 ÷ 1.0550.5) as of December 31, 2010, and the balance of the minimum required contribution is $25,528 ($45,000 − $19,472). This balance will be covered by the plan sponsor's election to use the prefunding balance to offset any portion of the minimum required contribution not covered by cash contributions.

(iii) Under section (b)(4)(ii) of this section, the amount used to offset the 2010 minimum required contribution for the purpose of adjusting the prefunding balance is discounted to January 1, 2010, using the effective interest rate for 2010. This amount is calculated as $24,197 ($25,528 ÷ 1.055).

(iv) The prefunding balance as of January 1, 2011, is reduced by the deemed election of $15,000 and the discounted amount used to offset the 2010 minimum required contribution ($24,197), and adjusted for investment experience for 2010 using the actual rate of return of 10%. Accordingly, the prefunding balance as of January 1, 2011 is $94,383 [($125,000 − $15,000 − $24,197) × 1.10].

Example 12. (i) The facts are the same as in *Example 11*, except that the enrolled actuary's certification of the AFTAP as of March 31, 2011, results in a deemed reduction of the prefunding balance as of January 1, 2011, of $75,000.

(ii) Under paragraph (d)(1)(ii) of this section, the deemed reduction of the prefunding balance is applied before the election to use the prefunding balance to offset the balance of the minimum required contribution for 2010. To determine the amount of the prefunding balance available to cover the remaining minimum required contribution for 2010, the deemed reduction is adjusted for investment experience to January 1, 2010, using the actual rate of return of 10% for 2010. Accordingly, the adjusted deemed reduction is $68,182 ($75,000 ÷ 1.10) and the available prefunding balance as of January 1, 2010, is $41,818 ($125,000 – $15,000 adjusted deemed reduction for 2010 – $68,182 adjusted deemed reduction for 2011).

(iii) This amount is then adjusted to December 31, 2010, using the effective interest rate of 5.5%. The amount of the prefunding balance available to offset the 2009 minimum required contribution as of December 31, 2010, is $44,118 ($41,818 × 1.055). This amount is larger than the election made by Plan V's sponsor to offset the minimum required contribution for 2010 ($25,528) and so the election remains valid.

(h) *Effective/applicability date and transition rules.*—(1) *Statutory effective date/applicability date.*—Section 430 generally applies to plan years beginning on or after January 1, 2008. The applicability of section 430 for purposes of determining the minimum required contribution is delayed for certain plans in accordance with sections 104 through 106 of PPA '06.

(2) *Effective date/applicability date of regulations.*—This section applies to plan years beginning on or after January 1, 2010. For plan years beginning before January 1, 2010, plans are permitted to rely on the provisions set forth in this section for purposes of satisfying the requirements of section 430.

(3) *Special lookback rule for 2007 plan year's funding ratio.*—(i) *Plan assets.*—For purposes of determining a plan's prior plan year funding ratio under paragraph (d)(3) of this section with respect to the first plan year beginning on or after January 1, 2008, the value of plan assets on the valuation date of the preceding plan year (the "2007 plan year") is determined under section 412(c)(2) as in effect for the 2007 plan year, except that, for this purpose—

(A) If the value of plan assets is less than 90 percent of the fair market value of plan assets for the 2007 plan year on that date, such value is considered to be 90 percent of the fair market value; and

(B) If the value of plan assets is greater than 110 percent of the fair market value of plan assets for the 2007 plan year on that date, such value is considered to be 110 percent of the fair market value.

(ii) *Funding target.*—For purposes of determining a plan's prior plan year funding ratio under paragraph (d)(3) of this section with respect to the first plan year beginning on or after January 1, 2008, the funding target of the plan for the preceding plan year is equal to the plan's current liability under section 412(l)(7) (as in effect prior to amendment by PPA '06) on the valuation date for the 2007 plan year.

(iii) *Special rules for new plans, mergers, and spinoffs.*—In the case of a plan described in paragraph (d)(3)(ii), (d)(3)(iii), or (d)(3)(iv) of this section, the plan's prior plan year funding ratio with respect to the first plan year beginning on or after January 1, 2008 is determined using rules similar to the rules of paragraphs (d)(3)(ii), (d)(3)(iii), and (d)(3)(iv) of this section.

(4) *First effective plan year.*—For purposes of this section, the term *first effective plan year* means the first plan year beginning on or after the date section 430 applies for purposes of determining the minimum required contribution for the plan.

(5) *Pre-effective plan year.*—For purposes of this section, the term *pre-effective plan year* means the plan year immediately preceding the first effective plan year. [Reg. § 1.430(f)-1.]

☐ [*T.D. 9467*, 10-14-2009. Amended by *T.D. 9732*, 9-8-2015.]

[Reg. § 1.430(g)-1]

§ 1.430(g)-1. Valuation date and valuation of plan assets.—(a) *In general.*—(1) *Overview.*—This section provides rules relating to a plan's valuation date and the valuation of a plan's assets for a plan year under section 430(g). Section 430 and this section apply to single employer defined benefit plans (including multiple employer plans as defined in section 413(c)) that are subject to the rules of section 412, but do not apply to multiemployer plans (as defined in section 414(f)). Paragraph (b) of this section describes valuation date rules. Paragraph (c) of this section describes rules regarding the determination of the asset value for purposes of a plan's actuarial valuation. Paragraph (d) of this section contains rules for taking employer contributions into account in the determination of the value of plan assets. Paragraph (e) of this section contains examples. Paragraph (f) of this section sets forth effective/applicability dates and transition rules.

(2) *Special rules for multiple employer plans.*—In the case of a multiple employer plan to which section 413(c)(4)(A) applies, the rules of section 430 and this section are applied separately for each employer under the plan as if each employer maintained a separate plan. Thus, in such a case, the value of plan assets is determined separately for each employer under the plan. In the case of a multiple employer plan to which section 413(c)(4)(A) does not apply (that is, a plan described in section 413(c)(4)(B) that has not made the election for section 413(c)(4)(A) to apply), the rules of section 430 and this section are applied as if all participants in the plan were employed by a single employer.

(b) *Valuation date.*—(1) *In general.*—The determination of the funding target, target normal cost, and value of plan assets for a plan year is made as of the valuation date for that plan year. Except as otherwise provided in paragraph (b)(2) of this section, the valuation date for any plan year is the first day of the plan year.

(2) *Exception for small plans.*—(i) *In general.*—If, on each day during the preceding plan year, a plan had 100 or fewer participants determined by applying the rules of § 1.430(d)-1(e)(1) and (2) (including active and inactive participants and all other individuals entitled to future benefits), then the plan may designate any day during the plan year as its valuation date for that plan year and succeeding plan years. For purposes of this paragraph (b)(2)(i), all defined benefit plans (other than multiemployer plans as defined in section 414(f)) maintained by an employer are treated as one plan, but only participants with respect to that employer are taken into account.

(ii) *Employer determination.*—For purposes of this paragraph (b)(2), the employer includes all members of the employer's controlled group determined pursuant to section 414(b), (c), (m), and (o) and includes any predecessor of the employer that, during the prior year, employed any employees of the employer who are covered by the plan.

(iii) *Application of exception in first plan year.*—In the case of the first plan year of any plan, the exception for small plans under paragraph (b)(2)(i) of this section is applied by taking into account the number of participants that the plan is reasonably expected to have on each day during the first plan year.

(iv) *Valuation date is part of funding method.*—The selection of a plan's valuation date is part of the plan's funding method and, accordingly, may only be changed with the consent of the Commissioner. A change of a plan's valuation date that is required by section 430 is treated as having been approved by the Commissioner and does not require the Commissioner's prior specific approval. Thus, if a plan that ceases to be eligible for the small plan exception under this paragraph (b)(2) for a plan year because the number of participants exceeded 100 in the prior plan year, then the resulting change in the valuation date to the first day of the plan year is automatically approved by the Commissioner.

(c) *Determination of asset value.*—(1) *In general.*—(i) *General use of fair market value.*—Except as otherwise provided in this paragraph (c), the value of plan assets for purposes of section 430 is equal to the fair market value of plan assets on the valuation date. Prior year contributions made after the valuation date and current year contributions made before the valuation date are taken into account to the extent provided in paragraph (d) of this section.

(ii) *Fair market value.*—The fair market value of an asset is determined as the price at which the asset would change hands between a willing buyer and a willing seller, neither being under any compulsion to buy or sell and both having reasonable knowledge of relevant facts. Except as otherwise provided by the Commissioner, any guidance on the valuation of insurance contracts under Subchapter D of Chapter 1 the Internal Revenue Code applies for purposes of this paragraph (c)(1)(ii).

(2) *Averaging of fair market values.*—(i) *In general.*—Subject to the plan asset corridor rules of paragraph (c)(2)(iii) of this section, a plan is permitted to determine the value of plan assets on the valuation date as the average of the fair market value of assets on the valuation date and the adjusted fair market value of assets determined for one or more earlier determination dates (adjusted using the method described in paragraph (c)(2)(ii) of this section). The method of determining the value of assets is part of the plan's funding method and, accordingly, may only be changed with the consent of the Commissioner.

(ii) *Adjusted fair market value.*—(A) *Determination dates.*—The period of time between each determination date (treating the valuation date as a determination date) must be equal and that period of time cannot exceed 12 months. In addition, the earliest determination date with respect to a plan year cannot be earlier than the last day of the 25th month before the valuation date of the plan year (or a similar period in the case of a valuation date that is not the first day of a month). In a typical situation, the earlier determination dates will be the two immediately preceding valuation dates. However, these rules also permit the use of more frequent determination dates. For example, monthly or quarterly determination dates may be used.

(B) *Adjustments for contributions and distributions.*—The adjusted fair market value of plan assets for a prior determination date is the fair market value of plan assets on that date, increased for contributions included in the plan's asset balance on the valuation date that were not included in the plan's asset balance on the earlier determination date, reduced for benefits and all other amounts paid from plan assets during the period beginning with the prior determination date and ending immediately before the valuation date, and adjusted for expected earnings as described in paragraph (c)(2)(ii)(D) of this section. For this purpose, the fair market value of assets as of a determination date includes any contribution for a plan year that ends with or prior to the determination date that is receivable as of the determination date (but only if the contribution is actually made within 8½ months after the end of the applicable plan year). If the contribution that is receivable as of the determination date is for a plan year beginning on or after January 1, 2008, then only the present value as of the determination date (determined using the effective interest rate under section 430(h)(2)(A) for the plan year for which the contribution is made) is included in the fair market value of assets.

(C) *Treatment of spin-offs and plan-to-plan transfers.*—For purposes of determining the adjusted fair market value of plan assets, assets spun-off from a plan as a result of a spin-off described in §1.414(l)-1(b)(4) are treated as an amount paid from plan assets. Except as otherwise provided by the Commissioner, for purposes of determining the adjusted fair market value of plan assets, assets that are added to a plan as a result of a plan-to-plan transfer described in §1.414(l)-1(b)(3) are treated in the same manner as contributions.

(D) *Adjustments for expected earnings.*—[Reserved.]

(E) *Assumed rate of return.*—[Reserved.]

(F) *Limitation on the assumed rate of return for periods within plan years for which the three segment rates were used.*—[Reserved.]

(G) *Limitation on the assumed rate of return for periods within plan years for which the full yield curve was used.*—[Reserved.]

(iii) *Restriction to 90-110 percent corridor.*—(A) *In general.*—This paragraph (c)(2)(iii) provides rules for applying the 90 to 110 percent corridor set forth in section 430(g)(3)(B)(iii). The rules for accounting for contribution receipts under paragraphs (d)(1) and (d)(2) of this section are applied prior to the application of the 90 to 110 percent corridor under this paragraph (c)(2)(iii).

(B) *Asset value less than 90 percent of fair market value.*—If the value of plan assets determined under paragraph (c)(2)(i) of this section is less than 90 percent of the fair market value of plan assets, then the value of plan assets under this paragraph (c)(2) is equal to 90 percent of the fair market value of plan assets.

(C) *Asset value greater than 110 percent of fair market value.*—If the value of plan assets determined under paragraph (c)(2)(i) of this section is greater than 110 percent of the fair market value of plan assets, then the value of plan assets under this paragraph (c)(2) is equal to 110 percent of the fair market value of plan assets.

(3) *Qualified transfers to health benefit accounts.*—In the case of a qualified transfer (as defined in section 420), any assets so transferred are not treated as plan assets for purposes of section 430 and this section.

(d) *Accounting for contribution receipts.*—(1) *Prior year contributions.*—(i) *In general.*—For purposes of determining the value of plan assets under paragraph (c) of this section, if an employer makes a contribution to the plan after the valuation date for the current plan year and the contribution is for an earlier plan year, then the present value of the contribution determined as of that valuation date is taken into account as an asset of the plan as of the valuation date, but only if the contribution is made before the deadline for contributions as described in section 430(j)(1) for the plan year immediately preceding the current plan year. For this purpose, the present value is determined using the effective interest rate under section 430(h)(2)(A) for the plan year for which the contribution is made.

(ii) *Special rule for contributions for the 2007 plan year.*—(A) *Timely contributions.*—Notwithstanding paragraph (d)(1)(i) of this section, if the employer makes a contribution to the plan after the valuation date for the first plan year that begins on or after January 1, 2008, and the contribution is for the immediately preceding plan year and is made by the deadline for contributions for that preceding plan

year under section 412(c)(10) (as in effect before amendment by the Pension Protection Act of 2006 (PPA '06), Public Law 109-280 (120 Stat. 780)), then the contribution is taken into account as a plan asset under paragraph (d)(1)(i) of this section without applying any present value discount.

(B) *Late contributions.*—If a contribution is for the plan year that immediately precedes the first plan year that begins on or after January 1, 2008, and is not described in paragraph (d)(1)(ii)(A) of this section, then the rules of paragraph (d)(1)(i) apply to the contribution except that the present value is determined using the valuation interest rate under section 412(c)(2) for that plan year.

(iii) *Ordering rules.*—For purposes of this paragraph (d)(1), the ordering rules of section 4971(c)(4)(B) apply for purposes of determining the plan year for which a contribution is made.

(2) *Current year contributions made before valuation date.*—In the case of a plan with a valuation date that is not the first day of the plan year, for purposes of determining the value of plan assets under paragraph (c) of this section, if an employer makes a contribution for a plan year before that year's valuation date, that contribution (and any interest on the contribution for the period between the contribution date and the valuation date, determined using the effective interest rate under section 430(h)(2)(A) for the plan year) must be subtracted from plan assets in determining the value of plan assets as of the valuation date. If the result of this subtraction is a number less than zero, the value of plan assets as of the valuation date is equal to zero.

(e) *Examples.*—[Reserved.]

(f) *Effective/applicability dates and transition rules.*—(1) *Statutory effective date/applicability date.*—Section 430 generally applies to plan years beginning on or after January 1, 2008. The applicability of section 430 for purposes of determining the minimum required contribution is delayed for certain plans in accordance with sections 104 through 106 of PPA '06.

(2) *Effective date/applicability date of regulations.*—(i) *In general.*—This section applies to plan years beginning on or after January 1, 2010, regardless of whether section 430 applies to determine the minimum required contribution for the plan year. For plan years beginning before January 1, 2010, plans are permitted to rely on the provisions set forth in this section for purposes of satisfying the requirements of section 430.

(ii) *Permission to use averaging for 2008.*—For purposes of determining the actuarial value of assets for a plan year beginning during 2008 using the averaging rules of paragraph (c)(2) of this section, a plan is permitted to apply an assumed earnings rate of zero under paragraph (c)(2)(ii)(E) of this section (even if zero is not the actuary's best estimate of the anticipated annual rate of return on plan assets).

(3) *Approval for changes in the valuation date and valuation method.*—Any change in a plan's valuation date or asset valuation method that satisfies the rules of this section and is made for either the first plan year beginning in 2008, the first plan year beginning in 2009, or the first plan year beginning in 2010 is treated as having been approved by the Commissioner and does not require the Commissioner's specific prior approval. In addition, a change in a plan's valuation date or asset valuation method for the first plan year to which section 430 applies to determine the plan's minimum required contribution (even if that plan year begins after December 31, 2010) that satisfies the rules of this section is treated as having been approved by the Commissioner and does not require the Commissioner's specific prior approval. [Reg. §1.430(g)-1.]

☐ [*T.D.* 9467, 10-14-2009.]

[Reg. §1.430(h)(2)-1]

§1.430(h)(2)-1. Interest rates used to determine present value.—(a) *In general.*—(1) *Overview.*—This section provides rules relating to the interest rates to be applied for a plan year under section 430(h)(2). Section 430(h)(2) and this section apply to single employer defined benefit plans (including multiple employer plans as defined in section 413(c)) that are subject to section 412 but do not apply to multiemployer plans (as defined in section 414(f)). Paragraph (b) of this section describes how the segment interest rates are used for a plan year. Paragraph (c) of this section describes those segment rates. Paragraph (d) of this section describes the monthly corporate bond yield curve that is used to develop the segment rates. Paragraph (e) of this section describes certain elections that are permitted to be made under this section. Paragraph (f) of this section describes other rules related to interest rates. Paragraph (g) of this section contains examples. Paragraph (h) of this section contains effective/applicability dates and transition rules.

(2) *Special rules for multiple employer plans.*—In the case of a multiple employer plan to which section 413(c)(4)(A) applies, the rules of section 430 and this section are applied separately for each employer under the plan as if each employer maintained a separate plan. Thus, each employer under such a multiple employer plan may make elections with respect to the interest rate rules under this section that are independent of the elections of other employers under the plan. In the case of a multiple employer plan to which section 413(c)(4)(A) does not apply (that is, a plan described in section 413(c)(4)(B) that has not made the election for section 413(c)(4)(A) to apply), the rules of section 430 and this section are applied as if all participants in the plan were employed by a single employer.

(b) *Interest rates for determining plan liabilities.*—(1) *In general.*—The interest rates used in determining the present value of the benefits that are included in the target normal cost and the funding target for the plan for a plan year are determined as set forth in this paragraph (b).

(2) *Benefits payable within 5 years.*—(i) *In general.*—In the case of benefits expected to be payable during the 5-year period beginning on the valuation date for the plan year, the interest rate used in determining the present value of the benefits that are included in the target normal cost and the funding target for the plan is the first segment rate with respect to the applicable month, as described in paragraph (c)(2)(i) of this section.

(ii) *Special rule for plan years beginning before January 1, 2014.*—With respect to a plan year beginning before January 1, 2014, for a plan with a valuation date other than the first day of the plan year, the 5-year period beginning on the first day of the plan year is permitted to be used in lieu of the 5-year period beginning on the valuation date for the plan year under paragraph (b)(2)(i) of this section.

(3) *Benefits payable after 5 years and within 20 years.*—In the case of benefits expected to be payable during the 15-year period beginning after the end of the period described in paragraph (b)(2) of this section, the interest rate used in determining the present value of the benefits that are included in the target normal cost and the funding target for the plan is the second segment rate with respect to the applicable month, as described in paragraph (c)(2)(ii) of this section.

(4) *Benefits payable after 20 years.*—In the case of benefits expected to be payable after the period described in paragraph (b)(3) of this section, the interest rate used in determining the present value of the benefits that are included in the target normal cost and the funding target for the plan is the third segment rate with respect to the applicable month, as described in paragraph (c)(2)(iii) of this section.

(5) *Applicable month.*—Except as otherwise provided in paragraph (e) of this section, the term *applicable month* for purposes of this paragraph (b) means the month that includes the valuation date of the plan for the plan year.

(6) *Special rule for certain airlines.*—(i) *In general.*—Pursuant to section 6615 of the U.S. Troop Readiness, Veterans' Care, Katrina Recovery, and Iraq Accountability Appropriations Act, 2007, Public Law 110-28 (121 Stat. 112), for a plan sponsor that makes the election described in section 402(a)(2) of the Pension Protection Act of 2006 (PPA '06), Public Law 109-280 (120 Stat. 780), the interest rate required to be used to determine the plan's funding target for each of the 10 years under that election is 8.25 percent (rather than the segment rates otherwise described in this paragraph (b) or the full yield curve as permitted under paragraph (e)(4) of this section).

(ii) *Special interest rate not applicable for other purposes.*—The special interest rate described in paragraph (b)(6)(i) of this section does not apply for other purposes such as the determination of the plan's target normal cost.

(c) *Segment rates.*—(1) *Overview.*—This paragraph (c) sets forth rules for determining the first, second, and third segment rates for purposes of paragraph (b) of this section. The first, second, and third segment rates are set forth in revenue rulings, notices, or other guidance published in the Internal Revenue Bulletin. See § 601.601(d)(2) relating to objectives and standards for publishing regulations, revenue rulings and revenue procedures in the Internal Revenue Bulletin. See paragraph (h)(4) of this section for a transition rule under which the definition of the segment rates is modified for plan years beginning in 2008 and 2009.

(2) *Definition of segment rates.*—(i) *First segment rate.*—For purposes of this section, except as otherwise provided under the transition rule of paragraph (h)(4) of this section, the *first segment rate* is, with respect to any month, the single rate of interest determined by

the Commissioner on the basis of the average of the monthly corporate bond yield curves (described in paragraph (d) of this section) for the 24-month period ending with the month preceding that month, taking into account only the first 5 years of each of those yield curves.

(ii) *Second segment rate.*—For purposes of this section, except as otherwise provided under the transition rule of paragraph (h)(4) of this section, the *second segment rate* is, with respect to any month, the single rate of interest determined by the Commissioner on the basis of the average of the monthly corporate bond yield curves (described in paragraph (d) of this section) for the 24-month period ending with the month preceding that month, taking into account only the portion of each of those yield curves corresponding to the 15-year period that follows the end of the 5-year period described in paragraph (c)(2)(i) of this section.

(iii) *Third segment rate.*—For purposes of this section, except as otherwise provided under the transition rule of paragraph (h)(4) of this section, the *third segment rate* is, with respect to any month, the single rate of interest determined by the Commissioner on the basis of the average of the monthly corporate bond yield curves (described in paragraph (d) of this section) for the 24-month period ending with the month preceding that month, taking into account only the portion of each of those yield curves corresponding to the 40-year period that follows the end of the 15-year period described in paragraph (c)(2)(ii) of this section.

(d) *Monthly corporate bond yield curve.*—(1) *In general.*—For purposes of this section, the monthly corporate bond yield curve is, with respect to any month, a yield curve that is prescribed by the Commissioner for that month based on yields for that month on investment grade corporate bonds with varying maturities that are in the top three quality levels available.

(2) *Determination and publication of yield curve.*—A description of the methodology for determining the monthly corporate bond yield curve is provided in guidance issued by the Commissioner that is published in the Internal Revenue Bulletin. The yield curve for a month will be set forth in revenue rulings, notices, or other guidance published in the Internal Revenue Bulletin. See § 601.601(d)(2) relating to objectives and standards for publishing regulations, revenue rulings and revenue procedures in the Internal Revenue Bulletin.

(e) *Elections.*—(1) *In general.*—This paragraph (e) describes elections for a plan year that a plan sponsor can make to use alternative interest rates under this section. Any election under this paragraph (e) must be made by providing written notification of the election to the plan's enrolled actuary. Any election in this paragraph (e) may be adopted for a plan year without obtaining the consent of the Commissioner, but, once adopted, that election will apply for that plan year and all future plan years and may be changed only with the consent of the Commissioner.

(2) *Election for alternative applicable month.*—As an alternative to defining the applicable month as the month that includes the valuation date for the plan year, a plan sponsor that is using segment rates as provided under paragraph (b) of this section may elect to use one of the 4 months preceding that month as the applicable month.

(3) *Election not to apply transition rule.*—The plan sponsor may elect not to apply the transition rule in paragraph (h)(4) of this section.

(4) *Election to use full yield curve.*—(i) *In general.*—For purposes of determining the plan's funding target and target normal cost, and for all other purposes under section 430 (including the determination of shortfall amortization installments, waiver installments, and the present values of those installments as described in paragraph (f)(2) of this section), the plan sponsor may elect to use interest rates under the monthly corporate bond yield curve described in paragraph (d) of this section for the month preceding the month that includes the valuation date in lieu of the segment rates determined under paragraph (c) of this section. In order to address the timing of benefit payments during a year, reasonable approximations are permitted to be used to value benefit payments that are expected to be made during a plan year.

(ii) *Reasonable techniques permitted.*—In the case of a plan sponsor using the monthly corporate bond yield curve under this paragraph (e)(4), if with respect to a decrement the benefit is only expected to be paid for one-half of a year (because the decrement was assumed to occur in the middle of the year), the interest rate for that year can be determined as if the benefit were being paid for the entire year. See § 1.430(d)-1(f)(7) for additional reasonable techniques that can be used in determining present value.

(5) *Plan sponsor.*—For purposes of the elections described in this section, any reference to the plan sponsor generally means the em-

ployer or employers responsible for making contributions to or under the plan. In the case of plans that are multiple employer plans to which section 413(c)(4)(A) does not apply, any reference to the plan sponsor means the plan administrator within the meaning of section 414(g).

(f) *Interest rates used for other purposes.*—(1) *Effective interest rate.*—(i) *In general.*—Except as otherwise provided in paragraph (f)(2) of this section, the effective interest rate determined under section 430(h)(2)(A) for the plan year is the single interest rate that, if used to determine the present value of the benefits that are taken into account in determining the plan's funding target for the plan year, would result in an amount equal to the plan's funding target determined for the plan year under section 430(d) as described in § 1.430(d)-1(b)(2) (without regard to calculations for plans in at-risk status under section 430(i)).

(ii) *Zero funding target.*—If, for the plan year, the plan's funding target is equal to zero, then the effective interest rate determined under section 430(h)(2)(A) for the plan year is the single interest rate that, if used to determine the present value of the benefits that are taken into account in determining the plan's target normal cost for the plan year, would result in an amount equal to the plan's target normal cost determined for the plan year under section 430(b) as described in § 1.430(d)-1(b)(1) (without regard to calculations for plans in at-risk status under section 430(i)).

(2) *Interest rates used for determining shortfall amortization installments and waiver amortization installments.*—The interest rates used to determine the amount of shortfall amortization installments and waiver amortization installments and the present value of those installments are determined based on the dates those installments are assumed to be paid, using the same timing rules that apply in determining target normal cost as described in paragraph (b) of this section. Thus, for a plan that uses the segment rates described in paragraph (c) of this section, the first segment rate applies to the installments assumed to be paid during the first 5 year period beginning on the valuation date for the plan year, and the second segment rate applies to the installments assumed to be paid during the subsequent 15-year period. For purposes of this paragraph (f)(2), the shortfall amortization installments for a plan year are assumed to be paid on the valuation date for that plan year. For example, for a plan that uses the segment rates described in paragraph (c) of this section, the shortfall amortization installment for the fifth plan year following the current plan year (the sixth installment) is assumed to be paid on the valuation date for that year so that such shortfall amortization installment will be determined using the second segment rate.

(g) *Examples.*—The following examples illustrate the rules of this section:

Example 1. (i) The January 1, 2009, valuation of Plan P is performed using the segment rates applicable for September 2008 (determined without regard to the transition rule of section 430(h)(2)(G)), and the 2009 annuitant and nonannuitant (male and female) mortality tables as published in Notice 2008-85. See § 601.601(d)(2) relating to objectives and standards for publishing regulations, revenue rulings and revenue procedures in the Internal Revenue Bulletin. Plan P provides for early retirement benefits as early as age 50, and offers a single-sum distribution payable immediately at retirement. The single-sum payment is equal to the present value of the participant's accrued benefit, based on the applicable interest rates and the applicable mortality table under section 417(e)(3). Participant E is the only participant in the plan, and is a male age 46 as of January 1, 2009, with an annual accrued benefit of $23,000 payable beginning at age 65. The actuary assumes a 100% probability that Participant E will terminate at age 50 and will elect to receive his benefit in the form of a single-sum payment.

(ii) Plan P's funding target is $68,908 as of January 1, 2009. This figure is based on the male nonannuitant rates for ages prior to age 50, the applicable mortality rates under section 417(e)(3) for ages 50 and later, and segment interest rates of 5.07% for the first 5 years after the valuation date, 6.09% for the next 15 years, and 6.56% for periods more than 20 years after the valuation date. (See § 1.430(d)-1(f)(9), *Example 10*, for additional details.)

(iii) The present value of Participant E's benefits as of January 1, 2009, is $68,908 if a single interest rate of 6.52805% is substituted for the segment interest rates but all other assumptions remain the same. Thus (rounded), the effective interest rate for Plan P is 6.53% for 2009.

Example 2. (i) The facts are the same as for *Example 1*, except that *Plan P offers a single-sum distribution equal to the present value of the accrued benefit based on the applicable interest rates under section 417(e)(3) or an interest rate of 6.25%, whichever produces the higher amount. The applicable mortality table under section 417(e)(3) is used for both calculations.

(ii) The present value of Participant E's age-50 single-sum distribution as of January 1, 2009 (when Participant E is age 46) is $77,392. This amount is determined by calculating the projected single-sum distribution at age 50 using the applicable mortality table under section 417(e)(3) and an interest rate of 6.25%, and discounting the result to January 1, 2009, using the first segment rate of 5.07% and male nonannuitant mortality rates for 2009. Because this amount is larger than the present value of Participant E's single-sum payment based on the applicable interest rates under section 417(e)(3) (that is, $68,908), the funding target for Plan P is $77,392 as of January 1, 2009. (See § 1.430(d)-1(f)(9), *Example 12* for additional details.)

(iii) The effective interest rate is the single interest rate that will produce the same funding target if substituted for the segment interest rates keeping all other assumptions the same, including the fixed interest rate used by the plan to determine single-sum payments. The only segment interest rate used to develop the funding target of $77,392 was the first segment rate of 5.07%. Therefore, considering only this calculation, the single interest rate that would produce the same funding target would be 5.07%.

(iv) However, the effective interest rate must also reflect the fact that the single-sum payment under Plan P is equal to the greater of the present value of Participant E's accrued benefit based on the fixed rate of 6.25% or the applicable interest rates under section 417(e)(3). If the single rate of 5.07% is substituted for the segment rates used to calculate the present value of the single-sum payment based on the applicable interest rates, the resulting funding target would be higher than $77,392.

(v) Using a single interest rate of 6.0771%, the January 1, 2009, present value of Participant E's single-sum payment based on the applicable interest rates is $77,392, and the present value of Participant E's single sum payment based on the plan's interest rate of 6.25% is $74,494. Plan P's funding target is the larger of the two, or $77,392, which is the same as the funding target based on the segment interest rates used for the 2009 valuation. Therefore, Plan P's effective interest rate for 2009 (rounded) is 6.08%.

(h) *Effective/applicability dates and transition rules.*—(1) *Statutory effective date/applicability date.*—Section 430 generally applies to plan years beginning on or after January 1, 2008. The applicability of section 430 for purposes of determining the minimum required contribution is delayed for certain plans in accordance with sections 104 through 106 of PPA '06.

(2) *Effective date/applicability date of regulations.*—This section applies to plan years beginning on or after January 1, 2010, regardless of whether section 430 applies to determine the minimum required contribution for the plan year. For plan years beginning before January 1, 2010, plans are permitted to rely on the provisions set forth in this section for purposes of satisfying the requirements of section 430.

(3) *Approval for changes in interest rate.*—Any change to an election under paragraph (e) of this section that is made for the first plan year beginning in 2009 or the first plan year beginning in 2010 is treated as having been approved by the Commissioner and does not require the Commissioner's specific prior approval.

(4) *Transition rule.*—(i) *In general.*—Notwithstanding the general rules for determination of segment rates under paragraph (c)(2) of this section, for plan years beginning in 2008 or 2009, the first, second, or third segment rate for a plan with respect to any month is equal to the sum of—

(A) The product of that rate for that month determined without regard to this paragraph (h)(4), multiplied by the applicable percentage; and

(B) The product of the weighted average interest rate determined under the rules of paragraph (h)(4)(iii) of this section, multiplied by a percentage equal to 100 percent minus the applicable percentage.

(ii) *Applicable percentage.*—For purposes of this paragraph (h)(4), the applicable percentage is 33-1/3 percent for plan years beginning in 2008 and 66-2/3 percent for plan years beginning in 2009.

(iii) *Weighted average interest rate.*—The weighted average interest rate for purposes of paragraph (h)(4)(i)(B) of this section is the weighted average interest rate under section 412(b)(5)(B)(ii)(II) (as that provision was in effect for plan years beginning in 2007) as of—

(A) The month which contains the first day of the plan year;

(B) The month which contains the valuation date (if the applicable month is determined under paragraph (b)(5) of this section); or

(C) The applicable month (if the applicable month is determined under paragraph (e)(2) of this section).

(iv) *New plans ineligible.*—The transition rule of this paragraph (h)(4) does not apply if the first plan year of the plan begins on or after January 1, 2008. [Reg. § 1.430(h)(2)-1.]

⬦➤ *Caution: Reg. §1.430(h)(3)-1, below, prior to amendment by T.D. 9826, is generally applicable to plans years beginning before January 1, 2018.*

[Reg. §1.430(h)(3)-1]

§1.430(h)(3)-1. Mortality tables used to determine present value.—(a) *Basis for mortality tables.*—(1) *In general.*—This section sets forth rules for the mortality tables to be used in determining present value or making any computation under section 430. Generally applicable mortality tables for participants and beneficiaries are set forth in this section pursuant to section 430(h)(3)(A). In lieu of using the mortality tables provided under this section with respect to participants and beneficiaries, plan-specific substitute mortality tables are permitted to be used for this purpose pursuant to section 430(h)(3)(C) provided that the requirements of §1.430(h)(3)-2 are satisfied. Mortality tables that may be used with respect to disabled individuals are to be provided in guidance published in the Internal Revenue Bulletin. See §601.601(d)(2)(ii)(*b*) of this chapter.

(2) *Static tables or generational tables permitted.*—The generally applicable mortality tables provided under section 430(h)(3)(A) are the static tables described in paragraph (a)(3) of this section and the generational mortality tables described in paragraph (a)(4) of this section. A plan is permitted to use either of those sets of mortality tables with respect to participants and beneficiaries pursuant to this section.

(3) *Static tables.*—The static mortality tables that are permitted to be used pursuant to paragraph (a)(2) of this section are updated annually to reflect expected improvements in mortality experience as described in paragraph (c)(2) of this section. Static mortality tables that are to be used with respect to valuation dates occurring during 2008 are provided in paragraph (e) of this section. The mortality tables to be used with respect to valuation dates occurring in later years are to be provided in guidance published in the Internal Revenue Bulletin. See §601.601(d)(2)(ii)(*b*) of this chapter.

(4) *Generational mortality tables.*—(i) *In general.*—The generational mortality tables that are permitted to be used pursuant to paragraph (a)(2) of this section are determined pursuant to this paragraph (a)(4) using the base mortality tables and projection factors set forth in paragraph (d) of this section. Under the generational mortality tables, the probability of an individual's death at a particular age is determined as the individual's base mortality rate (that is, the applicable mortality rate from the table set forth in paragraph (d) of this section for the age for which the probability of death is being determined) multiplied by the mortality improvement factor. The mortality improvement factor is equal to (1 - projection factor for that age)^n, where n is equal to the projection period. For this purpose, the projection period is the number of years between 2000 and the year for which the probability of death is being determined.

(ii) *Examples of calculation.*—As an example of the use of generational mortality tables under paragraph (a)(4)(i) of this section, for purposes of determining the probability of death at age 54 for a male annuitant born in 1974, the base mortality rate is .005797, the projection factor is .020, and the projection period (the period from the year 2000 until the year the participant will attain age 54) is 28 years, so that the mortality improvement factor is .567976, and the probability of death at age 54 is .003293. Similarly, under these generational mortality tables, the probability of death at age 55 for the same male annuitant would be determined by using the base mortality rate and projection factor at age 55, and a projection period of 29 years (the period from the year 2000 until the year the participant will attain age 55). Thus, the base mortality rate is .005905, the projection factor is .019, so that the mortality improvement factor is .573325 ((1-.019)^{29}), and the probability of death at age 55 is .003385 (.573325 times .005905). Because these generational mortality tables reflect expected improvements in mortality experience, no periodic updates are needed.

(b) *Use of the tables.*—(1) *Separate tables for annuitants and nonannuitants.*—(i) *In general.*—Separate tables are provided for use for annuitants and nonannuitants. The nonannuitant mortality table is applied to determine the probability of survival for a nonannuitant for the period before the nonannuitant is projected to commence receiving benefits. The annuitant mortality table is applied to determine the present value of benefits for each annuitant, and for each nonannuitant for the period beginning when the nonannuitant is projected to commence receiving benefits. For purposes of this section, an annuitant means a plan participant who has commenced receiving benefits and a nonannuitant means a plan participant who has not yet commenced receiving benefits (for example, an active employee or a terminated vested participant). A participant whose benefit has par-

⬜ [*T.D. 9467,* 10-14-2009. Amended by *T.D. 9732,* 9-8-2015]

tially commenced is treated as an annuitant with respect to the portion of the benefit which has commenced and a nonannuitant with respect to the balance of the benefit. In addition, for any period in which an annuitant is projected to be receiving benefits, any beneficiary with respect to that annuitant is also treated as an annuitant for purposes of this paragraph (b)(1).

(ii) *Examples of calculation.*—As an example of the use of separate annuitant and nonannuitant tables under paragraph (b)(1)(i) of this section, with respect to a 45-year-old active participant who is projected to commence receiving an annuity at age 55, the funding target would be determined using the nonannuitant mortality table for the period before the participant attains age 55 (so that, if the static mortality tables are used pursuant to paragraph (a)(3) of this section, the probability of an active male participant living from age 45 to age 55 using the table that applies for a plan year beginning in 2008 is 98.61%) and the annuitant mortality table for the period ages 55 and above. Similarly, if a 45-year-old terminated vested participant is projected to commence an annuity at age 65, the funding target would be determined using the nonannuitant mortality table for the period before the participant attains age 65 and the annuitant mortality table for ages 65 and above.

(2) *Small plan tables.*—If static mortality tables are used pursuant to paragraph (a)(3) of this section, as an alternative to the separate static tables specified for annuitants and nonannuitants pursuant to paragraph (b)(1) of this section, a combined static table that applies the same mortality rates to both annuitants and nonannuitants is permitted to be used for a small plan. For this purpose, a small plan is defined as a plan with 500 or fewer participants (including both active and inactive participants) on the valuation date.

(c) *Construction of static tables.*—(1) *Source of basic rates.*—The static mortality tables that are used pursuant to paragraph (a)(3) of this section are based on the base mortality tables set forth in paragraph (d) of this section.

(2) *Projected mortality improvements.*—The mortality rates under the base mortality tables are projected to improve using the projection factors provided in Projection Scale AA, as set forth in paragraph (d) of this section. Using these projection factors, the mortality rate for an individual at each age is determined as the individual's base mortality rate (that is, the applicable base mortality rate from the table set forth in paragraph (d) of this section for the individual at that age) multiplied by the mortality improvement factor. The mortality improvement factor is equal to (1 - projection factor for that age)^n, where n is equal to the projection period. The annuitant mortality rates for a plan year are determined using a projection period that runs from the calendar year 2000 until 7 years after the calendar year that contains the valuation date for the plan year. The nonannuitant mortality rates for a plan year are determined using a projection period that runs from the calendar year 2000 until 15 years after the calendar year that contains the valuation date for the plan year. Thus, for example, for a plan year with a January 1, 2012, valuation date, the annuitant mortality rates are determined using a projection period that runs from 2000 until 2019 (19 years) and the nonannuitant mortality rates are determined using a projection period that runs from 2000 until 2027 (27 years).

(3) *Construction of combined tables for small plans.*—The combined mortality tables that are permitted to be used for small plans pursuant to paragraph (b)(2) of this section are constructed from the separate nonannuitant and annuitant tables using the weighting factors for small plans that are set forth in paragraph (d) of this section. The weighting factors are applied to develop these mortality tables using the following equation: Combined mortality rate = [nonannuitant rate * (1- weighting factor)] + [annuitant rate * weighting factor].

(d) *Base mortality tables and projection factors.*—The following base mortality tables and projection factors are used to determine generational mortality tables for purposes of determining present value or making any computation under section 430 as set forth in paragraph (a)(4) of this section. In addition, the following base mortality tables and projection factors are used to determine the static mortality tables that are used for purposes of determining present value or making any computation under section 430 as set forth in paragraphs (a)(3) and (c) of this section. See §1.430(h)(3)-2(c)(3) for rules regarding the required use of the projection factors set forth in this paragraph (d) in connection with a plan-specific substitute mortality table.

>>>→ *Caution: Reg. §1.430(h)(3)-1, below, prior to amendment by T.D. 9826, is generally applicable to plans years beginning before January 1, 2018.*

Age	MALE Base Non-Annuitant Mortality Rates (Year 2000)	MALE Base Annuitant Mortality Rates (Year 2000)	MALE Scale AA Projection Factors	MALE Weighting Factors for Small Plans	FEMALE Base Non-Annuitant Mortality Rates (Year 2000)	FEMALE Base Annuitant Mortality Rates (Year 2000)	FEMALE Scale AA Projection Factors	FEMALE Weighting Factors for Small Plans
1	0.000637	0.000637	0.020	-	0.000571	0.000571	0.020	-
2	0.000430	0.000430	0.020	-	0.000372	0.000372	0.020	-
3	0.000357	0.000357	0.020	-	0.000278	0.000278	0.020	-
4	0.000278	0.000278	0.020	-	0.000208	0.000208	0.020	-
5	0.000255	0.000255	0.020	-	0.000188	0.000188	0.020	-
6	0.000244	0.000244	0.020	-	0.000176	0.000176	0.020	-
7	0.000234	0.000234	0.020	-	0.000165	0.000165	0.020	-
8	0.000216	0.000216	0.020	-	0.000147	0.000147	0.020	-
9	0.000209	0.000209	0.020	-	0.000140	0.000140	0.020	-
10	0.000212	0.000212	0.020	-	0.000141	0.000141	0.020	-
11	0.000219	0.000219	0.020	-	0.000143	0.000143	0.020	-
12	0.000228	0.000228	0.020	-	0.000148	0.000148	0.020	-
13	0.000240	0.000240	0.020	-	0.000155	0.000155	0.020	-
14	0.000254	0.000254	0.019	-	0.000162	0.000162	0.018	-
15	0.000269	0.000269	0.019	-	0.000170	0.000170	0.016	-
16	0.000284	0.000284	0.019	-	0.000177	0.000177	0.015	-
17	0.000301	0.000301	0.019	-	0.000184	0.000184	0.014	-
18	0.000316	0.000316	0.019	-	0.000188	0.000188	0.014	-
19	0.000331	0.000331	0.019	-	0.000190	0.000190	0.015	-
20	0.000345	0.000345	0.019	-	0.000191	0.000191	0.016	-
21	0.000357	0.000357	0.018	-	0.000192	0.000192	0.017	-
22	0.000366	0.000366	0.017	-	0.000194	0.000194	0.017	-
23	0.000373	0.000373	0.015	-	0.000197	0.000197	0.016	-
24	0.000376	0.000376	0.013	-	0.000201	0.000201	0.015	-
25	0.000376	0.000376	0.010	-	0.000207	0.000207	0.014	-
26	0.000378	0.000378	0.006	-	0.000214	0.000214	0.012	-
27	0.000382	0.000382	0.005	-	0.000223	0.000223	0.012	-
28	0.000393	0.000393	0.005	-	0.000235	0.000235	0.012	-
29	0.000412	0.000412	0.005	-	0.000248	0.000248	0.012	-
30	0.000444	0.000444	0.005	-	0.000264	0.000264	0.010	-
31	0.000499	0.000499	0.005	-	0.000307	0.000307	0.008	-
32	0.000562	0.000562	0.005	-	0.000350	0.000350	0.008	-
33	0.000631	0.000631	0.005	-	0.000394	0.000394	0.009	-
34	0.000702	0.000702	0.005	-	0.000435	0.000435	0.010	-
35	0.000773	0.000773	0.005	-	0.000475	0.000475	0.011	-
36	0.000841	0.000841	0.005	-	0.000514	0.000514	0.012	-
37	0.000904	0.000904	0.005	-	0.000554	0.000554	0.013	-
38	0.000964	0.000964	0.006	-	0.000598	0.000598	0.014	-
39	0.001021	0.001021	0.007	-	0.000648	0.000648	0.015	-
40	0.001079	0.001079	0.008	-	0.000706	0.000706	0.015	-
41	0.001142	0.001157	0.009	0.0045	0.000774	0.000774	0.015	-
42	0.001215	0.001312	0.010	0.0091	0.000852	0.000852	0.015	-
43	0.001299	0.001545	0.011	0.0136	0.000937	0.000937	0.015	-
44	0.001397	0.001855	0.012	0.0181	0.001029	0.001029	0.015	-
45	0.001508	0.002243	0.013	0.0226	0.001124	0.001124	0.016	0.0084
46	0.001616	0.002709	0.014	0.0272	0.001223	0.001223	0.017	0.0167
47	*0.001734*	*0.003252*	*0.015*	0.0317	0.001326	0.001335	0.018	0.0251
48	0.001860	0.003873	0.016	0.0362	0.001434	0.001559	0.018	0.0335
49	0.001995	0.004571	0.017	0.0407	0.001550	0.001896	0.018	0.0419

Reg. §1.430(h)(3)-1(d)

⋙→ *Caution: Reg. §1.430(h)(3)-1, below, prior to amendment by T.D. 9826, is generally applicable to plans years beginning before January 1, 2018.*

Age	MALE Base Non-Annuitant Mortality Rates (Year 2000)	MALE Base Annuitant Mortality Rates (Year 2000)	MALE Scale AA Projection Factors	MALE Weighting Factors for Small Plans	FEMALE Base Non-Annuitant Mortality Rates (Year 2000)	FEMALE Base Annuitant Mortality Rates (Year 2000)	FEMALE Scale AA Projection Factors	FEMALE Weighting Factors for Small Plans
50	0.002138	0.005347	0.018	0.0453	0.001676	0.002344	0.017	0.0502
51	0.002288	0.005528	0.019	0.0498	0.001814	0.002459	0.016	0.0586
52	0.002448	0.005644	0.020	0.0686	0.001967	0.002647	0.014	0.0744
53	0.002621	0.005722	0.020	0.0953	0.002135	0.002895	0.012	0.0947
54	0.002812	0.005797	0.020	0.1288	0.002321	0.003190	0.010	0.1189
55	0.003029	0.005905	0.019	0.2066	0.002526	0.003531	0.008	0.1897
56	0.003306	0.006124	0.018	0.3173	0.002756	0.003925	0.006	0.2857
57	0.003628	0.006444	0.017	0.3780	0.003010	0.004385	0.005	0.3403
58	0.003997	0.006895	0.016	0.4401	0.003291	0.004921	0.005	0.3878
59	0.004414	0.007485	0.016	0.4986	0.003599	0.005531	0.005	0.4360
60	0.004878	0.008196	0.016	0.5633	0.003931	0.006200	0.005	0.4954
61	0.005382	0.009001	0.015	0.6338	0.004285	0.006919	0.005	0.5805
62	0.005918	0.009915	0.015	0.7103	0.004656	0.007689	0.005	0.6598
63	0.006472	0.010951	0.014	0.7902	0.005039	0.008509	0.005	0.7520
64	0.007028	0.012117	0.014	0.8355	0.005429	0.009395	0.005	0.8043
65	0.007573	0.013419	0.014	0.8832	0.005821	0.010364	0.005	0.8552
66	0.008099	0.014868	0.013	0.9321	0.006207	0.011413	0.005	0.9118
67	0.008598	0.016460	0.013	0.9510	0.006583	0.012540	0.005	0.9367
68	0.009069	0.018200	0.014	0.9639	0.006945	0.013771	0.005	0.9523
69	0.009510	0.020105	0.014	0.9714	0.007289	0.015153	0.005	0.9627
70	0.009922	0.022206	0.015	0.9740	0.007613	0.016742	0.005	0.9661
71	0.010912	0.024570	0.015	0.9766	0.008309	0.018579	0.006	0.9695
72	0.012892	0.027281	0.015	0.9792	0.009700	0.020665	0.006	0.9729
73	0.015862	0.030387	0.015	0.9818	0.011787	0.022970	0.007	0.9763
74	0.019821	0.033900	0.015	0.9844	0.014570	0.025458	0.007	0.9797
75	0.024771	0.037834	0.014	0.9870	0.018049	0.028106	0.008	0.9830
76	0.030710	0.042169	0.014	0.9896	0.022224	0.030966	0.008	0.9864
77	0.037640	0.046906	0.013	0.9922	0.027094	0.034105	0.007	0.9898
78	0.045559	0.052123	0.012	0.9948	0.032660	0.037595	0.007	0.9932
79	0.054469	0.057927	0.011	0.9974	0.038922	0.041506	0.007	0.9966
80	0.064368	0.064368	0.010	1.0000	0.045879	0.045879	0.007	1.0000
81	0.072041	0.072041	0.009	1.0000	0.050780	0.050780	0.007	1.0000
82	0.080486	0.080486	0.008	1.0000	0.056294	0.056294	0.007	1.0000
83	0.089718	0.089718	0.008	1.0000	0.062506	0.062506	0.007	1.0000
84	0.099779	0.099779	0.007	1.0000	0.069517	0.069517	0.007	1.0000
85	0.110757	0.110757	0.007	1.0000	0.077446	0.077446	0.006	1.0000
86	0.122797	0.122797	0.007	1.0000	0.086376	0.086376	0.005	1.0000
87	0.136043	0.136043	0.006	1.0000	0.096337	0.096337	0.004	1.0000
88	0.150590	0.150590	0.005	1.0000	0.107303	0.107303	0.004	1.0000
89	0.166420	0.166420	0.005	1.0000	0.119154	0.119154	0.003	1.0000
90	0.183408	0.183408	0.004	1.0000	0.131682	0.131682	0.003	1.0000
91	0.199769	0.199769	0.004	1.0000	0.144604	0.144604	0.003	1.0000
92	0.216605	0.216605	0.003	1.0000	0.157618	0.157618	0.003	1.0000
93	0.233662	0.233662	0.003	1.0000	0.170433	0.170433	0.002	1.0000
94	0.250693	0.250693	0.003	1.0000	0.182799	0.182799	0.002	1.0000
95	0.267491	0.267491	0.002	1.0000	0.194509	0.194509	0.002	1.0000
96	0.283905	0.283905	0.002	1.0000	0.205379	0.205379	0.002	1.0000
97	0.299852	0.299852	0.002	1.0000	0.215240	0.215240	0.001	1.0000
98	0.315296	0.315296	0.001	1.0000	0.223947	0.223947	0.001	1.0000

⟫⟶ *Caution: Reg. §1.430(h)(3)-1, below, prior to amendment by T.D. 9826, is generally applicable to plans years beginning before January 1, 2018.*

Age	MALE Base Non-Annuitant Mortality Rates (Year 2000)	MALE Base Annuitant Mortality Rates (Year 2000)	MALE Scale AA Projection Factors	MALE Weighting Factors for Small Plans	FEMALE Base Non-Annuitant Mortality Rates (Year 2000)	FEMALE Base Annuitant Mortality Rates (Year 2000)	FEMALE Scale AA Projection Factors	FEMALE Weighting Factors for Small Plans
99	0.330207	0.330207	0.001	1.0000	0.231387	0.231387	0.001	1.0000
100	0.344556	0.344556	0.001	1.0000	0.237467	0.237467	0.001	1.0000
101	0.358628	0.358628	0.000	1.0000	0.244834	0.244834	0.000	1.0000
102	0.371685	0.371685	0.000	1.0000	0.254498	0.254498	0.000	1.0000
103	0.383040	0.383040	0.000	1.0000	0.266044	0.266044	0.000	1.0000
104	0.392003	0.392003	0.000	1.0000	0.279055	0.279055	0.000	1.0000
105	0.397886	0.397886	0.000	1.0000	0.293116	0.293116	0.000	1.0000
106	0.400000	0.400000	0.000	1.0000	0.307811	0.307811	0.000	1.0000
107	0.400000	0.400000	0.000	1.0000	0.322725	0.322725	0.000	1.0000
108	0.400000	0.400000	0.000	1.0000	0.337441	0.337441	0.000	1.0000
109	0.400000	0.400000	0.000	1.0000	0.351544	0.351544	0.000	1.0000
110	0.400000	0.400000	0.000	1.0000	0.364617	0.364617	0.000	1.0000
111	0.400000	0.400000	0.000	1.0000	0.376246	0.376246	0.000	1.0000
112	0.400000	0.400000	0.000	1.0000	0.386015	0.386015	0.000	1.0000
113	0.400000	0.400000	0.000	1.0000	0.393507	0.393507	0.000	1.0000
114	0.400000	0.400000	0.000	1.0000	0.398308	0.398308	0.000	1.0000
115	0.400000	0.400000	0.000	1.0000	0.400000	0.400000	0.000	1.0000
116	0.400000	0.400000	0.000	1.0000	0.400000	0.400000	0.000	1.0000
117	0.400000	0.400000	0.000	1.0000	0.400000	0.400000	0.000	1.0000
118	0.400000	0.400000	0.000	1.0000	0.400000	0.400000	0.000	1.0000
119	0.400000	0.400000	0.000	1.0000	0.400000	0.400000	0.000	1.0000
120	1.000000	1.000000	0.000	1.0000	1.000000	1.000000	0.000	1.0000

(e) *Static mortality tables with respect to valuation dates occurring during 2008.*—The following static mortality tables are used pursuant to paragraph (a)(3) of this section for determining present value or making any computation under section 430 with respect to valuation dates occurring during 2008.

Age	MALE Non-Annuitant Mortality Rates	MALE Annuitant Mortality Rates	MALE Optional Combined Table for Small Plans	FEMALE Non-Annuitant Mortality Rates	FEMALE Annuitant Mortality Rates	FEMALE Optional Combined Table for Small Plans
1	0.000400	0.000400	0.000400	0.000359	0.000359	0.000359
2	0.000270	0.000270	0.000270	0.000234	0.000234	0.000234
3	0.000224	0.000224	0.000224	0.000175	0.000175	0.000175
4	0.000175	0.000175	0.000175	0.000131	0.000131	0.000131
5	0.000160	0.000160	0.000160	0.000118	0.000118	0.000118
6	0.000153	0.000153	0.000153	0.000111	0.000111	0.000111
7	0.000147	0.000147	0.000147	0.000104	0.000104	0.000104
8	0.000136	0.000136	0.000136	0.000092	0.000092	0.000092
9	0.000131	0.000131	0.000131	0.000088	0.000088	0.000088
10	0.000133	0.000133	0.000133	0.000089	0.000089	0.000089
11	0.000138	0.000138	0.000138	0.000090	0.000090	0.000090
12	0.000143	0.000143	0.000143	0.000093	0.000093	0.000093
13	0.000151	0.000151	0.000151	0.000097	0.000097	0.000097
14	0.000163	0.000163	0.000163	0.000107	0.000107	0.000107
15	0.000173	0.000173	0.000173	0.000117	0.000117	0.000117
16	*0.000183*	*0.000183*	0.000183	0.000125	0.000125	0.000125
17	0.000194	0.000194	0.000194	0.000133	0.000133	0.000133
18	0.000203	0.000203	0.000203	0.000136	0.000136	0.000136

>>> *Caution: Reg. §1.430(h)(3)-1, below, prior to amendment by T.D. 9826, is generally applicable to plans years beginning before January 1, 2018.*

Age	MALE Non-Annuitant Mortality Rates	MALE Annuitant Mortality Rates	MALE Optional Combined Table for Small Plans	FEMALE Non-Annuitant Mortality Rates	FEMALE Annuitant Mortality Rates	FEMALE Optional Combined Table for Small Plans
19	0.000213	0.000213	0.000213	0.000134	0.000134	0.000134
20	0.000222	0.000222	0.000222	0.000132	0.000132	0.000132
21	0.000235	0.000235	0.000235	0.000129	0.000129	0.000129
22	0.000247	0.000247	0.000247	0.000131	0.000131	0.000131
23	0.000263	0.000263	0.000263	0.000136	0.000136	0.000136
24	0.000278	0.000278	0.000278	0.000142	0.000142	0.000142
25	0.000298	0.000298	0.000298	0.000150	0.000150	0.000150
26	0.000329	0.000329	0.000329	0.000162	0.000162	0.000162
27	0.000340	0.000340	0.000340	0.000169	0.000169	0.000169
28	0.000350	0.000350	0.000350	0.000178	0.000178	0.000178
29	0.000367	0.000367	0.000367	0.000188	0.000188	0.000188
30	0.000396	0.000396	0.000396	0.000210	0.000210	0.000210
31	0.000445	0.000445	0.000445	0.000255	0.000255	0.000255
32	0.000501	0.000501	0.000501	0.000291	0.000291	0.000291
33	0.000562	0.000562	0.000562	0.000320	0.000320	0.000320
34	0.000626	0.000626	0.000626	0.000345	0.000345	0.000345
35	0.000689	0.000689	0.000689	0.000368	0.000368	0.000368
36	0.000749	0.000749	0.000749	0.000389	0.000389	0.000389
37	0.000806	0.000806	0.000806	0.000410	0.000410	0.000410
38	0.000839	0.000839	0.000839	0.000432	0.000432	0.000432
39	0.000869	0.000869	0.000869	0.000458	0.000453	0.000458
40	0.000897	0.000897	0.000897	0.000499	0.000499	0.000499
41	0.000928	0.000955	0.000928	0.000547	0.000547	0.000547
42	0.000964	0.001070	0.000965	0.000602	0.000602	0.000602
43	0.001007	0.001243	0.001010	0.000662	0.000662	0.000662
44	0.001058	0.001474	0.001066	0.000727	0.000727	0.000727
45	0.001116	0.001763	0.001131	0.000776	0.000779	0.000776
46	0.001168	0.002109	0.001194	0.000824	0.000882	0.000825
47	0.001225	0.002513	0.001266	0.000873	0.001037	0.000877
48	0.001284	0.002975	0.001345	0.000944	0.001244	0.000954
49	0.001345	0.003495	0.001433	0.001021	0.001502	0.001041
50	0.001408	0.004072	0.001529	0.001130	0.001812	0.001164
51	0.001472	0.004146	0.001605	0.001252	0.001931	0.001292
52	0.001538	0.004168	0.001718	0.001422	0.002142	0.001476
53	0.001647	0.004226	0.001893	0.001617	0.002415	0.001693
54	0.001767	0.004281	0.002091	0.001842	0.002744	0.001949
55	0.001948	0.004428	0.002460	0.002100	0.003130	0.002295
56	0.002177	0.004663	0.002966	0.002400	0.003586	0.002739
57	0.002446	0.004983	0.003405	0.002682	0.004067	0.003153
58	0.002758	0.005413	0.003926	0.002933	0.004565	0.003566
59	0.003046	0.005876	0.004457	0.003207	0.005130	0.004045
60	0.003366	0.006435	0.005095	0.003503	0.005751	0.004617
61	0.003802	0.007175	0.005940	0.003818	0.006418	0.005327
62	0.004180	0.007904	0.006825	0.004149	0.007132	0.006117
63	0.004680	0.008864	0.007986	0.004490	0.007893	0.007049
64	0.005082	0.009807	0.009030	0.004838	0.008715	0.007956
65	0.005476	0.010861	0.010232	0.005187	0.009613	0.008972
66	0.005994	0.012218	0.011795	0.005531	0.010586	0.010140
67	0.006363	0.013527	0.013176	0.005866	0.011632	0.011267

>>> *Caution: Reg. §1.430(h)(3)-1, below, prior to amendment by T.D. 9826, is generally applicable to plans years beginning before January 1, 2018.*

Age	MALE Non-Annuitant Mortality Rates	MALE Annuitant Mortality Rates	MALE Optional Combined Table for Small Plans	FEMALE Non-Annuitant Mortality Rates	FEMALE Annuitant Mortality Rates	FEMALE Optional Combined Table for Small Plans
68	0.006557	0.014731	0.014436	0.006189	0.012774	0.012460
69	0.006876	0.016273	0.016004	0.006495	0.014055	0.013773
70	0.007009	0.017702	0.017424	0.006784	0.015529	0.015233
71	0.007888	0.019586	0.019312	0.007411	0.016975	0.016683
72	0.009646	0.021747	0.021495	0.008666	0.018881	0.018604
73	0.012283	0.024223	0.024006	0.010548	0.020673	0.020433
74	0.015799	0.027024	0.026849	0.013058	0.022912	0.022712
75	0.020195	0.030622	0.030486	0.016195	0.024916	0.024768
76	0.025470	0.034131	0.034041	0.019959	0.027451	0.027349
77	0.031624	0.038547	0.038493	0.024351	0.030694	0.030629
78	0.038657	0.043489	0.043464	0.029370	0.033835	0.033805
79	0.046569	0.049071	0.049064	0.035017	0.037355	0.037347
80	0.055360	0.055360	0.055360	0.041291	0.041291	0.041291
81	0.062905	0.062905	0.062905	0.045702	0.045702	0.045702
82	0.071350	0.071350	0.071350	0.050664	0.050664	0.050664
83	0.079534	0.079534	0.079534	0.056255	0.056255	0.056255
84	0.089800	0.089800	0.089800	0.062565	0.062565	0.062565
85	0.099680	0.099680	0.099680	0.070761	0.070761	0.070761
86	0.110516	0.110516	0.110516	0.080120	0.080120	0.080120
87	0.124300	0.124300	0.124300	0.090716	0.090716	0.090716
88	0.139683	0.139683	0.139683	0.101042	0.101042	0.101042
89	0.154366	0.154366	0.154366	0.113903	0.113903	0.113903
90	0.172706	0.172706	0.172706	0.125879	0.125879	0.125879
91	0.188113	0.188113	0.188113	0.138232	0.138232	0.138232
92	0.207060	0.207060	0.207060	0.150672	0.150672	0.150672
93	0.223365	0.223365	0.223365	0.165391	0.165391	0.165391
94	0.239646	0.239646	0.239646	0.177391	0.177391	0.177391
95	0.259578	0.259578	0.259578	0.188755	0.188755	0.188755
96	0.275506	0.275506	0.275506	0.199303	0.199303	0.199303
97	0.290981	0.290981	0.290981	0.212034	0.212034	0.212034
98	0.310600	0.310600	0.310600	0.220611	0.220611	0.220611
99	0.325288	0.325288	0.325288	0.227940	0.227940	0.227940
100	0.339424	0.339424	0.339424	0.233930	0.233930	0.233930
101	0.358628	0.358628	0.358628	0.244834	0.244834	0.244834
102	0.371685	0.371685	0.371685	0.254498	0.254498	0.254498
103	0.383040	0.383040	0.383040	0.266044	0.266044	0.266044
104	0.392003	0.392003	0.392003	0.279055	0.279055	0.279055
105	0.397886	0.397886	0.397886	0.293116	0.293116	0.293116
106	0.400000	0.400000	0.400000	0.307811	0.307811	0.307811
107	0.400000	0.400000	0.400000	0.322725	0.322725	0.322725
108	0.400000	0.400000	0.400000	0.337441	0.337441	0.337441
109	0.400000	0.400000	0.400000	0.351544	0.351544	0.351544
110	0.400000	0.400000	0.400000	0.364617	0.364617	0.364617
111	0.400000	0.400000	0.400000	0.376246	0.376246	0.376246
112	0.400000	0.400000	0.400000	0.386015	0.386015	0.386015
113	0.400000	0.400000	0.400000	0.393507	0.393507	0.393507
114	0.400000	0.400000	0.400000	0.398308	0.398308	0.398308
115	*0.400000*	*0.400000*	0.400000	0.400000	0.400000	0.400000
116	0.400000	0.400000	0.400000	0.400000	0.400000	0.400000

»»→ *Caution: Reg. §1.430(h)(3)-1, below, prior to amendment by T.D. 9826, is generally applicable to plans years beginning before January 1, 2018.*

Age	MALE Non-Annuitant Mortality Rates	MALE Annuitant Mortality Rates	MALE Optional Combined Table for Small Plans	FEMALE Non-Annuitant Mortality Rates	FEMALE Annuitant Mortality Rates	FEMALE Optional Combined Table for Small Plans
117	0.400000	0.400000	0.400000	0.400000	0.400000	0.400000
118	0.400000	0.400000	0.400000	0.400000	0.400000	0.400000
119	0.400000	0.400000	0.400000	0.400000	0.400000	0.400000
120	1.000000	1.000000	1.000000	1.000000	1.000000	1.000000

(f) *Effective/Applicability date.*—This section applies for plan years beginning on or after January 1, 2008. [Reg. §1.430(h)(3)-1.]

☐ [*T.D. 9419, 7-30-2008.*]

»»→ *Caution: Reg. §1.430(h)(3)-1, below, as amended by T.D. 9826, is generally applicable to plans years beginning on or after January 1, 2018.*

[Reg. §1.430(h)(3)-1]

§1.430(h)(3)-1. Mortality tables used to determine present value.—(a) *Basis for mortality tables.*—(1) *In general.*—Pursuant to section 430(h)(3)(A), this section provides generally applicable mortality tables that are used to determine present value for purposes of section 430, and rules regarding the use of those mortality tables. Either the generational mortality tables under paragraph (a)(2) of this section or the static mortality tables under paragraph (a)(3) of this section may be used for a plan. In lieu of using the mortality tables provided under this section, plan-specific substitute mortality tables may be used pursuant to section 430(h)(3)(C), provided that the requirements of §1.430(h)(3)-2 are satisfied. Mortality tables that may be used with respect to disabled individuals are provided in guidance published in the Internal Revenue Bulletin. See §601.601(d)(2)(ii)(b) of this chapter.

(2) *Generational mortality tables.*—(i) *In general.*—(A) *Use of generational mortality tables.*—The generational mortality tables that are permitted to be used under section 430(h)(3)(A) and paragraph (a)(1) of this section are determined using the base mortality tables described in paragraph (a)(2)(i)(B) of this section and the mortality improvement rates described in paragraph (a)(2)(i)(C) of this section.

(B) *Base mortality tables.*—The base mortality tables are set forth in paragraph (d) of this section. The base year for those tables is 2006.

(C) *Mortality improvement rates.*—The mortality improvement rates for valuation dates occurring during 2018 are the mortality improvement rates contained in the Mortality Improvement Scale MP-2016 Report (issued by the Retirement Plans Experience Committee (RPEC) of the Society of Actuaries and available at *www.soa.org/Research/Experience-Study/Pension/research-2016-mp.aspx*). For later years, updated mortality improvement rates that take into account new data for mortality improvement trends of the general population

will be provided in guidance published in the Internal Revenue Bulletin. See §601.601(d)(2)(ii)(b) of this chapter.

(D) *Application of mortality improvement rates.*—Under the generational mortality tables described in this paragraph (a)(2), the probability of an individual's death at a particular age in the future is determined as the individual's base mortality rate that applies at that age (that is, the applicable mortality rate from the table set forth in paragraph (d) of this section for that age, gender, and status as an annuitant or a nonannuitant) multiplied by the cumulative mortality improvement factor for the individual's gender and for that age for the period from 2006 through the calendar year in which the individual is projected to reach the particular age. Paragraph (a)(2)(ii) of this section shows how the base mortality tables in paragraph (d) of this section and the mortality improvement rates for valuation dates occurring during 2018 are combined to determine projected mortality rates.

(E) *Cumulative mortality improvement factor.*—The cumulative mortality improvement factor for an age and gender for a period is the product of the annual mortality improvement factors for that age and gender for each year within that period.

(F) *Annual mortality improvement factor.*—The annual mortality improvement factor for an age and gender for a year is 1 minus the mortality improvement rate that applies for that age and gender for that year.

(ii) *Example of calculation.*—(A) *Calculation of mortality rate.*—The mortality rate for 2018 that is applied to male annuitants who are age 66 in 2018 is equal to the product of the mortality rate for 2006 that applied to male annuitants who were age 66 in 2006 (0.013855) and the cumulative mortality improvement factor for age 66 males from 2006 to 2018. The cumulative mortality improvement factor for age 66 males for the period from 2006 to 2018 is 0.8929, and the mortality rate for 2018 for male annuitants who are age 66 in that year would be 0.012371, as shown in the following table.

Calendar Year	Scale MP-2016 Mortality Improvement Rate	Annual Mortality improvement factor (1-Scale MP-2016 Rate)	Cumulative Mortality Improvement Factor	Mortality Rate
2006	n/a	n/a	n/a	0.013855
2007	0.0237	0.9763	0.9763	
2008	0.0211	0.9789	0.9557	
2009	0.0180	0.9820	0.9385	
2010	0.0142	0.9858	0.9252	
2011	0.0099	0.9901	0.9160	
2012	0.0053	0.9947	0.9112	
2013	0.0043	0.9957	0.9072	
2014	0.0035	0.9965	0.9041	
2015	0.0030	0.9970	0.9014	
2016	0.0028	0.9972	0.8988	
2017	0.0030	0.9970	0.8961	
2018	0.0036	0.9964	0.8929	0.012371

(B) *Probability of survival for an individual.*—After the projected mortality rates are derived for each age for each year, the rates are used to calculate the present value of a benefit stream that depends on the probability of survival year-by-year. For example, for purposes of calculating the present value (for a 2018 valuation date)

of future payments in a benefit stream payable for a male annuitant who is age 66 in 2018, the probability of survival for the annuitant is based on the mortality rate for a male annuitant who is age 66 in 2018 (0.012371), and the projected mortality rate for a male annuitant who will be age 67 in 2019 (0.013302), age 68 in 2020 (0.014321), and so on.

Reg. §1.430(h)(3)-1(a)(2)(ii)(B)

>>>→ *Caution: Reg. §1.430(h)(3)-1, below, as amended by T.D. 9826, is generally applicable to plans years beginning on or after January 1, 2018.*

(3) *Static mortality tables.*—The static mortality tables that are permitted to be used under section 430(h)(3)(A) and paragraph (a)(1) of this section are updated annually by the IRS according to the methodology described in paragraph (c)(2) of this section. Paragraph (e) of this section sets forth static tables that are permitted to be used for valuation dates in 2018. For valuation dates in later years, static mortality tables will be provided in guidance published in the Internal Revenue Bulletin. See §601.601(d)(2)(ii)(b) of this chapter.

(b) *Use of the tables.*—(1) *Separate tables for annuitants and nonannuitants.*—(i) *In general.*—Separate tables are provided for use for annuitants and nonannuitants. The nonannuitant mortality table is applied to determine the probability of survival for a nonannuitant for the period before the nonannuitant is projected to commence receiving benefits. The annuitant mortality table is applied to determine the present value of benefits for each annuitant. In addition, the annuitant mortality table is applied for each nonannuitant with respect to each assumed commencement of benefits for the period beginning with that assumed commencement. For purposes of this section, an annuitant means a plan participant who has commenced receiving benefits, and a nonannuitant means a plan participant who has not yet commenced receiving benefits (for example, an active employee or a terminated vested participant). A participant whose benefit has partially commenced is treated as an annuitant with respect to the portion of the benefit that has commenced and treated as a nonannuitant with respect to the balance of the benefit. In addition, with respect to a beneficiary of a participant, the annuitant mortality table applies for the period beginning with each assumed commencement of benefits for the participant. If the participant has died (or to the extent the participant is assumed to die before commencing benefits), the annuitant mortality table applies with respect to the beneficiary for the period beginning with each assumed commencement of benefits for the beneficiary.

(ii) *Examples of calculation using separate annuitant and nonannuitant tables.*—With respect to a 45-year-old active participant who is projected to commence receiving an annuity at age 55, the funding target is determined using the nonannuitant mortality table for the period before the participant attains age 55 (so that, if the static mortality tables are used pursuant to paragraph (a)(3) of this section, the probability of an active male participant living from age 45 to age 55 using the table that applies for a valuation date in 2018 is 0.988857) and using the annuitant mortality table for the period ages 55 and above. Similarly, for a 45-year-old terminated vested participant who is projected to commence an annuity at age 65, the funding target is determined using the nonannuitant mortality table for the period before the participant attains age 65 and using the annuitant mortality table for ages 65 and above.

(2) *Small plan tables.*—If static mortality tables are used pursuant to paragraph (a)(3) of this section, as an alternative to the separate static tables specified for annuitants and nonannuitants pursuant to paragraph (b)(1) of this section, combined static tables that apply the same mortality rates to both annuitants and nonannuitants are permitted to be used for a small plan. For this purpose, a small plan is defined as a plan with 500 or fewer total participants (including both active and inactive participants and beneficiaries of deceased participants) on the valuation date. The combined static tables that are permitted to be used for small plans pursuant to this paragraph (b)(2) are constructed from the separate nonannuitant and annuitant static mortality tables using the weighting factors for small plans that are set forth in paragraph (d) of this section. The weighting factors are applied to develop these combined static tables using the following equation: Combined mortality rate = [nonannuitant rate * (1-weighting factor)] + [annuitant rate * weighting factor].

(c) *Static tables.*—(1) *Source of rates.*—The static mortality tables that are used pursuant to paragraph (a)(3) of this section are determined using the base mortality tables described in paragraph (a)(2)(i)(B) of this section taking into account the mortality improvement rates described in paragraph (a)(2)(i)(C) of this section, in accordance with the rules of paragraph (c)(3) of this section.

(2) *Selection of static tables.*—The static mortality tables that are used for a valuation date are the static mortality tables for the calendar year that contains the valuation date.

(3) *Projection of mortality improvements.*—(i) *General rule.*—Except as provided in paragraph (c)(3)(iii) of this section, the static mortality tables for a calendar year are determined by multiplying the applicable mortality rate for each age from the base mortality tables by both—

(A) The cumulative mortality improvement factor (determined under the rules of paragraph (a)(2) of this section) for the period from 2006 through that calendar year; and

(B) The cumulative mortality improvement factor (determined under the rules of paragraph (a)(2) of this section) for the period beginning in that calendar year and continuing beyond that calendar year for the number of years in the projection period described in paragraph (c)(3)(ii) of this section.

(ii) *Projection period for static mortality tables.*—(A) *In general.*—The projection period is 8 years for males and 9 years for females, as adjusted based on age as provided in paragraph (c)(3)(ii)(B) of this section.

(B) *Age adjustment.*—For ages below 80, the projection period is increased by 1 year for each year below age 80. For ages above 80, the projection period is reduced (but not below zero) by $1/3$ year for each year above 80.

(iii) *Fractional projection periods.*—If for an age the number of years in the projection period determined under this paragraph (c)(3) is not a whole number, then the mortality rate for that age is determined by using linear interpolation between—

(A) The mortality rate for that age that would be determined under paragraph (c)(3)(i) of this section if the number of years in the projection period were the next lower whole number; and

(B) The mortality rate for that age that would be determined under paragraph (c)(3)(i) of this section if the number of years in the projection period were the next higher whole number.

(iv) *Example.*—The following example illustrates how the mortality rates in the static mortality tables issued under the provisions of this paragraph (c) are calculated:

Example. At age 85, the projection period for a male is $6^{1/3}$ years (8 years minus $1/3$ year for each of the 5 years above age 80). For a valuation date in 2018, the mortality rate in the static mortality table for an 85-year-old male is based on a projection of mortality improvement for $6^{1/3}$ years beyond 2018. Under paragraph (c)(3)(iii) of this section, the mortality rate for an 85-year-old male annuitant in the static mortality table for 2018 is $2/3$ times the projected mortality rate for a male annuitant that age in 2024 plus $1/3$ times the projected mortality rate for a male annuitant that age in 2025. Accordingly, the mortality rate for an 85-year-old male annuitant in the static mortality table for 2018 is 0.075196 ($2/3$ times the projected mortality rate for an 85-year old male annuitant in 2024 (0.075447) plus $1/3$ times the projected mortality rate for an 85-year old male annuitant in 2025 (0.074693)).

(d) *Base mortality tables.*—The following are the base mortality tables. The base year for these tables is 2006.

	Males			Females		
Age	Non-Annuitant	Annuitant	Weighting Factor For Small Plans	Non-Annuitant	Annuitant	Weighting Factor For Small Plans
0	0.008878	0.008878	0	0.007278	0.007278	0
1	0.000515	0.000515	0	0.000451	0.000451	0
2	0.000348	0.000348	0	0.000295	0.000295	0
3	0.000289	0.000289	0	0.000220	0.000220	0
4	0.000225	0.000225	0	0.000165	0.000165	0
5	0.000197	0.000197	0	0.000149	0.000149	0
6	0.000177	0.000177	0	0.000137	0.000137	0
7	0.000156	0.000156	0	0.000127	0.000127	0
8	0.000132	0.000132	0	0.000117	0.000117	0
9	0.000107	0.000107	0	0.000109	0.000109	0

⯈⯈⯈→ *Caution: Reg. §1.430(h)(3)-1, below, as amended by T.D. 9826, is generally applicable to plans years beginning on or after January 1, 2018.*

	Males			Females		
Age	Non-Annuitant	Annuitant	Weighting Factor For Small Plans	Non-Annuitant	Annuitant	Weighting Factor For Small Plans
10	0.000090	0.000090	0	0.000102	0.000102	0
11	0.000095	0.000095	0	0.000105	0.000105	0
12	0.000142	0.000142	0	0.000121	0.000121	0
13	0.000187	0.000187	0	0.000137	0.000137	0
14	0.000230	0.000230	0	0.000151	0.000151	0
15	0.000274	0.000274	0	0.000165	0.000165	0
16	0.000318	0.000318	0	0.000177	0.000177	0
17	0.000364	0.000364	0	0.000187	0.000187	0
18	0.000412	0.000412	0	0.000196	0.000196	0
19	0.000463	0.000463	0	0.000202	0.000202	0
20	0.000510	0.000510	0	0.000202	0.000202	0
21	0.000552	0.000552	0	0.000197	0.000197	0
22	0.000587	0.000587	0	0.000191	0.000191	0
23	0.000599	0.000599	0	0.000190	0.000190	0
24	0.000594	0.000594	0	0.000188	0.000188	0
25	0.000545	0.000545	0	0.000186	0.000186	0
26	0.000510	0.000510	0	0.000186	0.000186	0
27	0.000486	0.000486	0	0.000188	0.000188	0
28	0.000472	0.000472	0	0.000192	0.000192	0
29	0.000468	0.000468	0	0.000198	0.000198	0
30	0.000470	0.000470	0	0.000209	0.000209	0
31	0.000480	0.000480	0	0.000222	0.000222	0
32	0.000495	0.000495	0	0.000238	0.000238	0
33	0.000514	0.000514	0	0.000257	0.000257	0
34	0.000534	0.000534	0	0.000278	0.000278	0
35	0.000557	0.000557	0	0.000301	0.000301	0
36	0.000581	0.000581	0	0.000325	0.000325	0
37	0.000611	0.000611	0	0.000355	0.000355	0
38	0.000648	0.000648	0	0.000389	0.000389	0
39	0.000694	0.000694	0	0.000428	0.000428	0
40	0.000750	0.000750	0	0.000471	0.000471	0
41	0.000814	0.000823	.0045	0.000518	0.000515	0
42	0.000890	0.000969	.0091	0.000570	0.000603	0
43	0.000982	0.001188	.0136	0.000628	0.000735	0
44	0.001088	0.001480	.0181	0.000691	0.000911	0
45	0.001207	0.001846	.0226	0.000758	0.001131	.0084
46	0.001342	0.002285	.0272	0.000831	0.001395	.0167
47	0.001487	0.002797	.0317	0.000908	0.001703	.0251
48	0.001643	0.003382	.0362	0.000986	0.002055	.0335
49	0.001807	0.004040	.0407	0.001065	0.002431	.0419
50	0.001979	0.004771	.0453	0.001151	0.002831	.0502
51	0.002159	0.005059	.0498	0.001242	0.002993	.0586
52	0.002351	0.005343	.0686	0.001344	0.003124	.0744
53	0.002539	0.005592	.0953	0.001458	0.003291	.0947
54	0.002741	0.005839	.1288	0.001588	0.003499	.1189
55	0.002967	0.006102	.2066	0.001735	0.003755	.1897
56	0.003231	0.006399	.3173	0.001902	0.004065	.2857
57	0.003548	0.006746	.3780	0.002091	0.004435	.3403
58	0.003932	0.007155	.4401	0.002302	0.004869	.3878
59	0.004396	0.007639	.4986	0.002537	0.005373	.4360
60	0.004954	0.008211	.5633	0.002795	0.005942	.4954
61	0.005616	0.008878	.6338	0.003080	0.006581	.5805
62	0.006392	0.009646	.7103	0.003388	0.007283	.6598
63	0.007291	0.010523	.7902	0.003724	0.008043	.7520
64	0.008320	0.011514	.8355	0.004089	0.008870	.8043
65	0.009486	0.012621	.8832	0.004482	0.009760	.8552

»»→ *Caution: Reg. §1.430(h)(3)-1, below, as amended by T.D. 9826, is generally applicable to plans years beginning on or after January 1, 2018.*

Age	Males			Females		
	Non-Annuitant	Annuitant	Weighting Factor For Small Plans	Non-Annuitant	Annuitant	Weighting Factor For Small Plans
66	0.010668	0.013855	.9321	0.005004	0.010731	.9118
67	0.011973	0.015221	.9510	0.005575	0.011790	.9367
68	0.013414	0.016736	.9639	0.006205	0.012952	.9523
69	0.015006	0.018421	.9714	0.006898	0.014226	.9627
70	0.016761	0.020288	.9740	0.007662	0.015628	.9661
71	0.018690	0.022348	.9766	0.008507	0.017170	.9695
72	0.020824	0.024638	.9792	0.009438	0.018861	.9729
73	0.023176	0.027176	.9818	0.010470	0.020723	.9763
74	0.025770	0.029992	.9844	0.011615	0.022780	.9797
75	0.028623	0.033113	.9870	0.012887	0.025057	.9830
76	0.031761	0.036585	.9896	0.014301	0.027590	.9864
77	0.035214	0.040457	.9922	0.015885	0.030438	.9898
78	0.039007	0.044778	.9948	0.017656	0.033653	.9932
79	0.043169	0.049605	.9974	0.019639	0.037296	.9966
80	0.047750	0.055022	1.0	0.021859	0.041440	1.0
81	0.049804	0.061087	1.0	0.023791	0.046181	1.0
82	0.053911	0.067902	1.0	0.027655	0.051564	1.0
83	0.060072	0.075550	1.0	0.033451	0.057714	1.0
84	0.068286	0.084162	1.0	0.041179	0.064709	1.0
85	0.078554	0.093775	1.0	0.050838	0.072601	1.0
86	0.090876	0.104507	1.0	0.062429	0.081490	1.0
87	0.105251	0.116487	1.0	0.075952	0.091444	1.0
88	0.121680	0.129770	1.0	0.091407	0.102470	1.0
89	0.140162	0.144470	1.0	0.108794	0.114635	1.0
90	0.160698	0.160698	1.0	0.128113	0.128113	1.0
91	0.177741	0.177741	1.0	0.142619	0.142619	1.0
92	0.195154	0.195154	1.0	0.157939	0.157939	1.0
93	0.212642	0.212642	1.0	0.173886	0.173886	1.0
94	0.230055	0.230055	1.0	0.190319	0.190319	1.0
95	0.247257	0.247257	1.0	0.207191	0.207191	1.0
96	0.265940	0.265940	1.0	0.225057	0.225057	1.0
97	0.284940	0.284940	1.0	0.243507	0.243507	1.0
98	0.304432	0.304432	1.0	0.262587	0.262587	1.0
99	0.324272	0.324272	1.0	0.282171	0.282171	1.0
100	0.344364	0.344364	1.0	0.302162	0.302162	1.0
101	0.364420	0.364420	1.0	0.322282	0.322282	1.0
102	0.384058	0.384058	1.0	0.342371	0.342371	1.0
103	0.403188	0.403188	1.0	0.362210	0.362210	1.0
104	0.421533	0.421533	1.0	0.381534	0.381534	1.0
105	0.438903	0.438903	1.0	0.400321	0.400321	1.0
106	0.455492	0.455492	1.0	0.418418	0.418418	1.0
107	0.470810	0.470810	1.0	0.435390	0.435390	1.0
108	0.484965	0.484965	1.0	0.451459	0.451459	1.0
109	0.498023	0.498023	1.0	0.466408	0.466408	1.0
110	0.509768	0.509768	1.0	0.480123	0.480123	1.0
111	0.512472	0.512472	1.0	0.492664	0.492664	1.0
112	0.509296	0.509296	1.0	0.503970	0.503970	1.0
113	0.506193	0.506193	1.0	0.507361	0.507361	1.0
114	0.503061	0.503061	1.0	0.503564	0.503564	1.0
115	0.500000	0.500000	1.0	0.500000	0.500000	1.0
116	0.500000	0.500000	1.0	0.500000	0.500000	1.0
117	0.500000	0.500000	1.0	0.500000	0.500000	1.0
118	0.500000	0.500000	1.0	0.500000	0.500000	1.0
119	0.500000	0.500000	1.0	0.500000	0.500000	1.0
120	1.000000	1.000000	1.0	1.000000	1.000000	1.0

(e) *Static tables for 2018.*—The following static mortality tables are used pursuant to paragraph (a)(3) of this section for determining present value or making any computation under section 430 with respect to valuation dates occurring during 2018.

Reg. §1.430(h)(3)-1(e)

⨠⟶ *Caution: Reg. §1.430(h)(3)-1, below, as amended by T.D. 9826, is generally applicable to plans years beginning on or after January 1, 2018.*

Age	Males			Females		
	Non-Annuitant	Annuitant	Optional Combined Table for Small Plans	Non-Annuitant	Annuitant	Optional Combined Table for Small Plans
0	0.002420	0.002420	0.002420	0.002234	0.002234	0.002234
1	0.000142	0.000142	0.000142	0.000140	0.000140	0.000140
2	0.000097	0.000097	0.000097	0.000092	0.000092	0.000092
3	0.000081	0.000081	0.000081	0.000070	0.000070	0.000070
4	0.000064	0.000064	0.000064	0.000053	0.000053	0.000053
5	0.000056	0.000056	0.000056	0.000048	0.000048	0.000048
6	0.000051	0.000051	0.000051	0.000045	0.000045	0.000045
7	0.000046	0.000046	0.000046	0.000042	0.000042	0.000042
8	0.000039	0.000039	0.000039	0.000039	0.000039	0.000039
9	0.000032	0.000032	0.000032	0.000037	0.000037	0.000037
10	0.000027	0.000027	0.000027	0.000035	0.000035	0.000035
11	0.000029	0.000029	0.000029	0.000036	0.000036	0.000036
12	0.000044	0.000044	0.000044	0.000042	0.000042	0.000042
13	0.000058	0.000058	0.000058	0.000048	0.000048	0.000048
14	0.000072	0.000072	0.000072	0.000053	0.000053	0.000053
15	0.000087	0.000087	0.000087	0.000059	0.000059	0.000059
16	0.000102	0.000102	0.000102	0.000064	0.000064	0.000064
17	0.000118	0.000118	0.000118	0.000068	0.000068	0.000068
18	0.000135	0.000135	0.000135	0.000072	0.000072	0.000072
19	0.000153	0.000153	0.000153	0.000075	0.000075	0.000075
20	0.000170	0.000170	0.000170	0.000076	0.000076	0.000076
21	0.000192	0.000192	0.000192	0.000078	0.000078	0.000078
22	0.000214	0.000214	0.000214	0.000080	0.000080	0.000080
23	0.000229	0.000229	0.000229	0.000084	0.000084	0.000084
24	0.000238	0.000238	0.000238	0.000087	0.000087	0.000087
25	0.000230	0.000230	0.000230	0.000090	0.000090	0.000090
26	0.000226	0.000226	0.000226	0.000094	0.000094	0.000094
27	0.000226	0.000226	0.000226	0.000099	0.000099	0.000099
28	0.000230	0.000230	0.000230	0.000105	0.000105	0.000105
29	0.000238	0.000238	0.000238	0.000111	0.000111	0.000111
30	0.000249	0.000249	0.000249	0.000120	0.000120	0.000120
31	0.000263	0.000263	0.000263	0.000130	0.000130	0.000130
32	0.000278	0.000278	0.000278	0.000142	0.000142	0.000142
33	0.000294	0.000294	0.000294	0.000155	0.000155	0.000155
34	0.000309	0.000309	0.000309	0.000168	0.000168	0.000168
35	0.000323	0.000323	0.000323	0.000182	0.000182	0.000182
36	0.000336	0.000336	0.000336	0.000196	0.000196	0.000196
37	0.000350	0.000350	0.000350	0.000213	0.000213	0.000213
38	0.000366	0.000366	0.000366	0.000231	0.000231	0.000231
39	0.000385	0.000385	0.000385	0.000251	0.000251	0.000251
40	0.000410	0.000410	0.000410	0.000273	0.000273	0.000273
41	0.000438	0.000443	0.000438	0.000298	0.000296	0.000298
42	0.000474	0.000516	0.000474	0.000326	0.000344	0.000326
43	0.000518	0.000627	0.000519	0.000358	0.000419	0.000358
44	0.000573	0.000779	0.000577	0.000395	0.000520	0.000395
45	0.000636	0.000973	0.000644	0.000436	0.000651	0.000438
46	0.000712	0.001213	0.000726	0.000484	0.000813	0.000489
47	0.000798	0.001502	0.000820	0.000538	0.001010	0.000550
48	0.000896	0.001844	0.000930	0.000597	0.001245	0.000619
49	*0.001005*	0.002248	0.001056	0.000661	0.001522	0.000697
50	0.001128	0.002719	0.001200	0.000734	0.001844	0.000790
51	0.001265	0.002963	0.001350	0.000814	0.001961	0.000881
52	0.001418	0.003224	0.001542	0.000903	0.002099	0.000992
53	0.001580	0.003481	0.001761	0.001003	0.002263	0.001122
54	0.001761	0.003751	0.002017	0.001114	0.002454	0.001273
55	0.001964	0.004040	0.002393	0.001235	0.002673	0.001508
56	0.002200	0.004357	0.002884	0.001367	0.002921	0.001811

➤➤➤ *Caution: Reg. §1.430(h)(3)-1, below, as amended by T.D. 9826, is generally applicable to plans years beginning on or after January 1, 2018.*

	Males			Females		
Age	Non-Annuitant	Annuitant	Optional Combined Table for Small Plans	Non-Annuitant	Annuitant	Optional Combined Table for Small Plans
57	0.002474	0.004704	0.003317	0.001509	0.003200	0.002084
58	0.002796	0.005088	0.003805	0.001661	0.003512	0.002379
59	0.003174	0.005515	0.004341	0.001823	0.003860	0.002711
60	0.003613	0.005989	0.004951	0.001994	0.004238	0.003106
61	0.004122	0.006516	0.005639	0.002181	0.004659	0.003619
62	0.004705	0.007100	0.006406	0.002381	0.005119	0.004188
63	0.005364	0.007742	0.007243	0.002600	0.005616	0.004868
64	0.006111	0.008457	0.008071	0.002842	0.006165	0.005515
65	0.006940	0.009234	0.008966	0.003107	0.006766	0.006236
66	0.007779	0.010103	0.009945	0.003465	0.007430	0.007080
67	0.008697	0.011056	0.010940	0.003863	0.008170	0.007897
68	0.009709	0.012114	0.012027	0.004308	0.008993	0.008770
69	0.010836	0.013302	0.013231	0.004806	0.009912	0.009722
70	0.012093	0.014637	0.014571	0.005366	0.010945	0.010756
71	0.013486	0.016126	0.016064	0.006001	0.012111	0.011925
72	0.015044	0.017799	0.017742	0.006711	0.013412	0.013230
73	0.016794	0.019693	0.019640	0.007521	0.014886	0.014711
74	0.018751	0.021823	0.021775	0.008439	0.016552	0.016387
75	0.020950	0.024237	0.024194	0.009485	0.018443	0.018291
76	0.023428	0.026986	0.026949	0.010678	0.020600	0.020465
77	0.026183	0.030081	0.030051	0.012035	0.023061	0.022949
78	0.029308	0.033645	0.033622	0.013582	0.025888	0.025804
79	0.032774	0.037661	0.037648	0.015347	0.029144	0.029097
80	0.036705	0.042295	0.042295	0.017347	0.032886	0.032886
81	0.038556	0.047291	0.047291	0.019058	0.036992	0.036992
82	0.042087	0.053009	0.053009	0.022345	0.041662	0.041662
83	0.047283	0.059466	0.059466	0.027251	0.047017	0.047017
84	0.054248	0.066860	0.066860	0.033811	0.053130	0.053130
85	0.062990	0.075196	0.075196	0.042053	0.060056	0.060056
86	0.073605	0.084646	0.084646	0.052009	0.067888	0.067888
87	0.086115	0.095308	0.095308	0.063725	0.076724	0.076724
88	0.100513	0.107196	0.107196	0.077205	0.086549	0.086549
89	0.116840	0.120431	0.120431	0.092462	0.097426	0.097426
90	0.135087	0.135087	0.135087	0.109484	0.109484	0.109484
91	0.150610	0.150610	0.150610	0.122541	0.122541	0.122541
92	0.166534	0.166534	0.166534	0.136397	0.136397	0.136397
93	0.182546	0.182546	0.182546	0.150811	0.150811	0.150811
94	0.198598	0.198598	0.198598	0.165818	0.165818	0.165818
95	0.214442	0.214442	0.214442	0.181360	0.181360	0.181360
96	0.232944	0.232944	0.232944	0.198746	0.198746	0.198746
97	0.251903	0.251903	0.251903	0.216930	0.216930	0.216930
98	0.271612	0.271612	0.271612	0.235921	0.235921	0.235921
99	0.291889	0.291889	0.291889	0.255617	0.255617	0.255617
100	0.312680	0.312680	0.312680	0.275938	0.275938	0.275938
101	0.333720	0.333720	0.333720	0.296628	0.296628	0.296628
102	0.354570	0.354570	0.354570	0.317471	0.317471	0.317471
103	0.375136	0.375136	0.375136	0.338385	0.338385	0.338385
104	0.395172	0.395172	0.395172	0.358868	0.358868	0.358868
105	0.413945	0.413945	0.413945	0.379183	0.379183	0.379183
106	0.432145	0.432145	0.432145	0.398878	0.398878	0.398878
107	0.449197	0.449197	0.449197	0.417703	0.417703	0.417703
108	0.465497	0.465497	0.465497	0.435384	0.435384	0.435384
109	0.480869	0.480869	0.480869	0.452108	0.452108	0.452108
110	0.495080	0.495080	0.495080	0.467928	0.467928	0.467928
111	*0.500557*	*0.500557*	*0.500557*	0.482562	0.482562	0.482562
112	0.500454	0.500454	0.500454	0.496164	0.496164	0.496164
113	0.500352	0.500352	0.500352	0.502110	0.502110	0.502110

→ *Caution: Reg. §1.430(h)(3)-1, below, as amended by T.D. 9826, is generally applicable to plans years beginning on or after January 1, 2018.*

Age	Males			Females		
	Non-Annuitant	Annuitant	Optional Combined Table for Small Plans	Non-Annuitant	Annuitant	Optional Combined Table for Small Plans
114	0.500201	0.500201	0.500201	0.500952	0.500952	0.500952
115	0.500000	0.500000	0.500000	0.500000	0.500000	0.500000
116	0.500000	0.500000	0.500000	0.500000	0.500000	0.500000
117	0.500000	0.500000	0.500000	0.500000	0.500000	0.500000
118	0.500000	0.500000	0.500000	0.500000	0.500000	0.500000
119	0.500000	0.500000	0.500000	0.500000	0.500000	0.500000
120	1.000000	1.000000	1.000000	1.000000	1.000000	1.000000

(f) *Effective/applicability date.*—(1) *In general.*—Except as provided in paragraph (f)(2) of this section, this section applies to plan years beginning or after January 1, 2018.

(2) *Option to apply prior regulations in certain circumstances.*—For a plan for which substitute mortality tables are not used pursuant to §1.430(h)(3)-2 for a plan year beginning during 2018, mortality tables determined in accordance with §1.430(h)(3)-1 as in effect on December 31, 2017 (as contained in 26 CFR part 1 revised April 1, 2017) may be used for purposes of applying the rules of section 430 for a valuation date occurring during 2018 if the plan sponsor—

(i) Concludes that the use of mortality tables determined in accordance with this section for the plan year would be administratively impracticable or would result in an adverse business impact that is greater than *de minimis*; and

(ii) Informs the actuary of the intent to apply the option under this paragraph (f)(2). [Reg. §1.430(h)(3)-1.]

☐ [T.D. 9419, 7-30-2008. Amended by T.D. 9826, 10-3-2017.]

→ *Caution: Reg. §1.430(h)(3)-2, below, prior to amendment by T.D. 9826, is generally applicable to plans years beginning before January 1, 2018.*

[Reg. §1.430(h)(3)-2]

§1.430(h)(3)-2. Plan-specific substitute mortality tables used to determine present value.—(a) *In general.*—This section sets forth rules for the use of substitute mortality tables under section 430(h)(3)(C) in determining any present value or making any computation under section 430 in accordance with §1.430(h)(3)-1(a)(1). In order to use substitute mortality tables, a plan sponsor must obtain approval to use substitute mortality tables for the plan in accordance with the procedures set forth in paragraph (b) of this section. Paragraph (c) of this section sets forth rules for the development of substitute mortality tables, including guidelines for determining whether a plan has sufficient credible mortality experience to use substitute mortality tables. Paragraph (d) of this section sets forth special rules regarding the use of substitute mortality tables. The Commissioner may, in revenue rulings and procedures, notices or other guidance published in the Internal Revenue Bulletin (see §601.601(d)(2)(ii)(*b*) of this chapter), provide additional guidance regarding approval and use of substitute mortality tables under section 430(h)(3)(C) and related matters.

(b) *Procedures for obtaining approval to use substitute mortality tables.*—(1) *Written request to use substitute mortality tables.*—(i) *General requirements.*—In order to use substitute mortality tables, a plan sponsor must submit a written request to the Commissioner that demonstrates that those substitute mortality tables meet the requirements of section 430(h)(3)(C) and this section. This request must state the first plan year and the term of years (not more than 10) that the tables are requested to be used.

(ii) *Time for written request.*—(A) *In general.*—Except as provided in this paragraph (b)(1)(ii), substitute mortality tables cannot be used for a plan year unless the plan sponsor submits the written request described in paragraph (b)(1)(i) of this section at least 7 months prior to the first day of the first plan year for which the substitute mortality tables are to apply.

(B) *Special rule for requests submitted on or before October 1, 2007.*—Notwithstanding the rule of paragraph (b)(1)(ii)(A) of this section, the timing of the written request described in paragraph (b)(1)(i) of this section does not prevent a plan from using substitute mortality tables for a plan year provided that the written request is submitted no later than October 1, 2007.

(C) *Special rule for requests submitted on or before October 1, 2008, with respect to plan years beginning during 2009.*—Notwithstanding the rule of paragraph (b)(1)(ii)(A) of this section, the timing of the written request described in paragraph (b)(1)(i) of this section does not prevent a plan from using substitute mortality tables for a plan year that begins during 2009 provided that the written request is submitted no later than October 1, 2008.

(2) *Commissioner's review of request.*—(i) *In general.*—During the 180-day period that begins on the date the plan sponsor submits a request to use substitute mortality tables for a plan year pursuant to this section, the Commissioner will determine whether the request to use substitute mortality tables satisfies the requirements of this section (including any published guidance issued pursuant to paragraph (a) of this section), and will either approve or deny the request. The Commissioner will deny a request if the request fails to meet the requirements of this section or if the Commissioner determines that a substitute mortality table does not sufficiently reflect the mortality experience of the applicable plan population.

(ii) *Request for additional information.*—The Commissioner may request additional information with respect to the submission. Failure to provide that information on a timely basis constitutes grounds for denial of the request.

(iii) *Deemed approval.*—Except as provided in paragraph (b)(2)(iv) of this section, if the Commissioner does not issue a denial within the 180-day review period, the request is deemed to have been approved.

(iv) *Extension of time permitted.*—The Commissioner and a plan sponsor may, before the expiration of the 180-day review period, agree in writing to extend that period, provided that any such agreement also specifies any revisions in the plan sponsor's request, including any change in the requested term of use of the substitute mortality tables.

(c) *Development of substitute mortality tables.*—(1) *Mortality experience requirements.*—(i) *In general.*—Substitute mortality tables must reflect the actual mortality experience of the pension plan for which the tables are to be used and that mortality experience must be credible mortality experience as described in paragraph (c)(1)(ii) of this section. Separate mortality tables must be established for each gender under the plan, and a substitute mortality table is permitted to be established for a gender only if the plan has credible mortality experience with respect to that gender.

(ii) *Credible mortality experience.*—There is credible mortality experience for a gender within a plan if and only if, over the period covered by the experience study described in paragraph (c)(2)(ii) of this section, there are at least 1,000 deaths within that gender.

(iii) *Gender without credible mortality experience.*—(A) *In general.*—If, for the first year for which a plan uses substitute mortality tables, one gender has credible mortality experience but the other gender does not have credible mortality experience, the substitute mortality tables are used for the gender that does have credible mortality experience and the mortality tables under §1.430(h)(3)-2 are used for the gender that does not have credible mortality experience. For a subsequent plan year, the plan sponsor may continue to use substitute mortality tables for the gender with credible mortality experience without using substitute mortality tables for the other gender only if the other gender continues to lack credible mortality experience for that subsequent plan year.

(B) *Demonstration of lack of credible mortality experience for a gender.*—In general, in order to demonstrate that a gender within a plan does not have credible mortality experience for a plan year, the demonstration that the gender population within the plan has fewer than 1,000 deaths over a 4-year period must be made using a 4-year period that ends less than 3 years before the first day of that plan year. For example, if a plan uses substitute mortality tables based on credible mortality experience obtained over a 4-year experience study period for its male population and the standard mortality tables under §1.430(h)(3)-2 for its female population, there must be a

Reg. §1.430(h)(3)-2(c)(1)(iii)(B)

>>>→ *Caution: Reg. §1.430(h)(3)-2, below, prior to amendment by T.D. 9826, is generally applicable to plans years beginning before January 1, 2018.*

demonstration that the plan's female population does not have at least 1,000 deaths in a 4-year period that ends less than 3 years before the first day of that plan year. However, if the experience study period described in paragraph (c)(2)(ii)(A) of this section exceeds 4 years then, in order to demonstrate that a gender within a plan does not have credible mortality experience for a plan year, the mortality experience of that population must be analyzed over a period that is the same length as the experience study on which the substitute mortality tables are based and that ends less than 3 years before the first day of that plan year.

(iv) *Disabled individuals.*—Under section 430(h)(3)(D), separate mortality tables are permitted to be used for certain disabled individuals. If such separate mortality tables are used for those disabled individuals, then those individuals are disregarded for all purposes under this section. Thus, if the mortality tables under section 430(h)(3)(D) are used for disabled individuals under a plan, mortality experience with respect to those individuals must be excluded in developing mortality rates for substitute mortality tables under this section.

(2) *Base table and base year.*—(i) *In general.*—Development of a substitute mortality table under this section requires creation of a base table and identification of a base year under this paragraph (c)(2). The base table and base year are then used to determine a substitute mortality table under paragraph (c)(3) of this section.

(ii) *Experience study and base table requirements.*—(A) *In general.*—The base table for a plan population must be developed from an experience study of the mortality experience of that plan population that generates amounts-weighted mortality rates based on experience data for the plan that is collected over an experience study period. The minimum length of the experience study period is 2 years. The maximum length of the experience study period is 5 years, but can be extended by the Commissioner in revenue rulings, notices, or other guidance published in the Internal Revenue Bulletin (see §601.601(d)(2)(ii)(*b*) of this chapter). The last day of the final year reflected in the experience data must be less than 3 years before the first day of the first plan year for which the substitute mortality tables are to apply. For example, if July 1, 2009, is the first day of the first plan year for which the substitute mortality tables will be used, then an experience study using calendar year data must include data collected for a period that ends no earlier than December 31, 2006.

(B) *Amounts-weighted mortality rates.*—The amounts-weighted mortality rate for an age is equal to the quotient determined by dividing the sum of the accrued benefits (or payable benefits, in the case of individuals in pay status) for all individuals at that age at the beginning of the year who died during the year, by the sum of the accrued benefits (or payable benefits, in the case of individuals in pay status) for all individuals at that age at the beginning of the year, with appropriate adjustments for individuals who left the relevant plan population during the year for reasons other than death. Because amounts-weighted mortality rates for a plan cannot be determined without accrued (or payable) benefits, the mortality experience study used to develop a base table cannot include periods before the plan was established.

(C) *Grouping of ages.*—Amounts-weighted mortality rates may be derived from amounts-weighted mortality rates for age groups. The Commissioner, in revenue rulings, notices, or other guidance published in the Internal Revenue Bulletin (see §601.601(d)(2)(ii)(b) of this chapter), may specify grouping rules (for example, 5-year age groups, except for extreme ages such as ages above 100 or below 20) and methods for developing amounts-weighted mortality rates for individual ages from amounts-weighted mortality rates initially determined for each age group.

(D) *Base table construction.*—The base tables must be constructed from the amounts-weighted mortality rates determined in paragraph (c)(2)(ii)(B) of this section. The base tables must be constructed either directly through graduation of the amounts-weighted mortality rates or indirectly by applying a level percentage to the applicable mortality table set forth in §1.430(h)(3)-1, provided that the adjusted table sufficiently reflects the mortality experience of the plan. The Commissioner also may permit the use of other recognized mortality tables in the construction of base tables, applying a similar mortality experience standard.

(iii) *Base year requirements.*—The base year is the calendar year that contains the day before the midpoint of the experience study period. If the base table is constructed by applying a level percentage to a table set forth in §1.430(h)(3)-1, then the percentage must be applied to the table under §1.430(h)(3)-1 after it has been projected to the base year using Projection Scale AA, as set forth in

§1.430(h)(3)-1(d). Thus, for example, if the base year of the mortality experience study is 2005, the applicable base (year 2000) mortality rates must be projected 5 years prior to determining the level percentage to be applied to the applicable projected base (year 2000) mortality rates.

(iv) *Change in number of individuals covered by table.*—Experience data cannot be used to develop a base table if the number of individuals in the population covered by the table (for example, the male annuitant population) as of the last day of the plan year before the year the request to use substitute mortality tables is made, compared to the average number of individuals in that population over the years covered by the experience study on which the substitute mortality tables are based, reflects a difference of 20 percent or more, unless it is demonstrated to the satisfaction of the Commissioner that the experience data is accurately predictive of future mortality of that plan population (taking into account the effect of the change in individuals) after appropriate adjustments to the data are made (for example, excluding data from individuals with respect to a spun-off portion of the plan). For this purpose, a reasonable estimate of the number of individuals in the population covered by the table may be used, such as the estimated number of participants and beneficiaries used for purposes of the PBGC Form 1-ES.

(3) *Determination of substitute mortality tables.*—(i) *In general.*—A plan's substitute mortality tables must be generational mortality tables. Substitute mortality tables are determined using the base mortality tables developed pursuant to paragraph (c)(2) of this section and the projection factors provided in Projection Scale AA, as set forth in §1.430(h)(3)-1(d). Under the generational mortality tables, the probability of an individual's death at a particular age is determined as the individual's base mortality rate (that is, the applicable mortality rate from the base mortality table for the age for which the probability of death is being determined) multiplied by the mortality improvement factor. The mortality improvement factor is equal to (1 - projection factor for that age)^n, where n is equal to the projection period (the number of years between the base year for the base mortality table and the calendar year in which the individual attains the age for which the probability of death is being determined).

(ii) *Example of calculation.*—As an example of the use of generational mortality tables under paragraph (c)(3)(i) of this section, if approved substitute mortality tables are based on data collected during 2005 and 2006, the base year would be 2005 because 2005 would be the year that contains the day before the midpoint of the experience study period. If the tables show a base mortality rate of .006000 for male annuitants at age 54, the probability of death at age 54 for a male annuitant born in 1974 would be determined using the base mortality rate of .006000, the age-54 projection factor of .020 (pursuant to the Scale AA Projection Factors set forth in §1.430(h)(3)-1(d)) and a projection period of 23 years. The projection period is the number of years between the base year of 2005 and the calendar year in which the individual reaches age 54. Accordingly, the mortality improvement factor would be .628347 and the probability of death at age 54 would be .003770.

(4) *Separate tables for specified populations.*—(i) *In general.*—Except as provided in this paragraph (c)(4), separate substitute mortality tables are permitted to be used for separate populations within a gender under a plan only if—

(A) All individuals of that gender in the plan are divided into separate populations;

(B) Each separate population has credible mortality experience as provided in paragraph (c)(4)(iii) of this section; and

(C) The separate substitute mortality table for each separate population is developed using mortality experience data for that population.

(ii) *Annuitant and nonannuitant separate populations.*—Notwithstanding paragraph (c)(4)(i)(B) of this section, substitute mortality tables for separate populations of annuitants and nonannuitants within a gender may be used even if only one of those separate populations has credible mortality experience. Similarly, if separate populations that satisfy paragraph (c)(4)(i)(B) of this section are established, then any of those populations may be further subdivided into separate annuitant and nonannuitant subpopulations, provided that at least one of the two resulting subpopulations has credible mortality experience. The standard mortality tables under §1.430(h)(3)-1 are used for a resulting subpopulation that does not have credible mortality experience. For example, in the case of a plan that has credible mortality experience for both its male hourly and salaried individuals, if the male salaried annuitant population has credible mortality experience, the plan may use substitute mortality tables with respect to that population even if the standard mortality tables under §1.430(h)(3)-1 are used for the male salaried nonannui-

⫸→ *Caution: Reg. §1.430(h)(3)-2, below, prior to amendment by T.D. 9826, is generally applicable to plans years beginning before January 1, 2018.*

tant population (because that nonannuitant population does not have credible mortality experience).

(iii) *Credible mortality experience for separate populations.*—In determining whether a separate population within a gender has credible mortality experience, the requirements of paragraph (c)(1)(ii) of this section must be satisfied but, in applying that paragraph (c)(1)(ii), the separate population should be substituted for the particular gender. In demonstrating that an annuitant or nonannuitant population within a gender or within a separate population does not have credible mortality experience, the requirements of paragraph (c)(1)(iii) of this section must be satisfied but, in applying that paragraph, the annuitant (or nonannuitant) population should be substituted for the particular gender.

(d) *Special rules.*—(1) *All plans in controlled group must use substitute mortality tables.*—(i) *In general.*—Except as otherwise provided in this paragraph (d)(1), substitute mortality tables are permitted to be used for a plan for a plan year only if, for that plan year (or any portion of that plan year), substitute mortality tables are also approved and used for each other pension plan subject to the requirements of section 430 that is maintained by the sponsor and by each member of the plan sponsor's controlled group. For purposes of this section, the term *controlled group* means any group treated as a single employer under paragraph (b), (c), (m), or (o) of section 414.

(ii) *Plans without credible experience.*—(A) *In general.*—For the first year for which a plan uses substitute mortality tables, the use of substitute mortality tables for the plan is not prohibited merely because another plan described in paragraph (d)(1)(i) of this section cannot use substitute mortality tables because neither the males nor the females under that other plan have credible mortality experience for a plan year. For each subsequent plan year, the plan sponsor may continue to use substitute mortality tables for the plan with credible mortality experience without using substitute mortality tables for the other plan only if neither the males nor the females under that other plan have credible mortality experience for that subsequent plan year.

(B) *Analysis of mortality experience.*—For each plan year in which a plan uses substitute mortality tables, in order to demonstrate that the male and female populations of another plan maintained by the plan sponsor (or by a member of the plan sponsor's controlled group) do not have credible mortality experience, the requirements of paragraph (c)(1)(iii)(B) of this section must be satisfied for that plan year. Thus, a plan is not prohibited from using substitute mortality tables for a plan year merely because another plan in the controlled group of the plan sponsor does not have at least 1,000 male deaths and does not have at least 1,000 female deaths in a 4-year period (or a period that is the length of the experience study period if the experience study period under paragraph (c)(2)(ii)(A) of this section is longer than 4 years) that ends less than 3 years before the first day of that plan year.

(iii) *Newly affiliated plans not using substitute mortality tables.*— (A) *In general.*—The use of substitute mortality tables for a plan is not prohibited merely because a newly affiliated plan does not use substitute mortality tables, but only through the last day of the plan year of the plan using substitute mortality tables that contains the last day of the period described in section 410(b)(6)(C)(ii) for either the newly affiliated plan or the plan using substitute mortality tables, whichever is later. Thus, for the following plan year, the mortality tables prescribed under §1.430(h)(3)-1 apply with respect to the plan (and all other plans within the plan sponsor's controlled group, including the newly affiliated plan) unless—

(1) Approval to use substitute mortality tables has been obtained with respect to the newly affiliated plan pursuant to paragraph (b)(1) of this section; or

(2) The newly affiliated plan cannot use substitute mortality tables because neither the males nor the females under the plan have credible mortality experience as described in paragraph (c)(1)(ii) of this section (as determined in accordance with the rules of paragraph (d)(1)(iv) of this section).

(B) *Definition of newly affiliated plan.*—For purposes of this section, a plan is treated as a newly affiliated plan if it becomes maintained by the plan sponsor (or by a member of the plan sponsor's controlled group) in connection with a merger, acquisition, or similar transaction described in §1.410(b)-2(f). A plan also is treated as a newly affiliated plan for purposes of this section if the plan is established in connection with a transfer of assets and liabilities from another employer's plan in connection with a merger, acquisition, or similar transaction described in §1.410(b)-2(f).

(iv) *Demonstration of credible mortality experience for newly affiliated plan.*—(A) *In general.*—In general, in the case of a newly affili-

ated plan described in paragraph (d)(1)(iii) of this section, the demonstration of whether credible mortality experience exists for the plan for a plan year may be made by either including or excluding mortality experience data for the period prior to the date the plan becomes maintained by a member of the new plan sponsor's controlled group. If a plan sponsor excludes mortality experience data for the period prior to the date the plan becomes maintained within the new plan sponsor's controlled group, the exclusion must apply for all populations within the plan.

(B) *Demonstration of credible mortality experience.*—Regardless of whether mortality experience data for the period prior to the date a newly affiliated plan becomes maintained within the new plan sponsor's controlled group is included or excluded for a plan year, the provisions of this section, including the demonstration of credible mortality experience in accordance with paragraph (c)(1)(ii) of this section, must be satisfied before substitute mortality tables may be used with respect to the plan. Thus, for example, the plan must meet the rule in paragraph (c)(2)(ii)(A) of this section that the base table be based on mortality experience data for the plan over a 2-year or longer consecutive period that ends less than 3 years before the first day of the plan year for which substitute mortality tables will be used.

(C) *Demonstration of lack of credible mortality experience.*—In the case of a newly affiliated plan described in paragraph (d)(1)(iii) of this section, in order to demonstrate a lack of credible mortality experience with respect to a gender for a plan year, the rules of paragraph (c)(1)(iii)(B) of this section generally will apply. However, a special rule applies if the plan's mortality experience demonstration for a plan year is made by excluding mortality experience for the period prior to the date the plan becomes maintained by a member of the new plan sponsor's controlled group. In such a case, an employer is permitted to demonstrate a plan's lack of credible mortality experience using an experience study period of less than four years, provided that the experience study period begins with the date the plan becomes maintained within the sponsor's controlled group and ends not more than one year and one day before the first day of the plan year with respect to which the lack of credible mortality experience demonstration is made.

(D) *Example.*—The following example illustrates the application of this paragraph (d)(1):

Example. (i) Employer A is a corporation and maintains Plan M, which has a calendar year plan year and has obtained approval to use substitute mortality tables for 10 years beginning with the plan year that begins on January 1, 2009. Employer B is a corporation and maintains Plan N, which does not use substitute mortality tables and has a calendar year plan year. On July 1, 2010, Employer A acquires 100% of the stock of Employer B.

(ii) Pursuant to paragraph (d)(1)(iii) of this section, the maintenance of Plan N within the controlled group that maintains Plan M does not impair the use of substitute mortality tables by Plan M through the end of the plan year that ends on December 31, 2011.

(iii) Pursuant to paragraph (d)(1)(iii) of this section, beginning with the plan year that begins on January 1, 2012, Plan M continues to use substitute mortality tables only if either Plan N obtains approval to use substitute mortality tables or Employer A can demonstrate that Plan N does not have credible mortality experience. Pursuant to paragraph (d)(1)(iv)(C) of this section, Employer A is permitted to either exclude mortality experience date for the period of time before July 1, 2010 (the date Plan N became maintained with Employer A's controlled group), or include that mortality experience data for purposes of demonstrating that Plan N does not have credible mortality experience. Thus, if there is an experience study that shows that the male and female populations of Plan N each do not have 1,000 deaths during the period from July 1, 2010, through December 31, 2010, then the maintenance of Plan N within the Employer A's controlled group does not impair Plan M's use of substitute mortality tables for Plan M's 2012 plan year.

(iv) For Plan M's 2013 plan year, pursuant to paragraph (d)(1)(iv)(C) of this section, the maintenance of Plan N within Employer A's controlled group does not impair Plan M's use of substitute mortality tables if there is an experience study that shows that the male and female populations of Plan N each do not have 1,000 deaths during the period from July 1, 2010, through December 31, 2011.

(2) *Duration of use of tables.*—Except as provided in paragraph (d)(4) of this section, substitute mortality tables are used with respect to a plan for the term of consecutive plan years specified in the plan sponsor's written request to use such tables under paragraph (b)(1) of this section and approved by the Commissioner, or such shorter period prescribed by the Commissioner in the approval to use substitute mortality tables. Following the end of such term of use, or

>>>→ *Caution: Reg. §1.430(h)(3)-2, below, prior to amendment by T.D. 9826, is generally applicable to plans years beginning before January 1, 2018.*

following any early termination of use described in paragraph (d)(4) of this section, the mortality tables specified in §1.430(h)(3)-1 apply with respect to the plan unless approval under paragraph (b)(1) of this section has been received by the plan sponsor to use substitute mortality tables for a further term.

(3) *Aggregation.*—(i) *Permissive aggregation of plans.*—In order for a plan sponsor to use a set of substitute mortality tables with respect to two or more plans, the rules of this section are applied by treating those plans as a single plan. In such a case, the substitute mortality tables must be used for the aggregated plans and must be based on data collected with respect to those aggregated plans.

(ii) *Required aggregation of plans.*—In general, plans are not required to be aggregated for purposes of applying the rules of this section. However, for purposes of this section, a plan is required to be aggregated with any plan that was previously spun off from that plan for purposes of this section if the Commissioner determines that one purpose of the spinoff is to avoid the use of substitute mortality tables for any of the plans that were involved in the spinoff.

(4) *Early termination of use of tables.*—(i) *General rule.*—A plan's substitute mortality tables cannot be used as of the earliest of—

(A) The plan year in which the plan fails to satisfy the requirements of paragraph (c)(1) of this section (regarding credible mortality experience requirements and demonstrations);

(B) The plan year in which the plan fails to satisfy the requirements of paragraph (d)(1) of this section (regarding use of substitute mortality tables by controlled group members);

(C) The second plan year following the plan year in which there is a significant change in individuals covered by the plan as described in paragraph (d)(4)(ii) of this section;

(D) The plan year following the plan year in which a substitute mortality table used for a plan population is no longer accurately predictive of future mortality of that population, as determined by the Commissioner or as certified by the plan's actuary to the satisfaction of the Commissioner; or

(E) The date specified in guidance published in the Internal Revenue Bulletin (see §601.601(d)(2)(ii)(b) of this chapter) pursuant to a replacement of mortality tables specified under section 430(h)(3)(A) and §1.430(h)(3)-1 (other than annual updates to the static mortality tables issued pursuant to §1.430(h)(3)-1(a)(3)).

(ii) *Significant change in coverage.*—(A) *Change in coverage from time of experience study.*—For purposes of applying the rules of paragraph (d)(4)(i)(C) of this section, a significant change in the individuals covered by a substitute mortality table occurs if there is an increase or decrease in the number of individuals of at least 20 percent compared to the average number of individuals in that population over the years covered by the experience study on which the substitute mortality tables are based. However, a change in coverage is not treated as significant if the plan's actuary certifies in writing to the satisfaction of the Commissioner that the substitute mortality tables used for the plan population continue to be accurately predictive of future mortality of that population (taking into account the effect of the change in the population).

(B) *Change in coverage from time of certification.*—For purposes of applying the rules of paragraph (d)(4)(i)(C) of this section, a significant change in the individuals covered by a substitute mortality table occurs if there is an increase or decrease in the number of individuals covered by a substitute mortality table of at least 20 percent compared to the number of individuals in a plan year for which a certification described in paragraph (d)(4)(ii)(A) of this section was made on account of a prior change in coverage. However, a change in coverage is not treated as significant if the plan's actuary certifies in writing to the satisfaction of the Commissioner that the substitute mortality tables used by the plan with respect to the covered population continue to be accurately predictive of future mortality of that population (taking into account the effect of the change in the plan population).

(e) *Effective/Applicability date.*—This section applies for plan years beginning on or after January 1, 2009. [Reg. §1.430(h)(3)-2.]

☐ [T.D. 9419, 7-30-2008.]

>>>→ *Caution: Reg. §1.430(h)(3)-2, below, as amended by T.D. 9826, is generally applicable to plans years beginning on or after January 1, 2018.*

[Reg. §1.430(h)(3)-2]

§1.430(h)(3)-2. Plan-specific substitute mortality tables used to determine present value.—(a) *In general.*—This section provides rules for the use of substitute mortality tables under section 430(h)(3)(C) in determining any present value or making any computation under section 430 in accordance with §1.430(h)(3)-1(a)(1). To use substitute mortality tables for a plan, a plan sponsor must first obtain approval to use the tables in accordance with the procedures described in paragraph (b) of this section. Paragraph (c) of this section provides rules for the development of substitute mortality tables, including guidelines providing that a plan must have either fully or partially credible mortality information in order to use substitute mortality tables. Paragraph (d) of this section describes the requirements for full credibility. Paragraph (e) of this section describes the requirements for partial credibility. Paragraph (f) of this section provides special rules for newly-affiliated plans. Paragraph (g) of this section specifies the effective date and applicability date of this section. The Commissioner may, in revenue rulings and procedures, notices, or other guidance published in the Internal Revenue Bulletin (see §601.601(d)(2)(ii)(b) of this chapter), provide additional guidance regarding approval and use of substitute mortality tables under section 430(h)(3)(C) and related matters.

(b) *Procedures for obtaining approval to use substitute mortality tables.*—(1) *Written request for approval to use substitute mortality tables.*—(i) *General requirements.*—To use substitute mortality tables, a plan sponsor must first submit a written request to the Commissioner demonstrating that those substitute mortality tables meet the requirements of section 430(h)(3)(C) and this section. This request must specify the first plan year, and the term of years (not more than 10), for which the tables are to apply.

(ii) *Time for written request.*—Substitute mortality tables may not be used for a plan year unless the plan sponsor submits the written request described in paragraph (b)(1)(i) of this section at least 7 months before the first day of the first plan year for which the substitute mortality tables are to apply.

(2) *Commissioner's review of request.*—(i) *In general.*—During the 180-day period that begins on the date the plan sponsor submits a request for approval to use substitute mortality tables for a plan pursuant to this section, the Commissioner will determine whether the request for approval to use substitute mortality tables satisfies the requirements of this section (including any published guidance is-

sued pursuant to paragraph (a) of this section), and will either approve or deny the request. The Commissioner will deny a request if the request fails to meet the requirements of this section or if the Commissioner determines that a substitute mortality table does not reflect the actual mortality experience of the applicable population.

(ii) *Request for additional information.*—The Commissioner may request additional information with respect to the submission and deny a request to use substitute mortality tables if the additional information is not provided in a timely manner.

(iii) *Deemed approval.*—Except as provided in paragraph (b)(2)(iv) of this section, if the Commissioner does not issue a denial within the 180-day review period, the request is deemed to have been approved.

(iv) *Extension of time permitted.*—The Commissioner and a plan sponsor may, before the expiration of the 180-day review period, agree in writing to extend that period.

(c) *Development of substitute mortality tables.*—(1) *Substitute mortality tables must be used for all plans in controlled group.*—(i) *General rule.*—Except as otherwise provided in this paragraph (c), substitute mortality tables are permitted to be used for a plan for a plan year only if, for that plan year (or any portion of that plan year), substitute mortality tables are also approved and used for each other pension plan subject to the requirements of section 430 that is maintained by the plan sponsor and by each member of the plan sponsor's controlled group. For purposes of this section, the term controlled group means any group that is treated as a single employer under paragraph (b), (c), (m), or (o) of section 414. See paragraph (c)(7) of this section for special rules applicable to multiple-employer plans.

(ii) *Treatment of plans without credible mortality information.*—The rule of paragraph (c)(1)(i) of this section does not prohibit use of substitute mortality tables for one plan for a plan year if the only other plan or plans maintained by the plan sponsor (or by a member of the plan sponsor's controlled group) for which substitute mortality tables are not used are too small to have fully or partially credible mortality information for the plan year. For this purpose, the demonstration that neither males nor females under a plan have credible mortality information for a plan year must be made by analyzing the actual number of deaths over a period that is the same length as the longest experience study period used for any plan within the controlled group and that ends less than three years before the first day of the plan year.

>>>→ *Caution: Reg. §1.430(h)(3)-2, below, as amended by T.D. 9826, is generally applicable to plans years beginning on or after January 1, 2018.*

(2) *Mortality experience requirements.*—(i) *In general.*—Substitute mortality tables must reflect the actual mortality experience of the pension plan for which the tables will be used, and that mortality experience must consist of credible mortality information as described in paragraph (c)(2)(ii) of this section. Separate substitute mortality tables must be established for each gender and, except as provided in paragraph (d)(6) of this section, a substitute mortality table is permitted to be established for a gender only if the plan has credible mortality information for that gender. See paragraph (d)(5) of this section for rules permitting the use of substitute mortality tables for separate populations within a gender in certain circumstances.

(ii) *Credible mortality information.*—(A) *In general.*—A plan has credible mortality information for a gender if and only if the mortality experience with respect to that gender satisfies the requirement for either full credibility (as described in paragraph (d) of this section) or partial credibility (as described in paragraph (e) of this section).

(B) *Simplified rule.*—Whether there is credible mortality information for a gender may be determined by only taking into account people who are at least age 50 and less than age 100. If there is credible mortality information for a gender using this simplified rule, the entire gender (not just those who are at least age 50 and less than age 100) has credible mortality information.

(iii) *Gender without credible mortality information.*—(A) *In general.*—If, for the first plan year substitute mortality tables will be used for a plan, one gender has credible mortality information but the other gender does not have credible mortality information, then substitute mortality tables are established for the gender that has credible mortality information, and the mortality tables under §1.430(h)(3)-1 are used for the gender that does not have credible mortality information. For a subsequent plan year, the plan sponsor may continue to use substitute mortality tables for the gender with credible mortality information without using substitute mortality tables for the other gender only if the other gender continues to lack credible mortality information for that subsequent plan year.

(B) *Demonstration of lack of credible mortality information for a gender.*—The demonstration that a gender does not have credible mortality information (that is, the individuals of that gender had fewer than the minimum number of actual deaths to have partial credibility, as described in paragraph (e)(1) of this section) for a plan year must be made by analyzing the actual number of deaths over a period that is the same length as the period for the experience study on which the substitute mortality tables are based and that ends less than three years before the first day of the plan year.

(3) *Determination of substitute mortality tables.*—(i) *Requirement to use generational mortality table.*—A plan's substitute mortality tables must be generational mortality tables. A plan's substitute mortality tables are determined using the plan's base substitute mortality tables developed pursuant to paragraph (d) or (e) of this section and the mortality improvement factors described in paragraph (c)(3)(ii) of this section.

(ii) *Determination of mortality improvement factors.*—The mortality improvement factor for an age and gender is the cumulative mortality improvement factor determined under §1.430(h)(3)-1(a)(2)(i)(E) for that age and gender for the applicable period. The applicable period is the period beginning with the base year for the base substitute mortality table determined under paragraph (d) or (e) of this section and ending in the calendar year in which the individual attains the age for which the probability of death is being determined. The base year for the base substitute mortality table is the calendar year that contains the day before the midpoint of the experience study period.

(4) *Disabled individuals.*—Under section 430(h)(3)(D), separate mortality tables are permitted to be used for certain disabled individuals. If the separate mortality tables issued under section 430(h)(3)(D) for certain disabled individuals are used, then those disabled individuals are disregarded for all purposes under this section. Thus, if the mortality tables under section 430(h)(3)(D) are used for disabled individuals under a plan, mortality experience with respect to those individuals must be excluded in developing mortality rates for substitute mortality tables under this section.

(5) *Aggregation.*—(i) *Permissive aggregation of plans.*—A plan sponsor may use the same substitute mortality tables for two or more of its plans provided that the rules of this section are applied by treating those plans as a single plan. In such a case, the substitute mortality tables must be based on data collected with respect to those aggregated plans.

(ii) *Required aggregation of plans.*—In general, plans are not required to be aggregated for purposes of applying the rules of this section. However, for purposes of this section, a plan is required to be aggregated with any plan that was previously spun off from that plan if a purpose of the spinoff is to avoid the use of substitute mortality tables for any of the plans that were involved in the spinoff.

(iii) *Special rule regarding experience study if aggregated plans have different plan years.*—If two or more plans are aggregated pursuant to this paragraph (c)(5) and not all of the plans have the same plan year, then the experience study period may be a period that is not a multiple of 12 months, provided that—

(A) The period over which mortality experience is collected for each plan (the data study period) is a multiple of 12 months and is based on the plan year for that plan;

(B) The data study periods for all of the plans consist of the same number of years;

(C) The data study periods for all of the plans satisfy the experience study period requirements of paragraph (d)(2)(ii) of this section; and

(D) The data study periods for all of the plans have been selected to minimize the total period of time covered by the experience study period by overlapping (to the greatest extent possible) those data study periods.

(6) *Duration of use of tables.*—(i) *General rule.*—Except as provided in this paragraph (c)(6), substitute mortality tables are used for a plan for the term of consecutive plan years specified in the plan sponsor's written request for approval to use such tables under paragraph (b)(1) of this section and approved by the Commissioner, or a shorter period prescribed by the Commissioner in the approval to use substitute mortality tables. Following the end of the approved term of use, or following any early termination of use described in this paragraph (c)(6), the mortality tables specified in §1.430(h)(3)-1 must be used for the plan unless approval under paragraph (b)(1) of this section has been received by the plan sponsor to use substitute mortality tables based on an updated experience study for a further term.

(ii) *Early termination of use of tables.*—A plan's substitute mortality tables must not be used beginning with the earliest of—

(A) For a plan using a substitute mortality table for only one gender because of a lack of credible mortality information with respect to the other gender, the first plan year for which there is credible mortality information with respect to the gender that had lacked credible mortality information (unless an approved substitute mortality table is used for that gender);

(B) The first plan year for which the plan fails to satisfy the requirements of paragraph (c)(1) of this section (regarding use of substitute mortality tables for all plans in the controlled group), taking into account the rules of paragraph (f)(3) of this section (regarding the transition period for newly-affiliated plans);

(C) The second plan year following the plan year for which there is a significant change in individuals covered by the plan as described in paragraph (c)(6)(iii) of this section;

(D) The first plan year following the plan year for which a substitute mortality table used for a population is no longer accurately predictive of future mortality of that population, as determined by the Commissioner or as certified by the plan's actuary to the satisfaction of the Commissioner; cr

(E) The date specified in guidance published in the Internal Revenue Bulletin (see §601.601(d)(2)(ii)(b) of this chapter) in conjunction with a replacement of mortality tables specified under section 430(h)(3)(A) and §1.430(h)(3)-1 (other than annual updates to the static mortality tables issued pursuant to §1.430(h)(3)-1(a)(3) or changes to the mortality improvement rates pursuant to §1.430(h)(3)-1(a)(2)(i)(C)).

(iii) *Significant change in coverage.*—(A) *Change in coverage from time of experience study.*—For purposes of applying the rules of paragraph (c)(6)(ii)(C) of this section, a significant change in the individuals covered by a substitute mortality table for a plan year occurs if the number of individuals covered by the substitute mortality table for the plan year is less than 80 percent or more than 120 percent of the average number of individuals in that population over the years covered by the experience study on which the substitute mortality tables are based. However, a change in coverage is not treated as significant if the plan's actuary certifies in writing to the satisfaction of the Commissioner that the substitute mortality tables used for the population continue to be accurately predictive of future mortality of that population (taking into account the effect of the change in the population).

(B) *Change in coverage from time of certification.*—For purposes of applying the rules of paragraph (c)(6)(ii)(C) of this section, a

»»→ *Caution: Reg. §1.430(h)(3)-2, below, as amended by T.D. 9826, is generally applicable to plans years beginning on or after January 1, 2018.*

significant change in the individuals covered by a substitute mortality table for a plan year occurs if the number of individuals covered by the substitute mortality table for the plan year is less than 80 percent or more than 120 percent of the number of individuals covered by the substitute mortality table in a plan year for which a certification described in paragraph (c)(6)(iii)(A) of this section was made on account of a prior change in coverage. However, a change in coverage is not treated as significant if the plan's actuary certifies in writing to the satisfaction of the Commissioner that the substitute mortality tables used by the plan with respect to the covered population continue to be accurately predictive of future mortality of that population (taking into account the effect of the change in the population).

(7) *Multiple-employer plans.*—(i) *General rule.*—In the case of a multiple-employer plan described in section 413(c), the plan administrator (as described in section 414(g)) is treated as the plan sponsor for purposes of this section. If approval is received to use substitute mortality tables by a plan, those tables must apply on a plan-wide basis (even if the plan is subject to the rules of section 413(c)(4)(A)).

(ii) *Application of controlled group consistency rules.*—In the case of an employer that participates in a multiple-employer plan, if the proportion of the plan's funding target attributable to the employees and former employees of the employer and members of its controlled group represents more than 50 percent of the plan's funding target, then the employer is treated as maintaining the plan for purposes of paragraph (c)(1) of this section. Thus, for a multiple-employer plan with credible mortality information that is treated as maintained by an employer under this paragraph (c)(7), unless substitute mortality tables are used for that plan, substitute mortality tables may not be used for any plan maintained by that employer or a member of its controlled group (and if substitute mortality tables are used for any other plan maintained by any member of the employer's controlled group, they must be used for the multiple-employer plan). By contrast, if the proportion of the plan's funding target attributable to the employees and former employees of the employer and members of its controlled group represents 50 percent or less of the funding target for a multiple-employer plan in which it participates, then the employer is not treated as maintaining the plan for purposes of paragraph (c)(1) of this section. Accordingly, whether substitute mortality tables may be used for other plans in such an employer's controlled group is independent of whether substitute mortality tables are used for the multiple-employer plan.

(d) *Full credibility.*—(1) *In general.*—The mortality experience with respect to a gender or other population within a plan has full credibility if the actual number of deaths for that population during the experience study period described in paragraph (d)(2) of this section is at least the full credibility threshold described in paragraph (d)(3) of this section. Paragraph (d)(4) of this section provides rules for the creation of a base substitute mortality table from the experience study, which apply if the mortality experience for the population has full credibility. Paragraph (d)(5) of this section provides rules regarding the use of separate substitute mortality tables for plan populations within a gender. Paragraph (d)(6) of this section provides an option to use the combined mortality experience of both genders to determine the existence and extent of credible mortality information and to develop a single mortality ratio for use in constructing substitute mortality tables.

(2) *Experience study period requirements.*—(i) *General rule.*—The base substitute mortality table for a gender or other population must be developed from an experience study of the mortality experience of that population that is collected over an experience study period. The experience study period must consist of 2, 3, 4, or 5 consecutive

12-month periods, and must be the same period for all populations except as provided in paragraph (c)(5)(iii) of this section.

(ii) *Requirement to use recent experience data.*—(A) *General rule.*—Except as provided in paragraph (d)(2)(ii)(B) of this section, the last day of the experience study period must be less than 3 years before the first day of the first plan year for which the substitute mortality tables are to apply. For example, if January 1, 2019, is the first day of the first plan year for which the substitute mortality tables will be used, then an experience study using calendar year data generally must include data collected for a period that ends no earlier than December 31, 2016.

(B) *Exception for submission between 1 and 2 years before effective date of table.*—If the plan sponsor submits a request for approval to use of substitute mortality tables more than 1 year (and less than 2 years) before the first day of the first plan year for which the substitute mortality tables are to apply, then the experience study is not treated as failing to satisfy the rule in paragraph (d)(2)(ii)(A) of this section if the last day of the final year reflected in the experience data is less than 2 years before the date of submission. For example, if an application for approval to use of substitute mortality tables that would apply for plan years beginning on or after January 1, 2019 year is submitted in 2017, then an experience study using calendar year data may be based on data collected for a period that ends as early as December 31, 2015.

(iii) *Experience study based on benefit amount.*—As provided in paragraph (d)(4)(i) of this section, the mortality rates under the base substitute mortality tables are amounts-weighted mortality rates that are derived from the experience study. An individual's benefit amount (which is used to determine amounts-weighted mortality rates and for other purposes under this paragraph (d)) is the individual's accrued benefit expressed in the form of an annual benefit commencing at normal retirement age (or at the current age, if later) if an individual has not commenced benefits and the individual's annual payment if the individual has commenced benefits. Because amounts-weighted mortality rates for a plan are determined using benefit amounts, the experience study used to develop a base substitute mortality table may not include periods before the plan was established.

(3) *Full credibility threshold.*—(i) *Threshold number of deaths.*—The full credibility threshold for a gender or other population is the product of 1,082 and the population's benefit dispersion factor. In calculating the population's benefit dispersion factor, for purposes of paragraphs (d)(3)(iii), (iv), and (v) of this section, the population is adjusted, as appropriate, for individuals who leave the population on account of a reason other than death.

(ii) *Population's benefit dispersion factor.*—The population's benefit dispersion factor is equal to—
(A) The number of expected deaths for the population during the experience study period (as defined in paragraph (d)(3)(iii) of this section); multiplied by
(B) The sum of the mortality-weighted squares of the benefits (as defined in paragraph (d)(3)(iv) of this section); divided by
(C) The square of the sum of the mortality-weighted benefits (as defined in paragraph (d)(3)(v) of this section).

(iii) *Number of expected deaths.*—For a population, the number of expected deaths during the experience study period is equal to the sum, for all years in the experience study period, of the expected number of deaths in the population during the year using the mortality rates from the standard mortality tables determined under paragraph (d)(4)(iii) of this section. This amount is equal to:

$$\sum_{t=1}^{E} \sum_{x=1}^{N_t} q_{xt}$$

Where E is equal to the number of years in the experience study period, t represents each year during the experience study period, x represents an individual in the population during year t, q_{xt} is the mortality rate for that individual's age and gender for the calendar year in which *year t begins under the applicable standard mortality table determined under paragraph (d)(4)(iii)* of this section, and Nt is equal to the number of individuals in the population in year t.

(iv) *Sum of the mortality-weighted squares of the benefits.*—(A) *Determination.*—For a population, the sum of the mortality-weighted squares of the benefits is the sum, for all years in the experience study period, for all individuals in the population at the beginning of the year, of the product of—
(1) The probability of death for the individual using the mortality rate for the individual's age and gender from the standard mortality table determined under paragraph (d)(4)(iii) of this section; and

⋙→ *Caution: Reg. §1.430(h)(3)-2, below, as amended by T.D. 9826, is generally applicable to plans years beginning on or after January 1, 2018.*

(2) The square of the benefit amount for the individual.

$$\sum_{t=1}^{E} \sum_{x=1}^{N_t} q_{xt} b_{xt}^2$$

Where E is equal to the number of years in the experience study period, t represents each year during the experience study period, x represents an individual in the population during year t, q_{xt} is the mortality rate for that individual's age and gender for the calendar year in which year t begins under the applicable standard mortality table determined under paragraph (d)(4)(iii) of this section, b_{xt} is equal to the benefit amount for that individual for year t, and Nt is equal to the number of individuals in the population in year t.

(v) *Square of the sum of the mortality-weighted benefits.*— (A) *Determination.*—For a population, the square of the sum of the mortality-weighted benefits is equal to the square of the sum, for all

(B) *Expression as formula.*—The sum of the mortality-weighted squares of the benefits for a population determined pursuant to paragraph (d)(3)(iv)(A) of this section is equal to:

years in the experience study period, for all individuals in the population at the beginning of the year, of the product of—

(1) The probability of death of the individual using the mortality rate for the individual's age and gender from the standard mortality table determined under paragraph (d)(4)(iii) of this section; and

(2) The benefit amount for the individual.

(B) *Expression as formula.*—The square of the sum of the mortality-weighted benefits for a population determined pursuant to paragraph (d)(3)(v)(A) of this section is equal to:

$$\left(\sum_{t=1}^{E} \sum_{x=1}^{N_t} q_{xt} b_{xt} \right)^2$$

Where E is equal to the number of years in the experience study period, t represents each year during the experience study period, x represents an individual in the population during year t, q_{xt} is the mortality rate for that individual's age and gender for the calendar year in which t begins under the applicable standard mortality table determined under paragraph (d)(4)(iii) of this section, b_{xt} is equal to the benefit amount for that individual for year t, and Nt is equal to the number of individuals in the population in year t.

(4) *Development of mortality rates.*—(i) *In general.*—The mortality rates under the base substitute mortality tables must be amounts-weighted mortality rates that are derived from the experience study. Except as provided in paragraph (d)(4)(iv) of this section, the mortality rate for an age and gender is determined by multiplying the mortality rate for that age and gender from the standard mortality table determined under paragraph (d)(4)(iii) of this section by the mortality ratio determined under paragraph (d)(4)(ii) of this section. If the simplified rule of paragraph (c)(2)(ii)(B) of this section is used for the population, then the mortality ratio is determined only taking into account people who are at least 50 years old and less than 100 years old, but the mortality ratio is applied to all ages.

(ii) *Mortality ratio.*—(A) *In general.*—Except as provided in paragraph (d)(6) of this section, a mortality ratio is determined for a gender or other population within a gender, and is equal to the quotient determined by dividing—

(1) The sum, for all years in the experience study period, of the benefit amount for all individuals in the population at the beginning of the year who died during the year, by

(2) The sum, for all years in the experience study period, for all individuals in the population at the beginning of the year (adjusted, as appropriate, for individuals who leave on account of reason other than death), of the product of—

(i) The probability of death of the individual using the mortality rate for the individual's age and gender from the standard mortality table determined under paragraph (d)(4)(iii) of this section; and

(ii) The benefit amount for the individual.

(B) *Expression as formula.*—For purposes of determining a mortality ratio as described in paragraph (d)(4)(ii)(A) of this section, the amount described in paragraph (d)(4)(ii)(A)(2) of this section is equal to:

$$\sum_{t=1}^{E} \sum_{x=1}^{N_t} q_{xt} b_{xt}$$

Where E is equal to the number of years in the experience study period, t represents each year during the experience study period, x represents an individual in the population during year t, q_{xt} is the mortality rate for that individual's age and gender for the calendar year in which t begins under the applicable standard mortality table determined under paragraph (d)(4)(iii) of this section, b_{xt} is equal to the benefit amount for that individual for year t, and Nt is equal to the number of individuals in the population in year t.

(iii) *Standard mortality table.*—(A) *Projection of base table.*—The standard mortality table for a year is the mortality table determined by applying cumulative mortality improvement factors determined under §1.430(h)(3)-1(a)(2)(i)(E) to the base mortality table under

§1.430(h)(3)-1(d) for the period beginning with 2006 and ending in the base year for the base substitute mortality table determined under paragraph (c)(3)(ii) of this section. For purposes of the previous sentence, the cumulative mortality improvement factors are determined using the mortality improvement rates described in §1.430(h)(3)-1(a)(2)(i)(C) that apply for the calendar year during which the plan sponsor submits the request for approval to use substitute mortality tables. If the plan sponsor submits such a request during 2017, then the cumulative mortality improvement factors are determined using the mortality improvement rates contained in the Mortality Improvement Scale MP-2016 Report (issued by the Retirement Plans Experience Committee (RPEC) of the Society of Actuaries

⋙→ *Caution: Reg. §1.430(h)(3)-2, below, as amended by T.D. 9826, is generally applicable to plans years beginning on or after January 1, 2018.*

and available at *www.soa.org/Research/Experience-Study/Pension/research-2016-mp.aspx*).

(B) *Selection of base table.*—If the population consists solely of annuitants, the annuitant base mortality table set forth in §1.430(h)(3)-1(d) must be used for purposes of paragraph (d)(4)(iii)(A) of this section. If the population consists solely of nonannuitants, the nonannuitant base mortality table set forth in §1.430(h)(3)-1(d) must be used for that purpose. If the population includes both annuitants and nonannuitants, a combination of the annuitant and nonannuitant base mortality tables set forth in §1.430(h)(3)-1(d) must be used for that purpose. The combined table is constructed using the weighting factors for small plans that are set forth in §1.430(h)(3)-1(d). The weighting factors are applied to develop the combined table using the following equation:

Combined mortality rate = [nonannuitant rate * (1-weighting factor)] + [annuitant rate * weighting factor].

(iv) *Modification for ages 96 and older.*—Mortality rates for ages 96 and older under the base substitute mortality table are determined using the rules of paragraph (d)(4)(i) of this section but substituting a modified mortality ratio for the mortality ratio determined under paragraph (d)(4)(ii) of this section. The modified mortality ratio is determined as follows—

(A) For ages 96 through 109, if the mortality ratio is greater than 1.0, the modified mortality ratio is equal to the mortality ratio for the population reduced by 1/15th of the excess of the mortality ratio over 1.0 for each year that the age exceeds 95.

(B) For ages 96 through 109, if the mortality ratio is less than 1.0, the modified mortality ratio is equal to the mortality ratio for the population increased by 1/15th of the excess of 1.0 over the mortality ratio for each year that the age exceeds 95.

(C) For ages 110 and older, the modified mortality ratio is equal to 1.0.

(v) *Change in number of individuals covered by table.*—Experience data may not be used to develop a base table if the number of individuals in the population covered by the table (for example, the male annuitant population) as of the last day of the plan year before the year the request for approval to use the substitute mortality table is made is less than 80 percent or more than 120 percent of the average number of individuals in that population over the years covered by the experience study on which the substitute mortality tables are based, unless it is demonstrated to the satisfaction of the Commissioner that the experience data is accurately predictive of future mortality of that population (taking into account the effect of the change in individuals) after appropriate adjustments to the data are made (for example, excluding data from individuals with respect to a spun-off portion of the plan). For this purpose, a reasonable estimate of the number of individuals in the population covered by the table may be used.

(5) *Separate tables for specified populations.*—(i) *In general.*—Except as provided in this paragraph (d)(5), separate substitute mortality tables are permitted to be used for separate populations within a gender only if—

(A) All individuals of that gender are divided into separate populations;

(B) Each separate population has mortality experience that has full credibility as determined under the rules of paragraph (d)(5)(iii) of this section; and

(C) The separate base substitute mortality table for each separate population is developed applying the rules of paragraphs (d)(1) through (4) of this section using an experience study that takes into account solely members of that population.

(ii) *Annuitant and nonannuitant separate populations.*—Notwithstanding paragraph (d)(5)(i)(B) of this section, a gender may be separated into separate populations of annuitants and nonannuitants for the purpose of developing and using substitute mortality tables, even if only one of those separate populations has credible mortality information. Similarly, if separate populations that satisfy paragraph (d)(5)(i)(B) of this section are established, then any of those populations may be further subdivided into separate annuitant and nonannuitant subpopulations, provided that at least one of the two resulting subpopulations has credible mortality information. The standard mortality tables under §1.430(h)(3)-1 are used for a resulting subpopulation that does not have credible mortality information. For example, if the male hourly and salaried populations under a plan each have mortality experience with full credibility and the male salaried annuitant population has credible mortality information, then substitute mortality tables may be used for the plan with respect to the male salaried annuitant population even if the standard mortality tables under §1.430(h)(3)-1 are used with respect to

the male salaried nonannuitant population (because that nonannuitant population does not have credible mortality information).

(iii) *Credible mortality information for separate populations.*—In determining whether the mortality experience for a separate population within a gender has full credibility, the rules of paragraph (d)(1) of this section must be applied to that separate population. In demonstrating that an annuitant (or nonannuitant) population within a gender or within a separate population does not have credible mortality information, the rules of paragraph (c)(2)(iii)(B) of this section are applied by substituting the annuitant (or nonannuitant) population for the gender.

(6) *Option to determine a single mortality ratio for both genders.*—Base substitute mortality tables for a plan may be constructed by developing and applying a single mortality ratio for both genders, but only if the substitute mortality tables used for all plans maintained by members of the plan sponsor's controlled group (except for plans for which both the male and female populations, considered separately, have mortality experience with full credibility) are constructed in this manner. If the option under this paragraph (d)(6) is applied for a plan then, for all plans maintained by members of the plan sponsor's controlled group, whether both the male and female populations within the plan have credible mortality information (and, if that combined population's mortality experience does not have full credibility, the partial credibility weighting factor for the plan) is determined using the combined mortality experience for both genders.

(e) *Partial credibility.*—(1) *In general.*—The mortality experience with respect to a population has partial credibility if the actual number of deaths for that population during the experience study period described in paragraph (d)(2) of this section is at least equal to 100 and is less than the full credibility threshold described for the population in paragraph (d)(3) of this section. If the mortality experience for the population has partial credibility, then in lieu of creating a base substitute mortality table as described in paragraph (d) of this section, the base substitute mortality table is created as the sum of—

(i) The product of—

(A) The partial credibility weighting factor determined under paragraph (e)(2) of this section; and

(B) The mortality rates that are derived from the experience study determined under paragraph (d)(4)(i) of this section, and

(ii) The product of—

(A) One minus the partial credibility weighting factor described in paragraph (e)(2) of this section; and

(B) The mortality rate from the standard mortality tables described in paragraph (d)(4)(iii) of this section.

(2) *Partial credibility weighting factor.*—The partial credibility weighting factor is equal to the square root of the fraction—

(i) The numerator of which is the actual number of deaths for the population during the experience study period, and

(ii) The denominator of which is the full credibility threshold for the population described in paragraph (d)(3) of this section.

(f) *Special rules for newly-affiliated plans.*—(1) *In general.*—This paragraph (f) provides special rules that provide temporary relief from certain rules in this section in the case of a controlled group that includes a newly-affiliated plan (as defined in paragraph (f)(2) of this section). Paragraph (f)(3) of this section provides a transition period during which the requirement in paragraph (c)(1) of this section (that is, the requirement that all plans within the controlled group that have credible mortality information must use substitute mortality tables) is not applicable. Paragraph (f)(4) of this section provides special rules that permit the use of a shorter experience study period in the case of a newly-affiliated plan that excludes the mortality experience data for the period before the date the plan becomes a newly-affiliated plan.

(2) *Definition of newly-affiliated plan.*—For purposes of this paragraph (f), a plan is a newly-affiliated plan if the plan sponsor becomes a member of the new controlled group in connection with a merger, acquisition, or similar transaction described in §1.410(b)-2(f). A plan also is treated as a newly-affiliated plan for purposes of this section if the plan is established in connection with a transfer of assets and liabilities from another employer's plan in connection with a merger, acquisition, or similar transaction described in §1.410(b)-2(f).

(3) *Transition period for newly-affiliated plans.*—The use of substitute mortality tables for a plan within a controlled group is not prohibited merely because, during the transition period, substitute mortality tables are not used for a newly-affiliated plan that fails to demonstrate a lack of credible mortality information during that

»»→ *Caution: Reg. §1.430(h)(3)-2, below, as amended by T.D. 9826, is generally applicable to plans years beginning on or after January 1, 2018.*

period. Similarly, during the transition period, the use of substitute mortality tables for a newly-affiliated plan is not prohibited merely because substitute mortality tables are not used for another plan within the controlled group that fails to demonstrate a lack of credible mortality information during that period. The transition period begins on the date of the transaction that results in the plan becoming a newly-affiliated plan and ends on the last day of the plan year that immediately follows the latest ending period described in section 410(b)(6)(C)(ii) with respect to that transaction for any of the plans in the controlled group.

(4) *Experience study period for newly-affiliated plan.*—(i) *In general.*—The mortality experience data for a newly-affiliated plan may either include or exclude mortality experience data for the period before the date the plan becomes a newly-affiliated plan. If a plan sponsor excludes mortality experience data for the period before the date the plan becomes a newly-affiliated plan, the exclusion must apply for all populations within the plan.

(ii) *Demonstration relating to lack of credible mortality information.*—If the experience study for a newly-affiliated plan excludes mortality experience data for the period prior to the date the plan becomes a newly-affiliated plan, then the demonstration that the plan does not have credible mortality information for a plan year that begins after the transition period can be made using a shorter experience study period than would otherwise be permitted under paragraph (c)(2)(iii)(B) of this section, provided that the experience study period begins with the date the plan becomes a newly-affiliated plan and ends not more than one year and one day before the first day of the plan year.

(iii) *Demonstration relating to credible mortality information.*—If the experience study for a newly-affiliated plan excludes mortality experience data for the period before the date the plan becomes a newly-affiliated plan and the plan fails to demonstrate that it does not have credible mortality information for the plan year under the rules of paragraph (f)(4)(ii) of this section, then other plans within the controlled group may continue to use substitute mortality tables only if substitute mortality tables are used for the newly-affiliated plan for the plan year. In such a case, the experience study period for the newly-affiliated plan may consist of a 12-month period.

(g) *Effective/applicability date.*—(1) *General rule.*—This section applies for plan years beginning on or after January 1, 2018. Except as provided in paragraph (g)(2) of this section, the substitute mortality table used for a plan for such a plan year must comply with the rules of paragraphs (a) through (f) of this section.

(2) *Transition rule for previously approved substitute mortality tables.*—(i) *Applicability for 2018.*—If a plan sponsor has received approval from the Commissioner to use substitute mortality tables for a plan year beginning in 2017, then that previous approval applies to a plan year beginning in 2018 provided that—

(A) The previous approval period had not ended;

(B) Substitute mortality tables are used for all plans in the plan sponsor's controlled group in accordance with the terms of that approval; and

(C) The projection factors provided in Projection Scale AA, as set forth in §1.430(h)(3)-1(d) as in effect on December 31, 2017 (as contained in 26 CFR part 1 revised April 1, 2017) are applied to the base substitute mortality table.

(ii) *Applicability for later plan years.*—If a plan sponsor is described in paragraph (g)(2)(i) of this section, then that previous approval applies to a later plan year provided that—

(A) The previous approval period had not ended;

(B) Substitute mortality tables are used for all plans in the plan sponsor's controlled group that have credible mortality information within the meaning of paragraph (c)(2)(ii) of this section; and

(C) The mortality improvement factors described in paragraph (c)(3)(ii) of this section are applied to the base substitute mortality table.

(3) *Transition rule for requests for approval to use substitute mortality tables.*—A written request described in paragraph (b)(1)(i) of this section to use substitute mortality tables for a plan year that begins during 2018 does not fail to satisfy the timing requirement of paragraph (b)(1)(ii) of this section if it is submitted no later than February 28, 2018, provided that the plan sponsor agrees to a 90-day extension of the 180-day review period in accordance with paragraph (b)(2)(iv) of this section. [Reg. §1.430(h)(3)-2.]

☐ [*T.D. 9419, 7-30-2008. Amended by T.D. 9826, 10-3-2017.*]

[Reg. §1.430(i)-1]

§1.430(i)-1. Special rules for plans in at-risk status.—(a) *In general.*—(1) *Overview.*—This section provides special rules related to determining the funding target and making other computations for certain defined benefit plans that are in at-risk status for the plan year. Section 430(i) and this section apply to single employer defined benefit plans (including multiple employer plans) but do not apply to multiemployer plans (as defined in section 414(f)). Paragraph (b) of this section describes rules for determining whether a plan is in at-risk status for a plan year, including the determination of a plan's funding target attainment percentage and at-risk funding target attainment percentage. Paragraph (c) of this section describes the funding target for a plan in at-risk status. Paragraph (d) of this section describes the target normal cost for a plan in at-risk status. Paragraph (e) of this section describes rules regarding how the funding target and the target normal cost are determined for a plan that has been in at-risk status for fewer than 5 consecutive plan years. Paragraph (f) of this section sets forth effective/applicability dates and transition rules.

(2) *Special rules for multiple employer plans.*—In the case of a multiple employer plan to which section 413(c)(4)(A) applies, the rules of section 430 and this section are applied separately for each employer under the plan, as if each employer maintained a separate plan. For example, at-risk status is determined separately for each employer under such a multiple employer plan. In the case of a multiple employer plan to which section 413(c)(4)(A) does not apply (that is, a plan described in section 413(c)(4)(B) that has not made the election for section 413(c)(4)(A) to apply), the rules of section 430 and this section are applied as if all participants in the plan were employed by a single employer.

(b) *Determination of at-risk status of a plan.*—(1) *General rule.*—Except as otherwise provided in this section, a plan is in at-risk status for a plan year if—

(i) The funding target attainment percentage for the preceding plan year (determined under paragraph (b)(3) of this section) is less than 80 percent; and

(ii) The at-risk funding target attainment percentage for the preceding plan year (determined under paragraph (b)(4) of this section) is less than 70 percent.

(2) *Small plan exception.*—If, on each day during the preceding plan year, a plan had 500 or fewer participants (including both active and inactive participants), determined in accordance with the same rules that apply for purposes of §1.430(g)-1(b)(2)(ii), then the plan is not treated as being in at-risk status for the plan year.

(3) *Funding target attainment percentage.*—For purposes of this section, except as otherwise provided in paragraph (b)(5) of this section, the funding target attainment percentage of a plan for a plan year is the funding target attainment percentage as defined in §1.430(d)-1(b)(3).

(4) *At-risk funding target attainment percentage.*—Except as otherwise provided in paragraph (b)(5) of this section, the at-risk funding target attainment percentage of a plan for a plan year is a fraction (expressed as a percentage)—

(i) The numerator of which is the value of plan assets for the plan year after subtraction of the prefunding balance and the funding standard carryover balance under section 430(f)(4)(B); and

(ii) The denominator of which is the at-risk funding target of the plan for the plan year (determined under paragraph (c) of this section, but without regard to the loading factor imposed under paragraph (c)(2)(ii) of this section).

(5) *Special rules.*—(i) *Special rule for new plans.*—Except as otherwise provided in paragraph (b)(5)(iii) of this section, in the case of a new plan that was neither the result of a merger nor involved in a spinoff, the funding target attainment percentage under paragraph (b)(3) of this section and the at-risk funding target attainment percentage under paragraph (b)(4) of this section are equal to 100 percent for years before the plan exists.

(ii) *Special rule for plans with zero funding target.*—Except as otherwise provided in paragraph (b)(5)(iii) of this section, if the funding target of the plan is equal to zero for a plan year, then the funding target attainment percentage under paragraph (b)(3) of this section and the at-risk funding target attainment percentage under paragraph (b)(4) of this section are equal to 100 percent for that plan year.

(iii) *Exception when plan has predecessor plan that was in at-risk status.*—[Reserved.]

(iv) *Special rules for plans that are the result of a merger.*—[Reserved.]

(v) *Special rules for plans that are involved in a spinoff.*—[Reserved.]

(6) *Special rule for determining at-risk status of plans of specified automobile manufacturers.*—See section 430(i)(4)(C) for special rules for determining the at-risk status of plans of specified automobile and automobile parts manufacturers.

(c) *Funding target for plans in at-risk status.*—(1) *In general.*—If the plan has been in at-risk status for 5 consecutive years, including the current plan year, then the funding target for the plan is the at-risk funding target determined under paragraph (c)(2) of this section. See paragraph (e) of this section for the determination of the funding target where the plan is in at-risk status for the plan year but was not in at-risk status for one or more of the 4 preceding plan years.

(2) *At-risk funding target.*—(i) *Use of modified actuarial assumptions.*—Except as otherwise provided in this paragraph (c)(2), the at-risk funding target of the plan under this paragraph (c)(2) for the plan year is equal to the present value of all benefits accrued or earned under the plan as of the beginning of the plan year, as determined in accordance with §1.430(d)-1 but using the additional actuarial assumptions described in paragraph (c)(3) of this section.

(ii) *Funding target includes load.*—The at-risk funding target is increased by the sum of—

(A) $700 multiplied by the number of participants in the plan (including active participants, inactive participants, and beneficiaries); plus

(B) Four percent of the funding target (determined under §1.430(d)-1(b)(2) as if the plan was not in at-risk status) of the plan for the plan year.

(iii) *Minimum amount.*—Notwithstanding any otherwise applicable provisions of this section, the at-risk funding target of a plan for a plan year is not less than the plan's funding target for the plan year determined without regard to this section.

(3) *Additional actuarial assumptions.*—(i) *In general.*—The actuarial assumptions used to determine a plan's at-risk funding target for a plan year are the actuarial assumptions that are applied under section 430, with the modifications described in this paragraph (c)(3).

(ii) *Special retirement age assumption.*—(A) *Participants eligible to retire and collect benefits within 11 years.*—Subject to paragraph (c)(3)(ii)(B) of this section, if a participant would be eligible to commence an immediate distribution by the end of the 10th plan year after the current plan year (that is, the end of the 11th plan year beginning with the current plan year), that participant is assumed to commence an immediate distribution at the earliest retirement age under the plan, or, if later, at the end of the current plan year. The rule of this paragraph (c)(3)(ii)(A) does not affect the application of plan assumptions regarding an employee's termination of employment prior to the employee's earliest retirement age.

(B) *Participants otherwise assumed to retire immediately.*—The special retirement age assumption of paragraph (c)(3)(ii)(A) of this section does not apply to a participant to the extent the participant is otherwise assumed to commence benefits during the current plan year under the actuarial assumptions for the plan. For example, if generally applicable retirement assumptions would provide for a 25 percent probability that a participant will commence benefits during the current plan year, the special retirement age assumption of paragraph (c)(3)(ii)(A) of this section requires the plan's enrolled actuary to assume a 75 percent probability that the participant will commence benefits at the end of the plan year.

(C) *Definition of earliest retirement date.*—For purposes of this paragraph (c)(3)(ii), a plan's earliest retirement date for an employee is the earliest date on which the employee can commence receiving an immediate distribution of a fully vested benefit under the plan. See §1.401(a)-20, Q&A-17(b).

(iii) *Requirement to assume most valuable benefit.*—All participants and beneficiaries who are assumed to retire on a particular date are assumed to elect the optional form of benefit available under the plan that would result in the highest present value of benefits commencing at that date.

(iv) *Reasonable techniques permitted.*—The plan's actuary is permitted to use reasonable techniques in determining the actuarial assumptions that are required to be used pursuant to this paragraph (c)(3). For example, the plan's actuary is permitted to use reasonable assumptions in determining the optional form of benefit under the plan that would result in the highest present value of benefits for this purpose.

(d) *Target normal cost of plans in at-risk status.*—(1) *General rule.*—If the plan has been in at-risk status for 5 consecutive years, including the current plan year, then the target normal cost for the plan is the at-risk target normal cost determined under paragraph (d)(2) of this section. See paragraph (e) of this section for the determination of the target normal cost where the plan is in at-risk status for the plan year but was not in at-risk status for one or more of the 4 preceding plan years.

(2) *At-risk target normal cost.*—(i) *Use of modified actuarial assumptions.*—(A) *In general.*—Except as otherwise provided in this paragraph (d)(2), the at-risk target normal cost of a plan for the plan year is equal to the present value (determined as of the valuation date) of all benefits that accrue during, are earned during, or are otherwise allocated to service in the plan year, as determined in accordance with §1.430(d)-1 but using the additional actuarial assumptions described in paragraph (c)(3) of this section.

(B) *Special adjustments.*—The target normal cost of the plan for the plan year (determined under paragraph (d)(2)(i)(A) of this section) is adjusted (not below zero) by adding the amount of plan-related expenses expected to be paid from plan assets during the plan year and subtracting the amount of any mandatory employee contributions expected to be made during the plan year.

(C) *Plan-related expenses.*—For purposes of this paragraph (d)(2), plan-related expenses are determined using the rules of §1.430(d)-1(b)(1)(iii)(B).

(ii) *Loading factor.*—The at-risk target normal cost is increased by a loading factor equal to 4 percent of the present value (determined as of the valuation date) of all benefits under the plan that accrue, are earned, or are otherwise allocated to service for the plan year under the applicable rules of §1.430(d)-1(c)(1)(ii)(B), (C), or (D), determined as if the plan were not in at-risk status.

(iii) *Minimum amount.*—The at-risk target normal cost of a plan for a plan year is not less than the plan's target normal cost determined without regard to section 430(i) and this section.

(e) *Transition between applicable funding targets and applicable target normal costs.*—(1) *Funding target.*—If a plan that is in at-risk status for the plan year has not been in at-risk status for one or more of the preceding 4 plan years, the plan's funding target for the plan year is determined as the sum of—

(i) The funding target determined without regard to section 430(i) and this section; plus

(ii) The phase-in percentage for the plan year multiplied by the excess of—

(A) The at-risk funding target determined under paragraph (c)(2) of this section (determined taking into account paragraph (e)(4) of this section); over

(B) The funding target determined without regard to section 430(i) and this section.

(2) *Target normal cost.*—If a plan that is in at-risk status for the plan year has not been in at-risk status for one or more of the preceding 4 plan years, the plan's target normal cost for the plan year is determined as the sum of—

(i) The target normal cost determined without regard to section 430(i) and this section; plus

(ii) The phase-in percentage for the plan year multiplied by the excess of—

(A) The at-risk target normal cost determined under paragraph (d)(2) of this section (determined taking into account paragraph (e)(4) of this section); over

(B) The target normal cost determined without regard to section 430(i) and this section.

(3) *Phase-in percentage.*—For purposes of this paragraph (e), the phase-in percentage is 20 percent multiplied by the number of consecutive plan years that the plan has been in at-risk status (including the current plan year) and not taking into account years before the first effective plan year for a plan.

(4) *Transition funding target and target normal cost determined without load.*—Notwithstanding paragraph (c)(2)(ii) of this section, if a plan has not been in at-risk status for 2 or more of the preceding 4 plan years (not taking into account years before the first effective plan year for a plan), then the plan's at-risk funding target that is used for purposes of paragraph (e)(1)(ii)(A) of this section (to calculate the plan's funding target where the plan has been in at-risk status for fewer than 5 plan years) is determined without regard to the loading factor set forth in paragraph (c)(2)(ii) of this section. Similarly, if a plan has not been in at-risk status for 2 or more of the preceding 4 plan years (not taking into account years before the first effective plan year for a plan), then the plan's at-risk target normal

cost that is used for purposes of paragraph (e)(2)(ii)(A) of this section (to calculate the plan's target normal cost where the plan has been in at-risk status for fewer than 5 plan years) is determined without regard to the loading factor set forth in paragraph (d)(2)(ii) of this section.

(f) *Effective/applicability dates and transition rules.*—(1) *Statutory effective date/applicability date.*—(i) *General rule.*—Section 430 generally applies to plan years beginning on or after January 1, 2008. The applicability of section 430 for purposes of determining the minimum required contribution is delayed for certain plans in accordance with sections 104 through 106 of the Pension Protection Act of 2006 (PPA '06), Public Law 109-280 (120 Stat. 780).

(ii) *Applicability of special adjustments to target normal cost.*—The special adjustments of paragraph (d)(2)(i)(B) of this section (relating to adjustments to the target normal cost for plan-related expenses and mandatory employee contributions) apply to plan years beginning after December 31, 2008. In addition, a plan sponsor may elect to make the special adjustments of paragraph (d)(2)(i)(B) of this section for plan years beginning in 2008. This election is made in the same manner and is subject to the same rules as an election to add an amount to the plan's prefunding balance pursuant to § 1.430(f)-1(f). Thus, the election can be made no later than the last day for making the minimum required contribution for the plan year to which the election relates.

(2) *Effective date/applicability date of regulations.*—This section applies to plan years beginning on or after January 1, 2010. For plan years beginning before January 1, 2010, plans are permitted to rely on the provisions set forth in this section for purposes of satisfying the requirements of section 430.

(3) *First effective plan year.*—For purposes of this section, the first effective plan year for a plan is the first plan year to which section 430 applies to the plan for purposes of determining the minimum required contribution.

(4) *Transition rule for determining at-risk status.*—In the case of plan years beginning in 2008, 2009, and 2010, paragraph (b)(1)(i) of this section is applied by substituting the following percentages for "80 percent"

(i) 65 percent in the case of 2008;

(ii) 70 percent in the case of 2009; and

(iii) 75 percent in the case of 2010. [Reg. § 1.430(i)-1.]

☐ *[T.D. 9467, 10-14-2009.]*

[Reg. § 1.430(j)-1]

§ 1.430(j)-1. Payment of minimum required contributions.—(a) *In general.*—(1) *Overview.*—This section provides rules related to the payment of minimum required contributions, including the payment of required installments. Section 430(j) and this section apply to single-employer defined benefit plans (including multiple employer plans as defined in section 413(c)) but do not apply to multiemployer plans (as defined in section 414(f)). Paragraph (b) of this section describes the general timing requirement for minimum required contributions. Paragraph (c) of this section describes the accelerated required installment schedule for plans with a funding shortfall in the preceding plan year. Paragraph (d) of this section provides rules regarding liquidity requirements. Paragraph (e) of this section provides definitions. Paragraph (f) of this section provides examples that illustrate the rules of this section. Paragraph (g) of this section sets forth effective/applicability dates and transition rules.

(2) *Special rules for multiple employer plans.*—(i) *In general.*—In the case of a multiple employer plan to which section 413(c)(4)(A) applies, the rules of section 430 and this section are applied separately for each employer under the plan, as if each employer maintained a separate plan. Thus, for example, required installments are determined separately for each employer under such a multiple employer plan. In the case of a multiple employer plan to which section 413(c)(4)(A) does not apply (that is, a plan described in section 413(c)(4)(B) that has not made the election for section 413(c)(4)(A) to apply), the rules of section 430 and this section are applied as if all participants in the plan were employed by a single employer.

(ii) *CSEC plans.*—A CSEC plan (that is, a plan that fits within the definition of a CSEC plan in section 414(y) for plan years beginning on or after January 1, 2014 and for which the election under section 414(y)(3)(A) has not been made) is not subject to the rules of section 430. See section 433 for the minimum funding rules that apply to CSEC plans.

(3) *Applicability of section 430(j) to plans of commercial passenger airlines.*—(i) *In general.*—Except as otherwise provided in this section, the rules of section 430(j) and this section apply to a plan for which an election described in section 402 of the Pension Protection Act of 2006, Public Law 109-280 (120 Stat. 780 (2006)), as amended (PPA '06), has been made in the same manner as those rules apply to any other plan subject to section 430.

(ii) *Special rules for plans for which election was made pursuant to section 402(a)(1) of PPA '06.*—For purposes of applying the rules of section 430(j) and this section to a plan with respect to which the election under section 402(a)(1) of PPA '06 has been made, the effective interest rate for the plan is deemed to be 8.85 percent during the period for which the election applies. In addition, see paragraph (e)(4)(ii) of this section for a special determination of the funding shortfall for a plan for which the election in section 402(a)(1) of PPA '06 has been made.

(b) *General timing requirement for minimum required contributions.*—(1) *Earliest date for contributions.*—A payment made before the first day of the plan year cannot be applied toward the minimum required contribution under section 430 for that plan year.

(2) *Deadline for contributions.*—The deadline for any payment of any minimum required contribution for a plan year is 8¹/₂ months after the close of the plan year. See section 4971 and the regulations thereunder regarding an excise tax that applies with respect to minimum required contributions not paid by this deadline. For additional rules that may apply in the case of a failure to pay minimum required contributions by this deadline, see also section 430(k) of the Code and sections 101(d) and 4043 of the Employee Retirement Income Security Act of 1974, as amended (ERISA).

(3) *Allocation of contribution to a plan year.*—(i) *Plans with unpaid minimum required contributions that have not been corrected.*—If a plan has unpaid minimum required contributions within the meaning of § 54.4971(c)-1(c) of this chapter that have not yet been corrected within the meaning of § 54.4971(c)-1(d)(2) of this chapter at the time a contribution is made, then the contribution is treated as a late contribution for the earliest plan year for which there is an unpaid minimum required contribution (to the extent necessary to correct that unpaid minimum required contribution). To the extent the contribution exceeds the amount necessary to correct the earlier unpaid minimum required contribution, the excess is treated as a late contribution for the next earliest plan year for which there is an unpaid minimum required contribution (to the extent necessary to correct that next earliest unpaid minimum required contribution). The allocation of the contribution under the preceding sentence is repeated until all unpaid minimum required contributions have been corrected, or until the entire contribution is allocated, whichever comes first.

(ii) *Plans without unpaid minimum required contributions.*—If a contribution is made during the current plan year but before the deadline under paragraph (b)(2) of this section for contributions for a prior plan year, and the plan has no unpaid minimum required contribution for any plan year at the time the contribution is made, then the contribution may be designated as a contribution for either that prior plan year or the current plan year. Similarly, if a contribution made during the current plan year but before the deadline under paragraph (b)(2) of this section for contributions for a prior plan year is more than enough to correct a plan's unpaid minimum required contributions for all plan years, the portion of a contribution that was not used to correct unpaid minimum required contributions may be designated as a contribution for either that prior plan year or the current plan year.

(iii) *Method of allocating contributions.*—(A) *Reporting for contributions to correct unpaid minimum required contributions.*—The allocation of a contribution under the rules of paragraph (b)(3)(i) of this section to correct unpaid minimum required contributions is automatic and must be shown on the actuarial report (Schedule SB, "Single-Employer Defined Benefit Plan Actuarial Information" of Form 5500, "Annual Return/Report of Employee Benefit Plan") for the earliest plan year with respect to which, as of the date of the contribution, the deadline for making contributions under paragraph (b)(2) of this section has not passed. See § 1.430(g)-1(d)(1) for the rules for determining the plan year for which these contributions are taken into account in determining the value of plan assets.

(B) *Designation of plan year if no unpaid minimum contribution.*—In the case of a contribution described in paragraph (b)(3)(ii) of this section, the designation is established by the completion (and filing, if required) of the actuarial report (Schedule SB, "Single-Employer Defined Benefit Plan Actuarial Information" of Form 5500, "Annual Return/Report of Employee Benefit Plan") for the plan year for which the contribution is designated and cannot be changed after the actuarial report that reflects the contribution is completed (and filed, if required) except as provided in guidance published in the Internal Revenue Bulletin. Thus, a contribution that has been designated for a plan year on an actuarial report pursuant to this paragraph (b)(3)(iii)(B) generally cannot be redesignated as a contribution for either an earlier or later plan year.

(4) *Adjustment for interest.*—(i) *In general.*—Except as provided in this paragraph (b)(4), any payment toward the minimum required contribution under section 430 for a plan year that is paid on a date other than the valuation date for that plan year is adjusted for interest for the period between the valuation date and the payment date, at the plan's effective interest rate for that plan year determined pursuant to § 1.430(h)(2)-1(f)(1). The direction of the adjustment depends on whether the contribution is paid before or after the valuation date for the plan year. If the contribution is paid after the valuation date for the plan year, the contribution is discounted to the valuation date using the plan's effective interest rate. By contrast, if the contribution is paid before the valuation date for the plan year (which could only occur in the case of a small plan described in section 430(g)(2)(B)), the contribution is increased for interest using the plan's effective interest rate.

(ii) *Interest adjustment for late quarterly installments.*—In the case of a plan that must make required installments under the rules of paragraph (c) of this section, to the extent a contribution for a plan year constitutes a late required installment, the adjustment for interest for the period between the valuation date and the payment date is made in two steps. In the first step, the portion of the contribution that constitutes a late required installment is adjusted for interest from the date of the contribution to the due date for the installment by discounting it using the plan's effective interest rate for that plan year determined pursuant to § 1.430(h)(2)-1(f)(1) plus 5 percentage points. In the second step, this discounted amount is treated as if it were contributed on the installment due date for purposes of the interest adjustment under paragraph (b)(4)(i) of this section. However, a contribution made toward the unpaid liquidity amount (as defined in paragraph (d)(3) of this section) that is made before the close of the quarter in which it is due is adjusted under paragraph (b)(4)(iii) of this section.

(iii) *Interest adjustment for unpaid liquidity amounts.*—In the case of a plan that is subject to the liquidity requirement rules of paragraph (d) of this section, to the extent a contribution made during a quarter constitutes a payment of the unpaid liquidity amount for that quarter as described in paragraph (d)(3) of this section, the adjustment for interest for the period between the valuation date and the payment date is made in two steps. In the first step, the portion of the contribution that constitutes a payment of the unpaid liquidity amount is increased for interest from the date of the contribution to the last day of the quarter, at the plan's effective interest rate for that plan year determined pursuant to § 1.430(h)(2)-1(f)(1). In the second step, this adjusted amount is treated as if it were contributed on the last day of that quarter for purposes of the interest adjustment for late required installments under the rules of paragraph (b)(4)(ii) of this section. See paragraph (d)(3)(iv)(B) of this section for an increase to the minimum required contribution that gives effect to this interest adjustment for unpaid liquidity amounts in the event a portion of the required installment is no longer treated as unpaid after the close of the quarter under paragraph (d)(3)(iv)(A) of this section.

(c) *Accelerated quarterly installments required for underfunded plans.*—(1) *Plans subject to quarterly installment requirement.*—The plan sponsor of a plan that has a funding shortfall for the preceding plan year is required to pay the installments described in paragraph (c)(5) of this section by the due dates described in paragraph (c)(6) of this section. See paragraph (b)(4)(ii) of this section, section 430(k) of the Internal Revenue Code (Code) (regarding the imposition of a lien), and sections 101(d) and 4043 of ERISA (regarding notice to participants and beneficiaries and to the Pension Benefit Guaranty Corporation) for examples of consequences that generally apply following a failure to make required installments.

(2) *Satisfaction of quarterly installment requirement.*—A plan sponsor may satisfy the requirement to pay an installment under paragraph (c)(1) of this section by one or a combination of the following—

(i) Making a contribution for the plan year which is allocated among the required installments under the rules of paragraph (c)(3) of this section; and

(ii) Making an election to use some or all of the plan's prefunding balance or funding standard carryover balance in accordance with the rules of paragraph (c)(4) of this section.

(3) *Satisfaction of quarterly installment requirement with contributions.*—(i) *Contributions allocated to earliest quarterly installments.*—For purposes of this section, a contribution for a plan year is allocated among the required installments for the plan year under the rules of paragraph (c)(3)(ii) or (iii) of this section, whichever is applicable. Which rule applies depends on whether, at the time the contribution is made, the plan sponsor has unpaid required installments (that is, the plan sponsor has not fully satisfied all required installments for

which the due date has passed, taking into account the special rule with respect to the unpaid liquidity amounts in paragraph (d)(3)(iv)(A) of this section).

(ii) *Early contributions increased with interest.*—If a plan has no unpaid required installments for a plan year at the time a contribution for the plan year is made, then the contribution is allocated to the required installments (if any) for the plan year due on or after the date of the contribution under the rules of this paragraph (c)(3)(ii). The contribution is allocated in the order in which those installments occur, and the amount allocated to each required installment is limited to the amount necessary to satisfy the required installment (including satisfaction of the liquidity requirement under paragraph (d)(1) of this section, taking into account the special rule with respect to the unpaid liquidity amounts in paragraph (d)(3)(iv)(A) of this section) taking into account any interest as described in the next sentence. If the contribution is made before the due date of the installment to which it is allocated, then the amount credited toward the installment includes interest on the contribution from the date of the contribution to the due date of the required installment (except as provided in paragraph (d)(2) of this section). This interest adjustment is made using an interest rate equal to the plan's effective interest rate under § 1.430(h)(2)-1(f)(1) for the plan year.

(iii) *Allocation of contributions to late required installments without interest.*—(A) *In general.*—If a plan has any unpaid required installments for a plan year at the time a contribution for the plan year is made, then the contribution is allocated to those unpaid required installments under the rules of this paragraph (c)(3)(iii). The contribution is allocated in the order in which those unpaid required installments occur, and the amount allocated to each required installment is limited to the amount that satisfies the required installment without any adjustment for interest. If a contribution is allocated to an unpaid required installment under this paragraph (c)(3)(iii), then that contribution is adjusted for interest under the rules of paragraph (b)(4) of this section (regarding interest adjustments for late quarterly installments) for purposes of determining the extent to which that contribution satisfies the minimum required contribution for the plan year.

(B) *Bifurcation of contributions that exceed unpaid required installments.*—Any amount of a contribution described in paragraph (c)(3)(iii)(A) of this section that is not used to satisfy the unpaid required installments for the plan year is allocated toward any remaining required installments for the plan year under the rules of paragraph (c)(3)(ii) of this section.

(4) *Satisfaction of quarterly installment requirements through use of funding balances.*—A plan sponsor may satisfy the requirement to pay an installment under paragraph (c)(1) of this section by making an election to use some or all of the plan's prefunding balance or funding standard carryover balance under section 430(f). Such an election is subject to the rules of § 1.430(f)-1 and cannot exceed the available amount of the plan's prefunding balance and funding standard carryover balance determined under § 1.430(f)-1(d)(1)(ii) as of the date of the election. The amount elected is allocated toward satisfaction of the required installments in the same manner as a contribution made on the date of the election. Thus, the amount of an election to use the plan's prefunding balance or funding standard carryover balance is increased with interest under the rules of paragraph (c)(3)(ii) of this section or is credited against the earliest unpaid required installment under the rules of paragraph (c)(3)(iii) of this section. See § 1.430(f)-1(f)(1)(iii) for rules permitting the use of a standing election for purposes of satisfying required installments through use of funding balances. See § 1.430(f)-1(d)(1)(i)(B) for rules relating to late elections to use the funding standard carryover balance or prefunding balance to satisfy the required installment rules.

(5) *Amount of required installment.*—(i) *In general.*—For purposes of this section, the amount of any required installment due for a plan year is equal to 25 percent of the required annual payment for the plan year as described in paragraph (c)(5)(ii) of this section.

(ii) *Required annual payment.*—The required annual payment for a plan year is equal to the lesser of—

(A) 90 percent of the minimum required contribution under section 430 for the plan year; or

(B) 100 percent of the minimum required contribution under section 430 (determined without regard to any funding waiver under section 412) for the preceding plan year.

(iii) *Treatment of funding balances.*—For purposes of paragraph (c)(5)(ii) of this section, the minimum required contribution for a plan year is determined without regard to the use of the prefunding balance or funding standard carryover balance for the current year or the prior year. However, see paragraph (c)(4) of this section regarding a plan sponsor's election to use the plan's prefunding balance or funding standard carryover balance for the current year in order to satisfy the requirement to pay an installment.

(iv) *Disregard of certain amounts.*—For purposes of paragraph (c)(5)(ii) of this section, the minimum required contribution for a plan year is determined without regard to the installment acceleration amount for the plan year determined under section 430(c)(7) or any

increase to the minimum required contribution under paragraph (d)(3)(iv)(B) of this section (relating to an unpaid liquidity amount).

(6) *Due dates for installments.*—For purposes of this section, there is a required installment for each quarter of the plan year, and the due dates for the required installments with respect to a full plan year are set forth in the following table:

Installment	Due date
First required installment	15th day of 4th plan month
Second required installment	15th day of 7th plan month
Third required installment	15th day of 10th plan month
Fourth required installment	15th day after the end of the plan year

(7) *Special rules for short plan years.*—(i) *In general.*—In the case of a short plan year, the rules of this paragraph (c) are modified as provided in this paragraph (c)(7).

(ii) *Current plan year is short plan year.*—(A) *Amount of required annual payment.*—In determining the required annual payment pursuant to paragraph (c)(5)(ii) of this section for a short plan year, the amount otherwise determined under paragraph (c)(5)(ii)(B) of this section (based on the prior year's minimum required contribution) is multiplied by a fraction, the numerator of which is the duration of the short plan year and the denominator of which is 1 year. This rule applies to the year that contains the plan's termination date if that date is before the date that would otherwise be the end of the plan year (because the plan is treated as having a short plan year for purposes of section 430 pursuant to § 1.430(a)-1(b)(5)).

(B) *Number and due dates of installments.*—If the plan has a short plan year, then an installment is due 15 days after the end of that short plan year. In addition, an installment is required for each due date determined under paragraph (c)(6) of this section that falls within the short plan year. Thus, for example, if the short plan year ends before the 15th day of the 4th plan month of the plan year, there will be only one installment for that short plan year, and that installment will be due on the 15th day after the end of the short plan year.

(C) *Amount of installments.*—The amount of each installment required to be paid for the short plan year is equal to the required annual payment determined pursuant to paragraph (c)(5)(ii) of this section (as modified by paragraph (c)(7)(ii)(A) of this section) divided by the number of installments determined pursuant to paragraph (c)(7)(ii)(B) of this section.

(D) *No increase in prior required installments.*—If a plan is amended to have a short plan year (including as a result of plan termination) and the required installments determined under paragraph (c)(7)(ii)(C) of this section are greater than the required installments determined without regard to the amendment, then—

(1) The required installments for which the due dates occur before the end of the short plan year are determined without regard to the amendment, and

(2) The required installment due on the 15th day after the end of the short plan year is increased to the extent necessary so that the total of the required installments for the year is the required annual payment determined under paragraph (c)(5)(ii) of this section, determined taking into account the rules of paragraph (c)(7)(ii)(A) of this section.

(iii) *Prior plan year is short plan year.*—If the prior plan year is a short plan year, the amount otherwise determined under paragraph (c)(5)(ii)(B) of this section (based on the prior year's minimum required contribution) is multiplied by a fraction, the numerator of which is 1 year and the denominator of which is the duration of the short plan year.

(d) *Liquidity requirement in connection with quarterly installments.*—(1) *In general.*—(i) *Additional requirement with respect to quarterly installments.*—Except as provided in this paragraph (d)(1), if a plan sponsor is required to pay the installments described in paragraph (c) of this section, then the plan sponsor is treated as failing to pay the full amount of the required installment for a quarter to the extent that the value of the liquid assets paid in the required installment after the end of that quarter and on or before the due date for the installment is less than the liquidity shortfall for that quarter. If the amount of any required installment is increased by reason of this paragraph (d)(1)(i), in no event shall this increase exceed the amount which, when added to the current required installment (determined without regard to the increase) and prior required installments for the plan year (not including any portion of a required installment that is no longer treated as unpaid under paragraph (d)(3)(iv)(A) of this section), is necessary to increase the funding target attainment percent-

age for the plan year to 100 percent (taking into account the expected increase in the funding target due to benefits accruing or earned during the plan year).

(ii) *Small plan exception.*—The liquidity requirement of this paragraph (d) does not apply to a plan for any plan year for which the plan is a small plan described in § 1.430(g)-1(b)(2).

(2) *Satisfaction of liquidity requirement.*—The additional requirement with respect to a required installment under paragraph (d)(1) of this section can be satisfied only with an actual contribution of liquid assets that, after application of paragraph (c)(3) of this section, is allocated to satisfy the required installment for the quarter. The liquidity requirement cannot be satisfied through the use of funding balances, and satisfaction of this requirement is determined without taking into account the increase for interest for early contributions set forth in paragraph (c)(3)(ii) of this section. Any contribution of liquid assets that is allocated to satisfy the required installment for a quarter applies for purposes of determining whether the requirements of paragraph (d)(1) of this section are satisfied, even if the contribution is less than the total amount needed to satisfy the requirements of paragraph (c) of this section for the quarter (taking into account any increase in the required installment under this paragraph (d)).

(3) *Failure to satisfy liquidity requirement.*—(i) *Treatment as failure to satisfy quarterly installment.*—If an employer fails to satisfy the additional requirement with respect to a required installment for a quarter under paragraph (d)(1) of this section, the portion of that required installment that is treated as not paid by reason of paragraph (d)(1) of this section (the unpaid liquidity amount for that quarter) is treated as an underpayment of the required installment. See paragraph (c)(1) of this section for examples of consequences of underpayment of a required installment.

(ii) *Late satisfaction of liquidity requirement.*—The rules of paragraph (d)(2) of this section apply to determine whether a contribution made after the deadline for a required installment satisfies the liquidity requirement of paragraph (d)(1) of this section. However, pursuant to section 430(j)(4)(C), the unpaid liquidity amount is treated as unpaid until the end of the quarter in which the due date for that installment occurs, even if liquid assets in that amount are contributed during that quarter (but after the due date for the installment). See paragraph (b)(4)(iii) of this section for the application of this rule for purposes of applying the additional interest for late required installments.

(iii) *Additional consequences of failure to pay liquidity shortfall.*—See section 206(e) of ERISA and section 401(a)(32) of the Code (regarding suspension of accelerated distributions for a plan with an unpaid liquidity amount). See also section 4971(f) regarding an excise tax imposed in the event of a failure to pay a liquidity shortfall.

(iv) *Treatment in subsequent quarter.*—(A) *Adjustment to required installment.*—After the close of the quarter in which the due date of a required installment occurs, any portion of the installment that was treated as unpaid solely by reason of paragraph (d)(1) of this section, and that was not satisfied with a contribution of liquid assets during that quarter, is no longer treated as unpaid (but any portion of the installment that would be treated as unpaid without regard to paragraph (d)(1) of this section must be satisfied in accordance with the rules of paragraph (c) of this section).

(B) *Increase to minimum required contribution for additional interest.*—If a portion of the required installment is no longer treated as unpaid by reason of paragraph (d)(3)(iv)(A) of this section, then the minimum required contribution for the plan year for which the installment was due is increased by an amount equal to—

(1) The portion of the required installment that is no longer treated as unpaid by reason of paragraph (d)(3)(iv)(A) of this section, discounted for interest for the period from the last day of the quarter that includes the due date of the required installment to the

valuation date, using the plan's effective interest rate for the plan year (determined pursuant to § 1.430(h)(2)-1(f)(1)); minus

(2) The portion of the required installment that is no longer treated as unpaid by reason of paragraph (d)(3)(iv)(A) of this section, discounted for interest for the period from the last day of the quarter that includes the due date of the required installment to the due date of the installment, using the plan's effective interest rate for the plan year plus 5 percentage points, and further discounted for interest for the period from the due date of the required installment to the valuation date using the plan's effective interest rate for the plan year.

(e) *Definitions.*—(1) *In general.*—The definitions set forth in this paragraph (e) apply for purposes of this section.

(2) *Adjusted disbursements.*—(i) *In general.*—The term *adjusted disbursements* means, with respect to a time period, the amount described in paragraph (e)(2)(ii) of this section if the time period is within a single plan year, or the amount described in paragraph (e)(2)(iii) of this section if the time period spans more than one plan year.

(ii) *Period within a single plan year.*—With respect to a period within a plan year, the adjusted disbursements are the disbursements from the plan during that period reduced by the product of—

(A) The plan's funding target attainment percentage determined under section 430(d)(2) for the plan year that contains that period; and

(B) The sum of the purchases of annuities and payments of single sums for that period.

(iii) *Period spanning more than one plan year.*—With respect to a period of time that spans more than one plan year, the adjusted disbursements are the sum of the adjusted disbursements determined separately under paragraph (e)(2)(ii) of this section for each portion of a plan year that is included in the time period for which adjusted disbursements are determined.

(3) *Disbursements from the plan.*—The term *disbursements from the plan* means all disbursements from the plan's trust, including purchases of annuities, payments of single sums and other benefits, and payments of administrative expenses.

(4) *Funding shortfall.*—(i) *In general.*—Except as otherwise provided in this paragraph (e)(4), the term *funding shortfall* has the same meaning as under § 1.430(a)-1(f)(2).

(ii) *Special rule for plans of commercial passenger airlines.*—In the case of a plan year for which an election described in section 402(a)(1) of PPA '06 is in effect, the term *funding shortfall* means the unfunded liability for that plan year determined under § 1.430(a)-1(b)(4)(ii).

(iii) *Special rule for first effective plan year.*—See paragraph (g)(5)(ii) of this section for a calculation of the funding shortfall for the plan's pre-effective plan year.

(iv) *Special rule for plan spinoffs and mergers.*—[Reserved]

(5) *Liquid assets.*—(i) *In general.*—The term *liquid assets* means cash, marketable securities, and other assets described in this paragraph (e)(5)(i). For this purpose, marketable securities include financial instruments such as stocks and other equity interests, evidences of indebtedness (including certificates of deposit), options, futures contracts, and other derivatives, for which there is a liquid financial market, and other interests in entities (such as partnerships, trusts, or regulated investment companies) for which there is a liquid financial market. For purposes of the preceding sentence, a liquid financial market is an established financial market described in § 1.1092(d)-1(b) (other than an interbank market or an interdealer market described in § 1.1092(d)-1(b)(1)(v) and (vi), respectively). Any security that is issued or guaranteed by the government of the United States or an agency or instrumentality thereof for which there is an established financial market described in § 1.1092(d)-1(b) is a marketable security. Finally, any financial instrument or other interest in an entity that, under its terms, contains a right by which the instrument or other interest may immediately be redeemed, exchanged, or converted into cash or a marketable security, is a marketable security, provided there are no restrictions on the exercise of that right.

(ii) *Insurance and annuity contracts.*—Other assets that are treated as liquid assets of a plan are insurance, annuity, or other contracts issued by an insurance company that is licensed to do business under the laws of any State, but only if the insurance, annuity, or other contract—

(A) Contains an unrestricted right by which the insurance, annuity or other contract may immediately be redeemed, exchanged, or converted into cash or a marketable security;

(B) Provides for substantially equal monthly disbursements to the extent provided in paragraph (e)(5)(iii) of this section; or

(C) Is benefit responsive within the meaning of paragraph (e)(5)(iv) of this section.

(iii) *Insurance and annuity contracts providing for substantially equal periodic payments.*—If the contract provides for substantially equal monthly disbursements (for example, an annuity contract in pay status), the only portion of the contract that may be treated as liquid assets for a quarter is the amount equal to 36 times the monthly disbursement (in the month containing the last day of the quarter) which is available under the terms of the contract, provided there are no restrictions on the right to disbursements.

(iv) *Benefit responsive insurance and annuity contracts.*—A contract is considered benefit responsive if, under applicable law and contractual provisions, the plan has the right to receive disbursements from the contract in order to pay plan benefits for any participant in the plan, without restrictions on that right.

(v) *Restrictions.*—For purposes of this paragraph (e)(5), a restriction on a redemption, exchange, or conversion right, or a restriction on a right to receive a disbursement, may result not only from applicable law or contractual provisions, but also from rehabilitation, conservatorship, receivership, insolvency, bankruptcy, or similar proceedings.

(6) *Liquidity shortfall.*—(i) *In general.*—Except as modified in paragraph (e)(6)(iii) of this section with respect to multiple employer plans, the term *liquidity shortfall* means, with respect to any required installment, an amount equal to the excess (as of the last day of the quarter for which that installment is due) of—

(A) The base amount with respect to the quarter, over

(B) The value (as of the last day of the quarter) of the plan's liquid assets.

(ii) *Base amount.*—(A) *In general.*—For purposes of this paragraph (e)(6), the term *base amount* means, with respect to any quarter, an amount equal to 3 times the sum of the adjusted disbursements from the plan for the 12 months ending on the last day of that quarter.

(B) *Special rule.*—If the generally applicable base amount for a quarter (as determined under paragraph (e)(6)(ii)(A) of this section) exceeds an amount equal to 2 times the sum of the adjusted disbursements from the plan for the 36 months ending on the last day of the quarter and the enrolled actuary for the plan certifies to the satisfaction of the Commissioner that such excess is the result of nonrecurring circumstances, then the base amount with respect to that quarter is determined without regard to amounts related to those nonrecurring circumstances.

(iii) *Multiple employer plans.*—(A) *Satisfaction of liquidity requirement as if plan were not a multiple employer plan.*—For a multiple employer plan to which section 413(c)(4)(A) applies, the liquidity requirement of paragraph (d)(1)(i) of this section is satisfied if the liquidity requirement would be satisfied if the plan were a single-employer plan that is not a multiple employer plan to which section 413(c)(4)(A) applies.

(B) *Failure to satisfy the liquidity requirement on a plan-wide basis.*—For a multiple employer plan to which section 413(c)(4)(A) applies, if the plan does not satisfy the liquidity requirement in accordance with paragraph (e)(6)(iii)(A) of this section, then the liquidity requirement must be applied separately for each employer under the plan, as if each employer maintained a separate plan. Thus, the value of plan assets as of the end of each quarter under such a multiple employer plan must be allocated among the employers sponsoring the plan, and the liquidity shortfall must be determined for each employer based on that allocation. See section 413(c)(7)(B) and paragraph (a)(2) of this section.

(7) *Plan month.*—(i) *Plan year begins on the first day of a calendar month.*—For a plan year that begins with the first day of a calendar month, the term *plan month* means any calendar month that begins during the plan year.

(ii) *Plan year begins on a date other than the first day of a calendar month.*—For a plan year that begins on a date other than the first day of a calendar month, the first day of each plan month is the day of the calendar month that corresponds to the day of the calendar month that is the first day of the plan year. Thus, for example, if the first day of a plan year is January 15, then a plan month starts on the 15th of each calendar month. However, if a calendar month does not contain a day that corresponds to the day of the calendar month that is the first day of the plan year (for example, if a calendar month has only 30 days and the first day of the plan year is the 31st day of a calendar month), then the first day of the plan month that begins during that calendar month is the last day of that calendar month.

(8) *Quarter.*—The term *quarter* means, with respect to any required installment, the 3-plan-month period preceding the plan month in which the due date for that installment occurs.

(9) *Short plan year.*—The term *short plan year* means a plan year that is shorter than 12 months (and is not a 52-week plan year of a plan that uses a 52-53 week plan year).

(f) *Examples.*—The following examples illustrate the rules of this section. Unless otherwise indicated, these examples are based on the following assumptions: section 430 applies to determine the minimum required contribution for plan years beginning on or after January 1, 2008; the plan year is the calendar year; the valuation date is January 1; the plan sponsor is required to pay the installments described in paragraph (c) of this section; the plan does not have a liquidity shortfall; and the plan sponsor has not elected any funding relief under section 430(c)(2)(D) for any plan year. In addition, these examples assume that, under the funding method used for the plan, interest adjustments are calculated to the nearest half month (rather than days) for transactions that occur on the 1st and 15th of a calendar month.

Example 1. (i) Plan A has a funding standard carryover balance of $15,000 and a prefunding balance of zero as of January 1, 2016, and the plan's funding ratio for 2015 (determined under § 1.430(f)-1(d)(3)) was over 80%. The minimum required contribution for Plan A (determined prior to any offset for the funding standard carryover balance) is $100,000 for 2016 and is $125,000 for 2017. The effective interest rate for the 2017 plan year is 5.90%.

(ii) The required annual payment for 2017 is equal to the lesser of (a) 100% of the 2016 minimum required contribution ($100,000) or (b) 90% of the 2017 minimum required contribution (90% of $125,000, or $112,500). Therefore, each required installment for 2017 is 25% of $100,000, or $25,000.

(iii) Installments of $25,000 each are due by April 15, 2017, July 15, 2017, October 15, 2017, and January 15, 2018. The final contribution for the 2017 plan year is due by September 15, 2018. The amount of this final contribution is equal to $125,000, less the contributions made prior to that date, with all contributions adjusted to the valuation date using the effective interest rate for the 2017 plan year. If the plan sponsor makes each required installment on the date due, the remaining amount due is determined as follows:

(A) The contribution paid April 15, 2017 is adjusted by discounting the contribution amount for $3^1/2$ months at the effective interest rate ($25,000 \div 1.0590^{(3.5/12)} = $24,585$).

(B) The contribution paid July 15, 2017 is discounted for $6^1/2$ months at the effective interest rate ($25,000 \div 1.0590^{(6.5/12)} = $24,236$).

(C) The contribution paid October 15, 2017 is discounted for $9^1/2$ months at the effective interest rate ($25,000 \div 1.0590^{(9.5/12)} = $23,891$).

(D) The contribution paid January 15, 2018 is discounted for $12^1/2$ months at the effective interest rate ($25,000 \div 1.0590^{(12.5/12)} = $23,551$).

(E) The sum of the above contributions for the 2017 plan year paid through January 15, 2018, adjusted for interest to the valuation date, is $96,263. The remaining amount due for the 2017 plan year is $125,000 minus $96,263, or $28,737, as of January 1, 2017.

(iv) If the final contribution is made on September 15, 2018, the remaining amount due must be increased for interest at the plan's effective interest rate for the $20^1/2$ months between January 1, 2017 and September 15, 2018 (so that, when it is discounted with interest for those $20^1/2$ months, the resulting amount will equal $28,737). Therefore, the remaining contribution due on September 15, 2018 is $28,737 x 1.0590^{(20.5/12)} = $31,694$.

Example 2. (i) The facts are the same as in *Example 1*, except that the plan sponsor elects to use the $15,000 funding standard carryover balance as of January 1, 2016, to offset the minimum required contribution for the 2016 plan year. The plan sponsor makes a contribution on January 1, 2016 of $85,000, which satisfies the minimum contribution requirement for 2016.

(ii) The required installments for 2017 are unaffected by the plan sponsor's election to offset the minimum required contribution by the funding standard carryover balance for 2016. Therefore, the required annual payment for 2017 is $100,000 (determined as the lesser of (a) 100% of $100,000 or (b) 90% of $125,000) and the amount of each required installment for the 2017 plan year is 25% of the required annual payment, or $25,000.

Example 3. (i) The facts are the same as in *Example 1*. Plan A's funding standard carryover balance has increased to $17,000 as of January 1, 2017, based on the actual rate of return of plan assets during the 2016 plan year. Plan A's funding ratio for 2016 (determined under § 1.430(f)-1(d)(3)) is over 80%. On March 15, 2017, the plan sponsor elects to use the entire amount of the funding standard carryover balance to offset the minimum required contribution for 2017.

(ii) The plan sponsor's election to use the funding standard carryover balance to offset the minimum required contribution is treated as satisfying the requirement to make a required installment to the extent of the amount elected, adjusted with interest for the period from the beginning of the plan year to the due date of the installment using the plan's effective interest rate for the 2017 plan year. This adjustment is made for the 2.5-month period from the beginning of the plan year to the date of the election as provided in § 1.430(f)-1(b)(5), and for the one-month period from the date of the election to the due date for the installment, as provided in paragraphs (c)(3)(ii) and (c)(4) of this section. Therefore, the $17,000 funding standard carryover balance as of January 1, 2017 offsets $17,000 x 1.0590^{(2.5/12)} x 1.0590^{(1/12)} or $17,287 of the $25,000 required installment due April 15, 2017, and the remaining contribution due on April 15, 2017 is $25,000 minus $17,287, or $7,713.

(iii) The interest adjustments in paragraph (ii) of this *Example 3* are based on the effective interest rate even if that rate is not determined by the time that the required installment is due. If the plan's effective interest rate for the plan year has not been determined at the time that the required installment is due, the actual amount of the required installment satisfied by the use of the funding standard carryover balance is determined after the effective interest rate is determined. If the extent to which the funding standard carryover balance satisfies the required installment is overestimated and the result is that the full amount of the required installment is not paid by the due date, the plan is subject to the consequences for late or unpaid required installments as described in paragraph (c)(1) of this section.

Example 4. (i) The facts are the same as in *Example 3*. The plan sponsor makes a contribution of $7,713 (which is equal to the remaining portion of the first required installment) on April 15, 2017. For the 2017 plan year, the plan sponsor makes another contribution of $200,000 on June 30, 2017. No further contributions are made for the 2017 plan year.

(ii) The contributions made for the 2017 plan year are adjusted to the valuation date using the plan's effective interest rate for the 2017 plan year. The contribution paid April 15, 2017 is discounted for the $3^1/2$ months between January 1, 2017 and the date of payment, using the effective interest rate of 5.90% ($7,713 \div 1.0590^{(3.5/12)} = $7,585$). The contribution paid June 30, 2017 is discounted for 6 months using the effective interest rate ($200,000 \div 1.0590^{(6/12)} = $194,349$), for a total interest-adjusted contribution of $201,934.

(iii) The present value of the excess contribution for 2017 is based on the net contribution required for that year, which is the minimum required contribution minus the offset for the funding standard carryover balance, or $108,000 (that is, $125,000 minus $17,000). Accordingly, the present value of the excess contribution for 2017 is $201,934 minus $108,000, or $93,934. All or a portion of this amount may be credited to the prefunding balance at the election of the plan sponsor.

Example 5. (i) The facts are the same as in *Example 3*. The plan sponsor pays the required installment of $7,713 on April 15, 2017 and installments of $25,000 each on July 15, 2017 and October 15, 2017. However, only $10,000 of the installment due on January 15, 2018 is paid. No additional contributions are made until the final contribution for the plan year of $55,000 is paid on September 15, 2018.

(ii) The 2017 Schedule SB shows that the contributions for the plan year exceed the minimum required contribution. This is determined by comparing the net contribution requirement of $108,000 (equal to the minimum required contribution of $125,000 offset by $17,000 for the amount of funding standard carryover balance used) and the interest-adjusted contributions made for the 2017 plan year, developed as shown:

(A) The contribution paid April 15, 2017 is adjusted by discounting the contribution amount for $3^1/2$ months at the effective interest rate ($7,713 \div 1.0590^{(3.5/12)} = $7,585$).

(B) The contribution paid July 15, 2017 is discounted for $6^1/2$ months at the effective interest rate ($25,000 \div 1.0590^{(6.5/12)} = $24,236$).

(C) The contribution paid October 15, 2017 is discounted for $9^1/2$ months at the effective interest rate ($25,000 \div 1.0590^{(9.5/12)} = $23,891$).

(D) The contribution paid January 15, 2018 is discounted for $12^1/2$ months at the effective interest rate ($10,000 \div 1.0590^{(12.5/12)} = $9,420$).

(E) Pursuant to paragraph (b)(4)(ii) of this section, the interest rate used to adjust the $15,000 underpayment of the required installment due January 15, 2018 is increased by 5 percentage points for the 8-month period of underpayment (January 15, 2018 through September 15, 2018). Accordingly, $15,000 of the contribution paid on September 15, 2018 is discounted using a rate of 10.90% for 8 months to the due date of January 15, 2018, and is then further adjusted using the 5.90% effective interest rate for the $12\frac{1}{2}$ months between the required installment due date of January 15, 2018 and the valuation date of January 1, 2017. This portion of the September 15, 2018 contribution results in an adjusted amount of $13,189 as of January 1, 2017 ($15,000 ÷ $1.1090^{(8/12)}$ ÷ $1.0590^{(12.5/12)}$).

(F) The remaining $40,000 of the contribution paid on September 15, 2018 is discounted using the effective interest rate of 5.90% for the $20\frac{1}{2}$-month period between the date of payment and the valuation date. This portion of the payment is therefore adjusted to $36,268 as of the valuation date (that is, $40,000 ÷ $1.0590^{(20.5/12)}$).

(G) The sum of the contributions (as calculated in paragraphs (ii)(A) through (F) of this *Example 5* for the 2017 plan year paid through September 15, 2018, adjusted for interest to the valuation date, is $114,589. This is greater than the net contribution required for the 2017 plan year of $108,000.

Example 6. (i) The facts are the same as in *Example 5*, except that the plan sponsor does not make the contribution on September 15, 2018.

(ii) The 2017 Schedule SB shows an unpaid minimum required contribution of $42,868 as of January 1, 2017. This is equal to the difference between the net contribution required for 2017 of $108,000 (the minimum required contribution of $125,000, offset by $17,000 for the amount of the funding standard carryover balance used) and $65,132 (the interest-adjusted contributions made for the 2017 plan year before the $8\frac{1}{2}$ month deadline, as illustrated in paragraphs (ii)(A) through (ii)(D) of *Example 5*.

Example 7. (i) The facts are the same as in *Example 1*, except that the plan year is changed to an August 1 – July 31 plan year effective August 1, 2017. This results in a short plan year beginning January 1, 2017 and ending July 31, 2017. The minimum required contribution for the 7-month period covered by the plan year is calculated as $72,917 in accordance with §1.430(a)-1(b)(2)(ii).

(ii) As provided in paragraph (c)(7) of this section, a required installment is due 15 days after the end of the short plan year (August 15, 2017), and required installments are also due on the regularly scheduled due dates for required installments that occur within the short plan year (April 15, 2017 and July 15, 2017).

(iii) The required installments are determined based on the lesser of (a) 90% of the minimum required contribution for the short plan year ending July 31, 2017 (90% of $72,917, or $65,625) or (b) 7/12 of 100% of the 2016 minimum required contribution ($100,000 x 7/12, or $58,333). The required installments are thus based on $58,333 because that is the smaller amount.

(iv) The amount of each required installment is determined by dividing the amount determined in paragraph (iii) of this *Example 7* by the number of required installments for the short plan year. This calculation results in required installments of $19,444 each (that is, $58,333 divided by 3 installments).

(v) The deadline for the remaining payment is $8\frac{1}{2}$ months after the end of the short plan year, or April 15, 2018. If the plan sponsor pays the minimum required amount at each installment date, does not elect to offset any amounts by any funding standard carryover or prefunding balance, and makes a final payment on April 15, 2018, then the remaining payment is $17,429, determined as follows:

(A) The contribution paid April 15, 2017 is adjusted by discounting the contribution amount for $3\frac{1}{2}$ months at the effective interest rate ($19,444 ÷ $1.0590^{(3.5/12)}$ = $19,122).

(B) The contribution paid July 15, 2017 is discounted for $6\frac{1}{2}$ months at the effective interest rate ($19,444 ÷ $1.0590^{(6.5/12)}$ = $18,850).

(C) The contribution paid August 15, 2017 is discounted for $7\frac{1}{2}$ months at the effective interest rate ($19,444 ÷ $1.0590^{(7.5/12)}$ = $18,760).

(D) The sum of the contributions for the 2017 plan year paid through August 15, 2017, adjusted for interest to the valuation date, is $56,732. The remaining amount paid April 15, 2018 for the 2017 plan year is ($72,917 - $56,732) x $1.059^{(15.5/12)}$ = $17,429.

Example 8. (i) Plan B has an August 10 to August 9 plan year.

(ii) For the plan year that begins on August 10, 2017, a plan month begins on the 10th day of each calendar month. Accordingly, the due dates for the required installments for that plan year are November 24, 2017, February 24, 2018, May 24, 2018 and August 24, 2018. The deadline for the final contribution for the plan year is April 24, 2019.

Example 9. (i) Plan C has a funding standard carryover balance of $0 and a prefunding balance of $65,000 as of January 1, 2017. Plan C's funding ratio for 2016 (determined under §1.430(f)-1(d)(3)) was over 80%. The minimum required contribution for Plan C (determined prior to any offset for the funding standard carryover balance) is $120,000 for 2016. Required installments for the 2016 plan year were made timely, and the final installment of the minimum required contribution for the 2016 plan year is due on September 15, 2017 in the amount of $40,000.

(ii) Prior to April 15, 2017, the plan sponsor makes a standing election to use Plan C's funding balances to offset any otherwise unpaid required installments and any otherwise unpaid minimum required contribution. On June 1, 2017, the actuary completes the 2017 valuation and notifies the plan sponsor that the minimum required contribution for the 2017 plan year is $100,000. The effective interest rate for the 2017 plan year is 5.90%. No contributions are made for the 2017 plan year until September 15, 2018.

(iii) The first required installment for the 2017 plan year is due on April 15, 2017. Under §1.430(f)-1(f)(1)(iii)(B), the amount of the prefunding balance used as of April 15, 2017 pursuant to the standing election is 25% of the $120,000 required annual payment for the 2016 plan year ($30,000). The prefunding balance is reduced by this amount, adjusted for the $3\frac{1}{2}$-month period between the January 1, 2017 valuation date and the April 15, 2017 due date, using the effective rate for Plan C for 2017 ($30,000 ÷ $1.0590^{(3.5/12)}$, or $29,503). The prefunding balance is available to offset the April 15, 2017 required installment even though the minimum required contribution for the 2016 plan year has not yet been made, because the standing election to use Plan C's balances to offset the minimum required contribution for the 2016 plan year does not take effect until the due date for that contribution, or September 15, 2017. Therefore, as of April 15, 2017, the prefunding balance still exists and may be used to offset the required installment due as of that date.

(iv) The second required installment for the 2017 plan year is due on July 15, 2017, after the actuary determined the minimum required contribution for the 2017 plan year. The required annual payment for 2017 is equal to the lesser of (a) 100% of the 2017 minimum required contribution ($120,000) or (b) 90% of the 2017 minimum required contribution (90% of $100,000, or $90,000). Therefore, each required installment for 2017 is 25% of $90,000, or $22,500.

(v) Although the amount of the required installments for 2017 ($22,500) is smaller than the amount based on the 2016 minimum required contribution ($30,000), under §1.430(f)-1(f)(1)(iii)(B), the amount of the prefunding balance used under the standing election continues to be the $30,000 based on the minimum required contribution for the 2016 plan year. Alternatively, the plan sponsor can make a replacement formula election to use the prefunding balance to cover the remaining required installments for the 2017 plan year as described in §1.430(f)-1(f)(1)(iii)(C), based on required installments of $22,500 each.

(vi) The use of $30,000 of the prefunding balance as of April 15, 2017 pursuant to the standing election is irrevocable, and therefore the prefunding balance is not adjusted to reflect the fact that the first required installment for the 2017 plan year (based on the actual 2017 minimum required contribution) is lower than $30,000.

(vii) However, the excess of the $30,000 of prefunding balance used on April 15, 2017 over the first required installment is allocated toward the second required installment. In addition, if the plan sponsor makes a replacement formula election in accordance with §1.430(f)-1(f)(1)(iii)(C), the amount of prefunding balance used pursuant to that election takes into account the actual required installment. In this case, the amount of the prefunding balance used to satisfy the July 15, 2017 required installment is $14,437. This amount is determined by (1) calculating the excess of the amount of the prefunding balance used on April 15, 2017 over the amount of the required installment due on that date ($30,000 minus $22,500 = $7,500), and adjusting it for the 3 months from April 15, 2017 to July 15, 2017, using the effective interest rate ($7,500 x $1.0590^{(3/12)}$ = $7,608), (2) deducting that amount from the required installment due July 15, 2017, to determine the net amount due as of that date ($22,500 - $7,608 = $14,892), and (3) adjusting the net amount to the valuation date of January 1, 2017 for the $6\frac{1}{2}$-month period between the valuation date and the due date for the required installment, using the effective interest rate for Plan C for 2017 ($14,892 ÷ $1.0590^{(6.5/12)}$ = $14,437).

Example 10. (i) The facts are the same as in *Example 9*, except that Plan C's prefunding balance as of January 1, 2017 is only $20,000, and Plan C's sponsor makes a contribution larger than the minimum required contribution for the 2016 plan year on March 1, 2017.

(ii) The amount of the April 15, 2017 required installment that is satisfied by the plan sponsor's election to offset the prefunding balance is calculated by increasing the January 1, 2017 prefunding balance with interest for $3\frac{1}{2}$ months to April 15, 2017, using the effective interest rate for Plan C for 2017. This results in an offset of $20,337 ($20,000 x $1.0590^{(3.5/12)}$). A cash contribution of $2,163 ($22,500 minus $20,337) is needed to satisfy the required installment on that date.

(iii) The excess contribution made for the 2016 plan year cannot be used to offset the remainder of the April 15, 2017 required installment even though it was contributed prior to the date the installment is due, because the sponsor had not yet elected to credit the excess contribution to the prefunding balance. If the plan sponsor elects at a later date to credit the excess contribution to the prefunding balance, the amount can be used to offset required installments due on or after the date of that election. However, note that if Plan C's actuary reflected the excess contribution for 2016 in certifying the 2017 adjusted funding target attainment percentage (AFTAP) used to apply benefit restrictions under section 436, a later election to credit the excess contribution to the prefunding balance would reduce the AFTAP and could cause Plan C to violate section 436.

Example 11. (i) Plan D is not a small plan described in §1.430(g)-1(b)(2). The valuation date for Plan D is January 1, and Plan D's funding target attainment percentage (FTAP) was 82% as of January 1, 2016 and is 90% as of January 1, 2017. The amount needed to increase the plan's FTAP for the 2017 plan year to 100% (including the expected increase in the funding target due to benefits accruing or earned during the plan year) is $500,000. Before taking the liquidity requirement of paragraph (d) of this section into account, the plan sponsor of Plan D is required to pay installments for the 2017 plan year in the amount of $50,000 each. During the 12-month period ending March 31, 2017, periodic annuity payments of $425,000 and single sum payments of $200,000 were made by Plan D. Of the single sum payments, $125,000 were made during the 2016 plan year and $75,000 were made during the 2017 plan year. None of these payments were due to nonrecurring circumstances. In addition, administrative expenses of $25,000 were paid from the plan trust during the 12-month period ending March 31, 2017. As of March 31, 2017, the reported value of Plan D's assets is $1,500,000, and the fair market value of Plan D's liquid assets is $1,300,000.

(ii) The amount of the adjusted disbursements from Plan D for the 12-month period ending March 31, 2017 is calculated as the sum of the annuity benefits, single sum payments, and administrative expenses paid during the 12-month period, reduced by the product of the plan's FTAP and the sum of the single sum payments and any payments for annuities purchased during the plan year. This results in adjusted disbursements for the period of $480,000 (that is, $425,000 plus $200,000 plus $25,000, reduced by 82% of $125,000 in single sum payments during 2016 and 90% of $75,000 in single sum payments during 2017).

(iii) The base amount is calculated in accordance with paragraph (e)(6)(ii) of this section as three times the adjusted disbursements determined in paragraph (ii) of this *Example 11*, or $1,440,000.

(iv) The liquidity shortfall is the difference between the base amount of $1,440,000 determined in paragraph (iii) of this *Example 11* and the $1,300,000 in liquid assets as of March 31, 2017, or $140,000. The required installment due on April 15, 2017 is therefore $140,000, since this amount is larger than the $50,000 installment otherwise required, but less than the $500,000 needed to increase the plan's FTAP (including the expected increase in the funding target due to benefits accruing or earned during the plan year) to 100%.

(v) Note that any contributions of liquid assets made through March 31, 2017 are reflected for purposes of determining the fair market value of Plan D's liquid assets as of March 31, 2017 and are not applied toward satisfying the liquidity requirement as of April 15, 2017. Similarly, any funding standard carryover balance or prefunding balance as of January 1, 2017 cannot be applied to offset the liquidity requirement. Only contributions made in cash or other liquid assets made after March 31, 2017 and by April 15, 2017 can be used to timely satisfy this requirement.

Example 12. (i) The facts are the same as in *Example 11*. The plan sponsor makes a cash contribution for the 2017 plan year of $30,000 on April 15, 2017, and makes an additional cash contribution for the 2017 plan year of $110,000 on April 30, 2017. The effective interest rate for Plan D for the 2017 plan year is 5.90%.

(ii) Under paragraph (d)(3)(i) of this section, the underpayment of the required installment due April 15, 2017 is $110,000 (that is, $140,000 minus $30,000).

(iii) Because the $110,000 contribution was made after the due date for the required installment (which reflects an unpaid liquidity amount) but during the quarter in which the installment was due, and because that contribution does not exceed the unpaid liquidity amount for the quarter, the special interest adjustment under paragraph (b)(4)(iii) of this section applies to the entire amount of the contribution. Accordingly, the contribution is adjusted for interest in two steps for the purpose of determining the portion of the minimum required contribution that is satisfied by the contribution. In the first step, the contribution is adjusted using the effective interest rate for the 2-month period from the payment date of April 30, 2017 to June 30, 2017, the last day of the quarter during which the liquidity requirement was due ($110,000 x $1.0590^{(2/12)}$ = $111,056). In the second step, this amount is adjusted as if that amount had been paid on June 30, 2017. Accordingly, this amount ($111,056) is discounted for interest at a rate of 10.90% (the effective interest rate for the 2017 plan year of 5.90%, increased by 5 percentage points) for the $2^{1/2}$-month period from June 30, 2017 to the April 15, 2017 due date for the installment, and is further discounted using the effective interest rate of 5.90% for the $3^{1/2}$-month period between April 15, 2017 and the valuation date of January 1, 2017. Therefore, the April 30, 2017 contribution is adjusted to $106,886 as of January 1, 2017 ($111,056 ÷ $1.1090^{(2.5/12)}$ ÷ $1.0590^{(3.5/12)}$).

(iv) The $140,000 contributed during April 2017 is needed to satisfy the required installment due April 15, 2017 (determined taking into account the liquidity shortfall as of March 31, 2017), and so the full amount is applied to satisfy that installment. No portion of those contributions is applied to the required installments for subsequent quarters, and no additional payments are needed to satisfy the required installment due April 15, 2017 (because the $110,000 payment satisfies both the unpaid liquidity amount and the remaining amount of the required installment described under paragraph (c)(5) of this section).

Example 13. (i) The facts are the same as in *Example 12*, except that the plan sponsor does not make the second cash contribution of $110,000 on April 30, 2017, but instead makes a second cash contribution of $75,000 for the 2017 plan year on July 15, 2017. The base amount as of June 30, 2017 calculated in accordance with paragraph (e)(6)(ii) of this section is $1,500,000, and the fair market value of liquid assets as of that date is $1,400,000.

(ii) Under paragraph (d)(3)(i) of this section, the underpayment of the required installment due April 15, 2017 is $110,000 (that is, $140,000 minus $30,000).

(iii) As of June 30, 2017, no portion of the $110,000 underpayment of the required installment due April 15, 2017 has been satisfied. Under paragraph (d)(3)(iv)(A) of this section, to the extent that the amount due April 15, 2017 solely because of the liquidity requirement under paragraph (d)(1) of this section is not satisfied with a contribution of liquid assets during the quarter, this amount is no longer considered unpaid. Of the $110,000 underpayment of the required installment that was due on April 15, 2017, $20,000 would have been due without regard to the liquidity requirement under paragraph (d)(1) of this section and $90,000 was due solely because of that liquidity requirement. Accordingly, as of July 1, 2017, $90,000 of the required installment due on April 15, 2017 is no longer treated as unpaid and $20,000 of that required installment continues to be treated as unpaid.

(iv) Under paragraph (d)(3)(iv)(B) of this section, the interest adjustment in paragraph (b)(4)(iii) of this section for the $90,000 portion of the installment due April 15, 2017 that is no longer treated as unpaid is given effect through an increase in the minimum required contribution. This increase to the minimum required contribution is $837, which is determined as the difference between:

(A) The $90,000 portion of the required installment that is no longer treated as unpaid by reason of paragraph (d)(3)(iv)(A) of this section, discounted for the 6-month period between June 30, 2017 (the last day of the quarter in which the liquidity amount was due) to January 1, 2017 (the valuation date) using the plan's effective interest rate for 2017 (5.90%), resulting in $87,457 (that is, $90,000 ÷ $1.0590^{(6/12)}$), and

(B) The $90,000 portion of the required installment that is no longer treated as unpaid by reason of paragraph (d)(3)(iv)(A) of this section, discounted for the $2^{1/2}$-month period between June 30, 2017 and the April 15, 2017 due date using the plan's effective interest rate increased by 5 percentage points (10.90%), and further discounted for the $3^{1/2}$-month period between April 15, 2017 and January 1, 2017 valuation date using the plan's effective interest rate, for a result of $86,620 (that is, $90,000 ÷ $1.1090^{(2.5/12)}$ ÷ $1.0590^{(3.5/12)}$).

(v) The remainder of the required installment that was due on April 15, 2017 without regard to the liquidity requirement ($20,000) remains unpaid until the July 15, 2017 contribution is made. Under paragraph (c) of this section, $20,000 of the July 15, 2017 contribution must be allocated to the required installment due on April 15, 2017. The interest adjustment under paragraph (b)(4)(ii) of this section applies to that $20,000 portion of the contribution because it is a late payment of a required installment. Accordingly, $20,000 of the July 15, 2017 contribution is adjusted to April 15, 2017, using an interest rate of 10.90% for the 3-month period between July 15, 2017 and the April 15, 2017 due date, and further adjusted using the effective interest rate of 5.90% for $3^{1/2}$ months between April 15, 2017 and the January 1, 2017 valuation date. Therefore, the portion of the July 15, 2017 contribution attributable to the April 15, 2017 required installment is adjusted to $19,166 as of January 1, 2017 ($20,000 ÷ $1.1090^{(3/12)}$ ÷ $1.0590^{(3.5/12)}$).

(vi) The liquidity shortfall is recalculated as of June 30, 2017 as $100,000 (that is, the base amount of $1,500,000 minus the value of liquid assets of $1,400,000). This amount is larger than the $50,000 required installment otherwise applicable, and so the amount of the required installment due on July 15, 2017 is $100,000. Of the $75,000 contribution made on July 15, 2017, $20,000 is applied to satisfy the remainder of the required installment due April 15, 2017, and the remaining $55,000 is applied toward the required installment due July 15, 2017. An additional contribution of $45,000 in liquid assets is needed to satisfy the required installment due July 15, 2017.

(vii) If instead there were no liquidity shortfall as of June 30, 2017, the required installment due July 15, 2017 would be $50,000. Of the $75,000 contribution made on July 15, 2017, $20,000 would be applied to satisfy the remainder of the required installment due April 15, 2017, $50,000 would be applied to satisfy the required installment due on July 15, 2017, and the remaining $5,000 would be applied toward the next required installment.

Example 14. (i) Plan E, which is a small plan described in section 430(g)(2)(B), has a calendar year plan year and a valuation date of December 31. The required installments for the 2017 plan year are $30,000 each and each of the required installments is paid on the due date. The effective interest rate for Plan E for the 2017 plan year is 5.90%.

(ii) The total contributions made for the plan year and before the valuation date, adjusted with interest to the valuation date, equal $92,402. This is developed as shown below:

(A) The contribution paid April 15, 2017 is adjusted by increasing the contribution amount for $8^{1}/_{2}$ months at the effective interest rate ($30,000 x $1.0590^{(8.5/12)}$ = $31,243).

(B) The contribution paid July 15, 2017 is increased for $5^{1}/_{2}$ months at the effective interest rate ($30,000 x $1.0590^{(5.5/12)}$ = $30,799).

(C) The contribution paid October 15, 2017 is increased for $2^{1}/_{2}$ months at the effective interest rate ($30,000 x $1.0590^{(2.5/12)}$ = $30,360).

(iii) Pursuant to § 1.430(g)-1(d)(2), the interest-adjusted value of the contributions for the 2017 plan year that are made before the valuation date is subtracted from the December 31, 2017 plan assets in determining the value of plan assets for the December 31, 2017 actuarial valuation.

Example 15. (i) The facts are the same as in *Example 14*, except that the first contribution for the 2017 plan year is made on May 15, 2017 in the amount of $40,000. The remaining amount of each required installment is paid on the date it is due.

(ii) In accordance with paragraph (c)(3)(iii) of this section, the amount of the required installment due on April 15, 2017 remains at $30,000, even though the associated contribution was not paid until May 15, 2017. Therefore, $30,000 of the payment is allocated to the April 15, 2017 required installment and the remaining $10,000 is allocated to the installment due on July 15, 2017.

(iii) Under paragraph (c)(3)(ii) of this section, the portion of the May 15, 2017 contribution allocated to the July 15, 2017 required installment is increased for interest for the 2 months between the date of the contribution and the due date, using the effective interest rate for 2017. Therefore, the amount allocated to the July 15, 2017 installment is $10,096 (that is, $10,000 x $1.0590^{(2/12)}$). The remaining installment due July 15, 2017 is $30,000 minus $10,096, or $19,904.

(iv) The total amount credited against the minimum required contribution is $122,062 as of December 31, 2017. This amount is calculated as shown below:

(A) The portion of the May 15, 2017 contribution allocated to the April 15, 2017 required installment is first adjusted for the 1 month between the due date and the payment date using the effective interest rate plus 5% ($30,000 ÷ $1.1090^{(1/12)}$ = $29,742). This amount is then adjusted using the effective interest rate, for the $8^{1}/_{2}$ months between the due date of April 15, 2017 and the valuation date of December 31, 2017 ($29,742 x $1.0590^{(8.5/12)}$ = $30,975).

(B) The remaining portion of the May 15, 2017 contribution ($10,000) is increased for the $7^{1}/_{2}$ months between the date of the contribution and the valuation date at the effective interest rate ($10,000 x $1.0590^{(7.5/12)}$ = $10,365).

(C) The contribution paid July 15, 2017 is increased for $5^{1}/_{2}$ months at the effective interest rate ($19,904 x $1.0590^{(5.5/12)}$ = $20,434).

(D) The contribution paid October 15, 2017 is increased for $2^{1}/_{2}$ months at the effective interest rate ($30,000 x $1.0590^{(2.5/12)}$ = $30,360).

(E) The contribution paid January 15, 2018 is discounted for $^{1}/_{2}$ month at the effective interest rate ($30,000 ÷ $1.0590^{(0.5/12)}$ = $29,928).

(v) The amount deducted from valuation assets as of December 31, 2017 for contributions made before the valuation date is determined without regard to the special interest adjustment for late payment of the required installment due April 15, 2017 (and without regard to the contribution paid on January 15, 2018).

Example 16. (i) Plan F has a required installment of $10,000 per quarter for the 2016 plan year. The plan sponsor makes a contribution of $9,993 on April 10, 2016. The effective interest rate for Plan F for the 2016 plan year is 5.90%.

(ii) In accordance with paragraph (c)(3)(ii) of this section, the contribution is increased for interest at the effective interest rate, for the 5 days between the contribution date and the due date for the required installment. Therefore, the amount credited against the required installment due April 15, 2016 is $10,001 ($9,993 x $1.0590^{(5/365)}$), and the required installment is satisfied.

Example 17. (i) The facts are the same as in *Example 16*, except that a contribution of $8,000 is made on April 20, 2016.

(ii) In accordance with paragraph (c)(3)(iii) of this section, the amount of the required installment due on April 15, 2016 remains at $10,000, even though the associated contribution was not paid until

after the due date, and so $2,000 ($10,000 - $8,000) of the required installment remains unpaid as of April 20, 2016.

(iii) The amount of the April 20, 2016 contribution credited against the minimum required contribution for 2016 is $7,858. This amount is determined by first adjusting the contribution for the 5 days between the due date for the required installment and the date of the contribution using the effective interest rate for Plan F for the 2016 plan year, plus 5% ($8,000 ÷ $1.1090^{(5/365)}$ = $7,989). The result is further adjusted for the 105 days from the due date for the required installment to the valuation date of January 1, 2016 using the effective interest rate of 5.90% ($7,989 ÷ $1.0590^{(105/365)}$ = $7,858).

(iv) Alternatively, the amount of the April 20, 2016 contribution credited against the minimum required contribution for 2016 could be determined using $3^{1}/_{2}$ months between the due date for the required installment and the January 1, 2016 valuation date, as long as the calculation is done consistently for each contribution and for each plan year. Using this approach, the amount adjusted to the April 15, 2016 due date (using the effective interest rate for Plan F for the 2016 plan year plus 5%) is adjusted to January 1, 2016 for $3^{1}/_{2}$ months at the effective interest rate for Plan F for the 2016 plan year. Under this approach, the amount credited against the minimum required contribution is $7,856 ($8,000 ÷ $1.1090^{(5/365)}$ ÷ $1.0590^{(3.5/12)}$).

Example 18. (i) Plan G has a funding standard carryover balance of $15,000 and a prefunding balance of $50,000 as of January 1, 2016. Plan G's required installments are $25,000 each for the 2017 plan year, and the final installment of the minimum required contribution for the 2016 plan year is due on September 15, 2017, in the amount of $40,000. Plan G's funding ratios for both 2015 and 2016 (determined under § 1.430(f)-1(d)(3)) were over 80%. No elections were made to reduce or use Plan G's funding balances during 2016. The effective interest rate for Plan G for the 2016 and 2017 plan years are 5.40% and 5.90%, respectively.

(ii) On April 15, 2017, Plan G's sponsor elected to use the balances to offset the required installment due on that date. The amount of the required installment is adjusted to January 1, 2017, using the effective interest rate for 2017 to determine the amount by which the balances are reduced. Accordingly, this election results in a reduction of $24,585 ($25,000 ÷ $1.0590^{(3.5/12)}$) in the funding balances as of January 1, 2017.

(iii) On September 15, 2017, Plan G's sponsor elected to use the balances to offset the remaining minimum required contribution for the 2016 plan year due on that date. This amount is adjusted to January 1, 2016, using the effective interest rate for 2016 to determine the amount by which the balances are reduced. Accordingly, this election results in a reduction of $36,563 ($40,000 ÷ $1.0540^{(20.5/12)}$) in Plan G's funding balances as of January 1, 2016.

(iv) Section 430(f)(3)(B) and § 1.430(f)-1(d)(2) require that the funding standard carryover balance be exhausted before the prefunding balance is used to offset required contribution amounts. Although the due date for the April 15, 2017 required installment occurs earlier than the due date for the 2016 minimum required contribution, for this purpose contributions for the 2016 plan year are deemed to occur before those for the 2017 plan year. Therefore, the election to offset the 2016 minimum required contribution will eliminate Plan G's funding standard carryover balance, and the 2017 required installment due April 15, 2017 will be offset by the prefunding balance.

(g) *Effective/applicability dates and transition rules.*—(1) *Statutory effective date/applicability date.*—Section 430 generally applies to plan years beginning on or after January 1, 2008. The applicability of section 430 for purposes of determining the minimum required contribution is delayed for certain plans in accordance with sections 104 through 106 of PPA '06.

(2) *Effective date/applicability date of regulations.*—This section applies to plan years beginning on or after January 1, 2016. For plan years beginning before January 1, 2016, plans are permitted to rely on the provisions set forth in this section for purposes of satisfying the requirements of section 430(j).

(3) *First effective plan year.*—For purposes of this section, the *first effective plan year* for a plan is the first plan year after the pre-effective plan year.

(4) *Pre-effective plan year.*—For purposes of this section, the *pre-effective plan year* is the plan year described in § 1.430(a)-1(h)(5).

(5) *Special rules relating to first effective plan year.*—(i) *Determination of minimum required contribution for pre-effective plan year.*—In the case of the plan's first effective plan year, the minimum required contribution for the preceding plan year for purposes of paragraph (c)(5)(ii)(B) of this section is equal to the minimum required contribution under section 412 for the pre-effective plan year (determined without regard to any funding waiver under section 412), determined as of the last day of the pre-effective plan year and without regard to the plan's credit balance.

(ii) *Determination of funding shortfall for pre-effective plan year.*—(A) *First effective plan year that begins during 2008.*—In general, in the case of a plan with a first effective plan year that begins during 2008, the funding shortfall for the pre-effective plan year that precedes it is determined pursuant to paragraph (e)(4) of this section. However, for this purpose, the plan's current liability for the pre-effective plan year under section 412(l)(7) (as in effect for the pre-effective plan year) is permitted to be used in place of the plan's funding target for the pre-effective plan year. In addition, for this purpose, the value of plan assets that was used for the pre-effective plan year is permitted to be used in place of the value of plan assets computed pursuant to §1.430(g)-1(c) for the pre-effective plan year, provided that the value of plan assets that was used for the pre-effective plan year was not less than 90 percent nor more than 110 percent of the value of plan assets computed pursuant to §1.430(g)-1(c). If the value of plan assets that was used for the pre-effective plan year was less than 90 percent of the value of plan assets computed pursuant to §1.430(g)-1(c), then 90 percent of the value of plan assets computed pursuant to §1.430(g)-1(c) is permitted to be used as the value of plan assets for the pre-effective plan year. If the value of plan assets that was used for the pre-effective plan year was more than 110 percent of the value of plan assets computed pursuant to §1.430(g)-1(c), then 110 percent of the value of plan assets computed pursuant to §1.430(g)-1(c) is permitted to be used as the value of plan assets for the pre-effective plan year. Finally, for this purpose, the value of plan assets is permitted to be determined without subtraction for the plan's credit balance for the pre-effective plan year.

(B) *First effective plan year begins after 2008.*—In the case of a plan with a first effective plan year that begins after December 31, 2008, the determination of the funding shortfall for the pre-effective plan year that immediately precedes it is made in accordance with paragraph (e)(4)(i) of this section. Thus, the funding shortfall for the pre-effective plan year is based on the funding target for the pre-effective plan year and the value of plan assets is determined under §1.430(g)-1(c) for the pre-effective plan year, even though section 430(g) did not apply to the plan for purposes of determining the minimum required contribution for the pre-effective plan year. [Reg. §1.430(j)-1.]

☐ [T.D. 9732, 9-8-2015.]

⫸→ Caution: Reg. §1.431(c)(6)-1, below, prior to amendment by T.D. 9826, is generally applicable to plans years beginning before January 1, 2018.

[Reg. §1.431(c)(6)-1]

§1.431(c)(6)-1. Mortality tables used to determine current liability.—(a) *Mortality tables used to determine current liability.*—The mortality assumptions that apply to a defined benefit plan for the plan year pursuant to section 430(h)(3)(A) and §1.430(h)(3)-1(a)(2) are used to determine a multiemployer plan's current liability for purposes of applying the rules of section 431(c)(6). A multiemployer plan is permitted to apply either the static mortality tables used pursuant to §1.430(h)(3)-1(a)(3) or generational mortality tables used pursuant to §1.430(h)(3)-1(a)(4) for this purpose. However, for this purpose, a multiemployer plan is not permitted to use substitute mortality tables under §1.430(h)(3)-2.

(b) *Effective/applicability date.*—This section applies for plan years beginning on or after January 1, 2008. [Reg. §1.431(c)(6)-1.]

☐ [T.D. 9419, 7-30-2008.]

⫸→ Caution: Reg. §1.431(c)(6)-1, below, as amended by T.D. 9826, is generally applicable to plans years beginning on or after January 1, 2018.

[Reg. §1.431(c)(6)-1]

§1.431(c)(6)-1. Mortality tables used to determine current liability.—(a) *Mortality tables used to determine current liability.*—The mortality assumptions that apply to a defined benefit plan for the plan year pursuant to section 430(h)(3)(A) and §1.430(h)(3)-1(a) are used to determine a multiemployer plan's current liability for purposes of applying the rules of section 431(c)(6). Either the generational mortality tables used pursuant to §1.430(h)(3)-1(a)(2) or the static mortality tables used pursuant to §1.430(h)(3)-1(a)(3) may be used for a multiemployer plan for this purpose. However, for this purpose, substitute mortality tables under §1.430(h)(3)-2 may not be used for a multiemployer plan.

(b) *Effective/applicability date.*—This section applies for plan years beginning on or after January 1, 2018. For rules that apply to plan years beginning before January 1, 2018 and on or after January 1, 2008, see §1.431(c)(6)-1 (as contained in 26 CFR part 1 revised April 1, 2015). [Reg. §1.431(c)(6)-1.]

☐ [T.D. 9419, 7-30-2008. Amended by T.D. 9826, 10-3-2017.]

[Reg. §1.432(e)(9)-1]

§1.432(e)(9)-1. Benefit suspensions for multiemployer plans in critical and declining status.—(a) *General rules on suspension of benefits.*—(1) *General rule.*—Subject to section 432(e)(9)(B) through (I) and this section, the plan sponsor of a multiemployer plan that is in critical and declining status (within the meaning of section 432(b)(6)) for a plan year may, by plan amendment adopted in the plan year, implement a suspension of benefits that the plan sponsor deems appropriate. Such an amendment is permitted notwithstanding the anti-cutback provisions of section 411(d)(6). As amended, the terms of the plan must satisfy the requirements of section 401(a).

(2) *Adoption of plan terms inconsistent with suspension requirements.*—(i) *General rule.*—A plan may implement (or continue to implement) a reduction of benefits pursuant to a suspension of benefits only if the terms of the plan are consistent with the requirements of section 432(e)(9) and this section.

(ii) *Changes in level of suspension.*—(A) *Phased-in suspension.*—A plan's terms are consistent with the requirements of section 432(e)(9) even if the plan provides that, instead of a suspension of benefits occurring in full on a specified effective date, the amount of a suspension will phase in or otherwise change in a definite, pre-determined manner as of a specified future effective date or dates.

(B) *Level of suspension contingent on future events.*—Except as otherwise provided in this paragraph (a)(2)(ii), a plan's terms are inconsistent with the requirements of section 432(e)(9) if they provide that the amount of a suspension will change contingent upon the occurrence of any other specified future event, condition, or development. For example, a plan is not permitted to provide that an additional or larger suspension of benefits is triggered if the plan's funded status deteriorates. Similarly, a plan is not permitted to provide that a suspension of benefits is decreased if the plan's funded status improves (except upon a failure to satisfy the annual plan sponsor determinations requirement of paragraph (c)(4) of this section).

(C) *Level of suspension contingent on future status of individual.*—A plan's terms are not inconsistent with the requirements of section 432(e)(9) merely because they provide that, for a participant who has not commenced benefits before the effective date of the suspension, the amount of the suspension will change upon the occurrence of a specified future event, condition or development (such as retirement, death, or disability) with respect to the participant.

(3) *Organization of the regulation.*—This paragraph (a) contains definitions and general rules relating to a suspension of benefits by a multiemployer plan under section 432(e)(9). Paragraph (b) of this section defines a suspension of benefits and describes the length of a suspension, the treatment of beneficiaries and alternate payees under this section, and the requirement to select a retiree representative. Paragraph (c) of this section prescribes certain rules for the actuarial certification and plan sponsor determinations that must be made in order for a plan to suspend benefits. Paragraph (d) of this section describes certain limitations on suspensions of benefits. Paragraph (e) of this section prescribes rules relating to benefit improvements. Paragraph (f) of this section describes the requirement to provide notice in connection with an application to suspend benefits. Paragraph (g) of this section describes certain requirements with respect to the approval or denial of an application for a suspension of benefits. Paragraph (h) of this section contains certain rules relating to the vote on an approved suspension systemically important plans, and the issuance of a final authorization to suspend benefits. Paragraph (j) of this section provides the effective/applicability date of this section.

(4) *Definitions.*—The following definitions apply for purposes of this section—

(i) *Pay status.*—A person is in pay status under a multiemployer plan if, as described in section 432(j)(6), at any time during the current plan year, the person is a participant, beneficiary, or alternate payee under the plan and is paid an early, late, normal, or disability retirement benefit under the plan (or a death benefit under the plan related to a retirement benefit).

(ii) *Plan sponsor.*—The term plan sponsor means the association, committee, joint board of trustees, or other similar group of representatives of the parties that establishes or maintains the multiemployer plan. However, in the case of a plan described in section 404(c), or a continuation of such a plan, the term plan sponsor means the association of employers that is the employer settlor of the plan.

(iii) *Effective date of suspension of benefits.*—(A) *Individuals who are receiving benefits.*—In the case of a suspension affecting an individual who is receiving benefits when the suspension is implemented, the effective date of a suspension of benefits is the first date as of which any portion of the individual's benefits are not paid as a result of the suspension.

(B) *Individuals who are not receiving benefits.*—In the case of a suspension affecting individuals other than individuals described in paragraph (a)(4)(iii)(A) of this section, the effective date of the suspension is the first date as of which the individual's entitlement to benefits is reduced as a result of the implementation of the suspension, regardless of whether the individual is eligible to commence benefits at that date.

(C) *Phased-in suspension.*—If a suspension of benefits provides for more than one reduction in benefits over time, such that benefits are scheduled to be reduced by an additional amount after benefits are first reduced pursuant to the suspension, then each date as of which benefits are reduced is treated as a separate effective date of the suspension. However, if the effective date of the final scheduled reduction in benefits in a series of reductions pursuant to a suspension is less than three years later than the effective date of the first reduction, then the effective date of the first reduction will be treated as the effective date of all subsequent reductions pursuant to that suspension.

(D) *Effective date may not be retroactive.*—The effective date of a suspension may not precede the date on which a final authorization to suspend benefits is issued pursuant to paragraph (h)(6) of this section.

(b) *Definition of suspension of benefits and related rules.*—(1) *In general.*—(i) *Definition.*—For purposes of this section, the term suspension of benefits means the temporary or permanent reduction, pursuant to the terms of the plan, of any current or future payment obligation of the plan with respect to any plan participant. A suspension of benefits may apply with respect to a plan participant regardless of whether the participant, beneficiary, or alternate payee commenced receiving benefits before the effective date of the suspension of benefits.

(ii) *Plan not liable for suspended benefits.*—If a plan pays a reduced level of benefits pursuant to a suspension of benefits that complies with the requirements of section 432(e)(9) and this section, then the plan is not liable for any benefits not paid as a result of the suspension.

(2) *Length of suspension.*—(i) *In general.*—A suspension of benefits may be of indefinite duration or may expire as of a date that is specified in the plan amendment implementing the suspension.

(ii) *Effect of a benefit improvement.*—A plan sponsor may amend the plan to eliminate some or all of a suspension of benefits, provided that the amendment satisfies the requirements that apply to a benefit improvement under section 432(e)(9)(E), in accordance with the rules of paragraph (e) of this section.

(3) *Treatment of beneficiaries and alternate payees.*—Except as otherwise specified in this section, all references to suspensions of benefits, increases in benefits, or resumptions of suspended benefits with respect to participants also apply with respect to benefits of beneficiaries or alternate payees (as defined in section 414(p)(8)) of participants.

(4) *Retiree representative.*—(i) *In general.*—(A) *Requirement to select retiree representative.*—The plan sponsor of a plan that intends to submit an application for a suspension of benefits and that has reported a total of 10,000 or more participants as of the end of the plan year for the most recently filed Form 5500, Annual Return/ Report of Employee Benefit Plan, must select a retiree representative. The plan sponsor must select the retiree representative at least 60 days before the date the plan sponsor submits an application to suspend benefits. The retiree representative must be a plan participant who is in pay status. The retiree representative may or may not be a plan trustee.

(B) *Role of retiree representative.*—The role of the retiree representative is to advocate for the interests of the retired and deferred vested participants and beneficiaries of the plan, beginning when the retiree representative is selected and continuing throughout the suspension approval process. In the discretion of the plan sponsor, the retiree representative may continue in this role throughout the period of the benefit suspension.

(ii) *Reasonable expenses from plan.*—The plan must pay reasonable expenses incurred by the retiree representative, including reasonable expenses for legal and actuarial support and communication with retired and deferred vested participants and beneficiaries, commensurate with the plan's size and funded status.

(iii) *Disclosure of information.*—Upon request, the plan sponsor must promptly provide the retiree representative with relevant information, such as plan documents and data, that is reasonably necessary to enable the retiree representative to perform the role described in paragraph (b)(4)(i)(B) of this section.

(iv) *Special rules relating to fiduciary status.*—See section 432(e)(9)(B)(v)(III) for rules relating to the fiduciary status of a retiree representative.

(v) *Retiree representative for other plans.*—The plan sponsor of a plan that has reported fewer than 10,000 participants as of the end of the plan year for the most recently filed Form 5500, Annual Return/ Report of Employee Benefit Plan is permitted to select a retiree representative. The rules in this paragraph (b)(4) (other than the rules in the first two sentences of paragraph (b)(4)(i)(A) of this section concerning the size of the plan and the timing of the appointment of the retiree representative) apply to such a representative.

(c) *Conditions for suspension.*—(1) *In general.*—(i) *Actuarial certification and initial plan sponsor determinations.*—The plan sponsor of a plan in critical and declining status for a plan year may suspend benefits only if the actuarial certification requirement in paragraph (c)(2) of this section and the initial plan sponsor determinations requirement in paragraph (c)(3) of this section are met.

(ii) *Annual requirement to make plan sponsor determinations.*—As provided in paragraph (c)(5) of this section, the suspension will continue only if the plan sponsor continues to make the annual plan sponsor determinations described in paragraph (c)(4) of this section.

(2) *Actuarial certification.*—A plan satisfies the actuarial certification requirement of this paragraph (c)(2) if, taking into account the proposed suspension of benefits (and, if applicable, a proposed partition of the plan under section 4233 of the Employee Retirement Income Security Act of 1974, Public Law 93-406 (88 Stat. 829 (1974)), as amended (ERISA)), the plan's actuary certifies that the plan is projected to avoid insolvency within the meaning of section 418E, assuming the suspension of benefits continues until it expires by its own terms or if no such expiration date is set, indefinitely.

(3) *Initial plan sponsor determinations.*—(i) *General rule.*—A plan satisfies the initial plan sponsor determinations requirement of this paragraph (c)(3) only if the plan sponsor determines that—
(A) All reasonable measures to avoid insolvency, within the meaning of section 418E, have been taken; and
(B) The plan would not be projected to avoid insolvency (determined using the standards described in paragraphs (d)(5)(ii), (iv), and (v) of this section) if no suspension of benefits were applied under the plan.

(ii) *Factors.*—In making its determination that all reasonable measures to avoid insolvency, within the meaning of section 418E, have been taken, the plan sponsor may take into account the following non-exclusive list of factors—
(A) Current and past contribution levels;
(B) Levels of benefit accruals (including any prior reductions in the rate of benefit accruals);
(C) Prior reductions (if any) of adjustable benefits;
(D) Prior suspensions (if any) of benefits under this section;
(E) The impact on plan solvency of the subsidies and ancillary benefits available to active participants;
(F) Compensation levels of active participants relative to employees in the participants' industry generally;
(G) Competitive and other economic factors facing contributing employers;
(H) The impact of benefit and contribution levels on retaining active participants and bargaining groups under the plan;
(I) The impact of past and anticipated contribution increases under the plan on employer attrition and retention levels; and
(J) Measures undertaken by the plan sponsor to retain or attract contributing employers.

(iii) *Reliance on certification of critical and declining status.*—For purposes of the insolvency projection under paragraph (c)(3)(i)(B) of this section, a plan sponsor may rely on the actuarial certification made pursuant to section 432(b)(3)(A)(i) that the plan is in critical and declining status for the plan year in making the determination that the plan is projected to become insolvent unless benefits are suspended.

(4) *Annual plan sponsor determinations.*—(i) *General rule.*—A plan satisfies the annual plan sponsor determinations requirement of this paragraph (c)(4) for a plan year only if the plan sponsor determines, no later than the last day of the plan year, that—
(A) All reasonable measures to avoid insolvency have been and continue to be taken; and

(B) The plan would not be projected to avoid insolvency (determined using the standards described in paragraphs (d)(5)(ii), (iv), and (v) of this section, substituting the current plan year for the plan year that includes the effective date of the suspension) if no suspension of benefits were applied under the plan.

(ii) *Factors.*—In making its determination that all reasonable measures to avoid insolvency have been and continue to be taken, the plan sponsor may take into account the non-exclusive list of factors in paragraph (c)(3)(ii) of this section.

(iii) *Requirement to maintain written record.*—The plan sponsor must maintain a written record of the annual plan sponsor determinations made under this paragraph (c)(4). The written record must be included in an update to the rehabilitation plan, whether or not there is otherwise an update for that year (or, if the plan is no longer in critical status, must be included in the documents under which the plain is maintained). The written record of the determinations must describe the plan sponsor's consideration of factors, as described in paragraph (c)(4)(ii) of this section.

(5) *Failure to make annual plan sponsor determinations.*—If a plan sponsor fails to satisfy the annual plan sponsor determinations requirement of paragraph (c)(4) of this section for a plan year (including maintaining the written record described in paragraph (c)(4)(iii) of this section), then the suspension of benefits will cease to be in effect beginning as of the first day of the next plan year.

(d) *Limitations on suspension.*—(1) *In general.*—Any suspension of benefits with respect to a participant made by a plan sponsor pursuant to this section is subject to the individual limitations of sections 432(e)(9)(D)(i) through (iii) and paragraphs (d)(2) through (d)(4) of this section. After applying those provisions, the overall size and distribution of the suspension is subject to the aggregate limitations of sections 432(e)(9)(D)(iv) and (vi) and paragraphs (d)(5) and (d)(6) of this section. See section 432(e)(9)(D)(vii) and paragraph (d)(8) of this section for additional rules applicable to certain plans.

(2) *Guarantee-based limitation.*—(i) *General rule.*—The reduction with respect to a participant under a suspension of benefits must be limited so that, on and after the effective date of the suspension, the monthly benefit is not less than the guarantee-based limitation. The guarantee-based limitation is 110 percent of the monthly benefit payable to a participant, beneficiary, or alternate payee that would be guaranteed by the Pension Benefit Guaranty Corporation (PBGC) under section 4022A of ERISA if the plan were to become insolvent as of the effective date of the suspension.

(ii) *PBGC guarantee.*—Under section 4022A of ERISA, the monthly benefit of a participant or beneficiary that would be guaranteed by PBGC with respect to a plan if the plan were to become insolvent as of the effective date of the suspension is generally based on section 4022A(c)(1) of ERISA. Under that section, the monthly benefit that would be guaranteed if the plan were to become insolvent as of the date as of which the guarantee is determined is the product of—

(A) 100 percent of the accrual rate up to $11, plus 75 percent of the lesser of—

(1) $33; or

(2) The accrual rate, if any, in excess of $11; and

(B) The number of the participant's years and months of credited service as of that date.

(iii) *Calculation of accrual rate.*—The accrual rate, as defined in section 4022A(c)(2) of ERISA, is calculated by dividing—

(A) The participant's or beneficiary's monthly benefit, described in section 4022A(c)(2)(A) of ERISA; by

(B) The participant's years of credited service, described in section 4022A(c)(3) of ERISA, as of the effective date of the suspension.

(iv) *Special rule for non-vested participants.*—For purposes of this paragraph (d)(2), a participant's nonforfeitable benefits under section 4022A(a) of ERISA include benefits that are forfeitable as of the effective date of the suspension, provided that the participant would have a nonforfeitable right to those benefits if the participant continued to earn vesting service following that date.

(v) *Examples.*—The following examples illustrate the limitation on a suspension of benefits under this paragraph (d)(2). Unless otherwise stated, the amount of guarantee payable by PBGC in these examples is based on section 4022A(c) of ERISA, and the rules under section 4022A(d) of ERISA (guarantee for benefits reduced under section 411(a)(3)(E)), section 4022A(e) of ERISA (benefits ineligible for guarantee), and section 4022A(h) of ERISA (guarantee for benefits accrued as of July 30, 1980) do not apply. In these examples, unless otherwise stated, the monthly benefits are nonforfeitable, are based on benefits that have been in effect for at least 60 months as of the

effective date of the suspension, and are no greater than the monthly benefit that would be payable at normal retirement age in the form of a single life annuity.

Example 1. (i) *Facts.* A participant is receiving a benefit of $1,500 per month immediately prior to the effective date of the suspension. The participant has 30 years of credited service under the plan.

(ii) *Calculation of accrual rate.* The participant's accrual rate is $50, calculated by dividing the participant's monthly benefit payment ($1,500) by the participant's years of credited service (30).

(iii) *Calculation of monthly PBGC-guaranteed benefit.* The first $11 of the accrual rate is fully guaranteed, and the next $33 of the accrual rate is 75% guaranteed ($33 x .75 = $24.75). The participant's monthly guaranteed benefit per year of credited service is $35.75 ($11 + $24.75 = $35.75). The PBGC guarantee formula is then applied to produce the amount of guarantee payable by PBGC, which is $1,072.50 ($35.75 x 30 years = $1,072.50).

(iv) *Calculation of guarantee-based limitation.* A suspension of benefits may not reduce the participant's benefits, determined on and after the effective date of the suspension, below the guarantee-based limitation, which is equal to 110% of the amount of guarantee payable by PBGC. That monthly amount is $1,179.75 ($1,072.50 x 1.1 = $1,179.75).

Example 2. (i) *Facts.* The facts are the same as in *Example 1*, except that the participant is deceased and, immediately prior to the effective date of the suspension, the participant's beneficiary is receiving a monthly benefit of $750 under a 50% joint and survivor annuity.

(ii) *Calculation of accrual rate.* The beneficiary's accrual rate is $25, calculated by dividing the beneficiary's monthly benefit payment ($750) by the participant's years of credited service (30).

(iii) *Calculation of monthly PBGC-guaranteed benefit.* The first $11 of the accrual rate is fully guaranteed, and the next $14 ($25 - $11 = $14) of the accrual rate is 75% guaranteed ($14 x .75 = $10.50). The beneficiary's monthly guaranteed benefit is $21.50 per year of credited service ($11 + $10.50 = $21.50). The PBGC guarantee formula is then applied to produce the amount of guarantee payable by PBGC, which is $645 ($21.50 x 30 years = $645).

(iv) *Calculation of guarantee-based limitation.* A suspension of benefits may not reduce the beneficiary's benefits, determined on and after the effective date of the suspension, below the guarantee-based limitation, which is equal to 110% of the monthly amount of guarantee payable by PBGC. That monthly guarantee-based limitation amount is $709.50 ($645 x 1.1 = $709.50).

Example 3. (i) *Facts.* A participant would be eligible for a monthly benefit of $1,000 payable as a single life annuity at normal retirement age, based on the participant's 25 years of credited service. The plan also permits a participant to receive a benefit on an unreduced basis as a single life annuity at a particular early retirement age and permits participants to receive an early retirement benefit beginning at that age in the form of a social security level income option. The participant has elected the social security level income option under which the participant receives a monthly benefit of $1,600 prior to normal retirement age (which is the plan's assumed social security retirement age) and $900 after normal retirement age.

(ii) *Calculation of accrual rate.* For purposes of calculating the accrual rate, the monthly benefit that is used to calculate the PBGC guarantee does not exceed the monthly benefit of $1,000 that would be payable at normal retirement age. In calculating the accrual rate, the amount of guarantee payable by PBGC would be based on a monthly benefit of $1,000 prior to normal retirement age and $900 after normal retirement age. Before normal retirement age, the participant's accrual rate is $40, determined by dividing the participant's monthly benefit payment ($1,000) by years of credited service (25). After normal retirement age, the participant's accrual rate is $36, calculated by dividing the participant's monthly benefit payment ($900) by the participant's years of credited service (25).

(iii) *Calculation of monthly PBGC-guaranteed benefit.* Before normal retirement age, the first $11 of the accrual rate is fully guaranteed, and the next $29 of the accrual rate is 75% guaranteed ($29 x .75 = $21.75). The participant's monthly guaranteed benefit per year of credited service is $32.75 ($11 + $21.75 = $32.75). The PBGC guarantee formula is then applied to produce the amount of guarantee payable by PBGC, which is $818.75 ($32.75 x 25 years = $818.75). After normal retirement age, the first $11 of the accrual rate is fully guaranteed, and the next $25 of the accrual rate is 75% guaranteed ($25 x .75 = $18.75). The participant's monthly guaranteed benefit per year of credited service is $29.75 ($11 + $18.75 = $29.75). The PBGC guarantee formula is then applied to produce the amount of guarantee payable by PBGC, which is $743.75 after normal retirement age ($29.75 x 25 years = $743.75).

(iv) *Calculation of guarantee-based limitation.* A suspension of benefits may not reduce the participant's benefits, determined on and after the effective date of the suspension, below the guarantee-based limitation, which is equal to 110% of the monthly amount of guarantee payable by PBGC. That monthly guarantee-based limitation amount is $900.63 ($818.75 x 1.1 = $900.63) before normal retirement age and $818.13 ($743.75 x 1.1 = $818.13) after normal retirement age.

Example 4. (i) *Facts.* A participant would be eligible for a monthly benefit of $1,000 payable as a single life annuity at normal retirement age, based on the participant's 20 years of credited service. The plan provides an actuarial increase for delaying benefits until after normal retirement age. The participant delays commencement of benefits until after normal retirement age and the monthly benefit the participant is receiving immediately before the effective date of the suspension is $1,200 instead of $1,000.

(ii) *Calculation of accrual rate.* For purposes of calculating the accrual rate, the monthly benefit that is used to calculate the PBGC guarantee does not exceed the monthly benefit of $1,000 that would be payable at normal retirement age. Thus, in determining the accrual rate, the PBGC guarantee would be based on a monthly benefit of $1,000, whether benefits are paid at or after normal retirement age. The participant's accrual rate is $50, calculated by dividing the participant's monthly benefit payment ($1,000) by the participant's years of credited service (20).

(iii) *Calculation of monthly PBGC-guaranteed benefit.* The first $11 of the accrual rate is fully guaranteed, and the next $33 of the accrual rate is 75% guaranteed ($33 x .75 = $24.75). The participant's monthly guaranteed benefit per year of credited service is $35.75 ($11 + $24.75 = $35.75). The PBGC guarantee formula is then applied to produce the amount of guarantee payable by PBGC, which is $715 ($35.75 x 20 years = $715).

(iv) *Calculation of guarantee-based limitation.* A suspension of benefits may not reduce the participant's benefits, determined on and after the effective date of the suspension, below the guarantee-based limitation, which is equal to 110% of the monthly amount of guarantee payable by PBGC. That monthly guarantee-based limitation amount is $786.50 ($715 x 1.1 = $786.50).

Example 5. (i) *Facts.* A plan provides that a participant who has completed at least five years of service will have a nonforfeitable right to 100% of an accrued benefit (and will not have a nonforfeitable right to any portion of the accrued benefit prior to completing five years of service). The plan implements a suspension of benefits on January 1, 2017. As of that date, a participant has three years of vesting service, and none of the participant's benefits are nonforfeitable under the terms of the plan.

(ii) *Calculation of nonforfeitable benefits.* For purposes of applying the guarantee-based limitation, the participant is considered to have a nonforfeitable right to 100% of the accrued benefit under the plan as of January 1, 2017.

(3) *Age-based limitation.*—(i) *No suspension for participants or beneficiaries who are age 80 and older.*—Pursuant to the age-based limitation of this paragraph (d)(3), no suspension of benefits is permitted to apply to a participant or beneficiary who—

(A) Has commenced benefits as of the effective date of the suspension; and

(B) Has attained 80 years of age no later than the end of the month that includes the effective date of the suspension.

(ii) *Limited suspension for participants and beneficiaries between ages 75 and 80.*—Pursuant to the age-based limitation of this paragraph (d)(3), no more than the applicable percentage of the maximum suspendable benefit may be suspended for a participant or beneficiary who—

(A) Has commenced benefits as of the effective date of the suspension; and

(B) Has attained 75 years of age no later than the end of the month that includes the effective date of the suspension.

(iii) *Maximum suspendable benefit.*—(A) *In general.*—For purposes of this paragraph (d)(3), the maximum suspendable benefit with respect to a participant, beneficiary, or alternate payee is the portion of the individual's benefits that would otherwise be suspended pursuant to this section (that is, the amount that would be suspended without regard to the limitation of this paragraph (d)(3)).

(B) *Coordination of limitations.*—An individual's maximum suspendable benefit is calculated after the application of the guarantee-based limitation under paragraph (d)(2) of this section and the disability-based limitation under paragraph (d)(4) of this section.

(iv) *Applicable percentage.*—For purposes of this paragraph (d)(3), the applicable percentage is the percentage obtained by dividing—

(A) The number of months during the period beginning with the month after the month in which the suspension of benefits is effective and ending with the month during which the participant or beneficiary attains the age of 80, by

(B) 60.

(v) *Applicability of age-based limitation to benefits paid to beneficiaries.*—If the age-based limitation of this paragraph (d)(3) applies to a participant on the effective date of the suspension, then the age-based limitation also applies to the beneficiary of the participant, based on the age of the participant as of the end of the month that includes the effective date of the suspension.

(vi) *Rule for benefits that have not commenced at the time of the suspension.*—If benefits have not commenced to either a participant or beneficiary as of the effective date of the suspension, then in applying this paragraph (d)(3)—

(A) If the participant is alive on the effective date of the suspension, the participant is treated as having commenced benefits on that date; and

(B) If the participant dies before the effective date of the suspension, the beneficiary is treated as having commenced benefits on that date.

(vii) *Rules for alternate payees.*—The age-based limitation of this paragraph (d)(3) applies to a suspension of benefits in which an alternate payee has an interest, whether or not the alternate payee has commenced benefits as of the effective date of the suspension. For purposes of this paragraph (d)(3), the applicable percentage for an alternate payee is calculated by—

(A) Using the participant's age as of the end of the month that includes the effective date of the suspension, if the alternate payee's right to the suspended benefits derives from a qualified domestic relations order within the meaning of section 414(p)(1)(A) (QDRO) under which the alternate payee shares in each benefit payment but the participant retains the right to choose the time and form of payment with respect to the benefit to which the suspension applies (shared payment QDRO); or

(B) Substituting the alternate payee's age as of the end of the month that includes the effective date of the suspension for the participant's age, if the alternate payee's right to the suspended benefits derives from a QDRO under which the alternate payee has a separate right to receive a portion of the participant's retirement benefit to be paid at a time and in a form different from that chosen by the participant (separate interest QDRO).

(viii) *Examples.*—The following examples illustrate the rules of this paragraph (d)(3):

Example 1. (i) *Facts.* The plan sponsor of a plan in critical and declining status is implementing a suspension of benefits, effective December 1, 2017, that generally would reduce all benefit payments under the plan by 30%. On that date, a retiree is receiving a monthly benefit of $1,500 (which is not a benefit based on disability) and has 28 years of credited service under the plan. If none of the limitations in section 432(e)(9)(D)(i), (ii), and (iii) were to apply, a 30% suspension would reduce the retiree's monthly benefit by $450, to $1,050. Under the guarantee-based limitation in section 432(e)(9)(D)(i), the retiree's monthly benefit could not be reduced by more than $398.90, to $1,101.10 (1.1 x (28 x ($11 + (.75 x $33)))). The retiree is 77 years old on the effective date of the suspension, turns 78 on December 10, 2017, and turns 80 on December 10, 2019.

(ii) *Maximum suspendable benefit.* Because the retiree is not receiving a benefit based on disability under section 432(e)(9)(D)(iii), the retiree's maximum suspendable benefit is $398.90 (which is equal to the lesser of the amount of reduction that would apply pursuant to the 30% suspension ($450) or the amount of reduction that would be permitted under the guarantee-based limitation ($398.90)).

(iii) *Applicable percentage.* Because the retiree is between ages 75 and 80 on the effective date of the suspension, the reduction is not permitted to exceed the applicable percentage of the retiree's maximum suspendable benefit. The number of months during the period beginning with January 2018 (the month after the month that includes the effective date of the suspension) and ending with December 2019 (the month in which the retiree turns 80) is 24. The applicable percentage is equal to 40% (24 months divided by 60).

(iv) *Age-based limitation.* The retiree's maximum suspendable benefit is $398.90 and the applicable percentage is 40%. Thus, under the age-based limitation, the retiree's benefit may not be reduced by more than $159.56 ($398.90 x .40 = $159.56). Because the retiree was receiving a monthly benefit of $1,500, the suspension of benefits may not reduce the retiree's monthly benefit below $1,340.44 ($1,500 - $159.56 = $1,340.44).

Example 2. (i) *Facts.* The facts are the same as *Example 1*, except that the retiree is 79 years old on December 1, 2017, and turns 80 on December 20, 2017.

(ii) *Age-based limitation.* The suspension is not permitted to apply to the retiree because the retiree will turn 80 by the end of the month (December 2017) in which the suspension is effective.

Example 3. (i) *Facts.* The facts are the same as *Example 1*, but on the effective date of the suspension, the retiree is receiving a benefit in the form of a 50% joint and survivor annuity for himself and a contingent beneficiary who is age 71. The retiree dies in October 2018.

(ii) *Application of age-based limitation to contingent beneficiary.* Because the retiree had attained age 78 in the month that included the effective date of the suspension, the age-based limitation on the suspension of benefits for a 78-year-old individual applies to the retiree. The age-based limitation also applies to the contingent beneficiary, even though the contingent beneficiary had not commenced benefits under the plan as of the effective date of the suspension and had not attained age 75 by the end of the month containing the effective date of the suspension.

(iii) *Maximum suspendable benefit.* The contingent beneficiary's amount of guarantee payable by PBGC is based on the benefit the beneficiary would have received from the plan before the suspension ($750). The beneficiary's accrual rate is $26.7857 (calculated by dividing the monthly benefit payment ($750) by years of credited service (28)) and the beneficiary's amount of guarantee payable by PBGC is $639.50 (28 x ($11 + (.75 x $15.7857))). The beneficiary's maximum suspendable benefit is $46.55 (which is equal to the lesser of the amount of reduction that would apply pursuant to the 30% suspension ($225) or the amount of reduction that would be permitted under the guarantee-based limitation ($46.55, which is equal to ($750 − 1.1 x $639.50)).

(iv) *Applicable percentage.* The applicable percentage for the beneficiary is based on the retiree's age of 78 as of the end of the month that includes the effective date of the suspension. Accordingly, the applicable percentage for the beneficiary is 40%.

(v) *Age-based limitation.* The beneficiary's maximum suspendable benefit is $46.55 and the applicable percentage is 40%. Thus, under the age-based limitation, the beneficiary's benefit may not be reduced by more than $18.62 ($46.55 x .40 = $18.62). Therefore, as a result of the retiree's age-based limitation, the suspension of benefits may not reduce the beneficiary's monthly benefit below $731.38 ($750 - $18.62 = $731.38).

Example 4. (i) *Facts.* The facts are the same as *Example 3,* except that on the effective date of the suspension the retiree is age 71 and the retiree's contingent beneficiary is age 77.

(ii) *Application of age-based limitation to contingent beneficiary.* Because the retiree had not reached age 75 as of the end of the month that includes the effective date of the suspension, the age-based limitation on the suspension of benefits does not apply to the retiree. The age-based limitation also does not apply to the retiree's contingent beneficiary, even though the contingent beneficiary had attained age 77 as of the end of the month that includes the effective date of the suspension, because the contingent beneficiary had not yet commenced benefits on that date. The beneficiary's post-suspension benefit may not be less than the minimum benefit payable pursuant to the guarantee-based limitation, which is $703.45 ($639.50 x 1.1 = $703.45).

Example 5. (i) *Facts.* The facts are the same as in *Example 4,* except that the retiree died in October 2017, prior to the December 1, 2017 effective date of the suspension of benefits. The retiree's beneficiary commenced benefits on November 1, 2017.

(ii) *Application of age-based limitation to contingent beneficiary.* Because the retiree's beneficiary had commenced benefits before the effective date of the suspension and had reached age 75 as of the end of the month that includes the effective date of the suspension, the age-based limitation applies to the beneficiary based on the beneficiary's age as of the end of the month that includes the effective date of the suspension.

(4) *Disability-based limitation.*—(i) *General rule.*—Pursuant to the disability-based limitation of this paragraph (d)(4), benefits based on disability (as defined under the plan) may not be suspended.

(ii) *Benefits based on disability.*—(A) *In general.*—For purposes of this section, benefits based on disability means the entire amount paid to a participant pursuant to the participant becoming disabled, without regard to whether a portion of that amount would have been paid if the participant had not become disabled.

(B) *Rule for auxiliary or other temporary disability benefits.*—If a participant begins receiving an auxiliary or other temporary disability benefit and the sole reason the participant ceases receiving that benefit is commencement of retirement benefits, then the benefit based on disability after commencement of retirement benefits is the lesser of—

(1) The periodic payment the participant was receiving immediately before the participant's retirement benefits commenced; or

(2) The periodic payment to the participant of retirement benefits under the plan.

(C) *Examples.*—The following examples illustrate the disability-based limitation on a suspension of benefits under this paragraph (d)(4):

Example 1. (i) *Facts.* A participant with a vested accrued benefit of $1,000 per month, payable at age 65, becomes disabled at age 55. The plan applies a reduction to the monthly benefit for early commencement if the participant commences benefits before age 65. For a participant who commences receiving benefits at age 55, the actuarially adjusted early retirement benefit is 60% of the accrued benefit. However, the plan also provides that if a participant becomes entitled to an early retirement benefit on account of disability, as defined in the plan, the benefit is not reduced. On account of a disability, the participant commences an unreduced early retirement benefit of $1,000 per month at age 55 (instead of the $600 monthly benefit the participant would receive if the participant were not disabled). The participant continues to receive $1,000 per month after reaching age 65.

(ii) *Conclusion.* The participant's disability benefit payment of $1,000 per month commencing at age 55 is a benefit based on disability, even though the participant would have received a portion of these benefits at retirement regardless of the disability. Thus, both before and after attaining age 65, the participant's entire monthly payment amount ($1,000) is a benefit based on disability. A suspension of benefits is not permitted to apply to any portion of the participant's benefit at any time.

Example 2. (i) *Facts.* The facts are the same as *Example 1,* except that the terms of the plan provide that when a disabled participant reaches age 65, the disability pension is discontinued by reason of reaching age 65, and the retirement benefits commence. In this case, the amount of the participant's retirement benefits is the same as the amount that the participant was receiving immediately before commencing retirement benefits, or $1,000.

(ii) *Conclusion.* Before age 65, the participant's disability benefit payment of $1,000 per month commencing at age 55 is a benefit based on disability. After age 65, the periodic retirement benefit of $1,000 per month is a benefit based on disability because it does not exceed the benefit based on disability that the participant was receiving immediately before commencing retirement benefits. Thus, both before and after attaining age 65, the participant's entire monthly payment amount ($1,000) is a benefit based on disability. A suspension of benefits is not permitted to apply to any portion of the participant's benefit at any time.

Example 3. (i) *Facts.* The facts are the same as *Example 2,* except that upon reaching age 65, the participant elects to commence payment of retirement benefits not in the form of a single life annuity payable in the amount of $1,000 per month but instead in the form of an actuarially equivalent joint and survivor annuity payable in the amount of $850 per month.

(ii) *Conclusion.* Before age 65, the participant's benefit based on disability is $1,000 per month. After age 65, the participant's entire retirement benefit of $850 per month is a benefit based on disability because it does not exceed the benefit based on disability that the participant was receiving immediately before commencing retirement benefits. Thus, a suspension of benefits is not permitted to apply to any portion of those benefits at any time.

Example 4. (i) *Facts.* A participant's disability pension is a specified amount unrelated to the participant's accrued benefit. The participant's disability benefit commencing at age 55 is $750 per month. Upon reaching age 65, the participant's disability pension is discontinued by reason of reaching age 65 and the participant elects to receive an accrued benefit payable in the amount of $1,000 per month.

(ii) *Conclusion.* Before age 65, the participant's benefit based on disability is $750 per month. After age 65, the participant's benefit based on disability continues to be $750 per month (even though the participant's payment is $1,000 per month), because the benefit based on disability is the lesser of the periodic disability pension the participant was receiving immediately before retirement benefits commenced ($750) and the periodic payment of retirement benefits to the participant under the plan determined without regard to the suspension ($1,000). Thus, a suspension of benefits is not permitted to reduce the participant's benefit based on disability ($750 per month) at any time.

Example 5. (i) *Facts.* The facts are the same as *Example 2,* except that when the participant attains age 65, the participant's monthly benefit payment increases from $1,000 to $1,300 as a result of the plan providing additional accruals during the period of disability, as if the participant were not disabled.

(ii) *Conclusion.* As in *Example 2,* before age 65, the participant's benefit payment of $1,000 per month commencing at age 55 is a benefit based on disability. After age 65, the participant's benefit payment of $1,300 per month is a benefit based on disability because the $1,300 is payable based on additional accruals earned pursuant to the participant becoming disabled. Thus, both before and after attaining age 65, the participant's entire monthly payment amount is a benefit based on disability. A suspension of benefits is not permitted to apply to any portion of the participant's benefit at any time.

Example 6. (i) *Facts.* The facts are the same as *Example 3* of paragraph (d)(2)(v) of this section, except that the social security level income option is only available to a participant who incurs a disability as defined in the plan.

(ii) *Conclusion.* Before normal retirement age, the participant's benefit payment of $1,600 per month is a benefit based on disability. After normal retirement age, the participant's benefit based on disability is $900, which is the lesser of the $1,600 periodic payment that the participant was receiving immediately before the participant's normal retirement benefit commenced and the participant's $900 periodic payment of retirement benefits determined without regard to the suspension. Thus, a suspension of benefits is not permitted to apply to any portion of those benefits ($1,600 per month before and $900 per month after normal retirement age) at any time.

Example 7. (i) *Facts.* A plan applies a reduction to the monthly benefit for early commencement if a participant commences benefits before age 65. The plan also provides that if a participant becomes disabled, as defined in the plan, the benefit that is paid before normal retirement age is not reduced for early retirement. Under the plan, when a disabled participant reaches age 65, the disability pension is discontinued by reason of reaching age 65 and the retirement benefits commence. A participant with a vested accrued benefit of $1,000 per month, payable at age 65, becomes disabled at age 55. On account of the disability, the participant commences benefits at age 55 in the amount of $1,000 per month (instead of the $600 monthly benefit the participant could have received at that age if the participant were not disabled). The participant recovers from the disability at age 60, and the participant's disability benefits cease. At age 60, the participant immediately elects to begin an early retirement benefit of $800.

(ii) *Conclusion.* The participant's disability benefit payment of $1,000 per month commencing at age 55 is a benefit based on disability, even though the participant would have received a portion of these benefits at retirement regardless of the disability. Because the participant ceased receiving disability benefits on account of the participant no longer being disabled (and not solely on account of commencing retirement benefits), the participant's early retirement benefit of $800 per month that began after the disability benefit ended is not a benefit based on disability.

(5) *Limitation on aggregate size of suspension.*—(i) *General rule.*—Any suspension of benefits (considered, if applicable, in combination with a partition of the plan under section 4233 of ERISA (partition)) must be at a level that is reasonably estimated to—

(A) Enable the plan to avoid insolvency; and

(B) Not materially exceed the level that is necessary to enable the plan to avoid insolvency.

(ii) *Suspension sufficient to avoid insolvency.*—(A) *General rule.*—A suspension of benefits (considered, if applicable, in combination with a partition of the plan) will satisfy the requirement that it is at a level that is reasonably estimated to enable the plan to avoid insolvency if—

(1) For each plan year throughout an extended period (as described in paragraph (d)(5)(ii)(C) of this section) beginning on the first day of the plan year that includes the effective date of the suspension, the plan's solvency ratio is projected on a deterministic basis to be at least 1.0;

(2) Based on stochastic projections reflecting variance in investment return, the probability that the plan will avoid insolvency throughout the extended period is more than 50 percent; and

(3) Unless the plan's projected funded percentage (within the meaning of section 432(j)(2)) at the end of the extended period using the deterministic projection described in paragraph (d)(5)(ii)(A)(1) of this section exceeds 100 percent, that projection shows that, during each of the last five plan years of that period, neither the plan's solvency ratio nor its available resources (as defined in section 418E(b)(3)) is projected to decrease.

(B) *Solvency ratio.*—For purposes of this section, a plan's solvency ratio for a plan year means the ratio of—

(1) The plan's available resources (as defined in section 418E(b)(3)) for the plan year; to

(2) The scheduled benefit payments under the plan for the plan year.

(C) *Extended period.*—For purposes of this section, an extended period means a period of at least 30 plan years. However, in the case of a temporary suspension of benefits that is scheduled to cease as of a date that is more than 25 years after the effective date, the extended period must be lengthened so that it ends no earlier than five plan years after the cessation of the suspension.

(iii) *Suspension not materially in excess of level necessary to avoid insolvency.*—(A) *General rule.*—A suspension of benefits will satisfy the requirement under paragraph (d)(5)(i)(B) of this section that the

suspension be at a level that is reasonably estimated to not materially exceed the level necessary for the plan to avoid insolvency only if an alternative, similar but smaller suspension of benefits would not be sufficient to enable the plan to satisfy the requirement to avoid insolvency under paragraph (d)(5)(i)(A) of this section (determined using an extended period that is no shorter than the extended period used to satisfy the requirements of paragraph (d)(5)(i)(A) of this section). The alternative suspension of benefits that is used for this purpose is a suspension of benefits under which, for each participant or beneficiary, the amount of the reduction in the periodic payment (determined after application of the individual limitations) is equal to the amount of the reduction proposed for that participant or beneficiary in the application submitted pursuant to paragraph (g) of this section, decreased (but not below zero) by the greater of—

(1) Five percent of the amount of the reduction in the periodic payment proposed for that participant or beneficiary; or

(2) Two percent of the amount of the participant's or beneficiary's periodic payment determined without regard to the reduction proposed in the application.

(B) *Special rule for partitions.*—If PBGC issues an order partitioning the plan, then a suspension of benefits with respect to the plan will be deemed to satisfy the requirement under paragraph (d)(5)(i)(B) of this section that the suspension be at a level that is reasonably estimated to not materially exceed the level necessary for the plan to avoid insolvency.

(iv) *Actuarial basis for projections.*—(A) *In general.*—This paragraph (d)(5)(iv) sets forth rules for the actuarial projections that are required under this paragraph (d)(5). The projections must reflect the assumption that the suspension of benefits continues indefinitely (or, if the suspension expires on a specified date by its own terms, until that date).

(B) *Reasonable actuarial assumptions and methods.*—Each of the actuarial assumptions and methods used for the actuarial projections that are required under this paragraph (d)(5), and the combination of those actuarial assumptions and methods, must be reasonable, taking into account the experience of the plan and reasonable expectations. To be reasonable, the actuarial assumptions and methods must also be appropriate for the purpose of the measurement (this means that factors specific to the measurements must be taken into account). The actuary's selection of assumptions about future covered employment and contribution levels (including contribution base units and average contribution rate) may be based on information provided by the plan sponsor, which must act in good faith in providing the information. In addition, to the extent that an actuarial assumption used for the deterministic projection in paragraph (d)(5)(ii)(A)(1) of this section differs from that used to certify whether the plan is in critical and declining status pursuant to section 432(b)(3)(B)(iv), an explanation of the information and analysis that led to the selection of that different assumption must be provided. Similarly, to the extent that an actuarial assumption used for the stochastic projection in paragraph (d)(5)(ii)(A)(2) of this section differs from that used for the deterministic projection, an explanation of the information and analysis that led to the selection of that different assumption must be provided.

(C) *Initial value of plan assets and cash flow projections.*—Except as provided in paragraph (d)(5)(iv)(D) of this section, the cash flow projections must be based on—

(1) The fair market value of plan assets as of the end of the calendar quarter immediately preceding the date the application is submitted;

(2) Projected benefit payments that are consistent with the projected benefit payments under the most recent actuarial valuation; and

(3) Appropriate adjustments to projected benefit payments to include benefits for new hires who are reflected in the projected contribution amounts.

(D) *Requirement to reflect significant events.*—The projected cash flows relating to contributions, withdrawal liability payments, and benefit payments must also be adjusted to reflect significant events that occurred after the most recent actuarial valuation. Significant events include—

(1) A plan merger or transfer;

(2) The withdrawal or the addition of employers that changed projected cash flows relating to contributions, withdrawal liability payments, or benefit payments by more than five percent;

(3) A plan amendment, a change in a collective bargaining agreement, or a change in a rehabilitation plan that changed projected cash flows relating to contributions, withdrawal liability payments, or benefit payments by more than five percent; or

(4) Any other event or trend that resulted in a material change in those projected cash flows.

Reg. §1.432(e)(9)-1(d)(5)(i)

(v) *Simplified determination for smaller plans.*—In the case of a plan that is not large enough to be required to select a retiree representative under paragraph (b)(4) of this section, the determination of whether the benefit suspension (or a benefit suspension in combination with a partition of the plan) will satisfy the requirement that it is at a level that is reasonably estimated to enable the plan to avoid insolvency is permitted to be made without regard to paragraph (d)(5)(ii)(A)(2) of this section.

(vi) *Additional disclosure.*—(A) *Disclosure of past experience for critical assumptions.*—The application for suspension must include a disclosure of the total contributions, total contribution base units and average contribution rate, withdrawal liability payments, and the rate of return on plan assets for each of the 10 plan years preceding the plan year in which the application is submitted.

(B) *Sensitivity of results to investment return assumptions.*— The application must include deterministic projections of the plan's solvency ratio over the extended period using two alternative assumptions for the plan's rate of return. These alternatives are that the plan's future rate of return will be lower than the assumed rate of return used under paragraph (d)(5)(iv)(B) of this section by—

(1) One percentage point; and

(2) Two percentage points.

(C) *Sensitivity of results to industry level assumptions.*—The application must include deterministic projections of the plan's solvency ratio over the extended period using two alternative assumptions for future contribution base units. These alternatives are that future contribution base units—

(1) Continue under the same trend as the plan experienced over the past 10 years; and

(2) Continue under the trend identified in paragraph (d)(5)(vi)(C)(1) of this section reduced by one percentage point.

(D) *Projection of funded percentage.*—The application must include an illustration, prepared on a deterministic basis, of the projected value of plan assets, the accrued liability of the plan (calculated using the unit credit funding method), and the funded percentage for each year in the extended period.

(E) *Permitted simplification of certain projections.*—It is permissible for the projections described in paragraph (d)(5)(vi)(C) of this section to be made without reflecting any adjustments to the projected benefit payments that result from the alternative assumptions regarding future contribution base units.

(6) *Equitable distribution.*—(i) *In general.*—Any suspension of benefits must be equitably distributed across the participant and beneficiary population, taking into account factors, with respect to participants and beneficiaries and their benefits, that may include one or more of the factors described in paragraph (d)(6)(ii) of this section. If a suspension of benefits provides for different treatment for different participants and beneficiaries (other than as a result of application of the individual limitations), then the suspension of benefits is equitably distributed across the participant and beneficiary population only if—

(A) Under the suspension, the participants and beneficiaries are divided into separate categories or groups that are defined by the consistent treatment of individuals within each separate category or group;

(B) Any difference in treatment under the suspension of benefits among the different categories or groups is based on relevant factors reasonably selected by the plan sponsor, such as the factors described in paragraph (d)(6)(ii) of this section; and

(C) Any such difference in treatment is based on a reasonable application of those relevant factors.

(ii) *Factors that may be considered.*—(A) *In general.*—In accordance with paragraph (d)(6)(i)(B) and (C) of this section, if, under the suspension, there is any difference between the treatment of one category or group of participants and beneficiaries and another category or group of participants and beneficiaries, that difference must be based on a reasonable application of relevant statutory factors described in paragraph (d)(6)(ii)(B) of this section and any other factors reasonably selected by the plan sponsor. For example, it would be reasonable for a plan sponsor to conclude that the statutory factor described in paragraph (d)(6)(ii)(B)(3) of this section (amount of benefit) is a factor that should be taken into account as justifying a lesser benefit reduction for participants or beneficiaries whose benefits are closer to the level of the PBGC guarantee than for others. In addition, it would be reasonable for a plan sponsor to conclude that the presumed financial vulnerability of certain participants or beneficiaries who are reasonably deemed to be in greater need of protection than other participants or beneficiaries is a factor that should be taken into account as justifying a lesser benefit reduction (as a

percentage or otherwise) for those participants or beneficiaries than for others.

(B) *Statutory factors.*—Factors that may be selected as a basis for differences in treatment under a suspension of benefits include, when reasonable under the circumstances, the following statutory factors:

(1) The age and life expectancy of the participant or beneficiary;

(2) The length of time that benefits have been in pay status;

(3) The amount of benefits;

(4) The type of benefit, such as survivor benefit, normal retirement benefit, or early retirement benefit;

(5) The extent to which a participant or beneficiary is receiving a subsidized benefit;

(6) The extent to which a participant or beneficiary has received post-retirement benefit increases;

(7) The history of benefit increases and reductions for participants and beneficiaries;

(8) The number of years to retirement for active employees;

(9) Any differences between active and retiree benefits;

(10) The extent to which active participants are reasonably likely to withdraw support for the plan, accelerating employer withdrawals from the plan and increasing the risk of additional benefit reductions for participants in and out of pay status; and

(11) The extent to which a participant's or beneficiary's benefits are attributable to service with an employer that failed to pay its full withdrawal liability.

(iii) *Reasonable application of factors.*—An application of a factor referred to in paragraph (d)(6)(ii) of this section is unreasonable if it is inconsistent with the protections provided by the individual limitations described in paragraphs (d)(2) through (d)(4) of this section. For example, it would constitute an unreasonable application of the factor described in paragraph (d)(6)(ii)(B)(3) of this section (amount of benefit) if that factor were used to justify a larger suspension for participants whose benefits are closer to the guarantee-based limitation. Similarly, it would constitute an unreasonable application of the factors described in paragraph (d)(6)(ii)(B)(1) of this section (age and life expectancy of the participant or beneficiary) if those factors were used to justify a greater suspension for older participants.

(iv) *Special rule for identification of categories or groups.*— (A) *New post-suspension benefit formula.*—This paragraph (d)(6)(iv) applies in the case of a proposed suspension of benefits under which an individual's benefits after suspension are calculated under a new benefit formula (rather than by reference to the individual's benefits before suspension). In this case, the evaluation of whether the proposed suspension is equitably distributed across the participant and beneficiary population is based on a comparison of an individual's pre-suspension benefit to the individual's post-suspension benefit (determined without regard to the application of the individual limitations). Accordingly, all individuals whose pre-suspension benefits are determined under a uniform pre-suspension benefit formula and whose post-suspension benefits are determined under a different uniform post-suspension benefit formula are treated as a single group.

(B) *Blended pre-suspension benefit formula.*—If a plan applies different pre-suspension benefit formulas with respect to different plan years, then all individuals to whom more than one such formula applied may be treated as having a uniform pre-suspension benefit formula for purposes of paragraph (d)(6)(iv)(A) of this section (even though those individuals have different proportions of their pre-suspension benefits calculated under the different benefit formulas).

(C) *Changes in early retirement factors.*—For purposes of paragraph (d)(6)(iv)(A) of this section, two individuals are not treated as having different pre-suspension or post-suspension benefit formulas merely because, as a result of the application of a uniform set of early retirement factors, their benefits differ because of retirement at different ages.

(v) *Examples.*—The following examples illustrate the rules on equitable distribution of a suspension of benefits of this paragraph (d)(6). As a simplifying assumption for purposes of these examples, it is assumed that the facts of each example describe all of the factors that are included in the application discussed in the example (provided, however, that, in the case of a plan described in section 432(e)(9)(D)(vii), the examples are not intended to illustrate the application of section 432(e)(9)(D)(vii) or its effect on the analysis or conclusions in the examples).

Example 1. (i) *Facts.* The plan sponsor applies for approval of a suspension of benefits on March 15, 2017. Under the plan terms applicable prior to the suspension, one group of participants benefitted only under Benefit Formula A and the remaining participants benefitted only under Benefit Formula B. Each of these benefit formulas is uniform. Under the suspension of benefits, subject to the individual limitations on benefit suspensions, benefits for all participants are reduced so that a uniform post-suspension benefit formula (Benefit Formula C) applies to all participants.

(ii) *Conclusion*. Because the reduction in benefits under the suspension formula is different for participants who benefitted only under Benefit Formula A than for participants who benefitted only under Benefit Formula B, the suspension of benefits provides for different treatment for different participants and beneficiaries (other than as a result of application of the individual limitations). In addition, the suspension of benefits provides for consistent treatment of participants within the following two categories: (1) participants who benefitted only under Benefit Formula A; and (2) participants who benefitted only under Benefit Formula B. Therefore, pursuant to paragraph (d)(6)(iv)(A) of this section, these two categories of participants are each treated as a single group for purposes of evaluating whether the proposed suspension is equitably distributed across the participant and beneficiary population. In order to demonstrate that the distribution of the suspension satisfies the equitable distribution requirement, the plan sponsor must reasonably select and apply factors that are the basis for the different treatment of these two groups of participants.

Example 2. (i) *Facts*. The facts are the same as in *Example 1*, except that the plan terms applicable prior to the suspension did not provide for different benefit formulas for different groups of participants at any given time. Instead, the plan terms provided that different uniform benefit formulas applied for service prior to January 1, 2000, and for service on or after January 1, 2000.

(ii) *Conclusion*. The reduction in benefits under the suspension formula is different for participants who had service only prior to January 1, 2000, participants who had service only after January 1, 2000, and participants who had service during both of those periods. The suspension of benefits provides for different treatment for different participants and beneficiaries (other than as a result of application of the individual limitations). In addition, the suspension of benefits provides for consistent treatment of participants within the following three categories of participants: (1) participants whose entire service was prior to January 1, 2000, (2) participants whose entire service was on or after January 1, 2000, and (3) participants who have some service before January 1, 2000 and some service on or after January 1, 2000. Therefore, pursuant to paragraph (d)(6)(iv)(A) of this section, the two categories of participants whose entire service was either before or on or after January 1, 2000 are each treated as a single group for purposes of evaluating whether the proposed suspension is equitably distributed across the participant and beneficiary population. In addition, pursuant to paragraph (d)(6)(iv)(B) of this section, the category of participants with some service before January 1, 2000 and some service on or after January 1, 2000 is treated as a single group for purposes of this evaluation. In order to demonstrate that the distribution of the suspension satisfies the equitable distribution requirement, the plan sponsor must reasonably select and apply factors that are the basis for the different treatment of these three categories of participants.

Example 3. (i) *Facts*. The plan sponsor applies for approval of a suspension of benefits. Under the suspension of benefits, subject to the individual limitations on benefit suspensions, benefits for all participants and beneficiaries are reduced by the same percentage, and the suspension application indicates the rationale for this reduction.

(ii) *Conclusion*. The suspension of benefits is equitably distributed across the participant and beneficiary populations.

Example 4. (i) *Facts*. The plan sponsor applies for approval of a suspension of benefits. Under the suspension of benefits, subject to the age-based and disability-based limitations of section 432(e)(9)(D)(ii) and (iii), the portion of each participant's and beneficiary's benefit that exceeds the guarantee-based limitation of section 432(e)(9)(D)(i) is reduced by the same percentage, and the suspension application indicates the rationale for this reduction.

(ii) *Conclusion*. The suspension of benefits is equitably distributed across the participant and beneficiary populations. The result would be the same if, instead, the suspension of benefits applies only to benefits that exceed a multiple (in excess of 100%) of the guarantee-based limitation.

Example 5. (i) *Facts*. A plan was previously amended to provide an ad hoc 15% increase to the benefits of all participants and beneficiaries (including participants who, at the time, were no longer *earning service under the plan, which therefore included retirees and* deferred vested participants). The plan sponsor applies for approval of a suspension of benefits. Under the suspension of benefits, subject to the individual limitations on benefit suspensions, benefits for all participants and beneficiaries who were no longer earning service

under the plan at the time of the ad hoc amendment are reduced by eliminating the amendment for those individuals. The suspension application indicates why the benefit reduction is based on the statutory factors in paragraph (d)(6)(ii)(B)(6) of this section (the extent to which a participant or beneficiary has received post-retirement benefit increases), including application of the reduction to those who, at the time of the previous benefit increase, were either retired participants or deferred vested participants, and in paragraph (d)(6)(ii)(B)(7) of this section (the history of benefit increases and reductions), and why it is reasonable to apply the factors in this manner.

(ii) *Conclusion*. The suspension of benefits is equitably distributed across the participant and beneficiary populations. This is because the difference in treatment between the two groups of participants is based on whether a participant has received post-retirement benefit increases (in this case, whether a participant was earning service under the plan at the time of the benefit increase amendment), which under these facts is a relevant factor that may be reasonably selected by the plan sponsor, and the difference in treatment between the two groups of participants (eliminating the amendment only for benefits with respect to participants who were no longer earning service at the time of the amendment) is based on a reasonable application of that factor.

Example 6. (i) *Facts*. A plan contains a provision that provides a "thirteenth check" in plan years for which the investment return is greater than 7% (which was the assumed rate of return under the plan's actuarial valuation). The plan sponsor applies for approval of a suspension of benefits. Under the suspension of benefits, subject to the individual limitations on benefit suspensions, benefits for all participants and beneficiaries are reduced by eliminating the "thirteenth check" for all of those individuals. The suspension application indicates why the benefit reduction is based on the statutory factors in paragraph (d)(6)(ii)(B)(6) of this section (the extent to which a participant or beneficiary has received post-retirement benefit increases) and in paragraph (d)(6)(ii)(B)(7) of this section (the history of benefit increases and reductions), and why it is reasonable to apply the factors in this manner.

(ii) *Conclusion*. The suspension of benefits is equitably distributed across the participant and beneficiary populations.

Example 7. (i) *Facts*. A plan was previously amended to reduce future accruals from $60 per year of service to $50 per year of service. The plan sponsor applies for approval of a suspension of benefits. Under the suspension of benefits, subject to the individual limitations on benefit suspensions, the accrued benefits for all participants and beneficiaries are reduced to $50 per year of service (and the plan's generally applicable adjustments for early retirement and form of benefit apply). The suspension application indicates why the benefit reduction is based on the statutory factor in paragraph (d)(6)(ii)(B)(7) of this section (the history of benefit increases and reductions), and why it is reasonable to apply the factors in this manner.

(ii) *Conclusion*. The suspension of benefits is equitably distributed across the participant and beneficiary populations. This is because the difference in treatment among the different groups of participants is based on the history of benefit reductions and a discrepancy between active and retiree benefits, which under these facts are relevant factors that may be reasonably selected by the plan sponsor, and the difference in treatment between the three groups of participants (reducing the $60 benefit multiplier to $50 per year of service for two groups of participants—those who had accrued all of their benefits under the $60 multiplier and those who had accrued some of their benefits under the $60 multiplier—and not reducing benefits for the group of participants who had accrued all of their benefits under the $50 multiplier) is based on a reasonable application of those factors.

Example 8. (i) *Facts*. The facts are the same as in *Example 7*, except that no plan amendments have previously reduced future accruals or other benefits for active participants. Under the suspension of benefits, subject to the individual limitations on benefit suspensions, benefits for deferred vested participants, retirees, and beneficiaries who have commenced benefits are reduced, but no reduction applies to active participants. The suspension of benefits is not accompanied by any reductions in future accruals or other benefits for active participants.

(ii) *Conclusion*. The suspension of benefits is not equitably distributed across the participant and beneficiary populations. This is because, under these facts, no relevant factor (such as a previous reduction in benefits applicable only to active participants) has been reasonably selected by the plan sponsor to justify the proposed difference in treatment among the categories.

Example 9. (i) *Facts*. The facts are the same as in *Example 8*, except that the suspension of benefits provides for a reduction that applies to both active and inactive participants. However, the reduction that applies to active participants is smaller than the reduction that applies to inactive participants because the plan sponsor concludes, as explained and supported in the application for suspension, that active participants are reasonably likely to withdraw support for the plan if any larger reduction is applied.

(ii) *Conclusion.* The suspension of benefits is equitably distributed across the participant and beneficiary populations. This is because the difference in treatment between the different groups of participants is based on the extent to which active participants are reasonably likely to withdraw support for the plan, which under these facts is a relevant factor that may reasonably be selected by the plan sponsor, and the difference in treatment between the two groups of participants (applying a greater suspension to inactive than to active participants) is based on a reasonable application of that factor.

Example 10. (i) *Facts.* The plan sponsor applies for approval of a suspension of benefits. Under the suspension of benefits, subject to the individual limitations on benefit suspensions, the benefits for participants and beneficiaries attributable to service with an employer that failed to pay its full withdrawal liability are reduced by 50%. As indicated in the suspension application, the present value of the benefit reduction with respect to the former employees of one such employer is significantly greater than the unpaid withdrawal liability for that employer. Benefits for participants and beneficiaries attributable to service with all other employers are reduced by 10%.

(ii) *Conclusion.* The suspension of benefits is not equitably distributed across the participant and beneficiary populations. This is because, although the difference in treatment between the different groups of participants is based on a relevant factor that may reasonably be selected by the plan sponsor, the difference in treatment between the groups of participants is not based on a reasonable application of that factor.

Example 11. (i) *Facts.* The plan sponsor applies for approval of a suspension of benefits. Under the suspension of benefits, subject to the individual limitations on benefit suspensions, the benefits for all participants and beneficiaries are reduced by the same percentage, except that the benefits for employees and former employees of a particular employer that is actively represented on the plan's Board of Trustees are reduced by a specified lesser percentage.

(ii) *Conclusion.* The suspension of benefits is not equitably distributed across the participant and beneficiary populations. This is because, under these facts, no relevant factor has been reasonably selected by the plan sponsor to justify the difference in treatment between the two groups of participants.

Example 12. (i) *Facts.* The facts are the same as in *Example 11,* except that the particular employer whose employees and former employees are subject to the lesser benefit reduction is the union that also participates in the plan.

(ii) *Conclusion.* The suspension of benefits is not equitably distributed across the participant and beneficiary populations. This is because, under these facts, no relevant factor has been reasonably selected by the plan sponsor to justify the difference in treatment between the two groups of participants.

Example 13. (i) *Facts.* The plan sponsor applies for approval of a suspension of benefits. Under the suspension of benefits, subject to the individual limitations on benefit suspensions, the monthly benefit of all participants and beneficiaries is reduced to 110% of the monthly benefit that is guaranteed by PBGC under section 4022A of ERISA. As indicated in the suspension application, this is because the plan sponsor is applying to PBGC for a partition of the plan, which requires the plan sponsor to have implemented the maximum benefit suspensions under section 432(e)(9).

(ii) *Conclusion.* The suspension of benefits is equitably distributed across the participant and beneficiary populations.

Example 14. (i) *Facts.* The plan sponsor applies for approval of a suspension of benefits. Under the suspension of benefits, subject to the individual limitations on benefit suspensions, benefits for all participants and beneficiaries are reduced by the same percentage, except that the protection for benefits based on disability goes beyond the required disability-based limitations and also includes payments to a beneficiary of a participant who had been receiving benefits based on disability at the time of death. The suspension application indicates the rationale for this protection from reduction.

(ii) *Conclusion.* The suspension of benefits is equitably distributed across the participant and beneficiary populations because this suspension design is a reasonable application of the statutory factor in paragraph (d)(6)(ii)(B)(4) of this section (type of benefit).

Example 15. (i) *Facts.* The facts are the same as in *Example 3,* except that the plan does not provide for benefits based on disability. Under the suspension of benefits, less of a reduction is applied to a participant who has become disabled within the meaning of title II of the Social Security Act than to otherwise similarly situated participants and the suspension application indicates the rationale for this reduction.

(ii) *Conclusion.* The suspension of benefits is equitably distributed across the participant and beneficiary populations because a

participant's disability within the meaning of title II of the Social Security Act is a factor that can reasonably be taken into account in designing a suspension of benefits and applying less of a reduction to an individual in this group is a reasonable application of that factor.

(7) *Effective date of suspension made in combination with partition.*— In any case in which a suspension of benefits with respect to a plan is made in combination with a partition of the plan, the suspension of benefits may not take effect prior to the effective date of the partition. This requirement will not be satisfied if the partition order under section 4233 of ERISA has not been provided to the Secretary of the Treasury by the last day of the 225-day period described in paragraph (g)(3)(i) of this section. For purposes of the preceding sentence, a conditional approval by PBGC (within the meaning of 29 CFR 4233.12(c)) of a partition application that is conditioned only on the Secretary's issuing a final authorization to suspend is treated as a partition order.

(8) *Additional rules for plans described in section 432(e)(9)(D)(vii).*— (i) *In general.*—In the case of a plan that includes the benefits described in paragraph (d)(8)(i)(C) of this section, any suspension of benefits under this section shall—

(A) First, be applied to the maximum extent permissible to benefits attributable to a participant's service for an employer that withdrew from the plan and failed to pay (or is delinquent with respect to paying) the full amount of its withdrawal liability under section 4201(b)(1) of ERISA or an agreement with the plan;

(B) Second, except as provided by paragraph (d)(8)(i)(C) of this section, be applied to all other benefits that may be suspended under this section; and

(C) Third, be applied to benefits under a plan that are directly attributable to a participant's service with any employer that has, prior to December 16, 2014—

(1) Withdrawn from the plan in a complete withdrawal under section 4203 of ERISA and paid the full amount of the employer's withdrawal liability under section 4201(b)(1) of ERISA or an agreement with the plan; and

(2) Pursuant to a collective bargaining agreement, assumed liability for providing benefits to participants and beneficiaries of the plan under a separate, single-employer plan sponsored by the employer, in an amount equal to any amount of benefits for such participants and beneficiaries reduced as a result of the financial status of the plan.

(ii) *Application of suspensions to benefits that are directly attributable to a participant's service with certain employers.*—(A) *Greater reduction in certain benefits not permitted.*—A suspension of benefits under this section must not be applied to provide for a greater reduction in benefits described in paragraph (d)(8)(i)(C) of this section than the reduction that is applied to benefits described in paragraph (d)(8)(i)(B) of this section. The requirement in the preceding sentence is satisfied if no individual's benefits that are directly attributable to service with an employer described in paragraph (d)(8)(i)(C) of this section are reduced more than that individual's benefits would have been reduced if, holding the benefit formula, work history, and all other relevant factors used to compute benefits constant, those benefits were attributable to service with an employer that is not described in paragraph (d)(8)(i)(C) of this section.

(B) *Application of limitation to benefits of participants with respect to which the employer has not assumed liability.*—Benefits described in paragraph (d)(8)(i)(C) of this section include all benefits of a participant or beneficiary that are directly attributable to service with an employer described in paragraph (d)(8)(i)(C) of this section without regard to whether the employer has assumed liability for providing benefits to that participant or beneficiary that are reduced as a result of the financial status of the plan as described in paragraph (d)(8)(i)(C)(2) of this section. Thus, the rule of paragraph (d)(8)(ii)(A) of this section limits the amount by which a suspension of benefits is permitted to reduce benefits under a plan that are directly attributable to a participant's service with such an employer, even if the employer has not, pursuant to a collective bargaining agreement that satisfies the requirements of paragraph (d)(8)(i)(C)(2) of this section, assumed liability with respect to that participant's benefits.

(e) *Benefit improvements.*—(1) *Limitations on benefit improvements.*— This paragraph (e) sets forth rules for the application of section 432(e)(9)(E). A plan satisfies the criteria in section 432(e)(9)(E) only if, during the period that any suspension of benefits remains in effect, the plan sponsor does not implement any benefit improvement with respect to the plan except as provided in this paragraph (e). Paragraph (e)(2) of this section describes limitations on a benefit improvement for participants and beneficiaries who are not yet in pay status. Paragraph (e)(3) of this section describes limitations on a benefit improvement for participants and beneficiaries who are in pay status. Paragraph (e)(4) of this section provides that the limitations of this paragraph (e) generally apply in addition to other limitations on benefit increases that apply to a plan. Paragraph (e)(5) of this section defines benefit improvement.

(2) *Limitations on benefit improvements for those not in pay status.*—(i) *Equitable distribution for those in pay status and solvency projection.*—During the period that any suspension of benefits under a plan remains in effect, the plan sponsor may not increase the liabilities of the plan by reason of any benefit improvement for any participant or beneficiary who was not in pay status by the first day of the plan year for which the benefit improvement takes effect; unless—

(A) The present value of the total liabilities for a benefit improvement for participants and beneficiaries whose benefit commencement dates were before the first day of the plan year for which the benefit improvement takes effect is not less than the present value of the total liabilities for a benefit improvement for participants and beneficiaries who were not in pay status by that date;

(B) The plan sponsor equitably distributes the benefit improvement among the participants and beneficiaries whose benefit commencement dates were before the first day of the plan year in which the benefit improvement is proposed to take effect; and

(C) The plan actuary certifies that after taking into account the benefit improvement, the plan is projected to avoid insolvency indefinitely.

(ii) *Rules of application.*—(A) *Present value determination.*—(1) *Actuarial assumptions and methods.*—For purposes of paragraph (e)(2)(i)(A) of this section, the present value of the total liabilities for a benefit improvement is the present value as of the first day of the plan year in which the benefit improvement is proposed to take effect. The actuarial assumptions and methods used for the calculation for present values and the actuarial projections that are required under this paragraph (e)(2) must each be reasonable, and the combination of the actuarial assumptions and methods must be reasonable, taking into account the experience of the plan and reasonable expectations.

(2) *Increase in future accrual rate.*—In the case of a benefit improvement that is an increase in the rate of future accrual, the present value determined under paragraph (e)(2)(i)(A) of this section must take into account the increase in accruals for participants and beneficiaries not yet in pay status for all future years.

(B) *Factors relevant to equitable distribution.*—The evaluation of whether a benefit improvement is equitably distributed for purposes of paragraph (e)(2)(i)(B) of this section must take into account the relevant factors described in paragraph (d)(6)(ii)(B) of this section and the extent to which the benefits of the participants and beneficiaries were suspended.

(C) *Actuarial certification.*—The certification in paragraph (e)(2)(i)(C) of this section must be made using the standards described in paragraphs (d)(5)(ii), (iv), and (v) of this section, substituting the plan year that includes the effective date of the benefit improvement for the plan year that includes the effective date of the suspension.

(iii) *Special rule for certain benefit increases.*—The limitations of this paragraph (e) do not apply to a resumption of suspended benefits or plan amendment that increases liabilities with respect to participants and beneficiaries not in pay status by the first day of the plan year in which the benefit improvement took effect that—

(A) The Secretary of the Treasury, in consultation with PBGC and the Secretary of Labor, determines to be reasonable and which provides for only *de minimis* increases in the liabilities of the plan; or

(B) Is required as a condition of qualification under section 401 or to comply with other applicable law, as determined by the Secretary of the Treasury.

(3) *Limitation on resumption of suspended benefits only for those in pay status.*—The plan sponsor may increase liabilities of the plan by eliminating some or all of the suspension that applies solely to participants and beneficiaries in pay status at the time of the resumption, provided that the plan sponsor equitably distributes the value of those resumed benefits among participants and beneficiaries in pay status, taking into account the relevant factors described in paragraph (d)(6)(ii)(B) of this section. A resumption of benefits that is described in this paragraph (e)(3) is not subject to the limitations on a benefit improvement under section 432(f) (relating to restrictions on benefit increases for plans in critical status).

(4) *Additional limitations.*—Except as provided in paragraph (e)(3) of this section, the limitations on a benefit improvement under this paragraph (e) are in addition to the limitations in section 432(f) and any other applicable limitations on increases in benefits imposed on a plan.

(5) *Definition of benefit improvement.*—(i) *In general.*—For purposes of this paragraph (e), the term benefit improvement means, with respect to a plan, a resumption of suspended benefits, an increase in benefits, an increase in the rate at which benefits accrue, or an increase in the rate at which benefits become nonforfeitable, under the plan.

(ii) *Effect of expiration of suspension.*—In the case of a suspension of benefits that expires as of a date that is specified in the plan amendment implementing the suspension, the resumption of benefits solely from the expiration of that period is not treated as a benefit improvement.

(f) *Notice requirements.*—(1) *In general.*—No suspension of benefits may be made pursuant to this section unless notice of the proposed suspension has been given by the plan sponsor to—

(i) All participants, beneficiaries of deceased participants, and alternate payees under the plan (regardless of whether their benefits are proposed to be suspended), except those who cannot be contacted by reasonable efforts;

(ii) Each employer who has an obligation to contribute (within the meaning of section 4212(a) of ERISA) under the plan; and

(iii) Each employee organization which, for purposes of collective bargaining, represents plan participants employed by an employer described in paragraph (f)(1)(ii) of this section.

(2) *Content of notice.*—(i) *In general.*—The notice described under paragraph (f)(1) of this section must contain—

(A) Sufficient information to enable a participant or beneficiary to understand the effect of any suspension of benefits, including an individualized estimate (on an annual or monthly basis) of the effect on that participant or beneficiary;

(B) A description of the factors considered by the plan sponsor in designing the benefit suspension;

(C) A statement that the application for approval of any suspension of benefits will be available on the website of the Department of the Treasury and that comments on the application will be accepted;

(D) Information as to the rights and remedies of plan participants and beneficiaries;

(E) If applicable, a statement describing the appointment of a retiree representative, the date of appointment of the representative, the role and responsibilities of the retiree representative, identifying information about the retiree representative (including whether the representative is a plan trustee), and how to contact the retiree representative; and

(F) Information on how to contact the Department of the Treasury for further information and assistance where appropriate.

(ii) *Description of suspension of benefits.*—The notice described under paragraph (f)(1) of this section will not satisfy the requirements of paragraph (f)(2)(i) of this section unless it includes the following—

(A) To the extent that it is not possible to provide an individualized estimate on an annual or monthly basis of the quantitative effect of the suspension on a participant or beneficiary, such as in the case of a suspension that affects the payment of any future cost-of-living adjustment, that effect may be reflected in a narrative description;

(B) A statement that the plan sponsor has determined that the plan will become insolvent unless the proposed suspension takes effect, and the year in which insolvency is projected to occur without a suspension of benefits;

(C) A statement that insolvency of the plan could result in benefits lower than benefits paid under the proposed suspension and a description of the projected benefit payments upon insolvency;

(D) A description of the proposed suspension and its effect, including a description of the different categories or groups affected by the suspension, how those categories or groups are defined, and the formula that is used to calculate the amount of the proposed suspension for individuals in each category or group;

(E) A description of the effect of the proposed suspension on the plan's projected insolvency;

(F) A description of whether the suspension will remain in effect indefinitely, or the date the suspension expires if it expires by its own terms; and

(G) A statement describing the right to vote on the suspension application.

(iii) *Readability requirement.*—A notice given under paragraph (f)(1) of this section must be written in a manner so as to be understood by the average plan participant.

(iv) *Model notice.*—The Secretary of the Treasury will provide a model notice. The use of the model notice will satisfy the content and readability requirements of this paragraph (f)(2) with respect to the language provided in the model.

(3) *Form and manner.*—(i) *Timing.*—(A) *In general.*—A notice under paragraph (f)(1) of this section must be given no earlier than four business days before the date on which an application is submitted and no later than two business days after the Secretary of the Treasury notifies the plan sponsor that it has submitted a complete application, as described in paragraph (g)(1)(ii) of this section.

(B) *Timing for lost participants.*—If additional individuals who are entitled to notice are located after the time period in paragraph (f)(3)(i)(A) of this section has elapsed, then the plan sponsor must give notice to these individuals as soon as practicable thereafter.

(ii) *Method of delivery of notice.*—(A) *Written or electronic delivery.*—A notice given under paragraph (f)(1) of this section may be provided in writing. It may also be provided in electronic form to the extent that the form is reasonably accessible to persons to whom the notice is required to be provided. Permissible electronic methods include those permitted under regulations of the Department of Labor at 29 CFR § 2520.104b-1(c) and those described at § 54.4980F-1, Q&A-13(c) of the Excise Tax Regulations.

(B) *No alternative method of delivery.*—A notice under this paragraph (f) must be provided in written or electronic form.

(iii) *Additional information in notice.*—A notice given under paragraph (f)(1) of this section is permitted to include information in addition to the information that is required under paragraph (f)(2) of this section, including, if applicable, information relating to an application for partition under section 4233 of ERISA (such as the model notice at Appendix A of 29 CFR part 4233), provided that the requirements of paragraph (f)(3)(iv) of this section are satisfied.

(iv) *No false or misleading information.*—A notice given under paragraph (f)(1) of this section may not include false or misleading information (or omit information in a manner that causes the information provided to be misleading).

(4) *Other notice requirement.*—Any notice given under paragraph (f)(1) of this section satisfies the requirement for notice of a significant reduction in benefits described in section 4980F that would otherwise be required as a result of that suspension of benefits. To the extent that there are other reductions that accompany a suspension of benefits, such as a reduction in the future accrual rate described in section 4980F for active participants or a reduction in adjustable benefits under section 432(e)(8), notice that satisfies the requirements (including the applicable timing requirements) of section 4980F or section 432(e)(8), as applicable, must be provided.

(5) *Examples.*—The following examples illustrate the requirement in paragraph (f)(1)(i) of this section to give notice to all participants, beneficiaries of deceased participants, and alternate payees, except those who cannot be contacted by reasonable efforts.

Example 1. (i) *Facts.* A plan sponsor distributes notice of a proposed suspension of benefits to plan participants, beneficiaries of deceased participants, and alternate payees by mailing the notice to their last known mailing addresses, using the same information that it used to send the most recent annual funding notice. Of 5,000 such notices, 300 were returned as undeliverable. The plan sponsor takes no additional steps to contact the individuals for whom the notice was returned as undeliverable.

(ii) *Conclusion.* The plan sponsor did not make any effort beyond the initial mailing to locate the 300 individuals for whom the notice was returned as undeliverable. Therefore, the plan sponsor did not satisfy the requirement to provide notice to all participants, beneficiaries of deceased participants, and alternate payees under the plan (regardless of whether their benefits are proposed to be suspended), except those who cannot be contacted by reasonable efforts.

Example 2. (i) *Facts.* The facts are the same as *Example 1*, but the plan sponsor contacts the bargaining parties for the plan and the plan administrators of any other employee benefit plans that the plan sponsor reasonably believes may have information useful for locating the missing individuals, and the plan sponsor requests contact information for the missing individuals. *The plan sponsor* then uses an Internet search tool, a credit reporting agency, and a commercial locator service to search for individuals for whom it was not able to obtain updated information from bargaining parties. Through these efforts, the plan sponsor locates the updated addresses of 250 of the 300 individuals whom it previously failed to contact. The plan sponsor mails notices to those individuals within one week of locating them.

(ii) *Conclusion.* By using effective search methods to find the previously missing individuals and promptly mailing the notice of suspension to them, the plan sponsor has satisfied the requirement to

provide notice to all participants, beneficiaries of deceased participants, and alternate payees under the plan (regardless of whether their benefits are proposed to be suspended), except those who cannot be contacted by reasonable efforts.

(g) *Approval or denial of an application for suspension of benefits.*—(1) *Application.*—(i) *In general.*—The plan sponsor of a plan in critical and declining status for a plan year that seeks to suspend benefits must submit an application for approval of the proposed suspension of benefits to the Secretary of the Treasury. The Secretary of the Treasury, in consultation with PBGC and the Secretary of Labor, will approve a complete application described in paragraph (g)(1)(ii) of this section upon finding that—

(A) The plan is eligible for the proposed suspension described in the application;

(B) The plan actuary and plan sponsor satisfy the requirements of section 432(e)(9)(C) in accordance with the rules of paragraph (c) of this section;

(C) The design of the proposed suspension described in the application satisfies the criteria of section 432(e)(9)(D) in accordance with the rules of paragraphs (d) of this section; and

(D) The plan sponsor satisfies the requirements of section 432(e)(9)(E) and (F) in accordance with the rules of paragraphs (e) and (f) of this section.

(ii) *Complete application.*—After receiving a submission, the plan sponsor will be notified within two business days whether the submission constitutes a complete application. A complete application will be treated as submitted on the date that it was originally submitted to the Secretary of the Treasury. If a submission is incomplete, the notification will inform the plan sponsor of the information that is needed to complete the submission and give the plan sponsor a reasonable opportunity to submit a complete application. In such a case, the complete application will be treated as submitted on the date on which the additional information needed to complete the application is submitted to the Secretary of the Treasury.

(iii) *Submission of application.*—An application described in this paragraph (g)(1) must be submitted electronically in a searchable format.

(iv) *Requirements for application.*—Additional guidance that may be necessary or appropriate with respect to applications described in this paragraph (g)(1), including procedures for submitting applications and the information required to be included in a complete application, may be published in the form of revenue procedures, notices, or other guidance in the Internal Revenue Bulletin.

(v) *Requirement to provide adequate time to process application.*—(A) *General rule.*—An application for suspension that is not submitted in combination with an application to PBGC for a plan partition under section 4233 of ERISA generally will not be accepted unless the proposed effective date of the suspension is at least nine months from the date on which the application is submitted.

(B) *Earlier effective date in appropriate circumstances.*—Notwithstanding paragraph (g)(1)(v)(A) of this section, in appropriate circumstances the Secretary of the Treasury, in consultation with PBGC and the Secretary of Labor, may permit a proposed suspension to have an earlier effective date.

(vi) *Plan sponsors that also apply for partition.*—See part 4233 of the PBGC regulations for a coordinated application process that applies in the case of a plan sponsor that is submitting an application for suspension in combination with an application to PBGC for a plan partition under section 4233 of ERISA.

(2) *Solicitation of comments.*—(i) *In general.*—Not later than 30 days after receipt of a complete application described in paragraph (g)(1) of this section—

(A) The application for approval of the suspension of benefits will be published on the website of the Department of the Treasury; and

(B) The Secretary of the Treasury will publish a notice in the **Federal Register** soliciting comments from contributing employers, employee organizations, and participants and beneficiaries of the plan for which an application was made, and other interested parties.

(ii) *Public comments.*—The notice described in paragraph (g)(2)(i)(B) of this section will generally request that comments be submitted no later than 45 days after publication of that notice in the **Federal Register**, but the notice may specify a different deadline for comments in appropriate circumstances. Comments received in response to this notice will be made publicly available.

(3) *Special rules in the case of revision to proposed suspension.*—(i) *Resubmission review available in certain circumstances.*—The Secretary of the Treasury (in consultation with PBGC and the Secretary of

Labor) has the discretion, in appropriate circumstances, to permit the plan sponsor to submit a revision of a proposed suspension that had been withdrawn for resubmission review. With respect to an application that is accepted for resubmission review—

(A) The rules of paragraph (g)(1)(v)(B) of this section will apply;

(B) The limitations of paragraph (d) of this section with respect to the revised proposed suspension may be applied using the same actuarial data (including the same fair market value of the plan assets) as was used in the initial application;

(C) The revision to the proposed suspension will be published, and comments solicited, in accordance with paragraph (g)(2) of this section; and

(D) The plan sponsor must provide notice of the revised proposed suspension in accordance with the requirements of paragraph (g)(3)(ii) of this section.

(ii) *Requirement to provide updated notice to affected participants.*—(A) *General rule.*—Except as provided in paragraph (g)(3)(ii)(B) of this section, a plan sponsor that revises a proposed suspension in accordance with this paragraph (g)(3) must provide notice of the suspension in accordance with the rules of paragraph (f) of this section.

(B) *Treatment of participants who are not affected by the revision.*—If the revision to the proposed suspension changes neither the amount of the suspension as initially proposed nor the effective date of the proposed suspension for an affected individual, then the Secretary of the Treasury (in consultation with PBGC and the Secretary of Labor) may permit the plan sponsor to provide a simplified version of the notice of the suspension to that individual. For this purpose, the effective date of a suspension is determined without taking into account the second sentence of paragraph (a)(4)(iii)(C) of this section.

(4) *Approval or denial.*—(i) *Deemed approval.*—A complete application described in paragraph (g)(1)(ii) of this section will be deemed approved unless, within 225 days following the date that the complete application is submitted, the Secretary of the Treasury notifies the plan sponsor that its application does not satisfy one or more of the requirements described in this paragraph (g).

(ii) *Notice of denial.*—If the Secretary of the Treasury denies a plan sponsor's application, the notification of the denial will detail the specific reasons for the denial, including reference to the specific requirement not satisfied.

(iii) *Special rules for systemically important plans.*—If the Secretary of the Treasury approves a plan sponsor's application and the Secretary expects that the plan is or may be a systemically important plan (as defined in paragraph (h)(5)(iv) of this section), the Secretary will so notify the plan sponsor. In that case, and in the event of a vote to reject the suspension (as described in paragraph (h)(4) of this section), the plan sponsor may be required to supply individual participant data and any actuarial analyses that the Secretary may request, in order to assist the Secretary in determining whether to permit the implementation of the suspension that was approved by the Secretary but rejected by a majority of the eligible voters or the implementation of a modification of that suspension.

(iv) *Agreement to stay 225-day period.*—The Secretary of the Treasury and the plan sponsor may mutually agree in writing to stay the 225-day period described in paragraph (g)(3)(i) of this section.

(5) *Consideration of certain factors.*—In evaluating whether the plan sponsor has satisfied the requirement of paragraph (c)(3)(i)(A) of this section, the Secretary of the Treasury, in consultation with PBGC and the Secretary of Labor, will review the plan sponsor's consideration of each of the factors under paragraph (c)(3)(ii) of this section (and any other factor that the plan sponsor considered).

(6) *Standard for accepting plan sponsor determinations.*—In evaluating the plan sponsor's application, the Secretary of the Treasury will accept the plan sponsor's determinations in paragraph (c)(3) of this section unless the Secretary concludes, in consultation with PBGC and the Secretary of Labor, that the determinations were clearly erroneous.

(7) *Plan sponsor certifications with respect to plan amendments.*—The plan sponsor will not satisfy the requirements of paragraph (g)(1)(i)(B) and (D) of this section unless the plan sponsor certifies that if the plan sponsor receives final authorization to suspend as described in paragraph (h)(6) of this section with respect to the *proposed benefit suspension (or, in the case of a systemically important plan, a proposed or modified benefit suspension)*, the plan sponsor chooses to implement the suspension, and the plan sponsor adopts the amendment described in paragraph (a)(1) of this section, then it will timely amend the plan to provide that—

(i) If the plan sponsor fails to make the annual determinations under section 432(e)(9)(C)(ii), then the suspension of benefits will cease as of the first day of the first plan year following the plan year in which the plan sponsor fails to make the annual plan sponsor determinations in paragraph (c)(4) of this section; and

(ii) Any future benefit improvement must satisfy the requirements of section 432(e)(9)(E).

(8) *Special Master.*—The Secretary of the Treasury may appoint a Special Master for purposes of this section. If a Special Master is appointed, the Special Master will coordinate the implementation of this section and the review of applications for the suspension of benefits and other appropriate documents, and will provide recommendations to the Secretary of the Treasury with respect to decisions required under this section.

(h) *Participant vote on proposed benefit reduction.*—(1) *Requirement for vote.*—(i) *In general.*—If an application for suspension is approved under paragraph (g) of this section, then the Secretary of the Treasury, in consultation with PBGC and the Secretary of Labor, will administer a vote as described in section 432(e)(9)(H) and this paragraph (h). A suspension of benefits may not take effect before the vote and may only take effect after a final authorization to suspend benefits under paragraph (h)(6) of this section.

(ii) *Communication by plan sponsor.*—The plan sponsor must take reasonable steps to inform eligible voters about the proposed suspension. This includes all eligible voters who may be contacted by reasonable efforts in accordance with paragraph (f)(1) of this section. Any eligible voter whom the plan sponsor has been able to locate through these means (or who has otherwise been located by the plan sponsor) must be—

(A) Included on the voting roster described in paragraph (h)(3)(iii)(B) of this section; and

(B) Sent a ballot described in paragraph (h)(3) of this section.

(iii) *Eligible voters.*—(A) *General definition.*—For purpose of this paragraph (h), the term "eligible voters" means all plan participants (that is, active plan participants, deferred vested participants, and retirees) and beneficiaries of deceased participants.

(B) *Voting roster.*—The voting roster includes those eligible voters to whom the notices described in paragraph (f) of this section were sent. If there is a plan participant or beneficiary who did not receive a notice but who is subsequently located by the plan sponsor, that individual must be included on the roster. Similarly, if an individual becomes a plan participant after the date the notices were sent, then the individual must be included on the roster. If a plan sponsor learns after the date the notices described in paragraph (f) of this section were sent that an eligible voter has died, then that deceased individual must not be included on the roster (but if that participant has a beneficiary entitled to benefits under the plan, the beneficiary must be added to the roster).

(2) *Participant vote.*—(i) *In general.*—The participant vote described in paragraph (h)(1)(i) of this section requires completion of the following steps—

(A) Distribution of the ballot package described in paragraph (h)(2)(iii) of this section to the eligible voters;

(B) Voting by eligible voters and collection and tabulation of the votes, as described in paragraph (h)(2)(iv) of this section; and

(C) Determination of whether a majority of the eligible voters has voted to reject the suspension, as described in paragraph (h)(2)(v) of this section.

(ii) *Designation of service provider for limited functions.*—The Secretary of the Treasury is permitted to designate one or more service providers to perform, under the supervision of the Secretary, any of the functions of the Secretary described in paragraphs (h)(2)(i)(A) and (B) of this section. If the Secretary designates a service provider to perform these functions then the service provider will provide the Secretary with a written report of the results of the vote, including (as applicable)—

(A) The number of ballot packages distributed to eligible voters;

(B) The number of eligible voters to whom ballot packages have not been provided (because the individuals could not be located);

(C) The number of eligible voters who voted (specifying the number of affirmative votes and the number of negative votes cast); and

(D) Any other information that the Secretary requires.

(iii) *Distribution of the ballot package to the eligible voters.*—(A) *Ballot package.*—The ballot package distributed to each eligible voter consists of—

(1) A ballot, approved under paragraph (h)(3)(iii) of this section, which contains the items described in section 432(e)(9)(H)(iii) and paragraph (h)(3)(i) of this section; and

(2) A voter identification code assigned to the eligible voter for use in voting.

(B) *Plan sponsor responsibilities.*—(1) *In general.*—This paragraph (h)(2)(iii)(B) sets forth the responsibilities of the plan sponsor with respect to the distribution of the ballot package to the eligible voters.

(2) Furnish information regarding eligible voters.—No later than 7 days following the date the Secretary of the Treasury has approved an application for a suspension of benefits under paragraph (g) of this section, the plan sponsor must furnish the following—

(i) The voting roster described in paragraph (h)(1)(iii)(B) of this section;

(ii) Plan information (such as participant identification codes used by the plan) to enable the Secretary of the Treasury to verify the identity of each eligible voter;

(iii) For each eligible voter on the voting roster, the last known mailing address (or, if the plan sponsor has been unable to locate that individual using the standards that apply for purposes of paragraph (f)(1)(i) of this section, an indication that the individual could not be located through reasonable efforts);

(iv) Current electronic mailing addresses for those eligible voters identified in paragraph (h)(2)(iii)(B)(4) of this section; and

(v) The individualized estimates described in paragraph (f)(2)(i)(A) of this section (or, if an individualized estimate is no longer accurate for an eligible voter, a corrected version of that estimate).

(3) Communication with eligible voters.—In accordance with section 432(e)(9)(H)(iv) and paragraph (h)(1)(ii) of this section, the plan sponsor is responsible for communicating with eligible voters, which includes—

(i) Notifying the eligible voters described in paragraph (h)(2)(iii)(B)(4) of this section that a ballot package will be mailed to them by first-class U.S. mail; and

(ii) Making reasonable efforts (using the standards that apply for purposes of paragraph (f)(1)(i) of this section) as necessary to locate eligible voters for whom the plan sponsor has received notification that the mailed ballot packages are returned as undeliverable (so that ballot packages can be sent to those eligible voters).

(4) Eligible voters to receive electronic notification.—Those eligible voters whom the plan sponsor must notify electronically are—

(i) Eligible voters who previously received the notice described in paragraph (f) of this section in electronic form (as permitted under paragraph (f)(3)(ii) of this section), and

(ii) Any other eligible voters who regularly receive plan-related communications from the plan sponsor in electronic form.

(5) Method of notifying certain eligible voters.—The notification described in paragraph (h)(2)(iii)(B)(3)(*i*) of this section for an eligible voter must be made using the electronic form normally used to send plan-related communications to that voter (or the form used to provide the notice in paragraph (f) of this section, if different). The plan sponsor must send this notification promptly after being informed of the ballot distribution date (within the meaning of paragraph (h)(2)(iii)(D) of this section) and the notification must include the ballot distribution date.

(6) Pay costs associated with distribution.—The plan sponsor is responsible for paying all costs associated with printing, assembling, and distributing the ballot package, including postage.

(C) *Required method of distributing ballot package.*—Ballot packages must be distributed to eligible voters by first-class U.S. mail. A supplemental copy of the mailed ballot package may also be sent by an electronic communication to an eligible voter who has consented to receive electronic communications.

(D) *Timing.*—Ballot packages will be distributed to eligible voters no later than 30 days after the Secretary of the Treasury has approved an application for a suspension of benefits under paragraph (g) of this section. The date on which the ballot packages are mailed to the eligible voters is referred to as the ballot distribution date.

(iv) *Collection and tabulation of votes cast by eligible voters.*—(A) *Voting period.*—The voting period is the period during which a vote received from an eligible voter will be counted. The voting

period begins on the ballot distribution date. The voting period generally remains open until the 30th day following the date the Secretary of the Treasury has approved an application for a suspension of benefits under paragraph (g) of this section. However, the voting period will not close earlier than 21 days after the ballot distribution date. In addition, the Secretary (in consultation with PBGC and the Secretary of Labor) may specify a later date to end the voting period in appropriate circumstances.

(B) *Automated voting system must be provided.*—An automated voting system that meets the requirements of paragraph (h)(2)(iv)(C) of this section must be made available to voters for casting their votes. In appropriate circumstances, the Secretary may, in consultation with PBGC and the Secretary of Labor, allow voters to cast votes by mail in lieu of using the automated voting system.

(C) *Automated voting system.*—An automated voting system meets the requirements of this paragraph (h)(2)(iv)(C) only if the system—

(1) Collects votes cast by eligible voters both electronically (through a website) and telephonically (through a toll-free number allowing voters to cast their votes using both a touch-tone voting system and an interactive voice response system); and

(2) Accepts only votes cast during the voting period by an eligible voter who provides the eligible voter's identification code described in paragraph (h)(2)(iii)(A)(2) of this section.

(D) *Policies and procedures.*—The Secretary of the Treasury (in consultation with PBGC and the Secretary of Labor) may establish such policies and procedures as may be necessary to facilitate the administration of the vote under this paragraph (h)(2). These policies and procedures may include, but are not limited to, establishing a process for an eligible voter to challenge the vote.

(v) *Determination of whether a majority of the eligible voters has voted to reject the suspension.*—Within 7 calendar days after the end of the voting period, the Secretary of the Treasury (in consultation with PBGC and the Secretary of Labor) will—

(A) Certify that a majority of all eligible voters has voted to reject the suspension that was approved under paragraph (g) of this section, or

(B) Issue a final authorization to suspend as described in paragraph (h)(6) of this section.

(3) *Ballots.*—(i) *In general.*—The plan sponsor must provide a ballot for the vote that includes the following—

(A) A description of the proposed suspension and its effect, including the effect of the suspension on each category or group of individuals affected by the suspension and the extent to which they are affected;

(B) A description of the factors considered by the plan sponsor in designing the benefit suspension, including but not limited to the factors in paragraph (d)(6)(iii) of this section;

(C) A description of whether the suspension will remain in effect indefinitely or will expire by its own terms (and, if it will expire by its own terms, when that will occur);

(D) A statement from the plan sponsor in support of the proposed suspension;

(E) A statement in opposition to the proposed suspension compiled from comments received pursuant to the solicitation of comments pursuant to paragraph (g)(2) of this section;

(F) A statement that the proposed suspension has been approved by the Secretary of the Treasury, in consultation with PBGC and the Secretary of Labor;

(G) A statement that the plan sponsor has determined that the plan will become insolvent unless the proposed suspension takes effect (including the year in which insolvency is projected to occur without a suspension of benefits), and an accompanying statement that this determination is subject to uncertainty;

(H) A statement that insolvency of the plan could result in benefits lower than benefits paid under the proposed suspension and a description of the projected benefit payments in the event of plan insolvency;

(I) A statement that insolvency of PBGC would result in benefits lower than benefits otherwise paid in the case of plan insolvency;

(J) A statement that the plan's actuary has certified that the plan is projected to avoid insolvency, taking into account the proposed suspension of benefits (and, if applicable, a proposed partition of the plan), and an accompanying statement that the actuary's projection is subject to uncertainty;

(K) A statement that the suspension will go into effect unless a majority of all eligible voters vote to reject the suspension and that, therefore, a failure to vote has the same effect on the outcome of the vote as a vote in favor of the suspension;

Reg. §1.432(e)(9)-1(h)(3)(i)(K)

(L) A copy of the individualized estimate described in paragraph (f)(2)(i)(A) of this section (or, if that individualized estimate is no longer accurate, a corrected version of that estimate); and

(M) A description of the voting procedures, including the deadline for voting.

(ii) *Additional rules.*—(A) *Readability requirement.*—A ballot provided under section 432(e)(9)(H)(iii), in accordance with the rules of paragraph (h)(3)(i) of this section, must be written in a manner that is readily understandable by the average plan participant.

(B) *No false or misleading information.*—A ballot provided under section 432(e)(9)(H)(iii), in accordance with the rules of paragraph (h)(3)(i) of this section, may not include false or misleading information (or omit information in a manner that causes the information provided to be misleading).

(iii) *Ballot must be approved.*—Any ballot provided under section 432(e)(9)(H)(iii), in accordance with the rules of paragraph (h)(3)(i) of this section, must be approved by the Secretary of the Treasury, in consultation with PBGC and the Secretary of Labor, before it is provided.

(iv) *Statement in opposition to the proposed suspension.*—The statement in opposition to the proposed suspension that is prepared from comments received on the application, as required under section 432(e)(9)(H)(iii)(II), will be compiled by the Secretary of Labor and will be written in accordance with the rules of paragraph (h)(3)(ii) of this section. If no comments in opposition are received, the statement in opposition to the proposed suspension will include a statement indicating that there were no such comments.

(v) *Model ballot.*—Model language for use in the ballot may be published in the Internal Revenue Bulletin.

(4) *Implementing suspension following vote.*—(i) *In general.*—Unless a majority of all eligible voters vote to reject the suspension that was approved under paragraph (g) of this section, the suspension will be permitted to take effect. If a majority of all eligible voters vote to reject the suspension that was approved under paragraph (g) of this section, a suspension of benefits will not be permitted to take effect except as provided under paragraph (h)(5)(iii) of this section relating to the implementation of a suspension for a systemically important plan (as defined in paragraph (h)(5)(iv) of this section).

(ii) *Effect of not sending ballot.*—Any eligible voters to whom ballots have not been provided (because the individuals could not be located) will be treated as voting to reject the suspension at the same rate (in other words, in the same percentage) as those to whom ballots have been provided.

(5) *Systemically important plans.*—(i) *In general.*—If a majority of all eligible voters vote to reject the suspension that was approved under paragraph (g) of this section, the Secretary of the Treasury will consult with PBGC and the Secretary of Labor to determine if the plan is a systemically important plan. This determination will be made no later than 14 days after the results of the vote are certified.

(ii) *Recommendations from Participant and Plan Sponsor Advocate.*—If the plan is determined to be a systemically important plan, then, no later than 44 days after the results of the vote are certified, the Participant and Plan Sponsor Advocate selected under section 4004 of ERISA may submit recommendations to the Secretary of the Treasury with respect to the suspension that was approved under paragraph (g) of this section or any modifications to the suspension.

(iii) *Implementation of original or modified suspension by systemically important plans.*—If a plan is a systemically important plan for which a majority of all eligible voters vote to reject the suspension that was approved under paragraph (g) of this section, then the Secretary of the Treasury must determine whether to permit the implementation of the suspension that was approved under paragraph (g) of this section or whether to permit the implementation of a modification of that suspension. Under any such modification, the plan must be projected to avoid insolvency in accordance with section 432(e)(9)(D)(iv). No later than 60 days after the results of a vote to reject a suspension are certified, the Secretary of the Treasury will notify the plan sponsor that the suspension or modified suspension is permitted to be implemented.

(iv) *Systemically important plan defined.*—(A) *In general.*—For purposes of this paragraph (h)(5), a systemically important plan is a *plan with respect to which PBGC projects that the present value of its* financial assistance payments will exceed $1.0 billion (adjusted in accordance with paragraph (h)(5)(iv)(B) of this section to the calendar year in which the application is submitted) if the suspension is not implemented.

(B) *Indexing.*—For calendar years beginning after 2015, the dollar amount specified in paragraph (h)(5)(iv)(A) of this section will be replaced with an amount equal to the product of the dollar amount and a fraction, the numerator of which is the contribution and benefit base (determined under section 230 of the Social Security Act) for the preceding calendar year and the denominator of which is the contribution and benefit base for calendar year 2014. If the amount otherwise determined under this paragraph (h)(5)(iv)(B) is not a multiple of $1.0 million, the amount will be rounded to the next lowest multiple of $1.0 million.

(6) *Final authorization to suspend.*—(i) *In general.*—In any case in which a suspension is permitted to take effect following a vote pursuant to section 432(e)(9)(H)(ii) and paragraph (h)(4) of this section, the Secretary of the Treasury, in consultation with PBGC and the Secretary of Labor, will issue a final authorization to suspend with respect to the suspension not later than seven days after the vote.

(ii) *Systemically important plans.*—In any case in which a suspension is permitted to take effect following a determination under paragraph (h)(5) of this section that the plan is a systemically important plan, the Secretary of the Treasury, in consultation with PBGC and the Secretary of Labor, will issue a final authorization to suspend, at a time sufficient to allow the implementation of the suspension prior to the end of the 90-day period beginning on the date the results of the vote are certified.

(iii) *Plan partitions.*—Notwithstanding any other provision of this section, in any case in which a suspension of benefits with respect to a plan is made in combination with a partition of the plan, the suspension of benefits is not permitted to take effect prior to the effective date of the partition.

(i) [*Reserved*].

(j) *Effective/applicability date.*—This section applies with respect to suspensions for which the approval or denial is issued on or after April 26, 2016, and, in the case of a systemically important plan, any modification described in paragraph (h)(5)(iii) of this section that is implemented on or after April 26, 2016. [Reg. § 1.432(e)(9)-1.]

☐ [*T.D. 9765, 4-26-2016. Amended by T.D. 9767, 5-3-2016.*]

[Reg. § 1.433(h)(3)-1]

§ 1.433(h)(3)-1. Mortality tables used to determine current liability.—(a) *Mortality tables used to determine current liability.*—In accordance with section 433(h)(3)(B), the mortality assumptions that apply to a defined benefit plan for the plan year pursuant to section 430(h)(3)(A) and § 1.430(h)(3)-1(a) are used to determine a CSEC plan's current liability for purposes of applying the rules of section 433(c)(7)(C). Either the static mortality tables used pursuant to § 1.430(h)(3)-1(a)(3) or generational mortality tables used pursuant to § 1.430(h)(3)-1(a)(2) may be used for a CSEC plan for this purpose, but substitute mortality tables under § 1.430(h)(3)-2 may not be used for this purpose.

(b) *Effective/applicability date.*—This section applies for plan years beginning on or after January 1, 2018. [Reg. § 1.433(h)(3)-1.]

☐ [T.D. 9826, 10-3-2017.]

[Reg. § 1.436-0]

§ 1.436-0. Table of contents.—This section contains a listing of the major headings of § 1.436-1.

§ 1.436-1 Limits on benefits and benefit accruals under single employer defined benefit plans.

(a) General rules.

  (1) Qualification requirement.

  (2) Organization of the regulation.

  (3) Special rules for certain plans.

  (4) Treatment of plan as of close of prohibited or cessation period.

  (5) Deemed election to reduce funding balances.

(b) Limitation on shutdown benefits and other unpredictable contingent event benefits.

  (1) In general.

  (2) Exemption if section 436 contribution is made.

  (3) Rules of application.

  (4) Prior unpredictable contingent event.

(c) Limitations on plan amendments increasing liability for benefits.

  (1) In general.

  (2) Exemption if section 436 contribution is made.

  (3) Rules of application regarding pre-existing plan provisions.

  (4) Exceptions.

  (5) Rule for determining when an amendment takes effect.

(6) Treatment of mergers, consolidations, and transfers of plan assets into a plan. [Reserved.]

(d) Limitations on prohibited payments.

(1) AFTAP less than 60 percent.

(2) Bankruptcy.

(3) Limited payment if AFTAP at least 60 percent but less than 80 percent.

(4) Exception for cessation of benefit accruals.

(5) Right to delay commencement.

(6) Plan alternative for special optional forms.

(7) Exception for distributions permitted without consent of the participant under section 411(a)(11).

(e) Limitation on benefit accruals for plans with severe funding shortfalls.

(1) In general.

(2) Exemption if section 436 contribution is made.

(3) Special rule under section 203 of the Worker, Retiree, and Employer Recovery Act of 2008. [Reserved]

(f) Methods to avoid or terminate benefit limitations.

(1) In general.

(2) Current year contributions to avoid or terminate benefit limitations.

(3) Security to increase adjusted funding target attainment percentage.

(4) Examples.

(g) Rules of operation for periods prior to and after certification.

(1) In general.

(2) Periods prior to certification during which a presumption applies.

(3) Periods prior to certification during which no presumption applies.

(4) Modification of the presumed AFTAP.

(5) Periods after certification of AFTAP.

(6) Examples.

(h) Presumed underfunding for purposes of benefit limitations.

(1) Presumption of continued underfunding.

(2) Presumption of underfunding beginning on first day of 4th month for certain underfunded plans.

(3) Presumption of underfunding beginning on first day of 10th month.

(4) Certification of AFTAP.

(5) Examples of rules of paragraphs (h)(1), (h)(2), and (h)(3) of this section.

(6) Examples of application of paragraph (h)(4) of this section.

(i) [Reserved]

(j) Definitions.

(1) Adjusted funding target attainment percentage.

(2) Annuity starting date.

(3) First effective plan year.

(4) Funding target.

(5) Prior year adjusted funding target attainment percentage.

(6) Prohibited payment.

(7) Section 436 contributions.

(8) Section 436 measurement date.

(9) Unpredictable contingent event.

(10) Examples.

(k) Effective/applicability dates.

(1) Statutory effective date.

(2) Collectively bargained plan exception.

(3) Effective date/applicability date of regulations. [Reg. § 1.436-0.]

☐ [*T.D. 9467, 10-14-2009.*]

[Reg. § 1.436-1]

§ 1.436-1. Limits on benefits and benefit accruals under single employer defined benefit plans.—(a) *General rules.*—(1) *Qualification requirement.*—Section 401(a)(29) provides that a defined benefit pension plan that is subject to section 412 and that is not a multiemployer plan (within the meaning of section 414(f)) is a qualified plan *only if it satisfies the requirements of section 436.* This section provides rules relating to funding-based limitations on certain benefits under section 436, and the requirements of section 436 are satisfied only if the plan meets the requirements of this section beginning with the plan's first effective plan year. This section applies to single employer defined benefit plans (including multiple employer plans), but does not apply to multiemployer plans.

(2) *Organization of the regulation.*—Paragraph (b) of this section describes limitations on shutdown benefits and other unpredictable contingent event benefits. Paragraph (c) of this section describes limitations on plan amendments increasing liabilities. Paragraph (d)

of this section describes limitations on prohibited payments. Paragraph (e) of this section describes limitations on benefit accruals. Paragraph (f) of this section provides rules relating to methods to avoid or terminate benefit limitations. Paragraph (g) of this section provides rules for the operation of the plan in relation to benefit limitations under section 436. Paragraph (h) of this section describes related presumptions regarding underfunding that apply for purposes of the benefit limitations under section 436 and requirements relating to certifications. Paragraph (j) of this section contains definitions. Paragraph (k) of this section contains effective/applicability date provisions.

(3) *Special rules for certain plans.*—(i) *New plans.*—The limitations described in paragraphs (b), (c), and (e) of this section do not apply to a plan for the first 5 plan years of the plan. Except as otherwise provided by the Commissioner in guidance of general applicability, plan years of the plan include the following (in addition to plan years during which the plan was maintained by the employer or plan sponsor):

(A) Plan years when the plan was maintained by a predecessor employer within the meaning of § 1.415(f)-1(c)(1).

(B) Plan years of another defined benefit plan maintained by a predecessor employer within the meaning of § 1.415(f)-1(c)(2) within the preceding five years if any participants in the plan participated in that other defined benefit plan (even if the plan maintained by the employer is not the plan that was maintained by the predecessor employer).

(C) Plan years of another defined benefit plan maintained by the employer within the preceding five years if any participants in the plan participated in that other defined benefit plan.

(ii) *Application of section 436 after termination of a plan.*—(A) *In general.*—Except as otherwise provided in paragraph (a)(3)(ii)(B) of this section, any section 436 limitations in effect immediately before the termination of a plan do not cease to apply thereafter.

(B) *Exception for payments pursuant to plan termination.*—The limitations under section 436(d) and paragraph (d) of this section do not apply to prohibited payments (within the meaning of paragraph (j)(6) of this section) that are made to carry out the termination of a plan in accordance with applicable law. For example, a plan sponsor's purchase of an irrevocable commitment from an insurer to pay benefit liabilities in connection with the standard termination of a plan in accordance with section 4041(b)(3) of the Employee Retirement Income Security Act of 1974, as amended (ERISA), and in accordance with 29 CFR § 4041.28, does not violate section 436(d) or this section.

(iii) *Multiple employer plans.*—In the case of a multiple employer plan to which section 413(c)(4)(A) applies, this section applies separately with respect to each employer under the plan, as if each employer maintained a separate plan. Thus, the benefit limitations under section 436 and this section could apply differently to participants who are employees of different employers under such a multiple employer plan. In the case of a multiple employer plan to which section 413(c)(4)(A) does not apply (that is, a plan described in section 413(c)(4)(B) that has not made the election for section 413(c)(4)(A) to apply), this section applies as if all participants in the plan were employed by a single employer.

(4) *Treatment of plan as of close of prohibited or cessation period.*—(i) *Application to prohibited payments and accruals.*—(A) *Resumption of prohibited payments.*—If a limitation on prohibited payments under paragraph (d) of this section applied to a plan as of a section 436 measurement date (as defined in paragraph (j)(8) of this section), but that limit no longer applies to the plan as of a later section 436 measurement date, then the limitation on prohibited payments under the plan does not apply to benefits with annuity starting dates (as defined in paragraph (j)(2) of this section) that are on or after that later section 436 measurement date. Any amendment to eliminate an optional form of benefit that contains a prohibited payment with respect to an annuity starting date during a period in which the limitations of section 436(d) and paragraph (d) of this section do not apply to the plan is subject to the rules of section 411(d)(6).

(B) *Resumption of benefit accruals.*—If a limitation on benefit accruals under paragraph (e) of this section applied to a plan as of a section 436 measurement date, but that limit no longer applies to the plan as of a later section 436 measurement date, then that limitation does not apply to benefit accruals that are based on service on or after that later section 436 measurement date, except to the extent that the plan provides that benefit accruals will not resume when the limitation ceases to apply. The plan must comply with the rules relating to partial years of participation and the prohibition on double proration under Department of Labor regulation 29 CFR § 2530.204-2(c) and (d).

(ii) *Restoration of options and missed benefit accruals.*—
(A) *Option to amend plan.*—A plan is permitted to be amended to provide participants who had an annuity starting date within a period during which a limitation under paragraph (d) of this section applied to the plan with the opportunity to make a new election under which the form of benefit previously elected is modified, subject to applicable qualification requirements. A participant who makes such a new election is treated as having a new annuity starting date under sections 415 and 417. Similarly, a plan is permitted to be amended to provide that any benefit accruals which were limited under the rules of paragraph (e) of this section are credited under the plan when the limitation no longer applies, subject to applicable qualification requirements. Any such plan amendment with respect to a new annuity starting date or crediting of benefit accruals is subject to the requirements of section 436(c) and paragraph (c) of this section.

(B) *Automatic plan provisions.*—A plan is permitted to provide that participants who had an annuity starting date within a period during which a limitation under paragraph (d) of this section applied to the plan will be provided with the opportunity to have a new annuity starting date (which would constitute a new annuity starting date under sections 415 and 417) under which the form of benefit previously elected may be modified, subject to applicable qualification requirements, once the limitations of paragraph (d) of this section cease to apply. In addition, subject to the rules of paragraph (c)(3) of this section, a plan is permitted to provide for the automatic restoration of benefit accruals that had been limited under section 436(e) as of the section 436 measurement date that the limitation ceases to apply.

(iii) *Shutdown and other unpredictable contingent event benefits.*—If unpredictable contingent event benefits with respect to an unpredictable contingent event that occurs during the plan year are not permitted to be paid after the occurrence of the event because of the limitations of section 436(b) and paragraph (b) of this section, but are permitted to be paid later in the plan year as a result of additional contributions under paragraph (f)(2) of this section or pursuant to the enrolled actuary's certification of the adjusted funding target attainment percentage for the plan year that meets the requirements of paragraph (g)(5)(ii)(B) of this section, then those unpredictable contingent event benefits must automatically become payable, retroactive to the period those benefits would have been payable under the terms of the plan (other than plan terms implementing the requirements of section 436(b)). If the benefits do not become payable during the plan year in accordance with the preceding sentence, then the plan is treated as if it does not provide for those benefits. However, all or any portion of those benefits can be restored pursuant to a plan amendment that meets the requirements of section 436(c) and paragraph (c) of this section and other applicable qualification requirements.

(iv) *Treatment of plan amendments that do not take effect.*—If a plan amendment does not take effect as of the effective date of the amendment because of the limitations of section 436(c) and paragraph (c) of this section, but is permitted to take effect later in the plan year as a result of additional contributions under paragraph (f)(2) of this section or pursuant to the enrolled actuary's certification of the adjusted funding target attainment percentage for the plan year that meets the requirements of paragraph (g)(5)(ii)(C) of this section, then the plan amendment must automatically take effect as of the first day of the plan year (or, if later, the original effective date of the amendment). If the plan amendment cannot take effect during the plan year, then it must be treated as if it were never adopted, unless the plan amendment provides otherwise.

(v) *Example.*—The following example illustrates the rules of this paragraph (a)(4):

Example. (i) Plan T is a non-collectively bargained defined benefit plan with a plan year that is the calendar year and a valuation date of January 1. As of January 1, 2011, Plan T does not have a funding standard carryover balance or a prefunding balance. Plan T's sponsor is not in bankruptcy. Beginning January 1, 2011, Plan T is subject to the restriction on prohibited payments under paragraph (d)(3) of this section based on a presumed adjusted funding target attainment percentage (AFTAP) of 75%.

(ii) U is a participant in Plan T. Participant U retires on February 1, 2011, and elects to receive benefits in the form of a single sum. Plan T may pay only a portion (generally, 50%) of the prohibited payment. Accordingly, U elects in accordance with paragraph (d)(3)(ii) of this section to receive 50% of U's benefit in a single sum (*up to the 2011 PBGC maximum benefit guarantee amount described in paragraph (d)(3)(iii)(C) of this section*) and the remainder as an immediately commencing straight life annuity.

(iii) On March 1, 2011, the enrolled actuary for the Plan certifies that the AFTAP for 2011 is 80%. Accordingly, beginning

March 1, 2011, Plan T is no longer subject to the restriction under paragraph (d)(3) of this section.

(iv) Effective March 1, 2011, Plan T is amended to provide that a participant whose benefits were restricted under paragraph (d)(3) of this section with respect to an annuity starting date between January 1, 2011, and February 28, 2011, may elect, within a specified period on or after March 1, 2011, a new annuity starting date and receive the remainder of his or her pension benefits in an accelerated form of payment. Plan T's enrolled actuary determines that the AFTAP, taking into account the amendment, would still be 80%. The amendment is permitted to take effect because Plan T would have an AFTAP of 80% taking into account the amendment and is therefore neither subject to the restriction on plan amendments in paragraph (c) of this section nor the restrictions on prohibited payments under paragraphs (d)(1) and (d)(3) of this section. Accordingly, Participant U may elect, within the specified period and subject to otherwise applicable qualification rules, including spousal consent, to receive the remainder of U's benefits in the form of a single sum on or after March 1, 2011.

(5) *Deemed election to reduce funding balances.*—(i) *Limitations on accelerated benefit payments.*—If a benefit limitation under paragraph (d)(1) or (d)(3) of this section would (but for this paragraph (a)(5)) apply to a plan, the employer is treated as having made an election under section 430(f) to reduce the prefunding balance or funding standard carryover balance by such amount as is necessary for the adjusted funding target attainment percentage to be at the applicable threshold (60 or 80 percent, as the case may be) in order for the benefit limitation not to apply to the plan. The determination of whether a benefit limitation under paragraph (d) of this section would apply to a plan is based on whether the plan provides for an optional form of benefit that would be limited under section 436(d) and is not based on whether any participant elects payment of benefits in such a form.

(ii) *Other limitations for collectively bargained plans.*—(A) *General rule.*—In the case of a collectively bargained plan to which a benefit limitation under paragraph (b), (c), or (e) of this section would (but for this paragraph (a)(5)) apply, the employer is treated as having made an election under section 430(f) to reduce the prefunding balance or funding standard carryover balance by such amount as is necessary for the adjusted funding target attainment percentage to be at the applicable threshold (60 or 80 percent, as the case may be) in order for the benefit limitation not to apply to the plan, taking into account the adjustments described in paragraph (g)(2)(iii)(A), (g)(3)(ii)(A), or (g)(5)(i)(B) of this section, whichever applies.

(B) *Collectively bargained plans.*—A plan is considered a collectively bargained plan for purposes of this paragraph (a)(5)(ii) if—

(1) At least 50 percent of the employees benefiting under the plan (within the meaning of §1.410(b)-3(a)) are members of collective bargaining units for which the benefit levels under the plan are specified under a collective bargaining agreement; or

(2) At least 25 percent of the participants in the plan are members of collective bargaining units for which the benefit levels under the plan are specified under a collective bargaining agreement.

(iii) *Exception for insufficient funding balances.*—(A) *In general.*—Paragraphs (a)(5)(i) and (a)(5)(ii) of this section apply with respect to a benefit limitation for any plan year only if the application of those paragraphs would result in the corresponding benefit limitation not applying for such plan year. Thus, if the plan's prefunding and funding standard carryover balances were reduced to zero and the resulting increase in plan assets taken into account would still not increase the plan's adjusted funding target attainment percentage enough to reach the threshold percentage applicable to the benefit limitation, the deemed election to reduce those balances pursuant to paragraph (a)(5)(i) or (a)(5)(ii) of this section does not apply.

(B) *Presumed adjusted funding target attainment percentage less than 60 percent.*—During any period when a plan is presumed to have an adjusted funding target attainment percentage of less than 60 percent as a result of paragraph (h)(3) of this section, the plan is treated as if the prefunding balance and the funding standard carryover balance are insufficient to increase the adjusted funding target attainment percentage to the threshold percentage of 60 percent. Accordingly, the deemed election to reduce those balances pursuant to paragraphs (a)(5)(i) and (a)(5)(ii) of this section does not apply to the plan.

(iv) *Other rules.*—(A) *Date of deemed election.*—If an election is deemed to be made pursuant to this paragraph (a)(5), then the plan sponsor is treated as having made that election on the date as of which the applicable benefit limitation would otherwise apply.

(B) *Coordination with section 436 contributions.*—The determination of whether one of the benefit limitations described in paragraph (a)(5)(ii)(A) of this section would otherwise apply is made without regard to any contribution described in paragraph (f)(2) of this section. Thus, the requirement to reduce the prefunding balance or funding standard carryover balance under paragraph (a)(5)(ii) of this section cannot be avoided through the use of a section 436 contribution.

(C) *Coordination with elections to offset minimum required contribution.*—See § 1.430(f)-1(d)(1)(ii) for rules on the coordination of elections to offset the minimum required contribution and the deemed election to reduce the prefunding and funding standard carryover balances under this paragraph (a)(5).

(v) *Example.*—The following example illustrates the rules of this paragraph (a)(5):

Example. (i) Plan W is a collectively bargained, single employer defined benefit plan sponsored by Sponsor X, with a plan year that is the calendar year and a valuation date of January 1.

(ii) The enrolled actuary for Plan W issues a certification on March 1, 2010, that the 2010 AFTAP is 81%. Sponsor X adopts an amendment on March 25, 2010, to increase benefits under a formula based on participant compensation, with an effective date of May 1, 2010. (Because the formula is based on compensation, the exception in paragraph (c)(4)(i) of this section does not apply.) The plan's enrolled actuary determines that the plan's AFTAP for 2010 would be 75% if the benefits attributable to the plan amendment were taken into account in determining the funding target.

(iii) Because the AFTAP would be below the 80% threshold if the benefits attributable to the plan amendment were taken into account in determining the funding target, Sponsor X is deemed pursuant to paragraph (a)(5)(ii) of this section to have made an election to reduce Plan W's prefunding and funding standard carryover balances by the amount necessary for the AFTAP to reach the 80% threshold (reflecting the increase in funding target attributable to the plan amendment), provided that the amount of those balances is sufficient for this purpose.

(iv) If the deemed election described in paragraph (iii) of this example occurs, the plan amendment takes effect on its effective date (May 1, 2010). See paragraph (f) of this section for other methods to avoid or terminate benefit limitations (where, for example, the amount necessary for a benefit limitation not to apply for a plan year exceeds the sum of the prefunding balance and the funding standard carryover balance).

(6) *Notice requirements.*—See section 101(j) of ERISA for rules requiring the plan administrator of a single employer plan to provide a written notice to participants and beneficiaries within 30 days after certain specified dates, which depend on whether the plan has become subject to a restriction described in the ERISA provisions that are parallel to Internal Revenue Code sections 436(b), 436(d), and 436(e) (ERISA sections 206(g)(1), 206(g)(3), and 206(g)(4), respectively).

(b) *Limitation on shutdown benefits and other unpredictable contingent event benefits.*—(1) *In general.*—Except as otherwise provided in this paragraph (b), a plan satisfies section 436(b) and this paragraph (b) only if it provides that unpredictable contingent event benefits with respect to any unpredictable contingent events occurring during a plan year will not be paid if the adjusted funding target attainment percentage for the plan year is—

(i) Less than 60 percent; or

(ii) 60 percent or more, but would be less than 60 percent if the adjusted funding target attainment percentage were redetermined applying an actuarial assumption that the likelihood of occurrence of the unpredictable contingent event during the plan year is 100 percent.

(2) *Exemption if section 436 contribution is made.*—The prohibition on payment of unpredictable contingent event benefits under paragraph (b)(1) of this section ceases to apply with respect to benefits attributable to an unpredictable contingent event occurring during the plan year upon payment by the plan sponsor of the contribution described in paragraph (f)(2)(iii) of this section with respect to that event. If the prior sentence applies with respect to an unpredictable contingent event, then all benefits with respect to the unpredictable contingent event must be paid, including benefits for periods prior to the contribution. See paragraph (f) of this section for additional rules.

(3) *Rules of application.*—(i) *Participant-by-participant application.*—The limitations of section 436(b) and this paragraph (b) apply on a participant-by-participant basis. Thus, whether payment or commencement of an unpredictable contingent event benefit under a plan is restricted with respect to a participant is determined based on whether the participant satisfies the plan's eligibility requirements (other than the attainment of any age, performance of any service,

receipt or derivation of any compensation, or the occurrence of death or disability) for such a benefit in a plan year in which the limitations of section 436(b) and this paragraph (b) apply.

(ii) *Multiple contingencies.*—In the case of a plan that provides for a benefit that depends upon the occurrence of more than one unpredictable contingent event with respect to a participant, the unpredictable contingent event for purposes of section 436(b) and this paragraph (b) occurs upon the last to occur of those unpredictable contingent events.

(iii) *Cessation of benefits.*—Cessation of a benefit under a plan upon the occurrence of a specified event is not an unpredictable contingent event for purposes of section 436(b) and this paragraph (b). Thus, section 436(b) and this paragraph (b) do not prohibit provisions of a plan that provide for cessation, suspension, or reduction of any benefits upon occurrence of any event. However, upon any subsequent recommencement of benefits (including any restoration of benefits), the rules of section 436 and this section will apply.

(4) *Prior unpredictable contingent event.*—Unpredictable contingent event benefits attributable to an unpredictable contingent event that occurred within a period during which no limitation under this paragraph (b) applied to the plan are not affected by the limitation described in this paragraph (b) as it applies in a subsequent period. For example, if a plant shutdown occurs in 2010 and the plan's funded status is such that benefits contingent upon that plant shutdown are not subject to the limitation described in this paragraph (b) for that calendar plan year, this paragraph (b) does not apply to restrict payment of those benefits even if another plant shutdown occurs in 2012 that results in the restriction of benefits that are contingent upon that later plant shutdown under this paragraph (b) (where the plan's adjusted funding target attainment percentage for 2012 would be less than 60 percent taking into account the liability attributable to those shutdown benefits)

(c) *Limitations on plan amendments increasing liability for benefits.*—(1) *In general.*—Except as otherwise provided in this paragraph (c), a plan satisfies section 436(c) and this paragraph (c) only if the plan provides that no amendment to the plan that has the effect of increasing liabilities of the plan by reason of increases in benefits, establishment of new benefits, changing the rate of benefit accrual, or changing the rate at which benefits become nonforfeitable will take effect in a plan year if the adjusted funding target attainment percentage for the plan year is—

(i) Less than 80 percent; or

(ii) 80 percent or more, but would be less than 80 percent if the benefits attributable to the amendment were taken into account in determining the adjusted funding target attainment percentage.

(2) *Exemption if section 436 contribution is made.*—(i) *General rule.*—The limitations on plan amendments in paragraph (c)(1) of this section cease to apply with respect to an amendment upon payment by the plan sponsor of the contribution described in paragraph (f)(2)(iv) of this section, so that the amendment is permitted to take effect as of the later of the first day of the plan year or the effective date of the amendment. See paragraph (f) of this section for additional rules.

(ii) *Amendments that do not increase funding target.*—If the amount of the contribution described in paragraph (f)(2)(iv) of this section is $0 (because the amendment increases benefits solely for future periods), the amendment is permitted to take effect without regard to this paragraph (c). However, see § 1.430(d)-1(d)(2) for a rule that requires such an amendment to be taken into account in determining the funding target and the target normal cost in certain situations.

(3) *Rules of application regarding pre-existing plan provisions.*—If a plan contains a provision that provides for the automatic restoration of benefit accruals that were not permitted to accrue because of the application of section 436(e) and paragraph (e) of this section, the restoration of those accruals is generally treated as a plan amendment that is subject to section 436(c). However, such a provision is permitted to take effect without regard to the limits of section 436(c) and this paragraph (c) if—

(i) The continuous period of the limitation is 12 months or less; and

(ii) The plan's enrolled actuary certifies that the adjusted funding target attainment percentage for the plan would not be less than 60 percent taking into account the restored benefit accruals for the prior plan year.

(4) *Exceptions.*—(i) *Benefit increases based on compensation.*—(A) *In general.*—In accordance with section 436(c)(3), section 436(c) and this paragraph (c) do not apply to any amendment that provides for an increase in benefits under a formula that is not based on a

Reg. § 1.436-1(c)(4)(i)(A)

participant's compensation, but only if the rate of increase in benefits does not exceed the contemporaneous rate of increase in average wages of participants covered by the amendment. The determination of the rate of increase in average wages is made by taking into consideration the net increase in average wages from the period of time beginning with the effective date of the most recent benefit increase applicable to all of those participants who are covered by the current amendment and ending on the effective date of the current amendment.

(B) *Application to participants who are not currently employed.*—If an amendment applies to both currently employed participants and other participants, all participants to whom the amendment applies are included in determining the increase in average wages of the participants covered by the amendment for purposes of this paragraph (c)(4)(i). For this purpose, participants who are not employees at any time during the period from the effective date of the most recent earlier benefit increase applicable to all of the participants who are covered by the current amendment and ending on the effective date of the current amendment are treated as having no increase or decrease in wages for the period after severance from employment.

(C) *Separate amendments for different plan populations.*—In lieu of a single amendment that applies to both currently employed participants and other participants as described in paragraph (c)(4)(i)(B) of this section, the employer can adopt multiple amendments — such as one that increases benefits for participants currently employed on the effective date of the current amendment and another one that increases benefits for other participants. In that case, the two amendments are considered separately in determining the increase in average wages, and the exception in this paragraph (c)(4)(i) applies separately to each amendment. Thus, the increase in benefits for currently employed participants takes effect if it satisfies the exception under this paragraph (c)(4), but the amendment increasing benefits for other participants who received no increase in wages from the employer during the period over which the increase in average wages is separately subject to the rules of this paragraph (c) without regard to the rules of this paragraph (c)(4).

(ii) *Plan provisions providing for accelerated vesting.*—To the extent that any amendment provides for (or any pre-existing plan provision results in) a mandatory increase in the vesting of benefits under the Code or ERISA (such as vesting rate increases pursuant to statute, plan termination amendments or partial terminations under section 411(d)(3), and vesting increases required by the rules for top-heavy plans under section 416), that amendment (or pre-existing plan provision) does not constitute an amendment that changes the rate at which benefits become nonforfeitable for purposes of section 436(c) and this paragraph (c). However, this paragraph (c)(4)(ii) applies only to the extent the increase in vesting is necessary to enable the plan to continue to satisfy the requirements for qualified plans.

(iii) *Authority for additional exceptions.*—The Commissioner may, in guidance of general applicability, issue additional rules under which other amendments to a plan are not treated as amendments to which section 436(c) and this paragraph (c) apply. See §601.601(d)(2) relating to objectives and standards for publishing regulations, revenue rulings and revenue procedures in the Internal Revenue Bulletin.

(5) *Rule for determining when an amendment takes effect.*—For purposes of section 436(c) and this paragraph (c), in the case of an amendment that increases benefits, the amendment takes effect under a plan on the first date on which any individual who is or could be a participant or beneficiary under the plan would obtain a legal right to the increased benefit if the individual were on that date to satisfy the applicable requirements for entitlement to the benefit (such as the attainment of any age, performance of any service, receipt or derivation of any compensation, or the occurrence of death, disability, or severance from employment).

(6) *Treatment of mergers, consolidations, and transfers of plan assets into a plan.*—[Reserved.]

(d) *Limitations on prohibited payments.*—(1) *AFTAP less than 60 percent.*—A plan satisfies the requirements of section 436(d)(1) and this paragraph (d)(1) only if the plan provides that, if the plan's adjusted funding target attainment percentage for a plan year is less than 60 percent, a participant or beneficiary is not permitted to elect an optional form of benefit that includes a prohibited payment, and the plan will not pay any prohibited payment, with an annuity starting date on or after the applicable section 436 measurement date.

(2) *Bankruptcy.*—A plan satisfies the requirements of section 436(d)(2) and this paragraph (d)(2) only if the plan provides that a participant or beneficiary is not permitted to elect an optional form of benefit that includes a prohibited payment, and the plan will not pay

any prohibited payment, with an annuity starting date that occurs during any period in which the plan sponsor is a debtor in a case under title 11, United States Code, or similar Federal or State law, except for payments made within a plan year with an annuity starting date that occurs on or after the date on which the enrolled actuary of the plan certifies that the plan's adjusted funding target attainment percentage for that plan year is not less than 100 percent.

(3) *Limited payment if AFTAP at least 60 percent but less than 80 percent.*—(i) *In general.*—A plan satisfies the requirements of section 436(d)(3) and this paragraph (d)(3) only if the plan provides that, in any case in which the plan's adjusted funding target attainment percentage for a plan year is 60 percent or more but is less than 80 percent, a participant or beneficiary is not permitted to elect the payment of an optional form of benefit that includes a prohibited payment, and the plan will not pay any prohibited payment, with an annuity starting date on or after the applicable section 436 measurement date, unless the present value, determined in accordance with section 417(e)(3), of the portion of the benefit that is being paid in a prohibited payment (which portion is determined under paragraph (d)(3)(iii)(B) of this section) does not exceed the lesser of—

(A) 50 percent of the present value (determined in accordance with section 417(e)(3)) of the benefit payable in the optional form of benefit that includes the prohibited payment; or

(B) 100 percent of the PBGC maximum benefit guarantee amount described in paragraph (d)(3)(iii)(C) of this section.

(ii) *Bifurcation if optional form unavailable.*—(A) *Requirement to offer bifurcation.*—If an optional form of benefit that is otherwise available under the terms of the plan is not available as of the annuity starting date because of the application of paragraph (d)(3)(i) of this section, then the plan must permit the participant or beneficiary to elect to—

(1) Receive the unrestricted portion of that optional form of benefit (determined under the rules of paragraph (d)(3)(iii)(D) of this section) at that annuity starting date, determined by treating the unrestricted portion of the benefit as if it were the participant's or beneficiary's entire benefit under the plan;

(2) Commence benefits with respect to the participant's or beneficiary's entire benefit under the plan in any other optional form of benefit available under the plan at the same annuity starting date that satisfies paragraph (d)(3)(i) of this section; or

(3) Defer commencement of the payments to the extent described in paragraph (d)(5) of this section.

(B) *Rules relating to bifurcation.*—If the participant or beneficiary elects payment of the unrestricted portion of the benefit as described in paragraph (d)(3)(ii)(A)(1) of this section, then the plan must permit the participant or beneficiary to elect payment of the remainder of the participant's or beneficiary's benefits under the plan in any optional form of benefit at that annuity starting date otherwise available under the plan that would not have included a prohibited payment if that optional form applied to the entire benefit of the participant or beneficiary. The rules of §1.417(e)-1 are applied separately to the separate optional forms for the unrestricted portion of the benefit and the remainder of the benefit (the restricted portion).

(C) *Plan alternative that anticipates election of payment that includes a prohibited payment.*—With respect to an optional form of benefit that includes a prohibited payment and that is not permitted to be paid under paragraph (d)(3)(i) of this section, for which no additional information from the participant or beneficiary (such as information regarding a social security leveling optional form of benefit) is needed to make that determination, rather than wait for the participant or beneficiary to elect such optional form of benefit, a plan is permitted to provide for separate elections with respect to the restricted and unrestricted portions of that optional form of benefit. However, the rule in the preceding sentence applies only if—

(1) The plan applies the rule to all such optional forms; and

(2) The plan identifies the option that the bifurcation election replaces.

(iii) *Definitions applicable to limited payment option.*—(A) *In general.*—The definitions in this paragraph (d)(3)(iii) apply for purposes of this paragraph (d)(3).

(B) *Portion of benefit being paid in a prohibited payment.*—If a benefit is being paid in an optional form for which any of the payments is greater than the amount payable under a straight life annuity to the participant or beneficiary (plus any social security supplements described in the last sentence of section 411(a)(9) payable to the participant or beneficiary) with the same annuity starting date, then the portion of the benefit that is being paid in a prohibited payment is the excess of each payment over the smallest payment during the participant's lifetime under the optional form of benefit (treating a period after the annuity starting date and during the participant's lifetime in which no payments are made as a payment of zero).

(C) *PBGC maximum benefit guarantee amount.*—The PBGC maximum benefit guarantee amount described in this paragraph (d)(3)(iii)(C) is the present value (determined under guidance prescribed by the Pension Benefit Guaranty Corporation, using the interest and mortality assumptions under section 417(e)) of the maximum benefit guarantee with respect to a participant (based on the participant's age or the beneficiary's age at the annuity starting date) under section 4022 of ERISA for the year in which the annuity starting date occurs.

(D) *Unrestricted portion of the benefit.*—(1) *General rule.*—Except as otherwise provided in this paragraph (d)(3)(iii)(D), the unrestricted portion of the benefit with respect to any optional form of benefit is 50 percent of the amount payable under the optional form of benefit.

(2) *Special rule for forms which include social security leveling or a refund of employee contributions.*—For an optional form of benefit that is a prohibited payment on account of a social security leveling feature (as defined in §1.411(d)-3(g)(16)) or a refund of employee contributions feature (as defined in §1.411(d)-3(g)(11)), the unrestricted portion of the benefit is the optional form of benefit that would apply if the participant's or beneficiary's accrued benefit were 50 percent smaller.

(3) *Limited to PBGC maximum benefit guarantee amount.*—After the application of the preceding rules of this paragraph (d)(3)(iii)(D), the unrestricted portion of the benefit with respect to the optional form of benefit is reduced, to the extent necessary, so that the present value (determined in accordance with section 417(e)) of the unrestricted portion of that optional form of benefit does not exceed the PBGC maximum benefit guarantee amount (described in paragraph (d)(3)(iii)(C) of this section).

(iv) *Other rules.*—(A) *One time application.*—A plan satisfies the requirements of this paragraph (d)(3) only if the plan provides that, in the case of a participant with respect to whom a prohibited payment (or series of prohibited payments under a single optional form of benefit) is made pursuant to paragraph (d)(3)(i) or (ii) of this section, no additional prohibited payment may be made with respect to that participant during any period of consecutive plan years for which prohibited payments are limited under this paragraph (d).

(B) *Treatment of beneficiaries.*—For purposes of this paragraph (d)(3), benefits provided with respect to a participant and any beneficiary of the participant (including an alternate payee, as defined in section 414(p)(8)) are aggregated. If the only benefits paid under the plan with respect to the participant are death benefits payable to the beneficiary, then paragraph (d)(3)(iii)(B) of this section is applied by substituting the lifetime of the beneficiary for the lifetime of the participant. If the accrued benefit of a participant is allocated to such an alternate payee and one or more other persons, then the unrestricted amount under paragraph (d)(3)(iii)(D) of this section is allocated among such persons in the same manner as the accrued benefit is allocated, unless a qualified domestic relations order (as defined in section 414(p)(1)(A)) with respect to the participant or the alternate payee provides otherwise. See paragraphs (j)(2)(ii) and (j)(6)(ii) of this section for other special rules relating to beneficiaries.

(C) *Treatment of annuity purchases and plan transfers.*—This paragraph (d)(3)(iv)(C) applies for purposes of applying paragraphs (d)(3)(i) and (iii)(D) of this section. In the case of a prohibited payment described in paragraph (j)(6)(i)(B) of this section (relating to purchase from an insurer), the present value of the portion of the benefit that is being paid in a prohibited payment is the cost to the plan of the irrevocable commitment and, in the case of a prohibited payment described in paragraph (j)(6)(i)(C) of this section (relating to certain plan transfers), the present value of the portion of the benefit that is being paid in a prohibited payment is the present value of the liabilities transferred (determined in accordance with section 414(l)). In addition, the present value of the accrued benefit is substituted for the present value of the benefit payable in the optional form of benefit that includes the prohibited payment in paragraph (d)(3)(i)(A) of this section. (Further, see §1.411(d)-4, A-2(a)(3)(ii), for a rule under section 411(d)(6) that applies to an optional form of benefit that includes a prohibited payment described in paragraph (j)(6)(i)(B) of this section.)

(v) *Examples.*—The following examples illustrate the rules of this paragraph (d)(3):

Example 1. (i) Plan A has a plan year that is the calendar year, and is subject to the restriction on prohibited payments under paragraph (d)(3) of this section for the 2010 plan year. Participant P is not married, and retires at age 65 during 2010, while the restriction under paragraph (d)(3) of this section applies to Plan A. P's accrued benefit is $10,000 per month, payable commencing at age 65 as a straight life annuity. Plan A provides for an optional single-sum payment (subject to the restrictions under section 436) equal to the present value of the participant's accrued benefit using actuarial assumptions under section 417(e). P's single-sum payment, determined without regard to this paragraph (d), is calculated to be $1,416,000, payable at age 65.

(ii) The PBGC guaranteed monthly benefit for a straight life annuity payable at age 65 in 2010 (for purposes of this example) is assumed to be $4,500. The PBGC maximum benefit guarantee amount at age 65 is assumed to be $637,200 for 2010.

(iii) Because Participant P retires during a period when the restriction in paragraph (d)(3) of this section applies to Plan A, only a portion of the benefit can be paid in the form of a single sum. P elects a single-sum payment. Because a single sum payment is a prohibited payment, a determination must be made whether the payment can be paid under paragraph (d)(3)(i) of this section. In this case, because the present value of the portion of Participant P's benefit that is being paid in a prohibited payment exceeds the lesser of 50% of the benefit or the PBGC maximum benefit guarantee amount, it cannot be paid under paragraph (d)(3)(i) of this section. Accordingly, the maximum single sum that P can receive is $637,200 (that is, the lesser of 50% of $1,416,000 or $637,200).

(iv) Pursuant to paragraph (d)(3)(ii) of this section, Plan A must offer P the option to bifurcate the benefit into unrestricted and restricted portions. The unrestricted portion is a monthly straight life annuity of $4,500, which can be paid in a single sum of $637,200. If P elects to receive the unrestricted portion of the benefit in the form of a single sum, then, with respect to the $5,500 restricted portion, Plan A must permit P to elect any form of benefit that would otherwise be permitted with respect to the full $10,000 and that is not a prohibited payment. Alternatively, Plan A may provide that P is permitted to elect to defer commencement of the restricted portion, subject to applicable qualification rules.

Example 2. (i) The facts are the same as in *Example 1.* In addition, Plan A provides an optional form of payment (subject to any benefit restrictions under section 436) that consists of a partial payment equal to the total return of employee contributions to the plan accumulated with interest, with an annuity payment for the remainder of the participant's benefit.

(ii) Participant Q is not married, and retires at age 65 during 2010, while Plan A is subject to the restriction under paragraph (d)(3) of this section. Participant Q has an accrued benefit equal to a straight life annuity of $3,000 per month. Under the optional form described in paragraph (i) of this *Example 2*, Q may elect a partial payment of $99,120 (representing the return of employee contributions accumulated with interest), plus a straight life annuity of $2,300 per month. The present value of Participant Q's accrued benefit, using actuarial assumptions under section 417(e), is $424,800.

(iii) Because the present value of the portion of Q's benefit that is being paid in a prohibited payment ($99,120) does not exceed the lesser of 50% of the present value of benefits (50% of $424,800) or 100% of the PBGC maximum benefit guarantee amount ($637,200 at age 65 for 2010), the optional form described in paragraph (i) of this *Example 2* is permitted to be paid under paragraph (d)(3)(i) of this section.

Example 3. (i) The facts are the same as in *Example 1.* In addition, Plan A provides an optional form of payment under a social security leveling option (subject to any benefit restrictions under section 436) that consists of an increased temporary benefit payable until age 62, with reduced payments beginning at age 62. The benefit is structured so that the combination of the participant's pension benefit and Social Security benefit provides an approximately level income for the participant's lifetime. The PBGC maximum benefit guarantee amount at age 55 is assumed to be $362,776 for 2010.

(ii) Participant R retires at age 55 in 2010 and is eligible to receive a level lifetime annuity of $1,200 per month beginning immediately. Instead, Participant R elects to receive a benefit under the social security leveling optional form of payment. Participant R's Social Security benefit payable at age 62 is projected, under the terms specified in Plan A, to be $1,500 per month. The Plan A adjustment factor for the social security leveling option using the minimum present value requirements of section 417(e)(3) is .590 at age 55. Therefore, Participant R's benefit payable from age 55 to age 62 is $2,085 per month ($1,200 + .590 × $1,500), and the benefit payable for Participant's lifetime, beginning after age 62, is $585 per month ($2,085 × $1,500).

(iii) Because the optional form provides some payments which are greater than payments described in paragraph (j)(6)(i)(A) of this section ($1,200), the portion of the benefit that is being paid in a prohibited payment is $1,500 per month which is payable from age 55 to age 62. Using the applicable interest and mortality rates under section 417(e) as in effect for Plan A at the time the benefit commences, the present value of a temporary benefit of $1,500 per month ($2,085 × $585) payable from age 55 to age 62 is $106,417, and the present value of the entire benefit (a temporary benefit of $2,085 per month payable from age 55 to age 62 plus a deferred lifetime benefit of $585 commencing at age 62) is $207,458.

(iv) Because $106,417 is more than 50% of $207,468 (and because 50% of Participant R's benefit is less than $362,776, which is the PBGC maximum guaranteed benefit amount at age 55 for 2010), Participant R can only receive 50% of the benefit in the form of the social security leveling option. Pursuant to paragraph (d)(3)(ii) of this section, Plan A must offer Participant R the option to bifurcate the benefit into unrestricted and restricted portions. Participant R elects to receive the restricted portion of the early retirement benefit as a level lifetime annuity of $600 commencing at age 55.

(v) Participant R elects to receive the unrestricted portion of the early retirement benefit in the social security leveling form of payment. This portion of the benefit is determined under the social security leveling form of payment as if Participant R's benefit was one-half of the early retirement benefit, or $600. However, using a monthly level lifetime benefit of $600 and a monthly social security benefit of $1,500, Participant R would have a negative benefit after age 62 ($600 + .590 × $1,500 is only $1,485; offsetting $1,500 at age 62 would produce a negative amount). Plan A provides that in this situation, the benefit under the social security leveling option is an actuarially equivalent monthly annuity payable until age 62, with zero payable thereafter. Using the actuarial equivalence factor of .590 at age 55, the plan administrator determines that the unrestricted portion of Participant R's benefit is $1,463 per month, payable from age 55 to age 62 ($600 + .590 × $1,463 = $1,463 payable until age 62; $1,463 × $1,463 = zero payable after age 62).

(vi) Combining the unrestricted and restricted portions of the benefit, Participant R will receive a total of $2,063 per month from age 55 to age 62 ($1,463 from the unrestricted portion of the benefit plus $600 from the restricted portion of the benefit), and $600 per month beginning at age 62 (zero from the unrestricted portion of the benefit plus $600 from the restricted portion of the benefit).

(4) *Exception for cessation of benefit accruals.*—This paragraph (d) does not apply to a plan for a plan year if the terms of the plan, as in effect for the period beginning on September 1, 2005, provided for no benefit accruals with respect to any participants. If a plan that is described in this paragraph (d)(4) provides for benefit accruals during any time on or after September 1, 2005 (treating benefit increases pursuant to a plan amendment as benefit accruals), this paragraph (d)(4) ceases to apply for the plan as of the date any benefits accrue under the plan (or the date the amendment takes effect). For example, the exception in this paragraph (d)(4) does not apply to a plan after the plan increases benefits to take into account increases in the limitations under section 415(b) on or after September 1, 2005.

(5) *Right to delay commencement.*—If a participant or beneficiary requests a distribution in an optional form of benefit that includes a prohibited payment that is not permitted to be paid under paragraph (d)(1), (d)(2), or (d)(3) of this section, the participant retains the right to delay commencement of benefits in accordance with the terms of the plan and applicable qualification requirements (such as sections 411(a)(11) and 401(a)(9)).

(6) *Plan alternative for special optional forms.*—A plan is permitted to offer optional forms of benefit that are solely available during the period in which paragraph (d)(1), (d)(2), or (d)(3) of this section applies to limit prohibited payments under the plan. For example, a plan may permit participants or beneficiaries who commence benefits during the period in which paragraph (d)(1) of this section (or paragraph (d)(2) of this section) applies to limit prohibited payments under the plan to elect, within a specified period after the date on which that paragraph ceases to apply to limit prohibited payments under the plan, to receive the remaining benefit in the form of a single-sum payment equal to the present value of the remaining benefit, but only to the extent then permitted under this paragraph (d). As another example, during a period when paragraph (d)(3) of this section applies to a plan, the plan may permit participants and beneficiaries to elect payment in an optional form of benefit that provides for the current payment of the unrestricted portion of the benefit, with a delayed commencement for the restricted portion of the benefit (subject to other applicable qualification requirements, such as sections 411(a)(11) and 401(a)(9)), or may satisfy paragraph (d)(3)(i) of this section by permitting participants and beneficiaries to elect an optional form of benefit that combines an unsubsidized *single-sum payment for over 50 percent of the accrued benefit* with a subsidized early retirement life annuity for the remainder of the accrued benefit. Any such optional forms must satisfy this paragraph (d) and applicable qualification requirements, including satisfaction of section 417(e) and section 415 (at each annuity starting date).

(7) *Exception for distributions permitted without consent of the participant under section 411(a)(11).*—[Reserved.]

(e) *Limitation on benefit accruals for plans with severe funding shortfalls.*—(1) *In general.*—Except as otherwise provided in this paragraph (e), a plan satisfies the requirements of section 436(e) and this paragraph (e) only if it provides that, in any case in which the plan's adjusted funding target attainment percentage for a plan year is less than 60 percent, benefit accruals under the plan will cease as of the applicable section 436 measurement date. If a plan is required to cease benefit accruals under this paragraph (e), then the plan is not permitted to be amended in a manner that would increase the liabilities of the plan by reason of an increase in benefits or establishment of new benefits. The preceding sentence applies regardless of whether an amendment would otherwise be permissible under paragraph (c)(2) or (c)(3) of this section.

(2) *Exemption if section 436 contribution is made.*—The prohibition on additional benefit accruals under a plan described in paragraph (e)(1) of this section ceases to apply with respect to a plan year, effective as of the first day of the plan year, upon payment by the plan sponsor of the contribution described in paragraph (f)(2)(v) of this section. See paragraph (f) of this section for additional rules.

(3) *Special rule under section 203 of the Worker, Retiree, and Employer Recovery Act of 2008.*—[Reserved.]

(f) *Methods to avoid or terminate benefit limitations.*—(1) *In general.*—This paragraph (f) sets forth rules relating to employer contributions and other methods to avoid or terminate the application of section 436 limitations under a plan for a plan year. In general, there are four methods a plan sponsor may utilize to avoid or terminate one or more of the benefit limitations under this section for a plan year. Two of these methods (where the plan sponsor elects to reduce the prefunding balance or funding standard carryover balance and where the plan sponsor makes additional contributions under section 430 for the prior plan year within the time period provided by section 430(j)(1) that are not added to the prefunding balance) involve increasing the amount of plan assets which are taken into account in determining the adjusted funding target attainment percentage. The other two methods (making a contribution that is specifically designated as a current year contribution to avoid or terminate application of a benefit limitation under paragraph (b), (c), or (e) of this section, and providing security under section 436(f)(1)) are described in paragraphs (f)(2) and (f)(3) of this section, respectively.

(2) *Current year contributions to avoid or terminate benefit limitations.*—(i) *General rules.*—(A) *Amount of contribution.*—(1) *In general.*—This paragraph (f)(2) sets forth rules regarding contributions to avoid or terminate the application of section 436 limitations under a plan for a plan year that apply to unpredictable contingent event benefits, plan amendments that increase liabilities for benefits, and benefit accruals.

(2) *Interest adjustment.*—Any contribution made by a plan sponsor pursuant to this paragraph (f)(2) on a date other than the valuation date for the plan year must be adjusted with interest at the plan's effective interest rate under section 430(h)(2)(A) for the plan year. If the plan's effective interest rate for the plan year has not been determined at the time of the contribution, then this interest adjustment must be made using the highest of the three segment rates as applicable for the plan year under section 430(h)(2)(C). In such a case, if the effective interest rate for the plan year under section 430(h)(2)(A) is subsequently determined to be less than that highest rate, the excess is recharacterized as an employer contribution taken into account under section 430 for the current plan year.

(B) *Timing requirement for section 436 contributions.*—Any contribution described in this paragraph (f)(2) must be paid before the unpredictable contingent event benefits are permitted to be paid, the plan amendment is permitted to take effect, or the benefit accruals are permitted to resume. In addition, any contribution described in this paragraph (f)(2) must be paid during the plan year.

(C) *Prefunding balance or funding standard carryover balance may not be used.*—No prefunding balance or funding standard carryover balance under section 430(f) may be used as a contribution described in this paragraph (f)(2). However, a plan sponsor is permitted to elect to reduce the funding standard carryover balance or the prefunding balance in order to increase the adjusted funding target attainment percentage for a plan year. See paragraph (a)(5) of this section for a rule mandating such a reduction in certain situations.

(ii) *Section 436 contributions separate from minimum required contributions.*—(A) *In general.*—The contributions described in this paragraph (f)(2) are contributions described in sections 436(b)(2), 436(c)(2), and 436(e)(2), and are separate from any minimum required contributions under section 430. Thus, if a plan sponsor makes a contribution described in this paragraph (f)(2) for a plan year but does not make the minimum required contribution for the plan year, the plan fails to satisfy the minimum funding requirements under section 430 for the plan year. In addition, a contribution described in this paragraph (f)(2) is disregarded in determining the maximum addition to the prefunding balance under section 430(f)(6) and §1.430(f)-1(b)(1)(ii).

(B) *Designation requirement.*—Any contribution made by a plan sponsor pursuant to this paragraph (f)(2) must be designated as such at the time the contribution is used to avoid or terminate the limitations under this paragraph (f)(2), including designation of the benefits or amendments to which the limits do not apply because of the contribution. Except as specifically provided in paragraph (f)(2)(i)(A)(2), (g) or (h) of this section, such a contribution cannot be subsequently recharacterized with respect to any plan year as a contribution to satisfy a minimum required contribution obligation, or otherwise. The designation must be made in accordance with the rules and procedures that otherwise apply to elections under §1.430(f)-1(f) with respect to the prefunding and funding standard carryover balances.

(C) *Requirement to recertify AFTAP.*—If the plan's enrolled actuary has already certified the adjusted funding target attainment percentage for the plan year, a plan sponsor is treated as making the contribution described in paragraph (f)(2)(iii)(B), (f)(2)(iv)(B), or (f)(2)(v) of this section for the plan year only after the plan's enrolled actuary certifies an updated adjusted funding target attainment percentage for the plan year that takes into account the increased liability for the unpredictable contingent event benefits, the plan amendments, or restored accruals, and the associated section 436 contribution, under the rules of paragraph (h)(4)(v) of this section. See also paragraph (g)(4)(i) of this section for a requirement to modify the presumed adjusted funding target attainment percentage to take the liability for the unpredictable contingent event benefits or plan amendments, and the associated section 436 contribution, into account (if the contribution described in paragraph (f)(2)(iii)(B), (f)(2)(iv)(B), or (f)(2)(v) of this section is made before the plan's enrolled actuary certifies the adjusted funding target attainment percentage for the plan year).

(iii) *Contribution for unpredictable contingent event benefits.*—In the case of a contribution to avoid or terminate the application of the limitation on benefits attributable to an unpredictable contingent event under section 436(b)—

(A) In the event that the adjusted funding target attainment percentage for the plan year determined without taking into account the liability attributable to the unpredictable contingent event benefits is less than 60 percent, the amount of the contribution under section 436(b)(2) is equal to the amount of the increase in the funding target of the plan for the plan year if the benefits attributable to the unpredictable contingent event were included in the determination of the funding target.

(B) In the event that the adjusted funding target attainment percentage for the plan year determined without taking into account the liability attributable to the unpredictable contingent event benefits is 60 percent or more, the amount of the contribution under section 436(b)(2) is the amount that would be sufficient to result in an adjusted funding target attainment percentage for the plan year of 60 percent if the contribution (and any prior section 436 contributions made for the plan year) were included as part of the plan assets and the funding target were to take into account the adjustments described in paragraph (g)(2)(iii)(A), (g)(3)(ii)(A), or (g)(5)(i)(B) of this section, whichever applies.

(iv) *Contribution for plan amendments increasing liability for benefits.*—In the case of a contribution to avoid or terminate the application of the limitation on benefits attributable to a plan amendment under section 436(c)—

(A) In the event that the adjusted funding target attainment percentage for the plan year determined without taking into account the liability attributable to the plan amendment is less than 80 percent, the amount of the contribution under section 436(c)(2) is equal to the amount of the increase in the funding target of the plan for the plan year if the liabilities attributable to the amendment were included in the determination of the funding target.

(B) In the event that the adjusted funding target attainment percentage for the plan year determined without taking into account the liability attributable to the plan amendment is 80 percent or more, the amount of the contribution under section 436(c)(2) is the amount that would be sufficient to result in an adjusted funding target attainment percentage for the plan year of 80 percent if the contribution (and any prior section 436 contributions made for the plan year) were included as part of the plan assets and the funding target were to take into account the adjustments described in paragraph

(g)(2)(iii)(A), (g)(3)(ii)(A), or (g)(5)(i)(B) of this section, whichever applies.

(v) *Contribution required for continued benefit accruals.*—In the case of a contribution to avoid or terminate the application of the limitation on accruals under section 436(e), the amount of the contribution under section 436(e)(2) is equal to the amount sufficient to result in an adjusted funding target attainment percentage for the plan year of 60 percent if the contribution (and any prior section 436 contributions made for the plan year) were included as part of the plan assets and the funding target were to take into account the adjustments described in paragraph (g)(2)(iii)(A) or (g)(5)(i)(B) of this section, whichever applies.

(3) *Security to increase adjusted funding target attainment percentage.*—(i) *In general.*—For purposes of avoiding benefit limitations under section 436, a plan sponsor may provide security in the form described in paragraph (f)(3)(ii) of this section. In such a case, the adjusted funding target attainment percentage for the plan year is determined by treating as an asset of the plan any security provided by a plan sponsor by the valuation date for the plan year in a form meeting the requirements of paragraph (f)(3)(ii) of this section. However, this security is not taken into account as a plan asset for any other purpose, including section 430.

(ii) *Form of security.*—The forms of security permitted under paragraph (f)(3)(i) of this section are limited to—

(A) A bond issued by a corporate surety company that is an acceptable surety for purposes of section 412 of ERISA; or

(B) Cash, or United States obligations which mature in 3 years or less, held in escrow by a bank or an insurance company.

(iii) *Enforcement.*—Any form of security provided under paragraph (f)(3)(i) of this section must provide—

(A) That it will be paid to the plan upon the earliest of—

(1) The plan termination date as defined in section 4048 of ERISA;

(2) If there is a failure to make a payment of the minimum required contribution for any plan year beginning after the security is provided, the due date for the payment under section 430(j)(1) or 430(j)(3); or

(3) If the plan's adjusted funding target attainment percentage is less than 60 percent (without regard to any security provided under this paragraph (f)(3)) for a consecutive period of 7 plan years, the valuation date for the last plan year in the 7-year period; and

(B) That the plan administrator must notify the surety, bank, or insurance company that issued or holds the security of any event described in paragraph (f)(3)(iii)(A) of this section within 10 days of its occurrence.

(iv) *Release of security.*—The form of security is permitted to provide that it will be released (and any amounts thereunder will be refunded to the plan sponsor together with any interest accrued thereon) as provided in the agreement governing the security, but such release is not permitted until the plan's enrolled actuary has certified that the plan's adjusted funding target attainment percentage for a plan year is at least 90 percent (without regard to any security provided under this paragraph (f)(3)) or until replacement security has been provided in accordance with paragraph (f)(3)(vi) of this section.

(v) *Contribution of security to plan.*—Any security provided under this paragraph (f)(3) that is subsequently turned over to the plan (whether pursuant to the enforcement mechanism of paragraph (f)(3)(iii) of this section or after its release under paragraph (f)(3)(iv) of this section) is treated as a contribution by the plan sponsor taken into account under section 430 when contributed and, if turned over pursuant to paragraph (f)(3)(iii) of this section, is not a contribution under paragraph (f)(2) of this section.

(vi) *Replacement security.*—If security has been provided to a plan pursuant to this paragraph (f)(3), the plan sponsor may provide new security to the plan and subsequently or simultaneously have the original security released, but only if—

(A) The new security is in a form that satisfies the requirements of paragraph (f)(3)(ii) of this section;

(B) The amount of the new security is no less than the amount of the original security, determined at the time the original security is released; and

(C) The period described in paragraph (f)(3)(iii)(A)(3) of this section with respect to the new security is the same as the period that applied under that paragraph to the original security.

(4) *Examples.*—The following examples illustrate the rules of this paragraph (f):

Example 1. (i) Plan Z is a non-collectively bargained defined benefit plan with a plan year that is the calendar year and a valuation date of January 1. Plan Z's sponsor is not in bankruptcy, and Plan Z did not purchase any annuities in 2009 or 2010. As of January 1, 2011, Plan Z does not have a funding standard carryover balance or a prefunding balance, and is not in at-risk status. As of that date, Plan Z has plan assets (and adjusted plan assets) of $2,000,000 and a funding target (and an adjusted funding target) of $2,550,000. On March 1, 2011, the enrolled actuary for the plan certifies that the AFTAP as of January 1, 2011, is 78.43%. The effective interest rate for Plan Z for the 2011 plan year is 5.5%.

(ii) On May 1, 2011, the plan sponsor amends Plan Z to increase benefits. The enrolled actuary for the plan determines that the present value, as of January 1, 2011, of the increase in the funding target due to the amendment is $400,000. Because the AFTAP prior to the plan amendment is less than 80%, Plan Z is subject to the restriction on plan amendments in paragraph (c) of this section, and the amendment cannot take effect unless the employer utilizes one of the methods described in paragraph (f) of this section to avoid benefit limitations.

(iii) In order for the amendment to be permitted to take effect, the plan sponsor makes a contribution described in paragraph (f)(2) of this section. Because the AFTAP prior to the amendment was less than 80%, the provisions of paragraph (f)(2)(iv)(A) of this section apply. The amount of the contribution as of January 1, 2011, needed to avoid the restriction on plan amendments under paragraph (c) of this section is equal to the amount of the increase in funding target attributable to the amendment, or $400,000. Under the provisions of paragraph (f)(2)(iv)(A) of this section, this contribution is required even though, if the contribution were included as part of the plan assets and the liabilities attributable to the plan amendment were included in the funding target, the AFTAP would be 81.36% (that is, adjusted plan assets of $2,000,000 plus the contribution of $400,000 as of January 1, 2011; divided by the adjusted funding target of $2,550,000 increased to reflect the additional $400,000 in the funding target attributable to the plan amendment).

(iv) However, because the contribution is not paid until May 1, 2011, the necessary contribution amount must be adjusted to reflect interest from the valuation date to the date of the contribution, at Plan Z's effective interest rate for the 2011 plan year. The amount of the required contribution after adjustment is $407,203, determined as $400,000 increased for 4 months of compound interest at an effective annual interest rate of 5.5%.

(v) A contribution of $407,203 is made on May 1, 2011, and is designated as a contribution under paragraph (f)(2) of this section with respect to the May 1, 2011, plan amendment. Accordingly, the contribution is not applied toward minimum funding requirements under section 430, and is not eligible for inclusion in the prefunding balance under §1.430(f)-1(b)(1). Since this contribution meets the requirements of paragraph (f)(2) of this section, the plan amendment takes effect in accordance with its terms.

Example 2. (i) The facts are the same as in *Example 1*, except that the plan is in at-risk status under section 430(i). The funding target determined under section 430(i) is $2,600,000, and the funding target determined without regard to section 430(i) is $2,550,000.

(ii) On May 1, 2011, the plan sponsor amends Plan Z to increase benefits. The plan's enrolled actuary determines that the present value as of January 1, 2011 of the increase in the funding target due to the amendment (taking into account the at-risk status of the plan) is $440,000. Because the AFTAP prior to the plan amendment is 78.43% (determined taking into account the at-risk status of Plan Z), Plan Z is subject to the restriction on plan amendments in paragraph (c) of this section, and the amendment cannot take effect unless the employer utilizes one of the methods described in this paragraph (f) to avoid benefit limitations.

(iii) In order for this amendment to be permitted to take effect, the plan sponsor makes a contribution described in paragraph (f)(2) of this section. Because the AFTAP prior to the amendment was less than 80%, the provisions of paragraph (f)(2)(iv)(A) of this section apply. The amount of the contribution as of January 1, 2011, needed to avoid the restriction on plan amendments under paragraph (c) of this section is equal to the amount of the increase in funding target attributable to the amendment, or $440,000. Under the provisions of paragraph (f)(2)(iv)(A) of this section, this contribution is required even though, if the contribution were included as part of the plan assets and the liability attributable to the plan amendment were included in the funding target, the AFTAP would exceed 80%.

(iv) However, because the contribution is not paid until May 1, 2011, the necessary contribution amount must be adjusted to reflect interest from the valuation date to the date of the contribution, at Plan Z's effective interest rate for the 2011 plan year. The amount of the required contribution after adjustment is $447,923, determined as $440,000 increased for 4 months of compound interest at an effective annual interest rate of 5.5%.

(v) A contribution of $447,923 is made on May 1, 2011, and is designated as a contribution under paragraph (f)(2) of this section with respect to the May 1, 2011, plan amendment. Accordingly, the contribution is not applied toward minimum funding requirements under section 430, and is not eligible for inclusion in the prefunding balance under §1.430(f)-1(b)(1). Since this contribution meets the requirements of paragraph (f)(2) of this section, the plan amendment takes effect in accordance with its terms.

Example 3. (i) The facts are the same as in *Example 1*, except that the enrolled actuary for the plan does not issue the certification of the 2011 AFTAP until September 1, 2011. Prior to October 1, 2010, the enrolled actuary had certified the 2010 AFTAP to be 82%. Other than this amendment, no other amendment or unpredictable contingent event has occurred that requires a recertification. As of May 1, 2011, the plan's effective interest rate for the 2011 plan year has not yet been determined. The highest of the three segment rates applicable to the 2011 plan year under section 430(h)(2)(C) is 6%.

(ii) Because the enrolled actuary has not certified the actual AFTAP as of January 1, 2011, and the amendment is scheduled to take effect after April 1, 2011, the rules of paragraph (h)(2)(iii) of this section apply. Accordingly, the AFTAP for 2011 (prior to reflecting the effect of the amendment) is presumed to be 10 percentage points lower than the 2010 AFTAP, or 72%. Because this presumed AFTAP is less than 80%, the restriction on plan amendments in paragraph (c) of this section applies, and the plan amendment cannot take effect.

(iii) In order to allow the plan amendment to take effect, the plan sponsor decides to make a contribution under paragraph (f)(2) of this section on May 1, 2011. Because the presumed AFTAP was less than 80% prior to reflecting the plan amendment, the rules of paragraph (f)(2)(iv)(A) of this section apply, and the amount of the contribution under section 436(c)(2) is the amount of the increase in the funding target for the year if the plan amendment were included in the determination of the funding target. Accordingly, an additional contribution of $400,000 is required as of January 1, 2011, to avoid the restriction on plan amendments under paragraph (c) of this section.

(iv) However, since the contribution is not made until May 1, 2011, the amount of the required contribution must be adjusted to reflect interest from the valuation date to the date of the contribution. Since the effective interest rate has not yet been determined, the interest adjustment is based on the highest of the three segment rates applicable for the 2011 plan year under section 430(h)(2)(C), or 6%. The amount of the required contribution after adjustment is $407,845, determined as $400,000 increased for 4 months of compound interest at the highest segment interest rate for 2011, or 6%.

(v) A contribution of $407,845 is made on May 1, 2011, and is designated as a contribution under paragraph (f)(2) of this section with respect to the May 1, 2011, plan amendment. Accordingly, the contribution is not applied toward minimum funding requirements under section 430, and is not eligible for inclusion in the prefunding balance under §1.430(f)-1(b)(1). Since this contribution meets the requirements of paragraph (f)(2) of this section, the plan amendment takes effect in accordance with its terms.

(vi) After the plan's effective interest rate for 2011 has been determined to be 5.5%, the amount of excess interest previously contributed is recharacterized as an employer contribution taken into account under section 430 for 2011 (because that rate for the year is less than 6%).

(g) *Rules of operation for periods prior to and after certification.*—(1) *In general.*—Section 436(h) and paragraph (h) of this section set forth a series of presumptions that apply before the enrolled actuary for a plan issues a certification of the plan's adjusted funding target attainment percentage for the plan year. This paragraph (g) sets forth rules for the application of limitations under sections 436(b), 436(c), 436(d), and 436(e) prior to and during the period those presumptions apply to the plan, and describes the interaction of those presumptions with plan operations after the plan's enrolled actuary has issued a certification of the plan's adjusted funding target attainment percentage for the plan year. Paragraph (g)(2) of this section sets forth rules that apply to periods during which a presumption under section 436(h) and paragraph (h) of this section applies. Paragraph (g)(3) of this section sets forth rules that apply to periods during which no presumptions under section 436(h) and paragraph (h) of this section apply but which are prior to the enrolled actuary's certification of the plan's adjusted funding target attainment percentage for the plan year. Paragraph (g)(4) of this section sets forth rules for modifying the plan's presumed adjusted funding target attainment percentage in certain situations. Paragraph (g)(5) of this section sets forth rules that apply after the enrolled actuary's certification of the plan's adjusted funding target attainment percentage for a plan year. Paragraph (g)(6) of this section sets forth examples illustrating the rules in this paragraph (g).

(2) *Periods prior to certification during which a presumption applies.*—(i) *Plan must follow presumptions.*—A plan must provide that,

for any period during which a presumption under section 436(h) and paragraph (h)(1), (2), or (3) of this section applies to the plan, the limitations applicable under section 436 and paragraphs (b), (c), (d), and (e) of this section are applied to the plan as if the adjusted funding target attainment percentage for the year were the presumed adjusted funding target attainment percentage determined under the rules of section 436(h) and paragraph (h)(1), (2), or (3) of this section, as applicable, updated to take into account certain unpredictable contingent event benefits and plan amendments in accordance with section 436 and the rules of this paragraph (g).

(ii) *Determination of amount of reduction in balances.*—(A) *In general.*—During the period described in this paragraph (g)(2), the rules of paragraph (a)(5) of this section (relating to the deemed election to reduce the funding standard carryover balance and the prefunding balance) must be applied based on the presumed adjusted funding target attainment percentage. This paragraph (g)(2)(ii) provides rules for the determination of the reduction that applies as of the first day of the plan year, and, in certain circumstances, that applies later in the plan year. Paragraph (g)(2)(iii) of this section provides additional rules that apply with respect to unpredictable contingent event benefits or plan amendments, which rules must be applied prior to the application of paragraph (g)(2)(iv) of this section relating to section 436 contributions. The reapplication of the rules under this paragraph (g)(2) regarding the deemed election in paragraph (a)(5) of this section may require an additional reduction in the prefunding and funding standard carryover balances if the amount of the reduction in those balances that is necessary to reach the applicable threshold to avoid the application of a section 436 limitation exceeds the amount that was initially reduced. Prior reductions of the prefunding and funding standard carryover balances continue to apply.

(B) *Reduction in balances at the first day of plan year.*—(1) *Plans with a certified AFTAP for the prior plan year.*—If section 436(h)(1) and paragraph (h)(1) of this section apply to determine the presumed adjusted funding target attainment percentage as of the first day of the current plan year based on the plan's enrolled actuary certification of the adjusted funding target attainment percentage for the prior plan year made during that prior plan year, then, in order to determine the amount of the reduction (if any) in the funding standard carryover balance and prefunding balance under this paragraph (g)(2)(ii), a presumed adjusted funding target must be established as of the first day of the plan year, and that amount is then compared to the interim value of adjusted plan assets as of that date. For this purpose, the interim value of adjusted plan assets is equal to the value of adjusted plan assets (within the meaning of paragraph (j)(1)(ii) of this section) as of the first day of the plan year, determined without regard to future contributions and future elections with respect to the plan's prefunding and funding standard carryover balances under section 430(f) (for example, elections to add to the prefunding balance for the prior plan year, elections to use the prefunding and funding standard carryover balances to offset the minimum required contribution for a year, and elections (including deemed elections under paragraph (a)(5) of this section) to reduce the prefunding and funding standard carryover balances for the current plan year), and the presumed adjusted funding target is equal to the interim value of adjusted plan assets for the plan year divided by the presumed adjusted funding target attainment percentage. As provided in §1.430(f)-1(e)(1), the rules of §1.430(f)-1(d)(1)(ii) apply for purposes of determining the amount of the prefunding balance or the funding standard carryover balance that is available for reduction.

(2) *Plans with presumed AFTAP deemed under 60 percent.*—If paragraph (g)(2)(ii)(B)(1) of this section does not apply to the plan for a plan year and the last day of the plan year is on or after the first day of the 10th month of the plan year, such that the presumed adjusted funding target attainment percentage for the prior plan year is conclusively presumed to be less than 60 percent under section 436(h)(2) and paragraph (h)(3) of this section, then no reduction in the funding standard carryover balance and prefunding balance is required under this paragraph (g)(2)(ii)(B). However, see paragraph (g)(2)(iv)(A) of this section for rules for determining the amount of a section 436 contribution that would permit unpredictable contingent event benefits to be paid in such a case.

(3) *Treatment of short plan years.*—If paragraph (g)(2)(ii)(B)(1) of this section does not apply to the plan for a plan year but the last day of the plan year is before the first day of the 10th month of the plan year, such that section 436(h)(2) and paragraph (h)(3) of this section did not apply for that plan year, then paragraph (g)(2)(ii)(B)(1) of this section must be applied as of the first day of the next plan year based on the presumed adjusted funding target attainment percentage as of that last day of the prior short plan year.

(C) *Change in presumed AFTAP later in the plan year.*—If the presumed adjusted funding target attainment percentage for the plan year changes during the year, the rules regarding the deemed election to reduce the prefunding and funding standard carryover balances described in paragraph (a)(5) of this section must be reapplied based on the new presumed adjusted funding target attainment percentage. This will typically occur on the first day of the 4th month of a plan year, but could happen at a different date if the enrolled actuary certifies the adjusted funding target attainment percentage for the prior plan year during the current plan year. In order to determine the amount of any reduction in the prefunding and funding standard carryover balances that would apply in such a situation, a new presumed adjusted funding target must be established, which is then compared to the updated interim value of adjusted plan assets. For this purpose, the updated interim value of adjusted plan assets for the plan year is determined as the interim value of adjusted plan assets as of the first day of the plan year updated to take into account contributions for the prior plan year and section 430(f) elections with respect to the plan's prefunding and funding standard carryover balances made before the date of the change in the presumed adjusted funding target attainment percentage, and the new presumed adjusted funding target is equal to the updated interim value of adjusted plan assets divided by the new presumed adjusted funding target attainment percentage.

(D) *Plans funded below the threshold.*—If, after application of paragraph (g)(2)(ii)(B) and (C) of this section, the presumed adjusted funding target attainment percentage under this paragraph (g)(2)(ii) is less than the 60 percent threshold under section 436(e), then no benefit accruals are permitted under the plan unless the plan sponsor makes a section 436 contribution as provided in paragraph (g)(2)(iv)(A) of this section. See paragraph (g)(5)(ii) of this section for rules that apply on and after the date the enrolled actuary for the plan issues a certification of the adjusted funding target attainment percentage of the plan for the current plan year.

(iii) *Calculation of inclusive presumed AFTAP for application to unpredictable contingent event benefits and plan amendments.*—(A) *Requirement to calculate inclusive presumed AFTAP.*—For purposes of applying the limitations under paragraphs (b) and (c) of this section during the period described in this paragraph (g)(2), an inclusive presumed adjusted funding target attainment percentage must be calculated. The inclusive presumed adjusted funding target attainment percentage is the ratio (expressed as a percentage) of the interim value of adjusted plan assets (updated to take into account contributions for the prior plan year, any prior section 436 contributions made for the plan year to the extent not previously taken into account in the interim value of adjusted plan assets for the plan year, and section 430(f) elections with respect to the plan's prefunding and funding standard carryover balances made before the date of the unpredictable contingent event or the date the plan amendment would take effect) to the inclusive presumed adjusted funding target. The inclusive presumed adjusted funding target is calculated as the presumed adjusted funding target determined under paragraph (g)(2)(ii)(B) or (C) of this section, increased to take into account—

(1) The unpredictable contingent event benefits or plan amendment;

(2) Any unpredictable contingent event benefits that are permitted to be paid as a result of any unpredictable contingent event that occurred, or plan amendment that has taken effect, in the prior plan year to the extent not taken into account in the prior plan year adjusted funding target attainment percentage; and

(3) Any other unpredictable contingent event benefits that are permitted to be paid as a result of any unpredictable contingent event that occurred, or plan amendment that has taken effect, in the current plan year to the extent not previously taken into account in the presumed adjusted funding target for the plan year.

(B) *Mandatory reduction for collectively bargained plans.*—During the period described in this paragraph (g)(2), the rules of paragraph (a)(5)(ii) of this section (relating to the deemed election to reduce the funding standard carryover balance and the prefunding balance) must be applied by treating the inclusive presumed adjusted funding target attainment percentage determined under this paragraph (g)(2)(iii) as if it were the adjusted funding target attainment percentage.

(C) *Optional reduction for plans that are not collectively bargained plans.*—A plan sponsor of a plan that is not a collectively bargained plan (and, thus, is not required to reduce the funding standard carryover balance and the prefunding balance under the rules of paragraph (a)(5)(ii) of this section) is permitted to elect to reduce those balances in order to increase the updated interim value of adjusted plan assets that is used to determine the inclusive presumed adjusted funding target attainment percentage under this paragraph (g)(2)(iii).

Reg. §1.436-1(g)(2)(iii)(C)

(D) *Plans funded below the threshold.*—If, after application of paragraph (g)(2)(iii)(B) and (C) of this section, the inclusive presumed adjusted funding target attainment percentage determined under this paragraph (g)(2)(iii) is less than the applicable threshold under section 436(b) or 436(c), then the plan is not permitted to provide any benefits attributable to the unpredictable contingent event, nor is the plan amendment permitted to take effect, unless the plan sponsor makes a section 436 contribution as provided in paragraph (g)(2)(iv) of this section. See paragraph (g)(5)(ii) of this section for rules that apply on and after the date the enrolled actuary for the plan issues a certification of the adjusted funding target attainment percentage of the plan for the current plan year.

(E) *Plans funded at or above the threshold.*—If, after application of paragraph (g)(2)(iii)(B) or (C) of this section, the inclusive presumed adjusted funding target attainment percentage is greater than or equal to the applicable threshold under section 436(b) or 436(c), then the plan is not permitted to limit the payment of unpredictable contingent event benefits described in paragraph (b) of this section, nor is the plan permitted to restrict a plan amendment increasing benefit liabilities described in paragraph (c) of this section from taking effect, based on an expectation that the limitations under paragraph (b) or (c) of this section will apply following the enrolled actuary's certification of the adjusted funding target attainment percentage for the plan year.

(iv) *Section 436 contributions.*—(A) *Plans with presumed AFTAP below 60 percent.*—(1) *Unpredictable contingent event benefits.*—If the presumed adjusted funding target attainment percentage for a plan is less than 60 percent, then unpredictable contingent event benefits are permitted to be paid as a result of an unpredictable contingent event occurring during the period described in this paragraph (g)(2) if the plan sponsor makes the section 436 contribution described in paragraph (f)(2)(iii)(A) of this section.

(2) *Plan amendments.*—If the presumed adjusted funding target attainment percentage for a plan is less than 60 percent, then no plan amendment increasing plan liabilities is permitted to take effect during the period described in this paragraph (g)(2). See paragraph (e)(1) of this section.

(3) *Benefit accruals.*—If the presumed adjusted funding target attainment percentage for a plan year of less than 60 percent is determined based on the plan's enrolled actuary certification of the adjusted funding target attainment percentage for the prior plan year made during that prior plan year (as opposed to being presumed to be less than 60 percent under the rules of section 436(h)(2) and paragraph (h)(3) of this section because the actuary has not certified the adjusted funding target attainment percentage for the prior plan year before the first day of the 10th month of the prior plan year), then benefits are permitted to accrue if the plan sponsor makes a section 436 contribution in the amount necessary to bring the ratio of the updated interim value of adjusted plan assets to the presumed adjusted funding target up to 60 percent, as described in paragraph (f)(2)(v) of this section.

(B) *Plan amendments for plans with presumed AFTAP below 80 percent.*—If the presumed adjusted funding target attainment percentage for a plan is less than 80 percent, but is not less than 60 percent, then a plan amendment increasing plan liabilities is permitted to take effect during the period described in this paragraph (g)(2) if the plan sponsor makes a section 436 contribution described in paragraph (f)(2)(iv)(A) of this section.

(C) *Contributions required to reach threshold.*—If a plan is described in paragraph (g)(2)(iii)(D) of this section and neither paragraph (g)(2)(iv)(A) nor (B) of this section apply to the plan, then unpredictable contingent event benefits are permitted to be paid or the plan amendment is permitted to become effective during the period this paragraph (g)(2) applies to the plan only if the plan sponsor makes a section 436 contribution in the amount necessary to bring the ratio of the updated interim value of adjusted plan assets to the inclusive presumed adjusted funding target up to the applicable threshold under section 436(b) or (c), as described in paragraph (f)(2)(iii)(B) or (f)(2)(iv)(B) of this section. This paragraph (g)(2)(iv)(C) applies, for example, if an unpredictable contingent event occurs in the case of a plan with a presumed adjusted funding target attainment percentage of more than 60 percent where taking into account the unpredictable contingent event benefit in the inclusive presumed adjusted funding target would cause the ratio of the interim value of adjusted plan assets to the inclusive presumed adjusted funding target to be less than 60 percent.

(v) *Bankruptcy of plan sponsor.*—Pursuant to section 436(d)(2), during any period in which the plan sponsor of a plan is a debtor in a case under title 11, United States Code, or any similar Federal or State law (as described in paragraph (d)(2) of this section), no prohib-

ited payment within the meaning of paragraph (j)(6) of this section may be paid if the plan's enrolled actuary has not yet certified the plan's adjusted funding target attainment percentage for the plan year to be at least 100 percent. Thus, the presumption rules of paragraph (h) of this section do not apply for purposes of section 436(d)(2) and this paragraph (g)(2)(v).

(3) *Periods prior to certification during which no presumption applies.*—(i) *Prohibited payments and benefit accruals.*—If no presumptions under section 436(h) apply to a plan during a period and the plan's enrolled actuary has not yet issued the certification of the plan's actual adjusted funding target attainment percentage for the plan year, the plan is not permitted to limit prohibited payments under paragraph (d) of this section or the accrual of benefits under paragraph (e) of this section based on an expectation that those paragraphs will apply to the plan once an actuarial certification is issued. However, see paragraph (g)(2)(v) of this section for a restriction on prohibited payments during any period in which the plan sponsor of a plan is a debtor in a case under title 11, United States Code, or any similar Federal or State law.

(ii) *Unpredictable contingent event benefits and plan amendments increasing benefit liability.*—(A) *In general.*—If no presumptions under section 436(h) apply to a plan during a period and the plan's enrolled actuary has not yet issued a certification of the plan's adjusted funding target attainment percentage for the plan year, the limitations on unpredictable contingent event benefits under paragraph (b) of this section and plan amendments increasing benefit liabilities under paragraph (c) of this section must be applied during that period by following the rules of paragraphs (g)(2)(iii) of this section, based on the inclusive presumed adjusted funding target determined using the prior plan year adjusted funding target attainment percentage. Thus, whether unpredictable contingent event benefits are permitted to be paid or a plan amendment is permitted to take effect during a plan year is determined by calculating the ratio of the interim value of adjusted plan assets to the inclusive presumed adjusted funding target, where the inclusive presumed adjusted funding target is determined by dividing the interim value of adjusted plan assets by the prior plan year adjusted funding target attainment percentage and then adding the adjustments described in paragraphs (g)(2)(iii)(A)(*1*), (*2*) and (*3*) of this section. If, after application of paragraphs (g)(2)(iii)(B) and (C) of this section, that ratio is less than the applicable threshold under section 436(b) or 436(c), then the plan is not permitted to provide any benefits attributable to the unpredictable contingent event, nor is the plan amendment permitted to take effect, unless the plan sponsor makes the contribution described in paragraph of (g)(2)(iv)(C) of this section.

(B) *Recharacterization of contributions made to avoid benefit limitations.*—In any case where, pursuant to paragraph (g)(3)(ii)(A) of this section, the plan sponsor makes section 436 contributions to avoid the application of the applicable benefit limitation, to the extent those contributions would not be needed to permit the payment of the unpredictable contingent event benefits or for the plan amendment to go into effect based on a subsequent certification of the adjusted funding target attainment percentage for the current plan year that takes into account the increase in the liability attributable to the unpredictable contingent event benefits or plan amendment, the excess section 436 contributions are recharacterized as employer contributions taken into account under section 430 for the current plan year.

(4) *Modification of the presumed AFTAP.*—(i) *Section 436 contributions.*—If, in accordance with the rules of paragraph (g)(2)(iv) of this section, unpredictable contingent event benefits are permitted to be paid, or a plan amendment takes effect, during the plan year because the plan sponsor makes a contribution described in paragraph (f)(2)(iii)(B) or (f)(2)(iv)(B) of this section, then the presumed adjusted funding target must be adjusted to reflect any increase in the funding target attributable to the unpredictable contingent event benefits or the plan amendment and the interim value of plan assets must be increased by the present value of the contribution. Similarly, if benefit accruals are permitted to resume in a plan year because the plan sponsor makes the contribution described in paragraph (f)(2)(v) of this section, then the presumed adjusted funding target must be adjusted to reflect any increase in the funding target attributable to the benefit accruals for the prior plan year and the interim value of adjusted plan assets must be increased by the present value of the contribution. The adjustment to the presumed adjusted funding target is made as of the date of the contribution, and that date is a section 436 measurement date.

(ii) *Modification of the presumed AFTAP for reduction in balances.*—If a plan's funding standard carryover balance or prefunding balance is reduced under the rules of paragraph (g)(2) or (g)(3) of this section, then the presumed adjusted funding target attainment percentage for the plan year is increased to reflect the higher interim value of adjusted plan assets resulting from the reduction in the funding standard carryover balance or prefunding balance. The date of the event that causes the reduction is a section 436 measurement date.

(5) *Periods after certification of AFTAP.*—(i) *Plan must follow certified AFTAP.*—(A) *In general.*—The rules of paragraphs (g)(2) and (g)(3) of this section no longer apply for a plan year on and after the date the enrolled actuary for the plan issues a certification of the adjusted funding target attainment percentage of the plan for the current plan year, provided that the certification is issued before the first day of the 10th month of the plan year. For example, the plan must provide that the limitations on prohibited payments apply for distributions with annuity starting dates on and after the date of that certification using the certified adjusted funding target attainment percentage of the plan for the plan year. Similarly, the plan must provide that any prohibition on accruals under paragraph (e) of this section as a result of the enrolled actuary's certification that the adjusted funding target attainment percentage of the plan for the plan year is less than 60 percent is effective as of the date of the certification and that any prohibition on accruals ceases to be effective on the date the enrolled actuary issues a certification that the adjusted funding target attainment percentage of the plan for the plan year is at least 60 percent.

(B) *Unpredictable contingent events and plan amendments.*—In the case of a plan that has been issued a certification of the plan's adjusted funding target attainment percentage for a plan year by the plan's enrolled actuary, the plan sponsor must comply with the requirements of paragraphs (b) and (c) of this section for an unpredictable contingent event that occurs or a plan amendment that takes effect on or after the date of the enrolled actuary's certification. Thus, the plan administrator must determine if the adjusted funding target attainment percentage would be at or above the applicable threshold if it were modified to take into account—

(1) The unpredictable contingent event or plan amendment;

(2) Any other unpredictable contingent event benefits that were permitted to be paid as a result of any unpredictable contingent event that occurred, and any other plan amendment that took effect, earlier during the plan year to the extent not taken into account in the certified adjusted funding target attainment percentage for the plan year; and

(3) Any earlier section 436 contributions made for the plan year to the extent those contributions were not taken into account in the certified adjusted funding target attainment percentage.

(C) *Application of rule for deemed election to reduce funding balances.*—After the adjusted funding target attainment percentage for a plan year is certified by the plan's enrolled actuary, the deemed election to reduce the prefunding and funding standard carryover balances under paragraph (a)(5) of this section must be reapplied based on the actual funding target for the year (provided the certification is issued before the first day of the 10th month of the plan year). The reapplication of the rules under this paragraph (g)(5) regarding the deemed election in paragraph (a)(5) of this section may require an additional reduction in the prefunding and funding standard carryover balances if the amount of the reduction in the prefunding and funding standard carryover balances that is necessary to reach the applicable threshold to avoid the application of a section 436 limitation exceeds the amount that was initially reduced. Prior reductions of the prefunding and funding standard carryover balances continue to apply.

(ii) *Applicability to prior periods.*—(A) *In general.*—Except as otherwise provided in this paragraph (g)(5)(ii), the enrolled actuary's certification of the adjusted funding target attainment percentage for the plan for the plan year does not affect prior periods. For example, the certification does not affect the application of the limitation under paragraph (d) of this section for distributions with annuity starting dates before the certification or the application of the limitation under paragraph (e) of this section prior to the date of that certification. See paragraph (a)(4) of this section for rules relating to the period of time after benefits cease to be limited. Except as otherwise provided in this paragraph (g)(5)(ii), the enrolled actuary's certification of the adjusted funding target attainment percentage for the plan for the plan year does not affect the application of the limitation under paragraph (b) or (c) of this section to unpredictable contingent event benefits, or a plan amendment that increases the liability for benefits, where the unpredictable contingent event occurs or the amendment takes effect during the periods to which paragraphs (g)(2) and (g)(3) of this section apply.

(B) *Special rule for unpredictable contingent event benefits.*—If a plan does not pay benefits attributable to an unpredictable contin-

gent event because of the application of paragraph (g)(2)(iii)(D) or (g)(3)(ii)(A) of this section, then the plan must pay the benefits attributable to that event that were not previously paid if such benefits would be permitted under the rules of section 436 based on a certified adjusted funding target attainment percentage for the plan year that takes into account the increase in the funding target that would be attributable to those unpredictable contingent event benefits.

(C) *Special rule for plan amendments that increase liability.*—If a plan amendment does not take effect because of the application of paragraph (g)(2)(iii)(D) or (g)(3)(ii)(A) of this section, the plan amendment must go into effect if it would be permitted under the rules of section 436 based on a certified actual adjusted funding target attainment percentage for the plan year that takes into account the increase in the funding target attributable to the plan amendment, unless the plan amendment provides otherwise.

(D) *Ordering rule for multiple unpredictable contingent events or plan amendments.*—[Reserved]

(6) *Examples.*—The following examples illustrate the rules of this paragraph (g). Unless otherwise indicated, these examples are based on the following facts: each plan has a plan year that is the calendar year and a valuation date of January 1; section 436 applies to the plan beginning in 2008; the plan has no funding standard carryover balance; the plan sponsor is not in bankruptcy; no annuity purchases have been made from the plan; and the plan offers a lump sum form of payment. No plan is in at-risk status for the years discussed in the examples. The examples read as follows:

Example 1. (i) The plan's certified AFTAP as of January 1, 2010, is 75%. As of January 1, 2011, Plan A has assets of $3,300,000 and a prefunding balance of $300,000. Beginning on January 1, 2011, Plan A's AFTAP for 2011 is presumed to be 75%, under the rules of paragraph (h) of this section and based on the certified AFTAP for 2010.

(ii) Based on Plan A's presumed AFTAP of 75%, Plan A would continue to be subject to the restriction on prohibited payments in paragraph (d)(3) of this section as of January 1, 2011. However, under the provisions of paragraph (a)(5) of this section, if the prefunding balance is large enough, Plan A's sponsor is deemed to elect to reduce the prefunding balance to the extent needed to avoid this restriction.

(iii) The amount needed to avoid the restriction in paragraph (d)(3) of this section is determined by comparing the presumed adjusted funding target for Plan A with the interim value of adjusted plan assets as of the valuation date. The interim value of adjusted plan assets for Plan A is $3,000,000 (that is, the asset value of $3,300,000 reduced by the prefunding balance of $300,000). The presumed adjusted funding target for Plan A is the interim value of the adjusted plan assets divided by the presumed AFTAP, or $4,000,000 (that is, $3,000,000 divided by 75%).

(iv) In order to avoid the restriction on prohibited payments in paragraph (d)(3) of this section, Plan A's presumed AFTAP must be increased to 80%. This requires an increase in Plan A's adjusted plan assets of $200,000 (that is, 80% of the presumed adjusted funding target of $4,000,000, minus the interim value of the adjusted plan assets of $3,000,000). Plan A's prefunding balance as of January 1, 2011, is reduced by $200,000 under the deemed election provisions of paragraph (a)(5) of this section. Accordingly, Plan A's prefunding balance is $100,000 (that is, $300,000 minus $200,000) and the interim value of adjusted plan assets is increased to $3,200,000 (that is, $3,300,000 minus the reduced prefunding balance of $100,000). Pursuant to paragraph (g)(4)(ii) of this section, the presumed adjusted funding target attainment percentage for Plan A is redetermined as 80% and Plan A must pay the full amount of the accelerated benefit distributions elected by participants with an annuity starting date of January 1, 2011, or later.

Example 2. (i) The facts are the same as in *Example 1.* As of April 1, 2011, the enrolled actuary for Plan A has not certified the 2011 AFTAP. Therefore, beginning April 1, 2011, Plan A's AFTAP is presumed to be reduced by 10 percentage points to 70%, in accordance with paragraph (h)(2) of this section. Under the provisions of paragraph (g)(2)(ii)(B) of this section, the deemed election to reduce the prefunding and funding standard carryover balances described in paragraph (a)(5) of this section must be reapplied based on the new presumed AFTAP.

(ii) In accordance with paragraph (g)(2)(ii)(C) of this section, a new presumed adjusted funding target must be determined based on the new presumed AFTAP and must be compared to an updated interim value of adjusted plan assets. The new presumed adjusted funding target is $3,200,000 divided by the new presumed AFTAP of 70%, or $4,571,429.

(iii) In order to avoid the restriction on prohibited payments in paragraph (d)(3) of this section, Plan A's presumed AFTAP must be increased to 80%. This requires an additional increase in Plan A's adjusted plan assets of $457,143 (that is, 80% of the new presumed adjusted funding target of $4,571,429, minus the updated interim value of the adjusted plan assets of $3,200,000 reflecting the deemed reduction in Plan A's prefunding balance).

(iv) Plan A's remaining prefunding balance as of January 1, 2011, is only $100,000, which is not enough to avoid the restriction on prohibited payments under paragraph (d)(3) of this section. Accordingly, unless Plan A's sponsor utilizes one of the methods described in paragraph (f) of this section to avoid the restriction, Plan A is subject to the restriction on prohibited payments in paragraph (d)(3) of this section and cannot pay accelerated benefit distributions elected by participants with an annuity starting date of April 1, 2011, or later.

(v) Plan A's prefunding balance remains at $100,000 because, under paragraph (a)(5)(iii) of this section, the deemed reduction rules do not apply if the prefunding balance is not large enough to increase the adjusted value of plan assets enough to avoid the restriction. However, the earlier deemed reduction of $200,000 continues to apply because all elections (including deemed elections) to reduce a plan's funding standard carryover balance or prefunding balance are irrevocable and must be unconditional in accordance with paragraph (g)(2)(ii)(A) of this section.

Example 3. (i) The facts are the same as in *Example 1.* On July 1, 2011, the enrolled actuary for Plan A calculates the actual adjusted funding target as $3,700,000 as of January 1, 2011. Therefore, the 2011 AFTAP would have been 81.08% without reducing the prefunding balance (that is, plan assets of $3,300,000 minus the prefunding balance of $300,000, divided by the adjusted funding target of $3,700,000), and Plan A would not have been subject to the restrictions under paragraph (d)(3) of this section.

(ii) However, paragraph (g)(5)(i)(C) of this section requires that any prior reductions in the prefunding or funding standard carryover balances continue to apply, and so Plan A's prefunding balance remains at the reduced amount of $100,000 as of January 1, 2011. The enrolled actuary certifies that the 2011 AFTAP is 86.49% (that is, plan assets of $3,300,000 reduced by the prefunding balance of $100,000, divided by the adjusted funding target of $3,700,000).

Example 4. (i) Plan B is a collectively bargained plan with assets of $2,500,000 and a prefunding balance of $150,000 as of January 1, 2011. On August 14, 2010, the enrolled actuary for Plan B certified the AFTAP for 2010 to be 83%. No unpredictable contingent events giving rise to unpredictable contingent event benefits occurred during 2010 and no plan amendments took effect in 2010 that were not taken into account in the certified AFTAP.

(ii) On January 10, 2011, Plan B's sponsor amends the plan to increase benefits effective on February 1, 2011. The amendment would increase Plan B's funding target by $350,000. Under the rules of paragraph (g)(3) of this section, the determination of whether the amendment is permitted to take effect is based on a comparison of the inclusive presumed adjusted funding target with the updated interim value of adjusted plan assets.

(iii) Plan B's interim value of adjusted plan assets as of the valuation date is $2,350,000 (that is, $2,500,000 minus the prefunding balance of $150,000). Prior to reflecting the amendment, Plan B's presumed adjusted funding target as of January 1, 2011, is $2,831,325, which is equal to the interim value of adjusted plan assets as of the valuation date of $2,350,000, divided by the presumed AFTAP of 83%. Increasing Plan B's presumed adjusted funding target by $350,000 to reflect the amendment results in an inclusive presumed adjusted funding target of $3,181,325 and would result in a presumed AFTAP of 73.87% (that is, the interim value of adjusted plan assets as of the valuation date of $2,350,000 divided by the inclusive presumed adjusted funding target of $3,181,325).

(iv) Because Plan B's presumed AFTAP was over 80% prior to taking the amendment into account but would be less than 80% if the amendment were taken into account, section 436(c) and paragraph (c) of this section prohibit the plan amendment from taking effect unless the adjusted plan assets are increased so that the inclusive presumed AFTAP would be increased to 80%. This would require an additional amount of $195,060 (that is, 80% of the inclusive presumed adjusted funding target of $3,181,325 less the interim value of adjusted plan assets of $2,350,000).

(v) Plan B's prefunding balance of $150,000 is not large enough for Plan B to avoid the restriction on plan amendments, and therefore the deemed election to reduce the prefunding balance under paragraph (a)(5) of this section does not apply, and the amendment cannot take effect unless the plan sponsor makes a contribution described in paragraph (f)(2) of this section.

Example 5. (i) The facts are the same as in *Example 4,* except that Plan B's sponsor decides to make a contribution on February 1, 2011, to avoid the benefit limitation as provided in paragraph (f)(2) of this section. As of February 1, 2011, Plan B's effective interest rate for the 2011 plan year has not yet been determined. Pursuant to paragraph

(f)(2)(i)(A)(2) of this section, Plan B's effective interest rate for 2011 is treated as 6.25%, which is the largest of the three segment interest rates applicable to the 2011 plan year, as provided in paragraph (f)(2)(i)(A)(2) of this section.

(ii) The amount of the contribution as of January 1, 2011, needed to avoid the restriction on plan amendments under paragraph (c) of this section is $195,060. However, because the contribution is not paid until February 1, 2011, the necessary contribution amount must be adjusted to reflect interest that would otherwise have accrued between the valuation date and the date of the contribution, at Plan B's effective interest rate for the 2011 plan year. The amount of the required contribution after adjustment is $196,048, determined as $195,060 increased for one month of compound interest at an effective annual interest rate of 6.25%.

(iii) In accordance with paragraph (g)(4)(i) of this section, the inclusive presumed AFTAP as of February 1, 2011, is 80 percent.

Example 6. (i) The facts are the same as in *Example 5.* As of April 1, 2011, the enrolled actuary for the plan has not certified the 2011 AFTAP. Beginning April 1, 2011, Plan A's presumed AFTAP is equal to be 70%, 10 percentage points lower than the inclusive presumed AFTAP as of February 1, 2011, in accordance with paragraphs (g)(2)(iii)(A) and (h)(2) of this section. On July 1, 2011, the enrolled actuary for the plan calculates the actual adjusted funding target, prior to taking the plan amendment into account, as $2,700,000, and determines the actual effective interest rate for 2011 to be 5.25%. On this basis, the actual AFTAP for 2011 (prior to taking the amendment into account) as 87.04% (that is, adjusted assets of $2,350,000 divided by the adjusted funding target of $2,700,000). Reflecting the $350,000 increase in funding target due to the plan amendment would increase the adjusted funding target to $3,050,000 and would decrease Plan B's AFTAP to 77.05%.

(ii) Based on the calculated adjusted funding target, the amount that was necessary to avoid the benefit restriction under paragraph (c) of this section was $90,000 (that is, 80% of the adjusted funding target reflecting the plan amendment (or $3,050,000), minus the adjusted value of plan assets of $2,350,000). This amount must be adjusted for interest between the valuation date and the date the contribution was made using the effective interest rate for Plan B. Therefore, the amount required on the payment date of February 1, 2011, was $90,385 (that is, $90,000 adjusted for compound interest for one month at Plan B's effective interest rate of 5.25% per year).

(iii) Under paragraph (g)(3)(ii)(B) of this section, the contribution made on February 1, 2011, is recharacterized as an employer contribution under section 430 to the extent that it exceeded the amount necessary to avoid application of the restriction on plan amendments under paragraph (c) of this section. Therefore, $105,663 (that is, the $196,048 actual contribution paid on February 1, 2011, minus the $90,385 required contribution based on the actual AFTAP) is recharacterized as an employer contribution under section 430 for the 2011 plan year. As such, it may be applied toward the minimum required contribution for 2011, or the plan sponsor can elect to credit the contribution to Plan B's prefunding balance to the extent that the contributions for the 2011 plan year exceed the minimum required contribution.

(iv) This recharacterization applied only because the 436 contribution was made during a period prior to the certification of Plan B's actual AFTAP for 2011 and during which no presumption applied (that is, when section 436 is applied based on the 2010 AFTAP, which was high enough that no restrictions applied for 2010). If the contribution had been made during a time when the presumptions applied (for instance, after April 1, 2011, when the presumed AFTAP was under 80%) then the only portion of the 436 contribution that would be recharacterized as an employer contribution under section 430 would be the portion of the interest adjustment attributable to the difference between the highest segment rate (6.25%) and the plan's actual effective interest rate (5.25%), in accordance with paragraph (f)(2)(i)(A)(2) of this section.

(v) After reflecting the plan amendment and the present value of the portion of the section 436 contribution that is not recharacterized as an employer contribution under section 430, the adjusted assets as of January 1, 2011, for purposes of section 436 are $2,440,000 ($2,350,000 plus $90,000) and the inclusive adjusted funding target is $3,050,000. Accordingly, the enrolled actuary certifies the inclusive AFTAP for 2011 as 80% ($2,440,000 ÷ $3,050,000). Note that assets for section 430 purposes are not increased to reflect the section 436 contribution as of January 1, 2011.

Example 7. (i) The facts are the same as in *Example 6,* except that on July 1, 2011, the enrolled actuary for Plan B calculates the actual adjusted funding target (before reflecting the plan amendment) as $3,000,000 and certifies the actual AFTAP as 78.33% prior to reflecting the plan amendment (that is, adjusted plan assets of $2,350,000 divided by the actual adjusted funding target of $3,000,000). Based on the provisions of paragraph (c) of this section, because the AFTAP prior to reflecting the amendment is less than 80%, the contribution required to avoid the restriction on plan amendments would have been the amount equal to the increase in funding target due to the plan amendment, or $350,000.

(ii) However, according to paragraph (g)(5)(ii)(A) of this section, the enrolled actuary's certification of the 2011 AFTAP does not affect the application of the limitation under paragraph (c) of this section to the amendment, because the amendment to Plan B took effect prior to the date of the certification. Therefore, it is not necessary for Plan B's sponsor to contribute an additional amount in order for the plan amendment to remain in effect regardless of the extent to which the certified AFTAP for the plan year is less than the presumed inclusive AFTAP.

(h) *Presumed underfunding for purposes of benefit limitations.*— (1) *Presumption of continued underfunding.*—(i) *In general.*—This paragraph (h)(1) applies to a plan for a plan year if a limitation under paragraph (b), (c), (d), or (e) of this section applied to the plan on the last day of the preceding plan year. If this paragraph (h)(1) applies to a plan, the first day of the plan year is a section 436 measurement date and the presumed adjusted funding target attainment percentage for the plan is the percentage under paragraph (h)(1)(ii) or (iii) of this section, whichever applies to the plan, beginning on that first day of the plan year and ending on the date specified in paragraph (h)(1)(iv) of this section.

(ii) *Rule where preceding year certification issued during preceding year.*—(A) *General rule.*—In any case in which the plan's enrolled actuary has issued a certification under paragraph (h)(4) of this section of the adjusted funding target attainment percentage for the plan year preceding the current plan year before the first day of the current plan year, the presumed adjusted funding target attainment percentage of the plan for the current plan year is equal to the prior plan year adjusted funding target attainment percentage until it is changed under paragraph (h)(1)(iv) of this section.

(B) *Special rule for late certifications.*—If the certification of the adjusted funding target attainment percentage for the prior plan year occurred after the first day of the 10th month of that prior plan year, the plan is treated as if no such certification was made, unless the certification took into account the effect of any unpredictable contingent event benefits that are permitted to be paid based on unpredictable contingent events that occurred, and any plan amendments that became effective, during the prior plan year but before the certification (and any associated section 436 contributions).

(iii) *No certification for preceding year issued during preceding year.*—(A) *Deemed percentage continues.*—In any case in which the plan's enrolled actuary has not issued a certification under paragraph (h)(4) of this section of the adjusted funding target attainment percentage of the plan for the plan year preceding the current plan year during that prior plan year, the presumed adjusted funding target attainment percentage of the plan for the current plan year is equal to the presumed adjusted funding target attainment percentage that applied on the last day of the preceding plan year until the presumed adjusted funding target attainment percentage is changed under paragraph (h)(1)(iii)(B) or (h)(1)(iv) of this section. Thus, if the prior plan year was a 12-month plan year (so that the last day of the plan year was after the first day of the 10th month of the plan year and the rules of section 436(h)(2) and paragraph (h)(3) of this section applied to the plan for that plan year), then the presumed adjusted funding target attainment percentage for the current plan year is presumed to be less than 60 percent. By contrast, if the prior plan year was less than 9 months, the presumed adjusted funding target attainment percentage for the current plan year is the presumed adjusted funding target attainment percentage at the last day of the preceding plan year.

(B) *Enrolled actuary's certification in following year.*—In any case in which the plan's enrolled actuary has issued the certification under paragraph (h)(4) of this section of the adjusted funding target attainment percentage of the plan for the plan year preceding the current plan year on or after the first day of the current plan year, the date of that prior plan year certification is a new section 436 measurement date for the current plan year. In such a case, the presumed *adjusted funding target attainment* percentage for the current plan year is equal to the prior plan year adjusted funding target attainment percentage (reduced by 10 percentage points if paragraph (h)(2)(iv) of this section applies to the plan) until it is changed under paragraph (h)(1)(iv) of this section. The rules of paragraph (h)(1)(ii)(B) of this section apply for purposes of determining whether the enrolled actuary has issued a certification of the adjusted funding target attainment percentage for the prior plan year during the current plan year.

(iv) *Duration of use of presumed adjusted funding target attainment percentage.*—If this paragraph (h)(1) applies to a plan for a plan year, the presumed adjusted funding target attainment percentage determined under this paragraph (h)(1) applies until the earliest of—

(A) The first day of the 4th month of the plan year if paragraph (h)(2) of this section applies;

(B) The first day of the 10th month of the plan year if paragraph (h)(3) of this section applies;

(C) The date of a change in the presumed adjusted funding target attainment percentage under paragraph (g)(4) of this section; or

(D) The date the enrolled actuary issues a certification under paragraph (h)(4) of this section of the adjusted funding target attainment percentage for the plan year.

(2) *Presumption of underfunding beginning on first day of 4th month for certain underfunded plans.*—(i) *In general.*—This paragraph (h)(2) applies to a plan for a plan year if—

(A) The enrolled actuary for the plan has not issued a certification of the adjusted funding target attainment percentage for the plan year before the first day of the 4th month of the plan year; and

(B) The plan's adjusted funding target attainment percentage for the preceding plan year was either—

(1) At least 60 percent but less than 70 percent; or

(2) At least 80 percent but less than 90 percent.

(ii) *Special rule for first plan year a plan is subject to section 436.*—This paragraph (h)(2) also applies to a plan for the first effective plan year if—

(A) The enrolled actuary for the plan has not issued a certification of the adjusted funding target attainment percentage for the plan year before the first day of the 4th month of the plan year; and

(B) The prior plan year adjusted funding target attainment percentage is at least 70 percent but less than 80 percent.

(iii) *Presumed adjusted funding target attainment percentage.*—If this paragraph (h)(2) applies to a plan for a plan year and the date of the enrolled actuary's certification of the adjusted funding target attainment percentage under paragraph (h)(4) of this section for the prior plan year (taking into account the special rules for late certifications under paragraph (h)(1)(ii)(B) of this section) occurred before the first day of the 4th month of the current plan year, then, commencing on the first day of the 4th month of the current plan year—

(A) The presumed adjusted funding target attainment percentage of the plan for the plan year is reduced by 10 percentage points; and

(B) The first day of the 4th month of the plan year is a section 436 measurement date.

(iv) *Certification for prior plan year.*—If this paragraph (h)(2) applies to a plan and the date of the enrolled actuary's certification of the adjusted funding target attainment percentage under paragraph (h)(4) of this section for the prior plan year (taking into account the rules for late certifications under paragraph (h)(1)(ii)(B) of this section) occurs on or after the first day of the 4th month of the current plan year, then, commencing on the date of that prior plan year certification—

(A) The presumed adjusted funding target attainment percentage of the plan for the current plan year is equal to 10 percentage points less than the prior plan year adjusted funding target attainment percentage; and

(B) The date of the prior plan year certification is a section 436 measurement date.

(v) *Duration of use of presumed adjusted funding target attainment percentage.*—If this paragraph (h)(2) applies to a plan for a plan year, the presumed adjusted funding target attainment percentage determined under this paragraph (h)(2) applies until the earliest of—

(A) The first day of the 10th month of the plan year if paragraph (h)(3) of this section applies;

(B) The date of a change in the presumed adjusted funding target attainment percentage under paragraph (g)(4) of this section; or

(C) The date the enrolled actuary issues a certification under paragraph (h)(4) of this section of the adjusted funding target attainment percentage for the plan year.

(3) *Presumption of underfunding beginning on first day of 10th month.*—In any case in which no certification of the specific adjusted funding target attainment percentage for the current plan year under paragraph (h)(4) of this section is made with respect to the plan before the first day of the 10th month of the plan year, then, commencing on the first day of the 10th month of the current plan year—

(i) The presumed adjusted funding target attainment percentage of the plan for the plan year is presumed to be less than 60 percent; and

(ii) The first day of the 10th month of the plan year is a section 436 measurement date.

(4) *Certification of AFTAP.*—(i) *Rules generally applicable to certifications.*—(A) *In general.*—The enrolled actuary's certification referred to in this section must be made in writing, must be signed and dated to show the date of the signature, must be provided to the plan administrator, and, except as otherwise provided in paragraph (h)(4)(ii) of this section, must certify the plan's adjusted funding target attainment percentage for the plan year. Except in the case of a range certification described in paragraph (h)(4)(ii) of this section, the certification must set forth the value of plan assets, the prefunding balance, the funding standard carryover balance, the value of the funding target used in the determination, the aggregate amount of annuity purchases included in the adjusted value of plan assets and the adjusted funding target, the unpredictable contingent event benefits permitted to be paid for unpredictable contingent events that occurred during the current plan year that were taken into account for the current plan year (including any associated section 436 contributions), the plan amendments that took effect in the current plan year that were taken into account for the current plan year (including any associated section 436 contributions), any benefit accruals that were restored for the plan year (including any section 436 contributions), and any other relevant factors. The actuarial assumptions and funding methods used in the calculation for the certification must be the actuarial assumptions and funding methods used for the plan for purposes of determining the minimum required contributions under section 430 for the plan year.

(B) *Determination of plan assets.*—For purposes of making any determination of the adjusted funding target attainment percentage under this section, the determination is not permitted to include in plan assets contributions that have not been made to the plan by the certification date. Thus, the enrolled actuary's certification of the adjusted funding target attainment percentage for a plan year cannot take into account contributions that are expected to be made after the certification date. Notwithstanding the foregoing, for plan years beginning before January 1, 2009, the enrolled actuary's certification of the adjusted funding target attainment percentage is permitted to take into account employer contributions for the prior plan year that are reasonably expected to be made for that prior plan year but have not been contributed by the date of the enrolled actuary's certification. See paragraphs (h)(4)(iii) and (v) of this section for rules relating to changes in the certified percentage.

(ii) *Special rules for certification within range.*—(A) *In general.*— Under this paragraph (h)(4)(ii), the plan's enrolled actuary is permitted to certify during a plan year that the plan's adjusted funding target attainment percentage for that plan year either is less than 60 percent, is 60 percent or higher (but is less than 80 percent), is 80 percent or higher, or is 100 percent or higher. If the enrolled actuary has issued such a range certification for a plan year and the enrolled actuary subsequently issues a certification of the specific adjusted funding target attainment percentage for the plan before the end of that plan year, then the certification of the specific adjusted funding target attainment percentage is treated as a change in the applicable percentage to which paragraph (h)(4)(iii) of this section applies.

(B) *Effect of range certification before certification of specific percentage.*—If a plan's enrolled actuary issues a range certification pursuant to this paragraph (h)(4)(ii), then, for purposes of this section (including application of the limitations of sections 436(b) and (c), contributions described in sections 436(b)(2), 436(c)(2), and 436(e)(2), and the mandatory reduction of the prefunding and funding standard carryover balances under paragraph (a)(5) of this section), the plan is treated as having a certified percentage at the smallest value within the applicable range until a certification of the plan's specific adjusted funding target attainment percentage for the plan year has been issued under paragraph (h)(4)(i) of this section. However, if the plan's enrolled actuary has issued a range certification for the plan year but does not issue a certification of the specific adjusted funding target attainment percentage for the plan by the last day of that plan year, the adjusted funding target attainment percentage for the plan is retroactively deemed to be less than 60 percent as of the first day of the 10th month of the plan year.

(C) *Effect of range certification on and after certification of specific percentage.*—Once the certification of the specific adjusted funding target attainment percentage is issued by the plan's enrolled actuary, the certified percentage applies for all purposes of this section on and after the date of that certification. If the plan sponsor made section 436 contributions to avoid application of a benefit limitation during the period a range certification was in effect, those section 436 contributions are recharacterized as employer contributions under section 430 to the extent the contributions exceed the amount necessary to avoid application of a limitation based on the

specific adjusted funding target attainment percentage as certified by the plan's enrolled actuary on or before the last day of the plan year.

(iii) *Change of certified percentage.*—(A) *Application of new percentage.*—If the enrolled actuary for the plan provides a certification of the adjusted funding target attainment percentage of the plan for the plan year under this paragraph (h)(4) (including a range certification) and that certified percentage is superseded by a subsequent determination of the adjusted funding target attainment percentage for that plan year, then, except to the extent provided in paragraph (h)(4)(iv)(B) of this section, that later percentage must be applied for the portion of the plan year beginning on the date of the earlier certification. The subsequent determination could be the correction of a prior incorrect certification or it could be an update of a prior correct certification to take into account subsequent facts under the rules of paragraph (h)(4)(v) of this section. The implications of such a change depend on whether the change is a material change or an immaterial change. See paragraph (h)(4)(iv) of this section.

(B) *Material change.*—A change in a plan's certified adjusted funding target attainment percentage constitutes a material change for a plan year if plan operations with respect to benefits that are addressed by section 436, taking into account any actual contributions and elections under section 430(f) made by the plan sponsor based on the prior certified percentage, would have been different based on the subsequent determination of the plan's adjusted funding target attainment percentage for the plan year. A change in a plan's adjusted funding target attainment percentage for a plan year can be a material change even if the only impact of the change occurs in the following plan year under the rules for determining the presumed adjusted funding target attainment percentage in that following year.

(C) *Immaterial change.*—In general, an immaterial change is any change in an adjusted funding target attainment percentage for a plan year that is not a material change. In addition, subject to the requirement to recertify the adjusted funding target attainment percentage in paragraph (h)(4)(v)(B) of this section, a change in adjusted funding target attainment percentage is deemed to be an immaterial change if it merely reflects a change in the funding target for the plan year or the value of the adjusted plan assets after the date of the enrolled actuary's certification resulting from—

(1) Additional contributions for the preceding year that are made by the plan sponsor;

(2) The plan sponsor's election to reduce the prefunding balance or funding standard carryover balance;

(3) The plan sponsor's election to apply the prefunding balance or funding standard carryover balance to offset the prior plan year's minimum required contribution;

(4) A change in funding method or actuarial assumptions, where such change required actual approval of the Commissioner (rather than deemed approval);

(5) Unpredictable contingent event benefits which are permitted to be paid because the employer makes the section 436 contribution described in paragraph (f)(2)(iii)(A) of this section;

(6) Unpredictable contingent event benefits which are permitted to be paid because the plan's enrolled actuary determines that the increase in the funding target attributable to the occurrence of the unpredictable contingent event would not cause the plan's adjusted funding target attainment percentage to fall below 60 percent;

(7) A plan amendment which takes effect because the employer makes the section 436 contribution described in paragraph (f)(2)(iv)(A) of this section, the liability for which was not taken into account in the certification of the adjusted funding target attainment percentage;

(8) A plan amendment which takes effect because the plan's enrolled actuary determines that the increase in the funding target attributable to the plan amendment would not cause the plan's adjusted funding target attainment percentage; or to fall below 80 percent, the liability for which was not taken into account in the certification of the adjusted funding target attainment percentage; or

(9) Any other event prescribed in guidance published in the Internal Revenue Bulletin.

(iv) *Effect of change in percentage.*—(A) *Material change.*—In the case of a material change, if the plan's prior operations were in accordance with the prior certification of the adjusted funding target attainment percentage for the plan year (rather than the actual adjusted funding target attainment percentage for the plan year), then the plan will not have satisfied the requirements of section 401(a)(29) and section 436. Even if the plan's prior operations were in accordance with the subsequent certification of the adjusted funding target attainment percentage, the plan will not have satisfied the qualification requirements of section 401(a) because the plan will not have been operated in accordance with its terms during the period of time the prior certification applied. In addition, in the case of a material change, the rules requiring application of a presumed adjusted funding target attainment percentage under paragraphs (h)(1) through (h)(3) of this section continue to apply from and after the date of the prior certification until the date of the subsequent certification.

(B) *Immaterial change.*—An immaterial change in the adjusted funding target attainment percentage applies prospectively only and does not change the inapplicability of the presumptions under paragraphs (h)(1), (2), and (3) of this section prior to the date of the later certification.

(v) *Rules relating to updated certification.*—(A) *In general.*—This paragraph (h)(4)(v) sets forth rules relating to updates of an actuary's certification of the plan's adjusted funding target attainment percentage for a plan year. Paragraphs (h)(4)(v)(B) and (D) of this section require that an updated adjusted funding target attainment percentage be certified in certain situations. Even if the updated adjusted funding target attainment percentage is not required to be certified, plan administrators may request that the actuary prepare an updated certification of the adjusted funding target attainment percentage, as described in paragraphs (h)(4)(v)(C) and (E) of this section. Any updated adjusted funding target attainment percentage determined under this paragraph (h)(4)(v) will apply beginning as of the date of the event that gave rise to the need for the update which is a section 436 measurement date. Thus, pursuant to this paragraph (h)(4)(v), the updated funding target attainment percentage applies thereafter for all purposes of section 436, including application with respect to unpredictable contingent events occurring on or after the measurement date (but not for unpredictable contingent events that occurred before such measurement date or for benefits with annuity starting dates before that measurement date). The updated adjusted funding target attainment percentage will continue to apply for the remainder of the plan year and will be used for the presumed adjusted funding target attainment percentage for the next plan year, unless there is a later updated certification of adjusted funding target attainment percentage for the plan year.

(B) *Requirement to recertify AFTAP if plan sponsor contributes to threshold.*—If, during the plan year, unpredictable contingent event benefits are permitted to be paid, a plan amendment takes effect, or benefits are permitted to accrue because the plan sponsor makes a contribution described in paragraph (f)(2)(iii)(B), (f)(2)(iv)(B), or (f)(2)(v) of this section, then, in accordance with paragraph (f)(2)(ii)(C) of this section, the plan's enrolled actuary must issue an updated certification of the adjusted funding target attainment percentage that takes into account such contribution as well as the liability for unpredictable contingent event benefits that are permitted to be paid, plan amendments that take effect during the plan year, and restored benefits.

(C) *Optional recertification of AFTAP after other unpredictable contingent event or plan amendment.*—Except as provided in paragraph (h)(4)(v)(D) of this section, if, during a plan year, unpredictable contingent event benefits are permitted to be paid, or a plan amendment takes effect, because either the plan sponsor makes a contribution described in paragraph (f)(2)(iii)(A) or (f)(2)(iv)(A) of this section, or the plan's enrolled actuary determines that the increase in the funding target attributable to the occurrence of the unpredictable contingent event or the plan amendment would not cause the plan's adjusted funding target attainment percentage to fall below the applicable 60 percent or 80 percent threshold (taking into account the occurrence of all previous unpredictable contingent event benefits and plan amendments to the extent not already reflected in the certified adjusted funding target attainment percentage for the plan year (or update)), then the plan administrator may request that the plan actuary issue an updated certification of the adjusted funding target attainment percentage that takes into account the unpredictable contingent event benefits or plan amendments and any associated section 436 contribution.

(D) *Requirement to recertify AFTAP after deemed immaterial change.*—If a change in the adjusted funding target attainment percentage as a result of one of the items listed in paragraph (h)(4)(iii)(C) of this section would be a material change, then the change is treated as an immaterial change only if the plan's enrolled actuary recertifies the adjusted funding target attainment percentage for the plan year as soon as practicable after the event that gives rise to the change.

(E) *Optional recertification after other immaterial change.*—If a change in the adjusted funding target attainment percentage is immaterial, then the plan administrator may request that the plan actuary issue an updated certification of the adjusted funding target attainment percentage that takes into account the unpredictable contingent event benefits or plan amendments and any associated section 436 contribution.

(5) *Examples of rules of paragraphs (h)(1), (h)(2), and (h)(3) of this section.*—The following examples illustrate the rules of paragraphs (h)(1), (h)(2), and (h)(3) of this section. Unless otherwise indicated, the examples in this section are based on the information in this paragraph (h)(5). Each plan is a non-collectively bargained defined benefit plan with a plan year that is the calendar year and a valuation date of January 1. The plan year is subject to section 436 in 2008. The plan does not have a funding standard carryover balance or a prefunding balance as of any of the dates mentioned, and the plan sponsor does not elect to utilize any of the methods in paragraph (f) of this section to avoid applicable benefit restrictions. No range certification under paragraph (h)(4) of this section has been issued. The plan sponsor is not in bankruptcy. The examples read as follows:

Example 1. (i) On July 15, 2010, the adjusted funding target attainment percentage ("AFTAP") for Plan T for 2010 is certified to be 65%. Based on this AFTAP, Plan T is subject to the restriction on prohibited payments in paragraph (d)(3) of this section for the remainder of 2010.

(ii) Beginning January 1, 2011, Plan T's AFTAP for 2011 is presumed to be equal to the AFTAP for 2010, or 65%, under the provisions of paragraph (h)(1)(ii) of this section. Accordingly, the restriction on prohibited payments in paragraph (d)(3) of this section continues to apply.

(iii) On March 1, 2011, the enrolled actuary for the plan certifies that the actual AFTAP for 2011 is 80%. Therefore, beginning March 1, 2011, Plan T is no longer subject to the restriction under paragraph (d)(3) of this section, and so Plan T resumes paying the full amount of any prohibited payments elected by participants with an annuity starting date of March 1, 2011, or later.

Example 2. (i) The facts are the same as in *Example 1*, except that the enrolled actuary for the plan does not certify the AFTAP for 2011 until June 1, 2011, when it is certified to be 66%.

(ii) Beginning January 1, 2011, Plan T's AFTAP for 2011 is presumed to be equal to the AFTAP for 2010, or 65%, under the provisions of paragraph (h)(1)(ii) of this section. Accordingly, the restriction on prohibited payments in paragraph (d)(3) of this section continues to apply.

(iii) Pursuant to paragraph (h)(2)(iv) of this section, beginning April 1, 2011, the AFTAP for 2011 is presumed to be 55% (10 percentage points less than the AFTAP for 2010). Plan T is subject to the restriction on prohibited payments under paragraph (d)(1) of this section for annuity starting dates on or after April 1, 2011. In addition, Plan T is subject to the restriction on unpredictable contingent event benefits under paragraph (b) of this section for unpredictable contingent events occurring on or after April 1, 2011 and benefits are required to be frozen on and after April 1, 2011 under paragraph (e) of this section.

(iv) Once the enrolled actuary for the plan certifies that the AFTAP for 2011 for Plan T is 66%, Plan T is no longer subject to the restriction under paragraph (d)(1) of this section, but it is subject to the restriction under paragraph (d)(3) of this section. Plan T must resume paying prohibited payments, as restricted under paragraph (d)(3) of this section, for participants who elect benefits in accelerated forms of payment and who have an annuity starting date of June 1, 2011, or later. In addition, Plan T must provide benefits for any unpredictable contingent event occurring on or after January 1, 2011, to the extent permitted under paragraph (b) of this section. Similarly, Plan T is no longer subject to the restriction on benefit accruals under paragraph (e) of this section, and benefit accruals resume under Plan T beginning June 1, 2011, unless Plan T provides otherwise.

Example 3. (i) The facts are the same as in *Example 1*, except that the enrolled actuary for the plan does not certify the 2011 AFTAP until November 15, 2011. Beginning October 1, 2011, Plan T is conclusively presumed to have an AFTAP of less than 60%, in accordance with the provisions of paragraph (h)(3) of this section. Accordingly, Plan T is subject to the restrictions in paragraphs (b), (d)(1), and (e) of this section commencing on October 1, 2011.

(ii) On November 15, 2011, the enrolled actuary for the plan certifies that the AFTAP for 2011 is 72%. However, because the certification occurred after September 30, 2011, the certification does not constitute a new section 436 measurement date, and Plan T continues to be subject to the restrictions on unpredictable contingent event benefits, prohibited payments, and benefit accruals under paragraphs (b), (d)(1), and (e) of this section.

(iii) Beginning January 1, 2012, the 2012 AFTAP for Plan T is presumed to be equal to the 2011 AFTAP of 72%. Because the presumed 2012 AFTAP is between 70% and 80% and, therefore, paragraph (h)(2) of this section (which provides for a 10 percentage point reduction in a plan's AFTAP in certain cases) will not apply, the presumed AFTAP will remain at 72% until the plan's enrolled actuary certifies the AFTAP for 2012 or until paragraph (h)(3) of this section applies on the first day of the 10th month of the plan year. Because the presumed AFTAP is 72%, Plan T is no longer subject to the restrictions on prohibited payments under paragraph (d)(1) of this section, and Plan T must provide benefits for any unpredictable contingent event occurring on or after January 1, 2012, to the extent permitted under paragraph (b) of this section and must resume paying prohibited payments, as restricted under paragraph (d)(3) of this section, that are elected by participants with annuity starting dates on or after January 1, 2012. Similarly, Plan T is no longer subject to the restriction on benefit accruals under paragraph (e) of this section, and benefit accruals resume under Plan T beginning January 1, 2012, unless Plan T provides otherwise.

Example 4. (i) The facts are the same as in *Example 3,* except that the enrolled actuary for the plan does not issue a certification of the AFTAP for 2011 for Plan T until February 1, 2012.

(ii) Beginning on January 1, 2012, the presumptions in paragraph (h)(1)(iii) of this section apply for the 2012 plan year. Because the enrolled actuary for the plan has not certified the AFTAP for 2011, the presumed AFTAP as of October 1, 2011, continues to apply for the period beginning January 1, 2012. Therefore, the AFTAP as of January 1, 2012, is presumed to be less than 60%, and Plan T continues to be subject to the restrictions on unpredictable contingent event benefits under paragraph (b) of this section, prohibited payments under paragraph (d)(1) of this section, and benefit accruals under paragraph (e) of this section.

(iii) On February 1, 2012, the enrolled actuary for the plan certifies that the AFTAP for 2011 for Plan T is 65%. Because the enrolled actuary for the plan has not issued a certification of the AFTAP for 2012, the provisions of paragraph (h)(1)(iii)(B) of this section apply. Accordingly, the certification date for the 2011 AFTAP (February 1, 2012) is a section 436 measurement date and 65% is the presumed AFTAP for 2012 beginning on that date.

(iv) Because the presumed AFTAP is over 60% but less than 80%, the full restriction on prohibited payments under paragraph (d)(1) of this section no longer applies; however, the partial restriction on prohibited payments under paragraph (d)(3) of this section applies beginning on February 1, 2012. Therefore, Plan T must pay a portion of the prohibited payments elected by participants with annuity starting dates on or after February 1, 2012. Furthermore, based on the presumed AFTAP of 65%, the restriction on unpredictable contingent event benefits under paragraph (b) of this section ceases to apply for events occurring on or after February 1, 2012, to the extent permitted under paragraph (b) of this section and the restriction on benefit accruals under paragraph (e) of this section no longer applies so that, unless Plan T provides otherwise, benefit accruals will resume as of February 1, 2012.

Example 5. (i) The facts are the same as in *Example 3,* except that the enrolled actuary for the plan does not issue a certification of the actual AFTAP for Plan T as of January 1, 2011, until May 1, 2012.

(ii) Beginning on January 1, 2012, the presumptions in paragraph (h)(1)(iii) of this section apply for the 2012 plan year. Because the enrolled actuary for the plan has not certified the actual AFTAP as of January 1, 2011, the presumed AFTAP as of October 1, 2011, continues to apply for the period beginning January 1, 2012. Therefore, the AFTAP as of January 1, 2012, is presumed to be less than 60%, and Plan T continues to be subject to the restrictions on unpredictable contingent event benefits under paragraph (b) of this section, on prohibited payments under paragraph (d)(1) of this section, and on benefit accruals under paragraph (e) of this section.

(iii) Since the enrolled actuary for the plan has not issued a certification of the actual AFTAP as of January 1, 2011, the rules of paragraph (h)(1)(iii) of this section apply beginning April 1, 2012, and the AFTAP is presumed to remain less than 60%. Plan T continues to be subject to the restrictions on unpredictable contingent event benefits under paragraph (b) of this section, on prohibited payments under paragraph (d)(1) of this section, and on benefit accruals under paragraph (e) of this section.

(iv) On May 1, 2012, the enrolled actuary for the plan certifies that the actual AFTAP for 2011 for Plan T is 65%. Because the enrolled actuary for the plan has not issued a certification of the actual AFTAP as of January 1, 2012, the provisions of paragraph (h)(2)(iv) of this section apply. Accordingly, on May 1, 2012, the 2012 AFTAP is presumed to be 10 percentage points less than the 2011 AFTAP, or 55%, so that the restrictions under paragraphs (b), (d), and (e) of this section continue to apply.

Example 6. (i) The enrolled actuary for Plan V certifies the plan's AFTAP for 2010 to be 69%. Based on this AFTAP, Plan V is subject to the restriction in paragraph (d)(3) of this section, and can only pay a portion (generally 50%) of the prohibited payments otherwise due to plan participants who commence benefits while the restriction is in effect. The enrolled actuary for the plan does not issue a certification of the AFTAP for 2011 until June 1, 2011.

(ii) Beginning January 1, 2011, Plan V's 2011 AFTAP is presumed *to be equal to the 2010 AFTAP,* or 69%, under the provisions of paragraph (h)(1)(ii) of this section. Accordingly, the restriction on prohibited payments in paragraph (d)(3) of this section continues to apply from January 1, 2011, through March 31, 2011, and Plan T may

only pay a portion of the prohibited payments otherwise due to participants who commence benefit payments during this period.

(iii) Beginning April 1, 2011, the provisions of paragraph (h)(2)(ii) of this section apply. Under those provisions, the AFTAP beginning April 1, 2011, is presumed to be 10 percentage points lower than the presumed 2011 AFTAP, or 59%. Because Plan V's presumed AFTAP for 2011 is less than 60%, the restrictions on unpredictable contingent event benefits under paragraph (b) of this section, on the payment of accelerated benefit distributions under paragraph (d)(1) of this section, and on benefit accruals under paragraph (e) of this section apply. Accordingly, Plan V cannot pay any unpredictable contingent event benefits for events occurring on or after April 1, 2011, or prohibited payments to participants with an annuity starting date on or after April 1, 2011, and benefit accruals cease as of April 1, 2011.

(iv) On June 1, 2011, Plan V's enrolled actuary certifies that the plan's AFTAP for 2011 is 71%. Therefore, the restrictions on unpredictable contingent event benefits, prohibited payments, and benefit accruals in paragraphs (b), (d)(1), and (e) of this section no longer apply, but the partial restriction on benefit payments in paragraph (d)(3) of this section does apply. Accordingly, Plan V begins paying unpredictable contingent event benefits for events occurring on or after January 1, 2011, to the extent permitted under paragraph (b) of this section and a portion of the prohibited payments elected by participants with an annuity starting date on or after June 1, 2011. Benefit accruals previously restricted under paragraph (e) of this section resume effective June 1, 2011, unless Plan V provides otherwise.

(v) Participants who were not able to elect an accelerated form of payment during the period from April 1, 2011, through May 31, 2011, would be able to elect a new annuity starting date with a partial distribution of accelerated benefits effective June 1, 2011, if Plan V contained a preexisting provision permitting such an election after the restriction in paragraph (d)(1) of this section no longer applies. This is permitted because, under paragraph (a)(4)(ii)(B) of this section, a preexisting provision of this type is not considered a plan amendment and is therefore not subject to the plan amendment restriction in paragraph (c) of this section even though Plan V's AFTAP for 2011 is less than 80%.

(vi) Benefit accruals for the period beginning April 1, 2011, through May 31, 2011, would be automatically restored if Plan V contained a preexisting provision to retroactively restore benefit accruals restricted under paragraph (e) of this section after the restriction no longer applies. This is permitted because under paragraph (a)(4)(ii)(B) of this section, a preexisting provision of this type is not considered to be a plan amendment and is therefore not subject to the plan amendment restriction in paragraph (c) of this section even though Plan V's AFTAP for 2011 is less than 80%, because the period of the restriction did not exceed 12 months.

(6) *Examples of rules of paragraph (h)(4) of this section.*—The following examples illustrate the rules of paragraph (h)(4) of this section:

Example 1. (i) Plan Y is a non-collectively bargained defined benefit plan with a plan year that is the calendar year and a valuation date of January 1. Plan Y does not have a funding standard carryover balance or a prefunding balance. Plan Y's sponsor is not in bankruptcy. In June of 2010, the actual AFTAP for 2010 for Plan Y is certified as 65%. On the last day of the 2010 plan year, Plan Y is subject to the restrictions in paragraph (d)(3) of this section.

(ii) The enrolled actuary for the plan issues a range certification on March 21, 2011, certifying that the AFTAP for 2011 is at least 60% and less than 80%. Because the certification was issued before the first day of the 4th month of the plan year, the 10 percentage point reduction in the presumed AFTAP under paragraph (h)(2) of this section does not apply. In addition, because the enrolled actuary for the plan has certified that the AFTAP is within this range, Plan Y is not subject to the full restriction on accelerated benefit payments in paragraph (d)(1) of this section or the restriction on benefit accruals under paragraph (e) of this section.

(iii) On August 1, 2011, the enrolled actuary for the plan certifies that the actual AFTAP as of January 1, 2011, is 75.86%. This AFTAP falls within the previously certified range. Thus, the change is immaterial under paragraph (h)(4)(iii) of this section and the new certification does not change the applicability or inapplicability of the restrictions in this section.

Example 2. (i) The facts are the same as in *Example 1,* except that the plan sponsor makes an additional contribution for the 2010 plan year on September 1, 2011, that is not added to the prefunding balance. Reflecting this contribution, the enrolled actuary for the plan issues a revised certification stating that the AFTAP for 2011 is 81%, and Plan Y is no longer subject to the restriction on accelerated benefit payments under paragraph (d)(3) of this section on that date.

(ii) Although the revised certification changes the applicability of the restriction under paragraph (d)(3) of this section, the change is not a material change under paragraph (h)(4)(iii)(C)(*1*) of this section because the AFTAP changed only because of additional contributions for the preceding year made by the plan sponsor after the date of the enrolled actuary's initial certification.

(i) [Reserved.]

(j) *Definitions.*—For purposes of this section—

(1) *Adjusted funding target attainment percentage.*—(i) *In general.*—Except as otherwise provided in this paragraph (j)(1), the *adjusted funding target attainment percentage* for a plan year is the fraction (expressed as a percentage)—

(A) The numerator of which is the adjusted plan assets for the plan year described in paragraph (j)(1)(ii) of this section; and

(B) The denominator of which is the adjusted funding target for the plan year described in paragraph (j)(1)(iii) of this section.

(ii) *Adjusted plan assets.*—(A) *General rule.*—The adjusted plan assets for a plan year is generally determined by—

(1) Subtracting the plan's funding standard carryover balance and prefunding balance as of the valuation date from the value of plan assets for the plan year under section 430(g) (but treating the resulting value as zero if it is below zero); and

(2) Increasing the resulting value by the aggregate amount of purchases of annuities for participants and beneficiaries (other than participants who, at the time of the purchase, were highly compensated employees as defined in section 414(q), which definition includes highly compensated former employees under §1.414(q)-1T, Q&A-4) which were made by the plan during the

preceding 2 plan years, to the extent not included in plan assets for purposes of section 430.

(B) *Special rule for plans that are fully funded without regard to subtraction of funding balances from plan assets.*—If for a plan year the value of plan assets determined without subtracting the funding standard carryover balance and the prefunding balance is not less than 100 percent of the plan's funding target determined under section 430 without regard to section 430(i), then the adjusted value of plan assets used in the calculation of the adjusted funding target attainment percentage for the plan year is determined without subtracting the plan's funding standard carryover balance and prefunding balance from the value of plan assets for the plan year.

(C) *Special rule for plans with section 436 contributions.*—If an employer makes a contribution described in paragraph (f)(2) of this section after the valuation date in order to avoid or terminate limitations under section 436, then the present value of that contribution (determined using the effective interest rate under section 430(h)(2)(A) for the plan year) is permitted to be added to the plan assets as of the valuation date for purposes of determining or redetermining the adjusted funding target attainment percentage for a plan year, but only if the liability for the benefits, amendment, or accruals that would have been limited (but for the contribution) is included in determining the adjusted funding target for the plan year.

(D) *Transition rule.*—Paragraph (j)(1)(ii)(B) of this section is applied to plan years beginning after 2007 and before 2011 by substituting for "100 percent" the applicable percentage determined in accordance with the following table:

In the case of a plan year beginning in calendar year:	The applicable percentage is:
2008	92
2009	94
2010	96

(E) *Limitation on transition rule.*—Paragraph (j)(1)(ii)(D) of this section does not apply with respect to the current plan year unless, for each plan year beginning after December 31, 2007, and before the current plan year, the value of plan assets determined without subtracting the funding standard carryover balance and prefunding balance is not less than the product of—

(1) The applicable percentage determined under paragraph (j)(1)(ii)(D) of this section for that plan year; and

(2) The funding target (determined without regard to the at-risk rules of section 430(i)) for that plan year.

(iii) *Adjusted funding target.*—(A) *In general.*—Except as otherwise provided in this paragraph (j)(1)(iii), the adjusted funding target equals the funding target for the plan year, determined in accordance with the rules set forth in §1.430(d)-1, but without regard to the at-risk rules under section 430(i), increased by the aggregate amount of purchases of annuities that were added to assets for purposes of determining the plan's adjusted plan assets under paragraph (j)(1)(ii)(A)(2) of this section. The definition of adjusted funding target for a plan maintained by a commercial airline for which the plan sponsor has made the election described in section 402(a)(1) of Pension Protection Act of 2006 (PPA '06), Public Law 109-280 (120 Stat. 780), is the same as if it did not make such an election.

(B) *Adjusted funding target after updated certification.*—After the plan's enrolled actuary prepares an updated certification of the adjusted funding target attainment percentage under paragraph (h)(4)(v) of this section, the adjusted funding target will also be updated to reflect unpredictable contingent event benefits and plan amendments not already taken into account.

(iv) *Plans with zero adjusted funding target.*—If the adjusted funding target for the plan year is zero, then the adjusted funding target attainment percentage for the plan year is 100 percent.

(v) *Plans with end of year valuation dates.*—[Reserved.]

(vi) *Special rule for plans that are the result of a merger.*—[Reserved.]

(vii) *Special rule for plans that are involved in a spinoff.*—[Reserved.]

(2) *Annuity starting date.*—(i) *General rule.*—The term *annuity starting date* means, as applicable—

(A) The first day of the first period for which an amount is payable as an annuity as described in section 417(f)(2)(A)(i);

(B) In the case of a benefit not payable in the form of an annuity, the annuity starting date is the annuity starting date for the

qualified joint and survivor annuity that is payable under the plan at the same time as the benefit that is not payable as an annuity;

(C) In the case of an amount payable under a retroactive annuity starting date, the benefit commencement date (instead of the date determined under paragraphs (j)(2)(i)(A) and (B) of this section);

(D) The date of the purchase of an irrevocable commitment from an insurer to pay benefits under the plan; and

(E) The date of any transfer to another plan described in paragraph (j)(6)(i)(C) of this section.

(ii) *Special rule for beneficiaries.*—If a participant commences benefits at an annuity starting date (as defined in paragraph (j)(2)(i) of this section) and, after the death of the participant, payments continue to a beneficiary, the annuity starting date for the payments to the participant constitutes the annuity starting date for payments to the beneficiary, except that a new annuity starting date occurs (determined by applying paragraph (j)(2)(i)(A), (B), and (C) of this section to the payments to the beneficiary) if the amounts payable to all beneficiaries of the participant in the aggregate at any future date can exceed the monthly amount that would have been paid to the participant had he or she not died.

(3) *First effective plan year.*—The *first effective plan year* for a plan is the first plan year to which section 436 applies to the plan under paragraph (k)(1) or (k)(2) of this section.

(4) *Funding target.*—In general, the *funding target* means the funding target under §1.430(d)-1, without regard to the at-risk rules under section 430(i) and §1.430(i)-1. However, solely for purposes of sections 436(b)(2)(A) and (c)(2)(A), the funding target means the funding target under §1.430(i)-1 if the plan is in at-risk status for the plan year.

(5) *Prior plan year adjusted funding target attainment percentage.*—(i) *In general.*—Except as otherwise provided in this paragraph (j)(5), the *prior plan year adjusted funding target attainment percentage* is the adjusted funding target attainment percentage determined under paragraph (j)(1) of this section for the immediately preceding plan year.

(ii) *Special rules.*—(A) *Special rule for new plans.*—In the case of a plan established during the plan year that was not the result of a merger or spinoff, the adjusted funding target attainment percentage is equal to 100 percent for plan years before the plan was established. Except as otherwise provided in paragraph (j)(5)(ii)(B) of this section, a plan that has a predecessor plan in accordance with §1.415(f)-1(c) is not a plan established during the plan year under this paragraph (j)(5)(ii)(A). Instead, if the plan has a predecessor plan, the adjusted funding target attainment percentage for the prior plan year is the adjusted funding target attainment percentage for the prior plan year for the predecessor plan (and that predecessor plan's adjusted funding target attainment percentage is treated as equal to 100 percent on any date on which it is terminated, other than in a distress termination).

(B) *Special rules for plans that are the result of a merger.*—[Reserved.]

(C) *Special rules for plans that are involved in a spinoff.*—[Reserved.]

(iii) *Special rules for 2007 plan year.*—(A) *General determination of 2007 adjusted funding target attainment percentage.*—In the case of the first plan year beginning in 2008, except as otherwise provided in this paragraph (j)(5), the adjusted funding target attainment percentage for the immediately preceding plan year (the 2007 plan year) is determined as the fraction (expressed as a percentage)—

(1) The numerator of which is the value of plan assets determined under paragraph (j)(5)(iii)(B) of this section increased by the aggregate amount of purchases of annuities for participants and beneficiaries (other than participants who, at the time of the purchase, were highly compensated employees as defined in section 414(q), which definition includes highly compensated former employees under §1.414(q)-1T, Q&A-4) which were made by the plan during the preceding 2 plan years, to the extent not included in plan assets under section 412(c)(2) (as in effect prior to amendment by PPA '06); and

(2) The denominator of which is the plan's current liability determined pursuant to section 412(l)(7) (as in effect prior to amendment by PPA '06) on the valuation date for the 2007 plan year increased by the aggregate amount of purchases of annuities that were added to the plan assets under the rules of paragraph (j)(5)(iii)(A)(1) of this section.

(B) *General determination of value of plan assets.*—(1) *In general.*—The value of plan assets for purposes of this paragraph (j)(5)(iii) is determined under section 412(c)(2) as in effect for the 2007 plan year, except that the value of plan assets prior to subtracting the plan's funding standard account credit balance described in paragraph (j)(5)(iii)(B)(2) of this section must be adjusted so that the value of plan assets is neither less than 90 percent of the fair market value of plan assets nor greater than 110 percent of the fair market value of plan assets on the valuation date for that plan year.

(2) *Subtraction of credit balance.*—If a plan has a funding standard account credit balance as of the valuation date for the 2007 plan year, that balance is subtracted from the value of plan assets described in paragraph (j)(5)(iii)(B)(1) of this section as of that valuation date. However, the subtraction does not apply if the value of plan assets prior to adjustment under paragraph (j)(5)(iii)(B)(1) of this section is greater than or equal to 90 percent of the plan's current liability as of the valuation date for the 2007 plan year.

(3) *Effect of funding standard carryover balance reduction for 2007 plan year.*—Notwithstanding paragraph (j)(5)(iii)(B)(2) of this section, if, for the first plan year beginning in 2008, the employer has made an election to reduce some or all of the funding standard carryover balance as of the first day of that year in accordance with §1.430(f)-1(e), then the present value (determined as of the valuation date for the 2007 plan year using the valuation interest rate for that plan year) of the amount so reduced is not treated as part of the funding standard account credit balance when that balance is subtracted from the asset value under paragraph (j)(5)(iii)(B)(2) of this section.

(C) *Plan with end-of-year valuation date.*—With respect to the first plan year beginning in 2008, if the plan had a valuation date under section 412 that was the last day of the plan year for each of the plan years beginning in 2006 and 2007, the adjusted funding target attainment percentage for the 2007 plan year may be determined as the fraction (expressed as a percentage)—

(1) The numerator of which is the value of plan assets determined under paragraph (j)(5)(iii)(D) of this section increased by the aggregate amount of purchases of annuities for participants and beneficiaries (other than participants who, at the time of the purchase, were highly compensated employees as defined in section 414(q), which definition includes highly compensated former employees under §1.414(q)-1T, Q&A-4) which were made by the plan during the preceding 2 plan years, to the extent not included in plan assets under section 412(c)(2) (as in effect prior to amendment by PPA '06); and

(2) The denominator of which is the plan's current liability determined pursuant to section 412(l)(7) (as in effect prior to amendment by PPA '06) on the valuation date for the second plan year that begins before 2008 (the 2006 plan year), including the increase in current liability for the 2006 plan year, increased by the aggregate amount of purchases of annuities that were added to the

plan assets under the rules of paragraph (j)(5)(iii)(C)(1) of this section.

(D) *Special asset determinations for 2006 adjusted funding target attainment percentage.*—(1) *General rule.*—If the adjusted funding target attainment percentage for the 2007 plan year is determined under the rules of paragraph (j)(5)(iii)(C) of this section, then the value of plan assets is determined as the value of plan assets under section 412(c)(2) as in effect for the 2006 plan year, adjusted as provided in this paragraph (j)(5)(iii)(D).

(2) *Inclusion of contributions for 2006.*—Contributions made for the 2006 plan year are taken into account in determining the value of plan assets, regardless of whether those contributions are made during the plan year or after the end of the plan year and within the period specified under section 412(c)(10) (as in effect prior to amendment by PPA '06).

(3) *Restriction to 90-110 percent corridor.*—The value of plan assets taking into account the amount of contributions made for the 2006 plan year is increased or decreased, as necessary, so that it is neither less than 90 percent of the fair market value of plan assets nor greater than 110 percent of the fair market value of plan assets on the valuation date for the 2006 plan year (taking into account assets attributable to contributions for the 2006 plan year).

(4) *Subtraction of credit balance.*—The plan's funding standard account credit balance as of the end of the 2006 plan year is generally subtracted from the value of plan assets determined after application of paragraph (j)(5)(iii)(D)(3) of this section. However, this subtraction does not apply if the value of plan assets is greater than or equal to 90 percent of the plan's current liability determined under section 412(l)(7) (as in effect prior to amendment by PPA '06) on the valuation date for the 2006 plan year.

(E) *Special rules for mergers and spinoffs.*—Rules similar to the rules of paragraph (j)(5)(ii) of this section apply for purposes of determining the adjusted funding target attainment percentage for the 2007 plan year in the case of a newly established plan, a plan that is the result of a merger of two plans, or a plan that is in involved in a spinoff.

(6) *Prohibited payment.*—(i) *General rule.*—The term *prohibited payment* means—

(A) Any payment for a month that is in excess of the monthly amount paid under a straight life annuity (plus any social security supplements described in the last sentence of section 411(a)(9)) to a participant or beneficiary whose annuity starting date occurs during any period that a limitation under paragraph (d) of this section is in effect;

(B) Any payment for the purchase of an irrevocable commitment from an insurer to pay benefits;

(C) Any transfer of assets and liabilities to another plan maintained by the same employer (or by any member of the employer's controlled group) that is made in order to avoid or terminate the application of section 436 benefit limitations; and

(D) Any other amount that is identified as a prohibited payment by the Commissioner in revenue rulings and procedures, notices, and other guidance published in the Internal Revenue Bulletin (see §601.601(d)(2) relating to objectives and standards for publishing regulations, revenue rulings and revenue procedures in the Internal Revenue Bulletin).

(ii) *Special rule for beneficiaries.*—In the case of a beneficiary that is not an individual, the amount that is a prohibited payment is determined by substituting for the amount in paragraph (j)(1)(i)(A) of this section the monthly amount payable in installments over 240 months that is actuarially equivalent to the benefit payable to the beneficiary.

(7) *Section 436 contributions.*—*Section 436 contributions* are the contributions described in paragraph (f)(2) of this section that are made in order to avoid the application of section 436 limitations under a plan for a plan year.

(8) *Section 436 measurement date.*—A *section 436 measurement date* is the date that is used to determine when the limitations of sections 436(d) and 436(e) apply or cease to apply, and is also used for calculations with respect to applying the limitations of paragraphs (b) and (c) of this section. See paragraphs (h)(1)(i), (h)(2)(iii)(B), (h)(2)(iv)(B), and (h)(3)(i) of this section regarding section 436 measurement dates that result from application of the presumptions under paragraph (h) of this section.

(9) *Unpredictable contingent event.*—An *unpredictable contingent event benefit* means any benefit or increase in benefits to the extent the benefit or increase would not be payable but for the occurrence of an unpredictable contingent event. For this purpose, an *unpredictable*

contingent event means a plant shutdown (whether full or partial) or similar event, or an event (including the absence of an event) other than the attainment of any age, performance of any service, receipt or derivation of any compensation, or the occurrence of death or disability. For example, if a plan provides for an unreduced early retirement benefit upon the occurrence of an event other than the attainment of any age, performance of any service, receipt or derivation of any compensation, or the occurrence of death or disability, then that unreduced early retirement benefit is an unpredictable contingent event benefit to the extent of any portion of the benefit that would not be payable but for the occurrence of the event, even if the remainder of the benefit is payable without regard to the occurrence of the event. Similarly, if a plan includes a benefit payable upon the presence (including the absence) of circumstances specified in the plan (other than the attainment of any age, performance of any service, receipt or derivation of any compensation, or the occurrence of death or disability), but not upon a severance from employment that does not include those circumstances, that benefit is an unpredictable contingent event benefit.

(10) *Examples.*—The following examples illustrate the rules of this paragraph (j):

Example 1. (i) Plan S is a non-collectively bargained defined benefit plan with a plan year that is the calendar year and a valuation date of January 1. The first effective plan year is 2008. Plan S is not in at-risk status for 2008.

(ii) As of January 1, 2008, Plan S has a value of plan assets (equal to the market value of assets) of $2,100,000 and a funding standard carryover balance of $200,000. During 2006, assets from Plan S were used to purchase a total of $100,000 in annuities for employees other than highly compensated employees. No annuities were purchased during 2007. On May 1, 2008, the enrolled actuary for the plan determines that the funding target as of January 1, 2008, is $2,500,000.

(iii) The adjusted value of assets for Plan S as of January 1, 2008, is $2,000,000 (that is, plan assets of $2,100,000, plus annuity purchases of $100,000, and minus the funding standard carryover balance of $200,000). The adjusted funding target is $2,600,000 (that is, the funding target of $2,500,000, increased by the annuity purchases of $100,000).

(iv) Based on the above adjusted plan assets and adjusted funding target, the adjusted funding target attainment percentage (AFTAP) as of January 1, 2008, would be 76.92%. Since the AFTAP is less than 80% but is at least 60%, Plan S is subject to the restrictions in paragraph (d)(3) of this section.

Example 2. (i) The facts are the same as in *Example 1*, except that it is reasonable to expect that the plan sponsor will make a contribution of $80,000 to Plan S for the 2007 plan year by September 15, 2008. This amount is in excess of the minimum required contribution for 2007. The plan sponsor elects to reduce the funding standard carryover balance by $80,000.

(ii) Because it is reasonable to expect that the $80,000 will be contributed by the plan sponsor, that amount is taken into account when the enrolled actuary certifies the 2008 AFTAP under the special rule in paragraph (h)(4)(i)(B) of this section for plan years beginning before 2009. Accordingly, the enrolled actuary for the plan certifies the 2008 AFTAP as 80% (that is, adjusted plan assets of $2,080,000, reflecting the $80,000 in contributions receivable, divided by the adjusted funding target of $2,600,000).

(iii) The ability to take contributions into account before they are actually paid to the plan is available only for plan years beginning before 2009. Furthermore, if the employer does not actually make the contribution and the difference between the incorrect certification and the corrected AFTAP constitutes a material change, the plan will have violated section 401(a)(29) or will not have been operated in accordance with its terms.

Example 3. (i) Plan R is a defined benefit plan with a plan year that is the calendar year and a valuation date of January 1. Section 436 applies to Plan R for 2008. The valuation interest rate for the 2007 plan year for Plan R is 7%. The fair market value of assets of Plan R as of January 1, 2007, is $1,000,000. The actuarial value of assets of Plan R as of January 1, 2007, is $1,200,000. The current liability of Plan R as of January 1, 2007, is $1,500,000. The funding standard account credit balance as of January 1, 2007, is $80,000. The funding standard carryover balance of Plan R is $50,000 as of the beginning of the 2008 plan year. The sponsor of Plan R, Sponsor T, elects in 2008 to reduce the funding standard carryover balance in accordance with § 1.430(f)-1 by $45,000. No annuities were purchased using plan assets during 2005 or 2006.

(ii) Pursuant to paragraph (j)(5)(iii)(B)(*1*) of this section, the asset value used to determine the AFTAP for the 2007 plan year is limited to 110% of the fair market value of assets on January 1, 2007, or $1,100,000 (110% of $1,000,000).

(iii) Pursuant to paragraph (j)(5)(iii)(B)(2) of this section, the funding standard account credit balance as of January 1, 2007, is subtracted from the asset value used to determine the AFTAP for the 2007 plan year. However, pursuant to paragraph (j)(5)(iii)(B)(3) of this section, the present value of the amount by which Sponsor T

elected to reduce the funding standard carryover balance in 2008 is not subtracted.

(iv) The present value, determined at an interest rate of 7%, of the $45,000 reduction in the funding standard carryover balance elected by Sponsor T in 2008 is $42,056. Thus, $42,056 is not subtracted from the 2007 plan year asset value. Accordingly, the funding standard account credit balance that is subtracted from the 2007 plan year asset value is $37,944 (that is, $80,000 less $42,056).

(v) Thus, the asset value that is used to determine the FTAP for the 2007 plan year is $1,100,000 less $37,944, or $1,062,056. Accordingly, for purposes of this section, the FTAP for the 2007 plan year for Plan R is 70.8% (that is, $1,062,056 divided by $1,500,000).

Example 4. (i) Plan T is a non-collectively bargained defined benefit plan that was established prior to 2007. Plan T has a plan year that is the calendar year and a valuation date of January 1. The first effective plan year is 2008; the plan met the conditions of paragraph (j)(1)(ii)(E) of this section for 2008. As of January 1, 2009, Plan T has a value of plan assets (equal to the market value of assets) of $3,000,000, a funding standard carryover balance of $150,000, and a prefunding balance of $50,000. During 2007 and 2008, assets from Plan T were used to purchase a total of $400,000 in annuities for employees other than highly compensated employees. The funding target for Plan T (without regard to the at-risk rules of section 430(i)) is $3,200,000 as of January 1, 2009.

(ii) The plan's funding status is calculated in accordance with paragraph (j)(1)(ii)(B) of this section to determine whether the special rule for fully-funded plans applies to Plan T. Accordingly, the value of plan assets determined without subtracting the funding standard carryover balance and the prefunding balance is 93.75% of the plan's funding target ($3,000,000 ÷ $3,200,000). The applicable transitional percentage in paragraph (j)(1)(ii)(D) of this section is 94% for 2009. Because the percentage calculated above is less than 94%, the transition rule does not apply to Plan T.

(iii) Accordingly, the January 1, 2009, AFTAP for Plan T is calculated without reflecting the special rule in paragraph (j)(1)(ii)(B) of this section. The AFTAP as of January 1, 2009, is calculated by dividing the adjusted assets by the adjusted funding target. For this purpose, the value of assets is increased by the annuities purchased for nonhighly compensated employees during 2007 and 2008, and decreased by the funding standard carryover balance and the prefunding balance as of January 1, 2009, resulting in an adjusted asset value of $3,200,000 (that is, $3,000,000 + $400,000 - $150,000 - $50,000). The funding target is increased by the annuities purchased for nonhighly compensated employees during 2007 and 2008, resulting in an adjusted funding target of $3,600,000 (that is, $3,200,000 + $400,000). The AFTAP for Plan T for 2009 is therefore $3,200,000 ÷ $3,600,000, or 88.89%.

(k) *Effective/applicability dates.*—(1) *Statutory effective date.*—Section 436 generally applies to plan years beginning on or after January 1, 2008. The applicability of section 436 for purposes of determining the minimum required contribution is delayed for certain plans in accordance with sections 104 through 106 of PPA '06.

(2) *Collectively bargained plan exception.*—(i) *In general.*—In the case of a collectively bargained plan that is maintained pursuant to one or more collective bargaining agreements between employee representatives and one or more employers ratified before January 1, 2008, section 436 does not apply to plan years beginning before the earlier of—

(A) January 1, 2010; or

(B) The later of—

(*1*) The date on which the last such collective bargaining agreement relating to the plan terminates (determined without regard to any extension thereof agreed to after August 17, 2006); or

(*2*) The first day of the first plan year to which section 436 would (but for this paragraph (k)(2)) apply.

(ii) *Treatment of certain plan amendments.*—For purposes of this paragraph (k)(2), any plan amendment made pursuant to a collective bargaining agreement relating to the plan which amends the plan solely to conform to any requirement added by section 436 is not treated as a termination of the collective bargaining agreement.

(iii) *Treatment of plans with both collectively bargained and non-collectively bargained employees.*—In the case of a plan with respect to which a collective bargaining agreement applies to some, but not all, of the plan participants, the plan is considered a collectively bargained plan for purposes of this paragraph (k)(2) if it is considered a collectively bargained plan under the rules of paragraph (a)(5)(ii)(B) of this section.

(3) *Effective date/applicability date of regulations.*—This section applies to plan years beginning on or after January 1, 2010. For plan years beginning before January 1, 2010, plans are permitted to rely on the provisions set forth in this section for purposes of satisfying the requirements of section 436. [Reg. § 1.436-1.]

☐ [*T.D.* 9467, 10-14-2009. Amended by *T.D.* 9732, 9-8-2015.]